Quick Index

P9-BYE-107

Loan Payment and Amortization

1 Constant Annual Percent

2 Debt Service

3 Total Interest

4 Percent Paid Off

5 Amortization Schedules Per $100

6 Points on Monthly Payment Loan

Compound Interest and Annuity

7 Scan Table

8 Compound Interest and Annuity

Interest

9 Days of the Year

10 Days Between Dates

11 Simple Interest on $100

12 Daily Compound Interest on $100

13 Compensating Balances, Effective Rate

14 Construction Loan, Average Interest

Savings and Withdrawal

15 Growth of 1

16 Savings Growth

17 Savings and Withdrawal

Installment Loan

18 Installment Loan Payments

19 APR Scan Table

20 Lease Payments

21 Monthly Rebate and Earnings, Rule of 78

22 Actuarial Rebate and Earnings

23 Daily Rebate

Investment

24 Discount Price

25 Mortgage Price and Yield

26 Prepayment Mortgage Price and Yield

27 Bond Price and Yield

Appendix

Calculating an Interest Rate

Thorndike Encyclopedia
of
Banking and Financial Tables

THIRD EDITION

by

DAVID THORNDIKE

Containing Tables for

Loan Payment and Amortization
Compound Interest and Annuity
Interest • Savings and Withdrawal
Installment Loan • Investment

WARREN, GORHAM & LAMONT
Boston • New York

The tables in this book have been prepared in accordance with generally accepted computing standards. However, they are not warranted by the publisher or the author.

Table of Contents

Introduction   v

LOAN PAYMENT AND AMORTIZATION

1   Constant Annual Percent   1-1.1
    Monthly Payment, in Arrears   1-2
    Quarterly Payment, in Arrears   1-4
    Monthly Payment, in Advance   1-6
    Quarterly Payment, in Advance   1-8

2   Debt Service   2-1
    Monthly Payment   2-2
    Quarterly Payment   2-4

3   Total Interest   3-1
    Monthly Payment   3-2
    Quarterly Payment   3-4

4   Percent Paid Off   4-1
    15 Year Loan   4-2
    20 Year Loan   4-4
    25 Year Loan   4-6
    30 Year Loan   4-8

5   Amortization Schedules Per $100   5-1.1
    Monthly Payment   5-2
    Quarterly Payment   5-350

6   Points on Monthly Payment Loan   6-1
    1–3 Year   6-2
    4–6 Year   6-3
    7–9 Year   6-4
    10–12 Year   6-5
    13–15 Year   6-6
    16–18 Year   6-7
    19–21 Year   6-8
    22–24 Year   6-9
    25–27 Year   6-10
    28–30 Year   6-11

COMPOUND INTEREST AND ANNUITY

7   Scan Tables   7-1
    Amount of 1   7-2
    Amount of 1 Per Period   7-4
    Sinking Fund Payment   7-6

    Present Worth of 1   7-8
    Present Worth of 1 Per Period   7-10
    Periodic Payment to Amortize 1   7-12
    Constant Annual Percent   7-14
    Total Interest   7-16
    Annual Add on Rate   7-18

8   Compound Interest and Annuity   8-1.1
    Monthly   8-2
    Quarterly   8-262
    Semiannual   8-362
    Annual   8-422

INTEREST

9   Days of the Year   9-1
    Table   9-1

10   Days Between Dates   10-1.1
    Jan & Feb   10-2
    Mar & Apr   10-3
    May & Jun   10-4
    Jul & Aug   10-5
    Sep & Oct   10-6
    Nov & Dec   10-7

11   Simple Interest on $100   11-1.1
    360 Day Year   11-2
    365 Day Year   11-8

12   Daily Compound Interest on $100   12-1
    360 Day Year   12-2
    365 Day Year   12-8

13   Compensating Balances, Effective Rate   13-1
    5%   13-2
    10%   13-3
    15%   13-4
    20%   13-5

14   Construction Loan, Average Interest   14-1
    1 Point   14-2
    2 Points   14-3
    3 Points   14-4
    4 Points   14-5
    5 Points   14-6

TABLE OF CONTENTS

SAVINGS AND WITHDRAWAL

15 Growth of 1 .... 15-1.1
- Continuous Compounding, 360 Day Year 15-2
- Daily Compounding, 360 Day Year 15-4
- Daily Compounding, 365 Day Year 15-6
- Monthly Compounding 15-8
- Quarterly Compounding 15-10
- Semiannual Compounding 15-12
- Annual Compounding 15-14

16 Savings Growth 16-1.1
- Daily Compounding, 360 Day Year 16-2
- Daily Compounding, 365 Day Year 16-12
- Monthly Compounding 16-22
- Quarterly Compounding 16-32
- Semiannual Compounding 16-42
- Annual Compounding 16-52

17 Savings and Withdrawal 17-1
- Tables 17-2

INSTALLMENT LOAN

18 Installment Loan Payments 18-1
- Monthly 18-2
- Semimonthly 18-5
- Biweekly 18-8
- Weekly 18-11

19 APR Scan Table 19-1
- Monthly Payment 19-2
- Semimonthly Payment 19-4
- Biweekly Payment 19-6
- Weekly Payment 19-8

20 Lease Payments 20-1
- Payments in Arrears 20-2
- 1 Payment in Advance 20-12
- 2 Payments in Advance 20-22
- 3 Payments in Advance 20-32

21 Monthly Rebate and Earnings, Rule of 78 .... 21-1.1
- Tables 21-2

22 Actuarial Rebate and Earnings 22-1.1
- Tables 22-2

23 Daily Rebate 23-1
- 365 Day Year 23-2
- 366 Day Year 23-3

INVESTMENT

24 Discount Price 24-1
- 91 Days 24-2
- 181 Days 24-3
- 240 Days 24-4
- 366 Days 24-5

25 Mortgage Price and Yield 25-1.1
- Tables 25-2

26 Prepayment Mortgage Price and Yield 26-1.1
- Tables 26-2

27 Bond Price and Yield 27-1.1
- Tables 27-2
- Current Yield 27-182

APPENDIX   Calculating an Interest Rate A-1

INDEX I-1

Introduction

The *Thorndike Encyclopedia of Banking and Financial Tables*, Third Edition, is a compilation of tables for use by bankers, attorneys, accountants, investors, entrepreneurs, lenders, and borrowers. Previous editions have found their way into corporations, universities, libraries, and government agencies at all levels. The Encyclopedia has even traveled abroad, to Toronto, London, Paris, Caracas, Poona, and Beijing.

Organization of Encyclopedia. The Encyclopedia is divided into the following 6 parts, with relevant tables grouped under each part:

- Loan Payment and Amortization
- Compound Interest and Annuity
- Interest
- Savings and Withdrawal
- Installment Loan, Leasing, and Rebate
- Investment

At the beginning of each table there is a synopsis of interest rates, terms, and other applicable data (except at Tables 9 and 10, where such data do not apply). Following the synopsis is an explanation of how the table is to be used, with one or more examples illustrating use of the table in specific circumstances. Where appropriate, formulae are given to show how the values are computed.

Most of the tables carry a Description and an Example on the top of each page. Independent variables are shown in the running heads, in the boldface index going down the left sides of the tables, and in the column heads. The table pages are designed to be self-explanatory. Many users have reported that they remember the appearance of a table, and when they use the book, they simply thumb through the pages until they come to a page arrangement that is familiar.

Inside the front cover, the black leaders on the edge of the Quick Index line up the tables vertically with corresponding leaders on the edges of the pages where the tables begin. In addition, the Table of Contents lists all the variations covered by each table. This edition also carries an Appendix listing two computer programs that calculate an interest rate.

Elements of a Financial Transaction. Most financial transactions have 4 elements that require numerical values. These elements are:

- Amount
- Rate
- Term
- Payment

"Amount" is the mortgage loan or the price to pay for a loan; "rate" is the interest rate on the loan or the yield on an investment; "term" is the original term or the time remaining to maturity; and "payment" includes all future payments. When 3 of these elements are given, the tables can supply the fourth.

United States Rule. Under this rule, interest on a loan is computed on the unpaid balance. The origin of the rule is the 1839 Supreme Court case of Story v. Livingston (38 US 359):

> The correct rule as to interest is, that the creditor shall calculate interest, whenever a payment is made. To this extent the payment is first to be applied, and if it exceeds the interest due, the balance is to be applied to diminish the principal. This rule is equally applicable, whether the debt be one which expressly draws interest, or on which interest is given as damages.

Annual Percentage Rate. The term "Annual Percentage Rate" was created by the Truth in Lending Act of 1969:

> The annual percentage rate is that nominal annual interest rate which will yield a sum equal to the amount of finance charge when it is applied to the unpaid balance of the amount financed, calculated according to the actuarial method of allocating payments made on a debt between the amount financed and the amount of the finance charge, pursuant to which a payment is applied first to the accumulated finance charge and the balance is applied to the unpaid amount financed.

Amortization Schedule. Whenever a calculation is made to find an interest rate or yield or to compute the present worth of a series of future payments, an amortization schedule should be prepared to show the amount being amortized at the given rate over the term by the payments. The calculation is proved by an amortization schedule.

The schedule provides all the required information "in black and white," that is, it verifies the assumptions and confirms what each party—lender and borrower, lessor and lessee, mortgagor and mortgagee, investor and investee—receives and gives. Schedules and sample tables are used throughout this book to describe, demonstrate, and illustrate calculations and concepts.

Nominal Rate. The nominal rate is the named annual interest rate (e.g., a 6% bond, an 8% mortgage, a 5% interest rate on savings, and an 18% rate on revolving credit).

Effective Rate. When interest on savings is compounded more frequently than once a year (e.g., daily or monthly),

then, by the end of a year, interest has been computed on interest. When interest is compounded, there is more money in the account at the end of the year than there would be if simple interest had been paid for the same period of time. This greater amount, when expressed as a rate per year, is known as the effective rate. For example, a nominal rate of 6% with interest compounded daily produces an effective rate of 6.27%. Compounded monthly, the rate is 6.17%, and quarterly, 6.13%. Nominal and effective rates are shown on each page of Table 8, Compound Interest and Annuity.

Finding a Payment. To find the payment that amortizes a loan, turn to Table 8, Compound Interest and Annuity, for the appropriate rate. Scan down the term index and then read the payment per $1 in the sixth column. Multiply the loan amount by this factor and round the product to the next higher cent.

A Book of Tables. In a marketplace that makes mortgage loans, issues bonds, pays interest, and encourages savings, reference to a table is an easy and efficient way to find a payment, a rate, a term, a price, a yield, and an amount. The tables on the following pages apply to borrowing, lending, saving, investing, and issuing mortgages and bonds. The boldface running heads, column heads, and indexes in the left columns of the tables make it easy to find the known elements. The answer, in clear, readable type, is provided in the body of the table. A few minutes taken to look through the book will show the scope, contents, and ease with which these tables are used.

TABLE **1**

Constant Annual Percent

Interest Rates: 0, 1, 2, 3%;
4 to 19% by .25%;
20, 25, 30%.

Terms: 1 to 30 years, each year.

Payments: Monthly and quarterly, in arrears and in advance.

This table shows the percent of the principal amount of a loan needed each year to amortize a loan over the term. The first and second tables are for monthly and quarterly payments made in arrears; the third and fourth tables are for payments made in advance.

Example: The Constant Annual Percent (Constant) to amortize a loan at 8%, for 30 years, monthly payment in arrears, is 8.81%. For a loan of $100,000, the annual debt service is $8,810 and the monthly payment is $743.17. An amortization schedule for this loan is shown on page 5-115.

Payments in Arrears and in Advance. Payments to repay a loan may be made in arrears at the end of the period or in advance at the beginning of the period. Payments on residential mortgage loans are usually made in arrears.

Payments in Arrears. The Constant is the periodic payment per $100 times the number of periods in the year. The formula is:

$$\text{Constant} = \frac{1}{A_{\overline{n}|}} \times 100 \times 12$$

where:

$1/A_{\overline{n}|}$ = actuarial symbol for a periodic payment

n = number of periods

For monthly payments and a term of 30 years, n = 360. (The text accompanying Table 8 explains the actuarial symbol in detail.) To compute the Constant for an 8%, 30 year loan, turn to page 8-88. On the 30 year line and in the column Periodic Payment to Amortize 1, the number is .007 337 6457. The calculation is:

$$\text{Constant} = .007\ 337\ 6457 \times 100 \times 12$$

$$= 8.805$$

$$= 8.81\%$$

Payments in Advance. The payment in advance is computed from the payment in arrears. The payment in arrears is divided by 1 plus the periodic interest factor $(1 + i)$. The payment in advance for an 8%, 30 year loan is:

$$.007\ 337\ 6457 \div 1.0066666667 = .0072890520$$

The Constant for a monthly payment made in advance is:

$$\text{Constant} = .007\ 289\ 0520 \times 100 \times 12$$

$$= 8.746$$

$$= 8.75\%$$

Dividing the payment by $(1 + i)$ thus moves all payments up 1 period.

Example: The Constant is used to measure the cost of a loan. The lowest Constant represents the lowest cost if all the other elements of a loan are the same.

The Constant is 8.81% for loan *A* and 8.75% for loan *B*. Turn to page 1-3. In the 30 year column, the 8.81% is equivalent to an 8% interest rate, and, by interpolation, the 8.75% is equivalent to a 7.93% interest rate.

The 8.75% Constant appears to be the lowest cost; however, payments for loan *B* are made in advance. Turn to the In Advance table on page 1-7, which shows that the 8.75% Constant is also equivalent to an 8% interest rate. Thus, the cost of the 2 loans is the same.

There is, however, a difference. When payments are made in advance, the first payment is made immediately, which reduces the proceeds from the loan.

For simplicity's sake, suppose the Constant is 8% and payments are made quarterly in advance. Then, immediately after closing, the first payment is due. At closing, a loan of $100 less the first quarterly payment of $2 leaves proceeds of $98. If the payments are in arrears, then, at closing, the proceeds are still $100.

The Constant is used to find the interest rate when the amount, term, and payment are known. The payment is converted to a Constant. In the appropriate table, scan down the

CONSTANT ANNUAL PERCENT

column for the appropriate term until the Constant is read directly or is bracketed between 2 values. The interest rate is read from the rate index.

Example: A machine costing $100,000 is financed by an 8 year lease. Monthly payments of $1,800 are made in advance.

What is the interest rate for the 8 year term?

The annual payment is $1,800 × 12, or $21,600, which produces a Constant of 21.60%. Turn to page 1-6, to the 8 year column. Scanning the column to where 21.60% is bracketed between 2 given values, the interest rate, 15.50%, is found in the rate index.

CONSTANT ANNUAL PERCENT

CONSTANT ANNUAL PERCENT

MONTHLY PAYMENT, IN ARREARS

Description: This table shows the percent of the principal amount needed to amortize a loan over the term. Divide this constant by 12 to get the monthly payment per $100.

Example: The constant needed to amortize an 8% 15 year loan is 11.47 %. The annual debt service for a $50,000 loan is $ 5735.00. Divide by 12 to get the monthly payment.

RATE	1 yr	2 yr	3 yr	4 yr	5 yr	6 yr	7 yr	8 yr	9 yr	10 yr	11 yr	12 yr	13 yr	14 yr	15 yr
0.00	100.00	50.00	33.34	25.00	20.00	16.67	14.29	12.50	11.12	10.00	9.10	8.34	7.70	7.15	6.67
1.00	100.55	50.53	33.85	25.52	20.52	17.18	14.80	13.02	11.63	10.52	9.61	8.85	8.21	7.66	7.19
2.00	101.09	51.05	34.38	26.04	21.04	17.71	15.33	13.54	12.16	11.05	10.14	9.39	8.75	8.20	7.73
3.00	101.64	51.58	34.90	26.57	21.57	18.24	15.86	14.08	12.70	11.59	10.69	9.94	9.30	8.76	8.29
4.00	102.18	52.11	35.43	27.10	22.10	18.78	16.41	14.63	13.25	12.15	11.26	10.51	9.88	9.35	8.88
4.25	102.32	52.25	35.57	27.23	22.24	18.92	16.55	14.77	13.40	12.30	11.40	10.66	10.03	9.49	9.03
4.50	102.46	52.38	35.70	27.37	22.38	19.05	16.69	14.91	13.54	12.44	11.55	10.81	10.18	9.65	9.18
4.75	102.60	52.52	35.84	27.50	22.51	19.19	16.83	15.05	13.68	12.59	11.69	10.95	10.33	9.80	9.34
5.00	102.73	52.65	35.97	27.64	22.65	19.33	16.97	15.20	13.83	12.73	11.84	11.10	10.48	9.95	9.49
5.25	102.87	52.79	36.10	27.78	22.79	19.47	17.11	15.34	13.97	12.88	11.99	11.25	10.63	10.11	9.65
5.50	103.01	52.92	36.24	27.91	22.93	19.61	17.25	15.48	14.12	13.03	12.14	11.41	10.79	10.26	9.81
5.75	103.15	53.05	36.38	28.05	23.07	19.75	17.39	15.63	14.26	13.18	12.29	11.56	10.94	10.42	9.97
6.00	103.28	53.19	36.51	28.19	23.20	19.89	17.54	15.77	14.41	13.33	12.45	11.72	11.10	10.58	10.13
6.25	103.42	53.33	36.65	28.32	23.34	20.03	17.68	15.92	14.56	13.48	12.60	11.87	11.26	10.74	10.29
6.50	103.56	53.46	36.78	28.46	23.48	20.18	17.82	16.07	14.71	13.63	12.75	12.03	11.42	10.90	10.46
6.75	103.70	53.60	36.92	28.60	23.63	20.32	17.97	16.22	14.86	13.78	12.91	12.19	11.58	11.07	10.62
7.00	103.84	53.73	37.06	28.74	23.77	20.46	18.12	16.37	15.01	13.94	13.07	12.35	11.74	11.23	10.79
7.25	103.98	53.87	37.19	28.88	23.91	20.61	18.26	16.52	15.16	14.09	13.22	12.51	11.91	11.40	10.96
7.50	104.11	54.00	37.33	29.02	24.05	20.75	18.41	16.67	15.32	14.25	13.38	12.67	12.07	11.56	11.13
7.75	104.25	54.14	37.47	29.16	24.19	20.90	18.56	16.82	15.47	14.41	13.54	12.83	12.24	11.73	11.30
8.00	104.39	54.28	37.61	29.30	24.34	21.04	18.71	16.97	15.63	14.56	13.70	12.99	12.40	11.90	11.47
8.25	104.53	54.41	37.75	29.44	24.48	21.19	18.86	17.12	15.78	14.72	13.87	13.16	12.57	12.07	11.65
8.50	104.67	54.55	37.89	29.58	24.62	21.34	19.01	17.28	15.94	14.88	14.03	13.33	12.74	12.24	11.82
8.75	104.81	54.69	38.03	29.72	24.77	21.49	19.16	17.43	16.10	15.04	14.19	13.49	12.91	12.42	12.00
9.00	104.95	54.83	38.16	29.87	24.92	21.64	19.31	17.59	16.26	15.21	14.36	13.66	13.08	12.59	12.18
9.25	105.09	54.96	38.30	30.01	25.06	21.78	19.46	17.74	16.42	15.37	14.52	13.83	13.25	12.77	12.36
9.50	105.23	55.10	38.44	30.15	25.21	21.93	19.62	17.90	16.58	15.53	14.69	14.00	13.43	12.95	12.54
9.75	105.36	55.24	38.58	30.30	25.35	22.09	19.77	18.06	16.74	15.70	14.86	14.17	13.60	13.12	12.72
10.00	105.50	55.38	38.73	30.44	25.50	22.24	19.93	18.21	16.90	15.86	15.03	14.35	13.78	13.30	12.90
10.25	105.64	55.52	38.87	30.58	25.65	22.39	20.08	18.37	17.06	16.03	15.20	14.52	13.96	13.48	13.08
10.50	105.78	55.66	39.01	30.73	25.80	22.54	20.24	18.53	17.23	16.20	15.37	14.69	14.14	13.67	13.27
10.75	105.92	55.80	39.15	30.87	25.95	22.69	20.39	18.69	17.39	16.37	15.54	14.87	14.31	13.85	13.46
11.00	106.06	55.93	39.29	31.02	26.10	22.85	20.55	18.86	17.56	16.54	15.72	15.05	14.50	14.03	13.64
11.25	106.20	56.07	39.43	31.17	26.25	23.00	20.71	19.02	17.72	16.71	15.89	15.23	14.68	14.22	13.83
11.50	106.34	56.21	39.58	31.31	26.40	23.15	20.87	19.18	17.89	16.88	16.07	15.40	14.86	14.41	14.02
11.75	106.48	56.35	39.72	31.46	26.55	23.31	21.03	19.34	18.06	17.05	16.24	15.58	15.04	14.59	14.21
12.00	106.62	56.49	39.86	31.61	26.70	23.47	21.19	19.51	18.23	17.22	16.42	15.77	15.23	14.78	14.41
12.25	106.76	56.63	40.01	31.75	26.85	23.62	21.35	19.67	18.40	17.40	16.60	15.95	15.42	14.97	14.60
12.50	106.90	56.77	40.15	31.90	27.00	23.78	21.51	19.84	18.57	17.57	16.78	16.13	15.60	15.16	14.80
12.75	107.05	56.91	40.29	32.05	27.16	23.94	21.67	20.01	18.74	17.75	16.96	16.32	15.79	15.36	14.99
13.00	107.19	57.06	40.44	32.20	27.31	24.09	21.84	20.17	18.91	17.92	17.14	16.50	15.98	15.55	15.19
13.25	107.33	57.20	40.58	32.35	27.46	24.25	22.00	20.34	19.08	18.10	17.32	16.69	16.17	15.74	15.39
13.50	107.47	57.34	40.73	32.50	27.62	24.41	22.16	20.51	19.26	18.28	17.50	16.87	16.36	15.94	15.58
13.75	107.61	57.48	40.87	32.65	27.77	24.57	22.33	20.68	19.43	18.46	17.68	17.06	16.55	16.13	15.78
14.00	107.75	57.62	41.02	32.80	27.93	24.73	22.49	20.85	19.61	18.64	17.87	17.25	16.75	16.33	15.99
14.25	107.89	57.76	41.16	32.95	28.08	24.89	22.66	21.02	19.78	18.82	18.05	17.44	16.94	16.53	16.19
14.50	108.03	57.90	41.31	33.10	28.24	25.05	22.83	21.19	19.96	19.00	18.24	17.63	17.14	16.73	16.39
14.75	108.17	58.05	41.46	33.25	28.40	25.22	22.99	21.37	20.14	19.18	18.43	17.82	17.33	16.93	16.60
15.00	108.31	58.19	41.60	33.40	28.55	25.38	23.16	21.54	20.31	19.37	18.62	18.02	17.53	17.13	16.80
15.25	108.46	58.33	41.75	33.55	28.71	25.54	23.33	21.71	20.49	19.55	18.80	18.21	17.73	17.33	17.01
15.50	108.60	58.47	41.90	33.71	28.87	25.71	23.50	21.89	20.67	19.73	18.99	18.40	17.93	17.53	17.21
15.75	108.74	58.62	42.05	33.86	29.03	25.87	23.67	22.06	20.85	19.92	19.19	18.60	18.12	17.74	17.42
16.00	108.88	58.76	42.19	34.01	29.19	26.04	23.84	22.24	21.04	20.11	19.38	18.79	18.33	17.94	17.63
16.25	109.02	58.90	42.34	34.17	29.35	26.20	24.01	22.42	21.22	20.29	19.57	18.99	18.53	18.15	17.84
16.50	109.17	59.05	42.49	34.32	29.51	26.37	24.18	22.59	21.40	20.48	19.76	19.19	18.73	18.36	18.05
16.75	109.31	59.19	42.64	34.48	29.67	26.53	24.35	22.77	21.58	20.67	19.96	19.39	18.93	18.56	18.26
17.00	109.45	59.34	42.79	34.63	29.83	26.70	24.53	22.95	21.77	20.86	20.15	19.59	19.14	18.77	18.47
17.25	109.59	59.48	42.94	34.79	29.99	26.87	24.70	23.13	21.95	21.05	20.35	19.79	19.34	18.98	18.69
17.50	109.74	59.62	43.09	34.94	30.15	27.04	24.88	23.31	22.14	21.24	20.54	19.99	19.55	19.19	18.90
17.75	109.88	59.77	43.24	35.10	30.31	27.21	25.05	23.49	22.33	21.43	20.74	20.19	19.75	19.40	19.11
18.00	110.02	59.91	43.39	35.25	30.48	27.37	25.23	23.67	22.51	21.63	20.94	20.39	19.96	19.61	19.33
18.25	110.16	60.06	43.54	35.41	30.64	27.54	25.40	23.86	22.70	21.82	21.14	20.60	20.17	19.82	19.55
18.50	110.31	60.20	43.69	35.57	30.80	27.71	25.58	24.04	22.89	22.01	21.34	20.80	20.38	20.04	19.76
18.75	110.45	60.35	43.84	35.73	30.97	27.89	25.76	24.22	23.08	22.21	21.54	21.01	20.59	20.25	19.98
19.00	110.59	60.50	43.99	35.89	31.13	28.06	25.93	24.41	23.27	22.41	21.74	21.21	20.80	20.47	20.20
20.00	111.17	61.08	44.60	36.52	31.80	28.75	26.65	25.15	24.04	23.20	22.55	22.04	21.65	21.33	21.08
25.00	114.06	64.05	47.72	39.79	35.23	32.33	30.38	29.01	28.03	27.30	26.76	26.36	26.05	25.81	25.63
30.00	116.99	67.10	50.95	43.21	38.83	36.11	34.32	33.10	32.24	31.64	31.20	30.89	30.66	30.49	30.36

CONSTANT ANNUAL PERCENT

MONTHLY PAYMENT, IN ARRE

Description: This table shows the percent of the principal amount needed to amortize a loan over the term. Divide this constant by 12 to get the monthly payment per $100.

Example: The constant needed to amortize an 8% 30 year is 8.81 %. The annual debt service for a $50,000 lo $ 4405.00. Divide by 12 to get the monthly payment.

RATE	16 yr	17 yr	18 yr	19 yr	20 yr	21 yr	22 yr	23 yr	24 yr	25 yr	26 yr	27 yr	28 yr	29 yr	30
0.00	6.25	5.89	5.56	5.27	5.00	4.77	4.55	4.35	4.17	4.00	3.85	3.71	3.58	3.45	3.34
1.00	6.77	6.40	6.08	5.79	5.52	5.29	5.07	4.87	4.69	4.53	4.37	4.23	4.10	3.98	3.86
2.00	7.31	6.95	6.63	6.34	6.08	5.84	5.63	5.43	5.25	5.09	4.94	4.80	4.67	4.55	4.44
3.00	7.88	7.52	7.20	6.92	6.66	6.43	6.22	6.03	5.86	5.70	5.55	5.41	5.29	5.17	5.06
4.00	8.48	8.12	7.81	7.53	7.28	7.05	6.85	6.66	6.49	6.34	6.20	6.07	5.95	5.84	5.73
4.25	8.63	8.28	7.96	7.68	7.44	7.21	7.01	6.83	6.66	6.51	6.37	6.24	6.12	6.01	5.91
4.50	8.78	8.43	8.12	7.84	7.60	7.37	7.17	6.99	6.83	6.67	6.54	6.41	6.29	6.18	6.09
4.75	8.94	8.59	8.28	8.01	7.76	7.54	7.34	7.16	7.00	6.85	6.71	6.58	6.47	6.36	6.26
5.00	9.10	8.75	8.44	8.17	7.92	7.71	7.51	7.33	7.17	7.02	6.89	6.76	6.65	6.54	6.45
5.25	9.26	8.91	8.60	8.33	8.09	7.87	7.68	7.50	7.34	7.20	7.06	6.94	6.83	6.73	6.63
5.50	9.42	9.07	8.77	8.50	8.26	8.04	7.85	7.68	7.52	7.37	7.24	7.12	7.01	6.91	6.82
5.75	9.58	9.24	8.94	8.67	8.43	8.22	8.03	7.85	7.70	7.55	7.42	7.31	7.20	7.10	7.01
6.00	9.74	9.40	9.10	8.84	8.60	8.39	8.20	8.03	7.88	7.74	7.61	7.49	7.39	7.29	7.20
6.25	9.91	9.57	9.27	9.01	8.78	8.57	8.38	8.21	8.06	7.92	7.80	7.68	7.58	7.48	7.39
6.50	10.07	9.74	9.44	9.18	8.95	8.75	8.56	8.39	8.24	8.11	7.98	7.87	7.77	7.68	7.59
6.75	10.24	9.91	9.62	9.36	9.13	8.93	8.74	8.58	8.43	8.30	8.17	8.06	7.96	7.87	7.79
7.00	10.41	10.08	9.79	9.54	9.31	9.11	8.93	8.76	8.62	8.49	8.37	8.26	8.16	8.07	7.99
7.25	10.58	10.25	9.97	9.71	9.49	9.29	9.11	8.95	8.81	8.68	8.56	8.46	8.36	8.27	8.19
7.50	10.75	10.43	10.14	9.89	9.67	9.47	9.30	9.14	9.00	8.87	8.76	8.65	8.56	8.47	8.40
7.75	10.93	10.61	10.32	10.08	9.86	9.66	9.49	9.33	9.19	9.07	8.96	8.85	8.76	8.68	8.60
8.00	11.10	10.78	10.50	10.26	10.04	9.85	9.68	9.53	9.39	9.27	9.16	9.06	8.97	8.88	8.81
8.25	11.28	10.96	10.69	10.44	10.23	10.04	9.87	9.72	9.59	9.47	9.36	9.26	9.17	9.09	9.02
8.50	11.46	11.14	10.87	10.63	10.42	10.23	10.07	9.92	9.79	9.67	9.56	9.47	9.38	9.30	9.23
8.75	11.64	11.33	11.06	10.82	10.61	10.43	10.26	10.12	9.99	9.87	9.77	9.67	9.59	9.51	9.45
9.00	11.82	11.51	11.24	11.01	10.80	10.62	10.46	10.32	10.19	10.08	9.97	9.88	9.80	9.73	9.66
9.25	12.00	11.70	11.43	11.20	11.00	10.82	10.66	10.52	10.39	10.28	10.18	10.09	10.01	9.94	9.88
9.50	12.18	11.88	11.62	11.39	11.19	11.01	10.86	10.72	10.60	10.49	10.39	10.31	10.23	10.16	10.10
9.75	12.37	12.07	11.81	11.58	11.39	11.21	11.06	10.93	10.81	10.70	10.60	10.52	10.44	10.38	10.31
10.00	12.56	12.26	12.00	11.78	11.59	11.41	11.26	11.13	11.01	10.91	10.82	10.73	10.66	10.59	10.54
10.25	12.74	12.45	12.20	11.98	11.78	11.62	11.47	11.34	11.22	11.12	11.03	10.95	10.88	10.82	10.76
10.50	12.93	12.64	12.39	12.17	11.99	11.82	11.68	11.55	11.43	11.34	11.25	11.17	11.10	11.04	10.98
10.75	13.12	12.84	12.59	12.37	12.19	12.03	11.88	11.76	11.65	11.55	11.46	11.39	11.32	11.26	11.21
11.00	13.31	13.03	12.79	12.57	12.39	12.23	12.09	11.97	11.86	11.77	11.68	11.61	11.54	11.48	11.43
11.25	13.51	13.23	12.98	12.78	12.60	12.44	12.30	12.18	12.08	11.98	11.90	11.83	11.77	11.71	11.66
11.50	13.70	13.42	13.18	12.98	12.80	12.65	12.51	12.40	12.29	12.20	12.12	12.05	11.99	11.94	11.89
11.75	13.89	13.62	13.39	13.18	13.01	12.86	12.73	12.61	12.51	12.42	12.35	12.28	12.22	12.16	12.12
12.00	14.09	13.82	13.59	13.39	13.22	13.07	12.94	12.83	12.73	12.64	12.57	12.50	12.44	12.39	12.35
12.25	14.29	14.02	13.79	13.60	13.43	13.28	13.16	13.05	12.95	12.87	12.79	12.73	12.67	12.62	12.58
12.50	14.49	14.22	14.00	13.80	13.64	13.50	13.37	13.26	13.17	13.09	13.02	12.96	12.90	12.85	12.81
12.75	14.68	14.42	14.20	14.01	13.85	13.71	13.59	13.48	13.39	13.31	13.24	13.18	13.13	13.09	13.05
13.00	14.88	14.63	14.41	14.22	14.06	13.93	13.81	13.71	13.62	13.54	13.47	13.41	13.36	13.32	13.28
13.25	15.09	14.83	14.62	14.44	14.28	14.14	14.03	13.93	13.84	13.77	13.70	13.64	13.59	13.55	13.51
13.50	15.29	15.04	14.83	14.65	14.49	14.36	14.25	14.15	14.07	13.99	13.93	13.87	13.83	13.79	13.75
13.75	15.49	15.25	15.04	14.86	14.71	14.58	14.47	14.37	14.29	14.22	14.16	14.11	14.06	14.02	13.99
14.00	15.70	15.45	15.25	15.08	14.93	14.80	14.69	14.60	14.52	14.45	14.39	14.34	14.30	14.26	14.22
14.25	15.90	15.66	15.46	15.29	15.15	15.02	14.92	14.82	14.75	14.68	14.62	14.57	14.53	14.49	14.46
14.50	16.11	15.87	15.68	15.51	15.36	15.24	15.14	15.05	14.98	14.91	14.86	14.81	14.77	14.73	14.70
14.75	16.32	16.09	15.89	15.72	15.59	15.47	15.37	15.28	15.21	15.14	15.09	15.04	15.00	14.97	14.94
15.00	16.53	16.30	16.11	15.94	15.81	15.69	15.59	15.51	15.44	15.37	15.32	15.28	15.24	15.21	15.18
15.25	16.74	16.51	16.32	16.16	16.03	15.92	15.82	15.74	15.67	15.61	15.56	15.51	15.48	15.45	15.42
15.50	16.95	16.72	16.54	16.38	16.25	16.14	16.05	15.97	15.90	15.84	15.79	15.75	15.72	15.69	15.66
15.75	17.16	16.94	16.76	16.60	16.48	16.37	16.28	16.20	16.13	16.08	16.03	15.99	15.95	15.93	15.90
16.00	17.37	17.16	16.98	16.83	16.70	16.59	16.50	16.43	16.37	16.31	16.27	16.23	16.19	16.17	16.14
16.25	17.58	17.37	17.20	17.05	16.93	16.82	16.74	16.66	16.60	16.55	16.50	16.47	16.43	16.41	16.38
16.50	17.80	17.59	17.42	17.27	17.15	17.05	16.97	16.89	16.83	16.78	16.74	16.71	16.67	16.65	16.63
16.75	18.01	17.81	17.64	17.50	17.38	17.28	17.20	17.13	17.07	17.02	16.98	16.94	16.92	16.89	16.87
17.00	18.23	18.03	17.86	17.72	17.61	17.51	17.43	17.36	17.31	17.26	17.22	17.19	17.16	17.13	17.11
17.25	18.45	18.25	18.08	17.95	17.84	17.74	17.66	17.60	17.54	17.50	17.46	17.43	17.40	17.38	17.36
17.50	18.66	18.47	18.31	18.17	18.06	17.97	17.90	17.83	17.78	17.74	17.70	17.67	17.64	17.62	17.60
17.75	18.88	18.69	18.53	18.40	18.29	18.20	18.13	18.07	18.02	17.97	17.94	17.91	17.88	17.86	17.85
18.00	19.10	18.91	18.76	18.63	18.52	18.44	18.37	18.31	18.26	18.21	18.18	18.15	18.13	18.11	18.09
18.25	19.32	19.13	18.98	18.86	18.76	18.67	18.60	18.54	18.49	18.45	18.42	18.39	18.37	18.35	18.34
18.50	19.54	19.36	19.21	19.09	18.99	18.91	18.84	18.78	18.73	18.69	18.66	18.64	18.61	18.60	18.58
18.75	19.76	19.58	19.44	19.32	19.22	19.14	19.07	19.02	18.97	18.94	18.90	18.88	18.86	18.84	18.83
19.00	19.98	19.81	19.67	19.55	19.45	19.37	19.31	19.26	19.21	19.18	19.15	19.12	19.10	19.09	19.09
20.00	20.88	20.72	20.58	20.48	20.39	20.32	20.26	20.22	20.18	20.15	20.12	20.10	20.08	20.07	20.06
25.00	25.49	25.38	25.30	25.23	25.18	25.14	25.11	25.09	25.07	25.06	25.05	25.04	25.03	25.02	25.02
30.00	30.27	30.20	30.15	30.11	30.09	30.06	30.05	30.04	30.03	30.02	30.02	30.02	30.01	30.01	30.01

iption: This table shows the percent of the principal
unt needed to amortize a loan over the term. Divide this
stant by 4 to get the quarter payment per $100.

Example: The constant needed to amortize an 8% 15 year loan is 11.51 %. The annual debt service for a $50,000 loan is $ 5755.00. Divide by 4 to get the quarter payment.

ATE	1 yr	2 yr	3 yr	4 yr	5 yr	6 yr	7 yr	8 yr	9 yr	10 yr	11 yr	12 yr	13 yr	14 yr	15 yr
0.00	100.00	50.00	33.34	25.00	20.00	16.67	14.29	12.50	11.12	10.00	9.10	8.34	7.70	7.15	6.67
1.00	100.63	50.57	33.88	25.54	20.53	17.20	14.81	13.03	11.64	10.53	9.62	8.86	8.22	7.67	7.19
2.00	101.26	51.14	34.43	26.08	21.07	17.73	15.35	13.56	12.17	11.06	10.16	9.40	8.76	8.21	7.74
3.00	101.89	51.71	34.99	26.63	21.62	18.28	15.90	14.11	12.72	11.62	10.71	9.96	9.32	8.76	8.31
4.00	102.52	52.28	35.54	27.18	22.17	18.83	16.45	14.67	13.29	12.19	11.29	10.54	9.91	9.37	8.90
4.25	102.68	52.43	35.69	27.32	22.31	18.97	16.60	14.82	13.43	12.33	11.43	10.69	10.06	9.52	9.06
4.50	102.83	52.57	35.83	27.46	22.45	19.12	16.74	14.96	13.58	12.48	11.58	10.84	10.21	9.67	9.21
4.75	102.99	52.71	35.97	27.60	22.59	19.26	16.88	15.10	13.72	12.63	11.73	10.99	10.36	9.82	9.36
5.00	103.15	52.86	36.11	27.74	22.73	19.40	17.02	15.25	13.87	12.77	11.88	11.14	10.51	9.98	9.52
5.25	103.31	53.00	36.25	27.88	22.87	19.54	17.17	15.39	14.02	12.92	12.03	11.29	10.67	10.14	9.68
5.50	103.47	53.15	36.39	28.03	23.02	19.69	17.31	15.54	14.17	13.07	12.18	11.44	10.82	10.29	9.84
5.75	103.62	53.29	36.53	28.17	23.16	19.83	17.46	15.69	14.32	13.22	12.34	11.60	10.98	10.45	10.00
6.00	103.78	53.44	36.68	28.31	23.30	19.97	17.61	15.84	14.47	13.38	12.49	11.75	11.14	10.61	10.16
6.25	103.94	53.58	36.82	28.45	23.45	20.12	17.75	15.98	14.62	13.53	12.64	11.91	11.30	10.78	10.33
6.50	104.10	53.73	36.96	28.60	23.59	20.27	17.90	16.13	14.77	13.68	12.80	12.07	11.46	10.94	10.49
6.75	104.26	53.88	37.11	28.74	23.74	20.41	18.05	16.28	14.92	13.84	12.96	12.23	11.62	11.10	10.66
7.00	104.42	54.02	37.25	28.88	23.88	20.56	18.20	16.44	15.08	13.99	13.12	12.39	11.78	11.27	10.83
7.25	104.58	54.17	37.39	29.03	24.03	20.71	18.35	16.59	15.23	14.15	13.28	12.55	11.95	11.44	11.00
7.50	104.74	54.32	37.54	29.17	24.17	20.86	18.50	16.74	15.38	14.31	13.44	12.72	12.11	11.60	11.17
7.75	104.90	54.46	37.68	29.32	24.32	21.00	18.65	16.89	15.54	14.47	13.60	12.88	12.28	11.77	11.34
8.00	105.05	54.61	37.83	29.47	24.47	21.15	18.80	17.05	15.70	14.63	13.76	13.05	12.45	11.94	11.51
8.25	105.21	54.76	37.97	29.61	24.62	21.30	18.95	17.20	15.86	14.79	13.92	13.21	12.62	12.12	11.69
8.50	105.37	54.90	38.12	29.76	24.76	21.45	19.11	17.36	16.01	14.95	14.09	13.38	12.79	12.29	11.86
8.75	105.53	55.05	38.27	29.90	24.91	21.61	19.26	17.52	16.17	15.11	14.25	13.55	12.96	12.46	12.04
9.00	105.69	55.20	38.41	30.05	25.06	21.76	19.42	17.67	16.34	15.28	14.42	13.72	13.13	12.64	12.22
9.25	105.85	55.35	38.56	30.20	25.21	21.91	19.57	17.83	16.50	15.44	14.59	13.89	13.31	12.82	12.40
9.50	106.01	55.49	38.71	30.35	25.36	22.06	19.73	17.99	16.66	15.61	14.76	14.06	13.48	12.99	12.58
9.75	106.17	55.64	38.85	30.50	25.51	22.22	19.88	18.15	16.82	15.77	14.93	14.23	13.66	13.17	12.76
10.00	106.33	55.79	39.00	30.64	25.66	22.37	20.04	18.31	16.99	15.94	15.10	14.41	13.83	13.35	12.95
10.25	106.49	55.94	39.15	30.79	25.82	22.52	20.20	18.47	17.15	16.11	15.27	14.58	14.01	13.54	13.13
10.50	106.65	56.09	39.30	30.94	25.97	22.68	20.36	18.64	17.32	16.28	15.44	14.76	14.19	13.72	13.32
10.75	106.81	56.24	39.44	31.09	26.12	22.84	20.52	18.80	17.48	16.45	15.61	14.94	14.37	13.90	13.50
11.00	106.97	56.39	39.59	31.24	26.27	22.99	20.68	18.96	17.65	16.62	15.79	15.11	14.55	14.09	13.69
11.25	107.13	56.54	39.74	31.39	26.43	23.15	20.84	19.13	17.82	16.79	15.96	15.29	14.74	14.27	13.88
11.50	107.29	56.69	39.89	31.55	26.58	23.31	21.00	19.29	17.99	16.96	16.14	15.47	14.92	14.46	14.07
11.75	107.46	56.84	40.04	31.70	26.74	23.47	21.16	19.46	18.16	17.14	16.32	15.65	15.11	14.65	14.27
12.00	107.62	56.99	40.19	31.85	26.89	23.62	21.32	19.62	18.33	17.31	16.50	15.84	15.29	14.84	14.46
12.25	107.78	57.14	40.34	32.00	27.05	23.78	21.49	19.79	18.50	17.49	16.68	16.02	15.48	15.03	14.65
12.50	107.94	57.29	40.49	32.15	27.20	23.94	21.65	19.96	18.67	17.66	16.86	16.20	15.67	15.22	14.85
12.75	108.10	57.44	40.64	32.31	27.36	24.10	21.81	20.13	18.84	17.84	17.04	16.39	15.86	15.41	15.04
13.00	108.26	57.59	40.79	32.46	27.52	24.26	21.98	20.30	19.02	18.02	17.22	16.57	16.05	15.61	15.24
13.25	108.42	57.74	40.94	32.61	27.67	24.43	22.14	20.47	19.19	18.19	17.40	16.76	16.24	15.80	15.44
13.50	108.58	57.89	41.09	32.77	27.83	24.59	22.31	20.64	19.37	18.37	17.59	16.95	16.43	16.00	15.64
13.75	108.74	58.04	41.25	32.92	27.99	24.75	22.48	20.81	19.54	18.55	17.77	17.14	16.62	16.19	15.84
14.00	108.91	58.20	41.40	33.08	28.15	24.91	22.65	20.98	19.72	18.74	17.96	17.33	16.81	16.39	16.04
14.25	109.07	58.35	41.55	33.23	28.31	25.08	22.81	21.15	19.90	18.92	18.14	17.52	17.01	16.59	16.24
14.50	109.23	58.50	41.70	33.39	28.47	25.24	22.98	21.33	20.07	19.10	18.33	17.71	17.21	16.79	16.45
14.75	109.39	58.65	41.86	33.55	28.63	25.41	23.15	21.50	20.25	19.28	18.52	17.90	17.40	16.99	16.65
15.00	109.55	58.80	42.01	33.70	28.79	25.57	23.32	21.68	20.43	19.47	18.71	18.10	17.60	17.19	16.86
15.25	109.71	58.96	42.16	33.86	28.95	25.74	23.49	21.85	20.61	19.65	18.90	18.29	17.80	17.39	17.06
15.50	109.88	59.11	42.32	34.02	29.11	25.91	23.67	22.03	20.80	19.84	19.09	18.48	18.00	17.60	17.27
15.75	110.04	59.26	42.47	34.17	29.28	26.07	23.84	22.21	20.98	20.03	19.28	18.68	18.20	17.80	17.48
16.00	110.20	59.42	42.63	34.33	29.44	26.24	24.01	22.38	21.16	20.21	19.47	18.88	18.40	18.01	17.69
16.25	110.36	59.57	42.78	34.49	29.60	26.41	24.18	22.56	21.34	20.40	19.66	19.07	18.60	18.21	17.90
16.50	110.53	59.72	42.94	34.65	29.76	26.58	24.36	22.74	21.53	20.59	19.86	19.27	18.80	18.42	18.11
16.75	110.69	59.88	43.09	34.81	29.93	26.75	24.53	22.92	21.71	20.78	20.05	19.47	19.01	18.63	18.32
17.00	110.85	60.03	43.25	34.97	30.09	26.92	24.71	23.10	21.90	20.97	20.25	19.67	19.21	18.84	18.53
17.25	111.01	60.19	43.40	35.13	30.26	27.09	24.88	23.28	22.08	21.16	20.44	19.87	19.42	19.04	18.74
17.50	111.18	60.34	43.56	35.29	30.42	27.26	25.06	23.46	22.27	21.36	20.64	20.07	19.62	19.25	18.96
17.75	111.34	60.49	43.71	35.45	30.59	27.43	25.24	23.65	22.46	21.55	20.84	20.28	19.83	19.47	19.17
18.00	111.50	60.65	43.87	35.61	30.76	27.60	25.41	23.83	22.65	21.74	21.04	20.48	20.04	19.68	19.39
18.25	111.67	60.80	44.03	35.77	30.92	27.77	25.59	24.01	22.84	21.94	21.24	20.68	20.24	19.89	19.60
18.50	111.83	60.96	44.19	35.93	31.09	27.95	25.77	24.20	23.03	22.13	21.44	20.89	20.45	20.10	19.82
18.75	111.99	61.11	44.34	36.10	31.26	28.12	25.95	24.38	23.22	22.33	21.64	21.09	20.66	20.32	20.04
19.00	112.16	61.27	44.50	36.26	31.43	28.29	26.13	24.57	23.41	22.52	21.84	21.30	20.87	20.53	20.26
20.00	112.81	61.89	45.14	36.91	32.10	28.99	26.85	25.32	24.18	23.32	22.65	22.13	21.72	21.40	21.14
25.00	116.10	65.06	48.37	40.27	35.59	32.62	30.61	29.20	28.18	27.43	26.87	26.45	26.12	25.87	25.68
30.00	119.43	68.30	51.72	43.76	39.24	36.43	34.57	33.30	32.40	31.77	31.30	30.97	30.72	30.54	30.40

CONSTANT ANNUAL PERCENT

QUARTERLY PAYMENT, IN ARREARS

Description: This table shows the percent of the principal amount needed to amortize a loan over the term. Divide this constant by 4 to get the quarter payment per $100.

Example: The constant needed to amortize an 8% 30 year loan is 8.82 %. The annual debt service for a $50,000 loan is $ 4410.00. Divide by 4 to get the quarter payment.

RATE	16 yr	17 yr	18 yr	19 yr	20 yr	21 yr	22 yr	23 yr	24 yr	25 yr	26 yr	27 yr	28 yr	29 yr	30 yr
0.00	6.25	5.89	5.56	5.27	5.00	4.77	4.55	4.35	4.17	4.00	3.85	3.71	3.58	3.45	3.34
1.00	6.78	6.41	6.08	5.79	5.53	5.29	5.07	4.88	4.70	4.53	4.38	4.24	4.10	3.98	3.87
2.00	7.32	6.96	6.63	6.34	6.08	5.85	5.63	5.44	5.26	5.10	4.95	4.81	4.68	4.56	4.45
3.00	7.90	7.54	7.22	6.93	6.67	6.44	6.23	6.04	5.87	5.71	5.56	5.42	5.30	5.18	5.07
4.00	8.50	8.14	7.83	7.54	7.29	7.07	6.86	6.68	6.51	6.35	6.21	6.08	5.96	5.85	5.74
4.25	8.65	8.30	7.98	7.70	7.45	7.23	7.02	6.84	6.67	6.52	6.38	6.25	6.13	6.02	5.92
4.50	8.81	8.45	8.14	7.86	7.61	7.39	7.19	7.01	6.84	6.69	6.55	6.42	6.30	6.20	6.10
4.75	8.96	8.61	8.30	8.02	7.78	7.56	7.36	7.18	7.01	6.86	6.72	6.60	6.48	6.37	6.28
5.00	9.12	8.77	8.46	8.19	7.94	7.72	7.53	7.35	7.18	7.03	6.90	6.77	6.66	6.56	6.46
5.25	9.28	8.93	8.63	8.35	8.11	7.89	7.70	7.52	7.36	7.21	7.08	6.95	6.84	6.74	6.64
5.50	9.44	9.10	8.79	8.52	8.28	8.06	7.87	7.69	7.53	7.39	7.26	7.14	7.03	6.92	6.83
5.75	9.61	9.26	8.96	8.69	8.45	8.24	8.04	7.87	7.71	7.57	7.44	7.32	7.21	7.11	7.02
6.00	9.77	9.43	9.13	8.86	8.62	8.41	8.22	8.05	7.89	7.75	7.62	7.51	7.40	7.30	7.21
6.25	9.94	9.60	9.30	9.03	8.80	8.59	8.40	8.23	8.08	7.94	7.81	7.70	7.59	7.49	7.41
6.50	10.10	9.77	9.47	9.21	8.98	8.77	8.58	8.41	8.26	8.12	8.00	7.89	7.78	7.69	7.60
6.75	10.27	9.94	9.64	9.38	9.15	8.95	8.76	8.60	8.45	8.31	8.19	8.08	7.98	7.89	7.80
7.00	10.44	10.11	9.82	9.56	9.33	9.13	8.95	8.78	8.64	8.50	8.38	8.27	8.18	8.08	8.00
7.25	10.62	10.29	10.00	9.74	9.51	9.31	9.13	8.97	8.83	8.70	8.58	8.47	8.37	8.29	8.20
7.50	10.79	10.46	10.17	9.92	9.70	9.50	9.32	9.16	9.02	8.89	8.78	8.67	8.58	8.49	8.41
7.75	10.96	10.64	10.35	10.10	9.88	9.69	9.51	9.35	9.21	9.09	8.97	8.87	8.78	8.69	8.62
8.00	11.14	10.82	10.54	10.29	10.07	9.88	9.70	9.55	9.41	9.29	9.17	9.07	8.98	8.90	8.82
8.25	11.32	11.00	10.72	10.47	10.26	10.07	9.90	9.74	9.61	9.49	9.38	9.28	9.19	9.11	9.03
8.50	11.50	11.18	10.90	10.66	10.45	10.26	10.09	9.94	9.81	9.69	9.58	9.48	9.40	9.32	9.25
8.75	11.68	11.36	11.09	10.85	10.64	10.45	10.29	10.14	10.01	9.89	9.79	9.69	9.61	9.53	9.46
9.00	11.86	11.55	11.28	11.04	10.83	10.65	10.48	10.34	10.21	10.10	9.99	9.90	9.82	9.74	9.67
9.25	12.04	11.73	11.46	11.23	11.02	10.84	10.68	10.54	10.41	10.30	10.20	10.11	10.03	9.96	9.89
9.50	12.23	11.92	11.65	11.42	11.22	11.04	10.88	10.74	10.62	10.51	10.41	10.32	10.24	10.17	10.11
9.75	12.41	12.11	11.85	11.62	11.42	11.24	11.09	10.95	10.83	10.72	10.62	10.54	10.46	10.39	10.33
10.00	12.60	12.30	12.04	11.81	11.62	11.44	11.29	11.15	11.04	10.93	10.84	10.75	10.68	10.61	10.55
10.25	12.79	12.49	12.23	12.01	11.82	11.64	11.49	11.36	11.25	11.14	11.05	10.97	10.90	10.83	10.77
10.50	12.98	12.68	12.43	12.21	12.02	11.85	11.70	11.57	11.46	11.36	11.27	11.19	11.12	11.05	11.00
10.75	13.17	12.88	12.62	12.41	12.22	12.05	11.91	11.78	11.67	11.57	11.48	11.41	11.34	11.27	11.22
11.00	13.36	13.07	12.82	12.61	12.42	12.26	12.12	11.99	11.88	11.79	11.70	11.63	11.56	11.50	11.45
11.25	13.55	13.27	13.02	12.81	12.63	12.47	12.33	12.21	12.10	12.00	11.92	11.85	11.78	11.72	11.67
11.50	13.74	13.46	13.22	13.01	12.83	12.68	12.54	12.42	12.32	12.22	12.14	12.07	12.01	11.95	11.90
11.75	13.94	13.66	13.42	13.22	13.04	12.89	12.75	12.64	12.53	12.44	12.36	12.29	12.23	12.18	12.13
12.00	14.14	13.86	13.63	13.42	13.25	13.10	12.97	12.85	12.75	12.66	12.59	12.52	12.46	12.41	12.36
12.25	14.33	14.06	13.83	13.63	13.46	13.31	13.18	13.07	12.97	12.89	12.81	12.75	12.69	12.64	12.59
12.50	14.53	14.26	14.04	13.84	13.67	13.52	13.40	13.29	13.19	13.11	13.04	12.97	12.92	12.87	12.82
12.75	14.73	14.47	14.24	14.05	13.88	13.74	13.62	13.51	13.41	13.33	13.26	13.20	13.15	13.10	13.06
13.00	14.93	14.67	14.45	14.26	14.10	13.96	13.83	13.73	13.64	13.56	13.49	13.43	13.38	13.33	13.29
13.25	15.13	14.88	14.66	14.47	14.31	14.17	14.05	13.95	13.86	13.78	13.72	13.66	13.61	13.56	13.53
13.50	15.34	15.08	14.87	14.68	14.53	14.39	14.27	14.17	14.09	14.01	13.95	13.89	13.84	13.80	13.76
13.75	15.54	15.29	15.08	14.90	14.74	14.61	14.50	14.40	14.31	14.24	14.18	14.12	14.07	14.03	14.00
14.00	15.75	15.50	15.29	15.11	14.96	14.83	14.72	14.62	14.54	14.47	14.41	14.35	14.31	14.27	14.23
14.25	15.95	15.71	15.50	15.33	15.18	15.05	14.94	14.85	14.77	14.70	14.64	14.59	14.54	14.50	14.47
14.50	16.16	15.92	15.71	15.54	15.40	15.27	15.17	15.07	15.00	14.93	14.87	14.82	14.78	14.74	14.71
14.75	16.37	16.13	15.93	15.76	15.62	15.49	15.39	15.30	15.23	15.16	15.10	15.06	15.02	14.98	14.95
15.00	16.58	16.34	16.14	15.98	15.84	15.72	15.62	15.53	15.46	15.39	15.34	15.29	15.25	15.22	15.19
15.25	16.79	16.55	16.36	16.20	16.06	15.94	15.84	15.76	15.69	15.63	15.57	15.53	15.49	15.46	15.43
15.50	17.00	16.77	16.58	16.42	16.28	16.17	16.07	15.99	15.92	15.86	15.81	15.76	15.73	15.70	15.67
15.75	17.21	16.98	16.80	16.64	16.51	16.39	16.30	16.22	16.15	16.09	16.04	16.00	15.97	15.94	15.91
16.00	17.42	17.20	17.01	16.86	16.73	16.62	16.53	16.45	16.38	16.33	16.28	16.24	16.21	16.18	16.15
16.25	17.63	17.42	17.23	17.08	16.96	16.85	16.76	16.68	16.62	16.56	16.52	16.48	16.45	16.42	16.39
16.50	17.85	17.63	17.46	17.31	17.18	17.08	16.99	16.92	16.85	16.80	16.76	16.72	16.69	16.66	16.64
16.75	18.06	17.85	17.68	17.53	17.41	17.31	17.22	17.15	17.09	17.04	16.99	16.96	16.93	16.90	16.88
17.00	18.28	18.07	17.90	17.76	17.64	17.54	17.45	17.38	17.32	17.27	17.23	17.20	17.17	17.14	17.12
17.25	18.49	18.29	18.12	17.98	17.86	17.77	17.69	17.62	17.56	17.51	17.47	17.44	17.41	17.38	17.36
17.50	18.71	18.51	18.35	18.21	18.09	18.00	17.92	17.85	17.80	17.75	17.71	17.68	17.65	17.63	17.61
17.75	18.93	18.73	18.57	18.43	18.32	18.23	18.15	18.09	18.03	17.99	17.95	17.92	17.89	17.87	17.85
18.00	19.15	18.95	18.79	18.66	18.55	18.46	18.39	18.32	18.27	18.23	18.19	18.16	18.14	18.11	18.10
18.25	19.37	19.18	19.02	18.89	18.78	18.70	18.62	18.56	18.51	18.47	18.43	18.40	18.38	18.36	18.34
18.50	19.59	19.40	19.25	19.12	19.02	18.93	18.86	18.80	18.75	18.71	18.67	18.65	18.62	18.60	18.59
18.75	19.81	19.63	19.47	19.35	19.25	19.16	19.09	19.04	18.99	18.95	18.92	18.89	18.87	18.85	18.83
19.00	20.03	19.85	19.70	19.58	19.48	19.40	19.33	19.27	19.23	19.19	19.16	19.13	19.11	19.09	19.08
20.00	20.93	20.76	20.62	20.51	20.42	20.34	20.28	20.23	20.19	20.16	20.13	20.11	20.09	20.07	20.06
25.00	25.53	25.42	25.33	25.26	25.20	25.16	25.13	25.10	25.08	25.06	25.05	25.04	25.03	25.03	25.02
30.00	30.30	30.23	30.17	30.13	30.10	30.07	30.06	30.04	30.03	30.03	30.02	30.02	30.01	30.01	30.01

CONSTANT ANNUAL PERCENT

MONTHLY PAYMENT, IN ADVANCE

Description: This table shows the percent of the principal amount needed to amortize a loan over the term. Divide this constant by 12 to get the advance monthly payment per $100.

Example: The constant needed to amortize an 8% 15 year loan is 11.40 %. The annual debt service for a $50,000 loan is $ 5700.00. Divide by 12 to get the advance monthly payment.

RATE	1 yr	2 yr	3 yr	4 yr	5 yr	6 yr	7 yr	8 yr	9 yr	10 yr	11 yr	12 yr	13 yr	14 yr	15 yr
0.00	100.00	50.00	33.34	25.00	20.00	16.67	14.29	12.50	11.12	10.00	9.10	8.34	7.70	7.15	6.67
1.00	100.46	50.49	33.83	25.50	20.50	17.17	14.79	13.01	11.62	10.51	9.60	8.84	8.20	7.66	7.18
2.00	100.92	50.97	34.32	26.00	21.00	17.68	15.30	13.52	12.14	11.03	10.12	9.37	8.73	8.19	7.71
3.00	101.38	51.45	34.82	26.50	21.51	18.19	15.82	14.05	12.67	11.56	10.66	9.91	9.28	8.74	8.27
4.00	101.85	51.94	35.32	27.01	22.03	18.72	16.35	14.58	13.21	12.11	11.22	10.48	9.85	9.31	8.85
4.25	101.96	52.06	35.44	27.14	22.16	18.85	16.49	14.72	13.35	12.25	11.36	10.62	9.99	9.46	9.00
4.50	102.08	52.19	35.57	27.27	22.29	18.98	16.62	14.86	13.49	12.40	11.50	10.76	10.14	9.61	9.15
4.75	102.19	52.31	35.69	27.40	22.42	19.12	16.76	15.00	13.63	12.54	11.65	10.91	10.29	9.76	9.30
5.00	102.31	52.43	35.82	27.53	22.56	19.25	16.90	15.13	13.77	12.68	11.79	11.06	10.44	9.91	9.46
5.25	102.42	52.56	35.95	27.66	22.69	19.39	17.03	15.27	13.91	12.82	11.94	11.21	10.59	10.06	9.61
5.50	102.54	52.68	36.07	27.79	22.82	19.52	17.17	15.41	14.05	12.97	12.09	11.36	10.74	10.22	9.77
5.75	102.66	52.80	36.20	27.92	22.96	19.66	17.31	15.55	14.20	13.11	12.23	11.51	10.89	10.37	9.92
6.00	102.77	52.93	36.33	28.05	23.09	19.79	17.45	15.70	14.34	13.26	12.38	11.66	11.05	10.53	10.08
6.25	102.89	53.05	36.46	28.18	23.22	19.93	17.59	15.84	14.49	13.41	12.53	11.81	11.20	10.68	10.24
6.50	103.00	53.17	36.59	28.31	23.36	20.07	17.73	15.98	14.63	13.56	12.68	11.96	11.36	10.84	10.40
6.75	103.12	53.30	36.71	28.44	23.49	20.21	17.87	16.13	14.78	13.71	12.84	12.12	11.52	11.00	10.56
7.00	103.23	53.42	36.84	28.57	23.63	20.35	18.01	16.27	14.93	13.86	12.99	12.27	11.67	11.16	10.73
7.25	103.35	53.54	36.97	28.71	23.76	20.48	18.15	16.42	15.07	14.01	13.14	12.43	11.83	11.33	10.89
7.50	103.47	53.67	37.10	28.84	23.90	20.62	18.30	16.56	15.22	14.16	13.30	12.59	11.99	11.49	11.06
7.75	103.58	53.79	37.23	28.97	24.04	20.76	18.44	16.71	15.37	14.31	13.46	12.75	12.16	11.66	11.23
8.00	103.70	53.92	37.36	29.11	24.18	20.91	18.58	16.86	15.52	14.47	13.61	12.91	12.32	11.82	11.40
8.25	103.82	54.04	37.49	29.24	24.31	21.05	18.73	17.01	15.68	14.62	13.77	13.07	12.48	11.99	11.57
8.50	103.93	54.17	37.62	29.37	24.45	21.19	18.88	17.15	15.83	14.78	13.93	13.23	12.65	12.16	11.74
8.75	104.05	54.29	37.75	29.51	24.59	21.33	19.02	17.30	15.98	14.94	14.09	13.40	12.82	12.33	11.91
9.00	104.17	54.42	37.88	29.64	24.73	21.47	19.17	17.45	16.14	15.09	14.25	13.56	12.98	12.50	12.09
9.25	104.28	54.54	38.01	29.78	24.87	21.62	19.32	17.61	16.29	15.25	14.41	13.73	13.15	12.67	12.26
9.50	104.40	54.67	38.14	29.92	25.01	21.76	19.46	17.76	16.45	15.41	14.58	13.89	13.32	12.84	12.44
9.75	104.52	54.80	38.27	30.05	25.15	21.91	19.61	17.91	16.60	15.57	14.74	14.06	13.49	13.02	12.61
10.00	104.63	54.92	38.41	30.19	25.29	22.05	19.76	18.06	16.76	15.73	14.90	14.23	13.67	13.19	12.79
10.25	104.75	55.05	38.54	30.33	25.43	22.20	19.91	18.22	16.92	15.89	15.07	14.40	13.84	13.37	12.97
10.50	104.87	55.17	38.67	30.46	25.57	22.34	20.06	18.37	17.08	16.06	15.24	14.57	14.01	13.55	13.15
10.75	104.98	55.30	38.80	30.60	25.72	22.49	20.21	18.53	17.24	16.22	15.40	14.74	14.19	13.73	13.34
11.00	105.10	55.43	38.93	30.74	25.86	22.64	20.37	18.68	17.40	16.38	15.57	14.91	14.36	13.91	13.52
11.25	105.22	55.55	39.07	30.88	26.00	22.79	20.52	18.84	17.56	16.55	15.74	15.08	14.54	14.09	13.70
11.50	105.33	55.68	39.20	31.01	26.15	22.93	20.67	19.00	17.72	16.72	15.91	15.26	14.72	14.27	13.89
11.75	105.45	55.81	39.33	31.15	26.29	23.08	20.82	19.16	17.88	16.88	16.08	15.43	14.90	14.45	14.08
12.00	105.57	55.93	39.47	31.29	26.43	23.23	20.98	19.32	18.05	17.05	16.26	15.61	15.08	14.64	14.26
12.25	105.69	56.06	39.60	31.43	26.58	23.38	21.13	19.47	18.21	17.22	16.43	15.79	15.26	14.82	14.45
12.50	105.80	56.19	39.74	31.57	26.72	23.53	21.29	19.64	18.37	17.39	16.60	15.97	15.44	15.01	14.64
12.75	105.92	56.32	39.87	31.71	26.87	23.68	21.44	19.80	18.54	17.56	16.78	16.14	15.62	15.19	14.83
13.00	106.04	56.44	40.00	31.85	27.02	23.84	21.60	19.96	18.71	17.73	16.95	16.32	15.81	15.38	15.03
13.25	106.15	56.57	40.14	31.99	27.16	23.99	21.76	20.12	18.87	17.90	17.13	16.50	15.99	15.57	15.22
13.50	106.27	56.70	40.27	32.14	27.31	24.14	21.92	20.28	19.04	18.07	17.31	16.69	16.18	15.76	15.41
13.75	106.39	56.83	40.41	32.28	27.46	24.29	22.07	20.45	19.21	18.25	17.48	16.87	16.37	15.95	15.61
14.00	106.51	56.96	40.55	32.42	27.60	24.45	22.23	20.61	19.38	18.42	17.66	17.05	16.55	16.14	15.80
14.25	106.62	57.08	40.68	32.56	27.75	24.60	22.39	20.78	19.55	18.60	17.84	17.24	16.74	16.34	16.00
14.50	106.74	57.21	40.82	32.70	27.90	24.76	22.55	20.94	19.72	18.77	18.02	17.42	16.93	16.53	16.20
14.75	106.86	57.34	40.95	32.85	28.05	24.91	22.71	21.11	19.89	18.95	18.20	17.61	17.12	16.72	16.39
15.00	106.98	57.47	41.09	32.99	28.20	25.07	22.88	21.27	20.06	19.13	18.39	17.79	17.31	16.92	16.59
15.25	107.10	57.60	41.23	33.13	28.35	25.22	23.04	21.44	20.24	19.30	18.57	17.98	17.50	17.11	16.79
15.50	107.21	57.73	41.36	33.28	28.50	25.38	23.20	21.61	20.41	19.48	18.75	18.17	17.70	17.31	16.99
15.75	107.33	57.86	41.50	33.42	28.65	25.54	23.36	21.78	20.58	19.66	18.94	18.36	17.89	17.51	17.20
16.00	107.45	57.99	41.64	33.57	28.80	25.69	23.53	21.95	20.76	19.84	19.12	18.55	18.08	17.71	17.40
16.25	107.57	58.12	41.78	33.71	28.95	25.85	23.69	22.12	20.93	20.02	19.31	18.74	18.28	17.91	17.60
16.50	107.69	58.25	41.91	33.86	29.11	26.01	23.85	22.29	21.11	20.20	19.49	18.93	18.48	18.11	17.80
16.75	107.80	58.38	42.05	34.00	29.26	26.17	24.02	22.46	21.29	20.39	19.68	19.12	18.67	18.31	18.01
17.00	107.92	58.51	42.19	34.15	29.41	26.33	24.19	22.63	21.46	20.57	19.87	19.31	18.87	18.51	18.22
17.25	108.04	58.64	42.33	34.29	29.56	26.49	24.35	22.80	21.64	20.75	20.06	19.51	19.07	18.71	18.42
17.50	108.16	58.77	42.47	34.44	29.72	26.65	24.52	22.98	21.82	20.94	20.25	19.70	19.27	18.91	18.63
17.75	108.28	58.90	42.61	34.59	29.87	26.81	24.69	23.15	22.00	21.12	20.44	19.90	19.47	19.12	18.84
18.00	108.40	59.03	42.75	34.73	30.03	26.97	24.85	23.32	22.18	21.31	20.63	20.09	19.67	19.32	19.04
18.25	108.51	59.16	42.89	34.88	30.18	27.13	25.02	23.50	22.36	21.49	20.82	20.29	19.87	19.53	19.25
18.50	108.63	59.29	43.03	35.03	30.34	27.29	25.19	23.67	22.54	21.68	21.01	20.49	20.07	19.73	19.46
18.75	108.75	59.42	43.17	35.18	30.49	27.46	25.36	23.85	22.72	21.87	21.21	20.68	20.27	19.94	19.67
19.00	108.87	59.55	43.31	35.33	30.65	27.62	25.53	24.03	22.91	22.06	21.40	20.88	20.47	20.15	19.88
20.00	109.34	60.08	43.87	35.92	31.28	28.28	26.22	24.74	23.64	22.82	22.18	21.68	21.29	20.98	20.74
25.00	111.73	62.74	46.74	38.98	34.51	31.67	29.76	28.42	27.46	26.75	26.22	25.82	25.52	25.29	25.11
30.00	114.14	65.46	49.70	42.16	37.88	35.23	33.48	32.29	31.46	30.87	30.44	30.13	29.91	29.74	29.62

CONSTANT ANNUAL PERCENT

MONTHLY PAYMENT, IN ADVANCE

Description: This table shows the percent of the principal amount needed to amortize a loan over the term. Divide this constant by 12 to get the advance monthly payment per $100.

Example: The constant needed to amortize an 8% 30 year loan is 8.75 %. The annual debt service for a $50,000 loan is $ 4375.00. Divide by 12 to get the advance monthly payment.

RATE	16 yr	17 yr	18 yr	19 yr	20 yr	21 yr	22 yr	23 yr	24 yr	25 yr	26 yr	27 yr	28 yr	29 yr	30 yr
0.00	6.25	5.89	5.56	5.27	5.00	4.77	4.55	4.35	4.17	4.00	3.85	3.71	3.58	3.45	3.34
1.00	6.77	6.40	6.07	5.78	5.52	5.28	5.07	4.87	4.69	4.52	4.37	4.23	4.10	3.98	3.86
2.00	7.30	6.94	6.61	6.33	6.07	5.83	5.62	5.42	5.25	5.08	4.93	4.79	4.66	4.54	4.43
3.00	7.86	7.50	7.18	6.90	6.64	6.41	6.20	6.01	5.84	5.68	5.53	5.40	5.28	5.16	5.05
4.00	8.45	8.09	7.78	7.50	7.25	7.03	6.82	6.64	6.47	6.32	6.18	6.05	5.93	5.82	5.71
4.25	8.60	8.25	7.94	7.66	7.41	7.19	6.98	6.80	6.64	6.48	6.34	6.22	6.10	5.99	5.89
4.50	8.75	8.40	8.09	7.81	7.57	7.35	7.15	6.97	6.80	6.65	6.51	6.39	6.27	6.16	6.06
4.75	8.90	8.56	8.25	7.97	7.73	7.51	7.31	7.13	6.97	6.82	6.68	6.56	6.44	6.34	6.24
5.00	9.06	8.71	8.41	8.13	7.89	7.67	7.48	7.30	7.14	6.99	6.86	6.73	6.62	6.52	6.42
5.25	9.22	8.87	8.57	8.30	8.06	7.84	7.65	7.47	7.31	7.16	7.03	6.91	6.80	6.70	6.60
5.50	9.37	9.03	8.73	8.46	8.22	8.01	7.82	7.64	7.48	7.34	7.21	7.09	6.98	6.88	6.79
5.75	9.53	9.19	8.89	8.63	8.39	8.18	7.99	7.82	7.66	7.52	7.39	7.27	7.16	7.07	6.97
6.00	9.69	9.36	9.06	8.79	8.56	8.35	8.16	7.99	7.84	7.70	7.57	7.46	7.35	7.25	7.16
6.25	9.86	9.52	9.22	8.96	8.73	8.52	8.34	8.17	8.02	7.88	7.76	7.64	7.54	7.44	7.36
6.50	10.02	9.69	9.39	9.13	8.90	8.70	8.51	8.35	8.20	8.06	7.94	7.83	7.73	7.63	7.55
6.75	10.18	9.85	9.56	9.31	9.08	8.88	8.69	8.53	8.38	8.25	8.13	8.02	7.92	7.83	7.74
7.00	10.35	10.02	9.73	9.48	9.25	9.05	8.87	8.71	8.57	8.44	8.32	8.21	8.11	8.02	7.94
7.25	10.52	10.19	9.91	9.66	9.43	9.23	9.06	8.90	8.76	8.63	8.51	8.40	8.31	8.22	8.14
7.50	10.69	10.36	10.08	9.83	9.61	9.42	9.24	9.08	8.94	8.82	8.70	8.60	8.51	8.42	8.34
7.75	10.86	10.54	10.26	10.01	9.79	9.60	9.43	9.27	9.14	9.01	8.90	8.80	8.71	8.62	8.55
8.00	11.03	10.71	10.44	10.19	9.98	9.78	9.62	9.46	9.33	9.21	9.10	9.00	8.91	8.83	8.75
8.25	11.20	10.89	10.61	10.37	10.16	9.97	9.80	9.66	9.52	9.40	9.29	9.20	9.11	9.03	8.96
8.50	11.38	11.07	10.79	10.56	10.35	10.16	10.00	9.85	9.72	9.60	9.49	9.40	9.31	9.24	9.17
8.75	11.55	11.24	10.98	10.74	10.53	10.35	10.19	10.04	9.91	9.80	9.70	9.60	9.52	9.44	9.38
9.00	11.73	11.42	11.16	10.93	10.72	10.54	10.38	10.24	10.11	10.00	9.90	9.81	9.73	9.65	9.59
9.25	11.91	11.61	11.34	11.11	10.91	10.73	10.58	10.44	10.31	10.20	10.10	10.02	9.94	9.87	9.80
9.50	12.09	11.79	11.53	11.30	11.10	10.93	10.77	10.64	10.52	10.41	10.31	10.22	10.15	10.08	10.02
9.75	12.27	11.97	11.72	11.49	11.30	11.12	10.97	10.84	10.72	10.61	10.52	10.43	10.36	10.29	10.23
10.00	12.45	12.16	11.90	11.68	11.49	11.32	11.17	11.04	10.92	10.82	10.73	10.65	10.57	10.51	10.45
10.25	12.64	12.34	12.09	11.88	11.68	11.52	11.37	11.24	11.13	11.03	10.94	10.86	10.79	10.72	10.67
10.50	12.82	12.53	12.28	12.07	11.88	11.72	11.57	11.45	11.34	11.24	11.15	11.07	11.00	10.94	10.89
10.75	13.01	12.72	12.48	12.26	12.08	11.92	11.78	11.65	11.54	11.45	11.36	11.29	11.22	11.16	11.11
11.00	13.19	12.91	12.67	12.46	12.28	12.12	11.98	11.86	11.75	11.66	11.58	11.50	11.44	11.38	11.33
11.25	13.38	13.10	12.86	12.66	12.48	12.32	12.19	12.07	11.96	11.87	11.79	11.72	11.66	11.60	11.55
11.50	13.57	13.29	13.06	12.86	12.68	12.53	12.39	12.28	12.18	12.09	12.01	11.94	11.88	11.82	11.78
11.75	13.76	13.49	13.26	13.06	12.88	12.73	12.60	12.49	12.39	12.30	12.23	12.16	12.10	12.05	12.00
12.00	13.95	13.68	13.45	13.26	13.09	12.94	12.81	12.70	12.60	12.52	12.44	12.38	12.32	12.27	12.23
12.25	14.14	13.88	13.65	13.46	13.29	13.15	13.02	12.91	12.82	12.74	12.66	12.60	12.54	12.50	12.45
12.50	14.34	14.08	13.85	13.66	13.50	13.36	13.23	13.13	13.04	12.95	12.88	12.82	12.77	12.72	12.68
12.75	14.53	14.27	14.05	13.87	13.71	13.57	13.45	13.34	13.25	13.17	13.11	13.05	12.99	12.95	12.91
13.00	14.73	14.47	14.26	14.07	13.91	13.78	13.66	13.56	13.47	13.39	13.33	13.27	13.22	13.18	13.14
13.25	14.92	14.67	14.46	14.28	14.12	13.99	13.87	13.78	13.69	13.62	13.55	13.49	13.45	13.40	13.37
13.50	15.12	14.87	14.66	14.48	14.33	14.20	14.09	13.99	13.91	13.84	13.77	13.72	13.67	13.63	13.60
13.75	15.32	15.07	14.87	14.69	14.54	14.42	14.31	14.21	14.13	14.06	14.00	13.95	13.90	13.86	13.83
14.00	15.52	15.28	15.07	14.90	14.76	14.63	14.52	14.43	14.35	14.28	14.22	14.17	14.13	14.09	14.06
14.25	15.72	15.48	15.28	15.11	14.97	14.85	14.74	14.65	14.57	14.51	14.45	14.40	14.36	14.32	14.29
14.50	15.92	15.68	15.49	15.32	15.18	15.06	14.96	14.87	14.80	14.73	14.68	14.63	14.59	14.55	14.52
14.75	16.12	15.89	15.70	15.53	15.40	15.28	15.18	15.09	15.02	14.96	14.91	14.86	14.82	14.79	14.76
15.00	16.32	16.10	15.91	15.75	15.61	15.50	15.40	15.32	15.25	15.19	15.13	15.09	15.05	15.02	14.99
15.25	16.53	16.30	16.12	15.96	15.83	15.72	15.62	15.54	15.47	15.41	15.36	15.32	15.28	15.25	15.23
15.50	16.73	16.51	16.33	16.17	16.04	15.93	15.84	15.76	15.70	15.64	15.59	15.55	15.52	15.49	15.46
15.75	16.94	16.72	16.54	16.39	16.26	16.16	16.06	15.99	15.92	15.87	15.82	15.78	15.75	15.72	15.69
16.00	17.14	16.93	16.75	16.60	16.48	16.38	16.29	16.21	16.15	16.10	16.05	16.01	15.98	15.95	15.93
16.25	17.35	17.14	16.97	16.82	16.70	16.60	16.51	16.44	16.38	16.33	16.28	16.25	16.21	16.19	16.17
16.50	17.56	17.35	17.18	17.04	16.92	16.82	16.74	16.67	16.61	16.56	16.51	16.48	16.45	16.42	16.40
16.75	17.76	17.56	17.40	17.26	17.14	17.04	16.96	16.89	16.84	16.79	16.75	16.71	16.68	16.66	16.64
17.00	17.97	17.78	17.61	17.47	17.36	17.27	17.19	17.12	17.06	17.02	16.98	16.95	16.92	16.89	16.87
17.25	18.18	17.99	17.83	17.69	17.58	17.49	17.41	17.35	17.29	17.25	17.21	17.18	17.15	17.13	17.11
17.50	18.39	18.20	18.04	17.91	17.80	17.71	17.64	17.58	17.52	17.48	17.44	17.41	17.39	17.37	17.35
17.75	18.61	18.42	18.26	18.13	18.03	17.94	17.87	17.81	17.75	17.71	17.68	17.65	17.62	17.60	17.59
18.00	18.82	18.63	18.48	18.35	18.25	18.17	18.09	18.04	17.99	17.95	17.91	17.88	17.86	17.84	17.82
18.25	19.03	18.85	18.70	18.58	18.48	18.39	18.32	18.26	18.22	18.18	18.15	18.12	18.10	18.08	18.06
18.50	19.24	19.06	18.92	18.80	18.70	18.62	18.55	18.50	18.45	18.41	18.38	18.35	18.33	18.31	18.30
18.75	19.46	19.28	19.14	19.02	18.92	18.85	18.78	18.73	18.68	18.64	18.61	18.59	18.57	18.55	18.54
19.00	19.67	19.50	19.36	19.24	19.15	19.07	19.01	18.96	18.91	18.88	18.85	18.82	18.80	18.79	18.77
20.00	20.54	20.38	20.25	20.14	20.06	19.99	19.93	19.88	19.85	19.82	19.79	19.77	19.75	19.74	19.73
25.00	24.97	24.87	24.78	24.72	24.67	24.63	24.60	24.58	24.56	24.55	24.53	24.53	24.52	24.51	24.51
30.00	29.53	29.46	29.42	29.38	29.35	29.33	29.32	29.31	29.30	29.29	29.29	29.28	29.28	29.28	29.28

CONSTANT ANNUAL PERCENT

QUARTERLY PAYMENT, IN ADVANCE

Description: This table shows the percent of the principal amount needed to amortize a loan over the term. Divide this constant by 4 to get the advance quarter payment per $100.

Example: The constant needed to amortize an 8% 15 year loan is 11.29 %. The annual debt service for a $50,000 loan is $ 5645.00. Divide by 4 to get the advance quarter payment.

RATE	1 yr	2 yr	3 yr	4 yr	5 yr	6 yr	7 yr	8 yr	9 yr	10 yr	11 yr	12 yr	13 yr	14 yr	15 yr
0.00	100.00	50.00	33.34	25.00	20.00	16.67	14.29	12.50	11.12	10.00	9.10	8.34	7.70	7.15	6.67
1.00	100.38	50.44	33.80	25.48	20.48	17.15	14.78	12.99	11.61	10.50	9.59	8.84	8.20	7.65	7.17
2.00	100.75	50.88	34.26	25.95	20.97	17.65	15.27	13.50	12.11	11.01	10.10	9.35	8.72	8.17	7.70
3.00	101.13	51.32	34.73	26.43	21.46	18.14	15.78	14.01	12.63	11.53	10.63	9.88	9.25	8.72	8.25
4.00	101.50	51.76	35.19	26.91	21.95	18.65	16.29	14.53	13.16	12.07	11.18	10.43	9.81	9.28	8.81
4.25	101.60	51.87	35.31	27.04	22.08	18.78	16.42	14.66	13.29	12.20	11.31	10.57	9.95	9.42	8.96
4.50	101.69	51.98	35.43	27.16	22.20	18.90	16.55	14.79	13.43	12.34	11.45	10.72	10.09	9.56	9.11
4.75	101.78	52.10	35.54	27.28	22.33	19.03	16.68	14.93	13.56	12.48	11.59	10.86	10.24	9.71	9.25
5.00	101.88	52.21	35.66	27.40	22.45	19.16	16.81	15.06	13.70	12.62	11.73	11.00	10.38	9.86	9.40
5.25	101.97	52.32	35.78	27.52	22.58	19.29	16.95	15.19	13.84	12.76	11.87	11.14	10.53	10.01	9.55
5.50	102.06	52.43	35.90	27.65	22.71	19.42	17.08	15.33	13.97	12.90	12.02	11.29	10.68	10.15	9.71
5.75	102.16	52.54	36.02	27.77	22.83	19.55	17.21	15.47	14.11	13.04	12.16	11.43	10.82	10.30	9.86
6.00	102.25	52.65	36.14	27.89	22.96	19.68	17.35	15.60	14.25	13.18	12.30	11.58	10.97	10.46	10.01
6.25	102.34	52.76	36.25	28.02	23.09	19.81	17.48	15.74	14.39	13.32	12.45	11.73	11.12	10.61	10.17
6.50	102.44	52.87	36.37	28.14	23.21	19.94	17.61	15.88	14.53	13.46	12.60	11.88	11.28	10.76	10.32
6.75	102.53	52.98	36.49	28.26	23.34	20.07	17.75	16.01	14.67	13.61	12.74	12.03	11.43	10.92	10.48
7.00	102.62	53.09	36.61	28.39	23.47	20.21	17.88	16.15	14.82	13.75	12.89	12.18	11.58	11.07	10.64
7.25	102.72	53.20	36.73	28.51	23.60	20.34	18.02	16.29	14.96	13.90	13.04	12.33	11.74	11.23	10.80
7.50	102.81	53.32	36.85	28.64	23.73	20.47	18.16	16.43	15.10	14.05	13.19	12.48	11.89	11.39	10.96
7.75	102.90	53.43	36.97	28.76	23.86	20.60	18.29	16.57	15.25	14.19	13.34	12.64	12.05	11.55	11.12
8.00	102.99	53.54	37.09	28.89	23.99	20.74	18.43	16.72	15.39	14.34	13.49	12.79	12.20	11.71	11.29
8.25	103.09	53.65	37.21	29.01	24.12	20.87	18.57	16.86	15.54	14.49	13.64	12.95	12.36	11.87	11.45
8.50	103.18	53.76	37.33	29.14	24.25	21.01	18.71	17.00	15.68	14.64	13.80	13.10	12.52	12.03	11.62
8.75	103.27	53.87	37.45	29.26	24.38	21.14	18.85	17.14	15.83	14.79	13.95	13.26	12.68	12.20	11.78
9.00	103.37	53.98	37.57	29.39	24.51	21.28	18.99	17.29	15.98	14.94	14.10	13.42	12.84	12.36	11.95
9.25	103.46	54.10	37.69	29.52	24.64	21.41	19.13	17.43	16.12	15.09	14.26	13.57	13.01	12.53	12.12
9.50	103.55	54.21	37.81	29.64	24.77	21.55	19.27	17.57	16.27	15.24	14.41	13.73	13.17	12.69	12.29
9.75	103.65	54.32	37.93	29.77	24.91	21.69	19.41	17.72	16.42	15.40	14.57	13.89	13.33	12.86	12.46
10.00	103.74	54.43	38.05	29.90	25.04	21.82	19.55	17.87	16.57	15.55	14.73	14.06	13.50	13.03	12.63
10.25	103.83	54.54	38.17	30.02	25.17	21.96	19.69	18.01	16.72	15.71	14.89	14.22	13.66	13.20	12.80
10.50	103.92	54.66	38.29	30.15	25.30	22.10	19.84	18.16	16.87	15.86	15.05	14.38	13.83	13.37	12.98
10.75	104.02	54.77	38.41	30.28	25.44	22.24	19.98	18.31	17.02	16.02	15.21	14.54	14.00	13.54	13.15
11.00	104.11	54.88	38.53	30.41	25.57	22.38	20.12	18.45	17.18	16.17	15.37	14.71	14.17	13.71	13.33
11.25	104.20	54.99	38.65	30.54	25.70	22.52	20.27	18.60	17.33	16.33	15.53	14.87	14.33	13.88	13.50
11.50	104.30	55.10	38.78	30.66	25.84	22.66	20.41	18.75	17.48	16.49	15.69	15.04	14.50	14.06	13.68
11.75	104.39	55.22	38.90	30.79	25.97	22.80	20.56	18.90	17.64	16.65	15.85	15.21	14.68	14.23	13.86
12.00	104.48	55.33	39.02	30.92	26.11	22.94	20.70	19.05	17.79	16.81	16.02	15.38	14.85	14.41	14.04
12.25	104.57	55.44	39.14	31.05	26.24	23.08	20.85	19.20	17.95	16.97	16.18	15.54	15.02	14.58	14.22
12.50	104.67	55.55	39.26	31.18	26.38	23.22	20.99	19.35	18.10	17.13	16.35	15.71	15.19	14.76	14.40
12.75	104.76	55.66	39.39	31.31	26.51	23.36	21.14	19.51	18.26	17.29	16.51	15.88	15.37	14.94	14.58
13.00	104.85	55.78	39.51	31.44	26.65	23.50	21.29	19.66	18.42	17.45	16.68	16.05	15.54	15.12	14.76
13.25	104.95	55.89	39.63	31.57	26.79	23.64	21.43	19.81	18.58	17.61	16.84	16.22	15.72	15.30	14.94
13.50	105.04	56.00	39.75	31.70	26.92	23.79	21.58	19.96	18.73	17.77	17.01	16.40	15.89	15.48	15.13
13.75	105.13	56.12	39.88	31.83	27.06	23.93	21.73	20.12	18.89	17.94	17.18	16.57	16.07	15.66	15.31
14.00	105.22	56.23	40.00	31.96	27.20	24.07	21.88	20.27	19.05	18.10	17.35	16.74	16.25	15.84	15.50
14.25	105.32	56.34	40.12	32.09	27.34	24.22	22.03	20.43	19.21	18.27	17.52	16.92	16.42	16.02	15.68
14.50	105.41	56.45	40.24	32.22	27.47	24.36	22.18	20.58	19.37	18.43	17.69	17.09	16.60	16.20	15.87
14.75	105.50	56.57	40.37	32.35	27.61	24.50	22.33	20.74	19.53	18.60	17.86	17.27	16.78	16.39	16.06
15.00	105.59	56.68	40.49	32.48	27.75	24.65	22.48	20.89	19.69	18.77	18.03	17.44	16.96	16.57	16.25
15.25	105.69	56.79	40.62	32.62	27.89	24.79	22.63	21.05	19.86	18.93	18.20	17.62	17.14	16.76	16.44
15.50	105.78	56.90	40.74	32.75	28.03	24.94	22.78	21.21	20.02	19.10	18.38	17.80	17.33	16.94	16.62
15.75	105.87	57.02	40.86	32.88	28.17	25.08	22.93	21.37	20.18	19.27	18.55	17.97	17.51	17.13	16.81
16.00	105.96	57.13	40.99	33.01	28.31	25.23	23.09	21.52	20.35	19.44	18.72	18.15	17.69	17.31	17.01
16.25	106.06	57.24	41.11	33.15	28.45	25.38	23.24	21.68	20.51	19.61	18.90	18.33	17.87	17.50	17.20
16.50	106.15	57.36	41.23	33.28	28.59	25.52	23.39	21.84	20.67	19.78	19.07	18.51	18.06	17.69	17.39
16.75	106.24	57.47	41.36	33.41	28.73	25.67	23.55	22.00	20.84	19.95	19.25	18.69	18.24	17.88	17.58
17.00	106.33	57.58	41.48	33.54	28.87	25.82	23.70	22.16	21.01	20.12	19.42	18.87	18.43	18.07	17.77
17.25	106.42	57.70	41.61	33.68	29.01	25.97	23.85	22.32	21.17	20.29	19.60	19.05	18.61	18.26	17.97
17.50	106.52	57.81	41.73	33.81	29.15	26.11	24.01	22.48	21.34	20.46	19.78	19.23	18.80	18.45	18.16
17.75	106.61	57.92	41.86	33.94	29.29	26.26	24.16	22.64	21.50	20.63	19.95	19.42	18.99	18.64	18.36
18.00	106.70	58.04	41.98	34.08	29.43	26.41	24.32	22.80	21.67	20.81	20.13	19.60	19.17	18.83	18.55
18.25	106.79	58.15	42.11	34.21	29.57	26.56	24.47	22.97	21.84	20.98	20.31	19.78	19.36	19.02	18.75
18.50	106.89	58.26	42.23	34.35	29.72	26.71	24.63	23.13	22.01	21.15	20.49	19.97	19.55	19.21	18.94
18.75	106.98	58.38	42.36	34.48	29.86	26.86	24.79	23.29	22.18	21.33	20.67	20.15	19.74	19.41	19.14
19.00	107.07	58.49	42.48	34.62	30.00	27.01	24.94	23.45	22.35	21.50	20.85	20.33	19.93	19.60	19.34
20.00	107.44	58.95	42.99	35.16	30.57	27.61	25.58	24.11	23.03	22.21	21.57	21.08	20.69	20.38	20.13
25.00	109.27	61.23	45.53	37.90	33.50	30.70	28.81	27.48	26.52	25.82	25.29	24.89	24.59	24.35	24.13
30.00	111.10	63.53	48.11	40.71	36.50	33.88	32.16	30.97	30.14	29.55	29.12	28.81	28.58	28.41	28.28

CONSTANT ANNUAL PERCENT

QUARTERLY PAYMENT, IN ADVANCE

Description: This table shows the percent of the principal amount needed to amortize a loan over the term. Divide this constant by 4 to get the advance quarter payment per $100.

Example: The constant needed to amortize an 8% 30 year loan is 8.65 %. The annual debt service for a $50,000 loan is $ 4325.00. Divide by 4 to get the advance quarter payment.

RATE	16 yr	17 yr	18 yr	19 yr	20 yr	21 yr	22 yr	23 yr	24 yr	25 yr	26 yr	27 yr	28 yr	29 yr	30 yr
0.00	6.25	5.89	5.56	5.27	5.00	4.77	4.55	4.35	4.17	4.00	3.85	3.71	3.58	3.45	3.34
1.00	6.76	6.39	6.07	5.78	5.51	5.28	5.06	4.87	4.69	4.52	4.37	4.23	4.09	3.97	3.86
2.00	7.29	6.92	6.60	6.31	6.05	5.82	5.61	5.41	5.24	5.07	4.92	4.78	4.65	4.54	4.42
3.00	7.84	7.48	7.16	6.88	6.62	6.39	6.18	5.99	5.82	5.66	5.52	5.38	5.26	5.14	5.03
4.00	8.41	8.06	7.75	7.47	7.22	7.00	6.79	6.61	6.44	6.29	6.15	6.02	5.90	5.79	5.69
4.25	8.56	8.21	7.90	7.62	7.37	7.15	6.95	6.77	6.60	6.45	6.31	6.18	6.07	5.96	5.86
4.50	8.71	8.36	8.05	7.78	7.53	7.31	7.11	6.93	6.76	6.61	6.48	6.35	6.23	6.13	6.03
4.75	8.86	8.51	8.20	7.93	7.69	7.47	7.27	7.09	6.93	6.78	6.64	6.52	6.41	6.30	6.20
5.00	9.01	8.66	8.36	8.09	7.85	7.63	7.43	7.26	7.09	6.95	6.81	6.69	6.58	6.47	6.38
5.25	9.16	8.82	8.52	8.25	8.01	7.79	7.60	7.42	7.26	7.12	6.99	6.86	6.75	6.65	6.56
5.50	9.32	8.97	8.67	8.41	8.17	7.95	7.76	7.59	7.43	7.29	7.16	7.04	6.93	6.83	6.74
5.75	9.47	9.13	8.83	8.57	8.33	8.12	7.93	7.76	7.60	7.46	7.33	7.22	7.11	7.01	6.92
6.00	9.63	9.29	8.99	8.73	8.50	8.29	8.10	7.93	7.78	7.64	7.51	7.40	7.29	7.19	7.11
6.25	9.78	9.45	9.16	8.90	8.66	8.46	8.27	8.10	7.95	7.82	7.69	7.58	7.47	7.38	7.29
6.50	9.94	9.61	9.32	9.06	8.83	8.63	8.44	8.28	8.13	8.00	7.87	7.76	7.66	7.57	7.48
6.75	10.10	9.77	9.48	9.23	9.00	8.80	8.62	8.46	8.31	8.18	8.06	7.95	7.85	7.76	7.67
7.00	10.26	9.94	9.65	9.40	9.17	8.97	8.79	8.63	8.49	8.36	8.24	8.13	8.04	7.95	7.86
7.25	10.43	10.10	9.82	9.57	9.35	9.15	8.97	8.81	8.67	8.54	8.43	8.32	8.23	8.14	8.06
7.50	10.59	10.27	9.99	9.74	9.52	9.32	9.15	8.99	8.85	8.73	8.61	8.51	8.42	8.33	8.25
7.75	10.76	10.44	10.16	9.91	9.70	9.50	9.33	9.18	9.04	8.92	8.80	8.70	8.61	8.53	8.45
8.00	10.92	10.61	10.33	10.09	9.87	9.68	9.51	9.36	9.23	9.10	8.99	8.90	8.81	8.72	8.65
8.25	11.09	10.78	10.50	10.26	10.05	9.86	9.70	9.55	9.41	9.29	9.19	9.09	9.00	8.92	8.85
8.50	11.26	10.95	10.68	10.44	10.23	10.04	9.88	9.73	9.60	9.49	9.38	9.29	9.20	9.12	9.05
8.75	11.43	11.12	10.85	10.62	10.41	10.23	10.07	9.92	9.79	9.68	9.58	9.48	9.40	9.33	9.26
9.00	11.60	11.29	11.03	10.80	10.59	10.41	10.25	10.11	9.99	9.87	9.77	9.68	9.60	9.53	9.46
9.25	11.77	11.47	11.21	10.98	10.78	10.60	10.44	10.30	10.18	10.07	9.97	9.88	9.80	9.73	9.67
9.50	11.94	11.64	11.38	11.16	10.96	10.79	10.63	10.50	10.37	10.27	10.17	10.08	10.01	9.94	9.87
9.75	12.12	11.82	11.56	11.34	11.15	10.97	10.82	10.69	10.57	10.46	10.37	10.29	10.21	10.14	10.08
10.00	12.29	12.00	11.75	11.52	11.33	11.16	11.01	10.88	10.77	10.66	10.57	10.49	10.42	10.35	10.29
10.25	12.47	12.18	11.93	11.71	11.52	11.35	11.21	11.08	10.96	10.86	10.77	10.69	10.62	10.56	10.50
10.50	12.64	12.36	12.11	11.90	11.71	11.55	11.40	11.28	11.16	11.07	10.98	10.90	10.83	10.77	10.71
10.75	12.82	12.54	12.29	12.08	11.90	11.74	11.60	11.47	11.36	11.27	11.18	11.11	11.04	10.98	10.93
11.00	13.00	12.72	12.48	12.27	12.09	11.93	11.79	11.67	11.57	11.47	11.39	11.31	11.25	11.19	11.14
11.25	13.18	12.90	12.67	12.46	12.28	12.13	11.99	11.87	11.77	11.68	11.59	11.52	11.46	11.40	11.35
11.50	13.36	13.09	12.85	12.65	12.48	12.32	12.19	12.07	11.97	11.88	11.80	11.73	11.67	11.62	11.57
11.75	13.54	13.27	13.04	12.84	12.67	12.52	12.39	12.27	12.18	12.09	12.01	11.94	11.88	11.83	11.78
12.00	13.72	13.46	13.23	13.03	12.86	12.72	12.59	12.48	12.38	12.29	12.22	12.15	12.10	12.05	12.00
12.25	13.91	13.64	13.42	13.23	13.06	12.92	12.79	12.68	12.59	12.50	12.43	12.37	12.31	12.26	12.22
12.50	14.09	13.83	13.61	13.42	13.26	13.11	12.99	12.89	12.79	12.71	12.64	12.58	12.53	12.48	12.44
12.75	14.28	14.02	13.80	13.61	13.45	13.32	13.19	13.09	13.00	12.92	12.85	12.79	12.74	12.69	12.65
13.00	14.46	14.21	13.99	13.81	13.65	13.52	13.40	13.30	13.21	13.13	13.07	13.01	12.96	12.91	12.87
13.25	14.65	14.40	14.19	14.01	13.85	13.72	13.60	13.50	13.42	13.34	13.28	13.22	13.17	13.13	13.09
13.50	14.84	14.59	14.38	14.20	14.05	13.92	13.81	13.71	13.63	13.55	13.49	13.44	13.39	13.35	13.31
13.75	15.02	14.78	14.58	14.40	14.25	14.12	14.01	13.92	13.84	13.77	13.71	13.65	13.61	13.57	13.53
14.00	15.21	14.97	14.77	14.60	14.45	14.33	14.22	14.13	14.05	13.98	13.92	13.87	13.82	13.79	13.75
14.25	15.40	15.17	14.97	14.80	14.66	14.53	14.43	14.34	14.26	14.19	14.14	14.09	14.04	14.01	13.97
14.50	15.59	15.36	15.17	15.00	14.86	14.74	14.64	14.55	14.47	14.41	14.35	14.30	14.26	14.23	14.20
14.75	15.79	15.56	15.36	15.20	15.06	14.94	14.84	14.76	14.68	14.62	14.57	14.52	14.48	14.45	14.42
15.00	15.98	15.75	15.56	15.40	15.27	15.15	15.05	14.97	14.90	14.84	14.78	14.74	14.70	14.67	14.64
15.25	16.17	15.95	15.76	15.60	15.47	15.36	15.26	15.18	15.11	15.05	15.00	14.96	14.92	14.89	14.86
15.50	16.36	16.14	15.96	15.81	15.68	15.57	15.47	15.39	15.33	15.27	15.22	15.18	15.14	15.11	15.08
15.75	16.56	16.34	16.16	16.01	15.88	15.77	15.68	15.61	15.54	15.48	15.44	15.40	15.36	15.33	15.31
16.00	16.75	16.54	16.36	16.21	16.09	15.98	15.89	15.82	15.75	15.70	15.65	15.62	15.58	15.55	15.53
16.25	16.95	16.74	16.56	16.42	16.29	16.19	16.10	16.03	15.97	15.92	15.87	15.84	15.80	15.78	15.75
16.50	17.14	16.94	16.76	16.62	16.50	16.40	16.32	16.25	16.19	16.13	16.09	16.06	16.02	16.00	15.98
16.75	17.34	17.13	16.97	16.83	16.71	16.61	16.53	16.46	16.40	16.35	16.31	16.28	16.25	16.22	16.20
17.00	17.53	17.33	17.17	17.03	16.92	16.82	16.74	16.67	16.62	16.57	16.53	16.50	16.47	16.44	16.42
17.25	17.73	17.53	17.37	17.24	17.13	17.03	16.95	16.89	16.83	16.79	16.75	16.72	16.69	16.67	16.65
17.50	17.93	17.74	17.58	17.44	17.34	17.24	17.17	17.10	17.05	17.01	16.97	16.94	16.91	16.89	16.87
17.75	18.13	17.94	17.78	17.65	17.54	17.46	17.38	17.32	17.27	17.22	17.19	17.16	17.13	17.11	17.09
18.00	18.33	18.14	17.99	17.86	17.75	17.67	17.60	17.54	17.49	17.44	17.41	17.38	17.36	17.33	17.32
18.25	18.52	18.34	18.19	18.07	17.96	17.88	17.81	17.75	17.70	17.66	17.63	17.60	17.58	17.56	17.54
18.50	18.72	18.54	18.40	18.28	18.18	18.09	18.02	17.97	17.92	17.88	17.85	17.82	17.80	17.78	17.77
18.75	18.92	18.75	18.60	18.48	18.39	18.31	18.24	18.18	18.14	18.10	18.07	18.04	18.02	18.00	17.99
19.00	19.12	18.95	18.81	18.69	18.60	18.52	18.45	18.40	18.36	18.32	18.29	18.27	18.24	18.23	18.21
20.00	19.93	19.77	19.64	19.53	19.44	19.37	19.32	19.27	19.23	19.20	19.17	19.15	19.13	19.12	19.11
25.00	24.03	23.92	23.84	23.77	23.72	23.68	23.65	23.62	23.60	23.59	23.58	23.57	23.56	23.56	23.55
30.00	28.19	28.12	28.07	28.03	28.00	27.98	27.96	27.95	27.94	27.93	27.93	27.92	27.92	27.92	27.92

TABLE **2**

Debt Service

Interest Rates:	0, 1, 2, 3%; 4 to 19% by .25%; 20, 25, 30%.
Terms:	1 to 30 years, each year.
Payments:	Monthly and quarterly.

This table shows the percent of the principal amount of a loan needed each month or quarter to amortize a loan over the term. The first table is for monthly payments, the second for quarterly payments. "Debt service" is payment that includes interest and principal and that amortizes the debt in the term. The debt service shown in Table 2 is the payment per $100, rounded to the next higher cent.

Example: The monthly payment needed to amortize an 8% loan over 30 years equals .74% of the principal amount. For a loan of $100,000, the monthly payment is $740. An amortization schedule for this loan is shown on page 5-115.

A loan payment, also called the Periodic Payment to Amortize 1, is represented by the actuarial symbol, $1/A_{\overline{n}|}$. The formula for calculating a loan payment is:

$$\frac{1}{A_{\overline{n}|}} = \frac{i}{1 - V^n}$$

where:

i = periodic interest factor (.08 ÷ 12 = .006 666 6667)
V^n = actuarial symbol for the Present Worth of 1
n = number of months

For 30 years, n = 360. (If payments were quarterly then n would be the number of quarters; for 30 years, n would equal 120.) The formula to compute the Present Worth of 1 is:

$$V^n = \frac{1}{(1 + i)^n}$$

$$= \frac{1}{(1.00666667)^{360}}$$

$$= \frac{1}{10.935730}$$

$$= .091443$$

Now, compute the payment:

$$\frac{1}{A_{\overline{n}|}} = \frac{i}{1 - V^n}$$

$$= \frac{.006666667}{1 - .091443}$$

$$= .00733764$$

The payment per $100 is $.74.

The Debt Service table, a quick reference for loan payments, shows the change in payment when the rate or term changes. A loan payment is higher by a small amount when calculated by the 2-decimal payments in the example. The exact payment to 10 decimal places is shown in Table 8.

DEBT SERVICE

Description: This table shows the monthly debt service to amortize a loan of $ 100 over the term. The debt service payment includes interest and principal.

Example: The debt service for an 8%, 15 year loan is .96%. The monthly payment of interest and principal for a $50,000 loan is $ 480.00.

RATE	1 yr	2 yr	3 yr	4 yr	5 yr	6 yr	7 yr	8 yr	9 yr	10 yr	11 yr	12 yr	13 yr	14 yr	15 yr
0.00	8.34	4.17	2.78	2.09	1.67	1.39	1.20	1.05	.93	.84	.76	.70	.65	.60	.56
1.00	8.38	4.22	2.83	2.13	1.71	1.44	1.24	1.09	.97	.88	.81	.74	.69	.64	.60
2.00	8.43	4.26	2.87	2.17	1.76	1.48	1.28	1.13	1.02	.93	.85	.79	.73	.69	.65
3.00	8.47	4.30	2.91	2.22	1.80	1.52	1.33	1.18	1.06	.97	.90	.83	.78	.73	.70
4.00	8.52	4.35	2.96	2.26	1.85	1.57	1.37	1.22	1.11	1.02	.94	.88	.83	.78	.74
4.25	8.53	4.36	2.97	2.27	1.86	1.58	1.38	1.24	1.12	1.03	.95	.89	.84	.80	.76
4.50	8.54	4.37	2.98	2.29	1.87	1.59	1.40	1.25	1.13	1.04	.97	.91	.85	.81	.77
4.75	8.55	4.38	2.99	2.30	1.88	1.60	1.41	1.26	1.14	1.05	.98	.92	.87	.82	.78
5.00	8.57	4.39	3.00	2.31	1.89	1.62	1.42	1.27	1.16	1.07	.99	.93	.88	.83	.80
5.25	8.58	4.40	3.01	2.32	1.90	1.63	1.43	1.28	1.17	1.08	1.00	.94	.89	.85	.81
5.50	8.59	4.41	3.02	2.33	1.92	1.64	1.44	1.29	1.18	1.09	1.02	.96	.90	.86	.82
5.75	8.60	4.43	3.04	2.34	1.93	1.65	1.45	1.31	1.19	1.10	1.03	.97	.92	.87	.84
6.00	8.61	4.44	3.05	2.35	1.94	1.66	1.47	1.32	1.21	1.12	1.04	.98	.93	.89	.85
6.25	8.62	4.45	3.06	2.36	1.95	1.67	1.48	1.33	1.22	1.13	1.05	.99	.94	.90	.86
6.50	8.63	4.46	3.07	2.38	1.96	1.69	1.49	1.34	1.23	1.14	1.07	1.01	.96	.91	.88
6.75	8.65	4.47	3.08	2.39	1.97	1.70	1.50	1.36	1.24	1.15	1.08	1.02	.97	.93	.89
7.00	8.66	4.48	3.09	2.40	1.99	1.71	1.51	1.37	1.26	1.17	1.09	1.03	.98	.94	.90
7.25	8.67	4.49	3.10	2.41	2.00	1.72	1.53	1.38	1.27	1.18	1.11	1.05	1.00	.95	.92
7.50	8.68	4.50	3.12	2.42	2.01	1.73	1.54	1.39	1.28	1.19	1.12	1.06	1.01	.97	.93
7.75	8.69	4.52	3.13	2.43	2.02	1.75	1.55	1.41	1.29	1.21	1.13	1.07	1.02	.98	.95
8.00	8.70	4.53	3.14	2.45	2.03	1.76	1.56	1.42	1.31	1.22	1.15	1.09	1.04	1.00	.96
8.25	8.72	4.54	3.15	2.46	2.04	1.77	1.58	1.43	1.32	1.23	1.16	1.10	1.05	1.01	.98
8.50	8.73	4.55	3.16	2.47	2.06	1.78	1.59	1.44	1.33	1.24	1.17	1.12	1.07	1.02	.99
8.75	8.74	4.56	3.17	2.48	2.07	1.80	1.60	1.46	1.35	1.26	1.19	1.13	1.08	1.04	1.00
9.00	8.75	4.57	3.18	2.49	2.08	1.81	1.61	1.47	1.36	1.27	1.20	1.14	1.09	1.05	1.02
9.25	8.76	4.58	3.20	2.51	2.09	1.82	1.63	1.48	1.37	1.29	1.21	1.16	1.11	1.07	1.03
9.50	8.77	4.60	3.21	2.52	2.11	1.83	1.64	1.50	1.39	1.30	1.23	1.17	1.12	1.08	1.05
9.75	8.78	4.61	3.22	2.53	2.12	1.85	1.65	1.51	1.40	1.31	1.24	1.19	1.14	1.10	1.06
10.00	8.80	4.62	3.23	2.54	2.13	1.86	1.67	1.52	1.41	1.33	1.26	1.20	1.15	1.11	1.08
10.25	8.81	4.63	3.24	2.55	2.14	1.87	1.68	1.54	1.43	1.34	1.27	1.21	1.17	1.13	1.09
10.50	8.82	4.64	3.26	2.57	2.15	1.88	1.69	1.55	1.44	1.35	1.29	1.23	1.18	1.14	1.11
10.75	8.83	4.65	3.27	2.58	2.17	1.90	1.70	1.56	1.45	1.37	1.30	1.24	1.20	1.16	1.13
11.00	8.84	4.67	3.28	2.59	2.18	1.91	1.72	1.58	1.47	1.38	1.31	1.26	1.21	1.17	1.14
11.25	8.85	4.68	3.29	2.60	2.19	1.92	1.73	1.59	1.48	1.40	1.33	1.27	1.23	1.19	1.16
11.50	8.87	4.69	3.30	2.61	2.20	1.93	1.74	1.60	1.50	1.41	1.34	1.29	1.24	1.21	1.17
11.75	8.88	4.70	3.31	2.63	2.22	1.95	1.76	1.62	1.51	1.43	1.36	1.30	1.26	1.22	1.19
12.00	8.89	4.71	3.33	2.64	2.23	1.96	1.77	1.63	1.52	1.44	1.37	1.32	1.27	1.24	1.21
12.25	8.90	4.72	3.34	2.65	2.24	1.97	1.78	1.64	1.54	1.45	1.39	1.33	1.29	1.25	1.22
12.50	8.91	4.74	3.35	2.66	2.25	1.99	1.80	1.66	1.55	1.47	1.40	1.35	1.30	1.27	1.24
12.75	8.93	4.75	3.36	2.68	2.27	2.00	1.81	1.67	1.57	1.48	1.42	1.36	1.32	1.28	1.25
13.00	8.94	4.76	3.37	2.69	2.28	2.01	1.82	1.69	1.58	1.50	1.43	1.38	1.34	1.30	1.27
13.25	8.95	4.77	3.39	2.70	2.29	2.03	1.84	1.70	1.59	1.51	1.45	1.40	1.35	1.32	1.29
13.50	8.96	4.78	3.40	2.71	2.31	2.04	1.85	1.71	1.61	1.53	1.46	1.41	1.37	1.33	1.30
13.75	8.97	4.79	3.41	2.73	2.32	2.05	1.87	1.73	1.62	1.54	1.48	1.43	1.38	1.35	1.32
14.00	8.98	4.81	3.42	2.74	2.33	2.07	1.88	1.74	1.64	1.56	1.49	1.44	1.40	1.37	1.34
14.25	9.00	4.82	3.43	2.75	2.34	2.08	1.89	1.76	1.65	1.57	1.51	1.46	1.42	1.38	1.35
14.50	9.01	4.83	3.45	2.76	2.36	2.09	1.91	1.77	1.67	1.59	1.52	1.47	1.43	1.40	1.37
14.75	9.02	4.84	3.46	2.78	2.37	2.11	1.92	1.79	1.68	1.60	1.54	1.49	1.45	1.42	1.39
15.00	9.03	4.85	3.47	2.79	2.38	2.12	1.93	1.80	1.70	1.62	1.56	1.51	1.47	1.43	1.40
15.25	9.04	4.87	3.48	2.80	2.40	2.13	1.95	1.81	1.71	1.63	1.57	1.52	1.48	1.45	1.42
15.50	9.05	4.88	3.50	2.81	2.41	2.15	1.96	1.83	1.73	1.65	1.59	1.54	1.50	1.47	1.44
15.75	9.07	4.89	3.51	2.83	2.42	2.16	1.98	1.84	1.74	1.66	1.60	1.55	1.51	1.48	1.46
16.00	9.08	4.90	3.52	2.84	2.44	2.17	1.99	1.86	1.76	1.68	1.62	1.57	1.53	1.50	1.47
16.25	9.09	4.91	3.53	2.85	2.45	2.19	2.01	1.87	1.77	1.70	1.64	1.59	1.55	1.52	1.49
16.50	9.10	4.93	3.55	2.86	2.46	2.20	2.02	1.89	1.79	1.71	1.65	1.60	1.57	1.53	1.51
16.75	9.11	4.94	3.56	2.88	2.48	2.22	2.03	1.90	1.80	1.73	1.67	1.62	1.58	1.55	1.53
17.00	9.13	4.95	3.57	2.89	2.49	2.23	2.05	1.92	1.82	1.74	1.68	1.64	1.60	1.57	1.54
17.25	9.14	4.96	3.58	2.90	2.50	2.24	2.06	1.93	1.83	1.76	1.70	1.65	1.62	1.59	1.56
17.50	9.15	4.97	3.60	2.92	2.52	2.26	2.08	1.95	1.85	1.77	1.72	1.67	1.63	1.60	1.58
17.75	9.16	4.99	3.61	2.93	2.53	2.27	2.09	1.96	1.87	1.79	1.73	1.69	1.65	1.62	1.60
18.00	9.17	5.00	3.62	2.94	2.54	2.29	2.11	1.98	1.88	1.81	1.75	1.70	1.67	1.64	1.62
18.25	9.18	5.01	3.63	2.96	2.56	2.30	2.12	1.99	1.90	1.82	1.77	1.72	1.69	1.66	1.63
18.50	9.20	5.02	3.65	2.97	2.57	2.31	2.14	2.01	1.91	1.84	1.78	1.74	1.70	1.67	1.65
18.75	9.21	5.03	3.66	2.98	2.59	2.33	2.15	2.02	1.93	1.86	1.80	1.76	1.72	1.69	1.67
19.00	9.22	5.05	3.67	3.00	2.60	2.34	2.17	2.04	1.94	1.87	1.82	1.77	1.74	1.71	1.69
20.00	9.27	5.09	3.72	3.05	2.65	2.40	2.23	2.10	2.01	1.94	1.88	1.84	1.81	1.78	1.76
25.00	9.51	5.34	3.98	3.32	2.94	2.70	2.54	2.42	2.34	2.28	2.23	2.20	2.18	2.16	2.14
30.00	9.75	5.60	4.25	3.61	3.24	3.01	2.86	2.76	2.69	2.64	2.60	2.58	2.56	2.55	2.53

DEBT SERVICE

MONTHLY PAYMENT

Description: This table shows the monthly debt service to amortize a loan of $ 100 over the term. The debt service payment includes interest and principal.

Example: The debt service for an 8%, 30 year loan is .74%. The monthly payment of interest and principal for a $50,000 loan is $ 370.00.

RATE	16 yr	17 yr	18 yr	19 yr	20 yr	21 yr	22 yr	23 yr	24 yr	25 yr	26 yr	27 yr	28 yr	29 yr	30 yr
0.00	.53	.50	.47	.44	.42	.40	.38	.37	.35	.34	.33	.31	.30	.29	.28
1.00	.57	.54	.51	.49	.46	.45	.43	.41	.40	.38	.37	.36	.35	.34	.33
2.00	.61	.58	.56	.53	.51	.49	.47	.46	.44	.43	.42	.40	.39	.38	.37
3.00	.66	.63	.60	.58	.56	.54	.52	.51	.49	.48	.47	.46	.45	.44	.43
4.00	.71	.68	.66	.63	.61	.59	.58	.56	.55	.53	.52	.51	.50	.49	.48
4.25	.72	.69	.67	.64	.62	.61	.59	.57	.56	.55	.54	.52	.51	.51	.50
4.50	.74	.71	.68	.66	.64	.62	.60	.59	.57	.56	.55	.54	.53	.52	.51
4.75	.75	.72	.69	.67	.65	.63	.62	.60	.59	.58	.56	.55	.54	.53	.53
5.00	.76	.73	.71	.69	.66	.65	.63	.62	.60	.59	.58	.57	.56	.55	.54
5.25	.78	.75	.72	.70	.68	.66	.64	.63	.62	.60	.59	.58	.57	.57	.56
5.50	.79	.76	.74	.71	.69	.67	.66	.64	.63	.62	.61	.60	.59	.58	.57
5.75	.80	.77	.75	.73	.71	.69	.67	.66	.65	.63	.62	.61	.60	.60	.59
6.00	.82	.79	.76	.74	.72	.70	.69	.67	.66	.65	.64	.63	.62	.61	.60
6.25	.83	.80	.78	.76	.74	.72	.70	.69	.68	.66	.65	.64	.64	.63	.62
6.50	.84	.82	.79	.77	.75	.73	.72	.70	.69	.68	.67	.66	.65	.64	.64
6.75	.86	.83	.81	.78	.77	.75	.73	.72	.71	.70	.69	.68	.67	.66	.65
7.00	.87	.84	.82	.80	.78	.76	.75	.73	.72	.71	.70	.69	.68	.68	.67
7.25	.89	.86	.84	.81	.80	.78	.76	.75	.74	.73	.72	.71	.70	.69	.69
7.50	.90	.87	.85	.83	.81	.79	.78	.77	.75	.74	.73	.72	.71	.71	.70
7.75	.92	.89	.86	.84	.83	.81	.80	.78	.77	.76	.75	.74	.73	.73	.72
8.00	.93	.90	.88	.86	.84	.83	.81	.80	.79	.78	.77	.76	.75	.74	.74
8.25	.94	.92	.90	.87	.86	.84	.83	.81	.80	.79	.78	.78	.77	.76	.76
8.50	.96	.93	.91	.89	.87	.86	.84	.83	.82	.81	.80	.79	.79	.78	.77
8.75	.97	.95	.93	.91	.89	.87	.86	.85	.84	.83	.82	.81	.80	.80	.79
9.00	.99	.96	.94	.92	.90	.89	.88	.86	.85	.84	.84	.83	.82	.82	.81
9.25	1.00	.98	.96	.94	.92	.91	.89	.88	.87	.86	.85	.85	.84	.83	.83
9.50	1.02	.99	.97	.95	.94	.92	.91	.90	.89	.88	.87	.86	.86	.85	.85
9.75	1.04	1.01	.99	.97	.95	.94	.93	.92	.91	.90	.89	.88	.87	.87	.86
10.00	1.05	1.03	1.00	.99	.97	.96	.94	.93	.92	.91	.91	.90	.89	.89	.88
10.25	1.07	1.04	1.02	1.00	.99	.97	.96	.95	.94	.93	.92	.92	.91	.91	.90
10.50	1.08	1.06	1.04	1.02	1.00	.99	.98	.97	.96	.95	.94	.94	.93	.92	.92
10.75	1.10	1.07	1.05	1.04	1.02	1.01	.99	.98	.98	.97	.96	.95	.95	.94	.94
11.00	1.11	1.09	1.07	1.05	1.04	1.02	1.01	1.00	.99	.99	.98	.97	.97	.96	.96
11.25	1.13	1.11	1.09	1.07	1.05	1.04	1.03	1.02	1.01	1.00	1.00	.99	.99	.98	.98
11.50	1.15	1.12	1.10	1.09	1.07	1.06	1.05	1.04	1.03	1.02	1.01	1.01	1.00	1.00	1.00
11.75	1.16	1.14	1.12	1.10	1.09	1.08	1.07	1.06	1.05	1.04	1.03	1.03	1.02	1.02	1.01
12.00	1.18	1.16	1.14	1.12	1.11	1.09	1.08	1.07	1.07	1.06	1.05	1.05	1.04	1.04	1.03
12.25	1.20	1.17	1.15	1.14	1.12	1.11	1.10	1.09	1.08	1.08	1.07	1.07	1.06	1.06	1.05
12.50	1.21	1.19	1.17	1.15	1.14	1.13	1.12	1.11	1.10	1.10	1.09	1.08	1.08	1.08	1.07
12.75	1.23	1.21	1.19	1.17	1.16	1.15	1.14	1.13	1.12	1.11	1.11	1.10	1.10	1.10	1.09
13.00	1.24	1.22	1.21	1.19	1.18	1.17	1.16	1.15	1.14	1.13	1.13	1.12	1.12	1.11	1.11
13.25	1.26	1.24	1.22	1.21	1.19	1.18	1.17	1.17	1.16	1.15	1.15	1.14	1.14	1.13	1.13
13.50	1.28	1.26	1.24	1.23	1.21	1.20	1.19	1.18	1.18	1.17	1.17	1.16	1.16	1.16	1.15
13.75	1.30	1.28	1.26	1.24	1.23	1.22	1.21	1.20	1.20	1.19	1.18	1.18	1.18	1.17	1.17
14.00	1.31	1.29	1.28	1.26	1.25	1.24	1.23	1.22	1.21	1.21	1.20	1.20	1.20	1.19	1.19
14.25	1.33	1.31	1.29	1.28	1.27	1.26	1.25	1.24	1.23	1.23	1.22	1.22	1.22	1.21	1.21
14.50	1.35	1.33	1.31	1.30	1.28	1.27	1.27	1.26	1.25	1.25	1.24	1.24	1.24	1.23	1.23
14.75	1.36	1.35	1.33	1.31	1.30	1.29	1.29	1.28	1.27	1.27	1.26	1.26	1.25	1.25	1.25
15.00	1.38	1.36	1.35	1.33	1.32	1.31	1.30	1.30	1.29	1.29	1.28	1.28	1.27	1.27	1.27
15.25	1.40	1.38	1.36	1.35	1.34	1.33	1.32	1.32	1.31	1.31	1.30	1.30	1.29	1.29	1.29
15.50	1.42	1.40	1.38	1.37	1.36	1.35	1.34	1.34	1.33	1.33	1.32	1.32	1.31	1.31	1.31
15.75	1.43	1.42	1.40	1.39	1.38	1.38	1.37	1.36	1.35	1.35	1.34	1.34	1.33	1.33	1.33
16.00	1.45	1.43	1.42	1.41	1.40	1.39	1.38	1.37	1.37	1.36	1.36	1.36	1.35	1.35	1.35
16.25	1.47	1.45	1.44	1.43	1.42	1.41	1.40	1.39	1.39	1.38	1.38	1.38	1.37	1.37	1.37
16.50	1.49	1.47	1.46	1.44	1.43	1.43	1.42	1.41	1.41	1.40	1.40	1.40	1.39	1.39	1.39
16.75	1.51	1.49	1.47	1.46	1.45	1.44	1.44	1.43	1.43	1.42	1.42	1.42	1.41	1.41	1.41
17.00	1.52	1.51	1.49	1.48	1.47	1.46	1.46	1.45	1.45	1.44	1.44	1.44	1.43	1.43	1.43
17.25	1.54	1.53	1.51	1.50	1.49	1.48	1.48	1.47	1.47	1.46	1.46	1.46	1.45	1.45	1.45
17.50	1.56	1.54	1.53	1.52	1.51	1.50	1.50	1.49	1.49	1.48	1.48	1.48	1.47	1.49	1.49
17.75	1.58	1.56	1.55	1.54	1.53	1.52	1.52	1.51	1.51	1.50	1.50	1.50	1.49	1.49	1.49
18.00	1.60	1.58	1.57	1.56	1.55	1.54	1.54	1.53	1.53	1.52	1.52	1.52	1.52	1.51	1.51
18.25	1.61	1.60	1.59	1.58	1.57	1.56	1.56	1.55	1.55	1.54	1.54	1.54	1.54	1.53	1.53
18.50	1.63	1.62	1.61	1.60	1.59	1.58	1.57	1.57	1.57	1.56	1.56	1.56	1.56	1.55	1.55
18.75	1.65	1.64	1.62	1.61	1.61	1.60	1.59	1.59	1.59	1.58	1.58	1.58	1.58	1.57	1.57
19.00	1.67	1.66	1.64	1.63	1.63	1.62	1.61	1.61	1.61	1.60	1.60	1.60	1.60	1.60	1.59
20.00	1.74	1.73	1.72	1.71	1.70	1.70	1.69	1.69	1.69	1.68	1.68	1.68	1.68	1.68	1.68
25.00	2.13	2.12	2.11	2.11	2.10	2.10	2.10	2.10	2.09	2.09	2.09	2.09	2.09	2.09	2.09
30.00	2.53	2.52	2.52	2.51	2.51	2.51	2.51	2.51	2.51	2.51	2.51	2.51	2.51	2.51	2.51

Description: This table shows the quarterly debt service to amortize a loan of $ 100 over the term. The debt service payment includes interest and principal.

Example: The debt service for an 8%, 15 year loan is 2.88%. The quarter payment of interest and principal for a $50,000 loan is $1440.00.

RATE	1 yr	2 yr	3 yr	4 yr	5 yr	6 yr	7 yr	8 yr	9 yr	10 yr	11 yr	12 yr	13 yr	14 yr	15 yr
0.00	25.00	12.51	8.34	6.26	5.01	4.17	3.58	3.13	2.78	2.51	2.28	2.09	1.93	1.79	1.67
1.00	25.16	12.65	8.47	6.39	5.14	4.30	3.71	3.26	2.91	2.64	2.41	2.22	2.06	1.92	1.80
2.00	25.32	12.79	8.61	6.52	5.27	4.44	3.84	3.39	3.05	2.77	2.54	2.35	2.19	2.06	1.94
3.00	25.48	12.93	8.75	6.66	5.41	4.57	3.98	3.53	3.18	2.91	2.68	2.49	2.33	2.20	2.08
4.00	25.63	13.07	8.89	6.80	5.55	4.71	4.12	3.67	3.33	3.05	2.83	2.64	2.48	2.35	2.23
4.25	25.67	13.11	8.93	6.83	5.58	4.75	4.15	3.71	3.36	3.09	2.86	2.68	2.52	2.38	2.27
4.50	25.71	13.15	8.96	6.87	5.62	4.78	4.19	3.74	3.40	3.12	2.90	2.71	2.56	2.42	2.31
4.75	25.75	13.18	9.00	6.90	5.65	4.82	4.22	3.78	3.43	3.16	2.94	2.75	2.59	2.46	2.34
5.00	25.79	13.22	9.03	6.94	5.69	4.85	4.26	3.82	3.47	3.20	2.97	2.79	2.63	2.50	2.38
5.25	25.83	13.25	9.07	6.97	5.72	4.89	4.30	3.85	3.51	3.23	3.01	2.83	2.67	2.54	2.42
5.50	25.87	13.29	9.10	7.01	5.76	4.93	4.33	3.89	3.55	3.27	3.05	2.86	2.71	2.58	2.46
5.75	25.91	13.33	9.14	7.05	5.79	4.96	4.37	3.93	3.58	3.31	3.09	2.90	2.75	2.62	2.50
6.00	25.95	13.36	9.17	7.08	5.83	5.00	4.41	3.96	3.62	3.35	3.13	2.94	2.79	2.66	2.54
6.25	25.99	13.40	9.21	7.12	5.87	5.03	4.44	4.00	3.66	3.39	3.16	2.98	2.83	2.70	2.59
6.50	26.03	13.44	9.24	7.15	5.90	5.07	4.48	4.04	3.70	3.42	3.20	3.02	2.87	2.74	2.63
6.75	26.07	13.47	9.28	7.19	5.94	5.11	4.52	4.07	3.73	3.46	3.24	3.06	2.91	2.78	2.67
7.00	26.11	13.51	9.32	7.22	5.97	5.14	4.55	4.11	3.77	3.50	3.28	3.10	2.95	2.82	2.71
7.25	26.15	13.55	9.35	7.26	6.01	5.18	4.59	4.15	3.81	3.54	3.32	3.14	2.99	2.86	2.75
7.50	26.19	13.58	9.39	7.30	6.05	5.22	4.63	4.19	3.85	3.58	3.36	3.18	3.03	2.90	2.80
7.75	26.23	13.62	9.42	7.33	6.08	5.25	4.67	4.23	3.89	3.62	3.40	3.22	3.07	2.95	2.84
8.00	26.27	13.66	9.46	7.37	6.12	5.29	4.70	4.27	3.93	3.66	3.44	3.27	3.12	2.99	2.88
8.25	26.31	13.69	9.50	7.41	6.16	5.33	4.74	4.30	3.97	3.70	3.48	3.31	3.16	3.03	2.93
8.50	26.35	13.73	9.53	7.44	6.19	5.37	4.78	4.34	4.01	3.74	3.53	3.35	3.20	3.08	2.97
8.75	26.39	13.77	9.57	7.48	6.23	5.41	4.82	4.38	4.05	3.78	3.57	3.39	3.24	3.12	3.01
9.00	26.43	13.80	9.61	7.52	6.27	5.44	4.86	4.42	4.09	3.82	3.61	3.43	3.29	3.16	3.06
9.25	26.47	13.84	9.64	7.55	6.31	5.48	4.90	4.46	4.13	3.86	3.65	3.48	3.33	3.21	3.10
9.50	26.51	13.88	9.68	7.59	6.34	5.52	4.94	4.50	4.17	3.91	3.69	3.52	3.37	3.25	3.15
9.75	26.55	13.91	9.72	7.63	6.38	5.56	4.97	4.54	4.21	3.95	3.74	3.56	3.42	3.30	3.19
10.00	26.59	13.95	9.75	7.66	6.42	5.60	5.01	4.58	4.25	3.99	3.78	3.61	3.46	3.34	3.24
10.25	26.63	13.99	9.79	7.70	6.46	5.63	5.05	4.62	4.29	4.03	3.82	3.65	3.51	3.39	3.29
10.50	26.67	14.03	9.83	7.74	6.50	5.67	5.09	4.66	4.33	4.07	3.86	3.69	3.55	3.43	3.33
10.75	26.71	14.06	9.86	7.78	6.53	5.71	5.13	4.70	4.37	4.12	3.91	3.74	3.60	3.48	3.38
11.00	26.75	14.10	9.90	7.81	6.57	5.75	5.17	4.74	4.42	4.16	3.95	3.78	3.64	3.53	3.43
11.25	26.79	14.14	9.94	7.85	6.61	5.79	5.21	4.79	4.46	4.20	3.99	3.83	3.69	3.57	3.47
11.50	26.83	14.18	9.98	7.89	6.65	5.83	5.25	4.83	4.50	4.24	4.04	3.87	3.73	3.62	3.52
11.75	26.87	14.21	10.01	7.93	6.69	5.87	5.29	4.87	4.54	4.29	4.08	3.92	3.78	3.67	3.57
12.00	26.91	14.25	10.05	7.97	6.73	5.91	5.33	4.91	4.59	4.33	4.13	3.96	3.83	3.71	3.62
12.25	26.95	14.29	10.09	8.00	6.77	5.95	5.38	4.95	4.63	4.38	4.17	4.01	3.87	3.76	3.67
12.50	26.99	14.33	10.13	8.04	6.80	5.99	5.42	4.99	4.67	4.42	4.22	4.05	3.92	3.81	3.72
12.75	27.03	14.36	10.16	8.08	6.84	6.03	5.46	5.04	4.71	4.46	4.26	4.10	3.97	3.86	3.76
13.00	27.07	14.40	10.20	8.12	6.88	6.07	5.50	5.08	4.76	4.51	4.31	4.15	4.02	3.91	3.81
13.25	27.11	14.44	10.24	8.16	6.92	6.11	5.54	5.12	4.80	4.55	4.35	4.19	4.06	3.95	3.86
13.50	27.15	14.48	10.28	8.20	6.96	6.15	5.58	5.16	4.85	4.60	4.40	4.24	4.11	4.00	3.91
13.75	27.19	14.51	10.32	8.23	7.00	6.19	5.62	5.21	4.89	4.64	4.45	4.29	4.16	4.05	3.96
14.00	27.23	14.55	10.35	8.27	7.04	6.23	5.67	5.25	4.93	4.69	4.49	4.34	4.21	4.10	4.01
14.25	27.27	14.59	10.39	8.31	7.08	6.27	5.71	5.29	4.98	4.73	4.54	4.38	4.26	4.15	4.06
14.50	27.31	14.63	10.43	8.35	7.12	6.31	5.75	5.34	5.02	4.78	4.59	4.43	4.31	4.20	4.12
14.75	27.35	14.67	10.47	8.39	7.16	6.36	5.79	5.38	5.07	4.82	4.63	4.48	4.35	4.25	4.17
15.00	27.39	14.70	10.51	8.43	7.20	6.40	5.83	5.42	5.11	4.87	4.68	4.53	4.40	4.30	4.22
15.25	27.43	14.74	10.54	8.47	7.24	6.44	5.88	5.47	5.16	4.92	4.73	4.58	4.45	4.35	4.27
15.50	27.47	14.78	10.58	8.51	7.28	6.48	5.92	5.51	5.20	4.96	4.78	4.62	4.50	4.40	4.32
15.75	27.51	14.82	10.62	8.55	7.32	6.52	5.96	5.56	5.25	5.01	4.82	4.67	4.55	4.45	4.37
16.00	27.55	14.86	10.66	8.59	7.36	6.56	6.01	5.60	5.29	5.06	4.87	4.72	4.60	4.51	4.43
16.25	27.59	14.90	10.70	8.63	7.40	6.61	6.05	5.64	5.34	5.10	4.92	4.77	4.65	4.56	4.48
16.50	27.64	14.93	10.74	8.67	7.44	6.65	6.09	5.69	5.39	5.15	4.97	4.82	4.70	4.61	4.53
16.75	27.68	14.97	10.78	8.71	7.49	6.69	6.14	5.73	5.43	5.20	5.02	4.87	4.76	4.66	4.58
17.00	27.72	15.01	10.82	8.75	7.53	6.73	6.18	5.78	5.48	5.25	5.07	4.92	4.81	4.71	4.64
17.25	27.76	15.05	10.85	8.79	7.57	6.78	6.22	5.82	5.52	5.29	5.11	4.97	4.86	4.76	4.69
17.50	27.80	15.09	10.89	8.83	7.61	6.82	6.27	5.87	5.57	5.34	5.16	5.02	4.91	4.82	4.74
17.75	27.84	15.13	10.93	8.87	7.65	6.86	6.31	5.92	5.62	5.39	5.21	5.07	4.96	4.87	4.80
18.00	27.88	15.17	10.97	8.91	7.69	6.90	6.36	5.96	5.67	5.44	5.26	5.12	5.01	4.92	4.85
18.25	27.92	15.20	11.01	8.95	7.73	6.95	6.40	6.01	5.71	5.49	5.31	5.17	5.06	4.98	4.90
18.50	27.96	15.24	11.05	8.99	7.78	6.99	6.45	6.05	5.76	5.54	5.36	5.23	5.12	5.03	4.96
18.75	28.00	15.28	11.09	9.03	7.82	7.03	6.49	6.10	5.81	5.59	5.41	5.28	5.17	5.08	5.01
19.00	28.04	15.32	11.13	9.07	7.86	7.08	6.54	6.15	5.86	5.63	5.46	5.33	5.22	5.14	5.07
20.00	28.21	15.48	11.29	9.23	8.03	7.25	6.72	6.33	6.05	5.83	5.67	5.54	5.43	5.35	5.27
25.00	29.03	16.27	12.10	10.07	8.90	8.16	7.66	7.30	7.05	6.86	6.72	6.62	6.53	6.47	6.42
30.00	29.86	17.08	12.93	10.94	9.81	9.11	8.65	8.33	8.10	7.95	7.83	7.75	7.68	7.64	7.60

Description: This table shows the quarterly debt service to amortize a loan of $ 100 over the term. The debt service payment includes interest and principal.

Example: The debt service for an 8%, 30 year loan is 2.21%. The quarter payment of interest and principal for a $50,000 loan is $1105.00.

RATE	16 yr	17 yr	18 yr	19 yr	20 yr	21 yr	22 yr	23 yr	24 yr	25 yr	26 yr	27 yr	28 yr	29 yr	30 yr
0.00	1.57	1.48	1.39	1.32	1.26	1.20	1.14	1.09	1.05	1.00	.97	.93	.90	.87	.84
1.00	1.70	1.61	1.52	1.45	1.39	1.33	1.27	1.22	1.18	1.14	1.10	1.06	1.03	1.00	.97
2.00	1.83	1.74	1.66	1.59	1.52	1.47	1.41	1.36	1.32	1.28	1.24	1.21	1.17	1.14	1.12
3.00	1.98	1.89	1.81	1.74	1.67	1.61	1.56	1.51	1.47	1.43	1.39	1.36	1.33	1.30	1.27
4.00	2.13	2.04	1.96	1.89	1.83	1.77	1.72	1.67	1.63	1.59	1.56	1.52	1.49	1.47	1.44
4.25	2.17	2.08	2.00	1.93	1.87	1.81	1.76	1.71	1.67	1.63	1.60	1.57	1.54	1.51	1.48
4.50	2.21	2.12	2.04	1.97	1.91	1.85	1.80	1.76	1.71	1.68	1.64	1.61	1.58	1.55	1.53
4.75	2.24	2.16	2.08	2.01	1.95	1.89	1.84	1.80	1.76	1.72	1.68	1.65	1.62	1.60	1.57
5.00	2.28	2.20	2.12	2.05	1.99	1.93	1.89	1.84	1.80	1.76	1.73	1.70	1.67	1.64	1.62
5.25	2.32	2.24	2.16	2.09	2.03	1.98	1.93	1.88	1.84	1.81	1.77	1.74	1.71	1.69	1.66
5.50	2.36	2.28	2.20	2.13	2.07	2.02	1.97	1.93	1.89	1.85	1.82	1.79	1.76	1.73	1.71
5.75	2.41	2.32	2.24	2.18	2.12	2.06	2.01	1.97	1.93	1.90	1.86	1.83	1.81	1.78	1.76
6.00	2.45	2.36	2.29	2.22	2.16	2.11	2.06	2.02	1.98	1.94	1.91	1.88	1.85	1.83	1.81
6.25	2.49	2.40	2.33	2.26	2.20	2.15	2.10	2.06	2.02	1.99	1.96	1.93	1.90	1.88	1.86
6.50	2.53	2.45	2.37	2.31	2.25	2.20	2.15	2.11	2.07	2.03	2.00	1.98	1.95	1.93	1.90
6.75	2.57	2.49	2.41	2.35	2.29	2.24	2.19	2.15	2.12	2.08	2.05	2.02	2.00	1.98	1.95
7.00	2.61	2.53	2.46	2.39	2.34	2.29	2.24	2.20	2.16	2.13	2.10	2.07	2.05	2.02	2.00
7.25	2.66	2.58	2.50	2.44	2.38	2.33	2.29	2.25	2.21	2.18	2.15	2.12	2.10	2.08	2.05
7.50	2.70	2.62	2.55	2.48	2.43	2.38	2.33	2.29	2.26	2.23	2.20	2.17	2.15	2.13	2.11
7.75	2.74	2.66	2.59	2.53	2.47	2.43	2.38	2.34	2.31	2.28	2.25	2.22	2.20	2.18	2.16
8.00	2.79	2.71	2.64	2.58	2.52	2.47	2.43	2.39	2.36	2.33	2.30	2.27	2.25	2.23	2.21
8.25	2.83	2.75	2.68	2.62	2.57	2.52	2.48	2.44	2.41	2.38	2.35	2.32	2.30	2.28	2.26
8.50	2.88	2.80	2.73	2.67	2.62	2.57	2.53	2.49	2.46	2.43	2.40	2.37	2.35	2.33	2.32
8.75	2.92	2.84	2.78	2.72	2.66	2.62	2.58	2.54	2.51	2.48	2.45	2.43	2.41	2.39	2.37
9.00	2.97	2.89	2.82	2.76	2.71	2.67	2.62	2.59	2.56	2.53	2.50	2.48	2.46	2.44	2.42
9.25	3.01	2.94	2.87	2.81	2.76	2.71	2.67	2.64	2.61	2.58	2.55	2.53	2.51	2.49	2.48
9.50	3.06	2.98	2.92	2.86	2.81	2.76	2.72	2.69	2.66	2.63	2.61	2.58	2.56	2.55	2.53
9.75	3.11	3.03	2.97	2.91	2.86	2.81	2.78	2.74	2.71	2.68	2.66	2.64	2.62	2.60	2.59
10.00	3.15	3.08	3.01	2.96	2.91	2.86	2.83	2.79	2.76	2.74	2.71	2.69	2.67	2.66	2.64
10.25	3.20	3.13	3.06	3.01	2.96	2.91	2.88	2.84	2.82	2.79	2.77	2.75	2.73	2.71	2.70
10.50	3.25	3.17	3.11	3.06	3.01	2.97	2.93	2.90	2.87	2.84	2.82	2.80	2.78	2.77	2.75
10.75	3.30	3.22	3.16	3.11	3.06	3.02	2.98	2.95	2.92	2.90	2.87	2.86	2.84	2.82	2.81
11.00	3.34	3.27	3.21	3.16	3.11	3.07	3.03	3.00	2.97	2.95	2.93	2.91	2.89	2.88	2.87
11.25	3.39	3.32	3.26	3.21	3.16	3.12	3.09	3.06	3.03	3.00	2.98	2.97	2.95	2.93	2.92
11.50	3.44	3.37	3.31	3.26	3.21	3.17	3.14	3.11	3.08	3.06	3.04	3.02	3.01	2.99	2.98
11.75	3.49	3.42	3.36	3.31	3.26	3.23	3.19	3.16	3.14	3.11	3.09	3.08	3.06	3.05	3.04
12.00	3.54	3.47	3.41	3.36	3.32	3.28	3.25	3.22	3.19	3.17	3.15	3.13	3.12	3.11	3.09
12.25	3.59	3.52	3.46	3.41	3.37	3.33	3.30	3.27	3.25	3.23	3.21	3.19	3.18	3.16	3.15
12.50	3.64	3.57	3.51	3.46	3.42	3.38	3.35	3.33	3.30	3.28	3.26	3.25	3.23	3.22	3.21
12.75	3.69	3.62	3.56	3.52	3.47	3.44	3.41	3.38	3.36	3.34	3.32	3.30	3.29	3.28	3.27
13.00	3.74	3.67	3.62	3.57	3.53	3.49	3.46	3.44	3.41	3.39	3.38	3.36	3.35	3.34	3.33
13.25	3.79	3.72	3.67	3.62	3.58	3.55	3.52	3.49	3.47	3.45	3.43	3.42	3.41	3.39	3.39
13.50	3.84	3.77	3.72	3.67	3.64	3.60	3.57	3.55	3.53	3.51	3.49	3.48	3.46	3.45	3.44
13.75	3.89	3.83	3.77	3.73	3.69	3.66	3.63	3.60	3.58	3.56	3.55	3.53	3.52	3.51	3.50
14.00	3.94	3.88	3.83	3.78	3.74	3.71	3.68	3.66	3.64	3.62	3.61	3.59	3.58	3.57	3.56
14.25	3.99	3.93	3.88	3.84	3.80	3.77	3.74	3.72	3.70	3.68	3.66	3.65	3.64	3.63	3.62
14.50	4.04	3.98	3.93	3.89	3.85	3.82	3.80	3.77	3.75	3.74	3.72	3.71	3.70	3.69	3.68
14.75	4.10	4.04	3.99	3.94	3.91	3.88	3.85	3.83	3.81	3.79	3.78	3.77	3.76	3.75	3.74
15.00	4.15	4.09	4.04	4.00	3.96	3.93	3.91	3.89	3.87	3.85	3.84	3.83	3.82	3.81	3.80
15.25	4.20	4.14	4.09	4.05	4.02	3.99	3.96	3.94	3.93	3.91	3.90	3.89	3.88	3.87	3.86
15.50	4.25	4.20	4.15	4.11	4.07	4.05	4.02	4.00	3.98	3.97	3.96	3.94	3.94	3.93	3.92
15.75	4.31	4.25	4.20	4.16	4.13	4.10	4.08	4.06	4.04	4.03	4.01	4.00	4.00	3.99	3.98
16.00	4.36	4.30	4.26	4.22	4.19	4.16	4.14	4.12	4.10	4.09	4.07	4.06	4.06	4.05	4.04
16.25	4.41	4.36	4.31	4.27	4.24	4.22	4.19	4.17	4.16	4.14	4.13	4.12	4.12	4.11	4.10
16.50	4.47	4.41	4.37	4.33	4.30	4.27	4.25	4.23	4.22	4.20	4.19	4.18	4.18	4.17	4.16
16.75	4.52	4.47	4.42	4.39	4.36	4.33	4.31	4.29	4.28	4.26	4.25	4.24	4.24	4.23	4.22
17.00	4.57	4.52	4.48	4.44	4.41	4.39	4.37	4.35	4.33	4.32	4.31	4.30	4.30	4.29	4.28
17.25	4.63	4.58	4.53	4.50	4.47	4.45	4.43	4.41	4.39	4.38	4.37	4.36	4.36	4.35	4.34
17.50	4.68	4.63	4.59	4.56	4.53	4.50	4.48	4.47	4.45	4.44	4.43	4.42	4.42	4.41	4.41
17.75	4.74	4.69	4.65	4.61	4.58	4.56	4.54	4.53	4.51	4.50	4.49	4.48	4.48	4.47	4.47
18.00	4.79	4.74	4.70	4.67	4.64	4.62	4.60	4.58	4.57	4.56	4.55	4.54	4.54	4.53	4.53
18.25	4.85	4.80	4.76	4.73	4.70	4.68	4.66	4.64	4.63	4.62	4.61	4.60	4.60	4.59	4.59
18.50	4.90	4.85	4.82	4.78	4.76	4.74	4.72	4.70	4.69	4.68	4.67	4.67	4.66	4.65	4.65
18.75	4.96	4.91	4.87	4.84	4.82	4.79	4.78	4.76	4.75	4.74	4.73	4.73	4.72	4.72	4.71
19.00	5.01	4.97	4.93	4.90	4.87	4.85	4.84	4.82	4.81	4.80	4.79	4.79	4.78	4.78	4.77
20.00	5.24	5.19	5.16	5.13	5.11	5.09	5.07	5.06	5.05	5.04	5.04	5.03	5.03	5.02	5.02
25.00	6.39	6.36	6.34	6.32	6.30	6.29	6.29	6.28	6.27	6.27	6.27	6.26	6.26	6.26	6.26
30.00	7.58	7.56	7.55	7.54	7.53	7.52	7.52	7.51	7.51	7.51	7.51	7.51	7.51	7.51	7.51

TABLE **3**

Total Interest

Interest Rates:	0, 1, 2, 3%; 4 to 19% by .25%; 20, 25, 30%.
Terms:	1 to 30 years, each year.
Payments:	Monthly and quarterly.

This table shows the total interest per $100 of amount financed, at the Annual Percentage Rate (APR), for the term of the loan. "Total interest" is the sum of all the loan payments less the amount of the loan. The first table is for monthly payments, the second for quarterly payments. Payments are made in arrears. The APRs are shown in the index.

Example: The total interest paid on a monthly payment loan at 8% for 30 years is 164.16% of the principal amount. For a loan of $100,000, the total interest paid is $164,160. An amortization schedule for this loan is shown on page 5-115; the total interest paid is the sum of the interest column.

To calculate the total interest, turn to page 8-88 for the 8%, 30 year payment. Using the number found under the column Periodic Payment to Amortize 1, the calculation is:

$$\text{Total interest} = (\text{Payment} \times \text{Periods}) - 1$$
$$= (.007\ 337\ 6457 \times 360) - 1$$
$$= 2.641552452 - 1$$
$$= 1.641552452$$

Total interest per $100 is $164.16.

The Total Interest table, a quick reference for interest amount, shows the change in interest when the rate or term changes.

Points. The table can also be used to find the APR for a loan when points are included in the finance charge and paid at closing.

Example: The following 6 steps are taken to find the APR on the proceeds of an 8%, 30 year loan when the borrower pays 2 points at closing.

1. Find the finance charge at the contract interest rate:
   Charge = 164.16

2. Add the points to determine the total finance charge:
   $$164.16 + 2.00 = 166.16$$

3. Compute the proceeds (loan minus points):
   $$100 - 2 = 98$$

4. Compute the new ratio of total finance charge to proceeds:
   $$\frac{166.16}{98} = 1.69551$$

5. Multiply the ratio by 100:
   $$1.69551 \times 100 = 169.55$$

6. Go to the Total Interest table for APR. The new ratio lies between the tabulated values in the Total Interest table:

Index	Value
8.00	164.16
—	169.55
8.25	170.46

By interpolation, the APR is 8.21%.

TOTAL INTEREST

MONTHLY PAYMENT

Description: This table shows the total interest per $ 100 of amount financed, at the Annual Percentage Rate, for the term of the loan. Loan payments are monthly in arrears.

Example: The total interest for a 15 year loan at an Annual Percentage Rate of 8 % is $ 72.02. The total interest for a $ 50,000 loan is $ 36010.00.

RATE	1 yr	2 yr	3 yr	4 yr	5 yr	6 yr	7 yr	8 yr	9 yr	10 yr	11 yr	12 yr	13 yr	14 yr	15 yr
0.00	0.00	0.00	0.00	0.00	0.00	0.00	0.00	0.00	0.00	0.00	0.00	0.00	0.00	0.00	0.00
1.00	.54	1.04	1.55	2.05	2.56	3.07	3.58	4.09	4.61	5.12	5.64	6.16	6.68	7.20	7.73
2.00	1.09	2.10	3.11	4.14	5.17	6.20	7.25	8.30	9.35	10.42	11.49	12.56	13.65	14.74	15.83
3.00	1.63	3.15	4.69	6.24	7.81	9.39	10.99	12.60	14.23	15.87	17.53	19.20	20.89	22.59	24.30
4.00	2.18	4.22	6.29	8.38	10.50	12.65	14.82	17.02	19.24	21.49	23.77	26.08	28.41	30.76	33.14
4.25	2.32	4.49	6.69	8.92	11.18	13.47	15.79	18.14	20.52	22.93	25.36	27.83	30.33	32.85	35.41
4.50	2.45	4.75	7.09	9.46	11.86	14.29	16.76	19.26	21.80	24.37	26.97	29.60	32.27	34.97	37.70
4.75	2.59	5.02	7.49	10.00	12.54	15.12	17.74	20.40	23.09	25.82	28.58	31.39	34.22	37.10	40.01
5.00	2.73	5.29	7.90	10.54	13.23	15.96	18.72	21.54	24.39	27.28	30.21	33.18	36.20	39.25	42.34
5.25	2.87	5.56	8.30	11.09	13.92	16.79	19.71	22.68	25.69	28.75	31.85	35.00	38.19	41.42	44.70
5.50	3.00	5.83	8.71	11.63	14.61	17.63	20.71	23.83	27.01	30.23	33.50	36.82	40.19	43.61	47.08
5.75	3.14	6.10	9.11	12.18	15.30	18.48	21.71	24.99	28.33	31.72	35.17	38.67	42.22	45.82	49.47
6.00	3.28	6.37	9.52	12.73	16.00	19.32	22.71	26.16	29.66	33.22	36.84	40.52	44.26	48.05	51.89
6.25	3.42	6.64	9.93	13.28	16.70	20.18	23.72	27.33	31.00	34.74	38.53	42.39	46.31	50.29	54.34
6.50	3.56	6.91	10.34	13.83	17.40	21.03	24.74	28.51	32.35	36.26	40.23	44.28	48.39	52.56	56.80
6.75	3.69	7.18	10.75	14.39	18.10	21.89	25.75	29.69	33.70	37.79	41.95	46.17	50.47	54.84	59.28
7.00	3.83	7.45	11.16	14.94	18.81	22.75	26.78	30.88	35.07	39.33	43.67	48.09	52.58	57.15	61.79
7.25	3.97	7.73	11.57	15.50	19.52	23.62	27.81	32.08	36.44	40.88	45.41	50.01	54.70	59.47	64.32
7.50	4.11	8.00	11.98	16.06	20.23	24.49	28.84	33.29	37.82	42.44	47.15	51.95	56.84	61.81	66.86
7.75	4.25	8.27	12.40	16.62	20.94	25.36	29.88	34.50	39.21	44.01	48.91	53.91	58.99	64.17	69.43
8.00	4.39	8.55	12.81	17.18	21.66	26.24	30.92	35.71	40.60	45.59	50.68	55.87	61.16	66.54	72.02
8.25	4.52	8.82	13.23	17.75	22.38	27.12	31.97	36.94	42.01	47.18	52.47	57.85	63.34	68.94	74.63
8.50	4.66	9.09	13.64	18.31	23.10	28.00	33.03	38.16	43.42	48.78	54.26	59.85	65.54	71.35	77.25
8.75	4.80	9.37	14.06	18.88	23.82	28.89	34.08	39.40	44.84	50.39	56.07	61.86	67.76	73.78	79.90
9.00	4.94	9.64	14.48	19.45	24.55	29.78	35.15	40.64	46.26	52.01	57.88	63.88	69.99	76.22	82.57
9.25	5.08	9.92	14.90	20.02	25.28	30.68	36.22	41.89	47.70	53.64	59.71	65.91	72.24	78.69	85.25
9.50	5.22	10.19	15.32	20.59	26.01	31.58	37.29	43.14	49.14	55.28	61.55	67.96	74.50	81.17	87.96
9.75	5.36	10.47	15.74	21.16	26.75	32.48	38.37	44.41	50.59	56.92	63.40	70.02	76.77	83.66	90.69
10.00	5.50	10.75	16.16	21.74	27.48	33.39	39.45	45.67	52.05	58.58	65.26	72.09	79.06	86.18	93.43
10.25	5.64	11.02	16.58	22.32	28.22	34.30	40.54	46.94	53.52	60.25	67.14	74.18	81.37	88.71	96.19
10.50	5.78	11.30	17.01	22.90	28.96	35.21	41.63	48.22	54.99	61.92	69.02	76.28	83.69	91.26	98.97
10.75	5.92	11.58	17.43	23.48	29.71	36.13	42.73	49.51	56.47	63.61	70.91	78.39	86.03	93.82	101.77
11.00	6.06	11.86	17.86	24.06	30.45	37.05	43.83	50.80	57.96	65.30	72.82	80.51	88.37	96.40	104.59
11.25	6.20	12.14	18.29	24.64	31.20	37.97	44.94	52.10	59.46	67.00	74.74	82.65	90.74	99.00	107.42
11.50	6.34	12.42	18.71	25.23	31.96	38.90	46.05	53.40	60.96	68.71	76.66	84.80	93.12	101.61	110.27
11.75	6.48	12.70	19.14	25.81	32.71	39.83	47.16	54.71	62.47	70.44	78.60	86.96	95.51	104.24	113.14
12.00	6.62	12.98	19.57	26.40	33.47	40.76	48.28	56.03	63.99	72.17	80.55	89.13	97.91	106.88	116.03
12.25	6.76	13.26	20.00	26.99	34.23	41.70	49.41	57.35	65.52	73.90	82.51	91.32	100.33	109.54	118.93
12.50	6.90	13.54	20.43	27.58	34.99	42.64	50.54	58.68	67.05	75.65	84.48	93.52	102.76	112.21	121.85
12.75	7.04	13.82	20.87	28.18	35.75	43.59	51.67	60.01	68.59	77.41	86.46	95.72	105.21	114.90	124.79
13.00	7.18	14.10	21.30	28.77	36.52	44.53	52.81	61.35	70.14	79.17	88.44	97.95	107.67	117.60	127.74
13.25	7.32	14.38	21.73	29.37	37.29	45.49	53.96	62.70	71.69	80.95	90.44	100.18	110.14	120.32	130.71
13.50	7.46	14.66	22.17	29.97	38.06	46.44	55.11	64.05	73.26	82.73	92.45	102.42	112.63	123.05	133.70
13.75	7.60	14.95	22.60	30.57	38.83	47.40	56.26	65.40	74.83	84.52	94.47	104.68	115.13	125.80	136.70
14.00	7.74	15.23	23.04	31.17	39.61	48.36	57.42	66.77	76.40	86.32	96.50	106.95	117.64	128.56	139.71
14.25	7.89	15.51	23.48	31.77	40.39	49.33	58.58	68.14	77.99	88.13	98.54	109.22	120.16	131.34	142.74
14.50	8.03	15.80	23.92	32.37	41.17	50.30	59.75	69.51	79.58	89.94	100.59	111.51	122.70	134.13	145.79
14.75	8.17	16.08	24.35	32.98	41.95	51.27	60.92	70.89	81.18	91.77	102.65	113.81	125.24	136.93	148.85
15.00	8.31	16.37	24.80	33.59	42.74	52.24	62.09	72.28	82.78	93.60	104.72	116.13	127.80	139.74	151.93
15.25	8.45	16.65	25.24	34.20	43.53	53.22	63.27	73.67	84.40	95.44	106.80	118.45	130.38	142.57	155.01
15.50	8.59	16.94	25.68	34.81	44.32	54.21	64.46	75.06	86.01	97.29	108.89	120.78	132.96	145.41	158.12
15.75	8.74	17.22	26.12	35.42	45.11	55.19	65.65	76.47	87.64	99.15	110.98	123.12	135.56	148.27	161.24
16.00	8.88	17.51	26.57	36.03	45.91	56.18	66.84	77.88	89.27	101.02	113.09	125.48	138.17	151.13	164.37
16.25	9.02	17.80	27.01	36.65	46.71	57.17	68.04	79.29	90.91	102.89	115.21	127.84	140.79	154.01	167.51
16.50	9.16	18.09	27.46	37.27	47.51	58.17	69.24	80.71	92.56	104.77	117.33	130.22	143.42	156.91	170.67
16.75	9.30	18.37	27.90	37.88	48.31	59.17	70.45	82.14	94.21	106.66	119.46	132.60	146.06	159.81	173.84
17.00	9.45	18.66	28.35	38.50	49.12	60.17	71.66	83.57	95.87	108.56	121.61	135.00	148.71	162.72	177.02
17.25	9.59	18.95	28.80	39.13	49.92	61.18	72.88	85.00	97.54	110.46	123.76	137.40	151.37	165.65	180.22
17.50	9.73	19.24	29.25	39.75	50.73	62.19	74.10	86.44	99.21	112.37	125.92	139.82	154.05	168.59	183.42
17.75	9.87	19.53	29.70	40.37	51.55	63.20	75.32	87.89	100.89	114.29	128.09	142.24	156.73	171.54	186.64
18.00	10.02	19.82	30.15	41.00	52.36	64.22	76.55	89.34	102.57	116.22	130.26	144.67	159.43	174.50	189.88
18.25	10.16	20.11	30.60	41.63	53.18	65.24	77.78	90.80	104.27	118.16	132.45	147.12	162.13	177.48	193.12
18.50	10.30	20.40	31.05	42.26	54.00	66.26	79.02	92.26	105.96	120.10	134.64	149.57	164.85	180.46	196.37
18.75	10.44	20.69	31.51	42.89	54.82	67.28	80.26	93.73	107.67	122.05	136.85	152.03	167.58	183.45	199.64
19.00	10.59	20.98	31.96	43.52	55.64	68.31	81.51	95.21	109.38	124.01	139.06	154.50	170.31	186.46	202.92
20.00	11.16	22.15	33.79	46.07	58.96	72.46	86.53	101.15	116.29	131.91	147.98	164.47	181.35	198.58	216.13
25.00	14.05	28.09	43.14	59.15	76.11	93.95	112.62	132.06	152.20	172.99	194.36	216.24	238.57	261.31	284.40
30.00	16.98	34.19	52.83	72.83	94.12	116.61	140.18	164.74	190.16	216.34	243.18	270.58	298.46	326.74	355.35

Description: This table shows the total interest per $ 100 of amount financed, at the Annual Percentage Rate, for the term of the loan. Loan payments are monthly in arrears.

Example: The total interest for a 30 year loan at an Annual Percentage Rate of 8 % is $ 164.16. The total interest for a $ 50,000 loan is $ 82080.00.

RATE	16 yr	17 yr	18 yr	19 yr	20 yr	21 yr	22 yr	23 yr	24 yr	25 yr	26 yr	27 yr	28 yr	29 yr	30 yr
0.00	0.00	0.00	0.00	0.00	0.00	0.00	0.00	0.00	0.00	0.00	0.00	0.00	0.00	0.00	0.00
1.00	8.25	8.78	9.31	9.84	10.37	10.91	11.44	11.98	12.52	13.06	13.60	14.15	14.69	15.24	15.79
2.00	16.93	18.04	19.16	20.28	21.41	22.55	23.69	24.84	25.99	27.16	28.32	29.50	30.68	31.87	33.06
3.00	26.04	27.78	29.54	31.31	33.10	34.91	36.72	38.56	40.40	42.26	44.14	46.03	47.93	49.85	51.78
4.00	35.55	37.98	40.44	42.93	45.44	47.97	50.53	53.11	55.72	58.35	61.01	63.69	66.39	69.12	71.87
4.25	37.99	40.61	43.25	45.92	48.62	51.34	54.10	56.88	59.69	62.52	65.38	68.27	71.19	74.13	77.10
4.50	40.46	43.26	46.09	48.95	51.84	54.76	57.71	60.69	63.71	66.75	69.82	72.93	76.06	79.22	82.41
4.75	42.96	45.94	48.96	52.01	55.09	58.21	61.37	64.56	67.78	71.04	74.32	77.64	80.99	84.38	87.79
5.00	45.47	48.65	51.86	55.10	58.39	61.71	65.07	68.47	71.91	75.38	78.88	82.42	86.00	89.61	93.26
5.25	48.02	51.38	54.79	58.23	61.72	65.25	68.82	72.43	76.08	79.77	83.50	87.27	91.07	94.92	98.79
5.50	50.59	54.14	57.75	61.40	65.09	68.83	72.62	76.44	80.31	84.23	88.18	92.18	96.21	100.29	104.40
5.75	53.18	56.93	60.74	64.60	68.50	72.45	76.45	80.50	84.59	88.73	92.92	97.14	101.42	105.73	110.09
6.00	55.80	59.75	63.76	67.83	71.94	76.11	80.33	84.60	88.92	93.29	97.71	102.17	106.68	111.24	115.84
6.25	58.44	62.60	66.82	71.09	75.42	79.81	84.25	88.75	93.30	97.90	102.55	107.26	112.01	116.81	121.66
6.50	61.10	65.47	69.90	74.39	78.94	83.55	88.22	92.94	97.72	102.56	107.45	112.40	117.40	122.45	127.54
6.75	63.79	68.37	73.01	77.72	82.49	87.32	92.22	97.18	102.20	107.27	112.41	117.60	122.84	128.14	133.50
7.00	66.50	71.29	76.15	81.08	86.07	91.13	96.26	101.46	106.71	112.03	117.41	122.85	128.35	133.90	139.51
7.25	69.24	74.24	79.32	84.47	89.69	94.98	100.35	105.78	111.28	116.84	122.47	128.16	133.91	139.72	145.58
7.50	72.00	77.22	82.51	87.89	93.34	98.87	104.47	110.14	115.89	121.70	127.58	133.52	139.52	145.59	151.72
7.75	74.78	80.22	85.74	91.34	97.03	102.79	108.63	114.55	120.54	126.60	132.73	138.93	145.19	151.52	157.91
8.00	77.59	83.24	88.99	94.83	100.75	106.75	112.83	118.99	125.23	131.54	137.93	144.39	150.91	157.50	164.16
8.25	80.41	86.30	92.27	98.34	104.50	110.74	117.07	123.48	129.97	136.54	143.18	149.89	156.68	163.54	170.46
8.50	83.26	89.37	95.58	101.88	108.28	114.76	121.34	128.00	134.74	141.57	148.47	155.45	162.50	169.62	176.81
8.75	86.13	92.47	98.91	105.45	112.09	118.82	125.65	132.56	139.56	146.64	153.81	161.05	168.36	175.75	183.21
9.00	89.03	95.60	102.27	109.05	115.93	122.91	129.99	137.16	144.42	151.76	159.19	166.69	174.28	181.93	189.66
9.25	91.94	98.74	105.66	112.68	119.81	127.04	134.37	141.79	149.31	156.91	164.61	172.38	180.23	188.16	196.16
9.50	94.88	101.92	109.07	116.34	123.71	131.19	138.78	146.46	154.24	162.11	170.07	178.11	186.23	194.43	202.71
9.75	97.84	105.11	112.51	120.02	127.64	135.38	143.22	151.16	159.21	167.34	175.57	183.88	192.27	200.75	209.30
10.00	100.81	108.33	115.97	123.73	131.61	139.60	147.70	155.90	164.21	172.61	181.10	189.69	198.35	207.10	215.93
10.25	103.81	111.57	119.45	127.46	135.59	143.84	152.20	160.67	169.24	177.91	186.68	195.53	204.48	213.50	222.60
10.50	106.83	114.83	122.96	131.22	139.61	148.12	156.74	165.48	174.31	183.25	192.29	201.42	210.63	219.93	229.31
10.75	109.87	118.11	126.49	135.01	143.65	152.42	161.31	170.31	179.42	188.63	197.94	207.34	216.83	226.40	236.05
11.00	112.93	121.42	130.05	138.82	147.73	156.76	165.91	175.17	184.55	194.03	203.62	213.29	223.06	232.91	242.84
11.25	116.01	124.74	133.63	142.66	151.82	161.12	170.53	180.07	189.72	199.47	209.33	219.28	229.32	239.45	249.65
11.50	119.10	128.09	137.23	146.52	155.94	165.50	175.19	184.99	194.91	204.94	215.07	225.30	235.62	246.02	256.50
11.75	122.22	131.46	140.86	150.40	160.09	169.91	179.87	189.94	200.14	210.44	220.85	231.35	241.94	252.63	263.39
12.00	125.36	134.85	144.50	154.31	164.26	174.35	184.58	194.92	205.39	215.97	226.65	237.43	248.30	259.26	270.30
12.25	128.51	138.26	148.17	158.24	168.46	178.82	189.31	199.93	210.67	221.52	232.48	243.54	254.69	265.93	277.24
12.50	131.68	141.68	151.86	162.19	172.67	183.30	194.07	204.96	215.98	227.11	238.34	249.68	261.10	272.62	284.21
12.75	134.87	145.13	155.56	166.16	176.91	187.81	198.85	210.02	221.31	232.72	244.23	255.84	267.55	279.34	291.21
13.00	138.08	148.60	159.29	170.16	181.18	192.35	203.66	215.10	226.67	238.35	250.14	262.03	274.01	286.08	298.23
13.25	141.30	152.08	163.04	174.17	185.46	196.91	208.49	220.21	232.05	244.01	256.08	268.24	280.51	292.85	305.28
13.50	144.54	155.59	166.81	178.21	189.77	201.49	213.34	225.34	237.46	249.69	262.04	274.48	287.02	299.65	312.35
13.75	147.80	159.11	170.60	182.26	194.10	206.09	218.22	230.49	242.89	255.40	268.02	280.74	293.56	306.46	319.44
14.00	151.08	162.65	174.40	186.34	198.44	210.71	223.12	235.66	248.34	261.13	274.03	287.03	300.12	313.30	326.55
14.25	154.37	166.20	178.23	190.43	202.81	215.35	228.04	240.86	253.81	266.88	280.06	293.33	306.70	320.16	333.69
14.50	157.68	169.77	182.07	194.55	207.20	220.01	232.97	246.07	259.30	272.65	286.10	299.66	313.30	327.03	340.84
14.75	161.00	173.36	185.93	198.68	211.61	224.69	237.93	251.31	264.82	278.44	292.17	306.00	319.93	333.93	348.01
15.00	164.34	176.97	189.81	202.83	216.03	229.39	242.91	256.56	270.35	284.25	298.26	312.37	326.57	340.85	355.20
15.25	167.69	180.59	193.70	207.00	220.47	234.11	247.90	261.84	275.90	290.08	304.36	318.75	333.22	347.78	362.41
15.50	171.06	184.23	197.61	211.18	224.93	238.85	252.92	267.13	281.47	295.92	310.49	325.15	339.90	354.73	369.63
15.75	174.45	187.89	201.54	215.38	229.41	243.60	257.95	272.44	287.05	301.79	316.63	331.56	346.59	361.69	376.86
16.00	177.85	191.55	205.48	219.60	233.90	248.37	263.00	277.76	292.66	307.67	322.78	337.99	353.29	368.67	384.11
16.25	181.26	195.24	209.43	223.83	238.41	253.16	268.06	283.10	298.28	313.56	328.95	344.44	360.01	375.66	391.38
16.50	184.68	198.94	213.41	228.08	242.94	257.96	273.14	288.46	303.91	319.47	335.14	350.90	366.75	382.67	398.65
16.75	188.12	202.65	217.39	232.34	247.48	262.78	278.24	293.84	309.56	325.40	341.34	357.38	373.49	389.68	405.94
17.00	191.58	206.38	221.40	236.62	252.03	267.61	283.35	299.22	315.22	331.34	347.56	363.86	380.25	396.72	413.24
17.25	195.04	210.12	225.41	240.91	256.60	272.46	288.47	304.63	320.90	337.29	353.78	370.36	387.03	403.76	420.55
17.50	198.52	213.87	229.44	245.22	261.19	277.32	293.61	310.04	326.59	343.26	360.02	376.88	393.81	410.81	427.88
17.75	202.02	217.64	233.49	249.54	265.78	282.20	298.76	315.47	332.30	349.24	366.28	383.40	400.60	417.88	435.21
18.00	205.52	221.42	237.54	253.87	270.39	287.09	303.93	320.91	338.02	355.23	372.54	389.94	407.41	424.95	442.55
18.25	209.04	225.21	241.61	258.22	275.02	291.99	309.11	326.37	343.74	361.23	378.81	396.48	414.23	432.03	449.90
18.50	212.57	229.01	245.69	262.58	279.66	296.90	314.30	331.83	349.48	367.25	385.10	403.04	421.05	439.13	457.26
18.75	216.11	232.83	249.79	266.95	284.30	301.83	319.50	337.31	355.24	373.27	391.40	409.60	427.88	446.23	464.63
19.00	219.66	236.66	253.89	271.33	288.96	306.76	324.71	342.80	361.00	379.30	397.70	416.18	434.73	453.34	472.00
20.00	233.98	252.08	270.43	288.98	307.72	326.62	345.67	364.85	384.15	403.54	423.01	442.56	462.18	481.85	501.57
25.00	307.78	331.43	355.30	379.35	403.57	427.92	452.39	476.95	501.59	526.29	551.05	575.85	600.69	625.56	650.45
30.00	384.23	413.33	442.62	472.05	501.61	531.25	560.98	590.76	620.59	650.46	680.35	710.27	740.21	770.16	800.12

Description: This table shows the total interest per $ 100 of amount financed, at the Annual Percentage Rate, for the term of the loan. Loan payments are quarterly in arrears.

Example: The total interest for a 15 year loan at an Annual Percentage Rate of 8 % is $ 72.61. The total interest for a $ 50,000 loan is $ 36305.00.

RATE	1 yr	2 yr	3 yr	4 yr	5 yr	6 yr	7 yr	8 yr	9 yr	10 yr	11 yr	12 yr	13 yr	14 yr	15 yr
0.00	0.00	0.00	0.00	0.00	0.00	0.00	0.00	0.00	0.00	0.00	0.00	0.00	0.00	0.00	0.00
1.00	.63	1.13	1.63	2.14	2.65	3.15	3.67	4.18	4.69	5.21	5.73	6.24	6.77	7.29	7.81
2.00	1.25	2.26	3.28	4.30	5.33	6.37	7.41	8.46	9.52	10.58	11.65	12.73	13.81	14.90	16.00
3.00	1.88	3.40	4.94	6.49	8.06	9.64	11.24	12.85	14.48	16.12	17.78	19.45	21.13	22.83	24.55
4.00	2.51	4.55	6.62	8.71	10.83	12.98	15.15	17.35	19.57	21.82	24.10	26.40	28.73	31.09	33.47
4.25	2.67	4.84	7.04	9.27	11.53	13.82	16.14	18.49	20.87	23.27	25.71	28.18	30.67	33.20	35.75
4.50	2.83	5.13	7.46	9.83	12.23	14.66	17.13	19.63	22.17	24.73	27.33	29.97	32.63	35.33	38.06
4.75	2.99	5.42	7.89	10.39	12.93	15.51	18.13	20.79	23.48	26.20	28.97	31.77	34.61	37.48	40.39
5.00	3.14	5.71	8.31	10.95	13.64	16.37	19.14	21.95	24.80	27.69	30.62	33.59	36.60	39.65	42.74
5.25	3.30	6.00	8.74	11.52	14.35	17.22	20.15	23.11	26.12	29.18	32.28	35.42	38.61	41.84	45.11
5.50	3.46	6.29	9.16	12.09	15.06	18.09	21.16	24.28	27.46	30.68	33.95	37.27	40.63	44.05	47.51
5.75	3.62	6.58	9.59	12.65	15.78	18.95	22.18	25.46	28.80	32.19	35.63	39.13	42.67	46.27	49.92
6.00	3.78	6.87	10.02	13.22	16.49	19.82	23.20	26.65	30.15	33.71	37.33	41.00	44.73	48.52	52.36
6.25	3.94	7.16	10.44	13.80	17.21	20.69	24.23	27.84	31.51	35.24	39.03	42.89	46.80	50.78	54.82
6.50	4.10	7.45	10.87	14.37	17.93	21.56	25.27	29.04	32.87	36.78	40.75	44.79	48.89	53.06	57.30
6.75	4.25	7.74	11.31	14.94	18.66	22.44	26.30	30.24	34.25	38.33	42.48	46.71	51.00	55.37	59.80
7.00	4.41	8.03	11.74	15.52	19.38	23.33	27.35	31.45	35.63	39.89	44.22	48.64	53.12	57.68	62.32
7.25	4.57	8.33	12.17	16.10	20.11	24.21	28.40	32.67	37.02	41.46	45.98	50.58	55.26	60.02	64.86
7.50	4.73	8.62	12.60	16.68	20.84	25.10	29.45	33.89	38.42	43.04	47.74	52.54	57.41	62.38	67.42
7.75	4.89	8.91	13.04	17.26	21.58	25.99	30.51	35.12	39.82	44.62	49.52	54.51	59.58	64.75	70.01
8.00	5.05	9.21	13.47	17.84	22.31	26.89	31.57	36.35	41.24	46.22	51.31	56.49	61.77	67.14	72.61
8.25	5.21	9.50	13.91	18.42	23.05	27.79	32.64	37.60	42.66	47.83	53.11	58.49	63.97	69.55	75.23
8.50	5.37	9.80	14.34	19.01	23.79	28.69	33.71	38.84	44.09	49.45	54.92	60.50	66.18	71.97	77.87
8.75	5.53	10.09	14.78	19.60	24.54	29.60	34.79	40.10	45.53	51.07	56.74	62.52	68.41	74.42	80.53
9.00	5.69	10.39	15.22	20.19	25.28	30.51	35.87	41.36	46.97	52.71	58.57	64.56	70.66	76.88	83.21
9.25	5.85	10.68	15.66	20.78	26.03	31.43	36.96	42.62	48.42	54.35	60.42	66.60	72.92	79.35	85.91
9.50	6.01	10.98	16.10	21.37	26.78	32.34	38.05	43.90	49.88	56.01	62.27	68.67	75.19	81.85	88.63
9.75	6.17	11.28	16.54	21.96	27.54	33.27	39.15	45.17	51.35	57.67	64.14	70.74	77.48	84.36	91.37
10.00	6.33	11.57	16.98	22.56	28.29	34.19	40.25	46.46	52.83	59.34	66.01	72.83	79.79	86.89	94.12
10.25	6.49	11.87	17.43	23.16	29.05	35.12	41.35	47.75	54.31	61.03	67.90	74.93	82.11	89.43	96.89
10.50	6.65	12.17	17.87	23.75	29.81	36.05	42.46	49.05	55.80	62.72	69.80	77.04	84.44	91.99	99.68
10.75	6.81	12.47	18.32	24.35	30.58	36.99	43.58	50.35	57.30	64.42	71.71	79.17	86.79	94.56	102.49
11.00	6.97	12.77	18.76	24.96	31.34	37.92	44.70	51.66	58.80	66.13	73.63	81.30	89.15	97.15	105.32
11.25	7.13	13.07	19.21	25.56	32.11	38.87	45.82	52.97	60.31	67.84	75.56	83.45	91.52	99.76	108.16
11.50	7.29	13.36	19.66	26.16	32.88	39.81	46.95	54.29	61.83	69.57	77.50	85.61	93.91	102.38	111.03
11.75	7.45	13.66	20.11	26.77	33.66	40.76	48.08	55.62	63.36	71.31	79.45	87.79	96.31	105.02	113.90
12.00	7.61	13.97	20.55	27.38	34.43	41.71	49.22	56.95	64.89	73.05	81.41	89.97	98.73	107.67	116.80
12.25	7.77	14.27	21.00	27.99	35.21	42.67	50.36	58.29	66.44	74.80	83.38	92.17	101.16	110.34	119.71
12.50	7.93	14.57	21.46	28.60	35.99	43.63	51.51	59.63	67.98	76.56	85.36	94.38	103.60	113.02	122.64
12.75	8.09	14.87	21.91	29.21	36.77	44.59	52.66	60.98	69.54	78.33	87.36	96.60	106.06	115.72	125.58
13.00	8.25	15.17	22.36	29.82	37.56	45.56	53.82	62.34	71.10	80.11	89.36	98.83	108.53	118.43	128.54
13.25	8.42	15.47	22.81	30.44	38.35	46.53	54.98	63.70	72.67	81.90	91.37	101.07	111.01	121.16	131.51
13.50	8.58	15.77	23.27	31.06	39.14	47.50	56.14	65.06	74.25	83.69	93.39	103.33	113.50	123.90	134.51
13.75	8.74	16.08	23.72	31.68	39.93	48.48	57.31	66.43	75.83	85.50	95.42	105.59	116.01	126.65	137.51
14.00	8.90	16.38	24.18	32.30	40.72	49.45	58.49	67.81	77.42	87.31	97.46	107.87	118.53	129.42	140.53
14.25	9.06	16.69	24.64	32.92	41.52	50.44	59.67	69.20	79.02	89.13	99.51	110.16	121.06	132.20	143.57
14.50	9.22	16.99	25.10	33.54	42.32	51.42	60.85	70.59	80.62	90.96	101.57	112.46	123.60	134.99	146.62
14.75	9.39	17.29	25.55	34.17	43.12	52.41	62.04	71.98	82.24	92.79	103.64	114.77	126.16	137.80	149.68
15.00	9.55	17.60	26.01	34.79	43.92	53.41	63.23	73.38	83.85	94.64	105.72	117.09	128.72	140.62	152.76
15.25	9.71	17.90	26.48	35.42	44.73	54.40	64.42	74.79	85.48	96.49	107.81	119.42	131.30	143.45	155.85
15.50	9.87	18.21	26.94	36.05	45.54	55.40	65.62	76.20	87.11	98.35	109.90	121.76	133.89	146.30	158.96
15.75	10.03	18.52	27.40	36.68	46.35	56.40	66.83	77.61	88.75	100.22	112.01	124.11	136.49	149.16	162.08
16.00	10.20	18.82	27.86	37.31	47.16	57.41	68.04	79.04	90.39	102.09	114.12	126.47	139.11	152.03	165.21
16.25	10.36	19.13	28.33	37.95	47.98	58.42	69.25	80.46	92.04	103.98	116.25	128.84	141.73	154.91	168.36
16.50	10.52	19.44	28.79	38.58	48.80	59.43	70.47	81.90	93.70	105.87	118.38	131.22	144.37	157.80	171.52
16.75	10.68	19.74	29.26	39.22	49.62	60.44	71.69	83.33	95.37	107.77	120.52	133.61	147.01	160.71	174.69
17.00	10.85	20.05	29.72	39.86	50.44	61.46	72.91	84.78	97.04	109.67	122.67	136.01	149.67	163.63	177.87
17.25	11.01	20.36	30.19	40.50	51.26	62.48	74.14	86.23	98.71	111.59	124.83	138.42	152.34	166.56	181.07
17.50	11.17	20.67	30.66	41.14	52.09	63.51	75.38	87.68	100.40	113.51	127.00	140.84	155.01	169.50	184.27
17.75	11.33	20.98	31.13	41.78	52.92	64.54	76.62	89.14	102.09	115.44	129.17	143.27	157.70	172.45	187.49
18.00	11.50	21.29	31.60	42.42	53.75	65.57	77.86	90.60	103.78	117.37	131.36	145.71	160.40	175.41	190.73
18.25	11.66	21.60	32.07	43.07	54.59	66.60	79.10	92.07	105.48	119.32	133.55	148.15	163.11	178.39	193.97
18.50	11.82	21.91	32.54	43.72	55.42	67.64	80.36	93.55	107.19	121.27	135.75	150.61	165.83	181.37	197.22
18.75	11.99	22.22	33.01	44.37	56.26	68.68	81.61	95.03	108.90	123.22	137.95	153.07	168.55	184.37	200.49
19.00	12.15	22.53	33.49	45.02	57.10	69.72	82.87	96.51	110.62	125.19	140.17	155.55	171.29	187.37	203.76
20.00	12.80	23.78	35.39	47.63	60.49	73.93	87.94	102.50	117.56	133.11	149.11	165.53	182.33	199.49	216.97
25.00	16.10	30.11	45.10	61.05	77.92	95.67	114.24	133.56	153.60	174.27	195.52	217.28	239.51	262.15	285.14
30.00	19.43	36.58	55.13	75.03	96.18	118.52	141.93	166.32	191.58	217.60	244.29	271.55	299.29	327.45	355.95

TOTAL INTEREST

QUARTERLY PAYMENT

Description: This table shows the total interest per $ 100 of amount financed, at the Annual Percentage Rate, for the term of the loan. Loan payments are quarterly in arrears.

Example: The total interest for a 30 year loan at an Annual Percentage Rate of 8 % is $ 164.58. The total interest for a $ 50,000 loan is $ 82290.00.

RATE	16 yr	17 yr	18 yr	19 yr	20 yr	21 yr	22 yr	23 yr	24 yr	25 yr	26 yr	27 yr	28 yr	29 yr	30 yr
0.00	0.00	0.00	0.00	0.00	0.00	0.00	0.00	0.00	0.00	0.00	0.00	0.00	0.00	0.00	0.00
1.00	8.34	8.87	9.39	9.93	10.46	10.99	11.53	12.06	12.60	13.14	13.69	14.23	14.78	15.32	15.87
2.00	17.10	18.21	19.32	20.45	21.58	22.71	23.85	25.00	26.16	27.32	28.49	29.66	30.84	32.03	33.22
3.00	26.28	28.02	29.78	31.56	33.35	35.15	36.97	38.80	40.64	42.50	44.38	46.26	48.17	50.08	52.01
4.00	35.87	38.30	40.76	43.24	45.75	48.28	50.84	53.42	56.03	58.66	61.31	63.99	66.69	69.42	72.17
4.25	38.33	40.95	43.59	46.25	48.95	51.67	54.42	57.20	60.01	62.84	65.70	68.59	71.50	74.44	77.41
4.50	40.82	43.61	46.44	49.30	52.19	55.11	58.06	61.04	64.05	67.09	70.16	73.26	76.39	79.54	82.73
4.75	43.33	46.31	49.33	52.38	55.46	58.58	61.73	64.92	68.14	71.39	74.67	77.99	81.34	84.72	88.13
5.00	45.87	49.04	52.24	55.49	58.77	62.09	65.45	68.84	72.28	75.74	79.25	82.78	86.36	89.96	93.60
5.25	48.43	51.79	55.19	58.64	62.12	65.65	69.21	72.82	76.47	80.15	83.88	87.64	91.44	95.28	99.15
5.50	51.02	54.57	58.17	61.82	65.51	69.24	73.02	76.84	80.71	84.62	88.57	92.56	96.59	100.66	104.77
5.75	53.62	57.38	61.18	65.03	68.93	72.88	76.87	80.91	85.00	89.14	93.31	97.54	101.80	106.11	110.46
6.00	56.26	60.21	64.22	68.28	72.39	76.55	80.76	85.03	89.34	93.71	98.12	102.57	107.08	111.63	116.22
6.25	58.92	63.07	67.28	71.55	75.88	80.26	84.70	89.19	93.73	98.33	102.97	107.67	112.42	117.21	122.05
6.50	61.60	65.96	70.38	74.86	79.41	84.01	88.67	93.39	98.17	103.00	107.88	112.82	117.81	122.85	127.94
6.75	64.30	68.87	73.51	78.21	82.97	87.80	92.69	97.64	102.65	107.72	112.85	118.03	123.27	128.56	133.90
7.00	67.03	71.81	76.66	81.58	86.57	91.62	96.74	101.93	107.18	112.49	117.86	123.29	128.78	134.32	139.92
7.25	69.78	74.77	79.84	84.98	90.20	95.48	100.84	106.26	111.75	117.30	122.92	128.60	134.34	140.14	146.00
7.50	72.55	77.76	83.05	88.42	93.86	99.38	104.97	110.63	116.37	122.17	128.03	133.97	139.96	146.02	152.13
7.75	75.35	80.78	86.29	91.88	97.56	103.31	109.14	115.05	121.03	127.08	133.19	139.38	145.63	151.95	158.33
8.00	78.17	83.82	89.55	95.38	101.29	107.28	113.35	119.50	125.73	132.03	138.40	144.85	151.36	157.94	164.58
8.25	81.01	86.88	92.84	98.90	105.05	111.28	117.59	123.99	130.47	137.02	143.65	150.36	157.13	163.97	170.88
8.50	83.87	89.97	96.16	102.45	108.84	115.31	121.87	128.52	135.25	142.06	148.95	155.91	162.95	170.06	177.23
8.75	86.75	93.08	99.51	106.03	112.66	119.38	126.19	133.09	140.07	147.14	154.29	161.52	168.82	176.19	183.64
9.00	89.66	96.21	102.88	109.64	116.51	123.48	130.54	137.69	144.93	152.26	159.67	167.16	174.73	182.37	190.09
9.25	92.58	99.37	106.27	113.28	120.39	127.61	134.92	142.33	149.83	157.42	165.09	172.85	180.69	188.60	196.59
9.50	95.53	102.55	109.69	116.94	124.30	131.77	139.33	147.00	154.76	162.61	170.56	178.58	186.69	194.87	203.13
9.75	98.50	105.76	113.14	120.63	128.24	135.96	143.78	151.71	159.73	167.85	176.06	184.35	192.73	201.18	209.71
10.00	101.49	108.98	116.61	124.35	132.21	140.18	148.26	156.45	164.74	173.12	181.59	190.16	198.81	207.54	216.34
10.25	104.50	112.23	120.10	128.09	136.20	144.43	152.77	161.22	169.77	178.42	187.17	196.00	204.93	213.93	223.01
10.50	107.52	115.50	123.62	131.86	140.22	148.71	157.31	166.03	174.84	183.76	192.78	201.89	211.08	220.36	229.71
10.75	110.57	118.79	127.16	135.65	144.27	153.02	161.88	170.86	179.95	189.14	198.42	207.80	217.27	226.83	236.46
11.00	113.64	122.11	130.72	139.47	148.35	157.35	166.48	175.73	185.08	194.54	204.10	213.76	223.50	233.33	243.24
11.25	116.73	125.44	134.30	143.31	152.45	161.72	171.11	180.62	190.25	199.98	209.81	219.74	229.76	239.86	250.05
11.50	119.83	128.79	137.91	147.17	156.57	166.11	175.77	185.55	195.44	205.45	215.55	225.76	236.05	246.43	256.89
11.75	122.95	132.17	141.54	151.06	160.72	170.52	180.45	190.50	200.66	210.94	221.32	231.80	242.37	253.03	263.77
12.00	126.10	135.56	145.19	154.97	164.89	174.96	185.15	195.48	205.92	216.47	227.12	237.88	248.73	259.66	270.68
12.25	129.26	138.98	148.86	158.90	169.09	179.42	189.89	200.48	211.19	222.02	232.95	243.98	255.11	266.32	277.62
12.50	132.43	142.41	152.55	162.85	173.31	183.91	194.65	205.51	216.50	227.60	238.81	250.12	261.52	273.01	284.58
12.75	135.63	145.86	156.26	166.83	177.55	188.42	199.43	210.57	221.83	233.20	244.69	256.27	267.95	279.72	291.57
13.00	138.84	149.33	159.99	170.83	181.82	192.95	204.23	215.65	227.18	238.84	250.60	262.46	274.42	286.46	298.58
13.25	142.07	152.82	163.75	174.84	186.10	197.51	209.06	220.75	232.56	244.49	256.53	268.67	280.90	293.22	305.62
13.50	145.32	156.32	167.51	178.88	190.41	202.09	213.91	225.88	237.96	250.17	262.48	274.90	287.41	300.01	312.69
13.75	148.58	159.85	171.30	182.93	194.73	206.69	218.79	231.02	243.39	255.87	268.46	281.16	293.94	306.82	319.77
14.00	151.86	163.39	175.11	187.01	199.08	211.31	223.68	236.19	248.83	261.59	274.46	287.43	300.50	313.65	326.88
14.25	155.15	166.95	178.93	191.10	203.44	215.95	228.60	241.38	254.30	267.34	280.48	293.73	307.07	320.50	334.00
14.50	158.46	170.52	182.78	195.22	207.83	220.60	233.53	246.59	259.79	273.10	286.53	300.05	313.67	327.37	341.15
14.75	161.79	174.11	186.64	199.35	212.23	225.28	238.48	251.82	265.30	278.89	292.59	306.39	320.28	334.26	348.31
15.00	165.13	177.72	190.51	203.50	216.65	229.98	243.46	257.07	270.82	284.69	298.67	312.74	326.91	341.17	355.49
15.25	168.49	181.34	194.41	207.66	221.09	234.69	248.45	262.34	276.37	290.51	304.76	319.12	333.56	348.09	362.69
15.50	171.86	184.98	198.31	211.84	225.55	239.43	253.46	267.63	281.93	296.35	310.88	325.51	340.23	355.03	369.91
15.75	175.24	188.64	202.24	216.04	230.02	244.17	258.48	272.93	287.51	302.21	317.01	331.92	346.91	361.99	377.13
16.00	178.64	192.30	206.18	220.25	234.51	248.94	263.52	278.25	293.11	308.08	323.16	338.34	353.61	368.96	384.38
16.25	182.05	195.99	210.13	224.48	239.02	253.72	268.58	283.59	298.72	313.97	329.33	344.78	360.32	375.94	391.63
16.50	185.48	199.68	214.10	228.73	243.54	258.52	273.66	288.94	304.35	319.87	335.51	351.23	367.05	382.94	398.90
16.75	188.92	203.39	218.09	232.99	248.07	263.33	278.75	294.30	309.99	325.79	341.70	357.70	373.79	389.95	406.18
17.00	192.37	207.12	222.09	237.26	252.62	268.16	283.85	299.68	315.65	331.72	347.91	364.18	380.54	396.98	413.48
17.25	195.84	210.86	226.10	241.55	257.19	273.00	288.97	305.08	321.32	337.67	354.13	370.67	387.31	404.01	420.78
17.50	199.32	214.61	230.13	245.85	261.77	277.86	294.10	310.49	327.00	343.63	360.36	377.18	394.08	411.06	428.10
17.75	202.81	218.37	234.17	250.17	266.36	282.72	299.25	315.91	332.70	349.60	366.60	383.70	400.87	418.12	435.42
18.00	206.31	222.15	238.22	254.50	270.97	287.61	304.41	321.34	338.41	355.58	372.86	390.23	407.67	425.18	442.76
18.25	209.83	225.94	242.28	258.84	275.58	292.50	309.58	326.79	344.13	361.58	379.13	396.76	414.48	432.26	450.10
18.50	213.35	229.74	246.36	263.19	280.21	297.41	314.76	332.25	349.86	367.59	385.41	403.31	421.30	439.35	457.45
18.75	216.89	233.55	250.45	267.56	284.86	302.33	319.96	337.72	355.61	373.60	391.69	409.87	428.12	446.44	464.81
19.00	220.44	237.38	254.55	271.93	289.51	307.26	325.16	343.20	361.36	379.63	397.99	416.44	434.96	453.54	472.18
20.00	234.74	252.78	271.06	289.55	308.24	327.09	346.09	365.23	384.48	403.83	423.27	442.79	462.38	482.03	501.72
25.00	308.43	332.00	355.80	379.79	403.95	428.24	452.66	477.18	501.79	526.46	551.19	575.97	600.79	625.64	650.52
30.00	384.74	413.76	442.97	472.35	501.85	531.45	561.14	590.89	620.70	650.54	680.42	710.33	740.26	770.20	800.15

TABLE **4**

Percent Paid Off

Interest Rates:	0, 1, 2, 3%; 4 to 20% by .25%; 20, 25, 30%.
Terms:	15, 20, 25, 30 years.
Payment:	Monthly.
Loan-To-Value Ratio:	100, 95, 90, 85, 80%.
Percent Paid Off:	5, 10, 15, 20, 25, 30, 40, 50%.

This table shows the term, in years and months, to pay off a percent of value. "Value" is usually appraised value.

Example: A 95% loan is written at 8% for 30 years. In 5 years and 4 months, 10% of the value is paid off. The 10% includes the down payment of 5% that was paid at closing.

The term, tabulated in years and months, shows when the loan-to-value ratio reaches a certain percent of original value. When mortgage insurance covers the top part of a loan, this table shows the term of the coverage.

In the 5 year, 4 month term, 5.3% of the loan is paid off: 5 ÷ 95 = 5.3% An amortization schedule for an 8%, 30 year loan is shown on page 5-115. To apply the schedule to the example, multiply the schedule figures by .95.

The years and months shown in this table are calculated from a schedule at the interest rate, testing for the percent of value and converting the periods to years and months. For a loan not covered by this table, the simplest way to find the term of a balance is to prepare a schedule and then, finding the future balance, to read directly the number of periods. Keep in mind the difference between percent of value and percent of loan.

PERCENT PAID OFF

15 YEAR LOAN

Description: This table shows the term in years and months when a percent of value is paid off for an original loan-to-value ratio.

Example: A 95 % L-T-V loan is written at 8 % for 15 years. 10% of the value is paid off in 1 years and 6 months. The percent of loan that is paid off is 5/95 = 5.3 %.

RATE	100 % LTV 5 % Yr-Mo	10 % Yr-Mo	15 % Yr-Mo	20 % Yr-Mo	25 % Yr-Mo	30 % Yr-Mo	40 % Yr-Mo	50 % Yr-Mo	95 % LTV 10 % Yr-Mo	15 % Yr-Mo	20 % Yr-Mo	25 % Yr-Mo	30 % Yr-Mo	40 % Yr-Mo	50 % Yr-Mo
0.00	0- 9	1- 6	2- 3	3- 0	3- 9	4- 6	6- 0	7- 6	0-10	1- 7	2- 5	3- 2	4- 0	5- 7	7- 2
1.00	0-10	1- 8	2- 5	3- 3	4- 0	4- 9	6- 4	7-10	0-11	1- 9	2- 7	3- 5	4- 3	5-10	7- 5
2.00	0-11	1- 9	2- 7	3- 5	4- 3	5- 0	6- 7	8- 1	0-11	1-10	2- 9	3- 7	4- 5	6- 1	7- 8
3.00	1- 0	1-11	2- 9	3- 8	4- 6	5- 3	6-10	8- 5	1- 0	2- 0	2-11	3-10	4- 8	6- 5	8- 0
4.00	1- 1	2- 0	2-11	3-10	4- 9	5- 7	7- 2	8- 8	1- 1	2- 1	3- 1	4- 0	4-11	6- 8	8- 3
4.25	1- 1	2- 1	3- 0	3-11	4- 9	5- 7	7- 3	8- 9	1- 1	2- 2	3- 2	4- 1	5- 0	6- 9	8- 4
4.50	1- 1	2- 1	3- 0	3-11	4-10	5- 8	7- 3	8- 9	1- 2	2- 2	3- 2	4- 2	5- 1	6-10	8- 5
4.75	1- 1	2- 1	3- 1	4- 0	4-11	5- 9	7- 4	8-10	1- 2	2- 3	3- 3	4- 2	5- 2	6-10	8- 6
5.00	1- 2	2- 2	3- 2	4- 1	5- 0	5-10	7- 5	8-11	1- 2	2- 3	3- 3	4- 3	5- 2	6-11	8- 6
5.25	1- 2	2- 2	3- 2	4- 2	5- 0	5-11	7- 6	9- 0	1- 2	2- 4	3- 4	4- 4	5- 3	7- 0	8- 7
5.50	1- 2	2- 3	3- 3	4- 2	5- 1	5-11	7- 7	9- 1	1- 3	2- 4	3- 5	4- 5	5- 4	7- 1	8- 8
5.75	1- 2	2- 3	3- 3	4- 3	5- 2	6- 0	7- 8	9- 1	1- 3	2- 5	3- 5	4- 5	5- 5	7- 2	8- 9
6.00	1- 3	2- 4	3- 4	4- 4	5- 3	6- 1	7- 8	9- 2	1- 3	2- 5	3- 6	4- 6	5- 5	7- 3	8-10
6.25	1- 3	2- 4	3- 5	4- 4	5- 3	6- 2	7- 9	9- 3	1- 4	2- 6	3- 7	4- 7	5- 6	7- 3	8-10
6.50	1- 3	2- 5	3- 5	4- 5	5- 4	6- 3	7-10	9- 4	1- 4	2- 6	3- 7	4- 8	5- 7	7- 4	8-11
6.75	1- 3	2- 5	3- 6	4- 6	5- 5	6- 4	7-11	9- 4	1- 4	2- 7	3- 8	4- 8	5- 8	7- 5	9- 0
7.00	1- 4	2- 6	3- 7	4- 7	5- 6	6- 4	8- 0	9- 5	1- 4	2- 7	3- 9	4- 9	5- 9	7- 6	9- 1
7.25	1- 4	2- 6	3- 7	4- 7	5- 7	6- 5	8- 0	9- 6	1- 5	2- 8	3- 9	4-10	5- 9	7- 7	9- 1
7.50	1- 4	2- 7	3- 8	4- 8	5- 7	6- 6	8- 1	9- 7	1- 5	2- 8	3-10	4-11	5-10	7- 7	9- 2
7.75	1- 5	2- 7	3- 9	4- 9	5- 8	6- 7	8- 2	9- 7	1- 5	2- 9	3-11	4-11	5-11	7- 8	9- 3
8.00	1- 5	2- 8	3- 9	4-10	5- 9	6- 8	8- 3	9- 8	1- 6	2- 9	3-11	5- 0	6- 0	7- 9	9- 4
8.25	1- 5	2- 8	3-10	4-10	5-10	6- 8	8- 4	9- 9	1- 6	2-10	4- 0	5- 1	6- 1	7-10	9- 4
8.50	1- 6	2- 9	3-11	4-11	5-11	6- 9	8- 4	9- 9	1- 6	2-10	4- 1	5- 2	6- 2	7-11	9- 5
8.75	1- 6	2- 9	3-11	5- 0	5-11	6-10	8- 5	9-10	1- 7	2-11	4- 1	5- 2	6- 2	7-11	9- 6
9.00	1- 6	2-10	4- 0	5- 1	6- 0	6-11	8- 6	9-11	1- 7	2-11	4- 2	5- 3	6- 3	8- 0	9- 7
9.25	1- 7	2-11	4- 1	5- 1	6- 1	7- 0	8- 7	9-11	1- 7	3- 0	4- 3	5- 4	6- 4	8- 1	9- 7
9.50	1- 7	2-11	4- 1	5- 2	6- 2	7- 1	8- 8	10- 0	1- 8	3- 1	4- 3	5- 5	6- 5	8- 2	9- 8
9.75	1- 7	3- 0	4- 2	5- 3	6- 3	7- 1	8- 8	10- 1	1- 8	3- 1	4- 4	5- 6	6- 6	8- 3	9- 9
10.00	1- 8	3- 0	4- 3	5- 4	6- 4	7- 2	8- 9	10- 1	1- 9	3- 2	4- 5	5- 6	6- 6	8- 3	9- 9
10.25	1- 8	3- 1	4- 4	5- 5	6- 4	7- 3	8-10	10- 2	1- 9	3- 2	4- 6	5- 7	6- 7	8- 4	9-10
10.50	1- 8	3- 1	4- 4	5- 5	6- 5	7- 4	8-11	10- 3	1- 9	3- 3	4- 6	5- 8	6- 8	8- 5	9-11
10.75	1- 9	3- 2	4- 5	5- 6	6- 6	7- 5	8-11	10- 3	1-10	3- 4	4- 7	5- 9	6- 9	8- 6	9-11
11.00	1- 9	3- 3	4- 6	5- 7	6- 7	7- 5	9- 0	10- 4	1-10	3- 4	4- 8	5-10	6-10	8- 6	10- 0
11.25	1-10	3- 3	4- 6	5- 8	6- 8	7- 6	9- 1	10- 5	1-11	3- 5	4- 9	5-10	6-10	8- 7	10- 1
11.50	1-10	3- 4	4- 7	5- 9	6- 8	7- 7	9- 1	10- 5	1-11	3- 6	4- 9	5-11	6-11	8- 8	10- 1
11.75	1-10	3- 5	4- 8	5- 9	6- 9	7- 8	9- 2	10- 6	2- 0	3- 6	4-10	6- 0	7- 0	8- 9	10- 2
12.00	1-11	3- 5	4- 9	5-10	6-10	7- 9	9- 3	10- 6	2- 0	3- 7	4-11	6- 1	7- 1	8- 9	10- 2
12.25	1-11	3- 6	4- 9	5-11	6-11	7- 9	9- 4	10- 7	2- 0	3- 8	5- 0	6- 2	7- 2	8-10	10- 3
12.50	2- 0	3- 7	4-10	6- 0	7- 0	7-10	9- 4	10- 8	2- 1	3- 8	5- 0	6- 2	7- 2	8-11	10- 4
12.75	2- 0	3- 7	4-11	6- 1	7- 0	7-11	9- 5	10- 8	2- 1	3- 9	5- 1	6- 3	7- 3	9- 0	10- 4
13.00	2- 1	3- 8	5- 0	6- 1	7- 1	8- 0	9- 6	10- 9	2- 2	3-10	5- 2	6- 4	7- 4	9- 0	10- 5
13.25	2- 1	3- 9	5- 1	6- 2	7- 2	8- 0	9- 6	10- 9	2- 2	3-10	5- 3	6- 5	7- 5	9- 1	10- 5
13.50	2- 2	3- 9	5- 1	6- 3	7- 3	8- 1	9- 7	10-10	2- 3	3-11	5- 4	6- 6	7- 6	9- 2	10- 6
13.75	2- 2	3-10	5- 2	6- 4	7- 3	8- 2	9- 8	10-10	2- 3	4- 0	5- 4	6- 6	7- 6	9- 2	10- 7
14.00	2- 3	3-11	5- 3	6- 4	7- 4	8- 3	9- 8	10-11	2- 4	4- 0	5- 5	6- 7	7- 7	9- 3	10- 7
14.25	2- 3	3-11	5- 4	6- 5	7- 5	8- 3	9- 9	10-11	2- 4	4- 1	5- 6	6- 8	7- 8	9- 4	10- 8
14.50	2- 4	4- 0	5- 4	6- 6	7- 6	8- 4	9- 9	11- 0	2- 5	4- 2	5- 7	6- 9	7- 9	9- 4	10- 8
14.75	2- 4	4- 1	5- 5	6- 7	7- 7	8- 5	9-10	11- 0	2- 5	4- 3	5- 7	6- 9	7- 9	9- 5	10- 9
15.00	2- 5	4- 1	5- 6	6- 8	7- 7	8- 6	9-11	11- 1	2- 6	4- 3	5- 8	6-10	7-10	9- 6	10- 9
15.25	2- 5	4- 2	5- 7	6- 8	7- 8	8- 6	9-11	11- 1	2- 6	4- 4	5- 9	6-11	7-11	9- 6	10-10
15.50	2- 6	4- 3	5- 7	6- 9	7- 9	8- 7	10- 0	11- 2	2- 7	4- 5	5-10	7- 0	8- 0	9- 7	10-10
15.75	2- 6	4- 4	5- 8	6-10	7-10	8- 8	10- 1	11- 2	2- 7	4- 5	5-11	7- 1	8- 0	9- 8	10-11
16.00	2- 7	4- 4	5- 9	6-11	7-10	8- 8	10- 1	11- 3	2- 8	4- 6	5-11	7- 1	8- 1	9- 8	10-11
16.25	2- 7	4- 5	5-10	6-11	7-11	8- 9	10- 2	11- 3	2- 9	4- 7	6- 0	7- 2	8- 2	9- 9	11- 0
16.50	2- 8	4- 6	5-11	7- 0	8- 0	8-10	10- 2	11- 4	2- 9	4- 8	6- 1	7- 3	8- 2	9- 9	11- 0
16.75	2- 8	4- 6	5-11	7- 1	8- 0	8-10	10- 3	11- 4	2-10	4- 8	6- 2	7- 4	8- 3	9-10	11- 1
17.00	2- 9	4- 7	6- 0	7- 2	8- 1	8-11	10- 3	11- 5	2-10	4- 9	6- 2	7- 4	8- 4	9-11	11- 1
17.25	2-10	4- 8	6- 1	7- 2	8- 2	9- 0	10- 4	11- 5	2-11	4-10	6- 3	7- 5	8- 5	9-11	11- 2
17.50	2-10	4- 9	6- 2	7- 3	8- 3	9- 0	10- 4	11- 6	3- 0	4-11	6- 4	7- 6	8- 5	10- 0	11- 2
17.75	2-11	4- 9	6- 2	7- 4	8- 3	9- 1	10- 5	11- 6	3- 0	4-11	6- 5	7- 6	8- 6	10- 0	11- 3
18.00	2-11	4-10	6- 3	7- 5	8- 4	9- 2	10- 6	11- 6	3- 1	5- 0	6- 5	7- 7	8- 7	10- 1	11- 3
18.25	3- 0	4-11	6- 4	7- 5	8- 5	9- 2	10- 6	11- 7	3- 1	5- 1	6- 6	7- 8	8- 7	10- 1	11- 4
18.50	3- 1	5- 0	6- 5	7- 6	8- 5	9- 3	10- 7	11- 7	3- 2	5- 2	6- 7	7- 9	8- 8	10- 2	11- 4
18.75	3- 1	5- 0	6- 5	7- 7	8- 6	9- 3	10- 7	11- 8	3- 3	5- 2	6- 8	7- 9	8- 9	10- 3	11- 5
19.00	3- 2	5- 1	6- 6	7- 8	8- 7	9- 4	10- 8	11- 8	3- 3	5- 3	6- 8	7-10	8- 9	10- 3	11- 5
20.00	3- 4	5- 4	6- 9	7-10	8- 9	9- 6	10-10	11-10	3- 6	5- 6	6-11	8- 1	9- 0	10- 5	11- 7
25.00	4- 6	6- 6	7-11	8-11	9- 9	10- 5	11- 6	12- 4	4- 7	6- 8	8- 1	9- 1	9-11	11- 2	12- 2
30.00	5- 7	7- 7	8-10	9- 9	10- 6	11- 1	12- 0	12- 9	5- 9	7- 9	9- 0	9-11	10- 8	11- 9	12- 7

Description: This table shows the term in years and months when a percent of value is paid off for an original loan-to-value ratio.

Example: An 85 % L-T-V loan is written at 8 % for 15 years. 30% of the value is paid off in 4 years and 4 months. The percent of loan that is paid off is 15/85 = 17.6 %.

| | 90 % LTV | | | | | | 85 % LTV | | | | | 80 % LTV | | | |
RATE	15 % Yr-Mo	20 % Yr-Mo	25 % Yr-Mo	30 % Yr-Mo	40 % Yr-Mo	50 % Yr-Mo	20 % Yr-Mo	25 % Yr-Mo	30 % Yr-Mo	40 % Yr-Mo	50 % Yr-Mo	25 % Yr-Mo	30 % Yr-Mo	40 % Yr-Mo	50 % Yr-Mo
0.00	0-10	1-8	2-6	3-4	5-0	6-8	0-11	1-10	2-8	4-5	6-3	1-0	1-11	3-9	5-8
1.00	0-11	1-10	2-8	3-7	5-4	7-0	1-0	1-11	2-10	4-8	6-6	1-1	2-1	4-0	5-11
2.00	1-0	1-11	2-11	3-9	5-7	7-3	1-1	2-1	3-0	4-11	6-9	1-1	2-2	4-3	6-2
3.00	1-1	2-1	3-1	4-0	5-10	7-7	1-2	2-2	3-3	5-2	7-1	1-2	2-4	4-6	6-6
4.00	1-2	2-3	3-3	4-3	6-1	7-10	1-3	2-4	3-5	5-5	7-4	1-4	2-6	4-9	6-9
4.25	1-2	2-3	3-4	4-4	6-2	7-11	1-3	2-5	3-6	5-6	7-5	1-4	2-6	4-9	6-10
4.50	1-2	2-4	3-4	4-4	6-3	8-0	1-3	2-5	3-6	5-7	7-6	1-4	2-7	4-10	6-11
4.75	1-3	2-4	3-5	4-5	6-4	8-0	1-3	2-6	3-7	5-8	7-6	1-4	2-7	4-11	7-0
5.00	1-3	2-5	3-5	4-6	6-4	8-1	1-4	2-6	3-8	5-9	7-7	1-5	2-8	5-0	7-0
5.25	1-3	2-5	3-6	4-6	6-5	8-2	1-4	2-7	3-8	5-9	7-8	1-5	2-8	5-0	7-1
5.50	1-3	2-6	3-7	4-7	6-6	8-3	1-4	2-7	3-9	5-10	7-9	1-5	2-9	5-1	7-2
5.75	1-4	2-6	3-7	4-8	6-7	8-4	1-5	2-8	3-10	5-11	7-10	1-6	2-9	5-2	7-3
6.00	1-4	2-7	3-8	4-9	6-8	8-4	1-5	2-8	3-10	6-0	7-11	1-6	2-10	5-3	7-4
6.25	1-4	2-7	3-9	4-9	6-9	8-5	1-5	2-9	3-11	6-1	7-11	1-6	2-11	5-3	7-5
6.50	1-5	2-8	3-9	4-10	6-9	8-6	1-6	2-9	4-0	6-2	8-0	1-7	2-11	5-4	7-5
6.75	1-5	2-8	3-10	4-11	6-10	8-7	1-6	2-10	4-0	6-2	8-1	1-7	3-0	5-5	7-6
7.00	1-5	2-9	3-11	5-0	6-11	8-8	1-6	2-10	4-1	6-3	8-2	1-7	3-0	5-6	7-7
7.25	1-6	2-9	3-11	5-0	7-0	8-8	1-7	2-11	4-2	6-4	8-3	1-8	3-1	5-7	7-8
7.50	1-6	2-10	4-0	5-1	7-1	8-9	1-7	2-11	4-2	6-5	8-3	1-8	3-1	5-7	7-9
7.75	1-6	2-10	4-1	5-2	7-2	8-10	1-7	3-0	4-3	6-6	8-4	1-8	3-2	5-8	7-10
8.00	1-7	2-11	4-1	5-3	7-2	8-11	1-8	3-1	4-4	6-6	8-5	1-9	3-3	5-9	7-10
8.25	1-7	2-11	4-2	5-4	7-3	8-11	1-8	3-1	4-5	6-7	8-6	1-9	3-3	5-10	7-11
8.50	1-7	3-0	4-3	5-4	7-4	9-0	1-8	3-2	4-5	6-8	8-7	1-10	3-4	5-11	8-0
8.75	1-8	3-1	4-4	5-5	7-5	9-1	1-9	3-2	4-6	6-9	8-7	1-10	3-4	5-11	8-1
9.00	1-8	3-1	4-4	5-6	7-6	9-2	1-9	3-3	4-7	6-10	8-8	1-10	3-5	6-0	8-1
9.25	1-8	3-2	4-5	5-7	7-6	9-2	1-10	3-4	4-8	6-11	8-9	1-11	3-6	6-1	8-2
9.50	1-9	3-2	4-6	5-8	7-7	9-3	1-10	3-4	4-8	6-11	8-10	1-11	3-6	6-2	8-3
9.75	1-9	3-3	4-7	5-8	7-8	9-4	1-10	3-5	4-9	7-0	8-10	2-0	3-7	6-3	8-4
10.00	1-10	3-4	4-7	5-9	7-9	9-5	1-11	3-6	4-10	7-1	8-11	2-0	3-8	6-4	8-5
10.25	1-10	3-4	4-8	5-10	7-10	9-5	1-11	3-6	4-11	7-2	9-0	2-0	3-8	6-4	8-5
10.50	1-10	3-5	4-9	5-11	7-10	9-6	2-0	3-7	4-11	7-3	9-1	2-1	3-9	6-5	8-6
10.75	1-11	3-6	4-10	6-0	7-11	9-7	2-0	3-8	5-0	7-3	9-1	2-1	3-10	6-6	8-7
11.00	1-11	3-6	4-10	6-0	8-0	9-7	2-1	3-8	5-1	7-4	9-2	2-2	3-10	6-7	8-8
11.25	2-0	3-7	4-11	6-1	8-1	9-8	2-1	3-9	5-2	7-5	9-3	2-2	3-11	6-8	8-8
11.50	2-0	3-8	5-0	6-2	8-1	9-9	2-1	3-10	5-2	7-6	9-3	2-3	4-0	6-8	8-9
11.75	2-1	3-8	5-1	6-3	8-2	9-9	2-2	3-10	5-3	7-7	9-4	2-3	4-1	6-9	8-10
12.00	2-1	3-9	5-1	6-4	8-3	9-10	2-2	3-11	5-4	7-8	9-5	2-4	4-1	6-10	8-11
12.25	2-2	3-10	5-2	6-4	8-4	9-11	2-3	4-0	5-5	7-8	9-5	2-4	4-2	6-11	8-11
12.50	2-2	3-10	5-3	6-5	8-5	9-11	2-3	4-0	5-6	7-9	9-6	2-5	4-3	7-0	9-0
12.75	2-3	3-11	5-4	6-6	8-5	10-0	2-4	4-1	5-6	7-10	9-7	2-5	4-3	7-0	9-1
13.00	2-3	4-0	5-4	6-7	8-6	10-1	2-4	4-2	5-7	7-10	9-7	2-6	4-4	7-1	9-1
13.25	2-4	4-0	5-5	6-8	8-7	10-1	2-5	4-2	5-8	7-11	9-8	2-6	4-5	7-2	9-2
13.50	2-4	4-1	5-6	6-8	8-7	10-2	2-5	4-3	5-9	8-0	9-9	2-7	4-6	7-3	9-3
13.75	2-5	4-2	5-7	6-9	8-8	10-2	2-6	4-4	5-10	8-1	9-9	2-7	4-6	7-3	9-3
14.00	2-5	4-2	5-8	6-10	8-9	10-3	2-6	4-5	5-10	8-1	9-10	2-8	4-7	7-4	9-4
14.25	2-6	4-3	5-8	6-11	8-10	10-4	2-7	4-5	5-11	8-2	9-11	2-9	4-8	7-5	9-5
14.50	2-6	4-4	5-9	6-11	8-10	10-4	2-8	4-6	6-0	8-3	9-11	2-9	4-9	7-6	9-5
14.75	2-7	4-5	5-10	7-0	8-11	10-5	2-8	4-7	6-1	8-4	10-0	2-10	4-9	7-7	9-6
15.00	2-7	4-5	5-11	7-1	9-0	10-5	2-9	4-8	6-1	8-4	10-1	2-10	4-10	7-7	9-7
15.25	2-8	4-6	6-0	7-2	9-0	10-6	2-9	4-8	6-2	8-5	10-1	2-11	4-11	7-8	9-7
15.50	2-8	4-7	6-0	7-3	9-1	10-6	2-10	4-9	6-3	8-6	10-2	3-0	5-0	7-9	9-8
15.75	2-9	4-8	6-1	7-3	9-2	10-7	2-10	4-10	6-4	8-6	10-2	3-0	5-0	7-10	9-9
16.00	2-9	4-8	6-2	7-4	9-2	10-8	2-11	4-11	6-5	8-7	10-3	3-1	5-1	7-10	9-9
16.25	2-10	4-9	6-3	7-5	9-3	10-8	3-0	4-11	6-5	8-8	10-3	3-1	5-2	7-11	9-10
16.50	2-11	4-10	6-3	7-6	9-4	10-9	3-0	5-0	6-6	8-9	10-4	3-2	5-3	8-0	9-10
16.75	2-11	4-11	6-4	7-6	9-4	10-9	3-1	5-1	6-7	8-9	10-5	3-3	5-3	8-0	9-11
17.00	3-0	4-11	6-5	7-7	9-5	10-10	3-1	5-2	6-8	8-10	10-5	3-3	5-4	8-1	10-0
17.25	3-0	5-0	6-6	7-8	9-6	10-10	3-2	5-2	6-8	8-11	10-6	3-4	5-5	8-2	10-0
17.50	3-1	5-1	6-6	7-8	9-6	10-11	3-3	5-3	6-9	8-11	10-6	3-4	5-6	8-3	10-1
17.75	3-2	5-2	6-7	7-9	9-7	10-11	3-3	5-4	6-10	9-0	10-7	3-5	5-6	8-3	10-1
18.00	3-2	5-2	6-8	7-10	9-7	11-0	3-4	5-5	6-11	9-1	10-7	3-6	5-7	8-4	10-2
18.25	3-3	5-3	6-9	7-11	9-8	11-0	3-5	5-5	6-11	9-1	10-8	3-6	5-8	8-5	10-2
18.50	3-4	5-4	6-9	7-11	9-9	11-1	3-5	5-6	7-0	9-2	10-8	3-7	5-9	8-5	10-3
18.75	3-4	5-5	6-10	8-0	9-9	11-1	3-6	5-7	7-1	9-2	10-9	3-8	5-9	8-6	10-4
19.00	3-5	5-5	6-11	8-1	9-10	11-1	3-7	5-8	7-2	9-3	10-9	3-8	5-10	8-7	10-4
20.00	3-7	5-8	7-2	8-3	10-0	11-3	3-9	5-11	7-4	9-5	10-11	3-11	6-1	8-9	10-6
25.00	4-9	6-11	8-3	9-4	10-10	11-11	4-11	7-1	8-6	10-4	11-7	5-1	7-3	9-9	11-3
30.00	5-11	7-11	9-2	10-1	11-5	12-4	6-1	8-1	9-4	11-0	12-1	6-3	8-3	10-6	11-10

Description: This table shows the term in years and months when a percent of value is paid off for an original loan-to-value ratio.

Example: A 95 % L-T-V loan is written at 8 % for 20 years. 10% of the value is paid off in 2 years and 5 months. The percent of loan that is paid off is 5/95 = 5.3 %.

RATE	100 % LTV 5 % Yr-Mo	10 % Yr-Mo	15 % Yr-Mo	20 % Yr-Mo	25 % Yr-Mo	30 % Yr-Mo	40 % Yr-Mo	50 % Yr-Mo	95 % LTV 10 % Yr-Mo	15 % Yr-Mo	20 % Yr-Mo	25 % Yr-Mo	30 % Yr-Mo	40 % Yr-Mo	50 % Yr-Mo
0.00	1- 0	2- 0	3- 0	4- 0	5- 0	6- 0	8- 0	10- 0	1- 1	2- 2	3- 2	4- 3	5- 4	7- 5	9- 6
1.00	1- 2	2- 3	3- 4	4- 4	5- 5	6- 6	8- 6	10- 6	1- 2	2- 4	3- 6	4- 7	5- 8	7-11	10- 0
2.00	1- 3	2- 5	3- 7	4- 9	5-10	6-11	9- 0	11- 0	1- 4	2- 7	3- 9	5- 0	6- 2	8- 4	10- 6
3.00	1- 5	2- 8	3-11	5- 1	6- 3	7- 5	9- 6	11- 6	1- 5	2-10	4- 1	5- 4	6- 7	8-10	11- 0
4.00	1- 6	2-11	4- 3	5- 6	6- 9	7-10	10- 0	12- 0	1- 7	3- 1	4- 6	5- 9	7- 0	9- 4	11- 6
4.25	1- 7	3- 0	4- 4	5- 7	6-10	8- 0	10- 2	12- 1	1- 8	3- 2	4- 7	5-11	7- 2	9- 6	11- 7
4.50	1- 7	3- 1	4- 5	5- 9	6-11	8- 1	10- 3	12- 3	1- 8	3- 3	4- 8	6- 0	7- 3	9- 7	11- 9
4.75	1- 8	3- 2	4- 6	5-10	7- 1	8- 3	10- 5	12- 4	1- 9	3- 3	4- 9	6- 1	7- 5	9- 9	11-10
5.00	1- 8	3- 3	4- 7	5-11	7- 2	8- 4	10- 6	12- 5	1- 9	3- 4	4-10	6- 3	7- 6	9-10	11-11
5.25	1- 9	3- 3	4- 9	6- 1	7- 4	8- 6	10- 7	12- 7	1-10	3- 5	4-11	6- 4	7- 7	10- 0	12- 1
5.50	1- 9	3- 4	4-10	6- 2	7- 5	8- 7	10- 9	12- 8	1-10	3- 6	5- 0	6- 5	7- 9	10- 1	12- 2
5.75	1-10	3- 5	4-11	6- 3	7- 6	8- 9	10-10	12- 9	1-11	3- 7	5- 2	6- 7	7-10	10- 3	12- 3
6.00	1-10	3- 6	5- 0	6- 5	7- 8	8-10	11- 0	12-10	2- 0	3- 8	5- 3	6- 8	8- 0	10- 4	12- 5
6.25	1-11	3- 7	5- 1	6- 6	7- 9	9- 0	11- 1	13- 0	2- 0	3- 9	5- 4	6- 9	8- 1	10- 5	12- 6
6.50	2- 0	3- 8	5- 3	6- 7	7-11	9- 1	11- 3	13- 1	2- 1	3-10	5- 5	6-11	8- 3	10- 7	12- 7
6.75	2- 0	3- 9	5- 4	6- 9	8- 0	9- 2	11- 4	13- 2	2- 1	3-11	5- 7	7- 0	8- 4	10- 8	12- 9
7.00	2- 1	3-10	5- 5	6-10	8- 2	9- 4	11- 5	13- 3	2- 2	4- 0	5- 8	7- 2	8- 6	10-10	12-10
7.25	2- 1	3-11	5- 6	7- 0	8- 3	9- 5	11- 7	13- 5	2- 3	4- 1	5- 9	7- 3	8- 7	10-11	12-11
7.50	2- 2	4- 0	5- 8	7- 1	8- 5	9- 7	11- 8	13- 6	2- 3	4- 2	5-10	7- 4	8- 8	11- 0	13- 0
7.75	2- 3	4- 1	5- 9	7- 2	8- 6	9- 8	11- 9	13- 7	2- 4	4- 3	6- 0	7- 6	8-10	11- 2	13- 1
8.00	2- 3	4- 2	5-10	7- 4	8- 7	9-10	11-11	13- 8	2- 5	4- 5	6- 1	7- 7	8-11	11- 3	13- 3
8.25	2- 4	4- 3	6- 0	7- 5	8- 9	9-11	12- 0	13- 9	2- 6	4- 6	6- 2	7- 9	9- 1	11- 5	13- 4
8.50	2- 5	4- 5	6- 1	7- 7	8-10	10- 0	12- 1	13-10	2- 6	4- 7	6- 4	7-10	9- 2	11- 6	13- 5
8.75	2- 6	4- 6	6- 2	7- 8	9- 0	10- 2	12- 2	13-11	2- 7	4- 8	6- 5	7-11	9- 4	11- 7	13- 6
9.00	2- 6	4- 7	6- 3	7- 9	9- 1	10- 3	12- 4	14- 0	2- 8	4- 9	6- 6	8- 1	9- 5	11- 8	13- 7
9.25	2- 7	4- 8	6- 5	7-11	9- 3	10- 5	12- 5	14- 1	2- 9	4-10	6- 8	8- 2	9- 6	11-10	13- 8
9.50	2- 8	4- 9	6- 6	8- 0	9- 4	10- 6	12- 6	14- 2	2- 9	5- 0	6- 9	8- 4	9- 8	11-11	13- 9
9.75	2- 9	4-10	6- 8	8- 2	9- 5	10- 7	12- 7	14- 3	2-10	5- 1	6-11	8- 5	9- 9	12- 0	13-10
10.00	2-10	5- 0	6- 9	8- 3	9- 7	10- 9	12- 9	14- 4	2-11	5- 2	7- 0	8- 7	9-11	12- 2	13-11
10.25	2-10	5- 1	6-10	8- 4	9- 8	10-10	12-10	14- 5	3- 0	5- 3	7- 1	8- 8	10- 0	12- 3	14- 0
10.50	2-11	5- 2	7- 0	8- 6	9-10	10-11	12-11	14- 6	3- 1	5- 5	7- 3	8- 9	10- 1	12- 4	14- 2
10.75	3- 0	5- 3	7- 1	8- 7	9-11	11- 1	13- 0	14- 7	3- 2	5- 6	7- 4	8-11	10- 3	12- 5	14- 2
11.00	3- 1	5- 5	7- 2	8- 9	10- 0	11- 2	13- 1	14- 8	3- 3	5- 7	7- 6	9- 0	10- 4	12- 6	14- 3
11.25	3- 2	5- 6	7- 4	8-10	10- 2	11- 3	13- 2	14- 9	3- 4	5- 8	7- 7	9- 2	10- 5	12- 7	14- 4
11.50	3- 3	5- 7	7- 5	8-11	10- 3	11- 5	13- 3	14-10	3- 5	5-10	7- 8	9- 3	10- 7	12- 9	14- 5
11.75	3- 4	5- 8	7- 7	9- 1	10- 4	11- 6	13- 4	14-11	3- 6	5-11	7-10	9- 4	10- 8	12-10	14- 6
12.00	3- 5	5-10	7- 8	9- 2	10- 6	11- 7	13- 5	15- 0	3- 7	6- 0	7-11	9- 6	10- 9	12-11	14- 7
12.25	3- 6	5-11	7- 9	9- 4	10- 7	11- 8	13- 6	15- 1	3- 8	6- 2	8- 0	9- 7	10-11	13- 0	14- 8
12.50	3- 7	6- 0	7-11	9- 5	10- 8	11- 9	13- 7	15- 1	3- 9	6- 3	8- 2	9- 8	11- 0	13- 1	14- 9
12.75	3- 8	6- 2	8- 0	9- 6	10- 9	11-11	13- 8	15- 2	3-10	6- 4	8- 3	9-10	11- 1	13- 2	14-10
13.00	3- 9	6- 3	8- 1	9- 8	10-11	12- 0	13- 9	15- 3	3-11	6- 5	8- 5	9-11	11- 2	13- 3	14-11
13.25	3-10	6- 4	8- 3	9- 9	11- 0	12- 1	13-10	15- 4	4- 0	6- 7	8- 6	10- 0	11- 4	13- 4	14-11
13.50	3-11	6- 5	8- 4	9-10	11- 1	12- 2	13-11	15- 4	4- 1	6- 8	8- 7	10- 2	11- 5	13- 5	15- 0
13.75	4- 0	6- 7	8- 5	10- 0	11- 2	12- 3	14- 0	15- 5	4- 2	6- 9	8- 9	10- 3	11- 6	13- 6	15- 1
14.00	4- 1	6- 8	8- 7	10- 1	11- 4	12- 4	14- 1	15- 6	4- 3	6-11	8-10	10- 4	11- 7	13- 7	15- 2
14.25	4- 2	6- 9	8- 8	10- 2	11- 5	12- 5	14- 2	15- 7	4- 4	7- 0	8-11	10- 5	11- 8	13- 8	15- 3
14.50	4- 3	6-11	8- 9	10- 3	11- 6	12- 6	14- 3	15- 7	4- 5	7- 1	9- 1	10- 7	11- 9	13- 9	15- 3
14.75	4- 5	7- 0	8-11	10- 5	11- 7	12- 8	14- 4	15- 8	4- 7	7- 3	9- 2	10- 8	11-11	13-10	15- 4
15.00	4- 6	7- 1	9- 0	10- 6	11- 8	12- 9	14- 5	15- 9	4- 8	7- 4	9- 3	10- 9	12- 0	13-11	15- 5
15.25	4- 7	7- 3	9- 1	10- 7	11- 9	12-10	14- 5	15- 9	4- 9	7- 5	9- 4	10-10	12- 1	14- 0	15- 5
15.50	4- 8	7- 4	9- 3	10- 8	11-11	12-11	14- 6	15-10	4-10	7- 7	9- 6	10-11	12- 2	14- 1	15- 6
15.75	4- 9	7- 5	9- 4	10- 9	12- 0	13- 0	14- 7	15-11	4-11	7- 8	9- 7	11- 1	12- 3	14- 1	15- 7
16.00	4-10	7- 7	9- 5	10-11	12- 1	13- 1	14- 8	15-11	5- 0	7- 9	9- 8	11- 2	12- 4	14- 2	15- 8
16.25	5- 0	7- 8	9- 7	11- 0	12- 2	13- 2	14- 9	16- 0	5- 2	7-11	9-10	11- 3	12- 5	14- 3	15- 8
16.50	5- 1	7- 9	9- 8	11- 1	12- 3	13- 3	14- 9	16- 0	5- 3	8- 0	9-11	11- 4	12- 6	14- 4	15- 9
16.75	5- 2	7-11	9- 9	11- 2	12- 4	13- 3	14-10	16- 1	5- 4	8- 1	10- 0	11- 5	12- 7	14- 5	15- 9
17.00	5- 3	8- 0	9-10	11- 3	12- 5	13- 4	14-11	16- 2	5- 5	8- 3	10- 1	11- 6	12- 8	14- 6	15-10
17.25	5- 4	8- 1	9-11	11- 4	12- 6	13- 5	15- 0	16- 2	5- 6	8- 4	10- 2	11- 7	12- 9	14- 6	15-11
17.50	5- 6	8- 2	10- 1	11- 5	12- 7	13- 6	15- 0	16- 3	5- 8	8- 5	10- 4	11- 8	12-10	14- 7	15-11
17.75	5- 7	8- 4	10- 2	11- 6	12- 8	13- 7	15- 1	16- 3	5- 9	8- 6	10- 5	11-10	12-11	14- 8	16- 0
18.00	5- 8	8- 5	10- 3	11- 8	12- 9	13- 8	15- 2	16- 4	5-10	8- 8	10- 6	11-11	13- 0	14- 9	16- 0
18.25	5- 9	8- 6	10- 4	11- 9	12-10	13- 9	15- 2	16- 4	5-11	8- 9	10- 7	12- 0	13- 1	14- 9	16- 1
18.50	5-10	8- 7	10- 5	11-10	12-11	13-10	15- 3	16- 5	6- 1	8-10	10- 8	12- 1	13- 2	14-10	16- 1
18.75	6- 0	8- 9	10- 6	11-11	13- 0	13-10	15- 4	16- 5	6- 2	8-11	10- 9	12- 2	13- 3	14-11	16- 2
19.00	6- 1	8-10	10- 8	12- 0	13- 1	13-11	15- 4	16- 6	6- 3	9- 1	10-10	12- 3	13- 3	14-11	16- 3
20.00	6- 6	9- 3	11- 0	12- 4	13- 4	14- 2	15- 7	16- 8	6- 8	9- 5	11- 3	12- 6	13- 7	15- 2	16- 5
25.00	8- 5	11- 0	12- 6	13- 8	14- 6	15- 3	16- 5	17- 3	8- 8	11- 2	12- 9	13-10	14- 9	16- 1	17- 1
30.00	10- 1	12- 4	13- 8	14- 8	15- 5	16- 0	17- 0	17- 9	10- 3	12- 6	13-10	14-10	15- 7	16- 8	17- 6

Description: This table shows the term in years and months when a percent of value is paid off for an original loan-to-value ratio.

Example: An 85 % L-T-V loan is written at 8 % for 20 years. 30% of the value is paid off in 6 years and 8 months. The percent of loan that is paid off is 15/85 = 17.6 %.

RATE	90 % LTV						85 % LTV					80 % LTV			
	15 % Yr-Mo	20 % Yr-Mo	25 % Yr-Mo	30 % Yr-Mo	40 % Yr-Mo	50 % Yr-Mo	20 % Yr-Mo	25 % Yr-Mo	30 % Yr-Mo	40 % Yr-Mo	50 % Yr-Mo	25 % Yr-Mo	30 % Yr-Mo	40 % Yr-Mo	50 % Yr-Mo
0.00	1-2	2-3	3-4	4-6	6-8	8-11	1-3	2-5	3-7	5-11	8-3	1-3	2-6	5-0	7-6
1.00	1-3	2-6	3-8	4-10	7-2	9-5	1-4	2-7	3-10	6-4	8-9	1-5	2-9	5-5	8-0
2.00	1-5	2-8	4-0	5-3	7-8	9-11	1-6	2-10	4-2	6-10	9-3	1-7	3-0	5-10	8-6
3.00	1-6	2-11	4-4	5-8	8-1	10-5	1-7	3-1	4-7	7-3	9-9	1-9	3-4	6-3	9-0
4.00	1-8	3-3	4-8	6-1	8-7	10-11	1-9	3-5	4-11	7-9	10-3	1-11	3-7	6-9	9-6
4.25	1-9	3-4	4-9	6-2	8-9	11-0	1-10	3-6	5-0	7-10	10-4	1-11	3-8	6-10	9-7
4.50	1-9	3-5	4-11	6-3	8-10	11-2	1-10	3-7	5-2	8-0	10-6	2-0	3-9	6-11	9-9
4.75	1-10	3-5	5-0	6-5	9-0	11-3	1-11	3-8	5-3	8-1	10-7	2-0	3-10	7-1	9-10
5.00	1-10	3-6	5-1	6-6	9-1	11-5	2-0	3-9	5-4	8-3	10-9	2-1	3-11	7-2	10-0
5.25	1-11	3-7	5-2	6-7	9-3	11-6	2-0	3-10	5-5	8-4	10-10	2-2	4-0	7-4	10-1
5.50	2-0	3-8	5-3	6-9	9-4	11-7	2-1	3-11	5-7	8-6	11-0	2-2	4-1	7-5	10-3
5.75	2-0	3-9	5-5	6-10	9-6	11-9	2-1	4-0	5-8	8-7	11-1	2-3	4-2	7-6	10-4
6.00	2-1	3-10	5-6	7-0	9-7	11-10	2-2	4-1	5-9	8-8	11-3	2-4	4-3	7-8	10-6
6.25	2-1	3-11	5-7	7-1	9-8	11-11	2-3	4-2	5-10	8-10	11-4	2-4	4-4	7-9	10-7
6.50	2-2	4-0	5-8	7-2	9-10	12-1	2-3	4-3	6-0	8-11	11-5	2-5	4-6	7-11	10-8
6.75	2-3	4-1	5-10	7-4	9-11	12-2	2-4	4-4	6-1	9-1	11-7	2-6	4-7	8-0	10-10
7.00	2-3	4-3	5-11	7-5	10-1	12-3	2-5	4-5	6-2	9-2	11-8	2-6	4-8	8-2	10-11
7.25	2-4	4-4	6-0	7-7	10-2	12-5	2-5	4-6	6-4	9-4	11-9	2-7	4-9	8-3	11-1
7.50	2-5	4-5	6-2	7-8	10-4	12-6	2-6	4-7	6-5	9-5	11-11	2-8	4-10	8-5	11-2
7.75	2-5	4-6	6-3	7-9	10-5	12-7	2-7	4-8	6-6	9-7	12-0	2-9	4-11	8-6	11-3
8.00	2-6	4-7	6-4	7-11	10-6	12-8	2-8	4-10	6-8	9-8	12-1	2-10	5-1	8-7	11-5
8.25	2-7	4-8	6-6	8-0	10-8	12-10	2-9	4-11	6-9	9-9	12-3	2-10	5-2	8-9	11-6
8.50	2-8	4-9	6-7	8-2	10-9	12-11	2-9	5-0	6-10	9-11	12-4	2-11	5-3	8-10	11-7
8.75	2-9	4-11	6-8	8-3	10-11	13-0	2-10	5-1	7-0	10-0	12-5	3-0	5-4	9-0	11-9
9.00	2-9	5-0	6-10	8-5	11-0	13-1	2-11	5-3	7-1	10-2	12-6	3-1	5-6	9-1	11-10
9.25	2-10	5-1	6-11	8-6	11-1	13-2	3-0	5-4	7-3	10-3	12-8	3-2	5-7	9-3	11-11
9.50	2-11	5-2	7-0	8-7	11-3	13-4	3-1	5-5	7-4	10-4	12-9	3-3	5-8	9-4	12-1
9.75	3-0	5-3	7-2	8-9	11-4	13-5	3-2	5-6	7-5	10-6	12-10	3-4	5-9	9-5	12-2
10.00	3-1	5-5	7-3	8-10	11-5	13-6	3-3	5-8	7-7	10-7	12-11	3-5	5-11	9-7	12-3
10.25	3-2	5-6	7-5	9-0	11-6	13-7	3-4	5-9	7-8	10-9	13-0	3-6	6-0	9-8	12-4
10.50	3-3	5-7	7-6	9-1	11-8	13-8	3-5	5-10	7-10	10-10	13-1	3-7	6-1	9-10	12-5
10.75	3-4	5-8	7-7	9-3	11-9	13-9	3-5	5-11	7-11	10-11	13-2	3-8	6-3	9-11	12-7
11.00	3-5	5-10	7-9	9-4	11-10	13-10	3-6	6-1	8-0	11-0	13-4	3-9	6-4	10-0	12-8
11.25	3-5	5-11	7-10	9-5	11-11	13-11	3-7	6-2	8-2	11-2	13-5	3-10	6-5	10-2	12-9
11.50	3-6	6-0	8-0	9-7	12-1	14-0	3-9	6-3	8-3	11-3	13-6	3-11	6-7	10-3	12-10
11.75	3-7	6-2	8-1	9-8	12-2	14-1	3-10	6-5	8-5	11-4	13-7	4-0	6-8	10-4	12-11
12.00	3-9	6-3	8-2	9-9	12-3	14-2	3-11	6-6	8-6	11-6	13-8	4-1	6-9	10-6	13-0
12.25	3-10	6-4	8-4	9-11	12-4	14-3	4-0	6-7	8-7	11-7	13-9	4-2	6-11	10-7	13-1
12.50	3-11	6-6	8-5	10-0	12-5	14-4	4-1	6-9	8-9	11-8	13-10	4-3	7-0	10-8	13-2
12.75	4-0	6-7	8-7	10-1	12-6	14-5	4-2	6-10	8-10	11-9	13-11	4-4	7-1	10-9	13-3
13.00	4-1	6-8	8-8	10-3	12-8	14-6	4-3	6-11	8-11	11-10	14-0	4-5	7-3	10-11	13-4
13.25	4-2	6-10	8-9	10-4	12-9	14-6	4-4	7-1	9-1	12-0	14-1	4-6	7-4	11-0	13-5
13.50	4-3	6-11	8-11	10-5	12-10	14-7	4-5	7-2	9-2	12-1	14-1	4-8	7-6	11-1	13-6
13.75	4-4	7-0	9-0	10-6	12-11	14-8	4-6	7-3	9-3	12-2	14-2	4-9	7-7	11-2	13-7
14.00	4-5	7-2	9-1	10-8	13-0	14-9	4-8	7-5	9-5	12-3	14-3	4-10	7-8	11-4	13-8
14.25	4-6	7-3	9-3	10-9	13-1	14-10	4-9	7-6	9-6	12-4	14-4	4-11	7-10	11-5	13-9
14.50	4-8	7-4	9-4	10-10	13-2	14-11	4-10	7-8	9-7	12-5	14-5	5-0	7-11	11-6	13-10
14.75	4-9	7-6	9-5	10-11	13-3	14-11	4-11	7-9	9-9	12-6	14-6	5-2	8-0	11-7	13-11
15.00	4-10	7-7	9-6	11-1	13-4	15-0	5-0	7-10	9-10	12-7	14-7	5-3	8-1	11-8	14-0
15.25	4-11	7-8	9-8	11-2	13-5	15-1	5-1	8-0	9-11	12-8	14-8	5-4	8-3	11-9	14-1
15.50	5-0	7-10	9-9	11-3	13-6	15-2	5-3	8-1	10-0	12-9	14-8	5-5	8-4	11-11	14-2
15.75	5-1	7-11	9-10	11-4	13-7	15-2	5-4	8-2	10-2	12-10	14-9	5-7	8-6	12-0	14-3
16.00	5-3	8-0	10-0	11-5	13-8	15-3	5-5	8-3	10-3	12-11	14-10	5-8	8-7	12-1	14-4
16.25	5-4	8-2	10-1	11-6	13-8	15-4	5-6	8-5	10-4	13-0	14-11	5-9	8-8	12-2	14-4
16.50	5-5	8-3	10-2	11-7	13-9	15-4	5-8	8-6	10-5	13-1	14-11	5-10	8-9	12-3	14-5
16.75	5-6	8-4	10-3	11-9	13-10	15-5	5-9	8-7	10-7	13-2	15-0	6-0	8-11	12-4	14-6
17.00	5-8	8-5	10-4	11-10	13-11	15-6	5-10	8-9	10-8	13-3	15-1	6-1	9-0	12-5	14-7
17.25	5-9	8-7	10-6	11-11	14-0	15-6	5-11	8-10	10-9	13-4	15-2	6-2	9-1	12-6	14-7
17.50	5-10	8-8	10-7	12-0	14-1	15-7	6-1	8-11	10-10	13-5	15-2	6-3	9-2	12-7	14-8
17.75	5-11	8-9	10-8	12-1	14-2	15-8	6-2	9-0	10-11	13-6	15-3	6-5	9-4	12-8	14-9
18.00	6-1	8-11	10-9	12-2	14-2	15-8	6-3	9-2	11-0	13-7	15-4	6-6	9-5	12-9	14-10
18.25	6-2	9-0	10-10	12-3	14-3	15-9	6-4	9-3	11-1	13-8	15-4	6-7	9-6	12-10	14-10
18.50	6-3	9-1	10-11	12-4	14-4	15-10	6-6	9-4	11-2	13-8	15-5	6-8	9-7	12-11	14-11
18.75	6-4	9-2	11-0	12-5	14-5	15-10	6-7	9-5	11-4	13-9	15-5	6-10	9-8	13-0	15-0
19.00	6-6	9-3	11-1	12-6	14-5	15-11	6-8	9-6	11-5	13-10	15-6	6-11	9-10	13-1	15-0
20.00	6-11	9-8	11-6	12-9	14-8	16-1	7-1	9-11	11-9	14-1	15-8	7-4	10-2	13-4	15-3
25.00	8-10	11-5	12-11	14-1	15-8	16-10	9-0	11-7	13-2	15-2	16-6	9-3	11-10	14-6	16-2
30.00	10-5	12-8	14-0	15-0	16-4	17-4	10-7	12-11	14-3	15-11	17-1	10-10	13-1	15-5	16-9

PERCENT PAID OFF   25 YEAR LOAN

Description: This table shows the term in years and months when a percent of value is paid off for an original loan-to-value ratio.

Example: A 95 % L-T-V loan is written at 8 % for 25 years. 10% of the value is paid off in 3 years and 8 months. The percent of loan that is paid off is 5/95 = 5.3 %.

RATE	100 % LTV 5 % Yr-Mo	10 % Yr-Mo	15 % Yr-Mo	20 % Yr-Mo	25 % Yr-Mo	30 % Yr-Mo	40 % Yr-Mo	50 % Yr-Mo	95 % LTV 10 % Yr-Mo	15 % Yr-Mo	20 % Yr-Mo	25 % Yr-Mo	30 % Yr-Mo	40 % Yr-Mo	50 % Yr-Mo
0.00	1- 3	2- 6	3- 9	5- 0	6- 3	7- 6	10- 0	12- 6	1- 4	2- 8	4- 0	5- 4	6- 7	9- 3	11-11
1.00	1- 5	2-10	4- 3	5- 7	6-11	8- 3	10-10	13- 4	1- 6	3- 0	4- 5	5-10	7- 3	10- 0	12- 8
2.00	1- 8	3- 2	4- 8	6- 2	7- 7	8-11	11- 7	14- 1	1- 9	3- 4	4-11	6- 5	7-11	10- 9	13- 5
3.00	1-10	3- 7	5- 2	6- 9	8- 3	9- 8	12- 4	14-10	1-11	3- 9	5- 5	7- 1	8- 8	11- 6	14- 2
4.00	2- 1	4- 0	5- 9	7- 5	9- 0	10- 5	13- 1	15- 6	2- 2	4- 2	6- 0	7- 9	9- 4	12- 4	14-11
4.25	2- 2	4- 1	5-11	7- 7	9- 2	10- 7	13- 4	15- 9	2- 3	4- 4	6- 2	7-11	9- 7	12- 6	15- 1
4.50	2- 3	4- 3	6- 1	7- 9	9- 4	10-10	13- 6	15-11	2- 4	4- 5	6- 4	8- 1	9- 9	12- 8	15- 3
4.75	2- 4	4- 4	6- 3	7-11	9- 6	11- 0	13- 8	16- 1	2- 5	4- 7	6- 6	8- 3	9-11	12-10	15- 5
5.00	2- 5	4- 6	6- 5	8- 1	9- 9	11- 2	13-10	16- 3	2- 6	4- 8	6- 8	8- 6	10- 1	13- 1	15- 7
5.25	2- 6	4- 7	6- 7	8- 4	9-11	11- 5	14- 0	16- 4	2- 7	4-10	6-10	8- 8	10- 4	13- 3	15- 9
5.50	2- 7	4- 9	6- 8	8- 6	10- 1	11- 7	14- 3	16- 6	2- 8	5- 0	7- 0	8-10	10- 6	13- 5	15-11
5.75	2- 8	4-11	6-10	8- 8	10- 3	11- 9	14- 5	16- 8	2- 9	5- 1	7- 2	9- 0	10- 8	13- 7	16- 1
6.00	2- 9	5- 0	7- 0	8-10	10- 6	11-11	14- 7	16-10	2-10	5- 3	7- 4	9- 2	10-10	13- 9	16- 3
6.25	2-10	5- 2	7- 2	9- 0	10- 8	12- 2	14- 9	17- 0	2-11	5- 5	7- 6	9- 5	11- 1	14- 0	16- 5
6.50	2-11	5- 4	7- 4	9- 2	10-10	12- 4	14-11	17- 2	3- 0	5- 6	7- 8	9- 7	11- 3	14- 2	16- 7
6.75	3- 0	5- 5	7- 7	9- 5	11- 0	12- 6	15- 1	17- 3	3- 1	5- 8	7-10	9- 9	11- 5	14- 4	16- 9
7.00	3- 1	5- 7	7- 9	9- 7	11- 3	12- 8	15- 3	17- 5	3- 3	5-10	8- 0	9-11	11- 7	14- 6	16-11
7.25	3- 2	5- 9	7-11	9- 9	11- 5	12-10	15- 5	17- 7	3- 4	6- 0	8- 2	10- 1	11-10	14- 8	17- 0
7.50	3- 3	5-11	8- 1	9-11	11- 7	13- 1	15- 7	17- 8	3- 5	6- 2	8- 5	10- 4	12- 0	14-10	17- 2
7.75	3- 5	6- 1	8- 3	10- 2	11- 9	13- 3	15- 9	17-10	3- 6	6- 4	8- 7	10- 6	12- 2	15- 0	17- 4
8.00	3- 6	6- 2	8- 5	10- 4	11-11	13- 5	15-11	17-11	3- 8	6- 5	8- 9	10- 8	12- 4	15- 2	17- 5
8.25	3- 7	6- 4	8- 7	10- 6	12- 2	13- 7	16- 0	18- 1	3- 9	6- 7	8-11	10-10	12- 6	15- 4	17- 7
8.50	3- 9	6- 6	8- 9	10- 8	12- 4	13- 9	16- 2	18- 2	3-11	6- 9	9- 1	11- 1	12- 9	15- 6	17- 8
8.75	3-10	6- 8	9- 0	10-10	12- 6	13-11	16- 4	18- 4	4- 0	6-11	9- 3	11- 3	12-11	15- 7	17-10
9.00	3-11	6-10	9- 2	11- 1	12- 8	14- 1	16- 6	18- 5	4- 2	7- 1	9- 6	11- 5	13- 1	15- 9	17-11
9.25	4- 1	7- 0	9- 4	11- 3	12-10	14- 3	16- 7	18- 7	4- 3	7- 3	9- 8	11- 7	13- 3	15-11	18- 1
9.50	4- 2	7- 2	9- 6	11- 5	13- 0	14- 5	16- 9	18- 8	4- 5	7- 5	9-10	11- 9	13- 5	16- 1	18- 2
9.75	4- 4	7- 4	9- 8	11- 7	13- 2	14- 7	16-11	18- 9	4- 6	7- 7	10- 0	11-11	13- 7	16- 3	18- 4
10.00	4- 6	7- 6	9-10	11- 9	13- 4	14- 9	17- 0	18-11	4- 8	7-10	10- 2	12- 1	13- 9	16- 4	18- 5
10.25	4- 7	7- 8	10- 0	11-11	13- 6	14-11	17- 2	19- 0	4- 9	8- 0	10- 4	12- 3	13-11	16- 6	18- 6
10.50	4- 9	7-10	10- 3	12- 1	13- 8	15- 0	17- 3	19- 1	4-11	8- 2	10- 6	12- 6	14- 1	16- 7	18- 8
10.75	4-10	8- 0	10- 5	12- 3	13-10	15- 2	17- 5	19- 2	5- 1	8- 4	10- 9	12- 8	14- 3	16- 9	18- 9
11.00	5- 0	8- 2	10- 7	12- 5	14- 0	15- 4	17- 6	19- 3	5- 2	8- 6	10-11	12-10	14- 4	16-11	18-10
11.25	5- 2	8- 5	10- 9	12- 7	14- 2	15- 6	17- 8	19- 5	5- 4	8- 8	11- 1	13- 0	14- 6	17- 0	18-11
11.50	5- 4	8- 7	10-11	12- 9	14- 4	15- 7	17- 9	19- 6	5- 6	8-10	11- 3	13- 2	14- 8	17- 2	19- 1
11.75	5- 5	8- 9	11- 1	12-11	14- 6	15- 9	17-10	19- 7	5- 8	9- 0	11- 5	13- 3	14-10	17- 3	19- 2
12.00	5- 7	8-11	11- 3	13- 1	14- 7	15-11	18- 0	19- 8	5-10	9- 2	11- 7	13- 5	15- 0	17- 4	19- 3
12.25	5- 9	9- 1	11- 5	13- 3	14- 9	16- 0	18- 1	19- 9	5-11	9- 4	11- 9	13- 7	15- 1	17- 6	19- 4
12.50	5-11	9- 3	11- 7	13- 5	14-11	16- 2	18- 2	19-10	6- 1	9- 6	11-11	13- 9	15- 3	17- 7	19- 5
12.75	6- 1	9- 5	11- 9	13- 7	15- 1	16- 3	18- 4	19-11	6- 3	9- 8	12- 1	13-11	15- 5	17- 9	19- 6
13.00	6- 2	9- 7	11-11	13- 9	15- 2	16- 5	18- 5	20- 0	6- 5	9-10	12- 3	14- 1	15- 6	17-10	19- 7
13.25	6- 4	9- 9	12- 1	13-11	15- 4	16- 6	18- 6	20- 1	6- 7	10- 0	12- 5	14- 2	15- 8	17-11	19- 8
13.50	6- 6	9-11	12- 3	14- 0	15- 5	16- 8	18- 7	20- 2	6- 9	10- 2	12- 7	14- 4	15- 9	18- 0	19- 9
13.75	6- 8	10- 1	12- 5	14- 2	15- 7	16- 9	18- 8	20- 2	6-11	10- 4	12- 9	14- 6	15-11	18- 2	19-10
14.00	6-10	10- 3	12- 7	14- 4	15- 9	16-11	18- 9	20- 3	7- 1	10- 6	12-10	14- 8	16- 1	18- 3	19-11
14.25	7- 0	10- 5	12- 9	14- 5	15-10	17- 0	18-10	20- 4	7- 3	10- 8	13- 0	14- 9	16- 2	18- 4	20- 0
14.50	7- 2	10- 7	12-10	14- 7	16- 0	17- 1	19- 0	20- 5	7- 5	10-10	13- 2	14-11	16- 3	18- 5	20- 1
14.75	7- 4	10- 9	13- 0	14- 9	16- 1	17- 3	19- 1	20- 6	7- 7	11- 0	13- 4	15- 0	16- 5	18- 6	20- 2
15.00	7- 6	10-11	13- 2	14-10	16- 3	17- 4	19- 2	20- 7	7- 8	11- 2	13- 6	15- 2	16- 6	18- 7	20- 2
15.25	7- 8	11- 1	13- 4	15- 0	16- 4	17- 5	19- 3	20- 7	7-10	11- 4	13- 7	15- 4	16- 8	18- 8	20- 3
15.50	7-10	11- 3	13- 6	15- 1	16- 5	17- 6	19- 4	20- 8	8- 0	11- 6	13- 9	15- 5	16- 9	18- 9	20- 4
15.75	7-11	11- 5	13- 7	15- 3	16- 7	17- 8	19- 4	20- 9	8- 2	11- 8	13-11	15- 7	16-10	18-11	20- 5
16.00	8- 1	11- 6	13- 9	15- 4	16- 8	17- 9	19- 5	20-10	8- 4	11-10	14- 0	15- 8	17- 0	19- 0	20- 6
16.25	8- 3	11- 8	13-11	15- 6	16- 9	17-10	19- 6	20-10	8- 6	12- 0	14- 2	15- 9	17- 1	19- 0	20- 6
16.50	8- 5	11-10	14- 0	15- 7	16-11	17-11	19- 7	20-11	8- 8	12- 1	14- 4	15-11	17- 2	19- 1	20- 7
16.75	8- 7	12- 0	14- 2	15- 9	17- 0	18- 0	19- 8	21- 0	8-10	12- 3	14- 5	16- 0	17- 3	19- 2	20- 8
17.00	8- 9	12- 2	14- 3	15-10	17- 1	18- 1	19- 9	21- 0	9- 0	12- 5	14- 7	16- 2	17- 4	19- 3	20- 9
17.25	8-11	12- 3	14- 5	16- 0	17- 2	18- 2	19-10	21- 1	9- 2	12- 7	14- 8	16- 3	17- 6	19- 4	20- 9
17.50	9- 1	12- 5	14- 6	16- 1	17- 3	18- 3	19-11	21- 2	9- 4	12- 8	14-10	16- 4	17- 7	19- 5	20-10
17.75	9- 3	12- 7	14- 8	16- 2	17- 5	18- 4	19-11	21- 2	9- 6	12-10	14-11	16- 5	17- 8	19- 6	20-11
18.00	9- 5	12- 8	14- 9	16- 3	17- 6	18- 5	20- 0	21- 3	9- 7	13- 0	15- 1	16- 7	17- 9	19- 7	20-11
18.25	9- 6	12-10	14-11	16- 5	17- 7	18- 6	20- 1	21- 3	9- 9	13- 1	15- 2	16- 8	17-10	19- 8	21- 0
18.50	9- 8	13- 0	15- 0	16- 6	17- 8	18- 7	20- 2	21- 4	9-11	13- 3	15- 4	16- 9	17-11	19- 8	21- 0
18.75	9-10	13- 1	15- 2	16- 7	17- 9	18- 8	20- 2	21- 4	10- 1	13- 4	15- 5	16-10	18- 0	19- 9	21- 1
19.00	10- 0	13- 3	15- 3	16- 8	17-10	18- 9	20- 3	21- 5	10- 3	13- 6	15- 6	16-11	18- 1	19-10	21- 2
20.00	10- 7	13- 9	15- 8	17- 1	18- 2	19- 1	20- 6	21- 7	10-10	14- 0	15-11	17- 4	18- 5	20- 1	21- 4
25.00	13- 1	15-10	17- 5	18- 7	19- 6	20- 2	21- 4	22- 3	13- 3	16- 0	17- 8	18- 9	19- 8	21- 0	22- 0
30.00	15- 0	17- 3	18- 8	19- 7	20- 4	21- 0	21-11	22- 8	15- 2	17- 6	18-10	19- 9	20- 7	21- 8	22- 6

PERCENT PAID OFF

Description: This table shows the term in years and months when a percent of value is paid off for an original loan-to-value ratio.

Example: An 85 % L-T-V loan is written at 8 % for 25 years. 30% of the value is paid off in 9 years and 6 months. The percent of loan that is paid off is 15/85 = 17.6 %.

RATE	90 % LTV 15% Yr-Mo	20% Yr-Mo	25% Yr-Mo	30% Yr-Mo	40% Yr-Mo	50% Yr-Mo	85 % LTV 20% Yr-Mo	25% Yr-Mo	30% Yr-Mo	40% Yr-Mo	50% Yr-Mo	80 % LTV 25% Yr-Mo	30% Yr-Mo	40% Yr-Mo	50% Yr-Mo
0.00	1- 5	2-10	4- 2	5- 7	8- 4	11- 2	1- 6	3- 0	4- 5	7- 5	10- 4	1- 7	3- 2	6- 3	9- 5
1.00	1- 7	3- 2	4- 8	6- 2	9- 1	11-11	1- 8	3- 4	4-11	8- 1	11- 1	1-10	3- 6	6-11	10- 2
2.00	1-10	3- 6	5- 2	6- 9	9-10	12- 8	1-11	3- 9	5- 6	8- 9	11-11	2- 0	3-11	7- 7	10-11
3.00	2- 1	3-11	5- 9	7- 5	10- 7	13- 6	2- 2	4- 2	6- 0	9- 6	12- 8	2- 3	4- 5	8- 3	11- 8
4.00	2- 4	4- 5	6- 4	8- 1	11- 4	14- 3	2- 5	4- 8	6- 8	10- 3	13- 5	2- 7	4-11	9- 0	12- 6
4.25	2- 5	4- 6	6- 6	8- 4	11- 7	14- 5	2- 6	4- 9	6-10	10- 5	13- 7	2- 8	5- 0	9- 2	12- 8
4.50	2- 6	4- 8	6- 8	8- 6	11- 9	14- 7	2- 7	4-11	7- 0	10- 8	13- 9	2- 9	5- 2	9- 4	12-10
4.75	2- 7	4- 9	6-10	8- 8	11-11	14- 9	2- 8	5- 0	7- 2	10-10	14- 0	2-10	5- 4	9- 6	13- 0
5.00	2- 8	4-11	7- 0	8-10	12- 1	14-11	2- 9	5- 2	7- 4	11- 0	14- 2	2-11	5- 5	9- 9	13- 3
5.25	2- 9	5- 1	7- 2	9- 0	12- 4	15- 1	2-10	5- 4	7- 6	11- 3	14- 4	3- 0	5- 7	9-11	13- 5
5.50	2-10	5- 2	7- 4	9- 3	12- 6	15- 3	2-11	5- 6	7- 8	11- 5	14- 6	3- 1	5- 9	10- 1	13- 7
5.75	2-11	5- 4	7- 6	9- 5	12- 8	15- 5	3- 1	5- 7	7-10	11- 7	14- 8	3- 3	5-11	10- 3	13- 9
6.00	3- 0	5- 6	7- 8	9- 7	12-10	15- 7	3- 2	5- 9	8- 0	11- 9	14-10	3- 4	6- 1	10- 6	13-11
6.25	3- 1	5- 8	7-10	9- 9	13- 1	15- 9	3- 3	5-11	8- 2	12- 0	15- 0	3- 5	6- 3	10- 8	14- 2
6.50	3- 2	5- 9	8- 0	9-11	13- 3	15-11	3- 4	6- 1	8- 4	12- 2	15- 2	3- 6	6- 4	10-10	14- 4
6.75	3- 3	5-11	8- 2	10- 2	13- 5	16- 1	3- 5	6- 3	8- 7	12- 4	15- 4	3- 8	6- 6	11- 0	14- 6
7.00	3- 5	6- 1	8- 4	10- 4	13- 7	16- 3	3- 7	6- 5	8- 9	12- 6	15- 6	3- 9	6- 8	11- 3	14- 8
7.25	3- 6	6- 3	8- 7	10- 6	13- 9	16- 5	3- 8	6- 6	8-11	12- 8	15- 8	3-10	6-10	11- 5	14-10
7.50	3- 7	6- 5	8- 9	10- 8	13-11	16- 7	3- 9	6- 8	9- 1	12-11	15-10	4- 0	7- 0	11- 7	15- 0
7.75	3- 9	6- 7	8-11	10-11	14- 1	16- 8	3-11	6-10	9- 3	13- 1	16- 0	4- 1	7- 2	11- 9	15- 2
8.00	3-10	6- 9	9- 1	11- 1	14- 3	16-10	4- 0	7- 0	9- 6	13- 3	16- 2	4- 3	7- 4	11-11	15- 4
8.25	3-11	6-11	9- 3	11- 3	14- 5	17- 0	4- 2	7- 2	9- 8	13- 5	16- 4	4- 4	7- 6	12- 2	15- 6
8.50	4- 1	7- 1	9- 5	11- 5	14- 7	17- 1	4- 3	7- 4	9-10	13- 7	16- 5	4- 6	7- 8	12- 4	15- 7
8.75	4- 2	7- 3	9- 8	11- 7	14- 9	17- 3	4- 5	7- 6	10- 0	13- 9	16- 7	4- 7	7-11	12- 6	15- 9
9.00	4- 4	7- 5	9-10	11-10	14-11	17- 5	4- 6	7- 9	10- 2	13-11	16- 9	4- 9	8- 1	12- 8	15-11
9.25	4- 5	7- 7	10- 0	12- 0	15- 1	17- 6	4- 8	7-11	10- 4	14- 1	16-10	4-11	8- 3	12-10	16- 1
9.50	4- 7	7- 9	10- 2	12- 2	15- 3	17- 8	4-10	8- 1	10- 7	14- 3	17- 0	5- 0	8- 5	13- 0	16- 3
9.75	4- 9	7-11	10- 4	12- 4	15- 5	17- 9	4-11	8- 3	10- 9	14- 5	17- 2	5- 2	8- 7	13- 2	16- 4
10.00	4-10	8- 1	10- 6	12- 6	15- 7	17-11	5- 1	8- 5	10-11	14- 7	17- 3	5- 4	8- 9	13- 4	16- 6
10.25	5- 0	8- 3	10- 9	12- 8	15- 8	18- 0	5- 3	8- 7	11- 1	14- 9	17- 5	5- 6	8-11	13- 6	16- 8
10.50	5- 2	8- 5	10-11	12-10	15-10	18- 1	5- 4	8- 9	11- 3	14-11	17- 6	5- 7	9- 1	13- 8	16- 9
10.75	5- 3	8- 7	11- 1	13- 0	16- 0	18- 3	5- 6	8-11	11- 5	15- 0	17- 8	5- 9	9- 3	13-10	16-11
11.00	5- 5	8- 9	11- 3	13- 2	16- 1	18- 4	5- 8	9- 1	11- 7	15- 2	17- 9	5-11	9- 6	14- 0	17- 0
11.25	5- 7	9- 0	11- 5	13- 4	16- 3	18- 5	5-10	9- 3	11- 9	15- 4	17-10	6- 1	9- 8	14- 2	17- 2
11.50	5- 9	9- 2	11- 7	13- 6	16- 5	18- 7	6- 0	9- 6	11-11	15- 6	18- 0	6- 3	9-10	14- 4	17- 3
11.75	5-10	9- 4	11- 9	13- 8	16- 6	18- 8	6- 1	9- 8	12- 1	15- 7	18- 1	6- 5	10- 0	14- 6	17- 5
12.00	6- 0	9- 6	11-11	13-10	16- 8	18- 9	6- 3	9-10	12- 3	15- 9	18- 2	6- 7	10- 2	14- 7	17- 6
12.25	6- 2	9- 8	12- 1	14- 0	16- 9	18-10	6- 5	10- 0	12- 5	15-11	18- 4	6- 8	10- 4	14- 9	17- 7
12.50	6- 4	9-10	12- 3	14- 1	16-11	18-11	6- 7	10- 2	12- 7	16- 0	18- 5	6-10	10- 6	14-11	17- 9
12.75	6- 6	10- 0	12- 5	14- 3	17- 0	19- 1	6- 9	10- 4	12- 9	16- 2	18- 7	7- 0	10- 8	15- 1	17-10
13.00	6- 8	10- 2	12- 7	14- 5	17- 2	19- 2	6-11	10- 6	12-11	16- 3	18- 7	7- 2	10-10	15- 2	17-11
13.25	6-10	10- 4	12- 9	14- 7	17- 3	19- 3	7- 1	10- 8	13- 1	16- 5	18- 8	7- 4	11- 0	15- 4	18- 1
13.50	7- 0	10- 6	12-11	14- 8	17- 4	19- 4	7- 3	10-10	13- 3	16- 6	18-10	7- 6	11- 2	15- 5	18- 2
13.75	7- 2	10- 8	13- 1	14-10	17- 6	19- 5	7- 5	11- 0	13- 5	16- 8	18-11	7- 8	11- 4	15- 7	18- 2
14.00	7- 4	10-10	13- 2	15- 0	17- 7	19- 6	7- 7	11- 2	13- 7	16- 9	19- 0	7-10	11- 6	15- 9	18- 4
14.25	7- 6	11- 0	13- 4	15- 1	17- 8	19- 7	7- 9	11- 4	13- 8	16-11	19- 1	8- 0	11- 8	15-10	18- 5
14.50	7- 8	11- 2	13- 6	15- 3	17- 9	19- 8	7-11	11- 6	13-10	17- 0	19- 2	8- 2	11-10	16- 0	18- 7
14.75	7- 9	11- 4	13- 8	15- 4	17-11	19- 9	8- 1	11- 8	14- 0	17- 1	19- 3	8- 4	12- 0	16- 1	18- 8
15.00	7-11	11- 6	13- 9	15- 6	18- 0	19-10	8- 3	11-10	14- 1	17- 3	19- 4	8- 6	12- 2	16- 3	18- 9
15.25	8- 1	11- 8	13-11	15- 7	18- 1	19-10	8- 5	11-11	14- 3	17- 4	19- 5	8- 8	12- 3	16- 4	18-10
15.50	8- 3	11-10	14- 1	15- 9	18- 2	19-11	8- 7	12- 1	14- 5	17- 5	19- 6	8-10	12- 5	16- 5	18-11
15.75	8- 5	11-11	14- 2	15-10	18- 3	20- 0	8- 9	12- 3	14- 6	17- 6	19- 7	9- 0	12- 7	16- 7	19- 0
16.00	8- 7	12- 1	14- 4	16- 0	18- 4	20- 1	8-10	12- 5	14- 8	17- 7	19- 8	9- 2	12- 9	16- 8	19- 1
16.25	8- 9	12- 3	14- 6	16- 1	18- 5	20- 2	9- 0	12- 7	14- 9	17- 9	19- 8	9- 4	12-11	16- 9	19- 2
16.50	8-11	12- 5	14- 7	16- 3	18- 6	20- 3	9- 2	12- 8	14-11	17-10	19- 9	9- 6	13- 0	16-11	19- 3
16.75	9- 1	12- 6	14- 9	16- 4	18- 7	20- 3	9- 4	12-10	15- 0	17-11	19-10	9- 8	13- 2	17- 0	19- 4
17.00	9- 3	12- 8	14-10	16- 5	18- 8	20- 4	9- 6	13- 0	15- 2	18- 0	19-11	9-10	13- 4	17- 1	19- 4
17.25	9- 5	12-10	15- 0	16- 6	18- 9	20- 5	9- 8	13- 1	15- 3	18- 1	20- 0	9-11	13- 5	17- 2	19- 5
17.50	9- 7	13- 0	15- 1	16- 8	18-10	20- 6	9-10	13- 3	15- 5	18- 2	20- 0	10- 1	13- 7	17- 3	19- 6
17.75	9- 9	13- 1	15- 3	16- 9	18-11	20- 6	10- 0	13- 5	15- 6	18- 3	20- 1	10- 3	13- 8	17- 5	19- 7
18.00	9-10	13- 3	15- 4	16-10	19- 0	20- 7	10- 2	13- 6	15- 8	18- 4	20- 2	10- 5	13-10	17- 6	19- 8
18.25	10- 0	13- 4	15- 5	16-11	19- 1	20- 8	10- 3	13- 8	15- 9	18- 5	20- 3	10- 7	14- 0	17- 7	19- 9
18.50	10- 2	13- 6	15- 7	17- 0	19- 2	20- 8	10- 5	13- 9	15-10	18- 6	20- 3	10- 9	14- 1	17- 8	19-10
18.75	10- 4	13- 8	15- 8	17- 2	19- 3	20- 9	10- 7	13-11	15-11	18- 7	20- 4	10-10	14- 3	17- 9	19-10
19.00	10- 6	13- 9	15- 9	17- 3	19- 4	20-10	10- 9	14- 0	16- 1	18- 8	20- 5	11- 0	14- 4	17-10	19-11
20.00	11- 0	14- 3	16- 2	17- 7	19- 7	21- 0	11- 4	14- 6	16- 6	18-11	20- 7	11- 7	14-10	18- 2	20- 2
25.00	13- 6	16- 3	17-10	19- 0	20- 7	21- 9	13- 9	16- 5	18- 1	20- 1	21- 6	14- 0	16- 8	19- 6	21- 1
30.00	15- 4	17- 8	19- 0	20- 0	21- 4	22- 4	15- 6	17-10	19- 2	20-11	22- 1	15- 9	18- 0	20- 4	21- 9

Description: This table shows the term in years and months when a percent of value is paid off for an original loan-to-value ratio.

Example: A 95 % L-T-V loan is written at 8 % for 30 years. 10% of the value is paid off in 5 years and 4 months. The percent of loan that is paid off is 5/95 = 5.3 %.

RATE	100 % LTV 5% Yr-Mo	10% Yr-Mo	15% Yr-Mo	20% Yr-Mo	25% Yr-Mo	30% Yr-Mo	40% Yr-Mo	50% Yr-Mo	95 % LTV 10% Yr-Mo	15% Yr-Mo	20% Yr-Mo	25% Yr-Mo	30% Yr-Mo	40% Yr-Mo	50% Yr-Mo
0.00	1-6	3-0	4-6	6-0	7-6	9-0	12-0	15-0	1-7	3-2	4-9	6-4	7-11	11-1	14-3
1.00	1-9	3-6	5-2	6-10	8-5	10-0	13-2	16-2	1-10	3-8	5-5	7-2	8-10	12-2	15-5
2.00	2-1	4-0	5-10	7-8	9-5	11-1	14-3	17-3	2-2	4-2	6-2	8-0	9-10	13-3	16-6
3.00	2-5	4-7	6-8	8-7	10-5	12-2	15-4	18-4	2-6	4-10	6-11	9-0	10-10	14-5	17-7
4.00	2-9	5-3	7-6	9-7	11-6	13-3	16-5	19-3	2-11	5-6	7-10	10-0	11-11	15-6	18-7
4.25	2-11	5-5	7-9	9-10	11-9	13-6	16-9	19-6	3-0	5-8	8-1	10-3	12-3	15-9	18-10
4.50	3-0	5-7	8-0	10-1	12-0	13-9	17-0	19-9	3-2	5-11	8-4	10-6	12-6	16-0	19-1
4.75	3-1	5-10	8-2	10-4	12-3	14-1	17-3	20-0	3-3	6-1	8-7	10-9	12-9	16-3	19-3
5.00	3-3	6-0	8-5	10-7	12-7	14-4	17-6	20-2	3-5	6-3	8-10	11-0	13-0	16-6	19-6
5.25	3-4	6-3	8-8	10-10	12-10	14-7	17-9	20-5	3-6	6-6	9-0	11-4	13-4	16-10	19-9
5.50	3-6	6-5	8-11	11-2	13-1	14-10	18-0	20-7	3-8	6-8	9-3	11-7	13-7	17-1	20-0
5.75	3-8	6-8	9-2	11-5	13-4	15-2	18-3	20-10	3-10	6-11	9-7	11-10	13-10	17-4	20-2
6.00	3-9	6-10	9-5	11-8	13-8	15-5	18-5	21-0	4-0	7-2	9-10	12-1	14-1	17-7	20-5
6.25	3-11	7-1	9-8	11-11	13-11	15-8	18-8	21-3	4-1	7-4	10-1	12-4	14-5	17-9	20-7
6.50	4-1	7-3	9-11	12-2	14-2	15-11	18-11	21-5	4-3	7-7	10-4	12-8	14-8	18-0	20-9
6.75	4-3	7-6	10-2	12-6	14-5	16-2	19-2	21-7	4-5	7-10	10-7	12-11	14-11	18-3	21-0
7.00	4-5	7-9	10-5	12-9	14-8	16-5	19-4	21-9	4-7	8-1	10-10	13-2	15-2	18-6	21-2
7.25	4-7	8-0	10-8	13-0	14-11	16-8	19-7	21-11	4-9	8-3	11-1	13-5	15-5	18-8	21-4
7.50	4-9	8-3	11-0	13-3	15-2	16-11	19-9	22-1	4-11	8-6	11-4	13-8	15-8	18-11	21-6
7.75	4-11	8-5	11-3	13-6	15-5	17-2	20-0	22-3	5-2	8-9	11-7	13-11	15-11	19-2	21-9
8.00	5-1	8-8	11-6	13-9	15-8	17-4	20-2	22-5	5-4	9-0	11-10	14-2	16-2	19-4	21-11
8.25	5-3	8-11	11-9	14-0	15-11	17-7	20-4	22-7	5-6	9-3	12-2	14-5	16-5	19-7	22-1
8.50	5-6	9-2	12-0	14-3	16-2	17-10	20-7	22-9	5-8	9-6	12-5	14-8	16-8	19-9	22-3
8.75	5-8	9-5	12-3	14-6	16-5	18-0	20-9	22-11	5-11	9-9	12-8	14-11	16-10	19-11	22-4
9.00	5-10	9-8	12-6	14-9	16-8	18-3	20-11	23-1	6-1	10-0	12-11	15-2	17-1	20-2	22-6
9.25	6-1	9-11	12-9	15-0	16-11	18-6	21-1	23-2	6-4	10-3	13-2	15-5	17-4	20-4	22-8
9.50	6-3	10-2	13-0	15-3	17-1	18-8	21-3	23-4	6-6	10-6	13-5	15-8	17-6	20-6	22-10
9.75	6-6	10-5	13-3	15-6	17-4	18-10	21-5	23-5	6-9	10-9	13-8	15-11	17-9	20-8	22-11
10.00	6-8	10-8	13-6	15-9	17-6	19-1	21-7	23-7	7-0	11-0	13-11	16-2	18-0	20-10	23-1
10.25	6-11	10-11	13-9	15-11	17-9	19-3	21-9	23-8	7-2	11-3	14-2	16-4	18-2	21-0	23-3
10.50	7-2	11-2	14-0	16-2	17-11	19-5	21-11	23-10	7-5	11-6	14-5	16-7	18-4	21-2	23-4
10.75	7-4	11-5	14-3	16-5	18-2	19-8	22-0	23-11	7-8	11-9	14-7	16-10	18-7	21-4	23-6
11.00	7-7	11-8	14-6	16-7	18-4	19-10	22-2	24-1	7-10	12-0	14-10	17-0	18-9	21-6	23-7
11.25	7-10	11-11	14-8	16-10	18-7	20-0	22-4	24-2	8-1	12-3	15-1	17-3	18-11	21-8	23-8
11.50	8-1	12-2	14-11	17-0	18-9	20-2	22-5	24-3	8-4	12-6	15-4	17-5	19-2	21-9	23-10
11.75	8-3	12-5	15-2	17-3	18-11	20-4	22-7	24-4	8-7	12-9	15-6	17-8	19-4	21-11	23-11
12.00	8-6	12-8	15-5	17-5	19-1	20-6	22-9	24-6	8-9	13-0	15-9	17-10	19-6	22-1	24-0
12.25	8-9	12-10	15-7	17-8	19-3	20-8	22-10	24-7	9-0	13-2	15-11	18-0	19-8	22-2	24-2
12.50	9-0	13-1	15-10	17-10	19-5	20-10	22-11	24-8	9-3	13-5	16-2	18-2	19-10	22-4	24-3
12.75	9-2	13-4	16-0	18-0	19-7	20-11	23-1	24-9	9-6	13-8	16-4	18-5	20-0	22-6	24-4
13.00	9-5	13-7	16-3	18-3	19-9	21-1	23-2	24-10	9-9	13-11	16-7	18-7	20-2	22-7	24-5
13.25	9-8	13-9	16-5	18-5	19-11	21-3	23-4	24-11	9-11	14-1	16-9	18-9	20-4	22-9	24-6
13.50	9-11	14-0	16-8	18-7	20-1	21-5	23-5	25-0	10-2	14-4	17-0	18-9	20-4	22-9	24-7
13.75	10-2	14-3	16-10	18-9	20-3	21-6	23-6	25-1	10-5	14-6	17-2	19-1	20-7	22-11	24-8
14.00	10-4	14-5	17-0	18-11	20-5	21-8	23-7	25-2	10-8	14-9	17-4	19-3	20-9	23-1	24-10
14.25	10-7	14-8	17-2	19-1	20-7	21-9	23-9	25-3	10-10	14-11	17-6	19-5	20-11	23-2	24-11
14.50	10-10	14-10	17-5	19-3	20-8	21-11	23-10	25-4	11-1	15-2	17-9	19-7	21-0	23-3	25-0
14.75	11-0	15-1	17-7	19-5	20-10	22-0	23-11	25-5	11-4	15-4	17-11	19-9	21-2	23-4	25-0
15.00	11-3	15-3	17-9	19-7	21-0	22-2	24-0	25-6	11-7	15-7	18-1	19-10	21-4	23-6	25-1
15.25	11-6	15-5	17-11	19-8	21-1	22-3	24-1	25-6	11-9	15-9	18-3	20-0	21-5	23-7	25-2
15.50	11-8	15-8	18-1	19-10	21-3	22-4	24-2	25-7	12-0	15-11	18-5	20-2	21-7	23-8	25-3
15.75	11-11	15-10	18-3	20-0	21-4	22-6	24-3	25-8	12-2	16-2	18-7	20-4	21-8	23-9	25-4
16.00	12-2	16-0	18-5	20-2	21-6	22-7	24-4	25-9	12-5	16-4	18-8	20-5	21-9	23-10	25-5
16.25	12-4	16-2	18-7	20-3	21-7	22-8	24-5	25-10	12-7	16-6	18-10	20-7	21-11	23-11	25-5
16.50	12-7	16-5	18-9	20-5	21-9	22-10	24-6	25-10	12-10	16-8	19-0	20-8	22-0	24-0	25-6
16.75	12-9	16-7	18-10	20-6	21-10	22-11	24-7	25-11	13-0	16-10	19-2	20-10	22-2	24-1	25-7
17.00	13-0	16-9	19-0	20-8	21-11	23-0	24-8	26-0	13-3	17-0	19-4	20-11	22-3	24-2	25-8
17.25	13-2	16-11	19-2	20-8	22-1	23-1	24-9	26-0	13-5	17-2	19-5	21-1	22-4	24-3	25-9
17.50	13-4	17-1	19-4	20-11	22-2	23-2	24-10	26-1	13-8	17-4	19-7	21-2	22-5	24-4	25-9
17.75	13-7	17-3	19-5	21-0	22-3	23-3	24-11	26-2	13-10	17-6	19-7	21-2	22-5	24-4	25-10
18.00	13-9	17-5	19-7	21-2	22-4	23-4	24-11	26-2	14-0	17-8	19-10	21-5	22-8	24-6	25-11
18.25	13-11	17-7	19-8	21-3	22-6	23-5	25-0	26-3	14-2	17-10	20-0	21-6	22-9	24-7	25-11
18.50	14-2	17-8	19-10	21-4	22-7	23-6	25-1	26-3	14-5	18-0	20-1	21-8	22-10	24-8	26-0
18.75	14-4	17-10	20-0	21-6	22-8	23-7	25-2	26-4	14-7	18-1	20-3	21-9	22-11	24-9	26-1
19.00	14-6	18-0	20-1	21-7	22-9	23-8	25-3	26-5	14-9	18-3	20-4	21-10	23-0	24-9	26-1
20.00	15-2	18-7	20-7	22-0	23-1	24-0	25-5	26-7	15-5	18-10	20-10	22-3	23-4	25-0	26-3
25.00	18-0	20-9	22-5	23-7	24-5	25-2	26-4	27-3	18-2	21-0	22-7	23-9	24-8	26-0	27-0
30.00	19-11	22-3	23-8	24-7	25-4	26-0	26-11	27-8	20-1	22-5	23-10	24-9	25-6	26-8	27-6

Description: This table shows the term in years and months when a percent of value is paid off for an original loan-to-value ratio.

Example: An 85 % L-T-V loan is written at 8 % for 30 years. 30% of the value is paid off in 12 years and 9 months. The percent of loan that is paid off is 15/85 = 17.6 %.

RATE	90 % LTV 15% Yr-Mo	20% Yr-Mo	25% Yr-Mo	30% Yr-Mo	40% Yr-Mo	50% Yr-Mo	85 % LTV 20% Yr-Mo	25% Yr-Mo	30% Yr-Mo	40% Yr-Mo	50% Yr-Mo	80 % LTV 25% Yr-Mo	30% Yr-Mo	40% Yr-Mo	50% Yr-Mo
0.00	1- 8	3- 4	5- 0	6- 8	10- 0	13- 4	1-10	3- 7	5- 4	8-10	12- 5	1-11	3- 9	7- 6	11- 3
1.00	2- 0	3-10	5- 9	7- 6	11- 1	14- 6	2- 1	4- 1	6- 0	9-10	13- 6	2- 2	4- 4	8- 5	12- 4
2.00	2- 3	4- 5	6- 6	8- 5	12- 2	15- 7	2- 5	4- 8	6-10	10-10	14- 7	2- 7	4-11	9- 5	13- 6
3.00	2- 8	5- 1	7- 4	9- 5	13- 3	16- 8	2- 9	5- 4	7- 8	11-11	15- 9	2-11	5- 8	10- 5	14- 7
4.00	3- 1	5- 9	8- 2	10- 5	14- 4	17- 9	3- 3	6- 1	8- 7	13- 0	16-10	3- 5	6- 5	11- 6	15- 8
4.25	3- 2	6- 0	8- 5	10- 8	14- 8	18- 0	3- 4	6- 3	8-10	13- 4	17- 1	3- 7	6- 7	11- 9	15-11
4.50	3- 4	6- 2	8- 8	10-11	14-11	18- 3	3- 6	6- 6	9- 1	13- 7	17- 4	3- 8	6-10	12- 0	16- 3
4.75	3- 5	6- 4	8-11	11- 3	15- 2	18- 6	3- 7	6- 8	9- 4	13-10	17- 7	3-10	7- 0	12- 3	16- 6
5.00	3- 7	6- 7	9- 2	11- 6	15- 5	18- 9	3- 9	6-11	9- 7	14- 2	17-10	4- 0	7- 3	12- 7	16- 9
5.25	3- 9	6- 9	9- 5	11- 9	15- 8	19- 0	3-11	7- 1	9-10	14- 5	18- 1	4- 1	7- 6	12-10	17- 0
5.50	3-10	7- 0	9- 8	12- 0	16- 0	19- 2	4- 1	7- 4	10- 1	14- 8	18- 4	4- 3	7- 9	13- 1	17- 3
5.75	4- 0	7- 3	9-11	12- 4	16- 3	19- 5	4- 2	7- 7	10- 5	14-11	18- 6	4- 5	7-11	13- 4	17- 6
6.00	4- 2	7- 5	10- 2	12- 7	16- 6	19- 8	4- 4	7-10	10- 8	15- 2	18- 9	4- 7	8- 2	13- 8	17- 9
6.25	4- 4	7- 8	10- 6	12-10	16- 9	19-10	4- 6	8- 0	10-11	15- 6	19- 0	4- 9	8- 5	13-11	18- 0
6.50	4- 6	7-11	10- 9	13- 1	17- 0	20- 1	4- 8	8- 3	11- 2	15- 9	19- 3	4-11	8- 8	14- 2	18- 3
6.75	4- 8	8- 2	11- 0	13- 4	17- 3	20- 3	4-10	8- 6	11- 5	16- 0	19- 5	5- 2	8-11	14- 5	18- 5
7.00	4-10	8- 5	11- 3	13- 8	17- 5	20- 6	5- 1	8- 9	11- 8	16- 3	19- 8	5- 4	9- 2	14- 8	18-11
7.25	5- 0	8- 8	11- 6	13-11	17- 8	20- 8	5- 3	9- 0	12- 0	16- 6	19-10	5- 6	9- 5	14-11	19- 1
7.50	5- 2	8-11	11- 9	14- 2	17-11	20-10	5- 5	9- 3	12- 3	16- 9	20- 1	5- 8	9- 8	15- 2	19- 1
7.75	5- 4	9- 1	12- 0	14- 5	18- 2	21- 1	5- 7	9- 6	12- 6	16-11	20- 3	5-11	9-11	15- 5	19- 4
8.00	5- 7	9- 4	12- 4	14- 8	18- 4	21- 3	5-10	9- 9	12- 9	17- 2	20- 5	6- 1	10- 2	15- 8	19- 6
8.25	5- 9	9- 7	12- 7	14-11	18- 7	21- 5	6- 0	10- 0	13- 0	17- 5	20- 8	6- 4	10- 5	15-11	19- 9
8.50	5-11	9-10	12-10	15- 2	18-10	21- 7	6- 3	10- 3	13- 3	17- 8	20-10	6- 6	10- 8	16- 2	19-11
8.75	6- 2	10- 1	13- 1	15- 5	19- 0	21- 9	6- 5	10- 6	13- 6	17-10	21- 0	6- 9	10-11	16- 5	20- 1
9.00	6- 4	10- 4	13- 4	15- 8	19- 3	21-11	6- 8	10- 9	13- 9	18- 1	21- 2	6-11	11- 2	16- 8	20- 4
9.25	6- 7	10- 8	13- 7	15-11	19- 5	22- 1	6-10	11- 0	14- 0	18- 3	21- 4	7- 2	11- 5	16-11	20- 6
9.50	6-10	10-11	13-10	16- 1	19- 7	22- 3	7- 1	11- 3	14- 3	18- 6	21- 6	7- 5	11- 8	17- 1	20- 8
9.75	7- 0	11- 2	14- 1	16- 4	19- 9	22- 4	7- 4	11- 6	14- 6	18- 8	21- 8	7- 8	11-11	17- 4	20-10
10.00	7- 3	11- 5	14- 4	16- 7	20- 0	22- 6	7- 6	11- 9	14- 9	18-11	21-10	7-10	12- 2	17- 6	21- 0
10.25	7- 5	11- 8	14- 7	16- 9	20- 2	22- 8	7- 9	12- 0	15- 0	19- 1	22- 0	8- 1	12- 5	17- 9	21- 2
10.50	7- 8	11-11	14- 9	17- 0	20- 4	22- 9	8- 0	12- 3	15- 3	19- 3	22- 2	8- 4	12- 8	17-11	21- 4
10.75	7-11	12- 1	15- 0	17- 3	20- 6	22-11	8- 3	12- 6	15- 5	19- 6	22- 3	8- 7	12-11	18- 2	21- 6
11.00	8- 2	12- 4	15- 3	17- 5	20- 8	23- 1	8- 5	12- 9	15- 8	19- 8	22- 5	8- 9	13- 2	18- 4	21- 8
11.25	8- 5	12- 7	15- 6	17- 8	20-10	23- 2	8- 8	13- 0	15-11	19-10	22- 7	9- 0	13- 5	18- 7	21- 9
11.50	8- 7	12-10	15- 8	17-10	21- 0	23- 4	8-11	13- 3	16- 1	20- 0	22- 8	9- 3	13- 8	18- 9	21-11
11.75	8-10	13- 1	15-11	18- 0	21- 2	23- 5	9- 2	13- 6	16- 4	20- 2	22-10	9- 6	13-11	18-11	22- 1
12.00	9- 1	13- 4	16- 2	18- 3	21- 4	23- 6	9- 5	13- 8	16- 6	20- 4	22-11	9- 9	14- 1	19- 1	22- 2
12.25	9- 4	13- 7	16- 4	18- 5	21- 5	23- 8	9- 8	13-11	16- 9	20- 6	23- 1	10- 0	14- 4	19- 3	22- 4
12.50	9- 7	13- 9	16- 7	18- 7	21- 7	23- 9	9-10	14- 2	16-11	20- 8	23- 2	10- 3	14- 7	19- 5	22- 6
12.75	9- 9	14- 0	16- 9	18- 9	21- 9	23-10	10- 1	14- 5	17- 2	20-10	23- 4	10- 5	14- 9	19- 7	22- 7
13.00	10- 0	14- 3	16-11	18-11	21-10	24- 0	10- 4	14- 7	17- 4	20-11	23- 5	10- 8	15- 0	19- 9	22- 9
13.25	10- 3	14- 5	17- 2	19- 1	22- 0	24- 1	10- 7	14-10	17- 6	21- 1	23- 6	10-11	15- 3	19-11	22-10
13.50	10- 6	14- 8	17- 4	19- 3	22- 1	24- 2	10-10	15- 0	17- 9	21- 3	23- 7	11- 2	15- 5	20- 1	22-11
13.75	10- 9	14-11	17- 6	19- 5	22- 3	24- 3	11- 0	15- 3	17-11	21- 5	23- 9	11- 5	15- 8	20- 3	23- 1
14.00	10-11	15- 1	17- 8	19- 7	22- 4	24- 4	11- 3	15- 5	18- 1	21- 6	23-10	11- 7	15-10	20- 5	23- 2
14.25	11- 2	15- 4	17-11	19- 9	22- 6	24- 5	11- 6	15- 8	18- 3	21- 8	23-11	11-10	16- 0	20- 7	23- 3
14.50	11- 5	15- 6	18- 1	19-11	22- 7	24- 6	11- 9	15-10	18- 5	21- 9	24- 0	12- 1	16- 3	20- 8	23- 5
14.75	11- 7	15- 8	18- 3	20- 1	22- 9	24- 7	11-11	16- 1	18- 7	21-11	24- 1	12- 3	16- 5	20-10	23- 6
15.00	11-10	15-11	18- 5	20- 3	22-10	24- 8	12- 2	16- 3	18- 9	22- 0	24- 2	12- 6	16- 7	21- 0	23- 7
15.25	12- 1	16- 1	18- 7	20- 4	22-11	24- 9	12- 5	16- 5	18-11	22- 2	24- 3	12- 9	16-10	21- 1	23- 8
15.50	12- 3	16- 3	18- 9	20- 6	23- 0	24-10	12- 7	16- 7	19- 1	22- 3	24- 4	12-11	17- 0	21- 3	23- 9
15.75	12- 6	16- 5	18-11	20- 8	23- 2	24-11	12-10	16- 9	19- 3	22- 4	24- 5	13- 2	17- 2	21- 4	23-10
16.00	12- 8	16- 8	19- 0	20- 9	23- 3	25- 0	13- 0	17- 0	19- 4	22- 6	24- 6	13- 4	17- 4	21- 6	24- 0
16.25	12-11	16-10	19- 2	20-11	23- 4	25- 1	13- 3	17- 2	19- 6	22- 7	24- 7	13- 7	17- 6	21- 7	24- 1
16.50	13- 1	17- 0	19- 4	21- 0	23- 5	25- 2	13- 5	17- 4	19- 8	22- 8	24- 8	13- 9	17- 8	21- 9	24- 2
16.75	13- 4	17- 2	19- 6	21- 2	23- 6	25- 3	13- 8	17- 6	19-10	22- 9	24- 9	13-11	17-10	21-10	24- 3
17.00	13- 6	17- 4	19- 7	21- 3	23- 7	25- 3	13-10	17- 8	19-11	22-11	24-10	14- 2	18- 0	21-11	24- 4
17.25	13- 9	17- 6	19- 9	21- 5	23- 8	25- 4	14- 0	17-10	20- 1	23- 0	24-11	14- 4	18- 2	22- 1	24- 4
17.50	13-11	17- 8	19-11	21- 6	23- 9	25- 5	14- 3	17-11	20- 2	23- 1	25- 0	14- 6	18- 3	22- 2	24- 5
17.75	14- 1	17-10	20- 0	21- 7	23-10	25- 6	14- 5	18- 1	20- 4	23- 2	25- 1	14- 9	18- 5	22- 3	24- 6
18.00	14- 4	17-11	20- 2	21- 9	23-11	25- 6	14- 7	18- 3	20- 5	23- 3	25- 1	14-11	18- 7	22- 4	24- 7
18.25	14- 6	18- 1	20- 3	21-10	24- 0	25- 7	14- 9	18- 5	20- 7	23- 4	25- 2	15- 1	18- 9	22- 6	24- 8
18.50	14- 8	18- 3	20- 5	21-11	24- 1	25- 8	14-11	18- 7	20- 8	23- 5	25- 3	15- 3	18-10	22- 7	24- 9
18.75	14-10	18- 5	20- 6	22- 0	24- 2	25- 8	15- 2	18- 8	20-10	23- 6	25- 4	15- 5	19- 0	22- 8	24-10
19.00	15- 0	18- 6	20- 8	22- 2	24- 3	25- 9	15- 4	18-10	20-11	23- 7	25- 4	15- 7	19- 2	22- 9	24-10
20.00	15- 8	19- 1	21- 1	22- 6	24- 6	26- 0	16- 0	19- 4	21- 4	23-11	25- 7	16- 3	19- 8	23- 1	25- 1
25.00	18- 5	21- 2	22-10	24- 0	25- 7	26- 9	18- 8	21- 5	23- 1	25- 1	26- 6	18-10	21- 8	24- 5	26- 1
30.00	20- 4	22- 8	24- 0	25- 0	26- 4	27- 4	20- 6	22-10	24- 2	25-11	27- 1	20- 8	23- 0	24- 9	26- 9

TABLE **5**

Amortization Schedules Per $100

Interest Rates:

Monthly: 0, 1, 2, 3%;
4 to 4.75% by .25%;
5 to 15% by .25%, .125%, .10%;
16 to 20% by 1%.

Quarterly: 0, 1, 2, 3%;
4 to 15% by .25%;
16 to 20% by 1%.

Terms: 1 to 30 years, each year.

Payments: Monthly and quarterly, in arrears.

This table shows how a loan of $100 is amortized by a level payment of interest and principal. While the actual payment is either monthly or quarterly, these schedules show the sum of the interest and principal payments for each year and the balance outstanding at year-end. Shown in the heading of each schedule are the terms in years, the monthly or quarterly payment per $100, and the Constant Annual Percent (Constant).

Example: A loan of $100,000 is written at 8% for 30 years. The monthly payment is $733.76, and the constant is 8.81%. In the first year, $7,969.80 is paid to interest and $835.40 to principal. The year-end balance is $99,164.60. These figures are shown on page 5-115.

For interest rates not shown, the balances can be computed by interpolation. A loan written at 8.15% for 30 years will, by interpolation, have a balance at the end of the fifth year of 95.1992% of the principal amount.

Amortization. Amortization is a very simple process of the repayment of a loan over time. The word literally means "death of a debt." An amortization schedule is the basic document for a loan. It shows the allocation of the payment, first to interest and then to principal, for each period during the life of the loan. To compute an amortization schedule, it is necessary to know the amount, the rate, the term, and the payment. The schedule is proof that the payment amortizes the amount over the term at the interest rate.

The first months of the 8%, 30 year loan are shown in this amortization schedule:

Amount: $100,000.00		Term: 30 years	
Rate: 8%		Payment: $733.76 monthly	
Payment	*Interest*	*Principal*	*Balance*
1	666.67	67.09	99,932.91
2	666.22	67.54	99,865.37
3	665.77	67.99	99,797.38

The process by which the amortization schedule is computed involves the following 3 steps:

1. Compute interest for the period, which in this case is 1 month. Multiply the balance by the factor for 1 period. The factor for 1 period is $8.00 \div 100 \div 12 = .00666666667$.

$$\text{Interest} = 100,000.00 \times .0066666667$$
$$= 666.67$$

2. Compute the principal by subtracting the interest from the payment.

$$\text{Principal} = 733.76 - 666.67$$
$$= 67.09$$

3. Compute the new balance by subtracting the principal from the balance.

$$\text{New balance} = 100,000.00 - 67.09$$
$$= 99,932.91$$

These steps are continued for each period until the balance is 0.

AMORTIZATION SCHEDULES PER $100

Average Life. The life of a mortgage is the weighted average of the payments to the principal. Weight is determined by the number of months each payment is outstanding. Where there is an amortization schedule, the weight is the payment number. Here, for example, are the monthly payments to principal of a loan of $100 at 8% for 1 year:

Payment	Principal	Weighted Value
1	8.0322	8.0322
2	8.0857	16.1714
3	8.1396	24.4189
4	8.1939	32.7756
5	8.2485	41.2426
6	8.3035	49.8211
7	8.3589	58.5121
8	8.4146	67.3167

Payment	Principal	Weighted Value
9	8.4707	76.2362
10	8.5272	85.2716
11	8.5840	94.4241
12	8.6412	103.6948
Total	100.0000	657.9173

To determine the average life in months, divide the sum of the weights by the sum of the payments:

$$657.9173 \div 100 = 6.579173$$

To determine the average life in years, divide the sum of the weights by 12:

$$6.579173 \div 12 = .54 \text{ years}$$

AMORTIZATION SCHEDULES PER $100

YEARS 2 — MO PAYT 4.1667 — AN CONST 50.00

#	INT	PRIN	BALANCE
1	0.0000	50.0000	50.0000
2	0.0000	50.0000	0.0000

YEARS 3 — MO PAYT 2.7778 — AN CONST 33.34

#	INT	PRIN	BALANCE
1	0.0000	33.3333	66.6667
2	0.0000	33.3333	33.3333
3	0.0000	33.3333	0.0000

YEARS 4 — MO PAYT 2.0833 — AN CONST 25.00

#	INT	PRIN	BALANCE
1	0.0000	25.0000	75.0000
2	0.0000	25.0000	50.0000
3	0.0000	25.0000	25.0000
4	0.0000	25.0000	0.0000

YEARS 5 — MO PAYT 1.6667 — AN CONST 20.00

#	INT	PRIN	BALANCE
1	0.0000	20.0000	80.0000
2	0.0000	20.0000	60.0000
3	0.0000	20.0000	40.0000
4	0.0000	20.0000	20.0000
5	0.0000	20.0000	0.0000

YEARS 6 — MO PAYT 1.3889 — AN CONST 16.67

#	INT	PRIN	BALANCE
1	0.0000	16.6667	83.3333
2	0.0000	16.6667	66.6667
3	0.0000	16.6667	50.0000
4	0.0000	16.6667	33.3333
5	0.0000	16.6667	16.6667
6	0.0000	16.6667	0.0000

YEARS 7 — MO PAYT 1.1905 — AN CONST 14.29

#	INT	PRIN	BALANCE
1	0.0000	14.2857	85.7143
2	0.0000	14.2857	71.4286
3	0.0000	14.2857	57.1429
4	0.0000	14.2857	42.8571
5	0.0000	14.2857	28.5714
6	0.0000	14.2857	14.2857
7	0.0000	14.2857	0.0000

YEARS 8 — MO PAYT 1.0417 — AN CONST 12.50

#	INT	PRIN	BALANCE
1	0.0000	12.5000	87.5000
2	0.0000	12.5000	75.0000
3	0.0000	12.5000	62.5000
4	0.0000	12.5000	50.0000
5	0.0000	12.5000	37.5000
6	0.0000	12.5000	25.0000
7	0.0000	12.5000	12.5000
8	0.0000	12.5000	0.0000

YEARS 9 — MO PAYT .9259 — AN CONST 11.12

#	INT	PRIN	BALANCE
1	0.0000	11.1111	88.8889
2	0.0000	11.1111	77.7778
3	0.0000	11.1111	66.6667
4	0.0000	11.1111	55.5556
5	0.0000	11.1111	44.4444
6	0.0000	11.1111	33.3333
7	0.0000	11.1111	22.2222
8	0.0000	11.1111	11.1111
9	0.0000	11.1111	0.0000

YEARS 10 — MO PAYT .8333 — AN CONST 10.00

#	INT	PRIN	BALANCE
1	0.0000	10.0000	90.0000
2	0.0000	10.0000	80.0000
3	0.0000	10.0000	70.0000
4	0.0000	10.0000	60.0000
5	0.0000	10.0000	50.0000
6	0.0000	10.0000	40.0000
7	0.0000	10.0000	30.0000
8	0.0000	10.0000	20.0000
9	0.0000	10.0000	10.0000
10	0.0000	10.0000	0.0000

YEARS 11 — MO PAYT .7576 — AN CONST 9.10

#	INT	PRIN	BALANCE
1	0.0000	9.0909	90.9091
2	0.0000	9.0909	81.8182
3	0.0000	9.0909	72.7273
4	0.0000	9.0909	63.6364
5	0.0000	9.0909	54.5455
6	0.0000	9.0909	45.4545
7	0.0000	9.0909	36.3636
8	0.0000	9.0909	27.2727
9	0.0000	9.0909	18.1818
10	0.0000	9.0909	9.0909
11	0.0000	9.0909	0.0000

YEARS 12 — MO PAYT .6944 — AN CONST 8.34

#	INT	PRIN	BALANCE
1	0.0000	8.3333	91.6667
2	0.0000	8.3333	83.3333
3	0.0000	8.3333	75.0000
4	0.0000	8.3333	66.6667
5	0.0000	8.3333	58.3333
6	0.0000	8.3333	50.0000
7	0.0000	8.3333	41.6667
8	0.0000	8.3333	33.3333
9	0.0000	8.3333	25.0000
10	0.0000	8.3333	16.6667
11	0.0000	8.3333	8.3333
12	0.0000	8.3333	0.0000

YEARS 13 — MO PAYT .6410 — AN CONST 7.70

#	INT	PRIN	BALANCE
1	0.0000	7.6923	92.3077
2	0.0000	7.6923	84.6154
3	0.0000	7.6923	76.9231
4	0.0000	7.6923	69.2308
5	0.0000	7.6923	61.5385
6	0.0000	7.6923	53.8462
7	0.0000	7.6923	46.1538
8	0.0000	7.6923	38.4615
9	0.0000	7.6923	30.7692
10	0.0000	7.6923	23.0769
11	0.0000	7.6923	15.3846
12	0.0000	7.6923	7.6923
13	0.0000	7.6923	0.0000

YEARS 14 — MO PAYT .5952 — AN CONST 7.15

#	INT	PRIN	BALANCE
1	0.0000	7.1429	92.8571
2	0.0000	7.1429	85.7143
3	0.0000	7.1429	78.5714
4	0.0000	7.1429	71.4286
5	0.0000	7.1429	64.2857
6	0.0000	7.1429	57.1429
7	0.0000	7.1429	50.0000
8	0.0000	7.1429	42.8571
9	0.0000	7.1429	35.7143
10	0.0000	7.1429	28.5714
11	0.0000	7.1429	21.4286
12	0.0000	7.1429	14.2857
13	0.0000	7.1429	7.1429
14	0.0000	7.1429	0.0000

YEARS 15 — MO PAYT .5556 — AN CONST 6.67

#	INT	PRIN	BALANCE
1	0.0000	6.6667	93.3333
2	0.0000	6.6667	86.6667
3	0.0000	6.6667	80.0000
4	0.0000	6.6667	73.3333
5	0.0000	6.6667	66.6667
6	0.0000	6.6667	60.0000
7	0.0000	6.6667	53.3333
8	0.0000	6.6667	46.6667
9	0.0000	6.6667	40.0000
10	0.0000	6.6667	33.3333
11	0.0000	6.6667	26.6667
12	0.0000	6.6667	20.0000
13	0.0000	6.6667	13.3333
14	0.0000	6.6667	6.6667
15	0.0000	6.6667	0.0000

YEARS 16 — MO PAYT .5208 — AN CONST 6.25

#	INT	PRIN	BALANCE
1	0.0000	6.2500	93.7500
2	0.0000	6.2500	87.5000
3	0.0000	6.2500	81.2500
4	0.0000	6.2500	75.0000
5	0.0000	6.2500	68.7500
6	0.0000	6.2500	62.5000
7	0.0000	6.2500	56.2500
8	0.0000	6.2500	50.0000
9	0.0000	6.2500	43.7500
10	0.0000	6.2500	37.5000
11	0.0000	6.2500	31.2500
12	0.0000	6.2500	25.0000
13	0.0000	6.2500	18.7500
14	0.0000	6.2500	12.5000
15	0.0000	6.2500	6.2500
16	0.0000	6.2500	0.0000

YEARS 17 — MO PAYT .4902 — AN CONST 5.89

#	INT	PRIN	BALANCE
1	0.0000	5.8824	94.1176
2	0.0000	5.8824	88.2353
3	0.0000	5.8824	82.3529
4	0.0000	5.8824	76.4706
5	0.0000	5.8824	70.5882
6	0.0000	5.8824	64.7059
7	0.0000	5.8824	58.8235
8	0.0000	5.8824	52.9412
9	0.0000	5.8824	47.0588
10	0.0000	5.8824	41.1765
11	0.0000	5.8824	35.2941
12	0.0000	5.8824	29.4118
13	0.0000	5.8824	23.5294
14	0.0000	5.8824	17.6471
15	0.0000	5.8824	11.7647
16	0.0000	5.8824	5.8824
17	0.0000	5.8824	0.0000

YEARS 18 — MO PAYT .4630 — AN CONST 5.56

#	INT	PRIN	BALANCE
1	0.0000	5.5556	94.4444
2	0.0000	5.5556	88.8889
3	0.0000	5.5556	83.3333
4	0.0000	5.5556	77.7778
5	0.0000	5.5556	72.2222
6	0.0000	5.5556	66.6667
7	0.0000	5.5556	61.1111
8	0.0000	5.5556	55.5556
9	0.0000	5.5556	50.0000
10	0.0000	5.5556	44.4444
11	0.0000	5.5556	38.8889
12	0.0000	5.5556	33.3333
13	0.0000	5.5556	27.7778
14	0.0000	5.5556	22.2222
15	0.0000	5.5556	16.6667
16	0.0000	5.5556	11.1111
17	0.0000	5.5556	5.5556
18	0.0000	5.5556	0.0000

YEARS 19 — MO PAYT .4386 — AN CONST 5.27

#	INT	PRIN	BALANCE
1	0.0000	5.2632	94.7368
2	0.0000	5.2632	89.4737
3	0.0000	5.2632	84.2105
4	0.0000	5.2632	78.9474
5	0.0000	5.2632	73.6842
6	0.0000	5.2632	68.4211
7	0.0000	5.2632	63.1579
8	0.0000	5.2632	57.8947
9	0.0000	5.2632	52.6316
10	0.0000	5.2632	47.3684
11	0.0000	5.2632	42.1053
12	0.0000	5.2632	36.8421
13	0.0000	5.2632	31.5789
14	0.0000	5.2632	26.3158
15	0.0000	5.2632	21.0526
16	0.0000	5.2632	15.7895
17	0.0000	5.2632	10.5263
18	0.0000	5.2632	5.2632
19	0.0000	5.2632	0.0000

YEARS 20 — MO PAYT .4167 — AN CONST 5.00

#	INT	PRIN	BALANCE
1	0.0000	5.0000	95.0000
2	0.0000	5.0000	90.0000
3	0.0000	5.0000	85.0000
4	0.0000	5.0000	80.0000
5	0.0000	5.0000	75.0000
6	0.0000	5.0000	70.0000
7	0.0000	5.0000	65.0000
8	0.0000	5.0000	60.0000
9	0.0000	5.0000	55.0000
10	0.0000	5.0000	50.0000
11	0.0000	5.0000	45.0000
12	0.0000	5.0000	40.0000
13	0.0000	5.0000	35.0000
14	0.0000	5.0000	30.0000
15	0.0000	5.0000	25.0000
16	0.0000	5.0000	20.0000
17	0.0000	5.0000	15.0000
18	0.0000	5.0000	10.0000
19	0.0000	5.0000	5.0000
20	0.0000	5.0000	0.0000

YEARS 21 — MO PAYT .3968 — AN CONST 4.77

#	INT	PRIN	BALANCE
1	0.0000	4.7619	95.2381
2	0.0000	4.7619	90.4762
3	0.0000	4.7619	85.7143

MONTHLY PAYMENT AMORTIZATION SCHEDULE PER $100   0.00 %

#	INT	PRIN	BALANCE
4	0.0000	4.7619	80.9524
5	0.0000	4.7619	76.1905
6	0.0000	4.7619	71.4286
7	0.0000	4.7619	66.6667
8	0.0000	4.7619	61.9048
9	0.0000	4.7619	57.1429
10	0.0000	4.7619	52.3810
11	0.0000	4.7619	47.6190
12	0.0000	4.7619	42.8571
13	0.0000	4.7619	38.0952
14	0.0000	4.7619	33.3333
15	0.0000	4.7619	28.5714
16	0.0000	4.7619	23.8095
17	0.0000	4.7619	19.0476
18	0.0000	4.7619	14.2857
19	0.0000	4.7619	9.5238
20	0.0000	4.7619	4.7619
21	0.0000	4.7619	0.0000

YEARS 22 — MO PAYT .3788 — AN CONST 4.55

#	INT	PRIN	BALANCE
1	0.0000	4.5455	95.4545
2	0.0000	4.5455	90.9091
3	0.0000	4.5455	86.3636
4	0.0000	4.5455	81.8182
5	0.0000	4.5455	77.2727
6	0.0000	4.5455	72.7273
7	0.0000	4.5455	68.1818
8	0.0000	4.5455	63.6364
9	0.0000	4.5455	59.0909
10	0.0000	4.5455	54.5455
11	0.0000	4.5455	50.0000
12	0.0000	4.5455	45.4545
13	0.0000	4.5455	40.9091
14	0.0000	4.5455	36.3636
15	0.0000	4.5455	31.8182
16	0.0000	4.5455	27.2727
17	0.0000	4.5455	22.7273
18	0.0000	4.5455	18.1818
19	0.0000	4.5455	13.6364
20	0.0000	4.5455	9.0909
21	0.0000	4.5455	4.5455
22	0.0000	4.5455	0.0000

YEARS 23 — MO PAYT .3623 — AN CONST 4.35

#	INT	PRIN	BALANCE
1	0.0000	4.3478	95.6522
2	0.0000	4.3478	91.3043
3	0.0000	4.3478	86.9565
4	0.0000	4.3478	82.6087
5	0.0000	4.3478	78.2609
6	0.0000	4.3478	73.9130
7	0.0000	4.3478	69.5652
8	0.0000	4.3478	65.2174
9	0.0000	4.3478	60.8696
10	0.0000	4.3478	56.5217
11	0.0000	4.3478	52.1739
12	0.0000	4.3478	47.8261
13	0.0000	4.3478	43.4783
14	0.0000	4.3478	39.1304
15	0.0000	4.3478	34.7826
16	0.0000	4.3478	30.4348
17	0.0000	4.3478	26.0870
18	0.0000	4.3478	21.7391
19	0.0000	4.3478	17.3913
20	0.0000	4.3478	13.0435
21	0.0000	4.3478	8.6957
22	0.0000	4.3478	4.3478
23	0.0000	4.3478	0.0000

YEARS 24 — MO PAYT .3472 — AN CONST 4.17

#	INT	PRIN	BALANCE
1	0.0000	4.1667	95.8333
2	0.0000	4.1667	91.6667
3	0.0000	4.1667	87.5000
4	0.0000	4.1667	83.3333
5	0.0000	4.1667	79.1667
6	0.0000	4.1667	75.0000
7	0.0000	4.1667	70.8333
8	0.0000	4.1667	66.6667
9	0.0000	4.1667	62.5000
10	0.0000	4.1667	58.3333
11	0.0000	4.1667	54.1667
12	0.0000	4.1667	50.0000
13	0.0000	4.1667	45.8333
14	0.0000	4.1667	41.6667
15	0.0000	4.1667	37.5000
16	0.0000	4.1667	33.3333
17	0.0000	4.1667	29.1667
18	0.0000	4.1667	25.0000
19	0.0000	4.1667	20.8333
20	0.0000	4.1667	16.6667
21	0.0000	4.1667	12.5000
22	0.0000	4.1667	8.3333
23	0.0000	4.1667	4.1667
24	0.0000	4.1667	0.0000

YEARS 25 — MO PAYT .3333 — AN CONST 4.00

#	INT	PRIN	BALANCE
1	0.0000	4.0000	96.0000
2	0.0000	4.0000	92.0000
3	0.0000	4.0000	88.0000
4	0.0000	4.0000	84.0000
5	0.0000	4.0000	80.0000
6	0.0000	4.0000	76.0000
7	0.0000	4.0000	72.0000
8	0.0000	4.0000	68.0000
9	0.0000	4.0000	64.0000
10	0.0000	4.0000	60.0000
11	0.0000	4.0000	56.0000
12	0.0000	4.0000	52.0000
13	0.0000	4.0000	48.0000
14	0.0000	4.0000	44.0000
15	0.0000	4.0000	40.0000
16	0.0000	4.0000	36.0000
17	0.0000	4.0000	32.0000
18	0.0000	4.0000	28.0000
19	0.0000	4.0000	24.0000
20	0.0000	4.0000	20.0000
21	0.0000	4.0000	16.0000
22	0.0000	4.0000	12.0000
23	0.0000	4.0000	8.0000
24	0.0000	4.0000	4.0000
25	0.0000	4.0000	0.0000

YEARS 26 — MO PAYT .3205 — AN CONST 3.85

#	INT	PRIN	BALANCE
1	0.0000	3.8462	96.1538
2	0.0000	3.8462	92.3077
3	0.0000	3.8462	88.4615
4	0.0000	3.8462	84.6154
5	0.0000	3.8462	80.7692
6	0.0000	3.8462	76.9231
7	0.0000	3.8462	73.0769
8	0.0000	3.8462	69.2308
9	0.0000	3.8462	65.3846
10	0.0000	3.8462	61.5385
11	0.0000	3.8462	57.6923
12	0.0000	3.8462	53.8462
13	0.0000	3.8462	50.0000
14	0.0000	3.8462	46.1538
15	0.0000	3.8462	42.3077
16	0.0000	3.8462	38.4615
17	0.0000	3.8462	34.6154
18	0.0000	3.8462	30.7692
19	0.0000	3.8462	26.9231
20	0.0000	3.8462	23.0769
21	0.0000	3.8462	19.2308
22	0.0000	3.8462	15.3846
23	0.0000	3.8462	11.5385
24	0.0000	3.8462	7.6923
25	0.0000	3.8462	3.8462
26	0.0000	3.8462	0.0000

YEARS 27 — MO PAYT .3086 — AN CONST 3.71

#	INT	PRIN	BALANCE
1	0.0000	3.7037	96.2963
2	0.0000	3.7037	92.5926
3	0.0000	3.7037	88.8889
4	0.0000	3.7037	85.1852
5	0.0000	3.7037	81.4815
6	0.0000	3.7037	77.7778
7	0.0000	3.7037	74.0741
8	0.0000	3.7037	70.3704
9	0.0000	3.7037	66.6667
10	0.0000	3.7037	62.9630
11	0.0000	3.7037	59.2593
12	0.0000	3.7037	55.5556
13	0.0000	3.7037	51.8519
14	0.0000	3.7037	48.1481
15	0.0000	3.7037	44.4444
16	0.0000	3.7037	40.7407
17	0.0000	3.7037	37.0370
18	0.0000	3.7037	33.3333
19	0.0000	3.7037	29.6296
20	0.0000	3.7037	25.9259
21	0.0000	3.7037	22.2222
22	0.0000	3.7037	18.5185
23	0.0000	3.7037	14.8148
24	0.0000	3.7037	11.1111
25	0.0000	3.7037	7.4074
26	0.0000	3.7037	3.7037
27	0.0000	3.7037	0.0000

YEARS 28 — MO PAYT .2976 — AN CONST 3.58

#	INT	PRIN	BALANCE
1	0.0000	3.5714	96.4286
2	0.0000	3.5714	92.8571
3	0.0000	3.5714	89.2857
4	0.0000	3.5714	85.7143
5	0.0000	3.5714	82.1429
6	0.0000	3.5714	78.5714
7	0.0000	3.5714	75.0000
8	0.0000	3.5714	71.4286
9	0.0000	3.5714	67.8571
10	0.0000	3.5714	64.2857
11	0.0000	3.5714	60.7143
12	0.0000	3.5714	57.1429
13	0.0000	3.5714	53.5714
14	0.0000	3.5714	50.0000
15	0.0000	3.5714	46.4286
16	0.0000	3.5714	42.8571
17	0.0000	3.5714	39.2857
18	0.0000	3.5714	35.7143
19	0.0000	3.5714	32.1429
20	0.0000	3.5714	28.5714
21	0.0000	3.5714	25.0000
22	0.0000	3.5714	21.4286
23	0.0000	3.5714	17.8571
24	0.0000	3.5714	14.2857
25	0.0000	3.5714	10.7143
26	0.0000	3.5714	7.1429
27	0.0000	3.5714	3.5714
28	0.0000	3.5714	0.0000

YEARS 29 — MO PAYT .2874 — AN CONST 3.45

#	INT	PRIN	BALANCE
1	0.0000	3.4483	96.5517
2	0.0000	3.4483	93.1034
3	0.0000	3.4483	89.6552
4	0.0000	3.4483	86.2069
5	0.0000	3.4483	82.7586
6	0.0000	3.4483	79.3103
7	0.0000	3.4483	75.8621
8	0.0000	3.4483	72.4138
9	0.0000	3.4483	68.9655
10	0.0000	3.4483	65.5172
11	0.0000	3.4483	62.0690
12	0.0000	3.4483	58.6207
13	0.0000	3.4483	55.1724
14	0.0000	3.4483	51.7241
15	0.0000	3.4483	48.2759
16	0.0000	3.4483	44.8276
17	0.0000	3.4483	41.3793
18	0.0000	3.4483	37.9310
19	0.0000	3.4483	34.4828
20	0.0000	3.4483	31.0345
21	0.0000	3.4483	27.5862
22	0.0000	3.4483	24.1379
23	0.0000	3.4483	20.6897
24	0.0000	3.4483	17.2414
25	0.0000	3.4483	13.7931
26	0.0000	3.4483	10.3448
27	0.0000	3.4483	6.8966
28	0.0000	3.4483	3.4483
29	0.0000	3.4483	0.0000

YEARS 30 — MO PAYT .2778 — AN CONST 3.34

#	INT	PRIN	BALANCE
1	0.0000	3.3333	96.6667
2	0.0000	3.3333	93.3333
3	0.0000	3.3333	90.0000
4	0.0000	3.3333	86.6667
5	0.0000	3.3333	83.3333
6	0.0000	3.3333	80.0000
7	0.0000	3.3333	76.6667
8	0.0000	3.3333	73.3333
9	0.0000	3.3333	70.0000
10	0.0000	3.3333	66.6667
11	0.0000	3.3333	63.3333
12	0.0000	3.3333	60.0000
13	0.0000	3.3333	56.6667
14	0.0000	3.3333	53.3333
15	0.0000	3.3333	50.0000
16	0.0000	3.3333	46.6667
17	0.0000	3.3333	43.3333
18	0.0000	3.3333	40.0000
19	0.0000	3.3333	36.6667
20	0.0000	3.3333	33.3333
21	0.0000	3.3333	30.0000
22	0.0000	3.3333	26.6667
23	0.0000	3.3333	23.3333
24	0.0000	3.3333	20.0000
25	0.0000	3.3333	16.6667
26	0.0000	3.3333	13.3333
27	0.0000	3.3333	10.0000
28	0.0000	3.3333	6.6667
29	0.0000	3.3333	3.3333
30	0.0000	3.3333	0.0000

YEARS 2 — MO PAYT 4.2102 — AN CONST 50.53

#	INT	PRIN	BALANCE
1	.7724	49.7501	50.2499
2	.2726	50.2499	0.0000

YEARS 3 — MO PAYT 2.8208 — AN CONST 33.85

#	INT	PRIN	BALANCE
1	.8490	33.0007	66.9993
2	.5175	33.3322	33.6671
3	.1826	33.6671	0.0000

YEARS 4 — MO PAYT 2.1261 — AN CONST 25.52

#	INT	PRIN	BALANCE
1	.8873	24.6264	75.3736
2	.6399	24.8738	50.4998
3	.3901	25.1237	25.3761
4	.1377	25.3761	0.0000

YEARS 5 — MO PAYT 1.7094 — AN CONST 20.52

#	INT	PRIN	BALANCE
1	.9103	19.6022	80.3978
2	.7134	19.7991	60.5987
3	.5145	19.9980	40.6007
4	.3136	20.1989	20.4018
5	.1107	20.4018	0.0000

YEARS 6 — MO PAYT 1.4316 — AN CONST 17.18

#	INT	PRIN	BALANCE
1	.9256	16.2530	83.7470
2	.7624	16.4162	67.3308
3	.5974	16.5812	50.7496
4	.4309	16.7477	34.0019
5	.2626	16.9160	17.0859
6	.0927	17.0859	0.0000

YEARS 7 — MO PAYT 1.2331 — AN CONST 14.80

#	INT	PRIN	BALANCE
1	.9366	13.8609	86.1391
2	.7973	14.0002	72.1389
3	.6567	14.1408	57.9981
4	.5146	14.2829	43.7153
5	.3712	14.4263	29.2889
6	.2262	14.5713	14.7177
7	.0798	14.7177	0.0000

YEARS 8 — MO PAYT 1.0843 — AN CONST 13.02

#	INT	PRIN	BALANCE
1	.9448	12.0671	87.9329
2	.8236	12.1883	75.7446
3	.7011	12.3107	63.4339
4	.5775	12.4344	50.9995
5	.4525	12.5593	38.4401
6	.3264	12.6855	25.7546
7	.1989	12.8129	12.9417
8	.0702	12.9417	0.0000

YEARS 9 — MO PAYT .9686 — AN CONST 11.63

#	INT	PRIN	BALANCE
1	.9512	10.6721	89.3279
2	.8440	10.7793	78.5487
3	.7357	10.8876	67.6611
4	.6263	10.9969	56.6642
5	.5158	11.1074	45.5568
6	.4042	11.2190	34.3378
7	.2915	11.3317	23.0061
8	.1777	11.4455	11.5605
9	.0627	11.5605	0.0000

YEARS 10 — MO PAYT .8760 — AN CONST 10.52

#	INT	PRIN	BALANCE
1	.9563	9.5562	90.4438
2	.8603	9.6522	80.7916
3	.7633	9.7492	71.0424
4	.6654	9.8471	61.1953
5	.5664	9.9460	51.2492
6	.4665	10.0460	41.2033
7	.3656	10.1469	31.0564
8	.2637	10.2488	20.8076
9	.1607	10.3518	10.4558
10	.0567	10.4558	0.0000

YEARS 11 — MO PAYT .8003 — AN CONST 9.61

#	INT	PRIN	BALANCE
1	.9605	8.6434	91.3566
2	.8736	8.7302	82.6264
3	.7859	8.8179	73.8084
4	.6973	8.9065	64.9019
5	.6079	8.9960	55.9059
6	.5175	9.0864	46.8195
7	.4262	9.1777	37.6419
8	.3340	9.2698	28.3720
9	.2409	9.3630	19.0091
10	.1468	9.4570	9.5520
11	.0518	9.5520	0.0000

YEARS 12 — MO PAYT .7372 — AN CONST 8.85

#	INT	PRIN	BALANCE
1	.9639	7.8829	92.1171
2	.8847	7.9621	84.1551
3	.8048	8.0420	76.1130
4	.7240	8.1228	67.9902
5	.6424	8.2044	59.7858
6	.5599	8.2869	51.4989
7	.4767	8.3701	43.1288
8	.3926	8.4542	34.6746
9	.3077	8.5391	26.1355
10	.2219	8.6249	17.5106
11	.1353	8.7115	8.7991
12	.0477	8.7991	0.0000

YEARS 13 — MO PAYT .6839 — AN CONST 8.21

#	INT	PRIN	BALANCE
1	.9669	7.2395	92.7605
2	.8942	7.3122	85.4484
3	.8207	7.3856	78.0627
4	.7465	7.4598	70.6029
5	.6716	7.5348	63.0681
6	.5959	7.6105	55.4576
7	.5194	7.6869	47.7707
8	.4422	7.7642	40.0065
9	.3642	7.8422	32.1644
10	.2854	7.9209	24.2434
11	.2058	8.0005	16.2429
12	.1255	8.0809	8.1621
13	.0443	8.1621	0.0000

YEARS 14 — MO PAYT .6381 — AN CONST 7.66

#	INT	PRIN	BALANCE
1	.9694	6.6881	93.3119
2	.9022	6.7553	86.5566
3	.8344	6.8231	79.7335

YEARS 15 — MO PAYT .5985 — AN CONST 7.19

#	INT	PRIN	BALANCE
1	.9716	6.2103	93.7897
2	.9092	6.2727	87.5169
3	.8462	6.3358	81.1812
4	.7825	6.3994	74.7818
5	.7182	6.4637	68.3181
6	.6533	6.5286	61.7895
7	.5877	6.5942	55.1952
8	.5215	6.6605	48.5348
9	.4546	6.7274	41.8074
10	.3870	6.7949	35.0125
11	.3187	6.8632	28.1493
12	.2498	6.9322	21.2171
13	.1801	7.0018	14.2153
14	.1098	7.0721	7.1432
15	.0388	7.1432	0.0000

YEARS 16 — MO PAYT .5638 — AN CONST 6.77

#	INT	PRIN	BALANCE
1	.9735	5.7924	94.2076
2	.9153	5.8506	88.3570
3	.8565	5.9094	82.4476
4	.7972	5.9688	76.4788
5	.7372	6.0287	70.4501
6	.6766	6.0893	64.3608
7	.6155	6.1505	58.2103
8	.5537	6.2122	51.9981
9	.4913	6.2747	45.7235
10	.4282	6.3377	39.3858
11	.3646	6.4014	32.9844
12	.3003	6.4657	26.5187
13	.2353	6.5306	19.9881
14	.1697	6.5962	13.3919
15	.1034	6.6625	6.7294
16	.0365	6.7294	0.0000

YEARS 17 — MO PAYT .5332 — AN CONST 6.40

#	INT	PRIN	BALANCE
1	.9752	5.4238	94.5762
2	.9207	5.4783	89.0980
3	.8657	5.5333	83.5647
4	.8101	5.5889	77.9758
5	.7539	5.6450	72.3308
6	.6972	5.7017	66.6290
7	.6399	5.7590	60.8700
8	.5821	5.8169	55.0532
9	.5237	5.8753	49.1778
10	.4646	5.9343	43.2435
11	.4050	5.9939	37.2496
12	.3448	6.0542	31.1954
13	.2840	6.1150	25.0804
14	.2225	6.1764	18.9040
15	.1605	6.2385	12.6656
16	.0978	6.3011	6.3644
17	.0345	6.3644	0.0000

YEARS 18 — MO PAYT .5061 — AN CONST 6.08

#	INT	PRIN	BALANCE
1	.9767	5.0962	94.9038
2	.9255	5.1474	89.7565
3	.8738	5.1991	84.5574
4	.8215	5.2513	79.3061
5	.7688	5.3041	74.0020
6	.7155	5.3573	68.6447
7	.6617	5.4112	63.2335
8	.6073	5.4655	57.7680
9	.5524	5.5204	52.2475
10	.4970	5.5759	46.6717
11	.4410	5.6319	41.0398
12	.3844	5.6885	35.3513
13	.3272	5.7456	29.6056
14	.2695	5.8034	23.8023
15	.2112	5.8617	17.9406
16	.1523	5.9205	12.0201
17	.0928	5.9800	6.0401
18	.0328	6.0401	0.0000

YEARS 19 — MO PAYT .4818 — AN CONST 5.79

#	INT	PRIN	BALANCE
1	.9780	4.8031	95.1969
2	.9298	4.8514	90.3455
3	.8810	4.9001	85.4453
4	.8318	4.9494	80.4960
5	.7821	4.9991	75.4969
6	.7319	5.0493	70.4476
7	.6811	5.1000	65.3476
8	.6299	5.1513	60.1963
9	.5782	5.2030	54.9933
10	.5259	5.2553	49.7380
11	.4731	5.3081	44.4300
12	.4198	5.3614	39.0686
13	.3659	5.4153	33.6533
14	.3115	5.4697	28.1836
15	.2566	5.5246	22.6590
16	.2011	5.5801	17.0789
17	.1450	5.6362	11.4428
18	.0884	5.6928	5.7500
19	.0312	5.7500	0.0000

YEARS 20 — MO PAYT .4599 — AN CONST 5.52

#	INT	PRIN	BALANCE
1	.9792	4.5395	95.4605
2	.9336	4.5851	90.8754
3	.8876	4.6312	86.2442
4	.8410	4.6777	81.5665
5	.7940	4.7247	76.8419
6	.7466	4.7721	72.0697
7	.6986	4.8201	67.2496
8	.6502	4.8685	62.3811
9	.6013	4.9174	57.4637
10	.5519	4.9668	52.4969
11	.5020	5.0167	47.4802
12	.4516	5.0671	42.4131
13	.4007	5.1180	37.2950
14	.3493	5.1694	32.1256
15	.2974	5.2214	26.9042
16	.2449	5.2738	21.6304
17	.1919	5.3268	16.3036
18	.1384	5.3803	10.9233
19	.0844	5.4344	5.4890
20	.0298	5.4890	0.0000

YEARS 21 — MO PAYT .4401 — AN CONST 5.29

#	INT	PRIN	BALANCE
1	.9803	4.3010	95.6990
2	.9371	4.3443	91.3547
3	.8935	4.3879	86.9668

MONTHLY PAYMENT AMORTIZATION SCHEDULE PER $100 — 1.00 %

#	INT	PRIN	BALANCE
4	.8494	4.4320	82.5348
5	.8049	4.4765	78.0583
6	.7599	4.5215	73.5369
7	.7145	4.5669	68.9700
8	.6686	4.6128	64.3572
9	.6223	4.6591	59.6981
10	.5755	4.7059	54.9922
11	.5282	4.7532	50.2390
12	.4804	4.8009	45.4380
13	.4322	4.8492	40.5888
14	.3835	4.8979	35.6910
15	.3343	4.9471	30.7439
16	.2846	4.9968	25.7471
17	.2344	5.0470	20.7001
18	.1837	5.0977	15.6024
19	.1325	5.1489	10.4535
20	.0807	5.2006	5.2529
21	.0285	5.2529	0.0000

YEARS 22 — MO PAYT .4221 — AN CONST 5.07

#	INT	PRIN	BALANCE
1	.9813	4.0843	95.9157
2	.9403	4.1254	91.7903
3	.8988	4.1668	87.6235
4	.8570	4.2087	83.4148
5	.8147	4.2510	79.1638
6	.7720	4.2937	74.8702
7	.7289	4.3368	70.5334
8	.6853	4.3804	66.1530
9	.6413	4.4244	61.7286
10	.5968	4.4688	57.2598
11	.5519	4.5137	52.7461
12	.5066	4.5591	48.1870
13	.4608	4.6049	43.5822
14	.4145	4.6511	38.9311
15	.3678	4.6978	34.2332
16	.3206	4.7450	29.4882
17	.2730	4.7927	24.6955
18	.2248	4.8409	19.8546
19	.1762	4.8895	14.9651
20	.1271	4.9386	10.0265
21	.0774	4.9882	5.0383
22	.0273	5.0383	0.0000

YEARS 23 — MO PAYT .4057 — AN CONST 4.87

#	INT	PRIN	BALANCE
1	.9822	3.8866	96.1134
2	.9432	3.9256	92.1878
3	.9037	3.9650	88.2228
4	.8639	4.0049	84.2179
5	.8237	4.0451	80.1728
6	.7830	4.0857	76.0871
7	.7420	4.1268	71.9603
8	.7005	4.1682	67.7920
9	.6587	4.2101	63.5819
10	.6164	4.2524	59.3295
11	.5736	4.2951	55.0344
12	.5305	4.3383	50.6961
13	.4869	4.3819	46.3142
14	.4429	4.4259	41.8883
15	.3984	4.4703	37.4180
16	.3535	4.5153	32.9027
17	.3082	4.5606	28.3421
18	.2623	4.6064	23.7357
19	.2161	4.6527	19.0830
20	.1693	4.6994	14.3835
21	.1221	4.7467	9.6369
22	.0744	4.7943	4.8425
23	.0263	4.8425	0.0000

YEARS 24 — MO PAYT .3907 — AN CONST 4.69

#	INT	PRIN	BALANCE
1	.9830	3.7053	96.2947
2	.9458	3.7426	92.5521
3	.9082	3.7801	88.7720
4	.8703	3.8181	84.9539
5	.8319	3.8565	81.0974
6	.7932	3.8952	77.2021
7	.7540	3.9344	73.2678
8	.7145	3.9739	69.2939
9	.6746	4.0138	65.2801
10	.6343	4.0541	61.2260
11	.5935	4.0948	57.1311
12	.5524	4.1360	52.9952
13	.5108	4.1775	48.8176
14	.4689	4.2195	44.5981
15	.4265	4.2619	40.3362
16	.3837	4.3047	36.0315
17	.3404	4.3480	31.6836
18	.2967	4.3916	27.2919
19	.2526	4.4357	22.8562
20	.2081	4.4803	18.3759
21	.1631	4.5253	13.8506
22	.1176	4.5708	9.2798
23	.0717	4.6167	4.6631
24	.0253	4.6631	0.0000

YEARS 25 — MO PAYT .3769 — AN CONST 4.53

#	INT	PRIN	BALANCE
1	.9838	3.5387	96.4613
2	.9483	3.5742	92.8871
3	.9124	3.6101	89.2770
4	.8761	3.6464	85.6306
5	.8395	3.6830	81.9476
6	.8025	3.7200	78.2276
7	.7651	3.7574	74.4702
8	.7273	3.7951	70.6751
9	.6892	3.8333	66.8418
10	.6507	3.8718	62.9701
11	.6118	3.9107	59.0594
12	.5725	3.9499	55.1095
13	.5328	3.9896	51.1198
14	.4928	4.0297	47.0901
15	.4523	4.0702	43.0199
16	.4114	4.1111	38.9089
17	.3701	4.1524	34.7565
18	.3284	4.1941	30.5624
19	.2862	4.2362	26.3262
20	.2437	4.2788	22.0474
21	.2007	4.3218	17.7256
22	.1573	4.3652	13.3604
23	.1134	4.4090	8.9514
24	.0691	4.4533	4.4981
25	.0244	4.4981	0.0000

YEARS 26 — MO PAYT .3641 — AN CONST 4.37

#	INT	PRIN	BALANCE
1	.9845	3.3849	96.6151
2	.9505	3.4189	93.1962
3	.9162	3.4532	89.7430
4	.8815	3.4879	86.2551
5	.8464	3.5230	82.7321
6	.8110	3.5583	79.1738
7	.7753	3.5941	75.5797
8	.7392	3.6302	71.9495
9	.7027	3.6667	68.2828
10	.6659	3.7035	64.5793
11	.6287	3.7407	60.8386
12	.5911	3.7783	57.0603
13	.5531	3.8162	53.2441
14	.5148	3.8546	49.3895
15	.4761	3.8933	45.4962
16	.4370	3.9324	41.5638
17	.3975	3.9719	37.5919
18	.3576	4.0118	33.5800
19	.3173	4.0521	29.5279
20	.2766	4.0928	25.4351
21	.2354	4.1340	21.3011
22	.1939	4.1755	17.1256
23	.1520	4.2174	12.9082
24	.1096	4.2598	8.6484
25	.0668	4.3026	4.3458
26	.0236	4.3458	0.0000

YEARS 27 — MO PAYT .3523 — AN CONST 4.23

#	INT	PRIN	BALANCE
1	.9852	3.2425	96.7575
2	.9526	3.2751	93.4823
3	.9197	3.3080	90.1743
4	.8865	3.3413	86.8331
5	.8529	3.3748	83.4582
6	.8190	3.4087	80.0495
7	.7847	3.4430	76.6066
8	.7502	3.4776	73.1290
9	.7152	3.5125	69.6165
10	.6799	3.5478	66.0687
11	.6443	3.5834	62.4853
12	.6083	3.6194	58.8659
13	.5719	3.6558	55.2101
14	.5352	3.6925	51.5176
15	.4981	3.7296	47.7880
16	.4606	3.7671	44.0210
17	.4228	3.8049	40.2161
18	.3846	3.8431	36.3729
19	.3460	3.8817	32.4912
20	.3070	3.9207	28.5704
21	.2676	3.9601	24.6103
22	.2278	3.9999	20.6104
23	.1876	4.0401	16.5703
24	.1470	4.0807	12.4896
25	.1060	4.1217	8.3680
26	.0646	4.1631	4.2049
27	.0228	4.2049	0.0000

YEARS 28 — MO PAYT .3414 — AN CONST 4.10

#	INT	PRIN	BALANCE
1	.9858	3.1104	96.8896
2	.9545	3.1417	93.7479
3	.9230	3.1732	90.5746
4	.8911	3.2051	87.3695
5	.8589	3.2373	84.1322
6	.8264	3.2698	80.8623
7	.7935	3.3027	77.5596
8	.7603	3.3359	74.2238
9	.7268	3.3694	70.8544
10	.6930	3.4032	67.4511
11	.6588	3.4374	64.0137
12	.6243	3.4720	60.5417
13	.5894	3.5068	57.0349
14	.5541	3.5421	53.4928
15	.5186	3.5776	49.9152
16	.4826	3.6136	46.3016
17	.4463	3.6499	42.6517
18	.4097	3.6866	38.9652
19	.3726	3.7236	35.2416
20	.3352	3.7610	31.4806
21	.2974	3.7988	27.6818
22	.2593	3.8369	23.8448
23	.2207	3.8755	19.9693
24	.1818	3.9144	16.0549
25	.1425	3.9537	12.1012
26	.1027	3.9935	8.1077
27	.0626	4.0336	4.0741
28	.0221	4.0741	0.0000

YEARS 29 — MO PAYT .3312 — AN CONST 3.98

#	INT	PRIN	BALANCE
1	.9863	2.9875	97.0125
2	.9563	3.0175	93.9950
3	.9260	3.0478	90.9472
4	.8954	3.0784	87.8687
5	.8645	3.1094	84.7593
6	.8332	3.1406	81.6187
7	.8017	3.1722	78.4466
8	.7698	3.2040	75.2425
9	.7376	3.2362	72.0063
10	.7051	3.2687	68.7376
11	.6723	3.3016	65.4360
12	.6391	3.3347	62.1013
13	.6056	3.3682	58.7331
14	.5718	3.4021	55.3310
15	.5376	3.4362	51.8947
16	.5031	3.4708	48.4240
17	.4682	3.5056	44.9183
18	.4330	3.5409	41.3775
19	.3974	3.5764	37.8011
20	.3615	3.6124	34.1887
21	.3252	3.6486	30.5401
22	.2885	3.6853	26.8548
23	.2515	3.7223	23.1325
24	.2141	3.7597	19.3728
25	.1764	3.7975	15.5753
26	.1382	3.8356	11.7396
27	.0997	3.8742	7.8655
28	.0608	3.9131	3.9524
29	.0214	3.9524	0.0000

YEARS 30 — MO PAYT .3216 — AN CONST 3.86

#	INT	PRIN	BALANCE
1	.9869	2.8728	97.1272
2	.9580	2.9017	94.2255
3	.9288	2.9308	91.2947
4	.8994	2.9603	88.3344
5	.8697	2.9900	85.3444
6	.8396	3.0200	82.3243
7	.8093	3.0504	79.2740
8	.7786	3.0810	76.1929
9	.7477	3.1120	73.0809
10	.7164	3.1432	69.9377
11	.6849	3.1748	66.7629
12	.6530	3.2067	63.5562
13	.6207	3.2389	60.3172
14	.5882	3.2715	57.0458
15	.5553	3.3043	53.7414
16	.5221	3.3375	50.4039
17	.4886	3.3711	47.0328
18	.4548	3.4049	43.6279
19	.4205	3.4391	40.1888
20	.3860	3.4737	36.7151
21	.3511	3.5086	33.2065
22	.3159	3.5438	29.6627
23	.2803	3.5794	26.0833
24	.2443	3.6154	22.4679
25	.2080	3.6517	18.8162
26	.1713	3.6884	15.1278
27	.1342	3.7254	11.4024
28	.0968	3.7629	7.6395
29	.0590	3.8007	3.8388
30	.0208	3.8388	0.0000

MONTHLY PAYMENT AMORTIZATION SCHEDULE PER $100

2.00 %

YEARS 2 — MO PAYT 4.2540 — AN CONST 51.05

#	INT	PRIN	BALANCE
1	1.5479	49.5004	50.4996
2	.5487	50.4996	0.0000

YEARS 3 — MO PAYT 2.8643 — AN CONST 34.38

#	INT	PRIN	BALANCE
1	1.7016	32.6695	67.3305
2	1.0422	33.3289	34.0016
3	.3695	34.0016	0.0000

YEARS 4 — MO PAYT 2.1695 — AN CONST 26.04

#	INT	PRIN	BALANCE
1	1.7785	24.2557	75.7443
2	1.2889	24.7453	50.9990
3	.7894	25.2447	25.7543
4	.2799	25.7543	0.0000

YEARS 5 — MO PAYT 1.7528 — AN CONST 21.04

#	INT	PRIN	BALANCE
1	1.8246	19.2088	80.7912
2	1.4368	19.5965	61.1948
3	1.0413	19.9920	41.2028
4	.6378	20.3955	20.8072
5	.2261	20.8072	0.0000

YEARS 6 — MO PAYT 1.4750 — AN CONST 17.71

#	INT	PRIN	BALANCE
1	1.8553	15.8453	84.1547
2	1.5354	16.1651	67.9897
3	1.2092	16.4914	51.4983
4	.8763	16.8242	34.6741
5	.5367	17.1638	17.5103
6	.1903	17.5103	0.0000

YEARS 7 — MO PAYT 1.2767 — AN CONST 15.33

#	INT	PRIN	BALANCE
1	1.8772	13.4437	86.5563
2	1.6059	13.7151	72.8412
3	1.3290	13.9919	58.8493
4	1.0466	14.2743	44.5750
5	.7585	14.5624	30.0126
6	.4646	14.8564	15.1562
7	.1647	15.1562	0.0000

YEARS 8 — MO PAYT 1.1281 — AN CONST 13.54

#	INT	PRIN	BALANCE
1	1.8937	11.6434	88.3566
2	1.6586	11.8784	76.4782
3	1.4189	12.1182	64.3600
4	1.1743	12.3628	51.9973
5	.9247	12.6123	39.3850
6	.6702	12.8669	26.5181
7	.4105	13.1266	13.3915
8	.1455	13.3915	0.0000

YEARS 9 — MO PAYT 1.0125 — AN CONST 12.16

#	INT	PRIN	BALANCE
1	1.9064	10.2439	89.7561
2	1.6997	10.4507	79.3055
3	1.4887	10.6616	68.6439
4	1.2735	10.8768	57.7671
5	1.0540	11.0963	46.6707
6	.8300	11.3203	35.3504
7	.6015	11.5488	23.8016
8	.3684	11.7819	12.0197
9	.1306	12.0197	0.0000

YEARS 10 — MO PAYT .9201 — AN CONST 11.05

#	INT	PRIN	BALANCE
1	1.9167	9.1250	90.8750
2	1.7325	9.3091	81.5659
3	1.5446	9.4970	72.0689
4	1.3529	9.6887	62.3801
5	1.1573	9.8843	52.4958
6	.9578	10.0838	42.4120
7	.7543	10.2873	32.1247
8	.5466	10.4950	21.6297
9	.3348	10.7068	10.9229
10	.1187	10.9229	0.0000

YEARS 11 — MO PAYT .8446 — AN CONST 10.14

#	INT	PRIN	BALANCE
1	1.9250	8.2101	91.7899
2	1.7593	8.3758	83.4141
3	1.5902	8.5449	74.8693
4	1.4178	8.7173	66.1520
5	1.2418	8.8933	57.2587
6	1.0623	9.0728	48.1859
7	.8792	9.2559	38.9300
8	.6924	9.4427	29.4872
9	.5018	9.6333	19.8539
10	.3073	9.8278	10.0261
11	.1089	10.0261	0.0000

YEARS 12 — MO PAYT .7817 — AN CONST 9.39

#	INT	PRIN	BALANCE
1	1.9320	7.4482	92.5518
2	1.7816	7.5986	84.9532
3	1.6283	7.7519	77.2013
4	1.4718	7.9084	69.2928
5	1.3122	8.0680	61.2248
6	1.1493	8.2309	52.9939
7	.9832	8.3970	44.5969
8	.8137	8.5665	36.0304
9	.6408	8.7394	27.2910
10	.4644	8.9158	18.3751
11	.2844	9.0958	9.2794
12	.1008	9.2794	0.0000

YEARS 13 — MO PAYT .7285 — AN CONST 8.75

#	INT	PRIN	BALANCE
1	1.9379	6.8041	93.1959
2	1.8005	6.9414	86.2544
3	1.6604	7.0816	79.1729
4	1.5175	7.2245	71.9484
5	1.3717	7.3703	64.5781
6	1.2229	7.5191	57.0590
7	1.0711	7.6708	49.3882
8	.9163	7.8257	41.5625
9	.7583	7.9836	33.5788
10	.5972	8.1448	25.4341
11	.4328	8.3092	17.1249
12	.2651	8.4769	8.6480
13	.0940	8.6480	0.0000

YEARS 14 — MO PAYT .6829 — AN CONST 8.20

#	INT	PRIN	BALANCE
1	1.9429	6.2525	93.7475
2	1.8167	6.3787	87.3688
3	1.6879	6.5074	80.8614
4	1.5566	6.6388	74.2226
5	1.4226	6.7728	67.4498
6	1.2859	6.9095	60.5403
7	1.1464	7.0490	53.4914
8	1.0041	7.1912	46.3002
9	.8590	7.3364	38.9638
10	.7109	7.4845	31.4793
11	.5598	7.6355	23.8438
12	.4057	7.7896	16.0542
13	.2485	7.9469	8.1073
14	.0881	8.1073	0.0000

YEARS 15 — MO PAYT .6435 — AN CONST 7.73

#	INT	PRIN	BALANCE
1	1.9473	5.7748	94.2252
2	1.8307	5.8914	88.3337
3	1.7118	6.0103	82.3234
4	1.5905	6.1316	76.1918
5	1.4667	6.2554	69.9364
6	1.3404	6.3817	63.5547
7	1.2116	6.5105	57.0442
8	1.0802	6.6419	50.4023
9	.9462	6.7759	43.6264
10	.8094	6.9127	36.7137
11	.6699	7.0522	29.6614
12	.5275	7.1946	22.4669
13	.3823	7.3398	15.1271
14	.2341	7.4880	7.6391
15	.0830	7.6391	0.0000

YEARS 16 — MO PAYT .6090 — AN CONST 7.31

#	INT	PRIN	BALANCE
1	1.9511	5.3573	94.6427
2	1.8429	5.4655	89.1772
3	1.7326	5.5758	83.6014
4	1.6201	5.6883	77.9131
5	1.5053	5.8031	72.1099
6	1.3881	5.9203	66.1896
7	1.2686	6.0398	60.1499
8	1.1467	6.1617	53.9882
9	1.0223	6.2861	47.7021
10	.8955	6.4129	41.2892
11	.7660	6.5424	34.7468
12	.6340	6.6744	28.0724
13	.4993	6.8091	21.2632
14	.3618	6.9466	14.3166
15	.2216	7.0868	7.2298
16	.0786	7.2298	0.0000

YEARS 17 — MO PAYT .5786 — AN CONST 6.95

#	INT	PRIN	BALANCE
1	1.9544	4.9893	95.0107
2	1.8537	5.0900	89.9206
3	1.7510	5.1928	84.7278
4	1.6462	5.2976	79.4302
5	1.5392	5.4045	74.0257
6	1.4302	5.5136	68.5121
7	1.3189	5.6249	62.8872
8	1.2053	5.7384	57.1488
9	1.0895	5.8543	51.2945
10	.9713	5.9724	45.3221
11	.8508	6.0930	39.2291
12	.7278	6.2160	33.0132
13	.6023	6.3414	26.6718
14	.4743	6.4694	20.2023
15	.3438	6.6000	13.6023
16	.2105	6.7332	6.8691
17	.0746	6.8691	0.0000

YEARS 18 — MO PAYT .5517 — AN CONST 6.63

#	INT	PRIN	BALANCE
1	1.9574	4.6626	95.3374
2	1.8633	4.7567	90.5807
3	1.7673	4.8527	85.7280
4	1.6693	4.9507	80.7773
5	1.5694	5.0506	75.7267
6	1.4675	5.1525	70.5742
7	1.3635	5.2565	65.3177
8	1.2574	5.3626	59.9550
9	1.1491	5.4709	54.4842
10	1.0387	5.5813	48.9029
11	.9261	5.6940	43.2089
12	.8111	5.8089	37.4000
13	.6939	5.9261	31.4739
14	.5743	6.0457	25.4282
15	.4522	6.1678	19.2604
16	.3277	6.2923	12.9681
17	.2007	6.4193	6.5488
18	.0712	6.5488	0.0000

YEARS 19 — MO PAYT .5276 — AN CONST 6.34

#	INT	PRIN	BALANCE
1	1.9601	4.3706	95.6294
2	1.8719	4.4588	91.1706
3	1.7819	4.5488	86.6218
4	1.6901	4.6406	81.9812
5	1.5964	4.7343	77.2469
6	1.5008	4.8298	72.4170
7	1.4033	4.9273	67.4897
8	1.3039	5.0268	62.4629
9	1.2024	5.1283	57.3347
10	1.0989	5.2318	52.1029
11	.9933	5.3374	46.7655
12	.8856	5.4451	41.3204
13	.7757	5.5550	35.7654
14	.6635	5.6671	30.0983
15	.5492	5.7815	24.3168
16	.4325	5.8982	18.4186
17	.3134	6.0173	12.4013
18	.1920	6.1387	6.2626
19	.0681	6.2626	0.0000

YEARS 20 — MO PAYT .5059 — AN CONST 6.08

#	INT	PRIN	BALANCE
1	1.9625	4.1081	95.8919
2	1.8796	4.1910	91.7008
3	1.7950	4.2756	87.4252
4	1.7087	4.3619	83.0633
5	1.6206	4.4500	78.6133
6	1.5308	4.5398	74.0735
7	1.4392	4.6314	69.4421
8	1.3457	4.7249	64.7171
9	1.2503	4.8203	59.8969
10	1.1530	4.9176	54.9793
11	1.0538	5.0168	49.9624
12	.9525	5.1181	44.8443
13	.8492	5.2214	39.6229
14	.7438	5.3268	34.2961
15	.6363	5.4343	28.8618
16	.5266	5.5440	23.3178
17	.4147	5.6559	17.6619
18	.3005	5.7701	11.8919
19	.1841	5.8865	6.0053
20	.0653	6.0053	0.0000

YEARS 21 — MO PAYT .4863 — AN CONST 5.84

#	INT	PRIN	BALANCE
1	1.9646	3.8710	96.1290
2	1.8865	3.9491	92.1799
3	1.8068	4.0288	88.1511

#	INT	PRIN	BALANCE
4	1.7255	4.1101	84.0410
5	1.6425	4.1931	79.8479
6	1.5579	4.2777	75.5702
7	1.4715	4.3641	71.2061
8	1.3835	4.4522	66.7540
9	1.2936	4.5420	62.2120
10	1.2019	4.6337	57.5783
11	1.1084	4.7272	52.8511
12	1.0130	4.8226	48.0284
13	.9156	4.9200	43.1084
14	.8163	5.0193	38.0892
15	.7150	5.1206	32.9686
16	.6117	5.2240	27.7446
17	.5062	5.3294	22.4152
18	.3986	5.4370	16.9782
19	.2889	5.5467	11.4315
20	.1769	5.6587	5.7729
21	.0627	5.7729	0.0000

YEARS 22 — MO PAYT .4685 — AN CONST 5.63

#	INT	PRIN	BALANCE
1	1.9666	3.6557	96.3443
2	1.8928	3.7295	92.6149
3	1.8175	3.8047	88.8101
4	1.7408	3.8815	84.9286
5	1.6624	3.9599	80.9687
6	1.5825	4.0398	76.9289
7	1.5009	4.1213	72.8076
8	1.4177	4.2045	68.6031
9	1.3329	4.2894	64.3137
10	1.2463	4.3760	59.9377
11	1.1580	4.4643	55.4734
12	1.0679	4.5544	50.9190
13	.9759	4.6463	46.2727
14	.8822	4.7401	41.5325
15	.7865	4.8358	36.6967
16	.6889	4.9334	31.7633
17	.5893	5.0330	26.7304
18	.4877	5.1346	21.5958
19	.3841	5.2382	16.3576
20	.2783	5.3439	11.0136
21	.1705	5.4518	5.5618
22	.0604	5.5618	0.0000

YEARS 23 — MO PAYT .4523 — AN CONST 5.43

#	INT	PRIN	BALANCE
1	1.9684	3.4594	96.5406
2	1.8986	3.5292	93.0114
3	1.8273	3.6004	89.4110
4	1.7547	3.6731	85.7379
5	1.6805	3.7473	81.9906
6	1.6049	3.8229	78.1677
7	1.5277	3.9000	74.2677
8	1.4490	3.9788	70.2889
9	1.3687	4.0591	66.2298
10	1.2868	4.1410	62.0888
11	1.2032	4.2246	57.8642
12	1.1179	4.3099	53.5544
13	1.0309	4.3969	49.1575
14	.9422	4.4856	44.6719
15	.8516	4.5761	40.0958
16	.7593	4.6685	35.4273
17	.6650	4.7627	30.6645
18	.5689	4.8589	25.8056
19	.4708	4.9569	20.8487
20	.3708	5.0570	15.7917
21	.2687	5.1591	10.6326
22	.1646	5.2632	5.3694
23	.0583	5.3694	0.0000

YEARS 24 — MO PAYT .4375 — AN CONST 5.25

#	INT	PRIN	BALANCE
1	1.9700	3.2797	96.7203
2	1.9038	3.3459	93.3744
3	1.8363	3.4135	89.9609
4	1.7674	3.4824	86.4785
5	1.6971	3.5526	82.9259
6	1.6254	3.6244	79.3015
7	1.5523	3.6975	75.6040
8	1.4776	3.7721	71.8319
9	1.4015	3.8483	67.9836
10	1.3238	3.9260	64.0577
11	1.2446	4.0052	60.0525
12	1.1637	4.0860	55.9664
13	1.0813	4.1685	51.7979
14	.9971	4.2526	47.5453
15	.9113	4.3385	43.2068
16	.8237	4.4261	38.7807
17	.7344	4.5154	34.2653
18	.6432	4.6065	29.6588
19	.5503	4.6995	24.9593
20	.4554	4.7944	20.1649
21	.3586	4.8911	15.2738
22	.2599	4.9899	10.2839
23	.1592	5.0906	5.1933
24	.0564	5.1933	0.0000

YEARS 25 — MO PAYT .4239 — AN CONST 5.09

#	INT	PRIN	BALANCE
1	1.9716	3.1147	96.8853
2	1.9087	3.1776	93.7077
3	1.8445	3.2417	90.4660
4	1.7791	3.3071	87.1589
5	1.7124	3.3739	83.7850
6	1.6443	3.4420	80.3430
7	1.5748	3.5115	76.8315
8	1.5039	3.5823	73.2492
9	1.4316	3.6546	69.5946
10	1.3578	3.7284	65.8661
11	1.2826	3.8037	62.0625
12	1.2058	3.8804	58.1820
13	1.1275	3.9588	54.2233
14	1.0476	4.0387	50.1846
15	.9661	4.1202	46.0644
16	.8829	4.2034	41.8610
17	.7981	4.2882	37.5728
18	.7115	4.3748	33.1981
19	.6232	4.4631	28.7350
20	.5331	4.5531	24.1819
21	.4412	4.6450	19.5368
22	.3475	4.7388	14.7981
23	.2518	4.8344	9.9636
24	.1542	4.9320	5.0316
25	.0547	5.0316	0.0000

YEARS 26 — MO PAYT .4113 — AN CONST 4.94

#	INT	PRIN	BALANCE
1	1.9729	2.9626	97.0374
2	1.9131	3.0224	94.0150
3	1.8521	3.0834	90.9315
4	1.7899	3.1457	87.7859
5	1.7264	3.2092	84.5767
6	1.6616	3.2739	81.3028
7	1.5955	3.3400	77.9627
8	1.5281	3.4074	74.5553
9	1.4594	3.4762	71.0791
10	1.3892	3.5464	67.5327
11	1.3176	3.6180	63.9148
12	1.2446	3.6910	60.2238
13	1.1701	3.7655	56.4583
14	1.0941	3.8415	52.6168
15	1.0165	3.9190	48.6978
16	.9374	3.9981	44.6997
17	.8567	4.0788	40.6208
18	.7744	4.1612	36.4597
19	.6904	4.2451	32.2145
20	.6047	4.3308	27.8837
21	.5173	4.4182	23.4655
22	.4281	4.5074	18.9580
23	.3372	4.5984	14.3596
24	.2443	4.6912	9.6684
25	.1497	4.7859	4.8825
26	.0531	4.8825	0.0000

YEARS 27 — MO PAYT .3997 — AN CONST 4.80

#	INT	PRIN	BALANCE
1	1.9742	2.8221	97.1779
2	1.9173	2.8790	94.2989
3	1.8592	2.9371	91.3618
4	1.7999	2.9964	88.3654
5	1.7394	3.0569	85.3085
6	1.6777	3.1186	82.1899
7	1.6147	3.1815	79.0084
8	1.5505	3.2458	75.7626
9	1.4850	3.3113	72.4513
10	1.4182	3.3781	69.0732
11	1.3500	3.4463	65.6269
12	1.2804	3.5159	62.1111
13	1.2095	3.5868	58.5242
14	1.1371	3.6592	54.8650
15	1.0632	3.7331	51.1319
16	.9879	3.8084	47.3235
17	.9110	3.8853	43.4382
18	.8326	3.9637	39.4745
19	.7526	4.0437	35.4308
20	.6709	4.1253	31.3054
21	.5877	4.2086	27.0968
22	.5027	4.2936	22.8033
23	.4161	4.3802	18.4230
24	.3276	4.4686	13.9544
25	.2374	4.5588	9.3956
26	.1454	4.6508	4.7447
27	.0516	4.7447	0.0000

YEARS 28 — MO PAYT .3889 — AN CONST 4.67

#	INT	PRIN	BALANCE
1	1.9754	2.6918	97.3082
2	1.9211	2.7461	94.5621
3	1.8657	2.8015	91.7606
4	1.8091	2.8581	88.9026
5	1.7514	2.9158	85.9868
6	1.6926	2.9746	83.0122
7	1.6325	3.0347	79.9775
8	1.5713	3.0959	76.8816
9	1.5088	3.1584	73.7232
10	1.4450	3.2221	70.5011
11	1.3800	3.2872	67.2139
12	1.3136	3.3535	63.8604
13	1.2460	3.4212	60.4392
14	1.1769	3.4903	56.9489
15	1.1065	3.5607	53.3882
16	1.0346	3.6326	49.7556
17	.9613	3.7059	46.0497
18	.8865	3.7807	42.2690
19	.8102	3.8570	38.4119
20	.7323	3.9349	34.4771
21	.6529	4.0143	30.4628
22	.5719	4.0953	26.3674
23	.4892	4.1780	22.1895
24	.4049	4.2623	17.9271
25	.3188	4.3483	13.5788
26	.2311	4.4361	9.1427
27	.1415	4.5257	4.6170
28	.0502	4.6170	0.0000

YEARS 29 — MO PAYT .3789 — AN CONST 4.55

#	INT	PRIN	BALANCE
1	1.9765	2.5707	97.4293
2	1.9246	2.6226	94.8068
3	1.8717	2.6755	92.1313
4	1.8177	2.7295	89.4018
5	1.7626	2.7846	86.6172
6	1.7064	2.8408	83.7764
7	1.6491	2.8981	80.8782
8	1.5906	2.9566	77.9216
9	1.5309	3.0163	74.9053
10	1.4700	3.0772	71.8281
11	1.4079	3.1393	68.6887
12	1.3445	3.2027	65.4861
13	1.2799	3.2673	62.2188
14	1.2139	3.3333	58.8855
15	1.1467	3.4005	55.4849
16	1.0780	3.4692	52.0157
17	1.0080	3.5392	48.4765
18	.9366	3.6106	44.8659
19	.8637	3.6835	41.1824
20	.7893	3.7579	37.4245
21	.7135	3.8337	33.5908
22	.6361	3.9111	29.6797
23	.5571	3.9900	25.6896
24	.4766	4.0706	21.6190
25	.3945	4.1527	17.4663
26	.3106	4.2366	13.2297
27	.2251	4.3221	8.9076
28	.1379	4.4093	4.4983
29	.0489	4.4983	0.0000

YEARS 30 — MO PAYT .3696 — AN CONST 4.44

#	INT	PRIN	BALANCE
1	1.9776	2.4579	97.5421
2	1.9279	2.5075	95.0346
3	1.8773	2.5581	92.4765
4	1.8257	2.6097	89.8668
5	1.7730	2.6624	87.2044
6	1.7193	2.7162	84.4882
7	1.6645	2.7710	81.7172
8	1.6085	2.8269	78.8903
9	1.5515	2.8840	76.0064
10	1.4933	2.9422	73.0642
11	1.4339	3.0016	70.0626
12	1.3733	3.0621	67.0005
13	1.3115	3.1240	63.8765
14	1.2484	3.1870	60.6895
15	1.1841	3.2513	57.4381
16	1.1185	3.3170	54.1212
17	1.0515	3.3839	50.7373
18	.9832	3.4522	47.2850
19	.9135	3.5219	43.7631
20	.8424	3.5930	40.1702
21	.7699	3.6655	36.5046
22	.6959	3.7395	32.7651
23	.6205	3.8150	28.9502
24	.5435	3.8920	25.0582
25	.4649	3.9705	21.0877
26	.3848	4.0507	17.0370
27	.3030	4.1324	12.9045
28	.2196	4.2158	8.6887
29	.1345	4.3009	4.3878
30	.0477	4.3878	0.0000

MONTHLY PAYMENT AMORTIZATION SCHEDULE PER $100   3.00 %

#	YEARS 2 — MO PAYT 4.2981 — AN CONST 51.58		
	INT	PRIN	BALANCE
1	2.3265	49.2510	50.7490
2	.8284	50.7490	0.0000

#	YEARS 3 — MO PAYT 2.9081 — AN CONST 34.90		
	INT	PRIN	BALANCE
1	2.5577	32.3397	67.6603
2	1.5741	33.3234	34.3369
3	.5605	34.3369	0.0000

#	YEARS 4 — MO PAYT 2.2134 — AN CONST 26.57		
	INT	PRIN	BALANCE
1	2.6733	23.8879	76.1121
2	1.9467	24.6144	51.4977
3	1.1981	25.3631	26.1346
4	.4266	26.1346	0.0000

#	YEARS 5 — MO PAYT 1.7969 — AN CONST 21.57		
	INT	PRIN	BALANCE
1	2.7426	18.8198	81.1802
2	2.1702	19.3922	61.7880
3	1.5804	19.9821	41.8059
4	.9726	20.5898	21.2161
5	.3463	21.2161	0.0000

#	YEARS 6 — MO PAYT 1.5194 — AN CONST 18.24		
	INT	PRIN	BALANCE
1	2.7888	15.4436	84.5564
2	2.3191	15.9133	68.6430
3	1.8350	16.3974	52.2457
4	1.3363	16.8961	35.3496
5	.8224	17.4100	17.9396
6	.2929	17.9396	0.0000

#	YEARS 7 — MO PAYT 1.3213 — AN CONST 15.86		
	INT	PRIN	BALANCE
1	2.8217	13.0342	86.9658
2	2.4253	13.4307	73.5351
3	2.0168	13.8392	59.6960
4	1.5959	14.2601	45.4359
5	1.1621	14.6938	30.7420
6	.7152	15.1408	15.6013
7	.2547	15.6013	0.0000

#	YEARS 8 — MO PAYT 1.1730 — AN CONST 14.08		
	INT	PRIN	BALANCE
1	2.8464	11.2291	88.7709
2	2.5049	11.5706	77.2004
3	2.1530	11.9225	65.2778
4	1.7903	12.2852	52.9927
5	1.4167	12.6588	40.3339
6	1.0316	13.0439	27.2900
7	.6349	13.4406	13.8494
8	.2261	13.8494	0.0000

#	YEARS 9 — MO PAYT 1.0577 — AN CONST 12.70		
	INT	PRIN	BALANCE
1	2.8656	9.8267	90.1733
2	2.5667	10.1256	80.0477
3	2.2587	10.4336	69.6141
4	1.9414	10.7509	58.8632
5	1.6144	11.0779	47.7852
6	1.2775	11.4149	36.3704
7	.9303	11.7621	24.6083
8	.5725	12.1198	12.4885
9	.2039	12.4885	0.0000

#	YEARS 10 — MO PAYT .9656 — AN CONST 11.59		
	INT	PRIN	BALANCE
1	2.8809	8.7064	91.2936
2	2.6161	8.9712	82.3225
3	2.3433	9.2440	73.0784
4	2.0621	9.5252	63.5532
5	1.7724	9.8149	53.7383
6	1.4738	10.1134	43.6249
7	1.1662	10.4211	33.2038
8	.8493	10.7380	22.4658
9	.5227	11.0646	11.4012
10	.1861	11.4012	0.0000

#	YEARS 11 — MO PAYT .8904 — AN CONST 10.69		
	INT	PRIN	BALANCE
1	2.8935	7.7911	92.2089
2	2.6565	8.0280	84.1809
3	2.4123	8.2722	75.9087
4	2.1607	8.5238	67.3849
5	1.9014	8.7831	58.6018
6	1.6343	9.0502	49.5515
7	1.3590	9.3255	40.2260
8	1.0754	9.6091	30.6169
9	.7831	9.9014	20.7155
10	.4819	10.2026	10.5129
11	.1716	10.5129	0.0000

#	YEARS 12 — MO PAYT .8278 — AN CONST 9.94		
	INT	PRIN	BALANCE
1	2.9039	7.0296	92.9704
2	2.6901	7.2434	85.7270
3	2.4697	7.4637	78.2633
4	2.2427	7.6907	70.5726
5	2.0088	7.9246	62.6480
6	1.7678	8.1657	54.4823
7	1.5194	8.4140	46.0683
8	1.2635	8.6700	37.3983
9	.9998	8.9337	28.4647
10	.7281	9.2054	19.2593
11	.4481	9.4854	9.7739
12	.1596	9.7739	0.0000

#	YEARS 13 — MO PAYT .7749 — AN CONST 9.30		
	INT	PRIN	BALANCE
1	2.9127	6.3864	93.6136
2	2.7184	6.5806	87.0330
3	2.5183	6.7808	80.2522
4	2.3120	6.9870	73.2651
5	2.0995	7.1996	66.0656
6	1.8805	7.4185	58.6470
7	1.6549	7.6442	51.0029
8	1.4224	7.8767	43.1262
9	1.1828	8.1163	35.0099
10	.9359	8.3631	26.6468
11	.6816	8.6175	18.0293
12	.4194	8.8796	9.1497
13	.1494	9.1497	0.0000

#	YEARS 14 — MO PAYT .7297 — AN CONST 8.76		
	INT	PRIN	BALANCE
1	2.9202	5.8362	94.1638
2	2.7427	6.0137	88.1502
3	2.5598	6.1966	81.9536
4	2.3713	6.3851	75.5685
5	2.1771	6.5793	68.9893
6	1.9770	6.7794	62.2099
7	1.7708	6.9856	55.2243
8	1.5583	7.1981	48.0263
9	1.3394	7.4170	40.6093
10	1.1138	7.6426	32.9667
11	.8813	7.8750	25.0916
12	.6418	8.1146	16.9771
13	.3950	8.3614	8.6157
14	.1406	8.6157	0.0000

#	YEARS 15 — MO PAYT .6906 — AN CONST 8.29		
	INT	PRIN	BALANCE
1	2.9267	5.3603	94.6397
2	2.7637	5.5233	89.1164
3	2.5957	5.6913	83.4251
4	2.4226	5.8644	77.5606
5	2.2442	6.0428	71.5178
6	2.0604	6.2266	65.2912
7	1.8710	6.4160	58.8753
8	1.6758	6.6111	52.2641
9	1.4748	6.8122	45.4519
10	1.2676	7.0194	38.4325
11	1.0541	7.2329	31.1996
12	.8341	7.4529	23.7467
13	.6074	7.6796	16.0671
14	.3738	7.9132	8.1539
15	.1331	8.1539	0.0000

#	YEARS 16 — MO PAYT .6564 — AN CONST 7.88		
	INT	PRIN	BALANCE
1	2.9324	4.9448	95.0552
2	2.7820	5.0952	89.9599
3	2.6270	5.2502	84.7097
4	2.4673	5.4099	79.2998
5	2.3028	5.5744	73.7254
6	2.1332	5.7440	67.9814
7	1.9585	5.9187	62.0627
8	1.7785	6.0987	55.9640
9	1.5930	6.2842	49.6798
10	1.4018	6.4754	43.2044
11	1.2049	6.6723	36.5321
12	1.0019	6.8753	29.6568
13	.7928	7.0844	22.5724
14	.5773	7.2999	15.2726
15	.3553	7.5219	7.7507
16	.1265	7.7507	0.0000

#	YEARS 17 — MO PAYT .6264 — AN CONST 7.52		
	INT	PRIN	BALANCE
1	2.9374	4.5791	95.4209
2	2.7981	4.7184	90.7025
3	2.6546	4.8619	85.8406
4	2.5067	5.0098	80.8308
5	2.3543	5.1622	75.6686
6	2.1973	5.3192	70.3494
7	2.0355	5.4810	64.8685
8	1.8688	5.6477	59.2208
9	1.6970	5.8195	53.4013
10	1.5200	5.9965	47.4049
11	1.3376	6.1789	41.2260
12	1.1497	6.3668	34.8592
13	.9561	6.5604	28.2988
14	.7565	6.7600	21.5388
15	.5509	6.9656	14.5732
16	.3390	7.1775	7.3958
17	.1207	7.3958	0.0000

#	YEARS 18 — MO PAYT .5997 — AN CONST 7.20		
	INT	PRIN	BALANCE
1	2.9418	4.2549	95.7451
2	2.8124	4.3843	91.3608
3	2.6790	4.5176	86.8432
4	2.5416	4.6550	82.1882
5	2.4000	4.7966	77.3915
6	2.2542	4.9425	72.4490
7	2.1038	5.0929	67.3562
8	1.9489	5.2478	62.1084
9	1.7893	5.4074	56.7010
10	1.6248	5.5718	51.1292
11	1.4554	5.7413	45.3879
12	1.2807	5.9159	39.4719
13	1.1008	6.0959	33.3760
14	.9154	6.2813	27.0947
15	.7243	6.4724	20.6224
16	.5275	6.6692	13.9531
17	.3246	6.8721	7.0811
18	.1156	7.0811	0.0000

#	YEARS 19 — MO PAYT .5759 — AN CONST 6.92		
	INT	PRIN	BALANCE
1	2.9458	3.9655	96.0345
2	2.8252	4.0861	91.9483
3	2.7009	4.2104	87.7379
4	2.5728	4.3385	83.3994
5	2.4408	4.4704	78.9290
6	2.3049	4.6064	74.3226
7	2.1648	4.7465	69.5760
8	2.0204	4.8909	64.6851
9	1.8716	5.0397	59.6455
10	1.7183	5.1929	54.4525
11	1.5604	5.3509	49.1016
12	1.3976	5.5136	43.5880
13	1.2299	5.6813	37.9066
14	1.0571	5.8542	32.0525
15	.8791	6.0322	26.0203
16	.6956	6.2157	19.8046
17	.5065	6.4047	13.3998
18	.3117	6.5996	6.8003
19	.1110	6.8003	0.0000

#	YEARS 20 — MO PAYT .5546 — AN CONST 6.66		
	INT	PRIN	BALANCE
1	2.9493	3.7059	96.2941
2	2.8366	3.8186	92.4756
3	2.7205	3.9347	88.5409
4	2.6008	4.0544	84.4865
5	2.4775	4.1777	80.3088
6	2.3504	4.3048	76.0040
7	2.2195	4.4357	71.5683
8	2.0845	4.5706	66.9976
9	1.9455	4.7096	62.2880
10	1.8023	4.8529	57.4351
11	1.6547	5.0005	52.4346
12	1.5026	5.1526	47.2820
13	1.3459	5.3093	41.9727
14	1.1844	5.4708	36.5019
15	1.0180	5.6372	30.8647
16	.8465	5.8087	25.0560
17	.6698	5.9853	19.0707
18	.4878	6.1674	12.9033
19	.3002	6.3550	6.5483
20	.1069	6.5483	0.0000

#	YEARS 21 — MO PAYT .5353 — AN CONST 6.43		
	INT	PRIN	BALANCE
1	2.9525	3.4716	96.5284
2	2.8469	3.5772	92.9512
3	2.7381	3.6860	89.2652

#	INT	PRIN	BALANCE
4	2.6260	3.7981	85.4671
5	2.5105	3.9136	81.5534
6	2.3915	4.0327	77.5208
7	2.2688	4.1553	73.3654
8	2.1424	4.2817	69.0837
9	2.0122	4.4120	64.6718
10	1.8780	4.5461	60.1256
11	1.7397	4.6844	55.4412
12	1.5972	4.8269	50.6143
13	1.4504	4.9737	45.6406
14	1.2991	5.1250	40.5156
15	1.1432	5.2809	35.2347
16	.9826	5.4415	29.7932
17	.8171	5.6070	24.1862
18	.6466	5.7776	18.4086
19	.4708	5.9533	12.4553
20	.2898	6.1344	6.3209
21	.1032	6.3209	0.0000

YEARS 22 — MO PAYT .5179 — AN CONST 6.22

#	INT	PRIN	BALANCE
1	2.9554	3.2593	96.7407
2	2.8563	3.3585	93.3822
3	2.7541	3.4606	89.9216
4	2.6489	3.5659	86.3558
5	2.5404	3.6743	82.6814
6	2.4287	3.7861	78.8954
7	2.3135	3.9012	74.9941
8	2.1948	4.0199	70.9742
9	2.0726	4.1422	66.8320
10	1.9466	4.2682	62.5639
11	1.8168	4.3980	58.1659
12	1.6830	4.5317	53.6342
13	1.5452	4.6696	48.9646
14	1.4031	4.8116	44.1530
15	1.2568	4.9580	39.1950
16	1.1060	5.1088	34.0863
17	.9506	5.2641	28.8221
18	.7905	5.4243	23.3978
19	.6255	5.5892	17.8086
20	.4555	5.7593	12.0493
21	.2803	5.9344	6.1149
22	.0998	6.1149	0.0000

YEARS 23 — MO PAYT .5020 — AN CONST 6.03

#	INT	PRIN	BALANCE
1	2.9581	3.0661	96.9339
2	2.8648	3.1594	93.7745
3	2.7687	3.2555	90.5190
4	2.6697	3.3545	87.1645
5	2.5677	3.4565	83.7080
6	2.4625	3.5617	80.1463
7	2.3542	3.6700	76.4763
8	2.2426	3.7816	72.6947
9	2.1276	3.8966	68.7981
10	2.0090	4.0152	64.7829
11	1.8869	4.1373	60.6456
12	1.7611	4.2631	56.3825
13	1.6314	4.3928	51.9897
14	1.4978	4.5264	47.4633
15	1.3601	4.6641	42.7992
16	1.2183	4.8059	37.9933
17	1.0721	4.9521	33.0411
18	.9215	5.1027	27.9384
19	.7662	5.2579	22.6804
20	.6063	5.4179	17.2626
21	.4415	5.5827	11.6799
22	.2717	5.7525	5.9274
23	.0968	5.9274	0.0000

YEARS 24 — MO PAYT .4875 — AN CONST 5.86

#	INT	PRIN	BALANCE
1	2.9605	2.8896	97.1104
2	2.8726	2.9775	94.1328
3	2.7820	3.0681	91.0647
4	2.6887	3.1614	87.9033
5	2.5926	3.2576	84.6458
6	2.4935	3.3566	81.2891
7	2.3914	3.4587	77.8304
8	2.2862	3.5639	74.2664
9	2.1778	3.6723	70.5941
10	2.0661	3.7840	66.8100
11	1.9510	3.8991	62.9109
12	1.8324	4.0177	58.8932
13	1.7102	4.1399	54.7532
14	1.5843	4.2659	50.4874
15	1.4545	4.3956	46.0918
16	1.3208	4.5293	41.5625
17	1.1830	4.6671	36.8954
18	1.0411	4.8090	32.0864
19	.8948	4.9553	27.1311
20	.7441	5.1060	22.0251
21	.5888	5.2613	16.7637
22	.4288	5.4213	11.3424
23	.2639	5.5862	5.7562
24	.0940	5.7562	0.0000

YEARS 25 — MO PAYT .4742 — AN CONST 5.70

#	INT	PRIN	BALANCE
1	2.9627	2.7278	97.2722
2	2.8797	2.8108	94.4613
3	2.7942	2.8963	91.5650
4	2.7061	2.9844	88.5806
5	2.6154	3.0752	85.5055
6	2.5218	3.1687	82.3368
7	2.4255	3.2651	79.0717
8	2.3261	3.3644	75.7073
9	2.2238	3.4667	72.2406
10	2.1184	3.5722	68.6684
11	2.0097	3.6808	64.9876
12	1.8978	3.7928	61.1948
13	1.7824	3.9081	57.2867
14	1.6635	4.0270	53.2596
15	1.5410	4.1495	49.1102
16	1.4148	4.2757	44.8345
17	1.2848	4.4058	40.4287
18	1.1508	4.5398	35.8889
19	1.0127	4.6778	31.2111
20	.8704	4.8201	26.3910
21	.7238	4.9667	21.4242
22	.5727	5.1178	16.3065
23	.4171	5.2735	11.0330
24	.2567	5.4339	5.5991
25	.0914	5.5991	0.0000

YEARS 26 — MO PAYT .4620 — AN CONST 5.55

#	INT	PRIN	BALANCE
1	2.9647	2.5790	97.4210
2	2.8863	2.6575	94.7635
3	2.8055	2.7383	92.0251
4	2.7222	2.8216	89.2035
5	2.6363	2.9074	86.2961
6	2.5479	2.9959	83.3003
7	2.4568	3.0870	80.2133
8	2.3629	3.1809	77.0324
9	2.2661	3.2776	73.7548
10	2.1665	3.3773	70.3774
11	2.0637	3.4800	66.8974
12	1.9579	3.5859	63.3115
13	1.8488	3.6950	59.6166
14	1.7364	3.8073	55.8092
15	1.6206	3.9231	51.8861
16	1.5013	4.0425	47.8436
17	1.3783	4.1654	43.6782
18	1.2516	4.2921	39.3860
19	1.1211	4.4227	34.9633
20	.9866	4.5572	30.4062
21	.8480	4.6958	25.7103
22	.7051	4.8386	20.8717
23	.5580	4.9858	15.8859
24	.4063	5.1375	10.7484
25	.2501	5.2937	5.4547
26	.0890	5.4547	0.0000

YEARS 27 — MO PAYT .4507 — AN CONST 5.41

#	INT	PRIN	BALANCE
1	2.9666	2.4418	97.5582
2	2.8923	2.5161	95.0421
3	2.8158	2.5926	92.4495
4	2.7370	2.6715	89.7781
5	2.6557	2.7527	87.0254
6	2.5720	2.8364	84.1889
7	2.4857	2.9227	81.2662
8	2.3968	3.0116	78.2546
9	2.3052	3.1032	75.1514
10	2.2108	3.1976	71.9538
11	2.1136	3.2949	68.6590
12	2.0133	3.3951	65.2639
13	1.9101	3.4983	61.7656
14	1.8037	3.6047	58.1608
15	1.6940	3.7144	54.4465
16	1.5811	3.8274	50.6191
17	1.4646	3.9438	46.6753
18	1.3447	4.0637	42.6116
19	1.2211	4.1873	38.4243
20	1.0937	4.3147	34.1096
21	.9625	4.4459	29.6637
22	.8273	4.5811	25.0825
23	.6879	4.7205	20.3621
24	.5443	4.8641	15.4980
25	.3964	5.0120	10.4860
26	.2440	5.1645	5.3215
27	.0869	5.3215	0.0000

YEARS 28 — MO PAYT .4403 — AN CONST 5.29

#	INT	PRIN	BALANCE
1	2.9683	2.3149	97.6851
2	2.8979	2.3853	95.2999
3	2.8254	2.4578	92.8420
4	2.7506	2.5326	90.3095
5	2.6736	2.6096	87.6998
6	2.5942	2.6890	85.0108
7	2.5124	2.7708	82.2401
8	2.4282	2.8551	79.3850
9	2.3413	2.9419	76.4431
10	2.2518	3.0314	73.4118
11	2.1596	3.1236	70.2882
12	2.0646	3.2186	67.0696
13	1.9667	3.3165	63.7531
14	1.8659	3.4173	60.3358
15	1.7619	3.5213	56.8145
16	1.6548	3.6284	53.1861
17	1.5445	3.7388	49.4473
18	1.4307	3.8525	45.5949
19	1.3136	3.9697	41.6252
20	1.1928	4.0904	37.5348
21	1.0684	4.2148	33.3200
22	.9402	4.3430	28.9770
23	.8081	4.4751	24.5019
24	.6720	4.6112	19.8907
25	.5317	4.7515	15.1392
26	.3872	4.8960	10.2433
27	.2383	5.0449	5.1983
28	.0849	5.1983	0.0000

YEARS 29 — MO PAYT .4306 — AN CONST 5.17

#	INT	PRIN	BALANCE
1	2.9700	2.1972	97.8028
2	2.9031	2.2640	95.5388
3	2.8343	2.3329	93.2060
4	2.7633	2.4038	90.8021
5	2.6902	2.4769	88.3252
6	2.6149	2.5523	85.7729
7	2.5372	2.6299	83.1430
8	2.4572	2.7099	80.4331
9	2.3748	2.7923	77.6408
10	2.2899	2.8773	74.7635
11	2.2024	2.9648	71.7988
12	2.1122	3.0549	68.7438
13	2.0193	3.1479	65.5960
14	1.9235	3.2436	62.3524
15	1.8249	3.3423	59.0101
16	1.7232	3.4439	55.5662
17	1.6185	3.5487	52.0175
18	1.5105	3.6566	48.3609
19	1.3993	3.7678	44.5931
20	1.2847	3.8824	40.7106
21	1.1666	4.0005	36.7101
22	1.0449	4.1222	32.5879
23	.9195	4.2476	28.3403
24	.7904	4.3768	23.9636
25	.6572	4.5099	19.4537
26	.5201	4.6471	14.8066
27	.3787	4.7884	10.0182
28	.2331	4.9341	5.0841
29	.0830	5.0841	0.0000

YEARS 30 — MO PAYT .4216 — AN CONST 5.06

#	INT	PRIN	BALANCE
1	2.9714	2.0878	97.9122
2	2.9079	2.1513	95.7609
3	2.8425	2.2167	93.5442
4	2.7751	2.2842	91.2600
5	2.7056	2.3536	88.9064
6	2.6340	2.4252	86.4811
7	2.5603	2.4990	83.9821
8	2.4842	2.5750	81.4072
9	2.4059	2.6533	78.7538
10	2.3252	2.7340	76.0198
11	2.2421	2.8172	73.2026
12	2.1564	2.9029	70.2998
13	2.0681	2.9912	67.3086
14	1.9771	3.0821	64.2265
15	1.8834	3.1759	61.0506
16	1.7868	3.2725	57.7781
17	1.6872	3.3720	54.4061
18	1.5847	3.4746	50.9315
19	1.4790	3.5803	47.3512
20	1.3701	3.6892	43.6621
21	1.2579	3.8014	39.8607
22	1.1423	3.9170	35.9437
23	1.0231	4.0361	31.9076
24	.9004	4.1589	27.7487
25	.7739	4.2854	23.4633
26	.6435	4.4157	19.0475
27	.5092	4.5500	14.4975
28	.3708	4.6884	9.8090
29	.2282	4.8310	4.9780
30	.0813	4.9780	0.0000

MONTHLY PAYMENT AMORTIZATION SCHEDULE PER $100 — 4.00 %

YEARS 2 — MO PAYT 4.3425 — AN CONST 52.11

#	INT	PRIN	BALANCE
1	3.1081	49.0018	50.9982
2	1.1117	50.9982	0.0000

YEARS 3 — MO PAYT 2.9524 — AN CONST 35.43

#	INT	PRIN	BALANCE
1	3.4174	32.0114	67.9886
2	2.1132	33.3156	34.6730
3	.7558	34.6730	0.0000

YEARS 4 — MO PAYT 2.2579 — AN CONST 27.10

#	INT	PRIN	BALANCE
1	3.5719	23.5230	76.4770
2	2.6135	24.4814	51.9956
3	1.6161	25.4788	26.5168
4	.5780	26.5168	0.0000

YEARS 5 — MO PAYT 1.8417 — AN CONST 22.10

#	INT	PRIN	BALANCE
1	3.6645	18.4354	81.5646
2	2.9134	19.1865	62.3782
3	2.1317	19.9681	42.4100
4	1.3182	20.7817	21.6284
5	.4715	21.6284	0.0000

YEARS 6 — MO PAYT 1.5645 — AN CONST 18.78

#	INT	PRIN	BALANCE
1	3.7261	15.0481	84.9519
2	3.1130	15.6612	69.2907
3	2.4750	16.2993	52.9914
4	1.8109	16.9633	36.0281
5	1.1198	17.6544	18.3737
6	.4005	18.3737	0.0000

YEARS 7 — MO PAYT 1.3669 — AN CONST 16.41

#	INT	PRIN	BALANCE
1	3.7701	12.6325	87.3675
2	3.2554	13.1472	74.2203
3	2.7198	13.6828	60.5375
4	2.1623	14.2403	46.2973
5	1.5821	14.8204	31.4769
6	.9783	15.4242	16.0526
7	.3499	16.0526	0.0000

YEARS 8 — MO PAYT 1.2189 — AN CONST 14.63

#	INT	PRIN	BALANCE
1	3.8030	10.8241	89.1759
2	3.3620	11.2651	77.9107
3	2.9030	11.7241	66.1866
4	2.4254	12.2018	53.9849
5	1.9283	12.6989	41.2860
6	1.4109	13.2162	28.0698
7	.8724	13.7547	14.3151
8	.3121	14.3151	0.0000

YEARS 9 — MO PAYT 1.1041 — AN CONST 13.25

#	INT	PRIN	BALANCE
1	3.8285	9.4206	90.5794
2	3.4447	9.8044	80.7749
3	3.0453	10.2039	70.5710
4	2.6296	10.6196	59.9514
5	2.1969	11.0523	48.8992
6	1.7466	11.5026	37.3966
7	1.2780	11.9712	25.4254
8	.7903	12.4589	12.9665
9	.2827	12.9665	0.0000

YEARS 10 — MO PAYT 1.0125 — AN CONST 12.15

#	INT	PRIN	BALANCE
1	3.8489	8.3005	91.6995
2	3.5107	8.6387	83.0608
3	3.1588	8.9906	74.0702
4	2.7925	9.3569	64.7133
5	2.4113	9.7381	54.9752
6	2.0145	10.1349	44.8403
7	1.6016	10.5478	34.2925
8	1.1719	10.9775	23.3150
9	.7247	11.4248	11.8902
10	.2592	11.8902	0.0000

YEARS 11 — MO PAYT .9377 — AN CONST 11.26

#	INT	PRIN	BALANCE
1	3.8656	7.3864	92.6136
2	3.5646	7.6874	84.9262
3	3.2514	8.0006	76.9256
4	2.9255	8.3265	68.5991
5	2.5862	8.6658	59.9333
6	2.2332	9.0188	50.9145
7	1.8657	9.3863	41.5282
8	1.4833	9.7687	31.7595
9	1.0853	10.1667	21.5928
10	.6711	10.5809	11.0120
11	.2400	11.0120	0.0000

YEARS 12 — MO PAYT .8755 — AN CONST 10.51

#	INT	PRIN	BALANCE
1	3.8794	6.6270	93.3730
2	3.6094	6.8970	86.4761
3	3.3284	7.1779	79.2981
4	3.0360	7.4704	71.8278
5	2.7316	7.7747	64.0530
6	2.4148	8.0915	55.9615
7	2.0852	8.4212	47.5404
8	1.7421	8.7642	38.7761
9	1.3850	9.1213	29.6548
10	1.0134	9.4929	20.1619
11	.6267	9.8797	10.2822
12	.2241	10.2822	0.0000

YEARS 13 — MO PAYT .8231 — AN CONST 9.88

#	INT	PRIN	BALANCE
1	3.8910	5.9864	94.0136
2	3.6471	6.2302	87.7834
3	3.3933	6.4841	81.2993
4	3.1291	6.7482	74.5511
5	2.8542	7.0232	67.5279
6	2.5681	7.3093	60.2186
7	2.2703	7.6071	52.6115
8	1.9604	7.9170	44.6944
9	1.6378	8.2396	36.4549
10	1.3021	8.5753	27.8796
11	.9527	8.9246	18.9549
12	.5891	9.2883	9.6667
13	.2107	9.6667	0.0000

YEARS 14 — MO PAYT .7783 — AN CONST 9.35

#	INT	PRIN	BALANCE
1	3.9010	5.4391	94.5609
2	3.6794	5.6607	88.9001
3	3.4488	5.8914	83.0087
4	3.2088	6.1314	76.8773
5	2.9589	6.3812	70.4961
6	2.6990	6.6412	63.8550
7	2.4284	6.9118	56.9432
8	2.1468	7.1933	49.7499
9	1.8537	7.4864	42.2634
10	1.5487	7.7914	34.4720
11	1.2313	8.1089	26.3632
12	.9009	8.4392	17.9239
13	.5571	8.7831	9.1409
14	.1993	9.1409	0.0000

YEARS 15 — MO PAYT .7397 — AN CONST 8.88

#	INT	PRIN	BALANCE
1	3.9096	4.9667	95.0333
2	3.7073	5.1690	89.8643
3	3.4967	5.3796	84.4847
4	3.2775	5.5988	78.8860
5	3.0494	5.8269	73.0591
6	2.8120	6.0643	66.9948
7	2.5649	6.3113	60.6835
8	2.3078	6.5685	54.1150
9	2.0402	6.8361	47.2790
10	1.7617	7.1146	40.1644
11	1.4718	7.4044	32.7599
12	1.1701	7.7061	25.0538
13	.8562	8.0201	17.0337
14	.5294	8.3468	8.6869
15	.1894	8.6869	0.0000

YEARS 16 — MO PAYT .7060 — AN CONST 8.48

#	INT	PRIN	BALANCE
1	3.9171	4.5549	95.4451
2	3.7315	4.7404	90.7047
3	3.5384	4.9336	85.7711
4	3.3374	5.1346	80.6366
5	3.1282	5.3438	75.2928
6	2.9105	5.5615	69.7314
7	2.6839	5.7880	63.9433
8	2.4481	6.0239	57.9195
9	2.2027	6.2693	51.6502
10	1.9472	6.5247	45.1255
11	1.6814	6.7905	38.3349
12	1.4048	7.0672	31.2677
13	1.1168	7.3551	23.9126
14	.8172	7.6548	16.2579
15	.5053	7.9666	8.2912
16	.1807	8.2912	0.0000

YEARS 17 — MO PAYT .6764 — AN CONST 8.12

#	INT	PRIN	BALANCE
1	3.9237	4.1930	95.8070
2	3.7529	4.3639	91.4431
3	3.5751	4.5417	86.9014
4	3.3900	4.7267	82.1747
5	3.1975	4.9193	77.2555
6	2.9970	5.1197	72.1358
7	2.7885	5.3283	66.8075
8	2.5714	5.5454	61.2621
9	2.3454	5.7713	55.4909
10	2.1103	6.0064	49.4845
11	1.8656	6.2511	43.2333
12	1.6109	6.5058	36.7275
13	1.3459	6.7709	29.9567
14	1.0700	7.0467	22.9100
15	.7829	7.3338	15.5762
16	.4841	7.6326	7.9436
17	.1732	7.9436	0.0000

YEARS 18 — MO PAYT .6502 — AN CONST 7.81

#	INT	PRIN	BALANCE
1	3.9295	3.8729	96.1271
2	3.7717	4.0306	92.0965
3	3.6075	4.1949	87.9016
4	3.4366	4.3658	83.5359
5	3.2587	4.5436	78.9922
6	3.0736	4.7288	74.2635
7	2.8810	4.9214	69.3421
8	2.6805	5.1219	64.2201
9	2.4718	5.3306	58.8896
10	2.2546	5.5478	53.3418
11	2.0286	5.7738	47.5680
12	1.7933	6.0090	41.5590
13	1.5485	6.2538	35.3051
14	1.2937	6.5086	28.7965
15	1.0286	6.7738	22.0227
16	.7526	7.0498	14.9729
17	.4654	7.3370	7.6359
18	.1665	7.6359	0.0000

YEARS 19 — MO PAYT .6269 — AN CONST 7.53

#	INT	PRIN	BALANCE
1	3.9347	3.5877	96.4123
2	3.7885	3.7339	92.6783
3	3.6364	3.8860	88.7923
4	3.4781	4.0444	84.7479
5	3.3133	4.2091	80.5388
6	3.1418	4.3806	76.1582
7	2.9633	4.5591	71.5991
8	2.7776	4.7448	66.8542
9	2.5843	4.9382	61.9161
10	2.3831	5.1393	56.7767
11	2.1737	5.3487	51.4280
12	1.9558	5.5666	45.8614
13	1.7290	5.7934	40.0679
14	1.4930	6.0295	34.0385
15	1.2473	6.2751	27.7634
16	.9917	6.5308	21.2326
17	.7256	6.7969	14.4357
18	.4487	7.0738	7.3620
19	.1605	7.3620	0.0000

YEARS 20 — MO PAYT .6060 — AN CONST 7.28

#	INT	PRIN	BALANCE
1	3.9393	3.3324	96.6676
2	3.8036	3.4682	93.1994
3	3.6623	3.6095	89.5899
4	3.5152	3.7565	85.8334
5	3.3622	3.9096	81.9238
6	3.2029	4.0689	77.8549
7	3.0371	4.2346	73.6203
8	2.8646	4.4072	69.2131
9	2.6850	4.5867	64.6264
10	2.4982	4.7736	59.8528
11	2.3037	4.9681	54.8847
12	2.1013	5.1705	49.7142
13	1.8906	5.3811	44.3331
14	1.6714	5.6004	38.7327
15	1.4432	5.8285	32.9042
16	1.2058	6.0660	26.8382
17	.9586	6.3131	20.5250
18	.7014	6.5704	13.9547
19	.4337	6.8380	7.1166
20	.1551	7.1166	0.0000

YEARS 21 — MO PAYT .5872 — AN CONST 7.05

#	INT	PRIN	BALANCE
1	3.9435	3.1026	96.8974
2	3.8171	3.2290	93.6684
3	3.6856	3.3606	90.3078

#	INT	PRIN	BALANCE
4	3.5487	3.4975	86.8103
5	3.4062	3.6400	83.1703
6	3.2579	3.7883	79.3820
7	3.1035	3.9426	75.4394
8	2.9429	4.1033	71.3361
9	2.7757	4.2704	67.0657
10	2.6017	4.4444	62.6213
11	2.4207	4.6255	57.9958
12	2.2322	4.8139	53.1818
13	2.0361	5.0101	48.1718
14	1.8320	5.2142	42.9576
15	1.6195	5.4266	37.5310
16	1.3984	5.6477	31.8833
17	1.1683	5.8778	26.0055
18	.9289	6.1173	19.8882
19	.6797	6.3665	13.5217
20	.4203	6.6259	6.8958
21	.1503	6.8958	0.0000

YEARS 22   MO PAYT .5702   AN CONST 6.85

#	INT	PRIN	BALANCE
1	3.9473	2.8949	97.1051
2	3.8294	3.0128	94.0923
3	3.7066	3.1355	90.9568
4	3.5789	3.2633	87.6935
5	3.4459	3.3962	84.2972
6	3.3076	3.5346	80.7626
7	3.1635	3.6786	77.0840
8	3.0137	3.8285	73.2555
9	2.8577	3.9845	69.2710
10	2.6954	4.1468	65.1242
11	2.5264	4.3158	60.8085
12	2.3506	4.4916	56.3169
13	2.1676	4.6746	51.6423
14	1.9771	4.8650	46.7773
15	1.7789	5.0632	41.7140
16	1.5726	5.2695	36.4445
17	1.3580	5.4842	30.9603
18	1.1345	5.7076	25.2527
19	.9020	5.9402	19.3125
20	.6600	6.1822	13.1303
21	.4081	6.4341	6.6962
22	.1460	6.6962	0.0000

YEARS 23   MO PAYT .5548   AN CONST 6.66

#	INT	PRIN	BALANCE
1	3.9507	2.7063	97.2937
2	3.8405	2.8165	94.4772
3	3.7257	2.9313	91.5459
4	3.6063	3.0507	88.4953
5	3.4820	3.1750	85.3203
6	3.3527	3.3043	82.0159
7	3.2180	3.4390	78.5770
8	3.0779	3.5791	74.9979
9	2.9321	3.7249	71.2730
10	2.7804	3.8766	67.3964
11	2.6224	4.0346	63.3618
12	2.4580	4.1990	59.1628
13	2.2870	4.3700	54.7928
14	2.1089	4.5481	50.2447
15	1.9236	4.7334	45.5114
16	1.7308	4.9262	40.5851
17	1.5301	5.1269	35.4582
18	1.3212	5.3358	30.1224
19	1.1038	5.5532	24.5693
20	.8776	5.7794	18.7898
21	.6421	6.0149	12.7749
22	.3971	6.2599	6.5150
23	.1420	6.5150	0.0000

YEARS 24   MO PAYT .5407   AN CONST 6.49

#	INT	PRIN	BALANCE
1	3.9539	2.5344	97.4656
2	3.8506	2.6377	94.8279
3	3.7432	2.7451	92.0828
4	3.6313	2.8570	89.2258
5	3.5149	2.9734	86.2524
6	3.3938	3.0945	83.1579
7	3.2677	3.2206	79.9373
8	3.1365	3.3518	76.5855
9	2.9999	3.4884	73.0971
10	2.8578	3.6305	69.4667
11	2.7099	3.7784	65.6883
12	2.5560	3.9323	61.7559
13	2.3957	4.0925	57.6634
14	2.2290	4.2593	53.4041
15	2.0555	4.4328	48.9713
16	1.8749	4.6134	44.3579
17	1.6869	4.8014	39.5565
18	1.4913	4.9970	34.5596
19	1.2877	5.2006	29.3590
20	1.0758	5.4124	23.9466
21	.8553	5.6330	18.3136
22	.6258	5.8624	12.4512
23	.3870	6.1013	6.3499
24	.1384	6.3499	0.0000

YEARS 25   MO PAYT .5278   AN CONST 6.34

#	INT	PRIN	BALANCE
1	3.9567	2.3773	97.6227
2	3.8599	2.4742	95.1485
3	3.7591	2.5750	92.5736
4	3.6542	2.6799	89.8937
5	3.5450	2.7891	87.1046
6	3.4314	2.9027	84.2019
7	3.3131	3.0209	81.1810
8	3.1900	3.1440	78.0369
9	3.0619	3.2721	74.7648
10	2.9286	3.4054	71.3594
11	2.7899	3.5442	67.8152
12	2.6455	3.6886	64.1267
13	2.4952	3.8388	60.2878
14	2.3388	3.9952	56.2926
15	2.1760	4.1580	52.1345
16	2.0066	4.3274	47.8071
17	1.8303	4.5037	43.3034
18	1.6468	4.6872	38.6162
19	1.4559	4.8782	33.7380
20	1.2571	5.0769	28.6610
21	1.0503	5.2838	23.3773
22	.8350	5.4990	17.8782
23	.6110	5.7231	12.1552
24	.3778	5.9562	6.1989
25	.1351	6.1989	0.0000

YEARS 26   MO PAYT .5160   AN CONST 6.20

#	INT	PRIN	BALANCE
1	3.9594	2.2332	97.7668
2	3.8684	2.3242	95.4425
3	3.7737	2.4189	93.0236
4	3.6751	2.5175	90.5062
5	3.5726	2.6200	87.8861
6	3.4658	2.7268	85.1594
7	3.3547	2.8379	82.3215
8	3.2391	2.9535	79.3680
9	3.1188	3.0738	76.2942
10	2.9935	3.1990	73.0952
11	2.8632	3.3294	69.7658
12	2.7276	3.4650	66.3007
13	2.5864	3.6062	62.6946
14	2.4395	3.7531	58.9414
15	2.2866	3.9060	55.0354
16	2.1274	4.0652	50.9703
17	1.9618	4.2308	46.7395
18	1.7894	4.4032	42.3363
19	1.6100	4.5825	37.7538
20	1.4233	4.7692	32.9845
21	1.2290	4.9635	28.0210
22	1.0268	5.1658	22.8552
23	.8164	5.3762	17.4790
24	.5973	5.5953	11.8837
25	.3694	5.8232	6.0605
26	.1321	6.0605	0.0000

YEARS 27   MO PAYT .5052   AN CONST 6.07

#	INT	PRIN	BALANCE
1	3.9618	2.1007	97.8993
2	3.8762	2.1863	95.7129
3	3.7871	2.2754	93.4375
4	3.6944	2.3681	91.0695
5	3.5979	2.4646	88.6049
6	3.4975	2.5650	86.0399
7	3.3930	2.6695	83.3704
8	3.2842	2.7782	80.5921
9	3.1711	2.8914	77.7007
10	3.0533	3.0092	74.6915
11	2.9307	3.1318	71.5596
12	2.8031	3.2594	68.3002
13	2.6703	3.3922	64.9079
14	2.5321	3.5304	61.3775
15	2.3882	3.6743	57.7032
16	2.2385	3.8240	53.8793
17	2.0827	3.9798	49.8995
18	1.9206	4.1419	45.7576
19	1.7518	4.3107	41.4469
20	1.5762	4.4863	36.9607
21	1.3934	4.6691	32.2916
22	1.2032	4.8593	27.4323
23	1.0052	5.0573	22.3751
24	.7992	5.2633	17.1118
25	.5848	5.4777	11.6341
26	.3616	5.7009	5.9332
27	.1293	5.9332	0.0000

YEARS 28   MO PAYT .4952   AN CONST 5.95

#	INT	PRIN	BALANCE
1	3.9640	1.9786	98.0214
2	3.8834	2.0592	95.9623
3	3.7995	2.1431	93.8192
4	3.7122	2.2304	91.5888
5	3.6213	2.3212	89.2676
6	3.5267	2.4158	86.8518
7	3.4283	2.5142	84.3375
8	3.3259	2.6167	81.7209
9	3.2193	2.7233	78.9976
10	3.1083	2.8342	76.1633
11	2.9928	2.9497	73.2136
12	2.8727	3.0699	70.1438
13	2.7476	3.1949	66.9488
14	2.6174	3.3251	63.6237
15	2.4820	3.4606	60.1631
16	2.3410	3.6016	56.5615
17	2.1942	3.7483	52.8132
18	2.0415	3.9010	48.9122
19	1.8826	4.0600	44.8523
20	1.7172	4.2254	40.6269
21	1.5450	4.3975	36.2294
22	1.3659	4.5767	31.6527
23	1.1794	4.7631	26.8896
24	.9854	4.9572	21.9324
25	.7834	5.1592	16.7732
26	.5732	5.3693	11.4039
27	.3544	5.5881	5.8158
28	.1268	5.8158	0.0000

YEARS 29   MO PAYT .4860   AN CONST 5.84

#	INT	PRIN	BALANCE
1	3.9660	1.8656	98.1344
2	3.8900	1.9416	96.1927
3	3.8109	2.0208	94.1720
4	3.7286	2.1031	92.0689
5	3.6429	2.1888	89.8801
6	3.5537	2.2779	87.6022
7	3.4609	2.3707	85.2314
8	3.3643	2.4673	82.7641
9	3.2638	2.5679	80.1962
10	3.1592	2.6725	77.5238
11	3.0503	2.7814	74.7424
12	2.9370	2.8947	71.8477
13	2.8191	3.0126	68.8351
14	2.6963	3.1353	65.6998
15	2.5686	3.2631	62.4367
16	2.4357	3.3960	59.0407
17	2.2973	3.5344	55.5063
18	2.1533	3.6784	51.8279
19	2.0034	3.8282	47.9997
20	1.8475	3.9842	44.0155
21	1.6851	4.1465	39.8689
22	1.5162	4.3155	35.5535
23	1.3404	4.4913	31.0622
24	1.1574	4.6743	26.3879
25	.9670	4.8647	21.5232
26	.7688	5.0629	16.4603
27	.5625	5.2692	11.1911
28	.3478	5.4838	5.7073
29	.1244	5.7073	0.0000

YEARS 30   MO PAYT .4774   AN CONST 5.73

#	INT	PRIN	BALANCE
1	3.9679	1.7610	98.2390
2	3.8962	1.8328	96.4062
3	3.8215	1.9075	94.4987
4	3.7438	1.9852	92.5136
5	3.6629	2.0660	90.4475
6	3.5788	2.1502	88.2973
7	3.4912	2.2378	86.0595
8	3.4000	2.3290	83.7305
9	3.3051	2.4239	81.3066
10	3.2063	2.5226	78.7840
11	3.1036	2.6254	76.1585
12	2.9966	2.7324	73.4262
13	2.8853	2.8437	70.5825
14	2.7694	2.9596	67.6229
15	2.6489	3.0801	64.5428
16	2.5234	3.2056	61.3372
17	2.3928	3.3362	58.0010
18	2.2568	3.4721	54.5288
19	2.1154	3.6136	50.9152
20	1.9682	3.7608	47.1544
21	1.8149	3.9140	43.2403
22	1.6555	4.0735	39.1668
23	1.4895	4.2395	34.9274
24	1.3168	4.4122	30.5152
25	1.1370	4.5920	25.9232
26	.9499	4.7790	21.1442
27	.7552	4.9737	16.1704
28	.5526	5.1764	10.9940
29	.3417	5.3873	5.6068
30	.1222	5.6068	0.0000

MONTHLY PAYMENT AMORTIZATION SCHEDULE PER $100   4.25 %

YEARS 2 — MO PAYT 4.3536 — AN CONST 52.25

#	INT	PRIN	BALANCE
1	3.3040	48.9395	51.0605
2	1.1831	51.0605	0.0000

YEARS 3 — MO PAYT 2.9635 — AN CONST 35.57

#	INT	PRIN	BALANCE
1	3.6328	31.9296	68.0704
2	2.2490	33.3133	34.7571
3	.8053	34.7571	0.0000

YEARS 4 — MO PAYT 2.2691 — AN CONST 27.23

#	INT	PRIN	BALANCE
1	3.7971	23.4323	76.5677
2	2.7816	24.4478	52.1200
3	1.7220	25.5073	26.6127
4	.6166	26.6127	0.0000

YEARS 5 — MO PAYT 1.8530 — AN CONST 22.24

#	INT	PRIN	BALANCE
1	3.8955	18.3400	81.6600
2	3.1007	19.1348	62.5252
3	2.2714	19.9640	42.5612
4	1.4062	20.8292	21.7319
5	.5035	21.7319	0.0000

YEARS 6 — MO PAYT 1.5759 — AN CONST 18.92

#	INT	PRIN	BALANCE
1	3.9610	14.9502	85.0498
2	3.3131	15.5981	69.4517
3	2.6371	16.2741	53.1776
4	1.9318	16.9794	36.1982
5	1.1960	17.7152	18.4830
6	.4283	18.4830	0.0000

YEARS 7 — MO PAYT 1.3784 — AN CONST 16.55

#	INT	PRIN	BALANCE
1	4.0077	12.5333	87.4667
2	3.4646	13.0765	74.3903
3	2.8979	13.6432	60.7471
4	2.3066	14.2344	46.5127
5	1.6897	14.8513	31.6614
6	1.0461	15.4949	16.1664
7	.3746	16.1664	0.0000

YEARS 8 — MO PAYT 1.2306 — AN CONST 14.77

#	INT	PRIN	BALANCE
1	4.0427	10.7244	89.2756
2	3.5779	11.1892	78.0864
3	3.0930	11.6741	66.4124
4	2.5871	12.1800	54.2323
5	2.0592	12.7079	41.5245
6	1.5085	13.2586	28.2659
7	.9339	13.8332	14.4327
8	.3344	14.4327	0.0000

YEARS 9 — MO PAYT 1.1159 — AN CONST 13.40

#	INT	PRIN	BALANCE
1	4.0698	9.3208	90.6792
2	3.6659	9.7248	80.9544
3	3.2444	10.1462	70.8081
4	2.8047	10.5860	60.2222
5	2.3459	11.0447	49.1774
6	1.8673	11.5234	37.6540
7	1.3679	12.0228	25.6313
8	.8469	12.5438	13.0874
9	.3032	13.0874	0.0000

YEARS 10 — MO PAYT 1.0244 — AN CONST 12.30

#	INT	PRIN	BALANCE
1	4.0915	8.2010	91.7990
2	3.7361	8.5564	83.2425
3	3.3652	8.9273	74.3153
4	2.9784	9.3141	65.0011
5	2.5747	9.7178	55.2833
6	2.1536	10.1389	45.1444
7	1.7142	10.5783	34.5660
8	1.2557	11.0368	23.5292
9	.7774	11.5151	12.0141
10	.2784	12.0141	0.0000

YEARS 11 — MO PAYT .9497 — AN CONST 11.40

#	INT	PRIN	BALANCE
1	4.1091	7.2875	92.7125
2	3.7933	7.6034	85.1091
3	3.4638	7.9329	77.1762
4	3.1200	8.2767	68.8995
5	2.7613	8.6354	60.2641
6	2.3871	9.0096	51.2545
7	1.9966	9.4001	41.8545
8	1.5892	9.8074	32.0470
9	1.1642	10.2325	21.8145
10	.7208	10.6759	11.1386
11	.2581	11.1386	0.0000

YEARS 12 — MO PAYT .8877 — AN CONST 10.66

#	INT	PRIN	BALANCE
1	4.1238	6.5288	93.4712
2	3.8409	6.8118	86.6594
3	3.5456	7.1070	79.5525
4	3.2376	7.4150	72.1375
5	2.9163	7.7363	64.4012
6	2.5810	8.0716	56.3296
7	2.2312	8.4214	47.9082
8	1.8663	8.7864	39.1219
9	1.4855	9.1671	29.9547
10	1.0882	9.5644	20.3903
11	.6737	9.9789	10.4114
12	.2412	10.4114	0.0000

YEARS 13 — MO PAYT .8354 — AN CONST 10.03

#	INT	PRIN	BALANCE
1	4.1362	5.8891	94.1109
2	3.8809	6.1443	87.9666
3	3.6147	6.4106	81.5560
4	3.3368	6.6884	74.8675
5	3.0470	6.9783	67.8892
6	2.7446	7.2807	60.6085
7	2.4290	7.5962	53.0123
8	2.0998	7.9254	45.0868
9	1.7564	8.2689	36.8179
10	1.3980	8.6273	28.1907
11	1.0241	9.0012	19.1895
12	.6340	9.3912	9.7982
13	.2270	9.7982	0.0000

YEARS 14 — MO PAYT .7908 — AN CONST 9.49

#	INT	PRIN	BALANCE
1	4.1467	5.3429	94.6571
2	3.9152	5.5745	89.0826
3	3.6736	5.8160	83.2666
4	3.4215	6.0681	77.1985
5	3.1586	6.3311	70.8674
6	2.8842	6.6054	64.2620
7	2.5979	6.8917	57.3703
8	2.2992	7.1904	50.1799
9	1.9876	7.5020	42.6779
10	1.6625	7.8271	34.8508
11	1.3233	8.1663	26.6845
12	.9694	8.5202	18.1642
13	.6001	8.8895	9.2747
14	.2149	9.2747	0.0000

YEARS 15 — MO PAYT .7523 — AN CONST 9.03

#	INT	PRIN	BALANCE
1	4.1558	4.8715	95.1285
2	3.9447	5.0826	90.0459
3	3.7244	5.3029	84.7430
4	3.4946	5.5327	79.2103
5	3.2549	5.7725	73.4378
6	3.0047	6.0227	67.4151
7	2.7437	6.2837	61.1315
8	2.4714	6.5560	54.5755
9	2.1872	6.8401	47.7354
10	1.8908	7.1365	40.5988
11	1.5815	7.4458	33.1530
12	1.2588	7.7685	25.3845
13	.9222	8.1052	17.2793
14	.5709	8.4564	8.8229
15	.2044	8.8229	0.0000

YEARS 16 — MO PAYT .7187 — AN CONST 8.63

#	INT	PRIN	BALANCE
1	4.1638	4.4609	95.5391
2	3.9704	4.6542	90.8849
3	3.7687	4.8559	86.0290
4	3.5583	5.0663	80.9627
5	3.3387	5.2859	75.6768
6	3.1097	5.5150	70.1618
7	2.8707	5.7540	64.4078
8	2.6213	6.0034	58.4045
9	2.3611	6.2635	52.1409
10	2.0897	6.5350	45.6060
11	1.8065	6.8182	38.7878
12	1.5110	7.1137	31.6741
13	1.2027	7.4220	24.2521
14	.8810	7.7436	16.5085
15	.5454	8.0792	8.4293
16	.1953	8.4293	0.0000

YEARS 17 — MO PAYT .6893 — AN CONST 8.28

#	INT	PRIN	BALANCE
1	4.1707	4.1003	95.8997
2	3.9930	4.2780	91.6218
3	3.8076	4.4634	87.1584
4	3.6142	4.6568	82.5016
5	3.4124	4.8586	77.6430
6	3.2018	5.0692	72.5738
7	2.9822	5.2889	67.2850
8	2.7529	5.5181	61.7669
9	2.5138	5.7572	56.0097
10	2.2643	6.0067	50.0030
11	2.0040	6.2670	43.7360
12	1.7324	6.5386	37.1974
13	1.4490	6.8220	30.3754
14	1.1534	7.1176	23.2577
15	.8449	7.4261	15.8316
16	.5231	7.7479	8.0837
17	.1873	8.0837	0.0000

YEARS 18 — MO PAYT .6632 — AN CONST 7.96

#	INT	PRIN	BALANCE
1	4.1769	3.7813	96.2187
2	4.0130	3.9452	92.2734
3	3.8421	4.1162	88.1572
4	3.6637	4.2946	83.8626
5	3.4776	4.4807	79.3819
6	3.2834	4.6749	74.7071
7	3.0808	4.8775	69.8296
8	2.8694	5.0889	64.7407
9	2.6488	5.3094	59.4313
10	2.4188	5.5395	53.8918
11	2.1787	5.7796	48.1122
12	1.9282	6.0300	42.0822
13	1.6669	6.2914	35.7908
14	1.3942	6.5640	29.2268
15	1.1098	6.8485	22.3783
16	.8130	7.1453	15.2330
17	.5033	7.4550	7.7780
18	.1802	7.7780	0.0000

YEARS 19 — MO PAYT .6400 — AN CONST 7.68

#	INT	PRIN	BALANCE
1	4.1824	3.4975	96.5025
2	4.0308	3.6491	92.8534
3	3.8727	3.8072	89.0461
4	3.7077	3.9722	85.0739
5	3.5355	4.1444	80.9295
6	3.3559	4.3240	76.6055
7	3.1685	4.5114	72.0942
8	2.9730	4.7069	67.3873
9	2.7690	4.9109	62.4764
10	2.5562	5.1237	57.3527
11	2.3342	5.3458	52.0069
12	2.1025	5.5774	46.4295
13	1.8608	5.8191	40.6104
14	1.6086	6.0713	34.5390
15	1.3455	6.3344	28.2046
16	1.0709	6.6090	21.5956
17	.7845	6.8954	14.7002
18	.4857	7.1942	7.5060
19	.1739	7.5060	0.0000

YEARS 20 — MO PAYT .6192 — AN CONST 7.44

#	INT	PRIN	BALANCE
1	4.1873	3.2435	96.7565
2	4.0467	3.3841	93.3724
3	3.9001	3.5307	89.8417
4	3.7471	3.6837	86.1579
5	3.5874	3.8434	82.3145
6	3.4209	4.0100	78.3046
7	3.2471	4.1837	74.1208
8	3.0658	4.3651	69.7558
9	2.8766	4.5542	65.2016
10	2.6792	4.7516	60.4500
11	2.4733	4.9575	55.4924
12	2.2584	5.1724	50.3201
13	2.0343	5.3965	44.9235
14	1.8004	5.6304	39.2932
15	1.5564	5.8744	33.4187
16	1.3018	6.1290	27.2898
17	1.0362	6.3946	20.8951
18	.7591	6.6717	14.2234
19	.4699	6.9609	7.2625
20	.1683	7.2625	0.0000

YEARS 21 — MO PAYT .6006 — AN CONST 7.21

#	INT	PRIN	BALANCE
1	4.1917	3.0151	96.9849
2	4.0611	3.1457	93.8392
3	3.9247	3.2820	90.5572

MONTHLY PAYMENT AMORTIZATION SCHEDULE PER $100   4.25 %

#	INT	PRIN	BALANCE
4	3.7825	3.4243	87.1329
5	3.6341	3.5727	83.5602
6	3.4793	3.7275	79.8327
7	3.3177	3.8891	75.9437
8	3.1492	4.0576	71.8861
9	2.9733	4.2334	67.6526
10	2.7899	4.4169	63.2357
11	2.5984	4.6083	58.6274
12	2.3987	4.8080	53.8193
13	2.1904	5.0164	48.8029
14	1.9730	5.2338	43.5691
15	1.7461	5.4606	38.1084
16	1.5095	5.6973	32.4112
17	1.2626	5.9442	26.4670
18	1.0050	6.2018	20.2651
19	.7362	6.4706	13.7946
20	.4558	6.7510	7.0436
21	.1632	7.0436	0.0000

YEARS 22   MO PAYT .5837   AN CONST 7.01

#	INT	PRIN	BALANCE
1	4.1957	2.8086	97.1914
2	4.0740	2.9304	94.2610
3	3.9470	3.0574	91.2036
4	3.8145	3.1899	88.0138
5	3.6763	3.3281	84.6856
6	3.5320	3.4723	81.2133
7	3.3815	3.6228	77.5905
8	3.2245	3.7798	73.8107
9	3.0607	3.9436	69.8670
10	2.8898	4.1145	65.7525
11	2.7115	4.2929	61.4596
12	2.5255	4.4789	56.9807
13	2.3314	4.6730	52.3077
14	2.1288	4.8755	47.4322
15	1.9175	5.0868	42.3454
16	1.6971	5.3073	37.0381
17	1.4671	5.5373	31.5008
18	1.2271	5.7772	25.7236
19	.9767	6.0276	19.6960
20	.7155	6.2888	13.4071
21	.4430	6.5614	6.8457
22	.1586	6.8457	0.0000

YEARS 23   MO PAYT .5684   AN CONST 6.83

#	INT	PRIN	BALANCE
1	4.1993	2.6214	97.3786
2	4.0857	2.7350	94.6436
3	3.9672	2.8536	91.7900
4	3.8435	2.9772	88.8128
5	3.7145	3.1062	85.7065
6	3.5799	3.2409	82.4657
7	3.4394	3.3813	79.0844
8	3.2929	3.5279	75.5565
9	3.1400	3.6807	71.8758
10	2.9805	3.8403	68.0355
11	2.8141	4.0067	64.0288
12	2.6404	4.1803	59.8485
13	2.4593	4.3615	55.4870
14	2.2702	4.5505	50.9365
15	2.0730	4.7477	46.1888
16	1.8673	4.9535	41.2353
17	1.6526	5.1681	36.0672
18	1.4286	5.3921	30.6751
19	1.1949	5.6258	25.0493
20	.9511	5.8696	19.1797
21	.6968	6.1240	13.0557
22	.4314	6.3894	6.6663
23	.1545	6.6663	0.0000

YEARS 24   MO PAYT .5545   AN CONST 6.66

#	INT	PRIN	BALANCE
1	4.2026	2.4509	97.5491
2	4.0964	2.5572	94.9919
3	3.9856	2.6680	92.3239
4	3.8700	2.7836	89.5403
5	3.7493	2.9042	86.6360
6	3.6235	3.0301	83.6059
7	3.4921	3.1614	80.4445
8	3.3551	3.2984	77.1461
9	3.2122	3.4414	73.7047
10	3.0630	3.5905	70.1141
11	2.9074	3.7461	66.3680
12	2.7451	3.9085	62.4595
13	2.5757	4.0779	58.3817
14	2.3990	4.2546	54.1271
15	2.2146	4.4390	49.6881
16	2.0222	4.6314	45.0567
17	1.8215	4.8321	40.2247
18	1.6121	5.0415	35.1832
19	1.3936	5.2600	29.9232
20	1.1657	5.4879	24.4353
21	.9278	5.7257	18.7096
22	.6797	5.9739	12.7357
23	.4208	6.2328	6.5029
24	.1507	6.5029	0.0000

YEARS 25   MO PAYT .5417   AN CONST 6.51

#	INT	PRIN	BALANCE
1	4.2056	2.2952	97.7048
2	4.1062	2.3947	95.3101
3	4.0024	2.4985	92.8116
4	3.8941	2.6068	90.2049
5	3.7811	2.7197	87.4851
6	3.6633	2.8376	84.6475
7	3.5403	2.9606	81.6870
8	3.4120	3.0889	78.5981
9	3.2781	3.2227	75.3754
10	3.1385	3.3624	72.0130
11	2.9927	3.5081	68.5049
12	2.8407	3.6602	64.8447
13	2.6821	3.8188	61.0259
14	2.5166	3.9843	57.0417
15	2.3439	4.1569	52.8847
16	2.1638	4.3371	48.5476
17	1.9758	4.5251	44.0226
18	1.7797	4.7212	39.3014
19	1.5751	4.9258	34.3757
20	1.3616	5.1392	29.2364
21	1.1389	5.3620	23.8745
22	.9065	5.5943	18.2801
23	.6641	5.8368	12.4434
24	.4111	6.0897	6.3536
25	.1472	6.3536	0.0000

YEARS 26   MO PAYT .5301   AN CONST 6.37

#	INT	PRIN	BALANCE
1	4.2084	2.1525	97.8475
2	4.1151	2.2458	95.6016
3	4.0178	2.3431	93.2585
4	3.9162	2.4447	90.8138
5	3.8103	2.5506	88.2632
6	3.6997	2.6612	85.6020
7	3.5844	2.7765	82.8255
8	3.4641	2.8968	79.9286
9	3.3385	3.0224	76.9063
10	3.2076	3.1534	73.7529
11	3.0709	3.2900	70.4629
12	2.9283	3.4326	67.0303
13	2.7796	3.5814	63.4489
14	2.6244	3.7366	59.7123
15	2.4624	3.8985	55.8138
16	2.2935	4.0675	51.7464
17	2.1172	4.2437	47.5026
18	1.9333	4.4276	43.0750
19	1.7414	4.6195	38.4555
20	1.5412	4.8197	33.6357
21	1.3323	5.0286	28.6071
22	1.1144	5.2465	23.3606
23	.8870	5.4739	17.8867
24	.6498	5.7111	12.1755
25	.4023	5.9586	6.2169
26	.1440	6.2169	0.0000

YEARS 27   MO PAYT .5194   AN CONST 6.24

#	INT	PRIN	BALANCE
1	4.2109	2.0214	97.9786
2	4.1233	2.1090	95.8696
3	4.0319	2.2004	93.6691
4	3.9366	2.2958	91.3734
5	3.8371	2.3953	88.9781
6	3.7333	2.4991	86.4790
7	3.6250	2.6074	83.8716
8	3.5120	2.7204	81.1512
9	3.3941	2.8383	78.3129
10	3.2711	2.9613	75.3517
11	3.1427	3.0896	72.2620
12	3.0088	3.2235	69.0385
13	2.8691	3.3632	65.6753
14	2.7234	3.5090	62.1663
15	2.5713	3.6610	58.5053
16	2.4126	3.8197	54.6856
17	2.2471	3.9852	50.7004
18	2.0744	4.1580	46.5424
19	1.8942	4.3381	42.2043
20	1.7062	4.5262	37.6781
21	1.5100	4.7223	32.9558
22	1.3054	4.9270	28.0288
23	1.0919	5.1405	22.8884
24	.8691	5.3633	17.5251
25	.6367	5.5957	11.9294
26	.3941	5.8382	6.0912
27	.1411	6.0912	0.0000

YEARS 28   MO PAYT .5095   AN CONST 6.12

#	INT	PRIN	BALANCE
1	4.2133	1.9006	98.0994
2	4.1309	1.9830	96.1164
3	4.0450	2.0689	94.0474
4	3.9553	2.1586	91.8888
5	3.8617	2.2521	89.6367
6	3.7641	2.3498	87.2869
7	3.6623	2.4516	84.8354
8	3.5561	2.5578	82.2775
9	3.4452	2.6687	79.6088
10	3.3296	2.7843	76.8245
11	3.2089	2.9050	73.9195
12	3.0830	3.0309	70.8886
13	2.9516	3.1622	67.7264
14	2.8146	3.2993	64.4271
15	2.6716	3.4423	60.9848
16	2.5224	3.5915	57.3933
17	2.3668	3.7471	53.6462
18	2.2044	3.9095	49.7367
19	2.0350	4.0789	45.6578
20	1.8582	4.2557	41.4021
21	1.6738	4.4401	36.9620
22	1.4813	4.6326	32.3294
23	1.2806	4.8333	27.4961
24	1.0711	5.0428	22.4533
25	.8526	5.2613	17.1920
26	.6246	5.4893	11.7027
27	.3867	5.7272	5.9754
28	.1385	5.9754	0.0000

YEARS 29   MO PAYT .5004   AN CONST 6.01

#	INT	PRIN	BALANCE
1	4.2154	1.7891	98.2109
2	4.1379	1.8666	96.3443
3	4.0570	1.9475	94.3968
4	3.9726	2.0319	92.3648
5	3.8845	2.1200	90.2449
6	3.7927	2.2119	88.0330
7	3.6968	2.3077	85.7253
8	3.5968	2.4077	83.3176
9	3.4924	2.5121	80.8055
10	3.3836	2.6209	78.1846
11	3.2700	2.7345	75.4501
12	3.1515	2.8530	72.5970
13	3.0278	2.9767	69.6204
14	2.8988	3.1057	66.5147
15	2.7642	3.2403	63.2744
16	2.6238	3.3807	59.8937
17	2.4773	3.5272	56.3665
18	2.3244	3.6801	52.6864
19	2.1650	3.8396	48.8469
20	1.9986	4.0059	44.8409
21	1.8249	4.1796	40.6614
22	1.6438	4.3607	36.3007
23	1.4548	4.5497	31.7510
24	1.2577	4.7468	27.0042
25	1.0519	4.9526	22.0516
26	.8373	5.1672	16.8844
27	.6134	5.3911	11.4933
28	.3797	5.6248	5.8685
29	.1360	5.8685	0.0000

YEARS 30   MO PAYT .4919   AN CONST 5.91

#	INT	PRIN	BALANCE
1	4.2174	1.6859	98.3141
2	4.1444	1.7589	96.5552
3	4.0681	1.8352	94.7200
4	3.9886	1.9147	92.8054
5	3.9056	1.9977	90.8077
6	3.8190	2.0842	88.7235
7	3.7287	2.1746	86.5489
8	3.6345	2.2688	84.2801
9	3.5361	2.3671	81.9130
10	3.4336	2.4697	79.4432
11	3.3265	2.5767	76.8665
12	3.2149	2.6884	74.1781
13	3.0983	2.8049	71.3731
14	2.9768	2.9265	68.4466
15	2.8500	3.0533	65.3933
16	2.7176	3.1856	62.2077
17	2.5796	3.3237	58.8840
18	2.4355	3.4677	55.4162
19	2.2853	3.6180	51.7982
20	2.1285	3.7748	48.0234
21	1.9649	3.9384	44.0850
22	1.7942	4.1091	39.9759
23	1.6161	4.2872	35.6887
24	1.4303	4.4730	31.2157
25	1.2365	4.6668	26.5489
26	1.0342	4.8691	21.6799
27	.8232	5.0801	16.5998
28	.6030	5.3002	11.2995
29	.3733	5.5299	5.7696
30	.1337	5.7696	0.0000

YEARS 2 — MO PAYT 4.3648 — AN CONST 52.38

#	INT	PRIN	BALANCE
1	3.5001	48.8773	51.1227
2	1.2547	51.1227	0.0000

YEARS 3 — MO PAYT 2.9747 — AN CONST 35.70

#	INT	PRIN	BALANCE
1	3.8485	31.8478	68.1522
2	2.3854	33.3109	34.8412
3	.8551	34.8412	0.0000

YEARS 4 — MO PAYT 2.2803 — AN CONST 27.37

#	INT	PRIN	BALANCE
1	4.0225	23.3417	76.6583
2	2.9502	24.4140	52.2443
3	1.8286	25.5356	26.7087
4	.6555	26.7087	0.0000

YEARS 5 — MO PAYT 1.8643 — AN CONST 22.38

#	INT	PRIN	BALANCE
1	4.1268	18.2449	81.7551
2	3.2886	19.0830	62.6721
3	2.4119	19.9597	42.7124
4	1.4950	20.8767	21.8357
5	.5359	21.8357	0.0000

YEARS 6 — MO PAYT 1.5874 — AN CONST 19.05

#	INT	PRIN	BALANCE
1	4.1961	14.8527	85.1473
2	3.5138	15.5350	69.6123
3	2.8001	16.2487	53.3636
4	2.0537	16.9952	36.3684
5	1.2729	17.7759	18.5925
6	.4563	18.5925	0.0000

YEARS 7 — MO PAYT 1.3900 — AN CONST 16.69

#	INT	PRIN	BALANCE
1	4.2456	12.4346	87.5654
2	3.6744	13.0058	74.5596
3	3.0769	13.6033	60.9563
4	2.4520	14.2282	46.7281
5	1.7983	14.8819	31.8462
6	1.1146	15.5656	16.2806
7	.3996	16.2806	0.0000

YEARS 8 — MO PAYT 1.2423 — AN CONST 14.91

#	INT	PRIN	BALANCE
1	4.2826	10.6252	89.3748
2	3.7945	11.1134	78.2614
3	3.2840	11.6239	66.6375
4	2.7500	12.1579	54.4795
5	2.1914	12.7165	41.7631
6	1.6072	13.3006	28.4624
7	.9962	13.9117	14.5508
8	.3571	14.5508	0.0000

YEARS 9 — MO PAYT 1.1278 — AN CONST 13.54

#	INT	PRIN	BALANCE
1	4.3113	9.2218	90.7782
2	3.8877	9.6454	81.1328
3	3.4446	10.0885	71.0443
4	2.9811	10.5520	60.4923
5	2.4964	11.0367	49.4556
6	1.9893	11.5438	37.9118
7	1.4590	12.0741	25.8377
8	.9043	12.6288	13.2089
9	.3242	13.2089	0.0000

YEARS 10 — MO PAYT 1.0364 — AN CONST 12.44

#	INT	PRIN	BALANCE
1	4.3342	8.1024	91.8976
2	3.9620	8.4746	83.4230
3	3.5727	8.8639	74.5591
4	3.1655	9.2711	65.2880
5	2.7396	9.6970	55.5910
6	2.2941	10.1425	45.4485
7	1.8282	10.6085	34.8400
8	1.3408	11.0958	23.7442
9	.8311	11.6055	12.1387
10	.2979	12.1387	0.0000

YEARS 11 — MO PAYT .9619 — AN CONST 11.55

#	INT	PRIN	BALANCE
1	4.3529	7.1896	92.8104
2	4.0226	7.5198	85.2906
3	3.6772	7.8653	77.4253
4	3.3158	8.2266	69.1987
5	2.9379	8.6046	60.5941
6	2.5426	8.9999	51.5943
7	2.1292	9.4133	42.1809
8	1.6967	9.8458	32.3352
9	1.2444	10.2981	22.0371
10	.7713	10.7712	11.2660
11	.2765	11.2660	0.0000

YEARS 12 — MO PAYT .9000 — AN CONST 10.81

#	INT	PRIN	BALANCE
1	4.3684	6.4317	93.5683
2	4.0730	6.7271	86.8412
3	3.7639	7.0362	79.8050
4	3.4407	7.3594	72.4456
5	3.1026	7.6975	64.7480
6	2.7490	8.0511	56.6969
7	2.3791	8.4210	48.2759
8	1.9922	8.8079	39.4680
9	1.5876	9.2125	30.2555
10	1.1644	9.6357	20.6198
11	.7217	10.0784	10.5414
12	.2587	10.5414	0.0000

YEARS 13 — MO PAYT .8479 — AN CONST 10.18

#	INT	PRIN	BALANCE
1	4.3815	5.7930	94.2070
2	4.1154	6.0591	88.1479
3	3.8370	6.3374	81.8105
4	3.5459	6.6286	75.1819
5	3.2414	6.9331	68.2488
6	2.9228	7.2516	60.9972
7	2.5897	7.5847	53.4125
8	2.2413	7.9332	45.4793
9	1.8768	8.2976	37.1816
10	1.4956	8.6788	28.5028
11	1.0969	9.0775	19.4253
12	.6799	9.4946	9.9307
13	.2437	9.9307	0.0000

YEARS 14 — MO PAYT .8034 — AN CONST 9.65

#	INT	PRIN	BALANCE
1	4.3926	5.2479	94.7521
2	4.1516	5.4890	89.2632
3	3.8994	5.7411	83.5221
4	3.6356	6.0049	77.5172
5	3.3598	6.2807	71.2365
6	3.0712	6.5693	64.6672
7	2.7695	6.8711	57.7962
8	2.4538	7.1867	50.6094
9	2.1236	7.5169	43.0926
10	1.7783	7.8622	35.2304
11	1.4171	8.2234	27.0070
12	1.0394	8.6012	18.4059
13	.6442	8.9963	9.4096
14	.2309	9.4096	0.0000

YEARS 15 — MO PAYT .7650 — AN CONST 9.18

#	INT	PRIN	BALANCE
1	4.4023	4.7777	95.2223
2	4.1828	4.9971	90.2252
3	3.9532	5.2267	84.9985
4	3.7131	5.4668	79.5317
5	3.4619	5.7180	73.8137
6	3.1993	5.9807	67.8330
7	2.9245	6.2554	61.5776
8	2.6371	6.5428	55.0348
9	2.3366	6.8434	48.1915
10	2.0222	7.1577	41.0338
11	1.6934	7.4866	33.5472
12	1.3494	7.8305	25.7167
13	.9897	8.1902	17.5265
14	.6134	8.5665	8.9600
15	.2199	8.9600	0.0000

YEARS 16 — MO PAYT .7316 — AN CONST 8.78

#	INT	PRIN	BALANCE
1	4.4106	4.3683	95.6317
2	4.2100	4.5690	91.0628
3	4.0001	4.7789	86.2839
4	3.7805	4.9984	81.2855
5	3.5509	5.2280	76.0575
6	3.3107	5.4682	70.5893
7	3.0595	5.7194	64.8699
8	2.7968	5.9822	58.8877
9	2.5219	6.2570	52.6308
10	2.2345	6.5444	46.0864
11	1.9339	6.8451	39.2413
12	1.6194	7.1595	32.0818
13	1.2905	7.4884	24.5933
14	.9465	7.8324	16.7609
15	.5866	8.1923	8.5686
16	.2103	8.5686	0.0000

YEARS 17 — MO PAYT .7022 — AN CONST 8.43

#	INT	PRIN	BALANCE
1	4.4180	4.0090	95.9910
2	4.2338	4.1932	91.7979
3	4.0412	4.3858	87.4121
4	3.8397	4.5873	82.8248
5	3.6290	4.7980	78.0268
6	3.4085	5.0184	73.0084
7	3.1780	5.2490	67.7594
8	2.9369	5.4901	62.2693
9	2.6846	5.7423	56.5269
10	2.4208	6.0061	50.5208
11	2.1449	6.2820	44.2388
12	1.8563	6.5706	37.6681
13	1.5545	6.8725	30.7956
14	1.2387	7.1882	23.6074
15	.9085	7.5184	16.0890
16	.5631	7.8638	8.2251
17	.2019	8.2251	0.0000

YEARS 18 — MO PAYT .6763 — AN CONST 8.12

#	INT	PRIN	BALANCE
1	4.4245	3.6914	96.3086
2	4.2549	3.8610	92.4476
3	4.0775	4.0384	88.4092
4	3.8920	4.2239	84.1853
5	3.6980	4.4179	79.7674
6	3.4950	4.6209	75.1465
7	3.2827	4.8332	70.3133
8	3.0607	5.0552	65.2581
9	2.8284	5.2874	59.9707
10	2.5855	5.5304	54.4403
11	2.3315	5.7844	48.6559
12	2.0657	6.0502	42.6057
13	1.7878	6.3281	36.2776
14	1.4971	6.6188	29.6588
15	1.1930	6.9229	22.7360
16	.8750	7.2409	15.4950
17	.5423	7.5736	7.9215
18	.1944	7.9215	0.0000

YEARS 19 — MO PAYT .6533 — AN CONST 7.84

#	INT	PRIN	BALANCE
1	4.4303	3.4090	96.5910
2	4.2737	3.5656	93.0255
3	4.1099	3.7294	89.2961
4	3.9385	3.9007	85.3954
5	3.7593	4.0799	81.3155
6	3.5719	4.2673	77.0481
7	3.3759	4.4634	72.5848
8	3.1708	4.6684	67.9164
9	2.9563	4.8829	63.0335
10	2.7320	5.1072	57.9263
11	2.4974	5.3418	52.5844
12	2.2520	5.5872	46.9972
13	1.9953	5.8439	41.1533
14	1.7269	6.1124	35.0409
15	1.4461	6.3932	28.6478
16	1.1524	6.6869	21.9609
17	.8452	6.9941	14.9668
18	.5239	7.3154	7.6514
19	.1878	7.6514	0.0000

YEARS 20 — MO PAYT .6326 — AN CONST 7.60

#	INT	PRIN	BALANCE
1	4.4354	3.1564	96.8436
2	4.2904	3.3014	93.5423
3	4.1388	3.4530	90.0892
4	3.9801	3.6117	86.4776
5	3.8142	3.7776	82.7000
6	3.6407	3.9511	78.7489
7	3.4592	4.1326	74.6162
8	3.2693	4.3225	70.2937
9	3.0707	4.5211	65.7727
10	2.8630	4.7288	61.0439
11	2.6458	4.9460	56.0979
12	2.4186	5.1732	50.9247
13	2.1809	5.4109	45.5138
14	1.9323	5.6595	39.8544
15	1.6723	5.9194	33.9349
16	1.4004	6.1914	27.7435
17	1.1160	6.4758	21.2677
18	.8185	6.7733	14.4944
19	.5073	7.0845	7.4099
20	.1819	7.4099	0.0000

YEARS 21 — MO PAYT .6141 — AN CONST 7.37

#	INT	PRIN	BALANCE
1	4.4401	2.9293	97.0707
2	4.3055	3.0639	94.0068
3	4.1647	3.2047	90.8021

#	INT	PRIN	BALANCE
4	4.0175	3.3519	87.4502
5	3.8635	3.5059	83.9444
6	3.7025	3.6669	80.2774
7	3.5340	3.8354	76.4421
8	3.3578	4.0116	72.4305
9	3.1735	4.1959	68.2346
10	2.9808	4.3886	63.8460
11	2.7792	4.5902	59.2557
12	2.5683	4.8011	54.4546
13	2.3477	5.0217	49.4329
14	2.1170	5.2524	44.1806
15	1.8757	5.4937	38.6869
16	1.6234	5.7460	32.9409
17	1.3594	6.0100	26.9308
18	1.0833	6.2861	20.6447
19	.7945	6.5749	14.0698
20	.4925	6.8769	7.1929
21	.1765	7.1929	0.0000

YEARS 22   MO PAYT .5974   AN CONST 7.17

#	INT	PRIN	BALANCE
1	4.4443	2.7244	97.2756
2	4.3191	2.8495	94.4261
3	4.1882	2.9804	91.4457
4	4.0513	3.1174	88.3283
5	3.9081	3.2606	85.0678
6	3.7583	3.4104	81.6574
7	3.6016	3.5670	78.0904
8	3.4377	3.7309	74.3595
9	3.2663	3.9023	70.4572
10	3.0871	4.0816	66.3756
11	2.8996	4.2691	62.1066
12	2.7034	4.4652	57.6414
13	2.4983	4.6703	52.9711
14	2.2838	4.8849	48.0862
15	2.0594	5.1093	42.9769
16	1.8246	5.3440	37.6329
17	1.5791	5.5895	32.0434
18	1.3224	5.8463	26.1971
19	1.0538	6.1149	20.0823
20	.7729	6.3958	13.6865
21	.4790	6.6896	6.9969
22	.1717	6.9969	0.0000

YEARS 23   MO PAYT .5822   AN CONST 6.99

#	INT	PRIN	BALANCE
1	4.4481	2.5386	97.4614
2	4.3314	2.6552	94.8062
3	4.2095	2.7772	92.0290
4	4.0819	2.9048	89.1242
5	3.9484	3.0382	86.0860
6	3.8089	3.1778	82.9082
7	3.6629	3.3238	79.5845
8	3.5102	3.4765	76.1080
9	3.3505	3.6362	72.4718
10	3.1834	3.8032	68.6686
11	3.0087	3.9779	64.6906
12	2.8260	4.1607	60.5299
13	2.6348	4.3518	56.1781
14	2.4349	4.5518	51.6264
15	2.2258	4.7609	46.8655
16	2.0071	4.9796	41.8859
17	1.7783	5.2083	36.6776
18	1.5390	5.4476	31.2300
19	1.2888	5.6979	25.5321
20	1.0270	5.9596	19.5725
21	.7532	6.2334	13.3391
22	.4669	6.5198	6.8193
23	.1674	6.8193	0.0000

YEARS 24   MO PAYT .5684   AN CONST 6.83

#	INT	PRIN	BALANCE
1	4.4515	2.3696	97.6304
2	4.3427	2.4784	95.1520
3	4.2288	2.5923	92.5597
4	4.1097	2.7114	89.8483
5	3.9852	2.8359	87.0124
6	3.8549	2.9662	84.0462
7	3.7186	3.1025	80.9437
8	3.5761	3.2450	77.6986
9	3.4270	3.3941	74.3046
10	3.2711	3.5500	70.7545
11	3.1080	3.7131	67.0414
12	2.9374	3.8837	63.1577
13	2.7590	4.0621	59.0956
14	2.5724	4.2487	54.8469
15	2.3772	4.4439	50.4030
16	2.1730	4.6481	45.7550
17	1.9595	4.8616	40.8934
18	1.7362	5.0849	35.8085
19	1.5026	5.3185	30.4900
20	1.2582	5.5629	24.9271
21	1.0027	5.8184	19.1087
22	.7354	6.0857	13.0230
23	.4558	6.3653	6.6577
24	.1634	6.6577	0.0000

YEARS 25   MO PAYT .5558   AN CONST 6.67

#	INT	PRIN	BALANCE
1	4.4547	2.2153	97.7847
2	4.3529	2.3171	95.4676
3	4.2465	2.4235	93.0441
4	4.1351	2.5349	90.5092
5	4.0187	2.6513	87.8579
6	3.8969	2.7731	85.0848
7	3.7695	2.9005	82.1843
8	3.6362	3.0338	79.1505
9	3.4969	3.1731	75.9774
10	3.3511	3.3189	72.6585
11	3.1986	3.4714	69.1871
12	3.0391	3.6308	65.5563
13	2.8723	3.7976	61.7586
14	2.6979	3.9721	57.7865
15	2.5154	4.1546	53.6319
16	2.3245	4.3455	49.2864
17	2.1249	4.5451	44.7414
18	1.9161	4.7539	39.9875
19	1.6977	4.9723	35.0152
20	1.4693	5.2007	29.8145
21	1.2304	5.4396	24.3749
22	.9805	5.6895	18.6854
23	.7191	5.9509	12.7345
24	.4457	6.2243	6.5102
25	.1598	6.5102	0.0000

YEARS 26   MO PAYT .5443   AN CONST 6.54

#	INT	PRIN	BALANCE
1	4.4576	2.0741	97.9259
2	4.3623	2.1694	95.7566
3	4.2626	2.2690	93.4875
4	4.1584	2.3733	91.1143
5	4.0494	2.4823	88.6320
6	3.9353	2.5963	86.0357
7	3.8160	2.7156	83.3201
8	3.6913	2.8404	80.4797
9	3.5608	2.9708	77.5089
10	3.4243	3.1073	74.4016
11	3.2816	3.2501	71.1515
12	3.1323	3.3994	67.7521
13	2.9761	3.5555	64.1966
14	2.8128	3.7189	60.4777
15	2.6419	3.8897	56.5880

#	INT	PRIN	BALANCE
16	2.4632	4.0684	52.5195
17	2.2763	4.2553	48.2642
18	2.0808	4.4508	43.8134
19	1.8764	4.6553	39.1581
20	1.6625	4.8691	34.2890
21	1.4388	5.0928	29.1961
22	1.2049	5.3268	23.8693
23	.9601	5.5715	18.2978
24	.7042	5.8275	12.4704
25	.4365	6.0952	6.3752
26	.1565	6.3752	0.0000

YEARS 27   MO PAYT .5337   AN CONST 6.41

#	INT	PRIN	BALANCE
1	4.4602	1.9444	98.0556
2	4.3709	2.0338	96.0218
3	4.2775	2.1272	93.8946
4	4.1797	2.2249	91.6697
5	4.0775	2.3271	89.3426
6	3.9706	2.4340	86.9086
7	3.8588	2.5458	84.3628
8	3.7418	2.6628	81.7000
9	3.6195	2.7851	78.9148
10	3.4916	2.9131	76.0018
11	3.3577	3.0469	72.9549
12	3.2178	3.1869	69.7680
13	3.0714	3.3333	66.4347
14	2.9182	3.4864	62.9483
15	2.7581	3.6466	59.3017
16	2.5906	3.8141	55.4876
17	2.4153	3.9893	51.4983
18	2.2321	4.1726	47.3257
19	2.0404	4.3643	42.9615
20	1.8399	4.5648	38.3967
21	1.6302	4.7745	33.6222
22	1.4108	4.9938	28.6284
23	1.1814	5.2232	23.4052
24	.9415	5.4632	17.9420
25	.6905	5.7142	12.2279
26	.4280	5.9767	6.2512
27	.1534	6.2512	0.0000

YEARS 28   MO PAYT .5240   AN CONST 6.29

#	INT	PRIN	BALANCE
1	4.4627	1.8251	98.1749
2	4.3788	1.9089	96.2660
3	4.2911	1.9966	94.2693
4	4.1994	2.0884	92.1810
5	4.1035	2.1843	89.9967
6	4.0031	2.2846	87.7120
7	3.8982	2.3896	85.3224
8	3.7884	2.4994	82.8231
9	3.6736	2.6142	80.2089
10	3.5535	2.7343	77.4746
11	3.4278	2.8599	74.6147
12	3.2965	2.9913	71.6234
13	3.1590	3.1287	68.4947
14	3.0153	3.2724	65.2222
15	2.8650	3.4228	61.7994
16	2.7077	3.5800	58.2194
17	2.5433	3.7445	54.4749
18	2.3712	3.9165	50.5584
19	2.1913	4.0964	46.4620
20	2.0031	4.2846	42.1774
21	1.8063	4.4815	37.6959
22	1.6004	4.6873	33.0086
23	1.3851	4.9027	28.1059
24	1.1599	5.1279	22.9780
25	.9243	5.3635	17.6146
26	.6779	5.6099	12.0047
27	.4202	5.8676	6.1371

#	INT	PRIN	BALANCE
28	.1506	6.1371	0.0000

YEARS 29   MO PAYT .5150   AN CONST 6.18

#	INT	PRIN	BALANCE
1	4.4649	1.7150	98.2850
2	4.3861	1.7938	96.4912
3	4.3037	1.8762	94.6150
4	4.2175	1.9624	92.6526
5	4.1274	2.0525	90.6001
6	4.0331	2.1468	88.4532
7	3.9345	2.2455	86.2078
8	3.8313	2.3486	83.8592
9	3.7234	2.4565	81.4026
10	3.6106	2.5694	78.8333
11	3.4925	2.6874	76.1459
12	3.3691	2.8109	73.3350
13	3.2399	2.9400	70.3950
14	3.1049	3.0751	67.3200
15	2.9636	3.2163	64.1037
16	2.8158	3.3641	60.7396
17	2.6613	3.5186	57.2210
18	2.4997	3.6803	53.5407
19	2.3306	3.8493	49.6914
20	2.1537	4.0262	45.6652
21	1.9688	4.2111	41.4540
22	1.7753	4.4046	37.0494
23	1.5730	4.6069	32.4425
24	1.3613	4.8186	27.6239
25	1.1400	5.0399	22.5840
26	.9084	5.2715	17.3125
27	.6663	5.5137	11.7988
28	.4130	5.7670	6.0319
29	.1480	6.0319	0.0000

YEARS 30   MO PAYT .5067   AN CONST 6.09

#	INT	PRIN	BALANCE
1	4.4670	1.6132	98.3868
2	4.3929	1.6873	96.6994
3	4.3154	1.7649	94.9346
4	4.2343	1.8459	93.0887
5	4.1495	1.9307	91.1579
6	4.0608	2.0194	89.1385
7	3.9680	2.1122	87.0263
8	3.8710	2.2092	84.8170
9	3.7695	2.3107	82.5063
10	3.6633	2.4169	80.0894
11	3.5523	2.5279	77.5615
12	3.4362	2.6440	74.9175
13	3.3147	2.7655	72.1520
14	3.1877	2.8926	69.2594
15	3.0548	3.0254	66.2340
16	2.9158	3.1644	63.0695
17	2.7704	3.3098	59.7597
18	2.6184	3.4619	56.2979
19	2.4593	3.6209	52.6770
20	2.2930	3.7872	48.8897
21	2.1190	3.9612	44.9285
22	1.9370	4.1432	40.7853
23	1.7467	4.3335	36.4518
24	1.5476	4.5326	31.9191
25	1.3394	4.7408	27.1783
26	1.1216	4.9586	22.2196
27	.8938	5.1864	17.0332
28	.6555	5.4247	11.6085
29	.4063	5.6739	5.9346
30	.1456	5.9346	0.0000

MONTHLY PAYMENT AMORTIZATION SCHEDULE PER $100   4.75 %

YEARS 2	MO PAYT 4.3760	AN CONST 52.52
# INT	PRIN	BALANCE
1 3.6964	48.8151	51.1849
2 1.3265	51.1849	0.0000

YEARS 3	MO PAYT 2.9859	AN CONST 35.84
# INT	PRIN	BALANCE
1 4.0643	31.7662	68.2338
2 2.5222	33.3084	34.9254
3 .9051	34.9254	0.0000

YEARS 4	MO PAYT 2.2916	AN CONST 27.50
# INT	PRIN	BALANCE
1 4.2481	23.2513	76.7487
2 3.1193	24.3801	52.3685
3 1.9357	25.5637	26.8048
4 .6947	26.8048	0.0000

YEARS 5	MO PAYT 1.8757	AN CONST 22.51
# INT	PRIN	BALANCE
1 4.3582	18.1501	81.8499
2 3.4771	19.0312	62.8187
3 2.5532	19.9551	42.8636
4 1.5844	20.9239	21.9397
5 .5686	21.9397	0.0000

YEARS 6	MO PAYT 1.5989	AN CONST 19.19
# INT	PRIN	BALANCE
1 4.4315	14.7556	85.2444
2 3.7152	15.4719	69.7725
3 2.9640	16.2230	53.5495
4 2.1764	17.0106	36.5389
5 1.3506	17.8365	18.7024
6 .4847	18.7024	0.0000

YEARS 7	MO PAYT 1.4017	AN CONST 16.83
# INT	PRIN	BALANCE
1 4.4837	12.3364	87.6636
2 3.8848	12.9353	74.7284
3 3.2568	13.5632	61.1651
4 2.5984	14.2217	46.9434
5 1.9079	14.9121	32.0313
6 1.1840	15.6361	16.3952
7 .4249	16.3952	0.0000

YEARS 8	MO PAYT 1.2541	AN CONST 15.05
# INT	PRIN	BALANCE
1 4.5228	10.5267	89.4733
2 4.0117	11.0377	78.4356
3 3.4759	11.5736	66.8619
4 2.9140	12.1355	54.7265
5 2.3249	12.7246	42.0018
6 1.7071	13.3424	28.6595
7 1.0594	13.9901	14.6693
8 .3802	14.6693	0.0000

YEARS 9	MO PAYT 1.1397	AN CONST 13.68
# INT	PRIN	BALANCE
1 4.5531	9.1234	90.8766
2 4.1102	9.5663	81.3103
3 3.6457	10.0307	71.2796
4 3.1588	10.5177	60.7619
5 2.6481	11.0283	49.7336
6 2.1127	11.5637	38.1698
7 1.5514	12.1251	26.0447
8 .9627	12.7138	13.3310
9 .3455	13.3310	0.0000

YEARS 10	MO PAYT 1.0485	AN CONST 12.59
# INT	PRIN	BALANCE
1 4.5772	8.0045	91.9955
2 4.1886	8.3931	83.6024
3 3.7812	8.8006	74.8018
4 3.3539	9.2278	65.5740
5 2.9059	9.6758	55.8982
6 2.4362	10.1456	45.7526
7 1.9436	10.6381	35.1145
8 1.4272	11.1546	23.9600
9 .8856	11.6961	12.2639
10 .3178	12.2639	0.0000

YEARS 11	MO PAYT .9741	AN CONST 11.69
# INT	PRIN	BALANCE
1 4.5969	7.0925	92.9075
2 4.2526	7.4368	85.4708
3 3.8915	7.7978	77.6729
4 3.5130	8.1764	69.4965
5 3.1160	8.5733	60.9232
6 2.6998	8.9896	51.9336
7 2.2634	9.4260	42.5076
8 1.8058	9.8836	32.6241
9 1.3260	10.3634	22.2606
10 .8228	10.8665	11.3941
11 .2953	11.3941	0.0000

YEARS 12	MO PAYT .9124	AN CONST 10.95
# INT	PRIN	BALANCE
1 4.6133	6.3355	93.6645
2 4.3057	6.6431	87.0213
3 3.9832	6.9656	80.0557
4 3.6450	7.3038	72.7519
5 3.2904	7.6584	65.0936
6 2.9186	8.0302	57.0634
7 2.5288	8.4200	48.6434
8 2.1200	8.8288	39.8146
9 1.6914	9.2574	30.5571
10 1.2419	9.7068	20.8503
11 .7707	10.1781	10.6722
12 .2766	10.6722	0.0000

YEARS 13	MO PAYT .8604	AN CONST 10.33
# INT	PRIN	BALANCE
1 4.6270	5.6979	94.3021
2 4.3504	5.9745	88.3275
3 4.0603	6.2646	82.0629
4 3.7562	6.5687	75.4942
5 3.4373	6.8876	68.6066
6 3.1029	7.2220	61.3846
7 2.7523	7.5726	53.8120
8 2.3847	7.9403	45.8717
9 1.9992	8.3257	37.5460
10 1.5950	8.7299	28.8160
11 1.1712	9.1538	19.6623
12 .7268	9.5981	10.0641
13 .2608	10.0641	0.0000

YEARS 14	MO PAYT .8161	AN CONST 9.80
# INT	PRIN	BALANCE
1 4.6388	5.1540	94.8460
2 4.3885	5.4043	89.4417
3 4.1262	5.6666	83.7751
4 3.8511	5.9417	77.8334
5 3.5626	6.2302	71.6032
6 3.2601	6.5326	65.0706
7 2.9430	6.8498	58.2208
8 2.6105	7.1823	51.0385
9 2.2618	7.5310	43.5075
10 1.8962	7.8966	35.6108
11 1.5128	8.2800	27.3308
12 1.1108	8.6820	18.6489
13 .6893	9.1035	9.5454
14 .2474	9.5454	0.0000

YEARS 15	MO PAYT .7778	AN CONST 9.34
# INT	PRIN	BALANCE
1 4.6489	4.6851	95.3149
2 4.4214	4.9126	90.4023
3 4.1829	5.1511	85.2513
4 3.9329	5.4011	79.8501
5 3.6706	5.6633	74.1868
6 3.3957	5.9383	68.2485
7 3.1074	6.2266	62.0219
8 2.8051	6.5289	55.4931
9 2.4882	6.8458	48.6473
10 2.1558	7.1782	41.4691
11 1.8073	7.5267	33.9424
12 1.4419	7.8921	26.0504
13 1.0588	8.2752	17.7751
14 .6570	8.6770	9.0982
15 .2358	9.0982	0.0000

YEARS 16	MO PAYT .7446	AN CONST 8.94
# INT	PRIN	BALANCE
1 4.6577	4.2771	95.7229
2 4.4500	4.4847	91.2382
3 4.2323	4.7024	86.5358
4 4.0040	4.9307	81.6050
5 3.7646	5.1701	76.4349
6 3.5136	5.4211	71.0138
7 3.2505	5.6843	65.3295
8 2.9745	5.9603	59.3692
9 2.6851	6.2496	53.1196
10 2.3817	6.5530	46.5666
11 2.0636	6.8712	39.6954
12 1.7300	7.2047	32.4907
13 1.3802	7.5545	24.9362
14 1.0135	7.9213	17.0149
15 .6289	8.3058	8.7091
16 .2257	8.7091	0.0000

YEARS 17	MO PAYT .7154	AN CONST 8.59
# INT	PRIN	BALANCE
1 4.6654	3.9192	96.0808
2 4.4751	4.1095	91.9714
3 4.2756	4.3090	87.6624
4 4.0664	4.5181	83.1443
5 3.8471	4.7375	78.4068
6 3.6171	4.9675	73.4393
7 3.3759	5.2087	68.2306
8 3.1231	5.4615	62.7691
9 2.8579	5.7267	57.0424
10 2.5799	6.0047	51.0377
11 2.2884	6.2962	44.7415
12 1.9827	6.6019	38.1397
13 1.6622	6.9224	31.2173
14 1.3262	7.2584	23.9589
15 .9738	7.6108	16.3480
16 .6043	7.9803	8.3677
17 .2169	8.3677	0.0000

YEARS 18	MO PAYT .6896	AN CONST 8.28
# INT	PRIN	BALANCE
1 4.6722	3.6031	96.3969
2 4.4973	3.7780	92.6190
3 4.3139	3.9614	88.6576
4 4.1216	4.1537	84.5039
5 3.9199	4.3554	80.1485
6 3.7085	4.5668	75.5817
7 3.4868	4.7885	70.7932
8 3.2543	5.0210	65.7722
9 3.0105	5.2647	60.5075
10 2.7550	5.5203	54.9872
11 2.4870	5.7883	49.1988
12 2.2059	6.0693	43.1295
13 1.9113	6.3640	36.7655
14 1.6023	6.6730	30.0925
15 1.2784	6.9969	23.0956
16 .9387	7.3366	15.7590
17 .5825	7.6928	8.0662
18 .2090	8.0662	0.0000

YEARS 19	MO PAYT .6667	AN CONST 8.01
# INT	PRIN	BALANCE
1 4.6783	3.3221	96.6779
2 4.5170	3.4834	93.1946
3 4.3479	3.6525	89.5421
4 4.1706	3.8298	85.7123
5 3.9847	4.0157	81.6966
6 3.7897	4.2107	77.4859
7 3.5853	4.4151	73.0708
8 3.3709	4.6294	68.4414
9 3.1462	4.8542	63.5872
10 2.9105	5.0898	58.4974
11 2.6634	5.3369	53.1604
12 2.4043	5.5960	47.5644
13 2.1327	5.8677	41.6967
14 1.8478	6.1526	35.5441
15 1.5491	6.4513	29.0928
16 1.2359	6.7645	22.3284
17 .9075	7.0929	15.2355
18 .5632	7.4372	7.7983
19 .2021	7.7983	0.0000

YEARS 20	MO PAYT .6462	AN CONST 7.76
# INT	PRIN	BALANCE
1 4.6837	3.0710	96.9290
2 4.5346	3.2201	93.7090
3 4.3783	3.3764	90.3326
4 4.2144	3.5403	86.7923
5 4.0425	3.7122	83.0801
6 3.8623	3.8924	79.1877
7 3.6733	4.0814	75.1064
8 3.4752	4.2795	70.8269
9 3.2674	4.4873	66.3396
10 3.0496	4.7051	61.6345
11 2.8212	4.9335	56.7009
12 2.5816	5.1730	51.5279
13 2.3305	5.4242	46.1037
14 2.0672	5.6875	40.4162
15 1.7910	5.9636	34.4526
16 1.5015	6.2532	28.1994
17 1.1979	6.5567	21.6427
18 .8796	6.8751	14.7676
19 .5459	7.2088	7.5588
20 .1959	7.5588	0.0000

YEARS 21	MO PAYT .6278	AN CONST 7.54
# INT	PRIN	BALANCE
1 4.6886	2.8454	97.1546
2 4.5504	2.9836	94.1710
3 4.4056	3.1284	91.0425

#	INT	PRIN	BALANCE
4	4.2537	3.2803	87.7622
5	4.0945	3.4396	84.3227
6	3.9275	3.6065	80.7161
7	3.7524	3.7816	76.9345
8	3.5688	3.9652	72.9692
9	3.3763	4.1577	68.8115
10	3.1744	4.3596	64.4519
11	2.9628	4.5712	59.8807
12	2.7409	4.7932	55.0876
13	2.5082	5.0258	50.0617
14	2.2642	5.2698	44.7919
15	2.0083	5.5257	39.2662
16	1.7401	5.7939	33.4722
17	1.4588	6.0752	27.3970
18	1.1639	6.3702	21.0268
19	.8546	6.6794	14.3474
20	.5303	7.0037	7.3437
21	.1903	7.3437	0.0000

YEARS 22 — MO PAYT .6112 — AN CONST 7.34

#	INT	PRIN	BALANCE
1	4.6930	2.6420	97.3580
2	4.5647	2.7703	94.5877
3	4.4302	2.9048	91.6830
4	4.2892	3.0458	88.6372
5	4.1413	3.1936	85.4435
6	3.9863	3.3487	82.0949
7	3.8237	3.5113	78.5836
8	3.6533	3.6817	74.9019
9	3.4745	3.8605	71.0414
10	3.2871	4.0479	66.9935
11	3.0906	4.2444	62.7491
12	2.8845	4.4505	58.2987
13	2.6685	4.6665	53.6321
14	2.4419	4.8931	48.7391
15	2.2044	5.1306	43.6085
16	1.9553	5.3797	38.2288
17	1.6941	5.6409	32.5879
18	1.4203	5.9147	26.6732
19	1.1331	6.2019	20.4713
20	.8320	6.5030	13.9684
21	.5163	6.8187	7.1497
22	.1853	7.1497	0.0000

YEARS 23 — MO PAYT .5962 — AN CONST 7.16

#	INT	PRIN	BALANCE
1	4.6970	2.4578	97.5422
2	4.5771	2.5771	94.9652
3	4.4525	2.7022	92.2630
4	4.3213	2.8334	89.4296
5	4.1838	2.9709	86.4587
6	4.0395	3.1152	83.3436
7	3.8883	3.2664	80.0772
8	3.7297	3.4250	76.6522
9	3.5635	3.5912	73.0610
10	3.3891	3.7656	69.2954
11	3.2063	3.9484	65.3470
12	3.0146	4.1401	61.2069
13	2.8136	4.3411	56.8658
14	2.6029	4.5518	52.3140
15	2.3819	4.7728	47.5412
16	2.1502	5.0045	42.5367
17	1.9072	5.2475	37.2892
18	1.6525	5.5022	31.7870
19	1.3854	5.7694	26.0176
20	1.1053	6.0494	19.9682
21	.8116	6.3431	13.6250
22	.5036	6.6511	6.9740
23	.1807	6.9740	0.0000

YEARS 24 — MO PAYT .5826 — AN CONST 7.00

#	INT	PRIN	BALANCE
1	4.7006	2.2903	97.7097
2	4.5894	2.4015	95.3083
3	4.4728	2.5180	92.7902
4	4.3505	2.6403	90.1499
5	4.2224	2.7685	87.3814
6	4.0880	2.9029	84.4786
7	3.9470	3.0438	81.4348
8	3.7993	3.1916	78.2432
9	3.6443	3.3465	74.8967
10	3.4819	3.5090	71.3877
11	3.3115	3.6793	67.7083
12	3.1329	3.8580	63.8504
13	2.9456	4.0453	59.8051
14	2.7492	4.2417	55.5634
15	2.5433	4.4476	51.1159
16	2.3273	4.6635	46.4524
17	2.1009	4.8899	41.5625
18	1.8635	5.1273	36.4352
19	1.6146	5.3762	31.0590
20	1.3536	5.6372	25.4217
21	1.0799	5.9109	19.5108
22	.7930	6.1979	13.3130
23	.4921	6.4987	6.8142
24	.1766	6.8142	0.0000

YEARS 25 — MO PAYT .5701 — AN CONST 6.85

#	INT	PRIN	BALANCE
1	4.7039	2.1375	97.8625
2	4.6001	2.2413	95.6211
3	4.4913	2.3501	93.2710
4	4.3772	2.4642	90.8068
5	4.2576	2.5839	88.2229
6	4.1321	2.7093	85.5136
7	4.0006	2.8408	82.6728
8	3.8627	2.9787	79.6940
9	3.7181	3.1234	76.5707
10	3.5664	3.2750	73.2957
11	3.4074	3.4340	69.8617
12	3.2407	3.6007	66.2610
13	3.0659	3.7755	62.4855
14	2.8826	3.9588	58.5267
15	2.6904	4.1510	54.3757
16	2.4889	4.3525	50.0232
17	2.2776	4.5638	45.4594
18	2.0560	4.7854	40.6740
19	1.8237	5.0177	35.6563
20	1.5801	5.2613	30.3951
21	1.3247	5.5167	24.8783
22	1.0569	5.7845	19.0938
23	.7760	6.0654	13.0284
24	.4816	6.3598	6.6686
25	.1728	6.6686	0.0000

YEARS 26 — MO PAYT .5587 — AN CONST 6.71

#	INT	PRIN	BALANCE
1	4.7069	1.9978	98.0022
2	4.6099	2.0948	95.9073
3	4.5082	2.1965	93.7108
4	4.4015	2.3032	91.4076
5	4.2897	2.4150	88.9926
6	4.1725	2.5322	86.4604
7	4.0496	2.6552	83.8052
8	3.9207	2.7841	81.0211
9	3.7855	2.9192	78.1019
10	3.6438	3.0610	75.0409
11	3.4952	3.2096	71.8314
12	3.3393	3.3654	68.4660
13	3.1760	3.5288	64.9372
14	3.0047	3.7001	61.2372
15	2.8250	3.8797	57.3574
16	2.6367	4.0681	53.2894
17	2.4392	4.2656	49.0238
18	2.2321	4.4726	44.5512
19	2.0150	4.6898	39.8614
20	1.7873	4.9174	34.9440
21	1.5485	5.1562	29.7878
22	1.2982	5.4065	24.3813
23	1.0357	5.6690	18.7123
24	.7605	5.9442	12.7681
25	.4720	6.2328	6.5354
26	.1694	6.5354	0.0000

YEARS 27 — MO PAYT .5483 — AN CONST 6.58

#	INT	PRIN	BALANCE
1	4.7096	1.8697	98.1303
2	4.6189	1.9605	96.1698
3	4.5237	2.0557	94.1141
4	4.4239	2.1555	91.9586
5	4.3193	2.2601	89.6985
6	4.2095	2.3698	87.3287
7	4.0945	2.4849	84.8438
8	3.9738	2.6055	82.2383
9	3.8473	2.7320	79.5062
10	3.7147	2.8647	76.6416
11	3.5756	3.0037	73.6379
12	3.4298	3.1496	70.4883
13	3.2769	3.3025	67.1859
14	3.1166	3.4628	63.7231
15	2.9485	3.6309	60.0922
16	2.7722	3.8072	56.2850
17	2.5874	3.9920	52.2930
18	2.3936	4.1858	48.1072
19	2.1904	4.3890	43.7182
20	1.9773	4.6021	39.1161
21	1.7539	4.8255	34.2906
22	1.5196	5.0598	29.2309
23	1.2740	5.3054	23.9254
24	1.0164	5.5630	18.3625
25	.7463	5.8331	12.5294
26	.4631	6.1162	6.4132
27	.1662	6.4132	0.0000

YEARS 28 — MO PAYT .5387 — AN CONST 6.47

#	INT	PRIN	BALANCE
1	4.7122	1.7519	98.2481
2	4.6271	1.8370	96.4111
3	4.5380	1.9261	94.4850
4	4.4444	2.0197	92.4653
5	4.3464	2.1177	90.3476
6	4.2436	2.2205	88.1271
7	4.1358	2.3283	85.7988
8	4.0227	2.4414	83.3574
9	3.9042	2.5599	80.7975
10	3.7799	2.6842	78.1134
11	3.6496	2.8145	75.2989
12	3.5130	2.9511	72.3478
13	3.3697	3.0944	69.2534
14	3.2195	3.2446	66.0088
15	3.0620	3.4021	62.6067
16	2.8968	3.5673	59.0394
17	2.7236	3.7405	55.2990
18	2.5420	3.9221	51.3769
19	2.3516	4.1125	47.2644
20	2.1520	4.3121	42.9523
21	1.9426	4.5215	38.4309
22	1.7231	4.7410	33.6899
23	1.4930	4.9711	28.7188
24	1.2516	5.2125	23.5063
25	.9986	5.4655	18.0408
26	.7332	5.7309	12.3099
27	.4550	6.0091	6.3008
28	.1633	6.3008	0.0000

YEARS 29 — MO PAYT .5298 — AN CONST 6.36

#	INT	PRIN	BALANCE
1	4.7145	1.6433	98.3567
2	4.6347	1.7231	96.6335
3	4.5511	1.8068	94.8267
4	4.4634	1.8945	92.9323
5	4.3714	1.9865	90.9458
6	4.2750	2.0829	88.8629
7	4.1738	2.1840	86.6788
8	4.0678	2.2901	84.3888
9	3.9566	2.4012	81.9875
10	3.8401	2.5178	79.4697
11	3.7178	2.6400	76.8297
12	3.5897	2.7682	74.0615
13	3.4553	2.9026	71.1589
14	3.3144	3.0435	68.1153
15	3.1666	3.1913	64.9241
16	3.0117	3.3462	61.5779
17	2.8492	3.5087	58.0692
18	2.6789	3.6790	54.3902
19	2.5003	3.8576	50.5326
20	2.3130	4.0449	46.4877
21	2.1166	4.2413	42.2465
22	1.9107	4.4472	37.7993
23	1.6948	4.6631	33.1362
24	1.4684	4.8894	28.2468
25	1.2311	5.1268	23.1200
26	.9822	5.3757	17.7443
27	.7212	5.6367	12.1076
28	.4475	5.9103	6.1973
29	.1606	6.1973	0.0000

YEARS 30 — MO PAYT .5216 — AN CONST 6.26

#	INT	PRIN	BALANCE
1	4.7167	1.5431	98.4569
2	4.6418	1.6180	96.8389
3	4.5632	1.6965	95.1424
4	4.4809	1.7789	93.3635
5	4.3945	1.8653	91.4982
6	4.3040	1.9558	89.5424
7	4.2090	2.0508	87.4917
8	4.1094	2.1503	85.3413
9	4.0050	2.2547	83.0866
10	3.8956	2.3642	80.7224
11	3.7808	2.4790	78.2435
12	3.6605	2.5993	75.6441
13	3.5343	2.7255	72.9186
14	3.4020	2.8578	70.0608
15	3.2632	2.9966	67.0643
16	3.1177	3.1420	63.9222
17	2.9652	3.2946	60.6277
18	2.8053	3.4545	57.1731
19	2.6375	3.6222	53.5509
20	2.4617	3.7981	49.7528
21	2.2773	3.9825	45.7704
22	2.0840	4.1758	41.5946
23	1.8812	4.3785	37.2160
24	1.6687	4.5911	32.6249
25	1.4458	4.8140	27.8109
26	1.2121	5.0477	22.7632
27	.9670	5.2928	17.4705
28	.7101	5.5497	11.9208
29	.4406	5.8191	6.1016
30	.1581	6.1016	0.0000

MONTHLY PAYMENT AMORTIZATION SCHEDULE PER $100   5.00 %

YEARS 2 — MO PAYT 4.3871 — AN CONST 52.65

#	INT	PRIN	BALANCE
1	3.8928	48.7529	51.2471
2	1.3985	51.2471	0.0000

YEARS 3 — MO PAYT 2.9971 — AN CONST 35.97

#	INT	PRIN	BALANCE
1	4.2804	31.6846	68.3154
2	2.6594	33.3057	35.0097
3	.9554	35.0097	0.0000

YEARS 4 — MO PAYT 2.3029 — AN CONST 27.64

#	INT	PRIN	BALANCE
1	4.4740	23.1611	76.8389
2	3.2890	24.3461	52.4927
3	2.0434	25.5917	26.9010
4	.7341	26.9010	0.0000

YEARS 5 — MO PAYT 1.8871 — AN CONST 22.65

#	INT	PRIN	BALANCE
1	4.5900	18.0555	81.9445
2	3.6662	18.9793	62.9652
3	2.6952	19.9503	43.0149
4	1.6745	20.9710	22.0439
5	.6016	22.0439	0.0000

YEARS 6 — MO PAYT 1.6105 — AN CONST 19.33

#	INT	PRIN	BALANCE
1	4.6671	14.6588	85.3412
2	3.9171	15.4088	69.9324
3	3.1288	16.1971	53.7352
4	2.3001	17.0258	36.7094
5	1.4290	17.8969	18.8125
6	.5134	18.8125	0.0000

YEARS 7 — MO PAYT 1.4134 — AN CONST 16.97

#	INT	PRIN	BALANCE
1	4.7221	12.2386	87.7614
2	4.0959	12.8648	74.8966
3	3.4377	13.5230	61.3736
4	2.7459	14.2148	47.1588
5	2.0186	14.9421	32.2167
6	1.2541	15.7066	16.5101
7	.4506	16.5101	0.0000

YEARS 8 — MO PAYT 1.2660 — AN CONST 15.20

#	INT	PRIN	BALANCE
1	4.7632	10.4287	89.5713
2	4.2296	10.9623	78.6090
3	3.6688	11.5231	67.0858
4	3.0792	12.1127	54.9731
5	2.4595	12.7324	42.2407
6	1.8081	13.3838	28.8569
7	1.1233	14.0686	14.7883
8	.4036	14.7883	0.0000

YEARS 9 — MO PAYT 1.1517 — AN CONST 13.83

#	INT	PRIN	BALANCE
1	4.7950	9.0257	90.9743
2	4.3333	9.4875	81.4868
3	3.8479	9.9729	71.5139
4	3.3376	10.4831	61.0308
5	2.8013	11.0194	50.0114
6	2.2375	11.5832	38.4282
7	1.6449	12.1758	26.2524
8	1.0220	12.7988	13.4536
9	.3671	13.4536	0.0000

YEARS 10 — MO PAYT 1.0607 — AN CONST 12.73

#	INT	PRIN	BALANCE
1	4.8204	7.9074	92.0926
2	4.4159	8.3120	83.7806
3	3.9906	8.7373	75.0433
4	3.5436	9.1843	65.8590
5	3.0737	9.6542	56.2049
6	2.5798	10.1481	46.0568
7	2.0606	10.6673	35.3895
8	1.5148	11.2130	24.1765
9	.9411	11.7867	12.3897
10	.3381	12.3897	0.0000

YEARS 11 — MO PAYT .9864 — AN CONST 11.84

#	INT	PRIN	BALANCE
1	4.8411	6.9963	93.0037
2	4.4832	7.3542	85.6495
3	4.1069	7.7305	77.9190
4	3.7114	8.1260	69.7931
5	3.2957	8.5417	61.2513
6	2.8587	8.9787	52.2726
7	2.3993	9.4381	42.8345
8	1.9164	9.9210	32.9136
9	1.4088	10.4285	22.4850
10	.8753	10.9621	11.5229
11	.3145	11.5229	0.0000

YEARS 12 — MO PAYT .9249 — AN CONST 11.10

#	INT	PRIN	BALANCE
1	4.8583	6.2404	93.7596
2	4.5390	6.5597	87.1999
3	4.2034	6.8953	80.3046
4	3.8506	7.2481	73.0566
5	3.4798	7.6189	65.4377
6	3.0900	8.0087	57.4290
7	2.6803	8.4184	49.0106
8	2.2496	8.8491	40.1615
9	1.7968	9.3019	30.8596
10	1.3209	9.7778	21.0819
11	.8207	10.2780	10.8039
12	.2948	10.8039	0.0000

YEARS 13 — MO PAYT .8731 — AN CONST 10.48

#	INT	PRIN	BALANCE
1	4.8727	5.6040	94.3960
2	4.5860	5.8907	88.5053
3	4.2846	6.1921	82.3132
4	3.9678	6.5089	75.8044
5	3.6348	6.8419	68.9625
6	3.2848	7.1919	61.7706
7	2.9168	7.5599	54.2107
8	2.5301	7.9467	46.2641
9	2.1235	8.3532	37.9108
10	1.6961	8.7806	29.1302
11	1.2469	9.2298	19.9004
12	.7747	9.7020	10.1984
13	.2783	10.1984	0.0000

YEARS 14 — MO PAYT .8289 — AN CONST 9.95

#	INT	PRIN	BALANCE
1	4.8851	5.0614	94.9386
2	4.6261	5.3203	89.6183
3	4.3539	5.5925	84.0257
4	4.0678	5.8787	78.1470
5	3.7670	6.1794	71.9676
6	3.4509	6.4956	65.4720
7	3.1185	6.8279	58.6441
8	2.7692	7.1772	51.4669
9	2.4020	7.5444	43.9224
10	2.0160	7.9304	35.9920
11	1.6103	8.3362	27.6559
12	1.1838	8.7627	18.8932
13	.7355	9.2110	9.6822
14	.2642	9.6822	0.0000

YEARS 15 — MO PAYT .7908 — AN CONST 9.49

#	INT	PRIN	BALANCE
1	4.8957	4.5939	95.4061
2	4.6606	4.8289	90.5773
3	4.4136	5.0759	85.5013
4	4.1539	5.3356	80.1657
5	3.8809	5.6086	74.5571
6	3.5940	5.8956	68.6615
7	3.2923	6.1972	62.4643
8	2.9753	6.5142	55.9501
9	2.6420	6.8475	49.1026
10	2.2917	7.1979	41.9047
11	1.9234	7.5661	34.3386
12	1.5363	7.9532	26.3854
13	1.1294	8.3601	18.0253
14	.7017	8.7878	9.2374
15	.2521	9.2374	0.0000

YEARS 16 — MO PAYT .7577 — AN CONST 9.10

#	INT	PRIN	BALANCE
1	4.9049	4.1873	95.8127
2	4.6907	4.4015	91.4112
3	4.4655	4.6267	86.7846
4	4.2288	4.8634	81.9212
5	3.9800	5.1122	76.8090
6	3.7184	5.3738	71.4352
7	3.4435	5.6487	65.7865
8	3.1545	5.9377	59.8488
9	2.8507	6.2415	53.6073
10	2.5314	6.5608	47.0465
11	2.1957	6.8965	40.1501
12	1.8429	7.2493	32.9007
13	1.4720	7.6202	25.2806
14	1.0821	8.0101	17.2705
15	.6723	8.4199	8.8506
16	.2415	8.8506	0.0000

YEARS 17 — MO PAYT .7287 — AN CONST 8.75

#	INT	PRIN	BALANCE
1	4.9130	3.8309	96.1691
2	4.7170	4.0269	92.1423
3	4.5110	4.2329	87.9094
4	4.2944	4.4494	83.4600
5	4.0668	4.6771	78.7829
6	3.8275	4.9164	73.8665
7	3.5760	5.1679	68.6986
8	3.3116	5.4323	63.2663
9	3.0336	5.7102	57.5561
10	2.7415	6.0024	51.5537
11	2.4344	6.3095	45.2442
12	2.1116	6.6323	38.6120
13	1.7723	6.9716	31.6404
14	1.4156	7.3283	24.3121
15	1.0407	7.7032	16.6089
16	.6466	8.0973	8.5116
17	.2323	8.5116	0.0000

YEARS 18 — MO PAYT .7030 — AN CONST 8.44

#	INT	PRIN	BALANCE
1	4.9201	3.5163	96.4837
2	4.7402	3.6962	92.7876
3	4.5511	3.8853	88.9023
4	4.3524	4.0840	84.8183
5	4.1434	4.2930	80.5253
6	3.9238	4.5126	76.0127
7	3.6929	4.7435	71.2692
8	3.4502	4.9862	66.2830
9	3.1951	5.2413	61.0417
10	2.9270	5.5094	55.5323
11	2.6451	5.7913	49.7409
12	2.3488	6.0876	43.6533
13	2.0373	6.3991	37.2543
14	1.7100	6.7265	30.5278
15	1.3658	7.0706	23.4572
16	1.0041	7.4323	16.0249
17	.6238	7.8126	8.2123
18	.2241	8.2123	0.0000

YEARS 19 — MO PAYT .6803 — AN CONST 8.17

#	INT	PRIN	BALANCE
1	4.9265	3.2368	96.7632
2	4.7609	3.4024	93.3607
3	4.5868	3.5765	89.7842
4	4.4038	3.7595	86.0247
5	4.2115	3.9518	82.0728
6	4.0093	4.1540	77.9188
7	3.7968	4.3666	73.5523
8	3.5734	4.5900	68.9623
9	3.3385	4.8248	64.1375
10	3.0917	5.0716	59.0659
11	2.8322	5.3311	53.7348
12	2.5595	5.6039	48.1309
13	2.2728	5.8906	42.2403
14	1.9714	6.1919	36.0484
15	1.6546	6.5087	29.5397
16	1.3216	6.8417	22.6979
17	.9716	7.1918	15.5062
18	.6036	7.5597	7.9465
19	.2169	7.9465	0.0000

YEARS 20 — MO PAYT .6600 — AN CONST 7.92

#	INT	PRIN	BALANCE
1	4.9322	2.9873	97.0127
2	4.7793	3.1401	93.8725
3	4.6187	3.3008	90.5717
4	4.4498	3.4697	87.1021
5	4.2723	3.6472	83.4549
6	4.0857	3.8338	79.6211
7	3.8895	4.0299	75.5911
8	3.6834	4.2361	71.3550
9	3.4666	4.4528	66.9022
10	3.2388	4.6807	62.2215
11	2.9993	4.9201	57.3014
12	2.7476	5.1719	52.1295
13	2.4830	5.4365	46.6931
14	2.2049	5.7146	40.9785
15	1.9125	6.0070	34.9715
16	1.6052	6.3143	28.6572
17	1.2821	6.6373	22.0199
18	.9425	6.9769	15.0430
19	.5856	7.3339	7.7091
20	.2104	7.7091	0.0000

YEARS 21 — MO PAYT .6417 — AN CONST 7.71

#	INT	PRIN	BALANCE
1	4.9372	2.7634	97.2366
2	4.7959	2.9048	94.3319
3	4.6473	3.0534	91.2785

#	INT	PRIN	BALANCE
4	4.4910	3.2096	88.0689
5	4.3268	3.3738	84.6951
6	4.1542	3.5464	81.1487
7	3.9728	3.7278	77.4208
8	3.7821	3.9186	73.5023
9	3.5816	4.1191	69.3832
10	3.3708	4.3298	65.0534
11	3.1493	4.5513	60.5021
12	2.9165	4.7842	55.7179
13	2.6717	5.0289	50.6890
14	2.4144	5.2862	45.4028
15	2.1439	5.5567	39.8461
16	1.8597	5.8410	34.0051
17	1.5608	6.1398	27.8653
18	1.2467	6.4539	21.4114
19	.9165	6.7841	14.6273
20	.5694	7.1312	7.4961
21	.2046	7.4961	0.0000

YEARS 22	MO PAYT .6253	AN CONST 7.51	
#	INT	PRIN	BALANCE
1	4.9418	2.5615	97.4385
2	4.8108	2.6926	94.7459
3	4.6730	2.8304	91.9155
4	4.5282	2.9752	88.9403
5	4.3760	3.1274	85.8130
6	4.2160	3.2874	82.5256
7	4.0478	3.4556	79.0700
8	3.8710	3.6324	75.4377
9	3.6852	3.8182	71.6195
10	3.4898	4.0135	67.6059
11	3.2845	4.2189	63.3870
12	3.0686	4.4347	58.9523
13	2.8417	4.6616	54.2907
14	2.6033	4.9001	49.3906
15	2.3526	5.1508	44.2398
16	2.0890	5.4143	38.8254
17	1.8120	5.6913	33.1341
18	1.5208	5.9825	27.1515
19	1.2148	6.2886	20.8629
20	.8930	6.6103	14.2526
21	.5548	6.9485	7.3040
22	.1993	7.3040	0.0000

YEARS 23	MO PAYT .6104	AN CONST 7.33	
#	INT	PRIN	BALANCE
1	4.9460	2.3789	97.6211
2	4.8243	2.5006	95.1205
3	4.6963	2.6285	92.4920
4	4.5618	2.7630	89.7289
5	4.4205	2.9044	86.8245
6	4.2719	3.0530	83.7716
7	4.1157	3.2092	80.5624
8	3.9515	3.3734	77.1890
9	3.7789	3.5459	73.6431
10	3.5975	3.7274	69.9157
11	3.4068	3.9181	65.9977
12	3.2064	4.1185	61.8791
13	2.9956	4.3292	57.5499
14	2.7741	4.5507	52.9992
15	2.5413	4.7835	48.2156
16	2.2966	5.0283	43.1873
17	2.0393	5.2855	37.9018
18	1.7689	5.5560	32.3458
19	1.4847	5.8402	26.5056
20	1.1859	6.1390	20.3666
21	.8718	6.4531	13.9135
22	.5416	6.7832	7.1303
23	.1946	7.1303	0.0000

YEARS 24	MO PAYT .5969	AN CONST 7.17	
#	INT	PRIN	BALANCE
1	4.9497	2.2130	97.7870
2	4.8365	2.3263	95.4607
3	4.7175	2.4453	93.0155
4	4.5924	2.5704	90.4451
5	4.4609	2.7019	87.7432
6	4.3227	2.8401	84.9031
7	4.1774	2.9854	81.9177
8	4.0246	3.1382	78.7795
9	3.8641	3.2987	75.4808
10	3.6953	3.4675	72.0133
11	3.5179	3.6449	68.3685
12	3.3314	3.8314	64.5371
13	3.1354	4.0274	60.5097
14	2.9293	4.2334	56.2763
15	2.7128	4.4500	51.8263
16	2.4851	4.6777	47.1486
17	2.2458	4.9170	42.2316
18	1.9942	5.1686	37.0630
19	1.7298	5.4330	31.6300
20	1.4518	5.7110	25.9191
21	1.1596	6.0032	19.9159
22	.8525	6.3103	13.6056
23	.5296	6.6331	6.9725
24	.1903	6.9725	0.0000

YEARS 25	MO PAYT .5846	AN CONST 7.02	
#	INT	PRIN	BALANCE
1	4.9532	2.0619	97.9381
2	4.8477	2.1674	95.7707
3	4.7368	2.2783	93.4924
4	4.6202	2.3948	91.0976
5	4.4977	2.5174	88.5802
6	4.3689	2.6462	85.9340
7	4.2335	2.7815	83.1525
8	4.0912	2.9239	80.2286
9	3.9416	3.0734	77.1552
10	3.7844	3.2307	73.9245
11	3.6191	3.3960	70.5285
12	3.4454	3.5697	66.9588
13	3.2627	3.7524	63.2064
14	3.0707	3.9443	59.2621
15	2.8689	4.1461	55.1159
16	2.6568	4.3583	50.7577
17	2.4338	4.5812	46.1764
18	2.1995	4.8156	41.3608
19	1.9531	5.0620	36.2988
20	1.6941	5.3210	30.9778
21	1.4219	5.5932	25.3846
22	1.1357	5.8794	19.5053
23	.8349	6.1802	13.3251
24	.5187	6.4964	6.8287
25	.1864	6.8287	0.0000

YEARS 26	MO PAYT .5733	AN CONST 6.89	
#	INT	PRIN	BALANCE
1	4.9563	1.9238	98.0762
2	4.8579	2.0222	96.0539
3	4.7544	2.1257	93.9282
4	4.6457	2.2345	91.6938
5	4.5313	2.3488	89.3450
6	4.4112	2.4689	86.8761
7	4.2849	2.5953	84.2808
8	4.1521	2.7280	81.5528
9	4.0125	2.8676	78.6852
10	3.8658	3.0143	75.6708
11	3.7116	3.1685	72.5023
12	3.5495	3.3306	69.1717
13	3.3791	3.5011	65.6706
14	3.2000	3.6802	61.9904
15	3.0117	3.8685	58.1220
16	2.8138	4.0664	54.0556
17	2.6057	4.2744	49.7812
18	2.3870	4.4931	45.2881
19	2.1571	4.7230	40.5651
20	1.9155	4.9646	35.6005
21	1.6615	5.2186	30.3819
22	1.3945	5.4856	24.8963
23	1.1139	5.7663	19.1300
24	.8188	6.0613	13.0687
25	.5087	6.3714	6.6974
26	.1828	6.6974	0.0000

YEARS 27	MO PAYT .5630	AN CONST 6.76	
#	INT	PRIN	BALANCE
1	4.9592	1.7973	98.2027
2	4.8672	1.8892	96.3135
3	4.7706	1.9859	94.3276
4	4.6690	2.0875	92.2401
5	4.5622	2.1943	90.0458
6	4.4499	2.3066	87.7392
7	4.3319	2.4246	85.3147
8	4.2079	2.5486	82.7660
9	4.0775	2.6790	80.0870
10	3.9404	2.8161	77.2710
11	3.7963	2.9601	74.3108
12	3.6449	3.1116	71.1992
13	3.4857	3.2708	67.9284
14	3.3183	3.4381	64.4903
15	3.1424	3.6140	60.8763
16	2.9575	3.7989	57.0774
17	2.7632	3.9933	53.0841
18	2.5589	4.1976	48.8865
19	2.3441	4.4123	44.4741
20	2.1184	4.6381	39.8360
21	1.8811	4.8754	34.9607
22	1.6316	5.1248	29.8358
23	1.3695	5.3870	24.4488
24	1.0938	5.6626	18.7862
25	.8041	5.9523	12.8339
26	.4996	6.2569	6.5770
27	.1795	6.5770	0.0000

YEARS 28	MO PAYT .5536	AN CONST 6.65	
#	INT	PRIN	BALANCE
1	4.9618	1.6811	98.3189
2	4.8758	1.7671	96.5519
3	4.7854	1.8575	94.6944
4	4.6904	1.9525	92.7419
5	4.5905	2.0524	90.6895
6	4.4855	2.1574	88.5321
7	4.3751	2.2678	86.2643
8	4.2591	2.3838	83.8805
9	4.1371	2.5058	81.3747
10	4.0089	2.6340	78.7407
11	3.8742	2.7687	75.9720
12	3.7325	2.9104	73.0616
13	3.5836	3.0593	70.0023
14	3.4271	3.2158	66.7865
15	3.2626	3.3803	63.4062
16	3.0896	3.5533	59.8529
17	2.9078	3.7351	56.1179
18	2.7167	3.9262	52.1917
19	2.5159	4.1270	48.0647
20	2.3047	4.3382	43.7265
21	2.0828	4.5601	39.1664
22	1.8495	4.7934	34.3729
23	1.6042	5.0387	29.3343
24	1.3464	5.2965	24.0378
25	1.0755	5.5674	18.4704
26	.7906	5.8523	12.6181
27	.4912	6.1517	6.4664
28	.1765	6.4664	0.0000

YEARS 29	MO PAYT .5449	AN CONST 6.54	
#	INT	PRIN	BALANCE
1	4.9643	1.5741	98.4259
2	4.8837	1.6546	96.7713
3	4.7991	1.7393	95.0321
4	4.7101	1.8282	93.2038
5	4.6165	1.9218	91.2821
6	4.5182	2.0201	89.2620
7	4.4149	2.1234	87.1385
8	4.3062	2.2321	84.9064
9	4.1920	2.3463	82.5601
10	4.0720	2.4663	80.0938
11	3.9458	2.5925	77.5013
12	3.8132	2.7251	74.7761
13	3.6738	2.8646	71.9116
14	3.5272	3.0111	68.9004
15	3.3731	3.1652	65.7353
16	3.2112	3.3271	62.4081
17	3.0410	3.4973	58.9108
18	2.8621	3.6763	55.2345
19	2.6740	3.8644	51.3702
20	2.4763	4.0621	47.3081
21	2.2684	4.2699	43.0382
22	2.0500	4.4883	38.5499
23	1.8203	4.7180	33.8319
24	1.5790	4.9594	28.8725
25	1.3252	5.2131	23.6594
26	1.0585	5.4798	18.1796
27	.7782	5.7602	12.4195
28	.4835	6.0549	6.3646
29	.1737	6.3646	0.0000

YEARS 30	MO PAYT .5368	AN CONST 6.45	
#	INT	PRIN	BALANCE
1	4.9665	1.4754	98.5246
2	4.8910	1.5508	96.9738
3	4.8117	1.6302	95.3436
4	4.7283	1.7136	93.6300
5	4.6406	1.8013	91.8287
6	4.5484	1.8934	89.9353
7	4.4516	1.9903	87.9450
8	4.3497	2.0921	85.8529
9	4.2427	2.1992	83.6537
10	4.1302	2.3117	81.3421
11	4.0119	2.4299	78.9121
12	3.8876	2.5543	76.3579
13	3.7569	2.6849	73.6729
14	3.6196	2.8223	70.8506
15	3.4752	2.9667	67.8839
16	3.3234	3.1185	64.7654
17	3.1638	3.2780	61.4874
18	2.9961	3.4457	58.0416
19	2.8198	3.6220	54.4196
20	2.6345	3.8073	50.6123
21	2.4397	4.0021	46.6101
22	2.2350	4.2069	42.4032
23	2.0197	4.4221	37.9811
24	1.7935	4.6484	33.3327
25	1.5557	4.8862	28.4466
26	1.3057	5.1362	23.3104
27	1.0429	5.3990	17.9114
28	.7667	5.6752	12.2363
29	.4763	5.9655	6.2707
30	.1711	6.2707	0.0000

YEARS 2 — MO PAYT 4.3916 — AN CONST 52.70

#	INT	PRIN	BALANCE
1	3.9714	48.7280	51.2720
2	1.4274	51.2720	0.0000

YEARS 3 — MO PAYT 3.0016 — AN CONST 36.02

#	INT	PRIN	BALANCE
1	4.3669	31.6520	68.3480
2	2.7144	33.3046	35.0434
3	.9756	35.0434	0.0000

YEARS 4 — MO PAYT 2.3075 — AN CONST 27.69

#	INT	PRIN	BALANCE
1	4.5644	23.1251	76.8749
2	3.3571	24.3325	52.5424
3	2.0867	25.6028	26.9396
4	.7500	26.9396	0.0000

YEARS 5 — MO PAYT 1.8917 — AN CONST 22.71

#	INT	PRIN	BALANCE
1	4.6827	18.0178	81.9822
2	3.7420	18.9585	63.0237
3	2.7522	19.9483	43.0754
4	1.7107	20.9898	22.0856
5	.6149	22.0856	0.0000

YEARS 6 — MO PAYT 1.6151 — AN CONST 19.39

#	INT	PRIN	BALANCE
1	4.7614	14.6202	85.3798
2	3.9981	15.3836	69.9962
3	3.1949	16.1867	53.8095
4	2.3498	17.0318	36.7777
5	1.4606	17.9210	18.8567
6	.5250	18.8567	0.0000

YEARS 7 — MO PAYT 1.4181 — AN CONST 17.02

#	INT	PRIN	BALANCE
1	4.8175	12.1997	87.8003
2	4.1805	12.8366	74.9637
3	3.5103	13.5068	61.4569
4	2.8051	14.2120	47.2449
5	2.0632	14.9540	32.2909
6	1.2824	15.7347	16.5562
7	.4609	16.5562	0.0000

YEARS 8 — MO PAYT 1.2708 — AN CONST 15.25

#	INT	PRIN	BALANCE
1	4.8594	10.3897	89.6103
2	4.3169	10.9322	78.6781
3	3.7462	11.5029	67.1752
4	3.1456	12.1035	55.0717
5	2.5137	12.7354	42.3363
6	1.8488	13.4003	28.9360
7	1.1492	14.0999	14.8361
8	.4130	14.8361	0.0000

YEARS 9 — MO PAYT 1.1566 — AN CONST 13.88

#	INT	PRIN	BALANCE
1	4.8919	8.9868	91.0132
2	4.4227	9.4560	81.5572
3	3.9290	9.9497	71.6074
4	3.4095	10.4692	61.1383
5	2.8629	11.0158	50.1225
6	2.2878	11.5909	38.5316
7	1.6826	12.1960	26.3356
8	1.0459	12.8328	13.5028
9	.3759	13.5028	0.0000

YEARS 10 — MO PAYT 1.0655 — AN CONST 12.79

#	INT	PRIN	BALANCE
1	4.9178	7.8688	92.1312
2	4.5069	8.2797	83.8515
3	4.0747	8.7119	75.1395
4	3.6198	9.1668	65.9728
5	3.1412	9.6454	56.3274
6	2.6376	10.1490	46.1784
7	2.1078	10.6788	35.4996
8	1.5507	11.2364	24.2633
9	.9636	11.8230	12.4403
10	.3463	12.4403	0.0000

YEARS 11 — MO PAYT .9914 — AN CONST 11.90

#	INT	PRIN	BALANCE
1	4.9389	6.9580	93.0420
2	4.5756	7.3213	85.7206
3	4.1933	7.7036	78.0171
4	3.7911	8.1058	69.9113
5	3.3679	8.5290	61.3823
6	2.9227	8.9742	52.4081
7	2.4541	9.4428	42.9653
8	1.9611	9.9358	33.0295
9	1.4424	10.4545	22.5750
10	.8966	11.0003	11.5747
11	.3222	11.5747	0.0000

YEARS 12 — MO PAYT .9299 — AN CONST 11.16

#	INT	PRIN	BALANCE
1	4.9563	6.2026	93.7974
2	4.6325	6.5265	87.2709
3	4.2918	6.8672	80.4037
4	3.9332	7.2257	73.1779
5	3.5560	7.6030	65.5750
6	3.1590	7.9999	57.5750
7	2.7414	8.4176	49.1574
8	2.3019	8.8571	40.3003
9	1.8395	9.3195	30.9808
10	1.3529	9.8061	21.1748
11	.8409	10.3180	10.8567
12	.3022	10.8567	0.0000

YEARS 13 — MO PAYT .8781 — AN CONST 10.54

#	INT	PRIN	BALANCE
1	4.9711	5.5667	94.4333
2	4.6804	5.8574	88.5759
3	4.3746	6.1632	82.4128
4	4.0529	6.4849	75.9278
5	3.7143	6.8235	69.1043
6	3.3580	7.1798	61.9246
7	2.9832	7.5546	54.3700
8	2.5888	7.9490	46.4210
9	2.1738	8.3640	38.0569
10	1.7371	8.8007	29.2562
11	1.2776	9.2602	19.9960
12	.7941	9.7437	10.2524
13	.2854	10.2524	0.0000

YEARS 14 — MO PAYT .8340 — AN CONST 10.01

#	INT	PRIN	BALANCE
1	4.9836	5.0247	94.9753
2	4.7213	5.2870	89.6883
3	4.4453	5.5630	84.1253
4	4.1548	5.8535	78.2718
5	3.8492	6.1591	72.1127
6	3.5277	6.4806	65.6321
7	3.1893	6.8190	58.8131
8	2.8333	7.1750	51.6381
9	2.4587	7.5496	44.0885
10	2.0645	7.9438	36.1447
11	1.6498	8.3585	27.7862
12	1.2134	8.7949	18.9913
13	.7542	9.2541	9.7372
14	.2711	9.7372	0.0000

YEARS 15 — MO PAYT .7960 — AN CONST 9.56

#	INT	PRIN	BALANCE
1	4.9944	4.5577	95.4423
2	4.7565	4.7957	90.6466
3	4.5061	5.0460	85.6006
4	4.2427	5.3095	80.2911
5	3.9655	5.5867	74.7044
6	3.6738	5.8784	68.8260
7	3.3669	6.1853	62.6408
8	3.0439	6.5082	56.1326
9	2.7042	6.8480	49.2846
10	2.3466	7.2055	42.0790
11	1.9704	7.5817	34.4973
12	1.5746	7.9775	26.5198
13	1.1581	8.3941	18.1257
14	.7199	8.8323	9.2934
15	.2587	9.2934	0.0000

YEARS 16 — MO PAYT .7630 — AN CONST 9.16

#	INT	PRIN	BALANCE
1	5.0038	4.1517	95.8483
2	4.7871	4.3685	91.4798
3	4.5590	4.5966	86.8832
4	4.3190	4.8365	82.0467
5	4.0665	5.0891	76.9576
6	3.8008	5.3548	71.6029
7	3.5213	5.6343	65.9686
8	3.2271	5.9285	60.0401
9	2.9176	6.2380	53.8021
10	2.5919	6.5637	47.2384
11	2.2492	6.9064	40.3320
12	1.8886	7.2669	33.0651
13	1.5092	7.6463	25.4187
14	1.1100	8.0456	17.3732
15	.6900	8.4656	8.9076
16	.2480	8.9076	0.0000

YEARS 17 — MO PAYT .7340 — AN CONST 8.81

#	INT	PRIN	BALANCE
1	5.0121	3.7959	96.2041
2	4.8139	3.9941	92.2099
3	4.6054	4.2027	88.0073
4	4.3860	4.4221	83.5852
5	4.1551	4.6530	78.9322
6	3.9122	4.8959	74.0364
7	3.6565	5.1515	68.8849
8	3.3876	5.4204	63.4644
9	3.1046	5.7034	57.7610
10	2.8068	6.0012	51.7598
11	2.4935	6.3145	45.4453
12	2.1638	6.6442	38.8010
13	1.8169	6.9911	31.8100
14	1.4519	7.3561	24.4539
15	1.0679	7.7401	16.7137
16	.6638	8.1443	8.5695
17	.2386	8.5695	0.0000

YEARS 18 — MO PAYT .7084 — AN CONST 8.51

#	INT	PRIN	BALANCE
1	5.0194	3.4820	96.5180
2	4.8376	3.6638	92.8542
3	4.6463	3.8551	88.9992
4	4.4450	4.0563	84.9429
5	4.2332	4.2681	80.6748
6	4.0104	4.4909	76.1838
7	3.7759	4.7254	71.4584
8	3.5292	4.9721	66.4863
9	3.2696	5.2317	61.2546
10	2.9965	5.5048	55.7498
11	2.7091	5.7922	49.9575
12	2.4067	6.0947	43.8629
13	2.0885	6.4129	37.4500
14	1.7537	6.7477	30.7023
15	1.4014	7.1000	23.6024
16	1.0307	7.4706	16.1317
17	.6407	7.8607	8.2711
18	.2303	8.2711	0.0000

YEARS 19 — MO PAYT .6858 — AN CONST 8.23

#	INT	PRIN	BALANCE
1	5.0258	3.2032	96.7968
2	4.8586	3.3704	93.4263
3	4.6826	3.5464	89.8799
4	4.4975	3.7316	86.1484
5	4.3026	3.9264	82.2220
6	4.0976	4.1314	78.0906
7	3.8819	4.3471	73.7435
8	3.6550	4.5740	69.1695
9	3.4162	4.8128	64.3566
10	3.1649	5.0641	59.2925
11	2.9005	5.3285	53.9640
12	2.6223	5.6067	48.3573
13	2.3296	5.8994	42.4578
14	2.0216	6.2074	36.2504
15	1.6975	6.5315	29.7189
16	1.3565	6.8725	22.8464
17	.9977	7.2313	15.6150
18	.6201	7.6089	8.0061
19	.2229	8.0061	0.0000

YEARS 20 — MO PAYT .6655 — AN CONST 7.99

#	INT	PRIN	BALANCE
1	5.0316	2.9543	97.0457
2	4.8773	3.1086	93.9371
3	4.7150	3.2709	90.6662
4	4.5443	3.4416	87.2246
5	4.3646	3.6213	83.6033
6	4.1755	3.8104	79.7929
7	3.9766	4.0093	75.7835
8	3.7673	4.2187	71.5649
9	3.5470	4.4389	67.1260
10	3.3153	4.6707	62.4553
11	3.0714	4.9145	57.5408
12	2.8148	5.1711	52.3697
13	2.5448	5.4411	46.9286
14	2.2608	5.7251	41.2035
15	1.9619	6.0240	35.1794
16	1.6473	6.3386	28.8409
17	1.3164	6.6695	22.1714
18	.9682	7.0177	15.1537
19	.6018	7.3841	7.7696
20	.2163	7.7696	0.0000

YEARS 21 — MO PAYT .6473 — AN CONST 7.77

#	INT	PRIN	BALANCE
1	5.0367	2.7311	97.2689
2	4.8942	2.8736	94.3953
3	4.7441	3.0237	91.3716

#	INT	PRIN	BALANCE
4	4.5863	3.1815	88.1901
5	4.4202	3.3476	84.8424
6	4.2454	3.5224	81.3200
7	4.0615	3.7063	77.6137
8	3.8680	3.8998	73.7138
9	3.6644	4.1034	69.6104
10	3.4501	4.3177	65.2927
11	3.2247	4.5431	60.7496
12	2.9875	4.7803	55.9693
13	2.7379	5.0299	50.9395
14	2.4753	5.2925	45.6470
15	2.1990	5.5688	40.0782
16	1.9083	5.8595	34.2187
17	1.6024	6.1655	28.0532
18	1.2805	6.4873	21.5659
19	.9418	6.8260	14.7398
20	.5854	7.1824	7.5574
21	.2104	7.5574	0.0000

YEARS 22   MO PAYT .6309   AN CONST 7.58

#	INT	PRIN	BALANCE
1	5.0414	2.5299	97.4701
2	4.9093	2.6620	94.8081
3	4.7703	2.8009	92.0072
4	4.6241	2.9472	89.0600
5	4.4702	3.1011	85.9590
6	4.3083	3.2630	82.6960
7	4.1380	3.4333	79.2627
8	3.9587	3.6126	75.6501
9	3.7701	3.8012	71.8490
10	3.5717	3.9996	67.8493
11	3.3628	4.2084	63.6409
12	3.1431	4.4282	59.2127
13	2.9119	4.6594	54.5534
14	2.6687	4.9026	49.6507
15	2.4127	5.1586	44.4922
16	2.1434	5.4279	39.0643
17	1.8600	5.7113	33.3530
18	1.5618	6.0095	27.3435
19	1.2481	6.3232	21.0203
20	.9179	6.6534	14.3669
21	.5706	7.0007	7.3662
22	.2051	7.3662	0.0000

YEARS 23   MO PAYT .6161   AN CONST 7.40

#	INT	PRIN	BALANCE
1	5.0456	2.3479	97.6521
2	4.9230	2.4705	95.1816
3	4.7941	2.5995	92.5821
4	4.6583	2.7352	89.8470
5	4.5155	2.8780	86.9690
6	4.3653	3.0282	83.9407
7	4.2072	3.1863	80.7544
8	4.0408	3.3527	77.4017
9	3.8658	3.5277	73.8739
10	3.6816	3.7119	70.1620
11	3.4878	3.9057	66.2563
12	3.2839	4.1096	62.1467
13	3.0693	4.3242	57.8225
14	2.8436	4.5500	53.2725
15	2.6060	4.7875	48.4850
16	2.3561	5.0375	43.4475
17	2.0931	5.3005	38.1471
18	1.8163	5.5772	32.5699
19	1.5252	5.8684	26.7015
20	1.2188	6.1748	20.5268
21	.8964	6.4971	14.0296
22	.5572	6.8363	7.1933
23	.2003	7.1933	0.0000

YEARS 24   MO PAYT .6027   AN CONST 7.24

#	INT	PRIN	BALANCE
1	5.0494	2.1827	97.8173
2	4.9355	2.2967	95.5206
3	4.8156	2.4166	93.1041
4	4.6894	2.5427	90.5614
5	4.5567	2.6755	87.8859
6	4.4170	2.8152	85.0707
7	4.2700	2.9621	82.1086
8	4.1154	3.1168	78.9918
9	3.9526	3.2795	75.7122
10	3.7814	3.4507	72.2615
11	3.6012	3.6309	68.6306
12	3.4117	3.8205	64.8101
13	3.2122	4.0199	60.7902
14	3.0023	4.2298	56.5604
15	2.7815	4.4506	52.1097
16	2.5491	4.6830	47.4267
17	2.3046	4.9275	42.4992
18	2.0474	5.1848	37.3144
19	1.7767	5.4555	31.8590
20	1.4919	5.7403	26.1187
21	1.1922	6.0400	20.0787
22	.8768	6.3553	13.7234
23	.5450	6.6871	7.0363
24	.1959	7.0363	0.0000

YEARS 25   MO PAYT .5904   AN CONST 7.09

#	INT	PRIN	BALANCE
1	5.0529	2.0322	97.9678
2	4.9468	2.1383	95.8294
3	4.8352	2.2500	93.5794
4	4.7177	2.3675	91.2120
5	4.5941	2.4911	88.7209
6	4.4641	2.6211	86.0998
7	4.3272	2.7580	83.3419
8	4.1832	2.9019	80.4399
9	4.0317	3.0535	77.3865
10	3.8723	3.2129	74.1736
11	3.7046	3.3806	70.7930
12	3.5281	3.5571	67.2359
13	3.3423	3.7428	63.4930
14	3.1469	3.9382	59.5548
15	2.9413	4.1439	55.4109
16	2.7250	4.3602	51.0507
17	2.4973	4.5878	46.4629
18	2.2578	4.8274	41.6355
19	2.0058	5.0794	36.5561
20	1.7406	5.3446	31.2115
21	1.4615	5.6236	25.5879
22	1.1679	5.9172	19.6707
23	.8590	6.2262	13.4445
24	.5339	6.5512	6.8933
25	.1919	6.8933	0.0000

YEARS 26   MO PAYT .5792   AN CONST 6.96

#	INT	PRIN	BALANCE
1	5.0561	1.8948	98.1052
2	4.9572	1.9937	96.1115
3	4.8531	2.0978	94.0136
4	4.7436	2.2073	91.8063
5	4.6283	2.3226	89.4837
6	4.5071	2.4439	87.0398
7	4.3795	2.5714	84.4684
8	4.2452	2.7057	81.7627
9	4.1040	2.8470	78.9157
10	3.9553	2.9956	75.9201
11	3.7989	3.1520	72.7681
12	3.6344	3.3166	69.4516
13	3.4612	3.4897	65.9619
14	3.2790	3.6719	62.2900
15	3.0873	3.8636	58.4263
16	2.8856	4.0653	54.3610
17	2.6733	4.2776	50.0834
18	2.4500	4.5009	45.5825
19	2.2150	4.7359	40.8466
20	1.9678	4.9832	35.8635
21	1.7076	5.2433	30.6201
22	1.4339	5.5171	25.1031
23	1.1458	5.8051	19.2979
24	.8427	6.1082	13.1898
25	.5238	6.4271	6.7627
26	.1883	6.7627	0.0000

YEARS 27   MO PAYT .5690   AN CONST 6.83

#	INT	PRIN	BALANCE
1	5.0590	1.7689	98.2311
2	4.9667	1.8613	96.3698
3	4.8695	1.9585	94.4113
4	4.7673	2.0607	92.3506
5	4.6597	2.1683	90.1823
6	4.5465	2.2815	87.9008
7	4.4273	2.4006	85.5002
8	4.3020	2.5260	82.9742
9	4.1701	2.6578	80.3164
10	4.0314	2.7966	77.5198
11	3.8854	2.9426	74.5772
12	3.7317	3.0962	71.4809
13	3.5701	3.2579	68.2230
14	3.4000	3.4280	64.7950
15	3.2210	3.6070	61.1881
16	3.0327	3.7953	57.3928
17	2.8345	3.9934	53.3994
18	2.6261	4.2019	49.1975
19	2.4067	4.4213	44.7762
20	2.1758	4.6521	40.1241
21	1.9330	4.8950	35.2291
22	1.6774	5.1506	30.0785
23	1.4085	5.4195	24.6590
24	1.1255	5.7024	18.9566
25	.8278	6.0001	12.9564
26	.5146	6.3134	6.6430
27	.1849	6.6430	0.0000

YEARS 28   MO PAYT .5596   AN CONST 6.72

#	INT	PRIN	BALANCE
1	5.0617	1.6534	98.3466
2	4.9754	1.7397	96.6069
3	4.8846	1.8305	94.7764
4	4.7890	1.9261	92.8503
5	4.6884	2.0266	90.8237
6	4.5826	2.1325	88.6912
7	4.4713	2.2438	86.4475
8	4.3541	2.3609	84.0865
9	4.2309	2.4842	81.6023
10	4.1012	2.6139	78.9884
11	3.9647	2.7504	76.2381
12	3.8211	2.8940	73.3441
13	3.6700	3.0450	70.2991
14	3.5110	3.2040	67.0950
15	3.3438	3.3713	63.7237
16	3.1678	3.5473	60.1764
17	2.9826	3.7325	56.4439
18	2.7877	3.9274	52.5165
19	2.5826	4.1324	48.3841
20	2.3669	4.3482	44.0359
21	2.1399	4.5752	39.4607
22	1.9010	4.8141	34.6466
23	1.6497	5.0654	29.5812
24	1.3852	5.3299	24.2513
25	1.1069	5.6081	18.6432
26	.8141	5.9009	12.7422
27	.5061	6.2090	6.5332
28	.1819	6.5332	0.0000

YEARS 29   MO PAYT .5509   AN CONST 6.62

#	INT	PRIN	BALANCE
1	5.0642	1.5470	98.4530
2	4.9834	1.6278	96.8252
3	4.8984	1.7128	95.1124
4	4.8090	1.8022	93.3102
5	4.7149	1.8963	91.4139
6	4.6159	1.9953	89.4186
7	4.5117	2.0995	87.3192
8	4.4021	2.2091	85.1101
9	4.2868	2.3244	82.7857
10	4.1654	2.4458	80.3399
11	4.0377	2.5735	77.7665
12	3.9034	2.7078	75.0587
13	3.7620	2.8492	72.2095
14	3.6133	2.9979	69.2115
15	3.4567	3.1545	66.0571
16	3.2920	3.3192	62.7379
17	3.1187	3.4924	59.2455
18	2.9364	3.6748	55.5707
19	2.7446	3.8666	51.7041
20	2.5427	4.0685	47.6356
21	2.3303	4.2809	43.3546
22	2.1068	4.5044	38.8502
23	1.8716	4.7396	34.1106
24	1.6241	4.9871	29.1235
25	1.3638	5.2474	23.8761
26	1.0898	5.5214	18.3547
27	.8015	5.8097	12.5451
28	.4982	6.1130	6.4321
29	.1791	6.4321	0.0000

YEARS 30   MO PAYT .5429   AN CONST 6.52

#	INT	PRIN	BALANCE
1	5.0664	1.4490	98.5510
2	4.9908	1.5246	97.0264
3	4.9112	1.6042	95.4222
4	4.8274	1.6880	93.7343
5	4.7393	1.7761	91.9582
6	4.6466	1.8688	90.0894
7	4.5490	1.9664	88.1230
8	4.4464	2.0690	86.0540
9	4.3383	2.1771	83.8769
10	4.2247	2.2907	81.5862
11	4.1051	2.4103	79.1758
12	3.9792	2.5362	76.6397
13	3.8468	2.6686	73.9711
14	3.7075	2.8079	71.1632
15	3.5609	2.9545	68.2087
16	3.4066	3.1088	65.0999
17	3.2443	3.2711	61.8289
18	3.0736	3.4418	58.3870
19	2.8939	3.6215	54.7655
20	2.7048	3.8106	50.9549
21	2.5058	4.0096	46.9453
22	2.2965	4.2189	42.7264
23	2.0762	4.4392	38.2873
24	1.8445	4.6709	33.6164
25	1.6006	4.9148	28.7016
26	1.3440	5.1714	23.5302
27	1.0740	5.4414	18.0888
28	.7899	5.7255	12.3633
29	.4910	6.0244	6.3389
30	.1765	6.3389	0.0000

YEARS 2 — MO PAYT 4.3927 — AN CONST 52.72

#	INT	PRIN	BALANCE
1	3.9911	48.7218	51.2782
2	1.4346	51.2782	0.0000

YEARS 3 — MO PAYT 3.0027 — AN CONST 36.04

#	INT	PRIN	BALANCE
1	4.3886	31.6439	68.3561
2	2.7282	33.3043	35.0518
3	.9807	35.0518	0.0000

YEARS 4 — MO PAYT 2.3086 — AN CONST 27.71

#	INT	PRIN	BALANCE
1	4.5870	23.1161	76.8839
2	3.3741	24.3291	52.5548
3	2.0975	25.6056	26.9492
4	.7540	26.9492	0.0000

YEARS 5 — MO PAYT 1.8929 — AN CONST 22.72

#	INT	PRIN	BALANCE
1	4.7059	18.0084	81.9916
2	3.7610	18.9553	63.0383
3	2.7665	19.9478	43.0906
4	1.7198	20.9945	22.0961
5	.6182	22.0961	0.0000

YEARS 6 — MO PAYT 1.6163 — AN CONST 19.40

#	INT	PRIN	BALANCE
1	4.7850	14.6106	85.3894
2	4.0183	15.3772	70.0122
3	3.2115	16.1841	53.8281
4	2.3623	17.0333	36.7948
5	1.4685	17.9271	18.8677
6	.5279	18.8677	0.0000

YEARS 7 — MO PAYT 1.4193 — AN CONST 17.04

#	INT	PRIN	BALANCE
1	4.8413	12.1900	87.8100
2	4.2017	12.8296	74.9805
3	3.5285	13.5028	61.4777
4	2.8200	14.2113	47.2664
5	2.0743	14.9569	32.3095
6	1.2895	15.7418	16.5677
7	.4635	16.5677	0.0000

YEARS 8 — MO PAYT 1.2720 — AN CONST 15.27

#	INT	PRIN	BALANCE
1	4.8834	10.3800	89.6200
2	4.3388	10.9246	78.6954
3	3.7656	11.4979	67.1975
4	3.1622	12.1012	55.0963
5	2.5273	12.7361	42.3602
6	1.8590	13.4044	28.9558
7	1.1557	14.1078	14.8480
8	.4154	14.8480	0.0000

YEARS 9 — MO PAYT 1.1578 — AN CONST 13.90

#	INT	PRIN	BALANCE
1	4.9161	8.9771	91.0229
2	4.4450	9.4482	81.5747
3	3.9493	9.9439	71.6308
4	3.4275	10.4657	61.1651
5	2.8784	11.0148	50.1503
6	2.3004	11.5928	38.5575
7	1.6921	12.2011	26.3564
8	1.0519	12.8413	13.5151
9	.3781	13.5151	0.0000

YEARS 10 — MO PAYT 1.0668 — AN CONST 12.81

#	INT	PRIN	BALANCE
1	4.9421	7.8592	92.1408
2	4.5297	8.2716	83.8692
3	4.0957	8.7056	75.1636
4	3.6389	9.1624	66.0012
5	3.1581	9.6432	56.3580
6	2.6521	10.1492	46.2088
7	2.1196	10.6817	35.5272
8	1.5591	11.2422	24.2850
9	.9692	11.8321	12.4529
10	.3484	12.4529	0.0000

YEARS 11 — MO PAYT .9927 — AN CONST 11.92

#	INT	PRIN	BALANCE
1	4.9633	6.9485	93.0515
2	4.5987	7.3131	85.7384
3	4.2150	7.6968	78.0415
4	3.8111	8.1007	69.9408
5	3.3861	8.5258	61.4151
6	2.9387	8.9731	52.4420
7	2.4679	9.4439	42.9980
8	1.9723	9.9395	33.0585
9	1.4508	10.4610	22.5975
10	.9019	11.0099	11.5876
11	.3242	11.5876	0.0000

YEARS 12 — MO PAYT .9312 — AN CONST 11.18

#	INT	PRIN	BALANCE
1	4.9809	6.1932	93.8068
2	4.6559	6.5182	87.2886
3	4.3139	6.8602	80.4284
4	3.9539	7.2202	73.2082
5	3.5751	7.5990	65.6092
6	3.1763	7.9977	57.6115
7	2.7567	8.4174	49.1941
8	2.3150	8.8591	40.3351
9	1.8502	9.3239	31.0112
10	1.3609	9.8131	21.1980
11	.8460	10.3280	10.8700
12	.3041	10.8700	0.0000

YEARS 13 — MO PAYT .8794 — AN CONST 10.56

#	INT	PRIN	BALANCE
1	4.9957	5.5574	94.4426
2	4.7041	5.8490	88.5935
3	4.3972	6.1559	82.4376
4	4.0741	6.4789	75.9587
5	3.7342	6.8189	69.1398
6	3.3764	7.1767	61.9631
7	2.9998	7.5533	54.4098
8	2.6035	7.9496	46.4602
9	2.1864	8.3667	38.0935
10	1.7474	8.8057	29.2877
11	1.2853	9.2678	20.0200
12	.7990	9.7541	10.2659
13	.2872	10.2659	0.0000

YEARS 14 — MO PAYT .8353 — AN CONST 10.03

#	INT	PRIN	BALANCE
1	5.0083	5.0155	94.9845
2	4.7451	5.2787	89.7058
3	4.4681	5.5557	84.1501
4	4.1766	5.8472	78.3029
5	3.8698	6.1540	72.1489
6	3.5469	6.4769	65.6720
7	3.2070	6.8168	58.8553
8	2.8494	7.1744	51.6809
9	2.4729	7.5509	44.1300
10	2.0767	7.9471	36.1829
11	1.6597	8.3641	27.8188
12	1.2208	8.8030	19.0158
13	.7589	9.2649	9.7510
14	.2728	9.7510	0.0000

YEARS 15 — MO PAYT .7973 — AN CONST 9.57

#	INT	PRIN	BALANCE
1	5.0191	4.5487	95.4513
2	4.7805	4.7874	90.6639
3	4.5293	5.0386	85.6253
4	4.2649	5.3030	80.3224
5	3.9866	5.5812	74.7412
6	3.6938	5.8741	68.8671
7	3.3856	6.1823	62.6848
8	3.0612	6.5067	56.1781
9	2.7198	6.8481	49.3300
10	2.3604	7.2074	42.1226
11	1.9822	7.5856	34.5370
12	1.5842	7.9836	26.5534
13	1.1653	8.4025	18.1509
14	.7244	8.8434	9.3074
15	.2604	9.3074	0.0000

YEARS 16 — MO PAYT .7643 — AN CONST 9.18

#	INT	PRIN	BALANCE
1	5.0286	4.1429	95.8571
2	4.8112	4.3603	91.4969
3	4.5824	4.5890	86.9078
4	4.3416	4.8298	82.0780
5	4.0882	5.0833	76.9947
6	3.8215	5.3500	71.6447
7	3.5408	5.6307	66.0140
8	3.2453	5.9262	60.0879
9	2.9343	6.2371	53.8507
10	2.6071	6.5644	47.2864
11	2.2626	6.9088	40.3775
12	1.9001	7.2713	33.1062
13	1.5186	7.6529	25.4533
14	1.1170	8.0544	17.3989
15	.6944	8.4771	8.9219
16	.2496	8.9219	0.0000

YEARS 17 — MO PAYT .7353 — AN CONST 8.83

#	INT	PRIN	BALANCE
1	5.0369	3.7873	96.2127
2	4.8381	3.9860	92.2268
3	4.6290	4.1951	88.0316
4	4.4089	4.4152	83.6164
5	4.1772	4.6469	78.9695
6	3.9334	4.8907	74.0787
7	3.6767	5.1474	68.9314
8	3.4067	5.4175	63.5139
9	3.1224	5.7017	57.8122
10	2.8232	6.0009	51.8113
11	2.5083	6.3158	45.4955
12	2.1769	6.6472	38.8483
13	1.8282	6.9960	31.8524
14	1.4611	7.3630	24.4893
15	1.0747	7.7494	16.7400
16	.6681	8.1560	8.5840
17	.2402	8.5840	0.0000

YEARS 18 — MO PAYT .7098 — AN CONST 8.52

#	INT	PRIN	BALANCE
1	5.0442	3.4734	96.5266
2	4.8619	3.6557	92.8708
3	4.6701	3.8475	89.0233
4	4.4682	4.0494	84.9739
5	4.2557	4.2619	80.7120
6	4.0321	4.4855	76.2265
7	3.7967	4.7209	71.5056
8	3.5490	4.9686	66.5371
9	3.2883	5.2293	61.3078
10	3.0139	5.5037	55.8041
11	2.7252	5.7925	50.0116
12	2.4212	6.0964	43.9152
13	2.1013	6.4163	37.4990
14	1.7647	6.7530	30.7460
15	1.4103	7.1073	23.6387
16	1.0374	7.4802	16.1585
17	.6449	7.8727	8.2858
18	.2318	8.2858	0.0000

YEARS 19 — MO PAYT .6871 — AN CONST 8.25

#	INT	PRIN	BALANCE
1	5.0506	3.1948	96.8052
2	4.8830	3.3625	93.4427
3	4.7066	3.5389	89.9038
4	4.5209	3.7246	86.1792
5	4.3255	3.9200	82.2591
6	4.1198	4.1257	78.1334
7	3.9033	4.3422	73.7912
8	3.6754	4.5700	69.2211
9	3.4356	4.8098	64.4113
10	3.1833	5.0622	59.3491
11	2.9176	5.3278	54.0212
12	2.6381	5.6074	48.4138
13	2.3439	5.9016	42.5122
14	2.0342	6.2113	36.3009
15	1.7083	6.5372	29.7637
16	1.3653	6.8802	22.8835
17	1.0043	7.2412	15.6423
18	.6243	7.6212	8.0211
19	.2244	8.0211	0.0000

YEARS 20 — MO PAYT .6669 — AN CONST 8.01

#	INT	PRIN	BALANCE
1	5.0564	2.9461	97.0539
2	4.9018	3.1007	93.9532
3	4.7392	3.2634	90.6897
4	4.5679	3.4347	87.2551
5	4.3877	3.6149	83.6402
6	4.1980	3.8045	79.8357
7	3.9984	4.0042	75.8315
8	3.7883	4.2143	71.6172
9	3.5672	4.4354	67.1818
10	3.3344	4.6681	62.5137
11	3.0895	4.9131	57.6006
12	2.8317	5.1709	52.4297
13	2.5604	5.4422	46.9875
14	2.2748	5.7278	41.2598
15	1.9743	6.0283	35.2315
16	1.6580	6.3446	28.8868
17	1.3250	6.6775	22.2093
18	.9747	7.0279	15.1814
19	.6059	7.3967	7.7848
20	.2178	7.7848	0.0000

YEARS 21 — MO PAYT .6487 — AN CONST 7.79

#	INT	PRIN	BALANCE
1	5.0616	2.7230	97.2770
2	4.9187	2.8659	94.4111
3	4.7684	3.0163	91.3948

#	INT	PRIN	BALANCE
4	4.6101	3.1746	88.2202
5	4.4435	3.3411	84.8791
6	4.2682	3.5164	81.3627
7	4.0837	3.7009	77.6617
8	3.8895	3.8951	73.7666
9	3.6851	4.0995	69.6671
10	3.4700	4.3146	65.3524
11	3.2436	4.5410	60.8114
12	3.0054	4.7793	56.0321
13	2.7546	5.0301	51.0020
14	2.4906	5.2940	45.7080
15	2.2129	5.5718	40.1362
16	1.9205	5.8641	34.2721
17	1.6128	6.1718	28.1002
18	1.2890	6.4957	21.6046
19	.9481	6.8365	14.7680
20	.5894	7.1952	7.5728
21	.2119	7.5728	0.0000

YEARS 22 — MO PAYT .6324 — AN CONST 7.59

#	INT	PRIN	BALANCE
1	5.0663	2.5220	97.4780
2	4.9340	2.6544	94.8236
3	4.7947	2.7936	92.0300
4	4.6481	2.9402	89.0898
5	4.4938	3.0945	85.9953
6	4.3315	3.2569	82.7384
7	4.1606	3.4278	79.3107
8	3.9807	3.6076	75.7031
9	3.7914	3.7969	71.9062
10	3.5922	3.9961	67.9100
11	3.3825	4.2058	63.7042
12	3.1618	4.4265	59.2777
13	2.9296	4.6588	54.6190
14	2.6851	4.9032	49.7158
15	2.4278	5.1605	44.5553
16	2.1571	5.4313	39.1240
17	1.8721	5.7163	33.4077
18	1.5721	6.0162	27.3916
19	1.2565	6.3319	21.0597
20	.9242	6.6641	14.3956
21	.5745	7.0138	7.3818
22	.2065	7.3818	0.0000

YEARS 23 — MO PAYT .6176 — AN CONST 7.42

#	INT	PRIN	BALANCE
1	5.0705	2.3402	97.6598
2	4.9477	2.4630	95.1968
3	4.8185	2.5922	92.6046
4	4.6825	2.7283	89.8763
5	4.5393	2.8714	87.0049
6	4.3887	3.0221	83.9828
7	4.2301	3.1806	80.8022
8	4.0632	3.3475	77.4547
9	3.8876	3.5232	73.9315
10	3.7027	3.7080	70.2234
11	3.5081	3.9026	66.3208
12	3.3034	4.1074	62.2134
13	3.0878	4.3229	57.8905
14	2.8610	4.5497	53.3408
15	2.6223	4.7885	48.5523
16	2.3710	5.0397	43.5126
17	2.1066	5.3042	38.2084
18	1.8283	5.5825	32.6259
19	1.5353	5.8754	26.7505
20	1.2271	6.1837	20.5668
21	.9026	6.5082	14.0587
22	.5611	6.8496	7.2091
23	.2017	7.2091	0.0000

YEARS 24 — MO PAYT .6041 — AN CONST 7.25

#	INT	PRIN	BALANCE
1	5.0744	2.1752	97.8248
2	4.9602	2.2893	95.5355
3	4.8401	2.4094	93.1261
4	4.7137	2.5358	90.5903
5	4.5806	2.6689	87.9214
6	4.4406	2.8089	85.1124
7	4.2932	2.9563	82.1561
8	4.1381	3.1115	79.0446
9	3.9748	3.2747	75.7699
10	3.8030	3.4465	72.3233
11	3.6222	3.6274	68.6959
12	3.4318	3.8177	64.8782
13	3.2315	4.0180	60.8602
14	3.0207	4.2289	56.6313
15	2.7988	4.4508	52.1805
16	2.5652	4.6843	47.4962
17	2.3194	4.9301	42.5661
18	2.0608	5.1888	37.3773
19	1.7885	5.4611	31.9163
20	1.5019	5.7476	26.1687
21	1.2004	6.0492	20.1195
22	.8830	6.3666	13.7529
23	.5489	6.7007	7.0522
24	.1973	7.0522	0.0000

YEARS 25 — MO PAYT .5919 — AN CONST 7.11

#	INT	PRIN	BALANCE
1	5.0779	2.0249	97.9751
2	4.9716	2.1311	95.8440
3	4.8598	2.2429	93.6011
4	4.7421	2.3606	91.2404
5	4.6183	2.4845	88.7559
6	4.4879	2.6149	86.1411
7	4.3507	2.7521	83.3890
8	4.2063	2.8965	80.4925
9	4.0543	3.0485	77.4441
10	3.8943	3.2084	74.2356
11	3.7260	3.3768	70.8589
12	3.5488	3.5539	67.3049
13	3.3623	3.7404	63.5645
14	3.1661	3.9367	59.6278
15	2.9595	4.1432	55.4846
16	2.7421	4.3607	51.1239
17	2.5133	4.5895	46.5345
18	2.2725	4.8303	41.7042
19	2.0190	5.0837	36.6205
20	1.7523	5.3505	31.2700
21	1.4715	5.6312	25.6388
22	1.1761	5.9267	19.7121
23	.8651	6.2377	13.4744
24	.5378	6.5650	6.9094
25	.1933	6.9094	0.0000

YEARS 26 — MO PAYT .5807 — AN CONST 6.97

#	INT	PRIN	BALANCE
1	5.0811	1.8876	98.1124
2	4.9820	1.9867	96.1257
3	4.8778	2.0909	94.0348
4	4.7681	2.2006	91.8342
5	4.6526	2.3161	89.5182
6	4.5311	2.4376	87.0806
7	4.4032	2.5655	84.5150
8	4.2686	2.7001	81.8149
9	4.1269	2.8418	78.9731
10	3.9778	2.9909	75.9822
11	3.8208	3.1478	72.8344
12	3.6557	3.3130	69.5213
13	3.4818	3.4869	66.0345
14	3.2989	3.6698	62.3647
15	3.1063	3.8624	58.5023
16	2.9036	4.0650	54.4372
17	2.6903	4.2783	50.1589
18	2.4659	4.5028	45.6561
19	2.2296	4.7391	40.9170
20	1.9809	4.9878	35.9292
21	1.7192	5.2495	30.6797
22	1.4438	5.5249	25.1548
23	1.1539	5.8148	19.3400
24	.8487	6.1199	13.2201
25	.5276	6.4411	6.7790
26	.1897	6.7790	0.0000

YEARS 27 — MO PAYT .5705 — AN CONST 6.85

#	INT	PRIN	BALANCE
1	5.0840	1.7619	98.2381
2	4.9915	1.8544	96.3837
3	4.8942	1.9517	94.4321
4	4.7918	2.0541	92.3780
5	4.6841	2.1618	90.2162
6	4.5706	2.2753	87.9409
7	4.4512	2.3947	85.5463
8	4.3256	2.5203	83.0260
9	4.1933	2.6525	80.3734
10	4.0542	2.7917	77.5817
11	3.9077	2.9382	74.6435
12	3.7535	3.0924	71.5511
13	3.5912	3.2546	68.2964
14	3.4205	3.4254	64.8710
15	3.2407	3.6052	61.2659
16	3.0516	3.7943	57.4715
17	2.8525	3.9934	53.4781
18	2.6429	4.2030	49.2752
19	2.4224	4.4235	44.8517
20	2.1903	4.6556	40.1961
21	1.9460	4.8999	35.2962
22	1.6889	5.1570	30.1392
23	1.4183	5.4276	24.7116
24	1.1335	5.7124	18.9993
25	.8338	6.0121	12.9871
26	.5183	6.3276	6.6596
27	.1863	6.6596	0.0000

YEARS 28 — MO PAYT .5611 — AN CONST 6.74

#	INT	PRIN	BALANCE
1	5.0867	1.6465	98.3535
2	5.0003	1.7329	96.6206
3	4.9094	1.8238	94.7968
4	4.8137	1.9195	92.8773
5	4.7129	2.0202	90.8570
6	4.6069	2.1262	88.7308
7	4.4954	2.2378	86.4930
8	4.3780	2.3552	84.1378
9	4.2544	2.4788	81.6590
10	4.1243	2.6089	79.0501
11	3.9874	2.7458	76.3043
12	3.8433	2.8898	73.4145
13	3.6917	3.0415	70.3730
14	3.5321	3.2011	67.1719
15	3.3642	3.3690	63.8029
16	3.1874	3.5458	60.2571
17	3.0013	3.7319	56.5253
18	2.8055	3.9277	52.5976
19	2.5994	4.1338	48.4638
20	2.3825	4.3507	44.1132
21	2.1542	4.5789	39.5342
22	1.9140	4.8192	34.7150
23	1.6611	5.0721	29.6430
24	1.3950	5.3382	24.3047
25	1.1149	5.6183	18.6864
26	.8201	5.9131	12.7733
27	.5098	6.2234	6.5499
28	.1832	6.5499	0.0000

YEARS 29 — MO PAYT .5525 — AN CONST 6.63

#	INT	PRIN	BALANCE
1	5.0892	1.5403	98.4597
2	5.0083	1.6211	96.8385
3	4.9233	1.7062	95.1323
4	4.8337	1.7957	93.3366
5	4.7395	1.8900	91.4467
6	4.6403	1.9891	89.4576
7	4.5360	2.0935	87.3641
8	4.4261	2.2033	85.1607
9	4.3105	2.3189	82.8418
10	4.1888	2.4406	80.4011
11	4.0608	2.5687	77.8325
12	3.9260	2.7035	75.1290
13	3.7841	2.8453	72.2837
14	3.6348	2.9946	69.2890
15	3.4777	3.1518	66.1373
16	3.3123	3.3171	62.8202
17	3.1383	3.4912	59.3290
18	2.9551	3.6744	55.6546
19	2.7623	3.8672	51.7874
20	2.5594	4.0701	47.7173
21	2.3458	4.2836	43.4337
22	2.1211	4.5084	38.9253
23	1.8845	4.7450	34.1803
24	1.6355	4.9939	29.1864
25	1.3735	5.2560	23.9304
26	1.0977	5.5318	18.3986
27	.8074	5.8220	12.5766
28	.5019	6.1275	6.4490
29	.1804	6.4490	0.0000

YEARS 30 — MO PAYT .5445 — AN CONST 6.54

#	INT	PRIN	BALANCE
1	5.0914	1.4424	98.5576
2	5.0157	1.5181	97.0395
3	4.9361	1.5978	95.4417
4	4.8523	1.6816	93.7601
5	4.7640	1.7698	91.9903
6	4.6712	1.8627	90.1276
7	4.5734	1.9604	88.1672
8	4.4706	2.0633	86.1039
9	4.3623	2.1716	83.9324
10	4.2483	2.2855	81.6469
11	4.1284	2.4054	79.2414
12	4.0022	2.5316	76.7098
13	3.8694	2.6645	74.0453
14	3.7296	2.8043	71.2410
15	3.5824	2.9514	68.2896
16	3.4276	3.1063	65.1833
17	3.2646	3.2693	61.9140
18	3.0930	3.4408	58.4732
19	2.9125	3.6214	54.8518
20	2.7225	3.8114	51.0404
21	2.5225	4.0114	47.0291
22	2.3120	4.2219	42.8072
23	2.0905	4.4434	38.3638
24	1.8573	4.6765	33.6873
25	1.6119	4.9219	28.7654
26	1.3537	5.1802	23.5852
27	1.0819	5.4520	18.1332
28	.7958	5.7381	12.3952
29	.4947	6.0391	6.3560
30	.1778	6.3560	0.0000

MONTHLY PAYMENT AMORTIZATION SCHEDULE PER $100   5.20 %

YEARS 2 — MO PAYT 4.3961 — AN CONST 52.76

#	INT	PRIN	BALANCE
1	4.0501	48.7031	51.2969
2	1.4563	51.2969	0.0000

YEARS 3 — MO PAYT 3.0061 — AN CONST 36.08

#	INT	PRIN	BALANCE
1	4.4535	31.6195	68.3805
2	2.7695	33.3034	35.0771
3	.9958	35.0771	0.0000

YEARS 4 — MO PAYT 2.3120 — AN CONST 27.75

#	INT	PRIN	BALANCE
1	4.6549	23.0891	76.9109
2	3.4252	24.3188	52.5921
3	2.1300	25.6140	26.9781
4	.7659	26.9781	0.0000

YEARS 5 — MO PAYT 1.8963 — AN CONST 22.76

#	INT	PRIN	BALANCE
1	4.7755	17.9801	82.0199
2	3.8179	18.9377	63.0822
3	2.8093	19.9463	43.1359
4	1.7471	21.0085	22.1274
5	.6282	22.1274	0.0000

YEARS 6 — MO PAYT 1.6198 — AN CONST 19.44

#	INT	PRIN	BALANCE
1	4.8557	14.5817	85.4183
2	4.0791	15.3583	70.0600
3	3.2612	16.1762	53.8837
4	2.3997	17.0378	36.8460
5	1.4923	17.9451	18.9008
6	.5366	18.9008	0.0000

YEARS 7 — MO PAYT 1.4228 — AN CONST 17.08

#	INT	PRIN	BALANCE
1	4.9129	12.1608	87.8392
2	4.2652	12.8085	75.0307
3	3.5831	13.4906	61.5401
4	2.8646	14.2091	47.3310
5	2.1079	14.9658	32.3652
6	1.3108	15.7629	16.6024
7	.4713	16.6024	0.0000

YEARS 8 — MO PAYT 1.2755 — AN CONST 15.31

#	INT	PRIN	BALANCE
1	4.9556	10.3508	89.6492
2	4.4044	10.9021	78.7471
3	3.8237	11.4827	67.2644
4	3.2122	12.0942	55.1702
5	2.5681	12.7383	42.4319
6	1.8897	13.4167	29.0152
7	1.1751	14.1313	14.8839
8	.4226	14.8839	0.0000

YEARS 9 — MO PAYT 1.1614 — AN CONST 13.94

#	INT	PRIN	BALANCE
1	4.9887	8.9481	91.0519
2	4.5122	9.4246	81.6273
3	4.0103	9.9265	71.7008
4	3.4816	10.4552	61.2456
5	2.9248	11.0120	50.2336
6	2.3383	11.5985	38.6351
7	1.7206	12.2162	26.4189
8	1.0700	12.8668	13.5521
9	.3847	13.5521	0.0000

YEARS 10 — MO PAYT 1.0705 — AN CONST 12.85

#	INT	PRIN	BALANCE
1	5.0151	7.8304	92.1696
2	4.5981	8.2474	83.9222
3	4.1589	8.6866	75.2356
4	3.6962	9.1493	66.0863
5	3.2090	9.6365	56.4498
6	2.6958	10.1497	46.3001
7	2.1552	10.6903	35.6098
8	1.5859	11.2596	24.3502
9	.9862	11.8593	12.4909
10	.3546	12.4909	0.0000

YEARS 11 — MO PAYT .9964 — AN CONST 11.96

#	INT	PRIN	BALANCE
1	5.0366	6.9200	93.0800
2	4.6681	7.2885	85.7915
3	4.2799	7.6767	78.1148
4	3.8711	8.0855	70.0293
5	3.4405	8.5161	61.5132
6	2.9869	8.9697	52.5435
7	2.5092	9.4474	43.0961
8	2.0061	9.9505	33.1456
9	1.4761	10.4805	22.6651
10	.9180	11.0386	11.6265
11	.3301	11.6265	0.0000

YEARS 12 — MO PAYT .9350 — AN CONST 11.22

#	INT	PRIN	BALANCE
1	5.0544	6.1650	93.8350
2	4.7261	6.4934	87.3416
3	4.3803	6.8392	80.5025
4	4.0161	7.2034	73.2990
5	3.6324	7.5870	65.7120
6	3.2284	7.9911	57.7209
7	2.8028	8.4167	49.3042
8	2.3545	8.8649	40.4392
9	1.8824	9.3371	31.1022
10	1.3851	9.8343	21.2678
11	.8614	10.3581	10.9097
12	.3097	10.9097	0.0000

YEARS 13 — MO PAYT .8833 — AN CONST 10.60

#	INT	PRIN	BALANCE
1	5.0694	5.5296	94.4704
2	4.7750	5.8241	88.6463
3	4.4648	6.1343	82.5120
4	4.1381	6.4610	76.0510
5	3.7940	6.8051	69.2459
6	3.4316	7.1675	62.0784
7	3.0498	7.5492	54.5291
8	2.6478	7.9513	46.5779
9	2.2243	8.3747	38.2031
10	1.7783	8.8208	29.3823
11	1.3085	9.2905	20.0918
12	.8137	9.7853	10.3065
13	.2926	10.3065	0.0000

YEARS 14 — MO PAYT .8392 — AN CONST 10.08

#	INT	PRIN	BALANCE
1	5.0822	4.9881	95.0119
2	4.8166	5.2538	89.7581
3	4.5368	5.5336	84.2245
4	4.2421	5.8283	78.3961
5	3.9317	6.1387	72.2574
6	3.6047	6.4656	65.7918
7	3.2604	6.8100	58.9818
8	2.8977	7.1727	51.8091
9	2.5157	7.5547	44.2545
10	2.1134	7.9570	36.2975
11	1.6896	8.3808	27.9167
12	1.2433	8.8271	19.0896
13	.7732	9.2972	9.7924
14	.2780	9.7924	0.0000

YEARS 15 — MO PAYT .8013 — AN CONST 9.62

#	INT	PRIN	BALANCE
1	5.0932	4.5218	95.4782
2	4.8524	4.7626	90.7156
3	4.5988	5.0162	85.6994
4	4.3316	5.2834	80.4160
5	4.0502	5.5648	74.8513
6	3.7539	5.8611	68.9901
7	3.4417	6.1733	62.8168
8	3.1130	6.5021	56.3148
9	2.7667	6.8483	49.4665
10	2.4020	7.2131	42.2534
11	2.0178	7.5972	34.6562
12	1.6132	8.0018	26.6544
13	1.1870	8.4280	18.2264
14	.7382	8.8768	9.3496
15	.2654	9.3496	0.0000

YEARS 16 — MO PAYT .7683 — AN CONST 9.22

#	INT	PRIN	BALANCE
1	5.1028	4.1164	95.8836
2	4.8836	4.3356	91.5480
3	4.6527	4.5665	86.9814
4	4.4095	4.8097	82.1717
5	4.1533	5.0659	77.1058
6	3.8835	5.3357	71.7701
7	3.5994	5.6199	66.1502
8	3.3001	5.9192	60.2310
9	2.9848	6.2344	53.9966
10	2.6528	6.5664	47.4302
11	2.3031	6.9161	40.5141
12	1.9347	7.2845	33.2296
13	1.5468	7.6724	25.5572
14	1.1382	8.0810	17.4761
15	.7078	8.5114	8.9647
16	.2545	8.9647	0.0000

YEARS 17 — MO PAYT .7394 — AN CONST 8.88

#	INT	PRIN	BALANCE
1	5.1112	3.7613	96.2387
2	4.9109	3.9616	92.2772
3	4.6999	4.1726	88.1046
4	4.4777	4.3948	83.7098
5	4.2436	4.6288	79.0810
6	3.9971	4.8754	74.2056
7	3.7375	5.1350	69.0706
8	3.4640	5.4085	63.6621
9	3.1759	5.6965	57.9656
10	2.8726	5.9999	51.9657
11	2.5530	6.3194	45.6462
12	2.2165	6.6560	38.9902
13	1.8620	7.0105	31.9797
14	1.4886	7.3838	24.5959
15	1.0954	7.7771	16.8188
16	.6812	8.1913	8.6275
17	.2449	8.6275	0.0000

YEARS 18 — MO PAYT .7139 — AN CONST 8.57

#	INT	PRIN	BALANCE
1	5.1186	3.4479	96.5521
2	4.9350	3.6316	92.9205
3	4.7416	3.8250	89.0955
4	4.5378	4.0287	85.0668
5	4.3233	4.2433	80.8235
6	4.0973	4.4692	76.3543
7	3.8593	4.7073	71.6470
8	3.6086	4.9580	66.6891
9	3.3445	5.2220	61.4671
10	3.0664	5.5001	55.9670
11	2.7735	5.7930	50.1739
12	2.4650	6.1016	44.0724
13	2.1400	6.4265	37.6459
14	1.7978	6.7688	30.8771
15	1.4373	7.1293	23.7478
16	1.0576	7.5089	16.2389
17	.6577	7.9088	8.3301
18	.2365	8.3301	0.0000

YEARS 19 — MO PAYT .6912 — AN CONST 8.30

#	INT	PRIN	BALANCE
1	5.1252	3.1698	96.8302
2	4.9563	3.3387	93.4915
3	4.7785	3.5165	89.9750
4	4.5913	3.7037	86.2713
5	4.3940	3.9010	82.3703
6	4.1862	4.1087	78.2616
7	3.9674	4.3276	73.9340
8	3.7370	4.5580	69.3759
9	3.4942	4.8008	64.5751
10	3.2385	5.0565	59.5187
11	2.9692	5.3258	54.1929
12	2.6856	5.6094	48.5835
13	2.3869	5.9081	42.6754
14	2.0722	6.2228	36.4526
15	1.7408	6.5542	29.8983
16	1.3917	6.9033	22.9951
17	1.0241	7.2709	15.7242
18	.6368	7.6582	8.0660
19	.2290	8.0660	0.0000

YEARS 20 — MO PAYT .6711 — AN CONST 8.06

#	INT	PRIN	BALANCE
1	5.1310	2.9216	97.0784
2	4.9754	3.0772	94.0011
3	4.8115	3.2411	90.7600
4	4.6389	3.4137	87.3463
5	4.4571	3.5955	83.7508
6	4.2656	3.7870	79.9638
7	4.0639	3.9887	75.9750
8	3.8515	4.2011	71.7739
9	3.6278	4.4249	67.3490
10	3.3921	4.6605	62.6885
11	3.1439	4.9087	57.7798
12	2.8825	5.1702	52.6096
13	2.6071	5.4455	47.1641
14	2.3171	5.7355	41.4285
15	2.0117	6.0410	35.3875
16	1.6899	6.3627	29.0248
17	1.3511	6.7016	22.3232
18	.9942	7.0585	15.2648
19	.6182	7.4344	7.8303
20	.2223	7.8303	0.0000

YEARS 21 — MO PAYT .6529 — AN CONST 7.84

#	INT	PRIN	BALANCE
1	5.1363	2.6990	97.3010
2	4.9925	2.8428	94.4582
3	4.8411	2.9942	91.4640

#	INT	PRIN	BALANCE
4	4.6817	3.1536	88.3104
5	4.5137	3.3216	84.9888
6	4.3368	3.4985	81.4903
7	4.1505	3.6848	77.8055
8	3.9543	3.8811	73.9245
9	3.7476	4.0877	69.8367
10	3.5299	4.3054	65.5313
11	3.3006	4.5347	60.9965
12	3.0591	4.7763	56.2203
13	2.8047	5.0306	51.1896
14	2.5368	5.2985	45.8911
15	2.2546	5.5807	40.3104
16	1.9574	5.8779	34.4324
17	1.6443	6.1910	28.2414
18	1.3146	6.5207	21.7207
19	.9673	6.8680	14.8528
20	.6016	7.2338	7.6190
21	.2163	7.6190	0.0000

YEARS 22	MO PAYT .6366	AN CONST 7.64	
#	INT	PRIN	BALANCE
1	5.1410	2.4985	97.5015
2	5.0079	2.6316	94.8699
3	4.8678	2.7717	92.0981
4	4.7202	2.9194	89.1788
5	4.5647	3.0748	86.1039
6	4.4009	3.2386	82.8653
7	4.2285	3.4111	79.4543
8	4.0468	3.5927	75.8615
9	3.8555	3.7841	72.0774
10	3.6539	3.9856	68.0918
11	3.4417	4.1979	63.8939
12	3.2181	4.4214	59.4725
13	2.9826	4.6569	54.8156
14	2.7346	4.9049	49.9107
15	2.4734	5.1662	44.7445
16	2.1982	5.4413	39.3032
17	1.9085	5.7311	33.5721
18	1.6032	6.0363	27.5358
19	1.2818	6.3578	21.1780
20	.9432	6.6964	14.4817
21	.5865	7.0530	7.4286
22	.2109	7.4286	0.0000

YEARS 23	MO PAYT .6219	AN CONST 7.47	
#	INT	PRIN	BALANCE
1	5.1453	2.3172	97.6828
2	5.0219	2.4406	95.2421
3	4.8919	2.5706	92.6715
4	4.7550	2.7075	89.9640
5	4.6108	2.8517	87.1123
6	4.4589	3.0036	84.1087
7	4.2990	3.1636	80.9452
8	4.1305	3.3320	77.6131
9	3.9530	3.5095	74.1036
10	3.7661	3.6964	70.4072
11	3.5693	3.8933	66.5140
12	3.3619	4.1006	62.4134
13	3.1435	4.3190	58.0944
14	2.9135	4.5490	53.5454
15	2.6712	4.7913	48.7541
16	2.4161	5.0464	43.7077
17	2.1473	5.3152	38.3925
18	1.8642	5.5983	32.7942
19	1.5661	5.8964	26.8978
20	1.2521	6.2105	20.6873
21	.9213	6.5412	14.1461
22	.5729	6.8896	7.2565
23	.2060	7.2565	0.0000

YEARS 24	MO PAYT .6085	AN CONST 7.31	
#	INT	PRIN	BALANCE
1	5.1492	2.1527	97.8473
2	5.0345	2.2673	95.5800
3	4.9138	2.3881	93.1919
4	4.7866	2.5153	90.6766
5	4.6526	2.6492	88.0274
6	4.5115	2.7903	85.2370
7	4.3629	2.9389	82.2981
8	4.2064	3.0954	79.2027
9	4.0416	3.2603	75.9424
10	3.8679	3.4339	72.5084
11	3.6850	3.6168	68.8916
12	3.4924	3.8094	65.0821
13	3.2895	4.0123	61.0698
14	3.0759	4.2260	56.8438
15	2.8508	4.4511	52.3927
16	2.6137	4.6881	47.7046
17	2.3641	4.9378	42.7668
18	2.1011	5.2008	37.5660
19	1.8241	5.4778	32.0882
20	1.5324	5.7695	26.3187
21	1.2251	6.0768	20.2420
22	.9015	6.4004	13.8416
23	.5606	6.7413	7.1003
24	.2016	7.1003	0.0000

YEARS 25	MO PAYT .5963	AN CONST 7.16	
#	INT	PRIN	BALANCE
1	5.1527	2.0029	97.9971
2	5.0460	2.1096	95.8875
3	4.9337	2.2219	93.6656
4	4.8154	2.3403	91.3253
5	4.6907	2.4649	88.8604
6	4.5594	2.5962	86.2643
7	4.4212	2.7344	83.5298
8	4.2756	2.8801	80.6498
9	4.1222	3.0335	77.6163
10	3.9606	3.1950	74.4213
11	3.7905	3.3652	71.0561
12	3.6112	3.5444	67.5118
13	3.4225	3.7331	63.7786
14	3.2237	3.9320	59.8466
15	3.0142	4.1414	55.7053
16	2.7937	4.3619	51.3433
17	2.5614	4.5942	46.7491
18	2.3167	4.8389	41.9102
19	2.0590	5.0966	36.8136
20	1.7876	5.3681	31.4455
21	1.5017	5.6539	25.7916
22	1.2006	5.9551	19.8365
23	.8834	6.2722	13.5643
24	.5494	6.6062	6.9581
25	.1975	6.9581	0.0000

YEARS 26	MO PAYT .5852	AN CONST 7.03	
#	INT	PRIN	BALANCE
1	5.1559	1.8661	98.1339
2	5.0566	1.9655	96.1683
3	4.9519	2.0702	94.0981
4	4.8416	2.1805	91.9177
5	4.7255	2.2966	89.6211
6	4.6032	2.4189	87.2022
7	4.4744	2.5477	84.6544
8	4.3387	2.6834	81.9710
9	4.1958	2.8263	79.1447
10	4.0452	2.9768	76.1679
11	3.8867	3.1354	73.0325
12	3.7197	3.3024	69.7301
13	3.5438	3.4782	66.2519
14	3.3586	3.6635	62.5884
15	3.1635	3.8586	58.7298
16	2.9580	4.0641	54.6657
17	2.7416	4.2805	50.3852
18	2.5136	4.5085	45.8767
19	2.2735	4.7486	41.1281
20	2.0206	5.0015	36.1266
21	1.7542	5.2679	30.8587
22	1.4737	5.5484	25.3103
23	1.1782	5.8439	19.4664
24	.8669	6.1552	13.3112
25	.5391	6.4830	6.8282
26	.1939	6.8282	0.0000

YEARS 27	MO PAYT .5750	AN CONST 6.90	
#	INT	PRIN	BALANCE
1	5.1589	1.7409	98.2591
2	5.0662	1.8337	96.4254
3	4.9685	1.9313	94.4941
4	4.8657	2.0342	92.4599
5	4.7573	2.1425	90.3174
6	4.6432	2.2566	88.0608
7	4.5230	2.3768	85.6840
8	4.3965	2.5034	83.1807
9	4.2631	2.6367	80.5440
10	4.1227	2.7771	77.7669
11	3.9748	2.9250	74.8418
12	3.8190	3.0808	71.7610
13	3.6550	3.2449	68.5162
14	3.4821	3.4177	65.0985
15	3.3001	3.5997	61.4988
16	3.1084	3.7914	57.7074
17	2.9065	3.9933	53.7140
18	2.6938	4.2060	49.5080
19	2.4698	4.4300	45.0780
20	2.2339	4.6659	40.4121
21	1.9854	4.9144	35.4976
22	1.7237	5.1762	30.3215
23	1.4480	5.4518	24.8696
24	1.1576	5.7422	19.1275
25	.8518	6.0480	13.0795
26	.5297	6.3701	6.7094
27	.1905	6.7094	0.0000

YEARS 28	MO PAYT .5656	AN CONST 6.79	
#	INT	PRIN	BALANCE
1	5.1616	1.6260	98.3740
2	5.0750	1.7126	96.6613
3	4.9838	1.8038	94.8575
4	4.8877	1.8999	92.9576
5	4.7865	2.0011	90.9565
6	4.6800	2.1077	88.8488
7	4.5677	2.2199	86.6289
8	4.4495	2.3381	84.2908
9	4.3250	2.4627	81.8281
10	4.1938	2.5938	79.2343
11	4.0557	2.7320	76.5023
12	3.9102	2.8775	73.6249
13	3.7569	3.0307	70.5942
14	3.5955	3.1921	67.4021
15	3.4255	3.3621	64.0400
16	3.2465	3.5412	60.4988
17	3.0579	3.7298	56.7690
18	2.8592	3.9284	52.8406
19	2.6500	4.1376	48.7030
20	2.4297	4.3580	44.3450
21	2.1976	4.5901	39.7550
22	1.9531	4.8345	34.9204
23	1.6956	5.0920	29.8284
24	1.4245	5.3632	24.4653
25	1.1388	5.6488	18.8164
26	.8380	5.9497	12.8668
27	.5211	6.2665	6.6003
28	.1874	6.6003	0.0000

YEARS 29	MO PAYT .5570	AN CONST 6.69	
#	INT	PRIN	BALANCE
1	5.1641	1.5203	98.4797
2	5.0831	1.6013	96.8783
3	4.9979	1.6866	95.1918
4	4.9080	1.7764	93.4153
5	4.8134	1.8710	91.5443
6	4.7138	1.9707	89.5737
7	4.6088	2.0756	87.4980
8	4.4983	2.1862	85.3119
9	4.3819	2.3026	83.0093
10	4.2592	2.4252	80.5841
11	4.1301	2.5544	78.0297
12	3.9940	2.6904	75.3392
13	3.8507	2.8337	72.5055
14	3.6998	2.9846	69.5209
15	3.5409	3.1436	66.3773
16	3.3734	3.3110	63.0663
17	3.1971	3.4873	59.5790
18	3.0114	3.6731	55.9059
19	2.8158	3.8687	52.0373
20	2.6097	4.0747	47.9626
21	2.3927	4.2917	43.6708
22	2.1642	4.5203	39.1506
23	1.9234	4.7610	34.3895
24	1.6699	5.0146	29.3749
25	1.4028	5.2816	24.0933
26	1.1215	5.5629	18.5304
27	.8252	5.8592	12.6712
28	.5132	6.1712	6.4999
29	.1845	6.4999	0.0000

YEARS 30	MO PAYT .5491	AN CONST 6.59	
#	INT	PRIN	BALANCE
1	5.1664	1.4229	98.5771
2	5.0906	1.4987	97.0784
3	5.0108	1.5785	95.4998
4	4.9267	1.6626	93.8372
5	4.8382	1.7511	92.0861
6	4.7449	1.8444	90.2417
7	4.6467	1.9426	88.2991
8	4.5432	2.0461	86.2530
9	4.4343	2.1551	84.0979
10	4.3195	2.2698	81.8281
11	4.1986	2.3907	79.4374
12	4.0713	2.5180	76.9194
13	3.9372	2.6521	74.2672
14	3.7959	2.7934	71.4738
15	3.6472	2.9422	68.5317
16	3.4905	3.0988	65.4328
17	3.3254	3.2639	62.1690
18	3.1516	3.4377	58.7312
19	2.9685	3.6208	55.1104
20	2.7757	3.8136	51.2968
21	2.5726	4.0167	47.2801
22	2.3587	4.2307	43.0494
23	2.1334	4.4560	38.5935
24	1.8961	4.6933	33.9002
25	1.6461	4.9432	28.9570
26	1.3828	5.2065	23.7505
27	1.1056	5.4838	18.2667
28	.8135	5.7758	12.4909
29	.5059	6.0834	6.4074
30	.1819	6.4074	0.0000

YEARS 2 — MO PAYT 4.3983 — AN CONST 52.79

#	INT	PRIN	BALANCE
1	4.0895	48.6907	51.3093
2	1.4708	51.3093	0.0000

YEARS 3 — MO PAYT 3.0083 — AN CONST 36.10

#	INT	PRIN	BALANCE
1	4.4967	31.6032	68.3968
2	2.7971	33.3029	35.0940
3	1.0060	35.0940	0.0000

YEARS 4 — MO PAYT 2.3143 — AN CONST 27.78

#	INT	PRIN	BALANCE
1	4.7001	23.0712	76.9288
2	3.4593	24.3120	52.6169
3	2.1517	25.6195	26.9974
4	.7739	26.9974	0.0000

YEARS 5 — MO PAYT 1.8986 — AN CONST 22.79

#	INT	PRIN	BALANCE
1	4.8219	17.9613	82.0387
2	3.8559	18.9273	63.1114
3	2.8380	19.9452	43.1662
4	1.7653	21.0179	22.1483
5	.6349	22.1483	0.0000

YEARS 6 — MO PAYT 1.6221 — AN CONST 19.47

#	INT	PRIN	BALANCE
1	4.9029	14.5625	85.4375
2	4.1197	15.3457	70.0918
3	3.2944	16.1710	53.9208
4	2.4247	17.0407	36.8801
5	1.5082	17.9572	18.9230
6	.5424	18.9230	0.0000

YEARS 7 — MO PAYT 1.4252 — AN CONST 17.11

#	INT	PRIN	BALANCE
1	4.9606	12.1414	87.8586
2	4.3076	12.7944	75.0642
3	3.6195	13.4825	61.5817
4	2.8944	14.2076	47.3741
5	2.1303	14.9717	32.4024
6	1.3251	15.7769	16.6254
7	.4766	16.6254	0.0000

YEARS 8 — MO PAYT 1.2779 — AN CONST 15.34

#	INT	PRIN	BALANCE
1	5.0038	10.3314	89.6686
2	4.4481	10.8870	78.7816
3	3.8626	11.4726	67.3090
4	3.2456	12.0896	55.2195
5	2.5954	12.7398	42.4797
6	1.9102	13.4249	29.0548
7	1.1882	14.1470	14.9078
8	.4273	14.9078	0.0000

YEARS 9 — MO PAYT 1.1638 — AN CONST 13.97

#	INT	PRIN	BALANCE
1	5.0372	8.9287	91.0713
2	4.5570	9.4089	81.6624
3	4.0510	9.9150	71.7474
4	3.5177	10.4482	61.2992
5	2.9558	11.0101	50.2891
6	2.3636	11.6023	38.6868

YEARS 9 (continued)

#	INT	PRIN	BALANCE
7	1.7396	12.2263	26.4605
8	1.0821	12.8838	13.5767
9	.3892	13.5767	0.0000

YEARS 10 — MO PAYT 1.0729 — AN CONST 12.88

#	INT	PRIN	BALANCE
1	5.0638	7.8112	92.1888
2	4.6437	8.2313	83.9575
3	4.2010	8.6740	75.2836
4	3.7345	9.1405	66.1431
5	3.2429	9.6321	56.5110
6	2.7249	10.1501	46.3609
7	2.1790	10.6960	35.6649
8	1.6038	11.2712	24.3937
9	.9976	11.8774	12.5162
10	.3588	12.5162	0.0000

YEARS 11 — MO PAYT .9989 — AN CONST 11.99

#	INT	PRIN	BALANCE
1	5.0855	6.9010	93.0990
2	4.7144	7.2721	85.8269
3	4.3233	7.6632	78.1636
4	3.9111	8.0754	70.0882
5	3.4768	8.5097	61.5786
6	3.0191	8.9674	52.6112
7	2.5369	9.4496	43.1615
8	2.0286	9.9579	33.2037
9	1.4931	10.4934	22.7103
10	.9287	11.0578	11.6525
11	.3340	11.6525	0.0000

YEARS 12 — MO PAYT .9375 — AN CONST 11.25

#	INT	PRIN	BALANCE
1	5.1035	6.1463	93.8537
2	4.7729	6.4768	87.3769
3	4.4246	6.8252	80.5517
4	4.0575	7.1922	73.3595
5	3.6707	7.5791	65.7804
6	3.2631	7.9867	57.7938
7	2.8336	8.4162	49.3776
8	2.3809	8.8688	40.5087
9	1.9040	9.3458	31.1629
10	1.4013	9.8485	21.3144
11	.8716	10.3781	10.9363
12	.3135	10.9363	0.0000

YEARS 13 — MO PAYT .8858 — AN CONST 10.63

#	INT	PRIN	BALANCE
1	5.1186	5.5111	94.4889
2	4.8222	5.8075	88.6813
3	4.5099	6.1199	82.5614
4	4.1808	6.4490	76.1124
5	3.8339	6.7959	69.3165
6	3.4684	7.1614	62.1552
7	3.0833	7.5465	54.6087
8	2.6774	7.9524	46.6563
9	2.2497	8.3801	38.2762
10	1.7990	8.8308	29.4455
11	1.3241	9.3057	20.1398
12	.8236	9.8062	10.3336
13	.2962	10.3336	0.0000

YEARS 14 — MO PAYT .8418 — AN CONST 10.11

#	INT	PRIN	BALANCE
1	5.1315	4.9700	95.0300
2	4.8642	5.2372	89.7928
3	4.5826	5.5189	84.2739

YEARS 14 (continued)

#	INT	PRIN	BALANCE
4	4.2858	5.8157	78.4582
5	3.9730	6.1285	72.3297
6	3.6434	6.4581	65.8715
7	3.2960	6.8054	59.0661
8	2.9300	7.1715	51.8946
9	2.5443	7.5571	44.3375
10	2.1379	7.9636	36.3739
11	1.7096	8.3919	27.9820
12	1.2583	8.8432	19.1388
13	.7827	9.3188	9.8200
14	.2815	9.8200	0.0000

YEARS 15 — MO PAYT .8039 — AN CONST 9.65

#	INT	PRIN	BALANCE
1	5.1427	4.5039	95.4961
2	4.9004	4.7461	90.7500
3	4.6452	5.0014	85.7486
4	4.3762	5.2703	80.4783
5	4.0927	5.5538	74.9245
6	3.7940	5.8525	69.0720
7	3.4793	6.1672	62.9048
8	3.1476	6.4989	56.4058
9	2.7981	6.8485	49.5574
10	2.4298	7.2168	42.3406
11	2.0416	7.6049	34.7357
12	1.6326	8.0139	26.7218
13	1.2016	8.4449	18.2768
14	.7474	8.8991	9.3777
15	.2688	9.3777	0.0000

YEARS 16 — MO PAYT .7709 — AN CONST 9.26

#	INT	PRIN	BALANCE
1	5.1523	4.0988	95.9012
2	4.9319	4.3193	91.5819
3	4.6996	4.5516	87.0303
4	4.4548	4.7964	82.2340
5	4.1968	5.0543	77.1796
6	3.9250	5.3262	71.8535
7	3.6385	5.6126	66.2409
8	3.3367	5.9145	60.3264
9	3.0186	6.2326	54.0938
10	2.6834	6.5678	47.5261
11	2.3302	6.9210	40.6051
12	1.9579	7.2932	33.3119
13	1.5657	7.6854	25.6265
14	1.1524	8.0988	17.5277
15	.7168	8.5343	8.9933
16	.2578	8.9933	0.0000

YEARS 17 — MO PAYT .7421 — AN CONST 8.91

#	INT	PRIN	BALANCE
1	5.1608	3.7440	96.2560
2	4.9594	3.9454	92.3106
3	4.7472	4.1576	88.1531
4	4.5236	4.3812	83.7719
5	4.2880	4.6168	79.1551
6	4.0397	4.8651	74.2900
7	3.7780	5.1267	69.1633
8	3.5023	5.4025	63.7608
9	3.2117	5.6930	58.0678
10	2.9056	5.9992	52.0686
11	2.5829	6.3219	45.7467
12	2.2429	6.6619	39.0849
13	1.8846	7.0201	32.0647
14	1.5071	7.3977	24.6670
15	1.1092	7.7956	16.8715
16	.6900	8.2148	8.6566
17	.2481	8.6566	0.0000

YEARS 18 — MO PAYT .7166 — AN CONST 8.60

#	INT	PRIN	BALANCE
1	5.1682	3.4310	96.5690
2	4.9837	3.6156	92.9534
3	4.7892	3.8100	89.1434
4	4.5843	4.0149	85.1285
5	4.3684	4.2308	80.8977
6	4.1409	4.4584	76.4393
7	3.9011	4.6982	71.7411
8	3.6484	4.9508	66.7903
9	3.3821	5.2171	61.5731
10	3.1016	5.4977	56.0755
11	2.8059	5.7934	50.2821
12	2.4943	6.1050	44.1771
13	2.1660	6.4333	37.7438
14	1.8200	6.7793	30.9646
15	1.4554	7.1439	23.8207
16	1.0712	7.5281	16.2926
17	.6663	7.9330	8.3596
18	.2396	8.3596	0.0000

YEARS 19 — MO PAYT .6940 — AN CONST 8.33

#	INT	PRIN	BALANCE
1	5.1748	3.1533	96.8467
2	5.0053	3.3228	93.5239
3	4.8265	3.5015	90.0224
4	4.6382	3.6899	86.3325
5	4.4398	3.8883	82.4442
6	4.2307	4.0974	78.3468
7	4.0103	4.3178	74.0289
8	3.7781	4.5500	69.4789
9	3.5334	4.7947	64.6842
10	3.2755	5.0526	59.6316
11	3.0038	5.3243	54.3073
12	2.7174	5.6107	48.6966
13	2.4156	5.9124	42.7841
14	2.0977	6.2304	36.5537
15	1.7626	6.5655	29.9882
16	1.4095	6.9186	23.0696
17	1.0374	7.2907	15.7788
18	.6453	7.6828	8.0960
19	.2321	8.0960	0.0000

YEARS 20 — MO PAYT .6738 — AN CONST 8.09

#	INT	PRIN	BALANCE
1	5.1808	2.9054	97.0946
2	5.0245	3.0616	94.0330
3	4.8598	3.2263	90.8067
4	4.6863	3.3998	87.4069
5	4.5035	3.5827	83.8242
6	4.3108	3.7753	80.0489
7	4.1077	3.9784	76.0705
8	3.8938	4.1924	71.8781
9	3.6683	4.4178	67.4603
10	3.4307	4.6554	62.8049
11	3.1803	4.9058	57.8991
12	2.9165	5.1696	52.7294
13	2.6384	5.4477	47.2817
14	2.3455	5.7407	41.5411
15	2.0367	6.0494	35.4917
16	1.7114	6.3748	29.1169
17	1.3685	6.7176	22.3993
18	1.0072	7.0789	15.3204
19	.6265	7.4596	7.8608
20	.2253	7.8608	0.0000

YEARS 21 — MO PAYT .6558 — AN CONST 7.87

#	INT	PRIN	BALANCE
1	5.1860	2.6831	97.3169
2	5.0417	2.8274	94.4895
3	4.8897	2.9795	91.5100

MONTHLY PAYMENT AMORTIZATION SCHEDULE PER $100   5.25 %

#	INT	PRIN	BALANCE
4	4.7294	3.1397	88.3702
5	4.5606	3.3086	85.0616
6	4.3826	3.4865	81.5751
7	4.1951	3.6740	77.9011
8	3.9975	3.8716	74.0294
9	3.7893	4.0799	69.9495
10	3.5699	4.2993	65.6503
11	3.3387	4.5305	61.1197
12	3.0950	4.7742	56.3456
13	2.8382	5.0309	51.3146
14	2.5677	5.3015	46.0131
15	2.2825	5.5866	40.4265
16	1.9821	5.8871	34.5394
17	1.6655	6.2037	28.3357
18	1.3318	6.5374	21.7983
19	.9802	6.8890	14.9093
20	.6097	7.2595	7.6499
21	.2193	7.6499	0.0000

YEARS 22 — MO PAYT .6395 — AN CONST 7.68

#	INT	PRIN	BALANCE
1	5.1908	2.4830	97.5170
2	5.0573	2.6165	94.9005
3	4.9166	2.7572	92.1433
4	4.7683	2.9055	89.2378
5	4.6120	3.0618	86.1760
6	4.4473	3.2264	82.9496
7	4.2738	3.4000	79.5496
8	4.0910	3.5828	75.9668
9	3.8983	3.7755	72.1913
10	3.6952	3.9786	68.2127
11	3.4812	4.1925	64.0202
12	3.2558	4.4180	59.6022
13	3.0181	4.6556	54.9465
14	2.7678	4.9060	50.0405
15	2.5039	5.1699	44.8706
16	2.2259	5.4479	39.4227
17	1.9329	5.7409	33.6818
18	1.6241	6.0497	27.6321
19	1.2987	6.3750	21.2571
20	.9559	6.7179	14.5391
21	.5946	7.0792	7.4599
22	.2138	7.4599	0.0000

YEARS 23 — MO PAYT .6248 — AN CONST 7.50

#	INT	PRIN	BALANCE
1	5.1951	2.3020	97.6980
2	5.0713	2.4258	95.2722
3	4.9409	2.5563	92.7159
4	4.8034	2.6937	90.0222
5	4.6585	2.8386	87.1836
6	4.5058	2.9913	84.1923
7	4.3450	3.1522	81.0401
8	4.1754	3.3217	77.7184
9	3.9968	3.5003	74.2181
10	3.8085	3.6886	70.5295
11	3.6102	3.8870	66.6425
12	3.4011	4.0960	62.5464
13	3.1808	4.3163	58.2301
14	2.9487	4.5485	53.6817
15	2.7040	4.7931	48.8886
16	2.4463	5.0509	43.8377
17	2.1746	5.3225	38.5152
18	1.8884	5.6088	32.9064
19	1.5867	5.9104	26.9960
20	1.2688	6.2283	20.7677
21	.9339	6.5633	14.2045
22	.5809	6.9162	7.2882
23	.2089	7.2882	0.0000

YEARS 24 — MO PAYT .6114 — AN CONST 7.34

#	INT	PRIN	BALANCE
1	5.1990	2.1378	97.8622
2	5.0841	2.2528	95.6094
3	4.9629	2.3739	93.2355
4	4.8352	2.5016	90.7338
5	4.7007	2.6362	88.0977
6	4.5589	2.7779	85.3197
7	4.4095	2.9273	82.3924
8	4.2521	3.0848	79.3076
9	4.0862	3.2507	76.0569
10	3.9113	3.4255	72.6314
11	3.7271	3.6097	69.0217
12	3.5330	3.8039	65.2178
13	3.3284	4.0085	61.2093
14	3.1128	4.2240	56.9853
15	2.8856	4.4512	52.5340
16	2.6462	4.6906	47.8434
17	2.3940	4.9429	42.9005
18	2.1281	5.2087	37.6918
19	1.8480	5.4889	32.2029
20	1.5528	5.7841	26.4189
21	1.2417	6.0951	20.3237
22	.9139	6.4230	13.9008
23	.5685	6.7684	7.1324
24	.2045	7.1324	0.0000

YEARS 25 — MO PAYT .5992 — AN CONST 7.20

#	INT	PRIN	BALANCE
1	5.2026	1.9884	98.0116
2	5.0957	2.0953	95.9163
3	4.9830	2.2080	93.7083
4	4.8642	2.3267	91.3816
5	4.7391	2.4519	88.9297
6	4.6072	2.5837	86.3460
7	4.4683	2.7227	83.6233
8	4.3218	2.8691	80.7541
9	4.1675	3.0234	77.7307
10	4.0049	3.1861	74.5446
11	3.8336	3.3574	71.1872
12	3.6530	3.5380	67.6493
13	3.4627	3.7282	63.9210
14	3.2622	3.9288	59.9923
15	3.0509	4.1401	55.8522
16	2.8283	4.3627	51.4895
17	2.5936	4.5974	46.8921
18	2.3464	4.8446	42.0475
19	2.0858	5.1052	36.9424
20	1.8112	5.3797	31.5626
21	1.5219	5.6691	25.8936
22	1.2170	5.9739	19.9196
23	.8957	6.2952	13.6244
24	.5572	6.6338	6.9906
25	.2004	6.9906	0.0000

YEARS 26 — MO PAYT .5882 — AN CONST 7.06

#	INT	PRIN	BALANCE
1	5.2059	1.8519	98.1481
2	5.1063	1.9515	96.1965
3	5.0013	2.0565	94.1400
4	4.8907	2.1671	91.9729
5	4.7741	2.2837	89.6893
6	4.6513	2.4065	87.2828
7	4.5219	2.5359	84.7469
8	4.3855	2.6723	82.0746
9	4.2418	2.8160	79.2586
10	4.0903	2.9675	76.2912
11	3.9308	3.1270	73.1641
12	3.7626	3.2952	69.8689
13	3.5854	3.4724	66.3964
14	3.3986	3.6592	62.7372
15	3.2018	3.8560	58.8812
16	2.9944	4.0634	54.8178
17	2.7759	4.2819	50.5359
18	2.5456	4.5122	46.0237
19	2.3029	4.7549	41.2688
20	2.0472	5.0106	36.2582
21	1.7777	5.2801	30.9781
22	1.4937	5.5641	25.4140
23	1.1945	5.8633	19.5507
24	.8791	6.1787	13.3721
25	.5468	6.5110	6.8611
26	.1967	6.8611	0.0000

YEARS 27 — MO PAYT .5780 — AN CONST 6.94

#	INT	PRIN	BALANCE
1	5.2088	1.7271	98.2729
2	5.1160	1.8200	96.4530
3	5.0181	1.9178	94.5351
4	4.9149	2.0210	92.5142
5	4.8062	2.1297	90.3845
6	4.6917	2.2442	88.1403
7	4.5710	2.3649	85.7754
8	4.4438	2.4921	83.2833
9	4.3098	2.6261	80.6571
10	4.1685	2.7674	77.8898
11	4.0197	2.9162	74.9736
12	3.8629	3.0730	71.9005
13	3.6976	3.2383	68.6622
14	3.5234	3.4125	65.2497
15	3.3399	3.5960	61.6537
16	3.1465	3.7894	57.8643
17	2.9427	3.9932	53.8711
18	2.7279	4.2080	49.6631
19	2.5016	4.4343	45.2288
20	2.2631	4.6728	40.5561
21	2.0118	4.9241	35.6320
22	1.7470	5.1889	30.4431
23	1.4679	5.4680	24.9751
24	1.1739	5.7621	19.2131
25	.8640	6.0719	13.1411
26	.5374	6.3985	6.7426
27	.1933	6.7426	0.0000

YEARS 28 — MO PAYT .5687 — AN CONST 6.83

#	INT	PRIN	BALANCE
1	5.2116	1.6125	98.3875
2	5.1248	1.6992	96.6883
3	5.0335	1.7906	94.8977
4	4.9372	1.8869	93.0108
5	4.8357	1.9884	91.0224
6	4.7287	2.0953	88.9270
7	4.6160	2.2080	86.7190
8	4.4973	2.3268	84.3922
9	4.3722	2.4519	81.9403
10	4.2403	2.5838	79.3565
11	4.1013	2.7227	76.6338
12	3.9549	2.8692	73.7646
13	3.8006	3.0235	70.7411
14	3.6380	3.1861	67.5550
15	3.4666	3.3575	64.1976
16	3.2860	3.5380	60.6596
17	3.0958	3.7283	56.9312
18	2.8952	3.9288	53.0024
19	2.6839	4.1401	48.8623
20	2.4613	4.3628	44.4995
21	2.2266	4.5974	39.9021
22	1.9794	4.8447	35.0574
23	1.7188	5.1052	29.9522
24	1.4443	5.3798	24.5724
25	1.1549	5.6691	18.9033
26	.8500	5.9740	12.9292
27	.5287	6.2953	6.6339
28	.1902	6.6339	0.0000

YEARS 29 — MO PAYT .5601 — AN CONST 6.73

#	INT	PRIN	BALANCE
1	5.2141	1.5071	98.4929
2	5.1330	1.5882	96.9047
3	5.0476	1.6736	95.2311
4	4.9576	1.7636	93.4674
5	4.8627	1.8585	91.6090
6	4.7628	1.9584	89.6505
7	4.6575	2.0638	87.5868
8	4.5465	2.1747	85.4120
9	4.4295	2.2917	83.1203
10	4.3063	2.4150	80.7054
11	4.1764	2.5448	78.1605
12	4.0395	2.6817	75.4788
13	3.8953	2.8259	72.6529
14	3.7433	2.9779	69.6750
15	3.5831	3.1381	66.5369
16	3.4144	3.3068	63.2300
17	3.2365	3.4847	59.7453
18	3.0491	3.6721	56.0732
19	2.8516	3.8696	52.2036
20	2.6435	4.0777	48.1259
21	2.4242	4.2970	43.8289
22	2.1931	4.5281	39.3007
23	1.9496	4.7717	34.5291
24	1.6929	5.0283	29.5008
25	1.4225	5.2987	24.2021
26	1.1375	5.5837	18.6184
27	.8372	5.8840	12.7344
28	.5208	6.2004	6.5339
29	.1873	6.5339	0.0000

YEARS 30 — MO PAYT .5522 — AN CONST 6.63

#	INT	PRIN	BALANCE
1	5.2164	1.4101	98.5899
2	5.1406	1.4859	97.1041
3	5.0606	1.5658	95.5383
4	4.9764	1.6500	93.8882
5	4.8877	1.7388	92.1495
6	4.7942	1.8323	90.3172
7	4.6956	1.9308	88.3864
8	4.5918	2.0347	86.3518
9	4.4824	2.1441	84.2077
10	4.3671	2.2594	81.9483
11	4.2455	2.3809	79.5674
12	4.1175	2.5090	77.0584
13	3.9825	2.6439	74.4145
14	3.8404	2.7861	71.6284
15	3.6905	2.9359	68.6925
16	3.5326	3.0938	65.5987
17	3.3662	3.2602	62.3384
18	3.1909	3.4356	58.9029
19	3.0061	3.6203	55.2826
20	2.8114	3.8150	51.4675
21	2.6062	4.0202	47.4473
22	2.3900	4.2364	43.2109
23	2.1622	4.4643	38.7466
24	1.9221	4.7044	34.0422
25	1.6691	4.9574	29.0848
26	1.4024	5.2240	23.8608
27	1.1215	5.5050	18.3558
28	.8254	5.8010	12.5548
29	.5134	6.1130	6.4418
30	.1847	6.4418	0.0000

MONTHLY PAYMENT AMORTIZATION SCHEDULE PER $100

5.30 %

YEARS 2 — MO PAYT 4.4006 — AN CONST 52.81

#	INT	PRIN	BALANCE
1	4.1288	48.6782	51.3218
2	1.4853	51.3218	0.0000

YEARS 3 — MO PAYT 3.0106 — AN CONST 36.13

#	INT	PRIN	BALANCE
1	4.5400	31.5869	68.4131
2	2.8247	33.3023	35.1108
3	1.0161	35.1108	0.0000

YEARS 4 — MO PAYT 2.3165 — AN CONST 27.80

#	INT	PRIN	BALANCE
1	4.7453	23.0532	76.9468
2	3.4934	24.3051	52.6417
3	2.1735	25.6250	27.0167
4	.7819	27.0167	0.0000

YEARS 5 — MO PAYT 1.9009 — AN CONST 22.82

#	INT	PRIN	BALANCE
1	4.8683	17.9425	82.0575
2	3.8939	18.9169	63.1407
3	2.8666	19.9442	43.1965
4	1.7835	21.0273	22.1692
5	.6416	22.1692	0.0000

YEARS 6 — MO PAYT 1.6244 — AN CONST 19.50

#	INT	PRIN	BALANCE
1	4.9501	14.5433	85.4567
2	4.1603	15.3331	70.1237
3	3.3276	16.1657	53.9579
4	2.4497	17.0436	36.9143
5	1.5241	17.9692	18.9451
6	.5483	18.9451	0.0000

YEARS 7 — MO PAYT 1.4275 — AN CONST 17.14

#	INT	PRIN	BALANCE
1	5.0083	12.1220	87.8780
2	4.3500	12.7803	75.0977
3	3.6560	13.4744	61.6233
4	2.9242	14.2061	47.4172
5	2.1528	14.9776	32.4395
6	1.3394	15.7910	16.6486
7	.4818	16.6486	0.0000

YEARS 8 — MO PAYT 1.2803 — AN CONST 15.37

#	INT	PRIN	BALANCE
1	5.0519	10.3120	89.6880
2	4.4919	10.8720	78.8160
3	3.9015	11.4624	67.3536
4	3.2790	12.0849	55.2687
5	2.6227	12.7412	42.5275
6	1.9308	13.4331	29.0944
7	1.2013	14.1626	14.9318
8	.4321	14.9318	0.0000

YEARS 9 — MO PAYT 1.1663 — AN CONST 14.00

#	INT	PRIN	BALANCE
1	5.0856	8.9094	91.0906
2	4.6018	9.3932	81.6973
3	4.0917	9.9034	71.7940
4	3.5539	10.4412	61.3528
5	2.9868	11.0082	50.3446
6	2.3890	11.6060	38.7386
7	1.7587	12.2363	26.5022
8	1.0942	12.9008	13.6014
9	.3936	13.6014	0.0000

YEARS 10 — MO PAYT 1.0754 — AN CONST 12.91

#	INT	PRIN	BALANCE
1	5.1125	7.7920	92.2080
2	4.6894	8.2152	83.9928
3	4.2432	8.6613	75.3315
4	3.7729	9.1317	66.1998
5	3.2770	9.6276	56.5722
6	2.7541	10.1504	46.4217
7	2.2029	10.7017	35.7200
8	1.6217	11.2829	24.4372
9	1.0090	11.8956	12.5416
10	.3630	12.5416	0.0000

YEARS 11 — MO PAYT 1.0014 — AN CONST 12.02

#	INT	PRIN	BALANCE
1	5.1344	6.8820	93.1180
2	4.7607	7.2558	85.8622
3	4.3666	7.6498	78.2124
4	3.9512	8.0652	70.1471
5	3.5132	8.5032	61.6439
6	3.0514	8.9650	52.6788
7	2.5646	9.4519	43.2270
8	2.0513	9.9652	33.2618
9	1.5101	10.5064	22.7554
10	.9395	11.0769	11.6785
11	.3380	11.6785	0.0000

YEARS 12 — MO PAYT .9400 — AN CONST 11.29

#	INT	PRIN	BALANCE
1	5.1526	6.1276	93.8724
2	4.8198	6.4603	87.4121
3	4.4690	6.8112	80.6009
4	4.0991	7.1811	73.4199
5	3.7091	7.5710	65.8488
6	3.2979	7.9822	57.8666
7	2.8645	8.4157	49.4509
8	2.4074	8.8727	40.5782
9	1.9256	9.3546	31.2236
10	1.4176	9.8626	21.3611
11	.8820	10.3982	10.9629
12	.3173	10.9629	0.0000

YEARS 13 — MO PAYT .8884 — AN CONST 10.67

#	INT	PRIN	BALANCE
1	5.1678	5.4927	94.5073
2	4.8696	5.7910	88.7163
3	4.5551	6.1055	82.6108
4	4.2235	6.4371	76.1737
5	3.8739	6.7866	69.3871
6	3.5054	7.1552	62.2319
7	3.1168	7.5438	54.6882
8	2.7071	7.9534	46.7347
9	2.2752	8.3854	38.3494
10	1.8198	8.8407	29.5086
11	1.3397	9.3209	20.1878
12	.8335	9.8270	10.3607
13	.2998	10.3607	0.0000

YEARS 14 — MO PAYT .8444 — AN CONST 10.14

#	INT	PRIN	BALANCE
1	5.1809	4.9518	95.0482
2	4.9119	5.2207	89.8275
3	4.6284	5.5042	84.3232
4	4.3295	5.8032	78.5201
5	4.0144	6.1183	72.4018
6	3.6821	6.4506	65.9512
7	3.3318	6.8009	59.1503
8	2.9625	7.1702	51.9801
9	2.5731	7.5596	44.4205
10	2.1625	7.9701	36.4504
11	1.7297	8.4030	28.0474
12	1.2734	8.8593	19.1881
13	.7922	9.3404	9.8477
14	.2850	9.8477	0.0000

YEARS 15 — MO PAYT .8065 — AN CONST 9.68

#	INT	PRIN	BALANCE
1	5.1921	4.4860	95.5140
2	4.9484	4.7297	90.7843
3	4.6916	4.9865	85.7978
4	4.4208	5.2573	80.5405
5	4.1353	5.5428	74.9976
6	3.8343	5.8438	69.1538
7	3.5169	6.1612	62.9926
8	3.1823	6.4958	56.4968
9	2.8296	6.8486	49.6483
10	2.4576	7.2205	42.4278
11	2.0655	7.6126	34.8152
12	1.6521	8.0260	26.7892
13	1.2162	8.4619	18.3273
14	.7567	8.9214	9.4059
15	.2722	9.4059	0.0000

YEARS 16 — MO PAYT .7736 — AN CONST 9.29

#	INT	PRIN	BALANCE
1	5.2018	4.0813	95.9187
2	4.9802	4.3030	91.6157
3	4.7465	4.5366	87.0791
4	4.5001	4.7830	82.2961
5	4.2404	5.0427	77.2534
6	3.9665	5.3166	71.9367
7	3.6778	5.6053	66.3314
8	3.3734	5.9097	60.4217
9	3.0524	6.2307	54.1910
10	2.7141	6.5690	47.6220
11	2.3573	6.9258	40.6962
12	1.9812	7.3019	33.3943
13	1.5847	7.6984	25.6958
14	1.1666	8.1165	17.5793
15	.7258	8.5573	9.0220
16	.2611	9.0220	0.0000

YEARS 17 — MO PAYT .7448 — AN CONST 8.94

#	INT	PRIN	BALANCE
1	5.2103	3.7268	96.2732
2	5.0079	3.9292	92.3440
3	4.7946	4.1426	88.2014
4	4.5696	4.3676	83.8338
5	4.3324	4.6047	79.2291
6	4.0823	4.8548	74.3743
7	3.8187	5.1185	69.2558
8	3.5407	5.3964	63.8594
9	3.2477	5.6895	58.1699
10	2.9387	5.9985	52.1714
11	2.6129	6.3242	45.8472
12	2.2695	6.6677	39.1795
13	1.9074	7.0298	32.1497
14	1.5256	7.4115	24.7382
15	1.1231	7.8140	16.9242
16	.6988	8.2384	8.6858
17	.2514	8.6858	0.0000

YEARS 18 — MO PAYT .7193 — AN CONST 8.64

#	INT	PRIN	BALANCE
1	5.2179	3.4142	96.5858
2	5.0324	3.5996	92.9863
3	4.8370	3.7951	89.1912
4	4.6309	4.0012	85.1900
5	4.4136	4.2184	80.9716
6	4.1845	4.4475	76.5241
7	3.9430	4.6891	71.8350
8	3.6883	4.9437	66.8913
9	3.4198	5.2122	61.6791
10	3.1368	5.4952	56.1839
11	2.8384	5.7937	50.3902
12	2.5237	6.1083	44.2819
13	2.1920	6.4400	37.8419
14	1.8423	6.7898	31.0521
15	1.4735	7.1585	23.8936
16	1.0848	7.5472	16.3463
17	.6749	7.9571	8.3892
18	.2428	8.3892	0.0000

YEARS 19 — MO PAYT .6968 — AN CONST 8.37

#	INT	PRIN	BALANCE
1	5.2245	3.1367	96.8633
2	5.0542	3.3071	93.5562
3	4.8746	3.4867	90.0695
4	4.6852	3.6760	86.3935
5	4.4856	3.8756	82.5179
6	4.2751	4.0861	78.4317
7	4.0532	4.3080	74.1237
8	3.8193	4.5420	69.5817
9	3.5726	4.7886	64.7931
10	3.3126	5.0487	59.7444
11	3.0384	5.3229	54.4215
12	2.7493	5.6119	48.8096
13	2.4446	5.9167	42.8929
14	2.1232	6.2380	36.6549
15	1.7845	6.5768	30.0781
16	1.4273	6.9340	23.1441
17	1.0507	7.3105	15.8336
18	.6537	7.7075	8.1261
19	.2352	8.1261	0.0000

YEARS 20 — MO PAYT .6766 — AN CONST 8.12

#	INT	PRIN	BALANCE
1	5.2305	2.8892	97.1108
2	5.0736	3.0461	94.0647
3	4.9082	3.2115	90.8532
4	4.7338	3.3859	87.4672
5	4.5499	3.5698	83.8974
6	4.3560	3.7637	80.1338
7	4.1516	3.9681	76.1657
8	3.9361	4.1836	71.9821
9	3.7089	4.4108	67.5714
10	3.4694	4.6503	62.9211
11	3.2169	4.9028	58.0183
12	2.9506	5.1691	52.8492
13	2.6699	5.4498	47.3994
14	2.3739	5.7458	41.6536
15	2.0619	6.0578	35.5958
16	1.7329	6.3868	29.2091
17	1.3861	6.7336	22.4754
18	1.0204	7.0993	15.3761
19	.6349	7.4848	7.8913
20	.2284	7.8913	0.0000

YEARS 21 — MO PAYT .6586 — AN CONST 7.91

#	INT	PRIN	BALANCE
1	5.2358	2.6673	97.3327
2	5.0910	2.8121	94.5206
3	4.9383	2.9649	91.5557

#	INT	PRIN	BALANCE
4	4.7772	3.1259	88.4299
5	4.6075	3.2956	85.1342
6	4.4285	3.4746	81.6596
7	4.2398	3.6633	77.9964
8	4.0409	3.8622	74.1341
9	3.8311	4.0720	70.0622
10	3.6100	4.2931	65.7691
11	3.3769	4.5263	61.2428
12	3.1311	4.7721	56.4707
13	2.8719	5.0312	51.4395
14	2.5987	5.3044	46.1351
15	2.3106	5.5925	40.5426
16	2.0069	5.8962	34.6464
17	1.6867	6.2164	28.4300
18	1.3491	6.5540	21.8760
19	.9932	6.9099	14.9660
20	.6179	7.2852	7.6808
21	.2223	7.6808	0.0000

YEARS 22   MO PAYT .6423   AN CONST 7.71

#	INT	PRIN	BALANCE
1	5.2406	2.4675	97.5325
2	5.1066	2.6015	94.9311
3	4.9654	2.7427	92.1883
4	4.8164	2.8917	89.2966
5	4.6594	3.0487	86.2479
6	4.4938	3.2143	83.0336
7	4.3192	3.3889	79.6447
8	4.1352	3.5729	76.0718
9	3.9412	3.7669	72.3049
10	3.7366	3.9715	68.3334
11	3.5209	4.1872	64.1462
12	3.2935	4.4146	59.7317
13	3.0538	4.6543	55.0773
14	2.8010	4.9071	50.1703
15	2.5346	5.1736	44.9967
16	2.2536	5.4545	39.5422
17	1.9574	5.7507	33.7915
18	1.6451	6.0630	27.7285
19	1.3158	6.3923	21.3362
20	.9687	6.7394	14.5967
21	.6027	7.1054	7.4913
22	.2168	7.4913	0.0000

YEARS 23   MO PAYT .6277   AN CONST 7.54

#	INT	PRIN	BALANCE
1	5.2450	2.2869	97.7131
2	5.1208	2.4110	95.3021
3	4.9899	2.5420	92.7601
4	4.8518	2.6800	90.0801
5	4.7063	2.8256	87.2545
6	4.5528	2.9790	84.2755
7	4.3910	3.1408	81.1347
8	4.2205	3.3114	77.8234
9	4.0406	3.4912	74.3322
10	3.8510	3.6808	70.6514
11	3.6512	3.8807	66.7707
12	3.4404	4.0914	62.6793
13	3.2182	4.3136	58.3657
14	2.9840	4.5479	53.8178
15	2.7370	4.7948	49.0230
16	2.4766	5.0552	43.9677
17	2.2021	5.3298	38.6379
18	1.9126	5.6192	33.0187
19	1.6075	5.9244	27.0944
20	1.2857	6.2461	20.8482
21	.9465	6.5853	14.2629
22	.5889	6.9429	7.3200
23	.2118	7.3200	0.0000

YEARS 24   MO PAYT .6143   AN CONST 7.38

#	INT	PRIN	BALANCE
1	5.2489	2.1230	97.8770
2	5.1336	2.2383	95.6387
3	5.0121	2.3599	93.2788
4	4.8839	2.4880	90.7908
5	4.7488	2.6231	88.1677
6	4.6063	2.7656	85.4021
7	4.4562	2.9158	82.4863
8	4.2978	3.0741	79.4122
9	4.1309	3.2411	76.1712
10	3.9549	3.4171	72.7541
11	3.7693	3.6026	69.1515
12	3.5736	3.7983	65.3532
13	3.3674	4.0046	61.3486
14	3.1499	4.2220	57.1266
15	2.9206	4.4513	52.6753
16	2.6789	4.6931	47.9822
17	2.4240	4.9479	43.0343
18	2.1553	5.2166	37.8177
19	1.8720	5.4999	32.3177
20	1.5733	5.7986	26.5191
21	1.2584	6.1135	20.4056
22	.9264	6.4455	13.9601
23	.5764	6.7955	7.1646
24	.2073	7.1646	0.0000

YEARS 25   MO PAYT .6022   AN CONST 7.23

#	INT	PRIN	BALANCE
1	5.2525	1.9739	98.0261
2	5.1453	2.0811	95.9450
3	5.0323	2.1941	93.7509
4	4.9131	2.3133	91.4376
5	4.7875	2.4389	88.9987
6	4.6551	2.5713	86.4273
7	4.5154	2.7110	83.7164
8	4.3682	2.8582	80.8581
9	4.2130	3.0134	77.8447
10	4.0493	3.1771	74.6676
11	3.8768	3.3496	71.3180
12	3.6949	3.5315	67.7865
13	3.5031	3.7233	64.0632
14	3.3009	3.9255	60.1376
15	3.0877	4.1387	55.9989
16	2.8630	4.3635	51.6355
17	2.6260	4.6004	47.0351
18	2.3762	4.8503	42.1848
19	2.1128	5.1137	37.0712
20	1.8351	5.3914	31.6798
21	1.5423	5.6841	25.9957
22	1.2336	5.9928	20.0028
23	.9081	6.3183	13.6846
24	.5650	6.6614	7.0232
25	.2033	7.0232	0.0000

YEARS 26   MO PAYT .5911   AN CONST 7.10

#	INT	PRIN	BALANCE
1	5.2558	1.8378	98.1622
2	5.1560	1.9376	96.2245
3	5.0508	2.0429	94.1817
4	4.9398	2.1538	92.0279
5	4.8228	2.2708	89.7571
6	4.6995	2.3941	87.3631
7	4.5695	2.5241	84.8390
8	4.4324	2.6612	82.1778
9	4.2879	2.8057	79.3721
10	4.1356	2.9581	76.4141
11	3.9749	3.1187	73.2954
12	3.8055	3.2881	70.0073
13	3.6270	3.4666	66.5407
14	3.4387	3.6549	62.8858
15	3.2402	3.8534	59.0324
16	3.0310	4.0626	54.9698
17	2.8103	4.2833	50.6865
18	2.5777	4.5159	46.1707
19	2.3325	4.7611	41.4095
20	2.0739	5.0197	36.3899
21	1.8013	5.2923	31.0976
22	1.5139	5.5797	25.5179
23	1.2109	5.8827	19.6352
24	.8914	6.2022	13.4331
25	.5546	6.5390	6.8941
26	.1995	6.8941	0.0000

YEARS 27   MO PAYT .5810   AN CONST 6.98

#	INT	PRIN	BALANCE
1	5.2588	1.7133	98.2867
2	5.1657	1.8063	96.4804
3	5.0676	1.9044	94.5759
4	4.9642	2.0079	92.5681
5	4.8552	2.1169	90.4512
6	4.7402	2.2319	88.2193
7	4.6190	2.3531	85.8663
8	4.4912	2.4808	83.3854
9	4.3565	2.6156	80.7699
10	4.2145	2.7576	78.0122
11	4.0647	2.9074	75.1049
12	3.9068	3.0653	72.0396
13	3.7403	3.2317	68.8079
14	3.5648	3.4072	65.4006
15	3.3798	3.5923	61.8084
16	3.1847	3.7874	58.0210
17	2.9790	3.9930	54.0280
18	2.7622	4.2099	49.8181
19	2.5336	4.4385	45.3794
20	2.2925	4.6795	40.7001
21	2.0384	4.9337	35.7664
22	1.7705	5.2016	30.5648
23	1.4880	5.4841	25.0807
24	1.1902	5.7819	19.2988
25	.8762	6.0959	13.2029
26	.5451	6.4269	6.7760
27	.1961	6.7760	0.0000

YEARS 28   MO PAYT .5717   AN CONST 6.87

#	INT	PRIN	BALANCE
1	5.2615	1.5991	98.4009
2	5.1747	1.6859	96.7150
3	5.0831	1.7775	94.9376
4	4.9866	1.8740	93.0636
5	4.8848	1.9757	91.0879
6	4.7775	2.0830	89.0048
7	4.6644	2.1962	86.8087
8	4.5452	2.3154	84.4932
9	4.4194	2.4412	82.0520
10	4.2868	2.5737	79.4783
11	4.1471	2.7135	76.7648
12	3.9997	2.8609	73.9039
13	3.8443	3.0162	70.8876
14	3.6805	3.1801	67.7076
15	3.5078	3.3527	64.3548
16	3.3258	3.5348	60.8200
17	3.1338	3.7268	57.0932
18	2.9314	3.9292	53.1641
19	2.7180	4.1426	49.0215
20	2.4931	4.3675	44.6540
21	2.2559	4.6047	40.0493
22	2.0058	4.8548	35.1945
23	1.7422	5.1184	30.0761
24	1.4642	5.3964	24.6797
25	1.1711	5.6894	18.9902
26	.8622	5.9984	12.9918
27	.5364	6.3242	6.6676
28	.1930	6.6676	0.0000

YEARS 29   MO PAYT .5632   AN CONST 6.76

#	INT	PRIN	BALANCE
1	5.2641	1.4940	98.5060
2	5.1829	1.5752	96.9308
3	5.0974	1.6607	95.2701
4	5.0072	1.7509	93.5192
5	4.9121	1.8460	91.6732
6	4.8119	1.9462	89.7270
7	4.7062	2.0519	87.6751
8	4.5947	2.1634	85.5117
9	4.4772	2.2808	83.2309
10	4.3534	2.4047	80.8262
11	4.2228	2.5353	78.2909
12	4.0851	2.6730	75.6179
13	3.9399	2.8181	72.7997
14	3.7869	2.9712	69.8286
15	3.6255	3.1325	66.6960
16	3.4554	3.3027	63.3934
17	3.2761	3.4820	59.9114
18	3.0870	3.6711	56.2402
19	2.8876	3.8705	52.3698
20	2.6774	4.0807	48.2891
21	2.4558	4.3023	43.9868
22	2.2222	4.5359	39.4509
23	1.9758	4.7822	34.6687
24	1.7161	5.0420	29.6267
25	1.4423	5.3158	24.3109
26	1.1536	5.6044	18.7065
27	.8493	5.9088	12.7977
28	.5284	6.2297	6.5680
29	.1901	6.5680	0.0000

YEARS 30   MO PAYT .5553   AN CONST 6.67

#	INT	PRIN	BALANCE
1	5.2664	1.3973	98.6027
2	5.1905	1.4732	97.1296
3	5.1105	1.5532	95.5764
4	5.0262	1.6375	93.9389
5	4.9372	1.7264	92.2125
6	4.8435	1.8202	90.3923
7	4.7446	1.9190	88.4733
8	4.6404	2.0233	86.4500
9	4.5305	2.1331	84.3169
10	4.4147	2.2490	82.0679
11	4.2926	2.3711	79.6968
12	4.1638	2.4999	77.1969
13	4.0280	2.6356	74.5613
14	3.8849	2.7788	71.7825
15	3.7340	2.9297	68.8529
16	3.5749	3.0888	65.7641
17	3.4071	3.2565	62.5076
18	3.2303	3.4334	59.0742
19	3.0438	3.6198	55.4544
20	2.8473	3.8164	51.6380
21	2.6400	4.0236	47.6144
22	2.4215	4.2422	43.3722
23	2.1911	4.4725	38.8997
24	1.9482	4.7154	34.1842
25	1.6922	4.9715	29.2127
26	1.4222	5.2415	23.9713
27	1.1375	5.5261	18.4451
28	.8374	5.8262	12.6189
29	.5210	6.1426	6.4762
30	.1874	6.4762	0.0000

YEARS 2 — MO PAYT 4.4040 — AN CONST 52.85

#	INT	PRIN	BALANCE
1	4.1879	48.6596	51.3404
2	1.5070	51.3404	0.0000

YEARS 3 — MO PAYT 3.0140 — AN CONST 36.17

#	INT	PRIN	BALANCE
1	4.6050	31.5625	68.4375
2	2.8661	33.3014	35.1361
3	1.0314	35.1361	0.0000

YEARS 4 — MO PAYT 2.3200 — AN CONST 27.84

#	INT	PRIN	BALANCE
1	4.8132	23.0262	76.9738
2	3.5446	24.2948	52.6789
3	2.2061	25.6333	27.0456
4	.7939	27.0456	0.0000

YEARS 5 — MO PAYT 1.9044 — AN CONST 22.86

#	INT	PRIN	BALANCE
1	4.9379	17.9143	82.0857
2	3.9510	18.9012	63.1845
3	2.9096	19.9426	43.2419
4	1.8109	21.0413	22.2006
5	.6517	22.2006	0.0000

YEARS 6 — MO PAYT 1.6279 — AN CONST 19.54

#	INT	PRIN	BALANCE
1	5.0209	14.5145	85.4855
2	4.2212	15.3141	70.1714
3	3.3775	16.1578	54.0136
4	2.4873	17.0480	36.9656
5	1.5481	17.9873	18.9783
6	.5571	18.9783	0.0000

YEARS 7 — MO PAYT 1.4311 — AN CONST 17.18

#	INT	PRIN	BALANCE
1	5.0800	12.0930	87.9070
2	4.4137	12.7592	75.1478
3	3.7108	13.4622	61.6856
4	2.9691	14.2039	47.4817
5	2.1865	14.9864	32.4953
6	1.3609	15.8121	16.6832
7	.4897	16.6832	0.0000

YEARS 8 — MO PAYT 1.2839 — AN CONST 15.41

#	INT	PRIN	BALANCE
1	5.1241	10.2829	89.7171
2	4.5576	10.8495	78.8676
3	3.9599	11.4472	67.4204
4	3.3292	12.0779	55.3425
5	2.6638	12.7433	42.5992
6	1.9617	13.4454	29.1539
7	1.2209	14.1861	14.9677
8	.4393	14.9677	0.0000

YEARS 9 — MO PAYT 1.1699 — AN CONST 14.04

#	INT	PRIN	BALANCE
1	5.1583	8.8805	91.1195
2	4.6691	9.3698	81.7497
3	4.1529	9.8860	71.8638
4	3.6082	10.4306	61.4331
5	3.0335	11.0053	50.4278
6	2.4272	11.6116	38.8162
7	1.7875	12.2514	26.5648
8	1.1125	12.9263	13.6385
9	.4003	13.6385	0.0000

YEARS 10 — MO PAYT 1.0791 — AN CONST 12.95

#	INT	PRIN	BALANCE
1	5.1856	7.7634	92.2366
2	4.7579	8.1911	84.0456
3	4.3066	8.6423	75.4032
4	3.8305	9.1185	66.2847
5	3.3281	9.6209	56.6639
6	2.7980	10.1509	46.5129
7	2.2388	10.7102	35.8028
8	1.6487	11.3002	24.5025
9	1.0261	11.9228	12.5797
10	.3693	12.5797	0.0000

YEARS 11 — MO PAYT 1.0051 — AN CONST 12.07

#	INT	PRIN	BALANCE
1	5.2078	6.8537	93.1463
2	4.8302	7.2313	85.9150
3	4.4318	7.6297	78.2854
4	4.0114	8.0500	70.2353
5	3.5679	8.4935	61.7418
6	3.1000	8.9615	52.7803
7	2.6063	9.4552	43.3251
8	2.0853	9.9761	33.3490
9	1.5357	10.5258	22.8232
10	.9558	11.1057	11.7175
11	.3439	11.7175	0.0000

YEARS 12 — MO PAYT .9438 — AN CONST 11.33

#	INT	PRIN	BALANCE
1	5.2262	6.0996	93.9004
2	4.8901	6.4356	87.4648
3	4.5356	6.7902	80.6746
4	4.1615	7.1643	73.5103
5	3.7668	7.5590	65.9513
6	3.3503	7.9755	57.9758
7	2.9109	8.4149	49.5609
8	2.4473	8.8785	40.6824
9	1.9581	9.3676	31.3148
10	1.4420	9.8837	21.4311
11	.8975	10.4283	11.0028
12	.3230	11.0028	0.0000

YEARS 13 — MO PAYT .8922 — AN CONST 10.71

#	INT	PRIN	BALANCE
1	5.2417	5.4651	94.5349
2	4.9406	5.7662	88.7686
3	4.6229	6.0839	82.6847
4	4.2877	6.4191	76.2656
5	3.9340	6.7728	69.4928
6	3.5609	7.1459	62.3469
7	3.1672	7.5396	54.8073
8	2.7518	7.9550	46.8524
9	2.3135	8.3933	38.4591
10	1.8511	8.8557	29.6034
11	1.3632	9.3436	20.2598
12	.8485	9.8584	10.4015
13	.3053	10.4015	0.0000

YEARS 14 — MO PAYT .8483 — AN CONST 10.18

#	INT	PRIN	BALANCE
1	5.2549	4.9247	95.0753
2	4.9835	5.1960	89.8793
3	4.6973	5.4823	84.3971
4	4.3952	5.7843	78.6128
5	4.0765	6.1030	72.5098
6	3.7403	6.4392	66.0705
7	3.3855	6.7940	59.2766
8	3.0112	7.1683	52.1083
9	2.6163	7.5632	44.5450
10	2.1996	7.9799	36.5651
11	1.7600	8.4196	28.1455
12	1.2961	8.8834	19.2621
13	.8067	9.3729	9.8892
14	.2903	9.8892	0.0000

YEARS 15 — MO PAYT .8105 — AN CONST 9.73

#	INT	PRIN	BALANCE
1	5.2662	4.4594	95.5406
2	5.0205	4.7051	90.8356
3	4.7613	4.9643	85.8713
4	4.4878	5.2378	80.6335
5	4.1992	5.5264	75.1071
6	3.8948	5.8308	69.2763
7	3.5735	6.1521	63.1242
8	3.2346	6.4910	56.6332
9	2.8769	6.8486	49.7846
10	2.4996	7.2260	42.5586
11	2.1015	7.6241	34.9345
12	1.6815	8.0441	26.8904
13	1.2383	8.4873	18.4031
14	.7707	8.9549	9.4482
15	.2773	9.4482	0.0000

YEARS 16 — MO PAYT .7776 — AN CONST 9.34

#	INT	PRIN	BALANCE
1	5.2761	4.0551	95.9449
2	5.0527	4.2785	91.6663
3	4.8169	4.5143	87.1521
4	4.5682	4.7630	82.3891
5	4.3058	5.0254	77.3637
6	4.0289	5.3023	72.0614
7	3.7368	5.5944	66.4670
8	3.4286	5.9026	60.5644
9	3.1034	6.2278	54.3366
10	2.7603	6.5709	47.7657
11	2.3983	6.9329	40.8328
12	2.0163	7.3149	33.5179
13	1.6133	7.7179	25.8000
14	1.1881	8.1431	17.6569
15	.7394	8.5918	9.0651
16	.2661	9.0651	0.0000

YEARS 17 — MO PAYT .7488 — AN CONST 8.99

#	INT	PRIN	BALANCE
1	5.2847	3.7011	96.2989
2	5.0808	3.9050	92.3938
3	4.8656	4.1202	88.2736
4	4.6386	4.3472	83.9264
5	4.3991	4.5867	79.3397
6	4.1464	4.8394	74.5003
7	3.8798	5.1060	69.3943
8	3.5985	5.3873	64.0070
9	3.3017	5.6841	58.3229
10	2.9885	5.9973	52.3256
11	2.6581	6.3277	45.9978
12	2.3095	6.6763	39.3215
13	1.9417	7.0442	32.2773
14	1.5536	7.4323	24.8451
15	1.1441	7.8417	17.0034
16	.7121	8.2738	8.7296
17	.2562	8.7296	0.0000

YEARS 18 — MO PAYT .7234 — AN CONST 8.69

#	INT	PRIN	BALANCE
1	5.2923	3.3890	96.6110
2	5.1056	3.5757	93.0353
3	4.9086	3.7727	89.2626
4	4.7008	3.9806	85.2820
5	4.4814	4.1999	81.0822
6	4.2501	4.4313	76.6509
7	4.0059	4.6754	71.9755
8	3.7483	4.9330	67.0426
9	3.4766	5.2048	61.8378
10	3.1898	5.4915	56.3463
11	2.8873	5.7941	50.5523
12	2.5680	6.1133	44.4390
13	2.2312	6.4501	37.9889
14	1.8759	6.8054	31.1835
15	1.5009	7.1804	24.0031
16	1.1053	7.5760	16.4271
17	.6879	7.9934	8.4338
18	.2476	8.4338	0.0000

YEARS 19 — MO PAYT .7009 — AN CONST 8.42

#	INT	PRIN	BALANCE
1	5.2991	3.1121	96.8879
2	5.1276	3.2835	93.6044
3	4.9467	3.4644	90.1400
4	4.7558	3.6553	86.4847
5	4.5545	3.8567	82.6280
6	4.3420	4.0692	78.5588
7	4.1178	4.2933	74.2655
8	3.8813	4.5299	69.7356
9	3.6317	4.7795	64.9562
10	3.3684	5.0428	59.9134
11	3.0905	5.3206	54.5928
12	2.7974	5.6137	48.9790
13	2.4881	5.9230	43.0560
14	2.1618	6.2493	36.8067
15	1.8175	6.5936	30.2130
16	1.4542	6.9569	23.2561
17	1.0709	7.3402	15.9159
18	.6665	7.7446	8.1713
19	.2399	8.1713	0.0000

YEARS 20 — MO PAYT .6808 — AN CONST 8.18

#	INT	PRIN	BALANCE
1	5.3051	2.8651	97.1349
2	5.1473	3.0229	94.1120
3	4.9807	3.1894	90.9226
4	4.8050	3.3652	87.5574
5	4.6196	3.5506	84.0069
6	4.4240	3.7462	80.2607
7	4.2176	3.9526	76.3081
8	3.9998	4.1703	72.1377
9	3.7701	4.4001	67.7376
10	3.5276	4.6425	63.0951
11	3.2719	4.8983	58.1968
12	3.0020	5.1682	53.0287
13	2.7173	5.4529	47.5758
14	2.4168	5.7533	41.8224
15	2.0999	6.0703	35.7521
16	1.7654	6.4047	29.3474
17	1.4126	6.7576	22.5898
18	1.0403	7.1299	15.4599
19	.6474	7.5227	7.9372
20	.2330	7.9372	0.0000

YEARS 21 — MO PAYT .6628 — AN CONST 7.96

#	INT	PRIN	BALANCE
1	5.3105	2.6437	97.3563
2	5.1649	2.7893	94.5670
3	5.0112	2.9430	91.6240

#	INT	PRIN	BALANCE
4	4.8490	3.1051	88.5189
5	4.6780	3.2762	85.2427
6	4.4975	3.4567	81.7860
7	4.3070	3.6471	78.1388
8	4.1061	3.8481	74.2908
9	3.8941	4.0601	70.2307
10	3.6704	4.2838	65.9469
11	3.4344	4.5198	61.4271
12	3.1854	4.7688	56.6583
13	2.9226	5.0315	51.6268
14	2.6454	5.3087	46.3180
15	2.3529	5.6012	40.7168
16	2.0443	5.9098	34.8070
17	1.7187	6.2354	28.5716
18	1.3752	6.5790	21.9926
19	1.0128	6.9414	15.0512
20	.6303	7.3238	7.7273
21	.2268	7.7273	0.0000

YEARS 22 — MO PAYT .6466 — AN CONST 7.76

#	INT	PRIN	BALANCE
1	5.3154	2.4444	97.5556
2	5.1807	2.5790	94.9766
3	5.0386	2.7211	92.2555
4	4.8887	2.8711	89.3844
5	4.7305	3.0292	86.3552
6	4.5636	3.1961	83.1591
7	4.3875	3.3722	79.7868
8	4.2017	3.5580	76.2288
9	4.0057	3.7540	72.4748
10	3.7989	3.9608	68.5140
11	3.5807	4.1791	64.3349
12	3.3504	4.4093	59.9256
13	3.1075	4.6522	55.2734
14	2.8512	4.9085	50.3648
15	2.5808	5.1790	45.1858
16	2.2954	5.4643	39.7215
17	1.9944	5.7654	33.9562
18	1.6767	6.0830	27.8732
19	1.3416	6.4181	21.4550
20	.9880	6.7717	14.6833
21	.6149	7.1448	7.5385
22	.2213	7.5385	0.0000

YEARS 23 — MO PAYT .6320 — AN CONST 7.59

#	INT	PRIN	BALANCE
1	5.3198	2.2643	97.7357
2	5.1950	2.3890	95.3467
3	5.0634	2.5206	92.8261
4	4.9245	2.6595	90.1665
5	4.7780	2.8060	87.3605
6	4.6234	2.9606	84.3999
7	4.4603	3.1238	81.2761
8	4.2882	3.2959	77.9802
9	4.1066	3.4774	74.5028
10	3.9150	3.6690	70.8338
11	3.7129	3.8712	66.9626
12	3.4996	4.0844	62.8782
13	3.2746	4.3095	58.5687
14	3.0371	4.5469	54.0218
15	2.7866	4.7974	49.2244
16	2.5223	5.0617	44.1627
17	2.2435	5.3406	38.8221
18	1.9492	5.6348	33.1873
19	1.6388	5.9453	27.2420
20	1.3112	6.2728	20.9692
21	.9656	6.6184	14.3508
22	.6010	6.9830	7.3678
23	.2163	7.3678	0.0000

YEARS 24 — MO PAYT .6187 — AN CONST 7.43

#	INT	PRIN	BALANCE
1	5.3237	2.1010	97.8990
2	5.2080	2.2167	95.6823
3	5.0859	2.3388	93.3435
4	4.9570	2.4677	90.8758
5	4.8211	2.6036	88.2722
6	4.6776	2.7471	85.5251
7	4.5263	2.8984	82.6266
8	4.3666	3.0581	79.5685
9	4.1981	3.2266	76.3419
10	4.0203	3.4044	72.9375
11	3.8328	3.5919	69.3456
12	3.6349	3.7898	65.5558
13	3.4261	3.9986	61.5571
14	3.2058	4.2189	57.3382
15	2.9733	4.4514	52.8868
16	2.7281	4.6966	48.1902
17	2.4693	4.9554	43.2349
18	2.1963	5.2284	38.0065
19	1.9083	5.5164	32.4900
20	1.6043	5.8204	26.6697
21	1.2837	6.1410	20.5287
22	.9453	6.4794	14.0493
23	.5884	6.8363	7.2130
24	.2117	7.2130	0.0000

YEARS 25 — MO PAYT .6066 — AN CONST 7.28

#	INT	PRIN	BALANCE
1	5.3274	1.9524	98.0476
2	5.2198	2.0599	95.9877
3	5.1063	2.1734	93.8143
4	4.9866	2.2932	91.5211
5	4.8602	2.4195	89.1016
6	4.7269	2.5528	86.5488
7	4.5863	2.6935	83.8553
8	4.4379	2.8418	81.0135
9	4.2813	2.9984	78.0151
10	4.1161	3.1636	74.8514
11	3.9418	3.3379	71.5135
12	3.7579	3.5218	67.9917
13	3.5639	3.7158	64.2759
14	3.3592	3.9206	60.3553
15	3.1432	4.1366	56.2188
16	2.9153	4.3645	51.8543
17	2.6748	4.6049	47.2494
18	2.4211	4.8586	42.3908
19	2.1534	5.1263	37.2645
20	1.8710	5.4087	31.8557
21	1.5730	5.7067	26.1490
22	1.2586	6.0211	20.1279
23	.9269	6.3529	13.7750
24	.5769	6.7029	7.0722
25	.2076	7.0722	0.0000

YEARS 26 — MO PAYT .5956 — AN CONST 7.15

#	INT	PRIN	BALANCE
1	5.3307	1.8168	98.1832
2	5.2306	1.9169	96.2663
3	5.1250	2.0225	94.2438
4	5.0135	2.1339	92.1098
5	4.8960	2.2515	89.8583
6	4.7719	2.3756	87.4828
7	4.6411	2.5064	84.9764
8	4.5030	2.6445	82.3318
9	4.3573	2.7902	79.5416
10	4.2035	2.9439	76.5977
11	4.0413	3.1061	73.4915
12	3.8702	3.2773	70.2143
13	3.6897	3.4578	66.7564
14	3.4992	3.6483	63.1081
15	3.2981	3.8493	59.2588

YEARS 27 — MO PAYT .5855 — AN CONST 7.03

#	INT	PRIN	BALANCE
1	5.3337	1.6928	98.3072
2	5.2404	1.7861	96.5212
3	5.1420	1.8845	94.6367
4	5.0382	1.9883	92.6484
5	4.9287	2.0978	90.5506
6	4.8131	2.2134	88.3372
7	4.6912	2.3353	86.0019
8	4.5625	2.4640	83.5379
9	4.4267	2.5998	80.9381
10	4.2835	2.7430	78.1951
11	4.1324	2.8941	75.3010
12	3.9729	3.0536	72.2475
13	3.8047	3.2218	69.0257
14	3.6272	3.3993	65.6264
15	3.4399	3.5866	62.0398
16	3.2423	3.7842	58.2557
17	3.0338	3.9927	54.2630
18	2.8139	4.2126	50.0504
19	2.5818	4.4447	45.6056
20	2.3369	4.6896	40.9160
21	2.0785	4.9480	35.9681
22	1.8059	5.2206	30.7475
23	1.5183	5.5082	25.2393
24	1.2148	5.8117	19.4277
25	.8946	6.1319	13.2958
26	.5568	6.4697	6.8261
27	.2004	6.8261	0.0000

YEARS 28 — MO PAYT .5763 — AN CONST 6.92

#	INT	PRIN	BALANCE
1	5.3365	1.5791	98.4209
2	5.2495	1.6661	96.7549
3	5.1577	1.7578	94.9970
4	5.0608	1.8547	93.1423
5	4.9587	1.9569	91.1855
6	4.8508	2.0647	89.1208
7	4.7371	2.1784	86.9423
8	4.6171	2.2985	84.6439
9	4.4904	2.4251	82.2188
10	4.3568	2.5587	79.6601
11	4.2159	2.6997	76.9604
12	4.0671	2.8484	74.1120
13	3.9102	3.0053	71.1066
14	3.7446	3.1709	67.9357
15	3.5699	3.3456	64.5901
16	3.3856	3.5299	61.0602
17	3.1911	3.7244	57.3358
18	2.9859	3.9296	53.4061
19	2.7694	4.1461	49.2600
20	2.5410	4.3745	44.8855
21	2.3000	4.6155	40.2700
22	2.0457	4.8698	35.4001
23	1.7774	5.1381	30.2620
24	1.4943	5.4212	24.8408
25	1.1956	5.7199	19.1209
26	.8805	6.0350	13.0859
27	.5480	6.3675	6.7183

#	INT	PRIN	BALANCE
16	3.0861	4.0614	55.1974
17	2.8623	4.2852	50.9122
18	2.6262	4.5213	46.3909
19	2.3771	4.7703	41.6206
20	2.1143	5.0332	36.5874
21	1.8370	5.3105	31.2770
22	1.5444	5.6030	25.6739
23	1.2357	5.9117	19.7622
24	.9100	6.2374	13.5247
25	.5664	6.5811	6.9437
26	.2038	6.9437	0.0000

#	INT	PRIN	BALANCE
28	.1972	6.7183	0.0000

YEARS 29 — MO PAYT .5678 — AN CONST 6.82

#	INT	PRIN	BALANCE
1	5.3390	1.4745	98.5255
2	5.2578	1.5558	96.9697
3	5.1721	1.6415	95.3282
4	5.0816	1.7319	93.5963
5	4.9862	1.8273	91.7689
6	4.8855	1.9280	89.8409
7	4.7793	2.0342	87.8066
8	4.6672	2.1463	85.6603
9	4.5490	2.2646	83.3958
10	4.4242	2.3893	81.0064
11	4.2926	2.5210	78.4854
12	4.1537	2.6599	75.8256
13	4.0072	2.8064	73.0192
14	3.8525	2.9610	70.0581
15	3.6894	3.1242	66.9340
16	3.5173	3.2963	63.6377
17	3.3357	3.4779	60.1598
18	3.1441	3.6695	56.4903
19	2.9419	3.8717	52.6187
20	2.7286	4.0850	48.5337
21	2.5035	4.3100	44.2237
22	2.2661	4.5475	39.6762
23	2.0155	4.7980	34.8781
24	1.7512	5.0624	29.8158
25	1.4723	5.3413	24.4745
26	1.1780	5.6356	18.8389
27	.8675	5.9460	12.8929
28	.5399	6.2736	6.6193
29	.1943	6.6193	0.0000

YEARS 30 — MO PAYT .5600 — AN CONST 6.72

#	INT	PRIN	BALANCE
1	5.3414	1.3783	98.6217
2	5.2654	1.4542	97.1675
3	5.1853	1.5343	95.6332
4	5.1008	1.6189	94.0143
5	5.0116	1.7081	92.3062
6	4.9175	1.8022	90.5041
7	4.8182	1.9014	88.6026
8	4.7134	2.0062	86.5964
9	4.6029	2.1167	84.4797
10	4.4863	2.2334	82.2463
11	4.3633	2.3564	79.8899
12	4.2334	2.4862	77.4037
13	4.0965	2.6232	74.7805
14	3.9519	2.7677	72.0128
15	3.7994	2.9202	69.0926
16	3.6386	3.0811	66.0115
17	3.4688	3.2508	62.7606
18	3.2897	3.4300	59.3306
19	3.1007	3.6189	55.7117
20	2.9014	3.8183	51.8934
21	2.6910	4.0287	47.8648
22	2.4690	4.2506	43.6141
23	2.2348	4.4848	39.1293
24	1.9878	4.7319	34.3974
25	1.7271	4.9926	29.4048
26	1.4520	5.2677	24.1372
27	1.1618	5.5579	18.5793
28	.8556	5.8641	12.7152
29	.5325	6.1872	6.5280
30	.1916	6.5280	0.0000

YEARS 2 — MO PAYT 4.4051 — AN CONST 52.87

#	INT	PRIN	BALANCE
1	4.2075	48.6534	51.3466
2	1.5143	51.3466	0.0000

YEARS 3 — MO PAYT 3.0151 — AN CONST 36.19

#	INT	PRIN	BALANCE
1	4.6266	31.5544	68.4456
2	2.8799	33.3011	35.1445
3	1.0364	35.1445	0.0000

YEARS 4 — MO PAYT 2.3211 — AN CONST 27.86

#	INT	PRIN	BALANCE
1	4.8359	23.0173	76.9827
2	3.5617	24.2914	52.6913
3	2.2170	25.6361	27.0552
4	.7979	27.0552	0.0000

YEARS 5 — MO PAYT 1.9055 — AN CONST 22.87

#	INT	PRIN	BALANCE
1	4.9612	17.9049	82.0951
2	3.9700	18.8960	63.1991
3	2.9240	19.9421	43.2570
4	1.8201	21.0460	22.2110
5	.6550	22.2110	0.0000

YEARS 6 — MO PAYT 1.6291 — AN CONST 19.55

#	INT	PRIN	BALANCE
1	5.0445	14.5049	85.4951
2	4.2416	15.3078	70.1873
3	3.3942	16.1552	54.0321
4	2.4999	17.0495	36.9826
5	1.5561	17.9933	18.9893
6	.5600	18.9893	0.0000

YEARS 7 — MO PAYT 1.4323 — AN CONST 17.19

#	INT	PRIN	BALANCE
1	5.1038	12.0833	87.9167
2	4.4350	12.7522	75.1645
3	3.7290	13.4581	61.7064
4	2.9840	14.2031	47.5033
5	2.1978	14.9894	32.5139
6	1.3680	15.8191	16.6948
7	.4923	16.6948	0.0000

YEARS 8 — MO PAYT 1.2851 — AN CONST 15.43

#	INT	PRIN	BALANCE
1	5.1482	10.2733	89.7267
2	4.5795	10.8420	78.8848
3	3.9793	11.4421	67.4427
4	3.3459	12.0755	55.3671
5	2.6775	12.7440	42.6231
6	1.9720	13.4495	29.1737
7	1.2275	14.1940	14.9797
8	.4418	14.9797	0.0000

YEARS 9 — MO PAYT 1.1711 — AN CONST 14.06

#	INT	PRIN	BALANCE
1	5.1826	8.8709	91.1291
2	4.6915	9.3619	81.7672
3	4.1733	9.8802	71.8870
4	3.6263	10.4271	61.4599
5	3.0491	11.0043	50.4556
6	2.4400	11.6135	38.8421
7	1.7971	12.2564	26.5857
8	1.1186	12.9348	13.6509
9	.4026	13.6509	0.0000

YEARS 10 — MO PAYT 1.0803 — AN CONST 12.97

#	INT	PRIN	BALANCE
1	5.2100	7.7538	92.2462
2	4.7807	8.1830	84.0631
3	4.3277	8.6360	75.4271
4	3.8497	9.1141	66.3130
5	3.3452	9.6186	56.6944
6	2.8127	10.1511	46.5434
7	2.2508	10.7130	35.8304
8	1.6577	11.3060	24.5243
9	1.0319	11.9319	12.5924
10	.3714	12.5924	0.0000

YEARS 11 — MO PAYT 1.0064 — AN CONST 12.08

#	INT	PRIN	BALANCE
1	5.2323	6.8442	93.1558
2	4.8534	7.2231	85.9326
3	4.4535	7.6230	78.3097
4	4.0315	8.0450	70.2647
5	3.5862	8.4903	61.7744
6	3.1162	8.9603	52.8141
7	2.6202	9.4563	43.3578
8	2.0967	9.9798	33.3780
9	1.5443	10.5322	22.8458
10	.9612	11.1153	11.7306
11	.3459	11.7306	0.0000

YEARS 12 — MO PAYT .9451 — AN CONST 11.35

#	INT	PRIN	BALANCE
1	5.2507	6.0903	93.9097
2	4.9136	6.4274	87.4823
3	4.5578	6.7832	80.6991
4	4.1823	7.1587	73.5404
5	3.7860	7.5550	65.9854
6	3.3678	7.9732	58.0122
7	2.9264	8.4146	49.5976
8	2.4606	8.8804	40.7172
9	1.9690	9.3720	31.3452
10	1.4502	9.8908	21.4544
11	.9027	10.4383	11.0161
12	.3249	11.0161	0.0000

YEARS 13 — MO PAYT .8935 — AN CONST 10.73

#	INT	PRIN	BALANCE
1	5.2663	5.4560	94.5440
2	4.9643	5.7580	88.7860
3	4.6455	6.0767	82.7093
4	4.3091	6.4131	76.2962
5	3.9541	6.7681	69.5280
6	3.5794	7.1428	62.3852
7	3.1840	7.5382	54.8470
8	2.7668	7.9555	46.8916
9	2.3264	8.3959	38.4957
10	1.8616	8.8606	29.6350
11	1.3711	9.3511	20.2839
12	.8535	9.8688	10.4151
13	.3071	10.4151	0.0000

YEARS 14 — MO PAYT .8496 — AN CONST 10.20

#	INT	PRIN	BALANCE
1	5.2795	4.9157	95.0843
2	5.0074	5.1878	89.8966
3	4.7202	5.4749	84.4216
4	4.4172	5.7780	78.6436
5	4.0973	6.0979	72.5457
6	3.7597	6.4354	66.1103
7	3.4035	6.7917	59.3186
8	3.0275	7.1676	52.1510
9	2.6308	7.5644	44.5865
10	2.2120	7.9832	36.6034
11	1.7701	8.4251	28.1783
12	1.3037	8.8915	19.2868
13	.8115	9.3837	9.9031
14	.2921	9.9031	0.0000

YEARS 15 — MO PAYT .8118 — AN CONST 9.75

#	INT	PRIN	BALANCE
1	5.2909	4.4505	95.5495
2	5.0446	4.6969	90.8526
3	4.7846	4.9569	85.8957
4	4.5102	5.2313	80.6644
5	4.2206	5.5209	75.1436
6	3.9149	5.8265	69.3171
7	3.5924	6.1490	63.1680
8	3.2520	6.4894	56.6786
9	2.8928	6.8486	49.8300
10	2.5137	7.2278	42.6022
11	2.1136	7.6279	34.9743
12	1.6913	8.0501	26.9242
13	1.2457	8.4958	18.4284
14	.7754	8.9661	9.4624
15	.2791	9.4624	0.0000

YEARS 16 — MO PAYT .7789 — AN CONST 9.35

#	INT	PRIN	BALANCE
1	5.3008	4.0464	95.9536
2	5.0768	4.2704	91.6831
3	4.8404	4.5068	87.1763
4	4.5909	4.7563	82.4200
5	4.3277	5.0196	77.4004
6	4.0498	5.2975	72.1029
7	3.7565	5.5907	66.5122
8	3.4470	5.9002	60.6120
9	3.1204	6.2268	54.3852
10	2.7757	6.5715	47.8136
11	2.4120	6.9353	40.8783
12	2.0280	7.3192	33.5591
13	1.6229	7.7244	25.8347
14	1.1953	8.1520	17.6827
15	.7440	8.6032	9.0795
16	.2678	9.0795	0.0000

YEARS 17 — MO PAYT .7502 — AN CONST 9.01

#	INT	PRIN	BALANCE
1	5.3095	3.6926	96.3074
2	5.1051	3.8970	92.4104
3	4.8894	4.1127	88.2976
4	4.6617	4.3404	83.9572
5	4.4214	4.5807	79.3766
6	4.1678	4.8343	74.5423
7	3.9002	5.1019	69.4404
8	3.6178	5.3843	64.0562
9	3.3198	5.6823	58.3738
10	3.0052	5.9969	52.3769
11	2.6732	6.3289	46.0481
12	2.3229	6.6792	39.3689
13	1.9532	7.0489	32.3199
14	1.5629	7.4392	24.8808
15	1.1511	7.8510	17.0298
16	.7165	8.2856	8.7442
17	.2579	8.7442	0.0000

YEARS 18 — MO PAYT .7248 — AN CONST 8.70

#	INT	PRIN	BALANCE
1	5.3171	3.3806	96.6194
2	5.1300	3.5678	93.0516
3	4.9325	3.7653	89.2863
4	4.7241	3.9737	85.3126
5	4.5041	4.1937	81.1189
6	4.2719	4.4258	76.6931
7	4.0270	4.6708	72.0223
8	3.7684	4.9294	67.0929
9	3.4955	5.2023	61.8907
10	3.2075	5.4902	56.4004
11	2.9036	5.7942	50.6063
12	2.5829	6.1149	44.4913
13	2.2444	6.4534	38.0379
14	1.8871	6.8106	31.2273
15	1.5101	7.1877	24.0396
16	1.1122	7.5855	16.4541
17	.6923	8.0055	8.4486
18	.2492	8.4486	0.0000

YEARS 19 — MO PAYT .7023 — AN CONST 8.43

#	INT	PRIN	BALANCE
1	5.3239	3.1039	96.8961
2	5.1521	3.2757	93.6204
3	4.9708	3.4570	90.1634
4	4.7794	3.6484	86.5150
5	4.5774	3.8504	82.6646
6	4.3643	4.0635	78.6011
7	4.1394	4.2885	74.3127
8	3.9020	4.5258	69.7868
9	3.6514	4.7764	65.0104
10	3.3870	5.0408	59.9696
11	3.1080	5.3198	54.6498
12	2.8135	5.6143	49.0355
13	2.5027	5.9251	43.1104
14	2.1747	6.2531	36.8573
15	1.8286	6.5993	30.2580
16	1.4632	6.9646	23.2935
17	1.0777	7.3501	15.9434
18	.6708	7.7570	8.1864
19	.2414	8.1864	0.0000

YEARS 20 — MO PAYT .6823 — AN CONST 8.19

#	INT	PRIN	BALANCE
1	5.3300	2.8570	97.1430
2	5.1718	3.0152	94.1278
3	5.0049	3.1821	90.9456
4	4.8288	3.3583	87.5874
5	4.6429	3.5442	84.0432
6	4.4467	3.7404	80.3029
7	4.2396	3.9474	76.3554
8	4.0211	4.1659	72.1895
9	3.7905	4.3965	67.7930
10	3.5471	4.6399	63.1531
11	3.2902	4.8968	58.2563
12	3.0192	5.1678	53.0884
13	2.7331	5.4539	47.6345
14	2.4312	5.7558	41.8787
15	2.1126	6.0744	35.8043
16	1.7763	6.4107	29.3935
17	1.4214	6.7656	22.6280
18	1.0469	7.1401	15.4879
19	.6517	7.5354	7.9525
20	.2345	7.9525	0.0000

YEARS 21 — MO PAYT .6643 — AN CONST 7.98

#	INT	PRIN	BALANCE
1	5.3354	2.6358	97.3642
2	5.1895	2.7817	94.5824
3	5.0355	2.9357	91.6467

#	INT	PRIN	BALANCE
4	4.8730	3.0982	88.5485
5	4.7015	3.2697	85.2787
6	4.5205	3.4507	81.8280
7	4.3295	3.6418	78.1862
8	4.1279	3.8434	74.3429
9	3.9151	4.0561	70.2867
10	3.6906	4.2807	66.0061
11	3.4536	4.5176	61.4885
12	3.2035	4.7677	56.7208
13	2.9396	5.0316	51.6891
14	2.6611	5.3102	46.3790
15	2.3671	5.6041	40.7749
16	2.0569	5.9143	34.8605
17	1.7295	6.2417	28.6188
18	1.3840	6.5873	22.0315
19	1.0193	6.9519	15.0796
20	.6345	7.3367	7.7429
21	.2283	7.7429	0.0000

YEARS 22	MO PAYT .6481	AN CONST 7.78	
#	INT	PRIN	BALANCE
1	5.3403	2.4367	97.5633
2	5.2054	2.5716	94.9917
3	5.0630	2.7140	92.2777
4	4.9128	2.8642	89.4135
5	4.7542	3.0227	86.3908
6	4.5869	3.1901	83.2007
7	4.4103	3.3667	79.8341
8	4.2240	3.5530	76.2810
9	4.0273	3.7497	72.5313
10	3.8197	3.9573	68.5740
11	3.6006	4.1763	64.3977
12	3.3695	4.4075	59.9902
13	3.1255	4.6515	55.3386
14	2.8680	4.9090	50.4296
15	2.5962	5.1808	45.2488
16	2.3094	5.4676	39.7813
17	2.0068	5.7702	34.0111
18	1.6873	6.0896	27.9214
19	1.3502	6.4267	21.4947
20	.9945	6.7825	14.7122
21	.6190	7.1580	7.5542
22	.2228	7.5542	0.0000

YEARS 23	MO PAYT .6335	AN CONST 7.61	
#	INT	PRIN	BALANCE
1	5.3447	2.2568	97.7432
2	5.2198	2.3817	95.3615
3	5.0879	2.5136	92.8479
4	4.9488	2.6527	90.1952
5	4.8019	2.7996	87.3957
6	4.6470	2.9545	84.4411
7	4.4834	3.1181	81.3231
8	4.3108	3.2907	78.0324
9	4.1286	3.4728	74.5595
10	3.9364	3.6651	70.8945
11	3.7335	3.8680	67.0265
12	3.5194	4.0821	62.9444
13	3.2934	4.3081	58.6363
14	3.0549	4.5465	54.0898
15	2.8032	4.7982	49.2915
16	2.5376	5.0638	44.2277
17	2.2573	5.3442	38.8835
18	1.9615	5.6400	33.2435
19	1.6493	5.9522	27.2913
20	1.3198	6.2817	21.0096
21	.9720	6.6294	14.3802
22	.6051	6.9964	7.3837
23	.2178	7.3837	0.0000

YEARS 24	MO PAYT .6202	AN CONST 7.45	
#	INT	PRIN	BALANCE
1	5.3487	2.0936	97.9064
2	5.2328	2.2095	95.6968
3	5.1105	2.3319	93.3650
4	4.9814	2.4609	90.9040
5	4.8452	2.5972	88.3069
6	4.7014	2.7409	85.5659
7	4.5497	2.8927	82.6733
8	4.3895	3.0528	79.6205
9	4.2205	3.2218	76.3987
10	4.0422	3.4001	72.9985
11	3.8540	3.5884	69.4102
12	3.6553	3.7870	65.6232
13	3.4457	3.9966	61.6265
14	3.2245	4.2179	57.4087
15	2.9910	4.4514	52.9573
16	2.7446	4.6978	48.2595
17	2.4845	4.9578	43.3017
18	2.2101	5.2323	38.0694
19	1.9204	5.5219	32.5475
20	1.6147	5.8276	26.7199
21	1.2921	6.1502	20.5697
22	.9517	6.4906	14.0791
23	.5924	6.8499	7.2291
24	.2132	7.2291	0.0000

YEARS 25	MO PAYT .6081	AN CONST 7.30	
#	INT	PRIN	BALANCE
1	5.3523	1.9452	98.0548
2	5.2446	2.0529	96.0018
3	5.1310	2.1666	93.8353
4	5.0111	2.2865	91.5488
5	4.8845	2.4131	89.1357
6	4.7509	2.5466	86.5891
7	4.6099	2.6876	83.9015
8	4.4612	2.8364	81.0651
9	4.3041	2.9934	78.0717
10	4.1384	3.1591	74.9125
11	3.9636	3.3340	71.5785
12	3.7790	3.5186	68.0600
13	3.5842	3.7133	64.3467
14	3.3787	3.9189	60.4278
15	3.1617	4.1358	56.2919
16	2.9328	4.3648	51.9272
17	2.6912	4.6064	47.3208
18	2.4362	4.8614	42.4594
19	2.1671	5.1305	37.3289
20	1.8831	5.4145	31.9144
21	1.5833	5.7142	26.2002
22	1.2670	6.0306	20.1696
23	.9332	6.3644	13.8052
24	.5809	6.7167	7.0885
25	.2090	7.0885	0.0000

YEARS 26	MO PAYT .5971	AN CONST 7.17	
#	INT	PRIN	BALANCE
1	5.3556	1.8098	98.1902
2	5.2555	1.9100	96.2801
3	5.1497	2.0158	94.2644
4	5.0381	2.1273	92.1370
5	4.9204	2.2451	89.8919
6	4.7961	2.3694	87.5225
7	4.6649	2.5006	85.0220
8	4.5265	2.6390	82.3830
9	4.3804	2.7851	79.5979
10	4.2262	2.9392	76.6587
11	4.0635	3.1019	73.5567
12	3.8918	3.2737	70.2831
13	3.7106	3.4549	66.8282
14	3.5194	3.6461	63.1821
15	3.3175	3.8480	59.3341
16	3.1045	4.0610	55.2731
17	2.8797	4.2858	50.9874
18	2.6425	4.5230	46.4643
19	2.3921	4.7734	41.6909
20	2.1278	5.0376	36.6533
21	1.8490	5.3165	31.3368
22	1.5547	5.6108	25.7260
23	1.2441	5.9214	19.8046
24	.9163	6.2492	13.5554
25	.5703	6.5951	6.9602
26	.2053	6.9602	0.0000

YEARS 27	MO PAYT .5871	AN CONST 7.05	
#	INT	PRIN	BALANCE
1	5.3587	1.6860	98.3140
2	5.2653	1.7793	96.5347
3	5.1668	1.8778	94.6568
4	5.0629	1.9818	92.6751
5	4.9532	2.0915	90.5836
6	4.8374	2.2073	88.3763
7	4.7152	2.3294	86.0469
8	4.5863	2.4584	83.5885
9	4.4502	2.5945	80.9940
10	4.3066	2.7381	78.2559
11	4.1550	2.8897	75.3662
12	3.9950	3.0496	72.3166
13	3.8262	3.2185	69.0981
14	3.6480	3.3966	65.7015
15	3.4600	3.5847	62.1168
16	3.2616	3.7831	58.3337
17	3.0522	3.9925	54.3412
18	2.8312	4.2135	50.1277
19	2.5979	4.4468	45.6810
20	2.3518	4.6929	40.9880
21	2.0920	4.9527	36.0353
22	1.8178	5.2269	30.8085
23	1.5285	5.5162	25.2922
24	1.2231	5.8216	19.4707
25	.9008	6.1438	13.3268
26	.5607	6.4839	6.8429
27	.2018	6.8429	0.0000

YEARS 28	MO PAYT .5778	AN CONST 6.94	
#	INT	PRIN	BALANCE
1	5.3615	1.5724	98.4276
2	5.2744	1.6595	96.7681
3	5.1826	1.7513	95.0167
4	5.0856	1.8483	93.1684
5	4.9833	1.9506	91.2178
6	4.8753	2.0586	89.1592
7	4.7614	2.1726	86.9867
8	4.6411	2.2928	84.6938
9	4.5142	2.4197	82.2741
10	4.3802	2.5537	79.7204
11	4.2388	2.6951	77.0254
12	4.0897	2.8442	74.1811
13	3.9322	3.0017	71.1794
14	3.7660	3.1679	68.0116
15	3.5907	3.3432	64.6684
16	3.4056	3.5283	61.1401
17	3.2103	3.7236	57.4165
18	3.0042	3.9297	53.4868
19	2.7866	4.1473	49.3395
20	2.5571	4.3768	44.9626
21	2.3148	4.6191	40.3435
22	2.0591	4.8748	35.4687
23	1.7892	5.1447	30.3240
24	1.5044	5.4295	24.8945
25	1.2039	5.7300	19.1645
26	.8867	6.0472	13.1173
27	.5519	6.3820	6.7353
28	.1986	6.7353	0.0000

YEARS 29	MO PAYT .5693	AN CONST 6.84	
#	INT	PRIN	BALANCE
1	5.3640	1.4681	98.5319
2	5.2827	1.5494	96.9826
3	5.1970	1.6351	95.3474
4	5.1065	1.7256	93.6218
5	5.0109	1.8212	91.8006
6	4.9101	1.9220	89.8787
7	4.8037	2.0284	87.8503
8	4.6914	2.1407	85.7096
9	4.5729	2.2592	83.4505
10	4.4479	2.3842	81.0663
11	4.3159	2.5162	78.5501
12	4.1766	2.6555	75.8946
13	4.0296	2.8025	73.0921
14	3.8745	2.9576	70.1345
15	3.7108	3.1213	67.0131
16	3.5380	3.2941	63.7190
17	3.3556	3.4765	60.2425
18	3.1632	3.6689	56.5736
19	2.9601	3.8720	52.7015
20	2.7457	4.0864	48.6151
21	2.5195	4.3126	44.3026
22	2.2808	4.5513	39.7512
23	2.0288	4.8033	34.9480
24	1.7629	5.0692	29.8788
25	1.4823	5.3498	24.5291
26	1.1862	5.6459	18.8831
27	.8737	5.9585	12.9247
28	.5438	6.2883	6.6364
29	.1957	6.6364	0.0000

YEARS 30	MO PAYT .5615	AN CONST 6.74	
#	INT	PRIN	BALANCE
1	5.3664	1.3720	98.6280
2	5.2904	1.4479	97.1801
3	5.2103	1.5281	95.6520
4	5.1257	1.6127	94.0393
5	5.0364	1.7020	92.3373
6	4.9422	1.7962	90.5411
7	4.8428	1.8956	88.6455
8	4.7378	2.0005	86.6450
9	4.6271	2.1113	84.5337
10	4.5102	2.2282	82.3055
11	4.3869	2.3515	79.9540
12	4.2567	2.4817	77.4724
13	4.1193	2.6191	74.8533
14	3.9743	2.7640	72.0893
15	3.8213	2.9170	69.1722
16	3.6598	3.0785	66.0937
17	3.4894	3.2489	62.8448
18	3.3096	3.4288	59.4160
19	3.1198	3.6186	55.7974
20	2.9195	3.8189	51.9785
21	2.7081	4.0303	47.9481
22	2.4850	4.2534	43.6947
23	2.2495	4.4889	39.2059
24	2.0010	4.7374	34.4685
25	1.7388	4.9996	29.4689
26	1.4620	5.2764	24.1925
27	1.1699	5.5685	18.6241
28	.8617	5.8767	12.7474
29	.5364	6.2020	6.5453
30	.1930	6.5453	0.0000

MONTHLY PAYMENT AMORTIZATION SCHEDULE PER $100

5.50 %

YEARS 2 — MO PAYT 4.4096 — AN CONST 52.92

#	INT	PRIN	BALANCE
1	4.2863	48.6285	51.3715
2	1.5433	51.3715	0.0000

YEARS 3 — MO PAYT 3.0196 — AN CONST 36.24

#	INT	PRIN	BALANCE
1	4.7133	31.5218	68.4782
2	2.9352	33.2999	35.1783
3	1.0568	35.1783	0.0000

YEARS 4 — MO PAYT 2.3256 — AN CONST 27.91

#	INT	PRIN	BALANCE
1	4.9264	22.9814	77.0186
2	3.6301	24.2777	52.7410
3	2.2606	25.6471	27.0938
4	.8139	27.0938	0.0000

YEARS 5 — MO PAYT 1.9101 — AN CONST 22.93

#	INT	PRIN	BALANCE
1	5.0541	17.8673	82.1327
2	4.0462	18.8752	63.2575
3	2.9815	19.9399	43.3176
4	1.8567	21.0647	22.2529
5	.6685	22.2529	0.0000

YEARS 6 — MO PAYT 1.6338 — AN CONST 19.61

#	INT	PRIN	BALANCE
1	5.1389	14.4665	85.5335
2	4.3229	15.2826	70.2509
3	3.4609	16.1446	54.1063
4	2.5502	17.0553	37.0510
5	1.5881	18.0173	19.0337
6	.5718	19.0337	0.0000

YEARS 7 — MO PAYT 1.4370 — AN CONST 17.25

#	INT	PRIN	BALANCE
1	5.1994	12.0447	87.9553
2	4.5200	12.7241	75.2312
3	3.8022	13.4418	61.7894
4	3.0440	14.2000	47.5894
5	2.2430	15.0010	32.5883
6	1.3968	15.8472	16.7411
7	.5029	16.7411	0.0000

YEARS 8 — MO PAYT 1.2899 — AN CONST 15.48

#	INT	PRIN	BALANCE
1	5.2446	10.2346	89.7654
2	4.6672	10.8119	78.9534
3	4.0574	11.4218	67.5316
4	3.4131	12.0661	55.4655
5	2.7325	12.7467	42.7188
6	2.0134	13.4657	29.2530
7	1.2539	14.2253	15.0277
8	.4515	15.0277	0.0000

YEARS 9 — MO PAYT 1.1760 — AN CONST 14.12

#	INT	PRIN	BALANCE
1	5.2796	8.8324	91.1676
2	4.7813	9.3307	81.8369
3	4.2550	9.8570	71.9799
4	3.6990	10.4130	61.5669
5	3.1116	11.0004	50.5665
6	2.4911	11.6209	38.9457
7	1.8356	12.2764	26.6693
8	1.1431	12.9689	13.7004
9	.4116	13.7004	0.0000

YEARS 10 — MO PAYT 1.0853 — AN CONST 13.03

#	INT	PRIN	BALANCE
1	5.3074	7.7157	92.2843
2	4.8722	8.1510	84.1333
3	4.4124	8.6107	75.5226
4	3.9267	9.0964	66.4261
5	3.4136	9.6096	56.8166
6	2.8715	10.1516	46.6650
7	2.2989	10.7242	35.9407
8	1.6940	11.3292	24.6116
9	1.0549	11.9682	12.6433
10	.3798	12.6433	0.0000

YEARS 11 — MO PAYT 1.0114 — AN CONST 12.14

#	INT	PRIN	BALANCE
1	5.3301	6.8066	93.1934
2	4.9462	7.1905	86.0028
3	4.5406	7.5962	78.4067
4	4.1121	8.0246	70.3821
5	3.6594	8.4773	61.9048
6	3.1812	8.9555	52.9493
7	2.6761	9.4606	43.4887
8	2.1424	9.9943	33.4944
9	1.5787	10.5580	22.9363
10	.9831	11.1536	11.7827
11	.3540	11.7827	0.0000

YEARS 12 — MO PAYT .9502 — AN CONST 11.41

#	INT	PRIN	BALANCE
1	5.3489	6.0531	93.9469
2	5.0075	6.3946	87.5523
3	4.6468	6.7553	80.7970
4	4.2657	7.1363	73.6606
5	3.8632	7.5389	66.1217
6	3.4379	7.9641	58.1576
7	2.9887	8.4134	49.7442
8	2.5141	8.8880	40.8562
9	2.0127	9.3893	31.4669
10	1.4831	9.9189	21.5480
11	.9236	10.4785	11.0695
12	.3325	11.0695	0.0000

YEARS 13 — MO PAYT .8987 — AN CONST 10.79

#	INT	PRIN	BALANCE
1	5.3647	5.4194	94.5806
2	5.0590	5.7251	88.8555
3	4.7361	6.0480	82.8075
4	4.3949	6.3892	76.4183
5	4.0345	6.7496	69.6687
6	3.6538	7.1303	62.5383
7	3.2516	7.5325	55.0058
8	2.8267	7.9574	47.0484
9	2.3779	8.4063	38.6421
10	1.9037	8.8805	29.7616
11	1.4027	9.3814	20.3802
12	.8736	9.9106	10.4696
13	.3145	10.4696	0.0000

YEARS 14 — MO PAYT .8548 — AN CONST 10.26

#	INT	PRIN	BALANCE
1	5.3782	4.8797	95.1203
2	5.1030	5.1550	89.9653
3	4.8122	5.4457	84.5196
4	4.5050	5.7529	78.7667
5	4.1805	6.0774	72.6893
6	3.8377	6.4202	66.2690
7	3.4755	6.7824	59.4867
8	3.0929	7.1650	52.3217
9	2.6888	7.5691	44.7525
10	2.2618	7.9961	36.7565
11	1.8108	8.4471	28.3093
12	1.3343	8.9236	19.3857
13	.8309	9.4270	9.9587
14	.2992	9.9587	0.0000

YEARS 15 — MO PAYT .8171 — AN CONST 9.81

#	INT	PRIN	BALANCE
1	5.3898	4.4152	95.5848
2	5.1408	4.6643	90.9206
3	4.8777	4.9274	85.9932
4	4.5997	5.2053	80.7879
5	4.3061	5.4989	75.2890
6	3.9959	5.8091	69.4799
7	3.6682	6.1368	63.3431
8	3.3221	6.4829	56.8602
9	2.9564	6.8486	50.0116
10	2.5701	7.2349	42.7766
11	2.1620	7.6430	35.1336
12	1.7308	8.0742	27.0594
13	1.2754	8.5296	18.5298
14	.7942	9.0108	9.5190
15	.2860	9.5190	0.0000

YEARS 16 — MO PAYT .7843 — AN CONST 9.42

#	INT	PRIN	BALANCE
1	5.3999	4.0118	95.9882
2	5.1736	4.2381	91.7502
3	4.9345	4.4771	87.2730
4	4.6820	4.7297	82.5433
5	4.4152	4.9965	77.5469
6	4.1333	5.2783	72.2686
7	3.8356	5.5760	66.6925
8	3.5211	5.8906	60.8019
9	3.1888	6.2229	54.5791
10	2.8378	6.5739	48.0052
11	2.4670	6.9447	41.0605
12	2.0752	7.3364	33.7241
13	1.6614	7.7503	25.9739
14	1.2242	8.1874	17.7864
15	.7624	8.6493	9.1372
16	.2745	9.1372	0.0000

YEARS 17 — MO PAYT .7556 — AN CONST 9.07

#	INT	PRIN	BALANCE
1	5.4087	3.6586	96.3414
2	5.2023	3.8650	92.4764
3	4.9843	4.0830	88.3934
4	4.7540	4.3133	84.0800
5	4.5107	4.5566	79.5234
6	4.2536	4.8137	74.7097
7	3.9821	5.0852	69.6245
8	3.6953	5.3720	64.2525
9	3.3922	5.6751	58.5774
10	3.0721	5.9952	52.5822
11	2.7340	6.3334	46.2489
12	2.3767	6.6906	39.5583
13	1.9993	7.0680	32.4903
14	1.6006	7.4667	25.0236
15	1.1794	7.8879	17.1357
16	.7345	8.3328	8.8029
17	.2645	8.8029	0.0000

YEARS 18 — MO PAYT .7303 — AN CONST 8.77

#	INT	PRIN	BALANCE
1	5.4165	3.3473	96.6527
2	5.2276	3.5362	93.1165
3	5.0282	3.7356	89.3809
4	4.8175	3.9463	85.4345
5	4.5948	4.1689	81.2656
6	4.3597	4.4041	76.8615
7	4.1113	4.6525	72.2089
8	3.8488	4.9150	67.2940
9	3.5716	5.1922	62.1017
10	3.2787	5.4851	56.6166
11	2.9693	5.7945	50.8221
12	2.6424	6.1214	44.7008
13	2.2971	6.4667	38.2341
14	1.9324	6.8314	31.4027
15	1.5470	7.2168	24.1859
16	1.1399	7.6238	16.5621
17	.7099	8.0539	8.5082
18	.2556	8.5082	0.0000

YEARS 19 — MO PAYT .7079 — AN CONST 8.50

#	INT	PRIN	BALANCE
1	5.4233	3.0713	96.9287
2	5.2501	3.2445	93.6842
3	5.0671	3.4276	90.2566
4	4.8737	3.6209	86.6357
5	4.6695	3.8251	82.8106
6	4.4537	4.0409	78.7697
7	4.2258	4.2688	74.5008
8	3.9850	4.5096	69.9912
9	3.7306	4.7640	65.2272
10	3.4619	5.0328	60.1944
11	3.1780	5.3166	54.8778
12	2.8781	5.6165	49.2612
13	2.5613	5.9334	43.3279
14	2.2266	6.2680	37.0599
15	1.8730	6.6216	30.4382
16	1.4995	6.9951	23.4431
17	1.1049	7.3897	16.0534
18	.6881	7.8065	8.2469
19	.2477	8.2469	0.0000

YEARS 20 — MO PAYT .6879 — AN CONST 8.26

#	INT	PRIN	BALANCE
1	5.4295	2.8252	97.1748
2	5.2701	2.9845	94.1903
3	5.1018	3.1529	91.0374
4	4.9239	3.3307	87.7067
5	4.7361	3.5186	84.1881
6	4.5376	3.7171	80.4711
7	4.3279	3.9267	76.5443
8	4.1064	4.1482	72.3961
9	3.8724	4.3822	68.0138
10	3.6252	4.6294	63.3844
11	3.3641	4.8906	58.4938
12	3.0882	5.1664	53.3274
13	2.7968	5.4579	47.8695
14	2.4889	5.7657	42.1038
15	2.1637	6.0910	36.0129
16	1.8201	6.4345	29.5783
17	1.4572	6.7975	22.7808
18	1.0737	7.1809	15.5999
19	.6687	7.5860	8.0139
20	.2407	8.0139	0.0000

YEARS 21 — MO PAYT .6700 — AN CONST 8.04

#	INT	PRIN	BALANCE
1	5.4350	2.6047	97.3953
2	5.2881	2.7516	94.6438
3	5.1329	2.9068	91.7370

#	INT	PRIN	BALANCE
4	4.9689	3.0708	88.6662
5	4.7957	3.2440	85.4223
6	4.6127	3.4269	81.9953
7	4.4194	3.6203	78.3751
8	4.2152	3.8245	74.5506
9	3.9994	4.0402	70.5104
10	3.7715	4.2681	66.2423
11	3.5308	4.5089	61.7335
12	3.2765	4.7632	56.9703
13	3.0078	5.0319	51.9384
14	2.7239	5.3157	46.6227
15	2.4241	5.6156	41.0072
16	2.1073	5.9323	35.0748
17	1.7727	6.2669	28.8079
18	1.4192	6.6204	22.1875
19	1.0458	6.9939	15.1936
20	.6512	7.3884	7.8052
21	.2345	7.8052	0.0000

YEARS 22	MO PAYT .6538	AN CONST 7.85	
#	INT	PRIN	BALANCE
1	5.4399	2.4062	97.5938
2	5.3042	2.5420	95.0518
3	5.1608	2.6854	92.3664
4	5.0093	2.8368	89.5296
5	4.8493	2.9969	86.5327
6	4.6803	3.1659	83.3668
7	4.5017	3.3445	80.0223
8	4.3130	3.5331	76.4892
9	4.1137	3.7324	72.7567
10	3.9032	3.9430	68.8138
11	3.6808	4.1654	64.6484
12	3.4458	4.4004	60.2480
13	3.1976	4.6486	55.5994
14	2.9354	4.9108	50.6886
15	2.6584	5.1878	45.5008
16	2.3658	5.4804	40.0204
17	2.0566	5.7896	34.2309
18	1.7300	6.1161	28.1147
19	1.3850	6.4611	21.6536
20	1.0206	6.8256	14.8280
21	.6356	7.2106	7.6174
22	.2288	7.6174	0.0000

YEARS 23	MO PAYT .6393	AN CONST 7.68	
#	INT	PRIN	BALANCE
1	5.4444	2.2270	97.7730
2	5.3188	2.3527	95.4203
3	5.1861	2.4854	92.9349
4	5.0459	2.6256	90.3094
5	4.8978	2.7737	87.5357
6	4.7413	2.9301	84.6056
7	4.5761	3.0954	81.5102
8	4.4014	3.2700	78.2402
9	4.2170	3.4545	74.7857
10	4.0221	3.6493	71.1364
11	3.8163	3.8552	67.2812
12	3.5988	4.0726	63.2086
13	3.3691	4.3024	58.9063
14	3.1264	4.5450	54.3612
15	2.8700	4.8014	49.5598
16	2.5992	5.0723	44.4875
17	2.3131	5.3584	39.1292
18	2.0108	5.6606	33.4685
19	1.6915	5.9799	27.4886
20	1.3542	6.3172	21.1713
21	.9979	6.6736	14.4977
22	.6214	7.0500	7.4477
23	.2237	7.4477	0.0000

YEARS 24	MO PAYT .6261	AN CONST 7.52	
#	INT	PRIN	BALANCE
1	5.4485	2.0646	97.9354
2	5.3320	2.1811	95.7543
3	5.2090	2.3041	93.4503
4	5.0790	2.4341	91.0162
5	4.9417	2.5714	88.4449
6	4.7967	2.7164	85.7285
7	4.6434	2.8696	82.8588
8	4.4816	3.0315	79.8273
9	4.3106	3.2025	76.6248
10	4.1299	3.3831	73.2417
11	3.9391	3.5740	69.6677
12	3.7375	3.7756	65.8922
13	3.5245	3.9885	61.9036
14	3.2995	4.2135	57.6901
15	3.0619	4.4512	53.2389
16	2.8108	4.7023	48.5366
17	2.5455	4.9675	43.5690
18	2.2653	5.2477	38.3213
19	1.9693	5.5438	32.7775
20	1.6566	5.8565	26.9211
21	1.3262	6.1868	20.7342
22	.9773	6.5358	14.1984
23	.6086	6.9045	7.2939
24	.2191	7.2939	0.0000

YEARS 25	MO PAYT .6141	AN CONST 7.37	
#	INT	PRIN	BALANCE
1	5.4522	1.9169	98.0831
2	5.3440	2.0250	96.0581
3	5.2298	2.1392	93.9188
4	5.1091	2.2599	91.6589
5	4.9817	2.3874	89.2715
6	4.8470	2.5221	86.7495
7	4.7047	2.6643	84.0851
8	4.5544	2.8146	81.2705
9	4.3957	2.9734	78.2971
10	4.2279	3.1411	75.1560
11	4.0508	3.3183	71.8377
12	3.8636	3.5055	68.3323
13	3.6658	3.7032	64.6291
14	3.4570	3.9121	60.7170
15	3.2363	4.1328	56.5842
16	3.0032	4.3659	52.2183
17	2.7569	4.6122	47.6062
18	2.4967	4.8723	42.7339
19	2.2219	5.1472	37.5867
20	1.9316	5.4375	32.1492
21	1.6248	5.7442	26.4050
22	1.3008	6.0682	20.3368
23	.9585	6.4105	13.9263
24	.5969	6.7721	7.1541
25	.2149	7.1541	0.0000

YEARS 26	MO PAYT .6031	AN CONST 7.24	
#	INT	PRIN	BALANCE
1	5.4555	1.7822	98.2178
2	5.3550	1.8827	96.3351
3	5.2488	1.9889	94.3461
4	5.1366	2.1011	92.2450
5	5.0181	2.2196	90.0254
6	4.8929	2.3448	87.6805
7	4.7606	2.4771	85.2034
8	4.6209	2.6168	82.5866
9	4.4733	2.7645	79.8221
10	4.3173	2.9204	76.9017
11	4.1526	3.0851	73.8166
12	3.9786	3.2591	70.5575
13	3.7947	3.4430	67.1145
14	3.6005	3.6372	63.4773
15	3.3953	3.8424	59.6349
16	3.1786	4.0591	55.5758
17	2.9496	4.2881	51.2877
18	2.7078	4.5300	46.7577
19	2.4522	4.7855	41.9723
20	2.1823	5.0554	36.9168
21	1.8971	5.3406	31.5763
22	1.5959	5.6418	25.9344
23	1.2776	5.9601	19.9743
24	.9414	6.2963	13.6781
25	.5863	6.6514	7.0266
26	.2111	7.0266	0.0000

YEARS 27	MO PAYT .5931	AN CONST 7.12	
#	INT	PRIN	BALANCE
1	5.4586	1.6590	98.3410
2	5.3650	1.7526	96.5883
3	5.2661	1.8515	94.7368
4	5.1617	1.9559	92.7809
5	5.0514	2.0663	90.7146
6	4.9348	2.1828	88.5318
7	4.8117	2.3059	86.2259
8	4.6816	2.4360	83.7898
9	4.5442	2.5734	81.2164
10	4.3991	2.7186	78.4978
11	4.2457	2.8719	75.6259
12	4.0837	3.0339	72.5919
13	3.9126	3.2051	69.3869
14	3.7318	3.3859	66.0010
15	3.5408	3.5769	62.4241
16	3.3390	3.7786	58.6455
17	3.1259	3.9918	54.6537
18	2.9007	4.2169	50.4368
19	2.6628	4.4548	45.9820
20	2.4116	4.7061	41.2759
21	2.1461	4.9715	36.3044
22	1.8657	5.2520	31.0524
23	1.5694	5.5482	25.5042
24	1.2564	5.8612	19.6430
25	.9258	6.1918	13.4511
26	.5766	6.5411	6.9101
27	.2076	6.9101	0.0000

YEARS 28	MO PAYT .5840	AN CONST 7.01	
#	INT	PRIN	BALANCE
1	5.4614	1.5462	98.4538
2	5.3742	1.6334	96.8204
3	5.2821	1.7255	95.0949
4	5.1847	1.8229	93.2720
5	5.0819	1.9257	91.3463
6	4.9733	2.0343	89.3120
7	4.8585	2.1491	87.1629
8	4.7373	2.2703	84.8927
9	4.6092	2.3984	82.4943
10	4.4740	2.5336	79.9607
11	4.3310	2.6766	77.2841
12	4.1801	2.8275	74.4566
13	4.0206	2.9870	71.4695
14	3.8521	3.1555	68.3140
15	3.6741	3.3335	64.9805
16	3.4860	3.5216	61.4589
17	3.2874	3.7202	57.7387
18	3.0775	3.9300	53.8087
19	2.8559	4.1517	49.6570
20	2.6217	4.3859	45.2710
21	2.3743	4.6333	40.6377
22	2.1129	4.8947	35.7430
23	1.8368	5.1708	30.5723
24	1.5451	5.4625	25.1098
25	1.2370	5.7706	19.3392
26	.9115	6.0961	13.2432
27	.5676	6.4399	6.8032
28	.2044	6.8032	0.0000

YEARS 29	MO PAYT .5755	AN CONST 6.91	
#	INT	PRIN	BALANCE
1	5.4640	1.4425	98.5575
2	5.3826	1.5239	97.0336
3	5.2967	1.6098	95.4238
4	5.2059	1.7006	93.7231
5	5.1099	1.7966	91.9266
6	5.0086	1.8979	90.0287
7	4.9015	2.0050	88.0237
8	4.7884	2.1181	85.9056
9	4.6690	2.2375	83.6681
10	4.5427	2.3638	81.3043
11	4.4094	2.4971	78.8072
12	4.2686	2.6379	76.1693
13	4.1198	2.7867	73.3825
14	3.9626	2.9439	70.4386
15	3.7965	3.1100	67.3286
16	3.6211	3.2854	64.0432
17	3.4357	3.4708	60.5724
18	3.2400	3.6665	56.9059
19	3.0331	3.8734	53.0325
20	2.8147	4.0918	48.9407
21	2.5838	4.3227	44.6180
22	2.3400	4.5665	40.0515
23	2.0824	4.8241	35.2274
24	1.8103	5.0962	30.1313
25	1.5229	5.3837	24.7476
26	1.2192	5.6873	19.0603
27	.8984	6.0081	13.0521
28	.5595	6.3471	6.7051
29	.2014	6.7051	0.0000

YEARS 30	MO PAYT .5678	AN CONST 6.82	
#	INT	PRIN	BALANCE
1	5.4664	1.3471	98.6529
2	5.3904	1.4231	97.2298
3	5.3101	1.5033	95.7265
4	5.2253	1.5881	94.1383
5	5.1357	1.6777	92.4606
6	5.0411	1.7724	90.6882
7	4.9411	1.8723	88.8159
8	4.8355	1.9780	86.8379
9	4.7239	2.0895	84.7484
10	4.6061	2.2074	82.5410
11	4.4816	2.3319	80.2091
12	4.3500	2.4635	77.7456
13	4.2111	2.6024	75.1432
14	4.0643	2.7492	72.3940
15	3.9092	2.9043	69.4897
16	3.7454	3.0681	66.4216
17	3.5723	3.2412	63.1804
18	3.3895	3.4240	59.7564
19	3.1963	3.6171	56.1393
20	2.9923	3.8212	52.3181
21	2.7767	4.0367	48.2814
22	2.5490	4.2644	44.0170
23	2.3085	4.5050	39.5120
24	2.0544	4.7591	34.7529
25	1.7859	5.0275	29.7254
26	1.5023	5.3111	24.4142
27	1.2027	5.6107	18.8035
28	.8863	5.9272	12.8763
29	.5519	6.2616	6.6148
30	.1987	6.6148	0.0000

YEARS 2 — MO PAYT 4.4141 — AN CONST 52.97

#	INT	PRIN	BALANCE
1	4.3651	48.6036	51.3964
2	1.5723	51.3964	0.0000

YEARS 3 — MO PAYT 3.0241 — AN CONST 36.29

#	INT	PRIN	BALANCE
1	4.7999	31.4893	68.5107
2	2.9906	33.2987	35.2120
3	1.0772	35.2120	0.0000

YEARS 4 — MO PAYT 2.3302 — AN CONST 27.97

#	INT	PRIN	BALANCE
1	5.0170	22.9455	77.0545
2	3.6986	24.2639	52.7906
3	2.3044	25.6581	27.1324
4	.8300	27.1324	0.0000

YEARS 5 — MO PAYT 1.9147 — AN CONST 22.98

#	INT	PRIN	BALANCE
1	5.1470	17.8298	82.1702
2	4.1225	18.8543	63.3158
3	3.0391	19.9377	43.3781
4	1.8935	21.0833	22.2948
5	.6820	22.2948	0.0000

YEARS 6 — MO PAYT 1.6385 — AN CONST 19.67

#	INT	PRIN	BALANCE
1	5.2334	14.4283	85.5717
2	4.4044	15.2573	70.3144
3	3.5277	16.1340	54.1804
4	2.6006	17.0610	37.1194
5	1.6203	18.0414	19.0780
6	.5836	19.0780	0.0000

YEARS 7 — MO PAYT 1.4418 — AN CONST 17.31

#	INT	PRIN	BALANCE
1	5.2950	12.0061	87.9939
2	4.6051	12.6960	75.2979
3	3.8756	13.4255	61.8724
4	3.1041	14.1969	47.6755
5	2.2884	15.0127	32.6628
6	1.4258	15.8753	16.7875
7	.5136	16.7875	0.0000

YEARS 8 — MO PAYT 1.2948 — AN CONST 15.54

#	INT	PRIN	BALANCE
1	5.3409	10.1961	89.8039
2	4.7551	10.7820	79.0219
3	4.1355	11.4015	67.6205
4	3.4804	12.0566	55.5638
5	2.7876	12.7494	42.8144
6	2.0551	13.4820	29.3325
7	1.2804	14.2566	15.0758
8	.4612	15.0758	0.0000

YEARS 9 — MO PAYT 1.1809 — AN CONST 14.18

#	INT	PRIN	BALANCE
1	5.3766	8.7941	91.2059
2	4.8713	9.2994	81.9064
3	4.3369	9.8338	72.0727
4	3.7719	10.3988	61.6738
5	3.1743	10.9963	50.6775
6	2.5425	11.6282	39.0493
7	1.8743	12.2963	26.7529
8	1.1678	13.0029	13.7500
9	.4206	13.7500	0.0000

YEARS 10 — MO PAYT 1.0902 — AN CONST 13.09

#	INT	PRIN	BALANCE
1	5.4049	7.6778	92.3222
2	4.9638	8.1189	84.2033
3	4.4972	8.5854	75.6179
4	4.0039	9.0788	66.5391
5	3.4823	9.6004	56.9387
6	2.9306	10.1521	46.7866
7	2.3473	10.7354	36.0512
8	1.7304	11.3523	24.6989
9	1.0781	12.0046	12.6943
10	.3883	12.6943	0.0000

YEARS 11 — MO PAYT 1.0164 — AN CONST 12.20

#	INT	PRIN	BALANCE
1	5.4280	6.7691	93.2309
2	5.0391	7.1581	86.0728
3	4.6278	7.5694	78.5035
4	4.1928	8.0043	70.4992
5	3.7329	8.4642	62.0350
6	3.2465	8.9506	53.0844
7	2.7322	9.4649	43.6196
8	2.1884	10.0087	33.6108
9	1.6133	10.5838	23.0270
10	1.0052	11.1920	11.8351
11	.3621	11.8351	0.0000

YEARS 12 — MO PAYT .9553 — AN CONST 11.47

#	INT	PRIN	BALANCE
1	5.4471	6.0162	93.9838
2	5.1015	6.3619	87.6220
3	4.7359	6.7274	80.8946
4	4.3493	7.1140	73.7806
5	3.9406	7.5227	66.2578
6	3.5083	7.9550	58.3029
7	3.0512	8.4121	49.8908
8	2.5679	8.8954	40.9953
9	2.0567	9.4066	31.5887
10	1.5162	9.9471	21.6417
11	.9447	10.5186	11.1230
12	.3403	11.1230	0.0000

YEARS 13 — MO PAYT .9039 — AN CONST 10.85

#	INT	PRIN	BALANCE
1	5.4632	5.3830	94.6170
2	5.1539	5.6923	88.9247
3	4.8268	6.0194	82.9053
4	4.4810	6.3653	76.5400
5	4.1152	6.7310	69.8090
6	3.7285	7.1178	62.6912
7	3.3195	7.5268	55.1644
8	2.8870	7.9593	47.2051
9	2.4296	8.4166	38.7885
10	1.9460	8.9002	29.8883
11	1.4346	9.4116	20.4767
12	.8938	9.9524	10.5243
13	.3220	10.5243	0.0000

YEARS 14 — MO PAYT .8601 — AN CONST 10.33

#	INT	PRIN	BALANCE
1	5.4769	4.8439	95.1561
2	5.1986	5.1223	90.0338
3	4.9043	5.4166	84.6172
4	4.5930	5.7278	78.8894
5	4.2639	6.0569	72.8324
6	3.9159	6.4050	66.4275
7	3.5479	6.7730	59.6545
8	3.1587	7.1622	52.4923
9	2.7471	7.5737	44.9186
10	2.3120	8.0089	36.9097
11	1.8518	8.4691	28.4406
12	1.3651	8.9557	19.4848
13	.8505	9.4703	10.0145
14	.3064	10.0145	0.0000

YEARS 15 — MO PAYT .8224 — AN CONST 9.87

#	INT	PRIN	BALANCE
1	5.4887	4.3801	95.6199
2	5.2370	4.6318	90.9882
3	4.9709	4.8979	86.0902
4	4.6895	5.1793	80.9109
5	4.3919	5.4769	75.4340
6	4.0771	5.7916	69.6423
7	3.7444	6.1244	63.5179
8	3.3925	6.4763	57.0415
9	3.0203	6.8485	50.1931
10	2.6268	7.2420	42.9511
11	2.2107	7.6581	35.2930
12	1.7707	8.0981	27.1948
13	1.3053	8.5635	18.6314
14	.8133	9.0555	9.5758
15	.2929	9.5758	0.0000

YEARS 16 — MO PAYT .7897 — AN CONST 9.48

#	INT	PRIN	BALANCE
1	5.4989	3.9773	96.0227
2	5.2704	4.2059	91.8168
3	5.0287	4.4475	87.3692
4	4.7732	4.7031	82.6662
5	4.5029	4.9733	77.6928
6	4.2172	5.2591	72.4337
7	3.9150	5.5613	66.8724
8	3.5954	5.8808	60.9916
9	3.2575	6.2188	54.7728
10	2.9002	6.5761	48.1967
11	2.5223	6.9539	41.2428
12	2.1228	7.3535	33.8893
13	1.7002	7.7761	26.1132
14	1.2534	8.2229	17.8903
15	.7809	8.6954	9.1950
16	.2813	9.1950	0.0000

YEARS 17 — MO PAYT .7611 — AN CONST 9.14

#	INT	PRIN	BALANCE
1	5.5079	3.6249	96.3751
2	5.2996	3.8332	92.5420
3	5.0794	4.0534	88.4885
4	4.8465	4.2863	84.2022
5	4.6002	4.5326	79.6696
6	4.3397	4.7931	74.8765
7	4.0643	5.0685	69.8081
8	3.7731	5.3597	64.4484
9	3.4651	5.6677	58.7807
10	3.1394	5.9933	52.7874
11	2.7951	6.3377	46.4497
12	2.4309	6.7019	39.7478
13	2.0458	7.0870	32.6608
14	1.6386	7.4942	25.1666
15	1.2080	7.9248	17.2418
16	.7526	8.3802	8.8617
17	.2711	8.8617	0.0000

YEARS 18 — MO PAYT .7358 — AN CONST 8.84

#	INT	PRIN	BALANCE
1	5.5158	3.3143	96.6857
2	5.3254	3.5047	93.1810
3	5.1240	3.7061	89.4748
4	4.9110	3.9191	85.5558
5	4.6858	4.1443	81.4115
6	4.4477	4.3824	77.0291
7	4.1959	4.6342	72.3949
8	3.9296	4.9005	67.4944
9	3.6480	5.1821	62.3124
10	3.3503	5.4798	56.8325
11	3.0354	5.7947	51.0378
12	2.7024	6.1277	44.9102
13	2.3503	6.4798	38.4304
14	1.9780	6.8521	31.5783
15	1.5843	7.2458	24.3325
16	1.1679	7.6621	16.6704
17	.7277	8.1024	8.5680
18	.2621	8.5680	0.0000

YEARS 19 — MO PAYT .7135 — AN CONST 8.57

#	INT	PRIN	BALANCE
1	5.5228	3.0390	96.9610
2	5.3482	3.2136	93.7475
3	5.1635	3.3982	90.3492
4	4.9683	3.5935	86.7557
5	4.7618	3.8000	82.9558
6	4.5434	4.0183	78.9374
7	4.3125	4.2492	74.6882
8	4.0684	4.4934	70.1949
9	3.8102	4.7516	65.4433
10	3.5372	5.0246	60.4187
11	3.2484	5.3133	55.1054
12	2.9431	5.6186	49.4868
13	2.6203	5.9414	43.5454
14	2.2789	6.2828	37.2625
15	1.9179	6.6439	30.6187
16	1.5361	7.0256	23.5931
17	1.1325	7.4293	16.1638
18	.7056	7.8562	8.3076
19	.2541	8.3076	0.0000

YEARS 20 — MO PAYT .6935 — AN CONST 8.33

#	INT	PRIN	BALANCE
1	5.5290	2.7935	97.2065
2	5.3685	2.9541	94.2524
3	5.1988	3.1238	91.1286
4	5.0193	3.3033	87.8253
5	4.8295	3.4931	84.3322
6	4.6288	3.6938	80.6384
7	4.4165	3.9061	76.7323
8	4.1921	4.1305	72.6018
9	3.9547	4.3678	68.2339
10	3.7037	4.6188	63.6151
11	3.4383	4.8842	58.7309
12	3.1577	5.1649	53.5660
13	2.8609	5.4616	48.1044
14	2.5471	5.7755	42.3289
15	2.2152	6.1073	36.2216
16	1.8643	6.4583	29.7633
17	1.4932	6.8293	22.9340
18	1.1008	7.2218	15.7122
19	.6859	7.6367	8.0755
20	.2470	8.0755	0.0000

YEARS 21 — MO PAYT .6757 — AN CONST 8.11

#	INT	PRIN	BALANCE
1	5.5346	2.5738	97.4262
2	5.3867	2.7216	94.7046
3	5.2303	2.8780	91.8266

#	INT	PRIN	BALANCE
4	5.0650	3.0434	88.7831
5	4.8901	3.2183	85.5649
6	4.7052	3.4032	82.1617
7	4.5096	3.5987	78.5629
8	4.3028	3.8055	74.7574
9	4.0842	4.0242	70.7332
10	3.8529	4.2554	66.4778
11	3.6084	4.4999	61.9778
12	3.3499	4.7585	57.2193
13	3.0764	5.0319	52.1874
14	2.7873	5.3211	46.8663
15	2.4815	5.6268	41.2395
16	2.1582	5.9501	35.2893
17	1.8163	6.2920	28.9973
18	1.4548	6.6536	22.3437
19	1.0725	7.0359	15.3078
20	.6682	7.4402	7.8677
21	.2407	7.8677	0.0000

YEARS 22 — MO PAYT .6596 — AN CONST 7.92

#	INT	PRIN	BALANCE
1	5.5396	2.3761	97.6239
2	5.4031	2.5126	95.1113
3	5.2587	2.6570	92.4543
4	5.1061	2.8097	89.6447
5	4.9446	2.9711	86.6736
6	4.7739	3.1418	83.5318
7	4.5934	3.3223	80.2094
8	4.4025	3.5132	76.6962
9	4.2006	3.7151	72.9811
10	3.9871	3.9286	69.0525
11	3.7614	4.1543	64.8982
12	3.5227	4.3930	60.5052
13	3.2703	4.6454	55.8597
14	3.0033	4.9124	50.9473
15	2.7211	5.1946	45.7527
16	2.4226	5.4931	40.2596
17	2.1069	5.8088	34.4508
18	1.7732	6.1425	28.3083
19	1.4202	6.4955	21.8128
20	1.0470	6.8687	14.9441
21	.6523	7.2634	7.6807
22	.2350	7.6807	0.0000

YEARS 23 — MO PAYT .6451 — AN CONST 7.75

#	INT	PRIN	BALANCE
1	5.5442	2.1976	97.8024
2	5.4179	2.3239	95.4786
3	5.2844	2.4574	93.0212
4	5.1432	2.5986	90.4226
5	4.9938	2.7479	87.6747
6	4.8360	2.9058	84.7689
7	4.6690	3.0728	81.6961
8	4.4924	3.2493	78.4468
9	4.3057	3.4360	75.0107
10	4.1083	3.6335	71.3773
11	3.8995	3.8422	67.5350
12	3.6787	4.0630	63.4720
13	3.4453	4.2965	59.1755
14	3.1984	4.5434	54.6322
15	2.9373	4.8044	49.8277
16	2.6613	5.0805	44.7473
17	2.3693	5.3724	39.3748
18	2.0606	5.6811	33.6937
19	1.7342	6.0075	27.6862
20	1.3890	6.3527	21.3335
21	1.0240	6.7178	14.6157
22	.6380	7.1038	7.5119
23	.2298	7.5119	0.0000

YEARS 24 — MO PAYT .6320 — AN CONST 7.59

#	INT	PRIN	BALANCE
1	5.5483	2.0359	97.9641
2	5.4313	2.1528	95.8113
3	5.3076	2.2765	93.5347
4	5.1768	2.4074	91.1274
5	5.0385	2.5457	88.5817
6	4.8922	2.6920	85.8897
7	4.7375	2.8466	83.0431
8	4.5739	3.0102	80.0329
9	4.4010	3.1832	76.8497
10	4.2181	3.3661	73.4836
11	4.0246	3.5595	69.9241
12	3.8201	3.7640	66.1601
13	3.6038	3.9803	62.1798
14	3.3751	4.2090	57.9708
15	3.1333	4.4509	53.5199
16	2.8775	4.7066	48.8133
17	2.6071	4.9771	43.8363
18	2.3211	5.2630	38.5732
19	2.0187	5.5654	33.0078
20	1.6989	5.8852	27.1225
21	1.3607	6.2234	20.8991
22	1.0031	6.5810	14.3182
23	.6250	6.9591	7.3590
24	.2251	7.3590	0.0000

YEARS 25 — MO PAYT .6201 — AN CONST 7.45

#	INT	PRIN	BALANCE
1	5.5520	1.8889	98.1111
2	5.4435	1.9974	96.1137
3	5.3287	2.1122	94.0015
4	5.2073	2.2335	91.7680
5	5.0790	2.3619	89.4061
6	4.9433	2.4976	86.9085
7	4.7998	2.6411	84.2674
8	4.6480	2.7929	81.4745
9	4.4875	2.9534	78.5212
10	4.3178	3.1230	75.3981
11	4.1384	3.3025	72.0956
12	3.9486	3.4923	68.6033
13	3.7480	3.6929	64.9104
14	3.5358	3.9051	61.0053
15	3.3114	4.1295	56.8758
16	3.0741	4.3668	52.5090
17	2.8232	4.6177	47.8913
18	2.5578	4.8830	43.0082
19	2.2773	5.1636	37.8446
20	1.9806	5.4603	32.3843
21	1.6668	5.7741	26.6102
22	1.3350	6.1058	20.5044
23	.9842	6.4567	14.0477
24	.6132	6.8277	7.2200
25	.2209	7.2200	0.0000

YEARS 26 — MO PAYT .6092 — AN CONST 7.32

#	INT	PRIN	BALANCE
1	5.5554	1.7549	98.2451
2	5.4546	1.8557	96.3894
3	5.3479	1.9624	94.4270
4	5.2352	2.0751	92.3519
5	5.1160	2.1944	90.1576
6	4.9899	2.3204	87.8371
7	4.8565	2.4538	85.3833
8	4.7155	2.5948	82.7886
9	4.5664	2.7439	80.0447
10	4.4088	2.9015	77.1432
11	4.2421	3.0682	74.0749
12	4.0658	3.2445	70.8304
13	3.8793	3.4310	67.3994
14	3.6822	3.6281	63.7713
15	3.4737	3.8366	59.9347

YEARS 27 — MO PAYT .5992 — AN CONST 7.20

#	INT	PRIN	BALANCE
1	5.5585	1.6324	98.3676
2	5.4647	1.7262	96.6413
3	5.3655	1.8254	94.8159
4	5.2606	1.9303	92.8855
5	5.1497	2.0412	90.8443
6	5.0324	2.1585	88.6858
7	4.9084	2.2826	86.4032
8	4.7773	2.4137	83.9895
9	4.6386	2.5524	81.4371
10	4.4919	2.6991	78.7380
11	4.3368	2.8542	75.8839
12	4.1728	3.0182	72.8657
13	3.9994	3.1916	69.6741
14	3.8160	3.3750	66.2992
15	3.6221	3.5689	62.7303
16	3.4170	3.7740	58.9563
17	3.2002	3.9908	54.9655
18	2.9708	4.2201	50.7454
19	2.7284	4.4626	46.2828
20	2.4719	4.7190	41.5637
21	2.2008	4.9902	36.5735
22	1.9140	5.2769	31.2966
23	1.6108	5.5801	25.7165
24	1.2902	5.9008	19.8157
25	.9511	6.2398	13.5759
26	.5926	6.5984	6.9775
27	.2135	6.9775	0.0000

YEARS 28 — MO PAYT .5901 — AN CONST 7.09

#	INT	PRIN	BALANCE
1	5.5614	1.5203	98.4797
2	5.4740	1.6076	96.8721
3	5.3816	1.7000	95.1721
4	5.2840	1.7977	93.3744
5	5.1807	1.9010	91.4734
6	5.0714	2.0102	89.4632
7	4.9559	2.1257	87.3375
8	4.8338	2.2479	85.0897
9	4.7046	2.3770	82.7126
10	4.5680	2.5136	80.1990
11	4.4236	2.6580	77.5410
12	4.2709	2.8108	74.7302
13	4.1094	2.9723	71.7580
14	3.9386	3.1431	68.6149
15	3.7580	3.3237	65.2912
16	3.5670	3.5146	61.7766
17	3.3651	3.7166	58.0600
18	3.1515	3.9301	54.1299
19	2.9257	4.1560	49.9739
20	2.6869	4.3948	45.5791
21	2.4344	4.6473	40.9318
22	2.1673	4.9143	36.0175
23	1.8849	5.1967	30.8208
24	1.5863	5.4953	25.3255
25	1.2706	5.8111	19.5145
26	.9367	6.1450	13.3695
27	.5836	6.4981	6.8714
28	.2102	6.8714	0.0000

YEARS 29 — MO PAYT .5818 — AN CONST 6.99

#	INT	PRIN	BALANCE
1	5.5640	1.4173	98.5827
2	5.4826	1.4987	97.0840
3	5.3964	1.5848	95.4991
4	5.3054	1.6759	93.8232
5	5.2091	1.7722	92.0510
6	5.1072	1.8740	90.1770
7	4.9996	1.9817	88.1953
8	4.8857	2.0956	86.0997
9	4.7653	2.2160	83.8837
10	4.6379	2.3433	81.5404
11	4.5033	2.4780	79.0624
12	4.3609	2.6204	76.4420
13	4.2103	2.7709	73.6711
14	4.0511	2.9301	70.7409
15	3.8828	3.0985	67.6424
16	3.7047	3.2766	64.3659
17	3.5165	3.4648	60.9011
18	3.3174	3.6639	57.2371
19	3.1068	3.8744	53.3627
20	2.8842	4.0971	49.2656
21	2.6488	4.3325	44.9332
22	2.3999	4.5814	40.3517
23	2.1366	4.8447	35.5071
24	1.8582	5.1230	30.3840
25	1.5639	5.4174	24.9666
26	1.2526	5.7287	19.2379
27	.9234	6.0579	13.1800
28	.5753	6.4060	6.7740
29	.2072	6.7740	0.0000

YEARS 30 — MO PAYT .5741 — AN CONST 6.89

#	INT	PRIN	BALANCE
1	5.5664	1.3226	98.6774
2	5.4904	1.3985	97.2789
3	5.4100	1.4789	95.8000
4	5.3251	1.5639	94.2361
5	5.2352	1.6537	92.5824
6	5.1402	1.7488	90.8336
7	5.0397	1.8493	88.9844
8	4.9334	1.9555	87.0288
9	4.8211	2.0679	84.9610
10	4.7023	2.1867	82.7743
11	4.5766	2.3123	80.4619
12	4.4437	2.4452	78.0167
13	4.3032	2.5857	75.4310
14	4.1547	2.7343	72.6967
15	3.9976	2.8914	69.8054
16	3.8314	3.0575	66.7478
17	3.6557	3.2332	63.5146
18	3.4699	3.4190	60.0956
19	3.2735	3.6155	56.4801
20	3.0657	3.8232	52.6569
21	2.8461	4.0429	48.6141
22	2.6138	4.2752	44.3389
23	2.3681	4.5208	39.8181
24	2.1083	4.7806	35.0375
25	1.8337	5.0553	29.9822
26	1.5432	5.3458	24.6364
27	1.2360	5.6529	18.9834
28	.9112	5.9778	13.0057
29	.5677	6.3212	6.6845
30	.2045	6.6845	0.0000

MONTHLY PAYMENT AMORTIZATION SCHEDULE PER $100

5.625%

YEARS 2	MO PAYT 4.4152	AN CONST 52.99
# INT	PRIN	BALANCE
1 4.3848	48.5974	51.4026
2 1.5796	51.4026	0.0000

YEARS 3	MO PAYT 3.0252	AN CONST 36.31
# INT	PRIN	BALANCE
1 4.8216	31.4812	68.5188
2 3.0044	33.2984	35.2205
3 1.0823	35.2205	0.0000

YEARS 4	MO PAYT 2.3313	AN CONST 27.98
# INT	PRIN	BALANCE
1 5.0397	22.9365	77.0635
2 3.7157	24.2605	52.8030
3 2.3153	25.6609	27.1421
4 .8341	27.1421	0.0000

YEARS 5	MO PAYT 1.9159	AN CONST 23.00
# INT	PRIN	BALANCE
1 5.1702	17.8205	82.1795
2 4.1416	18.8491	63.3304
3 3.0535	19.9372	43.3932
4 1.9027	21.0880	22.3053
5 .6854	22.3053	0.0000

YEARS 6	MO PAYT 1.6396	AN CONST 19.68
# INT	PRIN	BALANCE
1 5.2570	14.4187	85.5813
2 4.4247	15.2510	70.3303
3 3.5444	16.1313	54.1990
4 2.6133	17.0625	37.1365
5 1.6284	18.0474	19.0891
6 .5866	19.0891	0.0000

YEARS 7	MO PAYT 1.4429	AN CONST 17.32
# INT	PRIN	BALANCE
1 5.3188	11.9965	88.0035
2 4.6264	12.6890	75.3145
3 3.8939	13.4214	61.8931
4 3.1192	14.1961	47.6970
5 2.2998	15.0156	32.6814
6 1.4330	15.8823	16.7991
7 .5162	16.7991	0.0000

YEARS 8	MO PAYT 1.2960	AN CONST 15.56
# INT	PRIN	BALANCE
1 5.3650	10.1865	89.8135
2 4.7770	10.7745	79.0391
3 4.1551	11.3964	67.6427
4 3.4973	12.0542	55.5884
5 2.8015	12.7500	42.8384
6 2.0655	13.4860	29.3523
7 1.2870	14.2645	15.0879
8 .4636	15.0879	0.0000

YEARS 9	MO PAYT 1.1821	AN CONST 14.19
# INT	PRIN	BALANCE
1 5.4008	8.7846	91.2154
2 4.8937	9.2916	81.9238
3 4.3574	9.8280	72.0958
4 3.7901	10.3953	61.7005
5 3.1901	10.9953	50.7052
6 2.5554	11.6300	39.0752

#	INT	PRIN	BALANCE
7	1.8840	12.3013	26.7739
8	1.1740	13.0114	13.7625
9	.4229	13.7625	0.0000

YEARS 10	MO PAYT 1.0915	AN CONST 13.10
# INT	PRIN	BALANCE
1 5.4293	7.6683	92.3317
2 4.9867	8.1109	84.2208
3 4.5185	8.5791	75.6416
4 4.0233	9.0743	66.5673
5 3.4995	9.5981	56.9692
6 2.9454	10.1522	46.8170
7 2.3594	10.7382	36.0788
8 1.7396	11.3580	24.7208
9 1.0840	12.0137	12.7071
10 .3905	12.7071	0.0000

YEARS 11	MO PAYT 1.0177	AN CONST 12.22
# INT	PRIN	BALANCE
1 5.4525	6.7597	93.2403
2 5.0623	7.1499	86.0903
3 4.6496	7.5627	78.5277
4 4.2130	7.9992	70.5285
5 3.7513	8.4609	62.0675
6 3.2629	8.9493	53.1182
7 2.7463	9.4659	43.6523
8 2.1999	10.0123	33.6400
9 1.6220	10.5903	23.0497
10 1.0107	11.2016	11.8481
11 .3641	11.8481	0.0000

YEARS 12	MO PAYT .9566	AN CONST 11.48
# INT	PRIN	BALANCE
1 5.4717	6.0070	93.9930
2 5.1250	6.3537	87.6394
3 4.7582	6.7204	80.9189
4 4.3703	7.1084	73.8105
5 3.9600	7.5187	66.2918
6 3.5260	7.9527	58.3391
7 3.0669	8.4117	49.9274
8 2.5814	8.8973	41.0301
9 2.0678	9.4109	31.6192
10 1.5246	9.9541	21.6651
11 .9500	10.5287	11.1364
12 .3422	11.1364	0.0000

YEARS 13	MO PAYT .9051	AN CONST 10.87
# INT	PRIN	BALANCE
1 5.4879	5.3739	94.6261
2 5.1777	5.6841	88.9419
3 4.8495	6.0122	82.9297
4 4.5025	6.3593	76.5704
5 4.1354	6.7264	69.8440
6 3.7472	7.1146	62.7294
7 3.3365	7.5253	55.2040
8 2.9021	7.9597	47.2443
9 2.4426	8.4192	38.8252
10 1.9567	8.9051	29.9200
11 1.4426	9.4192	20.5008
12 .8989	9.9629	10.5380
13 .3238	10.5380	0.0000

YEARS 14	MO PAYT .8614	AN CONST 10.34
# INT	PRIN	BALANCE
1 5.5016	4.8350	95.1650
2 5.2225	5.1141	90.0509
3 4.9273	5.4093	84.6416

#	INT	PRIN	BALANCE
4	4.6151	5.7216	78.9200
5	4.2848	6.0518	72.8682
6	3.9355	6.4012	66.4670
7	3.5660	6.7706	59.6964
8	3.1752	7.1615	52.5349
9	2.7618	7.5749	44.9601
10	2.3245	8.0121	36.9480
11	1.8621	8.4746	28.4734
12	1.3729	8.9638	19.5096
13	.8555	9.4812	10.0285
14	.3082	10.0285	0.0000

YEARS 15	MO PAYT .8237	AN CONST 9.89
# INT	PRIN	BALANCE
1 5.5134	4.3713	95.6287
2 5.2611	4.6237	91.0050
3 4.9942	4.8906	86.1144
4 4.7119	5.1729	80.9416
5 4.4133	5.4714	75.4701
6 4.0975	5.7873	69.6829
7 3.7634	6.1213	63.5615
8 3.4101	6.4747	57.0868
9 3.0364	6.8484	50.2384
10 2.6411	7.2437	42.9947
11 2.2229	7.6619	35.3328
12 1.7807	8.1041	27.2287
13 1.3129	8.5719	18.6568
14 .8181	9.0667	9.5901
15 .2947	9.5901	0.0000

YEARS 16	MO PAYT .7910	AN CONST 9.50
# INT	PRIN	BALANCE
1 5.5237	3.9688	96.0312
2 5.2946	4.1978	91.8334
3 5.0523	4.4402	87.3932
4 4.7960	4.6965	82.6968
5 4.5249	4.9676	77.7292
6 4.2382	5.2543	72.4749
7 3.9349	5.5576	66.9173
8 3.6141	5.8784	61.0389
9 3.2748	6.2177	54.8212
10 2.9159	6.5766	48.2446
11 2.5362	6.9562	41.2883
12 2.1347	7.3578	33.9306
13 1.7100	7.7825	26.1481
14 1.2608	8.2317	17.9164
15 .7856	8.7069	9.2095
16 .2830	9.2095	0.0000

YEARS 17	MO PAYT .7624	AN CONST 9.15
# INT	PRIN	BALANCE
1 5.5327	3.6165	96.3835
2 5.3240	3.8252	92.5583
3 5.1031	4.0460	88.5123
4 4.8696	4.2796	84.2327
5 4.6226	4.5266	79.7061
6 4.3613	4.7879	74.9182
7 4.0849	5.0643	69.8539
8 3.7926	5.3566	64.4973
9 3.4834	5.6658	58.8315
10 3.1563	5.9929	52.8386
11 2.8104	6.3388	46.4998
12 2.4445	6.7047	39.7952
13 2.0575	7.0917	32.7035
14 1.6481	7.5010	25.2024
15 1.2152	7.9340	17.2684
16 .7572	8.3920	8.8764
17 .2728	8.8764	0.0000

YEARS 18	MO PAYT .7372	AN CONST 8.85
# INT	PRIN	BALANCE
1 5.5406	3.3061	96.6939
2 5.3498	3.4969	93.1970
3 5.1479	3.6988	89.4982
4 4.9344	3.9123	85.5860
5 4.7086	4.1381	81.4479
6 4.4697	4.3770	77.0709
7 4.2171	4.6296	72.4413
8 3.9499	4.8968	67.5445
9 3.6672	5.1795	62.3649
10 3.3682	5.4785	56.8865
11 3.0520	5.7947	51.0917
12 2.7175	6.1292	44.9625
13 2.3637	6.4830	38.4795
14 1.9895	6.8572	31.6223
15 1.5937	7.2531	24.3692
16 1.1750	7.6717	16.6975
17 .7322	8.1146	8.5830
18 .2638	8.5830	0.0000

YEARS 19	MO PAYT .7149	AN CONST 8.58
# INT	PRIN	BALANCE
1 5.5477	3.0309	96.9691
2 5.3727	3.2059	93.7632
3 5.1876	3.3909	90.3723
4 4.9919	3.5867	86.7856
5 4.7849	3.7937	82.9919
6 4.5659	4.0127	78.9793
7 4.3343	4.2443	74.7350
8 4.0893	4.4893	70.2457
9 3.8301	4.7484	65.4972
10 3.5560	5.0225	60.4747
11 3.2661	5.3124	55.1623
12 2.9595	5.6191	49.5432
13 2.6351	5.9434	43.5997
14 2.2921	6.2865	37.3132
15 1.9292	6.6494	30.6638
16 1.5454	7.0332	23.6306
17 1.1394	7.4392	16.1914
18 .7100	7.8686	8.3228
19 .2558	8.3228	0.0000

YEARS 20	MO PAYT .6950	AN CONST 8.34
# INT	PRIN	BALANCE
1 5.5539	2.7857	97.2143
2 5.3931	2.9465	94.2678
3 5.2230	3.1166	91.1513
4 5.0431	3.2965	87.8548
5 4.8529	3.4867	84.3681
6 4.6516	3.6880	80.6800
7 4.4387	3.9009	76.7791
8 4.2135	4.1261	72.6531
9 3.9754	4.3642	68.2888
10 3.7234	4.6162	63.6727
11 3.4570	4.8826	58.7901
12 3.1751	5.1645	53.6256
13 2.8770	5.4626	48.1631
14 2.5617	5.7779	42.3852
15 2.2282	6.1114	36.2738
16 1.8754	6.4642	29.8096
17 1.5023	6.8373	22.9723
18 1.1076	7.2320	15.7404
19 .6902	7.6494	8.0910
20 .2486	8.0910	0.0000

YEARS 21	MO PAYT .6771	AN CONST 8.13
# INT	PRIN	BALANCE
1 5.5595	2.5661	97.4339
2 5.4114	2.7142	94.7197
3 5.2547	2.8709	91.8488

#	INT	PRIN	BALANCE
4	5.0890	3.0366	88.8122
5	4.9137	3.2119	85.6004
6	4.7283	3.3973	82.2031
7	4.5322	3.5934	78.6097
8	4.3248	3.8008	74.8089
9	4.1054	4.0202	70.7887
10	3.8733	4.2522	66.5365
11	3.6279	4.4977	62.0388
12	3.3683	4.7573	57.2815
13	3.0937	5.0319	52.2495
14	2.8032	5.3224	46.9272
15	2.4960	5.6296	41.2975
16	2.1710	5.9546	35.3430
17	1.8273	6.2983	29.0447
18	1.4638	6.6618	22.3828
19	1.0792	7.0464	15.3365
20	.6725	7.4531	7.8833
21	.2423	7.8833	0.0000

YEARS 22 — MO PAYT .6611 — AN CONST 7.94

#	INT	PRIN	BALANCE
1	5.5646	2.3686	97.6314
2	5.4278	2.5053	95.1261
3	5.2832	2.6499	92.4762
4	5.1303	2.8029	89.6733
5	4.9685	2.9647	86.7087
6	4.7973	3.1358	83.5729
7	4.6163	3.3168	80.2561
8	4.4249	3.5083	76.7478
9	4.2224	3.7108	73.0370
10	4.0082	3.9250	69.1120
11	3.7816	4.1515	64.9605
12	3.5420	4.3912	60.5694
13	3.2885	4.6446	55.9247
14	3.0204	4.9127	51.0120
15	2.7368	5.1963	45.8156
16	2.4369	5.4963	40.3194
17	2.1196	5.8135	34.5058
18	1.7840	6.1491	28.3567
19	1.4291	6.5041	21.8527
20	1.0536	6.8795	14.9732
21	.6565	7.2766	7.6966
22	.2365	7.6966	0.0000

YEARS 23 — MO PAYT .6466 — AN CONST 7.76

#	INT	PRIN	BALANCE
1	5.5691	2.1903	97.8097
2	5.4427	2.3167	95.4930
3	5.3089	2.4504	93.0426
4	5.1675	2.5919	90.4507
5	5.0179	2.7415	87.7092
6	4.8596	2.8997	84.8095
7	4.6923	3.0671	81.7424
8	4.5152	3.2442	78.4982
9	4.3280	3.4314	75.0668
10	4.1299	3.6295	71.4373
11	3.9204	3.8390	67.5983
12	3.6988	4.0606	63.5377
13	3.4644	4.2950	59.2427
14	3.2165	4.5429	54.6998
15	2.9542	4.8051	49.8947
16	2.6769	5.0825	44.8122
17	2.3835	5.3759	39.4363
18	2.0732	5.6862	33.7501
19	1.7450	6.0144	27.7357
20	1.3978	6.3616	21.3741
21	1.0306	6.7288	14.6453
22	.6422	7.1172	7.5280
23	.2313	7.5280	0.0000

YEARS 24 — MO PAYT .6335 — AN CONST 7.61

#	INT	PRIN	BALANCE
1	5.5732	2.0287	97.9713
2	5.4561	2.1458	95.8254
3	5.3323	2.2697	93.5557
4	5.2012	2.4007	91.1550
5	5.0627	2.5393	88.6157
6	4.9161	2.6859	85.9298
7	4.7611	2.8409	83.0889
8	4.5971	3.0049	80.0840
9	4.4236	3.1783	76.9057
10	4.2402	3.3618	73.5439
11	4.0461	3.5559	69.9880
12	3.8408	3.7611	66.2269
13	3.6237	3.9782	62.2487
14	3.3941	4.2079	58.0408
15	3.1512	4.4507	53.5901
16	2.8943	4.7077	48.8824
17	2.6226	4.9794	43.9030
18	2.3351	5.2668	38.6362
19	2.0311	5.5708	33.0654
20	1.7096	5.8924	27.1730
21	1.3694	6.2325	20.9404
22	1.0097	6.5923	14.3481
23	.6291	6.9728	7.3753
24	.2266	7.3753	0.0000

YEARS 25 — MO PAYT .6216 — AN CONST 7.46

#	INT	PRIN	BALANCE
1	5.5770	1.8819	98.1181
2	5.4683	1.9906	96.1275
3	5.3534	2.1055	94.0221
4	5.2319	2.2270	91.7951
5	5.1034	2.3555	89.4395
6	4.9674	2.4915	86.9480
7	4.8236	2.6353	84.3127
8	4.6715	2.7874	81.5253
9	4.5106	2.9483	78.5769
10	4.3404	3.1185	75.4584
11	4.1604	3.2985	72.1599
12	3.9700	3.4889	68.6709
13	3.7686	3.6903	64.9806
14	3.5555	3.9034	61.0772
15	3.3302	4.1287	56.9486
16	3.0919	4.3670	52.5816
17	2.8398	4.6191	47.9625
18	2.5732	4.8857	43.0768
19	2.2912	5.1677	37.9091
20	1.9929	5.4660	32.4431
21	1.6774	5.7815	26.6616
22	1.3437	6.1152	20.5464
23	.9907	6.4682	14.0781
24	.6173	6.8416	7.2365
25	.2224	7.2365	0.0000

YEARS 26 — MO PAYT .6107 — AN CONST 7.33

#	INT	PRIN	BALANCE
1	5.5804	1.7481	98.2519
2	5.4795	1.8490	96.4029
3	5.3727	1.9558	94.4471
4	5.2599	2.0686	92.3784
5	5.1404	2.1881	90.1904
6	5.0141	2.3144	87.8760
7	4.8806	2.4480	85.4281
8	4.7393	2.5893	82.8388
9	4.5898	2.7387	80.1001
10	4.4317	2.8968	77.2033
11	4.2645	3.0640	74.1393
12	4.0876	3.2409	70.8984
13	3.9006	3.4280	67.4705
14	3.7027	3.6258	63.8446
15	3.4934	3.8351	60.0095
16	3.2720	4.0565	55.9530
17	3.0379	4.2906	51.6624
18	2.7902	4.5383	47.1241
19	2.5282	4.8003	42.3238
20	2.2511	5.0774	37.2464
21	1.9581	5.3704	31.8760
22	1.6481	5.6804	26.1955
23	1.3202	6.0083	20.1872
24	.9733	6.3552	13.8320
25	.6065	6.7220	7.1100
26	.2185	7.1100	0.0000

YEARS 27 — MO PAYT .6008 — AN CONST 7.21

#	INT	PRIN	BALANCE
1	5.5835	1.6258	98.3742
2	5.4897	1.7197	96.6545
3	5.3904	1.8190	94.8355
4	5.2854	1.9240	92.9115
5	5.1743	2.0350	90.8765
6	5.0569	2.1525	88.7240
7	4.9326	2.2767	86.4473
8	4.8012	2.4082	84.0391
9	4.6622	2.5472	81.4920
10	4.5152	2.6942	78.7978
11	4.3597	2.8497	75.9481
12	4.1952	3.0142	72.9339
13	4.0212	3.1882	69.7457
14	3.8371	3.3722	66.3735
15	3.6425	3.5669	62.8066
16	3.4366	3.7728	59.0339
17	3.2188	3.9905	55.0433
18	2.9885	4.2209	50.8224
19	2.7448	4.4645	46.3579
20	2.4871	4.7222	41.6357
21	2.2145	4.9948	36.6408
22	1.9262	5.2831	31.3577
23	1.6213	5.5881	25.7696
24	1.2987	5.9107	19.8590
25	.9575	6.2518	13.6071
26	.5966	6.6127	6.9944
27	.2149	6.9944	0.0000

YEARS 28 — MO PAYT .5917 — AN CONST 7.11

#	INT	PRIN	BALANCE
1	5.5864	1.5139	98.4861
2	5.4990	1.6012	96.8849
3	5.4066	1.6937	95.1913
4	5.3088	1.7914	93.3998
5	5.2054	1.8948	91.5050
6	5.0960	2.0042	89.5008
7	4.9803	2.1199	87.3809
8	4.8580	2.2423	85.1386
9	4.7285	2.3717	82.7669
10	4.5916	2.5086	80.2583
11	4.4468	2.6534	77.6049
12	4.2937	2.8066	74.7984
13	4.1316	2.9686	71.8298
14	3.9603	3.1399	68.6899
15	3.7790	3.3212	65.3687
16	3.5873	3.5129	61.8558
17	3.3846	3.7157	58.1402
18	3.1701	3.9301	54.2100
19	2.9432	4.1570	50.0531
20	2.7033	4.3969	45.6561
21	2.4495	4.6507	41.0054
22	2.1810	4.9192	36.0862
23	1.8971	5.2032	30.8830
24	1.5967	5.5035	25.3795
25	1.2790	5.8212	19.5583
26	.9430	6.1572	13.4011
27	.5876	6.5126	6.8885
28	.2117	6.8885	0.0000

YEARS 29 — MO PAYT .5833 — AN CONST 7.01

#	INT	PRIN	BALANCE
1	5.5890	1.4110	98.5890
2	5.5075	1.4925	97.0965
3	5.4214	1.5786	95.5178
4	5.3303	1.6698	93.8481
5	5.2339	1.7661	92.0819
6	5.1319	1.8681	90.2138
7	5.0241	1.9759	88.2379
8	4.9100	2.0900	86.1479
9	4.7894	2.2106	83.9373
10	4.6618	2.3382	81.5990
11	4.5268	2.4732	79.1258
12	4.3841	2.6160	76.5099
13	4.2331	2.7670	73.7429
14	4.0734	2.9267	70.8162
15	3.9044	3.0956	67.7206
16	3.7257	3.2743	64.4463
17	3.5367	3.4633	60.9830
18	3.3368	3.6632	57.3198
19	3.1254	3.8747	53.4451
20	2.9017	4.0983	49.3468
21	2.6651	4.3349	45.0119
22	2.4149	4.5851	40.4268
23	2.1502	4.8498	35.5770
24	1.8703	5.1297	30.4472
25	1.5742	5.4258	25.0214
26	1.2610	5.7390	19.2824
27	.9297	6.0703	13.2120
28	.5793	6.4207	6.7913
29	.2087	6.7913	0.0000

YEARS 30 — MO PAYT .5757 — AN CONST 6.91

#	INT	PRIN	BALANCE
1	5.5914	1.3165	98.6835
2	5.5154	1.3925	97.2911
3	5.4350	1.4728	95.8182
4	5.3500	1.5579	94.2604
5	5.2601	1.6478	92.6126
6	5.1650	1.7429	90.8697
7	5.0644	1.8435	89.0262
8	4.9580	1.9499	87.0763
9	4.8454	2.0625	85.0138
10	4.7264	2.1815	82.8323
11	4.6004	2.3074	80.5248
12	4.4672	2.4406	78.0842
13	4.3264	2.5815	75.5027
14	4.1773	2.7305	72.7721
15	4.0197	2.8882	69.8840
16	3.8530	3.0549	66.8291
17	3.6767	3.2312	63.5979
18	3.4902	3.4177	60.1802
19	3.2929	3.6150	56.5652
20	3.0842	3.8237	52.7415
21	2.8635	4.0444	48.6971
22	2.6300	4.2778	44.4193
23	2.3831	4.5248	39.8946
24	2.1219	4.7859	35.1086
25	1.8457	5.0622	30.0464
26	1.5535	5.3544	24.6920
27	1.2444	5.6635	19.0285
28	.9175	5.9904	13.0381
29	.5717	6.3362	6.7019
30	.2059	6.7019	0.0000

MONTHLY PAYMENT AMORTIZATION SCHEDULE PER $100   5.70 %

YEARS 2 — MO PAYT 4.4186 — AN CONST 53.03

#	INT	PRIN	BALANCE
1	4.4439	48.5788	51.4212
2	1.6014	51.4212	0.0000

YEARS 3 — MO PAYT 3.0286 — AN CONST 36.35

#	INT	PRIN	BALANCE
1	4.8866	31.4568	68.5432
2	3.0460	33.2974	35.2458
3	1.0977	35.2458	0.0000

YEARS 4 — MO PAYT 2.3348 — AN CONST 28.02

#	INT	PRIN	BALANCE
1	5.1076	22.9096	77.0904
2	3.7671	24.2502	52.8402
3	2.3482	25.6691	27.1711
4	.8462	27.1711	0.0000

YEARS 5 — MO PAYT 1.9194 — AN CONST 23.04

#	INT	PRIN	BALANCE
1	5.2399	17.7924	82.2076
2	4.1989	18.8335	63.3741
3	3.0969	19.9355	43.4387
4	1.9304	21.1020	22.3367
5	.6956	22.3367	0.0000

YEARS 6 — MO PAYT 1.6432 — AN CONST 19.72

#	INT	PRIN	BALANCE
1	5.3279	14.3901	85.6099
2	4.4859	15.2321	70.3779
3	3.5946	16.1233	54.2546
4	2.6512	17.0668	37.1878
5	1.6526	18.0654	19.1224
6	.5955	19.1224	0.0000

YEARS 7 — MO PAYT 1.4465 — AN CONST 17.36

#	INT	PRIN	BALANCE
1	5.3906	11.9676	88.0324
2	4.6903	12.6679	75.3645
3	3.9491	13.4091	61.9553
4	3.1644	14.1937	47.7616
5	2.3339	15.0243	32.7373
6	1.4548	15.9034	16.8339
7	.5243	16.8339	0.0000

YEARS 8 — MO PAYT 1.2996 — AN CONST 15.60

#	INT	PRIN	BALANCE
1	5.4374	10.1577	89.8423
2	4.8430	10.7520	79.0903
3	4.2139	11.3811	67.7092
4	3.5479	12.0471	55.6621
5	2.8430	12.7520	42.9101
6	2.0969	13.4982	29.4120
7	1.3070	14.2880	15.1240
8	.4710	15.1240	0.0000

YEARS 9 — MO PAYT 1.1858 — AN CONST 14.23

#	INT	PRIN	BALANCE
1	5.4736	8.7559	91.2441
2	4.9613	9.2683	81.9758
3	4.4190	9.8106	72.1652
4	3.8449	10.3846	61.7806
5	3.2373	10.9923	50.7884
6	2.5941	11.6354	39.1529
7	1.9133	12.3163	26.8367
8	1.1926	13.0369	13.7998
9	.4298	13.7998	0.0000

YEARS 10 — MO PAYT 1.0952 — AN CONST 13.15

#	INT	PRIN	BALANCE
1	5.5025	7.6399	92.3601
2	5.0554	8.0870	84.2731
3	4.5822	8.5602	75.7129
4	4.0813	9.0610	66.6519
5	3.5512	9.5912	57.0606
6	2.9899	10.1524	46.9082
7	2.3959	10.7465	36.1617
8	1.7671	11.3753	24.7864
9	1.1015	12.0409	12.7455
10	.3969	12.7455	0.0000

YEARS 11 — MO PAYT 1.0215 — AN CONST 12.26

#	INT	PRIN	BALANCE
1	5.5259	6.7317	93.2683
2	5.1320	7.1256	86.1426
3	4.7151	7.5426	78.6000
4	4.2738	7.9839	70.6161
5	3.8066	8.4511	62.1650
6	3.3121	8.9456	53.2195
7	2.7887	9.4690	43.7504
8	2.2346	10.0231	33.7274
9	1.6481	10.6096	23.1178
10	1.0273	11.2303	11.8875
11	.3702	11.8875	0.0000

YEARS 12 — MO PAYT .9604 — AN CONST 11.53

#	INT	PRIN	BALANCE
1	5.5454	5.9794	94.0206
2	5.1955	6.3292	87.6914
3	4.8252	6.6996	80.9918
4	4.4332	7.0916	73.9003
5	4.0182	7.5065	66.3937
6	3.5790	7.9458	58.4480
7	3.1141	8.4107	50.0373
8	2.6219	8.9028	41.1344
9	2.1010	9.4238	31.7107
10	1.5496	9.9752	21.7355
11	.9659	10.5588	11.1767
12	.3481	11.1767	0.0000

YEARS 13 — MO PAYT .9090 — AN CONST 10.91

#	INT	PRIN	BALANCE
1	5.5617	5.3468	94.6532
2	5.2489	5.6597	88.9935
3	4.9177	5.9908	83.0027
4	4.5672	6.3414	76.6614
5	4.1961	6.7124	69.9490
6	3.8034	7.1052	62.8438
7	3.3876	7.5209	55.3229
8	2.9476	7.9610	47.3619
9	2.4817	8.4268	38.9351
10	1.9887	8.9199	30.0152
11	1.4667	9.4418	20.5734
12	.9143	9.9943	10.5791
13	.3295	10.5791	0.0000

YEARS 14 — MO PAYT .8653 — AN CONST 10.39

#	INT	PRIN	BALANCE
1	5.5757	4.8084	95.1916
2	5.2943	5.0897	90.1019
3	4.9965	5.3875	84.7144
4	4.6813	5.7028	79.0117
5	4.3476	6.0364	72.9752
6	3.9944	6.3897	66.5856
7	3.6205	6.7635	59.8220
8	3.2247	7.1593	52.6627
9	2.8058	7.5782	45.0846
10	2.3624	8.0216	37.0629
11	1.8930	8.4910	28.5719
12	1.3962	8.9878	19.5841
13	.8703	9.5137	10.0704
14	.3136	10.0704	0.0000

YEARS 15 — MO PAYT .8277 — AN CONST 9.94

#	INT	PRIN	BALANCE
1	5.5876	4.3452	95.6548
2	5.3334	4.5994	91.0554
3	5.0643	4.8685	86.1869
4	4.7794	5.1534	81.0334
5	4.4779	5.4550	75.5785
6	4.1587	5.7741	69.8043
7	3.8208	6.1120	63.6923
8	3.4632	6.4696	57.2227
9	3.0846	6.8482	50.3745
10	2.6839	7.2489	43.1256
11	2.2598	7.6731	35.4525
12	1.8108	8.1220	27.3304
13	1.3355	8.5973	18.7332
14	.8325	9.1003	9.6328
15	.3000	9.6328	0.0000

YEARS 16 — MO PAYT .7951 — AN CONST 9.55

#	INT	PRIN	BALANCE
1	5.5980	3.9431	96.0569
2	5.3673	4.1738	91.8830
3	5.1231	4.4181	87.4650
4	4.8646	4.6766	82.7884
5	4.5909	4.9502	77.8382
6	4.3013	5.2399	72.5983
7	3.9947	5.5465	67.0519
8	3.6702	5.8710	61.1808
9	3.3266	6.2145	54.9663
10	2.9630	6.5782	48.3881
11	2.5781	6.9631	41.4251
12	2.1707	7.3705	34.0546
13	1.7394	7.8018	26.2528
14	1.2829	8.2583	17.9945
15	.7997	8.7415	9.2530
16	.2882	9.2530	0.0000

YEARS 17 — MO PAYT .7665 — AN CONST 9.20

#	INT	PRIN	BALANCE
1	5.6071	3.5914	96.4086
2	5.3970	3.8015	92.6071
3	5.1746	4.0239	88.5832
4	4.9391	4.2594	84.3238
5	4.6899	4.5086	79.8152
6	4.4261	4.7724	75.0427
7	4.1468	5.0517	69.9911
8	3.8512	5.3473	64.6438
9	3.5383	5.6602	58.9836
10	3.2071	5.9914	52.9923
11	2.8566	6.3419	46.6503
12	2.4855	6.7130	39.9373
13	2.0927	7.1058	32.8315
14	1.6769	7.5216	25.3099
15	1.2368	7.9617	17.3482
16	.7709	8.4276	8.9207
17	.2778	8.9207	0.0000

YEARS 18 — MO PAYT .7414 — AN CONST 8.90

#	INT	PRIN	BALANCE
1	5.6152	3.2815	96.7185
2	5.4231	3.4735	93.2450
3	5.2199	3.6768	89.5682
4	5.0048	3.8919	85.6763
5	4.7770	4.1196	81.5567
6	4.5360	4.3607	77.1960
7	4.2808	4.6158	72.5802
8	4.0107	4.8859	67.6943
9	3.7248	5.1718	62.5225
10	3.4222	5.4744	57.0481
11	3.1019	5.7947	51.2533
12	2.7628	6.1338	45.1195
13	2.4039	6.4927	38.6268
14	2.0240	6.8726	31.7542
15	1.6219	7.2748	24.4794
16	1.1962	7.7004	16.7790
17	.7456	8.1510	8.6280
18	.2687	8.6280	0.0000

YEARS 19 — MO PAYT .7191 — AN CONST 8.63

#	INT	PRIN	BALANCE
1	5.6223	3.0069	96.9931
2	5.4463	3.1828	93.8103
3	5.2601	3.3691	90.4412
4	5.0629	3.5662	86.8750
5	4.8543	3.7749	83.1001
6	4.6334	3.9957	79.1044
7	4.3996	4.2296	74.8748
8	4.1521	4.4770	70.3978
9	3.8901	4.7390	65.6588
10	3.6128	5.0163	60.6425
11	3.3193	5.3098	55.3327
12	3.0086	5.6205	49.7122
13	2.6798	5.9494	43.7628
14	2.3316	6.2975	37.4653
15	1.9632	6.6660	30.7994
16	1.5731	7.0560	23.7433
17	1.1602	7.4689	16.2744
18	.7232	7.9059	8.3685
19	.2606	8.3685	0.0000

YEARS 20 — MO PAYT .6992 — AN CONST 8.40

#	INT	PRIN	BALANCE
1	5.6286	2.7622	97.2378
2	5.4670	2.9238	94.3140
3	5.2959	3.0949	91.2190
4	5.1148	3.2760	87.9430
5	4.9231	3.4677	84.4753
6	4.7202	3.6706	80.8047
7	4.5054	3.8854	76.9194
8	4.2781	4.1127	72.8066
9	4.0374	4.3534	68.4533
10	3.7827	4.6081	63.8452
11	3.5131	4.8777	58.9674
12	3.2276	5.1631	53.8043
13	2.9255	5.4653	48.3390
14	2.6057	5.7850	42.5540
15	2.2672	6.1235	36.4305
16	1.9089	6.4818	29.9486
17	1.5297	6.8611	23.0875
18	1.1282	7.2626	15.8249
19	.7032	7.6875	8.1374
20	.2534	8.1374	0.0000

YEARS 21 — MO PAYT .6814 — AN CONST 8.18

#	INT	PRIN	BALANCE
1	5.6342	2.5432	97.4568
2	5.4854	2.6920	94.7649
3	5.3279	2.8495	91.9154

#	INT	PRIN	BALANCE
4	5.1612	3.0162	88.8992
5	4.9847	3.1927	85.7065
6	4.7979	3.3795	82.3270
7	4.6001	3.5773	78.7498
8	4.3908	3.7866	74.9632
9	4.1693	4.0081	70.9551
10	3.9347	4.2427	66.7124
11	3.6865	4.4909	62.2215
12	3.4237	4.7537	57.4678
13	3.1456	5.0318	52.4360
14	2.8511	5.3263	47.1097
15	2.5395	5.6379	41.4718
16	2.2096	5.9678	35.5040
17	1.8604	6.3170	29.1870
18	1.4908	6.6866	22.5003
19	1.0995	7.0779	15.4225
20	.6854	7.4920	7.9304
21	.2470	7.9304	0.0000

YEARS 22	MO PAYT .6655	AN CONST 7.99	
#	INT	PRIN	BALANCE
1	5.6393	2.3462	97.6538
2	5.5021	2.4835	95.1703
3	5.3567	2.6288	92.5415
4	5.2029	2.7826	89.7589
5	5.0401	2.9454	86.8135
6	4.8678	3.1178	83.6957
7	4.6853	3.3002	80.3955
8	4.4922	3.4933	76.9021
9	4.2878	3.6977	73.2044
10	4.0714	3.9141	69.2903
11	3.8424	4.1431	65.1472
12	3.6000	4.3855	60.7617
13	3.3434	4.6422	56.1195
14	3.0718	4.9138	51.2057
15	2.7842	5.2013	46.0044
16	2.4799	5.5056	40.4988
17	2.1577	5.8278	34.6710
18	1.8167	6.1688	28.5022
19	1.4558	6.5298	21.9724
20	1.0737	6.9118	15.0606
21	.6693	7.3163	7.7444
22	.2412	7.7444	0.0000

YEARS 23	MO PAYT .6510	AN CONST 7.82	
#	INT	PRIN	BALANCE
1	5.6439	2.1684	97.8316
2	5.5170	2.2953	95.5362
3	5.3827	2.4296	93.1066
4	5.2406	2.5718	90.5348
5	5.0901	2.7223	87.8125
6	4.9308	2.8816	84.9310
7	4.7622	3.0502	81.8808
8	4.5837	3.2287	78.6521
9	4.3948	3.4176	75.2345
10	4.1948	3.6175	71.6170
11	3.9832	3.8292	67.7878
12	3.7591	4.0533	63.7345
13	3.5219	4.2904	59.4441
14	3.2709	4.5415	54.9026
15	3.0051	4.8072	50.0954
16	2.7239	5.0885	45.0068
17	2.4261	5.3863	39.6206
18	2.1110	5.7014	33.9192
19	1.7773	6.0350	27.8841
20	1.4242	6.3882	21.4960
21	1.0504	6.7619	14.7340
22	.6548	7.1576	7.5764
23	.2360	7.5764	0.0000

YEARS 24	MO PAYT .6380	AN CONST 7.66	
#	INT	PRIN	BALANCE
1	5.6481	2.0075	97.9925
2	5.5306	2.1249	95.8676
3	5.4063	2.2492	93.6184
4	5.2747	2.3809	91.2375
5	5.1354	2.5202	88.7174
6	4.9879	2.6676	86.0497
7	4.8318	2.8237	83.2260
8	4.6666	2.9889	80.2371
9	4.4917	3.1638	77.0732
10	4.3066	3.3490	73.7243
11	4.1106	3.5449	70.1793
12	3.9032	3.7523	66.4270
13	3.6836	3.9719	62.4551
14	3.4512	4.2043	58.2508
15	3.2052	4.4503	53.8004
16	2.9448	4.7107	49.0897
17	2.6692	4.9864	44.1033
18	2.3774	5.2781	38.8252
19	2.0686	5.5870	33.2382
20	1.7417	5.9139	27.3244
21	1.3956	6.2599	21.0645
22	1.0293	6.6262	14.4382
23	.6416	7.0139	7.4243
24	.2312	7.4243	0.0000

YEARS 25	MO PAYT .6261	AN CONST 7.52	
#	INT	PRIN	BALANCE
1	5.6519	1.8612	98.1388
2	5.5430	1.9701	96.1687
3	5.4277	2.0854	94.0834
4	5.3057	2.2074	91.8760
5	5.1765	2.3365	89.5394
6	5.0398	2.4733	87.0662
7	4.8951	2.6180	84.4482
8	4.7419	2.7712	81.6770
9	4.5797	2.9333	78.7437
10	4.4081	3.1050	75.6387
11	4.2264	3.2866	72.3521
12	4.0341	3.4789	68.8732
13	3.8306	3.6825	65.1907
14	3.6151	3.8980	61.2927
15	3.3870	4.1261	57.1666
16	3.1456	4.3675	52.7991
17	2.8900	4.6230	48.1761
18	2.6195	4.8936	43.2825
19	2.3332	5.1799	38.1026
20	2.0301	5.4830	32.6196
21	1.7093	5.8038	26.8158
22	1.3697	6.1434	20.6724
23	1.0102	6.5029	14.1695
24	.6297	6.8834	7.2861
25	.2269	7.2861	0.0000

YEARS 26	MO PAYT .6153	AN CONST 7.39	
#	INT	PRIN	BALANCE
1	5.6553	1.7279	98.2721
2	5.5542	1.8290	96.4431
3	5.4472	1.9360	94.5070
4	5.3339	2.0493	92.4577
5	5.2140	2.1692	90.2884
6	5.0871	2.2962	87.9923
7	4.9527	2.4305	85.5617
8	4.8105	2.5727	82.9890
9	4.6600	2.7233	80.2657
10	4.5006	2.8826	77.3831
11	4.3319	3.0513	74.3318
12	4.1534	3.2298	71.1019
13	3.9644	3.4188	67.6831
14	3.7644	3.6189	64.0642
15	3.5526	3.8306	60.2336
16	3.3285	4.0548	56.1788
17	3.0912	4.2920	51.8868
18	2.8401	4.5432	47.3436
19	2.5742	4.8090	42.5346
20	2.2929	5.0904	37.4442
21	1.9950	5.3882	32.0560
22	1.6797	5.7035	26.3525
23	1.3460	6.0373	20.3152
24	.9927	6.3905	13.9247
25	.6188	6.7644	7.1602
26	.2230	7.1602	0.0000

YEARS 27	MO PAYT .6054	AN CONST 7.27	
#	INT	PRIN	BALANCE
1	5.6585	1.6062	98.3938
2	5.5645	1.7002	96.6936
3	5.4650	1.7996	94.8940
4	5.3597	1.9050	92.9891
5	5.2482	2.0164	90.9726
6	5.1303	2.1344	88.8382
7	5.0054	2.2593	86.5789
8	4.8732	2.3915	84.1875
9	4.7332	2.5314	81.6560
10	4.5851	2.6795	78.9765
11	4.4283	2.8363	76.1402
12	4.2624	3.0023	73.1379
13	4.0867	3.1780	69.9599
14	3.9007	3.3639	66.5960
15	3.7039	3.5608	63.0352
16	3.4956	3.7691	59.2661
17	3.2750	3.9896	55.2765
18	3.0416	4.2231	51.0534
19	2.7945	4.4702	46.5832
20	2.5329	4.7318	41.8514
21	2.2560	5.0086	36.8428
22	1.9630	5.3017	31.5411
23	1.6527	5.6119	25.9292
24	1.3244	5.9403	19.9889
25	.9768	6.2879	13.7010
26	.6089	6.6558	7.0452
27	.2194	7.0452	0.0000

YEARS 28	MO PAYT .5963	AN CONST 7.16	
#	INT	PRIN	BALANCE
1	5.6614	1.4947	98.5053
2	5.5739	1.5822	96.9231
3	5.4813	1.6748	95.2484
4	5.3833	1.7727	93.4756
5	5.2796	1.8765	91.5991
6	5.1698	1.9863	89.6129
7	5.0536	2.1025	87.5104
8	4.9305	2.2255	85.2848
9	4.8003	2.3557	82.9291
10	4.6625	2.4936	80.4355
11	4.5166	2.6395	77.7960
12	4.3621	2.7939	75.0021
13	4.1986	2.9574	72.0447
14	4.0256	3.1305	68.9142
15	3.8424	3.3136	65.6006
16	3.6485	3.5075	62.0930
17	3.4433	3.7128	58.3803
18	3.2261	3.9300	54.4502
19	2.9961	4.1600	50.2903
20	2.7527	4.4034	45.8869
21	2.4950	4.6610	41.2259
22	2.2223	4.9338	36.2921
23	1.9336	5.2225	31.0697
24	1.6280	5.5280	25.5416
25	1.3046	5.8515	19.6901
26	.9622	6.1939	13.4962
27	.5998	6.5563	6.9399
28	.2161	6.9399	0.0000

YEARS 29	MO PAYT .5880	AN CONST 7.06	
#	INT	PRIN	BALANCE
1	5.6640	1.3924	98.6076
2	5.5825	1.4739	97.1337
3	5.4963	1.5601	95.5735
4	5.4050	1.6514	93.9221
5	5.3084	1.7481	92.1740
6	5.2061	1.8503	90.3237
7	5.0978	1.9586	88.3651
8	4.9832	2.0732	86.2918
9	4.8619	2.1945	84.0973
10	4.7335	2.3229	81.7744
11	4.5976	2.4589	79.3155
12	4.4537	2.6027	76.7128
13	4.3014	2.7550	73.9577
14	4.1402	2.9162	71.0415
15	3.9695	3.0869	67.9546
16	3.7889	3.2675	64.6871
17	3.5977	3.4587	61.2284
18	3.3954	3.6611	57.5674
19	3.1811	3.8753	53.6921
20	2.9544	4.1020	49.5900
21	2.7144	4.3421	45.2480
22	2.4603	4.5961	40.6518
23	2.1914	4.8651	35.7868
24	1.9067	5.1497	30.6370
25	1.6054	5.4511	25.1860
26	1.2864	5.7700	19.4160
27	.9488	6.1076	13.3083
28	.5914	6.4650	6.8433
29	.2131	6.8433	0.0000

YEARS 30	MO PAYT .5804	AN CONST 6.97	
#	INT	PRIN	BALANCE
1	5.6664	1.2984	98.7016
2	5.5905	1.3743	97.3273
3	5.5100	1.4548	95.8725
4	5.4249	1.5399	94.3326
5	5.3348	1.6300	92.7026
6	5.2394	1.7254	90.9773
7	5.1385	1.8263	89.1509
8	5.0316	1.9332	87.2177
9	4.9185	2.0463	85.1714
10	4.7988	2.1660	83.0054
11	4.6720	2.2928	80.7126
12	4.5379	2.4269	78.2857
13	4.3959	2.5689	75.7167
14	4.2455	2.7193	72.9975
15	4.0864	2.8784	70.1191
16	3.9180	3.0468	67.0723
17	3.7397	3.2251	63.8472
18	3.5510	3.4138	60.4334
19	3.3513	3.6135	56.8199
20	3.1398	3.8250	52.9949
21	2.9160	4.0488	48.9462
22	2.6791	4.2857	44.6605
23	2.4283	4.5365	40.1240
24	2.1629	4.8019	35.3221
25	1.8819	5.0829	30.2392
26	1.5845	5.3803	24.8590
27	1.2697	5.6951	19.1639
28	.9365	6.0283	13.1355
29	.5837	6.3811	6.7544
30	.2104	6.7544	0.0000

YEARS 2 — MO PAYT 4.4208 — AN CONST 53.05

#	INT	PRIN	BALANCE
1	4.4833	48.5663	51.4337
2	1.6160	51.4337	0.0000

YEARS 3 — MO PAYT 3.0309 — AN CONST 36.38

#	INT	PRIN	BALANCE
1	4.9300	31.4406	68.5594
2	3.0737	33.2968	35.2626
3	1.1079	35.2626	0.0000

YEARS 4 — MO PAYT 2.3371 — AN CONST 28.05

#	INT	PRIN	BALANCE
1	5.1530	22.8917	77.1083
2	3.8014	24.2433	52.8650
3	2.3701	25.6746	27.1904
4	.8543	27.1904	0.0000

YEARS 5 — MO PAYT 1.9217 — AN CONST 23.07

#	INT	PRIN	BALANCE
1	5.2864	17.7737	82.2263
2	4.2371	18.8230	63.4033
3	3.1258	19.9343	43.4689
4	1.9489	21.1113	22.3577
5	.7025	22.3577	0.0000

YEARS 6 — MO PAYT 1.6455 — AN CONST 19.75

#	INT	PRIN	BALANCE
1	5.3752	14.3710	85.6290
2	4.5267	15.2194	70.4096
3	3.6282	16.1180	54.2916
4	2.6766	17.0696	37.2220
5	1.6688	18.0774	19.1447
6	.6015	19.1447	0.0000

YEARS 7 — MO PAYT 1.4489 — AN CONST 17.39

#	INT	PRIN	BALANCE
1	5.4384	11.9484	88.0516
2	4.7329	12.6539	75.3977
3	3.9859	13.4009	61.9968
4	3.1947	14.1921	47.8046
5	2.3568	15.0300	32.7746
6	1.4694	15.9174	16.8572
7	.5296	16.8572	0.0000

YEARS 8 — MO PAYT 1.3020 — AN CONST 15.63

#	INT	PRIN	BALANCE
1	5.4856	10.1385	89.8615
2	4.8870	10.7370	79.1245
3	4.2531	11.3710	67.7535
4	3.5818	12.0423	55.7112
5	2.8708	12.7533	42.9580
6	2.1178	13.5062	29.4517
7	1.3204	14.3036	15.1481
8	.4759	15.1481	0.0000

YEARS 9 — MO PAYT 1.1882 — AN CONST 14.26

#	INT	PRIN	BALANCE
1	5.5221	8.7369	91.2631
2	5.0063	9.2527	82.0105
3	4.4600	9.7990	72.2115
4	3.8815	10.3775	61.8340
5	3.2688	10.9902	50.8438
6	2.6200	11.6390	39.2048
7	1.9328	12.3262	26.8786
8	1.2051	13.0539	13.8246
9	.4344	13.8246	0.0000

YEARS 10 — MO PAYT 1.0977 — AN CONST 13.18

#	INT	PRIN	BALANCE
1	5.5512	7.6211	92.3789
2	5.1013	8.0710	84.3079
3	4.6248	8.5475	75.7604
4	4.1201	9.0522	66.7082
5	3.5857	9.5866	57.1216
6	3.0197	10.1526	46.9690
7	2.4203	10.7520	36.2170
8	1.7855	11.3868	24.8301
9	1.1132	12.0591	12.7711
10	.4013	12.7711	0.0000

YEARS 11 — MO PAYT 1.0240 — AN CONST 12.29

#	INT	PRIN	BALANCE
1	5.5749	6.7131	93.2869
2	5.1786	7.1095	86.1774
3	4.7588	7.5292	78.6482
4	4.3143	7.9737	70.6745
5	3.8435	8.4445	62.2300
6	3.3450	8.9431	53.2869
7	2.8170	9.4711	43.8159
8	2.2578	10.0302	33.7857
9	1.6656	10.6224	23.1633
10	1.0385	11.2495	11.9137
11	.3743	11.9137	0.0000

YEARS 12 — MO PAYT .9630 — AN CONST 11.56

#	INT	PRIN	BALANCE
1	5.5945	5.9610	94.0390
2	5.2426	6.3130	87.7260
3	4.8699	6.6857	81.0404
4	4.4752	7.0804	73.9600
5	4.0571	7.4984	66.4616
6	3.6144	7.9411	58.5205
7	3.1456	8.4100	50.1105
8	2.6491	8.9065	41.2040
9	2.1232	9.4323	31.7717
10	1.5663	9.9892	21.7825
11	.9766	10.5790	11.2035
12	.3520	11.2035	0.0000

YEARS 13 — MO PAYT .9116 — AN CONST 10.94

#	INT	PRIN	BALANCE
1	5.6110	5.3288	94.6712
2	5.2964	5.6434	89.0279
3	4.9632	5.9765	83.0513
4	4.6104	6.3294	76.7219
5	4.2367	6.7031	70.0188
6	3.8409	7.0988	62.9200
7	3.4218	7.5180	55.4020
8	2.9780	7.9618	47.4402
9	2.5079	8.4319	39.0084
10	2.0101	8.9297	30.0787
11	1.4829	9.4569	20.6218
12	.9245	10.0152	10.6065
13	.3332	10.6065	0.0000

YEARS 14 — MO PAYT .8680 — AN CONST 10.42

#	INT	PRIN	BALANCE
1	5.6251	4.7906	95.2094
2	5.3422	5.0735	90.1359
3	5.0427	5.3730	84.7629
4	4.7255	5.6902	79.0726
5	4.3895	6.0262	73.0465
6	4.0337	6.3820	66.6645
7	3.6569	6.7588	59.9057
8	3.2579	7.1578	52.7479
9	2.8353	7.5804	45.1675
10	2.3878	8.0279	37.1396
11	1.9138	8.5019	28.6377
12	1.4118	9.0039	19.6339
13	.8803	9.5354	10.0984
14	.3173	10.0984	0.0000

YEARS 15 — MO PAYT .8304 — AN CONST 9.97

#	INT	PRIN	BALANCE
1	5.6371	4.3278	95.6722
2	5.3816	4.5833	91.0889
3	5.1110	4.8539	86.2350
4	4.8244	5.1405	81.0945
5	4.5209	5.4440	75.6505
6	4.1995	5.7654	69.8852
7	3.8592	6.1058	63.7794
8	3.4987	6.4663	57.3131
9	3.1169	6.8480	50.4651
10	2.7126	7.2523	43.2128
11	2.2844	7.6805	35.5323
12	1.8310	8.1340	27.3983
13	1.3507	8.6142	18.7841
14	.8422	9.1228	9.6614
15	.3035	9.6614	0.0000

YEARS 16 — MO PAYT .7978 — AN CONST 9.58

#	INT	PRIN	BALANCE
1	5.6476	3.9261	96.0739
2	5.4158	4.1579	91.9160
3	5.1703	4.4034	87.5127
4	4.9104	4.6633	82.8493
5	4.6350	4.9387	77.9107
6	4.3435	5.2302	72.6804
7	4.0347	5.5390	67.1414
8	3.7076	5.8661	61.2754
9	3.3613	6.2124	55.0630
10	2.9945	6.5792	48.4838
11	2.6061	6.9676	41.5162
12	2.1947	7.3790	34.1373
13	1.7591	7.8146	26.3226
14	1.2977	8.2760	18.0467
15	.8091	8.7646	9.2821
16	.2916	9.2821	0.0000

YEARS 17 — MO PAYT .7693 — AN CONST 9.24

#	INT	PRIN	BALANCE
1	5.6568	3.5747	96.4253
2	5.4457	3.7857	92.6396
3	5.2222	4.0093	88.6303
4	4.9855	4.2460	84.3844
5	4.7348	4.4966	79.8877
6	4.4693	4.7621	75.1256
7	4.1882	5.0433	70.0823
8	3.8904	5.3410	64.7413
9	3.5751	5.6564	59.0849
10	3.2411	5.9903	53.0946
11	2.8875	6.3440	46.7507
12	2.5129	6.7185	40.0321
13	2.1163	7.1152	32.9170
14	1.6962	7.5353	25.3817
15	1.2513	7.9801	17.4015
16	.7802	8.4513	8.9503
17	.2812	8.9503	0.0000

YEARS 18 — MO PAYT .7442 — AN CONST 8.94

#	INT	PRIN	BALANCE
1	5.6648	3.2652	96.7348
2	5.4721	3.4580	93.2768
3	5.2679	3.6621	89.6147
4	5.0517	3.8783	85.7364
5	4.8227	4.1073	81.6290
6	4.5802	4.3498	77.2792
7	4.3234	4.6066	72.6726
8	4.0514	4.8786	67.7940
9	3.7634	5.1666	62.6274
10	3.4584	5.4717	57.1557
11	3.1353	5.7947	51.3610
12	2.7932	6.1368	45.2242
13	2.4309	6.4992	38.7250
14	2.0472	6.8829	31.8422
15	1.6408	7.2892	24.5529
16	1.2105	7.7196	16.8334
17	.7547	8.1753	8.6580
18	.2720	8.6580	0.0000

YEARS 19 — MO PAYT .7219 — AN CONST 8.67

#	INT	PRIN	BALANCE
1	5.6720	2.9909	97.0091
2	5.4954	3.1675	93.8415
3	5.3084	3.3545	90.4870
4	5.1103	3.5526	86.9344
5	4.9006	3.7623	83.1720
6	4.6785	3.9845	79.1876
7	4.4432	4.2197	74.9679
8	4.1941	4.4688	70.4990
9	3.9303	4.7327	65.7663
10	3.6508	5.0121	60.7542
11	3.3549	5.3080	55.4462
12	3.0415	5.6214	49.8248
13	2.7097	5.9533	43.8715
14	2.3582	6.3048	37.5668
15	1.9859	6.6770	30.8898
16	1.5917	7.0712	23.8186
17	1.1743	7.4887	16.3299
18	.7321	7.9308	8.3991
19	.2639	8.3991	0.0000

YEARS 20 — MO PAYT .7021 — AN CONST 8.43

#	INT	PRIN	BALANCE
1	5.6784	2.7466	97.2534
2	5.5162	2.9088	94.3446
3	5.3445	3.0805	91.2640
4	5.1626	3.2624	88.0016
5	4.9700	3.4550	84.5466
6	4.7660	3.6590	80.8876
7	4.5500	3.8750	77.0126
8	4.3212	4.1038	72.9088
9	4.0789	4.3461	68.5627
10	3.8223	4.6027	63.9600
11	3.5506	4.8744	59.0855
12	3.2628	5.1622	53.9233
13	2.9580	5.4670	48.4563
14	2.6352	5.7898	42.6665
15	2.2934	6.1316	36.5349
16	1.9314	6.4936	30.0413
17	1.5480	6.8770	23.1644
18	1.1420	7.2830	15.8814
19	.7120	7.7130	8.1684
20	.2566	8.1684	0.0000

YEARS 21 — MO PAYT .6843 — AN CONST 8.22

#	INT	PRIN	BALANCE
1	5.6841	2.5280	97.4720
2	5.5348	2.6772	94.7948
3	5.3768	2.8353	91.9596

#	INT	PRIN	BALANCE
4	5.2094	3.0027	88.9569
5	5.0321	3.1799	85.7770
6	4.8443	3.3677	82.4093
7	4.6455	3.5665	78.8428
8	4.4350	3.7771	75.0657
9	4.2120	4.0001	71.0657
10	3.9758	4.2362	66.8294
11	3.7257	4.4863	62.3431
12	3.4608	4.7512	57.5919
13	3.1803	5.0317	52.5601
14	2.8832	5.3288	47.2314
15	2.5686	5.6434	41.5879
16	2.2354	5.9766	35.6114
17	1.8826	6.3294	29.2819
18	1.5089	6.7031	22.5788
19	1.1131	7.0989	15.4799
20	.6940	7.5180	7.9619
21	.2502	7.9619	0.0000

YEARS 22   MO PAYT .6684   AN CONST 8.03

#	INT	PRIN	BALANCE
1	5.6892	2.3314	97.6686
2	5.5516	2.4690	95.1996
3	5.4058	2.6148	92.5848
4	5.2514	2.7692	89.8157
5	5.0879	2.9327	86.8830
6	4.9148	3.1058	83.7772
7	4.7314	3.2892	80.4880
8	4.5372	3.4834	77.0047
9	4.3316	3.6890	73.3157
10	4.1138	3.9068	69.4088
11	3.8831	4.1375	65.2714
12	3.6388	4.3817	60.8896
13	3.3801	4.6404	56.2492
14	3.1062	4.9144	51.3348
15	2.8160	5.2046	46.1302
16	2.5087	5.5118	40.6184
17	2.1833	5.8373	34.7811
18	1.8387	6.1819	28.5992
19	1.4737	6.5469	22.0524
20	1.0872	6.9334	15.1190
21	.6778	7.3427	7.7762
22	.2443	7.7762	0.0000

YEARS 23   MO PAYT .6540   AN CONST 7.85

#	INT	PRIN	BALANCE
1	5.6938	2.1540	97.8460
2	5.5667	2.2812	95.5649
3	5.4320	2.4158	93.1490
4	5.2893	2.5585	90.5906
5	5.1383	2.7095	87.8810
6	4.9783	2.8695	85.0116
7	4.8089	3.0389	81.9726
8	4.6295	3.2183	78.7543
9	4.4395	3.4083	75.3460
10	4.2383	3.6096	71.7365
11	4.0251	3.8227	67.9138
12	3.7995	4.0483	63.8654
13	3.5604	4.2874	59.5781
14	3.3073	4.5405	55.0376
15	3.0392	4.8086	50.2290
16	2.7554	5.0925	45.1366
17	2.4547	5.3931	39.7435
18	2.1363	5.7115	34.0319
19	1.7991	6.0487	27.9832
20	1.4420	6.4058	21.5774
21	1.0638	6.7840	14.7933
22	.6632	7.1846	7.6087
23	.2391	7.6087	0.0000

YEARS 24   MO PAYT .6409   AN CONST 7.70

#	INT	PRIN	BALANCE
1	5.6980	1.9934	98.0066
2	5.5803	2.1110	95.8956
3	5.4557	2.2357	93.6599
4	5.3237	2.3677	91.2922
5	5.1839	2.5075	88.7848
6	5.0359	2.6555	86.1293
7	4.8791	2.8123	83.3170
8	4.7130	2.9783	80.3386
9	4.5372	3.1542	77.1845
10	4.3510	3.3404	73.8441
11	4.1538	3.5376	70.3065
12	3.9449	3.7465	66.5600
13	3.7237	3.9677	62.5924
14	3.4895	4.2019	58.3905
15	3.2414	4.4500	53.9405
16	2.9787	4.7127	49.2278
17	2.7004	4.9909	44.2368
18	2.4058	5.2856	38.9512
19	2.0937	5.5977	33.3536
20	1.7632	5.9282	27.4254
21	1.4132	6.2782	21.1473
22	1.0426	6.6488	14.4984
23	.6500	7.0414	7.4571
24	.2343	7.4571	0.0000

YEARS 25   MO PAYT .6291   AN CONST 7.55

#	INT	PRIN	BALANCE
1	5.7018	1.8475	98.1525
2	5.5927	1.9565	96.1960
3	5.4772	2.0720	94.1240
4	5.3549	2.1944	91.9296
5	5.2253	2.3239	89.6056
6	5.0881	2.4611	87.1445
7	4.9428	2.6064	84.5380
8	4.7889	2.7603	81.7777
9	4.6260	2.9233	78.8544
10	4.4534	3.0959	75.7585
11	4.2706	3.2787	72.4798
12	4.0770	3.4722	69.0076
13	3.8720	3.6772	65.3304
14	3.6549	3.8944	61.4360
15	3.4250	4.1243	57.3117
16	3.1815	4.3678	52.9440
17	2.9236	4.6256	48.3183
18	2.6505	4.8987	43.4196
19	2.3613	5.1880	38.2316
20	2.0550	5.4943	32.7374
21	1.7306	5.8186	26.9187
22	1.3871	6.1622	20.7566
23	1.0233	6.5260	14.2306
24	.6380	6.9113	7.3193
25	.2300	7.3193	0.0000

YEARS 26   MO PAYT .6183   AN CONST 7.42

#	INT	PRIN	BALANCE
1	5.7053	1.7146	98.2854
2	5.6041	1.8158	96.4697
3	5.4969	1.9230	94.5467
4	5.3833	2.0365	92.5101
5	5.2631	2.1568	90.3534
6	5.1357	2.2841	88.0693
7	5.0009	2.4189	85.6504
8	4.8581	2.5618	83.0886
9	4.7068	2.7130	80.3756
10	4.5467	2.8732	77.5024
11	4.3770	3.0428	74.4596
12	4.1974	3.2225	71.2371
13	4.0071	3.4127	67.8244
14	3.8056	3.6142	64.2102
15	3.5923	3.8276	60.3826
16	3.3663	4.0536	56.3291
17	3.1270	4.2929	52.0362
18	2.8735	4.5463	47.4899
19	2.6051	4.8147	42.6751
20	2.3208	5.0990	37.5761
21	2.0198	5.4001	32.1761
22	1.7010	5.7189	26.4572
23	1.3633	6.0565	20.4007
24	1.0058	6.4141	13.9866
25	.6271	6.7928	7.1938
26	.2260	7.1938	0.0000

YEARS 27   MO PAYT .6085   AN CONST 7.31

#	INT	PRIN	BALANCE
1	5.7084	1.5932	98.4068
2	5.6144	1.6872	96.7196
3	5.5148	1.7869	94.9327
4	5.4093	1.8924	93.0404
5	5.2976	2.0041	91.0363
6	5.1792	2.1224	88.9139
7	5.0539	2.2477	86.6662
8	4.9212	2.3804	84.2858
9	4.7807	2.5209	81.7648
10	4.6318	2.6698	79.0951
11	4.4742	2.8274	76.2677
12	4.3073	2.9943	73.2733
13	4.1305	3.1711	70.1022
14	3.9433	3.3583	66.7439
15	3.7450	3.5566	63.1872
16	3.5350	3.7666	59.4206
17	3.3126	3.9890	55.4317
18	3.0771	4.2245	51.2072
19	2.8277	4.4739	46.7333
20	2.5636	4.7380	41.9952
21	2.2839	5.0178	36.9775
22	1.9876	5.3140	31.6634
23	1.6739	5.6278	26.0357
24	1.3416	5.9600	20.0757
25	.9897	6.3119	13.7638
26	.6171	6.6846	7.0792
27	.2224	7.0792	0.0000

YEARS 28   MO PAYT .5995   AN CONST 7.20

#	INT	PRIN	BALANCE
1	5.7113	1.4821	98.5179
2	5.6238	1.5696	96.9484
3	5.5312	1.6622	95.2861
4	5.4330	1.7604	93.5258
5	5.3291	1.8643	91.6614
6	5.2190	1.9744	89.6871
7	5.1025	2.0909	87.5961
8	4.9790	2.2144	85.3817
9	4.8483	2.3451	83.0366
10	4.7098	2.4836	80.5530
11	4.5632	2.6302	77.9228
12	4.4079	2.7855	75.1373
13	4.2435	2.9500	72.1874
14	4.0693	3.1241	69.0632
15	3.8848	3.3086	65.7547
16	3.6895	3.5039	62.2508
17	3.4826	3.7108	58.5400
18	3.2636	3.9299	54.6101
19	3.0315	4.1619	50.4483
20	2.7858	4.4076	46.0407
21	2.5256	4.6678	41.3728
22	2.2500	4.9434	36.4294
23	1.9582	5.2353	31.1942
24	1.6491	5.5444	25.6498
25	1.3217	5.8717	19.7781
26	.9751	6.2184	13.5598
27	.6079	6.5855	6.9743
28	.2191	6.9743	0.0000

YEARS 29   MO PAYT .5912   AN CONST 7.10

#	INT	PRIN	BALANCE
1	5.7140	1.3801	98.6199
2	5.6325	1.4616	97.1583
3	5.5462	1.5479	95.6103
4	5.4548	1.6393	93.9711
5	5.3581	1.7361	92.2350
6	5.2556	1.8386	90.3964
7	5.1470	1.9471	88.4493
8	5.0321	2.0621	86.3872
9	4.9103	2.1838	84.2034
10	4.7814	2.3128	81.8906
11	4.6448	2.4493	79.4413
12	4.5002	2.5939	76.8474
13	4.3471	2.7471	74.1003
14	4.1849	2.9092	71.1911
15	4.0131	3.0810	68.1101
16	3.8312	3.2629	64.8472
17	3.6386	3.4555	61.3916
18	3.4346	3.6596	57.7321
19	3.2185	3.8756	53.8564
20	2.9897	4.1044	49.7520
21	2.7474	4.3468	45.4052
22	2.4907	4.6034	40.8018
23	2.2190	4.8752	35.9267
24	1.9311	5.1630	30.7636
25	1.6263	5.4678	25.2958
26	1.3035	5.7907	19.5052
27	.9616	6.1325	13.3726
28	.5995	6.4946	6.8780
29	.2161	6.8780	0.0000

YEARS 30   MO PAYT .5836   AN CONST 7.01

#	INT	PRIN	BALANCE
1	5.7164	1.2864	98.7136
2	5.6405	1.3624	97.3512
3	5.5601	1.4428	95.9084
4	5.4749	1.5280	94.3804
5	5.3847	1.6182	92.7622
6	5.2891	1.7137	91.0484
7	5.1879	1.8149	89.2335
8	5.0808	1.9221	87.3114
9	4.9673	2.0356	85.2759
10	4.8471	2.1557	83.1201
11	4.7199	2.2830	80.8371
12	4.5851	2.4178	78.4193
13	4.4423	2.5605	75.8588
14	4.2912	2.7117	73.1471
15	4.1311	2.8718	70.2753
16	3.9615	3.0414	67.2339
17	3.7819	3.2209	64.0130
18	3.5918	3.4111	60.6019
19	3.3904	3.6125	56.9894
20	3.1771	3.8258	53.1636
21	2.9512	4.0516	49.1120
22	2.7120	4.2908	44.8211
23	2.4587	4.5442	40.2770
24	2.1904	4.8125	35.4645
25	1.9063	5.0966	30.3679
26	1.6054	5.3975	24.9704
27	1.2867	5.7162	19.2542
28	.9492	6.0536	13.2006
29	.5918	6.4110	6.7896
30	.2133	6.7896	0.0000

MONTHLY PAYMENT AMORTIZATION SCHEDULE PER $100   5.80 %

YEARS 2 — MO PAYT 4.4231 — AN CONST 53.08

#	INT	PRIN	BALANCE
1	4.5228	48.5539	51.4461
2	1.6306	51.4461	0.0000

YEARS 3 — MO PAYT 3.0331 — AN CONST 36.40

#	INT	PRIN	BALANCE
1	4.9734	31.4243	68.5757
2	3.1015	33.2962	35.2795
3	1.1182	35.2795	0.0000

YEARS 4 — MO PAYT 2.3393 — AN CONST 28.08

#	INT	PRIN	BALANCE
1	5.1983	22.8738	77.1262
2	3.8358	24.2364	52.8898
3	2.3921	25.6801	27.2097
4	.8624	27.2097	0.0000

YEARS 5 — MO PAYT 1.9240 — AN CONST 23.09

#	INT	PRIN	BALANCE
1	5.3329	17.7550	82.2450
2	4.2753	18.8126	63.4324
3	3.1547	19.9332	43.4992
4	1.9674	21.1206	22.3787
5	.7093	22.3787	0.0000

YEARS 6 — MO PAYT 1.6479 — AN CONST 19.78

#	INT	PRIN	BALANCE
1	5.4225	14.3519	85.6481
2	4.5676	15.2068	70.4413
3	3.6617	16.1126	54.3287
4	2.7020	17.0724	37.2562
5	1.6850	18.0894	19.1669
6	.6075	19.1669	0.0000

YEARS 7 — MO PAYT 1.4513 — AN CONST 17.42

#	INT	PRIN	BALANCE
1	5.4862	11.9292	88.0708
2	4.7756	12.6398	75.4309
3	4.0227	13.3927	62.0382
4	3.2249	14.1905	47.8477
5	2.3796	15.0358	32.8119
6	1.4840	15.9314	16.8804
7	.5350	16.8804	0.0000

YEARS 8 — MO PAYT 1.3044 — AN CONST 15.66

#	INT	PRIN	BALANCE
1	5.5338	10.1193	89.8807
2	4.9310	10.7221	79.1586
3	4.2923	11.3608	67.7978
4	3.6156	12.0375	55.7603
5	2.8986	12.7545	43.0058
6	2.1388	13.5157	29.4915
7	1.3338	14.3193	15.1722
8	.4809	15.1722	0.0000

YEARS 9 — MO PAYT 1.1907 — AN CONST 14.29

#	INT	PRIN	BALANCE
1	5.5707	8.7178	91.2822
2	5.0514	9.2371	82.0450
3	4.5011	9.7874	72.2577
4	3.9181	10.3704	61.8873
5	3.3004	10.9881	50.8992
6	2.6459	11.6426	39.2566
7	1.9524	12.3361	26.9205
8	1.2175	13.0710	13.8496
9	.4390	13.8496	0.0000

YEARS 10 — MO PAYT 1.1002 — AN CONST 13.21

#	INT	PRIN	BALANCE
1	5.6000	7.6022	92.3978
2	5.1472	8.0551	84.3427
3	4.6674	8.5349	75.8078
4	4.1590	9.0433	66.7645
5	3.6203	9.5820	57.1825
6	3.0495	10.1527	47.0298
7	2.4447	10.7575	36.2722
8	1.8040	11.3983	24.8739
9	1.1250	12.0773	12.7967
10	.4056	12.7967	0.0000

YEARS 11 — MO PAYT 1.0265 — AN CONST 12.32

#	INT	PRIN	BALANCE
1	5.6239	6.6945	93.3055
2	5.2251	7.0933	86.2122
3	4.8026	7.5158	78.6963
4	4.3549	7.9635	70.7328
5	3.8805	8.4379	62.2949
6	3.3779	8.9405	53.3544
7	2.8454	9.4731	43.8813
8	2.2811	10.0373	33.8440
9	1.6832	10.6352	23.2087
10	1.0497	11.2688	11.9400
11	.3784	11.9400	0.0000

YEARS 12 — MO PAYT .9655 — AN CONST 11.59

#	INT	PRIN	BALANCE
1	5.6437	5.9427	94.0573
2	5.2897	6.2967	87.7606
3	4.9146	6.6718	81.0888
4	4.5172	7.0692	74.0196
5	4.0961	7.4903	66.5294
6	3.6499	7.9365	58.5929
7	3.1772	8.4092	50.1837
8	2.6763	8.9101	41.2736
9	2.1455	9.4409	31.8327
10	1.5832	10.0032	21.8295
11	.9873	10.5991	11.2304
12	.3559	11.2304	0.0000

YEARS 13 — MO PAYT .9143 — AN CONST 10.98

#	INT	PRIN	BALANCE
1	5.6603	5.3108	94.6892
2	5.3440	5.6271	89.0621
3	5.0088	5.9623	83.0998
4	4.6536	6.3174	76.7824
5	4.2773	6.6938	70.0886
6	3.8786	7.0925	62.9961
7	3.4561	7.5150	55.4812
8	3.0084	7.9626	47.5186
9	2.5341	8.4369	39.0817
10	2.0316	8.9395	30.1422
11	1.4991	9.4720	20.6702
12	.9349	10.0362	10.6340
13	.3370	10.6340	0.0000

YEARS 14 — MO PAYT .8706 — AN CONST 10.45

#	INT	PRIN	BALANCE
1	5.6744	4.7730	95.2270
2	5.3901	5.0573	90.1698
3	5.0889	5.3585	84.8112
4	4.7697	5.6777	79.1335
5	4.4315	6.0159	73.1176
6	4.0731	6.3743	66.7433
7	3.6934	6.7540	59.9894
8	3.2911	7.1563	52.8331
9	2.8649	7.5826	45.2505
10	2.4132	8.0342	37.2163
11	1.9346	8.5128	28.7035
12	1.4275	9.0199	19.6836
13	.8902	9.5572	10.1265
14	.3210	10.1265	0.0000

YEARS 15 — MO PAYT .8331 — AN CONST 10.00

#	INT	PRIN	BALANCE
1	5.6866	4.3105	95.6895
2	5.4298	4.5672	91.1223
3	5.1578	4.8393	86.2830
4	4.8695	5.1275	81.1555
5	4.5641	5.4330	75.7225
6	4.2405	5.7566	69.9659
7	3.8976	6.0995	63.8664
8	3.5342	6.4628	57.4035
9	3.1493	6.8478	50.5557
10	2.7414	7.2557	43.3000
11	2.3092	7.6879	35.6121
12	1.8512	8.1459	27.4663
13	1.3660	8.6311	18.8352
14	.8519	9.1452	9.6900
15	.3071	9.6900	0.0000

YEARS 16 — MO PAYT .8005 — AN CONST 9.61

#	INT	PRIN	BALANCE
1	5.6972	3.9091	96.0909
2	5.4643	4.1420	91.9489
3	5.2176	4.3887	87.5602
4	4.9562	4.6501	82.9101
5	4.6792	4.9271	77.9830
6	4.3857	5.2206	72.7624
7	4.0747	5.5316	67.2308
8	3.7452	5.8611	61.3698
9	3.3961	6.2102	55.1596
10	3.0262	6.5801	48.5795
11	2.6342	6.9721	41.6074
12	2.2189	7.3874	34.2200
13	1.7789	7.8274	26.3926
14	1.3126	8.2937	18.0989
15	.8186	8.7877	9.3112
16	.2951	9.3112	0.0000

YEARS 17 — MO PAYT .7720 — AN CONST 9.27

#	INT	PRIN	BALANCE
1	5.7064	3.5581	96.4419
2	5.4945	3.7700	92.6719
3	5.2699	3.9946	88.6773
4	5.0319	4.2325	84.4448
5	4.7798	4.4847	79.9601
6	4.5127	4.7518	75.2083
7	4.2296	5.0348	70.1735
8	3.9297	5.3348	64.8387
9	3.6120	5.6525	59.1862
10	3.2752	5.9892	53.1970
11	2.9185	6.3460	46.8510
12	2.5405	6.7240	40.1270
13	2.1399	7.1245	33.0024
14	1.7156	7.5489	25.4535
15	1.2659	7.9986	17.4549
16	.7894	8.4750	8.9799
17	.2846	8.9799	0.0000

YEARS 18 — MO PAYT .7470 — AN CONST 8.97

#	INT	PRIN	BALANCE
1	5.7145	3.2489	96.7511
2	5.5210	3.4425	93.3086
3	5.3159	3.6475	89.6610
4	5.0987	3.8648	85.7962
5	4.8685	4.0950	81.7012
6	4.6245	4.3390	77.3622
7	4.3661	4.5974	72.7648
8	4.0922	4.8713	67.8936
9	3.8021	5.1614	62.7321
10	3.4946	5.4689	57.2633
11	3.1688	5.7946	51.4686
12	2.8237	6.1398	45.3288
13	2.4579	6.5055	38.8232
14	2.0704	6.8931	31.9302
15	1.6598	7.3037	24.6265
16	1.2248	7.7387	16.8878
17	.7638	8.1997	8.6881
18	.2754	8.6881	0.0000

YEARS 19 — MO PAYT .7247 — AN CONST 8.70

#	INT	PRIN	BALANCE
1	5.7217	2.9751	97.0249
2	5.5445	3.1523	93.8726
3	5.3568	3.3401	90.5326
4	5.1578	3.5390	86.9936
5	4.9470	3.7498	83.2437
6	4.7236	3.9732	79.2705
7	4.4869	4.2099	75.0607
8	4.2362	4.4606	70.6000
9	3.9705	4.7263	65.8737
10	3.6889	5.0079	60.8658
11	3.3906	5.3062	55.5596
12	3.0746	5.6223	49.9374
13	2.7397	5.9572	43.9802
14	2.3848	6.3120	37.6682
15	2.0088	6.6880	30.9802
16	1.6104	7.0864	23.8939
17	1.1883	7.5085	16.3854
18	.7411	7.9557	8.4296
19	.2672	8.4296	0.0000

YEARS 20 — MO PAYT .7049 — AN CONST 8.46

#	INT	PRIN	BALANCE
1	5.7282	2.7311	97.2689
2	5.5655	2.8938	94.3750
3	5.3931	3.0662	91.3088
4	5.2105	3.2488	88.0600
5	5.0169	3.4424	84.6176
6	4.8119	3.6474	80.9702
7	4.5946	3.8647	77.1055
8	4.3644	4.0949	73.0107
9	4.1205	4.3388	68.6718
10	3.8620	4.5973	64.0746
11	3.5882	4.8711	59.2035
12	3.2980	5.1613	54.0422
13	2.9906	5.4687	48.5735
14	2.6648	5.7945	42.7791
15	2.3197	6.1396	36.6395
16	1.9540	6.5053	30.1341
17	1.5665	6.8928	23.2413
18	1.1559	7.3034	15.9379
19	.7208	7.7385	8.1994
20	.2599	8.1994	0.0000

YEARS 21 — MO PAYT .6872 — AN CONST 8.25

#	INT	PRIN	BALANCE
1	5.7339	2.5128	97.4872
2	5.5842	2.6625	94.8247
3	5.4256	2.8211	92.0036

#	INT	PRIN	BALANCE
4	5.2576	2.9891	89.0144
5	5.0795	3.1672	85.8472
6	4.8909	3.3559	82.4913
7	4.6910	3.5558	78.9356
8	4.4792	3.7676	75.1680
9	4.2547	3.9920	71.1760
10	4.0169	4.2298	66.9462
11	3.7650	4.4817	62.4645
12	3.4980	4.7487	57.7158
13	3.2152	5.0316	52.6842
14	2.9154	5.3313	47.3530
15	2.5979	5.6488	41.7041
16	2.2614	5.9853	35.7188
17	1.9049	6.3419	29.3769
18	1.5271	6.7196	22.6573
19	1.1268	7.1199	15.5374
20	.7027	7.5440	7.9934
21	.2533	7.9934	0.0000

YEARS 22	MO PAYT .6713	AN CONST 8.06	
#	INT	PRIN	BALANCE
1	5.7391	2.3166	97.6834
2	5.6011	2.4546	95.2288
3	5.4549	2.6008	92.6279
4	5.2999	2.7558	89.8722
5	5.1358	2.9199	86.9523
6	4.9618	3.0938	83.8585
7	4.7776	3.2781	80.5803
8	4.5823	3.4734	77.1069
9	4.3754	3.6803	73.4267
10	4.1562	3.8995	69.5271
11	3.9239	4.1318	65.3954
12	3.6778	4.3779	61.0174
13	3.4170	4.6387	56.3787
14	3.1407	4.9150	51.4637
15	2.8479	5.2078	46.2560
16	2.5377	5.5180	40.7380
17	2.2090	5.8467	34.8913
18	1.8607	6.1949	28.6964
19	1.4917	6.5640	22.1324
20	1.1007	6.9550	15.1774
21	.6864	7.3692	7.8082
22	.2475	7.8082	0.0000

YEARS 23	MO PAYT .6569	AN CONST 7.89	
#	INT	PRIN	BALANCE
1	5.7437	2.1396	97.8604
2	5.6163	2.2671	95.5933
3	5.4812	2.4021	93.1912
4	5.3381	2.5452	90.6461
5	5.1865	2.6968	87.9493
6	5.0259	2.8574	85.0919
7	4.8557	3.0276	82.0642
8	4.6753	3.2080	78.8562
9	4.4842	3.3991	75.4572
10	4.2818	3.6015	71.8556
11	4.0672	3.8161	68.0395
12	3.8399	4.0434	63.9961
13	3.5991	4.2842	59.7119
14	3.3439	4.5394	55.1725
15	3.0735	4.8098	50.3626
16	2.7870	5.0964	45.2663
17	2.4834	5.3999	39.8663
18	2.1617	5.7216	34.1448
19	1.8209	6.0624	28.0824
20	1.4598	6.4235	21.6589
21	1.0772	6.8061	14.8527
22	.6718	7.2116	7.6411
23	.2422	7.6411	0.0000

YEARS 24	MO PAYT .6439	AN CONST 7.73	
#	INT	PRIN	BALANCE
1	5.7479	1.9793	98.0207
2	5.6300	2.0973	95.9234
3	5.5051	2.2222	93.7012
4	5.3727	2.3545	91.3467
5	5.2325	2.4948	88.8519
6	5.0839	2.6434	86.2085
7	4.9264	2.8009	83.4076
8	4.7596	2.9677	80.4399
9	4.5828	3.1445	77.2954
10	4.3955	3.3318	73.9636
11	4.1970	3.5303	70.4333
12	3.9867	3.7405	66.6928
13	3.7639	3.9634	62.7294
14	3.5278	4.1994	58.5300
15	3.2777	4.4496	54.0804
16	3.0126	4.7146	49.3658
17	2.7318	4.9955	44.3703
18	2.4342	5.2930	39.0773
19	2.1190	5.6083	33.4689
20	1.7849	5.9424	27.5265
21	1.4309	6.2964	21.2301
22	1.0559	6.6714	14.5587
23	.6585	7.0688	7.4899
24	.2374	7.4899	0.0000

YEARS 25	MO PAYT .6321	AN CONST 7.59	
#	INT	PRIN	BALANCE
1	5.7518	1.8338	98.1662
2	5.6425	1.9431	96.2231
3	5.5268	2.0588	94.1643
4	5.4041	2.1814	91.9829
5	5.2742	2.3114	89.6715
6	5.1365	2.4491	87.2225
7	4.9906	2.5949	84.6276
8	4.8361	2.7495	81.8780
9	4.6723	2.9133	78.9648
10	4.4988	3.0868	75.8779
11	4.3149	3.2707	72.6072
12	4.1201	3.4655	69.1417
13	3.9136	3.6719	65.4698
14	3.6949	3.8907	61.5791
15	3.4631	4.1224	57.4567
16	3.2176	4.3680	53.0887
17	2.9574	4.6282	48.4605
18	2.6817	4.9039	43.5566
19	2.3896	5.1960	38.3606
20	2.0801	5.5055	32.8552
21	1.7521	5.8334	27.0217
22	1.4047	6.1809	20.8408
23	1.0365	6.5491	14.2917
24	.6464	6.9392	7.3525
25	.2330	7.3525	0.0000

YEARS 26	MO PAYT .6214	AN CONST 7.46	
#	INT	PRIN	BALANCE
1	5.7552	1.7013	98.2987
2	5.6539	1.8026	96.4961
3	5.5465	1.9100	94.5861
4	5.4328	2.0238	92.5623
5	5.3122	2.1443	90.4180
6	5.1845	2.2720	88.1460
7	5.0491	2.4074	85.7386
8	4.9057	2.5508	83.1878
9	4.7538	2.7027	80.4851
10	4.5928	2.8637	77.6214
11	4.4222	3.0343	74.5870
12	4.2415	3.2151	71.3720
13	4.0500	3.4066	67.9654
14	3.8470	3.6095	64.3560
15	3.6320	3.8245	60.5315
16	3.4042	4.0523	56.4792
17	3.1628	4.2937	52.1855
18	2.9071	4.5494	47.6360
19	2.6361	4.8204	42.8156
20	2.3489	5.1076	37.7080
21	2.0447	5.4118	32.2962
22	1.7223	5.7342	26.5620
23	1.3808	6.0758	20.4863
24	1.0189	6.4377	14.0486
25	.6354	6.8211	7.2275
26	.2291	7.2275	0.0000

YEARS 27	MO PAYT .6116	AN CONST 7.34	
#	INT	PRIN	BALANCE
1	5.7584	1.5803	98.4197
2	5.6643	1.6744	96.7453
3	5.5646	1.7741	94.9712
4	5.4589	1.8798	93.0914
5	5.3469	1.9918	91.0996
6	5.2283	2.1104	88.9892
7	5.1025	2.2361	86.7530
8	4.9693	2.3693	84.3837
9	4.8282	2.5105	81.8732
10	4.6787	2.6600	79.2132
11	4.5202	2.8185	76.3947
12	4.3523	2.9864	73.4084
13	4.1744	3.1642	70.2441
14	3.9860	3.3527	66.8914
15	3.7863	3.5524	63.3390
16	3.5746	3.7640	59.5749
17	3.3504	3.9883	55.5867
18	3.1129	4.2258	51.3608
19	2.8611	4.4775	46.8833
20	2.5944	4.7443	42.1390
21	2.3118	5.0269	37.1121
22	2.0124	5.3263	31.7858
23	1.6951	5.6436	26.1423
24	1.3590	5.9797	20.1625
25	1.0028	6.3359	13.8266
26	.6253	6.7133	7.1132
27	.2254	7.1132	0.0000

YEARS 28	MO PAYT .6026	AN CONST 7.24	
#	INT	PRIN	BALANCE
1	5.7613	1.4695	98.5305
2	5.6738	1.5570	96.9735
3	5.5811	1.6498	95.3237
4	5.4828	1.7481	93.5756
5	5.3787	1.8522	91.7234
6	5.2683	1.9625	89.7609
7	5.1514	2.0794	87.6815
8	5.0276	2.2033	85.4782
9	4.8963	2.3345	83.1437
10	4.7573	2.4736	80.6701
11	4.6099	2.6209	78.0492
12	4.4538	2.7771	75.2721
13	4.2884	2.9425	72.3296
14	4.1131	3.1177	69.2119
15	3.9274	3.3035	65.9084
16	3.7306	3.5002	62.4082
17	3.5221	3.7087	58.6995
18	3.3012	3.9297	54.7698
19	3.0671	4.1637	50.6061
20	2.8191	4.4118	46.1943
21	2.5563	4.6745	41.5198
22	2.2779	4.9530	36.5668
23	1.9828	5.2480	31.3187
24	1.6702	5.5606	25.7581
25	1.3390	5.8919	19.8662
26	.9880	6.2428	13.6234
27	.6162	6.6147	7.0087
28	.2221	7.0087	0.0000

YEARS 29	MO PAYT .5943	AN CONST 7.14	
#	INT	PRIN	BALANCE
1	5.7640	1.3679	98.6321
2	5.6825	1.4494	97.1827
3	5.5962	1.5357	95.6469
4	5.5047	1.6272	94.0197
5	5.4078	1.7241	92.2956
6	5.3051	1.8269	90.4687
7	5.1963	1.9357	88.5330
8	5.0810	2.0510	86.4821
9	4.9588	2.1731	84.3089
10	4.8293	2.3026	82.0063
11	4.6922	2.4397	79.5666
12	4.5469	2.5851	76.9815
13	4.3929	2.7391	74.2424
14	4.2297	2.9022	71.3402
15	4.0568	3.0751	68.2651
16	3.8737	3.2583	65.0069
17	3.6796	3.4524	61.5545
18	3.4739	3.6580	57.8965
19	3.2560	3.8759	54.0206
20	3.0252	4.1068	49.9138
21	2.7805	4.3514	45.5624
22	2.5213	4.6106	40.9518
23	2.2467	4.8852	36.0666
24	1.9557	5.1762	30.8903
25	1.6474	5.4846	25.4058
26	1.3207	5.8113	19.5945
27	.9745	6.1574	13.4371
28	.6077	6.5242	6.9128
29	.2191	6.9128	0.0000

YEARS 30	MO PAYT .5868	AN CONST 7.05	
#	INT	PRIN	BALANCE
1	5.7665	1.2746	98.7254
2	5.6905	1.3505	97.3749
3	5.6101	1.4309	95.9440
4	5.5249	1.5162	94.4279
5	5.4346	1.6065	92.8214
6	5.3389	1.7022	91.1192
7	5.2375	1.8036	89.3156
8	5.1300	1.9110	87.4046
9	5.0162	2.0248	85.3798
10	4.8956	2.1454	83.2344
11	4.7678	2.2732	80.9611
12	4.6324	2.4087	78.5525
13	4.4889	2.5521	76.0003
14	4.3369	2.7042	73.2962
15	4.1758	2.8652	70.4309
16	4.0051	3.0359	67.3950
17	3.8243	3.2167	64.1783
18	3.6327	3.4084	60.7699
19	3.4297	3.6114	57.1586
20	3.2145	3.8265	53.3321
21	2.9866	4.0544	49.2776
22	2.7451	4.2959	44.9817
23	2.4892	4.5518	40.4299
24	2.2181	4.8230	35.6069
25	1.9308	5.1103	30.4966
26	1.6264	5.4147	25.0819
27	1.3038	5.7372	19.3447
28	.9621	6.0790	13.2658
29	.6000	6.4411	6.8247
30	.2163	6.8247	0.0000

MONTHLY PAYMENT AMORTIZATION SCHEDULE PER $100   5.875%

YEARS 2 — MO PAYT 4.4264 — AN CONST 53.12

#	INT	PRIN	BALANCE
1	4.5819	48.5353	51.4647
2	1.6524	51.4647	0.0000

YEARS 3 — MO PAYT 3.0365 — AN CONST 36.44

#	INT	PRIN	BALANCE
1	5.0384	31.4000	68.6000
2	3.1432	33.2952	35.3048
3	1.1336	35.3048	0.0000

YEARS 4 — MO PAYT 2.3428 — AN CONST 28.12

#	INT	PRIN	BALANCE
1	5.2663	22.8470	77.1530
2	3.8873	24.2260	52.9270
3	2.4251	25.6882	27.2387
4	.8746	27.2387	0.0000

YEARS 5 — MO PAYT 1.9275 — AN CONST 23.13

#	INT	PRIN	BALANCE
1	5.4027	17.7270	82.2730
2	4.3328	18.7969	63.4761
3	3.1982	19.9315	43.5446
4	1.9952	21.1345	22.4101
5	.7195	22.4101	0.0000

YEARS 6 — MO PAYT 1.6514 — AN CONST 19.82

#	INT	PRIN	BALANCE
1	5.4934	14.3233	85.6767
2	4.6289	15.1879	70.4888
3	3.7122	16.1046	54.3842
4	2.7401	17.0766	37.3076
5	1.7094	18.1073	19.2003
6	.6165	19.2003	0.0000

YEARS 7 — MO PAYT 1.4549 — AN CONST 17.46

#	INT	PRIN	BALANCE
1	5.5579	11.9005	88.0995
2	4.8397	12.6188	75.4807
3	4.0780	13.3804	62.1003
4	3.2704	14.1881	47.9122
5	2.4140	15.0444	32.8678
6	1.5060	15.9525	16.9153
7	.5431	16.9153	0.0000

YEARS 8 — MO PAYT 1.3081 — AN CONST 15.70

#	INT	PRIN	BALANCE
1	5.6062	10.0906	89.9094
2	4.9971	10.6997	79.2097
3	4.3513	11.3455	67.8642
4	3.6665	12.0303	55.8340
5	2.9404	12.7564	43.0776
6	2.1704	13.5263	29.5512
7	1.3540	14.3428	15.2085
8	.4883	15.2085	0.0000

YEARS 9 — MO PAYT 1.1944 — AN CONST 14.34

#	INT	PRIN	BALANCE
1	5.6435	8.6893	91.3107
2	5.1190	9.2138	82.0969
3	4.5629	9.7699	72.3269
4	3.9732	10.3596	61.9673
5	3.3479	10.9849	50.9824
6	2.6849	11.6479	39.3344
7	1.9818	12.3510	26.9834
8	1.2364	13.0965	13.8870
9	.4459	13.8870	0.0000

YEARS 10 — MO PAYT 1.1039 — AN CONST 13.25

#	INT	PRIN	BALANCE
1	5.6732	7.5740	92.4260
2	5.2161	8.0312	84.3948
3	4.7313	8.5160	75.8788
4	4.2173	9.0300	66.8488
5	3.6723	9.5750	57.2739
6	3.0943	10.1529	47.1209
7	2.4815	10.7657	36.3552
8	1.8317	11.4155	24.9397
9	1.1427	12.1045	12.8351
10	.4121	12.8351	0.0000

YEARS 11 — MO PAYT 1.0303 — AN CONST 12.37

#	INT	PRIN	BALANCE
1	5.6974	6.6667	93.3333
2	5.2950	7.0691	86.2642
3	4.8683	7.4958	78.7684
4	4.4159	7.9482	70.8202
5	3.9361	8.4280	62.3922
6	3.4275	8.9366	53.4556
7	2.8881	9.4760	43.9795
8	2.3161	10.0480	33.9315
9	1.7096	10.6545	23.2770
10	1.0665	11.2976	11.9795
11	.3846	11.9795	0.0000

YEARS 12 — MO PAYT .9694 — AN CONST 11.64

#	INT	PRIN	BALANCE
1	5.7174	5.9153	94.0847
2	5.3604	6.2724	87.8123
3	4.9818	6.6509	81.1614
4	4.5803	7.0524	74.1090
5	4.1547	7.4781	66.6309
6	3.7033	7.9294	58.7015
7	3.2247	8.4080	50.2935
8	2.7172	8.9155	41.3780
9	2.1791	9.4536	31.9244
10	1.6085	10.0242	21.9001
11	1.0034	10.6293	11.2708
12	.3619	11.2708	0.0000

YEARS 13 — MO PAYT .9182 — AN CONST 11.02

#	INT	PRIN	BALANCE
1	5.7342	5.2838	94.7162
2	5.4153	5.6028	89.1134
3	5.0771	5.9409	83.1725
4	4.7185	6.2995	76.8729
5	4.3383	6.6797	70.1932
6	3.9351	7.0829	63.1103
7	3.5076	7.5104	55.5998
8	3.0543	7.9638	47.6361
9	2.5736	8.4444	39.1916
10	2.0640	8.9541	30.2375
11	1.5235	9.4946	20.7430
12	.9504	10.0676	10.6753
13	.3428	10.6753	0.0000

YEARS 14 — MO PAYT .8746 — AN CONST 10.50

#	INT	PRIN	BALANCE
1	5.7485	4.7466	95.2534
2	5.4620	5.0330	90.2204
3	5.1583	5.3368	84.8836
4	4.8361	5.6589	79.2246
5	4.4946	6.0005	73.2241
6	4.1324	6.3627	66.8614
7	3.7484	6.7467	60.1147
8	3.3411	7.1539	52.9608
9	2.9093	7.5857	45.3750
10	2.4515	8.0436	37.3314
11	1.9660	8.5291	28.8023
12	1.4512	9.0439	19.7584
13	.9053	9.5898	10.1686
14	.3265	10.1686	0.0000

YEARS 15 — MO PAYT .8371 — AN CONST 10.05

#	INT	PRIN	BALANCE
1	5.7608	4.2846	95.7154
2	5.5022	4.5432	91.1722
3	5.2280	4.8174	86.3548
4	4.9373	5.1082	81.2467
5	4.6289	5.4165	75.8302
6	4.3020	5.7434	70.0868
7	3.9553	6.0901	63.9967
8	3.5878	6.4577	57.5390
9	3.1980	6.8474	50.6916
10	2.7847	7.2607	43.4309
11	2.3464	7.6990	35.7319
12	1.8818	8.1637	27.5682
13	1.3890	8.6564	18.9118
14	.8665	9.1789	9.7329
15	.3125	9.7329	0.0000

YEARS 16 — MO PAYT .8046 — AN CONST 9.66

#	INT	PRIN	BALANCE
1	5.7715	3.8838	96.1162
2	5.5371	4.1182	91.9981
3	5.2885	4.3667	87.6313
4	5.0250	4.6303	83.0010
5	4.7455	4.9098	78.0913
6	4.4492	5.2061	72.8851
7	4.1349	5.5204	67.3648
8	3.8017	5.8536	61.5112
9	3.4484	6.2069	55.3044
10	3.0738	6.5815	48.7229
11	2.6765	6.9787	41.7441
12	2.2553	7.4000	34.3442
13	1.8087	7.8466	26.4975
14	1.3351	8.3202	18.1773
15	.8329	8.8224	9.3549
16	.3004	9.3549	0.0000

YEARS 17 — MO PAYT .7762 — AN CONST 9.32

#	INT	PRIN	BALANCE
1	5.7809	3.5333	96.4667
2	5.5676	3.7465	92.7202
3	5.3415	3.9727	88.7475
4	5.1017	4.2124	84.5351
5	4.8474	4.4667	80.0684
6	4.5778	4.7363	75.3321
7	4.2920	5.0222	70.3099
8	3.9888	5.3253	64.9846
9	3.6674	5.6467	59.3379
10	3.3266	5.9876	53.3503
11	2.9652	6.3490	47.0014
12	2.5820	6.7322	40.2692
13	2.1756	7.1385	33.1307
14	1.7448	7.5694	25.5613
15	1.2879	8.0262	17.5351
16	.8034	8.5107	9.0244
17	.2898	9.0244	0.0000

YEARS 18 — MO PAYT .7511 — AN CONST 9.02

#	INT	PRIN	BALANCE
1	5.7891	3.2247	96.7753
2	5.5945	3.4193	93.3560
3	5.3881	3.6257	89.7303
4	5.1692	3.8446	85.8857
5	4.9372	4.0766	81.8091
6	4.6911	4.3227	77.4864
7	4.4302	4.5836	72.9029
8	4.1536	4.8602	68.0426
9	3.8602	5.1536	62.8890
10	3.5491	5.4646	57.4244
11	3.2193	5.7945	51.6299
12	2.8696	6.1442	45.4857
13	2.4987	6.5151	38.9706
14	2.1055	6.9083	32.0623
15	1.6885	7.3253	24.7370
16	1.2464	7.7674	16.9696
17	.7775	8.2362	8.7334
18	.2804	8.7334	0.0000

YEARS 19 — MO PAYT .7290 — AN CONST 8.75

#	INT	PRIN	BALANCE
1	5.7964	2.9514	97.0486
2	5.6182	3.1295	93.9191
3	5.4293	3.3184	90.6007
4	5.2290	3.5187	87.0820
5	5.0167	3.7311	83.3509
6	4.7915	3.9563	79.3946
7	4.5527	4.1951	75.1995
8	4.2995	4.4483	70.7512
9	4.0310	4.7168	66.0344
10	3.7463	5.0015	61.0330
11	3.4444	5.3034	55.7296
12	3.1243	5.6235	50.1061
13	2.7849	5.9629	44.1433
14	2.4250	6.3228	37.8205
15	2.0433	6.7044	31.1160
16	1.6387	7.1091	24.0070
17	1.2096	7.5382	16.4688
18	.7546	7.9932	8.4756
19	.2721	8.4756	0.0000

YEARS 20 — MO PAYT .7092 — AN CONST 8.52

#	INT	PRIN	BALANCE
1	5.8029	2.7080	97.2920
2	5.6394	2.8715	94.4205
3	5.4661	3.0448	91.3758
4	5.2823	3.2286	88.1472
5	5.0874	3.4234	84.7238
6	4.8808	3.6301	81.0937
7	4.6617	3.8492	77.2446
8	4.4294	4.0815	73.1631
9	4.1830	4.3278	68.8353
10	3.9218	4.5891	64.2462
11	3.6448	4.8660	59.3802
12	3.3511	5.1597	54.2204
13	3.0397	5.4712	48.7493
14	2.7095	5.8014	42.9478
15	2.3593	6.1516	36.7963
16	1.9880	6.5229	30.2734
17	1.5943	6.9166	23.3568
18	1.1768	7.3340	16.0228
19	.7342	7.7767	8.2461
20	.2648	8.2461	0.0000

YEARS 21 — MO PAYT .6916 — AN CONST 8.30

#	INT	PRIN	BALANCE
1	5.8087	2.4903	97.5097
2	5.6583	2.6406	94.8692
3	5.4990	2.8000	92.0692

#	INT	PRIN	BALANCE
4	5.3300	2.9690	89.1003
5	5.1508	3.1482	85.9521
6	4.9608	3.3382	82.6139
7	4.7593	3.5397	79.0743
8	4.5456	3.7533	75.3210
9	4.3191	3.9798	71.3411
10	4.0789	4.2201	67.1211
11	3.8241	4.4748	62.6463
12	3.5541	4.7449	57.9014
13	3.2677	5.0313	52.8702
14	2.9640	5.3349	47.5353
15	2.6420	5.6569	41.8783
16	2.3005	5.9984	35.8800
17	1.9385	6.3604	29.5195
18	1.5546	6.7443	22.7752
19	1.1475	7.1514	15.6238
20	.7159	7.5830	8.0407
21	.2582	8.0407	0.0000

	YEARS	MO PAYT	AN CONST
	22	.6757	8.11
#	INT	PRIN	BALANCE
1	5.8139	2.2946	97.7054
2	5.6754	2.4331	95.2723
3	5.5285	2.5800	92.6923
4	5.3728	2.7357	89.9566
5	5.2077	2.9008	87.0557
6	5.0326	3.0759	83.9798
7	4.8469	3.2616	80.7183
8	4.6501	3.4584	77.2598
9	4.4413	3.6672	73.5927
10	4.2200	3.8885	69.7041
11	3.9853	4.1232	65.5809
12	3.7364	4.3721	61.2088
13	3.4725	4.6360	56.5728
14	3.1927	4.9158	51.6570
15	2.8960	5.2125	46.4445
16	2.5814	5.5271	40.9174
17	2.2478	5.8607	35.0566
18	1.8940	6.2145	28.8422
19	1.5189	6.5896	22.2526
20	1.1212	6.9873	15.2653
21	.6994	7.4090	7.8562
22	.2522	7.8562	0.0000

	YEARS	MO PAYT	AN CONST
	23	.6614	7.94
#	INT	PRIN	BALANCE
1	5.8186	2.1182	97.8818
2	5.6907	2.2460	95.6358
3	5.5552	2.3816	93.2542
4	5.4114	2.5253	90.7289
5	5.2590	2.6778	88.0511
6	5.0974	2.8394	85.2118
7	4.9260	3.0108	82.2010
8	4.7443	3.1925	79.0085
9	4.5516	3.3852	75.6233
10	4.3472	3.5895	72.0338
11	4.1306	3.8062	68.2277
12	3.9009	4.0359	64.1918
13	3.6573	4.2795	59.9123
14	3.3990	4.5378	55.3745
15	3.1251	4.8117	50.5628
16	2.8346	5.1021	45.4607
17	2.5267	5.4101	40.0507
18	2.2001	5.7366	34.3141
19	1.8539	6.0828	28.2312
20	1.4867	6.4500	21.7812
21	1.0974	6.8393	14.9419
22	.6846	7.2521	7.6898
23	.2469	7.6898	0.0000

	YEARS	MO PAYT	AN CONST
	24	.6484	7.79
#	INT	PRIN	BALANCE
1	5.8228	1.9585	98.0415
2	5.7046	2.0767	95.9648
3	5.5793	2.2020	93.7628
4	5.4464	2.3349	91.4279
5	5.3054	2.4759	88.9520
6	5.1560	2.6253	86.3267
7	4.9975	2.7838	83.5429
8	4.8295	2.9518	80.5911
9	4.6513	3.1300	77.4611
10	4.4624	3.3189	74.1423
11	4.2621	3.5192	70.6231
12	4.0497	3.7316	66.8915
13	3.8245	3.9568	62.9346
14	3.5856	4.1957	58.7389
15	3.3324	4.4489	54.2900
16	3.0639	4.7174	49.5726
17	2.7791	5.0022	44.5704
18	2.4772	5.3041	39.2663
19	2.1571	5.6242	33.6421
20	1.8176	5.9637	27.6783
21	1.4576	6.3237	21.3547
22	1.0759	6.7054	14.6493
23	.6712	7.1101	7.5392
24	.2421	7.5392	0.0000

	YEARS	MO PAYT	AN CONST
	25	.6367	7.65
#	INT	PRIN	BALANCE
1	5.8267	1.8135	98.1865
2	5.7172	1.9230	96.2635
3	5.6012	2.0390	94.2245
4	5.4781	2.1621	92.0624
5	5.3476	2.2926	89.7698
6	5.2092	2.4310	87.3388
7	5.0625	2.5777	84.7611
8	4.9069	2.7333	82.0279
9	4.7419	2.8983	79.1296
10	4.5670	3.0732	76.0564
11	4.3815	3.2587	72.7977
12	4.1848	3.4554	69.3423
13	3.9762	3.6639	65.6784
14	3.7551	3.8851	61.7933
15	3.5206	4.1196	57.6737
16	3.2720	4.3682	53.3055
17	3.0083	4.6319	48.6736
18	2.7287	4.9115	43.7621
19	2.4323	5.2079	38.5542
20	2.1179	5.5223	33.0320
21	1.7846	5.8556	27.1764
22	1.4312	6.2090	20.9674
23	1.0564	6.5838	14.3836
24	.6590	6.9811	7.4025
25	.2377	7.4025	0.0000

	YEARS	MO PAYT	AN CONST
	26	.6260	7.52
#	INT	PRIN	BALANCE
1	5.8302	1.6815	98.3185
2	5.7287	1.7830	96.5355
3	5.6211	1.8906	94.6449
4	5.5070	2.0047	92.6401
5	5.3860	2.1257	90.5144
6	5.2577	2.2540	88.2603
7	5.1216	2.3901	85.8702
8	4.9774	2.5344	83.3359
9	4.8244	2.6873	80.6485
10	4.6622	2.8495	77.7990
11	4.4902	3.0215	74.7775
12	4.3078	3.2039	71.5736
13	4.1144	3.3973	68.1763
14	3.9094	3.6023	64.5740
15	3.6920	3.8198	60.7542
16	3.4614	4.0503	56.7039
17	3.2169	4.2948	52.4091
18	2.9577	4.5540	47.8551
19	2.6828	4.8289	43.0263
20	2.3914	5.1203	37.9059
21	2.0823	5.4294	32.4765
22	1.7546	5.7571	26.7194
23	1.4071	6.1046	20.6148
24	1.0387	6.4730	14.1418
25	.6480	6.8637	7.2780
26	.2337	7.2780	0.0000

	YEARS	MO PAYT	AN CONST
	27	.6162	7.40
#	INT	PRIN	BALANCE
1	5.8334	1.5610	98.4390
2	5.7392	1.6553	96.7837
3	5.6393	1.7552	95.0285
4	5.5333	1.8611	93.1674
5	5.4210	1.9734	91.1940
6	5.3019	2.0926	89.1014
7	5.1756	2.2189	86.8825
8	5.0417	2.3528	84.5298
9	4.8997	2.4948	82.0350
10	4.7491	2.6454	79.3896
11	4.5894	2.8050	76.5845
12	4.4201	2.9744	73.6102
13	4.2406	3.1539	70.4563
14	4.0502	3.3442	67.1121
15	3.8484	3.5461	63.5660
16	3.6343	3.7601	59.8058
17	3.4074	3.9871	55.8187
18	3.1667	4.2277	51.5910
19	2.9115	4.4829	47.1081
20	2.6410	4.7535	42.3546
21	2.3540	5.0404	37.3142
22	2.0498	5.3446	31.9695
23	1.7272	5.6672	26.3023
24	1.3852	6.0093	20.2930
25	1.0225	6.3720	13.9210
26	.6378	6.7566	7.1644
27	.2300	7.1644	0.0000

	YEARS	MO PAYT	AN CONST
	28	.6073	7.29
#	INT	PRIN	BALANCE
1	5.8363	1.4508	98.5492
2	5.7488	1.5384	97.0108
3	5.6559	1.6312	95.3795
4	5.5575	1.7297	93.6498
5	5.4531	1.8341	91.8157
6	5.3424	1.9448	89.8709
7	5.2250	2.0622	87.8087
8	5.1005	2.1867	85.6220
9	4.9685	2.3187	83.3034
10	4.8286	2.4586	80.8448
11	4.6802	2.6070	78.2378
12	4.5228	2.7644	75.4734
13	4.3560	2.9312	72.5422
14	4.1790	3.1081	69.4341
15	3.9914	3.2957	66.1384
16	3.7925	3.4946	62.6437
17	3.5816	3.7056	58.9382
18	3.3579	3.9292	55.0089
19	3.1208	4.1664	50.8425
20	2.8693	4.4179	46.4246
21	2.6026	4.6845	41.7401
22	2.3199	4.9673	36.7728
23	2.0201	5.2671	31.5057
24	1.7022	5.5850	25.9207
25	1.3651	5.9221	19.9986
26	1.0076	6.2796	13.7191
27	.6286	6.6586	7.0605
28	.2267	7.0605	0.0000

	YEARS	MO PAYT	AN CONST
	29	.5991	7.19
#	INT	PRIN	BALANCE
1	5.8390	1.3498	98.6502
2	5.7576	1.4312	97.2190
3	5.6712	1.5176	95.7014
4	5.5796	1.6092	94.0921
5	5.4825	1.7064	92.3858
6	5.3795	1.8094	90.5764
7	5.2702	1.9186	88.6578
8	5.1544	2.0344	86.6235
9	5.0317	2.1572	84.4663
10	4.9015	2.2874	82.1790
11	4.7634	2.4254	79.7536
12	4.6170	2.5718	77.1817
13	4.4618	2.7270	74.4547
14	4.2972	2.8916	71.5631
15	4.1226	3.0662	68.4969
16	3.9376	3.2512	65.2457
17	3.7413	3.4475	61.7982
18	3.5333	3.6556	58.1426
19	3.3126	3.8762	54.2664
20	3.0786	4.1102	50.1563
21	2.8306	4.3582	45.7980
22	2.5675	4.6213	41.1767
23	2.2886	4.9002	36.2765
24	1.9928	5.1960	31.0805
25	1.6792	5.5096	25.5708
26	1.3466	5.8422	19.7287
27	.9940	6.1948	13.5339
28	.6201	6.5687	6.9652
29	.2236	6.9652	0.0000

	YEARS	MO PAYT	AN CONST
	30	.5915	7.10
#	INT	PRIN	BALANCE
1	5.8415	1.2569	98.7431
2	5.7656	1.3328	97.4103
3	5.6852	1.4133	95.9970
4	5.5999	1.4986	94.4984
5	5.5094	1.5890	92.9094
6	5.4135	1.6849	91.2245
7	5.3118	1.7866	89.4379
8	5.2040	1.8944	87.5435
9	5.0897	2.0088	85.5347
10	4.9684	2.1300	83.4046
11	4.8398	2.2586	81.1460
12	4.7035	2.3949	78.7511
13	4.5590	2.5395	76.2116
14	4.4057	2.6928	73.5189
15	4.2432	2.8553	70.6636
16	4.0708	3.0276	67.6359
17	3.8881	3.2104	64.4256
18	3.6943	3.4041	61.0214
19	3.4888	3.6096	57.4118
20	3.2710	3.8275	53.5843
21	3.0400	4.0585	49.5258
22	2.7950	4.3035	45.2224
23	2.5352	4.5632	40.6591
24	2.2598	4.8386	35.8205
25	1.9678	5.1307	30.6898
26	1.6581	5.4404	25.2494
27	1.3297	5.7687	19.4807
28	.9815	6.1169	13.3638
29	.6123	6.4861	6.8776
30	.2208	6.8776	0.0000

YEARS 2 — MO PAYT 4.4276 — AN CONST 53.14

#	INT	PRIN	BALANCE
1	4.6016	48.5290	51.4710
2	1.6597	51.4710	0.0000

YEARS 3 — MO PAYT 3.0377 — AN CONST 36.46

#	INT	PRIN	BALANCE
1	5.0601	31.3918	68.6082
2	3.1571	33.2949	35.3133
3	1.1387	35.3133	0.0000

YEARS 4 — MO PAYT 2.3439 — AN CONST 28.13

#	INT	PRIN	BALANCE
1	5.2890	22.8381	77.1619
2	3.9045	24.2226	52.9394
3	2.4361	25.6910	27.2484
4	.8786	27.2484	0.0000

YEARS 5 — MO PAYT 1.9286 — AN CONST 23.15

#	INT	PRIN	BALANCE
1	5.4260	17.7176	82.2824
2	4.3519	18.7917	63.4907
3	3.2127	19.9309	43.5598
4	2.0045	21.1391	22.4206
5	.7230	22.4206	0.0000

YEARS 6 — MO PAYT 1.6526 — AN CONST 19.84

#	INT	PRIN	BALANCE
1	5.5170	14.3138	85.6862
2	4.6493	15.1816	70.5046
3	3.7290	16.1019	54.4027
4	2.7528	17.0780	37.3247
5	1.7175	18.1133	19.2114
6	.6195	19.2114	0.0000

YEARS 7 — MO PAYT 1.4561 — AN CONST 17.48

#	INT	PRIN	BALANCE
1	5.5819	11.8909	88.1091
2	4.8610	12.6118	75.4973
3	4.0965	13.3763	62.1210
4	3.2856	14.1872	47.9337
5	2.4255	15.0473	32.8865
6	1.5133	15.9595	16.9270
7	.5458	16.9270	0.0000

YEARS 8 — MO PAYT 1.3093 — AN CONST 15.72

#	INT	PRIN	BALANCE
1	5.6303	10.0811	89.9189
2	5.0192	10.6922	79.2267
3	4.3710	11.3404	67.8864
4	3.6835	12.0279	55.8585
5	2.9543	12.7570	43.1015
6	2.1810	13.5304	29.5711
7	1.3608	14.3506	15.2206
8	.4908	15.2206	0.0000

YEARS 9 — MO PAYT 1.1956 — AN CONST 14.35

#	INT	PRIN	BALANCE
1	5.6678	8.6799	91.3201
2	5.1416	9.2060	82.1141
3	4.5835	9.7641	72.3500
4	3.9916	10.3560	61.9939
5	3.3638	10.9839	51.0101
6	2.6979	11.6497	39.3604
7	1.9917	12.3559	27.0044
8	1.2426	13.1050	13.8994
9	.4482	13.8994	0.0000

YEARS 10 — MO PAYT 1.1052 — AN CONST 13.27

#	INT	PRIN	BALANCE
1	5.6976	7.5647	92.4353
2	5.2390	8.0233	84.4121
3	4.7526	8.5096	75.9024
4	4.2368	9.0255	66.8769
5	3.6896	9.5726	57.3043
6	3.1093	10.1530	47.1513
7	2.4938	10.7685	36.3829
8	1.8410	11.4213	24.9616
9	1.1486	12.1136	12.8480
10	.4143	12.8480	0.0000

YEARS 11 — MO PAYT 1.0316 — AN CONST 12.38

#	INT	PRIN	BALANCE
1	5.7219	6.6575	93.3425
2	5.3183	7.0611	86.2815
3	4.8902	7.4891	78.7924
4	4.4362	7.9431	70.8493
5	3.9547	8.4246	62.4246
6	3.4440	8.9354	53.4893
7	2.9023	9.4770	44.0122
8	2.3278	10.0515	33.9607
9	1.7185	10.6609	23.2998
10	1.0722	11.3072	11.9926
11	.3867	11.9926	0.0000

YEARS 12 — MO PAYT .9707 — AN CONST 11.65

#	INT	PRIN	BALANCE
1	5.7420	5.9062	94.0938
2	5.3839	6.2643	87.8295
3	5.0042	6.6440	81.1855
4	4.6014	7.0468	74.1387
5	4.1742	7.4740	66.6648
6	3.7211	7.9271	58.7377
7	3.2406	8.4076	50.3301
8	2.7309	8.9173	41.4128
9	2.1903	9.4579	31.9549
10	1.6170	10.0312	21.9237
11	1.0088	10.6393	11.2843
12	.3639	11.2843	0.0000

YEARS 13 — MO PAYT .9195 — AN CONST 11.04

#	INT	PRIN	BALANCE
1	5.7589	5.2749	94.7251
2	5.4391	5.5947	89.1304
3	5.0999	5.9338	83.1966
4	4.7402	6.2935	76.9031
5	4.3587	6.6751	70.2280
6	3.9540	7.0797	63.1483
7	3.5249	7.5089	55.6394
8	3.0696	7.9641	47.6752
9	2.5868	8.4469	39.2283
10	2.0748	8.9590	30.2693
11	1.5317	9.5021	20.7672
12	.9556	10.0781	10.6891
13	.3447	10.6891	0.0000

YEARS 14 — MO PAYT .8759 — AN CONST 10.52

#	INT	PRIN	BALANCE
1	5.7732	4.7378	95.2622
2	5.4860	5.0250	90.2373
3	5.1814	5.3296	84.9076
4	4.8583	5.6527	79.2550
5	4.5156	5.9954	73.2596
6	4.1522	6.3588	66.9008
7	3.7667	6.7443	60.1564
8	3.3579	7.1532	53.0033
9	2.9242	7.5868	45.4165
10	2.4643	8.0467	37.3698
11	1.9765	8.5345	28.8352
12	1.4591	9.0519	19.7833
13	.9104	9.6007	10.1827
14	.3283	10.1827	0.0000

YEARS 15 — MO PAYT .8385 — AN CONST 10.07

#	INT	PRIN	BALANCE
1	5.7856	4.2760	95.7240
2	5.5264	4.5352	91.1889
3	5.2515	4.8101	86.3787
4	4.9599	5.1017	81.2770
5	4.6506	5.4110	75.8660
6	4.3226	5.7390	70.1270
7	3.9746	6.0869	64.0401
8	3.6056	6.4559	57.5842
9	3.2143	6.8473	50.7369
10	2.7992	7.2624	43.4745
11	2.3589	7.7026	35.7718
12	1.8920	8.1696	27.6022
13	1.3967	8.6649	18.9374
14	.8714	9.1901	9.7473
15	.3143	9.7473	0.0000

YEARS 16 — MO PAYT .8060 — AN CONST 9.68

#	INT	PRIN	BALANCE
1	5.7963	3.8753	96.1247
2	5.5614	4.1103	92.0144
3	5.3122	4.3594	87.6550
4	5.0479	4.6237	83.0313
5	4.7676	4.9040	78.1273
6	4.4704	5.2013	72.9260
7	4.1550	5.5166	67.4094
8	3.8206	5.8510	61.5583
9	3.4659	6.2057	55.3526
10	3.0897	6.5819	48.7707
11	2.6907	6.9809	41.7897
12	2.2675	7.4041	34.3856
13	1.8186	7.8530	26.5326
14	1.3426	8.3291	18.2035
15	.8377	8.8340	9.3695
16	.3021	9.3695	0.0000

YEARS 17 — MO PAYT .7776 — AN CONST 9.34

#	INT	PRIN	BALANCE
1	5.8057	3.5250	96.4750
2	5.5920	3.7387	92.7363
3	5.3653	3.9654	88.7709
4	5.1250	4.2058	84.5651
5	4.8700	4.4607	80.1044
6	4.5996	4.7311	75.3733
7	4.3128	5.0179	70.3553
8	4.0086	5.3221	65.0332
9	3.6859	5.6448	59.3884
10	3.3437	5.9870	53.4014
11	2.9808	6.3499	47.0515
12	2.5959	6.7349	40.3166
13	2.1876	7.1431	33.1735
14	1.7545	7.5762	25.5973
15	1.2953	8.0355	17.5618
16	.8081	8.5226	9.0392
17	.2915	9.0392	0.0000

YEARS 18 — MO PAYT .7525 — AN CONST 9.04

#	INT	PRIN	BALANCE
1	5.8139	3.2166	96.7834
2	5.6189	3.4116	93.3717
3	5.4121	3.6185	89.7533
4	5.1928	3.8378	85.9154
5	4.9601	4.0705	81.8450
6	4.7133	4.3172	77.5277
7	4.4516	4.5790	72.9488
8	4.1740	4.8565	68.0922
9	3.8796	5.1510	62.9413
10	3.5674	5.4632	57.4781
11	3.2362	5.7944	51.6837
12	2.8849	6.1457	45.5380
13	2.5124	6.5182	39.0198
14	2.1172	6.9134	32.1064
15	1.6981	7.3325	24.7739
16	1.2536	7.7770	16.9969
17	.7821	8.2484	8.7485
18	.2821	8.7485	0.0000

YEARS 19 — MO PAYT .7304 — AN CONST 8.77

#	INT	PRIN	BALANCE
1	5.8212	2.9435	97.0565
2	5.6428	3.1220	93.9345
3	5.4535	3.3112	90.6233
4	5.2528	3.5120	87.1114
5	5.0399	3.7249	83.3865
6	4.8141	3.9507	79.4358
7	4.5746	4.1902	75.2457
8	4.3206	4.4442	70.8015
9	4.0512	4.7136	66.0879
10	3.7654	4.9993	61.0886
11	3.4624	5.3024	55.7862
12	3.1409	5.6238	50.1624
13	2.8000	5.9648	44.1976
14	2.4384	6.3264	37.8712
15	2.0549	6.7099	31.1613
16	1.6481	7.1166	24.0447
17	1.2167	7.5481	16.4966
18	.7591	8.0057	8.4910
19	.2738	8.4910	0.0000

YEARS 20 — MO PAYT .7107 — AN CONST 8.53

#	INT	PRIN	BALANCE
1	5.8278	2.7003	97.2997
2	5.6641	2.8640	94.4356
3	5.4904	3.0377	91.3980
4	5.3063	3.2218	88.1762
5	5.1110	3.4171	84.7591
6	4.9038	3.6243	81.1348
7	4.6841	3.8440	77.2908
8	4.4511	4.0770	73.2138
9	4.2039	4.3242	68.8896
10	3.9418	4.5863	64.3033
11	3.6638	4.8643	59.4390
12	3.3689	5.1592	54.2798
13	3.0561	5.4720	48.8078
14	2.7244	5.8037	43.0041
15	2.3726	6.1555	36.8486
16	1.9994	6.5287	30.3199
17	1.6036	6.9245	23.3954
18	1.1838	7.3442	16.0512
19	.7386	7.7895	8.2617
20	.2664	8.2617	0.0000

YEARS 21 — MO PAYT .6930 — AN CONST 8.32

#	INT	PRIN	BALANCE
1	5.8336	2.4828	97.5172
2	5.6831	2.6333	94.8839
3	5.5234	2.7929	92.0910

#	INT	PRIN	BALANCE
4	5.3541	2.9622	89.1288
5	5.1745	3.1418	85.9870
6	4.9841	3.3323	82.6547
7	4.7821	3.5343	79.1204
8	4.5678	3.7485	75.3719
9	4.3406	3.9758	71.3961
10	4.0996	4.2168	67.1793
11	3.8439	4.4724	62.7068
12	3.5728	4.7436	57.9633
13	3.2852	5.0311	52.9321
14	2.9802	5.3361	47.5960
15	2.6567	5.6596	41.9364
16	2.3136	6.0027	35.9337
17	1.9498	6.3666	29.5671
18	1.5638	6.7526	22.8145
19	1.1544	7.1619	15.6526
20	.7203	7.5961	8.0566
21	.2598	8.0566	0.0000

YEARS 22   MO PAYT .6772   AN CONST 8.13

#	INT	PRIN	BALANCE
1	5.8388	2.2873	97.7127
2	5.7001	2.4260	95.2867
3	5.5531	2.5731	92.7136
4	5.3971	2.7290	89.9846
5	5.2317	2.8945	87.0901
6	5.0562	3.0700	84.0202
7	4.8701	3.2561	80.7641
8	4.6727	3.4534	77.3106
9	4.4633	3.6628	73.6478
10	4.2413	3.8848	69.7630
11	4.0058	4.1204	65.6427
12	3.7560	4.3701	61.2725
13	3.4911	4.6351	56.6375
14	3.2101	4.9160	51.7214
15	2.9121	5.2141	46.5073
16	2.5960	5.5302	40.9772
17	2.2607	5.8654	35.1118
18	1.9052	6.2210	28.8908
19	1.5280	6.5981	22.2927
20	1.1280	6.9981	15.2946
21	.7038	7.4223	7.8723
22	.2538	7.8723	0.0000

YEARS 23   MO PAYT .6629   AN CONST 7.96

#	INT	PRIN	BALANCE
1	5.8435	2.1111	97.8889
2	5.7155	2.2390	95.6499
3	5.5798	2.3748	93.2751
4	5.4358	2.5187	90.7564
5	5.2832	2.6714	88.0849
6	5.1212	2.8334	85.2516
7	4.9494	3.0051	82.2464
8	4.7673	3.1873	79.0591
9	4.5740	3.3805	75.6786
10	4.3691	3.5855	72.0931
11	4.1518	3.8028	68.2903
12	3.9212	4.0334	64.2569
13	3.6767	4.2779	59.9790
14	3.4174	4.5372	55.4418
15	3.1423	4.8123	50.6295
16	2.8506	5.1040	45.5255
17	2.5412	5.4134	40.1121
18	2.2130	5.7416	34.3705
19	1.8649	6.0896	28.2809
20	1.4958	6.4588	21.8221
21	1.1042	6.8504	14.9717
22	.6889	7.2656	7.7061
23	.2485	7.7061	0.0000

YEARS 24   MO PAYT .6499   AN CONST 7.80

#	INT	PRIN	BALANCE
1	5.8478	1.9516	98.0484
2	5.7295	2.0699	95.9786
3	5.6040	2.1953	93.7832
4	5.4709	2.3284	91.4548
5	5.3298	2.4696	88.9852
6	5.1801	2.6193	86.3659
7	5.0213	2.7781	83.5878
8	4.8529	2.9465	80.6413
9	4.6742	3.1251	77.5162
10	4.4848	3.3146	74.2017
11	4.2838	3.5155	70.6862
12	4.0707	3.7286	66.9575
13	3.8447	3.9547	63.0029
14	3.6050	4.1944	58.8085
15	3.3507	4.4487	54.3598
16	3.0810	4.7184	49.6415
17	2.7950	5.0044	44.6371
18	2.4916	5.3078	39.3293
19	2.1698	5.6295	33.6998
20	1.8285	5.9708	27.7290
21	1.4666	6.3328	21.3962
22	1.0827	6.7167	14.6796
23	.6755	7.1238	7.5557
24	.2436	7.5557	0.0000

YEARS 25   MO PAYT .6382   AN CONST 7.66

#	INT	PRIN	BALANCE
1	5.8517	1.8068	98.1932
2	5.7421	1.9163	96.2769
3	5.6260	2.0325	94.2445
4	5.5027	2.1557	92.0888
5	5.3721	2.2864	89.8024
6	5.2335	2.4250	87.3775
7	5.0865	2.5720	84.8055
8	4.9305	2.7279	82.0776
9	4.7652	2.8933	79.1843
10	4.5898	3.0687	76.1157
11	4.4037	3.2547	72.8610
12	4.2064	3.4520	69.4090
13	3.9972	3.6613	65.7478
14	3.7752	3.8832	61.8646
15	3.5398	4.1186	57.7460
16	3.2901	4.3683	53.3777
17	3.0253	4.6331	48.7446
18	2.7445	4.9140	43.8306
19	2.4466	5.2119	38.6187
20	2.1306	5.5278	33.0909
21	1.7955	5.8629	27.2280
22	1.4401	6.2183	21.0096
23	1.0631	6.5953	14.4143
24	.6633	6.9951	7.4192
25	.2392	7.4192	0.0000

YEARS 26   MO PAYT .6275   AN CONST 7.54

#	INT	PRIN	BALANCE
1	5.8552	1.6750	98.3250
2	5.7536	1.7765	96.5485
3	5.6460	1.8842	94.6643
4	5.5317	1.9984	92.6659
5	5.4106	2.1196	90.5463
6	5.2821	2.2481	88.2983
7	5.1458	2.3843	85.9139
8	5.0013	2.5289	83.3850
9	4.8480	2.6822	80.7028
10	4.6854	2.8448	77.8580
11	4.5129	3.0173	74.8408
12	4.3300	3.2002	71.6406
13	4.1360	3.3942	68.2464
14	3.9302	3.5999	64.6465
15	3.7120	3.8182	60.8284
16	3.4805	4.0496	56.7787
17	3.2350	4.2951	52.4836
18	2.9747	4.5555	47.9281
19	2.6985	4.8317	43.0964
20	2.4056	5.1246	37.9719
21	2.0949	5.4352	32.5366
22	1.7654	5.7647	26.7719
23	1.4160	6.1142	20.6577
24	1.0453	6.4848	14.1729
25	.6522	6.8780	7.2949
26	.2352	7.2949	0.0000

YEARS 27   MO PAYT .6178   AN CONST 7.42

#	INT	PRIN	BALANCE
1	5.8584	1.5547	98.4453
2	5.7642	1.6489	96.7964
3	5.6642	1.7489	95.0475
4	5.5582	1.8549	93.1926
5	5.4457	1.9674	91.2252
6	5.3265	2.0866	89.1386
7	5.2000	2.2131	86.9255
8	5.0658	2.3473	84.5782
9	4.9235	2.4896	82.0887
10	4.7726	2.6405	79.4482
11	4.6125	2.8006	76.6476
12	4.4427	2.9703	73.6772
13	4.2627	3.1504	70.5268
14	4.0717	3.3414	67.1854
15	3.8691	3.5440	63.6415
16	3.6543	3.7588	59.8827
17	3.4264	3.9867	55.8960
18	3.1847	4.2283	51.6677
19	2.9284	4.4847	47.1830
20	2.6565	4.7565	42.4264
21	2.3682	5.0449	37.3815
22	2.0624	5.3507	32.0308
23	1.7380	5.6751	26.3557
24	1.3939	6.0191	20.3366
25	1.0291	6.3840	13.9525
26	.6420	6.7710	7.1815
27	.2316	7.1815	0.0000

YEARS 28   MO PAYT .6088   AN CONST 7.31

#	INT	PRIN	BALANCE
1	5.8613	1.4446	98.5554
2	5.7738	1.5322	97.0231
3	5.6809	1.6251	95.3980
4	5.5824	1.7236	93.6744
5	5.4779	1.8281	91.8463
6	5.3671	1.9389	89.9074
7	5.2495	2.0565	87.8509
8	5.1248	2.1811	85.6697
9	4.9926	2.3134	83.3564
10	4.8524	2.4536	80.9028
11	4.7036	2.6024	78.3004
12	4.5459	2.7601	75.5403
13	4.3786	2.9274	72.6129
14	4.2011	3.1049	69.5080
15	4.0129	3.2931	66.2148
16	3.8132	3.4928	62.7221
17	3.6015	3.7045	59.0176
18	3.3769	3.9291	55.0885
19	3.1387	4.1673	50.9212
20	2.8861	4.4199	46.5014
21	2.6182	4.6878	41.8135
22	2.3340	4.9720	36.8415
23	2.0326	5.2734	31.5681
24	1.7129	5.5931	25.9750
25	1.3738	5.9322	20.0428
26	1.0142	6.2918	13.7510
27	.6328	6.6732	7.0778
28	.2282	7.0778	0.0000

YEARS 29   MO PAYT .6007   AN CONST 7.21

#	INT	PRIN	BALANCE
1	5.8640	1.3438	98.6562
2	5.7826	1.4252	97.2310
3	5.6962	1.5116	95.7194
4	5.6045	1.6033	94.1161
5	5.5074	1.7005	92.4156
6	5.4043	1.8035	90.6121
7	5.2949	1.9129	88.6992
8	5.1790	2.0288	86.6704
9	5.0560	2.1518	84.5185
10	4.9255	2.2823	82.2363
11	4.7872	2.4206	79.8156
12	4.6404	2.5674	77.2482
13	4.4848	2.7230	74.5252
14	4.3197	2.8881	71.6371
15	4.1446	3.0632	68.5739
16	3.9589	3.2489	65.3251
17	3.7620	3.4458	61.8792
18	3.5531	3.6547	58.2245
19	3.3315	3.8763	54.3482
20	3.0966	4.1113	50.2370
21	2.8473	4.3605	45.8765
22	2.5830	4.6248	41.2516
23	2.3026	4.9052	36.3464
24	2.0052	5.2026	31.1439
25	1.6899	5.5180	25.6259
26	1.3554	5.8525	19.7735
27	1.0006	6.2073	13.5662
28	.6243	6.5835	6.9827
29	.2252	6.9827	0.0000

YEARS 30   MO PAYT .5931   AN CONST 7.12

#	INT	PRIN	BALANCE
1	5.8665	1.2511	98.7489
2	5.7907	1.3270	97.4219
3	5.7102	1.4074	96.0145
4	5.6249	1.4927	94.5218
5	5.5344	1.5832	92.9386
6	5.4385	1.6792	91.2594
7	5.3367	1.7810	89.4784
8	5.2287	1.8889	87.5895
9	5.1142	2.0035	85.5860
10	4.9927	2.1249	83.4611
11	4.8639	2.2537	81.2074
12	4.7273	2.3904	78.8170
13	4.5824	2.5353	76.2818
14	4.4287	2.6890	73.5928
15	4.2657	2.8520	70.7409
16	4.0928	3.0249	67.7160
17	3.9094	3.2082	64.5078
18	3.7149	3.4027	61.1051
19	3.5086	3.6090	57.4961
20	3.2899	3.8278	53.6683
21	3.0578	4.0598	49.6085
22	2.8117	4.3059	45.3025
23	2.5507	4.5670	40.7355
24	2.2738	4.8438	35.8917
25	1.9802	5.1375	30.7542
26	1.6687	5.4489	25.3053
27	1.3384	5.7792	19.5261
28	.9880	6.1296	13.3965
29	.6165	6.5012	6.8953
30	.2223	6.8953	0.0000

YEARS 2 — MO PAYT 4.4321 — AN CONST 53.19

#	INT	PRIN	BALANCE
1	4.6805	48.5042	51.4958
2	1.6889	51.4958	0.0000

YEARS 3 — MO PAYT 3.0422 — AN CONST 36.51

#	INT	PRIN	BALANCE
1	5.1469	31.3594	68.6406
2	3.2128	33.2936	35.3470
3	1.1593	35.3470	0.0000

YEARS 4 — MO PAYT 2.3485 — AN CONST 28.19

#	INT	PRIN	BALANCE
1	5.3797	22.8023	77.1977
2	3.9733	24.2087	52.9890
3	2.4802	25.7019	27.2871
4	.8949	27.2871	0.0000

YEARS 5 — MO PAYT 1.9333 — AN CONST 23.20

#	INT	PRIN	BALANCE
1	5.5190	17.6803	82.3197
2	4.4286	18.7708	63.5489
3	3.2708	19.9285	43.6203
4	2.0417	21.1577	22.4627
5	.7367	22.4627	0.0000

YEARS 6 — MO PAYT 1.6573 — AN CONST 19.89

#	INT	PRIN	BALANCE
1	5.6117	14.2758	85.7242
2	4.7312	15.1563	70.5679
3	3.7963	16.0911	54.4768
4	2.8039	17.0836	37.3932
5	1.7502	18.1373	19.2559
6	.6315	19.2559	0.0000

YEARS 7 — MO PAYT 1.4609 — AN CONST 17.54

#	INT	PRIN	BALANCE
1	5.6776	11.8527	88.1473
2	4.9465	12.5837	75.5636
3	4.1704	13.3599	62.2037
4	3.3464	14.1839	48.0198
5	2.4715	15.0587	32.9611
6	1.5428	15.9875	16.9736
7	.5567	16.9736	0.0000

YEARS 8 — MO PAYT 1.3141 — AN CONST 15.77

#	INT	PRIN	BALANCE
1	5.7268	10.0429	89.9571
2	5.1074	10.6623	79.2948
3	4.4497	11.3200	67.9748
4	3.7516	12.0182	55.9566
5	3.0103	12.7594	43.1972
6	2.2233	13.5464	29.6508
7	1.3878	14.3819	15.2689
8	.5008	15.2689	0.0000

YEARS 9 — MO PAYT 1.2006 — AN CONST 14.41

#	INT	PRIN	BALANCE
1	5.7649	8.6420	91.3580
2	5.2319	9.1750	82.1830
3	4.6660	9.7409	72.4421
4	4.0652	10.3417	62.1004
5	3.4273	10.9795	51.1209
6	2.7502	11.6567	39.4641
7	2.0312	12.3757	27.0884
8	1.2679	13.1390	13.9494
9	.4575	13.9494	0.0000

YEARS 10 — MO PAYT 1.1102 — AN CONST 13.33

#	INT	PRIN	BALANCE
1	5.7952	7.5272	92.4728
2	5.3310	7.9915	84.4813
3	4.8381	8.4844	75.9969
4	4.3148	9.0077	66.9892
5	3.7592	9.5633	57.4260
6	3.1694	10.1531	47.2729
7	2.5431	10.7793	36.4936
8	1.8783	11.4442	25.0494
9	1.1724	12.1500	12.8994
10	.4231	12.8994	0.0000

YEARS 11 — MO PAYT 1.0367 — AN CONST 12.45

#	INT	PRIN	BALANCE
1	5.8199	6.6205	93.3795
2	5.4116	7.0289	86.3506
3	4.9780	7.4624	78.8882
4	4.5178	7.9227	70.9655
5	4.0291	8.4113	62.5542
6	3.5103	8.9301	53.6241
7	2.9595	9.4809	44.1432
8	2.3748	10.0657	34.0775
9	1.7539	10.6865	23.3910
10	1.0948	11.3456	12.0454
11	.3951	12.0454	0.0000

YEARS 12 — MO PAYT .9759 — AN CONST 11.72

#	INT	PRIN	BALANCE
1	5.8403	5.8699	94.1301
2	5.4783	6.2319	87.8982
3	5.0939	6.6163	81.2819
4	4.6858	7.0244	74.2575
5	4.2526	7.4576	66.7999
6	3.7926	7.9176	58.8823
7	3.3043	8.4059	50.4764
8	2.7858	8.9244	41.5520
9	2.2354	9.4748	32.0772
10	1.6510	10.0592	22.0180
11	1.0306	10.6796	11.3383
12	.3719	11.3383	0.0000

YEARS 13 — MO PAYT .9247 — AN CONST 11.10

#	INT	PRIN	BALANCE
1	5.8575	5.2392	94.7608
2	5.5343	5.5623	89.1985
3	5.1913	5.9054	83.2930
4	4.8270	6.2697	77.0234
5	4.4403	6.6564	70.3670
6	4.0298	7.0669	63.3001
7	3.5939	7.5028	55.7974
8	3.1312	7.9655	47.8318
9	2.6399	8.4568	39.3750
10	2.1183	8.9784	30.3966
11	1.5645	9.5322	20.8644
12	.9766	10.1201	10.7443
13	.3524	10.7443	0.0000

YEARS 14 — MO PAYT .8812 — AN CONST 10.58

#	INT	PRIN	BALANCE
1	5.8721	4.7028	95.2972
2	5.5820	4.9928	90.3044
3	5.2741	5.3008	85.0037
4	4.9471	5.6277	79.3760
5	4.6000	5.9748	73.4012
6	4.2315	6.3433	67.0578
7	3.8403	6.7346	60.3233
8	3.4249	7.1499	53.1733
9	2.9839	7.5909	45.5824
10	2.5157	8.0591	37.5233
11	2.0186	8.5562	28.9671
12	1.4909	9.0839	19.8832
13	.9306	9.6442	10.2390
14	.3358	10.2390	0.0000

YEARS 15 — MO PAYT .8439 — AN CONST 10.13

#	INT	PRIN	BALANCE
1	5.8846	4.2417	95.7583
2	5.6230	4.5033	91.2550
3	5.3452	4.7810	86.4740
4	5.0504	5.0759	81.3981
5	4.7373	5.3890	76.0091
6	4.4049	5.7214	70.2877
7	4.0520	6.0743	64.2135
8	3.6774	6.4489	57.7646
9	3.2796	6.8467	50.9179
10	2.8573	7.2689	43.6490
11	2.4090	7.7173	35.9317
12	1.9330	8.1933	27.7384
13	1.4277	8.6986	19.0398
14	.8912	9.2351	9.8047
15	.3216	9.8047	0.0000

YEARS 16 — MO PAYT .8114 — AN CONST 9.74

#	INT	PRIN	BALANCE
1	5.8955	3.8418	96.1582
2	5.6585	4.0787	92.0795
3	5.4070	4.3303	87.7492
4	5.1399	4.5974	83.1519
5	4.8563	4.8809	78.2710
6	4.5553	5.1820	73.0890
7	4.2357	5.5016	67.5874
8	3.8964	5.8409	61.7465
9	3.5361	6.2012	55.5454
10	3.1536	6.5836	48.9618
11	2.7476	6.9897	41.9721
12	2.3165	7.4208	34.5513
13	1.8588	7.8785	26.6728
14	1.3728	8.3644	18.3084
15	.8569	8.8803	9.4280
16	.3092	9.4280	0.0000

YEARS 17 — MO PAYT .7831 — AN CONST 9.40

#	INT	PRIN	BALANCE
1	5.9050	3.4922	96.5078
2	5.6896	3.7076	92.8002
3	5.4609	3.9363	88.8639
4	5.2182	4.1791	84.6849
5	4.9604	4.4368	80.2481
6	4.6867	4.7105	75.5376
7	4.3962	5.0010	70.5366
8	4.0878	5.3094	65.2271
9	3.7603	5.6369	59.5902
10	3.4126	5.9846	53.6056
11	3.0435	6.3537	47.2519
12	2.6516	6.7456	40.5063
13	2.2356	7.1616	33.3447
14	1.7938	7.6034	25.7413
15	1.3249	8.0723	17.6690
16	.8270	8.5702	9.0988
17	.2984	9.0988	0.0000

YEARS 18 — MO PAYT .7582 — AN CONST 9.10

#	INT	PRIN	BALANCE
1	5.9134	3.1846	96.8154
2	5.7170	3.3810	93.4344
3	5.5084	3.5895	89.8449
4	5.2870	3.8109	86.0340
5	5.0520	4.0460	81.9880
6	4.8024	4.2955	77.6925
7	4.5375	4.5605	73.1320
8	4.2562	4.8417	68.2903
9	3.9576	5.1404	63.1499
10	3.6405	5.4574	57.6925
11	3.3039	5.7940	51.8985
12	2.9466	6.1514	45.7471
13	2.5672	6.5308	39.2164
14	2.1644	6.9336	32.2828
15	1.7367	7.3612	24.9216
16	1.2827	7.8153	17.1063
17	.8007	8.2973	8.8090
18	.2889	8.8090	0.0000

YEARS 19 — MO PAYT .7361 — AN CONST 8.84

#	INT	PRIN	BALANCE
1	5.9208	2.9122	97.0878
2	5.7412	3.0918	93.9959
3	5.5505	3.2825	90.7134
4	5.3480	3.4850	87.2284
5	5.1331	3.6999	83.5285
6	4.9049	3.9281	79.6003
7	4.6626	4.1704	75.4299
8	4.4054	4.4276	71.0023
9	4.1323	4.7007	66.3015
10	3.8423	4.9907	61.3109
11	3.5345	5.2985	56.0124
12	3.2077	5.6253	50.3871
13	2.8608	5.9722	44.4149
14	2.4924	6.3406	38.0743
15	2.1013	6.7317	31.3426
16	1.6861	7.1469	24.1958
17	1.2453	7.5877	16.6081
18	.7774	8.0556	8.5525
19	.2805	8.5525	0.0000

YEARS 20 — MO PAYT .7164 — AN CONST 8.60

#	INT	PRIN	BALANCE
1	5.9274	2.6698	97.3302
2	5.7627	2.8345	94.4957
3	5.5879	3.0093	91.4864
4	5.4023	3.1949	88.2915
5	5.2052	3.3920	84.8996
6	4.9960	3.6012	81.2984
7	4.7739	3.8233	77.4752
8	4.5381	4.0591	73.4161
9	4.2877	4.3094	69.1067
10	4.0219	4.5752	64.5314
11	3.7397	4.8574	59.6740
12	3.4402	5.1570	54.5170
13	3.1221	5.4751	49.0419
14	2.7844	5.8128	43.2291
15	2.4259	6.1713	37.0578
16	2.0452	6.5519	30.5059
17	1.6411	6.9560	23.5498
18	1.2121	7.3851	16.1647
19	.7566	7.8406	8.3242
20	.2730	8.3242	0.0000

YEARS 21 — MO PAYT .6989 — AN CONST 8.39

#	INT	PRIN	BALANCE
1	5.9333	2.4530	97.5470
2	5.7820	2.6043	94.9427
3	5.6213	2.7649	92.1777

#	INT	PRIN	BALANCE
4	5.4508	2.9355	89.2423
5	5.2698	3.1165	86.1257
6	5.0775	3.3087	82.8170
7	4.8735	3.5128	79.3042
8	4.6568	3.7295	75.5747
9	4.4268	3.9595	71.6152
10	4.1826	4.2037	67.4115
11	3.9233	4.4630	62.9485
12	3.6480	4.7383	58.2102
13	3.3558	5.0305	53.1797
14	3.0455	5.3408	47.8389
15	2.7161	5.6702	42.1687
16	2.3664	6.0199	36.1488
17	1.9951	6.3912	29.7575
18	1.6009	6.7854	22.9721
19	1.1824	7.2039	15.7682
20	.7380	7.6482	8.1200
21	.2663	8.1200	0.0000

YEARS 22 — MO PAYT .6831 — AN CONST 8.20

#	INT	PRIN	BALANCE
1	5.9386	2.2583	97.7417
2	5.7993	2.3976	95.3441
3	5.6514	2.5455	92.7986
4	5.4944	2.7025	90.0961
5	5.3277	2.8692	87.2269
6	5.1507	3.0461	84.1807
7	4.9629	3.2340	80.9467
8	4.7634	3.4335	77.5132
9	4.5516	3.6453	73.8680
10	4.3268	3.8701	69.9979
11	4.0881	4.1088	65.8891
12	3.8347	4.3622	61.5269
13	3.5656	4.6313	56.8956
14	3.2800	4.9169	51.9787
15	2.9767	5.2202	46.7585
16	2.6547	5.5421	41.2164
17	2.3129	5.8840	35.3324
18	1.9500	6.2469	29.0855
19	1.5647	6.6322	22.4534
20	1.1557	7.0412	15.4121
21	.7214	7.4755	7.9366
22	.2603	7.9366	0.0000

YEARS 23 — MO PAYT .6688 — AN CONST 8.03

#	INT	PRIN	BALANCE
1	5.9433	2.0828	97.9172
2	5.8149	2.2113	95.7059
3	5.6785	2.3477	93.3582
4	5.5337	2.4925	90.8657
5	5.3800	2.6462	88.2195
6	5.2167	2.8094	85.4101
7	5.0435	2.9827	82.4274
8	4.8595	3.1667	79.2607
9	4.6642	3.3620	75.8988
10	4.4568	3.5693	72.3294
11	4.2367	3.7895	68.5399
12	4.0030	4.0232	64.5167
13	3.7548	4.2714	60.2454
14	3.4914	4.5348	55.7106
15	3.2117	4.8145	50.8961
16	2.9147	5.1114	45.7846
17	2.5995	5.4267	40.3579
18	2.2647	5.7614	34.5965
19	1.9094	6.1168	28.4797
20	1.5321	6.4940	21.9857
21	1.1316	6.8946	15.0911
22	.7063	7.3198	7.7713
23	.2549	7.7713	0.0000

YEARS 24 — MO PAYT .6560 — AN CONST 7.88

#	INT	PRIN	BALANCE
1	5.9477	1.9241	98.0759
2	5.8290	2.0428	96.0332
3	5.7030	2.1687	93.8644
4	5.5692	2.3025	91.5619
5	5.4272	2.4445	89.1174
6	5.2764	2.5953	86.5221
7	5.1164	2.7554	83.7668
8	4.9464	2.9253	80.8414
9	4.7660	3.1057	77.7357
10	4.5744	3.2973	74.4384
11	4.3711	3.5007	70.9378
12	4.1552	3.7166	67.2212
13	3.9259	3.9458	63.2754
14	3.6826	4.1892	59.0862
15	3.4242	4.4476	54.6387
16	3.1499	4.7219	49.9168
17	2.8586	5.0131	44.9037
18	2.5494	5.3223	39.5814
19	2.2212	5.6506	33.9308
20	1.8727	5.9991	27.9318
21	1.5026	6.3691	21.5627
22	1.1098	6.7619	14.8007
23	.6928	7.1790	7.6218
24	.2500	7.6218	0.0000

YEARS 25 — MO PAYT .6443 — AN CONST 7.74

#	INT	PRIN	BALANCE
1	5.9516	1.7800	98.2200
2	5.8418	1.8898	96.3301
3	5.7252	2.0064	94.3237
4	5.6015	2.1301	92.1936
5	5.4701	2.2615	89.9321
6	5.3306	2.4010	87.5311
7	5.1825	2.5491	84.9820
8	5.0253	2.7063	82.2757
9	4.8584	2.8732	79.4024
10	4.6812	3.0505	76.3520
11	4.4930	3.2386	73.1134
12	4.2933	3.4383	69.6750
13	4.0812	3.6504	66.0246
14	3.8561	3.8756	62.1491
15	3.6170	4.1146	58.0345
16	3.3632	4.3684	53.6661
17	3.0938	4.6378	49.0283
18	2.8078	4.9239	44.1044
19	2.5041	5.2276	38.8768
20	2.1816	5.5500	33.3269
21	1.8393	5.8923	27.4346
22	1.4759	6.2557	21.1788
23	1.0901	6.6416	14.5373
24	.6804	7.0512	7.4861
25	.2455	7.4861	0.0000

YEARS 26 — MO PAYT .6337 — AN CONST 7.61

#	INT	PRIN	BALANCE
1	5.9551	1.6490	98.3510
2	5.8534	1.7507	96.6003
3	5.7455	1.8587	94.7417
4	5.6308	1.9733	92.7684
5	5.5091	2.0950	90.6734
6	5.3799	2.2242	88.4491
7	5.2427	2.3614	86.0877
8	5.0971	2.5071	83.5806
9	4.9424	2.6617	80.9190
10	4.7783	2.8259	78.0931
11	4.6040	3.0002	75.0930
12	4.4189	3.1852	71.9078
13	4.2225	3.3816	68.5261
14	4.0139	3.5902	64.9359
15	3.7925	3.8117	61.1242
16	3.5574	4.0468	57.0775
17	3.3078	4.2963	52.7811
18	3.0428	4.5613	48.2198
19	2.7615	4.8427	43.3771
20	2.4628	5.1414	38.2358
21	2.1457	5.4585	32.7773
22	1.8090	5.7951	26.9822
23	1.4516	6.1526	20.8296
24	1.0721	6.5320	14.2976
25	.6692	6.9349	7.3626
26	.2415	7.3626	0.0000

YEARS 27 — MO PAYT .6240 — AN CONST 7.49

#	INT	PRIN	BALANCE
1	5.9584	1.5294	98.4706
2	5.8641	1.6238	96.8468
3	5.7639	1.7239	95.1229
4	5.6576	1.8302	93.2927
5	5.5447	1.9431	91.3495
6	5.4249	2.0630	89.2866
7	5.2976	2.1902	87.0964
8	5.1625	2.3253	84.7711
9	5.0191	2.4687	82.3023
10	4.8668	2.6210	79.6814
11	4.7052	2.7826	76.8987
12	4.5336	2.9543	73.9445
13	4.3513	3.1365	70.8080
14	4.1579	3.3299	67.4781
15	3.9525	3.5353	63.9427
16	3.7345	3.7534	60.1894
17	3.5030	3.9849	56.2045
18	3.2572	4.2306	51.9739
19	2.9962	4.4916	47.4823
20	2.7192	4.7686	42.7137
21	2.4251	5.0627	37.6510
22	2.1128	5.3750	32.2760
23	1.7813	5.7065	26.5695
24	1.4294	6.0585	20.5110
25	1.0557	6.4321	14.0789
26	.6590	6.8289	7.2500
27	.2378	7.2500	0.0000

YEARS 28 — MO PAYT .6151 — AN CONST 7.39

#	INT	PRIN	BALANCE
1	5.9614	1.4201	98.5799
2	5.8738	1.5077	97.0722
3	5.7808	1.6007	95.4715
4	5.6821	1.6994	93.7720
5	5.5772	1.8042	91.9678
6	5.4660	1.9155	90.0523
7	5.3478	2.0337	88.0186
8	5.2224	2.1591	85.8595
9	5.0892	2.2923	83.5672
10	4.9478	2.4337	81.1336
11	4.7977	2.5838	78.5498
12	4.6384	2.7431	75.8067
13	4.4692	2.9123	72.8944
14	4.2896	3.0919	69.8024
15	4.0988	3.2826	66.5198
16	3.8964	3.4851	63.0347
17	3.6814	3.7001	59.3346
18	3.4532	3.9283	55.4063
19	3.2109	4.1706	51.2358
20	2.9537	4.4278	46.8080
21	2.6806	4.7009	42.1071
22	2.3907	4.9908	37.1163
23	2.0828	5.2986	31.8176
24	1.7560	5.6255	26.1922
25	1.4091	5.9724	20.2198
26	1.0407	6.3408	13.8790
27	.6496	6.7319	7.1471
28	.2344	7.1471	0.0000

YEARS 29 — MO PAYT .6070 — AN CONST 7.29

#	INT	PRIN	BALANCE
1	5.9641	1.3200	98.6800
2	5.8827	1.4014	97.2787
3	5.7962	1.4878	95.7909
4	5.7045	1.5796	94.2113
5	5.6071	1.6770	92.5343
6	5.5036	1.7804	90.7539
7	5.3938	1.8902	88.8636
8	5.2772	2.0068	86.8568
9	5.1534	2.1306	84.7262
10	5.0220	2.2620	82.4642
11	4.8825	2.4015	80.0626
12	4.7344	2.5497	77.5130
13	4.5771	2.7069	74.8060
14	4.4102	2.8739	71.9322
15	4.2329	3.0511	68.8811
16	4.0447	3.2393	65.6417
17	3.8450	3.4391	62.2026
18	3.6328	3.6512	58.5514
19	3.4076	3.8764	54.6750
20	3.1685	4.1155	50.5595
21	2.9147	4.3693	46.1901
22	2.6452	4.6388	41.5513
23	2.3591	4.9249	36.6264
24	2.0553	5.2287	31.3977
25	1.7329	5.5512	25.8464
26	1.3905	5.8936	19.9529
27	1.0270	6.2571	13.6958
28	.6410	6.6430	7.0527
29	.2313	7.0527	0.0000

YEARS 30 — MO PAYT .5996 — AN CONST 7.20

#	INT	PRIN	BALANCE
1	5.9666	1.2280	98.7720
2	5.8909	1.3038	97.4682
3	5.8104	1.3842	96.0841
4	5.7251	1.4695	94.6145
5	5.6344	1.5602	93.0544
6	5.5382	1.6564	91.3980
7	5.4360	1.7586	89.6394
8	5.3276	1.8670	87.7724
9	5.2124	1.9822	85.7902
10	5.0902	2.1044	83.6857
11	4.9604	2.2342	81.4515
12	4.8226	2.3720	79.0794
13	4.6763	2.5183	76.5611
14	4.5209	2.6737	73.8874
15	4.3560	2.8386	71.0488
16	4.1810	3.0137	68.0352
17	3.9951	3.1995	64.8357
18	3.7977	3.3969	61.4388
19	3.5882	3.6064	57.8324
20	3.3658	3.8288	54.0036
21	3.1296	4.0650	49.9386
22	2.8789	4.3157	45.6229
23	2.6127	4.5819	41.0411
24	2.3301	4.8645	36.1766
25	2.0301	5.1645	31.0121
26	1.7116	5.4830	25.5291
27	1.3734	5.8212	19.7078
28	1.0143	6.1803	13.5276
29	.6332	6.5614	6.9661
30	.2285	6.9661	0.0000

YEARS 2 — MO PAYT 4.4366 — AN CONST 53.24

#	INT	PRIN	BALANCE
1	4.7595	48.4793	51.5207
2	1.7182	51.5207	0.0000

YEARS 3 — MO PAYT 3.0467 — AN CONST 36.57

#	INT	PRIN	BALANCE
1	5.2338	31.3269	68.6731
2	3.2685	33.2922	35.3808
3	1.1799	35.3808	0.0000

YEARS 4 — MO PAYT 2.3531 — AN CONST 28.24

#	INT	PRIN	BALANCE
1	5.4705	22.7666	77.2334
2	4.0422	24.1949	53.0385
3	2.5244	25.7127	27.3258
4	.9113	27.3258	0.0000

YEARS 5 — MO PAYT 1.9379 — AN CONST 23.26

#	INT	PRIN	BALANCE
1	5.6121	17.6431	82.3569
2	4.5053	18.7499	63.6071
3	3.3290	19.9262	43.6809
4	2.0790	21.1762	22.5047
5	.7505	22.5047	0.0000

YEARS 6 — MO PAYT 1.6620 — AN CONST 19.95

#	INT	PRIN	BALANCE
1	5.7063	14.2379	85.7621
2	4.8131	15.1311	70.6311
3	3.8639	16.0803	54.5508
4	2.8551	17.0891	37.4617
5	1.7830	18.1612	19.3005
6	.6436	19.3005	0.0000

YEARS 7 — MO PAYT 1.4657 — AN CONST 17.59

#	INT	PRIN	BALANCE
1	5.7733	11.8145	88.1855
2	5.0321	12.5557	75.6297
3	4.2445	13.3434	62.2864
4	3.4074	14.1805	48.1059
5	2.5178	15.0701	33.0358
6	1.5723	16.0155	17.0202
7	.5676	17.0202	0.0000

YEARS 8 — MO PAYT 1.3190 — AN CONST 15.83

#	INT	PRIN	BALANCE
1	5.8234	10.0049	89.9951
2	5.1957	10.6325	79.3626
3	4.5287	11.2995	68.0631
4	3.8198	12.0084	56.0547
5	3.0665	12.7618	43.2929
6	2.2659	13.5624	29.7306
7	1.4150	14.4132	15.3174
8	.5108	15.3174	0.0000

YEARS 9 — MO PAYT 1.2055 — AN CONST 14.47

#	INT	PRIN	BALANCE
1	5.8621	8.6042	91.3958
2	5.3223	9.1440	82.2518
3	4.7487	9.7177	72.5341
4	4.1390	10.3273	62.2068
5	3.4911	10.9752	51.2316
6	2.8026	11.6637	39.5679
7	2.0709	12.3954	27.1725
8	1.2933	13.1730	13.9994
9	.4669	13.9994	0.0000

YEARS 10 — MO PAYT 1.1152 — AN CONST 13.39

#	INT	PRIN	BALANCE
1	5.8929	7.4899	92.5101
2	5.4230	7.9598	84.5503
3	4.9237	8.4591	76.0912
4	4.3930	8.9898	67.1014
5	3.8290	9.5538	57.5476
6	3.2297	10.1531	47.3944
7	2.5927	10.7901	36.6043
8	1.9158	11.4670	25.1373
9	1.1964	12.1864	12.9509
10	.4319	12.9509	0.0000

YEARS 11 — MO PAYT 1.0418 — AN CONST 12.51

#	INT	PRIN	BALANCE
1	5.9180	6.5838	93.4162
2	5.5049	6.9968	86.4195
3	5.0660	7.4357	78.9837
4	4.5995	7.9022	71.0815
5	4.1038	8.3980	62.6836
6	3.5769	8.9248	53.7588
7	3.0170	9.4847	44.2741
8	2.4220	10.0797	34.1944
9	1.7897	10.7121	23.4823
10	1.1176	11.3841	12.0982
11	.4035	12.0982	0.0000

YEARS 12 — MO PAYT .9810 — AN CONST 11.78

#	INT	PRIN	BALANCE
1	5.9387	5.8337	94.1663
2	5.5727	6.1997	87.9666
3	5.1838	6.5886	81.3780
4	4.7704	7.0020	74.3760
5	4.3312	7.4412	66.9348
6	3.8644	7.9080	59.0268
7	3.3682	8.4041	50.6226
8	2.8410	8.9314	41.6913
9	2.2807	9.4917	32.1996
10	1.6853	10.0871	22.1124
11	1.0524	10.7200	11.3925
12	.3799	11.3925	0.0000

YEARS 13 — MO PAYT .9300 — AN CONST 11.16

#	INT	PRIN	BALANCE
1	5.9561	5.2037	94.7963
2	5.6297	5.5301	89.2662
3	5.2827	5.8771	83.3891
4	4.9140	6.2458	77.1433
5	4.5222	6.6376	70.5057
6	4.1058	7.0540	63.4517
7	3.6633	7.4965	55.9552
8	3.1930	7.9668	47.9884
9	2.6932	8.4666	39.5218
10	2.1620	8.9978	30.5240
11	1.5976	9.5622	20.9618
12	.9977	10.1621	10.7996
13	.3602	10.7996	0.0000

YEARS 14 — MO PAYT .8866 — AN CONST 10.64

#	INT	PRIN	BALANCE
1	5.9709	4.6679	95.3321
2	5.6781	4.9608	90.3713
3	5.3669	5.2720	85.0993
4	5.0361	5.6027	79.4966
5	4.6846	5.9542	73.5423
6	4.3111	6.3278	67.2146
7	3.9141	6.7247	60.4899
8	3.4923	7.1466	53.3433
9	3.0439	7.5949	45.7483
10	2.5675	8.0714	37.6769
11	2.0611	8.5778	29.0992
12	1.5230	9.1159	19.9833
13	.9511	9.6878	10.2955
14	.3433	10.2955	0.0000

YEARS 15 — MO PAYT .8493 — AN CONST 10.20

#	INT	PRIN	BALANCE
1	5.9837	4.2076	95.7924
2	5.7197	4.4715	91.3209
3	5.4392	4.7521	86.5688
4	5.1411	5.0502	81.5187
5	4.8242	5.3670	76.1517
6	4.4875	5.7037	70.4480
7	4.1297	6.0615	64.3865
8	3.7495	6.4418	57.9447
9	3.3453	6.8459	51.0988
10	2.9159	7.2754	43.8234
11	2.4594	7.7318	36.0916
12	1.9744	8.2168	27.8748
13	1.4589	8.7323	19.1425
14	.9111	9.2801	9.8623
15	.3289	9.8623	0.0000

YEARS 16 — MO PAYT .8169 — AN CONST 9.81

#	INT	PRIN	BALANCE
1	5.9947	3.8084	96.1916
2	5.7558	4.0473	92.1443
3	5.5019	4.3012	87.8430
4	5.2320	4.5711	83.2719
5	4.9453	4.8578	78.4141
6	4.6405	5.1626	73.2515
7	4.3166	5.4865	67.7650
8	3.9724	5.8307	61.9344
9	3.6067	6.1964	55.7379
10	3.2179	6.5852	49.1528
11	2.8048	6.9983	42.1545
12	2.3658	7.4373	34.7171
13	1.8992	7.9039	26.8132
14	1.4033	8.3998	18.4135
15	.8764	8.9267	9.4867
16	.3164	9.4867	0.0000

YEARS 17 — MO PAYT .7887 — AN CONST 9.47

#	INT	PRIN	BALANCE
1	6.0043	3.4596	96.5404
2	5.7873	3.6767	92.8637
3	5.5566	3.9073	88.9564
4	5.3115	4.1524	84.8040
5	5.0510	4.4129	80.3911
6	4.7742	4.6898	75.7013
7	4.4800	4.9840	70.7173
8	4.1673	5.2967	65.4206
9	3.8350	5.6289	59.7917
10	3.4819	5.9821	53.8096
11	3.1066	6.3574	47.4523
12	2.7078	6.7562	40.6961
13	2.2839	7.1800	33.5160
14	1.8335	7.6305	25.8856
15	1.3548	8.1092	17.7764
16	.8461	8.6179	9.1585
17	.3054	9.1585	0.0000

YEARS 18 — MO PAYT .7638 — AN CONST 9.17

#	INT	PRIN	BALANCE
1	6.0128	3.1528	96.8472
2	5.8150	3.3505	93.4967
3	5.6048	3.5607	89.9360
4	5.3815	3.7841	86.1518
5	5.1441	4.0215	82.1303
6	4.8918	4.2738	77.8565
7	4.6237	4.5419	73.3146
8	4.3387	4.8269	68.4877
9	4.0359	5.1297	63.3581
10	3.7141	5.4515	57.9066
11	3.3721	5.7935	52.1131
12	3.0087	6.1569	45.9562
13	2.6224	6.5432	39.4130
14	2.2119	6.9537	32.4594
15	1.7757	7.3899	25.0695
16	1.3121	7.8535	17.2160
17	.8194	8.3462	8.8698
18	.2958	8.8698	0.0000

YEARS 19 — MO PAYT .7418 — AN CONST 8.91

#	INT	PRIN	BALANCE
1	6.0203	2.8812	97.1188
2	5.8396	3.0619	94.0569
3	5.6475	3.2540	90.8029
4	5.4434	3.4581	87.3448
5	5.2264	3.6751	83.6697
6	4.9959	3.9056	79.7640
7	4.7508	4.1507	75.6133
8	4.4904	4.4111	71.2023
9	4.2137	4.6878	66.5145
10	3.9196	4.9819	61.5326
11	3.6071	5.2944	56.2382
12	3.2750	5.6266	50.6117
13	2.9220	5.9795	44.6321
14	2.5468	6.3547	38.2775
15	2.1482	6.7533	31.5242
16	1.7245	7.1770	24.3472
17	1.2743	7.6272	16.7199
18	.7958	8.1057	8.6142
19	.2673	8.6142	0.0000

YEARS 20 — MO PAYT .7222 — AN CONST 8.67

#	INT	PRIN	BALANCE
1	6.0270	2.6395	97.3605
2	5.8614	2.8051	94.5553
3	5.6854	2.9811	91.5742
4	5.4984	3.1681	88.4061
5	5.2997	3.3669	85.0393
6	5.0885	3.5781	81.4612
7	4.8640	3.8026	77.6586
8	4.6254	4.0411	73.6175
9	4.3719	4.2946	69.3229
10	4.1025	4.5641	64.7588
11	3.8162	4.8504	59.9084
12	3.5119	5.1547	54.7538
13	3.1885	5.4780	49.2757
14	2.8448	5.8217	43.4540
15	2.4796	6.1869	37.2671
16	2.0915	6.5751	30.6921
17	1.6790	6.9875	23.7045
18	1.2406	7.4259	16.2786
19	.7748	7.8918	8.3869
20	.2797	8.3869	0.0000

YEARS 21 — MO PAYT .7047 — AN CONST 8.46

#	INT	PRIN	BALANCE
1	6.0330	2.4235	97.5765
2	5.8809	2.5756	95.0009
3	5.7194	2.7371	92.2638

#	INT	PRIN	BALANCE
4	5.5477	2.9089	89.3549
5	5.3652	3.0913	86.2636
6	5.1712	3.2853	82.9783
7	4.9651	3.4914	79.4869
8	4.7461	3.7104	75.7765
9	4.5133	3.9432	71.8334
10	4.2660	4.1905	67.6428
11	4.0031	4.4534	63.1894
12	3.7237	4.7328	58.4566
13	3.4268	5.0297	53.4268
14	3.1112	5.3453	48.0815
15	2.7759	5.6806	42.4009
16	2.4195	6.0370	36.3639
17	2.0408	6.4157	29.9482
18	1.6383	6.8182	23.1300
19	1.2106	7.2459	15.8841
20	.7560	7.7005	8.1836
21	.2729	8.1836	0.0000

YEARS 22 — MO PAYT .6890 — AN CONST 8.27

#	INT	PRIN	BALANCE
1	6.0383	2.2296	97.7704
2	5.8985	2.3695	95.4009
3	5.7498	2.5181	92.8828
4	5.5919	2.6761	90.2067
5	5.4240	2.8440	87.3627
6	5.2455	3.0224	84.3402
7	5.0559	3.2120	81.1282
8	4.8544	3.4135	77.7147
9	4.6403	3.6277	74.0870
10	4.4127	3.8553	70.2318
11	4.1708	4.0971	66.1346
12	3.9138	4.3541	61.7805
13	3.6407	4.6273	57.1532
14	3.3504	4.9176	52.2356
15	3.0419	5.2261	47.0095
16	2.7140	5.5540	41.4556
17	2.3656	5.9024	35.5532
18	1.9953	6.2727	29.2805
19	1.6018	6.6662	22.6143
20	1.1836	7.0844	15.5299
21	.7391	7.5288	8.0011
22	.2668	8.0011	0.0000

YEARS 23 — MO PAYT .6748 — AN CONST 8.10

#	INT	PRIN	BALANCE
1	6.0432	2.0549	97.9451
2	5.9143	2.1838	95.7613
3	5.7773	2.3208	93.4405
4	5.6317	2.4664	90.9741
5	5.4769	2.6211	88.3530
6	5.3125	2.7856	85.5675
7	5.1378	2.9603	82.6071
8	4.9520	3.1460	79.4611
9	4.7547	3.3434	76.1177
10	4.5449	3.5531	72.5646
11	4.3220	3.7760	68.7886
12	4.0851	4.0129	64.7757
13	3.8334	4.2647	60.5110
14	3.5658	4.5322	55.9788
15	3.2815	4.8165	51.1622
16	2.9794	5.1187	46.0435
17	2.6582	5.4398	40.6037
18	2.3170	5.7811	34.8226
19	1.9543	6.1438	28.6788
20	1.5689	6.5292	22.1496
21	1.1593	6.9388	15.2108
22	.7240	7.3741	7.8367
23	.2613	7.8367	0.0000

YEARS 24 — MO PAYT .6620 — AN CONST 7.95

#	INT	PRIN	BALANCE
1	6.0475	1.8969	98.1031
2	5.9285	2.0159	96.0872
3	5.8021	2.1424	93.9448
4	5.6677	2.2768	91.6680
5	5.5248	2.4196	89.2484
6	5.3731	2.5714	86.6770
7	5.2117	2.7327	83.9443
8	5.0403	2.9042	81.0402
9	4.8581	3.0863	77.9538
10	4.6645	3.2800	74.6739
11	4.4587	3.4857	71.1881
12	4.2400	3.7044	67.4837
13	4.0076	3.9368	63.5469
14	3.7607	4.1838	59.3631
15	3.4982	4.4462	54.9169
16	3.2193	4.7252	50.1917
17	2.9228	5.0216	45.1701
18	2.6078	5.3366	39.8335
19	2.2730	5.6714	34.1620
20	1.9172	6.0272	28.1348
21	1.5391	6.4053	21.7295
22	1.1373	6.8072	14.9223
23	.7102	7.2342	7.6881
24	.2564	7.6881	0.0000

YEARS 25 — MO PAYT .6504 — AN CONST 7.81

#	INT	PRIN	BALANCE
1	6.0515	1.7536	98.2464
2	5.9415	1.8636	96.3827
3	5.8246	1.9806	94.4022
4	5.7003	2.1048	92.2974
5	5.5683	2.2368	90.0605
6	5.4280	2.3772	87.6834
7	5.2788	2.5263	85.1570
8	5.1203	2.6848	82.4723
9	4.9519	2.8532	79.6190
10	4.7729	3.0322	76.5868
11	4.5827	3.2224	73.3644
12	4.3805	3.4246	69.9398
13	4.1657	3.6394	66.3003
14	3.9374	3.8678	62.4325
15	3.6947	4.1104	58.3221
16	3.4369	4.3683	53.9539
17	3.1628	4.6423	49.3116
18	2.8716	4.9336	44.3780
19	2.5621	5.2431	39.1349
20	2.2332	5.5720	33.5630
21	1.8836	5.9215	27.6414
22	1.5121	6.2930	21.3484
23	1.1173	6.6878	14.6606
24	.6978	7.1074	7.5532
25	.2519	7.5532	0.0000

YEARS 26 — MO PAYT .6399 — AN CONST 7.68

#	INT	PRIN	BALANCE
1	6.0551	1.6233	98.3767
2	5.9533	1.7252	96.6515
3	5.8450	1.8334	94.8181
4	5.7300	1.9484	92.8697
5	5.6078	2.0706	90.7991
6	5.4779	2.2005	88.5986
7	5.3398	2.3386	86.2600
8	5.1931	2.4853	83.7747
9	5.0372	2.6412	81.1335
10	4.8715	2.8069	78.3266
11	4.6954	2.9830	75.3436
12	4.5083	3.1701	72.1734
13	4.3094	3.3690	68.8044
14	4.0981	3.5804	65.2240
15	3.8735	3.8050	61.4191
16	3.6348	4.0437	57.3754
17	3.3811	4.2974	53.0780
18	3.1115	4.5670	48.5111
19	2.8250	4.8535	43.6576
20	2.5205	5.1579	38.4997
21	2.1969	5.4815	33.0181
22	1.8530	5.8254	27.1927
23	1.4876	6.1909	21.0019
24	1.0992	6.5792	14.4226
25	.6864	6.9920	7.4306
26	.2478	7.4306	0.0000

YEARS 27 — MO PAYT .6302 — AN CONST 7.57

#	INT	PRIN	BALANCE
1	6.0584	1.5045	98.4955
2	5.9640	1.5989	96.8966
3	5.8637	1.6992	95.1974
4	5.7571	1.8058	93.3916
5	5.6438	1.9191	91.4725
6	5.5234	2.0395	89.4330
7	5.3955	2.1674	87.2656
8	5.2595	2.3034	84.9622
9	5.1150	2.4479	82.5143
10	4.9614	2.6015	79.9128
11	4.7982	2.7647	77.1481
12	4.6248	2.9381	74.2100
13	4.4405	3.1224	71.0876
14	4.2446	3.3183	67.7692
15	4.0364	3.5265	64.2427
16	3.8152	3.7477	60.4950
17	3.5801	3.9828	56.5122
18	3.3302	4.2327	52.2795
19	3.0647	4.4982	47.7812
20	2.7825	4.7804	43.0008
21	2.4826	5.0803	37.9204
22	2.1639	5.3991	32.5214
23	1.8251	5.7378	26.7836
24	1.4652	6.0977	20.6859
25	1.0827	6.4803	14.2056
26	.6761	6.8868	7.3188
27	.2441	7.3188	0.0000

YEARS 28 — MO PAYT .6214 — AN CONST 7.46

#	INT	PRIN	BALANCE
1	6.0614	1.3959	98.6041
2	5.9738	1.4835	97.1206
3	5.8800	1.5766	95.5440
4	5.7819	1.6755	93.8685
5	5.6767	1.7806	92.0879
6	5.5650	1.8923	90.1956
7	5.4463	2.0110	88.1846
8	5.3202	2.1372	86.0474
9	5.1861	2.2712	83.7762
10	5.0436	2.4137	81.3624
11	4.8922	2.5652	78.7973
12	4.7313	2.7261	76.0712
13	4.5602	2.8971	73.1741
14	4.3785	3.0789	70.0952
15	4.1853	3.2720	66.8232
16	3.9801	3.4773	63.3460
17	3.7619	3.6954	59.6505
18	3.5301	3.9272	55.7233
19	3.2837	4.1736	51.5497
20	3.0219	4.4355	47.1142
21	2.7436	4.7137	42.4005
22	2.4479	5.0094	37.3911
23	2.1336	5.3237	32.0674
24	1.7997	5.6577	26.4097
25	1.4447	6.0126	20.3971
26	1.0675	6.3898	14.0073
27	.6667	6.7907	7.2167
28	.2407	7.2167	0.0000

YEARS 29 — MO PAYT .6134 — AN CONST 7.37

#	INT	PRIN	BALANCE
1	6.0642	1.2965	98.7035
2	5.9828	1.3778	97.3257
3	5.8964	1.4643	95.8614
4	5.8045	1.5561	94.3052
5	5.7069	1.6538	92.6515
6	5.6031	1.7575	90.8940
7	5.4929	1.8678	89.0262
8	5.3757	1.9849	87.0413
9	5.2512	2.1095	84.9318
10	5.1189	2.2418	82.6900
11	4.9782	2.3824	80.3076
12	4.8288	2.5319	77.7757
13	4.6699	2.6907	75.0849
14	4.5011	2.8595	72.2254
15	4.3217	3.0389	69.1864
16	4.1311	3.2296	65.9569
17	3.9285	3.4322	62.5247
18	3.7131	3.6475	58.8772
19	3.4843	3.8763	55.0008
20	3.2411	4.1195	50.8813
21	2.9827	4.3779	46.5034
22	2.7081	4.6526	41.8508
23	2.4162	4.9445	36.9063
24	2.1060	5.2547	31.6516
25	1.7763	5.5843	26.0673
26	1.4260	5.9346	20.1327
27	1.0537	6.3070	13.8257
28	.6580	6.7026	7.1231
29	.2375	7.1231	0.0000

YEARS 30 — MO PAYT .6060 — AN CONST 7.28

#	INT	PRIN	BALANCE
1	6.0667	1.2053	98.7947
2	5.9911	1.2809	97.5139
3	5.9107	1.3612	96.1526
4	5.8253	1.4466	94.7060
5	5.7346	1.5374	93.1686
6	5.6381	1.6338	91.5348
7	5.5356	1.7363	89.7985
8	5.4267	1.8453	87.9532
9	5.3109	1.9610	85.9922
10	5.1879	2.0840	83.9082
11	5.0572	2.2148	81.6934
12	4.9182	2.3537	79.3396
13	4.7706	2.5014	76.8383
14	4.6136	2.6583	74.1799
15	4.4469	2.8251	71.3549
16	4.2696	3.0023	68.3526
17	4.0813	3.1907	65.1619
18	3.8811	3.3908	61.7711
19	3.6684	3.6035	58.1675
20	3.4423	3.8296	54.3379
21	3.2021	4.0699	50.2681
22	2.9468	4.3252	45.9429
23	2.6754	4.5965	41.3464
24	2.3871	4.8849	36.4615
25	2.0806	5.1913	31.2702
26	1.7549	5.5170	25.7531
27	1.4088	5.8631	19.8900
28	1.0410	6.2309	13.6591
29	.6501	6.6218	7.0373
30	.2347	7.0373	0.0000

YEARS 2 — MO PAYT 4.4377 — AN CONST 53.26

#	INT	PRIN	BALANCE
1	4.7792	48.4731	51.5269
2	1.7255	51.5269	0.0000

YEARS 3 — MO PAYT 3.0479 — AN CONST 36.58

#	INT	PRIN	BALANCE
1	5.2555	31.3188	68.6812
2	3.2824	33.2919	35.3893
3	1.1851	35.3893	0.0000

YEARS 4 — MO PAYT 2.3542 — AN CONST 28.26

#	INT	PRIN	BALANCE
1	5.4932	22.7577	77.2423
2	4.0595	24.1914	53.0509
3	2.5354	25.7154	27.3355
4	.9154	27.3355	0.0000

YEARS 5 — MO PAYT 1.9391 — AN CONST 23.27

#	INT	PRIN	BALANCE
1	5.6354	17.6337	82.3663
2	4.5245	18.7447	63.6216
3	3.3436	19.9255	43.6961
4	2.0883	21.1808	22.5152
5	.7540	22.5152	0.0000

YEARS 6 — MO PAYT 1.6632 — AN CONST 19.96

#	INT	PRIN	BALANCE
1	5.7300	14.2284	85.7716
2	4.8336	15.1247	70.6469
3	3.8808	16.0776	54.5693
4	2.8679	17.0905	37.4788
5	1.7912	18.1672	19.3117
6	.6467	19.3117	0.0000

YEARS 7 — MO PAYT 1.4669 — AN CONST 17.61

#	INT	PRIN	BALANCE
1	5.7973	11.8050	88.1950
2	5.0535	12.5487	75.6463
3	4.2630	13.3393	62.3070
4	3.4226	14.1796	48.1274
5	2.5293	15.0729	33.0544
6	1.5797	16.0225	17.0319
7	.5703	17.0319	0.0000

YEARS 8 — MO PAYT 1.3202 — AN CONST 15.85

#	INT	PRIN	BALANCE
1	5.8475	9.9954	90.0046
2	5.2178	10.6251	79.3796
3	4.5484	11.2944	68.0852
4	3.8369	12.0060	56.0792
5	3.0805	12.7623	43.3169
6	2.2765	13.5663	29.7505
7	1.4218	14.4210	15.3295
8	.5133	15.3295	0.0000

YEARS 9 — MO PAYT 1.2068 — AN CONST 14.49

#	INT	PRIN	BALANCE
1	5.8864	8.5948	91.4052
2	5.3449	9.1363	82.2689
3	4.7693	9.7119	72.5571
4	4.1575	10.3237	62.2334
5	3.5071	10.9741	51.2593
6	2.8158	11.6654	39.5939
7	2.0809	12.4003	27.1935
8	1.2996	13.1816	14.0120
9	.4692	14.0120	0.0000

YEARS 10 — MO PAYT 1.1165 — AN CONST 13.40

#	INT	PRIN	BALANCE
1	5.9173	7.4806	92.5194
2	5.4460	7.9519	84.5675
3	4.9451	8.4528	76.1147
4	4.4126	8.9853	67.1294
5	3.8465	9.5514	57.5779
6	3.2448	10.1531	47.4248
7	2.6051	10.7928	36.6320
8	1.9252	11.4727	25.1593
9	1.2024	12.1955	12.9638
10	.4341	12.9638	0.0000

YEARS 11 — MO PAYT 1.0431 — AN CONST 12.52

#	INT	PRIN	BALANCE
1	5.9425	6.5746	93.4254
2	5.5283	6.9888	86.4366
3	5.0880	7.4291	79.0076
4	4.6200	7.8971	71.1105
5	4.1225	8.3946	62.7159
6	3.5936	8.9235	53.7924
7	3.0314	9.4856	44.3068
8	2.4338	10.0832	34.2236
9	1.7986	10.7184	23.5052
10	1.1234	11.3937	12.1115
11	.4056	12.1115	0.0000

YEARS 12 — MO PAYT .9823 — AN CONST 11.79

#	INT	PRIN	BALANCE
1	5.9633	5.8247	94.1753
2	5.5963	6.1916	87.9837
3	5.2063	6.5817	81.4020
4	4.7916	6.9963	74.4056
5	4.3509	7.4371	66.9685
6	3.8823	7.9056	59.0629
7	3.3843	8.4037	50.6592
8	2.8549	8.9331	41.7261
9	2.2921	9.4959	32.2302
10	1.6939	10.0941	22.1361
11	1.0579	10.7300	11.4060
12	.3820	11.4060	0.0000

YEARS 13 — MO PAYT .9313 — AN CONST 11.18

#	INT	PRIN	BALANCE
1	5.9808	5.1948	94.8052
2	5.6535	5.5221	89.2831
3	5.3056	5.8700	83.4131
4	4.9358	6.2398	77.1733
5	4.5427	6.6329	70.5404
6	4.1248	7.0508	63.4896
7	3.6807	7.4950	55.9947
8	3.2085	7.9671	48.0275
9	2.7066	8.4691	39.5585
10	2.1730	9.0026	30.5559
11	1.6059	9.5697	20.9861
12	1.0030	10.1726	10.8135
13	.3621	10.8135	0.0000

YEARS 14 — MO PAYT .8879 — AN CONST 10.66

#	INT	PRIN	BALANCE
1	5.9956	4.6593	95.3407
2	5.7021	4.9528	90.3879
3	5.3901	5.2648	85.1231
4	5.0584	5.5965	79.5266
5	4.7058	5.9491	73.5776
6	4.3311	6.3239	67.2537
7	3.9327	6.7222	60.5315
8	3.5092	7.1457	53.3857
9	3.0590	7.5959	45.7898
10	2.5805	8.0745	37.7153
11	2.0718	8.5831	29.1322
12	1.5310	9.1239	20.0083
13	.9562	9.6987	10.3097
14	.3452	10.3097	0.0000

YEARS 15 — MO PAYT .8506 — AN CONST 10.21

#	INT	PRIN	BALANCE
1	6.0084	4.1991	95.8009
2	5.7439	4.4636	91.3373
3	5.4627	4.7448	86.5925
4	5.1638	5.0437	81.5487
5	4.8460	5.3615	76.1872
6	4.5082	5.6993	70.4880
7	4.1492	6.0583	64.4297
8	3.7675	6.4400	57.9897
9	3.3618	6.8457	51.1440
10	2.9305	7.2770	43.8670
11	2.4721	7.7354	36.1316
12	1.9848	8.2227	27.9089
13	1.4667	8.7408	19.1682
14	.9161	9.2914	9.8768
15	.3307	9.8768	0.0000

YEARS 16 — MO PAYT .8183 — AN CONST 9.82

#	INT	PRIN	BALANCE
1	6.0195	3.8001	96.1999
2	5.7801	4.0395	92.1604
3	5.5256	4.2940	87.8664
4	5.2551	4.5645	83.3019
5	4.9675	4.8521	78.4498
6	4.6619	5.1577	73.2920
7	4.3369	5.4827	67.8094
8	3.9915	5.8281	61.9813
9	3.6244	6.1953	55.7860
10	3.2341	6.5855	49.2005
11	2.8192	7.0004	42.2001
12	2.3782	7.4414	34.7586
13	1.9094	7.9103	26.8484
14	1.4110	8.4086	18.4398
15	.8813	8.9383	9.5014
16	.3182	9.5014	0.0000

YEARS 17 — MO PAYT .7901 — AN CONST 9.49

#	INT	PRIN	BALANCE
1	6.0292	3.4515	96.5485
2	5.8117	3.6689	92.8795
3	5.5806	3.9001	88.9795
4	5.3349	4.1458	84.8337
5	5.0737	4.4070	80.4267
6	4.7961	4.6846	75.7421
7	4.5010	4.9797	70.7624
8	4.1872	5.2934	65.4689
9	3.8537	5.6269	59.8420
10	3.4993	5.9814	53.8606
11	3.1224	6.3582	47.5023
12	2.7219	6.7588	40.7435
13	2.2961	7.1846	33.5589
14	1.8434	7.6372	25.9217
15	1.3623	8.1184	17.8033
16	.8509	8.6298	9.1735
17	.3072	9.1735	0.0000

YEARS 18 — MO PAYT .7652 — AN CONST 9.19

#	INT	PRIN	BALANCE
1	6.0377	3.1448	96.8552
2	5.8396	3.3430	93.5122
3	5.6290	3.5536	89.9586
4	5.4051	3.7774	86.1812
5	5.1671	4.0154	82.1658
6	4.9142	4.2684	77.8974
7	4.6452	4.5373	73.3601
8	4.3594	4.8231	68.5370
9	4.0556	5.1270	63.4100
10	3.7326	5.4500	57.9601
11	3.3892	5.7933	52.1667
12	3.0242	6.1583	46.0085
13	2.6363	6.5463	39.4622
14	2.2239	6.9587	32.5035
15	1.7855	7.3971	25.1065
16	1.3195	7.8631	17.2434
17	.8241	8.3584	8.8850
18	.2975	8.8850	0.0000

YEARS 19 — MO PAYT .7432 — AN CONST 8.92

#	INT	PRIN	BALANCE
1	6.0452	2.8734	97.1266
2	5.8642	3.0545	94.0721
3	5.6718	3.2469	90.8252
4	5.4672	3.4515	87.3737
5	5.2498	3.6689	83.7048
6	5.0186	3.9000	79.8048
7	4.7729	4.1457	75.6591
8	4.5118	4.4069	71.2522
9	4.2341	4.6845	66.5676
10	3.9390	4.9797	61.5880
11	3.6253	5.2934	56.2946
12	3.2918	5.6268	50.6678
13	2.9373	5.9813	44.6864
14	2.5605	6.3582	38.3283
15	2.1600	6.7587	31.5696
16	1.7342	7.1845	24.3851
17	1.2816	7.6371	16.7479
18	.8004	8.1183	8.6297
19	.2890	8.6297	0.0000

YEARS 20 — MO PAYT .7237 — AN CONST 8.69

#	INT	PRIN	BALANCE
1	6.0519	2.6320	97.3680
2	5.8861	2.7978	94.5702
3	5.7099	2.9741	91.5961
4	5.5225	3.1614	88.4347
5	5.3233	3.3606	85.0740
6	5.1116	3.5723	81.5017
7	4.8866	3.7974	77.7043
8	4.6473	4.0366	73.6677
9	4.3930	4.2909	69.3768
10	4.1227	4.5612	64.8156
11	3.8353	4.8486	59.9670
12	3.5299	5.1540	54.8129
13	3.2052	5.4787	49.3342
14	2.8600	5.8239	43.5103
15	2.4931	6.1908	37.3195
16	2.1031	6.5808	30.7387
17	1.6885	6.9954	23.7432
18	1.2478	7.4361	16.3071
19	.7794	7.9046	8.4026
20	.2814	8.4026	0.0000

YEARS 21 — MO PAYT .7062 — AN CONST 8.48

#	INT	PRIN	BALANCE
1	6.0579	2.4162	97.5838
2	5.9057	2.5684	95.0154
3	5.7439	2.7302	92.2852

#	INT	PRIN	BALANCE
4	5.5719	2.9022	89.3830
5	5.3891	3.0851	86.2979
6	5.1947	3.2794	83.0185
7	4.9881	3.4860	79.5325
8	4.7685	3.7056	75.8268
9	4.5350	3.9391	71.8878
10	4.2869	4.1872	67.7005
11	4.0231	4.4510	63.2495
12	3.7427	4.7314	58.5181
13	3.4446	5.0295	53.4885
14	3.1277	5.3464	48.1422
15	2.7909	5.6832	42.4590
16	2.4329	6.0412	36.4178
17	2.0523	6.4218	29.9959
18	1.6477	6.8264	23.1696
19	1.2177	7.2564	15.9131
20	.7605	7.7136	8.1995
21	.2746	8.1995	0.0000

YEARS 22 — MO PAYT .6905 — AN CONST 8.29

#	INT	PRIN	BALANCE
1	6.0633	2.2225	97.7775
2	5.9233	2.3625	95.4150
3	5.7744	2.5113	92.9037
4	5.6162	2.6695	90.2342
5	5.4481	2.8377	87.3964
6	5.2693	3.0165	84.3799
7	5.0792	3.2065	81.1734
8	4.8772	3.4085	77.7649
9	4.6625	3.6233	74.1416
10	4.4342	3.8515	70.2901
11	4.1916	4.0942	66.1959
12	3.9337	4.3521	61.8438
13	3.6595	4.6263	57.2175
14	3.3680	4.9177	52.2998
15	3.0582	5.2275	47.0722
16	2.7289	5.5569	41.5153
17	2.3788	5.9070	35.6084
18	2.0067	6.2791	29.3293
19	1.6111	6.6747	22.6546
20	1.1906	7.0952	15.5595
21	.7436	7.5422	8.0173
22	.2685	8.0173	0.0000

YEARS 23 — MO PAYT .6763 — AN CONST 8.12

#	INT	PRIN	BALANCE
1	6.0681	2.0479	97.9521
2	5.9391	2.1770	95.7751
3	5.8020	2.3141	93.4610
4	5.6562	2.4599	91.0011
5	5.5012	2.6149	88.3862
6	5.3365	2.7796	85.6066
7	5.1614	2.9547	82.6519
8	4.9752	3.1409	79.5110
9	4.7774	3.3387	76.1723
10	4.5670	3.5491	72.6232
11	4.3434	3.7727	68.8506
12	4.1058	4.0103	64.8402
13	3.8531	4.2630	60.5773
14	3.5845	4.5315	56.0457
15	3.2991	4.8170	51.2287
16	2.9956	5.1205	46.1082
17	2.6730	5.4431	40.6651
18	2.3301	5.7860	34.8791
19	1.9656	6.1505	28.7286
20	1.5781	6.5380	22.1907
21	1.1662	6.9499	15.2408
22	.7284	7.3877	7.8531
23	.2630	7.8531	0.0000

YEARS 24 — MO PAYT .6636 — AN CONST 7.97

#	INT	PRIN	BALANCE
1	6.0725	1.8902	98.1098
2	5.9534	2.0092	96.1006
3	5.8269	2.1358	93.9648
4	5.6923	2.2704	91.6944
5	5.5493	2.4134	89.2810
6	5.3972	2.5654	86.7156
7	5.2356	2.7271	83.9885
8	5.0638	2.8989	81.0896
9	4.8812	3.0815	78.0081
10	4.6871	3.2756	74.7325
11	4.4807	3.4820	71.2505
12	4.2613	3.7013	67.5492
13	4.0282	3.9345	63.6147
14	3.7803	4.1824	59.4323
15	3.5168	4.4459	54.9864
16	3.2367	4.7260	50.2604
17	2.9390	5.0237	45.2367
18	2.6225	5.3402	39.8965
19	2.2861	5.6766	34.2199
20	1.9284	6.0342	28.1856
21	1.5483	6.4144	21.7712
22	1.1442	6.8185	14.9527
23	.7146	7.2481	7.7047
24	.2580	7.7047	0.0000

YEARS 25 — MO PAYT .6520 — AN CONST 7.83

#	INT	PRIN	BALANCE
1	6.0765	1.7471	98.2529
2	5.9664	1.8571	96.3958
3	5.8494	1.9741	94.4217
4	5.7251	2.0985	92.3232
5	5.5929	2.2307	90.0925
6	5.4523	2.3712	87.7212
7	5.3029	2.5206	85.2006
8	5.1441	2.6794	82.5212
9	4.9753	2.8482	79.6729
10	4.7959	3.0277	76.6453
11	4.6052	3.2184	73.4269
12	4.4024	3.4212	70.0057
13	4.1869	3.6367	66.3691
14	3.9578	3.8658	62.5033
15	3.7142	4.1093	58.3939
16	3.4554	4.3682	54.0257
17	3.1802	4.6434	49.3823
18	2.8876	4.9359	44.4464
19	2.5767	5.2469	39.1995
20	2.2461	5.5774	33.6220
21	1.8947	5.9288	27.6932
22	1.5212	6.3023	21.3909
23	1.1242	6.6994	14.6915
24	.7021	7.1214	7.5701
25	.2535	7.5701	0.0000

YEARS 26 — MO PAYT .6414 — AN CONST 7.70

#	INT	PRIN	BALANCE
1	6.0801	1.6170	98.3830
2	5.9782	1.7188	96.6642
3	5.8700	1.8271	94.8371
4	5.7549	1.9422	92.8949
5	5.6325	2.0646	90.8303
6	5.5024	2.1946	88.6357
7	5.3642	2.3329	86.3028
8	5.2172	2.4799	83.8229
9	5.0610	2.6361	81.1868
10	4.8949	2.8022	78.3847
11	4.7184	2.9787	75.4060
12	4.5307	3.1664	72.2396
13	4.3312	3.3658	68.8738
14	4.1192	3.5779	65.2959
15	3.8938	3.8033	61.4926
16	3.6542	4.0429	57.4497
17	3.3995	4.2976	53.1521
18	3.1287	4.5683	48.5838
19	2.8409	4.8561	43.7277
20	2.5350	5.1621	38.5656
21	2.2098	5.4873	33.0784
22	1.8641	5.8330	27.2454
23	1.4966	6.2004	21.0450
24	1.1060	6.5910	14.4539
25	.6908	7.0063	7.4477
26	.2494	7.4477	0.0000

YEARS 27 — MO PAYT .6318 — AN CONST 7.59

#	INT	PRIN	BALANCE
1	6.0834	1.4983	98.5017
2	5.9890	1.5927	96.9089
3	5.8887	1.6931	95.2159
4	5.7820	1.7997	93.4161
5	5.6686	1.9131	91.5030
6	5.5481	2.0336	89.4694
7	5.4200	2.1618	87.3076
8	5.2838	2.2979	85.0097
9	5.1390	2.4427	82.5670
10	4.9851	2.5966	79.9704
11	4.8216	2.7602	77.2102
12	4.6477	2.9341	74.2761
13	4.4628	3.1189	71.1572
14	4.2663	3.3154	67.8418
15	4.0575	3.5243	64.3175
16	3.8354	3.7463	60.5712
17	3.5994	3.9823	56.5889
18	3.3485	4.2332	52.3557
19	3.0819	4.4999	47.8559
20	2.7984	4.7834	43.0725
21	2.4970	5.0847	37.9878
22	2.1767	5.4050	32.5827
23	1.8362	5.7456	26.8372
24	1.4742	6.1075	20.7297
25	1.0894	6.4923	14.2374
26	.6804	6.9013	7.3361
27	.2457	7.3361	0.0000

YEARS 28 — MO PAYT .6230 — AN CONST 7.48

#	INT	PRIN	BALANCE
1	6.0864	1.3899	98.6101
2	5.9988	1.4775	97.1325
3	5.9058	1.5706	95.5620
4	5.8068	1.6695	93.8924
5	5.7016	1.7747	92.1177
6	5.5898	1.8865	90.2312
7	5.4710	2.0054	88.2258
8	5.3446	2.1317	86.0941
9	5.2104	2.2660	83.8281
10	5.0676	2.4088	81.4193
11	4.9158	2.5605	78.8588
12	4.7545	2.7218	76.1370
13	4.5831	2.8933	73.2437
14	4.4008	3.0756	70.1682
15	4.2070	3.2693	66.8989
16	4.0011	3.4753	63.4236
17	3.7821	3.6942	59.7293
18	3.5494	3.9270	55.8024
19	3.3020	4.1744	51.6280
20	3.0390	4.4373	47.1907
21	2.7595	4.7169	42.4738
22	2.4623	5.0140	37.4598
23	2.1464	5.3299	32.1299
24	1.8107	5.6657	26.4642
25	1.4537	6.0226	20.4415
26	1.0743	6.4021	14.0395
27	.6710	6.8054	7.2341
28	.2422	7.2341	0.0000

YEARS 29 — MO PAYT .6150 — AN CONST 7.38

#	INT	PRIN	BALANCE
1	6.0892	1.2907	98.7093
2	6.0079	1.3720	97.3373
3	5.9214	1.4584	95.8789
4	5.8295	1.5503	94.3285
5	5.7319	1.6480	92.6806
6	5.6280	1.7518	90.9288
7	5.5177	1.8622	89.0666
8	5.4004	1.9795	87.0871
9	5.2757	2.1042	84.9829
10	5.1431	2.2368	82.7461
11	5.0022	2.3777	80.3685
12	4.8524	2.5275	77.8410
13	4.6932	2.6867	75.1543
14	4.5239	2.8559	72.2984
15	4.3440	3.0359	69.2625
16	4.1527	3.2271	66.0354
17	3.9494	3.4304	62.6050
18	3.7333	3.6465	58.9584
19	3.5036	3.8763	55.0821
20	3.2594	4.1205	50.9617
21	2.9998	4.3801	46.5816
22	2.7239	4.6560	41.9256
23	2.4305	4.9493	36.9763
24	2.1187	5.2611	31.7152
25	1.7873	5.5926	26.1226
26	1.4350	5.9449	20.1777
27	1.0604	6.3194	13.8583
28	.6623	6.7175	7.1407
29	.2391	7.1407	0.0000

YEARS 30 — MO PAYT .6076 — AN CONST 7.30

#	INT	PRIN	BALANCE
1	6.0917	1.1996	98.8004
2	6.0161	1.2752	97.5252
3	5.9358	1.3555	96.1696
4	5.8504	1.4409	94.7287
5	5.7596	1.5317	93.1970
6	5.6631	1.6282	91.5687
7	5.5605	1.7308	89.8379
8	5.4515	1.8398	87.9981
9	5.3356	1.9557	86.0424
10	5.2124	2.0789	83.9634
11	5.0814	2.2099	81.7535
12	4.9422	2.3491	79.4044
13	4.7942	2.4971	76.9072
14	4.6369	2.6545	74.2528
15	4.4696	2.8217	71.4311
16	4.2919	2.9994	68.4316
17	4.1029	3.1884	65.2432
18	3.9020	3.3893	61.8539
19	3.6885	3.6028	58.2511
20	3.4616	3.8298	54.4214
21	3.2203	4.0710	50.3503
22	2.9638	4.3275	46.0228
23	2.6912	4.6001	41.4227
24	2.4014	4.8899	36.5327
25	2.0933	5.1980	31.3347
26	1.7658	5.5255	25.8092
27	1.4177	5.8736	19.9356
28	1.0477	6.2436	13.6920
29	.6544	6.6370	7.0551
30	.2363	7.0551	0.0000

MONTHLY PAYMENT AMORTIZATION SCHEDULE PER $100   6.20 %

YEARS 2 — MO PAYT 4.4411 — AN CONST 53.30

#	INT	PRIN	BALANCE
1	4.8385	48.4545	51.5455
2	1.7474	51.5455	0.0000

YEARS 3 — MO PAYT 3.0513 — AN CONST 36.62

#	INT	PRIN	BALANCE
1	5.3206	31.2945	68.7055
2	3.3243	33.2909	35.4146
3	1.2006	35.4146	0.0000

YEARS 4 — MO PAYT 2.3577 — AN CONST 28.30

#	INT	PRIN	BALANCE
1	5.5613	22.7309	77.2691
2	4.1112	24.1810	53.0881
3	2.5686	25.7236	27.3645
4	.9277	27.3645	0.0000

YEARS 5 — MO PAYT 1.9426 — AN CONST 23.32

#	INT	PRIN	BALANCE
1	5.7053	17.6058	82.3942
2	4.5822	18.7290	63.6652
3	3.3874	19.9237	43.7415
4	2.1164	21.1947	22.5468
5	.7643	22.5468	0.0000

YEARS 6 — MO PAYT 1.6667 — AN CONST 20.01

#	INT	PRIN	BALANCE
1	5.8010	14.2000	85.8000
2	4.8951	15.1058	70.6942
3	3.9315	16.0695	54.6248
4	2.9064	17.0946	37.5302
5	1.8159	18.1851	19.3451
6	.6558	19.3451	0.0000

YEARS 7 — MO PAYT 1.4705 — AN CONST 17.65

#	INT	PRIN	BALANCE
1	5.8691	11.7765	88.2235
2	5.1178	12.5277	75.6958
3	4.3187	13.3269	62.3689
4	3.4685	14.1770	48.1919
5	2.5641	15.0814	33.1105
6	1.6020	16.0435	17.0670
7	.5786	17.0670	0.0000

YEARS 8 — MO PAYT 1.3239 — AN CONST 15.89

#	INT	PRIN	BALANCE
1	5.9199	9.9669	90.0331
2	5.2841	10.6027	79.4304
3	4.6077	11.2791	68.1513
4	3.8882	11.9986	56.1527
5	3.1228	12.7640	43.3887
6	2.3086	13.5783	29.8104
7	1.4424	14.4445	15.3659
8	.5209	15.3659	0.0000

YEARS 9 — MO PAYT 1.2105 — AN CONST 14.53

#	INT	PRIN	BALANCE
1	5.9593	8.5666	91.4334
2	5.4128	9.1131	82.3203
3	4.8315	9.6944	72.6259
4	4.2130	10.3129	62.3131
5	3.5551	10.9707	51.3423
6	2.8553	11.6706	39.6717
7	2.1108	12.4151	27.2567
8	1.3188	13.2071	14.0496
9	.4763	14.0496	0.0000

YEARS 10 — MO PAYT 1.1203 — AN CONST 13.45

#	INT	PRIN	BALANCE
1	5.9906	7.4527	92.5473
2	5.5152	7.9281	84.6191
3	5.0094	8.4339	76.1852
4	4.4714	8.9719	67.2133
5	3.8990	9.5443	57.6690
6	3.2902	10.1531	47.5159
7	2.6425	10.8008	36.7151
8	1.9535	11.4898	25.2253
9	1.2205	12.2228	13.0025
10	.4408	13.0025	0.0000

YEARS 11 — MO PAYT 1.0469 — AN CONST 12.57

#	INT	PRIN	BALANCE
1	6.0160	6.5471	93.4529
2	5.5984	6.9648	86.4881
3	5.1541	7.4091	79.0790
4	4.6814	7.8817	71.1973
5	4.1786	8.3845	62.8128
6	3.6438	8.9194	53.8934
7	3.0748	9.4884	44.4050
8	2.4695	10.0937	34.3113
9	1.8256	10.7376	23.5738
10	1.1406	11.4225	12.1512
11	.4119	12.1512	0.0000

YEARS 12 — MO PAYT .9862 — AN CONST 11.84

#	INT	PRIN	BALANCE
1	6.0371	5.7977	94.2023
2	5.6672	6.1675	88.0348
3	5.2738	6.5610	81.4738
4	4.8553	6.9795	74.4943
5	4.4100	7.4248	67.0695
6	3.9364	7.8984	59.1711
7	3.4325	8.4023	50.7688
8	2.8965	8.9383	41.8305
9	2.3263	9.5085	32.3221
10	1.7197	10.1150	22.2070
11	1.0745	10.7603	11.4467
12	.3881	11.4467	0.0000

YEARS 13 — MO PAYT .9353 — AN CONST 11.23

#	INT	PRIN	BALANCE
1	6.0548	5.1683	94.8317
2	5.7251	5.4980	89.3336
3	5.3743	5.8488	83.4848
4	5.0012	6.2219	77.2629
5	4.6043	6.6188	70.6441
6	4.1821	7.0410	63.6031
7	3.7329	7.4902	56.1129
8	3.2551	7.9680	48.1449
9	2.7468	8.4763	39.6686
10	2.2061	9.0170	30.6516
11	1.6309	9.5923	21.0593
12	1.0189	10.2042	10.8551
13	.3680	10.8551	0.0000

YEARS 14 — MO PAYT .8919 — AN CONST 10.71

#	INT	PRIN	BALANCE
1	6.0698	4.6333	95.3667
2	5.7742	4.9289	90.4378
3	5.4598	5.2433	85.1945
4	5.1253	5.5778	79.6167
5	4.7695	5.9336	73.6831
6	4.3910	6.3121	67.3710
7	3.9883	6.7148	60.6562
8	3.5600	7.1432	53.5130
9	3.1043	7.5988	45.9142
10	2.6195	8.0836	37.8306
11	2.1039	8.5993	29.2314
12	1.5553	9.1478	20.0836
13	.9717	9.7314	10.3522
14	.3509	10.3522	0.0000

YEARS 15 — MO PAYT .8547 — AN CONST 10.26

#	INT	PRIN	BALANCE
1	6.0827	4.1737	95.8263
2	5.8165	4.4399	91.3864
3	5.5332	4.7232	86.6632
4	5.2319	5.0245	81.6388
5	4.9114	5.3450	76.2938
6	4.5704	5.6860	70.6078
7	4.2077	6.0487	64.5591
8	3.8219	6.4345	58.1246
9	3.4114	6.8450	51.2796
10	2.9747	7.2817	43.9979
11	2.5102	7.7462	36.2517
12	2.0161	8.2403	28.0113
13	1.4904	8.7660	19.2453
14	.9312	9.3252	9.9201
15	.3363	9.9201	0.0000

YEARS 16 — MO PAYT .8224 — AN CONST 9.87

#	INT	PRIN	BALANCE
1	6.0939	3.7753	96.2247
2	5.8531	4.0161	92.2086
3	5.5969	4.2723	87.9363
4	5.3243	4.5449	83.3915
5	5.0344	4.8348	78.5567
6	4.7260	5.1432	73.4135
7	4.3979	5.4713	67.9422
8	4.0489	5.8203	62.1218
9	3.6776	6.1916	55.9302
10	3.2826	6.5866	49.3436
11	2.8624	7.0068	42.3368
12	2.4154	7.4538	34.8831
13	1.9399	7.9292	26.9538
14	1.4341	8.4351	18.5188
15	.8960	8.9732	9.5456
16	.3236	9.5456	0.0000

YEARS 17 — MO PAYT .7942 — AN CONST 9.54

#	INT	PRIN	BALANCE
1	6.1037	3.4273	96.5727
2	5.8851	3.6459	92.9269
3	5.6525	3.8785	89.0484
4	5.4051	4.1259	84.9225
5	5.1419	4.3891	80.5334
6	4.8619	4.6691	75.8643
7	4.5640	4.9669	70.8974
8	4.2472	5.2838	65.6136
9	3.9101	5.6208	59.9928
10	3.5515	5.9794	54.0134
11	3.1701	6.3609	47.6525
12	2.7643	6.7666	40.8859
13	2.3327	7.1983	33.6876
14	1.8735	7.6575	26.0301
15	1.3850	8.1460	17.8841
16	.8653	8.6656	9.2184
17	.3125	9.2184	0.0000

YEARS 18 — MO PAYT .7695 — AN CONST 9.24

#	INT	PRIN	BALANCE
1	6.1123	3.1212	96.8788
2	5.9132	3.3203	93.5585
3	5.7014	3.5321	90.0264
4	5.4761	3.7574	86.2690
5	5.2364	3.9971	82.2719
6	4.9814	4.2521	78.0198
7	4.7101	4.5233	73.4965
8	4.4216	4.8119	68.6846
9	4.1146	5.1189	63.5657
10	3.7881	5.4454	58.1203
11	3.4407	5.7928	52.3275
12	3.0711	6.1623	46.1652
13	2.6780	6.5554	39.6097
14	2.2598	6.9736	32.6361
15	1.8150	7.4185	25.2176
16	1.3417	7.8917	17.3259
17	.8383	8.3952	8.9307
18	.3028	8.9307	0.0000

YEARS 19 — MO PAYT .7475 — AN CONST 8.98

#	INT	PRIN	BALANCE
1	6.1199	2.8504	97.1496
2	5.9381	3.0322	94.1174
3	5.7446	3.2256	90.8918
4	5.5389	3.4314	87.4603
5	5.3200	3.6503	83.8100
6	5.0871	3.8832	79.9269
7	4.8394	4.1309	75.7960
8	4.5759	4.3944	71.4015
9	4.2955	4.6747	66.7268
10	3.9973	4.9730	61.7538
11	3.6801	5.2902	56.4636
12	3.3426	5.6277	50.8360
13	2.9836	5.9867	44.8493
14	2.6017	6.3686	38.4807
15	2.1954	6.7749	31.7059
16	1.7632	7.2070	24.4988
17	1.3035	7.6668	16.8320
18	.8144	8.1559	8.6762
19	.2941	8.6762	0.0000

YEARS 20 — MO PAYT .7280 — AN CONST 8.74

#	INT	PRIN	BALANCE
1	6.1267	2.6095	97.3905
2	5.9602	2.7760	94.6145
3	5.7831	2.9531	91.6614
4	5.5947	3.1415	88.5199
5	5.3943	3.3419	85.1780
6	5.1811	3.5551	81.6230
7	4.9544	3.7818	77.8411
8	4.7131	4.0231	73.8180
9	4.4565	4.2797	69.5383
10	4.1834	4.5528	64.9855
11	3.8930	4.8432	60.1424
12	3.5841	5.1521	54.9902
13	3.2554	5.4808	49.5094
14	2.9057	5.8305	43.6789
15	2.5338	6.2024	37.4765
16	2.1381	6.5981	30.8785
17	1.7172	7.0190	23.8595
18	1.2695	7.4667	16.3928
19	.7932	7.9430	8.4498
20	.2865	8.4498	0.0000

YEARS 21 — MO PAYT .7106 — AN CONST 8.53

#	INT	PRIN	BALANCE
1	6.1327	2.3943	97.6057
2	5.9800	2.5470	95.0586
3	5.8175	2.7095	92.3491

#	INT	PRIN	BALANCE
4	5.6447	2.8824	89.4667
5	5.4608	3.0663	86.4005
6	5.2652	3.2619	83.1386
7	5.0571	3.4699	79.6687
8	4.8357	3.6913	75.9774
9	4.6003	3.9268	72.0506
10	4.3498	4.1773	67.8733
11	4.0833	4.4438	63.4296
12	3.7998	4.7272	58.7024
13	3.4982	5.0288	53.6736
14	3.1774	5.3496	48.3240
15	2.8362	5.6909	42.6331
16	2.4731	6.0539	36.5792
17	2.0870	6.4401	30.1392
18	1.6761	6.8509	23.2882
19	1.2391	7.2879	16.0003
20	.7742	7.7529	8.2474
21	.2796	8.2474	0.0000

YEARS 22	MO PAYT .6949	AN CONST 8.34	
#	INT	PRIN	BALANCE
1	6.1381	2.2012	97.7988
2	5.9977	2.3416	95.4572
3	5.8484	2.4910	92.9662
4	5.6894	2.6499	90.3163
5	5.5204	2.8189	87.4974
6	5.3406	2.9988	84.4986
7	5.1493	3.1901	81.3086
8	4.9458	3.3936	77.9150
9	4.7293	3.6100	74.3050
10	4.4990	3.8403	70.4646
11	4.2540	4.0853	66.3793
12	3.9934	4.3459	62.0334
13	3.7162	4.6232	57.4102
14	3.4212	4.9181	52.4921
15	3.1075	5.2318	47.2603
16	2.7737	5.5656	41.6947
17	2.4187	5.9206	35.7741
18	2.0410	6.2983	29.4757
19	1.6392	6.7001	22.7756
20	1.2118	7.1275	15.6481
21	.7571	7.5822	8.0659
22	.2734	8.0659	0.0000

YEARS 23	MO PAYT .6809	AN CONST 8.18	
#	INT	PRIN	BALANCE
1	6.1430	2.0272	97.9728
2	6.0137	2.1566	95.8162
3	5.8761	2.2941	93.5221
4	5.7298	2.4405	91.0816
5	5.5741	2.5962	88.4854
6	5.4085	2.7618	85.7236
7	5.2323	2.9380	82.7857
8	5.0449	3.1254	79.6603
9	4.8455	3.3248	76.3355
10	4.6334	3.5369	72.7986
11	4.4078	3.7625	69.0362
12	4.1678	4.0025	65.0337
13	3.9124	4.2578	60.7758
14	3.6408	4.5295	56.2464
15	3.3519	4.8184	51.4280
16	3.0445	5.1258	46.3022
17	2.7175	5.4528	40.8494
18	2.3697	5.8006	35.0488
19	1.9996	6.1706	28.8782
20	1.6060	6.5643	22.3139
21	1.1872	6.9830	15.3309
22	.7418	7.4285	7.9024
23	.2679	7.9024	0.0000

YEARS 24	MO PAYT .6681	AN CONST 8.02	
#	INT	PRIN	BALANCE
1	6.1475	1.8700	98.1300
2	6.0282	1.9893	96.1406
3	5.9013	2.1162	94.0244
4	5.7663	2.2512	91.7732
5	5.6226	2.3948	89.3783
6	5.4699	2.5476	86.8307
7	5.3073	2.7101	84.1206
8	5.1345	2.8830	81.2375
9	4.9505	3.0669	78.1706
10	4.7549	3.2626	74.9080
11	4.5468	3.4707	71.4373
12	4.3254	3.6921	67.7452
13	4.0898	3.9277	63.8175
14	3.8393	4.1782	59.6393
15	3.5727	4.4447	55.1945
16	3.2892	4.7283	50.4663
17	2.9876	5.0299	45.4363
18	2.6667	5.3508	40.0855
19	2.3254	5.6921	34.3934
20	1.9622	6.0552	28.3382
21	1.5760	6.4415	21.8966
22	1.1650	6.8524	15.0442
23	.7279	7.2896	7.7546
24	.2629	7.7546	0.0000

YEARS 25	MO PAYT .6566	AN CONST 7.88	
#	INT	PRIN	BALANCE
1	6.1515	1.7275	98.2725
2	6.0413	1.8377	96.4347
3	5.9240	1.9550	94.4798
4	5.7993	2.0797	92.4001
5	5.6666	2.2123	90.1878
6	5.5255	2.3535	87.8343
7	5.3754	2.5036	85.3307
8	5.2157	2.6633	82.6673
9	5.0458	2.8332	79.8341
10	4.8650	3.0140	76.8202
11	4.6728	3.2062	73.6139
12	4.4682	3.4108	70.2032
13	4.2506	3.6283	66.5748
14	4.0192	3.8598	62.7150
15	3.7730	4.1060	58.6090
16	3.5110	4.3680	54.2410
17	3.2324	4.6466	49.5944
18	2.9360	4.9430	44.6514
19	2.6206	5.2584	39.3931
20	2.2852	5.5938	33.7993
21	1.9283	5.9506	27.8486
22	1.5487	6.3302	21.5184
23	1.1449	6.7341	14.7843
24	.7153	7.1637	7.6206
25	.2583	7.6206	0.0000

YEARS 26	MO PAYT .6461	AN CONST 7.76	
#	INT	PRIN	BALANCE
1	6.1551	1.5980	98.4020
2	6.0532	1.6999	96.7021
3	5.9447	1.8084	94.8937
4	5.8294	1.9237	92.9700
5	5.7066	2.0464	90.9236
6	5.5761	2.1770	88.7466
7	5.4372	2.3159	86.4307
8	5.2895	2.4636	83.9671
9	5.1323	2.6208	81.3463
10	4.9651	2.7879	78.5584
11	4.7873	2.9658	75.5926
12	4.5981	3.1550	72.4376
13	4.3968	3.3563	69.0813
14	4.1827	3.5704	65.5110
15	3.9550	3.7981	61.7129
16	3.7127	4.0404	57.6724
17	3.4549	4.2982	53.3743
18	3.1807	4.5724	48.8019
19	2.8890	4.8640	43.9379
20	2.5788	5.1743	38.7636
21	2.2487	5.5044	33.2591
22	1.8975	5.8556	27.4036
23	1.5240	6.2291	21.1745
24	1.1266	6.6265	14.5480
25	.7039	7.0492	7.4989
26	.2542	7.4989	0.0000

YEARS 27	MO PAYT .6365	AN CONST 7.64	
#	INT	PRIN	BALANCE
1	6.1584	1.4799	98.5201
2	6.0640	1.5743	96.9457
3	5.9636	1.6748	95.2710
4	5.8567	1.7816	93.4894
5	5.7431	1.8953	91.5941
6	5.6222	2.0162	89.5780
7	5.4936	2.1448	87.4332
8	5.3567	2.2816	85.1516
9	5.2112	2.4271	82.7245
10	5.0564	2.5820	80.1425
11	4.8917	2.7467	77.3958
12	4.7164	2.9219	74.4739
13	4.5300	3.1083	71.3656
14	4.3318	3.3066	68.0590
15	4.1208	3.5175	64.5415
16	3.8964	3.7419	60.7996
17	3.6577	3.9806	56.8189
18	3.4038	4.2346	52.5844
19	3.1337	4.5047	48.0797
20	2.8463	4.7921	43.2876
21	2.5406	5.0978	38.1899
22	2.2154	5.4229	32.7669
23	1.8694	5.7689	26.9980
24	1.5014	6.1369	20.8611
25	1.1099	6.5284	14.3327
26	.6935	6.9449	7.3879
27	.2505	7.3879	0.0000

YEARS 28	MO PAYT .6278	AN CONST 7.54	
#	INT	PRIN	BALANCE
1	6.1614	1.3721	98.6279
2	6.0739	1.4596	97.1683
3	5.9808	1.5527	95.6156
4	5.8818	1.6518	93.9638
5	5.7764	1.7572	92.2066
6	5.6643	1.8693	90.3374
7	5.5450	1.9885	88.3489
8	5.4182	2.1153	86.2335
9	5.2832	2.2503	83.9832
10	5.1397	2.3938	81.5894
11	4.9870	2.5465	79.0428
12	4.8245	2.7090	76.3338
13	4.6517	2.8818	73.4520
14	4.4679	3.0657	70.3864
15	4.2723	3.2612	67.1252
16	4.0643	3.4693	63.6559
17	3.8430	3.6906	59.9653
18	3.6075	3.9260	56.0393
19	3.3571	4.1765	51.8629
20	3.0907	4.4429	47.4200
21	2.8072	4.7263	42.6937
22	2.5057	5.0278	37.6659
23	2.1850	5.3485	32.3173
24	1.8438	5.6897	26.6276
25	1.4808	6.0527	20.5749
26	1.0947	6.4388	14.1361
27	.6840	6.8496	7.2865
28	.2470	7.2865	0.0000

YEARS 29	MO PAYT .6198	AN CONST 7.44	
#	INT	PRIN	BALANCE
1	6.1642	1.2734	98.7266
2	6.0830	1.3546	97.3720
3	5.9966	1.4410	95.9310
4	5.9046	1.5330	94.3980
5	5.8069	1.6308	92.7673
6	5.7028	1.7348	91.0325
7	5.5922	1.8454	89.1870
8	5.4744	1.9632	87.2238
9	5.3492	2.0884	85.1354
10	5.2160	2.2216	82.9138
11	5.0742	2.3634	80.5504
12	4.9235	2.5141	78.0363
13	4.7631	2.6745	75.3618
14	4.5925	2.8451	72.5167
15	4.4110	3.0266	69.4901
16	4.2179	3.2197	66.2704
17	4.0125	3.4251	62.8453
18	3.7940	3.6436	59.2017
19	3.5616	3.8760	55.3257
20	3.3143	4.1233	51.2025
21	3.0513	4.3863	46.8162
22	2.7715	4.6661	42.1500
23	2.4738	4.9638	37.1863
24	2.1572	5.2804	31.9058
25	1.8203	5.6173	26.2885
26	1.4620	5.9756	20.3129
27	1.0808	6.3568	13.9561
28	.6753	6.7623	7.1937
29	.2439	7.1937	0.0000

YEARS 30	MO PAYT .6125	AN CONST 7.35	
#	INT	PRIN	BALANCE
1	6.1668	1.1829	98.8171
2	6.0913	1.2583	97.5588
3	6.0110	1.3386	96.2202
4	5.9256	1.4240	94.7962
5	5.8348	1.5148	93.2814
6	5.7382	1.6115	91.6699
7	5.6354	1.7143	89.9557
8	5.5260	1.8236	88.1321
9	5.4097	1.9400	86.1921
10	5.2859	2.0637	84.1284
11	5.1543	2.1954	81.9330
12	5.0142	2.3354	79.5976
13	4.8652	2.4844	77.1133
14	4.7068	2.6429	74.4704
15	4.5382	2.8115	71.6589
16	4.3588	2.9908	68.6681
17	4.1680	3.1816	65.4865
18	3.9651	3.3846	62.1019
19	3.7491	3.6005	58.5015
20	3.5195	3.8302	54.6713
21	3.2751	4.0745	50.5968
22	3.0152	4.3344	46.2624
23	2.7387	4.6109	41.6515
24	2.4446	4.9051	36.7464
25	2.1317	5.2180	31.5284
26	1.7988	5.5508	25.9776
27	1.4447	5.9049	20.0726
28	1.0680	6.2816	13.7910
29	.6673	6.6824	7.1086
30	.2410	7.1086	0.0000

YEARS 2 — MO PAYT 4.4433 — AN CONST 53.33

#	INT	PRIN	BALANCE
1	4.8780	48.4421	51.5579
2	1.7621	51.5579	0.0000

YEARS 3 — MO PAYT 3.0535 — AN CONST 36.65

#	INT	PRIN	BALANCE
1	5.3641	31.2783	68.7217
2	3.3522	33.2902	35.4315
3	1.2109	35.4315	0.0000

YEARS 4 — MO PAYT 2.3600 — AN CONST 28.32

#	INT	PRIN	BALANCE
1	5.6067	22.7131	77.2869
2	4.1457	24.1740	53.1129
3	2.5908	25.7290	27.3839
4	.9359	27.3839	0.0000

YEARS 5 — MO PAYT 1.9449 — AN CONST 23.34

#	INT	PRIN	BALANCE
1	5.7519	17.5872	82.4128
2	4.6206	18.7185	63.6943
3	3.4166	19.9225	43.7718
4	2.1352	21.2039	22.5678
5	.7713	22.5678	0.0000

YEARS 6 — MO PAYT 1.6691 — AN CONST 20.03

#	INT	PRIN	BALANCE
1	5.8483	14.1810	85.8190
2	4.9362	15.0932	70.7258
3	3.9654	16.0640	54.6618
4	2.9321	17.0973	37.5645
5	1.8324	18.1970	19.3675
6	.6619	19.3675	0.0000

YEARS 7 — MO PAYT 1.4729 — AN CONST 17.68

#	INT	PRIN	BALANCE
1	5.9170	11.7575	88.2425
2	5.1607	12.5137	75.7288
3	4.3558	13.3186	62.4102
4	3.4991	14.1753	48.2349
5	2.5874	15.0871	33.1479
6	1.6169	16.0575	17.0904
7	.5841	17.0904	0.0000

YEARS 8 — MO PAYT 1.3263 — AN CONST 15.92

#	INT	PRIN	BALANCE
1	5.9682	9.9480	90.0520
2	5.3284	10.5878	79.4642
3	4.6473	11.2689	68.1954
4	3.9225	11.9937	56.2017
5	3.1511	12.7651	43.4365
6	2.3300	13.5862	29.8503
7	1.4561	14.4601	15.3902
8	.5260	15.3902	0.0000

YEARS 9 — MO PAYT 1.2130 — AN CONST 14.56

#	INT	PRIN	BALANCE
1	6.0079	8.5478	91.4522
2	5.4581	9.0976	82.3546
3	4.8729	9.6828	72.6718
4	4.2501	10.3056	62.3662
5	3.5872	10.9685	51.3977
6	2.8817	11.6740	39.7237
7	2.1308	12.4249	27.2988
8	1.3316	13.2241	14.0747
9	.4810	14.0747	0.0000

YEARS 10 — MO PAYT 1.1228 — AN CONST 13.48

#	INT	PRIN	BALANCE
1	6.0394	7.4342	92.5658
2	5.5613	7.9124	84.6535
3	5.0523	8.4213	76.2322
4	4.5106	8.9630	67.2692
5	3.9341	9.5395	57.7297
6	3.3205	10.1531	47.5767
7	2.6675	10.8061	36.7705
8	1.9724	11.5012	25.2693
9	1.2326	12.2410	13.0283
10	.4453	13.0283	0.0000

YEARS 11 — MO PAYT 1.0495 — AN CONST 12.60

#	INT	PRIN	BALANCE
1	6.0651	6.5289	93.4711
2	5.6451	6.9488	86.5223
3	5.1982	7.3958	79.1266
4	4.7225	7.8715	71.2551
5	4.2162	8.3778	62.8773
6	3.6773	8.9167	53.9607
7	3.1037	9.4902	44.4705
8	2.4933	10.1006	34.3698
9	1.8436	10.7503	23.6195
10	1.1522	11.4418	12.1777
11	.4162	12.1777	0.0000

YEARS 12 — MO PAYT .9888 — AN CONST 11.87

#	INT	PRIN	BALANCE
1	6.0863	5.7797	94.2203
2	5.7145	6.1515	88.0687
3	5.3189	6.5472	81.5216
4	4.8977	6.9683	74.5533
5	4.4495	7.4165	67.1367
6	3.9725	7.8936	59.2432
7	3.4647	8.4013	50.8419
8	2.9244	8.9417	41.9002
9	2.3492	9.5168	32.3834
10	1.7371	10.1290	22.2544
11	1.0856	10.7805	11.4739
12	.3921	11.4739	0.0000

YEARS 13 — MO PAYT .9379 — AN CONST 11.26

#	INT	PRIN	BALANCE
1	6.1041	5.1507	94.8493
2	5.7728	5.4820	89.3672
3	5.4202	5.8347	83.5326
4	5.0449	6.2100	77.3226
5	4.6455	6.6094	70.7132
6	4.2203	7.0345	63.6787
7	3.7679	7.4870	56.1917
8	3.2863	7.9686	48.2231
9	2.7737	8.4811	39.7420
10	2.2282	9.0266	30.7154
11	1.6476	9.6073	21.1081
12	1.0296	10.2252	10.8829
13	.3719	10.8829	0.0000

YEARS 14 — MO PAYT .8946 — AN CONST 10.74

#	INT	PRIN	BALANCE
1	6.1193	4.6161	95.3839
2	5.8223	4.9130	90.4710
3	5.5063	5.2290	85.2420
4	5.1700	5.5653	79.6766
5	4.8120	5.9233	73.7533
6	4.4310	6.3043	67.4490
7	4.0255	6.7098	60.7392
8	3.5939	7.1414	53.5979
9	3.1346	7.6007	45.9971
10	2.6457	8.0896	37.9075
11	2.1254	8.6100	29.2975
12	1.5715	9.1638	20.1338
13	.9821	9.7532	10.3805
14	.3548	10.3805	0.0000

YEARS 15 — MO PAYT .8574 — AN CONST 10.29

#	INT	PRIN	BALANCE
1	6.1323	4.1568	95.8432
2	5.8649	4.4242	91.4190
3	5.5803	4.7088	86.7103
4	5.2774	5.0116	81.6986
5	4.9551	5.3340	76.3646
6	4.6120	5.6771	70.6876
7	4.2468	6.0422	64.6453
8	3.8582	6.4309	58.2144
9	3.4445	6.8445	51.3699
10	3.0043	7.2848	44.0851
11	2.5357	7.7534	36.3318
12	2.0370	8.2521	28.0797
13	1.5062	8.7829	19.2968
14	.9413	9.3478	9.9491
15	.3400	9.9491	0.0000

YEARS 16 — MO PAYT .8252 — AN CONST 9.91

#	INT	PRIN	BALANCE
1	6.1435	3.7588	96.2412
2	5.9018	4.0006	92.2406
3	5.6444	4.2579	87.9828
4	5.3706	4.5318	83.4510
5	5.0791	4.8233	78.6277
6	4.7688	5.1335	73.4942
7	4.4386	5.4637	68.0306
8	4.0872	5.8151	62.2154
9	3.7132	6.1892	56.0263
10	3.3151	6.5873	49.4390
11	2.8914	7.0110	42.4280
12	2.4404	7.4619	34.9661
13	1.9604	7.9419	27.0242
14	1.4496	8.4527	18.5715
15	.9059	8.9964	9.5751
16	.3272	9.5751	0.0000

YEARS 17 — MO PAYT .7970 — AN CONST 9.57

#	INT	PRIN	BALANCE
1	6.1534	3.4112	96.5888
2	5.9340	3.6306	92.9583
3	5.7004	3.8641	89.0942
4	5.4519	4.1126	84.9815
5	5.1874	4.3772	80.6043
6	4.9058	4.6587	75.9456
7	4.6062	4.9584	70.9872
8	4.2872	5.2773	65.7099
9	3.9478	5.6168	60.0932
10	3.5865	5.9780	54.1151
11	3.2020	6.3626	47.7526
12	2.7927	6.7718	40.9808
13	2.3572	7.2074	33.7734
14	1.8936	7.6710	26.1024
15	1.4002	8.1644	17.9380
16	.8750	8.6895	9.2485
17	.3161	9.2485	0.0000

YEARS 18 — MO PAYT .7723 — AN CONST 9.27

#	INT	PRIN	BALANCE
1	6.1620	3.1055	96.8945
2	5.9623	3.3052	93.5893
3	5.7497	3.5178	90.0715
4	5.5234	3.7441	86.3274
5	5.2826	3.9849	82.3424
6	5.0263	4.2412	78.1012
7	4.7535	4.5140	73.5871
8	4.4631	4.8044	68.7827
9	4.1541	5.1134	63.6693
10	3.8252	5.4423	58.2270
11	3.4751	5.7924	52.4346
12	3.1025	6.1650	46.2696
13	2.7060	6.5615	39.7081
14	2.2840	6.9836	32.7245
15	1.8348	7.4328	25.2918
16	1.3567	7.9108	17.3809
17	.8478	8.4197	8.9613
18	.3063	8.9613	0.0000

YEARS 19 — MO PAYT .7504 — AN CONST 9.01

#	INT	PRIN	BALANCE
1	6.1697	2.8351	97.1649
2	5.9873	3.0174	94.1475
3	5.7933	3.2115	90.9360
4	5.5867	3.4181	87.5179
5	5.3668	3.6380	83.8799
6	5.1328	3.8720	80.0080
7	4.8838	4.1210	75.8870
8	4.6187	4.3861	71.5009
9	4.3366	4.6682	66.8327
10	4.0363	4.9685	61.8642
11	3.7167	5.2880	56.5762
12	3.3766	5.6282	50.9480
13	3.0146	5.9902	44.9578
14	2.6293	6.3755	38.5824
15	2.2192	6.7856	31.7968
16	1.7827	7.2220	24.5747
17	1.3182	7.6866	16.8882
18	.8238	8.1810	8.7072
19	.2976	8.7072	0.0000

YEARS 20 — MO PAYT .7309 — AN CONST 8.78

#	INT	PRIN	BALANCE
1	6.1765	2.5946	97.4054
2	6.0096	2.7615	94.6439
3	5.8320	2.9391	91.7047
4	5.6429	3.1282	88.5765
5	5.4417	3.3294	85.2471
6	5.2276	3.5436	81.7035
7	4.9997	3.7715	77.9321
8	4.7571	4.0141	73.9180
9	4.4989	4.2723	69.6457
10	4.2241	4.5471	65.0986
11	3.9316	4.8395	60.2591
12	3.6203	5.1508	55.1083
13	3.2890	5.4821	49.6261
14	2.9364	5.8348	43.7914
15	2.5611	6.2101	37.5813
16	2.1616	6.6095	30.9718
17	1.7365	7.0346	23.9371
18	1.2840	7.4871	16.4500
19	.8024	7.9687	8.4813
20	.2899	8.4813	0.0000

YEARS 21 — MO PAYT .7135 — AN CONST 8.57

#	INT	PRIN	BALANCE
1	6.1826	2.3798	97.6202
2	6.0295	2.5329	95.0873
3	5.8666	2.6958	92.3915

MONTHLY PAYMENT AMORTIZATION SCHEDULE PER $100   6.25 %

#	INT	PRIN	BALANCE
4	5.6932	2.8692	89.5223
5	5.5087	3.0538	86.4686
6	5.3122	3.2502	83.2184
7	5.1032	3.4592	79.7592
8	4.8807	3.6817	76.0774
9	4.6439	3.9185	72.1589
10	4.3918	4.1706	67.9883
11	4.1235	4.4389	63.5494
12	3.8380	4.7244	58.8250
13	3.5341	5.0283	53.7968
14	3.2107	5.3517	48.4451
15	2.8665	5.6959	42.7492
16	2.5001	6.0623	36.6869
17	2.1102	6.4522	30.2347
18	1.6952	6.8672	23.3675
19	1.2535	7.3090	16.0585
20	.7833	7.7791	8.2794
21	.2830	8.2794	0.0000

YEARS 22   MO PAYT .6979   AN CONST 8.38

#	INT	PRIN	BALANCE
1	6.1881	2.1871	97.8129
2	6.0474	2.3278	95.4852
3	5.8977	2.4775	93.0077
4	5.7383	2.6368	90.3708
5	5.5687	2.8064	87.5644
6	5.3882	2.9870	84.5774
7	5.1960	3.1791	81.3983
8	4.9916	3.3836	78.0148
9	4.7739	3.6012	74.4136
10	4.5423	3.8328	70.5807
11	4.2958	4.0794	66.5013
12	4.0334	4.3418	62.1595
13	3.7541	4.6210	57.5385
14	3.4569	4.9183	52.6202
15	3.1405	5.2346	47.3856
16	2.8038	5.5713	41.8142
17	2.4454	5.9297	35.8845
18	2.0640	6.3111	29.5734
19	1.6581	6.7170	22.8564
20	1.2260	7.1491	15.7073
21	.7662	7.6089	8.0984
22	.2768	8.0984	0.0000

YEARS 23   MO PAYT .6839   AN CONST 8.21

#	INT	PRIN	BALANCE
1	6.1930	2.0135	97.9865
2	6.0635	2.1430	95.8434
3	5.9256	2.2809	93.5625
4	5.7789	2.4276	91.1349
5	5.6228	2.5837	88.5512
6	5.4566	2.7499	85.8013
7	5.2797	2.9268	82.8744
8	5.0914	3.1151	79.7594
9	4.8911	3.3154	76.4439
10	4.6778	3.5287	72.9152
11	4.4508	3.7557	69.1595
12	4.2093	3.9972	65.1623
13	3.9521	4.2544	60.9079
14	3.6785	4.5280	56.3799
15	3.3872	4.8193	51.5607
16	3.0773	5.1292	46.4315
17	2.7473	5.4592	40.9723
18	2.3962	5.8103	35.1620
19	2.0225	6.1840	28.9780
20	1.6247	6.5818	22.3962
21	1.2014	7.0051	15.3910
22	.7508	7.4557	7.9353
23	.2712	7.9353	0.0000

YEARS 24   MO PAYT .6712   AN CONST 8.06

#	INT	PRIN	BALANCE
1	6.1974	1.8567	98.1433
2	6.0780	1.9761	96.1671
3	5.9509	2.1033	94.0639
4	5.8156	2.2385	91.8253
5	5.6716	2.3825	89.4428
6	5.5184	2.5358	86.9070
7	5.3552	2.6989	84.2082
8	5.1817	2.8725	81.3357
9	4.9969	3.0572	78.2785
10	4.8002	3.2539	75.0246
11	4.5909	3.4632	71.5614
12	4.3682	3.6859	67.8754
13	4.1311	3.9230	63.9524
14	3.8788	4.1754	59.7771
15	3.6102	4.4439	55.3331
16	3.3244	4.7298	50.6034
17	3.0201	5.0340	45.5694
18	2.6963	5.3578	40.2116
19	2.3517	5.7024	34.5091
20	1.9849	6.0692	28.4399
21	1.5945	6.4596	21.9803
22	1.1790	6.8751	15.1053
23	.7368	7.3173	7.7880
24	.2662	7.7880	0.0000

YEARS 25   MO PAYT .6597   AN CONST 7.92

#	INT	PRIN	BALANCE
1	6.2014	1.7146	98.2854
2	6.0912	1.8249	96.4605
3	5.9738	1.9423	94.5183
4	5.8488	2.0672	92.4511
5	5.7159	2.2002	90.2509
6	5.5744	2.3417	87.9092
7	5.4237	2.4923	85.4169
8	5.2634	2.6526	82.7643
9	5.0928	2.8232	79.9411
10	4.9112	3.0048	76.9363
11	4.7179	3.1981	73.7382
12	4.5122	3.4038	70.3344
13	4.2933	3.6227	66.7117
14	4.0603	3.8558	62.8559
15	3.8123	4.1038	58.7521
16	3.5483	4.3677	54.3844
17	3.2674	4.6487	49.7357
18	2.9683	4.9477	44.7880
19	2.6501	5.2659	39.5221
20	2.3114	5.6046	33.9175
21	1.9509	5.9651	27.9523
22	1.5672	6.3488	21.6035
23	1.1588	6.7572	14.8463
24	.7242	7.1918	7.6544
25	.2616	7.6544	0.0000

YEARS 26   MO PAYT .6492   AN CONST 7.80

#	INT	PRIN	BALANCE
1	6.2051	1.5854	98.4146
2	6.1031	1.6874	96.7272
3	5.9946	1.7959	94.9312
4	5.8791	1.9115	93.0197
5	5.7561	2.0344	90.9853
6	5.6253	2.1653	88.8200
7	5.4860	2.3045	86.5155
8	5.3377	2.4528	84.0627
9	5.1800	2.6105	81.4522
10	5.0121	2.7785	78.6737
11	4.8333	2.9572	75.7165
12	4.6431	3.1474	72.5691
13	4.4407	3.3498	69.2193
14	4.2252	3.5653	65.6540
15	3.9959	3.7946	61.8594
16	3.7518	4.0387	57.8206
17	3.4920	4.2985	53.5222
18	3.2156	4.5750	48.9472
19	2.9213	4.8692	44.0779
20	2.6081	5.1824	38.8955
21	2.2747	5.5158	33.3797
22	1.9200	5.8706	27.5091
23	1.5424	6.2482	21.2610
24	1.1405	6.6501	14.6109
25	.7127	7.0778	7.5331
26	.2575	7.5331	0.0000

YEARS 27   MO PAYT .6397   AN CONST 7.68

#	INT	PRIN	BALANCE
1	6.2084	1.4678	98.5322
2	6.1140	1.5622	96.9701
3	6.0135	1.6626	95.3074
4	5.9066	1.7696	93.5378
5	5.7928	1.8834	91.6544
6	5.6716	2.0046	89.6499
7	5.5427	2.1335	87.5164
8	5.4055	2.2707	85.2457
9	5.2594	2.4168	82.8289
10	5.1040	2.5722	80.2566
11	4.9385	2.7377	77.5190
12	4.7624	2.9138	74.6052
13	4.5750	3.1012	71.5040
14	4.3755	3.3007	68.2033
15	4.1632	3.5130	64.6903
16	3.9372	3.7389	60.9514
17	3.6968	3.9794	56.9720
18	3.4408	4.2354	52.7366
19	3.1684	4.5078	48.2288
20	2.8784	4.7978	43.4310
21	2.5698	5.1064	38.3246
22	2.2414	5.4348	32.8898
23	1.8918	5.7844	27.1054
24	1.5197	6.1565	20.9489
25	1.1237	6.5525	14.3964
26	.7023	6.9739	7.4225
27	.2537	7.4225	0.0000

YEARS 28   MO PAYT .6310   AN CONST 7.58

#	INT	PRIN	BALANCE
1	6.2115	1.3603	98.6397
2	6.1240	1.4478	97.1919
3	6.0309	1.5409	95.6510
4	5.9317	1.6400	94.0110
5	5.8262	1.7455	92.2655
6	5.7140	1.8578	90.4077
7	5.5945	1.9773	88.4304
8	5.4673	2.1045	86.3259
9	5.3319	2.2398	84.0861
10	5.1879	2.3839	81.7022
11	5.0345	2.5372	79.1649
12	4.8713	2.7004	76.4645
13	4.6976	2.8741	73.5903
14	4.5128	3.0590	70.5313
15	4.3160	3.2558	67.2756
16	4.1066	3.4652	63.8104
17	3.8837	3.6881	60.1223
18	3.6465	3.9253	56.1970
19	3.3940	4.1778	52.0192
20	3.1253	4.4465	47.5727
21	2.8393	4.7325	42.8402
22	2.5348	5.0369	37.8033
23	2.2109	5.3609	32.4424
24	1.8660	5.7057	26.7367
25	1.4990	6.0727	20.6639
26	1.1084	6.4633	14.2006
27	.6927	6.8791	7.3215
28	.2502	7.3215	0.0000

YEARS 29   MO PAYT .6230   AN CONST 7.48

#	INT	PRIN	BALANCE
1	6.2143	1.2620	98.7380
2	6.1331	1.3431	97.3949
3	6.0467	1.4295	95.9654
4	5.9547	1.5215	94.4439
5	5.8569	1.6193	92.8246
6	5.7527	1.7235	91.1011
7	5.6419	1.8343	89.2668
8	5.5239	1.9523	87.3144
9	5.3983	2.0779	85.2365
10	5.2646	2.2116	83.0249
11	5.1224	2.3538	80.6711
12	4.9710	2.5052	78.1659
13	4.8098	2.6664	75.4995
14	4.6383	2.8379	72.6617
15	4.4558	3.0204	69.6413
16	4.2615	3.2147	66.4266
17	4.0548	3.4215	63.0051
18	3.8347	3.6415	59.3636
19	3.6004	3.8758	55.4878
20	3.3512	4.1251	51.3628
21	3.0858	4.3904	46.9724
22	2.8034	4.6728	42.2996
23	2.5029	4.9734	37.3262
24	2.1830	5.2932	32.0330
25	1.8425	5.6337	26.3993
26	1.4801	5.9961	20.4032
27	1.0944	6.3818	14.0214
28	.6840	6.7923	7.2291
29	.2471	7.2291	0.0000

YEARS 30   MO PAYT .6157   AN CONST 7.39

#	INT	PRIN	BALANCE
1	6.2168	1.1718	98.8282
2	6.1414	1.2472	97.5810
3	6.0612	1.3274	96.2536
4	5.9758	1.4128	94.8409
5	5.8850	1.5036	93.3372
6	5.7883	1.6004	91.7369
7	5.6853	1.7033	90.0336
8	5.5758	1.8129	88.2207
9	5.4591	1.9295	86.2913
10	5.3350	2.0536	84.2377
11	5.2030	2.1857	82.0521
12	5.0624	2.3262	79.7258
13	4.9127	2.4759	77.2500
14	4.7535	2.6351	74.6148
15	4.5840	2.8046	71.8102
16	4.4036	2.9850	68.8252
17	4.2116	3.1770	65.6482
18	4.0072	3.3814	62.2668
19	3.7897	3.5989	58.6680
20	3.5583	3.8303	54.8376
21	3.3119	4.0767	50.7609
22	3.0497	4.3389	46.4219
23	2.7706	4.6180	41.8039
24	2.4735	4.9151	36.8888
25	2.1574	5.2312	31.6576
26	1.8209	5.5677	26.0899
27	1.4628	5.9258	20.1641
28	1.0816	6.3070	13.8571
29	.6759	6.7127	7.1444
30	.2442	7.1444	0.0000

YEARS 2 — MO PAYT 4.4456 — AN CONST 53.35

#	INT	PRIN	BALANCE
1	4.9175	48.4296	51.5704
2	1.7767	51.5704	0.0000

YEARS 3 — MO PAYT 3.0558 — AN CONST 36.67

#	INT	PRIN	BALANCE
1	5.4075	31.2621	68.7379
2	3.3802	33.2895	35.4484
3	1.2213	35.4484	0.0000

YEARS 4 — MO PAYT 2.3623 — AN CONST 28.35

#	INT	PRIN	BALANCE
1	5.6521	22.6953	77.3047
2	4.1803	24.1671	53.1376
3	2.6130	25.7344	27.4033
4	.9441	27.4033	0.0000

YEARS 5 — MO PAYT 1.9473 — AN CONST 23.37

#	INT	PRIN	BALANCE
1	5.7985	17.5687	82.4313
2	4.6591	18.7080	63.7233
3	3.4459	19.9213	43.8021
4	2.1539	21.2132	22.5889
5	.7782	22.5889	0.0000

YEARS 6 — MO PAYT 1.6715 — AN CONST 20.06

#	INT	PRIN	BALANCE
1	5.8957	14.1621	85.8379
2	4.9773	15.0806	70.7573
3	3.9993	16.0586	54.6987
4	2.9579	17.1000	37.5988
5	1.8489	18.2089	19.3898
6	.6680	19.3898	0.0000

YEARS 7 — MO PAYT 1.4753 — AN CONST 17.71

#	INT	PRIN	BALANCE
1	5.9649	11.7385	88.2615
2	5.2036	12.4997	75.7618
3	4.3930	13.3103	62.4515
4	3.5298	14.1735	48.2779
5	2.6107	15.0927	33.1852
6	1.6319	16.0715	17.1137
7	.5896	17.1137	0.0000

YEARS 8 — MO PAYT 1.3288 — AN CONST 15.95

#	INT	PRIN	BALANCE
1	6.0166	9.9290	90.0710
2	5.3726	10.5729	79.4980
3	4.6870	11.2586	68.2394
4	3.9568	11.9888	56.2506
5	3.1793	12.7662	43.4844
6	2.3514	13.5941	29.8903
7	1.4698	14.4757	15.4145
8	.5311	15.4145	0.0000

YEARS 9 — MO PAYT 1.2155 — AN CONST 14.59

#	INT	PRIN	BALANCE
1	6.0565	8.5291	91.4709
2	5.5034	9.0822	82.3888
3	4.9144	9.6712	72.7176
4	4.2872	10.2984	62.4192
5	3.6194	10.9662	51.4530
6	2.9082	11.6774	39.7756
7	2.1509	12.4347	27.3409
8	1.3445	13.2411	14.0998
9	.4858	14.0998	0.0000

YEARS 10 — MO PAYT 1.1253 — AN CONST 13.51

#	INT	PRIN	BALANCE
1	6.0883	7.4157	92.5843
2	5.6074	7.8966	84.6878
3	5.0953	8.4087	76.2791
4	4.5500	8.9540	67.3251
5	3.9693	9.5347	57.7904
6	3.3510	10.1530	47.6374
7	2.6925	10.8114	36.8260
8	1.9914	11.5126	25.3134
9	1.2448	12.2592	13.0542
10	.4498	13.0542	0.0000

YEARS 11 — MO PAYT 1.0521 — AN CONST 12.63

#	INT	PRIN	BALANCE
1	6.1141	6.5106	93.4894
2	5.6919	6.9329	86.5565
3	5.2423	7.3825	79.1741
4	4.7635	7.8612	71.3128
5	4.2537	8.3710	62.9418
6	3.7109	8.9139	54.0279
7	3.1328	9.4920	44.5359
8	2.5172	10.1075	34.4284
9	1.8617	10.7630	23.6653
10	1.1637	11.4610	12.2043
11	.4205	12.2043	0.0000

YEARS 12 — MO PAYT .9914 — AN CONST 11.90

#	INT	PRIN	BALANCE
1	6.1355	5.7618	94.2382
2	5.7619	6.1355	88.1027
3	5.3640	6.5334	81.5693
4	4.9403	6.9571	74.6122
5	4.4891	7.4083	67.2039
6	4.0086	7.8887	59.3152
7	3.4971	8.4003	50.9149
8	2.9523	8.9451	41.9698
9	2.3722	9.5252	32.4447
10	1.7545	10.1429	22.3018
11	1.0967	10.8007	11.5011
12	.3962	11.5011	0.0000

YEARS 13 — MO PAYT .9406 — AN CONST 11.29

#	INT	PRIN	BALANCE
1	6.1535	5.1332	94.8668
2	5.8206	5.4661	89.4008
3	5.4661	5.8206	83.5802
4	5.0886	6.1980	77.3822
5	4.6867	6.6000	70.7822
6	4.2586	7.0280	63.7542
7	3.8029	7.4838	56.2704
8	3.3175	7.9691	48.3014
9	2.8007	8.4859	39.8154
10	2.2504	9.0362	30.7792
11	1.6644	9.6222	21.1570
12	1.0404	10.2463	10.9107
13	.3759	10.9107	0.0000

YEARS 14 — MO PAYT .8973 — AN CONST 10.77

#	INT	PRIN	BALANCE
1	6.1687	4.5989	95.4011
2	5.8705	4.8971	90.5040
3	5.5529	5.2147	85.2893
4	5.2147	5.5529	79.7365
5	4.8546	5.9130	73.8235
6	4.4711	6.2964	67.5270
7	4.0628	6.7048	60.8222
8	3.6280	7.1396	53.6826
9	3.1650	7.6026	46.0800
10	2.6719	8.0956	37.9844
11	2.1469	8.6207	29.3637
12	1.5879	9.1797	20.1840
13	.9925	9.7750	10.4090
14	.3586	10.4090	0.0000

YEARS 15 — MO PAYT .8602 — AN CONST 10.33

#	INT	PRIN	BALANCE
1	6.1818	4.1400	95.8600
2	5.9133	4.4085	91.4515
3	5.6274	4.6944	86.7572
4	5.3230	4.9988	81.7584
5	4.9988	5.3230	76.4354
6	4.6536	5.6682	70.7672
7	4.2860	6.0358	64.7314
8	3.8946	6.4272	58.3042
9	3.4778	6.8440	51.4602
10	3.0339	7.2879	44.1723
11	2.5613	7.7605	36.4118
12	2.0580	8.2638	28.1481
13	1.5221	8.7997	19.3484
14	.9514	9.3704	9.9780
15	.3438	9.9780	0.0000

YEARS 16 — MO PAYT .8280 — AN CONST 9.94

#	INT	PRIN	BALANCE
1	6.1932	3.7424	96.2576
2	5.9505	3.9851	92.2726
3	5.6920	4.2435	88.0291
4	5.4168	4.5187	83.5104
5	5.1238	4.8117	78.6987
6	4.8117	5.1238	73.5749
7	4.4795	5.4561	68.1188
8	4.1256	5.8099	62.3089
9	3.7488	6.1867	56.1223
10	3.3476	6.5879	49.5344
11	2.9204	7.0151	42.5192
12	2.4655	7.4701	35.0492
13	1.9810	7.9545	27.0947
14	1.4652	8.4704	18.6243
15	.9158	9.0197	9.6046
16	.3309	9.6046	0.0000

YEARS 17 — MO PAYT .7999 — AN CONST 9.60

#	INT	PRIN	BALANCE
1	6.2031	3.3951	96.6049
2	5.9829	3.6153	92.9896
3	5.7484	3.8498	89.1398
4	5.4988	4.0994	85.0404
5	5.2329	4.3653	80.6751
6	4.9498	4.6484	76.0268
7	4.6484	4.9498	71.0769
8	4.3274	5.2708	65.8061
9	3.9856	5.6126	60.1935
10	3.6216	5.9766	54.2168
11	3.2340	6.3642	47.8526
12	2.8213	6.7770	41.0757
13	2.3818	7.2164	33.8592
14	1.9138	7.6844	26.1748
15	1.4154	8.1828	17.9920
16	.8847	8.7135	9.2785
17	.3197	9.2785	0.0000

YEARS 18 — MO PAYT .7751 — AN CONST 9.31

#	INT	PRIN	BALANCE
1	6.2118	3.0898	96.9102
2	6.0114	3.2902	93.6199
3	5.7980	3.5036	90.1163
4	5.5708	3.7308	86.3855
5	5.3289	3.9728	82.4128
6	5.0712	4.2304	78.1824
7	4.7969	4.5047	73.6776
8	4.5048	4.7969	68.8808
9	4.1937	5.1080	63.7728
10	3.8624	5.4392	58.3336
11	3.5097	5.7920	52.5416
12	3.1341	6.1676	46.3740
13	2.7341	6.5676	39.8065
14	2.3082	6.9935	32.8130
15	1.8546	7.4470	25.3660
16	1.3717	7.9300	17.4361
17	.8574	8.4442	8.9918
18	.3098	8.9918	0.0000

YEARS 19 — MO PAYT .7533 — AN CONST 9.04

#	INT	PRIN	BALANCE
1	6.2195	2.8198	97.1802
2	6.0366	3.0027	94.1774
3	5.8419	3.1974	90.9800
4	5.6345	3.4048	87.5752
5	5.4137	3.6256	83.9496
6	5.1786	3.8607	80.0889
7	4.9282	4.1111	75.9778
8	4.6616	4.3777	71.6001
9	4.3777	4.6616	66.9384
10	4.0754	4.9639	61.9745
11	3.7535	5.2858	56.6887
12	3.4107	5.6286	51.0600
13	3.0457	5.9937	45.0664
14	2.6570	6.3824	38.6840
15	2.2431	6.7963	31.8877
16	1.8023	7.2370	24.6507
17	1.3330	7.7063	16.9444
18	.8332	8.2061	8.7383
19	.3011	8.7383	0.0000

YEARS 20 — MO PAYT .7338 — AN CONST 8.81

#	INT	PRIN	BALANCE
1	6.2264	2.5798	97.4202
2	6.0591	2.7471	94.6731
3	5.8809	2.9252	91.7479
4	5.6912	3.1150	88.6329
5	5.4892	3.3170	85.3160
6	5.2741	3.5321	81.7839
7	5.0450	3.7611	78.0227
8	4.8011	4.0050	74.0177
9	4.5414	4.2648	69.7529
10	4.2648	4.5414	65.2116
11	3.9703	4.8359	60.3757
12	3.6567	5.1495	55.2262
13	3.3227	5.4834	49.7428
14	2.9671	5.8390	43.9038
15	2.5884	6.2177	37.6860
16	2.1852	6.6209	31.0651
17	1.7558	7.0503	24.0148
18	1.2986	7.5075	16.5073
19	.8117	7.9944	8.5129
20	.2933	8.5129	0.0000

YEARS 21 — MO PAYT .7165 — AN CONST 8.60

#	INT	PRIN	BALANCE
1	6.2325	2.3654	97.6346
2	6.0791	2.5188	95.1159
3	5.9157	2.6821	92.4337

#	INT	PRIN	BALANCE
4	5.7418	2.8561	89.5777
5	5.5566	3.0413	86.5364
6	5.3593	3.2385	83.2979
7	5.1493	3.4485	79.8494
8	4.9257	3.6722	76.1772
9	4.6875	3.9103	72.2669
10	4.4339	4.1639	68.1030
11	4.1639	4.4339	63.6691
12	3.8764	4.7215	58.9476
13	3.5702	5.0277	53.9199
14	3.2441	5.3537	48.5662
15	2.8969	5.7009	42.8653
16	2.5272	6.0706	36.7946
17	2.1335	6.4643	30.3303
18	1.7143	6.8835	23.4468
19	1.2679	7.3300	16.1168
20	.7925	7.8053	8.3115
21	.2864	8.3115	0.0000

YEARS 22 MO PAYT .7009 AN CONST 8.42

#	INT	PRIN	BALANCE
1	6.2380	2.1730	97.8270
2	6.0970	2.3140	95.5130
3	5.9470	2.4640	93.0489
4	5.7872	2.6238	90.4251
5	5.6170	2.7940	87.6311
6	5.4358	2.9752	84.6559
7	5.2429	3.1681	81.4878
8	5.0374	3.3736	78.1142
9	4.8186	3.5924	74.5219
10	4.5857	3.8253	70.6965
11	4.3376	4.0734	66.6231
12	4.0734	4.3376	62.2855
13	3.7921	4.6189	57.6666
14	3.4926	4.9184	52.7482
15	3.1736	5.2374	47.5108
16	2.8340	5.5770	41.9338
17	2.4723	5.9387	35.9951
18	2.0872	6.3239	29.6712
19	1.6770	6.7340	22.9372
20	1.2403	7.1707	15.7666
21	.7753	7.6357	8.1309
22	.2801	8.1309	0.0000

YEARS 23 MO PAYT .6869 AN CONST 8.25

#	INT	PRIN	BALANCE
1	6.2429	1.9999	98.0001
2	6.1132	2.1296	95.8705
3	5.9751	2.2677	93.6028
4	5.8280	2.4148	91.1881
5	5.6714	2.5714	88.6167
6	5.5047	2.7381	85.8786
7	5.3271	2.9157	82.9629
8	5.1380	3.1048	79.8581
9	4.9367	3.3061	76.5520
10	4.7223	3.5205	73.0315
11	4.4940	3.7488	69.2827
12	4.2508	3.9920	65.2907
13	3.9920	4.2508	61.0399
14	3.7163	4.5265	56.5134
15	3.4227	4.8201	51.6933
16	3.1102	5.1326	46.5607
17	2.7773	5.4655	41.0952
18	2.4228	5.8200	35.2752
19	2.0454	6.1974	29.0778
20	1.6435	6.5993	22.4785
21	1.2155	7.0273	15.4513
22	.7598	7.4830	7.9683
23	.2745	7.9683	0.0000

YEARS 24 MO PAYT .6742 AN CONST 8.10

#	INT	PRIN	BALANCE
1	6.2474	1.8435	98.1565
2	6.1278	1.9630	96.1935
3	6.0005	2.0903	94.1032
4	5.8650	2.2259	91.8773
5	5.7206	2.3702	89.5070
6	5.5669	2.5240	86.9831
7	5.4032	2.6876	84.2954
8	5.2289	2.8619	81.4335
9	5.0433	3.0475	78.3860
10	4.8457	3.2452	75.1408
11	4.6352	3.4556	71.6852
12	4.4111	3.6797	68.0055
13	4.1725	3.9184	64.0871
14	3.9184	4.1725	59.9146
15	3.6478	4.4431	55.4716
16	3.3596	4.7312	50.7404
17	3.0528	5.0380	45.7023
18	2.7261	5.3648	40.3376
19	2.3782	5.7127	34.6249
20	2.0077	6.0831	28.5418
21	1.6132	6.4776	22.0641
22	1.1931	6.8977	15.1664
23	.7458	7.3450	7.8214
24	.2695	7.8214	0.0000

YEARS 25 MO PAYT .6628 AN CONST 7.96

#	INT	PRIN	BALANCE
1	6.2514	1.7017	98.2983
2	6.1411	1.8121	96.4862
3	6.0235	1.9296	94.5565
4	5.8984	2.0548	92.5018
5	5.7651	2.1880	90.3138
6	5.6233	2.3299	87.9839
7	5.4722	2.4810	85.5029
8	5.3113	2.6419	82.8610
9	5.1399	2.8132	80.0477
10	4.9575	2.9957	77.0521
11	4.7632	3.1899	73.8621
12	4.5563	3.3968	70.4653
13	4.3361	3.6171	66.8482
14	4.1015	3.8517	62.9965
15	3.8517	4.1015	58.8950
16	3.5857	4.3675	54.5276
17	3.3025	4.6507	49.8769
18	3.0009	4.9523	44.9246
19	2.6797	5.2735	39.6511
20	2.3377	5.6154	34.0357
21	1.9735	5.9796	28.0561
22	1.5858	6.3674	21.6887
23	1.1728	6.7803	14.9083
24	.7331	7.2201	7.6883
25	.2649	7.6883	0.0000

YEARS 26 MO PAYT .6523 AN CONST 7.83

#	INT	PRIN	BALANCE
1	6.2551	1.5730	98.4270
2	6.1531	1.6750	96.7521
3	6.0445	1.7836	94.9685
4	5.9288	1.8993	93.0692
5	5.8056	2.0224	91.0468
6	5.6745	2.1536	88.8932
7	5.5348	2.2933	86.5999
8	5.3861	2.4420	84.1579
9	5.2277	2.6003	81.5576
10	5.0591	2.7690	78.7886
11	4.8795	2.9486	75.8400
12	4.6883	3.1398	72.7003
13	4.4847	3.3434	69.3569
14	4.2678	3.5602	65.7967
15	4.0370	3.7911	62.0056
16	3.7911	4.0370	57.9686
17	3.5293	4.2988	53.6699
18	3.2505	4.5775	49.0923
19	2.9537	4.8744	44.2179
20	2.6376	5.1905	39.0274
21	2.3009	5.5271	33.5003
22	1.9425	5.8856	27.6148
23	1.5608	6.2672	21.3475
24	1.1544	6.6737	14.6738
25	.7216	7.1065	7.5673
26	.2607	7.5673	0.0000

YEARS 27 MO PAYT .6428 AN CONST 7.72

#	INT	PRIN	BALANCE
1	6.2584	1.4557	98.5443
2	6.1640	1.5501	96.9943
3	6.0635	1.6506	95.3437
4	5.9565	1.7576	93.5860
5	5.8425	1.8716	91.7144
6	5.7211	1.9930	89.7214
7	5.5919	2.1222	87.5992
8	5.4542	2.2599	85.3393
9	5.3077	2.4064	82.9329
10	5.1516	2.5625	80.3704
11	4.9854	2.7287	77.6417
12	4.8085	2.9056	74.7361
13	4.6200	3.0941	71.6420
14	4.4194	3.2947	68.3473
15	4.2057	3.5084	64.8389
16	3.9782	3.7359	61.1030
17	3.7359	3.9782	57.1248
18	3.4779	4.2362	52.8886
19	3.2032	4.5109	48.3777
20	2.9107	4.8034	43.5743
21	2.5992	5.1149	38.4593
22	2.2674	5.4467	33.0127
23	1.9142	5.7999	27.2128
24	1.5381	6.1760	21.0368
25	1.1376	6.5765	14.4602
26	.7111	7.0030	7.4572
27	.2569	7.4572	0.0000

YEARS 28 MO PAYT .6342 AN CONST 7.62

#	INT	PRIN	BALANCE
1	6.2615	1.3486	98.6514
2	6.1740	1.4360	97.2154
3	6.0809	1.5292	95.6862
4	5.9817	1.6283	94.0579
5	5.8761	1.7339	92.3240
6	5.7637	1.8464	90.4776
7	5.6440	1.9661	88.5115
8	5.5165	2.0936	86.4178
9	5.3807	2.2294	84.1884
10	5.2361	2.3740	81.8145
11	5.0821	2.5279	79.2865
12	4.9182	2.6919	76.5946
13	4.7436	2.8664	73.7282
14	4.5577	3.0523	70.6759
15	4.3598	3.2503	67.4256
16	4.1490	3.4611	63.9645
17	3.9246	3.6855	60.2790
18	3.6855	3.9245	56.3544
19	3.4310	4.1791	52.1754
20	3.1600	4.4501	47.7253
21	2.8714	4.7387	42.9866
22	2.5641	5.0460	37.9407
23	2.2369	5.3732	32.5675
24	1.8884	5.7217	26.8458
25	1.5174	6.0927	20.7531
26	1.1222	6.4878	14.2652
27	.7015	6.9086	7.3566
28	.2535	7.3566	0.0000

YEARS 29 MO PAYT .6262 AN CONST 7.52

#	INT	PRIN	BALANCE
1	6.2643	1.2506	98.7494
2	6.1832	1.3317	97.4177
3	6.0968	1.4181	95.9996
4	6.0049	1.5100	94.4896
5	5.9069	1.6080	92.8816
6	5.8027	1.7122	91.1693
7	5.6916	1.8233	89.3461
8	5.5734	1.9415	87.4045
9	5.4475	2.0674	85.3371
10	5.3134	2.2015	83.1356
11	5.1706	2.3443	80.7913
12	5.0186	2.4963	78.2950
13	4.8567	2.6582	75.6367
14	4.6843	2.8306	72.8061
15	4.5007	3.0142	69.7920
16	4.3053	3.2096	66.5823
17	4.0971	3.4178	63.1645
18	3.8755	3.6394	59.5251
19	3.6394	3.8755	55.6497
20	3.3881	4.1268	51.5229
21	3.1205	4.3944	47.1284
22	2.8355	4.6794	42.4490
23	2.5320	4.9829	37.4662
24	2.2089	5.3060	32.1602
25	1.8648	5.6501	26.5101
26	1.4984	6.0165	20.4935
27	1.1082	6.4067	14.0868
28	.6927	6.8222	7.2646
29	.2503	7.2646	0.0000

YEARS 30 MO PAYT .6190 AN CONST 7.43

#	INT	PRIN	BALANCE
1	6.2669	1.1608	98.8392
2	6.1916	1.2361	97.6031
3	6.1114	1.3163	96.2868
4	6.0261	1.4016	94.8852
5	5.9352	1.4925	93.3927
6	5.8384	1.5893	91.8034
7	5.7353	1.6924	90.1110
8	5.6255	1.8021	88.3089
9	5.5087	1.9190	86.3899
10	5.3842	2.0434	84.3465
11	5.2517	2.1760	82.1705
12	5.1106	2.3171	79.8534
13	4.9603	2.4673	77.3861
14	4.8003	2.6274	74.7587
15	4.6299	2.7977	71.9610
16	4.4485	2.9792	68.9818
17	4.2553	3.1724	65.8094
18	4.0496	3.3781	62.4313
19	3.8305	3.5972	58.8341
20	3.5972	3.8305	55.0037
21	3.3488	4.0789	50.9248
22	3.0843	4.3434	46.5814
23	2.8026	4.6251	41.9563
24	2.5026	4.9250	37.0313
25	2.1833	5.2444	31.7869
26	1.8431	5.5845	26.2023
27	1.4810	5.9467	20.2556
28	1.0953	6.3323	13.9233
29	.6847	6.7430	7.1803
30	.2474	7.1803	0.0000

MONTHLY PAYMENT AMORTIZATION SCHEDULE PER $100   6.375%

YEARS 2	MO PAYT 4.4490	AN CONST 53.39
# INT	PRIN	BALANCE
1 4.9767	48.4110	51.5890
2 1.7987	51.5890	0.0000

YEARS 3	MO PAYT 3.0592	AN CONST 36.72
# INT	PRIN	BALANCE
1 5.4727	31.2378	68.7622
2 3.4221	33.2885	35.4737
3 1.2368	35.4737	0.0000

YEARS 4	MO PAYT 2.3657	AN CONST 28.39
# INT	PRIN	BALANCE
1 5.7203	22.6686	77.3314
2 4.2322	24.1567	53.1748
3 2.6464	25.7424	27.4323
4 .9565	27.4323	0.0000

YEARS 5	MO PAYT 1.9508	AN CONST 23.41
# INT	PRIN	BALANCE
1 5.8684	17.5408	82.4592
2 4.7169	18.6923	63.7669
3 3.4898	19.9194	43.8475
4 2.1822	21.2270	22.6205
5 .7887	22.6205	0.0000

YEARS 6	MO PAYT 1.6750	AN CONST 20.11
# INT	PRIN	BALANCE
1 5.9668	14.1338	85.8662
2 5.0389	15.0616	70.8046
3 4.0502	16.0504	54.7542
4 2.9966	17.1040	37.6502
5 1.8737	18.2268	19.4233
6 .6772	19.4233	0.0000

YEARS 7	MO PAYT 1.4789	AN CONST 17.75
# INT	PRIN	BALANCE
1 6.0368	11.7100	88.2900
2 5.2681	12.4787	75.8112
3 4.4489	13.2979	62.5133
4 3.5759	14.1709	48.3425
5 2.6457	15.1011	33.2413
6 1.6543	16.0925	17.1489
7 .5979	17.1489	0.0000

YEARS 8	MO PAYT 1.3325	AN CONST 15.99
# INT	PRIN	BALANCE
1 6.0890	9.9007	90.0993
2 5.4391	10.5506	79.5487
3 4.7465	11.2433	68.3054
4 4.0084	11.9813	56.3241
5 3.2219	12.7679	43.5562
6 2.3837	13.6060	29.9502
7 1.4905	14.4992	15.4510
8 .5387	15.4510	0.0000

YEARS 9	MO PAYT 1.2192	AN CONST 14.64
# INT	PRIN	BALANCE
1 6.1295	8.5010	91.4990
2 5.5714	9.0590	82.4400
3 4.9767	9.6537	72.7862
4 4.3430	10.2875	62.4988
5 3.6677	10.9628	51.5360
6 2.9480	11.6825	39.8535

#	INT	PRIN	BALANCE
7	2.1811	12.4494	27.4041
8	1.3638	13.2666	14.1375
9	.4929	14.1375	0.0000

YEARS 10	MO PAYT 1.1291	AN CONST 13.55
# INT	PRIN	BALANCE
1 6.1616	7.3879	92.6121
2 5.6766	7.8729	84.7391
3 5.1598	8.3898	76.3493
4 4.6090	8.9405	67.4088
5 4.0221	9.5274	57.8814
6 3.3967	10.1529	47.7285
7 2.7302	10.8194	36.9092
8 2.0199	11.5296	25.3795
9 1.2631	12.2865	13.0930
10 .4565	13.0930	0.0000

YEARS 11	MO PAYT 1.0559	AN CONST 12.68
# INT	PRIN	BALANCE
1 6.1877	6.4834	93.5166
2 5.7621	6.9090	86.6077
3 5.3086	7.3625	79.2452
4 4.8253	7.8458	71.3993
5 4.3102	8.3609	63.0385
6 3.7614	8.9097	54.1287
7 3.1765	9.4946	44.6341
8 2.5532	10.1179	34.5162
9 1.8890	10.7821	23.7341
10 1.1812	11.4899	12.2442
11 .4269	12.2442	0.0000

YEARS 12	MO PAYT .9954	AN CONST 11.95
# INT	PRIN	BALANCE
1 6.2094	5.7350	94.2650
2 5.8329	6.1115	88.1534
3 5.4317	6.5127	81.6407
4 5.0041	6.9403	74.7004
5 4.5485	7.3959	67.3046
6 4.0630	7.8814	59.4232
7 3.5456	8.3988	51.0244
8 2.9943	8.9501	42.0743
9 2.4068	9.5376	32.5367
10 1.7807	10.1638	22.3729
11 1.1134	10.8310	11.5420
12 .4024	11.5420	0.0000

YEARS 13	MO PAYT .9445	AN CONST 11.34
# INT	PRIN	BALANCE
1 6.2275	5.1069	94.8931
2 5.8922	5.4422	89.4509
3 5.5350	5.7994	83.6515
4 5.1543	6.1801	77.4714
5 4.7486	6.5858	70.8855
6 4.3162	7.0182	63.8674
7 3.8555	7.4789	56.3885
8 3.3646	7.9698	48.4187
9 2.8414	8.4930	39.9256
10 2.2838	9.0506	30.8751
11 1.6897	9.6447	21.2304
12 1.0566	10.2778	10.9525
13 .3819	10.9525	0.0000

YEARS 14	MO PAYT .9013	AN CONST 10.82
# INT	PRIN	BALANCE
1 6.2429	4.5732	95.4268
2 5.9427	4.8734	90.5535
3 5.6228	5.1933	85.3602

#	INT	PRIN	BALANCE
4	5.2819	5.5342	79.8260
5	4.9186	5.8975	73.9285
6	4.5314	6.2847	67.6438
7	4.1189	6.6972	60.9466
8	3.6792	7.1369	53.8098
9	3.2107	7.6054	46.2044
10	2.7114	8.1046	38.0998
11	2.1794	8.6367	29.4631
12	1.6124	9.2036	20.2595
13	1.0083	9.8078	10.4517
14	.3644	10.4517	0.0000

YEARS 15	MO PAYT .8643	AN CONST 10.38
# INT	PRIN	BALANCE
1 6.2561	4.1149	95.8851
2 5.9860	4.3850	91.5002
3 5.6982	4.6728	86.8273
4 5.3914	4.9796	81.8477
5 5.0645	5.3065	76.5413
6 4.7162	5.6548	70.8864
7 4.3450	6.0260	64.8604
8 3.9494	6.4216	58.4388
9 3.5278	6.8432	51.5956
10 3.0786	7.2924	44.3031
11 2.5999	7.7711	36.5320
12 2.0897	8.2813	28.2507
13 1.5461	8.8249	19.4258
14 .9668	9.4042	10.0216
15 .3494	10.0216	0.0000

YEARS 16	MO PAYT .8321	AN CONST 9.99
# INT	PRIN	BALANCE
1 6.2676	3.7178	96.2822
2 6.0236	3.9619	92.3203
3 5.7635	4.2220	88.0984
4 5.4863	4.4991	83.5993
5 5.1910	4.7945	78.8048
6 4.8762	5.1092	73.6956
7 4.5408	5.4446	68.2510
8 4.1834	5.8020	62.4490
9 3.8025	6.1829	56.2661
10 3.3967	6.5888	49.6773
11 2.9641	7.0213	42.6560
12 2.5032	7.4822	35.1738
13 2.0120	7.9734	27.2004
14 1.4886	8.4968	18.7036
15 .9308	9.0546	9.6490
16 .3364	9.6490	0.0000

YEARS 17	MO PAYT .8041	AN CONST 9.65
# INT	PRIN	BALANCE
1 6.2776	3.3712	96.6288
2 6.0563	3.5925	93.0363
3 5.8205	3.8283	89.2080
4 5.5692	4.0796	85.1284
5 5.3014	4.3474	80.7810
6 5.0160	4.6328	76.1481
7 4.7118	4.9370	71.2112
8 4.3878	5.2610	65.9501
9 4.0424	5.6064	60.3437
10 3.6744	5.9745	54.3693
11 3.2822	6.3667	48.0026
12 2.8642	6.7846	41.2180
13 2.4188	7.2300	33.9880
14 1.9442	7.7046	26.2834
15 1.4384	8.2104	18.0731
16 .8994	8.7494	9.3237
17 .3251	9.3237	0.0000

YEARS 18	MO PAYT .7794	AN CONST 9.36
# INT	PRIN	BALANCE
1 6.2864	3.0665	96.9335
2 6.0851	3.2678	93.6657
3 5.8706	3.4823	90.1834
4 5.6420	3.7109	86.4725
5 5.3984	3.9545	82.5180
6 5.1388	4.2141	78.3038
7 4.8622	4.4908	73.8131
8 4.5674	4.7856	69.0275
9 4.2532	5.0997	63.9278
10 3.9184	5.4345	58.4933
11 3.5617	5.7912	52.7020
12 3.1815	6.1714	46.5306
13 2.7764	6.5765	39.9541
14 2.3447	7.0083	32.9458
15 1.8846	7.4683	25.4775
16 1.3943	7.9586	17.5189
17 .8719	8.4811	9.0378
18 .3151	9.0378	0.0000

YEARS 19	MO PAYT .7576	AN CONST 9.10
# INT	PRIN	BALANCE
1 6.2942	2.7971	97.2029
2 6.1106	2.9807	94.2222
3 5.9149	3.1764	91.0458
4 5.7064	3.3849	87.6609
5 5.4842	3.6071	84.0538
6 5.2474	3.8439	80.2098
7 4.9951	4.0962	76.1136
8 4.7262	4.3652	71.7484
9 4.4396	4.6517	67.0967
10 4.1342	4.9571	62.1397
11 3.8088	5.2825	56.8572
12 3.4621	5.6293	51.2279
13 3.0925	5.9988	45.2291
14 2.6987	6.3926	38.8365
15 2.2791	6.8122	32.0243
16 1.8319	7.2594	24.7648
17 1.3553	7.7360	17.0288
18 .8475	8.2438	8.7850
19 .3063	8.7850	0.0000

YEARS 20	MO PAYT .7382	AN CONST 8.86
# INT	PRIN	BALANCE
1 6.3011	2.5577	97.4423
2 6.1332	2.7256	94.7168
3 5.9543	2.9045	91.8123
4 5.7636	3.0952	88.7171
5 5.5605	3.2983	85.4188
6 5.3439	3.5149	81.9039
7 5.1132	3.7456	78.1583
8 4.8673	3.9915	74.1669
9 4.6053	4.2535	69.9134
10 4.3261	4.5327	65.3806
11 4.0285	4.8303	60.5503
12 3.7114	5.1474	55.4030
13 3.3735	5.4853	49.9177
14 3.0134	5.8454	44.0723
15 2.6297	6.2291	37.8432
16 2.2208	6.6380	31.2052
17 1.7850	7.0738	24.1314
18 1.3207	7.5381	16.5933
19 .8258	8.0330	8.5603
20 .2985	8.5603	0.0000

YEARS 21	MO PAYT .7209	AN CONST 8.66
# INT	PRIN	BALANCE
1 6.3073	2.3438	97.6562
2 6.1534	2.4977	95.1584
3 5.9895	2.6617	92.4968

#	INT	PRIN	BALANCE
4	5.8147	2.8364	89.6604
5	5.6285	3.0226	86.6377
6	5.4301	3.2210	83.4167
7	5.2187	3.4325	79.9842
8	4.9933	3.6578	76.3264
9	4.7532	3.8979	72.4285
10	4.4973	4.1538	68.2747
11	4.2247	4.4265	63.8482
12	3.9341	4.7171	59.1311
13	3.6244	5.0267	54.1044
14	3.2944	5.3567	48.7477
15	2.9428	5.7084	43.0393
16	2.5681	6.0831	36.9562
17	2.1687	6.4824	30.4738
18	1.7432	6.9080	23.5658
19	1.2897	7.3615	16.2044
20	.8064	7.8447	8.3597
21	.2915	8.3597	0.0000

YEARS 22   MO PAYT .7054   AN CONST 8.47

#	INT	PRIN	BALANCE
1	6.3128	2.1521	97.8479
2	6.1716	2.2934	95.5545
3	6.0210	2.4440	93.1105
4	5.8606	2.6044	90.5061
5	5.6896	2.7754	87.7307
6	5.5074	2.9576	84.7732
7	5.3133	3.1517	81.6215
8	5.1064	3.3586	78.2629
9	4.8859	3.5791	74.6838
10	4.6509	3.8140	70.8698
11	4.4006	4.0644	66.8053
12	4.1337	4.3312	62.4741
13	3.8494	4.6156	57.8586
14	3.5464	4.9185	52.9400
15	3.2235	5.2414	47.6986
16	2.8795	5.5855	42.1131
17	2.5128	5.9522	36.1609
18	2.1221	6.3429	29.8180
19	1.7057	6.7593	23.0587
20	1.2619	7.2030	15.8556
21	.7891	7.6759	8.1798
22	.2852	8.1798	0.0000

YEARS 23   MO PAYT .6914   AN CONST 8.30

#	INT	PRIN	BALANCE
1	6.3178	1.9796	98.0204
2	6.1879	2.1095	95.9109
3	6.0494	2.2480	93.6629
4	5.9018	2.3956	91.2673
5	5.7446	2.5528	88.7145
6	5.5770	2.7204	85.9941
7	5.3984	2.8990	83.0950
8	5.2081	3.0893	80.0057
9	5.0053	3.2921	76.7136
10	4.7892	3.5082	73.2054
11	4.5589	3.7385	69.4668
12	4.3134	3.9840	65.4829
13	4.0519	4.2455	61.2374
14	3.7732	4.5242	56.7132
15	3.4762	4.8212	51.8920
16	3.1597	5.1377	46.7543
17	2.8225	5.4749	41.2794
18	2.4630	5.8344	35.4451
19	2.0800	6.2174	29.2277
20	1.6719	6.6255	22.6022
21	1.2370	7.0604	15.5418
22	.7735	7.5239	8.0178
23	.2796	8.0178	0.0000

YEARS 24   MO PAYT .6788   AN CONST 8.15

#	INT	PRIN	BALANCE
1	6.3223	1.8237	98.1763
2	6.2026	1.9435	96.2328
3	6.0750	2.0711	94.1617
4	5.9391	2.2070	91.9547
5	5.7942	2.3519	89.6028
6	5.6398	2.5063	87.0965
7	5.4753	2.6708	84.4257
8	5.2999	2.8461	81.5796
9	5.1131	3.0330	78.5466
10	4.9140	3.2321	75.3145
11	4.7018	3.4443	71.8703
12	4.4757	3.6704	68.1999
13	4.2348	3.9113	64.2886
14	3.9780	4.1681	60.1206
15	3.7044	4.4417	55.6789
16	3.4128	4.7333	50.9456
17	3.1021	5.0440	45.9017
18	2.7710	5.3751	40.5266
19	2.4181	5.7279	34.7986
20	2.0421	6.1040	28.6947
21	1.6414	6.5047	22.1900
22	1.2144	6.9317	15.2583
23	.7594	7.3867	7.8716
24	.2745	7.8716	0.0000

YEARS 25   MO PAYT .6674   AN CONST 8.01

#	INT	PRIN	BALANCE
1	6.3264	1.6826	98.3174
2	6.2159	1.7931	96.5243
3	6.0982	1.9108	94.6136
4	5.9728	2.0362	92.5774
5	5.8391	2.1699	90.4075
6	5.6967	2.3123	88.0952
7	5.5449	2.4641	85.6311
8	5.3831	2.6259	83.0052
9	5.2108	2.7982	80.2069
10	5.0271	2.9819	77.2250
11	4.8313	3.1777	74.0473
12	4.6227	3.3863	70.6610
13	4.4004	3.6086	67.0524
14	4.1635	3.8455	63.2069
15	3.9111	4.0979	59.1090
16	3.6421	4.3669	54.7420
17	3.3554	4.6536	50.0884
18	3.0499	4.9591	45.1293
19	2.7244	5.2847	39.8447
20	2.3774	5.6316	34.2131
21	2.0077	6.0013	28.2118
22	1.6138	6.3952	21.8166
23	1.1940	6.8150	15.0016
24	.7466	7.2624	7.7392
25	.2698	7.7392	0.0000

YEARS 26   MO PAYT .6570   AN CONST 7.89

#	INT	PRIN	BALANCE
1	6.3301	1.5544	98.4456
2	6.2281	1.6565	96.7891
3	6.1193	1.7652	95.0239
4	6.0034	1.8811	93.1429
5	5.8800	2.0046	91.1383
6	5.7484	2.1361	89.0022
7	5.6081	2.2764	86.7258
8	5.4587	2.4258	84.3000
9	5.2995	2.5851	81.7149
10	5.1298	2.7548	78.9602
11	4.9489	2.9356	76.0246
12	4.7562	3.1283	72.8963
13	4.5509	3.3337	69.5626
14	4.3320	3.5525	66.0101
15	4.0988	3.7857	62.2244
16	3.8503	4.0342	58.1902
17	3.5855	4.2991	53.8911
18	3.3032	4.5813	49.3098
19	3.0025	4.8820	44.4278
20	2.6820	5.2025	39.2253
21	2.3405	5.5440	33.6813
22	1.9765	5.9080	27.7733
23	1.5887	6.2958	21.4775
24	1.1754	6.7091	14.7684
25	.7350	7.1495	7.6189
26	.2656	7.6189	0.0000

YEARS 27   MO PAYT .6476   AN CONST 7.78

#	INT	PRIN	BALANCE
1	6.3335	1.4377	98.5623
2	6.2391	1.5321	97.0303
3	6.1385	1.6326	95.3976
4	6.0313	1.7398	93.6578
5	5.9171	1.8540	91.8038
6	5.7954	1.9757	89.8280
7	5.6657	2.1054	87.7226
8	5.5275	2.2436	85.4790
9	5.3802	2.3909	83.0880
10	5.2233	2.5479	80.5401
11	5.0560	2.7151	77.8250
12	4.8778	2.8934	74.9316
13	4.6878	3.0833	71.8483
14	4.4854	3.2857	68.5625
15	4.2697	3.5014	65.0611
16	4.0399	3.7313	61.3298
17	3.7949	3.9762	57.3536
18	3.5339	4.2373	53.1163
19	3.2557	4.5154	48.6009
20	2.9593	4.8118	43.7891
21	2.6434	5.1277	38.6614
22	2.3068	5.4643	33.1971
23	1.9481	5.8230	27.3740
24	1.5659	6.2053	21.1687
25	1.1585	6.6126	14.5561
26	.7244	7.0467	7.5093
27	.2618	7.5093	0.0000

YEARS 28   MO PAYT .6390   AN CONST 7.67

#	INT	PRIN	BALANCE
1	6.3366	1.3312	98.6688
2	6.2492	1.4185	97.2503
3	6.1560	1.5117	95.7386
4	6.0568	1.6109	94.1277
5	5.9511	1.7167	92.4111
6	5.8384	1.8293	90.5817
7	5.7183	1.9494	88.6323
8	5.5903	2.0774	86.5549
9	5.4539	2.2138	84.3411
10	5.3086	2.3591	81.9820
11	5.1537	2.5140	79.4680
12	4.9887	2.6790	76.7890
13	4.8128	2.8549	73.9341
14	4.6254	3.0423	70.8919
15	4.4257	3.2420	67.6499
16	4.2129	3.4548	64.1950
17	3.9861	3.6816	60.5134
18	3.7444	3.9233	56.5901
19	3.4869	4.1808	52.4093
20	3.2124	4.4553	47.9540
21	2.9199	4.7478	43.2062
22	2.6083	5.0595	38.1467
23	2.2761	5.3916	32.7552
24	1.9222	5.7455	27.0096
25	1.5450	6.1227	20.8869
26	1.1431	6.5246	14.3623
27	.7148	6.9529	7.4094
28	.2583	7.4094	0.0000

YEARS 29   MO PAYT .6311   AN CONST 7.58

#	INT	PRIN	BALANCE
1	6.3394	1.2337	98.7663
2	6.2584	1.3147	97.4515
3	6.1721	1.4010	96.0505
4	6.0801	1.4930	94.5575
5	5.9821	1.5910	92.9664
6	5.8776	1.6955	91.2709
7	5.7663	1.8068	89.4642
8	5.6477	1.9254	87.5388
9	5.5213	2.0518	85.4870
10	5.3866	2.1865	83.3005
11	5.2431	2.3300	80.9705
12	5.0902	2.4830	78.4876
13	4.9272	2.6460	75.8416
14	4.7535	2.8196	73.0220
15	4.5684	3.0047	70.0172
16	4.3711	3.2020	66.8152
17	4.1609	3.4122	63.4030
18	3.9369	3.6362	59.7668
19	3.6982	3.8749	55.8919
20	3.4438	4.1293	51.7627
21	3.1728	4.4003	47.3623
22	2.8839	4.6892	42.6731
23	2.5761	4.9970	37.6761
24	2.2480	5.3251	32.3510
25	1.8985	5.6746	26.6764
26	1.5260	6.0472	20.6292
27	1.1290	6.4441	14.1851
28	.7060	6.8672	7.3180
29	.2552	7.3180	0.0000

YEARS 30   MO PAYT .6239   AN CONST 7.49

#	INT	PRIN	BALANCE
1	6.3419	1.1445	98.8555
2	6.2668	1.2196	97.6359
3	6.1867	1.2997	96.3362
4	6.1014	1.3850	94.9512
5	6.0105	1.4759	93.4752
6	5.9136	1.5728	91.9024
7	5.8104	1.6761	90.2264
8	5.7003	1.7861	88.4403
9	5.5831	1.9033	86.5369
10	5.4581	2.0283	84.5086
11	5.3250	2.1614	82.3472
12	5.1831	2.3033	80.0438
13	5.0319	2.4545	77.5893
14	4.8708	2.6157	74.9736
15	4.6991	2.7874	72.1862
16	4.5161	2.9704	69.2159
17	4.3211	3.1654	66.0505
18	4.1133	3.3731	62.6774
19	3.8919	3.5946	59.0828
20	3.6559	3.8305	55.2523
21	3.4044	4.0820	51.1703
22	3.1365	4.3500	46.8203
23	2.8509	4.6355	42.1847
24	2.5466	4.9398	37.2449
25	2.2223	5.2641	31.9808
26	1.8767	5.6097	26.3711
27	1.5085	5.9779	20.3931
28	1.1161	6.3704	14.0228
29	.6979	6.7886	7.2342
30	.2522	7.2342	0.0000

YEARS 2 — MO PAYT 4.4501 — AN CONST 53.41

#	INT	PRIN	BALANCE
1	4.9965	48.4048	51.5952
2	1.8061	51.5952	0.0000

YEARS 3 — MO PAYT 3.0604 — AN CONST 36.73

#	INT	PRIN	BALANCE
1	5.4945	31.2297	68.7703
2	3.4361	33.2881	35.4822
3	1.2420	35.4822	0.0000

YEARS 4 — MO PAYT 2.3669 — AN CONST 28.41

#	INT	PRIN	BALANCE
1	5.7430	22.6597	77.3403
2	4.2495	24.1532	53.1872
3	2.6575	25.7451	27.4420
4	.9606	27.4420	0.0000

YEARS 5 — MO PAYT 1.9519 — AN CONST 23.43

#	INT	PRIN	BALANCE
1	5.8917	17.5315	82.4685
2	4.7361	18.6871	63.7814
3	3.5045	19.9188	43.8626
4	2.1916	21.2316	22.6310
5	.7922	22.6310	0.0000

YEARS 6 — MO PAYT 1.6762 — AN CONST 20.12

#	INT	PRIN	BALANCE
1	5.9905	14.1244	85.8756
2	5.0595	15.0553	70.8203
3	4.0672	16.0476	54.7727
4	3.0095	17.1054	37.6673
5	1.8820	18.2328	19.4345
6	.6803	19.4345	0.0000

YEARS 7 — MO PAYT 1.4801 — AN CONST 17.77

#	INT	PRIN	BALANCE
1	6.0607	11.7005	88.2995
2	5.2895	12.4717	75.8277
3	4.4675	13.2938	62.5339
4	3.5913	14.1700	48.3640
5	2.6574	15.1039	33.2600
6	1.6618	16.0995	17.1606
7	.6007	17.1606	0.0000

YEARS 8 — MO PAYT 1.3337 — AN CONST 16.01

#	INT	PRIN	BALANCE
1	6.1132	9.8913	90.1087
2	5.4613	10.5432	79.5655
3	4.7663	11.2381	68.3274
4	4.0256	11.9788	56.3485
5	3.2361	12.7684	43.5802
6	2.3945	13.6100	29.9702
7	1.4975	14.5070	15.4632
8	.5413	15.4632	0.0000

YEARS 9 — MO PAYT 1.2205 — AN CONST 14.65

#	INT	PRIN	BALANCE
1	6.1538	8.4916	91.5084
2	5.5941	9.0513	82.4570
3	4.9975	9.6479	72.8091
4	4.3616	10.2838	62.5253
5	3.6838	10.9616	51.5636
6	2.9613	11.6841	39.8795
7	2.1912	12.4543	27.4252
8	1.3703	13.2751	14.1501
9	.4953	14.1501	0.0000

YEARS 10 — MO PAYT 1.1304 — AN CONST 13.57

#	INT	PRIN	BALANCE
1	6.1861	7.3787	92.6213
2	5.6997	7.8651	84.7562
3	5.1813	8.3835	76.3727
4	4.6288	8.9360	67.4367
5	4.0398	9.5250	57.9117
6	3.4120	10.1528	47.7589
7	2.7428	10.8220	36.9369
8	2.0295	11.5353	25.4016
9	1.2692	12.2956	13.1060
10	.4588	13.1060	0.0000

YEARS 11 — MO PAYT 1.0572 — AN CONST 12.69

#	INT	PRIN	BALANCE
1	6.2123	6.4743	93.5257
2	5.7855	6.9010	86.6247
3	5.3307	7.3559	79.2688
4	4.8459	7.8407	71.4282
5	4.3291	8.3575	63.0707
6	3.7782	8.9083	54.1623
7	3.1911	9.4955	44.6668
8	2.5652	10.1214	34.5455
9	1.8981	10.7885	23.7570
10	1.1870	11.4995	12.2575
11	.4291	12.2575	0.0000

YEARS 12 — MO PAYT .9967 — AN CONST 11.97

#	INT	PRIN	BALANCE
1	6.2340	5.7261	94.2739
2	5.8566	6.1036	88.1703
3	5.4543	6.5058	81.6645
4	5.0255	6.9347	74.7298
5	4.5684	7.3917	67.3381
6	4.0812	7.8789	59.4592
7	3.5619	8.3982	51.0609
8	3.0083	8.9518	42.1092
9	2.4183	9.5418	32.5674
10	1.7894	10.1707	22.3967
11	1.1190	10.8411	11.5556
12	.4045	11.5556	0.0000

YEARS 13 — MO PAYT .9459 — AN CONST 11.36

#	INT	PRIN	BALANCE
1	6.2522	5.0982	94.9018
2	5.9161	5.4342	89.4676
3	5.5580	5.7924	83.6752
4	5.1762	6.1742	77.5011
5	4.7692	6.5811	70.9199
6	4.3355	7.0149	63.9051
7	3.8731	7.4772	56.4278
8	3.3803	7.9701	48.4577
9	2.8550	8.4954	39.9624
10	2.2950	9.0553	30.9070
11	1.6982	9.6522	21.2548
12	1.0620	10.2884	10.9665
13	.3839	10.9665	0.0000

YEARS 14 — MO PAYT .9027 — AN CONST 10.84

#	INT	PRIN	BALANCE
1	6.2676	4.5646	95.4354
2	5.9668	4.8655	90.5699
3	5.6461	5.1862	85.3838
4	5.3043	5.5280	79.8558
5	4.9399	5.8923	73.9634
6	4.5515	6.2807	67.6827
7	4.1376	6.6947	60.9880
8	3.6963	7.1359	53.8521
9	3.2260	7.6063	46.2458
10	2.7247	8.1076	38.1382
11	2.1903	8.6420	29.4962
12	1.6207	9.2116	20.2846
13	1.0135	9.8187	10.4659
14	.3664	10.4659	0.0000

YEARS 15 — MO PAYT .8656 — AN CONST 10.39

#	INT	PRIN	BALANCE
1	6.2809	4.1065	95.8935
2	6.0103	4.3772	91.5163
3	5.7218	4.6657	86.8507
4	5.4142	4.9732	81.8775
5	5.0865	5.3010	76.5765
6	4.7371	5.6504	70.9261
7	4.3646	6.0228	64.9033
8	3.9677	6.4198	58.4836
9	3.5445	6.8429	51.6407
10	3.0935	7.2939	44.3468
11	2.6128	7.7747	36.5721
12	2.1003	8.2871	28.2850
13	1.5541	8.8333	19.4517
14	.9719	9.4155	10.0361
15	.3513	10.0361	0.0000

YEARS 16 — MO PAYT .8335 — AN CONST 10.01

#	INT	PRIN	BALANCE
1	6.2924	3.7097	96.2903
2	6.0479	3.9542	92.3362
3	5.7873	4.2148	88.1214
4	5.5095	4.4926	83.6288
5	5.2134	4.7887	78.8401
6	4.8978	5.1043	73.7358
7	4.5613	5.4408	68.2950
8	4.2027	5.7994	62.4956
9	3.8205	6.1816	56.3140
10	3.4130	6.5890	49.7250
11	2.9788	7.0233	42.7016
12	2.5158	7.4863	35.2154
13	2.0224	7.9797	27.2357
14	1.4965	8.5056	18.7301
15	.9358	9.0662	9.6638
16	.3383	9.6638	0.0000

YEARS 17 — MO PAYT .8055 — AN CONST 9.67

#	INT	PRIN	BALANCE
1	6.3025	3.3632	96.6368
2	6.0808	3.5849	93.0519
3	5.8445	3.8212	89.2307
4	5.5927	4.0730	85.1577
5	5.3242	4.3415	80.8162
6	5.0381	4.6276	76.1885
7	4.7330	4.9327	71.2559
8	4.4079	5.2578	65.9981
9	4.0614	5.6043	60.3938
10	3.6920	5.9737	54.4201
11	3.2983	6.3674	48.0526
12	2.8786	6.7871	41.2655
13	2.4312	7.2345	34.0310
14	1.9544	7.7113	26.3197
15	1.4461	8.2196	18.1001
16	.9044	8.7613	9.3388
17	.3269	9.3388	0.0000

YEARS 18 — MO PAYT .7808 — AN CONST 9.38

#	INT	PRIN	BALANCE
1	6.3113	3.0587	96.9413
2	6.1097	3.2603	93.6809
3	5.8948	3.4752	90.2057
4	5.6658	3.7043	86.5014
5	5.4216	3.9485	82.5529
6	5.1614	4.2087	78.3442
7	4.8840	4.4861	73.8581
8	4.5883	4.7818	69.0763
9	4.2731	5.0970	63.9794
10	3.9372	5.4329	58.5465
11	3.5791	5.7910	52.7555
12	3.1974	6.1727	46.5828
13	2.7905	6.5795	40.0033
14	2.3569	7.0132	32.9901
15	1.8946	7.4754	25.5146
16	1.4019	7.9682	17.5465
17	.8767	8.4933	9.0532
18	.3169	9.0532	0.0000

YEARS 19 — MO PAYT .7591 — AN CONST 9.11

#	INT	PRIN	BALANCE
1	6.3191	2.7896	97.2104
2	6.1353	2.9734	94.2370
3	5.9393	3.1694	91.0676
4	5.7304	3.3783	87.6893
5	5.5077	3.6010	84.0884
6	5.2704	3.8383	80.2501
7	5.0174	4.0913	76.1588
8	4.7477	4.3610	71.7978
9	4.4603	4.6484	67.1494
10	4.1539	4.9548	62.1946
11	3.8273	5.2813	56.9133
12	3.4792	5.6294	51.2838
13	3.1082	6.0005	45.2834
14	2.7127	6.3960	38.8874
15	2.2911	6.8176	32.0698
16	1.8418	7.2669	24.8029
17	1.3628	7.7459	17.0570
18	.8523	8.2564	8.8006
19	.3081	8.8006	0.0000

YEARS 20 — MO PAYT .7397 — AN CONST 8.88

#	INT	PRIN	BALANCE
1	6.3261	2.5503	97.4497
2	6.1580	2.7184	94.7313
3	5.9788	2.8976	91.8337
4	5.7878	3.0886	88.7451
5	5.5842	3.2921	85.4530
6	5.3672	3.5091	81.9438
7	5.1360	3.7404	78.2034
8	4.8894	3.9870	74.2165
9	4.6266	4.2497	69.9667
10	4.3465	4.5298	65.4369
11	4.0480	4.8284	60.6085
12	3.7297	5.1467	55.4618
13	3.3905	5.4859	49.9759
14	3.0289	5.8475	44.1285
15	2.6435	6.2329	37.8956
16	2.2327	6.6437	31.2519
17	1.7948	7.0816	24.1704
18	1.3280	7.5483	16.6220
19	.8305	8.0459	8.5762
20	.3002	8.5762	0.0000

YEARS 21 — MO PAYT .7224 — AN CONST 8.67

#	INT	PRIN	BALANCE
1	6.3322	2.3367	97.6633
2	6.1782	2.4907	95.1726
3	6.0141	2.6549	92.5177

MONTHLY PAYMENT AMORTIZATION SCHEDULE PER $100   6.40 %

#	INT	PRIN	BALANCE
4	5.8391	2.8299	89.6878
5	5.6526	3.0164	86.6714
6	5.4537	3.2152	83.4562
7	5.2418	3.4271	80.0291
8	5.0159	3.6530	76.3760
9	4.7752	3.8938	72.4823
10	4.5185	4.1504	68.3318
11	4.2450	4.4240	63.9078
12	3.9534	4.7156	59.1922
13	3.6426	5.0264	54.1658
14	3.3113	5.3577	48.8082
15	2.9581	5.7108	43.0973
16	2.5817	6.0872	37.0101
17	2.1805	6.4884	30.5217
18	1.7529	6.9161	23.6056
19	1.2970	7.3720	16.2336
20	.8111	7.8578	8.3758
21	.2932	8.3758	0.0000

YEARS 22	MO PAYT .7069	AN CONST 8.49	
#	INT	PRIN	BALANCE
1	6.3378	2.1452	97.8548
2	6.1964	2.2866	95.5682
3	6.0457	2.4373	93.1309
4	5.8851	2.5979	90.5330
5	5.7138	2.7692	87.7638
6	5.5313	2.9517	84.8121
7	5.3368	3.1462	81.6659
8	5.1294	3.3536	78.3123
9	4.9083	3.5747	74.7376
10	4.6727	3.8103	70.9274
11	4.4216	4.0614	66.8660
12	4.1539	4.3291	62.5369
13	3.8686	4.6144	57.9225
14	3.5644	4.9186	53.0039
15	3.2402	5.2428	47.7611
16	2.8947	5.5883	42.1728
17	2.5263	5.9566	36.2162
18	2.1337	6.3493	29.8669
19	1.7153	6.7677	23.0992
20	1.2692	7.2138	15.8854
21	.7937	7.6893	8.1961
22	.2869	8.1961	0.0000

YEARS 23	MO PAYT .6930	AN CONST 8.32	
#	INT	PRIN	BALANCE
1	6.3428	1.9728	98.0272
2	6.2128	2.1029	95.9243
3	6.0742	2.2415	93.6828
4	5.9264	2.3892	91.2936
5	5.7689	2.5467	88.7469
6	5.6011	2.7145	86.0324
7	5.4222	2.8935	83.1389
8	5.2315	3.0842	80.0548
9	5.0282	3.2875	76.7673
10	4.8115	3.5041	73.2632
11	4.5805	3.7351	69.5281
12	4.3344	3.9813	65.5468
13	4.0719	4.2437	61.3031
14	3.7922	4.5234	56.7797
15	3.4941	4.8215	51.9582
16	3.1763	5.1393	46.8189
17	2.8376	5.4781	41.3408
18	2.4765	5.8391	35.5017
19	2.0916	6.2240	29.2777
20	1.6814	6.6342	22.6435
21	1.2441	7.0715	15.5720
22	.7781	7.5376	8.0344
23	.2812	8.0344	0.0000

YEARS 24	MO PAYT .6804	AN CONST 8.17	
#	INT	PRIN	BALANCE
1	6.3473	1.8172	98.1828
2	6.2275	1.9370	96.2458
3	6.0999	2.0647	94.1811
4	5.9638	2.2007	91.9804
5	5.8187	2.3458	89.6346
6	5.6641	2.5004	87.1342
7	5.4993	2.6652	84.4690
8	5.3236	2.8409	81.6281
9	5.1364	3.0281	78.6000
10	4.9368	3.2277	75.3723
11	4.7241	3.4405	71.9318
12	4.4973	3.6672	68.2646
13	4.2556	3.9089	64.3557
14	3.9980	4.1666	60.1891
15	3.7233	4.4412	55.7479
16	3.4306	4.7339	51.0140
17	3.1186	5.0459	45.9681
18	2.7860	5.3785	40.5896
19	2.4315	5.7330	34.8565
20	2.0536	6.1109	28.7457
21	1.6509	6.5137	22.2320
22	1.2215	6.9430	15.2890
23	.7639	7.4006	7.8884
24	.2761	7.8884	0.0000

YEARS 25	MO PAYT .6690	AN CONST 8.03	
#	INT	PRIN	BALANCE
1	6.3514	1.6763	98.3237
2	6.2409	1.7868	96.5370
3	6.1231	1.9045	94.6325
4	5.9976	2.0300	92.6024
5	5.8638	2.1638	90.4386
6	5.7212	2.3065	88.1321
7	5.5692	2.4585	85.6736
8	5.4071	2.6205	83.0531
9	5.2344	2.7933	80.2598
10	5.0503	2.9774	77.2824
11	4.8541	3.1736	74.1088
12	4.6449	3.3828	70.7261
13	4.4219	3.6057	67.1203
14	4.1843	3.8434	63.2769
15	3.9309	4.0967	59.1802
16	3.6609	4.3667	54.8134
17	3.3731	4.6546	50.1589
18	3.0663	4.9613	45.1975
19	2.7393	5.2884	39.9092
20	2.3907	5.6369	34.2723
21	2.0192	6.0085	28.2638
22	1.6232	6.4045	21.8593
23	1.2011	6.8266	15.0327
24	.7511	7.2766	7.7562
25	.2715	7.7562	0.0000

YEARS 26	MO PAYT .6586	AN CONST 7.91	
#	INT	PRIN	BALANCE
1	6.3551	1.5483	98.4517
2	6.2531	1.6503	96.8014
3	6.1443	1.7591	95.0423
4	6.0283	1.8750	93.1673
5	5.9048	1.9986	91.1687
6	5.7730	2.1303	89.0383
7	5.6326	2.2708	86.7676
8	5.4829	2.4204	84.3472
9	5.3234	2.5800	81.7672
10	5.1534	2.7500	79.0172
11	4.9721	2.9313	76.0859
12	4.7789	3.1245	72.9614
13	4.5735	3.3304	69.6310
14	4.3535	3.5499	66.0811
15	4.1195	3.7839	62.2972
16	3.8701	4.0333	58.2639
17	3.6042	4.2991	53.9648
18	3.3209	4.5825	49.3823
19	3.0188	4.8845	44.4978
20	2.6969	5.2065	39.2913
21	2.3537	5.5496	33.7416
22	1.9879	5.9154	27.8262
23	1.5981	6.3053	21.5209
24	1.1825	6.7209	14.8000
25	.7395	7.1639	7.6361
26	.2673	7.6361	0.0000

YEARS 27	MO PAYT .6492	AN CONST 7.80	
#	INT	PRIN	BALANCE
1	6.3585	1.4317	98.5683
2	6.2641	1.5261	97.0422
3	6.1635	1.6267	95.4155
4	6.0563	1.7339	93.6816
5	5.9420	1.8482	91.8334
6	5.8202	1.9700	89.8634
7	5.6904	2.0998	87.7636
8	5.5520	2.2382	85.5253
9	5.4044	2.3858	83.1395
10	5.2472	2.5430	80.5965
11	5.0796	2.7106	77.8859
12	4.9009	2.8893	74.9966
13	4.7105	3.0797	71.9168
14	4.5075	3.2827	68.6341
15	4.2911	3.4991	65.1350
16	4.0605	3.7297	61.4053
17	3.8147	3.9756	57.4297
18	3.5526	4.2376	53.1922
19	3.2733	4.5169	48.6753
20	2.9756	4.8146	43.8607
21	2.6583	5.1319	38.7287
22	2.3200	5.4702	33.2585
23	1.9595	5.8307	27.4278
24	1.5752	6.2150	21.2128
25	1.1655	6.6247	14.5881
26	.7289	7.0613	7.5267
27	.2635	7.5267	0.0000

YEARS 28	MO PAYT .6406	AN CONST 7.69	
#	INT	PRIN	BALANCE
1	6.3616	1.3254	98.6746
2	6.2742	1.4128	97.2618
3	6.1811	1.5059	95.7560
4	6.0818	1.6051	94.1509
5	5.9760	1.7109	92.4399
6	5.8633	1.8237	90.6162
7	5.7431	1.9439	88.6723
8	5.6150	2.0720	86.6003
9	5.4784	2.2086	84.3918
10	5.3328	2.3542	82.0376
11	5.1776	2.5093	79.5283
12	5.0123	2.6747	76.8536
13	4.8360	2.8510	74.0026
14	4.6480	3.0389	70.9636
15	4.4478	3.2392	67.7244
16	4.2343	3.4527	64.2717
17	4.0067	3.6803	60.5914
18	3.7641	3.9229	56.6686
19	3.5055	4.1814	52.4871
20	3.2299	4.4570	48.0301
21	2.9362	4.7508	43.2793
22	2.6230	5.0639	38.2154
23	2.2893	5.3977	32.8177
24	1.9335	5.7535	27.0643
25	1.5543	6.1327	20.9316
26	1.1501	6.5369	14.3947
27	.7192	6.9677	7.4270
28	.2600	7.4270	0.0000

YEARS 29	MO PAYT .6327	AN CONST 7.60	
#	INT	PRIN	BALANCE
1	6.3644	1.2282	98.7718
2	6.2834	1.3091	97.4627
3	6.1972	1.3954	96.0673
4	6.1052	1.4874	94.5799
5	6.0071	1.5854	92.9945
6	5.9026	1.6899	91.3046
7	5.7913	1.8013	89.5033
8	5.6725	1.9200	87.5833
9	5.5460	2.0466	85.5367
10	5.4111	2.1815	83.3553
11	5.2673	2.3252	81.0300
12	5.1141	2.4785	78.5515
13	4.9507	2.6419	75.9097
14	4.7766	2.8160	73.0937
15	4.5910	3.0016	70.0921
16	4.3931	3.1994	66.8927
17	4.1822	3.4103	63.4824
18	3.9575	3.6351	59.8473
19	3.7179	3.8747	55.9726
20	3.4625	4.1301	51.8425
21	3.1903	4.4023	47.4402
22	2.9001	4.6924	42.7478
23	2.5908	5.0017	37.7461
24	2.2612	5.3314	32.4147
25	1.9098	5.6828	26.7319
26	1.5352	6.0574	20.6745
27	1.1360	6.4566	14.2179
28	.7104	6.8822	7.3358
29	.2568	7.3358	0.0000

YEARS 30	MO PAYT .6255	AN CONST 7.51	
#	INT	PRIN	BALANCE
1	6.3670	1.1391	98.8609
2	6.2919	1.2142	97.6467
3	6.2119	1.2942	96.3525
4	6.1266	1.3795	94.9730
5	6.0356	1.4704	93.5026
6	5.9387	1.5674	91.9352
7	5.8354	1.6707	90.2646
8	5.7253	1.7808	88.4838
9	5.6079	1.8981	86.5856
10	5.4828	2.0233	84.5624
11	5.3495	2.1566	82.4058
12	5.2073	2.2988	80.1070
13	5.0558	2.4503	77.6568
14	4.8943	2.6118	75.0450
15	4.7222	2.7839	72.2611
16	4.5387	2.9674	69.2937
17	4.3431	3.1630	66.1307
18	4.1346	3.3715	62.7592
19	3.9124	3.5937	59.1655
20	3.6755	3.8305	55.3350
21	3.4231	4.0830	51.2520
22	3.1539	4.3521	46.8998
23	2.8671	4.6390	42.2609
24	2.5613	4.9448	37.3161
25	2.2354	5.2707	32.0454
26	1.8880	5.6181	26.4274
27	1.5177	5.9884	20.4390
28	1.1230	6.3831	14.0560
29	.7023	6.8038	7.2522
30	.2539	7.2522	0.0000

YEARS 2 — MO PAYT 4.4546 — AN CONST 53.46

#	INT	PRIN	BALANCE
1	5.0755	48.3800	51.6200
2	1.8355	51.6200	0.0000

YEARS 3 — MO PAYT 3.0649 — AN CONST 36.78

#	INT	PRIN	BALANCE
1	5.5815	31.1973	68.8027
2	3.4921	33.2867	35.5160
3	1.2628	35.5160	0.0000

YEARS 4 — MO PAYT 2.3715 — AN CONST 28.46

#	INT	PRIN	BALANCE
1	5.8339	22.6241	77.3759
2	4.3187	24.1392	53.2367
3	2.7021	25.7559	27.4808
4	.9771	27.4808	0.0000

YEARS 5 — MO PAYT 1.9566 — AN CONST 23.48

#	INT	PRIN	BALANCE
1	5.9849	17.4945	82.5055
2	4.8133	18.6661	63.8394
3	3.5632	19.9162	43.9232
4	2.2293	21.2500	22.6732
5	.8062	22.6732	0.0000

YEARS 6 — MO PAYT 1.6810 — AN CONST 20.18

#	INT	PRIN	BALANCE
1	6.0852	14.0867	85.9133
2	5.1418	15.0301	70.8833
3	4.1352	16.0367	54.8466
4	3.0612	17.1107	37.7359
5	1.9153	18.2566	19.4793
6	.6926	19.4793	0.0000

YEARS 7 — MO PAYT 1.4849 — AN CONST 17.82

#	INT	PRIN	BALANCE
1	6.1566	11.6627	88.3373
2	5.3755	12.4438	75.8935
3	4.5422	13.2772	62.6163
4	3.6530	14.1664	48.4500
5	2.7042	15.1151	33.3349
6	1.6919	16.1274	17.2075
7	.6118	17.2075	0.0000

YEARS 8 — MO PAYT 1.3386 — AN CONST 16.07

#	INT	PRIN	BALANCE
1	6.2099	9.8536	90.1464
2	5.5500	10.5135	79.6329
3	4.8459	11.2176	68.4153
4	4.0946	11.9689	56.4464
5	3.2930	12.7705	43.6759
6	2.4378	13.6257	30.0502
7	1.5252	14.5383	15.5119
8	.5516	15.5119	0.0000

YEARS 9 — MO PAYT 1.2255 — AN CONST 14.71

#	INT	PRIN	BALANCE
1	6.2511	8.4543	91.5457
2	5.6849	9.0205	82.5251
3	5.0808	9.6247	72.9005
4	4.4362	10.2692	62.6312
5	3.7484	10.9570	51.6742
6	3.0146	11.6908	39.9834
7	2.2317	12.4738	27.5096
8	1.3963	13.3092	14.2005
9	.5049	14.2005	0.0000

YEARS 10 — MO PAYT 1.1355 — AN CONST 13.63

#	INT	PRIN	BALANCE
1	6.2838	7.3419	92.6581
2	5.7921	7.8336	84.8244
3	5.2675	8.3583	76.4662
4	4.7077	8.9180	67.5482
5	4.1105	9.5153	58.0329
6	3.4732	10.1525	47.8803
7	2.7933	10.8325	37.0479
8	2.0678	11.5579	25.4899
9	1.2938	12.3320	13.1579
10	.4679	13.1579	0.0000

YEARS 11 — MO PAYT 1.0624 — AN CONST 12.75

#	INT	PRIN	BALANCE
1	6.3104	6.4381	93.5619
2	5.8793	6.8692	86.6927
3	5.4192	7.3293	79.3634
4	4.9284	7.8201	71.5432
5	4.4046	8.3439	63.1994
6	3.8458	8.9027	54.2967
7	3.2496	9.4989	44.7978
8	2.6134	10.1351	34.6627
9	1.9347	10.8138	23.8488
10	1.2105	11.5381	12.3108
11	.4377	12.3108	0.0000

YEARS 12 — MO PAYT 1.0019 — AN CONST 12.03

#	INT	PRIN	BALANCE
1	6.3325	5.6906	94.3094
2	5.9513	6.0717	88.2377
3	5.5447	6.4783	81.7593
4	5.1108	6.9122	74.8471
5	4.6479	7.3751	67.4720
6	4.1540	7.8691	59.6029
7	3.6270	8.3961	51.2069
8	3.0647	8.9584	42.2485
9	2.4647	9.5583	32.6902
10	1.8246	10.1985	22.4917
11	1.1416	10.8815	11.6102
12	.4128	11.6102	0.0000

YEARS 13 — MO PAYT .9512 — AN CONST 11.42

#	INT	PRIN	BALANCE
1	6.3509	5.0634	94.9366
2	6.0118	5.4025	89.5342
3	5.6500	5.7643	83.7699
4	5.2640	6.1503	77.6196
5	4.8521	6.5622	71.0573
6	4.4126	7.0017	64.0556
7	3.9437	7.4706	56.5850
8	3.4433	7.9709	48.6141
9	2.9095	8.5048	40.1093
10	2.3399	9.0744	31.0349
11	1.7322	9.6821	21.3529
12	1.0838	10.3305	11.0224
13	.3919	11.0224	0.0000

YEARS 14 — MO PAYT .9081 — AN CONST 10.90

#	INT	PRIN	BALANCE
1	6.3666	4.5305	95.4695
2	6.0632	4.8340	90.6355
3	5.7394	5.1577	85.4778
4	5.3940	5.5031	79.9747
5	5.0255	5.8717	74.1030
6	4.6322	6.2649	67.8381
7	4.2127	6.6845	61.1536
8	3.7650	7.1322	54.0214
9	3.2873	7.6098	46.4116
10	2.7777	8.1195	38.2921
11	2.2339	8.6632	29.6289
12	1.6537	9.2434	20.3855
13	1.0347	9.8625	10.5230
14	.3742	10.5230	0.0000

YEARS 15 — MO PAYT .8711 — AN CONST 10.46

#	INT	PRIN	BALANCE
1	6.3801	4.0732	95.9268
2	6.1073	4.3460	91.5808
3	5.8162	4.6371	86.9437
4	5.5057	4.9476	81.9961
5	5.1743	5.2790	76.7171
6	4.8208	5.6325	71.0846
7	4.4436	6.0097	65.0749
8	4.0411	6.4122	58.6627
9	3.6116	6.8417	51.8210
10	3.1534	7.2999	44.5211
11	2.6646	7.7887	36.7324
12	2.1429	8.3104	28.4220
13	1.5864	8.8669	19.5551
14	.9925	9.4608	10.0944
15	.3589	10.0944	0.0000

YEARS 16 — MO PAYT .8391 — AN CONST 10.07

#	INT	PRIN	BALANCE
1	6.3917	3.6772	96.3228
2	6.1455	3.9234	92.3994
3	5.8827	4.1862	88.2132
4	5.6023	4.4666	83.7466
5	5.3032	4.7657	78.9810
6	4.9840	5.0849	73.8961
7	4.6435	5.4254	68.4707
8	4.2802	5.7887	62.6820
9	3.8925	6.1764	56.5055
10	3.4788	6.5901	49.9155
11	3.0375	7.0314	42.8840
12	2.5666	7.5023	35.3817
13	2.0641	8.0048	27.3769
14	1.5280	8.5409	18.8360
15	.9560	9.1129	9.7232
16	.3457	9.7232	0.0000

YEARS 17 — MO PAYT .8111 — AN CONST 9.74

#	INT	PRIN	BALANCE
1	6.4019	3.3315	96.6685
2	6.1788	3.5547	93.1138
3	5.9407	3.7927	89.3211
4	5.6867	4.0467	85.2743
5	5.4157	4.3177	80.9566
6	5.1265	4.6069	76.3497
7	4.8180	4.9155	71.4342
8	4.4888	5.2446	66.1896
9	4.1376	5.5959	60.5937
10	3.7628	5.9707	54.6230
11	3.3629	6.3705	48.2525
12	2.9363	6.7972	41.4553
13	2.4811	7.2524	34.2029
14	1.9954	7.7381	26.4648
15	1.4771	8.2563	18.2085
16	.9242	8.8093	9.3992
17	.3342	9.3992	0.0000

YEARS 18 — MO PAYT .7866 — AN CONST 9.44

#	INT	PRIN	BALANCE
1	6.4108	3.0279	96.9721
2	6.2081	3.2307	93.7414
3	5.9917	3.4470	90.2944
4	5.7608	3.6779	86.6165
5	5.5145	3.9242	82.6923
6	5.2517	4.1870	78.5053
7	4.9713	4.4674	74.0379
8	4.6721	4.7666	69.2713
9	4.3529	5.0858	64.1854
10	4.0123	5.4265	58.7590
11	3.6489	5.7899	52.9691
12	3.2611	6.1776	46.7915
13	2.8474	6.5914	40.2001
14	2.4059	7.0328	33.1673
15	1.9349	7.5038	25.6635
16	1.4324	8.0063	17.6572
17	.8962	8.5425	9.1146
18	.3241	9.1146	0.0000

YEARS 19 — MO PAYT .7649 — AN CONST 9.18

#	INT	PRIN	BALANCE
1	6.4188	2.7595	97.2405
2	6.2339	2.9443	94.2961
3	6.0368	3.1415	91.1546
4	5.8264	3.3519	87.8027
5	5.6019	3.5764	84.2263
6	5.3624	3.8159	80.4104
7	5.1068	4.0715	76.3389
8	4.8341	4.3441	71.9948
9	4.5432	4.6351	67.3597
10	4.2328	4.9455	62.4142
11	3.9016	5.2767	57.1375
12	3.5482	5.6301	51.5074
13	3.1711	6.0072	45.5002
14	2.7688	6.4095	39.0908
15	2.3395	6.8387	32.2521
16	1.8815	7.2967	24.9553
17	1.3929	7.7854	17.1699
18	.8715	8.3068	8.8631
19	.3151	8.8631	0.0000

YEARS 20 — MO PAYT .7456 — AN CONST 8.95

#	INT	PRIN	BALANCE
1	6.4258	2.5211	97.4789
2	6.2569	2.6899	94.7889
3	6.0768	2.8701	91.9188
4	5.8846	3.0623	88.8565
5	5.6795	3.2674	85.5891
6	5.4606	3.4862	82.1029
7	5.2272	3.7197	78.3832
8	4.9781	3.9688	74.4144
9	4.7123	4.2346	70.1797
10	4.4287	4.5182	65.6615
11	4.1261	4.8208	60.8407
12	3.8032	5.1437	55.6970
13	3.4587	5.4882	50.2089
14	3.0912	5.8557	44.3531
15	2.6990	6.2479	38.1053
16	2.2806	6.6663	31.4389
17	1.8341	7.1128	24.3262
18	1.3578	7.5891	16.7371
19	.8495	8.0974	8.6397
20	.3072	8.6397	0.0000

YEARS 21 — MO PAYT .7284 — AN CONST 8.75

#	INT	PRIN	BALANCE
1	6.4320	2.3083	97.6917
2	6.2774	2.4629	95.2288
3	6.1125	2.6279	92.6009

#	INT	PRIN	BALANCE
4	5.9365	2.8038	89.7971
5	5.7487	2.9916	86.8054
6	5.5484	3.1920	83.6135
7	5.3346	3.4058	80.2077
8	5.1065	3.6338	76.5738
9	4.8631	3.8772	72.6966
10	4.6035	4.1369	68.5598
11	4.3264	4.4139	64.1458
12	4.0308	4.7095	59.4363
13	3.7154	5.0249	54.4113
14	3.3789	5.3615	49.0499
15	3.0198	5.7205	43.3293
16	2.6367	6.1037	37.2257
17	2.2279	6.5124	30.7132
18	1.7918	6.9486	23.7647
19	1.3264	7.4139	16.3507
20	.8299	7.9105	8.4402
21	.3001	8.4402	0.0000

YEARS 22 MO PAYT .7129 AN CONST 8.56

#	INT	PRIN	BALANCE
1	6.4377	2.1176	97.8824
2	6.2958	2.2594	95.6229
3	6.1445	2.4108	93.2122
4	5.9831	2.5722	90.6400
5	5.8108	2.7445	87.8955
6	5.6270	2.9283	84.9672
7	5.4309	3.1244	81.8428
8	5.2216	3.3336	78.5092
9	4.9984	3.5569	74.9523
10	4.7602	3.7951	71.1572
11	4.5060	4.0493	67.1079
12	4.2348	4.3205	62.7875
13	3.9455	4.6098	58.1777
14	3.6367	4.9185	53.2591
15	3.3073	5.2479	48.0112
16	2.9559	5.5994	42.4118
17	2.5809	5.9744	36.4374
18	2.1807	6.3745	30.0628
19	1.7538	6.8014	23.2614
20	1.2983	7.2569	16.0045
21	.8123	7.7430	8.2615
22	.2938	8.2615	0.0000

YEARS 23 MO PAYT .6991 AN CONST 8.39

#	INT	PRIN	BALANCE
1	6.4427	1.9461	98.0539
2	6.3124	2.0764	95.9775
3	6.1733	2.2155	93.7621
4	6.0249	2.3638	91.3982
5	5.8666	2.5222	88.8761
6	5.6977	2.6911	86.1850
7	5.5175	2.8713	83.3137
8	5.3252	3.0636	80.2501
9	5.1200	3.2688	76.9814
10	4.9011	3.4877	73.4937
11	4.6675	3.7213	69.7724
12	4.4183	3.9705	65.8020
13	4.1524	4.2364	61.5656
14	3.8687	4.5201	57.0455
15	3.5660	4.8228	52.2227
16	3.2430	5.1458	47.0768
17	2.8983	5.4904	41.5864
18	2.5306	5.8581	35.7283
19	2.1383	6.2505	29.4778
20	1.7197	6.6691	22.8087
21	1.2731	7.1157	15.6930
22	.7965	7.5923	8.1007
23	.2880	8.1007	0.0000

YEARS 24 MO PAYT .6865 AN CONST 8.24

#	INT	PRIN	BALANCE
1	6.4473	1.7913	98.2087
2	6.3273	1.9112	96.2975
3	6.1993	2.0392	94.2583
4	6.0627	2.1758	92.0825
5	5.9170	2.3215	89.7610
6	5.7615	2.4770	87.2841
7	5.5957	2.6429	84.6412
8	5.4187	2.8199	81.8213
9	5.2298	3.0087	78.8126
10	5.0283	3.2102	75.6024
11	4.8133	3.4252	72.1772
12	4.5839	3.6546	68.5226
13	4.3392	3.8993	64.6233
14	4.0780	4.1605	60.4628
15	3.7994	4.4391	56.0236
16	3.5021	4.7364	51.2872
17	3.1849	5.0536	46.2336
18	2.8464	5.3921	40.8415
19	2.4853	5.7532	35.0883
20	2.1000	6.1385	28.9498
21	1.6889	6.5496	22.4002
22	1.2503	6.9883	15.4119
23	.7822	7.4563	7.9556
24	.2829	7.9556	0.0000

YEARS 25 MO PAYT .6752 AN CONST 8.11

#	INT	PRIN	BALANCE
1	6.4514	1.6511	98.3489
2	6.3408	1.7617	96.5872
3	6.2228	1.8797	94.7076
4	6.0969	2.0055	92.7020
5	5.9626	2.1399	90.5622
6	5.8193	2.2832	88.2790
7	5.6664	2.4361	85.8429
8	5.5033	2.5992	83.2437
9	5.3292	2.7733	80.4704
10	5.1435	2.9590	77.5114
11	4.9453	3.1572	74.3542
12	4.7338	3.3686	70.9855
13	4.5082	3.5943	67.3913
14	4.2675	3.8350	63.5563
15	4.0107	4.0918	59.4645
16	3.7366	4.3658	55.0986
17	3.4443	4.6582	50.4404
18	3.1323	4.9702	45.4702
19	2.7994	5.3031	40.1672
20	2.4443	5.6582	34.5089
21	2.0653	6.0372	28.4718
22	1.6610	6.4415	22.0303
23	1.2296	6.8729	15.1574
24	.7693	7.3332	7.8243
25	.2782	7.8243	0.0000

YEARS 26 MO PAYT .6649 AN CONST 7.98

#	INT	PRIN	BALANCE
1	6.4551	1.5239	98.4761
2	6.3531	1.6259	96.8502
3	6.2442	1.7348	95.1153
4	6.1280	1.8510	93.2643
5	6.0040	1.9750	91.2894
6	5.8718	2.1072	89.1821
7	5.7306	2.2484	86.9337
8	5.5801	2.3990	84.5348
9	5.4194	2.5596	81.9752
10	5.2480	2.7310	79.2441
11	5.0651	2.9139	76.3302
12	4.8699	3.1091	73.2211
13	4.6617	3.3173	69.9038
14	4.4395	3.5395	66.3643
15	4.2025	3.7765	62.5878
16	3.9496	4.0294	58.5583
17	3.6797	4.2993	54.2590
18	3.3918	4.5872	49.6718
19	3.0846	4.8945	44.7773
20	2.7568	5.2222	39.5551
21	2.4070	5.5720	33.9831
22	2.0339	5.9452	28.0379
23	1.6357	6.3433	21.6946
24	1.2109	6.7681	14.9265
25	.7576	7.2214	7.7050
26	.2740	7.7050	0.0000

YEARS 27 MO PAYT .6556 AN CONST 7.87

#	INT	PRIN	BALANCE
1	6.4585	1.4081	98.5919
2	6.3642	1.5024	97.0895
3	6.2636	1.6030	95.4864
4	6.1563	1.7104	93.7760
5	6.0417	1.8250	91.9511
6	5.9195	1.9472	90.0039
7	5.7891	2.0776	87.9263
8	5.6499	2.2167	85.7096
9	5.5015	2.3652	83.3444
10	5.3431	2.5236	80.8209
11	5.1741	2.6926	78.1283
12	4.9938	2.8729	75.2554
13	4.8013	3.0653	72.1900
14	4.5961	3.2706	68.9194
15	4.3770	3.4896	65.4298
16	4.1433	3.7233	61.7065
17	3.8940	3.9727	57.7337
18	3.6279	4.2388	53.4950
19	3.3440	4.5226	48.9723
20	3.0411	4.8255	44.1468
21	2.7179	5.1487	38.9981
22	2.3731	5.4935	33.5045
23	2.0052	5.8614	27.6431
24	1.6127	6.2540	21.3891
25	1.1938	6.6728	14.7163
26	.7469	7.1197	7.5965
27	.2701	7.5965	0.0000

YEARS 28 MO PAYT .6470 AN CONST 7.77

#	INT	PRIN	BALANCE
1	6.4616	1.3025	98.6975
2	6.3744	1.3898	97.3077
3	6.2813	1.4829	95.8248
4	6.1820	1.5822	94.2427
5	6.0761	1.6881	92.5545
6	5.9630	1.8012	90.7534
7	5.8424	1.9218	88.8316
8	5.7137	2.0505	86.7810
9	5.5764	2.1878	84.5932
10	5.4298	2.3344	82.2588
11	5.2735	2.4907	79.7681
12	5.1067	2.6575	77.1106
13	4.9287	2.8355	74.2751
14	4.7388	3.0254	71.2497
15	4.5362	3.2280	68.0217
16	4.3200	3.4442	64.5775
17	4.0893	3.6749	60.9027
18	3.8432	3.9210	56.9817
19	3.5806	4.1836	52.7982
20	3.3005	4.4637	48.3344
21	3.0015	4.7627	43.5718
22	2.6825	5.0816	38.4901
23	2.3422	5.4220	33.0681
24	1.9791	5.7851	27.2830
25	1.5917	6.1725	21.1105
26	1.1783	6.5859	14.5246
27	.7372	7.0270	7.4976
28	.2666	7.4976	0.0000

YEARS 29 MO PAYT .6392 AN CONST 7.68

#	INT	PRIN	BALANCE
1	6.4645	1.2061	98.7939
2	6.3837	1.2868	97.5071
3	6.2975	1.3730	96.1341
4	6.2056	1.4650	94.6691
5	6.1075	1.5631	93.1060
6	6.0028	1.6678	91.4383
7	5.8911	1.7795	89.6588
8	5.7719	1.8986	87.7602
9	5.6448	2.0258	85.7344
10	5.5091	2.1615	83.5729
11	5.3643	2.3062	81.2667
12	5.2099	2.4607	78.8061
13	5.0451	2.6255	76.1806
14	4.8693	2.8013	73.3793
15	4.6817	2.9889	70.3904
16	4.4815	3.1891	67.2014
17	4.2679	3.4026	63.7987
18	4.0400	3.6305	60.1682
19	3.7969	3.8737	56.2945
20	3.5375	4.1331	52.1614
21	3.2607	4.4099	47.7515
22	2.9653	4.7052	43.0463
23	2.6502	5.0204	38.0259
24	2.3140	5.3566	32.6693
25	1.9552	5.7153	26.9540
26	1.5725	6.0981	20.8559
27	1.1641	6.5065	14.3494
28	.7283	6.9422	7.4072
29	.2634	7.4072	0.0000

YEARS 30 MO PAYT .6321 AN CONST 7.59

#	INT	PRIN	BALANCE
1	6.4671	1.1177	98.8823
2	6.3922	1.1926	97.6897
3	6.3124	1.2725	96.4172
4	6.2271	1.3577	95.0596
5	6.1362	1.4486	93.6110
6	6.0392	1.5456	92.0654
7	5.9357	1.6491	90.4162
8	5.8252	1.7596	88.6567
9	5.7074	1.8774	86.7793
10	5.5817	2.0031	84.7761
11	5.4475	2.1373	82.6388
12	5.3044	2.2804	80.3584
13	5.1517	2.4332	77.9252
14	4.9887	2.5961	75.3291
15	4.8148	2.7700	72.5591
16	4.6293	2.9555	69.6037
17	4.4314	3.1534	66.4502
18	4.2202	3.3646	63.0856
19	3.9949	3.5900	59.4957
20	3.7544	3.8304	55.6653
21	3.4979	4.0869	51.5784
22	3.2242	4.3606	47.2178
23	2.9322	4.6526	42.5651
24	2.6206	4.9642	37.6009
25	2.2881	5.2967	32.3042
26	1.9334	5.6514	26.6527
27	1.5549	6.0299	20.6228
28	1.1511	6.4338	14.1890
29	.7202	6.8646	7.3244
30	.2604	7.3244	0.0000

MONTHLY PAYMENT AMORTIZATION SCHEDULE PER $100

YEARS 2 — MO PAYT 4.4591 — AN CONST 53.51

#	INT	PRIN	BALANCE
1	5.1546	48.3551	51.6449
2	1.8649	51.6449	0.0000

YEARS 3 — MO PAYT 3.0695 — AN CONST 36.84

#	INT	PRIN	BALANCE
1	5.6685	31.1650	68.8350
2	3.5482	33.2853	35.5498
3	1.2837	35.5498	0.0000

YEARS 4 — MO PAYT 2.3761 — AN CONST 28.52

#	INT	PRIN	BALANCE
1	5.9248	22.5885	77.4115
2	4.3880	24.1253	53.2862
3	2.7467	25.7666	27.5196
4	.9937	27.5196	0.0000

YEARS 5 — MO PAYT 1.9613 — AN CONST 23.54

#	INT	PRIN	BALANCE
1	6.0782	17.4574	82.5426
2	4.8905	18.6451	63.8974
3	3.6220	19.9136	43.9838
4	2.2672	21.2684	22.7154
5	.8202	22.7154	0.0000

YEARS 6 — MO PAYT 1.6858 — AN CONST 20.23

#	INT	PRIN	BALANCE
1	6.1801	14.0490	85.9510
2	5.2243	15.0048	70.9461
3	4.2034	16.0257	54.9205
4	3.1131	17.1160	37.8045
5	1.9487	18.2804	19.5241
6	.7050	19.5241	0.0000

YEARS 7 — MO PAYT 1.4898 — AN CONST 17.88

#	INT	PRIN	BALANCE
1	6.2525	11.6250	88.3750
2	5.4616	12.4158	75.9592
3	4.6169	13.2605	62.6987
4	3.7148	14.1627	48.5360
5	2.7512	15.1262	33.4098
6	1.7222	16.1553	17.2544
7	.6230	17.2544	0.0000

YEARS 8 — MO PAYT 1.3436 — AN CONST 16.13

#	INT	PRIN	BALANCE
1	6.3066	9.8160	90.1840
2	5.6388	10.4838	79.7001
3	4.9255	11.1971	68.5030
4	4.1637	11.9589	56.5442
5	3.3501	12.7725	43.7717
6	2.4812	13.6414	30.1302
7	1.5531	14.5695	15.5607
8	.5619	15.5607	0.0000

YEARS 9 — MO PAYT 1.2305 — AN CONST 14.77

#	INT	PRIN	BALANCE
1	6.3484	8.4171	91.5829
2	5.7758	8.9898	82.5931
3	5.1642	9.6014	72.9917
4	4.5109	10.2546	62.7370
5	3.8133	10.9523	51.7848
6	3.0682	11.6974	40.0874
7	2.2723	12.4932	27.5941
8	1.4224	13.3432	14.2510
9	.5146	14.2510	0.0000

YEARS 10 — MO PAYT 1.1406 — AN CONST 13.69

#	INT	PRIN	BALANCE
1	6.3816	7.3053	92.6947
2	5.8846	7.8023	84.8925
3	5.3538	8.3331	76.5594
4	4.7869	8.9000	67.6594
5	4.1814	9.5055	58.1539
6	3.5347	10.1522	48.0017
7	2.8440	10.8429	37.1589
8	2.1063	11.5806	25.5783
9	1.3185	12.3684	13.2099
10	.4770	13.2099	0.0000

YEARS 11 — MO PAYT 1.0676 — AN CONST 12.82

#	INT	PRIN	BALANCE
1	6.4086	6.4020	93.5980
2	5.9731	6.8376	86.7604
3	5.5079	7.3028	79.4577
4	5.0111	7.7996	71.6581
5	4.4804	8.3302	63.3279
6	3.9137	8.8970	54.4309
7	3.3084	9.5022	44.9287
8	2.6619	10.1487	34.7800
9	1.9715	10.8392	23.9408
10	1.2341	11.5766	12.3642
11	.4465	12.3642	0.0000

YEARS 12 — MO PAYT 1.0072 — AN CONST 12.09

#	INT	PRIN	BALANCE
1	6.4310	5.6552	94.3448
2	6.0462	6.0400	88.3048
3	5.6353	6.4509	81.8539
4	5.1964	6.8898	74.9642
5	4.7277	7.3585	67.6057
6	4.2271	7.8591	59.7465
7	3.6924	8.3938	51.3527
8	3.1213	8.9649	42.3879
9	2.5114	9.5748	32.8131
10	1.8600	10.2262	22.5869
11	1.1643	10.9219	11.6650
12	.4212	11.6650	0.0000

YEARS 13 — MO PAYT .9565 — AN CONST 11.48

#	INT	PRIN	BALANCE
1	6.4497	5.0287	94.9713
2	6.1076	5.3708	89.6004
3	5.7422	5.7362	83.8642
4	5.3519	6.1265	77.7377
5	4.9351	6.5433	71.1944
6	4.4899	6.9885	64.2060
7	4.0145	7.4639	56.7420
8	3.5067	7.9717	48.7703
9	2.9644	8.5141	40.2563
10	2.3851	9.0933	31.1630
11	1.7665	9.7119	21.4511
12	1.1057	10.3727	11.0784
13	.4000	11.0784	0.0000

YEARS 14 — MO PAYT .9135 — AN CONST 10.97

#	INT	PRIN	BALANCE
1	6.4656	4.4967	95.5033
2	6.1597	4.8026	90.7007
3	5.8329	5.1293	85.5714
4	5.4840	5.4783	80.0931
5	5.1113	5.8510	74.2421
6	4.7132	6.2491	67.9930
7	4.2880	6.6742	61.3188
8	3.8340	7.1283	54.1905
9	3.3490	7.6132	46.5773
10	2.8311	8.1312	38.4461
11	2.2779	8.6844	29.7617
12	1.6870	9.2752	20.4865
13	1.0560	9.9063	10.5802
14	.3820	10.5802	0.0000

YEARS 15 — MO PAYT .8766 — AN CONST 10.52

#	INT	PRIN	BALANCE
1	6.4792	4.0401	95.9599
2	6.2044	4.3150	91.6449
3	5.9108	4.6086	87.0363
4	5.5973	4.9221	82.1142
5	5.2624	5.2570	76.8573
6	4.9048	5.6146	71.2426
7	4.5228	5.9966	65.2460
8	4.1148	6.4046	58.8415
9	3.6791	6.8403	52.0012
10	3.2137	7.3057	44.6955
11	2.7167	7.8027	36.8928
12	2.1858	8.3335	28.5593
13	1.6189	8.9005	19.6588
14	1.0133	9.5060	10.1528
15	.3666	10.1528	0.0000

YEARS 16 — MO PAYT .8447 — AN CONST 10.14

#	INT	PRIN	BALANCE
1	6.4911	3.6449	96.3551
2	6.2431	3.8929	92.4622
3	5.9782	4.1577	88.3045
4	5.6954	4.4406	83.8639
5	5.3933	4.7427	79.1212
6	5.0706	5.0654	74.0559
7	4.7260	5.4100	68.6459
8	4.3579	5.7780	62.8679
9	3.9648	6.1711	56.6968
10	3.5450	6.5910	50.1058
11	3.0966	7.0394	43.0664
12	2.6177	7.5183	35.5481
13	2.1062	8.0298	27.5183
14	1.5599	8.5761	18.9422
15	.9764	9.1595	9.7827
16	.3532	9.7827	0.0000

YEARS 17 — MO PAYT .8168 — AN CONST 9.81

#	INT	PRIN	BALANCE
1	6.5014	3.3001	96.6999
2	6.2768	3.5246	93.1753
3	6.0370	3.7644	89.4109
4	5.7809	4.0205	85.3904
5	5.5074	4.2940	81.0963
6	5.2153	4.5862	76.5102
7	4.9033	4.8982	71.6120
8	4.5700	5.2314	66.3805
9	4.2141	5.5873	60.7932
10	3.8340	5.9675	54.8257
11	3.4280	6.3735	48.4522
12	2.9944	6.8071	41.6452
13	2.5313	7.2702	34.3750
14	2.0367	7.7648	26.6102
15	1.5084	8.2931	18.3171
16	.9442	8.8573	9.4599
17	.3416	9.4599	0.0000

YEARS 18 — MO PAYT .7923 — AN CONST 9.51

#	INT	PRIN	BALANCE
1	6.5104	2.9973	97.0027
2	6.3065	3.2012	93.8015
3	6.0887	3.4190	90.3826
4	5.8561	3.6516	86.7310
5	5.6077	3.9000	82.8310
6	5.3423	4.1653	78.6657
7	5.0590	4.4487	74.2169
8	4.7563	4.7514	69.4656
9	4.4330	5.0746	64.3909
10	4.0878	5.4199	58.9711
11	3.7191	5.7886	53.1824
12	3.3252	6.1824	47.0000
13	2.9046	6.6030	40.3970
14	2.4554	7.0523	33.3447
15	1.9756	7.5321	25.8126
16	1.4632	8.0445	17.7681
17	.9159	8.5918	9.1763
18	.3314	9.1763	0.0000

YEARS 19 — MO PAYT .7707 — AN CONST 9.25

#	INT	PRIN	BALANCE
1	6.5184	2.7297	97.2703
2	6.3327	2.9155	94.3548
3	6.1343	3.1138	91.2410
4	5.9225	3.3256	87.9154
5	5.6962	3.5519	84.3635
6	5.4546	3.7935	80.5699
7	5.1965	4.0516	76.5183
8	4.9209	4.3273	72.1910
9	4.6265	4.6217	67.5693
10	4.3120	4.9361	62.6332
11	3.9762	5.2719	57.3613
12	3.6175	5.6306	51.7307
13	3.2345	6.0137	45.7170
14	2.8253	6.4228	39.2942
15	2.3884	6.8598	32.4345
16	1.9217	7.3265	25.1080
17	1.4232	7.8249	17.2831
18	.8909	8.3573	8.9258
19	.3223	8.9258	0.0000

YEARS 20 — MO PAYT .7515 — AN CONST 9.02

#	INT	PRIN	BALANCE
1	6.5255	2.4922	97.5078
2	6.3560	2.6617	94.8461
3	6.1749	2.8428	92.0033
4	5.9815	3.0362	88.9671
5	5.7749	3.2428	85.7244
6	5.5543	3.4634	82.2610
7	5.3187	3.6990	78.5620
8	5.0670	3.9507	74.6113
9	4.7982	4.2194	70.3919
10	4.5112	4.5065	65.8854
11	4.2046	4.8131	61.0723
12	3.8771	5.1405	55.9318
13	3.5274	5.4903	50.4415
14	3.1539	5.8638	44.5777
15	2.7549	6.2627	38.3150
16	2.3289	6.6888	31.6261
17	1.8738	7.1439	24.4823
18	1.3878	7.6299	16.8524
19	.8687	8.1490	8.7034
20	.3143	8.7034	0.0000

YEARS 21 — MO PAYT .7343 — AN CONST 8.82

#	INT	PRIN	BALANCE
1	6.5318	2.2802	97.7198
2	6.3767	2.4353	95.2845
3	6.2110	2.6010	92.6835

#	INT	PRIN	BALANCE
4	6.0341	2.7780	89.9055
5	5.8451	2.9670	86.9385
6	5.6432	3.1688	83.7697
7	5.4276	3.3844	80.3853
8	5.1974	3.6147	76.7706
9	4.9515	3.8606	72.9101
10	4.6888	4.1232	68.7868
11	4.4083	4.4037	64.3831
12	4.1087	4.7033	59.6797
13	3.7887	5.0233	54.6564
14	3.4470	5.3651	49.2913
15	3.0820	5.7301	43.5612
16	2.6921	6.1199	37.4413
17	2.2758	6.5363	30.9050
18	1.8311	6.9810	23.9240
19	1.3561	7.4559	16.4681
20	.8489	7.9632	8.5049
21	.3071	8.5049	0.0000

YEARS 22 — MO PAYT .7190 — AN CONST 8.63

#	INT	PRIN	BALANCE
1	6.5375	2.0903	97.9097
2	6.3953	2.2325	95.6771
3	6.2434	2.3844	93.2927
4	6.0812	2.5466	90.7461
5	5.9079	2.7199	88.0262
6	5.7229	2.9049	85.1212
7	5.5253	3.1026	82.0186
8	5.3142	3.3137	78.7050
9	5.0887	3.5391	75.1659
10	4.8480	3.7799	71.3860
11	4.5908	4.0370	67.3490
12	4.3162	4.3117	63.0373
13	4.0228	4.6050	58.4322
14	3.7095	4.9183	53.5139
15	3.3749	5.2529	48.2610
16	3.0175	5.6103	42.6507
17	2.6358	5.9920	36.6587
18	2.2282	6.3997	30.2590
19	1.7928	6.8351	23.4239
20	1.3278	7.3001	16.1239
21	.8311	7.7967	8.3272
22	.3007	8.3272	0.0000

YEARS 23 — MO PAYT .7052 — AN CONST 8.47

#	INT	PRIN	BALANCE
1	6.5426	1.9196	98.0804
2	6.4120	2.0502	96.0302
3	6.2725	2.1897	93.8405
4	6.1236	2.3387	91.5019
5	5.9645	2.4978	89.0041
6	5.7945	2.6677	86.3364
7	5.6130	2.8492	83.4872
8	5.4192	3.0430	80.4442
9	5.2122	3.2501	77.1942
10	4.9911	3.4712	73.7230
11	4.7549	3.7073	70.0157
12	4.5027	3.9595	66.0561
13	4.2333	4.2289	61.8272
14	3.9456	4.5166	57.3106
15	3.6383	4.8239	52.4867
16	3.3101	5.1521	47.3346
17	2.9596	5.5026	41.8319
18	2.5852	5.8770	35.9550
19	2.1854	6.2768	29.6781
20	1.7584	6.7038	22.9743
21	1.3023	7.1599	15.8144
22	.8152	7.6471	8.1673
23	.2949	8.1673	0.0000

YEARS 24 — MO PAYT .6927 — AN CONST 8.32

#	INT	PRIN	BALANCE
1	6.5472	1.7656	98.2344
2	6.4271	1.8857	96.3487
3	6.2988	2.0140	94.3347
4	6.1618	2.1510	92.1837
5	6.0155	2.2974	89.8863
6	5.8592	2.4537	87.4327
7	5.6922	2.6206	84.8121
8	5.5139	2.7989	82.0132
9	5.3235	2.9893	79.0239
10	5.1201	3.1927	75.8312
11	4.9029	3.4099	72.4213
12	4.6710	3.6419	68.7795
13	4.4232	3.8896	64.8898
14	4.1586	4.1543	60.7356
15	3.8759	4.4369	56.2987
16	3.5741	4.7387	51.5600
17	3.2517	5.0611	46.4988
18	2.9073	5.4055	41.0934
19	2.5396	5.7732	35.3201
20	2.1468	6.1660	29.1541
21	1.7273	6.5855	22.5687
22	1.2793	7.0335	15.5351
23	.8008	7.5120	8.0231
24	.2897	8.0231	0.0000

YEARS 25 — MO PAYT .6815 — AN CONST 8.18

#	INT	PRIN	BALANCE
1	6.5514	1.6262	98.3738
2	6.4408	1.7369	96.6369
3	6.3226	1.8550	94.7818
4	6.1964	1.9812	92.8006
5	6.0616	2.1160	90.6846
6	5.9176	2.2600	88.4246
7	5.7639	2.4138	86.0108
8	5.5997	2.5780	83.4328
9	5.4243	2.7534	80.6795
10	5.2369	2.9407	77.7388
11	5.0369	3.1407	74.5980
12	4.8232	3.3544	71.2436
13	4.5950	3.5826	67.6610
14	4.3513	3.8264	63.8346
15	4.0909	4.0867	59.7479
16	3.8129	4.3647	55.3832
17	3.5159	4.6617	50.7215
18	3.1988	4.9788	45.7426
19	2.8601	5.3176	40.4251
20	2.4983	5.6793	34.7457
21	2.1119	6.0657	28.6800
22	1.6992	6.4784	22.2016
23	1.2585	6.9191	15.2825
24	.7878	7.3899	7.8926
25	.2850	7.8926	0.0000

YEARS 26 — MO PAYT .6712 — AN CONST 8.06

#	INT	PRIN	BALANCE
1	6.5552	1.4998	98.5002
2	6.4531	1.6018	96.8983
3	6.3442	1.7108	95.1875
4	6.2278	1.8272	93.3603
5	6.1034	1.9515	91.4088
6	5.9707	2.0843	89.3245
7	5.8289	2.2261	87.0984
8	5.6774	2.3776	84.7208
9	5.5157	2.5393	82.1815
10	5.3429	2.7121	79.4694
11	5.1584	2.8966	76.5728
12	4.9613	3.0936	73.4792
13	4.7509	3.3041	70.1751
14	4.5261	3.5289	66.6462
15	4.2860	3.7690	62.8772
16	4.0296	4.0254	58.8518
17	3.7557	4.2993	54.5525
18	3.4632	4.5918	49.9607
19	3.1508	4.9042	45.0566
20	2.8172	5.2378	39.8188
21	2.4608	5.5942	34.2246
22	2.0802	5.9747	28.2499
23	1.6738	6.3812	21.8687
24	1.2396	6.8154	15.0533
25	.7759	7.2790	7.7743
26	.2807	7.7743	0.0000

YEARS 27 — MO PAYT .6620 — AN CONST 7.95

#	INT	PRIN	BALANCE
1	6.5586	1.3848	98.6152
2	6.4644	1.4790	97.1361
3	6.3638	1.5797	95.5565
4	6.2563	1.6871	93.8693
5	6.1415	1.8019	92.0674
6	6.0189	1.9245	90.1429
7	5.8880	2.0554	88.0875
8	5.7482	2.1953	85.8922
9	5.5988	2.3446	83.5476
10	5.4393	2.5041	81.0434
11	5.2689	2.6745	78.3689
12	5.0870	2.8565	75.5124
13	4.8926	3.0508	72.4616
14	4.6851	3.2584	69.2033
15	4.4634	3.4800	65.7232
16	4.2266	3.7168	62.0064
17	3.9738	3.9697	58.0368
18	3.7037	4.2397	53.7971
19	3.4153	4.5282	49.2689
20	3.1072	4.8362	44.4326
21	2.7782	5.1653	39.2674
22	2.4267	5.5167	33.7507
23	2.0514	5.8920	27.8587
24	1.6506	6.2929	21.5658
25	1.2224	6.7210	14.8448
26	.7652	7.1782	7.6666
27	.2768	7.6666	0.0000

YEARS 28 — MO PAYT .6535 — AN CONST 7.85

#	INT	PRIN	BALANCE
1	6.5617	1.2800	98.7200
2	6.4747	1.3671	97.3529
3	6.3816	1.4601	95.8928
4	6.2823	1.5594	94.3333
5	6.1762	1.6655	92.6678
6	6.0629	1.7789	90.8889
7	5.9419	1.8999	88.9891
8	5.8126	2.0291	86.9599
9	5.6746	2.1672	84.7928
10	5.5271	2.3146	82.4781
11	5.3697	2.4721	80.0060
12	5.2015	2.6403	77.3658
13	5.0219	2.8199	74.5459
14	4.8300	3.0118	71.5341
15	4.6251	3.2167	68.3175
16	4.4063	3.4355	64.8820
17	4.1725	3.6692	61.2128
18	3.9229	3.9189	57.2939
19	3.6563	4.1855	53.1084
20	3.3715	4.4702	48.6382
21	3.0674	4.7743	43.8639
22	2.7426	5.0992	38.7647
23	2.3957	5.4461	33.3187
24	2.0252	5.8166	27.5021
25	1.6294	6.2123	21.2898
26	1.2068	6.6350	14.6548
27	.7554	7.0864	7.5685
28	.2733	7.5685	0.0000

YEARS 29 — MO PAYT .6457 — AN CONST 7.75

#	INT	PRIN	BALANCE
1	6.5646	1.1843	98.8157
2	6.4840	1.2649	97.5509
3	6.3980	1.3509	96.1999
4	6.3061	1.4428	94.7571
5	6.2079	1.5410	93.2162
6	6.1031	1.6458	91.5703
7	5.9911	1.7578	89.8126
8	5.8715	1.8774	87.9352
9	5.7438	2.0051	85.9301
10	5.6074	2.1415	83.7886
11	5.4617	2.2872	81.5014
12	5.3061	2.4428	79.0585
13	5.1399	2.6090	76.4495
14	4.9624	2.7865	73.6630
15	4.7728	2.9761	70.6869
16	4.5703	3.1786	67.5084
17	4.3541	3.3948	64.1136
18	4.1231	3.6258	60.4878
19	3.8764	3.8724	56.6154
20	3.6130	4.1359	52.4795
21	3.3316	4.4173	48.0622
22	3.0311	4.7178	43.3444
23	2.7101	5.0388	38.3056
24	2.3673	5.3816	32.9241
25	2.0012	5.7477	27.1764
26	1.6102	6.1387	21.0376
27	1.1925	6.5564	14.4813
28	.7465	7.0024	7.4788
29	.2701	7.4788	0.0000

YEARS 30 — MO PAYT .6387 — AN CONST 7.67

#	INT	PRIN	BALANCE
1	6.5672	1.0967	98.9033
2	6.4926	1.1713	97.7320
3	6.4129	1.2510	96.4810
4	6.3278	1.3361	95.1449
5	6.2369	1.4270	93.7179
6	6.1398	1.5241	92.1939
7	6.0361	1.6278	90.5661
8	5.9254	1.7385	88.8276
9	5.8071	1.8568	86.9708
10	5.6808	1.9831	84.9877
11	5.5459	2.1180	82.8697
12	5.4018	2.2621	80.6075
13	5.2479	2.4160	78.1915
14	5.0835	2.5804	75.6111
15	4.9080	2.7559	72.8552
16	4.7205	2.9434	69.9117
17	4.5202	3.1437	66.7680
18	4.3063	3.3576	63.4105
19	4.0779	3.5860	59.8245
20	3.8339	3.8300	55.9945
21	3.5734	4.0905	51.9040
22	3.2951	4.3688	47.5351
23	2.9978	4.6661	42.8691
24	2.6804	4.9835	37.8856
25	2.3414	5.3226	32.5630
26	1.9792	5.6847	26.8783
27	1.5925	6.0714	20.8069
28	1.1794	6.4845	14.3224
29	.7383	6.9256	7.3968
30	.2671	7.3968	0.0000

YEARS 2 — MO PAYT 4.4603 — AN CONST 53.53

#	INT	PRIN	BALANCE
1	5.1744	48.3489	51.6511
2	1.8722	51.6511	0.0000

YEARS 3 — MO PAYT 3.0706 — AN CONST 36.85

#	INT	PRIN	BALANCE
1	5.6902	31.1569	68.8431
2	3.5622	33.2849	35.5582
3	1.2889	35.5582	0.0000

YEARS 4 — MO PAYT 2.3773 — AN CONST 28.53

#	INT	PRIN	BALANCE
1	5.9476	22.5796	77.4204
2	4.4054	24.1218	53.2986
3	2.7579	25.7693	27.5293
4	.9979	27.5293	0.0000

YEARS 5 — MO PAYT 1.9625 — AN CONST 23.55

#	INT	PRIN	BALANCE
1	6.1015	17.4482	82.5518
2	4.9098	18.6399	63.9119
3	3.6367	19.9130	43.9990
4	2.2767	21.2730	22.7259
5	.8238	22.7259	0.0000

YEARS 6 — MO PAYT 1.6870 — AN CONST 20.25

#	INT	PRIN	BALANCE
1	6.2038	14.0396	85.9604
2	5.2449	14.9985	70.9618
3	4.2205	16.0229	54.9389
4	3.1261	17.1173	37.8217
5	1.9571	18.2864	19.5353
6	.7081	19.5353	0.0000

YEARS 7 — MO PAYT 1.4910 — AN CONST 17.90

#	INT	PRIN	BALANCE
1	6.2765	11.6155	88.3845
2	5.4832	12.4089	75.9756
3	4.6357	13.2564	62.7192
4	3.7303	14.1618	48.5575
5	2.7630	15.1290	33.4285
6	1.7297	16.1623	17.2662
7	.6259	17.2662	0.0000

YEARS 8 — MO PAYT 1.3448 — AN CONST 16.14

#	INT	PRIN	BALANCE
1	6.3308	9.8066	90.1934
2	5.6610	10.4764	79.7169
3	4.9455	11.1920	68.5250
4	4.1811	11.9564	56.5686
5	3.3644	12.7730	43.7956
6	2.4921	13.6454	30.1503
7	1.5601	14.5773	15.5729
8	.5645	15.5729	0.0000

YEARS 9 — MO PAYT 1.2317 — AN CONST 14.79

#	INT	PRIN	BALANCE
1	6.3727	8.4079	91.5921
2	5.7985	8.9821	82.6100
3	5.1850	9.5956	73.0144
4	4.5297	10.2510	62.7635
5	3.8295	10.9511	51.8124
6	3.0816	11.6990	40.1133
7	2.2825	12.4981	27.6153
8	1.4289	13.3517	14.2636
9	.5170	14.2636	0.0000

YEARS 10 — MO PAYT 1.1419 — AN CONST 13.71

#	INT	PRIN	BALANCE
1	6.4061	7.2961	92.7039
2	5.9078	7.7944	84.9095
3	5.3754	8.3268	76.5827
4	4.8067	8.8955	67.6872
5	4.1992	9.5030	58.1842
6	3.5501	10.1521	48.0321
7	2.8567	10.8455	37.1866
8	2.1160	11.5862	25.6004
9	1.3247	12.3775	13.2229
10	.4793	13.2229	0.0000

YEARS 11 — MO PAYT 1.0689 — AN CONST 12.83

#	INT	PRIN	BALANCE
1	6.4332	6.3930	93.6070
2	5.9966	6.8297	86.7773
3	5.5301	7.2961	79.4812
4	5.0318	7.7944	71.6868
5	4.4994	8.3268	63.3600
6	3.9307	8.8955	54.4645
7	3.3232	9.5031	44.9614
8	2.6741	10.1521	34.8093
9	1.9807	10.8455	23.9638
10	1.2400	11.5862	12.3776
11	.4487	12.3776	0.0000

YEARS 12 — MO PAYT 1.0085 — AN CONST 12.11

#	INT	PRIN	BALANCE
1	6.4556	5.6464	94.3536
2	6.0699	6.0320	88.3216
3	5.6580	6.4440	81.8775
4	5.2178	6.8842	74.9934
5	4.7477	7.3543	67.6390
6	4.2454	7.8566	59.7824
7	3.7088	8.3932	51.3892
8	3.1355	8.9665	42.4227
9	2.5231	9.5789	32.8438
10	1.8689	10.2331	22.6107
11	1.1700	10.9320	11.6787
12	.4233	11.6787	0.0000

YEARS 13 — MO PAYT .9579 — AN CONST 11.50

#	INT	PRIN	BALANCE
1	6.4744	5.0201	94.9799
2	6.1315	5.3629	89.6170
3	5.7652	5.7292	83.8877
4	5.3739	6.1205	77.7672
5	4.9559	6.5386	71.2286
6	4.5093	6.9851	64.2435
7	4.0322	7.4622	56.7813
8	3.5226	7.9719	48.8094
9	2.9781	8.5164	40.2930
10	2.3965	9.0980	31.1950
11	1.7751	9.7194	21.4756
12	1.1112	10.3832	11.0924
13	.4021	11.0924	0.0000

YEARS 14 — MO PAYT .9149 — AN CONST 10.98

#	INT	PRIN	BALANCE
1	6.4903	4.4882	95.5118
2	6.1838	4.7948	90.7170
3	5.8563	5.1222	85.5948
4	5.5065	5.4721	80.1227
5	5.1327	5.8458	74.2768
6	4.7335	6.2451	68.0317
7	4.3069	6.6716	61.3601
8	3.8513	7.1273	54.2328
9	3.3645	7.6141	46.6187
10	2.8444	8.1341	38.4846
11	2.2889	8.6897	29.7949
12	1.6954	9.2832	20.5117
13	1.0614	9.9172	10.5945
14	.3840	10.5945	0.0000

YEARS 15 — MO PAYT .8780 — AN CONST 10.54

#	INT	PRIN	BALANCE
1	6.5040	4.0319	95.9681
2	6.2287	4.3073	91.6608
3	5.9345	4.6014	87.0594
4	5.6202	4.9157	82.1437
5	5.2845	5.2515	76.8922
6	4.9258	5.6101	71.2821
7	4.5426	5.9933	65.2888
8	4.1333	6.4026	58.8861
9	3.6960	6.8399	52.0462
10	3.2288	7.3071	44.7391
11	2.7298	7.8062	36.9329
12	2.1966	8.3393	28.5936
13	1.6270	8.9089	19.6847
14	1.0186	9.5174	10.1674
15	.3685	10.1674	0.0000

YEARS 16 — MO PAYT .8461 — AN CONST 10.16

#	INT	PRIN	BALANCE
1	6.5159	3.6369	96.3631
2	6.2675	3.8853	92.4779
3	6.0021	4.1506	88.3273
4	5.7186	4.4341	83.8932
5	5.4158	4.7369	79.1562
6	5.0923	5.0605	74.0957
7	4.7466	5.4061	68.6896
8	4.3774	5.7753	62.9143
9	3.9830	6.1698	56.7445
10	3.5616	6.5912	50.1533
11	3.1114	7.0413	43.1120
12	2.6305	7.5223	35.5897
13	2.1167	8.0360	27.5537
14	1.5679	8.5849	18.9688
15	.9815	9.1712	9.7976
16	.3551	9.7976	0.0000

YEARS 17 — MO PAYT .8182 — AN CONST 9.82

#	INT	PRIN	BALANCE
1	6.5262	3.2923	96.7077
2	6.3014	3.5171	93.1906
3	6.0611	3.7573	89.4333
4	5.8045	4.0140	85.4193
5	5.5304	4.2881	81.1312
6	5.2375	4.5810	76.5502
7	4.9246	4.8939	71.6563
8	4.5904	5.2281	66.4282
9	4.2333	5.5852	60.8430
10	3.8518	5.9667	54.8763
11	3.4443	6.3742	48.5022
12	3.0090	6.8095	41.6926
13	2.5439	7.2746	34.4180
14	2.0470	7.7715	26.6466
15	1.5162	8.3022	18.3443
16	.9492	8.8693	9.4750
17	.3434	9.4750	0.0000

YEARS 18 — MO PAYT .7937 — AN CONST 9.53

#	INT	PRIN	BALANCE
1	6.5353	2.9897	97.0103
2	6.3311	3.1938	93.8165
3	6.1130	3.4120	90.4045
4	5.8799	3.6450	86.7595
5	5.6310	3.8940	82.8656
6	5.3650	4.1599	78.7056
7	5.0809	4.4440	74.2616
8	4.7774	4.7476	69.5140
9	4.4531	5.0718	64.4422
10	4.1067	5.4182	59.0240
11	3.7367	5.7883	53.2357
12	3.3413	6.1836	47.0521
13	2.9190	6.6059	40.4462
14	2.4678	7.0571	33.3891
15	1.9858	7.5391	25.8499
16	1.4709	8.0540	17.7959
17	.9208	8.6041	9.1918
18	.3332	9.1918	0.0000

YEARS 19 — MO PAYT .7721 — AN CONST 9.27

#	INT	PRIN	BALANCE
1	6.5433	2.7223	97.2777
2	6.3574	2.9083	94.3694
3	6.1588	3.1069	91.2625
4	5.9466	3.3191	87.9434
5	5.7199	3.5458	84.3976
6	5.4777	3.7880	80.6097
7	5.2190	4.0467	76.5630
8	4.9426	4.3231	72.2400
9	4.6473	4.6183	67.6216
10	4.3319	4.9337	62.6879
11	3.9949	5.2707	57.4172
12	3.6350	5.6307	51.7865
13	3.2504	6.0153	45.7712
14	2.8395	6.4261	39.3451
15	2.4006	6.8650	32.4801
16	1.9318	7.3339	25.1462
17	1.4309	7.8348	17.3114
18	.8958	8.3699	8.9415
19	.3241	8.9415	0.0000

YEARS 20 — MO PAYT .7530 — AN CONST 9.04

#	INT	PRIN	BALANCE
1	6.5504	2.4850	97.5150
2	6.3807	2.6547	94.8604
3	6.1994	2.8360	92.0244
4	6.0057	3.0297	88.9947
5	5.7988	3.2366	85.7581
6	5.5777	3.4577	82.3004
7	5.3416	3.6938	78.6066
8	5.0893	3.9461	74.6604
9	4.8198	4.2156	70.4448
10	4.5319	4.5036	65.9413
11	4.2243	4.8111	61.1301
12	3.8957	5.1397	55.9904
13	3.5446	5.4908	50.4996
14	3.1696	5.8658	44.6338
15	2.7690	6.2664	38.3674
16	2.3410	6.6944	31.6730
17	1.8838	7.1516	24.5213
18	1.3953	7.6401	16.8812
19	.8735	8.1619	8.7193
20	.3161	8.7193	0.0000

YEARS 21 — MO PAYT .7358 — AN CONST 8.84

#	INT	PRIN	BALANCE
1	6.5568	2.2732	97.7268
2	6.4015	2.4285	95.2983
3	6.2357	2.5943	92.7040

#	INT	PRIN	BALANCE
4	6.0585	2.7715	89.9325
5	5.8692	2.9608	86.9716
6	5.6670	3.1630	83.8086
7	5.4509	3.3791	80.4295
8	5.2202	3.6099	76.8197
9	4.9736	3.8564	72.9633
10	4.7102	4.1198	68.8435
11	4.4288	4.4012	64.4423
12	4.1282	4.7018	59.7405
13	3.8071	5.0229	54.7176
14	3.4640	5.3660	49.3516
15	3.0976	5.7325	43.6192
16	2.7060	6.1240	37.4952
17	2.2878	6.5422	30.9530
18	1.8409	6.9891	23.9639
19	1.3636	7.4664	16.4975
20	.8536	7.9764	8.5211
21	.3089	8.5211	0.0000

YEARS 22	MO PAYT .7205	AN CONST 8.65	
#	INT	PRIN	BALANCE
1	6.5625	2.0835	97.9165
2	6.4202	2.2258	95.6906
3	6.2682	2.3779	93.3127
4	6.1058	2.5403	90.7725
5	5.9323	2.7138	88.0587
6	5.7469	2.8991	85.1595
7	5.5489	3.0971	82.0624
8	5.3374	3.3087	78.7537
9	5.1114	3.5346	75.2191
10	4.8700	3.7761	71.4430
11	4.6121	4.0340	67.4091
12	4.3366	4.3095	63.0996
13	4.0422	4.6038	58.4958
14	3.7278	4.9182	53.5775
15	3.3919	5.2542	48.3234
16	3.0330	5.6130	42.7104
17	2.6497	5.9964	36.7140
18	2.2401	6.4059	30.3081
19	1.8026	6.8434	23.4646
20	1.3352	7.3108	16.1538
21	.8359	7.8102	8.3436
22	.3024	8.3436	0.0000

YEARS 23	MO PAYT .7067	AN CONST 8.49	
#	INT	PRIN	BALANCE
1	6.5676	1.9130	98.0870
2	6.4369	2.0437	96.0433
3	6.2974	2.1833	93.8600
4	6.1482	2.3324	91.5276
5	5.9889	2.4917	89.0359
6	5.8188	2.6619	86.3741
7	5.6370	2.8437	83.5304
8	5.4427	3.0379	80.4925
9	5.2353	3.2454	77.2472
10	5.0136	3.4670	73.7801
11	4.7768	3.7038	70.0763
12	4.5238	3.9568	66.1195
13	4.2536	4.2270	61.8925
14	3.9649	4.5157	57.3767
15	3.6565	4.8242	52.5526
16	3.3270	5.1536	47.3989
17	2.9750	5.5056	41.8933
18	2.5990	5.8817	36.0116
19	2.1973	6.2834	29.7283
20	1.7681	6.7125	23.0157
21	1.3096	7.1710	15.8447
22	.8199	7.6608	8.1840
23	.2966	8.1840	0.0000

YEARS 24	MO PAYT .6943	AN CONST 8.34	
#	INT	PRIN	BALANCE
1	6.5722	1.7592	98.2408
2	6.4521	1.8794	96.3614
3	6.3237	2.0077	94.3537
4	6.1866	2.1449	92.2088
5	6.0401	2.2914	89.9175
6	5.8836	2.4478	87.4696
7	5.7164	2.6150	84.8546
8	5.5378	2.7936	82.0609
9	5.3470	2.9844	79.0765
10	5.1432	3.1883	75.8882
11	4.9254	3.4060	72.4822
12	4.6928	3.6387	68.8435
13	4.4443	3.8872	64.9563
14	4.1788	4.1527	60.8037
15	3.8951	4.4363	56.3674
16	3.5921	4.7393	51.6281
17	3.2685	5.0630	46.5651
18	2.9227	5.4088	41.1563
19	2.5532	5.7782	35.3781
20	2.1586	6.1728	29.2053
21	1.7370	6.5944	22.6108
22	1.2866	7.0448	15.5660
23	.8054	7.5260	8.0400
24	.2914	8.0400	0.0000

YEARS 25	MO PAYT .6830	AN CONST 8.20	
#	INT	PRIN	BALANCE
1	6.5764	1.6201	98.3799
2	6.4657	1.7307	96.6492
3	6.3475	1.8489	94.8003
4	6.2213	1.9752	92.8251
5	6.0864	2.1101	90.7150
6	5.9422	2.2542	88.4607
7	5.7883	2.4082	86.0525
8	5.6238	2.5727	83.4799
9	5.4481	2.7484	80.7315
10	5.2604	2.9361	77.7954
11	5.0598	3.1366	74.6588
12	4.8456	3.3509	71.3079
13	4.6167	3.5797	67.7282
14	4.3723	3.8242	63.9040
15	4.1111	4.0854	59.8186
16	3.8320	4.3644	55.4542
17	3.5340	4.6625	50.7917
18	3.2155	4.9810	45.8107
19	2.8753	5.3212	40.4895
20	2.5119	5.6846	34.8050
21	2.1236	6.0728	28.7321
22	1.7089	6.4876	22.2445
23	1.2658	6.9307	15.3138
24	.7924	7.4041	7.9098
25	.2867	7.9098	0.0000

YEARS 26	MO PAYT .6728	AN CONST 8.08	
#	INT	PRIN	BALANCE
1	6.5802	1.4938	98.5062
2	6.4782	1.5959	96.9103
3	6.3692	1.7049	95.2054
4	6.2527	1.8213	93.3841
5	6.1283	1.9457	91.4384
6	5.9954	2.0786	89.3598
7	5.8535	2.2206	87.1393
8	5.7018	2.3722	84.7671
9	5.5398	2.5342	82.2328
10	5.3667	2.7073	79.5255
11	5.1818	2.8922	76.6333
12	4.9843	3.0898	73.5435
13	4.7732	3.3008	70.2427
14	4.5478	3.5262	66.7164
15	4.3069	3.7671	62.9494
16	4.0497	4.0244	58.9250
17	3.7748	4.2992	54.6258
18	3.4812	4.5929	50.0329
19	3.1675	4.9066	45.1264
20	2.8324	5.2417	39.8847
21	2.4744	5.5997	34.2850
22	2.0919	5.9821	28.3029
23	1.6833	6.3907	21.9122
24	1.2469	6.8272	15.0851
25	.7806	7.2935	7.7916
26	.2824	7.7916	0.0000

YEARS 27	MO PAYT .6636	AN CONST 7.97	
#	INT	PRIN	BALANCE
1	6.5836	1.3791	98.6209
2	6.4894	1.4732	97.1477
3	6.3888	1.5739	95.5738
4	6.2813	1.6814	93.8925
5	6.1665	1.7962	92.0963
6	6.0438	1.9189	90.1774
7	5.9128	2.0499	88.1275
8	5.7727	2.1899	85.9376
9	5.6232	2.3395	83.5981
10	5.4634	2.4993	81.0988
11	5.2927	2.6700	78.4288
12	5.1103	2.8523	75.5764
13	4.9155	3.0472	72.5293
14	4.7074	3.2553	69.2740
15	4.4851	3.4776	65.7964
16	4.2475	3.7151	62.0813
17	3.9938	3.9689	58.1124
18	3.7227	4.2399	53.8725
19	3.4332	4.5295	49.3429
20	3.1238	4.8389	44.5040
21	2.7933	5.1694	39.3347
22	2.4402	5.5224	33.8122
23	2.0631	5.8996	27.9126
24	1.6601	6.3026	21.6100
25	1.2297	6.7330	14.8770
26	.7698	7.1929	7.6841
27	.2785	7.6841	0.0000

YEARS 28	MO PAYT .6551	AN CONST 7.87	
#	INT	PRIN	BALANCE
1	6.5868	1.2744	98.7256
2	6.4997	1.3615	97.3641
3	6.4067	1.4545	95.9096
4	6.3074	1.5538	94.3558
5	6.2013	1.6599	92.6959
6	6.0879	1.7733	90.9226
7	5.9668	1.8944	89.0282
8	5.8374	2.0238	87.0044
9	5.6992	2.1620	84.8424
10	5.5515	2.3097	82.5327
11	5.3938	2.4674	80.0652
12	5.2252	2.6360	77.4293
13	5.0452	2.8160	74.6133
14	4.8529	3.0083	71.6049
15	4.6474	3.2138	68.3912
16	4.4279	3.4333	64.9579
17	4.1934	3.6678	61.2901
18	3.9429	3.9183	57.3718
19	3.6753	4.1859	53.1859
20	3.3894	4.4718	48.7141
21	3.0840	4.7772	43.9369
22	2.7577	5.1035	38.8334
23	2.4091	5.4521	33.3813
24	2.0368	5.8244	27.5569
25	1.6390	6.2222	21.3346
26	1.2140	6.6472	14.6874
27	.7600	7.1012	7.5862
28	.2750	7.5862	0.0000

YEARS 29	MO PAYT .6474	AN CONST 7.77	
#	INT	PRIN	BALANCE
1	6.5896	1.1789	98.8211
2	6.5091	1.2594	97.5617
3	6.4231	1.3454	96.2163
4	6.3312	1.4373	94.7790
5	6.2330	1.5355	93.2435
6	6.1282	1.6404	91.6031
7	6.0161	1.7524	89.8507
8	5.8964	1.8721	87.9786
9	5.7686	1.9999	85.9787
10	5.6320	2.1365	83.8422
11	5.4861	2.2825	81.5597
12	5.3302	2.4383	79.1213
13	5.1636	2.6049	76.5165
14	4.9857	2.7828	73.7337
15	4.7957	2.9729	70.7608
16	4.5926	3.1759	67.5849
17	4.3757	3.3928	64.1921
18	4.1440	3.6245	60.5675
19	3.8964	3.8721	56.6954
20	3.6320	4.1366	52.5589
21	3.3494	4.4191	48.1398
22	3.0476	4.7209	43.4189
23	2.7252	5.0433	38.3576
24	2.3807	5.3878	32.9878
25	2.0128	5.7558	27.2320
26	1.6196	6.1489	21.0831
27	1.1997	6.5688	14.5143
28	.7510	7.0175	7.4968
29	.2717	7.4968	0.0000

YEARS 30	MO PAYT .6403	AN CONST 7.69	
#	INT	PRIN	BALANCE
1	6.5923	1.0915	98.9085
2	6.5177	1.1660	97.7425
3	6.4381	1.2457	96.4968
4	6.3530	1.3307	95.1661
5	6.2621	1.4216	93.7445
6	6.1650	1.5187	92.2257
7	6.0613	1.6225	90.6033
8	5.9505	1.7333	88.8700
9	5.8321	1.8516	87.0184
10	5.7056	1.9781	85.0403
11	5.5705	2.1132	82.9270
12	5.4262	2.2575	80.6695
13	5.2720	2.4117	78.2578
14	5.1073	2.5765	75.6813
15	4.9313	2.7524	72.9289
16	4.7433	2.9404	69.9885
17	4.5425	3.1412	66.8472
18	4.3279	3.3558	63.4914
19	4.0987	3.5850	59.9065
20	3.8539	3.8298	56.0766
21	3.5923	4.0914	51.9852
22	3.3129	4.3708	47.6144
23	3.0144	4.6694	42.9450
24	2.6954	4.9883	37.9567
25	2.3547	5.3290	32.6277
26	1.9908	5.6929	26.9348
27	1.6020	6.0818	20.8530
28	1.1866	6.4971	14.3559
29	.7428	6.9409	7.4150
30	.2688	7.4150	0.0000

YEARS 2 — MO PAYT 4.4637 — AN CONST 53.57

#	INT	PRIN	BALANCE
1	5.2338	48.3303	51.6697
2	1.8943	51.6697	0.0000

YEARS 3 — MO PAYT 3.0740 — AN CONST 36.89

#	INT	PRIN	BALANCE
1	5.7555	31.1326	68.8674
2	3.6044	33.2838	35.5836
3	1.3046	35.5836	0.0000

YEARS 4 — MO PAYT 2.3807 — AN CONST 28.57

#	INT	PRIN	BALANCE
1	6.0158	22.5530	77.4470
2	4.4575	24.1113	53.3357
3	2.7915	25.7773	27.5584
4	1.0103	27.5584	0.0000

YEARS 5 — MO PAYT 1.9660 — AN CONST 23.60

#	INT	PRIN	BALANCE
1	6.1715	17.4205	82.5795
2	4.9678	18.6241	63.9554
3	3.6810	19.9110	44.0444
4	2.3052	21.2868	22.7576
5	.8343	22.7576	0.0000

YEARS 6 — MO PAYT 1.6905 — AN CONST 20.29

#	INT	PRIN	BALANCE
1	6.2749	14.0115	85.9885
2	5.3068	14.9796	71.0089
3	4.2717	16.0146	54.9943
4	3.1652	17.1212	37.8731
5	1.9822	18.3042	19.5689
6	.7174	19.5689	0.0000

YEARS 7 — MO PAYT 1.4946 — AN CONST 17.94

#	INT	PRIN	BALANCE
1	6.3485	11.5873	88.4127
2	5.5478	12.3879	76.0248
3	4.6919	13.2439	62.7809
4	3.7768	14.1590	48.6220
5	2.7984	15.1373	33.4847
6	1.7525	16.1832	17.3014
7	.6343	17.3014	0.0000

YEARS 8 — MO PAYT 1.3485 — AN CONST 16.19

#	INT	PRIN	BALANCE
1	6.4033	9.7785	90.2215
2	5.7277	10.4542	79.7672
3	5.0053	11.1766	68.5907
4	4.2331	11.9488	56.6419
5	3.4075	12.7744	43.8674
6	2.5248	13.6571	30.2104
7	1.5811	14.6007	15.6096
8	.5723	15.6096	0.0000

YEARS 9 — MO PAYT 1.2355 — AN CONST 14.83

#	INT	PRIN	BALANCE
1	6.4458	8.3801	91.6199
2	5.8667	8.9591	82.6608
3	5.2477	9.5781	73.0827
4	4.5859	10.2400	62.8427
5	3.8783	10.9475	51.8953
6	3.1219	11.7039	40.1913
7	2.3132	12.5126	27.6787
8	1.4486	13.3772	14.3015
9	.5243	14.3015	0.0000

YEARS 10 — MO PAYT 1.1457 — AN CONST 13.75

#	INT	PRIN	BALANCE
1	6.4795	7.2687	92.7313
2	5.9772	7.7709	84.9604
3	5.4403	8.3079	76.6525
4	4.8663	8.8819	67.7705
5	4.2525	9.4956	58.2749
6	3.5964	10.1518	48.1231
7	2.8950	10.8532	37.2699
8	2.1451	11.6031	25.6668
9	1.3433	12.4048	13.2620
10	.4862	13.2620	0.0000

YEARS 11 — MO PAYT 1.0727 — AN CONST 12.88

#	INT	PRIN	BALANCE
1	6.5069	6.3661	93.6339
2	6.0670	6.8060	86.8279
3	5.5967	7.2762	79.5517
4	5.0940	7.7790	71.7727
5	4.5565	8.3165	63.4562
6	3.9818	8.8911	54.5651
7	3.3675	9.5055	45.0596
8	2.7107	10.1623	34.8973
9	2.0085	10.8644	24.0328
10	1.2578	11.6151	12.4177
11	.4553	12.4177	0.0000

YEARS 12 — MO PAYT 1.0125 — AN CONST 12.15

#	INT	PRIN	BALANCE
1	6.5295	5.6200	94.3800
2	6.1412	6.0083	88.3717
3	5.7260	6.4235	81.9482
4	5.2822	6.8673	75.0809
5	4.8077	7.3418	67.7391
6	4.3004	7.8491	59.8900
7	3.7580	8.3915	51.4985
8	3.1782	8.9713	42.5272
9	2.5583	9.5912	32.9361
10	1.8956	10.2539	22.6822
11	1.1871	10.9624	11.7198
12	.4297	11.7198	0.0000

YEARS 13 — MO PAYT .9619 — AN CONST 11.55

#	INT	PRIN	BALANCE
1	6.5485	4.9942	95.0058
2	6.2034	5.3393	89.6664
3	5.8345	5.7083	83.9582
4	5.4401	6.1027	77.8555
5	5.0184	6.5243	71.3312
6	4.5676	6.9752	64.3560
7	4.0856	7.4571	56.8989
8	3.5704	7.9724	48.9265
9	3.0195	8.5232	40.4033
10	2.4306	9.1121	31.2912
11	1.8010	9.7418	21.5494
12	1.1278	10.4149	11.1345
13	.4082	11.1345	0.0000

YEARS 14 — MO PAYT .9190 — AN CONST 11.03

#	INT	PRIN	BALANCE
1	6.5646	4.4630	95.5370
2	6.2562	4.7714	90.7657
3	5.9265	5.1010	85.6646
4	5.5741	5.4535	80.2111
5	5.1973	5.8303	74.3808
6	4.7944	6.2332	68.1477
7	4.3637	6.6639	61.4838
8	3.9033	7.1243	54.3595
9	3.4110	7.6166	46.7430
10	2.8847	8.1428	38.6001
11	2.3221	8.7055	29.8946
12	1.7206	9.3070	20.5877
13	1.0775	9.9501	10.6376
14	.3900	10.6376	0.0000

YEARS 15 — MO PAYT .8821 — AN CONST 10.59

#	INT	PRIN	BALANCE
1	6.5784	4.0072	95.9928
2	6.3015	4.2841	91.7086
3	6.0055	4.5802	87.1285
4	5.6891	4.8966	82.2318
5	5.3507	5.2350	76.9969
6	4.9890	5.5967	71.4002
7	4.6023	5.9834	65.4168
8	4.1889	6.3968	59.0200
9	3.7469	6.8388	52.1812
10	3.2743	7.3113	44.8699
11	2.7691	7.8165	37.0533
12	2.2290	8.3566	28.6967
13	1.6516	8.9340	19.7627
14	1.0343	9.5513	10.2113
15	.3744	10.2113	0.0000

YEARS 16 — MO PAYT .8503 — AN CONST 10.21

#	INT	PRIN	BALANCE
1	6.5904	3.6128	96.3872
2	6.3408	3.8625	92.5247
3	6.0739	4.1294	88.3953
4	5.7886	4.4147	83.9807
5	5.4835	4.7197	79.2609
6	5.1574	5.0458	74.2151
7	4.8088	5.3945	68.8206
8	4.4360	5.7672	63.0534
9	4.0375	6.1657	56.8877
10	3.6115	6.5917	50.2960
11	3.1560	7.0472	43.2488
12	2.6691	7.5341	35.7146
13	2.1485	8.0547	27.6599
14	1.5920	8.6113	19.0487
15	.9970	9.2063	9.8424
16	.3608	9.8424	0.0000

YEARS 17 — MO PAYT .8225 — AN CONST 9.87

#	INT	PRIN	BALANCE
1	6.6008	3.2689	96.7311
2	6.3750	3.4947	93.2364
3	6.1335	3.7362	89.5002
4	5.8753	3.9944	85.5058
5	5.5993	4.2704	81.2354
6	5.3043	4.5654	76.6700
7	4.9888	4.8809	71.7891
8	4.6516	5.2181	66.5710
9	4.2910	5.5787	60.9923
10	3.9055	5.9642	55.0281
11	3.4934	6.3763	48.6519
12	3.0529	6.8168	41.8350
13	2.5818	7.2879	34.5472
14	2.0783	7.7914	26.7558
15	1.5399	8.3298	18.4260
16	.9644	8.9053	9.5207
17	.3490	9.5207	0.0000

YEARS 18 — MO PAYT .7981 — AN CONST 9.58

#	INT	PRIN	BALANCE
1	6.6100	2.9669	97.0331
2	6.4050	3.1719	93.8612
3	6.1858	3.3911	90.4702
4	5.9515	3.6254	86.8448
5	5.7010	3.8759	82.9689
6	5.4332	4.1437	78.8253
7	5.1469	4.4300	74.3953
8	4.8408	4.7361	69.6592
9	4.5136	5.0633	64.5959
10	4.1637	5.4132	59.1827
11	3.7897	5.7872	53.3955
12	3.3898	6.1871	47.2084
13	2.9623	6.6146	40.5938
14	2.5052	7.0716	33.5222
15	2.0166	7.5603	25.9619
16	1.4942	8.0826	17.8793
17	.9358	8.6411	9.2382
18	.3387	9.2382	0.0000

YEARS 19 — MO PAYT .7765 — AN CONST 9.32

#	INT	PRIN	BALANCE
1	6.6181	2.7002	97.2998
2	6.4315	2.8868	94.4130
3	6.2320	3.0862	91.3268
4	6.0188	3.2995	88.0273
5	5.7908	3.5275	84.4998
6	5.5471	3.7712	80.7286
7	5.2865	4.0318	76.6968
8	5.0079	4.3104	72.3865
9	4.7101	4.6082	67.7783
10	4.3917	4.9266	62.8517
11	4.0513	5.2670	57.5847
12	3.6873	5.6309	51.9537
13	3.2983	6.0200	45.9337
14	2.8823	6.4360	39.4977
15	2.4376	6.8807	32.6170
16	1.9622	7.3561	25.2609
17	1.4539	7.8644	17.3965
18	.9105	8.4078	8.9887
19	.3295	8.9887	0.0000

YEARS 20 — MO PAYT .7574 — AN CONST 9.09

#	INT	PRIN	BALANCE
1	6.6253	2.4635	97.5365
2	6.4550	2.6337	94.9028
3	6.2731	2.8157	92.0872
4	6.0785	3.0102	89.0770
5	5.8705	3.2182	85.8588
6	5.6482	3.4406	82.4182
7	5.4104	3.6783	78.7399
8	5.1563	3.9325	74.8074
9	4.8846	4.2042	70.6032
10	4.5941	4.4947	66.1086
11	4.2835	4.8052	61.3033
12	3.9515	5.1373	56.1661
13	3.5965	5.4922	50.6739
14	3.2170	5.8717	44.8021
15	2.8113	6.2774	38.5247
16	2.3776	6.7112	31.8135
17	1.9138	7.1749	24.6386
18	1.4181	7.6707	16.9680
19	.8881	8.2007	8.7673
20	.3214	8.7673	0.0000

YEARS 21 — MO PAYT .7403 — AN CONST 8.89

#	INT	PRIN	BALANCE
1	6.6317	2.2524	97.7476
2	6.4760	2.4080	95.3397
3	6.3097	2.5744	92.7653

#	INT	PRIN	BALANCE
4	6.1318	2.7522	90.0131
5	5.9416	2.9424	87.0706
6	5.7383	3.1457	83.9249
7	5.5209	3.3631	80.5618
8	5.2886	3.5955	76.9664
9	5.0401	3.8439	73.1225
10	4.7745	4.1095	69.0130
11	4.4906	4.3934	64.6196
12	4.1870	4.6970	59.9226
13	3.8625	5.0216	54.9010
14	3.5155	5.3685	49.5325
15	3.1446	5.7395	43.7930
16	2.7480	6.1360	37.6570
17	2.3240	6.5600	31.0970
18	1.8707	7.0133	24.0837
19	1.3861	7.4979	16.5858
20	.8681	8.0160	8.5698
21	.3142	8.5698	0.0000

YEARS 22	MO PAYT .7251	AN CONST 8.71	
#	INT	PRIN	BALANCE
1	6.6374	2.0633	97.9367
2	6.4948	2.2059	95.7308
3	6.3424	2.3583	93.3725
4	6.1795	2.5212	90.8513
5	6.0053	2.6955	88.1558
6	5.8190	2.8817	85.2741
7	5.6199	3.0808	82.1933
8	5.4070	3.2937	78.8996
9	5.1794	3.5213	75.3783
10	4.9361	3.7646	71.6138
11	4.6760	4.0247	67.5891
12	4.3979	4.3028	63.2863
13	4.1006	4.6001	58.6862
14	3.7828	4.9179	53.7682
15	3.4430	5.2578	48.5105
16	3.0797	5.6210	42.8894
17	2.6913	6.0094	36.8800
18	2.2760	6.4247	30.4553
19	1.8321	6.8686	23.5868
20	1.3575	7.3432	16.2436
21	.8501	7.8506	8.3930
22	.3077	8.3930	0.0000

YEARS 23	MO PAYT .7113	AN CONST 8.54	
#	INT	PRIN	BALANCE
1	6.6426	1.8934	98.1066
2	6.5117	2.0242	96.0823
3	6.3719	2.1641	93.9182
4	6.2223	2.3136	91.6046
5	6.0625	2.4735	89.1311
6	5.8916	2.6444	86.4867
7	5.7088	2.8271	83.6595
8	5.5135	3.0225	80.6370
9	5.3046	3.2313	77.4057
10	5.0814	3.4546	73.9511
11	4.8427	3.6933	70.2578
12	4.5875	3.9485	66.3093
13	4.3147	4.2213	62.0880
14	4.0230	4.5130	57.5750
15	3.7112	4.8248	52.7502
16	3.3778	5.1582	47.5920
17	3.0214	5.5146	42.0774
18	2.6403	5.8957	36.1817
19	2.2330	6.3030	29.8787
20	1.7974	6.7385	23.1402
21	1.3318	7.2041	15.9360
22	.8341	7.7019	8.2341
23	.3019	8.2341	0.0000

YEARS 24	MO PAYT .6990	AN CONST 8.39	
#	INT	PRIN	BALANCE
1	6.6472	1.7402	98.2598
2	6.5270	1.8605	96.3993
3	6.3984	1.9890	94.4103
4	6.2610	2.1265	92.2838
5	6.1140	2.2734	90.0105
6	5.9570	2.4305	87.5800
7	5.7890	2.5984	84.9816
8	5.6095	2.7779	82.2036
9	5.4175	2.9699	79.2338
10	5.2123	3.1751	76.0587
11	4.9929	3.3945	72.6642
12	4.7584	3.6290	69.0352
13	4.5077	3.8798	65.1554
14	4.2396	4.1479	61.0075
15	3.9530	4.4345	56.5731
16	3.6466	4.7409	51.8322
17	3.3190	5.0684	46.7638
18	2.9688	5.4186	41.3451
19	2.5944	5.7931	35.5521
20	2.1941	6.1933	29.3587
21	1.7662	6.6213	22.7375
22	1.3087	7.0788	15.6587
23	.8195	7.5679	8.0908
24	.2966	8.0908	0.0000

YEARS 25	MO PAYT .6878	AN CONST 8.26	
#	INT	PRIN	BALANCE
1	6.6514	1.6017	98.3983
2	6.5407	1.7124	96.6860
3	6.4224	1.8307	94.8553
4	6.2959	1.9572	92.8981
5	6.1607	2.0924	90.8057
6	6.0161	2.2370	88.5688
7	5.8616	2.3915	86.1772
8	5.6963	2.5568	83.6205
9	5.5196	2.7334	80.8870
10	5.3308	2.9223	77.9647
11	5.1289	3.1242	74.8405
12	4.9130	3.3401	71.5003
13	4.6822	3.5709	67.9294
14	4.4355	3.8176	64.1118
15	4.1717	4.0814	60.0304
16	3.8897	4.3634	55.6670
17	3.5882	4.6649	51.0020
18	3.2658	4.9873	46.0148
19	2.9212	5.3319	40.6829
20	2.5528	5.7003	34.9826
21	2.1590	6.0941	28.8885
22	1.7379	6.5152	22.3733
23	1.2877	6.9654	15.4079
24	.8064	7.4467	7.9612
25	.2919	7.9612	0.0000

YEARS 26	MO PAYT .6776	AN CONST 8.14	
#	INT	PRIN	BALANCE
1	6.6552	1.4761	98.5239
2	6.5532	1.5780	96.9459
3	6.4442	1.6871	95.2588
4	6.3276	1.8036	93.4552
5	6.2030	1.9283	91.5269
6	6.0698	2.0615	89.4654
7	5.9273	2.2040	87.2615
8	5.7750	2.3562	84.9052
9	5.6122	2.5190	82.3862
10	5.4382	2.6931	79.6931
11	5.2521	2.8792	76.8139
12	5.0531	3.0781	73.7358
13	4.8405	3.2908	70.4450
14	4.6131	3.5182	66.9268
15	4.3700	3.7613	63.1655
16	4.1101	4.0212	59.1443
17	3.8322	4.2990	54.8453
18	3.5352	4.5961	50.2492
19	3.2176	4.9136	45.3356
20	2.8781	5.2532	40.0824
21	2.5151	5.6161	34.4663
22	2.1271	6.0042	28.4621
23	1.7122	6.4191	22.0430
24	1.2687	6.8626	15.1805
25	.7945	7.3368	7.8437
26	.2876	7.8437	0.0000

YEARS 27	MO PAYT .6684	AN CONST 8.03	
#	INT	PRIN	BALANCE
1	6.6587	1.3619	98.6381
2	6.5646	1.4559	97.1822
3	6.4640	1.5565	95.6257
4	6.3564	1.6641	93.9616
5	6.2415	1.7791	92.1825
6	6.1185	1.9020	90.2805
7	5.9871	2.0334	88.2470
8	5.8466	2.1739	86.0731
9	5.6964	2.3241	83.7489
10	5.5358	2.4847	81.2642
11	5.3641	2.6564	78.6078
12	5.1806	2.8400	75.7678
13	4.9843	3.0362	72.7316
14	4.7745	3.2460	69.4856
15	4.5503	3.4703	66.0153
16	4.3105	3.7101	62.3053
17	4.0541	3.9664	58.3388
18	3.7801	4.2405	54.0984
19	3.4871	4.5335	49.5649
20	3.1738	4.8467	44.7182
21	2.8389	5.1816	39.5365
22	2.4809	5.5396	33.9969
23	2.0981	5.9224	28.0745
24	1.6889	6.3316	21.7429
25	1.2514	6.7691	14.9737
26	.7837	7.2368	7.7369
27	.2837	7.7369	0.0000

YEARS 28	MO PAYT .6600	AN CONST 7.92	
#	INT	PRIN	BALANCE
1	6.6618	1.2578	98.7422
2	6.5749	1.3447	97.3975
3	6.4820	1.4376	95.9598
4	6.3827	1.5370	94.4229
5	6.2765	1.6432	92.7797
6	6.1629	1.7567	91.0230
7	6.0416	1.8781	89.1449
8	5.9118	2.0079	87.1370
9	5.7731	2.1466	84.9904
10	5.6247	2.2949	82.6955
11	5.4662	2.4535	80.2420
12	5.2966	2.6230	77.6190
13	5.1154	2.8043	74.8148
14	4.9216	2.9980	71.8168
15	4.7145	3.2052	68.6116
16	4.4930	3.4266	65.1850
17	4.2563	3.6634	61.5216
18	4.0031	3.9165	57.6051
19	3.7325	4.1871	53.4179
20	3.4432	4.4765	48.9415
21	3.1339	4.7858	44.1557
22	2.8032	5.1164	39.0393
23	2.4497	5.4700	33.5693
24	2.0717	5.8479	27.7214
25	1.6677	6.2520	21.4694
26	1.2357	6.6840	14.7854
27	.7738	7.1458	7.6396
28	.2801	7.6396	0.0000

YEARS 29	MO PAYT .6523	AN CONST 7.83	
#	INT	PRIN	BALANCE
1	6.6647	1.1628	98.8372
2	6.5844	1.2432	97.5940
3	6.4985	1.3291	96.2649
4	6.4066	1.4209	94.8440
5	6.3085	1.5191	93.3249
6	6.2035	1.6241	91.7008
7	6.0913	1.7363	89.9645
8	5.9713	1.8562	88.1083
9	5.8430	1.9845	86.1238
10	5.7059	2.1216	84.0021
11	5.5593	2.2682	81.7339
12	5.4026	2.4250	79.3090
13	5.2350	2.5925	76.7165
14	5.0559	2.7716	73.9448
15	4.8644	2.9632	70.9817
16	4.6597	3.1679	67.8138
17	4.4408	3.3868	64.4270
18	4.2068	3.6208	60.8062
19	3.9566	3.8710	56.9352
20	3.6891	4.1385	52.7968
21	3.4032	4.4244	48.3723
22	3.0974	4.7301	43.6422
23	2.7706	5.0569	38.5853
24	2.4212	5.4064	33.1789
25	2.0476	5.7799	27.3990
26	1.6483	6.1793	21.2197
27	1.2213	6.6063	14.6135
28	.7648	7.0627	7.5507
29	.2768	7.5507	0.0000

YEARS 30	MO PAYT .6453	AN CONST 7.75	
#	INT	PRIN	BALANCE
1	6.6674	1.0760	98.9240
2	6.5930	1.1503	97.7737
3	6.5135	1.2298	96.5439
4	6.4286	1.3148	95.2291
5	6.3377	1.4056	93.8235
6	6.2406	1.5028	92.3207
7	6.1367	1.6066	90.7141
8	6.0257	1.7176	88.9965
9	5.9071	1.8363	87.1603
10	5.7802	1.9632	85.1971
11	5.6445	2.0988	83.0983
12	5.4995	2.2438	80.8545
13	5.3445	2.3989	78.4556
14	5.1787	2.5646	75.8910
15	5.0015	2.7418	73.1492
16	4.8121	2.9313	70.2179
17	4.6095	3.1338	67.0841
18	4.3930	3.3503	63.7338
19	4.1615	3.5818	60.1519
20	3.9140	3.8293	56.3226
21	3.6494	4.0939	52.2287
22	3.3665	4.3768	47.8519
23	3.0641	4.6792	43.1727
24	2.7408	5.0025	38.1701
25	2.3951	5.3482	32.8219
26	2.0256	5.7177	27.1042
27	1.6305	6.1128	20.9914
28	1.2082	6.5352	14.4562
29	.7566	6.9867	7.4695
30	.2738	7.4695	0.0000

YEARS 2 — MO PAYT 4.4659 — AN CONST 53.60

#	INT	PRIN	BALANCE
1	5.2733	48.3179	51.6821
2	1.9091	51.6821	0.0000

YEARS 3 — MO PAYT 3.0763 — AN CONST 36.92

#	INT	PRIN	BALANCE
1	5.7990	31.1165	68.8835
2	3.6325	33.2830	35.6005
3	1.3150	35.6005	0.0000

YEARS 4 — MO PAYT 2.3830 — AN CONST 28.60

#	INT	PRIN	BALANCE
1	6.0613	22.5352	77.4648
2	4.4922	24.1043	53.3605
3	2.8139	25.7826	27.5778
4	1.0187	27.5778	0.0000

YEARS 5 — MO PAYT 1.9683 — AN CONST 23.63

#	INT	PRIN	BALANCE
1	6.2182	17.4020	82.5980
2	5.0065	18.6136	63.9844
3	3.7105	19.9097	44.0747
4	2.3242	21.2959	22.7787
5	.8414	22.7787	0.0000

YEARS 6 — MO PAYT 1.6929 — AN CONST 20.32

#	INT	PRIN	BALANCE
1	6.3224	13.9927	86.0073
2	5.3481	14.9670	71.0403
3	4.3060	16.0091	55.0312
4	3.1913	17.1238	37.9075
5	1.9990	18.3161	19.5914
6	.7237	19.5914	0.0000

YEARS 7 — MO PAYT 1.4971 — AN CONST 17.97

#	INT	PRIN	BALANCE
1	6.3964	11.5685	88.4315
2	5.5910	12.3740	76.0576
3	4.7294	13.2355	62.8221
4	3.8078	14.1571	48.6650
5	2.8221	15.1428	33.5221
6	1.7677	16.1972	17.3250
7	.6400	17.3250	0.0000

YEARS 8 — MO PAYT 1.3510 — AN CONST 16.22

#	INT	PRIN	BALANCE
1	6.4517	9.7598	90.2402
2	5.7722	10.4394	79.8008
3	5.0453	11.1663	68.6345
4	4.2678	11.9438	56.6907
5	3.4362	12.7754	43.9153
6	2.5467	13.6649	30.2504
7	1.5952	14.6164	15.6341
8	.5775	15.6341	0.0000

YEARS 9 — MO PAYT 1.2380 — AN CONST 14.86

#	INT	PRIN	BALANCE
1	6.4945	8.3616	91.6384
2	5.9123	8.9438	82.6947
3	5.2895	9.5665	73.1282
4	4.6234	10.2326	62.8956
5	3.9110	10.9451	51.9505
6	3.1489	11.7072	40.2433
7	2.3337	12.5223	27.7210
8	1.4618	13.3942	14.3268
9	.5292	14.3268	0.0000

YEARS 10 — MO PAYT 1.1482 — AN CONST 13.78

#	INT	PRIN	BALANCE
1	6.5284	7.2505	92.7495
2	6.0236	7.7553	84.9942
3	5.4836	8.2953	76.6989
4	4.9060	8.8729	67.8260
5	4.2882	9.4907	58.3353
6	3.6274	10.1515	48.1838
7	2.9206	10.8583	37.3255
8	2.1645	11.6144	25.7111
9	1.3558	12.4231	13.2881
10	.4908	13.2881	0.0000

YEARS 11 — MO PAYT 1.0753 — AN CONST 12.91

#	INT	PRIN	BALANCE
1	6.5560	6.3482	93.6518
2	6.1140	6.7902	86.8616
3	5.6412	7.2630	79.5986
4	5.1355	7.7687	71.8299
5	4.5946	8.3096	63.5203
6	4.0160	8.8882	54.6321
7	3.3971	9.5071	45.1250
8	2.7352	10.1690	34.9560
9	2.0271	10.8771	24.0789
10	1.2698	11.6344	12.4445
11	.4597	12.4445	0.0000

YEARS 12 — MO PAYT 1.0151 — AN CONST 12.19

#	INT	PRIN	BALANCE
1	6.5788	5.6025	94.3975
2	6.1887	5.9925	88.4050
3	5.7714	6.4098	81.9952
4	5.3251	6.8561	75.1391
5	4.8478	7.3335	67.8057
6	4.3372	7.8441	59.9616
7	3.7910	8.3902	51.5714
8	3.2068	8.9744	42.5969
9	2.5819	9.5993	32.9976
10	1.9135	10.2677	22.7299
11	1.1986	10.9826	11.7473
12	.4339	11.7473	0.0000

YEARS 13 — MO PAYT .9646 — AN CONST 11.58

#	INT	PRIN	BALANCE
1	6.5979	4.9771	95.0229
2	6.2513	5.3236	89.6993
3	5.8807	5.6943	84.0050
4	5.4842	6.0908	77.9143
5	5.0601	6.5149	71.3994
6	4.6065	6.9685	64.4309
7	4.1213	7.4537	56.9773
8	3.6023	7.9727	49.0046
9	3.0472	8.5278	40.4768
10	2.4534	9.1215	31.3553
11	1.8183	9.7567	21.5986
12	1.1390	10.4360	11.1626
13	.4123	11.1626	0.0000

YEARS 14 — MO PAYT .9217 — AN CONST 11.07

#	INT	PRIN	BALANCE
1	6.6141	4.4462	95.5538
2	6.3045	4.7558	90.7980
3	5.9734	5.0869	85.7111
4	5.6192	5.4411	80.2700
5	5.2404	5.8200	74.4500
6	4.8351	6.2252	68.2248
7	4.4017	6.6586	61.5662
8	3.9381	7.1223	54.4439
9	3.4421	7.6182	46.8258
10	2.9117	8.1486	38.6772
11	2.3443	8.7160	29.9612
12	1.7375	9.3229	20.6383
13	1.0883	9.9720	10.6663
14	.3940	10.6663	0.0000

YEARS 15 — MO PAYT .8849 — AN CONST 10.62

#	INT	PRIN	BALANCE
1	6.6280	3.9909	96.0091
2	6.3502	4.2688	91.7404
3	6.0529	4.5660	87.1744
4	5.7350	4.8839	82.2905
5	5.3950	5.2240	77.0665
6	5.0312	5.5877	71.4788
7	4.6422	5.9768	65.5021
8	4.2260	6.3929	59.1092
9	3.7809	6.8380	52.2711
10	3.3048	7.3141	44.9570
11	2.7955	7.8234	37.1336
12	2.2508	8.3681	28.7655
13	1.6681	8.9508	19.8147
14	1.0449	9.5740	10.2406
15	.3783	10.2406	0.0000

YEARS 16 — MO PAYT .8531 — AN CONST 10.24

#	INT	PRIN	BALANCE
1	6.6401	3.5969	96.4031
2	6.3896	3.8473	92.5558
3	6.1217	4.1152	88.4406
4	5.8352	4.4017	84.0388
5	5.5287	4.7082	79.3306
6	5.2009	5.0361	74.2945
7	4.8503	5.3867	68.9078
8	4.4752	5.7618	63.1460
9	4.0740	6.1630	56.9831
10	3.6449	6.5921	50.3910
11	3.1859	7.0511	43.3400
12	2.6950	7.5420	35.7979
13	2.1698	8.0671	27.7308
14	1.6081	8.6288	19.1019
15	1.0073	9.2297	9.8723
16	.3647	9.8723	0.0000

YEARS 17 — MO PAYT .8253 — AN CONST 9.91

#	INT	PRIN	BALANCE
1	6.6506	3.2533	96.7467
2	6.4240	3.4799	93.2668
3	6.1818	3.7222	89.5446
4	5.9226	3.9813	85.5633
5	5.6454	4.2585	81.3047
6	5.3489	4.5551	76.7497
7	5.0317	4.8722	71.8775
8	4.6925	5.2115	66.6660
9	4.3296	5.5743	61.0917
10	3.9415	5.9625	55.1292
11	3.5263	6.3776	48.7516
12	3.0823	6.8217	41.9300
13	2.6073	7.2966	34.6333
14	2.0992	7.8047	26.8286
15	1.5558	8.3481	18.4805
16	.9745	8.9294	9.5511
17	.3528	9.5511	0.0000

YEARS 18 — MO PAYT .8010 — AN CONST 9.62

#	INT	PRIN	BALANCE
1	6.6598	2.9518	97.0482
2	6.4543	3.1573	93.8909
3	6.2344	3.3772	90.5137
4	5.9993	3.6123	86.9015
5	5.7478	3.8638	83.0376
6	5.4787	4.1328	78.9048
7	5.1910	4.4206	74.4842
8	4.8832	4.7284	69.7558
9	4.5539	5.0576	64.6982
10	4.2018	5.4098	59.2884
11	3.8251	5.7865	53.5019
12	3.4222	6.1894	47.3126
13	2.9913	6.6203	40.6923
14	2.5303	7.0813	33.6110
15	2.0373	7.5743	26.0367
16	1.5099	8.1017	17.9350
17	.9458	8.6658	9.2692
18	.3424	9.2692	0.0000

YEARS 19 — MO PAYT .7795 — AN CONST 9.36

#	INT	PRIN	BALANCE
1	6.6679	2.6855	97.3145
2	6.4809	2.8725	94.4420
3	6.2809	3.0725	91.3694
4	6.0670	3.2865	88.0830
5	5.8382	3.5153	84.5677
6	5.5934	3.7600	80.8076
7	5.3316	4.0219	76.7858
8	5.0516	4.3019	72.4839
9	4.7520	4.6014	67.8825
10	4.4316	4.9218	62.9607
11	4.0890	5.2645	57.6962
12	3.7224	5.6311	52.0651
13	3.3303	6.0231	46.0420
14	2.9109	6.4425	39.5995
15	2.4624	6.8911	32.7084
16	1.9825	7.3709	25.3375
17	1.4693	7.8841	17.4533
18	.9204	8.4331	9.0203
19	.3332	9.0203	0.0000

YEARS 20 — MO PAYT .7604 — AN CONST 9.13

#	INT	PRIN	BALANCE
1	6.6751	2.4492	97.5508
2	6.5046	2.6198	94.9310
3	6.3222	2.8022	92.1289
4	6.1271	2.9973	89.1316
5	5.9184	3.2060	85.9256
6	5.6952	3.4292	82.4964
7	5.4564	3.6680	78.8285
8	5.2010	3.9233	74.9051
9	4.9278	4.1965	70.7086
10	4.6356	4.4887	66.2199
11	4.3231	4.8013	61.4186
12	3.9888	5.1356	56.2831
13	3.6312	5.4931	50.7899
14	3.2488	5.8756	44.9143
15	2.8396	6.2847	38.6296
16	2.4021	6.7223	31.9073
17	1.9340	7.1904	24.7169
18	1.4333	7.6910	17.0259
19	.8978	8.2265	8.7993
20	.3250	8.7993	0.0000

YEARS 21 — MO PAYT .7433 — AN CONST 8.93

#	INT	PRIN	BALANCE
1	6.6816	2.2385	97.7615
2	6.5257	2.3944	95.3671
3	6.3590	2.5611	92.8060

#	INT	PRIN	BALANCE
4	6.1807	2.7394	90.0665
5	5.9899	2.9302	87.1364
6	5.7859	3.1342	84.0022
7	5.5677	3.3524	80.6497
8	5.3343	3.5858	77.0639
9	5.0846	3.8355	73.2284
10	4.8175	4.1026	69.1258
11	4.5319	4.3882	64.7375
12	4.2263	4.6938	60.0438
13	3.8995	5.0206	55.0232
14	3.5499	5.3702	49.6530
15	3.1760	5.7441	43.9089
16	2.7761	6.1440	37.7649
17	2.3483	6.5718	31.1930
18	1.8907	7.0294	24.1636
19	1.4013	7.5189	16.6447
20	.8777	8.0424	8.6024
21	.3178	8.6024	0.0000

	YEARS	MO PAYT	AN CONST
	22	.7281	8.74
#	INT	PRIN	BALANCE
1	6.6874	2.0499	97.9501
2	6.5446	2.1926	95.7574
3	6.3920	2.3453	93.4121
4	6.2287	2.5086	90.9035
5	6.0540	2.6833	88.2202
6	5.8672	2.8701	85.3501
7	5.6673	3.0700	82.2802
8	5.4536	3.2837	78.9965
9	5.2249	3.5123	75.4841
10	4.9804	3.7569	71.7272
11	4.7188	4.0185	67.7088
12	4.4390	4.2983	63.4105
13	4.1397	4.5976	58.8129
14	3.8196	4.9177	53.8952
15	3.4772	5.2601	48.6351
16	3.1109	5.6263	43.0088
17	2.7192	6.0181	36.9907
18	2.3001	6.4371	30.5536
19	1.8519	6.8853	23.6683
20	1.3725	7.3647	16.3035
21	.8597	7.8775	8.4260
22	.3112	8.4260	0.0000

	YEARS	MO PAYT	AN CONST
	23	.7144	8.58
#	INT	PRIN	BALANCE
1	6.6925	1.8804	98.1196
2	6.5616	2.0114	96.1082
3	6.4216	2.1514	93.9568
4	6.2718	2.3012	91.6556
5	6.1115	2.4614	89.1941
6	5.9401	2.6328	86.5613
7	5.7568	2.8161	83.7452
8	5.5607	3.0122	80.7330
9	5.3510	3.2220	77.5110
10	5.1267	3.4463	74.0647
11	4.8867	3.6863	70.3785
12	4.6300	3.9429	66.4355
13	4.3555	4.2175	62.2181
14	4.0619	4.5111	57.7070
15	3.7478	4.8252	52.8818
16	3.4118	5.1612	47.7206
17	3.0524	5.5205	42.2000
18	2.6680	5.9049	36.2951
19	2.2569	6.3161	29.9791
20	1.8171	6.7558	23.2232
21	1.3467	7.2262	15.9970
22	.8436	7.7294	8.2676
23	.3054	8.2676	0.0000

	YEARS	MO PAYT	AN CONST
	24	.7021	8.43
#	INT	PRIN	BALANCE
1	6.6972	1.7277	98.2723
2	6.5769	1.8479	96.4244
3	6.4482	1.9766	94.4478
4	6.3106	2.1142	92.3335
5	6.1634	2.2615	90.0721
6	6.0059	2.4189	87.6532
7	5.8375	2.5873	85.0658
8	5.6574	2.7675	82.2984
9	5.4647	2.9602	79.3382
10	5.2586	3.1663	76.1719
11	5.0381	3.3868	72.7851
12	4.8023	3.6226	69.1626
13	4.5501	3.8748	65.2878
14	4.2803	4.1446	61.1432
15	3.9917	4.4332	56.7100
16	3.6830	4.7418	51.9682
17	3.3528	5.0720	46.8961
18	2.9997	5.4252	41.4710
19	2.6219	5.8029	35.6681
20	2.2179	6.2070	29.4611
21	1.7857	6.6391	22.8220
22	1.3235	7.1014	15.7206
23	.8290	7.5959	8.1247
24	.3001	8.1247	0.0000

	YEARS	MO PAYT	AN CONST
	25	.6909	8.30
#	INT	PRIN	BALANCE
1	6.7014	1.5895	98.4105
2	6.5907	1.7002	96.7103
3	6.4724	1.8186	94.8917
4	6.3457	1.9452	92.9465
5	6.2103	2.0806	90.8659
6	6.0654	2.2255	88.6404
7	5.9105	2.3805	86.2599
8	5.7447	2.5462	83.7137
9	5.5674	2.7235	80.9902
10	5.3778	2.9131	78.0771
11	5.1750	3.1160	74.9611
12	4.9580	3.3329	71.6282
13	4.7260	3.5650	68.0632
14	4.4777	3.8132	64.2500
15	4.2122	4.0787	60.1713
16	3.9282	4.3627	55.8086
17	3.6245	4.6665	51.1421
18	3.2995	4.9914	46.1507
19	2.9520	5.3389	40.8118
20	2.5803	5.7107	35.1011
21	2.1826	6.1083	28.9928
22	1.7573	6.5336	22.4592
23	1.3024	6.9885	15.4707
24	.8158	7.4751	7.9956
25	.2953	7.9956	0.0000

	YEARS	MO PAYT	AN CONST
	26	.6808	8.17
#	INT	PRIN	BALANCE
1	6.7052	1.4643	98.5357
2	6.6033	1.5662	96.9695
3	6.4942	1.6753	95.2942
4	6.3776	1.7919	93.5022
5	6.2528	1.9167	91.5855
6	6.1194	2.0502	89.5354
7	5.9766	2.1929	87.3424
8	5.8239	2.3456	84.9968
9	5.6606	2.5089	82.4879
10	5.4859	2.6836	79.8043
11	5.2991	2.8705	76.9338
12	5.0992	3.0703	73.8635
13	4.8854	3.2841	70.5794
14	4.6568	3.5128	67.0666
15	4.4122	3.7574	63.3092
16	4.1505	4.0190	59.2902
17	3.8707	4.2988	54.9914
18	3.5714	4.5981	50.3932
19	3.2512	4.9183	45.4749
20	2.9088	5.2608	40.2142
21	2.5425	5.6270	34.5871
22	2.1507	6.0188	28.5683
23	1.7316	6.4379	22.1304
24	1.2833	6.8862	15.2442
25	.8039	7.3657	7.8785
26	.2910	7.8785	0.0000

	YEARS	MO PAYT	AN CONST
	27	.6716	8.06
#	INT	PRIN	BALANCE
1	6.7087	1.3505	98.6495
2	6.6147	1.4445	97.2050
3	6.5141	1.5451	95.6599
4	6.4065	1.6527	94.0072
5	6.2915	1.7677	92.2395
6	6.1684	1.8908	90.3487
7	6.0367	2.0225	88.3262
8	5.8959	2.1633	86.1629
9	5.7453	2.3139	83.8490
10	5.5842	2.4750	81.3739
11	5.4118	2.6474	78.7265
12	5.2275	2.8317	75.8948
13	5.0303	3.0289	72.8660
14	4.8194	3.2398	69.6262
15	4.5939	3.4653	66.1609
16	4.3526	3.7066	62.4542
17	4.0945	3.9647	58.4895
18	3.8184	4.2408	54.2487
19	3.5232	4.5360	49.7127
20	3.2073	4.8519	44.8608
21	2.8695	5.1897	39.6711
22	2.5082	5.5511	34.1200
23	2.1216	5.9376	28.1825
24	1.7082	6.3510	21.8315
25	1.2660	6.7932	15.0383
26	.7930	7.2662	7.7721
27	.2871	7.7721	0.0000

	YEARS	MO PAYT	AN CONST
	28	.6632	7.96
#	INT	PRIN	BALANCE
1	6.7119	1.2468	98.7532
2	6.6251	1.3336	97.4195
3	6.5322	1.4265	95.9930
4	6.4329	1.5258	94.4672
5	6.3267	1.6321	92.8351
6	6.2130	1.7457	91.0894
7	6.0915	1.8673	89.2222
8	5.9615	1.9973	87.2249
9	5.8224	2.1363	85.0886
10	5.6736	2.2851	82.8035
11	5.5145	2.4442	80.3593
12	5.3444	2.6144	77.7450
13	5.1623	2.7964	74.9486
14	4.9676	2.9911	71.9575
15	4.7594	3.1994	68.7581
16	4.5366	3.4221	65.3359
17	4.2983	3.6604	61.6755
18	4.0434	3.9153	57.7602
19	3.7708	4.1879	53.5724
20	3.4792	4.4795	49.0929
21	3.1673	4.7914	44.3015
22	2.8337	5.1250	39.1765
23	2.4769	5.4818	33.6946
24	2.0952	5.8635	27.8311
25	1.6869	6.2718	21.5593
26	1.2502	6.7085	14.8508
27	.7831	7.1756	7.6752
28	.2835	7.6752	0.0000

	YEARS	MO PAYT	AN CONST
	29	.6556	7.87
#	INT	PRIN	BALANCE
1	6.7148	1.1522	98.8478
2	6.6346	1.2325	97.6153
3	6.5487	1.3183	96.2970
4	6.4570	1.4101	94.8870
5	6.3588	1.5082	93.3787
6	6.2538	1.6133	91.7655
7	6.1414	1.7256	90.0399
8	6.0213	1.8457	88.1941
9	5.8928	1.9743	86.2199
10	5.7553	2.1117	84.1082
11	5.6083	2.2587	81.8494
12	5.4510	2.4160	79.4334
13	5.2828	2.5842	76.8492
14	5.1028	2.7642	74.0850
15	4.9104	2.9566	71.1283
16	4.7045	3.1625	67.9658
17	4.4843	3.3827	64.5831
18	4.2488	3.6182	60.9649
19	3.9969	3.8702	57.0947
20	3.7274	4.1396	52.9551
21	3.4391	4.4279	48.5272
22	3.1308	4.7362	43.7910
23	2.8011	5.0659	38.7251
24	2.4483	5.4187	33.3064
25	2.0710	5.7960	27.5104
26	1.6675	6.1995	21.3109
27	1.2358	6.6312	14.6797
28	.7741	7.0929	7.5868
29	.2802	7.5868	0.0000

	YEARS	MO PAYT	AN CONST
	30	.6486	7.79
#	INT	PRIN	BALANCE
1	6.7174	1.0657	98.9343
2	6.6432	1.1400	97.7943
3	6.5639	1.2193	96.5750
4	6.4790	1.3042	95.2707
5	6.3881	1.3950	93.8757
6	6.2910	1.4922	92.3835
7	6.1871	1.5961	90.7875
8	6.0760	1.7072	89.0803
9	5.9571	1.8261	87.2542
10	5.8300	1.9532	85.3010
11	5.6940	2.0892	83.2118
12	5.5485	2.2347	80.9771
13	5.3929	2.3903	78.5868
14	5.2265	2.5567	76.0301
15	5.0485	2.7347	73.2954
16	4.8580	2.9251	70.3703
17	4.6544	3.1288	67.2415
18	4.4365	3.3467	63.8948
19	4.2035	3.5797	60.3151
20	3.9543	3.8289	56.4862
21	3.6877	4.0955	52.3907
22	3.4025	4.3807	48.0100
23	3.0975	4.6857	43.3243
24	2.7712	5.0120	38.3124
25	2.4222	5.3609	32.9514
26	2.0490	5.7342	27.2172
27	1.6497	6.1335	21.0838
28	1.2227	6.5605	14.5232
29	.7659	7.0173	7.5059
30	.2773	7.5059	0.0000

YEARS 2 — MO PAYT 4.4682 — AN CONST 53.62

#	INT	PRIN	BALANCE
1	5.3129	48.3054	51.6946
2	1.9238	51.6946	0.0000

YEARS 3 — MO PAYT 3.0786 — AN CONST 36.95

#	INT	PRIN	BALANCE
1	5.8426	31.1003	68.8997
2	3.6606	33.2823	35.6174
3	1.3255	35.6174	0.0000

YEARS 4 — MO PAYT 2.3854 — AN CONST 28.63

#	INT	PRIN	BALANCE
1	6.1068	22.5175	77.4825
2	4.5270	24.0973	53.3852
3	2.8363	25.7880	27.5972
4	1.0270	27.5972	0.0000

YEARS 5 — MO PAYT 1.9707 — AN CONST 23.65

#	INT	PRIN	BALANCE
1	6.2648	17.3835	82.6165
2	5.0452	18.6031	64.0133
3	3.7400	19.9083	44.1050
4	2.3433	21.3051	22.7999
5	.8485	22.7999	0.0000

YEARS 6 — MO PAYT 1.6953 — AN CONST 20.35

#	INT	PRIN	BALANCE
1	6.3698	13.9739	86.0261
2	5.3894	14.9544	71.0717
3	4.3402	16.0036	55.0681
4	3.2174	17.1264	37.9418
5	2.0158	18.3279	19.6138
6	.7299	19.6138	0.0000

YEARS 7 — MO PAYT 1.4995 — AN CONST 18.00

#	INT	PRIN	BALANCE
1	6.4444	11.5497	88.4503
2	5.6341	12.3600	76.0903
3	4.7669	13.2272	62.8631
4	3.8389	14.1552	48.7079
5	2.8458	15.1483	33.5596
6	1.7830	16.2111	17.3485
7	.6456	17.3485	0.0000

YEARS 8 — MO PAYT 1.3534 — AN CONST 16.25

#	INT	PRIN	BALANCE
1	6.5001	9.7412	90.2588
2	5.8167	10.4246	79.8342
3	5.0853	11.1560	68.6782
4	4.3026	11.9387	56.7395
5	3.4650	12.7763	43.9632
6	2.5686	13.6727	30.2905
7	1.6093	14.6320	15.6586
8	.5827	15.6586	0.0000

YEARS 9 — MO PAYT 1.2405 — AN CONST 14.89

#	INT	PRIN	BALANCE
1	6.5432	8.3431	91.6569
2	5.9578	8.9285	82.7284
3	5.3314	9.5549	73.1736
4	4.6610	10.2252	62.9483
5	3.9436	10.9426	52.0057
6	3.1759	11.7104	40.2953
7	2.3543	12.5320	27.7634
8	1.4750	13.4112	14.3521
9	.5341	14.3521	0.0000

YEARS 10 — MO PAYT 1.1508 — AN CONST 13.81

#	INT	PRIN	BALANCE
1	6.5774	7.2323	92.7677
2	6.0699	7.7397	85.0280
3	5.5269	8.2827	76.7453
4	4.9458	8.8638	67.8815
5	4.3239	9.4857	58.3957
6	3.6584	10.1512	48.2445
7	2.9462	10.8634	37.3811
8	2.1840	11.6256	25.7554
9	1.3684	12.4413	13.3142
10	.4955	13.3142	0.0000

YEARS 11 — MO PAYT 1.0780 — AN CONST 12.94

#	INT	PRIN	BALANCE
1	6.6051	6.3303	93.6697
2	6.1610	6.7745	86.8952
3	5.6857	7.2498	79.6455
4	5.1770	7.7584	71.8871
5	4.6327	8.3027	63.5843
6	4.0502	8.8852	54.6991
7	3.4268	9.5086	45.1905
8	2.7597	10.1758	35.0147
9	2.0458	10.8897	24.1250
10	1.2817	11.6537	12.4713
11	.4641	12.4713	0.0000

YEARS 12 — MO PAYT 1.0178 — AN CONST 12.22

#	INT	PRIN	BALANCE
1	6.6281	5.5849	94.4151
2	6.2362	5.9768	88.4383
3	5.8169	6.3961	82.0422
4	5.3681	6.8449	75.1973
5	4.8879	7.3251	67.8722
6	4.3740	7.8390	60.0332
7	3.8240	8.3890	51.6442
8	3.2354	8.9776	42.6666
9	2.6056	9.6074	33.0592
10	1.9315	10.2815	22.7777
11	1.2102	11.0029	11.7748
12	.4382	11.7748	0.0000

YEARS 13 — MO PAYT .9673 — AN CONST 11.61

#	INT	PRIN	BALANCE
1	6.6473	4.9599	95.0401
2	6.2993	5.3079	89.7321
3	5.9269	5.6803	84.0518
4	5.5284	6.0789	77.9729
5	5.1019	6.5054	71.4676
6	4.6455	6.9618	64.5058
7	4.1570	7.4502	57.0556
8	3.6343	7.9729	49.0827
9	3.0750	8.5323	40.5504
10	2.4763	9.1309	31.4194
11	1.8357	9.7715	21.6479
12	1.1501	10.4571	11.1908
13	.4165	11.1908	0.0000

YEARS 14 — MO PAYT .9244 — AN CONST 11.10

#	INT	PRIN	BALANCE
1	6.6636	4.4295	95.5705
2	6.3529	4.7402	90.8303
3	6.0203	5.0728	85.7575
4	5.6644	5.4287	80.3287
5	5.2835	5.8096	74.5191
6	4.8759	6.2172	68.3019
7	4.4397	6.6534	61.6485
8	3.9729	7.1202	54.5283
9	3.4734	7.6198	46.9086
10	2.9387	8.1544	38.7542
11	2.3666	8.7265	30.0277
12	1.7544	9.3387	20.6890
13	1.0992	9.9939	10.6951
14	.3980	10.6951	0.0000

YEARS 15 — MO PAYT .8877 — AN CONST 10.66

#	INT	PRIN	BALANCE
1	6.6776	3.9746	96.0254
2	6.3988	4.2534	91.7720
3	6.1004	4.5518	87.2202
4	5.7810	4.8712	82.3490
5	5.4392	5.2130	77.1360
6	5.0735	5.5787	71.5573
7	4.6821	5.9701	65.5872
8	4.2632	6.3890	59.1983
9	3.8150	6.8372	52.3611
10	3.3353	7.3169	45.0442
11	2.8219	7.8303	37.2139
12	2.2726	8.3796	28.8343
13	1.6847	8.9675	19.8667
14	1.0555	9.5967	10.2700
15	.3822	10.2700	0.0000

YEARS 16 — MO PAYT .8559 — AN CONST 10.28

#	INT	PRIN	BALANCE
1	6.6898	3.5810	96.4190
2	6.4385	3.8322	92.5868
3	6.1696	4.1011	88.4857
4	5.8819	4.3888	84.0968
5	5.5740	4.6968	79.4001
6	5.2445	5.0263	74.3738
7	4.8918	5.3789	68.9949
8	4.5144	5.7563	63.2386
9	4.1106	6.1602	57.0784
10	3.6784	6.5924	50.4860
11	3.2159	7.0549	43.4311
12	2.7209	7.5499	35.8813
13	2.1912	8.0796	27.8017
14	1.6243	8.6464	19.1553
15	1.0177	9.2530	9.9022
16	.3685	9.9022	0.0000

YEARS 17 — MO PAYT .8282 — AN CONST 9.94

#	INT	PRIN	BALANCE
1	6.7003	3.2379	96.7621
2	6.4732	3.4650	93.2971
3	6.2300	3.7082	89.5889
4	5.9699	3.9683	85.6206
5	5.6915	4.2467	81.3739
6	5.3935	4.5447	76.8292
7	5.0747	4.8635	71.9657
8	4.7334	5.2048	66.7609
9	4.3683	5.5699	61.1910
10	3.9775	5.9607	55.2303
11	3.5593	6.3789	48.8513
12	3.1117	6.8265	42.0249
13	2.6328	7.3054	34.7195
14	2.1202	7.8180	26.9015
15	1.5717	8.3665	18.5351
16	.9848	8.9534	9.5816
17	.3566	9.5816	0.0000

YEARS 18 — MO PAYT .8039 — AN CONST 9.65

#	INT	PRIN	BALANCE
1	6.7096	2.9367	97.0633
2	6.5036	3.1428	93.9205
3	6.2831	3.3633	90.5572
4	6.0471	3.5993	86.9579
5	5.7946	3.8518	83.1061
6	5.5243	4.1220	78.9841
7	5.2351	4.4112	74.5729
8	4.9256	4.7207	69.8522
9	4.5944	5.0519	64.8003
10	4.2400	5.4064	59.3939
11	3.8607	5.7857	53.6083
12	3.4548	6.1916	47.4167
13	3.0204	6.6260	40.7907
14	2.5555	7.0909	33.6998
15	2.0580	7.5884	26.1115
16	1.5256	8.1208	17.9907
17	.9558	8.6905	9.3002
18	.3461	9.3002	0.0000

YEARS 19 — MO PAYT .7824 — AN CONST 9.39

#	INT	PRIN	BALANCE
1	6.7178	2.6709	97.3291
2	6.5304	2.8583	94.4708
3	6.3298	3.0588	91.4119
4	6.1152	3.2735	88.1385
5	5.8856	3.5031	84.6354
6	5.6398	3.7489	80.8865
7	5.3768	4.0119	76.8745
8	5.0953	4.2934	72.5811
9	4.7941	4.5946	67.9865
10	4.4717	4.9170	63.0695
11	4.1267	5.2620	57.8076
12	3.7576	5.6311	52.1764
13	3.3625	6.0262	46.1502
14	2.9397	6.4490	39.7012
15	2.4872	6.9015	32.7998
16	2.0030	7.3857	25.4141
17	1.4848	7.9039	17.5102
18	.9303	8.4584	9.0518
19	.3369	9.0518	0.0000

YEARS 20 — MO PAYT .7633 — AN CONST 9.17

#	INT	PRIN	BALANCE
1	6.7250	2.4350	97.5650
2	6.5542	2.6059	94.9591
3	6.3714	2.7887	92.1704
4	6.1757	2.9844	89.1860
5	5.9663	3.1937	85.9923
6	5.7423	3.4178	82.5744
7	5.5025	3.6576	78.9168
8	5.2458	3.9142	75.0026
9	4.9712	4.1889	70.8138
10	4.6773	4.4827	66.3310
11	4.3628	4.7972	61.5338
12	4.0263	5.1338	56.3999
13	3.6661	5.4940	50.9059
14	3.2806	5.8795	45.0265
15	2.8681	6.2920	38.7345
16	2.4267	6.7334	32.0011
17	1.9542	7.2058	24.7952
18	1.4487	7.7114	17.0838
19	.9076	8.2524	8.8314
20	.3287	8.8314	0.0000

YEARS 21 — MO PAYT .7464 — AN CONST 8.96

#	INT	PRIN	BALANCE
1	6.7315	2.2248	97.7752
2	6.5754	2.3809	95.3944
3	6.4084	2.5479	92.8465

#	INT	PRIN	BALANCE
4	6.2296	2.7267	90.1198
5	6.0383	2.9180	87.2018
6	5.8336	3.1227	84.0791
7	5.6145	3.3418	80.7374
8	5.3800	3.5762	77.1611
9	5.1291	3.8271	73.3340
10	4.8606	4.0957	69.2383
11	4.5733	4.3830	64.8553
12	4.2658	4.6905	60.1648
13	3.9367	5.0196	55.1452
14	3.5845	5.3718	49.7734
15	3.2076	5.7487	44.0247
16	2.8043	6.1520	37.8727
17	2.3727	6.5836	31.2891
18	1.9108	7.0455	24.2436
19	1.4164	7.5398	16.7038
20	.8875	8.0688	8.6349
21	.3213	8.6349	0.0000

YEARS 22 — MO PAYT .7312 — AN CONST 8.78

#	INT	PRIN	BALANCE
1	6.7373	2.0366	97.9634
2	6.5944	2.1795	95.7840
3	6.4415	2.3324	93.4516
4	6.2779	2.4960	90.9556
5	6.1027	2.6711	88.2844
6	5.9153	2.8585	85.4259
7	5.7148	3.0591	82.3668
8	5.5002	3.2737	79.0931
9	5.2705	3.5034	75.5897
10	5.0247	3.7492	71.8405
11	4.7616	4.0122	67.8282
12	4.4801	4.2937	63.5345
13	4.1789	4.5950	58.9395
14	3.8565	4.9174	54.0221
15	3.5115	5.2624	48.7597
16	3.1423	5.6316	43.1281
17	2.7472	6.0267	37.1014
18	2.3243	6.4495	30.6519
19	1.8718	6.9020	23.7499
20	1.3876	7.3863	16.3636
21	.8694	7.9045	8.4591
22	.3148	8.4591	0.0000

YEARS 23 — MO PAYT .7175 — AN CONST 8.62

#	INT	PRIN	BALANCE
1	6.7425	1.8675	98.1325
2	6.6115	1.9985	96.1339
3	6.4713	2.1388	93.9952
4	6.3212	2.2888	91.7064
5	6.1606	2.4494	89.2570
6	5.9888	2.6213	86.6357
7	5.8049	2.8052	83.8305
8	5.6081	3.0020	80.8286
9	5.3974	3.2126	77.6160
10	5.1720	3.4380	74.1780
11	4.9308	3.6792	70.4988
12	4.6727	3.9373	66.5615
13	4.3965	4.2136	62.3480
14	4.1008	4.5092	57.8388
15	3.7845	4.8255	53.0132
16	3.4459	5.1641	47.8491
17	3.0836	5.5264	42.3227
18	2.6959	5.9142	36.4085
19	2.2809	6.3291	30.0795
20	1.8369	6.7731	23.3063
21	1.3617	7.2483	16.0580
22	.8531	7.7569	8.3011
23	.3089	8.3011	0.0000

YEARS 24 — MO PAYT .7052 — AN CONST 8.47

#	INT	PRIN	BALANCE
1	6.7472	1.7152	98.2848
2	6.6269	1.8355	96.4494
3	6.4981	1.9643	94.4851
4	6.3603	2.1021	92.3830
5	6.2128	2.2496	90.1335
6	6.0550	2.4074	87.7261
7	5.8861	2.5763	85.1498
8	5.7053	2.7570	82.3927
9	5.5119	2.9505	79.4422
10	5.3049	3.1575	76.2848
11	5.0833	3.3790	72.9058
12	4.8463	3.6161	69.2897
13	4.5926	3.8698	65.4199
14	4.3211	4.1413	61.2786
15	4.0305	4.4318	56.8467
16	3.7196	4.7428	52.1040
17	3.3868	5.0755	47.0284
18	3.0307	5.4316	41.5968
19	2.6496	5.8127	35.7841
20	2.2418	6.2205	29.5636
21	1.8054	6.6570	22.9066
22	1.3383	7.1240	15.7826
23	.8385	7.6238	8.1587
24	.3036	8.1587	0.0000

YEARS 25 — MO PAYT .6941 — AN CONST 8.33

#	INT	PRIN	BALANCE
1	6.7514	1.5774	98.4226
2	6.6408	1.6881	96.7345
3	6.5223	1.8065	94.9279
4	6.3956	1.9333	92.9947
5	6.2599	2.0689	90.9257
6	6.1148	2.2141	88.7117
7	5.9595	2.3694	86.3422
8	5.7932	2.5357	83.8066
9	5.6153	2.7136	81.0930
10	5.4249	2.9039	78.1891
11	5.2212	3.1077	75.0814
12	5.0032	3.3257	71.7557
13	4.7698	3.5590	68.1967
14	4.5201	3.8087	64.3879
15	4.2529	4.0760	60.3120
16	3.9669	4.3619	55.9500
17	3.6609	4.6680	51.2821
18	3.3334	4.9955	46.2866
19	2.9829	5.3460	40.9406
20	2.6078	5.7210	35.2196
21	2.2065	6.1224	29.0972
22	1.7769	6.5520	22.5452
23	1.3172	7.0116	15.5336
24	.8253	7.5036	8.0300
25	.2988	8.0300	0.0000

YEARS 26 — MO PAYT .6840 — AN CONST 8.21

#	INT	PRIN	BALANCE
1	6.7553	1.4526	98.5474
2	6.6534	1.5545	96.9929
3	6.5443	1.6636	95.3293
4	6.4276	1.7803	93.5490
5	6.3027	1.9052	91.6438
6	6.1690	2.0389	89.6050
7	6.0260	2.1819	87.4230
8	5.8729	2.3350	85.0880
9	5.7091	2.4988	82.5892
10	5.5337	2.6741	79.9151
11	5.3461	2.8618	77.0533
12	5.1453	3.0625	73.9908
13	4.9305	3.2774	70.7134
14	4.7005	3.5073	67.2061
15	4.4545	3.7534	63.4526
16	4.1911	4.0168	59.4359
17	3.9093	4.2986	55.1373
18	3.6077	4.6002	50.5371
19	3.2850	4.9229	45.6142
20	2.9396	5.2683	40.3459
21	2.5700	5.6379	34.7080
22	2.1744	6.0335	28.6745
23	1.7511	6.4568	22.2178
24	1.2981	6.9098	15.3080
25	.8133	7.3946	7.9134
26	.2945	7.9134	0.0000

YEARS 27 — MO PAYT .6748 — AN CONST 8.10

#	INT	PRIN	BALANCE
1	6.7588	1.3392	98.6608
2	6.6648	1.4331	97.2277
3	6.5643	1.5337	95.6940
4	6.4567	1.6413	94.0527
5	6.3415	1.7565	92.2962
6	6.2183	1.8797	90.4165
7	6.0864	2.0116	88.4050
8	5.9453	2.1527	86.2523
9	5.7942	2.3037	83.9486
10	5.6326	2.4654	81.4832
11	5.4596	2.6383	78.8449
12	5.2745	2.8234	76.0214
13	5.0764	3.0215	72.9999
14	4.8645	3.2335	69.7664
15	4.6376	3.4604	66.3060
16	4.3948	3.7032	62.6029
17	4.1350	3.9630	58.6399
18	3.8570	4.2410	54.3989
19	3.5594	4.5386	49.8604
20	3.2410	4.8570	45.0034
21	2.9002	5.1977	39.8056
22	2.5355	5.5624	34.2432
23	2.1453	5.9527	28.2905
24	1.7276	6.3703	21.9202
25	1.2807	6.8173	15.1030
26	.8024	7.2956	7.8074
27	.2906	7.8074	0.0000

YEARS 28 — MO PAYT .6665 — AN CONST 8.00

#	INT	PRIN	BALANCE
1	6.7620	1.2359	98.7641
2	6.6752	1.3226	97.4414
3	6.5824	1.4154	96.0260
4	6.4831	1.5147	94.5113
5	6.3769	1.6210	92.8903
6	6.2631	1.7347	91.1555
7	6.1414	1.8565	89.2991
8	6.0112	1.9867	87.3124
9	5.8718	2.1261	85.1863
10	5.7226	2.2753	82.9110
11	5.5630	2.4349	80.4761
12	5.3922	2.6057	77.8704
13	5.2093	2.7885	75.0819
14	5.0137	2.9842	72.0977
15	4.8043	3.1935	68.9041
16	4.5803	3.4176	65.4865
17	4.3405	3.6574	61.8292
18	4.0839	3.9140	57.9152
19	3.8093	4.1886	53.7266
20	3.5154	4.4825	49.2441
21	3.2009	4.7970	44.4472
22	2.8644	5.1335	39.3137
23	2.5042	5.4937	33.8200
24	2.1188	5.8791	27.9409
25	1.7063	6.2916	21.6493
26	1.2649	6.7330	14.9163
27	.7925	7.2054	7.7109
28	.2870	7.7109	0.0000

YEARS 29 — MO PAYT .6589 — AN CONST 7.91

#	INT	PRIN	BALANCE
1	6.7649	1.1417	98.8583
2	6.6847	1.2218	97.6365
3	6.5990	1.3075	96.3289
4	6.5073	1.3993	94.9297
5	6.4091	1.4974	93.4322
6	6.3041	1.6025	91.8297
7	6.1916	1.7149	90.1148
8	6.0713	1.8353	88.2795
9	5.9425	1.9640	86.3155
10	5.8047	2.1018	84.2137
11	5.6573	2.2493	81.9644
12	5.4995	2.4071	79.5573
13	5.3306	2.5760	76.9814
14	5.1499	2.7567	74.2247
15	4.9565	2.9501	71.2745
16	4.7495	3.1571	68.1175
17	4.5280	3.3786	64.7389
18	4.2909	3.6156	61.1232
19	4.0373	3.8693	57.2539
20	3.7658	4.1408	53.1132
21	3.4753	4.4313	48.6819
22	3.1644	4.7422	43.9397
23	2.8317	5.0749	38.8648
24	2.4756	5.4309	33.4339
25	2.0946	5.8120	27.6219
26	1.6868	6.2198	21.4021
27	1.2504	6.6561	14.7460
28	.7834	7.1231	7.6229
29	.2837	7.6229	0.0000

YEARS 30 — MO PAYT .6519 — AN CONST 7.83

#	INT	PRIN	BALANCE
1	6.7675	1.0556	98.9444
2	6.6934	1.1297	97.8147
3	6.6142	1.2089	96.6058
4	6.5294	1.2937	95.3121
5	6.4386	1.3845	93.9276
6	6.3415	1.4816	92.4460
7	6.2375	1.5856	90.8604
8	6.1263	1.6968	89.1635
9	6.0072	1.8159	87.3476
10	5.8798	1.9433	85.4044
11	5.7435	2.0796	83.3247
12	5.5976	2.2255	81.0992
13	5.4414	2.3817	78.7175
14	5.2743	2.5488	76.1687
15	5.0955	2.7276	73.4411
16	4.9041	2.9190	70.5222
17	4.6993	3.1238	67.3984
18	4.4802	3.3429	64.0555
19	4.2456	3.5775	60.4780
20	3.9946	3.8285	56.6496
21	3.7260	4.0971	52.5525
22	3.4386	4.3845	48.1680
23	3.1310	4.6921	43.4759
24	2.8018	5.0213	38.4546
25	2.4495	5.3736	33.0809
26	2.0725	5.7506	27.3303
27	1.6690	6.1541	21.1762
28	1.2372	6.5859	14.5903
29	.7752	7.0479	7.5424
30	.2807	7.5424	0.0000

YEARS 2 — MO PAYT 4.4716 — AN CONST 53.66

#	INT	PRIN	BALANCE
1	5.3723	48.2868	51.7132
2	1.9459	51.7132	0.0000

YEARS 3 — MO PAYT 3.0820 — AN CONST 36.99

#	INT	PRIN	BALANCE
1	5.9079	31.0761	68.9239
2	3.7028	33.2812	35.6428
3	1.3412	35.6428	0.0000

YEARS 4 — MO PAYT 2.3888 — AN CONST 28.67

#	INT	PRIN	BALANCE
1	6.1751	22.4909	77.5091
2	4.5792	24.0868	53.4223
3	2.8700	25.7959	27.6264
4	1.0396	27.6264	0.0000

YEARS 5 — MO PAYT 1.9742 — AN CONST 23.70

#	INT	PRIN	BALANCE
1	6.3349	17.3559	82.6441
2	5.1033	18.5874	64.0568
3	3.7844	19.9063	44.1504
4	2.3719	21.3188	22.8316
5	.8591	22.8316	0.0000

YEARS 6 — MO PAYT 1.6989 — AN CONST 20.39

#	INT	PRIN	BALANCE
1	6.4410	13.9459	86.0541
2	5.4514	14.9354	71.1187
3	4.3916	15.9952	55.1235
4	3.2566	17.1302	37.9933
5	2.0411	18.3457	19.6475
6	.7393	19.6475	0.0000

YEARS 7 — MO PAYT 1.5032 — AN CONST 18.04

#	INT	PRIN	BALANCE
1	6.5164	11.5215	88.4785
2	5.6989	12.3391	76.1394
3	4.8233	13.2146	62.9247
4	3.8856	14.1523	48.7724
5	2.8814	15.1566	33.6159
6	1.8059	16.2320	17.3838
7	.6541	17.3838	0.0000

YEARS 8 — MO PAYT 1.3572 — AN CONST 16.29

#	INT	PRIN	BALANCE
1	6.5727	9.7132	90.2868
2	5.8835	10.4024	79.8844
3	5.1454	11.1406	68.7438
4	4.3548	11.9311	56.8127
5	3.5082	12.7777	44.0351
6	2.6015	13.6844	30.3507
7	1.6305	14.6554	15.6953
8	.5906	15.6953	0.0000

YEARS 9 — MO PAYT 1.2443 — AN CONST 14.94

#	INT	PRIN	BALANCE
1	6.6162	8.3154	91.6846
2	6.0262	8.9055	82.7791
3	5.3943	9.5374	73.2416
4	4.7175	10.2142	63.0275
5	3.9927	10.9390	52.0885
6	3.2165	11.7152	40.3733
7	2.3852	12.5465	27.8269
8	1.4949	13.4367	14.3902
9	.5415	14.3902	0.0000

YEARS 10 — MO PAYT 1.1547 — AN CONST 13.86

#	INT	PRIN	BALANCE
1	6.6508	7.2051	92.7949
2	6.1395	7.7163	85.0786
3	5.5920	8.2639	76.8148
4	5.0056	8.8502	67.9645
5	4.3776	9.4782	58.4863
6	3.7050	10.1508	48.3355
7	2.9848	10.8711	37.4644
8	2.2134	11.6425	25.8220
9	1.3872	12.4686	13.3534
10	.5025	13.3534	0.0000

YEARS 11 — MO PAYT 1.0819 — AN CONST 12.99

#	INT	PRIN	BALANCE
1	6.6788	6.3036	93.6964
2	6.2315	6.7509	86.9455
3	5.7525	7.2299	79.7156
4	5.2395	7.7429	71.9727
5	4.6901	8.2924	63.6803
6	4.1016	8.8808	54.7996
7	3.4715	9.5109	45.2886
8	2.7966	10.1858	35.1028
9	2.0738	10.9086	24.1942
10	1.2998	11.6826	12.5116
11	.4708	12.5116	0.0000

YEARS 12 — MO PAYT 1.0217 — AN CONST 12.27

#	INT	PRIN	BALANCE
1	6.7020	5.5587	94.4413
2	6.3076	5.9532	88.4881
3	5.8851	6.3756	82.1124
4	5.4327	6.8280	75.2844
5	4.9482	7.3125	67.9719
6	4.4294	7.8314	60.1405
7	3.8736	8.3871	51.7534
8	3.2785	8.9822	42.7712
9	2.6412	9.6196	33.1515
10	1.9586	10.3022	22.8493
11	1.2275	11.0332	11.8161
12	.4446	11.8161	0.0000

YEARS 13 — MO PAYT .9713 — AN CONST 11.66

#	INT	PRIN	BALANCE
1	6.7214	4.9343	95.0657
2	6.3713	5.2845	89.7812
3	5.9963	5.6594	84.1218
4	5.5948	6.0610	78.0607
5	5.1647	6.4911	71.5696
6	4.7041	6.9517	64.6180
7	4.2108	7.4450	57.1730
8	3.6825	7.9733	49.1997
9	3.1167	8.5390	40.6607
10	2.5108	9.1449	31.5157
11	1.8619	9.7939	21.7219
12	1.1670	10.4888	11.2331
13	.4227	11.2331	0.0000

YEARS 14 — MO PAYT .9285 — AN CONST 11.15

#	INT	PRIN	BALANCE
1	6.7379	4.4045	95.5955
2	6.4254	4.7170	90.8785
3	6.0907	5.0517	85.8268
4	5.7322	5.4102	80.4167
5	5.3483	5.7941	74.6226
6	4.9372	6.2052	68.4174
7	4.4969	6.6455	61.7719
8	4.0253	7.1171	54.6548
9	3.5203	7.6221	47.0327
10	2.9795	8.1629	38.8698
11	2.4002	8.7422	30.1276
12	1.7799	9.3625	20.7652
13	1.1156	10.0268	10.7383
14	.4041	10.7383	0.0000

YEARS 15 — MO PAYT .8919 — AN CONST 10.71

#	INT	PRIN	BALANCE
1	6.7521	3.9502	96.0498
2	6.4718	4.2305	91.8193
3	6.1716	4.5307	87.2887
4	5.8501	4.8522	82.4365
5	5.5058	5.1965	77.2401
6	5.1371	5.5652	71.6749
7	4.7422	5.9601	65.7148
8	4.3192	6.3830	59.3318
9	3.8663	6.8359	52.4958
10	3.3813	7.3210	45.1748
11	2.8618	7.8405	37.3344
12	2.3054	8.3968	28.9375
13	1.7096	8.9927	19.9449
14	1.0715	9.6308	10.3141
15	.3881	10.3141	0.0000

YEARS 16 — MO PAYT .8601 — AN CONST 10.33

#	INT	PRIN	BALANCE
1	6.7643	3.5572	96.4428
2	6.5119	3.8097	92.6331
3	6.2416	4.0800	88.5531
4	5.9520	4.3695	84.1836
5	5.6420	4.6796	79.5040
6	5.3099	5.0116	74.4924
7	4.9543	5.3672	69.1252
8	4.5735	5.7481	63.3771
9	4.1656	6.1559	57.2212
10	3.7288	6.5928	50.6284
11	3.2610	7.0606	43.5679
12	2.7600	7.5616	36.0063
13	2.2234	8.0981	27.9082
14	1.6488	8.6728	19.2354
15	1.0334	9.2882	9.9472
16	.3743	9.9472	0.0000

YEARS 17 — MO PAYT .8325 — AN CONST 9.99

#	INT	PRIN	BALANCE
1	6.7750	3.2148	96.7852
2	6.5468	3.4429	93.3423
3	6.3025	3.6872	89.6551
4	6.0409	3.9488	85.7063
5	5.7607	4.2290	81.4773
6	5.4606	4.5291	76.9482
7	5.1392	4.8505	72.0977
8	4.7951	5.1947	66.9030
9	4.4264	5.5633	61.3397
10	4.0317	5.9580	55.3817
11	3.6089	6.3808	49.0008
12	3.1561	6.8336	42.1673
13	2.6712	7.3185	34.8488
14	2.1519	7.8378	27.0110
15	1.5958	8.3940	18.6170
16	1.0002	8.9896	9.6275
17	.3623	9.6275	0.0000

YEARS 18 — MO PAYT .8082 — AN CONST 9.70

#	INT	PRIN	BALANCE
1	6.7843	2.9143	97.0857
2	6.5775	3.1211	93.9646
3	6.3560	3.3426	90.6221
4	6.1189	3.5797	87.0423
5	5.8649	3.8337	83.2086
6	5.5928	4.1058	79.1028
7	5.3015	4.3971	74.7057
8	4.9895	4.7091	69.9965
9	4.6553	5.0433	64.9532
10	4.2974	5.4012	59.5521
11	3.9142	5.7844	53.7677
12	3.5037	6.1949	47.5728
13	3.0642	6.6344	40.9384
14	2.5934	7.1052	33.8332
15	2.0892	7.6094	26.2238
16	1.5493	8.1493	18.0745
17	.9710	8.7276	9.3469
18	.3517	9.3469	0.0000

YEARS 19 — MO PAYT .7868 — AN CONST 9.45

#	INT	PRIN	BALANCE
1	6.7926	2.6491	97.3509
2	6.6046	2.8371	94.5138
3	6.4033	3.0384	91.4754
4	6.1877	3.2540	88.2214
5	5.9568	3.4849	84.7365
6	5.7095	3.7322	81.0043
7	5.4447	3.9970	77.0073
8	5.1610	4.2806	72.7266
9	4.8573	4.5844	68.1422
10	4.5320	4.9097	63.2325
11	4.1836	5.2581	57.9745
12	3.8105	5.6312	52.3433
13	3.4109	6.0308	46.3126
14	2.9830	6.4587	39.8539
15	2.5247	6.9170	32.9369
16	2.0339	7.4078	25.5291
17	1.5082	7.9334	17.5957
18	.9453	8.4964	9.0993
19	.3424	9.0993	0.0000

YEARS 20 — MO PAYT .7678 — AN CONST 9.22

#	INT	PRIN	BALANCE
1	6.7999	2.4139	97.5861
2	6.6286	2.5852	95.0009
3	6.4452	2.7686	92.2323
4	6.2487	2.9651	89.2673
5	6.0383	3.1755	86.0918
6	5.8130	3.4008	82.6910
7	5.5717	3.6421	79.0489
8	5.3132	3.9005	75.1484
9	5.0365	4.1773	70.9711
10	4.7400	4.4737	66.4974
11	4.4226	4.7912	61.7062
12	4.0826	5.1311	56.5750
13	3.7185	5.4952	51.0798
14	3.3286	5.8852	45.1946
15	2.9110	6.3028	38.8918
16	2.4638	6.7500	32.1418
17	1.9848	7.2290	24.9129
18	1.4718	7.7419	17.1709
19	.9225	8.2913	8.8796
20	.3341	8.8796	0.0000

YEARS 21 — MO PAYT .7509 — AN CONST 9.02

#	INT	PRIN	BALANCE
1	6.8064	2.2043	97.7957
2	6.6500	2.3607	95.4351
3	6.4825	2.5282	92.9069

MONTHLY PAYMENT AMORTIZATION SCHEDULE PER $100   6.875%

#	INT	PRIN	BALANCE
4	6.3031	2.7076	90.1993
5	6.1110	2.8997	87.2996
6	5.9052	3.1055	84.1941
7	5.6848	3.3258	80.8683
8	5.4489	3.5618	77.3065
9	5.1961	3.8146	73.4919
10	4.9254	4.0852	69.4067
11	4.6356	4.3751	65.0316
12	4.3251	4.6856	60.3460
13	3.9926	5.0180	55.3280
14	3.6366	5.3741	49.9539
15	3.2552	5.7555	44.1984
16	2.8468	6.1638	38.0346
17	2.4094	6.6012	31.4333
18	1.9410	7.0696	24.3637
19	1.4394	7.5713	16.7924
20	.9021	8.1085	8.6839
21	.3268	8.6839	0.0000

YEARS 22 — MO PAYT .7357 — AN CONST 8.83

#	INT	PRIN	BALANCE
1	6.8122	2.0167	97.9833
2	6.6691	2.1598	95.8235
3	6.5159	2.3131	93.5104
4	6.3517	2.4772	91.0332
5	6.1760	2.6530	88.3802
6	5.9877	2.8412	85.5390
7	5.7861	3.0428	82.4962
8	5.5702	3.2588	79.2374
9	5.3390	3.4900	75.7474
10	5.0913	3.7376	72.0098
11	4.8261	4.0028	68.0070
12	4.5421	4.2869	63.7201
13	4.2379	4.5911	59.1290
14	3.9121	4.9168	54.2122
15	3.5632	5.2657	48.9464
16	3.1896	5.6394	43.3071
17	2.7894	6.0395	37.2675
18	2.3609	6.4681	30.7994
19	1.9019	6.9271	23.8724
20	1.4104	7.4186	16.4538
21	.8839	7.9450	8.5088
22	.3202	8.5088	0.0000

YEARS 23 — MO PAYT .7221 — AN CONST 8.67

#	INT	PRIN	BALANCE
1	6.8175	1.8483	98.1517
2	6.6863	1.9794	96.1723
3	6.5459	2.1199	94.0524
4	6.3954	2.2703	91.7821
5	6.2344	2.4314	89.3507
6	6.0618	2.6039	86.7467
7	5.8771	2.7887	83.9580
8	5.6792	2.9866	80.9714
9	5.4672	3.1985	77.7729
10	5.2403	3.4255	74.3474
11	4.9972	3.6685	70.6789
12	4.7369	3.9289	66.7500
13	4.4581	4.2076	62.5424
14	4.1596	4.5062	58.0361
15	3.8398	4.8260	53.2102
16	3.4974	5.1684	48.0418
17	3.1306	5.5351	42.5066
18	2.7379	5.9279	36.5787
19	2.3172	6.3485	30.2302
20	1.8667	6.7990	23.4311
21	1.3843	7.2815	16.1497
22	.8676	7.7982	8.3515
23	.3143	8.3515	0.0000

YEARS 24 — MO PAYT .7099 — AN CONST 8.52

#	INT	PRIN	BALANCE
1	6.8222	1.6965	98.3035
2	6.7018	1.8169	96.4865
3	6.5729	1.9459	94.5407
4	6.4348	2.0839	92.4568
5	6.2869	2.2318	90.2250
6	6.1286	2.3902	87.8348
7	5.9590	2.5598	85.2750
8	5.7773	2.7414	82.5336
9	5.5828	2.9359	79.5977
10	5.3745	3.1443	76.4534
11	5.1514	3.3674	73.0861
12	4.9124	3.6063	69.4798
13	4.6565	3.8622	65.6176
14	4.3825	4.1363	61.4813
15	4.0890	4.4298	57.0515
16	3.7747	4.7441	52.3074
17	3.4380	5.0807	47.2267
18	3.0775	5.4412	41.7855
19	2.6914	5.8273	35.9581
20	2.2779	6.2408	29.7173
21	1.8351	6.6837	23.0336
22	1.3608	7.1579	15.8757
23	.8529	7.6659	8.2098
24	.3089	8.2098	0.0000

YEARS 25 — MO PAYT .6988 — AN CONST 8.39

#	INT	PRIN	BALANCE
1	6.8265	1.5594	98.4406
2	6.7158	1.6701	96.7705
3	6.5973	1.7886	94.9819
4	6.4704	1.9155	93.0664
5	6.3345	2.0514	91.0150
6	6.1889	2.1970	88.8180
7	6.0330	2.3529	86.4651
8	5.8661	2.5198	83.9452
9	5.6873	2.6987	81.2466
10	5.4958	2.8901	78.3564
11	5.2907	3.0952	75.2612
12	5.0710	3.3149	71.9463
13	4.8358	3.5501	68.3963
14	4.5839	3.8020	64.5943
15	4.3141	4.0718	60.5225
16	4.0252	4.3607	56.1619
17	3.7158	4.6701	51.4917
18	3.3844	5.0015	46.4903
19	3.0295	5.3564	41.1339
20	2.6494	5.7365	35.3974
21	2.2424	6.1435	29.2539
22	1.8064	6.5795	22.6744
23	1.3396	7.0463	15.6281
24	.8396	7.5463	8.0818
25	.3041	8.0818	0.0000

YEARS 26 — MO PAYT .6888 — AN CONST 8.27

#	INT	PRIN	BALANCE
1	6.8303	1.4352	98.5648
2	6.7285	1.5371	97.0277
3	6.6194	1.6461	95.3816
4	6.5026	1.7629	93.6187
5	6.3775	1.8880	91.7307
6	6.2436	2.0220	89.7087
7	6.1001	2.1655	87.5432
8	5.9464	2.3191	85.2241
9	5.7819	2.4837	82.7404
10	5.6056	2.6599	80.0805
11	5.4169	2.8487	77.2318
12	5.2147	3.0508	74.1810
13	4.9983	3.2673	70.9138
14	4.7664	3.4991	67.4146
15	4.5181	3.7474	63.6672
16	4.2522	4.0133	59.6539
17	3.9674	4.2981	55.3558
18	3.6625	4.6031	50.7527
19	3.3358	4.9297	45.8230
20	2.9860	5.2795	40.5435
21	2.6114	5.6541	34.8894
22	2.2102	6.0553	28.8340
23	1.7805	6.4850	22.3490
24	1.3204	6.9452	15.4038
25	.8275	7.4380	7.9658
26	.2997	7.9658	0.0000

YEARS 27 — MO PAYT .6797 — AN CONST 8.16

#	INT	PRIN	BALANCE
1	6.8338	1.3224	98.6776
2	6.7400	1.4162	97.2614
3	6.6395	1.5167	95.7446
4	6.5319	1.6243	94.1203
5	6.4166	1.7396	92.3807
6	6.2932	1.8630	90.5176
7	6.1610	1.9952	88.5224
8	6.0194	2.1368	86.3856
9	5.8678	2.2885	84.0971
10	5.7054	2.4508	81.6463
11	5.5315	2.6247	79.0215
12	5.3453	2.8110	76.2105
13	5.1458	3.0105	73.2001
14	4.9322	3.2241	69.9760
15	4.7034	3.4528	66.5232
16	4.4584	3.6979	62.8253
17	4.1960	3.9602	58.8651
18	3.9150	4.2413	54.6238
19	3.6140	4.5422	50.0816
20	3.2917	4.8645	45.2171
21	2.9465	5.2097	40.0074
22	2.5769	5.5794	34.4280
23	2.1810	5.9753	28.4527
24	1.7570	6.3993	22.0535
25	1.3029	6.8533	15.2001
26	.8166	7.3396	7.8605
27	.2958	7.8605	0.0000

YEARS 28 — MO PAYT .6714 — AN CONST 8.06

#	INT	PRIN	BALANCE
1	6.8370	1.2197	98.7803
2	6.7505	1.3063	97.4740
3	6.6578	1.3990	96.0751
4	6.5585	1.4982	94.5768
5	6.4522	1.6045	92.9723
6	6.3384	1.7184	91.2539
7	6.2164	1.8403	89.4136
8	6.0858	1.9709	87.4427
9	5.9460	2.1108	85.3319
10	5.7962	2.2605	83.0714
11	5.6358	2.4209	80.6504
12	5.4640	2.5927	78.0577
13	5.2801	2.7767	75.2810
14	5.0830	2.9737	72.3072
15	4.8720	3.1847	69.1225
16	4.6460	3.4107	65.7118
17	4.4040	3.6528	62.0590
18	4.1448	3.9119	58.1471
19	3.8672	4.1895	53.9575
20	3.5699	4.4868	49.4707
21	3.2516	4.8052	44.6655
22	2.9106	5.1462	39.5194
23	2.5454	5.5113	34.0081
24	2.1544	5.9024	28.1057
25	1.7355	6.3212	21.7845
26	1.2870	6.7698	15.0147
27	.8066	7.2501	7.7646
28	.2922	7.7646	0.0000

YEARS 29 — MO PAYT .6638 — AN CONST 7.97

#	INT	PRIN	BALANCE
1	6.8400	1.1261	98.8739
2	6.7601	1.2060	97.6679
3	6.6745	1.2916	96.3764
4	6.5828	1.3832	94.9932
5	6.4847	1.4814	93.5118
6	6.3796	1.5865	91.9254
7	6.2670	1.6990	90.2263
8	6.1464	1.8196	88.4067
9	6.0173	1.9487	86.4580
10	5.8790	2.0870	84.3710
11	5.7309	2.2351	82.1359
12	5.5724	2.3937	79.7422
13	5.4025	2.5635	77.1787
14	5.2206	2.7454	74.4333
15	5.0258	2.9403	71.4930
16	4.8171	3.1489	68.3441
17	4.5937	3.3723	64.9718
18	4.3544	3.6116	61.3602
19	4.0981	3.8679	57.4923
20	3.8237	4.1424	53.3499
21	3.5297	4.4363	48.9136
22	3.2150	4.7511	44.1626
23	2.8778	5.0882	39.0744
24	2.5168	5.4493	33.6251
25	2.1301	5.8359	27.7892
26	1.7160	6.2500	21.5392
27	1.2725	6.6935	14.8456
28	.7976	7.1685	7.6771
29	.2889	7.6771	0.0000

YEARS 30 — MO PAYT .6569 — AN CONST 7.89

#	INT	PRIN	BALANCE
1	6.8426	1.0405	98.9595
2	6.7688	1.1144	97.8451
3	6.6897	1.1934	96.6517
4	6.6050	1.2781	95.3736
5	6.5143	1.3688	94.0047
6	6.4172	1.4659	92.5388
7	6.3132	1.5700	90.9688
8	6.2018	1.6814	89.2875
9	6.0825	1.8007	87.4868
10	5.9547	1.9284	85.5584
11	5.8179	2.0653	83.4931
12	5.6713	2.2118	81.2813
13	5.5144	2.3688	78.9125
14	5.3463	2.5369	76.3756
15	5.1663	2.7169	73.6588
16	4.9735	2.9097	70.7491
17	4.7670	3.1161	67.6330
18	4.5459	3.3372	64.2957
19	4.3091	3.5740	60.7217
20	4.0555	3.8276	56.8941
21	3.7839	4.0992	52.7948
22	3.4930	4.3901	48.4047
23	3.1815	4.7016	43.7030
24	2.8479	5.0353	38.6678
25	2.4906	5.3926	33.2752
26	2.1079	5.7752	27.5000
27	1.6981	6.1850	21.3150
28	1.2593	6.6239	14.6912
29	.7893	7.0939	7.5973
30	.2859	7.5973	0.0000

MONTHLY PAYMENT AMORTIZATION SCHEDULE PER $100   6.90 %

YEARS 2	MO PAYT 4.4727	AN CONST 53.68
# INT	PRIN	BALANCE
1 5.3921	48.2806	51.7194
2 1.9533	51.7194	0.0000

YEARS 3	MO PAYT 3.0831	AN CONST 37.00
# INT	PRIN	BALANCE
1 5.9297	31.0680	68.9320
2 3.7169	33.2808	35.6512
3 1.3465	35.6512	0.0000

YEARS 4	MO PAYT 2.3900	AN CONST 28.68
# INT	PRIN	BALANCE
1 6.1978	22.4820	77.5180
2 4.5966	24.0833	53.4347
3 2.8812	25.7986	27.6361
4 1.0438	27.6361	0.0000

YEARS 5	MO PAYT 1.9754	AN CONST 23.71
# INT	PRIN	BALANCE
1 6.3582	17.3466	82.6534
2 5.1227	18.5821	64.0712
3 3.7992	19.9056	44.1656
4 2.3814	21.3234	22.8422
5 .8627	22.8422	0.0000

YEARS 6	MO PAYT 1.7001	AN CONST 20.41
# INT	PRIN	BALANCE
1 6.4647	13.9365	86.0635
2 5.4721	14.9291	71.1344
3 4.4088	15.9924	55.1419
4 3.2697	17.1315	38.0104
5 2.0496	18.3517	19.6588
6 .7425	19.6588	0.0000

YEARS 7	MO PAYT 1.5044	AN CONST 18.06
# INT	PRIN	BALANCE
1 6.5405	11.5122	88.4878
2 5.7205	12.3321	76.1557
3 4.8422	13.2105	62.9453
4 3.9012	14.1514	48.7939
5 2.8933	15.1593	33.6346
6 1.8136	16.2390	17.3956
7 .6570	17.3956	0.0000

YEARS 8	MO PAYT 1.3584	AN CONST 16.31
# INT	PRIN	BALANCE
1 6.5969	9.7039	90.2961
2 5.9058	10.3950	79.9011
3 5.1654	11.1354	68.7657
4 4.3723	11.9285	56.8371
5 3.5227	12.7781	44.0590
6 2.6126	13.6882	30.3708
7 1.6376	14.6632	15.7076
8 .5932	15.7076	0.0000

YEARS 9	MO PAYT 1.2456	AN CONST 14.95
# INT	PRIN	BALANCE
1 6.6406	8.3062	91.6938
2 6.0490	8.8979	82.7959
3 5.4152	9.5316	73.2643
4 4.7363	10.2105	63.0538
5 4.0091	10.9377	52.1161
6 3.2301	11.7168	40.3994

# INT	PRIN	BALANCE
7 2.3956	12.5513	27.8481
8 1.5016	13.4452	14.4029
9 .5440	14.4029	0.0000

YEARS 10	MO PAYT 1.1559	AN CONST 13.88
# INT	PRIN	BALANCE
1 6.6753	7.1960	92.8040
2 6.1627	7.7085	85.0955
3 5.6137	8.2576	76.8379
4 5.0255	8.8457	67.9922
5 4.3955	9.4757	58.5165
6 3.7206	10.1506	48.3658
7 2.9976	10.8736	37.4922
8 2.2232	11.6481	25.8441
9 1.3935	12.4777	13.3664
10 .5048	13.3664	0.0000

YEARS 11	MO PAYT 1.0832	AN CONST 13.00
# INT	PRIN	BALANCE
1 6.7034	6.2947	93.7053
2 6.2551	6.7430	86.9623
3 5.7748	7.2233	79.7390
4 5.2603	7.7378	72.0012
5 4.7092	8.2889	63.7123
6 4.1188	8.8793	54.8330
7 3.4864	9.5117	45.3214
8 2.8089	10.1892	35.1322
9 2.0832	10.9149	24.2173
10 1.3058	11.6923	12.5251
11 .4730	12.5251	0.0000

YEARS 12	MO PAYT 1.0231	AN CONST 12.28
# INT	PRIN	BALANCE
1 6.7267	5.5500	94.4500
2 6.3314	5.9453	88.5046
3 5.9079	6.3688	82.1358
4 5.4543	6.8224	75.3134
5 4.9684	7.3083	68.0051
6 4.4478	7.8289	60.1763
7 3.8902	8.3865	51.7898
8 3.2929	8.9838	42.8060
9 2.6530	9.6237	33.1823
10 1.9676	10.3091	22.8733
11 1.2333	11.0434	11.8299
12 .4468	11.8299	0.0000

YEARS 13	MO PAYT .9727	AN CONST 11.68
# INT	PRIN	BALANCE
1 6.7462	4.9258	95.0742
2 6.3953	5.2767	89.7975
3 6.0195	5.6525	84.1451
4 5.6169	6.0551	78.0900
5 5.1856	6.4863	71.6036
6 4.7236	6.9483	64.6553
7 4.2287	7.4432	57.2121
8 3.6986	7.9734	49.2387
9 3.1307	8.5413	40.6975
10 2.5224	9.1496	31.5478
11 1.8707	9.8013	21.7466
12 1.1726	10.4994	11.2472
13 .4248	11.2472	0.0000

YEARS 14	MO PAYT .9299	AN CONST 11.16
# INT	PRIN	BALANCE
1 6.7627	4.3962	95.6038
2 6.4496	4.7093	90.8946
3 6.1142	5.0447	85.8499

# INT	PRIN	BALANCE
4 5.7549	5.4040	80.4459
5 5.3700	5.7889	74.6570
6 4.9577	6.2012	68.4558
7 4.5160	6.6429	61.8130
8 4.0428	7.1160	54.6969
9 3.5360	7.6228	47.0741
10 2.9931	8.1658	38.9083
11 2.4115	8.7474	30.1610
12 1.7884	9.3704	20.7906
13 1.1210	10.0378	10.7527
14 .4061	10.7527	0.0000

YEARS 15	MO PAYT .8932	AN CONST 10.72
# INT	PRIN	BALANCE
1 6.7769	3.9421	96.0579
2 6.4961	4.2229	91.8351
3 6.1953	4.5236	87.3114
4 5.8731	4.8458	82.4656
5 5.5280	5.1910	77.2747
6 5.1583	5.5607	71.7140
7 4.7622	5.9567	65.7572
8 4.3380	6.3810	59.3762
9 3.8835	6.8355	52.5408
10 3.3966	7.3223	45.2184
11 2.8751	7.8439	37.3745
12 2.3164	8.4025	28.9720
13 1.7179	9.0010	19.9710
14 1.0769	9.6421	10.3289
15 .3901	10.3289	0.0000

YEARS 16	MO PAYT .8615	AN CONST 10.34
# INT	PRIN	BALANCE
1 6.7891	3.5494	96.4506
2 6.5363	3.8022	92.6485
3 6.2655	4.0730	88.5755
4 5.9754	4.3631	84.2124
5 5.6647	4.6738	79.5386
6 5.3318	5.0067	74.5319
7 4.9752	5.3633	69.1686
8 4.5932	5.7453	63.4233
9 4.1840	6.1545	57.2688
10 3.7456	6.5929	50.6759
11 3.2761	7.0624	43.6134
12 2.7730	7.5655	36.0480
13 2.2342	8.1043	27.9437
14 1.6570	8.6815	19.2621
15 1.0386	9.2999	9.9623
16 .3763	9.9623	0.0000

YEARS 17	MO PAYT .8339	AN CONST 10.01
# INT	PRIN	BALANCE
1 6.7998	3.2071	96.7929
2 6.5714	3.4355	93.3574
3 6.3267	3.6802	89.6771
4 6.0646	3.9423	85.7348
5 5.7838	4.2231	81.5117
6 5.4830	4.5239	76.9877
7 5.1608	4.8461	72.1416
8 4.8156	5.1913	66.9503
9 4.4459	5.5611	61.3892
10 4.0498	5.9571	55.4321
11 3.6255	6.3814	49.0507
12 3.1710	6.8359	42.2147
13 2.6841	7.3228	34.8919
14 2.1625	7.8444	27.0475
15 1.6038	8.4031	18.6444
16 1.0053	9.0016	9.6428
17 .3642	9.6428	0.0000

YEARS 18	MO PAYT .8097	AN CONST 9.72
# INT	PRIN	BALANCE
1 6.8092	2.9068	97.0932
2 6.6022	3.1139	93.9793
3 6.3804	3.3357	90.6436
4 6.1428	3.5732	87.0704
5 5.8883	3.8277	83.2426
6 5.6157	4.1004	79.1422
7 5.3236	4.3924	74.7498
8 5.0108	4.7053	70.0445
9 4.6757	5.0404	65.0041
10 4.3167	5.3994	59.6047
11 3.9321	5.7840	53.8208
12 3.5201	6.1959	47.6248
13 3.0788	6.6372	40.9876
14 2.6061	7.1100	33.8776
15 2.0997	7.6164	26.2613
16 1.5572	8.1588	18.1024
17 .9761	8.7400	9.3625
18 .3536	9.3625	0.0000

YEARS 19	MO PAYT .7883	AN CONST 9.46
# INT	PRIN	BALANCE
1 6.8175	2.6419	97.3581
2 6.6293	2.8300	94.5281
3 6.4278	3.0316	91.4965
4 6.2118	3.2475	88.2489
5 5.9805	3.4788	84.7701
6 5.7327	3.7266	81.0435
7 5.4673	3.9920	77.0514
8 5.1830	4.2764	72.7750
9 4.8784	4.5810	68.1941
10 4.5521	4.9072	63.2868
11 4.2026	5.2568	58.0301
12 3.8282	5.6312	52.3989
13 3.4271	6.0322	46.3666
14 2.9975	6.4619	39.9048
15 2.5372	6.9221	32.9826
16 2.0442	7.4152	25.5675
17 1.5161	7.9433	17.6242
18 .9503	8.5091	9.1151
19 .3443	9.1151	0.0000

YEARS 20	MO PAYT .7693	AN CONST 9.24
# INT	PRIN	BALANCE
1 6.8248	2.4069	97.5931
2 6.6534	2.5783	95.0148
3 6.4698	2.7619	92.2529
4 6.2730	2.9586	89.2943
5 6.0623	3.1694	86.1249
6 5.8366	3.3951	82.7298
7 5.5948	3.6369	79.0928
8 5.3357	3.8960	75.1969
9 5.0582	4.1735	71.0234
10 4.7610	4.4707	66.5527
11 4.4426	4.7891	61.7636
12 4.1015	5.1302	56.6334
13 3.7361	5.4956	51.1377
14 3.3446	5.8871	45.2507
15 2.9253	6.3064	38.9443
16 2.4762	6.7555	32.1888
17 1.9950	7.2367	24.9521
18 1.4796	7.7521	17.2000
19 .9274	8.3043	8.8957
20 .3360	8.8957	0.0000

YEARS 21	MO PAYT .7524	AN CONST 9.03
# INT	PRIN	BALANCE
1 6.8314	2.1975	97.8025
2 6.6749	2.3540	95.4486
3 6.5072	2.5216	92.9269

#	INT	PRIN	BALANCE
4	6.3276	2.7012	90.2257
5	6.1352	2.8936	87.3321
6	5.9291	3.0997	84.2323
7	5.7083	3.3205	80.9118
8	5.4718	3.5570	77.3548
9	5.2185	3.8104	73.5445
10	4.9471	4.0817	69.4627
11	4.6564	4.3725	65.0902
12	4.3449	4.6839	60.4064
13	4.0113	5.0175	55.3889
14	3.6540	5.3749	50.0140
15	3.2711	5.7577	44.2563
16	2.8611	6.1678	38.0885
17	2.4218	6.6071	31.4814
18	1.9512	7.0777	24.4038
19	1.4471	7.5818	16.8220
20	.9071	8.1218	8.7002
21	.3286	8.7002	0.0000

YEARS 22 — MO PAYT .7373 — AN CONST 8.85

#	INT	PRIN	BALANCE
1	6.8372	2.0101	97.9899
2	6.6942	2.1533	95.8366
3	6.5407	2.3067	93.5299
4	6.3764	2.4709	91.0590
5	6.2004	2.6469	88.4120
6	6.0119	2.8355	85.5766
7	5.8099	3.0374	82.5392
8	5.5936	3.2538	79.2854
9	5.3618	3.4855	75.7999
10	5.1136	3.7338	72.0661
11	4.8476	3.9997	68.0664
12	4.5628	4.2846	63.7819
13	4.2576	4.5897	59.1921
14	3.9307	4.9166	54.2755
15	3.5805	5.2668	49.0086
16	3.2054	5.6420	43.3667
17	2.8035	6.0438	37.3229
18	2.3731	6.4743	30.8486
19	1.9119	6.9354	23.9132
20	1.4180	7.4294	16.4839
21	.8888	7.9585	8.5254
22	.3220	8.5254	0.0000

YEARS 23 — MO PAYT .7237 — AN CONST 8.69

#	INT	PRIN	BALANCE
1	6.8425	1.8419	98.1581
2	6.7113	1.9731	96.1850
3	6.5708	2.1136	94.0714
4	6.4202	2.2642	91.8072
5	6.2589	2.4254	89.3818
6	6.0862	2.5982	86.7836
7	5.9011	2.7832	84.0003
8	5.7029	2.9815	81.0189
9	5.4906	3.1938	77.8250
10	5.2631	3.4213	74.4037
11	5.0194	3.6650	70.7387
12	4.7584	3.9260	66.8127
13	4.4787	4.2057	62.6071
14	4.1792	4.5052	58.1019
15	3.8583	4.8261	53.2758
16	3.5146	5.1698	48.1060
17	3.1463	5.5380	42.5679
18	2.7519	5.9325	36.6354
19	2.3294	6.3550	30.2804
20	1.8767	6.8076	23.4728
21	1.3919	7.2925	16.1803
22	.8725	7.8119	8.3683
23	.3161	8.3683	0.0000

YEARS 24 — MO PAYT .7115 — AN CONST 8.54

#	INT	PRIN	BALANCE
1	6.8472	1.6904	98.3096
2	6.7268	1.8108	96.4989
3	6.5978	1.9397	94.5591
4	6.4597	2.0779	92.4812
5	6.3117	2.2259	90.2553
6	6.1531	2.3844	87.8709
7	5.9833	2.5543	85.3166
8	5.8014	2.7362	82.5804
9	5.6065	2.9311	79.6493
10	5.3977	3.1398	76.5095
11	5.1741	3.3635	73.1460
12	4.9345	3.6030	69.5430
13	4.6779	3.8597	65.6833
14	4.4030	4.1346	61.5488
15	4.1085	4.4290	57.1197
16	3.7931	4.7445	52.3752
17	3.4552	5.0824	47.2928
18	3.0932	5.4444	41.8484
19	2.7054	5.8322	36.0162
20	2.2900	6.2476	29.7686
21	1.8450	6.6926	23.0760
22	1.3683	7.1692	15.9067
23	.8577	7.6799	8.2269
24	.3107	8.2269	0.0000

YEARS 25 — MO PAYT .7004 — AN CONST 8.41

#	INT	PRIN	BALANCE
1	6.8515	1.5535	98.4465
2	6.7408	1.6641	96.7824
3	6.6223	1.7826	94.9998
4	6.4953	1.9096	93.0902
5	6.3593	2.0456	91.0445
6	6.2136	2.1913	88.8532
7	6.0576	2.3474	86.5058
8	5.8904	2.5146	83.9912
9	5.7113	2.6937	81.2976
10	5.5194	2.8855	78.4120
11	5.3139	3.0911	75.3209
12	5.0937	3.3112	72.0097
13	4.8579	3.5471	68.4627
14	4.6053	3.7997	64.6629
15	4.3346	4.0703	60.5926
16	4.0447	4.3602	56.2324
17	3.7342	4.6708	51.5616
18	3.4015	5.0035	46.5581
19	3.0451	5.3598	41.1983
20	2.6634	5.7416	35.4567
21	2.2544	6.1505	29.3061
22	1.8163	6.5886	22.7175
23	1.3471	7.0579	15.6596
24	.8444	7.5606	8.0991
25	.3059	8.0991	0.0000

YEARS 26 — MO PAYT .6904 — AN CONST 8.29

#	INT	PRIN	BALANCE
1	6.8554	1.4295	98.5705
2	6.7535	1.5313	97.0393
3	6.6445	1.6403	95.3990
4	6.5276	1.7572	93.6418
5	6.4025	1.8823	91.7595
6	6.2684	2.0164	89.7431
7	6.1248	2.1600	87.5831
8	5.9710	2.3138	85.2693
9	5.8062	2.4786	82.7906
10	5.6296	2.6552	80.1354
11	5.4405	2.8443	77.2911
12	5.2379	3.0469	74.2443
13	5.0209	3.2639	70.9804
14	4.7884	3.4964	67.4840
15	4.5394	3.7454	63.7386
16	4.2727	4.0122	59.7265
17	3.9869	4.2979	55.4286
18	3.6808	4.6040	50.8245
19	3.3529	4.9320	45.8926
20	3.0016	5.2832	40.6093
21	2.6253	5.6595	34.9498
22	2.2222	6.0626	28.8872
23	1.7904	6.4944	22.3928
24	1.3278	6.9570	15.4358
25	.8323	7.4525	7.9833
26	.3015	7.9833	0.0000

YEARS 27 — MO PAYT .6813 — AN CONST 8.18

#	INT	PRIN	BALANCE
1	6.8589	1.3168	98.6832
2	6.7651	1.4106	97.2725
3	6.6646	1.5111	95.7614
4	6.5570	1.6187	94.1427
5	6.4417	1.7340	92.4087
6	6.3182	1.8575	90.5512
7	6.1859	1.9898	88.5613
8	6.0442	2.1316	86.4298
9	5.8923	2.2834	84.1464
10	5.7297	2.4460	81.7004
11	5.5555	2.6202	79.0802
12	5.3689	2.8068	76.2733
13	5.1690	3.0068	73.2666
14	4.9548	3.2209	70.0457
15	4.7254	3.4503	66.5954
16	4.4796	3.6961	62.8993
17	4.2164	3.9593	58.9400
18	3.9344	4.2413	54.6987
19	3.6323	4.5434	50.1552
20	3.3087	4.8670	45.2882
21	2.9621	5.2137	40.0746
22	2.5907	5.5850	34.4896
23	2.1929	5.9828	28.5068
24	1.7668	6.4089	22.0979
25	1.3103	6.8654	15.2325
26	.8214	7.3544	7.8782
27	.2975	7.8782	0.0000

YEARS 28 — MO PAYT .6730 — AN CONST 8.08

#	INT	PRIN	BALANCE
1	6.8621	1.2144	98.7856
2	6.7756	1.3008	97.4848
3	6.6829	1.3935	96.0913
4	6.5837	1.4928	94.5985
5	6.4774	1.5991	92.9995
6	6.3635	1.7130	91.2865
7	6.2415	1.8350	89.4515
8	6.1108	1.9657	87.4859
9	5.9708	2.1057	85.3802
10	5.8208	2.2556	83.1246
11	5.6601	2.4163	80.7083
12	5.4880	2.5884	78.1199
13	5.3037	2.7728	75.3471
14	5.1062	2.9702	72.3769
15	4.8946	3.1818	69.1951
16	4.6680	3.4084	65.7867
17	4.4252	3.6512	62.1355
18	4.1652	3.9112	58.2242
19	3.8866	4.1898	54.0344
20	3.5882	4.4882	49.5462
21	3.2685	4.8079	44.7383
22	2.9261	5.1503	39.5879
23	2.5593	5.5172	34.0708
24	2.1663	5.9101	28.1606
25	1.7454	6.3311	21.8296
26	1.2944	6.7820	15.0476
27	.8114	7.2651	7.7825
28	.2939	7.7825	0.0000

YEARS 29 — MO PAYT .6655 — AN CONST 7.99

#	INT	PRIN	BALANCE
1	6.8650	1.1209	98.8791
2	6.7852	1.2007	97.6783
3	6.6996	1.2863	96.3921
4	6.6080	1.3779	95.0142
5	6.5099	1.4760	93.5382
6	6.4048	1.5811	91.9570
7	6.2921	1.6938	90.2633
8	6.1715	1.8144	88.4489
9	6.0423	1.9436	86.5052
10	5.9038	2.0821	84.4232
11	5.7555	2.2304	82.1928
12	5.5967	2.3892	79.8036
13	5.4265	2.5594	77.2442
14	5.2442	2.7417	74.5025
15	5.0489	2.9370	71.5656
16	4.8398	3.1461	68.4195
17	4.6157	3.3702	65.0492
18	4.3756	3.6103	61.4390
19	4.1185	3.8674	57.5716
20	3.8430	4.1428	53.4287
21	3.5480	4.4379	48.9908
22	3.2319	4.7540	44.2368
23	2.8933	5.0926	39.1442
24	2.5306	5.4553	33.6889
25	2.1420	5.8439	27.8450
26	1.7258	6.2601	21.5849
27	1.2799	6.7060	14.8789
28	.8023	7.1836	7.6953
29	.2906	7.6953	0.0000

YEARS 30 — MO PAYT .6586 — AN CONST 7.91

#	INT	PRIN	BALANCE
1	6.8677	1.0355	98.9645
2	6.7939	1.1093	97.8552
3	6.7149	1.1883	96.6668
4	6.6303	1.2729	95.3939
5	6.5396	1.3636	94.0303
6	6.4425	1.4607	92.5696
7	6.3384	1.5648	91.0048
8	6.2270	1.6762	89.3286
9	6.1076	1.7956	87.5329
10	5.9797	1.9235	85.6094
11	5.8427	2.0605	83.5489
12	5.6959	2.2073	81.3417
13	5.5387	2.3645	78.9772
14	5.3703	2.5329	76.4443
15	5.1899	2.7133	73.7310
16	4.9967	2.9065	70.8245
17	4.7896	3.1136	67.7109
18	4.5679	3.3353	64.3756
19	4.3303	3.5729	60.8028
20	4.0759	3.8273	56.9754
21	3.8033	4.0999	52.8755
22	3.5112	4.3920	48.4835
23	3.1984	4.7048	43.7787
24	2.8633	5.0399	38.7388
25	2.5044	5.3988	33.3400
26	2.1198	5.7834	27.5566
27	1.7079	6.1953	21.3613
28	1.2667	6.6365	14.7248
29	.7940	7.1092	7.6156
30	.2876	7.6156	0.0000

MONTHLY PAYMENT AMORTIZATION SCHEDULE PER $100   7.00 %

YEARS 2 — MO PAYT 4.4773 — AN CONST 53.73

#	INT	PRIN	BALANCE
1	5.4713	48.2558	51.7442
2	1.9829	51.7442	0.0000

YEARS 3 — MO PAYT 3.0877 — AN CONST 37.06

#	INT	PRIN	BALANCE
1	6.0168	31.0357	68.9643
2	3.7732	33.2793	35.6850
3	1.3675	35.6850	0.0000

YEARS 4 — MO PAYT 2.3946 — AN CONST 28.74

#	INT	PRIN	BALANCE
1	6.2889	22.4466	77.5534
2	4.6662	24.0692	53.4842
3	2.9263	25.8092	27.6750
4	1.0605	27.6750	0.0000

YEARS 5 — MO PAYT 1.9801 — AN CONST 23.77

#	INT	PRIN	BALANCE
1	6.4516	17.3098	82.6902
2	5.2003	18.5611	64.1291
3	3.8585	19.9029	44.2262
4	2.4197	21.3417	22.8845
5	.8770	22.8845	0.0000

YEARS 6 — MO PAYT 1.7049 — AN CONST 20.46

#	INT	PRIN	BALANCE
1	6.5597	13.8991	86.1009
2	5.5549	14.9039	71.1970
3	4.4775	15.9813	55.2157
4	3.3222	17.1366	38.0791
5	2.0834	18.3754	19.7037
6	.7551	19.7037	0.0000

YEARS 7 — MO PAYT 1.5093 — AN CONST 18.12

#	INT	PRIN	BALANCE
1	6.6365	11.4747	88.5253
2	5.8070	12.3042	76.2210
3	4.9175	13.1937	63.0273
4	3.9637	14.1475	48.8799
5	2.9410	15.1702	33.7097
6	1.8444	16.2669	17.4428
7	.6684	17.4428	0.0000

YEARS 8 — MO PAYT 1.3634 — AN CONST 16.37

#	INT	PRIN	BALANCE
1	6.6938	9.6667	90.3333
2	5.9950	10.3655	79.9678
3	5.2456	11.1148	68.8530
4	4.4421	11.9183	56.9347
5	3.5806	12.7799	44.1548
6	2.6567	13.7037	30.4510
7	1.6661	14.6944	15.7567
8	.6038	15.7567	0.0000

YEARS 9 — MO PAYT 1.2506 — AN CONST 15.01

#	INT	PRIN	BALANCE
1	6.7380	8.2695	91.7305
2	6.1402	8.8673	82.8632
3	5.4992	9.5083	73.3549
4	4.8119	10.1957	63.1592
5	4.0748	10.9327	52.2265
6	3.2845	11.7231	40.5034
7	2.4370	12.5705	27.9329
8	1.5283	13.4792	14.4537
9	.5539	14.4537	0.0000

YEARS 10 — MO PAYT 1.1611 — AN CONST 13.94

#	INT	PRIN	BALANCE
1	6.7732	7.1598	92.8402
2	6.2556	7.6774	85.1627
3	5.7006	8.2324	76.9303
4	5.1055	8.8275	68.1028
5	4.4673	9.4657	58.6371
6	3.7831	10.1500	48.4871
7	3.0493	10.8837	37.6034
8	2.2625	11.6705	25.9329
9	1.4189	12.5141	13.4188
10	.5142	13.4188	0.0000

YEARS 11 — MO PAYT 1.0884 — AN CONST 13.07

#	INT	PRIN	BALANCE
1	6.8017	6.2592	93.7408
2	6.3492	6.7117	87.0291
3	5.8640	7.1969	79.8322
4	5.3438	7.7171	72.1151
5	4.7859	8.2750	63.8401
6	4.1877	8.8732	54.9669
7	3.5463	9.5147	45.4522
8	2.8585	10.2025	35.2498
9	2.1209	10.9400	24.3097
10	1.3301	11.7309	12.5789
11	.4820	12.5789	0.0000

YEARS 12 — MO PAYT 1.0284 — AN CONST 12.35

#	INT	PRIN	BALANCE
1	6.8253	5.5153	94.4847
2	6.4266	5.9140	88.5707
3	5.9991	6.3415	82.2292
4	5.5406	6.7999	75.4293
5	5.0491	7.2915	68.1377
6	4.5220	7.8186	60.3191
7	3.9567	8.3838	51.9353
8	3.3507	8.9899	42.9454
9	2.7008	9.6398	33.3056
10	2.0039	10.3366	22.9690
11	1.2567	11.0839	11.8851
12	.4554	11.8851	0.0000

YEARS 13 — MO PAYT .9781 — AN CONST 11.74

#	INT	PRIN	BALANCE
1	6.8450	4.8919	95.1081
2	6.4914	5.2455	89.8626
3	6.1122	5.6247	84.2380
4	5.7056	6.0313	78.2067
5	5.2696	6.4673	71.7394
6	4.8021	6.9348	64.8045
7	4.3007	7.4361	57.3684
8	3.7632	7.9737	49.3947
9	3.1868	8.5501	40.8446
10	2.5687	9.1682	31.6764
11	1.9059	9.8310	21.8454
12	1.1952	10.5417	11.3037
13	.4332	11.3037	0.0000

YEARS 14 — MO PAYT .9354 — AN CONST 11.23

#	INT	PRIN	BALANCE
1	6.8618	4.3630	95.6370
2	6.5464	4.6784	90.9586
3	6.2082	5.0166	85.9419
4	5.8455	5.3793	80.5626
5	5.4567	5.7682	74.7945
6	5.0397	6.1851	68.6094
7	4.5926	6.6323	61.9771
8	4.1131	7.1117	54.8654
9	3.5990	7.6258	47.2396
10	3.0477	8.1771	39.0625
11	2.4566	8.7682	30.2943
12	1.8228	9.4021	20.8923
13	1.1431	10.0817	10.8105
14	.4143	10.8105	0.0000

YEARS 15 — MO PAYT .8988 — AN CONST 10.79

#	INT	PRIN	BALANCE
1	6.8761	3.9098	96.0902
2	6.5935	4.1924	91.8978
3	6.2904	4.4955	87.4023
4	5.9654	4.8205	82.5818
5	5.6170	5.1690	77.4128
6	5.2433	5.5426	71.8702
7	4.8426	5.9433	65.9269
8	4.4130	6.3729	59.5539
9	3.9523	6.8336	52.7203
10	3.4583	7.3277	45.3926
11	2.9286	7.8574	37.5352
12	2.3606	8.4254	29.1099
13	1.7515	9.0345	20.0754
14	1.0984	9.6876	10.3879
15	.3981	10.3879	0.0000

YEARS 16 — MO PAYT .8672 — AN CONST 10.41

#	INT	PRIN	BALANCE
1	6.8886	3.5179	96.4821
2	6.6342	3.7723	92.7098
3	6.3615	4.0450	88.6649
4	6.0691	4.3374	84.3275
5	5.7556	4.6509	79.6766
6	5.4194	4.9871	74.6895
7	5.0589	5.3476	69.3418
8	4.6723	5.7342	63.6076
9	4.2577	6.1488	57.4588
10	3.8133	6.5932	50.8656
11	3.3366	7.0699	43.7957
12	2.8255	7.5810	36.2148
13	2.2775	8.1290	28.0858
14	1.6899	8.7166	19.3692
15	1.0597	9.3467	10.0224
16	.3841	10.0224	0.0000

YEARS 17 — MO PAYT .8397 — AN CONST 10.08

#	INT	PRIN	BALANCE
1	6.8994	3.1766	96.8234
2	6.6697	3.4062	93.4173
3	6.4235	3.6524	89.7648
4	6.1595	3.9165	85.8484
5	5.8763	4.1996	81.6488
6	5.5728	4.5032	77.1456
7	5.2472	4.8287	72.3169
8	4.8982	5.1778	67.1391
9	4.5239	5.5521	61.5871
10	4.1225	5.9534	55.6336
11	3.6921	6.3838	49.2498
12	3.2306	6.8453	42.4045
13	2.7358	7.3401	35.0644
14	2.2052	7.8708	27.1936
15	1.6362	8.4397	18.7539
16	1.0261	9.0498	9.7041
17	.3719	9.7041	0.0000

YEARS 18 — MO PAYT .8155 — AN CONST 9.79

#	INT	PRIN	BALANCE
1	6.9089	2.8772	97.1228
2	6.7009	3.0852	94.0377
3	6.4778	3.3082	90.7295
4	6.2387	3.5473	87.1821
5	5.9822	3.8038	83.3784
6	5.7073	4.0788	79.2996
7	5.4124	4.3736	74.9260
8	5.0963	4.6898	70.2362
9	4.7572	5.0288	65.2074
10	4.3937	5.3923	59.8151
11	4.0039	5.7821	54.0330
12	3.5859	6.2001	47.8328
13	3.1377	6.6483	41.1845
14	2.6571	7.1290	34.0555
15	2.1417	7.6443	26.4112
16	1.5891	8.1969	18.2143
17	.9966	8.7895	9.4249
18	.3612	9.4249	0.0000

YEARS 19 — MO PAYT .7942 — AN CONST 9.54

#	INT	PRIN	BALANCE
1	6.9172	2.6131	97.3869
2	6.7283	2.8020	94.5849
3	6.5258	3.0045	91.5804
4	6.3086	3.2217	88.3586
5	6.0757	3.4546	84.9040
6	5.8259	3.7044	81.1996
7	5.5581	3.9722	77.2274
8	5.2710	4.2593	72.9681
9	4.9631	4.5672	68.4009
10	4.6329	4.8974	63.5035
11	4.2789	5.2514	58.2521
12	3.8993	5.6310	52.6210
13	3.4922	6.0381	46.5829
14	3.0557	6.4746	40.1083
15	2.5876	6.9427	33.1656
16	2.0858	7.4446	25.7211
17	1.5476	7.9827	17.7384
18	.9705	8.5598	9.1786
19	.3517	9.1786	0.0000

YEARS 20 — MO PAYT .7753 — AN CONST 9.31

#	INT	PRIN	BALANCE
1	6.9246	2.3790	97.6210
2	6.7527	2.5509	95.0701
3	6.5683	2.7353	92.3348
4	6.3705	2.9331	89.4017
5	6.1585	3.1451	86.2566
6	5.9311	3.3725	82.8842
7	5.6873	3.6163	79.2679
8	5.4259	3.8777	75.3902
9	5.1456	4.1580	71.2322
10	4.8450	4.4586	66.7737
11	4.5227	4.7809	61.9928
12	4.1771	5.1265	56.8663
13	3.8065	5.4971	51.3692
14	3.4091	5.8945	45.4747
15	2.9830	6.3206	39.1541
16	2.5261	6.7775	32.3766
17	2.0361	7.2674	25.1092
18	1.5108	7.7928	17.3164
19	.9474	8.3562	8.9602
20	.3434	8.9602	0.0000

YEARS 21 — MO PAYT .7585 — AN CONST 9.11

#	INT	PRIN	BALANCE
1	6.9312	2.1704	97.8296
2	6.7743	2.3273	95.5023
3	6.6061	2.4956	93.0067

#	INT	PRIN	BALANCE
4	6.4257	2.6760	90.3307
5	6.2323	2.8694	87.4613
6	6.0248	3.0768	84.3845
7	5.8024	3.2993	81.0852
8	5.5639	3.5378	77.5475
9	5.3081	3.7935	73.7540
10	5.0339	4.0677	69.6862
11	4.7399	4.3618	65.3244
12	4.4245	4.6771	60.6473
13	4.0864	5.0152	55.6321
14	3.7239	5.3778	50.2543
15	3.3351	5.7665	44.4877
16	2.9183	6.1834	38.3043
17	2.4713	6.6304	31.6739
18	1.9919	7.1097	24.5642
19	1.4780	7.6237	16.9405
20	.9269	8.1748	8.7657
21	.3359	8.7657	0.0000

YEARS 22   MO PAYT .7434   AN CONST 8.93

#	INT	PRIN	BALANCE
1	6.9372	1.9839	98.0161
2	6.7937	2.1274	95.8887
3	6.6399	2.2811	93.6076
4	6.4750	2.4460	91.1615
5	6.2982	2.6229	88.5386
6	6.1086	2.8125	85.7262
7	5.9053	3.0158	82.7104
8	5.6873	3.2338	79.4766
9	5.4535	3.4676	76.0090
10	5.2028	3.7183	72.2907
11	4.9340	3.9870	68.3037
12	4.6458	4.2753	64.0284
13	4.3368	4.5843	59.4441
14	4.0054	4.9157	54.5284
15	3.6500	5.2711	49.2573
16	3.2690	5.6521	43.6051
17	2.8604	6.0607	37.5444
18	2.4222	6.4989	31.0455
19	1.9524	6.9687	24.0769
20	1.4487	7.4724	16.6045
21	.9085	8.0126	8.5918
22	.3292	8.5918	0.0000

YEARS 23   MO PAYT .7299   AN CONST 8.76

#	INT	PRIN	BALANCE
1	6.9425	1.8166	98.1834
2	6.8111	1.9479	96.2355
3	6.6703	2.0887	94.1468
4	6.5193	2.2397	91.9071
5	6.3574	2.4016	89.5055
6	6.1838	2.5752	86.9303
7	5.9976	2.7614	84.1689
8	5.7980	2.9610	81.2079
9	5.5840	3.1751	78.0328
10	5.3544	3.4046	74.6282
11	5.1083	3.6507	70.9775
12	4.8444	3.9146	67.0629
13	4.5614	4.1976	62.8653
14	4.2580	4.5010	58.3642
15	3.9326	4.8264	53.5378
16	3.5837	5.1753	48.3625
17	3.2096	5.5495	42.8130
18	2.8084	5.9506	36.8624
19	2.3782	6.3808	30.4816
20	1.9170	6.8421	23.6395
21	1.4223	7.3367	16.3028
22	.8920	7.8671	8.4358
23	.3233	8.4358	0.0000

YEARS 24   MO PAYT .7178   AN CONST 8.62

#	INT	PRIN	BALANCE
1	6.9472	1.6659	98.3341
2	6.8268	1.7863	96.5478
3	6.6977	1.9154	94.6323
4	6.5592	2.0539	92.5784
5	6.4107	2.2024	90.3760
6	6.2515	2.3616	88.0144
7	6.0808	2.5323	85.4821
8	5.8977	2.7154	82.7667
9	5.7014	2.9117	79.8550
10	5.4909	3.1222	76.7329
11	5.2652	3.3479	73.3850
12	5.0232	3.5899	69.7951
13	4.7637	3.8494	65.9457
14	4.4854	4.1277	61.8180
15	4.1870	4.4261	57.3919
16	3.8671	4.7460	52.6459
17	3.5240	5.0891	47.5568
18	3.1561	5.4570	42.0998
19	2.7616	5.8515	36.2483
20	2.3386	6.2745	29.9738
21	1.8850	6.7281	23.2457
22	1.3987	7.2145	16.0312
23	.8771	7.7360	8.2952
24	.3179	8.2952	0.0000

YEARS 25   MO PAYT .7068   AN CONST 8.49

#	INT	PRIN	BALANCE
1	6.9515	1.5298	98.4702
2	6.8409	1.6404	96.8298
3	6.7224	1.7590	95.0708
4	6.5952	1.8861	93.1846
5	6.4589	2.0225	91.1622
6	6.3126	2.1687	88.9935
7	6.1559	2.3255	86.6680
8	5.9878	2.4936	84.1744
9	5.8075	2.6738	81.5005
10	5.6142	2.8671	78.6334
11	5.4069	3.0744	75.5590
12	5.1847	3.2967	72.2623
13	4.9464	3.5350	68.7274
14	4.6908	3.7905	64.9368
15	4.4168	4.0645	60.8723
16	4.1230	4.3584	56.5140
17	3.8079	4.6734	51.8405
18	3.4701	5.0113	46.8293
19	3.1078	5.3735	41.4557
20	2.7194	5.7620	35.6938
21	2.3028	6.1785	29.5152
22	1.8562	6.6252	22.8901
23	1.3773	7.1041	15.7860
24	.8637	7.6177	8.1683
25	.3130	8.1683	0.0000

YEARS 26   MO PAYT .6968   AN CONST 8.37

#	INT	PRIN	BALANCE
1	6.9554	1.4066	98.5934
2	6.8538	1.5083	97.0851
3	6.7447	1.6173	95.4678
4	6.6278	1.7342	93.7335
5	6.5024	1.8596	91.8739
6	6.3680	1.9940	89.8799
7	6.2239	2.1382	87.7417
8	6.0693	2.2928	85.4489
9	5.9035	2.4585	82.9904
10	5.7258	2.6362	80.3541
11	5.5352	2.8268	77.5273
12	5.3309	3.0312	74.4962
13	5.1118	3.2503	71.2459
14	4.8768	3.4852	67.7606
15	4.6249	3.7372	64.0234
16	4.3547	4.0074	60.0161
17	4.0650	4.2971	55.7190
18	3.7544	4.6077	51.1113
19	3.4213	4.9408	46.1706
20	3.0641	5.2979	40.8726
21	2.6811	5.6809	35.1917
22	2.2704	6.0916	29.1001
23	1.8301	6.5320	22.5681
24	1.3579	7.0042	15.5639
25	.8516	7.5105	8.0534
26	.3086	8.0534	0.0000

YEARS 27   MO PAYT .6878   AN CONST 8.26

#	INT	PRIN	BALANCE
1	6.9590	1.2948	98.7052
2	6.8654	1.3884	97.3168
3	6.7650	1.4888	95.8280
4	6.6574	1.5964	94.2317
5	6.5420	1.7118	92.5199
6	6.4182	1.8355	90.6843
7	6.2856	1.9682	88.7161
8	6.1433	2.1105	86.6056
9	5.9907	2.2631	84.3425
10	5.8271	2.4267	81.9158
11	5.6517	2.6021	79.3137
12	5.4636	2.7902	76.5235
13	5.2619	2.9919	73.5316
14	5.0456	3.2082	70.3234
15	4.8137	3.4401	66.8833
16	4.5650	3.6888	63.1945
17	4.2983	3.9555	59.2390
18	4.0124	4.2414	54.9976
19	3.7058	4.5480	50.4496
20	3.3770	4.8768	45.5727
21	3.0244	5.2293	40.3434
22	2.6464	5.6074	34.7360
23	2.2410	6.0127	28.7233
24	1.8064	6.4474	22.2759
25	1.3403	6.9135	15.3624
26	.8405	7.4133	7.9492
27	.3046	7.9492	0.0000

YEARS 28   MO PAYT .6796   AN CONST 8.16

#	INT	PRIN	BALANCE
1	6.9622	1.1931	98.8069
2	6.8760	1.2793	97.5276
3	6.7835	1.3718	96.1557
4	6.6843	1.4710	94.6847
5	6.5780	1.5773	93.1074
6	6.4639	1.6914	91.4160
7	6.3417	1.8136	89.6024
8	6.2106	1.9447	87.6576
9	6.0700	2.0853	85.5723
10	5.9192	2.2361	83.3362
11	5.7576	2.3977	80.9385
12	5.5842	2.5711	78.3674
13	5.3984	2.7569	75.6105
14	5.1991	2.9562	72.6543
15	4.9854	3.1699	69.4844
16	4.7562	3.3991	66.0853
17	4.5105	3.6448	62.4405
18	4.2470	3.9083	58.5322
19	3.9645	4.1908	54.3414
20	3.6615	4.4938	49.8476
21	3.3367	4.8186	45.0290
22	2.9883	5.1670	39.8621
23	2.6148	5.5405	34.3216
24	2.2143	5.9410	28.3806
25	1.7848	6.3705	22.0101
26	1.3243	6.8310	15.1791
27	.8305	7.3248	7.8543
28	.3010	7.8543	0.0000

YEARS 29   MO PAYT .6721   AN CONST 8.07

#	INT	PRIN	BALANCE
1	6.9651	1.1004	98.8996
2	6.8856	1.1800	97.7196
3	6.8003	1.2653	96.4543
4	6.7088	1.3567	95.0976
5	6.6107	1.4548	93.6428
6	6.5056	1.5600	92.0828
7	6.3928	1.6728	90.4100
8	6.2719	1.7937	88.6164
9	6.1422	1.9233	86.6930
10	6.0032	2.0624	84.6306
11	5.8541	2.2115	82.4192
12	5.6942	2.3713	80.0478
13	5.5228	2.5428	77.5051
14	5.3390	2.7266	74.7785
15	5.1419	2.9237	71.8548
16	4.9305	3.1350	68.7197
17	4.7039	3.3617	65.3581
18	4.4609	3.6047	61.7534
19	4.2003	3.8653	57.8881
20	3.9209	4.1447	53.7434
21	3.6212	4.4443	49.2991
22	3.3000	4.7656	44.5335
23	2.9555	5.1101	39.4234
24	2.5861	5.4795	33.9439
25	2.1899	5.8756	28.0683
26	1.7652	6.3004	21.7679
27	1.3097	6.7558	15.0121
28	.8214	7.2442	7.7679
29	.2977	7.7679	0.0000

YEARS 30   MO PAYT .6653   AN CONST 7.99

#	INT	PRIN	BALANCE
1	6.9678	1.0158	98.9842
2	6.8944	1.0892	97.8949
3	6.8156	1.1680	96.7270
4	6.7312	1.2524	95.4745
5	6.6407	1.3430	94.1316
6	6.5436	1.4400	92.6916
7	6.4395	1.5441	91.1474
8	6.3279	1.6558	89.4917
9	6.2082	1.7755	87.7162
10	6.0798	1.9038	85.8124
11	5.9422	2.0414	83.7709
12	5.7946	2.1890	81.5819
13	5.6364	2.3473	79.2347
14	5.4667	2.5169	76.7178
15	5.2847	2.6989	74.0189
16	5.0896	2.8940	71.1249
17	4.8804	3.1032	68.0217
18	4.6561	3.3275	64.6942
19	4.4156	3.5681	61.1261
20	4.1576	3.8260	57.3001
21	3.8810	4.1026	53.1975
22	3.5845	4.3992	48.7983
23	3.2664	4.7172	44.0811
24	2.9254	5.0582	39.0229
25	2.5598	5.4238	33.5991
26	2.1677	5.8159	27.7832
27	1.7473	6.2364	21.5468
28	1.2964	6.6872	14.8596
29	.8130	7.1706	7.6890
30	.2946	7.6890	0.0000

YEARS 2 — MO PAYT 4.4818 — AN CONST 53.79

#	INT	PRIN	BALANCE
1	5.5505	48.2310	51.7690
2	2.0125	51.7690	0.0000

YEARS 3 — MO PAYT 3.0923 — AN CONST 37.11

#	INT	PRIN	BALANCE
1	6.1040	31.0034	68.9966
2	3.8297	33.2777	35.7189
3	1.3885	35.7189	0.0000

YEARS 4 — MO PAYT 2.3993 — AN CONST 28.80

#	INT	PRIN	BALANCE
1	6.3800	22.4112	77.5888
2	4.7360	24.0552	53.5336
3	2.9714	25.8198	27.7138
4	1.0774	27.7138	0.0000

YEARS 5 — MO PAYT 1.9848 — AN CONST 23.82

#	INT	PRIN	BALANCE
1	6.5451	17.2730	82.7270
2	5.2780	18.5401	64.1869
3	3.9180	19.9001	44.2868
4	2.4582	21.3599	22.9268
5	.8913	22.9268	0.0000

YEARS 6 — MO PAYT 1.7097 — AN CONST 20.52

#	INT	PRIN	BALANCE
1	6.6547	13.8618	86.1382
2	5.6378	14.8787	71.2595
3	4.5464	15.9701	55.2894
4	3.3749	17.1416	38.1478
5	2.1174	18.3991	19.7488
6	.7677	19.7488	0.0000

YEARS 7 — MO PAYT 1.5142 — AN CONST 18.17

#	INT	PRIN	BALANCE
1	6.7326	11.4374	88.5626
2	5.8936	12.2764	76.2863
3	4.9930	13.1769	63.1093
4	4.0264	14.1435	48.9658
5	2.9889	15.1811	33.7847
6	1.8752	16.2947	17.4900
7	.6799	17.4900	0.0000

YEARS 8 — MO PAYT 1.3684 — AN CONST 16.43

#	INT	PRIN	BALANCE
1	6.7906	9.6296	90.3704
2	6.0842	10.3360	80.0344
3	5.3260	11.0942	68.9402
4	4.5122	11.9080	57.0322
5	3.6387	12.7816	44.2506
6	2.7011	13.7192	30.5314
7	1.6947	14.7256	15.8058
8	.6144	15.8058	0.0000

YEARS 9 — MO PAYT 1.2557 — AN CONST 15.07

#	INT	PRIN	BALANCE
1	6.8355	8.2329	91.7671
2	6.2316	8.8368	82.9303
3	5.5833	9.4850	73.4453
4	4.8875	10.1808	63.2644
5	4.1407	10.9277	52.3368
6	3.3391	11.7293	40.6075
7	2.4787	12.5897	28.0178
8	1.5551	13.5132	14.5045
9	.5639	14.5045	0.0000

YEARS 10 — MO PAYT 1.1662 — AN CONST 14.00

#	INT	PRIN	BALANCE
1	6.8711	7.1238	92.8762
2	6.3486	7.6464	85.2298
3	5.7877	8.2073	77.0225
4	5.1856	8.8094	68.2132
5	4.5394	9.4556	58.7576
6	3.8457	10.1492	48.6084
7	3.1012	10.8937	37.7147
8	2.3021	11.6928	26.0218
9	1.4444	12.5506	13.4713
10	.5237	13.4713	0.0000

YEARS 11 — MO PAYT 1.0937 — AN CONST 13.13

#	INT	PRIN	BALANCE
1	6.9001	6.2239	93.7761
2	6.4435	6.6804	87.0957
3	5.9534	7.1705	79.9252
4	5.4274	7.6965	72.2288
5	4.8628	8.2611	63.9677
6	4.2568	8.8671	55.1006
7	3.6064	9.5175	45.5831
8	2.9082	10.2157	35.3674
9	2.1588	10.9651	24.4023
10	1.3545	11.7695	12.6328
11	.4911	12.6328	0.0000

YEARS 12 — MO PAYT 1.0337 — AN CONST 12.41

#	INT	PRIN	BALANCE
1	6.9239	5.4807	94.5193
2	6.5219	5.8828	88.6365
3	6.0903	6.3143	82.3223
4	5.6271	6.7775	75.5448
5	5.1300	7.2747	68.2701
6	4.5963	7.8083	60.4618
7	4.0235	8.3811	52.0807
8	3.4087	8.9959	43.0848
9	2.7488	9.6558	33.4290
10	2.0405	10.3641	23.0649
11	1.2802	11.1244	11.9405
12	.4642	11.9405	0.0000

YEARS 13 — MO PAYT .9835 — AN CONST 11.81

#	INT	PRIN	BALANCE
1	6.9439	4.8581	95.1419
2	6.5876	5.2144	89.9275
3	6.2050	5.5970	84.3305
4	5.7945	6.0075	78.3230
5	5.3538	6.4482	71.8747
6	4.8808	6.9213	64.9535
7	4.3730	7.4290	57.5245
8	3.8281	7.9739	49.5506
9	3.2431	8.5589	40.9917
10	2.6153	9.1867	31.8050
11	1.9414	9.8606	21.9444
12	1.2180	10.5840	11.3604
13	.4416	11.3604	0.0000

YEARS 14 — MO PAYT .9409 — AN CONST 11.30

#	INT	PRIN	BALANCE
1	6.9609	4.3301	95.6699
2	6.6433	4.6477	91.0222
3	6.3023	4.9887	86.0335
4	5.9364	5.3546	80.6789
5	5.5436	5.7474	74.9315
6	5.1220	6.1690	68.7625
7	4.6694	6.6216	62.1410
8	4.1837	7.1073	55.0337
9	3.6623	7.6287	47.4050
10	3.1027	8.1883	39.2167
11	2.5020	8.7889	30.4278
12	1.8573	9.4337	20.9941
13	1.1653	10.1257	10.8685
14	.4225	10.8685	0.0000

YEARS 15 — MO PAYT .9044 — AN CONST 10.86

#	INT	PRIN	BALANCE
1	6.9754	3.8777	96.1223
2	6.6910	4.1622	91.9601
3	6.3856	4.4675	87.4926
4	6.0579	4.7952	82.6974
5	5.7062	5.1470	77.5504
6	5.3286	5.5245	72.0259
7	4.9233	5.9298	66.0961
8	4.4883	6.3648	59.7313
9	4.0214	6.8317	52.8996
10	3.5203	7.3328	45.5668
11	2.9824	7.8708	37.6960
12	2.4050	8.4481	29.2479
13	1.7853	9.0678	20.1801
14	1.1201	9.7330	10.4470
15	.4061	10.4470	0.0000

YEARS 16 — MO PAYT .8729 — AN CONST 10.48

#	INT	PRIN	BALANCE
1	6.9880	3.4867	96.5133
2	6.7322	3.7425	92.7708
3	6.4577	4.0170	88.7537
4	6.1630	4.3117	84.4420
5	5.8467	4.6280	79.8140
6	5.5072	4.9675	74.8465
7	5.1428	5.3319	69.5145
8	4.7517	5.7230	63.7915
9	4.3319	6.1429	57.6486
10	3.8812	6.5935	51.0552
11	3.3976	7.0772	43.9780
12	2.8784	7.5963	36.3817
13	2.3212	8.1536	28.2281
14	1.7230	8.7517	19.4764
15	1.0810	9.3937	10.0828
16	.3920	10.0828	0.0000

YEARS 17 — MO PAYT .8454 — AN CONST 10.15

#	INT	PRIN	BALANCE
1	6.9989	3.1462	96.8538
2	6.7681	3.3770	93.4767
3	6.5204	3.6248	89.8520
4	6.2545	3.8907	85.9613
5	5.9691	4.1761	81.7852
6	5.6628	4.4824	77.3028
7	5.3339	4.8112	72.4916
8	4.9810	5.1642	67.3275
9	4.6022	5.5430	61.7845
10	4.1956	5.9496	55.8349
11	3.7591	6.3860	49.4488
12	3.2907	6.8545	42.5943
13	2.7878	7.3573	35.2370
14	2.2481	7.8970	27.3400
15	1.6688	8.4763	18.8637
16	1.0470	9.0981	9.7655
17	.3796	9.7655	0.0000

YEARS 18 — MO PAYT .8214 — AN CONST 9.86

#	INT	PRIN	BALANCE
1	7.0085	2.8477	97.1523
2	6.7996	3.0566	94.0956
3	6.5754	3.2809	90.8148
4	6.3347	3.5215	87.2932
5	6.0764	3.7799	83.5134
6	5.7991	4.0571	79.4562
7	5.5015	4.3548	75.1015
8	5.1820	4.6742	70.4272
9	4.8392	5.0171	65.4101
10	4.4711	5.3851	60.0250
11	4.0761	5.7802	54.2448
12	3.6521	6.2042	48.0407
13	3.1970	6.6593	41.3814
14	2.7084	7.1478	34.2336
15	2.1841	7.6721	26.5614
16	1.6213	8.2349	18.3265
17	1.0172	8.8390	9.4874
18	.3688	9.4874	0.0000

YEARS 19 — MO PAYT .8001 — AN CONST 9.61

#	INT	PRIN	BALANCE
1	7.0170	2.5845	97.4155
2	6.8274	2.7741	94.6413
3	6.6239	2.9776	91.6637
4	6.4054	3.1961	88.4676
5	6.1710	3.4305	85.0371
6	5.9193	3.6822	81.3549
7	5.6492	3.9523	77.4026
8	5.3593	4.2422	73.1604
9	5.0481	4.5534	68.6070
10	4.7141	4.8874	63.7196
11	4.3556	5.2460	58.4736
12	3.9707	5.6308	52.8429
13	3.5577	6.0438	46.7990
14	3.1143	6.4872	40.3118
15	2.6384	6.9631	33.3488
16	2.1277	7.4739	25.8749
17	1.5794	8.0221	17.8528
18	.9909	8.6106	9.2422
19	.3593	9.2422	0.0000

YEARS 20 — MO PAYT .7813 — AN CONST 9.38

#	INT	PRIN	BALANCE
1	7.0245	2.3513	97.6487
2	6.8520	2.5238	95.1249
3	6.6668	2.7089	92.4160
4	6.4681	2.9076	89.5084
5	6.2548	3.1209	86.3875
6	6.0259	3.3499	83.0376
7	5.7802	3.5956	79.4420
8	5.5164	3.8594	75.5827
9	5.2333	4.1425	71.4402
10	4.9294	4.4463	66.9939
11	4.6032	4.7725	62.2214
12	4.2531	5.1226	57.0988
13	3.8774	5.4984	51.6004
14	3.4740	5.9017	45.6986
15	3.0411	6.3347	39.3640
16	2.5764	6.7993	32.5647
17	2.0776	7.2981	25.2665
18	1.5423	7.8335	17.4330
19	.9676	8.4081	9.0249
20	.3508	9.0249	0.0000

YEARS 21 — MO PAYT .7646 — AN CONST 9.18

#	INT	PRIN	BALANCE
1	7.0311	2.1436	97.8564
2	6.8739	2.3009	95.5555
3	6.7051	2.4697	93.0858

#	INT	PRIN	BALANCE
4	6.5239	2.6508	90.4350
5	6.3295	2.8453	87.5897
6	6.1208	3.0540	84.5356
7	5.8967	3.2781	81.2576
8	5.6563	3.5185	77.7391
9	5.3981	3.7766	73.9625
10	5.1211	4.0537	69.9088
11	4.8237	4.3510	65.5578
12	4.5046	4.6702	60.8876
13	4.1620	5.0128	55.8748
14	3.7943	5.3805	50.4942
15	3.3996	5.7752	44.7190
16	2.9759	6.1989	38.5202
17	2.5212	6.6536	31.8666
18	2.0331	7.1417	24.7249
19	1.5092	7.6656	17.0593
20	.9469	8.2279	8.8315
21	.3433	8.8315	0.0000

	YEARS 22	MO PAYT .7496	AN CONST 9.00
#	INT	PRIN	BALANCE
1	7.0371	1.9580	98.0420
2	6.8935	2.1017	95.9403
3	6.7393	2.2558	93.6845
4	6.5738	2.4213	91.2632
5	6.3962	2.5989	88.6642
6	6.2055	2.7896	85.8746
7	6.0009	2.9942	82.8804
8	5.7813	3.2139	79.6665
9	5.5455	3.4496	76.2169
10	5.2925	3.7027	72.5142
11	5.0208	3.9743	68.5400
12	4.7293	4.2658	64.2741
13	4.4164	4.5788	59.6954
14	4.0805	4.9146	54.7807
15	3.7200	5.2752	49.5056
16	3.3330	5.6621	43.8434
17	2.9176	6.0775	37.7659
18	2.4718	6.5233	31.2426
19	1.9933	7.0018	24.2408
20	1.4797	7.5155	16.7253
21	.9283	8.0668	8.6585
22	.3366	8.6585	0.0000

	YEARS 23	MO PAYT .7362	AN CONST 8.84
#	INT	PRIN	BALANCE
1	7.0424	1.7915	98.2085
2	6.9110	1.9230	96.2855
3	6.7700	2.0640	94.2215
4	6.6186	2.2154	92.0061
5	6.4560	2.3779	89.6281
6	6.2816	2.5524	87.0758
7	6.0944	2.7396	84.3362
8	5.8934	2.9406	81.3956
9	5.6777	3.1563	78.2393
10	5.4462	3.3878	74.8515
11	5.1976	3.6363	71.2151
12	4.9309	3.9031	67.3120
13	4.6446	4.1894	63.1226
14	4.3372	4.4967	58.6259
15	4.0074	4.8266	53.7993
16	3.6533	5.1807	48.6186
17	3.2733	5.5607	43.0580
18	2.8654	5.9686	37.0893
19	2.4275	6.4064	30.6829
20	1.9576	6.8764	23.8065
21	1.4531	7.3808	16.4257
22	.9117	7.9223	8.5034
23	.3306	8.5034	0.0000

	YEARS 24	MO PAYT .7241	AN CONST 8.69
#	INT	PRIN	BALANCE
1	7.0473	1.6417	98.3583
2	6.9268	1.7621	96.5962
3	6.7976	1.8914	94.7048
4	6.6588	2.0301	92.6747
5	6.5099	2.1791	90.4956
6	6.3501	2.3389	88.1567
7	6.1785	2.5105	85.6463
8	5.9943	2.6946	82.9516
9	5.7966	2.8923	80.0593
10	5.5845	3.1045	76.9549
11	5.3567	3.3322	73.6226
12	5.1123	3.5766	70.0460
13	4.8499	3.8390	66.2070
14	4.5683	4.1206	62.0864
15	4.2660	4.4229	57.6634
16	3.9416	4.7474	52.9161
17	3.5933	5.0956	47.8205
18	3.2195	5.4694	42.3511
19	2.8183	5.8706	36.4805
20	2.3877	6.3013	30.1792
21	1.9254	6.7635	23.4157
22	1.4293	7.2597	16.1560
23	.8967	7.7922	8.3638
24	.3251	8.3638	0.0000

	YEARS 25	MO PAYT .7132	AN CONST 8.56
#	INT	PRIN	BALANCE
1	7.0516	1.5065	98.4935
2	6.9411	1.6170	96.8766
3	6.8225	1.7356	95.1410
4	6.6952	1.8629	93.2781
5	6.5585	1.9995	91.2786
6	6.4118	2.1462	89.1324
7	6.2544	2.3037	86.8287
8	6.0854	2.4727	84.3560
9	5.9040	2.6540	81.7020
10	5.7093	2.8487	78.8533
11	5.5004	3.0577	75.7956
12	5.2760	3.2820	72.5136
13	5.0353	3.5228	68.9908
14	4.7769	3.7812	65.2096
15	4.4995	4.0586	61.1511
16	4.2018	4.3563	56.7948
17	3.8822	4.6758	52.1189
18	3.5392	5.0188	47.1001
19	3.1710	5.3870	41.7131
20	2.7759	5.7822	35.9309
21	2.3517	6.2063	29.7246
22	1.8964	6.6616	23.0629
23	1.4078	7.1503	15.9126
24	.8832	7.6748	8.2378
25	.3202	8.2378	0.0000

	YEARS 26	MO PAYT .7033	AN CONST 8.44
#	INT	PRIN	BALANCE
1	7.0555	1.3841	98.6159
2	6.9540	1.4856	97.1304
3	6.8450	1.5946	95.5358
4	6.7281	1.7116	93.8242
5	6.6025	1.8371	91.9871
6	6.4677	1.9719	90.0152
7	6.3231	2.1165	87.8987
8	6.1678	2.2718	85.6269
9	6.0012	2.4384	83.1885
10	5.8223	2.6173	80.5712
11	5.6303	2.8093	77.7619
12	5.4242	3.0154	74.7465
13	5.2030	3.2366	71.5099
14	4.9656	3.4740	68.0359
15	4.7108	3.7288	64.3071

#	INT	PRIN	BALANCE
16	4.4372	4.0024	60.3047
17	4.1436	4.2960	56.0087
18	3.8285	4.6111	51.3976
19	3.4902	4.9494	46.4482
20	3.1272	5.3125	41.1357
21	2.7375	5.7022	35.4336
22	2.3192	6.1204	29.3131
23	1.8702	6.5694	22.7437
24	1.3883	7.0513	15.6924
25	.8710	7.5686	8.1238
26	.3158	8.1238	0.0000

	YEARS 27	MO PAYT .6943	AN CONST 8.34
#	INT	PRIN	BALANCE
1	7.0591	1.2731	98.7269
2	6.9657	1.3664	97.3605
3	6.8655	1.4667	95.8938
4	6.7579	1.5743	94.3195
5	6.6424	1.6898	92.6298
6	6.5184	1.8137	90.8160
7	6.3854	1.9468	88.8693
8	6.2426	2.0896	86.7797
9	6.0893	2.2429	84.5368
10	5.9248	2.4074	82.1295
11	5.7482	2.5840	79.5455
12	5.5586	2.7735	76.7719
13	5.3552	2.9770	73.7949
14	5.1368	3.1954	70.5996
15	4.9024	3.4298	67.1698
16	4.6508	3.6814	63.4884
17	4.3807	3.9514	59.5370
18	4.0909	4.2413	55.2957
19	3.7797	4.5524	50.7432
20	3.4458	4.8864	45.8569
21	3.0873	5.2448	40.6121
22	2.7026	5.6296	34.9825
23	2.2896	6.0425	28.9400
24	1.8464	6.4858	22.4542
25	1.3706	6.9616	15.4926
26	.8599	7.4722	8.0204
27	.3118	8.0204	0.0000

	YEARS 28	MO PAYT .6862	AN CONST 8.24
#	INT	PRIN	BALANCE
1	7.0623	1.1722	98.8278
2	6.9764	1.2581	97.5697
3	6.8841	1.3504	96.2193
4	6.7850	1.4495	94.7698
5	6.6787	1.5558	93.2140
6	6.5645	1.6700	91.5440
7	6.4420	1.7925	89.7515
8	6.3106	1.9239	87.8276
9	6.1694	2.0651	85.7625
10	6.0179	2.2166	83.5459
11	5.8553	2.3792	81.1668
12	5.6808	2.5537	78.6131
13	5.4935	2.7410	75.8720
14	5.2924	2.9421	72.9299
15	5.0766	3.1579	69.7720
16	4.8449	3.3896	66.3824
17	4.5963	3.6382	62.7442
18	4.3294	3.9051	58.8391
19	4.0429	4.1916	54.6475
20	3.7354	4.4991	50.1485
21	3.4054	4.8291	45.3194
22	3.0512	5.1833	40.1360
23	2.6709	5.5636	34.5724
24	2.2628	5.9717	28.6007
25	1.8247	6.4098	22.1910
26	1.3545	6.8800	15.3110
27	.8498	7.3847	7.9264

#	INT	PRIN	BALANCE
28	.3081	7.9264	0.0000

	YEARS 29	MO PAYT .6788	AN CONST 8.15
#	INT	PRIN	BALANCE
1	7.0653	1.0802	98.9198
2	6.9861	1.1595	97.7603
3	6.9010	1.2445	96.5157
4	6.8097	1.3358	95.1799
5	6.7117	1.4338	93.7460
6	6.6065	1.5390	92.2070
7	6.4936	1.6519	90.5551
8	6.3724	1.7731	88.7820
9	6.2424	1.9032	86.8788
10	6.1028	2.0428	84.8361
11	5.9529	2.1926	82.6434
12	5.7921	2.3535	80.2900
13	5.6194	2.5261	77.7639
14	5.4341	2.7114	75.0524
15	5.2352	2.9103	72.1421
16	5.0217	3.1238	69.0183
17	4.7926	3.3530	65.6653
18	4.5466	3.5989	62.0664
19	4.2826	3.8629	58.2035
20	3.9992	4.1463	54.0572
21	3.6951	4.4505	49.6067
22	3.3686	4.7769	44.8298
23	3.0182	5.1273	39.7025
24	2.6421	5.5035	34.1990
25	2.2384	5.9072	28.2918
26	1.8050	6.3405	21.9513
27	1.3399	6.8056	15.1456
28	.8407	7.3049	7.8407
29	.3048	7.8407	0.0000

	YEARS 30	MO PAYT .6720	AN CONST 8.07
#	INT	PRIN	BALANCE
1	7.0680	.9964	99.0036
2	6.9949	1.0695	97.9341
3	6.9164	1.1479	96.7862
4	6.8322	1.2321	95.5540
5	6.7418	1.3225	94.2315
6	6.6448	1.4196	92.8119
7	6.5407	1.5237	91.2883
8	6.4289	1.6355	89.6528
9	6.3090	1.7554	87.8974
10	6.1802	1.8842	86.0132
11	6.0420	2.0224	83.9908
12	5.8936	2.1708	81.8200
13	5.7344	2.3300	79.4900
14	5.5634	2.5009	76.9890
15	5.3800	2.6844	74.3046
16	5.1831	2.8813	71.4233
17	4.9717	3.0927	68.3306
18	4.7448	3.3196	65.0111
19	4.5013	3.5631	61.4480
20	4.2399	3.8244	57.6236
21	3.9594	4.1050	53.5186
22	3.6583	4.4061	49.1125
23	3.3351	4.7293	44.3831
24	2.9881	5.0763	39.3069
25	2.6157	5.4486	33.8582
26	2.2161	5.8483	28.0099
27	1.7870	6.2773	21.7325
28	1.3266	6.7378	14.9947
29	.8323	7.2321	7.7626
30	.3018	7.7626	0.0000

YEARS 2 — MO PAYT 4.4829 — AN CONST 53.80

#	INT	PRIN	BALANCE
1	5.5704	48.2248	51.7752
2	2.0199	51.7752	0.0000

YEARS 3 — MO PAYT 3.0934 — AN CONST 37.13

#	INT	PRIN	BALANCE
1	6.1258	30.9953	69.0047
2	3.8438	33.2773	35.7273
3	1.3938	35.7273	0.0000

YEARS 4 — MO PAYT 2.4004 — AN CONST 28.81

#	INT	PRIN	BALANCE
1	6.4028	22.4023	77.5977
2	4.7535	24.0517	53.5460
3	2.9827	25.8224	27.7236
4	1.0816	27.7236	0.0000

YEARS 5 — MO PAYT 1.9860 — AN CONST 23.84

#	INT	PRIN	BALANCE
1	6.5685	17.2638	82.7362
2	5.2974	18.5348	64.2014
3	3.9328	19.8994	44.3019
4	2.4678	21.3645	22.9374
5	.8948	22.9374	0.0000

YEARS 6 — MO PAYT 1.7109 — AN CONST 20.54

#	INT	PRIN	BALANCE
1	6.6784	13.8525	86.1475
2	5.6586	14.8723	71.2752
3	4.5636	15.9673	55.3079
4	3.3880	17.1429	38.1650
5	2.1259	18.4050	19.7600
6	.7709	19.7600	0.0000

YEARS 7 — MO PAYT 1.5154 — AN CONST 18.19

#	INT	PRIN	BALANCE
1	6.7566	11.4280	88.5720
2	5.9152	12.2694	76.3025
3	5.0119	13.1727	63.1298
4	4.0421	14.1426	48.9873
5	3.0009	15.1838	33.8035
6	1.8830	16.3017	17.5018
7	.6828	17.5018	0.0000

YEARS 8 — MO PAYT 1.3696 — AN CONST 16.44

#	INT	PRIN	BALANCE
1	6.8149	9.6203	90.3797
2	6.1066	10.3286	80.0510
3	5.3462	11.0891	68.9620
4	4.5297	11.9055	57.0565
5	3.6532	12.7820	44.2745
6	2.7122	13.7230	30.5515
7	1.7018	14.7334	15.8181
8	.6171	15.8181	0.0000

YEARS 9 — MO PAYT 1.2570 — AN CONST 15.09

#	INT	PRIN	BALANCE
1	6.8599	8.2237	91.7763
2	6.2544	8.8292	82.9471
3	5.6044	9.4792	73.4679
4	4.9065	10.1771	63.2907
5	4.1572	10.9264	52.3643
6	3.3528	11.7308	40.6335
7	2.4891	12.5945	28.0390
8	1.5619	13.5217	14.5173
9	.5664	14.5173	0.0000

YEARS 10 — MO PAYT 1.1675 — AN CONST 14.02

#	INT	PRIN	BALANCE
1	6.8956	7.1148	92.8852
2	6.3718	7.6386	85.2466
3	5.8094	8.2010	77.0455
4	5.2057	8.8048	68.2408
5	4.5574	9.4530	58.7877
6	3.8614	10.1490	48.6387
7	3.1142	10.8962	37.7425
8	2.3120	11.6984	26.0441
9	1.4507	12.5597	13.4844
10	.5261	13.4844	0.0000

YEARS 11 — MO PAYT 1.0950 — AN CONST 13.14

#	INT	PRIN	BALANCE
1	6.9246	6.2150	93.7850
2	6.4671	6.6726	87.1123
3	5.9758	7.1639	79.9484
4	5.4484	7.6913	72.2571
5	4.8821	8.2576	63.9996
6	4.2742	8.8655	55.1340
7	3.6215	9.5182	45.6158
8	2.9207	10.2190	35.3968
9	2.1683	10.9714	24.4254
10	1.3606	11.7791	12.6463
11	.4934	12.6463	0.0000

YEARS 12 — MO PAYT 1.0351 — AN CONST 12.43

#	INT	PRIN	BALANCE
1	6.9486	5.4721	94.5279
2	6.5457	5.8750	88.6530
3	6.1132	6.3075	82.3455
4	5.6488	6.7719	75.5736
5	5.1502	7.2704	68.3032
6	4.6150	7.8057	60.4974
7	4.0403	8.3804	52.1171
8	3.4233	8.9974	43.1197
9	2.7609	9.6598	33.4599
10	2.0497	10.3710	23.0889
11	1.2861	11.1345	11.9543
12	.4664	11.9543	0.0000

YEARS 13 — MO PAYT .9849 — AN CONST 11.82

#	INT	PRIN	BALANCE
1	6.9687	4.8497	95.1503
2	6.6116	5.2067	89.9436
3	6.2283	5.5900	84.3536
4	5.8167	6.0016	78.3520
5	5.3749	6.4435	71.9085
6	4.9005	6.9178	64.9907
7	4.3912	7.4272	57.5635
8	3.8443	7.9740	49.5896
9	3.2573	8.5610	41.0285
10	2.6270	9.1913	31.8372
11	1.9503	9.8680	21.9691
12	1.2238	10.5946	11.3746
13	.4438	11.3746	0.0000

YEARS 14 — MO PAYT .9423 — AN CONST 11.31

#	INT	PRIN	BALANCE
1	6.9857	4.3219	95.6781
2	6.6675	4.6401	91.0381
3	6.3259	4.9817	86.0564
4	5.9591	5.3484	80.7079
5	5.5653	5.7422	74.9657
6	5.1426	6.1650	68.8007
7	4.6887	6.6189	62.1819
8	4.2014	7.1062	55.0757
9	3.6782	7.6294	47.4464
10	3.1165	8.1911	39.2553
11	2.5134	8.7941	30.4612
12	1.8660	9.4416	21.0196
13	1.1709	10.1367	10.8830
14	.4246	10.8830	0.0000

YEARS 15 — MO PAYT .9058 — AN CONST 10.87

#	INT	PRIN	BALANCE
1	7.0003	3.8697	96.1303
2	6.7153	4.1546	91.9757
3	6.4095	4.4605	87.5151
4	6.0811	4.7889	82.7262
5	5.7285	5.1415	77.5848
6	5.3500	5.5200	72.0648
7	4.9436	5.9264	66.1383
8	4.5072	6.3627	59.7756
9	4.0388	6.8312	52.9444
10	3.5359	7.3341	45.6103
11	2.9959	7.8741	37.7362
12	2.4162	8.4538	29.2824
13	1.7938	9.0762	20.2062
14	1.1256	9.7444	10.4618
15	.4081	10.4618	0.0000

YEARS 16 — MO PAYT .8743 — AN CONST 10.50

#	INT	PRIN	BALANCE
1	7.0128	3.4790	96.5210
2	6.7567	3.7351	92.7859
3	6.4817	4.0101	88.7759
4	6.1865	4.3053	84.4705
5	5.8695	4.6223	79.8482
6	5.5292	4.9626	74.8856
7	5.1638	5.3280	69.5577
8	4.7716	5.7202	63.8374
9	4.3504	6.1414	57.6960
10	3.8983	6.5935	51.1025
11	3.4128	7.0790	44.0235
12	2.8917	7.6001	36.4234
13	2.3321	8.1597	28.2637
14	1.7314	8.7604	19.5033
15	1.0864	9.4054	10.0979
16	.3939	10.0979	0.0000

YEARS 17 — MO PAYT .8469 — AN CONST 10.17

#	INT	PRIN	BALANCE
1	7.0238	3.1387	96.8613
2	6.7927	3.3698	93.4915
3	6.5446	3.6179	89.8737
4	6.2783	3.8842	85.9895
5	5.9923	4.1702	81.8193
6	5.6853	4.4772	77.3420
7	5.3557	4.8068	72.5352
8	5.0018	5.1607	67.3745
9	4.6218	5.5407	61.8338
10	4.2139	5.9486	55.8851
11	3.7759	6.3866	49.4986
12	3.3057	6.8568	42.6418
13	2.8009	7.3616	35.2802
14	2.2589	7.9036	27.3766
15	1.6770	8.4855	18.8911
16	1.0523	9.1102	9.7809
17	.3816	9.7809	0.0000

YEARS 18 — MO PAYT .8228 — AN CONST 9.88

#	INT	PRIN	BALANCE
1	7.0334	2.8404	97.1596
2	6.8243	3.0495	94.1100
3	6.5998	3.2741	90.8360
4	6.3587	3.5151	87.3209
5	6.1000	3.7739	83.5470
6	5.8221	4.0517	79.4953
7	5.5238	4.3500	75.1452
8	5.2035	4.6703	70.4749
9	4.8597	5.0142	65.4607
10	4.4905	5.3833	60.0774
11	4.0942	5.7797	54.2978
12	3.6687	6.2052	48.0926
13	3.2118	6.6620	41.4306
14	2.7214	7.1525	34.2781
15	2.1948	7.6791	26.5990
16	1.6294	8.2445	18.3545
17	1.0224	8.8514	9.5031
18	.3707	9.5031	0.0000

YEARS 19 — MO PAYT .8016 — AN CONST 9.62

#	INT	PRIN	BALANCE
1	7.0419	2.5774	97.4226
2	6.8521	2.7672	94.6553
3	6.6484	2.9709	91.6844
4	6.4297	3.1897	88.4947
5	6.1949	3.4245	85.0702
6	5.9427	3.6766	81.3936
7	5.6720	3.9473	77.4463
8	5.3814	4.2379	73.2084
9	5.0694	4.5499	68.6584
10	4.7344	4.8849	63.7735
11	4.3748	5.2446	58.5290
12	3.9887	5.6307	52.8983
13	3.5741	6.0452	46.8530
14	3.1290	6.4903	40.3627
15	2.6512	6.9681	33.3946
16	2.1382	7.4812	25.9134
17	1.5874	8.0320	17.8815
18	.9961	8.6233	9.2582
19	.3612	9.2582	0.0000

YEARS 20 — MO PAYT .7828 — AN CONST 9.40

#	INT	PRIN	BALANCE
1	7.0494	2.3444	97.6556
2	6.8768	2.5170	95.1386
3	6.6915	2.7023	92.4362
4	6.4926	2.9013	89.5349
5	6.2789	3.1149	86.4201
6	6.0496	3.3442	83.0758
7	5.8034	3.5904	79.4854
8	5.5391	3.8548	75.6306
9	5.2553	4.1386	71.4921
10	4.9506	4.4433	67.0488
11	4.6234	4.7704	62.2784
12	4.2722	5.1216	57.1568
13	3.8952	5.4987	51.6581
14	3.4903	5.9035	45.7546
15	3.0557	6.3381	39.4165
16	2.5891	6.8048	32.6117
17	2.0881	7.3058	25.3059
18	1.5502	7.8437	17.4622
19	.9727	8.4211	9.0411
20	.3527	9.0411	0.0000

YEARS 21 — MO PAYT .7661 — AN CONST 9.20

#	INT	PRIN	BALANCE
1	7.0561	2.1370	97.8630
2	6.8988	2.2943	95.5687
3	6.7299	2.4632	93.1055

MONTHLY PAYMENT AMORTIZATION SCHEDULE PER $100   7.125%

#	INT	PRIN	BALANCE
4	6.5485	2.6446	90.4609
5	6.3538	2.8393	87.6216
6	6.1448	3.0483	84.5733
7	5.9203	3.2728	81.3005
8	5.6794	3.5137	77.7868
9	5.4207	3.7724	74.0144
10	5.1430	4.0501	69.9643
11	4.8448	4.3483	65.6160
12	4.5246	4.6685	60.9475
13	4.1809	5.0122	55.9354
14	3.8119	5.3812	50.5542
15	3.4157	5.7774	44.7768
16	2.9904	6.2027	38.5741
17	2.5337	6.6594	31.9148
18	2.0434	7.1497	24.7651
19	1.5171	7.6760	17.0891
20	.9519	8.2412	8.8479
21	.3452	8.8479	0.0000

YEARS 22 — MO PAYT .7511 — AN CONST 9.02

#	INT	PRIN	BALANCE
1	7.0621	1.9516	98.0484
2	6.9184	2.0953	95.9531
3	6.7641	2.2495	93.7036
4	6.5985	2.4152	91.2884
5	6.4207	2.5930	88.6955
6	6.2298	2.7839	85.9116
7	6.0248	2.9888	82.9227
8	5.8048	3.2089	79.7139
9	5.5686	3.4451	76.2687
10	5.3149	3.6988	72.5700
11	5.0426	3.9711	68.5989
12	4.7502	4.2635	64.3354
13	4.4363	4.5773	59.7581
14	4.0993	4.9143	54.8437
15	3.7375	5.2762	49.5676
16	3.3491	5.6646	43.9030
17	2.9320	6.0817	37.8213
18	2.4843	6.5294	31.2919
19	2.0036	7.0101	24.2818
20	1.4875	7.5262	16.7556
21	.9333	8.0803	8.6752
22	.3384	8.6752	0.0000

YEARS 23 — MO PAYT .7377 — AN CONST 8.86

#	INT	PRIN	BALANCE
1	7.0674	1.7853	98.2147
2	6.9360	1.9168	96.2979
3	6.7949	2.0579	94.2401
4	6.6434	2.2094	92.0307
5	6.4807	2.3720	89.6586
6	6.3061	2.5467	87.1120
7	6.1186	2.7342	84.3778
8	5.9173	2.9355	81.4423
9	5.7012	3.1516	78.2907
10	5.4691	3.3836	74.9071
11	5.2200	3.6327	71.2744
12	4.9526	3.9002	67.3742
13	4.6654	4.1873	63.1868
14	4.3571	4.4956	58.6912
15	4.0262	4.8266	53.8646
16	3.6708	5.1820	48.6826
17	3.2893	5.5635	43.1192
18	2.8797	5.9731	37.1461
19	2.4399	6.4128	30.7333
20	1.9678	6.8850	23.8483
21	1.4609	7.3919	16.4564
22	.9167	7.9361	8.5204
23	.3324	8.5204	0.0000

YEARS 24 — MO PAYT .7257 — AN CONST 8.71

#	INT	PRIN	BALANCE
1	7.0723	1.6357	98.3643
2	6.9518	1.7561	96.6082
3	6.8226	1.8854	94.7228
4	6.6837	2.0242	92.6986
5	6.5347	2.1732	90.5254
6	6.3747	2.3332	88.1921
7	6.2029	2.5050	85.6871
8	6.0185	2.6895	82.9976
9	5.8205	2.8875	80.1102
10	5.6079	3.1000	77.0101
11	5.3797	3.3283	73.6819
12	5.1346	3.5733	70.1085
13	4.8716	3.8364	66.2721
14	4.5891	4.1188	62.1533
15	4.2859	4.4221	57.7312
16	3.9603	4.7477	52.9835
17	3.6108	5.0972	47.8863
18	3.2355	5.4725	42.4139
19	2.8326	5.8754	36.5385
20	2.4000	6.3079	30.2306
21	1.9356	6.7724	23.4582
22	1.4370	7.2710	16.1873
23	.9017	7.8063	8.3810
24	.3270	8.3810	0.0000

YEARS 25 — MO PAYT .7148 — AN CONST 8.58

#	INT	PRIN	BALANCE
1	7.0766	1.5007	98.4993
2	6.9661	1.6111	96.8882
3	6.8475	1.7298	95.1584
4	6.7202	1.8571	93.3013
5	6.5834	1.9938	91.3075
6	6.4367	2.1406	89.1669
7	6.2791	2.2982	86.8686
8	6.1098	2.4674	84.4012
9	5.9282	2.6491	81.7521
10	5.7332	2.8441	78.9080
11	5.5238	3.0535	75.8545
12	5.2989	3.2783	72.5761
13	5.0576	3.5197	69.0565
14	4.7985	3.7788	65.2776
15	4.5202	4.0570	61.2206
16	4.2215	4.3557	56.8649
17	3.9009	4.6764	52.1884
18	3.5566	5.0207	47.1677
19	3.1869	5.3903	41.7774
20	2.7901	5.7872	35.9902
21	2.3640	6.2133	29.7769
22	1.9066	6.6707	23.1062
23	1.4154	7.1618	15.9443
24	.8882	7.6891	8.2552
25	.3221	8.2552	0.0000

YEARS 26 — MO PAYT .7049 — AN CONST 8.46

#	INT	PRIN	BALANCE
1	7.0806	1.3785	98.6215
2	6.9791	1.4800	97.1415
3	6.8701	1.5889	95.5526
4	6.7531	1.7059	93.8467
5	6.6275	1.8315	92.0152
6	6.4927	1.9663	90.0488
7	6.3479	2.1111	87.9377
8	6.1925	2.2665	85.6712
9	6.0256	2.4334	83.2378
10	5.8465	2.6126	80.6252
11	5.6541	2.8049	77.8203
12	5.4476	3.0114	74.8088
13	5.2259	3.2331	71.5757
14	4.9879	3.4712	68.1045
15	4.7323	3.7267	64.3778
16	4.4579	4.0011	60.3767
17	4.1634	4.2957	56.0810
18	3.8471	4.6119	51.4690
19	3.5075	4.9515	46.5175
20	3.1430	5.3160	41.2015
21	2.7516	5.7074	35.4941
22	2.3314	6.1276	29.3664
23	1.8803	6.5788	22.7877
24	1.3959	7.0631	15.7246
25	.8759	7.5831	8.1414
26	.3176	8.1414	0.0000

YEARS 27 — MO PAYT .6960 — AN CONST 8.36

#	INT	PRIN	BALANCE
1	7.0841	1.2677	98.7323
2	6.9908	1.3610	97.3713
3	6.8906	1.4612	95.9101
4	6.7830	1.5688	94.3413
5	6.6675	1.6843	92.6570
6	6.5435	1.8083	90.8487
7	6.4104	1.9414	88.9073
8	6.2675	2.0844	86.8230
9	6.1140	2.2378	84.5851
10	5.9492	2.4026	82.1826
11	5.7724	2.5795	79.6031
12	5.5824	2.7694	76.8338
13	5.3786	2.9733	73.8605
14	5.1597	3.1922	70.6683
15	4.9246	3.4272	67.2412
16	4.6723	3.6795	63.5617
17	4.4014	3.9504	59.6113
18	4.1106	4.2412	55.3701
19	3.7983	4.5535	50.8166
20	3.4631	4.8887	45.9278
21	3.1032	5.2487	40.6792
22	2.7167	5.6351	35.0441
23	2.3019	6.0500	28.9942
24	1.8564	6.4954	22.4988
25	1.3782	6.9736	15.5252
26	.8648	7.4870	8.0382
27	.3136	8.0382	0.0000

YEARS 28 — MO PAYT .6879 — AN CONST 8.26

#	INT	PRIN	BALANCE
1	7.0874	1.1670	98.8330
2	7.0015	1.2529	97.5802
3	6.9092	1.3451	96.2350
4	6.8102	1.4442	94.7909
5	6.7039	1.5505	93.2404
6	6.5897	1.6646	91.5758
7	6.4672	1.7872	89.7886
8	6.3356	1.9188	87.8698
9	6.1943	2.0600	85.8098
10	6.0426	2.2117	83.5981
11	5.8798	2.3745	81.2235
12	5.7050	2.5494	78.6742
13	5.5173	2.7370	75.9371
14	5.3158	2.9386	72.9986
15	5.0994	3.1549	69.8437
16	4.8672	3.3872	66.4565
17	4.6178	3.6366	62.8199
18	4.3501	3.9043	58.9156
19	4.0626	4.1917	54.7239
20	3.7540	4.5003	50.2236
21	3.4227	4.8317	45.3919
22	3.0669	5.1874	40.2045
23	2.6850	5.5693	34.6352
24	2.2750	5.9793	28.6558
25	1.8348	6.4196	22.2362
26	1.3621	6.8922	15.3440
27	.8547	7.3996	7.9444
28	.3099	7.9444	0.0000

YEARS 29 — MO PAYT .6805 — AN CONST 8.17

#	INT	PRIN	BALANCE
1	7.0903	1.0753	98.9247
2	7.0112	1.1544	97.7703
3	6.9262	1.2394	96.5309
4	6.8349	1.3307	95.2003
5	6.7370	1.4286	93.7716
6	6.6318	1.5338	92.2378
7	6.5189	1.6467	90.5911
8	6.3976	1.7680	88.8231
9	6.2675	1.8981	86.9250
10	6.1277	2.0379	84.8871
11	5.9777	2.1879	82.6992
12	5.8166	2.3490	80.3502
13	5.6436	2.5219	77.8282
14	5.4580	2.7076	75.1206
15	5.2586	2.9070	72.2137
16	5.0446	3.1210	69.0927
17	4.8148	3.3508	65.7419
18	4.5681	3.5975	62.1445
19	4.3033	3.8623	58.2822
20	4.0189	4.1467	54.1355
21	3.7136	4.4520	49.6835
22	3.3859	4.7797	44.9038
23	3.0340	5.1316	39.7722
24	2.6562	5.5094	34.2627
25	2.2505	5.9151	28.3477
26	1.8150	6.3505	21.9971
27	1.3475	6.8181	15.1791
28	.8455	7.3201	7.8590
29	.3066	7.8590	0.0000

YEARS 30 — MO PAYT .6737 — AN CONST 8.09

#	INT	PRIN	BALANCE
1	7.0930	.9916	99.0084
2	7.0200	1.0646	97.9438
3	6.9417	1.1430	96.8008
4	6.8575	1.2271	95.5737
5	6.7672	1.3175	94.2563
6	6.6702	1.4145	92.8418
7	6.5660	1.5186	91.3232
8	6.4542	1.6304	89.6928
9	6.3342	1.7504	87.9424
10	6.2053	1.8793	86.0630
11	6.0669	2.0177	84.0454
12	5.9184	2.1662	81.8791
13	5.7589	2.3257	79.5534
14	5.5877	2.4969	77.0565
15	5.4039	2.6808	74.3757
16	5.2065	2.8781	71.4976
17	4.9946	3.0900	68.4076
18	4.7671	3.3175	65.0900
19	4.5228	3.5618	61.5282
20	4.2606	3.8240	57.7042
21	3.9791	4.1055	53.5987
22	3.6768	4.4078	49.1909
23	3.3523	4.7323	44.4585
24	3.0039	5.0807	39.3778
25	2.6298	5.4548	33.9230
26	2.2282	5.8564	28.0666
27	1.7971	6.2876	21.7790
28	1.3341	6.7505	15.0285
29	.8371	7.2475	7.7811
30	.3036	7.7811	0.0000

YEARS 2 — MO PAYT 4.4863 — AN CONST 53.84

#	INT	PRIN	BALANCE
1	5.6298	48.2061	51.7939
2	2.0421	51.7939	0.0000

YEARS 3 — MO PAYT 3.0969 — AN CONST 37.17

#	INT	PRIN	BALANCE
1	6.1912	30.9711	69.0289
2	3.8862	33.2762	35.7527
3	1.4096	35.7527	0.0000

YEARS 4 — MO PAYT 2.4039 — AN CONST 28.85

#	INT	PRIN	BALANCE
1	6.4712	22.3758	77.6242
2	4.8059	24.0411	53.5831
3	3.0166	25.8303	27.7527
4	1.0942	27.7527	0.0000

YEARS 5 — MO PAYT 1.9896 — AN CONST 23.88

#	INT	PRIN	BALANCE
1	6.6386	17.2363	82.7637
2	5.3558	18.5191	64.2447
3	3.9775	19.8973	44.3474
4	2.4967	21.3782	22.9692
5	.9056	22.9692	0.0000

YEARS 6 — MO PAYT 1.7145 — AN CONST 20.58

#	INT	PRIN	BALANCE
1	6.7497	13.8245	86.1755
2	5.7208	14.8534	71.3220
3	4.6154	15.9589	55.3632
4	3.4276	17.1466	38.2165
5	2.1515	18.4227	19.7938
6	.7804	19.7938	0.0000

YEARS 7 — MO PAYT 1.5191 — AN CONST 18.23

#	INT	PRIN	BALANCE
1	6.8287	11.4001	88.5999
2	5.9802	12.2485	76.3514
3	5.0686	13.1601	63.1913
4	4.0892	14.1396	49.0517
5	3.0369	15.1919	33.8598
6	1.9062	16.3225	17.5373
7	.6915	17.5373	0.0000

YEARS 8 — MO PAYT 1.3733 — AN CONST 16.49

#	INT	PRIN	BALANCE
1	6.8875	9.5926	90.4074
2	6.1736	10.3065	80.1009
3	5.4066	11.0736	69.0273
4	4.5824	11.8977	57.1296
5	3.6970	12.7832	44.3464
6	2.7456	13.7346	30.6118
7	1.7234	14.7568	15.8550
8	.6251	15.8550	0.0000

YEARS 9 — MO PAYT 1.2608 — AN CONST 15.13

#	INT	PRIN	BALANCE
1	6.9330	8.1964	91.8036
2	6.3230	8.8064	82.9973
3	5.6676	9.4618	73.5355
4	4.9634	10.1660	63.3696
5	4.2068	10.9225	52.4470
6	3.3939	11.7354	40.7116
7	2.5205	12.6088	28.1027
8	1.5821	13.5472	14.5555
9	.5739	14.5555	0.0000

YEARS 10 — MO PAYT 1.1714 — AN CONST 14.06

#	INT	PRIN	BALANCE
1	6.9691	7.0879	92.9121
2	6.4416	7.6154	85.2967
3	5.8749	8.1822	77.1145
4	5.2659	8.7911	68.3234
5	4.6116	9.4454	58.8780
6	3.9087	10.1484	48.7296
7	3.1534	10.9036	37.8260
8	2.3419	11.7151	26.1108
9	1.4700	12.5870	13.5238
10	.5332	13.5238	0.0000

YEARS 11 — MO PAYT 1.0989 — AN CONST 13.19

#	INT	PRIN	BALANCE
1	6.9984	6.1887	93.8113
2	6.5378	6.6492	87.1621
3	6.0430	7.1441	80.0180
4	5.5113	7.6758	72.3422
5	4.9400	8.2471	64.0951
6	4.3262	8.8609	55.2342
7	3.6668	9.5203	45.7139
8	2.9582	10.2289	35.4851
9	2.1970	10.9901	24.4949
10	1.3790	11.8081	12.6869
11	.5002	12.6869	0.0000

YEARS 12 — MO PAYT 1.0391 — AN CONST 12.47

#	INT	PRIN	BALANCE
1	7.0226	5.4463	94.5537
2	6.6173	5.8516	88.7021
3	6.1818	6.2871	82.4150
4	5.7139	6.7550	75.6600
5	5.2111	7.2578	68.4022
6	4.6710	7.7979	60.6043
7	4.0906	8.3783	52.2260
8	3.4671	9.0018	43.2242
9	2.7971	9.6718	33.5525
10	2.0773	10.3916	23.1609
11	1.3039	11.1650	11.9959
12	.4730	11.9959	0.0000

YEARS 13 — MO PAYT .9889 — AN CONST 11.87

#	INT	PRIN	BALANCE
1	7.0429	4.8245	95.1755
2	6.6838	5.1835	89.9920
3	6.2980	5.5693	84.4227
4	5.8835	5.9838	78.4389
5	5.4382	6.4291	72.0098
6	4.9597	6.9076	65.1022
7	4.4456	7.4217	57.6805
8	3.8933	7.9741	49.7064
9	3.2998	8.5675	41.1389
10	2.6622	9.2052	31.9337
11	1.9771	9.8902	22.0435
12	1.2410	10.6263	11.4172
13	.4502	11.4172	0.0000

YEARS 14 — MO PAYT .9464 — AN CONST 11.36

#	INT	PRIN	BALANCE
1	7.0600	4.2973	95.7027
2	6.7402	4.6171	91.0855
3	6.3966	4.9608	86.1248
4	6.0274	5.3300	80.7948
5	5.6307	5.7266	75.0681
6	5.2045	6.1529	68.9153
7	4.7466	6.6108	62.3045
8	4.2546	7.1028	55.2018
9	3.7260	7.6314	47.5704
10	3.1580	8.1994	39.3710
11	2.5478	8.8096	30.5614
12	1.8921	9.4652	21.0962
13	1.1877	10.1697	10.9265
14	.4308	10.9265	0.0000

YEARS 15 — MO PAYT .9100 — AN CONST 10.93

#	INT	PRIN	BALANCE
1	7.0747	3.8458	96.1542
2	6.7885	4.1321	92.0221
3	6.4810	4.4396	87.5825
4	6.1506	4.7700	82.8126
5	5.7956	5.1250	77.6876
6	5.4141	5.5064	72.1812
7	5.0043	5.9162	66.2649
8	4.5640	6.3565	59.9084
9	4.0909	6.8296	53.0788
10	3.5827	7.3379	45.7409
11	3.0365	7.8840	37.8569
12	2.4498	8.4708	29.3861
13	1.8194	9.1012	20.2849
14	1.1420	9.7786	10.5063
15	.4142	10.5063	0.0000

YEARS 16 — MO PAYT .8786 — AN CONST 10.55

#	INT	PRIN	BALANCE
1	7.0874	3.4557	96.5443
2	6.8302	3.7129	92.8313
3	6.5539	3.9893	88.8421
4	6.2570	4.2862	84.5559
5	5.9380	4.6051	79.9508
6	5.5953	4.9479	75.0029
7	5.2270	5.3161	69.6868
8	4.8314	5.7118	63.9750
9	4.4063	6.1369	57.8381
10	3.9496	6.5936	51.2445
11	3.4589	7.0843	44.1602
12	2.9316	7.6116	36.5486
13	2.3651	8.1781	28.3706
14	1.7565	8.7867	19.5839
15	1.1025	9.4406	10.1433
16	.3999	10.1433	0.0000

YEARS 17 — MO PAYT .8512 — AN CONST 10.22

#	INT	PRIN	BALANCE
1	7.0985	3.1161	96.8839
2	6.8666	3.3481	93.5358
3	6.6174	3.5972	89.9386
4	6.3497	3.8649	86.0736
5	6.0620	4.1526	81.9210
6	5.7530	4.4616	77.4594
7	5.4209	4.7937	72.6657
8	5.0642	5.1505	67.5152
9	4.6808	5.5338	61.9814
10	4.2690	5.9456	56.0358
11	3.8265	6.3881	49.6477
12	3.3511	6.8636	42.7841
13	2.8403	7.3744	35.4097
14	2.2914	7.9232	27.4865
15	1.7017	8.5129	18.9736
16	1.0682	9.1465	9.8272
17	.3875	9.8272	0.0000

YEARS 18 — MO PAYT .8272 — AN CONST 9.93

#	INT	PRIN	BALANCE
1	7.1082	2.8185	97.1815
2	6.8984	3.0283	94.1532
3	6.6730	3.2537	90.8995
4	6.4309	3.4958	87.4036
5	6.1707	3.7560	83.6476
6	5.8912	4.0356	79.6121
7	5.5908	4.3359	75.2762
8	5.2681	4.6586	70.6176
9	4.9214	5.0053	65.6123
10	4.5489	5.3778	60.2345
11	4.1487	5.7781	54.4564
12	3.7187	6.2081	48.2483
13	3.2566	6.6701	41.5782
14	2.7602	7.1665	34.4117
15	2.2268	7.6999	26.7118
16	1.6538	8.2730	18.4388
17	1.0381	8.8887	9.5502
18	.3765	9.5502	0.0000

YEARS 19 — MO PAYT .8061 — AN CONST 9.68

#	INT	PRIN	BALANCE
1	7.1167	2.5562	97.4438
2	6.9265	2.7465	94.6973
3	6.7221	2.9509	91.7464
4	6.5025	3.1705	88.5759
5	6.2665	3.4065	85.1694
6	6.0130	3.6600	81.5094
7	5.7406	3.9324	77.5770
8	5.4479	4.2251	73.3519
9	5.1335	4.5395	68.8124
10	4.7956	4.8774	63.9351
11	4.4326	5.2403	58.6947
12	4.0426	5.6304	53.0644
13	3.6236	6.0494	47.0150
14	3.1734	6.4996	40.5154
15	2.6896	6.9833	33.5320
16	2.1699	7.5031	26.0290
17	1.6115	8.0615	17.9675
18	1.0115	8.6614	9.3061
19	.3669	9.3061	0.0000

YEARS 20 — MO PAYT .7873 — AN CONST 9.45

#	INT	PRIN	BALANCE
1	7.1243	2.3239	97.6761
2	6.9514	2.4968	95.1793
3	6.7655	2.6827	92.4966
4	6.5659	2.8823	89.6143
5	6.3514	3.0968	86.5175
6	6.1209	3.3273	83.1901
7	5.8732	3.5749	79.6152
8	5.6072	3.8410	75.7742
9	5.3213	4.1269	71.6473
10	5.0142	4.4340	67.2133
11	4.6842	4.7640	62.4493
12	4.3296	5.1186	57.3307
13	3.9487	5.4995	51.8312
14	3.5394	5.9088	45.9224
15	3.0996	6.3486	39.5739
16	2.6271	6.8211	32.7528
17	2.1195	7.3287	25.4241
18	1.5741	7.8741	17.5500
19	.9880	8.4602	9.0898
20	.3584	9.0898	0.0000

YEARS 21 — MO PAYT .7707 — AN CONST 9.25

#	INT	PRIN	BALANCE
1	7.1310	2.1171	97.8829
2	6.9735	2.2747	95.6082
3	6.8042	2.4440	93.1642

MONTHLY PAYMENT AMORTIZATION SCHEDULE PER $100   7.20 %

#	INT	PRIN	BALANCE
4	6.6223	2.6259	90.5383
5	6.4269	2.8213	87.7170
6	6.2169	3.0313	84.6858
7	5.9913	3.2569	81.4289
8	5.7489	3.4993	77.9296
9	5.4885	3.7597	74.1700
10	5.2087	4.0395	70.1305
11	4.9080	4.3401	65.7903
12	4.5850	4.6631	61.1272
13	4.2380	5.0102	56.1170
14	3.8651	5.3831	50.7339
15	3.4645	5.7837	44.9502
16	3.0340	6.2142	38.7360
17	2.5715	6.6766	32.0594
18	2.0746	7.1735	24.8858
19	1.5407	7.7074	17.1784
20	.9671	8.2810	8.8974
21	.3508	8.8974	0.0000

YEARS 22   MO PAYT .7558   AN CONST 9.07

#	INT	PRIN	BALANCE
1	7.1371	1.9324	98.0676
2	6.9932	2.0762	95.9914
3	6.8387	2.2307	93.7607
4	6.6727	2.3968	91.3639
5	6.4943	2.5751	88.7888
6	6.3027	2.7668	86.0220
7	6.0968	2.9727	83.0493
8	5.8755	3.1939	79.8554
9	5.6378	3.4316	76.4237
10	5.3824	3.6870	72.7367
11	5.1080	3.9614	68.7753
12	4.8132	4.2563	64.5190
13	4.4964	4.5730	59.9460
14	4.1561	4.9134	55.0326
15	3.7904	5.2791	49.7535
16	3.3975	5.6719	44.0816
17	2.9754	6.0941	37.9875
18	2.5218	6.5476	31.4399
19	2.0345	7.0349	24.4049
20	1.5110	7.5585	16.8465
21	.9484	8.1210	8.7254
22	.3440	8.7254	0.0000

YEARS 23   MO PAYT .7424   AN CONST 8.91

#	INT	PRIN	BALANCE
1	7.1425	1.7668	98.2332
2	7.0110	1.8983	96.3350
3	6.8697	2.0395	94.2955
4	6.7179	2.1913	92.1041
5	6.5548	2.3544	89.7497
6	6.3796	2.5296	87.2201
7	6.1913	2.7179	84.5022
8	5.9890	2.9202	81.5820
9	5.7717	3.1375	78.4445
10	5.5382	3.3710	75.0735
11	5.2873	3.6219	71.4516
12	5.0178	3.8915	67.5602
13	4.7281	4.1811	63.3791
14	4.4170	4.4922	58.8869
15	4.0826	4.8266	54.0603
16	3.7234	5.1858	48.8745
17	3.3375	5.5717	43.3028
18	2.9228	5.9864	37.3163
19	2.4773	6.4319	30.8844
20	1.9986	6.9106	23.9738
21	1.4843	7.4250	16.5488
22	.9317	7.9775	8.5713
23	.3379	8.5713	0.0000

YEARS 24   MO PAYT .7304   AN CONST 8.77

#	INT	PRIN	BALANCE
1	7.1473	1.6178	98.3822
2	7.0269	1.7382	96.6440
3	6.8975	1.8675	94.7765
4	6.7586	2.0065	92.7700
5	6.6092	2.1559	90.6141
6	6.4488	2.3163	88.2978
7	6.2764	2.4887	85.8091
8	6.0912	2.6739	83.1351
9	5.8922	2.8729	80.2622
10	5.6783	3.0867	77.1755
11	5.4486	3.3165	73.8590
12	5.2018	3.5633	70.2957
13	4.9366	3.8285	66.4672
14	4.6517	4.1134	62.3538
15	4.3455	4.4196	57.9342
16	4.0166	4.7485	53.1857
17	3.6632	5.1019	48.0838
18	3.2835	5.4816	42.6022
19	2.8755	5.8896	36.7126
20	2.4372	6.3279	30.3848
21	1.9662	6.7988	23.5859
22	1.4603	7.3048	16.2811
23	.9166	7.8485	8.4326
24	.3325	8.4326	0.0000

YEARS 25   MO PAYT .7196   AN CONST 8.64

#	INT	PRIN	BALANCE
1	7.1517	1.4834	98.5166
2	7.0413	1.5938	96.9228
3	6.9227	1.7124	95.2104
4	6.7952	1.8398	93.3706
5	6.6583	1.9768	91.3938
6	6.5112	2.1239	89.2699
7	6.3531	2.2820	86.9880
8	6.1833	2.4518	84.5362
9	6.0008	2.6343	81.9019
10	5.8047	2.8303	79.0716
11	5.5941	3.0410	76.0307
12	5.3678	3.2673	72.7634
13	5.1246	3.5104	69.2529
14	4.8634	3.7717	65.4812
15	4.5827	4.0524	61.4288
16	4.2811	4.3540	57.0748
17	3.9570	4.6781	52.3968
18	3.6089	5.0262	47.3705
19	3.2348	5.4003	41.9703
20	2.8329	5.8022	36.1681
21	2.4010	6.2340	29.9340
22	1.9371	6.6980	23.2361
23	1.4386	7.1965	16.0396
24	.9030	7.7321	8.3075
25	.3275	8.3075	0.0000

YEARS 26   MO PAYT .7098   AN CONST 8.52

#	INT	PRIN	BALANCE
1	7.1556	1.3618	98.6382
2	7.0543	1.4632	97.1750
3	6.9454	1.5721	95.6029
4	6.8284	1.6891	93.9138
5	6.7027	1.8148	92.0991
6	6.5676	1.9498	90.1492
7	6.4225	2.0950	88.0542
8	6.2666	2.2509	85.8034
9	6.0991	2.4184	83.3850
10	5.9191	2.5984	80.7866
11	5.7257	2.7918	77.9948
12	5.5179	2.9995	74.9953
13	5.2947	3.2228	71.7725
14	5.0548	3.4626	68.3098
15	4.7971	3.7203	64.5895
16	4.5202	3.9972	60.5923
17	4.2228	4.2947	56.2975
18	3.9031	4.6143	51.6832
19	3.5597	4.9578	46.7254
20	3.1907	5.3267	41.3987
21	2.7943	5.7232	35.6755
22	2.3683	6.1491	29.5264
23	1.9107	6.6068	22.9196
24	1.4190	7.0985	15.8212
25	.8907	7.6268	8.1944
26	.3231	8.1944	0.0000

YEARS 27   MO PAYT .7009   AN CONST 8.42

#	INT	PRIN	BALANCE
1	7.1592	1.2516	98.7484
2	7.0661	1.3448	97.4036
3	6.9660	1.4449	95.9587
4	6.8585	1.5524	94.4063
5	6.7429	1.6679	92.7384
6	6.6188	1.7921	90.9463
7	6.4854	1.9254	89.0209
8	6.3421	2.0687	86.9521
9	6.1882	2.2227	84.7294
10	6.0227	2.3881	82.3413
11	5.8450	2.5659	79.7754
12	5.6540	2.7568	77.0186
13	5.4489	2.9620	74.0566
14	5.2284	3.1824	70.8741
15	4.9916	3.4193	67.4548
16	4.7371	3.6738	63.7811
17	4.4637	3.9472	59.8339
18	4.1699	4.2410	55.5929
19	3.8543	4.5566	51.0363
20	3.5152	4.8957	46.1406
21	3.1508	5.2601	40.8805
22	2.7593	5.6515	35.2290
23	2.3387	6.0722	29.1568
24	1.8868	6.5241	22.6328
25	1.4012	7.0096	15.6231
26	.8796	7.5313	8.0918
27	.3190	8.0918	0.0000

YEARS 28   MO PAYT .6928   AN CONST 8.32

#	INT	PRIN	BALANCE
1	7.1625	1.1515	98.8485
2	7.0768	1.2372	97.6113
3	6.9847	1.3293	96.2820
4	6.8858	1.4282	94.8537
5	6.7795	1.5345	93.3192
6	6.6653	1.6487	91.6705
7	6.5426	1.7714	89.8991
8	6.4107	1.9033	87.9958
9	6.2691	2.0449	85.9509
10	6.1169	2.1971	83.7537
11	5.9534	2.3606	81.3931
12	5.7777	2.5363	78.8568
13	5.5889	2.7251	76.1317
14	5.3861	2.9279	73.2038
15	5.1682	3.1458	70.0580
16	4.9341	3.3799	66.6781
17	4.6825	3.6315	63.0466
18	4.4123	3.9017	59.1449
19	4.1219	4.1921	54.9527
20	3.8099	4.5041	50.4486
21	3.4747	4.8393	45.6093
22	3.1145	5.1995	40.4098
23	2.7275	5.5865	34.8233
24	2.3118	6.0022	28.8211
25	1.8651	6.4489	22.3721
26	1.3851	6.9289	15.4432
27	.8694	7.4446	7.9986
28	.3154	7.9986	0.0000

YEARS 29   MO PAYT .6855   AN CONST 8.23

#	INT	PRIN	BALANCE
1	7.1655	1.0604	98.9396
2	7.0865	1.1393	97.8003
3	7.0018	1.2241	96.5762
4	6.9106	1.3152	95.2610
5	6.8128	1.4131	93.8479
6	6.7076	1.5183	92.3297
7	6.5946	1.6312	90.6984
8	6.4732	1.7527	88.9458
9	6.3428	1.8831	87.0627
10	6.2026	2.0232	85.0394
11	6.0520	2.1738	82.8656
12	5.8902	2.3356	80.5300
13	5.7164	2.5094	78.0206
14	5.5297	2.6962	75.3244
15	5.3290	2.8968	72.4276
16	5.1134	3.1124	69.3151
17	4.8818	3.3441	65.9710
18	4.6329	3.5930	62.3781
19	4.3655	3.8604	58.5177
20	4.0782	4.1477	54.3700
21	3.7695	4.4564	49.9137
22	3.4378	4.7880	45.1257
23	3.0815	5.1444	39.9813
24	2.6986	5.5272	34.4541
25	2.2873	5.9386	28.5155
26	1.8453	6.3806	22.1349
27	1.3704	6.8554	15.2795
28	.8602	7.3656	7.9138
29	.3120	7.9138	0.0000

YEARS 30   MO PAYT .6788   AN CONST 8.15

#	INT	PRIN	BALANCE
1	7.1682	.9773	99.0227
2	7.0954	1.0500	97.9727
3	7.0173	1.1282	96.8445
4	6.9333	1.2121	95.6324
5	6.8431	1.3023	94.3300
6	6.7462	1.3993	92.9308
7	6.6420	1.5034	91.4273
8	6.5302	1.6153	89.8120
9	6.4099	1.7355	88.0765
10	6.2808	1.8647	86.2118
11	6.1420	2.0035	84.2084
12	5.9929	2.1526	82.0558
13	5.8327	2.3128	79.7430
14	5.6606	2.4849	77.2581
15	5.4756	2.6698	74.5883
16	5.2769	2.8685	71.7197
17	5.0634	3.0820	68.6377
18	4.8341	3.3114	65.3263
19	4.5876	3.5579	61.7685
20	4.3228	3.8226	57.9458
21	4.0383	4.1071	53.8387
22	3.7326	4.4128	49.4259
23	3.4042	4.7412	44.6846
24	3.0514	5.0941	39.5906
25	2.6722	5.4732	34.1173
26	2.2649	5.8806	28.2368
27	1.8273	6.3182	21.9186
28	1.3570	6.7884	15.1301
29	.8518	7.2937	7.8365
30	.3090	7.8365	0.0000

MONTHLY PAYMENT AMORTIZATION SCHEDULE PER $100

7.25 %

YEARS 2 — MO PAYT 4.4886 — AN CONST 53.87

#	INT	PRIN	BALANCE
1	5.6695	48.1937	51.8063
2	2.0569	51.8063	0.0000

YEARS 3 — MO PAYT 3.0992 — AN CONST 37.19

#	INT	PRIN	BALANCE
1	6.2348	30.9550	69.0450
2	3.9145	33.2754	35.7696
3	1.4202	35.7696	0.0000

YEARS 4 — MO PAYT 2.4062 — AN CONST 28.88

#	INT	PRIN	BALANCE
1	6.5168	22.3581	77.6419
2	4.8408	24.0341	53.6078
3	3.0393	25.8356	27.7722
4	1.1027	27.7722	0.0000

YEARS 5 — MO PAYT 1.9919 — AN CONST 23.91

#	INT	PRIN	BALANCE
1	6.6853	17.2179	82.7821
2	5.3947	18.5085	64.2736
3	4.0073	19.8959	44.3777
4	2.5160	21.3873	22.9904
5	.9128	22.9904	0.0000

YEARS 6 — MO PAYT 1.7169 — AN CONST 20.61

#	INT	PRIN	BALANCE
1	6.7972	13.8059	86.1941
2	5.7624	14.8408	71.3532
3	4.6499	15.9533	55.4000
4	3.4541	17.1491	38.2509
5	2.1686	18.4345	19.8164
6	.7868	19.8164	0.0000

YEARS 7 — MO PAYT 1.5215 — AN CONST 18.26

#	INT	PRIN	BALANCE
1	6.8767	11.3815	88.6185
2	6.0236	12.2346	76.3839
3	5.1065	13.1517	63.2322
4	4.1207	14.1375	49.0947
5	3.0610	15.1973	33.8974
6	1.9218	16.3364	17.5610
7	.6972	17.5610	0.0000

YEARS 8 — MO PAYT 1.3758 — AN CONST 16.52

#	INT	PRIN	BALANCE
1	6.9360	9.5741	90.4259
2	6.2183	10.2918	80.1341
3	5.4469	11.0633	69.0708
4	4.6176	11.8925	57.1783
5	3.7262	12.7840	44.3943
6	2.7679	13.7423	30.6520
7	1.7378	14.7723	15.8797
8	.6305	15.8797	0.0000

YEARS 9 — MO PAYT 1.2633 — AN CONST 15.16

#	INT	PRIN	BALANCE
1	6.9818	8.1781	91.8219
2	6.3688	8.7912	83.0307
3	5.7098	9.4501	73.5806
4	5.0014	10.1585	63.4221
5	4.2400	10.9200	52.5021
6	3.4214	11.7385	40.7636
7	2.5415	12.6184	28.1452
8	1.5957	13.5642	14.5810
9	.5789	14.5810	0.0000

YEARS 10 — MO PAYT 1.1740 — AN CONST 14.09

#	INT	PRIN	BALANCE
1	7.0181	7.0700	92.9300
2	6.4882	7.5999	85.3301
3	5.9185	8.1696	77.1604
4	5.3061	8.7820	68.3784
5	4.6478	9.4403	58.9382
6	3.9402	10.1479	48.7902
7	3.1795	10.9086	37.8817
8	2.3619	11.7263	26.1554
9	1.4829	12.6053	13.5501
10	.5380	13.5501	0.0000

YEARS 11 — MO PAYT 1.1016 — AN CONST 13.22

#	INT	PRIN	BALANCE
1	7.0476	6.1711	93.8289
2	6.5850	6.6337	87.1952
3	6.0878	7.1309	80.0643
4	5.5533	7.6655	72.3988
5	4.9787	8.2401	64.1587
6	4.3610	8.8577	55.3010
7	3.6971	9.5217	45.7793
8	2.9833	10.2354	35.5439
9	2.2161	11.0026	24.5413
10	1.3914	11.8274	12.7139
11	.5048	12.7139	0.0000

YEARS 12 — MO PAYT 1.0418 — AN CONST 12.51

#	INT	PRIN	BALANCE
1	7.0719	5.4291	94.5709
2	6.6650	5.8361	88.7348
3	6.2275	6.2735	82.4613
4	5.7573	6.7438	75.7175
5	5.2518	7.2493	68.4682
6	4.7084	7.7927	60.6755
7	4.1242	8.3768	52.2987
8	3.4963	9.0047	43.2939
9	2.8214	9.6797	33.6142
10	2.0958	10.4053	23.2089
11	1.3158	11.1852	12.0237
12	.4774	12.0237	0.0000

YEARS 13 — MO PAYT .9917 — AN CONST 11.91

#	INT	PRIN	BALANCE
1	7.0923	4.8077	95.1923
2	6.7319	5.1681	90.0242
3	6.3446	5.5555	84.4687
4	5.9281	5.9719	78.4968
5	5.4805	6.4196	72.0772
6	4.9993	6.9008	65.1764
7	4.4820	7.4180	57.7584
8	3.9260	7.9741	49.7843
9	3.3282	8.5718	41.2125
10	2.6857	9.2143	31.9981
11	1.9950	9.9050	22.0931
12	1.2526	10.6475	11.4456
13	.4544	11.4456	0.0000

YEARS 14 — MO PAYT .9492 — AN CONST 11.40

#	INT	PRIN	BALANCE
1	7.1096	4.2810	95.7190
2	6.7887	4.6019	91.1171
3	6.4438	4.9469	86.1702

YEARS 15 — MO PAYT .9129 — AN CONST 10.96

#	INT	PRIN	BALANCE
1	7.1244	3.8300	96.1700
2	6.8373	4.1170	92.0530
3	6.5287	4.4257	87.6273
4	6.1970	4.7574	82.8699
5	5.8404	5.1140	77.7559
6	5.4570	5.4973	72.2586
7	5.0449	5.9094	66.3492
8	4.6020	6.3524	59.9968
9	4.1258	6.8285	53.1683
10	3.6140	7.3404	45.8279
11	3.0637	7.8906	37.9373
12	2.4723	8.4821	29.4552
13	1.8365	9.1179	20.3374
14	1.1530	9.8013	10.5360
15	.4183	10.5360	0.0000

YEARS 16 — MO PAYT .8815 — AN CONST 10.58

#	INT	PRIN	BALANCE
1	7.1372	3.4403	96.5597
2	6.8793	3.6982	92.8615
3	6.6021	3.9754	88.8861
4	6.3041	4.2734	84.6127
5	5.9838	4.5937	80.0190
6	5.6394	4.9381	75.0809
7	5.2693	5.3082	69.7727
8	4.8714	5.7061	64.0666
9	4.4437	6.1338	57.9328
10	3.9839	6.5936	51.3391
11	3.4896	7.0879	44.2513
12	2.9583	7.6191	36.6321
13	2.3872	8.1903	28.4419
14	1.7733	8.8042	19.6377
15	1.1134	9.4641	10.1736
16	.4039	10.1736	0.0000

YEARS 17 — MO PAYT .8541 — AN CONST 10.25

#	INT	PRIN	BALANCE
1	7.1483	3.1012	96.8988
2	6.9158	3.3336	93.5652
3	6.6660	3.5835	89.9817
4	6.3973	3.8521	86.1296
5	6.1086	4.1409	81.9887
6	5.7982	4.4513	77.5374
7	5.4645	4.7849	72.7525
8	5.1059	5.1436	67.6089
9	4.7203	5.5291	62.0798
10	4.3059	5.9436	56.1362
11	3.8603	6.3891	49.7470
12	3.3814	6.8680	42.8790
13	2.8666	7.3829	35.4961
14	2.3132	7.9363	27.5599
15	1.7183	8.5312	19.0287
16	1.0788	9.1706	9.8581
17	.3914	9.8581	0.0000

YEARS 18 — MO PAYT .8302 — AN CONST 9.97

#	INT	PRIN	BALANCE
1	7.1580	2.8040	97.1960
2	6.9479	3.0142	94.1818
3	6.7219	3.2402	90.9416
4	6.4790	3.4830	87.4586
5	6.2180	3.7441	83.7145
6	5.9373	4.0248	79.6897
7	5.6356	4.3265	75.3633
8	5.3113	4.6508	70.7125
9	4.9627	4.9994	65.7131
10	4.5880	5.3741	60.3390
11	4.1851	5.7769	54.5621
12	3.7521	6.2100	48.3521
13	3.2866	6.6755	41.6766
14	2.7862	7.1758	34.5008
15	2.2483	7.7137	26.7871
16	1.6701	8.2919	18.4951
17	1.0486	8.9135	9.5816
18	.3804	9.5816	0.0000

YEARS 19 — MO PAYT .8091 — AN CONST 9.71

#	INT	PRIN	BALANCE
1	7.1666	2.5422	97.4578
2	6.9761	2.7327	94.7251
3	6.7712	2.9376	91.7875
4	6.5510	3.1578	88.6297
5	6.3143	3.3945	85.2352
6	6.0599	3.6489	81.5863
7	5.7864	3.9224	77.6639
8	5.4923	4.2165	73.4474
9	5.1763	4.5325	68.9149
10	4.8365	4.8723	64.0426
11	4.4713	5.2375	58.8051
12	4.0787	5.6301	53.1750
13	3.6567	6.0521	47.1229
14	3.2031	6.5058	40.6172
15	2.7154	6.9934	33.6237
16	2.1912	7.5176	26.1061
17	1.6277	8.0811	18.0249
18	1.0219	8.6869	9.3381
19	.3708	9.3381	0.0000

YEARS 20 — MO PAYT .7904 — AN CONST 9.49

#	INT	PRIN	BALANCE
1	7.1742	2.3103	97.6897
2	7.0011	2.4835	95.2063
3	6.8149	2.6696	92.5367
4	6.6148	2.8697	89.6669
5	6.3997	3.0848	86.5821
6	6.1685	3.3161	83.2661
7	5.9199	3.5646	79.7014
8	5.6527	3.8318	75.8696
9	5.3655	4.1191	71.7505
10	5.0567	4.4278	67.3227
11	4.7248	4.7597	62.5630
12	4.3680	5.1165	57.4465
13	3.9845	5.5000	51.9465
14	3.5722	5.9123	46.0342
15	3.1291	6.3555	39.6788
16	2.6527	6.8319	32.8469
17	2.1406	7.3440	25.5030
18	1.5901	7.8944	17.6085
19	.9983	8.4862	9.1223
20	.3622	9.1223	0.0000

YEARS 21 — MO PAYT .7737 — AN CONST 9.29

#	INT	PRIN	BALANCE
1	7.1810	2.1040	97.8960
2	7.0233	2.2617	95.6344
3	6.8538	2.4312	93.2032

#	INT	PRIN	BALANCE
4	6.6715	2.6134	90.5897
5	6.4756	2.8093	87.7804
6	6.2650	3.0199	84.7605
7	6.0387	3.2463	81.5142
8	5.7953	3.4896	78.0245
9	5.5338	3.7512	74.2733
10	5.2526	4.0324	70.2409
11	4.9503	4.3346	65.9063
12	4.6254	4.6596	61.2467
13	4.2761	5.0088	56.2379
14	3.9007	5.3843	50.8536
15	3.4971	5.7879	45.0657
16	3.0632	6.2217	38.8440
17	2.5968	6.6881	32.1558
18	2.0955	7.1894	24.9664
19	1.5566	7.7284	17.2380
20	.9773	8.3077	8.9304
21	.3546	8.9304	0.0000

YEARS 22	MO PAYT .7589	AN CONST 9.11	
#	INT	PRIN	BALANCE
1	7.1870	1.9197	98.0803
2	7.0431	2.0636	96.0168
3	6.8885	2.2183	93.7985
4	6.7222	2.3845	91.4140
5	6.5434	2.5633	88.8507
6	6.3513	2.7554	86.0953
7	6.1448	2.9620	83.1333
8	5.9227	3.1840	79.9494
9	5.6841	3.4226	76.5267
10	5.4275	3.6792	72.8475
11	5.1517	3.9550	68.8925
12	4.8553	4.2514	64.6411
13	4.5366	4.5701	60.0710
14	4.1940	4.9127	55.1583
15	3.8258	5.2809	49.8774
16	3.4299	5.6768	44.2006
17	3.0044	6.1023	38.0983
18	2.5470	6.5597	31.5386
19	2.0553	7.0514	24.4871
20	1.5267	7.5800	16.9071
21	.9585	8.1482	8.7590
22	.3478	8.7590	0.0000

YEARS 23	MO PAYT .7456	AN CONST 8.95	
#	INT	PRIN	BALANCE
1	7.1925	1.7545	98.2455
2	7.0609	1.8860	96.3595
3	6.9196	2.0274	94.3322
4	6.7676	2.1793	92.1528
5	6.6042	2.3427	89.8101
6	6.4286	2.5183	87.2918
7	6.2399	2.7071	84.5848
8	6.0370	2.9100	81.6748
9	5.8188	3.1281	78.5467
10	5.5844	3.3626	75.1841
11	5.3323	3.6146	71.5694
12	5.0614	3.8856	67.6838
13	4.7701	4.1768	63.5070
14	4.4550	4.4899	59.0171
15	4.1204	4.8265	54.1906
16	3.7587	5.1883	49.0023
17	3.3698	5.5772	43.4251
18	2.9517	5.9952	37.4298
19	2.5023	6.4446	30.9852
20	2.0192	6.9277	24.0575
21	1.4999	7.4470	16.6105
22	.9417	8.0052	8.6053
23	.3417	8.6053	0.0000

YEARS 24	MO PAYT .7336	AN CONST 8.81	
#	INT	PRIN	BALANCE
1	7.1973	1.6059	98.3941
2	7.0770	1.7263	96.6678
3	6.9476	1.8557	94.8121
4	6.8085	1.9948	92.8172
5	6.6589	2.1443	90.6729
6	6.4982	2.3051	88.3678
7	6.3254	2.4779	85.8900
8	6.1397	2.6636	83.2264
9	5.9400	2.8633	80.3631
10	5.7254	3.0779	77.2853
11	5.4947	3.3086	73.9767
12	5.2467	3.5566	70.4201
13	4.9801	3.8232	66.5969
14	4.6935	4.1098	62.4871
15	4.3854	4.4178	58.0693
16	4.0543	4.7490	53.3203
17	3.6983	5.1050	48.2153
18	3.3156	5.4876	42.7277
19	2.9043	5.8990	36.8288
20	2.4621	6.3411	30.4876
21	1.9868	6.8165	23.6712
22	1.4759	7.3274	16.3437
23	.9266	7.8767	8.4671
24	.3362	8.4671	0.0000

YEARS 25	MO PAYT .7228	AN CONST 8.68	
#	INT	PRIN	BALANCE
1	7.2017	1.4720	98.5280
2	7.0914	1.5823	96.9458
3	6.9728	1.7009	95.2449
4	6.8453	1.8284	93.4165
5	6.7082	1.9654	91.4510
6	6.5609	2.1128	89.3382
7	6.4025	2.2711	87.0671
8	6.2323	2.4414	84.6257
9	6.0493	2.6244	82.0013
10	5.8526	2.8211	79.1802
11	5.6411	3.0326	76.1477
12	5.4138	3.2599	72.8878
13	5.1694	3.5042	69.3835
14	4.9068	3.7669	65.6166
15	4.6244	4.0493	61.5673
16	4.3209	4.3528	57.2145
17	3.9946	4.6791	52.5354
18	3.6439	5.0298	47.5056
19	3.2668	5.4068	42.0988
20	2.8615	5.8121	36.2866
21	2.4259	6.2478	30.0388
22	1.9576	6.7161	23.3227
23	1.4541	7.2196	16.1032
24	.9130	7.7607	8.3424
25	.3312	8.3424	0.0000

YEARS 26	MO PAYT .7130	AN CONST 8.56	
#	INT	PRIN	BALANCE
1	7.2057	1.3508	98.6492
2	7.1044	1.4521	97.1971
3	6.9956	1.5609	95.6362
4	6.8786	1.6779	93.9583
5	6.7528	1.8037	92.1546
6	6.6176	1.9389	90.2157
7	6.4723	2.0842	88.1314
8	6.3161	2.2405	85.8910
9	6.1481	2.4084	83.4826
10	5.9676	2.5889	80.8936
11	5.7735	2.7830	78.1106
12	5.5649	2.9916	75.1190
13	5.3407	3.2159	71.9032
14	5.0996	3.4569	68.4463
15	4.8405	3.7160	64.7302
16	4.5619	3.9946	60.7357
17	4.2625	4.2940	56.4417
18	3.9406	4.6159	51.8258
19	3.5946	4.9619	46.8639
20	3.2227	5.3338	41.5301
21	2.8229	5.7336	35.7965
22	2.3931	6.1634	29.6331
23	1.9311	6.6254	23.0077
24	1.4345	7.1220	15.8856
25	.9006	7.6559	8.2298
26	.3268	8.2298	0.0000

YEARS 27	MO PAYT .7042	AN CONST 8.46	
#	INT	PRIN	BALANCE
1	7.2093	1.2410	98.7590
2	7.1163	1.3341	97.4249
3	7.0163	1.4341	95.9909
4	6.9088	1.5415	94.4493
5	6.7932	1.6571	92.7922
6	6.6690	1.7813	91.0109
7	6.5355	1.9148	89.0961
8	6.3920	2.0584	87.0377
9	6.2377	2.2127	84.8251
10	6.0718	2.3785	82.4465
11	5.8935	2.5568	79.8897
12	5.7019	2.7485	77.1413
13	5.4958	2.9545	74.1868
14	5.2744	3.1759	71.0108
15	5.0363	3.4140	67.5968
16	4.7804	3.6699	63.9269
17	4.5053	3.9450	59.9819
18	4.2096	4.2407	55.7412
19	3.8917	4.5586	51.1826
20	3.5500	4.9003	46.2823
21	3.1827	5.2676	41.0147
22	2.7879	5.6625	35.3522
23	2.3634	6.0869	29.2653
24	1.9071	6.5432	22.7221
25	1.4167	7.0336	15.6885
26	.8895	7.5609	8.1276
27	.3227	8.1276	0.0000

YEARS 28	MO PAYT .6962	AN CONST 8.36	
#	INT	PRIN	BALANCE
1	7.2126	1.1413	98.8587
2	7.1270	1.2269	97.6318
3	7.0351	1.3188	96.3130
4	6.9362	1.4177	94.8953
5	6.8299	1.5240	93.3714
6	6.7157	1.6382	91.7332
7	6.5929	1.7610	89.9722
8	6.4609	1.8930	88.0792
9	6.3190	2.0349	86.0443
10	6.1665	2.1874	83.8569
11	6.0025	2.3514	81.5056
12	5.8263	2.5276	78.9779
13	5.6368	2.7171	76.2608
14	5.4331	2.9208	73.3401
15	5.2142	3.1397	70.2004
16	4.9788	3.3750	66.8253
17	4.7259	3.6280	63.1973
18	4.4539	3.9000	59.2973
19	4.1616	4.1923	55.1050
20	3.8473	4.5066	50.5985
21	3.5095	4.8444	45.7541
22	3.1464	5.2075	40.5466
23	2.7560	5.5978	34.9488
24	2.3364	6.0174	28.9313
25	1.8854	6.4685	22.4628
26	1.4005	6.9534	15.5094
27	.8793	7.4746	8.0349
28	.3190	8.0349	0.0000

YEARS 29	MO PAYT .6888	AN CONST 8.27	
#	INT	PRIN	BALANCE
1	7.2155	1.0506	98.9494
2	7.1368	1.1293	97.8201
3	7.0521	1.2140	96.6061
4	6.9611	1.3050	95.3012
5	6.8633	1.4028	93.8984
6	6.7582	1.5079	92.3904
7	6.6451	1.6210	90.7694
8	6.5236	1.7425	89.0270
9	6.3930	1.8731	87.1539
10	6.2526	2.0135	85.1404
11	6.1017	2.1644	82.9760
12	5.9395	2.3267	80.6493
13	5.7650	2.5011	78.1482
14	5.5776	2.6885	75.4597
15	5.3760	2.8901	72.5696
16	5.1594	3.1067	69.4629
17	4.9265	3.3396	66.1233
18	4.6762	3.5899	62.5334
19	4.4071	3.8590	58.6744
20	4.1178	4.1483	54.5261
21	3.8069	4.4592	50.0669
22	3.4726	4.7935	45.2734
23	3.1133	5.1528	40.1206
24	2.7271	5.5390	34.5816
25	2.3119	5.9542	28.6274
26	1.8656	6.4005	22.2268
27	1.3858	6.8803	15.3465
28	.8701	7.3961	7.9505
29	.3157	7.9505	0.0000

YEARS 30	MO PAYT .6822	AN CONST 8.19	
#	INT	PRIN	BALANCE
1	7.2183	.9679	99.0321
2	7.1457	1.0404	97.9917
3	7.0677	1.1184	96.8733
4	6.9839	1.2022	95.6711
5	6.8938	1.2923	94.3788
6	6.7969	1.3892	92.9896
7	6.6928	1.4933	91.4962
8	6.5808	1.6053	89.8909
9	6.4605	1.7256	88.1653
10	6.3312	1.8550	86.3104
11	6.1921	1.9940	84.3163
12	6.0426	2.1435	82.1729
13	5.8820	2.3041	79.8687
14	5.7093	2.4769	77.3919
15	5.5236	2.6625	74.7293
16	5.3240	2.8621	71.8672
17	5.1095	3.0766	68.7906
18	4.8789	3.3073	65.4833
19	4.6309	3.5552	61.9282
20	4.3645	3.8217	58.1065
21	4.0780	4.1081	53.9984
22	3.7701	4.4161	49.5823
23	3.4390	4.7471	44.8352
24	3.0832	5.1029	39.7323
25	2.7007	5.4854	34.2469
26	2.2895	5.8966	28.3503
27	1.8475	6.3386	22.0117
28	1.3724	6.8137	15.1980
29	.8616	7.3245	7.8735
30	.3126	7.8735	0.0000

YEARS 2 — MO PAYT 4.4909 — AN CONST 53.90

#	INT	PRIN	BALANCE
1	5.7091	48.1813	51.8187
2	2.0718	51.8187	0.0000

YEARS 3 — MO PAYT 3.1014 — AN CONST 37.22

#	INT	PRIN	BALANCE
1	6.2784	30.9389	69.0611
2	3.9428	33.2746	35.7865
3	1.4308	35.7865	0.0000

YEARS 4 — MO PAYT 2.4086 — AN CONST 28.91

#	INT	PRIN	BALANCE
1	6.5623	22.3405	77.6595
2	4.8758	24.0270	53.6325
3	3.0619	25.8409	27.7917
4	1.1111	27.7917	0.0000

YEARS 5 — MO PAYT 1.9943 — AN CONST 23.94

#	INT	PRIN	BALANCE
1	6.7321	17.1996	82.8004
2	5.4337	18.4980	64.3024
3	4.0372	19.8945	44.4080
4	2.5353	21.3964	23.0116
5	.9200	23.0116	0.0000

YEARS 6 — MO PAYT 1.7193 — AN CONST 20.64

#	INT	PRIN	BALANCE
1	6.8448	13.7874	86.2126
2	5.8039	14.8282	71.3845
3	4.6845	15.9476	55.4368
4	3.4806	17.1515	38.2853
5	2.1858	18.4464	19.8389
6	.7932	19.8389	0.0000

YEARS 7 — MO PAYT 1.5240 — AN CONST 18.29

#	INT	PRIN	BALANCE
1	6.9248	11.3629	88.6371
2	6.0670	12.2207	76.4164
3	5.1444	13.1433	63.2731
4	4.1522	14.1355	49.1376
5	3.0851	15.2026	33.9350
6	1.9374	16.3503	17.5846
7	.7031	17.5846	0.0000

YEARS 8 — MO PAYT 1.3783 — AN CONST 16.55

#	INT	PRIN	BALANCE
1	6.9845	9.5557	90.4443
2	6.2631	10.2771	80.1672
3	5.4873	11.0529	69.1143
4	4.6528	11.8874	57.2269
5	3.7554	12.7848	44.4422
6	2.7903	13.7499	30.6922
7	1.7523	14.7879	15.9043
8	.6359	15.9043	0.0000

YEARS 9 — MO PAYT 1.2659 — AN CONST 15.20

#	INT	PRIN	BALANCE
1	7.0306	8.1599	91.8401
2	6.4146	8.7760	83.0641
3	5.7520	9.4385	73.6256
4	5.0395	10.1510	63.4746
5	4.2732	10.9173	52.5572
6	3.4490	11.7415	40.8157
7	2.5626	12.6279	28.1878
8	1.6093	13.5812	14.6065
9	.5840	14.6065	0.0000

YEARS 10 — MO PAYT 1.1766 — AN CONST 14.12

#	INT	PRIN	BALANCE
1	7.0671	7.0521	92.9479
2	6.5348	7.5845	85.3634
3	5.9622	8.1571	77.2063
4	5.3464	8.7729	68.4334
5	4.6841	9.4352	58.9983
6	3.9718	10.1474	48.8508
7	3.2058	10.9135	37.9373
8	2.3819	11.7374	26.1999
9	1.4958	12.6235	13.5765
10	.5428	13.5765	0.0000

YEARS 11 — MO PAYT 1.1042 — AN CONST 13.26

#	INT	PRIN	BALANCE
1	7.0968	6.1536	93.8464
2	6.6323	6.6182	87.2282
3	6.1326	7.1178	80.1105
4	5.5953	7.6551	72.4553
5	5.0174	8.2330	64.2223
6	4.3959	8.8546	55.3678
7	3.7274	9.5230	45.8447
8	3.0085	10.2419	35.6028
9	2.2353	11.0151	24.5877
10	1.4037	11.8467	12.7410
11	.5094	12.7410	0.0000

YEARS 12 — MO PAYT 1.0444 — AN CONST 12.54

#	INT	PRIN	BALANCE
1	7.1213	5.4120	94.5880
2	6.7127	5.8206	88.7674
3	6.2733	6.2600	82.5074
4	5.8007	6.7326	75.7749
5	5.2925	7.2408	68.5341
6	4.7459	7.7875	60.7466
7	4.1580	8.3753	52.3713
8	3.5257	9.0076	43.3636
9	2.8457	9.6876	33.6760
10	2.1143	10.4190	23.2570
11	1.3278	11.2055	12.0515
12	.4818	12.0515	0.0000

YEARS 13 — MO PAYT .9944 — AN CONST 11.94

#	INT	PRIN	BALANCE
1	7.1418	4.7910	95.2090
2	6.7801	5.1527	90.0563
3	6.3911	5.5417	84.5146
4	5.9721	5.9601	78.5545
5	5.5228	6.4100	72.1445
6	5.0389	6.8939	65.2506
7	4.5185	7.4144	57.8362
8	3.9587	7.9741	49.8621
9	3.3568	8.5761	41.2861
10	2.7093	9.2235	32.0626
11	2.0130	9.9198	22.1428
12	1.2642	10.6687	11.4741
13	.4587	11.4741	0.0000

YEARS 14 — MO PAYT .9520 — AN CONST 11.43

#	INT	PRIN	BALANCE
1	7.1592	4.2647	95.7353
2	6.8372	4.5867	91.1486
3	6.4910	4.9330	86.2156
4	6.1186	5.3054	80.9102
5	5.7180	5.7059	75.2043
6	5.2873	6.1366	69.0677
7	4.8240	6.5999	62.4678
8	4.3258	7.0982	55.3696
9	3.7899	7.6340	47.7356
10	3.2136	8.2103	39.5253
11	2.5938	8.8301	30.6952
12	1.9272	9.4968	21.1984
13	1.2102	10.2137	10.9847
14	.4392	10.9847	0.0000

YEARS 15 — MO PAYT .9157 — AN CONST 10.99

#	INT	PRIN	BALANCE
1	7.1741	3.8141	96.1859
2	6.8861	4.1021	92.0838
3	6.5764	4.4118	87.6720
4	6.2434	4.7448	82.9272
5	5.8852	5.1030	77.8242
6	5.5000	5.4883	72.3359
7	5.0856	5.9026	66.4334
8	4.6400	6.3482	60.0852
9	4.1608	6.8274	53.2578
10	3.6454	7.3428	45.9149
11	3.0910	7.8972	38.0178
12	2.4949	8.4933	29.5244
13	1.8537	9.1345	20.3899
14	1.1641	9.8241	10.5658
15	.4224	10.5658	0.0000

YEARS 16 — MO PAYT .8843 — AN CONST 10.62

#	INT	PRIN	BALANCE
1	7.1869	3.4250	96.5750
2	6.9284	3.6835	92.8915
3	6.6503	3.9616	88.9300
4	6.3512	4.2607	84.6693
5	6.0296	4.5823	80.0870
6	5.6836	4.9282	75.1588
7	5.3116	5.3003	69.8585
8	4.9114	5.7004	64.1581
9	4.4811	6.1308	58.0273
10	4.0183	6.5936	51.4337
11	3.5205	7.0913	44.3424
12	2.9852	7.6267	36.7157
13	2.4094	8.2025	28.5132
14	1.7902	8.8217	19.6915
15	1.1242	9.4876	10.2039
16	.4080	10.2039	0.0000

YEARS 17 — MO PAYT .8570 — AN CONST 10.29

#	INT	PRIN	BALANCE
1	7.1981	3.0863	96.9137
2	6.9651	3.3192	93.5945
3	6.7145	3.5698	90.0247
4	6.4450	3.8393	86.1853
5	6.1552	4.1292	82.0562
6	5.8435	4.4409	77.6153
7	5.5082	4.7761	72.8392
8	5.1477	5.1367	67.7025
9	4.7599	5.5245	62.1780
10	4.3428	5.9415	56.2364
11	3.8943	6.3901	49.8463
12	3.4119	6.8725	42.9739
13	2.8930	7.3913	35.5825
14	2.3350	7.9493	27.6332
15	1.7349	8.5494	19.0838
16	1.0895	9.1948	9.8890
17	.3954	9.8890	0.0000

YEARS 18 — MO PAYT .8331 — AN CONST 10.00

#	INT	PRIN	BALANCE
1	7.2079	2.7896	97.2104
2	6.9973	3.0002	94.2103
3	6.7708	3.2267	90.9836
4	6.5272	3.4702	87.5134
5	6.2652	3.7322	83.7811
6	5.9835	4.0140	79.7672
7	5.6805	4.3170	75.4502
8	5.3546	4.6429	70.8073
9	5.0041	4.9934	65.8138
10	4.6271	5.3704	60.4435
11	4.2217	5.7758	54.6677
12	3.7856	6.2118	48.4558
13	3.3167	6.6808	41.7751
14	2.8123	7.1851	34.5899
15	2.2699	7.7276	26.8624
16	1.6865	8.3109	18.5515
17	1.0591	8.9383	9.6131
18	.3843	9.6131	0.0000

YEARS 19 — MO PAYT .8121 — AN CONST 9.75

#	INT	PRIN	BALANCE
1	7.2165	2.5282	97.4718
2	7.0257	2.7190	94.7528
3	6.8204	2.9243	91.8285
4	6.5996	3.1451	88.6834
5	6.3622	3.3825	85.3009
6	6.1068	3.6379	81.6630
7	5.8322	3.9125	77.7505
8	5.5368	4.2079	73.5426
9	5.2192	4.5255	69.0171
10	4.8775	4.8672	64.1500
11	4.5101	5.2346	58.9153
12	4.1149	5.6298	53.2856
13	3.6899	6.0548	47.2308
14	3.2328	6.5119	40.7189
15	2.7412	7.0035	33.7154
16	2.2125	7.5322	26.1833
17	1.6439	8.1008	18.0824
18	1.0323	8.7124	9.3701
19	.3746	9.3701	0.0000

YEARS 20 — MO PAYT .7934 — AN CONST 9.53

#	INT	PRIN	BALANCE
1	7.2242	2.2967	97.7033
2	7.0508	2.4701	95.2331
3	6.8643	2.6566	92.5765
4	6.6637	2.8572	89.7194
5	6.4481	3.0728	86.6466
6	6.2161	3.3048	83.3417
7	5.9666	3.5543	79.7874
8	5.6983	3.8226	75.9648
9	5.4097	4.1112	71.8536
10	5.0993	4.4216	67.4320
11	4.7655	4.7554	62.6766
12	4.4065	5.1144	57.5622
13	4.0204	5.5005	52.0617
14	3.6052	5.9157	46.1460
15	3.1586	6.3623	39.7837
16	2.6783	6.8426	32.9411
17	2.1617	7.3592	25.5819
18	1.6061	7.9148	17.6671
19	1.0086	8.5123	9.1549
20	.3660	9.1549	0.0000

YEARS 21 — MO PAYT .7768 — AN CONST 9.33

#	INT	PRIN	BALANCE
1	7.2310	2.0909	97.9091
2	7.0731	2.2487	95.6604
3	6.9034	2.4185	93.2419

MONTHLY PAYMENT AMORTIZATION SCHEDULE PER $100   7.30 %

#	INT	PRIN	BALANCE
4	6.7208	2.6011	90.6409
5	6.5244	2.7974	87.8435
6	6.3132	3.0086	84.8349
7	6.0861	3.2357	81.5992
8	5.8418	3.4800	78.1192
9	5.5791	3.7427	74.3765
10	5.2966	4.0253	70.3512
11	4.9927	4.3291	66.0221
12	4.6659	4.6560	61.3661
13	4.3144	5.0074	56.3587
14	3.9364	5.3855	50.9732
15	3.5298	5.7920	45.1812
16	3.0925	6.2293	38.9519
17	2.6223	6.6996	32.2523
18	2.1165	7.2053	25.0470
19	1.5726	7.7493	17.2977
20	.9875	8.3343	8.9635
21	.3584	8.9635	0.0000

YEARS 22   MO PAYT .7620   AN CONST 9.15

#	INT	PRIN	BALANCE
1	7.2370	1.9070	98.0930
2	7.0931	2.0510	96.0420
3	6.9382	2.2058	93.8361
4	6.7717	2.3724	91.4638
5	6.5926	2.5514	88.9123
6	6.4000	2.7441	86.1683
7	6.1928	2.9512	83.2171
8	5.9700	3.1740	80.0430
9	5.7304	3.4136	76.6294
10	5.4727	3.6713	72.9581
11	5.1956	3.9485	69.0096
12	4.8975	4.2466	64.7630
13	4.5769	4.5672	60.1958
14	4.2321	4.9119	55.2839
15	3.8613	5.2828	50.0011
16	3.4625	5.6816	44.3196
17	3.0336	6.1105	38.2091
18	2.5723	6.5718	31.6373
19	2.0761	7.0679	24.5694
20	1.5426	7.6015	16.9679
21	.9687	8.1753	8.7925
22	.3515	8.7925	0.0000

YEARS 23   MO PAYT .7487   AN CONST 8.99

#	INT	PRIN	BALANCE
1	7.2425	1.7423	98.2577
2	7.1109	1.8738	96.3839
3	6.9695	2.0153	94.3687
4	6.8173	2.1674	92.2013
5	6.6537	2.3310	89.8702
6	6.4778	2.5070	87.3633
7	6.2885	2.6963	84.6670
8	6.0849	2.8998	81.7672
9	5.8660	3.1187	78.6485
10	5.6306	3.3542	75.2943
11	5.3774	3.6074	71.6869
12	5.1050	3.8797	67.8072
13	4.8122	4.1726	63.6347
14	4.4972	4.4876	59.1471
15	4.1584	4.8264	54.3207
16	3.7940	5.1907	49.1300
17	3.4022	5.5826	43.5474
18	2.9807	6.0040	37.5434
19	2.5275	6.4573	31.0861
20	2.0400	6.9448	24.1413
21	1.5157	7.4690	16.6722
22	.9518	8.0329	8.6393
23	.3454	8.6393	0.0000

YEARS 24   MO PAYT .7368   AN CONST 8.85

#	INT	PRIN	BALANCE
1	7.2474	1.5942	98.4058
2	7.1270	1.7145	96.6913
3	6.9976	1.8439	94.8474
4	6.8584	1.9831	92.8643
5	6.7087	2.1328	90.7314
6	6.5477	2.2939	88.4376
7	6.3745	2.4670	85.9705
8	6.1882	2.6533	83.3173
9	5.9879	2.8536	80.4637
10	5.7725	3.0690	77.3947
11	5.5408	3.3007	74.0940
12	5.2917	3.5499	70.5442
13	5.0237	3.8179	66.7263
14	4.7354	4.1061	62.6202
15	4.4255	4.4161	58.2042
16	4.0921	4.7494	53.4547
17	3.7335	5.1080	48.3468
18	3.3479	5.4936	42.8532
19	2.9332	5.9083	36.9449
20	2.4872	6.3544	30.5905
21	2.0075	6.8341	23.7564
22	1.4915	7.3500	16.4065
23	.9367	7.9049	8.5016
24	.3399	8.5016	0.0000

YEARS 25   MO PAYT .7260   AN CONST 8.72

#	INT	PRIN	BALANCE
1	7.2518	1.4606	98.5394
2	7.1415	1.5709	96.9685
3	7.0229	1.6895	95.2791
4	6.8954	1.8170	93.4621
5	6.7582	1.9542	91.5079
6	6.6107	2.1017	89.4062
7	6.4520	2.2604	87.1459
8	6.2814	2.4310	84.7149
9	6.0979	2.6145	82.1003
10	5.9005	2.8119	79.2884
11	5.6882	3.0242	76.2643
12	5.4599	3.2525	73.0118
13	5.2144	3.4980	69.5138
14	4.9503	3.7621	65.7517
15	4.6663	4.0461	61.7056
16	4.3608	4.3515	57.3540
17	4.0323	4.6801	52.6740
18	3.6790	5.0334	47.6406
19	3.2990	5.4134	42.2273
20	2.8904	5.8220	36.4052
21	2.4508	6.2615	30.1437
22	1.9781	6.7342	23.4095
23	1.4697	7.2426	16.1668
24	.9230	7.7894	8.3774
25	.3349	8.3774	0.0000

YEARS 26   MO PAYT .7163   AN CONST 8.60

#	INT	PRIN	BALANCE
1	7.2558	1.3399	98.6601
2	7.1546	1.4410	97.2191
3	7.0458	1.5498	95.6693
4	6.9288	1.6668	94.0024
5	6.8030	1.7927	92.2098
6	6.6677	1.9280	90.2818
7	6.5221	2.0735	88.2083
8	6.3656	2.2301	85.9782
9	6.1972	2.3984	83.5798
10	6.0162	2.5795	81.0003
11	5.8214	2.7742	78.2261
12	5.6120	2.9837	75.2424
13	5.3867	3.2089	72.0335
14	5.1445	3.4511	68.5824
15	4.8840	3.7117	64.8707
16	4.6038	3.9919	60.8788
17	4.3024	4.2932	56.5856
18	3.9783	4.6174	51.9682
19	3.6297	4.9659	47.0023
20	3.2548	5.3408	41.6615
21	2.8516	5.7440	35.9175
22	2.4180	6.1776	29.7398
23	1.9516	6.6440	23.0958
24	1.4501	7.1456	15.9502
25	.9106	7.6850	8.2652
26	.3305	8.2652	0.0000

YEARS 27   MO PAYT .7075   AN CONST 8.49

#	INT	PRIN	BALANCE
1	7.2594	1.2305	98.7695
2	7.1665	1.3234	97.4461
3	7.0666	1.4233	96.0228
4	6.9591	1.5307	94.4921
5	6.8436	1.6463	92.8457
6	6.7193	1.7706	91.0752
7	6.5856	1.9043	89.1709
8	6.4419	2.0480	87.1229
9	6.2872	2.2026	84.9202
10	6.1210	2.3689	82.5513
11	5.9421	2.5477	80.0036
12	5.7498	2.7401	77.2635
13	5.5429	2.9469	74.3166
14	5.3205	3.1694	71.1472
15	5.0812	3.4087	67.7385
16	4.8239	3.6660	64.0725
17	4.5471	3.9428	60.1297
18	4.2495	4.2404	55.8893
19	3.9293	4.5605	51.3287
20	3.5850	4.9048	46.4239
21	3.2148	5.2751	41.1488
22	2.8165	5.6733	35.4755
23	2.3882	6.1016	29.3739
24	1.9276	6.5623	22.8116
25	1.4322	7.0577	15.7539
26	.8994	7.5905	8.1635
27	.3264	8.1635	0.0000

YEARS 28   MO PAYT .6995   AN CONST 8.40

#	INT	PRIN	BALANCE
1	7.2626	1.1312	98.8688
2	7.1773	1.2166	97.6522
3	7.0854	1.3084	96.3438
4	6.9866	1.4072	94.9366
5	6.8804	1.5134	93.4232
6	6.7661	1.6277	91.7955
7	6.6433	1.7506	90.0449
8	6.5111	1.8827	88.1622
9	6.3690	2.0249	86.1374
10	6.2161	2.1777	83.9596
11	6.0517	2.3421	81.6175
12	5.8749	2.5189	79.0986
13	5.6847	2.7091	76.3895
14	5.4802	2.9136	73.4759
15	5.2603	3.1336	70.3423
16	5.0237	3.3701	66.9722
17	4.7693	3.6245	63.3477
18	4.4957	3.8982	59.4495
19	4.2014	4.1924	55.2571
20	3.8849	4.5089	50.7481
21	3.5445	4.8493	45.8988
22	3.1784	5.2154	40.6834
23	2.7847	5.6092	35.0742
24	2.3612	6.0326	29.0416
25	1.9058	6.4880	22.5536
26	1.4160	6.9778	15.5757
27	.8892	7.5046	8.0711
28	.3227	8.0711	0.0000

YEARS 29   MO PAYT .6922   AN CONST 8.31

#	INT	PRIN	BALANCE
1	7.2656	1.0408	98.9592
2	7.1871	1.1194	97.8398
3	7.1026	1.2039	96.6358
4	7.0117	1.2948	95.3410
5	6.9139	1.3926	93.9485
6	6.8088	1.4977	92.4508
7	6.6957	1.6107	90.8400
8	6.5741	1.7323	89.1077
9	6.4433	1.8631	87.2446
10	6.3027	2.0038	85.2408
11	6.1514	2.1550	83.0858
12	5.9887	2.3177	80.7680
13	5.8138	2.4927	78.2753
14	5.6256	2.6809	75.5944
15	5.4232	2.8833	72.7111
16	5.2055	3.1009	69.6102
17	4.9714	3.3350	66.2752
18	4.7197	3.5868	62.6883
19	4.4489	3.8576	58.8307
20	4.1577	4.1488	54.6819
21	3.8445	4.4620	50.2199
22	3.5076	4.7989	45.4211
23	3.1453	5.1611	40.2599
24	2.7557	5.5508	34.7091
25	2.3367	5.9698	28.7393
26	1.8860	6.4205	22.3188
27	1.4013	6.9052	15.4136
28	.8800	7.4265	7.9871
29	.3193	7.9871	0.0000

YEARS 30   MO PAYT .6856   AN CONST 8.23

#	INT	PRIN	BALANCE
1	7.2684	.9585	99.0415
2	7.1960	1.0309	98.0106
3	7.1182	1.1087	96.9020
4	7.0345	1.1924	95.7096
5	6.9445	1.2824	94.4272
6	6.8476	1.3792	93.0480
7	6.7435	1.4833	91.5647
8	6.6315	1.5953	89.9693
9	6.5111	1.7157	88.2536
10	6.3816	1.8453	86.4083
11	6.2423	1.9846	84.4238
12	6.0925	2.1344	82.2894
13	5.9313	2.2955	79.9939
14	5.7580	2.4688	77.5250
15	5.5717	2.6552	74.8698
16	5.3712	2.8556	72.0142
17	5.1556	3.0712	68.9430
18	4.9238	3.3031	65.6399
19	4.6744	3.5524	62.0875
20	4.4062	3.8206	58.2669
21	4.1178	4.1090	54.1578
22	3.8076	4.4192	49.7386
23	3.4740	4.7529	44.9857
24	3.1152	5.1117	39.8740
25	2.7293	5.4976	34.3764
26	2.3143	5.9126	28.4638
27	1.8679	6.3590	22.1049
28	1.3878	6.8390	15.2659
29	.8715	7.3553	7.9106
30	.3163	7.9106	0.0000

YEARS 2 — MO PAYT 4.4943 — AN CONST 53.94

#	INT	PRIN	BALANCE
1	5.7686	48.1627	51.8373
2	2.0941	51.8373	0.0000

YEARS 3 — MO PAYT 3.1049 — AN CONST 37.26

#	INT	PRIN	BALANCE
1	6.3439	30.9147	69.0853
2	3.9853	33.2733	35.8119
3	1.4467	35.8119	0.0000

YEARS 4 — MO PAYT 2.4121 — AN CONST 28.95

#	INT	PRIN	BALANCE
1	6.6308	22.3140	77.6860
2	4.9283	24.0164	53.6696
3	3.0960	25.8487	27.8209
4	1.1239	27.8209	0.0000

YEARS 5 — MO PAYT 1.9979 — AN CONST 23.98

#	INT	PRIN	BALANCE
1	6.8023	17.1721	82.8279
2	5.4921	18.4831	64.3457
3	4.0820	19.8923	44.4534
4	2.5643	21.4100	23.0434
5	.9309	23.0434	0.0000

YEARS 6 — MO PAYT 1.7230 — AN CONST 20.68

#	INT	PRIN	BALANCE
1	6.9161	13.7595	86.2405
2	5.8663	14.8093	71.4312
3	4.7364	15.9391	55.4921
4	3.5204	17.1552	38.3369
5	2.2115	18.4641	19.8728
6	.8028	19.8728	0.0000

YEARS 7 — MO PAYT 1.5277 — AN CONST 18.34

#	INT	PRIN	BALANCE
1	6.9969	11.3351	88.6649
2	6.1321	12.1999	76.4651
3	5.2013	13.1306	63.3345
4	4.1996	14.1324	49.2020
5	3.1213	15.2107	33.9914
6	1.9608	16.3712	17.6202
7	.7118	17.6202	0.0000

YEARS 8 — MO PAYT 1.3821 — AN CONST 16.59

#	INT	PRIN	BALANCE
1	7.0572	9.5281	90.4719
2	6.3303	10.2550	80.2169
3	5.5479	11.0374	69.1794
4	4.7058	11.8795	57.2999
5	3.7994	12.7859	44.5140
6	2.8239	13.7614	30.7526
7	1.7740	14.8113	15.9413
8	.6440	15.9413	0.0000

YEARS 9 — MO PAYT 1.2697 — AN CONST 15.24

#	INT	PRIN	BALANCE
1	7.1037	8.1327	91.8673
2	6.4833	8.7532	83.1141
3	5.8154	9.4210	73.6931
4	5.0967	10.1398	63.5533
5	4.3231	10.9134	52.6399
6	3.4904	11.7460	40.8938
7	2.5943	12.6422	28.2516
8	1.6297	13.6067	14.6449
9	.5916	14.6449	0.0000

YEARS 10 — MO PAYT 1.1805 — AN CONST 14.17

#	INT	PRIN	BALANCE
1	7.1407	7.0254	92.9746
2	6.6047	7.5614	85.4133
3	6.0278	8.1383	77.2750
4	5.4069	8.7592	68.5159
5	4.7386	9.4274	59.0884
6	4.0193	10.1467	48.9417
7	3.2452	10.9208	38.0209
8	2.4120	11.7540	26.2668
9	1.5152	12.6508	13.6160
10	.5500	13.6160	0.0000

YEARS 11 — MO PAYT 1.1082 — AN CONST 13.30

#	INT	PRIN	BALANCE
1	7.1706	6.1274	93.8726
2	6.7031	6.5949	87.2777
3	6.2000	7.0980	80.1797
4	5.6584	7.6396	72.5401
5	5.0756	8.2225	64.3176
6	4.4483	8.8498	55.4678
7	3.7731	9.5250	45.9429
8	3.0464	10.2517	35.6912
9	2.2642	11.0338	24.6573
10	1.4224	11.8756	12.7817
11	.5163	12.7817	0.0000

YEARS 12 — MO PAYT 1.0485 — AN CONST 12.59

#	INT	PRIN	BALANCE
1	7.1953	5.3864	94.6136
2	6.7844	5.7974	88.8162
3	6.3421	6.2397	82.5766
4	5.8660	6.7157	75.8609
5	5.3537	7.2281	68.6328
6	4.8022	7.7796	60.8532
7	4.2087	8.3731	52.4801
8	3.5698	9.0119	43.4682
9	2.8823	9.6995	33.7687
10	2.1422	10.4395	23.3292
11	1.3458	11.2360	12.0932
12	.4885	12.0932	0.0000

YEARS 13 — MO PAYT .9985 — AN CONST 11.99

#	INT	PRIN	BALANCE
1	7.2160	4.7661	95.2339
2	6.8524	5.1297	90.1043
3	6.4610	5.5211	84.5832
4	6.0398	5.9423	78.6409
5	5.5865	6.3956	72.2453
6	5.0985	6.8836	65.3617
7	4.5733	7.4088	57.9529
8	4.0081	7.9740	49.9789
9	3.3997	8.5824	41.3965
10	2.7449	9.2372	32.1593
11	2.0401	9.9419	22.2173
12	1.2816	10.7005	11.5169
13	.4652	11.5169	0.0000

YEARS 14 — MO PAYT .9562 — AN CONST 11.48

#	INT	PRIN	BALANCE
1	7.2336	4.2404	95.7596
2	6.9100	4.5640	91.1956
3	6.5618	4.9122	86.2834
4	6.1871	5.2869	80.9965
5	5.7837	5.6903	75.3062
6	5.3496	6.1244	69.1818
7	4.8823	6.5917	62.5901
8	4.3794	7.0946	55.4954
9	3.8381	7.6359	47.8595
10	3.2555	8.2185	39.6411
11	2.6285	8.8455	30.7956
12	1.9536	9.5204	21.2752
13	1.2273	10.2467	11.0285
14	.4455	11.0285	0.0000

YEARS 15 — MO PAYT .9199 — AN CONST 11.04

#	INT	PRIN	BALANCE
1	7.2486	3.7905	96.2095
2	6.9594	4.0797	92.1298
3	6.6481	4.3910	87.7388
4	6.3131	4.7260	83.0129
5	5.9525	5.0865	77.9263
6	5.5645	5.4746	72.4517
7	5.1468	5.8923	66.5594
8	4.6972	6.3418	60.2176
9	4.2134	6.8257	53.3919
10	3.6926	7.3465	46.0454
11	3.1321	7.9070	38.1385
12	2.5289	8.5102	29.6283
13	1.8976	9.1595	20.4688
14	1.1808	9.8583	10.6105
15	.4286	10.6105	0.0000

YEARS 16 — MO PAYT .8886 — AN CONST 10.67

#	INT	PRIN	BALANCE
1	7.2615	3.4020	96.5980
2	7.0020	3.6616	92.9364
3	6.7226	3.9409	88.9955
4	6.4219	4.2416	84.7540
5	6.0983	4.5652	80.1888
6	5.7500	4.9135	75.2753
7	5.3752	5.2884	69.9869
8	4.9717	5.6918	64.2951
9	4.5374	6.1261	58.1690
10	4.0700	6.5935	51.5755
11	3.5670	7.0965	44.4790
12	3.0256	7.6380	36.8410
13	2.4428	8.2207	28.6203
14	1.8156	8.8479	19.7724
15	1.1406	9.5229	10.2495
16	.4140	10.2495	0.0000

YEARS 17 — MO PAYT .8614 — AN CONST 10.34

#	INT	PRIN	BALANCE
1	7.2728	3.0640	96.9360
2	7.0390	3.2978	93.6382
3	6.7874	3.5494	90.0889
4	6.5166	3.8202	86.2687
5	6.2252	4.1116	82.1571
6	5.9115	4.4253	77.7318
7	5.5739	4.7629	72.9688
8	5.2105	5.1263	67.8425
9	4.8194	5.5174	62.3251
10	4.3984	5.9384	56.3867
11	3.9453	6.3915	49.9952
12	3.4577	6.8791	43.1161
13	2.9329	7.4039	35.7122
14	2.3680	7.9688	27.7434
15	1.7600	8.5768	19.1666
16	1.1056	9.2312	9.9354
17	.4014	9.9354	0.0000

YEARS 18 — MO PAYT .8376 — AN CONST 10.06

#	INT	PRIN	BALANCE
1	7.2827	2.7680	97.2320
2	7.0715	2.9792	94.2528
3	6.8442	3.2065	91.0463
4	6.5996	3.4511	87.5952
5	6.3363	3.7144	83.8808
6	6.0529	3.9978	79.8830
7	5.7479	4.3028	75.5802
8	5.4196	4.6311	70.9491
9	5.0662	4.9844	65.9646
10	4.6860	5.3647	60.5999
11	4.2767	5.7740	54.8259
12	3.8361	6.2145	48.6114
13	3.3620	6.6887	41.9227
14	2.8517	7.1990	34.7237
15	2.3024	7.7482	26.9755
16	1.7113	8.3394	18.6361
17	1.0750	8.9756	9.6604
18	.3902	9.6604	0.0000

YEARS 19 — MO PAYT .8166 — AN CONST 9.80

#	INT	PRIN	BALANCE
1	7.2914	2.5073	97.4927
2	7.1001	2.6986	94.7941
3	6.8942	2.9045	91.8896
4	6.6726	3.1261	88.7635
5	6.4341	3.3646	85.3989
6	6.1774	3.6213	81.7777
7	5.9011	3.8976	77.8801
8	5.6037	4.1949	73.6851
9	5.2837	4.5150	69.1702
10	4.9392	4.8595	64.3107
11	4.5685	5.2302	59.0805
12	4.1694	5.6292	53.4512
13	3.7400	6.0587	47.3925
14	3.2777	6.5210	40.8715
15	2.7802	7.0185	33.8531
16	2.2447	7.5540	26.2991
17	1.6684	8.1303	18.1688
18	1.0481	8.7506	9.4182
19	.3805	9.4182	0.0000

YEARS 20 — MO PAYT .7980 — AN CONST 9.58

#	INT	PRIN	BALANCE
1	7.2991	2.2765	97.7235
2	7.1254	2.4502	95.2732
3	6.9384	2.6372	92.6361
4	6.7372	2.8384	89.7977
5	6.5207	3.0549	86.7428
6	6.2876	3.2880	83.4548
7	6.0368	3.5388	79.9160
8	5.7668	3.8088	76.1071
9	5.4762	4.0994	72.0077
10	5.1634	4.4122	67.5955
11	4.8268	4.7488	62.8466
12	4.4645	5.1111	57.7355
13	4.0745	5.5011	52.2344
14	3.6548	5.9208	46.3136
15	3.2031	6.3725	39.9411
16	2.7169	6.8587	33.0824
17	2.1936	7.3820	25.7004
18	1.6304	7.9452	17.7552
19	1.0242	8.5514	9.2038
20	.3718	9.2038	0.0000

YEARS 21 — MO PAYT .7814 — AN CONST 9.38

#	INT	PRIN	BALANCE
1	7.3059	2.0713	97.9287
2	7.1479	2.2294	95.6993
3	6.9778	2.3995	93.2998

MONTHLY PAYMENT AMORTIZATION SCHEDULE PER $100   7.375%

#	INT	PRIN	BALANCE
4	6.7947	2.5825	90.7173
5	6.5977	2.7796	87.9377
6	6.3856	2.9916	84.9460
7	6.1574	3.2199	81.7262
8	5.9117	3.4655	78.2606
9	5.6473	3.7299	74.5307
10	5.3627	4.0145	70.5161
11	5.0565	4.3208	66.1953
12	4.7268	4.6505	61.5449
13	4.3720	5.0053	56.5396
14	3.9901	5.3871	51.1525
15	3.5791	5.7982	45.3543
16	3.1367	6.2405	39.1138
17	2.6606	6.7166	32.3971
18	2.1482	7.2291	25.1680
19	1.5966	7.7806	17.3874
20	1.0030	8.3743	9.0132
21	.3641	9.0132	0.0000

YEARS 22	MO PAYT .7667	AN CONST 9.21	
#	INT	PRIN	BALANCE
1	7.3120	1.8882	98.1118
2	7.1680	2.0322	96.0796
3	7.0129	2.1873	93.8923
4	6.8460	2.3542	91.5381
5	6.6664	2.5338	89.0044
6	6.4731	2.7271	86.2773
7	6.2651	2.9352	83.3421
8	6.0411	3.1591	80.1830
9	5.8001	3.4001	76.7829
10	5.5407	3.6595	73.1234
11	5.2615	3.9387	69.1847
12	4.9610	4.2392	64.9455
13	4.6375	4.5627	60.3828
14	4.2894	4.9108	55.4720
15	3.9148	5.2854	50.1866
16	3.5115	5.6887	44.4979
17	3.0775	6.1227	38.3752
18	2.6104	6.5898	31.7854
19	2.1076	7.0926	24.6928
20	1.5665	7.6337	17.0591
21	.9841	8.2161	8.8430
22	.3572	8.8430	0.0000

YEARS 23	MO PAYT .7535	AN CONST 9.05	
#	INT	PRIN	BALANCE
1	7.3175	1.7241	98.2759
2	7.1860	1.8556	96.4203
3	7.0444	1.9972	94.4231
4	6.8920	2.1496	92.2735
5	6.7280	2.3136	89.9599
6	6.5515	2.4901	87.4698
7	6.3615	2.6801	84.7898
8	6.1570	2.8845	81.9052
9	5.9370	3.1046	78.8006
10	5.7001	3.3415	75.4591
11	5.4452	3.5964	71.8627
12	5.1708	3.8708	67.9919
13	4.8754	4.1661	63.8257
14	4.5576	4.4840	59.3417
15	4.2155	4.8261	54.5156
16	3.8473	5.1943	49.3213
17	3.4510	5.5906	43.7307
18	3.0245	6.0171	37.7136
19	2.5654	6.4762	31.2374
20	2.0713	6.9703	24.2671
21	1.5395	7.5021	16.7650
22	.9671	8.0745	8.6905
23	.3511	8.6905	0.0000

YEARS 24	MO PAYT .7416	AN CONST 8.90	
#	INT	PRIN	BALANCE
1	7.3224	1.5766	98.4234
2	7.2021	1.6969	96.7265
3	7.0727	1.8264	94.9001
4	6.9333	1.9657	92.9344
5	6.7833	2.1157	90.8187
6	6.6219	2.2771	88.5416
7	6.4482	2.4508	86.0908
8	6.2612	2.6378	83.4530
9	6.0600	2.8391	80.6139
10	5.8434	3.0557	77.5582
11	5.6102	3.2888	74.2694
12	5.3593	3.5397	70.7297
13	5.0892	3.8098	66.9199
14	4.7986	4.1005	62.8194
15	4.4857	4.4133	58.4062
16	4.1490	4.7500	53.6561
17	3.7866	5.1124	48.5437
18	3.3966	5.5025	43.0413
19	2.9768	5.9223	37.1190
20	2.5249	6.3741	30.7449
21	2.0386	6.8604	23.8845
22	1.5152	7.3838	16.5007
23	.9519	7.9472	8.5535
24	.3455	8.5535	0.0000

YEARS 25	MO PAYT .7309	AN CONST 8.78	
#	INT	PRIN	BALANCE
1	7.3268	1.4437	98.5563
2	7.2167	1.5539	97.0024
3	7.0981	1.6724	95.3300
4	6.9706	1.8000	93.5300
5	6.8332	1.9373	91.5927
6	6.6854	2.0851	89.5076
7	6.5263	2.2442	87.2633
8	6.3551	2.4154	84.8479
9	6.1708	2.5997	82.2481
10	5.9725	2.7981	79.4501
11	5.7590	3.0116	76.4385
12	5.5292	3.2413	73.1972
13	5.2819	3.4886	69.7086
14	5.0158	3.7548	65.9538
15	4.7293	4.0413	61.9125
16	4.4210	4.3496	57.5629
17	4.0891	4.6814	52.8815
18	3.7320	5.0386	47.8429
19	3.3475	5.4230	42.4199
20	2.9338	5.8368	36.5831
21	2.4885	6.2821	30.3010
22	2.0092	6.7614	23.5397
23	1.4933	7.2772	16.2625
24	.9381	7.8324	8.4300
25	.3405	8.4300	0.0000

YEARS 26	MO PAYT .7212	AN CONST 8.66	
#	INT	PRIN	BALANCE
1	7.3309	1.3236	98.6764
2	7.2299	1.4246	97.2518
3	7.1212	1.5333	95.7185
4	7.0042	1.6503	94.0682
5	6.8783	1.7762	92.2921
6	6.7428	1.9117	90.3804
7	6.5969	2.0575	88.3228
8	6.4399	2.2145	86.1083
9	6.2710	2.3835	83.7248
10	6.0891	2.5653	81.1595
11	5.8934	2.7610	78.3984
12	5.6828	2.9717	75.4268
13	5.4560	3.1984	72.2283
14	5.2120	3.4424	68.7859
15	4.9494	3.7051	65.0808

#	INT	PRIN	BALANCE
16	4.6667	3.9878	61.0930
17	4.3625	4.2920	56.8010
18	4.0350	4.6195	52.1816
19	3.6826	4.9719	47.2096
20	3.3032	5.3512	41.8584
21	2.8950	5.7595	36.0989
22	2.4555	6.1989	29.9000
23	1.9826	6.6719	23.2281
24	1.4736	7.1809	16.0472
25	.9257	7.7288	8.3184
26	.3360	8.3184	0.0000

YEARS 27	MO PAYT .7124	AN CONST 8.55	
#	INT	PRIN	BALANCE
1	7.3345	1.2148	98.7852
2	7.2418	1.3075	97.4776
3	7.1420	1.4073	96.0703
4	7.0347	1.5147	94.5557
5	6.9191	1.6302	92.9254
6	6.7947	1.7546	91.1708
7	6.6609	1.8885	89.2824
8	6.5168	2.0325	87.2498
9	6.3617	2.1876	85.0622
10	6.1948	2.3545	82.7077
11	6.0152	2.5342	80.1735
12	5.8218	2.7275	77.4460
13	5.6137	2.9356	74.5104
14	5.3898	3.1596	71.3509
15	5.1487	3.4006	67.9502
16	4.8893	3.6601	64.2902
17	4.6100	3.9393	60.3508
18	4.3095	4.2399	56.1110
19	3.9860	4.5633	51.5476
20	3.6378	4.9115	46.6361
21	3.2631	5.2862	41.3499
22	2.8598	5.6895	35.6604
23	2.4257	6.1236	29.5367
24	1.9585	6.5908	22.9459
25	1.4557	7.0937	15.8522
26	.9145	7.6349	8.2174
27	.3320	8.2174	0.0000

YEARS 28	MO PAYT .7045	AN CONST 8.46	
#	INT	PRIN	BALANCE
1	7.3378	1.1161	98.8839
2	7.2526	1.2013	97.6826
3	7.1610	1.2929	96.3896
4	7.0623	1.3916	94.9981
5	6.9562	1.4978	93.5003
6	6.8419	1.6120	91.8883
7	6.7189	1.7350	90.1533
8	6.5865	1.8674	88.2859
9	6.4440	2.0099	86.2760
10	6.2907	2.1632	84.1128
11	6.1257	2.3282	81.7846
12	5.9480	2.5059	79.2787
13	5.7568	2.6971	76.5816
14	5.5511	2.9028	73.6788
15	5.3296	3.1243	70.5545
16	5.0912	3.3627	67.1918
17	4.8347	3.6192	63.5726
18	4.5586	3.8954	59.6772
19	4.2614	4.1925	55.4847
20	3.9415	4.5124	50.9723
21	3.5972	4.8567	46.1156
22	3.2267	5.2272	40.8884
23	2.8279	5.6260	35.2623
24	2.3986	6.0553	29.2071
25	1.9366	6.5173	22.6898
26	1.4394	7.0145	15.6753
27	.9042	7.5497	8.1257

#	INT	PRIN	BALANCE
28	.3282	8.1257	0.0000

YEARS 29	MO PAYT .6973	AN CONST 8.37	
#	INT	PRIN	BALANCE
1	7.3408	1.0264	98.9736
2	7.2625	1.1047	97.8690
3	7.1782	1.1890	96.6800
4	7.0875	1.2797	95.4003
5	6.9898	1.3773	94.0230
6	6.8848	1.4824	92.5406
7	6.7717	1.5955	90.9452
8	6.6499	1.7172	89.2279
9	6.5189	1.8482	87.3797
10	6.3779	1.9892	85.3905
11	6.2261	2.1410	83.2495
12	6.0628	2.3043	80.9451
13	5.8870	2.4802	78.4650
14	5.6978	2.6694	75.7956
15	5.4941	2.8730	72.9226
16	5.2749	3.0922	69.8303
17	5.0390	3.3282	66.5022
18	4.7851	3.5821	62.9201
19	4.5118	3.8554	59.0647
20	4.2176	4.1495	54.9152
21	3.9010	4.4661	50.4491
22	3.5603	4.8068	45.6423
23	3.1936	5.1736	40.4687
24	2.7988	5.5683	34.9004
25	2.3740	5.9931	28.9073
26	1.9168	6.4504	22.4569
27	1.4246	6.9425	15.5144
28	.8950	7.4722	8.0423
29	.3249	8.0423	0.0000

YEARS 30	MO PAYT .6907	AN CONST 8.29	
#	INT	PRIN	BALANCE
1	7.3435	.9446	99.0554
2	7.2714	1.0167	98.0387
3	7.1939	1.0942	96.9445
4	7.1104	1.1777	95.7667
5	7.0205	1.2676	94.4992
6	6.9238	1.3643	93.1349
7	6.8197	1.4684	91.6665
8	6.7077	1.5804	90.0861
9	6.5871	1.7010	88.3851
10	6.4573	1.8308	86.5543
11	6.3177	1.9704	84.5839
12	6.1673	2.1208	82.4631
13	6.0055	2.2826	80.1805
14	5.8314	2.4567	77.7238
15	5.6439	2.6442	75.0796
16	5.4422	2.8459	72.2337
17	5.2251	3.0630	69.1707
18	4.9914	3.2967	65.8740
19	4.7399	3.5482	62.3258
20	4.4691	3.8190	58.5068
21	4.1778	4.1103	54.3965
22	3.8642	4.4239	49.9726
23	3.5267	4.7614	45.2111
24	3.1634	5.1247	40.0864
25	2.7724	5.5157	34.5707
26	2.3516	5.9365	28.6342
27	1.8987	6.3894	22.2448
28	1.4112	6.8769	15.3679
29	.8865	7.4016	7.9663
30	.3218	7.9663	0.0000

MONTHLY PAYMENT AMORTIZATION SCHEDULE PER $100   7.40 %

YEARS 2 — MO PAYT 4.4954 — AN CONST 53.95

#	INT	PRIN	BALANCE
1	5.7884	48.1565	51.8435
2	2.1015	51.8435	0.0000

YEARS 3 — MO PAYT 3.1060 — AN CONST 37.28

#	INT	PRIN	BALANCE
1	6.3657	30.9067	69.0933
2	3.9994	33.2729	35.8204
3	1.4520	35.8204	0.0000

YEARS 4 — MO PAYT 2.4132 — AN CONST 28.96

#	INT	PRIN	BALANCE
1	6.6536	22.3052	77.6948
2	4.9458	24.0129	53.6820
3	3.1074	25.8514	27.8306
4	1.1281	27.8306	0.0000

YEARS 5 — MO PAYT 1.9990 — AN CONST 23.99

#	INT	PRIN	BALANCE
1	6.8256	17.1629	82.8371
2	5.5116	18.4769	64.3601
3	4.0970	19.8916	44.4686
4	2.5740	21.4145	23.0541
5	.9345	23.0541	0.0000

YEARS 6 — MO PAYT 1.7242 — AN CONST 20.70

#	INT	PRIN	BALANCE
1	6.9398	13.7502	86.2498
2	5.8871	14.8030	71.4468
3	4.7538	15.9363	55.5105
4	3.5336	17.1564	38.3540
5	2.2201	18.4700	19.8841
6	.8060	19.8841	0.0000

YEARS 7 — MO PAYT 1.5289 — AN CONST 18.35

#	INT	PRIN	BALANCE
1	7.0210	11.3258	88.6742
2	6.1539	12.1929	76.4813
3	5.2203	13.1264	63.3549
4	4.2154	14.1314	49.2235
5	3.1334	15.2133	34.0102
6	1.9687	16.3781	17.6320
7	.7147	17.6320	0.0000

YEARS 8 — MO PAYT 1.3834 — AN CONST 16.61

#	INT	PRIN	BALANCE
1	7.0815	9.5189	90.4811
2	6.3527	10.2477	80.2334
3	5.5681	11.0323	69.2011
4	4.7234	11.8769	57.3242
5	3.8141	12.7863	44.5380
6	2.8352	13.7652	30.7728
7	1.7813	14.8191	15.9537
8	.6467	15.9537	0.0000

YEARS 9 — MO PAYT 1.2710 — AN CONST 15.26

#	INT	PRIN	BALANCE
1	7.1281	8.1237	91.8763
2	6.5062	8.7456	83.1307
3	5.8366	9.4152	73.7155
4	5.1157	10.1361	63.5795
5	4.3397	10.9121	52.6674
6	3.5043	11.7475	40.9198
7	2.6048	12.6470	28.2729
8	1.6366	13.6152	14.6576
9	.5941	14.6576	0.0000

YEARS 10 — MO PAYT 1.1818 — AN CONST 14.19

#	INT	PRIN	BALANCE
1	7.1652	7.0165	92.9835
2	6.6280	7.5537	85.4299
3	6.0497	8.1320	77.2979
4	5.4271	8.7546	68.5433
5	4.7568	9.4249	59.1184
6	4.0352	10.1464	48.9720
7	3.2584	10.9233	38.0487
8	2.4221	11.7596	26.2891
9	1.5217	12.6599	13.6292
10	.5525	13.6292	0.0000

YEARS 11 — MO PAYT 1.1095 — AN CONST 13.32

#	INT	PRIN	BALANCE
1	7.1952	6.1187	93.8813
2	6.7268	6.5871	87.2942
3	6.2225	7.0915	80.2027
4	5.6795	7.6344	72.5683
5	5.0950	8.2189	64.3493
6	4.4657	8.8482	55.5012
7	3.7883	9.5256	45.9756
8	3.0590	10.2549	35.7206
9	2.2739	11.0401	24.6806
10	1.4286	11.8853	12.7953
11	.5187	12.7953	0.0000

YEARS 12 — MO PAYT 1.0498 — AN CONST 12.60

#	INT	PRIN	BALANCE
1	7.2200	5.3779	94.6221
2	6.8083	5.7896	88.8325
3	6.3650	6.2329	82.5996
4	5.8878	6.7101	75.8895
5	5.3741	7.2238	68.6656
6	4.8210	7.7769	60.8887
7	4.2256	8.3723	52.5164
8	3.5846	9.0133	43.5030
9	2.8945	9.7034	33.7996
10	2.1516	10.4463	23.3533
11	1.3518	11.2461	12.1072
12	.4908	12.1072	0.0000

YEARS 13 — MO PAYT .9999 — AN CONST 12.00

#	INT	PRIN	BALANCE
1	7.2408	4.7578	95.2422
2	6.8765	5.1220	90.1202
3	6.4844	5.5142	84.6060
4	6.0622	5.9364	78.6697
5	5.6077	6.3909	72.2788
6	5.1184	6.8802	65.3987
7	4.5916	7.4069	57.9918
8	4.0245	7.9740	50.0178
9	3.4140	8.5845	41.4333
10	2.7568	9.2418	32.1915
11	2.0492	9.9493	22.2422
12	1.2875	10.7111	11.5311
13	.4674	11.5311	0.0000

YEARS 14 — MO PAYT .9576 — AN CONST 11.50

#	INT	PRIN	BALANCE
1	7.2584	4.2324	95.7676
2	6.9343	4.5564	91.2113
3	6.5855	4.9052	86.3060
4	6.2099	5.2808	81.0252
5	5.8056	5.6851	75.3401
6	5.3704	6.1204	69.2197
7	4.9018	6.5890	62.6308
8	4.3973	7.0934	55.5374
9	3.8542	7.6365	47.9008
10	3.2695	8.2212	39.6797
11	2.6401	8.8506	30.8291
12	1.9625	9.5282	21.3008
13	1.2330	10.2577	11.0431
14	.4476	11.0431	0.0000

YEARS 15 — MO PAYT .9213 — AN CONST 11.06

#	INT	PRIN	BALANCE
1	7.2734	3.7827	96.2173
2	6.9838	4.0723	92.1451
3	6.6720	4.3840	87.7610
4	6.3364	4.7197	83.0414
5	5.9750	5.0810	77.9603
6	5.5860	5.4701	72.4903
7	5.1672	5.8889	66.6014
8	4.7163	6.3397	60.2617
9	4.2310	6.8251	53.4366
10	3.7084	7.3476	46.0889
11	3.1459	7.9102	38.1787
12	2.5402	8.5158	29.6629
13	1.8883	9.1678	20.4951
14	1.1863	9.8697	10.6254
15	.4307	10.6254	0.0000

YEARS 16 — MO PAYT .8901 — AN CONST 10.69

#	INT	PRIN	BALANCE
1	7.2864	3.3944	96.6056
2	7.0265	3.6543	92.9514
3	6.7467	3.9340	89.0173
4	6.4456	4.2352	84.7821
5	6.1213	4.5595	80.2226
6	5.7722	4.9086	75.3140
7	5.3964	5.2844	70.0297
8	4.9918	5.6890	64.3407
9	4.5563	6.1245	58.2162
10	4.0873	6.5934	51.6227
11	3.5825	7.0982	44.5245
12	3.0391	7.6417	36.8828
13	2.4540	8.2268	28.6560
14	1.8242	8.8566	19.7994
15	1.1461	9.5347	10.2647
16	.4161	10.2647	0.0000

YEARS 17 — MO PAYT .8629 — AN CONST 10.36

#	INT	PRIN	BALANCE
1	7.2977	3.0566	96.9434
2	7.0637	3.2906	93.6528
3	6.8118	3.5426	90.1102
4	6.5405	3.8138	86.2964
5	6.2485	4.1058	82.1907
6	5.9342	4.4201	77.7705
7	5.5958	4.7585	73.0120
8	5.2315	5.1229	67.8891
9	4.8392	5.5151	62.3741
10	4.4170	5.9373	56.4367
11	3.9624	6.3919	50.0448
12	3.4730	6.8813	43.1636
13	2.9462	7.4081	35.7554
14	2.3790	7.9753	27.7801
15	1.7684	8.5859	19.1942
16	1.1110	9.2433	9.9510
17	.4034	9.9510	0.0000

YEARS 18 — MO PAYT .8390 — AN CONST 10.07

#	INT	PRIN	BALANCE
1	7.3076	2.7608	97.2392
2	7.0962	2.9722	94.2669
3	6.8687	3.1998	91.0672
4	6.6237	3.4448	87.6224
5	6.3600	3.7085	83.9139
6	6.0760	3.9924	79.9215
7	5.7704	4.2981	75.6234
8	5.4413	4.6272	70.9963
9	5.0870	4.9814	66.0148
10	4.7056	5.3628	60.6520
11	4.2950	5.7734	54.8786
12	3.8530	6.2154	48.6632
13	3.3772	6.6913	41.9719
14	2.8649	7.2036	34.7683
15	2.3133	7.7551	27.0132
16	1.7196	8.3489	18.6643
17	1.0804	8.9881	9.6762
18	.3922	9.6762	0.0000

YEARS 19 — MO PAYT .8181 — AN CONST 9.82

#	INT	PRIN	BALANCE
1	7.3163	2.5004	97.4996
2	7.1249	2.6918	94.8078
3	6.9188	2.8979	91.9099
4	6.6969	3.1198	88.7902
5	6.4581	3.3586	85.4315
6	6.2009	3.6158	81.8158
7	5.9241	3.8926	77.9232
8	5.6261	4.1906	73.7325
9	5.3052	4.5115	69.2211
10	4.9598	4.8569	64.3642
11	4.5880	5.2287	59.1355
12	4.1876	5.6290	53.5064
13	3.7567	6.0600	47.4464
14	3.2927	6.5240	40.9224
15	2.7932	7.0235	33.8989
16	2.2555	7.5612	26.3377
17	1.6766	8.1401	18.1976
18	1.0534	8.7633	9.4343
19	.3824	9.4343	0.0000

YEARS 20 — MO PAYT .7995 — AN CONST 9.60

#	INT	PRIN	BALANCE
1	7.3240	2.2698	97.7302
2	7.1503	2.4436	95.2865
3	6.9632	2.6307	92.6558
4	6.7618	2.8321	89.8237
5	6.5449	3.0490	86.7748
6	6.3115	3.2824	83.4924
7	6.0602	3.5337	79.9587
8	5.7896	3.8042	76.1544
9	5.4984	4.0955	72.0589
10	5.1848	4.4091	67.6499
11	4.8472	4.7466	62.9032
12	4.4838	5.1100	57.7932
13	4.0926	5.5013	52.2919
14	3.6714	5.9225	46.3695
15	3.2180	6.3759	39.9936
16	2.7298	6.8641	33.1295
17	2.2043	7.3896	25.7399
18	1.6385	7.9553	17.7846
19	1.0294	8.5644	9.2201
20	.3737	9.2201	0.0000

YEARS 21 — MO PAYT .7830 — AN CONST 9.40

#	INT	PRIN	BALANCE
1	7.3309	2.0649	97.9351
2	7.1728	2.2230	95.7122
3	7.0026	2.3932	93.3190

#	INT	PRIN	BALANCE
4	6.8194	2.5764	90.7426
5	6.6221	2.7736	87.9690
6	6.4098	2.9860	84.9830
7	6.1812	3.2146	81.7684
8	5.9350	3.4607	78.3076
9	5.6701	3.7257	74.5819
10	5.3848	4.0109	70.5710
11	5.0778	4.3180	66.2530
12	4.7472	4.6486	61.6044
13	4.3912	5.0045	56.5998
14	4.0081	5.3877	51.2122
15	3.5956	5.8002	45.4120
16	3.1515	6.2443	39.1677
17	2.6735	6.7223	32.4454
18	2.1588	7.2370	25.2084
19	1.6047	7.7911	17.4173
20	1.0082	8.3876	9.0298
21	.3660	9.0298	0.0000

YEARS 22 — MO PAYT .7682 — AN CONST 9.22

#	INT	PRIN	BALANCE
1	7.3370	1.8819	98.1181
2	7.1929	2.0260	96.0921
3	7.0378	2.1811	93.9109
4	6.8708	2.3481	91.5628
5	6.6911	2.5279	89.0349
6	6.4975	2.7214	86.3135
7	6.2892	2.9298	83.3837
8	6.0648	3.1541	80.2295
9	5.8234	3.3956	76.8339
10	5.5634	3.6556	73.1784
11	5.2835	3.9355	69.2429
12	4.9822	4.2368	65.0062
13	4.6578	4.5611	60.4450
14	4.3086	4.9103	55.5347
15	3.9327	5.2863	50.2484
16	3.5279	5.6910	44.5574
17	3.0922	6.1267	38.4306
18	2.6231	6.5958	31.8348
19	2.1181	7.1008	24.7340
20	1.5745	7.6445	17.0896
21	.9892	8.2297	8.8598
22	.3591	8.8598	0.0000

YEARS 23 — MO PAYT .7550 — AN CONST 9.07

#	INT	PRIN	BALANCE
1	7.3425	1.7181	98.2819
2	7.2110	1.8496	96.4323
3	7.0694	1.9912	94.4411
4	6.9169	2.1437	92.2975
5	6.7528	2.3078	89.9897
6	6.5761	2.4845	87.5052
7	6.3859	2.6747	84.8305
8	6.1811	2.8795	81.9511
9	5.9606	3.0999	78.8511
10	5.7233	3.3373	75.5139
11	5.4678	3.5928	71.9211
12	5.1927	3.8678	68.0533
13	4.8966	4.1640	63.8893
14	4.5778	4.4828	59.4065
15	4.2346	4.8260	54.5806
16	3.8651	5.1955	49.3851
17	3.4673	5.5932	43.7918
18	3.0391	6.0215	37.7704
19	2.5781	6.4825	31.2879
20	2.0818	6.9788	24.3091
21	1.5474	7.5131	16.7959
22	.9722	8.0883	8.7076
23	.3530	8.7076	0.0000

YEARS 24 — MO PAYT .7432 — AN CONST 8.92

#	INT	PRIN	BALANCE
1	7.3474	1.5708	98.4292
2	7.2272	1.6911	96.7381
3	7.0977	1.8205	94.9176
4	6.9583	1.9599	92.9576
5	6.8083	2.1100	90.8477
6	6.6467	2.2715	88.5761
7	6.4728	2.4454	86.1307
8	6.2856	2.6327	83.4980
9	6.0840	2.8342	80.6638
10	5.8670	3.0512	77.6125
11	5.6334	3.2848	74.3277
12	5.3819	3.5363	70.7914
13	5.1112	3.8071	66.9843
14	4.8197	4.0986	62.8857
15	4.5059	4.4124	58.4734
16	4.1681	4.7502	53.7232
17	3.8044	5.1139	48.6093
18	3.4129	5.5054	43.1040
19	2.9913	5.9269	37.1771
20	2.5376	6.3807	30.7964
21	2.0491	6.8692	23.9272
22	1.5231	7.3951	16.5321
23	.9570	7.9613	8.5708
24	.3474	8.5708	0.0000

YEARS 25 — MO PAYT .7325 — AN CONST 8.79

#	INT	PRIN	BALANCE
1	7.3519	1.4381	98.5619
2	7.2418	1.5482	97.0137
3	7.1232	1.6668	95.3469
4	6.9956	1.7944	93.5526
5	6.8582	1.9317	91.6208
6	6.7103	2.0796	89.5412
7	6.5511	2.2389	87.3023
8	6.3797	2.4103	84.8920
9	6.1952	2.5948	82.2972
10	5.9965	2.7935	79.5037
11	5.7826	3.0074	76.4964
12	5.5524	3.2376	73.2588
13	5.3045	3.4855	69.7733
14	5.0377	3.7523	66.0210
15	4.7504	4.0396	61.9814
16	4.4411	4.3489	57.6325
17	4.1081	4.6819	52.9506
18	3.7497	5.0403	47.9103
19	3.3638	5.4262	42.4841
20	2.9483	5.8417	36.6424
21	2.5011	6.2889	30.3535
22	2.0196	6.7704	23.5831
23	1.5012	7.2888	16.2944
24	.9432	7.8468	8.4476
25	.3424	8.4476	0.0000

YEARS 26 — MO PAYT .7228 — AN CONST 8.68

#	INT	PRIN	BALANCE
1	7.3559	1.3182	98.6818
2	7.2550	1.4192	97.2626
3	7.1463	1.5278	95.7348
4	7.0293	1.6448	94.0900
5	6.9034	1.7707	92.3193
6	6.7678	1.9063	90.4130
7	6.6219	2.0522	88.3608
8	6.4648	2.2093	86.1515
9	6.2956	2.3785	83.7730
10	6.1135	2.5606	81.2124
11	5.9175	2.7567	78.4557
12	5.7064	2.9677	75.4880
13	5.4792	3.1949	72.2931
14	5.2346	3.4395	68.8535
15	4.9712	3.7029	65.1507
16	4.6877	3.9864	61.1643
17	4.3825	4.2916	56.8727
18	4.0540	4.6201	52.2526
19	3.7002	4.9739	47.2787
20	3.3194	5.3547	41.9240
21	2.9095	5.7646	36.1594
22	2.4681	6.2060	29.9534
23	1.9930	6.6811	23.2722
24	1.4814	7.1927	16.0796
25	.9308	7.7434	8.3362
26	.3379	8.3362	0.0000

YEARS 27 — MO PAYT .7141 — AN CONST 8.57

#	INT	PRIN	BALANCE
1	7.3595	1.2097	98.7903
2	7.2669	1.3023	97.4880
3	7.1672	1.4020	96.0861
4	7.0599	1.5093	94.5767
5	6.9443	1.6249	92.9518
6	6.8199	1.7493	91.2026
7	6.6860	1.8832	89.3193
8	6.5418	2.0274	87.2919
9	6.3866	2.1826	85.1093
10	6.2195	2.3497	82.7596
11	6.0396	2.5296	80.2300
12	5.8459	2.7233	77.5066
13	5.6374	2.9318	74.5748
14	5.4129	3.1563	71.4186
15	5.1713	3.3979	68.0206
16	4.9111	3.6581	64.3626
17	4.6310	3.9381	60.4244
18	4.3295	4.2397	56.1848
19	4.0049	4.5643	51.6205
20	3.6555	4.9137	46.7068
21	3.2793	5.2899	41.4169
22	2.8743	5.6949	35.7220
23	2.4383	6.1309	29.5910
24	1.9689	6.6003	22.9907
25	1.4635	7.1057	15.8851
26	.9195	7.6497	8.2354
27	.3338	8.2354	0.0000

YEARS 28 — MO PAYT .7062 — AN CONST 8.48

#	INT	PRIN	BALANCE
1	7.3628	1.1112	98.8888
2	7.2777	1.1962	97.6926
3	7.1862	1.2878	96.4048
4	7.0876	1.3864	95.0184
5	6.9814	1.4926	93.5258
6	6.8671	1.6068	91.9190
7	6.7441	1.7299	90.1892
8	6.6117	1.8623	88.3269
9	6.4691	2.0049	86.3220
10	6.3156	2.1584	84.1636
11	6.1503	2.3236	81.8400
12	5.9724	2.5015	79.3385
13	5.7809	2.6930	76.6454
14	5.5747	2.8992	73.7462
15	5.3528	3.1212	70.6250
16	5.1138	3.3602	67.2648
17	4.8565	3.6174	63.6474
18	4.5796	3.8944	59.7530
19	4.2814	4.1925	55.5605
20	3.9604	4.5135	51.0469
21	3.6149	4.8591	46.1878
22	3.2428	5.2311	40.9567
23	2.8423	5.6316	35.3251
24	2.4112	6.0628	29.2622
25	1.9470	6.5270	22.7353
26	1.4473	7.0267	15.7085
27	.9093	7.5647	8.1439
28	.3301	8.1439	0.0000

YEARS 29 — MO PAYT .6990 — AN CONST 8.39

#	INT	PRIN	BALANCE
1	7.3658	1.0216	98.9784
2	7.2876	1.0998	97.8786
3	7.2034	1.1840	96.6946
4	7.1127	1.2747	95.4199
5	7.0152	1.3722	94.0477
6	6.9101	1.4773	92.5704
7	6.7970	1.5904	90.9800
8	6.6752	1.7122	89.2678
9	6.5441	1.8433	87.4245
10	6.4030	1.9844	85.4401
11	6.2511	2.1363	83.3038
12	6.0875	2.2999	81.0039
13	5.9114	2.4760	78.5280
14	5.7219	2.6655	75.8624
15	5.5178	2.8696	72.9928
16	5.2981	3.0893	69.9035
17	5.0616	3.3258	66.5777
18	4.8069	3.5805	62.9972
19	4.5328	3.8546	59.1426
20	4.2377	4.1497	54.9929
21	3.9200	4.4674	50.5254
22	3.5779	4.8095	45.7160
23	3.2097	5.1777	40.5383
24	2.8133	5.5741	34.9642
25	2.3865	6.0009	28.9633
26	1.9271	6.4603	22.5030
27	1.4325	6.9549	15.5481
28	.9000	7.4874	8.0607
29	.3267	8.0607	0.0000

YEARS 30 — MO PAYT .6924 — AN CONST 8.31

#	INT	PRIN	BALANCE
1	7.3685	.9400	99.0600
2	7.2966	1.0120	98.0480
3	7.2191	1.0895	96.9585
4	7.1357	1.1729	95.7857
5	7.0459	1.2627	94.5230
6	6.9492	1.3593	93.1636
7	6.8451	1.4634	91.7002
8	6.7331	1.5755	90.1248
9	6.6125	1.6961	88.4287
10	6.4826	1.8259	86.6027
11	6.3428	1.9657	84.6370
12	6.1923	2.1162	82.5207
13	6.0303	2.2783	80.2425
14	5.8559	2.4527	77.7898
15	5.6681	2.6405	75.1493
16	5.4659	2.8426	72.3067
17	5.2483	3.0603	69.2464
18	5.0140	3.2946	65.9518
19	4.7617	3.5468	62.4050
20	4.4902	3.8184	58.5866
21	4.1978	4.1107	54.4759
22	3.8831	4.4254	50.0505
23	3.5443	4.7643	45.2862
24	3.1795	5.1290	40.1572
25	2.7869	5.5217	34.6355
26	2.3641	5.9445	28.6910
27	1.9090	6.3996	22.2915
28	1.4190	6.8895	15.4019
29	.8915	7.4170	7.9849
30	.3237	7.9849	0.0000

YEARS 2 — MO PAYT 4.5000 — AN CONST 54.00

#	INT	PRIN	BALANCE
1	5.8678	48.1317	51.8683
2	2.1312	51.8683	0.0000

YEARS 3 — MO PAYT 3.1106 — AN CONST 37.33

#	INT	PRIN	BALANCE
1	6.4530	30.8744	69.1256
2	4.0562	33.2713	35.8542
3	1.4732	35.8542	0.0000

YEARS 4 — MO PAYT 2.4179 — AN CONST 29.02

#	INT	PRIN	BALANCE
1	6.7448	22.2699	77.7301
2	5.0159	23.9987	53.7314
3	3.1529	25.8618	27.8696
4	1.1451	27.8696	0.0000

YEARS 5 — MO PAYT 2.0038 — AN CONST 24.05

#	INT	PRIN	BALANCE
1	6.9192	17.1263	82.8737
2	5.5897	18.4559	64.4178
3	4.1569	19.8886	44.5292
4	2.6129	21.4327	23.0965
5	.9490	23.0965	0.0000

YEARS 6 — MO PAYT 1.7290 — AN CONST 20.75

#	INT	PRIN	BALANCE
1	7.0350	13.7132	86.2868
2	5.9704	14.7778	71.5091
3	4.8231	15.9250	55.5841
4	3.5869	17.1613	38.4228
5	2.2546	18.4936	19.9293
6	.8189	19.9293	0.0000

YEARS 7 — MO PAYT 1.5338 — AN CONST 18.41

#	INT	PRIN	BALANCE
1	7.1172	11.2887	88.7113
2	6.2408	12.1651	76.5461
3	5.2964	13.1095	63.4366
4	4.2787	14.1273	49.3094
5	3.1819	15.2240	34.0854
6	2.0001	16.4059	17.6795
7	.7264	17.6795	0.0000

YEARS 8 — MO PAYT 1.3884 — AN CONST 16.67

#	INT	PRIN	BALANCE
1	7.1784	9.4822	90.5178
2	6.4423	10.2183	80.2995
3	5.6490	11.0116	69.2879
4	4.7942	11.8665	57.4214
5	3.8730	12.7877	44.6337
6	2.8802	13.7804	30.8533
7	1.8104	14.8502	16.0031
8	.6576	16.0031	0.0000

YEARS 9 — MO PAYT 1.2761 — AN CONST 15.32

#	INT	PRIN	BALANCE
1	7.2257	8.0875	91.9125
2	6.5979	8.7153	83.1972
3	5.9213	9.3919	73.8053
4	5.1922	10.1210	63.6842
5	4.4065	10.9068	52.7775
6	3.5597	11.7535	41.0240
7	2.6473	12.6659	28.3581
8	1.6640	13.6492	14.7088
9	.6044	14.7088	0.0000

YEARS 10 — MO PAYT 1.1870 — AN CONST 14.25

#	INT	PRIN	BALANCE
1	7.2633	6.9809	93.0191
2	6.7213	7.5229	85.4962
3	6.1373	8.1069	77.3893
4	5.5079	8.7363	68.6530
5	4.8297	9.4145	59.2385
6	4.0988	10.1454	49.0931
7	3.3112	10.9330	38.1601
8	2.4625	11.7817	26.3784
9	1.5478	12.6964	13.6820
10	.5622	13.6820	0.0000

YEARS 11 — MO PAYT 1.1148 — AN CONST 13.38

#	INT	PRIN	BALANCE
1	7.2937	6.0839	93.9161
2	6.8214	6.5562	87.3599
3	6.3124	7.0652	80.2946
4	5.7639	7.6137	72.6810
5	5.1728	8.2048	64.4762
6	4.5359	8.8417	55.6345
7	3.8495	9.5281	46.1063
8	3.1098	10.2678	35.8385
9	2.3127	11.0649	24.7736
10	1.4537	11.9239	12.8496
11	.5280	12.8496	0.0000

YEARS 12 — MO PAYT 1.0552 — AN CONST 12.67

#	INT	PRIN	BALANCE
1	7.3188	5.3439	94.6561
2	6.9039	5.7588	88.8973
3	6.4568	6.2059	82.6914
4	5.9751	6.6876	76.0038
5	5.4559	7.2068	68.7969
6	4.8964	7.7663	61.0306
7	4.2935	8.3692	52.6614
8	3.6438	9.0190	43.6424
9	2.9436	9.7191	33.9233
10	2.1891	10.4736	23.4497
11	1.3760	11.2867	12.1630
12	.4998	12.1630	0.0000

YEARS 13 — MO PAYT 1.0054 — AN CONST 12.07

#	INT	PRIN	BALANCE
1	7.3398	4.7247	95.2753
2	6.9730	5.0915	90.1839
3	6.5777	5.4867	84.6972
4	6.1518	5.9127	78.7845
5	5.6928	6.3717	72.4128
6	5.1981	6.8663	65.5465
7	4.6651	7.3994	58.1471
8	4.0906	7.9738	50.1733
9	3.4716	8.5928	41.5805
10	2.8045	9.2599	32.3206
11	2.0857	9.9788	22.3418
12	1.3110	10.7535	11.5883
13	.4762	11.5883	0.0000

YEARS 14 — MO PAYT .9631 — AN CONST 11.56

#	INT	PRIN	BALANCE
1	7.3576	4.2002	95.7998
2	7.0315	4.5262	91.2736
3	6.6801	4.8776	86.3960
4	6.3015	5.2563	81.1398
5	5.8934	5.6643	75.4754
6	5.4537	6.1041	69.3714
7	4.9798	6.5779	62.7935
8	4.4691	7.0886	55.7049
9	3.9188	7.6389	48.0660
10	3.3258	8.2319	39.8340
11	2.6867	8.8710	30.9630
12	1.9981	9.5597	21.4034
13	1.2559	10.3018	11.1016
14	.4562	11.1016	0.0000

YEARS 15 — MO PAYT .9270 — AN CONST 11.13

#	INT	PRIN	BALANCE
1	7.3728	3.7514	96.2486
2	7.0816	4.0426	92.2061
3	6.7677	4.3564	87.8496
4	6.4295	4.6946	83.1550
5	6.0651	5.0591	78.0959
6	5.6723	5.4518	72.6441
7	5.2491	5.8751	66.7690
8	4.7930	6.3312	60.4378
9	4.3015	6.8227	53.6152
10	3.7718	7.3523	46.2628
11	3.2010	7.9231	38.3397
12	2.5859	8.5382	29.8015
13	1.9231	9.2011	20.6005
14	1.2088	9.9154	10.6851
15	.4390	10.6851	0.0000

YEARS 16 — MO PAYT .8958 — AN CONST 10.75

#	INT	PRIN	BALANCE
1	7.3859	3.3640	96.6360
2	7.1248	3.6252	93.0108
3	6.8433	3.9066	89.1042
4	6.5401	4.2099	84.8944
5	6.2132	4.5367	80.3577
6	5.8610	4.8889	75.4688
7	5.4815	5.2684	70.2003
8	5.0725	5.6774	64.5229
9	4.6317	6.1182	58.4047
10	4.1568	6.5932	51.8116
11	3.6449	7.1050	44.7066
12	3.0933	7.6566	37.0500
13	2.4989	8.2510	28.7990
14	1.8584	8.8915	19.9075
15	1.1681	9.5818	10.3257
16	.4243	10.3257	0.0000

YEARS 17 — MO PAYT .8687 — AN CONST 10.43

#	INT	PRIN	BALANCE
1	7.3973	3.0272	96.9728
2	7.1623	3.2622	93.7107
3	6.9091	3.5154	90.1952
4	6.6362	3.7883	86.4069
5	6.3421	4.0824	82.3245
6	6.0251	4.3994	77.9251
7	5.6836	4.7409	73.1842
8	5.3156	5.1089	68.0753
9	4.9189	5.5056	62.5697
10	4.4915	5.9330	56.6367
11	4.0309	6.3936	50.2431
12	3.5346	6.8899	43.3532
13	2.9997	7.4248	35.9284
14	2.4233	8.0012	27.9272
15	1.8021	8.6224	19.3048
16	1.1328	9.2917	10.0131
17	.4114	10.0131	0.0000

YEARS 18 — MO PAYT .8450 — AN CONST 10.14

#	INT	PRIN	BALANCE
1	7.4073	2.7323	97.2677
2	7.1952	2.9445	94.3232
3	6.9666	3.1730	91.1502
4	6.7203	3.4194	87.7308
5	6.4549	3.6848	84.0460
6	6.1688	3.9709	80.0751
7	5.8605	4.2792	75.7959
8	5.5283	4.6114	71.1846
9	5.1703	4.9694	66.2152
10	4.7845	5.3551	60.8601
11	4.3688	5.7709	55.0892
12	3.9208	6.2189	48.8703
13	3.4380	6.7017	42.1687
14	2.9177	7.2219	34.9467
15	2.3571	7.7826	27.1641
16	1.7529	8.3868	18.7774
17	1.1018	9.0379	9.7395
18	.4002	9.7395	0.0000

YEARS 19 — MO PAYT .8241 — AN CONST 9.89

#	INT	PRIN	BALANCE
1	7.4161	2.4728	97.5272
2	7.2242	2.6648	94.8624
3	7.0173	2.8716	91.9908
4	6.7944	3.0946	88.8962
5	6.5541	3.3348	85.5614
6	6.2952	3.5937	81.9677
7	6.0162	3.8727	78.0950
8	5.7156	4.1733	73.9216
9	5.3916	4.4973	69.4243
10	5.0425	4.8465	64.5778
11	4.6662	5.2227	59.3551
12	4.2608	5.6282	53.7270
13	3.8238	6.0651	47.6619
14	3.3530	6.5359	41.1259
15	2.8456	7.0433	34.0826
16	2.2988	7.5901	26.4924
17	1.7096	8.1794	18.3130
18	1.0746	8.8144	9.4987
19	.3903	9.4987	0.0000

YEARS 20 — MO PAYT .8056 — AN CONST 9.67

#	INT	PRIN	BALANCE
1	7.4239	2.2432	97.7568
2	7.2498	2.4173	95.3395
3	7.0621	2.6050	92.7345
4	6.8599	2.8072	89.9273
5	6.6420	3.0252	86.9021
6	6.4071	3.2600	83.6421
7	6.1540	3.5131	80.1290
8	5.8813	3.7858	76.3432
9	5.5874	4.0797	72.2634
10	5.2707	4.3964	67.8670
11	4.9294	4.7378	63.1292
12	4.5616	5.1056	58.0237
13	4.1652	5.5019	52.5218
14	3.7381	5.9290	46.5927
15	3.2778	6.3893	40.2034
16	2.7818	6.8854	33.3180
17	2.2472	7.4199	25.8981
18	1.6712	7.9959	17.9022
19	1.0505	8.6167	9.2856
20	.3815	9.2856	0.0000

YEARS 21 — MO PAYT .7892 — AN CONST 9.47

#	INT	PRIN	BALANCE
1	7.4309	2.0391	97.9609
2	7.2725	2.1974	95.7634
3	7.1020	2.3680	93.3954

#	INT	PRIN	BALANCE
4	6.9181	2.5519	90.8435
5	6.7200	2.7500	88.0935
6	6.5065	2.9635	85.1300
7	6.2765	3.1935	81.9365
8	6.0285	3.4415	78.4950
9	5.7614	3.7086	74.7864
10	5.4735	3.9965	70.7899
11	5.1632	4.3068	66.4831
12	4.8288	4.6411	61.8419
13	4.4685	5.0015	56.8405
14	4.0803	5.3897	51.4508
15	3.6618	5.8081	45.6426
16	3.2109	6.2590	39.3836
17	2.7250	6.7450	32.6386
18	2.2014	7.2686	25.3700
19	1.6371	7.8329	17.5372
20	1.0290	8.4409	9.0962
21	.3738	9.0962	0.0000

YEARS 22 — MO PAYT .7745 — AN CONST 9.30

#	INT	PRIN	BALANCE
1	7.4370	1.8571	98.1429
2	7.2929	2.0013	96.1416
3	7.1375	2.1566	93.9850
4	6.9701	2.3241	91.6609
5	6.7896	2.5045	89.1564
6	6.5952	2.6989	86.4575
7	6.3857	2.9084	83.5491
8	6.1599	3.1342	80.4149
9	5.9166	3.3775	77.0373
10	5.6544	3.6398	73.3976
11	5.3718	3.9223	69.4752
12	5.0673	4.2268	65.2484
13	4.7392	4.5550	60.6935
14	4.3856	4.9086	55.7849
15	4.0045	5.2896	50.4953
16	3.5938	5.7003	44.7950
17	3.1513	6.1428	38.6522
18	2.6744	6.6197	32.0325
19	2.1605	7.1336	24.8989
20	1.6067	7.6874	17.2115
21	1.0099	8.2842	8.9273
22	.3668	8.9273	0.0000

YEARS 23 — MO PAYT .7614 — AN CONST 9.14

#	INT	PRIN	BALANCE
1	7.4426	1.6941	98.3059
2	7.3110	1.8256	96.4802
3	7.1693	1.9674	94.5129
4	7.0166	2.1201	92.3928
5	6.8520	2.2847	90.1081
6	6.6746	2.4621	87.6460
7	6.4835	2.6532	84.9928
8	6.2775	2.8592	82.1337
9	6.0555	3.0811	79.0525
10	5.8163	3.3203	75.7322
11	5.5586	3.5781	72.1541
12	5.2808	3.8559	68.2983
13	4.9815	4.1552	64.1430
14	4.6589	4.4778	59.6653
15	4.3113	4.8254	54.8398
16	3.9367	5.2000	49.6398
17	3.5330	5.6037	44.0361
18	3.0979	6.0387	37.9974
19	2.6291	6.5075	31.4898
20	2.1239	7.0127	24.4771
21	1.5795	7.5572	16.9199
22	.9928	8.1438	8.7761
23	.3606	8.7761	0.0000

YEARS 24 — MO PAYT .7496 — AN CONST 9.00

#	INT	PRIN	BALANCE
1	7.4475	1.5477	98.4523
2	7.3274	1.6679	96.7844
3	7.1979	1.7974	94.9870
4	7.0583	1.9369	93.0501
5	6.9080	2.0873	90.9628
6	6.7459	2.2493	88.7134
7	6.5713	2.4239	86.2895
8	6.3831	2.6121	83.6774
9	6.1803	2.8149	80.8624
10	5.9618	3.0334	77.8290
11	5.7263	3.2689	74.5601
12	5.4725	3.5227	71.0374
13	5.1991	3.7962	67.2412
14	4.9044	4.0909	63.1503
15	4.5868	4.4085	58.7418
16	4.2445	4.7507	53.9911
17	3.8757	5.1195	48.8715
18	3.4783	5.5170	43.3545
19	3.0500	5.9453	37.4093
20	2.5884	6.4068	31.0024
21	2.0911	6.9042	24.0982
22	1.5551	7.4402	16.6580
23	.9775	8.0178	8.6402
24	.3550	8.6402	0.0000

YEARS 25 — MO PAYT .7390 — AN CONST 8.87

#	INT	PRIN	BALANCE
1	7.4520	1.4159	98.5841
2	7.3421	1.5258	97.0583
3	7.2236	1.6443	95.4140
4	7.0960	1.7719	93.6420
5	6.9584	1.9095	91.7325
6	6.8102	2.0577	89.6748
7	6.6504	2.2175	87.4573
8	6.4783	2.3896	85.0677
9	6.2928	2.5751	82.4926
10	6.0928	2.7751	79.7175
11	5.8774	2.9905	76.7270
12	5.6452	3.2227	73.5044
13	5.3951	3.4728	70.0315
14	5.1255	3.7424	66.2891
15	4.8349	4.0330	62.2561
16	4.5218	4.3461	57.9101
17	4.1844	4.6835	53.2266
18	3.8208	5.0470	48.1795
19	3.4290	5.4389	42.7407
20	3.0068	5.8611	36.8796
21	2.5518	6.3161	30.5635
22	2.0614	6.8064	23.7570
23	1.5330	7.3348	16.4222
24	.9636	7.9043	8.5179
25	.3500	8.5179	0.0000

YEARS 26 — MO PAYT .7294 — AN CONST 8.76

#	INT	PRIN	BALANCE
1	7.4560	1.2969	98.7031
2	7.3553	1.3975	97.3056
3	7.2468	1.5060	95.7995
4	7.1299	1.6230	94.1766
5	7.0039	1.7490	92.4276
6	6.8682	1.8847	90.5429
7	6.7218	2.0310	88.5119
8	6.5642	2.1887	86.3231
9	6.3943	2.3586	83.9645
10	6.2111	2.5417	81.4227
11	6.0138	2.7391	78.6837
12	5.8012	2.9517	75.7320
13	5.5720	3.1809	72.5511
14	5.3251	3.4278	69.1233
15	5.0590	3.6939	65.4294
16	4.7722	3.9807	61.4487
17	4.4632	4.2897	57.1590
18	4.1302	4.6227	52.5363
19	3.7713	4.9816	47.5547
20	3.3846	5.3683	42.1864
21	2.9678	5.7851	36.4013
22	2.5187	6.2342	30.1671
23	2.0347	6.7182	23.4489
24	1.5132	7.2397	16.2092
25	.9511	7.8018	8.4074
26	.3455	8.4074	0.0000

YEARS 27 — MO PAYT .7207 — AN CONST 8.65

#	INT	PRIN	BALANCE
1	7.4597	1.1891	98.8109
2	7.3674	1.2814	97.5294
3	7.2679	1.3809	96.1485
4	7.1607	1.4881	94.6604
5	7.0451	1.6037	93.0567
6	6.9206	1.7282	91.3285
7	6.7865	1.8623	89.4662
8	6.6419	2.0069	87.4593
9	6.4861	2.1627	85.2966
10	6.3182	2.3306	82.9660
11	6.1373	2.5115	80.4545
12	5.9423	2.7065	77.7480
13	5.7322	2.9166	74.8314
14	5.5058	3.1430	71.6884
15	5.2618	3.3870	68.3014
16	4.9988	3.6500	64.6514
17	4.7155	3.9333	60.7180
18	4.4101	4.2387	56.4793
19	4.0811	4.5678	51.9116
20	3.7264	4.9224	46.9892
21	3.3443	5.3045	41.6847
22	2.9325	5.7163	35.9684
23	2.4887	6.1601	29.8084
24	2.0105	6.6383	23.1701
25	1.4952	7.1536	16.0165
26	.9398	7.7090	8.3075
27	.3413	8.3075	0.0000

YEARS 28 — MO PAYT .7129 — AN CONST 8.56

#	INT	PRIN	BALANCE
1	7.4630	1.0914	98.9086
2	7.3783	1.1762	97.7324
3	7.2870	1.2675	96.4650
4	7.1886	1.3659	95.0991
5	7.0825	1.4719	93.6272
6	6.9683	1.5862	92.0411
7	6.8451	1.7093	90.3318
8	6.7124	1.8420	88.4898
9	6.5694	1.9850	86.5048
10	6.4153	2.1391	84.3657
11	6.2493	2.3052	82.0605
12	6.0703	2.4841	79.5764
13	5.8775	2.6770	76.8995
14	5.6696	2.8848	74.0147
15	5.4457	3.1087	70.9060
16	5.2043	3.3501	67.5559
17	4.9443	3.6101	63.9458
18	4.6640	3.8904	60.0553
19	4.3620	4.1924	55.8629
20	4.0365	4.5179	51.3450
21	3.6858	4.8686	46.4764
22	3.3078	5.2466	41.2298
23	2.9005	5.6539	35.5759
24	2.4616	6.0928	29.4830
25	1.9886	6.5658	22.9172
26	1.4789	7.0756	15.8416
27	.9296	7.6249	8.2168
28	.3376	8.2168	0.0000

YEARS 29 — MO PAYT .7057 — AN CONST 8.47

#	INT	PRIN	BALANCE
1	7.4660	1.0026	98.9974
2	7.3882	1.0805	97.9169
3	7.3043	1.1644	96.7525
4	7.2139	1.2548	95.4978
5	7.1165	1.3522	94.1456
6	7.0115	1.4571	92.6885
7	6.8984	1.5703	91.1182
8	6.7765	1.6922	89.4261
9	6.6451	1.8235	87.6025
10	6.5036	1.9651	85.6374
11	6.3510	2.1176	83.5198
12	6.1866	2.2820	81.2378
13	6.0094	2.4592	78.7786
14	5.8185	2.6501	76.1284
15	5.6128	2.8559	73.2726
16	5.3911	3.0776	70.1950
17	5.1522	3.3165	66.8786
18	4.8947	3.5739	63.3046
19	4.6172	3.8514	59.4532
20	4.3182	4.1504	55.3028
21	3.9960	4.4726	50.8302
22	3.6488	4.8198	46.0104
23	3.2746	5.1940	40.8164
24	2.8714	5.5972	35.2192
25	2.4369	6.0317	29.1874
26	1.9686	6.5000	22.6874
27	1.4640	7.0046	15.6828
28	.9202	7.5484	8.1344
29	.3342	8.1344	0.0000

YEARS 30 — MO PAYT .6992 — AN CONST 8.40

#	INT	PRIN	BALANCE
1	7.4687	.9218	99.0782
2	7.3972	.9934	98.0848
3	7.3201	1.0705	97.0142
4	7.2369	1.1536	95.8606
5	7.1474	1.2432	94.6174
6	7.0509	1.3397	93.2777
7	6.9469	1.4437	91.8340
8	6.8348	1.5558	90.2783
9	6.7140	1.6766	88.6017
10	6.5839	1.8067	86.7950
11	6.4436	1.9470	84.8480
12	6.2925	2.0981	82.7499
13	6.1296	2.2610	80.4889
14	5.9540	2.4365	78.0524
15	5.7649	2.6257	75.4267
16	5.5610	2.8295	72.5971
17	5.3414	3.0492	69.5479
18	5.1047	3.2859	66.2620
19	4.8496	3.5410	62.7210
20	4.5747	3.8159	58.9051
21	4.2784	4.1121	54.7930
22	3.9592	4.4314	50.3616
23	3.6152	4.7754	45.5863
24	3.2445	5.1461	40.4401
25	2.8450	5.5456	34.8945
26	2.4144	5.9761	28.9184
27	1.9505	6.4401	22.4783
28	1.4505	6.9400	15.5382
29	.9118	7.4788	8.0594
30	.3312	8.0594	0.0000

YEARS	MO PAYT	AN CONST
2	4.5045	54.06

#	INT	PRIN	BALANCE
1	5.9472	48.1069	51.8931
2	2.1610	51.8931	0.0000

YEARS	MO PAYT	AN CONST
3	3.1152	37.39

#	INT	PRIN	BALANCE
1	6.5404	30.8422	69.1578
2	4.1129	33.2697	35.8881
3	1.4945	35.8881	0.0000

YEARS	MO PAYT	AN CONST
4	2.4226	29.08

#	INT	PRIN	BALANCE
1	6.8361	22.2346	77.7654
2	5.0861	23.9846	53.7808
3	3.1984	25.8723	27.9085
4	1.1622	27.9085	0.0000

YEARS	MO PAYT	AN CONST
5	2.0086	24.11

#	INT	PRIN	BALANCE
1	7.0128	17.0898	82.9102
2	5.6678	18.4348	64.4755
3	4.2169	19.8857	44.5898
4	2.6518	21.4508	23.1390
5	.9636	23.1390	0.0000

YEARS	MO PAYT	AN CONST
6	1.7339	20.81

#	INT	PRIN	BALANCE
1	7.1301	13.6762	86.3238
2	6.0538	14.7525	71.5713
3	4.8927	15.9136	55.6577
4	3.6402	17.1661	38.4916
5	2.2892	18.5171	19.9745
6	.8318	19.9745	0.0000

YEARS	MO PAYT	AN CONST
7	1.5388	18.47

#	INT	PRIN	BALANCE
1	7.2134	11.2518	88.7482
2	6.3279	12.1373	76.6109
3	5.3726	13.0926	63.5183
4	4.3422	14.1230	49.3952
5	3.2306	15.2346	34.1606
6	2.0316	16.4336	17.7270
7	.7382	17.7270	0.0000

YEARS	MO PAYT	AN CONST
8	1.3934	16.73

#	INT	PRIN	BALANCE
1	7.2755	9.4456	90.5544
2	6.5321	10.1890	80.3654
3	5.7302	10.9909	69.3745
4	4.8651	11.8559	57.5186
5	3.9320	12.7890	44.7295
6	2.9255	13.7956	30.9339
7	1.8397	14.8814	16.0526
8	.6685	16.0526	0.0000

YEARS	MO PAYT	AN CONST
9	1.2812	15.38

#	INT	PRIN	BALANCE
1	7.3234	8.0514	91.9486
2	6.6897	8.6851	83.2635
3	6.0061	9.3686	73.8949
4	5.2688	10.1060	63.7889
5	4.4734	10.9014	52.8875
6	3.6154	11.7593	41.1282
7	2.6899	12.6849	28.4433
8	1.6916	13.6832	14.7601
9	.6147	14.7601	0.0000

YEARS	MO PAYT	AN CONST
10	1.1922	14.31

#	INT	PRIN	BALANCE
1	7.3614	6.9455	93.0545
2	6.8147	7.4922	85.5623
3	6.2251	8.0819	77.4804
4	5.5890	8.7179	68.7625
5	4.9029	9.4041	59.3584
6	4.1627	10.1442	49.2142
7	3.3643	10.9426	38.2716
8	2.5031	11.8038	26.4678
9	1.5741	12.7328	13.7350
10	.5720	13.7350	0.0000

YEARS	MO PAYT	AN CONST
11	1.1201	13.45

#	INT	PRIN	BALANCE
1	7.3922	6.0493	93.9507
2	6.9161	6.5254	87.4253
3	6.4025	7.0390	80.3864
4	5.8485	7.5930	72.7934
5	5.2509	8.1906	64.6028
6	4.6063	8.8352	55.7676
7	3.9109	9.5306	46.2371
8	3.1608	10.2806	35.9564
9	2.3517	11.0898	24.8667
10	1.4789	11.9626	12.9041
11	.5374	12.9041	0.0000

YEARS	MO PAYT	AN CONST
12	1.0606	12.73

#	INT	PRIN	BALANCE
1	7.4176	5.3101	94.6899
2	6.9996	5.7281	88.9618
3	6.5488	6.1789	82.7829
4	6.0625	6.6652	76.1177
5	5.5379	7.1898	68.9280
6	4.9721	7.7556	61.1723
7	4.3617	8.3660	52.8063
8	3.7032	9.0245	43.7818
9	2.9930	9.7347	34.0471
10	2.2268	10.5009	23.5462
11	1.4003	11.3274	12.2189
12	.5088	12.2189	0.0000

YEARS	MO PAYT	AN CONST
13	1.0109	12.14

#	INT	PRIN	BALANCE
1	7.4388	4.6917	95.3083
2	7.0695	5.0610	90.2473
3	6.6712	5.4593	84.7879
4	6.2416	5.8890	78.8990
5	5.7781	6.3525	72.5465
6	5.2781	6.8524	65.6940
7	4.7388	7.3918	58.3023
8	4.1570	7.9735	50.3288
9	3.5295	8.6011	41.7277
10	2.8525	9.2780	32.4497
11	2.1223	10.0082	22.4415
12	1.3346	10.7959	11.6456
13	.4850	11.6456	0.0000

YEARS	MO PAYT	AN CONST
14	.9687	11.63

#	INT	PRIN	BALANCE
1	7.4568	4.1681	95.8319
2	7.1287	4.4962	91.3357
3	6.7749	4.8500	86.4856
4	6.3932	5.2318	81.2539
5	5.9814	5.6435	75.6103
6	5.5372	6.0877	69.5227
7	5.0581	6.5668	62.9558
8	4.5413	7.0837	55.8722
9	3.9838	7.6412	48.2310
10	3.3824	8.2426	39.9884
11	2.7336	8.8913	31.0972
12	2.0339	9.5911	21.5061
13	1.2790	10.3459	11.1602
14	.4647	11.1602	0.0000

YEARS	MO PAYT	AN CONST
15	.9327	11.20

#	INT	PRIN	BALANCE
1	7.4722	3.7203	96.2797
2	7.1794	4.0131	92.2667
3	6.8635	4.3289	87.9378
4	6.5228	4.6696	83.2681
5	6.1553	5.0371	78.2310
6	5.7589	5.4336	72.7974
7	5.3312	5.8612	66.9362
8	4.8699	6.3225	60.6137
9	4.3723	6.8201	53.7936
10	3.8356	7.3569	46.4367
11	3.2565	7.9359	38.5008
12	2.6319	8.5605	29.9403
13	1.9582	9.2342	20.7060
14	1.2314	9.9610	10.7450
15	.4475	10.7450	0.0000

YEARS	MO PAYT	AN CONST
16	.9016	10.82

#	INT	PRIN	BALANCE
1	7.4855	3.3339	96.6661
2	7.2231	3.5962	93.0699
3	6.9400	3.8793	89.1906
4	6.6347	4.1846	85.0060
5	6.3054	4.5139	80.4921
6	5.9501	4.8692	75.6229
7	5.5669	5.2524	70.3705
8	5.1535	5.6658	64.7047
9	4.7076	6.1117	58.5929
10	4.2266	6.5928	52.0002
11	3.7077	7.1116	44.8886
12	3.1480	7.6713	37.2172
13	2.5442	8.2751	28.9421
14	1.8929	8.9264	20.0157
15	1.1904	9.6289	10.3868
16	.4325	10.3868	0.0000

YEARS	MO PAYT	AN CONST
17	.8746	10.50

#	INT	PRIN	BALANCE
1	7.4970	2.9980	97.0020
2	7.2610	3.2339	93.7681
3	7.0065	3.4884	90.2797
4	6.7320	3.7630	86.5167
5	6.4358	4.0591	82.4576
6	6.1163	4.3786	78.0790
7	5.7717	4.7232	73.3558
8	5.4000	5.0950	68.2608
9	4.9990	5.4960	62.7649
10	4.5664	5.9285	56.8363
11	4.0998	6.3951	50.4412
12	3.5965	6.8984	43.5428
13	3.0536	7.4414	36.1015
14	2.4679	8.0270	28.0744
15	1.8362	8.6588	19.4156
16	1.1547	9.3403	10.0754
17	.4196	10.0754	0.0000

YEARS	MO PAYT	AN CONST
18	.8509	10.22

#	INT	PRIN	BALANCE
1	7.5071	2.7041	97.2959
2	7.2943	2.9169	94.3790
3	7.0647	3.1465	91.2326
4	6.8171	3.3941	87.8385
5	6.5499	3.6612	84.1773
6	6.2618	3.9494	80.2279
7	5.9510	4.2602	75.9677
8	5.6157	4.5955	71.3722
9	5.2540	4.9572	66.4150
10	4.8638	5.3473	61.0677
11	4.4430	5.7682	55.2995
12	3.9890	6.2222	49.0773
13	3.4993	6.7119	42.3654
14	2.9710	7.2401	35.1252
15	2.4012	7.8100	27.3153
16	1.7865	8.4246	18.8906
17	1.1235	9.0877	9.8029
18	.4082	9.8029	0.0000

YEARS	MO PAYT	AN CONST
19	.8301	9.97

#	INT	PRIN	BALANCE
1	7.5160	2.4455	97.5545
2	7.3235	2.6379	94.9166
3	7.1159	2.8456	92.0710
4	6.8919	3.0695	89.0015
5	6.6504	3.3111	85.6904
6	6.3898	3.5717	82.1187
7	6.1087	3.8528	78.2659
8	5.8054	4.1560	74.1099
9	5.4783	4.4831	69.6268
10	5.1255	4.8360	64.7908
11	4.7449	5.2166	59.5743
12	4.3343	5.6271	53.9471
13	3.8914	6.0700	47.8771
14	3.4137	6.5478	41.3294
15	2.8984	7.0631	34.2663
16	2.3425	7.6190	26.6473
17	1.7428	8.2186	18.4287
18	1.0960	8.8655	9.5632
19	.3982	9.5632	0.0000

YEARS	MO PAYT	AN CONST
20	.8117	9.75

#	INT	PRIN	BALANCE
1	7.5238	2.2168	97.7832
2	7.3494	2.3913	95.3920
3	7.1612	2.5795	92.8125
4	6.9582	2.7825	90.0300
5	6.7392	3.0015	87.0286
6	6.5029	3.2377	83.7909
7	6.2481	3.4925	80.2983
8	5.9732	3.7674	76.5310
9	5.6767	4.0639	72.4671
10	5.3569	4.3837	68.0833
11	5.0119	4.7288	63.3546
12	4.6397	5.1009	58.2536
13	4.2382	5.5024	52.7512
14	3.8052	5.9355	46.8158
15	3.3380	6.4026	40.4132
16	2.8341	6.9065	33.5067
17	2.2905	7.4501	26.0566
18	1.7042	8.0364	18.0201
19	1.0717	8.6689	9.3512
20	.3894	9.3512	0.0000

YEARS	MO PAYT	AN CONST
21	.7954	9.55

#	INT	PRIN	BALANCE
1	7.5308	2.0137	97.9863
2	7.3723	2.1721	95.8142
3	7.2014	2.3431	93.4711

#	INT	PRIN	BALANCE
4	7.0170	2.5275	90.9436
5	6.8180	2.7264	88.2171
6	6.6035	2.9410	85.2761
7	6.3720	3.1725	82.1036
8	6.1223	3.4222	78.6814
9	5.8530	3.6915	74.9899
10	5.5624	3.9821	71.0078
11	5.2490	4.2955	66.7123
12	4.9109	4.6335	62.0788
13	4.5463	4.9982	57.0806
14	4.1529	5.3916	51.6890
15	3.7285	5.8159	45.8731
16	3.2708	6.2737	39.5994
17	2.7770	6.7674	32.8319
18	2.2444	7.3001	25.5319
19	1.6699	7.8746	17.6573
20	1.0501	8.4944	9.1629
21	.3816	9.1629	0.0000

YEARS 22	MO PAYT .7808	AN CONST 9.37	
#	INT	PRIN	BALANCE
1	7.5370	1.8325	98.1675
2	7.3928	1.9768	96.1907
3	7.2372	2.1323	94.0584
4	7.0694	2.3002	91.7582
5	6.8884	2.4812	89.2770
6	6.6931	2.6765	86.6005
7	6.4824	2.8871	83.7134
8	6.2552	3.1144	80.5990
9	6.0101	3.3595	77.2395
10	5.7457	3.6239	73.6157
11	5.4605	3.9091	69.7066
12	5.1528	4.2168	65.4898
13	4.8209	4.5486	60.9412
14	4.4630	4.9066	56.0346
15	4.0768	5.2928	50.7418
16	3.6602	5.7094	45.0324
17	3.2109	6.1587	38.8737
18	2.7262	6.6434	32.2303
19	2.2033	7.1663	25.0640
20	1.6393	7.7303	17.3337
21	1.0309	8.3387	8.9950
22	.3746	8.9950	0.0000

YEARS 23	MO PAYT .7678	AN CONST 9.22	
#	INT	PRIN	BALANCE
1	7.5426	1.6705	98.3295
2	7.4111	1.8019	96.5276
3	7.2693	1.9437	94.5839
4	7.1163	2.0967	92.4872
5	6.9513	2.2617	90.2254
6	6.7733	2.4398	87.7857
7	6.5813	2.6318	85.1539
8	6.3742	2.8389	82.3150
9	6.1507	3.0623	79.2526
10	5.9097	3.3034	75.9493
11	5.6497	3.5633	72.3859
12	5.3693	3.8438	68.5422
13	5.0667	4.1463	64.3958
14	4.7404	4.4726	59.9232
15	4.3884	4.8247	55.0985
16	4.0087	5.2044	49.8942
17	3.5991	5.6140	44.2802
18	3.1572	6.0558	38.2243
19	2.6806	6.5324	31.6919
20	2.1665	7.0466	24.6453
21	1.6119	7.6012	17.0442
22	1.0136	8.1994	8.8447
23	.3683	8.8447	0.0000

YEARS 24	MO PAYT .7560	AN CONST 9.08	
#	INT	PRIN	BALANCE
1	7.5476	1.5250	98.4750
2	7.4276	1.6450	96.8301
3	7.2981	1.7744	95.0556
4	7.1585	1.9141	93.1415
5	7.0078	2.0648	91.0768
6	6.8453	2.2273	88.8495
7	6.6700	2.4025	86.4470
8	6.4809	2.5916	83.8553
9	6.2770	2.7956	81.0597
10	6.0569	3.0156	78.0441
11	5.8196	3.2530	74.7911
12	5.5636	3.5090	71.2821
13	5.2874	3.7852	67.4969
14	4.9895	4.0831	63.4138
15	4.6681	4.4044	59.0094
16	4.3215	4.7511	54.2583
17	3.9476	5.1250	49.1333
18	3.5442	5.5284	43.6049
19	3.1091	5.9635	37.6414
20	2.6397	6.4328	31.2086
21	2.1334	6.9391	24.2695
22	1.5873	7.4853	16.7842
23	.9982	8.0744	8.7099
24	.3627	8.7099	0.0000

YEARS 25	MO PAYT .7455	AN CONST 8.95	
#	INT	PRIN	BALANCE
1	7.5521	1.3940	98.6060
2	7.4424	1.5037	97.1023
3	7.3240	1.6220	95.4803
4	7.1964	1.7497	93.7305
5	7.0587	1.8874	91.8431
6	6.9101	2.0360	89.8072
7	6.7499	2.1962	87.6110
8	6.5770	2.3691	85.2419
9	6.3906	2.5555	82.6864
10	6.1895	2.7566	79.9297
11	5.9725	2.9736	76.9561
12	5.7385	3.2076	73.7485
13	5.4860	3.4601	70.2884
14	5.2137	3.7324	66.5560
15	4.9199	4.0262	62.5299
16	4.6031	4.3430	58.1868
17	4.2612	4.6849	53.5020
18	3.8925	5.0536	48.4484
19	3.4948	5.4513	42.9971
20	3.0657	5.8803	37.1167
21	2.6029	6.3432	30.7736
22	2.1037	6.8424	23.9312
23	1.5652	7.3809	16.5503
24	.9843	7.9618	8.5884
25	.3576	8.5884	0.0000

YEARS 26	MO PAYT .7360	AN CONST 8.84	
#	INT	PRIN	BALANCE
1	7.5562	1.2758	98.7242
2	7.4558	1.3762	97.3480
3	7.3474	1.4845	95.8635
4	7.2306	1.6014	94.2621
5	7.1046	1.7274	92.5347
6	6.9686	1.8633	90.6714
7	6.8220	2.0100	88.6614
8	6.6638	2.1682	86.4932
9	6.4931	2.3388	84.1544
10	6.3091	2.5229	81.6315
11	6.1105	2.7215	78.9100
12	5.8963	2.9357	75.9743
13	5.6653	3.1667	72.8076
14	5.4160	3.4159	69.3917
15	5.1472	3.6848	65.7069
16	4.8572	3.9748	61.7321
17	4.5443	4.2876	57.4445
18	4.2069	4.6251	52.8194
19	3.8429	4.9891	47.8303
20	3.4502	5.3818	42.4485
21	3.0266	5.8053	36.6432
22	2.5697	6.2622	30.3810
23	2.0769	6.7551	23.6259
24	1.5452	7.2867	16.3391
25	.9717	7.8602	8.4789
26	.3531	8.4789	0.0000

YEARS 27	MO PAYT .7274	AN CONST 8.73	
#	INT	PRIN	BALANCE
1	7.5598	1.1689	98.8311
2	7.4678	1.2609	97.5702
3	7.3686	1.3601	96.2101
4	7.2616	1.4672	94.7429
5	7.1461	1.5826	93.1603
6	7.0215	1.7072	91.4531
7	6.8872	1.8416	89.6116
8	6.7422	1.9865	87.6251
9	6.5859	2.1428	85.4822
10	6.4172	2.3115	83.1707
11	6.2353	2.4934	80.6773
12	6.0391	2.6897	77.9876
13	5.8274	2.9013	75.0863
14	5.5990	3.1297	71.9566
15	5.3527	3.3760	68.5806
16	5.0870	3.6417	64.9389
17	4.8004	3.9283	61.0105
18	4.4912	4.2375	56.7730
19	4.1577	4.5710	52.2020
20	3.7979	4.9308	47.2712
21	3.4099	5.3189	41.9523
22	2.9913	5.7375	36.2149
23	2.5397	6.1890	30.0258
24	2.0526	6.6761	23.3497
25	1.5272	7.2016	16.1481
26	.9604	7.7684	8.3798
27	.3490	8.3798	0.0000

YEARS 28	MO PAYT .7196	AN CONST 8.64	
#	INT	PRIN	BALANCE
1	7.5632	1.0720	98.9280
2	7.4788	1.1564	97.7717
3	7.3878	1.2474	96.5243
4	7.2896	1.3455	95.1788
5	7.1837	1.4514	93.7273
6	7.0695	1.5657	92.1616
7	6.9463	1.6889	90.4727
8	6.8133	1.8218	88.6509
9	6.6700	1.9652	86.6857
10	6.5153	2.1199	84.5659
11	6.3484	2.2867	82.2791
12	6.1685	2.4667	79.8124
13	5.9743	2.6608	77.1516
14	5.7649	2.8702	74.2814
15	5.5390	3.0961	71.1852
16	5.2953	3.3398	67.8454
17	5.0325	3.6027	64.2427
18	4.7489	3.8862	60.3565
19	4.4431	4.1921	56.1644
20	4.1131	4.5220	51.6424
21	3.7572	4.8779	46.7645
22	3.3733	5.2618	41.5026
23	2.9592	5.6760	35.8267
24	2.5125	6.1227	29.7040
25	2.0306	6.6046	23.0994
26	1.5108	7.1244	15.9750
27	.9501	7.6851	8.2899
28	.3452	8.2899	0.0000

YEARS 29	MO PAYT .7125	AN CONST 8.56	
#	INT	PRIN	BALANCE
1	7.5662	.9840	99.0160
2	7.4887	1.0614	97.9546
3	7.4052	1.1450	96.8096
4	7.3151	1.2351	95.5745
5	7.2179	1.3323	94.2422
6	7.1130	1.4372	92.8050
7	6.9999	1.5503	91.2548
8	6.8779	1.6723	89.5825
9	6.7463	1.8039	87.7786
10	6.6043	1.9459	85.8327
11	6.4512	2.0990	83.7337
12	6.2860	2.2642	81.4695
13	6.1078	2.4424	79.0271
14	5.9155	2.6346	76.3925
15	5.7082	2.8420	73.5505
16	5.4845	3.0657	70.4848
17	5.2432	3.3070	67.1778
18	4.9830	3.5672	63.6106
19	4.7022	3.8480	59.7626
20	4.3993	4.1508	55.6118
21	4.0727	4.4775	51.1342
22	3.7203	4.8299	46.3043
23	3.3401	5.2101	41.0942
24	2.9301	5.6201	35.4741
25	2.4877	6.0624	29.4117
26	2.0106	6.5396	22.8721
27	1.4959	7.0543	15.8178
28	.9407	7.6095	8.2084
29	.3418	8.2084	0.0000

YEARS 30	MO PAYT .7061	AN CONST 8.48	
#	INT	PRIN	BALANCE
1	7.5689	.9040	99.0960
2	7.4978	.9751	98.1209
3	7.4211	1.0518	97.0691
4	7.3383	1.1346	95.9345
5	7.2490	1.2239	94.7106
6	7.1526	1.3203	93.3903
7	7.0487	1.4242	91.9661
8	6.9366	1.5363	90.4299
9	6.8157	1.6572	88.7727
10	6.6853	1.7876	86.9851
11	6.5446	1.9283	85.0569
12	6.3929	2.0800	82.9768
13	6.2291	2.2437	80.7331
14	6.0526	2.4203	78.3127
15	5.8621	2.6108	75.7019
16	5.6566	2.8163	72.8856
17	5.4349	3.0380	69.8476
18	5.1958	3.2771	66.5706
19	4.9379	3.5350	63.0356
20	4.6597	3.8132	59.2224
21	4.3596	4.1133	55.1090
22	4.0358	4.4371	50.6720
23	3.6866	4.7863	45.8857
24	3.3099	5.1630	40.7228
25	2.9036	5.5693	35.1535
26	2.4653	6.0076	29.1458
27	1.9924	6.4805	22.6654
28	1.4824	6.9905	15.6748
29	.9322	7.5407	8.1342
30	.3387	8.1342	0.0000

YEARS 2	MO PAYT 4.5056	AN CONST 54.07
# INT	PRIN	BALANCE
1 5.9670	48.1007	51.8993
2 2.1684	51.8993	0.0000

YEARS 3	MO PAYT 3.1164	AN CONST 37.40
# INT	PRIN	BALANCE
1 6.5622	30.8342	69.1658
2 4.1272	33.2692	35.8966
3 1.4998	35.8966	0.0000

YEARS 4	MO PAYT 2.4237	AN CONST 29.09
# INT	PRIN	BALANCE
1 6.8589	22.2258	77.7742
2 5.1037	23.9810	53.7931
3 3.2099	25.8749	27.9183
4 1.1665	27.9183	0.0000

YEARS 5	MO PAYT 2.0097	AN CONST 24.12
# INT	PRIN	BALANCE
1 7.0363	17.0806	82.9194
2 5.6874	18.4295	64.4899
3 4.2320	19.8849	44.6049
4 2.6616	21.4553	23.1497
5 .9672	23.1497	0.0000

YEARS 6	MO PAYT 1.7351	AN CONST 20.83
# INT	PRIN	BALANCE
1 7.1539	13.6669	86.3331
2 6.0746	14.7462	71.5869
3 4.9101	15.9108	55.6761
4 3.6536	17.1673	38.5088
5 2.2978	18.5230	19.9858
6 .8350	19.9858	0.0000

YEARS 7	MO PAYT 1.5400	AN CONST 18.49
# INT	PRIN	BALANCE
1 7.2375	11.2426	88.7574
2 6.3496	12.1304	76.6270
3 5.3917	13.0884	63.5387
4 4.3581	14.1220	49.4167
5 3.2428	15.2372	34.1794
6 2.0395	16.4405	17.7389
7 .7412	17.7389	0.0000

YEARS 8	MO PAYT 1.3947	AN CONST 16.74
# INT	PRIN	BALANCE
1 7.2997	9.4364	90.5636
2 6.5545	10.1817	80.3819
3 5.7505	10.9857	69.3962
4 4.8829	11.8533	57.5429
5 3.9468	12.7894	44.7535
6 2.9368	13.7994	30.9541
7 1.8470	14.8891	16.0650
8 .6712	16.0650	0.0000

YEARS 9	MO PAYT 1.2825	AN CONST 15.40
# INT	PRIN	BALANCE
1 7.3478	8.0424	91.9576
2 6.7127	8.6775	83.2801
3 6.0274	9.3628	73.9173
4 5.2880	10.1022	63.8150
5 4.4902	10.9000	52.9150
6 3.6294	11.7608	41.1542
7 2.7006	12.6896	28.4647
8 1.6985	13.6917	14.7730
9 .6172	14.7730	0.0000

YEARS 10	MO PAYT 1.1936	AN CONST 14.33
# INT	PRIN	BALANCE
1 7.3859	6.9367	93.0633
2 6.8381	7.4845	85.5788
3 6.2470	8.0756	77.5032
4 5.6093	8.7133	68.7898
5 4.9212	9.4015	59.3884
6 4.1787	10.1439	49.2445
7 3.3776	10.9450	38.2995
8 2.5133	11.8093	26.4901
9 1.5807	12.7419	13.7482
10 .5744	13.7482	0.0000

YEARS 11	MO PAYT 1.1215	AN CONST 13.46
# INT	PRIN	BALANCE
1 7.4168	6.0407	93.9593
2 6.9397	6.5177	87.4417
3 6.4250	7.0324	80.4092
4 5.8697	7.5878	72.8215
5 5.2704	8.1870	64.6345
6 4.6239	8.8335	55.8009
7 3.9263	9.5311	46.2698
8 3.1736	10.2838	35.9859
9 2.3615	11.0960	24.8900
10 1.4852	11.9722	12.9177
11 .5397	12.9177	0.0000

YEARS 12	MO PAYT 1.0620	AN CONST 12.75
# INT	PRIN	BALANCE
1 7.4423	5.3017	94.6983
2 7.0236	5.7204	88.9779
3 6.5718	6.1721	82.8057
4 6.0844	6.6596	76.1462
5 5.5585	7.1855	68.9607
6 4.9910	7.7529	61.2077
7 4.3788	8.3652	52.8425
8 3.7181	9.0258	43.8167
9 3.0053	9.7386	34.0781
10 2.2363	10.5077	23.5704
11 1.4065	11.3375	12.2329
12 .5111	12.2329	0.0000

YEARS 13	MO PAYT 1.0123	AN CONST 12.15
# INT	PRIN	BALANCE
1 7.4636	4.6835	95.3165
2 7.0937	5.0534	90.2631
3 6.6946	5.4525	84.8106
4 6.2640	5.8831	78.9275
5 5.7994	6.3477	72.5798
6 5.2981	6.8490	65.7309
7 4.7573	7.3898	58.3410
8 4.1737	7.9734	50.3676
9 3.5440	8.6031	41.7645
10 2.8646	9.2825	32.4820
11 2.1315	10.0156	22.4664
12 1.3406	10.8065	11.6599
13 .4872	11.6599	0.0000

YEARS 14	MO PAYT .9701	AN CONST 11.65
# INT	PRIN	BALANCE
1 7.4816	4.1602	95.8398
2 7.1531	4.4887	91.3512
3 6.7986	4.8432	86.5080
4 6.4161	5.2256	81.2823
5 6.0034	5.6383	75.6440
6 5.5582	6.0836	69.5604
7 5.0777	6.5640	62.9964
8 4.5594	7.0824	55.9140
9 4.0000	7.6417	48.2723
10 3.3966	8.2452	40.0271
11 2.7454	8.8963	31.1307
12 2.0429	9.5989	21.5318
13 1.2848	10.3569	11.1749
14 .4669	11.1749	0.0000

YEARS 15	MO PAYT .9341	AN CONST 11.21
# INT	PRIN	BALANCE
1 7.4970	3.7125	96.2875
2 7.2038	4.0057	92.2818
3 6.8875	4.3220	87.9597
4 6.5462	4.6634	83.2964
5 6.1779	5.0316	78.2647
6 5.7806	5.4290	72.8357
7 5.3518	5.8577	66.9780
8 4.8892	6.3203	60.6576
9 4.3901	6.8195	53.8382
10 3.8515	7.3580	46.4801
11 3.2705	7.9391	38.5410
12 2.6435	8.5661	29.9750
13 1.9670	9.2425	20.7324
14 1.2371	9.9724	10.7600
15 .4496	10.7600	0.0000

YEARS 16	MO PAYT .9031	AN CONST 10.84
# INT	PRIN	BALANCE
1 7.5103	3.3263	96.6737
2 7.2477	3.5890	93.0846
3 6.9642	3.8725	89.2122
4 6.6584	4.1783	85.0339
5 6.3284	4.5082	80.5256
6 5.9724	4.8643	75.6614
7 5.5883	5.2484	70.4129
8 5.1738	5.6629	64.7500
9 4.7266	6.1101	58.6399
10 4.2441	6.5926	52.0473
11 3.7234	7.1133	44.9340
12 3.1617	7.6750	37.2590
13 2.5556	8.2811	28.9779
14 1.9016	8.9351	20.0428
15 1.1960	9.6407	10.4021
16 .4346	10.4021	0.0000

YEARS 17	MO PAYT .8760	AN CONST 10.52
# INT	PRIN	BALANCE
1 7.5219	2.9907	97.0093
2 7.2857	3.2269	93.7825
3 7.0309	3.4817	90.3008
4 6.7559	3.7567	86.5441
5 6.4593	4.0533	82.4908
6 6.1392	4.3734	78.1174
7 5.7938	4.7188	73.3986
8 5.4201	5.0915	68.3071
9 5.0191	5.4935	62.8136
10 4.5852	5.9274	56.8862
11 4.1171	6.3955	50.4907
12 3.6121	6.9005	43.5902
13 3.0671	7.4455	36.1447
14 2.4791	8.0335	28.1113
15 1.8447	8.6679	19.4434
16 1.1602	9.3524	10.0910
17 .4216	10.0910	0.0000

YEARS 18	MO PAYT .8524	AN CONST 10.23
# INT	PRIN	BALANCE
1 7.5320	2.6970	97.3030
2 7.3190	2.9100	94.3929
3 7.0892	3.1398	91.2531
4 6.8413	3.3878	87.8653
5 6.5737	3.6553	84.2100
6 6.2851	3.9440	80.2660
7 5.9736	4.2555	76.0105
8 5.6375	4.5915	71.4190
9 5.2749	4.9541	66.4648
10 4.8837	5.3454	61.1195
11 4.4616	5.7675	55.3520
12 4.0061	6.2230	49.1290
13 3.5147	6.7144	42.4146
14 2.9844	7.2447	35.1699
15 2.4123	7.8168	27.3531
16 1.7950	8.4341	18.9190
17 1.1289	9.1002	9.8188
18 .4102	9.8188	0.0000

YEARS 19	MO PAYT .8316	AN CONST 9.98
# INT	PRIN	BALANCE
1 7.5409	2.4387	97.5613
2 7.3484	2.6313	94.9301
3 7.1406	2.8391	92.0910
4 6.9164	3.0633	89.0277
5 6.6744	3.3052	85.7226
6 6.4134	3.5662	82.1564
7 6.1318	3.8478	78.3086
8 5.8279	4.1517	74.1569
9 5.5001	4.4796	69.6773
10 5.1463	4.8333	64.8440
11 4.7646	5.2150	59.6290
12 4.3528	5.6269	54.0021
13 3.9084	6.0712	47.9309
14 3.4289	6.5507	41.3802
15 2.9116	7.0680	34.3122
16 2.3534	7.6262	26.6860
17 1.7512	8.2284	18.4576
18 1.1014	8.8782	9.5794
19 .4002	9.5794	0.0000

YEARS 20	MO PAYT .8133	AN CONST 9.76
# INT	PRIN	BALANCE
1 7.5488	2.2102	97.7898
2 7.3743	2.3848	95.4050
3 7.1859	2.5731	92.8319
4 6.9827	2.7763	90.0556
5 6.7635	2.9956	87.0600
6 6.5269	3.2321	83.8279
7 6.2717	3.4874	80.3405
8 5.9963	3.7628	76.5778
9 5.6991	4.0599	72.5178
10 5.3785	4.3806	68.1373
11 5.0326	4.7265	63.4108
12 4.6593	5.0998	58.3110
13 4.2566	5.5025	52.8065
14 3.8220	5.9370	46.8715
15 3.3532	6.4059	40.4656
16 2.8473	6.9118	33.5538
17 2.3014	7.4576	26.0962
18 1.7125	8.0466	18.0497
19 1.0770	8.6820	9.3676
20 .3914	9.3676	0.0000

YEARS 21	MO PAYT .7969	AN CONST 9.57
# INT	PRIN	BALANCE
1 7.5558	2.0073	97.9927
2 7.3973	2.1659	95.8268
3 7.2262	2.3369	93.4899

#	INT	PRIN	BALANCE
4	7.0417	2.5215	90.9684
5	6.8426	2.7206	88.2479
6	6.6277	2.9354	85.3124
7	6.3959	3.1672	82.1452
8	6.1458	3.4174	78.7278
9	5.8759	3.6872	75.0406
10	5.5847	3.9784	71.0622
11	5.2705	4.2926	66.7695
12	4.9315	4.6316	62.1379
13	4.5658	4.9974	57.1405
14	4.1711	5.3920	51.7485
15	3.7453	5.8179	45.9306
16	3.2858	6.2773	39.6533
17	2.7901	6.7730	32.8803
18	2.2552	7.3079	25.5724
19	1.6781	7.8850	17.6873
20	1.0554	8.5077	9.1796
21	.3835	9.1796	0.0000

YEARS 22 — MO PAYT .7824 — AN CONST 9.39

#	INT	PRIN	BALANCE
1	7.5620	1.8264	98.1736
2	7.4178	1.9707	96.2029
3	7.2622	2.1263	94.0766
4	7.0943	2.2942	91.7824
5	6.9131	2.4754	89.3070
6	6.7176	2.6709	86.6361
7	6.5067	2.8818	83.7543
8	6.2791	3.1094	80.6449
9	6.0335	3.3550	77.2899
10	5.7686	3.6199	73.6700
11	5.4827	3.9058	69.7642
12	5.1743	4.2142	65.5500
13	4.8415	4.5470	61.0030
14	4.4824	4.9061	56.0969
15	4.0949	5.2936	50.8033
16	3.6769	5.7116	45.0917
17	3.2258	6.1627	38.9291
18	2.7392	6.6493	32.2798
19	2.2140	7.1744	25.1053
20	1.6475	7.7410	17.3643
21	1.0361	8.3523	9.0119
22	.3765	9.0119	0.0000

YEARS 23 — MO PAYT .7694 — AN CONST 9.24

#	INT	PRIN	BALANCE
1	7.5676	1.6646	98.3354
2	7.4362	1.7960	96.5394
3	7.2943	1.9379	94.6015
4	7.1413	2.0909	92.5106
5	6.9762	2.2560	90.2546
6	6.7980	2.4342	87.8204
7	6.6058	2.6264	85.1939
8	6.3984	2.8338	82.3601
9	6.1746	3.0576	79.3025
10	5.9331	3.2991	76.0034
11	5.6726	3.5596	72.4437
12	5.3914	3.8408	68.6030
13	5.0881	4.1441	64.4589
14	4.7609	4.4713	59.9876
15	4.4078	4.8244	55.1631
16	4.0268	5.2054	49.9577
17	3.6157	5.6165	44.3412
18	3.1721	6.0601	38.2811
19	2.6936	6.5386	31.7424
20	2.1772	7.0550	24.6874
21	1.6200	7.6122	17.0753
22	1.0189	8.2133	8.8619
23	.3703	8.8619	0.0000

YEARS 24 — MO PAYT .7577 — AN CONST 9.10

#	INT	PRIN	BALANCE
1	7.5726	1.5193	98.4807
2	7.4526	1.6393	96.8414
3	7.3232	1.7687	95.0727
4	7.1835	1.9084	93.1642
5	7.0328	2.0591	91.1051
6	6.8702	2.2218	88.8833
7	6.6947	2.3972	86.4861
8	6.5054	2.5865	83.8996
9	6.3011	2.7908	81.1088
10	6.0808	3.0112	78.0976
11	5.8430	3.2490	74.8486
12	5.5864	3.5056	71.3431
13	5.3095	3.7824	67.5607
14	5.0108	4.0811	63.4796
15	4.6885	4.4034	59.0762
16	4.3408	4.7511	54.3250
17	3.9656	5.1264	49.1987
18	3.5607	5.5312	43.6675
19	3.1239	5.9680	37.6995
20	2.6526	6.4393	31.2602
21	2.1441	6.9478	24.3123
22	1.5954	7.4965	16.8158
23	1.0034	8.0885	8.7273
24	.3646	8.7273	0.0000

YEARS 25 — MO PAYT .7471 — AN CONST 8.97

#	INT	PRIN	BALANCE
1	7.5771	1.3886	98.6114
2	7.4675	1.4982	97.1132
3	7.3492	1.6165	95.4967
4	7.2215	1.7442	93.7525
5	7.0838	1.8819	91.8706
6	6.9351	2.0305	89.8400
7	6.7748	2.1909	87.6491
8	6.6018	2.3639	85.2852
9	6.4151	2.5506	82.7346
10	6.2137	2.7520	79.9826
11	5.9963	2.9694	77.0132
12	5.7618	3.2039	73.8093
13	5.5088	3.4569	70.3524
14	5.2358	3.7299	66.6226
15	4.9413	4.0244	62.5981
16	4.6234	4.3423	58.2559
17	4.2805	4.6852	53.5707
18	3.9105	5.0552	48.5155
19	3.5113	5.4544	43.0611
20	3.0806	5.8851	37.1760
21	2.6158	6.3499	30.8261
22	2.1143	6.8514	23.9748
23	1.5733	7.3924	16.5823
24	.9895	7.9762	8.6061
25	.3596	8.6061	0.0000

YEARS 26 — MO PAYT .7376 — AN CONST 8.86

#	INT	PRIN	BALANCE
1	7.5812	1.2706	98.7294
2	7.4809	1.3709	97.3585
3	7.3726	1.4792	95.8793
4	7.2558	1.5960	94.2834
5	7.1298	1.7220	92.5613
6	6.9938	1.8580	90.7033
7	6.8470	2.0047	88.6986
8	6.6887	2.1631	86.5355
9	6.5179	2.3339	84.2016
10	6.3336	2.5182	81.6834
11	6.1347	2.7171	78.9663
12	5.9201	2.9316	76.0347
13	5.6886	3.1632	72.8715
14	5.4388	3.4130	69.4586
15	5.1693	3.6825	65.7761
16	4.8785	3.9733	61.8028
17	4.5647	4.2871	57.5157
18	4.2261	4.6256	52.8900
19	3.8608	4.9909	47.8991
20	3.4667	5.3851	42.5140
21	3.0414	5.8104	36.7037
22	2.5826	6.2692	30.4344
23	2.0875	6.7643	23.6701
24	1.5533	7.2985	16.3716
25	.9769	7.8749	8.4968
26	.3550	8.4968	0.0000

YEARS 27 — MO PAYT .7291 — AN CONST 8.75

#	INT	PRIN	BALANCE
1	7.5849	1.1639	98.8361
2	7.4930	1.2558	97.5803
3	7.3938	1.3550	96.2254
4	7.2868	1.4620	94.7634
5	7.1713	1.5774	93.1860
6	7.0468	1.7020	91.4840
7	6.9124	1.8364	89.6476
8	6.7673	1.9814	87.6662
9	6.6109	2.1379	85.5283
10	6.4420	2.3067	83.2216
11	6.2599	2.4889	80.7327
12	6.0633	2.6854	78.0473
13	5.8512	2.8975	75.1497
14	5.6224	3.1263	72.0234
15	5.3755	3.3732	68.6502
16	5.1091	3.6396	65.0105
17	4.8217	3.9271	61.0835
18	4.5116	4.2372	56.8463
19	4.1769	4.5718	52.2745
20	3.8159	4.9329	47.3416
21	3.4263	5.3224	42.0192
22	3.0060	5.7427	36.2765
23	2.5525	6.1962	30.0802
24	2.0632	6.6856	23.3946
25	1.5352	7.2136	16.1811
26	.9655	7.7832	8.3979
27	.3509	8.3979	0.0000

YEARS 28 — MO PAYT .7213 — AN CONST 8.66

#	INT	PRIN	BALANCE
1	7.5882	1.0672	98.9328
2	7.5039	1.1514	97.7814
3	7.4130	1.2424	96.5390
4	7.3149	1.3405	95.1985
5	7.2090	1.4464	93.7521
6	7.0948	1.5606	92.1916
7	6.9716	1.6838	90.5077
8	6.8386	1.8168	88.6909
9	6.6951	1.9603	86.7307
10	6.5403	2.1151	84.6156
11	6.3733	2.2821	82.3335
12	6.1931	2.4623	79.8712
13	5.9986	2.6568	77.2144
14	5.7888	2.8666	74.3478
15	5.5624	3.0930	71.2548
16	5.3181	3.3372	67.9175
17	5.0546	3.6008	64.3167
18	4.7702	3.8852	60.4316
19	4.4634	4.1920	56.2396
20	4.1324	4.5230	51.7166
21	3.7752	4.8802	46.8364
22	3.3898	5.2656	41.5708
23	2.9739	5.6814	35.8893
24	2.5253	6.1301	29.7592
25	2.0412	6.6142	23.1450
26	1.5188	7.1366	16.0084
27	.9552	7.7002	8.3083
28	.3471	8.3083	0.0000

YEARS 29 — MO PAYT .7142 — AN CONST 8.58

#	INT	PRIN	BALANCE
1	7.5912	.9794	99.0206
2	7.5139	1.0567	97.9639
3	7.4304	1.1402	96.8237
4	7.3404	1.2302	95.5935
5	7.2433	1.3274	94.2661
6	7.1384	1.4322	92.8340
7	7.0253	1.5453	91.2887
8	6.9033	1.6673	89.6213
9	6.7716	1.7990	87.8223
10	6.6295	1.9411	85.8813
11	6.4763	2.0944	83.7869
12	6.3109	2.2598	81.5271
13	6.1324	2.4382	79.0889
14	5.9399	2.6308	76.4581
15	5.7321	2.8385	73.6196
16	5.5079	3.0627	70.5569
17	5.2661	3.3046	67.2524
18	5.0051	3.5655	63.6868
19	4.7235	3.8471	59.8397
20	4.4197	4.1509	55.6888
21	4.0919	4.4787	51.2101
22	3.7382	4.8324	46.3777
23	3.3566	5.2140	41.1637
24	2.9448	5.6258	35.5378
25	2.5005	6.0701	29.4678
26	2.0212	6.5495	22.9183
27	1.5039	7.0667	15.8516
28	.9459	7.6247	8.2269
29	.3437	8.2269	0.0000

YEARS 30 — MO PAYT .7078 — AN CONST 8.50

#	INT	PRIN	BALANCE
1	7.5940	.8995	99.1005
2	7.5230	.9706	98.1299
3	7.4463	1.0472	97.0827
4	7.3636	1.1299	95.9528
5	7.2744	1.2191	94.7336
6	7.1781	1.3154	93.4182
7	7.0742	1.4193	91.9989
8	6.9621	1.5314	90.4675
9	6.8412	1.6523	88.8152
10	6.7107	1.7828	87.0323
11	6.5699	1.9236	85.1087
12	6.4180	2.0755	83.0332
13	6.2541	2.2394	80.7938
14	6.0772	2.4163	78.3775
15	5.8864	2.6071	75.7704
16	5.6805	2.8130	72.9574
17	5.4584	3.0351	69.9222
18	5.2187	3.2748	66.6474
19	4.9601	3.5335	63.1140
20	4.6810	3.8125	59.3015
21	4.3799	4.1136	55.1879
22	4.0551	4.4384	50.7495
23	3.7046	4.7889	45.9605
24	3.3264	5.1671	40.7934
25	2.9183	5.5752	35.2182
26	2.4780	6.0155	29.2027
27	2.0030	6.4905	22.7122
28	1.4904	7.0031	15.7090
29	.9374	7.5562	8.1529
30	.3406	8.1529	0.0000

YEARS 2 — MO PAYT 4.5091 — AN CONST 54.11

#	INT	PRIN	BALANCE
1	6.0266	48.0821	51.9179
2	2.1908	51.9179	0.0000

YEARS 3 — MO PAYT 3.1198 — AN CONST 37.44

#	INT	PRIN	BALANCE
1	6.6277	30.8101	69.1899
2	4.1698	33.2680	35.9220
3	1.5158	35.9220	0.0000

YEARS 4 — MO PAYT 2.4272 — AN CONST 29.13

#	INT	PRIN	BALANCE
1	6.9274	22.1994	77.8006
2	5.1564	23.9704	53.8302
3	3.2441	25.8827	27.9475
4	1.1793	27.9475	0.0000

YEARS 5 — MO PAYT 2.0133 — AN CONST 24.16

#	INT	PRIN	BALANCE
1	7.1065	17.0532	82.9468
2	5.7461	18.4137	64.5331
3	4.2771	19.8827	44.6504
4	2.6909	21.4688	23.1815
5	.9782	23.1815	0.0000

YEARS 6 — MO PAYT 1.7387 — AN CONST 20.87

#	INT	PRIN	BALANCE
1	7.2253	13.6392	86.3608
2	6.1372	14.7273	71.6335
3	4.9623	15.9022	55.7313
4	3.6937	17.1708	38.5604
5	2.3239	18.5407	20.0198
6	.8448	20.0198	0.0000

YEARS 7 — MO PAYT 1.5437 — AN CONST 18.53

#	INT	PRIN	BALANCE
1	7.3097	11.2149	88.7851
2	6.4150	12.1096	76.6755
3	5.4489	13.0757	63.5998
4	4.4058	14.1188	49.4810
5	3.2795	15.2451	34.2359
6	2.0633	16.4613	17.7746
7	.7500	17.7746	0.0000

YEARS 8 — MO PAYT 1.3985 — AN CONST 16.79

#	INT	PRIN	BALANCE
1	7.3725	9.4091	90.5909
2	6.6219	10.1597	80.4312
3	5.8114	10.9702	69.4610
4	4.9363	11.8454	57.6157
5	3.9913	12.7903	44.8253
6	2.9709	13.8107	31.0146
7	1.8691	14.9125	16.1021
8	.6795	16.1021	0.0000

YEARS 9 — MO PAYT 1.2864 — AN CONST 15.44

#	INT	PRIN	BALANCE
1	7.4210	8.0154	91.9846
2	6.7816	8.6549	83.3297
3	6.0911	9.3453	73.9843
4	5.3456	10.0909	63.8934
5	4.5406	10.8959	52.9975
6	3.6714	11.7651	41.2324
7	2.7328	12.7037	28.5287
8	1.7193	13.7172	14.8115
9	.6250	14.8115	0.0000

YEARS 10 — MO PAYT 1.1975 — AN CONST 14.37

#	INT	PRIN	BALANCE
1	7.4595	6.9103	93.0897
2	6.9082	7.4616	85.6282
3	6.3130	8.0568	77.5713
4	5.6702	8.6996	68.8718
5	4.9762	9.3936	59.4782
6	4.2268	10.1430	49.3352
7	3.4177	10.9521	38.3831
8	2.5439	11.8259	26.5573
9	1.6005	12.7693	13.7880
10	.5818	13.7880	0.0000

YEARS 11 — MO PAYT 1.1255 — AN CONST 13.51

#	INT	PRIN	BALANCE
1	7.4907	6.0148	93.9852
2	7.0108	6.4946	87.4906
3	6.4927	7.0128	80.4778
4	5.9333	7.5722	72.9056
5	5.3292	8.1763	64.7293
6	4.6769	8.8286	55.9007
7	3.9726	9.5329	46.3678
8	3.2121	10.2934	36.0744
9	2.3909	11.1146	24.9599
10	1.5042	12.0012	12.9587
11	.5468	12.9587	0.0000

YEARS 12 — MO PAYT 1.0661 — AN CONST 12.80

#	INT	PRIN	BALANCE
1	7.5164	5.2765	94.7235
2	7.0954	5.6974	89.0261
3	6.6409	6.1520	82.8741
4	6.1501	6.6427	76.2314
5	5.6202	7.1727	69.0587
6	5.0480	7.7449	61.3138
7	4.4301	8.3627	52.9511
8	3.7630	9.0299	43.9212
9	3.0426	9.7503	34.1710
10	2.2648	10.5281	23.6429
11	1.4249	11.3680	12.2749
12	.5180	12.2749	0.0000

YEARS 13 — MO PAYT 1.0164 — AN CONST 12.20

#	INT	PRIN	BALANCE
1	7.5379	4.6590	95.3410
2	7.1662	5.0307	90.3104
3	6.7648	5.4320	84.8784
4	6.3315	5.8653	79.0130
5	5.8636	6.3332	72.6798
6	5.3583	6.8385	65.8413
7	4.8128	7.3840	58.4572
8	4.2237	7.9731	50.4841
9	3.5877	8.6092	41.8749
10	2.9008	9.2960	32.5790
11	2.1592	10.0376	22.5414
12	1.3585	10.8384	11.7030
13	.4938	11.7030	0.0000

YEARS 14 — MO PAYT .9744 — AN CONST 11.70

#	INT	PRIN	BALANCE
1	7.5560	4.1363	95.8637
2	7.2261	4.4663	91.3974
3	6.8698	4.8226	86.5749
4	6.4850	5.2073	81.3675
5	6.0696	5.6227	75.7448
6	5.6211	6.0713	69.6735
7	5.1367	6.5556	63.1179
8	4.6137	7.0786	56.0393
9	4.0490	7.6433	48.3960
10	3.4393	8.2531	40.1429
11	2.7809	8.9115	31.2314
12	2.0699	9.6224	21.6090
13	1.3023	10.3901	11.2189
14	.4734	11.2189	0.0000

YEARS 15 — MO PAYT .9384 — AN CONST 11.27

#	INT	PRIN	BALANCE
1	7.5716	3.6894	96.3106
2	7.2773	3.9837	92.3269
3	6.9595	4.3015	88.0254
4	6.6163	4.6447	83.3808
5	6.2458	5.0152	78.3656
6	5.8457	5.4153	72.9503
7	5.4137	5.8473	67.1030
8	4.9472	6.3138	60.7892
9	4.4435	6.8175	53.9718
10	3.8996	7.3613	46.6105
11	3.3124	7.9486	38.6619
12	2.6783	8.5827	30.0792
13	1.9936	9.2674	20.8117
14	1.2542	10.0067	10.8050
15	.4559	10.8050	0.0000

YEARS 16 — MO PAYT .9074 — AN CONST 10.89

#	INT	PRIN	BALANCE
1	7.5850	3.3039	96.6961
2	7.2314	3.5675	93.1286
3	7.0368	3.8521	89.2765
4	6.7295	4.1594	85.1172
5	6.3977	4.4912	80.6260
6	6.0394	4.8495	75.7765
7	5.6525	5.2364	70.5401
8	5.2348	5.6541	64.8860
9	4.7837	6.1052	58.7808
10	4.2967	6.5922	52.1886
11	3.7708	7.1181	45.0705
12	3.2029	7.6860	37.3845
13	2.5898	8.2991	29.0854
14	1.9277	8.9612	20.1241
15	1.2128	9.6761	10.4480
16	.4409	10.4480	0.0000

YEARS 17 — MO PAYT .8805 — AN CONST 10.57

#	INT	PRIN	BALANCE
1	7.5967	2.9690	97.0310
2	7.3598	3.2058	93.8252
3	7.1041	3.4616	90.3637
4	6.8279	3.7377	86.6260
5	6.5297	4.0359	82.5901
6	6.2078	4.3579	78.2322
7	5.8601	4.7055	73.5267
8	5.4847	5.0809	68.4458
9	5.0794	5.4862	62.9596
10	4.6417	5.9239	57.0357
11	4.1691	6.3965	50.6392
12	3.6588	6.9068	43.7324
13	3.1078	7.4578	36.2746
14	2.5129	8.0527	28.2218
15	1.8705	8.6952	19.5267
16	1.1768	9.3888	10.1378
17	.4278	10.1378	0.0000

YEARS 18 — MO PAYT .8569 — AN CONST 10.29

#	INT	PRIN	BALANCE
1	7.6069	2.6760	97.3240
2	7.3934	2.8895	94.4345
3	7.1629	3.1200	91.3144
4	6.9140	3.3689	87.9455
5	6.6452	3.6377	84.3078
6	6.3550	3.9279	80.3799
7	6.0416	4.2412	76.1387
8	5.7033	4.5796	71.5591
9	5.3380	4.9449	66.6142
10	4.9435	5.3394	61.2748
11	4.5175	5.7654	55.5094
12	4.0576	6.2253	49.2840
13	3.5609	6.7220	42.5621
14	3.0247	7.2582	35.3039
15	2.4456	7.8373	27.4666
16	1.8204	8.4625	19.0041
17	1.1453	9.1376	9.8665
18	.4163	9.8665	0.0000

YEARS 19 — MO PAYT .8362 — AN CONST 10.04

#	INT	PRIN	BALANCE
1	7.6158	2.4184	97.5816
2	7.4229	2.6113	94.9703
3	7.2146	2.8196	92.1507
4	6.9896	3.0446	89.1061
5	6.7468	3.2875	85.8187
6	6.4845	3.5497	82.2690
7	6.2013	3.8329	78.4361
8	5.8955	4.1387	74.2974
9	5.5654	4.4688	69.8285
10	5.2089	4.8253	65.0032
11	4.8239	5.2103	59.7929
12	4.4083	5.6260	54.1669
13	3.9594	6.0748	48.0922
14	3.4748	6.5594	41.5328
15	2.9515	7.0827	34.4501
16	2.3865	7.6477	26.8024
17	1.7764	8.2578	18.5445
18	1.1176	8.9166	9.6279
19	.4063	9.6279	0.0000

YEARS 20 — MO PAYT .8179 — AN CONST 9.82

#	INT	PRIN	BALANCE
1	7.6238	2.1906	97.8094
2	7.4490	2.3654	95.4440
3	7.2603	2.5541	92.8899
4	7.0565	2.7579	90.1320
5	6.8365	2.9779	87.1541
6	6.5990	3.2154	83.9387
7	6.3424	3.4720	80.4667
8	6.0655	3.7489	76.7178
9	5.7664	4.0480	72.6698
10	5.4435	4.3709	68.2989
11	5.0948	4.7196	63.5792
12	4.7182	5.0962	58.4831
13	4.3117	5.5027	52.9803
14	3.8727	5.9417	47.0386
15	3.3987	6.4157	40.6229
16	2.8869	6.9275	33.6954
17	2.3342	7.4802	26.2152
18	1.7375	8.0769	18.1383
19	1.0931	8.7213	9.4170
20	.3974	9.4170	0.0000

YEARS 21 — MO PAYT .8016 — AN CONST 9.62

#	INT	PRIN	BALANCE
1	7.6308	1.9884	98.0116
2	7.4722	2.1471	95.8645
3	7.3009	2.3184	93.5461

#	INT	PRIN	BALANCE
4	7.1159	2.5033	91.0428
5	6.9162	2.7030	88.3398
6	6.7006	2.9187	85.4211
7	6.4677	3.1515	82.2696
8	6.2163	3.4029	78.8667
9	5.9449	3.6744	75.1923
10	5.6517	3.9675	71.2248
11	5.3352	4.2840	66.9408
12	4.9934	4.6258	62.3150
13	4.6244	4.9948	57.3201
14	4.2260	5.3933	51.9269
15	3.7957	5.8236	46.1033
16	3.3311	6.2881	39.8152
17	2.8295	6.7898	33.0254
18	2.2878	7.3314	25.6939
19	1.7029	7.9163	17.7776
20	1.0714	8.5479	9.2298
21	.3895	9.2298	0.0000

YEARS 22 — MO PAYT .7871 — AN CONST 9.45

#	INT	PRIN	BALANCE
1	7.6371	1.8082	98.1918
2	7.4928	1.9525	96.2393
3	7.3371	2.1083	94.1310
4	7.1689	2.2764	91.8546
5	6.9873	2.4580	89.3965
6	6.7912	2.6541	86.7424
7	6.5794	2.8659	83.8765
8	6.3508	3.0945	80.7820
9	6.1039	3.3414	77.4406
10	5.8374	3.6079	73.8327
11	5.5495	3.8958	69.9369
12	5.2387	4.2066	65.7303
13	4.9032	4.5421	61.1882
14	4.5408	4.9045	56.2837
15	4.1495	5.2958	50.9879
16	3.7271	5.7182	45.2696
17	3.2709	6.1744	39.0952
18	2.7783	6.6670	32.4282
19	2.2464	7.1989	25.2293
20	1.6721	7.7732	17.4562
21	1.0520	8.3933	9.0629
22	.3824	9.0629	0.0000

YEARS 23 — MO PAYT .7741 — AN CONST 9.29

#	INT	PRIN	BALANCE
1	7.6427	1.6471	98.3529
2	7.5113	1.7785	96.5745
3	7.3694	1.9203	94.6542
4	7.2162	2.0735	92.5806
5	7.0508	2.2389	90.3417
6	6.8722	2.4176	87.9241
7	6.6793	2.6104	85.3137
8	6.4711	2.8187	82.4950
9	6.2462	3.0435	79.4515
10	6.0034	3.2863	76.1651
11	5.7412	3.5485	72.6166
12	5.4581	3.8316	68.7850
13	5.1525	4.1373	64.6477
14	4.8224	4.4673	60.1804
15	4.4660	4.8237	55.3566
16	4.0812	5.2085	50.1481
17	3.6657	5.6241	44.5240
18	3.2170	6.0727	38.4513
19	2.7325	6.5572	31.8941
20	2.2094	7.0803	24.8138
21	1.6446	7.6451	17.1687
22	1.0347	8.2550	8.9136
23	.3761	8.9136	0.0000

YEARS 24 — MO PAYT .7625 — AN CONST 9.16

#	INT	PRIN	BALANCE
1	7.6477	1.5025	98.4975
2	7.5279	1.6223	96.8752
3	7.3984	1.7517	95.1235
4	7.2587	1.8915	93.2320
5	7.1078	2.0424	91.1896
6	6.9449	2.2053	88.9843
7	6.7689	2.3812	86.6031
8	6.5790	2.5712	84.0319
9	6.3738	2.7763	81.2556
10	6.1523	2.9978	78.2577
11	5.9132	3.2370	75.0208
12	5.6550	3.4952	71.5256
13	5.3761	3.7740	67.7515
14	5.0750	4.0751	63.6764
15	4.7499	4.4002	59.2762
16	4.3989	4.7513	54.5249
17	4.0199	5.1303	49.3946
18	3.6106	5.5396	43.8551
19	3.1687	5.9815	37.8736
20	2.6915	6.4587	31.4149
21	2.1762	6.9739	24.4410
22	1.6199	7.5303	16.9107
23	1.0191	8.1310	8.7797
24	.3705	8.7797	0.0000

YEARS 25 — MO PAYT .7520 — AN CONST 9.03

#	INT	PRIN	BALANCE
1	7.6522	1.3724	98.6276
2	7.5428	1.4818	97.1458
3	7.4245	1.6000	95.5458
4	7.2969	1.7277	93.8181
5	7.1591	1.8655	91.9526
6	7.0102	2.0143	89.9382
7	6.8495	2.1750	87.7632
8	6.6760	2.3486	85.4146
9	6.4887	2.5359	82.8787
10	6.2864	2.7382	80.1404
11	6.0679	2.9567	77.1838
12	5.8320	3.1925	73.9912
13	5.5774	3.4472	70.5440
14	5.3023	3.7222	66.8217
15	5.0054	4.0192	62.8025
16	4.6848	4.3398	58.4627
17	4.3385	4.6860	53.7767
18	3.9647	5.0599	48.7168
19	3.5610	5.4635	43.2532
20	3.1252	5.8994	37.3538
21	2.6546	6.3700	30.9838
22	2.1464	6.8782	24.1056
23	1.5977	7.4269	16.6786
24	1.0052	8.0194	8.6592
25	.3654	8.6592	0.0000

YEARS 26 — MO PAYT .7426 — AN CONST 8.92

#	INT	PRIN	BALANCE
1	7.6563	1.2550	98.7450
2	7.5562	1.3551	97.3899
3	7.4481	1.4632	95.9266
4	7.3314	1.5800	94.3467
5	7.2053	1.7060	92.6407
6	7.0692	1.8421	90.7985
7	6.9223	1.9891	88.8095
8	6.7636	2.1477	86.6617
9	6.5922	2.3191	84.3426
10	6.4072	2.5041	81.8385
11	6.2075	2.7039	79.1347
12	5.9918	2.9196	76.2151
13	5.7588	3.1525	73.0626
14	5.5074	3.4040	69.6586
15	5.2358	3.6755	65.9831
16	4.9426	3.9688	62.0144
17	4.6260	4.2854	57.7290
18	4.2841	4.6272	53.1018
19	3.9149	4.9964	48.1054
20	3.5164	5.3950	42.7104
21	3.0860	5.8254	36.8850
22	2.6212	6.2901	30.5949
23	2.1194	6.7919	23.8030
24	1.5776	7.3337	16.4693
25	.9925	7.9188	8.5505
26	.3608	8.5505	0.0000

YEARS 27 — MO PAYT .7341 — AN CONST 8.81

#	INT	PRIN	BALANCE
1	7.6600	1.1489	98.8511
2	7.5684	1.2406	97.6105
3	7.4694	1.3396	96.2709
4	7.3625	1.4464	94.8245
5	7.2471	1.5618	93.2627
6	7.1225	1.6864	91.5763
7	6.9880	1.8209	89.7553
8	6.8427	1.9662	87.7891
9	6.6859	2.1231	85.6660
10	6.5165	2.2924	83.3736
11	6.3336	2.4753	80.8983
12	6.1361	2.6728	78.2255
13	5.9229	2.8860	75.3394
14	5.6927	3.1163	72.2232
15	5.4441	3.3649	68.8583
16	5.1756	3.6333	65.2250
17	4.8858	3.9232	61.3019
18	4.5728	4.2361	57.0657
19	4.2349	4.5741	52.4917
20	3.8700	4.9390	47.5527
21	3.4760	5.3330	42.2197
22	3.0505	5.7584	36.4612
23	2.5911	6.2178	30.2434
24	2.0951	6.7139	23.5296
25	1.5595	7.2495	16.2801
26	.9811	7.8278	8.4523
27	.3567	8.4523	0.0000

YEARS 28 — MO PAYT .7264 — AN CONST 8.72

#	INT	PRIN	BALANCE
1	7.6634	1.0528	98.9472
2	7.5794	1.1368	97.8103
3	7.4887	1.2275	96.5828
4	7.3907	1.3255	95.2573
5	7.2850	1.4312	93.8261
6	7.1708	1.5454	92.2808
7	7.0475	1.6687	90.6121
8	6.9144	1.8018	88.8103
9	6.7707	1.9455	86.8648
10	6.6155	2.1007	84.7641
11	6.4479	2.2683	82.4958
12	6.2669	2.4493	80.0465
13	6.0715	2.6447	77.4019
14	5.8606	2.8556	74.5462
15	5.6327	3.0835	71.4628
16	5.3868	3.3294	68.1333
17	5.1212	3.5951	64.5383
18	4.8344	3.8819	60.6564
19	4.5247	4.1915	56.4649
20	4.1903	4.5259	51.9390
21	3.8292	4.8870	47.0520
22	3.4394	5.2768	41.7752
23	3.0184	5.6978	36.0774
24	2.5638	6.1524	29.9250
25	2.0730	6.6432	23.2818
26	1.5431	7.1731	16.1087
27	.9708	7.7454	8.3633
28	.3529	8.3633	0.0000

YEARS 29 — MO PAYT .7193 — AN CONST 8.64

#	INT	PRIN	BALANCE
1	7.6664	.9656	99.0344
2	7.5894	1.0427	97.9917
3	7.5062	1.1259	96.8658
4	7.4164	1.2157	95.6502
5	7.3194	1.3127	94.3375
6	7.2147	1.4174	92.9201
7	7.1016	1.5304	91.3897
8	6.9795	1.6525	89.7371
9	6.8477	1.7844	87.9528
10	6.7053	1.9267	86.0260
11	6.5516	2.0804	83.9456
12	6.3856	2.2464	81.6992
13	6.2064	2.4256	79.2736
14	6.0129	2.6191	76.6545
15	5.8040	2.8281	73.8264
16	5.5784	3.0537	70.7727
17	5.3347	3.2973	67.4754
18	5.0717	3.5603	63.9151
19	4.7877	3.8444	60.0707
20	4.4810	4.1511	55.9197
21	4.1498	4.4822	51.4375
22	3.7922	4.8398	46.5977
23	3.4061	5.2259	41.3718
24	2.9892	5.6428	35.7290
25	2.5391	6.0930	29.6360
26	2.0530	6.5790	23.0570
27	1.5282	7.1039	15.9531
28	.9614	7.6706	8.2825
29	.3495	8.2825	0.0000

YEARS 30 — MO PAYT .7130 — AN CONST 8.56

#	INT	PRIN	BALANCE
1	7.6692	.8864	99.1136
2	7.5984	.9571	98.1565
3	7.5221	1.0334	97.1231
4	7.4396	1.1159	96.0072
5	7.3506	1.2049	94.8023
6	7.2545	1.3010	93.5013
7	7.1507	1.4048	92.0965
8	7.0386	1.5169	90.5796
9	6.9176	1.6379	88.9417
10	6.7870	1.7686	87.1732
11	6.6459	1.9096	85.2635
12	6.4935	2.0620	83.2015
13	6.3290	2.2265	80.9750
14	6.1514	2.4041	78.5709
15	5.9596	2.5959	75.9750
16	5.7525	2.8030	73.1720
17	5.5289	3.0266	70.1454
18	5.2875	3.2681	66.8773
19	5.0267	3.5288	63.3486
20	4.7452	3.8103	59.5383
21	4.4413	4.1143	55.4240
22	4.1130	4.4425	50.9815
23	3.7586	4.7969	46.1846
24	3.3760	5.1796	41.0051
25	2.9627	5.5928	35.4123
26	2.5166	6.0389	29.3734
27	2.0348	6.5207	22.8526
28	1.5146	7.0409	15.8117
29	.9529	7.6026	8.2091
30	.3464	8.2091	0.0000

YEARS 2 — MO PAYT 4.5113 — AN CONST 54.14

#	INT	PRIN	BALANCE
1	6.0663	48.0697	51.9303
2	2.2057	51.9303	0.0000

YEARS 3 — MO PAYT 3.1221 — AN CONST 37.47

#	INT	PRIN	BALANCE
1	6.6714	30.7940	69.2060
2	4.1983	33.2671	35.9389
3	1.5265	35.9389	0.0000

YEARS 4 — MO PAYT 2.4296 — AN CONST 29.16

#	INT	PRIN	BALANCE
1	6.9731	22.1818	77.8182
2	5.1916	23.9633	53.8549
3	3.2670	25.8879	27.9670
4	1.1879	27.9670	0.0000

YEARS 5 — MO PAYT 2.0157 — AN CONST 24.19

#	INT	PRIN	BALANCE
1	7.1533	17.0350	82.9650
2	5.7852	18.4031	64.5618
3	4.3072	19.8812	44.6807
4	2.7105	21.4779	23.2028
5	.9855	23.2028	0.0000

YEARS 6 — MO PAYT 1.7411 — AN CONST 20.90

#	INT	PRIN	BALANCE
1	7.2729	13.6208	86.3792
2	6.1790	14.7147	71.6645
3	4.9972	15.8965	55.7680
4	3.7205	17.1732	38.5948
5	2.3413	18.5524	20.0424
6	.8513	20.0424	0.0000

YEARS 7 — MO PAYT 1.5462 — AN CONST 18.56

#	INT	PRIN	BALANCE
1	7.3578	11.1965	88.8035
2	6.4586	12.0957	76.7078
3	5.4872	13.0672	63.6406
4	4.4377	14.1166	49.5239
5	3.3040	15.2504	34.2736
6	2.0791	16.4752	17.7984
7	.7560	17.7984	0.0000

YEARS 8 — MO PAYT 1.4010 — AN CONST 16.82

#	INT	PRIN	BALANCE
1	7.4211	9.3909	90.6091
2	6.6669	10.1451	80.4641
3	5.8521	10.9598	69.5043
4	4.9719	11.8401	57.6642
5	4.0210	12.7910	44.8732
6	2.9937	13.8182	31.0550
7	1.8839	14.9280	16.1269
8	.6850	16.1269	0.0000

YEARS 9 — MO PAYT 1.2889 — AN CONST 15.47

#	INT	PRIN	BALANCE
1	7.4699	7.9975	92.0025
2	6.8276	8.6398	83.3627
3	6.1337	9.3337	74.0290
4	5.3841	10.0833	63.9456
5	4.5742	10.8931	53.0525
6	3.6994	11.7680	41.2845
7	2.7543	12.7131	28.5714
8	1.7332	13.7342	14.8372
9	.6302	14.8372	0.0000

YEARS 10 — MO PAYT 1.2001 — AN CONST 14.41

#	INT	PRIN	BALANCE
1	7.5086	6.8927	93.1073
2	6.9550	7.4463	85.6610
3	6.3570	8.0443	77.6167
4	5.7109	8.6904	68.9264
5	5.0130	9.3883	59.5381
6	4.2590	10.1423	49.3957
7	3.4444	10.9569	38.4389
8	2.5644	11.8369	26.6020
9	1.6138	12.7875	13.8145
10	.5868	13.8145	0.0000

YEARS 11 — MO PAYT 1.1281 — AN CONST 13.54

#	INT	PRIN	BALANCE
1	7.5399	5.9976	94.0024
2	7.0582	6.4793	87.5231
3	6.5379	6.9997	80.5234
4	5.9757	7.5618	72.9616
5	5.3684	8.1691	64.7924
6	4.7123	8.8252	55.9672
7	4.0035	9.5340	46.4332
8	3.2378	10.2997	36.1335
9	2.4106	11.1269	25.0065
10	1.5170	12.0206	12.9860
11	.5516	12.9860	0.0000

YEARS 12 — MO PAYT 1.0688 — AN CONST 12.83

#	INT	PRIN	BALANCE
1	7.5658	5.2597	94.7403
2	7.1434	5.6822	89.0581
3	6.6870	6.1385	82.9196
4	6.1940	6.6315	76.2881
5	5.6614	7.1641	69.1240
6	5.0860	7.7395	61.3845
7	4.4645	8.3611	53.0235
8	3.7930	9.0326	43.9909
9	3.0675	9.7580	34.2329
10	2.2838	10.5417	23.6913
11	1.4372	11.3883	12.3029
12	.5226	12.3029	0.0000

YEARS 13 — MO PAYT 1.0192 — AN CONST 12.24

#	INT	PRIN	BALANCE
1	7.5874	4.6427	95.3573
2	7.2145	5.0155	90.3418
3	6.8117	5.4184	84.9234
4	6.3765	5.8535	79.0699
5	5.9064	6.3236	72.7463
6	5.3986	6.8315	65.9148
7	4.8499	7.3802	58.5346
8	4.2572	7.9729	50.5618
9	3.6169	8.6132	41.9486
10	2.9251	9.3050	32.6436
11	2.1778	10.0523	22.5913
12	1.3705	10.8596	11.7318
13	.4983	11.7318	0.0000

YEARS 14 — MO PAYT .9772 — AN CONST 11.73

#	INT	PRIN	BALANCE
1	7.6057	4.1204	95.8796
2	7.2748	4.4514	91.4282
3	6.9173	4.8089	86.6193
4	6.5310	5.1951	81.4242
5	6.1138	5.6123	75.8119
6	5.6631	6.0631	69.7488
7	5.1761	6.5500	63.1988
8	4.6501	7.0761	56.1228
9	4.0818	7.6444	48.4784
10	3.4678	8.2583	40.2201
11	2.8046	8.9215	31.2986
12	2.0881	9.6381	21.6605
13	1.3140	10.4121	11.2484
14	.4778	11.2484	0.0000

YEARS 15 — MO PAYT .9413 — AN CONST 11.30

#	INT	PRIN	BALANCE
1	7.6213	3.6740	96.3260
2	7.3262	3.9691	92.3569
3	7.0075	4.2878	88.0691
4	6.6631	4.6322	83.4369
5	6.2911	5.0042	78.4327
6	5.8892	5.4061	73.0266
7	5.4550	5.8403	67.1863
8	4.9859	6.3094	60.8769
9	4.4792	6.8161	54.0608
10	3.9318	7.3635	46.6973
11	3.3404	7.9549	38.7424
12	2.7015	8.5938	30.1486
13	2.0113	9.2840	20.8647
14	1.2657	10.0296	10.8351
15	.4602	10.8351	0.0000

YEARS 16 — MO PAYT .9103 — AN CONST 10.93

#	INT	PRIN	BALANCE
1	7.6348	3.2890	96.7110
2	7.3707	3.5532	93.1578
3	7.0853	3.8385	89.3193
4	6.7770	4.1468	85.1725
5	6.4440	4.4798	80.6927
6	6.0842	4.8396	75.8530
7	5.6955	5.2283	70.6247
8	5.2756	5.6482	64.9765
9	4.8220	6.1018	58.8747
10	4.3319	6.5919	52.2828
11	3.8025	7.1213	45.1614
12	3.2306	7.6933	37.4682
13	2.6127	8.3111	29.1571
14	1.9452	8.9786	20.1784
15	1.2241	9.6997	10.4787
16	.4451	10.4787	0.0000

YEARS 17 — MO PAYT .8834 — AN CONST 10.61

#	INT	PRIN	BALANCE
1	7.6465	2.9545	97.0455
2	7.4092	3.1918	93.8536
3	7.1529	3.4482	90.4055
4	6.8759	3.7251	86.6803
5	6.5768	4.0243	82.6561
6	6.2536	4.3475	78.3086
7	5.9044	4.6966	73.6119
8	5.5272	5.0738	68.5381
9	5.1197	5.4813	63.0567
10	4.6795	5.9216	57.1352
11	4.2039	6.3971	50.7380
12	3.6901	6.9109	43.8271
13	3.1351	7.4660	36.3612
14	2.5355	8.0656	28.2956
15	1.8877	8.7133	19.5823
16	1.1879	9.4131	10.1691
17	.4319	10.1691	0.0000

YEARS 18 — MO PAYT .8599 — AN CONST 10.32

#	INT	PRIN	BALANCE
1	7.6568	2.6621	97.3379
2	7.4430	2.8759	94.4620
3	7.2120	3.1069	91.3552
4	6.9625	3.3564	87.9988
5	6.6929	3.6259	84.3728
6	6.4017	3.9172	80.4557
7	6.0871	4.2318	76.2239
8	5.7472	4.5716	71.6523
9	5.3801	4.9388	66.7135
10	4.9834	5.3354	61.3781
11	4.5549	5.7639	55.6142
12	4.0920	6.2268	49.3873
13	3.5919	6.7269	42.6604
14	3.0516	7.2672	35.3932
15	2.4680	7.8509	27.5423
16	1.8375	8.4814	19.0610
17	1.1563	9.1625	9.8984
18	.4204	9.8984	0.0000

YEARS 19 — MO PAYT .8392 — AN CONST 10.08

#	INT	PRIN	BALANCE
1	7.6658	2.4049	97.5951
2	7.4726	2.5981	94.9970
3	7.2640	2.8067	92.1903
4	7.0385	3.0321	89.1581
5	6.7950	3.2757	85.8825
6	6.5319	3.5387	82.3437
7	6.2477	3.8229	78.5208
8	5.9407	4.1300	74.3908
9	5.6090	4.4617	69.9291
10	5.2507	4.8200	65.1091
11	4.8636	5.2071	59.9020
12	4.4454	5.6253	54.2767
13	3.9936	6.0771	48.1996
14	3.5055	6.5652	41.6345
15	2.9783	7.0924	34.5420
16	2.4086	7.6620	26.8800
17	1.7933	8.2774	18.6026
18	1.1285	8.9422	9.6604
19	.4103	9.6604	0.0000

YEARS 20 — MO PAYT .8209 — AN CONST 9.86

#	INT	PRIN	BALANCE
1	7.6737	2.1777	97.8223
2	7.4988	2.3526	95.4698
3	7.3099	2.5415	92.9283
4	7.1058	2.7456	90.1827
5	6.8853	2.9661	87.2166
6	6.6471	3.2043	84.0123
7	6.3897	3.4617	80.5506
8	6.1117	3.7397	76.8109
9	5.8113	4.0400	72.7708
10	5.4869	4.3645	68.4063
11	5.1363	4.7150	63.6913
12	4.7577	5.0937	58.5976
13	4.3486	5.5028	53.0948
14	3.9066	5.9448	47.1500
15	3.4292	6.4222	40.7278
16	2.9134	6.9380	33.7898
17	2.3562	7.4952	26.2946
18	1.7542	8.0972	18.1975
19	1.1039	8.7475	9.4500
20	.4014	9.4500	0.0000

YEARS 21 — MO PAYT .8047 — AN CONST 9.66

#	INT	PRIN	BALANCE
1	7.6808	1.9759	98.0241
2	7.5221	2.1346	95.8894
3	7.3507	2.3061	93.5834

MONTHLY PAYMENT AMORTIZATION SCHEDULE PER $100   7.75 %

#	INT	PRIN	BALANCE
4	7.1655	2.4913	91.0921
5	6.9654	2.6914	88.4007
6	6.7492	2.9075	85.4932
7	6.5157	3.1410	82.3522
8	6.2634	3.3933	78.9589
9	5.9909	3.6658	75.2931
10	5.6965	3.9602	71.3329
11	5.3785	4.2783	67.0547
12	5.0349	4.6219	62.4328
13	4.6637	4.9931	57.4397
14	4.2626	5.3941	52.0456
15	3.8294	5.8273	46.2183
16	3.3614	6.2953	39.9230
17	2.8558	6.8009	33.1221
18	2.3096	7.3471	25.7751
19	1.7196	7.9372	17.8379
20	1.0821	8.5746	9.2633
21	.3935	9.2633	0.0000

YEARS 22	MO PAYT .7903	AN CONST 9.49	
#	INT	PRIN	BALANCE
1	7.6871	1.7962	98.2038
2	7.5428	1.9404	96.2634
3	7.3870	2.0963	94.1671
4	7.2186	2.2646	91.9024
5	7.0367	2.4465	89.4559
6	6.8403	2.6430	86.8129
7	6.6280	2.8553	83.9576
8	6.3987	3.0846	80.8730
9	6.1509	3.3323	77.5407
10	5.8833	3.6000	73.9407
11	5.5942	3.8891	70.0517
12	5.2818	4.2014	65.8502
13	4.9444	4.5389	61.3114
14	4.5799	4.9034	56.4080
15	4.1861	5.2972	51.1108
16	3.7606	5.7226	45.3882
17	3.3010	6.1822	39.2060
18	2.8045	6.6787	32.5272
19	2.2681	7.2151	25.3121
20	1.6887	7.7946	17.5175
21	1.0627	8.4206	9.0969
22	.3864	9.0969	0.0000

YEARS 23	MO PAYT .7773	AN CONST 9.33	
#	INT	PRIN	BALANCE
1	7.6927	1.6355	98.3645
2	7.5614	1.7668	96.5977
3	7.4195	1.9087	94.6890
4	7.2662	2.0620	92.6270
5	7.1006	2.2276	90.3994
6	6.9217	2.4065	87.9929
7	6.7284	2.5998	85.3931
8	6.5196	2.8086	82.5845
9	6.2940	3.0341	79.5504
10	6.0503	3.2778	76.2726
11	5.7871	3.5411	72.7315
12	5.5027	3.8255	68.9060
13	5.1955	4.1327	64.7733
14	4.8636	4.4646	60.3087
15	4.5050	4.8232	55.4855
16	4.1176	5.2106	50.2749
17	3.6991	5.6290	44.6459
18	3.2471	6.0811	38.5648
19	2.7587	6.5695	31.9952
20	2.2311	7.0971	24.8981
21	1.6611	7.6671	17.2310
22	1.0453	8.2829	8.9481
23	.3801	8.9481	0.0000

YEARS 24	MO PAYT .7658	AN CONST 9.19	
#	INT	PRIN	BALANCE
1	7.6978	1.4913	98.5087
2	7.5780	1.6111	96.8976
3	7.4486	1.7405	95.1572
4	7.3088	1.8802	93.2769
5	7.1578	2.0313	91.2457
6	6.9947	2.1944	89.0513
7	6.8184	2.3706	86.6807
8	6.6281	2.5610	84.1196
9	6.4224	2.7667	81.3529
10	6.2002	2.9889	78.3640
11	5.9601	3.2289	75.1351
12	5.7008	3.4883	71.6468
13	5.4206	3.7684	67.8784
14	5.1180	4.0711	63.8073
15	4.7910	4.3980	59.4093
16	4.4378	4.7513	54.6580
17	4.0562	5.1329	49.5252
18	3.6440	5.5451	43.9801
19	3.1986	5.9904	37.9896
20	2.7175	6.4715	31.5181
21	2.1978	6.9913	24.5268
22	1.6363	7.5528	16.9740
23	1.0297	8.1594	8.8147
24	.3744	8.8147	0.0000

YEARS 25	MO PAYT .7553	AN CONST 9.07	
#	INT	PRIN	BALANCE
1	7.7023	1.3616	98.6384
2	7.5930	1.4710	97.1674
3	7.4748	1.5891	95.5782
4	7.3472	1.7168	93.8615
5	7.2093	1.8546	92.0068
6	7.0604	2.0036	90.0032
7	6.8994	2.1645	87.8387
8	6.7256	2.3383	85.5004
9	6.5378	2.5261	82.9742
10	6.3349	2.7290	80.2452
11	6.1157	2.9482	77.2970
12	5.8790	3.1850	74.1120
13	5.6232	3.4408	70.6713
14	5.3468	3.7171	66.9541
15	5.0483	4.0156	62.9385
16	4.7258	4.3382	58.6003
17	4.3774	4.6866	53.9138
18	4.0010	5.0630	48.8508
19	3.5944	5.4696	43.3812
20	3.1551	5.9089	37.4724
21	2.6805	6.3834	31.0889
22	2.1679	6.8961	24.1928
23	1.6140	7.4499	16.7429
24	1.0157	8.0483	8.6946
25	.3693	8.6946	0.0000

YEARS 26	MO PAYT .7459	AN CONST 8.96	
#	INT	PRIN	BALANCE
1	7.7064	1.2447	98.7553
2	7.6064	1.3447	97.4106
3	7.4984	1.4527	95.9579
4	7.3818	1.5694	94.3886
5	7.2557	1.6954	92.6932
6	7.1196	1.8316	90.8616
7	6.9725	1.9787	88.8829
8	6.8136	2.1376	86.7454
9	6.6419	2.3092	84.4361
10	6.4564	2.4947	81.9414
11	6.2561	2.6951	79.2464
12	6.0396	2.9115	76.3349
13	5.8058	3.1453	73.1895
14	5.5532	3.3979	69.7916
15	5.2803	3.6708	66.1207
16	4.9855	3.9657	62.1551
17	4.6670	4.2842	57.8709
18	4.3229	4.6282	53.2427
19	3.9512	4.9999	48.2427
20	3.5496	5.4015	42.8412
21	3.1158	5.8353	37.0059
22	2.6472	6.3040	30.7020
23	2.1409	6.8103	23.8917
24	1.5939	7.3572	16.5345
25	1.0030	7.9481	8.5864
26	.3647	8.5864	0.0000

YEARS 27	MO PAYT .7374	AN CONST 8.85	
#	INT	PRIN	BALANCE
1	7.7101	1.1391	98.8609
2	7.6186	1.2305	97.6304
3	7.5198	1.3294	96.3010
4	7.4130	1.4361	94.8649
5	7.2977	1.5515	93.3134
6	7.1731	1.6761	91.6373
7	7.0385	1.8107	89.8266
8	6.8931	1.9561	87.8705
9	6.7359	2.1132	85.7573
10	6.5662	2.2829	83.4744
11	6.3829	2.4663	81.0081
12	6.1848	2.6644	78.3437
13	5.9708	2.8783	75.4654
14	5.7397	3.1095	72.3559
15	5.4899	3.3592	68.9966
16	5.2201	3.6290	65.3676
17	4.9287	3.9205	61.4471
18	4.6138	4.2354	57.2117
19	4.2736	4.5755	52.6362
20	3.9062	4.9430	47.6932
21	3.5092	5.3400	42.3533
22	3.0803	5.7688	36.5844
23	2.6170	6.2322	30.3523
24	2.1165	6.7327	23.6196
25	1.5758	7.2734	16.3462
26	.9916	7.8576	8.4886
27	.3606	8.4886	0.0000

YEARS 28	MO PAYT .7297	AN CONST 8.76	
#	INT	PRIN	BALANCE
1	7.7135	1.0434	98.9566
2	7.6297	1.1272	97.8294
3	7.5391	1.2177	96.6117
4	7.4413	1.3155	95.2962
5	7.3357	1.4212	93.8751
6	7.2215	1.5353	92.3398
7	7.0982	1.6586	90.6812
8	6.9650	1.7918	88.8894
9	6.8211	1.9357	86.9537
10	6.6657	2.0912	84.8625
11	6.4977	2.2591	82.6034
12	6.3163	2.4406	80.1629
13	6.1203	2.6366	77.5263
14	5.9085	2.8483	74.6780
15	5.6798	3.0771	71.6009
16	5.4326	3.3242	68.2767
17	5.1657	3.5912	64.6856
18	4.8772	3.8796	60.8060
19	4.5657	4.1912	56.6148
20	4.2291	4.5278	52.0870
21	3.8654	4.8914	47.1956
22	3.4726	5.2843	41.9113
23	3.0482	5.7087	36.2027
24	2.5897	6.1671	30.0356
25	2.0944	6.6624	23.3731
26	1.5593	7.1975	16.1756
27	.9813	7.7756	8.4000
28	.3568	8.4000	0.0000

YEARS 29	MO PAYT .7228	AN CONST 8.68	
#	INT	PRIN	BALANCE
1	7.7165	.9566	99.0434
2	7.6397	1.0334	98.0100
3	7.5567	1.1164	96.8936
4	7.4670	1.2061	95.6876
5	7.3702	1.3029	94.3847
6	7.2655	1.4076	92.9771
7	7.1525	1.5206	91.4565
8	7.0303	1.6427	89.8138
9	6.8984	1.7747	88.0391
10	6.7559	1.9172	86.1219
11	6.6019	2.0712	84.0508
12	6.4356	2.2375	81.8132
13	6.2559	2.4172	79.3960
14	6.0617	2.6113	76.7847
15	5.8520	2.8211	73.9636
16	5.6254	3.0476	70.9160
17	5.3807	3.2924	67.6236
18	5.1163	3.5568	64.0668
19	4.8306	3.8425	60.2243
20	4.5220	4.1511	56.0732
21	4.1886	4.4845	51.5888
22	3.8284	4.8446	46.7441
23	3.4394	5.2337	41.5104
24	3.0190	5.6540	35.8564
25	2.5649	6.1081	29.7482
26	2.0744	6.5987	23.1495
27	1.5444	7.1287	16.0209
28	.9719	7.7012	8.3197
29	.3534	8.3197	0.0000

YEARS 30	MO PAYT .7164	AN CONST 8.60	
#	INT	PRIN	BALANCE
1	7.7193	.8777	99.1223
2	7.6488	.9482	98.1741
3	7.5726	1.0243	97.1498
4	7.4904	1.1066	96.0432
5	7.4015	1.1955	94.8477
6	7.3055	1.2915	93.5563
7	7.2017	1.3952	92.1611
8	7.0897	1.5073	90.6538
9	6.9686	1.6283	89.0255
10	6.8379	1.7591	87.2664
11	6.6966	1.9004	85.3660
12	6.5440	2.0530	83.3131
13	6.3791	2.2179	81.0952
14	6.2010	2.3960	78.6992
15	6.0085	2.5884	76.1108
16	5.8006	2.7963	73.3145
17	5.5761	3.0209	70.2936
18	5.3334	3.2635	67.0301
19	5.0713	3.5256	63.5045
20	4.7882	3.8088	59.6957
21	4.4823	4.1146	55.5811
22	4.1518	4.4451	51.1360
23	3.7948	4.8021	46.3339
24	3.4092	5.1878	41.1461
25	2.9925	5.6044	35.5417
26	2.5424	6.0545	29.4872
27	2.0562	6.5408	22.9464
28	1.5309	7.0661	15.8803
29	.9634	7.6336	8.2467
30	.3503	8.2467	0.0000

YEARS 2 — MO PAYT 4.5136 — AN CONST 54.17

#	INT	PRIN	BALANCE
1	6.1061	48.0573	51.9427
2	2.2206	51.9427	0.0000

YEARS 3 — MO PAYT 3.1244 — AN CONST 37.50

#	INT	PRIN	BALANCE
1	6.7151	30.7779	69.2221
2	4.2267	33.2663	35.9558
3	1.5372	35.9558	0.0000

YEARS 4 — MO PAYT 2.4319 — AN CONST 29.19

#	INT	PRIN	BALANCE
1	7.0188	22.1642	77.8358
2	5.2268	23.9562	53.8796
3	3.2899	25.8931	27.9865
4	1.1965	27.9865	0.0000

YEARS 5 — MO PAYT 2.0181 — AN CONST 24.22

#	INT	PRIN	BALANCE
1	7.2002	17.0168	82.9832
2	5.8244	18.3926	64.5906
3	4.3373	19.8796	44.7110
4	2.7301	21.4869	23.2241
5	.9929	23.2241	0.0000

YEARS 6 — MO PAYT 1.7436 — AN CONST 20.93

#	INT	PRIN	BALANCE
1	7.3205	13.6024	86.3976
2	6.2208	14.7021	71.6955
3	5.0321	15.8908	55.8048
4	3.7474	17.1755	38.6292
5	2.3587	18.5642	20.0651
6	.8578	20.0651	0.0000

YEARS 7 — MO PAYT 1.5487 — AN CONST 18.59

#	INT	PRIN	BALANCE
1	7.4060	11.1781	88.8219
2	6.5022	12.0819	76.7400
3	5.5254	13.0587	63.6813
4	4.4696	14.1145	49.5669
5	3.3285	15.2556	34.3112
6	2.0951	16.4890	17.8222
7	.7619	17.8222	0.0000

YEARS 8 — MO PAYT 1.4035 — AN CONST 16.85

#	INT	PRIN	BALANCE
1	7.4696	9.3727	90.6273
2	6.7119	10.1304	80.4969
3	5.8928	10.9495	69.5474
4	5.0075	11.8347	57.7127
5	4.0507	12.7916	44.9211
6	3.0165	13.8258	31.0954
7	1.8987	14.9436	16.1518
8	.6905	16.1518	0.0000

YEARS 9 — MO PAYT 1.2915 — AN CONST 15.50

#	INT	PRIN	BALANCE
1	7.5187	7.9796	92.0204
2	6.8736	8.6248	83.3956
3	6.1763	9.3221	74.0736
4	5.4226	10.0758	63.9978
5	4.6080	10.8904	53.1075
6	3.7275	11.7709	41.3366
7	2.7758	12.7225	28.6141
8	1.7472	13.7511	14.8629
9	.6354	14.8629	0.0000

YEARS 10 — MO PAYT 1.2027 — AN CONST 14.44

#	INT	PRIN	BALANCE
1	7.5577	6.8751	93.1249
2	7.0018	7.4310	85.6939
3	6.4010	8.0318	77.6621
4	5.7516	8.6812	68.9809
5	5.0498	9.3830	59.5979
6	4.2912	10.1416	49.4562
7	3.4712	10.9616	38.4946
8	2.5850	11.8478	26.6468
9	1.6271	12.8057	13.8411
10	.5917	13.8411	0.0000

YEARS 11 — MO PAYT 1.1308 — AN CONST 13.57

#	INT	PRIN	BALANCE
1	7.5892	5.9805	94.0195
2	7.1057	6.4640	87.5556
3	6.5831	6.9866	80.5690
4	6.0182	7.5515	73.0175
5	5.4077	8.1620	64.8555
6	4.7478	8.8219	56.0337
7	4.0345	9.5351	46.4985
8	3.2636	10.3060	36.1925
9	2.4304	11.1393	25.0532
10	1.5298	12.0399	13.0133
11	.5563	13.0133	0.0000

YEARS 12 — MO PAYT 1.0715 — AN CONST 12.86

#	INT	PRIN	BALANCE
1	7.6152	5.2430	94.7570
2	7.1913	5.6669	89.0901
3	6.7331	6.1251	82.9650
4	6.2379	6.6203	76.3447
5	5.7027	7.1555	69.1892
6	5.1241	7.7341	61.4552
7	4.4989	8.3593	53.0958
8	3.8230	9.0352	44.0606
9	3.0925	9.7657	34.2949
10	2.3029	10.5552	23.7397
11	1.4496	11.4086	12.3310
12	.5272	12.3310	0.0000

YEARS 13 — MO PAYT 1.0219 — AN CONST 12.27

#	INT	PRIN	BALANCE
1	7.6369	4.6264	95.3736
2	7.2629	5.0004	90.3732
3	6.8586	5.4047	84.9684
4	6.4216	5.8417	79.1267
5	5.9493	6.3140	72.8127
6	5.4388	6.8245	65.9882
7	4.8871	7.3762	58.6120
8	4.2907	7.9726	50.6394
9	3.6461	8.6172	42.0222
10	2.9494	9.3139	32.7083
11	2.1964	10.0669	22.6414
12	1.3825	10.8808	11.7605
13	.5028	11.7605	0.0000

YEARS 14 — MO PAYT .9800 — AN CONST 11.76

#	INT	PRIN	BALANCE
1	7.6553	4.1046	95.8954
2	7.3235	4.4365	91.4589
3	6.9648	4.7952	86.6637
4	6.5771	5.1829	81.4808
5	6.1580	5.6019	75.8789
6	5.7051	6.0548	69.8240
7	5.2156	6.5444	63.2797
8	4.6865	7.0735	56.2062
9	4.1146	7.6454	48.5608
10	3.4965	8.2635	40.2973
11	2.8284	8.9316	31.3657
12	2.1063	9.6537	21.7120
13	1.3258	10.4342	11.2778
14	.4821	11.2778	0.0000

YEARS 15 — MO PAYT .9441 — AN CONST 11.33

#	INT	PRIN	BALANCE
1	7.6710	3.6587	96.3413
2	7.3752	3.9545	92.3869
3	7.0555	4.2742	88.1127
4	6.7100	4.6198	83.4929
5	6.3364	4.9933	78.4997
6	5.9327	5.3970	73.1027
7	5.4964	5.8333	67.2694
8	5.0248	6.3049	60.9645
9	4.5150	6.8147	54.1498
10	3.9641	7.3656	46.7841
11	3.3685	7.9612	38.8230
12	2.7249	8.6048	30.2182
13	2.0292	9.3005	20.9177
14	1.2772	10.0525	10.8652
15	.4645	10.8652	0.0000

YEARS 16 — MO PAYT .9132 — AN CONST 10.96

#	INT	PRIN	BALANCE
1	7.6846	3.2742	96.7258
2	7.4199	3.5389	93.1870
3	7.1338	3.8250	89.3620
4	6.8245	4.1342	85.2277
5	6.4903	4.4685	80.7592
6	6.1290	4.8298	75.9295
7	5.7385	5.2203	70.7092
8	5.3164	5.6423	65.0669
9	4.8603	6.0985	58.9684
10	4.3672	6.5916	52.3768
11	3.8343	7.1245	45.2524
12	3.2583	7.7005	37.5519
13	2.6357	8.3231	29.2288
14	1.9628	8.9960	20.2328
15	1.2354	9.7233	10.5095
16	.4493	10.5095	0.0000

YEARS 17 — MO PAYT .8864 — AN CONST 10.64

#	INT	PRIN	BALANCE
1	7.6964	2.9402	97.0598
2	7.4587	3.1779	93.8819
3	7.2017	3.4348	90.4471
4	6.9240	3.7125	86.7346
5	6.6239	4.0127	82.7219
6	6.2994	4.3371	78.3848
7	5.9488	4.6878	73.6970
8	5.5698	5.0668	68.6302
9	5.1601	5.4764	63.1538
10	4.7174	5.9192	57.2346
11	4.2388	6.3978	50.8369
12	3.7215	6.9150	43.9219
13	3.1625	7.4741	36.4478
14	2.5582	8.0784	28.3694
15	1.9050	8.7315	19.6379
16	1.1991	9.4374	10.2005
17	.4361	10.2005	0.0000

YEARS 18 — MO PAYT .8629 — AN CONST 10.36

#	INT	PRIN	BALANCE
1	7.7067	2.6482	97.3518
2	7.4925	2.8623	94.4895
3	7.2611	3.0937	91.3957
4	7.0110	3.3439	88.0519
5	6.7407	3.6142	84.4377
6	6.4484	3.9064	80.5312
7	6.1326	4.2223	76.3090
8	5.7912	4.5636	71.7453
9	5.4223	4.9326	66.8128
10	5.0235	5.3314	61.4814
11	4.5924	5.7624	55.7189
12	4.1265	6.2283	49.4906
13	3.6230	6.7319	42.7587
14	3.0787	7.2762	35.4826
15	2.4904	7.8644	27.6181
16	1.8546	8.5003	19.1178
17	1.1673	9.1875	9.9303
18	.4245	9.9303	0.0000

YEARS 19 — MO PAYT .8423 — AN CONST 10.11

#	INT	PRIN	BALANCE
1	7.7157	2.3915	97.6085
2	7.5223	2.5849	95.0236
3	7.3134	2.7939	92.2297
4	7.0875	3.0197	89.2100
5	6.8433	3.2639	85.9461
6	6.5794	3.5278	82.4183
7	6.2942	3.8130	78.6053
8	5.9859	4.1213	74.4840
9	5.6527	4.4545	70.0295
10	5.2926	4.8146	65.2149
11	4.9033	5.2039	60.0110
12	4.4826	5.6246	54.3864
13	4.0279	6.0794	48.3070
14	3.5363	6.5709	41.7361
15	3.0051	7.1021	34.6340
16	2.4309	7.6764	26.9576
17	1.8102	8.2970	18.6606
18	1.1394	8.9678	9.6928
19	.4144	9.6928	0.0000

YEARS 20 — MO PAYT .8240 — AN CONST 9.89

#	INT	PRIN	BALANCE
1	7.7237	2.1647	97.8353
2	7.5487	2.3398	95.4955
3	7.3595	2.5289	92.9666
4	7.1550	2.7334	90.2332
5	6.9341	2.9544	87.2788
6	6.6952	3.1932	84.0856
7	6.4370	3.4514	80.6342
8	6.1580	3.7305	76.9037
9	5.8564	4.0321	72.8716
10	5.5304	4.3581	68.5136
11	5.1780	4.7104	63.8032
12	4.7972	5.0912	58.7119
13	4.3856	5.5029	53.2091
14	3.9407	5.9478	47.2613
15	3.4598	6.4286	40.8326
16	2.9400	6.9484	33.8842
17	2.3783	7.5102	26.3741
18	1.7711	8.1174	18.2567
19	1.1148	8.7737	9.4830
20	.4054	9.4830	0.0000

YEARS 21 — MO PAYT .8079 — AN CONST 9.70

#	INT	PRIN	BALANCE
1	7.7308	1.9635	98.0365
2	7.5720	2.1222	95.9143
3	7.4005	2.2938	93.6205

#	INT	PRIN	BALANCE
4	7.2150	2.4793	91.1412
5	7.0146	2.6797	88.4615
6	6.7979	2.8964	85.5651
7	6.5637	3.1305	82.4346
8	6.3106	3.3836	79.0509
9	6.0371	3.6572	75.3937
10	5.7414	3.9529	71.4408
11	5.4218	4.2725	67.1683
12	5.0764	4.6179	62.5504
13	4.7030	4.9913	57.5591
14	4.2995	5.3948	52.1643
15	3.8633	5.8310	46.3333
16	3.3919	6.3024	40.0309
17	2.8823	6.8120	33.2189
18	2.3316	7.3627	25.8562
19	1.7363	7.9580	17.8982
20	1.0929	8.6014	9.2968
21	.3975	9.2968	0.0000

YEARS 22	MO PAYT .7934	AN CONST 9.53	
#	INT	PRIN	BALANCE
1	7.7371	1.7842	98.2158
2	7.5929	1.9285	96.2873
3	7.4369	2.0844	94.2030
4	7.2684	2.2529	91.9501
5	7.0863	2.4350	89.5151
6	6.8894	2.6319	86.8832
7	6.6766	2.8447	84.0385
8	6.4466	3.0747	80.9638
9	6.1980	3.3233	77.6405
10	5.9293	3.5920	74.0485
11	5.6389	3.8824	70.1662
12	5.3251	4.1963	65.9699
13	4.9858	4.5355	61.4344
14	4.6191	4.9022	56.5322
15	4.2227	5.2986	51.2336
16	3.7944	5.7270	45.5067
17	3.3313	6.1900	39.3167
18	2.8309	6.6904	32.6262
19	2.2900	7.2314	25.3949
20	1.7053	7.8160	17.5789
21	1.0734	8.4479	9.1309
22	.3904	9.1309	0.0000

YEARS 23	MO PAYT .7806	AN CONST 9.37	
#	INT	PRIN	BALANCE
1	7.7428	1.6239	98.3761
2	7.6115	1.7552	96.6208
3	7.4696	1.8971	94.7237
4	7.3162	2.0505	92.6732
5	7.1504	2.2163	90.4569
6	6.9712	2.3955	88.0614
7	6.7775	2.5892	85.4722
8	6.5682	2.7985	82.6737
9	6.3419	3.0248	79.6490
10	6.0974	3.2693	76.3797
11	5.8331	3.5336	72.8460
12	5.5474	3.8193	69.0267
13	5.2386	4.1281	64.8986
14	4.9048	4.4619	60.4367
15	4.5441	4.8226	55.6141
16	4.1542	5.2125	50.4016
17	3.7327	5.6340	44.7677
18	3.2772	6.0895	38.6782
19	2.7849	6.5818	32.0964
20	2.2528	7.1139	24.9825
21	1.6776	7.6891	17.2934
22	1.0559	8.3107	8.9827
23	.3840	8.9827	0.0000

YEARS 24	MO PAYT .7690	AN CONST 9.23	
#	INT	PRIN	BALANCE
1	7.7478	1.4802	98.5198
2	7.6281	1.5999	96.9199
3	7.4988	1.7292	95.1906
4	7.3590	1.8691	93.3216
5	7.2079	2.0202	91.3014
6	7.0445	2.1835	89.1179
7	6.8680	2.3600	86.7579
8	6.6772	2.5508	84.2071
9	6.4710	2.7571	81.4500
10	6.2481	2.9800	78.4700
11	6.0071	3.2209	75.2491
12	5.7467	3.4813	71.7678
13	5.4653	3.7628	68.0050
14	5.1610	4.0670	63.9380
15	4.8322	4.3958	59.5421
16	4.4768	4.7512	54.7909
17	4.0927	5.1354	49.6556
18	3.6775	5.5506	44.1050
19	3.2287	5.9993	38.1057
20	2.7437	6.4844	31.6213
21	2.2194	7.0086	24.6127
22	1.6528	7.5753	17.0374
23	1.0403	8.1877	8.8497
24	.3783	8.8497	0.0000

YEARS 25	MO PAYT .7586	AN CONST 9.11	
#	INT	PRIN	BALANCE
1	7.7524	1.3510	98.6490
2	7.6432	1.4602	97.1888
3	7.5251	1.5783	95.6105
4	7.3975	1.7059	93.9046
5	7.2596	1.8438	92.0608
6	7.1105	1.9929	90.0680
7	6.9494	2.1540	87.9140
8	6.7752	2.3281	85.5858
9	6.5870	2.5164	83.0694
10	6.3835	2.7198	80.3496
11	6.1636	2.9397	77.4099
12	5.9260	3.1774	74.2325
13	5.6691	3.4343	70.7982
14	5.3914	3.7120	67.0862
15	5.0913	4.0121	63.0742
16	4.7669	4.3364	58.7377
17	4.4163	4.6870	54.0507
18	4.0374	5.0660	48.9847
19	3.6278	5.4756	43.5091
20	3.1851	5.9183	37.5909
21	2.7066	6.3968	31.1941
22	2.1894	6.9139	24.2802
23	1.6304	7.4729	16.8073
24	1.0263	8.0771	8.7301
25	.3732	8.7301	0.0000

YEARS 26	MO PAYT .7492	AN CONST 9.00	
#	INT	PRIN	BALANCE
1	7.7565	1.2345	98.7655
2	7.6567	1.3343	97.4312
3	7.5488	1.4422	95.9890
4	7.4322	1.5588	94.4302
5	7.3062	1.6848	92.7454
6	7.1700	1.8210	90.9243
7	7.0227	1.9683	88.9561
8	6.8636	2.1274	86.8287
9	6.6916	2.2994	84.5292
10	6.5057	2.4853	82.0439
11	6.3047	2.6862	79.3577
12	6.0876	2.9034	76.4543
13	5.8528	3.1382	73.3161
14	5.5991	3.3919	69.9242
15	5.3249	3.6661	66.2581
16	5.0285	3.9625	62.2955
17	4.7081	4.2829	58.0126
18	4.3618	4.6292	53.3834
19	3.9875	5.0034	48.3800
20	3.5830	5.4080	42.9720
21	3.1458	5.8452	37.1268
22	2.6732	6.3178	30.8090
23	2.1624	6.8286	23.9804
24	1.6103	7.3807	16.5998
25	1.0136	7.9774	8.6224
26	.3686	8.6224	0.0000

YEARS 27	MO PAYT .7408	AN CONST 8.89	
#	INT	PRIN	BALANCE
1	7.7602	1.1293	98.8707
2	7.6689	1.2206	97.6502
3	7.5702	1.3192	96.3309
4	7.4636	1.4259	94.9050
5	7.3483	1.5412	93.3638
6	7.2237	1.6658	91.6980
7	7.0890	1.8005	89.8976
8	6.9434	1.9460	87.9515
9	6.7861	2.1034	85.8481
10	6.6160	2.2734	83.5747
11	6.4322	2.4572	81.1174
12	6.2335	2.6559	78.4615
13	6.0188	2.8706	75.5909
14	5.7867	3.1027	72.4881
15	5.5359	3.3536	69.1346
16	5.2647	3.6247	65.5098
17	4.9717	3.9178	61.5920
18	4.6549	4.2345	57.3575
19	4.3126	4.5769	52.7806
20	3.9425	4.9469	47.8337
21	3.5426	5.3469	42.4868
22	3.1103	5.7792	36.7076
23	2.6430	6.2464	30.4611
24	2.1380	6.7515	23.7096
25	1.5921	7.2973	16.4123
26	1.0021	7.8873	8.5250
27	.3645	8.5250	0.0000

YEARS 28	MO PAYT .7331	AN CONST 8.80	
#	INT	PRIN	BALANCE
1	7.7636	1.0340	98.9660
2	7.6800	1.1176	97.8484
3	7.5896	1.2079	96.6405
4	7.4919	1.3056	95.3349
5	7.3864	1.4112	93.9237
6	7.2723	1.5253	92.3985
7	7.1490	1.6486	90.7499
8	7.0157	1.7819	88.9680
9	6.8716	1.9259	87.0421
10	6.7159	2.0816	84.9605
11	6.5476	2.2499	82.7105
12	6.3657	2.4318	80.2787
13	6.1691	2.6285	77.6502
14	5.9566	2.8410	74.8093
15	5.7269	3.0707	71.7386
16	5.4786	3.3189	68.4197
17	5.2103	3.5872	64.8325
18	4.9203	3.8773	60.9552
19	4.6068	4.1908	56.7644
20	4.2680	4.5296	52.2349
21	3.9018	4.8958	47.3391
22	3.5059	5.2916	42.0474
23	3.0781	5.7194	36.3280
24	2.6157	6.1819	30.1461
25	2.1159	6.6817	23.4645
26	1.5757	7.2219	16.2426
27	.9918	7.8058	8.4369
28	.3607	8.4369	0.0000

YEARS 29	MO PAYT .7262	AN CONST 8.72	
#	INT	PRIN	BALANCE
1	7.7666	.9476	99.0524
2	7.6900	1.0242	98.0282
3	7.6072	1.1070	96.9212
4	7.5177	1.1965	95.7247
5	7.4209	1.2932	94.4315
6	7.3164	1.3978	93.0337
7	7.2034	1.5108	91.5229
8	7.0812	1.6330	89.8900
9	6.9492	1.7650	88.1250
10	6.8065	1.9077	86.2173
11	6.6523	2.0619	84.1554
12	6.4856	2.2286	81.9268
13	6.3054	2.4088	79.5180
14	6.1106	2.6035	76.9144
15	5.9001	2.8140	74.1004
16	5.6726	3.0416	71.0588
17	5.4267	3.2875	67.7714
18	5.1609	3.5533	64.2181
19	4.8736	3.8405	60.3776
20	4.5631	4.1510	56.2265
21	4.2275	4.4867	51.7399
22	3.8648	4.8494	46.8905
23	3.4727	5.2415	41.6490
24	3.0489	5.6652	35.9838
25	2.5909	6.1233	29.8605
26	2.0958	6.6183	23.2421
27	1.5607	7.1534	16.0887
28	.9824	7.7318	8.3569
29	.3573	8.3569	0.0000

YEARS 30	MO PAYT .7199	AN CONST 8.64	
#	INT	PRIN	BALANCE
1	7.7694	.8691	99.1309
2	7.6991	.9393	98.1916
3	7.6232	1.0153	97.1763
4	7.5411	1.0974	96.0789
5	7.4523	1.1861	94.8928
6	7.3565	1.2820	93.6108
7	7.2528	1.3856	92.2252
8	7.1408	1.4977	90.7275
9	7.0197	1.6188	89.1087
10	6.8888	1.7496	87.3591
11	6.7474	1.8911	85.4680
12	6.5945	2.0440	83.4240
13	6.4292	2.2092	81.2148
14	6.2506	2.3879	78.8269
15	6.0575	2.5809	76.2460
16	5.8489	2.7896	73.4564
17	5.6233	3.0151	70.4413
18	5.3796	3.2589	67.1824
19	5.1161	3.5224	63.6600
20	4.8313	3.8072	59.8529
21	4.5235	4.1150	55.7379
22	4.1908	4.4477	51.2902
23	3.8312	4.8073	46.4830
24	3.4425	5.1959	41.2870
25	3.0224	5.6160	35.6710
26	2.5684	6.0701	29.6010
27	2.0776	6.5608	23.0401
28	1.5472	7.0913	15.9489
29	.9738	7.6646	8.2843
30	.3542	8.2843	0.0000

YEARS 2 — MO PAYT 4.5170 — AN CONST 54.21

#	INT	PRIN	BALANCE
1	6.1657	48.0387	51.9613
2	2.2431	51.9613	0.0000

YEARS 3 — MO PAYT 3.1279 — AN CONST 37.54

#	INT	PRIN	BALANCE
1	6.7807	30.7538	69.2462
2	4.2695	33.2650	35.9813
3	1.5532	35.9813	0.0000

YEARS 4 — MO PAYT 2.4354 — AN CONST 29.23

#	INT	PRIN	BALANCE
1	7.0873	22.1379	77.8621
2	5.2796	23.9455	53.9166
3	3.3243	25.9008	28.0158
4	1.2094	28.0158	0.0000

YEARS 5 — MO PAYT 2.0217 — AN CONST 24.26

#	INT	PRIN	BALANCE
1	7.2705	16.9895	83.0105
2	5.8832	18.3768	64.6338
3	4.3826	19.8773	44.7565
4	2.7595	21.5004	23.2560
5	1.0039	23.2560	0.0000

YEARS 6 — MO PAYT 1.7472 — AN CONST 20.97

#	INT	PRIN	BALANCE
1	7.3920	13.5747	86.4253
2	6.2835	14.6832	71.7421
3	5.0846	15.8822	55.8599
4	3.7877	17.1790	38.6809
5	2.3849	18.5818	20.0991
6	.8676	20.0991	0.0000

YEARS 7 — MO PAYT 1.5524 — AN CONST 18.63

#	INT	PRIN	BALANCE
1	7.4782	11.1506	88.8494
2	6.5677	12.0611	76.7883
3	5.5829	13.0459	63.7424
4	4.5176	14.1112	49.6312
5	3.3653	15.2635	34.3677
6	2.1190	16.5098	17.8579
7	.7709	17.8579	0.0000

YEARS 8 — MO PAYT 1.4073 — AN CONST 16.89

#	INT	PRIN	BALANCE
1	7.5425	9.3454	90.6546
2	6.7794	10.1085	80.5461
3	5.9540	10.9339	69.6122
4	5.0611	11.8267	57.7854
5	4.0954	12.7925	44.9930
6	3.0508	13.8370	31.1559
7	1.9210	14.9669	16.1890
8	.6988	16.1890	0.0000

YEARS 9 — MO PAYT 1.2954 — AN CONST 15.55

#	INT	PRIN	BALANCE
1	7.5920	7.9528	92.0472
2	6.9426	8.6022	83.4450
3	6.2402	9.3046	74.1404
4	5.4804	10.0644	64.0760
5	4.6586	10.8862	53.1899
6	3.7697	11.7751	41.4148
7	2.8082	12.7366	28.6782
8	1.7682	13.7766	14.9016
9	.6433	14.9016	0.0000

YEARS 10 — MO PAYT 1.2067 — AN CONST 14.49

#	INT	PRIN	BALANCE
1	7.6313	6.8489	93.1511
2	7.0721	7.4081	85.7430
3	6.4671	8.0130	77.7300
4	5.8128	8.6673	69.0626
5	5.1051	9.3751	59.6876
6	4.3396	10.1406	49.5470
7	3.5115	10.9686	38.5783
8	2.6159	11.8643	26.7140
9	1.6471	12.8331	13.8810
10	.5992	13.8810	0.0000

YEARS 11 — MO PAYT 1.1348 — AN CONST 13.62

#	INT	PRIN	BALANCE
1	7.6631	5.9548	94.0452
2	7.1769	6.4410	87.6042
3	6.6509	6.9670	80.6372
4	6.0820	7.5359	73.1013
5	5.4667	8.1512	64.9501
6	4.8011	8.8168	56.1333
7	4.0812	9.5368	46.5965
8	3.3024	10.3155	36.2811
9	2.4601	11.1578	25.1233
10	1.5490	12.0689	13.0544
11	.5635	13.0544	0.0000

YEARS 12 — MO PAYT 1.0756 — AN CONST 12.91

#	INT	PRIN	BALANCE
1	7.6893	5.2180	94.7820
2	7.2633	5.6441	89.1379
3	6.8024	6.1049	83.0330
4	6.3039	6.6034	76.4295
5	5.7647	7.1427	69.2869
6	5.1814	7.7259	61.5610
7	4.5506	8.3567	53.2043
8	3.8682	9.0391	44.1651
9	3.1301	9.7772	34.3879
10	2.3317	10.5756	23.8123
11	1.4682	11.4391	12.3732
12	.5341	12.3732	0.0000

YEARS 13 — MO PAYT 1.0261 — AN CONST 12.32

#	INT	PRIN	BALANCE
1	7.7112	4.6021	95.3979
2	7.3355	4.9779	90.4201
3	6.9290	5.3843	85.0357
4	6.4893	5.8240	79.2118
5	6.0138	6.2995	72.9122
6	5.4994	6.8139	66.0983
7	4.9430	7.3703	58.7279
8	4.3412	7.9722	50.7558
9	3.6902	8.6231	42.1326
10	2.9861	9.3273	32.8054
11	2.2244	10.0889	22.7165
12	1.4006	10.9127	11.8038
13	.5095	11.8038	0.0000

YEARS 14 — MO PAYT .9842 — AN CONST 11.82

#	INT	PRIN	BALANCE
1	7.7298	4.0810	95.9190
2	7.3965	4.4143	91.5047
3	7.0361	4.7747	86.7300
4	6.6462	5.1646	81.5654
5	6.2245	5.5863	75.9791
6	5.7683	6.0425	69.9366
7	5.2749	6.5359	63.4008
8	4.7413	7.0696	56.3312
9	4.1640	7.6468	48.6844
10	3.5396	8.2712	40.4132
11	2.8642	8.9466	31.4666
12	2.1337	9.6772	21.7894
13	1.3435	10.4673	11.3221
14	.4887	11.3221	0.0000

YEARS 15 — MO PAYT .9484 — AN CONST 11.39

#	INT	PRIN	BALANCE
1	7.7456	3.6358	96.3642
2	7.4488	3.9326	92.4316
3	7.1276	4.2538	88.1778
4	6.7803	4.6011	83.5767
5	6.4046	4.9768	78.5999
6	5.9982	5.3832	73.2167
7	5.5586	5.8228	67.3939
8	5.0832	6.2982	61.0957
9	4.5689	6.8125	54.2832
10	4.0126	7.3688	46.9144
11	3.4109	7.9705	38.9439
12	2.7601	8.6213	30.3225
13	2.0561	9.3253	20.9972
14	1.2946	10.0868	10.9104
15	.4710	10.9104	0.0000

YEARS 16 — MO PAYT .9176 — AN CONST 11.02

#	INT	PRIN	BALANCE
1	7.7593	3.2520	96.7480
2	7.4937	3.5175	93.2305
3	7.2065	3.8048	89.4257
4	6.8958	4.1154	85.3103
5	6.5598	4.4515	80.8588
6	6.1963	4.8150	76.0438
7	5.8031	5.2081	70.8357
8	5.3779	5.6334	65.2023
9	4.9179	6.0934	59.1088
10	4.4203	6.5910	52.5179
11	3.8821	7.1292	45.3887
12	3.3000	7.7113	37.6774
13	2.6703	8.3410	29.3364
14	1.9892	9.0221	20.3144
15	1.2525	9.7588	10.5556
16	.4557	10.5556	0.0000

YEARS 17 — MO PAYT .8908 — AN CONST 10.69

#	INT	PRIN	BALANCE
1	7.7711	2.9187	97.0813
2	7.5328	3.1571	93.9242
3	7.2750	3.4149	90.5093
4	6.9962	3.6937	86.8156
5	6.6946	3.9953	82.8203
6	6.3683	4.3216	78.4987
7	6.0154	4.6744	73.8243
8	5.6338	5.0561	68.7682
9	5.2209	5.4690	63.2992
10	4.7743	5.9156	57.3836
11	4.2913	6.3986	50.9850
12	3.7688	6.9211	44.0639
13	3.2037	7.4862	36.5777
14	2.5924	8.0975	28.4802
15	1.9312	8.7587	19.7214
16	1.2160	9.4739	10.2475
17	.4424	10.2475	0.0000

YEARS 18 — MO PAYT .8674 — AN CONST 10.41

#	INT	PRIN	BALANCE
1	7.7815	2.6275	97.3725
2	7.5670	2.8421	94.5304
3	7.3349	3.0741	91.4563
4	7.0839	3.3251	88.1312
5	6.8124	3.5967	84.5345
6	6.5187	3.8903	80.6442
7	6.2010	4.2080	76.4362
8	5.8574	4.5516	71.8846
9	5.4857	4.9233	66.9613
10	5.0837	5.3253	61.6360
11	4.6489	5.7601	55.8759
12	4.1785	6.2305	49.6454
13	3.6698	6.7392	42.9061
14	3.1195	7.2895	35.6166
15	2.5243	7.8848	27.7319
16	1.8804	8.5286	19.2033
17	1.1840	9.2250	9.9783
18	.4307	9.9783	0.0000

YEARS 19 — MO PAYT .8468 — AN CONST 10.17

#	INT	PRIN	BALANCE
1	7.7906	2.3715	97.6285
2	7.5970	2.5652	95.0633
3	7.3875	2.7747	92.2886
4	7.1609	3.0012	89.2874
5	6.9159	3.2463	86.0411
6	6.6508	3.5114	82.5298
7	6.3641	3.7981	78.7317
8	6.0539	4.1082	74.6235
9	5.7185	4.4437	70.1798
10	5.3556	4.8065	65.3733
11	4.9632	5.1990	60.1743
12	4.5386	5.6235	54.5507
13	4.0794	6.0827	48.4680
14	3.5827	6.5794	41.8886
15	3.0455	7.1167	34.7720
16	2.4644	7.6978	27.0742
17	1.8358	8.3263	18.7479
18	1.1559	9.0062	9.7416
19	.4205	9.7416	0.0000

YEARS 20 — MO PAYT .8287 — AN CONST 9.95

#	INT	PRIN	BALANCE
1	7.7987	2.1455	97.8545
2	7.6235	2.3207	95.5339
3	7.4340	2.5102	93.0237
4	7.2290	2.7151	90.3086
5	7.0073	2.9368	87.3718
6	6.7675	3.1766	84.1951
7	6.5081	3.4360	80.7591
8	6.2275	3.7166	77.0425
9	5.9241	4.0201	73.0224
10	5.5958	4.3483	68.6741
11	5.2407	4.7034	63.9707
12	4.8567	5.0875	58.8832
13	4.4413	5.5029	53.3804
14	3.9919	5.9522	47.4282
15	3.5059	6.4382	40.9899
16	2.9802	6.9640	34.0259
17	2.4115	7.5326	26.4933
18	1.7964	8.1477	18.3456
19	1.1311	8.8130	9.5326
20	.4115	9.5326	0.0000

YEARS 21 — MO PAYT .8126 — AN CONST 9.76

#	INT	PRIN	BALANCE
1	7.8058	1.9449	98.0551
2	7.6470	2.1037	95.9513
3	7.4752	2.2755	93.6758

MONTHLY PAYMENT AMORTIZATION SCHEDULE PER $100 7.875%

#	INT	PRIN	BALANCE
4	7.2894	2.4613	91.2145
5	7.0884	2.6623	88.5522
6	6.8710	2.8797	85.6725
7	6.6359	3.1149	82.5576
8	6.3815	3.3692	79.1884
9	6.1064	3.6443	75.5441
10	5.8088	3.9419	71.6022
11	5.4870	4.2638	67.3384
12	5.1388	4.6119	62.7265
13	4.7622	4.9885	57.7380
14	4.3549	5.3959	52.3422
15	3.9143	5.8365	46.5057
16	3.4377	6.3130	40.1927
17	2.9222	6.8285	33.3642
18	2.3646	7.3861	25.9780
19	1.7615	7.9892	17.9888
20	1.1091	8.6416	9.3472
21	.4035	9.3472	0.0000

YEARS 22 MO PAYT .7982 AN CONST 9.58

#	INT	PRIN	BALANCE
1	7.8121	1.7663	98.2337
2	7.6679	1.9106	96.3231
3	7.5119	2.0666	94.2565
4	7.3432	2.2353	92.0212
5	7.1606	2.4179	89.6033
6	6.9632	2.6153	86.9880
7	6.7497	2.8288	84.1592
8	6.5187	3.0598	81.0994
9	6.2688	3.3097	77.7897
10	5.9986	3.5799	74.2097
11	5.7062	3.8723	70.3375
12	5.3900	4.1885	66.1490
13	5.0480	4.5305	61.6186
14	4.6781	4.9004	56.7182
15	4.2779	5.3005	51.4176
16	3.8451	5.7334	45.6843
17	3.3770	6.2015	39.4827
18	2.8706	6.7079	32.7748
19	2.3228	7.2556	25.5192
20	1.7304	7.8481	17.6711
21	1.0895	8.4890	9.1821
22	.3964	9.1821	0.0000

YEARS 23 MO PAYT .7854 AN CONST 9.43

#	INT	PRIN	BALANCE
1	7.8178	1.6068	98.3932
2	7.6866	1.7380	96.6553
3	7.5447	1.8799	94.7754
4	7.3912	2.0334	92.7420
5	7.2252	2.1994	90.5426
6	7.0456	2.3790	88.1636
7	6.8513	2.5733	85.5903
8	6.6412	2.7834	82.8069
9	6.4139	3.0107	79.7963
10	6.1681	3.2565	76.5398
11	5.9022	3.5224	73.0174
12	5.6145	3.8100	69.2073
13	5.3034	4.1212	65.0862
14	4.9669	4.4577	60.6285
15	4.6029	4.8217	55.8068
16	4.2092	5.2154	50.5915
17	3.7833	5.6412	44.9502
18	3.3227	6.1019	38.8483
19	2.8245	6.6001	32.2482
20	2.2855	7.1391	25.1091
21	1.7026	7.7220	17.3871
22	1.0720	8.3526	9.0346
23	.3900	9.0346	0.0000

YEARS 24 MO PAYT .7739 AN CONST 9.29

#	INT	PRIN	BALANCE
1	7.8229	1.4637	98.5363
2	7.7034	1.5832	96.9530
3	7.5741	1.7125	95.2405
4	7.4343	1.8524	93.3882
5	7.2830	2.0036	91.3845
6	7.1194	2.1672	89.2173
7	6.9425	2.3442	86.8731
8	6.7510	2.5356	84.3375
9	6.5440	2.7426	81.5949
10	6.3200	2.9666	78.6283
11	6.0778	3.2088	75.4194
12	5.8158	3.4709	71.9486
13	5.5324	3.7543	68.1943
14	5.2258	4.0608	64.1335
15	4.8942	4.3924	59.7411
16	4.5356	4.7511	54.9900
17	4.1476	5.1390	49.8509
18	3.7280	5.5587	44.2923
19	3.2741	6.0126	38.2797
20	2.7831	6.5035	31.7762
21	2.2521	7.0346	24.7416
22	1.6777	7.6090	17.1326
23	1.0563	8.2303	8.9023
24	.3843	8.9023	0.0000

YEARS 25 MO PAYT .7636 AN CONST 9.17

#	INT	PRIN	BALANCE
1	7.8275	1.3352	98.6648
2	7.7185	1.4442	97.2207
3	7.6005	1.5621	95.6586
4	7.4730	1.6897	93.9689
5	7.3350	1.8276	92.1413
6	7.1858	1.9769	90.1644
7	7.0244	2.1383	88.0261
8	6.8498	2.3129	85.7132
9	6.6609	2.5017	83.2115
10	6.4566	2.7060	80.5055
11	6.2357	2.9270	77.5785
12	5.9967	3.1660	74.4125
13	5.7381	3.4245	70.9880
14	5.4585	3.7041	67.2838
15	5.1560	4.0066	63.2772
16	4.8289	4.3338	58.9434
17	4.4750	4.6877	54.2558
18	4.0922	5.0704	49.1854
19	3.6782	5.4845	43.7009
20	3.2304	5.9323	37.7686
21	2.7460	6.4167	31.3519
22	2.2220	6.9406	24.4113
23	1.6553	7.5074	16.9039
24	1.0422	8.1204	8.7835
25	.3792	8.7835	0.0000

YEARS 26 MO PAYT .7542 AN CONST 9.06

#	INT	PRIN	BALANCE
1	7.8316	1.2193	98.7807
2	7.7321	1.3189	97.4618
3	7.6244	1.4266	96.0352
4	7.5079	1.5431	94.4922
5	7.3819	1.6691	92.8231
6	7.2456	1.8053	91.0178
7	7.0982	1.9528	89.0650
8	6.9387	2.1122	86.9528
9	6.7662	2.2847	84.6681
10	6.5797	2.4712	82.1969
11	6.3779	2.6730	79.5239
12	6.1596	2.8913	76.6325
13	5.9235	3.1274	73.5052
14	5.6682	3.3828	70.1224
15	5.3919	3.6590	66.4634
16	5.0932	3.9578	62.5057
17	4.7700	4.2809	58.2247
18	4.4204	4.6305	53.5942
19	4.0423	5.0086	48.5856
20	3.6333	5.4176	43.1681
21	3.1910	5.8600	37.3081
22	2.7125	6.3384	30.9697
23	2.1949	6.8560	24.1136
24	1.6351	7.4159	16.6978
25	1.0295	8.0214	8.6764
26	.3745	8.6764	0.0000

YEARS 27 MO PAYT .7458 AN CONST 8.96

#	INT	PRIN	BALANCE
1	7.8353	1.1147	98.8853
2	7.7443	1.2057	97.6796
3	7.6459	1.3042	96.3754
4	7.5394	1.4107	94.9647
5	7.4242	1.5259	93.4389
6	7.2996	1.6505	91.7884
7	7.1648	1.7852	90.0032
8	7.0190	1.9310	88.0722
9	6.8614	2.0887	85.9836
10	6.6908	2.2592	83.7243
11	6.5063	2.4437	81.2806
12	6.3068	2.6432	78.6374
13	6.0910	2.8591	75.7783
14	5.8575	3.0925	72.6858
15	5.6050	3.3451	69.3407
16	5.3318	3.6182	65.7225
17	5.0364	3.9136	61.8089
18	4.7168	4.2332	57.5757
19	4.3712	4.5789	52.9968
20	3.9973	4.9528	48.0440
21	3.5928	5.3572	42.6869
22	3.1554	5.7946	36.8922
23	2.6822	6.2678	30.6244
24	2.1704	6.7796	23.8448
25	1.6168	7.3332	16.5117
26	1.0181	7.9320	8.5797
27	.3704	8.5797	0.0000

YEARS 28 MO PAYT .7382 AN CONST 8.86

#	INT	PRIN	BALANCE
1	7.8387	1.0200	98.9800
2	7.7554	1.1033	97.8766
3	7.6653	1.1934	96.6832
4	7.5679	1.2909	95.3923
5	7.4625	1.3963	93.9961
6	7.3485	1.5103	92.4858
7	7.2251	1.6336	90.8522
8	7.0917	1.7670	89.0851
9	6.9474	1.9113	87.1739
10	6.7914	2.0674	85.1065
11	6.6226	2.2362	82.8703
12	6.4400	2.4188	80.4515
13	6.2425	2.6163	77.8353
14	6.0288	2.8299	75.0054
15	5.7978	3.0610	71.9444
16	5.5478	3.3109	68.6334
17	5.2775	3.5813	65.0522
18	4.9850	3.8737	61.1784
19	4.6687	4.1900	56.9884
20	4.3266	4.5322	52.4562
21	3.9565	4.9022	47.5540
22	3.5562	5.3025	42.2514
23	3.1232	5.7355	36.5159
24	2.6549	6.2039	30.3121
25	2.1483	6.7104	23.6016
26	1.6004	7.2584	16.3432
27	1.0077	7.8511	8.4922
28	.3666	8.4922	0.0000

YEARS 29 MO PAYT .7313 AN CONST 8.78

#	INT	PRIN	BALANCE
1	7.8418	.9342	99.0658
2	7.7655	1.0105	98.0553
3	7.6830	1.0930	96.9622
4	7.5937	1.1823	95.7800
5	7.4972	1.2788	94.5012
6	7.3927	1.3832	93.1179
7	7.2798	1.4962	91.6217
8	7.1576	1.6184	90.0034
9	7.0255	1.7505	88.2529
10	6.8825	1.8934	86.3595
11	6.7279	2.0480	84.3114
12	6.5607	2.2153	82.0961
13	6.3798	2.3962	79.6999
14	6.1841	2.5918	77.1081
15	5.9725	2.8035	74.3046
16	5.7436	3.0324	71.2723
17	5.4960	3.2800	67.9923
18	5.2281	3.5478	64.4444
19	4.9384	3.8375	60.6069
20	4.6251	4.1509	56.4560
21	4.2862	4.4898	51.9662
22	3.9195	4.8564	47.1097
23	3.5230	5.2530	41.8567
24	3.0940	5.6819	36.1748
25	2.6301	6.1459	30.0289
26	2.1282	6.6478	23.3811
27	1.5854	7.1906	16.1905
28	.9983	7.7777	8.4128
29	.3632	8.4128	0.0000

YEARS 30 MO PAYT .7251 AN CONST 8.71

#	INT	PRIN	BALANCE
1	7.8445	.8563	99.1437
2	7.7746	.9262	98.2175
3	7.6990	1.0019	97.2156
4	7.6172	1.0837	96.1320
5	7.5287	1.1721	94.9598
6	7.4330	1.2679	93.6919
7	7.3294	1.3714	92.3206
8	7.2175	1.4834	90.8372
9	7.0963	1.6045	89.2327
10	6.9653	1.7355	87.4972
11	6.8236	1.8772	85.6200
12	6.6703	2.0305	83.5894
13	6.5045	2.1963	81.3931
14	6.3252	2.3757	79.0175
15	6.1312	2.5696	76.4478
16	5.9214	2.7795	73.6684
17	5.6944	3.0064	70.6619
18	5.4489	3.2519	67.4100
19	5.1834	3.5175	63.8926
20	4.8962	3.8047	60.0879
21	4.5855	4.1153	55.9726
22	4.2494	4.4514	51.5212
23	3.8860	4.8149	46.7063
24	3.4928	5.2080	41.4983
25	3.0675	5.6333	35.8650
26	2.6076	6.0933	29.7717
27	2.1100	6.5908	23.1809
28	1.5718	7.1290	16.0519
29	.9897	7.7111	8.3408
30	.3601	8.3408	0.0000

MONTHLY PAYMENT AMORTIZATION SCHEDULE PER $100   7.90 %

#	YEARS 2 / INT	MO PAYT 4.5182 / PRIN	AN CONST 54.22 / BALANCE
1	6.1855	48.0325	51.9675
2	2.2505	51.9675	0.0000

#	YEARS 3 / INT	MO PAYT 3.1290 / PRIN	AN CONST 37.55 / BALANCE
1	6.8026	30.7457	69.2543
2	4.2838	33.2645	35.9897
3	1.5586	35.9897	0.0000

#	YEARS 4 / INT	MO PAYT 2.4366 / PRIN	AN CONST 29.24 / BALANCE
1	7.1101	22.1291	77.8709
2	5.2972	23.9420	53.9289
3	3.3358	25.9034	28.0255
4	1.2137	28.0255	0.0000

#	YEARS 5 / INT	MO PAYT 2.0229 / PRIN	AN CONST 24.28 / BALANCE
1	7.2939	16.9804	83.0196
2	5.9028	18.3715	64.6481
3	4.3977	19.8765	44.7716
4	2.7694	21.5049	23.2667
5	1.0076	23.2667	0.0000

#	YEARS 6 / INT	MO PAYT 1.7484 / PRIN	AN CONST 20.99 / BALANCE
1	7.4158	13.5655	86.4345
2	6.3045	14.6769	71.7576
3	5.1021	15.8793	55.8783
4	3.8012	17.1802	38.6981
5	2.3937	18.5877	20.1104
6	.8709	20.1104	0.0000

#	YEARS 7 / INT	MO PAYT 1.5536 / PRIN	AN CONST 18.65 / BALANCE
1	7.5023	11.1414	88.8586
2	6.5896	12.0542	76.8044
3	5.6020	13.0417	63.7628
4	4.5336	14.1101	49.6526
5	3.3777	15.2661	34.3866
6	2.1270	16.5167	17.8698
7	.7739	17.8698	0.0000

#	YEARS 8 / INT	MO PAYT 1.4086 / PRIN	AN CONST 16.91 / BALANCE
1	7.5668	9.3363	90.6637
2	6.8019	10.1012	80.5625
3	5.9743	10.9287	69.6337
4	5.0790	11.8241	57.8097
5	4.1103	12.7927	45.0169
6	3.0623	13.8408	31.1761
7	1.9284	14.9747	16.2015
8	.7016	16.2015	0.0000

#	YEARS 9 / INT	MO PAYT 1.2967 / PRIN	AN CONST 15.57 / BALANCE
1	7.6165	7.9439	92.0561
2	6.9657	8.5947	83.4615
3	6.2615	9.2988	74.1627
4	5.4998	10.0606	64.1021
5	4.6755	10.8848	53.2173
6	3.7838	11.7765	41.4408

(YEARS 2, continued)

#	INT	PRIN	BALANCE
7	2.8190	12.7413	28.6995
8	1.7752	13.7851	14.9144
9	.6459	14.9144	0.0000

#	YEARS 10 / INT	MO PAYT 1.2080 / PRIN	AN CONST 14.50 / BALANCE
1	7.6559	6.8401	93.1599
2	7.0955	7.4005	85.7594
3	6.4892	8.0068	77.7526
4	5.8333	8.6627	69.0899
5	5.1236	9.3724	59.7174
6	4.3557	10.1402	49.5772
7	3.5250	10.9710	38.6062
8	2.6262	11.8698	26.7365
9	1.6538	12.8422	13.8943
10	.6017	13.8943	0.0000

#	YEARS 11 / INT	MO PAYT 1.1362 / PRIN	AN CONST 13.64 / BALANCE
1	7.6878	5.9463	94.0537
2	7.2006	6.4334	87.6203
3	6.6736	6.9604	80.6599
4	6.1033	7.5307	73.1292
5	5.4864	8.1476	64.9816
6	4.8189	8.8151	56.1665
7	4.0967	9.5373	46.6292
8	3.3154	10.3186	36.3106
9	2.4701	11.1640	25.1466
10	1.5555	12.0786	13.0681
11	.5659	13.0681	0.0000

#	YEARS 12 / INT	MO PAYT 1.0770 / PRIN	AN CONST 12.93 / BALANCE
1	7.7140	5.2097	94.7903
2	7.2872	5.6365	89.1538
3	6.8255	6.0982	83.0556
4	6.3259	6.5978	76.4578
5	5.7854	7.1384	69.3194
6	5.2006	7.7232	61.5963
7	4.5679	8.3559	53.2404
8	3.8833	9.0404	44.2000
9	3.1427	9.7810	34.4189
10	2.3414	10.5824	23.8366
11	1.4744	11.4493	12.3873
12	.5364	12.3873	0.0000

#	YEARS 13 / INT	MO PAYT 1.0275 / PRIN	AN CONST 12.34 / BALANCE
1	7.7360	4.5940	95.4060
2	7.3597	4.9703	90.4357
3	6.9525	5.3775	85.0581
4	6.5119	5.8181	79.2400
5	6.0353	6.2947	72.9453
6	5.5196	6.8104	66.1349
7	4.9617	7.3684	58.7665
8	4.3580	7.9720	50.7945
9	3.7049	8.6251	42.1694
10	2.9983	9.3317	32.8377
11	2.2338	10.0962	22.7415
12	1.4067	10.9233	11.8182
13	.5118	11.8182	0.0000

#	YEARS 14 / INT	MO PAYT .9856 / PRIN	AN CONST 11.83 / BALANCE
1	7.7546	4.0732	95.9268
2	7.4209	4.4069	91.5200
3	7.0599	4.7679	86.7521

(YEARS 14, continued)

#	INT	PRIN	BALANCE
4	6.6693	5.1585	81.5936
5	6.2467	5.5811	76.0125
6	5.7895	6.0383	69.9741
7	5.2948	6.5330	63.4411
8	4.7596	7.0682	56.3729
9	4.1805	7.6473	48.7256
10	3.5540	8.2738	40.4518
11	2.8762	8.9516	31.5002
12	2.1428	9.6850	21.8152
13	1.3494	10.4784	11.3368
14	.4910	11.3368	0.0000

#	YEARS 15 / INT	MO PAYT .9499 / PRIN	AN CONST 11.40 / BALANCE
1	7.7705	3.6282	96.3718
2	7.4733	3.9254	92.4464
3	7.1517	4.2470	88.1995
4	6.8037	4.5949	83.6046
5	6.4273	4.9713	78.6332
6	6.0200	5.3786	73.2546
7	5.5794	5.8193	67.4354
8	5.1027	6.2960	61.1394
9	4.5869	6.8118	54.3276
10	4.0288	7.3698	46.9577
11	3.4251	7.9736	38.9841
12	2.7718	8.6268	30.3573
13	2.0651	9.3336	21.0237
14	1.3004	10.0982	10.9255
15	.4731	10.9255	0.0000

#	YEARS 16 / INT	MO PAYT .9191 / PRIN	AN CONST 11.03 / BALANCE
1	7.7842	3.2446	96.7554
2	7.5184	3.5104	93.2449
3	7.2308	3.7980	89.4469
4	6.9196	4.1092	85.3377
5	6.5830	4.4458	80.8919
6	6.2188	4.8100	76.0819
7	5.8247	5.2041	70.8778
8	5.3984	5.6304	65.2473
9	4.9371	6.0917	59.1556
10	4.4380	6.5908	52.5649
11	3.8981	7.1307	45.4341
12	3.3139	7.7149	37.7193
13	2.6819	8.3469	29.3723
14	1.9981	9.0307	20.3416
15	1.2582	9.7706	10.5710
16	.4578	10.5710	0.0000

#	YEARS 17 / INT	MO PAYT .8923 / PRIN	AN CONST 10.71 / BALANCE
1	7.7961	2.9116	97.0884
2	7.5575	3.1502	93.9382
3	7.2995	3.4082	90.5300
4	7.0203	3.6874	86.8426
5	6.7182	3.9895	82.8530
6	6.3913	4.3164	78.5366
7	6.0377	4.6700	73.8667
8	5.6551	5.0526	68.8141
9	5.2412	5.4665	63.3476
10	4.7934	5.9143	57.4332
11	4.3088	6.3989	51.0344
12	3.7846	6.9231	44.1113
13	3.2174	7.4903	36.6210
14	2.6038	8.1039	28.5171
15	1.9399	8.7678	19.7493
16	1.2216	9.4861	10.2632
17	.4445	10.2632	0.0000

#	YEARS 18 / INT	MO PAYT .8689 / PRIN	AN CONST 10.43 / BALANCE
1	7.8065	2.6206	97.3794
2	7.5918	2.8353	94.5441
3	7.3595	3.0676	91.4765
4	7.1082	3.3189	88.1575
5	6.8363	3.5908	84.5667
6	6.5421	3.8850	80.6817
7	6.2238	4.2033	76.4785
8	5.8795	4.5476	71.9309
9	5.5069	4.9202	67.0107
10	5.1038	5.3232	61.6875
11	4.6677	5.7593	55.9281
12	4.1959	6.2312	49.6969
13	3.6854	6.7417	42.9553
14	3.1331	7.2940	35.6613
15	2.5356	7.8915	27.7698
16	1.8891	8.5380	19.2318
17	1.1896	9.2375	9.9943
18	.4328	9.9943	0.0000

#	YEARS 19 / INT	MO PAYT .8484 / PRIN	AN CONST 10.19 / BALANCE
1	7.8156	2.3649	97.6351
2	7.6218	2.5587	95.0764
3	7.4122	2.7683	92.3082
4	7.1854	2.9951	89.3131
5	6.9401	3.2404	86.0727
6	6.6746	3.5059	82.5668
7	6.3874	3.7931	78.7737
8	6.0766	4.1039	74.6698
9	5.7404	4.4401	70.2298
10	5.3767	4.8038	65.4260
11	4.9831	5.1974	60.2286
12	4.5574	5.6231	54.6055
13	4.0967	6.0838	48.5217
14	3.5983	6.5822	41.9394
15	3.0590	7.1215	34.8180
16	2.4756	7.7049	27.1131
17	1.8444	8.3361	18.7770
18	1.1615	9.0190	9.7579
19	.4226	9.7579	0.0000

#	YEARS 20 / INT	MO PAYT .8302 / PRIN	AN CONST 9.97 / BALANCE
1	7.8236	2.1391	97.8609
2	7.6484	2.3143	95.5466
3	7.4588	2.5039	93.0427
4	7.2537	2.7091	90.3336
5	7.0317	2.9310	87.4026
6	6.7916	3.1711	84.2315
7	6.5318	3.4309	80.8006
8	6.2508	3.7120	77.0887
9	5.9467	4.0161	73.0726
10	5.6176	4.3451	68.7275
11	5.2617	4.7011	64.0265
12	4.8765	5.0862	58.9403
13	4.4599	5.5029	53.4374
14	4.0090	5.9537	47.4837
15	3.5213	6.4414	41.0423
16	2.9936	6.9691	34.0732
17	2.4226	7.5401	26.5331
18	1.8049	8.1578	18.3753
19	1.1366	8.8261	9.5492
20	.4135	9.5492	0.0000

#	YEARS 21 / INT	MO PAYT .8141 / PRIN	AN CONST 9.77 / BALANCE
1	7.8308	1.9388	98.0612
2	7.6720	2.0976	95.9636
3	7.5001	2.2695	93.6942

#	INT	PRIN	BALANCE
4	7.3142	2.4554	91.2388
5	7.1130	2.6565	88.5823
6	6.8954	2.8742	85.7081
7	6.6599	3.1096	82.5985
8	6.4052	3.3644	79.2341
9	6.1296	3.6400	75.5941
10	5.8314	3.9382	71.6559
11	5.5087	4.2608	67.3950
12	5.1597	4.6099	62.7851
13	4.7820	4.9876	57.7976
14	4.3734	5.3962	52.4014
15	3.9313	5.8383	46.5631
16	3.4530	6.3165	40.2466
17	2.9356	6.8340	33.4126
18	2.3757	7.3939	26.0187
19	1.7699	7.9996	18.0190
20	1.1146	8.6550	9.3640
21	.4055	9.3640	0.0000

YEARS 22 — MO PAYT .7998 — AN CONST 9.60

#	INT	PRIN	BALANCE
1	7.8372	1.7604	98.2396
2	7.6929	1.9046	96.3349
3	7.5369	2.0607	94.2743
4	7.3681	2.2295	92.0448
5	7.1854	2.4121	89.6326
6	6.9878	2.6098	87.0228
7	6.7740	2.8236	84.1993
8	6.5427	3.0549	81.1444
9	6.2924	3.3052	77.8392
10	6.0217	3.5759	74.2633
11	5.7287	3.8689	70.3944
12	5.4118	4.1858	66.2086
13	5.0688	4.5288	61.6799
14	4.6978	4.8998	56.7801
15	4.2964	5.3012	51.4789
16	3.8621	5.7355	45.7434
17	3.3922	6.2053	39.5381
18	2.8839	6.7137	32.8244
19	2.3339	7.2637	25.5606
20	1.7388	7.8588	17.7018
21	1.0950	8.5026	9.1992
22	.3984	9.1992	0.0000

YEARS 23 — MO PAYT .7870 — AN CONST 9.45

#	INT	PRIN	BALANCE
1	7.8429	1.6011	98.3989
2	7.7117	1.7322	96.6667
3	7.5698	1.8741	94.7925
4	7.4162	2.0277	92.7649
5	7.2501	2.1938	90.5711
6	7.0704	2.3735	88.1975
7	6.8759	2.5680	85.6295
8	6.6656	2.7784	82.8512
9	6.4379	3.0060	79.8452
10	6.1917	3.2522	76.5930
11	5.9253	3.5187	73.0743
12	5.6370	3.8069	69.2674
13	5.3251	4.1188	65.1486
14	4.9877	4.4562	60.6923
15	4.6226	4.8213	55.8710
16	4.2276	5.2163	50.6547
17	3.8003	5.6436	45.0110
18	3.3379	6.1060	38.9051
19	2.8377	6.6062	32.2988
20	2.2965	7.1474	25.1514
21	1.7109	7.7330	17.4184
22	1.0774	8.3665	9.0519
23	.3920	9.0519	0.0000

YEARS 24 — MO PAYT .7755 — AN CONST 9.31

#	INT	PRIN	BALANCE
1	7.8479	1.4583	98.5417
2	7.7285	1.5777	96.9640
3	7.5992	1.7070	95.2570
4	7.4594	1.8468	93.4102
5	7.3081	1.9981	91.4121
6	7.1444	2.1618	89.2503
7	6.9673	2.3389	86.9114
8	6.7757	2.5305	84.3808
9	6.5684	2.7378	81.6430
10	6.3441	2.9621	78.6809
11	6.1014	3.2048	75.4761
12	5.8388	3.4674	72.0087
13	5.5548	3.7514	68.2573
14	5.2475	4.0588	64.1985
15	4.9149	4.3913	59.8073
16	4.5552	4.7510	55.0563
17	4.1660	5.1402	49.9160
18	3.7449	5.5613	44.3547
19	3.2893	6.0170	38.3377
20	2.7963	6.5099	31.8278
21	2.2630	7.0432	24.7846
22	1.6860	7.6202	17.1644
23	1.0617	8.2445	8.9199
24	.3863	8.9199	0.0000

YEARS 25 — MO PAYT .7652 — AN CONST 9.19

#	INT	PRIN	BALANCE
1	7.8525	1.3299	98.6701
2	7.7436	1.4389	97.2312
3	7.6257	1.5567	95.6745
4	7.4982	1.6843	93.9902
5	7.3602	1.8223	92.1680
6	7.2109	1.9715	90.1964
7	7.0494	2.1331	88.0633
8	6.8746	2.3078	85.7555
9	6.6856	2.4969	83.2587
10	6.4810	2.7014	80.5572
11	6.2597	2.9227	77.6345
12	6.0203	3.1622	74.4723
13	5.7612	3.4212	71.0510
14	5.4809	3.7015	67.3495
15	5.1777	4.0048	63.3447
16	4.8496	4.3329	59.0119
17	4.4946	4.6878	54.3241
18	4.1106	5.0719	49.2522
19	3.6951	5.4874	43.7648
20	3.2455	5.9369	37.8279
21	2.7591	6.4233	31.4045
22	2.2329	6.9495	24.4550
23	1.6636	7.5189	16.9361
24	1.0476	8.1348	8.8013
25	.3812	8.8013	0.0000

YEARS 26 — MO PAYT .7559 — AN CONST 9.08

#	INT	PRIN	BALANCE
1	7.8567	1.2143	98.7857
2	7.7572	1.3138	97.4720
3	7.6495	1.4214	96.0506
4	7.5331	1.5378	94.5127
5	7.4071	1.6638	92.8489
6	7.2708	1.8001	91.0488
7	7.1233	1.9476	89.1012
8	6.9638	2.1072	86.9940
9	6.7912	2.2798	84.7142
10	6.6044	2.4666	82.2477
11	6.4023	2.6686	79.5790
12	6.1837	2.8873	76.6918
13	5.9472	3.1238	73.5680
14	5.6912	3.3797	70.1883
15	5.4144	3.6566	66.5317
16	5.1148	3.9561	62.5756
17	4.7907	4.2802	58.2953
18	4.4400	4.6309	53.6644
19	4.0607	5.0103	48.6541
20	3.6502	5.4208	43.2334
21	3.2061	5.8648	37.3685
22	2.7256	6.3453	31.0232
23	2.2058	6.8651	24.1581
24	1.6434	7.4276	16.7305
25	1.0349	8.0361	8.6944
26	.3765	8.6944	0.0000

YEARS 27 — MO PAYT .7475 — AN CONST 8.98

#	INT	PRIN	BALANCE
1	7.8604	1.1099	98.8901
2	7.7695	1.2008	97.6893
3	7.6711	1.2992	96.3901
4	7.5646	1.4056	94.9845
5	7.4495	1.5208	93.4637
6	7.3249	1.6454	91.8184
7	7.1901	1.7802	90.0382
8	7.0443	1.9260	88.1123
9	6.8865	2.0838	86.0285
10	6.7158	2.2545	83.7740
11	6.5311	2.4392	81.3348
12	6.3313	2.6390	78.6958
13	6.1151	2.8552	75.8406
14	5.8811	3.0891	72.7515
15	5.6281	3.3422	69.4093
16	5.3543	3.6160	65.7933
17	5.0580	3.9122	61.8810
18	4.7375	4.2327	57.6483
19	4.3908	4.5795	53.0688
20	4.0156	4.9547	48.1141
21	3.6097	5.3606	42.7535
22	3.1705	5.7997	36.9538
23	2.6954	6.2749	30.6789
24	2.1813	6.7890	23.8899
25	1.6251	7.3451	16.5448
26	1.0234	7.9469	8.5979
27	.3723	8.5979	0.0000

YEARS 28 — MO PAYT .7399 — AN CONST 8.88

#	INT	PRIN	BALANCE
1	7.8638	1.0154	98.9846
2	7.7806	1.0986	97.8860
3	7.6906	1.1886	96.6974
4	7.5932	1.2860	95.4114
5	7.4878	1.3913	94.0200
6	7.3739	1.5053	92.5147
7	7.2505	1.6286	90.8860
8	7.1171	1.7621	89.1240
9	6.9727	1.9064	87.2175
10	6.8166	2.0626	85.1549
11	6.6476	2.2316	82.9233
12	6.4648	2.4144	80.5089
13	6.2670	2.6122	77.8967
14	6.0530	2.8262	75.0705
15	5.8214	3.0578	72.0127
16	5.5709	3.3083	68.7045
17	5.2999	3.5793	65.1252
18	5.0067	3.8725	61.2527
19	4.6894	4.1898	57.0629
20	4.3462	4.5330	52.5299
21	3.9748	4.9044	47.6256
22	3.5750	5.3062	42.3194
23	3.1383	5.7409	36.5785
24	2.6680	6.2112	30.3674
25	2.1592	6.7200	23.6473
26	1.6086	7.2705	16.3768
27	1.0130	7.8662	8.5106
28	.3686	8.5106	0.0000

YEARS 29 — MO PAYT .7331 — AN CONST 8.80

#	INT	PRIN	BALANCE
1	7.8668	.9298	99.0702
2	7.7906	1.0060	98.0642
3	7.7082	1.0884	96.9758
4	7.6191	1.1776	95.7983
5	7.5226	1.2740	94.5242
6	7.4182	1.3784	93.1458
7	7.3053	1.4913	91.6545
8	7.1831	1.6135	90.0410
9	7.0509	1.7457	88.2953
10	6.9079	1.8887	86.4066
11	6.7532	2.0434	84.3631
12	6.5858	2.2108	82.1523
13	6.4047	2.3920	79.7603
14	6.2087	2.5879	77.1724
15	5.9967	2.7999	74.3725
16	5.7673	3.0293	71.3432
17	5.5191	3.2775	68.0657
18	5.2506	3.5460	64.5197
19	4.9601	3.8365	60.6832
20	4.6458	4.1508	56.5324
21	4.3058	4.4909	52.0415
22	3.9379	4.8588	47.1827
23	3.5398	5.2568	41.9259
24	3.1091	5.6875	36.2384
25	2.6432	6.1534	30.0850
26	2.1391	6.6575	23.4275
27	1.5937	7.2029	16.2245
28	1.0036	7.7930	8.4315
29	.3651	8.4315	0.0000

YEARS 30 — MO PAYT .7268 — AN CONST 8.73

#	INT	PRIN	BALANCE
1	7.8696	.8521	99.1479
2	7.7998	.9219	98.2260
3	7.7243	.9974	97.2286
4	7.6425	1.0791	96.1495
5	7.5541	1.1675	94.9820
6	7.4585	1.2632	93.7188
7	7.3550	1.3667	92.3521
8	7.2430	1.4786	90.8735
9	7.1219	1.5998	89.2738
10	6.9908	1.7308	87.5429
11	6.8491	1.8726	85.6703
12	6.6956	2.0260	83.6443
13	6.5297	2.1920	81.4523
14	6.3501	2.3716	79.0807
15	6.1558	2.5659	76.5148
16	5.9456	2.7761	73.7388
17	5.7182	3.0035	70.7353
18	5.4721	3.2496	67.4857
19	5.2059	3.5158	63.9699
20	4.9179	3.8038	60.1661
21	4.6062	4.1154	56.0507
22	4.2691	4.4526	51.5981
23	3.9043	4.8174	46.7807
24	3.5096	5.2120	41.5687
25	3.0826	5.6390	35.9296
26	2.6207	6.1010	29.8287
27	2.1209	6.6008	23.2279
28	1.5801	7.1416	16.0863
29	.9950	7.7266	8.3596
30	.3620	8.3596	0.0000

YEARS 2 — MO PAYT 4.5227 — AN CONST 54.28

#	INT	PRIN	BALANCE
1	6.2651	48.0077	51.9923
2	2.2804	51.9923	0.0000

YEARS 3 — MO PAYT 3.1336 — AN CONST 37.61

#	INT	PRIN	BALANCE
1	6.8900	30.7136	69.2864
2	4.3408	33.2628	36.0236
3	1.5800	36.0236	0.0000

YEARS 4 — MO PAYT 2.4413 — AN CONST 29.30

#	INT	PRIN	BALANCE
1	7.2015	22.0940	77.9060
2	5.3677	23.9277	53.9783
3	3.3818	25.9137	28.0646
4	1.2309	28.0646	0.0000

YEARS 5 — MO PAYT 2.0276 — AN CONST 24.34

#	INT	PRIN	BALANCE
1	7.3877	16.9440	83.0560
2	5.9813	18.3504	64.7056
3	4.4582	19.8734	44.8322
4	2.8088	21.5229	23.3093
5	1.0224	23.3093	0.0000

YEARS 6 — MO PAYT 1.7533 — AN CONST 21.04

#	INT	PRIN	BALANCE
1	7.5111	13.5288	86.4712
2	6.3882	14.6517	71.8195
3	5.1721	15.8678	55.9517
4	3.8551	17.1848	38.7669
5	2.4288	18.6111	20.1558
6	.8841	20.1558	0.0000

YEARS 7 — MO PAYT 1.5586 — AN CONST 18.71

#	INT	PRIN	BALANCE
1	7.5987	11.1048	88.8952
2	6.6770	12.0265	76.8688
3	5.6788	13.0247	63.8441
4	4.5978	14.1057	49.7384
5	3.4270	15.2765	34.4620
6	2.1591	16.5444	17.9176
7	.7859	17.9176	0.0000

YEARS 8 — MO PAYT 1.4137 — AN CONST 16.97

#	INT	PRIN	BALANCE
1	7.6639	9.3001	90.6999
2	6.8920	10.0720	80.6279
3	6.0560	10.9080	69.7199
4	5.1507	11.8133	57.9065
5	4.1702	12.7938	45.1127
6	3.1083	13.8557	31.2570
7	1.9583	15.0057	16.2512
8	.7128	16.2512	0.0000

YEARS 9 — MO PAYT 1.3019 — AN CONST 15.63

#	INT	PRIN	BALANCE
1	7.7142	7.9083	92.0917
2	7.0578	8.5646	83.5271
3	6.3470	9.2755	74.2516
4	5.5771	10.0454	64.2063
5	4.7433	10.8791	53.3271
6	3.8404	11.7821	41.5451
7	2.8625	12.7600	28.7851
8	1.8034	13.8191	14.9660
9	.6564	14.9660	0.0000

YEARS 10 — MO PAYT 1.2133 — AN CONST 14.56

#	INT	PRIN	BALANCE
1	7.7541	6.8052	93.1948
2	7.1892	7.3701	85.8247
3	6.5775	7.9818	77.8429
4	5.9150	8.6443	69.1986
5	5.1976	9.3617	59.8369
6	4.4205	10.1388	49.6981
7	3.5790	10.9803	38.7119
8	2.6677	11.8916	26.8262
9	1.6807	12.8786	13.9476
10	.6118	13.9476	0.0000

YEARS 11 — MO PAYT 1.1415 — AN CONST 13.70

#	INT	PRIN	BALANCE
1	7.7863	5.9122	94.0878
2	7.2956	6.4029	87.6849
3	6.7642	6.9343	80.7506
4	6.1886	7.5099	73.2407
5	5.5653	8.1332	65.1075
6	4.8903	8.8083	56.2992
7	4.1592	9.5393	46.7599
8	3.3674	10.3311	36.4288
9	2.5100	11.1886	25.2402
10	1.5813	12.1172	13.1229
11	.5756	13.1229	0.0000

YEARS 12 — MO PAYT 1.0825 — AN CONST 12.99

#	INT	PRIN	BALANCE
1	7.8129	5.1765	94.8235
2	7.3833	5.6062	89.2173
3	6.9180	6.0715	83.1459
4	6.4140	6.5754	76.5705
5	5.8683	7.1211	69.4494
6	5.2772	7.7122	61.7372
7	4.6371	8.3523	53.3849
8	3.9439	9.0455	44.3393
9	3.1931	9.7963	34.5430
10	2.3800	10.6094	23.9336
11	1.4995	11.4900	12.4436
12	.5458	12.4436	0.0000

YEARS 13 — MO PAYT 1.0331 — AN CONST 12.40

#	INT	PRIN	BALANCE
1	7.8351	4.5617	95.4383
2	7.4565	4.9404	90.4979
3	7.0465	5.3504	85.1475
4	6.6024	5.7945	79.3530
5	6.1215	6.2754	73.0775
6	5.6006	6.7963	66.2813
7	5.0365	7.3604	58.9209
8	4.4256	7.9713	50.9496
9	3.7640	8.6329	42.3167
10	3.0475	9.3494	32.9673
11	2.2715	10.1254	22.8418
12	1.4311	10.9658	11.8760
13	.5209	11.8760	0.0000

YEARS 14 — MO PAYT .9913 — AN CONST 11.90

#	INT	PRIN	BALANCE
1	7.8539	4.0419	95.9581
2	7.5185	4.3774	91.5808
3	7.1551	4.7407	86.8401

YEARS 15 — MO PAYT .9557 — AN CONST 11.47

#	INT	PRIN	BALANCE
1	7.8700	3.5978	96.4022
2	7.5714	3.8965	92.5057
3	7.2480	4.2199	88.2858
4	6.8977	4.5701	83.7157
5	6.5184	4.9494	78.7663
6	6.1076	5.3602	73.4060
7	5.6627	5.8051	67.6009
8	5.1809	6.2870	61.3139
9	4.6591	6.8088	54.5052
10	4.0939	7.3739	47.1313
11	3.4819	7.9859	39.1453
12	2.8191	8.6488	30.4966
13	2.1012	9.3666	21.1300
14	1.3238	10.1440	10.9860
15	.4819	10.9860	0.0000

YEARS 16 — MO PAYT .9249 — AN CONST 11.10

#	INT	PRIN	BALANCE
1	7.8838	3.2153	96.7847
2	7.6169	3.4822	93.3025
3	7.3279	3.7712	89.5314
4	7.0149	4.0842	85.4472
5	6.6759	4.4232	81.0240
6	6.3088	4.7903	76.2337
7	5.9112	5.1879	71.0458
8	5.4806	5.6185	65.4273
9	5.0143	6.0848	59.3425
10	4.5093	6.5898	52.7527
11	3.9623	7.1368	45.6159
12	3.3699	7.7292	37.8867
13	2.7284	8.3707	29.5160
14	2.0337	9.0654	20.4506
15	1.2812	9.8179	10.6327
16	.4664	10.6327	0.0000

YEARS 17 — MO PAYT .8983 — AN CONST 10.78

#	INT	PRIN	BALANCE
1	7.8958	2.8833	97.1167
2	7.6565	3.1226	93.9941
3	7.3973	3.3818	90.6124
4	7.1166	3.6624	86.9499
5	6.8127	3.9664	82.9835
6	6.4834	4.2956	78.6878
7	6.1269	4.6522	74.0357
8	5.7408	5.0383	68.9974
9	5.3226	5.4565	63.5409
10	4.8697	5.9094	57.6315
11	4.3792	6.3998	51.2316
12	3.8481	6.9310	44.3006
13	3.2728	7.5063	36.7943
14	2.6498	8.1293	28.6650
15	1.9750	8.8041	19.8609
16	1.2443	9.5348	10.3262
17	.4529	10.3262	0.0000

YEARS 18 — MO PAYT .8750 — AN CONST 10.50

#	INT	PRIN	BALANCE
1	7.9063	2.5933	97.4067
2	7.6910	2.8085	94.5982
3	7.4579	3.0416	91.5566
4	7.2055	3.2941	88.2625
5	6.9321	3.5675	84.6951
6	6.6360	3.8636	80.8315
7	6.3153	4.1842	76.6473
8	5.9680	4.5315	72.1157
9	5.5919	4.9077	67.2081
10	5.1846	5.3150	61.8931
11	4.7434	5.7561	56.1370
12	4.2657	6.2339	49.9031
13	3.7483	6.7513	43.1518
14	3.1879	7.3116	35.8401
15	2.5810	7.9185	27.9216
16	1.9238	8.5757	19.3459
17	1.2120	9.2875	10.0584
18	.4412	10.0584	0.0000

YEARS 19 — MO PAYT .8545 — AN CONST 10.26

#	INT	PRIN	BALANCE
1	7.9155	2.3385	97.6615
2	7.7214	2.5326	95.1288
3	7.5112	2.7428	92.3860
4	7.2835	2.9705	89.4155
5	7.0370	3.2170	86.1985
6	6.7700	3.4840	82.7144
7	6.4808	3.7732	78.9412
8	6.1676	4.0864	74.8548
9	5.8285	4.4256	70.4293
10	5.4611	4.7929	65.6364
11	5.0633	5.1907	60.4457
12	4.6325	5.6215	54.8242
13	4.1659	6.0881	48.7361
14	3.6606	6.5934	42.1427
15	3.1134	7.1407	35.0020
16	2.5207	7.7333	27.2687
17	1.8788	8.3752	18.8935
18	1.1837	9.0703	9.8232
19	.4309	9.8232	0.0000

YEARS 20 — MO PAYT .8364 — AN CONST 10.04

#	INT	PRIN	BALANCE
1	7.9236	2.1137	97.8863
2	7.7482	2.2891	95.5972
3	7.5582	2.4791	93.1181
4	7.3524	2.6849	90.4333
5	7.1296	2.9077	87.5256
6	6.8882	3.1490	84.3765
7	6.6269	3.4104	80.9661
8	6.3438	3.6935	77.2727
9	6.0373	4.0000	73.2727
10	5.7053	4.3320	68.9406
11	5.3457	4.6916	64.2491
12	4.9563	5.0810	59.1681
13	4.5346	5.5027	53.6654
14	4.0779	5.9594	47.7060
15	3.5832	6.4540	41.2519
16	3.0476	6.9897	34.2622
17	2.4674	7.5699	26.6923
18	1.8391	8.1982	18.4941
19	1.1587	8.8786	9.6155
20	.4217	9.6155	0.0000

YEARS 21 — MO PAYT .8204 — AN CONST 9.85

#	INT	PRIN	BALANCE
1	7.9308	1.9143	98.0857
2	7.7719	2.0732	96.0125
3	7.5999	2.2453	93.7672

#	INT	PRIN	BALANCE
4	7.4135	2.4316	91.3356
5	7.2117	2.6335	88.7021
6	6.9931	2.8520	85.8501
7	6.7564	3.0888	82.7613
8	6.5000	3.3451	79.4162
9	6.2224	3.6228	75.7934
10	5.9217	3.9234	71.8700
11	5.5960	4.2491	67.6209
12	5.2434	4.6018	63.0191
13	4.8614	4.9837	58.0354
14	4.4478	5.3974	52.6381
15	3.9998	5.8453	46.7927
16	3.5146	6.3305	40.4622
17	2.9892	6.8559	33.6063
18	2.4202	7.4250	26.1813
19	1.8039	8.0412	18.1401
20	1.1365	8.7086	9.4315
21	.4137	9.4315	0.0000

YEARS 22 — MO PAYT .8062 — AN CONST 9.68

#	INT	PRIN	BALANCE
1	7.9372	1.7369	98.2631
2	7.7931	1.8811	96.3820
3	7.6369	2.0372	94.3448
4	7.4679	2.2063	92.1386
5	7.2847	2.3894	89.7492
6	7.0864	2.5877	87.1614
7	6.8716	2.8025	84.3589
8	6.6390	3.0351	81.3238
9	6.3871	3.2870	78.0368
10	6.1143	3.5598	74.4770
11	5.8188	3.8553	70.6217
12	5.4988	4.1753	66.4464
13	5.1523	4.5218	61.9245
14	4.7770	4.8971	57.0274
15	4.3705	5.3036	51.7238
16	3.9303	5.7438	45.9800
17	3.4536	6.2205	39.7594
18	2.9373	6.7368	33.0226
19	2.3781	7.2960	25.7266
20	1.7726	7.9016	17.8250
21	1.1167	8.5574	9.2676
22	.4065	9.2676	0.0000

YEARS 23 — MO PAYT .7935 — AN CONST 9.53

#	INT	PRIN	BALANCE
1	7.9430	1.5785	98.4215
2	7.8119	1.7095	96.7120
3	7.6701	1.8514	94.8607
4	7.5164	2.0050	92.8556
5	7.3500	2.1715	90.6842
6	7.1697	2.3517	88.3325
7	6.9746	2.5469	85.7856
8	6.7632	2.7583	83.0273
9	6.5342	2.9872	80.0402
10	6.2863	3.2351	76.8050
11	6.0178	3.5036	73.3014
12	5.7270	3.7944	69.5069
13	5.4120	4.1094	65.3975
14	5.0710	4.4505	60.9471
15	4.7016	4.8198	56.1272
16	4.3015	5.2199	50.9073
17	3.8683	5.6531	45.2542
18	3.3991	6.1224	39.1318
19	2.8909	6.6305	32.5013
20	2.3406	7.1808	25.3205
21	1.7446	7.7768	17.5437
22	1.0991	8.4223	9.1214
23	.4001	9.1214	0.0000

YEARS 24 — MO PAYT .7821 — AN CONST 9.39

#	INT	PRIN	BALANCE
1	7.9481	1.4366	98.5634
2	7.8288	1.5558	97.0076
3	7.6997	1.6849	95.3227
4	7.5599	1.8248	93.4979
5	7.4084	1.9762	91.5217
6	7.2444	2.1403	89.3814
7	7.0667	2.3179	87.0635
8	6.8744	2.5103	84.5532
9	6.6660	2.7186	81.8346
10	6.4404	2.9443	78.8903
11	6.1960	3.1887	75.7017
12	5.9313	3.4533	72.2483
13	5.6447	3.7399	68.5084
14	5.3343	4.0504	64.4581
15	4.9981	4.3865	60.0715
16	4.6340	4.7506	55.3209
17	4.2397	5.1449	50.1760
18	3.8127	5.5719	44.6041
19	3.3503	6.0344	38.5697
20	2.8494	6.5353	32.0344
21	2.3070	7.0777	24.9568
22	1.7195	7.6651	17.2916
23	1.0833	8.3013	8.9903
24	.3943	8.9903	0.0000

YEARS 25 — MO PAYT .7718 — AN CONST 9.27

#	INT	PRIN	BALANCE
1	7.9527	1.3091	98.6909
2	7.8440	1.4178	97.2731
3	7.7264	1.5354	95.7377
4	7.5989	1.6629	94.0748
5	7.4609	1.8009	92.2739
6	7.3114	1.9504	90.3236
7	7.1496	2.1122	88.2113
8	6.9742	2.2876	85.9238
9	6.7844	2.4774	83.4464
10	6.5787	2.6830	80.7633
11	6.3561	2.9057	77.8576
12	6.1149	3.1469	74.7107
13	5.8537	3.4081	71.3025
14	5.5708	3.6910	67.6116
15	5.2645	3.9973	63.6142
16	4.9327	4.3291	59.2851
17	4.5734	4.6884	54.5967
18	4.1842	5.0776	49.5192
19	3.7628	5.4990	44.0202
20	3.3064	5.9554	38.0648
21	2.8121	6.4497	31.6151
22	2.2768	6.9850	24.6300
23	1.6970	7.5648	17.0653
24	1.0691	8.1926	8.8726
25	.3892	8.8726	0.0000

YEARS 26 — MO PAYT .7626 — AN CONST 9.16

#	INT	PRIN	BALANCE
1	7.9568	1.1943	98.8057
2	7.8577	1.2935	97.5122
3	7.7504	1.4008	96.1114
4	7.6341	1.5171	94.5943
5	7.5082	1.6430	92.9513
6	7.3718	1.7794	91.1719
7	7.2241	1.9271	89.2448
8	7.0642	2.0870	87.1578
9	6.8909	2.2602	84.8976
10	6.7033	2.4478	82.4497
11	6.5002	2.6510	79.7987
12	6.2801	2.8710	76.9277
13	6.0418	3.1093	73.8184
14	5.7838	3.3674	70.4509
15	5.5043	3.6469	66.8041
16	5.2016	3.9496	62.8545
17	4.8738	4.2774	58.5771
18	4.5188	4.6324	53.9446
19	4.1343	5.0169	48.9277
20	3.7179	5.4333	43.4944
21	3.2669	5.8843	37.6101
22	2.7785	6.3727	31.2375
23	2.2496	6.9016	24.3359
24	1.6768	7.4744	16.8615
25	1.0564	8.0948	8.7667
26	.3845	8.7667	0.0000

YEARS 27 — MO PAYT .7543 — AN CONST 9.06

#	INT	PRIN	BALANCE
1	7.9606	1.0908	98.9092
2	7.8700	1.1813	97.7279
3	7.7720	1.2794	96.4486
4	7.6658	1.3855	95.0630
5	7.5508	1.5005	93.5625
6	7.4263	1.6251	91.9374
7	7.2914	1.7600	90.1774
8	7.1453	1.9060	88.2713
9	6.9871	2.0643	86.2071
10	6.8158	2.2356	83.9715
11	6.6302	2.4211	81.5504
12	6.4293	2.6221	78.9283
13	6.2116	2.8397	76.0886
14	5.9759	3.0754	73.0132
15	5.7207	3.3307	69.6825
16	5.4442	3.6071	66.0754
17	5.1449	3.9065	62.1689
18	4.8206	4.2307	57.9381
19	4.4695	4.5819	53.3562
20	4.0892	4.9622	48.3940
21	3.6773	5.3740	43.0200
22	3.2313	5.8201	37.1999
23	2.7482	6.3032	30.8967
24	2.2250	6.8263	24.0704
25	1.6585	7.3929	16.6775
26	1.0449	8.0065	8.6710
27	.3803	8.6710	0.0000

YEARS 28 — MO PAYT .7468 — AN CONST 8.97

#	INT	PRIN	BALANCE
1	7.9640	.9971	99.0029
2	7.8812	1.0799	97.9230
3	7.7916	1.1695	96.7534
4	7.6945	1.2666	95.4868
5	7.5894	1.3717	94.1151
6	7.4755	1.4856	92.6295
7	7.3522	1.6089	91.0206
8	7.2187	1.7424	89.2782
9	7.0741	1.8870	87.3912
10	6.9174	2.0437	85.3475
11	6.7478	2.2133	83.1342
12	6.5641	2.3970	80.7372
13	6.3652	2.5959	78.1413
14	6.1497	2.8114	75.3299
15	5.9164	3.0447	72.2851
16	5.6636	3.2975	68.9877
17	5.3900	3.5711	65.4165
18	5.0936	3.8676	61.5490
19	4.7725	4.1886	57.3604
20	4.4249	4.5362	52.8242
21	4.0484	4.9127	47.9115
22	3.6406	5.3205	42.5910
23	3.1990	5.7621	36.8290
24	2.7208	6.2403	30.5887
25	2.2029	6.7582	23.8304
26	1.6419	7.3192	16.5112
27	1.0344	7.9267	8.5846
28	.3765	8.5846	0.0000

YEARS 29 — MO PAYT .7399 — AN CONST 8.88

#	INT	PRIN	BALANCE
1	7.9670	.9123	99.0877
2	7.8913	.9880	98.0996
3	7.8093	1.0700	97.0296
4	7.7205	1.1589	95.8707
5	7.6243	1.2550	94.6157
6	7.5201	1.3592	93.2565
7	7.4073	1.4720	91.7844
8	7.2851	1.5942	90.1902
9	7.1528	1.7265	88.4637
10	7.0095	1.8698	86.5939
11	6.8543	2.0250	84.5688
12	6.6863	2.1931	82.3758
13	6.5042	2.3751	80.0006
14	6.3071	2.5723	77.4284
15	6.0936	2.7858	74.6426
16	5.8624	3.0170	71.6256
17	5.6120	3.2674	68.3583
18	5.3408	3.5386	64.8197
19	5.0471	3.8323	60.9874
20	4.7290	4.1503	56.8371
21	4.3845	4.4948	52.3423
22	4.0115	4.8679	47.4744
23	3.6074	5.2719	42.2025
24	3.1699	5.7095	36.4930
25	2.6960	6.1834	30.3096
26	2.1828	6.6966	23.6130
27	1.6269	7.2524	16.3606
28	1.0250	7.8543	8.5063
29	.3731	8.5063	0.0000

YEARS 30 — MO PAYT .7338 — AN CONST 8.81

#	INT	PRIN	BALANCE
1	7.9698	.8354	99.1646
2	7.9005	.9047	98.2599
3	7.8254	.9798	97.2801
4	7.7441	1.0611	96.2190
5	7.6560	1.1492	95.0699
6	7.5606	1.2446	93.8253
7	7.4573	1.3479	92.4774
8	7.3454	1.4597	91.0177
9	7.2243	1.5809	89.4368
10	7.0931	1.7121	87.7247
11	6.9510	1.8542	85.8705
12	6.7971	2.0081	83.8624
13	6.6304	2.1748	81.6876
14	6.4499	2.3553	79.3323
15	6.2544	2.5508	76.7816
16	6.0427	2.7625	74.0191
17	5.8134	2.9918	71.0273
18	5.5651	3.2401	67.7872
19	5.2962	3.5090	64.2782
20	5.0049	3.8003	60.4780
21	4.6895	4.1157	56.3623
22	4.3479	4.4573	51.9050
23	3.9780	4.8272	47.0778
24	3.5773	5.2279	41.8499
25	3.1434	5.6618	36.1881
26	2.6735	6.1317	30.0564
27	2.1645	6.6406	23.4158
28	1.6134	7.1918	16.2239
29	1.0164	7.7887	8.4352
30	.3700	8.4352	0.0000

MONTHLY PAYMENT AMORTIZATION SCHEDULE PER $100

8.10 %

YEARS 2	MO PAYT 4.5273	AN CONST 54.33
# INT	PRIN	BALANCE
1 6.3446	47.9829	52.0171
2 2.3104	52.0171	0.0000

YEARS 3	MO PAYT 3.1383	AN CONST 37.66
# INT	PRIN	BALANCE
1 6.9776	30.6815	69.3185
2 4.3980	33.2610	36.0575
3 1.6015	36.0575	0.0000

YEARS 4	MO PAYT 2.4460	AN CONST 29.36
# INT	PRIN	BALANCE
1 7.2930	22.0589	77.9411
2 5.4384	23.9135	54.0276
3 3.4278	25.9240	28.1036
4 1.2483	28.1036	0.0000

YEARS 5	MO PAYT 2.0324	AN CONST 24.39
# INT	PRIN	BALANCE
1 7.4815	16.9077	83.0923
2 6.0599	18.3292	64.7631
3 4.5189	19.8703	44.8928
4 2.8483	21.5409	23.3519
5 1.0372	23.3519	0.0000

YEARS 6	MO PAYT 1.7582	AN CONST 21.10
# INT	PRIN	BALANCE
1 7.6064	13.4921	86.5079
2 6.4720	14.6265	71.8814
3 5.2423	15.8562	56.0252
4 3.9092	17.1893	38.8358
5 2.4640	18.6346	20.2013
6 .8973	20.2013	0.0000

YEARS 7	MO PAYT 1.5636	AN CONST 18.77
# INT	PRIN	BALANCE
1 7.6951	11.0682	88.9318
2 6.7645	11.9988	76.9330
3 5.7557	13.0076	63.9254
4 4.6621	14.1012	49.8242
5 3.4765	15.2868	34.5374
6 2.1913	16.5720	17.9653
7 .7980	17.9653	0.0000

YEARS 8	MO PAYT 1.4188	AN CONST 17.03
# INT	PRIN	BALANCE
1 7.7611	9.2640	90.7360
2 6.9822	10.0429	80.6932
3 6.1378	10.8872	69.8059
4 5.2225	11.8026	58.0034
5 4.2302	12.7949	45.2085
6 3.1544	13.8706	31.3379
7 1.9883	15.0368	16.3010
8 .7240	16.3010	0.0000

YEARS 9	MO PAYT 1.3071	AN CONST 15.69
# INT	PRIN	BALANCE
1 7.8120	7.8727	92.1273
2 7.1501	8.5347	83.5926
3 6.4325	9.2522	74.3404
4 5.6546	10.0301	64.3103
5 4.8113	10.8734	53.4369
6 3.8972	11.7876	41.6493

#	INT	PRIN	BALANCE
7	2.9061	12.7786	28.8707
8	1.8317	13.8530	15.0177
9	.6670	15.0177	0.0000

YEARS 10	MO PAYT 1.2186	AN CONST 14.63
# INT	PRIN	BALANCE
1 7.8523	6.7705	93.2295
2 7.2831	7.3397	85.8898
3 6.6660	7.9568	77.9330
4 5.9970	8.6258	69.3072
5 5.2718	9.3510	59.9562
6 4.4856	10.1372	49.8190
7 3.6333	10.9895	38.8295
8 2.7093	11.9135	26.9160
9 1.7077	12.9151	14.0009
10 .6219	14.0009	0.0000

YEARS 11	MO PAYT 1.1469	AN CONST 13.77
# INT	PRIN	BALANCE
1 7.8849	5.8783	94.1217
2 7.3907	6.3725	87.7492
3 6.8550	6.9083	80.8409
4 6.2741	7.4891	73.3519
5 5.6445	8.1187	65.2331
6 4.9619	8.8013	56.4318
7 4.2219	9.5413	46.8905
8 3.4197	10.3435	36.5470
9 2.5501	11.2131	25.3338
10 1.6073	12.1559	13.1779
11 .5853	13.1779	0.0000

YEARS 12	MO PAYT 1.0879	AN CONST 13.06
# INT	PRIN	BALANCE
1 7.9118	5.1435	94.8565
2 7.4794	5.5759	89.2806
3 7.0106	6.0447	83.2359
4 6.5024	6.5529	76.6829
5 5.9514	7.1039	69.5790
6 5.3542	7.7012	61.8779
7 4.7067	8.3486	53.5292
8 4.0048	9.0506	44.4787
9 3.2438	9.8115	34.6672
10 2.4189	10.6364	24.0308
11 1.5247	11.5307	12.5001
12 .5552	12.5001	0.0000

YEARS 13	MO PAYT 1.0387	AN CONST 12.47
# INT	PRIN	BALANCE
1 7.9343	4.5297	95.4703
2 7.5535	4.9105	90.5598
3 7.1406	5.3234	85.2365
4 6.6930	5.7709	79.4655
5 6.2078	6.2561	73.2094
6 5.6818	6.7821	66.4273
7 5.1116	7.3523	59.0750
8 4.4935	7.9705	51.1045
9 3.8234	8.6406	42.4639
10 3.0969	9.3671	33.0969
11 2.3094	10.1546	22.9423
12 1.4556	11.0084	11.9339
13 .5301	11.9339	0.0000

YEARS 14	MO PAYT .9970	AN CONST 11.97
# INT	PRIN	BALANCE
1 7.9533	4.0108	95.9892
2 7.6161	4.3480	91.6412
3 7.2505	4.7136	86.9277

#	INT	PRIN	BALANCE
4	6.8542	5.1099	81.8178
5	6.4246	5.5395	76.2784
6	5.9589	6.0052	70.2732
7	5.4540	6.5101	63.7631
8	4.9066	7.0574	56.7056
9	4.3133	7.6508	49.0548
10	3.6700	8.2940	40.7608
11	2.9727	8.9914	31.7694
12	2.2167	9.7473	22.0221
13	1.3972	10.5668	11.4553
14	.5088	11.4553	0.0000

YEARS 15	MO PAYT .9614	AN CONST 11.54
# INT	PRIN	BALANCE
1 7.9695	3.5677	96.4323
2 7.6695	3.8677	92.5646
3 7.3443	4.1929	88.3717
4 6.9918	4.5454	83.8263
5 6.6097	4.9275	78.8988
6 6.1954	5.3418	73.5569
7 5.7463	5.7910	67.7660
8 5.2594	6.2778	61.4882
9 4.7316	6.8056	54.6825
10 4.1594	7.3778	47.3047
11 3.5391	7.9981	39.3066
12 2.8666	8.6706	30.6360
13 2.1376	9.3996	21.2364
14 1.3474	10.1898	11.0466
15 .4906	11.0466	0.0000

YEARS 16	MO PAYT .9308	AN CONST 11.17
# INT	PRIN	BALANCE
1 7.9834	3.1862	96.8138
2 7.7156	3.4541	93.3598
3 7.4252	3.7445	89.6153
4 7.1103	4.0593	85.5560
5 6.7690	4.4006	81.1555
6 6.3991	4.7705	76.3849
7 5.9980	5.1716	71.2133
8 5.5632	5.6064	65.6069
9 5.0918	6.0778	59.5290
10 4.5808	6.5888	52.9402
11 4.0268	7.1428	45.7975
12 3.4263	7.7433	38.0542
13 2.7753	8.3943	29.6599
14 2.0695	9.1001	20.5598
15 1.3044	9.8652	10.6946
16 .4750	10.6946	0.0000

YEARS 17	MO PAYT .9042	AN CONST 10.86
# INT	PRIN	BALANCE
1 7.9955	2.8552	97.1448
2 7.7555	3.0952	94.0496
3 7.4953	3.3554	90.6942
4 7.2132	3.6375	87.0567
5 6.9073	3.9434	83.1133
6 6.5758	4.2749	78.8384
7 6.2164	4.6343	74.2040
8 5.8267	5.0240	69.1800
9 5.4043	5.4464	63.7337
10 4.9464	5.9043	57.8294
11 4.4500	6.4007	51.4287
12 3.9119	6.9388	44.4899
13 3.3285	7.5222	36.9677
14 2.6961	8.1547	28.8130
15 2.0104	8.8403	19.9728
16 1.2672	9.5835	10.3893
17 .4614	10.3893	0.0000

YEARS 18	MO PAYT .8810	AN CONST 10.58
# INT	PRIN	BALANCE
1 8.0061	2.5661	97.4339
2 7.7904	2.7819	94.6520
3 7.5565	3.0158	91.6362
4 7.3029	3.2693	88.3669
5 7.0281	3.5442	84.8227
6 6.7301	3.8422	80.9805
7 6.4070	4.1652	76.8153
8 6.0568	4.5154	72.2998
9 5.6772	4.8951	67.4048
10 5.2657	5.3066	62.0982
11 4.8195	5.7528	56.3454
12 4.3358	6.2364	50.1090
13 3.8115	6.7608	43.3482
14 3.2431	7.3292	36.0190
15 2.6269	7.9454	28.0736
16 1.9589	8.6134	19.4602
17 1.2347	9.3376	10.1227
18 .4496	10.1227	0.0000

YEARS 19	MO PAYT .8606	AN CONST 10.33
# INT	PRIN	BALANCE
1 8.0154	2.3124	97.6876
2 7.8210	2.5068	95.1808
3 7.6102	2.7176	92.4633
4 7.3817	2.9460	89.5172
5 7.1341	3.1937	86.3235
6 6.8655	3.4622	82.8612
7 6.5744	3.7533	79.1079
8 6.2589	4.0689	75.0390
9 5.9168	4.4110	70.6280
10 5.5459	4.7819	65.8461
11 5.1439	5.1839	60.6622
12 4.7080	5.6197	55.0425
13 4.2356	6.0922	48.9503
14 3.7234	6.6044	42.3458
15 3.1681	7.1597	35.1861
16 2.5661	7.7617	27.4245
17 1.9136	8.4142	19.0102
18 1.2061	9.1217	9.8886
19 .4392	9.8886	0.0000

YEARS 20	MO PAYT .8427	AN CONST 10.12
# INT	PRIN	BALANCE
1 8.0236	2.0885	97.9115
2 7.8480	2.2641	95.6474
3 7.6576	2.4544	93.1930
4 7.4513	2.6608	90.5322
5 7.2276	2.8845	87.6477
6 6.9851	3.1270	84.5206
7 6.7222	3.3899	81.1307
8 6.4371	3.6750	77.4557
9 6.1282	3.9839	73.4718
10 5.7932	4.3189	69.1529
11 5.4301	4.6820	64.4709
12 5.0365	5.0756	59.3953
13 4.6097	5.5024	53.8929
14 4.1471	5.9650	47.9279
15 3.6456	6.4665	41.4614
16 3.1019	7.0102	34.4513
17 2.5125	7.5996	26.8517
18 1.8736	8.2385	18.6132
19 1.1809	8.9312	9.6821
20 .4300	9.6821	0.0000

YEARS 21	MO PAYT .8267	AN CONST 9.93
# INT	PRIN	BALANCE
1 8.0309	1.8901	98.1099
2 7.8719	2.0490	96.0609
3 7.6997	2.2213	93.8396

#	INT	PRIN	BALANCE
4	7.5129	2.4081	91.4315
5	7.3105	2.6105	88.8210
6	7.0910	2.8300	85.9910
7	6.8530	3.0679	82.9231
8	6.5951	3.3259	79.5972
9	6.3155	3.6055	75.9917
10	6.0123	3.9086	72.0831
11	5.6837	4.2372	67.8459
12	5.3275	4.5935	63.2524
13	4.9413	4.9797	58.2727
14	4.5226	5.3984	52.8743
15	4.0687	5.8522	47.0221
16	3.5767	6.3443	40.6778
17	3.0433	6.8777	33.8001
18	2.4650	7.4559	26.3442
19	1.8382	8.0828	18.2614
20	1.1586	8.7623	9.4991
21	.4219	9.4991	0.0000

YEARS 22   MO PAYT .8126   AN CONST 9.76

#	INT	PRIN	BALANCE
1	8.0373	1.7136	98.2864
2	7.8932	1.8577	96.4286
3	7.7370	2.0139	94.4147
4	7.5677	2.1832	92.2315
5	7.3842	2.3668	89.8647
6	7.1852	2.5658	87.2989
7	6.9695	2.7815	84.5174
8	6.7356	3.0154	81.5021
9	6.4821	3.2689	78.2332
10	6.2072	3.5437	74.6895
11	5.9093	3.8416	70.8479
12	5.5863	4.1646	66.6832
13	5.2362	4.5148	62.1684
14	4.8566	4.8944	57.2741
15	4.4451	5.3059	51.9682
16	3.9990	5.7520	46.2163
17	3.5154	6.2356	39.9807
18	2.9911	6.7598	33.2209
19	2.4228	7.3282	25.8927
20	1.8067	7.9443	17.9485
21	1.1388	8.6122	9.3363
22	.4147	9.3363	0.0000

YEARS 23   MO PAYT .7999   AN CONST 9.60

#	INT	PRIN	BALANCE
1	8.0431	1.5561	98.4439
2	7.9122	1.6870	96.7569
3	7.7704	1.8288	94.9281
4	7.6166	1.9826	92.9455
5	7.4500	2.1493	90.7962
6	7.2693	2.3300	88.4663
7	7.0734	2.5259	85.9404
8	6.8610	2.7382	83.2022
9	6.6308	2.9684	80.2338
10	6.3812	3.2180	77.0158
11	6.1107	3.4886	73.5272
12	5.8173	3.7819	69.7454
13	5.4994	4.0998	65.6455
14	5.1547	4.4445	61.2010
15	4.7810	4.8182	56.3828
16	4.3759	5.2233	51.1595
17	3.9368	5.6624	45.4971
18	3.4607	6.1385	39.3586
19	2.9446	6.6546	32.7039
20	2.3851	7.2141	25.4898
21	1.7786	7.8206	17.6692
22	1.1210	8.4782	9.1910
23	.4082	9.1910	0.0000

YEARS 24   MO PAYT .7886   AN CONST 9.47

#	INT	PRIN	BALANCE
1	8.0482	1.4151	98.5849
2	7.9292	1.5341	97.0507
3	7.8003	1.6631	95.3876
4	7.6604	1.8029	93.5847
5	7.5089	1.9545	91.6302
6	7.3445	2.1188	89.5113
7	7.1664	2.2970	87.2144
8	6.9733	2.4901	84.7243
9	6.7639	2.6995	82.0248
10	6.5369	2.9264	79.0984
11	6.2909	3.1725	75.9259
12	6.0242	3.4392	72.4867
13	5.7350	3.7283	68.7584
14	5.4216	4.0418	64.7166
15	5.0817	4.3816	60.3349
16	4.7134	4.7500	55.5849
17	4.3140	5.1494	50.4355
18	3.8811	5.5823	44.8532
19	3.4117	6.0517	38.8016
20	2.9029	6.5605	32.2411
21	2.3513	7.1120	25.1291
22	1.7534	7.7100	17.4191
23	1.1052	8.3582	9.0609
24	.4025	9.0609	0.0000

YEARS 25   MO PAYT .7785   AN CONST 9.35

#	INT	PRIN	BALANCE
1	8.0529	1.2886	98.7114
2	7.9445	1.3969	97.3145
3	7.8271	1.5144	95.8002
4	7.6998	1.6417	94.1585
5	7.5617	1.7797	92.3788
6	7.4121	1.9293	90.4495
7	7.2499	2.0915	88.3579
8	7.0740	2.2674	86.0905
9	6.8834	2.4580	83.6325
10	6.6767	2.6647	80.9678
11	6.4527	2.8887	78.0791
12	6.2098	3.1316	74.9475
13	5.9466	3.3949	71.5527
14	5.6611	3.6803	67.8724
15	5.3517	3.9897	63.8826
16	5.0163	4.3252	59.5575
17	4.6526	4.6888	54.8687
18	4.2584	5.0830	49.7856
19	3.8310	5.5104	44.2753
20	3.3678	5.9737	38.3016
21	2.8655	6.4759	31.8257
22	2.3210	7.0204	24.8053
23	1.7308	7.6106	17.1947
24	1.0909	8.2505	8.9442
25	.3973	8.9442	0.0000

YEARS 26   MO PAYT .7693   AN CONST 9.24

#	INT	PRIN	BALANCE
1	8.0570	1.1747	98.8253
2	7.9583	1.2734	97.5519
3	7.8512	1.3805	96.1714
4	7.7351	1.4966	94.6748
5	7.6093	1.6224	93.0524
6	7.4729	1.7588	91.2936
7	7.3250	1.9067	89.3870
8	7.1647	2.0670	87.3200
9	6.9909	2.2408	85.0793
10	6.8026	2.4291	82.6501
11	6.5983	2.6334	80.0167
12	6.3769	2.8548	77.1620
13	6.1369	3.0948	74.0672
14	5.8767	3.3550	70.7122
15	5.5946	3.6371	67.0751
16	5.2888	3.9429	63.1322
17	4.9573	4.2744	58.8579
18	4.5980	4.6337	54.2241
19	4.2084	5.0233	49.2008
20	3.7860	5.4457	43.7552
21	3.3282	5.9035	37.8517
22	2.8319	6.3998	31.4518
23	2.2938	6.9379	24.5139
24	1.7105	7.5212	16.9927
25	1.0781	8.1536	8.8391
26	.3926	8.8391	0.0000

YEARS 27   MO PAYT .7611   AN CONST 9.14

#	INT	PRIN	BALANCE
1	8.0608	1.0720	98.9280
2	7.9707	1.1621	97.7660
3	7.8730	1.2598	96.5062
4	7.7670	1.3657	95.1405
5	7.6522	1.4805	93.6600
6	7.5277	1.6050	92.0550
7	7.3928	1.7399	90.3150
8	7.2465	1.8862	88.4288
9	7.0879	2.0448	86.3840
10	6.9160	2.2167	84.1673
11	6.7296	2.4031	81.7641
12	6.5276	2.6051	79.1590
13	6.3086	2.8242	76.3348
14	6.0711	3.0616	73.2732
15	5.8137	3.3190	69.9542
16	5.5347	3.5981	66.3561
17	5.2321	3.9006	62.4555
18	4.9042	4.2285	58.2269
19	4.5487	4.5841	53.6429
20	4.1633	4.9695	48.6734
21	3.7455	5.3873	43.2861
22	3.2925	5.8402	37.4459
23	2.8015	6.3312	31.1147
24	2.2692	6.8635	24.2511
25	1.6921	7.4406	16.8105
26	1.0666	8.0662	8.7443
27	.3884	8.7443	0.0000

YEARS 28   MO PAYT .7536   AN CONST 9.05

#	INT	PRIN	BALANCE
1	8.0642	.9791	99.0209
2	7.9819	1.0615	97.9594
3	7.8926	1.1507	96.8087
4	7.7959	1.2474	95.5613
5	7.6910	1.3523	94.2089
6	7.5773	1.4660	92.7429
7	7.4540	1.5893	91.1536
8	7.3204	1.7229	89.4307
9	7.1756	1.8678	87.5630
10	7.0185	2.0248	85.5382
11	6.8483	2.1950	83.3431
12	6.6637	2.3796	80.9636
13	6.4637	2.5796	78.3839
14	6.2468	2.7965	75.5874
15	6.0117	3.0316	72.5557
16	5.7568	3.2865	69.2692
17	5.4805	3.5629	65.7064
18	5.1809	3.8624	61.8440
19	4.8562	4.1871	57.6568
20	4.5041	4.5392	53.1176
21	4.1225	4.9208	48.1968
22	3.7088	5.3345	42.8623
23	3.2603	5.7830	37.0793
24	2.7741	6.2692	30.8100
25	2.2470	6.7963	24.0137
26	1.6756	7.3677	16.6459
27	1.0561	7.9872	8.6587
28	.3846	8.6587	0.0000

YEARS 29   MO PAYT .7469   AN CONST 8.97

#	INT	PRIN	BALANCE
1	8.0673	.8951	99.1049
2	7.9920	.9704	98.1345
3	7.9104	1.0520	97.0826
4	7.8220	1.1404	95.9422
5	7.7261	1.2363	94.7059
6	7.6221	1.3402	93.3656
7	7.5095	1.4529	91.9127
8	7.3873	1.5751	90.3377
9	7.2549	1.7075	88.6302
10	7.1113	1.8510	86.7792
11	6.9557	2.0067	84.7725
12	6.7870	2.1754	82.5971
13	6.6041	2.3583	80.2388
14	6.4058	2.5566	77.6823
15	6.1909	2.7715	74.9108
16	5.9579	3.0045	71.9063
17	5.7053	3.2571	68.6492
18	5.4314	3.5310	65.1182
19	5.1345	3.8278	61.2904
20	4.8127	4.1497	57.1407
21	4.4638	4.4985	52.6422
22	4.0856	4.8768	47.7654
23	3.6756	5.2868	42.4786
24	3.2311	5.7313	36.7474
25	2.7492	6.2131	30.5342
26	2.2269	6.7355	23.7987
27	1.6606	7.3018	16.4969
28	1.0467	7.9157	8.5812
29	.3811	8.5812	0.0000

YEARS 30   MO PAYT .7407   AN CONST 8.89

#	INT	PRIN	BALANCE
1	8.0700	.8189	99.1811
2	8.0012	.8878	98.2933
3	7.9265	.9624	97.3309
4	7.8456	1.0433	96.2875
5	7.7579	1.1311	95.1565
6	7.6628	1.2262	93.9303
7	7.5597	1.3292	92.6010
8	7.4480	1.4410	91.1600
9	7.3268	1.5622	89.5979
10	7.1955	1.6935	87.9044
11	7.0531	1.8359	86.0685
12	6.8987	1.9902	84.0783
13	6.7314	2.1576	81.9207
14	6.5500	2.3390	79.5817
15	6.3534	2.5356	77.0461
16	6.1402	2.7488	74.2973
17	5.9091	2.9799	71.3174
18	5.6585	3.2304	68.0870
19	5.3869	3.5020	64.5849
20	5.0925	3.7965	60.7885
21	4.7733	4.1157	56.6728
22	4.4273	4.4617	52.2111
23	4.0521	4.8368	47.3743
24	3.6455	5.2435	42.1308
25	3.2046	5.6843	36.4464
26	2.7267	6.1623	30.2842
27	2.2086	6.6803	23.6038
28	1.6470	7.2420	16.3618
29	1.0381	7.8509	8.5109
30	.3780	8.5109	0.0000

YEARS 2 — MO PAYT 4.5284 — AN CONST 54.35

#	INT	PRIN	BALANCE
1	6.3645	47.9767	52.0233
2	2.3179	52.0233	0.0000

YEARS 3 — MO PAYT 3.1394 — AN CONST 37.68

#	INT	PRIN	BALANCE
1	6.9994	30.6734	69.3266
2	4.4123	33.2606	36.0660
3	1.6069	36.0660	0.0000

YEARS 4 — MO PAYT 2.4472 — AN CONST 29.37

#	INT	PRIN	BALANCE
1	7.3159	22.0501	77.9499
2	5.4561	23.9099	54.0400
3	3.4394	25.9266	28.1134
4	1.2526	28.1134	0.0000

YEARS 5 — MO PAYT 2.0336 — AN CONST 24.41

#	INT	PRIN	BALANCE
1	7.5049	16.8986	83.1014
2	6.0796	18.3239	64.7774
3	4.5341	19.8695	44.9080
4	2.8582	21.5454	23.3626
5	1.0409	23.3626	0.0000

YEARS 6 — MO PAYT 1.7594 — AN CONST 21.12

#	INT	PRIN	BALANCE
1	7.6302	13.4830	86.5170
2	6.4930	14.6202	71.8968
3	5.2599	15.8533	56.0435
4	3.9227	17.1905	38.8530
5	2.4728	18.6404	20.2126
6	.9006	20.2126	0.0000

YEARS 7 — MO PAYT 1.5649 — AN CONST 18.78

#	INT	PRIN	BALANCE
1	7.7192	11.0591	88.9409
2	6.7864	11.9919	76.9490
3	5.7749	13.0033	63.9457
4	4.6782	14.1001	49.8456
5	3.4889	15.2894	34.5562
6	2.1993	16.5789	17.9773
7	.8010	17.9773	0.0000

YEARS 8 — MO PAYT 1.4200 — AN CONST 17.05

#	INT	PRIN	BALANCE
1	7.7854	9.2550	90.7450
2	7.0048	10.0356	80.7095
3	6.1583	10.8820	69.8274
4	5.2405	11.7999	58.0276
5	4.2452	12.7951	45.2324
6	3.1660	13.8743	31.3581
7	1.9958	15.0446	16.3135
8	.7268	16.3135	0.0000

YEARS 9 — MO PAYT 1.3084 — AN CONST 15.71

#	INT	PRIN	BALANCE
1	7.8364	7.8639	92.1361
2	7.1732	8.5272	83.6089
3	6.4539	9.2464	74.3626
4	5.6740	10.0263	64.3363
5	4.8284	10.8719	53.4643
6	3.9114	11.7889	41.6754
7	2.9170	12.7833	28.8921
8	1.8388	13.8615	15.0306
9	.6697	15.0306	0.0000

YEARS 10 — MO PAYT 1.2199 — AN CONST 14.64

#	INT	PRIN	BALANCE
1	7.8769	6.7618	93.2382
2	7.3065	7.3321	85.9060
3	6.6881	7.9506	77.9555
4	6.0175	8.6212	69.3343
5	5.2904	9.3483	59.9860
6	4.5019	10.1368	49.8492
7	3.6469	10.9918	38.8574
8	2.7198	11.9189	26.9385
9	1.7145	12.9242	14.0143
10	.6244	14.0143	0.0000

YEARS 11 — MO PAYT 1.1483 — AN CONST 13.78

#	INT	PRIN	BALANCE
1	7.9096	5.8698	94.1302
2	7.4145	6.3649	87.7653
3	6.8777	6.9018	80.8635
4	6.2955	7.4839	73.3796
5	5.6643	8.1151	65.2645
6	4.9798	8.7996	56.4649
7	4.2376	9.5418	46.9231
8	3.4328	10.3466	36.5765
9	2.5601	11.2193	25.3572
10	1.6139	12.1656	13.1917
11	.5878	13.1917	0.0000

YEARS 12 — MO PAYT 1.0893 — AN CONST 13.08

#	INT	PRIN	BALANCE
1	7.9366	5.1353	94.8647
2	7.5034	5.5684	89.2964
3	7.0338	6.0381	83.2583
4	6.5245	6.5473	76.7110
5	5.9722	7.0996	69.6114
6	5.3734	7.6984	61.9130
7	4.7241	8.3477	53.5653
8	4.0200	9.0518	44.5135
9	3.2565	9.8153	34.6982
10	2.4287	10.6431	24.0551
11	1.5310	11.5408	12.5142
12	.5576	12.5142	0.0000

YEARS 13 — MO PAYT 1.0401 — AN CONST 12.49

#	INT	PRIN	BALANCE
1	7.9591	4.5217	95.4783
2	7.5777	4.9031	90.5753
3	7.1641	5.3166	85.2587
4	6.7157	5.7650	79.4936
5	6.2295	6.2513	73.2423
6	5.7022	6.7786	66.4638
7	5.1305	7.3503	59.1135
8	4.5105	7.9703	51.1432
9	3.8383	8.6425	42.5007
10	3.1093	9.3715	33.1293
11	2.3189	10.1619	22.9674
12	1.4618	11.0190	11.9484
13	.5324	11.9484	0.0000

YEARS 14 — MO PAYT .9984 — AN CONST 11.99

#	INT	PRIN	BALANCE
1	7.9781	4.0030	95.9970
2	7.6405	4.3407	91.6563
3	7.2744	4.7068	86.9495
4	6.8774	5.1038	81.8457
5	6.4469	5.5343	76.3115
6	5.9801	6.0010	70.3104
7	5.4739	6.5072	63.8032
8	4.9251	7.0561	56.7472
9	4.3299	7.6512	49.0960
10	3.6846	8.2965	40.7994
11	2.9848	8.9963	31.8031
12	2.2260	9.7551	22.0480
13	1.4032	10.5779	11.4701
14	.5110	11.4701	0.0000

YEARS 15 — MO PAYT .9629 — AN CONST 11.56

#	INT	PRIN	BALANCE
1	7.9944	3.5602	96.4398
2	7.6941	3.8605	92.5793
3	7.3685	4.1861	88.3931
4	7.0154	4.5392	83.8539
5	6.6325	4.9221	78.9318
6	6.2174	5.3372	73.5946
7	5.7672	5.7874	67.8072
8	5.2791	6.2755	61.5317
9	4.7497	6.8048	54.7268
10	4.1758	7.3788	47.3480
11	3.5534	8.0012	39.3469
12	2.8786	8.6760	30.6708
13	2.1468	9.4078	21.2630
14	1.3533	10.2013	11.0617
15	.4929	11.0617	0.0000

YEARS 16 — MO PAYT .9323 — AN CONST 11.19

#	INT	PRIN	BALANCE
1	8.0083	3.1789	96.8211
2	7.7402	3.4471	93.3740
3	7.4495	3.7378	89.6362
4	7.1342	4.0531	85.5832
5	6.7924	4.3949	81.1882
6	6.4217	4.7656	76.4226
7	6.0197	5.1676	71.2551
8	5.5839	5.6034	65.6517
9	5.1112	6.0760	59.5756
10	4.5988	6.5885	52.9871
11	4.0430	7.1442	45.8429
12	3.4405	7.7468	38.0961
13	2.7871	8.4002	29.6958
14	2.0785	9.1087	20.5871
15	1.3103	9.8770	10.7101
16	.4772	10.7101	0.0000

YEARS 17 — MO PAYT .9057 — AN CONST 10.87

#	INT	PRIN	BALANCE
1	8.0205	2.8482	97.1518
2	7.7803	3.0884	94.0635
3	7.5198	3.3489	90.7146
4	7.2373	3.6313	87.0832
5	6.9310	3.9376	83.1456
6	6.5989	4.2697	78.8759
7	6.2388	4.6299	74.2460
8	5.8483	5.0204	69.2256
9	5.4248	5.4438	63.7818
10	4.9657	5.9030	57.8788
11	4.4678	6.4009	51.4779
12	3.9279	6.9408	44.5372
13	3.3425	7.5262	37.0110
14	2.7077	8.1610	28.8501
15	2.0193	8.8493	20.0007
16	1.2729	9.5957	10.4050
17	.4636	10.4050	0.0000

YEARS 18 — MO PAYT .8825 — AN CONST 10.60

#	INT	PRIN	BALANCE
1	8.0311	2.5594	97.4406
2	7.8152	2.7753	94.6653
3	7.5811	3.0093	91.6560
4	7.3273	3.2632	88.3928
5	7.0521	3.5384	84.8544
6	6.7536	3.8368	81.0176
7	6.4300	4.1605	76.8571
8	6.0791	4.5114	72.3458
9	5.6986	4.8919	67.4539
10	5.2860	5.3045	62.1494
11	4.8386	5.7519	56.3975
12	4.3534	6.2370	50.1604
13	3.8274	6.7631	43.3973
14	3.2569	7.3335	36.0638
15	2.6384	7.9521	28.1117
16	1.9677	8.6228	19.4889
17	1.2404	9.3501	10.1387
18	.4517	10.1387	0.0000

YEARS 19 — MO PAYT .8622 — AN CONST 10.35

#	INT	PRIN	BALANCE
1	8.0404	2.3059	97.6941
2	7.8459	2.5004	95.1937
3	7.6350	2.7113	92.4825
4	7.4063	2.9400	89.5425
5	7.1583	3.1879	86.3546
6	6.8895	3.4568	82.8978
7	6.5979	3.7484	79.1494
8	6.2817	4.0645	75.0849
9	5.9389	4.4073	70.6776
10	5.5672	4.7791	65.8985
11	5.1641	5.1822	60.7163
12	4.7270	5.6193	55.0970
13	4.2530	6.0932	49.0038
14	3.7391	6.6072	42.3966
15	3.1818	7.1644	35.2322
16	2.5775	7.7687	27.4634
17	1.9223	8.4240	19.0395
18	1.2118	9.1345	9.9050
19	.4413	9.9050	0.0000

YEARS 20 — MO PAYT .8442 — AN CONST 10.14

#	INT	PRIN	BALANCE
1	8.0486	2.0822	97.9178
2	7.8730	2.2579	95.6599
3	7.6825	2.4483	93.2116
4	7.4760	2.6548	90.5568
5	7.2521	2.8787	87.6780
6	7.0093	3.1215	84.5565
7	6.7460	3.3848	81.1717
8	6.4605	3.6703	77.5013
9	6.1509	3.9799	73.5215
10	5.8153	4.3156	69.2059
11	5.4513	4.6796	64.5263
12	5.0566	5.0743	59.4520
13	4.6286	5.5023	53.9498
14	4.1645	5.9664	47.9834
15	3.6612	6.4696	41.5138
16	3.1156	7.0153	34.4986
17	2.5239	7.6070	26.8916
18	1.8823	8.2486	18.6430
19	1.1865	8.9443	9.6987
20	.4321	9.6987	0.0000

YEARS 21 — MO PAYT .8283 — AN CONST 9.94

#	INT	PRIN	BALANCE
1	8.0559	1.8841	98.1159
2	7.8969	2.0430	96.0729
3	7.7246	2.2153	93.8576

#	INT	PRIN	BALANCE
4	7.5378	2.4022	91.4554
5	7.3352	2.6048	88.8506
6	7.1155	2.8245	86.0261
7	6.8772	3.0627	82.9634
8	6.6189	3.3211	79.6423
9	6.3388	3.6012	76.0411
10	6.0351	3.9049	72.1362
11	5.7057	4.2343	67.9020
12	5.3486	4.5914	63.3106
13	4.9613	4.9787	58.3319
14	4.5414	5.3986	52.9333
15	4.0860	5.8539	47.0794
16	3.5923	6.3477	40.7317
17	3.0569	6.8831	33.8486
18	2.4763	7.4636	26.3849
19	1.8468	8.0932	18.2918
20	1.1642	8.7758	9.5160
21	.4240	9.5160	0.0000

YEARS 22	MO PAYT .8142	AN CONST 9.78	
#	INT	PRIN	BALANCE
1	8.0623	1.7079	98.2921
2	7.9183	1.8519	96.4402
3	7.7621	2.0081	94.4321
4	7.5927	2.1775	92.2546
5	7.4090	2.3612	89.8934
6	7.2099	2.5603	87.3331
7	6.9939	2.7763	84.5569
8	6.7598	3.0104	81.5465
9	6.5059	3.2643	78.2821
10	6.2305	3.5397	74.7425
11	5.9320	3.8382	70.9042
12	5.6082	4.1620	66.7423
13	5.2572	4.5130	62.2293
14	4.8766	4.8936	57.3357
15	4.4638	5.3064	52.0293
16	4.0162	5.7540	46.2753
17	3.5309	6.2393	40.0360
18	3.0047	6.7655	33.2705
19	2.4340	7.3362	25.9343
20	1.8153	7.9549	17.9794
21	1.1443	8.6259	9.3535
22	.4167	9.3535	0.0000

YEARS 23	MO PAYT .8016	AN CONST 9.62	
#	INT	PRIN	BALANCE
1	8.0681	1.5506	98.4494
2	7.9373	1.6814	96.7680
3	7.7955	1.8232	94.9448
4	7.6417	1.9770	92.9678
5	7.4750	2.1437	90.8241
6	7.2942	2.3245	88.4996
7	7.0981	2.5206	85.9789
8	6.8855	2.7332	83.2457
9	6.6550	2.9637	80.2820
10	6.4050	3.2137	77.0683
11	6.1339	3.4848	73.5835
12	5.8400	3.7787	69.8048
13	5.5213	4.0974	65.7074
14	5.1757	4.4430	61.2644
15	4.8009	4.8178	56.4466
16	4.3946	5.2241	51.2225
17	3.9540	5.6647	45.5578
18	3.4762	6.1425	39.4152
19	2.9581	6.6606	32.7546
20	2.3963	7.2224	25.5322
21	1.7871	7.8316	17.7006
22	1.1266	8.4922	9.2084
23	.4103	9.2084	0.0000

YEARS 24	MO PAYT .7903	AN CONST 9.49	
#	INT	PRIN	BALANCE
1	8.0733	1.4098	98.5902
2	7.9544	1.5287	97.0614
3	7.8254	1.6577	95.4037
4	7.6856	1.7975	93.6062
5	7.5340	1.9491	91.6571
6	7.3696	2.1135	89.5436
7	7.1913	2.2918	87.2519
8	6.9980	2.4851	84.7668
9	6.7884	2.6947	82.0721
10	6.5611	2.9220	79.1502
11	6.3147	3.1684	75.9818
12	6.0474	3.4356	72.5461
13	5.7577	3.7254	68.8207
14	5.4434	4.0397	64.7810
15	5.1027	4.3804	60.4006
16	4.7333	4.7498	55.6508
17	4.3326	5.1505	50.5003
18	3.8982	5.5849	44.9155
19	3.4272	6.0559	38.8595
20	2.9164	6.5667	32.2928
21	2.3625	7.1206	25.1722
22	1.7619	7.7212	17.4510
23	1.1107	8.3724	9.0786
24	.4045	9.0786	0.0000

YEARS 25	MO PAYT .7801	AN CONST 9.37	
#	INT	PRIN	BALANCE
1	8.0779	1.2835	98.7165
2	7.9696	1.3917	97.3248
3	7.8523	1.5091	95.8157
4	7.7250	1.6364	94.1793
5	7.5870	1.7744	92.4048
6	7.4373	1.9241	90.4807
7	7.2750	2.0864	88.3944
8	7.0990	2.2624	86.1320
9	6.9082	2.4532	83.6788
10	6.7013	2.6601	81.0187
11	6.4769	2.8845	78.1343
12	6.2336	3.1277	75.0065
13	5.9698	3.3916	71.6150
14	5.6838	3.6776	67.9374
15	5.3736	3.9878	63.9496
16	5.0372	4.3242	59.6254
17	4.6725	4.6889	54.9365
18	4.2770	5.0844	49.8522
19	3.8482	5.5132	44.3390
20	3.3832	5.9782	38.3608
21	2.8789	6.4824	31.8783
22	2.3322	7.0292	24.8491
23	1.7393	7.6221	17.2270
24	1.0964	8.2650	8.9621
25	.3993	8.9621	0.0000

YEARS 26	MO PAYT .7710	AN CONST 9.26	
#	INT	PRIN	BALANCE
1	8.0821	1.1698	98.8302
2	7.9834	1.2685	97.5617
3	7.8764	1.3755	96.1863
4	7.7604	1.4915	94.6948
5	7.6346	1.6173	93.0776
6	7.4982	1.7537	91.3239
7	7.3503	1.9016	89.4223
8	7.1899	2.0620	87.3603
9	7.0160	2.2359	85.1244
10	6.8274	2.4245	82.7000
11	6.6229	2.6290	80.0710
12	6.4012	2.8507	77.2203
13	6.1607	3.0912	74.1291
14	5.9000	3.3519	70.7772
15	5.6173	3.6346	67.1426
16	5.3107	3.9412	63.2015
17	4.9783	4.2736	58.9279
18	4.6178	4.6340	54.2939
19	4.2270	5.0249	49.2690
20	3.8032	5.4487	43.8203
21	3.3436	5.9083	37.9120
22	2.8453	6.4066	31.5054
23	2.3049	6.9470	24.5584
24	1.7190	7.5329	17.0255
25	1.0836	8.1683	8.8572
26	.3946	8.8572	0.0000

YEARS 27	MO PAYT .7628	AN CONST 9.16	
#	INT	PRIN	BALANCE
1	8.0858	1.0673	98.9327
2	7.9958	1.1573	97.7754
3	7.8982	1.2549	96.5205
4	7.7924	1.3608	95.1597
5	7.6776	1.4755	93.6841
6	7.5531	1.6000	92.0841
7	7.4182	1.7350	90.3492
8	7.2718	1.8813	88.4679
9	7.1132	2.0400	86.4279
10	6.9411	2.2120	84.2159
11	6.7545	2.3986	81.8173
12	6.5522	2.6009	79.2164
13	6.3328	2.8203	76.3961
14	6.0950	3.0582	73.3379
15	5.8370	3.3161	70.0218
16	5.5573	3.5958	66.4260
17	5.2540	3.8991	62.5269
18	4.9252	4.2280	58.2990
19	4.5686	4.5846	53.7144
20	4.1819	4.9713	48.7432
21	3.7626	5.3906	43.3526
22	3.3079	5.8452	37.5074
23	2.8149	6.3382	31.1692
24	2.2803	6.8728	24.2963
25	1.7006	7.4525	16.8438
26	1.0720	8.0811	8.7627
27	.3904	8.7627	0.0000

YEARS 28	MO PAYT .7553	AN CONST 9.07	
#	INT	PRIN	BALANCE
1	8.0892	.9747	99.0253
2	8.0070	1.0569	97.9684
3	7.9179	1.1460	96.8224
4	7.8212	1.2427	95.5797
5	7.7164	1.3475	94.2322
6	7.6027	1.4612	92.7710
7	7.4795	1.5844	91.1866
8	7.3459	1.7180	89.4686
9	7.2010	1.8630	87.6056
10	7.0438	2.0201	85.5855
11	6.8734	2.1905	83.3951
12	6.6887	2.3752	81.0198
13	6.4884	2.5756	78.4443
14	6.2711	2.7928	75.6515
15	6.0356	3.0284	72.6231
16	5.7801	3.2838	69.3393
17	5.5032	3.5608	65.7786
18	5.2028	3.8611	61.9175
19	4.8772	4.1867	57.7308
20	4.5240	4.5399	53.1909
21	4.1411	4.9228	48.2681
22	3.7259	5.3380	42.9301
23	3.2757	5.7882	37.1418
24	2.7875	6.2765	30.8654
25	2.2581	6.8058	24.0595
26	1.6840	7.3799	16.6796
27	1.0616	8.0023	8.6773
28	.3866	8.6773	0.0000

YEARS 29	MO PAYT .7486	AN CONST 8.99	
#	INT	PRIN	BALANCE
1	8.0923	.8909	99.1091
2	8.0172	.9660	98.1431
3	7.9357	1.0475	97.0957
4	7.8473	1.1358	95.9598
5	7.7515	1.2316	94.7282
6	7.6477	1.3355	93.3927
7	7.5350	1.4481	91.9446
8	7.4129	1.5703	90.3743
9	7.2804	1.7027	88.6715
10	7.1368	1.8464	86.8252
11	6.9811	2.0021	84.8231
12	6.8122	2.1710	82.6521
13	6.6291	2.3541	80.2981
14	6.4305	2.5526	77.7455
15	6.2152	2.7679	74.9775
16	5.9818	3.0014	71.9762
17	5.7286	3.2545	68.7216
18	5.4541	3.5290	65.1926
19	5.1565	3.8267	61.3659
20	4.8337	4.1495	57.2165
21	4.4837	4.4994	52.7170
22	4.1042	4.8789	47.8381
23	3.6927	5.2905	42.5476
24	3.2465	5.7367	36.8109
25	2.7626	6.2205	30.5904
26	2.2380	6.7452	23.8452
27	1.6690	7.3141	16.5310
28	1.0521	7.9311	8.6000
29	.3832	8.6000	0.0000

YEARS 30	MO PAYT .7425	AN CONST 8.91	
#	INT	PRIN	BALANCE
1	8.0951	.8149	99.1851
2	8.0264	.8836	98.3015
3	7.9518	.9581	97.3434
4	7.8710	1.0389	96.3045
5	7.7834	1.1266	95.1779
6	7.6884	1.2216	93.9563
7	7.5853	1.3246	92.6317
8	7.4736	1.4363	91.1953
9	7.3525	1.5575	89.6378
10	7.2211	1.6889	87.9490
11	7.0787	1.8313	86.1177
12	6.9242	1.9858	84.1319
13	6.7567	2.1533	81.9786
14	6.5751	2.3349	79.6438
15	6.3781	2.5318	77.1119
16	6.1646	2.7454	74.3666
17	5.9330	2.9769	71.3897
18	5.6820	3.2280	68.1616
19	5.4097	3.5003	64.6614
20	5.1145	3.7955	60.8659
21	4.7943	4.1156	56.7502
22	4.4472	4.4628	52.2874
23	4.0708	4.8392	47.4483
24	3.6626	5.2473	42.2009
25	3.2200	5.6899	36.5110
26	2.7401	6.1699	30.3411
27	2.2197	6.6902	23.6509
28	1.6554	7.2545	16.3963
29	1.0435	7.8664	8.5299
30	.3800	8.5299	0.0000

MONTHLY PAYMENT AMORTIZATION SCHEDULE PER $100   8.20 %

YEARS 2 — MO PAYT 4.5319 — AN CONST 54.39

#	INT	PRIN	BALANCE
1	6.4242	47.9581	52.0419
2	2.3404	52.0419	0.0000

YEARS 3 — MO PAYT 3.1429 — AN CONST 37.72

#	INT	PRIN	BALANCE
1	7.0651	30.6494	69.3506
2	4.4552	33.2593	36.0914
3	1.6231	36.0914	0.0000

YEARS 4 — MO PAYT 2.4507 — AN CONST 29.41

#	INT	PRIN	BALANCE
1	7.3845	22.0238	77.9762
2	5.5091	23.8992	54.0770
3	3.4740	25.9343	28.1427
4	1.2656	28.1427	0.0000

YEARS 5 — MO PAYT 2.0372 — AN CONST 24.45

#	INT	PRIN	BALANCE
1	7.5753	16.8714	83.1286
2	6.1386	18.3081	64.8205
3	4.5796	19.8671	44.9534
4	2.8879	21.5588	23.3946
5	1.0521	23.3946	0.0000

YEARS 6 — MO PAYT 1.7631 — AN CONST 21.16

#	INT	PRIN	BALANCE
1	7.7018	13.4555	86.5445
2	6.5560	14.6013	71.9432
3	5.3126	15.8446	56.0986
4	3.9634	17.1939	38.9047
5	2.4993	18.6580	20.2467
6	.9105	20.2467	0.0000

YEARS 7 — MO PAYT 1.5686 — AN CONST 18.83

#	INT	PRIN	BALANCE
1	7.7915	11.0317	88.9683
2	6.8521	11.9711	76.9971
3	5.8327	12.9905	64.0066
4	4.7266	14.0967	49.9099
5	3.5262	15.2971	34.6128
6	2.2236	16.5997	18.0132
7	.8101	18.0132	0.0000

YEARS 8 — MO PAYT 1.4239 — AN CONST 17.09

#	INT	PRIN	BALANCE
1	7.8583	9.2280	90.7720
2	7.0725	10.0137	80.7583
3	6.2198	10.8664	69.8919
4	5.2945	11.7918	58.1001
5	4.2904	12.7959	45.3043
6	3.2008	13.8855	31.4188
7	2.0184	15.0679	16.3509
8	.7353	16.3509	0.0000

YEARS 9 — MO PAYT 1.3123 — AN CONST 15.75

#	INT	PRIN	BALANCE
1	7.9098	7.8374	92.1626
2	7.2424	8.5047	83.6579
3	6.5182	9.2289	74.4290
4	5.7323	10.0148	64.4142
5	4.8795	10.8676	53.5466
6	3.9541	11.7930	41.7536
7	2.9499	12.7972	28.9564
8	1.8602	13.8869	15.0695
9	.6777	15.0695	0.0000

YEARS 10 — MO PAYT 1.2239 — AN CONST 14.69

#	INT	PRIN	BALANCE
1	7.9506	6.7359	93.2641
2	7.3770	7.3094	85.9547
3	6.7546	7.9319	78.0228
4	6.0792	8.6073	69.4156
5	5.3462	9.3402	60.0753
6	4.5509	10.1356	49.9398
7	3.6878	10.9986	38.9411
8	2.7512	11.9352	27.0059
9	1.7349	12.9515	14.0544
10	.6320	14.0544	0.0000

YEARS 11 — MO PAYT 1.1523 — AN CONST 13.83

#	INT	PRIN	BALANCE
1	7.9836	5.8445	94.1555
2	7.4859	6.3422	87.8133
3	6.9459	6.8822	80.9311
4	6.3598	7.4683	73.4628
5	5.7239	8.1042	65.3586
6	5.0338	8.7943	56.5642
7	4.2849	9.5432	47.0210
8	3.4723	10.3558	36.6652
9	2.5904	11.2377	25.4276
10	1.6335	12.1946	13.2330
11	.5951	13.2330	0.0000

YEARS 12 — MO PAYT 1.0934 — AN CONST 13.13

#	INT	PRIN	BALANCE
1	8.0108	5.1106	94.8894
2	7.5756	5.5458	89.3436
3	7.1033	6.0181	83.3255
4	6.5909	6.5305	76.7950
5	6.0348	7.0866	69.7084
6	5.4313	7.6901	62.0183
7	4.7765	8.3449	53.6735
8	4.0659	9.0555	44.6180
9	3.2948	9.8266	34.7914
10	2.4580	10.6633	24.1281
11	1.5500	11.5714	12.5567
12	.5647	12.5567	0.0000

YEARS 13 — MO PAYT 1.0443 — AN CONST 12.54

#	INT	PRIN	BALANCE
1	8.0335	4.4978	95.5022
2	7.6505	4.8808	90.6215
3	7.2348	5.2964	85.3251
4	6.7838	5.7474	79.5777
5	6.2944	6.2368	73.3409
6	5.7634	6.7679	66.5731
7	5.1870	7.3442	59.2289
8	4.5617	7.9696	51.2593
9	3.8830	8.6482	42.6112
10	3.1466	9.3846	33.2266
11	2.3475	10.1837	23.0428
12	1.4803	11.0509	11.9919
13	.5393	11.9919	0.0000

YEARS 14 — MO PAYT 1.0027 — AN CONST 12.04

#	INT	PRIN	BALANCE
1	8.0526	3.9799	96.0201
2	7.7137	4.3188	91.7014
3	7.3460	4.6865	87.0149
4	6.9469	5.0856	81.9293
5	6.5139	5.5186	76.4106
6	6.0439	5.9886	70.4221
7	5.5340	6.4985	63.9236
8	4.9806	7.0519	56.8717
9	4.3801	7.6524	49.2193
10	3.7285	8.3040	40.9153
11	3.0214	9.0111	31.9042
12	2.2541	9.7784	22.1258
13	1.4214	10.6111	11.5147
14	.5178	11.5147	0.0000

YEARS 15 — MO PAYT .9672 — AN CONST 11.61

#	INT	PRIN	BALANCE
1	8.0690	3.5378	96.4622
2	7.7677	3.8391	92.6231
3	7.4408	4.1660	88.4572
4	7.0861	4.5207	83.9364
5	6.7011	4.9057	79.0308
6	6.2834	5.3234	73.7074
7	5.8301	5.7767	67.9307
8	5.3382	6.2686	61.6621
9	4.8044	6.8024	54.8597
10	4.2252	7.3816	47.4780
11	3.5966	8.0102	39.4678
12	2.9145	8.6923	30.7755
13	2.1743	9.4325	21.3430
14	1.3711	10.2357	11.1073
15	.4995	11.1073	0.0000

YEARS 16 — MO PAYT .9367 — AN CONST 11.25

#	INT	PRIN	BALANCE
1	8.0831	3.1573	96.8427
2	7.8142	3.4261	93.4166
3	7.5225	3.7179	89.6988
4	7.2059	4.0344	85.6643
5	6.8624	4.3780	81.2864
6	6.4896	4.7508	76.5356
7	6.0850	5.1553	71.3802
8	5.6460	5.5943	65.7859
9	5.1697	6.0707	59.7152
10	4.6527	6.5876	53.1276
11	4.0918	7.1486	45.9790
12	3.4830	7.7573	38.2217
13	2.8225	8.4179	29.8038
14	2.1057	9.1347	20.6691
15	1.3278	9.9125	10.7566
16	.4837	10.7566	0.0000

YEARS 17 — MO PAYT .9102 — AN CONST 10.93

#	INT	PRIN	BALANCE
1	8.0953	2.8272	97.1728
2	7.8546	3.0680	94.1048
3	7.5933	3.3292	90.7755
4	7.3098	3.6127	87.1628
5	7.0022	3.9204	83.2424
6	6.6683	4.2542	78.9882
7	6.3061	4.6165	74.3717
8	5.9130	5.0096	69.3622
9	5.4864	5.4362	63.9260
10	5.0235	5.8991	58.0269
11	4.5212	6.4014	51.6256
12	3.9761	6.9465	44.6791
13	3.3846	7.5380	37.1411
14	2.7427	8.1799	28.9612
15	2.0461	8.8764	20.0848
16	1.2903	9.6323	10.4525
17	.4701	10.4525	0.0000

YEARS 18 — MO PAYT .8871 — AN CONST 10.65

#	INT	PRIN	BALANCE
1	8.1060	2.5392	97.4608
2	7.8898	2.7555	94.7053
3	7.6551	2.9901	91.7152
4	7.4005	3.2447	88.4705
5	7.1242	3.5210	84.9495
6	6.8244	3.8208	81.1287
7	6.4990	4.1462	76.9825
8	6.1460	4.4992	72.4833
9	5.7628	4.8824	67.6009
10	5.3471	5.2981	62.3028
11	4.8959	5.7493	56.5535
12	4.4064	6.2388	50.3147
13	3.8751	6.7701	43.5446
14	3.2986	7.3466	36.1980
15	2.6730	7.9722	28.2258
16	1.9942	8.6510	19.5748
17	1.2575	9.3877	10.1871
18	.4581	10.1871	0.0000

YEARS 19 — MO PAYT .8668 — AN CONST 10.41

#	INT	PRIN	BALANCE
1	8.1153	2.2865	97.7135
2	7.9206	2.4812	95.2324
3	7.7094	2.6925	92.5399
4	7.4801	2.9217	89.6182
5	7.2313	3.1705	86.4477
6	6.9613	3.4405	83.0072
7	6.6683	3.7335	79.2737
8	6.3504	4.0514	75.2223
9	6.0054	4.3964	70.8259
10	5.6311	4.7707	66.0552
11	5.2248	5.1770	60.8782
12	4.7840	5.6178	55.2604
13	4.3056	6.0962	49.1642
14	3.7865	6.6153	42.5489
15	3.2232	7.1786	35.3703
16	2.6119	7.7899	27.5804
17	1.9486	8.4532	19.1272
18	1.2288	9.1730	9.9542
19	.4476	9.9542	0.0000

YEARS 20 — MO PAYT .8489 — AN CONST 10.19

#	INT	PRIN	BALANCE
1	8.1236	2.0636	97.9364
2	7.9479	2.2393	95.6971
3	7.7572	2.4300	93.2672
4	7.5503	2.6369	90.6303
5	7.3257	2.8614	87.7688
6	7.0821	3.1051	84.6638
7	6.8177	3.3695	81.2943
8	6.5307	3.6564	77.6378
9	6.2194	3.9678	73.6700
10	5.8815	4.3056	69.3644
11	5.5149	4.6723	64.6921
12	5.1170	5.0701	59.6220
13	4.6853	5.5019	54.1201
14	4.2168	5.9704	48.1497
15	3.7084	6.4788	41.6709
16	3.1567	7.0305	34.6404
17	2.5580	7.6291	27.0113
18	1.9084	8.2788	18.7325
19	1.2034	8.9838	9.7487
20	.4384	9.7487	0.0000

YEARS 21 — MO PAYT .8331 — AN CONST 10.00

#	INT	PRIN	BALANCE
1	8.1309	1.8662	98.1338
2	7.9720	2.0251	96.1088
3	7.7995	2.1975	93.9113

MONTHLY PAYMENT AMORTIZATION SCHEDULE PER $100

8.20 %

#	INT	PRIN	BALANCE
4	7.6124	2.3846	91.5267
5	7.4094	2.5877	88.9390
6	7.1890	2.8080	86.1309
7	6.9499	3.0471	83.0838
8	6.6904	3.3066	79.7772
9	6.4089	3.5882	76.1890
10	6.1033	3.8937	72.2953
11	5.7718	4.2253	68.0700
12	5.4120	4.5851	63.4849
13	5.0215	4.9755	58.5093
14	4.5978	5.3992	53.1101
15	4.1381	5.8590	47.2511
16	3.6392	6.3579	40.8933
17	3.0978	6.8993	33.9940
18	2.5103	7.4868	26.5072
19	1.8728	8.1243	18.3829
20	1.1809	8.8161	9.5668
21	.4302	9.5668	0.0000

YEARS 22	MO PAYT .8190	AN CONST 9.83
# **INT**	**PRIN**	**BALANCE**

#	INT	PRIN	BALANCE
1	8.1374	1.6906	98.3094
2	7.9934	1.8346	96.4748
3	7.8372	1.9908	94.4839
4	7.6677	2.1603	92.3236
5	7.4837	2.3443	89.9793
6	7.2841	2.5439	87.4353
7	7.0675	2.7606	84.6748
8	6.8324	2.9956	81.6791
9	6.5773	3.2507	78.4284
10	6.3005	3.5275	74.9009
11	6.0001	3.8279	71.0730
12	5.6742	4.1539	66.9191
13	5.3205	4.5076	62.4116
14	4.9366	4.8914	57.5201
15	4.5201	5.3079	52.2122
16	4.0681	5.7599	46.4523
17	3.5776	6.2504	40.2019
18	3.0454	6.7826	33.4193
19	2.4678	7.3602	26.0591
20	1.8411	7.9869	18.0721
21	1.1610	8.6671	9.4051
22	.4230	9.4051	0.0000

YEARS 23	MO PAYT .8064	AN CONST 9.68
# **INT**	**PRIN**	**BALANCE**

#	INT	PRIN	BALANCE
1	8.1432	1.5341	98.4659
2	8.0126	1.6647	96.8012
3	7.8708	1.8065	94.9948
4	7.7170	1.9603	93.0345
5	7.5501	2.1272	90.9073
6	7.3689	2.3083	88.5989
7	7.1724	2.5049	86.0940
8	6.9591	2.7182	83.3758
9	6.7276	2.9497	80.4261
10	6.4764	3.2008	77.2253
11	6.2039	3.4734	73.7519
12	5.9081	3.7692	69.9827
13	5.5871	4.0901	65.8925
14	5.2388	4.4384	61.4541
15	4.8609	4.8164	56.6377
16	4.4508	5.2265	51.4112
17	4.0057	5.6716	45.7397
18	3.5228	6.1545	39.5852
19	2.9987	6.6786	32.9066
20	2.4300	7.2473	25.6593
21	1.8129	7.8644	17.7949
22	1.1432	8.5341	9.2608
23	.4165	9.2608	0.0000

YEARS 24	MO PAYT .7952	AN CONST 9.55
# **INT**	**PRIN**	**BALANCE**

#	INT	PRIN	BALANCE
1	8.1484	1.3940	98.6060
2	8.0297	1.5127	97.0933
3	7.9009	1.6415	95.4518
4	7.7611	1.7813	93.6706
5	7.6094	1.9330	91.7376
6	7.4448	2.0976	89.6400
7	7.2662	2.2762	87.3639
8	7.0724	2.4700	84.8939
9	6.8620	2.6803	82.2136
10	6.6338	2.9086	79.3050
11	6.3861	3.1562	76.1488
12	6.1174	3.4250	72.7238
13	5.8257	3.7166	69.0071
14	5.5092	4.0331	64.9740
15	5.1658	4.3766	60.5975
16	4.7931	4.7492	55.8482
17	4.3887	5.1536	50.6946
18	3.9499	5.5925	45.1021
19	3.4737	6.0687	39.0334
20	2.9569	6.5855	32.4479
21	2.3961	7.1463	25.3016
22	1.7876	7.7548	17.5468
23	1.1272	8.4151	9.1317
24	.4107	9.1317	0.0000

YEARS 25	MO PAYT .7851	AN CONST 9.43
# **INT**	**PRIN**	**BALANCE**

#	INT	PRIN	BALANCE
1	8.1530	1.2683	98.7317
2	8.0450	1.3763	97.3554
3	7.9278	1.4935	95.8619
4	7.8007	1.6207	94.2412
5	7.6627	1.7587	92.4825
6	7.5129	1.9084	90.5741
7	7.3504	2.0710	88.5031
8	7.1740	2.2473	86.2558
9	6.9827	2.4387	83.8172
10	6.7750	2.6463	81.1708
11	6.5497	2.8717	78.2992
12	6.3051	3.1162	75.1830
13	6.0398	3.3816	71.8014
14	5.7518	3.6695	68.1319
15	5.4394	3.9820	64.1499
16	5.1003	4.3210	59.8289
17	4.7323	4.6890	55.1399
18	4.3331	5.0883	50.0516
19	3.8998	5.5216	44.5300
20	3.4296	5.9917	38.5383
21	2.9194	6.5020	32.0363
22	2.3657	7.0556	24.9807
23	1.7649	7.6564	17.3243
24	1.1129	8.3084	9.0159
25	.4055	9.0159	0.0000

YEARS 26	MO PAYT .7760	AN CONST 9.32
# **INT**	**PRIN**	**BALANCE**

#	INT	PRIN	BALANCE
1	8.1572	1.1553	98.8447
2	8.0588	1.2537	97.5911
3	7.9521	1.3604	96.2307
4	7.8363	1.4762	94.7544
5	7.7105	1.6020	93.1525
6	7.5741	1.7384	91.4141
7	7.4261	1.8864	89.5277
8	7.2655	2.0470	87.4807
9	7.0912	2.2213	85.2593
10	6.9020	2.4105	82.8488
11	6.6967	2.6158	80.2331
12	6.4740	2.8385	77.3946
13	6.2323	3.0802	74.3144
14	5.9700	3.3425	70.9719
15	5.6854	3.6271	67.3448

#	INT	PRIN	BALANCE
16	5.3765	3.9360	63.4088
17	5.0414	4.2711	59.1377
18	4.6777	4.6348	54.5029
19	4.2830	5.0295	49.4734
20	3.8547	5.4578	44.0156
21	3.3900	5.9225	38.0931
22	2.8857	6.4268	31.6662
23	2.3384	6.9741	24.6921
24	1.7445	7.5680	17.1241
25	1.1001	8.2124	8.9117
26	.4008	8.9117	0.0000

YEARS 27	MO PAYT .7679	AN CONST 9.22
# **INT**	**PRIN**	**BALANCE**

#	INT	PRIN	BALANCE
1	8.1610	1.0534	98.9466
2	8.0713	1.1431	97.8035
3	7.9740	1.2404	96.5630
4	7.8683	1.3461	95.2170
5	7.7537	1.4607	93.7563
6	7.6293	1.5851	92.1712
7	7.4943	1.7201	90.4511
8	7.3479	1.8665	88.5846
9	7.1889	2.0255	86.5591
10	7.0165	2.1979	84.3612
11	6.8293	2.3851	81.9761
12	6.6262	2.5882	79.3879
13	6.4058	2.8086	76.5793
14	6.1666	3.0478	73.5316
15	5.9071	3.3073	70.2243
16	5.6255	3.5889	66.6354
17	5.3199	3.8945	62.7409
18	4.9883	4.2261	58.5147
19	4.6284	4.5860	53.9287
20	4.2379	4.9765	48.9522
21	3.8141	5.4003	43.5519
22	3.3543	5.8601	37.6918
23	2.8553	6.3591	31.3327
24	2.3138	6.9006	24.4320
25	1.7261	7.4883	16.9438
26	1.0885	8.1259	8.8179
27	.3965	8.8179	0.0000

YEARS 28	MO PAYT .7605	AN CONST 9.13
# **INT**	**PRIN**	**BALANCE**

#	INT	PRIN	BALANCE
1	8.1644	.9614	99.0386
2	8.0825	1.0433	97.9953
3	7.9937	1.1321	96.8632
4	7.8973	1.2285	95.6347
5	7.7927	1.3331	94.3015
6	7.6792	1.4467	92.8549
7	7.5560	1.5698	91.2850
8	7.4223	1.7035	89.5815
9	7.2772	1.8486	87.7329
10	7.1198	2.0060	85.7270
11	6.9490	2.1768	83.5501
12	6.7636	2.3622	81.1880
13	6.5625	2.5633	78.6247
14	6.3442	2.7816	75.8431
15	6.1074	3.0184	72.8246
16	5.8503	3.2755	69.5491
17	5.5714	3.5544	65.9948
18	5.2687	3.8571	62.1377
19	4.9403	4.1855	57.9522
20	4.5839	4.5419	53.4103
21	4.1971	4.9287	48.4816
22	3.7774	5.3484	43.1332
23	3.3220	5.8038	37.3294
24	2.8278	6.2980	31.0314
25	2.2915	6.8343	24.1971
26	1.7095	7.4163	16.7809
27	1.0780	8.0478	8.7331

#	INT	PRIN	BALANCE
28	.3927	8.7331	0.0000

YEARS 29	MO PAYT .7538	AN CONST 9.05
# **INT**	**PRIN**	**BALANCE**

#	INT	PRIN	BALANCE
1	8.1675	.8782	99.1218
2	8.0927	.9530	98.1688
3	8.0116	1.0341	97.1347
4	7.9235	1.1222	96.0125
5	7.8279	1.2177	94.7948
6	7.7242	1.3214	93.4734
7	7.6117	1.4339	92.0394
8	7.4896	1.5561	90.4834
9	7.3571	1.6886	88.7948
10	7.2133	1.8323	86.9625
11	7.0573	1.9884	84.9741
12	6.8880	2.1577	82.8164
13	6.7042	2.3414	80.4750
14	6.5049	2.5408	77.9342
15	6.2885	2.7572	75.1770
16	6.0537	2.9919	72.1851
17	5.7990	3.2467	68.9384
18	5.5225	3.5232	65.4152
19	5.2225	3.8232	61.5920
20	4.8969	4.1487	57.4433
21	4.5436	4.5020	52.9412
22	4.1603	4.8854	48.0558
23	3.7443	5.3014	42.7544
24	3.2928	5.7528	37.0016
25	2.8030	6.2427	30.7589
26	2.2714	6.7743	23.9846
27	1.6945	7.3511	16.6335
28	1.0686	7.9771	8.6564
29	.3893	8.6564	0.0000

YEARS 30	MO PAYT .7478	AN CONST 8.98
# **INT**	**PRIN**	**BALANCE**

#	INT	PRIN	BALANCE
1	8.1703	.8028	99.1972
2	8.1019	.8711	98.3261
3	8.0277	.9453	97.3808
4	7.9472	1.0258	96.3549
5	7.8599	1.1132	95.2418
6	7.7651	1.2080	94.0338
7	7.6622	1.3108	92.7230
8	7.5506	1.4224	91.3006
9	7.4295	1.5436	89.7570
10	7.2981	1.6750	88.0820
11	7.1554	1.8176	86.2644
12	7.0006	1.9724	84.2920
13	6.8327	2.1404	82.1516
14	6.6504	2.3226	79.8290
15	6.4526	2.5204	77.3086
16	6.2380	2.7350	74.5735
17	6.0051	2.9679	71.6056
18	5.7524	3.2207	68.3850
19	5.4782	3.4949	64.8901
20	5.1806	3.7925	61.0976
21	4.8576	4.1154	56.9821
22	4.5072	4.4659	52.5162
23	4.1269	4.8462	47.6700
24	3.7142	5.2588	42.4112
25	3.2664	5.7066	36.7046
26	2.7805	6.1926	30.5120
27	2.2532	6.7199	23.7921
28	1.6809	7.2921	16.5000
29	1.0600	7.9131	8.5869
30	.3862	8.5869	0.0000

YEARS 2 — MO PAYT 4.5341 — AN CONST 54.41

#	INT	PRIN	BALANCE
1	6.4640	47.9457	52.0543
2	2.3554	52.0543	0.0000

YEARS 3 — MO PAYT 3.1452 — AN CONST 37.75

#	INT	PRIN	BALANCE
1	7.1089	30.6333	69.3667
2	4.4838	33.2584	36.1083
3	1.6339	36.1083	0.0000

YEARS 4 — MO PAYT 2.4530 — AN CONST 29.44

#	INT	PRIN	BALANCE
1	7.4302	22.0063	77.9937
2	5.5445	23.8921	54.1016
3	3.4971	25.9394	28.1622
4	1.2743	28.1622	0.0000

YEARS 5 — MO PAYT 2.0396 — AN CONST 24.48

#	INT	PRIN	BALANCE
1	7.6222	16.8533	83.1467
2	6.1780	18.2975	64.8492
3	4.6100	19.8655	44.9837
4	2.9077	21.5678	23.4160
5	1.0595	23.4160	0.0000

YEARS 6 — MO PAYT 1.7656 — AN CONST 21.19

#	INT	PRIN	BALANCE
1	7.7494	13.4372	86.5628
2	6.5980	14.5887	71.9741
3	5.3478	15.8388	56.1353
4	3.9906	17.1961	38.9392
5	2.5170	18.6697	20.2695
6	.9172	20.2695	0.0000

YEARS 7 — MO PAYT 1.5711 — AN CONST 18.86

#	INT	PRIN	BALANCE
1	7.8397	11.0135	88.9865
2	6.8960	11.9573	77.0291
3	5.8713	12.9820	64.0472
4	4.7589	14.0944	49.9528
5	3.5511	15.3022	34.6506
6	2.2398	16.6135	18.0371
7	.8162	18.0371	0.0000

YEARS 8 — MO PAYT 1.4264 — AN CONST 17.12

#	INT	PRIN	BALANCE
1	7.9069	9.2100	90.7900
2	7.1177	9.9992	80.7908
3	6.2608	10.8560	69.9348
4	5.3306	11.7863	58.1485
5	4.3206	12.7963	45.3521
6	3.2240	13.8929	31.4593
7	2.0335	15.0834	16.3759
8	.7410	16.3759	0.0000

YEARS 9 — MO PAYT 1.3149 — AN CONST 15.78

#	INT	PRIN	BALANCE
1	7.9587	7.8197	92.1803
2	7.2886	8.4898	83.6905
3	6.5611	9.2173	74.4732
4	5.7713	10.0071	64.4661
5	4.9137	10.8647	53.6014
6	3.9827	11.7957	41.8057
7	2.9719	12.8065	28.9993
8	1.8745	13.9039	15.0954
9	.6830	15.0954	0.0000

YEARS 10 — MO PAYT 1.2265 — AN CONST 14.72

#	INT	PRIN	BALANCE
1	7.9997	6.7186	93.2814
2	7.4240	7.2943	85.9871
3	6.7989	7.9194	78.0677
4	6.1203	8.5980	69.4697
5	5.3835	9.3348	60.1349
6	4.5836	10.1347	50.0002
7	3.7151	11.0032	38.9970
8	2.7722	11.9461	27.0509
9	1.7486	12.9698	14.0812
10	.6372	14.0812	0.0000

YEARS 11 — MO PAYT 1.1550 — AN CONST 13.87

#	INT	PRIN	BALANCE
1	8.0329	5.8277	94.1723
2	7.5335	6.3271	87.8453
3	6.9913	6.8692	80.9760
4	6.4027	7.4579	73.5182
5	5.7636	8.0970	65.4212
6	5.0698	8.7908	56.6304
7	4.3165	9.5441	47.0863
8	3.4986	10.3620	36.7244
9	2.6107	11.2499	25.4745
10	1.6467	12.2139	13.2606
11	.6000	13.2606	0.0000

YEARS 12 — MO PAYT 1.0962 — AN CONST 13.16

#	INT	PRIN	BALANCE
1	8.0602	5.0943	94.9057
2	7.6237	5.5308	89.3750
3	7.1497	6.0047	83.3702
4	6.6352	6.5193	76.8509
5	6.0765	7.0779	69.7730
6	5.4700	7.6845	62.0885
7	4.8115	8.3430	53.7455
8	4.0966	9.0579	44.6876
9	3.3204	9.8341	34.8535
10	2.4777	10.6768	24.1767
11	1.5628	11.5917	12.5850
12	.5695	12.5850	0.0000

YEARS 13 — MO PAYT 1.0471 — AN CONST 12.57

#	INT	PRIN	BALANCE
1	8.0830	4.4819	95.5181
2	7.6990	4.8659	90.6522
3	7.2820	5.2829	85.3693
4	6.8293	5.7356	79.6337
5	6.3378	6.2271	73.4066
6	5.8042	6.7607	66.6458
7	5.2249	7.3401	59.3058
8	4.5959	7.9691	51.3367
9	3.9130	8.6519	42.6848
10	3.1716	9.3933	33.2914
11	2.3666	10.1983	23.0932
12	1.4927	11.0722	12.0210
13	.5439	12.0210	0.0000

YEARS 14 — MO PAYT 1.0056 — AN CONST 12.07

#	INT	PRIN	BALANCE
1	8.1023	3.9645	96.0355
2	7.7626	4.3042	91.7313
3	7.3938	4.6730	87.0583
4	6.9933	5.0735	81.9848
5	6.5586	5.5082	76.4766
6	6.0865	5.9802	70.4964
7	5.5741	6.4927	64.0037
8	5.0177	7.0491	56.9546
9	4.4137	7.6531	49.3015
10	3.7579	8.3089	40.9926
11	3.0458	9.0209	31.9716
12	2.2728	9.7940	22.1776
13	1.4336	10.6332	11.5444
14	.5224	11.5444	0.0000

YEARS 15 — MO PAYT .9701 — AN CONST 11.65

#	INT	PRIN	BALANCE
1	8.1188	3.5229	96.4771
2	7.8169	3.8248	92.6523
3	7.4891	4.1526	88.4997
4	7.1333	4.5084	83.9913
5	6.7469	4.8947	79.0966
6	6.3275	5.3142	73.7824
7	5.8721	5.7696	68.0128
8	5.3777	6.2640	61.7489
9	4.8409	6.8007	54.9481
10	4.2582	7.3835	47.5646
11	3.6255	8.0162	39.5484
12	2.9385	8.7031	30.8453
13	2.1928	9.4489	21.3963
14	1.3831	10.2586	11.1377
15	.5040	11.1377	0.0000

YEARS 16 — MO PAYT .9397 — AN CONST 11.28

#	INT	PRIN	BALANCE
1	8.1329	3.1429	96.8571
2	7.8636	3.4122	93.4449
3	7.5712	3.7046	89.7403
4	7.2538	4.0220	85.7183
5	6.9091	4.3667	81.3516
6	6.5349	4.7409	76.6107
7	6.1286	5.1472	71.4635
8	5.6876	5.5882	65.8753
9	5.2087	6.0671	59.8082
10	4.6888	6.5870	53.2212
11	4.1243	7.1515	46.0697
12	3.5115	7.7643	38.3055
13	2.8462	8.4296	29.8759
14	2.1238	9.1520	20.7239
15	1.3396	9.9362	10.7877
16	.4881	10.7877	0.0000

YEARS 17 — MO PAYT .9132 — AN CONST 10.96

#	INT	PRIN	BALANCE
1	8.1452	2.8134	97.1866
2	7.9041	3.0545	94.1322
3	7.6424	3.3162	90.8160
4	7.3582	3.6004	87.2156
5	7.0497	3.9089	83.3067
6	6.7147	4.2439	79.0629
7	6.3510	4.6075	74.4553
8	5.9562	5.0023	69.4530
9	5.5276	5.4310	64.0220
10	5.0622	5.8964	58.1256
11	4.5569	6.4017	51.7239
12	4.0083	6.9503	44.7736
13	3.4127	7.5458	37.2278
14	2.7661	8.1925	29.0353
15	2.0641	8.8945	20.1408
16	1.3019	9.6567	10.4842
17	.4744	10.4842	0.0000

YEARS 18 — MO PAYT .8901 — AN CONST 10.69

#	INT	PRIN	BALANCE
1	8.1559	2.5259	97.4741
2	7.9395	2.7423	94.7318
3	7.7045	2.9773	91.7545
4	7.4493	3.2324	88.5221
5	7.1723	3.5094	85.0127
6	6.8716	3.8102	81.2025
7	6.5451	4.1367	77.0658
8	6.1906	4.4911	72.5747
9	5.8058	4.8760	67.6987
10	5.3879	5.2938	62.4049
11	4.9343	5.7475	56.6574
12	4.4418	6.2400	50.4174
13	3.9071	6.7747	43.6427
14	3.3265	7.3552	36.2875
15	2.6962	7.9855	28.3019
16	2.0119	8.6698	19.6321
17	1.2690	9.4128	10.2194
18	.4624	10.2194	0.0000

YEARS 19 — MO PAYT .8699 — AN CONST 10.44

#	INT	PRIN	BALANCE
1	8.1653	2.2736	97.7264
2	7.9705	2.4684	95.2580
3	7.7589	2.6800	92.5780
4	7.5293	2.9096	89.6684
5	7.2800	3.1589	86.5094
6	7.0093	3.4296	83.0798
7	6.7154	3.7235	79.3563
8	6.3963	4.0426	75.3137
9	6.0499	4.3890	70.9246
10	5.6738	4.7651	66.1595
11	5.2654	5.1735	60.9860
12	4.8221	5.6168	55.3692
13	4.3408	6.0981	49.2711
14	3.8182	6.6207	42.6504
15	3.2509	7.1880	35.4624
16	2.6349	7.8040	27.6585
17	1.9662	8.4727	19.1858
18	1.2402	9.1988	9.9870
19	.4519	9.9870	0.0000

YEARS 20 — MO PAYT .8521 — AN CONST 10.23

#	INT	PRIN	BALANCE
1	8.1736	2.0512	97.9488
2	7.9978	2.2270	95.7218
3	7.8070	2.4178	93.3040
4	7.5998	2.6250	90.6790
5	7.3749	2.8499	87.8291
6	7.1306	3.0941	84.7350
7	6.8655	3.3593	81.3757
8	6.5776	3.6472	77.7285
9	6.2651	3.9597	73.7688
10	5.9258	4.2990	69.4698
11	5.5574	4.6674	64.8024
12	5.1574	5.0674	59.7351
13	4.7232	5.5016	54.2335
14	4.2518	5.9730	48.2605
15	3.7399	6.4849	41.7756
16	3.1842	7.0406	34.7350
17	2.5809	7.6439	27.0911
18	1.9259	8.2989	18.7922
19	1.2147	9.0101	9.7822
20	.4426	9.7822	0.0000

YEARS 21 — MO PAYT .8363 — AN CONST 10.04

#	INT	PRIN	BALANCE
1	8.1809	1.8543	98.1457
2	8.0220	2.0132	96.1326
3	7.8495	2.1857	93.9469

#	INT	PRIN	BALANCE
4	7.6622	2.3730	91.5739
5	7.4589	2.5763	88.9976
6	7.2381	2.7971	86.2005
7	6.9984	3.0368	83.1638
8	6.7382	3.2970	79.8668
9	6.4557	3.5795	76.2872
10	6.1489	3.8863	72.4010
11	5.8159	4.2193	68.1817
12	5.4543	4.5808	63.6008
13	5.0618	4.9734	58.6274
14	4.6356	5.3996	53.2279
15	4.1729	5.8623	47.3656
16	3.6706	6.3646	41.0010
17	3.1252	6.9100	34.0909
18	2.5330	7.5022	26.5888
19	1.8902	8.1450	18.4438
20	1.1922	8.8430	9.6008
21	.4344	9.6008	0.0000

YEARS 22   MO PAYT .8222   AN CONST 9.87

#	INT	PRIN	BALANCE
1	8.1874	1.6792	98.3208
2	8.0435	1.8231	96.4976
3	7.8873	1.9794	94.5183
4	7.7177	2.1490	92.3693
5	7.5336	2.3331	90.0362
6	7.3336	2.5331	87.5031
7	7.1166	2.7501	84.7530
8	6.8809	2.9858	81.7672
9	6.6250	3.2416	78.5256
10	6.3473	3.5194	75.0062
11	6.0457	3.8210	71.1852
12	5.7182	4.1484	67.0367
13	5.3628	4.5039	62.5328
14	4.9768	4.8899	57.6429
15	4.5578	5.3089	52.3340
16	4.1028	5.7638	46.5702
17	3.6089	6.2577	40.3125
18	3.0727	6.7940	33.5185
19	2.4905	7.3762	26.1423
20	1.8584	8.0083	18.1341
21	1.1722	8.6945	9.4396
22	.4271	9.4396	0.0000

YEARS 23   MO PAYT .8097   AN CONST 9.72

#	INT	PRIN	BALANCE
1	8.1933	1.5231	98.4769
2	8.0627	1.6537	96.8232
3	7.9210	1.7954	95.0278
4	7.7672	1.9492	93.0786
5	7.6002	2.1162	90.9624
6	7.4188	2.2976	88.6648
7	7.2219	2.4945	86.1703
8	7.0082	2.7082	83.4621
9	6.7761	2.9403	80.5218
10	6.5241	3.1923	77.3296
11	6.2506	3.4658	73.8637
12	5.9536	3.7628	70.1009
13	5.6311	4.0852	66.0157
14	5.2814	4.4353	61.5804
15	4.9010	4.8154	56.7650
16	4.4884	5.2280	51.5369
17	4.0404	5.6760	45.8609
18	3.5540	6.1624	39.6985
19	3.0259	6.6905	33.0080
20	2.4526	7.2638	25.7441
21	1.8301	7.8863	17.8578
22	1.1543	8.5621	9.2958
23	.4206	9.2958	0.0000

YEARS 24   MO PAYT .7985   AN CONST 9.59

#	INT	PRIN	BALANCE
1	8.1985	1.3835	98.6165
2	8.0799	1.5021	97.1144
3	7.9512	1.6308	95.4837
4	7.8114	1.7705	93.7131
5	7.6597	1.9222	91.7909
6	7.4950	2.0870	89.7039
7	7.3162	2.2658	87.4381
8	7.1220	2.4600	84.9782
9	6.9112	2.6708	82.3074
10	6.6823	2.8996	79.4078
11	6.4339	3.1481	76.2597
12	6.1641	3.4179	72.8418
13	5.8712	3.7107	69.1311
14	5.5532	4.0287	65.1024
15	5.2080	4.3740	60.7284
16	4.8332	4.7488	55.9796
17	4.4263	5.1557	50.8239
18	3.9845	5.5975	45.2264
19	3.5048	6.0772	39.1492
20	2.9840	6.5979	32.5513
21	2.4186	7.1633	25.3880
22	1.8048	7.7772	17.6108
23	1.1384	8.4436	9.1672
24	.4148	9.1672	0.0000

YEARS 25   MO PAYT .7885   AN CONST 9.47

#	INT	PRIN	BALANCE
1	8.2031	1.2583	98.7417
2	8.0953	1.3661	97.3756
3	7.9782	1.4832	95.8925
4	7.8511	1.6103	94.2822
5	7.7132	1.7482	92.5340
6	7.5633	1.8981	90.6359
7	7.4007	2.0607	88.5752
8	7.2241	2.2373	86.3379
9	7.0324	2.4290	83.9089
10	6.8242	2.6372	81.2718
11	6.5983	2.8631	78.4086
12	6.3529	3.1085	75.3001
13	6.0865	3.3749	71.9253
14	5.7973	3.6641	68.2612
15	5.4834	3.9780	64.2832
16	5.1425	4.3189	59.9643
17	4.7724	4.6890	55.2752
18	4.3706	5.0908	50.1844
19	3.9343	5.5271	44.6573
20	3.4607	6.0007	38.6566
21	2.9465	6.5149	32.1417
22	2.3882	7.0732	25.0685
23	1.7821	7.6793	17.3892
24	1.1240	8.3374	9.0518
25	.4096	9.0518	0.0000

YEARS 26   MO PAYT .7794   AN CONST 9.36

#	INT	PRIN	BALANCE
1	8.2073	1.1457	98.8543
2	8.1091	1.2439	97.6105
3	8.0026	1.3504	96.2600
4	7.8868	1.4662	94.7938
5	7.7612	1.5918	93.2020
6	7.6248	1.7282	91.4738
7	7.4767	1.8763	89.5975
8	7.3159	2.0371	87.5604
9	7.1413	2.2117	85.3488
10	6.9518	2.4012	82.9476
11	6.7461	2.6069	80.3406
12	6.5227	2.8303	77.5103
13	6.2801	3.0729	74.4374
14	6.0168	3.3362	71.1012
15	5.7309	3.6221	67.4792

#	INT	PRIN	BALANCE
16	5.4205	3.9325	63.5467
17	5.0836	4.2694	59.2773
18	4.7177	4.6353	54.6420
19	4.3205	5.0325	49.6095
20	3.8892	5.4638	44.1457
21	3.4210	5.9320	38.2137
22	2.9127	6.4403	31.7735
23	2.3608	6.9922	24.7813
24	1.7617	7.5913	17.1900
25	1.1112	8.2419	8.9481
26	.4049	8.9481	0.0000

YEARS 27   MO PAYT .7713   AN CONST 9.26

#	INT	PRIN	BALANCE
1	8.2111	1.0442	98.9558
2	8.1216	1.1337	97.8220
3	8.0245	1.2309	96.5912
4	7.9190	1.3363	95.2548
5	7.8045	1.4509	93.8040
6	7.6802	1.5752	92.2288
7	7.5452	1.7102	90.5186
8	7.3986	1.8567	88.6619
9	7.2395	2.0158	86.6461
10	7.0668	2.1886	84.4575
11	6.8792	2.3761	82.0814
12	6.6756	2.5797	79.5017
13	6.4546	2.8008	76.7009
14	6.2146	3.0408	73.6601
15	5.9540	3.3014	70.3588
16	5.6711	3.5843	66.7745
17	5.3639	3.8914	62.8831
18	5.0305	4.2249	58.6583
19	4.6684	4.5869	54.0714
20	4.2754	4.9800	49.0914
21	3.8486	5.4067	43.6847
22	3.3853	5.8700	37.8147
23	2.8823	6.3730	31.4417
24	2.3362	6.9191	24.5225
25	1.7433	7.5121	17.0105
26	1.0995	8.1558	8.8547
27	.4007	8.8547	0.0000

YEARS 28   MO PAYT .7639   AN CONST 9.17

#	INT	PRIN	BALANCE
1	8.2145	.9527	99.0473
2	8.1329	1.0343	98.0131
3	8.0442	1.1229	96.8901
4	7.9480	1.2191	95.6710
5	7.8436	1.3236	94.3474
6	7.7301	1.4370	92.9103
7	7.6070	1.5602	91.3502
8	7.4733	1.6939	89.6563
9	7.3281	1.8390	87.8173
10	7.1705	1.9966	85.8206
11	6.9995	2.1677	83.6529
12	6.8137	2.3535	81.2995
13	6.6120	2.5551	78.7443
14	6.3931	2.7741	75.9702
15	6.1553	3.0118	72.9584
16	5.8973	3.2699	69.6885
17	5.6171	3.5501	66.1384
18	5.3128	3.8543	62.2841
19	4.9826	4.1846	58.0995
20	4.6240	4.5432	53.5563
21	4.2346	4.9325	48.6237
22	3.8120	5.3552	43.2685
23	3.3531	5.8141	37.4545
24	2.8549	6.3123	31.1421
25	2.3139	6.8532	24.2889
26	1.7267	7.4405	16.8484
27	1.0891	8.0781	8.7703
28	.3968	8.7703	0.0000

YEARS 29   MO PAYT .7573   AN CONST 9.09

#	INT	PRIN	BALANCE
1	8.2176	.8698	99.1302
2	8.1431	.9444	98.1858
3	8.0621	1.0253	97.1605
4	7.9743	1.1132	96.0474
5	7.8789	1.2085	94.8388
6	7.7753	1.3121	93.5267
7	7.6629	1.4245	92.1022
8	7.5408	1.5466	90.5556
9	7.4083	1.6791	88.8764
10	7.2644	1.8230	87.0534
11	7.1082	1.9793	85.0742
12	6.9386	2.1489	82.9253
13	6.7544	2.3330	80.5923
14	6.5545	2.5329	78.0594
15	6.3375	2.7500	75.3094
16	6.1018	2.9856	72.3238
17	5.8460	3.2415	69.0823
18	5.5682	3.5192	65.5631
19	5.2666	3.8208	61.7423
20	4.9392	4.1482	57.5941
21	4.5837	4.5037	53.0904
22	4.1978	4.8896	48.2008
23	3.7788	5.3086	42.8922
24	3.3239	5.7635	37.1287
25	2.8300	6.2574	30.8713
26	2.2938	6.7936	24.0776
27	1.7116	7.3758	16.7019
28	1.0796	8.0078	8.6940
29	.3934	8.6940	0.0000

YEARS 30   MO PAYT .7513   AN CONST 9.02

#	INT	PRIN	BALANCE
1	8.2204	.7948	99.2052
2	8.1523	.8629	98.3423
3	8.0783	.9369	97.4054
4	7.9981	1.0171	96.3883
5	7.9109	1.1043	95.2840
6	7.8163	1.1989	94.0850
7	7.7135	1.3017	92.7834
8	7.6020	1.4132	91.3702
9	7.4809	1.5343	89.8358
10	7.3494	1.6658	88.1700
11	7.2067	1.8085	86.3615
12	7.0517	1.9635	84.3980
13	6.8834	2.1318	82.2662
14	6.7007	2.3145	79.9517
15	6.5024	2.5128	77.4390
16	6.2871	2.7281	74.7108
17	6.0533	2.9619	71.7490
18	5.7995	3.2157	68.5333
19	5.5239	3.4913	65.0420
20	5.2248	3.7904	61.2516
21	4.9000	4.1152	57.1363
22	4.5473	4.4679	52.6684
23	4.1645	4.8507	47.8177
24	3.7488	5.2664	42.5513
25	3.2975	5.7177	36.8336
26	2.8075	6.2077	30.6259
27	2.2756	6.7396	23.8863
28	1.6980	7.3172	16.5691
29	1.0710	7.9442	8.6249
30	.3903	8.6249	0.0000

YEARS 2 — MO PAYT 4.5364 — AN CONST 54.44

#	INT	PRIN	BALANCE
1	6.5038	47.9333	52.0667
2	2.3704	52.0667	0.0000

YEARS 3 — MO PAYT 3.1475 — AN CONST 37.77

#	INT	PRIN	BALANCE
1	7.1527	30.6173	69.3827
2	4.5125	33.2574	36.1253
3	1.6447	36.1253	0.0000

YEARS 4 — MO PAYT 2.4554 — AN CONST 29.47

#	INT	PRIN	BALANCE
1	7.4760	21.9888	78.0112
2	5.5799	23.8849	54.1263
3	3.5202	25.9445	28.1818
4	1.2830	28.1818	0.0000

YEARS 5 — MO PAYT 2.0420 — AN CONST 24.51

#	INT	PRIN	BALANCE
1	7.6691	16.8352	83.1648
2	6.2174	18.2869	64.8779
3	4.6405	19.8638	45.0140
4	2.9276	21.5767	23.4373
5	1.0670	23.4373	0.0000

YEARS 6 — MO PAYT 1.7680 — AN CONST 21.22

#	INT	PRIN	BALANCE
1	7.7971	13.4190	86.5810
2	6.6400	14.5761	72.0049
3	5.3831	15.8330	56.1719
4	4.0178	17.1983	38.9736
5	2.5348	18.6813	20.2923
6	.9238	20.2923	0.0000

YEARS 7 — MO PAYT 1.5736 — AN CONST 18.89

#	INT	PRIN	BALANCE
1	7.8880	10.9954	89.0046
2	6.9398	11.9435	77.0611
3	5.9099	12.9734	64.0877
4	4.7912	14.0921	49.9956
5	3.5760	15.3073	34.6883
6	2.2560	16.6273	18.0611
7	.8223	18.0611	0.0000

YEARS 8 — MO PAYT 1.4290 — AN CONST 17.15

#	INT	PRIN	BALANCE
1	7.9555	9.1920	90.8080
2	7.1629	9.9847	80.8233
3	6.3019	10.8456	69.9777
4	5.3667	11.7809	58.1968
5	4.3508	12.7968	45.4000
6	3.2473	13.9002	31.4998
7	2.0487	15.0989	16.4009
8	.7467	16.4009	0.0000

YEARS 9 — MO PAYT 1.3175 — AN CONST 15.81

#	INT	PRIN	BALANCE
1	8.0076	7.8021	92.1979
2	7.3348	8.4749	83.7231
3	6.6040	9.2056	74.5174
4	5.8102	9.9995	64.5180
5	4.9480	10.8617	53.6562
6	4.0113	11.7984	41.8579
7	2.9940	12.8157	29.0421
8	1.8888	13.9209	15.1213
9	.6884	15.1213	0.0000

YEARS 10 — MO PAYT 1.2292 — AN CONST 14.76

#	INT	PRIN	BALANCE
1	8.0489	6.7014	93.2986
2	7.4710	7.2792	86.0194
3	6.8433	7.9069	78.1125
4	6.1615	8.5887	69.5238
5	5.4209	9.3294	60.1944
6	4.6164	10.1338	50.0605
7	3.7425	11.0077	39.0528
8	2.7933	11.9569	27.0959
9	1.7623	12.9880	14.1079
10	.6423	14.1079	0.0000

YEARS 11 — MO PAYT 1.1578 — AN CONST 13.90

#	INT	PRIN	BALANCE
1	8.0822	5.8109	94.1891
2	7.5812	6.3119	87.8772
3	7.0369	6.8562	81.0209
4	6.4457	7.4475	73.5735
5	5.8035	8.0897	65.4838
6	5.1059	8.7872	56.6966
7	4.3481	9.5450	47.1516
8	3.5251	10.3681	36.7835
9	2.6310	11.2621	25.5214
10	1.6599	12.2333	13.2882
11	.6050	13.2882	0.0000

YEARS 12 — MO PAYT 1.0990 — AN CONST 13.19

#	INT	PRIN	BALANCE
1	8.1097	5.0779	94.9221
2	7.6718	5.5158	89.4063
3	7.1962	5.9914	83.4148
4	6.6796	6.5081	76.9068
5	6.1184	7.0693	69.8375
6	5.5088	7.6789	62.1586
7	4.8466	8.3410	53.8176
8	4.1273	9.0603	44.7573
9	3.3461	9.8416	34.9157
10	2.4974	10.6902	24.2255
11	1.5756	11.6121	12.6134
12	.5742	12.6134	0.0000

YEARS 13 — MO PAYT 1.0499 — AN CONST 12.60

#	INT	PRIN	BALANCE
1	8.1326	4.4660	95.5340
2	7.7475	4.8511	90.6828
3	7.3292	5.2695	85.4134
4	6.8748	5.7239	79.6895
5	6.3812	6.2174	73.4721
6	5.8451	6.7536	66.7185
7	5.2627	7.3359	59.3826
8	4.6301	7.9685	51.4141
9	3.9430	8.6557	42.7584
10	3.1966	9.4021	33.3563
11	2.3859	10.2128	23.1435
12	1.5052	11.0935	12.0501
13	.5486	12.0501	0.0000

YEARS 14 — MO PAYT 1.0084 — AN CONST 12.11

#	INT	PRIN	BALANCE
1	8.1520	3.9491	96.0509
2	7.8115	4.2897	91.7612
3	7.4416	4.6596	87.1017
4	7.0398	5.0614	82.0403
5	6.6033	5.4978	76.5425
6	6.1292	5.9719	70.5706
7	5.6143	6.4869	64.0837
8	5.0549	7.0462	57.0375
9	4.4473	7.6538	49.3837
10	3.7873	8.3138	41.0698
11	3.0704	9.0308	32.0391
12	2.2916	9.8095	22.2296
13	1.4458	10.6554	11.5742
14	.5269	11.5742	0.0000

YEARS 15 — MO PAYT .9731 — AN CONST 11.68

#	INT	PRIN	BALANCE
1	8.1685	3.5081	96.4919
2	7.8660	3.8106	92.6813
3	7.5374	4.1392	88.5422
4	7.1805	4.4961	84.0461
5	6.7928	4.8838	79.1623
6	6.3717	5.3049	73.8573
7	5.9142	5.7624	68.0949
8	5.4173	6.2593	61.8356
9	4.8776	6.7990	55.0366
10	4.2913	7.3853	47.6512
11	3.6544	8.0222	39.6291
12	2.9627	8.7139	30.9151
13	2.2113	9.4654	21.4497
14	1.3950	10.2816	11.1682
15	.5084	11.1682	0.0000

YEARS 16 — MO PAYT .9426 — AN CONST 11.32

#	INT	PRIN	BALANCE
1	8.1828	3.1285	96.8715
2	7.9130	3.3983	93.4731
3	7.6199	3.6914	89.7818
4	7.3016	4.0097	85.7721
5	6.9559	4.3554	81.4166
6	6.5803	4.7310	76.6856
7	6.1723	5.1390	71.5467
8	5.7292	5.5821	65.9646
9	5.2478	6.0635	59.9011
10	4.7250	6.5863	53.3147
11	4.1570	7.1543	46.1604
12	3.5401	7.7712	38.3892
13	2.8700	8.4413	29.9479
14	2.1421	9.1692	20.7787
15	1.3514	9.9599	10.8188
16	.4925	10.8188	0.0000

YEARS 17 — MO PAYT .9162 — AN CONST 11.00

#	INT	PRIN	BALANCE
1	8.1951	2.7996	97.2004
2	7.9537	3.0410	94.1595
3	7.6915	3.3032	90.8563
4	7.4066	3.5880	87.2683
5	7.0972	3.8974	83.3709
6	6.7611	4.2335	79.1373
7	6.3961	4.5986	74.5388
8	5.9995	4.9951	69.5437
9	5.5688	5.4258	64.1178
10	5.1009	5.8937	58.2241
11	4.5927	6.4019	51.8222
12	4.0406	6.9540	44.8682
13	3.4410	7.5536	37.3145
14	2.7896	8.2050	29.1095
15	2.0821	8.9125	20.1970
16	1.3136	9.6811	10.5159
17	.4788	10.5159	0.0000

YEARS 18 — MO PAYT .8932 — AN CONST 10.72

#	INT	PRIN	BALANCE
1	8.2058	2.5126	97.4874
2	7.9892	2.7292	94.7582
3	7.7538	2.9646	91.7937
4	7.4982	3.2202	88.5735
5	7.2205	3.4979	85.0756
6	6.9189	3.7995	81.2761
7	6.5913	4.1271	77.1490
8	6.2354	4.4830	72.6660
9	5.8488	4.8696	67.7963
10	5.4289	5.2895	62.5068
11	4.9728	5.7456	56.7612
12	4.4773	6.2411	50.5201
13	3.9391	6.7793	43.7408
14	3.3545	7.3639	36.3770
15	2.7195	7.9989	28.3781
16	2.0298	8.6886	19.6895
17	1.2806	9.4378	10.2517
18	.4667	10.2517	0.0000

YEARS 19 — MO PAYT .8730 — AN CONST 10.48

#	INT	PRIN	BALANCE
1	8.2153	2.2608	97.7392
2	8.0203	2.4557	95.2835
3	7.8086	2.6675	92.6159
4	7.5785	2.8975	89.7184
5	7.3287	3.1474	86.5710
6	7.0573	3.4188	83.1522
7	6.7625	3.7136	79.4386
8	6.4422	4.0338	75.4048
9	6.0944	4.3817	71.0231
10	5.7166	4.7595	66.2636
11	5.3061	5.1699	61.0937
12	4.8603	5.6157	55.4779
13	4.3761	6.1000	49.3779
14	3.8501	6.6260	42.7519
15	3.2787	7.1974	35.5546
16	2.6581	7.8180	27.7365
17	1.9839	8.4922	19.2444
18	1.2516	9.2245	10.0199
19	.4562	10.0199	0.0000

YEARS 20 — MO PAYT .8552 — AN CONST 10.27

#	INT	PRIN	BALANCE
1	8.2236	2.0389	97.9611
2	8.0478	2.2147	95.7464
3	7.8568	2.4057	93.3407
4	7.6494	2.6131	90.7276
5	7.4240	2.8385	87.8892
6	7.1793	3.0832	84.8059
7	6.9134	3.3491	81.4569
8	6.6246	3.6379	77.8190
9	6.3109	3.9516	73.8674
10	5.9701	4.2923	69.5750
11	5.6000	4.6625	64.9126
12	5.1980	5.0645	59.8481
13	4.7612	5.5012	54.3468
14	4.2869	5.9756	48.3712
15	3.7716	6.4909	41.8803
16	3.2119	7.0506	34.8296
17	2.6039	7.6586	27.1710
18	1.9435	8.3190	18.8520
19	1.2261	9.0364	9.8156
20	.4469	9.8156	0.0000

YEARS 21 — MO PAYT .8394 — AN CONST 10.08

#	INT	PRIN	BALANCE
1	8.2310	1.8424	98.1576
2	8.0721	2.0013	96.1562
3	7.8995	2.1739	93.9823

MONTHLY PAYMENT AMORTIZATION SCHEDULE PER $100

8.30 %

#	INT	PRIN	BALANCE
4	7.7120	2.3614	91.6210
5	7.5084	2.5650	89.0560
6	7.2872	2.7862	86.2699
7	7.0470	3.0264	83.2434
8	6.7860	3.2874	79.9561
9	6.5025	3.5709	76.3852
10	6.1946	3.8788	72.5064
11	5.8601	4.2133	68.2932
12	5.4968	4.5766	63.7166
13	5.1022	4.9712	58.7454
14	4.6735	5.3999	53.3455
15	4.2079	5.8655	47.4800
16	3.7021	6.3713	41.1087
17	3.1527	6.9207	34.1879
18	2.5559	7.5175	26.6704
19	1.9076	8.1658	18.5047
20	1.2035	8.8699	9.6348
21	.4386	9.6348	0.0000

YEARS 22 — MO PAYT .8254 — AN CONST 9.91

#	INT	PRIN	BALANCE
1	8.2375	1.6679	98.3321
2	8.0937	1.8117	96.5204
3	7.9374	1.9679	94.5525
4	7.7677	2.1376	92.4148
5	7.5834	2.3220	90.0929
6	7.3832	2.5222	87.5707
7	7.1657	2.7397	84.8310
8	6.9295	2.9759	81.8550
9	6.6728	3.2326	78.6225
10	6.3941	3.5113	75.1112
11	6.0913	3.8141	71.2971
12	5.7624	4.1430	67.1541
13	5.4052	4.5002	62.6539
14	5.0171	4.8883	57.7656
15	4.5956	5.3098	52.4558
16	4.1377	5.7677	46.6881
17	3.6403	6.2651	40.4230
18	3.1001	6.8053	33.6177
19	2.5133	7.3921	26.2256
20	1.8758	8.0296	18.1960
21	1.1834	8.7220	9.4741
22	.4313	9.4741	0.0000

YEARS 23 — MO PAYT .8130 — AN CONST 9.76

#	INT	PRIN	BALANCE
1	8.2433	1.5123	98.4877
2	8.1129	1.6427	96.8451
3	7.9713	1.7843	95.0608
4	7.8174	1.9382	93.1226
5	7.6503	2.1053	91.0173
6	7.4687	2.2869	88.7304
7	7.2715	2.4841	86.2464
8	7.0573	2.6983	83.5481
9	6.8247	2.9309	80.6172
10	6.5719	3.1837	77.4335
11	6.2974	3.4582	73.9753
12	5.9992	3.7564	70.2189
13	5.6753	4.0803	66.1386
14	5.3234	4.4322	61.7064
15	4.9412	4.8144	56.8920
16	4.5261	5.2295	51.6625
17	4.0751	5.6805	45.9820
18	3.5853	6.1703	39.8117
19	3.0532	6.7024	33.1093
20	2.4753	7.2803	25.8290
21	1.8475	7.9081	17.9209
22	1.1655	8.5901	9.3308
23	.4248	9.3308	0.0000

YEARS 24 — MO PAYT .8018 — AN CONST 9.63

#	INT	PRIN	BALANCE
1	8.2485	1.3731	98.6269
2	8.1301	1.4915	97.1354
3	8.0015	1.6201	95.5153
4	7.8618	1.7598	93.7555
5	7.7101	1.9116	91.8439
6	7.5452	2.0764	89.7675
7	7.3662	2.2555	87.5121
8	7.1717	2.4499	85.0621
9	6.9604	2.6612	82.4009
10	6.7310	2.8907	79.5102
11	6.4817	3.1400	76.3703
12	6.2109	3.4107	72.9596
13	5.9168	3.7048	69.2547
14	5.5973	4.0243	65.2304
15	5.2503	4.3713	60.8591
16	4.8734	4.7483	56.1108
17	4.4639	5.1577	50.9531
18	4.0192	5.6025	45.3506
19	3.5361	6.0856	39.2651
20	3.0113	6.6104	32.6547
21	2.4413	7.1804	25.4743
22	1.8221	7.7995	17.6748
23	1.1495	8.4721	9.2027
24	.4190	9.2027	0.0000

YEARS 25 — MO PAYT .7918 — AN CONST 9.51

#	INT	PRIN	BALANCE
1	8.2532	1.2483	98.7517
2	8.1456	1.3560	97.3957
3	8.0287	1.4729	95.9229
4	7.9016	1.5999	94.3230
5	7.7637	1.7378	92.5851
6	7.6138	1.8877	90.6974
7	7.4510	2.0505	88.6469
8	7.2742	2.2273	86.4196
9	7.0822	2.4194	84.0003
10	6.8735	2.6280	81.3723
11	6.6469	2.8546	78.5177
12	6.4008	3.1008	75.4169
13	6.1334	3.3681	72.0488
14	5.8429	3.6586	68.3902
15	5.5275	3.9741	64.4161
16	5.1848	4.3168	60.0994
17	4.8125	4.6890	55.4104
18	4.4082	5.0933	50.3171
19	3.9690	5.5325	44.7845
20	3.4919	6.0096	38.7749
21	2.9737	6.5278	32.2471
22	2.4108	7.0907	25.1563
23	1.7993	7.7022	17.4541
24	1.1352	8.3664	9.0878
25	.4137	9.0878	0.0000

YEARS 26 — MO PAYT .7828 — AN CONST 9.40

#	INT	PRIN	BALANCE
1	8.2574	1.1362	98.8638
2	8.1595	1.2341	97.6297
3	8.0530	1.3405	96.2892
4	7.9374	1.4561	94.8330
5	7.8119	1.5817	93.2513
6	7.6755	1.7181	91.5332
7	7.5273	1.8663	89.6670
8	7.3664	2.0272	87.6398
9	7.1916	2.2020	85.4378
10	7.0017	2.3919	83.0459
11	6.7954	2.5981	80.4478
12	6.5714	2.8222	77.6256
13	6.3280	3.0655	74.5601
14	6.0637	3.3299	71.2302
15	5.7766	3.6170	67.6132
16	5.4647	3.9289	63.6843
17	5.1259	4.2677	59.4166
18	4.7579	4.6357	54.7808
19	4.3581	5.0355	49.7454
20	3.9239	5.4697	44.2757
21	3.4522	5.9413	38.3344
22	2.9399	6.4537	31.8807
23	2.3834	7.0102	24.8705
24	1.7789	7.6147	17.2558
25	1.1223	8.2713	8.9845
26	.4090	8.9845	0.0000

YEARS 27 — MO PAYT .7747 — AN CONST 9.30

#	INT	PRIN	BALANCE
1	8.2612	1.0351	98.9649
2	8.1719	1.1244	97.8405
3	8.0750	1.2214	96.6191
4	7.9697	1.3267	95.2925
5	7.8553	1.4411	93.8514
6	7.7310	1.5653	92.2860
7	7.5960	1.7003	90.5857
8	7.4494	1.8469	88.7388
9	7.2901	2.0062	86.7326
10	7.1171	2.1792	84.5534
11	6.9292	2.3671	82.1863
12	6.7251	2.5712	79.6150
13	6.5034	2.7930	76.8221
14	6.2625	3.0338	73.7883
15	6.0009	3.2954	70.4929
16	5.7168	3.5796	66.9133
17	5.4081	3.8882	63.0251
18	5.0728	4.2235	58.8015
19	4.7086	4.5877	54.2138
20	4.3130	4.9833	49.2305
21	3.8833	5.4131	43.8174
22	3.4165	5.8798	37.9376
23	2.9095	6.3869	31.5507
24	2.3587	6.9376	24.6131
25	1.7605	7.5359	17.0772
26	1.1107	8.1857	8.8915
27	.4048	8.8915	0.0000

YEARS 28 — MO PAYT .7674 — AN CONST 9.21

#	INT	PRIN	BALANCE
1	8.2646	.9440	99.0560
2	8.1832	1.0254	98.0307
3	8.0948	1.1138	96.9169
4	7.9988	1.2098	95.7071
5	7.8944	1.3141	94.3929
6	7.7811	1.4275	92.9655
7	7.6580	1.5506	91.4149
8	7.5243	1.6843	89.7306
9	7.3791	1.8295	87.9011
10	7.2213	1.9873	85.9139
11	7.0500	2.1586	83.7552
12	6.8638	2.3448	81.4105
13	6.6616	2.5470	78.8635
14	6.4420	2.7666	76.0969
15	6.2034	3.0052	73.0917
16	5.9443	3.2643	69.8275
17	5.6628	3.5458	66.2817
18	5.3570	3.8515	62.4301
19	5.0249	4.1837	58.2465
20	4.6642	4.5444	53.7020
21	4.2723	4.9363	48.7657
22	3.8466	5.3620	43.4038
23	3.3843	5.8243	37.5794
24	2.8820	6.3266	31.2529
25	2.3365	6.8721	24.3807
26	1.7439	7.4647	16.9160
27	1.1002	8.1084	8.8076
28	.4010	8.8076	0.0000

YEARS 29 — MO PAYT .7608 — AN CONST 9.13

#	INT	PRIN	BALANCE
1	8.2677	.8615	99.1385
2	8.1934	.9358	98.2026
3	8.1127	1.0165	97.1861
4	8.0251	1.1042	96.0819
5	7.9299	1.1994	94.8825
6	7.8264	1.3028	93.5797
7	7.7141	1.4152	92.1645
8	7.5921	1.5372	90.6273
9	7.4595	1.6698	88.9576
10	7.3155	1.8137	87.1438
11	7.1591	1.9701	85.1737
12	6.9892	2.1400	83.0337
13	6.8047	2.3246	80.7091
14	6.6042	2.5250	78.1841
15	6.3865	2.7428	75.4413
16	6.1500	2.9793	72.4620
17	5.8931	3.2362	69.2259
18	5.6140	3.5152	65.7106
19	5.3109	3.8184	61.8923
20	4.9816	4.1476	57.7446
21	4.6240	4.5053	53.2394
22	4.2355	4.8938	48.3456
23	3.8135	5.3158	43.0298
24	3.3551	5.7742	37.2557
25	2.8572	6.2721	30.9836
26	2.3163	6.8129	24.1707
27	1.7288	7.4004	16.7703
28	1.0907	8.0386	8.7317
29	.3975	8.7317	0.0000

YEARS 30 — MO PAYT .7548 — AN CONST 9.06

#	INT	PRIN	BALANCE
1	8.2705	.7869	99.2131
2	8.2027	.8548	98.3583
3	8.1289	.9285	97.4299
4	8.0489	1.0085	96.4213
5	7.9619	1.0955	95.3259
6	7.8675	1.1900	94.1359
7	7.7648	1.2926	92.8433
8	7.6534	1.4040	91.4393
9	7.5323	1.5251	89.9142
10	7.4008	1.6566	88.2576
11	7.2579	1.7995	86.4581
12	7.1028	1.9546	84.5035
13	6.9342	2.1232	82.3803
14	6.7511	2.3063	80.0740
15	6.5523	2.5052	77.5688
16	6.3362	2.7212	74.8477
17	6.1016	2.9558	71.8918
18	5.8467	3.2107	68.6811
19	5.5698	3.4876	65.1935
20	5.2691	3.7883	61.4052
21	4.9424	4.1150	57.2903
22	4.5876	4.4698	52.8204
23	4.2022	4.8553	47.9652
24	3.7835	5.2739	42.6912
25	3.3287	5.7287	36.9625
26	2.8347	6.2227	30.7398
27	2.2981	6.7593	23.9805
28	1.7152	7.3422	16.6383
29	1.0821	7.9753	8.6630
30	.3944	8.6630	0.0000

YEARS 2 — MO PAYT 4.5399 — AN CONST 54.48

#	INT	PRIN	BALANCE
1	6.5635	47.9147	52.0853
2	2.3930	52.0853	0.0000

YEARS 3 — MO PAYT 3.1510 — AN CONST 37.82

#	INT	PRIN	BALANCE
1	7.2184	30.5932	69.4068
2	4.5555	33.2561	36.1507
3	1.6609	36.1507	0.0000

YEARS 4 — MO PAYT 2.4589 — AN CONST 29.51

#	INT	PRIN	BALANCE
1	7.5447	21.9625	78.0375
2	5.6330	23.8742	54.1633
3	3.5550	25.9522	28.2111
4	1.2961	28.2111	0.0000

YEARS 5 — MO PAYT 2.0456 — AN CONST 24.55

#	INT	PRIN	BALANCE
1	7.7395	16.8081	83.1919
2	6.2765	18.2711	64.9209
3	4.6862	19.8614	45.0595
4	2.9575	21.5901	23.4694
5	1.0783	23.4694	0.0000

YEARS 6 — MO PAYT 1.7717 — AN CONST 21.27

#	INT	PRIN	BALANCE
1	7.8687	13.3916	86.6084
2	6.7031	14.5572	72.0512
3	5.4360	15.8243	56.2269
4	4.0587	17.2016	39.0253
5	2.5614	18.6989	20.3264
6	.9339	20.3264	0.0000

YEARS 7 — MO PAYT 1.5774 — AN CONST 18.93

#	INT	PRIN	BALANCE
1	7.9603	10.9681	89.0319
2	7.0057	11.9228	77.1091
3	5.9679	12.9606	64.1486
4	4.8398	14.0886	50.0599
5	3.6135	15.3149	34.7450
6	2.2805	16.6480	18.0970
7	.8314	18.0970	0.0000

YEARS 8 — MO PAYT 1.4328 — AN CONST 17.20

#	INT	PRIN	BALANCE
1	8.0285	9.1651	90.8349
2	7.2308	9.9629	80.8720
3	6.3636	10.8300	70.0420
4	5.4209	11.7727	58.2693
5	4.3962	12.7974	45.4718
6	3.2823	13.9113	31.5605
7	2.0715	15.1222	16.4384
8	.7552	16.4384	0.0000

YEARS 9 — MO PAYT 1.3214 — AN CONST 15.86

#	INT	PRIN	BALANCE
1	8.0810	7.7757	92.2243
2	7.4042	8.4525	83.7718
3	6.6685	9.1882	74.5837
4	5.8688	9.9879	64.5957
5	4.9994	10.8573	53.7384
6	4.0544	11.8023	41.9361
7	3.0271	12.8296	29.1065
8	1.9104	13.9463	15.1602
9	.6965	15.1602	0.0000

YEARS 10 — MO PAYT 1.2332 — AN CONST 14.80

#	INT	PRIN	BALANCE
1	8.1226	6.6756	93.3244
2	7.5416	7.2566	86.0678
3	6.9100	7.8882	78.1796
4	6.2234	8.5748	69.6048
5	5.4770	9.3212	60.2836
6	4.6657	10.1325	50.1511
7	3.7837	11.0144	39.1366
8	2.8250	11.9732	27.1635
9	1.7829	13.0153	14.1482
10	.6500	14.1482	0.0000

YEARS 11 — MO PAYT 1.1618 — AN CONST 13.95

#	INT	PRIN	BALANCE
1	8.1563	5.7857	94.2143
2	7.6527	6.2893	87.9249
3	7.1052	6.8368	81.0882
4	6.5102	7.4318	73.6563
5	5.8633	8.0787	65.5776
6	5.1601	8.7819	56.7957
7	4.3957	9.5463	47.2495
8	3.5648	10.3772	36.8723
9	2.6616	11.2804	25.5919
10	1.6797	12.2623	13.3296
11	.6124	13.3296	0.0000

YEARS 12 — MO PAYT 1.1031 — AN CONST 13.24

#	INT	PRIN	BALANCE
1	8.1839	5.0535	94.9465
2	7.7441	5.4934	89.4532
3	7.2659	5.9715	83.4817
4	6.7462	6.4913	76.9904
5	6.1812	7.0563	69.9341
6	5.5670	7.6705	62.2637
7	4.8993	8.3381	53.9256
8	4.1736	9.0638	44.8617
9	3.3847	9.8528	35.0090
10	2.5271	10.7104	24.2986
11	1.5948	11.6426	12.6560
12	.5815	12.6560	0.0000

YEARS 13 — MO PAYT 1.0541 — AN CONST 12.65

#	INT	PRIN	BALANCE
1	8.2070	4.4423	95.5577
2	7.8204	4.8290	90.7287
3	7.4001	5.2493	85.4793
4	6.9432	5.7062	79.7731
5	6.4465	6.2029	73.5702
6	5.9066	6.7428	66.8274
7	5.3197	7.3297	59.4977
8	4.6817	7.9677	51.5300
9	3.9882	8.6612	42.8688
10	3.2343	9.4151	33.4537
11	2.4148	10.2346	23.2192
12	1.5240	11.1254	12.0938
13	.5556	12.0938	0.0000

YEARS 14 — MO PAYT 1.0127 — AN CONST 12.16

#	INT	PRIN	BALANCE
1	8.2266	3.9262	96.0738
2	7.8848	4.2679	91.8059
3	7.5133	4.6394	87.1665
4	7.1095	5.0432	82.1233
5	6.6706	5.4822	76.6411
6	6.1934	5.9594	70.6817
7	5.6747	6.4781	64.2036
8	5.1108	7.0419	57.1617
9	4.4979	7.6549	49.5069
10	3.8316	8.3211	41.1857
11	3.1073	9.0454	32.1403
12	2.3200	9.8327	22.3075
13	1.4642	10.6886	11.6189
14	.5338	11.6189	0.0000

YEARS 15 — MO PAYT .9774 — AN CONST 11.73

#	INT	PRIN	BALANCE
1	8.2432	3.4859	96.5141
2	7.9398	3.7893	92.7248
3	7.6100	4.1191	88.6056
4	7.2514	4.4777	84.1279
5	6.8617	4.8674	79.2605
6	6.4380	5.2911	73.9694
7	5.9775	5.7516	68.2178
8	5.4769	6.2523	61.9656
9	4.9327	6.7965	55.1691
10	4.3411	7.3880	47.7811
11	3.6980	8.0311	39.7500
12	2.9990	8.7301	31.0199
13	2.2391	9.4900	21.5299
14	1.4131	10.3160	11.2139
15	.5152	11.2139	0.0000

YEARS 16 — MO PAYT .9471 — AN CONST 11.37

#	INT	PRIN	BALANCE
1	8.2575	3.1071	96.8929
2	7.9871	3.3776	93.5153
3	7.6931	3.6716	89.8437
4	7.3735	3.9912	85.8525
5	7.0261	4.3386	81.5140
6	6.6485	4.7162	76.7978
7	6.2380	5.1267	71.6711
8	5.7918	5.5729	66.0982
9	5.3067	6.0580	60.0402
10	4.7794	6.5853	53.4549
11	4.2062	7.1585	46.2965
12	3.5831	7.7815	38.5149
13	2.9058	8.4589	30.0561
14	2.1696	9.1951	20.8609
15	1.3692	9.9955	10.8655
16	.4992	10.8655	0.0000

YEARS 17 — MO PAYT .9207 — AN CONST 11.05

#	INT	PRIN	BALANCE
1	8.2699	2.7789	97.2211
2	8.0281	3.0208	94.2003
3	7.7651	3.2837	90.9165
4	7.4793	3.5696	87.3470
5	7.1686	3.8802	83.4667
6	6.8309	4.2180	79.2488
7	6.4637	4.5851	74.6636
8	6.0646	4.9842	69.6794
9	5.6308	5.4180	64.2614
10	5.1592	5.8896	58.3717
11	4.6466	6.4023	51.9695
12	4.0893	6.9595	45.0099
13	3.4836	7.5653	37.4446
14	2.8251	8.2238	29.2208
15	2.1093	8.9396	20.2812
16	1.3312	9.7177	10.5635
17	.4853	10.5635	0.0000

YEARS 18 — MO PAYT .8978 — AN CONST 10.78

#	INT	PRIN	BALANCE
1	8.2808	2.4927	97.5073
2	8.0638	2.7097	94.7977
3	7.8279	2.9455	91.8522
4	7.5716	3.2019	88.6503
5	7.2929	3.4806	85.1697
6	6.9899	3.7835	81.3862
7	6.6606	4.1128	77.2733
8	6.3026	4.4708	72.8025
9	5.9135	4.8600	67.9425
10	5.4905	5.2830	62.6595
11	5.0306	5.7428	56.9167
12	4.5308	6.2427	50.6740
13	3.9874	6.7861	43.8880
14	3.3967	7.3767	36.5112
15	2.7546	8.0188	28.4924
16	2.0567	8.7168	19.7757
17	1.2980	9.4755	10.3002
18	.4732	10.3002	0.0000

YEARS 19 — MO PAYT .8777 — AN CONST 10.54

#	INT	PRIN	BALANCE
1	8.2902	2.2417	97.7583
2	8.0951	2.4368	95.3215
3	7.8830	2.6489	92.6726
4	7.6525	2.8795	89.7931
5	7.4018	3.1301	86.6630
6	7.1294	3.4026	83.2605
7	6.8332	3.6987	79.5618
8	6.5113	4.0206	75.5411
9	6.1613	4.3706	71.1705
10	5.7809	4.7510	66.4195
11	5.3674	5.1646	61.2549
12	4.9178	5.6141	55.6408
13	4.4292	6.1027	49.5381
14	3.8980	6.6339	42.9041
15	3.3206	7.2114	35.6928
16	2.6929	7.8390	27.8537
17	2.0106	8.5214	19.3324
18	1.2689	9.2631	10.0693
19	.4626	10.0693	0.0000

YEARS 20 — MO PAYT .8599 — AN CONST 10.32

#	INT	PRIN	BALANCE
1	8.2986	2.0205	97.9795
2	8.1227	2.1964	95.7831
3	7.9316	2.3876	93.3955
4	7.7237	2.5954	90.8001
5	7.4978	2.8213	87.9788
6	7.2523	3.0669	84.9120
7	6.9853	3.3338	81.5782
8	6.6952	3.6240	77.9542
9	6.3797	3.9394	74.0148
10	6.0368	4.2823	69.7325
11	5.6641	4.6550	65.0774
12	5.2589	5.0602	60.0172
13	4.8185	5.5007	54.5166
14	4.3397	5.9794	48.5371
15	3.8192	6.4999	42.0372
16	3.2535	7.0656	34.9716
17	2.6385	7.6806	27.2909
18	1.9700	8.3492	18.9418
19	1.2432	9.0759	9.8659
20	.4533	9.8659	0.0000

YEARS 21 — MO PAYT .8442 — AN CONST 10.14

#	INT	PRIN	BALANCE
1	8.3060	1.8248	98.1752
2	8.1472	1.9837	96.1915
3	7.9745	2.1563	94.0352

#	INT	PRIN	BALANCE
4	7.7868	2.3440	91.6912
5	7.5828	2.5480	89.1432
6	7.3610	2.7698	86.3734
7	7.1199	3.0109	83.3625
8	6.8579	3.2730	80.0895
9	6.5730	3.5578	76.5317
10	6.2633	3.8675	72.6641
11	5.9267	4.2042	68.4600
12	5.5607	4.5701	63.8899
13	5.1630	4.9679	58.9220
14	4.7306	5.4003	53.5217
15	4.2605	5.8703	47.6514
16	3.7495	6.3813	41.2701
17	3.1941	6.9367	34.3334
18	2.5903	7.5405	26.7929
19	1.9340	8.1968	18.5961
20	1.2206	8.9103	9.6858
21	.4450	9.6858	0.0000

YEARS 22 — MO PAYT .8303 — AN CONST 9.97

#	INT	PRIN	BALANCE
1	8.3126	1.6510	98.3490
2	8.1689	1.7947	96.5543
3	8.0127	1.9509	94.6034
4	7.8429	2.1207	92.4827
5	7.6583	2.3053	90.1774
6	7.4576	2.5060	87.6714
7	7.2395	2.7241	84.9474
8	7.0024	2.9612	81.9862
9	6.7446	3.2189	78.7672
10	6.4645	3.4991	75.2681
11	6.1599	3.8037	71.4645
12	5.8288	4.1347	67.3297
13	5.4689	4.4946	62.8351
14	5.0777	4.8859	57.9492
15	4.6524	5.3111	52.6381
16	4.1902	5.7734	46.8647
17	3.6876	6.2759	40.5888
18	3.1414	6.8222	33.7666
19	2.5476	7.4160	26.3506
20	1.9021	8.0615	18.2891
21	1.2004	8.7632	9.5259
22	.4376	9.5259	0.0000

YEARS 23 — MO PAYT .8179 — AN CONST 9.82

#	INT	PRIN	BALANCE
1	8.3184	1.4961	98.5039
2	8.1882	1.6263	96.8776
3	8.0467	1.7678	95.1098
4	7.8928	1.9217	93.1881
5	7.7255	2.0890	91.0991
6	7.5437	2.2708	88.8283
7	7.3460	2.4685	86.3598
8	7.1312	2.6833	83.6765
9	6.8976	2.9169	80.7596
10	6.6437	3.1708	77.5888
11	6.3678	3.4468	74.1421
12	6.0677	3.7468	70.3953
13	5.7416	4.0729	66.3224
14	5.3871	4.4274	61.8950
15	5.0018	4.8128	57.0823
16	4.5828	5.2317	51.8506
17	4.1275	5.6870	46.1636
18	3.6325	6.1820	39.9815
19	3.0944	6.7201	33.2614
20	2.5095	7.3050	25.9564
21	1.8736	7.9409	18.0155
22	1.1824	8.6321	9.3834
23	.4311	9.3834	0.0000

YEARS 24 — MO PAYT .8068 — AN CONST 9.69

#	INT	PRIN	BALANCE
1	8.3237	1.3576	98.6424
2	8.2055	1.4758	97.1666
3	8.0771	1.6042	95.5624
4	7.9374	1.7438	93.8186
5	7.7856	1.8956	91.9230
6	7.6206	2.0606	89.8623
7	7.4413	2.2400	87.6223
8	7.2463	2.4350	85.1874
9	7.0344	2.6469	82.5405
10	6.8040	2.8773	79.6632
11	6.5535	3.1277	76.5355
12	6.2813	3.4000	73.1355
13	5.9854	3.6959	69.4396
14	5.6637	4.0176	65.4220
15	5.3140	4.3673	61.0547
16	4.9338	4.7474	56.3073
17	4.5206	5.1606	51.1467
18	4.0714	5.6098	45.5369
19	3.5832	6.0981	39.4387
20	3.0524	6.6289	32.8099
21	2.4754	7.2059	25.6040
22	1.8482	7.8331	17.7709
23	1.1664	8.5149	9.2560
24	.4252	9.2560	0.0000

YEARS 25 — MO PAYT .7968 — AN CONST 9.57

#	INT	PRIN	BALANCE
1	8.3284	1.2335	98.7665
2	8.2210	1.3408	97.4257
3	8.1043	1.4576	95.9681
4	7.9774	1.5844	94.3837
5	7.8395	1.7223	92.6613
6	7.6896	1.8722	90.7891
7	7.5266	2.0352	88.7539
8	7.3495	2.2124	86.5415
9	7.1569	2.4049	84.1366
10	6.9476	2.6142	81.5224
11	6.7201	2.8418	78.6806
12	6.4727	3.0891	75.5914
13	6.2038	3.3580	72.2334
14	5.9115	3.6503	68.5831
15	5.5938	3.9680	64.6151
16	5.2484	4.3134	60.3016
17	4.8730	4.6889	55.6128
18	4.4649	5.0970	50.5158
19	4.0212	5.5406	44.9752
20	3.5390	6.0229	38.9523
21	3.0147	6.5471	32.4051
22	2.4449	7.1170	25.2882
23	1.8254	7.7365	17.5517
24	1.1520	8.4098	9.1418
25	.4200	9.1418	0.0000

YEARS 26 — MO PAYT .7879 — AN CONST 9.46

#	INT	PRIN	BALANCE
1	8.3326	1.1220	98.8780
2	8.2349	1.2196	97.6584
3	8.1288	1.3258	96.3326
4	8.0134	1.4412	94.8914
5	7.8879	1.5666	93.3247
6	7.7516	1.7030	91.6217
7	7.6033	1.8512	89.7705
8	7.4422	2.0124	87.7581
9	7.2670	2.1875	85.5705
10	7.0766	2.3779	83.1926
11	6.8697	2.5849	80.6077
12	6.6447	2.8099	77.7978
13	6.4001	3.0545	74.7433
14	6.1342	3.3203	71.4230
15	5.8452	3.6094	67.8136
16	5.5311	3.9235	63.8901
17	5.1895	4.2650	59.6251
18	4.8183	4.6363	54.9888
19	4.4148	5.0398	49.9490
20	3.9761	5.4785	44.4705
21	3.4993	5.9553	38.5152
22	2.9809	6.4737	32.0416
23	2.4174	7.0371	25.0044
24	1.8049	7.6497	17.3548
25	1.1391	8.3155	9.0393
26	.4153	9.0393	0.0000

YEARS 27 — MO PAYT .7798 — AN CONST 9.36

#	INT	PRIN	BALANCE
1	8.3364	1.0216	98.9784
2	8.2475	1.1105	97.8679
3	8.1508	1.2072	96.6607
4	8.0457	1.3123	95.3484
5	7.9315	1.4265	93.9219
6	7.8073	1.5506	92.3713
7	7.6724	1.6856	90.6857
8	7.5257	1.8323	88.8534
9	7.3662	1.9918	86.8615
10	7.1928	2.1652	84.6964
11	7.0043	2.3536	82.3427
12	6.7995	2.5585	79.7842
13	6.5768	2.7812	77.0030
14	6.3347	3.0233	73.9797
15	6.0716	3.2864	70.6933
16	5.7855	3.5725	67.1208
17	5.4745	3.8834	63.2374
18	5.1365	4.2215	59.0159
19	4.7691	4.5889	54.4270
20	4.3697	4.9883	49.4387
21	3.9355	5.4225	44.0162
22	3.4635	5.8945	38.1218
23	2.9504	6.4075	31.7142
24	2.3927	6.9652	24.7490
25	1.7865	7.5715	17.1775
26	1.1274	8.2305	8.9469
27	.4110	8.9469	0.0000

YEARS 28 — MO PAYT .7726 — AN CONST 9.28

#	INT	PRIN	BALANCE
1	8.3398	.9311	99.0689
2	8.2588	1.0121	98.0569
3	8.1707	1.1002	96.9567
4	8.0749	1.1959	95.7607
5	7.9708	1.3000	94.4607
6	7.8577	1.4132	93.0475
7	7.7346	1.5362	91.5113
8	7.6009	1.6699	89.8414
9	7.4556	1.8153	88.0261
10	7.2976	1.9733	86.0528
11	7.1258	2.1450	83.9078
12	6.9391	2.3317	81.5761
13	6.7362	2.5347	79.0414
14	6.5155	2.7553	76.2861
15	6.2757	2.9951	73.2909
16	6.0150	3.2558	70.0351
17	5.7316	3.5392	66.4959
18	5.4236	3.8473	62.6486
19	5.0887	4.1821	58.4665
20	4.7247	4.5462	53.9203
21	4.3290	4.9419	48.9784
22	3.8988	5.3720	43.6064
23	3.4313	5.8396	37.7668
24	2.9230	6.3479	31.4190
25	2.3705	6.9004	24.5186
26	1.7698	7.5010	17.0175
27	1.1169	8.1539	8.8636
28	.4072	8.8636	0.0000

YEARS 29 — MO PAYT .7660 — AN CONST 9.20

#	INT	PRIN	BALANCE
1	8.3429	.8492	99.1508
2	8.2690	.9231	98.2276
3	8.1886	1.0035	97.2241
4	8.1013	1.0908	96.1333
5	8.0063	1.1858	94.9475
6	7.9031	1.2890	93.6585
7	7.7909	1.4012	92.2573
8	7.6690	1.5232	90.7341
9	7.5364	1.6557	89.0784
10	7.3923	1.7999	87.2785
11	7.2356	1.9565	85.3220
12	7.0653	2.1268	83.1952
13	6.8802	2.3119	80.8833
14	6.6790	2.5132	78.3701
15	6.4602	2.7319	75.6382
16	6.2224	2.9697	72.6685
17	5.9639	3.2282	69.4403
18	5.6830	3.5092	65.9312
19	5.3775	3.8146	62.1166
20	5.0455	4.1466	57.9699
21	4.6846	4.5076	53.4624
22	4.2922	4.8999	48.5625
23	3.8657	5.3264	43.2361
24	3.4021	5.7900	37.4461
25	2.8982	6.2940	31.1521
26	2.3503	6.8418	24.3103
27	1.7548	7.4373	16.8730
28	1.1075	8.0847	8.7884
29	.4038	8.7884	0.0000

YEARS 30 — MO PAYT .7601 — AN CONST 9.13

#	INT	PRIN	BALANCE
1	8.3457	.7752	99.2248
2	8.2782	.8426	98.3822
3	8.2049	.9160	97.4662
4	8.1251	.9957	96.4705
5	8.0385	1.0824	95.3881
6	7.9443	1.1766	94.2115
7	7.8419	1.2790	92.9325
8	7.7305	1.3903	91.5421
9	7.6095	1.5114	90.0308
10	7.4780	1.6429	88.3879
11	7.3350	1.7859	86.6020
12	7.1795	1.9413	84.6606
13	7.0105	2.1103	82.5503
14	6.8269	2.2940	80.2563
15	6.6272	2.4937	77.7626
16	6.4101	2.7107	75.0519
17	6.1742	2.9467	72.1052
18	5.9177	3.2032	68.9021
19	5.6389	3.4820	65.4201
20	5.3358	3.7850	61.6351
21	5.0064	4.1145	57.5206
22	4.6483	4.4726	53.0480
23	4.2590	4.8619	48.1860
24	3.8358	5.2851	42.9009
25	3.3757	5.7451	37.1558
26	2.8757	6.2452	30.9107
27	2.3321	6.7888	24.1219
28	1.7412	7.3797	16.7422
29	1.0989	8.0220	8.7202
30	.4006	8.7202	0.0000

YEARS 2 — MO PAYT 4.5410 — AN CONST 54.50

#	INT	PRIN	BALANCE
1	6.5834	47.9085	52.0915
2	2.4005	52.0915	0.0000

YEARS 3 — MO PAYT 3.1521 — AN CONST 37.83

#	INT	PRIN	BALANCE
1	7.2403	30.5852	69.4148
2	4.5699	33.2556	36.1592
3	1.6663	36.1592	0.0000

YEARS 4 — MO PAYT 2.4601 — AN CONST 29.53

#	INT	PRIN	BALANCE
1	7.5676	21.9538	78.0462
2	5.6508	23.8706	54.1756
3	3.5666	25.9547	28.2209
4	1.3005	28.2209	0.0000

YEARS 5 — MO PAYT 2.0468 — AN CONST 24.57

#	INT	PRIN	BALANCE
1	7.7630	16.7990	83.2010
2	6.2963	18.2658	64.9352
3	4.7015	19.8606	45.0746
4	2.9674	21.5946	23.4800
5	1.0820	23.4800	0.0000

YEARS 6 — MO PAYT 1.7729 — AN CONST 21.28

#	INT	PRIN	BALANCE
1	7.8926	13.3825	86.6175
2	6.7241	14.5509	72.0666
3	5.4537	15.8214	56.2453
4	4.0723	17.2027	39.0425
5	2.5703	18.7047	20.3378
6	.9372	20.3378	0.0000

YEARS 7 — MO PAYT 1.5786 — AN CONST 18.95

#	INT	PRIN	BALANCE
1	7.9845	10.9590	89.0410
2	7.0276	11.9159	77.1251
3	5.9872	12.9563	64.1688
4	4.8560	14.0875	50.0813
5	3.6260	15.3175	34.7639
6	2.2886	16.6549	18.1090
7	.8345	18.1090	0.0000

YEARS 8 — MO PAYT 1.4341 — AN CONST 17.21

#	INT	PRIN	BALANCE
1	8.0528	9.1562	90.8438
2	7.2534	9.9556	80.8882
3	6.3842	10.8248	70.0634
4	5.4390	11.7700	58.2934
5	4.4114	12.7976	45.4958
6	3.2940	13.9150	31.5808
7	2.0791	15.1299	16.4509
8	.7581	16.4509	0.0000

YEARS 9 — MO PAYT 1.3227 — AN CONST 15.88

#	INT	PRIN	BALANCE
1	8.1055	7.7669	92.2331
2	7.4274	8.4450	83.7881
3	6.6900	9.1824	74.6057
4	5.8883	9.9841	64.6216
5	5.0166	10.8558	53.7658
6	4.0688	11.8036	41.9622
7	3.0382	12.8342	29.1280
8	1.9176	13.9548	15.1732
9	.6992	15.1732	0.0000

YEARS 10 — MO PAYT 1.2345 — AN CONST 14.82

#	INT	PRIN	BALANCE
1	8.1472	6.6670	93.3330
2	7.5651	7.2491	86.0839
3	6.9322	7.8820	78.2019
4	6.2440	8.5702	69.6318
5	5.4957	9.3185	60.3133
6	4.6821	10.1321	50.1813
7	3.7975	11.0167	39.1646
8	2.8356	11.9786	27.1860
9	1.7898	13.0244	14.1616
10	.6526	14.1616	0.0000

YEARS 11 — MO PAYT 1.1632 — AN CONST 13.96

#	INT	PRIN	BALANCE
1	8.1809	5.7774	94.2226
2	7.6765	6.2818	87.9408
3	7.1280	6.8303	81.1105
4	6.5317	7.4266	73.6839
5	5.8833	8.0751	65.6089
6	5.1782	8.7801	56.8288
7	4.4116	9.5467	47.2821
8	3.5781	10.3802	36.9019
9	2.6718	11.2865	25.6154
10	1.6864	12.2719	13.3434
11	.6149	13.3434	0.0000

YEARS 12 — MO PAYT 1.1045 — AN CONST 13.26

#	INT	PRIN	BALANCE
1	8.2087	5.0454	94.9546
2	7.7682	5.4859	89.4687
3	7.2892	5.9649	83.5039
4	6.7684	6.4857	77.0182
5	6.2021	7.0519	69.9663
6	5.5864	7.6676	62.2987
7	4.9170	8.3371	53.9616
8	4.1890	9.0650	44.8965
9	3.3976	9.8565	35.0400
10	2.5370	10.7171	24.3230
11	1.6013	11.6528	12.6702
12	.5839	12.6702	0.0000

YEARS 13 — MO PAYT 1.0555 — AN CONST 12.67

#	INT	PRIN	BALANCE
1	8.2319	4.4345	95.5655
2	7.8447	4.8216	90.7439
3	7.4237	5.2426	85.5013
4	6.9660	5.7004	79.8009
5	6.4683	6.1981	73.6029
6	5.9271	6.7392	66.8637
7	5.3387	7.3276	59.5360
8	4.6989	7.9674	51.5687
9	4.0033	8.6630	42.9056
10	3.2469	9.4194	33.4862
11	2.4245	10.2418	23.2444
12	1.5303	11.1360	12.1083
13	.5580	12.1083	0.0000

YEARS 14 — MO PAYT 1.0142 — AN CONST 12.17

#	INT	PRIN	BALANCE
1	8.2514	3.9186	96.0814
2	7.9093	4.2607	91.8207
3	7.5373	4.6327	87.1880
4	7.1328	5.0372	82.1509
5	6.6930	5.4770	76.6739
6	6.2148	5.9552	70.7187
7	5.6948	6.4751	64.2436
8	5.1295	7.0405	57.2031
9	4.5148	7.6552	49.5479
10	3.8464	8.3236	41.2243
11	3.1197	9.0503	32.1740
12	2.3295	9.8405	22.3335
13	1.4703	10.6997	11.6339
14	.5361	11.6339	0.0000

YEARS 15 — MO PAYT .9789 — AN CONST 11.75

#	INT	PRIN	BALANCE
1	8.2681	3.4785	96.5215
2	7.9644	3.7823	92.7392
3	7.6342	4.1125	88.6267
4	7.2751	4.4715	84.1552
5	6.8847	4.8620	79.2932
6	6.4602	5.2865	74.0068
7	5.9986	5.7480	68.2587
8	5.4967	6.2499	62.0088
9	4.9511	6.7956	55.2133
10	4.3577	7.3889	47.8244
11	3.7126	8.0340	39.7903
12	3.0112	8.7355	31.0548
13	2.2485	9.4982	21.5567
14	1.4192	10.3275	11.2292
15	.5175	11.2292	0.0000

YEARS 16 — MO PAYT .9485 — AN CONST 11.39

#	INT	PRIN	BALANCE
1	8.2825	3.1000	96.9000
2	8.0118	3.3707	93.5293
3	7.7175	3.6650	89.8643
4	7.3975	3.9850	85.8793
5	7.0496	4.3329	81.5463
6	6.6713	4.7112	76.8351
7	6.2599	5.1226	71.7125
8	5.8127	5.5698	66.1427
9	5.3263	6.0561	60.0865
10	4.7976	6.5849	53.5016
11	4.2226	7.1598	46.3418
12	3.5975	7.7850	38.5568
13	2.9178	8.4647	30.0921
14	2.1788	9.2037	20.8884
15	1.3752	10.0073	10.8811
16	.5014	10.8811	0.0000

YEARS 17 — MO PAYT .9222 — AN CONST 11.07

#	INT	PRIN	BALANCE
1	8.2949	2.7721	97.2279
2	8.0529	3.0141	94.2138
3	7.7897	3.2773	90.9366
4	7.5036	3.5634	87.3732
5	7.1924	3.8745	83.4986
6	6.8541	4.2128	79.2858
7	6.4863	4.5806	74.7052
8	6.0864	4.9806	69.7246
9	5.6515	5.4154	64.3092
10	5.1787	5.8883	58.4209
11	4.6646	6.4024	52.0185
12	4.1056	6.9614	45.0572
13	3.4978	7.5692	37.4880
14	2.8369	8.2300	29.2580
15	2.1184	8.9486	20.3094
16	1.3370	9.7299	10.5794
17	.4875	10.5794	0.0000

YEARS 18 — MO PAYT .8993 — AN CONST 10.80

#	INT	PRIN	BALANCE
1	8.3057	2.4861	97.5139
2	8.0887	2.7032	94.8108
3	7.8527	2.9392	91.8716
4	7.5960	3.1958	88.6758
5	7.3170	3.4748	85.2010
6	7.0136	3.7782	81.4228
7	6.6837	4.1081	77.3147
8	6.3251	4.4668	72.8479
9	5.9351	4.8568	67.9912
10	5.5110	5.2808	62.7104
11	5.0499	5.7419	56.9685
12	4.5486	6.2432	50.7253
13	4.0035	6.7883	43.9370
14	3.4108	7.3810	36.5560
15	2.7664	8.0254	28.5306
16	2.0657	8.7261	19.8044
17	1.3038	9.4880	10.3164
18	.4754	10.3164	0.0000

YEARS 19 — MO PAYT .8792 — AN CONST 10.56

#	INT	PRIN	BALANCE
1	8.3152	2.2353	97.7647
2	8.1201	2.4305	95.3341
3	7.9079	2.6427	92.6914
4	7.6771	2.8735	89.8179
5	7.4262	3.1244	86.6936
6	7.1534	3.3971	83.2964
7	6.8568	3.6937	79.6027
8	6.5343	4.0163	75.5864
9	6.1837	4.3669	71.2195
10	5.8024	4.7482	66.4713
11	5.3878	5.1628	61.3086
12	4.9371	5.6135	55.6951
13	4.4469	6.1036	49.5914
14	3.9140	6.6366	42.9549
15	3.3346	7.2160	35.7389
16	2.7046	7.8460	27.8928
17	2.0195	8.5311	19.3617
18	1.2747	9.2759	10.0858
19	.4648	10.0858	0.0000

YEARS 20 — MO PAYT .8615 — AN CONST 10.34

#	INT	PRIN	BALANCE
1	8.3236	2.0144	97.9856
2	8.1477	2.1903	95.7952
3	7.9565	2.3816	93.4137
4	7.7486	2.5895	90.8242
5	7.5225	2.8156	88.0086
6	7.2766	3.0614	84.9472
7	7.0093	3.3287	81.6185
8	6.7187	3.6193	77.9991
9	6.4027	3.9353	74.0638
10	6.0591	4.2789	69.7849
11	5.6855	4.6525	65.1323
12	5.2793	5.0588	60.0736
13	4.8376	5.5004	54.5731
14	4.3574	5.9807	48.5924
15	3.8352	6.5029	42.0896
16	3.2674	7.0706	35.0189
17	2.6501	7.6880	27.3309
18	1.9788	8.3592	18.9717
19	1.2490	9.0891	9.8826
20	.4554	9.8826	0.0000

YEARS 21 — MO PAYT .8458 — AN CONST 10.16

#	INT	PRIN	BALANCE
1	8.3310	1.8190	98.1810
2	8.1722	1.9778	96.2032
3	7.9995	2.1505	94.0527

#	INT	PRIN	BALANCE
4	7.8118	2.3382	91.7145
5	7.6076	2.5424	89.1721
6	7.3856	2.7644	86.4077
7	7.1443	3.0057	83.4020
8	6.8818	3.2682	80.1339
9	6.5965	3.5535	76.5804
10	6.2862	3.8638	72.7166
11	5.9489	4.2011	68.5155
12	5.5821	4.5679	63.9476
13	5.1833	4.9667	58.9908
14	4.7496	5.4004	53.5804
15	4.2781	5.8719	47.7085
16	3.7654	6.3846	41.3240
17	3.2080	6.9420	34.3819
18	2.6019	7.5481	26.8338
19	1.9428	8.2072	18.6266
20	1.2263	8.9237	9.7029
21	.4471	9.7029	0.0000

YEARS 22 — MO PAYT .8319 — AN CONST 9.99

#	INT	PRIN	BALANCE
1	8.3376	1.6454	98.3546
2	8.1939	1.7890	96.5656
3	8.0377	1.9453	94.6203
4	7.8679	2.1151	92.5052
5	7.6832	2.2998	90.2054
6	7.4824	2.5006	87.7049
7	7.2641	2.7189	84.9860
8	7.0267	2.9563	82.0297
9	6.7686	3.2144	78.8153
10	6.4880	3.4950	75.3203
11	6.1828	3.8002	71.5201
12	5.8510	4.1320	67.3881
13	5.4902	4.4928	62.8954
14	5.0980	4.8850	58.0104
15	4.6715	5.3115	52.6988
16	4.2077	5.7753	46.9235
17	3.7035	6.2795	40.6440
18	3.1552	6.8278	33.8162
19	2.5591	7.4239	26.3923
20	1.9109	8.0721	18.3201
21	1.2061	8.7769	9.5432
22	.4398	9.5432	0.0000

YEARS 23 — MO PAYT .8195 — AN CONST 9.84

#	INT	PRIN	BALANCE
1	8.3435	1.4907	98.5093
2	8.2133	1.6209	96.8884
3	8.0718	1.7624	95.1261
4	7.9179	1.9163	93.2098
5	7.7506	2.0836	91.1262
6	7.5687	2.2655	88.8607
7	7.3709	2.4633	86.3975
8	7.1558	2.6784	83.7191
9	6.9220	2.9122	80.8069
10	6.6677	3.1665	77.6404
11	6.3912	3.4429	74.1975
12	6.0906	3.7435	70.4540
13	5.7638	4.0704	66.3836
14	5.4084	4.4258	61.9578
15	5.0220	4.8122	57.1456
16	4.6018	5.2324	51.9132
17	4.1450	5.6892	46.2241
18	3.6483	6.1859	40.0381
19	3.1082	6.7260	33.3121
20	2.5209	7.3133	25.9988
21	1.8824	7.9518	18.0470
22	1.1881	8.6461	9.4010
23	.4332	9.4010	0.0000

YEARS 24 — MO PAYT .8084 — AN CONST 9.71

#	INT	PRIN	BALANCE
1	8.3487	1.3525	98.6475
2	8.2306	1.4705	97.1770
3	8.1022	1.5989	95.5781
4	7.9626	1.7385	93.8395
5	7.8108	1.8903	91.9492
6	7.6458	2.0554	89.8938
7	7.4663	2.2348	87.6589
8	7.2712	2.4300	85.2290
9	7.0590	2.6421	82.5868
10	6.8284	2.8728	79.7140
11	6.5775	3.1236	76.5904
12	6.3048	3.3964	73.1940
13	6.0083	3.6929	69.5011
14	5.6858	4.0153	65.4858
15	5.3353	4.3659	61.1198
16	4.9541	4.7471	56.3727
17	4.5396	5.1616	51.2111
18	4.0889	5.6122	45.5989
19	3.5989	6.1023	39.4966
20	3.0661	6.6351	32.8616
21	2.4868	7.2144	25.6472
22	1.8569	7.8443	17.8030
23	1.1720	8.5291	9.2738
24	.4274	9.2738	0.0000

YEARS 25 — MO PAYT .7985 — AN CONST 9.59

#	INT	PRIN	BALANCE
1	8.3534	1.2286	98.7714
2	8.2461	1.3358	97.4356
3	8.1295	1.4525	95.9831
4	8.0027	1.5793	94.4038
5	7.8648	1.7172	92.6866
6	7.7149	1.8671	90.8195
7	7.5519	2.0301	88.7894
8	7.3746	2.2074	86.5820
9	7.1819	2.4001	84.1819
10	6.9723	2.6097	81.5722
11	6.7445	2.8375	78.7347
12	6.4967	3.0853	75.6494
13	6.2273	3.3546	72.2948
14	5.9345	3.6475	68.6472
15	5.6160	3.9660	64.6812
16	5.2697	4.3123	60.3689
17	4.8932	4.6888	55.6801
18	4.4838	5.0982	50.5820
19	4.0387	5.5433	45.0387
20	3.5547	6.0273	39.0114
21	3.0285	6.5535	32.4578
22	2.4563	7.1257	25.3321
23	1.8341	7.7479	17.5842
24	1.1576	8.4244	9.1599
25	.4221	9.1599	0.0000

YEARS 26 — MO PAYT .7896 — AN CONST 9.48

#	INT	PRIN	BALANCE
1	8.3576	1.1173	98.8827
2	8.2601	1.2149	97.6679
3	8.1540	1.3209	96.3469
4	8.0387	1.4363	94.9107
5	7.9133	1.5617	93.3490
6	7.7769	1.6980	91.6510
7	7.6287	1.8463	89.8048
8	7.4675	2.0075	87.7973
9	7.2922	2.1827	85.6146
10	7.1016	2.3733	83.2413
11	6.8944	2.5805	80.6608
12	6.6691	2.8058	77.8550
13	6.4241	3.0508	74.8042
14	6.1578	3.3172	71.4870
15	5.8681	3.6068	67.8802
16	5.5532	3.9217	63.9585
17	5.2108	4.2641	59.6944
18	4.8385	4.6364	55.0580
19	4.4337	5.0412	50.0168
20	3.9936	5.4814	44.5355
21	3.5150	5.9599	38.5755
22	2.9946	6.4803	32.0952
23	2.4288	7.0461	25.0491
24	1.8136	7.6613	17.3878
25	1.1447	8.3302	9.0575
26	.4174	9.0575	0.0000

YEARS 27 — MO PAYT .7815 — AN CONST 9.38

#	INT	PRIN	BALANCE
1	8.3614	1.0171	98.9829
2	8.2726	1.1059	97.8769
3	8.1761	1.2025	96.6744
4	8.0711	1.3075	95.3670
5	7.9569	1.4216	93.9453
6	7.8328	1.5458	92.3995
7	7.6978	1.6807	90.7188
8	7.5511	1.8275	88.8913
9	7.3915	1.9870	86.9043
10	7.2180	2.1605	84.7438
11	7.0294	2.3492	82.3946
12	6.8243	2.5543	79.8404
13	6.6013	2.7773	77.0631
14	6.3588	3.0198	74.0433
15	6.0951	3.2834	70.7599
16	5.8085	3.5701	67.1898
17	5.4968	3.8818	63.3080
18	5.1578	4.2207	59.0873
19	4.7893	4.5892	54.4980
20	4.3886	4.9899	49.5081
21	3.9529	5.4256	44.0825
22	3.4792	5.8993	38.1831
23	2.9642	6.4144	31.7687
24	2.4041	6.9744	24.7943
25	1.7952	7.5834	17.2109
26	1.1331	8.2455	8.9654
27	.4131	8.9654	0.0000

YEARS 28 — MO PAYT .7743 — AN CONST 9.30

#	INT	PRIN	BALANCE
1	8.3649	.9268	99.0732
2	8.2839	1.0077	98.0655
3	8.1960	1.0957	96.9698
4	8.1003	1.1913	95.7785
5	7.9963	1.2954	94.4831
6	7.8832	1.4085	93.0746
7	7.7602	1.5314	91.5432
8	7.6265	1.6652	89.8781
9	7.4811	1.8105	88.0675
10	7.3230	1.9686	86.0989
11	7.1511	2.1405	83.9584
12	6.9643	2.3274	81.6310
13	6.7610	2.5306	79.1004
14	6.5401	2.7515	76.3489
15	6.2999	2.9918	73.3571
16	6.0386	3.2530	70.1041
17	5.7546	3.5370	66.5671
18	5.4458	3.8458	62.7213
19	5.1100	4.1816	58.5397
20	4.7449	4.5467	53.9929
21	4.3480	4.9437	49.0492
22	3.9163	5.3753	43.6739
23	3.4470	5.8447	37.8293
24	2.9367	6.3550	31.4743
25	2.3818	6.9098	24.5645
26	1.7785	7.5131	17.0514
27	1.1226	8.1691	8.8823
28	.4093	8.8823	0.0000

YEARS 29 — MO PAYT .7678 — AN CONST 9.22

#	INT	PRIN	BALANCE
1	8.3680	.8452	99.1548
2	8.2942	.9190	98.2359
3	8.2139	.9992	97.2367
4	8.1267	1.0864	96.1503
5	8.0318	1.1813	94.9690
6	7.9287	1.2844	93.6846
7	7.8165	1.3966	92.2880
8	7.6946	1.5185	90.7695
9	7.5620	1.6511	89.1184
10	7.4179	1.7952	87.3232
11	7.2611	1.9520	85.3712
12	7.0907	2.1224	83.2488
13	6.9054	2.3077	80.9411
14	6.7039	2.5092	78.4319
15	6.4848	2.7283	75.7036
16	6.2466	2.9665	72.7371
17	5.9876	3.2255	69.5116
18	5.7060	3.5071	66.0045
19	5.3998	3.8133	62.1912
20	5.0668	4.1463	58.0449
21	4.7048	4.5083	53.5366
22	4.3112	4.9019	48.6347
23	3.8832	5.3299	43.3048
24	3.4179	5.7953	37.5096
25	2.9119	6.3012	31.2083
26	2.3617	6.8514	24.3569
27	1.7635	7.4496	16.9073
28	1.1131	8.1000	8.8073
29	.4059	8.8073	0.0000

YEARS 30 — MO PAYT .7618 — AN CONST 9.15

#	INT	PRIN	BALANCE
1	8.3708	.7713	99.2287
2	8.3034	.8386	98.3901
3	8.2302	.9119	97.4782
4	8.1506	.9915	96.4867
5	8.0640	1.0780	95.4087
6	7.9699	1.1722	94.2365
7	7.8675	1.2745	92.9620
8	7.7563	1.3858	91.5762
9	7.6353	1.5068	90.0694
10	7.5037	1.6383	88.4311
11	7.3607	1.7814	86.6497
12	7.2051	1.9369	84.7128
13	7.0360	2.1060	82.6067
14	6.8521	2.2899	80.3168
15	6.6522	2.4899	77.8270
16	6.4348	2.7072	75.1197
17	6.1984	2.9436	72.1761
18	5.9414	3.2006	68.9755
19	5.6620	3.4801	65.4954
20	5.3581	3.7839	61.7115
21	5.0278	4.1143	57.5972
22	4.6685	4.4735	53.1237
23	4.2780	4.8641	48.2596
24	3.8533	5.2888	42.9708
25	3.3915	5.7506	37.2202
26	2.8894	6.2526	30.9676
27	2.3435	6.7986	24.1690
28	1.7499	7.3921	16.7769
29	1.1045	8.0376	8.7393
30	.4027	8.7393	0.0000

YEARS 2 — MO PAYT 4.5456 — AN CONST 54.55

#	INT	PRIN	BALANCE
1	6.6631	47.8838	52.1162
2	2.4306	52.1162	0.0000

YEARS 3 — MO PAYT 3.1568 — AN CONST 37.89

#	INT	PRIN	BALANCE
1	7.3279	30.5531	69.4469
2	4.6273	33.2538	36.1931
3	1.6880	36.1931	0.0000

YEARS 4 — MO PAYT 2.4648 — AN CONST 29.58

#	INT	PRIN	BALANCE
1	7.6591	21.9188	78.0812
2	5.7217	23.8563	54.2249
3	3.6130	25.9649	28.2600
4	1.3180	28.2600	0.0000

YEARS 5 — MO PAYT 2.0517 — AN CONST 24.62

#	INT	PRIN	BALANCE
1	7.8569	16.7629	83.2371
2	6.3752	18.2446	64.9925
3	4.7626	19.8573	45.1352
4	3.0074	21.6125	23.5228
5	1.0970	23.5228	0.0000

YEARS 6 — MO PAYT 1.7778 — AN CONST 21.34

#	INT	PRIN	BALANCE
1	7.9880	13.3461	86.6539
2	6.8083	14.5257	72.1282
3	5.5244	15.8097	56.3186
4	4.1270	17.2071	39.1115
5	2.6060	18.7280	20.3834
6	.9506	20.3834	0.0000

YEARS 7 — MO PAYT 1.5836 — AN CONST 19.01

#	INT	PRIN	BALANCE
1	8.0810	10.9228	89.0772
2	7.1155	11.8883	77.1889
3	6.0647	12.9391	64.2498
4	4.9210	14.0828	50.1670
5	3.6762	15.3276	34.8394
6	2.3214	16.6824	18.1570
7	.8468	18.1570	0.0000

YEARS 8 — MO PAYT 1.4392 — AN CONST 17.28

#	INT	PRIN	BALANCE
1	8.1501	9.1204	90.8796
2	7.3440	9.9266	80.9530
3	6.4665	10.8040	70.1489
4	5.5116	11.7590	58.3899
5	4.4722	12.7984	45.5915
6	3.3409	13.9297	31.6619
7	2.1096	15.1609	16.5010
8	.7696	16.5010	0.0000

YEARS 9 — MO PAYT 1.3279 — AN CONST 15.94

#	INT	PRIN	BALANCE
1	8.2034	7.7318	92.2682
2	7.5200	8.4153	83.8529
3	6.7761	9.1591	74.6938
4	5.9665	9.9687	64.7251
5	5.0854	10.8498	53.8753
6	4.1264	11.8088	42.0665
7	3.0826	12.8526	29.2139
8	1.9465	13.9887	15.2252
9	.7101	15.2252	0.0000

YEARS 10 — MO PAYT 1.2399 — AN CONST 14.88

#	INT	PRIN	BALANCE
1	8.2456	6.6327	93.3673
2	7.6593	7.2190	86.1483
3	7.0212	7.8571	78.2912
4	6.3267	8.5516	69.7396
5	5.5708	9.3075	60.4321
6	4.7481	10.1302	50.3019
7	3.8527	11.0256	39.2763
8	2.8781	12.0002	27.2762
9	1.8174	13.0609	14.2153
10	.6630	14.2153	0.0000

YEARS 11 — MO PAYT 1.1686 — AN CONST 14.03

#	INT	PRIN	BALANCE
1	8.2796	5.7440	94.2560
2	7.7719	6.2517	88.0042
3	7.2193	6.8043	81.1999
4	6.6179	7.4058	73.7941
5	5.9633	8.0604	65.7337
6	5.2508	8.7729	56.9609
7	4.4754	9.5483	47.4126
8	3.6314	10.3923	37.0203
9	2.7128	11.3109	25.7094
10	1.7130	12.3106	13.3988
11	.6249	13.3988	0.0000

YEARS 12 — MO PAYT 1.1101 — AN CONST 13.33

#	INT	PRIN	BALANCE
1	8.3077	5.0130	94.9870
2	7.8646	5.4561	89.5309
3	7.3823	5.9383	83.5926
4	6.8574	6.4632	77.1294
5	6.2861	7.0345	70.0948
6	5.6643	7.6563	62.4385
7	4.9876	8.3331	54.1054
8	4.2510	9.0696	45.0358
9	3.4494	9.8713	35.1645
10	2.5768	10.7438	24.4206
11	1.6272	11.6935	12.7271
12	.5936	12.7271	0.0000

YEARS 13 — MO PAYT 1.0612 — AN CONST 12.74

#	INT	PRIN	BALANCE
1	8.3311	4.4031	95.5969
2	7.9419	4.7923	90.8047
3	7.5183	5.2158	85.5888
4	7.0573	5.6769	79.9120
5	6.5555	6.1787	73.7333
6	6.0093	6.7248	67.0085
7	5.4149	7.3192	59.6893
8	4.7680	7.9662	51.7231
9	4.0639	8.6703	43.0528
10	3.2975	9.4367	33.6162
11	2.4634	10.2708	23.3454
12	1.5555	11.1786	12.1667
13	.5674	12.1667	0.0000

YEARS 14 — MO PAYT 1.0199 — AN CONST 12.24

#	INT	PRIN	BALANCE
1	8.3508	3.8882	96.1118
2	8.0072	4.2319	91.8800
3	7.6331	4.6059	87.2740
4	7.2260	5.0130	82.2610
5	6.7829	5.4562	76.8048
6	6.3006	5.9384	70.8664
7	5.7757	6.4633	64.4031
8	5.2044	7.0346	57.3685
9	4.5826	7.6564	49.7120
10	3.9058	8.3332	41.3789
11	3.1693	9.0698	32.3091
12	2.3676	9.8714	22.4377
13	1.4950	10.7440	11.6937
14	.5454	11.6937	0.0000

YEARS 15 — MO PAYT .9847 — AN CONST 11.82

#	INT	PRIN	BALANCE
1	8.3677	3.4492	96.5508
2	8.0628	3.7541	92.7967
3	7.7310	4.0859	88.7108
4	7.3698	4.4471	84.2638
5	6.9767	4.8401	79.4236
6	6.5489	5.2680	74.1557
7	6.0833	5.7336	68.4221
8	5.5765	6.2404	62.1817
9	5.0249	6.7920	55.3897
10	4.4245	7.3923	47.9974
11	3.7711	8.0458	39.9516
12	3.0599	8.7569	31.1947
13	2.2859	9.5310	21.6637
14	1.4435	10.3734	11.2903
15	.5266	11.2903	0.0000

YEARS 16 — MO PAYT .9545 — AN CONST 11.46

#	INT	PRIN	BALANCE
1	8.3822	3.0717	96.9283
2	8.1106	3.3432	93.5850
3	7.8151	3.6388	89.9463
4	7.4935	3.9604	85.9859
5	7.1434	4.3105	81.6754
6	6.7624	4.6915	76.9840
7	6.3478	5.1061	71.8778
8	5.8964	5.5575	66.3203
9	5.4052	6.0487	60.2716
10	4.8705	6.5834	53.6883
11	4.2886	7.1653	46.5230
12	3.6553	7.7986	38.7244
13	2.9660	8.4879	30.2365
14	2.2157	9.2382	20.9983
15	1.3991	10.0548	10.9435
16	.5104	10.9435	0.0000

YEARS 17 — MO PAYT .9283 — AN CONST 11.14

#	INT	PRIN	BALANCE
1	8.3947	2.7448	97.2552
2	8.1521	2.9874	94.2678
3	7.8880	3.2515	91.0163
4	7.6006	3.5389	87.4774
5	7.2878	3.8517	83.6257
6	6.9474	4.1921	79.4336
7	6.5768	4.5627	74.8709
8	6.1735	4.9660	69.9049
9	5.7346	5.4049	64.5000
10	5.2568	5.8827	58.6173
11	4.7368	6.4027	52.2146
12	4.1709	6.9686	45.2461
13	3.5550	7.5846	37.6615
14	2.8845	8.2550	29.4065
15	2.1549	8.9846	20.4219
16	1.3607	9.7788	10.6431
17	.4964	10.6431	0.0000

YEARS 18 — MO PAYT .9055 — AN CONST 10.87

#	INT	PRIN	BALANCE
1	8.4056	2.4599	97.5401
2	8.1882	2.6773	94.8629
3	7.9516	2.9139	91.9489
4	7.6940	3.1715	88.7774
5	7.4137	3.4518	85.3256
6	7.1085	3.7569	81.5687
7	6.7765	4.0890	77.4796
8	6.4150	4.4505	73.0292
9	6.0217	4.8438	68.1854
10	5.5935	5.2720	62.9134
11	5.1275	5.7380	57.1754
12	4.6203	6.2452	50.9302
13	4.0683	6.7972	44.1331
14	3.4675	7.3980	36.7351
15	2.8136	8.0519	28.6832
16	2.1019	8.7636	19.9196
17	1.3273	9.5382	10.3813
18	.4842	10.3813	0.0000

YEARS 19 — MO PAYT .8854 — AN CONST 10.63

#	INT	PRIN	BALANCE
1	8.4152	2.2101	97.7899
2	8.2199	2.4055	95.3844
3	8.0072	2.6181	92.7663
4	7.7758	2.8495	89.9167
5	7.5239	3.1014	86.8153
6	7.2498	3.3755	83.4398
7	6.9514	3.6739	79.7659
8	6.6267	3.9986	75.7672
9	6.2733	4.3521	71.4151
10	5.8886	4.7368	66.6784
11	5.4699	5.1555	61.5229
12	5.0142	5.6112	55.9118
13	4.5182	6.1071	49.8046
14	3.9784	6.6469	43.1577
15	3.3909	7.2345	35.9232
16	2.7514	7.8739	28.0492
17	2.0554	8.5699	19.4793
18	1.2979	9.3274	10.1519
19	.4735	10.1519	0.0000

YEARS 20 — MO PAYT .8678 — AN CONST 10.42

#	INT	PRIN	BALANCE
1	8.4236	1.9902	98.0098
2	8.2477	2.1661	95.8436
3	8.0563	2.3576	93.4860
4	7.8479	2.5660	90.9200
5	7.6211	2.7928	88.1272
6	7.3742	3.0397	85.0875
7	7.1055	3.3084	81.7791
8	6.8131	3.6008	78.1784
9	6.4948	3.9191	74.2593
10	6.1484	4.2655	69.9938
11	5.7714	4.6425	65.3513
12	5.3610	5.0529	60.2985
13	4.9144	5.4995	54.7990
14	4.4283	5.9856	48.8134
15	3.8992	6.5147	42.2987
16	3.3234	7.0905	35.2082
17	2.6966	7.7172	27.4910
18	2.0145	8.3994	19.0916
19	1.2721	9.1418	9.9498
20	.4640	9.9498	0.0000

YEARS 21 — MO PAYT .8522 — AN CONST 10.23

#	INT	PRIN	BALANCE
1	8.4311	1.7958	98.2042
2	8.2724	1.9545	96.2498
3	8.0996	2.1272	94.1225

#	INT	PRIN	BALANCE
4	7.9116	2.3153	91.8072
5	7.7069	2.5199	89.2873
6	7.4842	2.7427	86.5446
7	7.2418	2.9851	83.5595
8	6.9779	3.2489	80.3106
9	6.6907	3.5361	76.7745
10	6.3782	3.8487	72.9258
11	6.0380	4.1889	68.7369
12	5.6677	4.5591	64.1778
13	5.2648	4.9621	59.2156
14	4.8261	5.4007	53.8149
15	4.3488	5.8781	47.9368
16	3.8292	6.3977	41.5391
17	3.2637	6.9632	34.5760
18	2.6482	7.5786	26.9973
19	1.9783	8.2485	18.7488
20	1.2492	8.9776	9.7712
21	.4557	9.7712	0.0000

YEARS 22 — MO PAYT .8384 — AN CONST 10.07

#	INT	PRIN	BALANCE
1	8.4377	1.6231	98.3769
2	8.2943	1.7666	96.6102
3	8.1381	1.9228	94.6875
4	7.9682	2.0927	92.5948
5	7.7832	2.2777	90.3171
6	7.5818	2.4790	87.8380
7	7.3627	2.6981	85.1399
8	7.1242	2.9366	82.2032
9	6.8647	3.1962	79.0070
10	6.5821	3.4787	75.5283
11	6.2747	3.7862	71.7421
12	5.9400	4.1209	67.6212
13	5.5757	4.4851	63.1361
14	5.1793	4.8816	58.2545
15	4.7478	5.3131	52.9414
16	4.2782	5.7827	47.1587
17	3.7670	6.2938	40.8649
18	3.2107	6.8501	34.0148
19	2.6052	7.4556	26.5591
20	1.9462	8.1146	18.4445
21	1.2290	8.8319	9.6126
22	.4483	9.6126	0.0000

YEARS 23 — MO PAYT .8261 — AN CONST 9.92

#	INT	PRIN	BALANCE
1	8.4436	1.4694	98.5306
2	8.3137	1.5993	96.9313
3	8.1724	1.7407	95.1906
4	8.0185	1.8945	93.2961
5	7.8511	2.0620	91.2342
6	7.6688	2.2442	88.9899
7	7.4704	2.4426	86.5473
8	7.2545	2.6585	83.8888
9	7.0195	2.8935	80.9953
10	6.7638	3.1492	77.8461
11	6.4854	3.4276	74.4185
12	6.1825	3.7306	70.6879
13	5.8527	4.0603	66.6276
14	5.4938	4.4192	62.2083
15	5.1032	4.8098	57.3985
16	4.6780	5.2350	52.1635
17	4.2153	5.6977	46.4658
18	3.7117	6.2013	40.2644
19	3.1635	6.7495	33.5149
20	2.5670	7.3461	26.1689
21	1.9176	7.9954	18.1735
22	1.2109	8.7021	9.4713
23	.4417	9.4713	0.0000

YEARS 24 — MO PAYT .8151 — AN CONST 9.79

#	INT	PRIN	BALANCE
1	8.4489	1.3321	98.6679
2	8.3312	1.4498	97.2181
3	8.2030	1.5780	95.6401
4	8.0635	1.7175	93.9226
5	7.9117	1.8693	92.0533
6	7.7465	2.0345	90.0188
7	7.5667	2.2143	87.8045
8	7.3709	2.4101	85.3944
9	7.1579	2.6231	82.7714
10	6.9260	2.8549	79.9164
11	6.6737	3.1073	76.8091
12	6.3990	3.3820	73.4272
13	6.1001	3.6809	69.7463
14	5.7747	4.0062	65.7400
15	5.4206	4.3604	61.3797
16	5.0352	4.7458	56.6339
17	4.6157	5.1653	51.4686
18	4.1592	5.6218	45.8468
19	3.6622	6.1187	39.7281
20	3.1214	6.6596	33.0685
21	2.5328	7.2482	25.8203
22	1.8921	7.8889	17.9314
23	1.1948	8.5862	9.3452
24	.4358	9.3452	0.0000

YEARS 25 — MO PAYT .8052 — AN CONST 9.67

#	INT	PRIN	BALANCE
1	8.4536	1.2091	98.7909
2	8.3467	1.3160	97.4749
3	8.2304	1.4323	96.0426
4	8.1038	1.5589	94.4837
5	7.9660	1.6967	92.7870
6	7.8161	1.8467	90.9403
7	7.6528	2.0099	88.9304
8	7.4752	2.1876	86.7429
9	7.2818	2.3809	84.3619
10	7.0714	2.5914	81.7706
11	6.8423	2.8204	78.9501
12	6.5930	3.0697	75.8804
13	6.3217	3.3411	72.5393
14	6.0263	3.6364	68.9030
15	5.7049	3.9578	64.9452
16	5.3551	4.3076	60.6375
17	4.9743	4.6884	55.9491
18	4.5599	5.1028	50.8463
19	4.1089	5.5538	45.2925
20	3.6180	6.0448	39.2477
21	3.0837	6.5791	32.6687
22	2.5021	7.1606	25.5081
23	1.8692	7.7935	17.7146
24	1.1803	8.4824	9.2322
25	.4306	9.2322	0.0000

YEARS 26 — MO PAYT .7964 — AN CONST 9.56

#	INT	PRIN	BALANCE
1	8.4579	1.0987	98.9013
2	8.3607	1.1958	97.7055
3	8.2550	1.3015	96.4039
4	8.1400	1.4166	94.9874
5	8.0148	1.5418	93.4456
6	7.8785	1.6781	91.7675
7	7.7302	1.8264	89.9411
8	7.5687	1.9878	87.9533
9	7.3930	2.1635	85.7898
10	7.2018	2.3548	83.4350
11	6.9937	2.5629	80.8721
12	6.7671	2.7894	78.0827
13	6.5206	3.0360	75.0467
14	6.2522	3.3044	71.7424
15	5.9601	3.5964	68.1459
16	5.6422	3.9143	64.2316
17	5.2962	4.2603	59.9713
18	4.9197	4.6369	55.3344
19	4.5098	5.0467	50.2877
20	4.0637	5.4928	44.7948
21	3.5782	5.9783	38.8165
22	3.0498	6.5068	32.3097
23	2.4746	7.0819	25.2278
24	1.8487	7.7079	17.5199
25	1.1674	8.3892	9.1307
26	.4258	9.1307	0.0000

YEARS 27 — MO PAYT .7884 — AN CONST 9.47

#	INT	PRIN	BALANCE
1	8.4617	.9994	99.0006
2	8.3733	1.0877	97.9129
3	8.2772	1.1839	96.7290
4	8.1725	1.2885	95.4405
5	8.0586	1.4024	94.0381
6	7.9347	1.5264	92.5117
7	7.7998	1.6613	90.8504
8	7.6529	1.8081	89.0423
9	7.4931	1.9680	87.0743
10	7.3191	2.1419	84.9324
11	7.1298	2.3312	82.6012
12	6.9238	2.5373	80.0639
13	6.6995	2.7616	77.3024
14	6.4554	3.0057	74.2967
15	6.1897	3.2713	71.0254
16	5.9006	3.5605	67.4649
17	5.5859	3.8752	63.5897
18	5.2433	4.2177	59.3719
19	4.8705	4.5905	54.7814
20	4.4647	4.9963	49.7851
21	4.0231	5.4379	44.3472
22	3.5425	5.9186	38.4286
23	3.0193	6.4417	31.9868
24	2.4499	7.0111	24.9757
25	1.8302	7.6309	17.3448
26	1.1557	8.3054	9.0395
27	.4216	9.0395	0.0000

YEARS 28 — MO PAYT .7812 — AN CONST 9.38

#	INT	PRIN	BALANCE
1	8.4651	.9099	99.0901
2	8.3847	.9903	98.0998
3	8.2971	1.0778	97.0220
4	8.2019	1.1731	95.8489
5	8.0982	1.2768	94.5721
6	7.9853	1.3897	93.1824
7	7.8625	1.5125	91.6700
8	7.7288	1.6462	90.0238
9	7.5833	1.7917	88.2321
10	7.4249	1.9500	86.2821
11	7.2526	2.1224	84.1597
12	7.0650	2.3100	81.8496
13	6.8608	2.5142	79.3354
14	6.6385	2.7364	76.5990
15	6.3967	2.9783	73.6207
16	6.1334	3.2416	70.3791
17	5.8469	3.5281	66.8510
18	5.5350	3.8399	63.0111
19	5.1956	4.1794	58.8317
20	4.8262	4.5488	54.2830
21	4.4241	4.9508	49.3321
22	3.9865	5.3885	43.9437
23	3.5102	5.8647	38.0789
24	2.9918	6.3831	31.6958
25	2.4276	6.9473	24.7484
26	1.8135	7.5614	17.1870
27	1.1452	8.2298	8.9572
28	.4177	8.9572	0.0000

YEARS 29 — MO PAYT .7748 — AN CONST 9.30

#	INT	PRIN	BALANCE
1	8.4682	.8291	99.1709
2	8.3949	.9023	98.2686
3	8.3152	.9821	97.2865
4	8.2283	1.0689	96.2176
5	8.1339	1.1634	95.0543
6	8.0310	1.2662	93.7880
7	7.9191	1.3781	92.4099
8	7.7973	1.4999	90.9100
9	7.6647	1.6325	89.2775
10	7.5204	1.7768	87.5006
11	7.3634	1.9339	85.5667
12	7.1924	2.1048	83.4619
13	7.0064	2.2909	81.1711
14	6.8039	2.4934	78.6777
15	6.5835	2.7137	75.9640
16	6.3436	2.9536	73.0103
17	6.0826	3.2147	69.7956
18	5.7984	3.4988	66.2968
19	5.4891	3.8081	62.4887
20	5.1525	4.1447	58.3440
21	4.7862	4.5111	53.8329
22	4.3874	4.9098	48.9231
23	3.9535	5.3438	43.5794
24	3.4811	5.8161	37.7632
25	2.9670	6.3302	31.4330
26	2.4075	6.8897	24.5433
27	1.7985	7.4987	17.0445
28	1.1357	8.1616	8.8830
29	.4143	8.8830	0.0000

YEARS 30 — MO PAYT .7689 — AN CONST 9.23

#	INT	PRIN	BALANCE
1	8.4710	.7560	99.2440
2	8.4042	.8228	98.4213
3	8.3315	.8955	97.5257
4	8.2523	.9747	96.5511
5	8.1661	1.0608	95.4903
6	8.0724	1.1546	94.3357
7	7.9703	1.2566	93.0790
8	7.8593	1.3677	91.7113
9	7.7384	1.4886	90.2227
10	7.6068	1.6202	88.6025
11	7.4636	1.7634	86.8392
12	7.3077	1.9193	84.9199
13	7.1381	2.0889	82.8310
14	6.9534	2.2735	80.5574
15	6.7525	2.4745	78.0829
16	6.5337	2.6932	75.3897
17	6.2957	2.9313	72.4584
18	6.0366	3.1904	69.2680
19	5.7546	3.4724	65.7956
20	5.4476	3.7793	62.0163
21	5.1136	4.1134	57.9029
22	4.7500	4.4770	53.4260
23	4.3543	4.8727	48.5533
24	3.9236	5.3034	43.2499
25	3.4548	5.7722	37.4778
26	2.9446	6.2824	31.1954
27	2.3893	6.8377	24.3577
28	1.7849	7.4421	16.9157
29	1.1271	8.0999	8.8158
30	.4111	8.8158	0.0000

YEARS 2 — MO PAYT 4.5501 — AN CONST 54.61

#	INT	PRIN	BALANCE
1	6.7427	47.8590	52.1410
2	2.4607	52.1410	0.0000

YEARS 3 — MO PAYT 3.1614 — AN CONST 37.94

#	INT	PRIN	BALANCE
1	7.4156	30.5211	69.4789
2	4.6848	33.2519	36.2270
3	1.7097	36.2270	0.0000

YEARS 4 — MO PAYT 2.4696 — AN CONST 29.64

#	INT	PRIN	BALANCE
1	7.7508	21.8839	78.1161
2	5.7928	23.8419	54.2742
3	3.6596	25.9751	28.2991
4	1.3355	28.2991	0.0000

YEARS 5 — MO PAYT 2.0565 — AN CONST 24.68

#	INT	PRIN	BALANCE
1	7.9509	16.7268	83.2732
2	6.4543	18.2234	65.0498
3	4.8238	19.8539	45.1959
4	3.0474	21.6303	23.5656
5	1.1121	23.5656	0.0000

YEARS 6 — MO PAYT 1.7828 — AN CONST 21.40

#	INT	PRIN	BALANCE
1	8.0835	13.3097	86.6903
2	6.8926	14.5005	72.1898
3	5.5953	15.7979	56.3918
4	4.1818	17.2114	39.1804
5	2.6418	18.7514	20.4291
6	.9641	20.4291	0.0000

YEARS 7 — MO PAYT 1.5887 — AN CONST 19.07

#	INT	PRIN	BALANCE
1	8.1775	10.8867	89.1133
2	7.2035	11.8607	77.2526
3	6.1423	12.9219	64.3307
4	4.9861	14.0781	50.2526
5	3.7265	15.3377	34.9150
6	2.3542	16.7100	18.2050
7	.8592	18.2050	0.0000

YEARS 8 — MO PAYT 1.4444 — AN CONST 17.34

#	INT	PRIN	BALANCE
1	8.2474	9.0848	90.9152
2	7.4346	9.8976	81.0176
3	6.5490	10.7832	70.2344
4	5.5843	11.7480	58.4864
5	4.5331	12.7991	45.6873
6	3.3880	13.9443	31.7430
7	2.1404	15.1919	16.5511
8	.7811	16.5511	0.0000

YEARS 9 — MO PAYT 1.3332 — AN CONST 16.00

#	INT	PRIN	BALANCE
1	8.3013	7.6969	92.3031
2	7.6127	8.3855	83.9176
3	6.8624	9.1358	74.7817
4	6.0450	9.9532	64.8285
5	5.1544	10.8438	53.9848
6	4.1842	11.8140	42.1708
7	3.1272	12.8710	29.2998
8	1.9756	14.0226	15.2772
9	.7210	15.2772	0.0000

YEARS 10 — MO PAYT 1.2452 — AN CONST 14.95

#	INT	PRIN	BALANCE
1	8.3439	6.5986	93.4014
2	7.7535	7.1890	86.2124
3	7.1103	7.8322	78.3802
4	6.4096	8.5330	69.8472
5	5.6461	9.2964	60.5507
6	4.8143	10.1282	50.4225
7	3.9081	11.0344	39.3881
8	2.9209	12.0217	27.3664
9	1.8452	13.0973	14.2691
10	.6734	14.2691	0.0000

YEARS 11 — MO PAYT 1.1741 — AN CONST 14.09

#	INT	PRIN	BALANCE
1	8.3784	5.7108	94.2892
2	7.8674	6.2218	88.0674
3	7.3107	6.7785	81.2890
4	6.7043	7.3849	73.9040
5	6.0435	8.0457	65.8583
6	5.3237	8.7655	57.0928
7	4.5394	9.5498	47.5430
8	3.6849	10.4043	37.1387
9	2.7540	11.3351	25.8036
10	1.7399	12.3493	13.4542
11	.6349	13.4542	0.0000

YEARS 12 — MO PAYT 1.1156 — AN CONST 13.39

#	INT	PRIN	BALANCE
1	8.4067	4.9807	95.0193
2	7.9611	5.4264	89.5929
3	7.4756	5.9119	83.6810
4	6.9466	6.4408	77.2402
5	6.3703	7.0171	70.2231
6	5.7425	7.6449	62.5781
7	5.0585	8.3290	54.2492
8	4.3133	9.0742	45.1750
9	3.5014	9.8860	35.2889
10	2.6169	10.7706	24.5184
11	1.6532	11.7342	12.7841
12	.6033	12.7841	0.0000

YEARS 13 — MO PAYT 1.0668 — AN CONST 12.81

#	INT	PRIN	BALANCE
1	8.4303	4.3718	95.6282
2	8.0392	4.7630	90.8652
3	7.6130	5.1891	85.6760
4	7.1487	5.6534	80.0226
5	6.6429	6.1593	73.8634
6	6.0918	6.7103	67.1530
7	5.4915	7.3107	59.8423
8	4.8373	7.9648	51.8775
9	4.1247	8.6775	43.2000
10	3.3483	9.4538	33.7462
11	2.5025	10.2997	23.4465
12	1.5809	11.2212	12.2252
13	.5769	12.2252	0.0000

YEARS 14 — MO PAYT 1.0257 — AN CONST 12.31

#	INT	PRIN	BALANCE
1	8.4503	3.8580	96.1420
2	8.1051	4.2032	91.9388
3	7.7290	4.5792	87.3596
4	7.3193	4.9889	82.3707
5	6.8729	5.4353	76.9353
6	6.3866	5.9216	71.0137
7	5.8568	6.4514	64.5623
8	5.2796	7.0287	57.5336
9	4.6507	7.6575	49.8760
10	3.9656	8.3427	41.5334
11	3.2191	9.0891	32.4442
12	2.4059	9.9023	22.5419
13	1.5199	10.7883	11.7536
14	.5547	11.7536	0.0000

YEARS 15 — MO PAYT .9906 — AN CONST 11.89

#	INT	PRIN	BALANCE
1	8.4673	3.4200	96.5800
2	8.1613	3.7260	92.8539
3	7.8279	4.0594	88.7945
4	7.4647	4.4226	84.3719
5	7.0690	4.8183	79.5536
6	6.6379	5.2494	74.3041
7	6.1682	5.7191	68.5850
8	5.6565	6.2308	62.3542
9	5.0990	6.7883	55.5659
10	4.4917	7.3957	48.1703
11	3.8300	8.0574	40.1129
12	3.1091	8.7783	31.3346
13	2.3236	9.5637	21.7710
14	1.4680	10.4194	11.3516
15	.5357	11.3516	0.0000

YEARS 16 — MO PAYT .9605 — AN CONST 11.53

#	INT	PRIN	BALANCE
1	8.4819	3.0436	96.9564
2	8.2096	3.3159	93.6404
3	7.9129	3.6126	90.0278
4	7.5897	3.9359	86.0919
5	7.2375	4.2880	81.8039
6	6.8538	4.6717	77.1322
7	6.4359	5.0897	72.0426
8	5.9805	5.5450	66.4975
9	5.4844	6.0412	60.4564
10	4.9438	6.5817	53.8747
11	4.3550	7.1706	46.7041
12	3.7134	7.8121	38.8920
13	3.0144	8.5111	30.3809
14	2.2529	9.2726	21.1083
15	1.4233	10.1022	11.0061
16	.5194	11.0061	0.0000

YEARS 17 — MO PAYT .9344 — AN CONST 11.22

#	INT	PRIN	BALANCE
1	8.4945	2.7177	97.2823
2	8.2514	2.9609	94.3213
3	7.9865	3.2258	91.0955
4	7.6978	3.5145	87.5811
5	7.3834	3.8289	83.7522
6	7.0408	4.1715	79.5807
7	6.6676	4.5447	75.0360
8	6.2609	4.9513	70.0846
9	5.8179	5.3943	64.6903
10	5.3353	5.8770	58.8133
11	4.8095	6.4028	52.4105
12	4.2366	6.9757	45.4348
13	3.6125	7.5998	37.8350
14	2.9323	8.2798	29.5553
15	2.1917	9.0206	20.5347
16	1.3846	9.8277	10.7070
17	.5053	10.7070	0.0000

YEARS 18 — MO PAYT .9116 — AN CONST 10.94

#	INT	PRIN	BALANCE
1	8.5056	2.4338	97.5662
2	8.2878	2.6516	94.9146
3	8.0505	2.8888	92.0257
4	7.7921	3.1473	88.8784
5	7.5105	3.4289	85.4495
6	7.2037	3.7357	81.7138
7	6.8694	4.0699	77.6438
8	6.5053	4.4341	73.2097
9	6.1086	4.8308	68.3789
10	5.6763	5.2630	63.1159
11	5.2054	5.7339	57.3819
12	4.6924	6.2470	51.1349
13	4.1335	6.8059	44.3290
14	3.5245	7.4148	36.9142
15	2.8611	8.0783	28.8359
16	2.1383	8.8010	20.0349
17	1.3509	9.5885	10.4464
18	.4930	10.4464	0.0000

YEARS 19 — MO PAYT .8917 — AN CONST 10.71

#	INT	PRIN	BALANCE
1	8.5152	2.1851	97.8149
2	8.3197	2.3807	95.4342
3	8.1067	2.5937	92.8405
4	7.8746	2.8257	90.0148
5	7.6218	3.0785	86.9363
6	7.3464	3.3540	83.5823
7	7.0463	3.6541	79.9282
8	6.7193	3.9810	75.9472
9	6.3631	4.3372	71.6100
10	5.9751	4.7253	66.8847
11	5.5523	5.1480	61.7367
12	5.0917	5.6086	56.1280
13	4.5899	6.1105	50.0176
14	4.0432	6.6572	43.3604
15	3.4475	7.2528	36.1076
16	2.7986	7.9017	28.2058
17	2.0916	8.6087	19.5971
18	1.3214	9.3790	10.2181
19	.4822	10.2181	0.0000

YEARS 20 — MO PAYT .8742 — AN CONST 10.49

#	INT	PRIN	BALANCE
1	8.5237	1.9663	98.0337
2	8.3478	2.1422	95.8916
3	8.1561	2.3338	93.5577
4	7.9473	2.5427	91.0150
5	7.7198	2.7702	88.2449
6	7.4719	3.0180	85.2269
7	7.2019	3.2880	81.9388
8	6.9077	3.5822	78.3566
9	6.5872	3.9027	74.4539
10	6.2380	4.2519	70.2019
11	5.8576	4.6324	65.5696
12	5.4431	5.0468	60.5228
13	4.9916	5.4984	55.0244
14	4.4996	5.9903	49.0341
15	3.9637	6.5263	42.5078
16	3.3797	7.1102	35.3976
17	2.7436	7.7464	27.6512
18	2.0505	8.4395	19.2118
19	1.2954	9.1946	10.0172
20	.4727	10.0172	0.0000

YEARS 21 — MO PAYT .8587 — AN CONST 10.31

#	INT	PRIN	BALANCE
1	8.5312	1.7728	98.2272
2	8.3726	1.9314	96.2958
3	8.1998	2.1042	94.1916

#	INT	PRIN	BALANCE
4	8.0115	2.2925	91.8991
5	7.8064	2.4976	89.4015
6	7.5829	2.7211	86.6805
7	7.3395	2.9645	83.7160
8	7.0742	3.2298	80.4862
9	6.7853	3.5187	76.9675
10	6.4704	3.8336	73.1340
11	6.1274	4.1765	68.9574
12	5.7538	4.5502	64.4072
13	5.3466	4.9573	59.4498
14	4.9031	5.4009	54.0489
15	4.4199	5.8841	48.1648
16	3.8934	6.4106	41.7542
17	3.3198	6.9842	34.7701
18	2.6949	7.6090	27.1610
19	2.0141	8.2898	18.8712
20	1.2724	9.0316	9.8396
21	.4644	9.8396	0.0000

YEARS 22 — MO PAYT .8449 — AN CONST 10.14

#	INT	PRIN	BALANCE
1	8.5379	1.6011	98.3989
2	8.3946	1.7444	96.6545
3	8.2385	1.9005	94.7540
4	8.0685	2.0705	92.6835
5	7.8832	2.2558	90.4277
6	7.6814	2.4576	87.9701
7	7.4615	2.6775	85.2926
8	7.2220	2.9170	82.3756
9	6.9610	3.1780	79.1975
10	6.6766	3.4624	75.7352
11	6.3668	3.7722	71.9630
12	6.0293	4.1097	67.8533
13	5.6616	4.4774	63.3759
14	5.2610	4.8780	58.4980
15	4.8246	5.3144	53.1835
16	4.3491	5.7899	47.3936
17	3.8311	6.3079	41.0857
18	3.2667	6.8723	34.2134
19	2.6518	7.4872	26.7261
20	1.9819	8.1571	18.5690
21	1.2521	8.8869	9.6821
22	.4569	9.6821	0.0000

YEARS 23 — MO PAYT .8327 — AN CONST 10.00

#	INT	PRIN	BALANCE
1	8.5438	1.4484	98.5516
2	8.4142	1.5780	96.9737
3	8.2730	1.7191	95.2545
4	8.1192	1.8729	93.3816
5	7.9516	2.0405	91.3411
6	7.7691	2.2231	89.1180
7	7.5702	2.4220	86.6960
8	7.3535	2.6387	84.0573
9	7.1174	2.8748	81.1825
10	6.8601	3.1320	78.0505
11	6.5799	3.4122	74.6382
12	6.2746	3.7175	70.9207
13	5.9420	4.0502	66.8705
14	5.5796	4.4125	62.4580
15	5.1848	4.8073	57.6507
16	4.7547	5.2374	52.4132
17	4.2861	5.7061	46.7072
18	3.7756	6.2166	40.4906
19	3.2194	6.7728	33.7178
20	2.6134	7.3788	26.3390
21	1.9532	8.0390	18.3001
22	1.2339	8.7582	9.5418
23	.4503	9.5418	0.0000

YEARS 24 — MO PAYT .8218 — AN CONST 9.87

#	INT	PRIN	BALANCE
1	8.5491	1.3120	98.6880
2	8.4317	1.4294	97.2587
3	8.3038	1.5572	95.7014
4	8.1645	1.6966	94.0048
5	8.0127	1.8484	92.1565
6	7.8473	2.0138	90.1427
7	7.6671	2.1939	87.9488
8	7.4708	2.3902	85.5585
9	7.2550	2.6041	82.9545
10	7.0240	2.8371	80.1174
11	6.7701	3.0909	77.0265
12	6.4936	3.3675	73.6590
13	6.1923	3.6688	69.9902
14	5.8640	3.9970	65.9932
15	5.5064	4.3546	61.6386
16	5.1168	4.7443	56.8943
17	4.6923	5.1687	51.7256
18	4.2299	5.6312	46.0944
19	3.7260	6.1350	39.9594
20	3.1771	6.6839	33.2754
21	2.5791	7.2820	25.9935
22	1.9276	7.9335	18.0600
23	1.2177	8.6433	9.4167
24	.4444	9.4167	0.0000

YEARS 25 — MO PAYT .8120 — AN CONST 9.75

#	INT	PRIN	BALANCE
1	8.5538	1.1899	98.8101
2	8.4474	1.2964	97.5137
3	8.3314	1.4124	96.1014
4	8.2050	1.5387	94.5627
5	8.0673	1.6764	92.8863
6	7.9173	1.8264	91.0599
7	7.7539	1.9898	89.0701
8	7.5759	2.1678	86.9023
9	7.3819	2.3618	84.5405
10	7.1706	2.5731	81.9674
11	6.9404	2.8033	79.1641
12	6.6896	3.0541	76.1099
13	6.4163	3.3274	72.7825
14	6.1186	3.6251	69.1574
15	5.7943	3.9495	65.2080
16	5.4409	4.3028	60.9051
17	5.0559	4.6878	56.2173
18	4.6365	5.1072	51.1101
19	4.1795	5.5642	45.5459
20	3.6817	6.0620	39.4839
21	3.1393	6.6044	32.8795
22	2.5484	7.1953	25.6842
23	1.9046	7.8391	17.8451
24	1.2032	8.5405	9.3046
25	.4391	9.3046	0.0000

YEARS 26 — MO PAYT .8032 — AN CONST 9.64

#	INT	PRIN	BALANCE
1	8.5581	1.0804	98.9196
2	8.4614	1.1770	97.7426
3	8.3561	1.2824	96.4602
4	8.2414	1.3971	95.0631
5	8.1164	1.5221	93.5410
6	7.9802	1.6583	91.8827
7	7.8318	1.8067	90.0761
8	7.6702	1.9683	88.1078
9	7.4941	2.1444	85.9634
10	7.3022	2.3363	83.6271
11	7.0932	2.5453	81.0818
12	6.8654	2.7730	78.3088
13	6.6173	3.0211	75.2876
14	6.3470	3.2914	71.9962
15	6.0525	3.5859	68.4103
16	5.7317	3.9068	64.5035
17	5.3821	4.2563	60.2471
18	5.0013	4.6372	55.6100
19	4.5864	5.0521	50.5579
20	4.1344	5.5041	45.0539
21	3.6419	5.9965	39.0573
22	3.1054	6.5331	32.5243
23	2.5209	7.1176	25.4067
24	1.8841	7.7544	17.6523
25	1.1902	8.4482	9.2041
26	.4344	9.2041	0.0000

YEARS 27 — MO PAYT .7953 — AN CONST 9.55

#	INT	PRIN	BALANCE
1	8.5619	.9819	99.0181
2	8.4740	1.0698	97.9483
3	8.3783	1.1655	96.7828
4	8.2740	1.2698	95.5130
5	8.1604	1.3834	94.1297
6	8.0367	1.5072	92.6225
7	7.9018	1.6420	90.9805
8	7.7549	1.7889	89.1916
9	7.5948	1.9490	87.2426
10	7.4205	2.1233	85.1193
11	7.2305	2.3133	82.8060
12	7.0235	2.5203	80.2857
13	6.7980	2.7458	77.5399
14	6.5523	2.9915	74.5484
15	6.2847	3.2591	71.2893
16	5.9931	3.5507	67.7385
17	5.6754	3.8684	63.8701
18	5.3293	4.2145	59.6556
19	4.9522	4.5916	55.0639
20	4.5414	5.0024	50.0615
21	4.0938	5.4500	44.6115
22	3.6062	5.9376	38.6738
23	3.0749	6.4689	32.2049
24	2.4961	7.0477	25.1572
25	1.8656	7.6783	17.4790
26	1.1786	8.3653	9.1137
27	.4301	9.1137	0.0000

YEARS 28 — MO PAYT .7882 — AN CONST 9.46

#	INT	PRIN	BALANCE
1	8.5653	.8932	99.1068
2	8.4854	.9731	98.1336
3	8.3983	1.0602	97.0734
4	8.3035	1.1551	95.9183
5	8.2001	1.2584	94.6599
6	8.0875	1.3710	93.2889
7	7.9649	1.4937	91.7952
8	7.8312	1.6273	90.1679
9	7.6856	1.7729	88.3949
10	7.5270	1.9316	86.4634
11	7.3542	2.1044	84.3590
12	7.1659	2.2927	82.0663
13	6.9608	2.4978	79.5685
14	6.7373	2.7213	76.8473
15	6.4938	2.9648	73.8825
16	6.2285	3.2300	70.6525
17	5.9396	3.5190	67.1335
18	5.6247	3.8339	63.2996
19	5.2817	4.1769	59.1227
20	4.9080	4.5506	54.5721
21	4.5008	4.9578	49.6143
22	4.0572	5.4013	44.2130
23	3.5740	5.8846	38.3284
24	3.0474	6.4111	31.9173
25	2.4738	6.9847	24.9325
26	1.8489	7.6097	17.3228
27	1.1680	8.2905	9.0323
28	.4263	9.0323	0.0000

YEARS 29 — MO PAYT .7818 — AN CONST 9.39

#	INT	PRIN	BALANCE
1	8.5684	.8132	99.1868
2	8.4957	.8860	98.3008
3	8.4164	.9652	97.3356
4	8.3301	1.0516	96.2840
5	8.2360	1.1457	95.1383
6	8.1335	1.2482	93.8901
7	8.0218	1.3599	92.5302
8	7.9001	1.4815	91.0487
9	7.7676	1.6141	89.4346
10	7.6231	1.7585	87.6761
11	7.4658	1.9159	85.7602
12	7.2944	2.0873	83.6730
13	7.1076	2.2740	81.3990
14	6.9042	2.4775	78.9215
15	6.6825	2.6991	76.2223
16	6.4410	2.9406	73.2817
17	6.1779	3.2038	70.0779
18	5.8913	3.4904	66.5875
19	5.5790	3.8027	62.7848
20	5.2387	4.1429	58.6419
21	4.8680	4.5136	54.1283
22	4.4642	4.9174	49.2109
23	4.0242	5.3574	43.8534
24	3.5449	5.8368	38.0167
25	3.0227	6.3590	31.6577
26	2.4537	6.9279	24.7298
27	1.8339	7.5478	17.1820
28	1.1585	8.2231	8.9589
29	.4228	8.9589	0.0000

YEARS 30 — MO PAYT .7760 — AN CONST 9.32

#	INT	PRIN	BALANCE
1	8.5712	.7409	99.2591
2	8.5050	.8072	98.4519
3	8.4327	.8794	97.5725
4	8.3541	.9581	96.6144
5	8.2683	1.0438	95.5706
6	8.1749	1.1372	94.4334
7	8.0732	1.2389	93.1945
8	7.9623	1.3498	91.8447
9	7.8416	1.4706	90.3741
10	7.7100	1.6021	88.7720
11	7.5667	1.7455	87.0265
12	7.4105	1.9017	85.1249
13	7.2403	2.0718	83.0530
14	7.0550	2.2572	80.7959
15	6.8530	2.4591	78.3367
16	6.6330	2.6791	75.6576
17	6.3933	2.9189	72.7387
18	6.1321	3.1800	69.5587
19	5.8476	3.4645	66.0942
20	5.5376	3.7745	62.3197
21	5.1999	4.1122	58.2074
22	4.8320	4.4802	53.7273
23	4.4311	4.8810	48.8463
24	3.9944	5.3177	43.5285
25	3.5186	5.7935	37.7350
26	3.0003	6.3119	31.4231
27	2.4355	6.8766	24.5465
28	1.8203	7.4919	17.0547
29	1.1500	8.1622	8.8925
30	.4197	8.8925	0.0000

YEARS 2 — MO PAYT 4.5513 — AN CONST 54.62

#	INT	PRIN	BALANCE
1	6.7627	47.8528	52.1472
2	2.4682	52.1472	0.0000

YEARS 3 — MO PAYT 3.1625 — AN CONST 37.96

#	INT	PRIN	BALANCE
1	7.4375	30.5131	69.4869
2	4.6992	33.2514	36.2355
3	1.7151	36.2355	0.0000

YEARS 4 — MO PAYT 2.4707 — AN CONST 29.65

#	INT	PRIN	BALANCE
1	7.7737	21.8752	78.1248
2	5.8105	23.8383	54.2865
3	3.6712	25.9776	28.3089
4	1.3399	28.3089	0.0000

YEARS 5 — MO PAYT 2.0577 — AN CONST 24.70

#	INT	PRIN	BALANCE
1	7.9744	16.7178	83.2822
2	6.4741	18.2181	65.0641
3	4.8391	19.8531	45.2110
4	3.0575	21.6347	23.5763
5	1.1159	23.5763	0.0000

YEARS 6 — MO PAYT 1.7840 — AN CONST 21.41

#	INT	PRIN	BALANCE
1	8.1074	13.3006	86.6994
2	6.9137	14.4942	72.2051
3	5.6130	15.7950	56.4101
4	4.1955	17.2125	39.1977
5	2.6508	18.7572	20.4405
6	.9675	20.4405	0.0000

YEARS 7 — MO PAYT 1.5899 — AN CONST 19.08

#	INT	PRIN	BALANCE
1	8.2017	10.8776	89.1224
2	7.2255	11.8538	77.2685
3	6.1617	12.9176	64.3509
4	5.0024	14.0769	50.2741
5	3.7391	15.3402	34.9339
6	2.3625	16.7168	18.2170
7	.8623	18.2170	0.0000

YEARS 8 — MO PAYT 1.4456 — AN CONST 17.35

#	INT	PRIN	BALANCE
1	8.2718	9.0759	90.9241
2	7.4573	9.8904	81.0337
3	6.5697	10.7780	70.2557
4	5.6025	11.7452	58.5105
5	4.5484	12.7993	45.7112
6	3.3998	13.9479	31.7633
7	2.1480	15.1996	16.5637
8	.7840	16.5637	0.0000

YEARS 9 — MO PAYT 1.3345 — AN CONST 16.02

#	INT	PRIN	BALANCE
1	8.3258	7.6882	92.3118
2	7.6358	8.3781	83.9337
3	6.8840	9.1300	74.8037
4	6.0646	9.9494	64.8544
5	5.1717	10.8422	54.0121
6	4.1987	11.8152	42.1969
7	3.1384	12.8756	29.3213
8	1.9829	14.0311	15.2902
9	.7237	15.2902	0.0000

YEARS 10 — MO PAYT 1.2466 — AN CONST 14.96

#	INT	PRIN	BALANCE
1	8.3685	6.5901	93.4099
2	7.7771	7.1815	86.2284
3	7.1326	7.8260	78.4024
4	6.4303	8.5283	69.8741
5	5.6649	9.2937	60.5804
6	4.8309	10.1277	50.4527
7	3.9220	11.0366	39.4161
8	2.9316	12.0271	27.3890
9	1.8522	13.1064	14.2826
10	.6760	14.2826	0.0000

YEARS 11 — MO PAYT 1.1755 — AN CONST 14.11

#	INT	PRIN	BALANCE
1	8.4031	5.7025	94.2975
2	7.8913	6.2143	88.0832
3	7.3336	6.7720	81.3112
4	6.7259	7.3797	73.9315
5	6.0636	8.0420	65.8895
6	5.3419	8.7637	57.1258
7	4.5554	9.5502	47.5756
8	3.6984	10.4072	37.1683
9	2.7644	11.3412	25.8271
10	1.7466	12.3590	13.4681
11	.6375	13.4681	0.0000

YEARS 12 — MO PAYT 1.1170 — AN CONST 13.41

#	INT	PRIN	BALANCE
1	8.4315	4.9727	95.0273
2	7.9852	5.4190	89.6083
3	7.4989	5.9053	83.7031
4	6.9689	6.4352	77.2678
5	6.3914	7.0127	70.2551
6	5.7621	7.6421	62.6130
7	5.0763	8.3279	54.2851
8	4.3289	9.0753	45.2098
9	3.5145	9.8897	35.3201
10	2.6269	10.7772	24.5428
11	1.6598	11.7444	12.7984
12	.6058	12.7984	0.0000

YEARS 13 — MO PAYT 1.0683 — AN CONST 12.82

#	INT	PRIN	BALANCE
1	8.4552	4.3641	95.6359
2	8.0635	4.7557	90.8803
3	7.6367	5.1825	85.6978
4	7.1716	5.6476	80.0502
5	6.6648	6.1544	73.8958
6	6.1125	6.7067	67.1891
7	5.5106	7.3086	59.8805
8	4.8547	7.9645	51.9160
9	4.1400	8.6792	43.2368
10	3.3611	9.4581	33.7787
11	2.5123	10.3069	23.4718
12	1.5873	11.2319	12.2399
13	.5793	12.2399	0.0000

YEARS 14 — MO PAYT 1.0271 — AN CONST 12.33

#	INT	PRIN	BALANCE
1	8.4751	3.8505	96.1495
2	8.1296	4.1960	91.9535
3	7.7530	4.5726	87.3809
4	7.3427	4.9829	82.3980
5	6.8955	5.4301	76.9679
6	6.4082	5.9174	71.0505
7	5.8771	6.4485	64.6020
8	5.2984	7.0272	57.5748
9	4.6678	7.6578	49.9170
10	3.9806	8.3450	41.5720
11	3.2317	9.0939	32.4781
12	2.4156	9.9101	22.5680
13	1.5262	10.7994	11.7686
14	.5570	11.7686	0.0000

YEARS 15 — MO PAYT .9921 — AN CONST 11.91

#	INT	PRIN	BALANCE
1	8.4922	3.4128	96.5872
2	8.1859	3.7191	92.8682
3	7.8522	4.0528	88.8153
4	7.4884	4.4165	84.3988
5	7.0921	4.8129	79.5860
6	6.6602	5.2448	74.3412
7	6.1895	5.7155	68.6257
8	5.6766	6.2284	62.3973
9	5.1176	6.7873	55.6099
10	4.5085	7.3965	48.2135
11	3.8447	8.0602	40.1532
12	3.1214	8.7836	31.3696
13	2.3331	9.5718	21.7978
14	1.4741	10.4309	11.3669
15	.5380	11.3669	0.0000

YEARS 16 — MO PAYT .9620 — AN CONST 11.55

#	INT	PRIN	BALANCE
1	8.5068	3.0366	96.9634
2	8.2343	3.3091	93.6542
3	7.9373	3.6061	90.0481
4	7.6137	3.9297	86.1183
5	7.2610	4.2824	81.8359
6	6.8767	4.6667	77.1692
7	6.4579	5.0855	72.0837
8	6.0015	5.5419	66.5418
9	5.5042	6.0393	60.5025
10	4.9622	6.5812	53.9213
11	4.3716	7.1719	46.7494
12	3.7280	7.8155	38.9339
13	3.0266	8.5169	30.4171
14	2.2623	9.2812	21.1359
15	1.4293	10.1141	11.0218
16	.5217	11.0218	0.0000

YEARS 17 — MO PAYT .9359 — AN CONST 11.24

#	INT	PRIN	BALANCE
1	8.5195	2.7110	97.2890
2	8.2762	2.9543	94.3347
3	8.0111	3.2194	91.1152
4	7.7222	3.5084	87.6069
5	7.4073	3.8232	83.7837
6	7.0642	4.1663	79.6174
7	6.6903	4.5402	75.0771
8	6.2829	4.9477	70.1295
9	5.8388	5.3917	64.7378
10	5.3550	5.8755	58.8623
11	4.8277	6.4028	52.4595
12	4.2531	6.9774	45.4820
13	3.6269	7.6036	37.8784
14	2.9445	8.2860	29.5925
15	2.2009	9.0296	20.5629
16	1.3906	9.8399	10.7230
17	.5075	10.7230	0.0000

YEARS 18 — MO PAYT .9132 — AN CONST 10.96

#	INT	PRIN	BALANCE
1	8.5305	2.4274	97.5726
2	8.3127	2.6452	94.9274
3	8.0753	2.8826	92.0448
4	7.8166	3.1413	88.9035
5	7.5347	3.4232	85.4803
6	7.2275	3.7304	81.7499
7	6.8927	4.0652	77.6847
8	6.5279	4.4300	73.2547
9	6.1303	4.8276	68.4272
10	5.6971	5.2608	63.1664
11	5.2250	5.7329	57.4335
12	4.7105	6.2474	51.1861
13	4.1498	6.8081	44.3780
14	3.5389	7.4190	36.9590
15	2.8731	8.0848	28.8741
16	2.1475	8.8104	20.0637
17	1.3568	9.6011	10.4627
18	.4952	10.4627	0.0000

YEARS 19 — MO PAYT .8933 — AN CONST 10.72

#	INT	PRIN	BALANCE
1	8.5402	2.1789	97.8211
2	8.3447	2.3745	95.4466
3	8.1316	2.5876	92.8590
4	7.8993	2.8198	90.0392
5	7.6463	3.0728	86.9664
6	7.3705	3.3486	83.6178
7	7.0700	3.6491	79.9686
8	6.7425	3.9766	75.9920
9	6.3857	4.3335	71.6586
10	5.9968	4.7224	66.9362
11	5.5730	5.1462	61.7900
12	5.1111	5.6080	56.1820
13	4.6079	6.1113	50.0708
14	4.0594	6.6597	43.4110
15	3.4618	7.2574	36.1537
16	2.8105	7.9087	28.2450
17	2.1007	8.6184	19.6266
18	1.3273	9.3919	10.2347
19	.4844	10.2347	0.0000

YEARS 20 — MO PAYT .8758 — AN CONST 10.51

#	INT	PRIN	BALANCE
1	8.5487	1.9603	98.0397
2	8.3728	2.1362	95.9035
3	8.1811	2.3279	93.5755
4	7.9722	2.5368	91.0387
5	7.7445	2.7645	88.2742
6	7.4964	3.0126	85.2616
7	7.2260	3.2830	81.9786
8	6.9314	3.5776	78.4010
9	6.6104	3.8986	74.5024
10	6.2605	4.2485	70.2538
11	5.8792	4.6298	65.6240
12	5.4637	5.0453	60.5788
13	5.0109	5.4981	55.0807
14	4.5175	5.9915	49.0892
15	3.9798	6.5292	42.5600
16	3.3939	7.1151	35.4449
17	2.7554	7.7536	27.6913
18	2.0595	8.4495	19.2418
19	1.3013	9.2077	10.0341
20	.4749	10.0341	0.0000

YEARS 21 — MO PAYT .8603 — AN CONST 10.33

#	INT	PRIN	BALANCE
1	8.5562	1.7671	98.2329
2	8.3976	1.9257	96.3073
3	8.2248	2.0985	94.2088

#	INT	PRIN	BALANCE
4	8.0365	2.2868	91.9220
5	7.8313	2.4920	89.4300
6	7.6076	2.7157	86.7143
7	7.3639	2.9594	83.7549
8	7.0984	3.2250	80.5300
9	6.8089	3.5144	77.0156
10	6.4936	3.8298	73.1859
11	6.1499	4.1734	69.0124
12	5.7753	4.5480	64.4644
13	5.3672	4.9561	59.5083
14	4.9224	5.4009	54.1074
15	4.4377	5.8856	48.2218
16	3.9095	6.4138	41.8080
17	3.3339	6.9894	34.8186
18	2.7067	7.6166	27.2020
19	2.0231	8.3002	18.9018
20	1.2783	9.0450	9.8568
21	.4665	9.8568	0.0000

YEARS 22	MO PAYT .8465	AN CONST 10.16	
#	INT	PRIN	BALANCE
1	8.5629	1.5957	98.4043
2	8.4197	1.7389	96.6654
3	8.2636	1.8949	94.7705
4	8.0936	2.0650	92.7055
5	7.9083	2.2503	90.4552
6	7.7063	2.4523	88.0029
7	7.4863	2.6723	85.3306
8	7.2464	2.9121	82.4185
9	6.9851	3.1735	79.2450
10	6.7003	3.4583	75.7867
11	6.3899	3.7686	72.0180
12	6.0517	4.1069	67.9112
13	5.6832	4.4754	63.4358
14	5.2815	4.8771	58.5587
15	4.8439	5.3147	53.2440
16	4.3669	5.7917	47.4523
17	3.8471	6.3114	41.1409
18	3.2807	6.8779	34.2630
19	2.6635	7.4951	26.7679
20	1.9909	8.1677	18.6002
21	1.2579	8.9007	9.6995
22	.4591	9.6995	0.0000

YEARS 23	MO PAYT .8343	AN CONST 10.02	
#	INT	PRIN	BALANCE
1	8.5688	1.4431	98.5569
2	8.4393	1.5727	96.9842
3	8.2982	1.7138	95.2704
4	8.1444	1.8676	93.4028
5	7.9768	2.0352	91.3676
6	7.7941	2.2178	89.1498
7	7.5951	2.4169	86.7329
8	7.3782	2.6338	84.0992
9	7.1419	2.8701	81.2291
10	6.8843	3.1277	78.1014
11	6.6036	3.4084	74.6930
12	6.2977	3.7143	70.9787
13	5.9644	4.0476	66.9311
14	5.6011	4.4108	62.5203
15	5.2053	4.8067	57.7136
16	4.7739	5.2380	52.4756
17	4.3039	5.7081	46.7675
18	3.7916	6.2204	40.5471
19	3.2334	6.7786	33.7685
20	2.6251	7.3869	26.3816
21	1.9621	8.0498	18.3318
22	1.2397	8.7723	9.5595
23	.4525	9.5595	0.0000

YEARS 24	MO PAYT .8234	AN CONST 9.89	
#	INT	PRIN	BALANCE
1	8.5741	1.3070	98.6930
2	8.4568	1.4243	97.2687
3	8.3290	1.5521	95.7166
4	8.1897	1.6914	94.0252
5	8.0379	1.8432	92.1821
6	7.8725	2.0086	90.1735
7	7.6923	2.1888	87.9846
8	7.4958	2.3853	85.5994
9	7.2818	2.5993	83.0000
10	7.0485	2.8326	80.1674
11	6.7943	3.0868	77.0806
12	6.5173	3.3638	73.7168
13	6.2154	3.6657	70.0510
14	5.8864	3.9947	66.0563
15	5.5279	4.3532	61.7032
16	5.1373	4.7438	56.9593
17	4.7116	5.1696	51.7898
18	4.2476	5.6335	46.1563
19	3.7421	6.1391	40.0172
20	3.1911	6.6900	33.3272
21	2.5907	7.2904	26.0368
22	1.9365	7.9446	18.0922
23	1.2235	8.6576	9.4346
24	.4466	9.4346	0.0000

YEARS 25	MO PAYT .8137	AN CONST 9.77	
#	INT	PRIN	BALANCE
1	8.5789	1.1851	98.8149
2	8.4725	1.2915	97.5234
3	8.3566	1.4074	96.1160
4	8.2303	1.5337	94.5823
5	8.0927	1.6713	92.9109
6	7.9427	1.8213	91.0896
7	7.7792	1.9848	89.1048
8	7.6011	2.1629	86.9419
9	7.4070	2.3570	84.5849
10	7.1955	2.5685	82.0163
11	6.9650	2.7990	79.2173
12	6.7138	3.0502	76.1671
13	6.4400	3.3240	72.8431
14	6.1417	3.6223	69.2208
15	5.8167	3.9473	65.2735
16	5.4624	4.3016	60.9719
17	5.0764	4.6876	56.2843
18	4.6557	5.1083	51.1760
19	4.1973	5.5667	45.6092
20	3.6977	6.0663	39.5429
21	3.1533	6.6107	32.9322
22	2.5600	7.2040	25.7282
23	1.9135	7.8505	17.8778
24	1.2090	8.5550	9.3228
25	.4413	9.3228	0.0000

YEARS 26	MO PAYT .8049	AN CONST 9.66	
#	INT	PRIN	BALANCE
1	8.5831	1.0758	98.9242
2	8.4866	1.1724	97.7518
3	8.3814	1.2776	96.4742
4	8.2667	1.3923	95.0819
5	8.1418	1.5172	93.5647
6	8.0056	1.6534	91.9113
7	7.8572	1.8017	90.1096
8	7.6955	1.9634	88.1462
9	7.5193	2.1396	86.0065
10	7.3273	2.3317	83.6749
11	7.1181	2.5409	81.1340
12	6.8900	2.7689	78.3651
13	6.6416	3.0174	75.3476
14	6.3708	3.2882	72.0594
15	6.0757	3.5833	68.4761
16	5.7541	3.9049	64.5712
17	5.4037	4.2553	60.3159
18	5.0218	4.6372	55.6787
19	4.6056	5.0533	50.6254
20	4.1521	5.5068	45.1186
21	3.6579	6.0010	39.1175
22	3.1194	6.5396	32.5779
23	2.5325	7.1265	25.4514
24	1.8929	7.7660	17.6854
25	1.1960	8.4630	9.2225
26	.4365	9.2225	0.0000

YEARS 27	MO PAYT .7970	AN CONST 9.57	
#	INT	PRIN	BALANCE
1	8.5870	.9776	99.0224
2	8.4992	1.0653	97.9571
3	8.4036	1.1609	96.7962
4	8.2994	1.2651	95.5310
5	8.1859	1.3786	94.1524
6	8.0622	1.5024	92.6500
7	7.9273	1.6372	91.0128
8	7.7804	1.7841	89.2287
9	7.6203	1.9442	87.2845
10	7.4458	2.1187	85.1657
11	7.2557	2.3089	82.8569
12	7.0485	2.5161	80.3408
13	6.8227	2.7419	77.5990
14	6.5766	2.9879	74.6110
15	6.3085	3.2561	71.3550
16	6.0163	3.5483	67.8067
17	5.6978	3.8667	63.9400
18	5.3508	4.2137	59.7263
19	4.9727	4.5919	55.1344
20	4.5606	5.0039	50.1305
21	4.1115	5.4530	44.6775
22	3.6222	5.9424	38.7351
23	3.0889	6.4757	32.2594
24	2.5077	7.0568	25.2026
25	1.8744	7.6901	17.5125
26	1.1843	8.3802	9.1323
27	.4323	9.1323	0.0000

YEARS 28	MO PAYT .7900	AN CONST 9.48	
#	INT	PRIN	BALANCE
1	8.5904	.8891	99.1109
2	8.5106	.9689	98.1420
3	8.4237	1.0559	97.0861
4	8.3289	1.1506	95.9355
5	8.2256	1.2539	94.6817
6	8.1131	1.3664	93.3153
7	7.9905	1.4890	91.8263
8	7.8569	1.6226	90.2036
9	7.7112	1.7683	88.4354
10	7.5526	1.9270	86.5084
11	7.3796	2.0999	84.4085
12	7.1912	2.2883	82.1202
13	6.9858	2.4937	79.6265
14	6.7620	2.7175	76.9090
15	6.5182	2.9614	73.9477
16	6.2524	3.2271	70.7206
17	5.9628	3.5167	67.2038
18	5.6472	3.8323	63.3715
19	5.3033	4.1762	59.1953
20	4.9285	4.5510	54.6442
21	4.5201	4.9595	49.6848
22	4.0750	5.4045	44.2802
23	3.5900	5.8895	38.3907
24	3.0614	6.4181	31.9726
25	2.4854	6.9941	24.9786
26	1.8578	7.6217	17.3568
27	1.1738	8.3057	9.0511
28	.4284	9.0511	0.0000

YEARS 29	MO PAYT .7836	AN CONST 9.41	
#	INT	PRIN	BALANCE
1	8.5935	.8093	99.1907
2	8.5209	.8819	98.3088
3	8.4417	.9611	97.3477
4	8.3555	1.0473	96.3004
5	8.2615	1.1413	95.1591
6	8.1591	1.2437	93.9154
7	8.0475	1.3553	92.5601
8	7.9258	1.4770	91.0831
9	7.7933	1.6095	89.4736
10	7.6488	1.7540	87.7197
11	7.4914	1.9114	85.8083
12	7.3199	2.0829	83.7254
13	7.1330	2.2698	81.4556
14	6.9293	2.4735	78.9821
15	6.7073	2.6955	76.2866
16	6.4654	2.9374	73.3492
17	6.2018	3.2010	70.1482
18	5.9145	3.4883	66.6600
19	5.6015	3.8013	62.8587
20	5.2603	4.1424	58.7162
21	4.8886	4.5142	54.2020
22	4.4835	4.9193	49.2827
23	4.0420	5.3608	43.9219
24	3.5609	5.8419	38.0800
25	3.0366	6.3661	31.7139
26	2.4653	6.9375	24.7764
27	1.8427	7.5600	17.2164
28	1.1643	8.2385	8.9779
29	.4249	8.9779	0.0000

YEARS 30	MO PAYT .7778	AN CONST 9.34	
#	INT	PRIN	BALANCE
1	8.5963	.7372	99.2628
2	8.5302	.8033	98.4595
3	8.4581	.8754	97.5841
4	8.3795	.9540	96.6301
5	8.2939	1.0396	95.5905
6	8.2006	1.1329	94.4577
7	8.0989	1.2346	93.2231
8	7.9881	1.3453	91.8778
9	7.8674	1.4661	90.4117
10	7.7358	1.5976	88.8140
11	7.5925	1.7410	87.0730
12	7.4362	1.8973	85.1758
13	7.2659	2.0675	83.1082
14	7.0804	2.2531	80.8551
15	6.8782	2.4553	78.3999
16	6.6579	2.6756	75.7242
17	6.4177	2.9157	72.8085
18	6.1561	3.1774	69.6311
19	5.8709	3.4625	66.1686
20	5.5602	3.7733	62.3953
21	5.2216	4.1119	58.2834
22	4.8526	4.4809	53.8024
23	4.4504	4.8831	48.9194
24	4.0122	5.3213	43.5981
25	3.5347	5.7988	37.7993
26	3.0143	6.3192	31.4801
27	2.4472	6.8863	24.5938
28	1.8292	7.5043	17.0894
29	1.1557	8.1778	8.9117
30	.4218	8.9117	0.0000

MONTHLY PAYMENT AMORTIZATION SCHEDULE PER $100   8.70 %

YEARS 2	MO PAYT 4.5547	AN CONST 54.66
# INT	PRIN	BALANCE
1 6.8225	47.8342	52.1658
2 2.4909	52.1658	0.0000

YEARS 3	MO PAYT 3.1660	AN CONST 38.00
# INT	PRIN	BALANCE
1 7.5033	30.4891	69.5109
2 4.7424	33.2500	36.2609
3 1.7314	36.2609	0.0000

YEARS 4	MO PAYT 2.4743	AN CONST 29.70
# INT	PRIN	BALANCE
1 7.8424	21.8490	78.1510
2 5.8639	23.8275	54.3235
3 3.7062	25.9852	28.3383
4 1.3531	28.3383	0.0000

YEARS 5	MO PAYT 2.0613	AN CONST 24.74
# INT	PRIN	BALANCE
1 8.0449	16.6908	83.3092
2 6.5334	18.2022	65.1070
3 4.8852	19.8505	45.2565
4 3.0876	21.6481	23.6084
5 1.1273	23.6084	0.0000

YEARS 6	MO PAYT 1.7877	AN CONST 21.46
# INT	PRIN	BALANCE
1 8.1790	13.2734	86.7266
2 6.9770	14.4754	72.2512
3 5.6662	15.7862	56.4651
4 4.2367	17.2157	39.2494
5 2.6778	18.7746	20.4748
6 .9776	20.4748	0.0000

YEARS 7	MO PAYT 1.5937	AN CONST 19.13
# INT	PRIN	BALANCE
1 8.2741	10.8506	89.1494
2 7.2915	11.8332	77.3163
3 6.2200	12.9047	64.4116
4 5.0514	14.0733	50.3383
5 3.7770	15.3477	34.9906
6 2.3872	16.7375	18.2531
7 .8716	18.2531	0.0000

YEARS 8	MO PAYT 1.4495	AN CONST 17.40
# INT	PRIN	BALANCE
1 8.3448	9.0492	90.9508
2 7.5254	9.8687	81.0821
3 6.6317	10.7623	70.3197
4 5.6571	11.7369	58.5828
5 4.5943	12.7998	45.7830
6 3.4352	13.9588	31.8242
7 2.1712	15.2229	16.6014
8 .7927	16.6014	0.0000

YEARS 9	MO PAYT 1.3384	AN CONST 16.07
# INT	PRIN	BALANCE
1 8.3993	7.6621	92.3379
2 7.7054	8.3559	83.9821
3 6.9488	9.1125	74.8695
4 6.1236	9.9377	64.9318
5 5.2237	10.8376	54.0941
6 4.2423	11.8190	42.2751

# INT	PRIN	BALANCE
7 3.1720	12.8893	29.3858
8 2.0048	14.0565	15.3293
9 .7320	15.3293	0.0000

YEARS 10	MO PAYT 1.2506	AN CONST 15.01
# INT	PRIN	BALANCE
1 8.4423	6.5646	93.4354
2 7.8479	7.1591	86.2763
3 7.1996	7.8074	78.4690
4 6.4926	8.5143	69.9546
5 5.7216	9.2854	60.6693
6 4.8808	10.1262	50.5431
7 3.9638	11.0432	39.4999
8 2.9638	12.0432	27.4568
9 1.8732	13.1337	14.3230
10 .6839	14.3230	0.0000

YEARS 11	MO PAYT 1.1796	AN CONST 14.16
# INT	PRIN	BALANCE
1 8.4771	5.6777	94.3223
2 7.9630	6.1919	88.1304
3 7.4023	6.7526	81.3778
4 6.7908	7.3641	74.0137
5 6.1240	8.0309	65.9828
6 5.3967	8.7582	57.2246
7 4.6036	9.5512	47.6734
8 3.7387	10.4162	37.2572
9 2.7955	11.3594	25.8978
10 1.7669	12.3880	13.5098
11 .6451	13.5098	0.0000

YEARS 12	MO PAYT 1.1212	AN CONST 13.46
# INT	PRIN	BALANCE
1 8.5058	4.9487	95.0513
2 8.0576	5.3968	89.6546
3 7.5689	5.8855	83.7691
4 7.0360	6.4184	77.3507
5 6.4548	6.9997	70.3510
6 5.8209	7.6335	62.7175
7 5.1297	8.3247	54.3928
8 4.3758	9.0786	45.3142
9 3.5537	9.9007	35.4135
10 2.6572	10.7972	24.6162
11 1.6794	11.7750	12.8413
12 .6132	12.8413	0.0000

YEARS 13	MO PAYT 1.0725	AN CONST 12.88
# INT	PRIN	BALANCE
1 8.5296	4.3408	95.6592
2 8.1365	4.7338	90.9254
3 7.7079	5.1625	85.7629
4 7.2404	5.6300	80.1329
5 6.7306	6.1398	73.9930
6 6.1746	6.6958	67.2972
7 5.5682	7.3021	59.9951
8 4.9070	7.9634	52.0317
9 4.1859	8.6845	43.3472
10 3.3995	9.4709	33.8763
11 2.5418	10.3286	23.5477
12 1.6065	11.2639	12.2838
13 .5865	12.2838	0.0000

YEARS 14	MO PAYT 1.0315	AN CONST 12.38
# INT	PRIN	BALANCE
1 8.5497	3.8280	96.1720
2 8.2031	4.1746	91.9974
3 7.8251	4.5526	87.4448

# INT	PRIN	BALANCE
4 7.4128	4.9649	82.4799
5 6.9632	5.4145	77.0654
6 6.4729	5.9048	71.1606
7 5.9382	6.4395	64.7211
8 5.3551	7.0226	57.6985
9 4.7192	7.6586	50.0399
10 4.0256	8.3521	41.6879
11 3.2693	9.1084	32.5795
12 2.4445	9.9332	22.6463
13 1.5450	10.8327	11.8136
14 .5641	11.8136	0.0000

YEARS 15	MO PAYT .9965	AN CONST 11.96
# INT	PRIN	BALANCE
1 8.5669	3.3911	96.6089
2 8.2598	3.6982	92.9108
3 7.9249	4.0330	88.8777
4 7.5597	4.3983	84.4795
5 7.1614	4.7965	79.6829
6 6.7271	5.2309	74.4521
7 6.2534	5.7046	68.7475
8 5.7368	6.2211	62.5264
9 5.1735	6.7845	55.7419
10 4.5591	7.3988	48.3430
11 3.8891	8.0688	40.2742
12 3.1585	8.7995	31.4747
13 2.3616	9.5963	21.8784
14 1.4926	10.4653	11.4130
15 .5450	11.4130	0.0000

YEARS 16	MO PAYT .9664	AN CONST 11.60
# INT	PRIN	BALANCE
1 8.5816	3.0157	96.9843
2 8.3085	3.2888	93.6955
3 8.0107	3.5866	90.1088
4 7.6859	3.9114	86.1974
5 7.3317	4.2656	81.9318
6 6.9455	4.6519	77.2799
7 6.5242	5.0731	72.2068
8 6.0648	5.5325	66.6743
9 5.5638	6.0335	60.6407
10 5.0175	6.5799	54.0609
11 4.4216	7.1757	46.8852
12 3.7718	7.8255	39.0596
13 3.0632	8.5341	30.5255
14 2.2904	9.3069	21.2186
15 1.4476	10.1497	11.0688
16 .5285	11.0688	0.0000

YEARS 17	MO PAYT .9404	AN CONST 11.29
# INT	PRIN	BALANCE
1 8.5944	2.6909	97.3091
2 8.3507	2.9346	94.3745
3 8.0850	3.2003	91.1742
4 7.7952	3.4901	87.6841
5 7.4791	3.8062	83.8779
6 7.1345	4.1508	79.7271
7 6.7586	4.5267	75.2004
8 6.3487	4.9366	70.2638
9 5.9016	5.3836	64.8801
10 5.4141	5.8712	59.0090
11 4.8825	6.4028	52.6061
12 4.3027	6.9826	45.6235
13 3.6704	7.6149	38.0086
14 2.9808	8.3045	29.7041
15 2.2288	9.0565	20.6476
16 1.4087	9.8766	10.7710
17 .5143	10.7710	0.0000

YEARS 18	MO PAYT .9178	AN CONST 11.02
# INT	PRIN	BALANCE
1 8.6055	2.4080	97.5920
2 8.3874	2.6261	94.9658
3 8.1496	2.8639	92.1019
4 7.8903	3.1233	88.9787
5 7.6075	3.4061	85.5726
6 7.2990	3.7145	81.8581
7 6.9627	4.0509	77.8072
8 6.5958	4.4177	73.3895
9 6.1958	4.8177	68.5718
10 5.7595	5.2540	63.3178
11 5.2837	5.7298	57.5880
12 4.7649	6.2486	51.3394
13 4.1990	6.8145	44.5249
14 3.5820	7.4316	37.0933
15 2.9090	8.1045	28.9888
16 2.1751	8.8384	20.1504
17 1.3748	9.6388	10.5116
18 .5019	10.5116	0.0000

YEARS 19	MO PAYT .8980	AN CONST 10.78
# INT	PRIN	BALANCE
1 8.6152	2.1604	97.8396
2 8.4196	2.3560	95.4836
3 8.2062	2.5694	92.9142
4 7.9736	2.8020	90.1122
5 7.7198	3.0558	87.0564
6 7.4431	3.3325	83.7239
7 7.1413	3.6343	80.0896
8 6.8122	3.9634	76.1263
9 6.4533	4.3223	71.8040
10 6.0619	4.7137	67.0904
11 5.6351	5.1405	61.9499
12 5.1696	5.6060	56.3439
13 4.6620	6.1136	50.2302
14 4.1083	6.6673	43.5630
15 3.5046	7.2710	36.2920
16 2.8462	7.9294	28.3625
17 2.1281	8.6475	19.7151
18 1.3451	9.4305	10.2845
19 .4911	10.2845	0.0000

YEARS 20	MO PAYT .8805	AN CONST 10.57
# INT	PRIN	BALANCE
1 8.6238	1.9425	98.0575
2 8.4479	2.1184	95.9391
3 8.2560	2.3103	93.6288
4 8.0468	2.5195	91.1093
5 7.8187	2.7476	88.3617
6 7.5699	2.9964	85.3653
7 7.2985	3.2678	82.0976
8 7.0026	3.5637	78.5339
9 6.6799	3.8864	74.6475
10 6.3280	4.2383	70.4092
11 5.9442	4.6221	65.7871
12 5.5256	5.0406	60.7465
13 5.0692	5.4971	55.2494
14 4.5714	5.9949	49.2545
15 4.0285	6.5377	42.7168
16 3.4365	7.1298	35.5870
17 2.7909	7.7754	27.8116
18 2.0868	8.4795	19.3321
19 1.3189	9.2474	10.0847
20 .4815	10.0847	0.0000

YEARS 21	MO PAYT .8651	AN CONST 10.39
# INT	PRIN	BALANCE
1 8.6313	1.7501	98.2499
2 8.4728	1.9085	96.3414
3 8.3000	2.0814	94.2601

#	INT	PRIN	BALANCE
4	8.1115	2.2698	91.9902
5	7.9060	2.4754	89.5149
6	7.6818	2.6995	86.8154
7	7.4374	2.9440	83.8714
8	7.1708	3.2106	80.6608
9	6.8801	3.5013	77.1595
10	6.5630	3.8184	73.3411
11	6.2172	4.1641	69.1770
12	5.8402	4.5412	64.6358
13	5.4289	4.9524	59.6834
14	4.9805	5.4009	54.2825
15	4.4914	5.8900	48.3925
16	3.9580	6.4233	41.9692
17	3.3764	7.0050	34.9642
18	2.7420	7.6393	27.3249
19	2.0503	8.3311	18.9938
20	1.2958	9.0855	9.9083
21	.4731	9.9083	0.0000

YEARS 22   MO PAYT .8514   AN CONST 10.22

#	INT	PRIN	BALANCE
1	8.6380	1.5794	98.4206
2	8.4950	1.7224	96.6982
3	8.3390	1.8784	94.8198
4	8.1689	2.0485	92.7713
5	7.9834	2.2340	90.5374
6	7.7811	2.4363	88.1011
7	7.5605	2.6569	85.4442
8	7.3199	2.8975	82.5467
9	7.0575	3.1599	79.3869
10	6.7714	3.4460	75.9409
11	6.4593	3.7581	72.1828
12	6.1190	4.0984	68.0844
13	5.7479	4.4695	63.6150
14	5.3432	4.8742	58.7408
15	4.9018	5.3156	53.4252
16	4.4205	5.7969	47.6282
17	3.8955	6.3219	41.3063
18	3.3230	6.8944	34.4120
19	2.6987	7.5187	26.8933
20	2.0179	8.1995	18.6938
21	1.2754	8.9420	9.7518
22	.4656	9.7518	0.0000

YEARS 23   MO PAYT .8393   AN CONST 10.08

#	INT	PRIN	BALANCE
1	8.6440	1.4276	98.5724
2	8.5147	1.5568	97.0156
3	8.3737	1.6978	95.3178
4	8.2200	1.8516	93.4662
5	8.0523	2.0192	91.4470
6	7.8695	2.2021	89.2449
7	7.6700	2.4015	86.8434
8	7.4526	2.6190	84.2244
9	7.2154	2.8561	81.3683
10	6.9568	3.1148	78.2536
11	6.6747	3.3968	74.8567
12	6.3671	3.7044	71.1523
13	6.0317	4.0399	67.1125
14	5.6659	4.4057	62.7068
15	5.2669	4.8046	57.9022
16	4.8318	5.2397	52.6625
17	4.3573	5.7142	46.9483
18	3.8399	6.2316	40.7167
19	3.2756	6.7959	33.9207
20	2.6602	7.4113	26.5094
21	1.9891	8.0825	18.4269
22	1.2572	8.8144	9.6125
23	.4590	9.6125	0.0000

YEARS 24   MO PAYT .8285   AN CONST 9.95

#	INT	PRIN	BALANCE
1	8.6493	1.2921	98.7079
2	8.5323	1.4091	97.2988
3	8.4047	1.5367	95.7620
4	8.2655	1.6759	94.0861
5	8.1138	1.8276	92.2585
6	7.9483	1.9931	90.2654
7	7.7678	2.1736	88.0917
8	7.5709	2.3705	85.7213
9	7.3563	2.5851	83.1361
10	7.1222	2.8192	80.3169
11	6.8669	3.0745	77.2424
12	6.5885	3.3529	73.8895
13	6.2849	3.6565	70.2330
14	5.9537	3.9877	66.2453
15	5.5927	4.3488	61.8966
16	5.1989	4.7425	57.1540
17	4.7694	5.1720	51.9820
18	4.3010	5.6404	46.3417
19	3.7903	6.1511	40.1905
20	3.2333	6.7081	33.4824
21	2.6258	7.3156	26.1668
22	1.9634	7.9780	18.1888
23	1.2409	8.7005	9.4883
24	.4531	9.4883	0.0000

YEARS 25   MO PAYT .8187   AN CONST 9.83

#	INT	PRIN	BALANCE
1	8.6540	1.1710	98.8290
2	8.5480	1.2770	97.5521
3	8.4324	1.3926	96.1594
4	8.3063	1.5187	94.6407
5	8.1687	1.6563	92.9844
6	8.0187	1.8062	91.1782
7	7.8552	1.9698	89.2084
8	7.6768	2.1482	87.0602
9	7.4823	2.3427	84.7175
10	7.2701	2.5548	82.1627
11	7.0388	2.7862	79.3765
12	6.7865	3.0385	76.3380
13	6.5113	3.3137	73.0243
14	6.2113	3.6137	69.4106
15	5.8840	3.9410	65.4696
16	5.5272	4.2978	61.1718
17	5.1380	4.6870	56.4848
18	4.7135	5.1114	51.3733
19	4.2507	5.5743	45.7990
20	3.7459	6.0791	39.7199
21	3.1954	6.6296	33.0904
22	2.5951	7.2299	25.8604
23	1.9404	7.8846	17.9758
24	1.2264	8.5986	9.3772
25	.4478	9.3772	0.0000

YEARS 26   MO PAYT .8101   AN CONST 9.73

#	INT	PRIN	BALANCE
1	8.6583	1.0623	98.9377
2	8.5621	1.1585	97.7792
3	8.4572	1.2634	96.5157
4	8.3428	1.3778	95.1379
5	8.2180	1.5026	93.6353
6	8.0820	1.6387	91.9967
7	7.9336	1.7871	90.2096
8	7.7717	1.9489	88.2607
9	7.5953	2.1254	86.1354
10	7.4028	2.3178	83.8175
11	7.1929	2.5277	81.2898
12	6.9640	2.7566	78.5332
13	6.7144	3.0062	75.5270
14	6.4422	3.2785	72.2485
15	6.1453	3.5753	68.6732
16	5.8215	3.8991	64.7741
17	5.4684	4.2522	60.5220
18	5.0834	4.6372	55.8847
19	4.6635	5.0571	50.8276
20	4.2055	5.5151	45.3125
21	3.7061	6.0145	39.2980
22	3.1615	6.5591	32.7388
23	2.5675	7.1531	25.5857
24	1.9198	7.8009	17.7849
25	1.2134	8.5073	9.2776
26	.4430	9.2776	0.0000

YEARS 27   MO PAYT .8022   AN CONST 9.63

#	INT	PRIN	BALANCE
1	8.6621	.9647	99.0353
2	8.5748	1.0521	97.9832
3	8.4795	1.1473	96.8359
4	8.3756	1.2512	95.5847
5	8.2623	1.3645	94.2201
6	8.1387	1.4881	92.7320
7	8.0040	1.6229	91.1092
8	7.8570	1.7698	89.3393
9	7.6968	1.9301	87.4093
10	7.5220	2.1049	85.3044
11	7.3314	2.2955	83.0089
12	7.1235	2.5033	80.5056
13	6.8968	2.7300	77.7756
14	6.6496	2.9772	74.7984
15	6.3800	3.2468	71.5516
16	6.0860	3.5408	68.0107
17	5.7654	3.8615	64.1492
18	5.4157	4.2112	59.9381
19	5.0344	4.5925	55.3456
20	4.6185	5.0084	50.3372
21	4.1650	5.4619	44.8754
22	3.6704	5.9565	38.9189
23	3.1310	6.4959	32.4230
24	2.5427	7.0841	25.3389
25	1.9012	7.7256	17.6133
26	1.2017	8.4252	9.1881
27	.4387	9.1881	0.0000

YEARS 28   MO PAYT .7952   AN CONST 9.55

#	INT	PRIN	BALANCE
1	8.6656	.8768	99.1232
2	8.5862	.9563	98.1669
3	8.4996	1.0428	97.1241
4	8.4052	1.1373	95.9868
5	8.3022	1.2403	94.7465
6	8.1899	1.3526	93.3939
7	8.0674	1.4751	91.9189
8	7.9338	1.6086	90.3103
9	7.7881	1.7543	88.5560
10	7.6293	1.9132	86.6428
11	7.4560	2.0864	84.5564
12	7.2671	2.2753	82.2811
13	7.0611	2.4814	79.7997
14	6.8364	2.7061	77.0936
15	6.5913	2.9511	74.1425
16	6.3241	3.2184	70.9242
17	6.0326	3.5098	67.4144
18	5.7148	3.8276	63.5868
19	5.3682	4.1742	59.4125
20	4.9902	4.5522	54.8603
21	4.5780	4.9644	49.8959
22	4.1284	5.4140	44.4819
23	3.6382	5.9043	38.5776
24	3.1035	6.4389	32.1387
25	2.5204	7.0220	25.1167
26	1.8846	7.6579	17.4589
27	1.1911	8.3513	9.1076
28	.4349	9.1076	0.0000

YEARS 29   MO PAYT .7889   AN CONST 9.47

#	INT	PRIN	BALANCE
1	8.6687	.7976	99.2024
2	8.5965	.8699	98.3325
3	8.5177	.9486	97.3839
4	8.4318	1.0345	96.3494
5	8.3381	1.1282	95.2212
6	8.2359	1.2304	93.9908
7	8.1245	1.3418	92.6490
8	8.0030	1.4633	91.1857
9	7.8705	1.5958	89.5899
10	7.7260	1.7403	87.8496
11	7.5684	1.8979	85.9517
12	7.3966	2.0698	83.8820
13	7.2091	2.2572	81.6248
14	7.0047	2.4616	79.1632
15	6.7818	2.6845	76.4787
16	6.5387	2.9276	73.5511
17	6.2736	3.1927	70.3585
18	5.9845	3.4818	66.8767
19	5.6692	3.7971	63.0796
20	5.3254	4.1409	58.9386
21	4.9504	4.5159	54.4227
22	4.5415	4.9248	49.4979
23	4.0955	5.3708	44.1271
24	3.6092	5.8572	38.2699
25	3.0788	6.3876	31.8824
26	2.5003	6.9660	24.9164
27	1.8695	7.5968	17.3196
28	1.1816	8.2847	9.0349
29	.4314	9.0349	0.0000

YEARS 30   MO PAYT .7831   AN CONST 9.40

#	INT	PRIN	BALANCE
1	8.6715	.7261	99.2739
2	8.6058	.7918	98.4821
3	8.5340	.8635	97.6185
4	8.4558	.9417	96.6768
5	8.3706	1.0270	95.6498
6	8.2776	1.1200	94.5298
7	8.1761	1.2214	93.3083
8	8.0655	1.3320	91.9763
9	7.9449	1.4527	90.5236
10	7.8134	1.5842	88.9394
11	7.6699	1.7277	87.2118
12	7.5135	1.8841	85.3276
13	7.3429	2.0547	83.2729
14	7.1568	2.2408	81.0321
15	6.9539	2.4437	78.5884
16	6.7326	2.6650	75.9234
17	6.4913	2.9063	73.0171
18	6.2281	3.1695	69.8476
19	5.9411	3.4565	66.3911
20	5.6281	3.7695	62.6216
21	5.2867	4.1109	58.5107
22	4.9145	4.4831	54.0276
23	4.5085	4.8891	49.1385
24	4.0658	5.3318	43.8067
25	3.5830	5.8146	37.9920
26	3.0564	6.3412	31.6509
27	2.4822	6.9154	24.7355
28	1.8560	7.5416	17.1938
29	1.1730	8.2245	8.9693
30	.4283	8.9693	0.0000

YEARS 2 — MO PAYT 4.5570 — AN CONST 54.69

#	INT	PRIN	BALANCE
1	6.8623	47.8218	52.1782
2	2.5060	52.1782	0.0000

YEARS 3 — MO PAYT 3.1684 — AN CONST 38.03

#	INT	PRIN	BALANCE
1	7.5471	30.4731	69.5269
2	4.7712	33.2490	36.2779
3	1.7423	36.2779	0.0000

YEARS 4 — MO PAYT 2.4767 — AN CONST 29.72

#	INT	PRIN	BALANCE
1	7.8882	21.8316	78.1684
2	5.8995	23.8203	54.3481
3	3.7295	25.9903	28.3579
4	1.3619	28.3579	0.0000

YEARS 5 — MO PAYT 2.0637 — AN CONST 24.77

#	INT	PRIN	BALANCE
1	8.0919	16.6728	83.3272
2	6.5731	18.1916	65.1356
3	4.9159	19.8488	45.2868
4	3.1077	21.6570	23.6298
5	1.1349	23.6298	0.0000

YEARS 6 — MO PAYT 1.7902 — AN CONST 21.49

#	INT	PRIN	BALANCE
1	8.2268	13.2553	86.7447
2	7.0193	14.4628	72.2819
3	5.7018	15.7803	56.5017
4	4.2643	17.2178	39.2839
5	2.6958	18.7863	20.4976
6	.9844	20.4976	0.0000

YEARS 7 — MO PAYT 1.5962 — AN CONST 19.16

#	INT	PRIN	BALANCE
1	8.3224	10.8326	89.1674
2	7.3356	11.8194	77.3480
3	6.2589	12.8961	64.4519
4	5.0841	14.0709	50.3811
5	3.8023	15.3527	35.0284
6	2.4038	16.7512	18.2772
7	.8778	18.2772	0.0000

YEARS 8 — MO PAYT 1.4521 — AN CONST 17.43

#	INT	PRIN	BALANCE
1	8.3935	9.0315	90.9685
2	7.5708	9.8542	81.1143
3	6.6731	10.7519	70.3623
4	5.6936	11.7314	58.6310
5	4.6250	12.8001	45.8309
6	3.4589	13.9661	31.8648
7	2.1867	15.2383	16.6265
8	.7985	16.6265	0.0000

YEARS 9 — MO PAYT 1.3411 — AN CONST 16.10

#	INT	PRIN	BALANCE
1	8.4482	7.6447	92.3553
2	7.7518	8.3411	84.0142
3	6.9920	9.1009	74.9133
4	6.1630	9.9300	64.9834
5	5.2584	10.8345	54.1488
6	4.2714	11.8215	42.3273
7	3.1945	12.8984	29.4289
8	2.0195	14.0734	15.3554
9	.7375	15.3554	0.0000

YEARS 10 — MO PAYT 1.2533 — AN CONST 15.04

#	INT	PRIN	BALANCE
1	8.4915	6.5477	93.4523
2	7.8951	7.1441	86.3082
3	7.2443	7.7949	78.5133
4	6.5342	8.5050	70.0083
5	5.7594	9.2798	60.7285
6	4.9141	10.1251	50.6033
7	3.9917	11.0475	39.5558
8	2.9853	12.0539	27.5020
9	1.8873	13.1519	14.3500
10	.6892	14.3500	0.0000

YEARS 11 — MO PAYT 1.1823 — AN CONST 14.19

#	INT	PRIN	BALANCE
1	8.5265	5.6613	94.3387
2	8.0108	6.1770	88.1617
3	7.4481	6.7397	81.4221
4	6.8342	7.3536	74.0684
5	6.1643	8.0235	66.0449
6	5.4334	8.7544	57.2905
7	4.6359	9.5519	47.7385
8	3.7657	10.4221	37.3165
9	2.8163	11.3715	25.9450
10	1.7804	12.4074	13.5376
11	.6502	13.5376	0.0000

YEARS 12 — MO PAYT 1.1240 — AN CONST 13.49

#	INT	PRIN	BALANCE
1	8.5553	4.9327	95.0673
2	8.1059	5.3820	89.6853
3	7.6157	5.8723	83.8130
4	7.0807	6.4072	77.4058
5	6.4971	6.9909	70.4149
6	5.8602	7.6278	62.7871
7	5.1654	8.3226	54.4645
8	4.4072	9.0808	45.3838
9	3.5800	9.9080	35.4758
10	2.6774	10.8106	24.6652
11	1.6926	11.7954	12.8699
12	.6181	12.8699	0.0000

YEARS 13 — MO PAYT 1.0754 — AN CONST 12.91

#	INT	PRIN	BALANCE
1	8.5793	4.3253	95.6747
2	8.1853	4.7193	90.9554
3	7.7553	5.1492	85.8062
4	7.2863	5.6183	80.1879
5	6.7745	6.1301	74.0578
6	6.2160	6.6885	67.3692
7	5.6067	7.2978	60.0714
8	4.9419	7.9626	52.1088
9	4.2166	8.6880	43.4208
10	3.4251	9.4794	33.9413
11	2.5616	10.3430	23.5984
12	1.6194	11.2852	12.3132
13	.5914	12.3132	0.0000

YEARS 14 — MO PAYT 1.0344 — AN CONST 12.42

#	INT	PRIN	BALANCE
1	8.5995	3.8130	96.1870
2	8.2521	4.1604	92.0266
3	7.8731	4.5394	87.4872
4	7.4596	4.9529	82.5343
5	7.0084	5.4041	77.1303
6	6.5162	5.8964	71.2339
7	5.9790	6.4335	64.8004
8	5.3930	7.0196	57.7809
9	4.7535	7.6590	50.1218
10	4.0558	8.3567	41.7651
11	3.2945	9.1180	32.6471
12	2.4639	9.9486	22.6986
13	1.5577	10.8549	11.8437
14	.5688	11.8437	0.0000

YEARS 15 — MO PAYT .9994 — AN CONST 12.00

#	INT	PRIN	BALANCE
1	8.6167	3.3767	96.6233
2	8.3091	3.6843	92.9391
3	7.9735	4.0199	88.9192
4	7.6073	4.3861	84.5331
5	7.2077	4.7856	79.7474
6	6.7718	5.2216	74.5258
7	6.2961	5.6973	68.8286
8	5.7771	6.2163	62.6123
9	5.2109	6.7825	55.8298
10	4.5930	7.4004	48.4294
11	3.9188	8.0745	40.3549
12	3.1833	8.8101	31.5448
13	2.3807	9.6127	21.9321
14	1.5051	10.4883	11.4438
15	.5496	11.4438	0.0000

YEARS 16 — MO PAYT .9694 — AN CONST 11.64

#	INT	PRIN	BALANCE
1	8.6315	3.0019	96.9981
2	8.3581	3.2753	93.7228
3	8.0597	3.5737	90.1492
4	7.7341	3.8992	86.2499
5	7.3789	4.2544	81.9955
6	6.9914	4.6420	77.3535
7	6.5685	5.0649	72.2887
8	6.1071	5.5262	66.7624
9	5.6037	6.0297	60.7328
10	5.0544	6.5789	54.1539
11	4.4551	7.1782	46.9756
12	3.8012	7.8322	39.1435
13	3.0877	8.5456	30.5978
14	2.3093	9.3241	21.2737
15	1.4599	10.1735	11.1002
16	.5331	11.1002	0.0000

YEARS 17 — MO PAYT .9435 — AN CONST 11.33

#	INT	PRIN	BALANCE
1	8.6443	2.6776	97.3224
2	8.4004	2.9215	94.4010
3	8.1343	3.1876	91.2134
4	7.8439	3.4780	87.7354
5	7.5271	3.7948	83.9405
6	7.1814	4.1405	79.8000
7	6.8042	4.5177	75.2823
8	6.3926	4.9292	70.3531
9	5.9436	5.3783	64.9748
10	5.4537	5.8682	59.1066
11	4.9191	6.4028	52.7039
12	4.3358	6.9860	45.7178
13	3.6994	7.6224	38.0954
14	3.0051	8.3168	29.7786
15	2.2474	9.0744	20.7041
16	1.4208	9.9011	10.8030
17	.5188	10.8030	0.0000

YEARS 18 — MO PAYT .9209 — AN CONST 11.06

#	INT	PRIN	BALANCE
1	8.6555	2.3952	97.6048
2	8.4373	2.6134	94.9913
3	8.1992	2.8515	92.1398
4	7.9394	3.1113	89.0286
5	7.6560	3.3947	85.6339
6	7.3468	3.7039	81.9300
7	7.0093	4.0413	77.8886
8	6.6412	4.4095	73.4792
9	6.2395	4.8112	68.6680
10	5.8012	5.2494	63.4185
11	5.3230	5.7276	57.6909
12	4.8013	6.2494	51.4415
13	4.2320	6.8187	44.6228
14	3.6108	7.4399	37.1829
15	2.9331	8.1176	29.0653
16	2.1936	8.8571	20.2082
17	1.3868	9.6639	10.5443
18	.5064	10.5443	0.0000

YEARS 19 — MO PAYT .9011 — AN CONST 10.82

#	INT	PRIN	BALANCE
1	8.6652	2.1481	97.8519
2	8.4695	2.3438	95.5081
3	8.2560	2.5573	92.9508
4	8.0231	2.7902	90.1606
5	7.7689	3.0444	87.1162
6	7.4915	3.3218	83.7944
7	7.1889	3.6244	80.1700
8	6.8588	3.9545	76.2155
9	6.4985	4.3148	71.9008
10	6.1055	4.7078	67.1929
11	5.6766	5.1367	62.0562
12	5.2087	5.6046	56.4516
13	4.6981	6.1152	50.3365
14	4.1411	6.6722	43.6642
15	3.5333	7.2801	36.3842
16	2.8701	7.9432	28.4409
17	2.1465	8.6668	19.7741
18	1.3570	9.4563	10.3178
19	.4955	10.3178	0.0000

YEARS 20 — MO PAYT .8837 — AN CONST 10.61

#	INT	PRIN	BALANCE
1	8.6738	1.9307	98.0693
2	8.4979	2.1066	95.9626
3	8.3060	2.2985	93.6641
4	8.0966	2.5079	91.1562
5	7.8682	2.7364	88.4198
6	7.6189	2.9856	85.4342
7	7.3469	3.2576	82.1765
8	7.0501	3.5544	78.6222
9	6.7264	3.8782	74.7440
10	6.3731	4.2315	70.5125
11	5.9876	4.6169	65.8956
12	5.5670	5.0375	60.8581
13	5.1081	5.4964	55.3617
14	4.6074	5.9971	49.3646
15	4.0611	6.5434	42.8212
16	3.4650	7.1395	35.6817
17	2.8147	7.7899	27.8918
18	2.1050	8.4995	19.3923
19	1.3308	9.2738	10.1186
20	.4860	10.1186	0.0000

YEARS 21 — MO PAYT .8683 — AN CONST 10.43

#	INT	PRIN	BALANCE
1	8.6814	1.7388	98.2612
2	8.5230	1.8972	96.3641
3	8.3501	2.0700	94.2941

#	INT	PRIN	BALANCE
4	8.1616	2.2586	92.0355
5	7.9558	2.4643	89.5712
6	7.7313	2.6888	86.8824
7	7.4864	2.9337	83.9487
8	7.2192	3.2010	80.7477
9	6.9276	3.4926	77.2551
10	6.6094	3.8107	73.4444
11	6.2623	4.1579	69.2865
12	5.8835	4.5366	64.7498
13	5.4702	4.9499	59.7999
14	5.0193	5.4008	54.3991
15	4.5273	5.8929	48.5063
16	3.9905	6.4296	42.0766
17	3.4048	7.0154	35.0613
18	2.7657	7.6544	27.4068
19	2.0684	8.3517	19.0551
20	1.3076	9.1125	9.9426
21	.4775	9.9426	0.0000

YEARS 22 — MO PAYT .8547 — AN CONST 10.26

#	INT	PRIN	BALANCE
1	8.6881	1.5686	98.4314
2	8.5452	1.7115	96.7199
3	8.3893	1.8674	94.8525
4	8.2192	2.0375	92.8150
5	8.0336	2.2231	90.5918
6	7.8310	2.4257	88.1662
7	7.6101	2.6466	85.5196
8	7.3690	2.8877	82.6318
9	7.1059	3.1508	79.4811
10	6.8189	3.4378	76.0433
11	6.5057	3.7510	72.2923
12	6.1640	4.0927	68.1997
13	5.7912	4.4655	63.7342
14	5.3844	4.8723	58.8619
15	4.9406	5.3161	53.5458
16	4.4563	5.8004	47.7454
17	3.9279	6.3288	41.4166
18	3.3514	6.9053	34.5113
19	2.7223	7.5344	26.9769
20	2.0360	8.2207	18.7562
21	1.2871	8.9696	9.7867
22	.4700	9.7867	0.0000

YEARS 23 — MO PAYT .8426 — AN CONST 10.12

#	INT	PRIN	BALANCE
1	8.6941	1.4173	98.5827
2	8.5649	1.5464	97.0364
3	8.4241	1.6872	95.3491
4	8.2704	1.8409	93.5082
5	8.1027	2.0086	91.4995
6	7.9197	2.1916	89.3079
7	7.7201	2.3913	86.9166
8	7.5022	2.6091	84.3075
9	7.2645	2.8468	81.4607
10	7.0052	3.1061	78.3546
11	6.7223	3.3891	74.9655
12	6.4135	3.6978	71.2677
13	6.0767	4.0347	67.2331
14	5.7091	4.4022	62.8309
15	5.3081	4.8032	58.0277
16	4.8706	5.2408	52.7869
17	4.3931	5.7182	47.0687
18	3.8722	6.2391	40.8296
19	3.3039	6.8074	34.0222
20	2.6838	7.4276	26.5946
21	2.0071	8.1042	18.4904
22	1.2689	8.8425	9.6480
23	.4634	9.6480	0.0000

YEARS 24 — MO PAYT .8318 — AN CONST 9.99

#	INT	PRIN	BALANCE
1	8.6994	1.2823	98.7177
2	8.5826	1.3991	97.3186
3	8.4551	1.5265	95.7921
4	8.3161	1.6656	94.1265
5	8.1643	1.8173	92.3091
6	7.9988	1.9829	90.3262
7	7.8181	2.1635	88.1627
8	7.6211	2.3606	85.8021
9	7.4060	2.5757	83.2265
10	7.1714	2.8103	80.4162
11	6.9154	3.0663	77.3499
12	6.6361	3.3456	74.0043
13	6.3313	3.6504	70.3539
14	5.9987	3.9829	66.3710
15	5.6359	4.3457	62.0252
16	5.2400	4.7416	57.2836
17	4.8081	5.1736	52.1100
18	4.3368	5.6449	46.4652
19	3.8226	6.1591	40.3061
20	3.2615	6.7202	33.5859
21	2.6493	7.3323	26.2536
22	1.9814	8.0003	18.2533
23	1.2526	8.7291	9.5242
24	.4574	9.5242	0.0000

YEARS 25 — MO PAYT .8221 — AN CONST 9.87

#	INT	PRIN	BALANCE
1	8.7041	1.1616	98.8384
2	8.5983	1.2674	97.5710
3	8.4829	1.3828	96.1882
4	8.3569	1.5088	94.6794
5	8.2195	1.6463	93.0331
6	8.0695	1.7962	91.2369
7	7.9059	1.9599	89.2770
8	7.7273	2.1384	87.1386
9	7.5325	2.3332	84.8055
10	7.3200	2.5457	82.2597
11	7.0881	2.7776	79.4821
12	6.8351	3.0307	76.4514
13	6.5590	3.3068	73.1447
14	6.2577	3.6080	69.5367
15	5.9291	3.9367	65.6000
16	5.5705	4.2953	61.3047
17	5.1792	4.6866	56.6182
18	4.7522	5.1135	51.5047
19	4.2864	5.5793	45.9254
20	3.7782	6.0875	39.8379
21	3.2236	6.6421	33.1958
22	2.6186	7.2472	25.9486
23	1.9584	7.9073	18.0413
24	1.2381	8.6277	9.4136
25	.4521	9.4136	0.0000

YEARS 26 — MO PAYT .8135 — AN CONST 9.77

#	INT	PRIN	BALANCE
1	8.7084	1.0534	98.9466
2	8.6125	1.1493	97.7973
3	8.5078	1.2540	96.5432
4	8.3935	1.3683	95.1750
5	8.2689	1.4929	93.6820
6	8.1329	1.6289	92.0531
7	7.9845	1.7773	90.2758
8	7.8226	1.9392	88.3366
9	7.6459	2.1159	86.2207
10	7.4532	2.3086	83.9121
11	7.2429	2.5189	81.3932
12	7.0134	2.7484	78.6448
13	6.7631	2.9987	75.6461
14	6.4899	3.2719	72.3742
15	6.1918	3.5700	68.8042
16	5.8666	3.8952	64.9090
17	5.5118	4.2500	60.6590
18	5.1246	4.6372	56.0218
19	4.7022	5.0596	50.9622
20	4.2413	5.5205	45.4417
21	3.7384	6.0234	39.4182
22	3.1897	6.5721	32.8461
23	2.5910	7.1708	25.6753
24	1.9377	7.8241	17.8512
25	1.2250	8.5368	9.3145
26	.4473	9.3145	0.0000

YEARS 27 — MO PAYT .8057 — AN CONST 9.67

#	INT	PRIN	BALANCE
1	8.7123	.9562	99.0438
2	8.6251	1.0433	98.0005
3	8.5301	1.1383	96.8621
4	8.4264	1.2420	95.6201
5	8.3133	1.3552	94.2649
6	8.1898	1.4786	92.7863
7	8.0551	1.6133	91.1729
8	7.9081	1.7603	89.4126
9	7.7478	1.9207	87.4919
10	7.5728	2.0956	85.3963
11	7.3819	2.2865	83.1098
12	7.1736	2.4948	80.6149
13	6.9464	2.7221	77.8928
14	6.6984	2.9701	74.9228
15	6.4278	3.2406	71.6821
16	6.1326	3.5358	68.1463
17	5.8105	3.8579	64.2883
18	5.4591	4.2094	60.0789
19	5.0756	4.5928	55.4861
20	4.6572	5.0112	50.4749
21	4.2007	5.4677	45.0071
22	3.7026	5.9658	39.0413
23	3.1592	6.5093	32.5320
24	2.5662	7.1023	25.4298
25	1.9192	7.7492	17.6805
26	1.2133	8.4552	9.2254
27	.4431	9.2254	0.0000

YEARS 28 — MO PAYT .7987 — AN CONST 9.59

#	INT	PRIN	BALANCE
1	8.7157	.8688	99.1312
2	8.6366	.9479	98.1834
3	8.5502	1.0342	97.1491
4	8.4560	1.1285	96.0206
5	8.3532	1.2313	94.7894
6	8.2410	1.3434	93.4460
7	8.1187	1.4658	91.9802
8	7.9851	1.5993	90.3808
9	7.8394	1.7450	88.6358
10	7.6805	1.9040	86.7318
11	7.5070	2.0774	84.6544
12	7.3178	2.2667	82.3877
13	7.1113	2.4732	79.9146
14	6.8860	2.6985	77.2161
15	6.6402	2.9443	74.2719
16	6.3720	3.2125	71.0594
17	6.0793	3.5051	67.5543
18	5.7600	3.8244	63.7298
19	5.4116	4.1728	59.5570
20	5.0315	4.5529	55.0041
21	4.6168	4.9677	50.0364
22	4.1642	5.4202	44.6161
23	3.6705	5.9140	38.7021
24	3.1317	6.4527	32.2494
25	2.5439	7.0406	25.2089
26	1.9025	7.6819	17.5269
27	1.2028	8.3817	9.1452
28	.4392	9.1452	0.0000

YEARS 29 — MO PAYT .7924 — AN CONST 9.51

#	INT	PRIN	BALANCE
1	8.7188	.7899	99.2101
2	8.6469	.8619	98.3482
3	8.5683	.9404	97.4078
4	8.4827	1.0261	96.3817
5	8.3892	1.1195	95.2621
6	8.2872	1.2215	94.0406
7	8.1759	1.3328	92.7078
8	8.0545	1.4542	91.2536
9	7.9221	1.5867	89.6669
10	7.7775	1.7312	87.9357
11	7.6198	1.8889	86.0467
12	7.4477	2.0610	83.9857
13	7.2600	2.2488	81.7369
14	7.0551	2.4536	79.2833
15	6.8316	2.6771	76.6062
16	6.5877	2.9210	73.6852
17	6.3216	3.1871	70.4981
18	6.0313	3.4774	67.0206
19	5.7145	3.7942	63.2264
20	5.3689	4.1399	59.0865
21	4.9918	4.5170	54.5696
22	4.5803	4.9285	49.6411
23	4.1313	5.3774	44.2637
24	3.6415	5.8673	38.3964
25	3.1070	6.4018	31.9947
26	2.5238	6.9849	25.0097
27	1.8875	7.6212	17.3885
28	1.1933	8.3155	9.0730
29	.4357	9.0730	0.0000

YEARS 30 — MO PAYT .7867 — AN CONST 9.45

#	INT	PRIN	BALANCE
1	8.7216	.7188	99.2812
2	8.6562	.7843	98.4970
3	8.5847	.8557	97.6413
4	8.5068	.9336	96.7076
5	8.4217	1.0187	95.6889
6	8.3289	1.1115	94.5774
7	8.2277	1.2128	93.3647
8	8.1172	1.3232	92.0414
9	7.9966	1.4438	90.5977
10	7.8651	1.5753	89.0224
11	7.7216	1.7188	87.3036
12	7.5650	1.8754	85.4282
13	7.3942	2.0462	83.3820
14	7.2078	2.2326	81.1494
15	7.0044	2.4360	78.7134
16	6.7825	2.6579	76.0555
17	6.5404	2.9000	73.1555
18	6.2762	3.1642	69.9913
19	5.9880	3.4524	66.5389
20	5.6735	3.7669	62.7719
21	5.3303	4.1101	58.6618
22	4.9559	4.4845	54.1773
23	4.5474	4.8930	49.2843
24	4.1016	5.3388	43.9455
25	3.6153	5.8251	38.1204
26	3.0847	6.3557	31.7647
27	2.5057	6.9347	24.8300
28	1.8740	7.5665	17.2635
29	1.1847	8.2557	9.0078
30	.4326	9.0078	0.0000

YEARS 2 — MO PAYT 4.5593 — AN CONST 54.72

#	INT	PRIN	BALANCE
1	6.9022	47.8094	52.1906
2	2.5211	52.1906	0.0000

YEARS 3 — MO PAYT 3.1707 — AN CONST 38.05

#	INT	PRIN	BALANCE
1	7.5910	30.4571	69.5429
2	4.8000	33.2481	36.2949
3	1.7532	36.2949	0.0000

YEARS 4 — MO PAYT 2.4790 — AN CONST 29.75

#	INT	PRIN	BALANCE
1	7.9341	21.8141	78.1859
2	5.9351	23.8131	54.3727
3	3.7529	25.9953	28.3774
4	1.3708	28.3774	0.0000

YEARS 5 — MO PAYT 2.0661 — AN CONST 24.80

#	INT	PRIN	BALANCE
1	8.1389	16.6548	83.3452
2	6.6121	18.1810	65.1642
3	4.9466	19.8471	45.3171
4	3.1279	21.6658	23.6512
5	1.1425	23.6512	0.0000

YEARS 6 — MO PAYT 1.7926 — AN CONST 21.52

#	INT	PRIN	BALANCE
1	8.2746	13.2372	86.7628
2	7.0615	14.4502	72.3126
3	5.7373	15.7744	56.5383
4	4.2918	17.2199	39.3184
5	2.7138	18.7979	20.5205
6	.9912	20.5205	0.0000

YEARS 7 — MO PAYT 1.5988 — AN CONST 19.19

#	INT	PRIN	BALANCE
1	8.3707	10.8146	89.1854
2	7.3797	11.8056	77.3798
3	6.2979	12.8875	64.4923
4	5.1169	14.0684	50.4239
5	3.8277	15.3576	35.0662
6	2.4203	16.7650	18.3013
7	.8840	18.3013	0.0000

YEARS 8 — MO PAYT 1.4547 — AN CONST 17.46

#	INT	PRIN	BALANCE
1	8.4422	9.0138	90.9862
2	7.6162	9.8398	81.1464
3	6.7145	10.7415	70.4049
4	5.7302	11.7258	58.6791
5	4.6557	12.8003	45.8788
6	3.4827	13.9733	31.9054
7	2.2022	15.2538	16.6516
8	.8044	16.6516	0.0000

YEARS 9 — MO PAYT 1.3437 — AN CONST 16.13

#	INT	PRIN	BALANCE
1	8.4972	7.6273	92.3727
2	7.7983	8.3263	84.0464
3	7.0353	9.0893	74.9571
4	6.2024	9.9222	65.0349
5	5.2931	10.8314	54.2035
6	4.3006	11.8240	42.3794
7	3.2170	12.9075	29.4719
8	2.0342	14.0904	15.3816
9	.7430	15.3816	0.0000

YEARS 10 — MO PAYT 1.2560 — AN CONST 15.08

#	INT	PRIN	BALANCE
1	8.5408	6.5307	93.4693
2	7.9423	7.1292	86.3400
3	7.2890	7.7825	78.5575
4	6.5758	8.4957	70.0618
5	5.7973	9.2742	60.7876
6	4.9474	10.1241	50.6636
7	4.0197	11.0518	39.6118
8	3.0069	12.0646	27.5472
9	1.9014	13.1701	14.3770
10	.6945	14.3770	0.0000

YEARS 11 — MO PAYT 1.1851 — AN CONST 14.23

#	INT	PRIN	BALANCE
1	8.5759	5.6448	94.3552
2	8.0587	6.1621	88.1931
3	7.4940	6.7268	81.4663
4	6.8775	7.3432	74.1231
5	6.2046	8.0161	66.1070
6	5.4701	8.7507	57.3563
7	4.6682	9.5526	47.8037
8	3.7928	10.4280	37.3757
9	2.8372	11.3836	25.9922
10	1.7940	12.4267	13.5655
11	.6553	13.5655	0.0000

YEARS 12 — MO PAYT 1.1268 — AN CONST 13.53

#	INT	PRIN	BALANCE
1	8.6048	4.9167	95.0833
2	8.1543	5.3673	89.7160
3	7.6624	5.8591	83.8569
4	7.1255	6.3960	77.4608
5	6.5394	6.9822	70.4787
6	5.8996	7.6220	62.8567
7	5.2011	8.3204	54.5362
8	4.4386	9.0829	45.4533
9	3.6063	9.9152	35.5381
10	2.6977	10.8239	24.7142
11	1.7058	11.8157	12.8985
12	.6231	12.8985	0.0000

YEARS 13 — MO PAYT 1.0782 — AN CONST 12.94

#	INT	PRIN	BALANCE
1	8.6289	4.3099	95.6901
2	8.2340	4.7048	90.9853
3	7.8028	5.1360	85.8493
4	7.3322	5.6066	80.2427
5	6.8184	6.1204	74.1224
6	6.2576	6.6812	67.4411
7	5.6453	7.2935	60.1476
8	4.9769	7.9618	52.1858
9	4.2473	8.6914	43.4943
10	3.4509	9.4879	34.0064
11	2.5814	10.3574	23.6491
12	1.6323	11.3065	12.3426
13	.5962	12.3426	0.0000

YEARS 14 — MO PAYT 1.0373 — AN CONST 12.45

#	INT	PRIN	BALANCE
1	8.6492	3.7981	96.2019
2	8.3012	4.1462	92.0557
3	7.9212	4.5261	87.5296
4	7.5065	4.9409	82.5887
5	7.0537	5.3937	77.1950
6	6.5594	5.8879	71.3071
7	6.0199	6.4275	64.8796
8	5.4309	7.0165	57.8632
9	4.7879	7.6594	50.2037
10	4.0860	8.3613	41.8424
11	3.3198	9.1275	32.7148
12	2.4834	9.9640	22.7508
13	1.5703	10.8771	11.8738
14	.5736	11.8738	0.0000

YEARS 15 — MO PAYT 1.0024 — AN CONST 12.03

#	INT	PRIN	BALANCE
1	8.6665	3.3623	96.6377
2	8.3584	3.6704	92.9673
3	8.0221	4.0068	88.9605
4	7.6549	4.3739	84.5866
5	7.2541	4.7748	79.8118
6	6.8165	5.2123	74.5995
7	6.3389	5.6899	68.9095
8	5.8175	6.2114	62.6982
9	5.2483	6.7806	55.9176
10	4.6269	7.4019	48.5157
11	3.9486	8.0802	40.4355
12	3.2082	8.8207	31.6148
13	2.3999	9.6290	21.9859
14	1.5175	10.5113	11.4746
15	.5543	11.4746	0.0000

YEARS 16 — MO PAYT .9725 — AN CONST 11.67

#	INT	PRIN	BALANCE
1	8.6814	2.9880	97.0120
2	8.4076	3.2618	93.7501
3	8.1087	3.5607	90.1894
4	7.7824	3.8870	86.3023
5	7.4262	4.2432	82.0591
6	7.0373	4.6321	77.4270
7	6.6129	5.0566	72.3704
8	6.1495	5.5199	66.8505
9	5.6437	6.0258	60.8247
10	5.0915	6.5780	54.2468
11	4.4887	7.1807	47.0660
12	3.8307	7.8388	39.2273
13	3.1123	8.5571	30.6702
14	2.3282	9.3412	21.3289
15	1.4722	10.1972	11.1317
16	.5377	11.1317	0.0000

YEARS 17 — MO PAYT .9465 — AN CONST 11.36

#	INT	PRIN	BALANCE
1	8.6942	2.6643	97.3357
2	8.4501	2.9084	94.4273
3	8.1836	3.1749	91.2524
4	7.8926	3.4659	87.7865
5	7.5750	3.7835	84.0030
6	7.2283	4.1302	79.8728
7	6.8498	4.5087	75.3641
8	6.4367	4.9218	70.4423
9	5.9856	5.3729	65.0694
10	5.4933	5.8652	59.2042
11	4.9558	6.4027	52.8015
12	4.3691	6.9894	45.8121
13	3.7286	7.6299	38.1822
14	3.0294	8.3291	29.8531
15	2.2661	9.0924	20.7607
16	1.4329	9.9256	10.8351
17	.5234	10.8351	0.0000

YEARS 18 — MO PAYT .9240 — AN CONST 11.09

#	INT	PRIN	BALANCE
1	8.7054	2.3825	97.6175
2	8.4871	2.6008	95.0167
3	8.2488	2.8391	92.1776
4	7.9886	3.0993	89.0783
5	7.7046	3.3833	85.6950
6	7.3946	3.6933	82.0017
7	7.0561	4.0318	77.9699
8	6.6866	4.4013	73.5686
9	6.2833	4.8046	68.7640
10	5.8430	5.2449	63.5192
11	5.3624	5.7255	57.7937
12	4.8377	6.2502	51.5435
13	4.2650	6.8229	44.7206
14	3.6398	7.4481	37.2725
15	2.9572	8.1307	29.1418
16	2.2122	8.8757	20.2661
17	1.3988	9.6891	10.5770
18	.5109	10.5770	0.0000

YEARS 19 — MO PAYT .9043 — AN CONST 10.86

#	INT	PRIN	BALANCE
1	8.7152	2.1359	97.8641
2	8.5195	2.3316	95.5326
3	8.3058	2.5452	92.9873
4	8.0726	2.7785	90.2088
5	7.8180	3.0331	87.1757
6	7.5400	3.3110	83.8647
7	7.2366	3.6145	80.2502
8	6.9054	3.9457	76.3045
9	6.5438	4.3073	71.9973
10	6.1491	4.7020	67.2953
11	5.7182	5.1328	62.1625
12	5.2479	5.6032	56.5593
13	4.7344	6.1167	50.4426
14	4.1739	6.6772	43.7654
15	3.5620	7.2891	36.4764
16	2.8941	7.9570	28.5194
17	2.1649	8.6862	19.8332
18	1.3689	9.4821	10.3511
19	.5000	10.3511	0.0000

YEARS 20 — MO PAYT .8869 — AN CONST 10.65

#	INT	PRIN	BALANCE
1	8.7238	1.9190	98.0810
2	8.5480	2.0949	95.9861
3	8.3560	2.2868	93.6993
4	8.1464	2.4964	91.2029
5	7.9177	2.7252	88.4777
6	7.6679	2.9749	85.5028
7	7.3953	3.2475	82.2553
8	7.0977	3.5451	78.7102
9	6.7729	3.8700	74.8402
10	6.4182	4.2246	70.6156
11	6.0311	4.6117	66.0039
12	5.6085	5.0343	60.9696
13	5.1472	5.4957	55.4739
14	4.6436	5.9993	49.4746
15	4.0938	6.5490	42.9256
16	3.4937	7.1492	35.7764
17	2.8385	7.8043	27.9721
18	2.1234	8.5195	19.4526
19	1.3427	9.3002	10.1524
20	.4904	10.1524	0.0000

YEARS 21 — MO PAYT .8716 — AN CONST 10.46

#	INT	PRIN	BALANCE
1	8.7314	1.7276	98.2724
2	8.5731	1.8859	96.3866
3	8.4003	2.0587	94.3279

#	INT	PRIN	BALANCE
4	8.2116	2.2473	92.0806
5	8.0057	2.4533	89.6273
6	7.7809	2.6781	86.9492
7	7.5355	2.9235	84.0257
8	7.2676	3.1914	80.8343
9	6.9751	3.4839	77.3504
10	6.6559	3.8031	73.5473
11	6.3074	4.1516	69.3957
12	5.9269	4.5321	64.8637
13	5.5116	4.9474	59.9163
14	5.0583	5.4007	54.5156
15	4.5633	5.8956	48.6199
16	4.0231	6.4359	42.1840
17	3.4333	7.0257	35.1583
18	2.7895	7.6695	27.4889
19	2.0867	8.3723	19.1166
20	1.3195	9.1395	9.9770
21	.4819	9.9770	0.0000

	YEARS 22	MO PAYT .8580	AN CONST 10.30
#	INT	PRIN	BALANCE
1	8.7382	1.5579	98.4421
2	8.5954	1.7006	96.7415
3	8.4396	1.8565	94.8850
4	8.2694	2.0266	92.8584
5	8.0837	2.2123	90.6461
6	7.8810	2.4151	88.2310
7	7.6597	2.6364	85.5946
8	7.4181	2.8780	82.7167
9	7.1544	3.1417	79.5750
10	6.8665	3.4296	76.1454
11	6.5522	3.7439	72.4015
12	6.2091	4.0869	68.3146
13	5.8346	4.4615	63.8532
14	5.4258	4.8703	58.9829
15	4.9795	5.3166	53.6663
16	4.4923	5.8038	47.8625
17	3.9604	6.3356	41.5268
18	3.3798	6.9162	34.6106
19	2.7460	7.5500	27.0606
20	2.0542	8.2419	18.8187
21	1.2989	8.9971	9.8216
22	.4744	9.8216	0.0000

	YEARS 23	MO PAYT .8459	AN CONST 10.16
#	INT	PRIN	BALANCE
1	8.7441	1.4070	98.5930
2	8.6152	1.5360	97.0570
3	8.4745	1.6767	95.3803
4	8.3208	1.8304	93.5499
5	8.1531	1.9981	91.5518
6	7.9700	2.1812	89.3706
7	7.7701	2.3811	86.9896
8	7.5519	2.5993	84.3903
9	7.3137	2.8375	81.5528
10	7.0537	3.0975	78.4553
11	6.7698	3.3813	75.0740
12	6.4600	3.6912	71.3828
13	6.1217	4.0294	67.3534
14	5.7525	4.3987	62.9547
15	5.3494	4.8018	58.1530
16	4.9094	5.2418	52.9112
17	4.4290	5.7221	47.1890
18	3.9047	6.2465	40.9425
19	3.3323	6.8189	34.1236
20	2.7074	7.4438	26.6799
21	2.0253	8.1259	18.5540
22	1.2806	8.8705	9.6834
23	.4678	9.6834	0.0000

	YEARS 24	MO PAYT .8352	AN CONST 10.03
#	INT	PRIN	BALANCE
1	8.7495	1.2725	98.7275
2	8.6329	1.3891	97.3384
3	8.5056	1.5164	95.8219
4	8.3666	1.6554	94.1666
5	8.2149	1.8071	92.3595
6	8.0493	1.9727	90.3868
7	7.8686	2.1534	88.2334
8	7.6712	2.3508	85.8826
9	7.4558	2.5662	83.3164
10	7.2206	2.8014	80.5151
11	6.9639	3.0581	77.4570
12	6.6837	3.3383	74.1187
13	6.3778	3.6442	70.4745
14	6.0438	3.9782	66.4963
15	5.6793	4.3427	62.1536
16	5.2813	4.7407	57.4130
17	4.8469	5.1751	52.2379
18	4.3727	5.6493	46.5886
19	3.8550	6.1670	40.4215
20	3.2899	6.7321	33.6894
21	2.6729	7.3491	26.3404
22	1.9995	8.0225	18.3179
23	1.2643	8.7577	9.5602
24	.4618	9.5602	0.0000

	YEARS 25	MO PAYT .8255	AN CONST 9.91
#	INT	PRIN	BALANCE
1	8.7543	1.1523	98.8477
2	8.6487	1.2578	97.5899
3	8.5334	1.3731	96.2168
4	8.4076	1.4989	94.7178
5	8.2702	1.6363	93.0815
6	8.1203	1.7863	91.2953
7	7.9566	1.9499	89.3453
8	7.7779	2.1286	87.2167
9	7.5828	2.3237	84.8930
10	7.3699	2.5366	82.3564
11	7.1374	2.7691	79.5873
12	6.8837	3.0228	76.5645
13	6.6067	3.2998	73.2647
14	6.3043	3.6022	69.6624
15	5.9742	3.9323	65.7301
16	5.6139	4.2927	61.4374
17	5.2205	4.6860	56.7514
18	4.7911	5.1155	51.6360
19	4.3223	5.5842	46.0517
20	3.8106	6.0959	39.9558
21	3.2520	6.6546	33.3012
22	2.6421	7.2644	26.0368
23	1.9765	7.9301	18.1068
24	1.2498	8.6568	9.4500
25	.4565	9.4500	0.0000

	YEARS 26	MO PAYT .8169	AN CONST 9.81
#	INT	PRIN	BALANCE
1	8.7585	1.0445	98.9555
2	8.6628	1.1402	97.8153
3	8.5583	1.2447	96.5706
4	8.4443	1.3588	95.2118
5	8.3198	1.4833	93.7285
6	8.1838	1.6192	92.1093
7	8.0355	1.7676	90.3417
8	7.8735	1.9296	88.4121
9	7.6967	2.1064	86.3057
10	7.5036	2.2994	84.0063
11	7.2929	2.5101	81.4962
12	7.0629	2.7402	78.7560
13	6.8118	2.9913	75.7648
14	6.5377	3.2654	72.4994
15	6.2385	3.5646	68.9348
16	5.9118	3.8912	65.0436
17	5.5552	4.2478	60.7957
18	5.1660	4.6371	56.1586
19	4.7410	5.0620	51.0966
20	4.2772	5.5259	45.5707
21	3.7708	6.0323	39.5384
22	3.2180	6.5851	32.9534
23	2.6146	7.1885	25.7649
24	1.9558	7.8472	17.9177
25	1.2367	8.5663	9.3513
26	.4517	9.3513	0.0000

	YEARS 27	MO PAYT .8092	AN CONST 9.72
#	INT	PRIN	BALANCE
1	8.7624	.9478	99.0522
2	8.6755	1.0346	98.0176
3	8.5807	1.1294	96.8882
4	8.4772	1.2329	95.6553
5	8.3642	1.3459	94.3094
6	8.2409	1.4692	92.8402
7	8.1063	1.6039	91.2363
8	7.9593	1.7508	89.4855
9	7.7989	1.9113	87.5742
10	7.6237	2.0864	85.4878
11	7.4325	2.2776	83.2101
12	7.2238	2.4863	80.7238
13	6.9960	2.7142	78.0096
14	6.7472	2.9629	75.0467
15	6.4757	3.2344	71.8123
16	6.1793	3.5308	68.2815
17	5.8558	3.8544	64.4271
18	5.5026	4.2076	60.2195
19	5.1170	4.5931	55.6264
20	4.6961	5.0140	50.6123
21	4.2366	5.4735	45.1388
22	3.7350	5.9751	39.1637
23	3.1875	6.5226	32.6411
24	2.5898	7.1204	25.5207
25	1.9373	7.7729	17.7478
26	1.2250	8.4851	9.2627
27	.4474	9.2627	0.0000

	YEARS 28	MO PAYT .8022	AN CONST 9.63
#	INT	PRIN	BALANCE
1	8.7658	.8607	99.1393
2	8.6870	.9396	98.1997
3	8.6009	1.0257	97.1740
4	8.5069	1.1197	96.0543
5	8.4043	1.2223	94.8320
6	8.2922	1.3343	93.4977
7	8.1700	1.4566	92.0411
8	8.0365	1.5901	90.4510
9	7.8908	1.7358	88.7152
10	7.7317	1.8948	86.8204
11	7.5581	2.0685	84.7519
12	7.3685	2.2580	82.4939
13	7.1616	2.4649	80.0290
14	6.9357	2.6908	77.3382
15	6.6892	2.9374	74.4008
16	6.4200	3.2066	71.1942
17	6.1261	3.5004	67.6938
18	5.8054	3.8212	63.8726
19	5.4552	4.1714	59.7012
20	5.0730	4.5536	55.1476
21	4.6557	4.9709	50.1767
22	4.2001	5.4264	44.7503
23	3.7029	5.9237	38.8266
24	3.1601	6.4665	32.3601
25	2.5675	7.0591	25.3010
26	1.9206	7.7060	17.5951
27	1.2144	8.4121	9.1830
28	.4436	9.1830	0.0000

	YEARS 29	MO PAYT .7959	AN CONST 9.56
#	INT	PRIN	BALANCE
1	8.7689	.7823	99.2177
2	8.6973	.8540	98.3637
3	8.6190	.9323	97.4315
4	8.5336	1.0177	96.4138
5	8.4403	1.1109	95.3028
6	8.3385	1.2127	94.0901
7	8.2274	1.3239	92.7662
8	8.1061	1.4452	91.3210
9	7.9736	1.5776	89.7434
10	7.8291	1.7222	88.0212
11	7.6712	1.8800	86.1412
12	7.4990	2.0523	84.0889
13	7.3109	2.2404	81.8486
14	7.1056	2.4457	79.4029
15	6.8815	2.6698	76.7331
16	6.6368	2.9144	73.8187
17	6.3698	3.1815	70.6372
18	6.0782	3.4730	67.1642
19	5.7600	3.7913	63.3729
20	5.4125	4.1387	59.2342
21	5.0333	4.5180	54.7162
22	4.6192	4.9320	49.7842
23	4.1673	5.3840	44.4002
24	3.6739	5.8773	38.5229
25	3.1353	6.4159	32.1070
26	2.5474	7.0039	25.1031
27	1.9056	7.6457	17.4574
28	1.2049	8.3463	9.1111
29	.4401	9.1111	0.0000

	YEARS 30	MO PAYT .7903	AN CONST 9.49
#	INT	PRIN	BALANCE
1	8.7718	.7115	99.2885
2	8.7066	.7767	98.5117
3	8.6354	.8479	97.6638
4	8.5577	.9256	96.7382
5	8.4729	1.0104	95.7278
6	8.3803	1.1030	94.6247
7	8.2792	1.2041	93.4206
8	8.1688	1.3145	92.1062
9	8.0484	1.4349	90.6713
10	7.9169	1.5664	89.1049
11	7.7734	1.7099	87.3949
12	7.6167	1.8666	85.5283
13	7.4456	2.0377	83.4906
14	7.2589	2.2244	81.2662
15	7.0550	2.4283	78.8379
16	6.8325	2.6508	76.1872
17	6.5896	2.8937	73.2935
18	6.3244	3.1589	70.1346
19	6.0350	3.4483	66.6863
20	5.7190	3.7643	62.9220
21	5.3740	4.1093	58.8127
22	4.9975	4.4858	54.3268
23	4.5864	4.8969	49.4299
24	4.1376	5.3457	44.0843
25	3.6478	5.8355	38.2488
26	3.1130	6.3703	31.8785
27	2.5293	6.9540	24.9245
28	1.8920	7.5913	17.3332
29	1.1964	8.2869	9.0463
30	.4370	9.0463	0.0000

YEARS 2 — MO PAYT 4.5627 — AN CONST 54.76

#	INT	PRIN	BALANCE
1	6.9620	47.7909	52.2091
2	2.5437	52.2091	0.0000
7	3.2509	12.9212	29.5365
8	2.0563	14.1158	15.4208
9	.7513	15.4208	0.0000

YEARS 3 — MO PAYT 3.1742 — AN CONST 38.09

#	INT	PRIN	BALANCE
1	7.6568	30.4331	69.5669
2	4.8433	33.2466	36.3203
3	1.7696	36.3203	0.0000

YEARS 4 — MO PAYT 2.4826 — AN CONST 29.80

#	INT	PRIN	BALANCE
1	8.0029	21.7880	78.2120
2	5.9886	23.8023	54.4097
3	3.7880	26.0029	28.4068
4	1.3840	28.4068	0.0000

YEARS 5 — MO PAYT 2.0698 — AN CONST 24.84

#	INT	PRIN	BALANCE
1	8.2094	16.6279	83.3721
2	6.6722	18.1651	65.2070
3	4.9928	19.8445	45.3625
4	3.1582	21.6791	23.6834
5	1.1539	23.6834	0.0000

YEARS 6 — MO PAYT 1.7964 — AN CONST 21.56

#	INT	PRIN	BALANCE
1	8.3462	13.2100	86.7900
2	7.1250	14.4313	72.3586
3	5.7908	15.7655	56.5931
4	4.3332	17.2230	39.3701
5	2.7410	18.8153	20.5548
6	1.0015	20.5548	0.0000

YEARS 7 — MO PAYT 1.6026 — AN CONST 19.24

#	INT	PRIN	BALANCE
1	8.4432	10.7877	89.2123
2	7.4459	11.7850	77.4274
3	6.3563	12.8745	64.5528
4	5.1661	14.0648	50.4881
5	3.8658	15.3651	35.1230
6	2.4453	16.7856	18.3374
7	.8934	18.3374	0.0000

YEARS 8 — MO PAYT 1.4585 — AN CONST 17.51

#	INT	PRIN	BALANCE
1	8.5153	8.9873	91.0127
2	7.6844	9.8181	81.1944
3	6.7767	10.7258	70.4687
4	5.7851	11.7174	58.7513
5	4.7018	12.8007	45.9506
6	3.5184	13.9842	31.9664
7	2.2255	15.2770	16.6894
8	.8131	16.6894	0.0000

YEARS 9 — MO PAYT 1.3477 — AN CONST 16.18

#	INT	PRIN	BALANCE
1	8.5707	7.6014	92.3986
2	7.8680	8.3041	84.0945
3	7.1003	9.0718	75.0227
4	6.2616	9.9105	65.1122
5	5.3453	10.8268	54.2854
6	4.3444	11.8277	42.4577

YEARS 10 — MO PAYT 1.2600 — AN CONST 15.13

#	INT	PRIN	BALANCE
1	8.6146	6.5054	93.4946
2	8.0132	7.1069	86.3877
3	7.3561	7.7639	78.6238
4	6.6384	8.4817	70.1421
5	5.8542	9.2658	60.8763
6	4.9976	10.1224	50.7539
7	4.0618	11.0583	39.6956
8	3.0394	12.0806	27.6150
9	1.9226	13.1975	14.4176
10	.7025	14.4176	0.0000

YEARS 11 — MO PAYT 1.1892 — AN CONST 14.28

#	INT	PRIN	BALANCE
1	8.6500	5.6202	94.3798
2	8.1304	6.1398	88.2400
3	7.5628	6.7074	81.5325
4	6.9427	7.3275	74.2050
5	6.2653	8.0050	66.2000
6	5.5252	8.7450	57.4550
7	4.7167	9.5535	47.9014
8	3.8335	10.4368	37.4647
9	2.8686	11.4016	26.0630
10	1.8145	12.4557	13.6073
11	.6630	13.6073	0.0000

YEARS 12 — MO PAYT 1.1310 — AN CONST 13.58

#	INT	PRIN	BALANCE
1	8.6791	4.8929	95.1071
2	8.2268	5.3452	89.7619
3	7.7326	5.8394	83.9225
4	7.1928	6.3793	77.5432
5	6.6030	6.9690	70.5742
6	5.9587	7.6133	62.9609
7	5.2549	8.3172	54.6438
8	4.4859	9.0861	45.5577
9	3.6459	9.9261	35.6316
10	2.7282	10.8438	24.7878
11	1.7257	11.8463	12.9415
12	.6305	12.9415	0.0000

YEARS 13 — MO PAYT 1.0825 — AN CONST 13.00

#	INT	PRIN	BALANCE
1	8.7034	4.2868	95.7132
2	8.3071	4.6831	91.0301
3	7.8741	5.1161	85.9140
4	7.4011	5.5891	80.3249
5	6.8844	6.1058	74.2191
6	6.3200	6.6703	67.5488
7	5.7033	7.2869	60.2619
8	5.0296	7.9606	52.3013
9	4.2936	8.6966	43.6047
10	3.4896	9.5006	34.1041
11	2.6113	10.3789	23.7252
12	1.6518	11.3385	12.3867
13	.6035	12.3867	0.0000

YEARS 14 — MO PAYT 1.0416 — AN CONST 12.50

#	INT	PRIN	BALANCE
1	8.7239	3.7759	96.2241
2	8.3748	4.1249	92.0992
3	7.9934	4.5063	87.5929
4	7.5768	4.9229	82.6700
5	7.1217	5.3780	77.2919
6	6.6245	5.8752	71.4167
7	6.0813	6.4184	64.9983
8	5.4879	7.0118	57.9865
9	4.8397	7.6600	50.3265
10	4.1315	8.3682	41.9582
11	3.3579	9.1419	32.8164
12	2.5127	9.9870	22.8293
13	1.5894	10.9103	11.9190
14	.5807	11.9190	0.0000

YEARS 15 — MO PAYT 1.0068 — AN CONST 12.09

#	INT	PRIN	BALANCE
1	8.7413	3.3409	96.6591
2	8.4324	3.6497	93.0094
3	8.0950	3.9871	89.0223
4	7.7264	4.3558	84.6665
5	7.3237	4.7584	79.9081
6	6.8838	5.1984	74.7097
7	6.4032	5.6790	69.0308
8	5.8781	6.2040	62.8268
9	5.3046	6.7775	56.0492
10	4.6780	7.4041	48.6451
11	3.9935	8.0886	40.5565
12	3.2457	8.8364	31.7200
13	2.4287	9.6534	22.0666
14	1.5363	10.5458	11.5208
15	.5613	11.5208	0.0000

YEARS 16 — MO PAYT .9770 — AN CONST 11.73

#	INT	PRIN	BALANCE
1	8.7562	2.9674	97.0326
2	8.4819	3.2417	93.7909
3	8.1822	3.5414	90.2495
4	7.8548	3.8688	86.3807
5	7.4971	4.2265	82.1542
6	7.1064	4.6172	77.5369
7	6.6795	5.0441	72.4928
8	6.2132	5.5104	66.9824
9	5.7037	6.0199	60.9625
10	5.1472	6.5764	54.3861
11	4.5392	7.1844	47.2016
12	3.8750	7.8486	39.3530
13	3.1494	8.5742	30.7788
14	2.3567	9.3669	21.4118
15	1.4907	10.2329	11.1789
16	.5447	11.1789	0.0000

YEARS 17 — MO PAYT .9511 — AN CONST 11.42

#	INT	PRIN	BALANCE
1	8.7691	2.6444	97.3556
2	8.5247	2.8889	94.4667
3	8.2568	3.1560	91.3107
4	7.9658	3.4478	87.8629
5	7.6471	3.7665	84.0964
6	7.2988	4.1147	79.9816
7	6.9184	4.4951	75.4865
8	6.5029	4.9107	70.5758
9	6.0489	5.3647	65.2111
10	5.5529	5.8607	59.3504
11	5.0111	6.4025	52.9478
12	4.4192	6.9944	45.9534
13	3.7725	7.6411	38.3123
14	3.0661	8.3475	29.9648
15	2.2944	9.1192	20.8456
16	1.4513	9.9623	10.8833
17	.5303	10.8833	0.0000

YEARS 18 — MO PAYT .9287 — AN CONST 11.15

#	INT	PRIN	BALANCE
1	8.7804	2.3634	97.6366
2	8.5619	2.5819	95.0546
3	8.3232	2.8206	92.2340
4	8.0624	3.0814	89.1526
5	7.7775	3.3663	85.7863
6	7.4663	3.6775	82.1088
7	7.1263	4.0175	78.0913
8	6.7549	4.3889	73.7024
9	6.3492	4.7947	68.9078
10	5.9059	5.2379	63.6698
11	5.4217	5.7222	57.9477
12	4.8926	6.2512	51.6965
13	4.3147	6.8291	44.8673
14	3.6833	7.4605	37.4069
15	2.9936	8.1502	29.2567
16	2.2401	8.9037	20.3530
17	1.4170	9.7268	10.6261
18	.5177	10.6261	0.0000

YEARS 19 — MO PAYT .9090 — AN CONST 10.91

#	INT	PRIN	BALANCE
1	8.7902	2.1176	97.8824
2	8.5945	2.3134	95.5690
3	8.3806	2.5273	93.0417
4	8.1469	2.7609	90.2808
5	7.8917	3.0162	87.2647
6	7.6128	3.2950	83.9697
7	7.3082	3.5996	80.3701
8	6.9754	3.9324	76.4377
9	6.6119	4.2960	72.1417
10	6.2147	4.6931	67.4486
11	5.7808	5.1270	62.3216
12	5.3068	5.6010	56.7206
13	4.7890	6.1188	50.6017
14	4.2233	6.6845	43.9172
15	3.6054	7.3025	36.6147
16	2.9302	7.9776	28.6371
17	2.1927	8.7152	19.9220
18	1.3870	9.5209	10.4011
19	.5068	10.4011	0.0000

YEARS 20 — MO PAYT .8917 — AN CONST 10.71

#	INT	PRIN	BALANCE
1	8.7989	1.9015	98.0985
2	8.6231	2.0773	96.0211
3	8.4310	2.2694	93.7517
4	8.2212	2.4792	91.2725
5	7.9920	2.7084	88.5641
6	7.7416	2.9588	85.6053
7	7.4681	3.2323	82.3730
8	7.1693	3.5312	78.8418
9	6.8428	3.8576	74.9842
10	6.4862	4.2143	70.7699
11	6.0965	4.6039	66.1660
12	5.6709	5.0295	61.1365
13	5.2059	5.4945	55.6420
14	4.6980	6.0025	49.6395
15	4.1430	6.5574	43.0821
16	3.5368	7.1636	35.9185
17	2.8745	7.8259	28.0926
18	2.1510	8.5494	19.5431
19	1.3606	9.3398	10.2033
20	.4971	10.2033	0.0000

YEARS 21 — MO PAYT .8764 — AN CONST 10.52

#	INT	PRIN	BALANCE
1	8.8065	1.7108	98.2892
2	8.6484	1.8690	96.4201
3	8.4756	2.0418	94.3783

#	INT	PRIN	BALANCE
4	8.2868	2.2306	92.1478
5	8.0806	2.4368	89.7110
6	7.8553	2.6621	87.0489
7	7.6092	2.9082	84.1407
8	7.3403	3.1770	80.9637
9	7.0466	3.4708	77.4929
10	6.7257	3.7916	73.7013
11	6.3752	4.1422	69.5591
12	5.9922	4.5251	65.0340
13	5.5739	4.9435	60.0905
14	5.1169	5.4005	54.6900
15	4.6176	5.8998	48.7903
16	4.0721	6.4452	42.3450
17	3.4763	7.0411	35.3040
18	2.8253	7.6920	27.6119
19	2.1142	8.4032	19.2088
20	1.3373	9.1800	10.0287
21	.4886	10.0287	0.0000

YEARS 22 — MO PAYT .8629 — AN CONST 10.36

#	INT	PRIN	BALANCE
1	8.8133	1.5419	98.4581
2	8.6707	1.6845	96.7736
3	8.5150	1.8402	94.9334
4	8.3449	2.0103	92.9231
5	8.1590	2.1962	90.7269
6	7.9560	2.3992	88.3277
7	7.7342	2.6210	85.7067
8	7.4919	2.8633	82.8434
9	7.2271	3.1281	79.7153
10	6.9379	3.4172	76.2981
11	6.6220	3.7332	72.5649
12	6.2769	4.0783	68.4866
13	5.8998	4.4553	64.0312
14	5.4879	4.8672	59.1640
15	5.0380	5.3172	53.8468
16	4.5464	5.8088	48.0380
17	4.0094	6.3458	41.6921
18	3.4227	6.9325	34.7596
19	2.7818	7.5734	27.1862
20	2.0816	8.2736	18.9126
21	1.3167	9.0385	9.8741
22	.4811	9.8741	0.0000

YEARS 23 — MO PAYT .8509 — AN CONST 10.22

#	INT	PRIN	BALANCE
1	8.8193	1.3918	98.6082
2	8.6906	1.5205	97.0878
3	8.5501	1.6610	95.4267
4	8.3965	1.8146	93.6122
5	8.2287	1.9823	91.6298
6	8.0455	2.1656	89.4642
7	7.8453	2.3658	87.0984
8	7.6265	2.5845	84.5138
9	7.3876	2.8235	81.6904
10	7.1266	3.0845	78.6058
11	6.8414	3.3697	75.2362
12	6.5299	3.6812	71.5549
13	6.1895	4.0215	67.5334
14	5.8177	4.3933	63.1401
15	5.4116	4.7995	58.3406
16	4.9679	5.2432	53.0973
17	4.4831	5.7280	47.3694
18	3.9536	6.2575	41.1119
19	3.3750	6.8360	34.2758
20	2.7431	7.4680	26.8078
21	2.0526	8.1584	18.6494
22	1.2984	8.9127	9.7367
23	.4744	9.7367	0.0000

YEARS 24 — MO PAYT .8402 — AN CONST 10.09

#	INT	PRIN	BALANCE
1	8.8246	1.2580	98.7420
2	8.7083	1.3743	97.3678
3	8.5813	1.5013	95.8664
4	8.4425	1.6401	94.2263
5	8.2909	1.7918	92.4345
6	8.1252	1.9574	90.4771
7	7.9443	2.1384	88.3388
8	7.7466	2.3361	86.0027
9	7.5306	2.5520	83.4507
10	7.2947	2.7880	80.6627
11	7.0369	3.0457	77.6170
12	6.7553	3.3273	74.2897
13	6.4477	3.6349	70.6548
14	6.1117	3.9710	66.6838
15	5.7445	4.3381	62.3458
16	5.3435	4.7391	57.6066
17	4.9054	5.1773	52.4294
18	4.4267	5.6559	46.7735
19	3.9038	6.1788	40.5947
20	3.3326	6.7500	33.8447
21	2.7085	7.3741	26.4706
22	2.0268	8.0558	18.4148
23	1.2820	8.8006	9.6142
24	.4684	9.6142	0.0000

YEARS 25 — MO PAYT .8307 — AN CONST 9.97

#	INT	PRIN	BALANCE
1	8.8294	1.1384	98.8616
2	8.7242	1.2437	97.6179
3	8.6092	1.3586	96.2593
4	8.4836	1.4842	94.7751
5	8.3464	1.6215	93.1536
6	8.1965	1.7714	91.3823
7	8.0327	1.9351	89.4471
8	7.8538	2.1140	87.3331
9	7.6584	2.3095	85.0237
10	7.4449	2.5230	82.5007
11	7.2116	2.7562	79.7444
12	6.9568	3.0110	76.7334
13	6.6784	3.2894	73.4440
14	6.3743	3.5935	69.8505
15	6.0421	3.9257	65.9247
16	5.6792	4.2887	61.6360
17	5.2827	4.6852	56.9509
18	4.8495	5.1183	51.8325
19	4.3763	5.5915	46.2410
20	3.8594	6.1085	40.1326
21	3.2947	6.6732	33.4594
22	2.6777	7.2901	26.1692
23	2.0037	7.9641	18.2051
24	1.2674	8.7004	9.5047
25	.4631	9.5047	0.0000

YEARS 26 — MO PAYT .8221 — AN CONST 9.87

#	INT	PRIN	BALANCE
1	8.8337	1.0313	98.9687
2	8.7384	1.1267	97.8420
3	8.6342	1.2308	96.6112
4	8.5204	1.3446	95.2666
5	8.3961	1.4689	93.7976
6	8.2603	1.6047	92.1929
7	8.1119	1.7531	90.4398
8	7.9499	1.9152	88.5247
9	7.7728	2.0922	86.4324
10	7.5794	2.2856	84.1468
11	7.3681	2.4970	81.6498
12	7.1372	2.7278	78.9220
13	6.8850	2.9800	75.9420
14	6.6095	3.2555	72.6865
15	6.3086	3.5565	69.1301
16	5.9798	3.8853	65.2448
17	5.6206	4.2445	61.0004
18	5.2282	4.6369	56.3635
19	4.7995	5.0655	51.2980
20	4.3312	5.5339	45.7641
21	3.8196	6.0455	39.7187
22	3.2607	6.6044	33.1143
23	2.6501	7.2149	25.8994
24	1.9831	7.8820	18.0174
25	1.2544	8.6107	9.4067
26	.4583	9.4067	0.0000

YEARS 27 — MO PAYT .8144 — AN CONST 9.78

#	INT	PRIN	BALANCE
1	8.8376	.9352	99.0648
2	8.7511	1.0217	98.0431
3	8.6567	1.1161	96.9270
4	8.5535	1.2193	95.7077
5	8.4407	1.3320	94.3756
6	8.3176	1.4552	92.9204
7	8.1831	1.5897	91.3307
8	8.0361	1.7367	89.5940
9	7.8755	1.8973	87.6968
10	7.7001	2.0727	85.6241
11	7.5085	2.2643	83.3598
12	7.2992	2.4736	80.8862
13	7.0705	2.7023	78.1839
14	6.8207	2.9521	75.2318
15	6.5477	3.2250	72.0068
16	6.2496	3.5232	68.4836
17	5.9239	3.8489	64.6346
18	5.5680	4.2048	60.4299
19	5.1793	4.5935	55.8364
20	4.7546	5.0182	50.8182
21	4.2907	5.4821	45.3361
22	3.7839	5.9889	39.3472
23	3.2302	6.5426	32.8046
24	2.6253	7.1475	25.6571
25	1.9645	7.8083	17.8489
26	1.2426	8.5301	9.3187
27	.4540	9.3187	0.0000

YEARS 28 — MO PAYT .8075 — AN CONST 9.69

#	INT	PRIN	BALANCE
1	8.8410	.8488	99.1512
2	8.7626	.9273	98.2239
3	8.6768	1.0130	97.2109
4	8.5832	1.1067	96.1043
5	8.4809	1.2090	94.8953
6	8.3691	1.3207	93.5746
7	8.2470	1.4428	92.1317
8	8.1136	1.5762	90.5555
9	7.9679	1.7220	88.8335
10	7.8087	1.8811	86.9524
11	7.6348	2.0551	84.8973
12	7.4448	2.2451	82.6523
13	7.2372	2.4526	80.1997
14	7.0105	2.6794	77.5203
15	6.7628	2.9271	74.5932
16	6.4922	3.1977	71.3956
17	6.1965	3.4933	67.9023
18	5.8736	3.8163	64.0860
19	5.5208	4.1691	59.9170
20	5.1353	4.5545	55.3624
21	4.7143	4.9756	50.3869
22	4.2543	5.4356	44.9513
23	3.7517	5.9381	39.0132
24	3.2028	6.4871	32.5262
25	2.6030	7.0868	25.4394
26	1.9478	7.7420	17.6974
27	1.2321	8.4577	9.2397
28	.4502	9.2397	0.0000

YEARS 29 — MO PAYT .8013 — AN CONST 9.62

#	INT	PRIN	BALANCE
1	8.8441	.7710	99.2290
2	8.7729	.8423	98.3868
3	8.6950	.9201	97.4666
4	8.6099	1.0052	96.4614
5	8.5170	1.0981	95.3633
6	8.4155	1.1996	94.1637
7	8.3046	1.3106	92.8531
8	8.1834	1.4317	91.4214
9	8.0510	1.5641	89.8573
10	7.9064	1.7087	88.1487
11	7.7485	1.8666	86.2820
12	7.5759	2.0392	84.2428
13	7.3874	2.2277	82.0150
14	7.1814	2.4337	79.5813
15	6.9564	2.6587	76.9226
16	6.7106	2.9045	74.0181
17	6.4421	3.1730	70.8451
18	6.1488	3.4664	67.3788
19	5.8283	3.7868	63.5919
20	5.4782	4.1369	59.4550
21	5.0957	4.5194	54.9356
22	4.6779	4.9372	49.9984
23	4.2215	5.3937	44.6047
24	3.7228	5.8923	38.7124
25	3.1781	6.4371	32.2754
26	2.5830	7.0322	25.2432
27	1.9328	7.6823	17.5609
28	1.2226	8.3925	9.1684
29	.4467	9.1684	0.0000

YEARS 30 — MO PAYT .7956 — AN CONST 9.55

#	INT	PRIN	BALANCE
1	8.8469	.7008	99.2992
2	8.7822	.7656	98.5336
3	8.7114	.8364	97.6973
4	8.6341	.9137	96.7836
5	8.5496	.9981	95.7854
6	8.4573	1.0904	94.6950
7	8.3565	1.1912	93.5038
8	8.2464	1.3014	92.2024
9	8.1261	1.4217	90.7807
10	7.9946	1.5531	89.2276
11	7.8510	1.6967	87.5309
12	7.6942	1.8536	85.6774
13	7.5228	2.0249	83.6524
14	7.3356	2.2121	81.4403
15	7.1311	2.4166	79.0236
16	6.9077	2.6401	76.3836
17	6.6636	2.8841	73.4994
18	6.3970	3.1508	70.3487
19	6.1057	3.4421	66.9066
20	5.7874	3.7603	63.1463
21	5.4398	4.1079	59.0383
22	5.0600	4.4877	54.5506
23	4.6451	4.9026	49.6480
24	4.1919	5.3559	44.2922
25	3.6967	5.8510	38.4411
26	3.1558	6.3919	32.0492
27	2.5649	6.9829	25.0663
28	1.9193	7.6285	17.4379
29	1.2140	8.3337	9.1042
30	.4436	9.1042	0.0000

YEARS 2 — MO PAYT 4.5639 — AN CONST 54.77

#	INT	PRIN	BALANCE
1	6.9820	47.7847	52.2153
2	2.5513	52.2153	0.0000

YEARS 3 — MO PAYT 3.1753 — AN CONST 38.11

#	INT	PRIN	BALANCE
1	7.6788	30.4251	69.5749
2	4.8577	33.2461	36.3288
3	1.7751	36.3288	0.0000

YEARS 4 — MO PAYT 2.4838 — AN CONST 29.81

#	INT	PRIN	BALANCE
1	8.0258	21.7793	78.2207
2	6.0064	23.7987	54.4220
3	3.7997	26.0054	28.4166
4	1.3885	28.4166	0.0000

YEARS 5 — MO PAYT 2.0710 — AN CONST 24.86

#	INT	PRIN	BALANCE
1	8.2329	16.6189	83.3811
2	6.6920	18.1598	65.2213
3	5.0082	19.8436	45.3777
4	3.1683	21.6836	23.6941
5	1.1577	23.6941	0.0000

YEARS 6 — MO PAYT 1.7976 — AN CONST 21.58

#	INT	PRIN	BALANCE
1	8.3701	13.2010	86.7990
2	7.1461	14.4250	72.3740
3	5.8086	15.7625	56.6114
4	4.3471	17.2241	39.3874
5	2.7500	18.8211	20.5662
6	1.0049	20.5662	0.0000

YEARS 7 — MO PAYT 1.6038 — AN CONST 19.25

#	INT	PRIN	BALANCE
1	8.4674	10.7787	89.2213
2	7.4679	11.7781	77.4432
3	6.3759	12.8702	64.5730
4	5.1825	14.0635	50.5095
5	3.8785	15.3675	35.1419
6	2.4536	16.7924	18.3495
7	.8966	18.3495	0.0000

YEARS 8 — MO PAYT 1.4598 — AN CONST 17.52

#	INT	PRIN	BALANCE
1	8.5396	8.9784	91.0216
2	7.7071	9.8109	81.2106
3	6.7974	10.7206	70.4900
4	5.8034	11.7147	58.7754
5	4.7172	12.8009	45.9745
6	3.5303	13.9878	31.9867
7	2.2333	15.2847	16.7020
8	.8161	16.7020	0.0000

YEARS 9 — MO PAYT 1.3490 — AN CONST 16.19

#	INT	PRIN	BALANCE
1	8.5952	7.5927	92.4073
2	7.8912	8.2967	84.1106
3	7.1219	9.0660	75.0445
4	6.2813	9.9066	65.1379
5	5.3628	10.8252	54.3127
6	4.3590	11.8289	42.4838
7	3.2622	12.9257	29.5581
8	2.0637	14.1242	15.4338
9	.7541	15.4338	0.0000

YEARS 10 — MO PAYT 1.2614 — AN CONST 15.14

#	INT	PRIN	BALANCE
1	8.6392	6.4970	93.5030
2	8.0368	7.0994	86.4036
3	7.3785	7.7577	78.6459
4	6.6592	8.4770	70.1689
5	5.8732	9.2630	60.9059
6	5.0143	10.1219	50.7840
7	4.0758	11.0604	39.7236
8	3.0503	12.0859	27.6377
9	1.9297	13.2066	14.4311
10	.7051	14.4311	0.0000

YEARS 11 — MO PAYT 1.1906 — AN CONST 14.29

#	INT	PRIN	BALANCE
1	8.6747	5.6120	94.3880
2	8.1544	6.1324	88.2556
3	7.5858	6.7010	81.5546
4	6.9644	7.3223	74.2322
5	6.2855	8.0013	66.2310
6	5.5436	8.7432	57.4878
7	4.7329	9.5538	47.9340
8	3.8471	10.4397	37.4943
9	2.8791	11.4077	26.0866
10	1.8214	12.4654	13.6212
11	.6656	13.6212	0.0000

YEARS 12 — MO PAYT 1.1324 — AN CONST 13.59

#	INT	PRIN	BALANCE
1	8.7039	4.8849	95.1151
2	8.2510	5.3379	89.7772
3	7.7560	5.8328	83.9443
4	7.2152	6.3737	77.5707
5	6.6242	6.9646	70.6060
6	5.9785	7.6104	62.9956
7	5.2728	8.3161	54.6796
8	4.5017	9.0871	45.5924
9	3.6592	9.9297	35.6627
10	2.7385	10.8504	24.8123
11	1.7324	11.8565	12.9558
12	.6330	12.9558	0.0000

YEARS 13 — MO PAYT 1.0839 — AN CONST 13.01

#	INT	PRIN	BALANCE
1	8.7282	4.2791	95.7209
2	8.3315	4.6759	91.0449
3	7.8979	5.1095	85.9355
4	7.4242	5.5832	80.3522
5	6.9065	6.1009	74.2513
6	6.3408	6.6666	67.5847
7	5.7226	7.2847	60.3000
8	5.0472	7.9602	52.3398
9	4.3091	8.6983	43.6415
10	3.5026	9.5048	34.1367
11	2.6213	10.3861	23.7506
12	1.6583	11.3491	12.4014
13	.6060	12.4014	0.0000

YEARS 14 — MO PAYT 1.0431 — AN CONST 12.52

#	INT	PRIN	BALANCE
1	8.7487	3.7685	96.2315
2	8.3993	4.1179	92.1136
3	8.0175	4.4997	87.6139
4	7.6003	4.9169	82.6970
5	7.1444	5.3728	77.3242
6	6.6462	5.8710	71.4532
7	6.1018	6.4154	65.0378
8	5.5070	7.0102	58.0276
9	4.8570	7.6602	50.3674
10	4.1467	8.3705	41.9969
11	3.3706	9.1466	32.8502
12	2.5225	9.9947	22.8555
13	1.5958	10.9214	11.9341
14	.5831	11.9341	0.0000

YEARS 15 — MO PAYT 1.0083 — AN CONST 12.10

#	INT	PRIN	BALANCE
1	8.7662	3.3337	96.6663
2	8.4571	3.6428	93.0234
3	8.1193	3.9806	89.0428
4	7.7502	4.3497	84.6931
5	7.3469	4.7530	79.9401
6	6.9062	5.1937	74.7464
7	6.4246	5.6753	69.0711
8	5.8984	6.2015	62.8696
9	5.3234	6.7765	56.0931
10	4.6951	7.4049	48.6882
11	4.0085	8.0914	40.5968
12	3.2582	8.8417	31.7551
13	2.4384	9.6615	22.0936
14	1.5426	10.5573	11.5362
15	.5637	11.5362	0.0000

YEARS 16 — MO PAYT .9785 — AN CONST 11.75

#	INT	PRIN	BALANCE
1	8.7812	2.9605	97.0395
2	8.5067	3.2350	93.8044
3	8.2067	3.5350	90.2694
4	7.8789	3.8628	86.4067
5	7.5208	4.2209	82.1858
6	7.1294	4.6123	77.5735
7	6.7017	5.0400	72.5335
8	6.2344	5.5073	67.0263
9	5.7238	6.0179	61.0083
10	5.1658	6.5759	54.4324
11	4.5561	7.1856	47.2468
12	3.8898	7.8519	39.3949
13	3.1618	8.5799	30.8150
14	2.3662	9.3755	21.4395
15	1.4969	10.2448	11.1947
16	.5470	11.1947	0.0000

YEARS 17 — MO PAYT .9527 — AN CONST 11.44

#	INT	PRIN	BALANCE
1	8.7941	2.6378	97.3622
2	8.5495	2.8824	94.4797
3	8.2823	3.1497	91.3300
4	7.9902	3.4417	87.8883
5	7.6711	3.7609	84.1274
6	7.3224	4.1096	80.0178
7	6.9413	4.4906	75.5272
8	6.5250	4.9070	70.6202
9	6.0700	5.3620	65.2582
10	5.5728	5.8592	59.3990
11	5.0295	6.4024	52.9966
12	4.4359	6.9961	46.0005
13	3.7872	7.6448	38.3557
14	3.0784	8.3536	30.0021
15	2.3038	9.1282	20.8740
16	1.4574	9.9746	10.8994
17	.5326	10.8994	0.0000

YEARS 18 — MO PAYT .9302 — AN CONST 11.17

#	INT	PRIN	BALANCE
1	8.8054	2.3571	97.6429
2	8.5868	2.5757	95.0672
3	8.3480	2.8145	92.2527
4	8.0870	3.0755	89.1773
5	7.8019	3.3606	85.8167
6	7.4903	3.6722	82.1444
7	7.1498	4.0127	78.1317
8	6.7777	4.3848	73.7469
9	6.3712	4.7913	68.9556
10	5.9269	5.2356	63.7200
11	5.4414	5.7211	57.9989
12	4.9110	6.2515	51.7474
13	4.3313	6.8312	44.9162
14	3.6979	7.4646	37.4517
15	3.0058	8.1567	29.2949
16	2.2495	8.9130	20.3819
17	1.4231	9.7394	10.6425
18	.5200	10.6425	0.0000

YEARS 19 — MO PAYT .9106 — AN CONST 10.93

#	INT	PRIN	BALANCE
1	8.8152	2.1116	97.8884
2	8.6195	2.3073	95.5811
3	8.4055	2.5213	93.0598
4	8.1717	2.7551	90.3048
5	7.9163	3.0105	87.2942
6	7.6371	3.2897	84.0046
7	7.3321	3.5947	80.4099
8	6.9988	3.9280	76.4819
9	6.6346	4.2922	72.1897
10	6.2366	4.6902	67.4996
11	5.8017	5.1251	62.3745
12	5.3265	5.6003	56.7743
13	4.8073	6.1195	50.6547
14	4.2399	6.6869	43.9678
15	3.6198	7.3070	36.6608
16	2.9423	7.9845	28.6764
17	2.2020	8.7248	19.9516
18	1.3930	9.5338	10.4178
19	.5090	10.4178	0.0000

YEARS 20 — MO PAYT .8933 — AN CONST 10.72

#	INT	PRIN	BALANCE
1	8.8239	1.8957	98.1043
2	8.6481	2.0715	96.0327
3	8.4561	2.2636	93.7691
4	8.2462	2.4735	91.2956
5	8.0168	2.7028	88.5928
6	7.7662	2.9534	85.6394
7	7.4924	3.2273	82.4121
8	7.1931	3.5265	78.8855
9	6.8661	3.8535	75.0320
10	6.5088	4.2108	70.8212
11	6.1184	4.6013	66.2199
12	5.6918	5.0279	61.1920
13	5.2256	5.4941	55.6980
14	4.7161	6.0035	49.6944
15	4.1595	6.5602	43.1343
16	3.5512	7.1684	35.9658
17	2.8865	7.8331	28.1327
18	2.1603	8.5594	19.5733
19	1.3666	9.3530	10.2203
20	.4994	10.2203	0.0000

YEARS 21 — MO PAYT .8781 — AN CONST 10.54

#	INT	PRIN	BALANCE
1	8.8316	1.7053	98.2947
2	8.6734	1.8634	96.4313
3	8.5007	2.0362	94.3951

#	INT	PRIN	BALANCE
4	8.3119	2.2250	92.1701
5	8.1055	2.4313	89.7388
6	7.8801	2.6567	87.0820
7	7.6338	2.9031	84.1790
8	7.3646	3.1723	81.0067
9	7.0705	3.4664	77.5403
10	6.7490	3.7878	73.7525
11	6.3978	4.1390	69.6135
12	6.0141	4.5228	65.0907
13	5.5947	4.9422	60.1485
14	5.1365	5.4004	54.7481
15	4.6357	5.9011	48.8470
16	4.0886	6.4483	42.3987
17	3.4907	7.0462	35.3525
18	2.8373	7.6995	27.6530
19	2.1234	8.4134	19.2395
20	1.3433	9.1936	10.0460
21	.4909	10.0460	0.0000

YEARS 22	MO PAYT .8646	AN CONST 10.38	
#	INT	PRIN	BALANCE
1	8.8383	1.5366	98.4634
2	8.6958	1.6791	96.7843
3	8.5402	1.8348	94.9495
4	8.3700	2.0049	92.9446
5	8.1841	2.1908	90.7538
6	7.9810	2.3939	88.3598
7	7.7590	2.6159	85.7439
8	7.5165	2.8585	82.8854
9	7.2514	3.1235	79.7619
10	6.9618	3.4131	76.3488
11	6.6453	3.7296	72.6192
12	6.2995	4.0754	68.5438
13	5.9216	4.4533	64.0905
14	5.5087	4.8662	59.2243
15	5.0575	5.3174	53.9069
16	4.5645	5.8105	48.0964
17	4.0257	6.3492	41.7472
18	3.4370	6.9379	34.8093
19	2.7937	7.5812	27.2281
20	2.0908	8.2842	18.9439
21	1.3227	9.0523	9.8916
22	.4833	9.8916	0.0000

YEARS 23	MO PAYT .8526	AN CONST 10.24	
#	INT	PRIN	BALANCE
1	8.8443	1.3867	98.6133
2	8.7158	1.5153	97.0980
3	8.5753	1.6558	95.4421
4	8.4217	1.8093	93.6328
5	8.2540	1.9771	91.6557
6	8.0706	2.1604	89.4953
7	7.8703	2.3607	87.1345
8	7.6514	2.5796	84.5549
9	7.4122	2.8188	81.7360
10	7.1509	3.0802	78.6558
11	6.8653	3.3658	75.2900
12	6.5532	3.6779	71.6122
13	6.2122	4.0189	67.5933
14	5.8395	4.3915	63.2017
15	5.4323	4.7987	58.4030
16	4.9874	5.2437	53.1593
17	4.5012	5.7299	47.4294
18	3.9699	6.2612	41.1683
19	3.3894	6.8417	34.3266
20	2.7550	7.4761	26.8505
21	2.0618	8.1693	18.6812
22	1.3043	8.9268	9.7545
23	.4766	9.7545	0.0000

YEARS 24	MO PAYT .8419	AN CONST 10.11	
#	INT	PRIN	BALANCE
1	8.8497	1.2532	98.7468
2	8.7335	1.3694	97.3775
3	8.6065	1.4963	95.8812
4	8.4678	1.6351	94.2461
5	8.3162	1.7867	92.4594
6	8.1505	1.9523	90.5071
7	7.9695	2.1334	88.3737
8	7.7717	2.3312	86.0426
9	7.5555	2.5473	83.4953
10	7.3194	2.7835	80.7118
11	7.0613	3.0416	77.6702
12	6.7792	3.3236	74.3465
13	6.4711	3.6318	70.7148
14	6.1343	3.9685	66.7462
15	5.7664	4.3365	62.4097
16	5.3643	4.7386	57.6711
17	4.9249	5.1780	52.4932
18	4.4448	5.6581	46.8351
19	3.9202	6.1827	40.6524
20	3.3469	6.7560	33.8964
21	2.7205	7.3824	26.5140
22	2.0360	8.0669	18.4471
23	1.2880	8.8149	9.6322
24	.4706	9.6322	0.0000

YEARS 25	MO PAYT .8324	AN CONST 9.99	
#	INT	PRIN	BALANCE
1	8.8545	1.1338	98.8662
2	8.7494	1.2389	97.6272
3	8.6345	1.3538	96.2734
4	8.5090	1.4794	94.7940
5	8.3718	1.6165	93.1775
6	8.2219	1.7664	91.4111
7	8.0581	1.9302	89.4809
8	7.8791	2.1092	87.3717
9	7.6836	2.3047	85.0670
10	7.4699	2.5184	82.5486
11	7.2364	2.7519	79.7966
12	6.9812	3.0071	76.7895
13	6.7024	3.2859	73.5036
14	6.3977	3.5906	69.9130
15	6.0648	3.9235	65.9894
16	5.7010	4.2873	61.7021
17	5.3034	4.6849	57.0172
18	4.8691	5.1193	51.8980
19	4.3944	5.5939	46.3041
20	3.8757	6.1126	40.1915
21	3.3089	6.6794	33.5121
22	2.6896	7.2987	26.2134
23	2.0129	7.9754	18.2379
24	1.2734	8.7149	9.5230
25	.4653	9.5230	0.0000

YEARS 26	MO PAYT .8238	AN CONST 9.89	
#	INT	PRIN	BALANCE
1	8.8588	1.0270	98.9730
2	8.7636	1.1222	97.8509
3	8.6595	1.2262	96.6246
4	8.5458	1.3399	95.2847
5	8.4216	1.4642	93.8206
6	8.2858	1.5999	92.2206
7	8.1375	1.7483	90.4724
8	7.9754	1.9104	88.5620
9	7.7982	2.0875	86.4745
10	7.6047	2.2811	84.1934
11	7.3932	2.4926	81.7008
12	7.1621	2.7237	78.9772
13	6.9095	2.9762	76.0009
14	6.6335	3.2522	72.7487
15	6.3320	3.5537	69.1950
16	6.0025	3.8832	65.3118
17	5.6424	4.2433	61.0684
18	5.2490	4.6368	56.4317
19	4.8191	5.0667	51.3650
20	4.3493	5.5365	45.8285
21	3.8359	6.0498	39.7787
22	3.2750	6.6108	33.1679
23	2.6620	7.2237	25.9442
24	1.9922	7.8935	18.0506
25	1.2603	8.6254	9.4252
26	.4605	9.4252	0.0000

YEARS 27	MO PAYT .8161	AN CONST 9.80	
#	INT	PRIN	BALANCE
1	8.8626	.9311	99.0689
2	8.7763	1.0174	98.0515
3	8.6820	1.1117	96.9398
4	8.5789	1.2148	95.7250
5	8.4662	1.3274	94.3976
6	8.3432	1.4505	92.9470
7	8.2087	1.5850	91.3620
8	8.0617	1.7320	89.6300
9	7.9011	1.8926	87.7374
10	7.7256	2.0681	85.6693
11	7.5339	2.2598	83.4095
12	7.3243	2.4694	80.9402
13	7.0954	2.6983	78.2418
14	6.8452	2.9485	75.2933
15	6.5718	3.2219	72.0714
16	6.2730	3.5207	68.5508
17	5.9466	3.8471	64.7037
18	5.5899	4.2038	60.4999
19	5.2001	4.5936	55.9063
20	4.7742	5.0195	50.8868
21	4.3088	5.4849	45.4018
22	3.8002	5.9935	39.4083
23	3.2445	6.5492	32.8591
24	2.6372	7.1565	25.7026
25	1.9736	7.8200	17.8826
26	1.2486	8.5451	9.3375
27	.4562	9.3375	0.0000

YEARS 28	MO PAYT .8092	AN CONST 9.72	
#	INT	PRIN	BALANCE
1	8.8661	.8449	99.1551
2	8.7878	.9232	98.2319
3	8.7022	1.0088	97.2231
4	8.6086	1.1023	96.1208
5	8.5064	1.2045	94.9163
6	8.3947	1.3162	93.6000
7	8.2727	1.4383	92.1618
8	8.1393	1.5716	90.5901
9	7.9936	1.7174	88.8728
10	7.8344	1.8766	86.9962
11	7.6603	2.0506	84.9456
12	7.4702	2.2407	82.7048
13	7.2624	2.4485	80.2563
14	7.0354	2.6755	77.5808
15	6.7873	2.9236	74.6572
16	6.5163	3.1947	71.4625
17	6.2200	3.4909	67.9716
18	5.8964	3.8146	64.1570
19	5.5427	4.1683	59.9887
20	5.1562	4.5548	55.4339
21	4.7338	4.9771	50.4568
22	4.2724	5.4386	45.0183
23	3.7681	5.9429	39.0754
24	3.2171	6.4939	32.5815
25	2.6149	7.0960	25.4855
26	1.9570	7.7540	17.7315
27	1.2380	8.4729	9.2586
28	.4524	9.2586	0.0000

YEARS 29	MO PAYT .8030	AN CONST 9.64	
#	INT	PRIN	BALANCE
1	8.8692	.7672	99.2328
2	8.7981	.8384	98.3944
3	8.7203	.9161	97.4783
4	8.6354	1.0011	96.4772
5	8.5426	1.0939	95.3833
6	8.4411	1.1953	94.1880
7	8.3303	1.3061	92.8819
8	8.2092	1.4272	91.4547
9	8.0769	1.5596	89.8951
10	7.9323	1.7042	88.1909
11	7.7742	1.8622	86.3287
12	7.6016	2.0349	84.2938
13	7.4129	2.2235	82.0703
14	7.2067	2.4297	79.6406
15	6.9814	2.6550	76.9856
16	6.7353	2.9012	74.0844
17	6.4663	3.1702	70.9142
18	6.1723	3.4641	67.4501
19	5.8511	3.7853	63.6648
20	5.5001	4.1363	59.5285
21	5.1166	4.5198	55.0086
22	4.6975	4.9389	50.0697
23	4.2396	5.3969	44.6729
24	3.7392	5.8973	38.7756
25	3.1924	6.4441	32.3315
26	2.5949	7.0416	25.2899
27	1.9420	7.6945	17.5955
28	1.2285	8.4079	9.1875
29	.4489	9.1875	0.0000

YEARS 30	MO PAYT .7974	AN CONST 9.57	
#	INT	PRIN	BALANCE
1	8.8720	.6972	99.3028
2	8.8074	.7619	98.5409
3	8.7367	.8325	97.7083
4	8.6595	.9097	96.7986
5	8.5752	.9941	95.8045
6	8.4830	1.0863	94.7183
7	8.3823	1.1870	93.5313
8	8.2722	1.2970	92.2343
9	8.1520	1.4173	90.8170
10	8.0205	1.5487	89.2683
11	7.8770	1.6923	87.5760
12	7.7200	1.8492	85.7268
13	7.5486	2.0207	83.7061
14	7.3612	2.2080	81.4981
15	7.1565	2.4128	79.0853
16	6.9328	2.6365	76.4488
17	6.6883	2.8809	73.5678
18	6.4212	3.1481	70.4198
19	6.1293	3.4400	66.9798
20	5.8103	3.7589	63.2209
21	5.4618	4.1075	59.1134
22	5.0809	4.4883	54.6251
23	4.6648	4.9045	49.7206
24	4.2100	5.3592	44.3614
25	3.7131	5.8561	38.5052
26	3.1701	6.3991	32.1061
27	2.5768	6.9925	25.1136
28	1.9284	7.6408	17.4728
29	1.2199	8.3493	9.1235
30	.4458	9.1235	0.0000

MONTHLY PAYMENT AMORTIZATION SCHEDULE PER $100   9.00 %

YEARS 2 — MO PAYT 4.5685 — AN CONST 54.83

#	INT	PRIN	BALANCE
1	7.0618	47.7599	52.2401
2	2.5816	52.2401	0.0000
7	3.3076	12.9439	29.6443
8	2.0934	14.1581	15.4862
9	.7653	15.4862	0.0000

YEARS 3 — MO PAYT 3.1800 — AN CONST 38.16

#	INT	PRIN	BALANCE
1	7.7666	30.3931	69.6069
2	4.9155	33.2442	36.3627
3	1.7970	36.3627	0.0000

YEARS 4 — MO PAYT 2.4885 — AN CONST 29.87

#	INT	PRIN	BALANCE
1	8.1176	21.7445	78.2555
2	6.0778	23.7843	54.4712
3	3.8466	26.0154	28.4558
4	1.4062	28.4558	0.0000

YEARS 5 — MO PAYT 2.0758 — AN CONST 24.92

#	INT	PRIN	BALANCE
1	8.3270	16.5830	83.4170
2	6.7714	18.1386	65.2784
3	5.0699	19.8401	45.4383
4	3.2088	21.7013	23.7370
5	1.1730	23.7370	0.0000

YEARS 6 — MO PAYT 1.8026 — AN CONST 21.64

#	INT	PRIN	BALANCE
1	8.4657	13.1649	86.8351
2	7.2308	14.3999	72.4352
3	5.8800	15.7507	56.6846
4	4.4025	17.2282	39.4564
5	2.7863	18.8443	20.6120
6	1.0186	20.6120	0.0000

YEARS 7 — MO PAYT 1.6089 — AN CONST 19.31

#	INT	PRIN	BALANCE
1	8.5640	10.7429	89.2571
2	7.5563	11.7506	77.5065
3	6.4540	12.8529	64.6536
4	5.2483	14.0586	50.5950
5	3.9295	15.3774	35.2176
6	2.4870	16.8199	18.3977
7	.9092	18.3977	0.0000

YEARS 8 — MO PAYT 1.4650 — AN CONST 17.59

#	INT	PRIN	BALANCE
1	8.6371	8.9432	91.0568
2	7.7981	9.7821	81.2747
3	6.8805	10.6997	70.5750
4	5.8768	11.7034	58.8715
5	4.7789	12.8013	46.0702
6	3.5781	14.0022	32.0680
7	2.2646	15.3157	16.7524
8	.8279	16.7524	0.0000

YEARS 9 — MO PAYT 1.3543 — AN CONST 16.26

#	INT	PRIN	BALANCE
1	8.6933	7.5582	92.4418
2	7.9843	8.2672	84.1745
3	7.2087	9.0428	75.1318
4	6.3605	9.8910	65.2408
5	5.4326	10.8194	54.4219
6	4.4177	11.8338	42.5881

YEARS 10 — MO PAYT 1.2668 — AN CONST 15.21

#	INT	PRIN	BALANCE
1	8.7377	6.4634	93.5366
2	8.1314	7.0697	86.4669
3	7.4682	7.7329	78.7340
4	6.7428	8.4583	70.2757
5	5.9494	9.2517	61.0240
6	5.0815	10.1196	50.9044
7	4.1322	11.0689	39.8355
8	3.0939	12.1072	27.7282
9	1.9581	13.2430	14.4853
10	.7158	14.4853	0.0000

YEARS 11 — MO PAYT 1.1961 — AN CONST 14.36

#	INT	PRIN	BALANCE
1	8.7736	5.5794	94.4206
2	8.2502	6.1028	88.3178
3	7.6777	6.6753	81.6426
4	7.0515	7.3014	74.3411
5	6.3666	7.9864	66.3548
6	5.6174	8.7355	57.6192
7	4.7980	9.5550	48.0642
8	3.9016	10.4513	37.6129
9	2.9212	11.4317	26.1812
10	1.8489	12.5041	13.6771
11	.6759	13.6771	0.0000

YEARS 12 — MO PAYT 1.1380 — AN CONST 13.66

#	INT	PRIN	BALANCE
1	8.8030	4.8533	95.1467
2	8.3478	5.3086	89.8381
3	7.8498	5.8066	84.0315
4	7.3051	6.3513	77.6802
5	6.7093	6.9471	70.7331
6	6.0576	7.5988	63.1344
7	5.3448	8.3116	54.8228
8	4.5651	9.0913	45.7315
9	3.7123	9.9441	35.7874
10	2.7795	10.8769	24.9105
11	1.7591	11.8972	13.0133
12	.6431	13.0133	0.0000

YEARS 13 — MO PAYT 1.0897 — AN CONST 13.08

#	INT	PRIN	BALANCE
1	8.8276	4.2486	95.7514
2	8.4290	4.6471	91.1043
3	7.9931	5.0831	86.0212
4	7.5163	5.5599	80.4613
5	6.9947	6.0814	74.3799
6	6.4242	6.6519	67.7280
7	5.8002	7.2759	60.4520
8	5.1177	7.9585	52.4936
9	4.3712	8.7050	43.7886
10	3.5546	9.5216	34.2670
11	2.6614	10.4148	23.8522
12	1.6844	11.3918	12.4604
13	.6158	12.4604	0.0000

YEARS 14 — MO PAYT 1.0489 — AN CONST 12.59

#	INT	PRIN	BALANCE
1	8.8483	3.7390	96.2610
2	8.4975	4.0897	92.1713
3	8.1139	4.4734	87.6979
4	7.6942	4.8930	82.8049
5	7.2352	5.3520	77.4529
6	6.7332	5.8541	71.5988
7	6.1840	6.4032	65.1956
8	5.5834	7.0039	58.1917
9	4.9264	7.6609	50.5309
10	4.2077	8.3795	42.1513
11	3.4217	9.1656	32.9857
12	2.5619	10.0254	22.9603
13	1.6214	10.9658	11.9945
14	.5927	11.9945	0.0000

YEARS 15 — MO PAYT 1.0143 — AN CONST 12.18

#	INT	PRIN	BALANCE
1	8.8659	3.3053	96.6947
2	8.5558	3.6154	93.0793
3	8.2166	3.9546	89.1247
4	7.8457	4.3255	84.7992
5	7.4399	4.7313	80.0679
6	6.9961	5.1751	74.8928
7	6.5106	5.6606	69.2323
8	5.9796	6.1916	63.0407
9	5.3988	6.7724	56.2683
10	4.7635	7.4077	48.8606
11	4.0686	8.1026	40.7581
12	3.3086	8.8626	31.8954
13	2.4772	9.6940	22.2014
14	1.5678	10.6034	11.5980
15	.5731	11.5980	0.0000

YEARS 16 — MO PAYT .9845 — AN CONST 11.82

#	INT	PRIN	BALANCE
1	8.8810	2.9332	97.0668
2	8.6058	3.2084	93.8584
3	8.3048	3.5094	90.3490
4	7.9756	3.8386	86.5105
5	7.6156	4.1986	82.3118
6	7.2217	4.5925	77.7193
7	6.7909	5.0233	72.6960
8	6.3197	5.4945	67.2015
9	5.8042	6.0100	61.1916
10	5.2405	6.5737	54.6178
11	4.6238	7.1904	47.4274
12	3.9493	7.8649	39.5626
13	3.2115	8.6027	30.9599
14	2.4045	9.4097	21.5502
15	1.5218	10.2924	11.2579
16	.5563	11.2579	0.0000

YEARS 17 — MO PAYT .9588 — AN CONST 11.51

#	INT	PRIN	BALANCE
1	8.8940	2.6116	97.3884
2	8.6490	2.8566	94.5317
3	8.3811	3.1246	91.4072
4	8.0879	3.4177	87.9895
5	7.7673	3.7383	84.2511
6	7.4167	4.0890	80.1622
7	7.0331	4.4726	75.6896
8	6.6135	4.8921	70.7975
9	6.1546	5.3510	65.4465
10	5.6527	5.8530	59.5935
11	5.1036	6.4020	53.1914
12	4.5030	7.0026	46.1888
13	3.8462	7.6595	38.5293
14	3.1276	8.3780	30.1513
15	2.3417	9.1639	20.9874
16	1.4821	10.0236	10.9638
17	.5418	10.9638	0.0000

YEARS 18 — MO PAYT .9364 — AN CONST 11.24

#	INT	PRIN	BALANCE
1	8.9054	2.3320	97.6680
2	8.6866	2.5507	95.1173
3	8.4473	2.7900	92.3273
4	8.1856	3.0517	89.2756
5	7.8993	3.3380	85.9376
6	7.5862	3.6511	82.2864
7	7.2437	3.9936	78.2928
8	6.8691	4.3683	73.9245
9	6.4593	4.7780	69.1465
10	6.0111	5.2262	63.9203
11	5.5208	5.7165	58.2038
12	4.9846	6.2528	51.9510
13	4.3980	6.8393	45.1117
14	3.7565	7.4809	37.6308
15	3.0547	8.1826	29.4482
16	2.2871	8.9502	20.4980
17	1.4475	9.7898	10.7082
18	.5292	10.7082	0.0000

YEARS 19 — MO PAYT .9169 — AN CONST 11.01

#	INT	PRIN	BALANCE
1	8.9153	2.0875	97.9125
2	8.7195	2.2833	95.6292
3	8.5053	2.4975	93.1317
4	8.2710	2.7318	90.4000
5	8.0147	2.9880	87.4120
6	7.7344	3.2683	84.1436
7	7.4278	3.5749	80.5687
8	7.0925	3.9103	76.6585
9	6.7257	4.2771	72.3814
10	6.3245	4.6783	67.7031
11	5.8856	5.1171	62.5859
12	5.4056	5.5972	56.9888
13	4.8805	6.1222	50.8665
14	4.3062	6.6965	44.1700
15	3.6780	7.3247	36.8453
16	2.9909	8.0118	28.8335
17	2.2394	8.7634	20.0701
18	1.4173	9.5855	10.4846
19	.5181	10.4846	0.0000

YEARS 20 — MO PAYT .8997 — AN CONST 10.80

#	INT	PRIN	BALANCE
1	8.9240	1.8727	98.1273
2	8.7483	2.0484	96.0789
3	8.5562	2.2405	93.8384
4	8.3460	2.4507	91.3877
5	8.1161	2.6806	88.7070
6	7.8646	2.9321	85.7750
7	7.5896	3.2071	82.5679
8	7.2887	3.5080	79.0599
9	6.9597	3.8370	75.2229
10	6.5997	4.1970	71.0259
11	6.2060	4.5907	66.4352
12	5.7754	5.0213	61.4139
13	5.3044	5.4924	55.9215
14	4.7891	6.0076	49.9140
15	4.2256	6.5711	43.3428
16	3.6092	7.1875	36.1553
17	2.9349	7.8618	28.2935
18	2.1974	8.5993	19.6942
19	1.3908	9.4059	10.2883
20	.5084	10.2883	0.0000

YEARS 21 — MO PAYT .8846 — AN CONST 10.62

#	INT	PRIN	BALANCE
1	8.9317	1.6833	98.3167
2	8.7738	1.8412	96.4755
3	8.6011	2.0139	94.4616

#	INT	PRIN	BALANCE
4	8.4122	2.2028	92.2588
5	8.2055	2.4095	89.8493
6	7.9795	2.6355	87.2139
7	7.7323	2.8827	84.3311
8	7.4618	3.1531	81.1780
9	7.1661	3.4489	77.7291
10	6.8425	3.7724	73.9567
11	6.4886	4.1263	69.8303
12	6.1016	4.5134	65.3169
13	5.6782	4.9368	60.3801
14	5.2151	5.3999	54.9802
15	4.7085	5.9064	49.0738
16	4.1545	6.4605	42.6133
17	3.5484	7.0666	35.5467
18	2.8855	7.7294	27.8172
19	2.1604	8.4545	19.3627
20	1.3674	9.2476	10.1151
21	.4999	10.1151	0.0000

YEARS 22	MO PAYT .8712	AN CONST 10.46	
#	INT	PRIN	BALANCE
1	8.9385	1.5156	98.4844
2	8.7963	1.6578	96.8266
3	8.6408	1.8133	95.0133
4	8.4707	1.9834	93.0300
5	8.2847	2.1694	90.8605
6	8.0811	2.3729	88.4876
7	7.8585	2.5955	85.8920
8	7.6151	2.8390	83.0530
9	7.3488	3.1053	79.9477
10	7.0574	3.3966	76.5510
11	6.7388	3.7153	72.8358
12	6.3903	4.0638	68.7720
13	6.0091	4.4450	64.3270
14	5.5921	4.8620	59.4650
15	5.1360	5.3181	54.1469
16	4.6372	5.8169	48.3300
17	4.0915	6.3626	41.9674
18	3.4946	6.9595	35.0080
19	2.8418	7.6123	27.3956
20	2.1277	8.3264	19.0693
21	1.3466	9.1075	9.9618
22	.4923	9.9618	0.0000

YEARS 23	MO PAYT .8593	AN CONST 10.32	
#	INT	PRIN	BALANCE
1	8.9445	1.3667	98.6333
2	8.8163	1.4949	97.1384
3	8.6761	1.6351	95.5033
4	8.5227	1.7885	93.7148
5	8.3549	1.9563	91.7585
6	8.1714	2.1398	89.6188
7	7.9707	2.3405	87.2782
8	7.7511	2.5601	84.7182
9	7.5110	2.8002	81.9180
10	7.2483	3.0629	78.8551
11	6.9610	3.3502	75.5048
12	6.6467	3.6645	71.8403
13	6.3030	4.0083	67.8321
14	5.9270	4.3843	63.4478
15	5.5157	4.7955	58.6523
16	5.0658	5.2454	53.4069
17	4.5738	5.7374	47.6695
18	4.0356	6.2756	41.3938
19	3.4469	6.8643	34.5295
20	2.8030	7.5083	27.0212
21	2.0986	8.2126	18.8086
22	1.3282	8.9830	9.8257
23	.4856	9.8257	0.0000

YEARS 24	MO PAYT .8487	AN CONST 10.19	
#	INT	PRIN	BALANCE
1	8.9499	1.2341	98.7659
2	8.8342	1.3498	97.4161
3	8.7075	1.4764	95.9397
4	8.5690	1.6149	94.3248
5	8.4175	1.7664	92.5583
6	8.2518	1.9321	90.6262
7	8.0706	2.1134	88.5128
8	7.8723	2.3116	86.2012
9	7.6555	2.5285	83.6727
10	7.4183	2.7657	80.9070
11	7.1589	3.0251	77.8819
12	6.8751	3.3089	74.5731
13	6.5647	3.6193	70.9538
14	6.2252	3.9588	66.9950
15	5.8538	4.3301	62.6648
16	5.4476	4.7363	57.9285
17	5.0033	5.1806	52.7479
18	4.5173	5.6666	47.0812
19	3.9858	6.1982	40.8830
20	3.4043	6.7796	34.1034
21	2.7684	7.4156	26.6878
22	2.0727	8.1112	18.5765
23	1.3118	8.8721	9.7044
24	.4796	9.7044	0.0000

YEARS 25	MO PAYT .8392	AN CONST 10.08	
#	INT	PRIN	BALANCE
1	8.9547	1.1156	98.8844
2	8.8501	1.2203	97.6641
3	8.7356	1.3348	96.3293
4	8.6104	1.4600	94.8694
5	8.4734	1.5969	93.2724
6	8.3236	1.7467	91.5257
7	8.1598	1.9106	89.6151
8	7.9806	2.0898	87.5253
9	7.7845	2.2858	85.2395
10	7.5701	2.5003	82.7392
11	7.3355	2.7348	80.0044
12	7.0790	2.9914	77.0131
13	6.7984	3.2720	73.7411
14	6.4915	3.5789	70.1622
15	6.1557	3.9146	66.2476
16	5.7885	4.2818	61.9657
17	5.3868	4.6835	57.2822
18	4.9475	5.1229	52.1594
19	4.4669	5.6034	46.5560
20	3.9413	6.1290	40.4269
21	3.3664	6.7040	33.7229
22	2.7375	7.3329	26.3900
23	2.0496	8.0208	18.3693
24	1.2972	8.7732	9.5961
25	.4742	9.5961	0.0000

YEARS 26	MO PAYT .8307	AN CONST 9.97	
#	INT	PRIN	BALANCE
1	8.9590	1.0097	98.9903
2	8.8643	1.1044	97.8860
3	8.7607	1.2080	96.6780
4	8.6474	1.3213	95.3567
5	8.5235	1.4452	93.9115
6	8.3879	1.5808	92.3307
7	8.2396	1.7291	90.6016
8	8.0774	1.8913	88.7103
9	7.9000	2.0687	86.6416
10	7.7059	2.2628	84.3789
11	7.4937	2.4750	81.9038
12	7.2615	2.7072	79.1967
13	7.0075	2.9612	76.2355
14	6.7298	3.2389	72.9966
15	6.4259	3.5428	69.4538
16	6.0936	3.8751	65.5787
17	5.7301	4.2386	61.3401
18	5.3325	4.6362	56.7039
19	4.8976	5.0711	51.6328
20	4.4218	5.5468	46.0859
21	3.9015	6.0672	40.0187
22	3.3324	6.6363	33.3824
23	2.7098	7.2588	26.1236
24	2.0289	7.9398	18.1838
25	1.2841	8.6846	9.4992
26	.4694	9.4992	0.0000

YEARS 27	MO PAYT .8231	AN CONST 9.88	
#	INT	PRIN	BALANCE
1	8.9629	.9146	99.0854
2	8.8771	1.0004	98.0850
3	8.7832	1.0943	96.9907
4	8.6806	1.1969	95.7938
5	8.5683	1.3092	94.4846
6	8.4455	1.4320	93.0526
7	8.3112	1.5663	91.4862
8	8.1642	1.7133	89.7730
9	8.0035	1.8740	87.8990
10	7.8277	2.0498	85.8492
11	7.6354	2.2421	83.6071
12	7.4251	2.4524	81.1547
13	7.1951	2.6824	78.4723
14	6.9434	2.9341	75.5382
15	6.6682	3.2093	72.3289
16	6.3671	3.5104	68.8186
17	6.0378	3.8397	64.9789
18	5.6777	4.1998	60.7791
19	5.2837	4.5938	56.1853
20	4.8528	5.0247	51.1605
21	4.3814	5.4961	45.6644
22	3.8658	6.0117	39.6527
23	3.3019	6.5756	33.0771
24	2.6851	7.1925	25.8847
25	2.0104	7.8672	18.0175
26	1.2724	8.6051	9.4124
27	.4651	9.4124	0.0000

YEARS 28	MO PAYT .8163	AN CONST 9.80	
#	INT	PRIN	BALANCE
1	8.9663	.8292	99.1708
2	8.8886	.9070	98.2637
3	8.8035	.9921	97.2716
4	8.7104	1.0852	96.1864
5	8.6086	1.1870	94.9994
6	8.4973	1.2983	93.7011
7	8.3755	1.4201	92.2809
8	8.2422	1.5533	90.7276
9	8.0965	1.6991	89.0285
10	7.9371	1.8584	87.1701
11	7.7628	2.0328	85.1373
12	7.5721	2.2235	82.9138
13	7.3635	2.4321	80.4818
14	7.1354	2.6602	77.8216
15	6.8859	2.9097	74.9118
16	6.6129	3.1827	71.7291
17	6.3143	3.4813	68.2479
18	5.9878	3.8078	64.4401
19	5.6306	4.1650	60.2751
20	5.2399	4.5557	55.7193
21	4.8125	4.9831	50.7363
22	4.3451	5.4505	45.2857
23	3.8338	5.9618	39.3239
24	3.2745	6.5211	32.8028
25	2.6628	7.1328	25.6700
26	1.9937	7.8019	17.8681
27	1.2618	8.5338	9.3343
28	.4613	9.3343	0.0000

YEARS 29	MO PAYT .8102	AN CONST 9.73	
#	INT	PRIN	BALANCE
1	8.9695	.7524	99.2476
2	8.8989	.8230	98.4246
3	8.8217	.9002	97.5244
4	8.7372	.9847	96.5397
5	8.6449	1.0770	95.4627
6	8.5438	1.1781	94.2846
7	8.4333	1.2886	92.9960
8	8.3124	1.4094	91.5866
9	8.1802	1.5417	90.0449
10	8.0356	1.6863	88.3586
11	7.8774	1.8445	86.5142
12	7.7044	2.0175	84.4967
13	7.5151	2.2067	82.2899
14	7.3081	2.4138	79.8762
15	7.0817	2.6402	77.2360
16	6.8340	2.8878	74.3482
17	6.5631	3.1587	71.1894
18	6.2668	3.4551	67.7344
19	5.9427	3.7792	63.9552
20	5.5882	4.1337	59.8215
21	5.2004	4.5214	55.3001
22	4.7763	4.9456	50.3545
23	4.3124	5.4095	44.9450
24	3.8049	5.9170	39.0280
25	3.2499	6.4720	32.5560
26	2.6428	7.0791	25.4769
27	1.9787	7.7432	17.7337
28	1.2523	8.4696	9.2641
29	.4578	9.2641	0.0000

YEARS 30	MO PAYT .8046	AN CONST 9.66	
#	INT	PRIN	BALANCE
1	8.9723	.6832	99.3168
2	8.9082	.7473	98.5695
3	8.8381	.8174	97.7521
4	8.7614	.8941	96.8581
5	8.6775	.9779	95.8801
6	8.5858	1.0697	94.8105
7	8.4855	1.1700	93.6405
8	8.3757	1.2798	92.3607
9	8.2557	1.3998	90.9609
10	8.1243	1.5311	89.4297
11	7.9807	1.6748	87.7550
12	7.8236	1.8319	85.9231
13	7.6518	2.0037	83.9194
14	7.4638	2.1917	81.7277
15	7.2582	2.3973	79.3305
16	7.0333	2.6221	76.7083
17	6.7874	2.8681	73.8402
18	6.5183	3.1372	70.7031
19	6.2240	3.4315	67.2716
20	5.9021	3.7533	63.5183
21	5.5500	4.1054	59.4128
22	5.1649	4.4906	54.9223
23	4.7437	4.9118	50.0105
24	4.2829	5.3726	44.6379
25	3.7789	5.8765	38.7614
26	3.2277	6.4278	32.3336
27	2.6247	7.0308	25.3028
28	1.9652	7.6903	17.6125
29	1.2438	8.4117	9.2008
30	.4547	9.2008	0.0000

MONTHLY PAYMENT AMORTIZATION SCHEDULE PER $100

YEARS 2 — MO PAYT 4.5731 — AN CONST 54.88

#	INT	PRIN	BALANCE
1	7.1416	47.7351	52.2649
2	2.6119	52.2649	0.0000

YEARS 3 — MO PAYT 3.1846 — AN CONST 38.22

#	INT	PRIN	BALANCE
1	7.8544	30.3611	69.6389
2	4.9734	33.2422	36.3967
3	1.8189	36.3967	0.0000

YEARS 4 — MO PAYT 2.4933 — AN CONST 29.92

#	INT	PRIN	BALANCE
1	8.2093	21.7097	78.2903
2	6.1492	23.7698	54.5205
3	3.8937	26.0254	28.4950
4	1.4240	28.4950	0.0000

YEARS 5 — MO PAYT 2.0807 — AN CONST 24.97

#	INT	PRIN	BALANCE
1	8.4211	16.5472	83.4528
2	6.8509	18.1174	65.3355
3	5.1317	19.8366	45.4989
4	3.2494	21.7189	23.7799
5	1.1884	23.7799	0.0000

YEARS 6 — MO PAYT 1.8075 — AN CONST 21.70

#	INT	PRIN	BALANCE
1	8.5614	13.1289	86.8711
2	7.3155	14.3747	72.4964
3	5.9515	15.7388	56.7576
4	4.4580	17.2323	39.5254
5	2.8228	18.8675	20.6579
6	1.0324	20.6579	0.0000

YEARS 7 — MO PAYT 1.6140 — AN CONST 19.37

#	INT	PRIN	BALANCE
1	8.6607	10.7071	89.2929
2	7.6447	11.7231	77.5697
3	6.5323	12.8356	64.7341
4	5.3142	14.0536	50.6805
5	3.9807	15.3872	35.2934
6	2.5205	16.8473	18.4460
7	.9218	18.4460	0.0000

YEARS 8 — MO PAYT 1.4702 — AN CONST 17.65

#	INT	PRIN	BALANCE
1	8.7345	8.9080	91.0920
2	7.8892	9.7533	81.3387
3	6.9637	10.6788	70.6598
4	5.9504	11.6922	58.9676
5	4.8409	12.8017	46.1659
6	3.6261	14.0165	32.1494
7	2.2960	15.3466	16.8028
8	.8397	16.8028	0.0000

YEARS 9 — MO PAYT 1.3596 — AN CONST 16.32

#	INT	PRIN	BALANCE
1	8.7913	7.5238	92.4762
2	8.0774	8.2378	84.2384
3	7.2957	9.0195	75.2189
4	6.4398	9.8754	65.3435
5	5.5027	10.8125	54.5310
6	4.4766	11.8385	42.6925
7	3.3532	12.9619	29.7305
8	2.1232	14.1919	15.5386
9	.7765	15.5386	0.0000

YEARS 10 — MO PAYT 1.2722 — AN CONST 15.27

#	INT	PRIN	BALANCE
1	8.8362	6.4299	93.5701
2	8.2261	7.0401	86.5300
3	7.5580	7.7081	78.8219
4	6.8266	8.4396	70.3824
5	6.0257	9.2404	61.1420
6	5.1489	10.1173	51.0247
7	4.1888	11.0773	39.9474
8	3.1376	12.1285	27.8189
9	1.9867	13.2794	14.5395
10	.7266	14.5395	0.0000

YEARS 11 — MO PAYT 1.2016 — AN CONST 14.42

#	INT	PRIN	BALANCE
1	8.8724	5.5469	94.4531
2	8.3461	6.0732	88.3799
3	7.7698	6.6496	81.7303
4	7.1388	7.2805	74.4498
5	6.4479	7.9714	66.4783
6	5.6915	8.7279	57.7505
7	4.8632	9.5561	48.1944
8	3.9564	10.4629	37.7315
9	2.9636	11.4557	26.2758
10	1.8765	12.5428	13.7330
11	.6863	13.7330	0.0000

YEARS 12 — MO PAYT 1.1437 — AN CONST 13.73

#	INT	PRIN	BALANCE
1	8.9022	4.8219	95.1781
2	8.4446	5.2794	89.8987
3	7.9436	5.7804	84.1183
4	7.3951	6.3289	77.7894
5	6.7945	6.9295	70.8599
6	6.1370	7.5871	63.2729
7	5.4170	8.3070	54.9658
8	4.6288	9.0953	45.8706
9	3.7657	9.9584	35.9122
10	2.8207	10.9033	25.0088
11	1.7860	11.9380	13.0708
12	.6532	13.0708	0.0000

YEARS 13 — MO PAYT 1.0954 — AN CONST 13.15

#	INT	PRIN	BALANCE
1	8.9269	4.2182	95.7818
2	8.5267	4.6185	91.1633
3	8.0884	5.0567	86.1066
4	7.6086	5.5366	80.5700
5	7.0832	6.0620	74.5081
6	6.5079	6.6372	67.8709
7	5.8871	7.2670	60.6039
8	5.1885	7.9566	52.6473
9	4.4335	8.7116	43.9356
10	3.6068	9.5383	34.3973
11	2.7017	10.4434	23.9539
12	1.7107	11.4344	12.5195
13	.6257	12.5195	0.0000

YEARS 14 — MO PAYT 1.0548 — AN CONST 12.66

#	INT	PRIN	BALANCE
1	8.9478	3.7097	96.2903
2	8.5958	4.0617	92.2286
3	8.2104	4.4471	87.7815
4	7.7884	4.8691	82.9123
5	7.3263	5.3312	77.5812
6	6.8204	5.8371	71.7441
7	6.2665	6.3910	65.3531
8	5.6601	6.9974	58.3557
9	4.9961	7.6614	50.6942
10	4.2690	8.3885	42.3058
11	3.4730	9.1845	33.1213
12	2.6015	10.0560	23.0653
13	1.6472	11.0103	12.0550
14	.6024	12.0550	0.0000

YEARS 15 — MO PAYT 1.0202 — AN CONST 12.25

#	INT	PRIN	BALANCE
1	8.9656	3.2771	96.7229
2	8.6546	3.5881	93.1348
3	8.3141	3.9286	89.2062
4	7.9413	4.3014	84.9048
5	7.5331	4.7096	80.1952
6	7.0862	5.1565	75.0387
7	6.5969	5.6458	69.3929
8	6.0612	6.1815	63.2114
9	5.4746	6.7681	56.4433
10	4.8323	7.4104	49.0329
11	4.1291	8.1136	40.9194
12	3.3592	8.8835	32.0359
13	2.5162	9.7265	22.3094
14	1.5933	10.6494	11.6600
15	.5827	11.6600	0.0000

YEARS 16 — MO PAYT .9906 — AN CONST 11.89

#	INT	PRIN	BALANCE
1	8.9808	2.9061	97.0939
2	8.7050	3.1819	93.9120
3	8.4031	3.4838	90.4281
4	8.0725	3.8144	86.6137
5	7.7105	4.1764	82.4373
6	7.3142	4.5727	77.8646
7	6.8803	5.0066	72.8580
8	6.4052	5.4817	67.3763
9	5.8850	6.0019	61.3744
10	5.3155	6.5714	54.8030
11	4.6919	7.1950	47.6080
12	4.0091	7.8778	39.7302
13	3.2616	8.6253	31.1049
14	2.4431	9.4438	21.6611
15	1.5470	10.3399	11.3211
16	.5658	11.3211	0.0000

YEARS 17 — MO PAYT .9650 — AN CONST 11.58

#	INT	PRIN	BALANCE
1	8.9939	2.5856	97.4144
2	8.7486	2.8310	94.5834
3	8.4799	3.0996	91.4838
4	8.1858	3.3938	88.0900
5	7.8637	3.7158	84.3742
6	7.5111	4.0684	80.3058
7	7.1251	4.4545	75.8513
8	6.7024	4.8772	70.9742
9	6.2396	5.3400	65.6342
10	5.7328	5.8467	59.7875
11	5.1780	6.4015	53.3860
12	4.5706	7.0090	46.3770
13	3.9055	7.6741	38.7029
14	3.1773	8.4023	30.3006
15	2.3799	9.1996	21.1010
16	1.5070	10.0726	11.0284
17	.5511	11.0284	0.0000

YEARS 18 — MO PAYT .9427 — AN CONST 11.32

#	INT	PRIN	BALANCE
1	9.0054	2.3071	97.6929
2	8.7864	2.5260	95.1670
3	8.5467	2.7657	92.4013
4	8.2843	3.0281	89.3732
5	7.9969	3.3155	86.0577
6	7.6823	3.6301	82.4276
7	7.3379	3.9745	78.4531
8	6.9607	4.3517	74.1014
9	6.5478	4.7646	69.3368
10	6.0956	5.2168	64.1200
11	5.6006	5.7118	58.4082
12	5.0586	6.2538	52.1543
13	4.4651	6.8473	45.3070
14	3.8154	7.4970	37.8100
15	3.1040	8.2084	29.6016
16	2.3250	8.9874	20.6142
17	1.4722	9.8402	10.7740
18	.5384	10.7740	0.0000

YEARS 19 — MO PAYT .9232 — AN CONST 11.08

#	INT	PRIN	BALANCE
1	9.0153	2.0636	97.9364
2	8.8195	2.2594	95.6769
3	8.6051	2.4738	93.2031
4	8.3704	2.7086	90.4945
5	8.1133	2.9656	87.5289
6	7.8319	3.2470	84.2818
7	7.5238	3.5552	80.7267
8	7.1864	3.8925	76.8341
9	6.8171	4.2619	72.5722
10	6.4126	4.6663	67.9059
11	5.9698	5.1091	62.7968
12	5.4850	5.5939	57.2028
13	4.9542	6.1248	51.0781
14	4.3730	6.7060	44.3721
15	3.7366	7.3423	37.0298
16	3.0399	8.0391	28.9907
17	2.2770	8.8019	20.1888
18	1.4418	9.6371	10.5516
19	.5273	10.5516	0.0000

YEARS 20 — MO PAYT .9062 — AN CONST 10.88

#	INT	PRIN	BALANCE
1	9.0241	1.8499	98.1501
2	8.8486	2.0254	96.1247
3	8.6564	2.2176	93.9070
4	8.4459	2.4281	91.4789
5	8.2155	2.6585	88.8204
6	7.9632	2.9108	85.9097
7	7.6870	3.1870	82.7227
8	7.3846	3.4894	79.2333
9	7.0535	3.8205	75.4128
10	6.6909	4.1831	71.2297
11	6.2940	4.5800	66.6497
12	5.8594	5.0146	61.6351
13	5.3835	5.4905	56.1446
14	4.8625	6.0115	50.1332
15	4.2921	6.5819	43.5512
16	3.6675	7.2065	36.3447
17	2.9837	7.8903	28.4544
18	2.2349	8.6391	19.8153
19	1.4151	9.4589	10.3565
20	.5176	10.3565	0.0000

YEARS 21 — MO PAYT .8911 — AN CONST 10.70

#	INT	PRIN	BALANCE
1	9.0318	1.6615	98.3385
2	8.8742	1.8192	96.5193
3	8.7015	1.9918	94.5275

#	INT	PRIN	BALANCE
4	8.5125	2.1808	92.3467
5	8.3056	2.3877	89.9590
6	8.0790	2.6143	87.3447
7	7.8309	2.8624	84.4823
8	7.5593	3.1340	81.3483
9	7.2619	3.4314	77.9168
10	6.9363	3.7570	74.1598
11	6.5798	4.1136	70.0462
12	6.1894	4.5039	65.5423
13	5.7620	4.9313	60.6110
14	5.2941	5.3992	55.2118
15	4.7817	5.9116	49.3002
16	4.2208	6.4726	42.8276
17	3.6066	7.0868	35.7409
18	2.9341	7.7592	27.9816
19	2.1978	8.4955	19.4861
20	1.3916	9.3017	10.1844
21	.5090	10.1844	0.0000

YEARS 22	MO PAYT .8778	AN CONST 10.54	
#	INT	PRIN	BALANCE
1	9.0387	1.4948	98.5052
2	8.8968	1.6367	96.8685
3	8.7415	1.7920	95.0765
4	8.5715	1.9620	93.1145
5	8.3853	2.1482	90.9663
6	8.1814	2.3520	88.6143
7	7.9582	2.5752	86.0390
8	7.7139	2.8196	83.2194
9	7.4463	3.0872	80.1322
10	7.1534	3.3801	76.7521
11	6.8326	3.7009	73.0512
12	6.4814	4.0521	68.9992
13	6.0969	4.4366	64.5626
14	5.6759	4.8576	59.7050
15	5.2150	5.3185	54.3865
16	4.7103	5.8232	48.5633
17	4.1577	6.3758	42.1874
18	3.5527	6.9808	35.2066
19	2.8902	7.6433	27.5634
20	2.1649	8.3686	19.1948
21	1.3708	9.1627	10.0321
22	.5013	10.0321	0.0000

YEARS 23	MO PAYT .8660	AN CONST 10.40	
#	INT	PRIN	BALANCE
1	9.0447	1.3469	98.6531
2	8.9169	1.4747	97.1784
3	8.7770	1.6146	95.5638
4	8.6238	1.7678	93.7960
5	8.4560	1.9356	91.8604
6	8.2724	2.1193	89.7411
7	8.0712	2.3204	87.4208
8	7.8511	2.5406	84.8802
9	7.6100	2.7816	82.0986
10	7.3460	3.0456	79.0530
11	7.0570	3.3346	75.7184
12	6.7406	3.6510	72.0673
13	6.3941	3.9975	68.0698
14	6.0148	4.3768	63.6930
15	5.5995	4.7922	58.9009
16	5.1447	5.2469	53.6540
17	4.6468	5.7448	47.9092
18	4.1017	6.2899	41.6192
19	3.5048	6.8868	34.7324
20	2.8513	7.5403	27.1921
21	2.1358	8.2558	18.9363
22	1.3524	9.0393	9.8970
23	.4946	9.8970	0.0000

YEARS 24	MO PAYT .8554	AN CONST 10.27	
#	INT	PRIN	BALANCE
1	9.0501	1.2152	98.7848
2	8.9348	1.3305	97.4543
3	8.8086	1.4568	95.9975
4	8.6703	1.5950	94.4025
5	8.5190	1.7464	92.6562
6	8.3533	1.9121	90.7441
7	8.1718	2.0935	88.6506
8	7.9732	2.2922	86.3584
9	7.7557	2.5097	83.8487
10	7.5175	2.7478	81.1009
11	7.2568	3.0086	78.0923
12	6.9713	3.2941	74.7982
13	6.6587	3.6067	71.1916
14	6.3164	3.9489	67.2427
15	5.9417	4.3236	62.9190
16	5.5314	4.7339	58.1851
17	5.0822	5.1831	53.0020
18	4.5904	5.6750	47.3270
19	4.0518	6.2135	41.1135
20	3.4622	6.8031	34.3104
21	2.8167	7.4487	26.8617
22	2.1098	8.1555	18.7062
23	1.3359	8.9294	9.7768
24	.4886	9.7768	0.0000

YEARS 25	MO PAYT .8461	AN CONST 10.16	
#	INT	PRIN	BALANCE
1	9.0550	1.0977	98.9023
2	8.9508	1.2019	97.7005
3	8.8368	1.3159	96.3846
4	8.7119	1.4408	94.9438
5	8.5752	1.5775	93.3663
6	8.4255	1.7272	91.6391
7	8.2616	1.8911	89.7480
8	8.0821	2.0705	87.6775
9	7.8856	2.2670	85.4105
10	7.6705	2.4821	82.9283
11	7.4350	2.7177	80.2107
12	7.1771	2.9756	77.2351
13	6.8947	3.2579	73.9772
14	6.5856	3.5671	70.4101
15	6.2471	3.9056	66.5045
16	5.8765	4.2762	62.2284
17	5.4707	4.6820	57.5464
18	5.0264	5.1262	52.4202
19	4.5400	5.6127	46.8075
20	4.0074	6.1453	40.6622
21	3.4242	6.7284	33.9337
22	2.7857	7.3669	26.5668
23	2.0867	8.0660	18.5008
24	1.3213	8.8314	9.6694
25	.4832	9.6694	0.0000

YEARS 26	MO PAYT .8377	AN CONST 10.06	
#	INT	PRIN	BALANCE
1	9.0593	.9926	99.0074
2	8.9651	1.0868	97.9206
3	8.8620	1.1899	96.7307
4	8.7490	1.3028	95.4278
5	8.6254	1.4265	94.0014
6	8.4900	1.5618	92.4395
7	8.3418	1.7100	90.7295
8	8.1796	1.8723	88.8572
9	8.0019	2.0500	86.8072
10	7.8074	2.2445	84.5627
11	7.5944	2.4575	82.1052
12	7.3612	2.6907	79.4145
13	7.1059	2.9460	76.4685
14	6.8263	3.2256	73.2429
15	6.5202	3.5317	69.7112
16	6.1851	3.8668	65.8444
17	5.8181	4.2337	61.6107
18	5.4164	4.6355	56.9752
19	4.9765	5.0754	51.8998
20	4.4949	5.5570	46.3429
21	3.9676	6.0843	40.2586
22	3.3902	6.6617	33.5969
23	2.7581	7.2938	26.3031
24	2.0660	7.9859	18.3172
25	1.3081	8.7437	9.5735
26	.4784	9.5735	0.0000

YEARS 27	MO PAYT .8301	AN CONST 9.97	
#	INT	PRIN	BALANCE
1	9.0631	.8984	99.1016
2	8.9779	.9837	98.1179
3	8.8845	1.0770	97.0409
4	8.7823	1.1792	95.8616
5	8.6704	1.2911	94.5705
6	8.5479	1.4137	93.1568
7	8.4138	1.5478	91.6090
8	8.2669	1.6947	89.9143
9	8.1061	1.8555	88.0589
10	7.9300	2.0316	86.0273
11	7.7372	2.2243	83.8029
12	7.5262	2.4354	81.3675
13	7.2950	2.6665	78.7010
14	7.0420	2.9196	75.7814
15	6.7650	3.1966	72.5848
16	6.4616	3.4999	69.0849
17	6.1295	3.8321	65.2528
18	5.7659	4.1957	61.0572
19	5.3677	4.5938	56.4633
20	4.9318	5.0298	51.4336
21	4.4545	5.5071	45.9265
22	3.9319	6.0296	39.8969
23	3.3598	6.6018	33.2951
24	2.7333	7.2283	26.0668
25	2.0474	7.9142	18.1526
26	1.2964	8.6652	9.4874
27	.4741	9.4874	0.0000

YEARS 28	MO PAYT .8234	AN CONST 9.89	
#	INT	PRIN	BALANCE
1	9.0666	.8139	99.1861
2	8.9894	.8911	98.2950
3	8.9048	.9757	97.3193
4	8.8122	1.0683	96.2510
5	8.7109	1.1696	95.0814
6	8.5999	1.2806	93.8008
7	8.4783	1.4021	92.3986
8	8.3453	1.5352	90.8634
9	8.1996	1.6809	89.1825
10	8.0401	1.8404	87.3422
11	7.8655	2.0150	85.3271
12	7.6743	2.2062	83.1209
13	7.4649	2.4156	80.7053
14	7.2357	2.6448	78.0605
15	6.9847	2.8958	75.1647
16	6.7099	3.1706	71.9941
17	6.4090	3.4715	68.5226
18	6.0796	3.8009	64.7218
19	5.7189	4.1615	60.5602
20	5.3240	4.5564	56.0038
21	4.8917	4.9888	51.0149
22	4.4183	5.4622	45.5527
23	3.8999	5.9806	39.5722
24	3.3324	6.5481	33.0241
25	2.7111	7.1694	25.8546
26	2.0307	7.8498	18.0049
27	1.2858	8.5947	9.4102
28	.4703	9.4102	0.0000

YEARS 29	MO PAYT .8173	AN CONST 9.81	
#	INT	PRIN	BALANCE
1	9.0697	.7379	99.2621
2	8.9997	.8079	98.4543
3	8.9230	.8845	97.5697
4	8.8391	.9685	96.6012
5	8.7472	1.0604	95.5408
6	8.6466	1.1610	94.3798
7	8.5364	1.2712	93.1087
8	8.4158	1.3918	91.7169
9	8.2837	1.5239	90.1930
10	8.1391	1.6685	88.5245
11	7.9808	1.8268	86.6977
12	7.8074	2.0002	84.6975
13	7.6176	2.1900	82.5076
14	7.4098	2.3978	80.1098
15	7.1823	2.6253	77.4845
16	6.9332	2.8744	74.6101
17	6.6604	3.1472	71.4629
18	6.3618	3.4458	68.0170
19	6.0348	3.7728	64.2442
20	5.6768	4.1308	60.1134
21	5.2848	4.5228	55.5905
22	4.8556	4.9520	50.6385
23	4.3857	5.4219	45.2166
24	3.8712	5.9364	39.2802
25	3.3078	6.4998	32.7804
26	2.6911	7.1165	25.6639
27	2.0157	7.7918	17.8720
28	1.2764	8.5312	9.3408
29	.4668	9.3408	0.0000

YEARS 30	MO PAYT .8118	AN CONST 9.75	
#	INT	PRIN	BALANCE
1	9.0725	.6694	99.3306
2	9.0090	.7329	98.5977
3	8.9395	.8025	97.7952
4	8.8633	.8786	96.9166
5	8.7799	.9620	95.9546
6	8.6887	1.0533	94.9013
7	8.5887	1.1532	93.7481
8	8.4793	1.2627	92.4854
9	8.3595	1.3825	91.1029
10	8.2283	1.5137	89.5892
11	8.0846	1.6573	87.9319
12	7.9274	1.8146	86.1173
13	7.7552	1.9868	84.1306
14	7.5666	2.1753	81.9553
15	7.3602	2.3817	79.5735
16	7.1342	2.6077	76.9658
17	6.8868	2.8552	74.1106
18	6.6158	3.1261	70.9845
19	6.3192	3.4228	67.5617
20	5.9944	3.7476	63.8142
21	5.6388	4.1032	59.7110
22	5.2494	4.4926	55.2184
23	4.8231	4.9189	50.2995
24	4.3563	5.3856	44.9139
25	3.8453	5.8967	39.0172
26	3.2857	6.4562	32.5610
27	2.6730	7.0689	25.4921
28	2.0023	7.7397	17.7524
29	1.2678	8.4741	9.2783
30	.4637	9.2783	0.0000

YEARS 2 — MO PAYT 4.5742 — AN CONST 54.90

#	INT	PRIN	BALANCE
1	7.1616	47.7289	52.2711
2	2.6195	52.2711	0.0000

YEARS 3 — MO PAYT 3.1858 — AN CONST 38.23

#	INT	PRIN	BALANCE
1	7.8764	30.3532	69.6468
2	4.9878	33.2417	36.4051
3	1.8244	36.4051	0.0000

YEARS 4 — MO PAYT 2.4944 — AN CONST 29.94

#	INT	PRIN	BALANCE
1	8.2323	21.7010	78.2990
2	6.1671	23.7662	54.5328
3	3.9054	26.0279	28.5049
4	1.4285	28.5049	0.0000

YEARS 5 — MO PAYT 2.0819 — AN CONST 24.99

#	INT	PRIN	BALANCE
1	8.4447	16.5382	83.4618
2	6.8708	18.1121	65.3497
3	5.1472	19.8357	45.5140
4	3.2595	21.7234	23.7907
5	1.1922	23.7907	0.0000

YEARS 6 — MO PAYT 1.8088 — AN CONST 21.71

#	INT	PRIN	BALANCE
1	8.5853	13.1199	86.8801
2	7.3367	14.3684	72.5117
3	5.9694	15.7358	56.7759
4	4.4719	17.2333	39.5426
5	2.8319	18.8733	20.6694
6	1.0358	20.6694	0.0000

YEARS 7 — MO PAYT 1.6153 — AN CONST 19.39

#	INT	PRIN	BALANCE
1	8.6849	10.6982	89.3018
2	7.6668	11.7163	77.5855
3	6.5518	12.8313	64.7543
4	5.3308	14.0523	50.7019
5	3.9935	15.3896	35.3123
6	2.5289	16.8542	18.4581
7	.9250	18.4581	0.0000

YEARS 8 — MO PAYT 1.4715 — AN CONST 17.66

#	INT	PRIN	BALANCE
1	8.7589	8.8992	91.1008
2	7.9120	9.7461	81.3546
3	6.9845	10.6736	70.6810
4	5.9688	11.6894	58.9916
5	4.8564	12.8018	46.1898
6	3.6381	14.0201	32.1698
7	2.3039	15.3543	16.8155
8	.8427	16.8155	0.0000

YEARS 9 — MO PAYT 1.3609 — AN CONST 16.34

#	INT	PRIN	BALANCE
1	8.8158	7.5153	92.4847
2	8.1007	8.2304	84.2543
3	7.3174	9.0137	75.2406
4	6.4596	9.8715	65.3691
5	5.5202	10.8109	54.5583
6	4.4914	11.8397	42.7186
7	3.3647	12.9664	29.7521
8	2.1307	14.2004	15.5517
9	.7794	15.5517	0.0000

YEARS 10 — MO PAYT 1.2735 — AN CONST 15.29

#	INT	PRIN	BALANCE
1	8.8608	6.4216	93.5784
2	8.2497	7.0327	86.5458
3	7.5805	7.7019	78.8439
4	6.8475	8.4349	70.4090
5	6.0448	9.2376	61.1714
6	5.1657	10.1167	51.0548
7	4.2030	11.0794	39.9754
8	3.1486	12.1338	27.8416
9	1.9939	13.2885	14.5531
10	.7293	14.5531	0.0000

YEARS 11 — MO PAYT 1.2030 — AN CONST 14.44

#	INT	PRIN	BALANCE
1	8.8972	5.5388	94.4612
2	8.3701	6.0659	88.3953
3	7.7928	6.6431	81.7522
4	7.1606	7.2753	74.4769
5	6.4683	7.9677	66.5092
6	5.7100	8.7259	57.7833
7	4.8796	9.5563	48.2270
8	3.9702	10.4657	37.7612
9	2.9742	11.4617	26.2995
10	1.8835	12.5525	13.7470
11	.6889	13.7470	0.0000

YEARS 12 — MO PAYT 1.1451 — AN CONST 13.75

#	INT	PRIN	BALANCE
1	8.9270	4.8140	95.1860
2	8.4688	5.2721	89.9138
3	7.9671	5.7739	84.1400
4	7.4177	6.3233	77.8166
5	6.8159	6.9251	70.8916
6	6.1569	7.5841	63.3074
7	5.4351	8.3059	55.0016
8	4.6447	9.0963	45.9053
9	3.7791	9.9619	35.9434
10	2.8310	10.9099	25.0334
11	1.7928	11.9482	13.0852
12	.6557	13.0852	0.0000

YEARS 13 — MO PAYT 1.0969 — AN CONST 13.17

#	INT	PRIN	BALANCE
1	8.9518	4.2106	95.7894
2	8.5511	4.6113	91.1781
3	8.1123	5.0502	86.1279
4	7.6317	5.5307	80.5972
5	7.1053	6.0571	74.5401
6	6.5289	6.6335	67.9066
7	5.8976	7.2648	60.6418
8	5.2063	7.9561	52.6857
9	4.4491	8.7133	43.9724
10	3.6199	9.5425	34.4299
11	2.7118	10.4506	23.9794
12	1.7173	11.4451	12.5343
13	.6281	12.5343	0.0000

YEARS 14 — MO PAYT 1.0563 — AN CONST 12.68

#	INT	PRIN	BALANCE
1	8.9727	3.7024	96.2976
2	8.6204	4.0547	92.2429
3	8.2345	4.4406	87.8023
4	7.8119	4.8632	82.9391
5	7.3491	5.3260	77.6131
6	6.8423	5.8328	71.7803
7	6.2872	6.3879	65.3924
8	5.6793	6.9958	58.3966
9	5.0135	7.6616	50.7351
10	4.2844	8.3907	42.3444
11	3.4859	9.1892	33.1552
12	2.6114	10.0637	23.0916
13	1.6537	11.0214	12.0702
14	.6049	12.0702	0.0000

YEARS 15 — MO PAYT 1.0217 — AN CONST 12.27

#	INT	PRIN	BALANCE
1	8.9905	3.2701	96.7299
2	8.6793	3.5813	93.1486
3	8.3385	3.9221	89.2264
4	7.9652	4.2954	84.9311
5	7.5564	4.7041	80.2269
6	7.1088	5.1518	75.0751
7	6.6185	5.6421	69.4330
8	6.0816	6.1790	63.2540
9	5.4936	6.7670	56.4870
10	4.8496	7.4110	49.0760
11	4.1443	8.1163	40.9597
12	3.3719	8.8887	32.0710
13	2.5260	9.7346	22.3364
14	1.5996	10.6609	11.6755
15	.5851	11.6755	0.0000

YEARS 16 — MO PAYT .9921 — AN CONST 11.91

#	INT	PRIN	BALANCE
1	9.0057	2.8994	97.1006
2	8.7298	3.1753	93.9253
3	8.4276	3.4775	90.4478
4	8.0967	3.8084	86.6394
5	7.7343	4.1708	82.4686
6	7.3374	4.5678	77.9008
7	6.9027	5.0024	72.8984
8	6.4266	5.4785	67.4199
9	5.9053	5.9999	61.4200
10	5.3343	6.5708	54.8492
11	4.7090	7.1961	47.6531
12	4.0241	7.8810	39.7721
13	3.2742	8.6310	31.1411
14	2.4528	9.4523	21.6888
15	1.5533	10.3518	11.3370
16	.5681	11.3370	0.0000

YEARS 17 — MO PAYT .9665 — AN CONST 11.60

#	INT	PRIN	BALANCE
1	9.0189	2.5792	97.4208
2	8.7735	2.8246	94.5962
3	8.5047	3.0934	91.5028
4	8.2103	3.3878	88.1150
5	7.8879	3.7102	84.4049
6	7.5348	4.0633	80.3416
7	7.1481	4.4499	75.8917
8	6.7246	4.8734	71.0182
9	6.2609	5.3372	65.6810
10	5.7529	5.8451	59.8359
11	5.1967	6.4014	53.4346
12	4.5875	7.0105	46.4240
13	3.9204	7.6777	38.7463
14	3.1897	8.4083	30.3380
15	2.3895	9.2085	21.1294
16	1.5132	10.0849	11.0446
17	.5535	11.0446	0.0000

YEARS 18 — MO PAYT .9443 — AN CONST 11.34

#	INT	PRIN	BALANCE
1	9.0304	2.3009	97.6991
2	8.8114	2.5198	95.1793
3	8.5716	2.7596	92.4197
4	8.3090	3.0222	89.3975
5	8.0214	3.3098	86.0876
6	7.7064	3.6248	82.4628
7	7.3614	3.9698	78.4931
8	6.9836	4.3476	74.1455
9	6.5699	4.7613	69.3842
10	6.1168	5.2144	64.1698
11	5.6206	5.7106	58.4592
12	5.0771	6.2541	52.2051
13	4.4820	6.8492	45.3559
14	3.8302	7.5010	37.8548
15	3.1163	8.2149	29.6399
16	2.3346	8.9967	20.6433
17	1.4784	9.8528	10.7905
18	.5407	10.7905	0.0000

YEARS 19 — MO PAYT .9248 — AN CONST 11.10

#	INT	PRIN	BALANCE
1	9.0404	2.0577	97.9423
2	8.8445	2.2535	95.6888
3	8.6301	2.4680	93.2208
4	8.3952	2.7028	90.5180
5	8.1380	2.9600	87.5580
6	7.8563	3.2417	84.3162
7	7.5478	3.5502	80.7660
8	7.2100	3.8881	76.8779
9	6.8399	4.2581	72.6198
10	6.4347	4.6633	67.9565
11	5.9909	5.1071	62.8494
12	5.5049	5.5931	57.2563
13	4.9727	6.1254	51.1309
14	4.3897	6.7083	44.4226
15	3.7513	7.3467	37.0759
16	3.0522	8.0458	29.0300
17	2.2865	8.8115	20.2185
18	1.4480	9.6501	10.5684
19	.5296	10.5684	0.0000

YEARS 20 — MO PAYT .9078 — AN CONST 10.90

#	INT	PRIN	BALANCE
1	9.0491	1.8442	98.1558
2	8.8736	2.0197	96.1360
3	8.6814	2.2119	93.9241
4	8.4709	2.4224	91.5016
5	8.2404	2.6530	88.8486
6	7.9879	2.9055	85.9432
7	7.7114	3.1819	82.7612
8	7.4086	3.4848	79.2765
9	7.0770	3.8164	75.4601
10	6.7138	4.1796	71.2805
11	6.3161	4.5773	66.7032
12	5.8805	5.0129	61.6903
13	5.4034	5.4900	56.2003
14	4.8810	6.0124	50.1879
15	4.3088	6.5846	43.6033
16	3.6822	7.2112	36.3921
17	2.9959	7.8975	28.4946
18	2.2443	8.6490	19.8456
19	1.4213	9.4721	10.3735
20	.5199	10.3735	0.0000

YEARS 21 — MO PAYT .8927 — AN CONST 10.72

#	INT	PRIN	BALANCE
1	9.0569	1.6561	98.3439
2	8.8993	1.8137	96.5302
3	8.7267	1.9863	94.5439

#	INT	PRIN	BALANCE
4	8.5376	2.1753	92.3686
5	8.3306	2.3823	89.9863
6	8.1039	2.6090	87.3772
7	7.8556	2.8573	84.5199
8	7.5837	3.1293	81.3906
9	7.2859	3.4270	77.9636
10	6.9598	3.7532	74.2104
11	6.6026	4.1104	70.1001
12	6.2115	4.5015	65.5986
13	5.7831	4.9299	60.6687
14	5.3139	5.3990	55.2696
15	4.8001	5.9128	49.3568
16	4.2374	6.4755	42.8812
17	3.6212	7.0918	35.7894
18	2.9463	7.7667	28.0228
19	2.2072	8.5058	19.5170
20	1.3977	9.3152	10.2017
21	.5112	10.2017	0.0000

YEARS 22	MO PAYT .8794	AN CONST 10.56
# INT	PRIN	BALANCE
1	9.0637	1.4897	98.5103
2	8.9220	1.6314	96.8789
3	8.7667	1.7867	95.0922
4	8.5967	1.9567	93.1355
5	8.4105	2.1429	90.9926
6	8.2065	2.3468	88.6458
7	7.9832	2.5702	86.0756
8	7.7386	2.8148	83.2608
9	7.4707	3.0826	80.1782
10	7.1774	3.3760	76.8022
11	6.8561	3.6973	73.1049
12	6.5043	4.0491	69.0558
13	6.1189	4.4345	64.6214
14	5.6969	4.8565	59.7649
15	5.2348	5.3186	54.4463
16	4.7286	5.8248	48.6215
17	4.1743	6.3791	42.2424
18	3.5672	6.9861	35.2563
19	2.9024	7.6510	27.6053
20	2.1743	8.3791	19.2262
21	1.3769	9.1765	10.0498
22	.5036	10.0498	0.0000

YEARS 23	MO PAYT .8676	AN CONST 10.42
# INT	PRIN	BALANCE
1	9.0698	1.3420	98.6580
2	8.9421	1.4697	97.1884
3	8.8022	1.6095	95.5788
4	8.6491	1.7627	93.8161
5	8.4813	1.9304	91.8857
6	8.2976	2.1142	89.7715
7	8.0964	2.3153	87.4562
8	7.8761	2.5357	84.9205
9	7.6348	2.7770	82.1435
10	7.3705	3.0413	79.1022
11	7.0811	3.3307	75.7715
12	6.7641	3.6477	72.1239
13	6.4170	3.9948	68.1291
14	6.0368	4.3749	63.7542
15	5.6205	4.7913	58.9629
16	5.1645	5.2472	53.7156
17	4.6652	5.7466	47.9690
18	4.1183	6.2935	41.6756
19	3.5192	6.8924	34.7832
20	2.8635	7.5483	27.2349
21	2.1451	8.2666	18.9682
22	1.3584	9.0533	9.9149
23	.4969	9.9149	0.0000

YEARS 24	MO PAYT .8571	AN CONST 10.29
# INT	PRIN	BALANCE
1	9.0752	1.2105	98.7895
2	8.9600	1.3257	97.4638
3	8.8338	1.4519	96.0119
4	8.6957	1.5900	94.4218
5	8.5444	1.7414	92.6805
6	8.3786	1.9071	90.7734
7	8.1972	2.0886	88.6848
8	7.9984	2.2873	86.3975
9	7.7807	2.5050	83.8925
10	7.5423	2.7434	81.1491
11	7.2813	3.0045	78.1447
12	6.9953	3.2904	74.8543
13	6.6822	3.6035	71.2508
14	6.3393	3.9464	67.3044
15	5.9637	4.3220	62.9824
16	5.5524	4.7333	58.2491
17	5.1020	5.1837	53.0654
18	4.6087	5.6770	47.3884
19	4.0684	6.2173	41.1711
20	3.4768	6.8090	34.3621
21	2.8288	7.4569	26.9052
22	2.1192	8.1666	18.7386
23	1.3420	8.9437	9.7949
24	.4909	9.7949	0.0000

YEARS 25	MO PAYT .8478	AN CONST 10.18
# INT	PRIN	BALANCE
1	9.0800	1.0932	98.9068
2	8.9760	1.1973	97.7095
3	8.8621	1.3112	96.3982
4	8.7373	1.4360	94.9622
5	8.6006	1.5727	93.3896
6	8.4509	1.7223	91.6673
7	8.2870	1.8862	89.7810
8	8.1075	2.0657	87.7153
9	7.9110	2.2623	85.4530
10	7.6957	2.4776	82.9754
11	7.4599	2.7134	80.2620
12	7.2017	2.9716	77.2904
13	6.9189	3.2544	74.0360
14	6.6092	3.5641	70.4719
15	6.2700	3.9033	66.5686
16	5.8985	4.2747	62.2939
17	5.4917	4.6815	57.6123
18	5.0462	5.1271	52.4853
19	4.5583	5.6150	46.8703
20	4.0240	6.1493	40.7210
21	3.4388	6.7345	33.9864
22	2.7979	7.3754	26.6110
23	2.0960	8.0773	18.5337
24	1.3273	8.8460	9.6878
25	.4855	9.6878	0.0000

YEARS 26	MO PAYT .8394	AN CONST 10.08
# INT	PRIN	BALANCE
1	9.0843	.9884	99.0116
2	8.9903	1.0824	97.9292
3	8.8873	1.1854	96.7437
4	8.7745	1.2983	95.4455
5	8.6509	1.4218	94.0237
6	8.5156	1.5571	92.4665
7	8.3674	1.7053	90.7612
8	8.2051	1.8676	88.8937
9	8.0274	2.0453	86.8483
10	7.8328	2.2400	84.6084
11	7.6196	2.4531	82.1553
12	7.3862	2.6866	79.4687
13	7.1305	2.9422	76.5265
14	6.8505	3.2222	73.3042
15	6.5438	3.5289	69.7753

#	INT	PRIN	BALANCE
16	6.2080	3.8647	65.9106
17	5.8402	4.2325	61.6782
18	5.4375	4.6353	57.0429
19	4.9963	5.0764	51.9665
20	4.5132	5.5595	46.4070
21	3.9842	6.0885	40.3185
22	3.4048	6.6680	33.6505
23	2.7702	7.3025	26.3480
24	2.0753	7.9975	18.3506
25	1.3142	8.7585	9.5920
26	.4807	9.5920	0.0000

YEARS 27	MO PAYT .8319	AN CONST 9.99
# INT	PRIN	BALANCE
1	9.0882	.8944	99.1056
2	9.0031	.9795	98.1260
3	8.9099	1.0728	97.0533
4	8.8078	1.1748	95.8784
5	8.6960	1.2867	94.5918
6	8.5735	1.4091	93.1827
7	8.4394	1.5432	91.6395
8	8.2926	1.6900	89.9494
9	8.1317	1.8509	88.0986
10	7.9556	2.0270	86.0715
11	7.7627	2.2199	83.8516
12	7.5515	2.4312	81.4204
13	7.3201	2.6625	78.7579
14	7.0667	2.9159	75.8420
15	6.7892	3.1934	72.6486
16	6.4853	3.4973	69.1513
17	6.1525	3.8301	65.3211
18	5.7880	4.1946	61.1265
19	5.3888	4.5938	56.5327
20	4.9517	5.0310	51.5017
21	4.4729	5.5098	45.9920
22	3.9485	6.0341	39.9579
23	3.3743	6.6083	33.3495
24	2.7454	7.2372	26.1124
25	2.0567	7.9259	18.1864
26	1.3024	8.6802	9.5062
27	.4764	9.5062	0.0000

YEARS 28	MO PAYT .8251	AN CONST 9.91
# INT	PRIN	BALANCE
1	9.0917	.8101	99.1899
2	9.0146	.8872	98.3027
3	8.9302	.9716	97.3311
4	8.8377	1.0641	96.2671
5	8.7364	1.1653	95.1017
6	8.6255	1.2762	93.8255
7	8.5041	1.3977	92.4278
8	8.3711	1.5307	90.8971
9	8.2254	1.6764	89.2208
10	8.0659	1.8359	87.3849
11	7.8912	2.0106	85.3743
12	7.6998	2.2019	83.1724
13	7.4903	2.4115	80.7609
14	7.2608	2.6410	78.1199
15	7.0095	2.8923	75.2276
16	6.7342	3.1675	72.0601
17	6.4328	3.4690	68.5911
18	6.1027	3.7991	64.7920
19	5.7411	4.1606	60.6313
20	5.3452	4.5566	56.0747
21	4.9115	4.9902	51.0845
22	4.4366	5.4651	45.6194
23	3.9166	5.9852	39.6342
24	3.3470	6.5548	33.0794
25	2.7232	7.1786	25.9008
26	2.0400	7.8617	18.0391
27	1.2919	8.6099	9.4292

#	INT	PRIN	BALANCE
28	.4725	9.4292	0.0000

YEARS 29	MO PAYT .8191	AN CONST 9.83
# INT	PRIN	BALANCE
1	9.0948	.7343	99.2657
2	9.0249	.8041	98.4616
3	8.9484	.8807	97.5809
4	8.8646	.9645	96.6165
5	8.7728	1.0563	95.5602
6	8.6723	1.1568	94.4034
7	8.5622	1.2669	93.1366
8	8.4416	1.3874	91.7492
9	8.3096	1.5195	90.2297
10	8.1650	1.6640	88.5657
11	8.0066	1.8224	86.7433
12	7.8332	1.9958	84.7474
13	7.6433	2.1858	82.5617
14	7.4353	2.3938	80.1679
15	7.2075	2.6216	77.5463
16	6.9580	2.8711	74.6752
17	6.6848	3.1443	71.5309
18	6.3855	3.4435	68.0874
19	6.0578	3.7712	64.3162
20	5.6990	4.1301	60.1861
21	5.3059	4.5231	55.6630
22	4.8755	4.9536	50.7094
23	4.4041	5.4250	45.2844
24	3.8878	5.9413	39.3432
25	3.3224	6.5067	32.8365
26	2.7032	7.1259	25.7106
27	2.0251	7.8040	17.9066
28	1.2824	8.5467	9.3600
29	.4691	9.3600	0.0000

YEARS 30	MO PAYT .8136	AN CONST 9.77
# INT	PRIN	BALANCE
1	9.0976	.6660	99.3340
2	9.0342	.7294	98.6046
3	8.9648	.7988	97.8059
4	8.8888	.8748	96.9311
5	8.8055	.9580	95.9730
6	8.7144	1.0492	94.9238
7	8.6145	1.1491	93.7747
8	8.5052	1.2584	92.5163
9	8.3854	1.3782	91.1381
10	8.2543	1.5093	89.6288
11	8.1106	1.6530	87.9758
12	7.9533	1.8103	86.1656
13	7.7811	1.9825	84.1830
14	7.5924	2.1712	82.0118
15	7.3858	2.3778	79.6340
16	7.1595	2.6041	77.0298
17	6.9117	2.8519	74.1779
18	6.6402	3.1233	71.0546
19	6.3430	3.4206	67.6340
20	6.0175	3.7461	63.8879
21	5.6610	4.1026	59.7853
22	5.2706	4.4930	55.2923
23	4.8430	4.9206	50.3717
24	4.3747	5.3889	44.9828
25	3.8619	5.9017	39.0811
26	3.3003	6.4633	32.6178
27	2.6852	7.0784	25.5394
28	2.0116	7.7520	17.7874
29	1.2739	8.4897	9.2977
30	.4659	9.2977	0.0000

#	YEARS 2 INT	MO PAYT 4.5777 PRIN	AN CONST 54.94 BALANCE
1	7.2215	47.7104	52.2896
2	2.6422	52.2896	0.0000

#	YEARS 3 INT	MO PAYT 3.1893 PRIN	AN CONST 38.28 BALANCE
1	7.9423	30.3292	69.6708
2	5.0313	33.2402	36.4306
3	1.8409	36.4306	0.0000

#	YEARS 4 INT	MO PAYT 2.4980 PRIN	AN CONST 29.98 BALANCE
1	8.3012	21.6750	78.3250
2	6.2208	23.7554	54.5697
3	3.9407	26.0354	28.5343
4	1.4419	28.5343	0.0000

#	YEARS 5 INT	MO PAYT 2.0856 PRIN	AN CONST 25.03 BALANCE
1	8.5153	16.5114	83.4886
2	6.9305	18.0961	65.3925
3	5.1937	19.8303	45.5595
4	3.2901	21.7366	23.8229
5	1.2038	23.8229	0.0000

#	YEARS 6 INT	MO PAYT 1.8125 PRIN	AN CONST 21.75 BALANCE
1	8.6571	13.0929	86.9071
2	7.4004	14.3496	72.5575
3	6.0231	15.7268	56.8307
4	4.5137	17.2363	39.5944
5	2.8593	18.8906	20.7038
6	1.0462	20.7038	0.0000

#	YEARS 7 INT	MO PAYT 1.6191 PRIN	AN CONST 19.43 BALANCE
1	8.7575	10.6714	89.3286
2	7.7332	11.6957	77.6329
3	6.6107	12.8183	64.8146
4	5.3804	14.0486	50.7660
5	4.0320	15.3969	35.3691
6	2.5542	16.8747	18.4944
7	.9345	18.4944	0.0000

#	YEARS 8 INT	MO PAYT 1.4754 PRIN	AN CONST 17.71 BALANCE
1	8.8320	8.8730	91.1270
2	7.9804	9.7246	81.4025
3	7.0471	10.6579	70.7445
4	6.0241	11.6809	59.0636
5	4.9030	12.8020	46.2616
6	3.6742	14.0308	32.2308
7	2.3275	15.3774	16.8534
8	.8516	16.8534	0.0000

#	YEARS 9 INT	MO PAYT 1.3649 PRIN	AN CONST 16.38 BALANCE
1	8.8894	7.4896	92.5104
2	8.1706	8.2084	84.3020
3	7.3827	8.9962	75.3058
4	6.5193	9.8597	65.4461
5	5.5729	10.8060	54.6400
6	4.5358	11.8432	42.7968

#	INT	PRIN	BALANCE
7	3.3990	12.9799	29.8169
8	2.1532	14.2257	15.5911
9	.7878	15.5911	0.0000

#	YEARS 10 INT	MO PAYT 1.2776 PRIN	AN CONST 15.34 BALANCE
1	8.9347	6.3965	93.6035
2	8.3208	7.0105	86.5930
3	7.6479	7.6834	78.9096
4	6.9105	8.4208	70.4888
5	6.1023	9.2290	61.2598
6	5.2164	10.1148	51.1450
7	4.2456	11.0857	40.0593
8	3.1816	12.1497	27.9096
9	2.0155	13.3158	14.5938
10	.7374	14.5938	0.0000

#	YEARS 11 INT	MO PAYT 1.2072 PRIN	AN CONST 14.49 BALANCE
1	8.9713	5.5145	94.4855
2	8.4420	6.0438	88.4417
3	7.8619	6.6239	81.8178
4	7.2262	7.2597	74.5581
5	6.5294	7.9564	66.6017
6	5.7657	8.7201	57.8816
7	4.9288	9.5571	48.3246
8	4.0115	10.4743	37.8502
9	3.0062	11.4797	26.3706
10	1.9043	12.5815	13.7891
11	.6968	13.7891	0.0000

#	YEARS 12 INT	MO PAYT 1.1493 PRIN	AN CONST 13.80 BALANCE
1	9.0013	4.7905	95.2095
2	8.5415	5.2503	89.9591
3	8.0376	5.7543	84.2048
4	7.4853	6.3066	77.8983
5	6.8800	6.9119	70.9864
6	6.2166	7.5753	63.4111
7	5.4895	8.3024	55.1088
8	4.6927	9.0992	46.0095
9	3.8193	9.9726	36.0370
10	2.8622	10.9297	25.1073
11	1.8131	11.9788	13.1285
12	.6634	13.1285	0.0000

#	YEARS 13 INT	MO PAYT 1.1012 PRIN	AN CONST 13.22 BALANCE
1	9.0263	4.1880	95.8120
2	8.6244	4.5899	91.2221
3	8.1838	5.0305	86.1917
4	7.7010	5.5133	80.6784
5	7.1718	6.0425	74.6359
6	6.5919	6.6224	68.0135
7	5.9563	7.2580	60.7555
8	5.2596	7.9547	52.8008
9	4.4961	8.7181	44.0827
10	3.6594	9.5549	34.5278
11	2.7423	10.4720	24.0558
12	1.7372	11.4771	12.5787
13	.6356	12.5787	0.0000

#	YEARS 14 INT	MO PAYT 1.0607 PRIN	AN CONST 12.73 BALANCE
1	9.0474	3.6806	96.3194
2	8.6941	4.0338	92.2856
3	8.3069	4.4210	87.8646

#	INT	PRIN	BALANCE
4	7.8826	4.8453	83.0193
5	7.4176	5.3104	77.7090
6	6.9079	5.8201	71.8889
7	6.3493	6.3787	65.5102
8	5.7370	6.9909	58.5193
9	5.0660	7.6619	50.8575
10	4.3307	8.3973	42.4602
11	3.5247	9.2032	33.2570
12	2.6414	10.0866	23.1704
13	1.6732	11.0547	12.1157
14	.6122	12.1157	0.0000

#	YEARS 15 INT	MO PAYT 1.0262 PRIN	AN CONST 12.32 BALANCE
1	9.0653	3.2491	96.7509
2	8.7534	3.5610	93.1899
3	8.4116	3.9028	89.2872
4	8.0370	4.2773	85.0098
5	7.6265	4.6879	80.3219
6	7.1766	5.1378	75.1841
7	6.6834	5.6310	69.5531
8	6.1430	6.1714	63.3817
9	5.5506	6.7637	56.6180
10	4.9014	7.4129	49.2050
11	4.1900	8.1244	41.0806
12	3.4102	8.9042	32.1764
13	2.5555	9.7588	22.4176
14	1.6189	10.6955	11.7221
15	.5923	11.7221	0.0000

#	YEARS 16 INT	MO PAYT .9967 PRIN	AN CONST 11.96 BALANCE
1	9.0806	2.8792	97.1208
2	8.8043	3.1556	93.9652
3	8.5014	3.4584	90.5068
4	8.1694	3.7904	86.7164
5	7.8056	4.1542	82.5622
6	7.4069	4.5529	78.0093
7	6.9699	4.9899	73.0194
8	6.4910	5.4688	67.5506
9	5.9661	5.9937	61.5568
10	5.3908	6.5690	54.9878
11	4.7603	7.1995	47.7883
12	4.0693	7.8905	39.8978
13	3.3120	8.6478	31.2500
14	2.4820	9.4779	21.7721
15	1.5723	10.3876	11.3846
16	.5753	11.3846	0.0000

#	YEARS 17 INT	MO PAYT .9711 PRIN	AN CONST 11.66 BALANCE
1	9.0938	2.5598	97.4402
2	8.8482	2.8055	94.6347
3	8.5789	3.0748	91.5599
4	8.2838	3.3699	88.1899
5	7.9603	3.6934	84.4966
6	7.6058	4.0478	80.4487
7	7.2173	4.4364	76.0124
8	6.7915	4.8622	71.1502
9	6.3248	5.3288	65.8214
10	5.8134	5.8403	59.9811
11	5.2528	6.4009	53.5802
12	4.6385	7.0152	46.5650
13	3.9651	7.6885	38.8765
14	3.2272	8.4265	30.4500
15	2.4184	9.2352	21.2148
16	1.5320	10.1216	11.0931
17	.5605	11.0931	0.0000

#	YEARS 18 INT	MO PAYT .9490 PRIN	AN CONST 11.39 BALANCE
1	9.1054	2.2823	97.7177
2	8.8863	2.5014	95.2163
3	8.6462	2.7415	92.4748
4	8.3831	3.0046	89.4701
5	8.0947	3.2930	86.1771
6	7.7786	3.6091	82.5681
7	7.4322	3.9555	78.6126
8	7.0526	4.3351	74.2775
9	6.6365	4.7512	69.5263
10	6.1805	5.2072	64.3191
11	5.6807	5.7070	58.6121
12	5.1329	6.2548	52.3573
13	4.5326	6.8551	45.5023
14	3.8746	7.5130	37.9892
15	3.1535	8.2342	29.7550
16	2.3632	9.0245	20.7306
17	1.4971	9.8906	10.8399
18	.5478	10.8399	0.0000

#	YEARS 19 INT	MO PAYT .9296 PRIN	AN CONST 11.16 BALANCE
1	9.1154	2.0400	97.9600
2	8.9196	2.2358	95.7242
3	8.7050	2.4504	93.2739
4	8.4698	2.6856	90.5883
5	8.2121	2.9433	87.6450
6	7.9296	3.2258	84.4191
7	7.6200	3.5354	80.8837
8	7.2806	3.8748	77.0089
9	6.9087	4.2467	72.7623
10	6.5011	4.6543	68.1080
11	6.0544	5.1010	63.0070
12	5.5648	5.5906	57.4164
13	5.0282	6.1272	51.2893
14	4.4401	6.7153	44.5740
15	3.7956	7.3598	37.2142
16	3.0892	8.0662	29.1481
17	2.3150	8.8404	20.3077
18	1.4665	9.6889	10.6188
19	.5366	10.6188	0.0000

#	YEARS 20 INT	MO PAYT .9126 PRIN	AN CONST 10.96 BALANCE
1	9.1242	1.8273	98.1727
2	8.9488	2.0027	96.1700
3	8.7566	2.1949	93.9750
4	8.5459	2.4056	91.5694
5	8.3151	2.6365	88.9330
6	8.0620	2.8895	86.0434
7	7.7847	3.1669	82.8765
8	7.4807	3.4708	79.4057
9	7.1476	3.8040	75.6017
10	6.7825	4.1691	71.4327
11	6.3823	4.5692	66.8634
12	5.9438	5.0078	61.8557
13	5.4631	5.4884	56.3672
14	4.9363	6.0152	50.3520
15	4.3590	6.5925	43.7595
16	3.7262	7.2253	36.5342
17	3.0328	7.9188	28.6154
18	2.2727	8.6788	19.9366
19	1.4397	9.5118	10.4248
20	.5268	10.4248	0.0000

#	YEARS 21 INT	MO PAYT .8977 PRIN	AN CONST 10.78 BALANCE
1	9.1320	1.6400	98.3600
2	8.9746	1.7974	96.5627
3	8.8021	1.9699	94.5928

#	INT	PRIN	BALANCE
4	8.6130	2.1589	92.4339
5	8.4058	2.3661	90.0677
6	8.1787	2.5933	87.4745
7	7.9298	2.8422	84.6323
8	7.6570	3.1149	81.5174
9	7.3580	3.4139	78.1035
10	7.0304	3.7416	74.3619
11	6.6712	4.1007	70.2612
12	6.2777	4.4943	65.7669
13	5.8463	4.9257	60.8413
14	5.3735	5.3984	55.4428
15	4.8554	5.9166	49.5263
16	4.2875	6.4844	43.0419
17	3.6651	7.1068	35.9351
18	2.9830	7.7889	28.1461
19	2.2354	8.5365	19.6096
20	1.4161	9.3558	10.2538
21	.5181	10.2538	0.0000

YEARS 22   MO PAYT .8844   AN CONST 10.62

#	INT	PRIN	BALANCE
1	9.1389	1.4743	98.5257
2	8.9974	1.6158	96.9100
3	8.8423	1.7709	95.1391
4	8.6723	1.9408	93.1983
5	8.4860	2.1271	91.0712
6	8.2819	2.3313	88.7399
7	8.0581	2.5550	86.1849
8	7.8129	2.8003	83.3846
9	7.5441	3.0690	80.3156
10	7.2496	3.3636	76.9520
11	6.9267	3.6864	73.2656
12	6.5729	4.0402	69.2254
13	6.1851	4.4280	64.7973
14	5.7601	4.8530	59.9443
15	5.2943	5.3188	54.6255
16	4.7838	5.8293	48.7961
17	4.2243	6.3888	42.4073
18	3.6111	7.0020	35.4053
19	2.9390	7.6741	27.7312
20	2.2025	8.4106	19.3205
21	1.3952	9.2179	10.1026
22	.5105	10.1026	0.0000

YEARS 23   MO PAYT .8727   AN CONST 10.48

#	INT	PRIN	BALANCE
1	9.1450	1.3273	98.6727
2	9.0176	1.4547	97.2180
3	8.8779	1.5943	95.6237
4	8.7249	1.7474	93.8763
5	8.5572	1.9151	91.9612
6	8.3734	2.0989	89.8624
7	8.1719	2.3003	87.5620
8	7.9512	2.5211	85.0409
9	7.7092	2.7631	82.2779
10	7.4440	3.0283	79.2496
11	7.1533	3.3189	75.9306
12	6.8348	3.6375	72.2931
13	6.4856	3.9866	68.3065
14	6.1030	4.3693	63.9373
15	5.6836	4.7886	59.1487
16	5.2240	5.2482	53.9004
17	4.7203	5.7520	48.1485
18	4.1682	6.3040	41.8444
19	3.5632	6.9091	34.9353
20	2.9000	7.5722	27.3631
21	2.1733	8.2990	19.0641
22	1.3767	9.0956	9.9685
23	.5037	9.9685	0.0000

YEARS 24   MO PAYT .8622   AN CONST 10.35

#	INT	PRIN	BALANCE
1	9.1504	1.1966	98.8034
2	9.0355	1.3114	97.4920
3	8.9097	1.4373	96.0547
4	8.7717	1.5753	94.4794
5	8.6205	1.7264	92.7530
6	8.4548	1.8921	90.8609
7	8.2732	2.0738	88.7871
8	8.0742	2.2728	86.5143
9	7.8560	2.4909	84.0234
10	7.6169	2.7300	81.2933
11	7.3549	2.9920	78.3013
12	7.0677	3.2792	75.0221
13	6.7530	3.5940	71.4281
14	6.4080	3.9389	67.4892
15	6.0300	4.3170	63.1722
16	5.6156	4.7313	58.4409
17	5.1615	5.1854	53.2555
18	4.6638	5.6831	47.5723
19	4.1184	6.2286	41.3437
20	3.5205	6.8264	34.5173
21	2.8653	7.4816	27.0357
22	2.1472	8.1997	18.8360
23	1.3602	8.9867	9.8493
24	.4977	9.8493	0.0000

YEARS 25   MO PAYT .8529   AN CONST 10.24

#	INT	PRIN	BALANCE
1	9.1552	1.0800	98.9200
2	9.0516	1.1837	97.7363
3	8.9379	1.2973	96.4391
4	8.8134	1.4218	95.0173
5	8.6770	1.5582	93.4591
6	8.5274	1.7078	91.7513
7	8.3635	1.8717	89.8796
8	8.1839	2.0514	87.8282
9	7.9870	2.2482	85.5799
10	7.7712	2.4640	83.1159
11	7.5347	2.7005	80.4154
12	7.2755	2.9597	77.4556
13	6.9914	3.2438	74.2118
14	6.6801	3.5552	70.6567
15	6.3388	3.8964	66.7603
16	5.9649	4.2704	62.4900
17	5.5550	4.6802	57.8097
18	5.1058	5.1294	52.6803
19	4.6135	5.6218	47.0586
20	4.0739	6.1613	40.8972
21	3.4825	6.7527	34.1445
22	2.8344	7.4008	26.7437
23	2.1241	8.1112	18.6326
24	1.3455	8.8897	9.7429
25	.4923	9.7429	0.0000

YEARS 26   MO PAYT .8446   AN CONST 10.14

#	INT	PRIN	BALANCE
1	9.1595	.9758	99.0242
2	9.0659	1.0695	97.9547
3	8.9632	1.1721	96.7826
4	8.8507	1.2846	95.4980
5	8.7274	1.4079	94.0901
6	8.5923	1.5430	92.5471
7	8.4442	1.6911	90.8560
8	8.2819	1.8534	89.0025
9	8.1040	2.0313	86.9712
10	7.9090	2.2263	84.7449
11	7.6953	2.4400	82.3049
12	7.4612	2.6742	79.6307
13	7.2045	2.9309	76.6998
14	6.9232	3.2122	73.4877
15	6.6149	3.5205	69.9672
16	6.2770	3.8584	66.1089
17	5.9067	4.2287	61.8802
18	5.5008	4.6346	57.2456
19	5.0560	5.0794	52.1662
20	4.5684	5.5669	46.5994
21	4.0341	6.1012	40.4981
22	3.4485	6.6868	33.8113
23	2.8067	7.3286	26.4827
24	2.1033	8.0320	18.4507
25	1.3324	8.8029	9.6478
26	.4875	9.6478	0.0000

YEARS 27   MO PAYT .8372   AN CONST 10.05

#	INT	PRIN	BALANCE
1	9.1634	.8825	99.1175
2	9.0787	.9672	98.1503
3	8.9859	1.0600	97.0903
4	8.8841	1.1618	95.9285
5	8.7726	1.2733	94.6553
6	8.6504	1.3955	93.2598
7	8.5165	1.5294	91.7304
8	8.3697	1.6762	90.0542
9	8.2088	1.8371	88.2171
10	8.0325	2.0134	86.2037
11	7.8392	2.2067	83.9970
12	7.6274	2.4185	81.5785
13	7.3953	2.6506	78.9279
14	7.1409	2.9050	76.0230
15	6.8621	3.1838	72.8391
16	6.5565	3.4894	69.3498
17	6.2216	3.8243	65.5255
18	5.8545	4.1914	61.3341
19	5.4522	4.5937	56.7404
20	5.0113	5.0346	51.7059
21	4.5281	5.5178	46.1881
22	3.9985	6.0474	40.1408
23	3.4181	6.6278	33.5130
24	2.7820	7.2639	26.2490
25	2.0848	7.9611	18.2879
26	1.3207	8.7252	9.5627
27	.4832	9.5627	0.0000

YEARS 28   MO PAYT .8305   AN CONST 9.97

#	INT	PRIN	BALANCE
1	9.1669	.7988	99.2012
2	9.0902	.8754	98.3258
3	9.0062	.9595	97.3663
4	8.9141	1.0516	96.3148
5	8.8132	1.1525	95.1623
6	8.7026	1.2631	93.8992
7	8.5813	1.3843	92.5149
8	8.4485	1.5172	90.9977
9	8.3028	1.6628	89.3348
10	8.1432	1.8224	87.5124
11	7.9683	1.9973	85.5151
12	7.7766	2.1890	83.3260
13	7.5665	2.3991	80.9269
14	7.3362	2.6294	78.2975
15	7.0839	2.8818	75.4157
16	6.8073	3.1584	72.2573
17	6.5041	3.4615	68.7958
18	6.1719	3.7938	65.0021
19	5.8078	4.1579	60.8442
20	5.4087	4.5570	56.2872
21	4.9713	4.9943	51.2929
22	4.4920	5.4737	45.8192
23	3.9666	5.9991	39.8201
24	3.3908	6.5749	33.2453
25	2.7597	7.2059	26.0394
26	2.0681	7.8975	18.1418
27	1.3101	8.6555	9.4863
28	.4794	9.4863	0.0000

YEARS 29   MO PAYT .8245   AN CONST 9.90

#	INT	PRIN	BALANCE
1	9.1700	.7235	99.2765
2	9.1005	.7930	98.4835
3	9.0244	.8691	97.6144
4	8.9410	.9525	96.6618
5	8.8496	1.0439	95.6179
6	8.7494	1.1441	94.4737
7	8.6396	1.2540	93.2198
8	8.5192	1.3743	91.8455
9	8.3873	1.5062	90.3392
10	8.2428	1.6508	88.6885
11	8.0843	1.8092	86.8792
12	7.9107	1.9829	84.8963
13	7.7203	2.1732	82.7231
14	7.5118	2.3818	80.3414
15	7.2832	2.6104	77.7310
16	7.0326	2.8609	74.8700
17	6.7580	3.1355	71.7345
18	6.4571	3.4365	68.2980
19	6.1272	3.7663	64.5317
20	5.7657	4.1278	60.4039
21	5.3696	4.5240	55.8799
22	4.9353	4.9582	50.9217
23	4.4595	5.4341	45.4877
24	3.9379	5.9557	39.5320
25	3.3663	6.5273	33.0047
26	2.7398	7.1538	25.8510
27	2.0532	7.8404	18.0106
28	1.3006	8.5929	9.4177
29	.4759	9.4177	0.0000

YEARS 30   MO PAYT .8191   AN CONST 9.83

#	INT	PRIN	BALANCE
1	9.1728	.6559	99.3441
2	9.1099	.7188	98.6253
3	9.0409	.7878	97.8376
4	8.9653	.8634	96.9741
5	8.8824	.9463	96.0279
6	8.7916	1.0371	94.9908
7	8.6920	1.1366	93.8541
8	8.5829	1.2457	92.6084
9	8.4634	1.3653	91.2431
10	8.3323	1.4963	89.7468
11	8.1887	1.6400	88.1068
12	8.0313	1.7974	86.3094
13	7.8588	1.9699	84.3395
14	7.6697	2.1589	82.1806
15	7.4625	2.3662	79.8144
16	7.2354	2.5933	77.2212
17	6.9865	2.8422	74.3790
18	6.7137	3.1150	71.2640
19	6.4147	3.4139	67.8501
20	6.0870	3.7416	64.1085
21	5.7279	4.1007	60.0078
22	5.3343	4.4943	55.5135
23	4.9030	4.9257	50.5878
24	4.4302	5.3984	45.1893
25	3.9121	5.9166	39.2727
26	3.3442	6.4845	32.7883
27	2.7218	7.1068	25.6814
28	2.0397	7.7890	17.8924
29	1.2921	8.5366	9.3559
30	.4728	9.3559	0.0000

YEARS 2 — MO PAYT 4.5800 — AN CONST 54.96

#	INT	PRIN	BALANCE
1	7.2614	47.6980	52.3020
2	2.6574	52.3020	0.0000

YEARS 3 — MO PAYT 3.1916 — AN CONST 38.30

#	INT	PRIN	BALANCE
1	7.9862	30.3132	69.6868
2	5.0603	33.2392	36.4476
3	1.8519	36.4476	0.0000

YEARS 4 — MO PAYT 2.5004 — AN CONST 30.01

#	INT	PRIN	BALANCE
1	8.3471	21.6576	78.3424
2	6.2566	23.7481	54.5943
3	3.9643	26.0404	28.5539
4	1.4508	28.5539	0.0000

YEARS 5 — MO PAYT 2.0880 — AN CONST 25.06

#	INT	PRIN	BALANCE
1	8.5624	16.4935	83.5065
2	6.9704	18.0855	65.4210
3	5.2247	19.8312	45.5898
4	3.3105	21.7454	23.8444
5	1.2115	23.8444	0.0000

YEARS 6 — MO PAYT 1.8150 — AN CONST 21.78

#	INT	PRIN	BALANCE
1	8.7049	13.0749	86.9251
2	7.4429	14.3370	72.5881
3	6.0590	15.7209	56.8672
4	4.5415	17.2383	39.6289
5	2.8776	18.9022	20.7267
6	1.0531	20.7267	0.0000

YEARS 7 — MO PAYT 1.6216 — AN CONST 19.46

#	INT	PRIN	BALANCE
1	8.8058	10.6536	89.3464
2	7.7775	11.6820	77.6644
3	6.6499	12.8096	64.8548
4	5.4135	14.0460	50.8088
5	4.0577	15.4018	35.4070
6	2.5711	16.8884	18.5186
7	.9409	18.5186	0.0000

YEARS 8 — MO PAYT 1.4780 — AN CONST 17.74

#	INT	PRIN	BALANCE
1	8.8808	8.8555	91.1445
2	8.0260	9.7102	81.4343
3	7.0888	10.6475	70.7868
4	6.0610	11.6752	59.1116
5	4.9341	12.8022	46.3094
6	3.6984	14.0379	32.2716
7	2.3434	15.3929	16.8787
8	.8576	16.8787	0.0000

YEARS 9 — MO PAYT 1.3676 — AN CONST 16.42

#	INT	PRIN	BALANCE
1	8.9385	7.4725	92.5275
2	8.2172	8.1937	84.3338
3	7.4263	8.9846	75.3492
4	6.5591	9.8519	65.4973
5	5.6081	10.8028	54.6945
6	4.5654	11.8455	42.8490
7	3.4220	12.9889	29.8601
8	2.1683	14.2427	15.6174
9	.7935	15.6174	0.0000

YEARS 10 — MO PAYT 1.2803 — AN CONST 15.37

#	INT	PRIN	BALANCE
1	8.9840	6.3799	93.6201
2	8.3682	6.9957	86.6244
3	7.6929	7.6710	78.9534
4	6.9525	8.4114	70.5420
5	6.1406	9.2233	61.3187
6	5.2503	10.1136	51.2051
7	4.2741	11.0898	40.1153
8	3.2037	12.1602	27.9550
9	2.0299	13.3340	14.6210
10	.7429	14.6210	0.0000

YEARS 11 — MO PAYT 1.2099 — AN CONST 14.52

#	INT	PRIN	BALANCE
1	9.0208	5.4984	94.5016
2	8.4900	6.0291	88.4725
3	7.9081	6.6111	81.8614
4	7.2700	7.2492	74.6122
5	6.5702	7.9489	66.6633
6	5.8030	8.7162	57.9471
7	4.9616	9.5575	48.3896
8	4.0391	10.4800	37.9096
9	3.0275	11.4916	26.4180
10	1.9183	12.6008	13.8171
11	.7020	13.8171	0.0000

YEARS 12 — MO PAYT 1.1522 — AN CONST 13.83

#	INT	PRIN	BALANCE
1	9.0509	4.7749	95.2251
2	8.5900	5.2358	89.9892
3	8.0846	5.7412	84.2480
4	7.5305	6.2954	77.9526
5	6.9228	6.9031	71.0495
6	6.2565	7.5694	63.4802
7	5.5259	8.3000	55.1802
8	4.7247	9.1011	46.0790
9	3.8463	9.9796	36.0994
10	2.8830	10.9429	25.1565
11	1.8267	11.9992	13.1574
12	.6685	13.1574	0.0000

YEARS 13 — MO PAYT 1.1041 — AN CONST 13.25

#	INT	PRIN	BALANCE
1	9.0760	4.1729	95.8271
2	8.6732	4.5757	91.2514
3	8.2316	5.0174	86.2340
4	7.7473	5.5017	80.7324
5	7.2162	6.0327	74.6997
6	6.6339	6.6150	68.0847
7	5.9954	7.2535	60.8312
8	5.2953	7.9536	52.8776
9	4.5276	8.7214	44.1562
10	3.6858	9.5632	34.5930
11	2.7627	10.4863	24.1068
12	1.7505	11.4984	12.6083
13	.6406	12.6083	0.0000

YEARS 14 — MO PAYT 1.0636 — AN CONST 12.77

#	INT	PRIN	BALANCE
1	9.0972	3.6661	96.3339
2	8.7433	4.0199	92.3140
3	8.3553	4.4079	87.9061
4	7.9298	4.8334	83.0727
5	7.4633	5.3000	77.7727
6	6.9517	5.8115	71.9612
7	6.3907	6.3725	65.5887
8	5.7756	6.9876	58.6011
9	5.1012	7.6621	50.9390
10	4.3616	8.4016	42.5374
11	3.5506	9.2126	33.3248
12	2.6614	10.1018	23.2230
13	1.6863	11.0769	12.1461
14	.6171	12.1461	0.0000

YEARS 15 — MO PAYT 1.0292 — AN CONST 12.36

#	INT	PRIN	BALANCE
1	9.1151	3.2352	96.7648
2	8.8028	3.5475	93.2174
3	8.4604	3.8899	89.3275
4	8.0850	4.2653	85.0621
5	7.6733	4.6770	80.3851
6	7.2218	5.1285	75.2566
7	6.7268	5.6235	69.6331
8	6.1840	6.1663	63.4668
9	5.5888	6.7615	56.7052
10	4.9361	7.4142	49.2911
11	4.2205	8.1298	41.1612
12	3.4358	8.9145	32.2467
13	2.5753	9.7750	22.4717
14	1.6318	10.7185	11.7531
15	.5972	11.7531	0.0000

YEARS 16 — MO PAYT .9997 — AN CONST 12.00

#	INT	PRIN	BALANCE
1	9.1305	2.8658	97.1342
2	8.8539	3.1425	93.9917
3	8.5506	3.4458	90.5459
4	8.2180	3.7784	86.7675
5	7.8533	4.1431	82.6244
6	7.4534	4.5430	78.0814
7	7.0148	4.9815	73.0999
8	6.5340	5.4624	67.6375
9	6.0068	5.9896	61.6479
10	5.4286	6.5677	55.0801
11	4.7947	7.2017	47.8785
12	4.0995	7.8968	39.9816
13	3.3373	8.6591	31.3226
14	2.5015	9.4949	21.8277
15	1.5850	10.4114	11.4163
16	.5801	11.4163	0.0000

YEARS 17 — MO PAYT .9742 — AN CONST 11.70

#	INT	PRIN	BALANCE
1	9.1438	2.5470	97.4530
2	8.8980	2.7929	94.6601
3	8.6284	3.0624	91.5977
4	8.3328	3.3580	88.2397
5	8.0087	3.6822	84.5575
6	7.6532	4.0376	80.5199
7	7.2635	4.4273	76.0926
8	6.8362	4.8546	71.2380
9	6.3676	5.3232	65.9148
10	5.8538	5.8371	60.0777
11	5.2904	6.4005	53.6773
12	4.6726	7.0183	46.6590
13	3.9951	7.6957	38.9633
14	3.2523	8.4385	30.5248
15	2.4378	9.2530	21.2717
16	1.5446	10.1462	11.1255
17	.5653	11.1255	0.0000

YEARS 18 — MO PAYT .9521 — AN CONST 11.43

#	INT	PRIN	BALANCE
1	9.1554	2.2701	97.7299
2	8.9362	2.4892	95.2407
3	8.6960	2.7295	92.5113
4	8.4325	2.9929	89.5184
5	8.1436	3.2818	86.2366
6	7.8269	3.5986	82.6380
7	7.4795	3.9459	78.6921
8	7.0986	4.3268	74.3653
9	6.6810	4.7444	69.6209
10	6.2230	5.2024	64.4185
11	5.7209	5.7045	58.7139
12	5.1703	6.2552	52.4587
13	4.5665	6.8589	45.5998
14	3.9044	7.5210	38.0788
15	3.1785	8.2470	29.8318
16	2.3824	9.0430	20.7888
17	1.5096	9.9159	10.8730
18	.5524	10.8730	0.0000

YEARS 19 — MO PAYT .9328 — AN CONST 11.20

#	INT	PRIN	BALANCE
1	9.1654	2.0283	97.9717
2	8.9697	2.2240	95.7477
3	8.7550	2.4387	93.3090
4	8.5196	2.6741	90.6349
5	8.2615	2.9322	87.7027
6	7.9785	3.2152	84.4875
7	7.6681	3.5256	80.9619
8	7.3278	3.8659	77.0960
9	6.9547	4.2390	72.8570
10	6.5455	4.6482	68.2088
11	6.0968	5.0969	63.1119
12	5.6048	5.5888	57.5231
13	5.0654	6.1283	51.3947
14	4.4739	6.7198	44.6749
15	3.8252	7.3685	37.3065
16	3.1140	8.0797	29.2268
17	2.3341	8.8596	20.3672
18	1.4790	9.7147	10.6524
19	.5412	10.6524	0.0000

YEARS 20 — MO PAYT .9159 — AN CONST 11.00

#	INT	PRIN	BALANCE
1	9.1743	1.8161	98.1839
2	8.9990	1.9914	96.1925
3	8.8068	2.1836	94.0088
4	8.5960	2.3944	91.6144
5	8.3649	2.6255	88.9889
6	8.1114	2.8790	86.1099
7	7.8336	3.1568	82.9531
8	7.5288	3.4616	79.4915
9	7.1947	3.7957	75.6959
10	6.8283	4.1621	71.5338
11	6.4266	4.5638	66.9700
12	5.9861	5.0043	61.9657
13	5.5031	5.4873	56.4784
14	4.9734	6.0170	50.4614
15	4.3926	6.5978	43.8636
16	3.7558	7.2346	36.6289
17	3.0574	7.9330	28.6960
18	2.2917	8.6987	19.9973
19	1.4521	9.5383	10.4590
20	.5314	10.4590	0.0000

YEARS 21 — MO PAYT .9009 — AN CONST 10.82

#	INT	PRIN	BALANCE
1	9.1821	1.6293	98.3707
2	9.0248	1.7865	96.5842
3	8.8524	1.9590	94.6252

#	INT	PRIN	BALANCE
4	8.6633	2.1481	92.4772
5	8.4559	2.3554	90.1218
6	8.2286	2.5828	87.5390
7	7.9793	2.8320	84.7070
8	7.7059	3.1054	81.6016
9	7.4062	3.4052	78.1964
10	7.0775	3.7338	74.4626
11	6.7171	4.0942	70.3683
12	6.3219	4.4894	65.8789
13	5.8886	4.9228	60.9561
14	5.4134	5.3979	55.5582
15	4.8924	5.9190	49.6392
16	4.3210	6.4903	43.1489
17	3.6946	7.1168	36.0321
18	3.0076	7.8037	28.2284
19	2.2544	8.5570	19.6715
20	1.4284	9.3829	10.2886
21	.5228	10.2886	0.0000

YEARS 22 — MO PAYT .8878 — AN CONST 10.66

#	INT	PRIN	BALANCE
1	9.1890	1.4641	98.5359
2	9.0476	1.6054	96.9305
3	8.8927	1.7604	95.1701
4	8.7228	1.9303	93.2398
5	8.5364	2.1166	91.1232
6	8.3321	2.3209	88.8023
7	8.1081	2.5449	86.2574
8	7.8625	2.7906	83.4668
9	7.5931	3.0599	80.4069
10	7.2977	3.3553	77.0515
11	6.9739	3.6792	73.3724
12	6.6188	4.0343	69.3381
13	6.2293	4.4237	64.9144
14	5.8024	4.8507	60.0637
15	5.3341	5.3189	54.7448
16	4.8207	5.8323	48.9124
17	4.2578	6.3953	42.5172
18	3.6405	7.0126	35.5046
19	2.9636	7.6895	27.8152
20	2.2214	8.4317	19.3835
21	1.4075	9.2455	10.1379
22	.5151	10.1379	0.0000

YEARS 23 — MO PAYT .8761 — AN CONST 10.52

#	INT	PRIN	BALANCE
1	9.1951	1.3176	98.6824
2	9.0679	1.4448	97.2376
3	8.9284	1.5843	95.6533
4	8.7755	1.7372	93.9161
5	8.6078	1.9049	92.0113
6	8.4240	2.0887	89.9226
7	8.2224	2.2903	87.6322
8	8.0013	2.5114	85.1208
9	7.7589	2.7538	82.3670
10	7.4931	3.0196	79.3474
11	7.2016	3.3111	76.0363
12	6.8820	3.6307	72.4056
13	6.5315	3.9811	68.4245
14	6.1473	4.3654	64.0590
15	5.7259	4.7868	59.2723
16	5.2639	5.2488	54.0234
17	4.7572	5.7555	48.2680
18	4.2017	6.3110	41.9570
19	3.5925	6.9202	35.0368
20	2.9245	7.5881	27.4487
21	2.1921	8.3206	19.1281
22	1.3890	9.1237	10.0044
23	.5083	10.0044	0.0000

YEARS 24 — MO PAYT .8657 — AN CONST 10.39

#	INT	PRIN	BALANCE
1	9.2005	1.1874	98.8126
2	9.0859	1.3020	97.5107
3	8.9602	1.4276	96.0830
4	8.8224	1.5654	94.5176
5	8.6713	1.7165	92.8010
6	8.5056	1.8822	90.9188
7	8.3239	2.0639	88.8549
8	8.1247	2.2631	86.5917
9	7.9063	2.4816	84.1101
10	7.6667	2.7211	81.3890
11	7.4041	2.9838	78.4053
12	7.1161	3.2718	75.1335
13	6.8003	3.5876	71.5459
14	6.4540	3.9339	67.6120
15	6.0743	4.3136	63.2984
16	5.6579	4.7300	58.5685
17	5.2014	5.1865	53.3820
18	4.7007	5.6871	47.6949
19	4.1518	6.2361	41.4588
20	3.5499	6.8380	34.6208
21	2.8898	7.4980	27.1227
22	2.1661	8.2218	18.9010
23	1.3725	9.0154	9.8856
24	.5023	9.8856	0.0000

YEARS 25 — MO PAYT .8564 — AN CONST 10.28

#	INT	PRIN	BALANCE
1	9.2053	1.0712	98.9288
2	9.1019	1.1746	97.7541
3	8.9886	1.2880	96.4661
4	8.8642	1.4124	95.0537
5	8.7279	1.5487	93.5051
6	8.5784	1.6982	91.8069
7	8.4145	1.8621	89.9448
8	8.2348	2.0418	87.9030
9	8.0377	2.2389	85.6641
10	7.8216	2.4550	83.2091
11	7.5846	2.6920	80.5172
12	7.3248	2.9518	77.5653
13	7.0399	3.2367	74.3286
14	6.7274	3.5492	70.7795
15	6.3849	3.8917	66.8877
16	6.0092	4.2674	62.6204
17	5.5973	4.6793	57.9411
18	5.1456	5.1309	52.8101
19	4.6504	5.6262	47.1839
20	4.1073	6.1693	41.0147
21	3.5118	6.7648	34.2499
22	2.8589	7.4177	26.8322
23	2.1429	8.1337	18.6985
24	1.3578	8.9188	9.7797
25	.4969	9.7797	0.0000

YEARS 26 — MO PAYT .8481 — AN CONST 10.18

#	INT	PRIN	BALANCE
1	9.2097	.9675	99.0325
2	9.1163	1.0609	97.9716
3	9.0139	1.1633	96.8083
4	8.9016	1.2756	95.5328
5	8.7785	1.3987	94.1341
6	8.6435	1.5337	92.6004
7	8.4954	1.6817	90.9187
8	8.3331	1.8441	89.0746
9	8.1551	2.0221	87.0526
10	7.9599	2.2172	84.8353
11	7.7459	2.4312	82.4041
12	7.5112	2.6659	79.7382
13	7.2539	2.9232	76.8149
14	6.9717	3.2054	73.6095
15	6.6623	3.5148	70.0947
16	6.3231	3.8541	66.2406
17	5.9511	4.2261	62.0145
18	5.5431	4.6340	57.3805
19	5.0959	5.0813	52.2992
20	4.6054	5.5718	46.7274
21	4.0676	6.1096	40.6178
22	3.4779	6.6993	33.9185
23	2.8312	7.3459	26.5726
24	2.1221	8.0550	18.5176
25	1.3446	8.8325	9.6851
26	.4921	9.6851	0.0000

YEARS 27 — MO PAYT .8407 — AN CONST 10.09

#	INT	PRIN	BALANCE
1	9.2135	.8746	99.1254
2	9.1291	.9590	98.1664
3	9.0365	1.0516	97.1148
4	8.9350	1.1531	95.9617
5	8.8237	1.2644	94.6972
6	8.7017	1.3865	93.3108
7	8.5679	1.5203	91.7905
8	8.4211	1.6670	90.1235
9	8.2602	1.8279	88.2956
10	8.0838	2.0044	86.2912
11	7.8903	2.1978	84.0933
12	7.6782	2.4100	81.6834
13	7.4455	2.6426	79.0408
14	7.1905	2.8977	76.1431
15	6.9108	3.1774	72.9657
16	6.6041	3.4841	69.4816
17	6.2678	3.8204	65.6613
18	5.8990	4.1891	61.4721
19	5.4947	4.5935	56.8786
20	5.0513	5.0369	51.8418
21	4.5651	5.5230	46.3187
22	4.0320	6.0561	40.2626
23	3.4474	6.6407	33.6219
24	2.8064	7.2817	26.3402
25	2.1036	7.9846	18.3556
26	1.3329	8.7553	9.6004
27	.4878	9.6004	0.0000

YEARS 28 — MO PAYT .8340 — AN CONST 10.01

#	INT	PRIN	BALANCE
1	9.2170	.7913	99.2087
2	9.1406	.8677	98.3410
3	9.0569	.9514	97.3896
4	8.9650	1.0433	96.3463
5	8.8643	1.1440	95.2023
6	8.7539	1.2544	93.9479
7	8.6328	1.3755	92.5724
8	8.5001	1.5082	91.0642
9	8.3545	1.6538	89.4103
10	8.1949	1.8135	87.5969
11	8.0198	1.9885	85.6084
12	7.8279	2.1804	83.4279
13	7.6174	2.3909	81.0370
14	7.3866	2.6217	78.4153
15	7.1336	2.8748	75.5405
16	6.8561	3.1522	72.3883
17	6.5518	3.4565	68.9318
18	6.2182	3.7901	65.1417
19	5.8523	4.1560	60.9857
20	5.4512	4.5571	56.4286
21	5.0113	4.9970	51.4316
22	4.5290	5.4793	45.9522
23	4.0001	6.0082	39.9440
24	3.4202	6.5882	33.3558
25	2.7842	7.2241	26.1318
26	2.0869	7.9214	18.2104
27	1.3223	8.6860	9.5244
28	.4839	9.5244	0.0000

YEARS 29 — MO PAYT .8281 — AN CONST 9.94

#	INT	PRIN	BALANCE
1	9.2201	.7165	99.2835
2	9.1510	.7856	98.4979
3	9.0751	.8615	97.6364
4	8.9920	.9446	96.6918
5	8.9008	1.0358	95.6560
6	8.8008	1.1358	94.5202
7	8.6912	1.2454	93.2748
8	8.5710	1.3656	91.9092
9	8.4392	1.4974	90.4117
10	8.2946	1.6420	88.7697
11	8.1361	1.8005	86.9693
12	7.9623	1.9743	84.9950
13	7.7718	2.1648	82.8302
14	7.5628	2.3738	80.4564
15	7.3337	2.6029	77.8535
16	7.0825	2.8542	74.9993
17	6.8070	3.1297	71.8697
18	6.5049	3.4317	68.4379
19	6.1736	3.7630	64.6749
20	5.8104	4.1262	60.5487
21	5.4121	4.5245	56.0243
22	4.9754	4.9612	51.0631
23	4.4965	5.4401	45.6230
24	3.9714	5.9652	39.6578
25	3.3957	6.5410	33.1168
26	2.7643	7.1723	25.9445
27	2.0720	7.8646	18.0799
28	1.3129	8.6237	9.4561
29	.4805	9.4561	0.0000

YEARS 30 — MO PAYT .8227 — AN CONST 9.88

#	INT	PRIN	BALANCE
1	9.2229	.6492	99.3508
2	9.1603	.7118	98.6390
3	9.0916	.7805	97.8585
4	9.0162	.8559	97.0026
5	8.9336	.9385	96.0641
6	8.8430	1.0291	95.0350
7	8.7437	1.1284	93.9066
8	8.6348	1.2373	92.6693
9	8.5153	1.3568	91.3125
10	8.3844	1.4877	89.8248
11	8.2408	1.6313	88.1935
12	8.0833	1.7888	86.4047
13	7.9107	1.9614	84.4432
14	7.7213	2.1508	82.2925
15	7.5137	2.3584	79.9341
16	7.2861	2.5860	77.3481
17	7.0365	2.8356	74.5124
18	6.7628	3.1093	71.4031
19	6.4626	3.4095	67.9936
20	6.1335	3.7386	64.2551
21	5.7727	4.0994	60.1557
22	5.3770	4.4951	55.6606
23	4.9431	4.9290	50.7316
24	4.4673	5.4048	45.3268
25	3.9457	5.9265	39.4004
26	3.3736	6.4985	32.9019
27	2.7463	7.1258	25.7761
28	2.0585	7.8136	17.9625
29	1.3043	8.5678	9.3948
30	.4773	9.3948	0.0000

YEARS 2 — MO PAYT 4.5823 — AN CONST 54.99

#	INT	PRIN	BALANCE
1	7.3014	47.6856	52.3144
2	2.6726	52.3144	0.0000

YEARS 3 — MO PAYT 3.1940 — AN CONST 38.33

#	INT	PRIN	BALANCE
1	8.0302	30.2973	69.7027
2	5.0893	33.2382	36.4646
3	1.8629	36.4646	0.0000

YEARS 4 — MO PAYT 2.5028 — AN CONST 30.04

#	INT	PRIN	BALANCE
1	8.3930	21.6403	78.3597
2	6.2924	23.7409	54.6189
3	3.9879	26.0453	28.5735
4	1.4598	28.5735	0.0000

YEARS 5 — MO PAYT 2.0904 — AN CONST 25.09

#	INT	PRIN	BALANCE
1	8.6095	16.4756	83.5244
2	7.0102	18.0749	65.4495
3	5.2557	19.8294	45.6201
4	3.3309	21.7542	23.8659
5	1.2193	23.8659	0.0000

YEARS 6 — MO PAYT 1.8175 — AN CONST 21.81

#	INT	PRIN	BALANCE
1	8.7528	13.0570	86.9430
2	7.4853	14.3244	72.6186
3	6.0949	15.7149	56.9037
4	4.5695	17.2403	39.6635
5	2.8960	18.9138	20.7497
6	1.0601	20.7497	0.0000

YEARS 7 — MO PAYT 1.6242 — AN CONST 19.50

#	INT	PRIN	BALANCE
1	8.8542	10.6359	89.3641
2	7.8218	11.6683	77.6958
3	6.6892	12.8009	64.8950
4	5.4466	14.0435	50.8515
5	4.0835	15.4066	35.4449
6	2.5880	16.9021	18.5428
7	.9473	18.5428	0.0000

YEARS 8 — MO PAYT 1.4806 — AN CONST 17.77

#	INT	PRIN	BALANCE
1	8.9296	8.8380	91.1620
2	8.0717	9.6959	81.4662
3	7.1305	10.6370	70.8291
4	6.0980	11.6695	59.1596
5	4.9653	12.8023	46.3573
6	3.7226	14.0450	32.3123
7	2.3592	15.4083	16.9040
8	.8636	16.9040	0.0000

YEARS 9 — MO PAYT 1.3702 — AN CONST 16.45

#	INT	PRIN	BALANCE
1	8.9875	7.4554	92.5446
2	8.2638	8.1791	84.3655
3	7.4699	8.9730	75.3925
4	6.5989	9.8440	65.5485
5	5.6434	10.7995	54.7490
6	4.5951	11.8478	42.9012
7	3.4450	12.9979	29.9033
8	2.1834	14.2596	15.6437
9	.7992	15.6437	0.0000

YEARS 10 — MO PAYT 1.2831 — AN CONST 15.40

#	INT	PRIN	BALANCE
1	9.0333	6.3633	93.6367
2	8.4156	6.9810	86.6557
3	7.7380	7.6586	78.9971
4	6.9946	8.4020	70.5951
5	6.1790	9.2176	61.3775
6	5.2843	10.1123	51.2651
7	4.3027	11.0939	40.1712
8	3.2258	12.1708	28.0004
9	2.0444	13.3522	14.6483
10	.7483	14.6483	0.0000

YEARS 11 — MO PAYT 1.2127 — AN CONST 14.56

#	INT	PRIN	BALANCE
1	9.0702	5.4823	94.5177
2	8.5381	6.0145	88.5033
3	7.9543	6.5983	81.9050
4	7.3138	7.2387	74.6662
5	6.6111	7.9414	66.7248
6	5.8403	8.7123	58.0126
7	4.9946	9.5579	48.4546
8	4.0668	10.4857	37.9689
9	3.0490	11.5035	26.4654
10	1.9323	12.6202	13.8452
11	.7073	13.8452	0.0000

YEARS 12 — MO PAYT 1.1550 — AN CONST 13.86

#	INT	PRIN	BALANCE
1	9.1005	4.7594	95.2406
2	8.6385	5.2214	90.0192
3	8.1317	5.7282	84.2910
4	7.5757	6.2842	78.0068
5	6.9657	6.8942	71.1126
6	6.2965	7.5634	63.5492
7	5.5623	8.2976	55.2515
8	4.7569	9.1030	46.1485
9	3.8732	9.9867	36.1618
10	2.9039	10.9560	25.2058
11	1.8404	12.0195	13.1863
12	.6737	13.1863	0.0000

YEARS 13 — MO PAYT 1.1070 — AN CONST 13.29

#	INT	PRIN	BALANCE
1	9.1257	4.1579	95.8421
2	8.7221	4.5615	91.2806
3	8.2794	5.0043	86.2763
4	7.7936	5.4900	80.7863
5	7.2607	6.0229	74.7634
6	6.6761	6.6076	68.1558
7	6.0347	7.2490	60.9068
8	5.3310	7.9526	52.9542
9	4.5591	8.7245	44.2297
10	3.7122	9.5714	34.6583
11	2.7831	10.5005	24.1578
12	1.7639	11.5198	12.6380
13	.6456	12.6380	0.0000

YEARS 14 — MO PAYT 1.0665 — AN CONST 12.80

#	INT	PRIN	BALANCE
1	9.1470	3.6516	96.3484
2	8.7925	4.0061	92.3423
3	8.4036	4.3949	87.9474
4	7.9770	4.8215	83.1259
5	7.5090	5.2896	77.8363
6	6.9956	5.8030	72.0333
7	6.4323	6.3663	65.6670
8	5.8143	6.9843	58.6828
9	5.1364	7.6622	51.0206
10	4.3926	8.4060	42.6146
11	3.5766	9.2219	33.3927
12	2.6815	10.1171	23.2756
13	1.6994	11.0991	12.1765
14	.6221	12.1765	0.0000

YEARS 15 — MO PAYT 1.0322 — AN CONST 12.39

#	INT	PRIN	BALANCE
1	9.1650	3.2213	96.7787
2	8.8523	3.5340	93.2447
3	8.5093	3.8770	89.3677
4	8.1329	4.2534	85.1144
5	7.7201	4.6662	80.4481
6	7.2671	5.1192	75.3290
7	6.7702	5.6161	69.7129
8	6.2251	6.1612	63.5517
9	5.6270	6.7593	56.7924
10	4.9709	7.4154	49.3770
11	4.2511	8.1352	41.2419
12	3.4614	8.9249	32.3170
13	2.5951	9.7912	22.5258
14	1.6447	10.7416	11.7843
15	.6020	11.7843	0.0000

YEARS 16 — MO PAYT 1.0027 — AN CONST 12.04

#	INT	PRIN	BALANCE
1	9.1804	2.8525	97.1475
2	8.9036	3.1294	94.0181
3	8.5998	3.4332	90.5849
4	8.2665	3.7664	86.8185
5	7.9009	4.1320	82.6865
6	7.4998	4.5331	78.1533
7	7.0598	4.9731	73.1802
8	6.5771	5.4559	67.7243
9	6.0475	5.9855	61.7389
10	5.4665	6.5665	55.1724
11	4.8291	7.2039	47.9685
12	4.1298	7.9031	40.0654
13	3.3627	8.6703	31.3952
14	2.5211	9.5119	21.8833
15	1.5978	10.4352	11.4481
16	.5849	11.4481	0.0000

YEARS 17 — MO PAYT .9773 — AN CONST 11.73

#	INT	PRIN	BALANCE
1	9.1938	2.5342	97.4658
2	8.9478	2.7802	94.6855
3	8.6779	3.0501	91.6354
4	8.3819	3.3462	88.2893
5	8.0570	3.6710	84.6183
6	7.7007	4.0273	80.5910
7	7.3098	4.4182	76.1727
8	6.8809	4.8471	71.3256
9	6.4104	5.3176	66.0080
10	5.8942	5.8338	60.1743
11	5.3280	6.4001	53.7742
12	4.7067	7.0213	46.7529
13	4.0252	7.7028	39.0501
14	3.2775	8.4505	30.5995
15	2.4572	9.2708	21.3287
16	1.5573	10.1707	11.1580
17	.5700	11.1580	0.0000

YEARS 18 — MO PAYT .9553 — AN CONST 11.47

#	INT	PRIN	BALANCE
1	9.2054	2.2578	97.7422
2	8.9862	2.4770	95.2651
3	8.7458	2.7175	92.5477
4	8.4820	2.9812	89.5664
5	8.1926	3.2706	86.2958
6	7.8751	3.5881	82.7077
7	7.5268	3.9364	78.7714
8	7.1447	4.3185	74.4529
9	6.7256	4.7377	69.7152
10	6.2657	5.1975	64.5177
11	5.7612	5.7021	58.8156
12	5.2077	6.2555	52.5601
13	4.6005	6.8628	45.6973
14	3.9343	7.5289	38.1684
15	3.2035	8.2597	29.9086
16	2.4017	9.0615	20.8471
17	1.5221	9.9411	10.9061
18	.5572	10.9061	0.0000

YEARS 19 — MO PAYT .9360 — AN CONST 11.24

#	INT	PRIN	BALANCE
1	9.2155	2.0166	97.9834
2	9.0197	2.2123	95.7711
3	8.8050	2.4271	93.3440
4	8.5694	2.6627	90.6814
5	8.3109	2.9211	87.7603
6	8.0274	3.2047	84.5556
7	7.7163	3.5157	81.0399
8	7.3751	3.8570	77.1829
9	7.0007	4.2314	72.9515
10	6.5899	4.6421	68.3094
11	6.1393	5.0927	63.2166
12	5.6450	5.5871	57.6296
13	5.1027	6.1294	51.5002
14	4.5077	6.7244	44.7758
15	3.8550	7.3771	37.3987
16	3.1389	8.0932	29.3055
17	2.3533	8.8788	20.4267
18	1.4914	9.7406	10.6861
19	.5459	10.6861	0.0000

YEARS 20 — MO PAYT .9191 — AN CONST 11.03

#	INT	PRIN	BALANCE
1	9.2243	1.8050	98.1950
2	9.0491	1.9802	96.2149
3	8.8569	2.1724	94.0425
4	8.6461	2.3833	91.6592
5	8.4147	2.6146	89.0446
6	8.1609	2.8684	86.1762
7	7.8825	3.1468	83.0294
8	7.5770	3.4523	79.5771
9	7.2419	3.7874	75.7898
10	6.8743	4.1550	71.6347
11	6.4710	4.5583	67.0764
12	6.0285	5.0008	62.0756
13	5.5431	5.4862	56.5894
14	5.0106	6.0188	50.5706
15	4.4263	6.6030	43.9676
16	3.7854	7.2439	36.7237
17	3.0822	7.9471	28.7766
18	2.3108	8.7185	20.0580
19	1.4645	9.5648	10.4932
20	.5361	10.4932	0.0000

YEARS 21 — MO PAYT .9042 — AN CONST 10.86

#	INT	PRIN	BALANCE
1	9.2322	1.6186	98.3814
2	9.0750	1.7758	96.6056
3	8.9027	1.9481	94.6575

MONTHLY PAYMENT AMORTIZATION SCHEDULE PER $100   9.30 %

#	INT	PRIN	BALANCE
4	8.7136	2.1372	92.5203
5	8.5061	2.3447	90.1756
6	8.2785	2.5723	87.6033
7	8.0288	2.8220	84.7814
8	7.7549	3.0959	81.6855
9	7.4544	3.3964	78.2891
10	7.1247	3.7261	74.5630
11	6.7630	4.0878	70.4752
12	6.3662	4.4846	65.9907
13	5.9309	4.9199	61.0708
14	5.4534	5.3974	55.6734
15	4.9294	5.9213	49.7520
16	4.3547	6.4961	43.2559
17	3.7241	7.1267	36.1292
18	3.0323	7.8185	28.3108
19	2.2734	8.5774	19.7334
20	1.4408	9.4100	10.3234
21	.5274	10.3234	0.0000

YEARS 22 — MO PAYT .8911 — AN CONST 10.70

#	INT	PRIN	BALANCE
1	9.2391	1.4540	98.5460
2	9.0979	1.5951	96.9509
3	8.9431	1.7499	95.2010
4	8.7732	1.9198	93.2812
5	8.5869	2.1061	91.1751
6	8.3824	2.3106	88.8645
7	8.1582	2.5349	86.3296
8	7.9121	2.7809	83.5487
9	7.6422	3.0509	80.4978
10	7.3460	3.3470	77.1508
11	7.0211	3.6719	73.4789
12	6.6647	4.0283	69.4505
13	6.2737	4.4194	65.0312
14	5.8447	4.8483	60.1829
15	5.3741	5.3189	54.8639
16	4.8578	5.8353	49.0287
17	4.2914	6.4017	42.6270
18	3.6700	7.0231	35.6039
19	2.9882	7.7048	27.8991
20	2.2404	8.4527	19.4465
21	1.4199	9.2732	10.1733
22	.5197	10.1733	0.0000

YEARS 23 — MO PAYT .8794 — AN CONST 10.56

#	INT	PRIN	BALANCE
1	9.2452	1.3080	98.6920
2	9.1182	1.4349	97.2571
3	8.9789	1.5742	95.6828
4	8.8261	1.7270	93.9558
5	8.6585	1.8947	92.0611
6	8.4746	2.0786	89.9825
7	8.2728	2.2804	87.7021
8	8.0514	2.5017	85.2004
9	7.8086	2.7446	82.4559
10	7.5422	3.0110	79.4449
11	7.2499	3.3032	76.1417
12	6.9293	3.6239	72.5178
13	6.5775	3.9756	68.5421
14	6.1916	4.3615	64.1806
15	5.7682	4.7849	59.3957
16	5.3038	5.2494	54.1463
17	4.7942	5.7589	48.3874
18	4.2352	6.3179	42.0694
19	3.6220	6.9312	35.1382
20	2.9492	7.6040	27.5342
21	2.2110	8.3421	19.1921
22	1.4013	9.1519	10.0402
23	.5129	10.0402	0.0000

YEARS 24 — MO PAYT .8691 — AN CONST 10.43

#	INT	PRIN	BALANCE
1	9.2506	1.1782	98.8218
2	9.1363	1.2926	97.5292
3	9.0108	1.4180	96.1112
4	8.8731	1.5557	94.5555
5	8.7221	1.7067	92.8488
6	8.5565	1.8724	90.9764
7	8.3747	2.0541	88.9223
8	8.1753	2.2535	86.6688
9	7.9566	2.4722	84.1966
10	7.7166	2.7122	81.4844
11	7.4533	2.9755	78.5089
12	7.1645	3.2643	75.2445
13	6.8476	3.5812	71.6634
14	6.5000	3.9288	67.7346
15	6.1187	4.3102	63.4244
16	5.7003	4.7285	58.6959
17	5.2413	5.1875	53.5083
18	4.7378	5.6911	47.8173
19	4.1853	6.2435	41.5738
20	3.5793	6.8495	34.7242
21	2.9144	7.5144	27.2098
22	2.1850	8.2438	18.9660
23	1.3848	9.0440	9.9219
24	.5069	9.9219	0.0000

YEARS 25 — MO PAYT .8598 — AN CONST 10.32

#	INT	PRIN	BALANCE
1	9.2555	1.0625	98.9375
2	9.1523	1.1657	97.7718
3	9.0392	1.2788	96.4929
4	8.9150	1.4030	95.0899
5	8.7789	1.5392	93.5508
6	8.6295	1.6886	91.8622
7	8.4655	1.8525	90.0098
8	8.2857	2.0323	87.9775
9	8.0885	2.2296	85.7479
10	7.8720	2.4460	83.3019
11	7.6346	2.6834	80.6185
12	7.3741	2.9439	77.6747
13	7.0884	3.2296	74.4450
14	6.7749	3.5431	70.9019
15	6.4310	3.8871	67.0149
16	6.0537	4.2644	62.7505
17	5.6397	4.6783	58.0722
18	5.1856	5.1324	52.9398
19	4.6874	5.6306	47.3092
20	4.1409	6.1772	41.1320
21	3.5413	6.7768	34.3553
22	2.8834	7.4346	26.9207
23	2.1618	8.1562	18.7645
24	1.3701	8.9479	9.8165
25	.5015	9.8165	0.0000

YEARS 26 — MO PAYT .8516 — AN CONST 10.22

#	INT	PRIN	BALANCE
1	9.2598	.9592	99.0408
2	9.1667	1.0524	97.9884
3	9.0645	1.1545	96.8339
4	8.9525	1.2666	95.5673
5	8.8295	1.3895	94.1778
6	8.6946	1.5244	92.6534
7	8.5467	1.6724	90.9810
8	8.3843	1.8347	89.1463
9	8.2062	2.0128	87.1336
10	8.0109	2.2082	84.9254
11	7.7965	2.4225	82.5029
12	7.5614	2.6577	79.8452
13	7.3034	2.9157	76.9296
14	7.0204	3.1987	73.7309
15	6.7099	3.5091	70.2218
16	6.3693	3.8498	66.3720
17	5.9956	4.2235	62.1486
18	5.5856	4.6334	57.5151
19	5.1359	5.0832	52.4320
20	4.6424	5.5766	46.8554
21	4.1011	6.1179	40.7375
22	3.5073	6.7118	34.0257
23	2.8558	7.3633	26.6625
24	2.1410	8.0780	18.5845
25	1.3569	8.8621	9.7223
26	.4967	9.7223	0.0000

YEARS 27 — MO PAYT .8442 — AN CONST 10.14

#	INT	PRIN	BALANCE
1	9.2637	.8668	99.1332
2	9.1795	.9509	98.1823
3	9.0872	1.0432	97.1390
4	8.9860	1.1445	95.9945
5	8.8749	1.2556	94.7390
6	8.7530	1.3775	93.3615
7	8.6193	1.5112	91.8503
8	8.4726	1.6579	90.1924
9	8.3117	1.8188	88.3736
10	8.1351	1.9953	86.3783
11	7.9414	2.1890	84.1893
12	7.7289	2.4015	81.7877
13	7.4958	2.6346	79.1531
14	7.2401	2.8904	76.2628
15	6.9595	3.1709	73.0918
16	6.6517	3.4787	69.6131
17	6.3141	3.8164	65.7967
18	5.9436	4.1868	61.6099
19	5.5372	4.5933	57.0166
20	5.0913	5.0391	51.9775
21	4.6022	5.5283	46.4492
22	4.0656	6.0649	40.3844
23	3.4769	6.6536	33.7308
24	2.8310	7.2994	26.4314
25	2.1225	8.0080	18.4234
26	1.3452	8.7853	9.6381
27	.4924	9.6381	0.0000

YEARS 28 — MO PAYT .8376 — AN CONST 10.06

#	INT	PRIN	BALANCE
1	9.2671	.7839	99.2161
2	9.1911	.8600	98.3561
3	9.1076	.9435	97.4126
4	9.0160	1.0351	96.3776
5	8.9155	1.1355	95.2420
6	8.8053	1.2458	93.9963
7	8.6844	1.3667	92.6296
8	8.5517	1.4993	91.1303
9	8.4062	1.6449	89.4854
10	8.2465	1.8045	87.6809
11	8.0713	1.9797	85.7012
12	7.8792	2.1719	83.5293
13	7.6684	2.3827	81.1466
14	7.4371	2.6140	78.5326
15	7.1833	2.8677	75.6649
16	6.9050	3.1461	72.5189
17	6.5996	3.4515	69.0674
18	6.2646	3.7865	65.2809
19	5.8970	4.1540	61.1269
20	5.4938	4.5573	56.5697
21	5.0514	4.9996	51.5700
22	4.5661	5.4849	46.0851
23	4.0337	6.0173	40.0678
24	3.4496	6.6014	33.4664
25	2.8088	7.2422	26.2242
26	2.1058	7.9452	18.2790
27	1.3346	8.7164	9.5625
28	.4885	9.5625	0.0000

YEARS 29 — MO PAYT .8316 — AN CONST 9.98

#	INT	PRIN	BALANCE
1	9.2703	.7095	99.2905
2	9.2014	.7783	98.5122
3	9.1258	.8539	97.6583
4	9.0430	.9368	96.7215
5	8.9520	1.0277	95.6938
6	8.8523	1.1275	94.5663
7	8.7428	1.2369	93.3294
8	8.6228	1.3570	91.9724
9	8.4910	1.4887	90.4837
10	8.3465	1.6332	88.8505
11	8.1880	1.7917	87.0588
12	8.0141	1.9657	85.0931
13	7.8233	2.1565	82.9367
14	7.6140	2.3658	80.5709
15	7.3843	2.5954	77.9755
16	7.1324	2.8474	75.1281
17	6.8560	3.1237	72.0044
18	6.5528	3.4270	68.5774
19	6.2201	3.7596	64.8178
20	5.8552	4.1246	60.6932
21	5.4548	4.5249	56.1683
22	5.0156	4.9641	51.2042
23	4.5337	5.4460	45.7582
24	4.0051	5.9746	39.7835
25	3.4252	6.5546	33.2289
26	2.7889	7.1908	26.0381
27	2.0909	7.8888	18.1493
28	1.3251	8.6546	9.4947
29	.4851	9.4947	0.0000

YEARS 30 — MO PAYT .8263 — AN CONST 9.92

#	INT	PRIN	BALANCE
1	9.2731	.6425	99.3575
2	9.2107	.7049	98.6525
3	9.1423	.7733	97.8792
4	9.0672	.8484	97.0308
5	8.9849	.9308	96.1000
6	8.8945	1.0211	95.0789
7	8.7954	1.1202	93.9587
8	8.6866	1.2290	92.7297
9	8.5674	1.3483	91.3815
10	8.4365	1.4791	89.9023
11	8.2929	1.6227	88.2796
12	8.1354	1.7802	86.4994
13	7.9626	1.9530	84.5464
14	7.7730	2.1426	82.4038
15	7.5650	2.3506	80.0532
16	7.3369	2.5787	77.4744
17	7.0866	2.8291	74.6454
18	6.8119	3.1037	71.5417
19	6.5107	3.4049	68.1368
20	6.1802	3.7355	64.4013
21	5.8176	4.0981	60.3032
22	5.4198	4.4958	55.8074
23	4.9834	4.9322	50.8752
24	4.5046	5.4110	45.4641
25	3.9794	5.9363	39.5279
26	3.4031	6.5125	33.0154
27	2.7710	7.1446	25.8708
28	2.0775	7.8381	18.0326
29	1.3166	8.5990	9.4337
30	.4819	9.4337	0.0000

YEARS 2 — MO PAYT 4.5857 — AN CONST 55.03

#	INT	PRIN	BALANCE
1	7.3613	47.6671	52.3329
2	2.6954	52.3329	0.0000
7	3.4797	13.0113	29.9681
8	2.2061	14.2849	15.6832
9	.8078	15.6832	0.0000

YEARS 3 — MO PAYT 3.1975 — AN CONST 38.37

#	INT	PRIN	BALANCE
1	8.0961	30.2733	69.7267
2	5.1328	33.2366	36.4900
3	1.8794	36.4900	0.0000

YEARS 4 — MO PAYT 2.5063 — AN CONST 30.08

#	INT	PRIN	BALANCE
1	8.4619	21.6143	78.3857
2	6.3462	23.7300	54.6558
3	4.0234	26.0528	28.6030
4	1.4732	28.6030	0.0000

YEARS 5 — MO PAYT 2.0941 — AN CONST 25.13

#	INT	PRIN	BALANCE
1	8.6801	16.4489	83.5511
2	7.0700	18.0590	65.4922
3	5.3023	19.8267	45.6655
4	3.3616	21.7674	23.8981
5	1.2309	23.8981	0.0000

YEARS 6 — MO PAYT 1.8212 — AN CONST 21.86

#	INT	PRIN	BALANCE
1	8.8246	13.0301	86.9699
2	7.5491	14.3056	72.6643
3	6.1488	15.7059	56.9585
4	4.6114	17.2432	39.7152
5	2.9236	18.9311	20.7842
6	1.0705	20.7842	0.0000

YEARS 7 — MO PAYT 1.6280 — AN CONST 19.54

#	INT	PRIN	BALANCE
1	8.9268	10.6092	89.3908
2	7.8883	11.6477	77.7431
3	6.7482	12.7879	64.9552
4	5.4965	14.0396	50.9156
5	4.1222	15.4139	35.5018
6	2.6134	16.9226	18.5791
7	.9569	18.5791	0.0000

YEARS 8 — MO PAYT 1.4845 — AN CONST 17.82

#	INT	PRIN	BALANCE
1	9.0028	8.8118	91.1882
2	8.1402	9.6744	81.5138
3	7.1932	10.6213	70.8925
4	6.1536	11.6610	59.2315
5	5.0121	12.8024	46.4290
6	3.7590	14.0556	32.3734
7	2.3831	15.4315	16.9420
8	.8726	16.9420	0.0000

YEARS 9 — MO PAYT 1.3742 — AN CONST 16.50

#	INT	PRIN	BALANCE
1	9.0611	7.4298	92.5702
2	8.3339	8.1571	84.4130
3	7.5354	8.9556	75.4575
4	6.6588	9.8322	65.6253
5	5.6964	10.7946	54.8307
6	4.6397	11.8512	42.9794

YEARS 10 — MO PAYT 1.2871 — AN CONST 15.45

#	INT	PRIN	BALANCE
1	9.1072	6.3385	93.6615
2	8.4868	6.9589	86.7026
3	7.8056	7.6401	79.0626
4	7.0578	8.3879	70.6746
5	6.2367	9.2090	61.4656
6	5.3353	10.1104	51.3552
7	4.3456	11.1001	40.2552
8	3.2591	12.1866	28.0686
9	2.0662	13.3795	14.6891
10	.7566	14.6891	0.0000

YEARS 11 — MO PAYT 1.2169 — AN CONST 14.61

#	INT	PRIN	BALANCE
1	9.1444	5.4582	94.5418
2	8.6101	5.9925	88.5493
3	8.0236	6.5791	81.9702
4	7.3796	7.2231	74.7471
5	6.6725	7.9301	66.8171
6	5.8963	8.7063	58.1107
7	5.0441	9.5586	48.5522
8	4.1084	10.4942	38.0580
9	3.0812	11.5214	26.5366
10	1.9534	12.6492	13.8874
11	.7153	13.8874	0.0000

YEARS 12 — MO PAYT 1.1593 — AN CONST 13.92

#	INT	PRIN	BALANCE
1	9.1749	4.7361	95.2639
2	8.7113	5.1997	90.0642
3	8.2024	5.7087	84.3555
4	7.6436	6.2675	78.0880
5	7.0301	6.8810	71.2070
6	6.3565	7.5545	63.6525
7	5.6170	8.2940	55.3585
8	4.8052	9.1058	46.2527
9	3.9139	9.9972	36.2555
10	2.9353	10.9758	25.2798
11	1.8609	12.0501	13.2296
12	.6814	13.2296	0.0000

YEARS 13 — MO PAYT 1.1113 — AN CONST 13.34

#	INT	PRIN	BALANCE
1	9.2003	4.1355	95.8645
2	8.7955	4.5403	91.3243
3	8.3511	4.9847	86.3396
4	7.8632	5.4726	80.8670
5	7.3275	6.0083	74.8587
6	6.7393	6.5964	68.2623
7	6.0937	7.2421	61.0202
8	5.3848	7.9510	53.0692
9	4.6065	8.7293	44.3399
10	3.7520	9.5837	34.7562
11	2.8139	10.5219	24.2343
12	1.7840	11.5518	12.6825
13	.6532	12.6825	0.0000

YEARS 14 — MO PAYT 1.0710 — AN CONST 12.86

#	INT	PRIN	BALANCE
1	9.2217	3.6300	96.3700
2	8.8663	3.9853	92.3846
3	8.4762	4.3754	88.0092
4	8.0479	4.8037	83.2055
5	7.5777	5.2739	77.9315
6	7.0615	5.7902	72.1413
7	6.4947	6.3570	65.7844
8	5.8725	6.9792	58.8052
9	5.1893	7.6624	51.1428
10	4.4393	8.4124	42.7304
11	3.6158	9.2359	33.4945
12	2.7118	10.1399	23.3546
13	1.7192	11.1325	12.2222
14	.6295	12.2222	0.0000

YEARS 15 — MO PAYT 1.0367 — AN CONST 12.45

#	INT	PRIN	BALANCE
1	9.2398	3.2005	96.7995
2	8.9265	3.5138	93.2856
3	8.5826	3.8578	89.4278
4	8.2049	4.2354	85.1924
5	7.7904	4.6500	80.5424
6	7.3352	5.1052	75.4373
7	6.8355	5.6049	69.8324
8	6.2868	6.1535	63.6789
9	5.6845	6.7558	56.9231
10	5.0232	7.4171	49.5059
11	4.2972	8.1432	41.3628
12	3.5001	8.9403	32.4225
13	2.6250	9.8154	22.6071
14	1.6642	10.7762	11.8310
15	.6094	11.8310	0.0000

YEARS 16 — MO PAYT 1.0073 — AN CONST 12.09

#	INT	PRIN	BALANCE
1	9.2553	2.8326	97.1674
2	8.9781	3.1099	94.0575
3	8.6737	3.4143	90.6432
4	8.3394	3.7485	86.8947
5	7.9725	4.1154	82.7793
6	7.5697	4.5183	78.2610
7	7.1274	4.9605	73.3004
8	6.6418	5.4461	67.8543
9	6.1088	5.9792	61.8751
10	5.5235	6.5645	55.3107
11	4.8809	7.2070	48.1036
12	4.1755	7.9125	40.1911
13	3.4009	8.6870	31.5041
14	2.5506	9.5373	21.9668
15	1.6170	10.4709	11.4959
16	.5921	11.4959	0.0000

YEARS 17 — MO PAYT .9820 — AN CONST 11.79

#	INT	PRIN	BALANCE
1	9.2687	2.5152	97.4848
2	9.0226	2.7614	94.7235
3	8.7523	3.0317	91.6918
4	8.4555	3.3284	88.3634
5	8.1297	3.6542	84.7091
6	7.7720	4.0119	80.6972
7	7.3793	4.4046	76.2926
8	6.9481	4.8358	71.4568
9	6.4748	5.3091	66.1477
10	5.9551	5.8288	60.3189
11	5.3846	6.3994	53.9195
12	4.7582	7.0258	46.8937
13	4.0704	7.7135	39.1802
14	3.3154	8.4685	30.7117
15	2.4865	9.2975	21.4143
16	1.5764	10.2075	11.2067
17	.5772	11.2067	0.0000

YEARS 18 — MO PAYT .9600 — AN CONST 11.53

#	INT	PRIN	BALANCE
1	9.2804	2.2396	97.7604
2	9.0612	2.4588	95.3015
3	8.8205	2.6995	92.6020
4	8.5562	2.9638	89.6382
5	8.2661	3.2539	86.3844
6	7.9476	3.5724	82.8120
7	7.5979	3.9221	78.8899
8	7.2140	4.3060	74.5839
9	6.7925	4.7275	69.8564
10	6.3298	5.1902	64.6662
11	5.8217	5.6983	58.9680
12	5.2640	6.2560	52.7119
13	4.6516	6.8684	45.8435
14	3.9793	7.5407	38.3028
15	3.2411	8.2789	30.0239
16	2.4308	9.0892	20.9347
17	1.5411	9.9789	10.9557
18	.5643	10.9557	0.0000

YEARS 19 — MO PAYT .9408 — AN CONST 11.29

#	INT	PRIN	BALANCE
1	9.2905	1.9992	98.0008
2	9.0949	2.1948	95.8060
3	8.8800	2.4097	93.3963
4	8.6441	2.6456	90.7507
5	8.3852	2.9045	87.8462
6	8.1009	3.1888	84.6574
7	7.7887	3.5010	81.1564
8	7.4460	3.8437	77.3128
9	7.0698	4.2199	73.0929
10	6.6567	4.6330	68.4599
11	6.2032	5.0865	63.3734
12	5.7054	5.5844	57.7891
13	5.1587	6.1310	51.6581
14	4.5586	6.7311	44.9270
15	3.8997	7.3900	37.5370
16	3.1764	8.1134	29.4237
17	2.3822	8.9075	20.5161
18	1.5103	9.7794	10.7367
19	.5530	10.7367	0.0000

YEARS 20 — MO PAYT .9240 — AN CONST 11.09

#	INT	PRIN	BALANCE
1	9.2995	1.7884	98.2116
2	9.1244	1.9634	96.2482
3	8.9322	2.1556	94.0926
4	8.7212	2.3666	91.7261
5	8.4896	2.5982	89.1278
6	8.2352	2.8526	86.2752
7	7.9560	3.1318	83.1434
8	7.6494	3.4384	79.7051
9	7.3129	3.7749	75.9301
10	6.9434	4.1444	71.7857
11	6.5377	4.5501	67.2356
12	6.0923	4.9955	62.2401
13	5.6033	5.4845	56.7556
14	5.0665	6.0213	50.7343
15	4.4771	6.6107	44.1236
16	3.8300	7.2578	36.8657
17	3.1195	7.9683	28.8975
18	2.3396	8.7482	20.1492
19	1.4833	9.6046	10.5447
20	.5431	10.5447	0.0000

YEARS 21 — MO PAYT .9092 — AN CONST 10.92

#	INT	PRIN	BALANCE
1	9.3073	1.6028	98.3972
2	9.1504	1.7597	96.6375
3	8.9782	1.9319	94.7056

#	INT	PRIN	BALANCE
4	8.7890	2.1210	92.5845
5	8.5814	2.3287	90.2559
6	8.3535	2.5566	87.6993
7	8.1032	2.8069	84.8924
8	7.8285	3.0816	81.8108
9	7.5268	3.3832	78.4276
10	7.1957	3.7144	74.7131
11	6.8321	4.0780	70.6351
12	6.4329	4.4772	66.1579
13	5.9947	4.9154	61.2425
14	5.5135	5.3966	55.8459
15	4.9853	5.9248	49.9211
16	4.4053	6.5048	43.4163
17	3.7686	7.1415	36.2748
18	3.0695	7.8405	28.4343
19	2.3021	8.6080	19.8263
20	1.4595	9.4506	10.3757
21	.5344	10.3757	0.0000

YEARS 22 — MO PAYT .8961 — AN CONST 10.76

#	INT	PRIN	BALANCE
1	9.3142	1.4389	98.5611
2	9.1734	1.5797	96.9814
3	9.0187	1.7344	95.2470
4	8.8490	1.9041	93.3429
5	8.6626	2.0905	91.2523
6	8.4579	2.2952	88.9572
7	8.2333	2.5198	86.4374
8	7.9866	2.7665	83.6709
9	7.7158	3.0373	80.6336
10	7.4185	3.3346	77.2991
11	7.0921	3.6610	73.6381
12	6.7338	4.0193	69.6188
13	6.3403	4.4128	65.2060
14	5.9084	4.8447	60.3613
15	5.4342	5.3189	55.0424
16	4.9135	5.8396	49.2028
17	4.3419	6.4112	42.7916
18	3.7144	7.0387	35.7529
19	3.0254	7.7277	28.0252
20	2.2690	8.4842	19.5410
21	1.4385	9.3146	10.2264
22	.5267	10.2264	0.0000

YEARS 23 — MO PAYT .8845 — AN CONST 10.62

#	INT	PRIN	BALANCE
1	9.3204	1.2936	98.7064
2	9.1937	1.4203	97.2861
3	9.0547	1.5593	95.7268
4	8.9021	1.7119	94.0148
5	8.7345	1.8795	92.1353
6	8.5505	2.0635	90.0719
7	8.3485	2.2655	87.8064
8	8.1268	2.4872	85.3192
9	7.8833	2.7307	82.5885
10	7.6160	2.9980	79.5905
11	7.3226	3.2914	76.2991
12	7.0004	3.6136	72.6855
13	6.6467	3.9673	68.7181
14	6.2583	4.3557	64.3625
15	5.8320	4.7820	59.5804
16	5.3639	5.2501	54.3303
17	4.8500	5.7640	48.5663
18	4.2858	6.3282	42.2381
19	3.6663	6.9477	35.2904
20	2.9862	7.6278	27.6626
21	2.2396	8.3744	19.2882
22	1.4199	9.1941	10.0941
23	.5199	10.0941	0.0000

YEARS 24 — MO PAYT .8742 — AN CONST 10.50

#	INT	PRIN	BALANCE
1	9.3258	1.1646	98.8354
2	9.2118	1.2786	97.5568
3	9.0867	1.4037	96.1531
4	8.9492	1.5411	94.6120
5	8.7984	1.6920	92.9200
6	8.6328	1.8576	91.0623
7	8.4509	2.0394	89.0229
8	8.2513	2.2391	86.7838
9	8.0321	2.4583	84.3256
10	7.7915	2.6989	81.6267
11	7.5273	2.9631	78.6636
12	7.2373	3.2531	75.4105
13	6.9189	3.5715	71.8390
14	6.5693	3.9211	67.9179
15	6.1854	4.3049	63.6129
16	5.7640	4.7263	58.8866
17	5.3014	5.1890	53.6976
18	4.7935	5.6969	48.0007
19	4.2358	6.2545	41.7462
20	3.6236	6.8668	34.8794
21	2.9515	7.5389	27.3405
22	2.2135	8.2769	19.0636
23	1.4033	9.0871	9.9765
24	.5138	9.9765	0.0000

YEARS 25 — MO PAYT .8650 — AN CONST 10.39

#	INT	PRIN	BALANCE
1	9.3307	1.0496	98.9504
2	9.2279	1.1524	97.7980
3	9.1151	1.2652	96.5329
4	8.9913	1.3890	95.1439
5	8.8553	1.5250	93.6189
6	8.7060	1.6742	91.9447
7	8.5422	1.8381	90.1065
8	8.3622	2.0180	88.0885
9	8.1647	2.2156	85.8729
10	7.9478	2.4325	83.4405
11	7.7097	2.6706	80.7699
12	7.4483	2.9320	77.8380
13	7.1613	3.2190	74.6190
14	6.8462	3.5340	71.0850
15	6.5003	3.8800	67.2050
16	6.1205	4.2598	62.9452
17	5.7035	4.6767	58.2685
18	5.2458	5.1345	53.1340
19	4.7432	5.6371	47.4969
20	4.1914	6.1889	41.3080
21	3.5856	6.7947	34.5133
22	2.9205	7.4598	27.0535
23	2.1903	8.1900	18.8635
24	1.3886	8.9917	9.8718
25	.5085	9.8718	0.0000

YEARS 26 — MO PAYT .8568 — AN CONST 10.29

#	INT	PRIN	BALANCE
1	9.3350	.9470	99.0530
2	9.2423	1.0397	98.0133
3	9.1405	1.1414	96.8719
4	9.0288	1.2532	95.6187
5	8.9061	1.3758	94.2429
6	8.7715	1.5105	92.7323
7	8.6236	1.6584	91.0740
8	8.4613	1.8207	89.2532
9	8.2830	1.9989	87.2543
10	8.0874	2.1946	85.0597
11	7.8726	2.4094	82.6503
12	7.6367	2.6453	80.0050
13	7.3778	2.9042	77.1008
14	7.0935	3.1885	73.9124
15	6.7814	3.5006	70.4118
16	6.4388	3.8432	66.5686
17	6.0626	4.2194	62.3491
18	5.6495	4.6324	57.7167
19	5.1961	5.0859	52.6308
20	4.6983	5.5837	47.0471
21	4.1517	6.1303	40.9168
22	3.5516	6.7303	34.1865
23	2.8928	7.3891	26.7973
24	2.1695	8.1124	18.6849
25	1.3755	8.9065	9.7783
26	.5036	9.7783	0.0000

YEARS 27 — MO PAYT .8495 — AN CONST 10.20

#	INT	PRIN	BALANCE
1	9.3389	.8552	99.1448
2	9.2552	.9389	98.2059
3	9.1633	1.0308	97.1751
4	9.0624	1.1317	96.0435
5	8.9516	1.2425	94.8010
6	8.8300	1.3641	93.4369
7	8.6964	1.4976	91.9393
8	8.5499	1.6442	90.2951
9	8.3889	1.8051	88.4900
10	8.2122	1.9818	86.5081
11	8.0182	2.1758	84.3323
12	7.8052	2.3888	81.9435
13	7.5714	2.6226	79.3208
14	7.3147	2.8794	76.4415
15	7.0328	3.1612	73.2803
16	6.7234	3.4706	69.8096
17	6.3837	3.8104	65.9993
18	6.0107	4.1833	61.8159
19	5.6012	4.5928	57.2231
20	5.1517	5.0424	52.1807
21	4.6581	5.5360	46.6448
22	4.1162	6.0779	40.5669
23	3.5213	6.6728	33.8941
24	2.8681	7.3260	26.5681
25	2.1510	8.0431	18.5251
26	1.3637	8.8304	9.6947
27	.4993	9.6947	0.0000

YEARS 28 — MO PAYT .8429 — AN CONST 10.12

#	INT	PRIN	BALANCE
1	9.3423	.7729	99.2271
2	9.2667	.8486	98.3785
3	9.1836	.9316	97.4469
4	9.0924	1.0228	96.4241
5	8.9923	1.1229	95.3011
6	8.8824	1.2329	94.0683
7	8.7617	1.3535	92.7147
8	8.6292	1.4860	91.2287
9	8.4838	1.6315	89.5972
10	8.3241	1.7912	87.8060
11	8.1487	1.9665	85.8395
12	7.9562	2.1590	83.6805
13	7.7449	2.3703	81.3101
14	7.5129	2.6024	78.7078
15	7.2582	2.8571	75.8507
16	6.9785	3.1368	72.7139
17	6.6714	3.4438	69.2701
18	6.3343	3.7809	65.4892
19	5.9643	4.1510	61.3382
20	5.5579	4.5573	56.7808
21	5.1118	5.0034	51.7774
22	4.6221	5.4932	46.2842
23	4.0844	6.0309	40.2533
24	3.4940	6.6212	33.6321
25	2.8459	7.2693	26.3628
26	2.1344	7.9809	18.3819
27	1.3532	8.7621	9.6198
28	.4955	9.6198	0.0000

YEARS 29 — MO PAYT .8370 — AN CONST 10.05

#	INT	PRIN	BALANCE
1	9.3455	.6991	99.3009
2	9.2770	.7675	98.5334
3	9.2019	.8426	97.6908
4	9.1194	.9251	96.7657
5	9.0289	1.0157	95.7500
6	8.9295	1.1151	94.6349
7	8.8203	1.2242	93.4107
8	8.7005	1.3441	92.0666
9	8.5689	1.4756	90.5909
10	8.4245	1.6201	88.9709
11	8.2659	1.7787	87.1922
12	8.0918	1.9528	85.2394
13	7.9006	2.1439	83.0955
14	7.6908	2.3538	80.7417
15	7.4604	2.5842	78.1575
16	7.2074	2.8371	75.3204
17	6.9297	3.1148	72.2056
18	6.6248	3.4197	68.7858
19	6.2901	3.7545	65.0313
20	5.9226	4.1220	60.9094
21	5.5191	4.5255	56.3839
22	5.0761	4.9684	51.4154
23	4.5898	5.4548	45.9607
24	4.0558	5.9887	39.9719
25	3.4696	6.5749	33.3970
26	2.8260	7.2185	26.1785
27	2.1194	7.9251	18.2534
28	1.3437	8.7009	9.5525
29	.4920	9.5525	0.0000

YEARS 30 — MO PAYT .8317 — AN CONST 9.99

#	INT	PRIN	BALANCE
1	9.3483	.6327	99.3673
2	9.2863	.6947	98.6726
3	9.2183	.7627	97.9100
4	9.1437	.8373	97.0727
5	9.0617	.9193	96.1534
6	8.9717	1.0092	95.1442
7	8.8730	1.1080	94.0361
8	8.7645	1.2165	92.8196
9	8.6454	1.3356	91.4841
10	8.5147	1.4663	90.0178
11	8.3712	1.6098	88.4079
12	8.2136	1.7674	86.6405
13	8.0406	1.9404	84.7001
14	7.8506	2.1304	82.5697
15	7.6421	2.3389	80.2308
16	7.4132	2.5678	77.6630
17	7.1618	2.8192	74.8438
18	6.8859	3.0951	71.7487
19	6.5829	3.3981	68.3506
20	6.2503	3.7307	64.6199
21	5.8851	4.0959	60.5240
22	5.4842	4.4968	56.0271
23	5.0440	4.9370	51.0901
24	4.5607	5.4203	45.6699
25	4.0302	5.9508	39.7190
26	3.4477	6.5333	33.1857
27	2.8081	7.1728	26.0129
28	2.1060	7.8750	18.1379
29	1.3352	8.6458	9.4921
30	.4889	9.4921	0.0000

MONTHLY PAYMENT AMORTIZATION SCHEDULE PER $100 — 9.40 %

YEARS 2 — MO PAYT 4.5868 — AN CONST 55.05

#	INT	PRIN	BALANCE
1	7.3813	47.6609	52.3391
2	2.7031	52.3391	0.0000

YEARS 3 — MO PAYT 3.1986 — AN CONST 38.39

#	INT	PRIN	BALANCE
1	8.1181	30.2654	69.7346
2	5.1473	33.2361	36.4985
3	1.8850	36.4985	0.0000

YEARS 4 — MO PAYT 2.5075 — AN CONST 30.10

#	INT	PRIN	BALANCE
1	8.4849	21.6056	78.3944
2	6.3641	23.7263	54.6681
3	4.0352	26.0553	28.6128
4	1.4777	28.6128	0.0000

YEARS 5 — MO PAYT 2.0953 — AN CONST 25.15

#	INT	PRIN	BALANCE
1	8.7037	16.4399	83.5601
2	7.0900	18.0536	65.5064
3	5.3179	19.8257	45.6807
4	3.3718	21.7718	23.9089
5	1.2348	23.9089	0.0000

YEARS 6 — MO PAYT 1.8225 — AN CONST 21.87

#	INT	PRIN	BALANCE
1	8.8485	13.0212	86.9788
2	7.5704	14.2993	72.6796
3	6.1668	15.7029	56.9767
4	4.6254	17.2442	39.7325
5	2.9328	18.9369	20.7957
6	1.0740	20.7957	0.0000

YEARS 7 — MO PAYT 1.6293 — AN CONST 19.56

#	INT	PRIN	BALANCE
1	8.9510	10.6004	89.3996
2	7.9105	11.6409	77.7588
3	6.7679	12.7835	64.9753
4	5.5131	14.0383	50.9370
5	4.1351	15.4163	35.5207
6	2.6219	16.9295	18.5912
7	.9601	18.5912	0.0000

YEARS 8 — MO PAYT 1.4859 — AN CONST 17.84

#	INT	PRIN	BALANCE
1	9.0271	8.8031	91.1969
2	8.1631	9.6672	81.5297
3	7.2141	10.6161	70.9136
4	6.1721	11.6582	59.2554
5	5.0278	12.8025	46.4529
6	3.7711	14.0592	32.3938
7	2.3911	15.4392	16.9546
8	.8756	16.9546	0.0000

YEARS 9 — MO PAYT 1.3756 — AN CONST 16.51

#	INT	PRIN	BALANCE
1	9.0857	7.4213	92.5787
2	8.3572	8.1498	84.4289
3	7.5572	8.9498	75.4791
4	6.6788	9.8282	65.6509
5	5.7140	10.7930	54.8579
6	4.6546	11.8524	43.0055
7	3.4912	13.0158	29.9897
8	2.2136	14.2934	15.6964
9	.8106	15.6964	0.0000

YEARS 10 — MO PAYT 1.2885 — AN CONST 15.47

#	INT	PRIN	BALANCE
1	9.1319	6.3302	93.6698
2	8.5105	6.9516	86.7182
3	7.8282	7.6339	79.0843
4	7.0789	8.3832	70.7011
5	6.2560	9.2061	61.4950
6	5.3523	10.1097	51.3853
7	4.3600	11.1021	40.2832
8	3.2702	12.1918	28.0913
9	2.0735	13.3886	14.7028
10	.7593	14.7028	0.0000

YEARS 11 — MO PAYT 1.2183 — AN CONST 14.62

#	INT	PRIN	BALANCE
1	9.1692	5.4502	94.5498
2	8.6342	5.9852	88.5646
3	8.0467	6.5727	81.9919
4	7.4015	7.2178	74.7741
5	6.6930	7.9263	66.8478
6	5.9150	8.7043	58.1434
7	5.0606	9.5587	48.5847
8	4.1224	10.4970	38.0877
9	3.0920	11.5274	26.5603
10	1.9605	12.6589	13.9014
11	.7179	13.9014	0.0000

YEARS 12 — MO PAYT 1.1607 — AN CONST 13.93

#	INT	PRIN	BALANCE
1	9.1997	4.7284	95.2716
2	8.7356	5.1925	90.0791
3	8.2259	5.7022	84.3769
4	7.6662	6.2619	78.1150
5	7.0516	6.8766	71.2385
6	6.3766	7.5515	63.6869
7	5.6353	8.2928	55.3942
8	4.8213	9.1068	46.2874
9	3.9274	10.0007	36.2867
10	2.9458	10.9823	25.3044
11	1.8678	12.0603	13.2441
12	.6840	13.2441	0.0000

YEARS 13 — MO PAYT 1.1128 — AN CONST 13.36

#	INT	PRIN	BALANCE
1	9.2252	4.1280	95.8720
2	8.8200	4.5332	91.3388
3	8.3750	4.9782	86.3607
4	7.8864	5.4668	80.8939
5	7.3497	6.0034	74.8904
6	6.7605	6.5927	68.2978
7	6.1133	7.2398	61.0580
8	5.4027	7.9504	53.1075
9	4.6223	8.7308	44.3767
10	3.7653	9.5878	34.7888
11	2.8242	10.5290	24.2599
12	1.7907	11.5625	12.6974
13	.6558	12.6974	0.0000

YEARS 14 — MO PAYT 1.0724 — AN CONST 12.87

#	INT	PRIN	BALANCE
1	9.2466	3.6228	96.3772
2	8.8909	3.9784	92.3987
3	8.5004	4.3690	88.0298
4	8.0716	4.7978	83.2319
5	7.6006	5.2687	77.9632
6	7.0835	5.7859	72.1773
7	6.5155	6.3538	65.8234
8	5.8919	6.9775	58.8459
9	5.2070	7.6624	51.1835
10	4.4549	8.4145	42.7690
11	3.6289	9.2405	33.5285
12	2.7219	10.1475	23.3810
13	1.7258	11.1436	12.2374
14	.6320	12.2374	0.0000

YEARS 15 — MO PAYT 1.0382 — AN CONST 12.46

#	INT	PRIN	BALANCE
1	9.2647	3.1937	96.8063
2	8.9513	3.5071	93.2992
3	8.6070	3.8514	89.4478
4	8.2290	4.2294	85.2184
5	7.8138	4.6446	80.5738
6	7.3579	5.1005	75.4733
7	6.8573	5.6011	69.8722
8	6.3075	6.1509	63.7213
9	5.7037	6.7547	56.9666
10	5.0407	7.4177	49.5489
11	4.3126	8.1458	41.4031
12	3.5130	8.9454	32.4577
13	2.6350	9.8234	22.6343
14	1.6707	10.7877	11.8466
15	.6118	11.8466	0.0000

YEARS 16 — MO PAYT 1.0089 — AN CONST 12.11

#	INT	PRIN	BALANCE
1	9.2803	2.8260	97.1740
2	9.0029	3.1034	94.0706
3	8.6983	3.4080	90.6626
4	8.3638	3.7425	86.9200
5	7.9964	4.1099	82.8101
6	7.5930	4.5133	78.2968
7	7.1500	4.9563	73.3404
8	6.6635	5.4428	67.8976
9	6.1292	5.9771	61.9205
10	5.5425	6.5638	55.3567
11	4.8982	7.2081	48.1486
12	4.1907	7.9156	40.2330
13	3.4137	8.6926	31.5404
14	2.5605	9.5458	21.9946
15	1.6235	10.4828	11.5118
16	.5945	11.5118	0.0000

YEARS 17 — MO PAYT .9835 — AN CONST 11.81

#	INT	PRIN	BALANCE
1	9.2937	2.5088	97.4912
2	9.0475	2.7551	94.7360
3	8.7770	3.0255	91.7105
4	8.4801	3.3225	88.3880
5	8.1539	3.6487	84.7393
6	7.7958	4.0068	80.7325
7	7.4025	4.4001	76.3324
8	6.9706	4.8320	71.5004
9	6.4963	5.3063	66.1942
10	5.9754	5.8271	60.3670
11	5.4035	6.3991	53.9679
12	4.7753	7.0272	46.9407
13	4.0856	7.7170	39.2236
14	3.3281	8.4745	30.7491
15	2.4962	9.3063	21.4428
16	1.5828	10.2198	11.2230
17	.5796	11.2230	0.0000

YEARS 18 — MO PAYT .9616 — AN CONST 11.54

#	INT	PRIN	BALANCE
1	9.3054	2.2336	97.7664
2	9.0862	2.4528	95.3136
3	8.8454	2.6936	92.6201
4	8.5810	2.9580	89.6621
5	8.2907	3.2483	86.4138
6	7.9718	3.5672	82.8466
7	7.6217	3.9173	78.9293
8	7.2372	4.3018	74.6275
9	6.8149	4.7241	69.9034
10	6.3512	5.1878	64.7157
11	5.8420	5.6970	59.0187
12	5.2828	6.2562	52.7625
13	4.6687	6.8703	45.8922
14	3.9943	7.5447	38.3475
15	3.2537	8.2852	30.0623
16	2.4405	9.0985	20.9639
17	1.5474	9.9916	10.9723
18	.5667	10.9723	0.0000

YEARS 19 — MO PAYT .9424 — AN CONST 11.31

#	INT	PRIN	BALANCE
1	9.3156	1.9934	98.0066
2	9.1199	2.1890	95.8176
3	8.9050	2.4039	93.4137
4	8.6691	2.6399	90.7738
5	8.4099	2.8990	87.8748
6	8.1254	3.1836	84.6912
7	7.8129	3.4961	81.1952
8	7.4697	3.8392	77.3560
9	7.0929	4.2161	73.1399
10	6.6791	4.6299	68.5100
11	6.2246	5.0844	63.4256
12	5.7255	5.5834	57.8422
13	5.1775	6.1315	51.7107
14	4.5756	6.7333	44.9774
15	3.9147	7.3943	37.5831
16	3.1889	8.1201	29.4631
17	2.3918	8.9171	20.5460
18	1.5166	9.7924	10.7536
19	.5554	10.7536	0.0000

YEARS 20 — MO PAYT .9256 — AN CONST 11.11

#	INT	PRIN	BALANCE
1	9.3245	1.7828	98.2172
2	9.1495	1.9578	96.2593
3	8.9573	2.1500	94.1093
4	8.7463	2.3611	91.7482
5	8.5145	2.5928	89.1554
6	8.2600	2.8473	86.3081
7	7.9805	3.1268	83.1813
8	7.6736	3.4337	79.7476
9	7.3366	3.7708	75.9768
10	6.9664	4.1409	71.8359
11	6.5600	4.5474	67.2886
12	6.1136	4.9937	62.2949
13	5.6234	5.4839	56.8110
14	5.0852	6.0222	50.7888
15	4.4940	6.6133	44.1755
16	3.8449	7.2624	36.9131
17	3.1320	7.9753	28.9378
18	2.3492	8.7581	20.1797
19	1.4895	9.6178	10.5619
20	.5455	10.5619	0.0000

YEARS 21 — MO PAYT .9108 — AN CONST 10.93

#	INT	PRIN	BALANCE
1	9.3323	1.5975	98.4025
2	9.1755	1.7544	96.6481
3	9.0033	1.9266	94.7215

#	INT	PRIN	BALANCE
4	8.8142	2.1157	92.6059
5	8.6065	2.3233	90.2825
6	8.3785	2.5514	87.7311
7	8.1281	2.8018	84.9293
8	7.8530	3.0769	81.8524
9	7.5510	3.3789	78.4736
10	7.2194	3.7105	74.7631
11	6.8551	4.0747	70.6883
12	6.4552	4.4747	66.2136
13	6.0159	4.9139	61.2997
14	5.5336	5.3963	55.9034
15	5.0039	5.9260	49.9774
16	4.4222	6.5076	43.4698
17	3.7835	7.1464	36.3234
18	3.0820	7.8479	28.4755
19	2.3117	8.6182	19.8573
20	1.4657	9.4642	10.3931
21	.5368	10.3931	0.0000

YEARS 22	MO PAYT .8978	AN CONST 10.78	
#	INT	PRIN	BALANCE
1	9.3393	1.4339	98.5661
2	9.1985	1.5746	96.9915
3	9.0440	1.7292	95.2623
4	8.8742	1.8989	93.3633
5	8.6878	2.0853	91.2780
6	8.4831	2.2900	88.9880
7	8.2584	2.5148	86.4732
8	8.0115	2.7617	83.7115
9	7.7404	3.0327	80.6788
10	7.4427	3.3304	77.3484
11	7.1158	3.6573	73.6910
12	6.7568	4.0163	69.6747
13	6.3626	4.4105	65.2642
14	5.9297	4.8435	60.4207
15	5.4543	5.3189	55.1018
16	4.9322	5.8410	49.2608
17	4.3588	6.4143	42.8465
18	3.7292	7.0439	35.8025
19	3.0378	7.7354	28.0672
20	2.2785	8.4946	19.5726
21	1.4447	9.3284	10.2441
22	.5291	10.2441	0.0000

YEARS 23	MO PAYT .8862	AN CONST 10.64	
#	INT	PRIN	BALANCE
1	9.3454	1.2889	98.7111
2	9.2189	1.4154	97.2957
3	9.0800	1.5543	95.7413
4	8.9274	1.7069	94.0344
5	8.7598	1.8745	92.1600
6	8.5759	2.0585	90.1015
7	8.3738	2.2605	87.8410
8	8.1519	2.4824	85.3586
9	7.9082	2.7261	82.6325
10	7.6407	2.9936	79.6389
11	7.3468	3.2875	76.3514
12	7.0241	3.6102	72.7412
13	6.6698	3.9645	68.7767
14	6.2806	4.3537	64.4230
15	5.8533	4.7810	59.6419
16	5.3840	5.2503	54.3916
17	4.8686	5.7657	48.6259
18	4.3027	6.3317	42.2942
19	3.6812	6.9531	35.3411
20	2.9987	7.6357	27.7054
21	2.2492	8.3851	19.3203
22	1.4261	9.2082	10.1121
23	.5222	10.1121	0.0000

YEARS 24	MO PAYT .8759	AN CONST 10.52	
#	INT	PRIN	BALANCE
1	9.3509	1.1601	98.8399
2	9.2370	1.2739	97.5660
3	9.1119	1.3990	96.1670
4	8.9746	1.5363	94.6307
5	8.8238	1.6871	92.9436
6	8.6582	1.8527	91.0908
7	8.4764	2.0346	89.0563
8	8.2767	2.2343	86.8220
9	8.0573	2.4536	84.3684
10	7.8165	2.6944	81.6739
11	7.5520	2.9589	78.7150
12	7.2616	3.2494	75.4657
13	6.9426	3.5683	71.8974
14	6.5924	3.9186	67.9788
15	6.2077	4.3032	63.6756
16	5.7854	4.7256	58.9500
17	5.3215	5.1894	53.7606
18	4.8121	5.6988	48.0618
19	4.2527	6.2582	41.8036
20	3.6385	6.8725	34.9311
21	2.9639	7.5471	27.3840
22	2.2231	8.2879	19.0962
23	1.4095	9.1014	9.9948
24	.5162	9.9948	0.0000

YEARS 25	MO PAYT .8668	AN CONST 10.41	
#	INT	PRIN	BALANCE
1	9.3557	1.0453	98.9547
2	9.2531	1.1479	97.8067
3	9.1404	1.2606	96.5461
4	9.0167	1.3844	95.1617
5	8.8808	1.5203	93.6415
6	8.7316	1.6695	91.9720
7	8.5677	1.8334	90.1386
8	8.3878	2.0133	88.1253
9	8.1901	2.2109	85.9144
10	7.9731	2.4279	83.4864
11	7.7348	2.6663	80.8202
12	7.4731	2.9280	77.8922
13	7.1857	3.2154	74.6768
14	6.8701	3.5310	71.1458
15	6.5235	3.8776	67.2682
16	6.1429	4.2582	63.0100
17	5.7249	4.6762	58.3338
18	5.2659	5.1352	53.1986
19	4.7618	5.6392	47.5594
20	4.2083	6.1928	41.3666
21	3.6004	6.8006	34.5660
22	2.9329	7.4682	27.0978
23	2.1998	8.2012	18.8965
24	1.3948	9.0063	9.8903
25	.5108	9.8903	0.0000

YEARS 26	MO PAYT .8586	AN CONST 10.31	
#	INT	PRIN	BALANCE
1	9.3601	.9429	99.0571
2	9.2675	1.0355	98.0216
3	9.1659	1.1371	96.8845
4	9.0542	1.2487	95.6357
5	8.9317	1.3713	94.2644
6	8.7971	1.5059	92.7585
7	8.6493	1.6537	91.1048
8	8.4869	1.8161	89.2887
9	8.3087	1.9943	87.2944
10	8.1129	2.1901	85.1043
11	7.8979	2.4051	82.6992
12	7.6619	2.6411	80.0581
13	7.4026	2.9004	77.1577
14	7.1179	3.1851	73.9727
15	6.8053	3.4977	70.4749

#	INT	PRIN	BALANCE
16	6.4620	3.8410	66.6339
17	6.0849	4.2181	62.4159
18	5.6709	4.6321	57.7838
19	5.2162	5.0868	52.6970
20	4.7169	5.5861	47.1109
21	4.1686	6.1344	40.9765
22	3.5665	6.7365	34.2400
23	2.9052	7.3978	26.8423
24	2.1791	8.1239	18.7184
25	1.3817	8.9213	9.7970
26	.5060	9.7970	0.0000

YEARS 27	MO PAYT .8513	AN CONST 10.22	
#	INT	PRIN	BALANCE
1	9.3639	.8513	99.1487
2	9.2804	.9349	98.2138
3	9.1886	1.0267	97.1871
4	9.0878	1.1274	96.0597
5	8.9772	1.2381	94.8215
6	8.8556	1.3596	93.4619
7	8.7222	1.4931	91.9688
8	8.5756	1.6397	90.3291
9	8.4147	1.8006	88.5285
10	8.2379	1.9773	86.5512
11	8.0438	2.1714	84.3798
12	7.8307	2.3846	81.9952
13	7.5966	2.6186	79.3765
14	7.3396	2.8757	76.5009
15	7.0573	3.1580	73.3429
16	6.7473	3.4679	69.8750
17	6.4069	3.8083	66.0666
18	6.0331	4.1821	61.8845
19	5.6226	4.5927	57.2918
20	5.1718	5.0435	52.2484
21	4.6768	5.5385	46.7099
22	4.1331	6.0822	40.6277
23	3.5361	6.6792	33.9485
24	2.8805	7.3348	26.6137
25	2.1605	8.0547	18.5590
26	1.3699	8.8454	9.7136
27	.5017	9.7136	0.0000

YEARS 28	MO PAYT .8447	AN CONST 10.14	
#	INT	PRIN	BALANCE
1	9.3674	.7693	99.2307
2	9.2919	.8448	98.3859
3	9.2090	.9277	97.4582
4	9.1179	1.0188	96.4395
5	9.0179	1.1188	95.3207
6	8.9081	1.2286	94.0921
7	8.7875	1.3492	92.7429
8	8.6551	1.4816	91.2613
9	8.5096	1.6270	89.6343
10	8.3499	1.7868	87.8475
11	8.1746	1.9621	85.8854
12	7.9820	2.1547	83.7306
13	7.7705	2.3662	81.3644
14	7.5382	2.5985	78.7659
15	7.2831	2.8536	75.9123
16	7.0030	3.1337	72.7787
17	6.6954	3.4413	69.3374
18	6.3577	3.7790	65.5584
19	5.9867	4.1500	61.4084
20	5.5794	4.5573	56.8511
21	5.1320	5.0047	51.8464
22	4.6408	5.4959	46.3505
23	4.1013	6.0354	40.3152
24	3.5089	6.6278	33.6874
25	2.8583	7.2784	26.4090
26	2.1439	7.9928	18.4162
27	1.3594	8.7773	9.6389

#	INT	PRIN	BALANCE
28	.4978	9.6389	0.0000

YEARS 29	MO PAYT .8388	AN CONST 10.07	
#	INT	PRIN	BALANCE
1	9.3705	.6956	99.3044
2	9.3023	.7639	98.5404
3	9.2273	.8389	97.7015
4	9.1449	.9213	96.7803
5	9.0545	1.0117	95.7686
6	8.9552	1.1110	94.6576
7	8.8461	1.2200	93.4376
8	8.7264	1.3398	92.0978
9	8.5949	1.4713	90.6265
10	8.4505	1.6157	89.0107
11	8.2919	1.7743	87.2364
12	8.1177	1.9485	85.2879
13	7.9264	2.1397	83.1482
14	7.7164	2.3498	80.7984
15	7.4858	2.5804	78.2180
16	7.2325	2.8337	75.3843
17	6.9543	3.1119	72.2724
18	6.6489	3.4173	68.8551
19	6.3134	3.7527	65.1024
20	5.9451	4.1211	60.9812
21	5.5406	4.5256	56.4556
22	5.0963	4.9698	51.4858
23	4.6085	5.4577	46.0281
24	4.0728	5.9934	40.0347
25	3.4845	6.5817	33.4530
26	2.8385	7.2277	26.2253
27	2.1290	7.9372	18.2881
28	1.3499	8.7163	9.5718
29	.4943	9.5718	0.0000

YEARS 30	MO PAYT .8336	AN CONST 10.01	
#	INT	PRIN	BALANCE
1	9.3733	.6295	99.3705
2	9.3116	.6913	98.6793
3	9.2437	.7591	97.9201
4	9.1692	.8336	97.0865
5	9.0874	.9155	96.1711
6	8.9975	1.0053	95.1657
7	8.8988	1.1040	94.0617
8	8.7905	1.2124	92.8494
9	8.6715	1.3314	91.5180
10	8.5408	1.4620	90.0560
11	8.3973	1.6056	88.4504
12	8.2397	1.7632	86.6873
13	8.0666	1.9362	84.7511
14	7.8765	2.1263	82.6248
15	7.6678	2.3350	80.2898
16	7.4386	2.5642	77.7256
17	7.1869	2.8159	74.9097
18	6.9105	3.0923	71.8175
19	6.6070	3.3958	68.4217
20	6.2737	3.7291	64.6925
21	5.9076	4.0952	60.5974
22	5.5057	4.4971	56.1002
23	5.0642	4.9386	51.1617
24	4.5795	5.4233	45.7384
25	4.0472	5.9557	39.7827
26	3.4626	6.5403	33.2424
27	2.8206	7.1822	26.0602
28	2.1156	7.8872	18.1730
29	1.3414	8.6614	9.5116
30	.4912	9.5116	0.0000

YEARS 2 — MO PAYT 4.5914 — AN CONST 55.10

#	INT	PRIN	BALANCE
1	7.4613	47.6361	52.3639
2	2.7335	52.3639	0.0000

YEARS 3 — MO PAYT 3.2033 — AN CONST 38.44

#	INT	PRIN	BALANCE
1	8.2061	30.2335	69.7665
2	5.2055	33.2341	36.5325
3	1.9071	36.5325	0.0000

YEARS 4 — MO PAYT 2.5123 — AN CONST 30.15

#	INT	PRIN	BALANCE
1	8.5768	21.5710	78.4290
2	6.4359	23.7118	54.7172
3	4.0826	26.0652	28.6521
4	1.4957	28.6521	0.0000

YEARS 5 — MO PAYT 2.1002 — AN CONST 25.21

#	INT	PRIN	BALANCE
1	8.7979	16.4043	83.5957
2	7.1698	18.0324	65.5633
3	5.3802	19.8221	45.7412
4	3.4129	21.7894	23.9519
5	1.2503	23.9519	0.0000

YEARS 6 — MO PAYT 1.8275 — AN CONST 21.93

#	INT	PRIN	BALANCE
1	8.9443	12.9854	87.0146
2	7.6555	14.2741	72.7405
3	6.2388	15.6908	57.0497
4	4.6815	17.2481	39.8016
5	2.9697	18.9599	20.8417
6	1.0880	20.8417	0.0000

YEARS 7 — MO PAYT 1.6344 — AN CONST 19.62

#	INT	PRIN	BALANCE
1	9.0478	10.5649	89.4351
2	7.9993	11.6135	77.8216
3	6.8467	12.7661	65.0555
4	5.5797	14.0331	51.0224
5	4.1869	15.4258	35.5966
6	2.6560	16.9568	18.6397
7	.9730	18.6397	0.0000

YEARS 8 — MO PAYT 1.4911 — AN CONST 17.90

#	INT	PRIN	BALANCE
1	9.1247	8.7683	91.2317
2	8.2545	9.6386	81.5931
3	7.2979	10.5952	70.9979
4	6.2463	11.6467	59.3512
5	5.0904	12.8026	46.5486
6	3.8198	14.0733	32.4753
7	2.4231	15.4700	17.0053
8	.8877	17.0053	0.0000

YEARS 9 — MO PAYT 1.3809 — AN CONST 16.58

#	INT	PRIN	BALANCE
1	9.1838	7.3874	92.6126
2	8.4507	8.1206	84.4920
3	7.6447	8.9265	75.5655
4	6.7588	9.8125	65.7530
5	5.7849	10.7863	54.9667
6	4.7144	11.8568	43.1099
7	3.5376	13.0336	30.0763
8	2.2441	14.3272	15.7491
9	.8221	15.7491	0.0000

YEARS 10 — MO PAYT 1.2940 — AN CONST 15.53

#	INT	PRIN	BALANCE
1	9.2305	6.2972	93.7028
2	8.6055	6.9222	86.7806
3	7.9185	7.6092	79.1714
4	7.1633	8.3644	70.8070
5	6.3332	9.1946	61.6124
6	5.4206	10.1071	51.5053
7	4.4175	11.1102	40.3951
8	3.3149	12.2129	28.1823
9	2.1028	13.4249	14.7573
10	.7704	14.7573	0.0000

YEARS 11 — MO PAYT 1.2239 — AN CONST 14.69

#	INT	PRIN	BALANCE
1	9.2681	5.4183	94.5817
2	8.7304	5.9560	88.6257
3	8.1392	6.5471	82.0786
4	7.4895	7.1969	74.8817
5	6.7752	7.9112	66.9705
6	5.9900	8.6964	58.2741
7	5.1269	9.5595	48.7146
8	4.1782	10.5082	38.2064
9	3.1352	11.5511	26.6553
10	1.9888	12.6975	13.9578
11	.7286	13.9578	0.0000

YEARS 12 — MO PAYT 1.1664 — AN CONST 14.00

#	INT	PRIN	BALANCE
1	9.2990	4.6975	95.3025
2	8.8327	5.1637	90.1387
3	8.3202	5.6762	84.4625
4	7.7569	6.2396	78.2229
5	7.1376	6.8588	71.3641
6	6.4569	7.5396	63.8245
7	5.7086	8.2879	55.5367
8	4.8861	9.1104	46.4263
9	3.9819	10.0146	36.4117
10	2.9880	11.0085	25.4032
11	1.8954	12.1011	13.3021
12	.6944	13.3021	0.0000

YEARS 13 — MO PAYT 1.1186 — AN CONST 13.43

#	INT	PRIN	BALANCE
1	9.3246	4.0983	95.9017
2	8.9179	4.5050	91.3967
3	8.4707	4.9521	86.4446
4	7.9793	5.4436	81.0010
5	7.4390	5.9839	75.0171
6	6.8451	6.5778	68.4394
7	6.1923	7.2306	61.2088
8	5.4747	7.9482	53.2606
9	4.6858	8.7370	44.5236
10	3.8187	9.6042	34.9194
11	2.8655	10.5574	24.3621
12	1.8177	11.6051	12.7569
13	.6659	12.7569	0.0000

YEARS 14 — MO PAYT 1.0784 — AN CONST 12.95

#	INT	PRIN	BALANCE
1	9.3462	3.5942	96.4058
2	8.9895	3.9510	92.4548
3	8.5973	4.3431	88.1117
4	8.1663	4.7741	83.3376
5	7.6925	5.2479	78.0896
6	7.1716	5.7688	72.3208
7	6.5991	6.3413	65.9795
8	5.9697	6.9707	59.0088
9	5.2779	7.6625	51.3463
10	4.5174	8.4230	42.9233
11	3.6814	9.2590	33.6643
12	2.7625	10.1779	23.4864
13	1.7524	11.1880	12.2984
14	.6420	12.2984	0.0000

YEARS 15 — MO PAYT 1.0442 — AN CONST 12.54

#	INT	PRIN	BALANCE
1	9.3645	3.1662	96.8338
2	9.0503	3.4804	93.3534
3	8.7048	3.8259	89.5275
4	8.3251	4.2056	85.3219
5	7.9077	4.6230	80.6989
6	7.4489	5.0818	75.6172
7	6.9446	5.5861	70.0310
8	6.3901	6.1406	63.8905
9	5.7807	6.7500	57.1405
10	5.1108	7.4199	49.7206
11	4.3744	8.1563	41.5643
12	3.5649	8.9658	32.5985
13	2.6751	9.8556	22.7428
14	1.6969	10.8338	11.9090
15	.6217	11.9090	0.0000

YEARS 16 — MO PAYT 1.0150 — AN CONST 12.18

#	INT	PRIN	BALANCE
1	9.3802	2.7997	97.2003
2	9.1023	3.0776	94.1227
3	8.7969	3.3830	90.7397
4	8.4611	3.7188	87.0210
5	8.0920	4.0878	82.9332
6	7.6863	4.4935	78.4396
7	7.2404	4.9395	73.5001
8	6.7501	5.4297	68.0704
9	6.2112	5.9686	62.1017
10	5.6189	6.5610	55.5407
11	4.9677	7.2122	48.3286
12	4.2519	7.9280	40.4006
13	3.4651	8.7148	31.6858
14	2.6002	9.5797	22.1061
15	1.6494	10.5305	11.5756
16	.6043	11.5756	0.0000

YEARS 17 — MO PAYT .9898 — AN CONST 11.88

#	INT	PRIN	BALANCE
1	9.3937	2.4837	97.5163
2	9.1472	2.7302	94.7862
3	8.8762	3.0011	91.7851
4	8.5784	3.2990	88.4861
5	8.2510	3.6264	84.8597
6	7.8911	3.9863	80.8734
7	7.4954	4.3819	76.4914
8	7.0605	4.8168	71.6746
9	6.5825	5.2949	66.3797
10	6.0570	5.8204	60.5593
11	5.4793	6.3981	54.1613
12	4.8443	7.0330	47.1282
13	4.1463	7.7311	39.3972
14	3.3790	8.4983	30.8988
15	2.5356	9.3418	21.5570
16	1.6084	10.2689	11.2881
17	.5893	11.2881	0.0000

YEARS 18 — MO PAYT .9679 — AN CONST 11.62

#	INT	PRIN	BALANCE
1	9.4054	2.2095	97.7905
2	9.1862	2.4288	95.3617
3	8.9451	2.6698	92.6919
4	8.6801	2.9348	89.7571
5	8.3889	3.2261	86.5310
6	8.0687	3.5463	82.9847
7	7.7167	3.8982	79.0865
8	7.3298	4.2851	74.8014
9	6.9045	4.7104	70.0910
10	6.4370	5.1779	64.9131
11	5.9231	5.6918	59.2213
12	5.3582	6.2567	52.9646
13	4.7373	6.8777	46.0869
14	4.0547	7.5602	38.5267
15	3.3044	8.3106	30.2161
16	2.4796	9.1354	21.0807
17	1.5729	10.0420	11.0387
18	.5762	11.0387	0.0000

YEARS 19 — MO PAYT .9488 — AN CONST 11.39

#	INT	PRIN	BALANCE
1	9.4157	1.9704	98.0296
2	9.2201	2.1660	95.8636
3	9.0051	2.3809	93.4827
4	8.7688	2.6172	90.8655
5	8.5091	2.8770	87.9885
6	8.2236	3.1625	84.8260
7	7.9097	3.4764	81.3496
8	7.5647	3.8214	77.5282
9	7.1854	4.2007	73.3275
10	6.7685	4.6176	68.7099
11	6.3102	5.0759	63.6340
12	5.8064	5.5796	58.0544
13	5.2527	6.1334	51.9210
14	4.6439	6.7421	45.1788
15	3.9748	7.4113	37.7676
16	3.2393	8.1468	29.6207
17	2.4307	8.9554	20.6654
18	1.5419	9.8442	10.8212
19	.5649	10.8212	0.0000

YEARS 20 — MO PAYT .9321 — AN CONST 11.19

#	INT	PRIN	BALANCE
1	9.4246	1.7609	98.2391
2	9.2499	1.9357	96.3034
3	9.0578	2.1278	94.1755
4	8.8466	2.3390	91.8365
5	8.6144	2.5711	89.2654
6	8.3593	2.8263	86.4391
7	8.0787	3.1068	83.3322
8	7.7704	3.4152	79.9171
9	7.4315	3.7541	76.1629
10	7.0589	4.1267	72.0362
11	6.6493	4.5363	67.5000
12	6.1991	4.9865	62.5135
13	5.7042	5.4814	57.0321
14	5.1602	6.0254	51.0067
15	4.5622	6.6234	44.3833
16	3.9048	7.2808	37.1025
17	3.1822	8.0034	29.0991
18	2.3879	8.7977	20.3015
19	1.5147	9.6708	10.6306
20	.5549	10.6306	0.0000

YEARS 21 — MO PAYT .9174 — AN CONST 11.01

#	INT	PRIN	BALANCE
1	9.4325	1.5767	98.4233
2	9.2760	1.7332	96.6901
3	9.1040	1.9052	94.7849

#	INT	PRIN	BALANCE
4	8.9149	2.0943	92.6907
5	8.7071	2.3021	90.3886
6	8.4786	2.5306	87.8579
7	8.2275	2.7818	85.0762
8	7.9514	3.0578	82.0183
9	7.6479	3.3613	78.6570
10	7.3143	3.6949	74.9621
11	6.9476	4.0616	70.9004
12	6.5445	4.4648	66.4357
13	6.1013	4.9079	61.5278
14	5.6142	5.3950	56.1329
15	5.0788	5.9304	50.2025
16	4.4902	6.5190	43.6835
17	3.8432	7.1660	36.5175
18	3.1320	7.8772	28.6403
19	2.3502	8.6590	19.9814
20	1.4909	9.5183	10.4630
21	.5462	10.4630	0.0000

YEARS 22   MO PAYT .9045   AN CONST 10.86

#	INT	PRIN	BALANCE
1	9.4395	1.4141	98.5859
2	9.2991	1.5544	97.0315
3	9.1449	1.7087	95.3229
4	8.9753	1.8782	93.4446
5	8.7889	2.0647	91.3800
6	8.5840	2.2696	89.1104
7	8.3587	2.4948	86.6156
8	8.1111	2.7424	83.8732
9	7.8389	3.0146	80.8586
10	7.5397	3.3138	77.5448
11	7.2109	3.6427	73.9021
12	6.8493	4.0042	69.8979
13	6.4519	4.4016	65.4962
14	6.0151	4.8385	60.6578
15	5.5349	5.3187	55.3391
16	5.0070	5.8465	49.4926
17	4.4267	6.4268	43.0658
18	3.7889	7.0646	36.0011
19	3.0877	7.7658	28.2353
20	2.3170	8.5365	19.6988
21	1.4698	9.3838	10.3151
22	.5385	10.3151	0.0000

YEARS 23   MO PAYT .8930   AN CONST 10.72

#	INT	PRIN	BALANCE
1	9.4456	1.2700	98.7300
2	9.3196	1.3961	97.3339
3	9.1810	1.5347	95.7992
4	9.0287	1.6870	94.1122
5	8.8613	1.8544	92.2578
6	8.6773	2.0384	90.2194
7	8.4749	2.2407	87.9787
8	8.2526	2.4631	85.5155
9	8.0081	2.7076	82.8079
10	7.7394	2.9763	79.8316
11	7.4440	3.2717	76.5599
12	7.1193	3.5964	72.9635
13	6.7623	3.9534	69.0101
14	6.3700	4.3457	64.6644
15	5.9387	4.7770	59.8874
16	5.4646	5.2511	54.6363
17	4.9434	5.7723	48.8640
18	4.3705	6.3452	42.5188
19	3.7408	6.9749	35.5439
20	3.0485	7.6672	27.8767
21	2.2876	8.4281	19.4486
22	1.4511	9.2646	10.1841
23	.5316	10.1841	0.0000

YEARS 24   MO PAYT .8828   AN CONST 10.60

#	INT	PRIN	BALANCE
1	9.4511	1.1422	98.8578
2	9.3378	1.2555	97.6023
3	9.2131	1.3801	96.2221
4	9.0762	1.5171	94.7050
5	8.9256	1.6677	93.0373
6	8.7601	1.8332	91.2041
7	8.5781	2.0152	89.1889
8	8.3781	2.2152	86.9738
9	8.1583	2.4350	84.5388
10	7.9166	2.6767	81.8621
11	7.6510	2.9423	78.9198
12	7.3590	3.2343	75.6855
13	7.0380	3.5553	72.1301
14	6.6851	3.9082	68.2219
15	6.2972	4.2961	63.9258
16	5.8708	4.7225	59.2034
17	5.4022	5.1911	54.0122
18	4.8869	5.7064	48.3059
19	4.3206	6.2727	42.0332
20	3.6980	6.8952	35.1379
21	3.0137	7.5796	27.5583
22	2.2615	8.3318	19.2265
23	1.4345	9.1588	10.0677
24	.5256	10.0677	0.0000

YEARS 25   MO PAYT .8737   AN CONST 10.49

#	INT	PRIN	BALANCE
1	9.4560	1.0284	98.9716
2	9.3539	1.1304	97.8412
3	9.2417	1.2426	96.5986
4	9.1184	1.3660	95.2326
5	8.9828	1.5015	93.7311
6	8.8338	1.6505	92.0805
7	8.6700	1.8144	90.2662
8	8.4899	1.9944	88.2717
9	8.2920	2.1924	86.0794
10	8.0744	2.4100	83.6694
11	7.8352	2.6491	81.0203
12	7.5723	2.9121	78.1082
13	7.2833	3.2011	74.9071
14	6.9656	3.5188	71.3883
15	6.6164	3.8680	67.5203
16	6.2325	4.2519	63.2684
17	5.8105	4.6739	58.5945
18	5.3466	5.1378	53.4568
19	4.8367	5.6477	47.8091
20	4.2762	6.2082	41.6009
21	3.6600	6.8243	34.7766
22	2.9827	7.5016	27.2749
23	2.2382	8.2462	19.0288
24	1.4198	9.0646	9.9642
25	.5202	9.9642	0.0000

YEARS 26   MO PAYT .8656   AN CONST 10.39

#	INT	PRIN	BALANCE
1	9.4603	.9269	99.0731
2	9.3683	1.0188	98.0543
3	9.2672	1.1200	96.9343
4	9.1561	1.2311	95.7032
5	9.0339	1.3533	94.3499
6	8.8996	1.4876	92.8623
7	8.7519	1.6352	91.2271
8	8.5896	1.7975	89.4295
9	8.4112	1.9759	87.4536
10	8.2151	2.1721	85.2815
11	7.9996	2.3876	82.8939
12	7.7626	2.6246	80.2693
13	7.5021	2.8851	77.3843
14	7.2158	3.1714	74.2128
15	6.9010	3.4862	70.7267
16	6.5550	3.8322	66.8945
17	6.1747	4.2125	62.6820
18	5.7566	4.6306	58.0515
19	5.2970	5.0901	52.9613
20	4.7919	5.5953	47.3660
21	4.2365	6.1507	41.2153
22	3.6261	6.7611	34.4542
23	2.9551	7.4321	27.0221
24	2.2175	8.1697	18.8524
25	1.4066	8.9806	9.8719
26	.5153	9.8719	0.0000

YEARS 27   MO PAYT .8584   AN CONST 10.31

#	INT	PRIN	BALANCE
1	9.4642	.8361	99.1639
2	9.3812	.9191	98.2448
3	9.2900	1.0103	97.2345
4	9.1897	1.1106	96.1239
5	9.0795	1.2208	94.9030
6	8.9584	1.3420	93.5611
7	8.8252	1.4752	92.0859
8	8.6788	1.6216	90.4643
9	8.5178	1.7825	88.6818
10	8.3409	1.9594	86.7224
11	8.1464	2.1539	84.5685
12	7.9327	2.3677	82.2008
13	7.6977	2.6026	79.5982
14	7.4394	2.8610	76.7372
15	7.1554	3.1449	73.5923
16	6.8433	3.4570	70.1353
17	6.5002	3.8001	66.3352
18	6.1231	4.1773	62.1579
19	5.7085	4.5919	57.5661
20	5.2528	5.0476	52.5185
21	4.7518	5.5485	46.9700
22	4.2011	6.0992	40.8707
23	3.5958	6.7046	34.1662
24	2.9304	7.3700	26.7962
25	2.1989	8.1014	18.6948
26	1.3949	8.9055	9.7893
27	.5110	9.7893	0.0000

YEARS 28   MO PAYT .8519   AN CONST 10.23

#	INT	PRIN	BALANCE
1	9.4677	.7549	99.2451
2	9.3928	.8298	98.4153
3	9.3104	.9122	97.5031
4	9.2199	1.0027	96.5004
5	9.1204	1.1022	95.3982
6	9.0110	1.2116	94.1866
7	8.8907	1.3319	92.8548
8	8.7585	1.4640	91.3907
9	8.6132	1.6093	89.7814
10	8.4535	1.7691	88.0124
11	8.2779	1.9446	86.0677
12	8.0849	2.1376	83.9301
13	7.8728	2.3498	81.5803
14	7.6396	2.5830	78.9973
15	7.3832	2.8394	76.1580
16	7.1014	3.1212	73.0368
17	6.7917	3.4309	69.6059
18	6.4511	3.7714	65.8344
19	6.0768	4.1457	61.6887
20	5.6654	4.5572	57.1315
21	5.2131	5.0095	52.1220
22	4.7159	5.5067	46.6154
23	4.1694	6.0532	40.5622
24	3.5686	6.6539	33.9083
25	2.9082	7.3143	26.5939
26	2.1823	8.0403	18.5537
27	1.3843	8.8382	9.7154
28	.5072	9.7154	0.0000

YEARS 29   MO PAYT .8461   AN CONST 10.16

#	INT	PRIN	BALANCE
1	9.4708	.6820	99.3180
2	9.4031	.7497	98.5682
3	9.3287	.8241	97.7441
4	9.2469	.9059	96.8381
5	9.1570	.9959	95.8423
6	9.0582	1.0947	94.7476
7	8.9495	1.2033	93.5442
8	8.8301	1.3228	92.2215
9	8.6988	1.4540	90.7674
10	8.5545	1.5984	89.1691
11	8.3959	1.7570	87.4121
12	8.2215	1.9314	85.4807
13	8.0298	2.1231	83.3576
14	7.8191	2.3338	81.0239
15	7.5875	2.5654	78.4585
16	7.3329	2.8200	75.6385
17	7.0530	3.0999	72.5387
18	6.7453	3.4075	69.1311
19	6.4071	3.7457	65.3854
20	6.0354	4.1175	61.2680
21	5.6267	4.5261	56.7419
22	5.1775	4.9753	51.7665
23	4.6838	5.4691	46.2974
24	4.1410	6.0119	40.2855
25	3.5443	6.6086	33.6770
26	2.8884	7.2644	26.4125
27	2.1674	7.9854	18.4271
28	1.3749	8.7780	9.6492
29	.5037	9.6492	0.0000

YEARS 30   MO PAYT .8409   AN CONST 10.10

#	INT	PRIN	BALANCE
1	9.4736	.6166	99.3834
2	9.4124	.6778	98.7055
3	9.3451	.7451	97.9604
4	9.2712	.8191	97.1413
5	9.1899	.9004	96.2410
6	9.1005	.9897	95.2513
7	9.0023	1.0879	94.1633
8	8.8943	1.1959	92.9674
9	8.7756	1.3146	91.6528
10	8.6452	1.4451	90.2077
11	8.5017	1.5885	88.6192
12	8.3441	1.7462	86.8731
13	8.1708	1.9195	84.9536
14	7.9803	2.1100	82.8436
15	7.7709	2.3194	80.5243
16	7.5407	2.5496	77.9747
17	7.2877	2.8026	75.1721
18	7.0095	3.0808	72.0913
19	6.7037	3.3865	68.7048
20	6.3676	3.7226	64.9822
21	5.9982	4.0921	60.8902
22	5.5921	4.4982	56.3920
23	5.1456	4.9446	51.4473
24	4.6549	5.4354	46.0120
25	4.1154	5.9748	40.0371
26	3.5224	6.5678	33.4693
27	2.8706	7.2197	26.2497
28	2.1541	7.9362	18.3135
29	1.3664	8.7238	9.5897
30	.5006	9.5897	0.0000

YEARS 2 — MO PAYT 4.5961 — AN CONST 55.16

#	INT	PRIN	BALANCE
1	7.5413	47.6114	52.3886
2	2.7640	52.3886	0.0000

YEARS 3 — MO PAYT 3.2080 — AN CONST 38.50

#	INT	PRIN	BALANCE
1	8.2941	30.2016	69.7984
2	5.2637	33.2320	36.5664
3	1.9292	36.5664	0.0000

YEARS 4 — MO PAYT 2.5171 — AN CONST 30.21

#	INT	PRIN	BALANCE
1	8.6688	21.5363	78.4637
2	6.5078	23.6973	54.7664
3	4.1301	26.0750	28.6914
4	1.5137	28.6914	0.0000

YEARS 5 — MO PAYT 2.1051 — AN CONST 25.27

#	INT	PRIN	BALANCE
1	8.8922	16.3687	83.6313
2	7.2498	18.0111	65.6202
3	5.4426	19.8183	45.8018
4	3.4540	21.8069	23.9950
5	1.2660	23.9950	0.0000

YEARS 6 — MO PAYT 1.8325 — AN CONST 21.99

#	INT	PRIN	BALANCE
1	9.0401	12.9497	87.0503
2	7.7407	14.2490	72.8013
3	6.3110	15.6787	57.1226
4	4.7378	17.2519	39.8707
5	3.0068	18.9830	20.8877
6	1.1020	20.8877	0.0000

YEARS 7 — MO PAYT 1.6395 — AN CONST 19.68

#	INT	PRIN	BALANCE
1	9.1447	10.5296	89.4704
2	8.0882	11.5861	77.8843
3	6.9256	12.7487	65.1356
4	5.6465	14.0278	51.1078
5	4.2389	15.4354	35.6724
6	2.6902	16.9841	18.6883
7	.9860	18.6883	0.0000

YEARS 8 — MO PAYT 1.4963 — AN CONST 17.96

#	INT	PRIN	BALANCE
1	9.2224	8.7337	91.2663
2	8.3460	9.6100	81.6564
3	7.3818	10.5742	71.0822
4	6.3208	11.6352	59.4469
5	5.1533	12.8027	46.6442
6	3.8687	14.0873	32.5569
7	2.4552	15.5008	17.0561
8	.8999	17.0561	0.0000

YEARS 9 — MO PAYT 1.3863 — AN CONST 16.64

#	INT	PRIN	BALANCE
1	9.2820	7.3536	92.6464
2	8.5442	8.0914	84.5550
3	7.7323	8.9033	75.6517
4	6.8390	9.7966	65.8551
5	5.8560	10.7796	55.0755
6	4.7744	11.8612	43.2142
7	3.5842	13.0514	30.1628
8	2.2747	14.3609	15.8019
9	.8337	15.8019	0.0000

YEARS 10 — MO PAYT 1.2995 — AN CONST 15.60

#	INT	PRIN	BALANCE
1	9.3291	6.2644	93.7356
2	8.7006	6.8929	86.8427
3	8.0089	7.5845	79.2582
4	7.2479	8.3456	70.9126
5	6.4105	9.1829	61.7297
6	5.4891	10.1044	51.6253
7	4.4753	11.1182	40.5071
8	3.3597	12.2338	28.2733
9	2.1322	13.4613	14.8120
10	.7815	14.8120	0.0000

YEARS 11 — MO PAYT 1.2295 — AN CONST 14.76

#	INT	PRIN	BALANCE
1	9.3671	5.3865	94.6135
2	8.8266	5.9269	88.6866
3	8.2319	6.5216	82.1650
4	7.5775	7.1760	74.9890
5	6.8575	7.8960	67.0929
6	6.0652	8.6883	58.4046
7	5.1935	9.5601	48.8446
8	4.2342	10.5193	38.3252
9	3.1787	11.5748	26.7504
10	2.0173	12.7362	14.0142
11	.7394	14.0142	0.0000

YEARS 12 — MO PAYT 1.1721 — AN CONST 14.07

#	INT	PRIN	BALANCE
1	9.3982	4.6668	95.3332
2	8.9299	5.1351	90.1981
3	8.4147	5.6503	84.5478
4	7.8477	6.2173	78.3305
5	7.2239	6.8411	71.4894
6	6.5375	7.5275	63.9618
7	5.7822	8.2828	55.6790
8	4.9511	9.1139	46.5651
9	4.0366	10.0284	36.5367
10	3.0304	11.0346	25.5020
11	1.9232	12.1419	13.3601
12	.7049	13.3601	0.0000

YEARS 13 — MO PAYT 1.1244 — AN CONST 13.50

#	INT	PRIN	BALANCE
1	9.4241	4.0687	95.9313
2	9.0158	4.4769	91.4544
3	8.5666	4.9262	86.5282
4	8.0723	5.4204	81.1078
5	7.5284	5.9643	75.1435
6	6.9300	6.5628	68.5807
7	6.2715	7.2213	61.3594
8	5.5469	7.9458	53.4136
9	4.7496	8.7431	44.6705
10	3.8724	9.6204	35.0501
11	2.9071	10.5857	24.4644
12	1.8449	11.6478	12.8166
13	.6762	12.8166	0.0000

YEARS 14 — MO PAYT 1.0843 — AN CONST 13.02

#	INT	PRIN	BALANCE
1	9.4458	3.5658	96.4342
2	9.0880	3.9236	92.5106
3	8.6943	4.3173	88.1933
4	8.2611	4.7505	83.4428
5	7.7845	5.2272	78.2156
6	7.2600	5.7516	72.4640
7	6.6829	6.3288	66.1352
8	6.0479	6.9638	59.1715
9	5.3491	7.6625	51.5090
10	4.5803	8.4314	43.0776
11	3.7343	9.2773	33.8003
12	2.8034	10.2082	23.5920
13	1.7791	11.2325	12.3596
14	.6521	12.3596	0.0000

YEARS 15 — MO PAYT 1.0503 — AN CONST 12.61

#	INT	PRIN	BALANCE
1	9.4643	3.1389	96.8611
2	9.1493	3.4539	93.4072
3	8.8028	3.8005	89.6067
4	8.4214	4.1818	85.4249
5	8.0018	4.6014	80.8236
6	7.5401	5.0631	75.7605
7	7.0321	5.5711	70.1894
8	6.4731	6.1301	64.0593
9	5.8580	6.7452	57.3141
10	5.1812	7.4220	49.8921
11	4.4365	8.1667	41.7254
12	3.6171	8.9861	32.7393
13	2.7154	9.8878	22.8515
14	1.7233	10.8799	11.9716
15	.6316	11.9716	0.0000

YEARS 16 — MO PAYT 1.0211 — AN CONST 12.26

#	INT	PRIN	BALANCE
1	9.4801	2.7736	97.2264
2	9.2018	3.0519	94.1745
3	8.8956	3.3581	90.8164
4	8.5586	3.6950	87.1214
5	8.1878	4.0658	83.0556
6	7.7799	4.4738	78.5818
7	7.3310	4.9226	73.6592
8	6.8371	5.4166	68.2426
9	6.2936	5.9601	62.2826
10	5.6955	6.5581	55.7245
11	5.0375	7.2161	48.5083
12	4.3135	7.9402	40.5681
13	3.5168	8.7369	31.8312
14	2.6401	9.6135	22.2177
15	1.6755	10.5782	11.6396
16	.6141	11.6396	0.0000

YEARS 17 — MO PAYT .9960 — AN CONST 11.96

#	INT	PRIN	BALANCE
1	9.4937	2.4587	97.5413
2	9.2470	2.7054	94.8359
3	8.9755	2.9768	91.8591
4	8.6768	3.2755	88.5836
5	8.3482	3.6042	84.9794
6	7.9865	3.9658	81.0135
7	7.5886	4.3638	76.6498
8	7.1508	4.8016	71.8482
9	6.6690	5.2834	66.5648
10	6.1388	5.8135	60.7512
11	5.5555	6.3969	54.3544
12	4.9137	7.0387	47.3157
13	4.2074	7.7450	39.5707
14	3.4303	8.5221	31.0486
15	2.5752	9.3772	21.6714
16	1.6343	10.3181	11.3534
17	.5990	11.3534	0.0000

YEARS 18 — MO PAYT .9743 — AN CONST 11.70

#	INT	PRIN	BALANCE
1	9.5055	2.1856	97.8144
2	9.2862	2.4049	95.4094
3	9.0449	2.6463	92.7632
4	8.7794	2.9118	89.8514
5	8.4872	3.2039	86.6474
6	8.1657	3.5254	83.1220
7	7.8120	3.8792	79.2429
8	7.4227	4.2684	74.9745
9	6.9945	4.6967	70.2778
10	6.5232	5.1679	65.1099
11	6.0047	5.6865	59.4234
12	5.4341	6.2570	53.1664
13	4.8063	6.8849	46.2815
14	4.1154	7.5757	38.7058
15	3.3553	8.3358	30.3700
16	2.5189	9.1722	21.1978
17	1.5986	10.0926	11.1052
18	.5859	11.1052	0.0000

YEARS 19 — MO PAYT .9553 — AN CONST 11.47

#	INT	PRIN	BALANCE
1	9.5158	1.9476	98.0524
2	9.3204	2.1431	95.9093
3	9.1053	2.3581	93.5512
4	8.8687	2.5947	90.9565
5	8.6084	2.8551	88.1014
6	8.3219	3.1415	84.9599
7	8.0067	3.4568	81.5031
8	7.6598	3.8036	77.6995
9	7.2782	4.1853	73.5142
10	6.8582	4.6052	68.9090
11	6.3962	5.0673	63.8418
12	5.8877	5.5757	58.2661
13	5.3283	6.1352	52.1309
14	4.7127	6.7508	45.3801
15	4.0353	7.4281	37.9520
16	3.2900	8.1735	29.7785
17	2.4698	8.9936	20.7849
18	1.5674	9.8960	10.8889
19	.5745	10.8889	0.0000

YEARS 20 — MO PAYT .9387 — AN CONST 11.27

#	INT	PRIN	BALANCE
1	9.5248	1.7393	98.2607
2	9.3503	1.9138	96.3470
3	9.1583	2.1058	94.2412
4	8.9470	2.3171	91.9241
5	8.7145	2.5496	89.3745
6	8.4586	2.8054	86.5691
7	8.1772	3.0869	83.4822
8	7.8674	3.3966	80.0855
9	7.5266	3.7374	76.3481
10	7.1516	4.1125	72.2356
11	6.7390	4.5251	67.7105
12	6.2849	4.9791	62.7314
13	5.7853	5.4787	57.2527
14	5.2356	6.0285	51.2242
15	4.6307	6.6334	44.5908
16	3.9651	7.2989	37.2919
17	3.2327	8.0313	29.2606
18	2.4269	8.8372	20.4234
19	1.5402	9.7239	10.6995
20	.5645	10.6995	0.0000

YEARS 21 — MO PAYT .9241 — AN CONST 11.09

#	INT	PRIN	BALANCE
1	9.5327	1.5561	98.4439
2	9.3766	1.7122	96.7317
3	9.2048	1.8840	94.8477

#	INT	PRIN	BALANCE
4	9.0157	2.0730	92.7747
5	8.8077	2.2810	90.4937
6	8.5789	2.5099	87.9838
7	8.3270	2.7618	85.2220
8	8.0499	3.0389	82.1831
9	7.7450	3.3438	78.8394
10	7.4095	3.6793	75.1601
11	7.0403	4.0485	71.1116
12	6.6341	4.4547	66.6569
13	6.1871	4.9017	61.7553
14	5.6953	5.3935	56.3618
15	5.1541	5.9347	50.4271
16	4.5586	6.5301	43.8970
17	3.9034	7.1854	36.7116
18	3.1824	7.9063	28.8053
19	2.3891	8.6996	20.1056
20	1.5162	9.5726	10.5331
21	.5557	10.5331	0.0000

YEARS 22	MO PAYT .9112	AN CONST 10.94	
#	INT	PRIN	BALANCE
1	9.5397	1.3944	98.6056
2	9.3998	1.5344	97.0712
3	9.2458	1.6883	95.3829
4	9.0764	1.8577	93.5251
5	8.8900	2.0441	91.4810
6	8.6849	2.2492	89.2318
7	8.4592	2.4749	86.7569
8	8.2109	2.7232	84.0336
9	7.9377	2.9965	81.0371
10	7.6370	3.2972	77.7400
11	7.3062	3.6280	74.1120
12	6.9421	3.9920	70.1200
13	6.5416	4.3926	65.7274
14	6.1008	4.8333	60.8941
15	5.6159	5.3183	55.5758
16	5.0822	5.8519	49.7239
17	4.4951	6.4391	43.2848
18	3.8490	7.0852	36.1997
19	3.1381	7.7961	28.4036
20	2.3558	8.5783	19.8253
21	1.4951	9.4391	10.3862
22	.5480	10.3862	0.0000

YEARS 23	MO PAYT .8998	AN CONST 10.80	
#	INT	PRIN	BALANCE
1	9.5459	1.2514	98.7486
2	9.4203	1.3770	97.3716
3	9.2822	1.5152	95.8564
4	9.1301	1.6672	94.1892
5	8.9628	1.8345	92.3547
6	8.7788	2.0185	90.3362
7	8.5762	2.2211	88.1151
8	8.3534	2.4439	85.6712
9	8.1082	2.6892	82.9820
10	7.8383	2.9590	80.0230
11	7.5414	3.2559	76.7671
12	7.2147	3.5826	73.1845
13	6.8553	3.9421	69.2425
14	6.4597	4.3376	64.9049
15	6.0245	4.7728	60.1321
16	5.5456	5.2517	54.8803
17	5.0186	5.7787	49.1017
18	4.4388	6.3585	42.7432
19	3.8008	6.9965	35.7467
20	3.0988	7.6985	28.0481
21	2.3263	8.4710	19.5772
22	1.4764	9.3210	10.2562
23	.5411	10.2562	0.0000

YEARS 24	MO PAYT .8897	AN CONST 10.68	
#	INT	PRIN	BALANCE
1	9.5514	1.1245	98.8755
2	9.4385	1.2374	97.6381
3	9.3144	1.3615	96.2766
4	9.1778	1.4981	94.7785
5	9.0275	1.6484	93.1300
6	8.8621	1.8138	91.3162
7	8.6801	1.9958	89.3204
8	8.4798	2.1961	87.1242
9	8.2594	2.4165	84.7078
10	8.0170	2.6589	82.0489
11	7.7502	2.9257	79.1231
12	7.4566	3.2193	75.9039
13	7.1336	3.5423	72.3616
14	6.7782	3.8977	68.4638
15	6.3871	4.2888	64.1750
16	5.9567	4.7192	59.4559
17	5.4832	5.1927	54.2632
18	4.9622	5.7137	48.5495
19	4.3889	6.2870	42.2625
20	3.7581	6.9178	35.3447
21	3.0639	7.6120	27.7327
22	2.3002	8.3757	19.3570
23	1.4598	9.2161	10.1409
24	.5350	10.1409	0.0000

YEARS 25	MO PAYT .8807	AN CONST 10.57	
#	INT	PRIN	BALANCE
1	9.5563	1.0116	98.9884
2	9.4547	1.1131	97.8752
3	9.3431	1.2248	96.6504
4	9.2202	1.3477	95.3026
5	9.0849	1.4830	93.8197
6	8.9361	1.6318	92.1879
7	8.7724	1.7955	90.3924
8	8.5922	1.9757	88.4168
9	8.3940	2.1739	86.2429
10	8.1759	2.3920	83.8509
11	7.9359	2.6320	81.2188
12	7.6718	2.8961	78.3227
13	7.3812	3.1867	75.1360
14	7.0614	3.5065	71.6295
15	6.7096	3.8583	67.7712
16	6.3225	4.2454	63.5258
17	5.8965	4.6714	58.8544
18	5.4278	5.1401	53.7143
19	4.9120	5.6559	48.0584
20	4.3445	6.2234	41.8350
21	3.7201	6.8478	34.9871
22	3.0329	7.5349	27.4522
23	2.2769	8.2910	19.1612
24	1.4450	9.1229	10.0383
25	.5296	10.0383	0.0000

YEARS 26	MO PAYT .8726	AN CONST 10.48	
#	INT	PRIN	BALANCE
1	9.5606	.9110	99.0890
2	9.4692	1.0024	98.0866
3	9.3686	1.1030	96.9836
4	9.2579	1.2137	95.7699
5	9.1362	1.3355	94.4344
6	9.0022	1.4695	92.9650
7	8.8547	1.6169	91.3481
8	8.6925	1.7791	89.5689
9	8.5140	1.9577	87.6113
10	8.3175	2.1541	85.4572
11	8.1014	2.3702	83.0870
12	7.8636	2.6080	80.4789
13	7.6019	2.8697	77.6092
14	7.3139	3.1577	74.4515
15	6.9971	3.4745	70.9770
16	6.6485	3.8231	67.1538
17	6.2649	4.2068	62.9471
18	5.8428	4.6289	58.3182
19	5.3783	5.0933	53.2249
20	4.8673	5.6044	47.6205
21	4.3049	6.1667	41.4538
22	3.6862	6.7855	34.6684
23	3.0053	7.4663	27.2021
24	2.2562	8.2155	18.9866
25	1.4318	9.0398	9.9468
26	.5248	9.9468	0.0000

YEARS 27	MO PAYT .8655	AN CONST 10.39	
#	INT	PRIN	BALANCE
1	9.5645	.8211	99.1789
2	9.4821	.9035	98.2753
3	9.3914	.9942	97.2811
4	9.2917	1.0939	96.1872
5	9.1819	1.2037	94.9835
6	9.0611	1.3245	93.6590
7	8.9282	1.4574	92.2016
8	8.7820	1.6036	90.5980
9	8.6211	1.7645	88.8334
10	8.4441	1.9416	86.8919
11	8.2492	2.1364	84.7555
12	8.0349	2.3508	82.4047
13	7.7990	2.5866	79.8181
14	7.5395	2.8462	76.9719
15	7.2539	3.1318	73.8401
16	6.9396	3.4460	70.3942
17	6.5939	3.7918	66.6024
18	6.2134	4.1722	62.4302
19	5.7948	4.5908	57.8393
20	5.3341	5.0515	52.7879
21	4.8273	5.5583	47.2295
22	4.2696	6.1161	41.1135
23	3.6559	6.7297	34.3837
24	2.9806	7.4050	26.9787
25	2.2376	8.1480	18.8307
26	1.4201	8.9656	9.8652
27	.5205	9.8652	0.0000

YEARS 28	MO PAYT .8591	AN CONST 10.31	
#	INT	PRIN	BALANCE
1	9.5680	.7407	99.2593
2	9.4936	.8151	98.4442
3	9.4119	.8968	97.5474
4	9.3219	.9868	96.5605
5	9.2229	1.0858	95.4747
6	9.1139	1.1948	94.2799
7	8.9940	1.3147	92.9652
8	8.8621	1.4466	91.5186
9	8.7170	1.5917	89.9269
10	8.5572	1.7515	88.1754
11	8.3815	1.9272	86.2482
12	8.1881	2.1206	84.1276
13	7.9754	2.3333	81.7943
14	7.7412	2.5675	79.2268
15	7.4836	2.8251	76.4017
16	7.2002	3.1086	73.2932
17	6.8882	3.4205	69.8727
18	6.5450	3.7637	66.1091
19	6.1674	4.1413	61.9678
20	5.7519	4.5568	57.4109
21	5.2946	5.0141	52.3968
22	4.7915	5.5172	46.8797
23	4.2379	6.0708	40.8089
24	3.6288	6.6799	34.1290
25	2.9586	7.3501	26.7789
26	2.2211	8.0876	18.6912
27	1.4096	8.8992	9.7921
28	.5166	9.7921	0.0000

YEARS 29	MO PAYT .8533	AN CONST 10.24	
#	INT	PRIN	BALANCE
1	9.5711	.6687	99.3313
2	9.5040	.7358	98.5955
3	9.4302	.8096	97.7859
4	9.3489	.8908	96.8951
5	9.2595	.9802	95.9149
6	9.1612	1.0786	94.8363
7	9.0530	1.1868	93.6495
8	8.9339	1.3059	92.3436
9	8.8028	1.4369	90.9066
10	8.6587	1.5811	89.3255
11	8.5000	1.7397	87.5858
12	8.3255	1.9143	85.6715
13	8.1334	2.1064	83.5651
14	7.9220	2.3177	81.2473
15	7.6895	2.5503	78.6970
16	7.4336	2.8062	75.8909
17	7.1520	3.0878	72.8031
18	6.8422	3.3976	69.4055
19	6.5013	3.7385	65.6670
20	6.1262	4.1136	61.5534
21	5.7134	4.5264	57.0270
22	5.2592	4.9805	52.0465
23	4.7595	5.4803	46.5662
24	4.2096	6.0302	40.5360
25	3.6045	6.6352	33.9008
26	2.9388	7.3010	26.5998
27	2.2062	8.0336	18.5662
28	1.4001	8.8396	9.7266
29	.5132	9.7266	0.0000

YEARS 30	MO PAYT .8482	AN CONST 10.18	
#	INT	PRIN	BALANCE
1	9.5739	.6040	99.3960
2	9.5133	.6646	98.7313
3	9.4466	.7313	98.0000
4	9.3732	.8047	97.1953
5	9.2925	.8855	96.3098
6	9.2036	.9743	95.3355
7	9.1059	1.0721	94.2634
8	8.9983	1.1796	93.0838
9	8.8799	1.2980	91.7858
10	8.7497	1.4282	90.3575
11	8.6064	1.5716	88.7860
12	8.4487	1.7292	87.0567
13	8.2752	1.9027	85.1540
14	8.0843	2.0937	83.0603
15	7.8742	2.3037	80.7566
16	7.6430	2.5349	78.2217
17	7.3887	2.7892	75.4324
18	7.1088	3.0691	72.3633
19	6.8009	3.3771	68.9863
20	6.4620	3.7159	65.2703
21	6.0892	4.0888	61.1816
22	5.6789	4.4990	56.6825
23	5.2275	4.9505	51.7321
24	4.7307	5.4472	46.2849
25	4.1842	5.9937	40.2912
26	3.5828	6.5951	33.6960
27	2.9210	7.2569	26.4391
28	2.1929	7.9850	18.4541
29	1.3917	8.7862	9.6678
30	.5101	9.6678	0.0000

YEARS 2 — MO PAYT 4.5972 — AN CONST 55.17

#	INT	PRIN	BALANCE
1	7.5613	47.6052	52.3948
2	2.7716	52.3948	0.0000

YEARS 3 — MO PAYT 3.2091 — AN CONST 38.51

#	INT	PRIN	BALANCE
1	8.3161	30.1936	69.8064
2	5.2782	33.2315	36.5749
3	1.9348	36.5749	0.0000

YEARS 4 — MO PAYT 2.5183 — AN CONST 30.22

#	INT	PRIN	BALANCE
1	8.6918	21.5277	78.4723
2	6.5258	23.6936	54.7787
3	4.1420	26.0775	28.7012
4	1.5183	28.7012	0.0000

YEARS 5 — MO PAYT 2.1063 — AN CONST 25.28

#	INT	PRIN	BALANCE
1	8.9158	16.3598	83.6402
2	7.2698	18.0058	65.6344
3	5.4582	19.8174	45.8170
4	3.4643	21.8113	24.0057
5	1.2699	24.0057	0.0000

YEARS 6 — MO PAYT 1.8337 — AN CONST 22.01

#	INT	PRIN	BALANCE
1	9.0640	12.9407	87.0593
2	7.7620	14.2427	72.8165
3	6.3290	15.6757	57.1408
4	4.7519	17.2529	39.8879
5	3.0160	18.9887	20.8992
6	1.1055	20.8992	0.0000

YEARS 7 — MO PAYT 1.6408 — AN CONST 19.69

#	INT	PRIN	BALANCE
1	9.1689	10.5208	89.4792
2	8.1104	11.5793	77.9000
3	6.9454	12.7443	65.1557
4	5.6632	14.0265	51.1292
5	4.2519	15.4377	35.6914
6	2.6987	16.9910	18.7004
7	.9892	18.7004	0.0000

YEARS 8 — MO PAYT 1.4976 — AN CONST 17.98

#	INT	PRIN	BALANCE
1	9.2468	8.7250	91.2750
2	8.3689	9.6028	81.6722
3	7.4028	10.5690	71.1032
4	6.3394	11.6324	59.4708
5	5.1691	12.8027	46.6681
6	3.8810	14.0908	32.5773
7	2.4633	15.5085	17.0688
8	.9029	17.0688	0.0000

YEARS 9 — MO PAYT 1.3876 — AN CONST 16.66

#	INT	PRIN	BALANCE
1	9.3066	7.3451	92.6549
2	8.5676	8.0841	84.5707
3	7.7542	8.8975	75.6732
4	6.8590	9.7927	65.8806
5	5.8738	10.7779	55.1026
6	4.7894	11.8623	43.2403

YEARS 10 — MO PAYT 1.3008 — AN CONST 15.61

#	INT	PRIN	BALANCE
7	3.5959	13.0558	30.1845
8	2.2823	14.3694	15.8151
9	.8366	15.8151	0.0000
1	9.3538	6.2562	93.7438
2	8.7243	6.8856	86.8582
3	8.0316	7.5784	79.2799
4	7.2691	8.3408	70.9390
5	6.4299	9.1800	61.7590
6	5.5063	10.1037	51.6553
7	4.4898	11.1202	40.5351
8	3.3709	12.2390	28.2961
9	2.1395	13.4704	14.8257
10	.7843	14.8257	0.0000

YEARS 11 — MO PAYT 1.2309 — AN CONST 14.78

#	INT	PRIN	BALANCE
1	9.3918	5.3785	94.6215
2	8.8507	5.9197	88.7018
3	8.2551	6.5153	82.1865
4	7.5996	7.1708	75.0158
5	6.8781	7.8922	67.1235
6	6.0841	8.6863	58.4372
7	5.2101	9.5602	48.8770
8	4.2483	10.5221	38.3549
9	3.1896	11.5807	26.7742
10	2.0245	12.7459	14.0283
11	.7421	14.0283	0.0000

YEARS 12 — MO PAYT 1.1735 — AN CONST 14.09

#	INT	PRIN	BALANCE
1	9.4230	4.6592	95.3408
2	8.9543	5.1279	90.2129
3	8.4383	5.6439	84.5690
4	7.8705	6.2117	78.3573
5	7.2455	6.8367	71.5207
6	6.5577	7.5245	63.9961
7	5.8006	8.2816	55.7146
8	4.9674	9.1148	46.5998
9	4.0503	10.0319	36.5679
10	3.0410	11.0412	25.5267
11	1.9301	12.1520	13.3747
12	.7075	13.3747	0.0000

YEARS 13 — MO PAYT 1.1259 — AN CONST 13.52

#	INT	PRIN	BALANCE
1	9.4489	4.0613	95.9387
2	9.0403	4.4699	91.4687
3	8.5906	4.9197	86.5491
4	8.0956	5.4146	81.1344
5	7.5508	5.9594	75.1750
6	6.9513	6.5590	68.6160
7	6.2913	7.2189	61.3970
8	5.5650	7.9452	53.4518
9	4.7656	8.7446	44.7072
10	3.8858	9.6244	35.0828
11	2.9175	10.5928	24.4900
12	1.8518	11.6585	12.8315
13	.6788	12.8315	0.0000

YEARS 14 — MO PAYT 1.0858 — AN CONST 13.03

#	INT	PRIN	BALANCE
1	9.4707	3.5587	96.4413
2	9.1127	3.9168	92.5245
3	8.7186	4.3109	88.2136
4	8.2849	4.7446	83.4690
5	7.8075	5.2220	78.2470
6	7.2821	5.7473	72.4997
7	6.7039	6.3256	66.1741
8	6.0674	6.9620	59.2121
9	5.3670	7.6625	51.5496
10	4.5961	8.4334	43.1162
11	3.7476	9.2819	33.8343
12	2.8137	10.2158	23.6185
13	1.7859	11.2436	12.3749
14	.6546	12.3749	0.0000

YEARS 15 — MO PAYT 1.0518 — AN CONST 12.63

#	INT	PRIN	BALANCE
1	9.4892	3.1321	96.8679
2	9.1741	3.4473	93.4206
3	8.8273	3.7941	89.6265
4	8.4455	4.1758	85.4506
5	8.0254	4.5960	80.8546
6	7.5630	5.0584	75.7962
7	7.0540	5.5673	70.2289
8	6.4939	6.1275	64.1014
9	5.8774	6.7440	57.3575
10	5.1989	7.4225	49.9350
11	4.4521	8.1693	41.7657
12	3.6302	8.9912	32.7745
13	2.7256	9.8958	22.8787
14	1.7299	10.8914	11.9873
15	.6341	11.9873	0.0000

YEARS 16 — MO PAYT 1.0227 — AN CONST 12.28

#	INT	PRIN	BALANCE
1	9.5050	2.7671	97.2329
2	9.2266	3.0455	94.1874
3	8.9202	3.3519	90.8356
4	8.5830	3.6891	87.1464
5	8.2118	4.0603	83.0861
6	7.8033	4.4688	78.6173
7	7.3537	4.9184	73.6989
8	6.8588	5.4133	68.2856
9	6.3142	5.9579	62.3277
10	5.7148	6.5574	55.7703
11	5.0550	7.2171	48.5532
12	4.3289	7.9432	40.6100
13	3.5297	8.7424	31.8676
14	2.6501	9.6220	22.2456
15	1.6821	10.5901	11.6556
16	.6166	11.6556	0.0000

YEARS 17 — MO PAYT .9976 — AN CONST 11.98

#	INT	PRIN	BALANCE
1	9.5187	2.4525	97.5475
2	9.2719	2.6992	94.8483
3	9.0004	2.9708	91.8775
4	8.7015	3.2697	88.6078
5	8.3725	3.5987	85.0092
6	8.0104	3.9607	81.0485
7	7.6119	4.3592	76.6892
8	7.1733	4.7978	71.8914
9	6.6906	5.2805	66.6109
10	6.1594	5.8118	60.7991
11	5.5746	6.3965	54.4026
12	4.9311	7.0401	47.3625
13	4.2227	7.7484	39.6141
14	3.4432	8.5280	31.0861
15	2.5851	9.3860	21.7001
16	1.6408	10.3304	11.3697
17	.6014	11.3697	0.0000

YEARS 18 — MO PAYT .9759 — AN CONST 11.72

#	INT	PRIN	BALANCE
1	9.5305	2.1797	97.8203
2	9.3112	2.3990	95.4213
3	9.0698	2.6404	92.7809
4	8.8042	2.9060	89.8749
5	8.5118	3.1984	86.6764
6	8.1900	3.5202	83.1562
7	7.8358	3.8744	79.2818
8	7.4460	4.2642	75.0176
9	7.0170	4.6932	70.3244
10	6.5448	5.1654	65.1590
11	6.0251	5.6851	59.4739
12	5.4531	6.2571	53.2168
13	4.8236	6.8866	46.3301
14	4.1307	7.5795	38.7506
15	3.3681	8.3421	30.4085
16	2.5288	9.1814	21.2271
17	1.6050	10.1052	11.1219
18	.5883	11.1219	0.0000

YEARS 19 — MO PAYT .9569 — AN CONST 11.49

#	INT	PRIN	BALANCE
1	9.5408	1.9420	98.0580
2	9.3454	2.1374	95.9206
3	9.1304	2.3524	93.5682
4	8.8937	2.5891	90.9791
5	8.6332	2.8496	88.1295
6	8.3465	3.1363	84.9932
7	8.0310	3.4519	81.5413
8	7.6837	3.7991	77.7422
9	7.3014	4.1814	73.5608
10	6.8807	4.6021	68.9587
11	6.4177	5.0651	63.8936
12	5.9081	5.5747	58.3189
13	5.3472	6.1356	52.1833
14	4.7299	6.7529	45.4304
15	4.0505	7.4323	37.9981
16	3.3027	8.1801	29.8180
17	2.4797	9.0031	20.8148
18	1.5739	9.9089	10.9059
19	.5769	10.9059	0.0000

YEARS 20 — MO PAYT .9403 — AN CONST 11.29

#	INT	PRIN	BALANCE
1	9.5498	1.7339	98.2661
2	9.3754	1.9083	96.3578
3	9.1834	2.1003	94.2575
4	8.9721	2.3116	91.9458
5	8.7395	2.5442	89.4016
6	8.4835	2.8002	86.6014
7	8.2018	3.0819	83.5195
8	7.8917	3.3920	80.1275
9	7.5504	3.7333	76.3942
10	7.1748	4.1089	72.2854
11	6.7614	4.5223	67.7631
12	6.3064	4.9773	62.7858
13	5.8057	5.4781	57.3077
14	5.2545	6.0292	51.2785
15	4.6479	6.6358	44.6427
16	3.9802	7.3035	37.3392
17	3.2454	8.0383	29.3010
18	2.4367	8.8470	20.4539
19	1.5466	9.7371	10.7168
20	.5669	10.7168	0.0000

YEARS 21 — MO PAYT .9257 — AN CONST 11.11

#	INT	PRIN	BALANCE
1	9.5578	1.5509	98.4491
2	9.4017	1.7070	96.7421
3	9.2300	1.8787	94.8634

MONTHLY PAYMENT AMORTIZATION SCHEDULE PER $100   9.625%

#	INT	PRIN	BALANCE
4	9.0410	2.0677	92.7956
5	8.8329	2.2758	90.5198
6	8.6039	2.5048	88.0151
7	8.3519	2.7568	85.2583
8	8.0746	3.0341	82.2242
9	7.7693	3.3394	78.8848
10	7.4333	3.6754	75.2094
11	7.0635	4.0452	71.1643
12	6.6566	4.4522	66.7121
13	6.2086	4.9001	61.8120
14	5.7156	5.3931	56.4189
15	5.1730	5.9357	50.4832
16	4.5758	6.5329	43.9503
17	3.9185	7.1902	36.7601
18	3.1951	7.9136	28.8465
19	2.3989	8.7098	20.1367
20	1.5226	9.5861	10.5506
21	.5581	10.5506	0.0000

YEARS 22 — MO PAYT .9129 — AN CONST 10.96

#	INT	PRIN	BALANCE
1	9.5648	1.3896	98.6104
2	9.4250	1.5294	97.0810
3	9.2711	1.6833	95.3978
4	9.1017	1.8526	93.5452
5	8.9153	2.0390	91.5061
6	8.7102	2.2442	89.2620
7	8.4844	2.4699	86.7920
8	8.2359	2.7185	84.0736
9	7.9624	2.9920	81.0816
10	7.6614	3.2930	77.7886
11	7.3300	3.6243	74.1643
12	6.9654	3.9890	70.1754
13	6.5641	4.3903	65.7851
14	6.1223	4.8320	60.9531
15	5.6362	5.3182	55.6349
16	5.1011	5.8532	49.7817
17	4.5122	6.4421	43.3396
18	3.8641	7.0903	36.2493
19	3.1507	7.8036	28.4457
20	2.3656	8.5888	19.8569
21	1.5014	9.4529	10.4040
22	.5504	10.4040	0.0000

YEARS 23 — MO PAYT .9015 — AN CONST 10.82

#	INT	PRIN	BALANCE
1	9.5709	1.2468	98.7532
2	9.4455	1.3723	97.3809
3	9.3074	1.5103	95.8706
4	9.1555	1.6623	94.2083
5	8.9882	1.8295	92.3788
6	8.8042	2.0136	90.3652
7	8.6016	2.2162	88.1491
8	8.3786	2.4392	85.7099
9	8.1332	2.6846	83.0253
10	7.8631	2.9547	80.0707
11	7.5658	3.2519	76.8187
12	7.2386	3.5791	73.2396
13	6.8785	3.9392	69.3004
14	6.4822	4.3355	64.9649
15	6.0460	4.7718	60.1931
16	5.5659	5.2518	54.9413
17	5.0375	5.7802	49.1610
18	4.4560	6.3618	42.7992
19	3.8159	7.0019	35.7973
20	3.1114	7.7063	28.0910
21	2.3361	8.4817	19.6093
22	1.4827	9.3350	10.2743
23	.5435	10.2743	0.0000

YEARS 24 — MO PAYT .8914 — AN CONST 10.70

#	INT	PRIN	BALANCE
1	9.5764	1.1201	98.8799
2	9.4637	1.2328	97.6470
3	9.3397	1.3569	96.2901
4	9.2032	1.4934	94.7967
5	9.0529	1.6437	93.1531
6	8.8876	1.8090	91.3440
7	8.7056	1.9910	89.3530
8	8.5052	2.1914	87.1617
9	8.2848	2.4118	84.7498
10	8.0421	2.6545	82.0953
11	7.7750	2.9216	79.1738
12	7.4811	3.2155	75.9583
13	7.1576	3.5390	72.4192
14	6.8015	3.8951	68.5241
15	6.4096	4.2870	64.2372
16	5.9783	4.7183	59.5189
17	5.5036	5.1930	54.3258
18	4.9811	5.7155	48.6103
19	4.4060	6.2905	42.3198
20	3.7731	6.9234	35.3964
21	3.0766	7.6200	27.7763
22	2.3099	8.3867	19.3897
23	1.4661	9.2305	10.1592
24	.5374	10.1592	0.0000

YEARS 25 — MO PAYT .8824 — AN CONST 10.59

#	INT	PRIN	BALANCE
1	9.5813	1.0075	98.9925
2	9.4800	1.1089	97.8836
3	9.3684	1.2204	96.6632
4	9.2456	1.3432	95.3200
5	9.1105	1.4784	93.8417
6	8.9617	1.6271	92.2146
7	8.7980	1.7908	90.4238
8	8.6178	1.9710	88.4528
9	8.4195	2.1693	86.2835
10	8.2013	2.3875	83.8960
11	7.9611	2.6277	81.2682
12	7.6967	2.8921	78.3761
13	7.4057	3.1831	75.1930
14	7.0855	3.5034	71.6896
15	6.7330	3.8558	67.8338
16	6.3450	4.2438	63.5900
17	5.9181	4.6708	58.9192
18	5.4481	5.1407	53.7785
19	4.9309	5.6579	48.1206
20	4.3617	6.2272	41.8934
21	3.7351	6.8537	35.0397
22	3.0456	7.5433	27.4965
23	2.2866	8.3022	19.1943
24	1.4513	9.1375	10.0568
25	.5320	10.0568	0.0000

YEARS 26 — MO PAYT .8744 — AN CONST 10.50

#	INT	PRIN	BALANCE
1	9.5857	.9071	99.0929
2	9.4944	.9984	98.0946
3	9.3940	1.0988	96.9958
4	9.2834	1.2094	95.7864
5	9.1617	1.3310	94.4554
6	9.0278	1.4649	92.9904
7	8.8804	1.6123	91.3781
8	8.7182	1.7746	89.6035
9	8.5397	1.9531	87.6504
10	8.3432	2.1496	85.5008
11	8.1269	2.3659	83.1350
12	7.8889	2.6039	80.5310
13	7.6269	2.8659	77.6652
14	7.3385	3.1542	74.5109
15	7.0212	3.4716	71.0393
16	6.6719	3.8209	67.2185
17	6.2875	4.2053	63.0132
18	5.8644	4.6284	58.3848
19	5.3987	5.0941	53.2907
20	4.8862	5.6066	47.6841
21	4.3221	6.1707	41.5134
22	3.7012	6.7915	34.7219
23	3.0179	7.4748	27.2471
24	2.2659	8.2269	19.0202
25	1.4382	9.0546	9.9656
26	.5272	9.9656	0.0000

YEARS 27 — MO PAYT .8672 — AN CONST 10.41

#	INT	PRIN	BALANCE
1	9.5896	.8174	99.1826
2	9.5073	.8997	98.2829
3	9.4168	.9902	97.2927
4	9.3172	1.0898	96.2029
5	9.2075	1.1995	95.0034
6	9.0868	1.3201	93.6833
7	8.9540	1.4530	92.2303
8	8.8078	1.5992	90.6311
9	8.6469	1.7601	88.8711
10	8.4699	1.9371	86.9340
11	8.2750	2.1320	84.8019
12	8.0605	2.3465	82.4554
13	7.8244	2.5826	79.8728
14	7.5645	2.8425	77.0303
15	7.2785	3.1285	73.9018
16	6.9638	3.4432	70.4586
17	6.6174	3.7896	66.6690
18	6.2361	4.1709	62.4981
19	5.8164	4.5906	57.9075
20	5.3546	5.0524	52.8551
21	4.8462	5.5608	47.2943
22	4.2868	6.1202	41.1741
23	3.6710	6.7360	34.4381
24	2.9933	7.4137	27.0244
25	2.2474	8.1596	18.8647
26	1.4264	8.9806	9.8841
27	.5229	9.8841	0.0000

YEARS 28 — MO PAYT .8609 — AN CONST 10.34

#	INT	PRIN	BALANCE
1	9.5930	.7372	99.2628
2	9.5189	.8114	98.4514
3	9.4372	.8930	97.5583
4	9.3474	.9829	96.5754
5	9.2485	1.0818	95.4936
6	9.1396	1.1906	94.3030
7	9.0199	1.3104	92.9926
8	8.8880	1.4423	91.5503
9	8.7429	1.5874	89.9630
10	8.5832	1.7471	88.2159
11	8.4074	1.9229	86.2930
12	8.2140	2.1163	84.1767
13	8.0010	2.3292	81.8475
14	7.7667	2.5636	79.2839
15	7.5088	2.8215	76.4624
16	7.2249	3.1054	73.3570
17	6.9124	3.4178	69.9392
18	6.5686	3.7617	66.1775
19	6.1901	4.1402	62.0373
20	5.7736	4.5567	57.4806
21	5.3151	5.0152	52.4654
22	4.8105	5.5198	46.9457
23	4.2552	6.0751	40.8705
24	3.6439	6.6863	34.1842
25	2.9712	7.3591	26.8251
26	2.2308	8.0995	18.7256
27	1.4159	8.9144	9.8113
28	.5190	9.8113	0.0000

YEARS 29 — MO PAYT .8551 — AN CONST 10.27

#	INT	PRIN	BALANCE
1	9.5962	.6654	99.3346
2	9.5292	.7323	98.6023
3	9.4555	.8060	97.7963
4	9.3744	.8871	96.9092
5	9.2852	.9764	95.9328
6	9.1870	1.0746	94.8582
7	9.0788	1.1827	93.6755
8	8.9598	1.3017	92.3738
9	8.8289	1.4327	90.9412
10	8.6847	1.5768	89.3644
11	8.5261	1.7354	87.6289
12	8.3515	1.9101	85.7189
13	8.1593	2.1022	83.6166
14	7.9478	2.3137	81.3029
15	7.7150	2.5465	78.7564
16	7.4588	2.8027	75.9536
17	7.1768	3.0847	72.8689
18	6.8665	3.3951	69.4738
19	6.5249	3.7367	65.7372
20	6.1489	4.1126	61.6245
21	5.7351	4.5264	57.0981
22	5.2797	4.9818	52.1163
23	4.7785	5.4830	46.6333
24	4.2268	6.0347	40.5986
25	3.6197	6.6419	33.9567
26	2.9514	7.3101	26.6466
27	2.2160	8.0456	18.6010
28	1.4065	8.8551	9.7460
29	.5156	9.7460	0.0000

YEARS 30 — MO PAYT .8500 — AN CONST 10.20

#	INT	PRIN	BALANCE
1	9.5989	.6009	99.3991
2	9.5385	.6614	98.7377
3	9.4719	.7279	98.0098
4	9.3987	.8012	97.2086
5	9.3181	.8818	96.3268
6	9.2294	.9705	95.3563
7	9.1317	1.0681	94.2882
8	9.0243	1.1756	93.1126
9	8.9060	1.2939	91.8187
10	8.7758	1.4241	90.3947
11	8.6325	1.5673	88.8274
12	8.4749	1.7250	87.1023
13	8.3013	1.8986	85.2038
14	8.1103	2.0896	83.1142
15	7.9000	2.2998	80.8143
16	7.6686	2.5312	78.2831
17	7.4140	2.7859	75.4972
18	7.1337	3.0662	72.4310
19	6.8252	3.3747	69.0563
20	6.4857	3.7142	65.3421
21	6.1120	4.0879	61.2542
22	5.7007	4.4992	56.7550
23	5.2480	4.9519	51.8031
24	4.7498	5.4501	46.3531
25	4.2014	5.9984	40.3546
26	3.5979	6.6019	33.7527
27	2.9337	7.2662	26.4865
28	2.2026	7.9972	18.4893
29	1.3980	8.8019	9.6874
30	.5125	9.6874	0.0000

YEARS 2 — MO PAYT 4.6007 — AN CONST 55.21

#	INT	PRIN	BALANCE
1	7.6213	47.5866	52.4134
2	2.7945	52.4134	0.0000

YEARS 3 — MO PAYT 3.2127 — AN CONST 38.56

#	INT	PRIN	BALANCE
1	8.3821	30.1697	69.8303
2	5.3220	33.2299	36.6004
3	1.9514	36.6004	0.0000

YEARS 4 — MO PAYT 2.5219 — AN CONST 30.27

#	INT	PRIN	BALANCE
1	8.7607	21.5018	78.4982
2	6.5798	23.6827	54.8155
3	4.1776	26.0849	28.7307
4	1.5318	28.7307	0.0000

YEARS 5 — MO PAYT 2.1100 — AN CONST 25.32

#	INT	PRIN	BALANCE
1	8.9865	16.3332	83.6668
2	7.3298	17.9898	65.6770
3	5.5051	19.8146	45.8624
4	3.4953	21.8244	24.0380
5	1.2816	24.0380	0.0000

YEARS 6 — MO PAYT 1.8375 — AN CONST 22.05

#	INT	PRIN	BALANCE
1	9.1359	12.9140	87.0860
2	7.8260	14.2239	72.8621
3	6.3833	15.6666	57.1955
4	4.7942	17.2557	39.9397
5	3.0439	19.0060	20.9338
6	1.1161	20.9338	0.0000

YEARS 7 — MO PAYT 1.6447 — AN CONST 19.74

#	INT	PRIN	BALANCE
1	9.2416	10.4943	89.5057
2	8.1771	11.5588	77.9469
3	7.0047	12.7312	65.2157
4	5.7134	14.0225	51.1932
5	4.2911	15.4448	35.7483
6	2.7245	17.0114	18.7369
7	.9990	18.7369	0.0000

YEARS 8 — MO PAYT 1.5016 — AN CONST 18.02

#	INT	PRIN	BALANCE
1	9.3200	8.6991	91.3009
2	8.4376	9.5814	81.7195
3	7.4658	10.5533	71.1662
4	6.3954	11.6237	59.5425
5	5.2164	12.8027	46.7398
6	3.9178	14.1013	32.6386
7	2.4875	15.5316	17.1070
8	.9121	17.1070	0.0000

YEARS 9 — MO PAYT 1.3917 — AN CONST 16.71

#	INT	PRIN	BALANCE
1	9.3802	7.3198	92.6802
2	8.6378	8.0623	84.6178
3	7.8200	8.8801	75.7378
4	6.9193	9.7808	65.9570
5	5.9272	10.7729	55.1841
6	4.8345	11.8656	43.3186
7	3.6310	13.0691	30.2495
8	2.3054	14.3947	15.8548
9	.8453	15.8548	0.0000

YEARS 10 — MO PAYT 1.3050 — AN CONST 15.66

#	INT	PRIN	BALANCE
1	9.4278	6.2316	93.7684
2	8.7957	6.8637	86.9047
3	8.0995	7.5599	79.3448
4	7.3327	8.3267	71.0181
5	6.4881	9.1713	61.8468
6	5.5579	10.1015	51.7453
7	4.5333	11.1261	40.6191
8	3.4047	12.2547	28.3644
9	2.1617	13.4977	14.8668
10	.7927	14.8668	0.0000

YEARS 11 — MO PAYT 1.2351 — AN CONST 14.83

#	INT	PRIN	BALANCE
1	9.4661	5.3548	94.6452
2	8.9229	5.8979	88.7473
3	8.3247	6.4962	82.2511
4	7.6658	7.1551	75.0960
5	6.9401	7.8808	67.2152
6	6.1407	8.6802	58.5350
7	5.2603	9.5606	48.9744
8	4.2905	10.5304	38.4440
9	3.2224	11.5985	26.8456
10	2.0460	12.7749	14.0707
11	.7502	14.0707	0.0000

YEARS 12 — MO PAYT 1.1778 — AN CONST 14.14

#	INT	PRIN	BALANCE
1	9.4975	4.6363	95.3637
2	9.0272	5.1065	90.2572
3	8.5093	5.6245	84.6327
4	7.9388	6.1950	78.4377
5	7.3104	6.8233	71.6144
6	6.6183	7.5154	64.0989
7	5.8560	8.2777	55.8212
8	5.0164	9.1174	46.7038
9	4.0916	10.0421	36.6617
10	3.0730	11.0607	25.6009
11	1.9511	12.1826	13.4183
12	.7154	13.4183	0.0000

YEARS 13 — MO PAYT 1.1302 — AN CONST 13.57

#	INT	PRIN	BALANCE
1	9.5236	4.0393	95.9607
2	9.1138	4.4490	91.5117
3	8.6626	4.9003	86.6114
4	8.1655	5.3973	81.2141
5	7.6181	5.9448	75.2694
6	7.0151	6.5477	68.7217
7	6.3510	7.2119	61.5098
8	5.6195	7.9434	53.5664
9	4.8138	8.7491	44.8173
10	3.9263	9.6365	35.1808
11	2.9489	10.6140	24.5668
12	1.8723	11.6905	12.8763
13	.6865	12.8763	0.0000

YEARS 14 — MO PAYT 1.0903 — AN CONST 13.09

#	INT	PRIN	BALANCE
1	9.5455	3.5376	96.4624
2	9.1866	3.8964	92.5660
3	8.7914	4.2916	88.2744
4	8.3561	4.7269	83.5475
5	7.8767	5.2064	78.3411
6	7.3486	5.7345	72.6067
7	6.7669	6.3161	66.2906
8	6.1263	6.9568	59.3338
9	5.4207	7.6624	51.6714
10	4.6435	8.4396	43.2319
11	3.7874	9.2956	33.9363
12	2.8446	10.2385	23.6978
13	1.8061	11.2770	12.4208
14	.6622	12.4208	0.0000

YEARS 15 — MO PAYT 1.0563 — AN CONST 12.68

#	INT	PRIN	BALANCE
1	9.5641	3.1119	96.8881
2	9.2484	3.4275	93.4607
3	8.9008	3.7751	89.6855
4	8.5179	4.1581	85.5274
5	8.0961	4.5798	80.9476
6	7.6316	5.0444	75.9033
7	7.1199	5.5560	70.3473
8	6.5564	6.1196	64.2277
9	5.9357	6.7403	57.4874
10	5.2520	7.4239	50.0635
11	4.4990	8.1770	41.8866
12	3.6696	9.0063	32.8802
13	2.7561	9.9199	22.9603
14	1.7499	10.9260	12.0343
15	.6416	12.0343	0.0000

YEARS 16 — MO PAYT 1.0273 — AN CONST 12.33

#	INT	PRIN	BALANCE
1	9.5800	2.7477	97.2523
2	9.3013	3.0264	94.2260
3	8.9943	3.3333	90.8927
4	8.6562	3.6714	87.2213
5	8.2838	4.0438	83.1774
6	7.8736	4.4540	78.7235
7	7.4219	4.9058	73.8177
8	6.9243	5.4033	68.4144
9	6.3762	5.9514	62.4630
10	5.7726	6.5551	55.9079
11	5.1077	7.2200	48.6879
12	4.3754	7.9523	40.7357
13	3.5687	8.7589	31.9768
14	2.6803	9.6473	22.3295
15	1.7018	10.6258	11.7036
16	.6240	11.7036	0.0000

YEARS 17 — MO PAYT 1.0023 — AN CONST 12.03

#	INT	PRIN	BALANCE
1	9.5937	2.4339	97.5661
2	9.3468	2.6808	94.8853
3	9.0749	2.9527	91.9326
4	8.7754	3.2522	88.6804
5	8.4455	3.5821	85.0984
6	8.0822	3.9454	81.1530
7	7.6820	4.3456	76.8074
8	7.2412	4.7863	72.0211
9	6.7558	5.2718	66.7492
10	6.2210	5.8066	60.9427
11	5.6321	6.3955	54.5471
12	4.9834	7.0442	47.5029
13	4.2689	7.7587	39.7442
14	3.4819	8.5457	31.1985
15	2.6151	9.4125	21.7860
16	1.6604	10.3672	11.4188
17	.6088	11.4188	0.0000

YEARS 18 — MO PAYT .9806 — AN CONST 11.77

#	INT	PRIN	BALANCE
1	9.6056	2.1620	97.8380
2	9.3863	2.3813	95.4567
3	9.1447	2.6228	92.8339
4	8.8787	2.8889	89.9450
5	8.5857	3.1819	86.7632
6	8.2629	3.5046	83.2586
7	7.9075	3.8601	79.3985
8	7.5159	4.2516	75.1468
9	7.0847	4.6829	70.4640
10	6.6097	5.1579	65.3061
11	6.0865	5.6810	59.6251
12	5.5103	6.2573	53.3678
13	4.8756	6.8919	46.4759
14	4.1766	7.5910	38.8849
15	3.4066	8.3609	30.5240
16	2.5585	9.2090	21.3150
17	1.6245	10.1431	11.1719
18	.5957	11.1719	0.0000

YEARS 19 — MO PAYT .9618 — AN CONST 11.55

#	INT	PRIN	BALANCE
1	9.6159	1.9251	98.0749
2	9.4206	2.1204	95.9545
3	9.2056	2.3354	93.6191
4	8.9687	2.5723	91.0467
5	8.7078	2.8332	88.2135
6	8.4204	3.1206	85.0929
7	8.1039	3.4371	81.6557
8	7.7552	3.7858	77.8700
9	7.3712	4.1698	73.7002
10	6.9483	4.5927	69.1075
11	6.4825	5.0586	64.0489
12	5.9694	5.5717	58.4772
13	5.4042	6.1368	52.3404
14	4.7818	6.7593	45.5812
15	4.0962	7.4448	38.1363
16	3.3410	8.2000	29.9364
17	2.5093	9.0317	20.9046
18	1.5932	9.9478	10.9568
19	.5842	10.9568	0.0000

YEARS 20 — MO PAYT .9452 — AN CONST 11.35

#	INT	PRIN	BALANCE
1	9.6250	1.7178	98.2822
2	9.4507	1.8920	96.3902
3	9.2588	2.0839	94.3062
4	9.0474	2.2953	92.0109
5	8.8146	2.5281	89.4827
6	8.5582	2.7846	86.6982
7	8.2757	3.0670	83.6312
8	7.9647	3.3781	80.2531
9	7.6220	3.7207	76.5323
10	7.2446	4.0981	72.4342
11	6.8289	4.5138	67.9203
12	6.3711	4.9717	62.9487
13	5.8668	5.4759	57.4727
14	5.3114	6.0314	51.4413
15	4.6996	6.6431	44.7982
16	4.0258	7.3170	37.4812
17	3.2836	8.0591	29.4221
18	2.4662	8.8766	20.5455
19	1.5658	9.7769	10.7686
20	.5742	10.7686	0.0000

YEARS 21 — MO PAYT .9307 — AN CONST 11.17

#	INT	PRIN	BALANCE
1	9.6329	1.5357	98.4643
2	9.4772	1.6914	96.7729
3	9.3056	1.8630	94.9099

#	INT	PRIN	BALANCE
4	9.1166	2.0519	92.8580
5	8.9085	2.2601	90.5979
6	8.6793	2.4893	88.1086
7	8.4268	2.7418	85.3668
8	8.1487	3.0199	82.3469
9	7.8423	3.3262	79.0206
10	7.5050	3.6636	75.3570
11	7.1334	4.0352	71.3218
12	6.7241	4.4445	66.8773
13	6.2733	4.8953	61.9820
14	5.7767	5.3919	56.5901
15	5.2298	5.9388	50.6514
16	4.6274	6.5411	44.1103
17	3.9640	7.2046	36.9057
18	3.2332	7.9354	28.9703
19	2.4283	8.7403	20.2300
20	1.5418	9.6268	10.6032
21	.5653	10.6032	0.0000

YEARS 22	MO PAYT .9179	AN CONST 11.02	
#	INT	PRIN	BALANCE
1	9.6399	1.3751	98.6249
2	9.5005	1.5145	97.1104
3	9.3468	1.6682	95.4422
4	9.1776	1.8374	93.6049
5	8.9913	2.0237	91.5811
6	8.7860	2.2290	89.3521
7	8.5599	2.4551	86.8970
8	8.3109	2.7041	84.1929
9	8.0366	2.9784	81.2145
10	7.7345	3.2805	77.9341
11	7.4018	3.6132	74.3208
12	7.0353	3.9797	70.3411
13	6.6316	4.3834	65.9577
14	6.1870	4.8280	61.1297
15	5.6973	5.3177	55.8120
16	5.1579	5.8571	49.9549
17	4.5638	6.4512	43.5037
18	3.9095	7.1055	36.3982
19	3.1887	7.8263	28.5719
20	2.3949	8.6201	19.9519
21	1.5206	9.4944	10.4574
22	.5576	10.4574	0.0000

YEARS 23	MO PAYT .9066	AN CONST 10.88	
#	INT	PRIN	BALANCE
1	9.6461	1.2330	98.7670
2	9.5211	1.3581	97.4088
3	9.3833	1.4959	95.9130
4	9.2316	1.6476	94.2654
5	9.0645	1.8147	92.4507
6	8.8804	1.9988	90.4519
7	8.6777	2.2015	88.2504
8	8.4544	2.4248	85.8256
9	8.2084	2.6708	83.1548
10	7.9375	2.9417	80.2131
11	7.6391	3.2400	76.9731
12	7.3105	3.5687	73.4044
13	6.9485	3.9307	69.4738
14	6.5498	4.3293	65.1444
15	6.1107	4.7685	60.3759
16	5.6270	5.2521	55.1238
17	5.0943	5.7849	49.3389
18	4.5075	6.3716	42.9673
19	3.8613	7.0179	35.9494
20	3.1494	7.7297	28.2196
21	2.3654	8.5138	19.7058
22	1.5018	9.3773	10.3285
23	.5507	10.3285	0.0000

YEARS 24	MO PAYT .8966	AN CONST 10.76	
#	INT	PRIN	BALANCE
1	9.6516	1.1071	98.8929
2	9.5393	1.2194	97.6735
3	9.4157	1.3431	96.3304
4	9.2794	1.4793	94.8511
5	9.1294	1.6294	93.2218
6	8.9641	1.7946	91.4272
7	8.7821	1.9766	89.4505
8	8.5816	2.1771	87.2734
9	8.3608	2.3980	84.8754
10	8.1175	2.6412	82.2342
11	7.8496	2.9091	79.3251
12	7.5546	3.2042	76.1209
13	7.2296	3.5292	72.5918
14	6.8716	3.8871	68.7046
15	6.4773	4.2814	64.4232
16	6.0431	4.7157	59.7075
17	5.5647	5.1940	54.5135
18	5.0379	5.7208	48.7927
19	4.4576	6.3011	42.4916
20	3.8185	6.9402	35.5514
21	3.1146	7.6442	27.9072
22	2.3392	8.4195	19.4877
23	1.4852	9.2735	10.2141
24	.5446	10.2141	0.0000

YEARS 25	MO PAYT .8876	AN CONST 10.66	
#	INT	PRIN	BALANCE
1	9.6565	.9951	99.0049
2	9.5556	1.0961	97.9088
3	9.4444	1.2073	96.7015
4	9.3220	1.3297	95.3718
5	9.1871	1.4646	93.9072
6	9.0385	1.6131	92.2941
7	8.8749	1.7768	90.5173
8	8.6947	1.9570	88.5603
9	8.4962	2.1555	86.4049
10	8.2776	2.3741	84.0308
11	8.0368	2.6149	81.4158
12	7.7715	2.8801	78.5357
13	7.4794	3.1723	75.3634
14	7.1576	3.4941	71.8694
15	6.8032	3.8485	68.0209
16	6.4129	4.2388	63.7821
17	5.9829	4.6688	59.1133
18	5.5094	5.1423	53.9710
19	4.9878	5.6639	48.3071
20	4.4133	6.2384	42.0687
21	3.7805	6.8712	35.1976
22	3.0836	7.5681	27.6295
23	2.3159	8.3357	19.2937
24	1.4704	9.1812	10.1125
25	.5392	10.1125	0.0000

YEARS 26	MO PAYT .8797	AN CONST 10.56	
#	INT	PRIN	BALANCE
1	9.6609	.8954	99.1046
2	9.5701	.9862	98.1184
3	9.4700	1.0863	97.0321
4	9.3598	1.1964	95.8356
5	9.2385	1.3178	94.5178
6	9.1048	1.4515	93.0664
7	8.9576	1.5987	91.4677
8	8.7954	1.7609	89.7068
9	8.6168	1.9395	87.7674
10	8.4201	2.1362	85.6312
11	8.2034	2.3528	83.2783
12	7.9648	2.5915	80.6868
13	7.7019	2.8544	77.8325
14	7.4124	3.1439	74.6886
15	7.0935	3.4628	71.2258
16	6.7423	3.8140	67.4118
17	6.3554	4.2009	63.2110
18	5.9293	4.6269	58.5840
19	5.4600	5.0963	53.4878
20	4.9431	5.6132	47.8746
21	4.3738	6.1825	41.6921
22	3.7467	6.8096	34.8824
23	3.0560	7.5003	27.3821
24	2.2952	8.2611	19.1210
25	1.4573	9.0990	10.0220
26	.5343	10.0220	0.0000

YEARS 27	MO PAYT .8726	AN CONST 10.48	
#	INT	PRIN	BALANCE
1	9.6648	.8064	99.1936
2	9.5830	.8882	98.3054
3	9.4929	.9783	97.3271
4	9.3937	1.0775	96.2496
5	9.2844	1.1868	95.0628
6	9.1640	1.3072	93.7557
7	9.0314	1.4398	92.3159
8	8.8854	1.5858	90.7301
9	8.7245	1.7467	88.9834
10	8.5474	1.9238	87.0596
11	8.3522	2.1189	84.9407
12	8.1373	2.3339	82.6068
13	7.9006	2.5706	80.0362
14	7.6398	2.8313	77.2048
15	7.3526	3.1185	74.0863
16	7.0363	3.4348	70.6515
17	6.6879	3.7832	66.8682
18	6.3042	4.1670	62.7013
19	5.8815	4.5896	58.1116
20	5.4160	5.0552	53.0565
21	4.9033	5.5679	47.4885
22	4.3385	6.1327	41.3559
23	3.7165	6.7547	34.6011
24	3.0313	7.4399	27.1613
25	2.2767	8.1945	18.9668
26	1.4455	9.0257	9.9411
27	.5300	9.9411	0.0000

YEARS 28	MO PAYT .8663	AN CONST 10.40	
#	INT	PRIN	BALANCE
1	9.6683	.7268	99.2732
2	9.5945	.8005	98.4727
3	9.5133	.8817	97.5909
4	9.4239	.9712	96.6197
5	9.3254	1.0697	95.5501
6	9.2169	1.1782	94.3719
7	9.0974	1.2977	93.0742
8	8.9658	1.4293	91.6449
9	8.8208	1.5743	90.0706
10	8.6611	1.7340	88.3367
11	8.4852	1.9098	86.4269
12	8.2915	2.1035	84.3233
13	8.0782	2.3169	82.0064
14	7.8431	2.5519	79.4545
15	7.5843	2.8108	76.6437
16	7.2992	3.0959	73.5478
17	6.9852	3.4099	70.1380
18	6.6393	3.7557	66.3822
19	6.2584	4.1367	62.2455
20	5.8388	4.5563	57.6893
21	5.3766	5.0184	52.6708
22	4.8676	5.5274	47.1434
23	4.3070	6.0881	41.0553
24	3.6894	6.7056	34.3497
25	3.0093	7.3858	26.9639
26	2.2601	8.1349	18.8289
27	1.4350	8.9601	9.8689
28	.5262	9.8689	0.0000

YEARS 29	MO PAYT .8606	AN CONST 10.33	
#	INT	PRIN	BALANCE
1	9.6714	.6556	99.3444
2	9.6049	.7220	98.6224
3	9.5316	.7953	97.8271
4	9.4510	.8760	96.9512
5	9.3621	.9648	95.9864
6	9.2643	1.0627	94.9237
7	9.1565	1.1705	93.7532
8	9.0377	1.2892	92.4641
9	8.9070	1.4199	91.0441
10	8.7630	1.5640	89.4802
11	8.6043	1.7226	87.7576
12	8.4296	1.8973	85.8603
13	8.2372	2.0898	83.7705
14	8.0252	2.3017	81.4688
15	7.7917	2.5352	78.9336
16	7.5346	2.7923	76.1413
17	7.2514	3.0756	73.0657
18	6.9394	3.3875	69.6782
19	6.5958	3.7311	65.9471
20	6.2173	4.1096	61.8375
21	5.8005	4.5264	57.3111
22	5.3414	4.9855	52.3255
23	4.8357	5.4912	46.8343
24	4.2787	6.0482	40.7861
25	3.6653	6.6617	34.1245
26	2.9896	7.3374	26.7871
27	2.2453	8.0816	18.7055
28	1.4256	8.9013	9.8042
29	.5227	9.8042	0.0000

YEARS 30	MO PAYT .8555	AN CONST 10.27	
#	INT	PRIN	BALANCE
1	9.6742	.5917	99.4083
2	9.6141	.6517	98.7567
3	9.5480	.7178	98.0389
4	9.4752	.7906	97.2483
5	9.3950	.8708	96.3775
6	9.3067	.9591	95.4184
7	9.2094	1.0564	94.3621
8	9.1023	1.1635	93.1985
9	8.9843	1.2815	91.9170
10	8.8543	1.4115	90.5055
11	8.7111	1.5547	88.9508
12	8.5534	1.7124	87.2384
13	8.3797	1.8861	85.3523
14	8.1884	2.0774	83.2749
15	7.9777	2.2881	80.9868
16	7.7456	2.5202	78.4666
17	7.4900	2.7758	75.6908
18	7.2084	3.0574	72.6334
19	6.8983	3.3675	69.2659
20	6.5568	3.7090	65.5569
21	6.1806	4.0853	61.4716
22	5.7662	4.4996	56.9720
23	5.3098	4.9560	52.0160
24	4.8071	5.4587	46.5572
25	4.2534	6.0124	40.5448
26	3.6436	6.6223	33.9226
27	2.9719	7.2940	26.6286
28	2.2320	8.0338	18.5948
29	1.4172	8.8487	9.7462
30	.5196	9.7462	0.0000

YEARS 2 — MO PAYT 4.6030 — AN CONST 55.24

#	INT	PRIN	BALANCE
1	7.6613	47.5743	52.4257
2	2.8098	52.4257	0.0000

YEARS 3 — MO PAYT 3.2150 — AN CONST 38.58

#	INT	PRIN	BALANCE
1	8.4261	30.1538	69.8462
2	5.3511	33.2288	36.6174
3	1.9625	36.6174	0.0000

YEARS 4 — MO PAYT 2.5243 — AN CONST 30.30

#	INT	PRIN	BALANCE
1	8.8067	21.4845	78.5155
2	6.6158	23.6754	54.8401
3	4.2015	26.0898	28.7503
4	1.5409	28.7503	0.0000

YEARS 5 — MO PAYT 2.1124 — AN CONST 25.35

#	INT	PRIN	BALANCE
1	9.0337	16.3154	83.6846
2	7.3699	17.9792	65.7054
3	5.5364	19.8127	45.8927
4	3.5160	21.8331	24.0596
5	1.2895	24.0596	0.0000

YEARS 6 — MO PAYT 1.8400 — AN CONST 22.09

#	INT	PRIN	BALANCE
1	9.1838	12.8962	87.1038
2	7.8687	14.2113	72.8924
3	6.4195	15.6606	57.2319
4	4.8224	17.2576	39.9743
5	3.0625	19.0175	20.9568
6	1.1232	20.9568	0.0000

YEARS 7 — MO PAYT 1.6472 — AN CONST 19.77

#	INT	PRIN	BALANCE
1	9.2900	10.4767	89.5233
2	8.2216	11.5451	77.9782
3	7.0443	12.7225	65.2557
4	5.7469	14.0199	51.2359
5	4.3172	15.4496	35.7863
6	2.7417	17.0251	18.7612
7	1.0055	18.7612	0.0000

YEARS 8 — MO PAYT 1.5042 — AN CONST 18.06

#	INT	PRIN	BALANCE
1	9.3688	8.6818	91.3182
2	8.4835	9.5672	81.7510
3	7.5079	10.5428	71.2082
4	6.4327	11.6179	59.5903
5	5.2480	12.8027	46.7877
6	3.9424	14.1083	32.6794
7	2.5037	15.5470	17.1324
8	.9182	17.1324	0.0000

YEARS 9 — MO PAYT 1.3944 — AN CONST 16.74

#	INT	PRIN	BALANCE
1	9.4294	7.3030	92.6970
2	8.6846	8.0478	84.6492
3	7.8639	8.8685	75.7807
4	6.9596	9.7728	66.0079
5	5.9629	10.7695	55.2384
6	4.8647	11.8677	43.3707
7	3.6545	13.0779	30.2928
8	2.3208	14.4116	15.8812
9	.8512	15.8812	0.0000

YEARS 10 — MO PAYT 1.3077 — AN CONST 15.70

#	INT	PRIN	BALANCE
1	9.4771	6.2153	93.7847
2	8.8433	6.8491	86.9356
3	8.1448	7.5476	79.3880
4	7.3752	8.3173	71.0707
5	6.5270	9.1654	61.9053
6	5.5923	10.1001	51.8052
7	4.5623	11.1301	40.6751
8	3.4273	12.2651	28.4100
9	2.1766	13.5159	14.8942
10	.7983	14.8942	0.0000

YEARS 11 — MO PAYT 1.2379 — AN CONST 14.86

#	INT	PRIN	BALANCE
1	9.5156	5.3390	94.6610
2	8.9711	5.8835	88.7775
3	8.3712	6.4835	82.2941
4	7.7100	7.1446	75.1495
5	6.9814	7.8732	67.2762
6	6.1785	8.6761	58.6002
7	5.2938	9.5609	49.0393
8	4.3188	10.5358	38.5035
9	3.2443	11.6103	26.8932
10	2.0604	12.7942	14.0990
11	.7556	14.0990	0.0000

YEARS 12 — MO PAYT 1.1807 — AN CONST 14.17

#	INT	PRIN	BALANCE
1	9.5471	4.6211	95.3789
2	9.0759	5.0923	90.2867
3	8.5566	5.6116	84.6751
4	7.9843	6.1838	78.4912
5	7.3537	6.8145	71.6768
6	6.6588	7.5094	64.1674
7	5.8930	8.2752	55.8922
8	5.0491	9.1190	46.7732
9	4.1192	10.0490	36.7242
10	3.0944	11.0737	25.6505
11	1.9652	12.2030	13.4474
12	.7207	13.4474	0.0000

YEARS 13 — MO PAYT 1.1332 — AN CONST 13.60

#	INT	PRIN	BALANCE
1	9.5733	4.0246	95.9754
2	9.1629	4.4351	91.5403
3	8.7106	4.8873	86.6529
4	8.2122	5.3857	81.2672
5	7.6630	5.9350	75.3322
6	7.0577	6.5402	68.7920
7	6.3908	7.2072	61.5849
8	5.6558	7.9421	53.6427
9	4.8459	8.7520	44.8907
10	3.9534	9.6445	35.2462
11	2.9699	10.6281	24.6181
12	1.8861	11.7119	12.9062
13	.6917	12.9062	0.0000

YEARS 14 — MO PAYT 1.0932 — AN CONST 13.12

#	INT	PRIN	BALANCE
1	9.5953	3.5235	96.4765
2	9.2360	3.8828	92.5936
3	8.8400	4.2788	88.3148
4	8.4037	4.7151	83.5997
5	7.9228	5.1960	78.4037
6	7.3930	5.7258	72.6779
7	6.8091	6.3098	66.3681
8	6.1656	6.9532	59.4149
9	5.4565	7.6623	51.7526
10	4.6752	8.4437	43.3090
11	3.8141	9.3047	34.0043
12	2.8652	10.2536	23.7507
13	1.8196	11.2992	12.4515
14	.6673	12.4515	0.0000

YEARS 15 — MO PAYT 1.0594 — AN CONST 12.72

#	INT	PRIN	BALANCE
1	9.6140	3.0984	96.9016
2	9.2980	3.4143	93.4873
3	8.9498	3.7625	89.7247
4	8.5661	4.1462	85.5785
5	8.1433	4.5690	81.0095
6	7.6774	5.0350	75.9745
7	7.1639	5.5484	70.4260
8	6.5981	6.1143	64.3118
9	5.9746	6.7378	57.5740
10	5.2875	7.4249	50.1491
11	4.5303	8.1820	41.9671
12	3.6959	9.0164	32.9507
13	2.7765	9.9359	23.0148
14	1.7632	10.9491	12.0657
15	.6467	12.0657	0.0000

YEARS 16 — MO PAYT 1.0304 — AN CONST 12.37

#	INT	PRIN	BALANCE
1	9.6299	2.7348	97.2652
2	9.3510	3.0137	94.2516
3	9.0437	3.3210	90.9306
4	8.7051	3.6596	87.2710
5	8.3319	4.0328	83.2381
6	7.9206	4.4441	78.7940
7	7.4674	4.8973	73.8967
8	6.9680	5.3967	68.5000
9	6.4177	5.9470	62.5530
10	5.8112	6.5535	55.9995
11	5.1429	7.2218	48.7777
12	4.4064	7.9583	40.8194
13	3.5949	8.7698	32.0496
14	2.7005	9.6642	22.3854
15	1.7150	10.6497	11.7357
16	.6290	11.7357	0.0000

YEARS 17 — MO PAYT 1.0054 — AN CONST 12.07

#	INT	PRIN	BALANCE
1	9.6437	2.4216	97.5784
2	9.3967	2.6685	94.9099
3	9.1246	2.9407	91.9692
4	8.8247	3.2406	88.7286
5	8.4943	3.5710	85.1576
6	8.1301	3.9352	81.2224
7	7.7288	4.3365	76.8860
8	7.2866	4.7787	72.1073
9	6.7993	5.2660	66.8413
10	6.2622	5.8030	61.0382
11	5.6705	6.3948	54.6434
12	5.0183	7.0469	47.5965
13	4.2997	7.7656	39.8309
14	3.5078	8.5575	31.2735
15	2.6351	9.4301	21.8433
16	1.6735	10.3918	11.4515
17	.6138	11.4515	0.0000

YEARS 18 — MO PAYT .9838 — AN CONST 11.81

#	INT	PRIN	BALANCE
1	9.6556	2.1502	97.8498
2	9.4363	2.3695	95.4802
3	9.1947	2.6112	92.8691
4	8.9284	2.8774	89.9916
5	8.6350	3.1709	86.8208
6	8.3116	3.4942	83.3265
7	7.9553	3.8506	79.4760
8	7.5626	4.2432	75.2327
9	7.1299	4.6759	70.5568
10	6.6531	5.1528	65.4040
11	6.1276	5.6783	59.7257
12	5.5485	6.2573	53.4684
13	4.9104	6.8954	46.5730
14	4.2073	7.5986	38.9745
15	3.4324	8.3735	30.6010
16	2.5785	9.2274	21.3736
17	1.6375	10.1683	11.2053
18	.6006	11.2053	0.0000

YEARS 19 — MO PAYT .9650 — AN CONST 11.58

#	INT	PRIN	BALANCE
1	9.6660	1.9139	98.0861
2	9.4708	2.1091	95.9770
3	9.2557	2.3242	93.6528
4	9.0187	2.5612	91.0916
5	8.7575	2.8224	88.2693
6	8.4697	3.1102	85.1591
7	8.1525	3.4274	81.7317
8	7.8030	3.7769	77.9549
9	7.4179	4.1620	73.7928
10	6.9934	4.5865	69.2064
11	6.5257	5.0542	64.1522
12	6.0103	5.5696	58.5826
13	5.4423	6.1375	52.4451
14	4.8165	6.7634	45.6817
15	4.1267	7.4531	38.2285
16	3.3667	8.2132	30.0153
17	2.5291	9.0508	20.9646
18	1.6062	9.9737	10.9908
19	.5891	10.9908	0.0000

YEARS 20 — MO PAYT .9485 — AN CONST 11.39

#	INT	PRIN	BALANCE
1	9.6750	1.7072	98.2928
2	9.5010	1.8812	96.4116
3	9.3091	2.0731	94.3385
4	9.0977	2.2845	92.0540
5	8.8647	2.5175	89.5366
6	8.6080	2.7742	86.7624
7	8.3251	3.0571	83.7053
8	8.0134	3.3688	80.3364
9	7.6698	3.7124	76.6240
10	7.2912	4.0910	72.5331
11	6.8740	4.5082	68.0249
12	6.4143	4.9679	63.0570
13	5.9077	5.4745	57.5826
14	5.3494	6.0328	51.5498
15	4.7342	6.6480	44.9018
16	4.0563	7.3259	37.5759
17	3.3092	8.0730	29.5029
18	2.4860	8.8963	20.6067
19	1.5787	9.8035	10.8032
20	.5790	10.8032	0.0000

YEARS 21 — MO PAYT .9340 — AN CONST 11.21

#	INT	PRIN	BALANCE
1	9.6830	1.5255	98.4745
2	9.5275	1.6811	96.7934
3	9.3560	1.8525	94.9408

MONTHLY PAYMENT AMORTIZATION SCHEDULE PER $100   9.75 %

#	INT	PRIN	BALANCE
4	9.1671	2.0415	92.8993
5	8.9589	2.2496	90.6497
6	8.7295	2.4791	88.1706
7	8.4767	2.7319	85.4388
8	8.1981	3.0105	82.4283
9	7.8911	3.3175	79.1109
10	7.5528	3.6558	75.4551
11	7.1800	4.0286	71.4266
12	6.7692	4.4394	66.9872
13	6.3165	4.8921	62.0951
14	5.8176	5.3910	56.7041
15	5.2678	5.9407	50.7634
16	4.6620	6.5466	44.2168
17	3.9944	7.2142	37.0027
18	3.2587	7.9498	29.0528
19	2.4480	8.7605	20.2923
20	1.5547	9.6539	10.6384
21	.5702	10.6384	0.0000

YEARS 22   MO PAYT .9213   AN CONST 11.06

#	INT	PRIN	BALANCE
1	9.6901	1.3655	98.6345
2	9.5508	1.5047	97.1298
3	9.3974	1.6582	95.4717
4	9.2283	1.8272	93.6444
5	9.0419	2.0136	91.6308
6	8.8366	2.2189	89.4119
7	8.6103	2.4452	86.9667
8	8.3610	2.6946	84.2721
9	8.0862	2.9693	81.3028
10	7.7834	3.2722	78.0306
11	7.4497	3.6058	74.4248
12	7.0820	3.9736	70.4513
13	6.6768	4.3788	66.0725
14	6.2302	4.8253	61.2472
15	5.7381	5.3174	55.9298
16	5.1959	5.8596	50.0702
17	4.5984	6.4572	43.6131
18	3.9399	7.1156	36.4974
19	3.2142	7.8413	28.6561
20	2.4146	8.6409	20.0152
21	1.5334	9.5221	10.4931
22	.5624	10.4931	0.0000

YEARS 23   MO PAYT .9100   AN CONST 10.93

#	INT	PRIN	BALANCE
1	9.6963	1.2239	98.7761
2	9.5715	1.3488	97.4273
3	9.4339	1.4863	95.9410
4	9.2823	1.6379	94.3032
5	9.1153	1.8049	92.4983
6	8.9313	1.9889	90.5093
7	8.7284	2.1918	88.3176
8	8.5049	2.4153	85.9023
9	8.2586	2.6616	83.2407
10	7.9872	2.9330	80.3077
11	7.6881	3.2321	77.0756
12	7.3585	3.5617	73.5139
13	6.9953	3.9249	69.5890
14	6.5950	4.3252	65.2638
15	6.1540	4.7662	60.4976
16	5.6679	5.2523	55.2453
17	5.1323	5.7879	49.4574
18	4.5421	6.3781	43.0793
19	3.8916	7.0286	36.0507
20	3.1749	7.7453	28.3054
21	2.3850	8.5352	19.7702
22	1.5147	9.4055	10.3647
23	.5555	10.3647	0.0000

YEARS 24   MO PAYT .9000   AN CONST 10.81

#	INT	PRIN	BALANCE
1	9.7018	1.0985	98.9015
2	9.5898	1.2105	97.6910
3	9.4663	1.3339	96.3571
4	9.3303	1.4700	94.8871
5	9.1804	1.6199	93.2673
6	9.0152	1.7851	91.4822
7	8.8332	1.9671	89.5151
8	8.6326	2.1677	87.3474
9	8.4115	2.3887	84.9587
10	8.1679	2.6323	82.3263
11	7.8995	2.9008	79.4255
12	7.6036	3.1966	76.2289
13	7.2777	3.5226	72.7064
14	6.9184	3.8818	68.8246
15	6.5226	4.2777	64.5469
16	6.0864	4.7139	59.8330
17	5.6057	5.1946	54.6384
18	5.0759	5.7243	48.9141
19	4.4922	6.3081	42.6060
20	3.8489	6.9513	35.6547
21	3.1400	7.6602	27.9945
22	2.3588	8.4414	19.5531
23	1.4980	9.3022	10.2508
24	.5494	10.2508	0.0000

YEARS 25   MO PAYT .8911   AN CONST 10.70

#	INT	PRIN	BALANCE
1	9.7067	.9870	99.0130
2	9.6060	1.0876	97.9254
3	9.4951	1.1985	96.7268
4	9.3729	1.3208	95.4061
5	9.2382	1.4555	93.9506
6	9.0898	1.6039	92.3467
7	8.9262	1.7674	90.5793
8	8.7460	1.9477	88.6316
9	8.5474	2.1463	86.4853
10	8.3285	2.3652	84.1201
11	8.0873	2.6064	81.5138
12	7.8215	2.8722	78.6416
13	7.5286	3.1650	75.4766
14	7.2058	3.4878	71.9888
15	6.8502	3.8435	68.1453
16	6.4582	4.2354	63.9098
17	6.0263	4.6674	59.2425
18	5.5503	5.1433	54.0992
19	5.0258	5.6678	48.4313
20	4.4478	6.2458	42.1855
21	3.8109	6.8827	35.3028
22	3.1090	7.5846	27.7182
23	2.3356	8.3581	19.3601
24	1.4832	9.2104	10.1497
25	.5440	10.1497	0.0000

YEARS 26   MO PAYT .8832   AN CONST 10.60

#	INT	PRIN	BALANCE
1	9.7110	.8877	99.1123
2	9.6205	.9782	98.1341
3	9.5207	1.0780	97.0561
4	9.4108	1.1879	95.8682
5	9.2897	1.3090	94.5592
6	9.1562	1.4425	93.1166
7	9.0091	1.5896	91.5270
8	8.8470	1.7518	89.7752
9	8.6683	1.9304	87.8448
10	8.4715	2.1272	85.7176
11	8.2545	2.3442	83.3734
12	8.0155	2.5832	80.7902
13	7.7521	2.8467	77.9435
14	7.4618	3.1370	74.8066
15	7.1419	3.4569	71.3497
16	6.7894	3.8094	67.5404
17	6.4009	4.1978	63.3425
18	5.9728	4.6259	58.7166
19	5.5011	5.0977	53.6189
20	4.9812	5.6175	48.0014
21	4.4084	6.1904	41.8111
22	3.7771	6.8216	34.9894
23	3.0814	7.5173	27.4721
24	2.3148	8.2839	19.1882
25	1.4701	9.1287	10.0596
26	.5392	10.0596	0.0000

YEARS 27   MO PAYT .8762   AN CONST 10.52

#	INT	PRIN	BALANCE
1	9.7149	.7991	99.2009
2	9.6334	.8806	98.3203
3	9.5436	.9704	97.3499
4	9.4447	1.0694	96.2805
5	9.3356	1.1784	95.1021
6	9.2154	1.2986	93.8035
7	9.0830	1.4310	92.3725
8	8.9371	1.5769	90.7956
9	8.7763	1.7378	89.0578
10	8.5991	1.9150	87.1429
11	8.4038	2.1102	85.0326
12	8.1886	2.3254	82.7072
13	7.9514	2.5626	80.1446
14	7.6901	2.8239	77.3207
15	7.4021	3.1119	74.2088
16	7.0848	3.4292	70.7796
17	6.7351	3.7789	67.0006
18	6.3497	4.1643	62.8363
19	5.9251	4.5890	58.2474
20	5.4571	5.0569	53.1905
21	4.9414	5.5726	47.6178
22	4.3731	6.1409	41.4769
23	3.7469	6.7671	34.7098
24	3.0568	7.4572	27.2526
25	2.2963	8.2177	19.0349
26	1.4583	9.0557	9.9792
27	.5348	9.9792	0.0000

YEARS 28   MO PAYT .8699   AN CONST 10.44

#	INT	PRIN	BALANCE
1	9.7184	.7199	99.2801
2	9.6450	.7934	98.4867
3	9.5641	.8743	97.6124
4	9.4749	.9634	96.6490
5	9.3767	1.0617	95.5874
6	9.2684	1.1699	94.4174
7	9.1491	1.2892	93.1282
8	9.0176	1.4207	91.7075
9	8.8727	1.5656	90.1419
10	8.7131	1.7252	88.4167
11	8.5372	1.9012	86.5155
12	8.3433	2.0951	84.4204
13	8.1296	2.3087	82.1117
14	7.8942	2.5441	79.5676
15	7.6348	2.8036	76.7640
16	7.3489	3.0895	73.6745
17	7.0338	3.4045	70.2700
18	6.6866	3.7517	66.5183
19	6.3040	4.1343	62.3840
20	5.8824	4.5559	57.8280
21	5.4178	5.0205	52.8075
22	4.9058	5.5325	47.2750
23	4.3416	6.0967	41.1783
24	3.7199	6.7184	34.4599
25	3.0348	7.4035	27.0564
26	2.2798	8.1585	18.8979
27	1.4478	8.9905	9.9073
28	.5310	9.9073	0.0000

YEARS 29   MO PAYT .8642   AN CONST 10.38

#	INT	PRIN	BALANCE
1	9.7215	.6491	99.3509
2	9.6553	.7153	98.6357
3	9.5824	.7882	97.8474
4	9.5020	.8686	96.9789
5	9.4134	.9572	96.0217
6	9.3158	1.0548	94.9669
7	9.2082	1.1623	93.8046
8	9.0897	1.2809	92.5237
9	8.9591	1.4115	91.1122
10	8.8152	1.5554	89.5568
11	8.6565	1.7140	87.8428
12	8.4817	1.8888	85.9539
13	8.2891	2.0815	83.8725
14	8.0769	2.2937	81.5788
15	7.8430	2.5276	79.0511
16	7.5852	2.7854	76.2658
17	7.3012	3.0694	73.1963
18	6.9881	3.3824	69.8139
19	6.6432	3.7274	66.0865
20	6.2631	4.1075	61.9790
21	5.8442	4.5263	57.4527
22	5.3826	4.9879	52.4648
23	4.8740	5.4966	46.9682
24	4.3135	6.0571	40.9110
25	3.6958	6.6748	34.2362
26	3.0151	7.3555	26.8808
27	2.2650	8.1056	18.7752
28	1.4384	8.9322	9.8430
29	.5275	9.8430	0.0000

YEARS 30   MO PAYT .8592   AN CONST 10.31

#	INT	PRIN	BALANCE
1	9.7243	.5856	99.4144
2	9.6646	.6453	98.7692
3	9.5988	.7111	98.0581
4	9.5263	.7836	97.2745
5	9.4464	.8635	96.4110
6	9.3583	.9516	95.4594
7	9.2613	1.0486	94.4108
8	9.1543	1.1555	93.2553
9	9.0365	1.2734	91.9819
10	8.9066	1.4032	90.5787
11	8.7635	1.5463	89.0324
12	8.6058	1.7040	87.3284
13	8.4321	1.8778	85.4506
14	8.2406	2.0693	83.3814
15	8.0296	2.2803	81.1011
16	7.7970	2.5128	78.5882
17	7.5408	2.7691	75.8192
18	7.2584	3.0515	72.7677
19	6.9472	3.3626	69.4051
20	6.6043	3.7055	65.6995
21	6.2264	4.0834	61.6161
22	5.8100	4.4998	57.1163
23	5.3511	4.9587	52.1575
24	4.8455	5.4644	46.6931
25	4.2882	6.0216	40.6715
26	3.6741	6.6357	34.0358
27	2.9974	7.3124	26.7234
28	2.2517	8.0581	18.6652
29	1.4300	8.8799	9.7854
30	.5245	9.7854	0.0000

YEARS 2 — MO PAYT 4.6053 — AN CONST 55.27

#	INT	PRIN	BALANCE
1	7.7013	47.5619	52.4381
2	2.8251	52.4381	0.0000

YEARS 3 — MO PAYT 3.2173 — AN CONST 38.61

#	INT	PRIN	BALANCE
1	8.4702	30.1379	69.8621
2	5.3803	33.2277	36.6344
3	1.9737	36.6344	0.0000

YEARS 4 — MO PAYT 2.5267 — AN CONST 30.32

#	INT	PRIN	BALANCE
1	8.8528	21.4672	78.5328
2	6.6519	23.6681	54.8647
3	4.2253	26.0947	28.7700
4	1.5500	28.7700	0.0000

YEARS 5 — MO PAYT 2.1149 — AN CONST 25.38

#	INT	PRIN	BALANCE
1	9.0809	16.2977	83.7023
2	7.4100	17.9686	65.7338
3	5.5678	19.8108	45.9230
4	3.5367	21.8418	24.0812
5	1.2974	24.0812	0.0000

YEARS 6 — MO PAYT 1.8425 — AN CONST 22.12

#	INT	PRIN	BALANCE
1	9.2317	12.8784	87.1216
2	7.9114	14.1988	72.9228
3	6.4557	15.6545	57.2683
4	4.8507	17.2595	40.0088
5	3.0812	19.0290	20.9799
6	1.1303	20.9799	0.0000

YEARS 7 — MO PAYT 1.6498 — AN CONST 19.80

#	INT	PRIN	BALANCE
1	9.3385	10.4591	89.5409
2	8.2662	11.5315	78.0094
3	7.0839	12.7137	65.2957
4	5.7805	14.0172	51.2785
5	4.3434	15.4543	35.8243
6	2.7589	17.0387	18.7856
7	1.0121	18.7856	0.0000

YEARS 8 — MO PAYT 1.5069 — AN CONST 18.09

#	INT	PRIN	BALANCE
1	9.4177	8.6646	91.3354
2	8.5293	9.5529	81.7825
3	7.5499	10.5323	71.2502
4	6.4701	11.6121	59.6381
5	5.2796	12.8026	46.8355
6	3.9670	14.1152	32.7202
7	2.5199	15.5624	17.1579
8	.9244	17.1579	0.0000

YEARS 9 — MO PAYT 1.3971 — AN CONST 16.77

#	INT	PRIN	BALANCE
1	9.4785	7.2862	92.7138
2	8.7315	8.0333	84.6805
3	7.9079	8.8569	75.8236
4	6.9998	9.7649	66.0587
5	5.9987	10.7660	55.2927
6	4.8949	11.8698	43.4229
7	3.6780	13.0867	30.3362
8	2.3363	14.4285	15.9077
9	.8570	15.9077	0.0000

YEARS 10 — MO PAYT 1.3105 — AN CONST 15.73

#	INT	PRIN	BALANCE
1	9.5265	6.1990	93.8010
2	8.8909	6.8346	86.9664
3	8.1902	7.5353	79.4311
4	7.4177	8.3078	71.1233
5	6.5659	9.1596	61.9638
6	5.6268	10.0986	51.8651
7	4.5915	11.1340	40.7311
8	3.4500	12.2755	28.4556
9	2.1915	13.5340	14.9216
10	.8039	14.9216	0.0000

YEARS 11 — MO PAYT 1.2407 — AN CONST 14.89

#	INT	PRIN	BALANCE
1	9.5651	5.3233	94.6767
2	9.0193	5.8690	88.8077
3	8.4176	6.4707	82.3370
4	7.7542	7.1342	75.2028
5	7.0228	7.8656	67.3372
6	6.2164	8.6720	58.6653
7	5.3273	9.5611	49.1042
8	4.3471	10.5413	38.5629
9	3.2663	11.6220	26.9408
10	2.0748	12.8136	14.1273
11	.7611	14.1273	0.0000

YEARS 12 — MO PAYT 1.1836 — AN CONST 14.21

#	INT	PRIN	BALANCE
1	9.5968	4.6059	95.3941
2	9.1246	5.0781	90.3160
3	8.6039	5.5987	84.7173
4	8.0299	6.1727	78.5446
5	7.3971	6.8056	71.7391
6	6.6993	7.5033	64.2358
7	5.9301	8.2726	55.9632
8	5.0819	9.1207	46.8425
9	4.1469	10.0558	36.7867
10	3.1159	11.0867	25.7000
11	1.9792	12.2234	13.4766
12	.7260	13.4766	0.0000

YEARS 13 — MO PAYT 1.1361 — AN CONST 13.64

#	INT	PRIN	BALANCE
1	9.6231	4.0100	95.9900
2	9.2119	4.4212	91.5688
3	8.7587	4.8745	86.6943
4	8.2589	5.3742	81.3201
5	7.7079	5.9252	75.3949
6	7.1004	6.5327	68.8623
7	6.4307	7.2024	61.6599
8	5.6923	7.9408	53.7191
9	4.8782	8.7550	44.9641
10	3.9806	9.6525	35.3116
11	2.9909	10.6422	24.6694
12	1.8999	11.7332	12.9362
13	.6969	12.9362	0.0000

YEARS 14 — MO PAYT 1.0962 — AN CONST 13.16

#	INT	PRIN	BALANCE
1	9.6451	3.5095	96.4905
2	9.2853	3.8693	92.6212
3	8.8886	4.2660	88.3552
4	8.4513	4.7034	83.6518
5	7.9691	5.1856	78.4662
6	7.4374	5.7172	72.7490
7	6.8513	6.3034	66.4456
8	6.2050	6.9496	59.4959
9	5.4925	7.6621	51.8338
10	4.7070	8.4477	43.3861
11	3.8409	9.3138	34.0723
12	2.8860	10.2687	23.8036
13	1.8332	11.3215	12.4822
14	.6725	12.4822	0.0000

YEARS 15 — MO PAYT 1.0624 — AN CONST 12.75

#	INT	PRIN	BALANCE
1	9.6639	3.0850	96.9150
2	9.3476	3.4012	93.5138
3	8.9989	3.7499	89.7639
4	8.6144	4.1344	85.6294
5	8.1906	4.5583	81.0712
6	7.7232	5.0256	76.0455
7	7.2080	5.5409	70.5047
8	6.6399	6.1089	64.3957
9	6.0136	6.7352	57.6605
10	5.3231	7.4258	50.2347
11	4.5617	8.1871	42.0476
12	3.7224	9.0265	33.0212
13	2.7969	9.9519	23.0693
14	1.7766	10.9722	12.0971
15	.6517	12.0971	0.0000

YEARS 16 — MO PAYT 1.0335 — AN CONST 12.41

#	INT	PRIN	BALANCE
1	9.6799	2.7219	97.2781
2	9.4008	3.0010	94.2771
3	9.0932	3.3087	90.9684
4	8.7539	3.6479	87.3205
5	8.3799	4.0219	83.2987
6	7.9676	4.4342	78.8645
7	7.5130	4.8888	73.9756
8	7.0118	5.3900	68.5856
9	6.4592	5.9427	62.6429
10	5.8499	6.5519	56.0910
11	5.1782	7.2236	48.8674
12	4.4376	7.9642	40.9031
13	3.6211	8.7808	32.1224
14	2.7208	9.6810	22.4414
15	1.7283	10.6735	11.7678
16	.6340	11.7678	0.0000

YEARS 17 — MO PAYT 1.0086 — AN CONST 12.11

#	INT	PRIN	BALANCE
1	9.6937	2.4093	97.5907
2	9.4467	2.6563	94.9343
3	9.1743	2.9287	92.0056
4	8.8741	3.2289	88.7767
5	8.5430	3.5600	85.2167
6	8.1780	3.9250	81.2917
7	7.7756	4.3274	76.9644
8	7.3320	4.7710	72.1933
9	6.8428	5.2602	66.9331
10	6.3035	5.7995	61.1337
11	5.7090	6.3941	54.7396
12	5.0534	7.0496	47.6900
13	4.3307	7.7724	39.9176
14	3.5338	8.5692	31.3484
15	2.6553	9.4478	21.9007
16	1.6866	10.4164	11.4843
17	.6187	11.4843	0.0000

YEARS 18 — MO PAYT .9870 — AN CONST 11.85

#	INT	PRIN	BALANCE
1	9.7056	2.1386	97.8614
2	9.4864	2.3578	95.5036
3	9.2447	2.5995	92.9041
4	8.9781	2.8661	90.0380
5	8.6843	3.1599	86.8782
6	8.3603	3.4839	83.3943
7	8.0032	3.8410	79.5533
8	7.6094	4.2348	75.3184
9	7.1752	4.6690	70.6494
10	6.6965	5.1477	65.5017
11	6.1687	5.6754	59.8263
12	5.5869	6.2573	53.5690
13	4.9453	6.8988	46.6701
14	4.2380	7.6061	39.0640
15	3.4582	8.3860	30.6780
16	2.5985	9.2457	21.4323
17	1.6506	10.1936	11.2387
18	.6055	11.2387	0.0000

YEARS 19 — MO PAYT .9682 — AN CONST 11.62

#	INT	PRIN	BALANCE
1	9.7160	1.9028	98.0972
2	9.5210	2.0979	95.9994
3	9.3059	2.3129	93.6864
4	9.0687	2.5501	91.1363
5	8.8073	2.8115	88.3248
6	8.5191	3.0998	85.2251
7	8.2013	3.4176	81.8075
8	7.8509	3.7679	78.0395
9	7.4646	4.1543	73.8853
10	7.0387	4.5802	69.3051
11	6.5691	5.0497	64.2554
12	6.0514	5.5675	58.6879
13	5.4806	6.1383	52.5497
14	4.8512	6.7676	45.7821
15	4.1574	7.4614	38.3207
16	3.3924	8.2264	30.0943
17	2.5490	9.0698	21.0245
18	1.6192	9.9997	11.0249
19	.5940	11.0249	0.0000

YEARS 20 — MO PAYT .9518 — AN CONST 11.43

#	INT	PRIN	BALANCE
1	9.7251	1.6966	98.3034
2	9.5512	1.8705	96.4329
3	9.3594	2.0623	94.3707
4	9.1480	2.2737	92.0970
5	8.9149	2.5068	89.5902
6	8.6579	2.7638	86.8263
7	8.3745	3.0472	83.7792
8	8.0621	3.3596	80.4196
9	7.7177	3.7040	76.7156
10	7.3379	4.0838	72.6318
11	6.9192	4.5025	68.1293
12	6.4576	4.9641	63.1653
13	5.9487	5.4730	57.6922
14	5.3876	6.0341	51.6581
15	4.7689	6.6528	45.0054
16	4.0869	7.3348	37.6706
17	3.3349	8.0868	29.5837
18	2.5058	8.9159	20.6678
19	1.5917	9.8300	10.8378
20	.5839	10.8378	0.0000

YEARS 21 — MO PAYT .9374 — AN CONST 11.25

#	INT	PRIN	BALANCE
1	9.7331	1.5155	98.4845
2	9.5778	1.6709	96.8137
3	9.4065	1.8422	94.9715

MONTHLY PAYMENT AMORTIZATION SCHEDULE PER $100   9.80 %

#	INT	PRIN	BALANCE
4	9.2176	2.0310	92.9405
5	9.0094	2.2392	90.7013
6	8.7798	2.4688	88.2324
7	8.5267	2.7219	85.5105
8	8.2476	3.0010	82.5095
9	7.9399	3.3087	79.2008
10	7.6007	3.6479	75.5529
11	7.2267	4.0219	71.5311
12	6.8144	4.4342	67.0968
13	6.3598	4.8888	62.2080
14	5.8585	5.3901	56.8179
15	5.3059	5.9427	50.8753
16	4.6967	6.5519	44.3233
17	4.0249	7.2237	37.0997
18	3.2843	7.9643	29.1354
19	2.4678	8.7808	20.3546
20	1.5676	9.6810	10.6736
21	.5750	10.6736	0.0000

YEARS 22 MO PAYT .9247 AN CONST 11.10

#	INT	PRIN	BALANCE
1	9.7402	1.3559	98.6441
2	9.6012	1.4949	97.1492
3	9.4479	1.6482	95.5010
4	9.2789	1.8172	93.6838
5	9.0926	2.0035	91.6803
6	8.8872	2.2089	89.4714
7	8.6607	2.4353	87.0361
8	8.4111	2.6850	84.3511
9	8.1358	2.9603	81.3907
10	7.8323	3.2638	78.1269
11	7.4977	3.5984	74.5285
12	7.1287	3.9674	70.5612
13	6.7220	4.3741	66.1871
14	6.2735	4.8225	61.3645
15	5.7791	5.3170	56.0475
16	5.2340	5.8621	50.1854
17	4.6330	6.4631	43.7223
18	3.9704	7.1257	36.5966
19	3.2398	7.8563	28.7403
20	2.4344	8.6617	20.0786
21	1.5463	9.5498	10.5288
22	.5672	10.5288	0.0000

YEARS 23 MO PAYT .9134 AN CONST 10.97

#	INT	PRIN	BALANCE
1	9.7464	1.2149	98.7851
2	9.6218	1.3394	97.4457
3	9.4845	1.4768	95.9689
4	9.3331	1.6282	94.3407
5	9.1662	1.7951	92.5456
6	8.9821	1.9791	90.5665
7	8.7792	2.1820	88.3844
8	8.5555	2.4058	85.9787
9	8.3089	2.6524	83.3263
10	8.0369	2.9243	80.4019
11	7.7371	3.2242	77.1778
12	7.4066	3.5547	73.6231
13	7.0421	3.9192	69.7039
14	6.6403	4.3210	65.3830
15	6.1973	4.7640	60.6190
16	5.7089	5.2524	55.3666
17	5.1704	5.7909	49.5757
18	4.5767	6.3846	43.1912
19	3.9221	7.0392	36.1520
20	3.2004	7.7608	28.3912
21	2.4048	8.5565	19.8347
22	1.5275	9.4337	10.4009
23	.5603	10.4009	0.0000

YEARS 24 MO PAYT .9035 AN CONST 10.85

#	INT	PRIN	BALANCE
1	9.7519	1.0899	98.9101
2	9.6402	1.2016	97.7084
3	9.5170	1.3248	96.3836
4	9.3811	1.4607	94.9229
5	9.2314	1.6104	93.3125
6	9.0663	1.7755	91.5370
7	8.8842	1.9576	89.5794
8	8.6835	2.1583	87.4211
9	8.4623	2.3795	85.0416
10	8.2183	2.6235	82.4181
11	7.9493	2.8925	79.5256
12	7.6528	3.1890	76.3366
13	7.3258	3.5160	72.8207
14	6.9654	3.8764	68.9442
15	6.5679	4.2739	64.6703
16	6.1298	4.7120	59.9583
17	5.6467	5.1951	54.7632
18	5.1141	5.7278	49.0354
19	4.5268	6.3150	42.7204
20	3.8794	6.9624	35.7580
21	3.1656	7.6762	28.0817
22	2.3786	8.4632	19.6185
23	1.5109	9.3309	10.2876
24	.5542	10.2876	0.0000

YEARS 25 MO PAYT .8946 AN CONST 10.74

#	INT	PRIN	BALANCE
1	9.7568	.9789	99.0211
2	9.6654	1.0792	97.9419
3	9.5458	1.1899	96.7520
4	9.4238	1.3119	95.4401
5	9.2893	1.4464	93.9938
6	9.1410	1.5947	92.3991
7	8.9775	1.7582	90.6409
8	8.7973	1.9384	88.7025
9	8.5985	2.1371	86.5654
10	8.3794	2.3562	84.2091
11	8.1379	2.5978	81.6113
12	7.8715	2.8642	78.7472
13	7.5779	3.1578	75.5894
14	7.2541	3.4816	72.1078
15	6.8972	3.8385	68.2693
16	6.5037	4.2320	64.0373
17	6.0698	4.6659	59.3714
18	5.5914	5.1443	54.2271
19	5.0640	5.6717	48.5554
20	4.4825	6.2532	42.3022
21	3.8414	6.8943	35.4080
22	3.1346	7.6011	27.8069
23	2.3553	8.3804	19.4265
24	1.4961	9.2396	10.1869
25	.5488	10.1869	0.0000

YEARS 26 MO PAYT .8868 AN CONST 10.65

#	INT	PRIN	BALANCE
1	9.7612	.8800	99.1200
2	9.6709	.9703	98.1497
3	9.5715	1.0697	97.0800
4	9.4618	1.1794	95.9005
5	9.3409	1.3003	94.6002
6	9.2076	1.4336	93.1666
7	9.0606	1.5806	91.5859
8	8.8985	1.7427	89.8433
9	8.7199	1.9213	87.9219
10	8.5229	2.1183	85.8036
11	8.3057	2.3355	83.4681
12	8.0663	2.5750	80.8931
13	7.8023	2.8390	78.0542
14	7.5112	3.1300	74.9242
15	7.1903	3.4509	71.4732
16	6.8365	3.8047	67.6685
17	6.4464	4.1948	63.4738
18	6.0164	4.6249	58.8489
19	5.5422	5.0990	53.7499
20	5.0194	5.6218	48.1281
21	4.4431	6.1981	41.9300
22	3.8076	6.8336	35.0964
23	3.1070	7.5342	27.5621
24	2.3346	8.3066	19.2555
25	1.4829	9.1583	10.0972
26	.5440	10.0972	0.0000

YEARS 27 MO PAYT .8797 AN CONST 10.56

#	INT	PRIN	BALANCE
1	9.7651	.7919	99.2081
2	9.6839	.8731	98.3350
3	9.5944	.9626	97.3725
4	9.4957	1.0613	96.3112
5	9.3869	1.1701	95.1411
6	9.2669	1.2900	93.8511
7	9.1346	1.4223	92.4288
8	8.9888	1.5681	90.8607
9	8.8281	1.7289	89.1318
10	8.6508	1.9061	87.2257
11	8.4554	2.1016	85.1241
12	8.2399	2.3170	82.8071
13	8.0024	2.5546	80.2525
14	7.7405	2.8165	77.4361
15	7.4517	3.1052	74.3308
16	7.1334	3.4236	70.9073
17	6.7824	3.7746	67.1327
18	6.3954	4.1616	62.9711
19	5.9687	4.5882	58.3829
20	5.4983	5.0586	53.3243
21	4.9797	5.5773	47.7470
22	4.4079	6.1491	41.5979
23	3.7775	6.7795	34.8184
24	3.0824	7.4745	27.3439
25	2.3161	8.2409	19.1030
26	1.4712	9.0858	10.0173
27	.5397	10.0173	0.0000

YEARS 28 MO PAYT .8735 AN CONST 10.49

#	INT	PRIN	BALANCE
1	9.7685	.7131	99.2869
2	9.6954	.7862	98.5006
3	9.6148	.8668	97.6338
4	9.5259	.9557	96.6781
5	9.4280	1.0537	95.6244
6	9.3199	1.1617	94.4627
7	9.2008	1.2808	93.1818
8	9.0695	1.4121	91.7697
9	8.9247	1.5569	90.2127
10	8.7651	1.7166	88.4962
11	8.5891	1.8925	86.6037
12	8.3951	2.0866	84.5171
13	8.1812	2.3005	82.2166
14	7.9453	2.5363	79.6802
15	7.6853	2.7964	76.8839
16	7.3986	3.0831	73.8008
17	7.0825	3.3992	70.4016
18	6.7340	3.7477	66.6539
19	6.3498	4.1319	62.5221
20	5.9261	4.5555	57.9665
21	5.4591	5.0226	52.9440
22	4.9442	5.5375	47.4065
23	4.3764	6.1052	41.3013
24	3.7505	6.7311	34.5701
25	3.0604	7.4212	27.1489
26	2.2996	8.1821	18.9668
27	1.4607	9.0210	9.9458
28	.5358	9.9458	0.0000

YEARS 29 MO PAYT .8679 AN CONST 10.42

#	INT	PRIN	BALANCE
1	9.7716	.6427	99.3573
2	9.7058	.7085	98.6488
3	9.6331	.7812	97.8676
4	9.5530	.8613	97.0064
5	9.4647	.9496	96.0568
6	9.3674	1.0469	95.0098
7	9.2600	1.1543	93.8556
8	9.1417	1.2726	92.5830
9	9.0112	1.4031	91.1799
10	8.8674	1.5469	89.6330
11	8.7088	1.7055	87.9275
12	8.5339	1.8804	86.0471
13	8.3411	2.0732	83.9739
14	8.1286	2.2857	81.6882
15	7.8942	2.5200	79.1682
16	7.6359	2.7784	76.3898
17	7.3510	3.0633	73.3265
18	7.0370	3.3773	69.9492
19	6.6907	3.7236	66.2256
20	6.3090	4.1053	62.1203
21	5.8881	4.5262	57.5940
22	5.4240	4.9903	52.6037
23	4.9124	5.5019	47.1018
24	4.3483	6.0660	41.0359
25	3.7264	6.6879	34.3480
26	3.0407	7.3736	26.9744
27	2.2848	8.1295	18.8449
28	1.4513	8.9630	9.8819
29	.5324	9.8819	0.0000

YEARS 30 MO PAYT .8628 AN CONST 10.36

#	INT	PRIN	BALANCE
1	9.7744	.5795	99.4205
2	9.7150	.6389	98.7816
3	9.6495	.7044	98.0771
4	9.5773	.7767	97.3005
5	9.4977	.8563	96.4442
6	9.4099	.9441	95.5001
7	9.3131	1.0409	94.4593
8	9.2064	1.1476	93.3117
9	9.0887	1.2652	92.0465
10	8.9590	1.3949	90.6515
11	8.8160	1.5380	89.1136
12	8.6583	1.6956	87.4179
13	8.4845	1.8695	85.5484
14	8.2928	2.0611	83.4873
15	8.0815	2.2725	81.2148
16	7.8485	2.5054	78.7094
17	7.5916	2.7623	75.9471
18	7.3084	3.0455	72.9016
19	6.9962	3.3578	69.5438
20	6.6519	3.7020	65.8418
21	6.2724	4.0815	61.7603
22	5.8539	4.5000	57.2603
23	5.3926	4.9614	52.2989
24	4.8839	5.4700	46.8289
25	4.3231	6.0308	40.7981
26	3.7048	6.6491	34.1489
27	3.0231	7.3308	26.8181
28	2.2715	8.0824	18.7357
29	1.4429	8.9110	9.8246
30	.5293	9.8246	0.0000

YEARS 2 — MO PAYT 4.6087 — AN CONST 55.31

#	INT	PRIN	BALANCE
1	7.7614	47.5433	52.4567
2	2.8480	52.4567	0.0000

YEARS 3 — MO PAYT 3.2209 — AN CONST 38.66

#	INT	PRIN	BALANCE
1	8.5362	30.1140	69.8860
2	5.4241	33.2261	36.6599
3	1.9904	36.6599	0.0000

YEARS 4 — MO PAYT 2.5303 — AN CONST 30.37

#	INT	PRIN	BALANCE
1	8.9218	21.4413	78.5587
2	6.7059	23.6572	54.9015
3	4.2611	26.1020	28.7995
4	1.5636	28.7995	0.0000

YEARS 5 — MO PAYT 2.1186 — AN CONST 25.43

#	INT	PRIN	BALANCE
1	9.1516	16.2711	83.7289
2	7.4701	17.9526	65.7763
3	5.6148	19.8079	45.9684
4	3.5678	21.8549	24.1135
5	1.3092	24.1135	0.0000

YEARS 6 — MO PAYT 1.8463 — AN CONST 22.16

#	INT	PRIN	BALANCE
1	9.3036	12.8518	87.1482
2	7.9755	14.1799	72.9683
3	6.5101	15.6454	57.3229
4	4.8932	17.2622	40.0607
5	3.1093	19.0462	21.0145
6	1.1409	21.0145	0.0000

YEARS 7 — MO PAYT 1.6537 — AN CONST 19.85

#	INT	PRIN	BALANCE
1	9.4112	10.4328	89.5672
2	8.3330	11.5110	78.0562
3	7.1434	12.7006	65.3556
4	5.8309	14.0131	51.3425
5	4.3827	15.4613	35.8812
6	2.7849	17.0591	18.8221
7	1.0219	18.8221	0.0000

YEARS 8 — MO PAYT 1.5108 — AN CONST 18.13

#	INT	PRIN	BALANCE
1	9.4909	8.6388	91.3612
2	8.5982	9.5315	81.8297
3	7.6131	10.5166	71.3131
4	6.5263	11.6034	59.7097
5	5.3272	12.8026	46.9071
6	4.0041	14.1256	32.7815
7	2.5443	15.5854	17.1961
8	.9336	17.1961	0.0000

YEARS 9 — MO PAYT 1.4011 — AN CONST 16.82

#	INT	PRIN	BALANCE
1	9.5522	7.2611	92.7389
2	8.8018	8.0115	84.7274
3	7.9739	8.8394	75.8879
4	7.0603	9.7530	66.1350
5	6.0524	10.7609	55.3741
6	4.9404	11.8729	43.5012
7	3.7134	13.0999	30.4012
8	2.3596	14.4538	15.9475
9	.8658	15.9475	0.0000

YEARS 10 — MO PAYT 1.3146 — AN CONST 15.78

#	INT	PRIN	BALANCE
1	9.6005	6.1746	93.8254
2	8.9624	6.8128	87.0126
3	8.2583	7.5168	79.4958
4	7.4815	8.2936	71.2021
5	6.6244	9.1507	62.0514
6	5.6787	10.0964	51.9550
7	4.6353	11.1398	40.8151
8	3.4841	12.2911	28.5241
9	2.2139	13.5613	14.9628
10	.8124	14.9628	0.0000

YEARS 11 — MO PAYT 1.2449 — AN CONST 14.94

#	INT	PRIN	BALANCE
1	9.6394	5.2997	94.7003
2	9.0917	5.8474	88.8529
3	8.4874	6.4517	82.4012
4	7.8207	7.1185	75.2827
5	7.0850	7.8541	67.4286
6	6.2733	8.6658	58.7628
7	5.3778	9.5613	49.2015
8	4.3897	10.5495	38.6520
9	3.2994	11.6397	27.0124
10	2.0965	12.8426	14.1698
11	.7693	14.1698	0.0000

YEARS 12 — MO PAYT 1.1879 — AN CONST 14.26

#	INT	PRIN	BALANCE
1	9.6712	4.5832	95.4168
2	9.1976	5.0568	90.3600
3	8.6750	5.5794	84.7806
4	8.0984	6.1560	78.6246
5	7.4622	6.7922	71.8324
6	6.7603	7.4941	64.3382
7	5.9858	8.2686	56.0696
8	5.1313	9.1231	46.9465
9	4.1885	10.0660	36.8805
10	3.1482	11.1062	25.7743
11	2.0004	12.2540	13.5204
12	.7341	13.5204	0.0000

YEARS 13 — MO PAYT 1.1405 — AN CONST 13.69

#	INT	PRIN	BALANCE
1	9.6977	3.9882	96.0118
2	9.2855	4.4004	91.6114
3	8.8308	4.8551	86.7562
4	8.3290	5.3569	81.3994
5	7.7754	5.9105	75.4889
6	7.1646	6.5213	68.9675
7	6.4907	7.1953	61.7723
8	5.7471	7.9388	53.8334
9	4.9266	8.7593	45.0742
10	4.0214	9.6645	35.4097
11	3.0226	10.6633	24.7464
12	1.9207	11.7653	12.9811
13	.7048	12.9811	0.0000

YEARS 14 — MO PAYT 1.1007 — AN CONST 13.21

#	INT	PRIN	BALANCE
1	9.7199	3.4886	96.5114
2	9.3594	3.8491	92.6623
3	8.9616	4.2469	88.4155
4	8.5227	4.6858	83.7297
5	8.0385	5.1700	78.5597
6	7.5042	5.7043	72.8554
7	6.9147	6.2938	66.5616
8	6.2642	6.9442	59.6173
9	5.5466	7.6619	51.9554
10	4.7548	8.4537	43.5017
11	3.8811	9.3273	34.1744
12	2.9172	10.2913	23.8831
13	1.8537	11.3548	12.5283
14	.6802	12.5283	0.0000

YEARS 15 — MO PAYT 1.0670 — AN CONST 12.81

#	INT	PRIN	BALANCE
1	9.7387	3.0649	96.9351
2	9.4220	3.3816	93.5534
3	9.0725	3.7311	89.8223
4	8.6869	4.1167	85.7056
5	8.2615	4.5422	81.1635
6	7.7921	5.0116	76.1519
7	7.2742	5.5295	70.6224
8	6.7027	6.1009	64.5215
9	6.0722	6.7314	57.7901
10	5.3766	7.4271	50.3630
11	4.6090	8.1946	42.1684
12	3.7622	9.0415	33.1270
13	2.8278	9.9759	23.1511
14	1.7968	11.0068	12.1443
15	.6594	12.1443	0.0000

YEARS 16 — MO PAYT 1.0381 — AN CONST 12.46

#	INT	PRIN	BALANCE
1	9.7548	2.7028	97.2972
2	9.4755	2.9821	94.3152
3	9.1673	3.2903	91.0249
4	8.8273	3.6303	87.3946
5	8.4522	4.0054	83.3892
6	8.0382	4.4194	78.9698
7	7.5815	4.8761	74.0937
8	7.0776	5.3800	68.7137
9	6.5216	5.9360	62.7777
10	5.9081	6.5495	56.2282
11	5.2313	7.2263	49.0019
12	4.4845	7.9731	41.0287
13	3.6605	8.7971	32.2316
14	2.7514	9.7062	22.5254
15	1.7483	10.7093	11.8161
16	.6415	11.8161	0.0000

YEARS 17 — MO PAYT 1.0133 — AN CONST 12.16

#	INT	PRIN	BALANCE
1	9.7687	2.3910	97.6090
2	9.5216	2.6381	94.9708
3	9.2490	2.9108	92.0601
4	8.9482	3.2116	88.8485
5	8.6163	3.5435	85.3050
6	8.2501	3.9097	81.3953
7	7.8460	4.3137	77.0816
8	7.4002	4.7595	72.3221
9	6.9083	5.2514	67.0707
10	6.3656	5.7941	61.2766
11	5.7669	6.3929	54.8837
12	5.1062	7.0535	47.8302
13	4.3772	7.7825	40.0477
14	3.5730	8.5868	31.4610
15	2.6856	9.4742	21.9868
16	1.7065	10.4533	11.5335
17	.6262	11.5335	0.0000

YEARS 18 — MO PAYT .9918 — AN CONST 11.91

#	INT	PRIN	BALANCE
1	9.7807	2.1211	97.8789
2	9.5615	2.3403	95.5386
3	9.3196	2.5822	92.9564
4	9.0528	2.8490	90.1074
5	8.7584	3.1435	86.9639
6	8.4335	3.4683	83.4956
7	8.0751	3.8267	79.6688
8	7.6796	4.2222	75.4466
9	7.2432	4.6586	70.7881
10	6.7618	5.1400	65.6481
11	6.2306	5.6712	59.9769
12	5.6445	6.2573	53.7196
13	4.9979	6.9039	46.8157
14	4.2844	7.6174	39.1983
15	3.4972	8.4046	30.7936
16	2.6286	9.2732	21.5204
17	1.6703	10.2315	11.2889
18	.6129	11.2889	0.0000

YEARS 19 — MO PAYT .9731 — AN CONST 11.68

#	INT	PRIN	BALANCE
1	9.7911	1.8862	98.1138
2	9.5962	2.0811	96.0327
3	9.3812	2.2962	93.7365
4	9.1439	2.5335	91.2031
5	8.8820	2.7953	88.4078
6	8.5932	3.0842	85.3236
7	8.2744	3.4029	81.9207
8	7.9228	3.7546	78.1662
9	7.5347	4.1426	74.0236
10	7.1066	4.5707	69.4529
11	6.6343	5.0431	64.4098
12	6.1131	5.5642	58.8456
13	5.5381	6.1393	52.7064
14	4.9036	6.7737	45.9326
15	4.2036	7.4737	38.4589
16	3.4312	8.2461	30.2128
17	2.5790	9.0983	21.1145
18	1.6388	10.0385	11.0760
19	.6013	11.0760	0.0000

YEARS 20 — MO PAYT .9568 — AN CONST 11.49

#	INT	PRIN	BALANCE
1	9.8003	1.6808	98.3192
2	9.6266	1.8545	96.4647
3	9.4349	2.0461	94.4186
4	9.2235	2.2576	92.1610
5	8.9902	2.4909	89.6702
6	8.7327	2.7483	86.9219
7	8.4487	3.0323	83.8895
8	8.1354	3.3457	80.5438
9	7.7896	3.6915	76.8524
10	7.4081	4.0730	72.7794
11	6.9872	4.4939	68.2855
12	6.5228	4.9583	63.3272
13	6.0104	5.4707	57.8565
14	5.4450	6.0361	51.8205
15	4.8212	6.6599	45.1606
16	4.1329	7.3481	37.8125
17	3.3736	8.1075	29.7050
18	2.5357	8.9454	20.7596
19	1.6112	9.8698	10.8898
20	.5912	10.8898	0.0000

YEARS 21 — MO PAYT .9424 — AN CONST 11.31

#	INT	PRIN	BALANCE
1	9.8083	1.5005	98.4995
2	9.6532	1.6556	96.8440
3	9.4821	1.8266	95.0173

#	INT	PRIN	BALANCE
4	9.2934	2.0154	93.0019
5	9.0851	2.2237	90.7782
6	8.8553	2.4535	88.3247
7	8.6017	2.7071	85.6176
8	8.3220	2.9868	82.6308
9	8.0133	3.2955	79.3353
10	7.6727	3.6361	75.6992
11	7.2969	4.0118	71.6874
12	6.8823	4.4264	67.2609
13	6.4249	4.8839	62.3770
14	5.9202	5.3886	56.9884
15	5.3633	5.9455	51.0429
16	4.7489	6.5599	44.4830
17	4.0709	7.2379	37.2451
18	3.3229	7.9859	29.2593
19	2.4976	8.8111	20.4481
20	1.5871	9.7217	10.7264
21	.5824	10.7264	0.0000

YEARS 22   MO PAYT .9298   AN CONST 11.16

#	INT	PRIN	BALANCE
1	9.8154	1.3417	98.6583
2	9.6747	1.4804	97.1779
3	9.5237	1.6333	95.5446
4	9.3549	1.8021	93.7425
5	9.1687	1.9884	91.7541
6	8.9632	2.1939	89.5602
7	8.7365	2.4206	87.1396
8	8.4863	2.6707	84.4689
9	8.2103	2.9468	81.5221
10	7.9058	3.2513	78.2708
11	7.5698	3.5873	74.6835
12	7.1990	3.9580	70.7255
13	6.7900	4.3671	66.3585
14	6.3387	4.8184	61.5401
15	5.8407	5.3163	56.2238
16	5.2913	5.8657	50.3581
17	4.6851	6.4719	43.8862
18	4.0163	7.1407	36.7454
19	3.2783	7.8787	28.8667
20	2.4641	8.6929	20.1738
21	1.5658	9.5913	10.5825
22	.5746	10.5825	0.0000

YEARS 23   MO PAYT .9186   AN CONST 11.03

#	INT	PRIN	BALANCE
1	9.8216	1.2014	98.7986
2	9.6974	1.3256	97.4730
3	9.5604	1.4626	96.0104
4	9.4093	1.6137	94.3967
5	9.2425	1.7805	92.6162
6	9.0585	1.9645	90.6517
7	8.8555	2.1675	88.4842
8	8.6315	2.3915	86.0927
9	8.3843	2.6387	83.4540
10	8.1117	2.9114	80.5427
11	7.8108	3.2122	77.3305
12	7.4788	3.5442	73.7863
13	7.1125	3.9105	69.8758
14	6.7084	4.3146	65.5612
15	6.2625	4.7605	60.8008
16	5.7706	5.2524	55.5483
17	5.2278	5.7953	49.7531
18	4.6289	6.3942	43.3589
19	3.9681	7.0550	36.3039
20	3.2390	7.7840	28.5199
21	2.4345	8.5885	19.9314
22	1.5470	9.4761	10.4554
23	.5677	10.4554	0.0000

YEARS 24   MO PAYT .9087   AN CONST 10.91

#	INT	PRIN	BALANCE
1	9.8271	1.0772	98.9228
2	9.7158	1.1885	97.7344
3	9.5930	1.3113	96.4231
4	9.4575	1.4468	94.9762
5	9.3079	1.5963	93.3799
6	9.1430	1.7613	91.6186
7	8.9609	1.9433	89.6753
8	8.7601	2.1442	87.5311
9	8.5385	2.3658	85.1653
10	8.2940	2.6102	82.5551
11	8.0243	2.8800	79.6751
12	7.7267	3.1776	76.4975
13	7.3983	3.5060	72.9915
14	7.0359	3.8683	69.1231
15	6.6362	4.2681	64.8550
16	6.1951	4.7092	60.1458
17	5.7084	5.1959	54.9500
18	5.1714	5.7328	49.2171
19	4.5790	6.3253	42.8919
20	3.9253	6.9790	35.9129
21	3.2041	7.7002	28.2127
22	2.4083	8.4960	19.7167
23	1.5303	9.3740	10.3427
24	.5615	10.3427	0.0000

YEARS 25   MO PAYT .8999   AN CONST 10.80

#	INT	PRIN	BALANCE
1	9.8320	.9668	99.0332
2	9.7321	1.0667	97.9664
3	9.6219	1.1770	96.7894
4	9.5002	1.2986	95.4908
5	9.3660	1.4328	94.0580
6	9.2179	1.5809	92.4771
7	9.0546	1.7443	90.7328
8	8.8743	1.9245	88.8083
9	8.6754	2.1234	86.6848
10	8.4560	2.3429	84.3419
11	8.2138	2.5850	81.7569
12	7.9467	2.8521	78.9048
13	7.6519	3.1469	75.7579
14	7.3267	3.4721	72.2858
15	6.9679	3.8309	68.4548
16	6.5720	4.2268	64.2280
17	6.1352	4.6637	59.5643
18	5.6532	5.1456	54.4187
19	5.1214	5.6774	48.7413
20	4.5347	6.2641	42.4772
21	3.8874	6.9115	35.5657
22	3.1731	7.6258	27.9399
23	2.3850	8.4138	19.5261
24	1.5155	9.2834	10.2427
25	.5561	10.2427	0.0000

YEARS 26   MO PAYT .8921   AN CONST 10.71

#	INT	PRIN	BALANCE
1	9.8364	.8687	99.1313
2	9.7466	.9584	98.1729
3	9.6476	1.0575	97.1154
4	9.5383	1.1668	95.9487
5	9.4177	1.2873	94.6613
6	9.2847	1.4204	93.2409
7	9.1379	1.5672	91.6738
8	8.9759	1.7291	89.9446
9	8.7972	1.9078	88.0368
10	8.6001	2.1050	85.9318
11	8.3825	2.3225	83.6093
12	8.1425	2.5625	81.0467
13	7.8777	2.8274	78.2194
14	7.5855	3.1196	75.0998
15	7.2631	3.4420	71.6579

#	INT	PRIN	BALANCE
16	6.9074	3.7977	67.8602
17	6.5149	4.1901	63.6701
18	6.0819	4.6232	59.0469
19	5.6041	5.1009	53.9460
20	5.0770	5.6281	48.3179
21	4.4953	6.2097	42.1082
22	3.8536	6.8515	35.2567
23	3.1455	7.5595	27.6972
24	2.3643	8.3407	19.3565
25	1.5023	9.2027	10.1538
26	.5513	10.1538	0.0000

YEARS 27   MO PAYT .8851   AN CONST 10.63

#	INT	PRIN	BALANCE
1	9.8403	.7811	99.2189
2	9.7595	.8619	98.3570
3	9.6705	.9509	97.4060
4	9.5722	1.0492	96.3568
5	9.4638	1.1577	95.1992
6	9.3441	1.2773	93.9219
7	9.2121	1.4093	92.5126
8	9.0665	1.5549	90.9577
9	8.9058	1.7156	89.2420
10	8.7285	1.8929	87.3491
11	8.5329	2.0885	85.2606
12	8.3170	2.3044	82.9562
13	8.0789	2.5425	80.4137
14	7.8161	2.8053	77.6084
15	7.5262	3.0952	74.5132
16	7.2064	3.4151	71.0981
17	6.8534	3.7680	67.3301
18	6.4640	4.1574	63.1727
19	6.0344	4.5870	58.5857
20	5.5603	5.0611	53.5246
21	5.0373	5.5841	47.9405
22	4.4602	6.1612	41.7793
23	3.8235	6.7979	34.9813
24	3.1210	7.5005	27.4809
25	2.3458	8.2756	19.2053
26	1.4906	9.1308	10.0744
27	.5470	10.0744	0.0000

YEARS 28   MO PAYT .8789   AN CONST 10.55

#	INT	PRIN	BALANCE
1	9.8437	.7030	99.2970
2	9.7711	.7757	98.5213
3	9.6909	.8558	97.6655
4	9.6025	.9443	96.7213
5	9.5049	1.0418	95.6794
6	9.3972	1.1495	94.5299
7	9.2784	1.2683	93.2616
8	9.1474	1.3994	91.8622
9	9.0028	1.5440	90.3182
10	8.8432	1.7036	88.6147
11	8.6671	1.8796	86.7350
12	8.4729	2.0739	84.6612
13	8.2586	2.2882	82.3730
14	8.0221	2.5247	79.8483
15	7.7612	2.7856	77.0628
16	7.4733	3.0734	73.9893
17	7.1557	3.3911	70.5983
18	6.8052	3.7415	66.8568
19	6.4186	4.1282	62.7286
20	5.9920	4.5548	58.1738
21	5.5212	5.0255	53.1483
22	5.0019	5.5449	47.6034
23	4.4289	6.1179	41.4855
24	3.7966	6.7501	34.7354
25	3.0990	7.4477	27.2877
26	2.3293	8.2174	19.0703
27	1.4801	9.0666	10.0036

#	INT	PRIN	BALANCE
28	.5431	10.0036	0.0000

YEARS 29   MO PAYT .8733   AN CONST 10.48

#	INT	PRIN	BALANCE
1	9.8469	.6331	99.3669
2	9.7814	.6986	98.6683
3	9.7092	.7707	97.8976
4	9.6296	.8504	97.0472
5	9.5417	.9383	96.1089
6	9.4447	1.0352	95.0737
7	9.3377	1.1422	93.9314
8	9.2197	1.2603	92.6711
9	9.0895	1.3905	91.2806
10	8.9458	1.5342	89.7464
11	8.7872	1.6928	88.0536
12	8.6123	1.8677	86.1859
13	8.4192	2.0607	84.1252
14	8.2063	2.2737	81.8515
15	7.9713	2.5087	79.3428
16	7.7120	2.7679	76.5749
17	7.4260	3.0540	73.5209
18	7.1104	3.3696	70.1513
19	6.7622	3.7178	66.4335
20	6.3779	4.1020	62.3315
21	5.9540	4.5260	57.8055
22	5.4863	4.9937	52.8118
23	4.9702	5.5098	47.3021
24	4.4008	6.0792	41.2229
25	3.7726	6.7074	34.5155
26	3.0794	7.4006	27.1149
27	2.3146	8.1654	18.9495
28	1.4707	9.0092	9.9403
29	.5397	9.9403	0.0000

YEARS 30   MO PAYT .8683   AN CONST 10.43

#	INT	PRIN	BALANCE
1	9.8496	.5705	99.4295
2	9.7907	.6295	98.7999
3	9.7256	.6946	98.1054
4	9.6538	.7663	97.3390
5	9.5746	.8455	96.4935
6	9.4873	.9329	95.5606
7	9.3908	1.0293	94.5312
8	9.2845	1.1357	93.3955
9	9.1671	1.2531	92.1424
10	9.0376	1.3826	90.7598
11	8.8947	1.5255	89.2344
12	8.7371	1.6831	87.5512
13	8.5631	1.8571	85.6942
14	8.3712	2.0490	83.6452
15	8.1595	2.2607	81.3845
16	7.9258	2.4944	78.8901
17	7.6680	2.7521	76.1380
18	7.3836	3.0366	73.1014
19	7.0698	3.3504	69.7511
20	6.7236	3.6966	66.0545
21	6.3416	4.0786	61.9758
22	5.9201	4.5001	57.4757
23	5.4550	4.9652	52.5105
24	4.9419	5.4783	47.0322
25	4.3757	6.0445	40.9877
26	3.7510	6.6691	34.3186
27	3.0618	7.3584	26.9602
28	2.3014	8.1188	18.8414
29	1.4624	8.9578	9.8836
30	.5366	9.8836	0.0000

YEARS 2 — MO PAYT 4.6099 — AN CONST 55.32

#	INT	PRIN	BALANCE
1	7.7814	47.5371	52.4629
2	2.8557	52.4629	0.0000

YEARS 3 — MO PAYT 3.2220 — AN CONST 38.67

#	INT	PRIN	BALANCE
1	8.5583	30.1061	69.8939
2	5.4387	33.2256	36.6684
3	1.9960	36.6684	0.0000

YEARS 4 — MO PAYT 2.5315 — AN CONST 30.38

#	INT	PRIN	BALANCE
1	8.9448	21.4327	78.5673
2	6.7240	23.6535	54.9138
3	4.2731	26.1044	28.8093
4	1.5682	28.8093	0.0000

YEARS 5 — MO PAYT 2.1198 — AN CONST 25.44

#	INT	PRIN	BALANCE
1	9.1752	16.2622	83.7378
2	7.4902	17.9473	65.7905
3	5.6305	19.8069	45.9836
4	3.5782	21.8593	24.1243
5	1.3131	24.1243	0.0000

YEARS 6 — MO PAYT 1.8475 — AN CONST 22.18

#	INT	PRIN	BALANCE
1	9.3276	12.8429	87.1571
2	7.9969	14.1737	72.9834
3	6.5282	15.6423	57.3411
4	4.9074	17.2631	40.0780
5	3.1186	19.0519	21.0260
6	1.1445	21.0260	0.0000

YEARS 7 — MO PAYT 1.6550 — AN CONST 19.86

#	INT	PRIN	BALANCE
1	9.4354	10.4240	89.5760
2	8.3553	11.5042	78.0718
3	7.1633	12.6962	65.3756
4	5.8477	14.0118	51.3638
5	4.3958	15.4636	35.9002
6	2.7935	17.0659	18.8343
7	1.0252	18.8343	0.0000

YEARS 8 — MO PAYT 1.5121 — AN CONST 18.15

#	INT	PRIN	BALANCE
1	9.5154	8.6302	91.3698
2	8.6211	9.5244	81.8454
3	7.6342	10.5113	71.3341
4	6.5451	11.6005	59.7336
5	5.3430	12.8025	46.9310
6	4.0165	14.1291	32.8020
7	2.5524	15.5931	17.2088
8	.9367	17.2088	0.0000

YEARS 9 — MO PAYT 1.4025 — AN CONST 16.83

#	INT	PRIN	BALANCE
1	9.5768	7.2527	92.7473
2	8.8252	8.0043	84.7430
3	7.9959	8.8336	75.9093
4	7.0805	9.7490	66.1604
5	6.0704	10.7591	55.4012
6	4.9555	11.8740	43.5273
7	3.7252	13.1043	30.4229
8	2.3673	14.4622	15.9607
9	.8688	15.9607	0.0000

YEARS 10 — MO PAYT 1.3160 — AN CONST 15.80

#	INT	PRIN	BALANCE
1	9.6252	6.1665	93.8335
2	8.9862	6.8055	87.0280
3	8.2810	7.5107	79.5173
4	7.5028	8.2889	71.2284
5	6.6439	9.1478	62.0806
6	5.6960	10.0957	51.9849
7	4.6499	11.1418	40.8431
8	3.4955	12.2963	28.5469
9	2.2213	13.5704	14.9765
10	.8152	14.9765	0.0000

YEARS 11 — MO PAYT 1.2463 — AN CONST 14.96

#	INT	PRIN	BALANCE
1	9.6642	5.2919	94.7081
2	9.1158	5.8402	88.8679
3	8.5107	6.4454	82.4225
4	7.8428	7.1132	75.3093
5	7.1058	7.8503	67.4590
6	6.2923	8.6637	58.7953
7	5.3946	9.5614	49.2339
8	4.4039	10.5522	38.6818
9	3.3105	11.6456	27.0362
10	2.1038	12.8522	14.1840
11	.7721	14.1840	0.0000

YEARS 12 — MO PAYT 1.1893 — AN CONST 14.28

#	INT	PRIN	BALANCE
1	9.6961	4.5756	95.4244
2	9.2220	5.0497	90.3746
3	8.6987	5.5730	84.8016
4	8.1213	6.1504	78.6512
5	7.4840	6.7877	71.8635
6	6.7806	7.4911	64.3724
7	6.0044	8.2673	56.1051
8	5.1478	9.1239	46.9812
9	4.2024	10.0693	36.9118
10	3.1590	11.1127	25.7991
11	2.0075	12.2642	13.5350
12	.7367	13.5350	0.0000

YEARS 13 — MO PAYT 1.1420 — AN CONST 13.71

#	INT	PRIN	BALANCE
1	9.7226	3.9810	96.0190
2	9.3101	4.3935	91.6256
3	8.8548	4.8487	86.7768
4	8.3554	5.3511	81.4257
5	7.7979	5.9056	75.5201
6	7.1860	6.5175	69.0026
7	6.5107	7.1929	61.8097
8	5.7654	7.9382	53.8716
9	4.9428	8.7607	45.1108
10	4.0351	9.6685	35.4424
11	3.0332	10.6703	24.7721
12	1.9276	11.7759	12.9961
13	.7074	12.9961	0.0000

YEARS 14 — MO PAYT 1.1022 — AN CONST 13.23

#	INT	PRIN	BALANCE
1	9.7448	3.4816	96.5184
2	9.3841	3.8424	92.6760
3	8.9859	4.2405	88.4355
4	8.5465	4.6799	83.7556
5	8.0616	5.1648	78.5908
6	7.5265	5.7000	72.8908
7	6.9358	6.2906	66.6002
8	6.2840	6.9424	59.6578
9	5.5647	7.6618	51.9960
10	4.7708	8.4557	43.5403
11	3.8946	9.3319	34.2084
12	2.9276	10.2988	23.9096
13	1.8605	11.3659	12.5437
14	.6828	12.5437	0.0000

YEARS 15 — MO PAYT 1.0685 — AN CONST 12.83

#	INT	PRIN	BALANCE
1	9.7637	3.0582	96.9418
2	9.4468	3.3751	93.5666
3	9.0971	3.7249	89.8418
4	8.7111	4.1108	85.7309
5	8.2852	4.5368	81.1942
6	7.8151	5.0069	76.1873
7	7.2963	5.5257	70.6616
8	6.7237	6.0982	64.5634
9	6.0918	6.7301	57.8333
10	5.3945	7.4275	50.4058
11	4.6249	8.1971	42.2087
12	3.7755	9.0465	33.1622
13	2.8381	9.9838	23.1784
14	1.8036	11.0183	12.1600
15	.6619	12.1600	0.0000

YEARS 16 — MO PAYT 1.0397 — AN CONST 12.48

#	INT	PRIN	BALANCE
1	9.7798	2.6964	97.3036
2	9.5004	2.9758	94.3278
3	9.1921	3.2841	91.0437
4	8.8518	3.6244	87.4193
5	8.4762	4.0000	83.4193
6	8.0618	4.4144	79.0048
7	7.6044	4.8719	74.1330
8	7.0995	5.3767	68.7563
9	6.5424	5.9338	62.8225
10	5.9276	6.5486	56.2739
11	5.2490	7.2272	49.0467
12	4.5001	7.9761	41.0706
13	3.6737	8.8025	32.2680
14	2.7616	9.7146	22.5534
15	1.7550	10.7212	11.8322
16	.6441	11.8322	0.0000

YEARS 17 — MO PAYT 1.0149 — AN CONST 12.18

#	INT	PRIN	BALANCE
1	9.7937	2.3850	97.6150
2	9.5466	2.6321	94.9830
3	9.2739	2.9048	92.0781
4	8.9729	3.2058	88.8723
5	8.6407	3.5380	85.3344
6	8.2741	3.9046	81.4298
7	7.8695	4.3092	77.1206
8	7.4230	4.7557	72.3649
9	6.9302	5.2484	67.1165
10	6.3864	5.7923	61.3242
11	5.7862	6.3925	54.9318
12	5.1238	7.0548	47.8769
13	4.3928	7.7858	40.0911
14	3.5861	8.5926	31.4985
15	2.6957	9.4829	22.0155
16	1.7131	10.4656	11.5500
17	.6287	11.5500	0.0000

YEARS 18 — MO PAYT .9934 — AN CONST 11.93

#	INT	PRIN	BALANCE
1	9.8057	2.1153	97.8847
2	9.5865	2.3345	95.5502
3	9.3446	2.5764	92.9738
4	9.0777	2.8434	90.1304
5	8.7831	3.1380	86.9924
6	8.4579	3.4631	83.5293
7	8.0991	3.8220	79.7073
8	7.7030	4.2180	75.4893
9	7.2660	4.6551	70.8342
10	6.7836	5.1374	65.6968
11	6.2513	5.6698	60.0270
12	5.6638	6.2572	53.7698
13	5.0154	6.9056	46.8642
14	4.2999	7.6212	39.2430
15	3.5102	8.4108	30.8322
16	2.6387	9.2824	21.5498
17	1.6769	10.2442	11.3057
18	.6154	11.3057	0.0000

YEARS 19 — MO PAYT .9747 — AN CONST 11.70

#	INT	PRIN	BALANCE
1	9.8162	1.8807	98.1193
2	9.6213	2.0755	96.0438
3	9.4062	2.2906	93.7532
4	9.1689	2.5280	91.2252
5	8.9070	2.7899	88.4353
6	8.6179	3.0790	85.3564
7	8.2988	3.3980	81.9584
8	7.9467	3.7501	78.2082
9	7.5582	4.1387	74.0696
10	7.1293	4.5675	69.5020
11	6.6560	5.0408	64.4612
12	6.1337	5.5631	58.8981
13	5.5573	6.1396	52.7585
14	4.9211	6.7757	45.9828
15	4.2190	7.4778	38.5050
16	3.4442	8.2527	30.2523
17	2.5891	9.1078	21.1445
18	1.6453	10.0515	11.0930
19	.6038	11.0930	0.0000

YEARS 20 — MO PAYT .9584 — AN CONST 11.51

#	INT	PRIN	BALANCE
1	9.8253	1.6755	98.3245
2	9.6517	1.8492	96.4753
3	9.4601	2.0408	94.4345
4	9.2486	2.2522	92.1823
5	9.0153	2.4856	89.6967
6	8.7577	2.7431	86.9536
7	8.4735	3.0274	83.9262
8	8.1598	3.3411	80.5851
9	7.8136	3.6873	76.8978
10	7.4315	4.0693	72.8285
11	7.0099	4.4910	68.3375
12	6.5445	4.9563	63.3812
13	6.0310	5.4699	57.9112
14	5.4642	6.0367	51.8745
15	4.8387	6.6622	45.2123
16	4.1483	7.3525	37.8598
17	3.3865	8.1144	29.7454
18	2.5457	8.9552	20.7903
19	1.6178	9.8831	10.9072
20	.5937	10.9072	0.0000

YEARS 21 — MO PAYT .9441 — AN CONST 11.33

#	INT	PRIN	BALANCE
1	9.8333	1.4955	98.5045
2	9.6784	1.6505	96.8540
3	9.5074	1.8215	95.0325

MONTHLY PAYMENT AMORTIZATION SCHEDULE PER $100   9.90 %

#	INT	PRIN	BALANCE
4	9.3186	2.0102	93.0222
5	9.1103	2.2185	90.8037
6	8.8804	2.4484	88.3553
7	8.6267	2.7021	85.6532
8	8.3468	2.9821	82.6711
9	8.0378	3.2911	79.3799
10	7.6967	3.6321	75.7478
11	7.3204	4.0085	71.7393
12	6.9050	4.4238	67.3155
13	6.4466	4.8822	62.4333
14	5.9408	5.3881	57.0452
15	5.3825	5.9464	51.0988
16	4.7663	6.5626	44.5362
17	4.0863	7.2426	37.2936
18	3.3358	7.9930	29.3006
19	2.5076	8.8213	20.4793
20	1.5936	9.7353	10.7440
21	.5848	10.7440	0.0000

YEARS 22 — MO PAYT .9315 — AN CONST 11.18

#	INT	PRIN	BALANCE
1	9.8404	1.3370	98.6630
2	9.7019	1.4755	97.1875
3	9.5490	1.6284	95.5591
4	9.3803	1.7971	93.7619
5	9.1940	1.9834	91.7786
6	8.9885	2.1889	89.5897
7	8.7617	2.4157	87.1740
8	8.5114	2.6660	84.5080
9	8.2352	2.9422	81.5658
10	7.9303	3.2471	78.3186
11	7.5938	3.5836	74.7351
12	7.2225	3.9549	70.7802
13	6.8127	4.3647	66.4155
14	6.3605	4.8169	61.5985
15	5.8613	5.3161	56.2825
16	5.3105	5.8669	50.4156
17	4.7026	6.4748	43.9407
18	4.0317	7.1457	36.7950
19	3.2912	7.8862	28.9088
20	2.4741	8.7033	20.2055
21	1.5723	9.6051	10.6004
22	.5770	10.6004	0.0000

YEARS 23 — MO PAYT .9203 — AN CONST 11.05

#	INT	PRIN	BALANCE
1	9.8467	1.1970	98.8030
2	9.7226	1.3210	97.4821
3	9.5858	1.4579	96.0242
4	9.4347	1.6089	94.4153
5	9.2680	1.7756	92.6396
6	9.0840	1.9596	90.6800
7	8.8809	2.1627	88.5173
8	8.6568	2.3868	86.1305
9	8.4095	2.6341	83.4965
10	8.1366	2.9070	80.5894
11	7.8354	3.2082	77.3812
12	7.5029	3.5407	73.8405
13	7.1361	3.9076	69.9330
14	6.7312	4.3124	65.6205
15	6.2843	4.7593	60.8612
16	5.7912	5.2524	55.6088
17	5.2469	5.7967	49.8121
18	4.6463	6.3973	43.4148
19	3.9834	7.0602	36.3546
20	3.2518	7.7918	28.5628
21	2.4445	8.5991	19.9637
22	1.5535	9.4902	10.4735
23	.5701	10.4735	0.0000

YEARS 24 — MO PAYT .9104 — AN CONST 10.93

#	INT	PRIN	BALANCE
1	9.8522	1.0729	98.9271
2	9.7410	1.1841	97.7429
3	9.6183	1.3068	96.4361
4	9.4829	1.4422	94.9939
5	9.3335	1.5917	93.4022
6	9.1685	1.7566	91.6457
7	8.9865	1.9386	89.7071
8	8.7856	2.1395	87.5676
9	8.5640	2.3612	85.2064
10	8.3193	2.6058	82.6006
11	8.0493	2.8758	79.7248
12	7.7513	3.1738	76.5509
13	7.4224	3.5027	73.0483
14	7.0595	3.8656	69.1826
15	6.6589	4.2662	64.9165
16	6.2169	4.7082	60.2082
17	5.7290	5.1961	55.0122
18	5.1906	5.7345	49.2777
19	4.5964	6.3287	42.9490
20	3.9407	6.9845	35.9645
21	3.2170	7.7082	28.2564
22	2.4182	8.5069	19.7495
23	1.5368	9.3883	10.3611
24	.5640	10.3611	0.0000

YEARS 25 — MO PAYT .9017 — AN CONST 10.82

#	INT	PRIN	BALANCE
1	9.8571	.9628	99.0372
2	9.7573	1.0626	97.9745
3	9.6472	1.1727	96.8018
4	9.5257	1.2942	95.5076
5	9.3916	1.4283	94.0793
6	9.2436	1.5763	92.5029
7	9.0803	1.7397	90.7633
8	8.9000	1.9199	88.8433
9	8.7011	2.1189	86.7244
10	8.4815	2.3384	84.3860
11	8.2392	2.5807	81.8053
12	7.9718	2.8481	78.9571
13	7.6767	3.1433	75.8139
14	7.3510	3.4690	72.3449
15	6.9915	3.8284	68.5165
16	6.5948	4.2251	64.2914
17	6.1570	4.6629	59.6285
18	5.6739	5.1461	54.4825
19	5.1407	5.6793	48.8032
20	4.5522	6.2678	42.5354
21	3.9027	6.9172	35.6182
22	3.1860	7.6340	27.9843
23	2.3950	8.4250	19.5593
24	1.5220	9.2979	10.2614
25	.5586	10.2614	0.0000

YEARS 26 — MO PAYT .8939 — AN CONST 10.73

#	INT	PRIN	BALANCE
1	9.8615	.8649	99.1351
2	9.7718	.9545	98.1806
3	9.6729	1.0534	97.1272
4	9.5638	1.1626	95.9646
5	9.4433	1.2830	94.6816
6	9.3104	1.4160	93.2656
7	9.1636	1.5627	91.7029
8	9.0017	1.7246	89.9782
9	8.8230	1.9033	88.0749
10	8.6258	2.1005	85.9744
11	8.4081	2.3182	83.6562
12	8.1679	2.5584	81.0978
13	7.9028	2.8235	78.2742
14	7.6103	3.1161	75.1582
15	7.2874	3.4390	71.7192

YEARS 26 (continued)

#	INT	PRIN	BALANCE
16	6.9311	3.7953	67.9239
17	6.5378	4.1886	63.7354
18	6.1038	4.6226	59.1128
19	5.6248	5.1015	54.0113
20	5.0962	5.6302	48.3811
21	4.5128	6.2135	42.1676
22	3.8690	6.8574	35.3102
23	3.1584	7.5679	27.7423
24	2.3743	8.3521	19.3902
25	1.5088	9.2175	10.1726
26	.5537	10.1726	0.0000

YEARS 27 — MO PAYT .8869 — AN CONST 10.65

#	INT	PRIN	BALANCE
1	9.8653	.7776	99.2224
2	9.7848	.8582	98.3642
3	9.6958	.9471	97.4171
4	9.5977	1.0452	96.3719
5	9.4894	1.1535	95.2184
6	9.3699	1.2731	93.9453
7	9.2380	1.4050	92.5403
8	9.0924	1.5506	90.9898
9	8.9317	1.7112	89.2786
10	8.7544	1.8885	87.3900
11	8.5587	2.0842	85.3058
12	8.3428	2.3002	83.0057
13	8.1044	2.5385	80.4671
14	7.8414	2.8016	77.6656
15	7.5511	3.0918	74.5737
16	7.2307	3.4122	71.1615
17	6.8772	3.7658	67.3957
18	6.4870	4.1560	63.2398
19	6.0563	4.5866	58.6531
20	5.5811	5.0619	53.5913
21	5.0566	5.5864	48.0049
22	4.4777	6.1652	41.8397
23	3.8389	6.8041	35.0356
24	3.1339	7.5091	27.5265
25	2.3558	8.2872	19.2394
26	1.4971	9.1459	10.0935
27	.5494	10.0935	0.0000

YEARS 28 — MO PAYT .8807 — AN CONST 10.57

#	INT	PRIN	BALANCE
1	9.8688	.6997	99.3003
2	9.7963	.7722	98.5282
3	9.7163	.8522	97.6760
4	9.6280	.9405	96.7356
5	9.5306	1.0379	95.6976
6	9.4230	1.1455	94.5522
7	9.3043	1.2642	93.2880
8	9.1733	1.3951	91.8929
9	9.0288	1.5397	90.3532
10	8.8692	1.6992	88.6539
11	8.6932	1.8753	86.7786
12	8.4988	2.0696	84.7090
13	8.2844	2.2841	82.4249
14	8.0477	2.5208	79.9041
15	7.7865	2.7820	77.1222
16	7.4983	3.0702	74.0520
17	7.1801	3.3883	70.6636
18	6.8290	3.7394	66.9242
19	6.4416	4.1269	62.7973
20	6.0139	4.5545	58.2428
21	5.5420	5.0265	53.2163
22	5.0212	5.5473	47.6690
23	4.4464	6.1221	41.5469
24	3.8120	6.7564	34.7905
25	3.1119	7.4565	27.3339
26	2.3393	8.2292	19.1048
27	1.4866	9.0819	10.0229
28	.5456	10.0229	0.0000

YEARS 29 — MO PAYT .8752 — AN CONST 10.51

#	INT	PRIN	BALANCE
1	9.8719	.6300	99.3700
2	9.8066	.6953	98.6748
3	9.7346	.7673	97.9075
4	9.6551	.8468	97.0607
5	9.5674	.9345	96.1261
6	9.4705	1.0314	95.0948
7	9.3637	1.1382	93.9565
8	9.2457	1.2562	92.7003
9	9.1155	1.3864	91.3140
10	8.9719	1.5300	89.7840
11	8.8134	1.6885	88.0954
12	8.6384	1.8635	86.2319
13	8.4453	2.0566	84.1753
14	8.2322	2.2697	81.9056
15	7.9970	2.5049	79.4008
16	7.7375	2.7644	76.6363
17	7.4510	3.0509	73.5855
18	7.1349	3.3670	70.2185
19	6.7860	3.7159	66.5026
20	6.4010	4.1009	62.4017
21	5.9761	4.5258	57.8759
22	5.5071	4.9948	52.8811
23	4.9896	5.5123	47.3687
24	4.4184	6.0835	41.2852
25	3.7880	6.7139	34.5713
26	3.0923	7.4096	27.1617
27	2.3246	8.1773	18.9844
28	1.4773	9.0246	9.9598
29	.5421	9.9598	0.0000

YEARS 30 — MO PAYT .8702 — AN CONST 10.45

#	INT	PRIN	BALANCE
1	9.8747	.5676	99.4324
2	9.8159	.6264	98.8060
3	9.7510	.6913	98.1147
4	9.6794	.7629	97.3518
5	9.6003	.8420	96.5098
6	9.5131	.9292	95.5805
7	9.4168	1.0255	94.5550
8	9.3105	1.1318	93.4232
9	9.1932	1.2491	92.1742
10	9.0638	1.3785	90.7957
11	8.9210	1.5213	89.2744
12	8.7633	1.6790	87.5954
13	8.5894	1.8529	85.7425
14	8.3974	2.0449	83.6976
15	8.1855	2.2568	81.4408
16	7.9516	2.4907	78.9501
17	7.6936	2.7487	76.2014
18	7.4087	3.0336	73.1678
19	7.0944	3.3479	69.8199
20	6.7475	3.6948	66.1251
21	6.3647	4.0776	62.0475
22	5.9421	4.5001	57.5474
23	5.4758	4.9664	52.5809
24	4.9612	5.4811	47.0999
25	4.3933	6.0490	41.0509
26	3.7665	6.6758	34.3751
27	3.0748	7.3675	27.0076
28	2.3114	8.1309	18.8767
29	1.4689	8.9734	9.9032
30	.5391	9.9032	0.0000

YEARS 2 — MO PAYT 4.6145 — AN CONST 55.38

#	INT	PRIN	BALANCE
1	7.8615	47.5124	52.4876
2	2.8863	52.4876	0.0000

YEARS 3 — MO PAYT 3.2267 — AN CONST 38.73

#	INT	PRIN	BALANCE
1	8.6464	30.0742	69.9258
2	5.4972	33.2234	36.7023
3	2.0183	36.7023	0.0000

YEARS 4 — MO PAYT 2.5363 — AN CONST 30.44

#	INT	PRIN	BALANCE
1	9.0369	21.3982	78.6018
2	6.7962	23.6389	54.9629
3	4.3209	26.1142	28.8487
4	1.5864	28.8487	0.0000

YEARS 5 — MO PAYT 2.1247 — AN CONST 25.50

#	INT	PRIN	BALANCE
1	9.2696	16.2268	83.7732
2	7.5705	17.9260	65.8472
3	5.6934	19.8031	46.0442
4	3.6198	21.8767	24.1675
5	1.3290	24.1675	0.0000

YEARS 6 — MO PAYT 1.8526 — AN CONST 22.24

#	INT	PRIN	BALANCE
1	9.4235	12.8075	87.1925
2	8.0824	14.1486	73.0440
3	6.6009	15.6301	57.4139
4	4.9642	17.2668	40.1471
5	3.1562	19.0748	21.0722
6	1.1588	21.0722	0.0000

YEARS 7 — MO PAYT 1.6601 — AN CONST 19.93

#	INT	PRIN	BALANCE
1	9.5324	10.3890	89.6110
2	8.4445	11.4769	78.1341
3	7.2427	12.6787	65.4554
4	5.9151	14.0063	51.4491
5	4.4485	15.4729	35.9762
6	2.8283	17.0932	18.8830
7	1.0384	18.8830	0.0000

YEARS 8 — MO PAYT 1.5174 — AN CONST 18.21

#	INT	PRIN	BALANCE
1	9.6131	8.5959	91.4041
2	8.7130	9.4960	81.9081
3	7.7186	10.4903	71.4178
4	6.6202	11.5888	59.8289
5	5.4067	12.8023	47.0266
6	4.0661	14.1429	32.8837
7	2.5852	15.6238	17.2599
8	.9491	17.2599	0.0000

YEARS 9 — MO PAYT 1.4079 — AN CONST 16.90

#	INT	PRIN	BALANCE
1	9.6751	7.2194	92.7806
2	8.9191	7.9753	84.8053
3	8.0840	8.8104	75.9949
4	7.1614	9.7330	66.2619
5	6.1422	10.7522	55.5097
6	5.0163	11.8781	43.6316
7	3.7726	13.1219	30.5097
8	2.3985	14.4959	16.0138
9	.8806	16.0138	0.0000

YEARS 10 — MO PAYT 1.3215 — AN CONST 15.86

#	INT	PRIN	BALANCE
1	9.7239	6.1342	93.8658
2	9.0816	6.7765	87.0893
3	8.3720	7.4861	79.6032
4	7.5881	8.2700	71.3332
5	6.7221	9.1360	62.1972
6	5.7655	10.0926	52.1046
7	4.7086	11.1495	40.9551
8	3.5411	12.3170	28.6382
9	2.2514	13.6067	15.0315
10	.8266	15.0315	0.0000

YEARS 11 — MO PAYT 1.2520 — AN CONST 15.03

#	INT	PRIN	BALANCE
1	9.7632	5.2606	94.7394
2	9.2124	5.8115	88.9279
3	8.6038	6.4200	82.5079
4	7.9316	7.0923	75.4156
5	7.1889	7.8349	67.5806
6	6.3685	8.6554	58.9253
7	5.4622	9.5617	49.3636
8	4.4609	10.5629	38.8006
9	3.3549	11.6690	27.1316
10	2.1330	12.8909	14.2407
11	.7831	14.2407	0.0000

YEARS 12 — MO PAYT 1.1951 — AN CONST 14.35

#	INT	PRIN	BALANCE
1	9.7954	4.5455	95.4545
2	9.3194	5.0215	90.4330
3	8.7936	5.5473	84.8856
4	8.2127	6.1282	78.7574
5	7.5710	6.7699	71.9875
6	6.8621	7.4788	64.5087
7	6.0790	8.2619	56.2468
8	5.2139	9.1271	47.1197
9	4.2582	10.0828	37.0370
10	3.2024	11.1386	25.8984
11	2.0360	12.3049	13.5934
12	.7475	13.5934	0.0000

YEARS 13 — MO PAYT 1.1478 — AN CONST 13.78

#	INT	PRIN	BALANCE
1	9.8221	3.9521	96.0479
2	9.4083	4.3659	91.6821
3	8.9511	4.8231	86.8590
4	8.4461	5.3281	81.5309
5	7.8882	5.8860	75.6449
6	7.2718	6.5024	69.1425
7	6.5909	7.1832	61.9593
8	5.8838	7.9354	54.0239
9	5.0078	8.7664	45.2575
10	4.0899	9.6843	35.5732
11	3.0758	10.6984	24.8748
12	1.9555	11.8186	13.0562
13	.7180	13.0562	0.0000

YEARS 14 — MO PAYT 1.1082 — AN CONST 13.30

#	INT	PRIN	BALANCE
1	9.8445	3.4539	96.5461
2	9.4829	3.8156	92.7306
3	9.0833	4.2151	88.5155
4	8.6420	4.6565	83.8590
5	8.1544	5.1441	78.7149
6	7.6157	5.6827	73.0322
7	7.0207	6.2778	66.7544
8	6.3633	6.9351	59.8193
9	5.6371	7.6613	52.1580
10	4.8349	8.4636	43.6944
11	3.9486	9.3498	34.3446
12	2.9696	10.3289	24.0157
13	1.8880	11.4104	12.6053
14	.6932	12.6053	0.0000

YEARS 15 — MO PAYT 1.0746 — AN CONST 12.90

#	INT	PRIN	BALANCE
1	9.8635	3.0317	96.9683
2	9.5461	3.3492	93.6191
3	9.1954	3.6999	89.9192
4	8.8080	4.0873	85.8319
5	8.3800	4.5153	81.3166
6	7.9072	4.9881	76.3285
7	7.3848	5.5104	70.8181
8	6.8078	6.0874	64.7306
9	6.1704	6.7249	58.0058
10	5.4662	7.4291	50.5767
11	4.6883	8.2070	42.3697
12	3.8289	9.0664	33.3033
13	2.8795	10.0157	23.2876
14	1.8308	11.0645	12.2231
15	.6722	12.2231	0.0000

YEARS 16 — MO PAYT 1.0459 — AN CONST 12.56

#	INT	PRIN	BALANCE
1	9.8798	2.6710	97.3290
2	9.6001	2.9507	94.3782
3	9.2911	3.2597	91.1185
4	8.9498	3.6011	87.5174
5	8.5727	3.9781	83.5393
6	8.1561	4.3947	79.1446
7	7.6959	4.8549	74.2897
8	7.1876	5.3632	68.9265
9	6.6260	5.9248	63.0016
10	6.0056	6.5453	56.4564
11	5.3202	7.2306	49.2258
12	4.5631	7.9878	41.2380
13	3.7266	8.8242	32.4138
14	2.8026	9.7482	22.6656
15	1.7819	10.7690	11.8966
16	.6542	11.8966	0.0000

YEARS 17 — MO PAYT 1.0212 — AN CONST 12.26

#	INT	PRIN	BALANCE
1	9.8937	2.3608	97.6392
2	9.6465	2.6080	95.0312
3	9.3734	2.8811	92.1502
4	9.0718	3.1828	88.9674
5	8.7385	3.5160	85.4513
6	8.3703	3.8842	81.5671
7	7.9636	4.2909	77.2762
8	7.5143	4.7403	72.5359
9	7.0179	5.2366	67.2993
10	6.4696	5.7850	61.5143
11	5.8638	6.3907	55.1236
12	5.1946	7.0599	48.0636
13	4.4553	7.7992	40.2644
14	3.6386	8.6159	31.6486
15	2.7365	9.5181	22.1305
16	1.7398	10.5147	11.6158
17	.6388	11.6158	0.0000

YEARS 18 — MO PAYT .9998 — AN CONST 12.00

#	INT	PRIN	BALANCE
1	9.9058	2.0923	97.9077
2	9.6867	2.3114	95.5963
3	9.4447	2.5534	93.0429
4	9.1773	2.8208	90.2221
5	8.8820	3.1162	87.1059
6	8.5556	3.4425	83.6634
7	8.1952	3.8029	79.8605
8	7.7970	4.2012	75.6593
9	7.3570	4.6411	71.0183
10	6.8711	5.1271	65.8912
11	6.3342	5.6639	60.2273
12	5.7411	6.2570	53.9702
13	5.0859	6.9122	47.0580
14	4.3621	7.6360	39.4220
15	3.5625	8.4356	30.9864
16	2.6792	9.3189	21.6675
17	1.7034	10.2947	11.3727
18	.6254	11.3727	0.0000

YEARS 19 — MO PAYT .9813 — AN CONST 11.78

#	INT	PRIN	BALANCE
1	9.9163	1.8588	98.1412
2	9.7217	2.0534	96.0878
3	9.5067	2.2684	93.8194
4	9.2691	2.5060	91.3134
5	9.0067	2.7684	88.5451
6	8.7169	3.0582	85.4868
7	8.3966	3.3785	82.1083
8	8.0428	3.7323	78.3761
9	7.6520	4.1231	74.2530
10	7.2203	4.5548	69.6982
11	6.7433	5.0318	64.6664
12	6.2165	5.5587	59.1078
13	5.6344	6.1407	52.9670
14	4.9914	6.7837	46.1833
15	4.2810	7.4941	38.6892
16	3.4963	8.2788	30.4104
17	2.6294	9.1457	21.2647
18	1.6717	10.1034	11.1613
19	.6138	11.1613	0.0000

YEARS 20 — MO PAYT .9650 — AN CONST 11.59

#	INT	PRIN	BALANCE
1	9.9255	1.6547	98.3453
2	9.7522	1.8280	96.5173
3	9.5608	2.0194	94.4978
4	9.3494	2.2309	92.2669
5	9.1158	2.4645	89.8024
6	8.8577	2.7226	87.0799
7	8.5726	3.0076	84.0722
8	8.2577	3.3226	80.7497
9	7.9098	3.6705	77.0792
10	7.5254	4.0548	73.0243
11	7.1008	4.4794	68.5449
12	6.6318	4.9485	63.5964
13	6.1136	5.4667	58.1297
14	5.5412	6.0391	52.0906
15	4.9088	6.6715	45.4191
16	4.2102	7.3701	38.0490
17	3.4384	8.1418	29.9072
18	2.5859	8.9944	20.9128
19	1.6441	9.9362	10.9766
20	.6036	10.9766	0.0000

YEARS 21 — MO PAYT .9508 — AN CONST 11.41

#	INT	PRIN	BALANCE
1	9.9336	1.4758	98.5242
2	9.7790	1.6303	96.8939
3	9.6083	1.8010	95.0929

#	INT	PRIN	BALANCE
4	9.4197	1.9896	93.1032
5	9.2114	2.1980	90.9053
6	8.9812	2.4281	88.4772
7	8.7270	2.6824	85.7948
8	8.4461	2.9633	82.8315
9	8.1358	3.2735	79.5580
10	7.7930	3.6163	75.9416
11	7.4144	3.9950	71.9466
12	6.9960	4.4133	67.5333
13	6.5339	4.8755	62.6578
14	6.0234	5.3860	57.2718
15	5.4594	5.9500	51.3218
16	4.8363	6.5730	44.7488
17	4.1481	7.2613	37.4875
18	3.3877	8.0217	29.4658
19	2.5477	8.8616	20.6042
20	1.6198	9.7896	10.8147
21	.5947	10.8147	0.0000

YEARS 22 — MO PAYT .9382 — AN CONST 11.26

#	INT	PRIN	BALANCE
1	9.9407	1.3183	98.6817
2	9.8026	1.4564	97.2254
3	9.6501	1.6088	95.6166
4	9.4817	1.7773	93.8393
5	9.2956	1.9634	91.8759
6	9.0900	2.1690	89.7069
7	8.8628	2.3961	87.3108
8	8.6119	2.6470	84.6638
9	8.3348	2.9242	81.7396
10	8.0286	3.2304	78.5092
11	7.6903	3.5687	74.9405
12	7.3166	3.9423	70.9982
13	6.9038	4.3552	66.6430
14	6.4478	4.8112	61.8318
15	5.9440	5.3150	56.5168
16	5.3874	5.8715	50.6453
17	4.7726	6.4864	44.1589
18	4.0934	7.1656	36.9933
19	3.3430	7.9159	29.0774
20	2.5141	8.7448	20.3326
21	1.5984	9.6605	10.6721
22	.5869	10.6721	0.0000

YEARS 23 — MO PAYT .9272 — AN CONST 11.13

#	INT	PRIN	BALANCE
1	9.9469	1.1793	98.8207
2	9.8234	1.3027	97.5180
3	9.6870	1.4392	96.0788
4	9.5363	1.5899	94.4890
5	9.3698	1.7563	92.7327
6	9.1859	1.9402	90.7924
7	8.9828	2.1434	88.6490
8	8.7583	2.3679	86.2812
9	8.5104	2.6158	83.6654
10	8.2365	2.8897	80.7756
11	7.9339	3.1923	77.5833
12	7.5996	3.5266	74.0568
13	7.2303	3.8959	70.1609
14	6.8224	4.3038	65.8571
15	6.3717	4.7545	61.1027
16	5.8739	5.2523	55.8503
17	5.3239	5.8023	50.0480
18	4.7163	6.4099	43.6381
19	4.0451	7.0811	36.5571
20	3.3036	7.8226	28.7345
21	2.4845	8.6417	20.0928
22	1.5796	9.5466	10.5462
23	.5799	10.5462	0.0000

YEARS 24 — MO PAYT .9174 — AN CONST 11.01

#	INT	PRIN	BALANCE
1	9.9525	1.0562	98.9438
2	9.8419	1.1668	97.7770
3	9.7197	1.2890	96.4880
4	9.5847	1.4240	95.0641
5	9.4356	1.5731	93.4910
6	9.2709	1.7378	91.7532
7	9.0889	1.9198	89.8335
8	8.8879	2.1208	87.7127
9	8.6658	2.3428	85.3698
10	8.4205	2.5882	82.7817
11	8.1495	2.8592	79.9225
12	7.8501	3.1586	76.7639
13	7.5193	3.4893	73.2746
14	7.1540	3.8547	69.4199
15	6.7503	4.2583	65.1615
16	6.3044	4.7042	60.4573
17	5.8118	5.1968	55.2604
18	5.2676	5.7410	49.5194
19	4.6665	6.3422	43.1772
20	4.0024	7.0063	36.1709
21	3.2687	7.7399	28.4310
22	2.4583	8.5504	19.8806
23	1.5629	9.4458	10.4348
24	.5738	10.4348	0.0000

YEARS 25 — MO PAYT .9087 — AN CONST 10.91

#	INT	PRIN	BALANCE
1	9.9574	.9470	99.0530
2	9.8582	1.0462	98.0068
3	9.7487	1.1558	96.8510
4	9.6276	1.2768	95.5742
5	9.4939	1.4105	94.1638
6	9.3462	1.5582	92.6056
7	9.1831	1.7213	90.8843
8	9.0028	1.9016	88.9827
9	8.8037	2.1007	86.8820
10	8.5838	2.3207	84.5614
11	8.3407	2.5637	81.9977
12	8.0723	2.8321	79.1656
13	7.7757	3.1287	76.0369
14	7.4481	3.4563	72.5806
15	7.0862	3.8182	68.7624
16	6.6864	4.2180	64.5444
17	6.2447	4.6597	59.8847
18	5.7568	5.1476	54.7371
19	5.2178	5.6867	49.0505
20	4.6223	6.2821	42.7683
21	3.9645	6.9399	35.8284
22	3.2378	7.6666	28.1618
23	2.4350	8.4694	19.6923
24	1.5481	9.3563	10.3360
25	.5684	10.3360	0.0000

YEARS 26 — MO PAYT .9010 — AN CONST 10.82

#	INT	PRIN	BALANCE
1	9.9617	.8500	99.1500
2	9.8727	.9390	98.2110
3	9.7744	1.0373	97.1737
4	9.6658	1.1459	96.0278
5	9.5458	1.2659	94.7619
6	9.4132	1.3985	93.3634
7	9.2668	1.5449	91.8185
8	9.1050	1.7067	90.1118
9	8.9263	1.8854	88.2264
10	8.7289	2.0828	86.1435
11	8.5108	2.3009	83.8426
12	8.2699	2.5419	81.3007
13	8.0037	2.8080	78.4927
14	7.7096	3.1021	75.3906
15	7.3848	3.4269	71.9637
16	7.0260	3.7857	68.1780
17	6.6296	4.1822	63.9958
18	6.1916	4.6201	59.3757
19	5.7079	5.1039	54.2718
20	5.1734	5.6383	48.6335
21	4.5830	6.2287	42.4048
22	3.9308	6.8809	35.5239
23	3.2102	7.6015	27.9224
24	2.4143	8.3974	19.5249
25	1.5350	9.2768	10.2482
26	.5636	10.2482	0.0000

YEARS 27 — MO PAYT .8941 — AN CONST 10.73

#	INT	PRIN	BALANCE
1	9.9656	.7635	99.2365
2	9.8857	.8435	98.3930
3	9.7974	.9318	97.4612
4	9.6998	1.0294	96.4318
5	9.5920	1.1372	95.2946
6	9.4729	1.2563	94.0383
7	9.3414	1.3878	92.6505
8	9.1960	1.5331	91.1174
9	9.0355	1.6937	89.4237
10	8.8582	1.8710	87.5527
11	8.6622	2.0669	85.4858
12	8.4458	2.2834	83.2024
13	8.2067	2.5225	80.6800
14	7.9426	2.7866	77.8934
15	7.6508	3.0784	74.8150
16	7.3284	3.4007	71.4143
17	6.9723	3.7568	67.6574
18	6.5789	4.1502	63.5072
19	6.1444	4.5848	58.9224
20	5.6643	5.0649	53.8575
21	5.1339	5.5953	48.2622
22	4.5480	6.1812	42.0810
23	3.9008	6.8284	35.2526
24	3.1857	7.5434	27.7092
25	2.3958	8.3333	19.3759
26	1.5232	9.2059	10.1699
27	.5593	10.1699	0.0000

YEARS 28 — MO PAYT .8880 — AN CONST 10.66

#	INT	PRIN	BALANCE
1	9.9691	.6864	99.3136
2	9.8972	.7583	98.5553
3	9.8178	.8377	97.7176
4	9.7301	.9254	96.7922
5	9.6332	1.0223	95.7698
6	9.5262	1.1294	94.6405
7	9.4079	1.2476	93.3928
8	9.2772	1.3783	92.0146
9	9.1329	1.5226	90.4920
10	8.9735	1.6820	88.8099
11	8.7974	1.8582	86.9518
12	8.6028	2.0527	84.8990
13	8.3878	2.2677	82.6313
14	8.1504	2.5051	80.1262
15	7.8881	2.7675	77.3587
16	7.5983	3.0573	74.3014
17	7.2781	3.3774	70.9240
18	6.9245	3.7311	67.1930
19	6.5338	4.1217	63.0713
20	6.1022	4.5533	58.5179
21	5.6254	5.0301	53.4878
22	5.0987	5.5569	47.9309
23	4.5168	6.1387	41.7922
24	3.8740	6.7815	35.0106
25	3.1639	7.4917	27.5190
26	2.3794	8.2761	19.2429
27	1.5128	9.1427	10.1001
28	.5554	10.1001	0.0000

YEARS 29 — MO PAYT .8825 — AN CONST 10.59

#	INT	PRIN	BALANCE
1	9.9722	.6175	99.3825
2	9.9075	.6822	98.7003
3	9.8361	.7536	97.9467
4	9.7572	.8325	97.1142
5	9.6700	.9197	96.1945
6	9.5737	1.0160	95.1784
7	9.4673	1.1224	94.0560
8	9.3498	1.2399	92.8161
9	9.2200	1.3698	91.4463
10	9.0765	1.5132	89.9332
11	8.9181	1.6716	88.2615
12	8.7430	1.8467	86.4148
13	8.5497	2.0401	84.3747
14	8.3360	2.2537	82.1211
15	8.1000	2.4897	79.6314
16	7.8393	2.7504	76.8810
17	7.5513	3.0384	73.8426
18	7.2332	3.3565	70.4861
19	6.8817	3.7080	66.7781
20	6.4934	4.0963	62.6818
21	6.0645	4.5252	58.1566
22	5.5907	4.9991	53.1575
23	5.0672	5.5225	47.6349
24	4.4889	6.1008	41.5341
25	3.8501	6.7397	34.7944
26	3.1443	7.4454	27.3491
27	2.3647	8.2250	19.1240
28	1.5034	9.0863	10.0377
29	.5520	10.0377	0.0000

YEARS 30 — MO PAYT .8776 — AN CONST 10.54

#	INT	PRIN	BALANCE
1	9.9750	.5559	99.4441
2	9.9168	.6141	98.8300
3	9.8525	.6784	98.1516
4	9.7814	.7494	97.4022
5	9.7030	.8279	96.5743
6	9.6163	.9146	95.6597
7	9.5205	1.0104	94.6494
8	9.4147	1.1162	93.5332
9	9.2978	1.2330	92.3002
10	9.1687	1.3622	90.9380
11	9.0261	1.5048	89.4332
12	8.8685	1.6624	87.7709
13	8.6944	1.8364	85.9344
14	8.5021	2.0287	83.9057
15	8.2897	2.2412	81.6646
16	8.0550	2.4758	79.1887
17	7.7958	2.7351	76.4536
18	7.5094	3.0215	73.4321
19	7.1930	3.3379	70.0943
20	6.8435	3.6874	66.4069
21	6.4573	4.0735	62.3333
22	6.0308	4.5001	57.8333
23	5.5596	4.9713	52.8620
24	5.0390	5.4918	47.3701
25	4.4639	6.0669	41.3032
26	3.8287	6.7022	34.6010
27	3.1269	7.4040	27.1970
28	2.3516	8.1793	19.0177
29	1.4951	9.0358	9.9819
30	.5489	9.9819	0.0000

YEARS 2 — MO PAYT 4.6191 — AN CONST 55.43

#	INT	PRIN	BALANCE
1	7.9416	47.4877	52.5123
2	2.9170	52.5123	0.0000

YEARS 3 — MO PAYT 3.2314 — AN CONST 38.78

#	INT	PRIN	BALANCE
1	8.7345	30.0425	69.9575
2	5.5558	33.2212	36.7363
3	2.0407	36.7363	0.0000

YEARS 4 — MO PAYT 2.5411 — AN CONST 30.50

#	INT	PRIN	BALANCE
1	9.1290	21.3638	78.6362
2	6.8685	23.6243	55.0120
3	4.3688	26.1239	28.8881
4	1.6047	28.8881	0.0000

YEARS 5 — MO PAYT 2.1296 — AN CONST 25.56

#	INT	PRIN	BALANCE
1	9.3641	16.1915	83.8085
2	7.6509	17.9047	65.9039
3	5.7564	19.7991	46.1047
4	3.6615	21.8941	24.2107
5	1.3449	24.2107	0.0000

YEARS 6 — MO PAYT 1.8576 — AN CONST 22.30

#	INT	PRIN	BALANCE
1	9.5195	12.7721	87.2279
2	8.1681	14.1235	73.1045
3	6.6737	15.6179	57.4866
4	5.0212	17.2704	40.2162
5	3.1938	19.0977	21.1185
6	1.1731	21.1185	0.0000

YEARS 7 — MO PAYT 1.6653 — AN CONST 19.99

#	INT	PRIN	BALANCE
1	9.6294	10.3541	89.6459
2	8.5338	11.4496	78.1963
3	7.3224	12.6611	65.5302
4	5.9827	14.0008	51.5344
5	4.5013	15.4822	36.0522
6	2.8631	17.1203	18.9318
7	1.0516	18.9318	0.0000

YEARS 8 — MO PAYT 1.5227 — AN CONST 18.28

#	INT	PRIN	BALANCE
1	9.7109	8.5617	91.4383
2	8.8050	9.4676	81.9707
3	7.8032	10.4694	71.5013
4	6.6954	11.5771	59.9242
5	5.4705	12.8021	47.1222
6	4.1159	14.1567	32.9655
7	2.6180	15.6546	17.3110
8	.9616	17.3110	0.0000

YEARS 9 — MO PAYT 1.4133 — AN CONST 16.96

#	INT	PRIN	BALANCE
1	9.7734	7.1861	92.8139
2	9.0130	7.9464	84.8675
3	8.1722	8.7872	76.0802
4	7.2425	9.7170	66.3632
5	6.2143	10.7452	55.6180
6	5.0774	11.8821	43.7359
7	3.8201	13.1393	30.5966
8	2.4299	14.5296	16.0670
9	.8925	16.0670	0.0000

YEARS 10 — MO PAYT 1.3271 — AN CONST 15.93

#	INT	PRIN	BALANCE
1	9.8227	6.1020	93.8980
2	9.1770	6.7476	87.1504
3	8.4631	7.4616	79.6889
4	7.6736	8.2511	71.4378
5	6.8005	9.1241	62.3137
6	5.8351	10.0895	52.2242
7	4.7675	11.1571	41.0672
8	3.5870	12.3376	28.7296
9	2.2816	13.6430	15.0866
10	.8380	15.0866	0.0000

YEARS 11 — MO PAYT 1.2577 — AN CONST 15.10

#	INT	PRIN	BALANCE
1	9.8623	5.2295	94.7705
2	9.3090	5.7829	88.9876
3	8.6971	6.3947	82.5929
4	8.0205	7.0714	75.5215
5	7.2723	7.8196	67.7020
6	6.4449	8.6469	59.0550
7	5.5300	9.5619	49.4932
8	4.5182	10.5736	38.9196
9	3.3994	11.6924	27.2272
10	2.1623	12.9296	14.2976
11	.7942	14.2976	0.0000

YEARS 12 — MO PAYT 1.2009 — AN CONST 14.42

#	INT	PRIN	BALANCE
1	9.8948	4.5156	95.4844
2	9.4170	4.9934	90.4910
3	8.8886	5.5217	84.9693
4	8.3044	6.1060	78.8633
5	7.6583	6.7520	72.1113
6	6.9439	7.4665	64.6448
7	6.1539	8.2565	56.3884
8	5.2803	9.1301	47.2583
9	4.3142	10.0961	37.1621
10	3.2459	11.1644	25.9977
11	2.0646	12.3457	13.6520
12	.7584	13.6520	0.0000

YEARS 13 — MO PAYT 1.1537 — AN CONST 13.85

#	INT	PRIN	BALANCE
1	9.9217	3.9233	96.0767
2	9.5066	4.3384	91.7383
3	9.0475	4.7975	86.9408
4	8.5399	5.3051	81.6357
5	7.9786	5.8664	75.7693
6	7.3579	6.4871	69.2822
7	6.6715	7.1735	62.1086
8	5.9124	7.9326	54.1761
9	5.0731	8.7719	45.4042
10	4.1449	9.7000	35.7041
11	3.1186	10.7264	24.9777
12	1.9836	11.8613	13.1164
13	.7286	13.1164	0.0000

YEARS 14 — MO PAYT 1.1142 — AN CONST 13.38

#	INT	PRIN	BALANCE
1	9.9443	3.4263	96.5737
2	9.5817	3.7889	92.7848
3	9.1808	4.1898	88.5950
4	8.7375	4.6331	83.9619
5	8.2473	5.1233	78.8386
6	7.7052	5.6654	73.1732
7	7.1057	6.2649	66.9083
8	6.4429	6.9277	59.9806
9	5.7098	7.6608	52.3198
10	4.8993	8.4713	43.8485
11	4.0029	9.3677	34.4808
12	3.0117	10.3589	24.1219
13	1.9157	11.4549	12.6670
14	.7036	12.6670	0.0000

YEARS 15 — MO PAYT 1.0807 — AN CONST 12.97

#	INT	PRIN	BALANCE
1	9.9634	3.0054	96.9946
2	9.6454	3.3234	93.6713
3	9.2938	3.6750	89.9963
4	8.9049	4.0639	85.9324
5	8.4749	4.4939	81.4385
6	7.9994	4.9693	76.4692
7	7.4736	5.4951	70.9741
8	6.8922	6.0766	64.8975
9	6.2492	6.7195	58.1779
10	5.5382	7.4305	50.7474
11	4.7520	8.2167	42.5307
12	3.8826	9.0862	33.4445
13	2.9212	10.0476	23.3970
14	1.8581	11.1107	12.2863
15	.6825	12.2863	0.0000

YEARS 16 — MO PAYT 1.0521 — AN CONST 12.63

#	INT	PRIN	BALANCE
1	9.9797	2.6459	97.3541
2	9.6998	2.9259	94.4283
3	9.3902	3.2354	91.1928
4	9.0479	3.5778	87.6150
5	8.6693	3.9563	83.6587
6	8.2507	4.3749	79.2838
7	7.7878	4.8379	74.4459
8	7.2759	5.3497	69.0962
9	6.7098	5.9158	63.1804
10	6.0839	6.5417	56.6386
11	5.3917	7.2339	49.4047
12	4.6263	7.9993	41.4053
13	3.7799	8.8457	32.5596
14	2.8439	9.7817	22.7779
15	1.8089	10.8167	11.9612
16	.6644	11.9612	0.0000

YEARS 17 — MO PAYT 1.0275 — AN CONST 12.34

#	INT	PRIN	BALANCE
1	9.9938	2.3368	97.6632
2	9.7465	2.5841	95.0791
3	9.4731	2.8575	92.2216
4	9.1708	3.1598	89.0618
5	8.8364	3.4942	85.5677
6	8.4667	3.8639	81.7038
7	8.0579	4.2727	77.4311
8	7.6058	4.7248	72.7062
9	7.1059	5.2247	67.4815
10	6.5530	5.7776	61.7040
11	5.9417	6.3889	55.3151
12	5.2657	7.0649	48.2502
13	4.5182	7.8124	40.4378
14	3.6916	8.6390	31.7987
15	2.7775	9.5531	22.2456
16	1.7667	10.5639	11.6817
17	.6489	11.6817	0.0000

YEARS 18 — MO PAYT 1.0063 — AN CONST 12.08

#	INT	PRIN	BALANCE
1	10.0059	2.0695	97.9305
2	9.7870	2.2884	95.6421
3	9.5448	2.5306	93.1115
4	9.2771	2.7983	90.3131
5	8.9810	3.0944	87.2187
6	8.6536	3.4219	83.7969
7	8.2915	3.7839	80.0129
8	7.8911	4.1843	75.8286
9	7.4484	4.6270	71.2016
10	6.9588	5.1166	66.0850
11	6.4174	5.6580	60.4270
12	5.8188	6.2567	54.1703
13	5.1567	6.9187	47.2517
14	4.4247	7.6507	39.6009
15	3.6152	8.4603	31.1407
16	2.7200	9.3554	21.7853
17	1.7301	10.3453	11.4399
18	.6355	11.4399	0.0000

YEARS 19 — MO PAYT .9878 — AN CONST 11.86

#	INT	PRIN	BALANCE
1	10.0165	1.8371	98.1629
2	9.8221	2.0315	96.1315
3	9.6072	2.2464	93.8851
4	9.3695	2.4841	91.4010
5	9.1066	2.7469	88.6540
6	8.8160	3.0376	85.6164
7	8.4946	3.3590	82.2574
8	8.1392	3.7144	78.5430
9	7.7462	4.1074	74.4356
10	7.3116	4.5420	69.8936
11	6.8310	5.0226	64.8710
12	6.2995	5.5541	59.3169
13	5.7119	6.1417	53.1752
14	5.0620	6.7916	46.3836
15	4.3434	7.5102	38.8734
16	3.5488	8.3048	30.5686
17	2.6700	9.1836	21.3850
18	1.6983	10.1553	11.2298
19	.6238	11.2298	0.0000

YEARS 20 — MO PAYT .9717 — AN CONST 11.66

#	INT	PRIN	BALANCE
1	10.0257	1.6342	98.3658
2	9.8528	1.8071	96.5588
3	9.6616	1.9983	94.5605
4	9.4502	2.2097	92.3508
5	9.2164	2.4435	89.9073
6	8.9578	2.7020	87.2053
7	8.6719	2.9879	84.2173
8	8.3558	3.3041	80.9132
9	8.0062	3.6537	77.2595
10	7.6196	4.0403	73.2192
11	7.1921	4.4678	68.7514
12	6.7193	4.9405	63.8109
13	6.1966	5.4633	58.3476
14	5.6185	6.0414	52.3062
15	4.9793	6.6806	45.6256
16	4.2724	7.3875	38.2382
17	3.4908	8.1691	30.0691
18	2.6264	9.0335	21.0356
19	1.6706	9.9893	11.0463
20	.6136	11.0463	0.0000

YEARS 21 — MO PAYT .9575 — AN CONST 11.50

#	INT	PRIN	BALANCE
1	10.0338	1.4563	98.5437
2	9.8797	1.6104	96.9334
3	9.7093	1.7807	95.1526

#	INT	PRIN	BALANCE
4	9.5209	1.9692	93.1835
5	9.3126	2.1775	91.0060
6	9.0822	2.4079	88.5980
7	8.8274	2.6627	85.9353
8	8.5456	2.9444	82.9909
9	8.2341	3.2560	79.7349
10	7.8896	3.6005	76.1344
11	7.5086	3.9815	72.1529
12	7.0873	4.4027	67.7502
13	6.6215	4.8686	62.8816
14	6.1063	5.3837	57.4979
15	5.5367	5.9534	51.5445
16	4.9068	6.5833	44.9612
17	4.2102	7.2799	37.6813
18	3.4399	8.0502	29.6312
19	2.5881	8.9019	20.7292
20	1.6462	9.8438	10.8854
21	.6047	10.8854	0.0000

YEARS 22 — MO PAYT .9451 — AN CONST 11.35

#	INT	PRIN	BALANCE
1	10.0409	1.2998	98.7002
2	9.9034	1.4373	97.2629
3	9.7513	1.5894	95.6734
4	9.5831	1.7576	93.9158
5	9.3972	1.9436	91.9723
6	9.1915	2.1492	89.8231
7	8.9641	2.3766	87.4464
8	8.7126	2.6281	84.8183
9	8.4346	2.9062	81.9122
10	8.1271	3.2137	78.6985
11	7.7870	3.5537	75.1448
12	7.4110	3.9297	71.2151
13	6.9952	4.3455	66.8696
14	6.5354	4.8053	62.0643
15	6.0270	5.3138	56.7505
16	5.4647	5.8760	50.8745
17	4.8430	6.4977	44.3768
18	4.1555	7.1853	37.1915
19	3.3952	7.9455	29.2460
20	2.5545	8.7862	20.4598
21	1.6248	9.7159	10.7439
22	.5968	10.7439	0.0000

YEARS 23 — MO PAYT .9341 — AN CONST 11.21

#	INT	PRIN	BALANCE
1	10.0472	1.1618	98.8382
2	9.9243	1.2847	97.5535
3	9.7883	1.4206	96.1329
4	9.6380	1.5710	94.5619
5	9.4718	1.7372	92.8247
6	9.2880	1.9210	90.9038
7	9.0847	2.1242	88.7795
8	8.8600	2.3490	86.4305
9	8.6114	2.5976	83.8329
10	8.3366	2.8724	80.9605
11	8.0326	3.1763	77.7842
12	7.6966	3.5124	74.2718
13	7.3249	3.8841	70.3877
14	6.9139	4.2950	66.0927
15	6.4595	4.7495	61.3432
16	5.9570	5.2520	56.0912
17	5.4012	5.8077	50.2835
18	4.7867	6.4222	43.8612
19	4.1072	7.1018	36.7595
20	3.3558	7.8532	28.9063
21	2.5248	8.6841	20.2221
22	1.6060	9.6030	10.6191
23	.5899	10.6191	0.0000

YEARS 24 — MO PAYT .9244 — AN CONST 11.10

#	INT	PRIN	BALANCE
1	10.0527	1.0397	98.9603
2	9.9427	1.1497	97.8106
3	9.8211	1.2713	96.5393
4	9.6866	1.4059	95.1334
5	9.5378	1.5546	93.5788
6	9.3733	1.7191	91.8596
7	9.1914	1.9010	89.9586
8	8.9903	2.1022	87.8565
9	8.7678	2.3246	85.5319
10	8.5219	2.5706	82.9613
11	8.2499	2.8425	80.1188
12	7.9491	3.1433	76.9755
13	7.6165	3.4759	73.4996
14	7.2488	3.8437	69.6559
15	6.8421	4.2504	65.4055
16	6.3923	4.7001	60.7054
17	5.8950	5.1974	55.5080
18	5.3451	5.7473	49.7607
19	4.7370	6.3555	43.4052
20	4.0645	7.0279	36.3773
21	3.3209	7.7716	28.6057
22	2.4986	8.5939	20.0119
23	1.5893	9.5032	10.5087
24	.5837	10.5087	0.0000

YEARS 25 — MO PAYT .9158 — AN CONST 10.99

#	INT	PRIN	BALANCE
1	10.0577	.9315	99.0685
2	9.9591	1.0300	98.0385
3	9.8501	1.1390	96.8995
4	9.7296	1.2595	95.6400
5	9.5963	1.3928	94.2473
6	9.4490	1.5401	92.7071
7	9.2860	1.7031	91.0040
8	9.1058	1.8833	89.1207
9	8.9065	2.0826	87.0381
10	8.6862	2.3029	84.7352
11	8.4425	2.5466	82.1886
12	8.1731	2.8161	79.3725
13	7.8751	3.1140	76.2585
14	7.5456	3.4435	72.8150
15	7.1812	3.8079	69.0071
16	6.7783	4.2108	64.7963
17	6.3328	4.6563	60.1400
18	5.8401	5.1490	54.9910
19	5.2953	5.6938	49.2972
20	4.6928	6.2963	43.0009
21	4.0266	6.9625	36.0384
22	3.2899	7.6992	28.3393
23	2.4753	8.5138	19.8255
24	1.5745	9.4147	10.4108
25	.5783	10.4108	0.0000

YEARS 26 — MO PAYT .9081 — AN CONST 10.90

#	INT	PRIN	BALANCE
1	10.0620	.8353	99.1647
2	9.9737	.9237	98.2410
3	9.8759	1.0214	97.2196
4	9.7678	1.1295	96.0902
5	9.6483	1.2490	94.8412
6	9.5162	1.3811	93.4600
7	9.3700	1.5273	91.9328
8	9.2084	1.6889	90.2439
9	9.0297	1.8676	88.3763
10	8.8321	2.0652	86.3111
11	8.6136	2.2837	84.0274
12	8.3720	2.5253	81.5021
13	8.1048	2.7925	78.7095
14	7.8093	3.0880	75.6215
15	7.4826	3.4148	72.2068
16	7.1213	3.7761	68.4307
17	6.7217	4.1756	64.2551
18	6.2799	4.6174	59.6377
19	5.7913	5.1060	54.5317
20	5.2511	5.6463	48.8854
21	4.6536	6.2437	42.6417
22	3.9930	6.9043	35.7374
23	3.2625	7.6349	28.1026
24	2.4546	8.4427	19.6599
25	1.5613	9.3360	10.3238
26	.5735	10.3238	0.0000

YEARS 27 — MO PAYT .9013 — AN CONST 10.82

#	INT	PRIN	BALANCE
1	10.0659	.7497	99.2503
2	9.9866	.8290	98.4213
3	9.8989	.9167	97.5045
4	9.8019	1.0137	96.4908
5	9.6946	1.1210	95.3698
6	9.5760	1.2396	94.1301
7	9.4448	1.3708	92.7594
8	9.2998	1.5158	91.2435
9	9.1394	1.6762	89.5673
10	8.9621	1.8536	87.7137
11	8.7659	2.0497	85.6640
12	8.5490	2.2666	83.3975
13	8.3092	2.5064	80.8911
14	8.0440	2.7716	78.1195
15	7.7508	3.0649	75.0546
16	7.4265	3.3892	71.6654
17	7.0679	3.7478	67.9177
18	6.6713	4.1443	63.7734
19	6.2328	4.5828	59.1906
20	5.7479	5.0677	54.1228
21	5.2117	5.6039	48.5189
22	4.6188	6.1969	42.3220
23	3.9631	6.8526	35.4695
24	3.2380	7.5776	27.8919
25	2.4362	8.3794	19.5125
26	1.5496	9.2660	10.2464
27	.5692	10.2464	0.0000

YEARS 28 — MO PAYT .8952 — AN CONST 10.75

#	INT	PRIN	BALANCE
1	10.0694	.6734	99.3266
2	9.9981	.7447	98.5819
3	9.9193	.8234	97.7585
4	9.8322	.9106	96.8479
5	9.7359	1.0069	95.8410
6	9.6293	1.1135	94.7275
7	9.5115	1.2313	93.4963
8	9.3812	1.3616	92.1347
9	9.2372	1.5056	90.6291
10	9.0779	1.6649	88.9642
11	8.9017	1.8411	87.1231
12	8.7069	2.0359	85.0872
13	8.4915	2.2513	82.8359
14	8.2533	2.4895	80.3463
15	7.9899	2.7529	77.5934
16	7.6986	3.0442	74.5492
17	7.3765	3.3663	71.1828
18	7.0203	3.7225	67.4603
19	6.6264	4.1164	63.3439
20	6.1908	4.5520	58.7920
21	5.7092	5.0336	53.7584
22	5.1766	5.5662	48.1922
23	4.5877	6.1551	42.0371
24	3.9364	6.8064	35.2306
25	3.2162	7.5266	27.7040
26	2.4198	8.3230	19.3811
27	1.5392	9.2036	10.1774
28	.5653	10.1774	0.0000

YEARS 29 — MO PAYT .8898 — AN CONST 10.68

#	INT	PRIN	BALANCE
1	10.0725	.6053	99.3947
2	10.0084	.6693	98.7254
3	9.9376	.7401	97.9852
4	9.8593	.8185	97.1668
5	9.7727	.9051	96.2617
6	9.6769	1.0008	95.2609
7	9.5710	1.1067	94.1542
8	9.4539	1.2238	92.9304
9	9.3245	1.3533	91.5770
10	9.1813	1.4965	90.0805
11	9.0229	1.6549	88.4257
12	8.8478	1.8299	86.5957
13	8.6542	2.0236	84.5722
14	8.4401	2.2377	82.3345
15	8.2033	2.4745	79.8600
16	7.9415	2.7363	77.1237
17	7.6520	3.0258	74.0979
18	7.3318	3.3460	70.7520
19	6.9778	3.7000	67.0520
20	6.5863	4.0915	62.9605
21	6.1534	4.5244	58.4361
22	5.6746	5.0031	53.4330
23	5.1453	5.5325	47.9005
24	4.5599	6.1179	41.7826
25	3.9126	6.7652	35.0174
26	3.1967	7.4810	27.5364
27	2.4052	8.2726	19.2638
28	1.5299	9.1479	10.1158
29	.5619	10.1158	0.0000

YEARS 30 — MO PAYT .8850 — AN CONST 10.62

#	INT	PRIN	BALANCE
1	10.0753	.5444	99.4556
2	10.0177	.6020	98.8536
3	9.9540	.6657	98.1879
4	9.8835	.7361	97.4518
5	9.8056	.8140	96.6378
6	9.7195	.9001	95.7377
7	9.6243	.9954	94.7423
8	9.5189	1.1007	93.6416
9	9.4025	1.2172	92.4245
10	9.2737	1.3459	91.0785
11	9.1313	1.4884	89.5901
12	8.9738	1.6458	87.9443
13	8.7997	1.8200	86.1243
14	8.6071	2.0126	84.1118
15	8.3941	2.2255	81.8863
16	8.1587	2.4610	79.4253
17	7.8983	2.7214	76.7039
18	7.6103	3.0093	73.6946
19	7.2919	3.3277	70.3668
20	6.9398	3.6798	66.6870
21	6.5504	4.0692	62.6178
22	6.1199	4.4998	58.1180
23	5.6438	4.9759	53.1421
24	5.1173	5.5024	47.6397
25	4.5351	6.0846	41.5551
26	3.8913	6.7284	34.8268
27	3.1793	7.4403	27.3865
28	2.3921	8.2276	19.1589
29	1.5215	9.0981	10.0608
30	.5589	10.0608	0.0000

YEARS 2 — MO PAYT 4.6203 — AN CONST 55.45

#	INT	PRIN	BALANCE
1	7.9617	47.4815	52.5185
2	2.9247	52.5185	0.0000

YEARS 3 — MO PAYT 3.2326 — AN CONST 38.80

#	INT	PRIN	BALANCE
1	8.7566	30.0345	69.9655
2	5.5704	33.2207	36.7448
3	2.0463	36.7448	0.0000

YEARS 4 — MO PAYT 2.5423 — AN CONST 30.51

#	INT	PRIN	BALANCE
1	9.1520	21.3552	78.6448
2	6.8866	23.6206	55.0242
3	4.3808	26.1263	28.8979
4	1.6093	28.8979	0.0000

YEARS 5 — MO PAYT 2.1309 — AN CONST 25.58

#	INT	PRIN	BALANCE
1	9.3877	16.1826	83.8174
2	7.6710	17.8993	65.9180
3	5.7722	19.7982	46.1199
4	3.6719	21.8984	24.2215
5	1.3489	24.2215	0.0000

YEARS 6 — MO PAYT 1.8589 — AN CONST 22.31

#	INT	PRIN	BALANCE
1	9.5435	12.7632	87.2368
2	8.1895	14.1172	73.1196
3	6.6919	15.6148	57.5048
4	5.0355	17.2713	40.2335
5	3.2033	19.1035	21.1300
6	1.1767	21.1300	0.0000

YEARS 7 — MO PAYT 1.6666 — AN CONST 20.00

#	INT	PRIN	BALANCE
1	9.6536	10.3454	89.6546
2	8.5562	11.4428	78.2118
3	7.3423	12.6567	65.5551
4	5.9996	13.9994	51.5557
5	4.5145	15.4845	36.0712
6	2.8719	17.1271	18.9440
7	1.0550	18.9440	0.0000

YEARS 8 — MO PAYT 1.5240 — AN CONST 18.29

#	INT	PRIN	BALANCE
1	9.7353	8.5532	91.4468
2	8.8280	9.4605	81.9863
3	7.8244	10.4641	71.5222
4	6.7143	11.5742	59.9480
5	5.4865	12.8020	47.1460
6	4.1284	14.1601	32.9860
7	2.6262	15.6622	17.3237
8	.9647	17.3237	0.0000

YEARS 9 — MO PAYT 1.4146 — AN CONST 16.98

#	INT	PRIN	BALANCE
1	9.7980	7.1778	92.8222
2	9.0365	7.9392	84.8830
3	8.1943	8.7815	76.1015
4	7.2627	9.7130	66.3885
5	6.2324	10.7434	55.6451
6	5.0927	11.8831	43.7620
7	3.8321	13.1437	30.6183
8	2.4377	14.5380	16.0803
9	.8955	16.0803	0.0000

YEARS 10 — MO PAYT 1.3284 — AN CONST 15.95

#	INT	PRIN	BALANCE
1	9.8474	6.0939	93.9061
2	9.2009	6.7404	87.1657
3	8.4858	7.4554	79.7103
4	7.6950	8.2463	71.4640
5	6.8202	9.1211	62.3429
6	5.8526	10.0887	52.2541
7	4.7823	11.1590	41.0952
8	3.5985	12.3427	28.7524
9	2.2892	13.6521	15.1004
10	.8409	15.1004	0.0000

YEARS 11 — MO PAYT 1.2591 — AN CONST 15.11

#	INT	PRIN	BALANCE
1	9.8871	5.2218	94.7782
2	9.3331	5.7757	89.0025
3	8.7204	6.3884	82.6141
4	8.0427	7.0661	75.5480
5	7.2931	7.8157	67.7323
6	6.4640	8.6448	59.0875
7	5.5469	9.5619	49.5256
8	4.5326	10.5763	38.9493
9	3.4106	11.6982	27.2511
10	2.1696	12.9392	14.3118
11	.7970	14.3118	0.0000

YEARS 12 — MO PAYT 1.2023 — AN CONST 14.43

#	INT	PRIN	BALANCE
1	9.9196	4.5081	95.4919
2	9.4414	4.9864	90.5055
3	8.9124	5.5153	84.9902
4	8.3273	6.1004	78.8898
5	7.6802	6.7476	72.1422
6	6.9644	7.4634	64.6788
7	6.1726	8.2551	56.4237
8	5.2969	9.1308	47.2929
9	4.3283	10.0995	37.1934
10	3.2569	11.1709	26.0226
11	2.0718	12.3559	13.6667
12	.7611	13.6667	0.0000

YEARS 13 — MO PAYT 1.1552 — AN CONST 13.87

#	INT	PRIN	BALANCE
1	9.9466	3.9161	96.0839
2	9.5311	4.3316	91.7523
3	9.0716	4.7911	86.9612
4	8.5634	5.2993	81.6618
5	8.0012	5.8615	75.8003
6	7.3794	6.4833	69.3170
7	6.6916	7.1711	62.1459
8	5.9309	7.9318	54.2141
9	5.0895	8.7733	45.4408
10	4.1588	9.7040	35.7369
11	3.1293	10.7334	25.0035
12	1.9907	11.8720	13.1314
13	.7313	13.1314	0.0000

YEARS 14 — MO PAYT 1.1157 — AN CONST 13.39

#	INT	PRIN	BALANCE
1	9.9692	3.4195	96.5805
2	9.6065	3.7822	92.7983
3	9.2052	4.1835	88.6148
4	8.7614	4.6273	83.9876
5	8.2706	5.1181	78.8694
6	7.7276	5.6611	73.2084
7	7.1271	6.2616	66.9467
8	6.4628	6.9259	60.0208
9	5.7281	7.6606	52.3602
10	4.9154	8.4733	43.8870
11	4.0165	9.3721	34.5148
12	3.0223	10.3664	24.1485
13	1.9226	11.4661	12.6824
14	.7063	12.6824	0.0000

YEARS 15 — MO PAYT 1.0823 — AN CONST 12.99

#	INT	PRIN	BALANCE
1	9.9884	2.9988	97.0012
2	9.6702	3.3169	93.6843
3	9.3184	3.6688	90.0154
4	8.9292	4.0580	85.9574
5	8.4987	4.4885	81.4689
6	8.0225	4.9646	76.5043
7	7.4959	5.4913	71.0130
8	6.9133	6.0739	64.9391
9	6.2690	6.7182	58.2209
10	5.5563	7.4309	50.7901
11	4.7680	8.2192	42.5709
12	3.8961	9.0911	33.4798
13	2.9371	10.0555	23.4243
14	1.8650	11.1222	12.3021
15	.6851	12.3021	0.0000

YEARS 16 — MO PAYT 1.0537 — AN CONST 12.65

#	INT	PRIN	BALANCE
1	10.0047	2.6396	97.3604
2	9.7247	2.9197	94.4407
3	9.4150	3.2294	91.2113
4	9.0724	3.5720	87.6394
5	8.6935	3.9509	83.6885
6	8.2744	4.3700	79.3185
7	7.8108	4.8336	74.4849
8	7.2980	5.3464	69.1385
9	6.7308	5.9135	63.2250
10	6.1035	6.5409	56.6841
11	5.4096	7.2347	49.4494
12	4.6422	8.0022	41.4472
13	3.7933	8.8511	32.5961
14	2.8543	9.7901	22.8060
15	1.8157	10.8286	11.9774
16	.6670	11.9774	0.0000

YEARS 17 — MO PAYT 1.0291 — AN CONST 12.35

#	INT	PRIN	BALANCE
1	10.0188	2.3308	97.6692
2	9.7715	2.5781	95.0910
3	9.4980	2.8516	92.2394
4	9.1955	3.1541	89.0853
5	8.8609	3.4887	85.5966
6	8.4908	3.8588	81.7378
7	8.0815	4.2682	77.4697
8	7.6287	4.7209	72.7487
9	7.1279	5.2217	67.5270
10	6.5740	5.7757	61.7513
11	5.9613	6.3884	55.3629
12	5.2836	7.0661	48.2968
13	4.5340	7.8157	40.4811
14	3.7048	8.6448	31.8363
15	2.7878	9.5619	22.2744
16	1.7734	10.5762	11.6982
17	.6515	11.6982	0.0000

YEARS 18 — MO PAYT 1.0079 — AN CONST 12.10

#	INT	PRIN	BALANCE
1	10.0310	2.0638	97.9362
2	9.8120	2.2827	95.6535
3	9.5699	2.5249	93.1286
4	9.3020	2.7928	90.3358
5	9.0058	3.0890	87.2468
6	8.6781	3.4167	83.8301
7	8.3156	3.7792	80.0509
8	7.9147	4.1801	75.8708
9	7.4713	4.6235	71.2473
10	6.9808	5.1140	66.1334
11	6.4383	5.6565	60.4769
12	5.8382	6.2566	54.2203
13	5.1745	6.9203	47.3000
14	4.4404	7.6544	39.6457
15	3.6284	8.4664	31.1793
16	2.7302	9.3645	21.8147
17	1.7368	10.3580	11.4568
18	.6380	11.4568	0.0000

YEARS 19 — MO PAYT .9894 — AN CONST 11.88

#	INT	PRIN	BALANCE
1	10.0415	1.8317	98.1683
2	9.8472	2.0260	96.1423
3	9.6323	2.2409	93.9014
4	9.3946	2.4787	91.4227
5	9.1316	2.7416	88.6811
6	8.8408	3.0324	85.6487
7	8.5191	3.3541	82.2946
8	8.1633	3.7099	78.5846
9	7.7697	4.1035	74.4811
10	7.3344	4.5388	69.9423
11	6.8529	5.0203	64.9220
12	6.3204	5.5529	59.3691
13	5.7313	6.1419	53.2272
14	5.0797	6.7935	46.4337
15	4.3590	7.5142	38.9195
16	3.5619	8.3113	30.6082
17	2.6802	9.1930	21.4151
18	1.7050	10.1682	11.2469
19	.6263	11.2469	0.0000

YEARS 20 — MO PAYT .9733 — AN CONST 11.68

#	INT	PRIN	BALANCE
1	10.0508	1.6290	98.3710
2	9.8780	1.8019	96.5691
3	9.6868	1.9930	94.5761
4	9.4754	2.2044	92.3717
5	9.2415	2.4383	89.9334
6	8.9829	2.6969	87.2365
7	8.6968	2.9830	84.2534
8	8.3803	3.2995	80.9540
9	8.0303	3.6495	77.3045
10	7.6432	4.0367	73.2678
11	7.2149	4.4649	68.8029
12	6.7413	4.9385	63.8644
13	6.2174	5.4624	58.4020
14	5.6379	6.0419	52.3601
15	4.9970	6.6828	45.6772
16	4.2880	7.3918	38.2855
17	3.5039	8.1759	30.1095
18	2.6366	9.0433	21.0663
19	1.6772	10.0026	11.0637
20	.6161	11.0637	0.0000

YEARS 21 — MO PAYT .9592 — AN CONST 11.52

#	INT	PRIN	BALANCE
1	10.0589	1.4514	98.5486
2	9.9049	1.6054	96.9432
3	9.7346	1.7757	95.1675

#	INT	PRIN	BALANCE
4	9.5462	1.9641	93.2034
5	9.3379	2.1724	91.0310
6	9.1074	2.4029	88.6281
7	8.8525	2.6578	85.9703
8	8.5706	2.9397	83.0306
9	8.2587	3.2516	79.7790
10	7.9138	3.5965	76.1824
11	7.5322	3.9781	72.2044
12	7.1102	4.4001	67.8043
13	6.6434	4.8668	62.9375
14	6.1272	5.3831	57.5543
15	5.5561	5.9542	51.6001
16	4.9244	6.5858	45.0143
17	4.2258	7.2845	37.7298
18	3.4530	8.0573	29.6725
19	2.5983	8.9120	20.7605
20	1.6529	9.8574	10.9031
21	.6072	10.9031	0.0000

YEARS 22 MO PAYT .9468 AN CONST 11.37

#	INT	PRIN	BALANCE
1	10.0660	1.2952	98.7048
2	9.9286	1.4326	97.2722
3	9.7766	1.5846	95.6876
4	9.6085	1.7527	93.9349
5	9.4226	1.9386	91.9962
6	9.2169	2.1443	89.8519
7	8.9894	2.3718	87.4802
8	8.7378	2.6234	84.8568
9	8.4595	2.9017	81.9551
10	8.1517	3.2095	78.7457
11	7.8113	3.5500	75.1957
12	7.4347	3.9265	71.2692
13	7.0181	4.3431	66.9261
14	6.5574	4.8038	62.1223
15	6.0478	5.3134	56.8089
16	5.4841	5.8771	50.9318
17	4.8607	6.5005	44.4312
18	4.1711	7.1901	37.2411
19	3.4083	7.9529	29.2882
20	2.5646	8.7966	20.4916
21	1.6315	9.7297	10.7619
22	.5993	10.7619	0.0000

YEARS 23 MO PAYT .9358 AN CONST 11.23

#	INT	PRIN	BALANCE
1	10.0723	1.1574	98.8426
2	9.9495	1.2802	97.5623
3	9.8137	1.4160	96.1463
4	9.6635	1.5663	94.5800
5	9.4973	1.7324	92.8476
6	9.3135	1.9162	90.9314
7	9.1102	2.1195	88.8119
8	8.8854	2.3443	86.4676
9	8.6367	2.5930	83.8746
10	8.3616	2.8681	81.0066
11	8.0574	3.1723	77.8342
12	7.7208	3.5089	74.3254
13	7.3486	3.8811	70.4443
14	6.9369	4.2928	66.1515
15	6.4815	4.7482	61.4032
16	5.9778	5.2519	56.1513
17	5.4207	5.8091	50.3423
18	4.8044	6.4253	43.9170
19	4.1228	7.1069	36.8100
20	3.3689	7.8608	28.9492
21	2.5350	8.6947	20.2545
22	1.6126	9.6171	10.6373
23	.5924	10.6373	0.0000

YEARS 24 MO PAYT .9261 AN CONST 11.12

#	INT	PRIN	BALANCE
1	10.0778	1.0356	98.9644
2	9.9680	1.1455	97.8189
3	9.8464	1.2670	96.5520
4	9.7120	1.4014	95.1506
5	9.5634	1.5500	93.6006
6	9.3989	1.7145	91.8861
7	9.2171	1.8963	89.9897
8	9.0159	2.0975	87.8922
9	8.7934	2.3200	85.5722
10	8.5473	2.5661	83.0060
11	8.2750	2.8384	80.1677
12	7.9739	3.1395	77.0282
13	7.6409	3.4725	73.5557
14	7.2725	3.8409	69.7147
15	6.8651	4.2484	65.4664
16	6.4144	4.6990	60.7674
17	5.9159	5.1975	55.5698
18	5.3645	5.7489	49.8209
19	4.7547	6.3588	43.4622
20	4.0801	7.0333	36.4288
21	3.3340	7.7794	28.6494
22	2.5087	8.6047	20.0447
23	1.5959	9.5175	10.5272
24	.5862	10.5272	0.0000

YEARS 25 MO PAYT .9175 AN CONST 11.02

#	INT	PRIN	BALANCE
1	10.0827	.9276	99.0724
2	9.9843	1.0260	98.0464
3	9.8755	1.1348	96.9116
4	9.7551	1.2552	95.6564
5	9.6220	1.3884	94.2680
6	9.4747	1.5357	92.7323
7	9.3118	1.6986	91.0338
8	9.1316	1.8788	89.1550
9	8.9323	2.0781	87.0769
10	8.7118	2.2985	84.7784
11	8.4680	2.5423	82.2361
12	8.1983	2.8120	79.4240
13	7.9000	3.1104	76.3137
14	7.5700	3.4403	72.8734
15	7.2051	3.8053	69.0681
16	6.8014	4.2090	64.8591
17	6.3549	4.6555	60.2037
18	5.8610	5.1493	55.0544
19	5.3148	5.6956	49.3588
20	4.7105	6.2998	43.0590
21	4.0422	6.9681	36.0909
22	3.3031	7.7073	28.3837
23	2.4854	8.5249	19.8588
24	1.5811	9.4292	10.4295
25	.5808	10.4295	0.0000

YEARS 26 MO PAYT .9099 AN CONST 10.92

#	INT	PRIN	BALANCE
1	10.0871	.8317	99.1683
2	9.9989	.9199	98.2485
3	9.9013	1.0175	97.2310
4	9.7934	1.1254	96.1056
5	9.6740	1.2448	94.8608
6	9.5419	1.3768	93.4840
7	9.3959	1.5229	91.9611
8	9.2343	1.6844	90.2767
9	9.0556	1.8631	88.4135
10	8.8580	2.0608	86.3528
11	8.6394	2.2794	84.0734
12	8.3976	2.5212	81.5522
13	8.1301	2.7887	78.7635
14	7.8343	3.0845	75.6790
15	7.5071	3.4117	72.2673
16	7.1451	3.7736	68.4937
17	6.7448	4.1739	64.3197
18	6.3020	4.6167	59.7030
19	5.8123	5.1065	54.5965
20	5.2706	5.6482	48.9483
21	4.6714	6.2474	42.7009
22	4.0086	6.9101	35.7908
23	3.2556	7.6432	28.1476
24	2.4648	8.4540	19.6936
25	1.5679	9.3508	10.3428
26	.5760	10.3428	0.0000

YEARS 27 MO PAYT .9031 AN CONST 10.84

#	INT	PRIN	BALANCE
1	10.0910	.7463	99.2537
2	10.0118	.8254	98.4283
3	9.9243	.9130	97.5153
4	9.8274	1.0099	96.5054
5	9.7203	1.1170	95.3884
6	9.6018	1.2355	94.1529
7	9.4707	1.3666	92.7864
8	9.3258	1.5115	91.2748
9	9.1654	1.6719	89.6030
10	8.9880	1.8492	87.7537
11	8.7919	2.0454	85.7083
12	8.5749	2.2624	83.4459
13	8.3349	2.5024	80.9436
14	8.0694	2.7678	78.1757
15	7.7758	3.0615	75.1142
16	7.4510	3.3862	71.7280
17	7.0918	3.7455	67.9825
18	6.6945	4.1428	63.8397
19	6.2550	4.5823	59.2574
20	5.7689	5.0684	54.1891
21	5.2312	5.6061	48.5830
22	4.6365	6.2008	42.3822
23	3.9787	6.8586	35.5237
24	3.2511	7.5861	27.9375
25	2.4464	8.3909	19.5466
26	1.5562	9.2810	10.2656
27	.5717	10.2656	0.0000

YEARS 28 MO PAYT .8971 AN CONST 10.77

#	INT	PRIN	BALANCE
1	10.0945	.6702	99.3298
2	10.0234	.7413	98.5885
3	9.9447	.8199	97.7686
4	9.8578	.9069	96.8617
5	9.7615	1.0031	95.8586
6	9.6551	1.1095	94.7491
7	9.5374	1.2272	93.5219
8	9.4072	1.3574	92.1645
9	9.2633	1.5014	90.6631
10	9.1040	1.6607	89.0025
11	8.9278	1.8368	87.1656
12	8.7330	2.0317	85.1339
13	8.5174	2.2472	82.8867
14	8.2790	2.4856	80.4011
15	8.0153	2.7493	77.6518
16	7.7237	3.0410	74.6108
17	7.4011	3.3635	71.2473
18	7.0443	3.7204	67.5269
19	6.6496	4.1150	63.4119
20	6.2131	4.5516	58.8603
21	5.7302	5.0344	53.8259
22	5.1962	5.5685	48.2574
23	4.6054	6.1592	42.0982
24	3.9521	6.8126	35.2856
25	3.2293	7.5353	27.7503
26	2.4300	8.3347	19.4156
27	1.5458	9.2188	10.1968
28	.5678	10.1968	0.0000

YEARS 29 MO PAYT .8917 AN CONST 10.70

#	INT	PRIN	BALANCE
1	10.0976	.6023	99.3977
2	10.0337	.6661	98.7316
3	9.9630	.7368	97.9948
4	9.8848	.8150	97.1798
5	9.7984	.9014	96.2784
6	9.7028	.9971	95.2813
7	9.5970	1.1028	94.1785
8	9.4800	1.2198	92.9587
9	9.3506	1.3492	91.6095
10	9.2075	1.4924	90.1171
11	9.0491	1.6507	88.4664
12	8.8740	1.8258	86.6407
13	8.6804	2.0195	84.6212
14	8.4661	2.2337	82.3875
15	8.2292	2.4706	79.9169
16	7.9671	2.7327	77.1841
17	7.6772	3.0226	74.1615
18	7.3565	3.3433	70.8182
19	7.0019	3.6980	67.1202
20	6.6096	4.0903	63.0300
21	6.1757	4.5242	58.5058
22	5.6957	5.0041	53.5017
23	5.1649	5.5349	47.9668
24	4.5777	6.1221	41.8447
25	3.9282	6.7716	35.0731
26	3.2099	7.4899	27.5832
27	2.4153	8.2845	19.2987
28	1.5365	9.1633	10.1354
29	.5644	10.1354	0.0000

YEARS 30 MO PAYT .8868 AN CONST 10.65

#	INT	PRIN	BALANCE
1	10.1003	.5415	99.4585
2	10.0429	.5990	98.8595
3	9.9793	.6625	98.1969
4	9.9090	.7328	97.4641
5	9.8313	.8106	96.6535
6	9.7453	.8965	95.7570
7	9.6502	.9917	94.7653
8	9.5450	1.0969	93.6685
9	9.4287	1.2132	92.4553
10	9.3000	1.3419	91.1133
11	9.1576	1.4843	89.6291
12	9.0001	1.6417	87.9873
13	8.8260	1.8159	86.1715
14	8.6333	2.0085	84.1629
15	8.4203	2.2216	81.9413
16	8.1846	2.4573	79.4841
17	7.9239	2.7179	76.7661
18	7.6356	3.0063	73.7599
19	7.3167	3.3252	70.4347
20	6.9639	3.6779	66.7567
21	6.5738	4.0681	62.6886
22	6.1422	4.4997	58.1890
23	5.6649	4.9770	53.2120
24	5.1369	5.5050	47.7070
25	4.5529	6.0890	41.6181
26	3.9070	6.7349	34.8832
27	3.1925	7.4494	27.4338
28	2.4023	8.2396	19.1942
29	1.5282	9.1137	10.0805
30	.5614	10.0805	0.0000

MONTHLY PAYMENT AMORTIZATION SCHEDULE PER $100   10.20 %

YEARS 2 — MO PAYT 4.6237 — AN CONST 55.49

#	INT	PRIN	BALANCE
1	8.0218	47.4630	52.5370
2	2.9477	52.5370	0.0000

YEARS 3 — MO PAYT 3.2361 — AN CONST 38.84

#	INT	PRIN	BALANCE
1	8.8227	30.0107	69.9893
2	5.6144	33.2190	36.7703
3	2.0631	36.7703	0.0000

YEARS 4 — MO PAYT 2.5459 — AN CONST 30.56

#	INT	PRIN	BALANCE
1	9.2211	21.3294	78.6706
2	6.9409	23.6096	55.0611
3	4.4169	26.1336	28.9275
4	1.6230	28.9275	0.0000

YEARS 5 — MO PAYT 2.1346 — AN CONST 25.62

#	INT	PRIN	BALANCE
1	9.4585	16.1562	83.8438
2	7.7314	17.8833	65.9605
3	5.8195	19.7952	46.1653
4	3.7033	21.9114	24.2539
5	1.3608	24.2539	0.0000

YEARS 6 — MO PAYT 1.8627 — AN CONST 22.36

#	INT	PRIN	BALANCE
1	9.6155	12.7367	87.2633
2	8.2538	14.0984	73.1649
3	6.7466	15.6056	57.5593
4	5.0783	17.2739	40.2853
5	3.2316	19.1206	21.1647
6	1.1875	21.1647	0.0000

YEARS 7 — MO PAYT 1.6705 — AN CONST 20.05

#	INT	PRIN	BALANCE
1	9.7264	10.3192	89.6808
2	8.6232	11.4224	78.2584
3	7.4021	12.6435	65.6148
4	6.0504	13.9952	51.6196
5	4.5543	15.4914	36.1282
6	2.8981	17.1475	18.9807
7	1.0650	18.9807	0.0000

YEARS 8 — MO PAYT 1.5280 — AN CONST 18.34

#	INT	PRIN	BALANCE
1	9.8086	8.5276	91.4724
2	8.8970	9.4392	82.0332
3	7.8879	10.4484	71.5848
4	6.7709	11.5654	60.0195
5	5.5345	12.8018	47.2177
6	4.1659	14.1703	33.0473
7	2.6510	15.6852	17.3621
8	.9741	17.3621	0.0000

YEARS 9 — MO PAYT 1.4187 — AN CONST 17.03

#	INT	PRIN	BALANCE
1	9.8717	7.1529	92.8471
2	9.1070	7.9176	84.9295
3	8.2606	8.7641	76.1654
4	7.3237	9.7010	66.4644
5	6.2866	10.7381	55.7263
6	5.1386	11.8861	43.8402
7	3.8679	13.1568	30.6835
8	2.4614	14.5633	16.1202
9	.9045	16.1202	0.0000

YEARS 10 — MO PAYT 1.3326 — AN CONST 16.00

#	INT	PRIN	BALANCE
1	9.9214	6.0698	93.9302
2	9.2725	6.7188	87.2114
3	8.5543	7.4370	79.7744
4	7.7592	8.2321	71.5423
5	6.8791	9.1122	62.4301
6	5.9050	10.0863	52.3438
7	4.8267	11.1646	41.1792
8	3.6331	12.3582	28.8211
9	2.3120	13.6793	15.1417
10	.8496	15.1417	0.0000

YEARS 11 — MO PAYT 1.2633 — AN CONST 15.16

#	INT	PRIN	BALANCE
1	9.9614	5.1985	94.8015
2	9.4057	5.7543	89.0471
3	8.7905	6.3695	82.6777
4	8.1096	7.0504	75.6273
5	7.3558	7.8041	67.8231
6	6.5215	8.6385	59.1846
7	5.5980	9.5620	49.6227
8	4.5758	10.5842	39.0385
9	3.4443	11.7157	27.3228
10	2.1918	12.9682	14.3546
11	.8054	14.3546	0.0000

YEARS 12 — MO PAYT 1.2067 — AN CONST 14.48

#	INT	PRIN	BALANCE
1	9.9941	4.4858	95.5142
2	9.5146	4.9654	90.5489
3	8.9837	5.4962	85.0527
4	8.3962	6.0838	78.9689
5	7.7458	6.7341	72.2348
6	7.0259	7.4541	64.7807
7	6.2290	8.2510	56.5297
8	5.3469	9.1330	47.3967
9	4.3705	10.1094	37.2873
10	3.2898	11.1902	26.0971
11	2.0935	12.3865	13.7107
12	.7693	13.7107	0.0000

YEARS 13 — MO PAYT 1.1597 — AN CONST 13.92

#	INT	PRIN	BALANCE
1	10.0213	3.8947	96.1053
2	9.6049	4.3111	91.7942
3	9.1440	4.7720	87.0222
4	8.6339	5.2821	81.7401
5	8.0692	5.8468	75.8933
6	7.4441	6.4719	69.4214
7	6.7522	7.1638	62.2577
8	5.9864	7.9296	54.3281
9	5.1386	8.7773	45.5507
10	4.2003	9.7157	35.8351
11	3.1616	10.7543	25.0807
12	2.0119	11.9041	13.1767
13	.7393	13.1767	0.0000

YEARS 14 — MO PAYT 1.1202 — AN CONST 13.45

#	INT	PRIN	BALANCE
1	10.0440	3.3990	96.6010
2	9.6806	3.7623	92.8387
3	9.2784	4.1646	88.6741
4	8.8332	4.6098	84.0644
5	8.3404	5.1026	78.9618
6	7.7949	5.6481	73.3137
7	7.1911	6.2519	67.0618
8	6.5227	6.9203	60.1416
9	5.7829	7.6601	52.4815
10	4.9640	8.4790	44.0025
11	4.0575	9.3854	34.6170
12	3.0542	10.3888	24.2282
13	1.9435	11.4994	12.7288
14	.7142	12.7288	0.0000

YEARS 15 — MO PAYT 1.0869 — AN CONST 13.05

#	INT	PRIN	BALANCE
1	10.0633	2.9792	97.0208
2	9.7448	3.2977	93.7231
3	9.3922	3.6502	90.0728
4	9.0020	4.0405	86.0324
5	8.5700	4.4724	81.5599
6	8.0919	4.9506	76.6094
7	7.5627	5.4798	71.1296
8	6.9768	6.0656	65.0639
9	6.3284	6.7141	58.3498
10	5.6106	7.4319	50.9180
11	4.8161	8.2264	42.6916
12	3.9366	9.1058	33.5857
13	2.9632	10.0793	23.5064
14	1.8856	11.1568	12.3496
15	.6929	12.3496	0.0000

YEARS 16 — MO PAYT 1.0584 — AN CONST 12.71

#	INT	PRIN	BALANCE
1	10.0797	2.6209	97.3791
2	9.7995	2.9011	94.4779
3	9.4894	3.2113	91.2667
4	9.1461	3.5546	87.7121
5	8.7661	3.9346	83.7775
6	8.3454	4.3552	79.4223
7	7.8798	4.8208	74.6015
8	7.3645	5.3362	69.2653
9	6.7940	5.9067	63.3586
10	6.1625	6.5381	56.8205
11	5.4636	7.2371	49.5834
12	4.6899	8.0108	41.5727
13	3.8335	8.8672	32.7055
14	2.8855	9.8151	22.8903
15	1.8362	10.8644	12.0259
16	.6747	12.0259	0.0000

YEARS 17 — MO PAYT 1.0339 — AN CONST 12.41

#	INT	PRIN	BALANCE
1	10.0938	2.3130	97.6870
2	9.8466	2.5603	95.1267
3	9.5729	2.8340	92.2926
4	9.2699	3.1370	89.1556
5	8.9345	3.4724	85.6833
6	8.5633	3.8436	81.8397
7	8.1524	4.2545	77.5852
8	7.6976	4.7093	72.8759
9	7.1941	5.2128	67.6632
10	6.6368	5.7700	61.8931
11	6.0200	6.3869	55.5062
12	5.3372	7.0697	48.4365
13	4.5814	7.8255	40.6111
14	3.7448	8.6621	31.9490
15	2.8188	9.5881	22.3609
16	1.7937	10.6131	11.7477
17	.6591	11.7477	0.0000

YEARS 18 — MO PAYT 1.0127 — AN CONST 12.16

#	INT	PRIN	BALANCE
1	10.1061	2.0469	97.9531
2	9.8872	2.2657	95.6875
3	9.6450	2.5079	93.1796
4	9.3769	2.7760	90.4035
5	9.0801	3.0728	87.3308
6	8.7516	3.4013	83.9295
7	8.3880	3.7649	80.1646
8	7.9855	4.1674	75.9972
9	7.5540	4.6129	71.3843
10	7.0469	5.1061	66.2782
11	6.5010	5.6519	60.6263
12	5.8968	6.2562	54.3701
13	5.2279	6.9250	47.4451
14	4.4876	7.6653	39.7798
15	3.6682	8.4848	31.2950
16	2.7611	9.3919	21.9032
17	1.7570	10.3959	11.5073
18	.6456	11.5073	0.0000

YEARS 19 — MO PAYT .9944 — AN CONST 11.94

#	INT	PRIN	BALANCE
1	10.1167	1.8156	98.1844
2	9.9226	2.0097	96.1747
3	9.7077	2.2245	93.9501
4	9.4699	2.4624	91.4878
5	9.2067	2.7256	88.7622
6	8.9153	3.0170	85.7452
7	8.5927	3.3395	82.4056
8	8.2357	3.6965	78.7091
9	7.8405	4.0917	74.6174
10	7.4031	4.5292	70.0882
11	6.9189	5.0134	65.0748
12	6.3830	5.5493	59.5255
13	5.7897	6.1426	53.3830
14	5.1330	6.7993	46.5837
15	4.4061	7.5261	39.0576
16	3.6016	8.3307	30.7268
17	2.7109	9.2213	21.5055
18	1.7251	10.2072	11.2984
19	.6339	11.2984	0.0000

YEARS 20 — MO PAYT .9783 — AN CONST 11.74

#	INT	PRIN	BALANCE
1	10.1259	1.6138	98.3862
2	9.9534	1.7863	96.5999
3	9.7624	1.9773	94.6227
4	9.5511	2.1887	92.4340
5	9.3171	2.4226	90.0114
6	9.0581	2.6816	87.3297
7	8.7714	2.9683	84.3614
8	8.4541	3.2856	81.0758
9	8.1028	3.6369	77.4389
10	7.7140	4.0257	73.4132
11	7.2836	4.4561	68.9571
12	6.8073	4.9325	64.0247
13	6.2800	5.4598	58.5649
14	5.6963	6.0434	52.5215
15	5.0502	6.6895	45.8319
16	4.3350	7.4047	38.4273
17	3.5434	8.1963	30.2310
18	2.6672	9.0725	21.1585
19	1.6973	10.0424	11.1160
20	.6237	11.1160	0.0000

YEARS 21 — MO PAYT .9643 — AN CONST 11.58

#	INT	PRIN	BALANCE
1	10.1341	1.4370	98.5630
2	9.9804	1.5906	96.9724
3	9.8104	1.7606	95.2118

#	INT	PRIN	BALANCE
4	9.6222	1.9489	93.2630
5	9.4138	2.1572	91.1058
6	9.1832	2.3878	88.7179
7	8.9279	2.6431	86.0748
8	8.6454	2.9257	83.1492
9	8.3326	3.2384	79.9108
10	7.9864	3.5846	76.3261
11	7.6032	3.9679	72.3583
12	7.1790	4.3920	67.9662
13	6.7094	4.8616	63.1047
14	6.1897	5.3813	57.7234
15	5.6144	5.9566	51.7668
16	4.9776	6.5934	45.1734
17	4.2727	7.2983	37.8751
18	3.4925	8.0785	29.7966
19	2.6289	8.9422	20.8544
20	1.6729	9.8981	10.9563
21	.6147	10.9563	0.0000

YEARS 22   MO PAYT .9519   AN CONST 11.43

#	INT	PRIN	BALANCE
1	10.1412	1.2815	98.7185
2	10.0042	1.4186	97.2999
3	9.8525	1.5702	95.7297
4	9.6847	1.7381	93.9916
5	9.4989	1.9239	92.0677
6	9.2932	2.1296	89.9382
7	9.0655	2.3572	87.5810
8	8.8135	2.6092	84.9718
9	8.5346	2.8882	82.0836
10	8.2258	3.1969	78.8867
11	7.8840	3.5387	75.3480
12	7.5057	3.9170	71.4310
13	7.0870	4.3358	67.0952
14	6.6235	4.7993	62.2960
15	6.1104	5.3123	56.9836
16	5.5425	5.8803	51.1033
17	4.9138	6.5089	44.5944
18	4.2180	7.2047	37.3897
19	3.4478	7.9750	29.4147
20	2.5952	8.8276	20.5872
21	1.6515	9.7713	10.8159
22	.6068	10.8159	0.0000

YEARS 23   MO PAYT .9410   AN CONST 11.30

#	INT	PRIN	BALANCE
1	10.1475	1.1445	98.8555
2	10.0251	1.2669	97.5886
3	9.8897	1.4023	96.1863
4	9.7398	1.5522	94.6340
5	9.5738	1.7182	92.9159
6	9.3901	1.9019	91.0140
7	9.1868	2.1052	88.9088
8	8.9618	2.3302	86.5786
9	8.7126	2.5794	83.9992
10	8.4369	2.8551	81.1441
11	8.1317	3.1603	77.9838
12	7.7938	3.4982	74.4856
13	7.4198	3.8722	70.6134
14	7.0059	4.2861	66.3273
15	6.5477	4.7443	61.5830
16	6.0405	5.2515	56.3314
17	5.4790	5.8130	50.5185
18	4.8576	6.4344	44.0840
19	4.1697	7.1223	36.9618
20	3.4083	7.8837	29.0781
21	2.5655	8.7265	20.3515
22	1.6326	9.6594	10.6921
23	.5999	10.6921	0.0000

YEARS 24   MO PAYT .9314   AN CONST 11.18

#	INT	PRIN	BALANCE
1	10.1530	1.0234	98.9766
2	10.0436	1.1328	97.8438
3	9.9225	1.2539	96.5899
4	9.7885	1.3880	95.2019
5	9.6401	1.5363	93.6656
6	9.4758	1.7006	91.9650
7	9.2940	1.8824	90.0826
8	9.0928	2.0836	87.9989
9	8.8700	2.3064	85.6925
10	8.6235	2.5530	83.1396
11	8.3505	2.8259	80.3137
12	8.0484	3.1280	77.1857
13	7.7140	3.4624	73.7233
14	7.3439	3.8325	69.8908
15	6.9342	4.2423	65.6485
16	6.4806	4.6958	60.9527
17	5.9786	5.1978	55.7549
18	5.4230	5.7535	50.0014
19	4.8079	6.3686	43.6329
20	4.1270	7.0494	36.5835
21	3.3734	7.8030	28.7805
22	2.5392	8.6372	20.1433
23	1.6159	9.5606	10.5827
24	.5938	10.5827	0.0000

YEARS 25   MO PAYT .9228   AN CONST 11.08

#	INT	PRIN	BALANCE
1	10.1580	.9161	99.0839
2	10.0600	1.0140	98.0699
3	9.9516	1.1224	96.9475
4	9.8316	1.2424	95.7050
5	9.6988	1.3753	94.3298
6	9.5518	1.5223	92.8075
7	9.3890	1.6850	91.1225
8	9.2089	1.8652	89.2573
9	9.0095	2.0645	87.1928
10	8.7888	2.2853	84.9075
11	8.5445	2.5296	82.3780
12	8.2741	2.8000	79.5780
13	7.9747	3.0993	76.4786
14	7.6434	3.4307	73.0479
15	7.2766	3.7974	69.2505
16	6.8706	4.2034	65.0471
17	6.4213	4.6528	60.3943
18	5.9239	5.1502	55.2442
19	5.3733	5.7008	49.5434
20	4.7638	6.3102	43.2332
21	4.0892	6.9848	36.2484
22	3.3425	7.7315	28.5168
23	2.5160	8.5581	19.9587
24	1.6010	9.4730	10.4857
25	.5883	10.4857	0.0000

YEARS 26   MO PAYT .9153   AN CONST 10.99

#	INT	PRIN	BALANCE
1	10.1623	.8208	99.1792
2	10.0746	.9086	98.2706
3	9.9774	1.0057	97.2649
4	9.8699	1.1132	96.1517
5	9.7509	1.2322	94.9195
6	9.6192	1.3640	93.5555
7	9.4734	1.5098	92.0457
8	9.3120	1.6712	90.3745
9	9.1333	1.8498	88.5247
10	8.9355	2.0476	86.4771
11	8.7166	2.2665	84.2106
12	8.4743	2.5088	81.7018
13	8.2061	2.7770	78.9248
14	7.9093	3.0739	75.8509
15	7.5806	3.4025	72.4484
16	7.2169	3.7663	68.6821
17	6.8143	4.1689	64.5132
18	6.3686	4.6146	59.8986
19	5.8752	5.1079	54.7907
20	5.3292	5.6540	49.1367
21	4.7247	6.2584	42.8783
22	4.0557	6.9275	35.9508
23	3.3151	7.6681	28.2827
24	2.4953	8.4878	19.7949
25	1.5879	9.3952	10.3997
26	.5835	10.3997	0.0000

YEARS 27   MO PAYT .9085   AN CONST 10.91

#	INT	PRIN	BALANCE
1	10.1662	.7361	99.2639
2	10.0875	.8148	98.4491
3	10.0004	.9019	97.5473
4	9.9040	.9983	96.5490
5	9.7973	1.1050	95.4439
6	9.6791	1.2232	94.2208
7	9.5484	1.3539	92.8668
8	9.4036	1.4987	91.3682
9	9.2434	1.6589	89.7093
10	9.0661	1.8362	87.8731
11	8.8698	2.0325	85.8405
12	8.6525	2.2498	83.5907
13	8.4120	2.4903	81.1004
14	8.1457	2.7566	78.3438
15	7.8510	3.0513	75.2925
16	7.5248	3.3775	71.9151
17	7.1638	3.7385	68.1765
18	6.7641	4.1382	64.0383
19	6.3217	4.5806	59.4577
20	5.8320	5.0703	54.3874
21	5.2899	5.6124	48.7750
22	4.6900	6.2124	42.5627
23	4.0258	6.8765	35.6862
24	3.2907	7.6116	28.0746
25	2.4769	8.4254	19.6492
26	1.5762	9.3261	10.3231
27	.5792	10.3231	0.0000

YEARS 28   MO PAYT .9025   AN CONST 10.84

#	INT	PRIN	BALANCE
1	10.1697	.6606	99.3394
2	10.0991	.7312	98.6082
3	10.0209	.8094	97.7988
4	9.9344	.8959	96.9029
5	9.8386	.9917	95.9111
6	9.7326	1.0977	94.8134
7	9.6152	1.2151	93.5983
8	9.4853	1.3450	92.2534
9	9.3415	1.4888	90.7646
10	9.1824	1.6479	89.1167
11	9.0062	1.8241	87.2926
12	8.8112	2.0191	85.2735
13	8.5953	2.2350	83.0385
14	8.3564	2.4739	80.5646
15	8.0919	2.7384	77.8263
16	7.7992	3.0311	74.7952
17	7.4751	3.3552	71.4400
18	7.1164	3.7138	67.7262
19	6.7194	4.1109	63.6153
20	6.2799	4.5504	59.0649
21	5.7935	5.0368	54.0281
22	5.2550	5.5753	48.4528
23	4.6590	6.1713	42.2815
24	3.9992	6.8311	35.4504
25	3.2689	7.5614	27.8891
26	2.4606	8.3697	19.5194
27	1.5658	9.2645	10.2549
28	.5754	10.2549	0.0000

YEARS 29   MO PAYT .8972   AN CONST 10.77

#	INT	PRIN	BALANCE
1	10.1728	.5933	99.4067
2	10.1094	.6567	98.7501
3	10.0391	.7269	98.0232
4	9.9614	.8046	97.2186
5	9.8754	.8906	96.3280
6	9.7802	.9858	95.3421
7	9.6748	1.0912	94.2509
8	9.5582	1.2079	93.0431
9	9.4290	1.3370	91.7061
10	9.2861	1.4799	90.2261
11	9.1279	1.6381	88.5880
12	8.9528	1.8133	86.7747
13	8.7589	2.0071	84.7676
14	8.5443	2.2217	82.5459
15	8.3068	2.4592	80.0867
16	8.0439	2.7221	77.3646
17	7.7529	3.0131	74.3514
18	7.4308	3.3353	71.0162
19	7.0742	3.6918	67.3244
20	6.6795	4.0865	63.2379
21	6.2427	4.5234	58.7145
22	5.7591	5.0069	53.7076
23	5.2238	5.5422	48.1654
24	4.6313	6.1347	42.0307
25	3.9755	6.7905	35.2401
26	3.2495	7.5165	27.7236
27	2.4460	8.3201	19.4036
28	1.5565	9.2095	10.1941
29	.5720	10.1941	0.0000

YEARS 30   MO PAYT .8924   AN CONST 10.71

#	INT	PRIN	BALANCE
1	10.1755	.5331	99.4669
2	10.1185	.5901	98.8768
3	10.0555	.6532	98.2236
4	9.9856	.7230	97.5006
5	9.9083	.8003	96.7003
6	9.8228	.8859	95.8144
7	9.7281	.9806	94.8339
8	9.6232	1.0854	93.7485
9	9.5072	1.2014	92.5470
10	9.3788	1.3299	91.2172
11	9.2366	1.4720	89.7451
12	9.0792	1.6294	88.1157
13	8.9050	1.8036	86.3121
14	8.7122	1.9964	84.3157
15	8.4988	2.2099	82.1058
16	8.2625	2.4461	79.6597
17	8.0010	2.7076	76.9521
18	7.7116	2.9971	73.9551
19	7.3912	3.3175	70.6376
20	7.0365	3.6721	66.9655
21	6.6439	4.0647	62.9008
22	6.2094	4.4992	58.4015
23	5.7284	4.9802	53.4213
24	5.1960	5.5127	47.9086
25	4.6066	6.1020	41.8066
26	3.9543	6.7543	35.0523
27	3.2322	7.4764	27.5758
28	2.4329	8.2757	19.3001
29	1.5482	9.1604	10.1397
30	.5689	10.1397	0.0000

YEARS 2 — MO PAYT 4.6260 — AN CONST 55.52

#	INT	PRIN	BALANCE
1	8.0619	47.4506	52.5494
2	2.9631	52.5494	0.0000

YEARS 3 — MO PAYT 3.2385 — AN CONST 38.87

#	INT	PRIN	BALANCE
1	8.8668	29.9948	70.0052
2	5.6437	33.2179	36.7873
3	2.0743	36.7873	0.0000

YEARS 4 — MO PAYT 2.5483 — AN CONST 30.58

#	INT	PRIN	BALANCE
1	9.2672	21.3122	78.6878
2	6.9771	23.6023	55.0856
3	4.4409	26.1384	28.9471
4	1.6322	28.9471	0.0000

YEARS 5 — MO PAYT 2.1370 — AN CONST 25.65

#	INT	PRIN	BALANCE
1	9.5058	16.1385	83.8615
2	7.7716	17.8727	65.9888
3	5.8511	19.7932	46.1956
4	3.7242	21.9201	24.2755
5	1.3688	24.2755	0.0000

YEARS 6 — MO PAYT 1.8652 — AN CONST 22.39

#	INT	PRIN	BALANCE
1	9.6635	12.7191	87.2809
2	8.2967	14.0858	73.1950
3	6.7831	15.5994	57.5956
4	5.1069	17.2757	40.3199
5	3.2505	19.1320	21.1879
6	1.1947	21.1879	0.0000

YEARS 7 — MO PAYT 1.6731 — AN CONST 20.08

#	INT	PRIN	BALANCE
1	9.7749	10.3018	89.6982
2	8.6680	11.4088	78.2894
3	7.4420	12.6347	65.6546
4	6.0844	13.9924	51.6622
5	4.5808	15.4960	36.1662
6	2.9157	17.1611	19.0051
7	1.0716	19.0051	0.0000

YEARS 8 — MO PAYT 1.5307 — AN CONST 18.37

#	INT	PRIN	BALANCE
1	9.8575	8.5106	91.4894
2	8.9430	9.4251	82.0643
3	7.9303	10.4379	71.6265
4	6.8087	11.5595	60.0670
5	5.5665	12.8016	47.2655
6	4.1909	14.1772	33.0883
7	2.6675	15.7006	17.3877
8	.9804	17.3877	0.0000

YEARS 9 — MO PAYT 1.4214 — AN CONST 17.06

#	INT	PRIN	BALANCE
1	9.9209	7.1364	92.8636
2	9.1541	7.9032	84.9604
3	8.3048	8.7525	76.2079
4	7.3643	9.6930	66.5149
5	6.3228	10.7345	55.7804
6	5.1693	11.8880	43.8924
7	3.8919	13.1654	30.7270
8	2.4772	14.5801	16.1468
9	.9105	16.1468	0.0000

YEARS 10 — MO PAYT 1.3354 — AN CONST 16.03

#	INT	PRIN	BALANCE
1	9.9708	6.0538	93.9462
2	9.3203	6.7044	87.2418
3	8.5999	7.4248	79.8170
4	7.8021	8.2226	71.5944
5	6.9185	9.1062	62.4882
6	5.9400	10.0847	52.4036
7	4.8564	11.1683	41.2352
8	3.6563	12.3684	28.8668
9	2.3272	13.6975	15.1693
10	.8553	15.1693	0.0000

YEARS 11 — MO PAYT 1.2662 — AN CONST 15.20

#	INT	PRIN	BALANCE
1	10.0110	5.1831	94.8169
2	9.4540	5.7401	89.0768
3	8.8372	6.3569	82.7200
4	8.1542	7.0399	75.6800
5	7.3977	7.7964	67.8836
6	6.5599	8.6342	59.2494
7	5.6321	9.5620	49.6874
8	4.6046	10.5895	39.0980
9	3.4668	11.7274	27.3706
10	2.2066	12.9875	14.3831
11	.8110	14.3831	0.0000

YEARS 12 — MO PAYT 1.2096 — AN CONST 14.52

#	INT	PRIN	BALANCE
1	10.0438	4.4710	95.5290
2	9.5634	4.9514	90.5777
3	9.0314	5.4834	85.0942
4	8.4421	6.0727	79.0216
5	7.7896	6.7252	72.2964
6	7.0669	7.4478	64.8485
7	6.2666	8.2482	56.6004
8	5.3803	9.1345	47.4659
9	4.3988	10.1160	37.3499
10	3.3118	11.2030	26.1469
11	2.1079	12.4069	13.7400
12	.7748	13.7400	0.0000

YEARS 13 — MO PAYT 1.1626 — AN CONST 13.96

#	INT	PRIN	BALANCE
1	10.0711	3.8805	96.1195
2	9.6541	4.2975	91.8221
3	9.1923	4.7592	87.0628
4	8.6809	5.2706	81.7922
5	8.1145	5.8370	75.9552
6	7.4873	6.4642	69.4909
7	6.7927	7.1588	62.3321
8	6.0234	7.9281	54.4040
9	5.1715	8.7800	45.6240
10	4.2281	9.7235	35.9006
11	3.1832	10.7683	25.1323
12	2.0261	11.9254	13.2069
13	.7447	13.2069	0.0000

YEARS 14 — MO PAYT 1.1233 — AN CONST 13.48

#	INT	PRIN	BALANCE
1	10.0939	3.3853	96.6147
2	9.7301	3.7491	92.8655
3	9.3273	4.1520	88.7136
4	8.8811	4.5981	84.1154
5	8.3870	5.0922	79.0232
6	7.8398	5.6394	73.3838
7	7.2338	6.2454	67.1384
8	6.5627	6.9165	60.2220
9	5.8195	7.6597	52.5623
10	4.9965	8.4828	44.0795
11	4.0849	9.3943	34.6852
12	3.0755	10.4038	24.2814
13	1.9575	11.5217	12.7598
14	.7195	12.7598	0.0000

YEARS 15 — MO PAYT 1.0900 — AN CONST 13.08

#	INT	PRIN	BALANCE
1	10.1132	2.9662	97.0338
2	9.7945	3.2849	93.7489
3	9.4415	3.6379	90.1110
4	9.0506	4.0288	86.0822
5	8.6177	4.4617	81.6204
6	8.1382	4.9412	76.6792
7	7.6073	5.4721	71.2071
8	7.0193	6.0601	65.1470
9	6.3681	6.7113	58.4357
10	5.6469	7.4325	51.0032
11	4.8483	8.2312	42.7720
12	3.9638	9.1156	33.6564
13	2.9843	10.0952	23.5612
14	1.8995	11.1799	12.3813
15	.6981	12.3813	0.0000

YEARS 16 — MO PAYT 1.0615 — AN CONST 12.74

#	INT	PRIN	BALANCE
1	10.1297	2.6085	97.3915
2	9.8494	2.8888	94.5027
3	9.5390	3.1992	91.3034
4	9.1952	3.5430	87.7604
5	8.8145	3.9237	83.8367
6	8.3929	4.3454	79.4913
7	7.9260	4.8123	74.6791
8	7.4088	5.3294	69.3497
9	6.8362	5.9021	63.4476
10	6.2020	6.5363	56.9113
11	5.4996	7.2386	49.6727
12	4.7218	8.0164	41.6563
13	3.8604	8.8779	32.7784
14	2.9064	9.8318	22.9466
15	1.8499	10.8883	12.0583
16	.6799	12.0583	0.0000

YEARS 17 — MO PAYT 1.0371 — AN CONST 12.45

#	INT	PRIN	BALANCE
1	10.1439	2.3012	97.6988
2	9.8966	2.5485	95.1503
3	9.6228	2.8223	92.3280
4	9.3195	3.1256	89.2023
5	8.9836	3.4615	85.7409
6	8.6117	3.8334	81.9074
7	8.1997	4.2454	77.6621
8	7.7436	4.7015	72.9605
9	7.2384	5.2067	67.7538
10	6.6789	5.7662	61.9875
11	6.0592	6.3858	55.6017
12	5.3731	7.0720	48.5297
13	4.6131	7.8320	40.6977
14	3.7715	8.6736	32.0241
15	2.8395	9.6056	22.4186
16	1.8074	10.6377	11.7808
17	.6643	11.7808	0.0000

YEARS 18 — MO PAYT 1.0160 — AN CONST 12.20

#	INT	PRIN	BALANCE
1	10.1561	2.0356	97.9644
2	9.9374	2.2544	95.7100
3	9.6951	2.4966	93.2134
4	9.4269	2.7649	90.4485
5	9.1298	3.0620	87.3865
6	8.8007	3.3910	83.9955
7	8.4364	3.7554	80.2401
8	8.0328	4.1589	76.0812
9	7.5859	4.6058	71.4753
10	7.0910	5.1008	66.3746
11	6.5429	5.6489	60.7257
12	5.9359	6.2559	54.4698
13	5.2637	6.9281	47.5418
14	4.5192	7.6725	39.8692
15	3.6948	8.4970	31.3722
16	2.7817	9.4100	21.9622
17	1.7706	10.4212	11.5410
18	.6508	11.5410	0.0000

YEARS 19 — MO PAYT .9976 — AN CONST 11.98

#	INT	PRIN	BALANCE
1	10.1668	1.8049	98.1951
2	9.9728	1.9989	96.1962
3	9.7580	2.2137	93.9825
4	9.5202	2.4516	91.5309
5	9.2567	2.7150	88.8160
6	8.9650	3.0067	85.8092
7	8.6419	3.3298	82.4794
8	8.2841	3.6876	78.7918
9	7.8878	4.0839	74.7079
10	7.4490	4.5227	70.1852
11	6.9630	5.0087	65.1765
12	6.4248	5.5469	59.6296
13	5.8288	6.1429	53.4867
14	5.1687	6.8030	46.6837
15	4.4377	7.5341	39.1496
16	3.6281	8.3436	30.8060
17	2.7315	9.2402	21.5658
18	1.7386	10.2331	11.3327
19	.6390	11.3327	0.0000

YEARS 20 — MO PAYT .9816 — AN CONST 11.78

#	INT	PRIN	BALANCE
1	10.1760	1.6037	98.3963
2	10.0037	1.7760	96.6203
3	9.8129	1.9668	94.6535
4	9.6015	2.1782	92.4753
5	9.3675	2.4122	90.0631
6	9.1083	2.6714	87.3916
7	8.8212	2.9585	84.4331
8	8.5033	3.2764	81.1567
9	8.1512	3.6285	77.5282
10	7.7613	4.0184	73.5099
11	7.3295	4.4502	69.0597
12	6.8514	4.9284	64.1313
13	6.3218	5.4579	58.6734
14	5.7353	6.0444	52.6289
15	5.0858	6.6939	45.9350
16	4.3665	7.4132	38.5218
17	3.5699	8.2098	30.3120
18	2.6877	9.0920	21.2200
19	1.7107	10.0690	11.1510
20	.6288	11.1510	0.0000

YEARS 21 — MO PAYT .9676 — AN CONST 11.62

#	INT	PRIN	BALANCE
1	10.1842	1.4274	98.5726
2	10.0308	1.5808	96.9918
3	9.8609	1.7506	95.2412

#	INT	PRIN	BALANCE
4	9.6728	1.9388	93.3024
5	9.4645	2.1471	91.1553
6	9.2338	2.3778	88.7775
7	8.9783	2.6333	86.1442
8	8.6953	2.9163	83.2279
9	8.3819	3.2296	79.9983
10	8.0349	3.5767	76.4216
11	7.6506	3.9610	72.4606
12	7.2249	4.3867	68.0739
13	6.7536	4.8580	63.2159
14	6.2315	5.3800	57.8359
15	5.6534	5.9582	51.8777
16	5.0132	6.5984	45.2793
17	4.3042	7.3074	37.9719
18	3.5189	8.0926	29.8793
19	2.6493	8.9622	20.9171
20	1.6863	9.9253	10.9918
21	.6198	10.9918	0.0000

YEARS 22	MO PAYT .9553	AN CONST 11.47	
#	INT	PRIN	BALANCE
1	10.1913	1.2725	98.7275
2	10.0546	1.4092	97.3183
3	9.9032	1.5607	95.7576
4	9.7355	1.7284	94.0292
5	9.5497	1.9141	92.1151
6	9.3441	2.1198	89.9954
7	9.1163	2.3475	87.6478
8	8.8640	2.5998	85.0480
9	8.5847	2.8792	82.1689
10	8.2753	3.1885	78.9803
11	7.9326	3.5312	75.4491
12	7.5532	3.9106	71.5385
13	7.1330	4.3308	67.2077
14	6.6676	4.7962	62.4115
15	6.1522	5.3116	57.0999
16	5.5815	5.8823	51.2176
17	4.9494	6.5144	44.7032
18	4.2494	7.2144	37.4887
19	3.4742	7.9897	29.4991
20	2.6156	8.8482	20.6509
21	1.6649	9.7990	10.8519
22	.6119	10.8519	0.0000

YEARS 23	MO PAYT .9445	AN CONST 11.34	
#	INT	PRIN	BALANCE
1	10.1976	1.1360	98.8640
2	10.0755	1.2580	97.6060
3	9.9404	1.3932	96.2128
4	9.7907	1.5429	94.6698
5	9.6249	1.7087	92.9611
6	9.4412	1.8923	91.0687
7	9.2379	2.0957	88.9730
8	9.0127	2.3209	86.6522
9	8.7633	2.5703	84.0819
10	8.4871	2.8465	81.2354
11	8.1813	3.1523	78.0831
12	7.8425	3.4911	74.5921
13	7.4674	3.8662	70.7259
14	7.0520	4.2816	66.4442
15	6.5919	4.7417	61.7025
16	6.0824	5.2512	56.4513
17	5.5181	5.8155	50.6358
18	4.8932	6.4404	44.1953
19	4.2011	7.1325	37.0629
20	3.4347	7.8989	29.1640
21	2.5859	8.7477	20.4163
22	1.6459	9.6877	10.7286
23	.6049	10.7286	0.0000

YEARS 24	MO PAYT .9349	AN CONST 11.22	
#	INT	PRIN	BALANCE
1	10.2032	1.0153	98.9847
2	10.0941	1.1244	97.8602
3	9.9732	1.2453	96.6149
4	9.8394	1.3791	95.2359
5	9.6912	1.5273	93.7086
6	9.5271	1.6914	92.0172
7	9.3454	1.8731	90.1441
8	9.1441	2.0744	88.0697
9	8.9212	2.2973	85.7724
10	8.6743	2.5442	83.2282
11	8.4010	2.8176	80.4106
12	8.0982	3.1203	77.2903
13	7.7629	3.4556	73.8347
14	7.3916	3.8269	70.0078
15	6.9804	4.2382	65.7696
16	6.5249	4.6936	61.0760
17	6.0206	5.1979	55.8781
18	5.4621	5.7565	50.1216
19	4.8435	6.3750	43.7466
20	4.1585	7.0601	36.6866
21	3.3998	7.8187	28.8679
22	2.5597	8.6589	20.2090
23	1.6292	9.5893	10.6197
24	.5988	10.6197	0.0000

YEARS 25	MO PAYT .9264	AN CONST 11.12	
#	INT	PRIN	BALANCE
1	10.2081	.9085	99.0915
2	10.1105	1.0061	98.0854
3	10.0024	1.1142	96.9712
4	9.8826	1.2340	95.7372
5	9.7500	1.3666	94.3707
6	9.6032	1.5134	92.8573
7	9.4406	1.6760	91.1812
8	9.2605	1.8561	89.3251
9	9.0610	2.0556	87.2696
10	8.8402	2.2764	84.9931
11	8.5955	2.5211	82.4721
12	8.3246	2.7920	79.6801
13	8.0246	3.0920	76.5881
14	7.6924	3.4242	73.1639
15	7.3244	3.7922	69.3717
16	6.9169	4.1997	65.1721
17	6.4657	4.6509	60.5211
18	5.9659	5.1507	55.3705
19	5.4124	5.7042	49.6663
20	4.7995	6.3171	43.3492
21	4.1207	6.9959	36.3533
22	3.3689	7.7477	28.6056
23	2.5364	8.5802	20.0254
24	1.6144	9.5022	10.5232
25	.5934	10.5232	0.0000

YEARS 26	MO PAYT .9188	AN CONST 11.03	
#	INT	PRIN	BALANCE
1	10.2125	.8137	99.1863
2	10.1250	.9011	98.2852
3	10.0282	.9979	97.2873
4	9.9210	1.1052	96.1821
5	9.8022	1.2239	94.9582
6	9.6707	1.3554	93.6028
7	9.5251	1.5011	92.1017
8	9.3638	1.6624	90.4393
9	9.1851	1.8410	88.5983
10	8.9873	2.0388	86.5595
11	8.7682	2.2579	84.3016
12	8.5256	2.5005	81.8010
13	8.2569	2.7692	79.0318
14	7.9593	3.0668	75.9650
15	7.6298	3.3964	72.5686
16	7.2648	3.7613	68.8073
17	6.8607	4.1655	64.6418
18	6.4131	4.6131	60.0287
19	5.9174	5.1088	54.9199
20	5.3684	5.6578	49.2622
21	4.7604	6.2657	42.9965
22	4.0872	6.9390	36.0575
23	3.3415	7.6846	28.3728
24	2.5158	8.5104	19.8625
25	1.6013	9.4249	10.4376
26	.5885	10.4376	0.0000

YEARS 27	MO PAYT .9121	AN CONST 10.95	
#	INT	PRIN	BALANCE
1	10.2164	.7294	99.2706
2	10.1380	.8077	98.4629
3	10.0512	.8945	97.5684
4	9.9551	.9907	96.5777
5	9.8486	1.0971	95.4806
6	9.7307	1.2150	94.2656
7	9.6002	1.3455	92.9201
8	9.4556	1.4901	91.4300
9	9.2955	1.6503	89.7797
10	9.1181	1.8276	87.9521
11	8.9218	2.0240	85.9281
12	8.7043	2.2415	83.6867
13	8.4634	2.4823	81.2044
14	8.1967	2.7490	78.4553
15	7.9013	3.0444	75.4109
16	7.5741	3.3716	72.0393
17	7.2118	3.7339	68.3054
18	6.8106	4.1351	64.1703
19	6.3363	4.5794	59.5909
20	5.8742	5.0715	54.5194
21	5.3292	5.6165	48.9029
22	4.7257	6.2200	42.6829
23	4.0573	6.8884	35.7945
24	3.3172	7.6286	28.1659
25	2.4974	8.4483	19.7176
26	1.5896	9.3561	10.3615
27	.5842	10.3615	0.0000

YEARS 28	MO PAYT .9062	AN CONST 10.88	
#	INT	PRIN	BALANCE
1	10.2198	.6543	99.3457
2	10.1495	.7246	98.6211
3	10.0717	.8024	97.8187
4	9.9854	.8887	96.9300
5	9.8899	.9842	95.9458
6	9.7842	1.0899	94.8559
7	9.6671	1.2070	93.6489
8	9.5374	1.3367	92.3121
9	9.3937	1.4804	90.8317
10	9.2347	1.6395	89.1923
11	9.0585	1.8156	87.3767
12	8.8634	2.0107	85.3659
13	8.6473	2.2268	83.1391
14	8.4080	2.4661	80.6731
15	8.1431	2.7311	77.9420
16	7.8496	3.0245	74.9175
17	7.5246	3.3495	71.5680
18	7.1647	3.7094	67.8585
19	6.7661	4.1080	63.7505
20	6.3246	4.5495	59.2010
21	5.8358	5.0383	54.1626
22	5.2944	5.5797	48.5829
23	4.6948	6.1793	42.4036
24	4.0308	6.8433	35.5603
25	3.2954	7.5787	27.9816
26	2.4811	8.3930	19.5886
27	1.5792	9.2949	10.2937
28	.5804	10.2937	0.0000

YEARS 29	MO PAYT .9009	AN CONST 10.82	
#	INT	PRIN	BALANCE
1	10.2229	.5873	99.4127
2	10.1598	.6504	98.7622
3	10.0899	.7203	98.0419
4	10.0125	.7977	97.2442
5	9.9268	.8835	96.3607
6	9.8319	.9784	95.3823
7	9.7267	1.0835	94.2988
8	9.6103	1.2000	93.0988
9	9.4814	1.3289	91.7700
10	9.3386	1.4717	90.2983
11	9.1804	1.6298	88.6684
12	9.0053	1.8050	86.8635
13	8.8113	1.9989	84.8646
14	8.5965	2.2137	82.6508
15	8.3587	2.4516	80.1993
16	8.0952	2.7150	77.4842
17	7.8035	3.0068	74.4775
18	7.4804	3.3299	71.1476
19	7.1226	3.6877	67.4600
20	6.7263	4.0839	63.3760
21	6.2875	4.5228	58.8533
22	5.8015	5.0088	53.8445
23	5.2633	5.5470	48.2976
24	4.6672	6.1430	42.1545
25	4.0071	6.8031	35.3514
26	3.2761	7.5341	27.8173
27	2.4665	8.3437	19.4735
28	1.5699	9.2403	10.2332
29	.5770	10.2332	0.0000

YEARS 30	MO PAYT .8961	AN CONST 10.76	
#	INT	PRIN	BALANCE
1	10.2257	.5275	99.4725
2	10.1690	.5842	98.8882
3	10.1062	.6470	98.2412
4	10.0367	.7165	97.5247
5	9.9597	.7935	96.7312
6	9.8744	.8788	95.8524
7	9.7800	.9732	94.8791
8	9.6754	1.0778	93.8013
9	9.5596	1.1936	92.6077
10	9.4313	1.3219	91.2858
11	9.2893	1.4639	89.8219
12	9.1320	1.6212	88.2007
13	8.9578	1.7954	86.4052
14	8.7648	1.9884	84.4169
15	8.5512	2.2020	82.2148
16	8.3146	2.4387	79.7762
17	8.0525	2.7007	77.0755
18	7.7623	2.9909	74.0846
19	7.4409	3.3123	70.7723
20	7.0850	3.6682	67.1041
21	6.6908	4.0624	63.0417
22	6.2543	4.4989	58.5428
23	5.7709	4.9823	53.5605
24	5.2355	5.5177	48.0428
25	4.6426	6.1106	41.9322
26	3.9860	6.7672	35.1649
27	3.2588	7.4944	27.6705
28	2.4535	8.2997	19.3708
29	1.5617	9.1916	10.1792
30	.5740	10.1792	0.0000

YEARS 2 — MO PAYT 4.6284 — AN CONST 55.55

#	INT	PRIN	BALANCE
1	8.1020	47.4382	52.5618
2	2.9784	52.5618	0.0000

YEARS 3 — MO PAYT 3.2408 — AN CONST 38.89

#	INT	PRIN	BALANCE
1	8.9109	29.9789	70.0211
2	5.6731	33.2168	36.8043
3	2.0855	36.8043	0.0000

YEARS 4 — MO PAYT 2.5507 — AN CONST 30.61

#	INT	PRIN	BALANCE
1	9.3133	21.2950	78.7050
2	7.0134	23.5949	55.1101
3	4.4650	26.1433	28.9669
4	1.6414	28.9669	0.0000

YEARS 5 — MO PAYT 2.1395 — AN CONST 25.68

#	INT	PRIN	BALANCE
1	9.5530	16.1209	83.8791
2	7.8119	17.8620	66.0171
3	5.8827	19.7912	46.2259
4	3.7452	21.9287	24.2971
5	1.3768	24.2971	0.0000

YEARS 6 — MO PAYT 1.8677 — AN CONST 22.42

#	INT	PRIN	BALANCE
1	9.7115	12.7015	87.2985
2	8.3397	14.0733	73.2252
3	6.8197	15.5933	57.6319
4	5.1356	17.2774	40.3545
5	3.2695	19.1435	21.2110
6	1.2019	21.2110	0.0000

YEARS 7 — MO PAYT 1.6757 — AN CONST 20.11

#	INT	PRIN	BALANCE
1	9.8235	10.2844	89.7156
2	8.7127	11.3952	78.3203
3	7.4820	12.6259	65.6944
4	6.1183	13.9896	51.7048
5	4.6074	15.5005	36.2043
6	2.9333	17.1747	19.0296
7	1.0783	19.0296	0.0000

YEARS 8 — MO PAYT 1.5333 — AN CONST 18.41

#	INT	PRIN	BALANCE
1	9.9065	8.4936	91.5064
2	8.9891	9.4109	82.0955
3	7.9727	10.4273	71.6681
4	6.8465	11.5535	60.1146
5	5.5987	12.8014	47.3132
6	4.2161	14.1840	33.1292
7	2.6841	15.7159	17.4133
8	.9867	17.4133	0.0000

YEARS 9 — MO PAYT 1.4242 — AN CONST 17.09

#	INT	PRIN	BALANCE
1	9.9701	7.1199	92.8801
2	9.2011	7.8889	84.9913
3	8.3491	8.7409	76.2504
4	7.4050	9.6849	66.5655
5	6.3590	10.7310	55.8345
6	5.2000	11.8899	43.9446
7	3.9159	13.1741	30.7705
8	2.4930	14.5970	16.1735
9	.9165	16.1735	0.0000

YEARS 10 — MO PAYT 1.3382 — AN CONST 16.06

#	INT	PRIN	BALANCE
1	10.0202	6.0379	93.9621
2	9.3681	6.6900	87.2721
3	8.6456	7.4125	79.8596
4	7.8450	8.2131	71.6465
5	6.9579	9.1002	62.5463
6	5.9751	10.0830	52.4633
7	4.8861	11.1720	41.2912
8	3.6794	12.3787	28.9126
9	2.3425	13.7156	15.1970
10	.8611	15.1970	0.0000

YEARS 11 — MO PAYT 1.2690 — AN CONST 15.23

#	INT	PRIN	BALANCE
1	10.0606	5.1677	94.8323
2	9.5024	5.7259	89.1064
3	8.8840	6.3443	82.7622
4	8.1988	7.0295	75.7327
5	7.4396	7.7887	67.9440
6	6.5984	8.6299	59.3141
7	5.6663	9.5620	49.7521
8	4.6336	10.5947	39.1574
9	3.4893	11.7390	27.4185
10	2.2214	13.0068	14.4116
11	.8166	14.4116	0.0000

YEARS 12 — MO PAYT 1.2125 — AN CONST 14.55

#	INT	PRIN	BALANCE
1	10.0935	4.4562	95.5438
2	9.6122	4.9374	90.6064
3	9.0790	5.4707	85.1357
4	8.4881	6.0616	79.0742
5	7.8334	6.7162	72.3579
6	7.1081	7.4416	64.9163
7	6.3043	8.2453	56.6710
8	5.4138	9.1359	47.5351
9	4.4271	10.1226	37.4125
10	3.3338	11.2159	26.1967
11	2.1224	12.4272	13.7694
12	.7803	13.7694	0.0000

YEARS 13 — MO PAYT 1.1656 — AN CONST 13.99

#	INT	PRIN	BALANCE
1	10.1209	3.8663	96.1337
2	9.7033	4.2839	91.8498
3	9.2406	4.7465	87.1033
4	8.7280	5.2592	81.8441
5	8.1599	5.8272	76.0169
6	7.5306	6.4566	69.5604
7	6.8332	7.1539	62.4065
8	6.0606	7.9266	54.4799
9	5.2045	8.7827	45.6973
10	4.2559	9.7312	35.9660
11	3.2049	10.7822	25.1838
12	2.0404	11.9468	13.2371
13	.7501	13.2371	0.0000

YEARS 14 — MO PAYT 1.1263 — AN CONST 13.52

#	INT	PRIN	BALANCE
1	10.1438	3.3718	96.6282
2	9.7796	3.7359	92.8923
3	9.3761	4.1394	88.7529
4	8.9290	4.5865	84.1664
5	8.4337	5.0819	79.0845
6	7.8848	5.6307	73.4538
7	7.2767	6.2389	67.2150
8	6.6028	6.9127	60.3023
9	5.8562	7.6593	52.6430
10	5.0290	8.4865	44.1565
11	4.1124	9.4031	34.7534
12	3.0969	10.4187	24.3347
13	1.9716	11.5439	12.7907
14	.7248	12.7907	0.0000

YEARS 15 — MO PAYT 1.0930 — AN CONST 13.12

#	INT	PRIN	BALANCE
1	10.1632	2.9532	97.0468
2	9.8442	3.2722	93.7746
3	9.4908	3.6256	90.1490
4	9.0992	4.0172	86.1318
5	8.6653	4.4510	81.6808
6	8.1846	4.9318	76.7490
7	7.6520	5.4644	71.2846
8	7.0618	6.0546	65.2299
9	6.4078	6.7085	58.5214
10	5.6833	7.4331	51.0883
11	4.8805	8.2359	42.8524
12	3.9910	9.1254	33.7270
13	3.0054	10.1110	23.6160
14	1.9134	11.2030	12.4130
15	.7034	12.4130	0.0000

YEARS 16 — MO PAYT 1.0647 — AN CONST 12.78

#	INT	PRIN	BALANCE
1	10.1797	2.5962	97.4038
2	9.8993	2.8766	94.5273
3	9.5886	3.1872	91.3401
4	9.2444	3.5315	87.8086
5	8.8630	3.9129	83.8957
6	8.4404	4.3355	79.5602
7	7.9721	4.8037	74.7565
8	7.4533	5.3226	69.4339
9	6.8784	5.8974	63.5365
10	6.2415	6.5344	57.0021
11	5.5358	7.2401	49.7620
12	4.7538	8.0221	41.7399
13	3.8874	8.8885	32.8514
14	2.9274	9.8485	23.0029
15	1.8637	10.9122	12.0907
16	.6851	12.0907	0.0000

YEARS 17 — MO PAYT 1.0403 — AN CONST 12.49

#	INT	PRIN	BALANCE
1	10.1939	2.2894	97.7106
2	9.9466	2.5367	95.1738
3	9.6727	2.8107	92.3631
4	9.3691	3.1143	89.2489
5	9.0328	3.4506	85.7983
6	8.6601	3.8233	81.9750
7	8.2471	4.2362	77.7387
8	7.7896	4.6938	73.0450
9	7.2827	5.2007	67.8442
10	6.7210	5.7624	62.0818
11	6.0986	6.3848	55.6971
12	5.4090	7.0744	48.6227
13	4.6450	7.8384	40.7843
14	3.7984	8.6850	32.0993
15	2.8604	9.6230	22.4763
16	1.8210	10.6623	11.8139
17	.6694	11.8139	0.0000

YEARS 18 — MO PAYT 1.0192 — AN CONST 12.24

#	INT	PRIN	BALANCE
1	10.2062	2.0245	97.9755
2	9.9875	2.2431	95.7324
3	9.7453	2.4854	93.2471
4	9.4769	2.7538	90.4933
5	9.1794	3.0512	87.4421
6	8.8499	3.3808	84.0613
7	8.4848	3.7459	80.3154
8	8.0802	4.1505	76.1649
9	7.6319	4.5987	71.5662
10	7.1352	5.0954	66.4708
11	6.5849	5.6458	60.8250
12	5.9751	6.2555	54.5695
13	5.2995	6.9311	47.6384
14	4.5509	7.6797	39.9586
15	3.7215	8.5092	31.4495
16	2.8024	9.4282	22.0212
17	1.7842	10.4465	11.5748
18	.6559	11.5748	0.0000

YEARS 19 — MO PAYT 1.0009 — AN CONST 12.02

#	INT	PRIN	BALANCE
1	10.2169	1.7943	98.2057
2	10.0231	1.9881	96.2175
3	9.8083	2.2029	94.0147
4	9.5704	2.4408	91.5739
5	9.3068	2.7044	88.8695
6	9.0147	2.9965	85.8731
7	8.6911	3.3201	82.5530
8	8.3325	3.6787	78.8743
9	7.9352	4.0760	74.7983
10	7.4950	4.5162	70.2821
11	7.0072	5.0040	65.2781
12	6.4667	5.5444	59.7336
13	5.8679	6.1433	53.5903
14	5.2044	6.8068	46.7836
15	4.4693	7.5419	39.2416
16	3.6547	8.3565	30.8851
17	2.7522	9.2590	21.6261
18	1.7521	10.2590	11.3671
19	.6441	11.3671	0.0000

YEARS 20 — MO PAYT .9850 — AN CONST 11.82

#	INT	PRIN	BALANCE
1	10.2262	1.5936	98.4064
2	10.0540	1.7657	96.6406
3	9.8633	1.9564	94.6842
4	9.6520	2.1677	92.5165
5	9.4179	2.4019	90.1146
6	9.1585	2.6613	87.4533
7	8.8711	2.9487	84.5046
8	8.5526	3.2672	81.2374
9	8.1997	3.6201	77.6173
10	7.8087	4.0110	73.6063
11	7.3755	4.4443	69.1620
12	6.8955	4.9243	64.2378
13	6.3637	5.4561	58.7817
14	5.7744	6.0454	52.7363
15	5.1215	6.6983	46.0380
16	4.3980	7.4217	38.6163
17	3.5965	8.2233	30.3930
18	2.7083	9.1115	21.2815
19	1.7242	10.0956	11.1859
20	.6339	11.1859	0.0000

YEARS 21 — MO PAYT .9710 — AN CONST 11.66

#	INT	PRIN	BALANCE
1	10.2343	1.4179	98.5821
2	10.0812	1.5710	97.0111
3	9.9115	1.7407	95.2704

MONTHLY PAYMENT AMORTIZATION SCHEDULE PER $100

10.30 %

#	INT	PRIN	BALANCE
4	9.7235	1.9287	93.3417
5	9.5152	2.1370	91.2047
6	9.2844	2.3678	88.8369
7	9.0286	2.6236	86.2133
8	8.7453	2.9069	83.3064
9	8.4313	3.2209	80.0855
10	8.0835	3.5687	76.5168
11	7.6980	3.9542	72.5626
12	7.2710	4.3812	68.1814
13	6.7978	4.8544	63.3270
14	6.2735	5.3787	57.9482
15	5.6925	5.9597	51.9886
16	5.0489	6.6033	45.3853
17	4.3357	7.3165	38.0687
18	3.5455	8.1067	29.9620
19	2.6699	8.9823	20.9797
20	1.6998	9.9524	11.0273
21	.6249	11.0273	0.0000

YEARS 22 — MO PAYT .9587 — AN CONST 11.51

#	INT	PRIN	BALANCE
1	10.2415	1.2635	98.7365
2	10.1050	1.4000	97.3365
3	9.9538	1.5512	95.7854
4	9.7863	1.7187	94.0666
5	9.6006	1.9043	92.1623
6	9.3950	2.1100	90.0523
7	9.1671	2.3379	87.7144
8	8.9146	2.5904	85.1240
9	8.6348	2.8702	82.2538
10	8.3248	3.1802	79.0737
11	7.9813	3.5236	75.5500
12	7.6008	3.9042	71.6458
13	7.1791	4.3259	67.3199
14	6.7119	4.7931	62.5268
15	6.1942	5.3108	57.2161
16	5.6206	5.8844	51.3317
17	4.9851	6.5199	44.8118
18	4.2809	7.2241	37.5877
19	3.5007	8.0043	29.5834
20	2.6362	8.8688	20.7147
21	1.6783	9.8267	10.8880
22	.6170	10.8880	0.0000

YEARS 23 — MO PAYT .9479 — AN CONST 11.38

#	INT	PRIN	BALANCE
1	10.2478	1.1275	98.8725
2	10.1260	1.2493	97.6233
3	9.9911	1.3842	96.2391
4	9.8416	1.5337	94.7054
5	9.6759	1.6993	93.0061
6	9.4924	1.8829	91.1232
7	9.2890	2.0862	89.0370
8	9.0637	2.3115	86.7254
9	8.8140	2.5612	84.1642
10	8.5374	2.8378	81.3264
11	8.2309	3.1443	78.1821
12	7.8913	3.4839	74.6982
13	7.5151	3.8602	70.8380
14	7.0981	4.2771	66.5609
15	6.6362	4.7391	61.8218
16	6.1244	5.2509	56.5710
17	5.5572	5.8180	50.7529
18	4.9289	6.4464	44.3066
19	4.2326	7.1426	37.1639
20	3.4612	7.9141	29.2499
21	2.6064	8.7688	20.4811
22	1.6594	9.7159	10.7652
23	.6100	10.7652	0.0000

YEARS 24 — MO PAYT .9384 — AN CONST 11.27

#	INT	PRIN	BALANCE
1	10.2533	1.0073	98.9927
2	10.1445	1.1161	97.8765
3	10.0240	1.2367	96.6399
4	9.8904	1.3702	95.2696
5	9.7424	1.5182	93.7514
6	9.5784	1.6822	92.0692
7	9.3968	1.8639	90.2053
8	9.1955	2.0652	88.1401
9	8.9724	2.2883	85.8518
10	8.7253	2.5354	83.3164
11	8.4514	2.8092	80.5072
12	8.1480	3.1126	77.3946
13	7.8118	3.4488	73.9457
14	7.4394	3.8213	70.1244
15	7.0266	4.2340	65.8904
16	6.5693	4.6913	61.1991
17	6.0627	5.1980	56.0011
18	5.5013	5.7594	50.2417
19	4.8792	6.3814	43.8603
20	4.1900	7.0707	36.7896
21	3.4263	7.8343	28.9553
22	2.5802	8.6805	20.2748
23	1.6427	9.6180	10.6568
24	.6039	10.6568	0.0000

YEARS 25 — MO PAYT .9299 — AN CONST 11.16

#	INT	PRIN	BALANCE
1	10.2583	.9010	99.0990
2	10.1609	.9983	98.1008
3	10.0531	1.1061	96.9947
4	9.9337	1.2255	95.7692
5	9.8013	1.3579	94.4113
6	9.6547	1.5046	92.9067
7	9.4922	1.6671	91.2397
8	9.3121	1.8471	89.3926
9	9.1126	2.0466	87.3460
10	8.8916	2.2676	85.0783
11	8.6467	2.5126	82.5658
12	8.3753	2.7839	79.7819
13	8.0746	3.0846	76.6973
14	7.7415	3.4177	73.2795
15	7.3723	3.7869	69.4926
16	6.9633	4.1959	65.2968
17	6.5102	4.6490	60.6477
18	6.0080	5.1512	55.4966
19	5.4517	5.7075	49.7890
20	4.8353	6.3240	43.4651
21	4.1522	7.0070	36.4581
22	3.3955	7.7637	28.6944
23	2.5569	8.6023	20.0921
24	1.6279	9.5313	10.5608
25	.5984	10.5608	0.0000

YEARS 26 — MO PAYT .9224 — AN CONST 11.07

#	INT	PRIN	BALANCE
1	10.2626	.8066	99.1934
2	10.1755	.8937	98.2997
3	10.0790	.9902	97.3095
4	9.9720	1.0972	96.2124
5	9.8535	1.2156	94.9967
6	9.7223	1.3469	93.6498
7	9.5768	1.4924	92.1574
8	9.4156	1.6536	90.5038
9	9.2370	1.8322	88.6716
10	9.0391	2.0301	86.6415
11	8.8198	2.2493	84.3921
12	8.5769	2.4923	81.8998
13	8.3077	2.7615	79.1384
14	8.0095	3.0597	76.0787
15	7.6790	3.3902	72.6885
16	7.3129	3.7563	68.9321
17	6.9072	4.1620	64.7701
18	6.4576	4.6116	60.1586
19	5.9596	5.1096	55.0489
20	5.4077	5.6615	49.3875
21	4.7963	6.2729	43.1145
22	4.1188	6.9504	36.1641
23	3.3681	7.7011	28.4629
24	2.5363	8.5329	19.9301
25	1.6147	9.4545	10.4756
26	.5936	10.4756	0.0000

YEARS 27 — MO PAYT .9158 — AN CONST 10.99

#	INT	PRIN	BALANCE
1	10.2665	.7227	99.2773
2	10.1885	.8007	98.4766
3	10.1020	.8872	97.5893
4	10.0062	.9830	96.6063
5	9.9000	1.0892	95.5171
6	9.7823	1.2069	94.3102
7	9.6520	1.3372	92.9730
8	9.5076	1.4816	91.4914
9	9.3475	1.6417	89.8497
10	9.1702	1.8190	88.0307
11	8.9738	2.0154	86.0153
12	8.7561	2.2331	83.7822
13	8.5149	2.4743	81.3080
14	8.2477	2.7415	78.5664
15	7.9516	3.0376	75.5288
16	7.6235	3.3657	72.1632
17	7.2600	3.7292	68.4340
18	6.8572	4.1320	64.3020
19	6.4110	4.5782	59.7238
20	5.9165	5.0727	54.6511
21	5.3686	5.6206	49.0305
22	4.7616	6.2276	42.8029
23	4.0890	6.9002	35.9027
24	3.3437	7.6455	28.2572
25	2.5180	8.4712	19.7860
26	1.6031	9.3861	10.3999
27	.5893	10.3999	0.0000

YEARS 28 — MO PAYT .9098 — AN CONST 10.92

#	INT	PRIN	BALANCE
1	10.2700	.6480	99.3520
2	10.2000	.7180	98.6340
3	10.1224	.7956	97.8384
4	10.0365	.8815	96.9569
5	9.9413	.9767	95.9803
6	9.8358	1.0822	94.8981
7	9.7189	1.1990	93.6991
8	9.5894	1.3285	92.3705
9	9.4460	1.4720	90.8985
10	9.2870	1.6310	89.2675
11	9.1108	1.8072	87.4603
12	8.9156	2.0024	85.4579
13	8.6994	2.2186	83.2393
14	8.4597	2.4582	80.7811
15	8.1942	2.7237	78.0573
16	7.9001	3.0179	75.0394
17	7.5741	3.3439	71.6955
18	7.2130	3.7050	67.9905
19	6.8128	4.1052	63.8853
20	6.3694	4.5486	59.3368
21	5.8782	5.0398	54.2970
22	5.3338	5.5841	48.7128
23	4.7307	6.1873	42.5256
24	4.0625	6.8555	35.6701
25	3.3221	7.5959	28.0741
26	2.5017	8.4163	19.6578
27	1.5927	9.3253	10.3325
28	.5855	10.3325	0.0000

YEARS 29 — MO PAYT .9045 — AN CONST 10.86

#	INT	PRIN	BALANCE
1	10.2731	.5814	99.4186
2	10.2103	.6442	98.7743
3	10.1407	.7138	98.0605
4	10.0636	.7909	97.2695
5	9.9782	.8764	96.3932
6	9.8835	.9710	95.4222
7	9.7786	1.0759	94.3463
8	9.6624	1.1921	93.1543
9	9.5337	1.3208	91.8334
10	9.3910	1.4635	90.3700
11	9.2330	1.6215	88.7484
12	9.0578	1.7967	86.9518
13	8.8638	1.9907	84.9610
14	8.6488	2.2057	82.7553
15	8.4106	2.4439	80.3114
16	8.1466	2.7079	77.6035
17	7.8541	3.0004	74.6031
18	7.5301	3.3244	71.2787
19	7.1710	3.6835	67.5952
20	6.7732	4.0813	63.5139
21	6.3324	4.5221	58.9918
22	5.8440	5.0105	53.9812
23	5.3028	5.5517	48.4296
24	4.7032	6.1513	42.2783
25	4.0389	6.8156	35.4627
26	3.3027	7.5518	27.9109
27	2.4871	8.3674	19.5435
28	1.5834	9.2711	10.2724
29	.5821	10.2724	0.0000

YEARS 30 — MO PAYT .8998 — AN CONST 10.80

#	INT	PRIN	BALANCE
1	10.2758	.5220	99.4780
2	10.2194	.5784	98.8996
3	10.1570	.6409	98.2587
4	10.0877	.7101	97.5486
5	10.0110	.7868	96.7618
6	9.9261	.8718	95.8900
7	9.8319	.9659	94.9241
8	9.7276	1.0703	93.8538
9	9.6120	1.1858	92.6680
10	9.4839	1.3139	91.3540
11	9.3420	1.4558	89.8982
12	9.1848	1.6131	88.2851
13	9.0106	1.7873	86.4978
14	8.8175	1.9803	84.5175
15	8.6036	2.1942	82.3233
16	8.3667	2.4312	79.8921
17	8.1041	2.6938	77.1983
18	7.8131	2.9847	74.2136
19	7.4908	3.3071	70.9066
20	7.1336	3.6642	67.2423
21	6.7378	4.0600	63.1823
22	6.2993	4.4985	58.6838
23	5.8135	4.9844	53.6994
24	5.2752	5.5227	48.1768
25	4.6787	6.1192	42.0576
26	4.0178	6.7801	35.2775
27	3.2855	7.5123	27.7652
28	2.4741	8.3237	19.4415
29	1.5751	9.2227	10.2188
30	.5791	10.2188	0.0000

YEARS 2 — MO PAYT 4.6318 — AN CONST 55.59

#	INT	PRIN	BALANCE
1	8.1621	47.4197	52.5803
2	3.0015	52.5803	0.0000

YEARS 3 — MO PAYT 3.2444 — AN CONST 38.94

#	INT	PRIN	BALANCE
1	8.9771	29.9551	70.0449
2	5.7172	33.2151	36.8298
3	2.1024	36.8298	0.0000

YEARS 4 — MO PAYT 2.5543 — AN CONST 30.66

#	INT	PRIN	BALANCE
1	9.3825	21.2692	78.7308
2	7.0678	23.5839	55.1469
3	4.5012	26.1505	28.9964
4	1.6553	28.9964	0.0000

YEARS 5 — MO PAYT 2.1432 — AN CONST 25.72

#	INT	PRIN	BALANCE
1	9.6239	16.0945	83.9055
2	7.8724	17.8460	66.0595
3	5.9302	19.7882	46.2713
4	3.7767	21.9417	24.3296
5	1.3888	24.3296	0.0000

YEARS 6 — MO PAYT 1.8716 — AN CONST 22.46

#	INT	PRIN	BALANCE
1	9.7835	12.6751	87.3249
2	8.4041	14.0545	73.2704
3	6.8746	15.5840	57.6864
4	5.1786	17.2800	40.4064
5	3.2980	19.1606	21.2458
6	1.2128	21.2458	0.0000

YEARS 7 — MO PAYT 1.6796 — AN CONST 20.16

#	INT	PRIN	BALANCE
1	9.8963	10.2584	89.7416
2	8.7799	11.3748	78.3668
3	7.5420	12.6127	65.7540
4	6.1693	13.9854	51.7687
5	4.6473	15.5074	36.2613
6	2.9597	17.1950	19.0663
7	1.0884	19.0663	0.0000

YEARS 8 — MO PAYT 1.5373 — AN CONST 18.45

#	INT	PRIN	BALANCE
1	9.9798	8.4681	91.5319
2	9.0583	9.3897	82.1421
3	8.0364	10.4116	71.7305
4	6.9033	11.5447	60.1859
5	5.6469	12.8011	47.3848
6	4.2538	14.1942	33.1907
7	2.7091	15.7389	17.4517
8	.9962	17.4517	0.0000

YEARS 9 — MO PAYT 1.4283 — AN CONST 17.14

#	INT	PRIN	BALANCE
1	10.0439	7.0952	92.9048
2	9.2717	7.8673	85.0375
3	8.4156	8.7235	76.3140
4	7.4662	9.6729	66.6412
5	6.4135	10.7256	55.9156
6	5.2463	11.8928	44.0228
7	3.9520	13.1871	30.8357
8	2.5169	14.6222	16.2135
9	.9255	16.2135	0.0000

YEARS 10 — MO PAYT 1.3424 — AN CONST 16.11

#	INT	PRIN	BALANCE
1	10.0944	6.0140	93.9860
2	9.4399	6.6685	87.3176
3	8.7141	7.3942	79.9234
4	7.9094	8.1989	71.7245
5	7.0172	9.0911	62.6334
6	6.0278	10.0805	52.5529
7	4.9308	11.1776	41.3753
8	3.7143	12.3940	28.9813
9	2.3655	13.7428	15.2384
10	.8699	15.2384	0.0000

YEARS 11 — MO PAYT 1.2733 — AN CONST 15.28

#	INT	PRIN	BALANCE
1	10.1349	5.1447	94.8553
2	9.5750	5.7046	89.1508
3	8.9542	6.3254	82.8254
4	8.2658	7.0138	75.8116
5	7.5025	7.7771	68.0345
6	6.6562	8.6234	59.4111
7	5.7177	9.5619	49.8492
8	4.6771	10.6025	39.2467
9	3.5232	11.7564	27.4903
10	2.2438	13.0358	14.4545
11	.8251	14.4545	0.0000

YEARS 12 — MO PAYT 1.2168 — AN CONST 14.61

#	INT	PRIN	BALANCE
1	10.1681	4.4340	95.5660
2	9.6855	4.9166	90.6494
3	9.1505	5.4516	85.1978
4	8.5572	6.0449	79.1529
5	7.8993	6.7028	72.4501
6	7.1699	7.4322	65.0179
7	6.3610	8.2411	56.7768
8	5.4642	9.1379	47.6389
9	4.4697	10.1324	37.5065
10	3.3670	11.2351	26.2714
11	2.1443	12.4578	13.8136
12	.7885	13.8136	0.0000

YEARS 13 — MO PAYT 1.1701 — AN CONST 14.05

#	INT	PRIN	BALANCE
1	10.1956	3.8451	96.1549
2	9.7771	4.2635	91.8914
3	9.3131	4.7275	87.1639
4	8.7986	5.2420	81.9219
5	8.2282	5.8125	76.1094
6	7.5956	6.4451	69.6643
7	6.8942	7.1465	62.5179
8	6.1164	7.9242	54.5937
9	5.2541	8.7866	45.8071
10	4.2978	9.7428	36.0643
11	3.2375	10.8031	25.2612
12	2.0619	11.9788	13.2824
13	.7582	13.2824	0.0000

YEARS 14 — MO PAYT 1.1308 — AN CONST 13.58

#	INT	PRIN	BALANCE
1	10.2186	3.3515	96.6485
2	9.8539	3.7162	92.9323
3	9.4494	4.1206	88.8117
4	9.0010	4.5691	84.2426
5	8.5037	5.0663	79.1763
6	7.9524	5.6177	73.5586
7	7.3410	6.2290	67.3296
8	6.6631	6.9069	60.4226
9	5.9115	7.6586	52.7640
10	5.0780	8.4921	44.2719
11	4.1538	9.4163	34.8556
12	3.1290	10.4410	24.4146
13	1.9928	11.5773	12.8373
14	.7328	12.8373	0.0000

YEARS 15 — MO PAYT 1.0977 — AN CONST 13.18

#	INT	PRIN	BALANCE
1	10.2381	2.9339	97.0661
2	9.9188	3.2531	93.8130
3	9.5648	3.6072	90.2058
4	9.1722	3.9997	86.2061
5	8.7369	4.4350	81.7711
6	8.2543	4.9177	76.8534
7	7.7191	5.4529	71.4005
8	7.1256	6.0463	65.3542
9	6.4676	6.7043	58.6499
10	5.7380	7.4339	51.2160
11	4.9290	8.2429	42.9730
12	4.0319	9.1400	33.8330
13	3.0372	10.1347	23.6983
14	1.9343	11.2377	12.4606
15	.7113	12.4606	0.0000

YEARS 16 — MO PAYT 1.0694 — AN CONST 12.84

#	INT	PRIN	BALANCE
1	10.2547	2.5777	97.4223
2	9.9742	2.8582	94.5641
3	9.6631	3.1693	91.3948
4	9.3182	3.5142	87.8806
5	8.9358	3.8966	83.9839
6	8.5117	4.3207	79.6632
7	8.0415	4.7909	74.8723
8	7.5201	5.3123	69.5600
9	6.9420	5.8904	63.6696
10	6.3009	6.5315	57.1381
11	5.5901	7.2423	49.8958
12	4.8019	8.0305	41.8653
13	3.9280	8.9044	32.9609
14	2.9589	9.8735	23.0874
15	1.8844	10.9480	12.1394
16	.6930	12.1394	0.0000

YEARS 17 — MO PAYT 1.0451 — AN CONST 12.55

#	INT	PRIN	BALANCE
1	10.2690	2.2719	97.7281
2	10.0217	2.5191	95.2090
3	9.7476	2.7933	92.4157
4	9.4436	3.0973	89.3184
5	9.1065	3.4344	85.8840
6	8.7328	3.8081	82.0759
7	8.3183	4.2225	77.8534
8	7.8588	4.6821	73.1713
9	7.3493	5.1916	67.9797
10	6.7843	5.7566	62.2231
11	6.1578	6.3831	55.8400
12	5.4631	7.0778	48.7622
13	4.6928	7.8480	40.9142
14	3.8388	8.7021	32.2121
15	2.8917	9.6492	22.5629
16	1.8416	10.6993	11.8636
17	.6772	11.8636	0.0000

YEARS 18 — MO PAYT 1.0241 — AN CONST 12.29

#	INT	PRIN	BALANCE
1	10.2813	2.0078	97.9922
2	10.0628	2.2263	95.7659
3	9.8205	2.4686	93.2974
4	9.5519	2.7372	90.5602
5	9.2540	3.0351	87.5251
6	8.9237	3.3654	84.1597
7	8.5574	3.7317	80.4280
8	8.1513	4.1378	76.2903
9	7.7010	4.5881	71.7022
10	7.2017	5.0874	66.6148
11	6.6480	5.6410	60.9738
12	6.0341	6.2549	54.7188
13	5.3534	6.9357	47.7832
14	4.5986	7.6905	40.0927
15	3.7617	8.5274	31.5653
16	2.8337	9.4554	22.1099
17	1.8046	10.4844	11.6254
18	.6636	11.6254	0.0000

YEARS 19 — MO PAYT 1.0059 — AN CONST 12.08

#	INT	PRIN	BALANCE
1	10.2920	1.7785	98.2215
2	10.0985	1.9721	96.2494
3	9.8838	2.1867	94.0627
4	9.6459	2.4247	91.6381
5	9.3820	2.6885	88.9495
6	9.0894	2.9811	85.9684
7	8.7650	3.3055	82.6629
8	8.4052	3.6653	78.9976
9	8.0063	4.0642	74.9334
10	7.5640	4.5065	70.4270
11	7.0736	4.9969	65.4300
12	6.5298	5.5407	59.8893
13	5.9268	6.1437	53.7456
14	5.2582	6.8123	46.9333
15	4.5168	7.5537	39.3797
16	3.6948	8.3757	31.0039
17	2.7833	9.2873	21.7167
18	1.7725	10.2980	11.4187
19	.6518	11.4187	0.0000

YEARS 20 — MO PAYT .9900 — AN CONST 11.88

#	INT	PRIN	BALANCE
1	10.3013	1.5786	98.4214
2	10.1295	1.7504	96.6709
3	9.9390	1.9409	94.7300
4	9.7278	2.1522	92.5778
5	9.4936	2.3864	90.1914
6	9.2339	2.6461	87.5454
7	8.9459	2.9341	84.6113
8	8.6266	3.2534	81.3579
9	8.2725	3.6074	77.7505
10	7.8800	4.0000	73.7505
11	7.4446	4.4353	69.3152
12	6.9619	4.9180	64.3971
13	6.4267	5.4532	58.9439
14	5.8333	6.0467	52.8972
15	5.1752	6.7048	46.1924
16	4.4455	7.4344	38.7580
17	3.6365	8.2435	30.5145
18	2.7393	9.1406	21.3738
19	1.7446	10.1354	11.2384
20	.6415	11.2384	0.0000

YEARS 21 — MO PAYT .9761 — AN CONST 11.72

#	INT	PRIN	BALANCE
1	10.3095	1.4037	98.5963
2	10.1567	1.5565	97.0398
3	9.9873	1.7259	95.3139

#	INT	PRIN	BALANCE
4	9.7995	1.9137	93.4003
5	9.5913	2.1220	91.2783
6	9.3603	2.3529	88.9254
7	9.1043	2.6089	86.3165
8	8.8203	2.8929	83.4236
9	8.5055	3.2077	80.2159
10	8.1564	3.5568	76.6591
11	7.7693	3.9439	72.7153
12	7.3401	4.3731	68.3422
13	6.8642	4.8490	63.4932
14	6.3365	5.3767	58.1165
15	5.7514	5.9618	52.1547
16	5.1026	6.6106	45.5440
17	4.3831	7.3301	38.2139
18	3.5854	8.1278	30.0861
19	2.7009	9.0123	21.0738
20	1.7201	9.9931	11.0807
21	.6325	11.0807	0.0000

YEARS 22	MO PAYT .9639	AN CONST 11.57	
#	INT	PRIN	BALANCE
1	10.3167	1.2501	98.7499
2	10.1806	1.3862	97.3637
3	10.0298	1.5370	95.8267
4	9.8625	1.7043	94.1224
5	9.6770	1.8898	92.2326
6	9.4714	2.0954	90.1372
7	9.2433	2.3235	87.8137
8	8.9905	2.5763	85.2374
9	8.7101	2.8567	82.3807
10	8.3992	3.1676	79.2131
11	8.0545	3.5123	75.7008
12	7.6722	3.8946	71.8062
13	7.2484	4.3184	67.4878
14	6.7784	4.7884	62.6995
15	6.2573	5.3095	57.3900
16	5.6795	5.8873	51.5027
17	5.0388	6.5280	44.9747
18	4.3283	7.2384	37.7362
19	3.5406	8.0262	29.7100
20	2.6671	8.8997	20.8104
21	1.6986	9.8682	10.9422
22	.6246	10.9422	0.0000

YEARS 23	MO PAYT .9532	AN CONST 11.44	
#	INT	PRIN	BALANCE
1	10.3230	1.1149	98.8851
2	10.2016	1.2362	97.6490
3	10.0671	1.3707	96.2783
4	9.9179	1.5199	94.7584
5	9.7525	1.6853	93.0731
6	9.5691	1.8687	91.2044
7	9.3658	2.0721	89.1323
8	9.1403	2.2976	86.8348
9	8.8902	2.5476	84.2871
10	8.6130	2.8249	81.4623
11	8.3055	3.1323	78.3300
12	7.9647	3.4732	74.8568
13	7.5867	3.8511	71.0057
14	7.1676	4.2703	66.7354
15	6.7028	4.7350	62.0004
16	6.1875	5.2503	56.7502
17	5.6162	5.8217	50.9285
18	4.9826	6.4552	44.4733
19	4.2801	7.1577	37.3155
20	3.5011	7.9367	29.3788
21	2.6374	8.8005	20.5784
22	1.6796	9.7582	10.8202
23	.6177	10.8202	0.0000

YEARS 24	MO PAYT .9437	AN CONST 11.33	
#	INT	PRIN	BALANCE
1	10.3285	.9954	99.0046
2	10.2202	1.1038	97.9008
3	10.1001	1.2239	96.6769
4	9.9669	1.3571	95.3199
5	9.8192	1.5048	93.8151
6	9.6555	1.6685	92.1466
7	9.4739	1.8501	90.2965
8	9.2725	2.0514	88.2451
9	9.0493	2.2747	85.9704
10	8.8017	2.5222	83.4481
11	8.5272	2.7967	80.6514
12	8.2229	3.1011	77.5503
13	7.8854	3.4386	74.1117
14	7.5112	3.8128	70.2989
15	7.0962	4.2278	66.0711
16	6.6361	4.6879	61.3833
17	6.1259	5.1980	56.1853
18	5.5603	5.7637	50.4215
19	4.9330	6.3910	44.0306
20	4.2375	7.0865	36.9441
21	3.4663	7.8577	29.0864
22	2.6111	8.7129	20.3735
23	1.6629	9.6611	10.7125
24	.6115	10.7125	0.0000

YEARS 25	MO PAYT .9353	AN CONST 11.23	
#	INT	PRIN	BALANCE
1	10.3335	.8897	99.1103
2	10.2367	.9866	98.1237
3	10.1293	1.0939	97.0298
4	10.0102	1.2130	95.8168
5	9.8782	1.3450	94.4718
6	9.7319	1.4914	92.9804
7	9.5695	1.6537	91.3267
8	9.3896	1.8336	89.4931
9	9.1900	2.0332	87.4599
10	8.9688	2.2545	85.2055
11	8.7234	2.4998	82.7057
12	8.4514	2.7719	79.9338
13	8.1497	3.0735	76.8603
14	7.8152	3.4080	73.4523
15	7.4443	3.7789	69.6734
16	7.0331	4.1901	65.4833
17	6.5771	4.6461	60.8371
18	6.0714	5.1518	55.6854
19	5.5108	5.7124	49.9729
20	4.8891	6.3341	43.6388
21	4.1998	7.0234	36.6154
22	3.4354	7.7878	28.8276
23	2.5879	8.6353	20.1922
24	1.6481	9.5751	10.6171
25	.6061	10.6171	0.0000

YEARS 26	MO PAYT .9278	AN CONST 11.14	
#	INT	PRIN	BALANCE
1	10.3379	.7960	99.2040
2	10.2512	.8827	98.3213
3	10.1552	.9787	97.3426
4	10.0487	1.0852	96.2574
5	9.9305	1.2033	95.0540
6	9.7996	1.3343	93.7198
7	9.6544	1.4795	92.2403
8	9.4934	1.6405	90.5998
9	9.3148	1.8190	88.7807
10	9.1169	2.0170	86.7637
11	8.8974	2.2365	84.5272
12	8.6540	2.4799	82.0473
13	8.3841	2.7498	79.2975
14	8.0848	3.0490	76.2485
15	7.7530	3.3809	72.8676
16	7.3851	3.7488	69.1188
17	6.9771	4.1568	64.9620
18	6.5247	4.6092	60.3529
19	6.0231	5.1108	55.2421
20	5.4669	5.6670	49.5751
21	4.8502	6.2837	43.2914
22	4.1663	6.9675	36.3239
23	3.4081	7.7258	28.5981
24	2.5673	8.5666	20.0315
25	1.6350	9.4989	10.5326
26	.6013	10.5326	0.0000

YEARS 27	MO PAYT .9212	AN CONST 11.06	
#	INT	PRIN	BALANCE
1	10.3417	.7128	99.2872
2	10.2642	.7904	98.4969
3	10.1782	.8764	97.6205
4	10.0828	.9717	96.6488
5	9.9770	1.0775	95.5713
6	9.8598	1.1948	94.3765
7	9.7297	1.3248	93.0517
8	9.5856	1.4689	91.5828
9	9.4257	1.6288	89.9540
10	9.2484	1.8061	88.1479
11	9.0519	2.0026	86.1453
12	8.8339	2.2206	83.9247
13	8.5923	2.4622	81.4625
14	8.3243	2.7302	78.7323
15	8.0272	3.0273	75.7050
16	7.6977	3.3568	72.3482
17	7.3324	3.7221	68.6261
18	6.9274	4.1272	64.4990
19	6.4782	4.5763	59.9227
20	5.9802	5.0743	54.8483
21	5.4279	5.6266	49.2218
22	4.8156	6.2389	42.9829
23	4.1366	6.9179	36.0650
24	3.3838	7.6707	28.3943
25	2.5490	8.5055	19.8887
26	1.6233	9.4312	10.4576
27	.5970	10.4576	0.0000

YEARS 28	MO PAYT .9153	AN CONST 10.99	
#	INT	PRIN	BALANCE
1	10.3452	.6387	99.3613
2	10.2757	.7082	98.6531
3	10.1986	.7853	97.8678
4	10.1131	.8708	96.9970
5	10.0184	.9655	96.0315
6	9.9133	1.0706	94.9608
7	9.7968	1.1871	93.7737
8	9.6676	1.3163	92.4574
9	9.5243	1.4596	90.9978
10	9.3655	1.6184	89.3794
11	9.1894	1.7945	87.5849
12	8.9941	1.9898	85.5951
13	8.7775	2.2064	83.3887
14	8.5374	2.4465	80.9422
15	8.2712	2.7128	78.2294
16	7.9759	3.0080	75.2214
17	7.6486	3.3353	71.8861
18	7.2856	3.6983	68.1878
19	6.8831	4.1008	64.0870
20	6.4368	4.5471	59.5399
21	5.9420	5.0419	54.4980
22	5.3933	5.5906	48.9074
23	4.7849	6.1991	42.7083
24	4.1102	6.8737	35.8346
25	3.3622	7.6217	28.2129
26	2.5327	8.4512	19.7617
27	1.6130	9.3709	10.3908
28	.5932	10.3908	0.0000

YEARS 29	MO PAYT .9101	AN CONST 10.93	
#	INT	PRIN	BALANCE
1	10.3483	.5727	99.4273
2	10.2859	.6351	98.7922
3	10.2168	.7042	98.0880
4	10.1402	.7808	97.3072
5	10.0552	.8658	96.4415
6	9.9610	.9600	95.4815
7	9.8565	1.0645	94.4170
8	9.7407	1.1803	93.2367
9	9.6122	1.3088	91.9279
10	9.4698	1.4512	90.4767
11	9.3119	1.6091	88.8675
12	9.1367	1.7843	87.0833
13	8.9426	1.9784	85.1048
14	8.7273	2.1937	82.9111
15	8.4885	2.4325	80.4786
16	8.2238	2.6972	77.7814
17	7.9303	2.9908	74.7906
18	7.6048	3.3162	71.4744
19	7.2439	3.6771	67.7973
20	6.8437	4.0773	63.7200
21	6.4000	4.5210	59.1989
22	5.9080	5.0131	54.1859
23	5.3624	5.5586	48.6273
24	4.7575	6.1635	42.4637
25	4.0867	6.8343	35.6294
26	3.3429	7.5781	28.0513
27	2.5182	8.4028	19.6485
28	1.6037	9.3173	10.3312
29	.5898	10.3312	0.0000

YEARS 30	MO PAYT .9054	AN CONST 10.87	
#	INT	PRIN	BALANCE
1	10.3510	.5139	99.4861
2	10.2951	.5698	98.9163
3	10.2331	.6318	98.2846
4	10.1643	.7006	97.5840
5	10.0881	.7768	96.8072
6	10.0036	.8613	95.9459
7	9.9098	.9551	94.9908
8	9.8059	1.0590	93.9318
9	9.6906	1.1743	92.7575
10	9.5628	1.3020	91.4555
11	9.4211	1.4437	90.0117
12	9.2640	1.6009	88.4109
13	9.0898	1.7751	86.6358
14	8.8966	1.9683	84.6675
15	8.6824	2.1825	82.4850
16	8.4449	2.4200	80.0650
17	8.1815	2.6834	77.3817
18	7.8895	2.9754	74.4063
19	7.5657	3.2992	71.1071
20	7.2067	3.6582	67.4489
21	6.8085	4.0564	63.3925
22	6.3671	4.4978	58.8947
23	5.8776	4.9873	53.9074
24	5.3348	5.5300	48.3774
25	4.7330	6.1319	42.2455
26	4.0657	6.7992	35.4463
27	3.3257	7.5391	27.9072
28	2.5053	8.3596	19.5475
29	1.5955	9.2694	10.2782
30	.5867	10.2782	0.0000

YEARS 2 — MO PAYT 4.6330 — AN CONST 55.60

#	INT	PRIN	BALANCE
1	8.1822	47.4135	52.5865
2	3.0092	52.5865	0.0000

YEARS 3 — MO PAYT 3.2455 — AN CONST 38.95

#	INT	PRIN	BALANCE
1	8.9992	29.9472	70.0528
2	5.7319	33.2145	36.8383
3	2.1081	36.8383	0.0000

YEARS 4 — MO PAYT 2.5555 — AN CONST 30.67

#	INT	PRIN	BALANCE
1	9.4055	21.2606	78.7394
2	7.0859	23.5802	55.1592
3	4.5132	26.1529	29.0063
4	1.6599	29.0063	0.0000

YEARS 5 — MO PAYT 2.1444 — AN CONST 25.74

#	INT	PRIN	BALANCE
1	9.6476	16.0857	83.9143
2	7.8926	17.8407	66.0736
3	5.9461	19.7872	46.2864
4	3.7873	21.9460	24.3404
5	1.3929	24.3404	0.0000

YEARS 6 — MO PAYT 1.8728 — AN CONST 22.48

#	INT	PRIN	BALANCE
1	9.8075	12.6663	87.3337
2	8.4256	14.0482	73.2855
3	6.8929	15.5809	57.7045
4	5.1929	17.2809	40.4237
5	3.3075	19.1663	21.2574
6	1.2164	21.2574	0.0000

YEARS 7 — MO PAYT 1.6809 — AN CONST 20.18

#	INT	PRIN	BALANCE
1	9.9206	10.2497	89.7503
2	8.8023	11.3680	78.3822
3	7.5620	12.6083	65.7739
4	6.1864	13.9839	51.7900
5	4.6607	15.5096	36.2803
6	2.9685	17.2018	19.0786
7	1.0918	19.0786	0.0000

YEARS 8 — MO PAYT 1.5387 — AN CONST 18.47

#	INT	PRIN	BALANCE
1	10.0043	8.4597	91.5403
2	9.0813	9.3827	82.1577
3	8.0576	10.4063	71.7513
4	6.9223	11.5417	60.2096
5	5.6630	12.8009	47.4087
6	4.2664	14.1976	33.2111
7	2.7174	15.7466	17.4646
8	.9994	17.4646	0.0000

YEARS 9 — MO PAYT 1.4296 — AN CONST 17.16

#	INT	PRIN	BALANCE
1	10.0685	7.0869	92.9131
2	9.2953	7.8601	85.0529
3	8.4377	8.7177	76.3352
4	7.4866	9.6688	66.6664
5	6.4317	10.7237	55.9426
6	5.2617	11.8937	44.0489

YEARS 9 (continued)

#	INT	PRIN	BALANCE
7	3.9640	13.1914	30.8575
8	2.5248	14.6306	16.2269
9	.9286	16.2269	0.0000

YEARS 10 — MO PAYT 1.3438 — AN CONST 16.13

#	INT	PRIN	BALANCE
1	10.1191	6.0060	93.9940
2	9.4638	6.6613	87.3327
3	8.7370	7.3881	79.9446
4	7.9310	8.1941	71.7505
5	7.0369	9.0881	62.6624
6	6.0454	10.0797	52.5827
7	4.9457	11.1794	41.4033
8	3.7260	12.3991	29.0042
9	2.3732	13.7519	15.2523
10	.8728	15.2523	0.0000

YEARS 11 — MO PAYT 1.2747 — AN CONST 15.30

#	INT	PRIN	BALANCE
1	10.1597	5.1370	94.8630
2	9.5992	5.6975	89.1655
3	8.9776	6.3191	82.8464
4	8.2882	7.0085	75.8379
5	7.5235	7.7732	68.0647
6	6.6755	8.6213	59.4434
7	5.7349	9.5619	49.8815
8	4.6916	10.6051	39.2764
9	3.5346	11.7622	27.5142
10	2.2513	13.0455	14.4688
11	.8280	14.4688	0.0000

YEARS 12 — MO PAYT 1.2183 — AN CONST 14.62

#	INT	PRIN	BALANCE
1	10.1929	4.4267	95.5733
2	9.7100	4.9096	90.6637
3	9.1743	5.4453	85.2184
4	8.5802	6.0394	79.1791
5	7.9213	6.6983	72.4808
6	7.1905	7.4291	65.0517
7	6.3800	8.2396	56.8120
8	5.4810	9.1386	47.6734
9	4.4839	10.1357	37.5378
10	3.3781	11.2415	26.2963
11	2.1516	12.4680	13.8283
12	.7913	13.8283	0.0000

YEARS 13 — MO PAYT 1.1715 — AN CONST 14.06

#	INT	PRIN	BALANCE
1	10.2205	3.8380	96.1620
2	9.8017	4.2568	91.9052
3	9.3373	4.7212	87.1840
4	8.8222	5.2363	81.9477
5	8.2509	5.8076	76.1402
6	7.6173	6.4412	69.6989
7	6.9145	7.1440	62.5550
8	6.1351	7.9234	54.6316
9	5.2706	8.7879	45.8437
10	4.3118	9.7467	36.0971
11	3.2484	10.8100	25.2870
12	2.0690	11.9895	13.2976
13	.7609	13.2976	0.0000

YEARS 14 — MO PAYT 1.1324 — AN CONST 13.59

#	INT	PRIN	BALANCE
1	10.2435	3.3447	96.6553
2	9.8786	3.7096	92.9456
3	9.4739	4.1144	88.8312
4	9.0250	4.5633	84.2680
5	8.5271	5.0611	79.2068
6	7.9749	5.6133	73.5935
7	7.3625	6.2258	67.3677
8	6.6833	6.9050	60.4627
9	5.9299	7.6584	52.8043
10	5.0943	8.4939	44.3104
11	4.1676	9.4207	34.8897
12	3.1398	10.4485	24.4412
13	1.9998	11.5884	12.8528
14	.7355	12.8528	0.0000

YEARS 15 — MO PAYT 1.0992 — AN CONST 13.20

#	INT	PRIN	BALANCE
1	10.2631	2.9274	97.0726
2	9.9437	3.2468	93.8258
3	9.5894	3.6011	90.2247
4	9.1966	3.9939	86.2308
5	8.7608	4.4297	81.8011
6	8.2775	4.9130	76.8881
7	7.7415	5.4490	71.4391
8	7.1470	6.0435	65.3956
9	6.4876	6.7029	58.6927
10	5.7563	7.4342	51.2585
11	4.9452	8.2453	43.0132
12	4.0456	9.1449	33.8683
13	3.0479	10.1426	23.7257
14	1.9413	11.2492	12.4765
15	.7140	12.4765	0.0000

YEARS 16 — MO PAYT 1.0709 — AN CONST 12.86

#	INT	PRIN	BALANCE
1	10.2797	2.5716	97.4284
2	9.9991	2.8521	94.5763
3	9.6880	3.1633	91.4130
4	9.3428	3.5084	87.9045
5	8.9601	3.8912	84.0133
6	8.5355	4.3158	79.6975
7	8.0646	4.7866	74.9109
8	7.5424	5.3089	69.6020
9	6.9632	5.8881	63.7139
10	6.3208	6.5305	57.1834
11	5.6083	7.2430	49.9403
12	4.8180	8.0333	41.9071
13	3.9416	8.9097	32.9974
14	2.9695	9.8818	23.1156
15	1.8914	10.9599	12.1557
16	.6956	12.1557	0.0000

YEARS 17 — MO PAYT 1.0467 — AN CONST 12.57

#	INT	PRIN	BALANCE
1	10.2940	2.2661	97.7339
2	10.0468	2.5133	95.2206
3	9.7726	2.7875	92.4331
4	9.4684	3.0916	89.3415
5	9.1311	3.4289	85.9125
6	8.7570	3.8031	82.1095
7	8.3421	4.2180	77.8915
8	7.8819	4.6782	73.2133
9	7.3715	5.1886	68.0248
10	6.8054	5.7547	62.2701
11	6.1775	6.3825	55.8876
12	5.4812	7.0789	48.8087
13	4.7089	7.8512	40.9575
14	3.8523	8.7078	32.2496
15	2.9022	9.6579	22.5918
16	1.8485	10.7116	11.8802
17	.6798	11.8802	0.0000

YEARS 18 — MO PAYT 1.0257 — AN CONST 12.31

#	INT	PRIN	BALANCE
1	10.3063	2.0022	97.9978
2	10.0879	2.2207	95.7771
3	9.8456	2.4630	93.3141
4	9.5769	2.7317	90.5824
5	9.2789	3.0297	87.5527
6	8.9483	3.3603	84.1924
7	8.5817	3.7269	80.4655
8	8.1751	4.1335	76.3319
9	7.7241	4.5845	71.7474
10	7.2239	5.0847	66.6627
11	6.6691	5.6395	61.0233
12	6.0539	6.2547	54.7685
13	5.3714	6.9371	47.8314
14	4.6146	7.6940	40.1374
15	3.7751	8.5335	31.6039
16	2.8441	9.4645	22.1394
17	1.8115	10.4971	11.6424
18	.6662	11.6424	0.0000

YEARS 19 — MO PAYT 1.0075 — AN CONST 12.10

#	INT	PRIN	BALANCE
1	10.3171	1.7733	98.2267
2	10.1236	1.9667	96.2600
3	9.9090	2.1813	94.0787
4	9.6710	2.4193	91.6594
5	9.4071	2.6833	88.9761
6	9.1143	2.9760	86.0001
7	8.7896	3.3007	82.6994
8	8.4295	3.6608	79.0386
9	8.0301	4.0602	74.9784
10	7.5871	4.5032	70.4751
11	7.0958	4.9945	65.4806
12	6.5509	5.5394	59.9412
13	5.9465	6.1438	53.7974
14	5.2762	6.8141	46.9832
15	4.5327	7.5576	39.4256
16	3.7082	8.3821	31.0435
17	2.7937	9.2967	21.7469
18	1.7794	10.3109	11.4359
19	.6544	11.4359	0.0000

YEARS 20 — MO PAYT .9917 — AN CONST 11.91

#	INT	PRIN	BALANCE
1	10.3264	1.5737	98.4263
2	10.1547	1.7454	96.6810
3	9.9643	1.9358	94.7452
4	9.7531	2.1470	92.5982
5	9.5188	2.3812	90.2170
6	9.2590	2.6410	87.5759
7	8.9709	2.9292	84.6468
8	8.6513	3.2488	81.3980
9	8.2968	3.6032	77.7948
10	7.9037	3.9963	73.7985
11	7.4677	4.4323	69.3661
12	6.9841	4.9159	64.4502
13	6.4478	5.4523	58.9979
14	5.8529	6.0471	52.9508
15	5.1932	6.7069	46.2439
16	4.4614	7.4386	38.8052
17	3.6498	8.2502	30.5550
18	2.7497	9.1504	21.4046
19	1.7514	10.1487	11.2559
20	.6441	11.2559	0.0000

YEARS 21 — MO PAYT .9778 — AN CONST 11.74

#	INT	PRIN	BALANCE
1	10.3346	1.3990	98.6010
2	10.1819	1.5517	97.0493
3	10.0126	1.7209	95.3284

#	INT	PRIN	BALANCE
4	9.8249	1.9087	93.4197
5	9.6166	2.1170	91.3027
6	9.3857	2.3479	88.9548
7	9.1295	2.6041	86.3507
8	8.8454	2.8882	83.4625
9	8.5303	3.2033	80.2592
10	8.1808	3.5528	76.7064
11	7.7932	3.9404	72.7660
12	7.3632	4.3703	68.3957
13	6.8864	4.8472	63.5485
14	6.3576	5.3760	58.1725
15	5.7710	5.9625	52.2100
16	5.1205	6.6131	45.5969
17	4.3990	7.3346	38.2623
18	3.5988	8.1348	30.1275
19	2.7112	9.0223	21.1052
20	1.7269	10.0067	11.0985
21	.6351	11.0985	0.0000

YEARS 22   MO PAYT .9656   AN CONST 11.59

#	INT	PRIN	BALANCE
1	10.3417	1.2457	98.7543
2	10.2058	1.3816	97.3727
3	10.0551	1.5323	95.8404
4	9.8879	1.6995	94.1409
5	9.7025	1.8849	92.2560
6	9.4968	2.0906	90.1654
7	9.2687	2.3187	87.8467
8	9.0158	2.5716	85.2751
9	8.7352	2.8522	82.4229
10	8.4240	3.1634	79.2595
11	8.0789	3.5085	75.7509
12	7.6961	3.8913	71.8596
13	7.2715	4.3159	67.5437
14	6.8006	4.7868	62.7569
15	6.2784	5.3090	57.4479
16	5.6992	5.8883	51.5596
17	5.0567	6.5307	45.0289
18	4.3442	7.2432	37.7857
19	3.5539	8.0335	29.7522
20	2.6775	8.9099	20.8423
21	1.7054	9.8821	10.9602
22	.6272	10.9602	0.0000

YEARS 23   MO PAYT .9549   AN CONST 11.46

#	INT	PRIN	BALANCE
1	10.3480	1.1107	98.8893
2	10.2269	1.2318	97.6575
3	10.0925	1.3662	96.2912
4	9.9434	1.5153	94.7759
5	9.7781	1.6806	93.0953
6	9.5947	1.8640	91.2313
7	9.3914	2.0674	89.1640
8	9.1658	2.2929	86.8710
9	8.9156	2.5431	84.3280
10	8.6382	2.8205	81.5074
11	8.3304	3.1283	78.3791
12	7.9891	3.4696	74.9096
13	7.6106	3.8481	71.0614
14	7.1908	4.2680	66.7935
15	6.7251	4.7336	62.0599
16	6.2087	5.2501	56.8098
17	5.6359	5.8229	50.9869
18	5.0006	6.4582	44.5288
19	4.2960	7.1628	37.3660
20	3.5145	7.9442	29.4218
21	2.6477	8.8110	20.6108
22	1.6864	9.7723	10.8385
23	.6202	10.8385	0.0000

YEARS 24   MO PAYT .9454   AN CONST 11.35

#	INT	PRIN	BALANCE
1	10.3536	.9915	99.0085
2	10.2454	1.0997	97.9089
3	10.1255	1.2196	96.6892
4	9.9924	1.3527	95.3365
5	9.8448	1.5003	93.8363
6	9.6811	1.6640	92.1723
7	9.4996	1.8455	90.3268
8	9.2982	2.0469	88.2799
9	9.0749	2.2702	86.0097
10	8.8272	2.5179	83.4919
11	8.5525	2.7926	80.6993
12	8.2478	3.0973	77.6020
13	7.9099	3.4352	74.1669
14	7.5351	3.8100	70.3569
15	7.1195	4.2256	66.1312
16	6.6584	4.6867	61.4446
17	6.1471	5.1980	56.2466
18	5.5800	5.7651	50.4814
19	4.9510	6.3941	44.0873
20	4.2534	7.0917	36.9955
21	3.4796	7.8655	29.1301
22	2.6215	8.7236	20.4064
23	1.6697	9.6754	10.7310
24	.6141	10.7310	0.0000

YEARS 25   MO PAYT .9370   AN CONST 11.25

#	INT	PRIN	BALANCE
1	10.3586	.8860	99.1140
2	10.2619	.9827	98.1313
3	10.1547	1.0899	97.0414
4	10.0358	1.2088	95.8325
5	9.9039	1.3407	94.4918
6	9.7576	1.4870	93.0048
7	9.5954	1.6492	91.3556
8	9.4154	1.8292	89.5265
9	9.2159	2.0287	87.4977
10	8.9945	2.2501	85.2477
11	8.7490	2.4956	82.7521
12	8.4768	2.7678	79.9843
13	8.1748	3.0698	76.9145
14	7.8398	3.4047	73.5097
15	7.4684	3.7762	69.7335
16	7.0564	4.1882	65.5453
17	6.5994	4.6452	60.9001
18	6.0926	5.1520	55.7482
19	5.5305	5.7141	50.0341
20	4.9071	6.3375	43.6967
21	4.2157	7.0289	36.6678
22	3.4488	7.7958	28.8720
23	2.5982	8.6463	20.2256
24	1.6549	9.5897	10.6359
25	.6086	10.6359	0.0000

YEARS 26   MO PAYT .9296   AN CONST 11.16

#	INT	PRIN	BALANCE
1	10.3629	.7925	99.2075
2	10.2765	.8790	98.3285
3	10.1806	.9749	97.3535
4	10.0742	1.0813	96.2723
5	9.9562	1.1992	95.0730
6	9.8254	1.3301	93.7429
7	9.6803	1.4752	92.2677
8	9.5193	1.6362	90.6316
9	9.3408	1.8147	88.8169
10	9.1428	2.0126	86.8043
11	8.9232	2.2322	84.5720
12	8.6797	2.4758	82.0963
13	8.4096	2.7459	79.3504
14	8.1100	3.0455	76.3049
15	7.7777	3.3778	72.9271
16	7.4092	3.7463	69.1808
17	7.0005	4.1550	65.0258
18	6.5471	4.6083	60.4175
19	6.0443	5.1111	55.3064
20	5.4867	5.6688	49.6376
21	4.8682	6.2872	43.3504
22	4.1823	6.9732	36.3772
23	3.4215	7.7340	28.6431
24	2.5777	8.5778	20.0653
25	1.6418	9.5137	10.5517
26	.6038	10.5517	0.0000

YEARS 27   MO PAYT .9230   AN CONST 11.08

#	INT	PRIN	BALANCE
1	10.3668	.7095	99.2905
2	10.2894	.7869	98.5036
3	10.2035	.8728	97.6308
4	10.1083	.9680	96.6628
5	10.0027	1.0736	95.5892
6	9.8856	1.1907	94.3985
7	9.7557	1.3206	93.0778
8	9.6116	1.4647	91.6131
9	9.4518	1.6245	89.9885
10	9.2745	1.8018	88.1868
11	9.0779	1.9984	86.1884
12	8.8599	2.2164	83.9720
13	8.6181	2.4582	81.5138
14	8.3499	2.7264	78.7874
15	8.0524	3.0239	75.7635
16	7.7225	3.3538	72.4097
17	7.3566	3.7197	68.6900
18	6.9508	4.1255	64.5645
19	6.5007	4.5756	59.9888
20	6.0015	5.0749	54.9140
21	5.4478	5.6285	49.2854
22	4.8337	6.2426	43.0428
23	4.1526	6.9237	36.1191
24	3.3972	7.6791	28.4399
25	2.5594	8.5170	19.9230
26	1.6301	9.4462	10.4768
27	.5995	10.4768	0.0000

YEARS 28   MO PAYT .9172   AN CONST 11.01

#	INT	PRIN	BALANCE
1	10.3703	.6356	99.3644
2	10.3009	.7050	98.6594
3	10.2240	.7819	97.8774
4	10.1387	.8672	97.0102
5	10.0441	.9618	96.0484
6	9.9391	1.0668	94.9816
7	9.8227	1.1832	93.7984
8	9.6937	1.3123	92.4862
9	9.5505	1.4554	91.0308
10	9.3917	1.6142	89.4165
11	9.2156	1.7903	87.6262
12	9.0202	1.9857	85.6405
13	8.8036	2.2023	83.4382
14	8.5633	2.4426	80.9956
15	8.2968	2.7091	78.2866
16	8.0013	3.0047	75.2819
17	7.6734	3.3325	71.9494
18	7.3099	3.6961	68.2534
19	6.9066	4.0993	64.1541
20	6.4594	4.5466	59.6075
21	5.9633	5.0426	54.5649
22	5.4131	5.5928	48.9721
23	4.8030	6.2030	42.7692
24	4.1262	6.8797	35.8895
25	3.3756	7.6303	28.2591
26	2.5431	8.4628	19.7963
27	1.6198	9.3861	10.4102
28	.5957	10.4102	0.0000

YEARS 29   MO PAYT .9119   AN CONST 10.95

#	INT	PRIN	BALANCE
1	10.3733	.5698	99.4302
2	10.3112	.6320	98.7981
3	10.2422	.7010	98.0972
4	10.1657	.7775	97.3197
5	10.0809	.8623	96.4574
6	9.9868	.9564	95.5011
7	9.8825	1.0607	94.4404
8	9.7668	1.1764	93.2639
9	9.6384	1.3048	91.9592
10	9.4961	1.4471	90.5120
11	9.3382	1.6050	88.9070
12	9.1631	1.7801	87.1269
13	8.9688	1.9744	85.1525
14	8.7534	2.1898	82.9628
15	8.5145	2.4287	80.5341
16	8.2495	2.6936	77.8404
17	7.9557	2.9875	74.8529
18	7.6297	3.3135	71.5394
19	7.2682	3.6750	67.8644
20	6.8672	4.0759	63.7885
21	6.4225	4.5206	59.2678
22	5.9293	5.0139	54.2540
23	5.3823	5.5609	48.6931
24	4.7756	6.1676	42.5255
25	4.1027	6.8405	35.6849
26	3.3564	7.5868	28.0981
27	2.5286	8.4146	19.6835
28	1.6105	9.3326	10.3509
29	.5923	10.3509	0.0000

YEARS 30   MO PAYT .9073   AN CONST 10.89

#	INT	PRIN	BALANCE
1	10.3761	.5112	99.4888
2	10.3203	.5669	98.9219
3	10.2585	.6288	98.2931
4	10.1899	.6974	97.5957
5	10.1138	.7735	96.8222
6	10.0294	.8579	95.9644
7	9.9358	.9515	95.0129
8	9.8320	1.0553	93.9576
9	9.7168	1.1704	92.7872
10	9.5891	1.2981	91.4891
11	9.4475	1.4397	90.0494
12	9.2904	1.5968	88.4525
13	9.1162	1.7710	86.6815
14	8.9230	1.9643	84.7172
15	8.7087	2.1786	82.5387
16	8.4710	2.4163	80.1224
17	8.2074	2.6799	77.4425
18	7.9150	2.9723	74.4703
19	7.5907	3.2965	71.1737
20	7.2310	3.6562	67.5175
21	6.8321	4.0551	63.4624
22	6.3897	4.4975	58.9649
23	5.8990	4.9882	53.9766
24	5.3548	5.5325	48.4442
25	4.7512	6.1361	42.3081
26	4.0817	6.8055	35.5025
27	3.3392	7.5481	27.9545
28	2.5157	8.3716	19.5829
29	1.6023	9.2849	10.2980
30	.5893	10.2980	0.0000

YEARS 2 — MO PAYT 4.6376 — AN CONST 55.66

#	INT	PRIN	BALANCE
1	8.2625	47.3888	52.6112
2	3.0400	52.6112	0.0000

YEARS 3 — MO PAYT 3.2502 — AN CONST 39.01

#	INT	PRIN	BALANCE
1	9.0875	29.9154	70.0846
2	5.7907	33.2122	36.8723
3	2.1306	36.8723	0.0000

YEARS 4 — MO PAYT 2.5603 — AN CONST 30.73

#	INT	PRIN	BALANCE
1	9.4978	21.2263	78.7737
2	7.1586	23.5655	55.2082
3	4.5616	26.1625	29.0457
4	1.6784	29.0457	0.0000

YEARS 5 — MO PAYT 2.1494 — AN CONST 25.80

#	INT	PRIN	BALANCE
1	9.7421	16.0505	83.9495
2	7.9733	17.8194	66.1301
3	6.0096	19.7831	46.3470
4	3.8294	21.9633	24.3837
5	1.4090	24.3837	0.0000

YEARS 6 — MO PAYT 1.8779 — AN CONST 22.54

#	INT	PRIN	BALANCE
1	9.9036	12.6312	87.3688
2	8.5116	14.0232	73.3457
3	6.9662	15.5686	57.7771
4	5.2505	17.2843	40.4928
5	3.3457	19.1891	21.3038
6	1.2310	21.3038	0.0000

YEARS 7 — MO PAYT 1.6861 — AN CONST 20.24

#	INT	PRIN	BALANCE
1	10.0177	10.2151	89.7849
2	8.8919	11.3409	78.4440
3	7.6421	12.5907	65.8533
4	6.2546	13.9782	51.8751
5	4.7141	15.5187	36.3564
6	3.0039	17.2289	19.1276
7	1.1053	19.1276	0.0000

YEARS 8 — MO PAYT 1.5440 — AN CONST 18.53

#	INT	PRIN	BALANCE
1	10.1022	8.4259	91.5741
2	9.1736	9.3544	82.2197
3	8.1427	10.3853	71.8344
4	6.9982	11.5298	60.3046
5	5.7276	12.8004	47.5042
6	4.3169	14.2111	33.2931
7	2.7508	15.7772	17.5159
8	1.0121	17.5159	0.0000

YEARS 9 — MO PAYT 1.4351 — AN CONST 17.23

#	INT	PRIN	BALANCE
1	10.1669	7.0541	92.9459
2	9.3895	7.8315	85.1144
3	8.5265	8.6945	76.4199
4	7.5683	9.6527	66.7671
5	6.5046	10.7165	56.0507
6	5.3236	11.8975	44.1532
7	4.0124	13.2086	30.9446
8	2.5568	14.6643	16.2803
9	.9407	16.2803	0.0000

YEARS 10 — MO PAYT 1.3493 — AN CONST 16.20

#	INT	PRIN	BALANCE
1	10.2179	5.9743	94.0257
2	9.5595	6.6327	87.3930
3	8.8286	7.3636	80.0294
4	8.0171	8.1751	71.8543
5	7.1162	9.0760	62.7783
6	6.1160	10.0762	52.7020
7	5.0055	11.1867	41.5153
8	3.7727	12.4195	29.0958
9	2.4040	13.7882	15.3077
10	.8845	15.3077	0.0000

YEARS 11 — MO PAYT 1.2804 — AN CONST 15.37

#	INT	PRIN	BALANCE
1	10.2589	5.1065	94.8935
2	9.6961	5.6692	89.2243
3	9.0714	6.2940	82.9303
4	8.3778	6.9876	75.9428
5	7.6077	7.7577	68.1851
6	6.7528	8.6126	59.5725
7	5.8036	9.5617	50.0108
8	4.7499	10.6154	39.3954
9	3.5801	11.7853	27.6101
10	2.2813	13.0841	14.5260
11	.8394	14.5260	0.0000

YEARS 12 — MO PAYT 1.2241 — AN CONST 14.69

#	INT	PRIN	BALANCE
1	10.2924	4.3973	95.6027
2	9.8078	4.8819	90.7208
3	9.2698	5.4199	85.3009
4	8.6725	6.0172	79.2836
5	8.0094	6.6803	72.6033
6	7.2732	7.4165	65.1868
7	6.4558	8.2339	56.9529
8	5.5484	9.1413	47.8117
9	4.5410	10.1486	37.6630
10	3.4226	11.2671	26.3960
11	2.1810	12.5087	13.8872
12	.8024	13.8872	0.0000

YEARS 13 — MO PAYT 1.1775 — AN CONST 14.14

#	INT	PRIN	BALANCE
1	10.3201	3.8099	96.1901
2	9.9002	4.2298	91.9603
3	9.4341	4.6959	87.2644
4	8.9166	5.2134	82.0510
5	8.3421	5.7880	76.2630
6	7.7042	6.4258	69.8372
7	6.9961	7.1340	62.7032
8	6.2099	7.9201	54.7831
9	5.3370	8.7930	45.9901
10	4.3680	9.7620	36.2281
11	3.2922	10.8378	25.3903
12	2.0979	12.0322	13.3581
13	.7719	13.3581	0.0000

YEARS 14 — MO PAYT 1.1384 — AN CONST 13.67

#	INT	PRIN	BALANCE
1	10.3433	3.3179	96.6821
2	9.9777	3.6835	92.9986
3	9.5718	4.0894	88.9092

YEARS 15 — MO PAYT 1.1054 — AN CONST 13.27

#	INT	PRIN	BALANCE
1	10.3630	2.9018	97.0982
2	10.0432	3.2216	93.8766
3	9.6882	3.5766	90.3000
4	9.2940	3.9708	86.3292
5	8.8564	4.4084	81.9208
6	8.3706	4.8942	77.0267
7	7.8312	5.4335	71.5931
8	7.2325	6.0323	65.5608
9	6.5677	6.6971	58.8637
10	5.8296	7.4352	51.4285
11	5.0102	8.2545	43.1739
12	4.1006	9.1642	34.0097
13	3.0906	10.1742	23.8356
14	1.9694	11.2954	12.5402
15	.7246	12.5402	0.0000

YEARS 16 — MO PAYT 1.0772 — AN CONST 12.93

#	INT	PRIN	BALANCE
1	10.3797	2.5472	97.4528
2	10.0990	2.8279	94.6249
3	9.7874	3.1395	91.4854
4	9.4414	3.4855	87.9999
5	9.0573	3.8696	84.1303
6	8.6308	4.2961	79.8342
7	8.1574	4.7695	75.0647
8	7.6318	5.2951	69.7695
9	7.0482	5.8787	63.8908
10	6.4004	6.5265	57.3643
11	5.6811	7.2458	50.1185
12	4.8826	8.0443	42.0742
13	3.9961	8.9308	33.1434
14	3.0119	9.9150	23.2284
15	1.9192	11.0077	12.2208
16	.7062	12.2208	0.0000

YEARS 17 — MO PAYT 1.0531 — AN CONST 12.64

#	INT	PRIN	BALANCE
1	10.3941	2.2429	97.7571
2	10.1469	2.4900	95.2671
3	9.8725	2.7645	92.5026
4	9.5679	3.0691	89.4335
5	9.2296	3.4073	86.0262
6	8.8541	3.7828	82.2433
7	8.4373	4.1997	78.0436
8	7.9744	4.6625	73.3810
9	7.4606	5.1764	68.2047
10	6.8901	5.7468	62.4578
11	6.2568	6.3802	56.0777
12	5.5537	7.0833	48.9944
13	4.7731	7.8639	41.1306
14	3.9065	8.7305	32.4001
15	2.9444	9.6926	22.7074
16	1.8762	10.7608	11.9467
17	.6903	11.9467	0.0000

YEARS 18 — MO PAYT 1.0322 — AN CONST 12.39

#	INT	PRIN	BALANCE
1	10.4065	1.9802	98.0198
2	10.1883	2.1985	95.8213
3	9.9460	2.4407	93.3806
4	9.6770	2.7097	90.6708
5	9.3784	3.0083	87.6625
6	9.0469	3.3399	84.3226
7	8.6788	3.7079	80.6147
8	8.2702	4.1166	76.4981
9	7.8165	4.5702	71.9279
10	7.3129	5.0739	66.8541
11	6.7537	5.6330	61.2210
12	6.1329	6.2538	54.9672
13	5.4437	6.9430	48.0242
14	4.6786	7.7081	40.3161
15	3.8291	8.5576	31.7585
16	2.8860	9.5007	22.2578
17	1.8390	10.5477	11.7101
18	.6766	11.7101	0.0000

YEARS 19 — MO PAYT 1.0141 — AN CONST 12.17

#	INT	PRIN	BALANCE
1	10.4173	1.7524	98.2476
2	10.2241	1.9455	96.3021
3	10.0097	2.1599	94.1421
4	9.7717	2.3980	91.7442
5	9.5074	2.6622	89.0819
6	9.2140	2.9556	86.1263
7	8.8883	3.2813	82.8450
8	8.5267	3.6430	79.2020
9	8.1252	4.0444	75.1576
10	7.6795	4.4901	70.6675
11	7.1847	4.9850	65.6825
12	6.6354	5.5343	60.1482
13	6.0254	6.1442	54.0040
14	5.3483	6.8213	47.1826
15	4.5966	7.5731	39.6096
16	3.7620	8.4076	31.2019
17	2.8355	9.3342	21.8677
18	1.8068	10.3629	11.5049
19	.6648	11.5049	0.0000

YEARS 20 — MO PAYT .9984 — AN CONST 11.99

#	INT	PRIN	BALANCE
1	10.4266	1.5539	98.4461
2	10.2554	1.7252	96.7209
3	10.0653	1.9153	94.8056
4	9.8542	2.1264	92.6792
5	9.6199	2.3607	90.3185
6	9.3597	2.6209	87.6977
7	9.0709	2.9097	84.7880
8	8.7502	3.2303	81.5576
9	8.3942	3.5863	77.9713
10	7.9990	3.9816	73.9897
11	7.5602	4.4204	69.5693
12	7.0731	4.9075	64.6618
13	6.5322	5.4483	59.2135
14	5.9318	6.0487	53.1648
15	5.2652	6.7153	46.4495
16	4.5252	7.4554	38.9941
17	3.7036	8.2770	30.7171
18	2.7914	9.1891	21.5279
19	1.7787	10.2018	11.3261
20	.6545	11.3261	0.0000

YEARS 21 — MO PAYT .9846 — AN CONST 11.82

#	INT	PRIN	BALANCE
1	10.4348	1.3804	98.6196
2	10.2827	1.5325	97.0872
3	10.1138	1.7014	95.3858

#	INT	PRIN	BALANCE
4	9.9263	1.8889	93.4969
5	9.7182	2.0970	91.3999
6	9.4871	2.3281	89.0718
7	9.2305	2.5847	86.4871
8	8.9457	2.8695	83.6176
9	8.6294	3.1858	80.4318
10	8.2783	3.5368	76.8950
11	7.8886	3.9266	72.9684
12	7.4558	4.3593	68.6090
13	6.9754	4.8398	63.7693
14	6.4421	5.3731	58.3962
15	5.8499	5.9652	52.4309
16	5.1925	6.6226	45.8083
17	4.4627	7.3525	38.4558
18	3.6524	8.1627	30.2931
19	2.7529	9.0623	21.2308
20	1.7542	10.0610	11.1698
21	.6454	11.1698	0.0000

YEARS 22 — MO PAYT .9725 — AN CONST 11.68

#	INT	PRIN	BALANCE
1	10.4420	1.2281	98.7719
2	10.3067	1.3634	97.4085
3	10.1564	1.5137	95.8949
4	9.9896	1.6805	94.2144
5	9.8044	1.8657	92.3487
6	9.5988	2.0713	90.2775
7	9.3706	2.2995	87.9779
8	9.1171	2.5529	85.4250
9	8.8358	2.8343	82.5907
10	8.5234	3.1466	79.4441
11	8.1767	3.4934	75.9507
12	7.7917	3.8784	72.0723
13	7.3643	4.3058	67.7665
14	6.8898	4.7803	62.9861
15	6.3630	5.3071	57.6790
16	5.7781	5.8920	51.7870
17	5.1288	6.5413	45.2457
18	4.4079	7.2622	37.9835
19	3.6076	8.0625	29.9210
20	2.7191	8.9510	20.9700
21	1.7326	9.9374	11.0326
22	.6375	11.0326	0.0000

YEARS 23 — MO PAYT .9619 — AN CONST 11.55

#	INT	PRIN	BALANCE
1	10.4483	1.0941	98.9059
2	10.3278	1.2146	97.6913
3	10.1939	1.3485	96.3428
4	10.0453	1.4971	94.8457
5	9.8803	1.6621	93.1836
6	9.6972	1.8453	91.3384
7	9.4938	2.0486	89.2898
8	9.2680	2.2744	87.0154
9	9.0174	2.5250	84.4904
10	8.7391	2.8033	81.6871
11	8.4302	3.1122	78.5749
12	8.0872	3.4552	75.1197
13	7.7064	3.8360	71.2837
14	7.2837	4.2587	67.0251
15	6.8144	4.7280	62.2970
16	6.2933	5.2491	57.0480
17	5.7149	5.8275	51.2204
18	5.0727	6.4697	44.7507
19	4.3597	7.1827	37.5680
20	3.5681	7.9743	29.5937
21	2.6893	8.8531	20.7406
22	1.7137	9.8287	10.9119
23	.6305	10.9119	0.0000

YEARS 24 — MO PAYT .9525 — AN CONST 11.43

#	INT	PRIN	BALANCE
1	10.4539	.9758	99.0242
2	10.3464	1.0834	97.9408
3	10.2270	1.2028	96.7380
4	10.0944	1.3353	95.4027
5	9.9473	1.4825	93.9202
6	9.7839	1.6459	92.2743
7	9.6025	1.8272	90.4470
8	9.4012	2.0286	88.4184
9	9.1776	2.2522	86.1663
10	8.9294	2.5004	83.6659
11	8.6538	2.7759	80.8900
12	8.3479	3.0818	77.8081
13	8.0083	3.4215	74.3867
14	7.6312	3.7985	70.5881
15	7.2126	4.2171	66.3710
16	6.7479	4.6819	61.6891
17	6.2319	5.1978	56.4913
18	5.6591	5.7707	50.7206
19	5.0232	6.4066	44.3140
20	4.3171	7.1126	37.2014
21	3.5333	7.8965	29.3049
22	2.6631	8.7667	20.5382
23	1.6970	9.7328	10.8054
24	.6244	10.8054	0.0000

YEARS 25 — MO PAYT .9442 — AN CONST 11.34

#	INT	PRIN	BALANCE
1	10.4589	.8713	99.1287
2	10.3628	.9673	98.1613
3	10.2562	1.0739	97.0874
4	10.1379	1.1923	95.8951
5	10.0065	1.3237	94.5714
6	9.8606	1.4696	93.1018
7	9.6987	1.6315	91.4703
8	9.5189	1.8113	89.6590
9	9.3192	2.0109	87.6480
10	9.0976	2.2326	85.4155
11	8.8516	2.4786	82.9369
12	8.5784	2.7517	80.1851
13	8.2752	3.0550	77.1302
14	7.9385	3.3917	73.7385
15	7.5648	3.7654	69.9731
16	7.1498	4.1804	65.7927
17	6.6891	4.6411	61.1516
18	6.1776	5.1525	55.9991
19	5.6098	5.7204	50.2787
20	4.9794	6.3508	43.9279
21	4.2795	7.0507	36.8772
22	3.5025	7.8277	29.0496
23	2.6399	8.6903	20.3593
24	1.6822	9.6480	10.7112
25	.6189	10.7112	0.0000

YEARS 26 — MO PAYT .9368 — AN CONST 11.25

#	INT	PRIN	BALANCE
1	10.4632	.7787	99.2213
2	10.3774	.8645	98.3567
3	10.2821	.9598	97.3969
4	10.1764	1.0656	96.3313
5	10.0589	1.1830	95.1483
6	9.9286	1.3134	93.8349
7	9.7838	1.4581	92.3768
8	9.6231	1.6188	90.7580
9	9.4447	1.7972	88.9608
10	9.2467	1.9953	86.9655
11	9.0268	2.2152	84.7503
12	8.7827	2.4593	82.2910
13	8.5116	2.7303	79.5607
14	8.2108	3.0312	76.5295
15	7.8767	3.3652	73.1643
16	7.5058	3.7361	69.4282
17	7.0941	4.1478	65.2803
18	6.6370	4.6049	60.6754
19	6.1295	5.1124	55.5630
20	5.5661	5.6758	49.8871
21	4.9406	6.3013	43.5858
22	4.2462	6.9958	36.5901
23	3.4752	7.7667	28.8233
24	2.6193	8.6226	20.2007
25	1.6691	9.5729	10.6278
26	.6141	10.6278	0.0000

YEARS 27 — MO PAYT .9303 — AN CONST 11.17

#	INT	PRIN	BALANCE
1	10.4671	.6965	99.3035
2	10.3904	.7733	98.5302
3	10.3051	.8585	97.6717
4	10.2105	.9531	96.7185
5	10.1055	1.0582	95.6604
6	9.9889	1.1748	94.4856
7	9.8594	1.3042	93.1813
8	9.7157	1.4480	91.7334
9	9.5561	1.6075	90.1258
10	9.3789	1.7847	88.3411
11	9.1823	1.9814	86.3597
12	8.9639	2.1997	84.1600
13	8.7215	2.4422	81.7179
14	8.4524	2.7113	79.0066
15	8.1536	3.0101	75.9965
16	7.8218	3.3418	72.6547
17	7.4536	3.7101	68.9446
18	7.0447	4.1189	64.8256
19	6.5908	4.5729	60.2528
20	6.0868	5.0768	55.1760
21	5.5273	5.6363	49.5397
22	4.9062	6.2574	43.2822
23	4.2166	6.9470	36.3352
24	3.4510	7.7126	28.6226
25	2.6011	8.5626	20.0600
26	1.6574	9.5062	10.5538
27	.6098	10.5538	0.0000

YEARS 28 — MO PAYT .9245 — AN CONST 11.10

#	INT	PRIN	BALANCE
1	10.4706	.6235	99.3765
2	10.4019	.6922	98.6843
3	10.3256	.7685	97.9159
4	10.2409	.8532	97.0627
5	10.1469	.9472	96.1155
6	10.0425	1.0516	95.0639
7	9.9266	1.1675	93.8965
8	9.7979	1.2961	92.6004
9	9.6551	1.4389	91.1614
10	9.4965	1.5975	89.5639
11	9.3205	1.7736	87.7903
12	9.1250	1.9690	85.8213
13	8.9080	2.1860	83.6353
14	8.6671	2.4269	81.2084
15	8.3997	2.6944	78.5140
16	8.1027	2.9913	75.5227
17	7.7731	3.3210	72.2017
18	7.4071	3.6870	68.5147
19	7.0008	4.0933	64.4215
20	6.5497	4.5444	59.8771
21	6.0489	5.0452	54.8319
22	5.4929	5.6012	49.2308
23	4.8756	6.2184	43.0124
24	4.1903	6.9037	36.1087
25	3.4295	7.6645	28.4441
26	2.5849	8.5092	19.9349
27	1.6471	9.4469	10.4880
28	.6060	10.4880	0.0000

YEARS 29 — MO PAYT .9193 — AN CONST 11.04

#	INT	PRIN	BALANCE
1	10.4736	.5585	99.4415
2	10.4121	.6200	98.8215
3	10.3438	.6883	98.1332
4	10.2679	.7642	97.3690
5	10.1837	.8484	96.5206
6	10.0902	.9419	95.5787
7	9.9864	1.0457	94.5331
8	9.8712	1.1609	93.3721
9	9.7432	1.2889	92.0832
10	9.6012	1.4309	90.6523
11	9.4435	1.5886	89.0637
12	9.2684	1.7637	87.3001
13	9.0741	1.9580	85.3420
14	8.8583	2.1738	83.1682
15	8.6187	2.4134	80.7548
16	8.3527	2.6793	78.0755
17	8.0575	2.9746	75.1009
18	7.7297	3.3024	71.7985
19	7.3657	3.6664	68.1321
20	6.9617	4.0704	64.0617
21	6.5131	4.5190	59.5427
22	6.0151	5.0170	54.5257
23	5.4622	5.5699	48.9559
24	4.8484	6.1837	42.7722
25	4.1669	6.8652	35.9070
26	3.4104	7.6217	28.2853
27	2.5704	8.4617	19.8236
28	1.6379	9.3942	10.4294
29	.6026	10.4294	0.0000

YEARS 30 — MO PAYT .9147 — AN CONST 10.98

#	INT	PRIN	BALANCE
1	10.4764	.5005	99.4995
2	10.4212	.5557	98.9438
3	10.3600	.6169	98.3269
4	10.2920	.6849	97.6421
5	10.2165	.7604	96.8817
6	10.1327	.8442	96.0375
7	10.0397	.9372	95.1004
8	9.9364	1.0405	94.0599
9	9.8217	1.1551	92.9048
10	9.6945	1.2824	91.6224
11	9.5531	1.4237	90.1986
12	9.3962	1.5806	88.6180
13	9.2220	1.7548	86.8631
14	9.0286	1.9482	84.9149
15	8.8139	2.1629	82.7520
16	8.5756	2.4013	80.3507
17	8.3109	2.6659	77.6847
18	8.0171	2.9597	74.7250
19	7.6910	3.2859	71.4391
20	7.3289	3.6480	67.7911
21	6.9268	4.0500	63.7411
22	6.4805	4.4964	59.2447
23	5.9850	4.9919	54.2528
24	5.4349	5.5420	48.7108
25	4.8241	6.1527	42.5581
26	4.1461	6.8308	35.7273
27	3.3933	7.5836	28.1437
28	2.5576	8.4193	19.7244
29	1.6297	9.3472	10.3772
30	.5996	10.3772	0.0000

YEARS 2 — MO PAYT 4.6422 — AN CONST 55.71

#	INT	PRIN	BALANCE
1	8.3427	47.3641	52.6359
2	3.0709	52.6359	0.0000

YEARS 3 — MO PAYT 3.2550 — AN CONST 39.06

#	INT	PRIN	BALANCE
1	9.1758	29.8837	70.1163
2	5.8496	33.2099	36.9063
3	2.1532	36.9063	0.0000

YEARS 4 — MO PAYT 2.5652 — AN CONST 30.79

#	INT	PRIN	BALANCE
1	9.5900	21.1920	78.8080
2	7.2313	23.5508	55.2572
3	4.6100	26.1721	29.0851
4	1.6969	29.0851	0.0000

YEARS 5 — MO PAYT 2.1543 — AN CONST 25.86

#	INT	PRIN	BALANCE
1	9.8367	16.0154	83.9846
2	8.0542	17.7980	66.1866
3	6.0732	19.7790	46.4075
4	3.8717	21.9805	24.4270
5	1.4251	24.4270	0.0000

YEARS 6 — MO PAYT 1.8830 — AN CONST 22.60

#	INT	PRIN	BALANCE
1	9.9997	12.5961	87.4039
2	8.5977	13.9981	73.4058
3	7.0396	15.5562	57.8496
4	5.3082	17.2876	40.5620
5	3.3840	19.2118	21.3502
6	1.2456	21.3502	0.0000

YEARS 7 — MO PAYT 1.6913 — AN CONST 20.30

#	INT	PRIN	BALANCE
1	10.1148	10.1806	89.8194
2	8.9817	11.3137	78.5057
3	7.7224	12.5730	65.9326
4	6.3230	13.9724	51.9602
5	4.7678	15.5276	36.4325
6	3.0395	17.2559	19.1766
7	1.1188	19.1766	0.0000

YEARS 8 — MO PAYT 1.5493 — AN CONST 18.60

#	INT	PRIN	BALANCE
1	10.2000	8.3921	91.6079
2	9.2660	9.3262	82.2816
3	8.2279	10.3643	71.9174
4	7.0743	11.5179	60.3995
5	5.7923	12.7999	47.5996
6	4.3676	14.2245	33.3751
7	2.7844	15.8078	17.5673
8	1.0249	17.5673	0.0000

YEARS 9 — MO PAYT 1.4406 — AN CONST 17.29

#	INT	PRIN	BALANCE
1	10.2654	7.0214	92.9786
2	9.4839	7.8029	85.1757
3	8.6154	8.6714	76.5043
4	7.6502	9.6366	66.8678
5	6.5776	10.7092	56.1586
6	5.3856	11.9011	44.2575
7	4.0610	13.2258	31.0317
8	2.5889	14.6979	16.3338
9	.9530	16.3338	0.0000

YEARS 10 — MO PAYT 1.3550 — AN CONST 16.26

#	INT	PRIN	BALANCE
1	10.3168	5.9427	94.0573
2	9.6553	6.6041	87.4532
3	8.9203	7.3392	80.1140
4	8.1034	8.1561	71.9579
5	7.1956	9.0639	62.8940
6	6.1867	10.0727	52.8213
7	5.0656	11.1939	41.6274
8	3.8196	12.4398	29.1876
9	2.4350	13.8244	15.3631
10	.8963	15.3631	0.0000

YEARS 11 — MO PAYT 1.2862 — AN CONST 15.44

#	INT	PRIN	BALANCE
1	10.3581	5.0760	94.9240
2	9.7931	5.6410	89.2829
3	9.1652	6.2689	83.0140
4	8.4675	6.9667	76.0474
5	7.6921	7.7421	68.3053
6	6.8303	8.6038	59.7015
7	5.8727	9.5614	50.1400
8	4.8084	10.6257	39.5144
9	3.6258	11.8084	27.7060
10	2.3114	13.1227	14.5833
11	.8508	14.5833	0.0000

YEARS 12 — MO PAYT 1.2300 — AN CONST 14.76

#	INT	PRIN	BALANCE
1	10.3918	4.3681	95.6319
2	9.9056	4.8543	90.7776
3	9.3653	5.3946	85.3829
4	8.7649	5.9951	79.3879
5	8.0976	6.6623	72.7255
6	7.3561	7.4039	65.3216
7	6.5320	8.2280	57.0937
8	5.6162	9.1438	47.9499
9	4.5984	10.1615	37.7883
10	3.4674	11.2926	26.4958
11	2.2105	12.5495	13.9463
12	.8137	13.9463	0.0000

YEARS 13 — MO PAYT 1.1835 — AN CONST 14.21

#	INT	PRIN	BALANCE
1	10.4198	3.7820	96.2180
2	9.9988	4.2029	92.0151
3	9.5310	4.6707	87.3444
4	9.0111	5.1906	82.1538
5	8.4334	5.7683	76.3855
6	7.7914	6.4104	69.9751
7	7.0778	7.1239	62.8512
8	6.2849	7.9168	54.9344
9	5.4038	8.7980	46.1364
10	4.4245	9.7772	36.3592
11	3.3362	10.8655	25.4937
12	2.1269	12.0749	13.4188
13	.7829	13.4188	0.0000

YEARS 14 — MO PAYT 1.1445 — AN CONST 13.74

#	INT	PRIN	BALANCE
1	10.4431	3.2912	96.7088
2	10.0768	3.6575	93.0513
3	9.6697	4.0646	88.9867
4	9.2173	4.5170	84.4697
5	8.7146	5.0198	79.4500
6	8.1558	5.5785	73.8715
7	7.5349	6.1994	67.6721
8	6.8449	6.8894	60.7826
9	6.0781	7.6562	53.1264
10	5.2259	8.5084	44.6180
11	4.2789	9.4554	35.1625
12	3.2264	10.5079	24.6547
13	2.0569	11.6775	12.9772
14	.7571	12.9772	0.0000

YEARS 15 — MO PAYT 1.1116 — AN CONST 13.34

#	INT	PRIN	BALANCE
1	10.4629	2.8764	97.1236
2	10.1428	3.1965	93.9271
3	9.7870	3.5523	90.3748
4	9.3916	3.9477	86.4272
5	8.9522	4.3871	82.0401
6	8.4639	4.8754	77.1647
7	7.9212	5.4180	71.7467
8	7.3182	6.0211	65.7256
9	6.6480	6.6913	59.0343
10	5.9033	7.4360	51.5983
11	5.0756	8.2637	43.3346
12	4.1558	9.1835	34.1511
13	3.1336	10.2056	23.9455
14	1.9977	11.3416	12.6039
15	.7353	12.6039	0.0000

YEARS 16 — MO PAYT 1.0836 — AN CONST 13.01

#	INT	PRIN	BALANCE
1	10.4798	2.5230	97.4770
2	10.1989	2.8038	94.6732
3	9.8869	3.1159	91.5574
4	9.5401	3.4627	88.0947
5	9.1546	3.8481	84.2466
6	8.7263	4.2764	79.9702
7	8.2504	4.7524	75.2179
8	7.7214	5.2813	69.9365
9	7.1336	5.8692	64.0673
10	6.4803	6.5224	57.5449
11	5.7543	7.2484	50.2965
12	4.9475	8.0552	42.2413
13	4.0510	8.9518	33.2895
14	3.0546	9.9481	23.3414
15	1.9473	11.0554	12.2859
16	.7168	12.2859	0.0000

YEARS 17 — MO PAYT 1.0595 — AN CONST 12.72

#	INT	PRIN	BALANCE
1	10.4942	2.2199	97.7801
2	10.2471	2.4670	95.3132
3	9.9725	2.7415	92.5716
4	9.6674	3.0467	89.5249
5	9.3283	3.3858	86.1391
6	8.9514	3.7627	82.3764
7	8.5326	4.1815	78.1950
8	8.0672	4.6469	73.5481
9	7.5500	5.1641	68.3840
10	6.9752	5.7389	62.6451
11	6.3364	6.3776	56.2675
12	5.6266	7.0875	49.1800
13	4.8377	7.8764	41.3036
14	3.9610	8.7531	32.5505
15	2.9868	9.7273	22.8232
16	1.9041	10.8100	12.0132
17	.7009	12.0132	0.0000

YEARS 18 — MO PAYT 1.0388 — AN CONST 12.47

#	INT	PRIN	BALANCE
1	10.5067	1.9584	98.0416
2	10.2887	2.1764	95.8652
3	10.0464	2.4187	93.4465
4	9.7772	2.6879	90.7587
5	9.4781	2.9870	87.7716
6	9.1456	3.3195	84.4521
7	8.7761	3.6890	80.7632
8	8.3655	4.0996	76.6636
9	7.9092	4.5559	72.1077
10	7.4021	5.0630	67.0448
11	6.8386	5.6265	61.4183
12	6.2123	6.2527	55.1655
13	5.5164	6.9487	48.2168
14	4.7430	7.7221	40.4947
15	3.8835	8.5816	31.9131
16	2.9283	9.5368	22.3762
17	1.8668	10.5983	11.7779
18	.6872	11.7779	0.0000

YEARS 19 — MO PAYT 1.0208 — AN CONST 12.25

#	INT	PRIN	BALANCE
1	10.5175	1.7318	98.2682
2	10.3247	1.9245	96.3437
3	10.1105	2.1387	94.2050
4	9.8725	2.3768	91.8283
5	9.6079	2.6413	89.1869
6	9.3139	2.9353	86.2516
7	8.9872	3.2620	82.9896
8	8.6241	3.6251	79.3645
9	8.2206	4.0286	75.3360
10	7.7722	4.4770	70.8590
11	7.2739	4.9753	65.8837
12	6.7202	5.5291	60.3547
13	6.1048	6.1445	54.2102
14	5.4209	6.8284	47.3818
15	4.6608	7.5884	39.7934
16	3.8162	8.4330	31.3604
17	2.8776	9.3717	21.9887
18	1.8345	10.4148	11.5740
19	.6753	11.5740	0.0000

YEARS 20 — MO PAYT 1.0051 — AN CONST 12.07

#	INT	PRIN	BALANCE
1	10.5269	1.5344	98.4656
2	10.3561	1.7052	96.7604
3	10.1663	1.8950	94.8654
4	9.9554	2.1059	92.7595
5	9.7210	2.3403	90.4192
6	9.4605	2.6008	87.8185
7	9.1710	2.8903	84.9282
8	8.8493	3.2120	81.7162
9	8.4918	3.5695	78.1468
10	8.0945	3.9668	74.1800
11	7.6530	4.4083	69.7717
12	7.1623	4.8989	64.8728
13	6.6171	5.4442	59.4286
14	6.0111	6.0502	53.3784
15	5.3377	6.7236	46.6548
16	4.5893	7.4720	39.1828
17	3.7576	8.3036	30.8792
18	2.8334	9.2279	21.6513
19	1.8063	10.2550	11.3964
20	.6649	11.3964	0.0000

YEARS 21 — MO PAYT .9914 — AN CONST 11.90

#	INT	PRIN	BALANCE
1	10.5351	1.3619	98.6381
2	10.3835	1.5135	97.1246
3	10.2150	1.6820	95.4426

#	INT	PRIN	BALANCE
4	10.0278	1.8692	93.5734
5	9.8198	2.0772	91.4962
6	9.5886	2.3084	89.1878
7	9.3316	2.5654	86.6224
8	9.0461	2.8509	83.7715
9	8.7288	3.1682	80.6033
10	8.3762	3.5209	77.0825
11	7.9843	3.9127	73.1697
12	7.5488	4.3482	68.8215
13	7.0648	4.8322	63.9893
14	6.5269	5.3701	58.6192
15	5.9292	5.9678	52.6514
16	5.2650	6.6320	46.0194
17	4.5268	7.3702	38.6492
18	3.7065	8.1905	30.4587
19	2.7948	9.1022	21.3565
20	1.7817	10.1153	11.2412
21	.6558	11.2412	0.0000

YEARS 22	MO PAYT .9794	AN CONST 11.76	
#	INT	PRIN	BALANCE
1	10.5423	1.2107	98.7893
2	10.4075	1.3454	97.4439
3	10.2578	1.4952	95.9487
4	10.0914	1.6616	94.2871
5	9.9064	1.8465	92.4406
6	9.7009	2.0521	90.3885
7	9.4725	2.2805	88.1080
8	9.2187	2.5343	85.5737
9	8.9366	2.8164	82.7573
10	8.6231	3.1299	79.6275
11	8.2747	3.4782	76.1493
12	7.8876	3.8654	72.2839
13	7.4574	4.2956	67.9883
14	6.9793	4.7737	63.2146
15	6.4479	5.3051	57.9095
16	5.8574	5.8955	52.0140
17	5.2012	6.5517	45.4622
18	4.4720	7.2810	38.1813
19	3.6616	8.0914	30.0899
20	2.7610	8.9920	21.0979
21	1.7601	9.9928	11.1051
22	.6479	11.1051	0.0000

YEARS 23	MO PAYT .9689	AN CONST 11.63	
#	INT	PRIN	BALANCE
1	10.5486	1.0777	98.9223
2	10.4287	1.1976	97.7247
3	10.2954	1.3309	96.3938
4	10.1473	1.4791	94.9147
5	9.9826	1.6437	93.2710
6	9.7997	1.8266	91.4444
7	9.5964	2.0300	89.4144
8	9.3704	2.2559	87.1585
9	9.1193	2.5070	84.6515
10	8.8403	2.7860	81.8655
11	8.5302	3.0961	78.7694
12	8.1856	3.4407	75.3286
13	7.8026	3.8237	71.5049
14	7.3770	4.2493	67.2556
15	6.9040	4.7223	62.5333
16	6.3784	5.2479	57.2854
17	5.7943	5.8320	51.4534
18	5.1452	6.4811	44.9723
19	4.4238	7.2025	37.7698
20	3.6221	8.0042	29.7656
21	2.7312	8.8951	20.8705
22	1.7412	9.8851	10.9854
23	.6409	10.9854	0.0000

YEARS 24	MO PAYT .9596	AN CONST 11.52	
#	INT	PRIN	BALANCE
1	10.5542	.9604	99.0396
2	10.4473	1.0673	97.9722
3	10.3285	1.1861	96.7861
4	10.1965	1.3181	95.4680
5	10.0498	1.4649	94.0031
6	9.8867	1.6279	92.3752
7	9.7056	1.8091	90.5661
8	9.5042	2.0105	88.5557
9	9.2804	2.2342	86.3214
10	9.0317	2.4829	83.8385
11	8.7554	2.7593	81.0792
12	8.4483	3.0664	78.0128
13	8.1070	3.4077	74.6051
14	7.7277	3.7870	70.8182
15	7.3062	4.2085	66.6097
16	6.8377	4.6769	61.9327
17	6.3172	5.1975	56.7353
18	5.7387	5.7760	50.9593
19	5.0958	6.4189	44.5404
20	4.3813	7.1333	37.4071
21	3.5874	7.9273	29.4797
22	2.7050	8.8096	20.6701
23	1.7245	9.7902	10.8799
24	.6348	10.8799	0.0000

YEARS 25	MO PAYT .9513	AN CONST 11.42	
#	INT	PRIN	BALANCE
1	10.5592	.8568	99.1432
2	10.4638	.9522	98.1910
3	10.3578	1.0582	97.1328
4	10.2400	1.1760	95.9568
5	10.1091	1.3069	94.6500
6	9.9637	1.4523	93.1977
7	9.8020	1.6140	91.5837
8	9.6224	1.7936	89.7901
9	9.4228	1.9932	87.7969
10	9.2009	2.2151	85.5818
11	8.9544	2.4616	83.1202
12	8.6804	2.7356	80.3845
13	8.3759	3.0401	77.3444
14	8.0375	3.3785	73.9659
15	7.6615	3.7545	70.2114
16	7.2436	4.1724	66.0389
17	6.7791	4.6368	61.4021
18	6.2630	5.1530	56.2491
19	5.6895	5.7265	50.5226
20	5.0521	6.3639	44.1588
21	4.3438	7.0722	37.0865
22	3.5566	7.8594	29.2272
23	2.6818	8.7342	20.4930
24	1.7097	9.7063	10.7867
25	.6293	10.7867	0.0000

YEARS 26	MO PAYT .9441	AN CONST 11.33	
#	INT	PRIN	BALANCE
1	10.5635	.7651	99.2349
2	10.4784	.8503	98.3846
3	10.3837	.9449	97.4397
4	10.2786	1.0501	96.3896
5	10.1617	1.1670	95.2227
6	10.0318	1.2969	93.9258
7	9.8875	1.4412	92.4846
8	9.7270	1.6016	90.8830
9	9.5488	1.7799	89.1031
10	9.3507	1.9780	87.1251
11	9.1305	2.1981	84.9270
12	8.8858	2.4428	82.4842
13	8.6139	2.7147	79.7695
14	8.3118	3.0169	76.7526
15	7.9760	3.3526	73.4000
16	7.6028	3.7258	69.6742
17	7.1881	4.1405	65.5337
18	6.7273	4.6014	60.9323
19	6.2151	5.1135	55.8188
20	5.6460	5.6827	50.1361
21	5.0135	6.3152	43.8209
22	4.3105	7.0181	36.8028
23	3.5294	7.7992	29.0035
24	2.6613	8.6673	20.3362
25	1.6966	9.6321	10.7041
26	.6245	10.7041	0.0000

YEARS 27	MO PAYT .9376	AN CONST 11.26	
#	INT	PRIN	BALANCE
1	10.5674	.6838	99.3162
2	10.4913	.7599	98.5563
3	10.4067	.8445	97.7119
4	10.3127	.9385	96.7734
5	10.2083	1.0429	95.7305
6	10.0922	1.1590	94.5716
7	9.9632	1.2880	93.2836
8	9.8198	1.4313	91.8522
9	9.6605	1.5907	90.2616
10	9.4835	1.7677	88.4939
11	9.2867	1.9645	86.5294
12	9.0681	2.1831	84.3463
13	8.8251	2.4261	81.9202
14	8.5550	2.6961	79.2241
15	8.2550	2.9962	76.2278
16	7.9215	3.3297	72.8981
17	7.5508	3.7003	69.1978
18	7.1390	4.1122	65.0856
19	6.6813	4.5699	60.5156
20	6.1726	5.0786	55.4371
21	5.6074	5.6438	49.7933
22	4.9792	6.2720	43.5213
23	4.2811	6.9701	36.5511
24	3.5053	7.7459	28.8052
25	2.6431	8.6081	20.1971
26	1.6850	9.5662	10.6310
27	.6202	10.6310	0.0000

YEARS 28	MO PAYT .9319	AN CONST 11.19	
#	INT	PRIN	BALANCE
1	10.5709	.6115	99.3885
2	10.5028	.6796	98.7089
3	10.4271	.7552	97.9536
4	10.3431	.8393	97.1144
5	10.2497	.9327	96.1816
6	10.1459	1.0365	95.1451
7	10.0305	1.1519	93.9932
8	9.9023	1.2801	92.7131
9	9.7598	1.4226	91.2905
10	9.6015	1.5809	89.7096
11	9.4255	1.7569	87.9527
12	9.2299	1.9524	86.0003
13	9.0126	2.1698	83.8305
14	8.7711	2.4113	81.4192
15	8.5027	2.6797	78.7396
16	8.2045	2.9779	75.7617
17	7.8730	3.3094	72.4523
18	7.5047	3.6777	68.7746
19	7.0953	4.0871	64.6875
20	6.6404	4.5420	60.1456
21	6.1349	5.0475	55.0981
22	5.5731	5.6093	49.4888
23	4.9487	6.2337	43.2551
24	4.2549	6.9275	36.3276
25	3.4838	7.6986	28.6291
26	2.6269	8.5554	20.0736
27	1.6747	9.5077	10.5659
28	.6164	10.5659	0.0000

YEARS 29	MO PAYT .9268	AN CONST 11.13	
#	INT	PRIN	BALANCE
1	10.5739	.5473	99.4527
2	10.5130	.6082	98.8446
3	10.4453	.6759	98.1687
4	10.3701	.7511	97.4176
5	10.2865	.8347	96.5829
6	10.1936	.9276	95.6553
7	10.0903	1.0309	94.6244
8	9.9756	1.1456	93.4788
9	9.8481	1.2731	92.2057
10	9.7064	1.4148	90.7909
11	9.5489	1.5723	89.2186
12	9.3739	1.7473	87.4714
13	9.1794	1.9418	85.5296
14	8.9633	2.1579	83.3717
15	8.7231	2.3981	80.9736
16	8.4562	2.6650	78.3087
17	8.1596	2.9616	75.3470
18	7.8299	3.2913	72.0558
19	7.4636	3.6576	68.3982
20	7.0565	4.0647	64.3335
21	6.6041	4.5171	59.8164
22	6.1013	5.0199	54.7965
23	5.5426	5.5786	49.2179
24	4.9216	6.1995	43.0184
25	4.2316	6.8896	36.1288
26	3.4648	7.6564	28.4724
27	2.6126	8.5086	19.9638
28	1.6655	9.4557	10.5081
29	.6131	10.5081	0.0000

YEARS 30	MO PAYT .9222	AN CONST 11.07	
#	INT	PRIN	BALANCE
1	10.5766	.4900	99.5100
2	10.5221	.5446	98.9654
3	10.4615	.6052	98.3602
4	10.3941	.6726	97.6876
5	10.3193	.7474	96.9402
6	10.2361	.8306	96.1096
7	10.1436	.9231	95.1865
8	10.0409	1.0258	94.1607
9	9.9267	1.1400	93.0207
10	9.7998	1.2669	91.7539
11	9.6588	1.4079	90.3460
12	9.5021	1.5646	88.7814
13	9.3280	1.7387	87.0427
14	9.1344	1.9322	85.1105
15	8.9194	2.1473	82.9632
16	8.6804	2.3863	80.5768
17	8.4148	2.6519	77.9249
18	8.1196	2.9471	74.9778
19	7.7916	3.2751	71.7027
20	7.4270	3.6397	68.0630
21	7.0219	4.0448	64.0183
22	6.5717	4.4950	59.5233
23	6.0714	4.9953	54.5280
24	5.5154	5.5513	48.9767
25	4.8975	6.1692	42.8076
26	4.2109	6.8558	35.9518
27	3.4478	7.6189	28.3329
28	2.5998	8.4669	19.8659
29	1.6574	9.4093	10.4566
30	.6101	10.4566	0.0000

YEARS 2 — MO PAYT 4.6434 — AN CONST 55.73

#	INT	PRIN	BALANCE
1	8.3628	47.3579	52.6421
2	3.0786	52.6421	0.0000

YEARS 3 — MO PAYT 3.2561 — AN CONST 39.08

#	INT	PRIN	BALANCE
1	9.1979	29.8758	70.1242
2	5.8644	33.2093	36.9148
3	2.1589	36.9148	0.0000

YEARS 4 — MO PAYT 2.5664 — AN CONST 30.80

#	INT	PRIN	BALANCE
1	9.6131	21.1834	78.8166
2	7.2495	23.5471	55.2695
3	4.6221	26.1745	29.0950
4	1.7015	29.0950	0.0000

YEARS 5 — MO PAYT 2.1556 — AN CONST 25.87

#	INT	PRIN	BALANCE
1	9.8604	16.0067	83.9933
2	8.0744	17.7927	66.2007
3	6.0891	19.7780	46.4227
4	3.8822	21.9848	24.4379
5	1.4292	24.4379	0.0000

YEARS 6 — MO PAYT 1.8843 — AN CONST 22.62

#	INT	PRIN	BALANCE
1	10.0237	12.5873	87.4127
2	8.6192	13.9918	73.4208
3	7.0580	15.5531	57.8678
4	5.3226	17.2885	40.5793
5	3.3936	19.2175	21.3618
6	1.2493	21.3618	0.0000

YEARS 7 — MO PAYT 1.6926 — AN CONST 20.32

#	INT	PRIN	BALANCE
1	10.1391	10.1720	89.8280
2	9.0041	11.3070	78.5211
3	7.7425	12.5686	65.9525
4	6.3401	13.9710	51.9815
5	4.7812	15.5299	36.4516
6	3.0484	17.2627	19.1889
7	1.1222	19.1889	0.0000

YEARS 8 — MO PAYT 1.5507 — AN CONST 18.61

#	INT	PRIN	BALANCE
1	10.2245	8.3837	91.6163
2	9.2891	9.3192	82.2971
3	8.2492	10.3590	71.9381
4	7.0934	11.5149	60.4232
5	5.8085	12.7997	47.6235
6	4.3804	14.2279	33.3956
7	2.7928	15.8154	17.5801
8	1.0281	17.5801	0.0000

YEARS 9 — MO PAYT 1.4419 — AN CONST 17.31

#	INT	PRIN	BALANCE
1	10.2900	7.0132	92.9868
2	9.5075	7.7958	85.1910
3	8.6376	8.6656	76.5254
4	7.6707	9.6325	66.8929
5	6.5959	10.7073	56.1856
6	5.4012	11.9020	44.2835
7	4.0732	13.2301	31.0535
8	2.5969	14.7063	16.3472
9	.9560	16.3472	0.0000

YEARS 10 — MO PAYT 1.3564 — AN CONST 16.28

#	INT	PRIN	BALANCE
1	10.3415	5.9348	94.0652
2	9.6793	6.5970	87.4682
3	8.9432	7.3331	80.1351
4	8.1250	8.1513	71.9838
5	7.2155	9.0608	62.9229
6	6.2044	10.0719	52.8511
7	5.0806	11.1957	41.6554
8	3.8314	12.4449	29.2105
9	2.4428	13.8335	15.3770
10	.8993	15.3770	0.0000

YEARS 11 — MO PAYT 1.2876 — AN CONST 15.46

#	INT	PRIN	BALANCE
1	10.3829	5.0685	94.9315
2	9.8174	5.6340	89.2975
3	9.1887	6.2626	83.0349
4	8.4899	6.9614	76.0735
5	7.7132	7.7382	68.3353
6	6.8497	8.6016	59.7337
7	5.8900	9.5614	50.1723
8	4.8231	10.6282	39.5441
9	3.6372	11.8141	27.7300
10	2.3190	13.1323	14.5976
11	.8537	14.5976	0.0000

YEARS 12 — MO PAYT 1.2315 — AN CONST 14.78

#	INT	PRIN	BALANCE
1	10.4167	4.3608	95.6392
2	9.9301	4.8474	90.7917
3	9.3892	5.3883	85.4034
4	8.7880	5.9895	79.4139
5	8.1197	6.6578	72.7560
6	7.3768	7.4007	65.3553
7	6.5510	8.2265	57.1288
8	5.6331	9.1444	47.9844
9	4.6128	10.1647	37.8197
10	3.4786	11.2989	26.5207
11	2.2179	12.5597	13.9611
12	.8165	13.9611	0.0000

YEARS 13 — MO PAYT 1.1850 — AN CONST 14.22

#	INT	PRIN	BALANCE
1	10.4447	3.7750	96.2250
2	10.0235	4.1962	92.0288
3	9.5552	4.6644	87.3643
4	9.0348	5.1849	82.1794
5	8.4563	5.7634	76.4160
6	7.8132	6.4065	70.0095
7	7.0983	7.1213	62.8881
8	6.3037	7.9159	54.9722
9	5.4205	8.7992	46.1730
10	4.4387	9.7810	36.3920
11	3.3473	10.8724	25.5196
12	2.1342	12.0855	13.4340
13	.7856	13.4340	0.0000

YEARS 14 — MO PAYT 1.1461 — AN CONST 13.76

#	INT	PRIN	BALANCE
1	10.4681	3.2845	96.7155
2	10.1016	3.6510	93.0645
3	9.6942	4.0584	89.0061
4	9.2414	4.5112	84.4948
5	8.7380	5.0146	79.4802
6	8.1785	5.5741	73.9061
7	7.5565	6.1961	67.7100
8	6.8652	6.8874	60.8226
9	6.0967	7.6559	53.1666
10	5.2424	8.5102	44.6564
11	4.2929	9.4598	35.1967
12	3.2374	10.5153	24.6814
13	2.0641	11.6886	12.9928
14	.7598	12.9928	0.0000

YEARS 15 — MO PAYT 1.1132 — AN CONST 13.36

#	INT	PRIN	BALANCE
1	10.4879	2.8700	97.1300
2	10.1677	3.1903	93.9397
3	9.8117	3.5462	90.3935
4	9.4160	3.9419	86.4516
5	8.9762	4.3818	82.0698
6	8.4873	4.8707	77.1991
7	7.9438	5.4141	71.7850
8	7.3397	6.0183	65.7667
9	6.6682	6.6898	59.0769
10	5.9217	7.4362	51.6407
11	5.0920	8.2660	43.3748
12	4.1697	9.1883	34.1865
13	3.1444	10.2135	23.9730
14	2.0048	11.3531	12.6199
15	.7380	12.6199	0.0000

YEARS 16 — MO PAYT 1.0851 — AN CONST 13.03

#	INT	PRIN	BALANCE
1	10.5048	2.5169	97.4831
2	10.2239	2.7978	94.6853
3	9.9118	3.1100	91.5753
4	9.5647	3.4570	88.1183
5	9.1790	3.8427	84.2756
6	8.7502	4.2715	80.0041
7	8.2736	4.7481	75.2561
8	7.7438	5.2779	69.9782
9	7.1549	5.8668	64.1114
10	6.5003	6.5214	57.5900
11	5.7727	7.2491	50.3409
12	4.9638	8.0579	42.2830
13	4.0647	8.9570	33.3260
14	3.0653	9.9564	23.3696
15	1.9544	11.0674	12.3023
16	.7195	12.3023	0.0000

YEARS 17 — MO PAYT 1.0611 — AN CONST 12.74

#	INT	PRIN	BALANCE
1	10.5192	2.2142	97.7858
2	10.2722	2.4612	95.3246
3	9.9976	2.7358	92.5888
4	9.6923	3.0411	89.5477
5	9.3530	3.3804	86.1672
6	8.9758	3.7576	82.4096
7	8.5565	4.1769	78.2327
8	8.0904	4.6430	73.5898
9	7.5724	5.1610	68.4287
10	6.9965	5.7369	62.6919
11	6.3564	6.3770	56.3149
12	5.6448	7.0885	49.2263
13	4.8539	7.8795	41.3468
14	3.9747	8.7587	32.5882
15	2.9974	9.7360	22.8522
16	1.9111	10.8223	12.0299
17	.7035	12.0299	0.0000

YEARS 18 — MO PAYT 1.0404 — AN CONST 12.49

#	INT	PRIN	BALANCE
1	10.5317	1.9530	98.0470
2	10.3138	2.1709	95.8761
3	10.0716	2.4132	93.4629
4	9.8023	2.6824	90.7805
5	9.5030	2.9817	87.7988
6	9.1703	3.3144	84.4844
7	8.8005	3.6842	80.8002
8	8.3894	4.0953	76.7048
9	7.9324	4.5523	72.1526
10	7.4245	5.0602	67.0923
11	6.8599	5.6248	61.4675
12	6.2323	6.2525	55.2150
13	5.5346	6.9501	48.2649
14	4.7591	7.7256	40.5393
15	3.8971	8.5876	31.9517
16	2.9389	9.5458	22.4059
17	1.8738	10.6110	11.7949
18	.6898	11.7949	0.0000

YEARS 19 — MO PAYT 1.0224 — AN CONST 12.27

#	INT	PRIN	BALANCE
1	10.5425	1.7266	98.2734
2	10.3499	1.9193	96.3541
3	10.1357	2.1334	94.2207
4	9.8977	2.3715	91.8492
5	9.6331	2.6361	89.2131
6	9.3389	2.9302	86.2828
7	9.0120	3.2572	83.0257
8	8.6485	3.6206	79.4050
9	8.2445	4.0246	75.3804
10	7.7955	4.4737	70.9067
11	7.2963	4.9728	65.9339
12	6.7414	5.5277	60.4062
13	6.1246	6.1445	54.2617
14	5.4390	6.8301	47.4316
15	4.6769	7.5922	39.8394
16	3.8298	8.4393	31.4000
17	2.8881	9.3810	22.0190
18	1.8414	10.4277	11.5913
19	.6779	11.5913	0.0000

YEARS 20 — MO PAYT 1.0068 — AN CONST 12.09

#	INT	PRIN	BALANCE
1	10.5519	1.5295	98.4705
2	10.3813	1.7002	96.7702
3	10.1916	1.8899	94.8803
4	9.9807	2.1008	92.7795
5	9.7463	2.3352	90.4443
6	9.4857	2.5958	87.8485
7	9.1961	2.8854	84.9631
8	8.8741	3.2074	81.7557
9	8.5162	3.5652	78.1905
10	8.1184	3.9631	74.2274
11	7.6762	4.4052	69.8222
12	7.1847	4.8968	64.9254
13	6.6383	5.4432	59.4822
14	6.0310	6.0505	53.4317
15	5.3559	6.7256	46.7061
16	4.6054	7.4761	39.2300
17	3.7712	8.3103	30.9197
18	2.8440	9.2375	21.6822
19	1.8132	10.2682	11.4140
20	.6675	11.4140	0.0000

YEARS 21 — MO PAYT .9931 — AN CONST 11.92

#	INT	PRIN	BALANCE
1	10.5602	1.3573	98.6427
2	10.4087	1.5088	97.1339
3	10.2404	1.6771	95.4567

#	INT	PRIN	BALANCE
4	10.0532	1.8643	93.5925
5	9.8452	2.0723	91.5202
6	9.6140	2.3035	89.2167
7	9.3570	2.5605	86.6561
8	9.0713	2.8462	83.8099
9	8.7537	3.1638	80.6460
10	8.4006	3.5169	77.1292
11	8.0082	3.9093	73.2199
12	7.5720	4.3455	68.8745
13	7.0872	4.8303	64.0442
14	6.5482	5.3693	58.6749
15	5.9491	5.9684	52.7065
16	5.2832	6.6343	46.0721
17	4.5429	7.3746	38.6975
18	3.7200	8.1975	30.5001
19	2.8054	9.1121	21.3879
20	1.7886	10.1289	11.2590
21	.6585	11.2590	0.0000

YEARS 22 — MO PAYT .9811 — AN CONST 11.78

#	INT	PRIN	BALANCE
1	10.5674	1.2064	98.7936
2	10.4328	1.3410	97.4527
3	10.2831	1.4906	95.9621
4	10.1168	1.6569	94.3052
5	9.9319	1.8418	92.4634
6	9.7264	2.0473	90.4161
7	9.4980	2.2757	88.1404
8	9.2441	2.5297	85.6107
9	8.9618	2.8119	82.7988
10	8.6481	3.1257	79.6732
11	8.2993	3.4744	76.1987
12	7.9116	3.8621	72.3366
13	7.4807	4.2930	68.0436
14	7.0017	4.7721	63.2716
15	6.4692	5.3045	57.9670
16	5.8773	5.8964	52.0706
17	5.2194	6.5543	45.5163
18	4.4881	7.2856	38.2307
19	3.6752	8.0986	30.1321
20	2.7715	9.0022	21.1299
21	1.7671	10.0067	11.1232
22	.6505	11.1232	0.0000

YEARS 23 — MO PAYT .9706 — AN CONST 11.65

#	INT	PRIN	BALANCE
1	10.5737	1.0736	98.9264
2	10.4539	1.1934	97.7330
3	10.3208	1.3266	96.4064
4	10.1727	1.4746	94.9318
5	10.0082	1.6391	93.2927
6	9.8253	1.8220	91.4707
7	9.6220	2.0253	89.4454
8	9.3960	2.2513	87.1941
9	9.1448	2.5025	84.6916
10	8.8656	2.7817	81.9099
11	8.5552	3.0921	78.8178
12	8.2102	3.4371	75.3807
13	7.8267	3.8206	71.5600
14	7.4004	4.2469	67.3131
15	6.9265	4.7208	62.5923
16	6.3998	5.2476	57.3447
17	5.8142	5.8331	51.5116
18	5.1634	6.4839	45.0277
19	4.4399	7.2074	37.8202
20	3.6357	8.0116	29.8086
21	2.7418	8.9056	20.9030
22	1.7481	9.8992	11.0038
23	.6435	11.0038	0.0000

YEARS 24 — MO PAYT .9613 — AN CONST 11.54

#	INT	PRIN	BALANCE
1	10.5793	.9566	99.0434
2	10.4726	1.0633	97.9801
3	10.3539	1.1820	96.7981
4	10.2220	1.3139	95.4842
5	10.0754	1.4605	94.0237
6	9.9125	1.6234	92.4003
7	9.7313	1.8046	90.5957
8	9.5300	2.0059	88.5898
9	9.3062	2.2298	86.3600
10	9.0574	2.4786	83.8814
11	8.7808	2.7551	81.1263
12	8.4734	3.0625	78.0638
13	8.1317	3.4042	74.6596
14	7.7518	3.7841	70.8755
15	7.3296	4.2063	66.6692
16	6.8603	4.6757	61.9935
17	6.3385	5.1974	56.7961
18	5.7586	5.7773	51.0188
19	5.1140	6.4219	44.5969
20	4.3974	7.1385	37.4584
21	3.6009	7.9350	29.5235
22	2.7155	8.8204	20.7031
23	1.7314	9.8045	10.8985
24	.6374	10.8985	0.0000

YEARS 25 — MO PAYT .9531 — AN CONST 11.44

#	INT	PRIN	BALANCE
1	10.5842	.8532	99.1468
2	10.4890	.9484	98.1983
3	10.3832	1.0543	97.1441
4	10.2656	1.1719	95.9721
5	10.1348	1.3027	94.6695
6	9.9895	1.4480	93.2215
7	9.8279	1.6096	91.6119
8	9.6483	1.7892	89.8227
9	9.4487	1.9888	87.8339
10	9.2267	2.2107	85.6231
11	8.9801	2.4574	83.1657
12	8.7059	2.7316	80.4341
13	8.4011	3.0364	77.3977
14	8.0623	3.3752	74.0225
15	7.6857	3.7518	70.2707
16	7.2671	4.1704	66.1003
17	6.8017	4.6358	61.4645
18	6.2845	5.1530	56.3115
19	5.7095	5.7280	50.5835
20	5.0704	6.3671	44.2164
21	4.3599	7.0776	37.1388
22	3.5702	7.8673	29.2716
23	2.6924	8.7451	20.5264
24	1.7166	9.7209	10.8055
25	.6319	10.8055	0.0000

YEARS 26 — MO PAYT .9459 — AN CONST 11.36

#	INT	PRIN	BALANCE
1	10.5886	.7617	99.2383
2	10.5036	.8467	98.3915
3	10.4091	.9412	97.4503
4	10.3041	1.0462	96.4041
5	10.1874	1.1630	95.2411
6	10.0576	1.2927	93.9483
7	9.9134	1.4370	92.5114
8	9.7530	1.5973	90.9140
9	9.5748	1.7756	89.1385
10	9.3767	1.9737	87.1648
11	9.1565	2.1939	84.9709
12	8.9117	2.4387	82.5322
13	8.6396	2.7108	79.8214
14	8.3371	3.0133	76.8082
15	8.0009	3.3495	73.4587
16	7.6271	3.7232	69.7355
17	7.2117	4.1387	65.5968
18	6.7499	4.6005	60.9963
19	6.2366	5.1138	55.8826
20	5.6660	5.6844	50.1982
21	5.0317	6.3186	43.8796
22	4.3267	7.0237	36.8559
23	3.5430	7.8074	29.0486
24	2.6719	8.6785	20.3701
25	1.7035	9.6468	10.7232
26	.6271	10.7232	0.0000

YEARS 27 — MO PAYT .9394 — AN CONST 11.28

#	INT	PRIN	BALANCE
1	10.5925	.6806	99.3194
2	10.5165	.7566	98.5628
3	10.4321	.8410	97.7219
4	10.3383	.9348	96.7870
5	10.2340	1.0391	95.7479
6	10.1180	1.1551	94.5929
7	9.9892	1.2839	93.3089
8	9.8459	1.4272	91.8817
9	9.6867	1.5865	90.2953
10	9.5096	1.7635	88.5318
11	9.3129	1.9602	86.5716
12	9.0941	2.1790	84.3926
13	8.8510	2.4221	81.9705
14	8.5808	2.6923	79.2782
15	8.2803	2.9928	76.2854
16	7.9464	3.3267	72.9587
17	7.5752	3.6979	69.2608
18	7.1626	4.1105	65.1503
19	6.7040	4.5691	60.5812
20	6.1941	5.0790	55.5022
21	5.6274	5.6457	49.8566
22	4.9975	6.2756	43.5809
23	4.2973	6.9759	36.6051
24	3.5189	7.7542	28.8509
25	2.6537	8.6194	20.2314
26	1.6919	9.5812	10.6503
27	.6228	10.6503	0.0000

YEARS 28 — MO PAYT .9337 — AN CONST 11.21

#	INT	PRIN	BALANCE
1	10.5959	.6086	99.3914
2	10.5280	.6765	98.7150
3	10.4525	.7520	97.9630
4	10.3686	.8359	97.1271
5	10.2754	.9291	96.1980
6	10.1717	1.0328	95.1652
7	10.0565	1.1480	94.0172
8	9.9284	1.2761	92.7411
9	9.7860	1.4185	91.3225
10	9.6277	1.5768	89.7457
11	9.4518	1.7527	87.9930
12	9.2562	1.9483	86.0447
13	9.0388	2.1657	83.8790
14	8.7971	2.4073	81.4717
15	8.5285	2.6760	78.7957
16	8.2300	2.9745	75.8211
17	7.8981	3.3064	72.5147
18	7.5291	3.6754	68.8393
19	7.1190	4.0855	64.7539
20	6.6632	4.5413	60.2125
21	6.1564	5.0481	55.1645
22	5.5932	5.6113	49.5531
23	4.9671	6.2374	43.3157
24	4.2711	6.9334	36.3823
25	3.4975	7.7070	28.6753
26	2.6375	8.5670	20.1083
27	1.6816	9.5229	10.5854
28	.6191	10.5854	0.0000

YEARS 29 — MO PAYT .9286 — AN CONST 11.15

#	INT	PRIN	BALANCE
1	10.5990	.5445	99.4555
2	10.5382	.6053	98.8502
3	10.4707	.6728	98.1775
4	10.3956	.7479	97.4296
5	10.3122	.8313	96.5983
6	10.2194	.9241	95.6742
7	10.1163	1.0272	94.6471
8	10.0017	1.1418	93.5053
9	9.8743	1.2692	92.2361
10	9.7327	1.4108	90.8253
11	9.5753	1.5682	89.2571
12	9.4003	1.7432	87.5139
13	9.2058	1.9377	85.5762
14	8.9896	2.1539	83.4223
15	8.7492	2.3942	81.0280
16	8.4821	2.6614	78.3666
17	8.1851	2.9583	75.4083
18	7.8550	3.2884	72.1199
19	7.4881	3.6554	68.4645
20	7.0803	4.0632	64.4013
21	6.6269	4.5166	59.8847
22	6.1229	5.0206	54.8641
23	5.5627	5.5808	49.2833
24	4.9400	6.2035	43.0799
25	4.2478	6.8956	36.1842
26	3.4784	7.6651	28.5192
27	2.6232	8.5203	19.9988
28	1.6725	9.4710	10.5278
29	.6157	10.5278	0.0000

YEARS 30 — MO PAYT .9241 — AN CONST 11.09

#	INT	PRIN	BALANCE
1	10.6017	.4875	99.5125
2	10.5473	.5418	98.9707
3	10.4869	.6023	98.3684
4	10.4197	.6695	97.6989
5	10.3450	.7442	96.9547
6	10.2619	.8273	96.1274
7	10.1696	.9196	95.2079
8	10.0670	1.0222	94.1857
9	9.9530	1.1362	93.0495
10	9.8262	1.2630	91.7865
11	9.6853	1.4039	90.3826
12	9.5286	1.5606	88.8220
13	9.3545	1.7347	87.0873
14	9.1609	1.9283	85.1590
15	8.9458	2.1434	83.0156
16	8.7066	2.3826	80.6331
17	8.4408	2.6484	77.9846
18	8.1452	2.9439	75.0407
19	7.8168	3.2724	71.7683
20	7.4516	3.6375	68.1308
21	7.0457	4.0434	64.0873
22	6.5946	4.4946	59.5927
23	6.0931	4.9961	54.5967
24	5.5356	5.5536	49.0431
25	4.9159	6.1732	42.8699
26	4.2271	6.8620	36.0078
27	3.4615	7.6277	28.3801
28	2.6104	8.4788	19.9013
29	1.6643	9.4249	10.4765
30	.6127	10.4765	0.0000

YEARS 2 — MO PAYT 4.6469 — AN CONST 55.77

#	INT	PRIN	BALANCE
1	8.4230	47.3394	52.6606
2	3.1018	52.6606	0.0000

YEARS 3 — MO PAYT 3.2597 — AN CONST 39.12

#	INT	PRIN	BALANCE
1	9.2642	29.8520	70.1480
2	5.9086	33.2076	36.9404
3	2.1758	36.9404	0.0000

YEARS 4 — MO PAYT 2.5700 — AN CONST 30.85

#	INT	PRIN	BALANCE
1	9.6823	21.1577	78.8423
2	7.3041	23.5360	55.3062
3	4.6585	26.1816	29.1246
4	1.7155	29.1246	0.0000

YEARS 5 — MO PAYT 2.1593 — AN CONST 25.92

#	INT	PRIN	BALANCE
1	9.9314	15.9804	84.0196
2	8.1351	17.7767	66.2430
3	6.1369	19.7749	46.4681
4	3.9140	21.9977	24.4704
5	1.4413	24.4704	0.0000

YEARS 6 — MO PAYT 1.8881 — AN CONST 22.66

#	INT	PRIN	BALANCE
1	10.0958	12.5611	87.4389
2	8.6839	13.9731	73.4658
3	7.1132	15.5437	57.9221
4	5.3660	17.2909	40.6312
5	3.4224	19.2345	21.3966
6	1.2603	21.3966	0.0000

YEARS 7 — MO PAYT 1.6965 — AN CONST 20.36

#	INT	PRIN	BALANCE
1	10.2120	10.1461	89.8539
2	9.0715	11.2866	78.5672
3	7.8028	12.5553	66.0119
4	6.3915	13.9666	52.0453
5	4.8216	15.5366	36.5087
6	3.0751	17.2830	19.2257
7	1.1324	19.2257	0.0000

YEARS 8 — MO PAYT 1.5547 — AN CONST 18.66

#	INT	PRIN	BALANCE
1	10.2980	8.3585	91.6415
2	9.3584	9.2981	82.3434
3	8.3132	10.3432	72.0002
4	7.1506	11.5059	60.4943
5	5.8573	12.7992	47.6950
6	4.4185	14.2379	33.4571
7	2.8181	15.8384	17.6187
8	1.0378	17.6187	0.0000

YEARS 9 — MO PAYT 1.4461 — AN CONST 17.36

#	INT	PRIN	BALANCE
1	10.3638	6.9888	93.0112
2	9.5783	7.7744	85.2369
3	8.7044	8.6483	76.5886
4	7.7323	9.6204	66.9682
5	6.6509	10.7018	56.2665
6	5.4479	11.9047	44.3617
7	4.1097	13.2429	31.1189
8	2.6212	14.7315	16.3874
9	.9652	16.3874	0.0000

YEARS 10 — MO PAYT 1.3606 — AN CONST 16.33

#	INT	PRIN	BALANCE
1	10.4157	5.9112	94.0888
2	9.7512	6.5757	87.5131
3	9.0121	7.3148	80.1983
4	8.1898	8.1370	72.0613
5	7.2752	9.0517	63.0096
6	6.2577	10.0692	52.9404
7	5.1259	11.2010	41.7394
8	3.8668	12.4601	29.2794
9	2.4662	13.8607	15.4187
10	.9082	15.4187	0.0000

YEARS 11 — MO PAYT 1.2919 — AN CONST 15.51

#	INT	PRIN	BALANCE
1	10.4573	5.0458	94.9542
2	9.8901	5.6129	89.3413
3	9.2592	6.2439	83.0974
4	8.5573	6.9457	76.1517
5	7.7766	7.7265	68.4253
6	6.9081	8.5950	59.8303
7	5.9420	9.5611	50.2692
8	4.8672	10.6358	39.6334
9	3.6717	11.8314	27.8020
10	2.3418	13.1613	14.6407
11	.8624	14.6407	0.0000

YEARS 12 — MO PAYT 1.2359 — AN CONST 14.84

#	INT	PRIN	BALANCE
1	10.4913	4.3391	95.6609
2	10.0036	4.8268	90.8341
3	9.4610	5.3694	85.4647
4	8.8574	5.9729	79.4918
5	8.1860	6.6443	72.8474
6	7.4392	7.3912	65.4562
7	6.6083	8.2220	57.2342
8	5.6841	9.1462	48.0880
9	4.6560	10.1743	37.9136
10	3.5124	11.3180	26.5956
11	2.2402	12.5902	14.0054
12	.8249	14.0054	0.0000

YEARS 13 — MO PAYT 1.1895 — AN CONST 14.28

#	INT	PRIN	BALANCE
1	10.5194	3.7542	96.2458
2	10.0974	4.1762	92.0696
3	9.6280	4.6456	87.4240
4	9.1058	5.1678	82.2562
5	8.5249	5.7487	76.5075
6	7.8787	6.3949	70.1126
7	7.1599	7.1137	62.9989
8	6.3603	7.9134	55.0855
9	5.4707	8.8029	46.2827
10	4.4812	9.7924	36.4903
11	3.3805	10.8931	25.5972
12	2.1561	12.1176	13.4796
13	.7940	13.4796	0.0000

YEARS 14 — MO PAYT 1.1506 — AN CONST 13.81

#	INT	PRIN	BALANCE
1	10.5430	3.2647	96.7353
2	10.1760	3.6316	93.1037
3	9.7678	4.0398	89.0639
4	9.3137	4.4939	84.5699
5	8.8085	4.9991	79.5708
6	8.2466	5.5610	74.0098
7	7.6215	6.1861	67.8237
8	6.9261	6.8815	60.9422
9	6.1526	7.6550	53.2872
10	5.2921	8.5155	44.7717
11	4.3349	9.4727	35.2990
12	3.2702	10.5375	24.7615
13	2.0857	11.7220	13.0396
14	.7680	13.0396	0.0000

YEARS 15 — MO PAYT 1.1178 — AN CONST 13.42

#	INT	PRIN	BALANCE
1	10.5629	2.8511	97.1489
2	10.2424	3.1716	93.9773
3	9.8859	3.5281	90.4492
4	9.4893	3.9247	86.5246
5	9.0481	4.3658	82.1588
6	8.5574	4.8566	77.3022
7	8.0115	5.4025	71.8997
8	7.4042	6.0098	65.8900
9	6.7287	6.6853	59.2047
10	5.9772	7.4368	51.7679
11	5.1413	8.2727	43.4952
12	4.2114	9.2026	34.2926
13	3.1769	10.2370	24.0556
14	2.0262	11.3878	12.6678
15	.7462	12.6678	0.0000

YEARS 16 — MO PAYT 1.0899 — AN CONST 13.08

#	INT	PRIN	BALANCE
1	10.5798	2.4989	97.5011
2	10.2989	2.7798	94.7212
3	9.9864	3.0923	91.6289
4	9.6388	3.4399	88.1890
5	9.2522	3.8266	84.3624
6	8.8220	4.2567	80.1057
7	8.3435	4.7352	75.3704
8	7.8113	5.2675	70.1030
9	7.2192	5.8596	64.2434
10	6.5605	6.5182	57.7252
11	5.8278	7.2509	50.4743
12	5.0128	8.0660	42.4083
13	4.1061	8.9726	33.4356
14	3.0975	9.9812	23.4544
15	1.9756	11.1032	12.3512
16	.7275	12.3512	0.0000

YEARS 17 — MO PAYT 1.0660 — AN CONST 12.80

#	INT	PRIN	BALANCE
1	10.5943	2.1971	97.8029
2	10.3474	2.4440	95.3589
3	10.0726	2.7188	92.6401
4	9.7670	3.0244	89.6157
5	9.4271	3.3643	86.2514
6	9.0489	3.7425	82.5089
7	8.6282	4.1632	78.3457
8	8.1602	4.6312	73.7145
9	7.6397	5.1517	68.5628
10	7.0606	5.7308	62.8319
11	6.4164	6.3750	56.4569
12	5.6998	7.0916	49.3653
13	4.9026	7.8888	41.4765
14	4.0159	8.7755	32.7010
15	3.0295	9.7619	22.9391
16	1.9322	10.8592	12.0799
17	.7115	12.0799	0.0000

YEARS 18 — MO PAYT 1.0453 — AN CONST 12.55

#	INT	PRIN	BALANCE
1	10.6068	1.9368	98.0632
2	10.3891	2.1545	95.9087
3	10.1469	2.3967	93.5119
4	9.8775	2.6661	90.8458
5	9.5779	2.9658	87.8800
6	9.2445	3.2992	84.5809
7	8.8736	3.6700	80.9108
8	8.4611	4.0826	76.8283
9	8.0022	4.5415	72.2868
10	7.4917	5.0520	67.2348
11	6.9238	5.6198	61.6150
12	6.2921	6.2515	55.3634
13	5.5894	6.9543	48.4092
14	4.8077	7.7360	40.6732
15	3.9381	8.6055	32.0677
16	2.9708	9.5729	22.4948
17	1.8947	10.6489	11.8459
18	.6977	11.8459	0.0000

YEARS 19 — MO PAYT 1.0274 — AN CONST 12.33

#	INT	PRIN	BALANCE
1	10.6177	1.7113	98.2887
2	10.4253	1.9037	96.3850
3	10.2113	2.1177	94.2674
4	9.9733	2.3557	91.9117
5	9.7085	2.6205	89.2912
6	9.4139	2.9150	86.3761
7	9.0863	3.2427	83.1334
8	8.7218	3.6072	79.5262
9	8.3163	4.0127	75.5135
10	7.8652	4.4638	71.0497
11	7.3635	4.9655	66.0842
12	6.8053	5.5237	60.5606
13	6.1844	6.1446	54.4160
14	5.4937	6.8353	47.5808
15	4.7254	7.6036	39.9772
16	3.8707	8.4583	31.5189
17	2.9200	9.4090	22.1099
18	1.8623	10.4667	11.6432
19	.6858	11.6432	0.0000

YEARS 20 — MO PAYT 1.0119 — AN CONST 12.15

#	INT	PRIN	BALANCE
1	10.6271	1.5151	98.4849
2	10.4568	1.6854	96.7995
3	10.2674	1.8748	94.9247
4	10.0566	2.0856	92.8391
5	9.8222	2.3200	90.5191
6	9.5614	2.5808	87.9384
7	9.2713	2.8709	85.0675
8	8.9486	3.1936	81.8739
9	8.5896	3.5526	78.3213
10	8.1903	3.9519	74.3694
11	7.7461	4.3961	69.9733
12	7.2519	4.8903	65.0830
13	6.7022	5.4400	59.6430
14	6.0907	6.0515	53.5916
15	5.4105	6.7317	46.8599
16	4.6538	7.4884	39.3715
17	3.8121	8.3301	31.0414
18	2.8757	9.2665	21.7749
19	1.8341	10.3081	11.4668
20	.6754	11.4668	0.0000

YEARS 21 — MO PAYT .9983 — AN CONST 11.98

#	INT	PRIN	BALANCE
1	10.6354	1.3437	98.6563
2	10.4843	1.4947	97.1616
3	10.3163	1.6627	95.4989

#	INT	PRIN	BALANCE
4	10.1294	1.8496	93.6492
5	9.9215	2.0575	91.5917
6	9.6902	2.2888	89.3029
7	9.4329	2.5461	86.7567
8	9.1467	2.8323	83.9244
9	8.8284	3.1507	80.7738
10	8.4742	3.5048	77.2689
11	8.0802	3.8988	73.3701
12	7.6420	4.3371	69.0331
13	7.1545	4.8246	64.2085
14	6.6122	5.3669	58.8416
15	6.0089	5.9702	52.8715
16	5.3378	6.6412	46.2302
17	4.5913	7.3878	38.8425
18	3.7609	8.2182	30.6243
19	2.8371	9.1420	21.4823
20	1.8095	10.1696	11.3127
21	.6663	11.3127	0.0000

YEARS 22   MO PAYT .9863   AN CONST 11.84

#	INT	PRIN	BALANCE
1	10.6426	1.1935	98.8065
2	10.5084	1.3276	97.4789
3	10.3592	1.4769	96.0020
4	10.1932	1.6429	94.3591
5	10.0085	1.8276	92.5315
6	9.8031	2.0330	90.4985
7	9.5746	2.2615	88.2370
8	9.3204	2.5157	85.7213
9	9.0376	2.7985	82.9228
10	8.7230	3.1131	79.8097
11	8.3731	3.4630	76.3467
12	7.9838	3.8523	72.4945
13	7.5508	4.2853	68.2092
14	7.0691	4.7670	63.4422
15	6.5333	5.3028	58.1393
16	5.9372	5.8989	52.2404
17	5.2741	6.5620	45.6785
18	4.5365	7.2996	38.3789
19	3.7160	8.1201	30.2588
20	2.8032	9.0329	21.2259
21	1.7879	10.0482	11.1777
22	.6584	11.1777	0.0000

YEARS 23   MO PAYT .9759   AN CONST 11.72

#	INT	PRIN	BALANCE
1	10.6489	1.0615	98.9385
2	10.5296	1.1808	97.7577
3	10.3969	1.3136	96.4441
4	10.2492	1.4612	94.9829
5	10.0850	1.6255	93.3575
6	9.9023	1.8082	91.5493
7	9.6990	2.0114	89.5379
8	9.4729	2.2375	87.3004
9	9.2214	2.4890	84.8114
10	8.9416	2.7688	82.0426
11	8.6304	3.0800	78.9626
12	8.2842	3.4262	75.5363
13	7.8991	3.8114	71.7249
14	7.4706	4.2398	67.4851
15	6.9941	4.7164	62.7687
16	6.4639	5.2465	57.5222
17	5.8742	5.8363	51.6859
18	5.2181	6.4923	45.1936
19	4.4883	7.2221	37.9715
20	3.6765	8.0339	29.9376
21	2.7735	8.9370	21.0006
22	1.7689	9.9416	11.0590
23	.6514	11.0590	0.0000

YEARS 24   MO PAYT .9666   AN CONST 11.60

#	INT	PRIN	BALANCE
1	10.6545	.9452	99.0548
2	10.5483	1.0515	98.0033
3	10.4301	1.1697	96.8337
4	10.2986	1.3011	95.5325
5	10.1524	1.4474	94.0851
6	9.9897	1.6101	92.4750
7	9.8087	1.7911	90.6840
8	9.6074	1.9924	88.6916
9	9.3834	2.2164	86.4752
10	9.1343	2.4655	84.0097
11	8.8571	2.7426	81.2671
12	8.5488	3.0509	78.2162
13	8.2059	3.3939	74.8223
14	7.8244	3.7754	71.0470
15	7.4000	4.1997	66.8472
16	6.9279	4.6718	62.1754
17	6.4028	5.1969	56.9785
18	5.8186	5.7811	51.1974
19	5.1688	6.4310	44.7664
20	4.4459	7.1538	37.6126
21	3.6418	7.9580	29.6546
22	2.7472	8.8525	20.8021
23	1.7522	9.8476	10.9545
24	.6452	10.9545	0.0000

YEARS 25   MO PAYT .9585   AN CONST 11.51

#	INT	PRIN	BALANCE
1	10.6595	.8425	99.1575
2	10.5648	.9373	98.2202
3	10.4594	1.0426	97.1776
4	10.3422	1.1598	96.0178
5	10.2118	1.2902	94.7276
6	10.0668	1.4352	93.2924
7	9.9055	1.5965	91.6959
8	9.7260	1.7760	89.9199
9	9.5264	1.9756	87.9443
10	9.3043	2.1977	85.7466
11	9.0573	2.4447	83.3019
12	8.7825	2.7195	80.5824
13	8.4768	3.0252	77.5572
14	8.1368	3.3653	74.1919
15	7.7585	3.7435	70.4484
16	7.3377	4.1643	66.2840
17	6.8696	4.6324	61.6516
18	6.3489	5.1532	56.4984
19	5.7696	5.7324	50.7660
20	5.1252	6.3768	44.3892
21	4.4085	7.0936	37.2957
22	3.6111	7.8909	29.4048
23	2.7241	8.7779	20.6268
24	1.7374	9.7646	10.8622
25	.6398	10.8622	0.0000

YEARS 26   MO PAYT .9513   AN CONST 11.42

#	INT	PRIN	BALANCE
1	10.6638	.7517	99.2483
2	10.5793	.8362	98.4121
3	10.4854	.9302	97.4819
4	10.3808	1.0348	96.4471
5	10.2645	1.1511	95.2960
6	10.1351	1.2805	94.0155
7	9.9912	1.4244	92.5911
8	9.8310	1.5845	91.0066
9	9.6529	1.7626	89.2440
10	9.4548	1.9608	87.2832
11	9.2344	2.1812	85.1021
12	8.9892	2.4263	82.6757
13	8.7165	2.6991	79.9766
14	8.4131	3.0025	76.9742
15	8.0756	3.3400	73.6342
16	7.7002	3.7154	69.9188
17	7.2825	4.1330	65.7858
18	6.8179	4.5976	61.1881
19	6.3011	5.1144	56.0737
20	5.7262	5.6893	50.3844
21	5.0867	6.3288	44.0556
22	4.3753	7.0402	37.0153
23	3.5839	7.8316	29.1837
24	2.7036	8.7119	20.4718
25	1.7243	9.6912	10.7806
26	.6350	10.7806	0.0000

YEARS 27   MO PAYT .9449   AN CONST 11.34

#	INT	PRIN	BALANCE
1	10.6677	.6712	99.3288
2	10.5923	.7467	98.5821
3	10.5083	.8306	97.7515
4	10.4150	.9240	96.8275
5	10.3111	1.0278	95.7997
6	10.1956	1.1434	94.6564
7	10.0671	1.2719	93.3845
8	9.9241	1.4148	91.9696
9	9.7651	1.5739	90.3958
10	9.5881	1.7508	88.6450
11	9.3913	1.9476	86.6974
12	9.1724	2.1665	84.5308
13	8.9289	2.4101	82.1208
14	8.6580	2.6810	79.4398
15	8.3566	2.9823	76.4575
16	8.0214	3.3176	73.1400
17	7.6485	3.6905	69.4495
18	7.2336	4.1053	65.3442
19	6.7722	4.5668	60.7774
20	6.2588	5.0801	55.6973
21	5.6878	5.6511	50.0462
22	5.0526	6.2864	43.7598
23	4.3460	6.9930	36.7669
24	3.5599	7.7790	28.9878
25	2.6855	8.6535	20.3344
26	1.7128	9.6262	10.7082
27	.6307	10.7082	0.0000

YEARS 28   MO PAYT .9392   AN CONST 11.28

#	INT	PRIN	BALANCE
1	10.6712	.5998	99.4002
2	10.6037	.6672	98.7330
3	10.5287	.7422	97.9908
4	10.4453	.8256	97.1652
5	10.3525	.9184	96.2468
6	10.2493	1.0217	95.2251
7	10.1344	1.1365	94.0886
8	10.0067	1.2642	92.8244
9	9.8646	1.4064	91.4180
10	9.7065	1.5644	89.8536
11	9.5306	1.7403	88.1133
12	9.3350	1.9359	86.1774
13	9.1174	2.1535	84.0238
14	8.8753	2.3956	81.6282
15	8.6060	2.6649	78.9634
16	8.3065	2.9644	75.9989
17	7.9733	3.2977	72.7013
18	7.6026	3.6683	69.0329
19	7.1903	4.0807	64.9523
20	6.7316	4.5394	60.4129
21	6.2213	5.0496	55.3633
22	5.6537	5.6172	49.7460
23	5.0223	6.2487	43.4974
24	4.3199	6.9510	36.5463
25	3.5385	7.7324	28.8140
26	2.6694	8.6016	20.2124
27	1.7025	9.5684	10.6440
28	.6269	10.6440	0.0000

YEARS 29   MO PAYT .9342   AN CONST 11.22

#	INT	PRIN	BALANCE
1	10.6742	.5363	99.4637
2	10.6139	.5966	98.8672
3	10.5469	.6636	98.2035
4	10.4723	.7382	97.4653
5	10.3893	.8212	96.6442
6	10.2970	.9135	95.7307
7	10.1943	1.0162	94.7145
8	10.0801	1.1304	93.5841
9	9.9530	1.2575	92.3266
10	9.8117	1.3988	90.9278
11	9.6544	1.5561	89.3717
12	9.4795	1.7310	87.6408
13	9.2849	1.9255	85.7152
14	9.0685	2.1420	83.5732
15	8.8277	2.3828	81.1905
16	8.5599	2.6506	78.5399
17	8.2619	2.9485	75.5914
18	7.9305	3.2800	72.3114
19	7.5618	3.6487	68.6627
20	7.1517	4.0588	64.6039
21	6.6955	4.5150	60.0889
22	6.1879	5.0225	55.0664
23	5.6234	5.5871	49.4793
24	4.9953	6.2151	43.2641
25	4.2967	6.9138	36.3504
26	3.5196	7.6909	28.6594
27	2.6551	8.5554	20.1040
28	1.6934	9.5171	10.5869
29	.6236	10.5869	0.0000

YEARS 30   MO PAYT .9297   AN CONST 11.16

#	INT	PRIN	BALANCE
1	10.6769	.4798	99.5202
2	10.6230	.5337	98.9865
3	10.5630	.5937	98.3928
4	10.4963	.6604	97.7324
5	10.4220	.7347	96.9977
6	10.3394	.8172	96.1805
7	10.2476	.9091	95.2714
8	10.1454	1.0113	94.2601
9	10.0317	1.1250	93.1351
10	9.9053	1.2514	91.8836
11	9.7646	1.3921	90.4915
12	9.6081	1.5486	88.9429
13	9.4340	1.7227	87.2203
14	9.2404	1.9163	85.3040
15	9.0250	2.1317	83.1723
16	8.7854	2.3713	80.8010
17	8.5188	2.6379	78.1631
18	8.2223	2.9344	75.2287
19	7.8925	3.2642	71.9645
20	7.5255	3.6312	68.3333
21	7.1174	4.0393	64.2940
22	6.6633	4.4934	59.8006
23	6.1582	4.9984	54.8022
24	5.5964	5.5603	49.2419
25	4.9714	6.1853	43.0566
26	4.2761	6.8806	36.1760
27	3.5027	7.6540	28.5219
28	2.6423	8.5144	20.0076
29	1.6852	9.4715	10.5361
30	.6206	10.5361	0.0000

YEARS 2 — MO PAYT 4.6492 — AN CONST 55.80

#	INT	PRIN	BALANCE
1	8.4632	47.3270	52.6730
2	3.1172	52.6730	0.0000

YEARS 3 — MO PAYT 3.2620 — AN CONST 39.15

#	INT	PRIN	BALANCE
1	9.3083	29.8362	70.1638
2	5.9381	33.2064	36.9574
3	2.1872	36.9574	0.0000

YEARS 4 — MO PAYT 2.5724 — AN CONST 30.87

#	INT	PRIN	BALANCE
1	9.7285	21.1406	78.8594
2	7.3405	23.5286	55.3307
3	4.6828	26.1864	29.1443
4	1.7248	29.1443	0.0000

YEARS 5 — MO PAYT 2.1618 — AN CONST 25.95

#	INT	PRIN	BALANCE
1	9.9787	15.9629	84.0371
2	8.1756	17.7660	66.2712
3	6.1687	19.7728	46.4984
4	3.9353	22.0063	24.4921
5	1.4495	24.4921	0.0000

YEARS 6 — MO PAYT 1.8906 — AN CONST 22.69

#	INT	PRIN	BALANCE
1	10.1439	12.5436	87.4564
2	8.7270	13.9605	73.4958
3	7.1500	15.5375	57.9584
4	5.3950	17.2926	40.6658
5	3.4416	19.2459	21.4199
6	1.2677	21.4199	0.0000

YEARS 7 — MO PAYT 1.6991 — AN CONST 20.39

#	INT	PRIN	BALANCE
1	10.2606	10.1289	89.8711
2	9.1164	11.2731	78.5980
3	7.8430	12.5465	66.0515
4	6.4258	13.9637	52.0878
5	4.8485	15.5410	36.5468
6	3.0930	17.2965	19.2503
7	1.1393	19.2503	0.0000

YEARS 8 — MO PAYT 1.5574 — AN CONST 18.69

#	INT	PRIN	BALANCE
1	10.3469	8.3417	91.6583
2	9.4047	9.2840	82.3742
3	8.3560	10.3327	72.0415
4	7.1888	11.4999	60.5416
5	5.8898	12.7989	47.7428
6	4.4441	14.2446	33.4981
7	2.8350	15.8537	17.6445
8	1.0442	17.6445	0.0000

YEARS 9 — MO PAYT 1.4488 — AN CONST 17.39

#	INT	PRIN	BALANCE
1	10.4131	6.9725	93.0275
2	9.6255	7.7601	85.2674
3	8.7489	8.6367	76.6307
4	7.7733	9.6123	67.0184
5	6.6876	10.6981	56.3204
6	5.4791	11.9065	44.4139

YEARS 9 (continued)

#	INT	PRIN	BALANCE
7	4.1342	13.2514	31.1625
8	2.6373	14.7483	16.4142
9	.9714	16.4142	0.0000

YEARS 10 — MO PAYT 1.3634 — AN CONST 16.37

#	INT	PRIN	BALANCE
1	10.4651	5.8955	94.1045
2	9.7992	6.5615	87.5430
3	9.0580	7.3026	80.2404
4	8.2331	8.1275	72.1129
5	7.3151	9.0456	63.0673
6	6.2933	10.0673	53.0000
7	5.1561	11.2045	41.7955
8	3.8905	12.4702	29.3253
9	2.4819	13.8788	15.4465
10	.9141	15.4465	0.0000

YEARS 11 — MO PAYT 1.2948 — AN CONST 15.54

#	INT	PRIN	BALANCE
1	10.5069	5.0307	94.9693
2	9.9387	5.5989	89.3704
3	9.3062	6.2314	83.1390
4	8.6023	6.9352	76.2038
5	7.8190	7.7186	68.4852
6	6.9471	8.5905	59.8946
7	5.9767	9.5609	50.3337
8	4.8967	10.6409	39.6929
9	3.6947	11.8428	27.8500
10	2.3570	13.1806	14.6694
11	.8682	14.6694	0.0000

YEARS 12 — MO PAYT 1.2388 — AN CONST 14.87

#	INT	PRIN	BALANCE
1	10.5410	4.3246	95.6754
2	10.0525	4.8131	90.8623
3	9.5089	5.3568	85.5055
4	8.9038	5.9619	79.5436
5	8.2303	6.6353	72.9083
6	7.4808	7.3848	65.5234
7	6.6466	8.2190	57.3044
8	5.7182	9.1474	48.1570
9	4.6850	10.1807	37.9763
10	3.5350	11.3307	26.6456
11	2.2551	12.6106	14.0350
12	.8306	14.0350	0.0000

YEARS 13 — MO PAYT 1.1925 — AN CONST 14.31

#	INT	PRIN	BALANCE
1	10.5693	3.7404	96.2596
2	10.1468	4.1629	92.0968
3	9.6765	4.6331	87.4637
4	9.1532	5.1564	82.3073
5	8.5707	5.7389	76.5684
6	7.9225	6.3871	70.1812
7	7.2010	7.1086	63.0726
8	6.3980	7.9116	55.1610
9	5.5043	8.8053	46.3558
10	4.5097	9.7999	36.5559
11	3.4027	10.9069	25.6490
12	2.1707	12.1389	13.5101
13	.7995	13.5101	0.0000

YEARS 14 — MO PAYT 1.1537 — AN CONST 13.85

#	INT	PRIN	BALANCE
1	10.5929	3.2515	96.7485
2	10.2256	3.6187	93.1298
3	9.8168	4.0275	89.1023
4	9.3619	4.4824	84.6199
5	8.8556	4.9888	79.6311
6	8.2921	5.5523	74.0788
7	7.6649	6.1795	67.8993
8	6.9669	6.8775	61.0218
9	6.1900	7.6544	53.3675
10	5.3254	8.5190	44.8485
11	4.3631	9.4813	35.3673
12	3.2921	10.5522	24.8150
13	2.1001	11.7442	13.0708
14	.7735	13.0708	0.0000

YEARS 15 — MO PAYT 1.1209 — AN CONST 13.46

#	INT	PRIN	BALANCE
1	10.6128	2.8385	97.1615
2	10.2922	3.1592	94.0023
3	9.9354	3.5160	90.4863
4	9.5382	3.9132	86.5731
5	9.0962	4.3552	82.2179
6	8.6042	4.8472	77.3707
7	8.0567	5.3947	71.9761
8	7.4473	6.0041	65.9720
9	6.7691	6.6823	59.2897
10	6.0143	7.4371	51.8526
11	5.1742	8.2772	43.5755
12	4.2392	9.2121	34.3633
13	3.1987	10.2527	24.1106
14	2.0405	11.4108	12.6998
15	.7516	12.6998	0.0000

YEARS 16 — MO PAYT 1.0931 — AN CONST 13.12

#	INT	PRIN	BALANCE
1	10.6298	2.4870	97.5130
2	10.3489	2.7679	94.7451
3	10.0362	3.0806	91.6645
4	9.6883	3.4286	88.2359
5	9.3010	3.8159	84.4200
6	8.8699	4.2469	80.1731
7	8.3902	4.7266	75.4465
8	7.8563	5.2605	70.1860
9	7.2621	5.8547	64.3313
10	6.6008	6.5161	57.8152
11	5.8647	7.2521	50.5631
12	5.0455	8.0713	42.4918
13	4.1338	8.9830	33.5087
14	3.1191	9.9977	23.5110
15	1.9898	11.1271	12.3839
16	.7329	12.3839	0.0000

YEARS 17 — MO PAYT 1.0692 — AN CONST 12.84

#	INT	PRIN	BALANCE
1	10.6444	2.1858	97.8142
2	10.3975	2.4326	95.3816
3	10.1227	2.7074	92.6742
4	9.8169	3.0133	89.6609
5	9.4765	3.3536	86.3073
6	9.0977	3.7325	82.5748
7	8.6761	4.1541	78.4207
8	8.2068	4.6233	73.7974
9	7.6846	5.1455	68.6519
10	7.1034	5.7268	62.9251
11	6.4565	6.3737	56.5515
12	5.7365	7.0936	49.4579
13	4.9352	7.8949	41.5630
14	4.0435	8.7867	32.7763
15	3.0509	9.7792	22.9971
16	1.9463	10.8838	12.1133
17	.7169	12.1133	0.0000

YEARS 18 — MO PAYT 1.0486 — AN CONST 12.59

#	INT	PRIN	BALANCE
1	10.6569	1.9261	98.0739
2	10.4394	2.1437	95.9303
3	10.1972	2.3858	93.5445
4	9.9277	2.6553	90.8892
5	9.6278	2.9552	87.9340
6	9.2940	3.2890	84.6449
7	8.9225	3.6606	80.9844
8	8.5090	4.0741	76.9103
9	8.0488	4.5343	72.3760
10	7.5366	5.0464	67.3296
11	6.9666	5.6165	61.7131
12	6.3321	6.2509	55.4623
13	5.6260	6.9570	48.5053
14	4.8402	7.7428	40.7625
15	3.9656	8.6174	32.1450
16	2.9922	9.5908	22.5542
17	1.9088	10.6742	11.8800
18	.7031	11.8800	0.0000

YEARS 19 — MO PAYT 1.0307 — AN CONST 12.37

#	INT	PRIN	BALANCE
1	10.6678	1.7012	98.2988
2	10.4756	1.8933	96.4055
3	10.2618	2.1072	94.2983
4	10.0238	2.3452	91.9531
5	9.7588	2.6101	89.3430
6	9.4640	2.9050	86.4381
7	9.1359	3.2331	83.2050
8	8.7707	3.5983	79.6067
9	8.3642	4.0047	75.6019
10	7.9118	4.4571	71.1448
11	7.4084	4.9606	66.1842
12	6.8480	5.5209	60.6633
13	6.2244	6.1446	54.5188
14	5.5303	6.8386	47.6801
15	4.7579	7.6111	40.0690
16	3.8981	8.4708	31.5982
17	2.9413	9.4277	22.1705
18	1.8763	10.4926	11.6779
19	.6911	11.6779	0.0000

YEARS 20 — MO PAYT 1.0152 — AN CONST 12.19

#	INT	PRIN	BALANCE
1	10.6773	1.5055	98.4945
2	10.5072	1.6755	96.8190
3	10.3179	1.8648	94.9541
4	10.1073	2.0755	92.8787
5	9.8728	2.3099	90.5688
6	9.6119	2.5708	87.9980
7	9.3215	2.8612	85.1367
8	8.9983	3.1844	81.9523
9	8.6386	3.5441	78.4082
10	8.2383	3.9445	74.4638
11	7.7927	4.3900	70.0737
12	7.2968	4.8859	65.1878
13	6.7449	5.4378	59.7500
14	6.1307	6.0520	53.6980
15	5.4471	6.7357	46.9623
16	4.6862	7.4965	39.4658
17	3.8394	8.3433	31.1225
18	2.8970	9.2858	21.8367
19	1.8481	10.3347	11.5020
20	.6807	11.5020	0.0000

YEARS 21 — MO PAYT 1.0017 — AN CONST 12.03

#	INT	PRIN	BALANCE
1	10.6855	1.3346	98.6654
2	10.5348	1.4854	97.1800
3	10.3670	1.6532	95.5268

#	INT	PRIN	BALANCE
4	10.1802	1.8399	93.6868
5	9.9724	2.0478	91.6391
6	9.7411	2.2791	89.3600
7	9.4836	2.5365	86.8235
8	9.1971	2.8230	84.0005
9	8.8782	3.1419	80.8586
10	8.5233	3.4968	77.3617
11	8.1283	3.8918	73.4699
12	7.6887	4.3314	69.1385
13	7.1995	4.8207	64.3178
14	6.6549	5.3652	58.9526
15	6.0489	5.9713	52.9813
16	5.3744	6.6458	46.3355
17	4.6237	7.3965	38.9391
18	3.7882	8.2320	30.7071
19	2.8583	9.1618	21.5453
20	1.8234	10.1967	11.3485
21	.6716	11.3485	0.0000

YEARS 22 — MO PAYT .9898 — AN CONST 11.88

#	INT	PRIN	BALANCE
1	10.6927	1.1850	98.8150
2	10.5589	1.3188	97.4962
3	10.4099	1.4678	96.0284
4	10.2441	1.6336	94.3948
5	10.0596	1.8181	92.5767
6	9.8542	2.0235	90.5532
7	9.6257	2.2521	88.3011
8	9.3713	2.5065	85.7947
9	9.0881	2.7896	83.0051
10	8.7730	3.1047	79.9004
11	8.4223	3.4554	76.4450
12	8.0320	3.8457	72.5993
13	7.5976	4.2801	68.3192
14	7.1141	4.7636	63.5557
15	6.5761	5.3017	58.2540
16	5.9772	5.9005	52.3535
17	5.3107	6.5670	45.7865
18	4.5689	7.3088	38.4776
19	3.7433	8.1344	30.3432
20	2.8245	9.0533	21.2900
21	1.8018	10.0759	11.2141
22	.6637	11.2141	0.0000

YEARS 23 — MO PAYT .9794 — AN CONST 11.76

#	INT	PRIN	BALANCE
1	10.6991	1.0535	98.9465
2	10.5801	1.1725	97.7740
3	10.4477	1.3049	96.4691
4	10.3003	1.4523	95.0168
5	10.1362	1.6164	93.4004
6	9.9536	1.7990	91.6014
7	9.7504	2.0022	89.5992
8	9.5242	2.2283	87.3709
9	9.2725	2.4800	84.8908
10	8.9924	2.7602	82.1306
11	8.6806	3.0720	79.0587
12	8.3336	3.4190	75.6397
13	7.9474	3.8052	71.8345
14	7.5176	4.2350	67.5995
15	7.0392	4.7134	62.8861
16	6.5068	5.2458	57.6403
17	5.9142	5.8384	51.8020
18	5.2547	6.4978	45.3041
19	4.5208	7.2318	38.0723
20	3.7039	8.0487	30.0236
21	2.7947	8.9579	21.0657
22	1.7828	9.9698	11.0959
23	.6567	11.0959	0.0000

YEARS 24 — MO PAYT .9702 — AN CONST 11.65

#	INT	PRIN	BALANCE
1	10.7047	.9377	99.0623
2	10.5988	1.0436	98.0187
3	10.4809	1.1615	96.8572
4	10.3497	1.2927	95.5645
5	10.2037	1.4387	94.1258
6	10.0412	1.6012	92.5246
7	9.8603	1.7821	90.7425
8	9.6590	1.9834	88.7591
9	9.4349	2.2074	86.5516
10	9.1856	2.4568	84.0948
11	8.9081	2.7343	81.3605
12	8.5992	3.0432	78.3173
13	8.2555	3.3869	74.9304
14	7.8729	3.7695	71.1609
15	7.4471	4.1953	66.9656
16	6.9732	4.6692	62.2964
17	6.4458	5.1966	57.0998
18	5.8588	5.7836	51.3162
19	5.2055	6.4369	44.8793
20	4.4784	7.1640	37.7153
21	3.6691	7.9732	29.7420
22	2.7685	8.8739	20.8681
23	1.7661	9.8763	10.9919
24	.6505	10.9919	0.0000

YEARS 25 — MO PAYT .9621 — AN CONST 11.55

#	INT	PRIN	BALANCE
1	10.7096	.8355	99.1645
2	10.6153	.9299	98.2347
3	10.5102	1.0349	97.1998
4	10.3933	1.1518	96.0480
5	10.2632	1.2819	94.7661
6	10.1184	1.4267	93.3394
7	9.9573	1.5879	91.7515
8	9.7779	1.7672	89.9843
9	9.5783	1.9668	88.0175
10	9.3561	2.1890	85.8285
11	9.1088	2.4363	83.3922
12	8.8336	2.7115	80.6808
13	8.5274	3.0177	77.6630
14	8.1865	3.3586	74.3044
15	7.8071	3.7380	70.5664
16	7.3849	4.1602	66.4061
17	6.9149	4.6302	61.7760
18	6.3919	5.1532	56.6228
19	5.8098	5.7353	50.8875
20	5.1620	6.3831	44.5043
21	4.4410	7.1042	37.4002
22	3.6385	7.9066	29.4935
23	2.7454	8.7998	20.6938
24	1.7514	9.7938	10.9000
25	.6451	10.9000	0.0000

YEARS 26 — MO PAYT .9549 — AN CONST 11.46

#	INT	PRIN	BALANCE
1	10.7140	.7451	99.2549
2	10.6298	.8293	98.4256
3	10.5362	.9229	97.5027
4	10.4319	1.0272	96.4755
5	10.3159	1.1432	95.3323
6	10.1867	1.2723	94.0600
7	10.0430	1.4161	92.6439
8	9.8831	1.5760	91.0679
9	9.7050	1.7540	89.3139
10	9.5069	1.9522	87.3617
11	9.2864	2.1727	85.1890
12	9.0410	2.4181	82.7709
13	8.7678	2.6913	80.0796
14	8.4638	2.9953	77.0844
15	8.1255	3.3336	73.7508
16	7.7489	3.7102	70.0406
17	7.3298	4.1292	65.9113
18	6.8634	4.5957	61.3157
19	6.3443	5.1148	56.2009
20	5.7665	5.6926	50.5083
21	5.1235	6.3356	44.1727
22	4.4079	7.0512	37.1215
23	3.6114	7.8477	29.2738
24	2.7249	8.7342	20.5396
25	1.7383	9.7208	10.8188
26	.6403	10.8188	0.0000

YEARS 27 — MO PAYT .9486 — AN CONST 11.39

#	INT	PRIN	BALANCE
1	10.7179	.6650	99.3350
2	10.6427	.7401	98.5948
3	10.5591	.8237	97.7711
4	10.4661	.9168	96.8543
5	10.3625	1.0203	95.8340
6	10.2473	1.1356	94.6984
7	10.1190	1.2639	93.4345
8	9.9762	1.4066	92.0278
9	9.8173	1.5655	90.4623
10	9.6405	1.7424	88.7199
11	9.4437	1.9392	86.7807
12	9.2246	2.1582	84.6225
13	8.9809	2.4020	82.2204
14	8.7095	2.6734	79.5471
15	8.4075	2.9753	76.5717
16	8.0715	3.3114	73.2603
17	7.6974	3.6855	69.5748
18	7.2811	4.1018	65.4730
19	6.8178	4.5651	60.9079
20	6.3021	5.0808	55.8271
21	5.7282	5.6547	50.1724
22	5.0894	6.2934	43.8790
23	4.3785	7.0043	36.8746
24	3.5874	7.7955	29.0791
25	2.7068	8.6761	20.4030
26	1.7267	9.6561	10.7469
27	.6360	10.7469	0.0000

YEARS 28 — MO PAYT .9429 — AN CONST 11.32

#	INT	PRIN	BALANCE
1	10.7213	.5940	99.4060
2	10.6542	.6611	98.7450
3	10.5795	.7357	98.0092
4	10.4964	.8188	97.1904
5	10.4039	.9113	96.2790
6	10.3010	1.0143	95.2647
7	10.1864	1.1289	94.1359
8	10.0589	1.2564	92.8795
9	9.9170	1.3983	91.4812
10	9.7590	1.5562	89.9250
11	9.5832	1.7320	88.1929
12	9.3876	1.9277	86.2653
13	9.1699	2.1454	84.1198
14	8.9275	2.3878	81.7321
15	8.6578	2.6575	79.0746
16	8.3576	2.9577	76.1169
17	8.0235	3.2918	72.8251
18	7.6517	3.6636	69.1616
19	7.2379	4.0774	65.0841
20	6.7773	4.5380	60.5461
21	6.2647	5.0506	55.4955
22	5.6942	5.6211	49.8744
23	5.0592	6.2561	43.6184
24	4.3525	6.9627	36.6556
25	3.5660	7.7492	28.9064
26	2.6907	8.6246	20.2818
27	1.7165	9.5988	10.6830
28	.6322	10.6830	0.0000

YEARS 29 — MO PAYT .9379 — AN CONST 11.26

#	INT	PRIN	BALANCE
1	10.7243	.5309	99.4691
2	10.6644	.5908	98.8783
3	10.5976	.6576	98.2208
4	10.5234	.7318	97.4889
5	10.4407	.8145	96.6744
6	10.3487	.9065	95.7679
7	10.2463	1.0089	94.7590
8	10.1323	1.1229	93.6361
9	10.0055	1.2497	92.3864
10	9.8643	1.3909	90.9956
11	9.7072	1.5480	89.4476
12	9.5324	1.7228	87.7248
13	9.3378	1.9174	85.8073
14	9.1212	2.1340	83.6733
15	8.8801	2.3751	81.2982
16	8.6118	2.6434	78.6548
17	8.3132	2.9420	75.7128
18	7.9809	3.2743	72.4386
19	7.6111	3.6441	68.7944
20	7.1994	4.0558	64.7386
21	6.7413	4.5139	60.2247
22	6.2314	5.0238	55.2009
23	5.6639	5.5913	49.6097
24	5.0324	6.2229	43.3868
25	4.3294	6.9258	36.4610
26	3.5471	7.7081	28.7529
27	2.6764	8.5788	20.1742
28	1.7074	9.5478	10.6263
29	.6289	10.6263	0.0000

YEARS 30 — MO PAYT .9335 — AN CONST 11.21

#	INT	PRIN	BALANCE
1	10.7271	.4747	99.5253
2	10.6734	.5283	98.9969
3	10.6138	.5880	98.4089
4	10.5473	.6544	97.7545
5	10.4734	.7284	97.0261
6	10.3911	.8106	96.2155
7	10.2996	.9022	95.3133
8	10.1977	1.0041	94.3092
9	10.0842	1.1175	93.1916
10	9.9580	1.2438	91.9479
11	9.8175	1.3843	90.5636
12	9.6611	1.5406	89.0230
13	9.4871	1.7147	87.3083
14	9.2934	1.9083	85.4000
15	9.0779	2.1239	83.2761
16	8.8380	2.3638	80.9122
17	8.5709	2.6308	78.2814
18	8.2738	2.9280	75.3534
19	7.9430	3.2587	72.0947
20	7.5749	3.6268	68.4678
21	7.1653	4.0365	64.4313
22	6.7093	4.4925	59.9388
23	6.2018	4.9999	54.9389
24	5.6370	5.5647	49.3741
25	5.0085	6.1933	43.1808
26	4.3089	6.8929	36.2879
27	3.5303	7.6715	28.6164
28	2.6637	8.5381	20.0784
29	1.6993	9.5025	10.5759
30	.6259	10.5759	0.0000

YEARS 2 — MO PAYT 4.6515 — AN CONST 55.82

#	INT	PRIN	BALANCE
1	8.5034	47.3147	52.6853
2	3.1327	52.6853	0.0000

YEARS 3 — MO PAYT 3.2644 — AN CONST 39.18

#	INT	PRIN	BALANCE
1	9.3525	29.8204	70.1796
2	5.9676	33.2053	36.9744
3	2.1985	36.9744	0.0000

YEARS 4 — MO PAYT 2.5749 — AN CONST 30.90

#	INT	PRIN	BALANCE
1	9.7747	21.1235	78.8765
2	7.3770	23.5212	55.3552
3	4.7071	26.1911	29.1641
4	1.7341	29.1641	0.0000

YEARS 5 — MO PAYT 2.1643 — AN CONST 25.98

#	INT	PRIN	BALANCE
1	10.0260	15.9454	84.0546
2	8.2161	17.7553	66.2993
3	6.2007	19.7707	46.5286
4	3.9565	22.0149	24.5138
5	1.4576	24.5138	0.0000

YEARS 6 — MO PAYT 1.8932 — AN CONST 22.72

#	INT	PRIN	BALANCE
1	10.1920	12.5262	87.4738
2	8.7701	13.9480	73.5258
3	7.1869	15.5312	57.9946
4	5.4240	17.2942	40.7004
5	3.4609	19.2572	21.4431
6	1.2750	21.4431	0.0000

YEARS 7 — MO PAYT 1.7017 — AN CONST 20.43

#	INT	PRIN	BALANCE
1	10.3092	10.1118	89.8882
2	9.1614	11.2596	78.6287
3	7.8833	12.5376	66.0911
4	6.4602	13.9608	52.1303
5	4.8755	15.5454	36.5849
6	3.1109	17.3100	19.2749
7	1.1461	19.2749	0.0000

YEARS 8 — MO PAYT 1.5601 — AN CONST 18.73

#	INT	PRIN	BALANCE
1	10.3959	8.3250	91.6750
2	9.4509	9.2700	82.4050
3	8.3987	10.3222	72.0828
4	7.2270	11.4939	60.5890
5	5.9224	12.7985	47.7905
6	4.4696	14.2513	33.5392
7	2.8520	15.8689	17.6702
8	1.0507	17.6702	0.0000

YEARS 9 — MO PAYT 1.4516 — AN CONST 17.42

#	INT	PRIN	BALANCE
1	10.4623	6.9563	93.0437
2	9.6727	7.7459	85.2978
3	8.7935	8.6251	76.6727
4	7.8145	9.6042	67.0686
5	6.7243	10.6943	56.3742
6	5.5104	11.9082	44.4660
7	4.1587	13.2599	31.2061
8	2.6536	14.7651	16.4410
9	.9776	16.4410	0.0000

YEARS 10 — MO PAYT 1.3662 — AN CONST 16.40

#	INT	PRIN	BALANCE
1	10.5146	5.8798	94.1202
2	9.8472	6.5473	87.5729
3	9.1040	7.2904	80.2825
4	8.2765	8.1180	72.1645
5	7.3550	9.0394	63.1250
6	6.3289	10.0655	53.0595
7	5.1864	11.2080	41.8515
8	3.9142	12.4803	29.3712
9	2.4975	13.8969	15.4743
10	.9201	15.4743	0.0000

YEARS 11 — MO PAYT 1.2977 — AN CONST 15.58

#	INT	PRIN	BALANCE
1	10.5565	5.0156	94.9844
2	9.9872	5.5849	89.3995
3	9.3533	6.2189	83.1806
4	8.6474	6.9248	76.2558
5	7.8613	7.7108	68.5450
6	6.9861	8.5861	59.9589
7	6.0115	9.5607	50.3983
8	4.9263	10.6459	39.7524
9	3.7179	11.8543	27.8981
10	2.3723	13.1999	14.6982
11	.8740	14.6982	0.0000

YEARS 12 — MO PAYT 1.2417 — AN CONST 14.91

#	INT	PRIN	BALANCE
1	10.5908	4.3102	95.6898
2	10.1015	4.7994	90.8904
3	9.5568	5.3442	85.5462
4	8.9501	5.9508	79.5953
5	8.2747	6.6263	72.9690
6	7.5225	7.3785	65.5906
7	6.6850	8.2160	57.3746
8	5.7524	9.1486	48.2260
9	4.7139	10.1870	38.0390
10	3.5576	11.3434	26.6956
11	2.2700	12.6309	14.0647
12	.8363	14.0647	0.0000

YEARS 13 — MO PAYT 1.1955 — AN CONST 14.35

#	INT	PRIN	BALANCE
1	10.6191	3.7266	96.2734
2	10.1961	4.1496	92.1239
3	9.7251	4.6206	87.5033
4	9.2006	5.1451	82.3582
5	8.6166	5.7291	76.6292
6	7.9663	6.3794	70.2498
7	7.2422	7.1035	63.1463
8	6.4359	7.9098	55.2365
9	5.5380	8.8077	46.4288
10	4.5383	9.8074	36.6214
11	3.4250	10.9206	25.7008
12	2.1854	12.1602	13.5405
13	.8051	13.5405	0.0000

YEARS 14 — MO PAYT 1.1568 — AN CONST 13.89

#	INT	PRIN	BALANCE
1	10.6428	3.2383	96.7617
2	10.2752	3.6059	93.1558
3	9.8659	4.0152	89.1406
4	9.4102	4.4709	84.6697
5	8.9027	4.9784	79.6912
6	8.3376	5.5435	74.1477
7	7.7083	6.1728	67.9749
8	7.0077	6.8735	61.1014
9	6.2275	7.6537	53.4478
10	5.3587	8.5224	44.9253
11	4.3913	9.4898	35.4355
12	3.3141	10.5670	24.8685
13	2.1147	11.7665	13.1021
14	.7791	13.1021	0.0000

YEARS 15 — MO PAYT 1.1241 — AN CONST 13.49

#	INT	PRIN	BALANCE
1	10.6628	2.8260	97.1740
2	10.3420	3.1468	94.0272
3	9.9849	3.5040	90.5232
4	9.5871	3.9017	86.6215
5	9.1442	4.3446	82.2769
6	8.6511	4.8378	77.4392
7	8.1020	5.3869	72.0523
8	7.4905	5.9983	66.0539
9	6.8096	6.6792	59.3747
10	6.0515	7.4374	51.9373
11	5.2072	8.2816	43.6557
12	4.2672	9.2216	34.4341
13	3.2205	10.2684	24.1657
14	2.0549	11.4339	12.7318
15	.7570	12.7318	0.0000

YEARS 16 — MO PAYT 1.0962 — AN CONST 13.16

#	INT	PRIN	BALANCE
1	10.6799	2.4751	97.5249
2	10.3989	2.7561	94.7688
3	10.0861	3.0689	91.6999
4	9.7377	3.4173	88.2827
5	9.3498	3.8051	84.4775
6	8.9179	4.2371	80.2405
7	8.4370	4.7180	75.5224
8	7.9014	5.2536	70.2689
9	7.3051	5.8499	64.4190
10	6.6411	6.5139	57.9051
11	5.9017	7.2533	50.6518
12	5.0784	8.0766	42.5752
13	4.1616	8.9934	33.5818
14	3.1408	10.0142	23.5676
15	2.0040	11.1509	12.4167
16	.7383	12.4167	0.0000

YEARS 17 — MO PAYT 1.0724 — AN CONST 12.87

#	INT	PRIN	BALANCE
1	10.6945	2.1745	97.8255
2	10.4476	2.4213	95.4042
3	10.1728	2.6961	92.7081
4	9.8668	3.0022	89.7059
5	9.5260	3.3429	86.3630
6	9.1465	3.7224	82.6406
7	8.7240	4.1449	78.4957
8	8.2535	4.6154	73.8802
9	7.7296	5.1393	68.7409
10	7.1462	5.7227	63.0182
11	6.4967	6.3723	56.6460
12	5.7734	7.0956	49.5504
13	4.9679	7.9010	41.6494
14	4.0711	8.7978	32.8516
15	3.0725	9.7965	23.0551
16	1.9605	10.9085	12.1467
17	.7223	12.1467	0.0000

YEARS 18 — MO PAYT 1.0519 — AN CONST 12.63

#	INT	PRIN	BALANCE
1	10.7070	1.9154	98.0846
2	10.4896	2.1328	95.9518
3	10.2475	2.3749	93.5769
4	9.9779	2.6445	90.9324
5	9.6778	2.9447	87.9877
6	9.3435	3.2789	84.7088
7	8.9713	3.6511	81.0577
8	8.5569	4.0655	76.9921
9	8.0954	4.5270	72.4651
10	7.5816	5.0409	67.4242
11	7.0094	5.6131	61.8112
12	6.3722	6.2502	55.5610
13	5.6628	6.9597	48.6013
14	4.8728	7.7497	40.8517
15	3.9931	8.6293	32.2224
16	3.0136	9.6088	22.6135
17	1.9229	10.6995	11.9140
18	.7084	11.9140	0.0000

YEARS 19 — MO PAYT 1.0341 — AN CONST 12.41

#	INT	PRIN	BALANCE
1	10.7179	1.6911	98.3089
2	10.5260	1.8830	96.4259
3	10.3122	2.0968	94.3292
4	10.0742	2.3348	91.9944
5	9.8092	2.5998	89.3946
6	9.5141	2.8949	86.4998
7	9.1855	3.2235	83.2763
8	8.8196	3.5894	79.6869
9	8.4122	3.9968	75.6902
10	7.9585	4.4505	71.2397
11	7.4533	4.9556	66.2841
12	6.8908	5.5181	60.7659
13	6.2645	6.1445	54.6214
14	5.5670	6.8420	47.7794
15	4.7904	7.6186	40.1608
16	3.9256	8.4834	31.6775
17	2.9626	9.4463	22.2311
18	1.8904	10.5186	11.7125
19	.6964	11.7125	0.0000

YEARS 20 — MO PAYT 1.0186 — AN CONST 12.23

#	INT	PRIN	BALANCE
1	10.7274	1.4960	98.5040
2	10.5576	1.6658	96.8383
3	10.3685	1.8548	94.9834
4	10.1580	2.0654	92.9180
5	9.9235	2.2998	90.6182
6	9.6625	2.5609	88.0573
7	9.3718	2.8516	85.2058
8	9.0481	3.1752	82.0305
9	8.6877	3.5357	78.4949
10	8.2863	3.9370	74.5579
11	7.8395	4.3839	70.1740
12	7.3418	4.8815	65.2925
13	6.7877	5.4356	59.8569
14	6.1708	6.0526	53.8043
15	5.4837	6.7396	47.0647
16	4.7187	7.5046	39.5600
17	3.8669	8.3565	31.2036
18	2.9183	9.3050	21.8986
19	1.8621	10.3612	11.5373
20	.6860	11.5373	0.0000

YEARS 21 — MO PAYT 1.0051 — AN CONST 12.07

#	INT	PRIN	BALANCE
1	10.7357	1.3257	98.6743
2	10.5852	1.4761	97.1982
3	10.4176	1.6437	95.5545

#	INT	PRIN	BALANCE
4	10.2311	1.8303	93.7243
5	10.0233	2.0380	91.6863
6	9.7920	2.2693	89.4169
7	9.5344	2.5269	86.8900
8	9.2475	2.8138	84.0762
9	8.9282	3.1332	80.9431
10	8.5725	3.4888	77.4543
11	8.1765	3.8848	73.5695
12	7.7355	4.3258	69.2437
13	7.2445	4.8168	64.4269
14	6.6978	5.3635	59.0634
15	6.0890	5.9724	53.0910
16	5.4110	6.6503	46.4408
17	4.6562	7.4051	39.0356
18	3.8156	8.2457	30.7899
19	2.8796	9.1817	21.6083
20	1.8374	10.2239	11.3844
21	.6769	11.3844	0.0000

YEARS 22	MO PAYT .9933	AN CONST 11.92	
#	INT	PRIN	BALANCE
1	10.7429	1.1765	98.8235
2	10.6093	1.3101	97.5134
3	10.4606	1.4588	96.0547
4	10.2951	1.6243	94.4303
5	10.1107	1.8087	92.6216
6	9.9054	2.0140	90.6076
7	9.6768	2.2426	88.3649
8	9.4222	2.4972	85.8677
9	9.1387	2.7807	83.0871
10	8.8231	3.0963	79.9908
11	8.4717	3.4477	76.5430
12	8.0803	3.8391	72.7039
13	7.6445	4.2749	68.4291
14	7.1593	4.7601	63.6689
15	6.6190	5.3004	58.3685
16	6.0173	5.9021	52.4664
17	5.3474	6.5720	45.8944
18	4.6014	7.3180	38.5764
19	3.7707	8.1487	30.4277
20	2.8458	9.0736	21.3540
21	1.8158	10.1036	11.2504
22	.6690	11.2504	0.0000

YEARS 23	MO PAYT .9829	AN CONST 11.80	
#	INT	PRIN	BALANCE
1	10.7493	1.0455	98.9545
2	10.6306	1.1642	97.7903
3	10.4984	1.2964	96.4939
4	10.3513	1.4435	95.0504
5	10.1874	1.6074	93.4430
6	10.0050	1.7898	91.6532
7	9.8018	1.9930	89.6602
8	9.5756	2.2192	87.4411
9	9.3237	2.4711	84.9700
10	9.0432	2.7516	82.2184
11	8.7309	3.0639	79.1545
12	8.3831	3.4117	75.7428
13	7.9958	3.7990	71.9438
14	7.5646	4.2302	67.7136
15	7.0844	4.7103	63.0033
16	6.5498	5.2450	57.7582
17	5.9544	5.8404	51.9179
18	5.2915	6.5033	45.4145
19	4.5533	7.2415	38.1730
20	3.7313	8.0635	30.1095
21	2.8160	8.9788	21.1308
22	1.7968	9.9980	11.1328
23	.6620	11.1328	0.0000

YEARS 24	MO PAYT .9738	AN CONST 11.69	
#	INT	PRIN	BALANCE
1	10.7548	.9302	99.0698
2	10.6493	1.0358	98.0340
3	10.5317	1.1534	96.8806
4	10.4008	1.2843	95.5963
5	10.2550	1.4301	94.1662
6	10.0927	1.5924	92.5738
7	9.9119	1.7732	90.8006
8	9.7106	1.9744	88.8262
9	9.4865	2.1986	86.6277
10	9.2370	2.4481	84.1796
11	8.9591	2.7260	81.4536
12	8.6496	3.0354	78.4182
13	8.3051	3.3800	75.0382
14	7.9214	3.7636	71.2746
15	7.4942	4.1908	67.0837
16	7.0185	4.6665	62.4172
17	6.4888	5.1962	57.2210
18	5.8990	5.7861	51.4349
19	5.2422	6.4428	44.9921
20	4.5109	7.1741	37.8179
21	3.6966	7.9885	29.8295
22	2.7898	8.8953	20.9342
23	1.7801	9.9049	11.0293
24	.6558	11.0293	0.0000

YEARS 25	MO PAYT .9657	AN CONST 11.59	
#	INT	PRIN	BALANCE
1	10.7598	.8285	99.1715
2	10.6657	.9225	98.2490
3	10.5610	1.0272	97.2218
4	10.4444	1.1438	96.0780
5	10.3146	1.2737	94.8043
6	10.1700	1.4182	93.3861
7	10.0090	1.5792	91.8069
8	9.8298	1.7585	90.0484
9	9.6302	1.9581	88.0903
10	9.4079	2.1803	85.9100
11	9.1604	2.4278	83.4822
12	8.8849	2.7034	80.7787
13	8.5780	3.0103	77.7685
14	8.2363	3.3520	74.4165
15	7.8558	3.7324	70.6841
16	7.4321	4.1561	66.5280
17	6.9604	4.6279	61.9001
18	6.4351	5.1532	56.7469
19	5.8501	5.7381	51.0088
20	5.1988	6.3894	44.6193
21	4.4735	7.1147	37.5046
22	3.6660	7.9223	29.5823
23	2.7667	8.8216	20.7608
24	1.7654	9.8229	10.9379
25	.6504	10.9379	0.0000

YEARS 26	MO PAYT .9586	AN CONST 11.51	
#	INT	PRIN	BALANCE
1	10.7642	.7385	99.2615
2	10.6803	.8224	98.4391
3	10.5870	.9157	97.5234
4	10.4830	1.0196	96.5038
5	10.3673	1.1354	95.3684
6	10.2384	1.2643	94.1042
7	10.0949	1.4078	92.6964
8	9.9351	1.5676	91.1288
9	9.7572	1.7455	89.3834
10	9.5591	1.9436	87.4397
11	9.3384	2.1642	85.2755
12	9.0928	2.4099	82.8656
13	8.8192	2.6834	80.1822
14	8.5146	2.9880	77.1941
15	8.1755	3.3272	73.8669

#	INT	PRIN	BALANCE
16	7.7978	3.7049	70.1621
17	7.3773	4.1254	66.0366
18	6.9090	4.5937	61.4429
19	6.3876	5.1151	56.3278
20	5.8069	5.6957	50.6321
21	5.1604	6.3423	44.2898
22	4.4405	7.0622	37.2277
23	3.6389	7.8638	29.3639
24	2.7463	8.7564	20.6075
25	1.7523	9.7503	10.8571
26	.6456	10.8571	0.0000

YEARS 27	MO PAYT .9522	AN CONST 11.43	
#	INT	PRIN	BALANCE
1	10.7680	.6589	99.3411
2	10.6932	.7337	98.6075
3	10.6100	.8169	97.7905
4	10.5172	.9097	96.8809
5	10.4140	1.0129	95.8680
6	10.2990	1.1279	94.7401
7	10.1710	1.2559	93.4841
8	10.0284	1.3985	92.0857
9	9.8697	1.5572	90.5284
10	9.6929	1.7340	88.7944
11	9.4961	1.9308	86.8636
12	9.2769	2.1500	84.7137
13	9.0329	2.3940	82.3196
14	8.7611	2.6658	79.6539
15	8.4585	2.9684	76.6855
16	8.1216	3.3053	73.3802
17	7.7464	3.6805	69.6998
18	7.3287	4.0982	65.6015
19	6.8635	4.5634	61.0381
20	6.3455	5.0814	55.9567
21	5.7687	5.6582	50.2985
22	5.1264	6.3005	43.9980
23	4.4113	7.0156	36.9824
24	3.6149	7.8120	29.1704
25	2.7282	8.6987	20.4717
26	1.7408	9.6861	10.7856
27	.6413	10.7856	0.0000

YEARS 28	MO PAYT .9466	AN CONST 11.36	
#	INT	PRIN	BALANCE
1	10.7714	.5882	99.4118
2	10.7047	.6550	98.7568
3	10.6303	.7293	98.0274
4	10.5475	.8121	97.2153
5	10.4554	.9043	96.3110
6	10.3527	1.0070	95.3040
7	10.2384	1.1213	94.1828
8	10.1111	1.2485	92.9342
9	9.9694	1.3903	91.5440
10	9.8116	1.5481	89.9959
11	9.6359	1.7238	88.2721
12	9.4402	1.9195	86.3527
13	9.2223	2.1373	84.2154
14	8.9797	2.3799	81.8354
15	8.7096	2.6501	79.1853
16	8.4088	2.9509	76.2344
17	8.0738	3.2858	72.9486
18	7.7009	3.6588	69.2898
19	7.2855	4.0741	65.2157
20	6.8231	4.5366	60.6791
21	6.3081	5.0515	55.6275
22	5.7347	5.6249	50.0026
23	5.0963	6.2634	43.7392
24	4.3853	6.9744	36.7648
25	3.5936	7.7660	28.9988
26	2.7121	8.6475	20.3513
27	1.7305	9.6291	10.7221

#	INT	PRIN	BALANCE
28	.6375	10.7221	0.0000

YEARS 29	MO PAYT .9417	AN CONST 11.30	
#	INT	PRIN	BALANCE
1	10.7745	.5255	99.4745
2	10.7148	.5851	98.8894
3	10.6484	.6516	98.2378
4	10.5745	.7255	97.5123
5	10.4921	.8079	96.7045
6	10.4004	.8996	95.8049
7	10.2983	1.0017	94.8032
8	10.1846	1.1154	93.6879
9	10.0580	1.2420	92.4459
10	9.9170	1.3830	91.0629
11	9.7600	1.5399	89.5230
12	9.5853	1.7147	87.8083
13	9.3906	1.9094	85.8989
14	9.1739	2.1261	83.7728
15	8.9326	2.3674	81.4054
16	8.6638	2.6362	78.7692
17	8.3646	2.9354	75.8338
18	8.0314	3.2686	72.5653
19	7.6604	3.6396	68.9257
20	7.2473	4.0527	64.8730
21	6.7872	4.5127	60.3602
22	6.2750	5.0250	55.3352
23	5.7046	5.5954	49.7399
24	5.0695	6.2305	43.5094
25	4.3623	6.9377	36.5716
26	3.5748	7.7252	28.8464
27	2.6979	8.6021	20.2443
28	1.7215	9.5785	10.6658
29	.6342	10.6658	0.0000

YEARS 30	MO PAYT .9372	AN CONST 11.25	
#	INT	PRIN	BALANCE
1	10.7772	.4697	99.5303
2	10.7239	.5230	99.0073
3	10.6645	.5824	98.4249
4	10.5984	.6485	97.7764
5	10.5248	.7221	97.0543
6	10.4428	.8041	96.2502
7	10.3516	.8953	95.3549
8	10.2499	.9970	94.3579
9	10.1368	1.1101	93.2478
10	10.0108	1.2361	92.0117
11	9.8704	1.3765	90.6352
12	9.7142	1.5327	89.1025
13	9.5402	1.7067	87.3958
14	9.3465	1.9004	85.4954
15	9.1308	2.1161	83.3793
16	8.8906	2.3563	81.0230
17	8.6231	2.6238	78.3993
18	8.3253	2.9216	75.4777
19	7.9937	3.2532	72.2244
20	7.6244	3.6225	68.6019
21	7.2132	4.0337	64.5682
22	6.7554	4.4915	60.0767
23	6.2455	5.0014	55.0753
24	5.6778	5.5691	49.5062
25	5.0457	6.2012	43.3050
26	4.3418	6.9051	36.3999
27	3.5580	7.6889	28.7109
28	2.6852	8.5617	20.1492
29	1.7134	9.5335	10.6157
30	.6312	10.6157	0.0000

MONTHLY PAYMENT AMORTIZATION SCHEDULE PER $100   10.875%

YEARS 2 — MO PAYT 4.6550 — AN CONST 55.86

#	INT	PRIN	BALANCE
1	8.5637	47.2961	52.7039
2	3.1559	52.7039	0.0000

YEARS 3 — MO PAYT 3.2680 — AN CONST 39.22

#	INT	PRIN	BALANCE
1	9.4188	29.7966	70.2034
2	6.0120	33.2035	36.9999
3	2.2156	36.9999	0.0000

YEARS 4 — MO PAYT 2.5785 — AN CONST 30.95

#	INT	PRIN	BALANCE
1	9.8440	21.0979	78.9021
2	7.4317	23.5102	55.3920
3	4.7436	26.1983	29.1937
4	1.7481	29.1937	0.0000

YEARS 5 — MO PAYT 2.1680 — AN CONST 26.02

#	INT	PRIN	BALANCE
1	10.0970	15.9191	84.0809
2	8.2769	17.7393	66.3416
3	6.2486	19.7675	46.5740
4	3.9884	22.0277	24.5463
5	1.4698	24.5463	0.0000

YEARS 6 — MO PAYT 1.8970 — AN CONST 22.77

#	INT	PRIN	BALANCE
1	10.2641	12.5000	87.5000
2	8.8349	13.9292	73.5708
3	7.2423	15.5219	58.0489
4	5.4675	17.2966	40.7523
5	3.4899	19.2743	21.4780
6	1.2861	21.4780	0.0000

YEARS 7 — MO PAYT 1.7057 — AN CONST 20.47

#	INT	PRIN	BALANCE
1	10.3821	10.0860	89.9140
2	9.2289	11.2393	78.6747
3	7.9438	12.5243	66.1504
4	6.5118	13.9563	52.1941
5	4.9161	15.5521	36.6420
6	3.1379	17.3302	19.3117
7	1.1564	19.3117	0.0000

YEARS 8 — MO PAYT 1.5641 — AN CONST 18.77

#	INT	PRIN	BALANCE
1	10.4694	8.2999	91.7001
2	9.5204	9.2489	82.4512
3	8.4629	10.3064	72.1448
4	7.2845	11.4848	60.6600
5	5.9713	12.7980	47.8620
6	4.5080	14.2613	33.6007
7	2.8775	15.8919	17.7089
8	1.0604	17.7089	0.0000

YEARS 9 — MO PAYT 1.4557 — AN CONST 17.47

#	INT	PRIN	BALANCE
1	10.5362	6.9320	93.0680
2	9.7437	7.7246	85.3435
3	8.8604	8.6078	76.7357
4	7.8762	9.5920	67.1437
5	6.7795	10.6887	56.4550
6	5.5574	11.9108	44.5442
7	4.1956	13.2727	31.2715
8	2.6780	14.7902	16.4813
9	.9869	16.4813	0.0000

YEARS 10 — MO PAYT 1.3704 — AN CONST 16.45

#	INT	PRIN	BALANCE
1	10.5888	5.8564	94.1436
2	9.9192	6.5260	87.6176
3	9.1730	7.2722	80.3454
4	8.3415	8.1037	72.2417
5	7.4150	9.0302	63.2115
6	6.3825	10.0627	53.1488
7	5.2319	11.2133	41.9355
8	3.9498	12.4954	29.4402
9	2.5212	13.9241	15.5161
10	.9291	15.5161	0.0000

YEARS 11 — MO PAYT 1.3020 — AN CONST 15.63

#	INT	PRIN	BALANCE
1	10.6310	4.9931	95.0069
2	10.0601	5.5640	89.4429
3	9.4239	6.2002	83.2427
4	8.7150	6.9091	76.3337
5	7.9250	7.6990	68.6346
6	7.0447	8.5793	60.0553
7	6.0638	9.5603	50.4950
8	4.9707	10.6534	39.8416
9	3.7526	11.8715	27.9702
10	2.3953	13.2288	14.7414
11	.8827	14.7414	0.0000

YEARS 12 — MO PAYT 1.2462 — AN CONST 14.96

#	INT	PRIN	BALANCE
1	10.6654	4.2886	95.7114
2	10.1751	4.7790	90.9324
3	9.6287	5.3254	85.6071
4	9.0198	5.9343	79.6728
5	8.3413	6.6128	73.0600
6	7.5852	7.3689	65.6912
7	6.7426	8.2114	57.4798
8	5.8038	9.1503	48.3295
9	4.7575	10.1965	38.1330
10	3.5917	11.3623	26.7706
11	2.2925	12.6615	14.1092
12	.8449	14.1092	0.0000

YEARS 13 — MO PAYT 1.2000 — AN CONST 14.40

#	INT	PRIN	BALANCE
1	10.6939	3.7059	96.2941
2	10.2702	4.1297	92.1644
3	9.7980	4.6019	87.5625
4	9.2718	5.1280	82.4345
5	8.6855	5.7143	76.7202
6	8.0321	6.3677	70.3525
7	7.3041	7.0958	63.2567
8	6.4927	7.9071	55.3496
9	5.5887	8.8112	46.5384
10	4.5812	9.8186	36.7198
11	3.4586	10.9413	25.7785
12	2.2076	12.1923	13.5863
13	.8136	13.5863	0.0000

YEARS 14 — MO PAYT 1.1614 — AN CONST 13.94

#	INT	PRIN	BALANCE
1	10.7177	3.2187	96.7813
2	10.3497	3.5867	93.1947
3	9.9396	3.9968	89.1979
4	9.4826	4.4537	84.7442
5	8.9734	4.9630	79.7812
6	8.4059	5.5304	74.2508
7	7.7736	6.1628	68.0881
8	7.0690	6.8674	61.2207
9	6.2838	7.6526	53.5681
10	5.4088	8.5276	45.0405
11	4.4338	9.5026	35.5379
12	3.3473	10.5891	24.9488
13	2.1365	11.7998	13.1490
14	.7874	13.1490	0.0000

YEARS 15 — MO PAYT 1.1288 — AN CONST 13.55

#	INT	PRIN	BALANCE
1	10.7378	2.8073	97.1927
2	10.4168	3.1283	94.0644
3	10.0591	3.4860	90.5784
4	9.6606	3.8846	86.6939
5	9.2164	4.3287	82.3652
6	8.7215	4.8236	77.5415
7	8.1700	5.3752	72.1664
8	7.5554	5.9897	66.1766
9	6.8705	6.6746	59.5020
10	6.1074	7.4378	52.0643
11	5.2569	8.2882	43.7761
12	4.3093	9.2358	34.5403
13	3.2533	10.2918	24.2484
14	2.0766	11.4686	12.7799
15	.7653	12.7799	0.0000

YEARS 16 — MO PAYT 1.1010 — AN CONST 13.22

#	INT	PRIN	BALANCE
1	10.7549	2.4574	97.5426
2	10.4739	2.7383	94.8043
3	10.1608	3.0514	91.7529
4	9.8120	3.4003	88.3526
5	9.4232	3.7891	84.5635
6	8.9899	4.2223	80.3411
7	8.5072	4.7051	75.6360
8	7.9692	5.2431	70.3930
9	7.3697	5.8426	64.5504
10	6.7017	6.5106	58.0398
11	5.9573	7.2550	50.7848
12	5.1278	8.0845	42.7003
13	4.2034	9.0089	33.6915
14	3.1733	10.0389	23.6526
15	2.0255	11.1867	12.4658
16	.7465	12.4658	0.0000

YEARS 17 — MO PAYT 1.0773 — AN CONST 12.93

#	INT	PRIN	BALANCE
1	10.7696	2.1576	97.8424
2	10.5229	2.4043	95.4380
3	10.2480	2.6792	92.7588
4	9.9416	2.9856	89.7732
5	9.6002	3.3269	86.4463
6	9.2199	3.7073	82.7389
7	8.7960	4.1312	78.6077
8	8.3236	4.6036	74.0041
9	7.7972	5.1299	68.8741
10	7.2107	5.7165	63.1576
11	6.5571	6.3701	56.7875
12	5.8287	7.0984	49.6891
13	5.0171	7.9101	41.7790
14	4.1127	8.8145	32.9645
15	3.1049	9.8223	23.1422
16	1.9818	10.9454	12.1968
17	.7304	12.1968	0.0000

YEARS 18 — MO PAYT 1.0568 — AN CONST 12.69

#	INT	PRIN	BALANCE
1	10.7822	1.8995	98.1005
2	10.5650	2.1167	95.9839
3	10.3230	2.3587	93.6252
4	10.0533	2.6284	90.9969
5	9.7528	2.9289	88.0680
6	9.4179	3.2638	84.8042
7	9.0447	3.6369	81.1673
8	8.6289	4.0528	77.1145
9	8.1655	4.5161	72.5984
10	7.6491	5.0325	67.5659
11	7.0737	5.6079	61.9580
12	6.4325	6.2491	55.7089
13	5.7180	6.9636	48.7453
14	4.9218	7.7598	40.9854
15	4.0346	8.6471	32.3384
16	3.0459	9.6357	22.7026
17	1.9442	10.7375	11.9652
18	.7165	11.9652	0.0000

YEARS 19 — MO PAYT 1.0391 — AN CONST 12.47

#	INT	PRIN	BALANCE
1	10.7931	1.6760	98.3240
2	10.6015	1.8676	96.4564
3	10.3879	2.0812	94.3752
4	10.1500	2.3191	92.0560
5	9.8848	2.5843	89.4717
6	9.5893	2.8798	86.5920
7	9.2600	3.2091	83.3829
8	8.8931	3.5760	79.8069
9	8.4843	3.9848	75.8221
10	8.0287	4.4405	71.3816
11	7.5209	4.9482	66.4335
12	6.9552	5.5139	60.9196
13	6.3247	6.1444	54.7752
14	5.6222	6.8469	47.9283
15	4.8393	7.6298	40.2985
16	3.9670	8.5021	31.7964
17	2.9949	9.4742	22.3221
18	1.9116	10.5575	11.7646
19	.7045	11.7646	0.0000

YEARS 20 — MO PAYT 1.0237 — AN CONST 12.29

#	INT	PRIN	BALANCE
1	10.8026	1.4818	98.5182
2	10.6332	1.6512	96.8671
3	10.4444	1.8400	95.0271
4	10.2340	2.0503	92.9768
5	9.9996	2.2848	90.6920
6	9.7383	2.5460	88.1460
7	9.4472	2.8371	85.3089
8	9.1228	3.1615	82.1474
9	8.7614	3.5230	78.6244
10	8.3586	3.9258	74.6986
11	7.9097	4.3747	70.3239
12	7.4095	4.8748	65.4491
13	6.8521	5.4322	60.0169
14	6.2310	6.0533	53.9636
15	5.5389	6.7455	47.2181
16	4.7676	7.5167	39.7014
17	3.9082	8.3762	31.3252
18	2.9505	9.3339	21.9914
19	1.8833	10.4011	11.5903
20	.6940	11.5903	0.0000

YEARS 21 — MO PAYT 1.0103 — AN CONST 12.13

#	INT	PRIN	BALANCE
1	10.8109	1.3123	98.6877
2	10.6608	1.4623	97.2254
3	10.4936	1.6295	95.5959

#	INT	PRIN	BALANCE
4	10.3073	1.8158	93.7801
5	10.0997	2.0234	91.7567
6	9.8683	2.2548	89.5019
7	9.6105	2.5126	86.9893
8	9.3233	2.7999	84.1894
9	9.0031	3.1200	81.0694
10	8.6464	3.4767	77.5926
11	8.2489	3.8743	73.7184
12	7.8059	4.3172	69.4011
13	7.3123	4.8109	64.5902
14	6.7622	5.3609	59.2293
15	6.1492	5.9739	53.2554
16	5.4662	6.6569	46.5985
17	4.7051	7.4181	39.1804
18	3.8569	8.2662	30.9142
19	2.9118	9.2114	21.7028
20	1.8586	10.2646	11.4382
21	.6849	11.4382	0.0000

YEARS 22 — MO PAYT .9985 — AN CONST 11.99

#	INT	PRIN	BALANCE
1	10.8181	1.1639	98.8361
2	10.6850	1.2970	97.5391
3	10.5367	1.4453	96.0938
4	10.3715	1.6105	94.4833
5	10.1873	1.7947	92.6886
6	9.9821	1.9999	90.6887
7	9.7535	2.2285	88.4601
8	9.4987	2.4834	85.9768
9	9.2147	2.7673	83.2095
10	8.8983	3.0837	80.1258
11	8.5458	3.4363	76.6895
12	8.1529	3.8292	72.8603
13	7.7150	4.2670	68.5933
14	7.2272	4.7549	63.8385
15	6.6835	5.2985	58.5399
16	6.0777	5.9044	52.6356
17	5.4026	6.5795	46.0561
18	4.6503	7.3317	38.7244
19	3.8120	8.1700	30.5544
20	2.8779	9.1042	21.4502
21	1.8369	10.1451	11.3051
22	.6770	11.3051	0.0000

YEARS 23 — MO PAYT .9882 — AN CONST 11.86

#	INT	PRIN	BALANCE
1	10.8245	1.0337	98.9663
2	10.7063	1.1519	97.8144
3	10.5746	1.2836	96.5308
4	10.4278	1.4303	95.1005
5	10.2643	1.5939	93.5066
6	10.0820	1.7761	91.7305
7	9.8790	1.9792	89.7513
8	9.6527	2.2055	87.5457
9	9.4005	2.4577	85.0881
10	9.1195	2.7387	82.3494
11	8.8064	3.0518	79.2975
12	8.4574	3.4008	75.8968
13	8.0686	3.7896	72.1072
14	7.6353	4.2229	67.8843
15	7.1525	4.7057	63.1786
16	6.6144	5.2438	57.9348
17	6.0148	5.8433	52.0915
18	5.3467	6.5114	45.5800
19	4.6022	7.2559	38.3241
20	3.7726	8.0856	30.2385
21	2.8481	9.0101	21.2285
22	1.8179	10.0402	11.1882
23	.6700	11.1882	0.0000

YEARS 24 — MO PAYT .9791 — AN CONST 11.75

#	INT	PRIN	BALANCE
1	10.8301	.9191	99.0809
2	10.7250	1.0242	98.0567
3	10.6079	1.1413	96.9154
4	10.4774	1.2718	95.6436
5	10.3320	1.4172	94.2264
6	10.1699	1.5792	92.6472
7	9.9894	1.7598	90.8874
8	9.7882	1.9610	88.9263
9	9.5639	2.1852	86.7411
10	9.3141	2.4351	84.3060
11	9.0357	2.7135	81.5925
12	8.7254	3.0238	78.5687
13	8.3797	3.3695	75.1992
14	7.9944	3.7548	71.4444
15	7.5651	4.1841	67.2604
16	7.0867	4.6625	62.5979
17	6.5536	5.1956	57.4023
18	5.9596	5.7896	51.6127
19	5.2976	6.4516	45.1611
20	4.5599	7.1893	37.9719
21	3.7379	8.0113	29.9606
22	2.8219	8.9272	21.0334
23	1.8012	9.9480	11.0854
24	.6638	11.0854	0.0000

YEARS 25 — MO PAYT .9711 — AN CONST 11.66

#	INT	PRIN	BALANCE
1	10.8350	.8181	99.1819
2	10.7415	.9116	98.2704
3	10.6373	1.0158	97.2546
4	10.5211	1.1320	96.1226
5	10.3917	1.2614	94.8612
6	10.2475	1.4056	93.4556
7	10.0868	1.5663	91.8893
8	9.9077	1.7454	90.1439
9	9.7081	1.9450	88.1989
10	9.4857	2.1674	86.0315
11	9.2379	2.4152	83.6163
12	8.9618	2.6913	80.9250
13	8.6540	2.9990	77.9260
14	8.3111	3.3419	74.5840
15	7.9290	3.7241	70.8600
16	7.5032	4.1499	66.7101
17	7.0287	4.6243	62.0858
18	6.5000	5.1531	56.9327
19	5.9108	5.7423	51.1905
20	5.2543	6.3988	44.7917
21	4.5226	7.1304	37.6612
22	3.7074	7.9457	29.7155
23	2.7989	8.8542	20.8613
24	1.7865	9.8666	10.9947
25	.6584	10.9947	0.0000

YEARS 26 — MO PAYT .9640 — AN CONST 11.57

#	INT	PRIN	BALANCE
1	10.8394	.7288	99.2712
2	10.7561	.8121	98.4591
3	10.6632	.9049	97.5542
4	10.5597	1.0084	96.5458
5	10.4444	1.1237	95.4221
6	10.3160	1.2522	94.1699
7	10.1728	1.3954	92.7745
8	10.0132	1.5549	91.2196
9	9.8355	1.7327	89.4869
10	9.6373	1.9308	87.5561
11	9.4166	2.1516	85.4046
12	9.1706	2.3976	83.0070
13	8.8964	2.6717	80.3353
14	8.5910	2.9772	77.3581
15	8.2506	3.3176	74.0405
16	7.8712	3.6969	70.3436
17	7.4485	4.1196	66.2240
18	6.9775	4.5906	61.6334
19	6.4526	5.1155	56.5178
20	5.8677	5.7004	50.8174
21	5.2160	6.3522	44.4652
22	4.4897	7.0785	37.3868
23	3.6803	7.8878	29.4989
24	2.7785	8.7897	20.7093
25	1.7735	9.7947	10.9146
26	.6536	10.9146	0.0000

YEARS 27 — MO PAYT .9577 — AN CONST 11.50

#	INT	PRIN	BALANCE
1	10.8432	.6497	99.3503
2	10.7690	.7240	98.6262
3	10.6862	.8068	97.8194
4	10.5939	.8991	96.9204
5	10.4911	1.0019	95.9185
6	10.3766	1.1164	94.8021
7	10.2489	1.2441	93.5580
8	10.1067	1.3863	92.1717
9	9.9482	1.5448	90.6269
10	9.7716	1.7214	88.9055
11	9.5747	1.9183	86.9872
12	9.3554	2.1376	84.8496
13	9.1110	2.3820	82.4677
14	8.8386	2.6543	79.8133
15	8.5351	2.9578	76.8555
16	8.1970	3.2960	73.5594
17	7.8201	3.6729	69.8865
18	7.4001	4.0928	65.7937
19	6.9322	4.5608	61.2329
20	6.4107	5.0823	56.1506
21	5.8296	5.6634	50.4872
22	5.1821	6.3109	44.1763
23	4.4605	7.0325	37.1438
24	3.6564	7.8366	29.3073
25	2.7604	8.7326	20.5747
26	1.7619	9.7310	10.8437
27	.6493	10.8437	0.0000

YEARS 28 — MO PAYT .9522 — AN CONST 11.43

#	INT	PRIN	BALANCE
1	10.8467	.5797	99.4203
2	10.7804	.6460	98.7743
3	10.7065	.7198	98.0545
4	10.6242	.8021	97.2524
5	10.5325	.8939	96.3585
6	10.4303	.9961	95.3625
7	10.3164	1.1099	94.2525
8	10.1895	1.2368	93.0157
9	10.0481	1.3783	91.6374
10	9.8905	1.5358	90.1016
11	9.7149	1.7115	88.3901
12	9.5192	1.9071	86.4830
13	9.3012	2.1252	84.3578
14	9.0582	2.3682	81.9896
15	8.7874	2.6390	79.3506
16	8.4857	2.9407	76.4099
17	8.1494	3.2769	73.1330
18	7.7748	3.6516	69.4814
19	7.3572	4.0691	65.4123
20	6.8920	4.5344	60.8779
21	6.3735	5.0528	55.8251
22	5.7958	5.6305	50.1946
23	5.1520	6.2743	43.9202
24	4.4346	6.9917	36.9285
25	3.6352	7.7911	29.1374
26	2.7444	8.6820	20.4554
27	1.7517	9.6746	10.7808
28	.6456	10.7808	0.0000

YEARS 29 — MO PAYT .9473 — AN CONST 11.37

#	INT	PRIN	BALANCE
1	10.8497	.5175	99.4825
2	10.7905	.5767	98.9058
3	10.7246	.6426	98.2632
4	10.6511	.7161	97.5471
5	10.5692	.7980	96.7491
6	10.4780	.8892	95.8598
7	10.3763	.9909	94.8689
8	10.2630	1.1042	93.7648
9	10.1368	1.2304	92.5343
10	9.9961	1.3711	91.1632
11	9.8393	1.5279	89.6353
12	9.6646	1.7026	87.9327
13	9.4700	1.8973	86.0354
14	9.2530	2.1142	83.9212
15	9.0113	2.3559	81.5653
16	8.7419	2.6253	78.9400
17	8.4418	2.9255	76.0145
18	8.1073	3.2600	72.7545
19	7.7345	3.6327	69.1218
20	7.3192	4.0481	65.0738
21	6.8563	4.5109	60.5629
22	6.3406	5.0267	55.5362
23	5.7658	5.6014	49.9348
24	5.1254	6.2419	43.6929
25	4.4117	6.9555	36.7374
26	3.6164	7.7508	28.9866
27	2.7302	8.6370	20.3496
28	1.7427	9.6246	10.7250
29	.6422	10.7250	0.0000

YEARS 30 — MO PAYT .9429 — AN CONST 11.32

#	INT	PRIN	BALANCE
1	10.8524	.4623	99.5377
2	10.7996	.5151	99.0226
3	10.7407	.5740	98.4486
4	10.6750	.6397	97.8089
5	10.6019	.7128	97.0961
6	10.5204	.7943	96.3018
7	10.4296	.8851	95.4167
8	10.3284	.9863	94.4304
9	10.2156	1.0991	93.3313
10	10.0899	1.2248	92.1065
11	9.9499	1.3648	90.7418
12	9.7938	1.5208	89.2209
13	9.6200	1.6947	87.5262
14	9.4262	1.8885	85.6377
15	9.2103	2.1044	83.5333
16	8.9696	2.3450	81.1882
17	8.7015	2.6132	78.5751
18	8.4027	2.9119	75.6631
19	8.0698	3.2449	72.4182
20	7.6988	3.6159	68.8023
21	7.2853	4.0293	64.7730
22	6.8246	4.4900	60.2829
23	6.3113	5.0034	55.2795
24	5.7392	5.5755	49.7040
25	5.1017	6.2130	43.4910
26	4.3913	6.9234	36.5676
27	3.5997	7.7150	28.8526
28	2.7176	8.5971	20.2555
29	1.7346	9.5801	10.6754
30	.6392	10.6754	0.0000

YEARS 2 — MO PAYT 4.6561 — AN CONST 55.88

#	INT	PRIN	BALANCE
1	8.5837	47.2900	52.7100
2	3.1637	52.7100	0.0000

YEARS 3 — MO PAYT 3.2691 — AN CONST 39.23

#	INT	PRIN	BALANCE
1	9.4410	29.7887	70.2113
2	6.0268	33.2029	37.0084
3	2.2213	37.0084	0.0000

YEARS 4 — MO PAYT 2.5797 — AN CONST 30.96

#	INT	PRIN	BALANCE
1	9.8670	21.0893	78.9107
2	7.4499	23.5065	55.4042
3	4.7558	26.2006	29.2036
4	1.7528	29.2036	0.0000

YEARS 5 — MO PAYT 2.1693 — AN CONST 26.04

#	INT	PRIN	BALANCE
1	10.1207	15.9104	84.0896
2	8.2972	17.7339	66.3557
3	6.2646	19.7665	46.5892
4	3.9991	22.0320	24.5572
5	1.4739	24.5572	0.0000

YEARS 6 — MO PAYT 1.8983 — AN CONST 22.78

#	INT	PRIN	BALANCE
1	10.2882	12.4913	87.5087
2	8.8565	13.9230	73.5857
3	7.2607	15.5187	58.0670
4	5.4821	17.2974	40.7696
5	3.4996	19.2799	21.4897
6	1.2898	21.4897	0.0000

YEARS 7 — MO PAYT 1.7070 — AN CONST 20.49

#	INT	PRIN	BALANCE
1	10.4064	10.0775	89.9225
2	9.2514	11.2325	78.6900
3	7.9640	12.5199	66.1701
4	6.5290	13.9548	52.2153
5	4.9296	15.5543	36.6610
6	3.1469	17.3370	19.3240
7	1.1598	19.3240	0.0000

YEARS 8 — MO PAYT 1.5655 — AN CONST 18.79

#	INT	PRIN	BALANCE
1	10.4939	8.2916	91.7084
2	9.5436	9.2419	82.4665
3	8.4843	10.3011	72.1654
4	7.3037	11.4818	60.6836
5	5.9877	12.7978	47.8858
6	4.5209	14.2646	33.6213
7	2.8860	15.8995	17.7218
8	1.0637	17.7218	0.0000

YEARS 9 — MO PAYT 1.4571 — AN CONST 17.49

#	INT	PRIN	BALANCE
1	10.5609	6.9239	93.0761
2	9.7673	7.7175	85.3586
3	8.8828	8.6020	76.7566
4	7.8969	9.5879	67.1687
5	6.7980	10.6868	56.4819
6	5.5731	11.9117	44.5703
7	4.2079	13.2769	31.2934
8	2.6861	14.7986	16.4947
9	.9900	16.4947	0.0000

YEARS 10 — MO PAYT 1.3718 — AN CONST 16.47

#	INT	PRIN	BALANCE
1	10.6135	5.8486	94.1514
2	9.9432	6.5189	87.6324
3	9.1960	7.2661	80.3663
4	8.3632	8.0989	72.2674
5	7.4350	9.0271	63.2403
6	6.4004	10.0618	53.1785
7	5.2472	11.2150	41.9635
8	3.9618	12.5004	29.4631
9	2.5290	13.9331	15.5300
10	.9321	15.5300	0.0000

YEARS 11 — MO PAYT 1.3035 — AN CONST 15.65

#	INT	PRIN	BALANCE
1	10.6558	4.9856	95.0144
2	10.0844	5.5570	89.4574
3	9.4475	6.1939	83.2634
4	8.7376	6.9038	76.3596
5	7.9463	7.6951	68.6645
6	7.0643	8.5771	60.0874
7	6.0813	9.5601	50.5273
8	4.9855	10.6559	39.8714
9	3.7642	11.8772	27.9942
10	2.4030	13.2385	14.7558
11	.8856	14.7558	0.0000

YEARS 12 — MO PAYT 1.2476 — AN CONST 14.98

#	INT	PRIN	BALANCE
1	10.6903	4.2814	95.7186
2	10.1996	4.7721	90.9464
3	9.6526	5.3191	85.6273
4	9.0430	5.9287	79.6986
5	8.3635	6.6083	73.0903
6	7.6061	7.3657	65.7247
7	6.7619	8.2099	57.5148
8	5.8209	9.1508	48.3640
9	4.7721	10.1996	38.1643
10	3.6031	11.3687	26.7957
11	2.3001	12.6717	14.1240
12	.8477	14.1240	0.0000

YEARS 13 — MO PAYT 1.2015 — AN CONST 14.42

#	INT	PRIN	BALANCE
1	10.7188	3.6991	96.3009
2	10.2949	4.1231	92.1778
3	9.8223	4.5956	87.5822
4	9.2956	5.1223	82.4599
5	8.7085	5.7094	76.7504
6	8.0541	6.3638	70.3866
7	7.3247	7.0932	63.2934
8	6.5117	7.9062	55.3873
9	5.6056	8.8123	46.5749
10	4.5956	9.8223	36.7526
11	3.4698	10.9481	25.8045
12	2.2150	12.2029	13.6015
13	.8164	13.6015	0.0000

YEARS 14 — MO PAYT 1.1629 — AN CONST 13.96

#	INT	PRIN	BALANCE
1	10.7427	3.2121	96.7879
2	10.3745	3.5803	93.2076
3	9.9642	3.9906	89.2170
4	9.5068	4.4480	84.7690
5	8.9970	4.9578	79.8112
6	8.4288	5.5260	74.2851
7	7.7954	6.1594	68.1257
8	7.0894	6.8654	61.2604
9	6.3026	7.6522	53.6082
10	5.4255	8.5293	45.0789
11	4.4480	9.5068	35.5721
12	3.3583	10.5965	24.9756
13	2.1438	11.8110	13.1646
14	.7901	13.1646	0.0000

YEARS 15 — MO PAYT 1.1303 — AN CONST 13.57

#	INT	PRIN	BALANCE
1	10.7628	2.8011	97.1989
2	10.4418	3.1221	94.0767
3	10.0839	3.4800	90.5968
4	9.6851	3.8788	86.7179
5	9.2405	4.3234	82.3945
6	8.7450	4.8189	77.5756
7	8.1927	5.3713	72.2043
8	7.5770	5.9869	66.2175
9	6.8909	6.6730	59.5444
10	6.1260	7.4379	52.1065
11	5.2736	8.2904	43.8162
12	4.3234	9.2405	34.5756
13	3.2643	10.2996	24.2760
14	2.0838	11.4801	12.7959
15	.7680	12.7959	0.0000

YEARS 16 — MO PAYT 1.1026 — AN CONST 13.24

#	INT	PRIN	BALANCE
1	10.7799	2.4515	97.5485
2	10.4990	2.7324	94.8161
3	10.1858	3.0456	91.7705
4	9.8367	3.3947	88.3758
5	9.4476	3.7838	84.5921
6	9.0140	4.2174	80.3746
7	8.5306	4.7008	75.6738
8	7.9918	5.2396	70.4343
9	7.3913	5.8401	64.5942
10	6.7219	6.5095	58.0847
11	5.9759	7.2555	50.8292
12	5.1443	8.0871	42.7420
13	4.2174	9.0140	33.7280
14	3.1842	10.0471	23.6809
15	2.0327	11.1987	12.4822
16	.7492	12.4822	0.0000

YEARS 17 — MO PAYT 1.0789 — AN CONST 12.95

#	INT	PRIN	BALANCE
1	10.7946	2.1521	97.8479
2	10.5479	2.3987	95.4492
3	10.2730	2.6736	92.7756
4	9.9666	2.9801	89.7955
5	9.6250	3.3216	86.4739
6	9.2443	3.7023	82.7716
7	8.8200	4.1267	78.6449
8	8.3470	4.5996	74.0453
9	7.8198	5.1268	68.9185
10	7.2322	5.7144	63.2041
11	6.5773	6.3694	56.8347
12	5.8473	7.0994	49.7353
13	5.0336	7.9131	41.8222
14	4.1266	8.8200	33.0022
15	3.1157	9.8309	23.1713
16	1.9890	10.9577	12.2136
17	.7331	12.2136	0.0000

YEARS 18 — MO PAYT 1.0585 — AN CONST 12.71

#	INT	PRIN	BALANCE
1	10.8072	1.8942	98.1058
2	10.5901	2.1113	95.9945
3	10.3481	2.3533	93.6413
4	10.0784	2.6230	91.0183
5	9.7778	2.9236	88.0946
6	9.4427	3.2587	84.8359
7	9.0692	3.6322	81.2037
8	8.6529	4.0485	77.1552
9	8.1889	4.5125	72.6427
10	7.6717	5.0297	67.6130
11	7.0952	5.6062	62.0069
12	6.4527	6.2487	55.7581
13	5.7365	6.9649	48.7932
14	4.9382	7.7632	41.0300
15	4.0485	8.6530	32.3771
16	3.0567	9.6447	22.7324
17	1.9513	10.7501	11.9822
18	.7192	11.9822	0.0000

YEARS 19 — MO PAYT 1.0408 — AN CONST 12.49

#	INT	PRIN	BALANCE
1	10.8182	1.6710	98.3290
2	10.6266	1.8625	96.4664
3	10.4132	2.0760	94.3904
4	10.1752	2.3139	92.0765
5	9.9100	2.5792	89.4973
6	9.6144	2.8748	86.6226
7	9.2849	3.2043	83.4183
8	8.9177	3.5715	79.8468
9	8.5083	3.9808	75.8660
10	8.0521	4.4371	71.4289
11	7.5435	4.9457	66.4832
12	6.9767	5.5125	60.9707
13	6.3449	6.1443	54.8264
14	5.6406	6.8485	47.9779
15	4.8557	7.6335	40.3444
16	3.9808	8.5084	31.8360
17	3.0056	9.4835	22.3525
18	1.9187	10.5705	11.7820
19	.7072	11.7820	0.0000

YEARS 20 — MO PAYT 1.0254 — AN CONST 12.31

#	INT	PRIN	BALANCE
1	10.8277	1.4770	98.5230
2	10.6584	1.6463	96.8766
3	10.4697	1.8350	95.0416
4	10.2594	2.0453	92.9963
5	10.0249	2.2798	90.7165
6	9.7636	2.5411	88.1754
7	9.4724	2.8323	85.3431
8	9.1478	3.1569	82.1862
9	8.7859	3.5188	78.6674
10	8.3827	3.9220	74.7454
11	7.9331	4.3716	70.3738
12	7.4321	4.8726	65.5012
13	6.8736	5.4311	60.0701
14	6.2511	6.0536	54.0166
15	5.5573	6.7474	47.2692
16	4.7840	7.5207	39.7485
17	3.9220	8.3827	31.3658
18	2.9612	9.3435	22.0223
19	1.8903	10.4144	11.6080
20	.6967	11.6080	0.0000

YEARS 21 — MO PAYT 1.0120 — AN CONST 12.15

#	INT	PRIN	BALANCE
1	10.8359	1.3078	98.6922
2	10.6860	1.4577	97.2344
3	10.5190	1.6248	95.6096

#	INT	PRIN	BALANCE
4	10.3327	1.8110	93.7986
5	10.1252	2.0186	91.7800
6	9.8938	2.2500	89.5301
7	9.6359	2.5078	87.0222
8	9.3485	2.7953	84.2270
9	9.0281	3.1156	81.1113
10	8.6710	3.4727	77.6386
11	8.2730	3.8708	73.7679
12	7.8294	4.3144	69.4535
13	7.3349	4.8089	64.6446
14	6.7837	5.3600	59.2845
15	6.1694	5.9744	53.3101
16	5.4846	6.6591	46.6510
17	4.7214	7.4224	39.2287
18	3.8707	8.2731	30.9556
19	2.9225	9.2213	21.7343
20	1.8656	10.2782	11.4562
21	.6876	11.4562	0.0000

YEARS 22	MO PAYT 1.0002	AN CONST 12.01	
#	INT	PRIN	BALANCE
1	10.8432	1.1597	98.8403
2	10.7103	1.2927	97.5476
3	10.5621	1.4408	96.1068
4	10.3970	1.6060	94.5008
5	10.2129	1.7900	92.7108
6	10.0078	1.9952	90.7156
7	9.7791	2.2239	88.4918
8	9.5242	2.4787	86.0130
9	9.2401	2.7628	83.2502
10	8.9234	3.0795	80.1707
11	8.5705	3.4325	76.7382
12	8.1771	3.8259	72.9123
13	7.7386	4.2644	68.6480
14	7.2498	4.7531	63.8949
15	6.7051	5.2979	58.5970
16	6.0978	5.9051	52.6919
17	5.4210	6.5819	46.1100
18	4.6667	7.3363	38.7737
19	3.8258	8.1771	30.5966
20	2.8886	9.1143	21.4823
21	1.8440	10.1590	11.3233
22	.6796	11.3233	0.0000

YEARS 23	MO PAYT .9899	AN CONST 11.88	
#	INT	PRIN	BALANCE
1	10.8496	1.0298	98.9702
2	10.7315	1.1478	97.8224
3	10.6000	1.2794	96.5431
4	10.4534	1.4260	95.1171
5	10.2899	1.5894	93.5277
6	10.1077	1.7716	91.7561
7	9.9047	1.9746	89.7814
8	9.6784	2.2010	87.5805
9	9.4261	2.4532	85.1273
10	9.1449	2.7344	82.3929
11	8.8315	3.0478	79.3451
12	8.4822	3.3971	75.9480
13	8.0929	3.7865	72.1615
14	7.6589	4.2204	67.9411
15	7.1752	4.7042	63.2369
16	6.6360	5.2433	57.9936
17	6.0350	5.8443	52.1493
18	5.3652	6.5141	45.6352
19	4.6186	7.2607	38.3744
20	3.7864	8.0929	30.2815
21	2.8589	9.0205	21.2610
22	1.8250	10.0543	11.2067
23	.6726	11.2067	0.0000

YEARS 24	MO PAYT .9809	AN CONST 11.78	
#	INT	PRIN	BALANCE
1	10.8552	.9154	99.0846
2	10.7502	1.0203	98.0642
3	10.6333	1.1373	96.9269
4	10.5029	1.2676	95.6593
5	10.3577	1.4129	94.2464
6	10.1957	1.5749	92.6715
7	10.0152	1.7554	90.9161
8	9.8140	1.9566	88.9596
9	9.5898	2.1808	86.7788
10	9.3398	2.4308	84.3480
11	9.0612	2.7094	81.6386
12	8.7507	3.0199	78.6187
13	8.4046	3.3660	75.2527
14	8.0188	3.7518	71.5009
15	7.5888	4.1818	67.3191
16	7.1095	4.6611	62.6580
17	6.5753	5.1953	57.4627
18	5.9798	5.7908	51.6719
19	5.3161	6.4545	45.2174
20	4.5763	7.1943	38.0231
21	3.7518	8.0188	30.0043
22	2.8327	8.9379	21.0664
23	1.8083	9.9623	11.1041
24	.6665	11.1041	0.0000

YEARS 25	MO PAYT .9729	AN CONST 11.68	
#	INT	PRIN	BALANCE
1	10.8601	.8146	99.1854
2	10.7667	.9080	98.2774
3	10.6627	1.0120	97.2654
4	10.5467	1.1280	96.1374
5	10.4174	1.2573	94.8801
6	10.2733	1.4014	93.4786
7	10.1127	1.5620	91.9166
8	9.9336	1.7411	90.1755
9	9.7341	1.9406	88.2349
10	9.5117	2.1630	86.0719
11	9.2637	2.4110	83.6609
12	8.9874	2.6873	80.9736
13	8.6794	2.9953	77.9783
14	8.3361	3.3386	74.6397
15	7.9535	3.7212	70.9185
16	7.5270	4.1477	66.7707
17	7.0516	4.6231	62.1476
18	6.5217	5.1530	56.9946
19	5.9311	5.7436	51.2510
20	5.2728	6.4019	44.8491
21	4.5390	7.1357	37.7134
22	3.7212	7.9535	29.7599
23	2.8096	8.8651	20.8948
24	1.7936	9.8811	11.0137
25	.6610	11.0137	0.0000

YEARS 26	MO PAYT .9658	AN CONST 11.60	
#	INT	PRIN	BALANCE
1	10.8645	.7255	99.2745
2	10.7813	.8087	98.4658
3	10.6886	.9014	97.5644
4	10.5853	1.0047	96.5597
5	10.4702	1.1198	95.4399
6	10.3418	1.2482	94.1917
7	10.1987	1.3913	92.8004
8	10.0393	1.5507	91.2497
9	9.8616	1.7284	89.5213
10	9.6635	1.9265	87.5947
11	9.4426	2.1474	85.4474
12	9.1965	2.3935	83.0539
13	8.9222	2.6678	80.3861
14	8.6164	2.9736	77.4125
15	8.2756	3.3144	74.0982
16	7.8958	3.6942	70.4039
17	7.4723	4.1177	66.2863
18	7.0004	4.5896	61.6967
19	6.4744	5.1156	56.5811
20	5.8881	5.7019	50.8791
21	5.2345	6.3555	44.5237
22	4.5061	7.0839	37.4398
23	3.6942	7.8958	29.5440
24	2.7892	8.8008	20.7432
25	1.7805	9.8095	10.9338
26	.6562	10.9338	0.0000

YEARS 27	MO PAYT .9596	AN CONST 11.52	
#	INT	PRIN	BALANCE
1	10.8683	.6467	99.3533
2	10.7942	.7208	98.6324
3	10.7116	.8035	97.8290
4	10.6195	.8956	96.9334
5	10.5169	.9982	95.9352
6	10.4024	1.1126	94.8226
7	10.2749	1.2401	93.5825
8	10.1328	1.3823	92.2003
9	9.9744	1.5407	90.6596
10	9.7978	1.7173	88.9423
11	9.6010	1.9141	87.0282
12	9.3816	2.1335	84.8948
13	9.1371	2.3780	82.5168
14	8.8645	2.6505	79.8662
15	8.5607	2.9543	76.9119
16	8.2221	3.2929	73.6190
17	7.8447	3.6704	69.9486
18	7.4240	4.0910	65.8576
19	6.9551	4.5599	61.2977
20	6.4325	5.0825	56.2151
21	5.8500	5.6651	50.5501
22	5.2007	6.3144	44.2357
23	4.4770	7.0381	37.1976
24	3.6703	7.8447	29.3529
25	2.7712	8.7438	20.6091
26	1.7690	9.7460	10.8630
27	.6520	10.8630	0.0000

YEARS 28	MO PAYT .9541	AN CONST 11.45	
#	INT	PRIN	BALANCE
1	10.8717	.5769	99.4231
2	10.8056	.6430	98.7801
3	10.7319	.7167	98.0635
4	10.6498	.7988	97.2646
5	10.5582	.8904	96.3742
6	10.4562	.9924	95.3818
7	10.3424	1.1062	94.2756
8	10.2157	1.2330	93.0427
9	10.0743	1.3743	91.6684
10	9.9168	1.5318	90.1366
11	9.7413	1.7074	88.4292
12	9.5456	1.9030	86.5262
13	9.3275	2.1212	84.4050
14	9.0843	2.3643	82.0408
15	8.8134	2.6352	79.4055
16	8.5113	2.9373	76.4682
17	8.1747	3.2739	73.1943
18	7.7994	3.6492	69.5451
19	7.3812	4.0674	65.4777
20	6.9150	4.5336	60.9441
21	6.3954	5.0532	55.8909
22	5.8162	5.6324	50.2585
23	5.1707	6.2779	43.9805
24	4.4511	6.9975	36.9831
25	3.6491	7.7995	29.1836
26	2.7552	8.6934	20.4902
27	1.7588	9.6898	10.8004
28	.6482	10.8004	0.0000

YEARS 29	MO PAYT .9491	AN CONST 11.39	
#	INT	PRIN	BALANCE
1	10.8748	.5149	99.4851
2	10.8158	.5739	98.9112
3	10.7500	.6397	98.2715
4	10.6767	.7130	97.5585
5	10.5950	.7947	96.7638
6	10.5039	.8858	95.8780
7	10.4023	.9873	94.8907
8	10.2892	1.1005	93.7902
9	10.1631	1.2266	92.5636
10	10.0225	1.3672	91.1964
11	9.8658	1.5239	89.6725
12	9.6911	1.6986	87.9739
13	9.4964	1.8932	86.0807
14	9.2794	2.1102	83.9704
15	9.0376	2.3521	81.6183
16	8.7680	2.6217	78.9967
17	8.4675	2.9222	76.0745
18	8.1326	3.2571	72.8174
19	7.7593	3.6304	69.1870
20	7.3432	4.0465	65.1405
21	6.8794	4.5103	60.6303
22	6.3625	5.0272	55.6031
23	5.7863	5.6034	49.9997
24	5.1441	6.2456	43.7541
25	4.4282	6.9614	36.7926
26	3.6303	7.7593	29.0333
27	2.7410	8.6486	20.3847
28	1.7498	9.6399	10.7448
29	.6449	10.7448	0.0000

YEARS 30	MO PAYT .9448	AN CONST 11.34	
#	INT	PRIN	BALANCE
1	10.8775	.4598	99.5402
2	10.8248	.5125	99.0277
3	10.7660	.5713	98.4564
4	10.7006	.6367	97.8197
5	10.6276	.7097	97.1099
6	10.5462	.7911	96.3189
7	10.4556	.8817	95.4372
8	10.3545	.9828	94.4544
9	10.2419	1.0954	93.3589
10	10.1163	1.2210	92.1380
11	9.9764	1.3609	90.7770
12	9.8204	1.5169	89.2601
13	9.6465	1.6908	87.5694
14	9.4528	1.8845	85.6849
15	9.2368	2.1005	83.5843
16	8.8960	2.3413	81.2430
17	8.7277	2.6096	78.6334
18	8.4286	2.9087	75.7247
19	8.0952	3.2421	72.4826
20	7.7236	3.6137	68.8689
21	7.3094	4.0279	64.8410
22	6.8478	4.4895	60.3515
23	6.3332	5.0041	55.3474
24	5.7597	5.5776	49.7698
25	5.1204	6.2169	43.5529
26	4.4079	6.9294	36.6235
27	3.6137	7.7236	28.8998
28	2.7284	8.6089	20.2909
29	1.7417	9.5956	10.6954
30	.6419	10.6954	0.0000

MONTHLY PAYMENT AMORTIZATION SCHEDULE PER $100   11.00 %

YEARS 2 — MO PAYT 4.6608 — AN CONST 55.93

#	INT	PRIN	BALANCE
1	8.6641	47.2653	52.7347
2	3.1947	52.7347	0.0000

YEARS 3 — MO PAYT 3.2739 — AN CONST 39.29

#	INT	PRIN	BALANCE
1	9.5294	29.7571	70.2429
2	6.0860	33.2005	37.0424
3	2.2440	37.0424	0.0000

YEARS 4 — MO PAYT 2.5846 — AN CONST 31.02

#	INT	PRIN	BALANCE
1	9.9595	21.0552	78.9448
2	7.5230	23.4917	55.4532
3	4.8045	26.2101	29.2431
4	1.7715	29.2431	0.0000

YEARS 5 — MO PAYT 2.1742 — AN CONST 26.10

#	INT	PRIN	BALANCE
1	10.2154	15.8755	84.1245
2	8.3783	17.7126	66.4120
3	6.3287	19.7622	46.6497
4	4.0418	22.0491	24.6006
5	1.4903	24.6006	0.0000

YEARS 6 — MO PAYT 1.9034 — AN CONST 22.85

#	INT	PRIN	BALANCE
1	10.3844	12.4565	87.5435
2	8.9429	13.8979	73.6456
3	7.3347	15.5062	58.1394
4	5.5403	17.3006	40.8388
5	3.5383	19.3026	21.5362
6	1.3047	21.5362	0.0000

YEARS 7 — MO PAYT 1.7122 — AN CONST 20.55

#	INT	PRIN	BALANCE
1	10.5037	10.0433	89.9567
2	9.3415	11.2055	78.7513
3	8.0448	12.5021	66.2491
4	6.5981	13.9489	52.3003
5	4.9839	15.5630	36.7372
6	3.1830	17.3640	19.3733
7	1.1736	19.3733	0.0000

YEARS 8 — MO PAYT 1.5708 — AN CONST 18.86

#	INT	PRIN	BALANCE
1	10.5919	8.2582	91.7418
2	9.6362	9.2139	82.5279
3	8.5700	10.2801	72.2478
4	7.3804	11.4697	60.7781
5	6.0532	12.7969	47.9812
6	4.5723	14.2778	33.7034
7	2.9201	15.9300	17.7734
8	1.0767	17.7734	0.0000

YEARS 9 — MO PAYT 1.4626 — AN CONST 17.56

#	INT	PRIN	BALANCE
1	10.6594	6.8916	93.1084
2	9.8619	7.6891	85.4193
3	8.9722	8.5789	76.8404
4	7.9794	9.5716	67.2688
5	6.8718	10.6792	56.5895
6	5.6360	11.9150	44.6745
7	4.2572	13.2938	31.3807
8	2.7189	14.8322	16.5485
9	1.0025	16.5485	0.0000

YEARS 10 — MO PAYT 1.3775 — AN CONST 16.54

#	INT	PRIN	BALANCE
1	10.7125	5.8175	94.1825
2	10.0393	6.4907	87.6918
3	9.2882	7.2418	80.4500
4	8.4502	8.0798	72.3702
5	7.5152	9.0148	63.3554
6	6.4720	10.0580	53.2974
7	5.3081	11.2219	42.0756
8	4.0096	12.5205	29.5551
9	2.5607	13.9693	15.5858
10	.9442	15.5858	0.0000

YEARS 11 — MO PAYT 1.3092 — AN CONST 15.72

#	INT	PRIN	BALANCE
1	10.7551	4.9557	95.0443
2	10.1816	5.5292	89.5151
3	9.5418	6.1690	83.3460
4	8.8279	6.8829	76.4631
5	8.0314	7.6794	68.7837
6	7.1428	8.5680	60.2157
7	6.1513	9.5595	50.6562
8	5.0451	10.6657	39.9904
9	3.8108	11.9000	28.0904
10	2.4338	13.2770	14.8134
11	.8974	14.8134	0.0000

YEARS 12 — MO PAYT 1.2536 — AN CONST 15.05

#	INT	PRIN	BALANCE
1	10.7898	4.2528	95.7472
2	10.2977	4.7450	91.0022
3	9.7486	5.2941	85.7081
4	9.1360	5.9067	79.8015
5	8.4525	6.5902	73.2113
6	7.6899	7.3528	65.8585
7	6.8390	8.2037	57.6548
8	5.8897	9.1530	48.5018
9	4.8305	10.2121	38.2897
10	3.6488	11.3939	26.8958
11	2.3303	12.7124	14.1834
12	.8592	14.1834	0.0000

YEARS 13 — MO PAYT 1.2075 — AN CONST 14.50

#	INT	PRIN	BALANCE
1	10.8185	3.6718	96.3282
2	10.3936	4.0967	92.2315
3	9.9196	4.5707	87.6608
4	9.3907	5.0997	82.5611
5	8.8005	5.6898	76.8713
6	8.1421	6.3482	70.5231
7	7.4075	7.0828	63.4403
8	6.5879	7.9024	55.5378
9	5.6734	8.8169	46.7209
10	4.6532	9.8372	36.8838
11	3.5148	10.9755	25.9082
12	2.2447	12.2456	13.6626
13	.8277	13.6626	0.0000

YEARS 14 — MO PAYT 1.1691 — AN CONST 14.03

#	INT	PRIN	BALANCE
1	10.8425	3.1861	96.8139
2	10.4738	3.5548	93.2591
3	10.0625	3.9662	89.2929
4	9.6035	4.4251	84.8678
5	9.0915	4.9372	79.9306
6	8.5201	5.5085	74.4221
7	7.8827	6.1460	68.2762
8	7.1715	6.8572	61.4190
9	6.3780	7.6507	53.7684
10	5.4927	8.5360	45.2324
11	4.5049	9.5238	35.7086
12	3.4028	10.6258	25.0828
13	2.1732	11.8554	13.2273
14	.8013	13.2273	0.0000

YEARS 15 — MO PAYT 1.1366 — AN CONST 13.64

#	INT	PRIN	BALANCE
1	10.8628	2.7764	97.2236
2	10.5415	3.0977	94.1260
3	10.1831	3.4561	90.6699
4	9.7831	3.8560	86.8138
5	9.3369	4.3023	82.5116
6	8.8391	4.8001	77.7115
7	8.2836	5.3556	72.3559
8	7.6638	5.9753	66.3806
9	6.9724	6.6668	59.7138
10	6.2009	7.4382	52.2755
11	5.3402	8.2990	43.9766
12	4.3798	9.2593	34.7172
13	3.3083	10.3308	24.3864
14	2.1129	11.5263	12.8601
15	.7791	12.8601	0.0000

YEARS 16 — MO PAYT 1.1090 — AN CONST 13.31

#	INT	PRIN	BALANCE
1	10.8800	2.4280	97.5720
2	10.5990	2.7090	94.8630
3	10.2856	3.0224	91.8406
4	9.9358	3.3722	88.4684
5	9.5456	3.7624	84.7060
6	9.1102	4.1978	80.5082
7	8.6244	4.6836	75.8246
8	8.0825	5.2255	70.5991
9	7.4778	5.8302	64.7688
10	6.8031	6.5049	58.2639
11	6.0504	7.2576	51.0063
12	5.2105	8.0975	42.9088
13	4.2735	9.0345	33.8743
14	3.2280	10.0800	23.7943
15	2.0616	11.2464	12.5479
16	.7601	12.5479	0.0000

YEARS 17 — MO PAYT 1.0854 — AN CONST 13.03

#	INT	PRIN	BALANCE
1	10.8947	2.1298	97.8702
2	10.6483	2.3763	95.4939
3	10.3733	2.6513	92.8426
4	10.0665	2.9581	89.8846
5	9.7242	3.3004	86.5842
6	9.3423	3.6823	82.9019
7	8.9162	4.1084	78.7935
8	8.4408	4.5838	74.2097
9	7.9103	5.1142	69.0954
10	7.3185	5.7061	63.3894
11	6.6582	6.3664	57.0230
12	5.9215	7.1031	49.9199
13	5.0995	7.9250	41.9949
14	4.1825	8.8421	33.1528
15	3.1593	9.8653	23.2875
16	2.0177	11.0069	12.2806
17	.7440	12.2806	0.0000

YEARS 18 — MO PAYT 1.0650 — AN CONST 12.79

#	INT	PRIN	BALANCE
1	10.9074	1.8732	98.1268
2	10.6907	2.0899	96.0369
3	10.4488	2.3318	93.7051
4	10.1790	2.6016	91.1035
5	9.8779	2.9027	88.2009
6	9.5420	3.2385	84.9623
7	9.1673	3.6133	81.3490
8	8.7492	4.0314	77.3176
9	8.2826	4.4980	72.8196
10	7.7621	5.0184	67.8012
11	7.1814	5.5992	62.2020
12	6.5335	6.2471	55.9549
13	5.8106	6.9700	48.9849
14	5.0040	7.7766	41.2083
15	4.1041	8.6765	32.5318
16	3.1001	9.6805	22.8513
17	1.9799	10.8007	12.0506
18	.7300	12.0506	0.0000

YEARS 19 — MO PAYT 1.0475 — AN CONST 12.57

#	INT	PRIN	BALANCE
1	10.9184	1.6512	98.3488
2	10.7273	1.8423	96.5066
3	10.5141	2.0554	94.4512
4	10.2763	2.2933	92.1579
5	10.0109	2.5586	89.5993
6	9.7148	2.8547	86.7445
7	9.3845	3.1851	83.5595
8	9.0159	3.5536	80.0058
9	8.6047	3.9649	76.0409
10	8.1459	4.4237	71.6172
11	7.6340	4.9356	66.6817
12	7.0628	5.5067	61.1749
13	6.4256	6.1440	55.0310
14	5.7146	6.8549	48.1760
15	4.9214	7.6482	40.5279
16	4.0364	8.5332	31.9947
17	3.0489	9.5207	22.4740
18	1.9472	10.6224	11.8516
19	.7180	11.8516	0.0000

YEARS 20 — MO PAYT 1.0322 — AN CONST 12.39

#	INT	PRIN	BALANCE
1	10.9279	1.4583	98.5417
2	10.7592	1.6271	96.9146
3	10.5709	1.8154	95.0992
4	10.3608	2.0254	93.0738
5	10.1264	2.2598	90.8139
6	9.8649	2.5213	88.2926
7	9.5732	2.8131	85.4795
8	9.2476	3.1386	82.3409
9	8.8844	3.5018	78.8391
10	8.4792	3.9071	74.9320
11	8.0271	4.3592	70.5728
12	7.5227	4.8636	65.7092
13	6.9598	5.4264	60.2828
14	6.3319	6.0544	54.2284
15	5.6313	6.7550	47.4735
16	4.8496	7.5366	39.9368
17	3.9775	8.4088	31.5281
18	3.0044	9.3818	22.1462
19	1.9188	10.4675	11.6788
20	.7075	11.6788	0.0000

YEARS 21 — MO PAYT 1.0189 — AN CONST 12.23

#	INT	PRIN	BALANCE
1	10.9362	1.2902	98.7098
2	10.7869	1.4395	97.2703
3	10.6204	1.6061	95.6642

#	INT	PRIN	BALANCE
4	10.4345	1.7920	93.8722
5	10.2271	1.9993	91.8729
6	9.9958	2.2307	89.6422
7	9.7376	2.4888	87.1534
8	9.4496	2.7768	84.3766
9	9.1283	3.0981	81.2785
10	8.7698	3.4566	77.8219
11	8.3698	3.8566	73.9652
12	7.9235	4.3029	69.6623
13	7.4256	4.8009	64.8614
14	6.8700	5.3564	59.5050
15	6.2502	5.9762	53.5288
16	5.5586	6.6678	46.8610
17	4.7871	7.4394	39.4216
18	3.9262	8.3003	31.1213
19	2.9657	9.2608	21.8605
20	1.8940	10.3324	11.5281
21	.6984	11.5281	0.0000

YEARS 22 — MO PAYT 1.0072 — AN CONST 12.09

#	INT	PRIN	BALANCE
1	10.9435	1.1432	98.8568
2	10.8112	1.2755	97.5814
3	10.6636	1.4231	96.1583
4	10.4989	1.5877	94.5706
5	10.3152	1.7715	92.7991
6	10.1102	1.9765	90.8226
7	9.8815	2.2052	88.6175
8	9.6263	2.4604	86.1571
9	9.3416	2.7451	83.4121
10	9.0240	3.0627	80.3493
11	8.6696	3.4171	76.9322
12	8.2741	3.8126	73.1197
13	7.8329	4.2537	68.8659
14	7.3407	4.7460	64.1199
15	6.7915	5.2952	58.8248
16	6.1788	5.9079	52.9168
17	5.4951	6.5916	46.3253
18	4.7323	7.3544	38.9709
19	3.8813	8.2054	30.7655
20	2.9318	9.1549	21.6106
21	1.8724	10.2143	11.3963
22	.6904	11.3963	0.0000

YEARS 23 — MO PAYT .9970 — AN CONST 11.97

#	INT	PRIN	BALANCE
1	10.9499	1.0142	98.9858
2	10.8325	1.1316	97.8542
3	10.7016	1.2625	96.5917
4	10.5555	1.4086	95.1830
5	10.3925	1.5716	93.6114
6	10.2106	1.7535	91.8579
7	10.0077	1.9564	89.9015
8	9.7813	2.1828	87.7187
9	9.5287	2.4354	85.2833
10	9.2469	2.7172	82.5661
11	8.9324	3.0317	79.5344
12	8.5816	3.3825	76.1520
13	8.1902	3.7739	72.3781
14	7.7535	4.2106	68.1675
15	7.2663	4.6978	63.4696
16	6.7226	5.2415	58.2282
17	6.1161	5.8480	52.3802
18	5.4394	6.5247	45.8554
19	4.6843	7.2798	38.5757
20	3.8419	8.1222	30.4535
21	2.9020	9.0621	21.3914
22	1.8534	10.1107	11.2807
23	.6834	11.2807	0.0000

YEARS 24 — MO PAYT .9880 — AN CONST 11.86

#	INT	PRIN	BALANCE
1	10.9555	.9008	99.0992
2	10.8512	1.0051	98.0941
3	10.7349	1.1214	96.9727
4	10.6052	1.2512	95.7215
5	10.4604	1.3959	94.3256
6	10.2988	1.5575	92.7681
7	10.1186	1.7377	91.0304
8	9.9175	1.9388	89.0916
9	9.6932	2.1631	86.9285
10	9.4429	2.4135	84.5150
11	9.1636	2.6927	81.8223
12	8.8520	3.0043	78.8180
13	8.5043	3.3520	75.4660
14	8.1164	3.7399	71.7261
15	7.6837	4.1727	67.5534
16	7.2008	4.6555	62.8979
17	6.6621	5.1943	57.7036
18	6.0610	5.7953	51.9083
19	5.3904	6.4660	45.4423
20	4.6421	7.2142	38.2282
21	3.8073	8.0490	30.1791
22	2.8759	8.9804	21.1987
23	1.8367	10.0196	11.1791
24	.6772	11.1791	0.0000

YEARS 25 — MO PAYT .9801 — AN CONST 11.77

#	INT	PRIN	BALANCE
1	10.9604	.8009	99.1991
2	10.8677	.8936	98.3054
3	10.7643	.9970	97.3084
4	10.6489	1.1124	96.1960
5	10.5202	1.2411	94.9549
6	10.3766	1.3848	93.5701
7	10.2164	1.5450	92.0251
8	10.0376	1.7238	90.3013
9	9.8381	1.9233	88.3781
10	9.6155	2.1458	86.2322
11	9.3672	2.3941	83.8381
12	9.0902	2.6712	81.1669
13	8.7811	2.9803	78.1867
14	8.4362	3.3252	74.8615
15	8.0514	3.7099	71.1516
16	7.6221	4.1392	67.0123
17	7.1431	4.6182	62.3941
18	6.6087	5.1527	57.2414
19	6.0124	5.7489	51.4925
20	5.3472	6.4142	45.0784
21	4.6050	7.1564	37.9220
22	3.7768	7.9845	29.9374
23	2.8529	8.9085	21.0289
24	1.8220	9.9394	11.0896
25	.6718	11.0896	0.0000

YEARS 26 — MO PAYT .9731 — AN CONST 11.68

#	INT	PRIN	BALANCE
1	10.9648	.7128	99.2872
2	10.8823	.7952	98.4920
3	10.7903	.8873	97.6048
4	10.6876	.9899	96.6148
5	10.5730	1.1045	95.5104
6	10.4452	1.2323	94.2781
7	10.3026	1.3749	92.9032
8	10.1435	1.5340	91.3692
9	9.9660	1.7115	89.6577
10	9.7680	1.9096	87.7481
11	9.5470	2.1305	85.6176
12	9.3005	2.3771	83.2406
13	9.0254	2.6521	80.5884
14	8.7185	2.9590	77.6294
15	8.3761	3.3015	74.3279
16	7.9940	3.6835	70.6444
17	7.5678	4.1097	66.5347
18	7.0922	4.5853	61.9494
19	6.5616	5.1159	56.8335
20	5.9696	5.7079	51.1255
21	5.3091	6.3684	44.7571
22	4.5721	7.1054	37.6517
23	3.7499	7.9276	29.7241
24	2.8325	8.8450	20.8790
25	1.8090	9.8685	11.0105
26	.6670	11.0105	0.0000

YEARS 27 — MO PAYT .9670 — AN CONST 11.61

#	INT	PRIN	BALANCE
1	10.9686	.6348	99.3652
2	10.8952	.7082	98.6570
3	10.8132	.7902	97.8668
4	10.7218	.8816	96.9852
5	10.6198	.9836	96.0016
6	10.5059	1.0975	94.9041
7	10.3789	1.2245	93.6796
8	10.2372	1.3662	92.3135
9	10.0792	1.5242	90.7892
10	9.9028	1.7006	89.0886
11	9.7060	1.8974	87.1911
12	9.4864	2.1170	85.0741
13	9.2414	2.3620	82.7122
14	8.9681	2.6353	80.0769
15	8.6631	2.9403	77.1366
16	8.3229	3.2805	73.8561
17	7.9433	3.6601	70.1960
18	7.5197	4.0837	66.1124
19	7.0472	4.5562	61.5561
20	6.5200	5.0835	56.4727
21	5.9317	5.6717	50.8010
22	5.2754	6.3280	44.4730
23	4.5431	7.0603	37.4127
24	3.7261	7.8773	29.5354
25	2.8145	8.7889	20.7465
26	1.7975	9.8059	10.9406
27	.6628	10.9406	0.0000

YEARS 28 — MO PAYT .9615 — AN CONST 11.54

#	INT	PRIN	BALANCE
1	10.9720	.5657	99.4343
2	10.9066	.6312	98.8031
3	10.8335	.7042	98.0989
4	10.7520	.7857	97.3132
5	10.6611	.8766	96.4365
6	10.5597	.9781	95.4585
7	10.4465	1.0913	94.3672
8	10.3202	1.2175	93.1497
9	10.1793	1.3584	91.7912
10	10.0221	1.5156	90.2756
11	9.8467	1.6910	88.5846
12	9.6511	1.8867	86.6979
13	9.4327	2.1050	84.5929
14	9.1891	2.3486	82.2443
15	8.9174	2.6204	79.6239
16	8.6141	2.9236	76.7002
17	8.2758	3.2619	73.4383
18	7.8984	3.6394	69.7989
19	7.4772	4.0606	65.7383
20	7.0073	4.5304	61.2079
21	6.4831	5.0547	56.1532
22	5.8981	5.6396	50.5136
23	5.2455	6.2922	44.2214
24	4.5174	7.0204	37.2010
25	3.7050	7.8327	29.3683
26	2.7986	8.7391	20.6291
27	1.7873	9.7504	10.8787
28	.6590	10.8787	0.0000

YEARS 29 — MO PAYT .9566 — AN CONST 11.48

#	INT	PRIN	BALANCE
1	10.9751	.5045	99.4955
2	10.9167	.5629	98.9327
3	10.8516	.6280	98.3047
4	10.7789	.7007	97.6040
5	10.6978	.7817	96.8222
6	10.6073	.8722	95.9500
7	10.5064	.9731	94.9769
8	10.3938	1.0858	93.8911
9	10.2682	1.2114	92.6797
10	10.1280	1.3516	91.3282
11	9.9716	1.5080	89.8202
12	9.7971	1.6825	88.1377
13	9.6024	1.8772	86.2605
14	9.3852	2.0944	84.1661
15	9.1428	2.3368	81.8293
16	8.8724	2.6072	79.2222
17	8.5707	2.9089	76.3133
18	8.2341	3.2455	73.0678
19	7.8585	3.6210	69.4468
20	7.4395	4.0401	65.4067
21	6.9720	4.5076	60.8991
22	6.4504	5.0292	55.8699
23	5.8684	5.6112	50.2588
24	5.2191	6.2605	43.9983
25	4.4946	6.9849	37.0134
26	3.6863	7.7932	29.2201
27	2.7845	8.6950	20.5251
28	1.7783	9.7012	10.8238
29	.6557	10.8238	0.0000

YEARS 30 — MO PAYT .9523 — AN CONST 11.43

#	INT	PRIN	BALANCE
1	10.9778	.4501	99.5499
2	10.9257	.5022	99.0477
3	10.8676	.5603	98.4873
4	10.8027	.6252	97.8622
5	10.7304	.6975	97.1646
6	10.6497	.7782	96.3864
7	10.5596	.8683	95.5181
8	10.4591	.9688	94.5494
9	10.3470	1.0809	93.4685
10	10.2219	1.2059	92.2626
11	10.0824	1.3455	90.9171
12	9.9267	1.5012	89.4159
13	9.7530	1.6749	87.7410
14	9.5592	1.8687	85.8722
15	9.3429	2.0850	83.7873
16	9.1016	2.3262	81.4610
17	8.8324	2.5954	78.8656
18	8.5321	2.8958	75.9698
19	8.1970	3.2309	72.7389
20	7.8231	3.6047	69.1342
21	7.4060	4.0219	65.1123
22	6.9406	4.4873	60.6250
23	6.4213	5.0066	55.6185
24	5.8420	5.5859	50.0325
25	5.1956	6.2323	43.8002
26	4.4744	6.9535	36.8467
27	3.6697	7.7581	29.0886
28	2.7720	8.6559	20.4327
29	1.7703	9.6576	10.7751
30	.6528	10.7751	0.0000

YEARS 2 — MO PAYT 4.6654 — AN CONST 55.99

#	INT	PRIN	BALANCE
1	8.7446	47.2406	52.7594
2	3.2257	52.7594	0.0000

YEARS 3 — MO PAYT 3.2786 — AN CONST 39.35

#	INT	PRIN	BALANCE
1	9.6179	29.7254	70.2746
2	6.1452	33.1981	37.0765
3	2.2668	37.0765	0.0000

YEARS 4 — MO PAYT 2.5894 — AN CONST 31.08

#	INT	PRIN	BALANCE
1	10.0519	21.0211	78.9789
2	7.5961	23.4768	55.5021
3	4.8534	26.2195	29.2826
4	1.7903	29.2826	0.0000

YEARS 5 — MO PAYT 2.1792 — AN CONST 26.16

#	INT	PRIN	BALANCE
1	10.3102	15.8406	84.1594
2	8.4596	17.6912	66.4682
3	6.3928	19.7580	46.7102
4	4.0846	22.0662	24.6441
5	1.5067	24.6441	0.0000

YEARS 6 — MO PAYT 1.9085 — AN CONST 22.91

#	INT	PRIN	BALANCE
1	10.4806	12.4218	87.5782
2	9.0295	13.8729	73.7053
3	7.4088	15.4936	58.2117
4	5.5987	17.3037	40.9080
5	3.5772	19.3252	21.5828
6	1.3196	21.5828	0.0000

YEARS 7 — MO PAYT 1.7175 — AN CONST 20.62

#	INT	PRIN	BALANCE
1	10.6009	10.0091	89.9909
2	9.4316	11.1784	78.8124
3	8.1257	12.4844	66.3281
4	6.6672	13.9429	52.3852
5	5.0383	15.5717	36.8135
6	3.2192	17.3909	19.4226
7	1.1875	19.4226	0.0000

YEARS 8 — MO PAYT 1.5762 — AN CONST 18.92

#	INT	PRIN	BALANCE
1	10.6899	8.2250	91.7750
2	9.7290	9.1859	82.5891
3	8.6559	10.2590	72.3301
4	7.4574	11.4575	60.8726
5	6.1188	12.7961	48.0765
6	4.6239	14.2910	33.7856
7	2.9544	15.9605	17.8251
8	1.0898	17.8251	0.0000

YEARS 9 — MO PAYT 1.4681 — AN CONST 17.62

#	INT	PRIN	BALANCE
1	10.7580	6.8595	93.1405
2	9.9566	7.6608	85.4797
3	9.0617	8.5558	76.9240
4	8.0621	9.5553	67.3687
5	6.9458	10.6716	56.6970
6	5.6991	11.9183	44.7787
7	4.3068	13.3107	31.4681
8	2.7517	14.8657	16.6024
9	1.0151	16.6024	0.0000

YEARS 10 — MO PAYT 1.3832 — AN CONST 16.60

#	INT	PRIN	BALANCE
1	10.8115	5.7865	94.2135
2	10.1355	6.4625	87.7510
3	9.3805	7.2175	80.5334
4	8.5373	8.0607	72.4727
5	7.5956	9.0024	63.4704
6	6.5439	10.0541	53.4163
7	5.3693	11.2287	42.1876
8	4.0576	12.5404	29.6472
9	2.5925	14.0055	15.6417
10	.9563	15.6417	0.0000

YEARS 11 — MO PAYT 1.3150 — AN CONST 15.79

#	INT	PRIN	BALANCE
1	10.8544	4.9260	95.0740
2	10.2789	5.5015	89.5725
3	9.6362	6.1442	83.4283
4	8.9184	6.8620	76.5664
5	8.1168	7.6636	68.9027
6	7.2215	8.5589	60.3438
7	6.2216	9.5588	50.7850
8	5.1048	10.6755	40.1094
9	3.8577	11.9227	28.1867
10	2.4648	13.3156	14.8712
11	.9092	14.8712	0.0000

YEARS 12 — MO PAYT 1.2595 — AN CONST 15.12

#	INT	PRIN	BALANCE
1	10.8894	4.2244	95.7756
2	10.3959	4.7179	91.0577
3	9.8447	5.2691	85.7886
4	9.2291	5.8846	79.9040
5	8.5417	6.5721	73.3319
6	7.7739	7.3399	65.9920
7	6.9164	8.1974	57.7947
8	5.9587	9.1550	48.6396
9	4.8892	10.2246	38.4151
10	3.6947	11.4190	26.9960
11	2.3607	12.7531	14.2429
12	.8708	14.2429	0.0000

YEARS 13 — MO PAYT 1.2136 — AN CONST 14.57

#	INT	PRIN	BALANCE
1	10.9183	3.6446	96.3554
2	10.4925	4.0704	92.2849
3	10.0170	4.5460	87.7390
4	9.4859	5.0770	82.6620
5	8.8928	5.6702	76.9918
6	8.2303	6.3326	70.6592
7	7.4905	7.0724	63.5868
8	6.6643	7.8986	55.6882
9	5.7416	8.8214	46.8669
10	4.7110	9.8519	37.0150
11	3.5601	11.0029	26.0121
12	2.2746	12.2883	13.7238
13	.8391	13.7238	0.0000

YEARS 14 — MO PAYT 1.1752 — AN CONST 14.11

#	INT	PRIN	BALANCE
1	10.9424	3.1603	96.8397
2	10.5732	3.5295	93.3103
3	10.1609	3.9418	89.3685
4	9.7004	4.4023	84.9662
5	9.1861	4.9166	80.0496
6	8.6117	5.4910	74.5587
7	7.9702	6.1324	68.4262
8	7.2538	6.8489	61.5773
9	6.4537	7.6490	53.9283
10	5.5601	8.5426	45.3858
11	4.5621	9.5406	35.8452
12	3.4475	10.6551	25.1901
13	2.2028	11.8999	13.2901
14	.8126	13.2901	0.0000

YEARS 15 — MO PAYT 1.1429 — AN CONST 13.72

#	INT	PRIN	BALANCE
1	10.9628	2.7518	97.2482
2	10.6413	3.0733	94.1749
3	10.2823	3.4323	90.7425
4	9.8813	3.8333	86.9092
5	9.4335	4.2811	82.6281
6	8.9333	4.7813	77.8468
7	8.3747	5.3399	72.5069
8	7.7509	5.9637	66.5432
9	7.0542	6.6604	59.8828
10	6.2761	7.4385	52.4443
11	5.4071	8.3075	44.1368
12	4.4366	9.2780	34.8588
13	3.3527	10.3619	24.4969
14	2.1421	11.5725	12.9244
15	.7902	12.9244	0.0000

YEARS 16 — MO PAYT 1.1154 — AN CONST 13.39

#	INT	PRIN	BALANCE
1	10.9801	2.4047	97.5953
2	10.6992	2.6856	94.9096
3	10.3854	2.9994	91.9102
4	10.0350	3.3498	88.5605
5	9.6437	3.7411	84.8193
6	9.2066	4.1782	80.6411
7	8.7185	4.6663	75.9748
8	8.1734	5.2115	70.7634
9	7.5645	5.8203	64.9431
10	6.8846	6.5002	58.4428
11	6.1252	7.2596	51.1832
12	5.2771	8.1077	43.0755
13	4.3299	9.0549	34.0206
14	3.2721	10.1128	23.9078
15	2.0906	11.2942	12.6136
16	.7712	12.6136	0.0000

YEARS 17 — MO PAYT 1.0919 — AN CONST 13.11

#	INT	PRIN	BALANCE
1	10.9949	2.1078	97.8922
2	10.7487	2.3540	95.5382
3	10.4737	2.6290	92.9092
4	10.1665	2.9362	89.9730
5	9.8235	3.2792	86.6938
6	9.4404	3.6623	83.0315
7	9.0126	4.0901	78.9414
8	8.5347	4.5680	74.3734
9	8.0011	5.1016	69.2718
10	7.4051	5.6976	63.5742
11	6.7395	6.3632	57.2110
12	5.9961	7.1066	50.1044
13	5.1659	7.9368	42.1675
14	4.2386	8.8641	33.3035
15	3.2031	9.8996	23.4039
16	2.0466	11.0561	12.3478
17	.7549	12.3478	0.0000

YEARS 18 — MO PAYT 1.0717 — AN CONST 12.86

#	INT	PRIN	BALANCE
1	11.0076	1.8523	98.1477
2	10.7912	2.0687	96.0789
3	10.5496	2.3104	93.7685
4	10.2796	2.5803	91.1882
5	9.9782	2.8818	88.3064
6	9.6415	3.2184	85.0879
7	9.2655	3.5944	81.4935
8	8.8456	4.0144	77.4791
9	8.3766	4.4833	72.9958
10	7.8529	5.0071	67.9887
11	7.2679	5.5921	62.3966
12	6.6146	6.2454	56.1512
13	5.8850	6.9750	49.1763
14	5.0702	7.7898	41.3864
15	4.1601	8.6999	32.6866
16	3.1438	9.7162	22.9704
17	2.0087	10.8513	12.1190
18	.7410	12.1190	0.0000

YEARS 19 — MO PAYT 1.0542 — AN CONST 12.66

#	INT	PRIN	BALANCE
1	11.0187	1.6315	98.3685
2	10.8280	1.8221	96.5464
3	10.6152	2.0350	94.5114
4	10.3774	2.2727	92.2386
5	10.1119	2.5382	89.7004
6	9.8154	2.8348	86.8656
7	9.4842	3.1659	83.6997
8	9.1144	3.5358	80.1639
9	8.7013	3.9489	76.2150
10	8.2400	4.4102	71.8048
11	7.7248	4.9254	66.8794
12	7.1493	5.5008	61.3786
13	6.5067	6.1435	55.2351
14	5.7890	6.8612	48.3739
15	4.9874	7.6627	40.7112
16	4.0922	8.5579	32.1533
17	3.0925	9.5577	22.5956
18	1.9759	10.6743	11.9213
19	.7289	11.9213	0.0000

YEARS 20 — MO PAYT 1.0390 — AN CONST 12.47

#	INT	PRIN	BALANCE
1	11.0282	1.4398	98.5602
2	10.8600	1.6080	96.9522
3	10.6721	1.7959	95.1563
4	10.4623	2.0057	93.1506
5	10.2280	2.2400	90.9106
6	9.9663	2.5017	88.4089
7	9.6741	2.7940	85.6149
8	9.3477	3.1204	82.4946
9	8.9831	3.4849	79.0097
10	8.5760	3.8920	75.1177
11	8.1213	4.3467	70.7710
12	7.6135	4.8545	65.9165
13	7.0464	5.4216	60.4948
14	6.4130	6.0550	54.4398
15	5.7056	6.7624	47.6774
16	4.9156	7.5524	40.1251
17	4.0333	8.4347	31.6903
18	3.0479	9.4201	22.2703
19	1.9474	10.5206	11.7497
20	.7184	11.7497	0.0000

YEARS 21 — MO PAYT 1.0258 — AN CONST 12.31

#	INT	PRIN	BALANCE
1	11.0365	1.2728	98.7272
2	10.8878	1.4215	97.3057
3	10.7218	1.5876	95.7181

#	INT	PRIN	BALANCE
4	10.5363	1.7730	93.9451
5	10.3292	1.9802	91.9650
6	10.0978	2.2115	89.7535
7	9.8395	2.4699	87.2836
8	9.5509	2.7584	84.5252
9	9.2287	3.0806	81.4446
10	8.8688	3.4405	78.0040
11	8.4669	3.8425	74.1616
12	8.0180	4.2914	69.8702
13	7.5166	4.7927	65.0775
14	6.9567	5.3526	59.7249
15	6.3314	5.9779	53.7469
16	5.6330	6.6763	47.0706
17	4.8531	7.4563	39.6143
18	3.9820	8.3274	31.2870
19	3.0091	9.3002	21.9868
20	1.9227	10.3867	11.6001
21	.7092	11.6001	0.0000

YEARS 22 — MO PAYT 1.0142 — AN CONST 12.18

#	INT	PRIN	BALANCE
1	11.0438	1.1268	98.8732
2	10.9122	1.2585	97.6147
3	10.7652	1.4055	96.2092
4	10.6010	1.5697	94.6396
5	10.4176	1.7530	92.8865
6	10.2128	1.9578	90.9287
7	9.9841	2.1866	88.7421
8	9.7286	2.4420	86.3001
9	9.4433	2.7273	83.5728
10	9.1247	3.0459	80.5268
11	8.7689	3.4018	77.1251
12	8.3715	3.7992	73.3259
13	7.9276	4.2430	69.0829
14	7.4319	4.7387	64.3442
15	6.8783	5.2923	59.0519
16	6.2601	5.9106	53.1413
17	5.5696	6.6011	46.5402
18	4.7984	7.3723	39.1680
19	3.9371	8.2335	30.9344
20	2.9752	9.1954	21.7390
21	1.9010	10.2696	11.4694
22	.7012	11.4694	0.0000

YEARS 23 — MO PAYT 1.0041 — AN CONST 12.05

#	INT	PRIN	BALANCE
1	11.0502	.9989	99.0011
2	10.9335	1.1156	97.8856
3	10.8032	1.2459	96.6397
4	10.6576	1.3914	95.2482
5	10.4951	1.5540	93.6942
6	10.3135	1.7355	91.9587
7	10.1108	1.9383	90.0204
8	9.8843	2.1647	87.8557
9	9.6314	2.4176	85.4381
10	9.3490	2.7001	82.7380
11	9.0336	3.0155	79.7225
12	8.6813	3.3678	76.3547
13	8.2878	3.7612	72.5935
14	7.8484	4.2006	68.3928
15	7.3577	4.6914	63.7015
16	6.8096	5.2394	58.4620
17	6.1975	5.8515	52.6105
18	5.5139	6.5351	46.0753
19	4.7505	7.2986	38.7767
20	3.8978	8.1513	30.6254
21	2.9455	9.1035	21.5219
22	1.8820	10.1671	11.3548
23	.6942	11.3548	0.0000

YEARS 24 — MO PAYT .9952 — AN CONST 11.95

#	INT	PRIN	BALANCE
1	11.0558	.8865	99.1135
2	10.9522	.9900	98.1235
3	10.8366	1.1057	97.0179
4	10.7074	1.2348	95.7830
5	10.5632	1.3791	94.4039
6	10.4020	1.5402	92.8637
7	10.2221	1.7202	91.1435
8	10.0211	1.9211	89.2224
9	9.7967	2.1455	87.0769
10	9.5461	2.3962	84.6807
11	9.2661	2.6761	82.0046
12	8.9535	2.9888	79.0158
13	8.6043	3.3379	75.6779
14	8.2144	3.7279	71.9500
15	7.7789	4.1634	67.7866
16	7.2925	4.6498	63.1368
17	6.7493	5.1930	57.9438
18	6.1426	5.7997	52.1441
19	5.4650	6.4772	45.6669
20	4.7083	7.2339	38.4330
21	3.8632	8.0790	30.3540
22	2.9194	9.0228	21.3311
23	1.8653	10.0769	11.2542
24	.6881	11.2542	0.0000

YEARS 25 — MO PAYT .9874 — AN CONST 11.85

#	INT	PRIN	BALANCE
1	11.0607	.7875	99.2125
2	10.9687	.8795	98.3330
3	10.8660	.9822	97.3508
4	10.7512	1.0970	96.2539
5	10.6231	1.2251	95.0287
6	10.4800	1.3682	93.6605
7	10.3201	1.5281	92.1324
8	10.1416	1.7066	90.4258
9	9.9422	1.9060	88.5198
10	9.7196	2.1286	86.3912
11	9.4709	2.3773	84.0138
12	9.1932	2.6551	81.3588
13	8.8830	2.9652	78.3936
14	8.5366	3.3116	75.0819
15	8.1497	3.6985	71.3834
16	7.7176	4.1306	67.2528
17	7.2350	4.6132	62.6396
18	6.6961	5.1521	57.4875
19	6.0942	5.7540	51.7335
20	5.4220	6.4262	45.3073
21	4.6713	7.1769	38.1303
22	3.8328	8.0154	30.1149
23	2.8964	8.9518	21.1631
24	1.8506	9.9976	11.1656
25	.6827	11.1656	0.0000

YEARS 26 — MO PAYT .9804 — AN CONST 11.77

#	INT	PRIN	BALANCE
1	11.0651	.7002	99.2998
2	10.9833	.7820	98.5179
3	10.8919	.8733	97.6446
4	10.7899	.9753	96.6692
5	10.6760	1.0893	95.5799
6	10.5487	1.2165	94.3634
7	10.4066	1.3587	93.0047
8	10.2479	1.5174	91.4873
9	10.0706	1.6947	89.7927
10	9.8726	1.8926	87.9000
11	9.6515	2.1137	85.7863
12	9.4046	2.3607	83.4256
13	9.1288	2.6365	80.7891
14	8.8208	2.9445	77.8447
15	8.4768	3.2885	74.5562
16	8.0926	3.6726	70.8836
17	7.6636	4.1017	66.7819
18	7.1844	4.5809	62.2010
19	6.6492	5.1160	57.0850
20	6.0515	5.7137	51.3713
21	5.3840	6.3812	44.9901
22	4.6386	7.1267	37.8634
23	3.8060	7.9593	29.9041
24	2.8761	8.8891	21.0150
25	1.8377	9.9276	11.0874
26	.6779	11.0874	0.0000

YEARS 27 — MO PAYT .9743 — AN CONST 11.70

#	INT	PRIN	BALANCE
1	11.0689	.6230	99.3770
2	10.9962	.6958	98.6812
3	10.9149	.7771	97.9041
4	10.8241	.8679	97.0362
5	10.7227	.9693	96.0669
6	10.6095	1.0825	94.9844
7	10.4830	1.2090	93.7755
8	10.3418	1.3502	92.4253
9	10.1840	1.5079	90.9173
10	10.0079	1.6841	89.2332
11	9.8111	1.8808	87.3524
12	9.5914	2.1006	85.2518
13	9.3460	2.3460	82.9059
14	9.0719	2.6200	80.2858
15	8.7658	2.9261	77.3597
16	8.4240	3.2680	74.0917
17	8.0422	3.6498	70.4420
18	7.6158	4.0761	66.3658
19	7.1396	4.5523	61.8135
20	6.6078	5.0842	56.7293
21	6.0138	5.6781	51.0512
22	5.3505	6.3415	44.7098
23	4.6097	7.0823	37.6275
24	3.7823	7.9097	29.7178
25	2.8582	8.8337	20.8840
26	1.8262	9.8657	11.0183
27	.6737	11.0183	0.0000

YEARS 28 — MO PAYT .9689 — AN CONST 11.63

#	INT	PRIN	BALANCE
1	11.0723	.5548	99.4452
2	11.0075	.6196	98.8257
3	10.9352	.6919	98.1337
4	10.8543	.7728	97.3610
5	10.7640	.8631	96.4979
6	10.6632	.9639	95.5340
7	10.5506	1.0765	94.4575
8	10.4248	1.2023	93.2553
9	10.2844	1.3427	91.9125
10	10.1275	1.4996	90.4130
11	9.9523	1.6748	88.7382
12	9.7567	1.8704	86.8678
13	9.5382	2.0889	84.7789
14	9.2941	2.3330	82.4459
15	9.0216	2.6055	79.8404
16	8.7172	2.9099	76.9305
17	8.3773	3.2498	73.6807
18	7.9976	3.6295	70.0512
19	7.5736	4.0535	65.9976
20	7.1000	4.5271	61.4706
21	6.5711	5.0560	56.4146
22	5.9805	5.6466	50.7680
23	5.3208	6.3063	44.4617
24	4.5841	7.0430	37.4187
25	3.7613	7.8658	29.5529
26	2.8424	8.7847	20.7682
27	1.8161	9.8110	10.9572
28	.6699	10.9572	0.0000

YEARS 29 — MO PAYT .9641 — AN CONST 11.57

#	INT	PRIN	BALANCE
1	11.0754	.4943	99.5057
2	11.0176	.5520	98.9537
3	10.9531	.6165	98.3372
4	10.8811	.6885	97.6487
5	10.8007	.7690	96.8797
6	10.7108	.8588	96.0209
7	10.6105	.9591	95.0618
8	10.4985	1.0712	93.9906
9	10.3733	1.1963	92.7943
10	10.2336	1.3361	91.4583
11	10.0775	1.4922	89.9661
12	9.9031	1.6665	88.2996
13	9.7085	1.8612	86.4384
14	9.4910	2.0786	84.3599
15	9.2482	2.3214	82.0384
16	8.9770	2.5926	79.4458
17	8.6741	2.8955	76.5503
18	8.3358	3.2338	73.3165
19	7.9581	3.6116	69.7049
20	7.5361	4.0335	65.6714
21	7.0649	4.5047	61.1667
22	6.5387	5.0310	56.1358
23	5.9509	5.6187	50.5171
24	5.2945	6.2751	44.2420
25	4.5614	7.0082	37.2338
26	3.7427	7.8269	29.4068
27	2.8283	8.7413	20.6655
28	1.8071	9.7625	10.9030
29	.6666	10.9030	0.0000

YEARS 30 — MO PAYT .9599 — AN CONST 11.52

#	INT	PRIN	BALANCE
1	11.0780	.4406	99.5594
2	11.0266	.4921	99.0673
3	10.9691	.5496	98.5177
4	10.9049	.6138	97.9039
5	10.8332	.6855	97.2184
6	10.7531	.7656	96.4529
7	10.6636	.8550	95.5979
8	10.5638	.9549	94.6430
9	10.4522	1.0665	93.5765
10	10.3276	1.1910	92.3855
11	10.1885	1.3302	91.0553
12	10.0331	1.4856	89.5697
13	9.8595	1.6591	87.9106
14	9.6657	1.8530	86.0576
15	9.4492	2.0694	83.9881
16	9.2074	2.3112	81.6769
17	8.9374	2.5812	79.0957
18	8.6359	2.8828	76.2130
19	8.2991	3.2195	72.9935
20	7.9230	3.5957	69.3978
21	7.5029	4.0157	65.3821
22	7.0338	4.4849	60.8972
23	6.5099	5.0088	55.8884
24	5.9247	5.5939	50.2945
25	5.2712	6.2475	44.0470
26	4.5413	6.9773	37.0697
27	3.7262	7.7924	29.2773
28	2.8159	8.7028	20.5745
29	1.7991	9.7195	10.8550
30	.6637	10.8550	0.0000

YEARS 2 — MO PAYT 4.6666 — AN CONST 56.00

#	INT	PRIN	BALANCE
1	8.7647	47.2344	52.7656
2	3.2335	52.7656	0.0000

YEARS 3 — MO PAYT 3.2798 — AN CONST 39.36

#	INT	PRIN	BALANCE
1	9.6400	29.7175	70.2825
2	6.1600	33.1975	37.0850
3	2.2726	37.0850	0.0000

YEARS 4 — MO PAYT 2.5906 — AN CONST 31.09

#	INT	PRIN	BALANCE
1	10.0750	21.0125	78.9875
2	7.6144	23.4731	55.5144
3	4.8657	26.2219	29.2925
4	1.7950	29.2925	0.0000

YEARS 5 — MO PAYT 2.1805 — AN CONST 26.17

#	INT	PRIN	BALANCE
1	10.3339	15.8319	84.1681
2	8.4799	17.6858	66.4823
3	6.4089	19.7569	46.7254
4	4.0953	22.0704	24.6549
5	1.5108	24.6549	0.0000

YEARS 6 — MO PAYT 1.9098 — AN CONST 22.92

#	INT	PRIN	BALANCE
1	10.5047	12.4131	87.5869
2	9.0511	13.8667	73.7202
3	7.4273	15.4905	58.2298
4	5.6134	17.3044	40.9253
5	3.5870	19.3308	21.5945
6	1.3233	21.5945	0.0000

YEARS 7 — MO PAYT 1.7188 — AN CONST 20.63

#	INT	PRIN	BALANCE
1	10.6253	10.0006	89.9994
2	9.4542	11.1717	78.8277
3	8.1460	12.4799	66.3478
4	6.6845	13.9413	52.4064
5	5.0520	15.5739	36.8325
6	3.2283	17.3976	19.4349
7	1.1910	19.4349	0.0000

YEARS 8 — MO PAYT 1.5776 — AN CONST 18.94

#	INT	PRIN	BALANCE
1	10.7144	8.2167	91.7833
2	9.7522	9.1789	82.6044
3	8.6774	10.2538	72.3507
4	7.4766	11.4545	60.8962
5	6.1353	12.7958	48.1003
6	4.6369	14.2942	33.8061
7	2.9630	15.9681	17.8380
8	1.0931	17.8380	0.0000

YEARS 9 — MO PAYT 1.4695 — AN CONST 17.64

#	INT	PRIN	BALANCE
1	10.7826	6.8514	93.1486
2	9.9803	7.6537	85.4948
3	9.0841	8.5500	76.9448
4	8.0828	9.5512	67.3936
5	6.9644	10.6697	56.7239
6	5.7149	11.9191	44.8048
7	4.3192	13.3149	31.4899
8	2.7600	14.8741	16.6158
9	1.0182	16.6158	0.0000

YEARS 10 — MO PAYT 1.3846 — AN CONST 16.62

#	INT	PRIN	BALANCE
1	10.8362	5.7788	94.2212
2	10.1595	6.4555	87.7657
3	9.4036	7.2114	80.5543
4	8.5591	8.0559	72.4983
5	7.6157	8.9993	63.4991
6	6.5619	10.0531	53.4460
7	5.3847	11.2303	42.2156
8	4.0696	12.5454	29.6702
9	2.6005	14.0145	15.6557
10	.9594	15.6557	0.0000

YEARS 11 — MO PAYT 1.3165 — AN CONST 15.80

#	INT	PRIN	BALANCE
1	10.8792	4.9186	95.0814
2	10.3032	5.4946	89.5869
3	9.6598	6.1380	83.4489
4	8.9411	6.8567	76.5921
5	8.1381	7.6597	68.9325
6	7.2412	8.5566	60.3758
7	6.2392	9.5586	50.8172
8	5.1198	10.6780	40.1392
9	3.8694	11.9284	28.2108
10	2.4726	13.3252	14.8856
11	.9122	14.8856	0.0000

YEARS 12 — MO PAYT 1.2610 — AN CONST 15.14

#	INT	PRIN	BALANCE
1	10.9143	4.2173	95.7827
2	10.4204	4.7112	91.0715
3	9.8687	5.2628	85.8087
4	9.2524	5.8791	79.9296
5	8.5640	6.5676	73.3620
6	7.7949	7.3366	66.0254
7	6.9358	8.1958	57.8296
8	5.9760	9.1555	48.6741
9	4.9039	10.2276	38.4464
10	3.7062	11.4253	27.0211
11	2.3683	12.7632	14.2578
12	.8737	14.2578	0.0000

YEARS 13 — MO PAYT 1.2151 — AN CONST 14.59

#	INT	PRIN	BALANCE
1	10.9432	3.6379	96.3621
2	10.5172	4.0639	92.2982
3	10.0413	4.5398	87.7585
4	9.5097	5.0714	82.6871
5	8.9158	5.6652	77.0219
6	8.2524	6.3287	70.6932
7	7.5113	7.0698	63.6234
8	6.6835	7.8976	55.7258
9	5.7586	8.8225	46.9034
10	4.7255	9.8556	37.0478
11	3.5714	11.0097	26.0381
12	2.2822	12.2989	13.7392
13	.8419	13.7392	0.0000

YEARS 14 — MO PAYT 1.1768 — AN CONST 14.13

#	INT	PRIN	BALANCE
1	10.9674	3.1538	96.8462
2	10.5981	3.5231	93.3230
3	10.1855	3.9357	89.3873
4	9.7246	4.3966	84.9907
5	9.2098	4.9114	80.0793
6	8.6347	5.4866	74.5927
7	7.9922	6.1291	68.4637
8	7.2744	6.8468	61.6169
9	6.4727	7.6486	53.9683
10	5.5770	8.5442	45.4241
11	4.5765	9.5448	35.8794
12	3.4588	10.6625	25.2169
13	2.2102	11.9110	13.3059
14	.8154	13.3059	0.0000

YEARS 15 — MO PAYT 1.1445 — AN CONST 13.74

#	INT	PRIN	BALANCE
1	10.9878	2.7457	97.2543
2	10.6663	3.0672	94.1871
3	10.3071	3.4264	90.7607
4	9.9059	3.8276	86.9330
5	9.4576	4.2759	82.6571
6	8.9569	4.7766	77.8805
7	8.3976	5.3359	72.5446
8	7.7727	5.9608	66.5838
9	7.0747	6.6588	59.9251
10	6.2950	7.4385	52.4865
11	5.4239	8.3096	44.1769
12	4.4508	9.2827	34.8942
13	3.3638	10.3697	24.5245
14	2.1495	11.5840	12.9405
15	.7930	12.9405	0.0000

YEARS 16 — MO PAYT 1.1170 — AN CONST 13.41

#	INT	PRIN	BALANCE
1	11.0051	2.3989	97.6011
2	10.7242	2.6798	94.9212
3	10.4104	2.9937	91.9276
4	10.0598	3.3442	88.5834
5	9.6682	3.7358	84.8475
6	9.2307	4.1733	80.6743
7	8.7420	4.6620	76.0123
8	8.1961	5.2079	70.8043
9	7.5863	5.8178	64.9866
10	6.9050	6.4991	58.4875
11	6.1439	7.2601	51.2274
12	5.2938	8.1103	43.1171
13	4.3440	9.0600	34.0571
14	3.2831	10.1209	23.9362
15	2.0979	11.3061	12.6301
16	.7740	12.6301	0.0000

YEARS 17 — MO PAYT 1.0935 — AN CONST 13.13

#	INT	PRIN	BALANCE
1	11.0199	2.1023	97.8977
2	10.7738	2.3485	95.5492
3	10.4988	2.6235	92.9257
4	10.1915	2.9307	89.9950
5	9.8483	3.2739	86.7211
6	9.4650	3.6573	83.0638
7	9.0367	4.0856	78.9782
8	8.5583	4.5640	74.4142
9	8.0238	5.0984	69.3158
10	7.4268	5.6955	63.6203
11	6.7598	6.3624	57.2579
12	6.0148	7.1075	50.1504
13	5.1825	7.9398	42.2107
14	4.2527	8.8695	33.3411
15	3.2141	9.9082	23.4330
16	2.0538	11.0684	12.3646
17	.7577	12.3646	0.0000

YEARS 18 — MO PAYT 1.0733 — AN CONST 12.88

#	INT	PRIN	BALANCE
1	11.0327	1.8472	98.1528
2	10.8164	2.0635	96.0894
3	10.5748	2.3051	93.7843
4	10.3048	2.5750	91.2092
5	10.0033	2.8766	88.3326
6	9.6664	3.2134	85.1192
7	9.2901	3.5897	81.5295
8	8.8698	4.0101	77.5194
9	8.4002	4.4797	73.0397
10	7.8756	5.0043	68.0354
11	7.2896	5.5903	62.4452
12	6.6350	6.2449	56.2003
13	5.9037	6.9762	49.2241
14	5.0868	7.7931	41.4310
15	4.1742	8.7057	32.7253
16	3.1547	9.7251	23.0001
17	2.0159	10.8640	12.1362
18	.7437	12.1362	0.0000

YEARS 19 — MO PAYT 1.0559 — AN CONST 12.68

#	INT	PRIN	BALANCE
1	11.0437	1.6266	98.3734
2	10.8532	1.8171	96.5562
3	10.6404	2.0299	94.5263
4	10.4027	2.2676	92.2587
5	10.1372	2.5332	89.7256
6	9.8406	2.8298	86.8958
7	9.5092	3.1612	83.7346
8	9.1390	3.5313	80.2033
9	8.7255	3.9449	76.2584
10	8.2635	4.4068	71.8516
11	7.7475	4.9229	66.9287
12	7.1710	5.4993	61.4294
13	6.5270	6.1433	55.2861
14	5.8076	6.8627	48.4234
15	5.0040	7.6663	40.7570
16	4.1063	8.5641	32.1930
17	3.1034	9.5670	22.6260
18	1.9831	10.6873	11.9388
19	.7316	11.9388	0.0000

YEARS 20 — MO PAYT 1.0407 — AN CONST 12.49

#	INT	PRIN	BALANCE
1	11.0533	1.4352	98.5648
2	10.8852	1.6033	96.9615
3	10.6975	1.7910	95.1704
4	10.4877	2.0008	93.1697
5	10.2534	2.2351	90.9346
6	9.9917	2.4968	88.4378
7	9.6993	2.7892	85.6486
8	9.3727	3.1158	82.5328
9	9.0078	3.4807	79.0522
10	8.6003	3.8882	75.1639
11	8.1449	4.3436	70.8204
12	7.6363	4.8522	65.9682
13	7.0681	5.4204	60.5478
14	6.4334	6.0551	54.4926
15	5.7243	6.7642	47.7284
16	4.9322	7.5563	40.1721
17	4.0473	8.4412	31.7309
18	3.0589	9.4296	22.3013
19	1.9546	10.5339	11.7674
20	.7211	11.7674	0.0000

YEARS 21 — MO PAYT 1.0275 — AN CONST 12.34

#	INT	PRIN	BALANCE
1	11.0616	1.2685	98.7315
2	10.9131	1.4170	97.3145
3	10.7471	1.5830	95.7315

#	INT	PRIN	BALANCE
4	10.5618	1.7683	93.9632
5	10.3547	1.9754	91.9878
6	10.1234	2.2067	89.7811
7	9.8650	2.4651	87.3160
8	9.5763	2.7538	84.5622
9	9.2538	3.0763	81.4859
10	8.8936	3.4365	78.0494
11	8.4912	3.8389	74.2105
12	8.0416	4.2885	69.9220
13	7.5394	4.7907	65.1314
14	6.9784	5.3517	59.7797
15	6.3518	5.9783	53.8014
16	5.6517	6.6784	47.1230
17	4.8696	7.4605	39.6625
18	3.9960	8.3341	31.3284
19	3.0201	9.3100	22.0184
20	1.9298	10.4002	11.6181
21	.7120	11.6181	0.0000

YEARS 22	MO PAYT 1.0160	AN CONST 12.20	
#	INT	PRIN	BALANCE
1	11.0689	1.1228	98.8772
2	10.9374	1.2542	97.6230
3	10.7905	1.4011	96.2219
4	10.6265	1.5652	94.6567
5	10.4432	1.7485	92.9082
6	10.2384	1.9532	90.9550
7	10.0097	2.1819	88.7731
8	9.7542	2.4374	86.3356
9	9.4688	2.7229	83.6128
10	9.1499	3.0417	80.5710
11	8.7937	3.3979	77.1731
12	8.3958	3.7958	73.3773
13	7.9513	4.2403	69.1370
14	7.4548	4.7369	64.4001
15	6.9001	5.2916	59.1085
16	6.2804	5.9112	53.1973
17	5.5882	6.6034	46.5939
18	4.8150	7.3767	39.2172
19	3.9511	8.2405	30.9767
20	2.9862	9.2055	21.7712
21	1.9082	10.2835	11.4877
22	.7040	11.4877	0.0000

YEARS 23	MO PAYT 1.0059	AN CONST 12.08	
#	INT	PRIN	BALANCE
1	11.0753	.9951	99.0049
2	10.9588	1.1116	97.8933
3	10.8286	1.2418	96.6516
4	10.6832	1.3872	95.2644
5	10.5207	1.5496	93.7148
6	10.3393	1.7311	91.9838
7	10.1366	1.9338	90.0500
8	9.9101	2.1602	87.8897
9	9.6571	2.4132	85.4766
10	9.3746	2.6958	82.7808
11	9.0589	3.0115	79.7693
12	8.7062	3.3641	76.4052
13	8.3123	3.7581	72.6471
14	7.8742	4.1981	68.4490
15	7.3806	4.6897	63.7593
16	6.8314	5.2389	58.5204
17	6.2179	5.8524	52.6680
18	5.5326	6.5377	46.1303
19	4.7670	7.3033	38.8270
20	3.9118	8.1585	30.6684
21	2.9564	9.1139	21.5545
22	1.8892	10.1812	11.3734
23	.6970	11.3734	0.0000

YEARS 24	MO PAYT .9970	AN CONST 11.97	
#	INT	PRIN	BALANCE
1	11.0809	.8829	99.1171
2	10.9775	.9863	98.1308
3	10.8620	1.1018	97.0291
4	10.7330	1.2308	95.7983
5	10.5889	1.3749	94.4233
6	10.4278	1.5359	92.8874
7	10.2480	1.7158	91.1716
8	10.0471	1.9167	89.2549
9	9.8226	2.1412	87.1138
10	9.5719	2.3919	84.7219
11	9.2918	2.6720	82.0499
12	8.9789	2.9849	79.0650
13	8.6294	3.3344	75.7306
14	8.2389	3.7249	72.0057
15	7.8027	4.1611	67.8447
16	7.3154	4.6483	63.1964
17	6.7711	5.1927	58.0037
18	6.1630	5.8007	52.2030
19	5.4838	6.4800	45.7230
20	4.7250	7.2388	38.4842
21	3.8773	8.0865	30.3977
22	2.9303	9.0334	21.3642
23	1.8725	10.0913	11.2730
24	.6908	11.2730	0.0000

YEARS 25	MO PAYT .9892	AN CONST 11.87	
#	INT	PRIN	BALANCE
1	11.0858	.7841	99.2159
2	10.9940	.8760	98.3399
3	10.8914	.9785	97.3613
4	10.7768	1.0931	96.2682
5	10.6448	1.2211	95.0471
6	10.5058	1.3641	93.6829
7	10.3461	1.5239	92.1591
8	10.1676	1.7023	90.4567
9	9.9683	1.9017	88.5550
10	9.7456	2.1244	86.4307
11	9.4968	2.3731	84.0575
12	9.2189	2.6510	81.4065
13	8.9085	2.9615	78.4450
14	8.5617	3.3083	75.1368
15	8.1743	3.6957	71.4411
16	7.7415	4.1284	67.3127
17	7.2581	4.6119	62.7008
18	6.7180	5.1519	57.5489
19	6.1147	5.7552	51.7936
20	5.4408	6.4292	45.3644
21	4.6879	7.1821	38.1824
22	3.8469	8.0231	30.1593
23	2.9074	8.9626	21.1967
24	1.8578	10.0121	11.1846
25	.6854	11.1846	0.0000

YEARS 26	MO PAYT .9823	AN CONST 11.79	
#	INT	PRIN	BALANCE
1	11.0902	.6971	99.3029
2	11.0085	.7787	98.5243
3	10.9174	.8699	97.6544
4	10.8155	.9717	96.6827
5	10.7017	1.0855	95.5972
6	10.5746	1.2126	94.3845
7	10.4326	1.3546	93.0299
8	10.2740	1.5133	91.5167
9	10.0968	1.6905	89.8262
10	9.8988	1.8884	87.9378
11	9.6777	2.1096	85.8282
12	9.4306	2.3566	83.4716
13	9.1547	2.6326	80.8391
14	8.8464	2.9408	77.8982
15	8.5020	3.2852	74.6130
16	8.1173	3.6699	70.9431
17	7.6876	4.0997	66.8435
18	7.2075	4.5797	62.2637
19	6.6712	5.1160	57.1477
20	6.0721	5.7151	51.4326
21	5.4028	6.3844	45.0482
22	4.6552	7.1320	37.9162
23	3.8201	7.9672	29.9491
24	2.8871	8.9001	21.0490
25	1.8449	9.9423	11.1066
26	.6806	11.1066	0.0000

YEARS 27	MO PAYT .9762	AN CONST 11.72	
#	INT	PRIN	BALANCE
1	11.0940	.6201	99.3799
2	11.0214	.6927	98.6872
3	10.9403	.7738	97.9133
4	10.8497	.8645	97.0488
5	10.7484	.9657	96.0831
6	10.6353	1.0788	95.0044
7	10.5090	1.2051	93.7993
8	10.3679	1.3462	92.4530
9	10.2102	1.5039	90.9491
10	10.0341	1.6800	89.2692
11	9.8374	1.8767	87.3925
12	9.6176	2.0965	85.2960
13	9.3721	2.3420	82.9540
14	9.0979	2.6162	80.3378
15	8.7915	2.9226	77.4152
16	8.4493	3.2648	74.1504
17	8.0670	3.6471	70.5032
18	7.6399	4.0742	66.4290
19	7.1628	4.5513	61.8776
20	6.6298	5.0843	56.7933
21	6.0344	5.6797	51.1137
22	5.3693	6.3448	44.7689
23	4.6264	7.0878	37.6811
24	3.7964	7.9178	29.7634
25	2.8692	8.8449	20.9184
26	1.8334	9.8807	11.0377
27	.6764	11.0377	0.0000

YEARS 28	MO PAYT .9708	AN CONST 11.65	
#	INT	PRIN	BALANCE
1	11.0974	.5520	99.4480
2	11.0328	.6167	98.8313
3	10.9606	.6889	98.1424
4	10.8799	.7696	97.3728
5	10.7898	.8597	96.5131
6	10.6891	.9604	95.5527
7	10.5766	1.0728	94.4799
8	10.4510	1.1985	93.2814
9	10.3107	1.3388	91.9426
10	10.1539	1.4956	90.4471
11	9.9788	1.6707	88.7764
12	9.7831	1.8663	86.9100
13	9.5646	2.0849	84.8251
14	9.3204	2.3290	82.4961
15	9.0477	2.6018	79.8943
16	8.7430	2.9065	76.9878
17	8.4027	3.2468	73.7410
18	8.0224	3.6270	70.1140
19	7.5977	4.0517	66.0623
20	7.1233	4.5262	61.5361
21	6.5932	5.0562	56.4798
22	6.0011	5.6483	50.8315
23	5.3397	6.3098	44.5217
24	4.6008	7.0486	37.4731
25	3.7754	7.8740	29.5991
26	2.8534	8.7961	20.8029
27	1.8233	9.8261	10.9768
28	.6727	10.9768	0.0000

YEARS 29	MO PAYT .9660	AN CONST 11.60	
#	INT	PRIN	BALANCE
1	11.1004	.4917	99.5083
2	11.0428	.5493	98.9589
3	10.9785	.6137	98.3453
4	10.9067	.6855	97.6598
5	10.8264	.7658	96.8940
6	10.7367	.8555	96.0385
7	10.6365	.9556	95.0828
8	10.5246	1.0676	94.0153
9	10.3996	1.1926	92.8227
10	10.2600	1.3322	91.4905
11	10.1040	1.4882	90.0023
12	9.9297	1.6625	88.3398
13	9.7350	1.8572	86.4826
14	9.5175	2.0747	84.4080
15	9.2746	2.3176	82.0904
16	9.0032	2.5890	79.5014
17	8.7000	2.8922	76.6092
18	8.3613	3.2308	73.3784
19	7.9830	3.6092	69.7692
20	7.5604	4.0318	65.7374
21	7.0882	4.5040	61.2335
22	6.5608	5.0314	56.2021
23	5.9716	5.6206	50.5815
24	5.3134	6.2787	44.3028
25	4.5782	7.0140	37.2888
26	3.7568	7.8353	29.4535
27	2.8393	8.7529	20.7007
28	1.8143	9.7778	10.9228
29	.6693	10.9228	0.0000

YEARS 30	MO PAYT .9618	AN CONST 11.55	
#	INT	PRIN	BALANCE
1	11.1031	.4383	99.5617
2	11.0518	.4896	99.0721
3	10.9944	.5469	98.5252
4	10.9304	.6110	97.9143
5	10.8589	.6825	97.2317
6	10.7789	.7624	96.4693
7	10.6896	.8517	95.6176
8	10.5899	.9515	94.6661
9	10.4785	1.0629	93.6033
10	10.3540	1.1873	92.4159
11	10.2150	1.3264	91.0895
12	10.0597	1.4817	89.6078
13	9.8862	1.6552	87.9526
14	9.6923	1.8490	86.1036
15	9.4758	2.0656	84.0381
16	9.2339	2.3074	81.7306
17	8.9637	2.5776	79.1530
18	8.6619	2.8795	76.2735
19	8.3247	3.2167	73.0568
20	7.9480	3.5934	69.4634
21	7.5272	4.0141	65.4493
22	7.0572	4.4842	60.9651
23	6.5320	5.0093	55.9558
24	5.9454	5.5959	50.3598
25	5.2902	6.2512	44.1086
26	4.5581	6.9832	37.1254
27	3.7404	7.8010	29.3244
28	2.8269	8.7145	20.6099
29	1.8064	9.7350	10.8750
30	.6664	10.8750	0.0000

MONTHLY PAYMENT AMORTIZATION SCHEDULE PER $100 — 11.20 %

YEARS 2	MO PAYT 4.6701	AN CONST 56.05
# INT	PRIN	BALANCE
1 8.8250	47.2159	52.7841
2 3.2568	52.7841	0.0000

YEARS 3	MO PAYT 3.2834	AN CONST 39.41
# INT	PRIN	BALANCE
1 9.7064	29.6938	70.3062
2 6.2045	33.1957	37.1105
3 2.2897	37.1105	0.0000

YEARS 4	MO PAYT 2.5943	AN CONST 31.14
# INT	PRIN	BALANCE
1 10.1443	20.9870	79.0130
2 7.6693	23.4620	55.5511
3 4.9024	26.2289	29.3221
4 1.8092	29.3221	0.0000

YEARS 5	MO PAYT 2.1842	AN CONST 26.22
# INT	PRIN	BALANCE
1 10.4050	15.8058	84.1942
2 8.5410	17.6698	66.5244
3 6.4571	19.7536	46.7708
4 4.1275	22.0832	24.6875
5 1.5232	24.6875	0.0000

YEARS 6	MO PAYT 1.9137	AN CONST 22.97
# INT	PRIN	BALANCE
1 10.5769	12.3871	87.6129
2 9.1161	13.8479	73.7650
3 7.4830	15.4810	58.2840
4 5.6573	17.3067	40.9772
5 3.6163	19.3478	21.6295
6 1.3345	21.6295	0.0000

YEARS 7	MO PAYT 1.7228	AN CONST 20.68
# INT	PRIN	BALANCE
1 10.6983	9.9751	90.0249
2 9.5219	11.1515	78.8735
3 8.2068	12.4666	66.4069
4 6.7365	13.9368	52.4701
5 5.0930	15.5804	36.8897
6 3.2555	17.4178	19.4719
7 1.2014	19.4719	0.0000

YEARS 8	MO PAYT 1.5817	AN CONST 18.98
# INT	PRIN	BALANCE
1 10.7879	8.1919	91.8081
2 9.8219	9.1579	82.6502
3 8.7419	10.2379	72.4123
4 7.5345	11.4453	60.9669
5 6.1847	12.7951	48.1718
6 4.6757	14.3041	33.8678
7 2.9888	15.9910	17.8768
8 1.1030	17.8768	0.0000

YEARS 9	MO PAYT 1.4737	AN CONST 17.69
# INT	PRIN	BALANCE
1 10.8566	6.8274	93.1726
2 10.0514	7.6326	85.5400
3 9.1513	8.5327	77.0074
4 8.1450	9.5390	67.4684
5 7.0201	10.6639	56.8045
6 5.7624	11.9215	44.8829
7 4.3565	13.3275	31.5555
8 2.7848	14.8992	16.6563
9 1.0277	16.6563	0.0000

YEARS 10	MO PAYT 1.3888	AN CONST 16.67
# INT	PRIN	BALANCE
1 10.9105	5.7557	94.2443
2 10.2317	6.4344	87.8099
3 9.4729	7.1933	80.6166
4 8.6246	8.0416	72.5751
5 7.6762	8.9899	63.5851
6 6.6160	10.0501	53.5350
7 5.4308	11.2354	42.2996
8 4.1058	12.5604	29.7393
9 2.6245	14.0416	15.6976
10 .9685	15.6976	0.0000

YEARS 11	MO PAYT 1.3208	AN CONST 15.86
# INT	PRIN	BALANCE
1 10.9537	4.8964	95.1036
2 10.3763	5.4738	89.6298
3 9.7307	6.1194	83.5104
4 9.0091	6.8410	76.6693
5 8.2023	7.6478	69.0215
6 7.3004	8.5498	60.4718
7 6.2921	9.5580	50.9137
8 5.1649	10.6852	40.2285
9 3.9047	11.9454	28.2831
10 2.4960	13.3541	14.9290
11 .9211	14.9290	0.0000

YEARS 12	MO PAYT 1.2654	AN CONST 15.19
# INT	PRIN	BALANCE
1 10.9889	4.1961	95.8039
2 10.4941	4.6909	91.1130
3 9.9409	5.2442	85.8688
4 9.3224	5.8626	80.0062
5 8.6310	6.5540	73.4522
6 7.8581	7.3269	66.1253
7 6.9940	8.1910	57.9343
8 6.0280	9.1570	48.7773
9 4.9481	10.2369	38.5405
10 3.7409	11.4441	27.0963
11 2.3913	12.7938	14.3026
12 .8825	14.3026	0.0000

YEARS 13	MO PAYT 1.2196	AN CONST 14.64
# INT	PRIN	BALANCE
1 11.0180	3.6176	96.3824
2 10.5914	4.0443	92.3381
3 10.1144	4.5212	87.8168
4 9.5812	5.0544	82.7624
5 8.9852	5.6505	77.1119
6 8.3188	6.3169	70.7950
7 7.5738	7.0619	63.7331
8 6.7410	7.8947	55.8385
9 5.8100	8.8257	47.0127
10 4.7691	9.8665	37.1462
11 3.6056	11.0301	26.1161
12 2.3048	12.3309	13.7851
13 .8505	13.7851	0.0000

YEARS 14	MO PAYT 1.1814	AN CONST 14.18
# INT	PRIN	BALANCE
1 11.0423	3.1346	96.8654
2 10.6727	3.5043	93.3612
3 10.2594	3.9175	89.4436
4 9.7974	4.3795	85.0641
5 9.2809	4.8960	80.1681
6 8.7035	5.4734	74.6947
7 8.0580	6.1189	68.5759
8 7.3364	6.8405	61.7354
9 6.5297	7.6472	54.0881
10 5.6279	8.5491	45.5391
11 4.6196	9.5573	35.9818
12 3.4925	10.6844	25.2974
13 2.2325	11.9444	13.3530
14 .8239	13.3530	0.0000

YEARS 15	MO PAYT 1.1492	AN CONST 13.80
# INT	PRIN	BALANCE
1 11.0628	2.7274	97.2726
2 10.7412	3.0491	94.2235
3 10.3816	3.4087	90.8148
4 9.9796	3.8107	87.0041
5 9.5302	4.2601	82.7441
6 9.0278	4.7625	77.9816
7 8.4661	5.3241	72.6575
8 7.8383	5.9520	66.7055
9 7.1363	6.6539	60.0516
10 6.3516	7.4386	52.6129
11 5.4744	8.3159	44.2970
12 4.4936	9.2966	35.0004
13 3.3973	10.3930	24.6075
14 2.1716	11.6186	12.9888
15 .8014	12.9888	0.0000

YEARS 16	MO PAYT 1.1218	AN CONST 13.47
# INT	PRIN	BALANCE
1 11.0802	2.3816	97.6184
2 10.7993	2.6625	94.9559
3 10.4853	2.9765	91.9794
4 10.1343	3.3275	88.6519
5 9.7419	3.7199	84.9320
6 9.3032	4.1586	80.7734
7 8.8128	4.6490	76.1244
8 8.2645	5.1973	70.9271
9 7.6516	5.8102	65.1168
10 6.9664	6.4955	58.6214
11 6.2003	7.2615	51.3599
12 5.3440	8.1178	43.2421
13 4.3866	9.0752	34.1669
14 3.3164	10.1454	24.0214
15 2.1199	11.3419	12.6795
16 .7823	12.6795	0.0000

YEARS 17	MO PAYT 1.0984	AN CONST 13.19
# INT	PRIN	BALANCE
1 11.0951	2.0859	97.9141
2 10.8491	2.3319	95.5821
3 10.5741	2.6069	92.9752
4 10.2666	2.9144	90.0608
5 9.9229	3.2581	86.8027
6 9.5387	3.6423	83.1604
7 9.1091	4.0719	79.0885
8 8.6289	4.5521	74.5365
9 8.0921	5.0889	69.4476
10 7.4920	5.6890	63.7585
11 6.8210	6.3600	57.3986
12 6.0710	7.1100	50.2886
13 5.2325	7.9485	42.3401
14 4.2951	8.8859	33.4542
15 3.2472	9.9338	23.5203
16 2.0757	11.1053	12.4150
17 .7660	12.4150	0.0000

YEARS 18	MO PAYT 1.0783	AN CONST 12.94
# INT	PRIN	BALANCE
1 11.1079	1.8317	98.1683
2 10.8918	2.0477	96.1206
3 10.6504	2.2892	93.8313
4 10.3804	2.5592	91.2722
5 10.0786	2.8610	88.4112
6 9.7412	3.1984	85.2127
7 9.3640	3.5756	81.6371
8 8.9423	3.9973	77.6399
9 8.4709	4.4687	73.1712
10 7.9439	4.9957	68.1755
11 7.3547	5.5848	62.5907
12 6.6961	6.2435	56.3472
13 5.9598	6.9798	49.3674
14 5.1367	7.8029	41.5645
15 4.2164	8.7231	32.8414
16 3.1877	9.7519	23.0895
17 2.0377	10.9019	12.1876
18 .7520	12.1876	0.0000

YEARS 19	MO PAYT 1.0609	AN CONST 12.74
# INT	PRIN	BALANCE
1 11.1189	1.6121	98.3879
2 10.9288	1.8022	96.5858
3 10.7163	2.0147	94.5710
4 10.4787	2.2523	92.3187
5 10.2130	2.5179	89.8008
6 9.9161	2.8149	86.9859
7 9.5841	3.1468	83.8391
8 9.2130	3.5180	80.3211
9 8.7981	3.9328	76.3883
10 8.3343	4.3966	71.9916
11 7.8158	4.9152	67.0765
12 7.2362	5.4948	61.5817
13 6.5882	6.1428	55.4388
14 5.8637	6.8673	48.5716
15 5.0539	7.6771	40.8945
16 4.1485	8.5825	32.3120
17 3.1363	9.5947	22.7173
18 2.0048	10.7262	11.9911
19 .7398	11.9911	0.0000

YEARS 20	MO PAYT 1.0458	AN CONST 12.56
# INT	PRIN	BALANCE
1 11.1285	1.4215	98.5785
2 10.9609	1.5892	96.9893
3 10.7734	1.7766	95.2128
4 10.5639	1.9861	93.2267
5 10.3297	2.2203	91.0064
6 10.0679	2.4821	88.5243
7 9.7751	2.7749	85.7494
8 9.4479	3.1021	82.6473
9 9.0821	3.4680	79.1793
10 8.6731	3.8769	75.3024
11 8.2159	4.3341	70.9682
12 7.7047	4.8453	66.1230
13 7.1333	5.4167	60.7063
14 6.4945	6.0555	54.6508
15 5.7804	6.7696	47.8811
16 4.9820	7.5680	40.3131
17 4.0895	8.4605	31.8526
18 3.0917	9.4583	22.3944
19 1.9763	10.5737	11.8207
20 .7293	11.8207	0.0000

YEARS 21	MO PAYT 1.0327	AN CONST 12.40
# INT	PRIN	BALANCE
1 11.1368	1.2556	98.7444
2 10.9888	1.4037	97.3408
3 10.8232	1.5692	95.7716

#	INT	PRIN	BALANCE
4	10.6382	1.7543	94.0173
5	10.4313	1.9611	92.0562
6	10.2000	2.1924	89.8637
7	9.9415	2.4510	87.4128
8	9.6524	2.7400	84.6727
9	9.3293	3.0632	81.6096
10	8.9680	3.4244	78.1852
11	8.5642	3.8283	74.3569
12	8.1127	4.2797	70.0772
13	7.6080	4.7844	65.2927
14	7.0437	5.3487	59.9440
15	6.4130	5.9795	53.9646
16	5.7078	6.6846	47.2799
17	4.9195	7.4730	39.8070
18	4.0382	8.3543	31.4527
19	3.0529	9.3395	22.1132
20	1.9515	10.4409	11.6723
21	.7202	11.6723	0.0000

YEARS 22	MO PAYT 1.0212	AN CONST 12.26	
#	INT	PRIN	BALANCE
1	11.1441	1.1107	98.8893
2	11.0132	1.2416	97.6477
3	10.8667	1.3881	96.2596
4	10.7030	1.5518	94.7079
5	10.5200	1.7348	92.9731
6	10.3154	1.9394	91.0337
7	10.0867	2.1681	88.8657
8	9.8310	2.4238	86.4419
9	9.5452	2.7096	83.7323
10	9.2257	3.0291	80.7032
11	8.8684	3.3864	77.3168
12	8.4691	3.7857	73.5311
13	8.0226	4.2322	69.2989
14	7.5235	4.7313	64.5676
15	6.9655	5.2893	59.2783
16	6.3417	5.9131	53.3652
17	5.6444	6.6104	46.7548
18	4.8648	7.3900	39.3649
19	3.9933	8.2615	31.1034
20	3.0190	9.2358	21.8676
21	1.9298	10.3250	11.5426
22	.7122	11.5426	0.0000

YEARS 23	MO PAYT 1.0112	AN CONST 12.14	
#	INT	PRIN	BALANCE
1	11.1505	.9837	99.0163
2	11.0345	1.0997	97.9165
3	10.9048	1.2294	96.6871
4	10.7598	1.3744	95.3127
5	10.5977	1.5365	93.7762
6	10.4165	1.7177	92.0585
7	10.2140	1.9203	90.1382
8	9.9875	2.1467	87.9915
9	9.7343	2.3999	85.5916
10	9.4513	2.6829	82.9086
11	9.1349	2.9993	79.9093
12	8.7812	3.3531	76.5562
13	8.3857	3.7485	72.8077
14	7.9437	4.1906	68.6172
15	7.4495	4.6848	63.9324
16	6.8970	5.2372	58.6951
17	6.2794	5.8549	52.8403
18	5.5889	6.5454	46.2949
19	4.8170	7.3173	38.9776
20	3.9540	8.1802	30.7974
21	2.9893	9.1449	21.6525
22	1.9108	10.2234	11.4291
23	.7052	11.4291	0.0000

YEARS 24	MO PAYT 1.0024	AN CONST 12.03	
#	INT	PRIN	BALANCE
1	11.1561	.8723	99.1277
2	11.0533	.9751	98.1526
3	10.9383	1.0901	97.0624
4	10.8097	1.2187	95.8437
5	10.6660	1.3624	94.4813
6	10.5053	1.5231	92.9582
7	10.3257	1.7027	91.2555
8	10.1249	1.9035	89.3520
9	9.9004	2.1280	87.2239
10	9.6494	2.3790	84.8450
11	9.3689	2.6595	82.1854
12	9.0552	2.9732	79.2122
13	8.7046	3.3238	75.8884
14	8.3126	3.7158	72.1726
15	7.8744	4.1540	68.0186
16	7.3845	4.6439	63.3747
17	6.8368	5.1916	58.1832
18	6.2246	5.8038	52.3793
19	5.5401	6.4883	45.8911
20	4.7749	7.2534	38.6376
21	3.9195	8.1089	30.5288
22	2.9632	9.0652	21.4636
23	1.8942	10.1342	11.3294
24	.6990	11.3294	0.0000

YEARS 25	MO PAYT .9946	AN CONST 11.94	
#	INT	PRIN	BALANCE
1	11.1611	.7742	99.2258
2	11.0698	.8655	98.3603
3	10.9677	.9676	97.3927
4	10.8536	1.0817	96.3110
5	10.7260	1.2093	95.1017
6	10.5834	1.3519	93.7498
7	10.4240	1.5113	92.2385
8	10.2457	1.6895	90.5490
9	10.0465	1.8888	88.6602
10	9.8237	2.1115	86.5486
11	9.5747	2.3606	84.1881
12	9.2963	2.6389	81.5491
13	8.9851	2.9502	78.5990
14	8.6372	3.2981	75.3009
15	8.2482	3.6870	71.6139
16	7.8134	4.1218	67.4920
17	7.3273	4.6079	62.8841
18	6.7839	5.1514	57.7327
19	6.1764	5.7589	51.9738
20	5.4972	6.4380	45.5358
21	4.7380	7.1973	38.3385
22	3.8892	8.0461	30.2924
23	2.9403	8.9950	21.2974
24	1.8795	10.0558	11.2417
25	.6936	11.2417	0.0000

YEARS 26	MO PAYT .9878	AN CONST 11.86	
#	INT	PRIN	BALANCE
1	11.1654	.6878	99.3122
2	11.0843	.7689	98.5433
3	10.9936	.8596	97.6838
4	10.8922	.9609	96.7228
5	10.7789	1.0743	95.6486
6	10.6522	1.2010	94.4476
7	10.5106	1.3426	93.1050
8	10.3523	1.5009	91.6041
9	10.1753	1.6779	89.9262
10	9.9774	1.8758	88.0504
11	9.7562	2.0970	85.9534
12	9.5089	2.3443	83.6091
13	9.2324	2.6208	80.9883
14	8.9233	2.9299	78.0584
15	8.5778	3.2754	74.7830
16	8.1915	3.6617	71.1213
17	7.7597	4.0935	67.0278
18	7.2769	4.5763	62.4516
19	6.7372	5.1159	57.3356
20	6.1339	5.7193	51.6163
21	5.4594	6.3938	45.2226
22	4.7054	7.1478	38.0748
23	3.8624	7.9907	30.0841
24	2.9201	8.9331	21.1510
25	1.8666	9.9866	11.1643
26	.6888	11.1643	0.0000

YEARS 27	MO PAYT .9817	AN CONST 11.79	
#	INT	PRIN	BALANCE
1	11.1692	.6115	99.3885
2	11.0971	.6836	98.7050
3	11.0165	.7642	97.9408
4	10.9264	.8543	97.0865
5	10.8256	.9551	96.1314
6	10.7130	1.0677	95.0637
7	10.5871	1.1936	93.8701
8	10.4463	1.3344	92.5357
9	10.2890	1.4917	91.0440
10	10.1130	1.6677	89.3763
11	9.9164	1.8643	87.5120
12	9.6965	2.0842	85.4278
13	9.4507	2.3300	83.0978
14	9.1759	2.6048	80.4930
15	8.8687	2.9120	77.5811
16	8.5253	3.2554	74.3257
17	8.1414	3.6393	70.6864
18	7.7122	4.0685	66.6180
19	7.2324	4.5483	62.0697
20	6.6960	5.0847	56.9850
21	6.0964	5.6843	51.3007
22	5.4260	6.3547	44.9461
23	4.6766	7.1041	37.8420
24	3.8388	7.9419	29.9001
25	2.9022	8.8785	21.0216
26	1.8552	9.9255	11.0961
27	.6846	11.0961	0.0000

YEARS 28	MO PAYT .9764	AN CONST 11.72	
#	INT	PRIN	BALANCE
1	11.1726	.5440	99.4560
2	11.1085	.6081	98.8479
3	11.0368	.6799	98.1680
4	10.9566	.7600	97.4080
5	10.8670	.8497	96.5583
6	10.7668	.9499	95.6085
7	10.6547	1.0619	94.5466
8	10.5295	1.1871	93.3595
9	10.3895	1.3271	92.0324
10	10.2330	1.4836	90.5487
11	10.0580	1.6586	88.8901
12	9.8624	1.8542	87.0360
13	9.6438	2.0729	84.9631
14	9.3993	2.3173	82.6458
15	9.1260	2.5906	80.0552
16	8.8205	2.8961	77.1591
17	8.4790	3.2377	73.9214
18	8.0971	3.6195	70.3019
19	7.6703	4.0463	66.2556
20	7.1931	4.5235	61.7320
21	6.6596	5.0570	56.6750
22	6.0632	5.6534	51.0217
23	5.3965	6.3201	44.7016
24	4.6512	7.0654	37.6361
25	3.8179	7.8987	29.7375
26	2.8864	8.8302	20.9073
27	1.8451	9.8715	11.0357
28	.6809	11.0357	0.0000

YEARS 29	MO PAYT .9717	AN CONST 11.66	
#	INT	PRIN	BALANCE
1	11.1756	.4842	99.5158
2	11.1185	.5413	98.9744
3	11.0547	.6052	98.3692
4	10.9833	.6766	97.6927
5	10.9035	.7564	96.9363
6	10.8143	.8455	96.0908
7	10.7146	.9453	95.1455
8	10.6031	1.0567	94.0888
9	10.4785	1.1814	92.9074
10	10.3392	1.3207	91.5867
11	10.1834	1.4764	90.1103
12	10.0093	1.6506	88.4597
13	9.8147	1.8452	86.6145
14	9.5971	2.0628	84.5517
15	9.3538	2.3061	82.2456
16	9.0818	2.5781	79.6675
17	8.7778	2.8821	76.7854
18	8.4379	3.2220	73.5634
19	8.0579	3.6020	69.9615
20	7.6331	4.0267	65.9347
21	7.1583	4.5016	61.4331
22	6.6274	5.0325	56.4006
23	6.0339	5.6260	50.7746
24	5.3704	6.2895	44.4851
25	4.6287	7.0312	37.4539
26	3.7995	7.8604	29.5935
27	2.8725	8.7874	20.8060
28	1.8361	9.8237	10.9823
29	.6776	10.9823	0.0000

YEARS 30	MO PAYT .9675	AN CONST 11.61	
#	INT	PRIN	BALANCE
1	11.1783	.4313	99.5687
2	11.1274	.4822	99.0866
3	11.0706	.5390	98.5475
4	11.0070	.6026	97.9450
5	10.9360	.6736	97.2713
6	10.8565	.7531	96.5182
7	10.7677	.8419	95.6763
8	10.6684	.9412	94.7351
9	10.5574	1.0522	93.6830
10	10.4333	1.1763	92.5067
11	10.2946	1.3150	91.1917
12	10.1395	1.4701	89.7216
13	9.9662	1.6434	88.0782
14	9.7723	1.8373	86.2409
15	9.5557	2.0539	84.1870
16	9.3134	2.2961	81.8909
17	9.0427	2.5669	79.3239
18	8.7399	2.8697	76.4543
19	8.4015	3.2081	73.2462
20	8.0232	3.5864	69.6597
21	7.6002	4.0094	65.6504
22	7.1274	4.4822	61.1682
23	6.5988	5.0108	56.1574
24	6.0079	5.6017	50.5556
25	5.3472	6.2624	44.2932
26	4.6087	7.0009	37.2923
27	3.7831	7.8265	29.4658
28	2.8601	8.7495	20.7163
29	1.8282	9.7814	10.9349
30	.6747	10.9349	0.0000

MONTHLY PAYMENT AMORTIZATION SCHEDULE PER $100   11.25 %

YEARS 2	MO PAYT 4.6724	AN CONST 56.07
# INT	PRIN	BALANCE
1 8.8653	47.2035	52.7965
2 3.2723	52.7965	0.0000

YEARS 3	MO PAYT 3.2857	AN CONST 39.43
# INT	PRIN	BALANCE
1 9.7507	29.6780	70.3220
2 6.2342	33.1945	37.1275
3 2.3012	37.1275	0.0000

YEARS 4	MO PAYT 2.5967	AN CONST 31.17
# INT	PRIN	BALANCE
1 10.1906	20.9699	79.0301
2 7.7060	23.4546	55.5755
3 4.9269	26.2336	29.3419
4 1.8186	29.3419	0.0000

YEARS 5	MO PAYT 2.1867	AN CONST 26.25
# INT	PRIN	BALANCE
1 10.4524	15.7884	84.2116
2 8.5817	17.6591	66.5525
3 6.4893	19.7515	46.8010
4 4.1490	22.0917	24.7093
5 1.5315	24.7093	0.0000

YEARS 6	MO PAYT 1.9162	AN CONST 23.00
# INT	PRIN	BALANCE
1 10.6251	12.3698	87.6302
2 9.1594	13.8354	73.7948
3 7.5201	15.4747	58.3201
4 5.6866	17.3083	41.0118
5 3.6358	19.3590	21.6528
6 1.3420	21.6528	0.0000

YEARS 7	MO PAYT 1.7254	AN CONST 20.71
# INT	PRIN	BALANCE
1 10.7469	9.9581	90.0419
2 9.5670	11.1380	78.9039
3 8.2473	12.4577	66.4463
4 6.7713	13.9337	52.5125
5 5.1203	15.5847	36.9279
6 3.2738	17.4312	19.4966
7 1.2084	19.4966	0.0000

YEARS 8	MO PAYT 1.5844	AN CONST 19.02
# INT	PRIN	BALANCE
1 10.8370	8.1753	91.8247
2 9.8683	9.1440	82.6807
3 8.7849	10.2274	72.4533
4 7.5731	11.4392	61.0141
5 6.2177	12.7946	48.2195
6 4.7017	14.3106	33.9089
7 3.0061	16.0062	17.9027
8 1.1096	17.9027	0.0000

YEARS 9	MO PAYT 1.4764	AN CONST 17.72
# INT	PRIN	BALANCE
1 10.9059	6.8114	93.1886
2 10.0988	7.6185	85.5701
3 9.1961	8.5211	77.0490
4 8.1865	9.5308	67.5182
5 7.0572	10.6600	56.8582
6 5.7942	11.9231	44.9350

# INT	PRIN	BALANCE
7 4.3815	13.3358	31.5992
8 2.8014	14.9159	16.6833
9 1.0340	16.6833	0.0000

YEARS 10	MO PAYT 1.3917	AN CONST 16.71
# INT	PRIN	BALANCE
1 10.9600	5.7403	94.2597
2 10.2799	6.4204	87.8393
3 9.5191	7.1811	80.6582
4 8.6683	8.0320	72.6262
5 7.7166	8.9837	63.6425
6 6.6521	10.0481	53.5943
7 5.4616	11.2387	42.3556
8 4.1300	12.5703	29.7853
9 2.6405	14.0597	15.7256
10 .9747	15.7256	0.0000

YEARS 11	MO PAYT 1.3238	AN CONST 15.89
# INT	PRIN	BALANCE
1 11.0034	4.8816	95.1184
2 10.4250	5.4601	89.6583
3 9.7780	6.1070	83.5513
4 9.0544	6.8306	76.7207
5 8.2451	7.6399	69.0808
6 7.3399	8.5451	60.5357
7 6.3274	9.5576	50.9781
8 5.1950	10.6901	40.2880
9 3.9283	11.9567	28.3313
10 2.5116	13.3734	14.9579
11 .9271	14.9579	0.0000

YEARS 12	MO PAYT 1.2684	AN CONST 15.23
# INT	PRIN	BALANCE
1 11.0387	4.1820	95.8180
2 10.5432	4.6775	91.1405
3 9.9890	5.2317	85.9088
4 9.3691	5.8516	80.0572
5 8.6758	6.5449	73.5123
6 7.9003	7.3204	66.1919
7 7.0329	8.1878	58.0041
8 6.0628	9.1579	48.8462
9 4.9777	10.2430	38.6032
10 3.7641	11.4567	27.1465
11 2.4066	12.8141	14.3324
12 .8883	14.3324	0.0000

YEARS 13	MO PAYT 1.2227	AN CONST 14.68
# INT	PRIN	BALANCE
1 11.0679	3.6042	96.3958
2 10.6409	4.0313	92.3645
3 10.1632	4.5089	87.8556
4 9.6290	5.0432	82.8125
5 9.0314	5.6407	77.1718
6 8.3631	6.3090	70.8627
7 7.6156	7.0566	63.8062
8 6.7795	7.8927	55.9135
9 5.8443	8.8278	47.0856
10 4.7983	9.8738	37.2118
11 3.6284	11.0437	26.1681
12 2.3199	12.3523	13.8158
13 .8563	13.8158	0.0000

YEARS 14	MO PAYT 1.1845	AN CONST 14.22
# INT	PRIN	BALANCE
1 11.0923	3.1218	96.8782
2 10.7224	3.4917	93.3865
3 10.3087	3.9054	89.4811
4 9.8459	4.3682	85.1129
5 9.3284	4.8857	80.2272
6 8.7495	5.4646	74.7626
7 8.1020	6.1121	68.6505
8 7.3778	6.8363	61.8143
9 6.5678	7.6463	54.1680
10 5.6618	8.5523	45.6157
11 4.6485	9.5656	36.0501
12 3.5151	10.6990	25.3512
13 2.2474	11.9666	13.3845
14 .8296	13.3845	0.0000

YEARS 15	MO PAYT 1.1523	AN CONST 13.83
# INT	PRIN	BALANCE
1 11.1128	2.7153	97.2847
2 10.7911	3.0370	94.2476
3 10.4312	3.3969	90.8508
4 10.0288	3.7994	87.0514
5 9.5786	4.2495	82.8018
6 9.0751	4.7531	78.0488
7 8.5119	5.3162	72.7326
8 7.8820	5.9461	66.7865
9 7.1775	6.6507	60.1358
10 6.3895	7.4387	52.6971
11 5.5081	8.3200	44.3771
12 4.5223	9.3058	35.0713
13 3.4197	10.4085	24.6628
14 2.1864	11.6417	13.0211
15 .8070	13.0211	0.0000

YEARS 16	MO PAYT 1.1250	AN CONST 13.51
# INT	PRIN	BALANCE
1 11.1303	2.3701	97.6299
2 10.8494	2.6510	94.9789
3 10.5353	2.9651	92.0139
4 10.1840	3.3164	88.6975
5 9.7911	3.7093	84.9882
6 9.3516	4.1488	80.8393
7 8.8600	4.6404	76.1989
8 8.3102	5.1902	71.0087
9 7.6952	5.8052	65.2035
10 7.0074	6.4930	58.7105
11 6.2380	7.2624	51.4482
12 5.3775	8.1228	43.3253
13 4.4151	9.0853	34.2400
14 3.3386	10.1618	24.0783
15 2.1346	11.3658	12.7125
16 .7879	12.7125	0.0000

YEARS 17	MO PAYT 1.1017	AN CONST 13.23
# INT	PRIN	BALANCE
1 11.1452	2.0751	97.9249
2 10.8993	2.3209	95.6040
3 10.6243	2.5959	93.0080
4 10.3167	2.9035	90.1045
5 9.9727	3.2476	86.8569
6 9.5879	3.6323	83.2246
7 9.1575	4.0627	79.1619
8 8.6761	4.5441	74.6177
9 8.1377	5.0825	69.5352
10 7.5355	5.6847	63.8505
11 6.8620	6.3583	57.4922
12 6.1086	7.1117	50.3806
13 5.2660	7.9543	42.4263
14 4.3235	8.8968	33.5295
15 3.2693	9.9509	23.5786
16 2.0903	11.1299	12.4487
17 .7716	12.4487	0.0000

YEARS 18	MO PAYT 1.0816	AN CONST 12.98
# INT	PRIN	BALANCE
1 11.1580	1.8215	98.1785
2 10.9422	2.0373	96.1413
3 10.7008	2.2787	93.8626
4 10.4308	2.5487	91.3139
5 10.1288	2.8506	88.4633
6 9.7910	3.1884	85.2749
7 9.4133	3.5662	81.7087
8 8.9907	3.9887	77.7200
9 8.5181	4.4613	73.2586
10 7.9895	4.9899	68.2687
11 7.3983	5.5812	62.6875
12 6.7370	6.2425	56.4450
13 5.9973	6.9821	49.4629
14 5.1700	7.8094	41.6535
15 4.2447	8.7347	32.9188
16 3.2098	9.7696	23.1491
17 2.0522	10.9272	12.2219
18 .7575	12.2219	0.0000

YEARS 19	MO PAYT 1.0643	AN CONST 12.78
# INT	PRIN	BALANCE
1 11.1690	1.6024	98.3976
2 10.9792	1.7923	96.6053
3 10.7668	2.0046	94.6007
4 10.5293	2.2422	92.3585
5 10.2636	2.5078	89.8507
6 9.9665	2.8050	87.0457
7 9.6341	3.1373	83.9084
8 9.2624	3.5090	80.3994
9 8.8466	3.9248	76.4746
10 8.3816	4.3898	72.0847
11 7.8615	4.9100	67.1747
12 7.2797	5.4917	61.6830
13 6.6290	6.1424	55.5405
14 5.9012	6.8702	48.6703
15 5.0872	7.6843	40.9860
16 4.1767	8.5947	32.3913
17 3.1584	9.6131	22.7782
18 2.0193	10.7521	12.0261
19 .7454	12.0261	0.0000

YEARS 20	MO PAYT 1.0493	AN CONST 12.60
# INT	PRIN	BALANCE
1 11.1786	1.4124	98.5876
2 11.0113	1.5798	97.0078
3 10.8241	1.7670	95.2408
4 10.6147	1.9763	93.2645
5 10.3806	2.2105	91.0540
6 10.1187	2.4724	88.5816
7 9.8257	2.7653	85.8163
8 9.4981	3.0930	82.7233
9 9.1316	3.4595	79.2638
10 8.7217	3.8694	75.3944
11 8.2632	4.3278	71.0666
12 7.7504	4.8406	66.2259
13 7.1769	5.4142	60.8117
14 6.5354	6.0557	54.7561
15 5.8179	6.7732	47.9829
16 5.0153	7.5757	40.4071
17 4.1177	8.4733	31.9338
18 3.1138	9.4773	22.4565
19 1.9908	10.6002	11.8562
20 .7348	11.8562	0.0000

YEARS 21	MO PAYT 1.0362	AN CONST 12.44
# INT	PRIN	BALANCE
1 11.1870	1.2471	98.7529
2 11.0392	1.3948	97.3581
3 10.8740	1.5601	95.7980

#	INT	PRIN	BALANCE
4	10.6891	1.7449	94.0531
5	10.4824	1.9517	92.1014
6	10.2511	2.1829	89.9185
7	9.9925	2.4416	87.4769
8	9.7032	2.7309	84.7461
9	9.3796	3.0544	81.6917
10	9.0177	3.4163	78.2753
11	8.6129	3.8211	74.4542
12	8.1602	4.2739	70.1803
13	7.6538	4.7803	65.4001
14	7.0874	5.3467	60.0534
15	6.4539	5.9802	54.0732
16	5.7453	6.6887	47.3845
17	4.9528	7.4813	39.9032
18	4.0664	8.3677	31.5356
19	3.0749	9.3591	22.1764
20	1.9660	10.4681	11.7084
21	.7257	11.7084	0.0000

YEARS 22 — MO PAYT 1.0247 — AN CONST 12.30

#	INT	PRIN	BALANCE
1	11.1943	1.1027	98.8973
2	11.0636	1.2333	97.6640
3	10.9175	1.3794	96.2846
4	10.7541	1.5429	94.7417
5	10.5713	1.7257	93.0160
6	10.3668	1.9302	91.0859
7	10.1381	2.1589	88.9270
8	9.8823	2.4146	86.5124
9	9.5962	2.7007	83.8116
10	9.2762	3.0208	80.7909
11	8.9183	3.3787	77.4122
12	8.5180	3.7790	73.6332
13	8.0702	4.2267	69.4065
14	7.5694	4.7276	64.6789
15	7.0092	5.2877	59.3912
16	6.3827	5.9142	53.4770
17	5.6820	6.6150	46.8620
18	4.8982	7.3988	39.4632
19	4.0215	8.2754	31.1878
20	3.0410	9.2559	21.9319
21	1.9443	10.3526	11.5793
22	.7177	11.5793	0.0000

YEARS 23 — MO PAYT 1.0147 — AN CONST 12.18

#	INT	PRIN	BALANCE
1	11.2007	.9762	99.0238
2	11.0850	1.0919	97.9319
3	10.9556	1.2213	96.7106
4	10.8109	1.3660	95.3447
5	10.6491	1.5278	93.8168
6	10.4681	1.7088	92.1080
7	10.2656	1.9113	90.1967
8	10.0391	2.1378	88.0589
9	9.7858	2.3911	85.6678
10	9.5025	2.6744	82.9934
11	9.1856	2.9913	80.0022
12	8.8312	3.3457	76.6565
13	8.4348	3.7421	72.9144
14	7.9914	4.1855	68.7289
15	7.4955	4.6814	64.0475
16	6.9408	5.2361	58.8114
17	6.3204	5.8565	52.9549
18	5.6265	6.5504	46.4045
19	4.8504	7.3265	39.0780
20	3.9823	8.1946	30.8834
21	3.0113	9.1656	21.7178
22	1.9253	10.2516	11.4662
23	.7107	11.4662	0.0000

YEARS 24 — MO PAYT 1.0060 — AN CONST 12.08

#	INT	PRIN	BALANCE
1	11.2063	.8653	99.1347
2	11.1038	.9678	98.1670
3	10.9891	1.0824	97.0845
4	10.8608	1.2107	95.8738
5	10.7174	1.3541	94.5197
6	10.5569	1.5146	93.0051
7	10.3775	1.6941	91.3110
8	10.1768	1.8948	89.4162
9	9.9523	2.1193	87.2970
10	9.7012	2.3704	84.9266
11	9.4203	2.6512	82.2753
12	9.1062	2.9654	79.3100
13	8.7548	3.3167	75.9932
14	8.3618	3.7097	72.2835
15	7.9223	4.1493	68.1342
16	7.4306	4.6409	63.4933
17	6.8808	5.1908	58.3025
18	6.2657	5.8058	52.4967
19	5.5778	6.4937	46.0030
20	4.8084	7.2631	38.7399
21	3.9478	8.1237	30.6161
22	2.9853	9.0863	21.5299
23	1.9087	10.1629	11.3670
24	.7045	11.3670	0.0000

YEARS 25 — MO PAYT .9982 — AN CONST 11.98

#	INT	PRIN	BALANCE
1	11.2112	.7677	99.2323
2	11.1203	.8586	98.3737
3	11.0185	.9603	97.4134
4	10.9047	1.0741	96.3392
5	10.7775	1.2014	95.1378
6	10.6351	1.3438	93.7941
7	10.4759	1.5030	92.2911
8	10.2978	1.6811	90.6101
9	10.0986	1.8802	88.7298
10	9.8759	2.1030	86.6268
11	9.6267	2.3522	84.2746
12	9.3480	2.6309	81.6437
13	9.0363	2.9426	78.7011
14	8.6876	3.2913	75.4099
15	8.2976	3.6812	71.7286
16	7.8615	4.1174	67.6112
17	7.3736	4.6053	63.0059
18	6.8279	5.1509	57.8550
19	6.2176	5.7612	52.0937
20	5.5350	6.4439	45.6499
21	4.7715	7.2074	38.4425
22	3.9175	8.0614	30.3811
23	2.9624	9.0165	21.3646
24	1.8940	10.0848	11.2798
25	.6991	11.2798	0.0000

YEARS 26 — MO PAYT .9914 — AN CONST 11.90

#	INT	PRIN	BALANCE
1	11.2156	.6817	99.3183
2	11.1348	.7624	98.5559
3	11.0445	.8528	97.7032
4	10.9434	.9538	96.7494
5	10.8304	1.0668	95.6825
6	10.7040	1.1932	94.4893
7	10.5626	1.3346	93.1547
8	10.4045	1.4927	91.6620
9	10.2276	1.6696	89.9924
10	10.0298	1.8674	88.1250
11	9.8085	2.0887	86.0363
12	9.5611	2.3362	83.7002
13	9.2843	2.6130	81.0872
14	8.9747	2.9226	78.1647
15	8.6284	3.2688	74.8958
16	8.2411	3.6561	71.2397
17	7.8079	4.0894	67.1503
18	7.3233	4.5739	62.5764
19	6.7814	5.1158	57.4606
20	6.1752	5.7220	51.7386
21	5.4973	6.4000	45.3387
22	4.7390	7.1583	38.1804
23	3.8908	8.0064	30.1740
24	2.9422	8.9551	21.2190
25	1.8811	10.0161	11.2029
26	.6944	11.2029	0.0000

YEARS 27 — MO PAYT .9854 — AN CONST 11.83

#	INT	PRIN	BALANCE
1	11.2194	.6058	99.3942
2	11.1476	.6775	98.7167
3	11.0673	.7578	97.9589
4	10.9776	.8476	97.1113
5	10.8771	.9480	96.1633
6	10.7648	1.0604	95.1029
7	10.6392	1.1860	93.9170
8	10.4986	1.3265	92.5904
9	10.3415	1.4837	91.1068
10	10.1657	1.6595	89.4473
11	9.9690	1.8561	87.5912
12	9.7491	2.0760	85.5152
13	9.5031	2.3220	83.1932
14	9.2280	2.5971	80.5960
15	8.9203	2.9049	77.6912
16	8.5761	3.2490	74.4421
17	8.1911	3.6340	70.8081
18	7.7606	4.0646	66.7436
19	7.2790	4.5462	62.1974
20	6.7403	5.0848	57.1125
21	6.1378	5.6873	51.4252
22	5.4640	6.3612	45.0640
23	4.7103	7.1149	37.9492
24	3.8672	7.9579	29.9912
25	2.9243	8.9008	21.0904
26	1.8697	9.9554	11.1350
27	.6901	11.1350	0.0000

YEARS 28 — MO PAYT .9801 — AN CONST 11.77

#	INT	PRIN	BALANCE
1	11.2228	.5387	99.4613
2	11.1590	.6025	98.8588
3	11.0876	.6739	98.1850
4	11.0077	.7537	97.4312
5	10.9184	.8430	96.5882
6	10.8185	.9429	95.6453
7	10.7068	1.0546	94.5907
8	10.5819	1.1796	93.4111
9	10.4421	1.3194	92.0917
10	10.2858	1.4757	90.6160
11	10.1109	1.6505	88.9655
12	9.9153	1.8461	87.1194
13	9.6966	2.0648	85.0545
14	9.4520	2.3095	82.7450
15	9.1783	2.5831	80.1619
16	8.8722	2.8892	77.2727
17	8.5299	3.2315	74.0411
18	8.1470	3.6144	70.4267
19	7.7188	4.0427	66.3840
20	7.2398	4.5217	61.8623
21	6.7040	5.0574	56.8049
22	6.1048	5.6567	51.1482
23	5.4345	6.3269	44.8213
24	4.6849	7.0766	37.7447
25	3.8464	7.9150	29.8297
26	2.9086	8.8529	20.9768
27	1.8597	9.9018	11.0750
28	.6864	11.0750	0.0000

YEARS 29 — MO PAYT .9754 — AN CONST 11.71

#	INT	PRIN	BALANCE
1	11.2258	.4793	99.5207
2	11.1690	.5361	98.9846
3	11.1055	.5996	98.3850
4	11.0344	.6706	97.7144
5	10.9550	.7501	96.9643
6	10.8661	.8390	96.1253
7	10.7667	.9384	95.1869
8	10.6555	1.0496	94.1373
9	10.5311	1.1739	92.9633
10	10.3920	1.3130	91.6503
11	10.2365	1.4686	90.1817
12	10.0625	1.6426	88.5391
13	9.8678	1.8373	86.7018
14	9.6501	2.0549	84.6469
15	9.4067	2.2984	82.3484
16	9.1343	2.5708	79.7777
17	8.8297	2.8754	76.9023
18	8.4890	3.2160	73.6863
19	8.1080	3.5971	70.0892
20	7.6818	4.0233	66.0659
21	7.2051	4.5000	61.5658
22	6.6719	5.0332	56.5326
23	6.0755	5.6296	50.9031
24	5.4085	6.2966	44.6065
25	4.6624	7.0426	37.5638
26	3.8280	7.8771	29.6867
27	2.8947	8.8104	20.8763
28	1.8507	9.8543	11.0219
29	.6831	11.0219	0.0000

YEARS 30 — MO PAYT .9713 — AN CONST 11.66

#	INT	PRIN	BALANCE
1	11.2284	.4267	99.5733
2	11.1779	.4773	99.0961
3	11.1213	.5338	98.5623
4	11.0581	.5970	97.9652
5	10.9873	.6678	97.2974
6	10.9082	.7469	96.5505
7	10.8197	.8354	95.7151
8	10.7207	.9344	94.7807
9	10.6100	1.0451	93.7356
10	10.4862	1.1689	92.5667
11	10.3477	1.3074	91.2592
12	10.1928	1.4624	89.7969
13	10.0195	1.6356	88.1613
14	9.8257	1.8294	86.3318
15	9.6090	2.0462	84.2857
16	9.3665	2.2886	81.9971
17	9.0953	2.5598	79.4373
18	8.7920	2.8631	76.5742
19	8.4528	3.2023	73.3718
20	8.0734	3.5818	69.7901
21	7.6490	4.0061	65.7840
22	7.1743	4.4808	61.3031
23	6.6434	5.0117	56.2914
24	6.0496	5.6055	50.6859
25	5.3854	6.2697	44.4161
26	4.6425	7.0126	37.4035
27	3.8116	7.8435	29.5600
28	2.8823	8.7728	20.7872
29	1.8428	9.8123	10.9749
30	.6802	10.9749	0.0000

YEARS 2 — MO PAYT 4.6747 — AN CONST 56.10

#	INT	PRIN	BALANCE
1	8.9055	47.1912	52.8088
2	3.2879	52.8088	0.0000

YEARS 3 — MO PAYT 3.2881 — AN CONST 39.46

#	INT	PRIN	BALANCE
1	9.7949	29.6622	70.3378
2	6.2639	33.1932	37.1445
3	2.3126	37.1445	0.0000

YEARS 4 — MO PAYT 2.5991 — AN CONST 31.19

#	INT	PRIN	BALANCE
1	10.2368	20.9529	79.0471
2	7.7426	23.4471	55.6000
3	4.9515	26.2383	29.3617
4	1.8281	29.3617	0.0000

YEARS 5 — MO PAYT 2.1892 — AN CONST 26.28

#	INT	PRIN	BALANCE
1	10.4998	15.7710	84.2290
2	8.6224	17.6484	66.5806
3	6.5215	19.7493	46.8313
4	4.1706	22.1002	24.7310
5	1.5398	24.7310	0.0000

YEARS 6 — MO PAYT 1.9188 — AN CONST 23.03

#	INT	PRIN	BALANCE
1	10.6732	12.3525	87.6475
2	9.2028	13.8229	73.8246
3	7.5573	15.4684	58.3562
4	5.7160	17.3098	41.0465
5	3.6554	19.3703	21.6762
6	1.3496	21.6762	0.0000

YEARS 7 — MO PAYT 1.7281 — AN CONST 20.74

#	INT	PRIN	BALANCE
1	10.7956	9.9411	90.0589
2	9.6122	11.1245	78.9344
3	8.2879	12.4488	66.4856
4	6.8060	13.9307	52.5550
5	5.1477	15.5890	36.9660
6	3.2920	17.4447	19.5213
7	1.2154	19.5213	0.0000

YEARS 8 — MO PAYT 1.5871 — AN CONST 19.05

#	INT	PRIN	BALANCE
1	10.8860	8.1588	91.8412
2	9.9148	9.1300	82.7112
3	8.8280	10.2169	72.4943
4	7.6117	11.4331	61.0612
5	6.2507	12.7941	48.2671
6	4.7277	14.3171	33.9500
7	3.0234	16.0214	17.9286
8	1.1162	17.9286	0.0000

YEARS 9 — MO PAYT 1.4792 — AN CONST 17.76

#	INT	PRIN	BALANCE
1	10.9552	6.7954	93.2046
2	10.1463	7.6044	85.6002
3	9.2410	8.5096	77.0906
4	8.2281	9.5226	67.5680
5	7.0945	10.6562	56.9118
6	5.8260	11.9247	44.9871
7	4.4065	13.3442	31.6429
8	2.8180	14.9327	16.7103
9	1.0404	16.7103	0.0000

YEARS 10 — MO PAYT 1.3945 — AN CONST 16.74

#	INT	PRIN	BALANCE
1	11.0095	5.7249	94.2751
2	10.3280	6.4064	87.8687
3	9.5654	7.1690	80.6996
4	8.7120	8.0224	72.6772
5	7.7570	8.9774	63.6998
6	6.6883	10.0461	53.6537
7	5.4924	11.2420	42.4117
8	4.1542	12.5802	29.8314
9	2.6566	14.0778	15.7536
10	.9808	15.7536	0.0000

YEARS 11 — MO PAYT 1.3267 — AN CONST 15.92

#	INT	PRIN	BALANCE
1	11.0531	4.8669	95.1331
2	10.4737	5.4463	89.6868
3	9.8254	6.0946	83.5922
4	9.0999	6.8201	76.7720
5	8.2880	7.6320	69.1400
6	7.3795	8.5405	60.5995
7	6.3628	9.5572	51.0424
8	5.2251	10.6949	40.3475
9	3.9520	11.9680	28.3795
10	2.5273	13.3926	14.9869
11	.9331	14.9869	0.0000

YEARS 12 — MO PAYT 1.2714 — AN CONST 15.26

#	INT	PRIN	BALANCE
1	11.0885	4.1679	95.8321
2	10.5924	4.6641	91.1680
3	10.0372	5.2193	85.9487
4	9.4158	5.8406	80.1081
5	8.7206	6.5359	73.5722
6	7.9426	7.3139	66.2583
7	7.0719	8.1845	58.0738
8	6.0976	9.1588	48.9150
9	5.0073	10.2491	38.6659
10	3.7873	11.4692	27.1967
11	2.4220	12.8344	14.3623
12	.8942	14.3623	0.0000

YEARS 13 — MO PAYT 1.2257 — AN CONST 14.71

#	INT	PRIN	BALANCE
1	11.1178	3.5908	96.4092
2	10.6904	4.0183	92.3909
3	10.2120	4.4966	87.8943
4	9.6767	5.0319	82.8624
5	9.0777	5.6309	77.2316
6	8.4074	6.3012	70.9304
7	7.6574	7.0513	63.8791
8	6.8180	7.8907	55.9885
9	5.8787	8.8300	47.1585
10	4.8275	9.8811	37.2774
11	3.6513	11.0573	26.2201
12	2.3350	12.3736	13.8465
13	.8621	13.8465	0.0000

YEARS 14 — MO PAYT 1.1876 — AN CONST 14.26

#	INT	PRIN	BALANCE
1	11.1422	3.1091	96.8909
2	10.7721	3.4792	93.4118
3	10.3580	3.8933	89.5184
4	9.8945	4.3568	85.1616
5	9.3759	4.8754	80.2862
6	8.7955	5.4558	74.8304
7	8.1461	6.1053	68.7251
8	7.4193	6.8320	61.8931
9	6.6060	7.6453	54.2477
10	5.6959	8.5554	45.6923
11	4.6775	9.5739	36.1185
12	3.5378	10.7135	25.4049
13	2.2624	11.9889	13.4160
14	.8353	13.4160	0.0000

YEARS 15 — MO PAYT 1.1555 — AN CONST 13.87

#	INT	PRIN	BALANCE
1	11.1628	2.7032	97.2968
2	10.8410	3.0250	94.2717
3	10.4809	3.3851	90.8866
4	10.0780	3.7881	87.0985
5	9.6270	4.2390	82.8595
6	9.1224	4.7436	78.1159
7	8.5577	5.3083	72.8075
8	7.9258	5.9402	66.8673
9	7.2187	6.6474	60.2200
10	6.4274	7.4387	52.7813
11	5.5419	8.3242	44.4571
12	4.5510	9.3151	35.1421
13	3.4421	10.4239	24.7182
14	2.2013	11.6648	13.0534
15	.8127	13.0534	0.0000

YEARS 16 — MO PAYT 1.1283 — AN CONST 13.54

#	INT	PRIN	BALANCE
1	11.1803	2.3587	97.6413
2	10.8995	2.6395	95.0018
3	10.5853	2.9537	92.0482
4	10.2337	3.3053	88.7429
5	9.8403	3.6987	85.0441
6	9.4000	4.1390	80.9051
7	8.9073	4.6318	76.2733
8	8.3559	5.1831	71.0902
9	7.7389	5.8001	65.2901
10	7.0485	6.4906	58.7996
11	6.2758	7.2632	51.5364
12	5.4112	8.1278	43.4085
13	4.4437	9.0953	34.3132
14	3.3610	10.1781	24.1351
15	2.1494	11.3897	12.7455
16	.7935	12.7455	0.0000

YEARS 17 — MO PAYT 1.1050 — AN CONST 13.26

#	INT	PRIN	BALANCE
1	11.1953	2.0643	97.9357
2	10.9495	2.3100	95.6257
3	10.6745	2.5850	93.0407
4	10.3668	2.8927	90.1480
5	10.0225	3.2371	86.9110
6	9.6371	3.6224	83.2886
7	9.2059	4.0536	79.2350
8	8.7234	4.5361	74.6989
9	8.1834	5.0761	69.6227
10	7.5791	5.6804	63.9423
11	6.9030	6.3566	57.5858
12	6.1463	7.1133	50.4725
13	5.2995	7.9600	42.5125
14	4.3519	8.9076	33.6049
15	3.2916	9.9680	23.6369
16	2.1050	11.1545	12.4824
17	.7772	12.4824	0.0000

YEARS 18 — MO PAYT 1.0849 — AN CONST 13.02

#	INT	PRIN	BALANCE
1	11.2081	1.8113	98.1887
2	10.9925	2.0269	96.1618
3	10.7512	2.2682	93.8937
4	10.4812	2.5382	91.3555
5	10.1791	2.8403	88.5152
6	9.8409	3.1784	85.3368
7	9.4626	3.5568	81.7800
8	9.0392	3.9802	77.7998
9	8.5654	4.4540	73.3459
10	8.0352	4.9842	68.3617
11	7.4419	5.5775	62.7842
12	6.7779	6.2414	56.5427
13	6.0349	6.9844	49.5583
14	5.2035	7.8159	41.7425
15	4.2731	8.7463	32.9962
16	3.2320	9.7874	23.2088
17	2.0669	10.9525	12.2563
18	.7631	12.2563	0.0000

YEARS 19 — MO PAYT 1.0677 — AN CONST 12.82

#	INT	PRIN	BALANCE
1	11.2192	1.5928	98.4072
2	11.0296	1.7824	96.6248
3	10.8174	1.9946	94.6302
4	10.5800	2.2320	92.3981
5	10.3143	2.4977	89.9004
6	10.0169	2.7951	87.1053
7	9.6842	3.1278	83.9775
8	9.3119	3.5001	80.4774
9	8.8952	3.9168	76.5606
10	8.4290	4.3830	72.1776
11	7.9072	4.9048	67.2728
12	7.3233	5.4887	61.7841
13	6.6700	6.1420	55.6421
14	5.9388	6.8732	48.7689
15	5.1206	7.6914	41.0776
16	4.2050	8.6069	32.4706
17	3.1805	9.6315	22.8391
18	2.0339	10.7781	12.0611
19	.7509	12.0611	0.0000

YEARS 20 — MO PAYT 1.0527 — AN CONST 12.64

#	INT	PRIN	BALANCE
1	11.2288	1.4034	98.5966
2	11.0617	1.5705	97.0261
3	10.8748	1.7574	95.2687
4	10.6656	1.9666	93.3021
5	10.4315	2.2007	91.1014
6	10.1695	2.4627	88.6387
7	9.8763	2.7558	85.8829
8	9.5483	3.0839	82.7990
9	9.1812	3.4510	79.3480
10	8.7704	3.8618	75.4862
11	8.3107	4.3215	71.1647
12	7.7962	4.8360	66.3287
13	7.2206	5.4116	60.9171
14	6.5764	6.0558	54.8612
15	5.8555	6.7767	48.0845
16	5.0488	7.5834	40.5011
17	4.1460	8.4862	32.0149
18	3.1358	9.4963	22.5186
19	2.0054	10.6268	11.8918
20	.7404	11.8918	0.0000

YEARS 21 — MO PAYT 1.0396 — AN CONST 12.48

#	INT	PRIN	BALANCE
1	11.2372	1.2386	98.7614
2	11.0897	1.3860	97.3754
3	10.9247	1.5510	95.8244

#	INT	PRIN	BALANCE
4	10.7401	1.7356	94.0888
5	10.5335	1.9422	92.1465
6	10.3023	2.1735	89.9731
7	10.0435	2.4322	87.5409
8	9.7540	2.7217	84.8192
9	9.4300	3.0457	81.7735
10	9.0675	3.4083	78.3652
11	8.6617	3.8140	74.5512
12	8.2077	4.2680	70.2832
13	7.6997	4.7761	65.5072
14	7.1311	5.3446	60.1626
15	6.4949	5.9808	54.1817
16	5.7829	6.6928	47.4890
17	4.9862	7.4895	39.9995
18	4.0947	8.3810	31.6184
19	3.0970	9.3787	22.2397
20	1.9806	10.4952	11.7445
21	.7312	11.7445	0.0000

YEARS 22	MO PAYT 1.0283	AN CONST 12.34	
#	INT	PRIN	BALANCE
1	11.2445	1.0947	98.9053
2	11.1141	1.1250	97.6803
3	10.9683	1.3708	96.3094
4	10.8051	1.5340	94.7754
5	10.6225	1.7166	93.0588
6	10.4182	1.9210	91.1378
7	10.1895	2.1497	88.9881
8	9.9336	2.4056	86.5826
9	9.6472	2.6919	83.8907
10	9.3268	3.0124	80.8783
11	8.9682	3.3710	77.5073
12	8.5669	3.7722	73.7351
13	8.1179	4.2213	69.5138
14	7.6154	4.7238	64.7901
15	7.0531	5.2861	59.5040
16	6.4238	5.9154	53.5886
17	5.7196	6.6195	46.9691
18	4.9316	7.4075	39.5616
19	4.0499	8.2893	31.2723
20	3.0631	9.2761	21.9962
21	1.9589	10.3803	11.6159
22	.7232	11.6159	0.0000

YEARS 23	MO PAYT 1.0183	AN CONST 12.22	
#	INT	PRIN	BALANCE
1	11.2508	.9688	99.0312
2	11.1355	1.0841	97.9471
3	11.0065	1.2131	96.7340
4	10.8621	1.3576	95.3764
5	10.7005	1.5192	93.8573
6	10.5196	1.7000	92.1572
7	10.3172	1.9024	90.2549
8	10.0908	2.1288	88.1260
9	9.8374	2.3823	85.7438
10	9.5538	2.6658	83.0779
11	9.2364	2.9832	80.0948
12	8.8813	3.3383	76.7565
13	8.4839	3.7357	73.0208
14	8.0392	4.1804	68.8404
15	7.5416	4.6780	64.1624
16	6.9847	5.2349	58.9275
17	6.3616	5.8580	53.0695
18	5.6642	6.5554	46.5141
19	4.8839	7.3357	39.1783
20	4.0106	8.2090	30.9693
21	3.0334	9.1862	21.7831
22	1.9399	10.2797	11.5034
23	.7162	11.5034	0.0000

YEARS 24	MO PAYT 1.0096	AN CONST 12.12	
#	INT	PRIN	BALANCE
1	11.2565	.8583	99.1417
2	11.1543	.9605	98.1813
3	11.0399	1.0748	97.1065
4	10.9120	1.2027	95.9037
5	10.7688	1.3459	94.5578
6	10.6086	1.5061	93.0517
7	10.4293	1.6854	91.3663
8	10.2287	1.8860	89.4802
9	10.0042	2.1106	87.3697
10	9.7529	2.3618	85.0079
11	9.4718	2.6430	82.3649
12	9.1572	2.9576	79.4073
13	8.8051	3.3096	76.0977
14	8.4111	3.7036	72.3941
15	7.9702	4.1445	68.2496
16	7.4769	4.6379	63.6117
17	6.9248	5.1900	58.4217
18	6.3070	5.8078	52.6140
19	5.6156	6.4991	46.1148
20	4.8420	7.2728	38.8421
21	3.9762	8.1385	30.7035
22	3.0074	9.1073	21.5962
23	1.9233	10.1915	11.4047
24	.7101	11.4047	0.0000

YEARS 25	MO PAYT 1.0019	AN CONST 12.03	
#	INT	PRIN	BALANCE
1	11.2614	.7611	99.2389
2	11.1708	.8518	98.3871
3	11.0694	.9531	97.4339
4	10.9559	1.0666	96.3673
5	10.8289	1.1936	95.1738
6	10.6869	1.3357	93.8381
7	10.5279	1.4947	92.3434
8	10.3499	1.6726	90.6708
9	10.1508	1.8717	88.7991
10	9.9280	2.0945	86.7046
11	9.6787	2.3438	84.3608
12	9.3997	2.6228	81.7380
13	9.0875	2.9351	78.8029
14	8.7381	3.2845	75.5185
15	8.3471	3.6754	71.8430
16	7.9096	4.1130	67.7301
17	7.4200	4.6026	63.1275
18	6.8721	5.1505	57.9771
19	6.2590	5.7636	52.2135
20	5.5729	6.4497	45.7638
21	4.8051	7.2174	38.5464
22	3.9459	8.0766	30.4698
23	2.9845	9.0380	21.4318
24	1.9086	10.1139	11.3179
25	.7046	11.3179	0.0000

YEARS 26	MO PAYT .9951	AN CONST 11.95	
#	INT	PRIN	BALANCE
1	11.2657	.6756	99.3244
2	11.1853	.7560	98.5684
3	11.0953	.8460	97.7224
4	10.9946	.9467	96.7757
5	10.8819	1.0594	95.7163
6	10.7558	1.1855	94.5308
7	10.6147	1.3266	93.2041
8	10.4567	1.4846	91.7196
9	10.2800	1.6613	90.0583
10	10.0823	1.8590	88.1992
11	9.8610	2.0803	86.1189
12	9.6133	2.3280	83.7909
13	9.3362	2.6051	81.1858
14	9.0261	2.9152	78.2705
15	8.6790	3.2623	75.0083
16	8.2907	3.6506	71.3577
17	7.8561	4.0852	67.2725
18	7.3698	4.5715	62.7010
19	6.8256	5.1157	57.5854
20	6.2167	5.7246	51.8608
21	5.5352	6.4061	45.4547
22	4.7726	7.1687	38.2860
23	3.9193	8.0220	30.2640
24	2.9643	8.9770	21.2870
25	1.8957	10.0456	11.2414
26	.6999	11.2414	0.0000

YEARS 27	MO PAYT .9891	AN CONST 11.87	
#	INT	PRIN	BALANCE
1	11.2696	.6001	99.3999
2	11.1981	.6715	98.7284
3	11.1182	.7515	97.9769
4	11.0287	.8409	97.1360
5	10.9286	.9410	96.1950
6	10.8166	1.0530	95.1419
7	10.6912	1.1784	93.9635
8	10.5510	1.3187	92.6448
9	10.3940	1.4757	91.1692
10	10.2183	1.6513	89.5178
11	10.0218	1.8479	87.6700
12	9.8018	2.0679	85.6021
13	9.5556	2.3140	83.2881
14	9.2802	2.5895	80.6986
15	8.9719	2.8977	77.8008
16	8.6270	3.2427	74.5582
17	8.2410	3.6287	70.9295
18	7.8090	4.0607	66.8688
19	7.3256	4.5440	62.3248
20	6.7847	5.0850	57.2398
21	6.1794	5.6903	51.5495
22	5.5020	6.3676	45.1819
23	4.7440	7.1256	38.0562
24	3.8958	7.9739	30.0824
25	2.9465	8.9231	21.1593
26	1.8843	9.9853	11.1740
27	.6957	11.1740	0.0000

YEARS 28	MO PAYT .9839	AN CONST 11.81	
#	INT	PRIN	BALANCE
1	11.2729	.5334	99.4666
2	11.2094	.5969	98.8697
3	11.1384	.6679	98.2018
4	11.0589	.7475	97.4543
5	10.9699	.8364	96.6179
6	10.8703	.9360	95.6819
7	10.7589	1.0474	94.6344
8	10.6342	1.1721	93.4623
9	10.4947	1.3116	92.1507
10	10.3385	1.4678	90.6829
11	10.1638	1.6425	89.0404
12	9.9683	1.8380	87.2023
13	9.7495	2.0568	85.1455
14	9.5047	2.3017	82.8438
15	9.2307	2.5757	80.2681
16	8.9241	2.8823	77.3859
17	8.5809	3.2254	74.1605
18	8.1970	3.6093	70.5511
19	7.7673	4.0390	66.5121
20	7.2865	4.5198	61.9923
21	6.7485	5.0578	56.9345
22	6.1464	5.6599	51.2746
23	5.4727	6.3337	44.9409
24	4.7187	7.0876	37.8533
25	3.8750	7.9314	29.9219
26	2.9308	8.8755	21.0464
27	1.8743	9.9320	11.1144
28	.6920	11.1144	0.0000

YEARS 29	MO PAYT .9792	AN CONST 11.76	
#	INT	PRIN	BALANCE
1	11.2759	.4744	99.5256
2	11.2195	.5309	98.9947
3	11.1563	.5941	98.4007
4	11.0855	.6648	97.7359
5	11.0064	.7439	96.9920
6	10.9179	.8325	96.1595
7	10.8188	.9316	95.2279
8	10.7079	1.0425	94.1855
9	10.5838	1.1666	93.0189
10	10.4449	1.3054	91.7135
11	10.2895	1.4608	90.2527
12	10.1156	1.6347	88.6180
13	9.9210	1.8293	86.7886
14	9.7032	2.0471	84.7416
15	9.4596	2.2908	82.4508
16	9.1869	2.5635	79.8873
17	8.8817	2.8686	77.0187
18	8.5402	3.2101	73.8087
19	8.1581	3.5922	70.2164
20	7.7305	4.0198	66.1966
21	7.2520	4.4984	61.6982
22	6.7165	5.0338	56.6644
23	6.1173	5.6331	51.0313
24	5.4467	6.3036	44.7277
25	4.6963	7.0540	37.6737
26	3.8566	7.8937	29.7800
27	2.9169	8.8334	20.9466
28	1.8654	9.8849	11.0616
29	.6887	11.0616	0.0000

YEARS 30	MO PAYT .9751	AN CONST 11.71	
#	INT	PRIN	BALANCE
1	11.2786	.4221	99.5779
2	11.2283	.4724	99.1055
3	11.1721	.5286	98.5768
4	11.1092	.5916	97.9853
5	11.0387	.6620	97.3233
6	10.9599	.7408	96.5825
7	10.8718	.8290	95.7536
8	10.7731	.9276	94.8259
9	10.6627	1.0381	93.7879
10	10.5391	1.1616	92.6262
11	10.4008	1.2999	91.3263
12	10.2461	1.4547	89.8717
13	10.0729	1.6278	88.2439
14	9.8791	1.8216	86.4223
15	9.6623	2.0384	84.3838
16	9.4196	2.2811	82.1027
17	9.1481	2.5526	79.5501
18	8.8442	2.8565	76.6936
19	8.5042	3.1965	73.4971
20	8.1237	3.5771	69.9200
21	7.6979	4.0029	65.9172
22	7.2214	4.4794	61.4378
23	6.6881	5.0126	56.4252
24	6.0914	5.6093	50.8159
25	5.4237	6.2770	44.5389
26	4.6765	7.0242	37.5146
27	3.8403	7.8604	29.6542
28	2.9046	8.7961	20.8581
29	1.8575	9.8432	11.0149
30	.6858	11.0149	0.0000

	YEARS 2	MO PAYT 4.6782	AN CONST 56.14
#	INT	PRIN	BALANCE
1	8.9659	47.1727	52.8273
2	3.3112	52.8273	0.0000

	YEARS 3	MO PAYT 3.2917	AN CONST 39.50
#	INT	PRIN	BALANCE
1	9.8614	29.6385	70.3615
2	6.3085	33.1914	37.1701
3	2.3298	37.1701	0.0000

	YEARS 4	MO PAYT 2.6028	AN CONST 31.24
#	INT	PRIN	BALANCE
1	10.3062	20.9274	79.0726
2	7.7976	23.4360	55.6367
3	4.9883	26.2453	29.3914
4	1.8423	29.3914	0.0000

	YEARS 5	MO PAYT 2.1930	AN CONST 26.32
#	INT	PRIN	BALANCE
1	10.5709	15.7450	84.2550
2	8.6835	17.6324	66.6227
3	6.5699	19.7460	46.8767
4	4.2029	22.1130	24.7637
5	1.5522	24.7637	0.0000

	YEARS 6	MO PAYT 1.9227	AN CONST 23.08
#	INT	PRIN	BALANCE
1	10.7455	12.3266	87.6734
2	9.2679	13.8042	73.8693
3	7.6131	15.4589	58.4104
4	5.7601	17.3120	41.0984
5	3.6848	19.3872	21.7112
6	1.3609	21.7112	0.0000

	YEARS 7	MO PAYT 1.7320	AN CONST 20.79
#	INT	PRIN	BALANCE
1	10.8686	9.9157	90.0843
2	9.6800	11.1043	78.9800
3	8.3489	12.4354	66.5446
4	6.8582	13.9260	52.6186
5	5.1889	15.5954	37.0232
6	3.3195	17.4648	19.5584
7	1.2259	19.5584	0.0000

	YEARS 8	MO PAYT 1.5911	AN CONST 19.10
#	INT	PRIN	BALANCE
1	10.9596	8.1341	91.8659
2	9.9845	9.1091	82.7568
3	8.8926	10.2011	72.5557
4	7.6698	11.4239	61.1318
5	6.3004	12.7933	48.3385
6	4.7668	14.3268	34.0117
7	3.0495	16.0442	17.9675
8	1.1262	17.9675	0.0000

	YEARS 9	MO PAYT 1.4834	AN CONST 17.81
#	INT	PRIN	BALANCE
1	11.0292	6.7716	93.2284
2	10.2175	7.5833	85.6452
3	9.3084	8.4923	77.1529
4	8.2904	9.5103	67.6426
5	7.1504	10.6503	56.9923
6	5.8738	11.9270	45.0653
7	4.4440	13.3567	31.7086
8	2.8430	14.9578	16.7508
9	1.0499	16.7508	0.0000

	YEARS 10	MO PAYT 1.3988	AN CONST 16.79
#	INT	PRIN	BALANCE
1	11.0838	5.7019	94.2981
2	10.4003	6.3855	87.9126
3	9.6349	7.1509	80.7617
4	8.7777	8.0081	72.7536
5	7.8177	8.9680	63.7856
6	6.7427	10.0430	53.7426
7	5.5388	11.2469	42.4957
8	4.1907	12.5951	29.9006
9	2.6809	14.1049	15.7957
10	.9901	15.7957	0.0000

	YEARS 11	MO PAYT 1.3310	AN CONST 15.98
#	INT	PRIN	BALANCE
1	11.1276	4.8449	95.1551
2	10.5468	5.4257	89.7294
3	9.8964	6.0761	83.6533
4	9.1681	6.8044	76.8489
5	8.3524	7.6201	69.2288
6	7.4390	8.5335	60.6953
7	6.4160	9.5565	51.1388
8	5.2705	10.7020	40.4368
9	3.9876	11.9849	28.4519
10	2.5510	13.4215	15.0304
11	.9421	15.0304	0.0000

	YEARS 12	MO PAYT 1.2758	AN CONST 15.32
#	INT	PRIN	BALANCE
1	11.1632	4.1469	95.8531
2	10.6661	4.6440	91.2091
3	10.1094	5.2007	86.0084
4	9.4860	5.8241	80.1843
5	8.7879	6.5223	73.6620
6	8.0060	7.3041	66.3579
7	7.1305	8.1796	58.1783
8	6.1500	9.1602	49.0181
9	5.0519	10.2582	38.7599
10	3.8223	11.4879	27.2720
11	2.4452	12.8649	14.4071
12	.9030	14.4071	0.0000

	YEARS 13	MO PAYT 1.2303	AN CONST 14.77
#	INT	PRIN	BALANCE
1	11.1926	3.5708	96.4292
2	10.7646	3.9988	92.4304
3	10.2853	4.4782	87.9522
4	9.7484	5.0150	82.9372
5	9.1473	5.6161	77.3211
6	8.4741	6.2894	71.0317
7	7.7202	7.0433	63.9884
8	6.8759	7.8876	56.1008
9	5.9304	8.8331	47.2678
10	4.8715	9.8919	37.3759
11	3.6858	11.0777	26.2982
12	2.3579	12.4056	13.8926
13	.8708	13.8926	0.0000

	YEARS 14	MO PAYT 1.1923	AN CONST 14.31
#	INT	PRIN	BALANCE
1	11.2172	3.0900	96.9100
2	10.8468	3.4605	93.4495
3	10.4320	3.8753	89.5742
4	9.9674	4.3398	85.2344
5	9.4472	4.8600	80.3744
6	8.8646	5.4426	74.9318
7	8.2122	6.0950	68.8368
8	7.4816	6.8256	62.0111
9	6.6634	7.6438	54.3673
10	5.7471	8.5601	45.8072
11	4.7210	9.5862	36.2209
12	3.5719	10.7354	25.4856
13	2.2850	12.0222	13.4634
14	.8439	13.4634	0.0000

	YEARS 15	MO PAYT 1.1603	AN CONST 13.93
#	INT	PRIN	BALANCE
1	11.2379	2.6852	97.3148
2	10.9160	3.0071	94.3077
3	10.5555	3.3675	90.9402
4	10.1519	3.7712	87.1690
5	9.6998	4.2233	82.9457
6	9.1935	4.7295	78.2162
7	8.6266	5.2965	72.9197
8	7.9917	5.9314	66.9884
9	7.2807	6.6424	60.3460
10	6.4845	7.4386	52.9074
11	5.5928	8.3303	44.5772
12	4.5942	9.3288	35.2483
13	3.4760	10.4471	24.8012
14	2.2237	11.6994	13.1018
15	.8212	13.1018	0.0000

	YEARS 16	MO PAYT 1.1331	AN CONST 13.60
#	INT	PRIN	BALANCE
1	11.2554	2.3416	97.6584
2	10.9747	2.6223	95.0361
3	10.6604	2.9367	92.0994
4	10.3084	3.2887	88.8107
5	9.9141	3.6829	85.1278
6	9.4727	4.1244	81.0034
7	8.9783	4.6188	76.3847
8	8.4246	5.1724	71.2122
9	7.8046	5.7925	65.4198
10	7.1102	6.4868	58.9329
11	6.3326	7.2644	51.6685
12	5.4618	8.1352	43.5333
13	4.4867	9.1104	34.4230
14	3.3946	10.2025	24.2205
15	2.1716	11.4255	12.7950
16	.8020	12.7950	0.0000

	YEARS 17	MO PAYT 1.1099	AN CONST 13.32
#	INT	PRIN	BALANCE
1	11.2704	2.0481	97.9519
2	11.0249	2.2937	95.6582
3	10.7499	2.5686	93.0896
4	10.4420	2.8765	90.2131
5	10.0972	3.2213	86.9917
6	9.7111	3.6075	83.3843
7	9.2786	4.0399	79.3444
8	8.7944	4.5242	74.8202
9	8.2521	5.0665	69.7537
10	7.6447	5.6738	64.0799
11	6.9646	6.3540	57.7259
12	6.2029	7.1156	50.6103
13	5.3500	7.9686	42.6417
14	4.3948	8.9238	33.7179
15	3.3250	9.9935	23.7244
16	2.1271	11.1914	12.5330
17	.7856	12.5330	0.0000

	YEARS 18	MO PAYT 1.0899	AN CONST 13.08
#	INT	PRIN	BALANCE
1	11.2833	1.7961	98.2039
2	11.0680	2.0114	96.1926
3	10.8269	2.2525	93.9401
4	10.5569	2.5225	91.4176
5	10.2545	2.8248	88.5928
6	9.9159	3.1635	85.4293
7	9.5367	3.5427	81.8866
8	9.1120	3.9673	77.9193
9	8.6364	4.4429	73.4764
10	8.1038	4.9755	68.5009
11	7.5074	5.5719	62.9290
12	6.8395	6.2398	56.6891
13	6.0915	6.9878	49.7013
14	5.2539	7.8255	41.8758
15	4.3158	8.7635	33.1123
16	3.2653	9.8140	23.2983
17	2.0889	10.9904	12.3079
18	.7715	12.3079	0.0000

	YEARS 19	MO PAYT 1.0727	AN CONST 12.88
#	INT	PRIN	BALANCE
1	11.2944	1.5785	98.4215
2	11.1052	1.7677	96.6538
3	10.8933	1.9796	94.6742
4	10.6560	2.2169	92.4573
5	10.3902	2.4827	89.9746
6	10.0926	2.7803	87.1944
7	9.7593	3.1135	84.0808
8	9.3861	3.4868	80.5941
9	8.9682	3.9047	76.6893
10	8.5001	4.3728	72.3166
11	7.9759	4.8970	67.4196
12	7.3889	5.4840	61.9356
13	6.7315	6.1413	55.7943
14	5.9954	6.8775	48.9168
15	5.1709	7.7019	41.2148
16	4.2477	8.6252	32.5897
17	3.2138	9.6591	22.9306
18	2.0559	10.8170	12.1136
19	.7593	12.1136	0.0000

	YEARS 20	MO PAYT 1.0578	AN CONST 12.70
#	INT	PRIN	BALANCE
1	11.3040	1.3899	98.6101
2	11.1374	1.5566	97.0535
3	10.9508	1.7431	95.3104
4	10.7419	1.9521	93.3583
5	10.5079	2.1861	91.1722
6	10.2458	2.4481	88.7240
7	9.9523	2.7416	85.9824
8	9.6237	3.0703	82.9121
9	9.2557	3.4383	79.4739
10	8.8435	3.8504	75.6234
11	8.3819	4.3120	71.3114
12	7.8651	4.8289	66.4825
13	7.2862	5.4077	61.0748
14	6.6380	6.0560	55.0188
15	5.9120	6.7819	48.2369
16	5.0991	7.5949	40.6420
17	4.1887	8.5053	32.1367
18	3.1691	9.5248	22.6118
19	2.0274	10.6666	11.9452
20	.7487	11.9452	0.0000

	YEARS 21	MO PAYT 1.0449	AN CONST 12.54
#	INT	PRIN	BALANCE
1	11.3124	1.2259	98.7741
2	11.1654	1.3729	97.4012
3	11.0009	1.5375	95.8637

#	INT	PRIN	BALANCE
4	10.8166	1.7218	94.1419
5	10.6102	1.9282	92.2137
6	10.3790	2.1593	90.0544
7	10.1202	2.4181	87.6363
8	9.8303	2.7080	84.9283
9	9.5057	3.0326	81.8957
10	9.1422	3.3961	78.4996
11	8.7351	3.8032	74.6963
12	8.2792	4.2591	70.4372
13	7.7686	4.7697	65.6675
14	7.1969	5.3414	60.3260
15	6.5566	5.9817	54.3443
16	5.8396	6.6988	47.6455
17	5.0366	7.5018	40.1437
18	4.1373	8.4010	31.7427
19	3.1303	9.4081	22.3346
20	2.0025	10.5358	11.7988
21	.7395	11.7988	0.0000

YEARS 22	MO PAYT 1.0335	AN CONST 12.41	
#	INT	PRIN	BALANCE
1	11.3197	1.0829	98.9171
2	11.1899	1.2127	97.7045
3	11.0445	1.3580	96.3464
4	10.8817	1.5208	94.8256
5	10.6994	1.7031	93.1225
6	10.4953	1.9073	91.2152
7	10.2666	2.1359	89.0793
8	10.0106	2.3920	86.6873
9	9.7239	2.6787	84.0086
10	9.4028	2.9998	81.0089
11	9.0432	3.3594	77.6495
12	8.6405	3.7621	73.8874
13	8.1895	4.2130	69.6744
14	7.6845	4.7180	64.9564
15	7.1190	5.2836	59.6728
16	6.4856	5.9170	53.7558
17	5.7763	6.6262	47.1296
18	4.9820	7.4205	39.7090
19	4.0925	8.3101	31.3990
20	3.0964	9.3062	22.0928
21	1.9808	10.4217	11.6710
22	.7315	11.6710	0.0000

YEARS 23	MO PAYT 1.0236	AN CONST 12.29	
#	INT	PRIN	BALANCE
1	11.3261	.9577	99.0423
2	11.2113	1.0725	97.9698
3	11.0827	1.2011	96.7688
4	10.9388	1.3450	95.4237
5	10.7775	1.5063	93.9175
6	10.5970	1.6868	92.2307
7	10.3948	1.8890	90.3416
8	10.1683	2.1155	88.2262
9	9.9147	2.3690	85.8571
10	9.6308	2.6530	83.2041
11	9.3127	2.9710	80.2331
12	8.9566	3.3272	76.9059
13	8.5578	3.7260	73.1798
14	8.1111	4.1727	69.0072
15	7.6109	4.6729	64.3343
16	7.0508	5.2330	59.1013
17	6.4235	5.8603	53.2410
18	5.7210	6.5628	46.6782
19	4.9343	7.3495	39.3287
20	4.0533	8.2305	31.0983
21	3.0667	9.2171	21.8812
22	1.9618	10.3219	11.5592
23	.7245	11.5592	0.0000

YEARS 24	MO PAYT 1.0150	AN CONST 12.18	
#	INT	PRIN	BALANCE
1	11.3317	.8479	99.1521
2	11.2301	.9496	98.2025
3	11.1162	1.0634	97.1391
4	10.9888	1.1909	95.9482
5	10.8460	1.3336	94.6146
6	10.6861	1.4935	93.1211
7	10.5071	1.6725	91.4486
8	10.3066	1.8730	89.5756
9	10.0821	2.0975	87.4781
10	9.8307	2.3490	85.1291
11	9.5491	2.6305	82.4986
12	9.2338	2.9459	79.5527
13	8.8806	3.2990	76.2538
14	8.4852	3.6944	72.5593
15	8.0423	4.1373	68.4220
16	7.5464	4.6332	63.7888
17	6.9910	5.1886	58.6001
18	6.3690	5.8106	52.7895
19	5.6725	6.5071	46.2824
20	4.8925	7.2872	38.9953
21	4.0189	8.1607	30.8346
22	3.0407	9.1389	21.6957
23	1.9452	10.2344	11.4612
24	.7184	11.4612	0.0000

YEARS 25	MO PAYT 1.0073	AN CONST 12.09	
#	INT	PRIN	BALANCE
1	11.3366	.7515	99.2485
2	11.2465	.8416	98.4070
3	11.1457	.9424	97.4645
4	11.0327	1.0554	96.4091
5	10.9062	1.1819	95.2272
6	10.7645	1.3236	93.9036
7	10.6058	1.4823	92.4213
8	10.4282	1.6599	90.7614
9	10.2292	1.8589	88.9025
10	10.0063	2.0818	86.8207
11	9.7568	2.3313	84.4894
12	9.4773	2.6108	81.8786
13	9.1644	2.9237	78.9549
14	8.8139	3.2742	75.6807
15	8.4214	3.6667	72.0141
16	7.9819	4.1062	67.9078
17	7.4897	4.5984	63.3094
18	6.9385	5.1496	58.1598
19	6.3212	5.7669	52.3928
20	5.6299	6.4582	45.9346
21	4.8557	7.2324	38.7022
22	3.9887	8.0994	30.6029
23	3.0179	9.0702	21.5326
24	1.9306	10.1575	11.3751
25	.7130	11.3751	0.0000

YEARS 26	MO PAYT 1.0006	AN CONST 12.01	
#	INT	PRIN	BALANCE
1	11.3410	.6666	99.3334
2	11.2611	.7465	98.5870
3	11.1716	.8359	97.7510
4	11.0714	.9362	96.8149
5	10.9592	1.0484	95.7665
6	10.8335	1.1740	94.5924
7	10.6927	1.3148	93.2777
8	10.5351	1.4724	91.8053
9	10.3586	1.6489	90.1564
10	10.1610	1.8465	88.3099
11	9.9396	2.0679	86.2420
12	9.6918	2.3158	83.9262
13	9.4142	2.5934	81.3329
14	9.1033	2.9042	78.4286
15	8.7552	3.2524	75.1763
16	8.3653	3.6422	71.5340
17	7.9287	4.0788	67.4552
18	7.4398	4.5678	62.8874
19	6.8922	5.1153	57.7721
20	6.2790	5.7285	52.0436
21	5.5923	6.4152	45.6284
22	4.8233	7.1842	38.4442
23	3.9622	8.0454	30.3989
24	2.9977	9.0098	21.3891
25	1.9177	10.0898	11.2993
26	.7082	11.2993	0.0000

YEARS 27	MO PAYT .9947	AN CONST 11.94	
#	INT	PRIN	BALANCE
1	11.3448	.5917	99.4083
2	11.2739	.6626	98.7457
3	11.1944	.7421	98.0036
4	11.1055	.8310	97.1726
5	11.0059	.9306	96.2420
6	10.8943	1.0422	95.1998
7	10.7694	1.1671	94.0327
8	10.6295	1.3070	92.7257
9	10.4728	1.4637	91.2621
10	10.2974	1.6391	89.6230
11	10.1009	1.8356	87.7873
12	9.8808	2.0556	85.7317
13	9.6344	2.3021	83.4296
14	9.3585	2.5780	80.8516
15	9.0494	2.8870	77.9646
16	8.7034	3.2331	74.7315
17	8.3158	3.6207	71.1108
18	7.8818	4.0547	67.0561
19	7.3957	4.5407	62.5153
20	6.8514	5.0851	57.4303
21	6.2419	5.6946	51.7357
22	5.5592	6.3772	45.3584
23	4.7948	7.1417	38.2168
24	3.9387	7.9978	30.2190
25	2.9800	8.9565	21.2625
26	1.9064	10.0301	11.2324
27	.7040	11.2324	0.0000

YEARS 28	MO PAYT .9895	AN CONST 11.88	
#	INT	PRIN	BALANCE
1	11.3482	.5256	99.4744
2	11.2852	.5886	98.8858
3	11.2146	.6591	98.2267
4	11.1356	.7382	97.4885
5	11.0471	.8266	96.6619
6	10.9480	.9257	95.7362
7	10.8370	1.0367	94.6995
8	10.7128	1.1610	93.5385
9	10.5736	1.3001	92.2384
10	10.4178	1.4560	90.7824
11	10.2432	1.6305	89.1519
12	10.0478	1.8260	87.3259
13	9.8289	2.0448	85.2811
14	9.5838	2.2900	82.9911
15	9.3093	2.5645	80.4267
16	9.0019	2.8719	77.5548
17	8.6576	3.2161	74.3387
18	8.2721	3.6017	70.7370
19	7.8404	4.0334	66.7036
20	7.3569	4.5169	62.1868
21	6.8154	5.0583	57.1284
22	6.2091	5.6647	51.4638
23	5.5300	6.3437	45.1200
24	4.7696	7.1041	38.0159
25	3.9180	7.9557	30.0602
26	2.9643	8.9094	21.1508
27	1.8964	9.9774	11.1734
28	.7003	11.1734	0.0000

YEARS 29	MO PAYT .9849	AN CONST 11.82	
#	INT	PRIN	BALANCE
1	11.3511	.4671	99.5329
2	11.2951	.5231	99.0097
3	11.2324	.5858	98.4239
4	11.1622	.6561	97.7678
5	11.0836	.7347	97.0331
6	10.9955	.8228	96.2104
7	10.8969	.9214	95.2890
8	10.7864	1.0319	94.2571
9	10.6627	1.1555	93.1016
10	10.5242	1.2941	91.8075
11	10.3691	1.4492	90.3583
12	10.1954	1.6229	88.7355
13	10.0008	1.8174	86.9180
14	9.7830	2.0353	84.8827
15	9.5390	2.2793	82.6035
16	9.2658	2.5525	80.0510
17	8.9598	2.8585	77.1925
18	8.6172	3.2011	73.9914
19	8.2334	3.5848	70.4066
20	7.8037	4.0145	66.3920
21	7.3225	4.4958	61.8963
22	6.7836	5.0347	56.8616
23	6.1801	5.6382	51.2234
24	5.5042	6.3141	44.9093
25	4.7473	7.0710	37.8383
26	3.8997	7.9186	29.9198
27	2.9505	8.8678	21.0520
28	1.8875	9.9308	11.1212
29	.6971	11.1212	0.0000

YEARS 30	MO PAYT .9808	AN CONST 11.77	
#	INT	PRIN	BALANCE
1	11.3538	.4154	99.5846
2	11.3040	.4652	99.1194
3	11.2482	.5210	98.5985
4	11.1858	.5834	98.0151
5	11.1158	.6533	97.3617
6	11.0375	.7317	96.6301
7	10.9498	.8194	95.8107
8	10.8516	.9176	94.8931
9	10.7416	1.0276	93.8656
10	10.6184	1.1507	92.7148
11	10.4805	1.2887	91.4262
12	10.3260	1.4432	89.9830
13	10.1530	1.6162	88.3669
14	9.9593	1.8099	86.5570
15	9.7423	2.0268	84.5301
16	9.4994	2.2698	82.2603
17	9.2273	2.5419	79.7185
18	8.9226	2.8466	76.8719
19	8.5814	3.1878	73.6841
20	8.1992	3.5699	70.1141
21	7.7713	3.9979	66.1163
22	7.2921	4.4771	61.6391
23	6.7554	5.0138	56.6254
24	6.1544	5.6148	51.0106
25	5.4813	6.2878	44.7227
26	4.7276	7.0416	37.6811
27	3.8835	7.8857	29.7955
28	2.9382	8.8309	20.9645
29	1.8797	9.8895	11.0750
30	.6942	11.0750	0.0000

YEARS 2 — MO PAYT 4.6794 — AN CONST 56.16

#	INT	PRIN	BALANCE
1	8.9860	47.1665	52.8335
2	3.3190	52.8335	0.0000

YEARS 3 — MO PAYT 3.2928 — AN CONST 39.52

#	INT	PRIN	BALANCE
1	9.8835	29.6307	70.3693
2	6.3234	33.1908	37.1786
3	2.3356	37.1786	0.0000

YEARS 4 — MO PAYT 2.6040 — AN CONST 31.25

#	INT	PRIN	BALANCE
1	10.3294	20.9189	79.0811
2	7.8160	23.4323	55.6489
3	5.0006	26.2476	29.4013
4	1.8470	29.4013	0.0000

YEARS 5 — MO PAYT 2.1942 — AN CONST 26.34

#	INT	PRIN	BALANCE
1	10.5946	15.7363	84.2637
2	8.7039	17.6270	66.6367
3	6.5860	19.7449	46.8918
4	4.2137	22.1172	24.7746
5	1.5563	24.7746	0.0000

YEARS 6 — MO PAYT 1.9240 — AN CONST 23.09

#	INT	PRIN	BALANCE
1	10.7696	12.3179	87.6821
2	9.2896	13.7979	73.8842
3	7.6318	15.4557	58.4284
4	5.7748	17.3127	41.1157
5	3.6947	19.3928	21.7229
6	1.3646	21.7229	0.0000

YEARS 7 — MO PAYT 1.7333 — AN CONST 20.81

#	INT	PRIN	BALANCE
1	10.8930	9.9072	90.0928
2	9.7026	11.0976	78.9952
3	8.3692	12.4309	66.5643
4	6.8757	13.9245	52.6398
5	5.2027	15.5975	37.0423
6	3.3286	17.4715	19.5707
7	1.2294	19.5707	0.0000

YEARS 8 — MO PAYT 1.5925 — AN CONST 19.11

#	INT	PRIN	BALANCE
1	10.9841	8.1259	91.8741
2	10.0078	9.1022	82.7720
3	8.9142	10.1958	72.5762
4	7.6892	11.4208	61.1554
5	6.3170	12.7930	48.3624
6	4.7799	14.3301	34.0323
7	3.0581	16.0518	17.9804
8	1.1295	17.9804	0.0000

YEARS 9 — MO PAYT 1.4848 — AN CONST 17.82

#	INT	PRIN	BALANCE
1	11.0538	6.7636	93.2364
2	10.2412	7.5763	85.6601
3	9.3309	8.4865	77.1736
4	8.3113	9.5062	67.6674
5	7.1691	10.6484	57.0191
6	5.8897	11.9277	45.0913
7	4.4566	13.3608	31.7305
8	2.8513	14.9661	16.7643
9	1.0531	16.7643	0.0000

YEARS 10 — MO PAYT 1.4002 — AN CONST 16.81

#	INT	PRIN	BALANCE
1	11.1086	5.6943	94.3057
2	10.4244	6.3785	87.9272
3	9.6580	7.1448	80.7824
4	8.7996	8.0033	72.7791
5	7.8380	8.9649	63.8142
6	6.7609	10.0420	53.7722
7	5.5543	11.2485	42.5237
8	4.2028	12.6000	29.9236
9	2.6889	14.1139	15.8097
10	.9932	15.8097	0.0000

YEARS 11 — MO PAYT 1.3325 — AN CONST 16.00

#	INT	PRIN	BALANCE
1	11.1524	4.8376	95.1624
2	10.5712	5.4188	89.7436
3	9.9201	6.0699	83.6736
4	9.1908	6.7992	76.8744
5	8.3739	7.6161	69.2583
6	7.4588	8.5312	60.7271
7	6.4338	9.5562	51.1709
8	5.2856	10.7044	40.4665
9	3.9995	11.9905	28.4760
10	2.5589	13.4312	15.0449
11	.9451	15.0449	0.0000

YEARS 12 — MO PAYT 1.2773 — AN CONST 15.33

#	INT	PRIN	BALANCE
1	11.1881	4.1399	95.8601
2	10.6907	4.6373	91.2227
3	10.1335	5.1945	86.0282
4	9.5094	5.8186	80.2096
5	8.8103	6.5177	73.6919
6	8.0272	7.3008	66.3911
7	7.1500	8.1780	58.2131
8	6.1675	9.1606	49.0525
9	5.0668	10.2612	38.7913
10	3.8339	11.4941	27.2972
11	2.4529	12.8751	14.4220
12	.9060	14.4220	0.0000

YEARS 13 — MO PAYT 1.2318 — AN CONST 14.79

#	INT	PRIN	BALANCE
1	11.2176	3.5641	96.4359
2	10.7894	3.9924	92.4435
3	10.3097	4.4721	87.9714
4	9.7724	5.0094	82.9621
5	9.1705	5.6112	77.3508
6	8.4963	6.2854	71.0654
7	7.7411	7.0406	64.0248
8	6.8952	7.8865	56.1383
9	5.9476	8.8341	47.3042
10	4.8862	9.8955	37.4087
11	3.6973	11.0844	26.3242
12	2.3655	12.4162	13.9080
13	.8737	13.9080	0.0000

YEARS 14 — MO PAYT 1.1938 — AN CONST 14.33

#	INT	PRIN	BALANCE
1	11.2422	3.0837	96.9163
2	10.8717	3.4542	93.4620
3	10.4566	3.8693	89.5928
4	9.9918	4.3341	85.2586
5	9.4710	4.8549	80.4038
6	8.8877	5.4382	74.9656
7	8.2343	6.0916	68.8740
8	7.5024	6.8235	62.0505
9	6.6826	7.6433	54.4071
10	5.7642	8.5617	45.8455
11	4.7355	9.5904	36.2551
12	3.5833	10.7426	25.5125
13	2.2926	12.0333	13.4791
14	.8468	13.4791	0.0000

YEARS 15 — MO PAYT 1.1618 — AN CONST 13.95

#	INT	PRIN	BALANCE
1	11.2629	2.6792	97.3208
2	10.9410	3.0011	94.3197
3	10.5804	3.3617	90.9580
4	10.1765	3.7656	87.1924
5	9.7241	4.2180	82.9744
6	9.2173	4.7248	78.2496
7	8.6496	5.2925	72.9571
8	8.0137	5.9284	67.0287
9	7.3014	6.6407	60.3880
10	6.5035	7.4386	52.9495
11	5.6098	8.3323	44.6172
12	4.6087	9.3334	35.2838
13	3.4873	10.4548	24.8290
14	2.2311	11.7109	13.1180
15	.8241	13.1180	0.0000

YEARS 16 — MO PAYT 1.1347 — AN CONST 13.62

#	INT	PRIN	BALANCE
1	11.2804	2.3360	97.6640
2	10.9998	2.6166	95.0474
3	10.6854	2.9310	92.1164
4	10.3332	3.2832	88.8333
5	9.9388	3.6776	85.1556
6	9.4969	4.1195	81.0361
7	9.0020	4.6144	76.4217
8	8.4475	5.1689	71.2528
9	7.8265	5.7899	65.4629
10	7.1308	6.4856	58.9774
11	6.3516	7.2648	51.7126
12	5.4788	8.1377	43.5749
13	4.5010	9.1154	34.4595
14	3.4058	10.2106	24.2490
15	2.1790	11.4374	12.8116
16	.8048	12.8116	0.0000

YEARS 17 — MO PAYT 1.1115 — AN CONST 13.34

#	INT	PRIN	BALANCE
1	11.2955	2.0428	97.9572
2	11.0500	2.2882	95.6690
3	10.7751	2.5632	93.1058
4	10.4671	2.8711	90.2347
5	10.1222	3.2161	87.0186
6	9.7357	3.6025	83.4161
7	9.3029	4.0353	79.3807
8	8.8181	4.5202	74.8606
9	8.2750	5.0633	69.7973
10	7.6666	5.6716	64.1257
11	6.9852	6.3531	57.7726
12	6.2219	7.1164	50.6562
13	5.3668	7.9714	42.6848
14	4.4091	8.9292	33.7556
15	3.3362	10.0020	23.7536
16	2.1345	11.2037	12.5499
17	.7884	12.5499	0.0000

YEARS 18 — MO PAYT 1.0916 — AN CONST 13.10

#	INT	PRIN	BALANCE
1	11.3083	1.7910	98.2090
2	11.0931	2.0062	96.2028
3	10.8521	2.2473	93.9555
4	10.5821	2.5173	91.4383
5	10.2796	2.8197	88.6186
6	9.9409	3.1585	85.4601
7	9.5614	3.5380	81.9221
8	9.1363	3.9631	77.9590
9	8.6601	4.4392	73.5198
10	8.1268	4.9726	68.5472
11	7.5293	5.5700	62.9772
12	6.8601	6.2393	56.7379
13	6.1104	6.9889	49.7489
14	5.2707	7.8286	41.9203
15	4.3301	8.7693	33.1510
16	3.2765	9.8229	23.3282
17	2.0963	11.0031	12.3251
18	.7743	12.3251	0.0000

YEARS 19 — MO PAYT 1.0744 — AN CONST 12.90

#	INT	PRIN	BALANCE
1	11.3195	1.5737	98.4263
2	11.1304	1.7628	96.6634
3	10.9186	1.9746	94.6888
4	10.6813	2.2119	92.4769
5	10.4156	2.4776	89.9993
6	10.1179	2.7753	87.2239
7	9.7844	3.1088	84.1151
8	9.4109	3.4823	80.6328
9	8.9925	3.9007	76.7321
10	8.5238	4.3694	72.3628
11	7.9989	4.8943	67.4684
12	7.4108	5.4824	61.9860
13	6.7521	6.1411	55.8450
14	6.0143	6.8789	48.9660
15	5.1878	7.7054	41.2606
16	4.2620	8.6312	32.6293
17	3.2249	9.6683	22.9610
18	2.0633	10.8299	12.1311
19	.7621	12.1311	0.0000

YEARS 20 — MO PAYT 1.0595 — AN CONST 12.72

#	INT	PRIN	BALANCE
1	11.3291	1.3855	98.6145
2	11.1626	1.5519	97.0626
3	10.9762	1.7384	95.3242
4	10.7673	1.9473	93.3769
5	10.5333	2.1812	91.1956
6	10.2713	2.4433	88.7523
7	9.9777	2.7369	86.0155
8	9.6489	3.0657	82.9497
9	9.2805	3.4341	79.5157
10	8.8679	3.8467	75.6690
11	8.4057	4.3088	71.3602
12	7.8880	4.8265	66.5337
13	7.3081	5.4064	61.1272
14	6.6586	6.0560	55.0712
15	5.9309	6.7836	48.2876
16	5.1159	7.5987	40.6889
17	4.2029	8.5117	32.1773
18	3.1802	9.5343	22.6429
19	2.0347	10.6799	11.9631
20	.7515	11.9631	0.0000

YEARS 21 — MO PAYT 1.0466 — AN CONST 12.56

#	INT	PRIN	BALANCE
1	11.3375	1.2218	98.7782
2	11.1907	1.3686	97.4097
3	11.0262	1.5330	95.8767

MONTHLY PAYMENT AMORTIZATION SCHEDULE PER $100   11.40 %

#	INT	PRIN	BALANCE
4	10.8421	1.7172	94.1595
5	10.6357	1.9235	92.2360
6	10.4046	2.1546	90.0815
7	10.1458	2.4135	87.6680
8	9.8558	2.7034	84.9646
9	9.5310	3.0283	81.9363
10	9.1671	3.3921	78.5442
11	8.7596	3.7997	74.7445
12	8.3030	4.2562	70.4884
13	7.7917	4.7676	65.7208
14	7.2189	5.3404	60.3804
15	6.5772	5.9820	54.3984
16	5.8585	6.7008	47.6976
17	5.0534	7.5058	40.1918
18	4.1516	8.4077	31.7841
19	3.1418	9.4178	22.3663
20	2.0098	10.5494	11.8169
21	.7423	11.8169	0.0000

YEARS 22 — MO PAYT 1.0353 — AN CONST 12.43

#	INT	PRIN	BALANCE
1	11.3448	1.0789	98.9211
2	11.2151	1.2086	97.7125
3	11.0699	1.3538	96.3587
4	10.9073	1.5164	94.8422
5	10.7251	1.6986	93.1436
6	10.5210	1.9027	91.2409
7	10.2924	2.1313	89.1095
8	10.0363	2.3874	86.7221
9	9.7495	2.6743	84.0478
10	9.4281	2.9956	81.0522
11	9.0682	3.3555	77.6967
12	8.6651	3.7587	73.9381
13	8.2135	4.2103	69.7278
14	7.7076	4.7161	65.0117
15	7.1410	5.2828	59.7289
16	6.5062	5.9175	53.8115
17	5.7953	6.6285	47.1830
18	4.9989	7.4249	39.7581
19	4.1068	8.3170	31.4412
20	3.1075	9.3162	22.1250
21	1.9882	10.4356	11.6894
22	.7343	11.6894	0.0000

YEARS 23 — MO PAYT 1.0254 — AN CONST 12.31

#	INT	PRIN	BALANCE
1	11.3512	.9540	99.0460
2	11.2365	1.0686	97.9773
3	11.1082	1.1970	96.7803
4	10.9643	1.3409	95.4394
5	10.8032	1.5020	93.9374
6	10.6228	1.6824	92.2550
7	10.4206	1.8846	90.3704
8	10.1942	2.1110	88.2594
9	9.9405	2.3646	85.8948
10	9.6564	2.6488	83.2460
11	9.3382	2.9670	80.2790
12	8.9817	3.3235	76.9555
13	8.5824	3.7228	73.2327
14	8.1351	4.1701	69.0626
15	7.6341	4.6711	64.3915
16	7.0728	5.2324	59.1591
17	6.4442	5.8610	53.2981
18	5.7400	6.5652	46.7329
19	4.9512	7.3540	39.3788
20	4.0676	8.2376	31.1412
21	3.0778	9.2274	21.9139
22	1.9692	10.3360	11.5779
23	.7273	11.5779	0.0000

YEARS 24 — MO PAYT 1.0168 — AN CONST 12.21

#	INT	PRIN	BALANCE
1	11.3568	.8445	99.1555
2	11.2553	.9460	98.2095
3	11.1417	1.0596	97.1499
4	11.0143	1.1869	95.9630
5	10.8717	1.3295	94.6334
6	10.7120	1.4893	93.1441
7	10.5331	1.6682	91.4759
8	10.3326	1.8687	89.6072
9	10.1081	2.0932	87.5141
10	9.8566	2.3447	85.1694
11	9.5749	2.6264	82.5430
12	9.2593	2.9419	79.6010
13	8.9059	3.2954	76.3056
14	8.5099	3.6914	72.6142
15	8.0664	4.1349	68.4794
16	7.5696	4.6317	63.8477
17	7.0131	5.1882	58.6595
18	6.3898	5.8115	52.8480
19	5.6915	6.5098	46.3382
20	4.9094	7.2919	39.0463
21	4.0332	8.1680	30.8782
22	3.0519	9.1494	21.7288
23	1.9526	10.2487	11.4801
24	.7212	11.4801	0.0000

YEARS 25 — MO PAYT 1.0092 — AN CONST 12.11

#	INT	PRIN	BALANCE
1	11.3617	.7483	99.2517
2	11.2718	.8382	98.4135
3	11.1711	.9389	97.4747
4	11.0583	1.0517	96.4230
5	10.9319	1.1781	95.2449
6	10.7904	1.3196	93.9253
7	10.6318	1.4781	92.4472
8	10.4542	1.6557	90.7914
9	10.2553	1.8547	88.9367
10	10.0325	2.0775	86.8592
11	9.7828	2.3271	84.5321
12	9.5032	2.6067	81.9253
13	9.1900	2.9199	79.0054
14	8.8392	3.2708	75.7346
15	8.4462	3.6637	72.0709
16	8.0060	4.1039	67.9670
17	7.5130	4.5970	63.3699
18	6.9606	5.1494	58.2206
19	6.3419	5.7680	52.4525
20	5.6489	6.4611	45.9915
21	4.8726	7.2374	38.7541
22	4.0031	8.1069	30.6472
23	3.0290	9.0810	21.5662
24	1.9379	10.1720	11.3942
25	.7158	11.3942	0.0000

YEARS 26 — MO PAYT 1.0025 — AN CONST 12.03

#	INT	PRIN	BALANCE
1	11.3660	.6636	99.3364
2	11.2863	.7433	98.5931
3	11.1970	.8326	97.7605
4	11.0970	.9327	96.8278
5	10.9849	1.0447	95.7831
6	10.8594	1.1702	94.6129
7	10.7188	1.3108	93.3020
8	10.5613	1.4683	91.8337
9	10.3849	1.6448	90.1889
10	10.1872	1.8424	88.3466
11	9.9659	2.0637	86.2828
12	9.7179	2.3117	83.9711
13	9.4402	2.5894	81.3817
14	9.1291	2.9006	78.4811
15	8.7806	3.2491	75.2321
16	8.3902	3.6394	71.5926
17	7.9529	4.0767	67.5159
18	7.4631	4.5665	62.9494
19	6.9144	5.1152	57.8342
20	6.2999	5.7298	52.1045
21	5.6114	6.4182	45.6863
22	4.8403	7.1893	38.4969
23	3.9765	8.0531	30.4438
24	3.0089	9.0207	21.4231
25	1.9251	10.1045	11.3186
26	.7110	11.3186	0.0000

YEARS 27 — MO PAYT .9966 — AN CONST 11.96

#	INT	PRIN	BALANCE
1	11.3699	.5889	99.4111
2	11.2991	.6597	98.7514
3	11.2198	.7389	98.0125
4	11.1311	.8277	97.1848
5	11.0316	.9272	96.2576
6	10.9202	1.0386	95.2190
7	10.7954	1.1633	94.0557
8	10.6557	1.3031	92.7526
9	10.4991	1.4597	91.2929
10	10.3237	1.6351	89.6578
11	10.1273	1.8315	87.8263
12	9.9072	2.0516	85.7747
13	9.6607	2.2981	83.4766
14	9.3846	2.5742	80.9024
15	9.0753	2.8835	78.0189
16	8.7289	3.2299	74.7890
17	8.3408	3.6180	71.1710
18	7.9061	4.0527	67.1183
19	7.4192	4.5396	62.5787
20	6.8737	5.0851	57.4936
21	6.2628	5.6960	51.7976
22	5.5784	6.3804	45.4172
23	4.8118	7.1470	38.2702
24	3.9531	8.0057	30.2645
25	2.9912	8.9676	21.2970
26	1.9138	10.0450	11.2519
27	.7068	11.2519	0.0000

YEARS 28 — MO PAYT .9914 — AN CONST 11.90

#	INT	PRIN	BALANCE
1	11.3732	.5230	99.4770
2	11.3104	.5858	98.8912
3	11.2400	.6562	98.2349
4	11.1612	.7351	97.4999
5	11.0728	.8234	96.6765
6	10.9739	.9223	95.7542
7	10.8631	1.0331	94.7210
8	10.7390	1.1573	93.5638
9	10.5999	1.2963	92.2675
10	10.4442	1.4521	90.8154
11	10.2697	1.6265	89.1889
12	10.0743	1.8219	87.3669
13	9.8554	2.0409	85.3261
14	9.6102	2.2861	83.0400
15	9.3355	2.5607	80.4793
16	9.0278	2.8684	77.6109
17	8.6832	3.2130	74.3979
18	8.2972	3.5991	70.7988
19	7.8647	4.0315	66.7673
20	7.3803	4.5159	62.2514
21	6.8378	5.0585	57.1930
22	6.2300	5.6662	51.5267
23	5.5492	6.3470	45.1797
24	4.7866	7.1096	38.0701
25	3.9324	7.9638	30.1062
26	2.9756	8.9207	21.1856
27	1.9037	9.9925	11.1931
28	.7032	11.1931	0.0000

YEARS 29 — MO PAYT .9867 — AN CONST 11.85

#	INT	PRIN	BALANCE
1	11.3762	.4647	99.5353
2	11.3204	.5206	99.0147
3	11.2578	.5831	98.4316
4	11.1878	.6532	97.7784
5	11.1093	.7317	97.0468
6	11.0214	.8196	96.2272
7	10.9229	.9180	95.3092
8	10.8126	1.0283	94.2808
9	10.6891	1.1519	93.1289
10	10.5507	1.2903	91.8387
11	10.3956	1.4453	90.3934
12	10.2220	1.6190	88.7744
13	10.0275	1.8135	86.9609
14	9.8096	2.0314	84.9295
15	9.5655	2.2754	82.6541
16	9.2921	2.5488	80.1053
17	8.9859	2.8551	77.2502
18	8.6428	3.1981	74.0521
19	8.2586	3.5823	70.4698
20	7.8282	4.0128	66.4570
21	7.3461	4.4949	61.9621
22	6.8060	5.0350	56.9272
23	6.2010	5.6399	51.2873
24	5.5234	6.3175	44.9697
25	4.7644	7.0766	37.8932
26	3.9141	7.9268	29.9663
27	2.9617	8.8792	21.0871
28	1.8949	9.9461	11.1411
29	.6999	11.1411	0.0000

YEARS 30 — MO PAYT .9827 — AN CONST 11.80

#	INT	PRIN	BALANCE
1	11.3789	.4132	99.5868
2	11.3292	.4628	99.1240
3	11.2736	.5184	98.6056
4	11.2113	.5807	98.0249
5	11.1415	.6505	97.3744
6	11.0634	.7286	96.6458
7	10.9758	.8162	95.8296
8	10.8778	.9142	94.9154
9	10.7679	1.0241	93.8913
10	10.6449	1.1471	92.7442
11	10.5071	1.2850	91.4592
12	10.3527	1.4393	90.0199
13	10.1798	1.6123	88.4076
14	9.9860	1.8060	86.6016
15	9.7690	2.0230	84.5786
16	9.5260	2.2660	82.3126
17	9.2537	2.5383	79.7743
18	8.9488	2.8433	76.9310
19	8.6071	3.1849	73.7462
20	8.2245	3.5675	70.1786
21	7.7958	3.9962	66.1824
22	7.3157	4.4763	61.7061
23	6.7779	5.0142	56.6920
24	6.1754	5.6166	51.0754
25	5.5006	6.2914	44.7839
26	4.7447	7.0473	37.7366
27	3.8980	7.8941	29.8425
28	2.9495	8.8425	21.0000
29	1.8871	9.9050	11.0950
30	.6970	11.0950	0.0000

MONTHLY PAYMENT AMORTIZATION SCHEDULE PER $100

11.50 %

YEARS 2 — MO PAYT 4.6840 — AN CONST 56.21

#	INT	PRIN	BALANCE
1	9.0666	47.1418	52.8582
2	3.3502	52.8582	0.0000

YEARS 3 — MO PAYT 3.2976 — AN CONST 39.58

#	INT	PRIN	BALANCE
1	9.9721	29.5991	70.4009
2	6.3829	33.1883	37.2126
3	2.3586	37.2126	0.0000

YEARS 4 — MO PAYT 2.6089 — AN CONST 31.31

#	INT	PRIN	BALANCE
1	10.4219	20.8849	79.1151
2	7.8895	23.4174	55.6978
3	5.0499	26.2569	29.4408
4	1.8660	29.4408	0.0000

YEARS 5 — MO PAYT 2.1993 — AN CONST 26.40

#	INT	PRIN	BALANCE
1	10.6895	15.7016	84.2984
2	8.7855	17.6056	66.6928
3	6.6507	19.7405	46.9523
4	4.2570	22.1342	24.8181
5	1.5730	24.8181	0.0000

YEARS 6 — MO PAYT 1.9291 — AN CONST 23.15

#	INT	PRIN	BALANCE
1	10.8659	12.2835	87.7165
2	9.3765	13.7729	73.9436
3	7.7064	15.4430	58.5006
4	5.8337	17.3156	41.1849
5	3.7341	19.4153	21.7696
6	1.3798	21.7696	0.0000

YEARS 7 — MO PAYT 1.7386 — AN CONST 20.87

#	INT	PRIN	BALANCE
1	10.9903	9.8734	90.1266
2	9.7931	11.0707	79.0559
3	8.4507	12.4131	66.6429
4	6.9455	13.9183	52.7246
5	5.2578	15.6060	37.1186
6	3.3654	17.4984	19.6202
7	1.2435	19.6202	0.0000

YEARS 8 — MO PAYT 1.5979 — AN CONST 19.18

#	INT	PRIN	BALANCE
1	11.0822	8.0930	91.9070
2	10.1009	9.0744	82.8326
3	9.0005	10.1747	72.6579
4	7.7668	11.4085	61.2494
5	6.3834	12.7919	48.4576
6	4.8322	14.3430	34.1146
7	3.0930	16.0822	18.0323
8	1.1429	18.0323	0.0000

YEARS 9 — MO PAYT 1.4904 — AN CONST 17.89

#	INT	PRIN	BALANCE
1	11.1525	6.7319	93.2681
2	10.3362	7.5482	85.7199
3	9.4209	8.4635	77.2564
4	8.3946	9.4898	67.7667
5	7.2439	10.6405	57.1262
6	5.9537	11.9307	45.1955
7	4.5069	13.3774	31.8180
8	2.8848	14.9996	16.8184
9	1.0660	16.8184	0.0000

YEARS 10 — MO PAYT 1.4060 — AN CONST 16.88

#	INT	PRIN	BALANCE
1	11.2076	5.6638	94.3362
2	10.5208	6.3506	87.9856
3	9.7508	7.1207	80.8649
4	8.8873	7.9841	72.8808
5	7.9192	8.9523	63.9285
6	6.8336	10.0378	53.8907
7	5.6165	11.2550	42.6357
8	4.2517	12.6198	30.0159
9	2.7214	14.1500	15.8659
10	1.0056	15.8659	0.0000

YEARS 11 — MO PAYT 1.3384 — AN CONST 16.07

#	INT	PRIN	BALANCE
1	11.2518	4.8084	95.1916
2	10.6687	5.3915	89.8001
3	10.0150	6.0452	83.7549
4	9.2819	6.7783	76.9766
5	8.4600	7.6002	69.3764
6	7.5384	8.5218	60.8546
7	6.5050	9.5552	51.2994
8	5.3464	10.7138	40.5856
9	4.0472	12.0130	28.5726
10	2.5906	13.4696	15.1030
11	.9572	15.1030	0.0000

YEARS 12 — MO PAYT 1.2833 — AN CONST 15.40

#	INT	PRIN	BALANCE
1	11.2877	4.1121	95.8879
2	10.7891	4.6107	91.2773
3	10.2300	5.1698	86.1075
4	9.6031	5.7967	80.3108
5	8.9002	6.4996	73.8113
6	8.1121	7.2877	66.5236
7	7.2284	8.1714	58.3522
8	6.2376	9.1622	49.1899
9	5.1265	10.2733	38.9167
10	3.8808	11.5190	27.3977
11	2.4840	12.9158	14.4819
12	.9179	14.4819	0.0000

YEARS 13 — MO PAYT 1.2379 — AN CONST 14.86

#	INT	PRIN	BALANCE
1	11.3174	3.5376	96.4624
2	10.8884	3.9666	92.4958
3	10.4074	4.4476	88.0482
4	9.8681	4.9869	83.0613
5	9.2634	5.5916	77.4697
6	8.5854	6.2696	71.2001
7	7.8251	7.0299	64.1702
8	6.9727	7.8823	56.2879
9	6.0169	8.8381	47.4498
10	4.9452	9.9098	37.5400
11	3.7435	11.1115	26.4285
12	2.3962	12.4589	13.9696
13	.8854	13.9696	0.0000

YEARS 14 — MO PAYT 1.2001 — AN CONST 14.41

#	INT	PRIN	BALANCE
1	11.3421	3.0585	96.9415
2	10.9712	3.4294	93.5120
3	10.5554	3.8453	89.6668
4	10.0891	4.3115	85.3552
5	9.5663	4.8344	80.5209
6	8.9801	5.4206	75.1003
7	8.3228	6.0779	69.0224
8	7.5858	6.8149	62.2075
9	6.7594	7.6412	54.5663
10	5.8329	8.5678	45.9985
11	4.7939	9.6067	36.3918
12	3.6290	10.7716	25.6201
13	2.3229	12.0778	13.5423
14	.8583	13.5423	0.0000

YEARS 15 — MO PAYT 1.1682 — AN CONST 14.02

#	INT	PRIN	BALANCE
1	11.3629	2.6553	97.3447
2	11.0409	2.9773	94.3673
3	10.6799	3.3384	91.0290
4	10.2751	3.7432	87.2858
5	9.8212	4.1971	83.0887
6	9.3123	4.7060	78.3827
7	8.7416	5.2766	73.1061
8	8.1018	5.9165	67.1896
9	7.3844	6.6339	60.5557
10	6.5799	7.4383	53.1174
11	5.6780	8.3403	44.7771
12	4.6666	9.3516	35.4254
13	3.5327	10.4856	24.9398
14	2.2612	11.7571	13.1827
15	.8355	13.1827	0.0000

YEARS 16 — MO PAYT 1.1412 — AN CONST 13.70

#	INT	PRIN	BALANCE
1	11.3806	2.3134	97.6866
2	11.1001	2.5939	95.0927
3	10.7855	2.9085	92.1842
4	10.4328	3.2611	88.9231
5	10.0374	3.6566	85.2665
6	9.5940	4.1000	81.1666
7	9.0969	4.5971	76.5694
8	8.5394	5.1546	71.4149
9	7.9144	5.7796	65.6353
10	7.2135	6.4804	59.1548
11	6.4277	7.2663	51.8886
12	5.5466	8.1474	43.7412
13	4.5587	9.1353	34.6059
14	3.4509	10.2430	24.3629
15	2.2089	11.4851	12.8778
16	.8162	12.8778	0.0000

YEARS 17 — MO PAYT 1.1181 — AN CONST 13.42

#	INT	PRIN	BALANCE
1	11.3957	2.0215	97.9785
2	11.1505	2.2666	95.7119
3	10.8757	2.5415	93.1704
4	10.5675	2.8497	90.3207
5	10.2219	3.1952	87.1255
6	9.8345	3.5827	83.5429
7	9.4021	4.0171	79.5258
8	8.9130	4.5042	75.0216
9	8.3668	5.0504	69.9712
10	7.7544	5.6628	64.3084
11	7.0677	6.3494	57.9590
12	6.2978	7.1194	50.8396
13	5.4345	7.9827	42.8570
14	4.4665	8.9506	33.9064
15	3.3812	10.0360	23.8704
16	2.1642	11.2529	12.6175
17	.7997	12.6175	0.0000

YEARS 18 — MO PAYT 1.0983 — AN CONST 13.18

#	INT	PRIN	BALANCE
1	11.4086	1.7710	98.2290
2	11.1938	1.9857	96.2433
3	10.9531	2.2265	94.0168
4	10.6831	2.4965	91.5204
5	10.3804	2.7992	88.7212
6	10.0409	3.1386	85.5826
7	9.6603	3.5192	82.0634
8	9.2336	3.9459	78.1174
9	8.7551	4.4244	73.6930
10	8.2186	4.9609	68.7321
11	7.6171	5.5625	63.1696
12	6.9426	6.2370	56.9326
13	6.1863	6.9933	49.9393
14	5.3383	7.8413	42.0980
15	4.3874	8.7921	33.3059
16	3.3213	9.8582	23.4476
17	2.1259	11.0536	12.3940
18	.7855	12.3940	0.0000

YEARS 19 — MO PAYT 1.0812 — AN CONST 12.98

#	INT	PRIN	BALANCE
1	11.4197	1.5549	98.4451
2	11.2312	1.7434	96.7017
3	11.0198	1.9548	94.7469
4	10.7827	2.1919	92.5550
5	10.5170	2.4577	90.0973
6	10.2189	2.7557	87.3417
7	9.8848	3.0898	84.2519
8	9.5101	3.4645	80.7874
9	9.0900	3.8846	76.9028
10	8.6190	4.3556	72.5472
11	8.0908	4.8838	67.6634
12	7.4986	5.4760	62.1874
13	6.8346	6.1400	56.0473
14	6.0901	6.8845	49.1628
15	5.2553	7.7194	41.4434
16	4.3192	8.6554	32.7880
17	3.2697	9.7050	23.0831
18	2.0928	10.8818	12.2013
19	.7733	12.2013	0.0000

YEARS 20 — MO PAYT 1.0664 — AN CONST 12.80

#	INT	PRIN	BALANCE
1	11.4294	1.3678	98.6322
2	11.2635	1.5336	97.0986
3	11.0776	1.7196	95.3791
4	10.8691	1.9281	93.4510
5	10.6353	2.1619	91.2891
6	10.3731	2.4240	88.8650
7	10.0792	2.7180	86.1471
8	9.7496	3.0476	83.0995
9	9.3801	3.4171	79.6824
10	8.9657	3.8315	75.8509
11	8.5011	4.2961	71.5549
12	7.9802	4.8170	66.7379
13	7.3961	5.4011	61.3368
14	6.7411	6.0560	55.2808
15	6.0068	6.7904	48.4904
16	5.1834	7.6138	40.8766
17	4.2601	8.5370	32.3396
18	3.2249	9.5722	22.7673
19	2.0642	10.7329	12.0344
20	.7627	12.0344	0.0000

YEARS 21 — MO PAYT 1.0536 — AN CONST 12.65

#	INT	PRIN	BALANCE
1	11.4378	1.2051	98.7949
2	11.2917	1.3513	97.4436
3	11.1278	1.5151	95.9285

MONTHLY PAYMENT AMORTIZATION SCHEDULE PER $100   11.50 %

#	INT	PRIN	BALANCE
4	10.9441	1.6989	94.2296
5	10.7381	1.9049	92.3247
6	10.5071	2.1358	90.1889
7	10.2481	2.3948	87.7941
8	9.9577	2.6852	85.1089
9	9.6321	3.0108	82.0980
10	9.2670	3.3759	78.7221
11	8.8576	3.7853	74.9368
12	8.3986	4.2443	70.6925
13	7.8840	4.7589	65.9336
14	7.3069	5.3360	60.5976
15	6.6599	5.9830	54.6145
16	5.9344	6.7086	47.9060
17	5.1209	7.5220	40.3840
18	4.2088	8.4341	31.9498
19	3.1861	9.4569	22.4930
20	2.0393	10.6036	11.8894
21	.7536	11.8894	0.0000

YEARS 22	MO PAYT 1.0424	AN CONST 12.51	
#	INT	PRIN	BALANCE
1	11.4451	1.0634	98.9366
2	11.3162	1.1923	97.7443
3	11.1716	1.3369	96.4074
4	11.0095	1.4990	94.9084
5	10.8277	1.6808	93.2276
6	10.6239	1.8846	91.3430
7	10.3954	2.1131	89.2299
8	10.1391	2.3694	86.8605
9	9.8518	2.6567	84.2038
10	9.5297	2.9788	81.2250
11	9.1685	3.3400	77.8850
12	8.7635	3.7450	74.1400
13	8.3093	4.1992	69.9408
14	7.8002	4.7083	65.2325
15	7.2292	5.2793	59.9532
16	6.5891	5.9194	54.0338
17	5.8713	6.6372	47.3966
18	5.0665	7.4420	39.9545
19	4.1640	8.3445	31.6101
20	3.1522	9.3563	22.2538
21	2.0177	10.4908	11.7629
22	.7455	11.7629	0.0000

YEARS 23	MO PAYT 1.0326	AN CONST 12.40	
#	INT	PRIN	BALANCE
1	11.4515	.9395	99.0605
2	11.3376	1.0534	98.0071
3	11.2099	1.1811	96.8260
4	11.0666	1.3243	95.5017
5	10.9060	1.4849	94.0167
6	10.7260	1.6650	92.3517
7	10.5241	1.8669	90.4848
8	10.2977	2.0933	88.3916
9	10.0439	2.3471	86.0445
10	9.7593	2.6317	83.4128
11	9.4401	2.9508	80.4619
12	9.0823	3.3086	77.1533
13	8.6811	3.7098	73.4434
14	8.2313	4.1597	69.2837
15	7.7269	4.6641	64.6196
16	7.1613	5.2297	59.3900
17	6.5272	5.8638	53.5261
18	5.8161	6.5749	46.9513
19	5.0189	7.3721	39.5792
20	4.1249	8.2661	31.3131
21	3.1226	9.2684	22.0447
22	1.9987	10.3923	11.6524
23	.7385	11.6524	0.0000

YEARS 24	MO PAYT 1.0240	AN CONST 12.29	
#	INT	PRIN	BALANCE
1	11.4571	.8309	99.1691
2	11.3564	.9317	98.2374
3	11.2434	1.0446	97.1928
4	11.1167	1.1713	96.0215
5	10.9747	1.3133	94.7081
6	10.8154	1.4726	93.2355
7	10.6369	1.6512	91.5844
8	10.4366	1.8514	89.7330
9	10.2121	2.0759	87.6571
10	9.9604	2.3276	85.3295
11	9.6782	2.6098	82.7197
12	9.3617	2.9263	79.7934
13	9.0069	3.2812	76.5122
14	8.6090	3.6790	72.8332
15	8.1629	4.1251	68.7081
16	7.6627	4.6253	64.0827
17	7.1018	5.1862	58.8965
18	6.4729	5.8151	53.0814
19	5.7678	6.5202	46.5612
20	4.9772	7.3109	39.2503
21	4.0906	8.1974	31.0529
22	3.0966	9.1914	21.8615
23	1.9821	10.3059	11.5556
24	.7324	11.5556	0.0000

YEARS 25	MO PAYT 1.0165	AN CONST 12.20	
#	INT	PRIN	BALANCE
1	11.4620	.7356	99.2644
2	11.3728	.8248	98.4396
3	11.2728	.9248	97.5148
4	11.1607	1.0370	96.4778
5	11.0349	1.1627	95.3151
6	10.8939	1.3037	94.0115
7	10.7359	1.4618	92.5497
8	10.5586	1.6390	90.9107
9	10.3599	1.8378	89.0729
10	10.1370	2.0606	87.0123
11	9.8872	2.3105	84.7018
12	9.6070	2.5906	82.1112
13	9.2928	2.9048	79.2064
14	8.9406	3.2570	75.9494
15	8.5457	3.6520	72.2974
16	8.1028	4.0948	68.2026
17	7.6063	4.5913	63.6113
18	7.0496	5.1481	58.4632
19	6.4253	5.7723	52.6909
20	5.7254	6.4723	46.2187
21	4.9405	7.2571	38.9616
22	4.0606	8.1371	30.8245
23	3.0739	9.1238	21.7007
24	1.9675	10.2301	11.4706
25	.7270	11.4706	0.0000

YEARS 26	MO PAYT 1.0098	AN CONST 12.12	
#	INT	PRIN	BALANCE
1	11.4664	.6518	99.3482
2	11.3873	.7308	98.6174
3	11.2987	.8194	97.7980
4	11.1993	.9188	96.8792
5	11.0879	1.0302	95.8490
6	10.9630	1.1551	94.6939
7	10.8229	1.2952	93.3987
8	10.6659	1.4522	91.9465
9	10.4898	1.6283	90.3182
10	10.2923	1.8258	88.4924
11	10.0709	2.0472	86.4452
12	9.8227	2.2954	84.1498
13	9.5444	2.5738	81.5760
14	9.2323	2.8859	78.6902
15	8.8823	3.2358	75.4544
16	8.4900	3.6282	71.8262
17	8.0500	4.0681	67.7581
18	7.5567	4.5614	63.1967
19	7.0036	5.1145	58.0822
20	6.3834	5.7347	52.3475
21	5.6880	6.4301	45.9174
22	4.9083	7.2098	38.7076
23	4.0341	8.0840	30.6236
24	3.0538	9.0643	21.5593
25	1.9547	10.1634	11.3959
26	.7223	11.3959	0.0000

YEARS 27	MO PAYT 1.0040	AN CONST 12.05	
#	INT	PRIN	BALANCE
1	11.4702	.5779	99.4221
2	11.4001	.6480	98.7741
3	11.3215	.7266	98.0475
4	11.2334	.8147	97.2328
5	11.1346	.9135	96.3193
6	11.0239	1.0242	95.2951
7	10.8997	1.1484	94.1466
8	10.7604	1.2877	92.8590
9	10.6042	1.4438	91.4151
10	10.4292	1.6189	89.7962
11	10.2329	1.8152	87.9809
12	10.0127	2.0353	85.9456
13	9.7659	2.2822	83.6635
14	9.4892	2.5589	81.1046
15	9.1789	2.8692	78.2354
16	8.8310	3.2171	75.0183
17	8.4409	3.6072	71.4111
18	8.0035	4.0446	67.3665
19	7.5131	4.5350	62.8315
20	6.9631	5.0850	57.7465
21	6.3465	5.7016	52.0450
22	5.6552	6.3929	45.6521
23	4.8800	7.1681	38.4839
24	4.0108	8.0373	30.4466
25	3.0362	9.0119	21.4347
26	1.9434	10.1047	11.3300
27	.7181	11.3300	0.0000

YEARS 28	MO PAYT .9989	AN CONST 11.99	
#	INT	PRIN	BALANCE
1	11.4735	.5128	99.4872
2	11.4114	.5750	98.9123
3	11.3416	.6447	98.2676
4	11.2635	.7229	97.5447
5	11.1758	.8105	96.7342
6	11.0775	.9088	95.8254
7	10.9673	1.0190	94.8064
8	10.8438	1.1426	93.6639
9	10.7052	1.2811	92.3828
10	10.5499	1.4364	90.9463
11	10.3757	1.6106	89.3357
12	10.1804	1.8059	87.5298
13	9.9614	2.0249	85.5049
14	9.7159	2.2704	83.2344
15	9.4405	2.5458	80.6887
16	9.1319	2.8545	77.8342
17	8.7857	3.2006	74.6336
18	8.3976	3.5887	71.0449
19	7.9625	4.0239	67.0211
20	7.4745	4.5118	62.5093
21	6.9274	5.0589	57.4504
22	6.3140	5.6723	51.7781
23	5.6262	6.3601	45.4180
24	4.8549	7.1314	38.2866
25	3.9902	7.9961	30.2905
26	3.0206	8.9657	21.3248
27	1.9334	10.0529	11.2719
28	.7144	11.2719	0.0000

YEARS 29	MO PAYT .9943	AN CONST 11.94	
#	INT	PRIN	BALANCE
1	11.4765	.4552	99.5448
2	11.4213	.5104	99.0343
3	11.3594	.5723	98.4620
4	11.2900	.6417	97.8202
5	11.2122	.7196	97.1007
6	11.1249	.8068	96.2938
7	11.0271	.9047	95.3892
8	10.9174	1.0143	94.3748
9	10.7944	1.1373	93.2375
10	10.6565	1.2753	91.9622
11	10.5018	1.4299	90.5323
12	10.3285	1.6033	88.9290
13	10.1340	1.7977	87.1313
14	9.9161	2.0157	85.1156
15	9.6716	2.2601	82.8555
16	9.3976	2.5342	80.3213
17	9.0903	2.8415	77.4799
18	8.7457	3.1860	74.2939
19	8.3594	3.5724	70.7215
20	7.9262	4.0055	66.7160
21	7.4405	4.4912	62.2247
22	6.8959	5.0358	57.1889
23	6.2853	5.6465	51.5424
24	5.6006	6.3312	45.2112
25	4.8328	7.0989	38.1123
26	3.9720	7.9597	30.1526
27	3.0069	8.9249	21.2277
28	1.9246	10.0071	11.2206
29	.7112	11.2206	0.0000

YEARS 30	MO PAYT .9903	AN CONST 11.89	
#	INT	PRIN	BALANCE
1	11.4791	.4044	99.5956
2	11.4301	.4534	99.1422
3	11.3751	.5084	98.6338
4	11.3135	.5700	98.0638
5	11.2443	.6392	97.4247
6	11.1668	.7167	96.7080
7	11.0799	.8036	95.9044
8	10.9825	.9010	95.0035
9	10.8732	1.0102	93.9932
10	10.7507	1.1328	92.8605
11	10.6134	1.2701	91.5904
12	10.4594	1.4241	90.1662
13	10.2867	1.5968	88.5694
14	10.0931	1.7904	86.7790
15	9.8760	2.0075	84.7714
16	9.6325	2.2510	82.5205
17	9.3596	2.5239	79.9965
18	9.0535	2.8300	77.1666
19	8.7104	3.1731	73.9934
20	8.3256	3.5579	70.4355
21	7.8942	3.9893	66.4462
22	7.4104	4.4731	61.9731
23	6.8680	5.0155	56.9576
24	6.2598	5.6237	51.3340
25	5.5779	6.3056	45.0284
26	4.8133	7.0702	37.9582
27	3.9560	7.9275	30.0307
28	2.9947	8.8888	21.1419
29	1.9168	9.9667	11.1752
30	.7083	11.1752	0.0000

MONTHLY PAYMENT AMORTIZATION SCHEDULE PER $100   11.60 %

YEARS 2 — MO PAYT 4.6887 — AN CONST 56.27

#	INT	PRIN	BALANCE
1	9.1471	47.1171	52.8829
2	3.3814	52.8829	0.0000

YEARS 3 — MO PAYT 3.3024 — AN CONST 39.63

#	INT	PRIN	BALANCE
1	10.0608	29.5676	70.4324
2	6.4426	33.1857	37.2467
3	2.3816	37.2467	0.0000

YEARS 4 — MO PAYT 2.6138 — AN CONST 31.37

#	INT	PRIN	BALANCE
1	10.5145	20.8509	79.1491
2	7.9630	23.4024	55.7466
3	5.0992	26.2662	29.4804
4	1.8850	29.4804	0.0000

YEARS 5 — MO PAYT 2.2043 — AN CONST 26.46

#	INT	PRIN	BALANCE
1	10.7844	15.6670	84.3330
2	8.8672	17.5842	66.7488
3	6.7154	19.7360	47.0128
4	4.3003	22.1511	24.8617
5	1.5897	24.8617	0.0000

YEARS 6 — MO PAYT 1.9343 — AN CONST 23.22

#	INT	PRIN	BALANCE
1	10.9623	12.2490	87.7510
2	9.4634	13.7480	74.0030
3	7.7811	15.4303	58.5727
4	5.8929	17.3185	41.2542
5	3.7736	19.4378	21.8164
6	1.3950	21.8164	0.0000

YEARS 7 — MO PAYT 1.7440 — AN CONST 20.93

#	INT	PRIN	BALANCE
1	11.0878	9.8397	90.1603
2	9.8837	11.0438	79.1165
3	8.5322	12.3952	66.7213
4	7.0154	13.9120	52.8093
5	5.3130	15.6144	37.1949
6	3.4023	17.5252	19.6697
7	1.2577	19.6697	0.0000

YEARS 8 — MO PAYT 1.6034 — AN CONST 19.25

#	INT	PRIN	BALANCE
1	11.1804	8.0602	91.9398
2	10.1941	9.0466	82.8932
3	9.0870	10.1536	72.7396
4	7.8445	11.3961	61.3434
5	6.4500	12.7907	48.5528
6	4.8848	14.3559	34.1969
7	3.1280	16.1126	18.0843
8	1.1563	18.0843	0.0000

YEARS 9 — MO PAYT 1.4960 — AN CONST 17.96

#	INT	PRIN	BALANCE
1	11.2512	6.7003	93.2997
2	10.4313	7.5202	85.7795
3	9.5110	8.4404	77.3391
4	8.4782	9.4733	67.8658
5	7.3189	10.6325	57.2333
6	6.0178	11.9337	45.2996
7	4.5575	13.3940	31.9056
8	2.9185	15.0330	16.8726
9	1.0789	16.8726	0.0000

YEARS 10 — MO PAYT 1.4117 — AN CONST 16.95

#	INT	PRIN	BALANCE
1	11.3067	5.6334	94.3666
2	10.6174	6.3228	88.0437
3	9.8436	7.0965	80.9472
4	8.9752	7.9649	72.9822
5	8.0006	8.9396	64.0426
6	6.9066	10.0336	54.0091
7	5.6788	11.2614	42.7477
8	4.3007	12.6394	30.1082
9	2.7540	14.1861	15.9221
10	1.0181	15.9221	0.0000

YEARS 11 — MO PAYT 1.3442 — AN CONST 16.14

#	INT	PRIN	BALANCE
1	11.3512	4.7794	95.2206
2	10.7663	5.3642	89.8564
3	10.1099	6.0206	83.8358
4	9.3732	6.7574	77.0784
5	8.5463	7.5843	69.4942
6	7.6182	8.5124	60.9818
7	6.5765	9.5540	51.4278
8	5.4074	10.7232	40.7046
9	4.0952	12.0354	28.6693
10	2.6224	13.5081	15.1611
11	.9694	15.1611	0.0000

YEARS 12 — MO PAYT 1.2893 — AN CONST 15.48

#	INT	PRIN	BALANCE
1	11.3874	4.0843	95.9157
2	10.8876	4.5841	91.3315
3	10.3266	5.1451	86.1864
4	9.6970	5.7747	80.4117
5	8.9903	6.4814	73.9303
6	8.1972	7.2745	66.6558
7	7.3070	8.1647	58.4911
8	6.3079	9.1638	49.3273
9	5.1865	10.2852	39.0421
10	3.9279	11.5438	27.4983
11	2.5153	12.9564	14.5419
12	.9298	14.5419	0.0000

YEARS 13 — MO PAYT 1.2440 — AN CONST 14.93

#	INT	PRIN	BALANCE
1	11.4172	3.5113	96.4887
2	10.9875	3.9409	92.5478
3	10.5053	4.4232	88.1246
4	9.9640	4.9645	83.1602
5	9.3565	5.5720	77.5882
6	8.6747	6.2538	71.3344
7	7.9094	7.0191	64.3153
8	7.0505	7.8780	56.4373
9	6.0864	8.8420	47.5953
10	5.0044	9.9240	37.6712
11	3.7900	11.1385	26.5328
12	2.4270	12.5015	14.0313
13	.8972	14.0313	0.0000

YEARS 14 — MO PAYT 1.2063 — AN CONST 14.48

#	INT	PRIN	BALANCE
1	11.4421	3.0335	96.9665
2	11.0709	3.4047	93.5617
3	10.6542	3.8214	89.7403
4	10.1866	4.2890	85.4513
5	9.6618	4.8139	80.6375
6	9.0727	5.4029	75.2345
7	8.4115	6.0641	69.1705
8	7.6695	6.8062	62.3643
9	6.8366	7.6390	54.7253
10	5.9018	8.5738	46.1515
11	4.8526	9.6230	36.5285
12	3.6750	10.8006	25.7279
13	2.3534	12.1222	13.6056
14	.8700	13.6056	0.0000

YEARS 15 — MO PAYT 1.1746 — AN CONST 14.10

#	INT	PRIN	BALANCE
1	11.4630	2.6317	97.3683
2	11.1410	2.9537	94.4146
3	10.7795	3.3151	91.0995
4	10.3738	3.7208	87.3787
5	9.9185	4.1761	83.2025
6	9.4075	4.6872	78.5154
7	8.8339	5.2607	73.2546
8	8.1902	5.9045	67.3501
9	7.4676	6.6270	60.7231
10	6.6567	7.4380	53.2851
11	5.7465	8.3482	44.9369
12	4.7249	9.3698	35.5672
13	3.5783	10.5163	25.0508
14	2.2914	11.8032	13.2476
15	.8471	13.2476	0.0000

YEARS 16 — MO PAYT 1.1476 — AN CONST 13.78

#	INT	PRIN	BALANCE
1	11.4807	2.2910	97.7090
2	11.2004	2.5714	95.1376
3	10.8857	2.8860	92.2516
4	10.5326	3.2392	89.0124
5	10.1362	3.6356	85.3768
6	9.6913	4.0805	81.2964
7	9.1920	4.5798	76.7166
8	8.6315	5.1402	71.5764
9	8.0025	5.7692	65.8071
10	7.2965	6.4752	59.3319
11	6.5042	7.2676	52.0643
12	5.6148	8.1569	43.9074
13	4.6167	9.1551	34.7523
14	3.4963	10.2754	24.4769
15	2.2389	11.5328	12.9441
16	.8277	12.9441	0.0000

YEARS 17 — MO PAYT 1.1247 — AN CONST 13.50

#	INT	PRIN	BALANCE
1	11.4959	2.0004	97.9996
2	11.2511	2.2452	95.7544
3	10.9763	2.5199	93.2345
4	10.6680	2.8283	90.4062
5	10.3219	3.1744	87.2318
6	9.9334	3.5628	83.6689
7	9.4974	3.9988	79.6701
8	9.0081	4.4882	75.1819
9	8.4589	5.0374	70.1445
10	7.8424	5.6538	64.4907
11	7.1506	6.3457	58.1450
12	6.3741	7.1222	51.0228
13	5.5025	7.9938	43.0291
14	4.5243	8.9720	34.0571
15	3.4264	10.0699	23.9873
16	2.1941	11.3021	12.6852
17	.8111	12.6852	0.0000

YEARS 18 — MO PAYT 1.1050 — AN CONST 13.26

#	INT	PRIN	BALANCE
1	11.5088	1.7511	98.2489
2	11.2946	1.9654	96.2835
3	11.0541	2.2059	94.0777
4	10.7841	2.4758	91.6019
5	10.4812	2.7788	88.8231
6	10.1411	3.1188	85.7043
7	9.7595	3.5005	82.2038
8	9.3311	3.9288	78.2750
9	8.8503	4.4096	73.8654
10	8.3107	4.9492	68.9163
11	7.7051	5.5548	63.3614
12	7.0254	6.2346	57.1269
13	6.2624	6.9975	50.1294
14	5.4061	7.8538	42.2756
15	4.4451	8.8148	33.4608
16	3.3664	9.8935	23.5672
17	2.1557	11.1042	12.4630
18	.7969	12.4630	0.0000

YEARS 19 — MO PAYT 1.0880 — AN CONST 13.06

#	INT	PRIN	BALANCE
1	11.5200	1.5362	98.4638
2	11.3320	1.7242	96.7396
3	11.1211	1.9352	94.8044
4	10.8842	2.1720	92.6325
5	10.6185	2.4378	90.1947
6	10.3201	2.7361	87.4586
7	9.9853	3.0709	84.3877
8	9.6095	3.4467	80.9410
9	9.1878	3.8685	77.0726
10	8.7144	4.3418	72.7307
11	8.1831	4.8732	67.8576
12	7.5867	5.4695	62.3881
13	6.9174	6.1388	56.2493
14	6.1662	6.8900	49.3593
15	5.3231	7.7331	41.6262
16	4.3768	8.6794	32.9467
17	3.3147	9.7415	23.2052
18	2.1226	10.9336	12.2716
19	.7847	12.2716	0.0000

YEARS 20 — MO PAYT 1.0733 — AN CONST 12.88

#	INT	PRIN	BALANCE
1	11.5297	1.3502	98.6498
2	11.3645	1.5155	97.1343
3	11.1790	1.7009	95.4334
4	10.9709	1.9090	93.5244
5	10.7373	2.1427	91.3817
6	10.4751	2.4049	88.9768
7	10.1808	2.6991	86.2777
8	9.8505	3.0294	83.2483
9	9.4798	3.4001	79.8481
10	9.0637	3.8162	76.0319
11	8.5967	4.2832	71.7487
12	8.0726	4.8074	66.9413
13	7.4843	5.3956	61.5457
14	6.8240	6.0559	55.4898
15	6.0830	6.7970	48.6928
16	5.2512	7.6287	41.0641
17	4.3177	8.5622	32.5019
18	3.2699	9.6100	22.8919
19	2.0940	10.7860	12.1059
20	.7741	12.1059	0.0000

YEARS 21 — MO PAYT 1.0606 — AN CONST 12.73

#	INT	PRIN	BALANCE
1	11.5381	1.1887	98.8113
2	11.3927	1.3342	97.4771
3	11.2294	1.4974	95.9797

#	INT	PRIN	BALANCE
4	11.0461	1.6807	94.2990
5	10.8405	1.8864	92.4126
6	10.6096	2.1172	90.2954
7	10.3506	2.3763	87.9192
8	10.0598	2.6671	85.2521
9	9.7334	2.9934	82.2587
10	9.3671	3.3597	78.8990
11	8.9560	3.7709	75.1281
12	8.4945	4.2323	70.8958
13	7.9766	4.7502	66.1456
14	7.3953	5.3315	60.8141
15	6.7429	5.9839	54.8302
16	6.0107	6.7162	48.1140
17	5.1888	7.5380	40.5760
18	4.2664	8.4605	32.1155
19	3.2311	9.4958	22.6197
20	2.0691	10.6578	11.9620
21	.7649	11.9620	0.0000

YEARS 22	MO PAYT 1.0495	AN CONST 12.60	
#	INT	PRIN	BALANCE
1	11.5454	1.0480	98.9520
2	11.4172	1.1763	97.7757
3	11.2733	1.3202	96.4555
4	11.1117	1.4818	94.9738
5	10.9304	1.6631	93.3107
6	10.7269	1.8666	91.4441
7	10.4985	2.0950	89.3491
8	10.2421	2.3514	86.9978
9	9.9544	2.6391	84.3587
10	9.6314	2.9621	81.3966
11	9.2689	3.3245	78.0721
12	8.8621	3.7313	74.3407
13	8.4055	4.1879	70.1528
14	7.8930	4.7004	65.4524
15	7.3178	5.2756	60.1767
16	6.6723	5.9212	54.2555
17	5.9477	6.6458	47.6098
18	5.1344	7.4590	40.1507
19	4.2217	8.3718	31.7789
20	3.1972	9.3963	22.3827
21	2.0474	10.5461	11.8366
22	.7568	11.8366	0.0000

YEARS 23	MO PAYT 1.0397	AN CONST 12.48	
#	INT	PRIN	BALANCE
1	11.5518	.9251	99.0749
2	11.4386	1.0383	98.0366
3	11.3116	1.1654	96.8712
4	11.1690	1.3080	95.5632
5	11.0089	1.4680	94.0952
6	10.8293	1.6477	92.4475
7	10.6276	1.8493	90.5982
8	10.4013	2.0756	88.5225
9	10.1473	2.3296	86.1929
10	9.8623	2.6147	83.5782
11	9.5423	2.9346	80.6436
12	9.1832	3.2938	77.3498
13	8.7801	3.6968	73.6530
14	8.3277	4.1492	69.5038
15	7.8200	4.6569	64.8469
16	7.2501	5.2268	59.6200
17	6.6105	5.8664	53.7536
18	5.8926	6.5843	47.1693
19	5.0869	7.3900	39.7793
20	4.1826	8.2943	31.4849
21	3.1676	9.3093	22.1756
22	2.0284	10.4485	11.7271
23	.7498	11.7271	0.0000

YEARS 24	MO PAYT 1.0312	AN CONST 12.38	
#	INT	PRIN	BALANCE
1	11.5574	.8175	99.1825
2	11.4574	.9175	98.2649
3	11.3451	1.0298	97.2351
4	11.2191	1.1558	96.0793
5	11.0777	1.2973	94.7820
6	10.9189	1.4560	93.3259
7	10.7407	1.6342	91.6917
8	10.5408	1.8342	89.8575
9	10.3163	2.0586	87.7989
10	10.0644	2.3106	85.4883
11	9.7816	2.5933	82.8950
12	9.4643	2.9107	79.9843
13	9.1081	3.2668	76.7175
14	8.7084	3.6666	73.0509
15	8.2597	4.1153	68.9356
16	7.7561	4.6189	64.3167
17	7.1909	5.1841	59.1326
18	6.5565	5.8185	53.3142
19	5.8445	6.5305	46.7837
20	5.0453	7.3296	39.4541
21	4.1484	8.2265	31.2276
22	3.1417	9.2332	21.9943
23	2.0119	10.3631	11.6312
24	.7437	11.6312	0.0000

YEARS 25	MO PAYT 1.0238	AN CONST 12.29	
#	INT	PRIN	BALANCE
1	11.5624	.7231	99.2769
2	11.4739	.8116	98.4653
3	11.3746	.9109	97.5544
4	11.2631	1.0224	96.5320
5	11.1380	1.1475	95.3845
6	10.9976	1.2879	94.0966
7	10.8400	1.4455	92.6511
8	10.6631	1.6224	91.0287
9	10.4645	1.8209	89.2077
10	10.2417	2.0438	87.1640
11	9.9916	2.2939	84.8701
12	9.7109	2.5746	82.2956
13	9.3959	2.8896	79.4060
14	9.0423	3.2432	76.1627
15	8.6454	3.6401	72.5227
16	8.1999	4.0855	68.4371
17	7.7000	4.5855	63.8517
18	7.1389	5.1466	58.7051
19	6.5091	5.7764	52.9287
20	5.8022	6.4833	46.4454
21	5.0089	7.2766	39.1688
22	4.1184	8.1671	31.0017
23	3.1190	9.1665	21.8353
24	1.9973	10.2882	11.5471
25	.7383	11.5471	0.0000

YEARS 26	MO PAYT 1.0172	AN CONST 12.21	
#	INT	PRIN	BALANCE
1	11.5667	.6401	99.3599
2	11.4883	.7185	98.6414
3	11.4004	.8064	97.8350
4	11.3017	.9051	96.9299
5	11.1910	1.0158	95.9141
6	11.0667	1.1401	94.7739
7	10.9272	1.2797	93.4942
8	10.7706	1.4363	92.0580
9	10.5948	1.6120	90.4460
10	10.3975	1.8093	88.6367
11	10.1761	2.0307	86.6060
12	9.9276	2.2792	84.3268
13	9.6487	2.5581	81.7687
14	9.3357	2.8711	78.8976
15	8.9844	3.2225	75.6752
16	8.5900	3.6168	72.0584
17	8.1474	4.0594	67.9990
18	7.6507	4.5561	63.4429
19	7.0932	5.1137	58.3293
20	6.4674	5.7394	52.5898
21	5.7651	6.4417	46.1481
22	4.9768	7.2300	38.9181
23	4.0921	8.1148	30.8033
24	3.0990	9.1078	21.6955
25	1.9845	10.2223	11.4732
26	.7336	11.4732	0.0000

YEARS 27	MO PAYT 1.0115	AN CONST 12.14	
#	INT	PRIN	BALANCE
1	11.5705	.5671	99.4329
2	11.5011	.6365	98.7964
3	11.4232	.7144	98.0820
4	11.3358	.8018	97.2801
5	11.2376	.8999	96.3802
6	11.1275	1.0101	95.3701
7	11.0039	1.1337	94.2364
8	10.8652	1.2724	92.9640
9	10.7095	1.4281	91.5359
10	10.5347	1.6029	89.9330
11	10.3386	1.7990	88.1340
12	10.1184	2.0192	86.1148
13	9.8713	2.2663	83.8486
14	9.5940	2.5436	81.3050
15	9.2828	2.8548	78.4502
16	8.9334	3.2042	75.2460
17	8.5413	3.5963	71.6497
18	8.1012	4.0364	67.6134
19	7.6073	4.5303	63.0831
20	7.0529	5.0847	57.9985
21	6.4307	5.7069	52.2916
22	5.7324	6.4052	45.8864
23	4.9486	7.1890	38.6973
24	4.0688	8.0688	30.6286
25	3.0815	9.0561	21.5725
26	1.9733	10.1643	11.4081
27	.7295	11.4081	0.0000

YEARS 28	MO PAYT 1.0064	AN CONST 12.08	
#	INT	PRIN	BALANCE
1	11.5738	.5027	99.4973
2	11.5123	.5643	98.9330
3	11.4433	.6333	98.2997
4	11.3658	.7108	97.5889
5	11.2788	.7978	96.7911
6	11.1811	.8954	95.8956
7	11.0716	1.0050	94.8906
8	10.9486	1.1280	93.7627
9	10.8106	1.2660	92.4966
10	10.6556	1.4209	91.0757
11	10.4818	1.5948	89.4809
12	10.2866	1.7900	87.6909
13	10.0676	2.0090	85.6819
14	9.8217	2.2549	83.4271
15	9.5458	2.5308	80.8963
16	9.2361	2.8405	78.0558
17	8.8885	3.1881	74.8677
18	8.4984	3.5782	71.2895
19	8.0605	4.0161	67.2735
20	7.5691	4.5075	62.7660
21	7.0175	5.0591	57.7069
22	6.3984	5.6782	52.0287
23	5.7036	6.3730	45.6557
24	4.9237	7.1529	38.5028
25	4.0484	8.0282	30.4746
26	3.0660	9.0106	21.4640
27	1.9633	10.1132	11.3508
28	.7258	11.3508	0.0000

YEARS 29	MO PAYT 1.0019	AN CONST 12.03	
#	INT	PRIN	BALANCE
1	11.5768	.4459	99.5541
2	11.5222	.5005	99.0536
3	11.4610	.5618	98.4918
4	11.3922	.6305	97.8613
5	11.3151	.7076	97.1537
6	11.2285	.7942	96.3594
7	11.1313	.8914	95.4680
8	11.0222	1.0005	94.4675
9	10.8998	1.1230	93.3445
10	10.7624	1.2604	92.0842
11	10.6081	1.4146	90.6696
12	10.4350	1.5877	89.0819
13	10.2407	1.7820	87.2999
14	10.0227	2.0001	85.2998
15	9.7779	2.2448	83.0550
16	9.5032	2.5195	80.5355
17	9.1949	2.8278	77.7077
18	8.8489	3.1739	74.5339
19	8.4605	3.5622	70.9716
20	8.0246	3.9981	66.9735
21	7.5353	4.4874	62.4861
22	6.9862	5.0365	57.4495
23	6.3699	5.6529	51.7967
24	5.6781	6.3446	45.4521
25	4.9017	7.1210	38.3311
26	4.0303	7.9924	30.3387
27	3.0523	8.9704	21.3683
28	1.9546	10.0681	11.3002
29	.7225	11.3002	0.0000

YEARS 30	MO PAYT .9979	AN CONST 11.98	
#	INT	PRIN	BALANCE
1	11.5794	.3957	99.6043
2	11.5310	.4442	99.1601
3	11.4766	.4985	98.6616
4	11.4156	.5595	98.1020
5	11.3471	.6280	97.4740
6	11.2703	.7048	96.7692
7	11.1840	.7911	95.9781
8	11.0872	.8879	95.0902
9	10.9786	.9966	94.0936
10	10.8566	1.1185	92.9751
11	10.7198	1.2554	91.7198
12	10.5661	1.4090	90.3108
13	10.3937	1.5814	88.7293
14	10.2002	1.7749	86.9544
15	9.9830	1.9921	84.9623
16	9.7392	2.2359	82.7263
17	9.4656	2.5095	80.2168
18	9.1585	2.8166	77.4002
19	8.8138	3.1613	74.2389
20	8.4270	3.5481	70.6908
21	7.9928	3.9823	66.7084
22	7.5055	4.4696	62.2388
23	6.9585	5.0166	57.2222
24	6.3447	5.6305	51.5917
25	5.6557	6.3195	45.2722
26	4.8823	7.0928	38.1794
27	4.0144	7.9608	30.2187
28	3.0402	8.9349	21.2837
29	1.9469	10.0283	11.2555
30	.7197	11.2555	0.0000

YEARS 2 — MO PAYT 4.6899 — AN CONST 56.28

#	INT	PRIN	BALANCE
1	9.1673	47.1110	52.8890
2	3.3892	52.8890	0.0000

YEARS 3 — MO PAYT 3.3035 — AN CONST 39.65

#	INT	PRIN	BALANCE
1	10.0829	29.5597	70.4403
2	6.4575	33.1851	37.2552
3	2.3874	37.2552	0.0000

YEARS 4 — MO PAYT 2.6150 — AN CONST 31.39

#	INT	PRIN	BALANCE
1	10.5377	20.8424	79.1576
2	7.9814	23.3987	55.7589
3	5.1116	26.2685	29.4903
4	1.8898	29.4903	0.0000

YEARS 5 — MO PAYT 2.2055 — AN CONST 26.47

#	INT	PRIN	BALANCE
1	10.8081	15.6584	84.3416
2	8.8877	17.5788	66.7628
3	6.7316	19.7349	47.0279
4	4.3112	22.1553	24.8726
5	1.5939	24.8726	0.0000

YEARS 6 — MO PAYT 1.9356 — AN CONST 23.23

#	INT	PRIN	BALANCE
1	10.9864	12.2404	87.7596
2	9.4852	13.7417	74.0178
3	7.7998	15.4271	58.5907
4	5.9077	17.3192	41.2715
5	3.7835	19.4434	21.8281
6	1.3988	21.8281	0.0000

YEARS 7 — MO PAYT 1.7453 — AN CONST 20.95

#	INT	PRIN	BALANCE
1	11.1121	9.8313	90.1687
2	9.9063	11.0371	79.1317
3	8.5527	12.3907	66.7410
4	7.0329	13.9104	52.8305
5	5.3269	15.6165	37.2140
6	3.4115	17.5319	19.6821
7	1.2613	19.6821	0.0000

YEARS 8 — MO PAYT 1.6048 — AN CONST 19.26

#	INT	PRIN	BALANCE
1	11.2049	8.0521	91.9479
2	10.2174	9.0396	82.9083
3	9.1087	10.1483	72.7599
4	7.8640	11.3930	61.3669
5	6.4667	12.7904	48.5766
6	4.8979	14.3591	34.2175
7	3.1368	16.1202	18.0973
8	1.1597	18.0973	0.0000

YEARS 9 — MO PAYT 1.4974 — AN CONST 17.97

#	INT	PRIN	BALANCE
1	11.2759	6.6924	93.3076
2	10.4551	7.5132	85.7944
3	9.5336	8.4347	77.3597
4	8.4991	9.4692	67.8906
5	7.3377	10.6306	57.2600
6	6.0339	11.9344	45.3256
7	4.5701	13.3981	31.9275
8	2.9269	15.0414	16.8862
9	1.0821	16.8862	0.0000

YEARS 10 — MO PAYT 1.4131 — AN CONST 16.96

#	INT	PRIN	BALANCE
1	11.3315	5.6259	94.3741
2	10.6415	6.3159	88.0582
3	9.8669	7.0905	80.9677
4	8.9972	7.9602	73.0076
5	8.0209	8.9365	64.0711
6	6.9249	10.0325	54.0386
7	5.6944	11.2630	42.7757
8	4.3130	12.6443	30.1313
9	2.7622	14.1952	15.9362
10	1.0212	15.9362	0.0000

YEARS 11 — MO PAYT 1.3457 — AN CONST 16.15

#	INT	PRIN	BALANCE
1	11.3760	4.7721	95.2279
2	10.7908	5.3574	89.8705
3	10.1337	6.0145	83.8560
4	9.3960	6.7521	77.1039
5	8.5679	7.5803	69.5236
6	7.6382	8.5100	61.0136
7	6.5944	9.5537	51.4599
8	5.4227	10.7255	40.7344
9	4.1072	12.0409	28.6934
10	2.6304	13.5177	15.1757
11	.9725	15.1757	0.0000

YEARS 12 — MO PAYT 1.2908 — AN CONST 15.49

#	INT	PRIN	BALANCE
1	11.4123	4.0774	95.9226
2	10.9122	4.5775	91.3450
3	10.3508	5.1390	86.2061
4	9.7205	5.7692	80.4368
5	9.0129	6.4768	73.9600
6	8.2185	7.2712	66.6888
7	7.3267	8.1630	58.5258
8	6.3255	9.1642	49.3616
9	5.2016	10.2882	39.0734
10	3.9397	11.5500	27.5235
11	2.5232	12.9666	14.5569
12	.9328	14.5569	0.0000

YEARS 13 — MO PAYT 1.2456 — AN CONST 14.95

#	INT	PRIN	BALANCE
1	11.4422	3.5047	96.4953
2	11.0123	3.9345	92.5608
3	10.5298	4.4171	88.1437
4	9.9880	4.9589	83.1848
5	9.3798	5.5670	77.6178
6	8.6970	6.2498	71.3679
7	7.9305	7.0164	64.3516
8	7.0699	7.8769	56.4746
9	6.1039	8.8430	47.6316
10	5.0193	9.9276	37.7040
11	3.8017	11.1452	26.5589
12	2.4347	12.5121	14.0467
13	.9001	14.0467	0.0000

YEARS 14 — MO PAYT 1.2079 — AN CONST 14.50

#	INT	PRIN	BALANCE
1	11.4671	3.0273	96.9727
2	11.0958	3.3986	93.5741
3	10.6789	3.8154	89.7587
4	10.2110	4.2834	85.4753
5	9.6856	4.8087	80.6666
6	9.0959	5.3985	75.2680
7	8.4337	6.0606	69.2074
8	7.6904	6.8040	62.4034
9	6.8559	7.6385	54.7650
10	5.9191	8.5753	46.1897
11	4.8673	9.6271	36.5626
12	3.6866	10.8078	25.7548
13	2.3610	12.1334	13.6215
14	.8729	13.6215	0.0000

YEARS 15 — MO PAYT 1.1761 — AN CONST 14.12

#	INT	PRIN	BALANCE
1	11.4880	2.6258	97.3742
2	11.1660	2.9478	94.4264
3	10.8044	3.3094	91.1171
4	10.3985	3.7152	87.4018
5	9.9429	4.1709	83.2309
6	9.4313	4.6825	78.5484
7	8.8570	5.2568	73.2917
8	8.2123	5.9015	67.3902
9	7.4885	6.6253	60.7649
10	6.6759	7.4379	53.3270
11	5.7636	8.3501	44.9768
12	4.7395	9.3743	35.6026
13	3.5898	10.5240	25.0786
14	2.2990	11.8148	13.2638
15	.8500	13.2638	0.0000

YEARS 16 — MO PAYT 1.1493 — AN CONST 13.80

#	INT	PRIN	BALANCE
1	11.5058	2.2854	97.7146
2	11.2255	2.5658	95.1488
3	10.9108	2.8804	92.2684
4	10.5575	3.2337	89.0346
5	10.1609	3.6303	85.4043
6	9.7156	4.0756	81.3287
7	9.2158	4.5755	76.7533
8	8.6546	5.1366	71.6166
9	8.0246	5.7666	65.8500
10	7.3173	6.4739	59.3761
11	6.5233	7.2679	52.1082
12	5.6319	8.1593	43.9489
13	4.6312	9.1600	34.7889
14	3.5077	10.2835	24.5054
15	2.2465	11.5447	12.9607
16	.8305	12.9607	0.0000

YEARS 17 — MO PAYT 1.1263 — AN CONST 13.52

#	INT	PRIN	BALANCE
1	11.5209	1.9951	98.0049
2	11.2762	2.2399	95.7650
3	11.0015	2.5146	93.2504
4	10.6931	2.8230	90.4275
5	10.3469	3.1692	87.2583
6	9.9582	3.5579	83.7004
7	9.5218	3.9943	79.7061
8	9.0319	4.4842	75.2219
9	8.4819	5.0341	70.1878
10	7.8645	5.6516	64.5362
11	7.1713	6.3447	58.1915
12	6.3932	7.1229	51.0686
13	5.5196	7.9965	43.0721
14	4.5388	8.9773	34.0948
15	3.4378	10.0783	24.0165
16	2.2017	11.3144	12.7021
17	.8140	12.7021	0.0000

YEARS 18 — MO PAYT 1.1067 — AN CONST 13.29

#	INT	PRIN	BALANCE
1	11.5339	1.7461	98.2539
2	11.3197	1.9603	96.2935
3	11.0793	2.2007	94.0928
4	10.8094	2.4707	91.6221
5	10.5064	2.7737	88.8485
6	10.1662	3.1139	85.7346
7	9.7843	3.4958	82.2388
8	9.3555	3.9245	78.3143
9	8.8742	4.4059	73.9084
10	8.3338	4.9462	68.9622
11	7.7272	5.5529	63.4093
12	7.0461	6.2339	57.1754
13	6.2815	6.9985	50.1769
14	5.4232	7.8569	42.3200
15	4.4595	8.8205	33.4995
16	3.3777	9.9023	23.5971
17	2.1632	11.1168	12.4803
18	.7998	12.4803	0.0000

YEARS 19 — MO PAYT 1.0897 — AN CONST 13.08

#	INT	PRIN	BALANCE
1	11.5451	1.5316	98.4684
2	11.3573	1.7194	96.7490
3	11.1464	1.9303	94.8187
4	10.9096	2.1670	92.6517
5	10.6438	2.4328	90.2189
6	10.3455	2.7312	87.4877
7	10.0105	3.0662	84.4215
8	9.6344	3.4422	80.9793
9	9.2122	3.8644	77.1149
10	8.7383	4.3384	72.7765
11	8.2062	4.8705	67.9060
12	7.6088	5.4678	62.4382
13	6.9382	6.1385	56.2997
14	6.1853	6.8913	49.4084
15	5.3401	7.7365	41.6718
16	4.3912	8.6854	32.9864
17	3.3260	9.7507	23.2357
18	2.1301	10.9466	12.2892
19	.7875	12.2892	0.0000

YEARS 20 — MO PAYT 1.0751 — AN CONST 12.91

#	INT	PRIN	BALANCE
1	11.5548	1.3459	98.6541
2	11.3897	1.5109	97.1432
3	11.2044	1.6963	95.4469
4	10.9964	1.9043	93.5426
5	10.7606	2.1379	91.4047
6	10.5006	2.4001	89.0047
7	10.2062	2.6944	86.3102
8	9.8758	3.0249	83.2853
9	9.5048	3.3959	79.8894
10	9.0883	3.8124	76.0770
11	8.6207	4.2800	71.7970
12	8.0957	4.8049	66.9921
13	7.5064	5.3942	61.5978
14	6.8448	6.0558	55.5420
15	6.1021	6.7986	48.7434
16	5.2682	7.6324	41.1110
17	4.3321	8.5685	32.5424
18	3.2812	9.6194	22.9230
19	2.1014	10.7992	12.1238
20	.7769	12.1238	0.0000

YEARS 21 — MO PAYT 1.0623 — AN CONST 12.75

#	INT	PRIN	BALANCE
1	11.5632	1.1846	98.8154
2	11.4179	1.3299	97.4854
3	11.2548	1.4930	95.9924

MONTHLY PAYMENT AMORTIZATION SCHEDULE PER $100   11.625%

#	INT	PRIN	BALANCE
4	11.0717	1.6762	94.3162
5	10.8661	1.8817	92.4345
6	10.6353	2.1125	90.3219
7	10.3762	2.3716	87.9503
8	10.0853	2.6625	85.2878
9	9.7588	2.9891	82.2987
10	9.3922	3.3557	78.9430
11	8.9806	3.7672	75.1758
12	8.5185	4.2293	70.9465
13	7.9998	4.7480	66.1984
14	7.4175	5.3303	60.8681
15	6.7637	5.9841	54.8840
16	6.0298	6.7180	48.1660
17	5.2058	7.5420	40.6240
18	4.2808	8.4670	32.1569
19	3.2424	9.5055	22.6515
20	2.0765	10.6713	11.9801
21	.7677	11.9801	0.0000

YEARS 22 — MO PAYT 1.0512 — AN CONST 12.62

#	INT	PRIN	BALANCE
1	11.5705	1.0442	98.9558
2	11.4425	1.1723	97.7835
3	11.2987	1.3160	96.4675
4	11.1373	1.4775	94.9900
5	10.9561	1.6587	93.3314
6	10.7526	1.8621	91.4693
7	10.5242	2.0905	89.3788
8	10.2678	2.3469	87.0319
9	9.9800	2.6347	84.3972
10	9.6569	2.9579	81.4393
11	9.2941	3.3206	78.1187
12	8.8868	3.7279	74.3908
13	8.4296	4.1851	70.2056
14	7.9163	4.6984	65.5072
15	7.3400	5.2747	60.2325
16	6.6931	5.9216	54.3109
17	5.9668	6.6479	47.6630
18	5.1515	7.4632	40.1998
19	4.2361	8.3786	31.8212
20	3.2085	9.4062	22.4149
21	2.0548	10.5599	11.8550
22	.7597	11.8550	0.0000

YEARS 23 — MO PAYT 1.0415 — AN CONST 12.50

#	INT	PRIN	BALANCE
1	11.5769	.9216	99.0784
2	11.4639	1.0346	98.0439
3	11.3370	1.1615	96.8824
4	11.1946	1.3039	95.5785
5	11.0346	1.4638	94.1146
6	10.8551	1.6434	92.4713
7	10.6535	1.8449	90.6263
8	10.4273	2.0712	88.5551
9	10.1732	2.3252	86.2299
10	9.8880	2.6104	83.6194
11	9.5679	2.9306	80.6888
12	9.2084	3.2900	77.3988
13	8.8049	3.6936	73.7052
14	8.3519	4.1466	69.5587
15	7.8433	4.6551	64.9035
16	7.2724	5.2261	59.6774
17	6.6314	5.8670	53.8104
18	5.9118	6.5866	47.2238
19	5.1040	7.3945	39.8293
20	4.1971	8.3014	31.5279
21	3.1789	9.3195	22.2084
22	2.0359	10.4626	11.7458
23	.7527	11.7458	0.0000

YEARS 24 — MO PAYT 1.0331 — AN CONST 12.40

#	INT	PRIN	BALANCE
1	11.5825	.8142	99.1858
2	11.4827	.9140	98.2718
3	11.3706	1.0262	97.2456
4	11.2447	1.1520	96.0936
5	11.1034	1.2933	94.8003
6	10.9448	1.4519	93.3484
7	10.7667	1.6300	91.7184
8	10.5668	1.8299	89.8885
9	10.3424	2.0544	87.8341
10	10.0904	2.3063	85.5278
11	9.8075	2.5892	82.9386
12	9.4900	2.9067	80.0319
13	9.1335	3.2633	76.7686
14	8.7332	3.6635	73.1051
15	8.2839	4.1128	68.9923
16	7.7795	4.6172	64.3751
17	7.2132	5.1835	59.1916
18	6.5774	5.8193	53.3723
19	5.8637	6.5330	46.8393
20	5.0624	7.3343	39.5050
21	4.1629	8.2338	31.2712
22	3.1530	9.2437	22.0275
23	2.0193	10.3774	11.6502
24	.7466	11.6502	0.0000

YEARS 25 — MO PAYT 1.0256 — AN CONST 12.31

#	INT	PRIN	BALANCE
1	11.5874	.7200	99.2800
2	11.4991	.8083	98.4717
3	11.4000	.9075	97.5642
4	11.2887	1.0188	96.5454
5	11.1637	1.1437	95.4017
6	11.0235	1.2840	94.1177
7	10.8660	1.4415	92.6762
8	10.6892	1.6183	91.0580
9	10.4907	1.8167	89.2412
10	10.2679	2.0396	87.2017
11	10.0177	2.2897	84.9120
12	9.7369	2.5705	82.3414
13	9.4216	2.8858	79.4556
14	9.0677	3.2398	76.2159
15	8.6704	3.6371	72.5787
16	8.2243	4.0832	68.4956
17	7.7235	4.5840	63.9116
18	7.1613	5.1462	58.7654
19	6.5301	5.7774	52.9880
20	5.8215	6.4860	46.5020
21	5.0260	7.2815	39.2206
22	4.1329	8.1745	31.0460
23	3.1303	9.1771	21.8689
24	2.0048	10.3027	11.5663
25	.7412	11.5663	0.0000

YEARS 26 — MO PAYT 1.0191 — AN CONST 12.23

#	INT	PRIN	BALANCE
1	11.5918	.6373	99.3627
2	11.5136	.7154	98.6473
3	11.4258	.8032	97.8441
4	11.3273	.9017	96.9424
5	11.2168	1.0123	95.9302
6	11.0926	1.1364	94.7937
7	10.9532	1.2758	93.5179
8	10.7967	1.4323	92.0856
9	10.6211	1.6080	90.4777
10	10.4239	1.8052	88.6725
11	10.2025	2.0266	86.6460
12	9.9539	2.2751	84.3708
13	9.6749	2.5542	81.8167
14	9.3616	2.8674	78.9493
15	9.0099	3.2191	75.7302
16	8.6151	3.6139	72.1162
17	8.1719	4.0572	68.0591
18	7.6742	4.5548	63.5043
19	7.1156	5.1134	58.3909
20	6.4885	5.7406	52.6503
21	5.7844	6.4446	46.2057
22	4.9940	7.2351	38.9706
23	4.1066	8.1224	30.8482
24	3.1104	9.1186	21.7296
25	1.9920	10.2370	11.4926
26	.7365	11.4926	0.0000

YEARS 27 — MO PAYT 1.0133 — AN CONST 12.16

#	INT	PRIN	BALANCE
1	11.5956	.5644	99.4356
2	11.5263	.6337	98.8019
3	11.4486	.7114	98.0905
4	11.3614	.7986	97.2919
5	11.2634	.8966	96.3953
6	11.1534	1.0066	95.3887
7	11.0300	1.1300	94.2587
8	10.8914	1.2686	92.9901
9	10.7358	1.4242	91.5659
10	10.5611	1.5989	89.9670
11	10.3650	1.7950	88.1720
12	10.1449	2.0151	86.1569
13	9.8977	2.2623	83.8946
14	9.6203	2.5397	81.3549
15	9.3088	2.8512	78.5036
16	8.9591	3.2009	75.3027
17	8.5665	3.5935	71.7092
18	8.1257	4.0343	67.6749
19	7.6309	4.5291	63.1458
20	7.0755	5.0845	58.0613
21	6.4518	5.7082	52.3531
22	5.7517	6.4083	45.9449
23	4.9658	7.1942	38.7507
24	4.0834	8.0766	30.6741
25	3.0928	9.0672	21.6069
26	1.9808	10.1792	11.4277
27	.7323	11.4277	0.0000

YEARS 28 — MO PAYT 1.0083 — AN CONST 12.10

#	INT	PRIN	BALANCE
1	11.5989	.5003	99.4997
2	11.5375	.5616	98.9381
3	11.4687	.6305	98.3076
4	11.3913	.7078	97.5998
5	11.3045	.7946	96.8051
6	11.2071	.8921	95.9130
7	11.0976	1.0015	94.9115
8	10.9748	1.1244	93.7871
9	10.8369	1.2623	92.5249
10	10.6821	1.4171	91.1078
11	10.5083	1.5909	89.5169
12	10.3132	1.7860	87.7309
13	10.0941	2.0050	85.7259
14	9.8482	2.2510	83.4749
15	9.5721	2.5270	80.9479
16	9.2622	2.8370	78.1109
17	8.9142	3.1849	74.9260
18	8.5236	3.5756	71.3504
19	8.0851	4.0141	67.3363
20	7.5928	4.5064	62.8299
21	7.0401	5.0591	57.7708
22	6.4196	5.6796	52.0912
23	5.7230	6.3762	45.7150
24	4.9409	7.1582	38.5568
25	4.0630	8.0362	30.5206
26	3.0774	9.0218	21.4988
27	1.9709	10.1283	11.3705
28	.7286	11.3705	0.0000

YEARS 29 — MO PAYT 1.0038 — AN CONST 12.05

#	INT	PRIN	BALANCE
1	11.6019	.4436	99.5564
2	11.5474	.4980	99.0583
3	11.4864	.5591	98.4992
4	11.4178	.6277	97.8715
5	11.3408	.7047	97.1668
6	11.2544	.7911	96.3757
7	11.1573	.8882	95.4875
8	11.0484	.9971	94.4904
9	10.9261	1.1194	93.3711
10	10.7888	1.2567	92.1144
11	10.6347	1.4108	90.7036
12	10.4617	1.5838	89.1198
13	10.2674	1.7781	87.3417
14	10.0493	1.9962	85.3456
15	9.8045	2.2410	83.1046
16	9.5297	2.5158	80.5888
17	9.2211	2.8244	77.7644
18	8.8747	3.1708	74.5936
19	8.4858	3.5597	71.0339
20	8.0492	3.9963	67.0376
21	7.5591	4.4864	62.5512
22	7.0088	5.0367	57.5145
23	6.3911	5.6544	51.8601
24	5.6976	6.3479	45.5122
25	4.9190	7.1265	38.3858
26	4.0450	8.0005	30.3852
27	3.0637	8.9818	21.4035
28	1.9621	10.0834	11.3201
29	.7254	11.3201	0.0000

YEARS 30 — MO PAYT .9998 — AN CONST 12.00

#	INT	PRIN	BALANCE
1	11.6045	.3936	99.6064
2	11.5562	.4419	99.1645
3	11.5020	.4961	98.6684
4	11.4411	.5569	98.1115
5	11.3728	.6252	97.4863
6	11.2962	.7019	96.7843
7	11.2101	.7880	95.9963
8	11.1134	.8847	95.1117
9	11.0049	.9932	94.1185
10	10.8831	1.1150	93.0035
11	10.7464	1.2517	91.7518
12	10.5928	1.4052	90.3466
13	10.4205	1.5776	88.7690
14	10.2270	1.7711	86.9979
15	10.0098	1.9883	85.0096
16	9.7659	2.2322	82.7775
17	9.4922	2.5059	80.2716
18	9.1848	2.8133	77.4583
19	8.8398	3.1583	74.3000
20	8.4524	3.5457	70.7543
21	8.0175	3.9805	66.7738
22	7.5293	4.4688	62.3050
23	6.9812	5.0168	57.2882
24	6.3659	5.6322	51.6560
25	5.6752	6.3229	45.3331
26	4.8997	7.0984	38.2347
27	4.0290	7.9690	30.2656
28	3.0517	8.9464	21.3192
29	1.9544	10.0437	11.2755
30	.7226	11.2755	0.0000

YEARS 2 — MO PAYT 4.6933 — AN CONST 56.33

#	INT	PRIN	BALANCE
1	9.2277	47.0925	52.9075
2	3.4126	52.9075	0.0000

YEARS 3 — MO PAYT 3.3071 — AN CONST 39.69

#	INT	PRIN	BALANCE
1	10.1494	29.5360	70.4640
2	6.5022	33.1832	37.2808
3	2.4047	37.2808	0.0000

YEARS 4 — MO PAYT 2.6187 — AN CONST 31.43

#	INT	PRIN	BALANCE
1	10.6072	20.8170	79.1830
2	8.0366	23.3875	55.7955
3	5.1487	26.2755	29.5200
4	1.9041	29.5200	0.0000

YEARS 5 — MO PAYT 2.2093 — AN CONST 26.52

#	INT	PRIN	BALANCE
1	10.8793	15.6324	84.3676
2	8.9490	17.5628	66.8048
3	6.7803	19.7315	47.0733
4	4.3438	22.1680	24.9053
5	1.6064	24.9053	0.0000

YEARS 6 — MO PAYT 1.9395 — AN CONST 23.28

#	INT	PRIN	BALANCE
1	11.0588	12.2147	87.7853
2	9.5505	13.7230	74.0623
3	7.8559	15.4175	58.6448
4	5.9521	17.3213	41.3234
5	3.8132	19.4602	21.8632
6	1.4102	21.8632	0.0000

YEARS 7 — MO PAYT 1.7493 — AN CONST 21.00

#	INT	PRIN	BALANCE
1	11.1852	9.8060	90.1940
2	9.9743	11.0169	79.1771
3	8.6139	12.3773	66.7997
4	7.0856	13.9057	52.8941
5	5.3684	15.6228	37.2712
6	3.4393	17.5519	19.7193
7	1.2719	19.7193	0.0000

YEARS 8 — MO PAYT 1.6088 — AN CONST 19.31

#	INT	PRIN	BALANCE
1	11.2786	8.0276	91.9724
2	10.2873	9.0188	82.9536
3	9.1736	10.1325	72.8210
4	7.9224	11.3837	61.4373
5	6.5168	12.7894	48.6479
6	4.9375	14.3687	34.2793
7	3.1632	16.1429	18.1363
8	1.1698	18.1363	0.0000

YEARS 9 — MO PAYT 1.5016 — AN CONST 18.02

#	INT	PRIN	BALANCE
1	11.3499	6.6688	93.3312
2	10.5264	7.4922	85.8390
3	9.6013	8.4174	77.4216
4	8.5619	9.4568	67.9648
5	7.3941	10.6246	57.3402
6	6.0822	11.9365	45.4037
7	4.6082	13.4105	31.9933
8	2.9523	15.0664	16.9269
9	1.0918	16.9269	0.0000

YEARS 10 — MO PAYT 1.4174 — AN CONST 17.01

#	INT	PRIN	BALANCE
1	11.4058	5.6032	94.3968
2	10.7139	6.2951	88.1017
3	9.9366	7.0724	81.0293
4	9.0633	7.9458	73.0835
5	8.0821	8.9269	64.1566
6	6.9798	10.0292	54.1273
7	5.7414	11.2677	42.8597
8	4.3500	12.6590	30.2006
9	2.7868	14.2222	15.9784
10	1.0306	15.9784	0.0000

YEARS 11 — MO PAYT 1.3501 — AN CONST 16.21

#	INT	PRIN	BALANCE
1	11.4506	4.7504	95.2496
2	10.8640	5.3370	89.9125
3	10.2050	5.9961	83.9165
4	9.4646	6.7365	77.1800
5	8.6327	7.5683	69.6117
6	7.6982	8.5029	61.1089
7	6.6482	9.5528	51.5561
8	5.4686	10.7324	40.8236
9	4.1434	12.0577	28.7660
10	2.6544	13.5466	15.2194
11	.9817	15.2194	0.0000

YEARS 12 — MO PAYT 1.2953 — AN CONST 15.55

#	INT	PRIN	BALANCE
1	11.4870	4.0568	95.9432
2	10.9861	4.5577	91.3855
3	10.4233	5.1205	86.2650
4	9.7910	5.7528	80.5122
5	9.0806	6.4632	74.0490
6	8.2825	7.2613	66.7877
7	7.3859	8.1579	58.6298
8	6.3785	9.1653	49.4645
9	5.2468	10.2970	39.1675
10	3.9753	11.5685	27.5990
11	2.5468	12.9970	14.6019
12	.9419	14.6019	0.0000

YEARS 13 — MO PAYT 1.2502 — AN CONST 15.01

#	INT	PRIN	BALANCE
1	11.5170	3.4851	96.5149
2	11.0867	3.9154	92.5996
3	10.6032	4.3989	88.2007
4	10.0600	4.9421	83.2586
5	9.4498	5.5523	77.7063
6	8.7642	6.2379	71.4684
7	7.9939	7.0082	64.4601
8	7.1285	7.8736	56.5865
9	6.1562	8.8459	47.7407
10	5.0639	9.9382	37.8025
11	3.8367	11.1654	26.6371
12	2.4580	12.5441	14.0931
13	.9090	14.0931	0.0000

YEARS 14 — MO PAYT 1.2126 — AN CONST 14.56

#	INT	PRIN	BALANCE
1	11.5421	3.0087	96.9913
2	11.1705	3.3802	93.6111
3	10.7531	3.7976	89.8135
4	10.2842	4.2665	85.5470
5	9.7574	4.7934	80.7536
6	9.1655	5.3853	75.3684
7	8.5005	6.0503	69.3181
8	7.7534	6.7974	62.5207
9	6.9140	7.6367	54.8840
10	5.9710	8.5797	46.3043
11	4.9116	9.6392	36.6652
12	3.7213	10.8294	25.8357
13	2.3841	12.1667	13.6690
14	.8817	13.6690	0.0000

YEARS 15 — MO PAYT 1.1809 — AN CONST 14.18

#	INT	PRIN	BALANCE
1	11.5631	2.6081	97.3919
2	11.2410	2.9302	94.4616
3	10.8792	3.2920	91.1696
4	10.4727	3.6985	87.4711
5	10.0160	4.1553	83.3158
6	9.5029	4.6684	78.6475
7	8.9264	5.2448	73.4026
8	8.2788	5.8925	67.5102
9	7.5512	6.6201	60.8901
10	6.7337	7.4375	53.4526
11	5.8153	8.3559	45.0966
12	4.7835	9.3878	35.7089
13	3.6242	10.5470	25.1619
14	2.3219	11.8494	13.3125
15	.8587	13.3125	0.0000

YEARS 16 — MO PAYT 1.1541 — AN CONST 13.85

#	INT	PRIN	BALANCE
1	11.5809	2.2688	97.7312
2	11.3007	2.5490	95.1822
3	10.9860	2.8637	92.3185
4	10.6324	3.2173	89.1011
5	10.2351	3.6146	85.4865
6	9.7887	4.0610	81.4255
7	9.2873	4.5624	76.8631
8	8.7239	5.1258	71.7373
9	8.0909	5.7588	65.9785
10	7.3798	6.4699	59.5086
11	6.5809	7.2688	52.2398
12	5.6833	8.1664	44.0735
13	4.6749	9.1748	34.8987
14	3.5420	10.3077	24.5910
15	2.2692	11.5805	13.0105
16	.8392	13.0105	0.0000

YEARS 17 — MO PAYT 1.1313 — AN CONST 13.58

#	INT	PRIN	BALANCE
1	11.5961	1.9795	98.0205
2	11.3517	2.2239	95.7966
3	11.0770	2.4985	93.2981
4	10.7685	2.8070	90.4911
5	10.4219	3.1537	87.3374
6	10.0325	3.5431	83.7943
7	9.5950	3.9806	79.8137
8	9.1034	4.4721	75.3416
9	8.5512	5.0244	70.3173
10	7.9308	5.6448	64.6725
11	7.2337	6.3418	58.3307
12	6.4506	7.1249	51.2058
13	5.5708	8.0047	43.2010
14	4.5824	8.9932	34.2079
15	3.4719	10.1037	24.1042
16	2.2243	11.3513	12.7530
17	.8226	12.7530	0.0000

YEARS 18 — MO PAYT 1.1117 — AN CONST 13.35

#	INT	PRIN	BALANCE
1	11.6091	1.7314	98.2686
2	11.3953	1.9452	96.3234
3	11.1551	2.1854	94.1380
4	10.8852	2.4553	91.6827
5	10.5821	2.7584	88.9243
6	10.2414	3.0991	85.8252
7	9.8588	3.4817	82.3435
8	9.4288	3.9117	78.4318
9	8.9458	4.3947	74.0371
10	8.4031	4.9374	69.0998
11	7.7935	5.5470	63.5527
12	7.1085	6.2320	57.3207
13	6.3390	7.0015	50.3192
14	5.4744	7.8661	42.4531
15	4.5031	8.8374	33.6156
16	3.4118	9.9287	23.6869
17	2.1858	11.1547	12.5322
18	.8084	12.5322	0.0000

YEARS 19 — MO PAYT 1.0948 — AN CONST 13.14

#	INT	PRIN	BALANCE
1	11.6203	1.5177	98.4823
2	11.4329	1.7051	96.7772
3	11.2224	1.9157	94.8615
4	10.9858	2.1522	92.7093
5	10.7200	2.4180	90.2913
6	10.4215	2.7166	87.5747
7	10.0860	3.0520	84.5227
8	9.7091	3.4289	81.0938
9	9.2857	3.8523	77.2415
10	8.8100	4.3280	72.9135
11	8.2756	4.8624	68.0510
12	7.6752	5.4629	62.5882
13	7.0006	6.1374	56.4508
14	6.2428	6.8953	49.5555
15	5.3913	7.7467	41.8087
16	4.4347	8.7033	33.1054
17	3.3600	9.7780	23.3274
18	2.1526	10.9854	12.3420
19	.7961	12.3420	0.0000

YEARS 20 — MO PAYT 1.0802 — AN CONST 12.97

#	INT	PRIN	BALANCE
1	11.6300	1.3329	98.6671
2	11.4654	1.4975	97.1696
3	11.2805	1.6824	95.4872
4	11.0728	1.8901	93.5971
5	10.8394	2.1235	91.4735
6	10.5772	2.3858	89.0878
7	10.2826	2.6804	86.4074
8	9.9516	3.0113	83.3961
9	9.5797	3.3832	80.0129
10	9.1620	3.8010	76.2119
11	8.6926	4.2703	71.9416
12	8.1653	4.7976	67.1440
13	7.5729	5.3900	61.7540
14	6.9073	6.0556	55.6983
15	6.1595	6.8034	48.8950
16	5.3194	7.6435	41.2515
17	4.3756	8.5873	32.6642
18	3.3152	9.6477	23.0165
19	2.1239	10.8390	12.1774
20	.7855	12.1774	0.0000

YEARS 21 — MO PAYT 1.0676 — AN CONST 12.82

#	INT	PRIN	BALANCE
1	11.6384	1.1725	98.8275
2	11.4937	1.3173	97.5102
3	11.3310	1.4799	96.0303

MONTHLY PAYMENT AMORTIZATION SCHEDULE PER $100

11.70 %

#	INT	PRIN	BALANCE
4	11.1483	1.6627	94.3677
5	10.9429	1.8680	92.4997
6	10.7123	2.0986	90.4010
7	10.4531	2.3578	88.0432
8	10.1620	2.6489	85.3943
9	9.8349	2.9760	82.4183
10	9.4674	3.3435	79.0747
11	9.0545	3.7564	75.3183
12	8.5907	4.2202	71.0981
13	8.0696	4.7414	66.3567
14	7.4841	5.3268	61.0299
15	6.8263	5.9846	55.0453
16	6.0873	6.7236	48.3217
17	5.2571	7.5539	40.7678
18	4.3243	8.4866	32.2812
19	3.2764	9.5346	22.7466
20	2.0990	10.7119	12.0347
21	.7763	12.0347	0.0000

YEARS 22 — MO PAYT 1.0566 — AN CONST 12.68

#	INT	PRIN	BALANCE
1	11.6458	1.0328	98.9672
2	11.5182	1.1604	97.8068
3	11.3750	1.3037	96.5031
4	11.2140	1.4646	95.0385
5	11.0331	1.6455	93.3930
6	10.8299	1.8487	91.5443
7	10.6016	2.0770	89.4673
8	10.3452	2.3334	87.1339
9	10.0570	2.6216	84.5123
10	9.7333	2.9453	81.5670
11	9.3696	3.3090	78.2580
12	8.9610	3.7176	74.5404
13	8.5020	4.1767	70.3638
14	7.9862	4.6924	65.6714
15	7.4068	5.2718	60.3996
16	6.7558	5.9228	54.4768
17	6.0245	6.6542	47.8226
18	5.2028	7.4758	40.3467
19	4.2796	8.3990	31.9478
20	3.2425	9.4361	22.5117
21	2.0773	10.6013	11.9104
22	.7682	11.9104	0.0000

YEARS 23 — MO PAYT 1.0469 — AN CONST 12.57

#	INT	PRIN	BALANCE
1	11.6522	.9109	99.0891
2	11.5397	1.0234	98.0656
3	11.4133	1.1498	96.9158
4	11.2713	1.2918	95.6240
5	11.1118	1.4513	94.1727
6	10.9326	1.6305	92.5422
7	10.7313	1.8318	90.7104
8	10.5051	2.0580	88.6523
9	10.2509	2.3122	86.3401
10	9.9654	2.5977	83.7424
11	9.6447	2.9185	80.8240
12	9.2843	3.2788	77.5451
13	8.8794	3.6837	73.8614
14	8.4245	4.1386	69.7228
15	7.9135	4.6497	65.0732
16	7.3393	5.2238	59.8493
17	6.6943	5.8688	53.9805
18	5.9696	6.5936	47.3869
19	5.1554	7.4077	39.9792
20	4.2407	8.3225	31.6567
21	3.2130	9.3501	22.3066
22	2.0584	10.5047	11.8019
23	.7612	11.8019	0.0000

YEARS 24 — MO PAYT 1.0385 — AN CONST 12.47

#	INT	PRIN	BALANCE
1	11.6578	.8043	99.1957
2	11.5585	.9036	98.2921
3	11.4469	1.0152	97.2769
4	11.3215	1.1406	96.1363
5	11.1807	1.2814	94.8549
6	11.0224	1.4396	93.4153
7	10.8447	1.6174	91.7979
8	10.6450	1.8171	89.9808
9	10.4206	2.0415	87.9393
10	10.1685	2.2936	85.6457
11	9.8853	2.5768	83.0689
12	9.5671	2.8950	80.1739
13	9.2096	3.2525	76.9214
14	8.8080	3.6541	73.2673
15	8.3568	4.1053	69.1620
16	7.8498	4.6123	64.5498
17	7.2803	5.1818	59.3680
18	6.6404	5.8216	53.5463
19	5.9216	6.5405	47.0058
20	5.1139	7.3482	39.6577
21	4.2065	8.2555	31.4021
22	3.1871	9.2749	22.1272
23	2.0418	10.4202	11.7070
24	.7551	11.7070	0.0000

YEARS 25 — MO PAYT 1.0311 — AN CONST 12.38

#	INT	PRIN	BALANCE
1	11.6627	.7108	99.2892
2	11.5749	.7986	98.4906
3	11.4763	.8972	97.5934
4	11.3655	1.0080	96.5854
5	11.2410	1.1324	95.4530
6	11.1012	1.2723	94.1807
7	10.9441	1.4294	92.7513
8	10.7676	1.6059	91.1454
9	10.5693	1.8042	89.3412
10	10.3465	2.0270	87.3142
11	10.0962	2.2773	85.0369
12	9.8150	2.5585	82.4784
13	9.4991	2.8744	79.6040
14	9.1441	3.2294	76.3747
15	8.7454	3.6281	72.7465
16	8.2974	4.0761	68.6704
17	7.7940	4.5795	64.0909
18	7.2285	5.1450	58.9460
19	6.5932	5.7803	53.1657
20	5.8795	6.4940	46.6717
21	5.0776	7.2959	39.3758
22	4.1766	8.1968	31.1789
23	3.1645	9.2090	21.9699
24	2.0273	10.3462	11.6237
25	.7498	11.6237	0.0000

YEARS 26 — MO PAYT 1.0246 — AN CONST 12.30

#	INT	PRIN	BALANCE
1	11.6670	.6287	99.3713
2	11.5894	.7063	98.6650
3	11.5021	.7936	97.8714
4	11.4041	.8916	96.9798
5	11.2941	1.0016	95.9782
6	11.1704	1.1253	94.8529
7	11.0314	1.2643	93.5886
8	10.8753	1.4204	92.1682
9	10.6999	1.5958	90.5724
10	10.5028	1.7929	88.7795
11	10.2815	2.0142	86.7653
12	10.0327	2.2630	84.5023
13	9.7533	2.5424	81.9599
14	9.4394	2.8563	79.1036
15	9.0866	3.2091	75.8945

#	INT	PRIN	BALANCE
16	8.6904	3.6053	72.2892
17	8.2452	4.0505	68.2387
18	7.7450	4.5507	63.6880
19	7.1831	5.1126	58.5754
20	6.5518	5.7439	52.8315
21	5.8425	6.4532	46.3783
22	5.0456	7.2501	39.1282
23	4.1504	8.1453	30.9829
24	3.1446	9.1511	21.8318
25	2.0146	10.2811	11.5507
26	.7450	11.5507	0.0000

YEARS 27 — MO PAYT 1.0189 — AN CONST 12.23

#	INT	PRIN	BALANCE
1	11.6708	.5565	99.4435
2	11.6021	.6252	98.8183
3	11.5249	.7024	98.1159
4	11.4381	.7891	97.3267
5	11.3407	.8866	96.4402
6	11.2312	.9961	95.4441
7	11.1082	1.1191	94.3250
8	10.9700	1.2573	93.0678
9	10.8148	1.4125	91.6553
10	10.6404	1.5869	90.0683
11	10.4444	1.7829	88.2855
12	10.2242	2.0030	86.2824
13	9.9769	2.2504	84.0321
14	9.6990	2.5283	81.5038
15	9.3868	2.8404	78.6633
16	9.0361	3.1912	75.4722
17	8.6420	3.5853	71.8869
18	8.1993	4.0280	67.8589
19	7.7019	4.5254	63.3336
20	7.1431	5.0842	58.2494
21	6.5153	5.7120	52.5375
22	5.8100	6.4173	46.1202
23	5.0176	7.2097	38.9105
24	4.1273	8.1000	30.8105
25	3.1271	9.1002	21.7103
26	2.0034	10.2239	11.4864
27	.7409	11.4864	0.0000

YEARS 28 — MO PAYT 1.0139 — AN CONST 12.17

#	INT	PRIN	BALANCE
1	11.6741	.4929	99.5071
2	11.6133	.5537	98.9534
3	11.5449	.6221	98.3312
4	11.4681	.6989	97.6323
5	11.3818	.7853	96.8470
6	11.2848	.8822	95.9648
7	11.1758	.9912	94.9737
8	11.0535	1.1136	93.8601
9	10.9160	1.2511	92.6090
10	10.7615	1.4055	91.2035
11	10.5879	1.5791	89.6244
12	10.3929	1.7741	87.8503
13	10.1738	1.9932	85.8572
14	9.9277	2.2393	83.6179
15	9.6512	2.5158	81.1021
16	9.3406	2.8264	78.2756
17	8.9915	3.1755	75.1002
18	8.5994	3.5676	71.5326
19	8.1589	4.0081	67.5245
20	7.6640	4.5030	63.0214
21	7.1079	5.0591	57.9623
22	6.4832	5.6838	52.2785
23	5.7814	6.3857	45.8929
24	4.9928	7.1742	38.7187
25	4.1069	8.0601	30.6586
26	3.1117	9.0553	21.6033
27	1.9935	10.1735	11.4298
28	.7372	11.4298	0.0000

YEARS 29 — MO PAYT 1.0095 — AN CONST 12.12

#	INT	PRIN	BALANCE
1	11.6771	.4368	99.5632
2	11.6231	.4907	99.0725
3	11.5625	.5513	98.5211
4	11.4945	.6194	97.9017
5	11.4180	.6959	97.2058
6	11.3320	.7818	96.4240
7	11.2355	.8784	95.5456
8	11.1270	.9868	94.5588
9	11.0052	1.1087	93.4501
10	10.8683	1.2456	92.2045
11	10.7145	1.3994	90.8051
12	10.5417	1.5722	89.2329
13	10.3475	1.7663	87.4666
14	10.1294	1.9845	85.4821
15	9.8844	2.2295	83.2526
16	9.6091	2.5048	80.7478
17	9.2998	2.8141	77.9337
18	8.9523	3.1616	74.7721
19	8.5619	3.5520	71.2201
20	8.1233	3.9906	67.2295
21	7.6305	4.4834	62.7461
22	7.0769	5.0370	57.7091
23	6.4549	5.6590	52.0502
24	5.7561	6.3578	45.6924
25	4.9710	7.1428	38.5496
26	4.0890	8.0249	30.5247
27	3.0981	9.0158	21.5089
28	1.9848	10.1291	11.3798
29	.7340	11.3798	0.0000

YEARS 30 — MO PAYT 1.0056 — AN CONST 12.07

#	INT	PRIN	BALANCE
1	11.6797	.3873	99.6127
2	11.6318	.4351	99.1776
3	11.5781	.4888	98.6888
4	11.5178	.5492	98.1396
5	11.4499	.6170	97.5226
6	11.3737	.6932	96.8294
7	11.2882	.7788	96.0506
8	11.1920	.8750	95.1756
9	11.0839	.9830	94.1926
10	10.9626	1.1044	93.0882
11	10.8262	1.2408	91.8474
12	10.6730	1.3940	90.4535
13	10.5008	1.5661	88.8873
14	10.3074	1.7595	87.1278
15	10.0902	1.9768	85.1511
16	9.8461	2.2209	82.9302
17	9.5718	2.4951	80.4351
18	9.2637	2.8032	77.6319
19	8.9176	3.1494	74.4825
20	8.5287	3.5382	70.9443
21	8.0918	3.9752	66.9692
22	7.6009	4.4660	62.5031
23	7.0495	5.0175	57.4856
24	6.4299	5.6371	51.8486
25	5.7338	6.3331	45.5154
26	4.9518	7.1152	38.4003
27	4.0732	7.9938	30.4065
28	3.0861	8.9809	21.4256
29	1.9771	10.0898	11.3358
30	.7312	11.3358	0.0000

YEARS 2	MO PAYT 4.6957	AN CONST 56.35
# INT	PRIN	BALANCE
1 9.2681	47.0801	52.9199
2 3.4283	52.9199	0.0000

YEARS 3	MO PAYT 3.3095	AN CONST 39.72
# INT	PRIN	BALANCE
1 10.1938	29.5203	70.4797
2 6.5321	33.1819	37.2978
3 2.4162	37.2978	0.0000

YEARS 4	MO PAYT 2.6211	AN CONST 31.46
# INT	PRIN	BALANCE
1 10.6535	20.8000	79.2000
2 8.0735	23.3800	55.8199
3 5.1734	26.2801	29.5398
4 1.9137	29.5398	0.0000

YEARS 5	MO PAYT 2.2118	AN CONST 26.55
# INT	PRIN	BALANCE
1 10.9268	15.6152	84.3848
2 8.9899	17.5521	66.8328
3 6.8128	19.7292	47.1035
4 4.3656	22.1764	24.9271
5 1.6148	24.9271	0.0000

YEARS 6	MO PAYT 1.9420	AN CONST 23.31
# INT	PRIN	BALANCE
1 11.1070	12.1975	87.8025
2 9.5940	13.7105	74.0920
3 7.8934	15.4111	58.6808
4 5.9818	17.3227	41.3581
5 3.8331	19.4714	21.8866
6 1.4179	21.8866	0.0000

YEARS 7	MO PAYT 1.7519	AN CONST 21.03
# INT	PRIN	BALANCE
1 11.2339	9.7892	90.2108
2 10.0197	11.0035	79.2073
3 8.6548	12.3684	66.8389
4 7.1207	13.9025	52.9364
5 5.3962	15.6270	37.3094
6 3.4579	17.5653	19.7441
7 1.2791	19.7441	0.0000

YEARS 8	MO PAYT 1.6116	AN CONST 19.34
# INT	PRIN	BALANCE
1 11.3277	8.0113	91.9887
2 10.3340	9.0050	82.9837
3 9.2170	10.1220	72.8617
4 7.9615	11.3775	61.4843
5 6.5502	12.7887	48.6955
6 4.9639	14.3750	34.3205
7 3.1808	16.1581	18.1623
8 1.1766	18.1623	0.0000

YEARS 9	MO PAYT 1.5044	AN CONST 18.06
# INT	PRIN	BALANCE
1 11.3993	6.6531	93.3469
2 10.5740	7.4783	85.8687
3 9.6464	8.4059	77.4628
4 8.6038	9.4486	68.0142
5 7.4318	10.6205	57.3937
6 6.1144	11.9379	45.4558

#	INT	PRIN	BALANCE
7	4.6337	13.4187	32.0371
8	2.9692	15.0831	16.9540
9	1.0983	16.9540	0.0000

YEARS 10	MO PAYT 1.4203	AN CONST 17.05
# INT	PRIN	BALANCE
1 11.4554	5.5881	94.4119
2 10.7623	6.2813	88.1306
3 9.9831	7.0604	81.0702
4 9.1074	7.9362	73.1340
5 8.1230	8.9206	64.2135
6 7.0165	10.0271	54.1864
7 5.7727	11.2708	42.9156
8 4.3747	12.6688	30.2468
9 2.8033	14.2402	16.0066
10 1.0369	16.0066	0.0000

YEARS 11	MO PAYT 1.3530	AN CONST 16.24
# INT	PRIN	BALANCE
1 11.5003	4.7360	95.2640
2 10.9129	5.3235	89.9405
3 10.2526	5.9838	83.9567
4 9.5103	6.7260	77.2307
5 8.6760	7.5603	69.6704
6 7.7383	8.4981	61.1723
7 6.6842	9.5522	51.6202
8 5.4993	10.7370	40.8832
9 4.1675	12.0688	28.8143
10 2.6705	13.5658	15.2485
11 .9878	15.2485	0.0000

YEARS 12	MO PAYT 1.2983	AN CONST 15.58
# INT	PRIN	BALANCE
1 11.5369	4.0430	95.9570
2 11.0354	4.5445	91.4124
3 10.4717	5.1082	86.3042
4 9.8380	5.7419	80.5623
5 9.1258	6.4541	74.1082
6 8.3253	7.2546	66.8536
7 7.4254	8.1545	58.6991
8 6.4139	9.1660	49.5331
9 5.2770	10.3029	39.2302
10 3.9990	11.5809	27.6494
11 2.5626	13.0173	14.6320
12 .9479	14.6320	0.0000

YEARS 13	MO PAYT 1.2532	AN CONST 15.04
# INT	PRIN	BALANCE
1 11.5670	3.4720	96.5280
2 11.1363	3.9027	92.6253
3 10.6522	4.3868	88.2386
4 10.1081	4.9309	83.3077
5 9.4965	5.5425	77.7652
6 8.8090	6.2300	71.5352
7 8.0362	7.0028	64.5324
8 7.1676	7.8714	56.6611
9 6.1912	8.8477	47.8133
10 5.0938	9.9452	37.8681
11 3.8602	11.1788	26.6894
12 2.4736	12.5654	14.1240
13 .9150	14.1240	0.0000

YEARS 14	MO PAYT 1.2157	AN CONST 14.59
# INT	PRIN	BALANCE
1 11.5920	2.9963	97.0037
2 11.2204	3.3680	93.6357
3 10.8026	3.7857	89.8500

#	INT	PRIN	BALANCE
4	10.3330	4.2553	85.5947
5	9.8052	4.7831	80.8115
6	9.2119	5.3764	75.4351
7	8.5450	6.0433	69.3918
8	7.7954	6.7929	62.5988
9	6.9528	7.6355	54.9633
10	6.0057	8.5826	46.3807
11	4.9412	9.6472	36.7335
12	3.7445	10.8438	25.8897
13	2.3995	12.1889	13.7008
14	.8876	13.7008	0.0000

YEARS 15	MO PAYT 1.1841	AN CONST 14.21
# INT	PRIN	BALANCE
1 11.6131	2.5965	97.4035
2 11.2911	2.9185	94.4850
3 10.9290	3.2805	91.2045
4 10.5221	3.6874	87.5171
5 10.0648	4.1448	83.3722
6 9.5506	4.6589	78.7133
7 8.9727	5.2368	73.4765
8 8.3232	5.8864	67.5900
9 7.5930	6.6166	60.9735
10 6.7723	7.4373	53.5362
11 5.8498	8.3598	45.1764
12 4.8129	9.3967	35.7797
13 3.6473	10.5623	25.2175
14 2.3372	11.8724	13.3451
15 .8645	13.3451	0.0000

YEARS 16	MO PAYT 1.1574	AN CONST 13.89
# INT	PRIN	BALANCE
1 11.6310	2.2578	97.7422
2 11.3509	2.5378	95.2044
3 11.0361	2.8526	92.3518
4 10.6823	3.2065	89.1453
5 10.2846	3.6042	85.5411
6 9.8375	4.0512	81.4899
7 9.3350	4.5538	76.9361
8 8.7702	5.1186	71.8175
9 8.1352	5.7535	66.0640
10 7.4216	6.4672	59.5968
11 6.6194	7.2693	52.3275
12 5.7177	8.1710	44.1565
13 4.7042	9.1846	34.9719
14 3.5650	10.3238	24.6481
15 2.2844	11.6044	13.0437
16 .8450	13.0437	0.0000

YEARS 17	MO PAYT 1.1346	AN CONST 13.62
# INT	PRIN	BALANCE
1 11.6462	1.9691	98.0309
2 11.4020	2.2133	95.8176
3 11.1274	2.4879	93.3297
4 10.8188	2.7965	90.5333
5 10.4720	3.1433	87.3900
6 10.0821	3.5332	83.8567
7 9.6438	3.9715	79.8853
8 9.1512	4.4641	75.4212
9 8.5975	5.0178	70.4034
10 7.9751	5.6402	64.7632
11 7.2755	6.3398	58.4233
12 6.4891	7.1262	51.2971
13 5.6051	8.0101	43.2870
14 4.6116	9.0037	34.2833
15 3.4948	10.1205	24.1628
16 2.2394	11.3759	12.7869
17 .8284	12.7869	0.0000

YEARS 18	MO PAYT 1.1151	AN CONST 13.39
# INT	PRIN	BALANCE
1 11.6592	1.7216	98.2784
2 11.4457	1.9352	96.3432
3 11.2057	2.1752	94.1680
4 10.9358	2.4450	91.7229
5 10.6326	2.7483	88.9746
6 10.2917	3.0892	85.8854
7 9.9085	3.4724	82.4130
8 9.4778	3.9031	78.5099
9 8.9936	4.3872	74.1227
10 8.4494	4.9314	69.1913
11 7.8378	5.5431	63.6482
12 7.1502	6.2307	57.4175
13 6.3773	7.0035	50.4140
14 5.5086	7.8722	42.5417
15 4.5322	8.8487	33.6930
16 3.4346	9.9463	23.7468
17 2.2009	11.1800	12.5668
18 .8141	12.5668	0.0000

YEARS 19	MO PAYT 1.0983	AN CONST 13.18
# INT	PRIN	BALANCE
1 11.6705	1.5085	98.4915
2 11.4834	1.6957	96.7958
3 11.2730	1.9060	94.8898
4 11.0366	2.1424	92.7474
5 10.7709	2.4081	90.3393
6 10.4722	2.7068	87.6324
7 10.1364	3.0426	84.5898
8 9.7590	3.4200	81.1698
9 9.3348	3.8442	77.3256
10 8.8580	4.3211	73.0045
11 8.3220	4.8570	68.1475
12 7.7195	5.4595	62.6880
13 7.0423	6.1367	56.5513
14 6.2811	6.8979	49.6535
15 5.4255	7.7535	41.9000
16 4.4638	8.7152	33.1848
17 3.3828	9.7962	23.3885
18 2.1677	11.0114	12.3772
19 .8018	12.3772	0.0000

YEARS 20	MO PAYT 1.0837	AN CONST 13.01
# INT	PRIN	BALANCE
1 11.6802	1.3243	98.6757
2 11.5159	1.4886	97.1871
3 11.3313	1.6732	95.5139
4 11.1237	1.8807	93.6332
5 10.8905	2.1140	91.5192
6 10.6282	2.3763	89.1429
7 10.3335	2.6710	86.4719
8 10.0022	3.0023	83.4696
9 9.6298	3.3747	80.0949
10 9.2112	3.7933	76.3016
11 8.7407	4.2638	72.0377
12 8.2118	4.7927	67.2450
13 7.6173	5.3872	61.8578
14 6.9491	6.0554	55.8024
15 6.1980	6.8065	48.9959
16 5.3537	7.6508	41.3451
17 4.4047	8.5998	32.7453
18 3.3380	9.6665	23.0788
19 2.1390	10.8655	12.2133
20 .7912	12.2133	0.0000

YEARS 21	MO PAYT 1.0711	AN CONST 12.86
# INT	PRIN	BALANCE
1 11.6886	1.1644	98.8356
2 11.5442	1.3089	97.5267
3 11.3818	1.4712	96.0555

#	INT	PRIN	BALANCE
4	11.1993	1.6537	94.4017
5	10.9942	1.8588	92.5429
6	10.7636	2.0894	90.4535
7	10.5045	2.3486	88.1049
8	10.2132	2.6399	85.4650
9	9.8857	2.9674	82.4976
10	9.5176	3.3354	79.1622
11	9.1039	3.7491	75.4131
12	8.6389	4.2142	71.1989
13	8.1162	4.7369	66.4620
14	7.5286	5.3245	61.1375
15	6.8682	5.9849	55.1526
16	6.1258	6.7273	48.4254
17	5.2913	7.5617	40.8637
18	4.3534	8.4997	32.3640
19	3.2991	9.5539	22.8101
20	2.1140	10.7390	12.0711
21	.7820	12.0711	0.0000

YEARS 22	MO PAYT 1.0601	AN CONST 12.73	
#	INT	PRIN	BALANCE
1	11.6959	1.0253	98.9747
2	11.5688	1.1525	97.8222
3	11.4258	1.2955	96.5267
4	11.2651	1.4561	95.0706
5	11.0845	1.6368	93.4338
6	10.8815	1.8398	91.5940
7	10.6533	2.0680	89.5260
8	10.3968	2.3245	87.2015
9	10.1084	2.6128	84.5887
10	9.7843	2.9369	81.6518
11	9.4201	3.3012	78.3506
12	9.0106	3.7107	74.6399
13	8.5503	4.1710	70.4689
14	8.0329	4.6883	65.7806
15	7.4514	5.2699	60.5107
16	6.7977	5.9235	54.5871
17	6.0630	6.6583	47.9289
18	5.2371	7.4842	40.4447
19	4.3088	8.4125	32.0322
20	3.2653	9.4560	22.5762
21	2.0924	10.6289	11.9473
22	.7740	11.9473	0.0000

YEARS 23	MO PAYT 1.0505	AN CONST 12.61	
#	INT	PRIN	BALANCE
1	11.7023	.9039	99.0961
2	11.5902	1.0161	98.0800
3	11.4642	1.1421	96.9379
4	11.3225	1.2837	95.6542
5	11.1633	1.4430	94.2112
6	10.9843	1.6220	92.5892
7	10.7831	1.8232	90.7661
8	10.5570	2.0493	88.7168
9	10.3028	2.3035	86.4133
10	10.0171	2.5892	83.8241
11	9.6959	2.9104	80.9137
12	9.3349	3.2714	77.6423
13	8.9291	3.6772	73.9652
14	8.4730	4.1333	69.8319
15	7.9603	4.6460	65.1859
16	7.3840	5.2222	59.9637
17	6.7363	5.8700	54.0937
18	6.0082	6.5981	47.4956
19	5.1898	7.4165	40.0791
20	4.2698	8.3365	31.7426
21	3.2358	9.3705	22.3721
22	2.0735	10.5328	11.8393
23	.7670	11.8393	0.0000

YEARS 24	MO PAYT 1.0421	AN CONST 12.51	
#	INT	PRIN	BALANCE
1	11.7079	.7978	99.2022
2	11.6090	.8967	98.3055
3	11.4978	1.0079	97.2976
4	11.3727	1.1330	96.1646
5	11.2322	1.2735	94.8911
6	11.0742	1.4315	93.4596
7	10.8967	1.6090	91.8506
8	10.6971	1.8086	90.0420
9	10.4728	2.0329	88.0090
10	10.2206	2.2851	85.7239
11	9.9372	2.5686	83.1554
12	9.6186	2.8872	80.2682
13	9.2604	3.2453	77.0229
14	8.8579	3.6478	73.3751
15	8.4054	4.1003	69.2748
16	7.8968	4.6089	64.6659
17	7.3251	5.1806	59.4853
18	6.6825	5.8232	53.6622
19	5.9602	6.5455	47.1167
20	5.1484	7.3574	39.7594
21	4.2358	8.2700	31.4894
22	3.2100	9.2958	22.1936
23	2.0569	10.4488	11.7448
24	.7609	11.7448	0.0000

YEARS 25	MO PAYT 1.0348	AN CONST 12.42	
#	INT	PRIN	BALANCE
1	11.7128	.7047	99.2953
2	11.6254	.7921	98.5031
3	11.5272	.8904	97.6127
4	11.4167	1.0008	96.6119
5	11.2926	1.1250	95.4869
6	11.1530	1.2645	94.2224
7	10.9962	1.4214	92.8010
8	10.8199	1.5977	91.2033
9	10.6217	1.7959	89.4074
10	10.3990	2.0186	87.3888
11	10.1486	2.2690	85.1198
12	9.8671	2.5505	82.5693
13	9.5508	2.8668	79.7025
14	9.1952	3.2224	76.4801
15	8.7955	3.6221	72.8580
16	8.3462	4.0714	68.7866
17	7.8412	4.5764	64.2102
18	7.2735	5.1441	59.0661
19	6.6355	5.7821	53.2840
20	5.9182	6.4993	46.7847
21	5.1121	7.3055	39.4792
22	4.2059	8.2117	31.2675
23	3.1873	9.2302	22.0372
24	2.0424	10.3752	11.6621
25	.7555	11.6621	0.0000

YEARS 26	MO PAYT 1.0284	AN CONST 12.35	
#	INT	PRIN	BALANCE
1	11.7172	.6231	99.3769
2	11.6399	.7003	98.6766
3	11.5530	.7872	97.8894
4	11.4554	.8849	97.0045
5	11.3456	.9946	96.0099
6	11.2222	1.1180	94.8920
7	11.0836	1.2567	93.6353
8	10.9277	1.4125	92.2228
9	10.7525	1.5877	90.6350
10	10.5555	1.7847	88.8504
11	10.3342	2.0060	86.8443
12	10.0853	2.2549	84.5894
13	9.8056	2.5346	82.0549
14	9.4913	2.8490	79.2059
15	9.1379	3.2023	76.0036
16	8.7407	3.5995	72.4041
17	8.2942	4.0460	68.3580
18	7.7923	4.5479	63.8101
19	7.2282	5.1120	58.6981
20	6.5941	5.7461	52.9520
21	5.8814	6.4588	46.4932
22	5.0802	7.2600	39.2332
23	4.1797	8.1605	31.0727
24	3.1675	9.1727	21.8999
25	2.0297	10.3105	11.5894
26	.7508	11.5894	0.0000

YEARS 27	MO PAYT 1.0227	AN CONST 12.28	
#	INT	PRIN	BALANCE
1	11.7209	.5512	99.4488
2	11.6526	.6196	98.8291
3	11.5757	.6965	98.1327
4	11.4895	.7829	97.3498
5	11.3922	.8800	96.4698
6	11.2831	.9891	95.4807
7	11.1604	1.1118	94.3689
8	11.0225	1.2497	93.1191
9	10.8674	1.4047	91.7144
10	10.6932	1.5790	90.1354
11	10.4973	1.7748	88.3606
12	10.2777	1.9950	86.3656
13	10.0297	2.2424	84.1232
14	9.7516	2.5206	81.6026
15	9.4389	2.8332	78.7693
16	9.0875	3.1847	75.5846
17	8.6925	3.5797	72.0049
18	8.2485	4.0237	67.9812
19	7.7494	4.5228	63.4584
20	7.1884	5.0838	58.3745
21	6.5578	5.7144	52.6601
22	5.8489	6.4232	46.2369
23	5.0522	7.2200	39.0169
24	4.1567	8.1155	30.9014
25	3.1500	9.1222	21.7792
26	2.0185	10.2537	11.5255
27	.7467	11.5255	0.0000

YEARS 28	MO PAYT 1.0177	AN CONST 12.22	
#	INT	PRIN	BALANCE
1	11.7243	.4880	99.5120
2	11.6637	.5486	98.9634
3	11.5957	.6166	98.3468
4	11.5192	.6931	97.6537
5	11.4332	.7790	96.8747
6	11.3366	.8757	95.9990
7	11.2280	.9843	95.0147
8	11.1059	1.1064	93.9083
9	10.9687	1.2436	92.6647
10	10.8144	1.3979	91.2668
11	10.6410	1.5713	89.6955
12	10.4461	1.7662	87.9294
13	10.2270	1.9853	85.9441
14	9.9808	2.2315	83.7126
15	9.7040	2.5083	81.2043
16	9.3929	2.8194	78.3849
17	9.0432	3.1691	75.2158
18	8.6501	3.5622	71.6535
19	8.2082	4.0041	67.6494
20	7.7115	4.5008	63.1487
21	7.1533	5.0590	58.0897
22	6.5258	5.6865	52.4031
23	5.8204	6.3919	46.0112
24	5.0276	7.1847	38.8265
25	4.1364	8.0759	30.7506
26	3.1346	9.0777	21.6729
27	2.0087	10.2036	11.4693
28	.7430	11.4693	0.0000

YEARS 29	MO PAYT 1.0133	AN CONST 12.16	
#	INT	PRIN	BALANCE
1	11.7272	.4323	99.5677
2	11.6736	.4859	99.0818
3	11.6133	.5462	98.5356
4	11.5456	.6139	97.9217
5	11.4694	.6901	97.2316
6	11.3838	.7757	96.4559
7	11.2876	.8719	95.5840
8	11.1795	.9800	94.6040
9	11.0579	1.1016	93.5024
10	10.9213	1.2383	92.2641
11	10.7677	1.3918	90.8723
12	10.5950	1.5645	89.3078
13	10.4010	1.7585	87.5493
14	10.1828	1.9767	85.5726
15	9.9376	2.2219	83.3507
16	9.6621	2.4974	80.8533
17	9.3523	2.8072	78.0460
18	9.0041	3.1554	74.8906
19	8.6127	3.5468	71.3438
20	8.1727	3.9868	67.3570
21	7.6782	4.4813	62.8757
22	7.1223	5.0372	57.8385
23	6.4975	5.6620	52.1766
24	5.7952	6.3643	45.8123
25	5.0058	7.1537	38.6587
26	4.1185	8.0410	30.6176
27	3.1211	9.0384	21.5792
28	2.0000	10.1595	11.4197
29	.7398	11.4197	0.0000

YEARS 30	MO PAYT 1.0094	AN CONST 12.12	
#	INT	PRIN	BALANCE
1	11.7298	.3831	99.6169
2	11.6823	.4306	99.1863
3	11.6289	.4841	98.7022
4	11.5688	.5441	98.1581
5	11.5013	.6116	97.5465
6	11.4255	.6874	96.8591
7	11.3402	.7727	96.0864
8	11.2444	.8686	95.2178
9	11.1366	.9763	94.2415
10	11.0155	1.0974	93.1442
11	10.8794	1.2335	91.9106
12	10.7264	1.3865	90.5241
13	10.5544	1.5585	88.9656
14	10.3611	1.7518	87.2138
15	10.1438	1.9691	85.2447
16	9.8996	2.2133	83.0314
17	9.6250	2.4879	80.5435
18	9.3164	2.7965	77.7470
19	8.9696	3.1433	74.6037
20	8.5797	3.5332	71.0704
21	8.1414	3.9715	67.0989
22	7.6488	4.4641	62.6348
23	7.0951	5.0179	57.6170
24	6.4727	5.6403	51.9767
25	5.7730	6.3399	45.6368
26	4.9866	7.1263	38.5105
27	4.1027	8.0102	30.5003
28	3.1091	9.0038	21.4966
29	1.9923	10.1206	11.3760
30	.7370	11.3760	0.0000

MONTHLY PAYMENT AMORTIZATION SCHEDULE PER $100   11.80 %

YEARS 2 — MO PAYT 4.6980 — AN CONST 56.38

#	INT	PRIN	BALANCE
1	9.3084	47.0678	52.9322
2	3.4439	52.9322	0.0000

YEARS 3 — MO PAYT 3.3119 — AN CONST 39.75

#	INT	PRIN	BALANCE
1	10.2381	29.5045	70.4955
2	6.5620	33.1807	37.3148
3	2.4278	37.3148	0.0000

YEARS 4 — MO PAYT 2.6236 — AN CONST 31.49

#	INT	PRIN	BALANCE
1	10.6998	20.7831	79.2169
2	8.1103	23.3726	55.8443
3	5.1982	26.2847	29.5597
4	1.9232	29.5597	0.0000

YEARS 5 — MO PAYT 2.2144 — AN CONST 26.58

#	INT	PRIN	BALANCE
1	10.9743	15.5979	84.4021
2	9.0309	17.5414	66.8607
3	6.8453	19.7269	47.1338
4	4.3874	22.1848	24.9490
5	1.6233	24.9490	0.0000

YEARS 6 — MO PAYT 1.9446 — AN CONST 23.34

#	INT	PRIN	BALANCE
1	11.1552	12.1804	87.8196
2	9.6376	13.6980	74.1216
3	7.9309	15.4047	58.7168
4	6.0115	17.3241	41.3927
5	3.8530	19.4826	21.9101
6	1.4255	21.9101	0.0000

YEARS 7 — MO PAYT 1.7546 — AN CONST 21.06

#	INT	PRIN	BALANCE
1	11.2827	9.7725	90.2275
2	10.0651	10.9901	79.2374
3	8.6958	12.3594	66.8781
4	7.1558	13.8993	52.9787
5	5.4240	15.6311	37.3476
6	3.4765	17.5787	19.7689
7	1.2862	19.7689	0.0000

YEARS 8 — MO PAYT 1.6143 — AN CONST 19.38

#	INT	PRIN	BALANCE
1	11.3768	7.9950	92.0050
2	10.3806	8.9912	83.0138
3	9.2604	10.1114	72.9024
4	8.0005	11.3713	61.5311
5	6.5837	12.7881	48.7431
6	4.9904	14.3814	34.3617
7	3.1985	16.1733	18.1884
8	1.1834	18.1884	0.0000

YEARS 9 — MO PAYT 1.5072 — AN CONST 18.09

#	INT	PRIN	BALANCE
1	11.4486	6.6374	93.3626
2	10.6217	7.4644	85.8983
3	9.6916	8.3944	77.5039
4	8.6457	9.4403	68.0636
5	7.4695	10.6165	57.4471
6	6.1467	11.9393	45.5078
7	4.6591	13.4269	32.0810
8	2.9862	15.0998	16.9812
9	1.1048	16.9812	0.0000

YEARS 10 — MO PAYT 1.4232 — AN CONST 17.08

#	INT	PRIN	BALANCE
1	11.5050	5.5731	94.4269
2	10.8106	6.2675	88.1595
3	10.0297	7.0484	81.1111
4	9.1515	7.9266	73.1845
5	8.1639	8.9142	64.2704
6	7.0532	10.0248	54.2455
7	5.8042	11.2739	42.9716
8	4.3995	12.6786	30.2931
9	2.8198	14.2583	16.0348
10	1.0433	16.0348	0.0000

YEARS 11 — MO PAYT 1.3560 — AN CONST 16.28

#	INT	PRIN	BALANCE
1	11.5501	4.7216	95.2784
2	10.9618	5.3099	89.9684
3	10.3002	5.9715	83.9969
4	9.5561	6.7156	77.2813
5	8.7194	7.5523	69.7290
6	7.7784	8.4933	61.2357
7	6.7202	9.5515	51.6842
8	5.5301	10.7416	40.9427
9	4.1918	12.0799	28.8627
10	2.6867	13.5850	15.2777
11	.9940	15.2777	0.0000

YEARS 12 — MO PAYT 1.3013 — AN CONST 15.62

#	INT	PRIN	BALANCE
1	11.5867	4.0294	95.9706
2	11.0847	4.5314	91.4393
3	10.5201	5.0960	86.3433
4	9.8851	5.7309	80.6124
5	9.1711	6.4450	74.1674
6	8.3681	7.2480	66.9194
7	7.4650	8.1511	58.7683
8	6.4494	9.1666	49.6017
9	5.3073	10.3088	39.2929
10	4.0229	11.5932	27.6997
11	2.5784	13.0377	14.6621
12	.9540	14.6621	0.0000

YEARS 13 — MO PAYT 1.2563 — AN CONST 15.08

#	INT	PRIN	BALANCE
1	11.6169	3.4590	96.5410
2	11.1859	3.8900	92.6510
3	10.7012	4.3747	88.2764
4	10.1562	4.9197	83.3567
5	9.5432	5.5327	77.8240
6	8.8539	6.2220	71.6019
7	8.0786	6.9973	64.6047
8	7.2068	7.8691	56.7355
9	6.2263	8.8496	47.8860
10	5.1237	9.9522	37.9338
11	3.8837	11.1922	26.7416
12	2.4892	12.5867	14.1549
13	.9210	14.1549	0.0000

YEARS 14 — MO PAYT 1.2188 — AN CONST 14.63

#	INT	PRIN	BALANCE
1	11.6420	2.9840	97.0160
2	11.2702	3.3558	93.6602
3	10.8521	3.7739	89.8863
4	10.3819	4.2441	85.6422
5	9.8531	4.7729	80.8693
6	9.2584	5.3676	75.5017
7	8.5897	6.0364	69.4653
8	7.8375	6.7885	62.6769
9	6.9917	7.6343	55.0426
10	6.0405	8.5855	46.4571
11	4.9708	9.6552	36.8019
12	3.7678	10.8582	25.9436
13	2.4149	12.2111	13.7325
14	.8935	13.7325	0.0000

YEARS 15 — MO PAYT 1.1873 — AN CONST 14.25

#	INT	PRIN	BALANCE
1	11.6632	2.5848	97.4152
2	11.3411	2.9069	94.5083
3	10.9789	3.2690	91.2393
4	10.5716	3.6764	87.5629
5	10.1136	4.1344	83.4285
6	9.5984	4.6495	78.7790
7	9.0191	5.2289	73.5501
8	8.3676	5.8803	67.6698
9	7.6350	6.6130	61.0568
10	6.8110	7.4370	53.6198
11	5.8844	8.3636	45.2562
12	4.8423	9.4056	35.8506
13	3.6704	10.5775	25.2731
14	2.3525	11.8955	13.3776
15	.8704	13.3776	0.0000

YEARS 16 — MO PAYT 1.1607 — AN CONST 13.93

#	INT	PRIN	BALANCE
1	11.6811	2.2468	97.7532
2	11.4011	2.5267	95.2265
3	11.0863	2.8415	92.3849
4	10.7323	3.1956	89.1893
5	10.3341	3.5938	85.5956
6	9.8863	4.0415	81.5541
7	9.3828	4.5451	77.0090
8	8.8165	5.1114	71.8976
9	8.1796	5.7482	66.1494
10	7.4634	6.4644	59.6850
11	6.6580	7.2699	52.4151
12	5.7522	8.1757	44.2394
13	4.7335	9.1943	35.0451
14	3.5880	10.3399	24.7052
15	2.2997	11.6282	13.0770
16	.8508	13.0770	0.0000

YEARS 17 — MO PAYT 1.1379 — AN CONST 13.66

#	INT	PRIN	BALANCE
1	11.6963	1.9587	98.0413
2	11.4523	2.2028	95.8385
3	11.1778	2.4772	93.3612
4	10.8692	2.7859	90.5754
5	10.5220	3.1330	87.4424
6	10.1317	3.5234	83.9190
7	9.6927	3.9624	79.9566
8	9.1990	4.4560	75.5006
9	8.6438	5.0113	70.4893
10	8.0194	5.6356	64.8537
11	7.3172	6.3378	58.5159
12	6.5276	7.1275	51.3884
13	5.6395	8.0155	43.3729
14	4.6408	9.0142	34.3587
15	3.5177	10.1374	24.2213
16	2.2546	11.4004	12.8209
17	.8342	12.8209	0.0000

YEARS 18 — MO PAYT 1.1184 — AN CONST 13.43

#	INT	PRIN	BALANCE
1	11.7094	1.7119	98.2881
2	11.4961	1.9252	96.3629
3	11.2562	2.1651	94.1978
4	10.9865	2.4348	91.7630
5	10.6831	2.7382	89.0248
6	10.3419	3.0794	85.9454
7	9.9582	3.4630	82.4824
8	9.5268	3.8945	78.5879
9	9.0415	4.3798	74.2081
10	8.4958	4.9255	69.2826
11	7.8821	5.5392	63.7435
12	7.1920	6.2293	57.5142
13	6.4158	7.0055	50.5087
14	5.5430	7.8783	42.6304
15	4.5614	8.8599	33.7705
16	3.4575	9.9638	23.8067
17	2.2160	11.2053	12.6014
18	.8199	12.6014	0.0000

YEARS 19 — MO PAYT 1.1017 — AN CONST 13.23

#	INT	PRIN	BALANCE
1	11.7206	1.4994	98.5006
2	11.5338	1.6862	96.8143
3	11.3237	1.8963	94.9180
4	11.0874	2.1326	92.7854
5	10.8217	2.3983	90.3871
6	10.5229	2.6971	87.6899
7	10.1868	3.0332	84.6567
8	9.8089	3.4111	81.2456
9	9.3839	3.8361	77.4095
10	8.9059	4.3141	73.0954
11	8.3684	4.8516	68.2438
12	7.7639	5.4561	62.7877
13	7.0841	6.1359	56.6518
14	6.3196	6.9004	49.7514
15	5.4599	7.7602	41.9912
16	4.4930	8.7271	33.2641
17	3.4056	9.8144	23.4497
18	2.1828	11.0373	12.4124
19	.8076	12.4124	0.0000

YEARS 20 — MO PAYT 1.0872 — AN CONST 13.05

#	INT	PRIN	BALANCE
1	11.7303	1.3157	98.6843
2	11.5664	1.4797	97.2046
3	11.3820	1.6640	95.5405
4	11.1747	1.8714	93.6691
5	10.9415	2.1045	91.5646
6	10.6793	2.3668	89.1978
7	10.3844	2.6617	86.5362
8	10.0528	2.9933	83.5429
9	9.6799	3.3662	80.1766
10	9.2604	3.7857	76.3910
11	8.7888	4.2573	72.1337
12	8.2583	4.7878	67.3459
13	7.6618	5.3843	61.9616
14	6.9909	6.0552	55.9064
15	6.2365	6.8096	49.0968
16	5.3880	7.6581	41.4387
17	4.4339	8.6122	32.8264
18	3.3608	9.6853	23.1412
19	2.1541	10.8920	12.2491
20	.7970	12.2491	0.0000

YEARS 21 — MO PAYT 1.0746 — AN CONST 12.90

#	INT	PRIN	BALANCE
1	11.7388	1.1564	98.8436
2	11.5947	1.3005	97.5430
3	11.4327	1.4626	96.0804

#	INT	PRIN	BALANCE
4	11.2504	1.6448	94.4356
5	11.0455	1.8497	92.5859
6	10.8150	2.0802	90.5057
7	10.5558	2.3394	88.1663
8	10.2644	2.6309	85.5354
9	9.9366	2.9587	82.5767
10	9.5679	3.3273	79.2494
11	9.1534	3.7419	75.5076
12	8.6871	4.2081	71.2995
13	8.1628	4.7324	66.5671
14	7.5732	5.3220	61.2450
15	6.9101	5.9852	55.2599
16	6.1644	6.7309	48.5290
17	5.3257	7.5695	40.9595
18	4.3826	8.5126	32.4468
19	3.3219	9.5733	22.8735
20	2.1292	10.7661	12.1075
21	.7877	12.1075	0.0000

YEARS 22	MO PAYT 1.0637	AN CONST 12.77	
#	INT	PRIN	BALANCE
1	11.7461	1.0179	98.9821
2	11.6193	1.1447	97.8375
3	11.4767	1.2873	96.5502
4	11.3163	1.4477	95.1025
5	11.1359	1.6281	93.4744
6	10.9331	1.8309	91.6435
7	10.7049	2.0590	89.5845
8	10.4484	2.3156	87.2689
9	10.1599	2.6041	84.6648
10	9.8354	2.9286	81.7362
11	9.4705	3.2934	78.4428
12	9.0602	3.7038	74.7390
13	8.5987	4.1653	70.5737
14	8.0797	4.6842	65.8895
15	7.4961	5.2679	60.6216
16	6.8397	5.9242	54.6974
17	6.1016	6.6624	48.0350
18	5.2715	7.4925	40.5426
19	4.3380	8.4260	32.1166
20	3.2881	9.4758	22.6407
21	2.1075	10.6565	11.9842
22	.7797	11.9842	0.0000

YEARS 23	MO PAYT 1.0541	AN CONST 12.65	
#	INT	PRIN	BALANCE
1	11.7525	.8970	99.1030
2	11.6408	1.0087	98.0943
3	11.5151	1.1344	96.9599
4	11.3737	1.2757	95.6842
5	11.2148	1.4347	94.2495
6	11.0360	1.6135	92.6360
7	10.8350	1.8145	90.8215
8	10.6089	2.0406	88.7809
9	10.3547	2.2948	86.4861
10	10.0687	2.5807	83.9054
11	9.7472	2.9023	81.0031
12	9.3856	3.2639	77.7392
13	8.9789	3.6706	74.0686
14	8.5216	4.1279	69.9407
15	8.0073	4.6422	65.2985
16	7.4289	5.2206	60.0779
17	6.7784	5.8711	54.2068
18	6.0469	6.6026	47.6042
19	5.2242	7.4253	40.1789
20	4.2991	8.3504	31.8285
21	3.2586	9.3908	22.4376
22	2.0886	10.5609	11.8767
23	.7727	11.8767	0.0000

YEARS 24	MO PAYT 1.0458	AN CONST 12.55	
#	INT	PRIN	BALANCE
1	11.7581	.7913	99.2087
2	11.6595	.8899	98.3189
3	11.5486	1.0007	97.3181
4	11.4240	1.1254	96.1927
5	11.2837	1.2657	94.9270
6	11.1260	1.4233	93.5037
7	10.9487	1.6007	91.9030
8	10.7493	1.8001	90.1028
9	10.5250	2.0244	88.0784
10	10.2727	2.2767	85.8018
11	9.9891	2.5603	83.2415
12	9.6701	2.8793	80.3621
13	9.3113	3.2381	77.1241
14	8.9079	3.6415	73.4825
15	8.4541	4.0952	69.3873
16	7.9439	4.6055	64.7818
17	7.3701	5.1793	59.6025
18	6.7248	5.8246	53.7779
19	5.9990	6.5504	47.2275
20	5.1829	7.3665	39.8610
21	4.2650	8.2843	31.5766
22	3.2329	9.3165	22.2601
23	2.0721	10.4773	11.7828
24	.7666	11.7828	0.0000

YEARS 25	MO PAYT 1.0385	AN CONST 12.47	
#	INT	PRIN	BALANCE
1	11.7630	.6987	99.3013
2	11.6760	.7858	98.5156
3	11.5781	.8837	97.6319
4	11.4680	.9938	96.6382
5	11.3441	1.1176	95.5206
6	11.2049	1.2568	94.2638
7	11.0483	1.4134	92.8504
8	10.8722	1.5895	91.2609
9	10.6742	1.7876	89.4733
10	10.4514	2.0103	87.4630
11	10.2010	2.2607	85.2023
12	9.9193	2.5424	82.6598
13	9.6025	2.8592	79.8006
14	9.2463	3.2154	76.5852
15	8.8456	3.6161	72.9691
16	8.3951	4.0666	68.9025
17	7.8884	4.5733	64.3292
18	7.3186	5.1431	59.1860
19	6.6778	5.7839	53.4021
20	5.9571	6.5046	46.8975
21	5.1467	7.3150	39.5825
22	4.2352	8.2265	31.3560
23	3.2103	9.2514	22.1046
24	2.0576	10.4041	11.7004
25	.7613	11.7004	0.0000

YEARS 26	MO PAYT 1.0321	AN CONST 12.39	
#	INT	PRIN	BALANCE
1	11.7673	.6174	99.3826
2	11.6904	.6944	98.6882
3	11.6039	.7809	97.9073
4	11.5066	.8782	97.0291
5	11.3971	.9876	96.0415
6	11.2741	1.1107	94.9308
7	11.1357	1.2491	93.6817
8	10.9801	1.4047	92.2771
9	10.8051	1.5797	90.6974
10	10.6082	1.7765	88.9209
11	10.3869	1.9979	86.9230
12	10.1380	2.2468	84.6762
13	9.8580	2.5267	82.1495
14	9.5432	2.8416	79.3079
15	9.1892	3.1956	76.1123

#	INT	PRIN	BALANCE
16	8.7910	3.5938	72.5186
17	8.3432	4.0415	68.4770
18	7.8397	4.5451	63.9320
19	7.2734	5.1114	58.8206
20	6.6365	5.7482	53.0724
21	5.9203	6.4644	46.6079
22	5.1149	7.2699	39.3381
23	4.2091	8.1757	31.1624
24	3.1904	9.1943	21.9681
25	2.0449	10.3399	11.6282
26	.7566	11.6282	0.0000

YEARS 27	MO PAYT 1.0264	AN CONST 12.32	
#	INT	PRIN	BALANCE
1	11.7711	.5460	99.4540
2	11.7031	.6141	98.8399
3	11.6265	.6906	98.1493
4	11.5405	.7766	97.3727
5	11.4437	.8734	96.4993
6	11.3349	.9822	95.5170
7	11.2125	1.1046	94.4124
8	11.0749	1.2422	93.1702
9	10.9201	1.3970	91.7732
10	10.7461	1.5711	90.2021
11	10.5503	1.7668	88.4353
12	10.3302	1.9870	86.4483
13	10.0826	2.2345	84.2138
14	9.8042	2.5129	81.7009
15	9.4911	2.8260	78.8749
16	9.1390	3.1781	75.6967
17	8.7430	3.5741	72.1226
18	8.2977	4.0195	68.1031
19	7.7969	4.5203	63.5829
20	7.2337	5.0835	58.4994
21	6.6003	5.7168	52.7826
22	5.8880	6.4291	46.3534
23	5.0870	7.2302	39.1233
24	4.1861	8.1310	30.9922
25	3.1730	9.1441	21.8481
26	2.0337	10.2834	11.5647
27	.7524	11.5647	0.0000

YEARS 28	MO PAYT 1.0215	AN CONST 12.26	
#	INT	PRIN	BALANCE
1	11.7744	.4832	99.5168
2	11.7142	.5434	98.9734
3	11.6465	.6111	98.3623
4	11.5704	.6873	97.6750
5	11.4847	.7729	96.9021
6	11.3884	.8692	96.0330
7	11.2801	.9775	95.0555
8	11.1584	1.0993	93.9562
9	11.0214	1.2362	92.7200
10	10.8674	1.3903	91.3297
11	10.6941	1.5635	89.7663
12	10.4993	1.7583	88.0080
13	10.2803	1.9774	86.0306
14	10.0339	2.2237	83.8069
15	9.7568	2.5008	81.3061
16	9.4452	2.8124	78.4937
17	9.0948	3.1628	75.3309
18	8.7008	3.5569	71.7741
19	8.2576	4.0000	67.7741
20	7.7592	4.4984	63.2756
21	7.1987	5.0589	58.2167
22	6.5684	5.6892	52.5275
23	5.8596	6.3981	46.1295
24	5.0624	7.1952	38.9342
25	4.1659	8.0917	30.8425
26	3.1577	9.0999	21.7426
27	2.0239	10.2337	11.5088

#	INT	PRIN	BALANCE
28	.7488	11.5088	0.0000

YEARS 29	MO PAYT 1.0171	AN CONST 12.21	
#	INT	PRIN	BALANCE
1	11.7774	.4278	99.5722
2	11.7240	.4811	99.0910
3	11.6641	.5411	98.5500
4	11.5967	.6085	97.9415
5	11.5209	.6843	97.2571
6	11.4356	.7696	96.4876
7	11.3397	.8655	95.6221
8	11.2319	.9733	94.6488
9	11.1106	1.0946	93.5543
10	10.9742	1.2309	92.3233
11	10.8209	1.3843	90.9390
12	10.6484	1.5568	89.3822
13	10.4544	1.7508	87.6315
14	10.2363	1.9689	85.6626
15	9.9910	2.2142	83.4484
16	9.7151	2.4901	80.9583
17	9.4048	2.8003	78.1579
18	9.0559	3.1493	75.0087
19	8.6635	3.5416	71.4670
20	8.2223	3.9829	67.4841
21	7.7260	4.4792	63.0049
22	7.1679	5.0373	57.9677
23	6.5403	5.6649	52.3028
24	5.8345	6.3707	45.9321
25	5.0407	7.1645	38.7677
26	4.1481	8.0571	30.7105
27	3.1442	9.0610	21.6495
28	2.0152	10.1900	11.4596
29	.7456	11.4596	0.0000

YEARS 30	MO PAYT 1.0132	AN CONST 12.16	
#	INT	PRIN	BALANCE
1	11.7799	.3790	99.6210
2	11.7327	.4262	99.1948
3	11.6796	.4793	98.7155
4	11.6199	.5390	98.1765
5	11.5527	.6062	97.5703
6	11.4772	.6817	96.8886
7	11.3923	.7667	96.1219
8	11.2967	.8622	95.2597
9	11.1893	.9696	94.2901
10	11.0685	1.0904	93.1997
11	10.9326	1.2263	91.9734
12	10.7799	1.3791	90.5944
13	10.6080	1.5509	89.0435
14	10.4148	1.7441	87.2994
15	10.1975	1.9614	85.3379
16	9.9531	2.2058	83.1321
17	9.6783	2.4807	80.6514
18	9.3692	2.7897	77.8617
19	9.0216	3.1373	74.7244
20	8.6307	3.5282	71.1962
21	8.1911	3.9678	67.2283
22	7.6967	4.4622	62.7662
23	7.1408	5.0182	57.7480
24	6.5155	5.6434	52.1046
25	5.8124	6.3465	45.7580
26	5.0216	7.1373	38.6207
27	4.1323	8.0266	30.5942
28	3.1323	9.0267	21.5675
29	2.0076	10.1513	11.4162
30	.7428	11.4162	0.0000

YEARS 2 — MO PAYT 4.7015 — AN CONST 56.42

#	INT	PRIN	BALANCE
1	9.3689	47.0493	52.9507
2	3.4674	52.9507	0.0000

YEARS 3 — MO PAYT 3.3155 — AN CONST 39.79

#	INT	PRIN	BALANCE
1	10.3047	29.4809	70.5191
2	6.6068	33.1787	37.3404
3	2.4452	37.3404	0.0000

YEARS 4 — MO PAYT 2.6273 — AN CONST 31.53

#	INT	PRIN	BALANCE
1	10.7693	20.7577	79.2423
2	8.1657	23.3613	55.8810
3	5.2354	26.2916	29.5894
4	1.9376	29.5894	0.0000

YEARS 5 — MO PAYT 2.2181 — AN CONST 26.62

#	INT	PRIN	BALANCE
1	11.0455	15.5721	84.4279
2	9.0923	17.5253	66.9027
3	6.8941	19.7235	47.1791
4	4.4202	22.1974	24.9817
5	1.6359	24.9817	0.0000

YEARS 6 — MO PAYT 1.9485 — AN CONST 23.39

#	INT	PRIN	BALANCE
1	11.2276	12.1547	87.8453
2	9.7030	13.6793	74.1659
3	7.9872	15.3951	58.7708
4	6.0561	17.3262	41.4446
5	3.8829	19.4994	21.9452
6	1.4371	21.9452	0.0000

YEARS 7 — MO PAYT 1.7586 — AN CONST 21.11

#	INT	PRIN	BALANCE
1	11.3558	9.7473	90.2527
2	10.1332	10.9700	79.2827
3	8.7572	12.3459	66.9367
4	7.2086	13.8945	53.0422
5	5.4658	15.6373	37.4049
6	3.5044	17.5987	19.8062
7	1.2970	19.8062	0.0000

YEARS 8 — MO PAYT 1.6184 — AN CONST 19.43

#	INT	PRIN	BALANCE
1	11.4504	7.9707	92.0293
2	10.4507	8.9704	83.0589
3	9.3255	10.0956	72.9633
4	8.0592	11.3619	61.6014
5	6.6341	12.7870	48.8144
6	5.0302	14.3909	34.4235
7	3.2251	16.1960	18.2275
8	1.1936	18.2275	0.0000

YEARS 9 — MO PAYT 1.5114 — AN CONST 18.14

#	INT	PRIN	BALANCE
1	11.5227	6.6139	93.3861
2	10.6931	7.4435	85.9426
3	9.7595	8.3771	77.5655
4	8.7087	9.4279	68.1376
5	7.5262	10.6104	57.5272
6	6.1953	11.9413	45.5859
7	4.6975	13.4391	32.1467
8	3.0118	15.1248	17.0219
9	1.1147	17.0219	0.0000

YEARS 10 — MO PAYT 1.4275 — AN CONST 17.13

#	INT	PRIN	BALANCE
1	11.5793	5.5506	94.4494
2	10.8831	6.2468	88.2026
3	10.0996	7.0303	81.1723
4	9.2178	7.9121	73.2602
5	8.2253	8.9046	64.3556
6	7.1084	10.0215	54.3341
7	5.8514	11.2785	43.0556
8	4.4367	12.6932	30.3624
9	2.8446	14.2853	16.0771
10	1.0528	16.0771	0.0000

YEARS 11 — MO PAYT 1.3604 — AN CONST 16.33

#	INT	PRIN	BALANCE
1	11.6246	4.7001	95.2999
2	11.0351	5.2897	90.0102
3	10.3716	5.9532	84.0570
4	9.6249	6.6999	77.3571
5	8.7845	7.5403	69.8168
6	7.8387	8.4861	61.3308
7	6.7743	9.5505	51.7803
8	5.5764	10.7484	41.0319
9	4.2282	12.0966	28.9353
10	2.7109	13.6139	15.3215
11	1.0033	15.3215	0.0000

YEARS 12 — MO PAYT 1.3059 — AN CONST 15.68

#	INT	PRIN	BALANCE
1	11.6615	4.0089	95.9911
2	11.1586	4.5117	91.4794
3	10.5927	5.0776	86.4018
4	9.9558	5.7145	80.6873
5	9.2390	6.4313	74.2560
6	8.4324	7.2380	67.0180
7	7.5245	8.1459	58.8721
8	6.5027	9.1676	49.7045
9	5.3528	10.3175	39.3870
10	4.0587	11.6116	27.7754
11	2.6022	13.0681	14.7073
12	.9631	14.7073	0.0000

YEARS 13 — MO PAYT 1.2609 — AN CONST 15.14

#	INT	PRIN	BALANCE
1	11.6918	3.4396	96.5604
2	11.2604	3.8710	92.6894
3	10.7748	4.3565	88.3329
4	10.2284	4.9030	83.4299
5	9.6134	5.5180	77.9120
6	8.9213	6.2101	71.7019
7	8.1423	6.9890	64.7128
8	7.2657	7.8657	56.8472
9	6.2791	8.8523	47.9949
10	5.1687	9.9626	38.0323
11	3.9191	11.2123	26.8200
12	2.5127	12.6186	14.2014
13	.9300	14.2014	0.0000

YEARS 14 — MO PAYT 1.2236 — AN CONST 14.69

#	INT	PRIN	BALANCE
1	11.7170	2.9656	97.0344
2	11.3451	3.3376	93.6969
3	10.9264	3.7562	89.9407
4	10.4553	4.2273	85.7133
5	9.9250	4.7576	80.9557
6	9.3283	5.3543	75.6014
7	8.6567	6.0259	69.5755
8	7.9009	6.7818	62.7937
9	7.0502	7.6324	55.1613
10	6.0929	8.5898	46.5716
11	5.0154	9.6672	36.9044
12	3.8029	10.8797	26.0246
13	2.4382	12.2444	13.7802
14	.9024	13.7802	0.0000

YEARS 15 — MO PAYT 1.1921 — AN CONST 14.31

#	INT	PRIN	BALANCE
1	11.7382	2.5674	97.4326
2	11.4162	2.8894	94.5431
3	11.0538	3.2519	91.2913
4	10.6459	3.6598	87.6315
5	10.1868	4.1188	83.5127
6	9.6702	4.6354	78.8773
7	9.0888	5.2169	73.6604
8	8.4344	5.8712	67.7892
9	7.6980	6.6077	61.1816
10	6.8692	7.4365	53.7451
11	5.9364	8.3692	45.3759
12	4.8867	9.4190	35.9569
13	3.7052	10.6004	25.3565
14	2.3756	11.9300	13.4264
15	.8792	13.4264	0.0000

YEARS 16 — MO PAYT 1.1655 — AN CONST 13.99

#	INT	PRIN	BALANCE
1	11.7562	2.2304	97.7696
2	11.4764	2.5101	95.2595
3	11.1616	2.8250	92.4345
4	10.8072	3.1793	89.2551
5	10.4085	3.5781	85.6770
6	9.9596	4.0269	81.6501
7	9.4545	4.5320	77.1180
8	8.8861	5.1005	72.0175
9	8.2463	5.7403	66.2772
10	7.5263	6.4603	59.8170
11	6.7160	7.2706	52.5464
12	5.8040	8.1826	44.3638
13	4.7777	9.2089	35.1549
14	3.6226	10.3640	24.7909
15	2.3226	11.6640	13.1270
16	.8596	13.1270	0.0000

YEARS 17 — MO PAYT 1.1429 — AN CONST 13.72

#	INT	PRIN	BALANCE
1	11.7715	1.9433	98.0567
2	11.5277	2.1870	95.8697
3	11.2534	2.4614	93.4083
4	10.9447	2.7701	90.6382
5	10.5972	3.1176	87.5206
6	10.2062	3.5086	84.0120
7	9.7661	3.9487	80.0634
8	9.2708	4.4440	75.6194
9	8.7134	5.0014	70.6180
10	8.0861	5.6287	64.9893
11	7.3801	6.3347	58.6545
12	6.5855	7.1293	51.5252
13	5.6912	8.0235	43.5017
14	4.6848	9.0299	34.4718
15	3.5522	10.1626	24.3092
16	2.2775	11.4373	12.8719
17	.8429	12.8719	0.0000

YEARS 18 — MO PAYT 1.1235 — AN CONST 13.49

#	INT	PRIN	BALANCE
1	11.7846	1.6974	98.3026
2	11.5717	1.9103	96.3923
3	11.3321	2.1499	94.2424
4	11.0624	2.4196	91.8228
5	10.7589	2.7231	89.0997
6	10.4173	3.0646	86.0351
7	10.0329	3.4490	82.5860
8	9.6003	3.8817	78.7044
9	9.1134	4.3685	74.3358
10	8.5655	4.9165	69.4193
11	7.9488	5.5332	63.8862
12	7.2548	6.2272	57.6589
13	6.4737	7.0083	50.6507
14	5.5946	7.8874	42.7633
15	4.6053	8.8767	33.8866
16	3.4919	9.9901	23.8965
17	2.2388	11.2432	12.6534
18	.8286	12.6534	0.0000

YEARS 19 — MO PAYT 1.1068 — AN CONST 13.29

#	INT	PRIN	BALANCE
1	11.7959	1.4858	98.5142
2	11.6095	1.6722	96.8420
3	11.3997	1.8819	94.9601
4	11.1637	2.1180	92.8421
5	10.8980	2.3836	90.4585
6	10.5990	2.6826	87.7758
7	10.2626	3.0191	84.7567
8	9.8839	3.3978	81.3589
9	9.4577	3.8240	77.5350
10	8.9780	4.3036	73.2313
11	8.4382	4.8434	68.3879
12	7.8307	5.4510	62.9369
13	7.1470	6.1347	56.8022
14	6.3775	6.9042	49.8981
15	5.5115	7.7702	42.1279
16	4.5369	8.7448	33.3831
17	3.4400	9.8416	23.5415
18	2.2056	11.0761	12.4654
19	.8163	12.4654	0.0000

YEARS 20 — MO PAYT 1.0924 — AN CONST 13.11

#	INT	PRIN	BALANCE
1	11.8056	1.3030	98.6970
2	11.6422	1.4665	97.2305
3	11.4582	1.6504	95.5801
4	11.2512	1.8574	93.7227
5	11.0182	2.0904	91.6324
6	10.7560	2.3526	89.2798
7	10.4609	2.6477	86.6321
8	10.1288	2.9798	83.6523
9	9.7551	3.3535	80.2988
10	9.3345	3.7742	76.5247
11	8.8611	4.2476	72.2771
12	8.3283	4.7803	67.4968
13	7.7287	5.3799	62.1168
14	7.0539	6.0547	56.0621
15	6.2944	6.8142	49.2479
16	5.4397	7.6689	41.5790
17	4.4778	8.6308	32.9482
18	3.3952	9.7134	23.2347
19	2.1768	10.9318	12.3030
20	.8056	12.3030	0.0000

YEARS 21 — MO PAYT 1.0799 — AN CONST 12.96

#	INT	PRIN	BALANCE
1	11.8140	1.1445	98.8555
2	11.6705	1.2881	97.5674
3	11.5089	1.4497	96.1177

Column 1

#	INT	PRIN	BALANCE
4	11.3271	1.6315	94.4862
5	11.1224	1.8361	92.6500
6	10.8921	2.0665	90.5836
7	10.6329	2.3257	88.2579
8	10.3412	2.6174	85.6406
9	10.0129	2.9457	82.6949
10	9.6434	3.3151	79.3798
11	9.2276	3.7310	75.6488
12	8.7596	4.1989	71.4499
13	8.2330	4.7256	66.7243
14	7.6402	5.3184	61.4059
15	6.9731	5.9854	55.4204
16	6.2224	6.7362	48.6842
17	5.3774	7.5811	41.1031
18	4.4265	8.5321	32.5710
19	3.3563	9.6022	22.9688
20	2.1519	10.8067	12.1622
21	.7964	12.1622	0.0000

YEARS 22   MO PAYT 1.0690   AN CONST 12.83

#	INT	PRIN	BALANCE
1	11.8214	1.0067	98.9933
2	11.6951	1.1330	97.8602
3	11.5530	1.2751	96.5851
4	11.3930	1.4351	95.1500
5	11.2130	1.6151	93.5350
6	11.0105	1.8177	91.7173
7	10.7825	2.0457	89.6716
8	10.5259	2.3022	87.3694
9	10.2371	2.5910	84.7784
10	9.9121	2.9160	81.8624
11	9.5464	3.2818	78.5806
12	9.1347	3.6934	74.8872
13	8.6714	4.1567	70.7306
14	8.1501	4.6780	66.0525
15	7.5633	5.2648	60.7877
16	6.9029	5.9252	54.8625
17	6.1597	6.6684	48.1941
18	5.3233	7.5048	40.6893
19	4.3820	8.4462	32.2431
20	3.3225	9.5056	22.7376
21	2.1303	10.6979	12.0397
22	.7884	12.0397	0.0000

YEARS 23   MO PAYT 1.0595   AN CONST 12.72

#	INT	PRIN	BALANCE
1	11.8278	.8866	99.1134
2	11.7166	.9978	98.1156
3	11.5914	1.1230	96.9926
4	11.4506	1.2638	95.7288
5	11.2920	1.4224	94.3064
6	11.1136	1.6008	92.7057
7	10.9128	1.8015	90.9041
8	10.6869	2.0275	88.8766
9	10.4326	2.2818	86.5948
10	10.1463	2.5680	84.0267
11	9.8242	2.8902	81.1366
12	9.4617	3.2527	77.8839
13	9.0537	3.6607	74.2233
14	8.5946	4.1198	70.1035
15	8.0778	4.6366	65.4669
16	7.4962	5.2181	60.2487
17	6.8417	5.8727	54.3761
18	6.1051	6.6093	47.7668
19	5.2761	7.4383	40.3285
20	4.3431	8.3713	31.9573
21	3.2931	9.4213	22.5360
22	2.1114	10.6030	11.9330
23	.7814	11.9330	0.0000

Column 2

YEARS 24   MO PAYT 1.0513   AN CONST 12.62

#	INT	PRIN	BALANCE
1	11.8334	.7816	99.2184
2	11.7353	.8797	98.3387
3	11.6250	.9900	97.3487
4	11.5008	1.1142	96.2345
5	11.3611	1.2539	94.9805
6	11.2038	1.4112	93.5693
7	11.0268	1.5882	91.9810
8	10.8275	1.7875	90.1936
9	10.6033	2.0117	88.1819
10	10.3510	2.2640	85.9179
11	10.0670	2.5480	83.3700
12	9.7474	2.8676	80.5024
13	9.3878	3.2272	77.2752
14	8.9830	3.6320	73.6431
15	8.5274	4.0876	69.5555
16	8.0147	4.6003	64.9552
17	7.4376	5.1774	59.7778
18	6.7882	5.8268	53.9511
19	6.0574	6.5576	47.3935
20	5.2349	7.3801	40.0133
21	4.3092	8.3058	31.7075
22	3.2674	9.3477	22.3598
23	2.0949	10.5201	11.8397
24	.7753	11.8397	0.0000

YEARS 25   MO PAYT 1.0440   AN CONST 12.53

#	INT	PRIN	BALANCE
1	11.8383	.6897	99.3103
2	11.7517	.7762	98.5340
3	11.6544	.8736	97.6604
4	11.5448	.9832	96.6772
5	11.4215	1.1065	95.5707
6	11.2827	1.2453	94.3254
7	11.1265	1.4015	92.9239
8	10.9507	1.5773	91.3466
9	10.7529	1.7751	89.5715
10	10.5302	1.9978	87.5737
11	10.2796	2.2484	85.3253
12	9.9976	2.5304	82.7949
13	9.6802	2.8478	79.9471
14	9.3230	3.2050	76.7422
15	8.9210	3.6070	73.1352
16	8.4686	4.0594	69.0758
17	7.9594	4.5686	64.5072
18	7.3863	5.1416	59.3655
19	6.7414	5.7866	53.5790
20	6.0156	6.5124	47.0666
21	5.1988	7.3292	39.7373
22	4.2794	8.2486	31.4888
23	3.2448	9.2832	22.2056
24	2.0804	10.4476	11.7580
25	.7700	11.7580	0.0000

YEARS 26   MO PAYT 1.0376   AN CONST 12.46

#	INT	PRIN	BALANCE
1	11.8426	.6091	99.3909
2	11.7662	.6855	98.7053
3	11.6802	.7715	97.9338
4	11.5834	.8683	97.0655
5	11.4745	.9772	96.0883
6	11.3519	1.0998	94.9886
7	11.2140	1.2377	93.7509
8	11.0587	1.3930	92.3579
9	10.8840	1.5677	90.7902
10	10.6874	1.7643	89.0259
11	10.4661	1.9856	87.0403
12	10.2170	2.2347	84.8056
13	9.9367	2.5150	82.2906
14	9.6212	2.8304	79.4602
15	9.2662	3.1855	76.2747

Column 3

#	INT	PRIN	BALANCE
16	8.8667	3.5850	72.6897
17	8.4170	4.0347	68.6550
18	7.9109	4.5408	64.1142
19	7.3414	5.1103	59.0039
20	6.7004	5.7513	53.2526
21	5.9790	6.4727	46.7799
22	5.1671	7.2846	39.4953
23	4.2534	8.1983	31.2970
24	3.2250	9.2266	22.0703
25	2.0677	10.3839	11.6864
26	.7653	11.6864	0.0000

YEARS 27   MO PAYT 1.0321   AN CONST 12.39

#	INT	PRIN	BALANCE
1	11.8463	.5383	99.4617
2	11.7788	.6058	98.8558
3	11.7028	.6818	98.1740
4	11.6173	.7674	97.4066
5	11.5210	.8636	96.5430
6	11.4127	.9719	95.5711
7	11.2908	1.0938	94.4772
8	11.1536	1.2311	93.2462
9	10.9992	1.3855	91.8607
10	10.8254	1.5592	90.3015
11	10.6298	1.7548	88.5466
12	10.4097	1.9749	86.5717
13	10.1620	2.2227	84.3491
14	9.8832	2.5014	81.8476
15	9.5694	2.8152	79.0324
16	9.2163	3.1683	75.8641
17	8.8189	3.5657	72.2984
18	8.3717	4.0130	68.2854
19	7.8683	4.5163	63.7691
20	7.3018	5.0828	58.6863
21	6.6643	5.7204	52.9659
22	5.9468	6.4379	46.5280
23	5.1393	7.2454	39.2827
24	4.2305	8.1542	31.1285
25	3.2077	9.1770	21.9515
26	2.0566	10.3280	11.6235
27	.7612	11.6235	0.0000

YEARS 28   MO PAYT 1.0271   AN CONST 12.33

#	INT	PRIN	BALANCE
1	11.8496	.4760	99.5240
2	11.7899	.5358	98.9882
3	11.7227	.6030	98.3852
4	11.6471	.6786	97.7066
5	11.5620	.7637	96.9429
6	11.4662	.8595	96.0834
7	11.3584	.9673	95.1161
8	11.2371	1.0886	94.0275
9	11.1005	1.2252	92.8023
10	10.9468	1.3789	91.4234
11	10.7739	1.5518	89.8716
12	10.5792	1.7465	88.1251
13	10.3602	1.9655	86.1596
14	10.1136	2.2121	83.9475
15	9.8362	2.4895	81.4580
16	9.5239	2.8018	78.6562
17	9.1725	3.1532	75.5030
18	8.7769	3.5487	71.9542
19	8.3318	3.9939	67.9603
20	7.8309	4.4948	63.4655
21	7.2671	5.0586	58.4069
22	6.6326	5.6931	52.7138
23	5.9185	6.4072	46.3066
24	5.1148	7.2109	39.0957
25	4.2103	8.1154	30.9803
26	3.1924	9.1333	21.8470
27	2.0468	10.2789	11.5682

Column 4

#	INT	PRIN	BALANCE
28	.7575	11.5682	0.0000

YEARS 29   MO PAYT 1.0228   AN CONST 12.28

#	INT	PRIN	BALANCE
1	11.8526	.4212	99.5788
2	11.7997	.4740	99.1047
3	11.7403	.5335	98.5712
4	11.6734	.6004	97.9708
5	11.5980	.6757	97.2951
6	11.5133	.7605	96.5346
7	11.4179	.8559	95.6787
8	11.3105	.9632	94.7155
9	11.1897	1.0841	93.6314
10	11.0537	1.2200	92.4114
11	10.9007	1.3731	91.0383
12	10.7285	1.5453	89.4930
13	10.5347	1.7391	87.7539
14	10.3165	1.9573	85.7967
15	10.0710	2.2028	83.5939
16	9.7947	2.4790	81.1149
17	9.4838	2.7900	78.3249
18	9.1338	3.1399	75.1849
19	8.7400	3.5338	71.6511
20	8.2967	3.9770	67.6741
21	7.7979	4.4759	63.1982
22	7.2365	5.0373	58.1609
23	6.6046	5.6691	52.4917
24	5.8935	6.3802	46.1115
25	5.0933	7.1805	38.9310
26	4.1926	8.0812	30.8498
27	3.1790	9.0948	21.7550
28	2.0382	10.2356	11.5194
29	.7543	11.5194	0.0000

YEARS 30   MO PAYT 1.0190   AN CONST 12.23

#	INT	PRIN	BALANCE
1	11.8551	.3729	99.6271
2	11.8084	.4196	99.2075
3	11.7557	.4723	98.7352
4	11.6965	.5315	98.2037
5	11.6298	.5982	97.6055
6	11.5548	.6732	96.9323
7	11.4704	.7577	96.1746
8	11.3753	.8527	95.3219
9	11.2684	.9596	94.3623
10	11.1480	1.0800	93.2823
11	11.0125	1.2155	92.0668
12	10.8601	1.3679	90.6989
13	10.6885	1.5395	89.1593
14	10.4954	1.7326	87.4267
15	10.2781	1.9500	85.4768
16	10.0335	2.1945	83.2822
17	9.7582	2.4698	80.8124
18	9.4484	2.7796	78.0328
19	9.0998	3.1282	74.9046
20	8.7074	3.5206	71.3840
21	8.2658	3.9622	67.4217
22	7.7688	4.4592	62.9625
23	7.2095	5.0185	57.9440
24	6.5800	5.6480	52.2960
25	5.8716	6.3564	45.9396
26	5.0743	7.1537	38.7858
27	4.1770	8.0510	30.7348
28	3.1671	9.0609	21.6739
29	2.0306	10.1974	11.4765
30	.7515	11.4765	0.0000

YEARS 2 — MO PAYT 4.7027 — AN CONST 56.44

#	INT	PRIN	BALANCE
1	9.3890	47.0431	52.9569
2	3.4753	52.9569	0.0000

YEARS 3 — MO PAYT 3.3167 — AN CONST 39.80

#	INT	PRIN	BALANCE
1	10.3269	29.4730	70.5270
2	6.6218	33.1781	37.3489
3	2.4510	37.3489	0.0000

YEARS 4 — MO PAYT 2.6285 — AN CONST 31.55

#	INT	PRIN	BALANCE
1	10.7925	20.7492	79.2508
2	8.1841	23.3576	55.8932
3	5.2478	26.2939	29.5993
4	1.9424	29.5993	0.0000

YEARS 5 — MO PAYT 2.2194 — AN CONST 26.64

#	INT	PRIN	BALANCE
1	11.0693	15.5634	84.4366
2	9.1128	17.5199	66.9166
3	6.9104	19.7224	47.1943
4	4.4311	22.2017	24.9926
5	1.6401	24.9926	0.0000

YEARS 6 — MO PAYT 1.9498 — AN CONST 23.40

#	INT	PRIN	BALANCE
1	11.2517	12.1462	87.8538
2	9.7248	13.6731	74.1807
3	8.0060	15.3919	58.7888
4	6.0710	17.3268	41.4620
5	3.8929	19.5050	21.9570
6	1.4409	21.9570	0.0000

YEARS 7 — MO PAYT 1.7599 — AN CONST 21.12

#	INT	PRIN	BALANCE
1	11.3802	9.7390	90.2610
2	10.1559	10.9633	79.2977
3	8.7777	12.3415	66.9563
4	7.2263	13.8929	53.0634
5	5.4798	15.6394	37.4240
6	3.5138	17.6054	19.8186
7	1.3006	19.8186	0.0000

YEARS 8 — MO PAYT 1.6198 — AN CONST 19.44

#	INT	PRIN	BALANCE
1	11.4750	7.9625	92.0375
2	10.4740	8.9635	83.0739
3	9.3472	10.0903	72.9836
4	8.0788	11.3588	61.6249
5	6.6509	12.7867	48.8382
6	5.0434	14.3941	34.4441
7	3.2340	16.2036	18.2405
8	1.1970	18.2405	0.0000

YEARS 9 — MO PAYT 1.5128 — AN CONST 18.16

#	INT	PRIN	BALANCE
1	11.5474	6.6061	93.3939
2	10.7169	7.4365	85.9574
3	9.7821	8.3714	77.5860
4	8.7297	9.4237	68.1623
5	7.5451	10.6084	57.5539
6	6.2115	11.9420	45.6119
7	4.7103	13.4432	32.1687
8	3.0203	15.1331	17.0355
9	1.1179	17.0355	0.0000

YEARS 10 — MO PAYT 1.4289 — AN CONST 17.15

#	INT	PRIN	BALANCE
1	11.6041	5.5431	94.4569
2	10.9073	6.2399	88.2170
3	10.1229	7.0243	81.1927
4	9.2399	7.9073	73.2854
5	8.2458	8.9014	64.3840
6	7.1268	10.0204	54.3636
7	5.8672	11.2800	43.0836
8	4.4492	12.6980	30.3855
9	2.8529	14.2943	16.0912
10	1.0560	16.0912	0.0000

YEARS 11 — MO PAYT 1.3619 — AN CONST 16.35

#	INT	PRIN	BALANCE
1	11.6495	4.6930	95.3070
2	11.0596	5.2829	90.0241
3	10.3954	5.9471	84.0770
4	9.6478	6.6947	77.3823
5	8.8062	7.5363	69.8461
6	7.8589	8.4836	61.3624
7	6.7924	9.5501	51.8123
8	5.5918	10.7507	41.0617
9	4.2404	12.1021	28.9596
10	2.7190	13.6235	15.3361
11	1.0064	15.3361	0.0000

YEARS 12 — MO PAYT 1.3074 — AN CONST 15.69

#	INT	PRIN	BALANCE
1	11.6864	4.0021	95.9979
2	11.1833	4.5052	91.4928
3	10.6169	5.0715	86.4212
4	9.9794	5.7091	80.7122
5	9.2617	6.4267	74.2854
6	8.4538	7.2346	67.0508
7	7.5443	8.1441	58.9067
8	6.5205	9.1679	49.7388
9	5.3681	10.3204	39.4184
10	4.0707	11.6178	27.8006
11	2.6102	13.0783	14.7223
12	.9661	14.7223	0.0000

YEARS 13 — MO PAYT 1.2625 — AN CONST 15.15

#	INT	PRIN	BALANCE
1	11.7168	3.4331	96.5669
2	11.2852	3.8647	92.7022
3	10.7994	4.3505	88.3517
4	10.2525	4.8974	83.4543
5	9.6368	5.5131	77.9412
6	8.9438	6.2061	71.7351
7	8.1636	6.9863	64.7489
8	7.2853	7.8645	56.8843
9	6.2967	8.8532	48.0312
10	5.1838	9.9661	38.0651
11	3.9309	11.2189	26.8462
12	2.5206	12.6293	14.2169
13	.9330	14.2169	0.0000

YEARS 14 — MO PAYT 1.2251 — AN CONST 14.71

#	INT	PRIN	BALANCE
1	11.7420	2.9595	97.0405
2	11.3700	3.3315	93.7090
3	10.9512	3.7503	89.9587
4	10.4797	4.2218	85.7370
5	9.9490	4.7525	80.9845
6	9.3516	5.3499	75.6346
7	8.6791	6.0224	69.6122
8	7.9220	6.7795	62.8326
9	7.0697	7.6318	55.2009
10	6.1103	8.5912	46.6097
11	5.0304	9.6712	36.9386
12	3.8146	10.8869	26.0516
13	2.4460	12.2555	13.7961
14	.9054	13.7961	0.0000

YEARS 15 — MO PAYT 1.1937 — AN CONST 14.33

#	INT	PRIN	BALANCE
1	11.7633	2.5616	97.4384
2	11.4412	2.8837	94.5547
3	11.0787	3.2462	91.3085
4	10.6707	3.6542	87.6543
5	10.2113	4.1136	83.5407
6	9.6942	4.6307	78.9100
7	9.1120	5.2129	73.6971
8	8.4567	5.8682	67.8290
9	7.7191	6.6059	61.2231
10	6.8886	7.4363	53.7868
11	5.9538	8.3711	45.4157
12	4.9015	9.4234	35.9923
13	3.7169	10.6080	25.3843
14	2.3833	11.9416	13.4427
15	.8822	13.4427	0.0000

YEARS 16 — MO PAYT 1.1672 — AN CONST 14.01

#	INT	PRIN	BALANCE
1	11.7812	2.2249	97.7751
2	11.5015	2.5046	95.2704
3	11.1867	2.8195	92.4509
4	10.8322	3.1739	89.2770
5	10.4333	3.5729	85.7041
6	9.9841	4.0221	81.6820
7	9.4785	4.5277	77.1543
8	8.9093	5.0969	72.0574
9	8.2686	5.7376	66.3198
10	7.5473	6.4589	59.8609
11	6.7354	7.2708	52.5901
12	5.8213	8.1848	44.4053
13	4.7924	9.2137	35.1915
14	3.6342	10.3720	24.8195
15	2.3303	11.6759	13.1436
16	.8625	13.1436	0.0000

YEARS 17 — MO PAYT 1.1446 — AN CONST 13.74

#	INT	PRIN	BALANCE
1	11.7965	1.9382	98.0618
2	11.5529	2.1818	95.8800
3	11.2786	2.4561	93.4239
4	10.9699	2.7649	90.6591
5	10.6223	3.1124	87.5466
6	10.2310	3.5037	84.0430
7	9.7906	3.9441	80.0988
8	9.2948	4.4399	75.6589
9	8.7366	4.9981	70.6608
10	8.1083	5.6264	65.0344
11	7.4010	6.3337	58.7007
12	6.6048	7.1299	51.5708
13	5.7085	8.0262	43.5446
14	4.6995	9.0352	34.5094
15	3.5637	10.1710	24.3385
16	2.2851	11.4496	12.8889
17	.8458	12.8889	0.0000

YEARS 18 — MO PAYT 1.1252 — AN CONST 13.51

#	INT	PRIN	BALANCE
1	11.8097	1.6926	98.3074
2	11.5969	1.9054	96.4020
3	11.3574	2.1449	94.2572
4	11.0877	2.4145	91.8426
5	10.7842	2.7181	89.1246
6	10.4425	3.0597	86.0648
7	10.0579	3.4444	82.6205
8	9.6249	3.8774	78.7431
9	9.1375	4.3648	74.3783
10	8.5888	4.9135	69.4648
11	7.9711	5.5312	63.9336
12	7.2758	6.2265	57.7072
13	6.4930	7.0092	50.6979
14	5.6119	7.8903	42.8076
15	4.6200	8.8822	33.9253
16	3.5034	9.9988	23.9265
17	2.2465	11.2558	12.6707
18	.8315	12.6707	0.0000

YEARS 19 — MO PAYT 1.1085 — AN CONST 13.31

#	INT	PRIN	BALANCE
1	11.8209	1.4813	98.5187
2	11.6347	1.6675	96.8512
3	11.4251	1.8771	94.9740
4	11.1891	2.1131	92.8609
5	10.9235	2.3788	90.4822
6	10.6244	2.6778	87.8044
7	10.2878	3.0144	84.7900
8	9.9089	3.3934	81.3966
9	9.4823	3.8199	77.5767
10	9.0021	4.3001	73.2765
11	8.4615	4.8407	68.4358
12	7.8530	5.4492	62.9866
13	7.1680	6.1343	56.8523
14	6.3968	6.9054	49.9469
15	5.5288	7.7735	42.1735
16	4.5516	8.7507	33.4228
17	3.4515	9.8507	23.5721
18	2.2132	11.0890	12.4830
19	.8192	12.4830	0.0000

YEARS 20 — MO PAYT 1.0941 — AN CONST 13.13

#	INT	PRIN	BALANCE
1	11.8307	1.2988	98.7012
2	11.6674	1.4621	97.2391
3	11.4836	1.6459	95.5933
4	11.2767	1.8528	93.7405
5	11.0438	2.0857	91.6548
6	10.7816	2.3479	89.3070
7	10.4865	2.6430	86.6640
8	10.1542	2.9753	83.6887
9	9.7802	3.3493	80.3394
10	9.3591	3.7703	76.5691
11	8.8852	4.2443	72.3248
12	8.3516	4.7778	67.5470
13	7.7510	5.3785	62.1685
14	7.0749	6.0546	56.1139
15	6.3138	6.8157	49.2982
16	5.4570	7.6725	41.6257
17	4.4925	8.6370	32.9887
18	3.4067	9.7228	23.2659
19	2.1844	10.9450	12.3209
20	.8086	12.3209	0.0000

YEARS 21 — MO PAYT 1.0816 — AN CONST 12.98

#	INT	PRIN	BALANCE
1	11.8391	1.1406	98.8594
2	11.6957	1.2840	97.5754
3	11.5343	1.4454	96.1300

#	INT	PRIN	BALANCE
4	11.3526	1.6271	94.5029
5	11.1481	1.8316	92.6713
6	10.9178	2.0619	90.6094
7	10.6586	2.3211	88.2884
8	10.3669	2.6129	85.6755
9	10.0384	2.9413	82.7342
10	9.6686	3.3111	79.4231
11	9.2524	3.7273	75.6958
12	8.7838	4.1959	71.4999
13	8.2564	4.7233	66.7765
14	7.6626	5.3171	61.4594
15	6.9942	5.9855	55.4739
16	6.2418	6.7380	48.7359
17	5.3947	7.5850	41.1509
18	4.4412	8.5385	32.6124
19	3.3678	9.6119	23.0006
20	2.1595	10.8202	12.1804
21	.7993	12.1804	0.0000

YEARS 22 — MO PAYT 1.0708 — AN CONST 12.85

#	INT	PRIN	BALANCE
1	11.8465	1.0031	98.9969
2	11.7204	1.1292	97.8678
3	11.5784	1.2711	96.5967
4	11.4186	1.4309	95.1658
5	11.2388	1.6108	93.5550
6	11.0363	1.8133	91.7418
7	10.8083	2.0412	89.7006
8	10.5517	2.2978	87.4028
9	10.2629	2.5867	84.8161
10	9.9377	2.9118	81.9043
11	9.5717	3.2779	78.6264
12	9.1596	3.6899	74.9365
13	8.6957	4.1538	70.7827
14	8.1736	4.6760	66.1067
15	7.5857	5.2638	60.8430
16	6.9240	5.9255	54.9175
17	6.1791	6.6704	48.2471
18	5.3406	7.5089	40.7382
19	4.3967	8.4529	32.2853
20	3.3341	9.5155	22.7699
21	2.1379	10.7117	12.0582
22	.7913	12.0582	0.0000

YEARS 23 — MO PAYT 1.0613 — AN CONST 12.74

#	INT	PRIN	BALANCE
1	11.8529	.8832	99.1168
2	11.7418	.9942	98.1226
3	11.6169	1.1192	97.0034
4	11.4762	1.2599	95.7436
5	11.3178	1.4183	94.3253
6	11.1395	1.5965	92.7288
7	10.9388	1.7972	90.9315
8	10.7129	2.0232	88.9084
9	10.4585	2.2775	86.6308
10	10.1722	2.5638	84.0670
11	9.8499	2.8861	81.1809
12	9.4871	3.2489	77.9320
13	9.0787	3.6573	74.2747
14	8.6189	4.1171	70.1576
15	8.1014	4.6347	65.5229
16	7.5187	5.2173	60.3056
17	6.8629	5.8732	54.4325
18	6.1246	6.6115	47.8210
19	5.2934	7.4426	40.3784
20	4.3578	8.3782	32.0002
21	3.3046	9.4314	22.5688
22	2.1190	10.6170	11.9517
23	.7843	11.9517	0.0000

YEARS 24 — MO PAYT 1.0531 — AN CONST 12.64

#	INT	PRIN	BALANCE
1	11.8584	.7784	99.2216
2	11.7606	.8763	98.3453
3	11.6504	.9865	97.3588
4	11.5264	1.1105	96.2483
5	11.3868	1.2501	94.9983
6	11.2297	1.4072	93.5910
7	11.0528	1.5841	92.0069
8	10.8536	1.7833	90.2237
9	10.6295	2.0074	88.2163
10	10.3771	2.2598	85.9565
11	10.0930	2.5439	83.4126
12	9.7733	2.8636	80.5490
13	9.4133	3.2236	77.3254
14	9.0080	3.6289	73.6965
15	8.5518	4.0851	69.6114
16	8.0383	4.5986	65.0128
17	7.4602	5.1767	59.8362
18	6.8095	5.8274	54.0087
19	6.0769	6.5600	47.4487
20	5.2522	7.3847	40.0641
21	4.3239	8.3130	31.7511
22	3.2789	9.3580	22.3931
23	2.1025	10.5344	11.8587
24	.7782	11.8587	0.0000

YEARS 25 — MO PAYT 1.0458 — AN CONST 12.56

#	INT	PRIN	BALANCE
1	11.8633	.6868	99.3132
2	11.7770	.7731	98.5401
3	11.6798	.8703	97.6699
4	11.5704	.9797	96.6902
5	11.4473	1.1028	95.5873
6	11.3086	1.2415	94.3458
7	11.1526	1.3975	92.9483
8	10.9769	1.5732	91.3751
9	10.7791	1.7710	89.6041
10	10.5565	1.9936	87.6104
11	10.3059	2.2443	85.3662
12	10.0237	2.5264	82.8398
13	9.7061	2.8440	79.9958
14	9.3486	3.2015	76.7943
15	8.9462	3.6039	73.1904
16	8.4931	4.0570	69.1334
17	7.9831	4.5670	64.5664
18	7.4090	5.1411	59.4252
19	6.7627	5.7874	53.6378
20	6.0352	6.5149	47.1229
21	5.2162	7.3339	39.7889
22	4.2942	8.2559	31.5330
23	3.2564	9.2937	22.2393
24	2.0881	10.4621	11.7772
25	.7729	11.7772	0.0000

YEARS 26 — MO PAYT 1.0395 — AN CONST 12.48

#	INT	PRIN	BALANCE
1	11.8676	.6064	99.3936
2	11.7914	.6826	98.7110
3	11.7056	.7684	97.9426
4	11.6090	.8650	97.0776
5	11.5003	.9737	96.1039
6	11.3779	1.0962	95.0077
7	11.2401	1.2340	93.7738
8	11.0849	1.3891	92.3847
9	10.9103	1.5637	90.8210
10	10.7137	1.7603	89.0607
11	10.4925	1.9815	87.0792
12	10.2434	2.2306	84.8485
13	9.9629	2.5111	82.3375
14	9.6473	2.8267	79.5107
15	9.2919	3.1821	76.3286
16	8.8919	3.5821	72.7466
17	8.4416	4.0324	68.7142
18	7.9347	4.5393	64.1748
19	7.3641	5.1099	59.0649
20	6.7217	5.7523	53.3126
21	5.9986	6.4754	46.8371
22	5.1845	7.2895	39.5477
23	4.2682	8.2058	31.3418
24	3.2366	9.2374	22.1044
25	2.0754	10.3986	11.7058
26	.7682	11.7058	0.0000

YEARS 27 — MO PAYT 1.0339 — AN CONST 12.41

#	INT	PRIN	BALANCE
1	11.8714	.5358	99.4642
2	11.8041	.6031	98.8611
3	11.7282	.6789	98.1822
4	11.6429	.7643	97.4179
5	11.5468	.8604	96.5575
6	11.4386	.9685	95.5890
7	11.3169	1.0903	94.4987
8	11.1798	1.2273	93.2713
9	11.0255	1.3816	91.8897
10	10.8519	1.5553	90.3344
11	10.6563	1.7508	88.5836
12	10.4362	1.9709	86.6126
13	10.1885	2.2187	84.3939
14	9.9096	2.4976	81.8963
15	9.5956	2.8116	79.0847
16	9.2421	3.1650	75.9197
17	8.8443	3.5629	72.3568
18	8.3964	4.0108	68.3460
19	7.8922	4.5110	63.8310
20	7.3246	5.0826	58.7484
21	6.6857	5.7215	53.0269
22	5.9664	6.4408	46.5862
23	5.1568	7.2504	39.3358
24	4.2453	8.1619	31.1739
25	3.2193	9.1879	21.9860
26	2.0643	10.3429	11.6431
27	.7641	11.6431	0.0000

YEARS 28 — MO PAYT 1.0290 — AN CONST 12.35

#	INT	PRIN	BALANCE
1	11.8747	.4737	99.5263
2	11.8152	.5332	98.9931
3	11.7481	.6003	98.3928
4	11.6727	.6757	97.7171
5	11.5877	.7607	96.9564
6	11.4921	.8563	96.1001
7	11.3845	.9639	95.1362
8	11.2633	1.0851	94.0511
9	11.1269	1.2215	92.8295
10	10.9733	1.3751	91.4544
11	10.8005	1.5479	89.9065
12	10.6059	1.7425	88.1639
13	10.3868	1.9616	86.2023
14	10.1402	2.2082	83.9942
15	9.8626	2.4858	81.5084
16	9.5501	2.7983	78.7101
17	9.1984	3.1500	75.5601
18	8.8024	3.5460	72.0141
19	8.3566	3.9918	68.0223
20	7.8548	4.4936	63.5286
21	7.2899	5.0585	58.4702
22	6.6540	5.6944	52.7758
23	5.9382	6.4102	46.3655
24	5.1323	7.2161	39.1494
25	4.2252	8.1232	31.0262
26	3.2040	9.1444	21.8819
27	2.0545	10.2939	11.5880
28	.7604	11.5880	0.0000

YEARS 29 — MO PAYT 1.0247 — AN CONST 12.30

#	INT	PRIN	BALANCE
1	11.8776	.4190	99.5810
2	11.8250	.4717	99.1093
3	11.7657	.5310	98.5783
4	11.6989	.5978	97.9805
5	11.6238	.6729	97.3076
6	11.5392	.7575	96.5501
7	11.4440	.8527	95.6974
8	11.3368	.9599	94.7375
9	11.2161	1.0806	93.6570
10	11.0803	1.2164	92.4405
11	10.9273	1.3693	91.0712
12	10.7552	1.5415	89.5298
13	10.5614	1.7352	87.7945
14	10.3433	1.9534	85.8411
15	10.0977	2.1989	83.6422
16	9.8213	2.4754	81.1668
17	9.5101	2.7865	78.3803
18	9.1598	3.1368	75.2435
19	8.7655	3.5312	71.7123
20	8.3216	3.9751	67.7372
21	7.8219	4.4748	63.2624
22	7.2594	5.0373	58.2251
23	6.6261	5.6705	52.5546
24	5.9133	6.3834	46.1712
25	5.1108	7.1858	38.9854
26	4.2075	8.0892	30.8962
27	3.1906	9.1061	21.7902
28	2.0459	10.2508	11.5394
29	.7573	11.5394	0.0000

YEARS 30 — MO PAYT 1.0209 — AN CONST 12.26

#	INT	PRIN	BALANCE
1	11.8802	.3709	99.6291
2	11.8336	.4175	99.2117
3	11.7811	.4700	98.7417
4	11.7220	.5290	98.2127
5	11.6555	.5955	97.6172
6	11.5807	.6704	96.9468
7	11.4964	.7547	96.1921
8	11.4015	.8495	95.3425
9	11.2947	.9563	94.3862
10	11.1745	1.0766	93.3096
11	11.0392	1.2119	92.0977
12	10.8868	1.3642	90.7335
13	10.7153	1.5357	89.1977
14	10.5223	1.7288	87.4689
15	10.3049	1.9461	85.5228
16	10.0603	2.1908	83.3320
17	9.7849	2.4662	80.8658
18	9.4749	2.7762	78.0896
19	9.1259	3.1252	74.9644
20	8.7330	3.5181	71.4463
21	8.2907	3.9603	67.4860
22	7.7929	4.4582	63.0278
23	7.2324	5.0186	58.0092
24	6.6015	5.6495	52.3597
25	5.8914	6.3597	46.0000
26	5.0919	7.1592	38.8408
27	4.1919	8.0592	30.7816
28	3.1788	9.0723	21.7094
29	2.0383	10.2128	11.4966
30	.7545	11.4966	0.0000

YEARS 2 — MO PAYT 4.7073 — AN CONST 56.49

#	INT	PRIN	BALANCE
1	9.4697	47.0184	52.9816
2	3.5066	52.9816	0.0000

YEARS 3 — MO PAYT 3.3214 — AN CONST 39.86

#	INT	PRIN	BALANCE
1	10.4156	29.4416	70.5584
2	6.6817	33.1755	37.3830
3	2.4742	37.3830	0.0000

YEARS 4 — MO PAYT 2.6334 — AN CONST 31.61

#	INT	PRIN	BALANCE
1	10.8852	20.7154	79.2846
2	8.2580	23.3426	55.9420
3	5.2976	26.3031	29.6389
4	1.9617	29.6389	0.0000

YEARS 5 — MO PAYT 2.2244 — AN CONST 26.70

#	INT	PRIN	BALANCE
1	11.1643	15.5290	84.4710
2	9.1948	17.4985	66.9725
3	6.9756	19.7177	47.2547
4	4.4749	22.2184	25.0363
5	1.6570	25.0363	0.0000

YEARS 6 — MO PAYT 1.9550 — AN CONST 23.47

#	INT	PRIN	BALANCE
1	11.3482	12.1120	87.8880
2	9.8121	13.6481	74.2398
3	8.0812	15.3791	58.8608
4	6.1307	17.3295	41.5312
5	3.9329	19.5273	22.0039
6	1.4563	22.0039	0.0000

YEARS 7 — MO PAYT 1.7653 — AN CONST 21.19

#	INT	PRIN	BALANCE
1	11.4777	9.7056	90.2944
2	10.2468	10.9365	79.3579
3	8.8598	12.3235	67.0344
4	7.2968	13.8864	53.1480
5	5.5357	15.6476	37.5004
6	3.5512	17.6321	19.8683
7	1.3150	19.8683	0.0000

YEARS 8 — MO PAYT 1.6253 — AN CONST 19.51

#	INT	PRIN	BALANCE
1	11.5732	7.9302	92.0698
2	10.5675	8.9359	83.1339
3	9.4342	10.0692	73.0647
4	8.1572	11.3462	61.7185
5	6.7182	12.7852	48.9333
6	5.0967	14.4067	34.5265
7	3.2696	16.2338	18.2927
8	1.2107	18.2927	0.0000

YEARS 9 — MO PAYT 1.5184 — AN CONST 18.23

#	INT	PRIN	BALANCE
1	11.6462	6.5749	93.4251
2	10.8123	7.4088	86.0163
3	9.8727	8.3484	77.6679
4	8.8139	9.4072	68.2608
5	7.6208	10.6002	57.6605
6	6.2765	11.9446	45.7159
7	4.7616	13.4595	32.2565
8	3.0546	15.1665	17.0900
9	1.1311	17.0900	0.0000

YEARS 10 — MO PAYT 1.4347 — AN CONST 17.22

#	INT	PRIN	BALANCE
1	11.7033	5.5132	94.4868
2	11.0041	6.2124	88.2744
3	10.2162	7.0003	81.2741
4	9.3284	7.8881	73.3860
5	8.3280	8.8885	64.4974
6	7.2007	10.0158	54.4816
7	5.9304	11.2861	43.1955
8	4.4991	12.7174	30.4781
9	2.8862	14.3303	16.1478
10	1.0687	16.1478	0.0000

YEARS 11 — MO PAYT 1.3678 — AN CONST 16.42

#	INT	PRIN	BALANCE
1	11.7490	4.6645	95.3355
2	11.1574	5.2560	90.0795
3	10.4908	5.9226	84.1568
4	9.7397	6.6738	77.4831
5	8.8933	7.5202	69.9629
6	7.9395	8.4739	61.4890
7	6.8648	9.5486	51.9403
8	5.6538	10.7596	41.1807
9	4.2892	12.1242	29.0564
10	2.7516	13.6619	15.3946
11	1.0189	15.3946	0.0000

YEARS 12 — MO PAYT 1.3134 — AN CONST 15.77

#	INT	PRIN	BALANCE
1	11.7861	3.9749	96.0251
2	11.2820	4.4791	91.5460
3	10.7139	5.0471	86.4989
4	10.0738	5.6872	80.8117
5	9.3525	6.4085	74.4032
6	8.5398	7.2213	67.1819
7	7.6239	8.1371	59.0448
8	6.5919	9.1691	49.8757
9	5.4291	10.3320	39.5438
10	4.1187	11.6423	27.9015
11	2.6422	13.1188	14.7826
12	.9784	14.7826	0.0000

YEARS 13 — MO PAYT 1.2687 — AN CONST 15.23

#	INT	PRIN	BALANCE
1	11.8166	3.4074	96.5926
2	11.3845	3.8395	92.7531
3	10.8976	4.3264	88.4267
4	10.3489	4.8751	83.5516
5	9.7306	5.4934	78.0581
6	9.0339	6.1901	71.8680
7	8.2488	6.9752	64.8928
8	7.3642	7.8598	57.0329
9	6.3673	8.8567	48.1763
10	5.2441	9.9799	38.1964
11	3.9784	11.2456	26.9508
12	2.5522	12.6718	14.2789
13	.9451	14.2789	0.0000

YEARS 14 — MO PAYT 1.2314 — AN CONST 14.78

#	INT	PRIN	BALANCE
1	11.8420	2.9351	97.0649
2	11.4698	3.3074	93.7575
3	11.0503	3.7268	90.0307
4	10.5777	4.1995	85.8313
5	10.0451	4.7321	81.0992
6	9.4450	5.3322	75.7670
7	8.7687	6.0085	69.7586
8	8.0067	6.7705	62.9881
9	7.1480	7.6291	55.3590
10	6.1804	8.5967	46.7623
11	5.0902	9.6870	37.0753
12	3.8616	10.9155	26.1597
13	2.4773	12.2999	13.8598
14	.9173	13.8598	0.0000

YEARS 15 — MO PAYT 1.2002 — AN CONST 14.41

#	INT	PRIN	BALANCE
1	11.8634	2.5386	97.4614
2	11.5414	2.8606	94.6008
3	11.1786	3.2234	91.3774
4	10.7698	3.6322	87.7452
5	10.3092	4.0928	83.6523
6	9.7901	4.6119	79.0404
7	9.2052	5.1968	73.8436
8	8.5461	5.8559	67.9877
9	7.8034	6.5986	61.3891
10	6.9666	7.4355	53.9536
11	6.0235	8.3785	45.5751
12	4.9609	9.4411	36.1341
13	3.7636	10.6384	25.4956
14	2.4144	11.9877	13.5080
15	.8940	13.5080	0.0000

YEARS 16 — MO PAYT 1.1737 — AN CONST 14.09

#	INT	PRIN	BALANCE
1	11.8814	2.2033	97.7967
2	11.6020	2.4827	95.3140
3	11.2871	2.7976	92.5165
4	10.9323	3.1524	89.3641
5	10.5325	3.5522	85.8119
6	10.0820	4.0027	81.8093
7	9.5744	4.5103	77.2989
8	9.0024	5.0823	72.2166
9	8.3578	5.7269	66.4897
10	7.6315	6.4532	60.0365
11	6.8131	7.2716	52.7649
12	5.8908	8.1939	44.5710
13	4.8516	9.2331	35.3379
14	3.6807	10.4040	24.9339
15	2.3612	11.7235	13.2104
16	.8743	13.2104	0.0000

YEARS 17 — MO PAYT 1.1512 — AN CONST 13.82

#	INT	PRIN	BALANCE
1	11.8968	1.9178	98.0822
2	11.6536	2.1610	95.9212
3	11.3795	2.4351	93.4861
4	11.0707	2.7439	90.7422
5	10.7227	3.0919	87.6503
6	10.3305	3.4840	84.1662
7	9.8887	3.9259	80.2403
8	9.3908	4.4238	75.8165
9	8.8297	4.9849	70.8316
10	8.1975	5.6171	65.2146
11	7.4851	6.3295	58.8851
12	6.6824	7.1322	51.7529
13	5.7779	8.0367	43.7162
14	4.7586	9.0560	34.6602
15	3.6101	10.2045	24.4557
16	2.3159	11.4987	12.9570
17	.8576	12.9570	0.0000

YEARS 18 — MO PAYT 1.1320 — AN CONST 13.59

#	INT	PRIN	BALANCE
1	11.9099	1.6735	98.3265
2	11.6977	1.8857	96.4408
3	11.4586	2.1249	94.3160
4	11.1891	2.3943	91.9217
5	10.8854	2.6980	89.2237
6	10.5432	3.0402	86.1835
7	10.1577	3.4257	82.7577
8	9.7232	3.8602	78.8975
9	9.2336	4.3498	74.5478
10	8.6820	4.9014	69.6463
11	8.0603	5.5231	64.1232
12	7.3599	6.2235	57.8997
13	6.5706	7.0128	50.8869
14	5.6812	7.9022	42.9846
15	4.6790	8.9044	34.0802
16	3.5497	10.0337	24.0465
17	2.2771	11.3063	12.7402
18	.8432	12.7402	0.0000

YEARS 19 — MO PAYT 1.1154 — AN CONST 13.39

#	INT	PRIN	BALANCE
1	11.9212	1.4634	98.5366
2	11.7357	1.6490	96.8876
3	11.5265	1.8581	95.0295
4	11.2909	2.0938	92.9358
5	11.0253	2.3593	90.5765
6	10.7261	2.6585	87.9180
7	10.3889	2.9957	84.9223
8	10.0090	3.3756	81.5467
9	9.5809	3.8037	77.7430
10	9.0985	4.2861	73.4568
11	8.5549	4.8297	68.6271
12	7.9424	5.4422	63.1849
13	7.2522	6.1325	57.0524
14	6.4744	6.9102	50.1422
15	5.5980	7.7866	42.3556
16	4.6105	8.7741	33.5815
17	3.4977	9.8869	23.6946
18	2.2438	11.1408	12.5538
19	.8309	12.5538	0.0000

YEARS 20 — MO PAYT 1.1011 — AN CONST 13.22

#	INT	PRIN	BALANCE
1	11.9310	1.2820	98.7180
2	11.7684	1.4446	97.2734
3	11.5852	1.6278	95.6455
4	11.3788	1.8343	93.8112
5	11.1461	2.0669	91.7443
6	10.8840	2.3291	89.4153
7	10.5886	2.6244	86.7908
8	10.2558	2.9573	83.8336
9	9.8807	3.3323	80.5012
10	9.4581	3.7550	76.7463
11	8.9819	4.2312	72.5151
12	8.4452	4.7678	67.7473
13	7.8406	5.3725	62.3748
14	7.1592	6.0538	56.3210
15	6.3914	6.8216	49.4994
16	5.5263	7.6868	41.8126
17	4.5514	8.6616	33.1510
18	3.4529	9.7602	23.3908
19	2.2150	10.9980	12.3928
20	.8202	12.3928	0.0000

YEARS 21 — MO PAYT 1.0887 — AN CONST 13.07

#	INT	PRIN	BALANCE
1	11.9395	1.1249	98.8751
2	11.7968	1.2676	97.6075
3	11.6360	1.4284	96.1791

#	INT	PRIN	BALANCE
4	11.4549	1.6095	94.5696
5	11.2507	1.8136	92.7559
6	11.0207	2.0437	90.7123
7	10.7615	2.3029	88.4094
8	10.4695	2.5949	85.8145
9	10.1404	2.9240	82.8905
10	9.7695	3.2948	79.5956
11	9.3517	3.7127	75.8829
12	8.8808	4.1836	71.6994
13	8.3502	4.7142	66.9852
14	7.7524	5.3120	61.6732
15	7.0787	5.9857	55.6874
16	6.3195	6.7449	48.9425
17	5.4641	7.6003	41.3422
18	4.5002	8.5642	32.7780
19	3.4140	9.6504	23.1277
20	2.1901	10.8743	12.2534
21	.8110	12.2534	0.0000

YEARS 22	MO PAYT 1.0779	AN CONST 12.94	
#	INT	PRIN	BALANCE
1	11.9468	.9885	99.0115
2	11.8214	1.1138	97.8977
3	11.6802	1.2551	96.6427
4	11.5210	1.4142	95.2284
5	11.3416	1.5936	93.6348
6	11.1395	1.7957	91.8391
7	10.9118	2.0235	89.8156
8	10.6552	2.2801	87.5355
9	10.3660	2.5693	84.9663
10	10.0402	2.8951	82.0712
11	9.6730	3.2623	78.8089
12	9.2592	3.6760	75.1329
13	8.7930	4.1422	70.9906
14	8.2677	4.6676	66.3231
15	7.6757	5.2595	61.0635
16	7.0087	5.9266	55.1370
17	6.2571	6.6782	48.4588
18	5.4101	7.5252	40.9336
19	4.4557	8.4796	32.4540
20	3.3803	9.5550	22.8991
21	2.1685	10.7668	12.1323
22	.8030	12.1323	0.0000

YEARS 23	MO PAYT 1.0686	AN CONST 12.83	
#	INT	PRIN	BALANCE
1	11.9532	.8696	99.1304
2	11.8429	.9799	98.1506
3	11.7186	1.1041	97.0464
4	11.5786	1.2442	95.8023
5	11.4208	1.4020	94.4003
6	11.2430	1.5798	92.8206
7	11.0427	1.7801	91.0405
8	10.8169	2.0059	89.0346
9	10.5625	2.2603	86.7743
10	10.2759	2.5469	84.2274
11	9.9528	2.8699	81.3575
12	9.5889	3.2339	78.1236
13	9.1787	3.6441	74.4795
14	8.7166	4.1062	70.3733
15	8.1958	4.6270	65.7463
16	7.6090	5.2138	60.5325
17	6.9477	5.8750	54.6575
18	6.2026	6.6201	48.0374
19	5.3630	7.4597	40.5776
20	4.4170	8.4058	32.1718
21	3.3509	9.4719	22.6999
22	2.1496	10.6732	12.0268
23	.7960	12.0268	0.0000

YEARS 24	MO PAYT 1.0604	AN CONST 12.73	
#	INT	PRIN	BALANCE
1	11.9588	.7658	99.2342
2	11.8617	.8629	98.3713
3	11.7522	.9724	97.3989
4	11.6289	1.0957	96.3033
5	11.4900	1.2346	95.0686
6	11.3334	1.3912	93.6774
7	11.1569	1.5677	92.1098
8	10.9581	1.7665	90.3433
9	10.7341	1.9905	88.3528
10	10.4816	2.2430	86.1098
11	10.1972	2.5274	83.5824
12	9.8766	2.8480	80.7345
13	9.5154	3.2091	77.5253
14	9.1084	3.6161	73.9092
15	8.6498	4.0748	69.8344
16	8.1330	4.5915	65.2429
17	7.5507	5.1739	60.0690
18	6.8945	5.8300	54.2389
19	6.1551	6.5694	47.6695
20	5.3220	7.4026	40.2669
21	4.3831	8.3414	31.9255
22	3.3252	9.3993	22.5261
23	2.1332	10.5914	11.9347
24	.7899	11.9347	0.0000

YEARS 25	MO PAYT 1.0532	AN CONST 12.64	
#	INT	PRIN	BALANCE
1	11.9637	.6750	99.3250
2	11.8781	.7606	98.5644
3	11.7816	.8571	97.7073
4	11.6729	.9658	96.7415
5	11.5504	1.0883	95.6532
6	11.4124	1.2263	94.4269
7	11.2569	1.3818	93.0451
8	11.0816	1.5571	91.4880
9	10.8841	1.7545	89.7335
10	10.6616	1.9771	87.7564
11	10.4109	2.2278	85.5286
12	10.1283	2.5104	83.0182
13	9.8100	2.8287	80.1895
14	9.4512	3.1875	77.0020
15	9.0470	3.5917	73.4103
16	8.5914	4.0473	69.3630
17	8.0781	4.5606	64.8025
18	7.4997	5.1389	59.6635
19	6.8480	5.7907	53.8728
20	6.1136	6.5251	47.3477
21	5.2860	7.3526	39.9951
22	4.3535	8.2851	31.7100
23	3.3028	9.3359	22.3740
24	2.1188	10.5199	11.8541
25	.7846	11.8541	0.0000

YEARS 26	MO PAYT 1.0470	AN CONST 12.57	
#	INT	PRIN	BALANCE
1	11.9680	.5955	99.4045
2	11.8924	.6710	98.7335
3	11.8073	.7561	97.9774
4	11.7114	.8520	97.1254
5	11.6034	.9600	96.1654
6	11.4816	1.0818	95.0836
7	11.3444	1.2190	93.8646
8	11.1898	1.3736	92.4910
9	11.0156	1.5478	90.9432
10	10.8193	1.7441	89.1991
11	10.5981	1.9653	87.2338
12	10.3489	2.2145	85.0193
13	10.0680	2.4954	82.5239
14	9.7515	2.8119	79.7120
15	9.3949	3.1685	76.5435
16	8.9931	3.5703	72.9731
17	8.5403	4.0232	68.9500
18	8.0300	4.5334	64.4166
19	7.4551	5.1083	59.3082
20	6.8072	5.7562	53.5520
21	6.0772	6.4862	47.0658
22	5.2546	7.3089	39.7569
23	4.3276	8.2358	31.5211
24	3.2831	9.2803	22.2408
25	2.1061	10.4573	11.7835
26	.7799	11.7835	0.0000

YEARS 27	MO PAYT 1.0414	AN CONST 12.50	
#	INT	PRIN	BALANCE
1	11.9717	.5257	99.4743
2	11.9050	.5923	98.8820
3	11.8299	.6675	98.2145
4	11.7453	.7521	97.4624
5	11.6499	.8475	96.6149
6	11.5424	.9550	95.6599
7	11.4213	1.0761	94.5838
8	11.2848	1.2126	93.3712
9	11.1310	1.3664	92.0048
10	10.9577	1.5397	90.4652
11	10.7625	1.7349	88.7302
12	10.5424	1.9550	86.7753
13	10.2945	2.2029	84.5723
14	10.0151	2.4823	82.0901
15	9.7003	2.7971	79.2930
16	9.3455	3.1518	76.1411
17	8.9458	3.5516	72.5895
18	8.4954	4.0020	68.5875
19	7.9878	4.5096	64.0780
20	7.4159	5.0815	58.9965
21	6.7714	5.7259	53.2705
22	6.0452	6.4521	46.8184
23	5.2269	7.2704	39.5479
24	4.3049	8.1925	31.3554
25	3.2659	9.2315	22.1239
26	2.0951	10.4023	11.7216
27	.7758	11.7216	0.0000

YEARS 28	MO PAYT 1.0366	AN CONST 12.44	
#	INT	PRIN	BALANCE
1	11.9750	.4643	99.5357
2	11.9161	.5232	99.0124
3	11.8498	.5896	98.4228
4	11.7750	.6644	97.7585
5	11.6907	.7486	97.0098
6	11.5958	.8436	96.1663
7	11.4888	.9506	95.2157
8	11.3687	1.0711	94.1446
9	11.2324	1.2070	92.9376
10	11.0793	1.3600	91.5776
11	10.9068	1.5325	90.0451
12	10.7125	1.7269	88.3182
13	10.4935	1.9459	86.3723
14	10.2467	2.1927	84.1796
15	9.9686	2.4708	81.7089
16	9.6552	2.7841	78.9248
17	9.3021	3.1372	75.7876
18	8.9043	3.5351	72.2525
19	8.4559	3.9834	68.2690
20	7.9507	4.4886	63.7804
21	7.3815	5.0579	58.7225
22	6.7400	5.6994	53.0232
23	6.0172	6.4222	46.6010
24	5.2027	7.2367	39.3643
25	4.2849	8.1545	31.2098
26	3.2507	9.1887	22.0212
27	2.0853	10.3540	11.6672
28	.7722	11.6672	0.0000

YEARS 29	MO PAYT 1.0324	AN CONST 12.39	
#	INT	PRIN	BALANCE
1	11.9779	.4104	99.5896
2	11.9259	.4624	99.1272
3	11.8672	.5211	98.6061
4	11.8011	.5872	98.0189
5	11.7267	.6616	97.3573
6	11.6428	.7456	96.6117
7	11.5482	.8401	95.7716
8	11.4416	.9467	94.8249
9	11.3216	1.0667	93.7582
10	11.1863	1.2020	92.5562
11	11.0339	1.3544	91.2018
12	10.8621	1.5262	89.6755
13	10.6685	1.7198	87.9558
14	10.4504	1.9379	86.0179
15	10.2046	2.1837	83.8342
16	9.9277	2.4606	81.3736
17	9.6156	2.7727	78.6009
18	9.2640	3.1243	75.4765
19	8.8677	3.5206	71.9559
20	8.4212	3.9671	67.9889
21	7.9181	4.4702	63.5187
22	7.3512	5.0371	58.4815
23	6.7123	5.6760	52.8056
24	5.9925	6.3958	46.4097
25	5.1813	7.2070	39.2028
26	4.2673	8.1210	31.0817
27	3.2374	9.1510	21.9308
28	2.0768	10.3115	11.6193
29	.7690	11.6193	0.0000

YEARS 30	MO PAYT 1.0286	AN CONST 12.35	
#	INT	PRIN	BALANCE
1	11.9805	.3629	99.6371
2	11.9344	.4089	99.2282
3	11.8826	.4608	98.7675
4	11.8242	.5192	98.2483
5	11.7583	.5850	97.6632
6	11.6841	.6592	97.0040
7	11.6005	.7429	96.2611
8	11.5063	.8371	95.4241
9	11.4001	.9432	94.4808
10	11.2805	1.0628	93.4180
11	11.1457	1.1976	92.2204
12	10.9938	1.3495	90.8708
13	10.8227	1.5207	89.3501
14	10.6298	1.7135	87.6366
15	10.4125	1.9309	85.7057
16	10.1676	2.1758	83.5300
17	9.8917	2.4517	81.0783
18	9.5807	2.7626	78.3156
19	9.2304	3.1130	75.2026
20	8.8355	3.5078	71.6948
21	8.3907	3.9527	67.7422
22	7.8894	4.4540	63.2882
23	7.3245	5.0189	58.2693
24	6.6880	5.6554	52.6139
25	5.9707	6.3726	46.2413
26	5.1625	7.1808	39.0605
27	4.2518	8.0915	30.9690
28	3.2256	9.1177	21.8512
29	2.0692	10.2741	11.5771
30	.7662	11.5771	0.0000

MONTHLY PAYMENT AMORTIZATION SCHEDULE PER $100

12.10 %

YEARS 2 — MO PAYT 4.7120 — AN CONST 56.55

#	INT	PRIN	BALANCE
1	9.5504	46.9938	53.0062
2	3.5380	53.0062	0.0000

YEARS 3 — MO PAYT 3.3262 — AN CONST 39.92

#	INT	PRIN	BALANCE
1	10.5044	29.4101	70.5899
2	6.7416	33.1729	37.4170
3	2.4975	37.4170	0.0000

YEARS 4 — MO PAYT 2.6383 — AN CONST 31.66

#	INT	PRIN	BALANCE
1	10.9780	20.6816	79.3184
2	8.3319	23.3276	55.9908
3	5.3474	26.3122	29.6786
4	1.9810	29.6786	0.0000

YEARS 5 — MO PAYT 2.2295 — AN CONST 26.76

#	INT	PRIN	BALANCE
1	11.2594	15.4946	84.5054
2	9.2770	17.4771	67.0283
3	7.0409	19.7131	47.3152
4	4.5188	22.2352	25.0800
5	1.6740	25.0800	0.0000

YEARS 6 — MO PAYT 1.9602 — AN CONST 23.53

#	INT	PRIN	BALANCE
1	11.4447	12.0779	87.9221
2	9.8995	13.6232	74.2988
3	8.1565	15.3662	58.9327
4	6.1905	17.3322	41.6005
5	3.9730	19.5496	22.0509
6	1.4718	22.0509	0.0000

YEARS 7 — MO PAYT 1.7706 — AN CONST 21.25

#	INT	PRIN	BALANCE
1	11.5753	9.6723	90.3277
2	10.3378	10.9097	79.4180
3	8.9420	12.3055	67.1125
4	7.3676	13.8799	53.2325
5	5.5918	15.6557	37.5768
6	3.5888	17.6588	19.9180
7	1.3295	19.9180	0.0000

YEARS 8 — MO PAYT 1.6308 — AN CONST 19.57

#	INT	PRIN	BALANCE
1	11.6715	7.8979	92.1021
2	10.6611	8.9084	83.1938
3	9.5213	10.0481	73.1457
4	8.2357	11.3337	61.8120
5	6.7857	12.7837	49.0283
6	5.1501	14.4193	34.6090
7	3.3053	16.2641	18.3449
8	1.2245	18.3449	0.0000

YEARS 9 — MO PAYT 1.5241 — AN CONST 18.29

#	INT	PRIN	BALANCE
1	11.7450	6.5438	93.4562
2	10.9078	7.3811	86.0751
3	9.9634	8.3254	77.7497
4	8.8982	9.3906	68.3591
5	7.6968	10.5920	57.7671
6	6.3417	11.9472	45.8200
7	4.8131	13.4757	32.3443
8	3.0890	15.1998	17.1445
9	1.1443	17.1445	0.0000

YEARS 10 — MO PAYT 1.4405 — AN CONST 17.29

#	INT	PRIN	BALANCE
1	11.8025	5.4834	94.5166
2	11.1009	6.1850	88.3315
3	10.3096	6.9763	81.3552
4	9.4171	7.8689	73.4863
5	8.4103	8.8756	64.6107
6	7.2748	10.0112	54.5995
7	5.9939	11.2920	43.3074
8	4.5492	12.7368	30.5707
9	2.9196	14.3663	16.2044
10	1.0816	16.2044	0.0000

YEARS 11 — MO PAYT 1.3737 — AN CONST 16.49

#	INT	PRIN	BALANCE
1	11.8485	4.6361	95.3639
2	11.2553	5.2292	90.1347
3	10.5863	5.8983	84.2364
4	9.8317	6.6529	77.5835
5	8.9805	7.5041	70.0794
6	8.0204	8.4642	61.6153
7	6.9375	9.5471	52.0682
8	5.7160	10.7685	41.2997
9	4.3383	12.1463	29.1534
10	2.7843	13.7003	15.4531
11	1.0314	15.4531	0.0000

YEARS 12 — MO PAYT 1.3195 — AN CONST 15.84

#	INT	PRIN	BALANCE
1	11.8858	3.9479	96.0521
2	11.3807	4.4531	91.5990
3	10.8110	5.0228	86.5762
4	10.1684	5.6654	80.9108
5	9.4435	6.3902	74.5206
6	8.6259	7.2078	67.3127
7	7.7038	8.1300	59.1827
8	6.6636	9.1702	50.0126
9	5.4904	10.3434	39.6692
10	4.1670	11.6667	28.0024
11	2.6744	13.1594	14.8430
12	.9907	14.8430	0.0000

YEARS 13 — MO PAYT 1.2749 — AN CONST 15.30

#	INT	PRIN	BALANCE
1	11.9165	3.3818	96.6182
2	11.4839	3.8144	92.8038
3	10.9958	4.3025	88.5013
4	10.4454	4.8529	83.6484
5	9.8245	5.4738	78.1746
6	9.1242	6.1741	72.0004
7	8.3342	6.9641	65.0364
8	7.4432	7.8551	57.1813
9	6.4383	8.8600	48.3213
10	5.3047	9.9936	38.3277
11	4.0261	11.2722	27.0555
12	2.5839	12.7144	14.3411
13	.9572	14.3411	0.0000

YEARS 14 — MO PAYT 1.2377 — AN CONST 14.86

#	INT	PRIN	BALANCE
1	11.9421	2.9109	97.0891
2	11.5696	3.2833	93.8058
3	11.1496	3.7034	90.1024
4	10.6758	4.1772	85.9251
5	10.1413	4.7117	81.2135
6	9.5385	5.3145	75.8990
7	8.8586	5.9944	69.9046
8	8.0916	6.7614	63.1432
9	7.2266	7.6264	55.5168
10	6.2508	8.6021	46.9147
11	5.1503	9.7027	37.2120
12	3.9089	10.9441	26.2679
13	2.5087	12.3443	13.9236
14	.9294	13.9236	0.0000

YEARS 15 — MO PAYT 1.2066 — AN CONST 14.48

#	INT	PRIN	BALANCE
1	11.9635	2.5158	97.4842
2	11.6416	2.8377	94.6465
3	11.2786	3.2007	91.4458
4	10.8691	3.6102	87.8356
5	10.4072	4.0721	83.7634
6	9.8862	4.5931	79.1703
7	9.2985	5.1808	73.9895
8	8.6357	5.8436	68.1459
9	7.8881	6.5912	61.5547
10	7.0448	7.4345	54.1201
11	6.0936	8.3857	45.7344
12	5.0207	9.4586	36.2758
13	3.8106	10.6687	25.6071
14	2.4456	12.0337	13.5733
15	.9060	13.5733	0.0000

YEARS 16 — MO PAYT 1.1803 — AN CONST 14.17

#	INT	PRIN	BALANCE
1	11.9816	2.1818	97.8182
2	11.7025	2.4609	95.3573
3	11.3876	2.7758	92.5816
4	11.0325	3.1309	89.4507
5	10.6319	3.5315	85.9192
6	10.1801	3.9833	81.9359
7	9.6705	4.4929	77.4430
8	9.0957	5.0677	72.3752
9	8.4473	5.7161	66.6591
10	7.7160	6.4474	60.2117
11	6.8911	7.2723	52.9394
12	5.9606	8.2028	44.7366
13	4.9112	9.2522	35.4843
14	3.7274	10.4360	25.0484
15	2.3922	11.7712	13.2772
16	.8862	13.2772	0.0000

YEARS 17 — MO PAYT 1.1579 — AN CONST 13.90

#	INT	PRIN	BALANCE
1	11.9970	1.8976	98.1024
2	11.7543	2.1404	95.9620
3	11.4804	2.4142	93.5478
4	11.1716	2.7231	90.8247
5	10.8232	3.0715	87.7533
6	10.4302	3.4645	84.2888
7	9.9869	3.9077	80.3811
8	9.4870	4.4077	75.9734
9	8.9231	4.9716	71.0019
10	8.2870	5.6076	65.3942
11	7.5695	6.3251	59.0691
12	6.7603	7.1343	51.9348
13	5.8475	8.0471	43.8877
14	4.8180	9.0767	34.8110
15	3.6567	10.2379	24.5731
16	2.3468	11.5478	13.0252
17	.8694	13.0252	0.0000

YEARS 18 — MO PAYT 1.1387 — AN CONST 13.67

#	INT	PRIN	BALANCE
1	12.0102	1.6545	98.3455
2	11.7986	1.8662	96.4793
3	11.5598	2.1050	94.3743
4	11.2905	2.3743	92.0001
5	10.9867	2.6780	89.3220
6	10.6441	3.0207	86.3014
7	10.2576	3.4071	82.8942
8	9.8217	3.8430	79.0512
9	9.3300	4.3347	74.7164
10	8.7754	4.8893	69.8271
11	8.1499	5.5149	64.3123
12	7.4443	6.2204	58.0918
13	6.6485	7.0163	51.0755
14	5.7508	7.9140	43.1615
15	4.7383	8.9265	34.2350
16	3.5962	10.0686	24.1665
17	2.3080	11.3567	12.8097
18	.8550	12.8097	0.0000

YEARS 19 — MO PAYT 1.1223 — AN CONST 13.47

#	INT	PRIN	BALANCE
1	12.0216	1.4456	98.5544
2	11.8366	1.6306	96.9238
3	11.6280	1.8392	95.0845
4	11.3927	2.0745	93.0100
5	11.1273	2.3399	90.6701
6	10.8279	2.6393	88.0308
7	10.4902	2.9770	85.0538
8	10.1093	3.3579	81.6959
9	9.6797	3.7875	77.9084
10	9.1951	4.2721	73.6363
11	8.6486	4.8186	68.8177
12	8.0321	5.4351	63.3825
13	7.3367	6.1305	57.2520
14	6.5523	6.9149	50.3371
15	5.6676	7.7996	42.5376
16	4.6698	8.7975	33.7401
17	3.5442	9.9230	23.8171
18	2.2746	11.1926	12.6246
19	.8427	12.6246	0.0000

YEARS 20 — MO PAYT 1.1081 — AN CONST 13.30

#	INT	PRIN	BALANCE
1	12.0313	1.2654	98.7346
2	11.8694	1.4273	97.3072
3	11.6868	1.6100	95.6973
4	11.4808	1.8159	93.8813
5	11.2485	2.0483	91.8330
6	10.9865	2.3103	89.5227
7	10.6909	2.6059	86.9168
8	10.3575	2.9393	83.9774
9	9.9814	3.3154	80.6621
10	9.5572	3.7396	76.9225
11	9.0788	4.2180	72.7045
12	8.5391	4.7577	67.9468
13	7.9304	5.3664	62.5805
14	7.2438	6.0529	56.5275
15	6.4694	6.8274	49.7002
16	5.5959	7.7009	41.9993
17	4.6107	8.6861	33.3132
18	3.4994	9.7974	23.5157
19	2.2459	11.0509	12.4648
20	.8320	12.4648	0.0000

YEARS 21 — MO PAYT 1.0958 — AN CONST 13.15

#	INT	PRIN	BALANCE
1	12.0398	1.1095	98.8905
2	11.8979	1.2514	97.6391
3	11.7378	1.4115	96.2276

#	INT	PRIN	BALANCE
4	11.5572	1.5921	94.6355
5	11.3535	1.7958	92.8397
6	11.1237	2.0256	90.8142
7	10.8646	2.2847	88.5295
8	10.5723	2.5770	85.9525
9	10.2426	2.9067	83.0458
10	9.8707	3.2786	79.7672
11	9.4512	3.6981	76.0691
12	8.9781	4.1712	71.8979
13	8.4444	4.7049	67.1930
14	7.8424	5.3068	61.8862
15	7.1635	5.9858	55.9004
16	6.3976	6.7516	49.1488
17	5.5338	7.6154	41.5333
18	4.5595	8.5898	32.9436
19	3.4605	9.6887	23.2548
20	2.2209	10.9283	12.3265
21	.8228	12.3265	0.0000

YEARS 22	MO PAYT 1.0851	AN CONST 13.03	
#	INT	PRIN	BALANCE
1	12.0472	.9740	99.0260
2	11.9225	1.0987	97.9273
3	11.7820	1.2392	96.6881
4	11.6234	1.3978	95.2903
5	11.4446	1.5766	93.7137
6	11.2429	1.7783	91.9354
7	11.0154	2.0058	89.9296
8	10.7587	2.2624	87.6672
9	10.4693	2.5519	85.1153
10	10.1428	2.8784	82.2369
11	9.7745	3.2467	78.9902
12	9.3591	3.6621	75.3281
13	8.8906	4.1306	71.1976
14	8.3621	4.6591	66.5385
15	7.7661	5.2551	61.2834
16	7.0937	5.9275	55.3559
17	6.3353	6.6859	48.6700
18	5.4799	7.5413	41.1288
19	4.5151	8.5061	32.6227
20	3.4268	9.5944	23.0283
21	2.1993	10.8219	12.2064
22	.8147	12.2064	0.0000

YEARS 23	MO PAYT 1.0758	AN CONST 12.91	
#	INT	PRIN	BALANCE
1	12.0536	.8562	99.1438
2	11.9440	.9657	98.1782
3	11.8205	1.0892	97.0889
4	11.6811	1.2286	95.8603
5	11.5239	1.3858	94.4745
6	11.3466	1.5631	92.9114
7	11.1466	1.7631	91.1483
8	10.9211	1.9886	89.1597
9	10.6666	2.2431	86.9166
10	10.3796	2.5301	84.3865
11	10.0559	2.8538	81.5328
12	9.6908	3.2189	78.3139
13	9.2790	3.6307	74.6832
14	8.8145	4.0952	70.5880
15	8.2905	4.6192	65.9688
16	7.6996	5.2101	60.7587
17	7.0330	5.8767	54.8820
18	6.2811	6.6286	48.2533
19	5.4330	7.4767	40.7767
20	4.4764	8.4333	32.3434
21	3.3975	9.5122	22.8312
22	2.1805	10.7292	12.1019
23	.8078	12.1019	0.0000

YEARS 24	MO PAYT 1.0677	AN CONST 12.82	
#	INT	PRIN	BALANCE
1	12.0591	.7533	99.2467
2	11.9627	.8497	98.3970
3	11.8540	.9584	97.4386
4	11.7314	1.0810	96.3575
5	11.5931	1.2193	95.1382
6	11.4371	1.3754	93.7628
7	11.2611	1.5513	92.2115
8	11.0627	1.7498	90.4617
9	10.8388	1.9737	88.4880
10	10.5863	2.2262	86.2618
11	10.3015	2.5110	83.7508
12	9.9802	2.8323	80.9186
13	9.6178	3.1946	77.7240
14	9.2091	3.6033	74.1206
15	8.7481	4.0644	70.0562
16	8.2281	4.5844	65.4719
17	7.6416	5.1709	60.3010
18	6.9800	5.8325	54.4685
19	6.2338	6.5787	47.8898
20	5.3921	7.4204	40.4695
21	4.4427	8.3697	32.0997
22	3.3719	9.4406	22.6592
23	2.1641	10.6484	12.0108
24	.8017	12.0108	0.0000

YEARS 25	MO PAYT 1.0606	AN CONST 12.73	
#	INT	PRIN	BALANCE
1	12.0640	.6634	99.3366
2	11.9791	.7483	98.5882
3	11.8834	.8441	97.7442
4	11.7754	.9521	96.7921
5	11.6536	1.0739	95.7182
6	11.5162	1.2113	94.5070
7	11.3612	1.3662	93.1407
8	11.1864	1.5410	91.5997
9	10.9893	1.7382	89.8615
10	10.7669	1.9606	87.9010
11	10.5160	2.2114	85.6895
12	10.2331	2.4943	83.1952
13	9.9140	2.8135	80.3817
14	9.5540	3.1734	77.2083
15	9.1480	3.5794	73.6289
16	8.6901	4.0374	69.5915
17	8.1735	4.5540	65.0375
18	7.5909	5.1366	59.9009
19	6.9337	5.7938	54.1071
20	6.1924	6.5350	47.5721
21	5.3563	7.3711	40.2010
22	4.4132	8.3142	31.8868
23	3.3495	9.3779	22.5088
24	2.1497	10.5778	11.9311
25	.7964	11.9311	0.0000

YEARS 26	MO PAYT 1.0544	AN CONST 12.66	
#	INT	PRIN	BALANCE
1	12.0683	.5848	99.4152
2	11.9935	.6596	98.7557
3	11.9091	.7440	98.0117
4	11.8139	.8391	97.1726
5	11.7065	.9465	96.2261
6	11.5854	1.0676	95.1585
7	11.4489	1.2042	93.9543
8	11.2948	1.3582	92.5961
9	11.1210	1.5320	91.0641
10	10.9250	1.7280	89.3361
11	10.7039	1.9491	87.3870
12	10.4545	2.1985	85.1885
13	10.1733	2.4798	82.7087
14	9.8560	2.7970	79.9117
15	9.4982	3.1549	76.7568
16	9.0945	3.5585	73.1983
17	8.6392	4.0138	69.1845
18	8.1257	4.5273	64.6572
19	7.5465	5.1066	59.5506
20	6.8931	5.7599	53.7908
21	6.1562	6.4968	47.2939
22	5.3250	7.3280	39.9659
23	4.3874	8.2656	31.7003
24	3.3299	9.3231	22.3772
25	2.1371	10.5159	11.8613
26	.7917	11.8613	0.0000

YEARS 27	MO PAYT 1.0490	AN CONST 12.59	
#	INT	PRIN	BALANCE
1	12.0720	.5158	99.4842
2	12.0060	.5817	98.9025
3	11.9316	.6562	98.2464
4	11.8477	.7401	97.5062
5	11.7530	.8348	96.6714
6	11.6462	.9416	95.7298
7	11.5257	1.0621	94.6677
8	11.3898	1.1980	93.4698
9	11.2365	1.3512	92.1185
10	11.0637	1.5241	90.5944
11	10.8687	1.7191	88.8753
12	10.6487	1.9391	86.9363
13	10.4006	2.1871	84.7491
14	10.1208	2.4670	82.2821
15	9.8052	2.7826	79.4996
16	9.4492	3.1386	76.3609
17	9.0476	3.5402	72.8208
18	8.5947	3.9931	68.8277
19	8.0838	4.5040	64.3237
20	7.5076	5.0802	59.2435
21	6.8576	5.7302	53.5133
22	6.1245	6.4633	47.0500
23	5.2975	7.2902	39.7598
24	4.3648	8.2230	31.5368
25	3.3128	9.2750	22.2618
26	2.1261	10.4617	11.8001
27	.7876	11.8001	0.0000

YEARS 28	MO PAYT 1.0442	AN CONST 12.54	
#	INT	PRIN	BALANCE
1	12.0753	.4552	99.5448
2	12.0171	.5134	99.0314
3	11.9514	.5791	98.4523
4	11.8773	.6532	97.7992
5	11.7937	.7367	97.0624
6	11.6995	.8310	96.2314
7	11.5931	.9373	95.2941
8	11.4732	1.0572	94.2368
9	11.3380	1.1925	93.0443
10	11.1854	1.3451	91.6992
11	11.0133	1.5172	90.1821
12	10.8192	1.7113	88.4708
13	10.6002	1.9302	86.5405
14	10.3533	2.1772	84.3634
15	10.0747	2.4557	81.9076
16	9.7605	2.7699	79.1377
17	9.4062	3.1243	76.0134
18	9.0064	3.5240	72.4893
19	8.5556	3.9749	68.5144
20	8.0470	4.4835	64.0309
21	7.4734	5.0571	58.9739
22	6.8264	5.7041	53.2698
23	6.0966	6.4339	46.8359
24	5.2734	7.2571	39.5788
25	4.3449	8.1855	31.3933
26	3.2977	9.2328	22.1605
27	2.1164	10.4140	11.7464
28	.7840	11.7464	0.0000

YEARS 29	MO PAYT 1.0400	AN CONST 12.49	
#	INT	PRIN	BALANCE
1	12.0782	.4019	99.5981
2	12.0268	.4533	99.1447
3	11.9688	.5113	98.6334
4	11.9034	.5768	98.0566
5	11.8296	.6506	97.4061
6	11.7463	.7338	96.6723
7	11.6524	.8277	95.8446
8	11.5466	.9336	94.9111
9	11.4271	1.0530	93.8581
10	11.2924	1.1877	92.6704
11	11.1404	1.3397	91.3307
12	10.9690	1.5111	89.8196
13	10.7757	1.7044	88.1152
14	10.5576	1.9225	86.1927
15	10.3117	2.1684	84.0243
16	10.0342	2.4459	81.5784
17	9.7213	2.7588	78.8196
18	9.3684	3.1118	75.7079
19	8.9702	3.5099	72.1980
20	8.5212	3.9589	68.2390
21	8.0147	4.4655	63.7736
22	7.4433	5.0368	58.7368
23	6.7989	5.6812	53.0557
24	6.0721	6.4080	46.6476
25	5.2522	7.2279	39.4197
26	4.3275	8.1526	31.2671
27	3.2844	9.1957	22.0714
28	2.1079	10.3722	11.6992
29	.7809	11.6992	0.0000

YEARS 30	MO PAYT 1.0363	AN CONST 12.44	
#	INT	PRIN	BALANCE
1	12.0807	.3551	99.6449
2	12.0353	.4005	99.2444
3	11.9841	.4517	98.7927
4	11.9263	.5095	98.2832
5	11.8611	.5747	97.7085
6	11.7876	.6482	97.0602
7	11.7046	.7312	96.3291
8	11.6111	.8247	95.5043
9	11.5056	.9302	94.5741
10	11.3865	1.0493	93.5248
11	11.2523	1.1835	92.3413
12	11.1009	1.3349	91.0064
13	10.9301	1.5057	89.5007
14	10.7374	1.6984	87.8023
15	10.5202	1.9156	85.8867
16	10.2751	2.1607	83.7260
17	9.9986	2.4372	81.2888
18	9.6868	2.7490	78.5398
19	9.3351	3.1007	75.4391
20	8.9384	3.4974	71.9416
21	8.4909	3.9449	67.9968
22	7.9862	4.4496	63.5472
23	7.4169	5.0189	58.5283
24	6.7748	5.6610	52.8673
25	6.0505	6.3853	46.4820
26	5.2336	7.2022	39.2798
27	4.3121	8.1237	31.1561
28	3.2728	9.1630	21.9931
29	2.1004	10.3354	11.6577
30	.7781	11.6577	0.0000

YEARS 2 — MO PAYT 4.7132 — AN CONST 56.56

#	INT	PRIN	BALANCE
1	9.5706	46.9876	53.0124
2	3.5459	53.0124	0.0000

YEARS 3 — MO PAYT 3.3274 — AN CONST 39.93

#	INT	PRIN	BALANCE
1	10.5266	29.4022	70.5978
2	6.7566	33.1722	37.4256
3	2.5033	37.4256	0.0000

YEARS 4 — MO PAYT 2.6395 — AN CONST 31.68

#	INT	PRIN	BALANCE
1	11.0012	20.6731	79.3269
2	8.3504	23.3239	56.0030
3	5.3598	26.3145	29.6885
4	1.9858	29.6885	0.0000

YEARS 5 — MO PAYT 2.2308 — AN CONST 26.77

#	INT	PRIN	BALANCE
1	11.2831	15.4861	84.5139
2	9.2975	17.4717	67.0422
3	7.0573	19.7119	47.3303
4	4.5298	22.2394	25.0909
5	1.6783	25.0909	0.0000

YEARS 6 — MO PAYT 1.9615 — AN CONST 23.54

#	INT	PRIN	BALANCE
1	11.4689	12.0694	87.9306
2	9.9213	13.6170	74.3136
3	8.1754	15.3630	58.9506
4	6.2055	17.3328	41.6178
5	3.9831	19.5552	22.0626
6	1.4757	22.0626	0.0000

YEARS 7 — MO PAYT 1.7720 — AN CONST 21.27

#	INT	PRIN	BALANCE
1	11.5996	9.6639	90.3361
2	10.3605	10.9031	79.4330
3	8.9625	12.3010	67.1320
4	7.3853	13.8783	53.2537
5	5.6058	15.6578	37.5959
6	3.5982	17.6654	19.9305
7	1.3331	19.9305	0.0000

YEARS 8 — MO PAYT 1.6322 — AN CONST 19.59

#	INT	PRIN	BALANCE
1	11.6961	7.8898	92.1102
2	10.6844	8.9015	83.2087
3	9.5431	10.0428	73.1659
4	8.2554	11.3305	61.8354
5	6.8026	12.7833	49.0520
6	5.1635	14.4224	34.6296
7	3.3143	16.2716	18.3580
8	1.2279	18.3580	0.0000

YEARS 9 — MO PAYT 1.5255 — AN CONST 18.31

#	INT	PRIN	BALANCE
1	11.7697	6.5361	93.4639
2	10.9316	7.3741	86.0898
3	9.9861	8.3197	77.7701
4	8.9194	9.3864	68.3837
5	7.7158	10.5899	57.7938
6	6.3580	11.9478	45.8460
7	4.8260	13.4797	32.3662
8	3.0977	15.2081	17.1581
9	1.1477	17.1581	0.0000

YEARS 10 — MO PAYT 1.4419 — AN CONST 17.31

#	INT	PRIN	BALANCE
1	11.8273	5.4760	94.5240
2	11.1252	6.1782	88.3458
3	10.3330	6.9703	81.3755
4	9.4393	7.8641	73.5114
5	8.4309	8.8724	64.6390
6	7.2933	10.0100	54.6289
7	6.0098	11.2935	43.3354
8	4.5618	12.7416	30.5938
9	2.9280	14.3753	16.2185
10	1.0848	16.2185	0.0000

YEARS 11 — MO PAYT 1.3752 — AN CONST 16.51

#	INT	PRIN	BALANCE
1	11.8734	4.6290	95.3710
2	11.2798	5.2225	90.1484
3	10.6102	5.8922	84.2563
4	9.8547	6.6477	77.6086
5	9.0023	7.5000	70.1085
6	8.0407	8.4617	61.6468
7	6.9557	9.5467	52.1002
8	5.7316	10.7707	41.3294
9	4.3506	12.1518	29.1776
10	2.7925	13.7099	15.4678
11	1.0346	15.4678	0.0000

YEARS 12 — MO PAYT 1.3210 — AN CONST 15.86

#	INT	PRIN	BALANCE
1	11.9107	3.9412	96.0588
2	11.4054	4.4466	91.6122
3	10.8353	5.0167	86.5955
4	10.1920	5.6600	80.9355
5	9.4663	6.3857	74.5499
6	8.6475	7.2045	67.3454
7	7.7238	8.1282	59.2172
8	6.6816	9.1704	50.0468
9	5.5057	10.3462	39.7005
10	4.1791	11.6728	28.0277
11	2.6824	13.1695	14.8581
12	.9938	14.8581	0.0000

YEARS 13 — MO PAYT 1.2764 — AN CONST 15.32

#	INT	PRIN	BALANCE
1	11.9415	3.3754	96.6246
2	11.5087	3.8082	92.8164
3	11.0204	4.2965	88.5199
4	10.4695	4.8474	83.6726
5	9.8480	5.4689	78.2036
6	9.1468	6.1701	72.0335
7	8.3556	6.9613	65.0722
8	7.4631	7.8539	57.2184
9	6.4560	8.8609	48.3575
10	5.3199	9.9970	38.3605
11	4.0381	11.2788	27.0816
12	2.5919	12.7250	14.3566
13	.9603	14.3566	0.0000

YEARS 14 — MO PAYT 1.2393 — AN CONST 14.88

#	INT	PRIN	BALANCE
1	11.9671	2.9049	97.0951
2	11.5946	3.2773	93.8178
3	11.1744	3.6976	90.1202
4	10.7003	4.1717	85.9485
5	10.1654	4.7066	81.2420
6	9.5619	5.3100	75.9319
7	8.8811	5.9909	69.9410
8	8.1129	6.7591	63.1820
9	7.2463	7.6257	55.5563
10	6.2685	8.6035	46.9528
11	5.1653	9.7066	37.2462
12	3.9208	10.9512	26.2950
13	2.5166	12.3554	13.9396
14	.9324	13.9396	0.0000

YEARS 15 — MO PAYT 1.2082 — AN CONST 14.50

#	INT	PRIN	BALANCE
1	11.9885	2.5101	97.4899
2	11.6667	2.8320	94.6579
3	11.3036	3.1951	91.4628
4	10.8939	3.6048	87.8581
5	10.4317	4.0670	83.7911
6	9.9102	4.5884	79.2027
7	9.3219	5.1768	74.0259
8	8.6581	5.8405	68.1854
9	7.9093	6.5894	61.5960
10	7.0644	7.4343	54.1617
11	6.1111	8.3875	45.7742
12	5.0357	9.4630	36.3112
13	3.8223	10.6763	25.6349
14	2.4534	12.0452	13.5897
15	.9090	13.5897	0.0000

YEARS 16 — MO PAYT 1.1819 — AN CONST 14.19

#	INT	PRIN	BALANCE
1	12.0067	2.1764	97.8236
2	11.7276	2.4555	95.3681
3	11.4128	2.7703	92.5978
4	11.0576	3.1255	89.4722
5	10.6568	3.5263	85.9459
6	10.2047	3.9784	81.9675
7	9.6945	4.4886	77.4789
8	9.1190	5.0641	72.4148
9	8.4697	5.7134	66.7014
10	7.7371	6.4460	60.2554
11	6.9106	7.2725	52.9829
12	5.9781	8.2050	44.7780
13	4.9261	9.2570	35.5210
14	3.7392	10.4440	25.0770
15	2.4000	11.7831	13.2939
16	.8892	13.2939	0.0000

YEARS 17 — MO PAYT 1.1596 — AN CONST 13.92

#	INT	PRIN	BALANCE
1	12.0221	1.8926	98.1074
2	11.7794	2.1352	95.9722
3	11.5057	2.4090	93.5632
4	11.1968	2.7179	90.8453
5	10.8483	3.0664	87.7789
6	10.4551	3.4596	84.3193
7	10.0115	3.9032	80.4162
8	9.5111	4.4036	76.0126
9	8.9464	4.9682	71.0443
10	8.3094	5.6053	65.4390
11	7.5907	6.3240	59.1151
12	6.7798	7.1349	51.9802
13	5.8650	8.0497	43.9305
14	4.8329	9.0818	34.8487
15	3.6684	10.2463	24.6024
16	2.3546	11.5601	13.0423
17	.8724	13.0423	0.0000

YEARS 18 — MO PAYT 1.1404 — AN CONST 13.69

#	INT	PRIN	BALANCE
1	12.0353	1.6498	98.3502
2	11.8238	1.8613	96.4888
3	11.5851	2.1000	94.3888
4	11.3158	2.3693	92.0196
5	11.0121	2.6731	89.3465
6	10.6693	3.0158	86.3307
7	10.2826	3.4025	82.9282
8	9.8464	3.8388	79.0895
9	9.3542	4.3310	74.7585
10	8.7988	4.8863	69.8722
11	8.1723	5.5128	64.3594
12	7.4655	6.2197	58.1398
13	6.6680	7.0171	51.1226
14	5.7682	7.9169	43.2057
15	4.7531	8.9320	34.2738
16	3.6079	10.0773	24.1965
17	2.3158	11.3694	12.8271
18	.8580	12.8271	0.0000

YEARS 19 — MO PAYT 1.1240 — AN CONST 13.49

#	INT	PRIN	BALANCE
1	12.0467	1.4412	98.5588
2	11.8619	1.6260	96.9327
3	11.6534	1.8345	95.0982
4	11.4181	2.0697	93.0285
5	11.1528	2.3351	90.6934
6	10.8533	2.6345	88.0588
7	10.5155	2.9723	85.0865
8	10.1344	3.3534	81.7330
9	9.7045	3.7834	77.9496
10	9.2193	4.2685	73.6811
11	8.6720	4.8159	68.8652
12	8.0545	5.4333	63.4319
13	7.3579	6.1300	57.3018
14	6.5719	6.9160	50.3858
15	5.6851	7.8028	42.5830
16	4.6846	8.8033	33.7798
17	3.5559	9.9320	23.8478
18	2.2824	11.2055	12.6423
19	.8456	12.6423	0.0000

YEARS 20 — MO PAYT 1.1098 — AN CONST 13.32

#	INT	PRIN	BALANCE
1	12.0564	1.2613	98.7387
2	11.8947	1.4231	97.3156
3	11.7122	1.6055	95.7101
4	11.5064	1.8114	93.8987
5	11.2741	2.0436	91.8551
6	11.0121	2.3057	89.5494
7	10.7165	2.6013	86.9481
8	10.3829	2.9348	84.0133
9	10.0066	3.3112	80.7021
10	9.5820	3.7357	76.9664
11	9.1031	4.2147	72.7517
12	8.5626	4.7551	67.9966
13	7.9529	5.3648	62.6318
14	7.2651	6.0527	56.5791
15	6.4890	6.8288	49.7503
16	5.6134	7.7044	42.0459
17	4.6255	8.6922	33.3537
18	3.5110	9.8067	23.5470
19	2.2536	11.0642	12.4828
20	.8349	12.4828	0.0000

YEARS 21 — MO PAYT 1.0975 — AN CONST 13.18

#	INT	PRIN	BALANCE
1	12.0649	1.1056	98.8944
2	11.9231	1.2474	97.6470
3	11.7632	1.4073	96.2397

#	INT	PRIN	BALANCE
4	11.5827	1.5878	94.6519
5	11.3792	1.7914	92.8606
6	11.1495	2.0210	90.8395
7	10.8903	2.2802	88.5593
8	10.5980	2.5725	85.9868
9	10.2681	2.9024	83.0844
10	9.8960	3.2745	79.8099
11	9.4761	3.6944	76.1155
12	9.0024	4.1681	71.9473
13	8.4680	4.7025	67.2448
14	7.8650	5.3055	61.9393
15	7.1847	5.9858	55.9535
16	6.4172	6.7533	49.2003
17	5.5513	7.6192	41.5811
18	4.5744	8.5961	32.9850
19	3.4722	9.6983	23.2866
20	2.2287	10.9418	12.3448
21	.8257	12.3448	0.0000

YEARS 22 — MO PAYT 1.0869 — AN CONST 13.05

#	INT	PRIN	BALANCE
1	12.0722	.9705	99.0295
2	11.9478	1.0949	97.9347
3	11.8074	1.2353	96.6994
4	11.6490	1.3937	95.3057
5	11.4703	1.5724	93.7334
6	11.2687	1.7740	91.9594
7	11.0413	2.0014	89.9580
8	10.7846	2.2581	87.6999
9	10.4951	2.5476	85.1523
10	10.1685	2.8742	82.2781
11	9.7999	3.2428	79.0353
12	9.3841	3.6586	75.3768
13	8.9150	4.1277	71.2491
14	8.3858	4.6569	66.5922
15	7.7887	5.2540	61.3382
16	7.1150	5.9277	55.4105
17	6.3550	6.6877	48.7228
18	5.4975	7.5452	41.1775
19	4.5300	8.5127	32.6648
20	3.4385	9.6042	23.0607
21	2.2070	10.8357	12.2250
22	.8177	12.2250	0.0000

YEARS 23 — MO PAYT 1.0776 — AN CONST 12.94

#	INT	PRIN	BALANCE
1	12.0786	.8528	99.1472
2	11.9693	.9622	98.1850
3	11.8459	1.0856	97.0994
4	11.7067	1.2247	95.8747
5	11.5497	1.3818	94.4929
6	11.3725	1.5589	92.9340
7	11.1726	1.7588	91.1751
8	10.9471	1.9844	89.1908
9	10.6927	2.2388	86.9520
10	10.4056	2.5259	84.4261
11	10.0817	2.8497	81.5764
12	9.7164	3.2151	78.3613
13	9.3041	3.6274	74.7339
14	8.8390	4.0925	70.6415
15	8.3143	4.6172	66.0243
16	7.7223	5.2092	60.8151
17	7.0543	5.8771	54.9380
18	6.3008	6.6307	48.3073
19	5.4506	7.4809	40.8264
20	4.4914	8.4401	32.3863
21	3.4092	9.5223	22.8640
22	2.1882	10.7432	12.1207
23	.8107	12.1207	0.0000

YEARS 24 — MO PAYT 1.0695 — AN CONST 12.84

#	INT	PRIN	BALANCE
1	12.0842	.7502	99.2498
2	11.9880	.8464	98.4033
3	11.8795	.9550	97.4484
4	11.7570	1.0774	96.3710
5	11.6189	1.2156	95.1554
6	11.4630	1.3714	93.7840
7	11.2872	1.5473	92.2367
8	11.0888	1.7456	90.4911
9	10.8650	1.9695	88.5216
10	10.6125	2.2220	86.2996
11	10.3275	2.5069	83.7927
12	10.0061	2.8283	80.9644
13	9.6435	3.1910	77.7734
14	9.2343	3.6001	74.1733
15	8.7727	4.0618	70.1115
16	8.2519	4.5825	65.5290
17	7.6643	5.1701	60.3588
18	7.0014	5.8330	54.5258
19	6.2535	6.5810	47.9448
20	5.4097	7.4248	40.5201
21	4.4577	8.3768	32.1433
22	3.3836	9.4508	22.6925
23	2.1718	10.6626	12.0298
24	.8046	12.0298	0.0000

YEARS 25 — MO PAYT 1.0625 — AN CONST 12.75

#	INT	PRIN	BALANCE
1	12.0891	.6606	99.3394
2	12.0044	.7453	98.5941
3	11.9088	.8408	97.7533
4	11.8010	.9487	96.8046
5	11.6794	1.0703	95.7344
6	11.5421	1.2075	94.5268
7	11.3873	1.3624	93.1645
8	11.2126	1.5370	91.6274
9	11.0156	1.7341	89.8933
10	10.7932	1.9565	87.9369
11	10.5424	2.2073	85.7296
12	10.2593	2.4903	83.2392
13	9.9400	2.8097	80.4296
14	9.5798	3.1699	77.2597
15	9.1733	3.5764	73.6833
16	8.7148	4.0349	69.6484
17	8.1974	4.5523	65.0961
18	7.6137	5.1360	59.9601
19	6.9552	5.7945	54.1656
20	6.2122	6.5375	47.6281
21	5.3739	7.3757	40.2524
22	4.4282	8.3214	31.9310
23	3.3613	9.3884	22.5425
24	2.1575	10.5922	11.9503
25	.7993	11.9503	0.0000

YEARS 26 — MO PAYT 1.0563 — AN CONST 12.68

#	INT	PRIN	BALANCE
1	12.0934	.5821	99.4179
2	12.0187	.6567	98.7612
3	11.9345	.7409	98.0202
4	11.8395	.8359	97.1843
5	11.7323	.9431	96.2411
6	11.6114	1.0641	95.1771
7	11.4750	1.2005	93.9766
8	11.3210	1.3544	92.6222
9	11.1474	1.5281	91.0941
10	10.9514	1.7240	89.3701
11	10.7304	1.9451	87.4250
12	10.4810	2.1945	85.2305
13	10.1996	2.4758	82.7547
14	9.8822	2.7933	79.9614
15	9.5240	3.1515	76.8099
16	9.1199	3.5555	73.2544
17	8.6640	4.0114	69.2430
18	8.1497	4.5258	64.7172
19	7.5694	5.1061	59.6111
20	6.9147	5.7608	53.8503
21	6.1760	6.4994	47.3509
22	5.3427	7.3328	40.0181
23	4.4025	8.2730	31.7451
24	3.3417	9.3338	22.4113
25	2.1449	10.5305	11.8808
26	.7947	11.8808	0.0000

YEARS 27 — MO PAYT 1.0509 — AN CONST 12.62

#	INT	PRIN	BALANCE
1	12.0971	.5133	99.4867
2	12.0313	.5791	98.9076
3	11.9570	.6534	98.2542
4	11.8733	.7371	97.5171
5	11.7787	.8317	96.6854
6	11.6721	.9383	95.7471
7	11.5518	1.0586	94.6885
8	11.4161	1.1943	93.4942
9	11.2629	1.3475	92.1467
10	11.0901	1.5202	90.6265
11	10.8952	1.7152	88.9113
12	10.6753	1.9351	86.9762
13	10.4272	2.1832	84.7930
14	10.1473	2.4631	82.3299
15	9.8314	2.7790	79.5509
16	9.4751	3.1353	76.4157
17	9.0731	3.5373	72.8784
18	8.6195	3.9908	68.8875
19	8.1078	4.5025	64.3850
20	7.5305	5.0799	59.3051
21	6.8792	5.7312	53.5739
22	6.1443	6.4661	47.1078
23	5.3152	7.2951	39.8127
24	4.3799	8.2305	31.5822
25	3.3245	9.2859	22.2963
26	2.1339	10.4765	11.8198
27	.7906	11.8198	0.0000

YEARS 28 — MO PAYT 1.0461 — AN CONST 12.56

#	INT	PRIN	BALANCE
1	12.1004	.4529	99.5471
2	12.0423	.5110	99.0361
3	11.9768	.5765	98.4596
4	11.9029	.6504	97.8092
5	11.8195	.7338	97.0754
6	11.7254	.8279	96.2475
7	11.6192	.9340	95.3135
8	11.4995	1.0538	94.2597
9	11.3644	1.1889	93.0708
10	11.2119	1.3414	91.7294
11	11.0399	1.5134	90.2161
12	10.8459	1.7074	88.5087
13	10.6270	1.9263	86.5823
14	10.3800	2.1733	84.4090
15	10.1013	2.4520	81.9570
16	9.7869	2.7664	79.1907
17	9.4322	3.1211	76.0696
18	9.0320	3.5213	72.5483
19	8.5805	3.9728	68.5755
20	8.0711	4.4822	64.0934
21	7.4964	5.0569	59.0365
22	6.8480	5.7053	53.3313
23	6.1165	6.4368	46.8945
24	5.2912	7.2621	39.6324
25	4.3600	8.1933	31.4391
26	3.3095	9.2438	22.1953
27	2.1242	10.4290	11.7663
28	.7870	11.7663	0.0000

YEARS 29 — MO PAYT 1.0419 — AN CONST 12.51

#	INT	PRIN	BALANCE
1	12.1033	.3998	99.6002
2	12.0520	.4511	99.1491
3	11.9942	.5089	98.6402
4	11.9289	.5742	98.0660
5	11.8553	.6478	97.4182
6	11.7722	.7309	96.6873
7	11.6785	.8246	95.8627
8	11.5728	.9303	94.9324
9	11.4535	1.0496	93.8828
10	11.3189	1.1842	92.6987
11	11.1671	1.3360	91.3627
12	10.9958	1.5073	89.8554
13	10.8025	1.7006	88.1548
14	10.5845	1.9186	86.2362
15	10.3385	2.1646	84.0715
16	10.0609	2.4422	81.6294
17	9.7478	2.7553	78.8740
18	9.3945	3.1086	75.7654
19	8.9959	3.5072	72.2582
20	8.5462	3.9569	68.3014
21	8.0389	4.4642	63.8371
22	7.4664	5.0366	58.8005
23	6.8206	5.6824	53.1180
24	6.0920	6.4110	46.7070
25	5.2700	7.2331	39.4739
26	4.3426	8.1605	31.3134
27	3.2962	9.2068	22.1066
28	2.1157	10.3874	11.7192
29	.7839	11.7192	0.0000

YEARS 30 — MO PAYT 1.0382 — AN CONST 12.46

#	INT	PRIN	BALANCE
1	12.1058	.3531	99.6469
2	12.0605	.3984	99.2485
3	12.0094	.4495	98.7990
4	11.9518	.5071	98.2918
5	11.8868	.5722	97.7197
6	11.8134	.6455	97.0742
7	11.7307	.7283	96.3459
8	11.6373	.8217	95.5242
9	11.5319	.9270	94.5972
10	11.4131	1.0459	93.5513
11	11.2789	1.1800	92.3713
12	11.1276	1.3313	91.0400
13	10.9570	1.5020	89.5380
14	10.7644	1.6946	87.8435
15	10.5471	1.9118	85.9316
16	10.3020	2.1570	83.7746
17	10.0254	2.4336	81.3411
18	9.7133	2.7456	78.5955
19	9.3613	3.0976	75.4979
20	8.9641	3.4948	72.0031
21	8.5160	3.9429	68.0602
22	8.0105	4.4485	63.6117
23	7.4401	5.0189	58.5928
24	6.7966	5.6624	52.9305
25	6.0705	6.3884	46.5421
26	5.2514	7.2075	39.3345
27	4.3273	8.1317	31.2028
28	3.2846	9.1743	22.0285
29	2.1083	10.3507	11.6778
30	.7811	11.6778	0.0000

MONTHLY PAYMENT AMORTIZATION SCHEDULE PER $100 — 12.20 %

YEARS 2 — MO PAYT 4.7167 — AN CONST 56.61

#	INT	PRIN	BALANCE
1	9.6312	46.9691	53.0309
2	3.5694	53.0309	0.0000

YEARS 3 — MO PAYT 3.3310 — AN CONST 39.98

#	INT	PRIN	BALANCE
1	10.5932	29.3787	70.6213
2	6.8017	33.1702	37.4511
3	2.5208	37.4511	0.0000

YEARS 4 — MO PAYT 2.6432 — AN CONST 31.72

#	INT	PRIN	BALANCE
1	11.0707	20.6478	79.3522
2	8.4060	23.3126	56.0396
3	5.3973	26.3213	29.7183
4	2.0003	29.7183	0.0000

YEARS 5 — MO PAYT 2.2346 — AN CONST 26.82

#	INT	PRIN	BALANCE
1	11.3545	15.4603	84.5397
2	9.3592	17.4556	67.0841
3	7.1064	19.7084	47.3757
4	4.5628	22.2519	25.1237
5	1.6910	25.1237	0.0000

YEARS 6 — MO PAYT 1.9654 — AN CONST 23.59

#	INT	PRIN	BALANCE
1	11.5413	12.0439	87.9561
2	9.9869	13.5983	74.3578
3	8.2320	15.3533	59.0045
4	6.2505	17.3347	41.6698
5	4.0133	19.5719	22.0979
6	1.4874	22.0979	0.0000

YEARS 7 — MO PAYT 1.7760 — AN CONST 21.32

#	INT	PRIN	BALANCE
1	11.6728	9.6390	90.3610
2	10.4288	10.8830	79.4780
3	9.0243	12.2876	67.1904
4	7.4385	13.8734	53.3171
5	5.6480	15.6638	37.6532
6	3.6265	17.6854	19.9678
7	1.3440	19.9678	0.0000

YEARS 8 — MO PAYT 1.6363 — AN CONST 19.64

#	INT	PRIN	BALANCE
1	11.7698	7.8657	92.1343
2	10.7547	8.8808	83.2535
3	9.6085	10.0270	73.2265
4	8.3145	11.3211	61.9054
5	6.8534	12.7821	49.1233
6	5.2037	14.4318	34.6915
7	3.3412	16.2943	18.3972
8	1.2383	18.3972	0.0000

YEARS 9 — MO PAYT 1.5297 — AN CONST 18.36

#	INT	PRIN	BALANCE
1	11.8438	6.5129	93.4871
2	11.0033	7.3534	86.1337
3	10.0542	8.3024	77.8313
4	8.9827	9.3739	68.4573
5	7.7730	10.5837	57.8736
6	6.4070	11.9496	45.9240
7	4.8648	13.4918	32.4321
8	3.1236	15.2331	17.1990
9	1.1576	17.1990	0.0000

YEARS 10 — MO PAYT 1.4463 — AN CONST 17.36

#	INT	PRIN	BALANCE
1	11.9017	5.4538	94.5462
2	11.1979	6.1577	88.3885
3	10.4032	6.9524	81.4361
4	9.5059	7.8496	73.5865
5	8.4928	8.8627	64.7238
6	7.3490	10.0065	54.7173
7	6.0576	11.2979	43.4194
8	4.5995	12.7560	30.6633
9	2.9532	14.4023	16.2610
10	1.0945	16.2610	0.0000

YEARS 11 — MO PAYT 1.3797 — AN CONST 16.56

#	INT	PRIN	BALANCE
1	11.9480	4.6078	95.3922
2	11.3533	5.2025	90.1897
3	10.6819	5.8739	84.3157
4	9.9238	6.6320	77.6837
5	9.0679	7.4879	70.1957
6	8.1015	8.4543	61.7414
7	7.0104	9.5454	52.1960
8	5.7785	10.7773	41.4187
9	4.3876	12.1682	29.2504
10	2.8172	13.7387	15.5118
11	1.0441	15.5118	0.0000

YEARS 12 — MO PAYT 1.3256 — AN CONST 15.91

#	INT	PRIN	BALANCE
1	11.9855	3.9211	96.0789
2	11.4795	4.4272	91.6517
3	10.9081	4.9985	86.6532
4	10.2630	5.6436	81.0096
5	9.5347	6.3720	74.6376
6	8.7123	7.1943	67.4433
7	7.7838	8.1228	59.3205
8	6.7355	9.1711	50.1493
9	5.5519	10.3548	39.7946
10	4.2155	11.6911	28.1035
11	2.7067	13.2000	14.9035
12	1.0031	14.9035	0.0000

YEARS 13 — MO PAYT 1.2811 — AN CONST 15.38

#	INT	PRIN	BALANCE
1	12.0164	3.3563	96.6437
2	11.5833	3.7895	92.8542
3	11.0942	4.2786	88.5756
4	10.5420	4.8308	83.7448
5	9.9186	5.4542	78.2907
6	9.2147	6.1581	72.1325
7	8.4199	6.9529	65.1797
8	7.5226	7.8502	57.3295
9	6.5094	8.8633	48.4662
10	5.3656	10.0072	38.4590
11	4.0740	11.2987	27.1602
12	2.6159	12.7569	14.4033
13	.9695	14.4033	0.0000

YEARS 14 — MO PAYT 1.2441 — AN CONST 14.93

#	INT	PRIN	BALANCE
1	12.0421	2.8869	97.1131
2	11.6695	3.2594	93.8537
3	11.2489	3.6801	90.1736
4	10.7739	4.1550	86.0185
5	10.2377	4.6913	81.3272
6	9.6322	5.2967	76.0305
7	8.9486	5.9803	70.0502
8	8.1768	6.7521	63.2980
9	7.3054	7.6236	55.6745
10	6.3215	8.6075	47.0670
11	5.2107	9.7183	37.3487
12	3.9564	10.9725	26.3761
13	2.5403	12.3886	13.9875
14	.9415	13.9875	0.0000

YEARS 15 — MO PAYT 1.2131 — AN CONST 14.56

#	INT	PRIN	BALANCE
1	12.0636	2.4931	97.5069
2	11.7419	2.8149	94.6920
3	11.3786	3.1782	91.5138
4	10.9684	3.5884	87.9254
5	10.5053	4.0515	83.8740
6	9.9824	4.5743	79.2996
7	9.3921	5.1647	74.1350
8	8.7255	5.8312	68.3037
9	7.9730	6.5838	61.7199
10	7.1233	7.4335	54.2864
11	6.1639	8.3929	45.8936
12	5.0808	9.4760	36.4175
13	3.8578	10.6990	25.7186
14	2.4770	12.0798	13.6388
15	.9180	13.6388	0.0000

YEARS 16 — MO PAYT 1.1869 — AN CONST 14.25

#	INT	PRIN	BALANCE
1	12.0818	2.1604	97.8396
2	11.8030	2.4393	95.4003
3	11.4882	2.7541	92.6462
4	11.1328	3.1095	89.5367
5	10.7315	3.5108	86.0259
6	10.2784	3.9639	82.0619
7	9.7668	4.4755	77.5864
8	9.1892	5.0531	72.5333
9	8.5370	5.7053	66.8281
10	7.8007	6.4416	60.3865
11	6.9694	7.2729	53.1136
12	6.0308	8.2115	44.9021
13	4.9710	9.2713	35.6308
14	3.7745	10.4678	25.1629
15	2.4235	11.8188	13.3441
16	.8982	13.3441	0.0000

YEARS 17 — MO PAYT 1.1646 — AN CONST 13.98

#	INT	PRIN	BALANCE
1	12.0973	1.8776	98.1224
2	11.8550	2.1199	96.0025
3	11.5814	2.3935	93.6091
4	11.2725	2.7024	90.9067
5	10.9237	3.0511	87.8556
6	10.5300	3.4449	84.4107
7	10.0854	3.8895	80.5212
8	9.5834	4.3915	76.1297
9	9.0166	4.9582	71.1715
10	8.3767	5.5981	65.5733
11	7.6543	6.3206	59.2527
12	6.8385	7.1363	52.1163
13	5.9175	8.0574	44.0590
14	4.8777	9.0972	34.9618
15	3.7036	10.2713	24.6905
16	2.3780	11.5969	13.0936
17	.8813	13.0936	0.0000

YEARS 18 — MO PAYT 1.1455 — AN CONST 13.75

#	INT	PRIN	BALANCE
1	12.1105	1.6357	98.3643
2	11.8994	1.8469	96.5174
3	11.6611	2.0852	94.4322
4	11.3920	2.3543	92.0779
5	11.0881	2.6582	89.4197
6	10.7451	3.0012	86.4185
7	10.3577	3.3886	83.0299
8	9.9204	3.8259	79.2040
9	9.4266	4.3196	74.8844
10	8.8692	4.8771	70.0073
11	8.2397	5.5066	64.5007
12	7.5291	6.2172	58.2835
13	6.7267	7.0196	51.2639
14	5.8207	7.9256	43.3383
15	4.7979	8.9484	34.3899
16	3.6430	10.1033	24.2866
17	2.3391	11.4072	12.8794
18	.8669	12.8794	0.0000

YEARS 19 — MO PAYT 1.1292 — AN CONST 13.55

#	INT	PRIN	BALANCE
1	12.1219	1.4281	98.5719
2	11.9376	1.6124	96.9595
3	11.7295	1.8205	95.1390
4	11.4945	2.0554	93.0836
5	11.2293	2.3207	90.7629
6	10.9298	2.6202	88.1427
7	10.5916	2.9584	85.1843
8	10.2098	3.3402	81.8442
9	9.7787	3.7712	78.0729
10	9.2920	4.2580	73.8150
11	8.7425	4.8075	69.0075
12	8.1221	5.4279	63.5796
13	7.4215	6.1284	57.4511
14	6.6306	6.9194	50.5318
15	5.7376	7.8124	42.7194
16	4.7294	8.8206	33.8988
17	3.5910	9.9590	23.9398
18	2.3057	11.2443	12.6955
19	.8545	12.6955	0.0000

YEARS 20 — MO PAYT 1.1151 — AN CONST 13.39

#	INT	PRIN	BALANCE
1	12.1317	1.2490	98.7510
2	11.9705	1.4102	97.3407
3	11.7885	1.5922	95.7485
4	11.5830	1.7977	93.9507
5	11.3510	2.0298	91.9210
6	11.0890	2.2917	89.6292
7	10.7933	2.5875	87.0418
8	10.4593	2.9214	84.1204
9	10.0823	3.2984	80.8219
10	9.6566	3.7241	77.0978
11	9.1760	4.2048	72.8930
12	8.6333	4.7474	68.1456
13	8.0206	5.3601	62.7854
14	7.3288	6.0519	56.7335
15	6.5478	6.8329	49.9006
16	5.6659	7.7148	42.1858
17	4.6703	8.7105	33.4754
18	3.5461	9.8346	23.6407
19	2.2769	11.1038	12.5369
20	.8438	12.5369	0.0000

YEARS 21 — MO PAYT 1.1029 — AN CONST 13.24

#	INT	PRIN	BALANCE
1	12.1402	1.0942	98.9058
2	11.9989	1.2354	97.6705
3	11.8395	1.3948	96.2756

MONTHLY PAYMENT AMORTIZATION SCHEDULE PER $100   12.20 %

#	INT	PRIN	BALANCE
4	11.6595	1.5748	94.7008
5	11.4563	1.7781	92.9227
6	11.2268	2.0075	90.9152
7	10.9677	2.2666	88.6486
8	10.6752	2.5592	86.0894
9	10.3449	2.8894	83.1999
10	9.9720	3.2624	79.9376
11	9.5509	3.6834	76.2542
12	9.0756	4.1588	72.0954
13	8.5388	4.6955	67.3999
14	7.9328	5.3015	62.0985
15	7.2486	5.9857	56.1128
16	6.4761	6.7582	49.3546
17	5.6039	7.6304	41.7242
18	4.6192	8.6151	33.1091
19	3.5073	9.7270	23.3821
20	2.2520	10.9824	12.3997
21	.8346	12.3997	0.0000

YEARS 22 — MO PAYT 1.0923 — AN CONST 13.11

#	INT	PRIN	BALANCE
1	12.1475	.9598	99.0402
2	12.0236	1.0837	97.9565
3	11.8838	1.2235	96.7330
4	11.7259	1.3814	95.3516
5	11.5476	1.5597	93.7919
6	11.3463	1.7610	92.0309
7	11.1190	1.9883	90.0426
8	10.8624	2.2449	87.7977
9	10.5727	2.5346	85.2631
10	10.2456	2.8617	82.4014
11	9.8763	3.2310	79.1703
12	9.4593	3.6480	75.5223
13	8.9885	4.1188	71.4035
14	8.4569	4.6504	66.7530
15	7.8567	5.2506	61.5024
16	7.1791	5.9282	55.5742
17	6.4140	6.6933	48.8809
18	5.5502	7.5571	41.3238
19	4.5748	8.5325	32.7913
20	3.4737	9.6336	23.1577
21	2.2304	10.8769	12.2807
22	.8266	12.2807	0.0000

YEARS 23 — MO PAYT 1.0831 — AN CONST 13.00

#	INT	PRIN	BALANCE
1	12.1539	.8429	99.1571
2	12.0451	.9517	98.2054
3	11.9223	1.0745	97.1308
4	11.7836	1.2132	95.9176
5	11.6270	1.3698	94.5479
6	11.4503	1.5466	93.0013
7	11.2507	1.7462	91.2551
8	11.0253	1.9715	89.2836
9	10.7709	2.2260	87.0576
10	10.4836	2.5132	84.5444
11	10.1592	2.8376	81.7068
12	9.7930	3.2038	78.5030
13	9.3975	3.6173	74.8857
14	8.9127	4.0841	70.8016
15	8.3856	4.6112	66.1904
16	7.7905	5.2063	60.9840
17	7.1186	5.8783	55.1058
18	6.3599	6.6369	48.4689
19	5.5034	7.4934	40.9754
20	4.5363	8.4605	32.5149
21	3.4444	9.5524	22.9625
22	2.2116	10.7853	12.1772
23	.8196	12.1772	0.0000

YEARS 24 — MO PAYT 1.0750 — AN CONST 12.91

#	INT	PRIN	BALANCE
1	12.1595	.7410	99.2590
2	12.0638	.8367	98.4223
3	11.9559	.9447	97.4776
4	11.8339	1.0666	96.4111
5	11.6963	1.2042	95.2069
6	11.5409	1.3596	93.8472
7	11.3654	1.5351	92.3121
8	11.1673	1.7332	90.5789
9	10.9436	1.9569	88.6220
10	10.6910	2.2095	86.4125
11	10.4059	2.4946	83.9179
12	10.0839	2.8166	81.1013
13	9.7204	3.1801	77.9213
14	9.3100	3.5905	74.3308
15	8.8466	4.0539	70.2769
16	8.3235	4.5770	65.6999
17	7.7328	5.1768	60.5321
18	7.0685	5.8347	54.6974
19	6.3128	6.5877	48.1097
20	5.4626	7.4379	40.6718
21	4.5027	8.3978	32.2739
22	3.4189	9.4817	22.7923
23	2.1952	10.7053	12.0870
24	.8136	12.0870	0.0000

YEARS 25 — MO PAYT 1.0680 — AN CONST 12.82

#	INT	PRIN	BALANCE
1	12.1643	.6521	99.3479
2	12.0802	.7362	98.6117
3	11.9852	.8312	97.7805
4	11.8779	.9385	96.8420
5	11.7568	1.0596	95.7824
6	11.6200	1.1964	94.5861
7	11.4656	1.3508	93.2353
8	11.2913	1.5251	91.7102
9	11.0945	1.7219	89.9883
10	10.8722	1.9441	88.0441
11	10.6213	2.1951	85.8491
12	10.3380	2.4783	83.3707
13	10.0182	2.7982	80.5725
14	9.6571	3.1593	77.4132
15	9.2493	3.5671	73.8461
16	8.7890	4.0274	69.8187
17	8.2692	4.5472	65.2715
18	7.6823	5.1341	60.1374
19	7.0197	5.7967	54.3408
20	6.2716	6.5448	47.7960
21	5.4270	7.3894	40.4066
22	4.4733	8.3431	32.0635
23	3.3966	9.4198	22.6437
24	2.1809	10.6355	12.0081
25	.8083	12.0081	0.0000

YEARS 26 — MO PAYT 1.0619 — AN CONST 12.75

#	INT	PRIN	BALANCE
1	12.1686	.5742	99.4258
2	12.0945	.6483	98.7775
3	12.0108	.7320	98.0455
4	11.9164	.8264	97.2191
5	11.8097	.9331	96.2860
6	11.6893	1.0535	95.2324
7	11.5533	1.1895	94.0429
8	11.3998	1.3430	92.6999
9	11.2265	1.5163	91.1836
10	11.0308	1.7120	89.4716
11	10.8098	1.9330	87.5386
12	10.5603	2.1825	85.3561
13	10.2787	2.4641	82.8920
14	9.9607	2.7821	80.1099
15	9.6016	3.1412	76.9687
16	9.1962	3.5466	73.4221
17	8.7385	4.0043	69.4178
18	8.2217	4.5211	64.8967
19	7.6382	5.1046	59.7921
20	6.9794	5.7634	54.0287
21	6.2356	6.5072	47.5216
22	5.3958	7.3470	40.1746
23	4.4476	8.2952	31.8794
24	3.3771	9.3657	22.5137
25	2.1683	10.5745	11.9392
26	.8036	11.9392	0.0000

YEARS 27 — MO PAYT 1.0565 — AN CONST 12.68

#	INT	PRIN	BALANCE
1	12.1723	.5060	99.4940
2	12.1070	.5713	98.9227
3	12.0333	.6450	98.2777
4	11.9500	.7283	97.5494
5	11.8561	.8223	96.7271
6	11.7499	.9284	95.7988
7	11.6301	1.0482	94.7506
8	11.4948	1.1835	93.5671
9	11.3421	1.3362	92.2309
10	11.1697	1.5087	90.7222
11	10.9749	1.7034	89.0188
12	10.7551	1.9232	87.0956
13	10.5069	2.1714	84.9242
14	10.2267	2.4517	82.4726
15	9.9103	2.7681	79.7045
16	9.5530	3.1253	76.5792
17	9.1497	3.5286	73.0506
18	8.6943	3.9840	69.0665
19	8.1801	4.4982	64.5683
20	7.5996	5.0788	59.4896
21	6.9441	5.7342	53.7554
22	6.2041	6.4743	47.2811
23	5.3685	7.3098	39.9713
24	4.4251	8.2532	31.7181
25	3.3600	9.3183	22.3997
26	2.1574	10.5210	11.8788
27	.7995	11.8788	0.0000

YEARS 28 — MO PAYT 1.0518 — AN CONST 12.63

#	INT	PRIN	BALANCE
1	12.1756	.4462	99.5538
2	12.1180	.5037	99.0501
3	12.0530	.5687	98.4814
4	11.9796	.6421	97.8392
5	11.8967	.7250	97.1142
6	11.8032	.8186	96.2956
7	11.6975	.9242	95.3714
8	11.5782	1.0435	94.3278
9	11.4436	1.1782	93.1496
10	11.2915	1.3303	91.8194
11	11.1198	1.5019	90.3174
12	10.9260	1.6958	88.6217
13	10.7071	1.9146	86.7070
14	10.4600	2.1617	84.5453
15	10.1810	2.4407	82.1046
16	9.8660	2.7557	79.3489
17	9.5104	3.1114	76.2376
18	9.1089	3.5129	72.7247
19	8.6555	3.9663	68.7584
20	8.1436	4.4781	64.2802
21	7.5657	5.0561	59.2241
22	6.9131	5.7086	53.5155
23	6.1764	6.4454	47.0702
24	5.3446	7.2772	39.7930
25	4.4054	8.2164	31.5766
26	3.3450	9.2768	22.2998
27	2.1477	10.4740	11.8258
28	.7960	11.8258	0.0000

YEARS 29 — MO PAYT 1.0477 — AN CONST 12.58

#	INT	PRIN	BALANCE
1	12.1785	.3936	99.6064
2	12.1277	.4444	99.1620
3	12.0703	.5018	98.6602
4	12.0056	.5665	98.0937
5	11.9325	.6396	97.4541
6	11.8499	.7222	96.7319
7	11.7567	.8154	95.9166
8	11.6515	.9206	94.9960
9	11.5327	1.0394	93.9566
10	11.3985	1.1736	92.7830
11	11.2471	1.3250	91.4580
12	11.0761	1.4960	89.9620
13	10.8830	1.6891	88.2729
14	10.6650	1.9071	86.3658
15	10.4189	2.1532	84.2126
16	10.1410	2.4311	81.7814
17	9.8272	2.7449	79.0366
18	9.4730	3.0991	75.9375
19	9.0730	3.4991	72.4384
20	8.6214	3.9507	68.4877
21	8.1116	4.4605	64.0272
22	7.5359	5.0362	58.9910
23	6.8859	5.6862	53.3049
24	6.1521	6.4200	46.8849
25	5.3235	7.2486	39.6363
26	4.3880	8.1840	31.4523
27	3.3318	9.2403	22.2120
28	2.1393	10.4328	11.7792
29	.7928	11.7792	0.0000

YEARS 30 — MO PAYT 1.0440 — AN CONST 12.53

#	INT	PRIN	BALANCE
1	12.1810	.3474	99.6526
2	12.1362	.3922	99.2604
3	12.0855	.4429	98.8175
4	12.0284	.5000	98.3175
5	11.9639	.5645	97.7530
6	11.8910	.6374	97.1156
7	11.8087	.7197	96.3959
8	11.7159	.8125	95.5834
9	11.6110	.9174	94.6660
10	11.4926	1.0358	93.6301
11	11.3589	1.1695	92.4607
12	11.2080	1.3204	91.1402
13	11.0376	1.4908	89.6494
14	10.8452	1.6832	87.9662
15	10.6279	1.9005	86.0657
16	10.3827	2.1457	83.9200
17	10.1057	2.4227	81.4973
18	9.7931	2.7353	78.7620
19	9.4401	3.0883	75.6737
20	9.0415	3.4869	72.1868
21	8.5915	3.9369	68.2498
22	8.0834	4.4450	63.8048
23	7.5097	5.0187	58.7861
24	6.8620	5.6664	53.1197
25	6.1307	6.3977	46.7220
26	5.3050	7.2234	39.4986
27	4.3728	8.1556	31.3430
28	3.3202	9.2082	22.1349
29	2.1319	10.3965	11.7383
30	.7901	11.7383	0.0000

MONTHLY PAYMENT AMORTIZATION SCHEDULE PER $100

12.25 %

YEARS 2 — MO PAYT 4.7190 — AN CONST 56.63

#	INT	PRIN	BALANCE
1	9.6716	46.9568	53.0432
2	3.5852	53.0432	0.0000

YEARS 3 — MO PAYT 3.3334 — AN CONST 40.01

#	INT	PRIN	BALANCE
1	10.6377	29.3629	70.6371
2	6.8317	33.1689	37.4682
3	2.5325	37.4682	0.0000

YEARS 4 — MO PAYT 2.6457 — AN CONST 31.75

#	INT	PRIN	BALANCE
1	11.1171	20.6310	79.3690
2	8.4430	23.3051	56.0640
3	5.4223	26.3258	29.7381
4	2.0100	29.7381	0.0000

YEARS 5 — MO PAYT 2.2371 — AN CONST 26.85

#	INT	PRIN	BALANCE
1	11.4020	15.4432	84.5568
2	9.4003	17.4449	67.1119
3	7.1391	19.7060	47.4059
4	4.5849	22.2603	25.1456
5	1.6996	25.1456	0.0000

YEARS 6 — MO PAYT 1.9680 — AN CONST 23.62

#	INT	PRIN	BALANCE
1	11.5896	12.0269	87.9731
2	10.0307	13.5858	74.3872
3	8.2697	15.3468	59.0404
4	6.2805	17.3360	41.7044
5	4.0335	19.5831	22.1214
6	1.4952	22.1214	0.0000

YEARS 7 — MO PAYT 1.7787 — AN CONST 21.35

#	INT	PRIN	BALANCE
1	11.7216	9.6224	90.3776
2	10.4744	10.8697	79.5079
3	9.0655	12.2786	67.2294
4	7.4740	13.8701	53.3593
5	5.6762	15.6679	37.6914
6	3.6454	17.6987	19.9928
7	1.3513	19.9928	0.0000

YEARS 8 — MO PAYT 1.6391 — AN CONST 19.67

#	INT	PRIN	BALANCE
1	11.8190	7.8496	92.1504
2	10.8015	8.8671	83.2833
3	9.6522	10.0164	73.2668
4	8.3539	11.3147	61.9521
5	6.8873	12.7813	49.1708
6	5.2306	14.4380	34.7328
7	3.3592	16.3094	18.4234
8	1.2452	18.4234	0.0000

YEARS 9 — MO PAYT 1.5326 — AN CONST 18.40

#	INT	PRIN	BALANCE
1	11.8932	6.4974	93.5026
2	11.0510	7.3396	86.1629
3	10.0997	8.2910	77.8720
4	9.0250	9.3656	68.5064
5	7.8111	10.5796	57.9268
6	6.4398	11.9509	45.9760
7	4.8908	13.4999	32.4761
8	3.1409	15.2497	17.2263
9	1.1643	17.2263	0.0000

YEARS 10 — MO PAYT 1.4492 — AN CONST 17.40

#	INT	PRIN	BALANCE
1	11.9513	5.4390	94.5610
2	11.2463	6.1440	88.4169
3	10.4500	6.9404	81.4765
4	9.5504	7.8400	73.6365
5	8.5342	8.8562	64.7803
6	7.3863	10.0041	54.7761
7	6.0895	11.3008	43.4753
8	4.6248	12.7656	30.7097
9	2.9701	14.4203	16.2894
10	1.1010	16.2894	0.0000

YEARS 11 — MO PAYT 1.3826 — AN CONST 16.60

#	INT	PRIN	BALANCE
1	11.9978	4.5938	95.4062
2	11.4023	5.1892	90.2171
3	10.7297	5.8618	84.3553
4	9.9699	6.6216	77.7337
5	9.1117	7.4799	70.2538
6	8.1421	8.4494	61.8044
7	7.0469	9.5446	52.2599
8	5.8098	10.7817	41.4781
9	4.4123	12.1792	29.2989
10	2.8337	13.7578	15.5411
11	1.0504	15.5411	0.0000

YEARS 12 — MO PAYT 1.3286 — AN CONST 15.95

#	INT	PRIN	BALANCE
1	12.0354	3.9077	96.0923
2	11.5289	4.4142	91.6780
3	10.9568	4.9864	86.6916
4	10.3104	5.6327	81.0589
5	9.5803	6.3628	74.6960
6	8.7556	7.1876	67.5085
7	7.8240	8.1192	59.3893
8	6.7716	9.1716	50.2177
9	5.5828	10.3604	39.8573
10	4.2399	11.7033	28.1540
11	2.7229	13.2202	14.9338
12	1.0094	14.9338	0.0000

YEARS 13 — MO PAYT 1.2842 — AN CONST 15.42

#	INT	PRIN	BALANCE
1	12.0664	3.3437	96.6563
2	11.6330	3.7771	92.8793
3	11.1434	4.2666	88.6126
4	10.5904	4.8197	83.7929
5	9.9657	5.4444	78.3485
6	9.2600	6.1501	72.1984
7	8.4628	6.9472	65.2512
8	7.5623	7.8477	57.4035
9	6.5451	8.8649	48.5386
10	5.3961	10.0140	38.5246
11	4.0981	11.3120	27.2126
12	2.6319	12.7782	14.4345
13	.9756	14.4345	0.0000

YEARS 14 — MO PAYT 1.2473 — AN CONST 14.97

#	INT	PRIN	BALANCE
1	12.0921	2.8749	97.1251
2	11.7195	3.2475	93.8775
3	11.2986	3.6685	90.2091
4	10.8231	4.1440	86.0651
5	10.2859	4.6811	81.3840
6	9.6792	5.2879	76.0961
7	8.9938	5.9733	70.1228
8	8.2195	6.7475	63.3753
9	7.3449	7.6221	55.7532
10	6.3570	8.6101	47.1431
11	5.2410	9.7261	37.4170
12	3.9803	10.9867	26.4303
13	2.5562	12.4108	14.0195
14	.9476	14.0195	0.0000

YEARS 15 — MO PAYT 1.2163 — AN CONST 14.60

#	INT	PRIN	BALANCE
1	12.1137	2.4819	97.5181
2	11.7920	2.8036	94.7146
3	11.4286	3.1669	91.5476
4	11.0181	3.5774	87.9702
5	10.5544	4.0411	83.9291
6	10.0306	4.5649	79.3641
7	9.4389	5.1566	74.2075
8	8.7706	5.8250	68.3825
9	8.0155	6.5800	61.8024
10	7.1626	7.4329	54.3695
11	6.1992	8.3964	45.9731
12	5.1109	9.4847	36.4884
13	3.8815	10.7141	25.7743
14	2.4928	12.1028	13.6715
15	.9241	13.6715	0.0000

YEARS 16 — MO PAYT 1.1902 — AN CONST 14.29

#	INT	PRIN	BALANCE
1	12.1320	2.1499	97.8501
2	11.8533	2.4285	95.4216
3	11.5385	2.7433	92.6784
4	11.1829	3.0989	89.5795
5	10.7813	3.5005	86.0790
6	10.3275	3.9543	82.1247
7	9.8150	4.4668	77.6579
8	9.2360	5.0458	72.6121
9	8.5820	5.6998	66.9123
10	7.8432	6.4386	60.4737
11	7.0087	7.2731	53.2006
12	6.0659	8.2159	44.9847
13	5.0010	9.2808	35.7040
14	3.7981	10.4837	25.2202
15	2.4392	11.8426	13.3776
16	.9042	13.3776	0.0000

YEARS 17 — MO PAYT 1.1679 — AN CONST 14.02

#	INT	PRIN	BALANCE
1	12.1474	1.8676	98.1324
2	11.9054	2.1097	96.0227
3	11.6319	2.3832	93.6395
4	11.3230	2.6921	90.9475
5	10.9741	3.0410	87.9065
6	10.5799	3.4352	84.4713
7	10.1347	3.8804	80.5909
8	9.6317	4.3834	76.2075
9	9.0635	4.9515	71.2560
10	8.4217	5.5933	65.6627
11	7.6967	6.3183	59.3443
12	6.8778	7.1373	52.2070
13	5.9526	8.0624	44.1446
14	4.9076	9.1075	35.0371
15	3.7271	10.2879	24.7492
16	2.3936	11.6214	13.1278
17	.8873	13.1278	0.0000

YEARS 18 — MO PAYT 1.1489 — AN CONST 13.79

#	INT	PRIN	BALANCE
1	12.1607	1.6264	98.3736
2	11.9499	1.8372	96.5363
3	11.7117	2.0754	94.4609
4	11.4427	2.3444	92.1165
5	11.1389	2.6483	89.4683
6	10.7956	2.9915	86.4767
7	10.4078	3.3793	83.0975
8	9.9698	3.8173	79.2802
9	9.4750	4.3121	74.9681
10	8.9161	4.8710	70.0971
11	8.2848	5.5024	64.5947
12	7.5716	6.2156	58.3791
13	6.7659	7.0212	51.3579
14	5.8558	7.9313	43.4266
15	4.8278	8.9593	34.4673
16	3.6665	10.1206	24.3467
17	2.3547	11.4324	12.9143
18	.8729	12.9143	0.0000

YEARS 19 — MO PAYT 1.1326 — AN CONST 13.60

#	INT	PRIN	BALANCE
1	12.1721	1.4194	98.5806
2	11.9881	1.6033	96.9773
3	11.7803	1.8112	95.1661
4	11.5455	2.0459	93.1202
5	11.2803	2.3111	90.8091
6	10.9808	2.6107	88.1984
7	10.6424	2.9491	85.2493
8	10.2601	3.3313	81.9180
9	9.8283	3.7631	78.1549
10	9.3406	4.2509	73.9040
11	8.7896	4.8019	69.1021
12	8.1672	5.4243	63.6779
13	7.4641	6.1274	57.5505
14	6.6699	6.9216	50.6289
15	5.7727	7.8187	42.8102
16	4.7593	8.8322	33.9781
17	3.6145	9.9770	24.0011
18	2.3213	11.2701	12.7310
19	.8605	12.7310	0.0000

YEARS 20 — MO PAYT 1.1186 — AN CONST 13.43

#	INT	PRIN	BALANCE
1	12.1819	1.2409	98.7591
2	12.0210	1.4018	97.3573
3	11.8393	1.5835	95.7739
4	11.6341	1.7887	93.9852
5	11.4022	2.0205	91.9646
6	11.1403	2.2824	89.6822
7	10.8445	2.5783	87.1039
8	10.5103	2.9125	84.1914
9	10.1328	3.2900	80.9015
10	9.7064	3.7164	77.1850
11	9.2246	4.1981	72.9869
12	8.6805	4.7423	68.2446
13	8.0658	5.3570	62.8877
14	7.3715	6.0513	56.8364
15	6.5871	6.8357	50.0007
16	5.7011	7.7217	42.2790
17	4.7002	8.7226	33.5564
18	3.5696	9.8532	23.7033
19	2.2925	11.1303	12.5730
20	.8498	12.5730	0.0000

YEARS 21 — MO PAYT 1.1064 — AN CONST 13.28

#	INT	PRIN	BALANCE
1	12.1903	1.0866	98.9134
2	12.0495	1.2274	97.6860
3	11.8904	1.3865	96.2994

MONTHLY PAYMENT AMORTIZATION SCHEDULE PER $100 12.25 %

#	INT	PRIN	BALANCE
4	11.7107	1.5662	94.7332
5	11.5077	1.7693	92.9639
6	11.2783	1.9986	90.9654
7	11.0193	2.2576	88.7077
8	10.7267	2.5503	86.1575
9	10.3961	2.8808	83.2766
10	10.0227	3.2542	80.0224
11	9.6009	3.6760	76.3464
12	9.1244	4.1525	72.1938
13	8.5862	4.6908	67.5031
14	7.9782	5.2988	62.2043
15	7.2914	5.9856	56.2188
16	6.5155	6.7614	49.4574
17	5.6391	7.6378	41.8196
18	4.6491	8.6278	33.1918
19	3.5308	9.7461	23.4457
20	2.2676	11.0094	12.4364
21	.8406	12.4364	0.0000

YEARS 22 MO PAYT 1.0959 AN CONST 13.16

#	INT	PRIN	BALANCE
1	12.1977	.9527	99.0473
2	12.0742	1.0762	97.9710
3	11.9347	1.2157	96.7553
4	11.7771	1.3733	95.3820
5	11.5991	1.5513	93.8306
6	11.3980	1.7524	92.0782
7	11.1709	1.9795	90.0987
8	10.9143	2.2361	87.8626
9	10.6245	2.5260	85.3366
10	10.2971	2.8534	82.4832
11	9.9272	3.2232	79.2600
12	9.5094	3.6410	75.6190
13	9.0375	4.1130	71.5060
14	8.5044	4.6461	66.8600
15	7.9022	5.2483	61.6117
16	7.2219	5.9285	55.6832
17	6.4535	6.6970	48.9862
18	5.5854	7.5650	41.4212
19	4.6048	8.5456	32.8756
20	3.4972	9.6532	23.2223
21	2.2460	10.9045	12.3179
22	.8326	12.3179	0.0000

YEARS 23 MO PAYT 1.0867 AN CONST 13.05

#	INT	PRIN	BALANCE
1	12.2041	.8364	99.1636
2	12.0957	.9448	98.2189
3	11.9732	1.0672	97.1516
4	11.8349	1.2056	95.9460
5	11.6786	1.3618	94.5842
6	11.5021	1.5383	93.0459
7	11.3027	1.7377	91.3081
8	11.0775	1.9630	89.3451
9	10.8230	2.2174	87.1277
10	10.5356	2.5048	84.6229
11	10.2109	2.8295	81.7933
12	9.8442	3.1963	78.5971
13	9.4299	3.6106	74.9865
14	8.9619	4.0786	70.9080
15	8.4332	4.6072	66.3008
16	7.8361	5.2044	61.0964
17	7.1615	5.8790	55.2174
18	6.3995	6.6410	48.5765
19	5.5387	7.5018	41.0747
20	4.5663	8.4741	32.6006
21	3.4679	9.5725	23.0281
22	2.2272	10.8133	12.2148
23	.8256	12.2148	0.0000

YEARS 24 MO PAYT 1.0787 AN CONST 12.95

#	INT	PRIN	BALANCE
1	12.2096	.7350	99.2650
2	12.1144	.8302	98.4348
3	12.0068	.9378	97.4970
4	11.8852	1.0594	96.4376
5	11.7479	1.1967	95.2409
6	11.5928	1.3518	93.8891
7	11.4176	1.5270	92.3620
8	11.2196	1.7250	90.6370
9	10.9960	1.9486	88.6885
10	10.7435	2.2011	86.4874
11	10.4582	2.4864	84.0009
12	10.1359	2.8087	81.1922
13	9.7718	3.1728	78.0194
14	9.3606	3.5840	74.4354
15	8.8960	4.0486	70.3868
16	8.3713	4.5733	65.8135
17	7.7785	5.1661	60.6474
18	7.1089	5.8357	54.8116
19	6.3524	6.5922	48.2195
20	5.4980	7.4466	40.7728
21	4.5328	8.4118	32.3610
22	3.4425	9.5021	22.8589
23	2.2108	10.7338	12.1251
24	.8195	12.1251	0.0000

YEARS 25 MO PAYT 1.0717 AN CONST 12.87

#	INT	PRIN	BALANCE
1	12.2145	.6464	99.3536
2	12.1307	.7302	98.6234
3	12.0361	.8249	97.7985
4	11.9292	.9318	96.8667
5	11.8084	1.0525	95.8142
6	11.6720	1.1890	94.6252
7	11.5178	1.3431	93.2821
8	11.3438	1.5172	91.7650
9	11.1471	1.7138	90.0511
10	10.9250	1.9360	88.1152
11	10.6740	2.1869	85.9283
12	10.3906	2.4704	83.4579
13	10.0704	2.7906	80.6674
14	9.7087	3.1523	77.5151
15	9.3001	3.5609	73.9542
16	8.8385	4.0224	69.9318
17	8.3171	4.5438	65.3881
18	7.7282	5.1327	60.2553
19	7.0629	5.7980	54.4573
20	6.3114	6.5495	47.9078
21	5.4624	7.3985	40.5093
22	4.5035	8.3575	32.1518
23	3.4202	9.4407	22.7111
24	2.1965	10.6644	12.0467
25	.8142	12.0467	0.0000

YEARS 26 MO PAYT 1.0656 AN CONST 12.79

#	INT	PRIN	BALANCE
1	12.2188	.5690	99.4310
2	12.1450	.6427	98.7883
3	12.0617	.7261	98.0622
4	11.9676	.8202	97.2421
5	11.8613	.9265	96.3156
6	11.7412	1.0466	95.2690
7	11.6055	1.1822	94.0868
8	11.4523	1.3354	92.7514
9	11.2792	1.5085	91.2428
10	11.0837	1.7041	89.5388
11	10.8628	1.9249	87.6138
12	10.6133	2.1745	85.4394
13	10.3314	2.4563	82.9831
14	10.0131	2.7747	80.2084
15	9.6534	3.1343	77.0740
16	9.2472	3.5406	73.5334
17	8.7882	3.9995	69.5339
18	8.2698	4.5179	65.0160
19	7.6842	5.1035	59.9125
20	7.0227	5.7650	54.1474
21	6.2755	6.5123	47.6352
22	5.4314	7.3564	40.2788
23	4.4778	8.3099	31.9689
24	3.4007	9.3870	22.5819
25	2.1840	10.6037	11.9782
26	.8096	11.9782	0.0000

YEARS 27 MO PAYT 1.0603 AN CONST 12.73

#	INT	PRIN	BALANCE
1	12.2225	.5012	99.4988
2	12.1575	.5661	98.9327
3	12.0841	.6395	98.2932
4	12.0012	.7224	97.5707
5	11.9076	.8161	96.7547
6	11.8018	.9218	95.8329
7	11.6823	1.0413	94.7916
8	11.5474	1.1763	93.6153
9	11.3949	1.3287	92.2865
10	11.2227	1.5010	90.7855
11	11.0281	1.6955	89.0900
12	10.8084	1.9153	87.1747
13	10.5601	2.1636	85.0112
14	10.2797	2.4440	82.5672
15	9.9629	2.7608	79.8064
16	9.6050	3.1186	76.6878
17	9.2008	3.5228	73.1649
18	8.7442	3.9795	69.1854
19	8.2284	4.4953	64.6902
20	7.6457	5.0779	59.6122
21	6.9875	5.7361	53.8761
22	6.2440	6.4796	47.3964
23	5.4041	7.3195	40.0769
24	4.4554	8.2683	31.8087
25	3.3837	9.3400	22.4687
26	2.1731	10.5506	11.9181
27	.8055	11.9181	0.0000

YEARS 28 MO PAYT 1.0556 AN CONST 12.67

#	INT	PRIN	BALANCE
1	12.2257	.4417	99.5583
2	12.1685	.4990	99.0593
3	12.1038	.5636	98.4957
4	12.0308	.6367	97.8590
5	11.9482	.7192	97.1398
6	11.8550	.8124	96.3273
7	11.7497	.9178	95.4096
8	11.6307	1.0367	94.3729
9	11.4964	1.1711	93.2018
10	11.3446	1.3229	91.8789
11	11.1731	1.4943	90.3845
12	10.9794	1.6880	88.6965
13	10.7606	1.9068	86.7896
14	10.5135	2.1540	84.6356
15	10.2343	2.4332	82.2024
16	9.9189	2.7486	79.4539
17	9.5626	3.1048	76.3490
18	9.1602	3.5073	72.8417
19	8.7056	3.9619	68.8798
20	8.1920	4.4754	64.4044
21	7.6119	5.0555	59.3489
22	6.9567	5.7108	53.6381
23	6.2164	6.4510	47.1871
24	5.3803	7.2872	39.8999
25	4.4357	8.2317	31.6682
26	3.3688	9.2987	22.3695
27	2.1635	10.5040	11.8655
28	.8020	11.8655	0.0000

YEARS 29 MO PAYT 1.0515 AN CONST 12.62

#	INT	PRIN	BALANCE
1	12.2286	.3895	99.6105
2	12.1781	.4400	99.1705
3	12.1211	.4970	98.6735
4	12.0567	.5614	98.1120
5	11.9839	.6342	97.4778
6	11.9017	.7164	96.7614
7	11.8088	.8093	95.9521
8	11.7039	.9142	95.0379
9	11.5854	1.0327	94.0053
10	11.4516	1.1665	92.8387
11	11.3004	1.3177	91.5210
12	11.1296	1.4885	90.0325
13	10.9366	1.6815	88.3510
14	10.7187	1.8994	86.4516
15	10.4725	2.1456	84.3060
16	10.1944	2.4237	81.8823
17	9.8802	2.7379	79.1444
18	9.5254	3.0928	76.0516
19	9.1245	3.4936	72.5580
20	8.6717	3.9465	68.6115
21	8.1601	4.4580	64.1536
22	7.5823	5.0358	59.1177
23	6.9296	5.6886	53.4292
24	6.1922	6.4259	47.0033
25	5.3593	7.2588	39.7445
26	4.4184	8.1997	31.5448
27	3.3556	9.2625	22.2823
28	2.1551	10.4631	11.8193
29	.7989	11.8193	0.0000

YEARS 30 MO PAYT 1.0479 AN CONST 12.58

#	INT	PRIN	BALANCE
1	12.2311	.3436	99.6564
2	12.1866	.3882	99.2682
3	12.1363	.4385	98.8297
4	12.0794	.4953	98.3344
5	12.0152	.5595	97.7749
6	11.9427	.6320	97.1429
7	11.8608	.7140	96.4289
8	11.7683	.8065	95.6224
9	11.6637	.9110	94.7114
10	11.5456	1.0291	93.6822
11	11.4122	1.1625	92.5197
12	11.2616	1.3132	91.2065
13	11.0913	1.4834	89.7231
14	10.8991	1.6757	88.0474
15	10.6819	1.8929	86.1545
16	10.4365	2.1382	84.0163
17	10.1594	2.4154	81.6009
18	9.8463	2.7285	78.8724
19	9.4926	3.0821	75.7903
20	9.0931	3.4816	72.3087
21	8.6419	3.9329	68.3758
22	8.1321	4.4427	63.9331
23	7.5562	5.0185	58.9146
24	6.9057	5.6690	53.2456
25	6.1709	6.4038	46.8418
26	5.3409	7.2339	39.6079
27	4.4033	8.1715	31.4364
28	3.3441	9.2307	22.2058
29	2.1476	10.4271	11.7786
30	.7961	11.7786	0.0000

YEARS 2 — MO PAYT 4.7214 — AN CONST 56.66

#	INT	PRIN	BALANCE
1	9.7120	46.9445	53.0555
2	3.6009	53.0555	0.0000

YEARS 3 — MO PAYT 3.3358 — AN CONST 40.03

#	INT	PRIN	BALANCE
1	10.6821	29.3472	70.6528
2	6.8618	33.1676	37.4852
3	2.5441	37.4852	0.0000

YEARS 4 — MO PAYT 2.6481 — AN CONST 31.78

#	INT	PRIN	BALANCE
1	11.1636	20.6141	79.3859
2	8.4801	23.2976	56.0883
3	5.4473	26.3304	29.7580
4	2.0197	29.7580	0.0000

YEARS 5 — MO PAYT 2.2396 — AN CONST 26.88

#	INT	PRIN	BALANCE
1	11.4496	15.4260	84.5740
2	9.4415	17.4342	67.1398
3	7.1719	19.7037	47.4361
4	4.6070	22.2686	25.1675
5	1.7081	25.1675	0.0000

YEARS 6 — MO PAYT 1.9707 — AN CONST 23.65

#	INT	PRIN	BALANCE
1	11.6379	12.0100	87.9900
2	10.0745	13.5734	74.4166
3	8.3075	15.3403	59.0763
4	6.3106	17.3373	41.7391
5	4.0537	19.5942	22.1449
6	1.5030	22.1449	0.0000

YEARS 7 — MO PAYT 1.7814 — AN CONST 21.38

#	INT	PRIN	BALANCE
1	11.7704	9.6059	90.3941
2	10.5200	10.8563	79.5378
3	9.1067	12.2695	67.2683
4	7.5095	13.8668	53.4015
5	5.7044	15.6719	37.7297
6	3.6643	17.7120	20.0177
7	1.3586	20.0177	0.0000

YEARS 8 — MO PAYT 1.6418 — AN CONST 19.71

#	INT	PRIN	BALANCE
1	11.8681	7.8336	92.1664
2	10.8484	8.8534	83.3130
3	9.6959	10.0059	73.3072
4	8.3934	11.3084	61.9988
5	6.9213	12.7805	49.2183
6	5.2575	14.4442	34.7741
7	3.3772	16.3245	18.4496
8	1.2522	18.4496	0.0000

YEARS 9 — MO PAYT 1.5354 — AN CONST 18.43

#	INT	PRIN	BALANCE
1	11.9426	6.4820	93.5180
2	11.0988	7.3258	86.1921
3	10.1452	8.2795	77.9126
4	9.0674	9.3573	68.5554
5	7.8493	10.5754	57.9800
6	6.4726	11.9520	46.0279
7	4.9167	13.5079	32.5200
8	3.1583	15.2663	17.2537
9	1.1710	17.2537	0.0000

YEARS 10 — MO PAYT 1.4521 — AN CONST 17.43

#	INT	PRIN	BALANCE
1	12.0010	5.4243	94.5757
2	11.2948	6.1304	88.4453
3	10.4968	6.9285	81.5168
4	9.5949	7.8304	73.6864
5	8.5755	8.8497	64.8367
6	7.4235	10.0017	54.8350
7	6.1215	11.3037	43.5312
8	4.6500	12.7752	30.7560
9	2.9870	14.4383	16.3178
10	1.1075	16.3178	0.0000

YEARS 11 — MO PAYT 1.3856 — AN CONST 16.63

#	INT	PRIN	BALANCE
1	12.0475	4.5797	95.4203
2	11.4513	5.1759	90.2444
3	10.7776	5.8497	84.3947
4	10.0161	6.6112	77.7836
5	9.1555	7.4718	70.3118
6	8.1828	8.4444	61.8674
7	7.0835	9.5437	52.3237
8	5.8412	10.7861	41.5376
9	4.4371	12.1901	29.3475
10	2.8502	13.7770	15.5705
11	1.0568	15.5705	0.0000

YEARS 12 — MO PAYT 1.3316 — AN CONST 15.98

#	INT	PRIN	BALANCE
1	12.0853	3.8944	96.1056
2	11.5783	4.4014	91.7042
3	11.0054	4.9743	86.7299
4	10.3578	5.6219	81.1081
5	9.6260	6.3537	74.7544
6	8.7989	7.1808	67.5736
7	7.8641	8.1156	59.4580
8	6.8077	9.1720	50.2860
9	5.6137	10.3660	39.9200
10	4.2643	11.7154	28.2046
11	2.7392	13.2405	14.9641
12	1.0156	14.9641	0.0000

YEARS 13 — MO PAYT 1.2873 — AN CONST 15.45

#	INT	PRIN	BALANCE
1	12.1164	3.3311	96.6689
2	11.6827	3.7647	92.9043
3	11.1927	4.2548	88.6495
4	10.6388	4.8086	83.8409
5	10.0128	5.4346	78.4063
6	9.3054	6.1420	72.2643
7	8.5058	6.9416	65.3227
8	7.6022	7.8452	57.4774
9	6.5809	8.8665	48.6109
10	5.4267	10.0207	38.5902
11	4.1222	11.3252	27.2651
12	2.6480	12.7994	14.4656
13	.9818	14.4656	0.0000

YEARS 14 — MO PAYT 1.2504 — AN CONST 15.01

#	INT	PRIN	BALANCE
1	12.1422	2.8630	97.1370
2	11.7695	3.2357	93.9013
3	11.3483	3.6569	90.2444
4	10.8722	4.1329	86.1115
5	10.3342	4.6709	81.4405
6	9.7262	5.2790	76.1615
7	9.0390	5.9662	70.1953
8	8.2623	6.7429	63.4525
9	7.3845	7.6206	55.8319
10	6.3925	8.6126	47.2192
11	5.2713	9.7338	37.4854
12	4.0042	11.0009	26.4845
13	2.5722	12.4330	14.0515
14	.9537	14.0515	0.0000

YEARS 15 — MO PAYT 1.2195 — AN CONST 14.64

#	INT	PRIN	BALANCE
1	12.1638	2.4706	97.5294
2	11.8422	2.7923	94.7371
3	11.4787	3.1557	91.5814
4	11.0679	3.5665	88.0148
5	10.6036	4.0308	83.9840
6	10.0789	4.5555	79.4284
7	9.4859	5.1486	74.2799
8	8.8156	5.8188	68.4611
9	8.0582	6.5763	61.8848
10	7.2021	7.4323	54.4525
11	6.2346	8.3999	46.0526
12	5.1411	9.4933	36.5593
13	3.9053	10.7291	25.8301
14	2.5086	12.1258	13.7043
15	.9301	13.7043	0.0000

YEARS 16 — MO PAYT 1.1934 — AN CONST 14.33

#	INT	PRIN	BALANCE
1	12.1821	2.1393	97.8607
2	11.9036	2.4178	95.4429
3	11.5888	2.7325	92.7104
4	11.2331	3.0882	89.6222
5	10.8311	3.4902	86.1319
6	10.3768	3.9446	82.1873
7	9.8633	4.4581	77.7292
8	9.2829	5.0384	72.6908
9	8.6270	5.6943	66.9965
10	7.8858	6.4356	60.5609
11	7.0480	7.2733	53.2876
12	6.1012	8.2202	45.0674
13	5.0311	9.2902	35.7772
14	3.8218	10.4996	25.2776
15	2.4549	11.8664	13.4111
16	.9102	13.4111	0.0000

YEARS 17 — MO PAYT 1.1713 — AN CONST 14.06

#	INT	PRIN	BALANCE
1	12.1976	1.8577	98.1423
2	11.9558	2.0996	96.0427
3	11.6824	2.3729	93.6699
4	11.3735	2.6818	90.9881
5	11.0244	3.0309	87.9572
6	10.6299	3.4254	84.5318
7	10.1840	3.8713	80.6605
8	9.6800	4.3753	76.2852
9	9.1105	4.9448	71.3404
10	8.4668	5.5885	65.7519
11	7.7393	6.3160	59.4358
12	6.9171	7.1382	52.2976
13	5.9879	8.0675	44.2302
14	4.9377	9.1176	35.1125
15	3.7508	10.3046	24.8080
16	2.4093	11.6460	13.1620
17	.8933	13.1620	0.0000

YEARS 18 — MO PAYT 1.1523 — AN CONST 13.83

#	INT	PRIN	BALANCE
1	12.2108	1.6172	98.3828
2	12.0003	1.8277	96.5552
3	11.7624	2.0656	94.4896
4	11.4935	2.3345	92.1551
5	11.1896	2.6384	89.5167
6	10.8462	2.9818	86.5348
7	10.4580	3.3700	83.1648
8	10.0193	3.8087	79.3561
9	9.5235	4.3045	75.0516
10	8.9631	4.8649	70.1867
11	8.3299	5.4982	64.6886
12	7.6141	6.2139	58.4747
13	6.8052	7.0228	51.4519
14	5.8910	7.9370	43.5149
15	4.8578	8.9702	34.5447
16	3.6901	10.1379	24.4068
17	2.3704	11.4576	12.9491
18	.8789	12.9491	0.0000

YEARS 19 — MO PAYT 1.1361 — AN CONST 13.64

#	INT	PRIN	BALANCE
1	12.2222	1.4107	98.5893
2	12.0386	1.5943	96.9949
3	11.8310	1.8019	95.1930
4	11.5965	2.0365	93.1566
5	11.3314	2.3016	90.8550
6	11.0318	2.6012	88.2539
7	10.6932	2.9398	85.3141
8	10.3105	3.3225	81.9916
9	9.8780	3.7550	78.2366
10	9.3891	4.2438	73.9928
11	8.8367	4.7962	69.1966
12	8.2123	5.4206	63.7760
13	7.5067	6.1262	57.6498
14	6.7092	6.9237	50.7260
15	5.8079	7.8250	42.9010
16	4.7893	8.8437	34.0574
17	3.6380	9.9949	24.0625
18	2.3369	11.2960	12.7665
19	.8665	12.7665	0.0000

YEARS 20 — MO PAYT 1.1221 — AN CONST 13.47

#	INT	PRIN	BALANCE
1	12.2320	1.2328	98.7672
2	12.0715	1.3933	97.3739
3	11.8902	1.5747	95.7992
4	11.6852	1.7797	94.0195
5	11.4535	2.0114	92.0081
6	11.1917	2.2732	89.7349
7	10.8958	2.5691	87.1658
8	10.5613	2.9035	84.2623
9	10.1834	3.2815	80.9808
10	9.7562	3.7087	77.2721
11	9.2734	4.1915	73.0806
12	8.7278	4.7371	68.3435
13	8.1111	5.3538	62.9897
14	7.4142	6.0507	56.9390
15	6.6265	6.8384	50.1007
16	5.7363	7.7286	42.3721
17	4.7302	8.7346	33.6375
18	3.5932	9.8717	23.7658
19	2.3081	11.1567	12.6091
20	.8558	12.6091	0.0000

YEARS 21 — MO PAYT 1.1100 — AN CONST 13.32

#	INT	PRIN	BALANCE
1	12.2405	1.0791	98.9209
2	12.1000	1.2195	97.7014
3	11.9413	1.3783	96.3231

#	INT	PRIN	BALANCE
4	11.7619	1.5577	94.7654
5	11.5591	1.7605	93.0049
6	11.3299	1.9897	91.0153
7	11.0709	2.2487	88.7666
8	10.7782	2.5414	86.2253
9	10.4474	2.8722	83.3530
10	10.0735	3.2461	80.1069
11	9.6509	3.6687	76.4383
12	9.1733	4.1462	72.2920
13	8.6536	4.6860	67.6060
14	8.0236	5.2960	62.3100
15	7.3342	5.9854	56.3246
16	6.5550	6.7646	49.5601
17	5.6744	7.6452	41.9149
18	4.6792	8.6404	33.2745
19	3.5544	9.7652	23.5094
20	2.2832	11.0363	12.4730
21	.8465	12.4730	0.0000

YEARS 22 — MO PAYT 1.0995 — AN CONST 13.20

#	INT	PRIN	BALANCE
1	12.2479	.9457	99.0543
2	12.1247	1.0689	97.9854
3	11.9856	1.2080	96.7774
4	11.8284	1.3652	95.4122
5	11.6506	1.5430	93.8692
6	11.4498	1.7438	92.1254
7	11.2228	1.9708	90.1545
8	10.9662	2.2274	87.9271
9	10.6763	2.5173	85.4098
10	10.3486	2.8450	82.5647
11	9.9782	3.2154	79.3493
12	9.5596	3.6340	75.7154
13	9.0866	4.1070	71.6083
14	8.5519	4.6417	66.9667
15	7.9477	5.2459	61.7208
16	7.2648	5.9288	55.7920
17	6.4930	6.7006	49.0914
18	5.6207	7.5729	41.5185
19	4.6349	8.5587	32.9598
20	3.5208	9.6728	23.2870
21	2.2616	10.9320	12.3551
22	.8385	12.3551	0.0000

YEARS 23 — MO PAYT 1.0903 — AN CONST 13.09

#	INT	PRIN	BALANCE
1	12.2542	.8299	99.1701
2	12.1462	.9379	98.2322
3	12.0241	1.0600	97.1723
4	11.8861	1.1980	95.9743
5	11.7302	1.3539	94.6204
6	11.5539	1.5302	93.0902
7	11.3548	1.7294	91.3608
8	11.1296	1.9545	89.4064
9	10.8752	2.2089	87.1975
10	10.5877	2.4965	84.7010
11	10.2627	2.8214	81.8796
12	9.8954	3.1887	78.6908
13	9.4803	3.6038	75.0870
14	9.0112	4.0729	71.0141
15	8.4810	4.6032	66.4109
16	7.8817	5.2024	61.2086
17	7.2045	5.8796	55.3290
18	6.4391	6.6450	48.6840
19	5.5741	7.5100	41.1740
20	4.5965	8.4876	32.6863
21	3.4916	9.5925	23.0938
22	2.2429	10.8413	12.2525
23	.8316	12.2525	0.0000

YEARS 24 — MO PAYT 1.0824 — AN CONST 12.99

#	INT	PRIN	BALANCE
1	12.2598	.7289	99.2711
2	12.1649	.8238	98.4473
3	12.0577	.9311	97.5162
4	11.9365	1.0523	96.4639
5	11.7995	1.1892	95.2747
6	11.6447	1.3440	93.9307
7	11.4697	1.5190	92.4116
8	11.2720	1.7168	90.6949
9	11.0485	1.9402	88.7547
10	10.7959	2.1928	86.5619
11	10.5105	2.4783	84.0836
12	10.1879	2.8009	81.2827
13	9.8233	3.1655	78.1173
14	9.4112	3.5775	74.5397
15	8.9455	4.0433	70.4964
16	8.4191	4.5696	65.9268
17	7.8243	5.1645	60.7624
18	7.1520	5.8367	54.9256
19	6.3922	6.5966	48.3291
20	5.5335	7.4553	40.8738
21	4.5630	8.4258	32.4481
22	3.4661	9.5226	22.9254
23	2.2265	10.7622	12.1632
24	.8255	12.1632	0.0000

YEARS 25 — MO PAYT 1.0755 — AN CONST 12.91

#	INT	PRIN	BALANCE
1	12.2647	.6408	99.3592
2	12.1812	.7243	98.6349
3	12.0870	.8185	97.8164
4	11.9804	.9251	96.8913
5	11.8600	1.0455	95.8458
6	11.7239	1.1816	94.6642
7	11.5701	1.3354	93.3287
8	11.3962	1.5093	91.8194
9	11.1998	1.7058	90.1137
10	10.9777	1.9278	88.1859
11	10.7268	2.1788	86.0071
12	10.4431	2.4624	83.5448
13	10.1226	2.7829	80.7618
14	9.7603	3.1452	77.6166
15	9.3509	3.5546	74.0620
16	8.8882	4.0174	70.0447
17	8.3652	4.5403	65.5044
18	7.7741	5.1314	60.3730
19	7.1062	5.7993	54.5737
20	6.3512	6.5543	48.0194
21	5.4980	7.4075	40.6119
22	4.5337	8.3718	32.2401
23	3.4439	9.4616	22.7785
24	2.2122	10.6933	12.0853
25	.8202	12.0853	0.0000

YEARS 26 — MO PAYT 1.0694 — AN CONST 12.84

#	INT	PRIN	BALANCE
1	12.2689	.5638	99.4362
2	12.1955	.6372	98.7990
3	12.1126	.7202	98.0788
4	12.0188	.8139	97.2649
5	11.9129	.9199	96.3450
6	11.7931	1.0396	95.3054
7	11.6578	1.1750	94.1304
8	11.5048	1.3279	92.8025
9	11.3320	1.5008	91.3017
10	11.1366	1.6961	89.6056
11	10.9158	1.9169	87.6887
12	10.6663	2.1665	85.5222
13	10.3842	2.4485	83.0737
14	10.0655	2.7672	80.3065
15	9.7053	3.1275	77.1790
16	9.2982	3.5346	73.6444
17	8.8380	3.9947	69.6497
18	8.3180	4.5147	65.1350
19	7.7303	5.1024	60.0326
20	7.0661	5.7666	54.2660
21	6.3154	6.5173	47.7486
22	5.4670	7.3657	40.3829
23	4.5082	8.3246	32.0583
24	3.4245	9.4082	22.6501
25	2.1998	10.6330	12.0171
26	.8156	12.0171	0.0000

YEARS 27 — MO PAYT 1.0641 — AN CONST 12.77

#	INT	PRIN	BALANCE
1	12.2726	.4964	99.5036
2	12.2080	.5610	98.9426
3	12.1350	.6341	98.3085
4	12.0524	.7166	97.5919
5	11.9592	.8099	96.7820
6	11.8537	.9153	95.8667
7	11.7346	1.0345	94.8323
8	11.5999	1.1691	93.6631
9	11.4477	1.3213	92.3418
10	11.2757	1.4933	90.8485
11	11.0813	1.6877	89.1608
12	10.8616	1.9074	87.2534
13	10.6133	2.1557	85.0977
14	10.3327	2.4363	82.6613
15	10.0155	2.7535	79.9078
16	9.6571	3.1119	76.7959
17	9.2520	3.5170	73.2789
18	8.7942	3.9749	69.3040
19	8.2767	4.4923	64.8117
20	7.6919	5.0771	59.7346
21	7.0310	5.7380	53.9966
22	6.2841	6.4850	47.5116
23	5.4399	7.3292	40.1825
24	4.4858	8.2832	31.8992
25	3.4075	9.3615	22.5377
26	2.1889	10.5802	11.9575
27	.8116	11.9575	0.0000

YEARS 28 — MO PAYT 1.0594 — AN CONST 12.72

#	INT	PRIN	BALANCE
1	12.2759	.4373	99.5627
2	12.2190	.4942	99.0685
3	12.1546	.5586	98.5099
4	12.0819	.6313	97.8786
5	11.9997	.7135	97.1651
6	11.9069	.8063	96.3588
7	11.8019	.9113	95.4475
8	11.6833	1.0299	94.4176
9	11.5492	1.1640	93.2536
10	11.3977	1.3155	91.9380
11	11.2264	1.4868	90.4512
12	11.0329	1.6803	88.7709
13	10.8141	1.8991	86.8718
14	10.5669	2.1463	84.7255
15	10.2875	2.4257	82.2999
16	9.9717	2.7415	79.5584
17	9.6149	3.0983	76.4601
18	9.2115	3.5017	72.9584
19	8.7557	3.9575	69.0009
20	8.2405	4.4727	64.5283
21	7.6583	5.0549	59.4734
22	7.0003	5.7129	53.7605
23	6.2566	6.4566	47.3038
24	5.4161	7.2971	40.0067
25	4.4662	8.2470	31.7597
26	3.3926	9.3206	22.4391
27	2.1793	10.5339	11.9052
28	.8080	11.9052	0.0000

YEARS 29 — MO PAYT 1.0553 — AN CONST 12.67

#	INT	PRIN	BALANCE
1	12.2788	.3854	99.6146
2	12.2286	.4356	99.1789
3	12.1719	.4923	98.6866
4	12.1078	.5564	98.1302
5	12.0353	.6289	97.5013
6	11.9535	.7107	96.7906
7	11.8610	.8032	95.9874
8	11.7564	.9078	95.0796
9	11.6382	1.0260	94.0536
10	11.5047	1.1595	92.8941
11	11.3537	1.3105	91.5836
12	11.1831	1.4811	90.1026
13	10.9903	1.6739	88.4287
14	10.7724	1.8918	86.5370
15	10.5262	2.1380	84.3990
16	10.2479	2.4163	81.9826
17	9.9333	2.7309	79.2517
18	9.5778	3.0864	76.1654
19	9.1760	3.4882	72.6772
20	8.7220	3.9422	68.7350
21	8.2088	4.4554	64.2796
22	7.6288	5.0354	59.2441
23	6.9733	5.6909	53.5532
24	6.2325	6.4317	47.1215
25	5.3952	7.2690	39.8525
26	4.4490	8.2152	31.6373
27	3.3795	9.2847	22.3526
28	2.1709	10.4933	11.8593
29	.8049	11.8593	0.0000

YEARS 30 — MO PAYT 1.0518 — AN CONST 12.63

#	INT	PRIN	BALANCE
1	12.2813	.3399	99.6601
2	12.2370	.3841	99.2760
3	12.1870	.4341	98.8418
4	12.1305	.4907	98.3512
5	12.0666	.5545	97.7967
6	11.9944	.6267	97.1699
7	11.9129	.7083	96.4616
8	11.8207	.8005	95.6611
9	11.7164	.9047	94.7564
10	11.5987	1.0225	93.7340
11	11.4656	1.1556	92.5784
12	11.3151	1.3060	91.2724
13	11.1451	1.4760	89.7963
14	10.9530	1.6682	88.1282
15	10.7358	1.8853	86.2429
16	10.4904	2.1307	84.1121
17	10.2130	2.4081	81.7040
18	9.8995	2.7216	78.9824
19	9.5453	3.0759	75.9065
20	9.1449	3.4763	72.4302
21	8.6923	3.9288	68.5014
22	8.1809	4.4403	64.0611
23	7.6029	5.0183	59.0428
24	6.9496	5.6716	53.3712
25	6.2113	6.4099	46.9614
26	5.3769	7.2443	39.7171
27	4.4338	8.1873	31.5298
28	3.3680	9.2531	22.2766
29	2.1635	10.4577	11.8190
30	.8022	11.8190	0.0000

MONTHLY PAYMENT AMORTIZATION SCHEDULE PER $100

12.375%

YEARS 2 — MO PAYT 4.7249 — AN CONST 56.70

#	INT	PRIN	BALANCE
1	9.7726	46.9260	53.0740
2	3.6245	53.0740	0.0000

YEARS 3 — MO PAYT 3.3394 — AN CONST 40.08

#	INT	PRIN	BALANCE
1	10.7488	29.3237	70.6763
2	6.9069	33.1656	37.5108
3	2.5617	37.5108	0.0000

YEARS 4 — MO PAYT 2.6518 — AN CONST 31.83

#	INT	PRIN	BALANCE
1	11.2332	20.5888	79.4112
2	8.5357	23.2863	56.1249
3	5.4848	26.3372	29.7877
4	2.0343	29.7877	0.0000

YEARS 5 — MO PAYT 2.2434 — AN CONST 26.93

#	INT	PRIN	BALANCE
1	11.5209	15.4004	84.5996
2	9.5032	17.4181	67.1816
3	7.2212	19.7001	47.4815
4	4.6402	22.2811	25.2003
5	1.7210	25.2003	0.0000

YEARS 6 — MO PAYT 1.9746 — AN CONST 23.70

#	INT	PRIN	BALANCE
1	11.7104	11.9845	88.0155
2	10.1402	13.5547	74.4608
3	8.3643	15.3306	59.1302
4	6.3558	17.3391	41.7910
5	4.0841	19.6108	22.1802
6	1.5147	22.1802	0.0000

YEARS 7 — MO PAYT 1.7854 — AN CONST 21.43

#	INT	PRIN	BALANCE
1	11.8437	9.5810	90.4190
2	10.5884	10.8363	79.5827
3	9.1687	12.2560	67.3266
4	7.5629	13.8618	53.4649
5	5.7468	15.6779	37.7870
6	3.6928	17.7319	20.0551
7	1.3696	20.0551	0.0000

YEARS 8 — MO PAYT 1.6460 — AN CONST 19.76

#	INT	PRIN	BALANCE
1	11.9419	7.8096	92.1904
2	10.9187	8.8328	83.3576
3	9.7615	9.9900	73.3676
4	8.4526	11.2989	62.0687
5	6.9723	12.7792	49.2895
6	5.2980	14.4535	34.8360
7	3.4044	16.3471	18.4889
8	1.2626	18.4889	0.0000

YEARS 9 — MO PAYT 1.5396 — AN CONST 18.48

#	INT	PRIN	BALANCE
1	12.0168	6.4590	93.5410
2	11.1706	7.3052	86.2359
3	10.2135	8.2623	77.9736
4	9.1310	9.3448	68.6288
5	7.9067	10.5691	58.0597
6	6.5220	11.9538	46.1059
7	4.9558	13.5199	32.5859
8	3.1845	15.2913	17.2947
9	1.1811	17.2947	0.0000

YEARS 10 — MO PAYT 1.4565 — AN CONST 17.48

#	INT	PRIN	BALANCE
1	12.0754	5.4023	94.5977
2	11.3676	6.1100	88.4877
3	10.5671	6.9105	81.5772
4	9.6617	7.8159	73.7612
5	8.6377	8.8399	64.9213
6	7.4795	9.9981	54.9232
7	6.1696	11.3080	43.6151
8	4.6881	12.7896	30.8256
9	3.0125	14.4652	16.3604
10	1.1173	16.3604	0.0000

YEARS 11 — MO PAYT 1.3901 — AN CONST 16.69

#	INT	PRIN	BALANCE
1	12.1222	4.5587	95.4413
2	11.5249	5.1560	90.2853
3	10.8494	5.8315	84.4538
4	10.0854	6.5955	77.8583
5	9.2213	7.4596	70.3987
6	8.2439	8.4370	61.9617
7	7.1386	9.5423	52.4194
8	5.8884	10.7925	41.6269
9	4.4744	12.2065	29.4203
10	2.8751	13.8058	15.6146
11	1.0663	15.6146	0.0000

YEARS 12 — MO PAYT 1.3362 — AN CONST 16.04

#	INT	PRIN	BALANCE
1	12.1601	3.8745	96.1255
2	11.6525	4.3821	91.7434
3	11.0784	4.9562	86.7872
4	10.4290	5.6056	81.1817
5	9.6946	6.3400	74.8417
6	8.8640	7.1706	67.6711
7	7.9245	8.1101	59.5610
8	6.8620	9.1726	50.3884
9	5.6602	10.3744	40.0140
10	4.3010	11.7336	28.2804
11	2.7637	13.2709	15.0096
12	1.0250	15.0096	0.0000

YEARS 13 — MO PAYT 1.2920 — AN CONST 15.51

#	INT	PRIN	BALANCE
1	12.1913	3.3122	96.6878
2	11.7574	3.7461	92.9417
3	11.2666	4.2369	88.7047
4	10.7115	4.7921	83.9127
5	10.0836	5.4199	78.4928
6	9.3735	6.1300	72.3628
7	8.5704	6.9331	65.4297
8	7.6621	7.8414	57.5883
9	6.6347	8.8688	48.7194
10	5.4727	10.0308	38.6887
11	4.1586	11.3449	27.3437
12	2.6722	12.8313	14.5124
13	.9911	14.5124	0.0000

YEARS 14 — MO PAYT 1.2552 — AN CONST 15.07

#	INT	PRIN	BALANCE
1	12.2172	2.8452	97.1548
2	11.8444	3.2180	93.9369
3	11.4228	3.6396	90.2973
4	10.9460	4.1164	86.1809
5	10.4067	4.6557	81.5252
6	9.7967	5.2657	76.2595
7	9.1068	5.9556	70.3039
8	8.3266	6.7358	63.5681
9	7.4441	7.6183	55.9498
10	6.4459	8.6165	47.3333
11	5.3170	9.7454	37.5879
12	4.0402	11.0222	26.5658
13	2.5962	12.4662	14.0995
14	.9629	14.0995	0.0000

YEARS 15 — MO PAYT 1.2244 — AN CONST 14.70

#	INT	PRIN	BALANCE
1	12.2389	2.4539	97.5461
2	11.9174	2.7754	94.7708
3	11.5538	3.1390	91.6318
4	11.1425	3.5502	88.0815
5	10.6774	4.0154	84.0661
6	10.1513	4.5415	79.5247
7	9.5563	5.1365	74.3882
8	8.8834	5.8094	68.5788
9	8.1222	6.5706	62.0082
10	7.2614	7.4314	54.5768
11	6.2878	8.4050	46.1718
12	5.1866	9.5062	36.6656
13	3.9411	10.7517	25.9139
14	2.5325	12.1603	13.7535
15	.9393	13.7535	0.0000

YEARS 16 — MO PAYT 1.1984 — AN CONST 14.39

#	INT	PRIN	BALANCE
1	12.2572	2.1235	97.8765
2	11.9790	2.4018	95.4747
3	11.6643	2.7164	92.7583
4	11.3084	3.0723	89.6859
5	10.9059	3.4749	86.2111
6	10.4507	3.9301	82.2810
7	9.9358	4.4450	77.8359
8	9.3534	5.0274	72.8085
9	8.6947	5.6861	67.1225
10	7.9498	6.4310	60.6915
11	7.1072	7.2736	53.4179
12	6.1542	8.2265	45.1913
13	5.0764	9.3044	35.8870
14	3.8574	10.5234	25.3636
15	2.4787	11.9021	13.4615
16	.9193	13.4615	0.0000

YEARS 17 — MO PAYT 1.1763 — AN CONST 14.12

#	INT	PRIN	BALANCE
1	12.2728	1.8430	98.1570
2	12.0313	2.0844	96.0726
3	11.7582	2.3575	93.7151
4	11.4494	2.6664	91.0488
5	11.1000	3.0157	88.0331
6	10.7049	3.4108	84.6222
7	10.2581	3.8577	80.7646
8	9.7526	4.3631	76.4014
9	9.1810	4.9347	71.4667
10	8.5345	5.5813	65.8854
11	7.8032	6.3125	59.5729
12	6.9762	7.1395	52.4334
13	6.0408	8.0749	44.3585
14	4.9829	9.1329	35.2256
15	3.7863	10.3294	24.8961
16	2.4330	11.6828	13.2134
17	.9024	13.2134	0.0000

YEARS 18 — MO PAYT 1.1575 — AN CONST 13.89

#	INT	PRIN	BALANCE
1	12.2861	1.6033	98.3967
2	12.0760	1.8134	96.5833
3	11.8384	2.0510	94.5323
4	11.5697	2.3197	92.2126
5	11.2658	2.6236	89.5889
6	10.9221	2.9674	86.6216
7	10.5333	3.3561	83.2655
8	10.0936	3.7958	79.4696
9	9.5963	4.2931	75.1765
10	9.0338	4.8556	70.3209
11	8.3976	5.4918	64.8291
12	7.6781	6.2113	58.6178
13	6.8644	7.0251	51.5927
14	5.9440	7.9455	43.6472
15	4.9030	8.9865	34.6608
16	3.7256	10.1638	24.4970
17	2.3940	11.4954	13.0015
18	.8879	13.0015	0.0000

YEARS 19 — MO PAYT 1.1413 — AN CONST 13.70

#	INT	PRIN	BALANCE
1	12.2975	1.3978	98.6022
2	12.1143	1.5809	97.0213
3	11.9072	1.7881	95.2332
4	11.6730	2.0223	93.2109
5	11.4080	2.2873	90.9236
6	11.1083	2.5869	88.3367
7	10.7694	2.9259	85.4108
8	10.3861	3.3092	82.1016
9	9.9525	3.7428	78.3588
10	9.4621	4.2331	74.1257
11	8.9075	4.7877	69.3379
12	8.2803	5.4150	63.9229
13	7.5708	6.1245	57.7984
14	6.7684	6.9269	50.8715
15	5.8609	7.8344	43.0371
16	4.8344	8.8608	34.1763
17	3.6735	10.0217	24.1545
18	2.3605	11.3348	12.8198
19	.8755	12.8198	0.0000

YEARS 20 — MO PAYT 1.1273 — AN CONST 13.53

#	INT	PRIN	BALANCE
1	12.3073	1.2208	98.7792
2	12.1474	1.3807	97.3985
3	11.9665	1.5616	95.8368
4	11.7619	1.7662	94.0706
5	11.5305	1.9976	92.0730
6	11.2687	2.2594	89.8136
7	10.9727	2.5554	87.2583
8	10.6379	2.8902	84.3681
9	10.2593	3.2688	81.0993
10	9.8310	3.6971	77.4022
11	9.3466	4.1815	73.2207
12	8.7988	4.7293	68.4914
13	8.1792	5.3489	63.1425
14	7.4784	6.0497	57.0928
15	6.6858	6.8423	50.2505
16	5.7893	7.7388	42.5117
17	4.7754	8.7527	33.7591
18	3.6287	9.8994	23.8597
19	2.3317	11.1964	12.6633
20	.8648	12.6633	0.0000

YEARS 21 — MO PAYT 1.1153 — AN CONST 13.39

#	INT	PRIN	BALANCE
1	12.3158	1.0678	98.9322
2	12.1759	1.2078	97.7244
3	12.0176	1.3660	96.3584

MONTHLY PAYMENT AMORTIZATION SCHEDULE PER $100

12.375%

#	INT	PRIN	BALANCE
4	11.8387	1.5450	94.8135
5	11.6363	1.7474	93.0661
6	11.4073	1.9763	91.0898
7	11.1484	2.2352	88.8546
8	10.8555	2.5281	86.3265
9	10.5243	2.8593	83.4672
10	10.1497	3.2339	80.2333
11	9.7260	3.6576	76.5757
12	9.2468	4.1368	72.4389
13	8.7048	4.6788	67.7601
14	8.0918	5.2918	62.4683
15	7.3985	5.9851	56.4832
16	6.6144	6.7692	49.7139
17	5.7275	7.6561	42.0578
18	4.7244	8.6592	33.3986
19	3.5899	9.7937	23.6049
20	2.3068	11.0768	12.5281
21	.8556	12.5281	0.0000

YEARS 22 — MO PAYT 1.1049 — AN CONST 13.26

#	INT	PRIN	BALANCE
1	12.3231	.9353	99.0647
2	12.2006	1.0579	98.0068
3	12.0620	1.1965	96.8104
4	11.9052	1.3532	95.4572
5	11.7279	1.5305	93.9266
6	11.5274	1.7310	92.1956
7	11.3006	1.9578	90.2378
8	11.0441	2.2143	88.0235
9	10.7540	2.5044	85.5190
10	10.4259	2.8326	82.6865
11	10.0548	3.2037	79.4828
12	9.6351	3.6234	75.8594
13	9.1603	4.0991	71.7613
14	8.6234	4.6350	67.1263
15	8.0161	5.2423	61.8840
16	7.3293	5.9291	55.9549
17	6.5525	6.7059	49.2489
18	5.6739	7.5845	41.6644
19	4.6802	8.5782	33.0862
20	3.5564	9.7021	23.3841
21	2.2852	10.9732	12.4109
22	.8476	12.4109	0.0000

YEARS 23 — MO PAYT 1.0958 — AN CONST 13.15

#	INT	PRIN	BALANCE
1	12.3295	.8202	99.1798
2	12.2221	.9276	98.2522
3	12.1005	1.0492	97.2030
4	11.9631	1.1866	96.0163
5	11.8076	1.3421	94.6742
6	11.6318	1.5180	93.1563
7	11.4329	1.7168	91.4394
8	11.2079	1.9418	89.4977
9	10.9535	2.1962	87.3015
10	10.6658	2.4839	84.8176
11	10.3404	2.8093	82.0083
12	9.9723	3.1774	78.8309
13	9.5560	3.5937	75.2372
14	9.0852	4.0645	71.1727
15	8.5527	4.5970	66.5757
16	7.9504	5.1993	61.3764
17	7.2692	5.8805	55.4959
18	6.4988	6.6509	48.8450
19	5.6274	7.5223	41.3227
20	4.6419	8.5079	32.8148
21	3.5272	9.6225	23.1923
22	2.2665	10.8832	12.3091
23	.8406	12.3091	0.0000

YEARS 24 — MO PAYT 1.0879 — AN CONST 13.06

#	INT	PRIN	BALANCE
1	12.3351	.7200	99.2800
2	12.2407	.8143	98.4658
3	12.1341	.9210	97.5448
4	12.0134	1.0416	96.5032
5	11.8769	1.1781	95.3251
6	11.7226	1.3325	93.9926
7	11.5480	1.5070	92.4856
8	11.3506	1.7045	90.7811
9	11.1273	1.9278	88.8533
10	10.8747	2.1803	86.6730
11	10.5890	2.4660	84.2070
12	10.2659	2.7891	81.4179
13	9.9005	3.1545	78.2634
14	9.4872	3.5678	74.6956
15	9.0198	4.0352	70.6603
16	8.4911	4.5639	66.0964
17	7.8932	5.1619	60.9345
18	7.2169	5.8382	55.0964
19	6.4520	6.6030	48.4933
20	5.5869	7.4682	41.0252
21	4.6084	8.4466	32.5786
22	3.5018	9.5532	23.0253
23	2.2502	10.8049	12.2205
24	.8346	12.2205	0.0000

YEARS 25 — MO PAYT 1.0810 — AN CONST 12.98

#	INT	PRIN	BALANCE
1	12.3399	.6325	99.3675
2	12.2570	.7154	98.6521
3	12.1633	.8091	97.8429
4	12.0573	.9151	96.9278
5	11.9374	1.0350	95.8927
6	11.8018	1.1706	94.7221
7	11.6484	1.3240	93.3981
8	11.4750	1.4975	91.9006
9	11.2788	1.6937	90.2069
10	11.0569	1.9156	88.2913
11	10.8059	2.1666	86.1248
12	10.5220	2.4504	83.6743
13	10.2010	2.7715	80.9029
14	9.8379	3.1346	77.7683
15	9.4272	3.5452	74.2231
16	8.9627	4.0097	70.2134
17	8.4374	4.5351	65.6783
18	7.8432	5.1292	60.5491
19	7.1712	5.8012	54.7479
20	6.4112	6.5613	48.1866
21	5.5515	7.4209	40.7657
22	4.5793	8.3932	32.3725
23	3.4796	9.4928	22.8797
24	2.2359	10.7365	12.1432
25	.8293	12.1432	0.0000

YEARS 26 — MO PAYT 1.0750 — AN CONST 12.91

#	INT	PRIN	BALANCE
1	12.3442	.5562	99.4438
2	12.2713	.6290	98.8148
3	12.1889	.7114	98.1034
4	12.0957	.8046	97.2988
5	11.9903	.9101	96.3887
6	11.8710	1.0293	95.3594
7	11.7362	1.1641	94.1953
8	11.5836	1.3167	92.8786
9	11.4111	1.4892	91.3895
10	11.2160	1.6843	89.7052
11	10.9954	1.9049	87.8003
12	10.7458	2.1545	85.6458
13	10.4635	2.4368	83.2090
14	10.1443	2.7560	80.4529
15	9.7832	3.1171	77.3358
16	9.3748	3.5255	73.8103
17	8.9129	3.9874	69.8229
18	8.3905	4.5098	65.3131
19	7.7996	5.1007	60.2124
20	7.1313	5.7690	54.4434
21	6.3755	6.5248	47.9186
22	5.5207	7.3796	40.5390
23	4.5538	8.3465	32.1925
24	3.4603	9.4400	22.7524
25	2.2235	10.6768	12.0756
26	.8247	12.0756	0.0000

YEARS 27 — MO PAYT 1.0698 — AN CONST 12.84

#	INT	PRIN	BALANCE
1	12.3479	.4893	99.5107
2	12.2838	.5534	98.9573
3	12.2112	.6259	98.3313
4	12.1292	.7079	97.6234
5	12.0365	.8007	96.8227
6	11.9316	.9056	95.9171
7	11.8129	1.0242	94.8928
8	11.6787	1.1584	93.7344
9	11.5270	1.3102	92.4242
10	11.3553	1.4819	90.9423
11	11.1612	1.6760	89.2663
12	10.9416	1.8956	87.3707
13	10.6932	2.1440	85.2267
14	10.4123	2.4249	82.8018
15	10.0946	2.7426	80.0593
16	9.7353	3.1019	76.9574
17	9.3289	3.5083	73.4491
18	8.8693	3.9679	69.4812
19	8.3494	4.4878	64.9935
20	7.7614	5.0757	59.9177
21	7.0964	5.7407	54.1770
22	6.3443	6.4929	47.6841
23	5.4937	7.3435	40.3406
24	4.5315	8.3057	32.0349
25	3.4434	9.3938	22.6411
26	2.2126	10.6246	12.0166
27	.8206	12.0166	0.0000

YEARS 28 — MO PAYT 1.0652 — AN CONST 12.79

#	INT	PRIN	BALANCE
1	12.3511	.4308	99.5692
2	12.2947	.4872	99.0820
3	12.2308	.5510	98.5310
4	12.1586	.6232	97.9077
5	12.0770	.7049	97.2028
6	11.9846	.7972	96.4056
7	11.8802	.9017	95.5039
8	11.7620	1.0198	94.4840
9	11.6284	1.1535	93.3306
10	11.4773	1.3046	92.0260
11	11.3064	1.4755	90.5505
12	11.1131	1.6688	88.8817
13	10.8944	1.8874	86.9943
14	10.6472	2.1347	84.8596
15	10.3675	2.4144	82.4451
16	10.0511	2.7307	79.7144
17	9.6934	3.0885	76.6259
18	9.2887	3.4932	73.1327
19	8.8311	3.9508	69.1819
20	8.3135	4.4684	64.7135
21	7.7280	5.0539	59.6596
22	7.0659	5.7160	53.9436
23	6.3170	6.4649	47.4787
24	5.4700	7.3119	40.1668
25	4.5120	8.2699	31.8969
26	3.4285	9.3534	22.5436
27	2.2031	10.5788	11.9648
28	.8171	11.9648	0.0000

YEARS 29 — MO PAYT 1.0611 — AN CONST 12.74

#	INT	PRIN	BALANCE
1	12.3540	.3794	99.6206
2	12.3042	.4291	99.1914
3	12.2480	.4854	98.7061
4	12.1844	.5490	98.1571
5	12.1125	.6209	97.5362
6	12.0312	.7022	96.8340
7	11.9392	.7942	96.0398
8	11.8351	.8983	95.1415
9	11.7174	1.0160	94.1255
10	11.5843	1.1491	92.9765
11	11.4338	1.2996	91.6769
12	11.2635	1.4699	90.2070
13	11.0709	1.6625	88.5445
14	10.8531	1.8803	86.6642
15	10.6068	2.1266	84.5376
16	10.3281	2.4053	82.1323
17	10.0130	2.7204	79.4119
18	9.6566	3.0768	76.3351
19	9.2535	3.4799	72.8552
20	8.7976	3.9358	68.9194
21	8.2819	4.4515	64.4679
22	7.6987	5.0347	59.4333
23	7.0391	5.6943	53.7389
24	6.2930	6.4404	47.2986
25	5.4492	7.2842	40.0144
26	4.4949	8.2385	31.7759
27	3.4155	9.3179	22.4580
28	2.1947	10.5387	11.9194
29	.8140	11.9194	0.0000

YEARS 30 — MO PAYT 1.0576 — AN CONST 12.70

#	INT	PRIN	BALANCE
1	12.3565	.3344	99.6656
2	12.3127	.3782	99.2875
3	12.2631	.4277	98.8598
4	12.2071	.4837	98.3760
5	12.1437	.5471	97.8289
6	12.0720	.6188	97.2101
7	11.9909	.6999	96.5102
8	11.8992	.7916	95.7187
9	11.7955	.8953	94.8234
10	11.6782	1.0126	93.8108
11	11.5456	1.1452	92.6656
12	11.3955	1.2953	91.3703
13	11.2258	1.4650	89.9053
14	11.0339	1.6569	88.2484
15	10.8168	1.8740	86.3744
16	10.5713	2.1195	84.2549
17	10.2936	2.3972	81.8577
18	9.9795	2.7113	79.1464
19	9.6243	3.0665	76.0799
20	9.2225	3.4683	72.6117
21	8.7681	3.9227	68.6890
22	8.2542	4.4366	64.2524
23	7.6730	5.0179	59.2345
24	7.0155	5.6753	53.5593
25	6.2720	6.4188	47.1404
26	5.4310	7.2598	39.8806
27	4.4799	8.2109	31.6697
28	3.4041	9.2867	22.3830
29	2.1874	10.5034	11.8795
30	.8113	11.8795	0.0000

YEARS 2 — MO PAYT 4.7260 — AN CONST 56.72

#	INT	PRIN	BALANCE
1	9.7928	46.9198	53.0802
2	3.6324	53.0802	0.0000

YEARS 3 — MO PAYT 3.3406 — AN CONST 40.09

#	INT	PRIN	BALANCE
1	10.7710	29.3158	70.6842
2	6.9219	33.1649	37.5193
3	2.5675	37.5193	0.0000

YEARS 4 — MO PAYT 2.6531 — AN CONST 31.84

#	INT	PRIN	BALANCE
1	11.2564	20.5804	79.4196
2	8.5543	23.2825	56.1371
3	5.4974	26.3394	29.7977
4	2.0391	29.7977	0.0000

YEARS 5 — MO PAYT 2.2447 — AN CONST 26.94

#	INT	PRIN	BALANCE
1	11.5447	15.3918	84.6082
2	9.5238	17.4127	67.1955
3	7.2376	19.6989	47.4966
4	4.6512	22.2853	25.2113
5	1.7253	25.2113	0.0000

YEARS 6 — MO PAYT 1.9759 — AN CONST 23.72

#	INT	PRIN	BALANCE
1	11.7345	11.9761	88.0239
2	10.1621	13.5485	74.4754
3	8.3832	15.3273	59.1481
4	6.3708	17.3398	41.8083
5	4.0942	19.6164	22.1919
6	1.5186	22.1919	0.0000

YEARS 7 — MO PAYT 1.7867 — AN CONST 21.45

#	INT	PRIN	BALANCE
1	11.8681	9.5728	90.4272
2	10.6112	10.8296	79.5976
3	9.1893	12.2515	67.3461
4	7.5807	13.8601	53.4860
5	5.7610	15.6799	37.8061
6	3.7023	17.7386	20.0676
7	1.3733	20.0676	0.0000

YEARS 8 — MO PAYT 1.6473 — AN CONST 19.77

#	INT	PRIN	BALANCE
1	11.9665	7.8016	92.1984
2	10.9422	8.8259	83.3724
3	9.7834	9.9847	73.3877
4	8.4724	11.2957	62.0920
5	6.9893	12.7788	49.3132
6	5.3115	14.4566	34.8566
7	3.4134	16.3547	18.5020
8	1.2661	18.5020	0.0000

YEARS 9 — MO PAYT 1.5411 — AN CONST 18.50

#	INT	PRIN	BALANCE
1	12.0415	6.4513	93.5487
2	11.1945	7.2983	86.2504
3	10.2363	8.2566	77.9938
4	9.1522	9.3406	68.6532
5	7.9258	10.5670	58.0863
6	6.5384	11.9544	46.1319
7	4.9689	13.5239	32.6079
8	3.1932	15.2996	17.3084
9	1.1844	17.3084	0.0000

YEARS 10 — MO PAYT 1.4579 — AN CONST 17.50

#	INT	PRIN	BALANCE
1	12.1002	5.3949	94.6051
2	11.3919	6.1032	88.5018
3	10.5906	6.9046	81.5973
4	9.6840	7.8111	73.7861
5	8.6584	8.8367	64.9495
6	7.4982	9.9969	54.9526
7	6.1857	11.3095	43.6431
8	4.7008	12.7943	30.8488
9	3.0209	14.4742	16.3746
10	1.1205	16.3746	0.0000

YEARS 11 — MO PAYT 1.3916 — AN CONST 16.70

#	INT	PRIN	BALANCE
1	12.1471	4.5517	95.4483
2	11.5494	5.1494	90.2989
3	10.8734	5.8254	84.4735
4	10.1085	6.5903	77.8832
5	9.2432	7.4556	70.4276
6	8.2643	8.4345	61.9931
7	7.1569	9.5419	52.4513
8	5.9041	10.7947	41.6566
9	4.4868	12.2120	29.4446
10	2.8834	13.8154	15.6293
11	1.0695	15.6293	0.0000

YEARS 12 — MO PAYT 1.3377 — AN CONST 16.06

#	INT	PRIN	BALANCE
1	12.1851	3.8678	96.1322
2	11.6772	4.3757	91.7565
3	11.1027	4.9502	86.8063
4	10.4528	5.6001	81.2062
5	9.7175	6.3354	74.8708
6	8.8857	7.1672	67.7036
7	7.9447	8.1082	59.5953
8	6.8801	9.1728	50.4225
9	5.6758	10.3772	40.0454
10	4.3133	11.7396	28.3057
11	2.7719	13.2810	15.0247
12	1.0282	15.0247	0.0000

YEARS 13 — MO PAYT 1.2935 — AN CONST 15.53

#	INT	PRIN	BALANCE
1	12.2163	3.3059	96.6941
2	11.7822	3.7400	92.9541
3	11.2912	4.2310	88.7231
4	10.7357	4.7865	83.9365
5	10.1072	5.4150	78.5216
6	9.3963	6.1260	72.3956
7	8.5920	6.9303	65.4653
8	7.6820	7.8402	57.6252
9	6.6527	8.8696	48.7556
10	5.4881	10.0341	38.7215
11	4.1707	11.3515	27.3700
12	2.6803	12.8419	14.5280
13	.9942	14.5280	0.0000

YEARS 14 — MO PAYT 1.2568 — AN CONST 15.09

#	INT	PRIN	BALANCE
1	12.2422	2.8393	97.1607
2	11.8694	3.2121	93.9487
3	11.4477	3.6338	90.3149
4	10.9706	4.1109	86.2040
5	10.4309	4.6506	81.5534
6	9.8203	5.2612	76.2921
7	9.1295	5.9520	70.3401
8	8.3480	6.7335	63.6066
9	7.4639	7.6176	55.9890
10	6.4638	8.6177	47.3713
11	5.3323	9.7492	37.6221
12	4.0523	11.0292	26.5929
13	2.6042	12.4773	14.1155
14	.9660	14.1155	0.0000

YEARS 15 — MO PAYT 1.2260 — AN CONST 14.72

#	INT	PRIN	BALANCE
1	12.2640	2.4483	97.5517
2	11.9425	2.7698	94.7819
3	11.5788	3.1334	91.6485
4	11.1674	3.5448	88.1037
5	10.7020	4.0102	84.0935
6	10.1755	4.5368	79.5567
7	9.5798	5.1324	74.4243
8	8.9060	5.8063	68.6180
9	8.1436	6.5686	62.0493
10	7.2812	7.4311	54.6182
11	6.3055	8.4067	46.2115
12	5.2017	9.5105	36.7010
13	3.9531	10.7592	25.9418
14	2.5404	12.1718	13.7700
15	.9423	13.7700	0.0000

YEARS 16 — MO PAYT 1.2001 — AN CONST 14.41

#	INT	PRIN	BALANCE
1	12.2823	2.1183	97.8817
2	12.0042	2.3964	95.4852
3	11.6895	2.7111	92.7742
4	11.3336	3.0670	89.7071
5	10.9309	3.4697	86.2374
6	10.4753	3.9253	82.3121
7	9.9599	4.4407	77.8714
8	9.3769	5.0237	72.8477
9	8.7173	5.6833	67.1644
10	7.9711	6.4295	60.7349
11	7.1269	7.2737	53.4613
12	6.1719	8.2287	45.2326
13	5.0916	9.3090	35.9235
14	3.8693	10.5313	25.3923
15	2.4866	11.9140	13.4783
16	.9223	13.4783	0.0000

YEARS 17 — MO PAYT 1.1780 — AN CONST 14.14

#	INT	PRIN	BALANCE
1	12.2979	1.8381	98.1619
2	12.0565	2.0794	96.0826
3	11.7835	2.3524	93.7302
4	11.4747	2.6613	91.0689
5	11.1252	3.0107	88.0582
6	10.7300	3.4060	84.6523
7	10.2828	3.8531	80.7991
8	9.7769	4.3590	76.4401
9	9.2045	4.9314	71.5087
10	8.5571	5.5788	65.9299
11	7.8246	6.3113	59.6186
12	6.9960	7.1400	52.4786
13	6.0585	8.0774	44.4012
14	4.9980	9.1379	35.2633
15	3.7982	10.3377	24.9255
16	2.4409	11.6950	13.2305
17	.9054	13.2305	0.0000

YEARS 18 — MO PAYT 1.1592 — AN CONST 13.91

#	INT	PRIN	BALANCE
1	12.3112	1.5988	98.4012
2	12.1013	1.8087	96.5926
3	11.8638	2.0461	94.5464
4	11.5951	2.3148	92.2317
5	11.2912	2.6187	89.6129
6	10.9474	2.9625	86.6504
7	10.5584	3.3515	83.2989
8	10.1184	3.7915	79.5074
9	9.6206	4.2894	75.2180
10	9.0574	4.8525	70.3655
11	8.4203	5.4896	64.8758
12	7.6995	6.2104	58.6654
13	6.8841	7.0258	51.6396
14	5.9616	7.9483	43.6913
15	4.9181	8.9918	34.6995
16	3.7375	10.1724	24.5270
17	2.4019	11.5080	13.0190
18	.8909	13.0190	0.0000

YEARS 19 — MO PAYT 1.1430 — AN CONST 13.72

#	INT	PRIN	BALANCE
1	12.3226	1.3935	98.6065
2	12.1396	1.5765	97.0300
3	11.9326	1.7835	95.2465
4	11.6985	2.0176	93.2289
5	11.4336	2.2825	90.9464
6	11.1339	2.5822	88.3642
7	10.7948	2.9213	85.4429
8	10.4113	3.3048	82.1381
9	9.9774	3.7387	78.3994
10	9.4865	4.2296	74.1698
11	8.9312	4.7849	69.3849
12	8.3029	5.4131	63.9718
13	7.5922	6.1239	57.8479
14	6.7882	6.9279	50.9200
15	5.8786	7.8375	43.0825
16	4.8495	8.8665	34.2159
17	3.6854	10.0307	24.1853
18	2.3684	11.3477	12.8376
19	.8785	12.8376	0.0000

YEARS 20 — MO PAYT 1.1291 — AN CONST 13.55

#	INT	PRIN	BALANCE
1	12.3324	1.2168	98.7832
2	12.1726	1.3766	97.4066
3	11.9919	1.5573	95.8493
4	11.7874	1.7618	94.0876
5	11.5561	1.9931	92.0945
6	11.2944	2.2548	89.8398
7	10.9984	2.5508	87.2890
8	10.6635	2.8857	84.4033
9	10.2846	3.2646	81.1387
10	9.8560	3.6932	77.4455
11	9.3711	4.1781	73.2673
12	8.8225	4.7267	68.5407
13	8.2019	5.3473	63.1934
14	7.4998	6.0494	57.1440
15	6.7056	6.8436	50.3004
16	5.8070	7.7421	42.5583
17	4.7905	8.7587	33.7996
18	3.6405	9.9086	23.8910
19	2.3396	11.2096	12.6814
20	.8678	12.6814	0.0000

YEARS 21 — MO PAYT 1.1171 — AN CONST 13.41

#	INT	PRIN	BALANCE
1	12.3409	1.0641	98.9359
2	12.2012	1.2039	97.7320
3	12.0431	1.3619	96.3701

MONTHLY PAYMENT AMORTIZATION SCHEDULE PER $100 — 12.40 %

#	INT	PRIN	BALANCE
4	11.8643	1.5407	94.8294
5	11.6620	1.7430	93.0864
6	11.4331	1.9719	91.1145
7	11.1742	2.2308	88.8837
8	10.8813	2.5237	86.3601
9	10.5500	2.8550	83.5051
10	10.1752	3.2298	80.2752
11	9.7511	3.6539	76.6213
12	9.2713	4.1337	72.4877
13	8.7286	4.6764	67.8113
14	8.1146	5.2904	62.5209
15	7.4200	5.9850	56.5359
16	6.6342	6.7708	49.7651
17	5.7452	7.6598	42.1054
18	4.7395	8.6655	33.4399
19	3.6018	9.8032	23.6367
20	2.3147	11.0903	12.5464
21	.8586	12.5464	0.0000

YEARS 22 — MO PAYT 1.1067 — AN CONST 13.29

#	INT	PRIN	BALANCE
1	12.3482	.9319	99.0681
2	12.2259	1.0542	98.0139
3	12.0875	1.1926	96.8213
4	11.9309	1.3492	95.4721
5	11.7537	1.5264	93.9457
6	11.5533	1.7268	92.2189
7	11.3266	1.9535	90.2654
8	11.0701	2.2100	88.0555
9	10.7800	2.5001	85.5553
10	10.4517	2.8284	82.7269
11	10.0803	3.1997	79.5272
12	9.6602	3.6199	75.9073
13	9.1850	4.0951	71.8122
14	8.6473	4.6328	67.1794
15	8.0390	5.2411	61.9383
16	7.3509	5.9292	56.0091
17	6.5724	6.7077	49.3014
18	5.6917	7.5884	41.7130
19	4.6954	8.5847	33.1283
20	3.5682	9.7118	23.4165
21	2.2931	10.9870	12.4295
22	.8506	12.4295	0.0000

YEARS 23 — MO PAYT 1.0976 — AN CONST 13.18

#	INT	PRIN	BALANCE
1	12.3546	.8170	99.1830
2	12.2473	.9243	98.2588
3	12.1260	1.0456	97.2132
4	11.9887	1.1829	96.0303
5	11.8334	1.3382	94.6921
6	11.6577	1.5139	93.1782
7	11.4589	1.7127	91.4655
8	11.2341	1.9375	89.5280
9	10.9797	2.1919	87.3361
10	10.6919	2.4797	84.8563
11	10.3663	2.8053	82.0511
12	9.9980	3.1736	78.8775
13	9.5813	3.5903	75.2872
14	9.1099	4.0617	71.2255
15	8.5766	4.5950	66.6305
16	7.9733	5.1983	61.4323
17	7.2908	5.8808	55.5515
18	6.5187	6.6529	48.8986
19	5.6452	7.5264	41.3722
20	4.6570	8.5146	32.8577
21	3.5391	9.6325	23.2252
22	2.2744	10.8972	12.3280
23	.8436	12.3280	0.0000

YEARS 24 — MO PAYT 1.0898 — AN CONST 13.08

#	INT	PRIN	BALANCE
1	12.3602	.7170	99.2830
2	12.2660	.8111	98.4719
3	12.1595	.9176	97.5543
4	12.0390	1.0381	96.5161
5	11.9027	1.1744	95.3417
6	11.7485	1.3286	94.0131
7	11.5741	1.5030	92.5101
8	11.3768	1.7004	90.8097
9	11.1535	1.9236	88.8861
10	10.9009	2.1762	86.7099
11	10.6152	2.4619	84.2479
12	10.2920	2.7852	81.4628
13	9.9263	3.1509	78.3119
14	9.5126	3.5645	74.7474
15	9.0446	4.0326	70.7148
16	8.5151	4.5620	66.1528
17	7.9162	5.1610	60.9918
18	7.2385	5.8386	55.1532
19	6.4720	6.6052	48.5480
20	5.6047	7.4724	41.0756
21	4.6236	8.4535	32.6221
22	3.5137	9.5634	23.0586
23	2.2581	10.8191	12.2396
24	.8376	12.2396	0.0000

YEARS 25 — MO PAYT 1.0829 — AN CONST 13.00

#	INT	PRIN	BALANCE
1	12.3650	.6298	99.3702
2	12.2823	.7125	98.6577
3	12.1888	.8060	97.8517
4	12.0829	.9118	96.9399
5	11.9632	1.0316	95.9083
6	11.8278	1.1670	94.7413
7	11.6746	1.3202	93.4211
8	11.5012	1.4936	91.9275
9	11.3051	1.6897	90.2378
10	11.0833	1.9115	88.3263
11	10.8323	2.1625	86.1638
12	10.5484	2.4464	83.7174
13	10.2272	2.7676	80.9497
14	9.8638	3.1310	77.8187
15	9.4527	3.5421	74.2766
16	8.9876	4.0072	70.2695
17	8.4615	4.5333	65.7362
18	7.8663	5.1285	60.6077
19	7.1930	5.8018	54.8059
20	6.4312	6.5636	48.2423
21	5.5694	7.4254	40.8169
22	4.5945	8.4003	32.4166
23	3.4916	9.5032	22.9134
24	2.2439	10.7509	12.1625
25	.8323	12.1625	0.0000

YEARS 26 — MO PAYT 1.0769 — AN CONST 12.93

#	INT	PRIN	BALANCE
1	12.3692	.5536	99.4464
2	12.2965	.6263	98.8201
3	12.2143	.7085	98.1116
4	12.1213	.8016	97.3100
5	12.0161	.9068	96.4032
6	11.8970	1.0259	95.3773
7	11.7623	1.1606	94.2168
8	11.6099	1.3129	92.9039
9	11.4375	1.4853	91.4186
10	11.2425	1.6803	89.7382
11	11.0219	1.9009	87.8373
12	10.7723	2.1505	85.6868
13	10.4900	2.4329	83.2539
14	10.1705	2.7523	80.5016
15	9.8092	3.1137	77.3879
16	9.4004	3.5225	73.8654
17	8.9379	3.9850	69.8804
18	8.4147	4.5082	65.3722
19	7.8228	5.1001	60.2722
20	7.1531	5.7697	54.5024
21	6.3956	6.5273	47.9752
22	5.5386	7.3843	40.5909
23	4.5691	8.3538	32.2372
24	3.4723	9.4506	22.7866
25	2.2314	10.6914	12.0952
26	.8277	12.0952	0.0000

YEARS 27 — MO PAYT 1.0717 — AN CONST 12.86

#	INT	PRIN	BALANCE
1	12.3729	.4870	99.5130
2	12.3090	.5509	98.9621
3	12.2367	.6233	98.3389
4	12.1548	.7051	97.6338
5	12.0623	.7977	96.8361
6	11.9575	.9024	95.9337
7	11.8391	1.0209	94.9129
8	11.7050	1.1549	93.7580
9	11.5534	1.3065	92.4514
10	11.3818	1.4781	90.9734
11	11.1878	1.6721	89.3012
12	10.9682	1.8917	87.4095
13	10.7199	2.1401	85.2695
14	10.4389	2.4210	82.8485
15	10.1210	2.7389	80.1095
16	9.7614	3.0985	77.0110
17	9.3546	3.5053	73.5057
18	8.8943	3.9656	69.5401
19	8.3737	4.4862	65.0539
20	7.7847	5.0753	59.9786
21	7.1183	5.7416	54.2370
22	6.3645	6.4955	47.7416
23	5.5116	7.3483	40.3933
24	4.5468	8.3131	32.0802
25	3.4554	9.4046	22.6756
26	2.2206	10.6393	12.0363
27	.8237	12.0363	0.0000

YEARS 28 — MO PAYT 1.0671 — AN CONST 12.81

#	INT	PRIN	BALANCE
1	12.3762	.4286	99.5714
2	12.3199	.4849	99.0865
3	12.2562	.5486	98.5379
4	12.1842	.6206	97.9174
5	12.1027	.7021	97.2153
6	12.0106	.7942	96.4211
7	11.9063	.8985	95.5225
8	11.7883	1.0165	94.5061
9	11.6549	1.1499	93.3561
10	11.5039	1.3009	92.0552
11	11.3331	1.4717	90.5834
12	11.1398	1.6650	88.9185
13	10.9212	1.8836	87.0349
14	10.6739	2.1309	84.9040
15	10.3941	2.4107	82.4934
16	10.0776	2.7272	79.7662
17	9.7196	3.0852	76.6810
18	9.3145	3.4903	73.1906
19	8.8562	3.9486	69.2421
20	8.3378	4.4670	64.7751
21	7.7513	5.0535	59.7216
22	7.0878	5.7170	54.0046
23	6.3372	6.4676	47.5369
24	5.4880	7.3168	40.2201
25	4.5273	8.2775	31.9427
26	3.4405	9.3643	22.5784
27	2.2111	10.5937	11.9847
28	.8201	11.9847	0.0000

YEARS 29 — MO PAYT 1.0630 — AN CONST 12.76

#	INT	PRIN	BALANCE
1	12.3790	.3774	99.6226
2	12.3295	.4270	99.1956
3	12.2734	.4831	98.7125
4	12.2100	.5465	98.1660
5	12.1382	.6182	97.5478
6	12.0571	.6994	96.8484
7	11.9652	.7912	96.0571
8	11.8613	.8951	95.1620
9	11.7438	1.0127	94.1493
10	11.6109	1.1456	93.0037
11	11.4604	1.2960	91.7077
12	11.2903	1.4662	90.2415
13	11.0978	1.6587	88.5828
14	10.8800	1.8765	86.7064
15	10.6336	2.1228	84.5835
16	10.3549	2.4016	82.1820
17	10.0396	2.7169	79.4651
18	9.6829	3.0736	76.3915
19	9.2793	3.4771	72.9144
20	8.8228	3.9337	68.9807
21	8.3063	4.4501	64.5306
22	7.7220	5.0344	59.4961
23	7.0610	5.6954	53.8007
24	6.3133	6.4432	47.3575
25	5.4673	7.2892	40.0683
26	4.5102	8.2462	31.8221
27	3.4276	9.3289	22.4932
28	2.2027	10.5538	11.9394
29	.8170	11.9394	0.0000

YEARS 30 — MO PAYT 1.0595 — AN CONST 12.72

#	INT	PRIN	BALANCE
1	12.3815	.3325	99.6675
2	12.3379	.3762	99.2913
3	12.2885	.4256	98.8657
4	12.2326	.4815	98.3843
5	12.1694	.5447	97.8396
6	12.0979	.6162	97.2234
7	12.0170	.6971	96.5263
8	11.9254	.7886	95.7377
9	11.8219	.8921	94.8456
10	11.7048	1.0093	93.8363
11	11.5723	1.1418	92.6945
12	11.4223	1.2917	91.4028
13	11.2527	1.4613	89.9415
14	11.0609	1.6532	88.2883
15	10.8438	1.8702	86.4181
16	10.5983	2.1158	84.3023
17	10.3205	2.3936	81.9087
18	10.0062	2.7078	79.2009
19	9.6507	3.0634	76.1375
20	9.2485	3.4656	72.6719
21	8.7935	3.9206	68.7513
22	8.2787	4.4353	64.3160
23	7.6964	5.0177	59.2983
24	7.0376	5.6765	53.6218
25	6.2923	6.4218	47.2000
26	5.4491	7.2649	39.9351
27	4.4953	8.2188	31.7163
28	3.4162	9.2979	22.4184
29	2.1954	10.5187	11.8997
30	.8143	11.8997	0.0000

MONTHLY PAYMENT AMORTIZATION SCHEDULE PER $100 — 12.50 %

YEARS 2 — MO PAYT 4.7307 — AN CONST 56.77

#	INT	PRIN	BALANCE
1	9.8736	46.8952	53.1048
2	3.6639	53.1048	0.0000

YEARS 3 — MO PAYT 3.3454 — AN CONST 40.15

#	INT	PRIN	BALANCE
1	10.8599	29.2844	70.7156
2	6.9822	33.1622	37.5534
3	2.5910	37.5534	0.0000

YEARS 4 — MO PAYT 2.6580 — AN CONST 31.90

#	INT	PRIN	BALANCE
1	11.3493	20.5467	79.4533
2	8.6286	23.2674	56.1858
3	5.5476	26.3484	29.8374
4	2.0586	29.8374	0.0000

YEARS 5 — MO PAYT 2.2498 — AN CONST 27.00

#	INT	PRIN	BALANCE
1	11.6399	15.3576	84.6424
2	9.6063	17.3912	67.2511
3	7.3034	19.6941	47.5570
4	4.6956	22.3019	25.2551
5	1.7425	25.2551	0.0000

YEARS 6 — MO PAYT 1.9811 — AN CONST 23.78

#	INT	PRIN	BALANCE
1	11.8312	11.9422	88.0578
2	10.2498	13.5236	74.5342
3	8.4541	15.3143	59.2198
4	6.4312	17.3422	41.8776
5	4.1348	19.6386	22.2390
6	1.5344	22.2390	0.0000

YEARS 7 — MO PAYT 1.7921 — AN CONST 21.51

#	INT	PRIN	BALANCE
1	11.9657	9.5398	90.4602
2	10.7025	10.8030	79.6572
3	9.2720	12.2335	67.4238
4	7.6521	13.8534	53.5704
5	5.8177	15.6878	37.8826
6	3.7404	17.7651	20.1175
7	1.3880	20.1175	0.0000

YEARS 8 — MO PAYT 1.6529 — AN CONST 19.84

#	INT	PRIN	BALANCE
1	12.0649	7.7697	92.2303
2	11.0360	8.7986	83.4317
3	9.8709	9.9636	73.4681
4	8.5516	11.2830	62.1851
5	7.0576	12.7770	49.4081
6	5.3657	14.4689	34.9392
7	3.4498	16.3848	18.5544
8	1.2802	18.5544	0.0000

YEARS 9 — MO PAYT 1.5468 — AN CONST 18.57

#	INT	PRIN	BALANCE
1	12.1404	6.4207	93.5793
2	11.2902	7.2709	86.3085
3	10.3274	8.2336	78.0749
4	9.2372	9.3239	68.7510
5	8.0025	10.5585	58.1924
6	6.6044	11.9566	46.2358
7	5.0212	13.5399	32.6959
8	3.2283	15.3328	17.3631
9	1.1980	17.3631	0.0000

YEARS 10 — MO PAYT 1.4638 — AN CONST 17.57

#	INT	PRIN	BALANCE
1	12.1995	5.3656	94.6344
2	11.4890	6.0761	88.5582
3	10.6844	6.8807	81.6775
4	9.7733	7.7918	73.8856
5	8.7415	8.8236	65.0620
6	7.5731	9.9920	55.0700
7	6.2500	11.3151	43.7549
8	4.7517	12.8134	30.9416
9	3.0550	14.5101	16.4315
10	1.1337	16.4315	0.0000

YEARS 11 — MO PAYT 1.3975 — AN CONST 16.78

#	INT	PRIN	BALANCE
1	12.2466	4.5239	95.4761
2	11.6476	5.1229	90.3532
3	10.9692	5.8013	84.5519
4	10.2011	6.5694	77.9825
5	9.3312	7.4393	70.5431
6	8.3461	8.4244	62.1187
7	7.2305	9.5400	52.5787
8	5.9673	10.8032	41.7755
9	4.5368	12.2337	29.5418
10	2.9168	13.8537	15.6881
11	1.0824	15.6881	0.0000

YEARS 12 — MO PAYT 1.3439 — AN CONST 16.13

#	INT	PRIN	BALANCE
1	12.2849	3.8414	96.1586
2	11.7762	4.3501	91.8085
3	11.2002	4.9261	86.8824
4	10.5479	5.5784	81.3039
5	9.8092	6.3171	74.9869
6	8.9727	7.1536	67.8333
7	8.0255	8.1008	59.7325
8	6.9528	9.1735	50.5590
9	5.7381	10.3882	40.1708
10	4.3625	11.7638	28.4070
11	2.8048	13.3215	15.0855
12	1.0408	15.0855	0.0000

YEARS 13 — MO PAYT 1.2998 — AN CONST 15.60

#	INT	PRIN	BALANCE
1	12.3162	3.2809	96.7191
2	11.8818	3.7154	93.0037
3	11.3898	4.2074	88.7963
4	10.8327	4.7645	84.0318
5	10.2018	5.3954	78.6364
6	9.4874	6.1098	72.5266
7	8.6783	6.9189	65.6077
8	7.7622	7.8350	57.7727
9	6.7247	8.8725	48.9002
10	5.5498	10.0474	38.8528
11	4.2194	11.3778	27.4750
12	2.7128	12.8844	14.5905
13	1.0067	14.5905	0.0000

YEARS 14 — MO PAYT 1.2632 — AN CONST 15.16

#	INT	PRIN	BALANCE
1	12.3423	2.8157	97.1843
2	11.9695	3.1886	93.9957
3	11.5472	3.6108	90.3849
4	11.0691	4.0889	86.2960
5	10.5277	4.6303	81.6657
6	9.9145	5.2435	76.4222
7	9.2202	5.9378	70.4844
8	8.4340	6.7241	63.7604
9	7.5436	7.6144	56.1460
10	6.5353	8.6227	47.5233
11	5.3935	9.7645	37.7588
12	4.1006	11.0575	26.7013
13	2.6364	12.5216	14.1797
14	.9783	14.1797	0.0000

YEARS 15 — MO PAYT 1.2325 — AN CONST 14.80

#	INT	PRIN	BALANCE
1	12.3641	2.4261	97.5739
2	12.0429	2.7474	94.8265
3	11.6791	3.1112	91.7153
4	11.2671	3.5232	88.1921
5	10.8006	3.9897	84.2024
6	10.2723	4.5180	79.6844
7	9.6740	5.1163	74.5681
8	8.9965	5.7937	68.7744
9	8.2293	6.5609	62.2135
10	7.3606	7.4297	54.7838
11	6.3768	8.4135	46.3703
12	5.2627	9.5276	36.8427
13	4.0011	10.7892	26.0535
14	2.5724	12.2178	13.8357
15	.9546	13.8357	0.0000

YEARS 16 — MO PAYT 1.2067 — AN CONST 14.49

#	INT	PRIN	BALANCE
1	12.3825	2.0975	97.9025
2	12.1048	2.3753	95.5272
3	11.7903	2.6898	92.8375
4	11.4341	3.0459	89.7915
5	11.0308	3.4493	86.3422
6	10.5740	3.9060	82.4362
7	10.0568	4.4232	78.0130
8	9.4711	5.0089	73.0040
9	8.8078	5.6722	67.3318
10	8.0567	6.4233	60.9085
11	7.2062	7.2738	53.6347
12	6.2430	8.2370	45.3977
13	5.1523	9.3277	36.0699
14	3.9172	10.5629	25.5070
15	2.5185	11.9616	13.5455
16	.9346	13.5455	0.0000

YEARS 17 — MO PAYT 1.1847 — AN CONST 14.22

#	INT	PRIN	BALANCE
1	12.3982	1.8186	98.1814
2	12.1573	2.0594	96.1221
3	11.8847	2.3321	93.7900
4	11.5758	2.6409	91.1492
5	11.2262	2.9906	88.1586
6	10.8302	3.3866	84.7721
7	10.3817	3.8350	80.9371
8	9.8739	4.3428	76.5943
9	9.2989	4.9179	71.6764
10	8.6477	5.5691	66.1074
11	7.9102	6.3065	59.8009
12	7.0751	7.1416	52.6593
13	6.1295	8.0872	44.5721
14	5.0586	9.1581	35.4140
15	3.8459	10.3708	25.0432
16	2.4727	11.7440	13.2991
17	.9176	13.2991	0.0000

YEARS 18 — MO PAYT 1.1660 — AN CONST 14.00

#	INT	PRIN	BALANCE
1	12.4115	1.5805	98.4195
2	12.2022	1.7898	96.6297
3	11.9652	2.0268	94.6028
4	11.6968	2.2952	92.3076
5	11.3929	2.5991	89.7085
6	11.0487	2.9433	86.7652
7	10.6590	3.3330	83.4322
8	10.2176	3.7744	79.6578
9	9.7179	4.2742	75.3837
10	9.1519	4.8401	70.5436
11	8.5110	5.4810	65.0625
12	7.7852	6.2068	58.8557
13	6.9633	7.0287	51.8270
14	6.0326	7.9594	43.8676
15	4.9787	9.0134	34.8542
16	3.7851	10.2069	24.6474
17	2.4336	11.5584	13.0889
18	.9031	13.0889	0.0000

YEARS 19 — MO PAYT 1.1500 — AN CONST 13.80

#	INT	PRIN	BALANCE
1	12.4229	1.3765	98.6235
2	12.2406	1.5588	97.0647
3	12.0342	1.7652	95.2995
4	11.8005	1.9989	93.3006
5	11.5358	2.2636	91.0370
6	11.2361	2.5633	88.4737
7	10.8966	2.9028	85.5709
8	10.5123	3.2871	82.2838
9	10.0770	3.7224	78.5613
10	9.5841	4.2153	74.3460
11	9.0259	4.7735	69.5725
12	8.3938	5.4056	64.1669
13	7.6780	6.1214	58.0456
14	6.8675	6.9319	51.1136
15	5.9496	7.8498	43.2638
16	4.9101	8.8893	34.3745
17	3.7330	10.0664	24.3081
18	2.4001	11.3993	12.9088
19	.8906	12.9088	0.0000

YEARS 20 — MO PAYT 1.1361 — AN CONST 13.64

#	INT	PRIN	BALANCE
1	12.4327	1.2009	98.7991
2	12.2737	1.3600	97.4391
3	12.0936	1.5401	95.8990
4	11.8897	1.7440	94.1550
5	11.6589	1.9749	92.1801
6	11.3973	2.2364	89.9437
7	11.1011	2.5326	87.4112
8	10.7658	2.8679	84.5432
9	10.3860	3.2477	81.2956
10	9.9560	3.6777	77.6179
11	9.4690	4.1647	73.4532
12	8.9175	4.7162	68.7370
13	8.2930	5.3407	63.3963
14	7.5858	6.0479	57.3485
15	6.7850	6.8487	50.4998
16	5.8781	7.7556	42.7442
17	4.8512	8.7825	33.9617
18	3.6882	9.9455	24.0162
19	2.3713	11.2624	12.7537
20	.8799	12.7537	0.0000

YEARS 21 — MO PAYT 1.1242 — AN CONST 13.50

#	INT	PRIN	BALANCE
1	12.4412	1.0494	98.9506
2	12.3023	1.1883	97.7623
3	12.1449	1.3457	96.4166

#	INT	PRIN	BALANCE
4	11.9667	1.5239	94.8927
5	11.7649	1.7257	93.1670
6	11.5364	1.9542	91.2128
7	11.2777	2.2130	88.9999
8	10.9846	2.5060	86.4939
9	10.6528	2.8378	83.6561
10	10.2770	3.2136	80.4425
11	9.8515	3.6391	76.8034
12	9.3696	4.1210	72.6824
13	8.8239	4.6667	68.0157
14	8.2060	5.2846	62.7310
15	7.5062	5.9844	56.7467
16	6.7138	6.7768	49.9698
17	5.8164	7.6742	42.2956
18	4.8002	8.6904	33.6053
19	3.6495	9.8411	23.7642
20	2.3464	11.1442	12.6199
21	.8707	12.6199	0.0000

YEARS 22	MO PAYT 1.1139	AN CONST 13.37	
#	INT	PRIN	BALANCE
1	12.4486	.9182	99.0818
2	12.3270	1.0398	98.0421
3	12.1893	1.1774	96.8646
4	12.0334	1.3333	95.5313
5	11.8568	1.5099	94.0214
6	11.6569	1.7098	92.3116
7	11.4305	1.9362	90.3753
8	11.1741	2.1926	88.1827
9	10.8838	2.4830	85.6997
10	10.5550	2.8118	82.8880
11	10.1827	3.1841	79.7039
12	9.7610	3.6057	76.0982
13	9.2836	4.0832	72.0150
14	8.7429	4.6238	67.3912
15	8.1306	5.2361	62.1551
16	7.4373	5.9294	56.2256
17	6.6521	6.7146	49.5110
18	5.7630	7.6037	41.9073
19	4.7562	8.6106	33.2967
20	3.6160	9.7508	23.5460
21	2.3248	11.0419	12.5040
22	.8627	12.5040	0.0000

YEARS 23	MO PAYT 1.1049	AN CONST 13.26	
#	INT	PRIN	BALANCE
1	12.4550	.8043	99.1957
2	12.3485	.9108	98.2849
3	12.2279	1.0314	97.2535
4	12.0913	1.1680	96.0856
5	11.9366	1.3226	94.7630
6	11.7615	1.4978	93.2652
7	11.5632	1.6961	91.5691
8	11.3386	1.9207	89.6484
9	11.0842	2.1750	87.4734
10	10.7962	2.4630	85.0104
11	10.4701	2.7891	82.2213
12	10.1008	3.1585	79.0628
13	9.6825	3.5767	75.4861
14	9.2089	4.0503	71.4358
15	8.6726	4.5866	66.8492
16	8.0653	5.1940	61.6552
17	7.3775	5.8818	55.7734
18	6.5986	6.6606	49.1128
19	5.7167	7.5426	41.5702
20	4.7179	8.5413	33.0289
21	3.5869	9.6723	23.3566
22	2.3061	10.9531	12.4035
23	.8558	12.4035	0.0000

YEARS 24	MO PAYT 1.0971	AN CONST 13.17	
#	INT	PRIN	BALANCE
1	12.4605	.7052	99.2948
2	12.3671	.7986	98.4962
3	12.2614	.9044	97.5918
4	12.1416	1.0241	96.5677
5	12.0060	1.1597	95.4079
6	11.8524	1.3133	94.0947
7	11.6785	1.4872	92.6075
8	11.4816	1.6841	90.9233
9	11.2586	1.9071	89.0162
10	11.0061	2.1597	86.8566
11	10.7201	2.4456	84.4109
12	10.3963	2.7695	81.6414
13	10.0295	3.1362	78.5052
14	9.6143	3.5515	74.9538
15	9.1440	4.0218	70.9320
16	8.6114	4.5543	66.3777
17	8.0084	5.1574	61.2204
18	7.3255	5.8403	55.3801
19	6.5521	6.6136	48.7664
20	5.6764	7.4894	41.2771
21	4.6846	8.4811	32.7960
22	3.5616	9.6041	23.1919
23	2.2899	10.8759	12.3160
24	.8497	12.3160	0.0000

YEARS 25	MO PAYT 1.0904	AN CONST 13.09	
#	INT	PRIN	BALANCE
1	12.4653	.6189	99.3811
2	12.3834	.7009	98.6802
3	12.2906	.7937	97.8865
4	12.1855	.8988	96.9878
5	12.0665	1.0178	95.9700
6	11.9317	1.1525	94.8175
7	11.7791	1.3052	93.5123
8	11.6063	1.4780	92.0343
9	11.4106	1.6737	90.3606
10	11.1889	1.8953	88.4653
11	10.9380	2.1463	86.3190
12	10.6538	2.4305	83.8885
13	10.3319	2.7523	81.1362
14	9.9675	3.1168	78.0194
15	9.5547	3.5295	74.4899
16	9.0874	3.9969	70.4930
17	8.5581	4.5261	65.9669
18	7.9588	5.1254	60.8415
19	7.2801	5.8041	55.0373
20	6.5116	6.5727	48.4646
21	5.6412	7.4430	41.0216
22	4.6557	8.4286	32.5930
23	3.5396	9.5447	23.0483
24	2.2757	10.8085	12.2398
25	.8445	12.2398	0.0000

YEARS 26	MO PAYT 1.0844	AN CONST 13.02	
#	INT	PRIN	BALANCE
1	12.4696	.5436	99.4564
2	12.3976	.6155	98.8409
3	12.3161	.6971	98.1438
4	12.2238	.7894	97.3545
5	12.1192	.8939	96.4606
6	12.0009	1.0122	95.4483
7	11.8668	1.1463	94.3021
8	11.7151	1.2981	93.0040
9	11.5432	1.4700	91.5340
10	11.3485	1.6646	89.8694
11	11.1281	1.8850	87.9844
12	10.8785	2.1346	85.8498
13	10.5958	2.4173	83.4325
14	10.2758	2.7374	80.6951
15	9.9133	3.0998	77.5953

#	INT	PRIN	BALANCE
16	9.5028	3.5103	74.0850
17	9.0380	3.9751	70.1098
18	8.5116	4.5015	65.6083
19	7.9155	5.0976	60.5107
20	7.2405	5.7726	54.7382
21	6.4762	6.5370	48.2012
22	5.6106	7.4026	40.7986
23	4.6303	8.3828	32.4158
24	3.5203	9.4928	22.9230
25	2.2633	10.7498	12.1732
26	.8399	12.1732	0.0000

YEARS 27	MO PAYT 1.0792	AN CONST 12.96	
#	INT	PRIN	BALANCE
1	12.4732	.4777	99.5223
2	12.4100	.5410	98.9813
3	12.3384	.6126	98.3687
4	12.2572	.6937	97.6750
5	12.1654	.7856	96.8894
6	12.0614	.8896	95.9998
7	11.9436	1.0074	94.9924
8	11.8102	1.1408	93.8516
9	11.6591	1.2919	92.5597
10	11.4880	1.4629	91.0968
11	11.2943	1.6566	89.4401
12	11.0749	1.8760	87.5641
13	10.8265	2.1244	85.4397
14	10.5452	2.4057	83.0339
15	10.2267	2.7243	80.3096
16	9.8659	3.0850	77.2246
17	9.4574	3.4935	73.7310
18	8.9948	3.9561	69.7749
19	8.4710	4.4800	65.2949
20	7.8777	5.0732	60.2217
21	7.2060	5.7450	54.4767
22	6.4452	6.5057	47.9709
23	5.5838	7.3672	40.6037
24	4.6082	8.3427	32.2610
25	3.5035	9.4474	22.8135
26	2.2525	10.6984	12.1151
27	.8359	12.1151	0.0000

YEARS 28	MO PAYT 1.0747	AN CONST 12.90	
#	INT	PRIN	BALANCE
1	12.4765	.4201	99.5799
2	12.4208	.4757	99.1042
3	12.3579	.5387	98.5655
4	12.2865	.6100	97.9555
5	12.2057	.6908	97.2647
6	12.1143	.7823	96.4824
7	12.0107	.8859	95.5965
8	11.8934	1.0032	94.5933
9	11.7605	1.1360	93.4573
10	11.6101	1.2864	92.1709
11	11.4398	1.4568	90.7141
12	11.2469	1.6497	89.0644
13	11.0284	1.8681	87.1963
14	10.7811	2.1155	85.0807
15	10.5009	2.3956	82.6851
16	10.1837	2.7129	79.9723
17	9.8245	3.0721	76.9002
18	9.4177	3.4789	73.4213
19	8.9570	3.9395	69.4818
20	8.4354	4.4612	65.0206
21	7.8446	5.0519	59.9687
22	7.1757	5.7209	54.2478
23	6.4181	6.4784	47.7694
24	5.5603	7.3363	40.4331
25	4.5889	8.3077	32.1255
26	3.4888	9.4078	22.7177
27	2.2431	10.6535	12.0642

#	INT	PRIN	BALANCE
28	.8324	12.0642	0.0000

YEARS 29	MO PAYT 1.0707	AN CONST 12.85	
#	INT	PRIN	BALANCE
1	12.4793	.3696	99.6304
2	12.4304	.4185	99.2119
3	12.3749	.4740	98.7379
4	12.3122	.5367	98.2012
5	12.2411	.6078	97.5934
6	12.1606	.6883	96.9052
7	12.0695	.7794	96.1258
8	11.9663	.8826	95.2432
9	11.8494	.9995	94.2437
10	11.7171	1.1318	93.1119
11	11.5672	1.2817	91.8302
12	11.3975	1.4514	90.3788
13	11.2053	1.6436	88.7352
14	10.9877	1.8612	86.8740
15	10.7412	2.1077	84.7663
16	10.4621	2.3868	82.3795
17	10.1461	2.7028	79.6767
18	9.7882	3.0607	76.6160
19	9.3829	3.4660	73.1500
20	8.9239	3.9250	69.2250
21	8.4042	4.4447	64.7803
22	7.8156	5.0332	59.7470
23	7.1492	5.6997	54.0473
24	6.3944	6.4545	47.5929
25	5.5398	7.3091	40.2837
26	4.5719	8.2770	32.0067
27	3.4759	9.3730	22.6337
28	2.2348	10.6141	12.0196
29	.8293	12.0196	0.0000

YEARS 30	MO PAYT 1.0673	AN CONST 12.81	
#	INT	PRIN	BALANCE
1	12.4818	.3253	99.6747
2	12.4387	.3684	99.3063
3	12.3899	.4172	98.8891
4	12.3347	.4724	98.4167
5	12.2721	.5350	97.8818
6	12.2013	.6058	97.2760
7	12.1211	.6860	96.5899
8	12.0302	.7769	95.8131
9	11.9274	.8797	94.9333
10	11.8109	.9962	93.9371
11	11.6790	1.1281	92.8090
12	11.5296	1.2775	91.5315
13	11.3604	1.4467	90.0848
14	11.1688	1.6382	88.4465
15	10.9519	1.8552	86.5914
16	10.7063	2.1008	84.4905
17	10.4281	2.3790	82.1115
18	10.1131	2.6940	79.4175
19	9.7563	3.0508	76.3667
20	9.3524	3.4547	72.9120
21	8.8949	3.9122	68.9998
22	8.3769	4.4302	64.5696
23	7.7902	5.0169	59.5527
24	7.1259	5.6812	53.8715
25	6.3736	6.4335	47.4380
26	5.5217	7.2854	40.1527
27	4.5570	8.2501	31.9026
28	3.4646	9.3425	22.5601
29	2.2275	10.5796	11.9805
30	.8266	11.9805	0.0000

#	YEARS 2 INT	MO PAYT 4.7354 PRIN	AN CONST 56.83 BALANCE
1	9.9545	46.8705	53.1295
2	3.6955	53.1295	0.0000

#	YEARS 3 INT	MO PAYT 3.3502 PRIN	AN CONST 40.21 BALANCE
1	10.9489	29.2531	70.7469
2	7.0425	33.1595	37.5875
3	2.6145	37.5875	0.0000

#	YEARS 4 INT	MO PAYT 2.6629 PRIN	AN CONST 31.96 BALANCE
1	11.4422	20.5131	79.4869
2	8.7029	23.2524	56.2345
3	5.5978	26.3574	29.8771
4	2.0782	29.8771	0.0000

#	YEARS 5 INT	MO PAYT 2.2549 PRIN	AN CONST 27.06 BALANCE
1	11.7351	15.3235	84.6765
2	9.6888	17.3698	67.3067
3	7.3693	19.6893	47.6174
4	4.7401	22.3185	25.2989
5	1.7597	25.2989	0.0000

#	YEARS 6 INT	MO PAYT 1.9864 PRIN	AN CONST 23.84 BALANCE
1	11.9278	11.9085	88.0915
2	10.3376	13.4987	74.5928
3	8.5350	15.3013	59.2915
4	6.4917	17.3446	41.9469
5	4.1756	19.6607	22.2862
6	1.5502	22.2862	0.0000

#	YEARS 7 INT	MO PAYT 1.7975 PRIN	AN CONST 21.58 BALANCE
1	12.0634	9.5068	90.4932
2	10.7939	10.7764	79.7168
3	9.3548	12.2154	67.5014
4	7.7236	13.8466	53.6548
5	5.8746	15.6957	37.9591
6	3.7786	17.7916	20.1675
7	1.4028	20.1675	0.0000

#	YEARS 8 INT	MO PAYT 1.6584 PRIN	AN CONST 19.91 BALANCE
1	12.1632	7.7379	92.2621
2	11.1299	8.7712	83.4909
3	9.9587	9.9425	73.5484
4	8.6310	11.2702	62.2782
5	7.1260	12.7752	49.5030
6	5.4200	14.4811	35.0218
7	3.4862	16.4149	18.6069
8	1.2942	18.6069	0.0000

#	YEARS 9 INT	MO PAYT 1.5525 PRIN	AN CONST 18.63 BALANCE
1	12.2393	6.3901	93.6099
2	11.3860	7.2435	86.3664
3	10.4187	8.2107	78.1557
4	9.3223	9.3072	68.8485
5	8.0794	10.5500	58.2985
6	6.6706	11.9588	46.3397

#	INT	PRIN	BALANCE
7	5.0737	13.5558	32.7839
8	3.2635	15.3660	17.4179
9	1.2115	17.4179	0.0000

#	YEARS 10 INT	MO PAYT 1.4696 PRIN	AN CONST 17.64 BALANCE
1	12.2988	5.3365	94.6635
2	11.5862	6.0491	88.6144
3	10.7784	6.8569	81.7575
4	9.8627	7.7726	73.9849
5	8.8248	8.8105	65.1744
6	7.6483	9.9870	55.1874
7	6.3146	11.3207	43.8668
8	4.8029	12.8324	31.0344
9	3.0893	14.5460	16.4884
10	1.1469	16.4884	0.0000

#	YEARS 11 INT	MO PAYT 1.4035 PRIN	AN CONST 16.85 BALANCE
1	12.3462	4.4962	95.5038
2	11.7458	5.0966	90.4073
3	11.0652	5.7771	84.6301
4	10.2938	6.5486	78.0815
5	9.4193	7.4231	70.6584
6	8.4280	8.4144	62.2441
7	7.3044	9.5380	52.7061
8	6.0307	10.8117	41.8945
9	4.5870	12.2554	29.6390
10	2.9504	13.8920	15.7471
11	1.0953	15.7471	0.0000

#	YEARS 12 INT	MO PAYT 1.3500 PRIN	AN CONST 16.20 BALANCE
1	12.3847	3.8152	96.1848
2	11.8752	4.3246	91.8602
3	11.2977	4.9021	86.9581
4	10.6431	5.5567	81.4014
5	9.9010	6.2988	75.1026
6	9.0599	7.1399	67.9627
7	8.1065	8.0933	59.8694
8	7.0257	9.1741	50.6953
9	5.8006	10.3992	40.2961
10	4.4120	11.7879	28.5083
11	2.8378	13.3620	15.1463
12	1.0535	15.1463	0.0000

#	YEARS 13 INT	MO PAYT 1.3060 PRIN	AN CONST 15.68 BALANCE
1	12.4162	3.2561	96.7439
2	11.9814	3.6909	93.0530
3	11.4885	4.1838	88.8691
4	10.9298	4.7425	84.1266
5	10.2965	5.3758	78.7508
6	9.5787	6.0937	72.6572
7	8.7649	6.9074	65.7498
8	7.8425	7.8298	57.9200
9	6.7970	8.8754	49.0446
10	5.6118	10.0606	38.9840
11	4.2683	11.4040	27.5800
12	2.7454	12.9269	14.6531
13	1.0192	14.6531	0.0000

#	YEARS 14 INT	MO PAYT 1.2696 PRIN	AN CONST 15.24 BALANCE
1	12.4424	2.7923	97.2077
2	12.0695	3.1652	94.0425
3	11.6468	3.5879	90.4546

#	INT	PRIN	BALANCE
4	11.1677	4.0670	86.3876
5	10.6246	4.6101	81.7776
6	10.0090	5.2257	76.5519
7	9.3112	5.9235	70.6283
8	8.5202	6.7145	63.9138
9	7.6235	7.6112	56.3027
10	6.6072	8.6275	47.6751
11	5.4551	9.7796	37.8955
12	4.1491	11.0856	26.8099
13	2.6688	12.5659	14.2439
14	.9908	14.2439	0.0000

#	YEARS 15 INT	MO PAYT 1.2390 PRIN	AN CONST 14.87 BALANCE
1	12.4643	2.4041	97.5959
2	12.1433	2.7252	94.8707
3	11.7793	3.0891	91.7816
4	11.3668	3.5016	88.2800
5	10.8992	3.9692	84.3108
6	10.3692	4.4992	79.8115
7	9.7684	5.1001	74.7115
8	9.0873	5.7811	68.9303
9	8.3153	6.5531	62.3772
10	7.4403	7.4282	54.9491
11	6.4483	8.4201	46.5289
12	5.3239	9.5445	36.9844
13	4.0494	10.8191	26.1653
14	2.6046	12.2638	13.9015
15	.9669	13.9015	0.0000

#	YEARS 16 INT	MO PAYT 1.2133 PRIN	AN CONST 14.56 BALANCE
1	12.4828	2.0769	97.9231
2	12.2054	2.3542	95.5689
3	11.8911	2.6686	92.9003
4	11.5347	3.0249	89.8754
5	11.1308	3.4289	86.4465
6	10.6729	3.8868	82.5597
7	10.1538	4.4058	78.1539
8	9.5655	4.9941	73.1598
9	8.8986	5.6610	67.4987
10	8.1426	6.4170	61.0817
11	7.2857	7.2739	53.8078
12	6.3144	8.2452	45.5626
13	5.2133	9.3463	36.2163
14	3.9653	10.5944	25.6219
15	2.5505	12.0091	13.6128
16	.9469	13.6128	0.0000

#	YEARS 17 INT	MO PAYT 1.1915 PRIN	AN CONST 14.30 BALANCE
1	12.4984	1.7992	98.2008
2	12.2582	2.0395	96.1613
3	11.9858	2.3119	93.8494
4	11.6771	2.6206	91.2288
5	11.3272	2.9705	88.2583
6	10.9305	3.3672	84.8911
7	10.4808	3.8168	81.0743
8	9.9712	4.3265	76.7478
9	9.3934	4.9043	71.8435
10	8.7385	5.5592	66.2843
11	7.9961	6.3015	59.9827
12	7.1546	7.1430	52.8397
13	6.2008	8.0969	44.7428
14	5.1195	9.1781	35.5647
15	3.8939	10.4038	25.1609
16	2.5046	11.7930	13.3679
17	.9298	13.3679	0.0000

#	YEARS 18 INT	MO PAYT 1.1729 PRIN	AN CONST 14.08 BALANCE
1	12.5118	1.5625	98.4375
2	12.3032	1.7711	96.6664
3	12.0666	2.0076	94.6588
4	11.7986	2.2757	92.3830
5	11.4947	2.5796	89.8034
6	11.1502	2.9241	86.8793
7	10.7597	3.3146	83.5647
8	10.3171	3.7572	79.8075
9	9.8154	4.2589	75.5486
10	9.2466	4.8277	70.7209
11	8.6020	5.4723	65.2486
12	7.8712	6.2031	59.0455
13	7.0429	7.0314	52.0141
14	6.1039	7.9704	44.0437
15	5.0396	9.0347	35.0090
16	3.8331	10.2412	24.7678
17	2.4655	11.6088	13.1590
18	.9153	13.1590	0.0000

#	YEARS 19 INT	MO PAYT 1.1569 PRIN	AN CONST 13.89 BALANCE
1	12.5233	1.3597	98.6403
2	12.3417	1.5412	97.0991
3	12.1359	1.7470	95.3521
4	11.9026	1.9803	93.3717
5	11.6381	2.2448	91.1269
6	11.3384	2.5446	88.5824
7	10.9986	2.8843	85.6980
8	10.6134	3.2695	82.4285
9	10.1768	3.7061	78.7224
10	9.6819	4.2010	74.5214
11	9.1209	4.7620	69.7594
12	8.4850	5.3979	64.3614
13	7.7642	6.1187	58.2427
14	6.9471	6.9358	51.3069
15	6.0209	7.8620	43.4449
16	4.9710	8.9119	34.5330
17	3.7810	10.1020	24.4310
18	2.4320	11.4509	12.9801
19	.9028	12.9801	0.0000

#	YEARS 20 INT	MO PAYT 1.1432 PRIN	AN CONST 13.72 BALANCE
1	12.5331	1.1853	98.8147
2	12.3748	1.3436	97.4712
3	12.1954	1.5230	95.9482
4	11.9920	1.7263	94.2219
5	11.7615	1.9569	92.2650
6	11.5002	2.2182	90.0468
7	11.2040	2.5144	87.5324
8	10.8682	2.8502	84.6823
9	10.4876	3.2308	81.4515
10	10.0562	3.6622	77.7893
11	9.5671	4.1512	73.6381
12	9.0128	4.7056	68.9325
13	8.3844	5.3339	63.5986
14	7.6722	6.0462	57.5524
15	6.8648	6.8536	50.6987
16	5.9495	7.7688	42.9299
17	4.9121	8.8063	34.1237
18	3.7362	9.9822	24.1414
19	2.4032	11.3152	12.8262
20	.8921	12.8262	0.0000

#	YEARS 21 INT	MO PAYT 1.1314 PRIN	AN CONST 13.58 BALANCE
1	12.5416	1.0348	98.9652
2	12.4034	1.1730	97.7922
3	12.2468	1.3296	96.4625

MONTHLY PAYMENT AMORTIZATION SCHEDULE PER $100 — 12.60 %

#	INT	PRIN	BALANCE
4	12.0692	1.5072	94.9553
5	11.8679	1.7085	93.2468
6	11.6398	1.9366	91.3102
7	11.3812	2.1952	89.1150
8	11.0880	2.4884	86.6266
9	10.7557	2.8207	83.8060
10	10.3791	3.1973	80.6086
11	9.9521	3.6243	76.9843
12	9.4681	4.1083	72.8761
13	8.9195	4.6569	68.2192
14	8.2977	5.2787	62.9405
15	7.5928	5.9837	56.9568
16	6.7937	6.7827	50.1741
17	5.8880	7.6884	42.4857
18	4.8613	8.7151	33.7705
19	3.6975	9.8789	23.8916
20	2.3783	11.1981	12.6935
21	.8829	12.6935	0.0000

YEARS 22 — MO PAYT 1.1211 — AN CONST 13.46

#	INT	PRIN	BALANCE
1	12.5489	.9047	99.0953
2	12.4281	1.0255	98.0699
3	12.2912	1.1624	96.9075
4	12.1360	1.3176	95.5899
5	11.9600	1.4936	94.0963
6	11.7606	1.6930	92.4033
7	11.5345	1.9191	90.4842
8	11.2782	2.1754	88.3088
9	10.9877	2.4659	85.8430
10	10.6584	2.7951	83.0478
11	10.2852	3.1684	79.8794
12	9.8621	3.5915	76.2879
13	9.3825	4.0711	72.2168
14	8.8388	4.6147	67.6020
15	8.2226	5.2310	62.3711
16	7.5241	5.9295	56.4415
17	6.7323	6.7213	49.7202
18	5.8347	7.6189	42.1013
19	4.8173	8.6363	33.4650
20	3.6640	9.7896	23.6755
21	2.3568	11.0968	12.5787
22	.8749	12.5787	0.0000

YEARS 23 — MO PAYT 1.1123 — AN CONST 13.35

#	INT	PRIN	BALANCE
1	12.5553	.7918	99.2082
2	12.4496	.8975	98.3107
3	12.3297	1.0173	97.2934
4	12.1939	1.1532	96.1402
5	12.0399	1.3072	94.8330
6	11.8653	1.4817	93.3513
7	11.6675	1.6796	91.6717
8	11.4432	1.9039	89.7678
9	11.1889	2.1581	87.6096
10	10.9007	2.4463	85.1633
11	10.5741	2.7730	82.3903
12	10.2038	3.1433	79.2469
13	9.7840	3.5631	75.6839
14	9.3082	4.0389	71.6450
15	8.7689	4.5782	67.0668
16	8.1575	5.1896	61.8772
17	7.4645	5.8826	55.9947
18	6.6790	6.6681	49.3265
19	5.7885	7.5586	41.7680
20	4.7792	8.5679	33.2001
21	3.6350	9.7120	23.4880
22	2.3381	11.0090	12.4791
23	.8680	12.4791	0.0000

YEARS 24 — MO PAYT 1.1045 — AN CONST 13.26

#	INT	PRIN	BALANCE
1	12.5608	.6936	99.3064
2	12.4682	.7863	98.5201
3	12.3632	.8913	97.6288
4	12.2442	1.0103	96.6185
5	12.1093	1.1452	95.4733
6	11.9564	1.2981	94.1752
7	11.7830	1.4715	92.7038
8	11.5865	1.6680	91.0358
9	11.3638	1.8907	89.1451
10	11.1113	2.1432	87.0019
11	10.8251	2.4294	84.5726
12	10.5007	2.7538	81.8188
13	10.1330	3.1215	78.6973
14	9.7161	3.5384	75.1589
15	9.2436	4.0109	71.1481
16	8.7080	4.5465	66.6016
17	8.1009	5.1536	61.4480
18	7.4127	5.8418	55.6063
19	6.6326	6.6219	48.9844
20	5.7484	7.5061	41.4783
21	4.7460	8.5085	32.9698
22	3.6098	9.6447	23.3251
23	2.3219	10.9326	12.3925
24	.8620	12.3925	0.0000

YEARS 25 — MO PAYT 1.0978 — AN CONST 13.18

#	INT	PRIN	BALANCE
1	12.5657	.6082	99.3918
2	12.4845	.6894	98.7024
3	12.3924	.7815	97.9209
4	12.2880	.8858	97.0350
5	12.1697	1.0041	96.0309
6	12.0356	1.1382	94.8927
7	11.8837	1.2902	93.6024
8	11.7114	1.4625	92.1399
9	11.5161	1.6578	90.4821
10	11.2947	1.8792	88.6029
11	11.0437	2.1301	86.4728
12	10.7593	2.4146	84.0582
13	10.4368	2.7370	81.3211
14	10.0713	3.1025	78.2186
15	9.6570	3.5168	74.7018
16	9.1874	3.9865	70.7153
17	8.6551	4.5188	66.1965
18	8.0516	5.1222	61.0743
19	7.3676	5.8062	55.2681
20	6.5923	6.5816	48.6865
21	5.7134	7.4605	41.2260
22	4.7171	8.4567	32.7693
23	3.5879	9.5860	23.1832
24	2.3078	10.8661	12.3171
25	.8567	12.3171	0.0000

YEARS 26 — MO PAYT 1.0920 — AN CONST 13.11

#	INT	PRIN	BALANCE
1	12.5699	.5337	99.4663
2	12.4986	.6050	98.8613
3	12.4178	.6857	98.1756
4	12.3263	.7773	97.3983
5	12.2225	.8811	96.5172
6	12.1048	.9988	95.5184
7	11.9714	1.1322	94.3862
8	11.8202	1.2833	93.1029
9	11.6489	1.4547	91.6482
10	11.4546	1.6490	89.9992
11	11.2344	1.8692	88.1300
12	10.9848	2.1188	86.0113
13	10.7019	2.4017	83.6096
14	10.3811	2.7224	80.8871
15	10.0176	3.0860	77.8012
16	9.6055	3.4981	74.3031
17	9.1384	3.9652	70.3379
18	8.6089	4.4947	65.8432
19	8.0087	5.0949	60.7483
20	7.3283	5.7753	54.9731
21	6.5571	6.5465	48.4266
22	5.6829	7.4207	41.0060
23	4.6920	8.4116	32.5944
24	3.5687	9.5349	23.0595
25	2.2955	10.8081	12.2514
26	.8522	12.2514	0.0000

YEARS 27 — MO PAYT 1.0868 — AN CONST 13.05

#	INT	PRIN	BALANCE
1	12.5735	.4686	99.5314
2	12.5110	.5312	99.0002
3	12.4400	.6021	98.3981
4	12.3596	.6825	97.7155
5	12.2685	.7737	96.9419
6	12.1652	.8770	96.0649
7	12.0481	.9941	95.0708
8	11.9153	1.1268	93.9439
9	11.7648	1.2773	92.6666
10	11.5943	1.4479	91.2187
11	11.4009	1.6412	89.5775
12	11.1818	1.8604	87.7171
13	10.9333	2.1088	85.6082
14	10.6517	2.3905	83.2178
15	10.3325	2.7097	80.5081
16	9.9707	3.0715	77.4366
17	9.5605	3.4817	73.9549
18	9.0956	3.9466	70.0083
19	8.5685	4.4736	65.5347
20	7.9711	5.0710	60.4637
21	7.2940	5.7482	54.7155
22	6.5264	6.5158	48.1997
23	5.6563	7.3859	40.8138
24	4.6700	8.3722	32.4416
25	3.5520	9.4902	22.9515
26	2.2847	10.7575	12.1940
27	.8482	12.1940	0.0000

YEARS 28 — MO PAYT 1.0824 — AN CONST 12.99

#	INT	PRIN	BALANCE
1	12.5768	.4117	99.5883
2	12.5218	.4667	99.1216
3	12.4595	.5290	98.5926
4	12.3888	.5996	97.9930
5	12.3087	.6797	97.3132
6	12.2180	.7705	96.5428
7	12.1151	.8734	95.6694
8	11.9985	.9900	94.6794
9	11.8663	1.1222	93.5572
10	11.7164	1.2721	92.2851
11	11.5465	1.4419	90.8432
12	11.3540	1.6345	89.2087
13	11.1357	1.8528	87.3559
14	10.8883	2.1002	85.2558
15	10.6079	2.3806	82.8752
16	10.2900	2.6985	80.1766
17	9.9296	3.0589	77.1178
18	9.5211	3.4673	73.6504
19	9.0581	3.9304	69.7201
20	8.5333	4.4552	65.2649
21	7.9383	5.0501	60.2147
22	7.2639	5.7245	54.4902
23	6.4995	6.4890	48.0013
24	5.6330	7.3555	40.6458
25	4.6508	8.3377	32.3081
26	3.5374	9.4511	22.8570
27	2.2753	10.7132	12.1438
28	.8447	12.1438	0.0000

YEARS 29 — MO PAYT 1.0785 — AN CONST 12.95

#	INT	PRIN	BALANCE
1	12.5796	.3619	99.6381
2	12.5312	.4102	99.2279
3	12.4765	.4650	98.7629
4	12.4144	.5271	98.2358
5	12.3440	.5975	97.6383
6	12.2642	.6773	96.9611
7	12.1738	.7677	96.1934
8	12.0712	.8702	95.3232
9	11.9550	.9864	94.3367
10	11.8233	1.1181	93.2186
11	11.6740	1.2675	91.9511
12	11.5047	1.4367	90.5144
13	11.3129	1.6286	88.8858
14	11.0954	1.8460	87.0398
15	10.8489	2.0926	84.9472
16	10.5695	2.3720	82.5752
17	10.2527	2.6887	79.8865
18	9.8937	3.0478	76.8387
19	9.4867	3.4548	73.3839
20	9.0253	3.9161	69.4678
21	8.5024	4.4391	65.0287
22	7.9096	5.0319	59.9968
23	7.2377	5.7038	54.2930
24	6.4760	6.4655	47.8275
25	5.6126	7.3289	40.4987
26	4.6339	8.3075	32.1911
27	3.5246	9.4169	22.7742
28	2.2671	10.6744	12.0998
29	.8416	12.0998	0.0000

YEARS 30 — MO PAYT 1.0750 — AN CONST 12.91

#	INT	PRIN	BALANCE
1	12.5820	.3182	99.6818
2	12.5395	.3607	99.3210
3	12.4914	.4089	98.9121
4	12.4368	.4635	98.4486
5	12.3749	.5254	97.9232
6	12.3047	.5956	97.3276
7	12.2252	.6751	96.6525
8	12.1350	.7653	95.8872
9	12.0328	.8674	95.0198
10	11.9170	.9833	94.0365
11	11.7857	1.1146	92.9219
12	11.6369	1.2634	91.6585
13	11.4681	1.4321	90.2264
14	11.2769	1.6234	88.6030
15	11.0601	1.8402	86.7628
16	10.8144	2.0859	84.6769
17	10.5358	2.3644	82.3124
18	10.2201	2.6802	79.6323
19	9.8622	3.0381	76.5942
20	9.4565	3.4438	73.1504
21	8.9966	3.9037	69.2467
22	8.4753	4.4250	64.8217
23	7.8844	5.0159	59.8059
24	7.2146	5.6857	54.1202
25	6.4554	6.4449	47.6753
26	5.5947	7.3055	40.3698
27	4.6192	8.2811	32.0887
28	3.5133	9.3869	22.7018
29	2.2598	10.6404	12.0613
30	.8389	12.0613	0.0000

YEARS 2 MO PAYT 4.7366 AN CONST 56.84		
# INT	PRIN	BALANCE
1 9.9747	46.8644	53.1356
2 3.7034	53.1356	0.0000

YEARS 3 MO PAYT 3.3514 AN CONST 40.22		
# INT	PRIN	BALANCE
1 10.9711	29.2452	70.7548
2 7.0576	33.1588	37.5960
3 2.6203	37.5960	0.0000

YEARS 4 MO PAYT 2.6642 AN CONST 31.98		
# INT	PRIN	BALANCE
1 11.4654	20.5047	79.4953
2 8.7215	23.2486	56.2467
3 5.6104	26.3597	29.8871
4 2.0830	29.8871	0.0000

YEARS 5 MO PAYT 2.2562 AN CONST 27.08		
# INT	PRIN	BALANCE
1 11.7589	15.3150	84.6850
2 9.7095	17.3644	67.3206
3 7.3858	19.6881	47.6325
4 4.7512	22.3227	25.3099
5 1.7640	25.3099	0.0000

YEARS 6 MO PAYT 1.9877 AN CONST 23.86		
# INT	PRIN	BALANCE
1 11.9520	11.9001	88.0999
2 10.3596	13.4925	74.6074
3 8.5540	15.2980	59.3094
4 6.5069	17.3452	41.9642
5 4.1858	19.6663	22.2980
6 1.5541	22.2980	0.0000

YEARS 7 MO PAYT 1.7989 AN CONST 21.59		
# INT	PRIN	BALANCE
1 12.0878	9.4986	90.5014
2 10.8167	10.7697	79.7317
3 9.3756	12.2109	67.5208
4 7.7415	13.8449	53.6758
5 5.8888	15.6976	37.9782
6 3.7882	17.7982	20.1800
7 1.4065	20.1800	0.0000

YEARS 8 MO PAYT 1.6598 AN CONST 19.92		
# INT	PRIN	BALANCE
1 12.1878	7.7300	92.2700
2 11.1534	8.7644	83.5056
3 9.8806	9.9372	73.5684
4 8.6508	11.2670	62.3014
5 7.1431	12.7747	49.5267
6 5.4336	14.4842	35.0425
7 3.4954	16.4224	18.6201
8 1.2978	18.6201	0.0000

YEARS 9 MO PAYT 1.5539 AN CONST 18.65		
# INT	PRIN	BALANCE
1 12.2641	6.3825	93.6175
2 11.4100	7.2366	86.3809
3 10.4416	8.2050	78.1759
4 9.3436	9.3030	68.8729
5 8.0987	10.5479	58.3250
6 6.6872	11.9594	46.3657
7 5.0868	13.5597	32.8059
8 3.2723	15.3743	17.4316
9 1.2149	17.4316	0.0000

YEARS 10 MO PAYT 1.4711 AN CONST 17.66		
# INT	PRIN	BALANCE
1 12.3236	5.3292	94.6708
2 11.6105	6.0424	88.6284
3 10.8019	6.8510	81.7774
4 9.8851	7.7677	74.0097
5 8.8457	8.8072	65.2025
6 7.6671	9.9858	55.2167
7 6.3308	11.3220	43.8947
8 4.8157	12.8371	31.0576
9 3.0979	14.5549	16.5027
10 1.1502	16.5027	0.0000

YEARS 11 MO PAYT 1.4050 AN CONST 16.87		
# INT	PRIN	BALANCE
1 12.3711	4.4892	95.5108
2 11.7704	5.0900	90.4208
3 11.0892	5.7711	84.6496
4 10.3170	6.5434	78.1062
5 9.4413	7.4190	70.6872
6 8.4485	8.4118	62.2754
7 7.3229	9.5375	52.7379
8 6.0466	10.8138	41.9242
9 4.5995	12.2608	29.6634
10 2.9588	13.9015	15.7618
11 1.0986	15.7618	0.0000

YEARS 12 MO PAYT 1.3515 AN CONST 16.22		
# INT	PRIN	BALANCE
1 12.4096	3.8086	96.1914
2 11.9000	4.3183	91.8731
3 11.3221	4.8961	86.9770
4 10.6669	5.5513	81.4257
5 9.9240	6.2942	75.1315
6 9.0818	7.1365	67.9950
7 8.1268	8.0914	59.9036
8 7.0440	9.1742	50.7294
9 5.8163	10.4019	40.3275
10 4.4244	11.7939	28.5336
11 2.8461	13.3721	15.1615
12 1.0567	15.1615	0.0000

YEARS 13 MO PAYT 1.3076 AN CONST 15.70		
# INT	PRIN	BALANCE
1 12.4412	3.2499	96.7501
2 12.0063	3.6848	93.0652
3 11.5132	4.1779	88.8873
4 10.9541	4.7370	84.1503
5 10.3202	5.3709	78.7794
6 9.6015	6.0896	72.6898
7 8.7866	6.9045	65.7852
8 7.8627	7.8285	57.9567
9 6.8151	8.8761	49.0807
10 5.6273	10.0638	39.0168
11 4.2806	11.4106	27.6063
12 2.7536	12.9375	14.6688
13 1.0224	14.6688	0.0000

YEARS 14 MO PAYT 1.2712 AN CONST 15.26		
# INT	PRIN	BALANCE
1 12.4674	2.7865	97.2135
2 12.0945	3.1594	94.0541
3 11.6718	3.5822	90.4720
4 11.1924	4.0615	86.4105
5 10.6489	4.6050	81.8055
6 10.0327	5.2212	76.5842
7 9.3340	5.9199	70.6643
8 8.5418	6.7121	63.9521
9 7.6436	7.6103	56.3418
10 6.6252	8.6287	47.7131
11 5.4705	9.7834	37.9296
12 4.1613	11.0926	26.8370
13 2.6769	12.5770	14.2600
14 .9939	14.2600	0.0000

YEARS 15 MO PAYT 1.2407 AN CONST 14.89		
# INT	PRIN	BALANCE
1 12.4893	2.3987	97.6013
2 12.1684	2.7197	94.8817
3 11.8044	3.0836	91.7981
4 11.3918	3.4962	88.3019
5 10.9239	3.9641	84.3378
6 10.3935	4.4946	79.8432
7 9.7920	5.0960	74.7472
8 9.1101	5.7779	68.9693
9 8.3369	6.5511	62.4181
10 7.4602	7.4278	54.9903
11 6.4663	8.4218	46.5686
12 5.3393	9.5487	37.0198
13 4.0615	10.8265	26.1933
14 2.6127	12.2753	13.9180
15 .9700	13.9180	0.0000

YEARS 16 MO PAYT 1.2150 AN CONST 14.58		
# INT	PRIN	BALANCE
1 12.5078	2.0717	97.9283
2 12.2306	2.3490	95.5793
3 11.9163	2.6633	92.9160
4 11.5599	3.0197	89.8963
5 11.1558	3.4238	86.4725
6 10.6976	3.8820	82.5905
7 10.1781	4.4014	78.1891
8 9.5891	4.9904	73.1986
9 8.9213	5.6582	67.5404
10 8.1642	6.4154	61.1250
11 7.3057	7.2739	53.8511
12 6.3323	8.2473	45.6038
13 5.2287	9.3509	36.2529
14 3.9773	10.6022	25.6506
15 2.5586	12.0210	13.6296
16 .9499	13.6296	0.0000

YEARS 17 MO PAYT 1.1932 AN CONST 14.32		
# INT	PRIN	BALANCE
1 12.5235	1.7944	98.2056
2 12.2834	2.0346	96.1710
3 12.0111	2.3068	93.8642
4 11.7024	2.6155	91.2487
5 11.3524	2.9655	88.2831
6 10.9556	3.3624	84.9208
7 10.5057	3.8123	81.1085
8 9.9955	4.3225	76.7860
9 9.4171	4.9009	71.8851
10 8.7613	5.5567	66.3284
11 8.0177	6.3003	60.0281
12 7.1746	7.1434	52.8848
13 6.2187	8.0993	44.7855
14 5.1348	9.1831	35.6023
15 3.9060	10.4120	25.1904
16 2.5127	11.8053	13.3851
17 .9329	13.3851	0.0000

YEARS 18 MO PAYT 1.1746 AN CONST 14.10		
# INT	PRIN	BALANCE
1 12.5369	1.5580	98.4420
2 12.3284	1.7665	96.6755
3 12.0920	2.0029	94.6727
4 11.8240	2.2709	92.4018
5 11.5201	2.5748	89.8270
6 11.1756	2.9193	86.9077
7 10.7849	3.3100	83.5977
8 10.3420	3.7529	79.8448
9 9.8398	4.2551	75.5897
10 9.2704	4.8245	70.7652
11 8.6248	5.4701	65.2950
12 7.8928	6.2021	59.0929
13 7.0628	7.0321	52.0608
14 6.1218	7.9731	44.0877
15 5.0548	9.0401	35.0477
16 3.8451	10.2498	24.7979
17 2.4735	11.6214	13.1765
18 .9184	13.1765	0.0000

YEARS 19 MO PAYT 1.1587 AN CONST 13.91		
# INT	PRIN	BALANCE
1 12.5483	1.3555	98.6445
2 12.3670	1.5369	97.1076
3 12.1613	1.7425	95.3651
4 11.9281	1.9757	93.3894
5 11.6637	2.2401	91.1493
6 11.3640	2.5399	88.6094
7 11.0241	2.8797	85.7297
8 10.6387	3.2651	82.4646
9 10.2018	3.7020	78.7625
10 9.7064	4.1974	74.5651
11 9.1447	4.7591	69.8060
12 8.5078	5.3960	64.4100
13 7.7858	6.1181	58.2919
14 6.9671	6.9368	51.3551
15 6.0388	7.8650	43.4901
16 4.9863	8.9175	34.5726
17 3.7930	10.1108	24.4618
18 2.4400	11.4638	12.9979
19 .9059	12.9979	0.0000

YEARS 20 MO PAYT 1.1450 AN CONST 13.74		
# INT	PRIN	BALANCE
1 12.5582	1.1814	98.8186
2 12.4001	1.3395	97.4791
3 12.2209	1.5187	95.9604
4 12.0176	1.7219	94.2385
5 11.7872	1.9524	92.2861
6 11.5259	2.2136	90.0725
7 11.2297	2.5099	87.5626
8 10.8938	2.8457	84.7169
9 10.5130	3.2265	81.4903
10 10.0813	3.6583	77.8320
11 9.5917	4.1478	73.6842
12 9.0367	4.7029	68.9813
13 8.4073	5.3322	63.6490
14 7.6938	6.0458	57.6033
15 6.8848	6.8548	50.7484
16 5.9675	7.7721	42.9763
17 4.9274	8.8122	34.1642
18 3.7482	9.9914	24.1728
19 2.4112	11.3284	12.8444
20 .8952	12.8444	0.0000

YEARS 21 MO PAYT 1.1332 AN CONST 13.60		
# INT	PRIN	BALANCE
1 12.5667	1.0312	98.9688
2 12.4287	1.1692	97.7996
3 12.2722	1.3257	96.4739

#	INT	PRIN	BALANCE
4	12.0948	1.5031	94.9709
5	11.8937	1.7042	93.2667
6	11.6656	1.9322	91.3344
7	11.4071	2.1908	89.1436
8	11.1139	2.4840	86.6597
9	10.7815	2.8164	83.8433
10	10.4046	3.1933	80.6500
11	9.9773	3.6206	77.0294
12	9.4928	4.1051	72.9244
13	8.9435	4.6544	68.2699
14	8.3206	5.2773	62.9927
15	7.6144	5.9834	57.0092
16	6.8138	6.7841	50.2251
17	5.9059	7.6920	42.5331
18	4.8766	8.7213	33.8119
19	3.7095	9.8884	23.9235
20	2.3863	11.2116	12.7119
21	.8860	12.7119	0.0000

YEARS 22 MO PAYT 1.1229 AN CONST 13.48

#	INT	PRIN	BALANCE
1	12.5740	.9013	99.0987
2	12.4534	1.0219	98.0768
3	12.3167	1.1587	96.9181
4	12.1616	1.3137	95.6044
5	11.9858	1.4895	94.1149
6	11.7865	1.6888	92.4261
7	11.5605	1.9148	90.5112
8	11.3043	2.1711	88.3402
9	11.0137	2.4616	85.8786
10	10.6843	2.7910	83.0876
11	10.3108	3.1645	79.9231
12	9.8874	3.5879	76.3352
13	9.4073	4.0681	72.2671
14	8.8629	4.6125	67.6546
15	8.2456	5.2297	62.4249
16	7.5458	5.9295	56.4954
17	6.7523	6.7230	49.7724
18	5.8527	7.6226	42.1498
19	4.8326	8.6427	33.5071
20	3.6761	9.7992	23.7079
21	2.3648	11.1105	12.5973
22	.8780	12.5973	0.0000

YEARS 23 MO PAYT 1.1141 AN CONST 13.37

#	INT	PRIN	BALANCE
1	12.5804	.7887	99.2113
2	12.4749	.8942	98.3171
3	12.3552	1.0139	97.3033
4	12.2195	1.1495	96.1538
5	12.0657	1.3034	94.8504
6	11.8913	1.4778	93.3727
7	11.6935	1.6755	91.6971
8	11.4693	1.8997	89.7974
9	11.2151	2.1539	87.6435
10	10.9269	2.4422	85.2013
11	10.6001	2.7690	82.4323
12	10.2295	3.1395	79.2928
13	9.8094	3.5597	75.7331
14	9.3331	4.0360	71.6971
15	8.7930	4.5761	67.1211
16	8.1806	5.1884	61.9326
17	7.4863	5.8827	56.0499
18	6.6991	6.6700	49.3799
19	5.8065	7.5625	41.8174
20	4.7945	8.5745	33.2429
21	3.6471	9.7219	23.5209
22	2.3461	11.0229	12.4980
23	.8711	12.4980	0.0000

YEARS 24 MO PAYT 1.1064 AN CONST 13.28

#	INT	PRIN	BALANCE
1	12.5859	.6908	99.3092
2	12.4935	.7832	98.5260
3	12.3887	.8880	97.6380
4	12.2699	1.0068	96.6312
5	12.1351	1.1416	95.4896
6	11.9824	1.2943	94.1952
7	11.8092	1.4676	92.7277
8	11.6128	1.6639	91.0637
9	11.3901	1.8866	89.1771
10	11.1376	2.1391	87.0381
11	10.8514	2.4253	84.6128
12	10.5268	2.7499	81.8629
13	10.1589	3.1178	78.7451
14	9.7416	3.5351	75.2100
15	9.2686	4.0081	71.2019
16	8.7322	4.5445	66.6574
17	8.1241	5.1526	61.5048
18	7.4346	5.8421	55.6627
19	6.6528	6.6239	49.0388
20	5.7664	7.5103	41.5285
21	4.7614	8.5153	33.0132
22	3.6219	9.6548	23.3584
23	2.3299	10.9468	12.4116
24	.8651	12.4116	0.0000

YEARS 25 MO PAYT 1.0997 AN CONST 13.20

#	INT	PRIN	BALANCE
1	12.5908	.6056	99.3944
2	12.5097	.6866	98.7079
3	12.4178	.7785	97.9294
4	12.3137	.8826	97.0468
5	12.1956	1.0008	96.0460
6	12.0616	1.1347	94.9113
7	11.9098	1.2865	93.6248
8	11.7376	1.4587	92.1662
9	11.5424	1.6539	90.5123
10	11.3211	1.8752	88.6371
11	11.0702	2.1261	86.5110
12	10.7857	2.4106	84.1004
13	10.4631	2.7332	81.3672
14	10.0974	3.0990	78.2682
15	9.6827	3.5137	74.7546
16	9.2125	3.9838	70.7707
17	8.6794	4.5170	66.2538
18	8.0749	5.1214	61.1324
19	7.3896	5.8067	55.3256
20	6.6125	6.5838	48.7418
21	5.7315	7.4648	41.2770
22	4.7326	8.4637	32.8133
23	3.6000	9.5963	23.2170
24	2.3158	10.8805	12.3365
25	.8598	12.3365	0.0000

YEARS 26 MO PAYT 1.0939 AN CONST 13.13

#	INT	PRIN	BALANCE
1	12.5950	.5312	99.4688
2	12.5239	.6023	98.8664
3	12.4433	.6829	98.1835
4	12.3519	.7743	97.4091
5	12.2483	.8780	96.5312
6	12.1308	.9954	95.5358
7	11.9976	1.1286	94.4071
8	11.8465	1.2797	93.1274
9	11.6753	1.4509	91.6765
10	11.4811	1.6451	90.0314
11	11.2610	1.8652	88.1662
12	11.0114	2.1148	86.0514
13	10.7284	2.3978	83.6536
14	10.4075	2.7187	80.9349
15	10.0437	3.0825	77.8524
16	9.6312	3.4950	74.3574
17	9.1635	3.9627	70.3947
18	8.6332	4.4930	65.9018
19	8.0320	5.0942	60.8076
20	7.3503	5.7759	55.0317
21	6.5774	6.5488	48.4829
22	5.7011	7.4252	41.0578
23	4.7074	8.4188	32.6390
24	3.5809	9.5453	23.0936
25	2.3035	10.8227	12.2710
26	.8553	12.2710	0.0000

YEARS 27 MO PAYT 1.0887 AN CONST 13.07

#	INT	PRIN	BALANCE
1	12.5986	.4664	99.5336
2	12.5362	.5288	99.0049
3	12.4655	.5995	98.4053
4	12.3852	.6798	97.7256
5	12.2943	.7707	96.9549
6	12.1911	.8739	96.0810
7	12.0742	.9908	95.0902
8	11.9416	1.1234	93.9668
9	11.7913	1.2737	92.6931
10	11.6208	1.4442	91.2490
11	11.4276	1.6374	89.6116
12	11.2085	1.8565	87.7551
13	10.9600	2.1050	85.6501
14	10.6784	2.3866	83.2635
15	10.3590	2.7060	80.5575
16	9.9969	3.0681	77.4893
17	9.5863	3.4787	74.0106
18	9.1208	3.9442	70.0665
19	8.5930	4.4720	65.5944
20	7.9946	5.0704	60.5240
21	7.3160	5.7490	54.7751
22	6.5467	6.5183	48.2568
23	5.6745	7.3905	40.8663
24	4.6855	8.3795	32.4868
25	3.5642	9.5008	22.9859
26	2.2928	10.7722	12.2137
27	.8513	12.2137	0.0000

YEARS 28 MO PAYT 1.0843 AN CONST 13.02

#	INT	PRIN	BALANCE
1	12.6018	.4096	99.5904
2	12.5470	.4645	99.1259
3	12.4849	.5266	98.5993
4	12.4144	.5971	98.0022
5	12.3345	.6770	97.3253
6	12.2439	.7676	96.5577
7	12.1412	.8703	95.6874
8	12.0247	.9867	94.7007
9	11.8927	1.1188	93.5819
10	11.7430	1.2685	92.3134
11	11.5732	1.4382	90.8752
12	11.3808	1.6307	89.2445
13	11.1626	1.8489	87.3956
14	10.9151	2.0963	85.2992
15	10.6346	2.3769	82.9224
16	10.3165	2.6949	80.2275
17	9.9559	3.0556	77.1719
18	9.5470	3.4644	73.7075
19	9.0834	3.9280	69.7794
20	8.5578	4.4537	65.3257
21	7.9618	5.0497	60.2761
22	7.2861	5.7254	54.5507
23	6.5199	6.4916	48.0591
24	5.6512	7.3602	40.6989
25	4.6663	8.3452	32.3537
26	3.5496	9.4619	22.8918
27	2.2834	10.7281	12.1637
28	.8478	12.1637	0.0000

YEARS 29 MO PAYT 1.0804 AN CONST 12.97

#	INT	PRIN	BALANCE
1	12.6046	.3600	99.6400
2	12.5565	.4082	99.2319
3	12.5018	.4628	98.7691
4	12.4399	.5247	98.2444
5	12.3697	.5949	97.6494
6	12.2901	.6745	96.9749
7	12.1998	.7648	96.2101
8	12.0975	.8671	95.3430
9	11.9814	.9832	94.3598
10	11.8499	1.1147	93.2450
11	11.7007	1.2639	91.9811
12	11.5316	1.4331	90.5480
13	11.3398	1.6248	88.9232
14	11.1224	1.8423	87.0810
15	10.8758	2.0888	84.9922
16	10.5963	2.3683	82.6239
17	10.2794	2.6852	79.9387
18	9.9201	3.0446	76.8941
19	9.5127	3.4520	73.4421
20	9.0507	3.9139	69.5282
21	8.5270	4.4377	65.0906
22	7.9331	5.0315	60.0591
23	7.2598	5.7048	54.3543
24	6.4964	6.4682	47.8861
25	5.6309	7.3338	40.5524
26	4.6495	8.3151	32.2372
27	3.5368	9.4279	22.8094
28	2.2752	10.6895	12.1199
29	.8447	12.1199	0.0000

YEARS 30 MO PAYT 1.0770 AN CONST 12.93

#	INT	PRIN	BALANCE
1	12.6071	.3165	99.6835
2	12.5647	.3588	99.3247
3	12.5167	.4069	98.9178
4	12.4623	.4613	98.4565
5	12.4005	.5230	97.9334
6	12.3306	.5930	97.3404
7	12.2512	.6724	96.6680
8	12.1612	.7624	95.9056
9	12.0592	.8644	95.0412
10	11.9435	.9801	94.0611
11	11.8124	1.1112	92.9499
12	11.6637	1.2599	91.6900
13	11.4951	1.4285	90.2615
14	11.3039	1.6197	88.6418
15	11.0872	1.8364	86.8054
16	10.8414	2.0822	84.7232
17	10.5628	2.3608	82.3624
18	10.2469	2.6767	79.6857
19	9.8887	3.0349	76.6507
20	9.4826	3.4410	73.2097
21	9.0221	3.9015	69.3082
22	8.5000	4.4236	64.8846
23	7.9080	5.0156	59.8690
24	7.2369	5.6867	54.1823
25	6.4759	6.4477	47.7346
26	5.6131	7.3105	40.4240
27	4.6348	8.2888	32.1352
28	3.5256	9.3980	22.7372
29	2.2680	10.6556	12.0815
30	.8421	12.0815	0.0000

YEARS 2 — MO PAYT 4.7401 — AN CONST 56.89

#	INT	PRIN	BALANCE
1	10.0354	46.8459	53.1541
2	3.7271	53.1541	0.0000

YEARS 3 — MO PAYT 3.3550 — AN CONST 40.26

#	INT	PRIN	BALANCE
1	11.0378	29.2217	70.7783
2	7.1029	33.1567	37.6216
3	2.6380	37.6216	0.0000

YEARS 4 — MO PAYT 2.6679 — AN CONST 32.02

#	INT	PRIN	BALANCE
1	11.5351	20.4795	79.5205
2	8.7773	23.2373	56.2832
3	5.6482	26.3664	29.9169
4	2.0977	29.9169	0.0000

YEARS 5 — MO PAYT 2.2600 — AN CONST 27.12

#	INT	PRIN	BALANCE
1	11.8303	15.2894	84.7106
2	9.7715	17.3483	67.3623
3	7.4353	19.6844	47.6779
4	4.7846	22.3351	25.3427
5	1.7770	25.3427	0.0000

YEARS 6 — MO PAYT 1.9916 — AN CONST 23.90

#	INT	PRIN	BALANCE
1	12.0246	11.8748	88.1252
2	10.4255	13.4738	74.6514
3	8.6111	15.2882	59.3631
4	6.5524	17.3469	42.0162
5	4.2165	19.6829	22.3333
6	1.5660	22.3333	0.0000

YEARS 7 — MO PAYT 1.8029 — AN CONST 21.64

#	INT	PRIN	BALANCE
1	12.1611	9.4740	90.5260
2	10.8853	10.7498	79.7762
3	9.4378	12.1973	67.5789
4	7.7953	13.8398	53.7391
5	5.9316	15.7035	38.0356
6	3.8170	17.8181	20.2175
7	1.4176	20.2175	0.0000

YEARS 8 — MO PAYT 1.6640 — AN CONST 19.97

#	INT	PRIN	BALANCE
1	12.2617	7.7062	92.2938
2	11.2239	8.7439	83.5499
3	10.0465	9.9214	73.6285
4	8.7105	11.2574	62.3711
5	7.1946	12.7733	49.5978
6	5.4745	14.4933	35.1045
7	3.5229	16.4450	18.6595
8	1.3084	18.6595	0.0000

YEARS 9 — MO PAYT 1.5582 — AN CONST 18.70

#	INT	PRIN	BALANCE
1	12.3383	6.3597	93.6403
2	11.4819	7.2161	86.4242
3	10.5101	8.1878	78.2363
4	9.4076	9.2904	68.9459
5	8.1565	10.5414	58.4045
6	6.7370	11.9609	46.4435
7	5.1264	13.5716	32.8719
8	3.2988	15.3992	17.4728
9	1.2252	17.4728	0.0000

YEARS 10 — MO PAYT 1.4755 — AN CONST 17.71

#	INT	PRIN	BALANCE
1	12.3981	5.3075	94.6925
2	11.6834	6.0222	88.6704
3	10.8725	6.8331	81.8372
4	9.9523	7.7533	74.0840
5	8.9083	8.7973	65.2867
6	7.7236	9.9820	55.3047
7	6.3795	11.3261	43.9786
8	4.8543	12.8513	31.1273
9	3.1237	14.5818	16.5454
10	1.1601	16.5454	0.0000

YEARS 11 — MO PAYT 1.4095 — AN CONST 16.92

#	INT	PRIN	BALANCE
1	12.4458	4.4686	95.5314
2	11.8441	5.0703	90.4611
3	11.1613	5.7531	84.7081
4	10.3866	6.5278	78.1803
5	9.5076	7.4068	70.7735
6	8.5102	8.4042	62.3693
7	7.3785	9.5359	52.8334
8	6.0944	10.8200	42.0134
9	4.6374	12.2770	29.7363
10	2.9841	13.9302	15.8061
11	1.1083	15.8061	0.0000

YEARS 12 — MO PAYT 1.3561 — AN CONST 16.28

#	INT	PRIN	BALANCE
1	12.4845	3.7890	96.2110
2	11.9742	4.2993	91.9117
3	11.3953	4.8782	87.0335
4	10.7384	5.5351	81.4984
5	9.9931	6.2804	75.2180
6	9.1473	7.1262	68.0918
7	8.1877	8.0858	60.0061
8	7.0989	9.1746	50.8315
9	5.8635	10.4100	40.4215
10	4.4617	11.8118	28.6096
11	2.8711	13.4024	15.2072
12	1.0663	15.2072	0.0000

YEARS 13 — MO PAYT 1.3123 — AN CONST 15.75

#	INT	PRIN	BALANCE
1	12.5162	3.2314	96.7686
2	12.0810	3.6666	93.1020
3	11.5873	4.1603	88.9416
4	11.0271	4.7206	84.2211
5	10.3914	5.3562	78.8649
6	9.6701	6.0775	72.7874
7	8.8518	6.8959	65.8915
8	7.9232	7.8245	58.0670
9	6.8695	8.8781	49.1889
10	5.6740	10.0736	39.1153
11	4.3175	11.4302	27.6851
12	2.7783	12.9693	14.7158
13	1.0319	14.7158	0.0000

YEARS 14 — MO PAYT 1.2760 — AN CONST 15.32

#	INT	PRIN	BALANCE
1	12.5425	2.7691	97.2309
2	12.1696	3.1420	94.0890
3	11.7465	3.5651	90.5239
4	11.2664	4.0451	86.4788
5	10.7217	4.5898	81.8889
6	10.1037	5.2079	76.6810
7	9.4024	5.9092	70.7718
8	8.6066	6.7049	64.0669
9	7.7038	7.6078	56.4591
10	6.6793	8.6323	47.8268
11	5.5169	9.7947	38.0321
12	4.1979	11.1136	26.9185
13	2.7014	12.6102	14.3083
14	1.0033	14.3083	0.0000

YEARS 15 — MO PAYT 1.2456 — AN CONST 14.95

#	INT	PRIN	BALANCE
1	12.5645	2.3823	97.6177
2	12.2437	2.7031	94.9146
3	11.8797	3.0671	91.8475
4	11.4667	3.4801	88.3673
5	10.9980	3.9488	84.4186
6	10.4663	4.4805	79.9381
7	9.8630	5.0838	74.8543
8	9.1784	5.7684	69.0858
9	8.4016	6.5452	62.5406
10	7.5202	7.4266	55.1141
11	6.5202	8.4266	46.6874
12	5.3854	9.5614	37.1261
13	4.0979	10.8489	26.2772
14	2.6370	12.3098	13.9674
15	.9794	13.9674	0.0000

YEARS 16 — MO PAYT 1.2200 — AN CONST 14.64

#	INT	PRIN	BALANCE
1	12.5830	2.0564	97.9436
2	12.3061	2.3333	95.6103
3	11.9919	2.6475	92.9628
4	11.6354	3.0040	89.9587
5	11.2309	3.4086	86.5502
6	10.7719	3.8676	82.6826
7	10.2511	4.3884	78.2942
8	9.6601	4.9793	73.3150
9	8.9896	5.6498	67.6652
10	8.2288	6.4106	61.2546
11	7.3656	7.2738	53.9807
12	6.3861	8.2533	45.7274
13	5.2747	9.3647	36.3626
14	4.0136	10.6258	25.7368
15	2.5828	12.0566	13.6802
16	.9592	13.6802	0.0000

YEARS 17 — MO PAYT 1.1982 — AN CONST 14.38

#	INT	PRIN	BALANCE
1	12.5987	1.7801	98.2199
2	12.3590	2.0198	96.2001
3	12.0871	2.2918	93.9083
4	11.7784	2.6004	91.3079
5	11.4283	2.9506	88.3574
6	11.0310	3.3479	85.0095
7	10.5801	3.7987	81.2108
8	10.0686	4.3102	76.9005
9	9.4882	4.8907	72.0099
10	8.8296	5.5492	66.4607
11	8.0824	6.2965	60.1642
12	7.2345	7.1444	53.0198
13	6.2724	8.1064	44.9134
14	5.1808	9.1980	35.7153
15	3.9422	10.4366	25.2787
16	2.5368	11.8420	13.4367
17	.9422	13.4367	0.0000

YEARS 18 — MO PAYT 1.1797 — AN CONST 14.16

#	INT	PRIN	BALANCE
1	12.6121	1.5446	98.4554
2	12.4041	1.7526	96.7028
3	12.1681	1.9886	94.7142
4	11.9004	2.2564	92.4578
5	11.5965	2.5602	89.8976
6	11.2518	2.9050	86.9926
7	10.8606	3.2962	83.6964
8	10.4167	3.7400	79.9564
9	9.9131	4.2437	75.7127
10	9.3416	4.8151	70.8976
11	8.6932	5.4635	65.4341
12	7.9575	6.1992	59.2349
13	7.1227	7.0340	52.2009
14	6.1755	7.9812	44.2196
15	5.1008	9.0560	35.1637
16	3.8813	10.2754	24.8882
17	2.4976	11.6591	13.2291
18	.9276	13.2291	0.0000

YEARS 19 — MO PAYT 1.1639 — AN CONST 13.97

#	INT	PRIN	BALANCE
1	12.6236	1.3430	98.6570
2	12.4428	1.5239	97.1331
3	12.2376	1.7291	95.4041
4	12.0047	1.9619	93.4422
5	11.7405	2.2261	91.2161
6	11.4408	2.5258	88.6903
7	11.1006	2.8660	85.8243
8	10.7147	3.2519	82.5724
9	10.2768	3.6898	78.8826
10	9.7799	4.1867	74.6959
11	9.2162	4.7504	69.9455
12	8.5765	5.3901	64.5553
13	7.8506	6.1160	58.4393
14	7.0271	6.9395	51.4998
15	6.0926	7.8740	43.6258
16	5.0323	8.9343	34.6914
17	3.8292	10.1374	24.5540
18	2.4641	11.5025	13.0515
19	.9152	13.0515	0.0000

YEARS 20 — MO PAYT 1.1503 — AN CONST 13.81

#	INT	PRIN	BALANCE
1	12.6335	1.1698	98.8302
2	12.4759	1.3273	97.5029
3	12.2972	1.5060	95.9969
4	12.0944	1.7088	94.2881
5	11.8643	1.9389	92.3491
6	11.6032	2.2000	90.1491
7	11.3069	2.4963	87.6528
8	10.9708	2.8324	84.8203
9	10.5894	3.2139	81.6065
10	10.1566	3.6466	77.9598
11	9.6655	4.1377	73.8221
12	9.1084	4.6949	69.1272
13	8.4762	5.3271	63.8002
14	7.7588	6.0444	57.7557
15	6.9449	6.8584	50.8974
16	6.0213	7.7819	43.1154
17	4.9734	8.8298	34.2856
18	3.7844	10.0188	24.2668
19	2.4353	11.3680	12.8988
20	.9045	12.8988	0.0000

YEARS 21 — MO PAYT 1.1385 — AN CONST 13.67

#	INT	PRIN	BALANCE
1	12.6420	1.0204	98.9796
2	12.5045	1.1578	97.8217
3	12.3486	1.3138	96.5080

#	INT	PRIN	BALANCE
4	12.1717	1.4907	95.0173
5	11.9710	1.6914	93.3259
6	11.7432	1.9192	91.4068
7	11.4848	2.1776	89.2292
8	11.1916	2.4708	86.7583
9	10.8588	2.8035	83.9548
10	10.4813	3.1811	80.7737
11	10.0530	3.6094	77.1643
12	9.5669	4.0955	73.0688
13	9.0154	4.6470	68.4219
14	8.3897	5.2727	63.1491
15	7.6796	5.9828	57.1664
16	6.8740	6.7884	50.3780
17	5.9599	7.7025	42.6755
18	4.9227	8.7397	33.9358
19	3.7458	9.9166	24.0191
20	2.4104	11.2520	12.7672
21	.8952	12.7672	0.0000

	YEARS 22	MO PAYT 1.1284	AN CONST 13.55
#	INT	PRIN	BALANCE
1	12.6493	.8913	99.1087
2	12.5293	1.0113	98.0974
3	12.3931	1.1475	96.9498
4	12.2386	1.3020	95.6478
5	12.0632	1.4774	94.1704
6	11.8643	1.6763	92.4941
7	11.6386	1.9021	90.5920
8	11.3824	2.1582	88.4339
9	11.0918	2.4488	85.9851
10	10.7621	2.7786	83.2065
11	10.3879	3.1527	80.0538
12	9.9634	3.5773	76.4765
13	9.4816	4.0590	72.4176
14	8.9351	4.6056	67.8120
15	8.3149	5.2257	62.5863
16	7.6112	5.9294	56.6568
17	6.8127	6.7279	49.9290
18	5.9068	7.6339	42.2951
19	4.8788	8.6618	33.6333
20	3.7124	9.8282	23.8051
21	2.3889	11.1517	12.6534
22	.8872	12.6534	0.0000

	YEARS 23	MO PAYT 1.1196	AN CONST 13.44
#	INT	PRIN	BALANCE
1	12.6557	.7794	99.2206
2	12.5507	.8844	98.3362
3	12.4316	1.0035	97.3328
4	12.2965	1.1386	96.1942
5	12.1432	1.2919	94.9023
6	11.9692	1.4659	93.4364
7	11.7718	1.6633	91.7732
8	11.5478	1.8872	89.8860
9	11.2937	2.1414	87.7446
10	11.0054	2.4297	85.3149
11	10.6782	2.7569	82.5580
12	10.3069	3.1281	79.4298
13	9.8857	3.5494	75.8805
14	9.4077	4.0273	71.8531
15	8.8654	4.5697	67.2835
16	8.2501	5.1850	62.0985
17	7.5519	5.8832	56.2153
18	6.7596	6.6754	49.5398
19	5.8607	7.5744	41.9655
20	4.8408	8.5943	33.3711
21	3.6835	9.7516	23.6195
22	2.3703	11.0648	12.5547
23	.8803	12.5547	0.0000

	YEARS 24	MO PAYT 1.1120	AN CONST 13.35
#	INT	PRIN	BALANCE
1	12.6612	.6822	99.3178
2	12.5693	.7741	98.5437
3	12.4651	.8783	97.6654
4	12.3468	.9966	96.6687
5	12.2126	1.1308	95.5379
6	12.0603	1.2831	94.2549
7	11.8876	1.4559	92.7990
8	11.6915	1.6519	91.1471
9	11.4691	1.8744	89.2727
10	11.2167	2.1268	87.1460
11	10.9303	2.4131	84.7328
12	10.6053	2.7381	81.9948
13	10.2366	3.1068	78.8879
14	9.8183	3.5252	75.3628
15	9.3436	3.9999	71.3629
16	8.8049	4.5385	66.8244
17	8.1938	5.1496	61.6748
18	7.5003	5.8431	55.8317
19	6.7135	6.6299	49.2018
20	5.8207	7.5227	41.6792
21	4.8077	8.5357	33.1435
22	3.6583	9.6851	23.4584
23	2.3541	10.9893	12.4691
24	.8743	12.4691	0.0000

	YEARS 25	MO PAYT 1.1053	AN CONST 13.27
#	INT	PRIN	BALANCE
1	12.6660	.5977	99.4023
2	12.5855	.6781	98.7242
3	12.4942	.7695	97.9547
4	12.3906	.8731	97.0816
5	12.2730	.9906	96.0910
6	12.1396	1.1240	94.9669
7	11.9883	1.2754	93.6915
8	11.8165	1.4472	92.2444
9	11.6216	1.6420	90.6023
10	11.4005	1.8632	88.7392
11	11.1496	2.1140	86.6251
12	10.8650	2.3987	84.2264
13	10.5419	2.7217	81.5047
14	10.1754	3.0882	78.4165
15	9.7596	3.5041	74.9124
16	9.2877	3.9760	70.9364
17	8.7523	4.5114	66.4251
18	8.1448	5.1189	61.3062
19	7.4555	5.8082	55.4981
20	6.6734	6.5903	48.9078
21	5.7859	7.4777	41.4301
22	4.7790	8.4847	32.9454
23	3.6365	9.6272	23.3182
24	2.3401	10.9236	12.3946
25	.8691	12.3946	0.0000

	YEARS 26	MO PAYT 1.0995	AN CONST 13.20
#	INT	PRIN	BALANCE
1	12.6702	.5240	99.4760
2	12.5996	.5945	98.8815
3	12.5196	.6746	98.2069
4	12.4287	.7654	97.4415
5	12.3257	.8685	96.5730
6	12.2087	.9855	95.5875
7	12.0760	1.1182	94.4693
8	11.9254	1.2687	93.2006
9	11.7546	1.4396	91.7610
10	11.5607	1.6334	90.1276
11	11.3408	1.8534	88.2742
12	11.0912	2.1030	86.1712
13	10.8080	2.3861	83.7851
14	10.4867	2.7075	81.0776
15	10.1221	3.0721	78.0056
16	9.7084	3.4857	74.5198
17	9.2390	3.9551	70.5647
18	8.7065	4.4877	66.0770
19	8.1021	5.0920	60.9850
20	7.4165	5.7777	55.2073
21	6.6384	6.5557	48.6515
22	5.7556	7.4385	41.2130
23	4.7540	8.4402	32.7728
24	3.6174	9.5768	23.1960
25	2.3278	10.8664	12.3296
26	.8645	12.3296	0.0000

	YEARS 27	MO PAYT 1.0945	AN CONST 13.14
#	INT	PRIN	BALANCE
1	12.6739	.4597	99.5403
2	12.6120	.5216	99.0188
3	12.5417	.5918	98.4270
4	12.4620	.6715	97.7555
5	12.3716	.7619	96.9936
6	12.2690	.8645	96.1290
7	12.1526	.9809	95.1481
8	12.0205	1.1130	94.0351
9	11.8706	1.2629	92.7722
10	11.7006	1.4330	91.3392
11	11.5076	1.6259	89.7133
12	11.2887	1.8449	87.8684
13	11.0402	2.0933	85.7751
14	10.7583	2.3752	83.4000
15	10.4385	2.6950	80.7049
16	10.0756	3.0579	77.6470
17	9.6638	3.4697	74.1773
18	9.1966	3.9369	70.2404
19	8.6664	4.4671	65.7733
20	8.0649	5.0686	60.7047
21	7.3824	5.7512	54.9535
22	6.6079	6.5256	48.4279
23	5.7292	7.4043	41.0235
24	4.7321	8.4014	32.6221
25	3.6008	9.5327	23.0894
26	2.3171	10.8164	12.2730
27	.8606	12.2730	0.0000

	YEARS 28	MO PAYT 1.0900	AN CONST 13.09
#	INT	PRIN	BALANCE
1	12.6770	.4035	99.5965
2	12.6227	.4578	99.1387
3	12.5611	.5195	98.6192
4	12.4911	.5894	98.0298
5	12.4117	.6688	97.3610
6	12.3217	.7588	96.6022
7	12.2195	.8610	95.7412
8	12.1036	.9770	94.7642
9	11.9720	1.1085	93.6557
10	11.8227	1.2578	92.3979
11	11.6534	1.4272	90.9707
12	11.4612	1.6194	89.3513
13	11.2431	1.8374	87.5139
14	10.9957	2.0849	85.4291
15	10.7149	2.3656	83.0635
16	10.3964	2.6841	80.3793
17	10.0349	3.0456	77.3337
18	9.6248	3.4557	73.8780
19	9.1595	3.9211	69.9570
20	8.6315	4.4491	65.5079
21	8.0324	5.0482	60.4597
22	7.3526	5.7280	54.7318
23	6.5812	6.4993	48.2325
24	5.7061	7.3745	40.8580
25	4.7130	8.3675	32.4905
26	3.5862	9.4943	22.9962
27	2.3078	10.7728	12.2234
28	.8571	12.2234	0.0000

	YEARS 29	MO PAYT 1.0862	AN CONST 13.04
#	INT	PRIN	BALANCE
1	12.6798	.3543	99.6457
2	12.6321	.4021	99.2436
3	12.5780	.4562	98.7874
4	12.5166	.5176	98.2698
5	12.4469	.5873	97.6825
6	12.3678	.6664	97.0161
7	12.2780	.7562	96.2599
8	12.1762	.8580	95.4019
9	12.0607	.9735	94.4284
10	11.9296	1.1046	93.3238
11	11.7808	1.2533	92.0705
12	11.6121	1.4221	90.6484
13	11.4206	1.6136	89.0347
14	11.2033	1.8309	87.2038
15	10.9567	2.0775	85.1264
16	10.6770	2.3572	82.7691
17	10.3595	2.6746	80.0945
18	9.9994	3.0348	77.0597
19	9.5907	3.4435	73.6162
20	9.1270	3.9072	69.7091
21	8.6009	4.4333	65.2758
22	8.0039	5.0303	60.2455
23	7.3265	5.7077	54.5378
24	6.5579	6.4763	48.0616
25	5.6858	7.3483	40.7132
26	4.6963	8.3379	32.3754
27	3.5735	9.4606	22.9147
28	2.2996	10.7346	12.1801
29	.8541	12.1801	0.0000

	YEARS 30	MO PAYT 1.0828	AN CONST 13.00
#	INT	PRIN	BALANCE
1	12.6823	.3113	99.6887
2	12.6404	.3532	99.3355
3	12.5928	.4008	98.9347
4	12.5388	.4548	98.4799
5	12.4776	.5160	97.9639
6	12.4081	.5855	97.3784
7	12.3293	.6643	96.7140
8	12.2398	.7538	95.9602
9	12.1383	.8553	95.1049
10	12.0231	.9705	94.1345
11	11.8924	1.1012	93.0333
12	11.7442	1.2494	91.7839
13	11.5759	1.4177	90.3662
14	11.3850	1.6086	88.7576
15	11.1684	1.8252	86.9323
16	10.9226	2.0710	84.8613
17	10.6437	2.3499	82.5115
18	10.3273	2.6663	79.8452
19	9.9683	3.0254	76.8198
20	9.5609	3.4327	73.3871
21	9.0986	3.8950	69.4921
22	8.5741	4.4195	65.0726
23	7.9790	5.0146	60.0579
24	7.3037	5.6899	54.3680
25	6.5375	6.4561	47.9120
26	5.6681	7.3255	40.5865
27	4.6817	8.3119	32.2746
28	3.5624	9.4312	22.8434
29	2.2924	10.7012	12.1422
30	.8514	12.1422	0.0000

YEARS 2 — MO PAYT 4.7424 — AN CONST 56.91

#	INT	PRIN	BALANCE
1	10.0758	46.8336	53.1664
2	3.7429	53.1664	0.0000

YEARS 3 — MO PAYT 3.3574 — AN CONST 40.29

#	INT	PRIN	BALANCE
1	11.0823	29.2061	70.7939
2	7.1331	33.1553	37.6386
3	2.6498	37.6386	0.0000

YEARS 4 — MO PAYT 2.6704 — AN CONST 32.05

#	INT	PRIN	BALANCE
1	11.5816	20.4627	79.5373
2	8.8146	23.2297	56.3076
3	5.6735	26.3708	29.9367
4	2.1076	29.9367	0.0000

YEARS 5 — MO PAYT 2.2625 — AN CONST 27.16

#	INT	PRIN	BALANCE
1	11.8780	15.2724	84.7276
2	9.8128	17.3376	67.3900
3	7.4684	19.6820	47.7081
4	4.8070	22.3434	25.3647
5	1.7857	25.3647	0.0000

YEARS 6 — MO PAYT 1.9942 — AN CONST 23.94

#	INT	PRIN	BALANCE
1	12.0729	11.8580	88.1420
2	10.4695	13.4614	74.6806
3	8.6492	15.2817	59.3989
4	6.5828	17.3481	42.0509
5	4.2370	19.6939	22.3569
6	1.5739	22.3569	0.0000

YEARS 7 — MO PAYT 1.8056 — AN CONST 21.67

#	INT	PRIN	BALANCE
1	12.2100	9.4576	90.5424
2	10.9311	10.7365	79.8059
3	9.4793	12.1883	67.6176
4	7.8312	13.8364	53.7812
5	5.9602	15.7074	38.0738
6	3.8363	17.8313	20.2425
7	1.4251	20.2425	0.0000

YEARS 8 — MO PAYT 1.6668 — AN CONST 20.01

#	INT	PRIN	BALANCE
1	12.3109	7.6904	92.3096
2	11.2710	8.7303	83.5793
3	10.0905	9.9108	73.6685
4	8.7503	11.2510	62.4176
5	7.2289	12.7723	49.6452
6	5.5019	14.4994	35.1458
7	3.5412	16.4600	18.6858
8	1.3155	18.6858	0.0000

YEARS 9 — MO PAYT 1.5610 — AN CONST 18.74

#	INT	PRIN	BALANCE
1	12.3877	6.3445	93.6555
2	11.5298	7.2025	86.4530
3	10.5559	8.1764	78.2766
4	9.4503	9.2820	68.9946
5	8.1951	10.5371	58.4574
6	6.7703	11.9620	46.4955
7	5.1528	13.5795	32.9160
8	3.3166	15.4157	17.5003
9	1.2320	17.5003	0.0000

YEARS 10 — MO PAYT 1.4784 — AN CONST 17.75

#	INT	PRIN	BALANCE
1	12.4478	5.2930	94.7070
2	11.7320	6.0087	88.6983
3	10.9195	6.8212	81.8770
4	9.9972	7.7436	74.1334
5	8.9501	8.7907	65.3427
6	7.7614	9.9794	55.3633
7	6.4119	11.3288	44.0345
8	4.8801	12.8607	31.1737
9	3.1410	14.5998	16.5740
10	1.1668	16.5740	0.0000

YEARS 11 — MO PAYT 1.4125 — AN CONST 16.96

#	INT	PRIN	BALANCE
1	12.4956	4.4548	95.5452
2	11.8932	5.0572	90.4880
3	11.2094	5.7411	84.7469
4	10.4331	6.5174	78.2295
5	9.5518	7.3986	70.8309
6	8.5514	8.3991	62.4318
7	7.4156	9.5348	52.8970
8	6.1263	10.8242	42.0728
9	4.6627	12.2878	29.7850
10	3.0011	13.9494	15.8356
11	1.1148	15.8356	0.0000

YEARS 12 — MO PAYT 1.3592 — AN CONST 16.32

#	INT	PRIN	BALANCE
1	12.5344	3.7760	96.2240
2	12.0238	4.2866	91.9374
3	11.4442	4.8663	87.0711
4	10.7861	5.5243	81.5469
5	10.0391	6.2713	75.2756
6	9.1911	7.1193	68.1563
7	8.2285	8.0820	60.0744
8	7.1356	9.1748	50.8996
9	5.8950	10.4154	40.4841
10	4.4866	11.8238	28.6603
11	2.8878	13.4226	15.2377
12	1.0727	15.2377	0.0000

YEARS 13 — MO PAYT 1.3154 — AN CONST 15.79

#	INT	PRIN	BALANCE
1	12.5662	3.2192	96.7808
2	12.1309	3.6545	93.1264
3	11.6367	4.1486	88.9778
4	11.0757	4.7096	84.2682
5	10.4389	5.3464	78.9217
6	9.7160	6.0694	72.8523
7	8.8953	6.8901	65.9622
8	7.9636	7.8218	58.1405
9	6.9059	8.8795	49.2610
10	5.7052	10.0801	39.1809
11	4.3422	11.4432	27.7377
12	2.7948	12.9905	14.7471
13	1.0382	14.7471	0.0000

YEARS 14 — MO PAYT 1.2792 — AN CONST 15.36

#	INT	PRIN	BALANCE
1	12.5925	2.7575	97.2425
2	12.2197	3.1304	94.1121
3	11.7964	3.5537	90.5584
4	11.3158	4.0342	86.5242
5	10.7703	4.5797	81.9445
6	10.1511	5.1990	76.7455
7	9.4480	5.9020	70.8434
8	8.6500	6.7001	64.1433
9	7.7440	7.6061	56.5372
10	6.7155	8.6346	47.9026
11	5.5479	9.8022	38.1005
12	4.2224	11.1276	26.9728
13	2.7177	12.6323	14.3405
14	1.0096	14.3405	0.0000

YEARS 15 — MO PAYT 1.2488 — AN CONST 14.99

#	INT	PRIN	BALANCE
1	12.6146	2.3715	97.6285
2	12.2939	2.6921	94.9364
3	11.9299	3.0562	91.8803
4	11.5166	3.4694	88.4109
5	11.0475	3.9385	84.4723
6	10.5149	4.4711	80.0012
7	9.9103	5.0757	74.9255
8	9.2240	5.7621	69.1634
9	8.4448	6.5412	62.6222
10	7.5603	7.4257	55.1965
11	6.5562	8.4298	46.7666
12	5.4163	9.5697	37.1969
13	4.1223	10.8638	26.3332
14	2.6533	12.3328	14.0004
15	.9856	14.0004	0.0000

YEARS 16 — MO PAYT 1.2233 — AN CONST 14.68

#	INT	PRIN	BALANCE
1	12.6332	2.0462	97.9538
2	12.3565	2.3229	95.6308
3	12.0424	2.6370	92.9938
4	11.6858	2.9936	90.0002
5	11.2810	3.3984	86.6018
6	10.8214	3.8580	82.7438
7	10.2998	4.3796	78.3642
8	9.7075	4.9719	73.3923
9	9.0352	5.6442	67.7482
10	8.2720	6.4074	61.3408
11	7.4056	7.2738	54.0670
12	6.4221	8.2573	45.8097
13	5.3055	9.3739	36.4358
14	4.0379	10.6415	25.7943
15	2.5990	12.0804	13.7139
16	.9655	13.7139	0.0000

YEARS 17 — MO PAYT 1.2016 — AN CONST 14.42

#	INT	PRIN	BALANCE
1	12.6489	1.7706	98.2294
2	12.4095	2.0100	96.2194
3	12.1377	2.2818	93.9376
4	11.8291	2.5903	91.3473
5	11.4789	2.9406	88.4067
6	11.0812	3.3382	85.0684
7	10.6298	3.7896	81.2788
8	10.1174	4.3021	76.9767
9	9.5357	4.8838	72.0928
10	8.8753	5.5442	66.5486
11	8.1256	6.2939	60.2547
12	7.2745	7.1450	53.1097
13	6.3083	8.1111	44.9986
14	5.2116	9.2079	35.7907
15	3.9664	10.4530	25.3376
16	2.5530	11.8665	13.4711
17	.9484	13.4711	0.0000

YEARS 18 — MO PAYT 1.1832 — AN CONST 14.20

#	INT	PRIN	BALANCE
1	12.6623	1.5357	98.4643
2	12.4546	1.7434	96.7209
3	12.2189	1.9791	94.7417
4	11.9513	2.2468	92.4950
5	11.6475	2.5506	89.9444
6	11.3026	2.8955	87.0490
7	10.9111	3.2870	83.7620
8	10.4666	3.7315	80.0305
9	9.9620	4.2360	75.7945
10	9.3892	4.8088	70.9857
11	8.7390	5.4591	65.5266
12	8.0008	6.1973	59.3294
13	7.1628	7.0353	52.2941
14	6.2115	7.9866	44.3075
15	5.1315	9.0665	35.2410
16	3.9055	10.2925	24.9485
17	2.5138	11.6843	13.2642
18	.9338	13.2642	0.0000

YEARS 19 — MO PAYT 1.1674 — AN CONST 14.01

#	INT	PRIN	BALANCE
1	12.6738	1.3347	98.6653
2	12.4933	1.5152	97.1500
3	12.2884	1.7201	95.4299
4	12.0558	1.9527	93.4772
5	11.7918	2.2168	91.2604
6	11.4920	2.5165	88.7439
7	11.1517	2.8568	85.8871
8	10.7654	3.2431	82.6440
9	10.3269	3.6816	78.9623
10	9.8291	4.1795	74.7829
11	9.2639	4.7446	70.0382
12	8.6223	5.3862	64.6520
13	7.8940	6.1145	58.5375
14	7.0672	6.9414	51.5961
15	6.1286	7.8800	43.7161
16	5.0630	8.9455	34.7706
17	3.8534	10.1551	24.6155
18	2.4802	11.5283	13.0872
19	.9213	13.0872	0.0000

YEARS 20 — MO PAYT 1.1538 — AN CONST 13.85

#	INT	PRIN	BALANCE
1	12.6836	1.1621	98.8379
2	12.5265	1.3192	97.5187
3	12.3481	1.4976	96.0210
4	12.1456	1.7001	94.3209
5	11.9157	1.9300	92.3909
6	11.6547	2.1910	90.1999
7	11.3585	2.4873	87.7126
8	11.0221	2.8236	84.8890
9	10.6403	3.2054	81.6836
10	10.2069	3.6389	78.0447
11	9.7148	4.1309	73.9138
12	9.1562	4.6895	69.2243
13	8.5221	5.3236	63.9007
14	7.8023	6.0435	57.8572
15	6.9851	6.8607	50.9965
16	6.0573	7.7884	43.2081
17	5.0042	8.8416	34.3666
18	3.8086	10.0371	24.3295
19	2.4514	11.3943	12.9351
20	.9106	12.9351	0.0000

YEARS 21 — MO PAYT 1.1421 — AN CONST 13.71

#	INT	PRIN	BALANCE
1	12.6921	1.0133	98.9867
2	12.5551	1.1503	97.8364
3	12.3996	1.3059	96.5305

MONTHLY PAYMENT AMORTIZATION SCHEDULE PER $100   12.75 %

#	INT	PRIN	BALANCE
4	12.2230	1.4824	95.0481
5	12.0225	1.6829	93.3652
6	11.7950	1.9105	91.4547
7	11.5366	2.1688	89.2859
8	11.2434	2.4621	86.8238
9	10.9104	2.7950	84.0288
10	10.5325	3.1729	80.8559
11	10.1035	3.6020	77.2539
12	9.6164	4.0891	73.1648
13	9.0635	4.6420	68.5229
14	8.4358	5.2697	63.2532
15	7.7232	5.9822	57.2709
16	6.9143	6.7912	50.4798
17	5.9960	7.7095	42.7703
18	4.9535	8.7520	34.0183
19	3.7700	9.9354	24.0829
20	2.4266	11.2789	12.8040
21	.9014	12.8040	0.0000

YEARS 22	MO PAYT 1.1320	AN CONST 13.59	
#	INT	PRIN	BALANCE
1	12.6995	.8847	99.1153
2	12.5799	1.0043	98.1110
3	12.4440	1.1401	96.9708
4	12.2899	1.2943	95.6765
5	12.1149	1.4693	94.2072
6	11.9162	1.6680	92.5392
7	11.6906	1.8936	90.6456
8	11.4346	2.1496	88.4960
9	11.1439	2.4403	86.0557
10	10.8139	2.7703	83.2854
11	10.4393	3.1449	80.1405
12	10.0141	3.5701	76.5704
13	9.5313	4.0529	72.5175
14	8.9833	4.6009	67.9166
15	8.3611	5.2231	62.6936
16	7.6549	5.9293	56.7643
17	6.8531	6.7311	50.0332
18	5.9429	7.6413	42.3919
19	4.9097	8.6745	33.7174
20	3.7367	9.8475	23.8699
21	2.4051	11.1791	12.6908
22	.8934	12.6908	0.0000

YEARS 23	MO PAYT 1.1233	AN CONST 13.48	
#	INT	PRIN	BALANCE
1	12.7058	.7733	99.2267
2	12.6013	.8779	98.3488
3	12.4826	.9966	97.3523
4	12.3478	1.1313	96.2209
5	12.1948	1.2843	94.9366
6	12.0212	1.4580	93.4787
7	11.8240	1.6551	91.8236
8	11.6002	1.8789	89.9446
9	11.3461	2.1330	87.8116
10	11.0577	2.4214	85.3902
11	10.7303	2.7488	82.6414
12	10.3586	3.1205	79.5208
13	9.9366	3.5425	75.9783
14	9.4576	4.0215	71.9568
15	8.9138	4.5653	67.3914
16	8.2965	5.1827	62.2088
17	7.5957	5.8835	56.3253
18	6.8001	6.6790	49.6463
19	5.8970	7.5822	42.0641
20	4.8717	8.6075	33.4566
21	3.7078	9.7714	23.6853
22	2.3865	11.0927	12.5926
23	.8865	12.5926	0.0000

YEARS 24	MO PAYT 1.1157	AN CONST 13.39	
#	INT	PRIN	BALANCE
1	12.7114	.6766	99.3234
2	12.6199	.7681	98.5554
3	12.5160	.8719	97.6834
4	12.3981	.9898	96.6936
5	12.2643	1.1237	95.5699
6	12.1123	1.2756	94.2943
7	11.9398	1.4481	92.8462
8	11.7440	1.6439	91.2023
9	11.5217	1.8662	89.3361
10	11.2694	2.1186	87.2175
11	10.9829	2.4050	84.8125
12	10.6577	2.7302	82.0822
13	10.2885	3.0994	78.9828
14	9.8694	3.5185	75.4643
15	9.3936	3.9943	71.4699
16	8.8535	4.5344	66.9355
17	8.2403	5.1476	61.7879
18	7.5443	5.8437	55.9442
19	6.7541	6.6338	49.3104
20	5.8571	7.5309	41.7795
21	4.8387	8.5492	33.2303
22	3.6827	9.7053	23.5250
23	2.3703	11.0176	12.5074
24	.8805	12.5074	0.0000

YEARS 25	MO PAYT 1.1091	AN CONST 13.31	
#	INT	PRIN	BALANCE
1	12.7162	.5925	99.4075
2	12.6361	.6726	98.7350
3	12.5451	.7635	97.9715
4	12.4419	.8668	97.1047
5	12.3247	.9840	96.1207
6	12.1916	1.1170	95.0037
7	12.0406	1.2681	93.7357
8	11.8691	1.4395	92.2961
9	11.6744	1.6342	90.6620
10	11.4535	1.8552	88.8068
11	11.2026	2.1060	86.7008
12	10.9178	2.3908	84.3100
13	10.5946	2.7141	81.5959
14	10.2276	3.0811	78.5149
15	9.8109	3.4977	75.0172
16	9.3380	3.9707	71.0465
17	8.8010	4.5076	66.5389
18	8.1915	5.1171	61.4218
19	7.4996	5.8090	55.6128
20	6.7141	6.5945	49.0182
21	5.8224	7.4863	41.5320
22	4.8101	8.4986	33.0334
23	3.6609	9.6478	23.3856
24	2.3563	10.9523	12.4333
25	.8753	12.4333	0.0000

YEARS 26	MO PAYT 1.1033	AN CONST 13.24	
#	INT	PRIN	BALANCE
1	12.7204	.5192	99.4808
2	12.6502	.5894	98.8914
3	12.5705	.6691	98.2224
4	12.4800	.7596	97.4628
5	12.3773	.8623	96.6006
6	12.2607	.9789	95.6217
7	12.1283	1.1112	94.5105
8	11.9781	1.2615	93.2490
9	11.8075	1.4321	91.8170
10	11.6138	1.6257	90.1913
11	11.3940	1.8455	88.3457
12	11.1445	2.0951	86.2507
13	10.8612	2.3784	83.8723
14	10.5395	2.7000	81.1723
15	10.1745	3.0651	78.1072
16	9.7600	3.4795	74.6277
17	9.2895	3.9500	70.6776
18	8.7554	4.4842	66.1935
19	8.1490	5.0905	61.1029
20	7.4607	5.7789	55.3240
21	6.6792	6.5603	48.7637
22	5.7921	7.4474	41.3163
23	4.7851	8.4544	32.8619
24	3.6419	9.5977	23.2642
25	2.3441	10.8955	12.3688
26	.8708	12.3688	0.0000

YEARS 27	MO PAYT 1.0983	AN CONST 13.18	
#	INT	PRIN	BALANCE
1	12.7240	.4553	99.5447
2	12.6624	.5168	99.0279
3	12.5926	.5867	98.4412
4	12.5132	.6660	97.7752
5	12.4232	.7561	97.0191
6	12.3209	.8583	96.1608
7	12.2049	.9744	95.1864
8	12.0731	1.1062	94.0802
9	11.9235	1.2557	92.8245
10	11.7537	1.4255	91.3990
11	11.5610	1.6183	89.7807
12	11.3421	1.8371	87.9435
13	11.0937	2.0855	85.8580
14	10.8117	2.3675	83.4905
15	10.4916	2.6877	80.8028
16	10.1281	3.0511	77.7516
17	9.7156	3.4637	74.2879
18	9.2472	3.9321	70.3559
19	8.7155	4.4638	65.8921
20	8.1119	5.0674	60.8248
21	7.4267	5.7526	55.0722
22	6.6488	6.5304	48.5417
23	5.7658	7.4135	41.1282
24	4.7633	8.4160	32.7123
25	3.6253	9.5540	23.1583
26	2.3334	10.8459	12.3125
27	.8668	12.3125	0.0000

YEARS 28	MO PAYT 1.0939	AN CONST 13.13	
#	INT	PRIN	BALANCE
1	12.7272	.3994	99.6006
2	12.6732	.4534	99.1471
3	12.6119	.5147	98.6324
4	12.5423	.5844	98.0480
5	12.4632	.6634	97.3847
6	12.3735	.7531	96.6316
7	12.2717	.8549	95.7767
8	12.1561	.9705	94.8062
9	12.0249	1.1017	93.7044
10	11.8759	1.2507	92.4537
11	11.7068	1.4198	91.0339
12	11.5148	1.6118	89.4221
13	11.2968	1.8298	87.5923
14	11.0494	2.0772	85.5151
15	10.7685	2.3581	83.1570
16	10.4497	2.6770	80.4800
17	10.0877	3.0389	77.4411
18	9.6768	3.4499	73.9912
19	9.2103	3.9164	70.0749
20	8.6807	4.4459	65.6289
21	8.0795	5.0471	60.5818
22	7.3970	5.7296	54.8522
23	6.6223	6.5044	48.3479
24	5.7427	7.3839	40.9640
25	4.7443	8.3823	32.5816
26	3.6108	9.5158	23.0658
27	2.3241	10.8025	12.2633
28	.8633	12.2633	0.0000

YEARS 29	MO PAYT 1.0900	AN CONST 13.09	
#	INT	PRIN	BALANCE
1	12.7300	.3506	99.6494
2	12.6826	.3980	99.2514
3	12.6287	.4518	98.7995
4	12.5676	.5129	98.2866
5	12.4983	.5823	97.7043
6	12.4195	.6610	97.0432
7	12.3302	.7504	96.2928
8	12.2287	.8519	95.4409
9	12.1135	.9671	94.4738
10	11.9827	1.0979	93.3759
11	11.8343	1.2463	92.1296
12	11.6657	1.4149	90.7147
13	11.4744	1.6062	89.1085
14	11.2577	1.8234	87.2852
15	11.0107	2.0699	85.2152
16	10.7308	2.3498	82.8654
17	10.4130	2.6676	80.1978
18	10.0523	3.0283	77.1696
19	9.6428	3.4378	73.7318
20	9.1780	3.9026	69.8292
21	8.6502	4.4303	65.3988
22	8.0512	5.0294	60.3694
23	7.3711	5.7095	54.6599
24	6.5990	6.4816	48.1783
25	5.7226	7.3580	40.8203
26	4.7276	8.3530	32.4674
27	3.5981	9.4824	22.9850
28	2.3159	10.7647	12.2203
29	.8603	12.2203	0.0000

YEARS 30	MO PAYT 1.0867	AN CONST 13.05	
#	INT	PRIN	BALANCE
1	12.7324	.3079	99.6921
2	12.6908	.3495	99.3426
3	12.6435	.3968	98.9458
4	12.5899	.4505	98.4953
5	12.5290	.5114	97.9839
6	12.4598	.5805	97.4034
7	12.3813	.6590	96.7444
8	12.2922	.7481	95.9963
9	12.1910	.8493	95.1470
10	12.0762	.9641	94.1829
11	11.9458	1.0945	93.0884
12	11.7978	1.2425	91.8459
13	11.6298	1.4105	90.4354
14	11.4391	1.6012	88.8342
15	11.2226	1.8178	87.0164
16	10.9768	2.0636	84.9529
17	10.6977	2.3426	82.6103
18	10.3810	2.6594	79.9509
19	10.0214	3.0190	76.9320
20	9.6131	3.4272	73.5048
21	9.1497	3.8906	69.6142
22	8.6236	4.4167	65.1975
23	8.0264	5.0139	60.1835
24	7.3484	5.6919	54.4916
25	6.5787	6.4616	48.0300
26	5.7050	7.3353	40.6947
27	4.7131	8.3272	32.3674
28	3.5871	9.4532	22.9142
29	2.3088	10.7315	12.1827
30	.8577	12.1827	0.0000

YEARS 2 — MO PAYT 4.7448 — AN CONST 56.94

#	INT	PRIN	BALANCE
1	10.1163	46.8212	53.1788
2	3.7588	53.1788	0.0000

YEARS 3 — MO PAYT 3.3598 — AN CONST 40.32

#	INT	PRIN	BALANCE
1	11.1269	29.1904	70.8096
2	7.1633	33.1539	37.6557
3	2.6616	37.6557	0.0000

YEARS 4 — MO PAYT 2.6728 — AN CONST 32.08

#	INT	PRIN	BALANCE
1	11.6281	20.4459	79.5541
2	8.8519	23.2221	56.3319
3	5.6987	26.3753	29.9566
4	2.1174	29.9566	0.0000

YEARS 5 — MO PAYT 2.2651 — AN CONST 27.19

#	INT	PRIN	BALANCE
1	11.9256	15.2554	84.7446
2	9.8542	17.3268	67.4178
3	7.5015	19.6795	47.7383
4	4.8293	22.3516	25.3866
5	1.7944	25.3866	0.0000

YEARS 6 — MO PAYT 1.9969 — AN CONST 23.97

#	INT	PRIN	BALANCE
1	12.1213	11.8412	88.1588
2	10.5135	13.4490	74.7099
3	8.6873	15.2751	59.4347
4	6.6132	17.3492	42.0855
5	4.2575	19.7050	22.3805
6	1.5819	22.3805	0.0000

YEARS 7 — MO PAYT 1.8083 — AN CONST 21.71

#	INT	PRIN	BALANCE
1	12.2588	9.4412	90.5588
2	10.9769	10.7232	79.8355
3	9.5209	12.1792	67.6563
4	7.8671	13.8330	53.8234
5	5.9888	15.7112	38.1121
6	3.8555	17.8446	20.2675
7	1.4325	20.2675	0.0000

YEARS 8 — MO PAYT 1.6696 — AN CONST 20.04

#	INT	PRIN	BALANCE
1	12.3601	7.6746	92.3254
2	11.3180	8.7167	83.6087
3	10.1345	9.9002	73.7085
4	8.7902	11.2445	62.4640
5	7.2634	12.7713	49.6926
6	5.5292	14.5055	35.1872
7	3.5596	16.4751	18.7121
8	1.3226	18.7121	0.0000

YEARS 9 — MO PAYT 1.5639 — AN CONST 18.77

#	INT	PRIN	BALANCE
1	12.4372	6.3294	93.6706
2	11.5778	7.1888	86.4818
3	10.6017	8.1650	78.3168
4	9.4930	9.2736	69.0432
5	8.2338	10.5328	58.5104
6	6.8036	11.9630	46.5474
7	5.1793	13.5874	32.9600
8	3.3343	15.4323	17.5277
9	1.2389	17.5277	0.0000

YEARS 10 — MO PAYT 1.4813 — AN CONST 17.78

#	INT	PRIN	BALANCE
1	12.4974	5.2786	94.7214
2	11.7807	5.9953	88.7261
3	10.9666	6.8094	81.9168
4	10.0420	7.7340	74.1828
5	8.9919	8.7841	65.3987
6	7.7992	9.9768	55.4219
7	6.4445	11.3315	44.0903
8	4.9059	12.8701	31.2202
9	3.1583	14.6177	16.6025
10	1.1735	16.6025	0.0000

YEARS 11 — MO PAYT 1.4155 — AN CONST 16.99

#	INT	PRIN	BALANCE
1	12.5454	4.4411	95.5589
2	11.9424	5.0441	90.5147
3	11.2575	5.7290	84.7857
4	10.4796	6.5070	78.2787
5	9.5961	7.3905	70.8883
6	8.5926	8.3940	62.4943
7	7.4528	9.5338	52.9605
8	6.1583	10.8283	42.1322
9	4.6880	12.2986	29.8337
10	3.0181	13.9685	15.8652
11	1.1214	15.8652	0.0000

YEARS 12 — MO PAYT 1.3623 — AN CONST 16.35

#	INT	PRIN	BALANCE
1	12.5843	3.7630	96.2370
2	12.0734	4.2740	91.9630
3	11.4930	4.8543	87.1086
4	10.8339	5.5135	81.5952
5	10.0852	6.2621	75.3331
6	9.2350	7.1124	68.2207
7	8.2692	8.0781	60.1426
8	7.1724	9.1750	50.9676
9	5.9265	10.4208	40.5468
10	4.5116	11.8358	28.7110
11	2.9045	13.4429	15.2682
12	1.0792	15.2682	0.0000

YEARS 13 — MO PAYT 1.3186 — AN CONST 15.83

#	INT	PRIN	BALANCE
1	12.6162	3.2069	96.7931
2	12.1807	3.6424	93.1507
3	11.6862	4.1369	89.0138
4	11.1244	4.6987	84.3151
5	10.4864	5.3367	78.9785
6	9.7618	6.0613	72.9172
7	8.9388	6.8843	66.0329
8	8.0040	7.8191	58.2139
9	6.9423	8.8808	49.3331
10	5.7365	10.0866	39.2465
11	4.3669	11.4562	27.7903
12	2.8113	13.0118	14.7785
13	1.0446	14.7785	0.0000

YEARS 14 — MO PAYT 1.2824 — AN CONST 15.39

#	INT	PRIN	BALANCE
1	12.6426	2.7460	97.2540
2	12.2697	3.1189	94.1352
3	11.8463	3.5423	90.5928
4	11.3653	4.0233	86.5695
5	10.8190	4.5696	81.9999
6	10.1985	5.1901	76.8097
7	9.4938	5.8948	70.9149
8	8.6933	6.6953	64.2197
9	7.7842	7.6044	56.6153
10	6.7517	8.6369	47.9784
11	5.5790	9.8096	38.1688
12	4.2470	11.1416	27.0272
13	2.7341	12.6545	14.3727
14	1.0159	14.3727	0.0000

YEARS 15 — MO PAYT 1.2521 — AN CONST 15.03

#	INT	PRIN	BALANCE
1	12.6647	2.3606	97.6394
2	12.3442	2.6812	94.9582
3	11.9801	3.0452	91.9130
4	11.5666	3.4587	88.4542
5	11.0970	3.9284	84.5259
6	10.5636	4.4618	80.0641
7	9.9577	5.0676	74.9965
8	9.2697	5.7557	69.2409
9	8.4881	6.5372	62.7037
10	7.6005	7.4248	55.2788
11	6.5923	8.4330	46.8458
12	5.4473	9.5781	37.2678
13	4.1467	10.8786	26.3892
14	2.6696	12.3557	14.0334
15	.9919	14.0334	0.0000

YEARS 16 — MO PAYT 1.2266 — AN CONST 14.72

#	INT	PRIN	BALANCE
1	12.6833	2.0361	97.9639
2	12.4068	2.3126	95.6513
3	12.0928	2.6266	93.0247
4	11.7362	2.9832	90.0415
5	11.3311	3.3883	86.6532
6	10.8710	3.8484	82.8049
7	10.3485	4.3709	78.4339
8	9.7550	4.9644	73.4695
9	9.0809	5.6385	67.8310
10	8.3153	6.4041	61.4270
11	7.4457	7.2737	54.1533
12	6.4581	8.2613	45.8920
13	5.3364	9.3830	36.5089
14	4.0623	10.6571	25.8518
15	2.6152	12.1042	13.7477
16	.9717	13.7477	0.0000

YEARS 17 — MO PAYT 1.2050 — AN CONST 14.47

#	INT	PRIN	BALANCE
1	12.6991	1.7611	98.2389
2	12.4599	2.0002	96.2386
3	12.1883	2.2718	93.9668
4	11.8798	2.5803	91.3865
5	11.5295	2.9307	88.4558
6	11.1315	3.3286	85.1272
7	10.6796	3.7806	81.3466
8	10.1662	4.2939	77.0526
9	9.5832	4.8770	72.1757
10	8.9210	5.5392	66.6365
11	8.1689	6.2913	60.3452
12	7.3146	7.1456	53.1996
13	6.3444	8.1158	45.0838
14	5.2424	9.2178	35.8660
15	3.9908	10.4694	25.3966
16	2.5692	11.8910	13.5056
17	.9546	13.5056	0.0000

YEARS 18 — MO PAYT 1.1866 — AN CONST 14.24

#	INT	PRIN	BALANCE
1	12.7125	1.5269	98.4731
2	12.5052	1.7342	96.7389
3	12.2697	1.9697	94.7692
4	12.0022	2.2372	92.5320
5	11.6985	2.5409	89.9911
6	11.3534	2.8859	87.1051
7	10.9616	3.2778	83.8274
8	10.5165	3.7229	80.1045
9	10.0110	4.2284	75.8761
10	9.4369	4.8025	71.0736
11	8.7848	5.4546	65.6190
12	8.0441	6.1953	59.4237
13	7.2029	7.0365	52.3873
14	6.2475	7.9919	44.3954
15	5.1623	9.0771	35.3183
16	3.9298	10.3096	25.0088
17	2.5300	11.7094	13.2994
18	.9400	13.2994	0.0000

YEARS 19 — MO PAYT 1.1709 — AN CONST 14.06

#	INT	PRIN	BALANCE
1	12.7240	1.3265	98.6735
2	12.5438	1.5066	97.1668
3	12.3393	1.7112	95.4556
4	12.1069	1.9436	93.5120
5	11.8430	2.2075	91.3046
6	11.5433	2.5072	88.7973
7	11.2028	2.8477	85.9497
8	10.8162	3.2343	82.7154
9	10.3770	3.6735	79.0419
10	9.8782	4.1723	74.8696
11	9.3117	4.7388	70.1308
12	8.6682	5.3823	64.7485
13	7.9374	6.1131	58.6355
14	7.1074	6.9431	51.6924
15	6.1646	7.8859	43.8065
16	5.0938	8.9566	34.8498
17	3.8777	10.1728	24.6770
18	2.4964	11.5541	13.1229
19	.9276	13.1229	0.0000

YEARS 20 — MO PAYT 1.1574 — AN CONST 13.89

#	INT	PRIN	BALANCE
1	12.7338	1.1545	98.8455
2	12.5771	1.3112	97.5343
3	12.3990	1.4893	96.0451
4	12.1968	1.6915	94.3536
5	11.9671	1.9211	92.4325
6	11.7063	2.1820	90.2505
7	11.4100	2.4783	87.7722
8	11.0735	2.8148	84.9574
9	10.6913	3.1970	81.7604
10	10.2572	3.6311	78.1294
11	9.7642	4.1241	74.0053
12	9.2042	4.6841	69.3212
13	8.5682	5.3201	64.0010
14	7.8458	6.0425	57.9586
15	7.0253	6.8630	51.0956
16	6.0934	7.7948	43.3007
17	5.0350	8.8532	34.4475
18	3.8329	10.0554	24.3921
19	2.4676	11.4207	12.9714
20	.9168	12.9714	0.0000

YEARS 21 — MO PAYT 1.1457 — AN CONST 13.75

#	INT	PRIN	BALANCE
1	12.7423	1.0062	98.9938
2	12.6057	1.1428	97.8509
3	12.4505	1.2980	96.5529

#	INT	PRIN	BALANCE
4	12.2743	1.4743	95.0787
5	12.0741	1.6744	93.4042
6	11.8467	1.9018	91.5024
7	11.5885	2.1600	89.3424
8	11.2952	2.4533	86.8890
9	10.9621	2.7865	84.1026
10	10.5837	3.1648	80.9378
11	10.1540	3.5945	77.3432
12	9.6659	4.0826	73.2606
13	9.1116	4.6370	68.6236
14	8.4820	5.2666	63.3571
15	7.7668	5.9817	57.3754
16	6.9546	6.7939	50.5815
17	6.0321	7.7164	42.8651
18	4.9844	8.7642	34.1009
19	3.7944	9.9542	24.1467
20	2.4427	11.3058	12.8409
21	.9076	12.8409	0.0000

YEARS 22	MO PAYT 1.1357	AN CONST 13.63	
#	INT	PRIN	BALANCE
1	12.7497	.8781	99.1219
2	12.6304	.9974	98.1245
3	12.4950	1.1328	96.9917
4	12.3412	1.2866	95.7051
5	12.1665	1.4613	94.2437
6	11.9681	1.6597	92.5840
7	11.7427	1.8851	90.6989
8	11.4867	2.1411	88.5578
9	11.1960	2.4318	86.1260
10	10.8658	2.7620	83.3640
11	10.4908	3.1370	80.2270
12	10.0648	3.5630	76.6640
13	9.5810	4.0468	72.6173
14	9.0316	4.5962	68.0210
15	8.4075	5.2203	62.8007
16	7.6986	5.9292	56.8715
17	6.8936	6.7342	50.1373
18	5.9792	7.6486	42.4886
19	4.9406	8.6872	33.8014
20	3.7610	9.8668	23.9347
21	2.4213	11.2065	12.7282
22	.8996	12.7282	0.0000

YEARS 23	MO PAYT 1.1269	AN CONST 13.53	
#	INT	PRIN	BALANCE
1	12.7560	.7672	99.2328
2	12.6518	.8714	98.3614
3	12.5335	.9897	97.3716
4	12.3991	1.1241	96.2475
5	12.2465	1.2767	94.9708
6	12.0731	1.4501	93.5207
7	11.8762	1.6470	91.8737
8	11.6526	1.8706	90.0030
9	11.3986	2.1246	87.8784
10	11.1101	2.4131	85.4652
11	10.7825	2.7408	82.7244
12	10.4103	3.1130	79.6115
13	9.9876	3.5356	76.0759
14	9.5075	4.0157	72.0601
15	8.9623	4.5610	67.4992
16	8.3430	5.1803	62.3189
17	7.6396	5.8837	56.4352
18	6.8407	6.6826	49.7526
19	5.9333	7.5900	42.1627
20	4.9027	8.6205	33.5421
21	3.7322	9.7911	23.7510
22	2.4027	11.1205	12.6305
23	.8927	12.6305	0.0000

YEARS 24	MO PAYT 1.1194	AN CONST 13.44	
#	INT	PRIN	BALANCE
1	12.7615	.6710	99.3290
2	12.6704	.7621	98.5669
3	12.5670	.8656	97.7014
4	12.4494	.9831	96.7183
5	12.3159	1.1166	95.6017
6	12.1643	1.2682	94.3336
7	11.9921	1.4404	92.8932
8	11.7966	1.6360	91.2572
9	11.5744	1.8581	89.3991
10	11.3221	2.1104	87.2887
11	11.0356	2.3969	84.8918
12	10.7101	2.7224	82.1694
13	10.3404	3.0921	79.0773
14	9.9206	3.5119	75.5654
15	9.4437	3.9888	71.5766
16	8.9021	4.5304	67.0463
17	8.2870	5.1455	61.9007
18	7.5883	5.8442	56.0565
19	6.7948	6.6377	49.4188
20	5.8935	7.5390	41.8798
21	4.8698	8.5627	33.3170
22	3.7071	9.7254	23.5917
23	2.3866	11.0459	12.5458
24	.8868	12.5458	0.0000

YEARS 25	MO PAYT 1.1128	AN CONST 13.36	
#	INT	PRIN	BALANCE
1	12.7663	.5873	99.4127
2	12.6866	.6670	98.7457
3	12.5960	.7576	97.9881
4	12.4932	.8605	97.1276
5	12.3763	.9773	96.1503
6	12.2436	1.1100	95.0403
7	12.0929	1.2607	93.7795
8	11.9217	1.4319	92.3476
9	11.7273	1.6263	90.7213
10	11.5064	1.8472	88.8741
11	11.2556	2.0980	86.7761
12	10.9708	2.3829	84.3932
13	10.6472	2.7064	81.6868
14	10.2797	3.0739	78.6129
15	9.8623	3.4913	75.1216
16	9.3883	3.9653	71.1563
17	8.8499	4.5038	66.6525
18	8.2383	5.1153	61.5372
19	7.5437	5.8099	55.7273
20	6.7549	6.5988	49.1286
21	5.8589	7.4948	41.6338
22	4.8412	8.5124	33.1214
23	3.6854	9.6683	23.4531
24	2.3726	10.9810	12.4721
25	.8815	12.4721	0.0000

YEARS 26	MO PAYT 1.1071	AN CONST 13.29	
#	INT	PRIN	BALANCE
1	12.7705	.5144	99.4856
2	12.7007	.5843	98.9013
3	12.6213	.6636	98.2377
4	12.5312	.7537	97.4840
5	12.4289	.8560	96.6280
6	12.3126	.9723	95.6557
7	12.1806	1.1043	94.5514
8	12.0307	1.2542	93.2971
9	11.8604	1.4246	91.8726
10	11.6669	1.6180	90.2546
11	11.4473	1.8377	88.4169
12	11.1977	2.0872	86.3297
13	10.9143	2.3706	83.9591
14	10.5924	2.6925	81.2666
15	10.2268	3.0581	78.2085
16	9.8116	3.4733	74.7352
17	9.3400	3.9449	70.7902
18	8.8043	4.4806	66.3096
19	8.1959	5.0890	61.2206
20	7.5049	5.7800	55.4406
21	6.7201	6.5648	48.8758
22	5.8287	7.4562	41.4196
23	4.8163	8.4686	32.9510
24	3.6664	9.6185	23.3325
25	2.3604	10.9246	12.4079
26	.8770	12.4079	0.0000

YEARS 27	MO PAYT 1.1021	AN CONST 13.23	
#	INT	PRIN	BALANCE
1	12.7742	.4509	99.5491
2	12.7129	.5121	99.0370
3	12.6434	.5816	98.4554
4	12.5644	.6606	97.7948
5	12.4747	.7503	97.0445
6	12.3728	.8522	96.1923
7	12.2571	.9679	95.2244
8	12.1257	1.0993	94.1251
9	11.9764	1.2486	92.8765
10	11.8069	1.4181	91.4583
11	11.6143	1.6107	89.8477
12	11.3956	1.8294	88.0183
13	11.1472	2.0778	85.9405
14	10.8651	2.3599	83.5805
15	10.5447	2.6804	80.9002
16	10.1807	3.0443	77.8559
17	9.7674	3.4577	74.3982
18	9.2979	3.9272	70.4711
19	8.7646	4.4604	66.0107
20	8.1590	5.0660	60.9446
21	7.4711	5.7539	55.1907
22	6.6898	6.5352	48.6555
23	5.8024	7.4226	41.2329
24	4.7946	8.4304	32.8024
25	3.6499	9.5752	23.2273
26	2.3497	10.8753	12.3520
27	.8731	12.3520	0.0000

YEARS 28	MO PAYT 1.0977	AN CONST 13.18	
#	INT	PRIN	BALANCE
1	12.7773	.3954	99.6046
2	12.7236	.4491	99.1555
3	12.6627	.5101	98.6454
4	12.5934	.5793	98.0661
5	12.5147	.6580	97.4081
6	12.4254	.7473	96.6608
7	12.3239	.8488	95.8119
8	12.2087	.9641	94.8479
9	12.0778	1.0950	93.7529
10	11.9291	1.2437	92.5092
11	11.7602	1.4125	91.0967
12	11.5684	1.6043	89.4924
13	11.3506	1.8222	87.6702
14	11.1032	2.0696	85.6007
15	10.8222	2.3506	83.2501
16	10.5030	2.6698	80.5803
17	10.1405	3.0323	77.5480
18	9.7287	3.4440	74.1040
19	9.2611	3.9116	70.1924
20	8.7300	4.4428	65.7496
21	8.1267	5.0460	60.7036
22	7.4416	5.7312	54.9724
23	6.6634	6.5094	48.4631
24	5.7795	7.3932	41.0698
25	4.7756	8.3971	32.6727
26	3.6354	9.5373	23.1354
27	2.3404	10.8323	12.3031
28	.8696	12.3031	0.0000

YEARS 29	MO PAYT 1.0939	AN CONST 13.13	
#	INT	PRIN	BALANCE
1	12.7801	.3469	99.6531
2	12.7330	.3940	99.2590
3	12.6795	.4475	98.8115
4	12.6187	.5083	98.3032
5	12.5497	.5773	97.7259
6	12.4713	.6557	97.0702
7	12.3823	.7447	96.3254
8	12.2812	.8459	95.4795
9	12.1663	.9607	94.5188
10	12.0359	1.0912	93.4276
11	11.8877	1.2393	92.1883
12	11.7194	1.4076	90.7807
13	11.5283	1.5988	89.1819
14	11.3112	1.8158	87.3661
15	11.0646	2.0624	85.3037
16	10.7846	2.3424	82.9612
17	10.4665	2.6605	80.3007
18	10.1053	3.0217	77.2790
19	9.6950	3.4320	73.8470
20	9.2290	3.8981	69.9489
21	8.6997	4.4274	65.5215
22	8.0985	5.0285	60.4930
23	7.4157	5.7113	54.7817
24	6.6402	6.4868	48.2949
25	5.7595	7.3676	40.9274
26	4.7591	8.3680	32.5594
27	3.6228	9.5042	23.0552
28	2.3323	10.7947	12.2605
29	.8666	12.2605	0.0000

YEARS 30	MO PAYT 1.0906	AN CONST 13.09	
#	INT	PRIN	BALANCE
1	12.7825	.3045	99.6955
2	12.7412	.3459	99.3496
3	12.6942	.3928	98.9568
4	12.6409	.4462	98.5106
5	12.5803	.5068	98.0038
6	12.5115	.5756	97.4283
7	12.4333	.6537	96.7746
8	12.3446	.7425	96.0321
9	12.2438	.8433	95.1888
10	12.1293	.9578	94.2310
11	11.9992	1.0879	93.1431
12	11.8515	1.2356	91.9076
13	11.6837	1.4033	90.5042
14	11.4932	1.5939	88.9103
15	11.2768	1.8103	87.1000
16	11.0310	2.0561	85.0439
17	10.7518	2.3353	82.7086
18	10.4347	2.6524	80.0562
19	10.0745	3.0125	77.0437
20	9.6655	3.4216	73.6221
21	9.2009	3.8862	69.7359
22	8.6732	4.4139	65.3220
23	8.0739	5.0132	60.3088
24	7.3932	5.6939	54.6149
25	6.6200	6.4670	48.1479
26	5.7419	7.3452	40.8027
27	4.7446	8.3425	32.4602
28	3.6118	9.4753	22.9850
29	2.3252	10.7618	12.2231
30	.8639	12.2231	0.0000

MONTHLY PAYMENT AMORTIZATION SCHEDULE PER $100   12.875%

YEARS 2	MO PAYT 4.7483	AN CONST 56.98
# INT	PRIN	BALANCE
1 10.1770	46.8028	53.1972
2 3.7825	53.1972	0.0000

YEARS 3	MO PAYT 3.3634	AN CONST 40.37
# INT	PRIN	BALANCE
1 11.1936	29.1669	70.8331
2 7.2087	33.1519	37.6813
3 2.6793	37.6813	0.0000

YEARS 4	MO PAYT 2.6765	AN CONST 32.12
# INT	PRIN	BALANCE
1 11.6978	20.4208	79.5792
2 8.9078	23.2108	56.3684
3 5.7366	26.3820	29.9864
4 2.1321	29.9864	0.0000

YEARS 5	MO PAYT 2.2689	AN CONST 27.23
# INT	PRIN	BALANCE
1 11.9971	15.2299	84.7701
2 9.9163	17.3107	67.4594
3 7.5512	19.6758	47.7836
4 4.8629	22.3640	25.4195
5 1.8074	25.4195	0.0000

YEARS 6	MO PAYT 2.0008	AN CONST 24.01
# INT	PRIN	BALANCE
1 12.1939	11.8160	88.1840
2 10.5795	13.4303	74.7537
3 8.7445	15.2653	59.4884
4 6.6589	17.3509	42.1375
5 4.2883	19.7215	22.4160
6 1.5939	22.4160	0.0000

YEARS 7	MO PAYT 1.8124	AN CONST 21.75
# INT	PRIN	BALANCE
1 12.3322	9.4167	90.5833
2 11.0456	10.7033	79.8800
3 9.5832	12.1656	67.7143
4 7.9211	13.8278	53.8865
5 6.0319	15.7170	38.1695
6 3.8845	17.8644	20.3051
7 1.4438	20.3051	0.0000

YEARS 8	MO PAYT 1.6737	AN CONST 20.09
# INT	PRIN	BALANCE
1 12.4340	7.6509	92.3491
2 11.3886	8.6963	83.6528
3 10.2005	9.8844	73.7684
4 8.8500	11.2349	62.5335
5 7.3151	12.7698	49.7637
6 5.5704	14.5145	35.2492
7 3.5873	16.4976	18.7516
8 1.3333	18.7516	0.0000

YEARS 9	MO PAYT 1.5682	AN CONST 18.82
# INT	PRIN	BALANCE
1 12.5114	6.3068	93.6932
2 11.6498	7.1684	86.5248
3 10.6704	8.1478	78.3770
4 9.5572	9.2610	69.1160
5 8.2919	10.5263	58.5897
6 6.8537	11.9645	46.6252
7 5.2191	13.5991	33.0261
8 3.3611	15.4571	17.5690
9 1.2492	17.5690	0.0000

YEARS 10	MO PAYT 1.4857	AN CONST 17.83
# INT	PRIN	BALANCE
1 12.5720	5.2570	94.7430
2 11.8537	5.9752	88.7678
3 11.0373	6.7916	81.9762
4 10.1094	7.7195	74.2568
5 9.0548	8.7742	65.4826
6 7.8560	9.9729	55.5097
7 6.4934	11.3355	44.1742
8 4.9447	12.8842	31.2899
9 3.1844	14.6446	16.6454
10 1.1835	16.6454	0.0000

YEARS 11	MO PAYT 1.4201	AN CONST 17.05
# INT	PRIN	BALANCE
1 12.6202	4.4206	95.5794
2 12.0162	5.0246	90.5548
3 11.3297	5.7111	84.8437
4 10.5494	6.4913	78.3524
5 9.6625	7.3782	70.9742
6 8.6545	8.3863	62.5879
7 7.5087	9.5321	53.0558
8 6.2064	10.8344	42.2214
9 4.7261	12.3147	29.9067
10 3.0436	13.9972	15.9095
11 1.1312	15.9095	0.0000

YEARS 12	MO PAYT 1.3669	AN CONST 16.41
# INT	PRIN	BALANCE
1 12.6592	3.7436	96.2564
2 12.1477	4.2551	92.0012
3 11.5664	4.8365	87.1648
4 10.9056	5.4973	81.6675
5 10.1545	6.2483	75.4192
6 9.3008	7.1020	68.3171
7 8.3305	8.0723	60.2448
8 7.2276	9.1752	51.0696
9 5.9740	10.4288	40.6408
10 4.5492	11.8537	28.7871
11 2.9297	13.4732	15.3140
12 1.0889	15.3140	0.0000

YEARS 13	MO PAYT 1.3233	AN CONST 15.88
# INT	PRIN	BALANCE
1 12.6912	3.1886	96.8114
2 12.2555	3.6243	93.1871
3 11.7604	4.1194	89.0677
4 11.1975	4.6823	84.3854
5 10.5578	5.3220	79.0634
6 9.8307	6.0491	73.0143
7 9.0042	6.8756	66.1388
8 8.0649	7.8149	58.3238
9 6.9971	8.8827	49.4412
10 5.7835	10.0963	39.3449
11 4.4041	11.4757	27.8692
12 2.8362	13.0436	14.8256
13 1.0542	14.8256	0.0000

YEARS 14	MO PAYT 1.2872	AN CONST 15.45
# INT	PRIN	BALANCE
1 12.7177	2.7288	97.2712
2 12.3449	3.1016	94.1696
3 11.9211	3.5254	90.6442
4 11.4395	4.0070	86.6372
5 10.8920	4.5545	82.0827
6 10.2697	5.1768	76.9060
7 9.5625	5.8840	71.0219
8 8.7585	6.6879	64.3340
9 7.8448	7.6017	56.7323
10 6.8062	8.6403	48.0920
11 5.6257	9.8208	38.2713
12 4.2839	11.1625	27.1087
13 2.7589	12.6876	14.4211
14 1.0254	14.4211	0.0000

YEARS 15	MO PAYT 1.2570	AN CONST 15.09
# INT	PRIN	BALANCE
1 12.7398	2.3445	97.6555
2 12.4195	2.6648	94.9907
3 12.0554	3.0289	91.9618
4 11.6416	3.4427	88.5191
5 11.1713	3.9131	84.6060
6 10.6366	4.4477	80.1583
7 10.0290	5.0554	75.1029
8 9.3383	5.7461	69.3568
9 8.5532	6.5311	62.8257
10 7.6609	7.4235	55.4022
11 6.6466	8.4377	46.9645
12 5.4938	9.5905	37.3740
13 4.1835	10.9008	26.4732
14 2.6942	12.3902	14.0830
15 1.0014	14.0830	0.0000

YEARS 16	MO PAYT 1.2316	AN CONST 14.78
# INT	PRIN	BALANCE
1 12.7585	2.0210	97.9790
2 12.4824	2.2971	95.6819
3 12.1685	2.6110	93.0709
4 11.8118	2.9677	90.1033
5 11.4063	3.3731	86.7301
6 10.9455	3.8340	82.8961
7 10.4217	4.3578	78.5383
8 9.8263	4.9532	73.5851
9 9.1495	5.6300	67.9551
10 8.3803	6.3992	61.5560
11 7.5060	7.2734	54.2825
12 6.5123	8.2672	46.0154
13 5.3828	9.3967	36.6187
14 4.0990	10.6805	25.9381
15 2.6397	12.1398	13.7984
16 .9811	13.7984	0.0000

YEARS 17	MO PAYT 1.2101	AN CONST 14.53
# INT	PRIN	BALANCE
1 12.7743	1.7470	98.2530
2 12.5356	1.9857	96.2673
3 12.2643	2.2570	94.0103
4 11.9559	2.5653	91.4450
5 11.6055	2.9158	88.5292
6 11.2071	3.3142	85.2150
7 10.7543	3.7670	81.4479
8 10.2396	4.2817	77.1662
9 9.6546	4.8667	72.2996
10 8.9897	5.5316	66.7680
11 8.2339	6.2874	60.4806
12 7.3749	7.1464	53.3342
13 6.3985	8.1228	45.2115
14 5.2888	9.2325	35.9789
15 4.0274	10.4939	25.4850
16 2.5936	11.9277	13.5573
17 .9640	13.5573	0.0000

YEARS 18	MO PAYT 1.1918	AN CONST 14.31
# INT	PRIN	BALANCE
1 12.7877	1.5137	98.4863
2 12.5809	1.7206	96.7657
3 12.3459	1.9556	94.8101
4 12.0787	2.2228	92.5873
5 11.7750	2.5265	90.0608
6 11.4298	2.8717	87.1891
7 11.0374	3.2640	83.9250
8 10.5915	3.7100	80.2150
9 10.0846	4.2169	75.9981
10 9.5085	4.7930	71.2051
11 8.8536	5.4479	65.7573
12 8.1093	6.1922	59.5651
13 7.2633	7.0382	52.5269
14 6.3017	7.9998	44.5271
15 5.2087	9.0928	35.4343
16 3.9664	10.3351	25.0992
17 2.5543	11.7471	13.3521
18 .9494	13.3521	0.0000

YEARS 19	MO PAYT 1.1761	AN CONST 14.12
# INT	PRIN	BALANCE
1 12.7992	1.3143	98.6857
2 12.6197	1.4938	97.1919
3 12.4156	1.6979	95.4939
4 12.1836	1.9299	93.5640
5 11.9199	2.1936	91.3704
6 11.6202	2.4933	88.8771
7 11.2796	2.8340	86.0432
8 10.8924	3.2211	82.8220
9 10.4523	3.6612	79.1608
10 9.9521	4.1615	74.9993
11 9.3835	4.7300	70.2693
12 8.7373	5.3763	64.8930
13 8.0027	6.1108	58.7822
14 7.1678	6.9457	51.8365
15 6.2189	7.8947	43.9419
16 5.1402	8.9733	34.9686
17 3.9143	10.1993	24.7693
18 2.5208	11.5927	13.1766
19 .9369	13.1766	0.0000

YEARS 20	MO PAYT 1.1627	AN CONST 13.96
# INT	PRIN	BALANCE
1 12.8091	1.1431	98.8569
2 12.6529	1.2993	97.5577
3 12.4754	1.4768	96.0809
4 12.2737	1.6785	94.4024
5 12.0443	1.9079	92.4945
6 11.7837	2.1685	90.3260
7 11.4874	2.4648	87.8612
8 11.1506	2.8016	85.0596
9 10.7679	3.1843	81.8753
10 10.3328	3.6194	78.2559
11 9.8383	4.1139	74.1420
12 9.2762	4.6760	69.4661
13 8.6374	5.3148	64.1513
14 7.9112	6.0410	58.1103
15 7.0859	6.8663	51.2440
16 6.1478	7.8044	43.4396
17 5.0815	8.8707	34.5689
18 3.8695	10.0827	24.4862
19 2.4920	11.4602	13.0260
20 .9262	13.0260	0.0000

YEARS 21	MO PAYT 1.1511	AN CONST 13.82
# INT	PRIN	BALANCE
1 12.8176	.9957	99.0043
2 12.6816	1.1317	97.8726
3 12.5270	1.2863	96.5863

#	INT	PRIN	BALANCE
4	12.3512	1.4621	95.1243
5	12.1515	1.6618	93.4624
6	11.9244	1.8889	91.5736
7	11.6663	2.1469	89.4266
8	11.3730	2.4403	86.9864
9	11.0396	2.7737	84.2127
10	10.6606	3.1526	81.0601
11	10.2299	3.5833	77.4767
12	9.7403	4.0729	73.4038
13	9.1839	4.6294	68.7744
14	8.5514	5.2619	63.5125
15	7.8325	5.9808	57.5317
16	7.0153	6.7979	50.7338
17	6.0866	7.7267	43.0071
18	5.0309	8.7824	34.2247
19	3.8310	9.9823	24.2424
20	2.4671	11.3461	12.8963
21	.9170	12.8963	0.0000

YEARS 22 — MO PAYT 1.1411 — AN CONST 13.70

#	INT	PRIN	BALANCE
1	12.8249	.8684	99.1316
2	12.7063	.9870	98.1446
3	12.5714	1.1219	97.0227
4	12.4182	1.2751	95.7476
5	12.2440	1.4494	94.2982
6	12.0459	1.6474	92.6508
7	11.8209	1.8725	90.7784
8	11.5650	2.1283	88.6501
9	11.2742	2.4191	86.2310
10	10.9437	2.7496	83.4814
11	10.5681	3.1252	80.3562
12	10.1411	3.5522	76.8039
13	9.6558	4.0376	72.7664
14	9.1041	4.5892	68.1772
15	8.4771	5.2162	62.9610
16	7.7645	5.9289	57.0321
17	6.9544	6.7389	50.2932
18	6.0337	7.6596	42.6336
19	4.9872	8.7061	33.9275
20	3.7977	9.8956	24.0319
21	2.4457	11.2476	12.7843
22	.9090	12.7843	0.0000

YEARS 23 — MO PAYT 1.1325 — AN CONST 13.59

#	INT	PRIN	BALANCE
1	12.8313	.7582	99.2418
2	12.7277	.8618	98.3800
3	12.6100	.9795	97.4005
4	12.4761	1.1134	96.2871
5	12.3240	1.2655	95.0216
6	12.1511	1.4384	93.5832
7	11.9546	1.6349	91.9483
8	11.7312	1.8583	90.0901
9	11.4773	2.1122	87.9779
10	11.1888	2.4007	85.5772
11	10.8608	2.7287	82.8485
12	10.4879	3.1015	79.7469
13	10.0642	3.5253	76.2216
14	9.5825	4.0069	72.2147
15	9.0351	4.5544	67.6603
16	8.4128	5.1766	62.4836
17	7.7056	5.8839	56.5997
18	6.9017	6.6878	49.9119
19	5.9880	7.6015	42.3104
20	4.9494	8.6401	33.6703
21	3.7689	9.8206	23.8497
22	2.4272	11.1623	12.6874
23	.9021	12.6874	0.0000

YEARS 24 — MO PAYT 1.1250 — AN CONST 13.50

#	INT	PRIN	BALANCE
1	12.8368	.6626	99.3374
2	12.7463	.7532	98.5842
3	12.6434	.8561	97.7281
4	12.5264	.9730	96.7551
5	12.3935	1.1060	95.6491
6	12.2424	1.2571	94.3920
7	12.0706	1.4288	92.9631
8	11.8754	1.6241	91.3391
9	11.6535	1.8460	89.4931
10	11.4013	2.0982	87.3949
11	11.1146	2.3848	85.0101
12	10.7888	2.7106	82.2995
13	10.4184	3.0810	79.2185
14	9.9975	3.5019	75.7165
15	9.5190	3.9804	71.7361
16	8.9752	4.5242	67.2119
17	8.3571	5.1423	62.0696
18	7.6545	5.8449	56.2247
19	6.8560	6.6435	49.5812
20	5.9483	7.5512	42.0300
21	4.9166	8.5829	33.4471
22	3.7440	9.7555	23.6917
23	2.4111	11.0883	12.6033
24	.8961	12.6033	0.0000

YEARS 25 — MO PAYT 1.1184 — AN CONST 13.43

#	INT	PRIN	BALANCE
1	12.8416	.5796	99.4204
2	12.7624	.6588	98.7616
3	12.6724	.7488	98.0128
4	12.5701	.8511	97.1617
5	12.4538	.9674	96.1942
6	12.3216	1.0996	95.0947
7	12.1714	1.2498	93.8449
8	12.0006	1.4206	92.4243
9	11.8065	1.6147	90.8096
10	11.5859	1.8353	88.9744
11	11.3352	2.0860	86.8884
12	11.0502	2.3710	84.5174
13	10.7263	2.6949	81.8225
14	10.3631	3.0631	78.7593
15	9.9396	3.4816	75.2777
16	9.4639	3.9573	71.3204
17	8.9232	4.4980	66.8224
18	8.3087	5.1125	61.7098
19	7.6102	5.8110	55.8988
20	6.8162	6.6050	49.2938
21	5.9138	7.5074	41.7864
22	4.8881	8.5331	33.2533
23	3.7223	9.6989	23.5543
24	2.3971	11.0241	12.5303
25	.8909	12.5303	0.0000

YEARS 26 — MO PAYT 1.1128 — AN CONST 13.36

#	INT	PRIN	BALANCE
1	12.8458	.5074	99.4926
2	12.7764	.5767	98.9160
3	12.6976	.6555	98.2605
4	12.6081	.7450	97.5155
5	12.5063	.8468	96.6687
6	12.3906	.9625	95.7062
7	12.2591	1.0940	94.6122
8	12.1096	1.2435	93.3687
9	11.9397	1.4134	91.9554
10	11.7466	1.6065	90.3489
11	11.5272	1.8259	88.5230
12	11.2777	2.0754	86.4476
13	10.9941	2.3590	84.0886
14	10.6718	2.6813	81.4073
15	10.3055	3.0476	78.3597
16	9.8891	3.4640	74.8958
17	9.4159	3.9372	70.9585
18	8.8779	4.4752	66.4833
19	8.2665	5.0866	61.3967
20	7.5715	5.7816	55.6152
21	6.7816	6.5715	49.0437
22	5.8838	7.4693	41.5744
23	4.8633	8.4898	33.0846
24	3.7034	9.6497	23.4348
25	2.3850	10.9681	12.4667
26	.8864	12.4667	0.0000

YEARS 27 — MO PAYT 1.1078 — AN CONST 13.30

#	INT	PRIN	BALANCE
1	12.8494	.4444	99.5556
2	12.7887	.5051	99.0505
3	12.7197	.5741	98.4764
4	12.6412	.6525	97.8239
5	12.5521	.7417	97.0822
6	12.4507	.8430	96.2391
7	12.3355	.9582	95.2809
8	12.2046	1.0891	94.1918
9	12.0558	1.2379	92.9538
10	11.8867	1.4071	91.5467
11	11.6944	1.5993	89.9474
12	11.4759	1.8178	88.1296
13	11.2276	2.0662	86.0634
14	10.9453	2.3485	83.7149
15	10.6244	2.6694	81.0456
16	10.2597	3.0341	78.0115
17	9.8452	3.4486	74.5629
18	9.3740	3.9197	70.6432
19	8.8385	4.4553	66.1879
20	8.2298	5.0640	61.1239
21	7.5379	5.7559	55.3680
22	6.7515	6.5423	48.8257
23	5.8577	7.4361	41.3896
24	4.8417	8.4521	32.9375
25	3.6869	9.6069	23.3307
26	2.3744	10.9194	12.4113
27	.8825	12.4113	0.0000

YEARS 28 — MO PAYT 1.1035 — AN CONST 13.25

#	INT	PRIN	BALANCE
1	12.8525	.3894	99.6106
2	12.7993	.4427	99.1679
3	12.7389	.5031	98.6648
4	12.6701	.5719	98.0929
5	12.5920	.6500	97.4429
6	12.5032	.7388	96.7041
7	12.4022	.8398	95.8643
8	12.2875	.9545	94.9098
9	12.1571	1.0849	93.8249
10	12.0089	1.2331	92.5918
11	11.8404	1.4016	91.1902
12	11.6489	1.5931	89.5971
13	11.4312	1.8107	87.7864
14	11.1839	2.0581	85.7282
15	10.9027	2.3393	83.3889
16	10.5830	2.6590	80.7299
17	10.2198	3.0222	77.7077
18	9.8068	3.4352	74.2725
19	9.3375	3.9045	70.3681
20	8.8041	4.4379	65.9301
21	8.1977	5.0443	60.8858
22	7.5085	5.7335	55.1524
23	6.7252	6.5168	48.6356
24	5.8348	7.4072	41.2284
25	4.8228	8.4192	32.8093
26	3.6726	9.5694	23.2398
27	2.3651	10.8769	12.3629
28	.8791	12.3629	0.0000

YEARS 29 — MO PAYT 1.0997 — AN CONST 13.20

#	INT	PRIN	BALANCE
1	12.8553	.3415	99.6585
2	12.8087	.3881	99.2704
3	12.7556	.4411	98.8293
4	12.6954	.5014	98.3279
5	12.6269	.5699	97.7579
6	12.5490	.6478	97.1102
7	12.4605	.7363	96.3739
8	12.3599	.8369	95.5370
9	12.2456	.9512	94.5857
10	12.1156	1.0812	93.5046
11	11.9679	1.2289	92.2756
12	11.8000	1.3968	90.8788
13	11.6091	1.5877	89.2912
14	11.3922	1.8046	87.4866
15	11.1457	2.0511	85.4355
16	10.8654	2.3314	83.1042
17	10.5469	2.6499	80.4543
18	10.1849	3.0119	77.4424
19	9.7734	3.4234	74.0189
20	9.3056	3.8912	70.1278
21	8.7740	4.4228	65.7050
22	8.1697	5.0271	60.6779
23	7.4829	5.7139	54.9641
24	6.7022	6.4945	48.4695
25	5.8149	7.3819	41.0877
26	4.8064	8.3904	32.6972
27	3.6600	9.5368	23.1605
28	2.3570	10.8397	12.3207
29	.8760	12.3207	0.0000

YEARS 30 — MO PAYT 1.0964 — AN CONST 13.16

#	INT	PRIN	BALANCE
1	12.8577	.2995	99.7005
2	12.8168	.3404	99.3600
3	12.7703	.3870	98.9731
4	12.7174	.4398	98.5333
5	12.6573	.4999	98.0334
6	12.5890	.5682	97.4651
7	12.5114	.6458	96.8193
8	12.4232	.7341	96.0852
9	12.3229	.8344	95.2508
10	12.2089	.9484	94.3024
11	12.0793	1.0780	93.2245
12	11.9320	1.2252	91.9993
13	11.7646	1.3926	90.6066
14	11.5744	1.5829	89.0237
15	11.3581	1.7992	87.2246
16	11.1123	2.0450	85.1796
17	10.8329	2.3244	82.8552
18	10.5153	2.6419	80.2133
19	10.1544	3.0029	77.2104
20	9.7441	3.4132	73.7972
21	9.2778	3.8795	69.9177
22	8.7477	4.4095	65.5082
23	8.1453	5.0120	60.4962
24	7.4605	5.6968	54.7994
25	6.6822	6.4751	48.3243
26	5.7975	7.3598	40.9646
27	4.7920	8.3653	32.5993
28	3.6490	9.5082	23.0911
29	2.3500	10.8073	12.2838
30	.8734	12.2838	0.0000

YEARS 2 — MO PAYT 4.7495 — AN CONST 57.00

#	INT	PRIN	BALANCE
1	10.1972	46.7966	53.2034
2	3.7904	53.2034	0.0000

YEARS 3 — MO PAYT 3.3646 — AN CONST 40.38

#	INT	PRIN	BALANCE
1	11.2159	29.1591	70.8409
2	7.2238	33.1512	37.6898
3	2.6852	37.6898	0.0000

YEARS 4 — MO PAYT 2.6778 — AN CONST 32.14

#	INT	PRIN	BALANCE
1	11.7211	20.4124	79.5876
2	8.9265	23.2070	56.3806
3	5.7493	26.3842	29.9964
4	2.1371	29.9964	0.0000

YEARS 5 — MO PAYT 2.2702 — AN CONST 27.25

#	INT	PRIN	BALANCE
1	12.0209	15.2214	84.7786
2	9.9370	17.3053	67.4732
3	7.5677	19.6746	47.7987
4	4.8741	22.3682	25.4305
5	1.8118	25.4305	0.0000

YEARS 6 — MO PAYT 2.0021 — AN CONST 24.03

#	INT	PRIN	BALANCE
1	12.2180	11.8076	88.1924
2	10.6015	13.4241	74.7683
3	8.7636	15.2620	59.5063
4	6.6742	17.3515	42.1548
5	4.2986	19.7270	22.4278
6	1.5979	22.4278	0.0000

YEARS 7 — MO PAYT 1.8138 — AN CONST 21.77

#	INT	PRIN	BALANCE
1	12.3566	9.4086	90.5914
2	11.0685	10.6967	79.8948
3	9.6041	12.1611	67.7336
4	7.9391	13.8261	53.9076
5	6.0462	15.7189	38.1886
6	3.8942	17.8710	20.3177
7	1.4475	20.3177	0.0000

YEARS 8 — MO PAYT 1.6751 — AN CONST 20.11

#	INT	PRIN	BALANCE
1	12.4586	7.6431	92.3569
2	11.4122	8.6895	83.6675
3	10.2225	9.8791	73.7884
4	8.8700	11.2316	62.5567
5	7.3323	12.7693	49.7874
6	5.5841	14.5175	35.2699
7	3.5965	16.5051	18.7648
8	1.3369	18.7648	0.0000

YEARS 9 — MO PAYT 1.5696 — AN CONST 18.84

#	INT	PRIN	BALANCE
1	12.5362	6.2992	93.7008
2	11.6738	7.1616	86.5392
3	10.6933	8.1421	78.3971
4	9.5786	9.2568	69.1403
5	8.3113	10.5241	58.6161
6	6.8704	11.9650	46.6512
7	5.2323	13.6030	33.0481
8	3.3700	15.4654	17.5827
9	1.2527	17.5827	0.0000

YEARS 10 — MO PAYT 1.4872 — AN CONST 17.85

#	INT	PRIN	BALANCE
1	12.5968	5.2498	94.7502
2	11.8781	5.9685	88.7817
3	11.0609	6.7856	81.9960
4	10.1319	7.7147	74.2814
5	9.0757	8.7708	65.5106
6	7.8749	9.9716	55.5389
7	6.5098	11.3368	44.2021
8	4.9577	12.8889	31.3132
9	3.1931	14.6535	16.6597
10	1.1869	16.6597	0.0000

YEARS 11 — MO PAYT 1.4216 — AN CONST 17.06

#	INT	PRIN	BALANCE
1	12.6451	4.4138	95.5862
2	12.0408	5.0181	90.5681
3	11.3538	5.7051	84.8631
4	10.5727	6.4861	78.3769
5	9.6847	7.3741	71.0028
6	8.6752	8.3837	62.6191
7	7.5274	9.5315	53.0875
8	6.2224	10.8364	42.2511
9	4.7388	12.3200	29.9311
10	3.0521	14.0067	15.9243
11	1.1345	15.9243	0.0000

YEARS 12 — MO PAYT 1.3684 — AN CONST 16.43

#	INT	PRIN	BALANCE
1	12.6842	3.7372	96.2628
2	12.1725	4.2488	92.0140
3	11.5908	4.8305	87.1834
4	10.9295	5.4919	81.6916
5	10.1776	6.2437	75.4478
6	9.3228	7.0986	68.3493
7	8.3509	8.0704	60.2789
8	7.2460	9.1753	51.1036
9	5.9899	10.4315	40.6721
10	4.5617	11.8596	28.8125
11	2.9381	13.4833	15.3292
12	1.0921	15.3292	0.0000

YEARS 13 — MO PAYT 1.3249 — AN CONST 15.90

#	INT	PRIN	BALANCE
1	12.7162	3.1825	96.8175
2	12.2805	3.6183	93.1992
3	11.7851	4.1136	89.0856
4	11.2219	4.6768	84.4088
5	10.5816	5.3171	79.0917
6	9.8537	6.0450	73.0467
7	9.0261	6.8726	66.1740
8	8.0852	7.8136	58.3605
9	7.0154	8.8833	49.4772
10	5.7993	10.0995	39.3777
11	4.4166	11.4822	27.8955
12	2.8446	13.0542	14.8414
13	1.0574	14.8414	0.0000

YEARS 14 — MO PAYT 1.2888 — AN CONST 15.47

#	INT	PRIN	BALANCE
1	12.7427	2.7231	97.2769
2	12.3699	3.0959	94.1811
3	11.9461	3.5197	90.6613
4	11.4642	4.0016	86.6597
5	10.9163	4.5494	82.1103
6	10.2935	5.1723	76.9380
7	9.5854	5.8804	71.0576
8	8.7803	6.6855	64.3721
9	7.8650	7.6008	56.7713
10	6.8244	8.6414	48.1299
11	5.6413	9.8245	38.3054
12	4.2963	11.1695	27.1359
13	2.7671	12.6987	14.4372
14	1.0286	14.4372	0.0000

YEARS 15 — MO PAYT 1.2587 — AN CONST 15.11

#	INT	PRIN	BALANCE
1	12.7649	2.3391	97.6609
2	12.4447	2.6594	95.0015
3	12.0806	3.0235	91.9780
4	11.6666	3.4374	88.5406
5	11.1960	3.9080	84.6326
6	10.6610	4.4430	80.1896
7	10.0527	5.0513	75.1383
8	9.3612	5.7429	69.3954
9	8.5749	6.5291	62.8663
10	7.6810	7.4230	55.4433
11	6.6648	8.4393	47.0041
12	5.5094	9.5947	37.4094
13	4.1958	10.9082	26.5012
14	2.7024	12.4016	14.0995
15	1.0045	14.0995	0.0000

YEARS 16 — MO PAYT 1.2333 — AN CONST 14.80

#	INT	PRIN	BALANCE
1	12.7836	2.0160	97.9840
2	12.5076	2.2920	95.6921
3	12.1938	2.6058	93.0863
4	11.8370	2.9625	90.1238
5	11.4314	3.3681	86.7557
6	10.9703	3.8292	82.9265
7	10.4461	4.3535	78.5730
8	9.8501	4.9495	73.6235
9	9.1724	5.6271	67.9964
10	8.4020	6.3975	61.5989
11	7.5262	7.2734	54.3256
12	6.5304	8.2691	46.0565
13	5.3983	9.4012	36.6552
14	4.1112	10.6883	25.9669
15	2.6479	12.1516	13.8153
16	.9843	13.8153	0.0000

YEARS 17 — MO PAYT 1.2118 — AN CONST 14.55

#	INT	PRIN	BALANCE
1	12.7994	1.7423	98.2577
2	12.5608	1.9808	96.2768
3	12.2896	2.2520	94.0248
4	11.9813	2.5604	91.4644
5	11.6308	2.9109	88.5535
6	11.2323	3.3094	85.2441
7	10.7792	3.7625	81.4816
8	10.2641	4.2776	77.2040
9	9.6784	4.8632	72.3408
10	9.0126	5.5291	66.8117
11	8.2557	6.2860	60.5257
12	7.3951	7.1466	53.3791
13	6.4166	8.1251	45.2540
14	5.3043	9.2374	36.0166
15	4.0396	10.5021	25.5145
16	2.6018	11.9399	13.5746
17	.9671	13.5746	0.0000

YEARS 18 — MO PAYT 1.1935 — AN CONST 14.33

#	INT	PRIN	BALANCE
1	12.8128	1.5094	98.4906
2	12.6062	1.7160	96.7746
3	12.3712	1.9509	94.8237
4	12.1041	2.2180	92.6056
5	11.8005	2.5217	90.0839
6	11.4552	2.8670	87.2169
7	11.0627	3.2595	83.9575
8	10.6165	3.7057	80.2518
9	10.1092	4.2130	76.0387
10	9.5324	4.7898	71.2489
11	8.8766	5.4456	65.8033
12	8.1311	6.1911	59.6121
13	7.2834	7.0388	52.5734
14	6.3198	8.0024	44.5710
15	5.2242	9.0980	35.4730
16	3.9786	10.3436	25.1294
17	2.5625	11.7597	13.3697
18	.9525	13.3697	0.0000

YEARS 19 — MO PAYT 1.1779 — AN CONST 14.14

#	INT	PRIN	BALANCE
1	12.8243	1.3102	98.6898
2	12.6449	1.4896	97.2002
3	12.4410	1.6935	95.5067
4	12.2092	1.9254	93.5813
5	11.9456	2.1890	91.3923
6	11.6459	2.4887	88.9036
7	11.3052	2.8294	86.0742
8	10.9178	3.2168	82.8575
9	10.4774	3.6572	79.2003
10	9.9767	4.1578	75.0425
11	9.4075	4.7271	70.3154
12	8.7603	5.3743	64.9411
13	8.0245	6.1100	58.8311
14	7.1880	6.9465	51.8846
15	6.2370	7.8976	43.9870
16	5.1557	8.9788	35.0082
17	3.9265	10.2081	24.8001
18	2.5289	11.6056	13.1945
19	.9400	13.1945	0.0000

YEARS 20 — MO PAYT 1.1645 — AN CONST 13.98

#	INT	PRIN	BALANCE
1	12.8342	1.1393	98.8607
2	12.6782	1.2953	97.5654
3	12.5009	1.4726	96.0928
4	12.2993	1.6742	94.4185
5	12.0701	1.9035	92.5151
6	11.8095	2.1640	90.3510
7	11.5132	2.4603	87.8907
8	11.1764	2.7972	85.0936
9	10.7934	3.1801	81.9135
10	10.3580	3.6155	78.2980
11	9.8630	4.1105	74.1875
12	9.3003	4.6732	69.5143
13	8.6605	5.3130	64.2012
14	7.9331	6.0404	58.1608
15	7.1061	6.8674	51.2934
16	6.1659	7.8076	43.4858
17	5.0970	8.8765	34.6093
18	3.8817	10.0918	24.5176
19	2.5001	11.4734	13.0442
20	.9293	13.0442	0.0000

YEARS 21 — MO PAYT 1.1529 — AN CONST 13.84

#	INT	PRIN	BALANCE
1	12.8427	.9922	99.0078
2	12.7069	1.1280	97.8798
3	12.5524	1.2824	96.5974

MONTHLY PAYMENT AMORTIZATION SCHEDULE PER $100

12.90 %

#	INT	PRIN	BALANCE
4	12.3769	1.4580	95.1394
5	12.1772	1.6576	93.4817
6	11.9503	1.8846	91.5972
7	11.6923	2.1426	89.4546
8	11.3990	2.4359	87.0187
9	11.0655	2.7694	84.2493
10	10.6863	3.1486	81.1007
11	10.2553	3.5796	77.5211
12	9.7652	4.0697	73.4514
13	9.2080	4.6269	68.8246
14	8.5746	5.2603	63.5643
15	7.8544	5.9805	57.5838
16	7.0356	6.7993	50.7845
17	6.1047	7.7301	43.0544
18	5.0464	8.7884	34.2660
19	3.8432	9.9916	24.2743
20	2.4753	11.3596	12.9148
21	.9201	12.9148	0.0000

YEARS 22 — MO PAYT 1.1429 — AN CONST 13.72

#	INT	PRIN	BALANCE
1	12.8500	.8651	99.1349
2	12.7316	.9836	98.1513
3	12.5969	1.1182	97.0330
4	12.4438	1.2713	95.7617
5	12.2698	1.4454	94.3163
6	12.0719	1.6433	92.6730
7	11.8469	1.8683	90.8047
8	11.5911	2.1240	88.6807
9	11.3003	2.4148	86.2659
10	10.9697	2.7454	83.5204
11	10.5939	3.1213	80.3991
12	10.1665	3.5486	76.8504
13	9.6807	4.0345	72.8160
14	9.1283	4.5868	68.2291
15	8.5004	5.2148	63.0143
16	7.7864	5.9287	57.0856
17	6.9747	6.7404	50.3452
18	6.0519	7.6632	42.6819
19	5.0028	8.7124	33.9695
20	3.8100	9.9052	24.0643
21	2.4539	11.2613	12.8030
22	.9121	12.8030	0.0000

YEARS 23 — MO PAYT 1.1343 — AN CONST 13.62

#	INT	PRIN	BALANCE
1	12.8564	.7552	99.2448
2	12.7530	.8586	98.3862
3	12.6354	.9762	97.4100
4	12.5018	1.1098	96.3002
5	12.3499	1.2617	95.0385
6	12.1771	1.4345	93.6040
7	11.9807	1.6309	91.9731
8	11.7574	1.8542	90.1190
9	11.5036	2.1080	88.0110
10	11.2150	2.3966	85.6144
11	10.8869	2.7247	82.8897
12	10.5139	3.0977	79.7919
13	10.0897	3.5218	76.2701
14	9.6076	4.0040	72.2660
15	9.0594	4.5522	67.7139
16	8.4362	5.1754	62.5384
17	7.7276	5.8840	56.6545
18	6.9221	6.6895	49.9649
19	6.0062	7.6054	42.3596
20	4.9650	8.6466	33.7130
21	3.7812	9.8304	23.8826
22	2.4354	11.1762	12.7063
23	.9053	12.7063	0.0000

YEARS 24 — MO PAYT 1.1268 — AN CONST 13.53

#	INT	PRIN	BALANCE
1	12.8619	.6599	99.3401
2	12.7715	.7502	98.5899
3	12.6688	.8529	97.7369
4	12.5521	.9697	96.7672
5	12.4193	1.1025	95.6647
6	12.2684	1.2534	94.4113
7	12.0968	1.4250	92.9863
8	11.9017	1.6201	91.3662
9	11.6799	1.8419	89.5243
10	11.4277	2.0941	87.4302
11	11.1410	2.3808	85.0494
12	10.8150	2.7067	82.3427
13	10.4445	3.0773	79.2654
14	10.0232	3.4986	75.7668
15	9.5442	3.9776	71.7892
16	8.9996	4.5222	67.2670
17	8.3805	5.1413	62.1258
18	7.6766	5.8451	56.2806
19	6.8764	6.6454	49.6352
20	5.9666	7.5552	42.0800
21	4.9322	8.5895	33.4905
22	3.7563	9.7655	23.7250
23	2.4193	11.1025	12.6225
24	.8993	12.6225	0.0000

YEARS 25 — MO PAYT 1.1203 — AN CONST 13.45

#	INT	PRIN	BALANCE
1	12.8667	.5771	99.4229
2	12.7877	.6561	98.7668
3	12.6978	.7459	98.0209
4	12.5957	.8480	97.1729
5	12.4796	.9641	96.2088
6	12.3476	1.0961	95.1127
7	12.1976	1.2462	93.8665
8	12.0270	1.4168	92.4497
9	11.8330	1.6108	90.8389
10	11.6125	1.8313	89.0077
11	11.3617	2.0820	86.9257
12	11.0767	2.3670	84.5586
13	10.7526	2.6911	81.8675
14	10.3842	3.0595	78.8080
15	9.9653	3.4784	75.3295
16	9.4891	3.9546	71.3749
17	8.9477	4.4961	66.8788
18	8.3321	5.1116	61.7672
19	7.6323	5.8114	55.9558
20	6.8367	6.6070	49.3488
21	5.9322	7.5116	41.8372
22	4.9038	8.5400	33.2972
23	3.7346	9.7092	23.5881
24	2.4053	11.0384	12.5497
25	.8941	12.5497	0.0000

YEARS 26 — MO PAYT 1.1147 — AN CONST 13.38

#	INT	PRIN	BALANCE
1	12.8708	.5050	99.4950
2	12.8017	.5742	98.9208
3	12.7231	.6528	98.2681
4	12.6337	.7421	97.5259
5	12.5321	.8437	96.6822
6	12.4166	.9593	95.7229
7	12.2853	1.0906	94.6323
8	12.1360	1.2399	93.3925
9	11.9662	1.4096	91.9828
10	11.7732	1.6026	90.3802
11	11.5538	1.8220	88.5582
12	11.3044	2.0715	86.4867
13	11.0208	2.3551	84.1316
14	10.6983	2.6775	81.4540
15	10.3318	3.0441	78.4100
16	9.9150	3.4609	74.9491
17	9.4412	3.9347	71.0144
18	8.9025	4.4733	66.5411
19	8.2901	5.0858	61.4553
20	7.5938	5.7821	55.6732
21	6.8022	6.5737	49.0996
22	5.9022	7.4737	41.6259
23	4.8790	8.4968	33.1291
24	3.7157	9.6601	23.4689
25	2.3932	10.9827	12.4863
26	.8896	12.4863	0.0000

YEARS 27 — MO PAYT 1.1097 — AN CONST 13.32

#	INT	PRIN	BALANCE
1	12.8745	.4422	99.5578
2	12.8139	.5028	99.0550
3	12.7451	.5716	98.4834
4	12.6668	.6499	97.8335
5	12.5778	.7389	97.0946
6	12.4767	.8400	96.2546
7	12.3617	.9550	95.2996
8	12.2309	1.0858	94.2138
9	12.0823	1.2344	92.9794
10	11.9133	1.4034	91.5760
11	11.7212	1.5955	89.9805
12	11.5027	1.8140	88.1665
13	11.2544	2.0623	86.1042
14	10.9720	2.3447	83.7595
15	10.6510	2.6657	81.0938
16	10.2861	3.0306	78.0632
17	9.8712	3.4455	74.6176
18	9.3994	3.9173	70.7004
19	8.8631	4.4536	66.2468
20	8.2534	5.0633	61.1835
21	7.5602	5.7565	55.4270
22	6.7721	6.5446	48.8824
23	5.8761	7.4406	41.4418
24	4.8574	8.4593	32.9826
25	3.6993	9.6174	23.3652
26	2.3826	10.9341	12.4311
27	.8856	12.4311	0.0000

YEARS 28 — MO PAYT 1.1054 — AN CONST 13.27

#	INT	PRIN	BALANCE
1	12.8776	.3875	99.6125
2	12.8246	.4405	99.1720
3	12.7643	.5008	98.6712
4	12.6957	.5694	98.1018
5	12.6177	.6474	97.4544
6	12.5291	.7360	96.7184
7	12.4283	.8368	95.8816
8	12.3138	.9513	94.9303
9	12.1835	1.0816	93.8488
10	12.0355	1.2296	92.6192
11	11.8671	1.3980	91.2212
12	11.6757	1.5894	89.6318
13	11.4581	1.8070	87.8249
14	11.2108	2.0543	85.7705
15	10.9295	2.3356	83.4350
16	10.6097	2.6554	80.7796
17	10.2462	3.0189	77.7607
18	9.8329	3.4322	74.3285
19	9.3630	3.9021	70.4264
20	8.8288	4.4363	65.9901
21	8.2214	5.0437	60.9465
22	7.5309	5.7342	55.2123
23	6.7459	6.5192	48.6930
24	5.8533	7.4118	41.2813
25	4.8386	8.4265	32.8548
26	3.6850	9.5801	23.2746
27	2.3734	10.8917	12.3829
28	.8822	12.3829	0.0000

YEARS 29 — MO PAYT 1.1017 — AN CONST 13.23

#	INT	PRIN	BALANCE
1	12.8804	.3397	99.6603
2	12.8339	.3862	99.2742
3	12.7810	.4390	98.8351
4	12.7209	.4991	98.3360
5	12.6526	.5675	97.7685
6	12.5749	.6452	97.1234
7	12.4866	.7335	96.3899
8	12.3861	.8339	95.5560
9	12.2720	.9481	94.6079
10	12.1422	1.0779	93.5300
11	11.9946	1.2254	92.3046
12	11.8268	1.3932	90.9114
13	11.6361	1.5840	89.3274
14	11.4192	1.8008	87.5266
15	11.1727	2.0474	85.4792
16	10.8924	2.3277	83.1516
17	10.5737	2.6463	80.5052
18	10.2114	3.0086	77.4966
19	9.7995	3.4205	74.0761
20	9.3312	3.8888	70.1872
21	8.7988	4.4212	65.7660
22	8.1935	5.0265	60.7394
23	7.5053	5.7147	55.0247
24	6.7229	6.4971	48.5276
25	5.8334	7.3866	41.1410
26	4.8222	8.3979	32.7432
27	3.6724	9.5476	23.1956
28	2.3653	10.8547	12.3408
29	.8792	12.3408	0.0000

YEARS 30 — MO PAYT 1.0984 — AN CONST 13.19

#	INT	PRIN	BALANCE
1	12.8828	.2979	99.7021
2	12.8420	.3386	99.3635
3	12.7957	.3850	98.9785
4	12.7429	.4377	98.5408
5	12.6830	.4976	98.0431
6	12.6149	.5658	97.4773
7	12.5374	.6432	96.8341
8	12.4494	.7313	96.1028
9	12.3492	.8314	95.2713
10	12.2354	.9453	94.3261
11	12.1060	1.0747	93.2514
12	11.9589	1.2218	92.0296
13	11.7916	1.3891	90.6406
14	11.6014	1.5792	89.0613
15	11.3852	1.7955	87.2659
16	11.1394	2.0413	85.2246
17	10.8599	2.3207	82.9039
18	10.5422	2.6384	80.2654
19	10.1810	2.9997	77.2658
20	9.7703	3.4103	73.8554
21	9.3034	3.8772	69.9782
22	8.7726	4.4081	65.5701
23	8.1691	5.0116	60.5585
24	7.4830	5.6977	54.8608
25	6.7029	6.4777	48.3831
26	5.8161	7.3646	41.0185
27	4.8078	8.3729	32.6456
28	3.6615	9.5192	23.1265
29	2.3583	10.8224	12.3041
30	.8766	12.3041	0.0000

YEARS 2 — MO PAYT 4.7542 — AN CONST 57.06

#	INT	PRIN	BALANCE
1	10.2782	46.7720	53.2280
2	3.8222	53.2280	0.0000

YEARS 3 — MO PAYT 3.3694 — AN CONST 40.44

#	INT	PRIN	BALANCE
1	11.3050	29.1278	70.8722
2	7.2844	33.1483	37.7239
3	2.7089	37.7239	0.0000

YEARS 4 — MO PAYT 2.6827 — AN CONST 32.20

#	INT	PRIN	BALANCE
1	11.8141	20.3789	79.6211
2	9.0011	23.1918	56.4293
3	5.7999	26.3931	30.0362
4	2.1568	30.0362	0.0000

YEARS 5 — MO PAYT 2.2753 — AN CONST 27.31

#	INT	PRIN	BALANCE
1	12.1162	15.1875	84.8125
2	10.0198	17.2839	67.5287
3	7.6341	19.6696	47.8591
4	4.9191	22.3846	25.4744
5	1.8293	25.4744	0.0000

YEARS 6 — MO PAYT 2.0074 — AN CONST 24.09

#	INT	PRIN	BALANCE
1	12.3148	11.7741	88.2259
2	10.6896	13.3993	74.8266
3	8.8401	15.2488	59.5778
4	6.7353	17.3537	42.2241
5	4.3399	19.7490	22.4751
6	1.6139	22.4751	0.0000

YEARS 7 — MO PAYT 1.8192 — AN CONST 21.84

#	INT	PRIN	BALANCE
1	12.4544	9.3760	90.6240
2	11.1602	10.6702	79.9539
3	9.6874	12.1430	67.8109
4	8.0112	13.8191	53.9918
5	6.1038	15.7266	38.2652
6	3.9330	17.8974	20.3678
7	1.4626	20.3678	0.0000

YEARS 8 — MO PAYT 1.6807 — AN CONST 20.17

#	INT	PRIN	BALANCE
1	12.5571	7.6116	92.3884
2	11.5064	8.6623	83.7260
3	10.3107	9.8580	73.8681
4	8.9500	11.2187	62.6494
5	7.4015	12.7672	49.8821
6	5.6392	14.5295	35.3526
7	3.6336	16.5351	18.8175
8	1.3512	18.8175	0.0000

YEARS 9 — MO PAYT 1.5754 — AN CONST 18.91

#	INT	PRIN	BALANCE
1	12.6352	6.2691	93.7309
2	11.7698	7.1345	86.5964
3	10.7851	8.1193	78.4772
4	9.6643	9.2400	69.2372
5	8.3889	10.5154	58.7218
6	6.9375	11.9669	46.7549
7	5.2856	13.6187	33.1363
8	3.4058	15.4985	17.6378
9	1.2665	17.6378	0.0000

YEARS 10 — MO PAYT 1.4931 — AN CONST 17.92

#	INT	PRIN	BALANCE
1	12.6962	5.2211	94.7789
2	11.9755	5.9418	88.8371
3	11.1553	6.7620	82.0751
4	10.2204	7.6953	74.3798
5	9.1597	8.7575	65.6222
6	7.9509	9.9664	55.6559
7	6.5752	11.3421	44.3138
8	5.0097	12.9076	31.4062
9	3.2280	14.6893	16.7169
10	1.2004	16.7169	0.0000

YEARS 11 — MO PAYT 1.4276 — AN CONST 17.14

#	INT	PRIN	BALANCE
1	12.7447	4.3866	95.6134
2	12.1392	4.9921	90.6213
3	11.4502	5.6812	84.9402
4	10.6660	6.4653	78.4748
5	9.7736	7.3578	71.1170
6	8.7579	8.3734	62.7436
7	7.6021	9.5292	53.2145
8	6.2868	10.8445	42.3699
9	4.7899	12.3414	30.0285
10	3.0864	14.0449	15.9836
11	1.1477	15.9836	0.0000

YEARS 12 — MO PAYT 1.3746 — AN CONST 16.50

#	INT	PRIN	BALANCE
1	12.7840	3.7115	96.2885
2	12.2717	4.2238	92.0647
3	11.6887	4.8068	87.2579
4	11.0252	5.4703	81.7876
5	10.2701	6.2254	75.5622
6	9.4108	7.0847	68.4775
7	8.4329	8.0626	60.4149
8	7.3200	9.1755	51.2394
9	6.0535	10.4420	40.7974
10	4.6121	11.8834	28.9140
11	2.9718	13.5237	15.3904
12	1.1051	15.3904	0.0000

YEARS 13 — MO PAYT 1.3312 — AN CONST 15.98

#	INT	PRIN	BALANCE
1	12.8162	3.1583	96.8417
2	12.3803	3.5943	93.2474
3	11.8841	4.0904	89.1570
4	11.3195	4.6550	84.5020
5	10.6770	5.2975	79.2045
6	9.9458	6.0288	73.1757
7	9.1136	6.8609	66.3148
8	8.1666	7.8080	58.5068
9	7.0888	8.8857	49.6211
10	5.8623	10.1122	39.5089
11	4.4665	11.5081	28.0008
12	2.8780	13.0965	14.9043
13	1.0702	14.9043	0.0000

YEARS 14 — MO PAYT 1.2953 — AN CONST 15.55

#	INT	PRIN	BALANCE
1	12.8429	2.7003	97.2997
2	12.4701	3.0730	94.2267
3	12.0460	3.4972	90.7295
4	11.5632	3.9799	86.7495
5	11.0139	4.5293	82.2202
6	10.3887	5.1545	77.0657
7	9.6772	5.8660	71.1998
8	8.8675	6.6757	64.5241
9	7.9460	7.5971	56.9270
10	6.8974	8.6458	48.2812
11	5.7040	9.8392	38.4420
12	4.3459	11.1973	27.2447
13	2.8003	12.7429	14.5018
14	1.0413	14.5018	0.0000

YEARS 15 — MO PAYT 1.2652 — AN CONST 15.19

#	INT	PRIN	BALANCE
1	12.8651	2.3178	97.6822
2	12.5452	2.6377	95.0445
3	12.1811	3.0018	92.0427
4	11.7668	3.4162	88.6265
5	11.2952	3.8877	84.7389
6	10.7586	4.4243	80.3145
7	10.1479	5.0350	75.2795
8	9.4529	5.7300	69.5495
9	8.6620	6.5209	63.0286
10	7.7619	7.4210	55.6075
11	6.7375	8.4454	47.1621
12	5.5718	9.6111	37.5510
13	4.2451	10.9378	26.6132
14	2.7354	12.4475	14.1657
15	1.0172	14.1657	0.0000

YEARS 16 — MO PAYT 1.2400 — AN CONST 14.88

#	INT	PRIN	BALANCE
1	12.8838	1.9960	98.0040
2	12.6083	2.2715	95.7325
3	12.2948	2.5851	93.1474
4	11.9380	2.9419	90.2055
5	11.5319	3.3480	86.8576
6	11.0698	3.8101	83.0475
7	10.5438	4.3360	78.7115
8	9.9453	4.9345	73.7769
9	9.2642	5.6156	68.1613
10	8.4891	6.3908	61.7705
11	7.6069	7.2729	54.4976
12	6.6030	8.2768	46.2208
13	5.4606	9.4193	36.8015
14	4.1604	10.7195	26.0820
15	2.6808	12.1991	13.8830
16	.9969	13.8830	0.0000

YEARS 17 — MO PAYT 1.2186 — AN CONST 14.63

#	INT	PRIN	BALANCE
1	12.8997	1.7237	98.2763
2	12.6618	1.9616	96.3147
3	12.3910	2.2324	94.0824
4	12.0829	2.5405	91.5418
5	11.7322	2.8912	88.6507
6	11.3331	3.2903	85.3604
7	10.8790	3.7444	81.6160
8	10.3621	4.2613	77.3547
9	9.7739	4.8495	72.5053
10	9.1045	5.5188	66.9864
11	8.3427	6.2806	60.7058
12	7.4758	7.1476	53.5582
13	6.4892	8.1342	45.4241
14	5.3664	9.2569	36.1672
15	4.0887	10.5347	25.6325
16	2.6346	11.9888	13.6437
17	.9797	13.6437	0.0000

YEARS 18 — MO PAYT 1.2004 — AN CONST 14.41

#	INT	PRIN	BALANCE
1	12.9132	1.4920	98.5080
2	12.7072	1.6980	96.8100
3	12.4729	1.9323	94.8777
4	12.2061	2.1991	92.6786
5	11.9026	2.5026	90.1760
6	11.5571	2.8480	87.3280
7	11.1640	3.2412	84.0868
8	10.7166	3.6886	80.3983
9	10.2075	4.1977	76.2006
10	9.6281	4.7771	71.4235
11	8.9687	5.4365	65.9870
12	8.2183	6.1869	59.8001
13	7.3643	7.0409	52.7591
14	6.3924	8.0128	44.7464
15	5.2864	9.1188	35.6275
16	4.0277	10.3775	25.2500
17	2.5953	11.8099	13.4401
18	.9651	13.4401	0.0000

YEARS 19 — MO PAYT 1.1849 — AN CONST 14.22

#	INT	PRIN	BALANCE
1	12.9247	1.2941	98.7059
2	12.7461	1.4727	97.2332
3	12.5428	1.6760	95.5572
4	12.3114	1.9073	93.6499
5	12.0482	2.1706	91.4793
6	11.7486	2.4702	89.0091
7	11.4076	2.8112	86.1979
8	11.0196	3.1992	82.9987
9	10.5780	3.6408	79.3579
10	10.0754	4.1434	75.2145
11	9.5035	4.7153	70.4992
12	8.8526	5.3662	65.1330
13	8.1119	6.1069	59.0262
14	7.2690	6.9498	52.0764
15	6.3097	7.9091	44.1673
16	5.2180	9.0008	35.1665
17	3.9756	10.2432	24.9233
18	2.5617	11.6571	13.2662
19	.9526	13.2662	0.0000

YEARS 20 — MO PAYT 1.1716 — AN CONST 14.06

#	INT	PRIN	BALANCE
1	12.9346	1.1243	98.8757
2	12.7794	1.2795	97.5961
3	12.6028	1.4561	96.1400
4	12.4018	1.6571	94.4828
5	12.1730	1.8859	92.5970
6	11.9127	2.1462	90.4508
7	11.6165	2.4424	88.0083
8	11.2793	2.7796	85.2287
9	10.8957	3.1633	82.0655
10	10.4590	3.5999	78.4656
11	9.9621	4.0968	74.3688
12	9.3966	4.6623	69.7065
13	8.7531	5.3058	64.4007
14	8.0207	6.0382	58.3625
15	7.1872	6.8717	51.4909
16	6.2387	7.8202	43.6707
17	5.1593	8.8996	34.7711
18	3.9309	10.1280	24.6431
19	2.5329	11.5260	13.1170
20	.9419	13.1170	0.0000

YEARS 21 — MO PAYT 1.1601 — AN CONST 13.93

#	INT	PRIN	BALANCE
1	12.9431	.9783	99.0217
2	12.8080	1.1133	97.9084
3	12.6544	1.2670	96.6413

#	INT	PRIN	BALANCE
4	12.4795	1.4419	95.1994
5	12.2804	1.6409	93.5585
6	12.0539	1.8674	91.6911
7	11.7962	2.1252	89.5659
8	11.5028	2.4185	87.1473
9	11.1690	2.7524	84.3949
10	10.7891	3.1323	81.2626
11	10.3567	3.5647	77.6980
12	9.8647	4.0567	73.6413
13	9.3047	4.6167	69.0246
14	8.6675	5.2539	63.7707
15	7.9422	5.9791	57.7916
16	7.1169	6.8044	50.9871
17	6.1777	7.7437	43.2435
18	5.1088	8.8125	34.4309
19	3.8924	10.0290	24.4020
20	2.5081	11.4133	12.9887
21	.9327	12.9887	0.0000

YEARS 22 — MO PAYT 1.1502 — AN CONST 13.81

#	INT	PRIN	BALANCE
1	12.9504	.8523	99.1477
2	12.8328	.9700	98.1777
3	12.6989	1.1038	97.0739
4	12.5465	1.2562	95.8177
5	12.3731	1.4296	94.3880
6	12.1758	1.6269	92.7611
7	11.9512	1.8515	90.9096
8	11.6956	2.1071	88.8025
9	11.4048	2.3979	86.4046
10	11.0738	2.7289	83.6756
11	10.6971	3.1056	80.5700
12	10.2684	3.5343	77.0357
13	9.7806	4.0221	73.0136
14	9.2254	4.5773	68.4363
15	8.5936	5.2091	63.2272
16	7.8746	5.9282	57.2990
17	7.0563	6.7464	50.5526
18	6.1251	7.6777	42.8749
19	5.0653	8.7374	34.1375
20	3.8592	9.9435	24.1940
21	2.4867	11.3160	12.8780
22	.9247	12.8780	0.0000

YEARS 23 — MO PAYT 1.1417 — AN CONST 13.71

#	INT	PRIN	BALANCE
1	12.9567	.7434	99.2566
2	12.8541	.8460	98.4107
3	12.7374	.9628	97.4479
4	12.6045	1.0956	96.3523
5	12.4532	1.2469	95.1054
6	12.2811	1.4190	93.6864
7	12.0853	1.6149	92.0715
8	11.8624	1.8378	90.2338
9	11.6087	2.0914	88.1424
10	11.3200	2.3801	85.7623
11	10.9915	2.7086	83.0536
12	10.6176	3.0825	79.9711
13	10.1921	3.5080	76.4631
14	9.7079	3.9922	72.4709
15	9.1568	4.5433	67.9276
16	8.5297	5.1704	62.7572
17	7.8160	5.8841	56.8731
18	7.0038	6.6963	50.1768
19	6.0795	7.6206	42.5562
20	5.0276	8.6725	33.8837
21	3.8305	9.8696	24.0141
22	2.4682	11.2319	12.7823
23	.9179	12.7823	0.0000

YEARS 24 — MO PAYT 1.1343 — AN CONST 13.62

#	INT	PRIN	BALANCE
1	12.9622	.6490	99.3510
2	12.8727	.7385	98.6125
3	12.7707	.8405	97.7720
4	12.6547	.9565	96.8155
5	12.5227	1.0885	95.7270
6	12.3724	1.2388	94.4882
7	12.2014	1.4098	93.0784
8	12.0068	1.6044	91.4740
9	11.7854	1.8258	89.6482
10	11.5334	2.0779	87.5703
11	11.2465	2.3647	85.2057
12	10.9201	2.6911	82.5146
13	10.5487	3.0625	79.4521
14	10.1260	3.4852	75.9669
15	9.6449	3.9663	72.0005
16	9.0974	4.5138	67.4867
17	8.4743	5.1369	62.3499
18	7.7653	5.8459	56.5040
19	6.9584	6.6528	49.8511
20	6.0401	7.5711	42.2800
21	4.9950	8.6162	33.6638
22	3.8057	9.8055	23.8583
23	2.4522	11.1590	12.6993
24	.9119	12.6993	0.0000

YEARS 25 — MO PAYT 1.1278 — AN CONST 13.54

#	INT	PRIN	BALANCE
1	12.9670	.5670	99.4330
2	12.8887	.6453	98.7877
3	12.7997	.7344	98.0533
4	12.6983	.8357	97.2176
5	12.5829	.9511	96.2665
6	12.4517	1.0824	95.1842
7	12.3023	1.2318	93.9524
8	12.1322	1.4018	92.5506
9	11.9387	1.5953	90.9554
10	11.7185	1.8155	89.1399
11	11.4680	2.0661	87.0738
12	11.1828	2.3513	84.7226
13	10.8582	2.6758	82.0467
14	10.4889	3.0452	79.0016
15	10.0685	3.4655	75.5361
16	9.5902	3.9438	71.5923
17	9.0458	4.4882	67.1041
18	8.4263	5.1077	61.9963
19	7.7213	5.8128	56.1836
20	6.9189	6.6151	49.5685
21	6.0058	7.5282	42.0403
22	4.9667	8.5673	33.4729
23	3.7841	9.7499	23.7230
24	2.4383	11.0957	12.6273
25	.9067	12.6273	0.0000

YEARS 26 — MO PAYT 1.1222 — AN CONST 13.47

#	INT	PRIN	BALANCE
1	12.9711	.4958	99.5042
2	12.9027	.5642	98.9400
3	12.8248	.6421	98.2979
4	12.7362	.7307	97.5672
5	12.6353	.8316	96.7356
6	12.5206	.9464	95.7893
7	12.3899	1.0770	94.7123
8	12.2413	1.2257	93.4866
9	12.0721	1.3948	92.0918
10	11.8796	1.5874	90.5044
11	11.6605	1.8065	88.6979
12	11.4111	2.0558	86.6421
13	11.1273	2.3396	84.3025
14	10.8044	2.6625	81.6400
15	10.4369	3.0301	78.6099
16	10.0186	3.4483	75.1616
17	9.5426	3.9243	71.2373
18	9.0010	4.4660	66.7714
19	8.3845	5.0824	61.6890
20	7.6830	5.7839	55.9050
21	6.8846	6.5823	49.3227
22	5.9760	7.4909	41.8318
23	4.9421	8.5249	33.3070
24	3.7653	9.7016	23.6054
25	2.4262	11.0407	12.5647
26	.9022	12.5647	0.0000

YEARS 27 — MO PAYT 1.1174 — AN CONST 13.41

#	INT	PRIN	BALANCE
1	12.9748	.4338	99.5662
2	12.9149	.4936	99.0726
3	12.8468	.5618	98.5109
4	12.7692	.6393	97.8716
5	12.6810	.7275	97.1440
6	12.5805	.8280	96.3160
7	12.4663	.9423	95.3738
8	12.3362	1.0723	94.3015
9	12.1882	1.2203	93.0811
10	12.0197	1.3888	91.6923
11	11.8280	1.5805	90.1119
12	11.6099	1.7986	88.3132
13	11.3616	2.0469	86.2663
14	11.0791	2.3294	83.9369
15	10.7575	2.6510	81.2859
16	10.3916	3.0169	78.2690
17	9.9752	3.4333	74.8356
18	9.5013	3.9073	70.9284
19	8.9619	4.4466	66.4818
20	8.3482	5.0604	61.4214
21	7.6497	5.7589	55.6626
22	6.8548	6.5538	49.1088
23	5.9501	7.4584	41.6504
24	4.9206	8.4879	33.1625
25	3.7490	9.6595	23.5030
26	2.4157	10.9928	12.5102
27	.8983	12.5102	0.0000

YEARS 28 — MO PAYT 1.1131 — AN CONST 13.36

#	INT	PRIN	BALANCE
1	12.9779	.3797	99.6203
2	12.9255	.4321	99.1882
3	12.8658	.4918	98.6964
4	12.7980	.5596	98.1368
5	12.7207	.6369	97.4999
6	12.6328	.7248	96.7752
7	12.5328	.8248	95.9503
8	12.4189	.9387	95.0116
9	12.2893	1.0683	93.9434
10	12.1419	1.2157	92.7277
11	11.9741	1.3835	91.3442
12	11.7831	1.5745	89.7697
13	11.5658	1.7918	87.9779
14	11.3185	2.0391	85.9388
15	11.0370	2.3206	83.6181
16	10.7167	2.6409	80.9772
17	10.3521	3.0055	77.9718
18	9.9373	3.4203	74.5515
19	9.4652	3.8924	70.6590
20	8.9279	4.4297	66.2293
21	8.3165	5.0411	61.1882
22	7.6206	5.7370	55.4512
23	6.8287	6.5289	48.9223
24	5.9275	7.4301	41.4923
25	4.9019	8.4557	33.0366
26	3.7348	9.6228	23.4138
27	2.4065	10.9511	12.4627
28	.8949	12.4627	0.0000

YEARS 29 — MO PAYT 1.1094 — AN CONST 13.32

#	INT	PRIN	BALANCE
1	12.9806	.3325	99.6675
2	12.9347	.3784	99.2890
3	12.8825	.4307	98.8584
4	12.8231	.4901	98.3682
5	12.7554	.5578	97.8105
6	12.6784	.6348	97.1757
7	12.5908	.7224	96.4533
8	12.4911	.8221	95.6313
9	12.3776	.9356	94.6957
10	12.2485	1.0647	93.6310
11	12.1015	1.2117	92.4193
12	11.9343	1.3789	91.0404
13	11.7439	1.5692	89.4712
14	11.5273	1.7859	87.6853
15	11.2808	2.0324	85.6530
16	11.0003	2.3129	83.3401
17	10.6810	2.6321	80.7079
18	10.3177	2.9955	77.7125
19	9.9042	3.4089	74.3036
20	9.4337	3.8795	70.4241
21	8.8982	4.4150	66.0091
22	8.2888	5.0244	60.9847
23	7.5953	5.7179	55.2668
24	6.8060	6.5072	48.7596
25	5.9078	7.4054	41.3543
26	4.8856	8.4275	32.9267
27	3.7224	9.5908	23.3359
28	2.3985	10.9147	12.4212
29	.8919	12.4212	0.0000

YEARS 30 — MO PAYT 1.1062 — AN CONST 13.28

#	INT	PRIN	BALANCE
1	12.9830	.2913	99.7087
2	12.9428	.3316	99.3771
3	12.8971	.3773	98.9998
4	12.8450	.4294	98.5703
5	12.7857	.4887	98.0817
6	12.7183	.5561	97.5255
7	12.6415	.6329	96.8926
8	12.5541	.7203	96.1723
9	12.4547	.8197	95.3526
10	12.3416	.9328	94.4198
11	12.2128	1.0616	93.3582
12	12.0663	1.2081	92.1501
13	11.8995	1.3749	90.7752
14	11.7097	1.5647	89.2105
15	11.4937	1.7806	87.4299
16	11.2480	2.0264	85.4034
17	10.9682	2.3061	83.0973
18	10.6499	2.6245	80.4728
19	10.2877	2.9867	77.4861
20	9.8754	3.3990	74.0871
21	9.4062	3.8682	70.2189
22	8.8723	4.4021	65.8168
23	8.2647	5.0097	60.8070
24	7.5731	5.7012	55.1058
25	6.7862	6.4882	48.6176
26	5.8906	7.3838	41.2338
27	4.8714	8.4030	32.8308
28	3.7115	9.5629	23.2679
29	2.3915	10.8829	12.3851
30	.8893	12.3851	0.0000

YEARS 2 — MO PAYT 4.7589 — AN CONST 57.11

#	INT	PRIN	BALANCE
1	10.3592	46.7473	53.2527
2	3.8539	53.2527	0.0000

YEARS 3 — MO PAYT 3.3742 — AN CONST 40.50

#	INT	PRIN	BALANCE
1	11.3941	29.0965	70.9035
2	7.3451	33.1455	37.7580
3	2.7326	37.7580	0.0000

YEARS 4 — MO PAYT 2.6877 — AN CONST 32.26

#	INT	PRIN	BALANCE
1	11.9072	20.3454	79.6546
2	9.0759	23.1767	56.4779
3	5.8507	26.4019	30.0760
4	2.1766	30.0760	0.0000

YEARS 5 — MO PAYT 2.2804 — AN CONST 27.37

#	INT	PRIN	BALANCE
1	12.2115	15.1536	84.8464
2	10.1028	17.2624	67.5840
3	7.7006	19.6646	47.9195
4	4.9641	22.4011	25.5184
5	1.8468	25.5184	0.0000

YEARS 6 — MO PAYT 2.0127 — AN CONST 24.16

#	INT	PRIN	BALANCE
1	12.4116	11.7407	88.2593
2	10.7778	13.3745	74.8849
3	8.9167	15.2356	59.6492
4	6.7965	17.3558	42.2934
5	4.3813	19.7710	22.5224
6	1.6300	22.5224	0.0000

YEARS 7 — MO PAYT 1.8246 — AN CONST 21.90

#	INT	PRIN	BALANCE
1	12.5522	9.3435	90.6565
2	11.2520	10.6437	80.0129
3	9.7708	12.1248	67.8880
4	8.0835	13.8121	54.0759
5	6.1615	15.7342	38.3417
6	3.9719	17.9237	20.4180
7	1.4777	20.4180	0.0000

YEARS 8 — MO PAYT 1.6863 — AN CONST 20.24

#	INT	PRIN	BALANCE
1	12.6556	7.5803	92.4197
2	11.6007	8.6352	83.7845
3	10.3990	9.8369	73.9476
4	9.0302	11.2057	62.7419
5	7.4708	12.7651	49.9768
6	5.6944	14.5415	35.4353
7	3.6708	16.5651	18.8702
8	1.3656	18.8702	0.0000

YEARS 9 — MO PAYT 1.5811 — AN CONST 18.98

#	INT	PRIN	BALANCE
1	12.7342	6.2391	93.7609
2	11.8660	7.1074	86.6535
3	10.8769	8.0964	78.5571
4	9.7502	9.2231	69.3339
5	8.4667	10.5066	58.8274
6	7.0047	11.9687	46.8587
7	5.3391	13.6342	33.2244
8	3.4418	15.5315	17.6929
9	1.2804	17.6929	0.0000

YEARS 10 — MO PAYT 1.4990 — AN CONST 17.99

#	INT	PRIN	BALANCE
1	12.7956	5.1926	94.8074
2	12.0730	5.9152	88.8923
3	11.2498	6.7383	82.1539
4	10.3121	7.6760	74.4779
5	9.2439	8.7442	65.7337
6	8.0271	9.9610	55.7727
7	6.6409	11.3472	44.4255
8	5.0619	12.9263	31.4992
9	3.2631	14.7251	16.7742
10	1.2140	16.7742	0.0000

YEARS 11 — MO PAYT 1.4337 — AN CONST 17.21

#	INT	PRIN	BALANCE
1	12.8444	4.3595	95.6405
2	12.2377	4.9662	90.6743
3	11.5466	5.6573	85.0170
4	10.7594	6.4446	78.5724
5	9.8626	7.3414	71.2310
6	8.8409	8.3630	62.8680
7	7.6772	9.5268	53.3413
8	6.3514	10.8525	42.4888
9	4.8412	12.3627	30.1260
10	3.1208	14.0831	16.0429
11	1.1610	16.0429	0.0000

YEARS 12 — MO PAYT 1.3808 — AN CONST 16.57

#	INT	PRIN	BALANCE
1	12.8839	3.6859	96.3141
2	12.3710	4.1988	92.1152
3	11.7867	4.7832	87.3321
4	11.1210	5.4488	81.8833
5	10.3628	6.2070	75.6763
6	9.4990	7.0708	68.6055
7	8.5151	8.0547	60.5508
8	7.3942	9.1756	51.3752
9	6.1173	10.4525	40.9227
10	4.6628	11.9071	29.0156
11	3.0058	13.5640	15.4516
12	1.1182	15.4516	0.0000

YEARS 13 — MO PAYT 1.3375 — AN CONST 16.06

#	INT	PRIN	BALANCE
1	12.9162	3.1342	96.8658
2	12.4801	3.5704	93.2954
3	11.9832	4.0672	89.2281
4	11.4172	4.6332	84.5949
5	10.7725	5.2780	79.3169
6	10.0380	6.0125	73.3044
7	9.2013	6.8492	66.4553
8	8.2482	7.8023	58.6530
9	7.1624	8.8880	49.7649
10	5.9256	10.1249	39.6400
11	4.5166	11.5339	28.1062
12	2.9116	13.1389	14.9673
13	1.0832	14.9673	0.0000

YEARS 14 — MO PAYT 1.3017 — AN CONST 15.63

#	INT	PRIN	BALANCE
1	12.9430	2.6777	97.3223
2	12.5704	3.0503	94.2720
3	12.1459	3.4748	90.7972
4	11.6624	3.9583	86.8389
5	11.1115	4.5092	82.3297
6	10.4840	5.1367	77.1930
7	9.7692	5.8515	71.3416
8	8.9549	6.6658	64.6758
9	8.0273	7.5934	57.0824
10	6.9706	8.6500	48.4324
11	5.7669	9.8538	38.5786
12	4.3957	11.2250	27.3536
13	2.8336	12.7871	14.5665
14	1.0542	14.5665	0.0000

YEARS 15 — MO PAYT 1.2718 — AN CONST 15.27

#	INT	PRIN	BALANCE
1	12.9654	2.2966	97.7034
2	12.6458	2.6162	95.0872
3	12.2817	2.9803	92.1070
4	11.8670	3.3950	88.7120
5	11.3945	3.8674	84.8445
6	10.8563	4.4056	80.4389
7	10.2433	5.0187	75.4202
8	9.5449	5.7171	69.7031
9	8.7493	6.5127	63.1904
10	7.8430	7.4190	55.7715
11	6.8106	8.4514	47.3201
12	5.6345	9.6275	37.6926
13	4.2947	10.9672	26.7254
14	2.7685	12.4934	14.2320
15	1.0300	14.2320	0.0000

YEARS 16 — MO PAYT 1.2467 — AN CONST 14.97

#	INT	PRIN	BALANCE
1	12.9841	1.9762	98.0238
2	12.7091	2.2512	95.7726
3	12.3959	2.5645	93.2081
4	12.0390	2.9214	90.2867
5	11.6324	3.3279	86.9588
6	11.1693	3.7910	83.1678
7	10.6418	4.3186	78.8493
8	10.0408	4.9195	73.9298
9	9.3562	5.6041	68.3256
10	8.5764	6.3840	61.9417
11	7.6880	7.2724	54.6693
12	6.6760	8.2844	46.3849
13	5.5231	9.4372	36.9477
14	4.2099	10.7505	26.1972
15	2.7138	12.2465	13.9507
16	1.0096	13.9507	0.0000

YEARS 17 — MO PAYT 1.2254 — AN CONST 14.71

#	INT	PRIN	BALANCE
1	13.0000	1.7052	98.2948
2	12.7627	1.9425	96.3523
3	12.4924	2.2128	94.1395
4	12.1845	2.5208	91.6187
5	11.8337	2.8715	88.7471
6	11.4341	3.2711	85.4760
7	10.9789	3.7264	81.7496
8	10.4603	4.2449	77.5047
9	9.8696	4.8356	72.6691
10	9.1967	5.5085	67.1605
11	8.4301	6.2751	60.8854
12	7.5569	7.1484	53.7371
13	6.5621	8.1431	45.5940
14	5.4289	9.2763	36.3177
15	4.1381	10.5672	25.7505
16	2.6676	12.0377	13.7128
17	.9924	13.7128	0.0000

YEARS 18 — MO PAYT 1.2074 — AN CONST 14.49

#	INT	PRIN	BALANCE
1	13.0135	1.4748	98.5252
2	12.8083	1.6801	96.8451
3	12.5745	1.9139	94.9312
4	12.3082	2.1802	92.7511
5	12.0048	2.4836	90.2675
6	11.6592	2.8292	87.4383
7	11.2655	3.2229	84.2154
8	10.8170	3.6714	80.5440
9	10.3061	4.1823	76.3617
10	9.7240	4.7643	71.5974
11	9.0611	5.4273	66.1700
12	8.3058	6.1826	59.9875
13	7.4454	7.0429	52.9446
14	6.4654	8.0230	44.9215
15	5.3489	9.1395	35.7821
16	4.0770	10.4113	25.3707
17	2.6282	11.8601	13.5106
18	.9778	13.5106	0.0000

YEARS 19 — MO PAYT 1.1919 — AN CONST 14.31

#	INT	PRIN	BALANCE
1	13.0251	1.2781	98.7219
2	12.8472	1.4560	97.2659
3	12.6446	1.6586	95.6073
4	12.4138	1.8894	93.7179
5	12.1509	2.1523	91.5656
6	11.8513	2.4518	89.1137
7	11.5101	2.7930	86.3207
8	11.1215	3.1817	83.1390
9	10.6787	3.6245	79.5145
10	10.1743	4.1289	75.3857
11	9.5998	4.7034	70.6823
12	8.9452	5.3579	65.3243
13	8.1996	6.1035	59.2208
14	7.3503	6.9529	52.2679
15	6.3827	7.9205	44.3474
16	5.2805	9.0227	35.3247
17	4.0249	10.2783	25.0465
18	2.5946	11.7086	13.3379
19	.9653	13.3379	0.0000

YEARS 20 — MO PAYT 1.1787 — AN CONST 14.15

#	INT	PRIN	BALANCE
1	13.0349	1.1095	98.8905
2	12.8805	1.2639	97.6265
3	12.7047	1.4398	96.1867
4	12.5043	1.6402	94.5465
5	12.2760	1.8684	92.6781
6	12.0160	2.1284	90.5496
7	11.7198	2.4246	88.1250
8	11.3824	2.7620	85.3630
9	10.9981	3.1464	82.2165
10	10.5602	3.5843	78.6323
11	10.0614	4.0830	74.5492
12	9.4933	4.6512	69.8980
13	8.8460	5.2985	64.5995
14	8.1087	6.0358	58.5637
15	7.2687	6.8758	51.6879
16	6.3119	7.8326	43.8553
17	5.2219	8.9226	34.9328
18	3.9803	10.1642	24.7686
19	2.5658	11.5787	13.1899
20	.9546	13.1899	0.0000

YEARS 21 — MO PAYT 1.1673 — AN CONST 14.01

#	INT	PRIN	BALANCE
1	13.0434	.9646	99.0354
2	12.9092	1.0988	97.9366
3	12.7563	1.2517	96.6848

#	INT	PRIN	BALANCE
4	12.5821	1.4259	95.2589
5	12.3837	1.6244	93.6345
6	12.1576	1.8504	91.7841
7	11.9001	2.1079	89.6762
8	11.6068	2.4012	87.2749
9	11.2726	2.7354	84.5395
10	10.8920	3.1161	81.4235
11	10.4584	3.5497	77.8738
12	9.9644	4.0437	73.8301
13	9.4017	4.6064	69.2238
14	8.7607	5.2474	63.9764
15	8.0304	5.9776	57.9988
16	7.1986	6.8094	51.1894
17	6.2510	7.7570	43.4323
18	5.1716	8.8365	34.5958
19	3.9419	10.0662	24.5297
20	2.5411	11.4670	13.0627
21	.9454	13.0627	0.0000

YEARS 22 — MO PAYT 1.1575 — AN CONST 13.90

#	INT	PRIN	BALANCE
1	13.0508	.8397	99.1603
2	12.9339	.9565	98.2038
3	12.8008	1.0896	97.1142
4	12.6492	1.2412	95.8730
5	12.4765	1.4140	94.4590
6	12.2797	1.6107	92.8483
7	12.0556	1.8349	91.0134
8	11.8002	2.0902	88.9232
9	11.5093	2.3811	86.5421
10	11.1780	2.7124	83.8297
11	10.8005	3.0899	80.7398
12	10.3705	3.5199	77.2199
13	9.8807	4.0097	73.2102
14	9.3227	4.5677	68.6425
15	8.6871	5.2033	63.4392
16	7.9630	5.9274	57.5118
17	7.1382	6.7523	50.7595
18	6.1985	7.6919	43.0676
19	5.1281	8.7623	34.3053
20	3.9088	9.9816	24.3237
21	2.5197	11.3707	12.9530
22	.9374	12.9530	0.0000

YEARS 23 — MO PAYT 1.1491 — AN CONST 13.79

#	INT	PRIN	BALANCE
1	13.0571	.7317	99.2683
2	12.9553	.8335	98.4348
3	12.8393	.9495	97.4853
4	12.7072	1.0816	96.4037
5	12.5566	1.2322	95.1715
6	12.3852	1.4036	93.7679
7	12.1898	1.5989	92.1690
8	11.9673	1.8214	90.3475
9	11.7139	2.0749	88.2726
10	11.4251	2.3637	85.9089
11	11.0962	2.6926	83.2163
12	10.7215	3.0673	80.1490
13	10.2947	3.4941	76.6549
14	9.8084	3.9804	72.6746
15	9.2545	4.5343	68.1403
16	8.6235	5.1653	62.9750
17	7.9048	5.8840	57.0910
18	7.0859	6.7029	50.3881
19	6.1532	7.6356	42.7525
20	5.0906	8.6982	34.0543
21	3.8802	9.9086	24.1457
22	2.5013	11.2875	12.8582
23	.9306	12.8582	0.0000

YEARS 24 — MO PAYT 1.1417 — AN CONST 13.71

#	INT	PRIN	BALANCE
1	13.0626	.6382	99.3618
2	12.9738	.7270	98.6348
3	12.8726	.8282	97.8066
4	12.7573	.9434	96.8631
5	12.6261	1.0747	95.7884
6	12.4765	1.2243	94.5641
7	12.3061	1.3947	93.1695
8	12.1121	1.5887	91.5807
9	11.8910	1.8098	89.7709
10	11.6391	2.0617	87.7092
11	11.3522	2.3486	85.3606
12	11.0254	2.6754	82.6852
13	10.6531	3.0477	79.6375
14	10.2290	3.4718	76.1657
15	9.7458	3.9550	72.2107
16	9.1955	4.5053	67.7054
17	8.5685	5.1323	62.5731
18	7.8543	5.8465	56.7266
19	7.0407	6.6601	50.0666
20	6.1139	7.5869	42.4797
21	5.0581	8.6427	33.8370
22	3.8554	9.8454	23.9916
23	2.4853	11.2154	12.7762
24	.9246	12.7762	0.0000

YEARS 25 — MO PAYT 1.1354 — AN CONST 13.63

#	INT	PRIN	BALANCE
1	13.0673	.5571	99.4429
2	12.9898	.6347	98.8082
3	12.9015	.7230	98.0853
4	12.8009	.8236	97.2617
5	12.6863	.9382	96.3235
6	12.5557	1.0687	95.2547
7	12.4070	1.2175	94.0373
8	12.2376	1.3869	92.6504
9	12.0446	1.5799	91.0705
10	11.8247	1.7997	89.2708
11	11.5743	2.0502	87.2206
12	11.2890	2.3355	84.8851
13	10.9640	2.6605	82.2246
14	10.5937	3.0307	79.1938
15	10.1720	3.4525	75.7414
16	9.6915	3.9329	71.8084
17	9.1442	4.4802	67.3282
18	8.5208	5.1037	62.2245
19	7.8105	5.8139	56.4106
20	7.0015	6.6230	49.7876
21	6.0798	7.5446	42.2430
22	5.0299	8.5945	33.6485
23	3.8339	9.7905	23.8580
24	2.4715	11.1530	12.7050
25	.9195	12.7050	0.0000

YEARS 26 — MO PAYT 1.1298 — AN CONST 13.56

#	INT	PRIN	BALANCE
1	13.0715	.4867	99.5133
2	13.0037	.5544	98.9589
3	12.9266	.6316	98.3273
4	12.8387	.7195	97.6079
5	12.7386	.8196	96.7883
6	12.6245	.9336	95.8547
7	12.4946	1.0635	94.7912
8	12.3466	1.2115	93.5796
9	12.1780	1.3801	92.1995
10	11.9860	1.5722	90.6273
11	11.7672	1.7910	88.8363
12	11.5179	2.0402	86.7961
13	11.2340	2.3241	84.4720
14	10.9106	2.6476	81.8244
15	10.5422	3.0160	78.8084

(continued)

#	INT	PRIN	BALANCE
16	10.1225	3.4357	75.3727
17	9.6444	3.9138	71.4590
18	9.0997	4.4584	67.0005
19	8.4793	5.0789	61.9217
20	7.7725	5.7856	56.1361
21	6.9674	6.5907	49.5453
22	6.0503	7.5079	42.0374
23	5.0055	8.5527	33.4847
24	3.8153	9.7429	23.7418
25	2.4595	11.0987	12.6432
26	.9150	12.6432	0.0000

YEARS 27 — MO PAYT 1.1250 — AN CONST 13.51

#	INT	PRIN	BALANCE
1	13.0751	.4254	99.5746
2	13.0159	.4846	99.0900
3	12.9484	.5521	98.5379
4	12.8716	.6289	97.9090
5	12.7841	.7164	97.1926
6	12.6844	.8161	96.3766
7	12.5708	.9296	95.4469
8	12.4415	1.0590	94.3879
9	12.2941	1.2064	93.1815
10	12.1262	1.3743	91.8072
11	11.9350	1.5655	90.2417
12	11.7171	1.7834	88.4584
13	11.4689	2.0315	86.4268
14	11.1862	2.3142	84.1126
15	10.8642	2.6363	81.4763
16	10.4973	3.0032	78.4732
17	10.0794	3.4211	75.0521
18	9.6033	3.8971	71.1550
19	9.0610	4.4395	66.7155
20	8.4432	5.0572	61.6582
21	7.7395	5.7610	55.8972
22	6.9378	6.5627	49.3345
23	6.0245	7.4760	41.8586
24	4.9842	8.5163	33.3423
25	3.7990	9.7014	23.6408
26	2.4490	11.0515	12.5894
27	.9111	12.5894	0.0000

YEARS 28 — MO PAYT 1.1209 — AN CONST 13.46

#	INT	PRIN	BALANCE
1	13.0782	.3721	99.6279
2	13.0264	.4238	99.2041
3	12.9674	.4828	98.7213
4	12.9002	.5500	98.1713
5	12.8237	.6265	97.5448
6	12.7365	.7137	96.8310
7	12.6372	.8130	96.0180
8	12.5241	.9262	95.0918
9	12.3952	1.0551	94.0367
10	12.2483	1.2019	92.8348
11	12.0811	1.3692	91.4657
12	11.8906	1.5597	89.9060
13	11.6735	1.7767	88.1293
14	11.4263	2.0240	86.1053
15	11.1446	2.3056	83.7996
16	10.8238	2.6265	81.1732
17	10.4583	2.9920	78.1812
18	10.0419	3.4083	74.7729
19	9.5676	3.8826	70.8902
20	9.0273	4.4229	66.4673
21	8.4118	5.0384	61.4288
22	7.7107	5.7396	55.6893
23	6.9120	6.5383	49.1510
24	6.0021	7.4481	41.7028
25	4.9656	8.4846	33.2182
26	3.7849	9.6653	23.5529
27	2.4399	11.0103	12.5425
28	.9077	12.5425	0.0000

YEARS 29 — MO PAYT 1.1172 — AN CONST 13.41

#	INT	PRIN	BALANCE
1	13.0809	.3255	99.6745
2	13.0356	.3708	99.3036
3	12.9840	.4225	98.8812
4	12.9252	.4812	98.3999
5	12.8582	.5482	97.8517
6	12.7820	.6245	97.2272
7	12.6951	.7114	96.5158
8	12.5961	.8104	95.7054
9	12.4833	.9232	94.7822
10	12.3548	1.0516	93.7306
11	12.2085	1.1980	92.5326
12	12.0418	1.3647	91.1679
13	11.8518	1.5546	89.6133
14	11.6355	1.7709	87.8424
15	11.3891	2.0174	85.8250
16	11.1083	2.2981	83.5268
17	10.7885	2.6179	80.9089
18	10.4242	2.9822	77.9267
19	10.0092	3.3972	74.5294
20	9.5365	3.8700	70.6594
21	8.9979	4.4085	66.2509
22	8.3844	5.0220	61.2289
23	7.6856	5.7209	55.5080
24	6.8895	6.5170	48.9910
25	5.9826	7.4239	41.5671
26	4.9495	8.4570	33.1101
27	3.7726	9.6339	23.4762
28	2.4320	10.9745	12.5017
29	.9048	12.5017	0.0000

YEARS 30 — MO PAYT 1.1140 — AN CONST 13.37

#	INT	PRIN	BALANCE
1	13.0833	.2850	99.7150
2	13.0436	.3246	99.3904
3	12.9985	.3698	99.0206
4	12.9470	.4212	98.5994
5	12.8884	.4799	98.1195
6	12.8216	.5466	97.5729
7	12.7455	.6227	96.9502
8	12.6589	.7094	96.2408
9	12.5602	.8081	95.4327
10	12.4477	.9205	94.5121
11	12.3196	1.0486	93.4635
12	12.1737	1.1946	92.2689
13	12.0074	1.3608	90.9081
14	11.8181	1.5502	89.3579
15	11.6024	1.7659	87.5920
16	11.3566	2.0116	85.5804
17	11.0767	2.2916	83.2888
18	10.7578	2.6105	80.6784
19	10.3945	2.9737	77.7046
20	9.9807	3.3876	74.3171
21	9.5093	3.8590	70.4581
22	8.9723	4.3960	66.0621
23	8.3605	5.0077	61.0544
24	7.6637	5.7046	55.3498
25	6.8698	6.4984	48.8514
26	5.9655	7.4027	41.4486
27	4.9354	8.4329	33.0157
28	3.7618	9.6064	23.4093
29	2.4250	10.9432	12.4661
30	.9022	12.4661	0.0000

YEARS 2 — MO PAYT 4.7601 — AN CONST 57.13

#	INT	PRIN	BALANCE
1	10.3795	46.7412	53.2588
2	3.8619	53.2588	0.0000

YEARS 3 — MO PAYT 3.3754 — AN CONST 40.51

#	INT	PRIN	BALANCE
1	11.4164	29.0887	70.9113
2	7.3602	33.1448	37.7665
3	2.7385	37.7665	0.0000

YEARS 4 — MO PAYT 2.6890 — AN CONST 32.27

#	INT	PRIN	BALANCE
1	11.9304	20.3371	79.6629
2	9.0946	23.1729	56.4900
3	5.8634	26.4041	30.0859
4	2.1816	30.0859	0.0000

YEARS 5 — MO PAYT 2.2817 — AN CONST 27.39

#	INT	PRIN	BALANCE
1	12.2354	15.1451	84.8549
2	10.1235	17.2570	67.5979
3	7.7172	19.6633	47.9346
4	4.9754	22.4052	25.5294
5	1.8512	25.5294	0.0000

YEARS 6 — MO PAYT 2.0140 — AN CONST 24.17

#	INT	PRIN	BALANCE
1	12.4359	11.7323	88.2677
2	10.7999	13.3683	74.8994
3	8.9358	15.2323	59.6671
4	6.8118	17.3564	42.3107
5	4.3916	19.7765	22.5342
6	1.6340	22.5342	0.0000

YEARS 7 — MO PAYT 1.8260 — AN CONST 21.92

#	INT	PRIN	BALANCE
1	12.5767	9.3353	90.6647
2	11.2749	10.6371	80.0276
3	9.7917	12.1203	67.9073
4	8.1016	13.8104	54.0970
5	6.1759	15.7361	38.3609
6	3.9817	17.9303	20.4305
7	1.4814	20.4305	0.0000

YEARS 8 — MO PAYT 1.6877 — AN CONST 20.26

#	INT	PRIN	BALANCE
1	12.6802	7.5725	92.4275
2	11.6243	8.6284	83.7991
3	10.4211	9.8316	73.9675
4	9.0502	11.2025	62.7650
5	7.4881	12.7646	50.0005
6	5.7082	14.5445	35.4560
7	3.6801	16.5726	18.8834
8	1.3693	18.8834	0.0000

YEARS 9 — MO PAYT 1.5826 — AN CONST 19.00

#	INT	PRIN	BALANCE
1	12.7590	6.2317	93.7683
2	11.8900	7.1006	86.6677
3	10.8999	8.0907	78.5770
4	9.7717	9.2189	69.3581
5	8.4862	10.5044	58.8537
6	7.0215	11.9691	46.8846
7	5.3525	13.6381	33.2465
8	3.4508	15.5398	17.7067
9	1.2839	17.7067	0.0000

YEARS 10 — MO PAYT 1.5005 — AN CONST 18.01

#	INT	PRIN	BALANCE
1	12.8204	5.1855	94.8145
2	12.0973	5.9085	88.9060
3	11.2735	6.7324	82.1736
4	10.3347	7.6712	74.5024
5	9.2650	8.7409	65.7616
6	8.0462	9.9597	55.8019
7	6.6574	11.3485	44.4534
8	5.0750	12.9309	31.5225
9	3.2719	14.7340	16.7885
10	1.2174	16.7885	0.0000

YEARS 11 — MO PAYT 1.4352 — AN CONST 17.23

#	INT	PRIN	BALANCE
1	12.8693	4.3528	95.6472
2	12.2624	4.9597	90.6875
3	11.5708	5.6513	85.0361
4	10.7828	6.4394	78.5968
5	9.8848	7.3373	71.2595
6	8.8617	8.3604	62.8991
7	7.6960	9.5262	53.3729
8	6.3676	10.8545	42.5185
9	4.8541	12.3681	30.1504
10	3.1295	14.0927	16.0577
11	1.1644	16.0577	0.0000

YEARS 12 — MO PAYT 1.3824 — AN CONST 16.59

#	INT	PRIN	BALANCE
1	12.9089	3.6795	96.3205
2	12.3958	4.1926	92.1278
3	11.8112	4.7773	87.3506
4	11.1450	5.4434	81.9072
5	10.3860	6.2024	75.7048
6	9.5211	7.0673	68.6375
7	8.5357	8.0528	60.5847
8	7.4128	9.1756	51.4091
9	6.1333	10.4551	40.9540
10	4.6755	11.9130	29.0410
11	3.0143	13.5741	15.4669
12	1.1215	15.4669	0.0000

YEARS 13 — MO PAYT 1.3391 — AN CONST 16.07

#	INT	PRIN	BALANCE
1	12.9413	3.1282	96.8718
2	12.5050	3.5644	93.3073
3	12.0080	4.0615	89.2458
4	11.4417	4.6278	84.6180
5	10.7964	5.2731	79.3449
6	10.0611	6.0084	73.3365
7	9.2233	6.8462	66.4903
8	8.2686	7.8008	58.6895
9	7.1809	8.8886	49.8009
10	5.9415	10.1280	39.6728
11	4.5292	11.5403	28.1325
12	2.9200	13.1495	14.9831
13	1.0864	14.9831	0.0000

YEARS 14 — MO PAYT 1.3033 — AN CONST 15.65

#	INT	PRIN	BALANCE
1	12.9680	2.6721	97.3279
2	12.5955	3.0447	94.2833
3	12.1709	3.4692	90.8141
4	11.6872	3.9529	86.8611
5	11.1360	4.5041	82.3570
6	10.5079	5.1322	77.2248
7	9.7923	5.8478	71.3769
8	8.9768	6.6633	64.7137
9	8.0477	7.5924	57.1213
10	6.9890	8.6511	48.4702
11	5.7827	9.8574	38.6127
12	4.4082	11.2319	27.3808
13	2.8420	12.7981	14.5827
14	1.0574	14.5827	0.0000

YEARS 15 — MO PAYT 1.2735 — AN CONST 15.29

#	INT	PRIN	BALANCE
1	12.9904	2.2913	97.7087
2	12.6709	2.6108	95.0978
3	12.3068	2.9749	92.1229
4	11.8920	3.3897	88.7332
5	11.4194	3.8624	84.8709
6	10.8808	4.4009	80.4699
7	10.2671	5.0146	75.4553
8	9.5679	5.7139	69.7415
9	8.7711	6.5106	63.2309
10	7.8633	7.4184	55.8124
11	6.8289	8.4529	47.3595
12	5.6502	9.6315	37.7280
13	4.3072	10.9746	26.7534
14	2.7769	12.5049	14.2486
15	1.0332	14.2486	0.0000

YEARS 16 — MO PAYT 1.2484 — AN CONST 14.99

#	INT	PRIN	BALANCE
1	13.0092	1.9713	98.0287
2	12.7343	2.2462	95.7826
3	12.4211	2.5594	93.2232
4	12.0642	2.9162	90.3069
5	11.6576	3.3229	86.9841
6	11.1943	3.7862	83.1978
7	10.6663	4.3142	78.8836
8	10.0647	4.9158	73.9679
9	9.3793	5.6012	68.3667
10	8.5982	6.3823	61.9844
11	7.7083	7.2722	54.7122
12	6.6943	8.2862	46.4260
13	5.5388	9.4417	36.9843
14	4.2223	10.7582	26.2260
15	2.7221	12.2584	13.9677
16	1.0128	13.9677	0.0000

YEARS 17 — MO PAYT 1.2271 — AN CONST 14.73

#	INT	PRIN	BALANCE
1	13.0251	1.7006	98.2994
2	12.7880	1.9378	96.3616
3	12.5178	2.2080	94.1537
4	12.2099	2.5158	91.6378
5	11.8591	2.8667	88.7712
6	11.4594	3.2664	85.5048
7	11.0039	3.7218	81.7829
8	10.4849	4.2408	77.5421
9	9.8936	4.8322	72.7100
10	9.2198	5.5060	67.2040
11	8.4520	6.2737	60.9303
12	7.5772	7.1485	53.7817
13	6.5804	8.1453	45.6364
14	5.4446	9.2811	36.3553
15	4.1505	10.5753	25.7800
16	2.6758	12.0499	13.7301
17	.9956	13.7301	0.0000

YEARS 18 — MO PAYT 1.2091 — AN CONST 14.51

#	INT	PRIN	BALANCE
1	13.0386	1.4706	98.5294
2	12.8336	1.6756	96.8538
3	12.5999	1.9093	94.9446
4	12.3337	2.1755	92.7691
5	12.0303	2.4788	90.2902
6	11.6847	2.8245	87.4657
7	11.2908	3.2183	84.2474
8	10.8421	3.6671	80.5803
9	10.3307	4.1785	76.4018
10	9.7481	4.7611	71.6407
11	9.0842	5.4250	66.2157
12	8.3277	6.1815	60.0343
13	7.4658	7.0434	52.9909
14	6.4836	8.0255	44.9653
15	5.3646	9.1446	35.8207
16	4.0894	10.4198	25.4009
17	2.6365	11.8727	13.5282
18	.9809	13.5282	0.0000

YEARS 19 — MO PAYT 1.1937 — AN CONST 14.33

#	INT	PRIN	BALANCE
1	13.0502	1.2742	98.7258
2	12.8725	1.4518	97.2740
3	12.6700	1.6543	95.6198
4	12.4394	1.8849	93.7348
5	12.1765	2.1478	91.5871
6	11.8771	2.4473	89.1398
7	11.5358	2.7885	86.3513
8	11.1470	3.1773	83.1739
9	10.7039	3.6204	79.5536
10	10.1991	4.1252	75.4283
11	9.6239	4.7004	70.7279
12	8.9684	5.3559	65.3720
13	8.2216	6.1027	59.2693
14	7.3707	6.9537	52.3157
15	6.4010	7.9233	44.3924
16	5.2962	9.0281	35.3643
17	4.0373	10.2870	25.0773
18	2.6029	11.7214	13.3559
19	.9684	13.3559	0.0000

YEARS 20 — MO PAYT 1.1805 — AN CONST 14.17

#	INT	PRIN	BALANCE
1	13.0600	1.1059	98.8941
2	12.9058	1.2601	97.6341
3	12.7301	1.4358	96.1983
4	12.5299	1.6360	94.5623
5	12.3018	1.8641	92.6982
6	12.0419	2.1240	90.5742
7	11.7457	2.4202	88.1540
8	11.4082	2.7577	85.3964
9	11.0237	3.1422	82.2542
10	10.5856	3.5804	78.6738
11	10.0863	4.0796	74.5942
12	9.5174	4.6485	69.9457
13	8.8693	5.2966	64.6491
14	8.1307	6.0352	58.6139
15	7.2891	6.8768	51.7371
16	6.3302	7.8357	43.9015
17	5.2376	8.9283	34.9732
18	3.9927	10.1732	24.8000
19	2.5741	11.5918	13.2082
20	.9577	13.2082	0.0000

YEARS 21 — MO PAYT 1.1691 — AN CONST 14.03

#	INT	PRIN	BALANCE
1	13.0685	.9612	99.0388
2	12.9345	1.0952	97.9436
3	12.7818	1.2480	96.6956

#	INT	PRIN	BALANCE
4	12.6078	1.4220	95.2737
5	12.4095	1.6202	93.6534
6	12.1836	1.8462	91.8072
7	11.9261	2.1036	89.7036
8	11.6328	2.3969	87.3067
9	11.2986	2.7312	84.5755
10	10.9177	3.1120	81.4635
11	10.4838	3.5459	77.9176
12	9.9894	4.0404	73.8772
13	9.4260	4.6038	69.2734
14	8.7840	5.2457	64.0277
15	8.0525	5.9772	58.0505
16	7.2191	6.8107	51.2398
17	6.2694	7.7603	43.4795
18	5.1873	8.8425	34.6370
19	3.9543	10.0755	24.5616
20	2.5494	11.4804	13.0812
21	.9485	13.0812	0.0000

YEARS 22 — MO PAYT 1.1594 — AN CONST 13.92

#	INT	PRIN	BALANCE
1	13.0759	.8365	99.1635
2	12.9592	.9532	98.2103
3	12.8263	1.0861	97.1243
4	12.6749	1.2375	95.8867
5	12.5023	1.4101	94.4767
6	12.3057	1.6067	92.8700
7	12.0816	1.8307	91.0392
8	11.8264	2.0860	88.9532
9	11.5355	2.3769	86.5764
10	11.2041	2.7083	83.8680
11	10.8264	3.0860	80.7821
12	10.3961	3.5163	77.2658
13	9.9058	4.0066	73.2592
14	9.3471	4.5653	68.6939
15	8.7105	5.2019	63.4921
16	7.9852	5.9272	57.5649
17	7.1587	6.7537	50.8112
18	6.2170	7.6954	43.1158
19	5.1439	8.7685	34.3473
20	3.9212	9.9912	24.3561
21	2.5280	11.3843	12.9718
22	.9406	12.9718	0.0000

YEARS 23 — MO PAYT 1.1509 — AN CONST 13.82

#	INT	PRIN	BALANCE
1	13.0822	.7288	99.2712
2	12.9806	.8304	98.4408
3	12.8648	.9462	97.4946
4	12.7328	1.0782	96.4164
5	12.5825	1.2285	95.1879
6	12.4112	1.3998	93.7881
7	12.2160	1.5950	92.1931
8	11.9936	1.8174	90.3758
9	11.7402	2.0708	88.3050
10	11.4514	2.3596	85.9454
11	11.1224	2.6886	83.2568
12	10.7475	3.0635	80.1933
13	10.3203	3.4906	76.7027
14	9.8336	3.9774	72.7253
15	9.2790	4.5320	68.1933
16	8.6470	5.1639	63.0294
17	7.9270	5.8840	57.1454
18	7.1065	6.7045	50.4409
19	6.1716	7.6393	42.8015
20	5.1064	8.7046	34.0970
21	3.8926	9.9184	24.1786
22	2.5096	11.3014	12.8772
23	.9337	12.8772	0.0000

YEARS 24 — MO PAYT 1.1436 — AN CONST 13.73

#	INT	PRIN	BALANCE
1	13.0877	.6355	99.3645
2	12.9990	.7242	98.6403
3	12.8981	.8251	97.8152
4	12.7830	.9402	96.8750
5	12.6519	1.0713	95.8036
6	12.5025	1.2207	94.5830
7	12.3323	1.3909	93.1921
8	12.1384	1.5848	91.6072
9	11.9174	1.8058	89.8014
10	11.6656	2.0576	87.7437
11	11.3786	2.3446	85.3992
12	11.0517	2.6715	82.7277
13	10.6792	3.0440	79.6837
14	10.2547	3.4685	76.2152
15	9.7711	3.9521	72.2631
16	9.2200	4.5032	67.7599
17	8.5921	5.1311	62.6288
18	7.8766	5.8466	56.7822
19	7.0614	6.6619	50.1203
20	6.1324	7.5908	42.5295
21	5.0740	8.6493	33.8803
22	3.8679	9.8553	24.0250
23	2.4937	11.2295	12.7954
24	.9278	12.7954	0.0000

YEARS 25 — MO PAYT 1.1373 — AN CONST 13.65

#	INT	PRIN	BALANCE
1	13.0924	.5547	99.4453
2	13.0151	.6320	98.8133
3	12.9269	.7201	98.0932
4	12.8265	.8206	97.2726
5	12.7121	.9350	96.3376
6	12.5817	1.0654	95.2722
7	12.4332	1.2139	94.0583
8	12.2639	1.3832	92.6752
9	12.0710	1.5761	91.0991
10	11.8513	1.7958	89.3033
11	11.6009	2.0462	87.2570
12	11.3155	2.3316	84.9255
13	10.9904	2.6567	82.2688
14	10.6200	3.0271	79.2417
15	10.1979	3.4492	75.7925
16	9.7169	3.9302	71.8623
17	9.1689	4.4782	67.3841
18	8.5444	5.1027	62.2814
19	7.8329	5.8142	56.4672
20	7.0222	6.6249	49.8423
21	6.0984	7.5487	42.2936
22	5.0458	8.6013	33.6923
23	3.8464	9.8007	23.8917
24	2.4798	11.1673	12.7244
25	.9227	12.7244	0.0000

YEARS 26 — MO PAYT 1.1317 — AN CONST 13.59

#	INT	PRIN	BALANCE
1	13.0965	.4844	99.5156
2	13.0290	.5520	98.9636
3	12.9520	.6290	98.3346
4	12.8643	.7167	97.6180
5	12.7644	.8166	96.8014
6	12.6505	.9305	95.8709
7	12.5208	1.0602	94.8107
8	12.3729	1.2080	93.6027
9	12.2045	1.3765	92.2262
10	12.0126	1.5684	90.6578
11	11.7939	1.7871	88.8707
12	11.5447	2.0363	86.8343
13	11.2607	2.3203	84.5141
14	10.9372	2.6438	81.8703
15	10.5685	3.0125	78.8578
16	10.1485	3.4325	75.4253
17	9.6698	3.9111	71.5141
18	9.1245	4.4565	67.0576
19	8.5030	5.0779	61.9797
20	7.7950	5.7860	56.1937
21	6.9882	6.5928	49.6009
22	6.0689	7.5121	42.0887
23	5.0214	8.5596	33.5291
24	3.8278	9.7532	23.7760
25	2.4678	11.1132	12.6628
26	.9182	12.6628	0.0000

YEARS 27 — MO PAYT 1.1270 — AN CONST 13.53

#	INT	PRIN	BALANCE
1	13.1001	.4234	99.5766
2	13.0411	.4824	99.0943
3	12.9738	.5497	98.5446
4	12.8972	.6263	97.9183
5	12.8099	.7136	97.2047
6	12.7104	.8131	96.3916
7	12.5970	.9265	95.4650
8	12.4678	1.0557	94.4093
9	12.3206	1.2029	93.2064
10	12.1528	1.3707	91.8358
11	11.9617	1.5618	90.2740
12	11.7439	1.7796	88.4944
13	11.4958	2.0277	86.4667
14	11.2130	2.3104	84.1563
15	10.8909	2.6326	81.5237
16	10.5238	2.9997	78.5240
17	10.1055	3.4180	75.1060
18	9.6289	3.8946	71.2114
19	9.0858	4.4377	66.7737
20	8.4670	5.0564	61.7173
21	7.7620	5.7615	55.9558
22	6.9586	6.5649	49.3909
23	6.0432	7.4803	41.9106
24	5.0001	8.5234	33.3872
25	3.8116	9.7119	23.6753
26	2.4574	11.0661	12.6092
27	.9143	12.6092	0.0000

YEARS 28 — MO PAYT 1.1228 — AN CONST 13.48

#	INT	PRIN	BALANCE
1	13.1033	.3702	99.6298
2	13.0516	.4218	99.2080
3	12.9928	.4806	98.7274
4	12.9258	.5476	98.1798
5	12.8495	.6240	97.5559
6	12.7624	.7110	96.8449
7	12.6633	.8101	96.0347
8	12.5503	.9231	95.1117
9	12.4216	1.0518	94.0599
10	12.2750	1.1985	92.8614
11	12.1078	1.3656	91.4958
12	11.9174	1.5560	89.9398
13	11.7005	1.7730	88.1668
14	11.4532	2.0202	86.1466
15	11.1715	2.3019	83.8448
16	10.8506	2.6229	81.2219
17	10.4848	2.9886	78.2333
18	10.0681	3.4053	74.8280
19	9.5933	3.8802	70.9478
20	9.0522	4.4212	66.5266
21	8.4357	5.0377	61.4888
22	7.7332	5.7402	55.7486
23	6.9328	6.5406	49.2080
24	6.0208	7.4526	41.7554
25	4.9816	8.4918	33.2636
26	3.7975	9.6759	23.5877
27	2.4483	11.0252	12.5625
28	.9109	12.5625	0.0000

YEARS 29 — MO PAYT 1.1191 — AN CONST 13.43

#	INT	PRIN	BALANCE
1	13.1060	.3238	99.6762
2	13.0608	.3690	99.3072
3	13.0094	.4204	98.8868
4	12.9508	.4790	98.4077
5	12.8840	.5458	97.8619
6	12.8078	.6220	97.2399
7	12.7211	.7087	96.5313
8	12.6223	.8075	95.7238
9	12.5097	.9201	94.8037
10	12.3814	1.0484	93.7553
11	12.2352	1.1946	92.5607
12	12.0686	1.3612	91.1995
13	11.8788	1.5510	89.6486
14	11.6626	1.7672	87.8813
15	11.4161	2.0137	85.8677
16	11.1354	2.2944	83.5733
17	10.8154	2.6144	80.9589
18	10.4509	2.9789	77.9800
19	10.0355	3.3943	74.5857
20	9.5622	3.8676	70.7180
21	9.0229	4.4069	66.3111
22	8.4084	5.0214	61.2897
23	7.7082	5.7216	55.5681
24	6.9104	6.5194	49.0487
25	6.0013	7.4285	41.6202
26	4.9655	8.4643	33.1559
27	3.7852	9.6446	23.5113
28	2.4403	10.9894	12.5218
29	.9080	12.5218	0.0000

YEARS 30 — MO PAYT 1.1160 — AN CONST 13.40

#	INT	PRIN	BALANCE
1	13.1084	.2834	99.7166
2	13.0688	.3229	99.3937
3	13.0238	.3679	99.0258
4	12.9725	.4192	98.6066
5	12.9141	.4777	98.1289
6	12.8474	.5443	97.5846
7	12.7715	.6202	96.9644
8	12.6851	.7067	96.2577
9	12.5865	.8052	95.4525
10	12.4742	.9175	94.5350
11	12.3463	1.0454	93.4896
12	12.2005	1.1912	92.2984
13	12.0344	1.3573	90.9411
14	11.8452	1.5466	89.3945
15	11.6295	1.7622	87.6323
16	11.3838	2.0079	85.6244
17	11.1038	2.2879	83.3364
18	10.7848	2.6070	80.7295
19	10.4213	2.9705	77.7590
20	10.0071	3.3847	74.3743
21	9.5351	3.8566	70.5176
22	8.9973	4.3944	66.1232
23	8.3846	5.0072	61.1160
24	7.6864	5.7054	55.4107
25	6.8908	6.5009	48.9097
26	5.9843	7.4074	41.5023
27	4.9514	8.4403	33.0619
28	3.7745	9.6173	23.4446
29	2.4334	10.9583	12.4863
30	.9054	12.4863	0.0000

YEARS 2 — MO PAYT 4.7636 — AN CONST 57.17

#	INT	PRIN	BALANCE
1	10.4403	46.7227	53.2773
2	3.8857	53.2773	0.0000

YEARS 3 — MO PAYT 3.3790 — AN CONST 40.55

#	INT	PRIN	BALANCE
1	11.4832	29.0652	70.9348
2	7.4058	33.1427	37.7921
3	2.7563	37.7921	0.0000

YEARS 4 — MO PAYT 2.6927 — AN CONST 32.32

#	INT	PRIN	BALANCE
1	12.0002	20.3120	79.6880
2	9.1508	23.1615	56.5265
3	5.9015	26.4107	30.1158
4	2.1965	30.1158	0.0000

YEARS 5 — MO PAYT 2.2856 — AN CONST 27.43

#	INT	PRIN	BALANCE
1	12.3069	15.1198	84.8802
2	10.1858	17.2409	67.6394
3	7.7672	19.6595	47.9798
4	5.0092	22.4175	25.5623
5	1.8644	25.5623	0.0000

YEARS 6 — MO PAYT 2.0180 — AN CONST 24.22

#	INT	PRIN	BALANCE
1	12.5085	11.7073	88.2927
2	10.8661	13.3497	74.9431
3	8.9933	15.2224	59.7206
4	6.8579	17.3579	42.3627
5	4.4228	19.7930	22.5697
6	1.6461	22.5697	0.0000

YEARS 7 — MO PAYT 1.8301 — AN CONST 21.97

#	INT	PRIN	BALANCE
1	12.6500	9.3110	90.6890
2	11.3438	10.6172	80.0718
3	9.8544	12.1067	67.9651
4	8.1560	13.8051	54.1600
5	6.2193	15.7417	38.4183
6	4.0110	17.9501	20.4682
7	1.4928	20.4682	0.0000

YEARS 8 — MO PAYT 1.6919 — AN CONST 20.31

#	INT	PRIN	BALANCE
1	12.7541	7.5491	92.4509
2	11.6951	8.6081	83.8428
3	10.4875	9.8157	74.0271
4	9.1105	11.1927	62.8344
5	7.5403	12.7629	50.0714
6	5.7498	14.5534	35.5181
7	3.7082	16.5950	18.9231
8	1.3801	18.9231	0.0000

YEARS 9 — MO PAYT 1.5869 — AN CONST 19.05

#	INT	PRIN	BALANCE
1	12.8332	6.2093	93.7907
2	11.9622	7.0803	86.7104
3	10.9689	8.0736	78.6368
4	9.8363	9.2062	69.4305
5	8.5448	10.4977	58.9328
6	7.0721	11.9704	46.9624
7	5.3928	13.6497	33.3127
8	3.4779	15.5646	17.7481
9	1.2944	17.7481	0.0000

YEARS 10 — MO PAYT 1.5049 — AN CONST 18.06

#	INT	PRIN	BALANCE
1	12.8950	5.1642	94.8358
2	12.1705	5.8886	88.9472
3	11.3444	6.7147	82.2325
4	10.4024	7.6567	74.5759
5	9.3283	8.7308	65.8450
6	8.1035	9.9556	55.8894
7	6.7069	11.3523	44.5372
8	5.1143	12.9448	31.5923
9	3.2983	14.7608	16.8315
10	1.2276	16.8315	0.0000

YEARS 11 — MO PAYT 1.4397 — AN CONST 17.28

#	INT	PRIN	BALANCE
1	12.9441	4.3326	95.6674
2	12.3363	4.9404	90.7270
3	11.6432	5.6335	85.0935
4	10.8529	6.4238	78.6697
5	9.9517	7.3249	71.3448
6	8.9242	8.3525	62.9922
7	7.7524	9.5243	53.4680
8	6.4163	10.8604	42.6075
9	4.8927	12.3840	30.2236
10	3.1554	14.1213	16.1023
11	1.1744	16.1023	0.0000

YEARS 12 — MO PAYT 1.3870 — AN CONST 16.65

#	INT	PRIN	BALANCE
1	12.9838	3.6605	96.3395
2	12.4703	4.1740	92.1655
3	11.8847	4.7596	87.4059
4	11.2170	5.4273	81.9787
5	10.4556	6.1886	75.7900
6	9.5875	7.0568	68.7332
7	8.5975	8.0468	60.6864
8	7.4686	9.1756	51.5108
9	6.1814	10.4629	41.0479
10	4.7136	11.9307	29.1172
11	3.0399	13.6044	15.5129
12	1.1314	15.5129	0.0000

YEARS 13 — MO PAYT 1.3439 — AN CONST 16.13

#	INT	PRIN	BALANCE
1	13.0163	3.1103	96.8897
2	12.5800	3.5466	93.3431
3	12.0824	4.0442	89.2989
4	11.5151	4.6115	84.6873
5	10.8681	5.2585	79.4289
6	10.1304	5.9962	73.4327
7	9.2893	6.8373	66.5954
8	8.3301	7.7965	58.7989
9	7.2363	8.8903	49.9086
10	5.9892	10.1374	39.7712
11	4.5670	11.5596	28.2116
12	2.9454	13.1812	15.0304
13	1.0962	15.0304	0.0000

YEARS 14 — MO PAYT 1.3082 — AN CONST 15.70

#	INT	PRIN	BALANCE
1	13.0432	2.6552	97.3448
2	12.6707	3.0277	94.3170
3	12.2459	3.4525	90.8646
4	11.7616	3.9368	86.9278
5	11.2093	4.4891	82.4387
6	10.5796	5.1188	77.3199
7	9.8615	5.8369	71.4829
8	9.0426	6.6558	64.8271
9	8.1089	7.5895	57.2376
10	7.0442	8.6542	48.5834
11	5.8301	9.8683	38.7152
12	4.4457	11.2526	27.4625
13	2.8672	12.8312	14.6313
14	1.0671	14.6313	0.0000

YEARS 15 — MO PAYT 1.2784 — AN CONST 15.35

#	INT	PRIN	BALANCE
1	13.0656	2.2756	97.7244
2	12.7464	2.5948	95.1296
3	12.3823	2.9588	92.1708
4	11.9673	3.3739	88.7969
5	11.4939	3.8472	84.9497
6	10.9542	4.3869	80.5627
7	10.3388	5.0024	75.5604
8	9.6370	5.7041	69.8563
9	8.8368	6.5043	63.3519
10	7.9244	7.4168	55.9351
11	6.8839	8.4573	47.4779
12	5.6975	9.6437	37.8342
13	4.3446	10.9966	26.8376
14	2.8019	12.5393	14.2983
15	1.0428	14.2983	0.0000

YEARS 16 — MO PAYT 1.2534 — AN CONST 15.05

#	INT	PRIN	BALANCE
1	13.0844	1.9566	98.0434
2	12.8100	2.2311	95.8124
3	12.4970	2.5440	93.2683
4	12.1401	2.9009	90.3674
5	11.7331	3.3079	87.0595
6	11.2691	3.7719	83.2876
7	10.7399	4.3011	78.9865
8	10.1365	4.9045	74.0820
9	9.4485	5.5925	68.4895
10	8.6639	6.3771	62.1124
11	7.7693	7.2717	54.8407
12	6.7492	8.2918	46.5489
13	5.5860	9.4550	37.0939
14	4.2596	10.7814	26.3125
15	2.7471	12.2939	14.0186
16	1.0224	14.0186	0.0000

YEARS 17 — MO PAYT 1.2323 — AN CONST 14.79

#	INT	PRIN	BALANCE
1	13.1004	1.6869	98.3131
2	12.8637	1.9236	96.3895
3	12.5939	2.1934	94.1961
4	12.2862	2.5011	91.6950
5	11.9353	2.8520	88.8430
6	11.5352	3.2521	85.5909
7	11.0790	3.7083	81.8826
8	10.5587	4.2285	77.6540
9	9.9655	4.8217	72.8323
10	9.2891	5.4982	67.3341
11	8.5178	6.2695	61.0646
12	7.6383	7.1490	53.9156
13	6.6354	8.1519	45.7637
14	5.4918	9.2955	36.4682
15	4.1877	10.5996	25.8686
16	2.7008	12.0865	13.7821
17	1.0052	13.7821	0.0000

YEARS 18 — MO PAYT 1.2143 — AN CONST 14.58

#	INT	PRIN	BALANCE
1	13.1139	1.4578	98.5422
2	12.9094	1.6623	96.8799
3	12.6762	1.8955	94.9843
4	12.4103	2.1614	92.8229
5	12.1070	2.4647	90.3582
6	11.7613	2.8104	87.5478
7	11.3670	3.2047	84.3431
8	10.9175	3.6543	80.6889
9	10.4048	4.1669	76.5220
10	9.8203	4.7515	71.7705
11	9.1537	5.4180	66.3525
12	8.3936	6.1781	60.1744
13	7.5269	7.0448	53.1296
14	6.5386	8.0331	45.0965
15	5.4117	9.1600	35.9365
16	4.1267	10.4450	25.4915
17	2.6614	11.9103	13.5812
18	.9905	13.5812	0.0000

YEARS 19 — MO PAYT 1.1990 — AN CONST 14.39

#	INT	PRIN	BALANCE
1	13.1254	1.2623	98.7377
2	12.9484	1.4394	97.2983
3	12.7464	1.6413	95.6569
4	12.5162	1.8716	93.7853
5	12.2536	2.1342	91.6512
6	11.9542	2.4335	89.2176
7	11.6128	2.7749	86.4427
8	11.2235	3.1642	83.2785
9	10.7796	3.6081	79.6703
10	10.2735	4.1143	75.5560
11	9.6963	4.6915	70.8646
12	9.0381	5.3496	65.5149
13	8.2877	6.1001	59.4148
14	7.4319	6.9559	52.4590
15	6.4561	7.9317	44.5273
16	5.3434	9.0444	35.4829
17	4.0746	10.3132	25.1697
18	2.6278	11.7600	13.4097
19	.9780	13.4097	0.0000

YEARS 20 — MO PAYT 1.1859 — AN CONST 14.24

#	INT	PRIN	BALANCE
1	13.1353	1.0949	98.9051
2	12.9817	1.2485	97.6566
3	12.8066	1.4237	96.2329
4	12.6069	1.6234	94.6096
5	12.3791	1.8511	92.7585
6	12.1194	2.1108	90.6477
7	11.8233	2.4069	88.2408
8	11.4857	2.7446	85.4962
9	11.1006	3.1296	82.3666
10	10.6616	3.5686	78.7980
11	10.1610	4.0692	74.7288
12	9.5901	4.6401	70.0887
13	8.9392	5.2911	64.7976
14	8.1969	6.0333	58.7643
15	7.3505	6.8797	51.8846
16	6.3854	7.8448	44.0398
17	5.2849	8.9454	35.0944
18	4.0300	10.2003	24.8941
19	2.5990	11.6312	13.2629
20	.9673	13.2629	0.0000

YEARS 21 — MO PAYT 1.1746 — AN CONST 14.10

#	INT	PRIN	BALANCE
1	13.1438	.9511	99.0489
2	13.0104	1.0845	97.9644
3	12.8583	1.2366	96.7278

#	INT	PRIN	BALANCE
4	12.6848	1.4101	95.3177
5	12.4870	1.6079	93.7098
6	12.2614	1.8335	91.8763
7	12.0042	2.0907	89.7856
8	11.7109	2.3840	87.4015
9	11.3764	2.7185	84.6831
10	10.9951	3.0998	81.5833
11	10.5602	3.5347	78.0486
12	10.0643	4.0305	74.0180
13	9.4989	4.5960	69.4221
14	8.8542	5.2407	64.1813
15	8.1190	5.9759	58.2054
16	7.2806	6.8143	51.3911
17	6.3247	7.7702	43.6209
18	5.2346	8.8603	34.7606
19	3.9916	10.1033	24.6574
20	2.5743	11.5206	13.1368
21	.9581	13.1368	0.0000

YEARS 22	MO PAYT 1.1649	AN CONST 13.98	
#	INT	PRIN	BALANCE
1	13.1511	.8272	99.1728
2	13.0351	.9432	98.2294
3	12.9028	1.0755	97.1541
4	12.7519	1.2264	95.9277
5	12.5799	1.3984	94.5293
6	12.3837	1.5946	92.9346
7	12.1600	1.8183	91.1163
8	11.9049	2.0734	89.0429
9	11.6140	2.3643	86.6786
10	11.2823	2.6960	83.9826
11	10.9041	3.0742	80.9084
12	10.4729	3.5054	77.4030
13	9.9811	3.9972	73.4058
14	9.4203	4.5580	68.8478
15	8.7809	5.1974	63.6504
16	8.0518	5.9265	57.7239
17	7.2204	6.7579	50.9660
18	6.2724	7.7059	43.2601
19	5.1913	8.7870	34.4731
20	3.9586	10.0197	24.4534
21	2.5530	11.4253	13.0281
22	.9502	13.0281	0.0000

YEARS 23	MO PAYT 1.1565	AN CONST 13.88	
#	INT	PRIN	BALANCE
1	13.1575	.7202	99.2798
2	13.0564	.8212	98.4586
3	12.9412	.9364	97.5222
4	12.8099	1.0678	96.4544
5	12.6601	1.2176	95.2369
6	12.4893	1.3884	93.8485
7	12.2945	1.5831	92.2654
8	12.0724	1.8052	90.4601
9	11.8191	2.0585	88.4016
10	11.5304	2.3473	86.0544
11	11.2011	2.6766	83.3778
12	10.8256	3.0520	80.3258
13	10.3974	3.4802	76.8456
14	9.9092	3.9684	72.8771
15	9.3525	4.5251	68.3520
16	8.7177	5.1600	63.1921
17	7.9938	5.8838	57.3082
18	7.1684	6.7092	50.5990
19	6.2272	7.6505	42.9485
20	5.1539	8.7237	34.2248
21	3.9301	9.9475	24.2773
22	2.5346	11.3430	12.9343
23	.9433	12.9343	0.0000

YEARS 24	MO PAYT 1.1492	AN CONST 13.80	
#	INT	PRIN	BALANCE
1	13.1629	.6276	99.3724
2	13.0749	.7157	98.6567
3	12.9745	.8161	97.8407
4	12.8600	.9305	96.9102
5	12.7295	1.0611	95.8491
6	12.5806	1.2099	94.6392
7	12.4109	1.3797	93.2595
8	12.2173	1.5732	91.6863
9	11.9966	1.7939	89.8924
10	11.7450	2.0456	87.8468
11	11.4580	2.3325	85.5143
12	11.1308	2.6598	82.8545
13	10.7577	3.0329	79.8216
14	10.3322	3.4584	76.3633
15	9.8470	3.9435	72.4198
16	9.2938	4.4967	67.9230
17	8.6630	5.1276	62.7955
18	7.9436	5.8469	56.9486
19	7.1234	6.6671	50.2814
20	6.1881	7.6024	42.6790
21	5.1216	8.6690	34.0100
22	3.9054	9.8851	24.1249
23	2.5187	11.2718	12.8531
24	.9374	12.8531	0.0000

YEARS 25	MO PAYT 1.1429	AN CONST 13.72	
#	INT	PRIN	BALANCE
1	13.1677	.5474	99.4526
2	13.0909	.6242	98.8284
3	13.0033	.7117	98.1167
4	12.9035	.8116	97.3051
5	12.7896	.9254	96.3797
6	12.6598	1.0553	95.3244
7	12.5111	1.2033	94.1211
8	12.3429	1.3721	92.7490
9	12.1505	1.5646	91.1844
10	11.9310	1.7841	89.4003
11	11.6807	2.0344	87.3659
12	11.3953	2.3198	85.0462
13	11.0699	2.6452	82.4010
14	10.6988	3.0163	79.3847
15	10.2756	3.4394	75.9453
16	9.7931	3.9219	72.0233
17	9.2429	4.4721	67.5512
18	8.6156	5.0995	62.4517
19	7.9002	5.8149	56.6368
20	7.0844	6.6306	50.0062
21	6.1542	7.5608	42.4454
22	5.0935	8.6215	33.8239
23	3.8841	9.8310	23.9929
24	2.5049	11.2101	12.7828
25	.9323	12.7828	0.0000

YEARS 26	MO PAYT 1.1375	AN CONST 13.65	
#	INT	PRIN	BALANCE
1	13.1718	.4777	99.5223
2	13.1048	.5448	98.9775
3	13.0283	.6212	98.3563
4	12.9412	.7083	97.6480
5	12.8418	.8077	96.8402
6	12.7285	.9210	95.9192
7	12.5993	1.0502	94.8690
8	12.4520	1.1976	93.6715
9	12.2840	1.3656	92.3059
10	12.0924	1.5571	90.7488
11	11.8740	1.7756	88.9732
12	11.6249	2.0247	86.9486
13	11.3408	2.3087	84.6399
14	11.0170	2.6326	82.0073
15	10.6477	3.0019	79.0054
16	10.2265	3.4230	75.5824
17	9.7463	3.9032	71.6793
18	9.1988	4.4508	67.2285
19	8.5744	5.0751	62.1534
20	7.8624	5.7871	56.3663
21	7.0506	6.5990	49.7673
22	6.1248	7.5247	42.2426
23	5.0692	8.5803	33.6623
24	3.8655	9.7840	23.8783
25	2.4930	11.1566	12.7217
26	.9278	12.7217	0.0000

YEARS 27	MO PAYT 1.1327	AN CONST 13.60	
#	INT	PRIN	BALANCE
1	13.1754	.4172	99.5828
2	13.1168	.4758	99.1070
3	13.0501	.5425	98.5645
4	12.9740	.6186	97.9459
5	12.8872	.7054	97.2405
6	12.7882	.8043	96.4362
7	12.6754	.9172	95.5190
8	12.5467	1.0458	94.4732
9	12.4000	1.1926	93.2806
10	12.2327	1.3599	91.9208
11	12.0420	1.5506	90.3702
12	11.8244	1.7682	88.6020
13	11.5764	2.0162	86.5858
14	11.2935	2.2991	84.2867
15	10.9710	2.6216	81.6652
16	10.6032	2.9893	78.6758
17	10.1839	3.4087	75.2671
18	9.7057	3.8869	71.3802
19	9.1604	4.4322	66.9480
20	8.5386	5.0540	61.8940
21	7.8296	5.7630	56.1311
22	7.0212	6.5714	49.5597
23	6.0993	7.4933	42.0663
24	5.0481	8.5445	33.5218
25	3.8494	9.7432	23.7786
26	2.4826	11.1100	12.6686
27	.9240	12.6686	0.0000

YEARS 28	MO PAYT 1.1286	AN CONST 13.55	
#	INT	PRIN	BALANCE
1	13.1785	.3646	99.6354
2	13.1273	.4157	99.2197
3	13.0690	.4740	98.7457
4	13.0025	.5405	98.2052
5	12.9267	.6163	97.5889
6	12.8402	.7028	96.8860
7	12.7416	.8014	96.0846
8	12.6292	.9138	95.1708
9	12.5010	1.0420	94.1288
10	12.3548	1.1882	92.9406
11	12.1881	1.3549	91.5857
12	11.9981	1.5450	90.0407
13	11.7813	1.7617	88.2790
14	11.5342	2.0089	86.2701
15	11.2524	2.2907	83.9795
16	10.9310	2.6120	81.3674
17	10.5646	2.9785	78.3890
18	10.1467	3.3963	74.9927
19	9.6703	3.8727	71.1200
20	9.1270	4.4160	66.7039
21	8.5075	5.0355	61.6684
22	7.8011	5.7420	55.9265
23	6.9956	6.5475	49.3790
24	6.0770	7.4660	41.9130
25	5.0297	8.5134	33.3996
26	3.8354	9.7077	23.6920
27	2.4735	11.0695	12.6224
28	.9206	12.6224	0.0000

YEARS 29	MO PAYT 1.1250	AN CONST 13.50	
#	INT	PRIN	BALANCE
1	13.1812	.3187	99.6813
2	13.1365	.3634	99.3179
3	13.0855	.4144	98.9035
4	13.0274	.4725	98.4310
5	12.9611	.5388	97.8922
6	12.8855	.6144	97.2779
7	12.7993	.7006	96.5773
8	12.7010	.7989	95.7784
9	12.5889	.9109	94.8675
10	12.4612	1.0387	93.8288
11	12.3154	1.1844	92.6444
12	12.1493	1.3506	91.2938
13	11.9598	1.5400	89.7537
14	11.7438	1.7561	87.9977
15	11.4974	2.0025	85.9952
16	11.2165	2.2834	83.7118
17	10.8962	2.6037	81.1081
18	10.5309	2.9690	78.1392
19	10.1144	3.3855	74.7537
20	9.6395	3.8604	70.8933
21	9.0979	4.4020	66.4914
22	8.4804	5.0195	61.4719
23	7.7762	5.7237	55.7482
24	6.9733	6.5266	49.2216
25	6.0577	7.4422	41.7794
26	5.0136	8.4862	33.2932
27	3.8231	9.6767	23.6164
28	2.4656	11.0342	12.5822
29	.9177	12.5822	0.0000

YEARS 30	MO PAYT 1.1219	AN CONST 13.47	
#	INT	PRIN	BALANCE
1	13.1835	.2787	99.7213
2	13.1444	.3178	99.4035
3	13.0999	.3624	99.0411
4	13.0490	.4132	98.6279
5	12.9910	.4712	98.1567
6	12.9249	.5373	97.6194
7	12.8496	.6127	97.0067
8	12.7636	.6986	96.3081
9	12.6656	.7966	95.5115
10	12.5539	.9084	94.6031
11	12.4264	1.0358	93.5673
12	12.2811	1.1811	92.3862
13	12.1154	1.3468	91.0394
14	11.9265	1.5358	89.5036
15	11.7110	1.7512	87.7524
16	11.4654	1.9969	85.7555
17	11.1852	2.2770	83.4785
18	10.8658	2.5964	80.8821
19	10.5016	2.9607	77.9214
20	10.0862	3.3760	74.5454
21	9.6126	3.8496	70.6957
22	9.0726	4.3897	66.3060
23	8.4567	5.0055	61.3005
24	7.7545	5.7077	55.5928
25	6.9538	6.5084	49.0844
26	6.0408	7.4215	41.6630
27	4.9997	8.4626	33.2004
28	3.8125	9.6498	23.5506
29	2.4587	11.0035	12.5471
30	.9151	12.5471	0.0000

YEARS 2 — MO PAYT 4.7659 — AN CONST 57.20

#	INT	PRIN	BALANCE
1	10.4808	46.7104	53.2896
2	3.9016	53.2896	0.0000

YEARS 3 — MO PAYT 3.3814 — AN CONST 40.58

#	INT	PRIN	BALANCE
1	11.5278	29.0496	70.9504
2	7.4362	33.1412	37.8092
3	2.7682	37.8092	0.0000

YEARS 4 — MO PAYT 2.6952 — AN CONST 32.35

#	INT	PRIN	BALANCE
1	12.0468	20.2953	79.7047
2	9.1882	23.1539	56.5508
3	5.9270	26.4151	30.1357
4	2.2064	30.1357	0.0000

YEARS 5 — MO PAYT 2.2881 — AN CONST 27.46

#	INT	PRIN	BALANCE
1	12.3546	15.1029	84.8971
2	10.2274	17.2301	67.6670
3	7.8005	19.6570	48.0100
4	5.0318	22.4257	25.5843
5	1.8732	25.5843	0.0000

YEARS 6 — MO PAYT 2.0206 — AN CONST 24.25

#	INT	PRIN	BALANCE
1	12.5569	11.6906	88.3094
2	10.9103	13.3373	74.9721
3	9.0317	15.2158	59.7563
4	6.8886	17.3590	42.3973
5	4.4436	19.8040	22.5934
6	1.6542	22.5934	0.0000

YEARS 7 — MO PAYT 1.8328 — AN CONST 22.00

#	INT	PRIN	BALANCE
1	12.6990	9.2948	90.7052
2	11.3898	10.6040	80.1012
3	9.8962	12.0976	68.0036
4	8.1923	13.8015	54.2021
5	6.2483	15.7455	38.4566
6	4.0306	17.9632	20.4934
7	1.5004	20.4934	0.0000

YEARS 8 — MO PAYT 1.6947 — AN CONST 20.34

#	INT	PRIN	BALANCE
1	12.8034	7.5335	92.4665
2	11.7423	8.5946	83.8719
3	10.5317	9.8052	74.0667
4	9.1507	11.1862	62.8805
5	7.5751	12.7618	50.1187
6	5.7776	14.5593	35.5595
7	3.7269	16.6100	18.9495
8	1.3874	18.9495	0.0000

YEARS 9 — MO PAYT 1.5898 — AN CONST 19.08

#	INT	PRIN	BALANCE
1	12.8828	6.1944	93.8056
2	12.0103	7.0668	86.7388
3	11.0149	8.0622	78.6766
4	9.8794	9.1978	69.4788
5	8.5838	10.4933	58.9855
6	7.1059	11.9713	47.0142
7	5.4197	13.6574	33.3568
8	3.4961	15.5811	17.7757
9	1.3015	17.7757	0.0000

YEARS 10 — MO PAYT 1.5079 — AN CONST 18.10

#	INT	PRIN	BALANCE
1	12.9447	5.1500	94.8500
2	12.2193	5.8754	88.9747
3	11.3918	6.7029	82.2717
4	10.4477	7.6470	74.6247
5	9.3706	8.7241	65.9006
6	8.1418	9.9529	55.9477
7	6.7399	11.3548	44.5930
8	5.1406	12.9541	31.6389
9	3.3160	14.7787	16.8602
10	1.2344	16.8602	0.0000

YEARS 11 — MO PAYT 1.4428 — AN CONST 17.32

#	INT	PRIN	BALANCE
1	12.9939	4.3192	95.6808
2	12.3856	4.9275	90.7533
3	11.6915	5.6216	85.1317
4	10.8997	6.4134	78.7183
5	9.9964	7.3167	71.4015
6	8.9658	8.3473	63.0543
7	7.7901	9.5230	53.5313
8	6.4488	10.8643	42.6669
9	4.9186	12.3946	30.2724
10	3.1728	14.1403	16.1320
11	1.1811	16.1320	0.0000

YEARS 12 — MO PAYT 1.3901 — AN CONST 16.69

#	INT	PRIN	BALANCE
1	13.0337	3.6478	96.3522
2	12.5199	4.1616	92.1905
3	11.9338	4.7478	87.4427
4	11.2650	5.4165	82.0262
5	10.5021	6.1794	75.8468
6	9.6317	7.0498	68.7969
7	8.6388	8.0428	60.7541
8	7.5060	9.1756	51.5785
9	6.2136	10.4680	41.1105
10	4.7391	11.9424	29.1681
11	3.0570	13.6245	15.5435
12	1.1380	15.5435	0.0000

YEARS 13 — MO PAYT 1.3471 — AN CONST 16.17

#	INT	PRIN	BALANCE
1	13.0663	3.0984	96.9016
2	12.6299	3.5348	93.3668
3	12.1320	4.0327	89.3341
4	11.5640	4.6007	84.7334
5	10.9160	5.2487	79.4847
6	10.1767	5.9880	73.4967
7	9.3333	6.8314	66.6653
8	8.3711	7.7936	58.8717
9	7.2734	8.8913	49.9804
10	6.0210	10.1437	39.8367
11	4.5923	11.5724	28.2643
12	2.9623	13.2024	15.0619
13	1.1028	15.0619	0.0000

YEARS 14 — MO PAYT 1.3114 — AN CONST 15.74

#	INT	PRIN	BALANCE
1	13.0932	2.6441	97.3559
2	12.7208	3.0165	94.3395
3	12.2960	3.4413	90.8981
4	11.8112	3.9261	86.9721
5	11.2583	4.4790	82.4930
6	10.6274	5.1099	77.3831
7	9.9076	5.8297	71.5534
8	9.0865	6.6508	64.9027
9	8.1498	7.5875	57.3151
10	7.0811	8.6562	48.6589
11	5.8618	9.8755	38.7834
12	4.4709	11.2664	27.5170
13	2.8840	12.8533	14.6637
14	1.0736	14.6637	0.0000

YEARS 15 — MO PAYT 1.2817 — AN CONST 15.39

#	INT	PRIN	BALANCE
1	13.1157	2.2651	97.7349
2	12.7967	2.5842	95.1507
3	12.4327	2.9481	92.2026
4	12.0174	3.3634	88.8392
5	11.5437	3.8371	85.0020
6	11.0032	4.3776	80.6244
7	10.3867	4.9942	75.6303
8	9.6832	5.6976	69.9327
9	8.8807	6.5001	63.4325
10	7.9652	7.4157	56.0169
11	6.9207	8.4602	47.5567
12	5.7291	9.6518	37.9049
13	4.3696	11.0112	26.8937
14	2.8187	12.5622	14.3315
15	1.0493	14.3315	0.0000

YEARS 16 — MO PAYT 1.2568 — AN CONST 15.09

#	INT	PRIN	BALANCE
1	13.1346	1.9468	98.0532
2	12.8604	2.2210	95.8322
3	12.5475	2.5339	93.2983
4	12.1906	2.8908	90.4075
5	11.7835	3.2979	87.1096
6	11.3190	3.7624	83.3472
7	10.7890	4.2924	79.0548
8	10.1845	4.8969	74.1579
9	9.4947	5.5867	68.5712
10	8.7078	6.3736	62.1976
11	7.8101	7.2713	54.9263
12	6.7859	8.2955	46.6309
13	5.6175	9.4639	37.1670
14	4.2845	10.7969	26.3701
15	2.7638	12.3176	14.0525
16	1.0289	14.0525	0.0000

YEARS 17 — MO PAYT 1.2357 — AN CONST 14.83

#	INT	PRIN	BALANCE
1	13.1505	1.6778	98.3222
2	12.9142	1.9142	96.4080
3	12.6446	2.1838	94.2243
4	12.3370	2.4913	91.7329
5	11.9861	2.8423	88.8907
6	11.5858	3.2426	85.6481
7	11.1291	3.6993	81.9488
8	10.6080	4.2203	77.7284
9	10.0136	4.8148	72.9136
10	9.3354	5.4930	67.4207
11	8.5617	6.2666	61.1541
12	7.6791	7.1493	54.0048
13	6.6721	8.1563	45.8485
14	5.5233	9.3051	36.5434
15	4.2127	10.6157	25.9277
16	2.7174	12.1109	13.8168
17	1.0116	13.8168	0.0000

YEARS 18 — MO PAYT 1.2178 — AN CONST 14.62

#	INT	PRIN	BALANCE
1	13.1641	1.4494	98.5506
2	12.9599	1.6535	96.8971
3	12.7270	1.8864	95.0107
4	12.4613	2.1521	92.8586
5	12.1582	2.4552	90.4034
6	11.8124	2.8011	87.6023
7	11.4179	3.1956	84.4067
8	10.9678	3.6457	80.7610
9	10.4543	4.1592	76.6019
10	9.8684	4.7450	71.8569
11	9.2001	5.4133	66.4435
12	8.4376	6.1758	60.2677
13	7.5678	7.0457	53.2220
14	6.5754	8.0381	45.1840
15	5.4432	9.1702	36.0138
16	4.1516	10.4618	25.5519
17	2.6780	11.9354	13.6165
18	.9969	13.6165	0.0000

YEARS 19 — MO PAYT 1.2025 — AN CONST 14.44

#	INT	PRIN	BALANCE
1	13.1756	1.2545	98.7455
2	12.9989	1.4312	97.3143
3	12.7973	1.6328	95.6816
4	12.5674	1.8627	93.8188
5	12.3050	2.1251	91.6937
6	12.0057	2.4244	89.2693
7	11.6642	2.7659	86.5033
8	11.2746	3.1555	83.3478
9	10.8302	3.6000	79.7479
10	10.3231	4.1070	75.6409
11	9.7446	4.6855	70.9554
12	9.0847	5.3454	65.6100
13	8.3318	6.0983	59.5117
14	7.4728	6.9573	52.5544
15	6.4929	7.9372	44.6171
16	5.3749	9.0552	35.5620
17	4.0995	10.3306	25.2314
18	2.6444	11.7857	13.4457
19	.9844	13.4457	0.0000

YEARS 20 — MO PAYT 1.1894 — AN CONST 14.28

#	INT	PRIN	BALANCE
1	13.1855	1.0877	98.9123
2	13.0323	1.2408	97.6715
3	12.8575	1.4156	96.2559
4	12.6582	1.6150	94.6409
5	12.4307	1.8425	92.7984
6	12.1712	2.1020	90.6964
7	11.8751	2.3981	88.2983
8	11.5373	2.7358	85.5625
9	11.1520	3.1212	82.4413
10	10.7124	3.5608	78.8805
11	10.2108	4.0623	74.8182
12	9.6387	4.6345	70.1837
13	8.9859	5.2873	64.8964
14	8.2412	6.0320	58.8644
15	7.3916	6.8816	51.9828
16	6.4223	7.8509	44.1319
17	5.3165	8.9567	35.1752
18	4.0549	10.2182	24.9569
19	2.6157	11.6575	13.2994
20	.9737	13.2994	0.0000

YEARS 21 — MO PAYT 1.1782 — AN CONST 14.14

#	INT	PRIN	BALANCE
1	13.1940	.9444	99.0556
2	13.0610	1.0774	97.9783
3	12.9093	1.2291	96.7491

#	INT	PRIN	BALANCE
4	12.7361	1.4023	95.3469
5	12.5386	1.5998	93.7471
6	12.3133	1.8251	91.9220
7	12.0562	2.0821	89.8399
8	11.7630	2.3754	87.4645
9	11.4284	2.7100	84.7545
10	11.0467	3.0917	81.6628
11	10.6112	3.5272	78.1356
12	10.1144	4.0240	74.1116
13	9.5476	4.5907	69.5209
14	8.9010	5.2374	64.2835
15	8.1633	5.9750	58.3085
16	7.3218	6.8166	51.4919
17	6.3616	7.7768	43.7151
18	5.2663	8.8721	34.8430
19	4.0166	10.1217	24.7212
20	2.5910	11.5474	13.1739
21	.9645	13.1739	0.0000

YEARS 22 — MO PAYT 1.1685 — AN CONST 14.03

#	INT	PRIN	BALANCE
1	13.2013	.8210	99.1790
2	13.0857	.9366	98.2424
3	12.9538	1.0685	97.1739
4	12.8033	1.2190	95.9548
5	12.6316	1.3907	94.5641
6	12.4357	1.5866	92.9775
7	12.2122	1.8101	91.1674
8	11.9573	2.0651	89.1023
9	11.6664	2.3559	86.7464
10	11.3346	2.6877	84.0587
11	10.9560	3.0663	80.9923
12	10.5241	3.4982	77.4941
13	10.0314	3.9909	73.5032
14	9.4692	4.5531	68.9501
15	8.8279	5.1944	63.7558
16	8.0963	5.9260	57.8298
17	7.2616	6.7607	51.0691
18	6.3094	7.7129	43.3562
19	5.2230	8.7993	34.5569
20	3.9837	10.0386	24.5183
21	2.5697	11.4526	13.0657
22	.9566	13.0657	0.0000

YEARS 23 — MO PAYT 1.1602 — AN CONST 13.93

#	INT	PRIN	BALANCE
1	13.2076	.7145	99.2855
2	13.1070	.8151	98.4704
3	12.9922	.9299	97.5405
4	12.8612	1.0609	96.4796
5	12.7118	1.2103	95.2693
6	12.5413	1.3808	93.8885
7	12.3468	1.5753	92.3132
8	12.1250	1.7972	90.5160
9	11.8718	2.0503	88.4657
10	11.5830	2.3391	86.1266
11	11.2536	2.6685	83.4581
12	10.8777	3.0444	80.4137
13	10.4489	3.4732	76.9404
14	9.9597	3.9624	72.9780
15	9.4016	4.5205	68.4575
16	8.7649	5.1572	63.3002
17	8.0385	5.8836	57.4166
18	7.2098	6.7124	50.7042
19	6.2643	7.6578	43.0464
20	5.1857	8.7364	34.3100
21	3.9552	9.9669	24.3431
22	2.5514	11.3708	12.9723
23	.9498	12.9723	0.0000

YEARS 24 — MO PAYT 1.1530 — AN CONST 13.84

#	INT	PRIN	BALANCE
1	13.2131	.6224	99.3776
2	13.1254	.7100	98.6676
3	13.0254	.8100	97.8576
4	12.9113	.9241	96.9334
5	12.7812	1.0543	95.8791
6	12.6327	1.2028	94.6763
7	12.4633	1.3722	93.3041
8	12.2700	1.5655	91.7386
9	12.0495	1.7860	89.9527
10	11.7979	2.0375	87.9151
11	11.5109	2.3245	85.5906
12	11.1835	2.6519	82.9387
13	10.8100	3.0255	79.9132
14	10.3839	3.4516	76.4616
15	9.8977	3.9378	72.5238
16	9.3431	4.4924	68.0314
17	8.7103	5.1252	62.9063
18	7.9884	5.8470	57.0593
19	7.1649	6.6706	50.3887
20	6.2253	7.6101	42.7785
21	5.1534	8.6820	34.0965
22	3.9306	9.9049	24.1916
23	2.5355	11.3000	12.8916
24	.9439	12.8916	0.0000

YEARS 25 — MO PAYT 1.1467 — AN CONST 13.77

#	INT	PRIN	BALANCE
1	13.2178	.5426	99.4574
2	13.1414	.6190	98.8384
3	13.0542	.7062	98.1323
4	12.9548	.8056	97.3266
5	12.8413	.9191	96.4075
6	12.7118	1.0486	95.3589
7	12.5641	1.1963	94.1627
8	12.3956	1.3648	92.7979
9	12.2034	1.5570	91.2409
10	11.9841	1.7763	89.4646
11	11.7339	2.0265	87.4381
12	11.4485	2.3119	85.1262
13	11.1229	2.6375	82.4887
14	10.7514	3.0090	79.4796
15	10.3275	3.4329	76.0467
16	9.8440	3.9164	72.1303
17	9.2924	4.4680	67.6623
18	8.6631	5.0973	62.5650
19	7.9451	5.8153	56.7497
20	7.1260	6.6344	50.1153
21	6.1916	7.5688	42.5464
22	5.1255	8.6349	33.9115
23	3.9093	9.8512	24.0604
24	2.5217	11.2387	12.8217
25	.9387	12.8217	0.0000

YEARS 26 — MO PAYT 1.1413 — AN CONST 13.70

#	INT	PRIN	BALANCE
1	13.2219	.4733	99.5267
2	13.1553	.5400	98.9867
3	13.0792	.6161	98.3706
4	12.9924	.7028	97.6678
5	12.8934	.8018	96.8659
6	12.7805	.9148	95.9512
7	12.6517	1.0436	94.9076
8	12.5047	1.1906	93.7169
9	12.3370	1.3583	92.3586
10	12.1457	1.5496	90.8090
11	11.9274	1.7679	89.0411
12	11.6784	2.0169	87.0242
13	11.3943	2.3010	84.7233
14	11.0702	2.6251	82.0982
15	10.7005	2.9948	79.1034
16	10.2786	3.4166	75.6868
17	9.7974	3.8979	71.7889
18	9.2484	4.4469	67.3420
19	8.6221	5.0732	62.2688
20	7.9075	5.7878	56.4811
21	7.0923	6.6030	49.8781
22	6.1623	7.5330	42.3450
23	5.1012	8.5940	33.7510
24	3.8907	9.8045	23.9465
25	2.5098	11.1855	12.7610
26	.9343	12.7610	0.0000

YEARS 27 — MO PAYT 1.1366 — AN CONST 13.64

#	INT	PRIN	BALANCE
1	13.2255	.4132	99.5868
2	13.1673	.4714	99.1154
3	13.1009	.5378	98.5777
4	13.0252	.6135	97.9642
5	12.9388	.6999	97.2642
6	12.8402	.7985	96.4657
7	12.7277	.9110	95.5547
8	12.5994	1.0393	94.5154
9	12.4530	1.1857	93.3297
10	12.2860	1.3527	91.9770
11	12.0955	1.5432	90.4338
12	11.8781	1.7606	88.6732
13	11.6301	2.0086	86.6647
14	11.3472	2.2915	84.3732
15	11.0245	2.6142	81.7590
16	10.6563	2.9824	78.7766
17	10.2362	3.4025	75.3741
18	9.7569	3.8818	71.4923
19	9.2102	4.4285	67.0638
20	8.5864	5.0523	62.0115
21	7.8748	5.7639	56.2477
22	7.0630	6.5757	49.6720
23	6.1368	7.5019	42.1701
24	5.0801	8.5585	33.6115
25	3.8747	9.7640	23.8475
26	2.4994	11.1393	12.7082
27	.9304	12.7082	0.0000

YEARS 28 — MO PAYT 1.1325 — AN CONST 13.59

#	INT	PRIN	BALANCE
1	13.2286	.3609	99.6391
2	13.1778	.4117	99.2274
3	13.1198	.4697	98.7578
4	13.0536	.5358	98.2219
5	12.9782	.6113	97.6106
6	12.8921	.6974	96.9132
7	12.7938	.7956	96.1176
8	12.6818	.9077	95.2099
9	12.5539	1.0356	94.1743
10	12.4081	1.1814	92.9929
11	12.2417	1.3478	91.6451
12	12.0518	1.5376	90.1075
13	11.8352	1.7542	88.3532
14	11.5882	2.0013	86.3519
15	11.3063	2.2832	84.0687
16	10.9847	2.6048	81.4640
17	10.6178	2.9717	78.4923
18	10.1992	3.3902	75.1021
19	9.7217	3.8677	71.2343
20	9.1770	4.4125	66.8218
21	8.5554	5.0340	61.7878
22	7.8464	5.7431	56.0447
23	7.0375	6.5520	49.4927
24	6.1146	7.4748	42.0179
25	5.0618	8.5277	33.4902
26	3.8607	9.7288	23.7615
27	2.4904	11.0991	12.6624
28	.9271	12.6624	0.0000

YEARS 29 — MO PAYT 1.1289 — AN CONST 13.55

#	INT	PRIN	BALANCE
1	13.2313	.3153	99.6847
2	13.1869	.3597	99.3250
3	13.1362	.4104	98.9146
4	13.0784	.4682	98.4464
5	13.0125	.5341	97.9122
6	12.9372	.6094	97.3029
7	12.8514	.6952	96.6076
8	12.7535	.7931	95.8145
9	12.6418	.9048	94.9097
10	12.5143	1.0323	93.8774
11	12.3689	1.1777	92.6997
12	12.2031	1.3436	91.3562
13	12.0138	1.5328	89.8234
14	11.7979	1.7487	88.0747
15	11.5516	1.9950	86.0797
16	11.2706	2.2760	83.8037
17	10.9500	2.5966	81.2071
18	10.5843	2.9623	78.2448
19	10.1671	3.3795	74.8652
20	9.6911	3.8555	71.0097
21	9.1480	4.3986	66.6111
22	8.5285	5.0181	61.5929
23	7.8217	5.7250	55.8680
24	7.0153	6.5313	49.3367
25	6.0954	7.4513	41.8854
26	5.0459	8.5008	33.3846
27	3.8485	9.6981	23.6865
28	2.4825	11.0641	12.6225
29	.9242	12.6225	0.0000

YEARS 30 — MO PAYT 1.1258 — AN CONST 13.51

#	INT	PRIN	BALANCE
1	13.2337	.2756	99.7244
2	13.1948	.3144	99.4099
3	13.1505	.3587	99.0512
4	13.1000	.4093	98.6419
5	13.0424	.4669	98.1750
6	12.9766	.5327	97.6424
7	12.9016	.6077	97.0347
8	12.8160	.6933	96.3414
9	12.7183	.7909	95.5504
10	12.6069	.9023	94.6481
11	12.4798	1.0294	93.6187
12	12.3348	1.1744	92.4442
13	12.1694	1.3399	91.1044
14	11.9807	1.5286	89.5758
15	11.7654	1.7439	87.8319
16	11.5198	1.9895	85.8424
17	11.2396	2.2697	83.5727
18	10.9199	2.5894	80.9833
19	10.5551	2.9541	78.0291
20	10.1391	3.3702	74.6589
21	9.6644	3.8449	70.8140
22	9.1228	4.3865	66.4275
23	8.5050	5.0043	61.4232
24	7.8001	5.7092	55.7140
25	6.9960	6.5133	49.2007
26	6.0786	7.4307	41.7700
27	5.0319	8.4773	33.2926
28	3.8379	9.6714	23.6213
29	2.4757	11.0336	12.5877
30	.9216	12.5877	0.0000

YEARS 2 — MO PAYT 4.7683 — AN CONST 57.22

#	INT	PRIN	BALANCE
1	10.5213	46.6981	53.3019
2	3.9175	53.3019	0.0000

YEARS 3 — MO PAYT 3.3839 — AN CONST 40.61

#	INT	PRIN	BALANCE
1	11.5724	29.0340	70.9660
2	7.4666	33.1398	37.8262
3	2.7801	37.8262	0.0000

YEARS 4 — MO PAYT 2.6977 — AN CONST 32.38

#	INT	PRIN	BALANCE
1	12.0934	20.2786	79.7214
2	9.2257	23.1463	56.5751
3	5.9525	26.4195	30.1556
4	2.2163	30.1556	0.0000

YEARS 5 — MO PAYT 2.2907 — AN CONST 27.49

#	INT	PRIN	BALANCE
1	12.4023	15.0860	84.9140
2	10.2690	17.2194	67.6946
3	7.8339	19.6544	48.0402
4	5.0545	22.4339	25.6063
5	1.8820	25.6063	0.0000

YEARS 6 — MO PAYT 2.0233 — AN CONST 24.28

#	INT	PRIN	BALANCE
1	12.6054	11.6740	88.3260
2	10.9545	13.3249	75.0012
3	9.0702	15.2092	59.7920
4	6.9194	17.3600	42.4320
5	4.4644	19.8149	22.6171
6	1.6623	22.6171	0.0000

YEARS 7 — MO PAYT 1.8355 — AN CONST 22.03

#	INT	PRIN	BALANCE
1	12.7479	9.2787	90.7213
2	11.4358	10.5908	80.1305
3	9.9381	12.0885	68.0421
4	8.2286	13.7980	54.2441
5	6.2773	15.7492	38.4949
6	4.0502	17.9764	20.5185
7	1.5080	20.5185	0.0000

YEARS 8 — MO PAYT 1.6976 — AN CONST 20.38

#	INT	PRIN	BALANCE
1	12.8527	7.5179	92.4821
2	11.7895	8.5811	83.9010
3	10.5760	9.7946	74.1064
4	9.1909	11.1797	62.9267
5	7.6100	12.7607	50.1660
6	5.8054	14.5652	35.6009
7	3.7457	16.6249	18.9759
8	1.3947	18.9759	0.0000

YEARS 9 — MO PAYT 1.5927 — AN CONST 19.12

#	INT	PRIN	BALANCE
1	12.9323	6.1795	93.8205
2	12.0584	7.0534	86.7671
3	11.0610	8.0508	78.7163
4	9.9225	9.1893	69.5270
5	8.6230	10.4888	59.0381
6	7.1397	11.9721	47.0660
7	5.4467	13.6651	33.4009
8	3.5142	15.5976	17.8033
9	1.3085	17.8033	0.0000

YEARS 10 — MO PAYT 1.5109 — AN CONST 18.14

#	INT	PRIN	BALANCE
1	12.9944	5.1358	94.8642
2	12.2681	5.8621	89.0020
3	11.4391	6.6911	82.3109
4	10.4929	7.6373	74.6736
5	9.4129	8.7174	65.9562
6	8.1801	9.9501	56.0060
7	6.7730	11.3572	44.6488
8	5.1669	12.9633	31.6855
9	3.3337	14.7965	16.8890
10	1.2413	16.8890	0.0000

YEARS 11 — MO PAYT 1.4458 — AN CONST 17.35

#	INT	PRIN	BALANCE
1	13.0438	4.3058	95.6942
2	12.4349	4.9147	90.7795
3	11.7399	5.6097	85.1698
4	10.9466	6.4030	78.7668
5	10.0411	7.3085	71.4583
6	9.0076	8.3420	63.1162
7	7.8279	9.5217	53.5945
8	6.4814	10.8682	42.7263
9	4.9445	12.4051	30.3212
10	3.1902	14.1594	16.1618
11	1.1878	16.1618	0.0000

YEARS 12 — MO PAYT 1.3932 — AN CONST 16.72

#	INT	PRIN	BALANCE
1	13.0837	3.6352	96.3648
2	12.5696	4.1493	92.2155
3	11.9829	4.7360	87.4795
4	11.3131	5.4058	82.0737
5	10.5486	6.1703	75.9034
6	9.6761	7.0428	68.8606
7	8.6801	8.0388	60.8218
8	7.5433	9.1756	51.6462
9	6.2458	10.4731	41.1731
10	4.7647	11.9542	29.2189
11	3.0742	13.6447	15.5742
12	1.1447	15.5742	0.0000

YEARS 13 — MO PAYT 1.3502 — AN CONST 16.21

#	INT	PRIN	BALANCE
1	13.1163	3.0865	96.9135
2	12.6799	3.5230	93.3905
3	12.1817	4.0212	89.3693
4	11.6130	4.5899	84.7794
5	10.9639	5.2389	79.5404
6	10.2231	5.9798	73.5606
7	9.3774	6.8254	66.7352
8	8.4122	7.7907	58.9445
9	7.3105	8.8924	50.0522
10	6.0530	10.1499	39.9023
11	4.6177	11.5852	28.3171
12	2.9793	13.2235	15.0935
13	1.1093	15.0935	0.0000

YEARS 14 — MO PAYT 1.3147 — AN CONST 15.78

#	INT	PRIN	BALANCE
1	13.1433	2.6329	97.3671
2	12.7710	3.0053	94.3618
3	12.3460	3.4302	90.9316
4	11.8609	3.9153	87.0162
5	11.3072	4.4690	82.5472
6	10.6753	5.1010	77.4462
7	9.9539	5.8224	71.6238
8	9.1305	6.6457	64.9781
9	8.1907	7.5855	57.3926
10	7.1180	8.6582	48.7343
11	5.8936	9.8826	38.8517
12	4.4961	11.2802	27.5715
13	2.9009	12.8754	14.6961
14	1.0801	14.6961	0.0000

YEARS 15 — MO PAYT 1.2850 — AN CONST 15.43

#	INT	PRIN	BALANCE
1	13.1658	2.2547	97.7453
2	12.8470	2.5736	95.1717
3	12.4830	2.9375	92.2342
4	12.0676	3.3529	88.8813
5	11.5935	3.8271	85.0543
6	11.0523	4.3683	80.6860
7	10.4346	4.9860	75.7000
8	9.7295	5.6911	70.0089
9	8.9247	6.4959	63.5130
10	8.0060	7.4145	56.0985
11	6.9575	8.4630	47.6355
12	5.7607	9.6598	37.9757
13	4.3947	11.0259	26.9499
14	2.8355	12.5851	14.3648
15	1.0558	14.3648	0.0000

YEARS 16 — MO PAYT 1.2602 — AN CONST 15.13

#	INT	PRIN	BALANCE
1	13.1847	1.9371	98.0629
2	12.9108	2.2110	95.8519
3	12.5981	2.5237	93.3282
4	12.2412	2.8806	90.4476
5	11.8339	3.2880	87.1596
6	11.3689	3.7529	83.4067
7	10.8382	4.2836	79.1230
8	10.2334	4.8894	74.2336
9	9.5410	5.5808	68.6528
10	8.7518	6.3701	62.2827
11	7.8510	7.2709	55.0119
12	6.8228	8.2991	46.7128
13	5.6491	9.4727	37.2401
14	4.3096	10.8123	26.4278
15	2.7806	12.3413	14.0865
16	1.0353	14.0865	0.0000

YEARS 17 — MO PAYT 1.2391 — AN CONST 14.87

#	INT	PRIN	BALANCE
1	13.2007	1.6688	98.3312
2	12.9647	1.9048	96.4264
3	12.6953	2.1741	94.2523
4	12.3879	2.4816	91.7707
5	12.0370	2.8325	88.9382
6	11.6364	3.2331	85.7051
7	11.1792	3.6903	82.0148
8	10.6573	4.2122	77.8026
9	10.0617	4.8078	72.9948
10	9.3818	5.4877	67.5071
11	8.6057	6.2638	61.2434
12	7.7199	7.1495	54.0938
13	6.7089	8.1606	45.9332
14	5.5549	9.3146	36.6186
15	4.2377	10.6318	25.9868
16	2.7342	12.1353	13.8514
17	1.0180	13.8514	0.0000

YEARS 18 — MO PAYT 1.2213 — AN CONST 14.66

#	INT	PRIN	BALANCE
1	13.2143	1.4410	98.5590
2	13.0105	1.6447	96.9143
3	12.7779	1.8773	95.0370
4	12.5124	2.1428	92.8942
5	12.2094	2.4458	90.4483
6	11.8635	2.7917	87.6566
7	11.4687	3.1865	84.4701
8	11.0181	3.6371	80.8330
9	10.5038	4.1515	76.6815
10	9.9167	4.7385	71.9430
11	9.2466	5.4086	66.5344
12	8.4817	6.1735	60.3609
13	7.6087	7.0465	53.3143
14	6.6122	8.0430	45.2714
15	5.4748	9.1804	36.0910
16	4.1766	10.4786	25.6123
17	2.6948	11.9605	13.6519
18	1.0034	13.6519	0.0000

YEARS 19 — MO PAYT 1.2060 — AN CONST 14.48

#	INT	PRIN	BALANCE
1	13.2258	1.2467	98.7533
2	13.0495	1.4230	97.3303
3	12.8483	1.6242	95.7061
4	12.6186	1.8539	93.8521
5	12.3564	2.1161	91.7360
6	12.0572	2.4153	89.3207
7	11.7156	2.7569	86.5638
8	11.3257	3.1468	83.4170
9	10.8807	3.5918	79.8252
10	10.3728	4.0997	75.7255
11	9.7931	4.6795	71.0461
12	9.1313	5.3412	65.7049
13	8.3760	6.0965	59.6083
14	7.5138	6.9587	52.6497
15	6.5298	7.9427	44.7070
16	5.4066	9.0659	35.6410
17	4.1245	10.3480	25.2930
18	2.6612	11.8114	13.4817
19	.9909	13.4817	0.0000

YEARS 20 — MO PAYT 1.1930 — AN CONST 14.32

#	INT	PRIN	BALANCE
1	13.2357	1.0804	98.9196
2	13.0829	1.2332	97.6863
3	12.9085	1.4076	96.2787
4	12.7095	1.6067	94.6720
5	12.4823	1.8339	92.8381
6	12.2229	2.0932	90.7449
7	11.9269	2.3892	88.3556
8	11.5890	2.7271	85.6285
9	11.2034	3.1128	82.5158
10	10.7632	3.5530	78.9628
11	10.2607	4.0554	74.9074
12	9.6872	4.6289	70.2785
13	9.0327	5.2835	64.9950
14	8.2855	6.0307	58.9643
15	7.4327	6.8835	52.0808
16	6.4592	7.8569	44.2239
17	5.3482	8.9680	35.2559
18	4.0800	10.2362	25.0197
19	2.6324	11.6837	13.3360
20	.9802	13.3360	0.0000

YEARS 21 — MO PAYT 1.1818 — AN CONST 14.19

#	INT	PRIN	BALANCE
1	13.2442	.9377	99.0623
2	13.1116	1.0703	97.9920
3	12.9602	1.2217	96.7703

MONTHLY PAYMENT AMORTIZATION SCHEDULE PER $100 — 13.30 %

#	INT	PRIN	BALANCE
4	12.7875	1.3944	95.3759
5	12.5903	1.5916	93.7843
6	12.3652	1.8167	91.9676
7	12.1083	2.0736	89.8940
8	11.8151	2.3668	87.5271
9	11.4804	2.7015	84.8256
10	11.0983	3.0836	81.7420
11	10.6623	3.5197	78.2223
12	10.1645	4.0174	74.2050
13	9.5964	4.5855	69.6165
14	8.9480	5.2340	64.3855
15	8.2078	5.9741	58.4114
16	7.3630	6.8189	51.5925
17	6.3987	7.7832	43.8092
18	5.2980	8.8839	34.9253
19	4.0417	10.1402	24.7851
20	2.6077	11.5742	13.2109
21	.9710	13.2109	0.0000

YEARS 22 — MO PAYT 1.1722 — AN CONST 14.07

#	INT	PRIN	BALANCE
1	13.2515	.8148	99.1852
2	13.1363	.9301	98.2551
3	13.0048	1.0616	97.1935
4	12.8546	1.2117	95.9818
5	12.6833	1.3831	94.5987
6	12.4877	1.5786	93.0201
7	12.2645	1.8019	91.2182
8	12.0096	2.0567	89.1615
9	11.7188	2.3476	86.8139
10	11.3868	2.6795	84.1344
11	11.0079	3.0585	81.0759
12	10.5754	3.4910	77.5850
13	10.0817	3.9846	73.6003
14	9.5182	4.5481	69.0522
15	8.8750	5.1913	63.8609
16	8.1409	5.9254	57.9354
17	7.3030	6.7634	51.1721
18	6.3465	7.7198	43.4523
19	5.2548	8.8115	34.6408
20	4.0088	10.0576	24.5832
21	2.5865	11.4799	13.1033
22	.9631	13.1033	0.0000

YEARS 23 — MO PAYT 1.1639 — AN CONST 13.97

#	INT	PRIN	BALANCE
1	13.2578	.7088	99.2912
2	13.1576	.8091	98.4821
3	13.0432	.9235	97.5587
4	12.9126	1.0541	96.5046
5	12.7635	1.2031	95.3015
6	12.5934	1.3733	93.9282
7	12.3992	1.5675	92.3607
8	12.1775	1.7891	90.5716
9	11.9245	2.0421	88.5295
10	11.6357	2.3309	86.1986
11	11.3061	2.6605	83.5380
12	10.9299	3.0368	80.5013
13	10.5004	3.4662	77.0350
14	10.0102	3.9564	73.0786
15	9.4507	4.5159	68.5627
16	8.8121	5.1545	63.4082
17	8.0832	5.8834	57.5248
18	7.2512	6.7154	50.8094
19	6.3015	7.6651	43.1443
20	5.2176	8.7491	34.3952
21	3.9803	9.9863	24.4089
22	2.5681	11.3985	13.0104
23	.9562	13.0104	0.0000

YEARS 24 — MO PAYT 1.1567 — AN CONST 13.89

#	INT	PRIN	BALANCE
1	13.2633	.6172	99.3828
2	13.1760	.7044	98.6784
3	13.0764	.8041	97.8743
4	12.9627	.9178	96.9566
5	12.8329	1.0476	95.9090
6	12.6847	1.1957	94.7133
7	12.5157	1.3648	93.3485
8	12.3227	1.5578	91.7907
9	12.1024	1.7781	90.0126
10	11.8509	2.0295	87.9831
11	11.5639	2.3165	85.6666
12	11.2363	2.6441	83.0225
13	10.8624	3.0180	80.0044
14	10.4356	3.4448	76.5596
15	9.9485	3.9320	72.6276
16	9.3924	4.4880	68.1396
17	8.7577	5.1227	63.0169
18	8.0333	5.8471	57.1698
19	7.2065	6.6740	50.4958
20	6.2627	7.6178	42.8780
21	5.1854	8.6951	34.1829
22	3.9558	9.9247	24.2583
23	2.5523	11.3282	12.9301
24	.9503	12.9301	0.0000

YEARS 25 — MO PAYT 1.1505 — AN CONST 13.81

#	INT	PRIN	BALANCE
1	13.2680	.5378	99.4622
2	13.1919	.6138	98.8484
3	13.1051	.7007	98.1477
4	13.0061	.7997	97.3480
5	12.8930	.9128	96.4351
6	12.7639	1.0419	95.3932
7	12.6165	1.1893	94.2039
8	12.4484	1.3574	92.8465
9	12.2564	1.5494	91.2971
10	12.0373	1.7685	89.5286
11	11.7872	2.0186	87.5099
12	11.5017	2.3041	85.2059
13	11.1759	2.6299	82.5760
14	10.8040	3.0018	79.5742
15	10.3795	3.4263	76.1479
16	9.8950	3.9108	72.2370
17	9.3419	4.4639	67.7731
18	8.7106	5.0951	62.6780
19	7.9901	5.8157	56.8623
20	7.1677	6.6381	50.2242
21	6.2290	7.5768	42.6474
22	5.1575	8.6483	33.9991
23	3.9345	9.8713	24.1278
24	2.5386	11.2672	12.8606
25	.9452	12.8606	0.0000

YEARS 26 — MO PAYT 1.1451 — AN CONST 13.75

#	INT	PRIN	BALANCE
1	13.2721	.4690	99.5310
2	13.2058	.5353	98.9958
3	13.1301	.6110	98.3848
4	13.0437	.6974	97.6874
5	12.9451	.7960	96.8914
6	12.8325	.9086	95.9829
7	12.7040	1.0370	94.9458
8	12.5574	1.1837	93.7622
9	12.3900	1.3511	92.4111
10	12.1989	1.5421	90.8689
11	11.9808	1.7602	89.1087
12	11.7319	2.0091	87.0996
13	11.4478	2.2933	84.8063
14	11.1235	2.6176	82.1887
15	10.7533	2.9877	79.2010
16	10.3308	3.4102	75.7908
17	9.8486	3.8925	71.8983
18	9.2981	4.4430	67.4553
19	8.6698	5.0713	62.3841
20	7.9527	5.7884	56.5956
21	7.1341	6.6070	49.9887
22	6.1998	7.5413	42.4474
23	5.1333	8.6077	33.8397
24	3.9161	9.8250	24.0147
25	2.5267	11.2144	12.8003
26	.9408	12.8003	0.0000

YEARS 27 — MO PAYT 1.1404 — AN CONST 13.69

#	INT	PRIN	BALANCE
1	13.2757	.4092	99.5908
2	13.2178	.4670	99.1238
3	13.1517	.5331	98.5907
4	13.0764	.6085	97.9822
5	12.9903	.6945	97.2877
6	12.8921	.7927	96.4950
7	12.7800	.9048	95.5901
8	12.6520	1.0328	94.5573
9	12.5060	1.1788	93.3785
10	12.3393	1.3456	92.0330
11	12.1490	1.5358	90.4971
12	11.9318	1.7530	88.7441
13	11.6839	2.0009	86.7432
14	11.4009	2.2839	84.4593
15	11.0780	2.6069	81.8524
16	10.7093	2.9755	78.8769
17	10.2885	3.3963	75.4806
18	9.8083	3.8766	71.6041
19	9.2601	4.4248	67.1793
20	8.6343	5.0505	62.1288
21	7.9201	5.7647	56.3641
22	7.1049	6.5799	49.7841
23	6.1744	7.5104	42.2737
24	5.1123	8.5725	33.7012
25	3.9000	9.7848	23.9164
26	2.5163	11.1685	12.7479
27	.9369	12.7479	0.0000

YEARS 28 — MO PAYT 1.1363 — AN CONST 13.64

#	INT	PRIN	BALANCE
1	13.2787	.3572	99.6428
2	13.2282	.4077	99.2351
3	13.1706	.4654	98.7697
4	13.1048	.5312	98.2385
5	13.0296	.6063	97.6322
6	12.9439	.6920	96.9402
7	12.8460	.7899	96.1503
8	12.7343	.9016	95.2487
9	12.6068	1.0291	94.2196
10	12.4613	1.1746	93.0450
11	12.2952	1.3407	91.7042
12	12.1056	1.5303	90.1739
13	11.8892	1.7468	88.4271
14	11.6422	1.9938	86.4333
15	11.3602	2.2757	84.1576
16	11.0384	2.5975	81.5601
17	10.6711	2.9649	78.5952
18	10.2518	3.3842	75.2110
19	9.7732	3.8627	71.3483
20	9.2270	4.4090	66.9393
21	8.6035	5.0325	61.9069
22	7.8918	5.7441	56.1627
23	7.0795	6.5564	49.6063
24	6.1523	7.4836	42.1227
25	5.0941	8.5419	33.5808
26	3.8861	9.7498	23.8310
27	2.5073	11.1286	12.7024
28	.9336	12.7024	0.0000

YEARS 29 — MO PAYT 1.1328 — AN CONST 13.60

#	INT	PRIN	BALANCE
1	13.2814	.3120	99.6880
2	13.2373	.3561	99.3319
3	13.1870	.4064	98.9255
4	13.1295	.4639	98.4616
5	13.0639	.5295	97.9321
6	12.9890	.6044	97.3277
7	12.9035	.6899	96.6378
8	12.8060	.7874	95.8503
9	12.6946	.8988	94.9515
10	12.5675	1.0259	93.9257
11	12.4224	1.1710	92.7547
12	12.2568	1.3366	91.4181
13	12.0678	1.5256	89.8925
14	11.8521	1.7413	88.1512
15	11.6058	1.9876	86.1637
16	11.3248	2.2686	83.8951
17	11.0040	2.5894	81.3056
18	10.6378	2.9556	78.3500
19	10.2198	3.3736	74.9764
20	9.7427	3.8507	71.1257
21	9.1982	4.3952	66.7305
22	8.5766	5.0168	61.7137
23	7.8672	5.7262	55.9875
24	7.0574	6.5360	49.4516
25	6.1331	7.4603	41.9913
26	5.0782	8.5152	33.4761
27	3.8740	9.7194	23.7566
28	2.4995	11.0939	12.6627
29	.9307	12.6627	0.0000

YEARS 30 — MO PAYT 1.1297 — AN CONST 13.56

#	INT	PRIN	BALANCE
1	13.2838	.2726	99.7274
2	13.2452	.3111	99.4163
3	13.2012	.3551	99.0612
4	13.1510	.4053	98.6559
5	13.0937	.4627	98.1932
6	13.0283	.5281	97.6651
7	12.9536	.6028	97.0624
8	12.8684	.6880	96.3744
9	12.7711	.7853	95.5891
10	12.6600	.8963	94.6927
11	12.5333	1.0231	93.6696
12	12.3886	1.1678	92.5019
13	12.2234	1.3329	91.1689
14	12.0349	1.5214	89.6475
15	11.8198	1.7366	87.9110
16	11.5742	1.9821	85.9288
17	11.2939	2.2624	83.6664
18	10.9740	2.5824	81.0840
19	10.6088	2.9476	78.1364
20	10.1920	3.3644	74.7720
21	9.7162	3.8402	70.9318
22	9.1731	4.3832	66.5486
23	8.5533	5.0031	61.5455
24	7.8458	5.7106	55.8349
25	7.0382	6.5182	49.3168
26	6.1164	7.4399	41.8768
27	5.0643	8.4920	33.3848
28	3.8634	9.6929	23.6919
29	2.4927	11.0637	12.6282
30	.9281	12.6282	0.0000

MONTHLY PAYMENT AMORTIZATION SCHEDULE PER $100

13.375%

YEARS 2 — MO PAYT 4.7718 — AN CONST 57.27

#	INT	PRIN	BALANCE
1	10.5821	46.6796	53.3204
2	3.9414	53.3204	0.0000

YEARS 3 — MO PAYT 3.3875 — AN CONST 40.65

#	INT	PRIN	BALANCE
1	11.6393	29.0105	70.9895
2	7.5122	33.1376	37.8518
3	2.7980	37.8518	0.0000

YEARS 4 — MO PAYT 2.7014 — AN CONST 32.42

#	INT	PRIN	BALANCE
1	12.1632	20.2536	79.7464
2	9.2819	23.1349	56.6116
3	5.9907	26.4261	30.1855
4	2.2313	30.1855	0.0000

YEARS 5 — MO PAYT 2.2945 — AN CONST 27.54

#	INT	PRIN	BALANCE
1	12.4739	15.0607	84.9393
2	10.3314	17.2032	67.7361
3	7.8840	19.6506	48.0855
4	5.0885	22.4461	25.6393
5	1.8953	25.6393	0.0000

YEARS 6 — MO PAYT 2.0273 — AN CONST 24.33

#	INT	PRIN	BALANCE
1	12.6780	11.6490	88.3510
2	11.0208	13.3063	75.0447
3	9.1279	15.1992	59.8455
4	6.9656	17.3615	42.4840
5	4.4957	19.8314	22.6526
6	1.6745	22.6526	0.0000

YEARS 7 — MO PAYT 1.8396 — AN CONST 22.08

#	INT	PRIN	BALANCE
1	12.8213	9.2544	90.7456
2	11.5048	10.5710	80.1746
3	10.0009	12.0748	68.0997
4	8.2831	13.7926	54.3071
5	6.3210	15.7548	38.5523
6	4.0797	17.9961	20.5562
7	1.5195	20.5562	0.0000

YEARS 8 — MO PAYT 1.7018 — AN CONST 20.43

#	INT	PRIN	BALANCE
1	12.9266	7.4947	92.5053
2	11.8604	8.5609	83.9445
3	10.6425	9.7787	74.1658
4	9.2514	11.1699	62.9959
5	7.6623	12.7589	50.2370
6	5.8472	14.5740	35.6630
7	3.7739	16.6473	19.0156
8	1.4056	19.0156	0.0000

YEARS 9 — MO PAYT 1.5970 — AN CONST 19.17

#	INT	PRIN	BALANCE
1	13.0066	6.1572	93.8428
2	12.1307	7.0332	86.8096
3	11.1301	8.0337	78.7758
4	9.9872	9.1766	69.5992
5	8.6817	10.4821	59.1171
6	7.1905	11.9733	47.1438
7	5.4872	13.6767	33.4671
8	3.5415	15.6223	17.8448
9	1.3191	17.8448	0.0000

YEARS 10 — MO PAYT 1.5153 — AN CONST 18.19

#	INT	PRIN	BALANCE
1	13.0690	5.1147	94.8853
2	12.3414	5.8423	89.0430
3	11.5102	6.6735	82.3695
4	10.5608	7.6228	74.7467
5	9.4764	8.7073	66.0394
6	8.2377	9.9460	56.0934
7	6.8228	11.3609	44.7325
8	5.2065	12.9771	31.7554
9	3.3604	14.8233	16.9321
10	1.2516	16.9321	0.0000

YEARS 11 — MO PAYT 1.4504 — AN CONST 17.41

#	INT	PRIN	BALANCE
1	13.1186	4.2858	95.7142
2	12.5089	4.8955	90.8187
3	11.8124	5.5919	85.2268
4	11.0169	6.3875	78.8393
5	10.1082	7.2961	71.5432
6	9.0703	8.3341	63.2091
7	7.8846	9.5197	53.6894
8	6.5304	10.8740	42.8154
9	4.9834	12.4210	30.3944
10	3.2164	14.1880	16.2064
11	1.1980	16.2064	0.0000

YEARS 12 — MO PAYT 1.3979 — AN CONST 16.78

#	INT	PRIN	BALANCE
1	13.1586	3.6163	96.3837
2	12.6442	4.1308	92.2529
3	12.0565	4.7185	87.5344
4	11.3853	5.3897	82.1447
5	10.6185	6.1565	75.9882
6	9.7427	7.0323	68.9559
7	8.7423	8.0327	60.9232
8	7.5995	9.1755	51.7478
9	6.2942	10.4808	41.2670
10	4.8032	11.9718	29.2952
11	3.1001	13.6749	15.6203
12	1.1546	15.6203	0.0000

YEARS 13 — MO PAYT 1.3550 — AN CONST 16.27

#	INT	PRIN	BALANCE
1	13.1914	3.0688	96.9312
2	12.7548	3.5054	93.4259
3	12.2561	4.0040	89.4218
4	11.6865	4.5737	84.8482
5	11.0359	5.2243	79.6238
6	10.2927	5.9675	73.6563
7	9.4437	6.8165	66.8398
8	8.4740	7.7862	59.0536
9	7.3663	8.8939	50.1598
10	6.1010	10.1591	40.0006
11	4.6558	11.6044	28.3962
12	3.0049	13.2553	15.1410
13	1.1192	15.1410	0.0000

YEARS 14 — MO PAYT 1.3196 — AN CONST 15.84

#	INT	PRIN	BALANCE
1	13.2185	2.6163	97.3837
2	12.8463	2.9885	94.3952
3	12.4211	3.4136	90.9816
4	11.9355	3.8993	87.0823
5	11.3808	4.4540	82.6283
6	10.7471	5.0876	77.5407
7	10.0234	5.8114	71.7292
8	9.1966	6.6381	65.0911
9	8.2523	7.5825	57.5086
10	7.1736	8.6612	48.8474
11	5.9414	9.8933	38.9541
12	4.5340	11.3008	27.6533
13	2.9263	12.9085	14.7448
14	1.0899	14.7448	0.0000

YEARS 15 — MO PAYT 1.2900 — AN CONST 15.49

#	INT	PRIN	BALANCE
1	13.2410	2.2392	97.7608
2	12.9225	2.5577	95.2031
3	12.5586	2.9216	92.2815
4	12.1430	3.3372	88.9443
5	11.6682	3.8120	85.1324
6	11.1259	4.3543	80.7781
7	10.5065	4.9737	75.8044
8	9.7989	5.6813	70.1231
9	8.9907	6.4895	63.6336
10	8.0675	7.4127	56.2209
11	7.0129	8.4673	47.7536
12	5.8084	9.6718	38.0818
13	4.4325	11.0477	27.0341
14	2.8608	12.6194	14.4147
15	1.0655	14.4147	0.0000

YEARS 16 — MO PAYT 1.2652 — AN CONST 15.19

#	INT	PRIN	BALANCE
1	13.2600	1.9226	98.0774
2	12.9865	2.1961	95.8813
3	12.6740	2.5085	93.3727
4	12.3172	2.8654	90.5073
5	11.9095	3.2730	87.2343
6	11.4439	3.7387	83.4956
7	10.9120	4.2705	79.2250
8	10.3045	4.8781	74.3470
9	9.6105	5.5720	68.7749
10	8.8178	6.3647	62.4102
11	7.9124	7.2702	55.1400
12	6.8781	8.3045	46.8355
13	5.6967	9.4859	37.3497
14	4.3472	10.8353	26.5143
15	2.8058	12.3768	14.1375
16	1.0450	14.1375	0.0000

YEARS 17 — MO PAYT 1.2443 — AN CONST 14.94

#	INT	PRIN	BALANCE
1	13.2760	1.6553	98.3447
2	13.0405	1.8908	96.4539
3	12.7715	2.1598	94.2942
4	12.4642	2.4670	91.8271
5	12.1133	2.8180	89.0092
6	11.7124	3.2189	85.7903
7	11.2545	3.6768	82.1135
8	10.7314	4.1999	77.9136
9	10.1339	4.7973	73.1163
10	9.4514	5.4798	67.6365
11	8.6719	6.2594	61.3771
12	7.7814	7.1498	54.2273
13	6.7643	8.1670	46.0603
14	5.6024	9.3288	36.7314
15	4.2753	10.6560	26.0754
16	2.7593	12.1719	13.9035
17	1.0277	13.9035	0.0000

YEARS 18 — MO PAYT 1.2265 — AN CONST 14.72

#	INT	PRIN	BALANCE
1	13.2895	1.4284	98.5716
2	13.0863	1.6317	96.9399
3	12.8542	1.8638	95.0761
4	12.5891	2.1289	92.9472
5	12.2862	2.4318	90.5154
6	11.9402	2.7777	87.7377
7	11.5451	3.1729	84.5648
8	11.0937	3.6243	80.9406
9	10.5781	4.1399	76.8007
10	9.9892	4.7288	72.0719
11	9.3164	5.4015	66.6703
12	8.5480	6.1700	60.5004
13	7.6703	7.0477	53.4527
14	6.6676	8.0503	45.4023
15	5.5224	9.1956	36.2067
16	4.2142	10.5038	25.7030
17	2.7199	11.9981	13.7049
18	1.0131	13.7049	0.0000

YEARS 19 — MO PAYT 1.2113 — AN CONST 14.54

#	INT	PRIN	BALANCE
1	13.3011	1.2351	98.7649
2	13.1254	1.4108	97.3541
3	12.9247	1.6115	95.7426
4	12.6954	1.8408	93.9019
5	12.4336	2.1026	91.7992
6	12.1345	2.4017	89.3975
7	11.7928	2.7434	86.6541
8	11.4025	3.1337	83.5204
9	10.9567	3.5795	79.9409
10	10.4475	4.0887	75.8521
11	9.8658	4.6704	71.1817
12	9.2014	5.3348	65.8469
13	8.4424	6.0938	59.7531
14	7.5755	6.9607	52.7925
15	6.5853	7.9509	44.8416
16	5.4542	9.0820	35.7595
17	4.1622	10.3740	25.3855
18	2.6863	11.8499	13.5356
19	1.0006	13.5356	0.0000

YEARS 20 — MO PAYT 1.1984 — AN CONST 14.39

#	INT	PRIN	BALANCE
1	13.3110	1.0697	98.9303
2	13.1588	1.2219	97.7084
3	12.9850	1.3957	96.3127
4	12.7864	1.5943	94.7185
5	12.5596	1.8211	92.8974
6	12.3006	2.0801	90.8173
7	12.0046	2.3761	88.4412
8	11.6666	2.7141	85.7271
9	11.2805	3.1002	82.6270
10	10.8395	3.5412	79.0857
11	10.3357	4.0450	75.0407
12	9.7603	4.6204	70.4203
13	9.1029	5.2778	65.1425
14	8.3521	6.0286	59.1140
15	7.4945	6.8862	52.2277
16	6.5148	7.8659	44.3619
17	5.3958	8.9849	35.3770
18	4.1176	10.2631	25.1140
19	2.6576	11.7231	13.3909
20	.9898	13.3909	0.0000

YEARS 21 — MO PAYT 1.1873 — AN CONST 14.25

#	INT	PRIN	BALANCE
1	13.3195	.9278	99.0722
2	13.1875	1.0598	98.0124
3	13.0367	1.2105	96.8019

#	INT	PRIN	BALANCE
4	12.8645	1.3828	95.4191
5	12.6678	1.5795	93.8397
6	12.4431	1.8042	92.0355
7	12.1864	2.0608	89.9747
8	11.8933	2.3540	87.6207
9	11.5584	2.6889	84.9318
10	11.1759	3.0714	81.8604
11	10.7389	3.5084	78.3520
12	10.2398	4.0075	74.3445
13	9.6697	4.5776	69.7669
14	9.0185	5.2288	64.5382
15	8.2746	5.9726	58.5655
16	7.4250	6.8223	51.7432
17	6.4544	7.7929	43.9503
18	5.3458	8.9015	35.0488
19	4.0794	10.1678	24.8810
20	2.6329	11.6143	13.2666
21	.9807	13.2666	0.0000

YEARS 22	MO PAYT 1.1777	AN CONST 14.14	
#	INT	PRIN	BALANCE
1	13.3268	.8057	99.1943
2	13.2122	.9203	98.2740
3	13.0813	1.0512	97.2228
4	12.9317	1.2008	96.0220
5	12.7609	1.3716	94.6503
6	12.5657	1.5667	93.0836
7	12.3429	1.7896	91.2940
8	12.0883	2.0442	89.2497
9	11.7974	2.3350	86.9147
10	11.4653	2.6672	84.2475
11	11.0858	3.0467	81.2008
12	10.6524	3.4801	77.7207
13	10.1573	3.9752	73.7455
14	9.5918	4.5407	69.2048
15	8.9458	5.1867	64.0182
16	8.2080	5.9245	58.0936
17	7.3651	6.7674	51.3263
18	6.4024	7.7301	43.5962
19	5.3027	8.8298	34.7664
20	4.0466	10.0859	24.6805
21	2.6117	11.5208	13.1597
22	.9728	13.1597	0.0000

YEARS 23	MO PAYT 1.1695	AN CONST 14.04	
#	INT	PRIN	BALANCE
1	13.3331	.7004	99.2996
2	13.2335	.8001	98.4995
3	13.1196	.9139	97.5857
4	12.9896	1.0439	96.5418
5	12.8411	1.1924	95.3494
6	12.6715	1.3620	93.9874
7	12.4777	1.5558	92.4316
8	12.2564	1.7771	90.6545
9	12.0036	2.0299	88.6246
10	11.7148	2.3187	86.3059
11	11.3850	2.6485	83.6574
12	11.0082	3.0253	80.6321
13	10.5778	3.4557	77.1763
14	10.0862	3.9473	73.2290
15	9.5246	4.5089	68.7201
16	8.8832	5.1503	63.5698
17	8.1505	5.8830	57.6868
18	7.3135	6.7200	50.9668
19	6.3576	7.6759	43.2908
20	5.2656	8.7679	34.5229
21	4.0182	10.0153	24.5076
22	2.5934	11.4401	13.0676
23	.9659	13.0676	0.0000

YEARS 24	MO PAYT 1.1623	AN CONST 13.95	
#	INT	PRIN	BALANCE
1	13.3385	.6094	99.3906
2	13.2518	.6961	98.6944
3	13.1528	.7952	97.8992
4	13.0397	.9083	96.9909
5	12.9105	1.0375	95.9534
6	12.7629	1.1851	94.7683
7	12.5943	1.3537	93.4146
8	12.4017	1.5463	91.8683
9	12.1817	1.7663	90.1021
10	11.9304	2.0175	88.0845
11	11.6434	2.3046	85.7800
12	11.3156	2.6324	83.1476
13	10.9411	3.0069	80.1407
14	10.5133	3.4347	76.7060
15	10.0247	3.9233	72.7827
16	9.4666	4.4814	68.3013
17	8.8290	5.1189	63.1824
18	8.1008	5.8472	57.3352
19	7.2690	6.6790	50.6562
20	6.3188	7.6292	43.0270
21	5.2335	8.7145	34.3125
22	3.9937	9.9542	24.3583
23	2.5776	11.3704	12.9879
24	.9601	12.9879	0.0000

YEARS 25	MO PAYT 1.1562	AN CONST 13.88	
#	INT	PRIN	BALANCE
1	13.3432	.5307	99.4693
2	13.2677	.6062	98.8631
3	13.1815	.6924	98.1706
4	13.0830	.7910	97.3797
5	12.9705	.9035	96.4762
6	12.8419	1.0320	95.4442
7	12.6951	1.1788	94.2654
8	12.5274	1.3465	92.9189
9	12.3359	1.5381	91.3808
10	12.1171	1.7569	89.6239
11	11.8671	2.0068	87.6170
12	11.5816	2.2923	85.3247
13	11.2555	2.6184	82.7063
14	10.8830	2.9909	79.7154
15	10.4575	3.4164	76.2989
16	9.9715	3.9025	72.3965
17	9.4163	4.4576	67.9388
18	8.7822	5.0918	62.8471
19	8.0578	5.8161	57.0309
20	7.2304	6.6436	50.3873
21	6.2853	7.5887	42.7987
22	5.2057	8.6683	34.1304
23	3.9725	9.9014	24.2290
24	2.5639	11.3100	12.9190
25	.9550	12.9190	0.0000

YEARS 26	MO PAYT 1.1508	AN CONST 13.81	
#	INT	PRIN	BALANCE
1	13.3473	.4625	99.5375
2	13.2815	.5283	99.0093
3	13.2064	.6034	98.4059
4	13.1205	.6892	97.7166
5	13.0225	.7873	96.9293
6	12.9105	.8993	96.0300
7	12.7826	1.0272	95.0028
8	12.6364	1.1734	93.8294
9	12.4695	1.3403	92.4891
10	12.2788	1.5310	90.9582
11	12.0610	1.7488	89.2094
12	11.8122	1.9975	87.2119
13	11.5281	2.2817	84.9301
14	11.2035	2.6063	82.3238
15	10.8327	2.9771	79.3467
16	10.4092	3.4006	75.9461
17	9.9254	3.8844	72.0617
18	9.3728	4.4370	67.6246
19	8.7416	5.0682	62.5564
20	8.0205	5.7892	56.7672
21	7.1970	6.6128	50.1543
22	6.2562	7.5536	42.6007
23	5.1816	8.6282	33.9726
24	3.9542	9.8556	24.1169
25	2.5521	11.2577	12.8592
26	.9506	12.8592	0.0000

YEARS 27	MO PAYT 1.1462	AN CONST 13.76	
#	INT	PRIN	BALANCE
1	13.3509	.4032	99.5968
2	13.2935	.4606	99.1362
3	13.2280	.5261	98.6100
4	13.1531	.6010	98.0091
5	13.0676	.6865	97.3226
6	12.9700	.7841	96.5385
7	12.8584	.8957	95.6428
8	12.7310	1.0231	94.6197
9	12.5855	1.1686	93.4511
10	12.4192	1.3349	92.1162
11	12.2293	1.5248	90.5914
12	12.0124	1.7417	88.8497
13	11.7646	1.9895	86.8602
14	11.4816	2.2725	84.5877
15	11.1583	2.5958	81.9918
16	10.7890	2.9651	79.0267
17	10.3672	3.3869	75.6398
18	9.8854	3.8687	71.7711
19	9.3350	4.4191	67.3520
20	8.7063	5.0478	62.3042
21	7.9882	5.7659	56.5383
22	7.1679	6.5862	49.9521
23	6.2310	7.5231	42.4290
24	5.1607	8.5934	33.8356
25	3.9382	9.8159	24.0197
26	2.5418	11.2123	12.8074
27	.9467	12.8074	0.0000

YEARS 28	MO PAYT 1.1421	AN CONST 13.71	
#	INT	PRIN	BALANCE
1	13.3540	.3518	99.6482
2	13.3039	.4018	99.2464
3	13.2467	.4590	98.7874
4	13.1815	.5243	98.2632
5	13.1069	.5989	97.6643
6	13.0217	.6841	96.9803
7	12.9244	.7814	96.1989
8	12.8132	.8925	95.3064
9	12.6862	1.0195	94.2869
10	12.5412	1.1645	93.1224
11	12.3755	1.3302	91.7922
12	12.1863	1.5194	90.2727
13	11.9701	1.7356	88.5371
14	11.7232	1.9825	86.5546
15	11.4412	2.2645	84.2901
16	11.1190	2.5867	81.7034
17	10.7511	2.9547	78.7488
18	10.3307	3.3750	75.3737
19	9.8506	3.8551	71.5186
20	9.3021	4.4036	67.1150
21	8.6757	5.0300	62.0850
22	7.9601	5.7456	56.3394
23	7.1427	6.5630	49.7764
24	6.2091	7.4967	42.2797
25	5.1426	8.5631	33.7166
26	3.9244	9.7814	23.9352
27	2.5329	11.1729	12.7623
28	.9434	12.7623	0.0000

YEARS 29	MO PAYT 1.1386	AN CONST 13.67	
#	INT	PRIN	BALANCE
1	13.3566	.3070	99.6930
2	13.3130	.3507	99.3423
3	13.2631	.4006	98.9417
4	13.2061	.4576	98.4841
5	13.1410	.5227	97.9615
6	13.0666	.5970	97.3645
7	12.9817	.6819	96.6825
8	12.8847	.7790	95.9036
9	12.7739	.8898	95.0138
10	12.6473	1.0164	93.9974
11	12.5027	1.1610	92.8365
12	12.3375	1.3261	91.5103
13	12.1489	1.5148	89.9956
14	11.9334	1.7303	88.2653
15	11.6872	1.9764	86.2889
16	11.4061	2.2576	84.0313
17	11.0849	2.5787	81.4526
18	10.7180	2.9456	78.5070
19	10.2990	3.3646	75.1423
20	9.8203	3.8433	71.2990
21	9.2736	4.3901	66.9090
22	8.6491	5.0146	61.8944
23	7.9357	5.7280	56.1664
24	7.1208	6.5429	49.6236
25	6.1900	7.4736	42.1499
26	5.1268	8.5369	33.6130
27	3.9123	9.7513	23.8617
28	2.5251	11.1386	12.7232
29	.9405	12.7232	0.0000

YEARS 30	MO PAYT 1.1356	AN CONST 13.63	
#	INT	PRIN	BALANCE
1	13.3590	.2681	99.7319
2	13.3208	.3062	99.4258
3	13.2773	.3498	99.0760
4	13.2275	.3995	98.6765
5	13.1707	.4563	98.2202
6	13.1058	.5213	97.6989
7	13.0316	.5954	97.1035
8	12.9469	.6801	96.4234
9	12.8501	.7769	95.6465
10	12.7396	.8874	94.7591
11	12.6134	1.0136	93.7454
12	12.4692	1.1578	92.5876
13	12.3045	1.3226	91.2650
14	12.1163	1.5107	89.7543
15	11.9014	1.7256	88.0287
16	11.6559	1.9711	86.0576
17	11.3755	2.2515	83.8061
18	11.0552	2.5718	81.2342
19	10.6893	2.9377	78.2965
20	10.2714	3.3556	74.9409
21	9.7940	3.8330	71.1079
22	9.2487	4.3783	66.7296
23	8.6259	5.0012	61.7285
24	7.9144	5.7126	56.0158
25	7.1017	6.5253	49.4905
26	6.1734	7.4536	42.0369
27	5.1130	8.5140	33.5229
28	3.9018	9.7252	23.7978
29	2.5183	11.1087	12.6890
30	.9380	12.6890	0.0000

MONTHLY PAYMENT AMORTIZATION SCHEDULE PER $100

13.40 %

YEARS 2 — MO PAYT 4.7730 — AN CONST 57.28

#	INT	PRIN	BALANCE
1	10.6024	46.6735	53.3265
2	3.9494	53.3265	0.0000

YEARS 3 — MO PAYT 3.3887 — AN CONST 40.67

#	INT	PRIN	BALANCE
1	11.6616	29.0027	70.9973
2	7.5274	33.1369	37.8604
3	2.8040	37.8604	0.0000

YEARS 4 — MO PAYT 2.7026 — AN CONST 32.44

#	INT	PRIN	BALANCE
1	12.1865	20.2452	79.7548
2	9.3007	23.1311	56.6237
3	6.0035	26.4283	30.1954
4	2.2363	30.1954	0.0000

YEARS 5 — MO PAYT 2.2958 — AN CONST 27.56

#	INT	PRIN	BALANCE
1	12.4978	15.0523	84.9477
2	10.3522	17.1979	67.7499
3	7.9007	19.6493	48.1006
4	5.0998	22.4502	25.6504
5	1.8997	25.6504	0.0000

YEARS 6 — MO PAYT 2.0286 — AN CONST 24.35

#	INT	PRIN	BALANCE
1	12.7023	11.6407	88.3593
2	11.0429	13.3001	75.0592
3	9.1471	15.1959	59.8633
4	6.9810	17.3620	42.5013
5	4.5062	19.8368	22.6645
6	1.6785	22.6645	0.0000

YEARS 7 — MO PAYT 1.8410 — AN CONST 22.10

#	INT	PRIN	BALANCE
1	12.8458	9.2464	90.7536
2	11.5278	10.5644	80.1892
3	10.0219	12.0703	68.1189
4	8.3013	13.7908	54.3281
5	6.3355	15.7566	38.5715
6	4.0895	18.0026	20.5688
7	1.5233	20.5688	0.0000

YEARS 8 — MO PAYT 1.7032 — AN CONST 20.44

#	INT	PRIN	BALANCE
1	12.9512	7.4869	92.5131
2	11.8840	8.5541	83.9590
3	10.6647	9.7735	74.1855
4	9.2715	11.1666	63.0189
5	7.6798	12.7583	50.2606
6	5.8612	14.5770	35.6837
7	3.7833	16.6548	19.0289
8	1.4093	19.0289	0.0000

YEARS 9 — MO PAYT 1.5984 — AN CONST 19.19

#	INT	PRIN	BALANCE
1	13.0314	6.1498	93.8502
2	12.1548	7.0265	86.8237
3	11.1532	8.0280	78.7956
4	10.0088	9.1724	69.6232
5	8.7014	10.4799	59.1434
6	7.2075	11.9737	47.1697
7	5.5007	13.6805	33.4892
8	3.5507	15.6306	17.8586
9	1.3226	17.8586	0.0000

YEARS 10 — MO PAYT 1.5168 — AN CONST 18.21

#	INT	PRIN	BALANCE
1	13.0938	5.1077	94.8923
2	12.3658	5.8357	89.0566
3	11.5339	6.6676	82.3890
4	10.5835	7.6180	74.7710
5	9.4976	8.7039	66.0671
6	8.2569	9.9446	56.1225
7	6.8394	11.3621	44.7604
8	5.2198	12.9817	31.7787
9	3.3693	14.8322	16.9464
10	1.2551	16.9464	0.0000

YEARS 11 — MO PAYT 1.4519 — AN CONST 17.43

#	INT	PRIN	BALANCE
1	13.1435	4.2791	95.7209
2	12.5335	4.8891	90.8318
3	11.8366	5.5860	85.2458
4	11.0404	6.3823	78.8635
5	10.1306	7.2920	71.5715
6	9.0912	8.3315	63.2400
7	7.9036	9.5190	53.7210
8	6.5467	10.8759	42.8450
9	4.9964	12.4262	30.4188
10	3.2251	14.1975	16.2213
11	1.2014	16.2213	0.0000

YEARS 12 — MO PAYT 1.3995 — AN CONST 16.80

#	INT	PRIN	BALANCE
1	13.1836	3.6101	96.3899
2	12.6690	4.1247	92.2653
3	12.0811	4.7126	87.5527
4	11.4093	5.3844	82.1683
5	10.6418	6.1519	76.0165
6	9.7649	7.0288	68.9877
7	8.7630	8.0307	60.9570
8	7.6183	9.1754	51.7816
9	6.3104	10.4833	41.2983
10	4.8160	11.9776	29.3207
11	3.1087	13.6850	15.6357
12	1.1580	15.6357	0.0000

YEARS 13 — MO PAYT 1.3566 — AN CONST 16.28

#	INT	PRIN	BALANCE
1	13.2164	3.0629	96.9371
2	12.7798	3.4995	93.4376
3	12.2810	3.9983	89.4393
4	11.7110	4.5683	84.8710
5	11.0599	5.2194	79.6516
6	10.3159	5.9634	73.6882
7	9.4658	6.8135	66.8747
8	8.4946	7.7847	59.0900
9	7.3849	8.8944	50.1956
10	6.1171	10.1622	40.0334
11	4.6685	11.6108	28.4226
12	3.0135	13.2658	15.1568
13	1.1225	15.1568	0.0000

YEARS 14 — MO PAYT 1.3212 — AN CONST 15.86

#	INT	PRIN	BALANCE
1	13.2435	2.6108	97.3892
2	12.8714	2.9829	94.4063
3	12.4462	3.4081	90.9982
4	11.9604	3.8939	87.1042
5	11.4053	4.4490	82.6552
6	10.7711	5.0832	77.5721
7	10.0465	5.8077	71.7643
8	9.2187	6.6356	65.1287
9	8.2728	7.5815	57.5473
10	7.1921	8.6622	48.8851
11	5.9574	9.8969	38.9882
12	4.5466	11.3076	27.6806
13	2.9348	12.9195	14.7611
14	1.0932	14.7611	0.0000

YEARS 15 — MO PAYT 1.2917 — AN CONST 15.51

#	INT	PRIN	BALANCE
1	13.2661	2.2340	97.7660
2	12.9477	2.5525	95.2135
3	12.5838	2.9163	92.2973
4	12.1681	3.3320	88.9653
5	11.6932	3.8069	85.1583
6	11.1505	4.3496	80.8087
7	10.5305	4.9696	75.8391
8	9.8221	5.6780	70.1611
9	9.0127	6.4874	63.6737
10	8.0880	7.4121	56.2616
11	7.0315	8.4686	47.7930
12	5.8243	9.6758	38.1172
13	4.4451	11.0550	27.0622
14	2.8692	12.6309	14.4313
15	1.0688	14.4313	0.0000

YEARS 16 — MO PAYT 1.2669 — AN CONST 15.21

#	INT	PRIN	BALANCE
1	13.2850	1.9178	98.0822
2	13.0117	2.1912	95.8910
3	12.6993	2.5035	93.3875
4	12.3425	2.8604	90.5272
5	11.9348	3.2681	87.2591
6	11.4689	3.7339	83.5252
7	10.9367	4.2662	79.2590
8	10.3285	4.8743	74.3847
9	9.6337	5.5691	68.8156
10	8.8399	6.3629	62.4526
11	7.9329	7.2699	55.1827
12	6.8966	8.3062	46.8764
13	5.7126	9.4902	37.3862
14	4.3598	10.8430	26.5432
15	2.8142	12.3886	14.1545
16	1.0483	14.1545	0.0000

YEARS 17 — MO PAYT 1.2460 — AN CONST 14.96

#	INT	PRIN	BALANCE
1	13.3011	1.6508	98.3492
2	13.0657	1.8861	96.4630
3	12.7969	2.1550	94.3081
4	12.4897	2.4622	91.8459
5	12.1387	2.8131	89.0327
6	11.7377	3.2141	85.8186
7	11.2796	3.6723	82.1463
8	10.7561	4.1958	77.9505
9	10.1580	4.7938	73.1567
10	9.4747	5.4772	67.6795
11	8.6940	6.2579	61.4216
12	7.8019	7.1499	54.2717
13	6.7828	8.1691	46.1026
14	5.6183	9.3336	36.7690
15	4.2879	10.6640	26.1050
16	2.7678	12.1841	13.9209
17	1.0310	13.9209	0.0000

YEARS 18 — MO PAYT 1.2282 — AN CONST 14.74

#	INT	PRIN	BALANCE
1	13.3146	1.4243	98.5757
2	13.1116	1.6273	96.9484
3	12.8796	1.8593	95.0891
4	12.6146	2.1243	92.9648
5	12.3118	2.4271	90.5377
6	11.9658	2.7731	87.7647
7	11.5706	3.1684	84.5963
8	11.1189	3.6200	80.9763
9	10.6029	4.1360	76.8403
10	10.0134	4.7256	72.1148
11	9.3398	5.3992	66.7156
12	8.5701	6.1688	60.5468
13	7.6908	7.0481	53.4987
14	6.6862	8.0528	45.4460
15	5.5383	9.2006	36.2453
16	4.2268	10.5121	25.7332
17	2.7283	12.0106	13.7226
18	1.0163	13.7226	0.0000

YEARS 19 — MO PAYT 1.2131 — AN CONST 14.56

#	INT	PRIN	BALANCE
1	13.3262	1.2312	98.7688
2	13.1507	1.4067	97.3620
3	12.9502	1.6073	95.7547
4	12.7211	1.8364	93.9184
5	12.4593	2.0981	91.8202
6	12.1602	2.3972	89.4230
7	11.8185	2.7389	86.6841
8	11.4281	3.1293	83.5547
9	10.9820	3.5754	79.9793
10	10.4724	4.0851	75.8942
11	9.8901	4.6674	71.2268
12	9.2248	5.3327	65.8942
13	8.4646	6.0928	59.8013
14	7.5961	6.9613	52.8400
15	6.6038	7.9536	44.8864
16	5.4701	9.0874	35.7990
17	4.1747	10.3827	25.4163
18	2.6947	11.8627	13.5537
19	1.0038	13.5537	0.0000

YEARS 20 — MO PAYT 1.2002 — AN CONST 14.41

#	INT	PRIN	BALANCE
1	13.3361	1.0661	98.9339
2	13.1841	1.2181	97.7157
3	13.0105	1.3918	96.3240
4	12.8121	1.5901	94.7339
5	12.5854	1.8168	92.9171
6	12.3265	2.0758	90.8413
7	12.0306	2.3717	88.4696
8	11.6925	2.7097	85.7599
9	11.3063	3.0960	82.6639
10	10.8649	3.5373	79.1266
11	10.3607	4.0415	75.0851
12	9.7846	4.6176	70.4675
13	9.1264	5.2758	65.1916
14	8.3744	6.0279	59.1638
15	7.5151	6.8871	52.2767
16	6.5334	7.8688	44.4078
17	5.4118	8.9905	35.4174
18	4.1302	10.2720	25.1454
19	2.6660	11.7362	13.4091
20	.9931	13.4091	0.0000

YEARS 21 — MO PAYT 1.1891 — AN CONST 14.27

#	INT	PRIN	BALANCE
1	13.3446	.9245	99.0755
2	13.2128	1.0563	98.0192
3	13.0622	1.2069	96.8124

#	INT	PRIN	BALANCE
4	12.8902	1.3789	95.4335
5	12.6937	1.5754	93.8580
6	12.4691	1.8000	92.0580
7	12.2125	2.0566	90.0014
8	11.9194	2.3497	87.6517
9	11.5844	2.6847	84.9670
10	11.2017	3.0674	81.8997
11	10.7645	3.5046	78.3951
12	10.2649	4.0042	74.3909
13	9.6942	4.5749	69.8160
14	9.0420	5.2271	64.5889
15	8.2970	5.9721	58.6168
16	7.4457	6.8234	51.7934
17	6.4730	7.7961	43.9973
18	5.3617	8.9074	35.0899
19	4.0920	10.1770	24.9129
20	2.6414	11.6277	13.2852
21	.9839	13.2852	0.0000

YEARS 22	MO PAYT 1.1795	AN CONST 14.16	
#	INT	PRIN	BALANCE
1	13.3519	.8027	99.1973
2	13.2375	.9171	98.2802
3	13.1067	1.0478	97.2324
4	12.9574	1.1972	96.0353
5	12.7867	1.3678	94.6675
6	12.5918	1.5628	93.1047
7	12.3690	1.7856	91.3191
8	12.1145	2.0401	89.2790
9	11.8237	2.3309	86.9482
10	11.4914	2.6631	84.2850
11	11.1118	3.0427	81.2423
12	10.6781	3.4765	77.7658
13	10.1825	3.9720	73.7938
14	9.6164	4.5382	69.2556
15	8.9695	5.1851	64.0705
16	8.2304	5.9242	58.1463
17	7.3859	6.7687	51.3776
18	6.4211	7.7335	43.6441
19	5.3187	8.8359	34.8083
20	4.0592	10.0954	24.7129
21	2.6202	11.5344	13.1785
22	.9760	13.1785	0.0000

YEARS 23	MO PAYT 1.1713	AN CONST 14.06	
#	INT	PRIN	BALANCE
1	13.3582	.6976	99.3024
2	13.2587	.7971	98.5053
3	13.1451	.9107	97.5946
4	13.0153	1.0405	96.5541
5	12.8670	1.1888	95.3653
6	12.6975	1.3583	94.0070
7	12.5039	1.5519	92.4551
8	12.2827	1.7731	90.6820
9	12.0300	2.0258	88.6562
10	11.7412	2.3146	86.3416
11	11.4113	2.6446	83.6970
12	11.0343	3.0215	80.6755
13	10.6036	3.4522	77.2233
14	10.1115	3.9443	73.2790
15	9.5493	4.5065	68.7725
16	8.9069	5.1489	63.6235
17	8.1729	5.8829	57.7407
18	7.3344	6.7214	51.0192
19	6.3763	7.6795	43.3397
20	5.2816	8.7742	34.5655
21	4.0309	10.0249	24.5405
22	2.6019	11.4539	13.0866
23	.9692	13.0866	0.0000

YEARS 24	MO PAYT 1.1642	AN CONST 13.98	
#	INT	PRIN	BALANCE
1	13.3636	.6069	99.3931
2	13.2771	.6934	98.6997
3	13.1783	.7922	97.9075
4	13.0653	.9052	97.0023
5	12.9363	1.0342	95.9682
6	12.7889	1.1816	94.7866
7	12.6205	1.3500	93.4365
8	12.4280	1.5425	91.8941
9	12.2082	1.7623	90.1317
10	11.9570	2.0135	88.1182
11	11.6699	2.3006	85.8176
12	11.3420	2.6285	83.1891
13	10.9673	3.0032	80.1859
14	10.5392	3.4313	76.7547
15	10.0501	3.9204	72.8343
16	9.4913	4.4792	68.3551
17	8.8528	5.1177	63.2374
18	8.1233	5.8472	57.3902
19	7.2899	6.6807	50.7096
20	6.3376	7.6329	43.0767
21	5.2495	8.7210	34.3557
22	4.0064	9.9641	24.3916
23	2.5861	11.3844	13.0072
24	.9633	13.0072	0.0000

YEARS 25	MO PAYT 1.1581	AN CONST 13.90	
#	INT	PRIN	BALANCE
1	13.3683	.5284	99.4716
2	13.2930	.6037	98.8680
3	13.2070	.6897	98.1782
4	13.1086	.7880	97.3902
5	12.9963	.9004	96.4898
6	12.8680	1.0287	95.4611
7	12.7213	1.1754	94.2857
8	12.5538	1.3429	92.9428
9	12.3624	1.5343	91.4085
10	12.1437	1.7530	89.6555
11	11.8938	2.0029	87.6526
12	11.6083	2.2884	85.3642
13	11.2821	2.6146	82.7496
14	10.9094	2.9873	79.7622
15	10.4836	3.4131	76.3491
16	9.9970	3.8997	72.4495
17	9.4412	4.4555	67.9939
18	8.8061	5.0906	62.9033
19	8.0804	5.8163	57.0870
20	7.2513	6.6454	50.4417
21	6.3041	7.5926	42.8490
22	5.2218	8.6749	34.1742
23	3.9853	9.9114	24.2627
24	2.5724	11.3243	12.9385
25	.9582	12.9385	0.0000

YEARS 26	MO PAYT 1.1527	AN CONST 13.84	
#	INT	PRIN	BALANCE
1	13.3724	.4603	99.5397
2	13.3068	.5259	99.0138
3	13.2318	.6009	98.4129
4	13.1462	.6866	97.7263
5	13.0483	.7844	96.9419
6	12.9365	.8962	96.0457
7	12.8087	1.0240	95.0217
8	12.6628	1.1699	93.8517
9	12.4960	1.3367	92.5150
10	12.3055	1.5273	90.9877
11	12.0878	1.7450	89.2428
12	11.8390	1.9937	87.2491
13	11.5548	2.2779	84.9712
14	11.2301	2.6026	82.3686
15	10.8592	2.9736	79.3951
16	10.4353	3.3974	75.9977
17	9.9510	3.8817	72.1160
18	9.3977	4.4350	67.6809
19	8.7655	5.0672	62.6137
20	8.0432	5.7895	56.8242
21	7.2180	6.6148	50.2095
22	6.2751	7.5577	42.6518
23	5.1978	8.6350	34.0169
24	3.9669	9.8658	24.1510
25	2.5606	11.2721	12.8789
26	.9538	12.8789	0.0000

YEARS 27	MO PAYT 1.1481	AN CONST 13.78	
#	INT	PRIN	BALANCE
1	13.3759	.4013	99.5987
2	13.3187	.4585	99.1403
3	13.2534	.5238	98.6164
4	13.1787	.5985	98.0180
5	13.0934	.6838	97.3342
6	12.9959	.7813	96.5529
7	12.8846	.8926	95.6603
8	12.7573	1.0199	94.6404
9	12.6120	1.1653	93.4751
10	12.4459	1.3314	92.1438
11	12.2561	1.5211	90.6226
12	12.0393	1.7380	88.8847
13	11.7915	1.9857	86.8990
14	11.5085	2.2687	84.6303
15	11.1851	2.5921	82.0381
16	10.8156	2.9616	79.0765
17	10.3934	3.3838	75.6927
18	9.9111	3.8661	71.8266
19	9.3600	4.4172	67.4094
20	8.7303	5.0469	62.3625
21	8.0109	5.7663	56.5962
22	7.1890	6.5882	50.0080
23	6.2499	7.5273	42.4807
24	5.1769	8.6003	33.8804
25	3.9510	9.8262	24.0541
26	2.5503	11.2269	12.8272
27	.9500	12.8272	0.0000

YEARS 28	MO PAYT 1.1441	AN CONST 13.73	
#	INT	PRIN	BALANCE
1	13.3790	.3500	99.6500
2	13.3291	.3999	99.2502
3	13.2721	.4569	98.7933
4	13.2070	.5220	98.2713
5	13.1326	.5964	97.6749
6	13.0476	.6814	96.9935
7	12.9505	.7785	96.2150
8	12.8395	.8895	95.3255
9	12.7127	1.0163	94.3092
10	12.5678	1.1612	93.1480
11	12.4023	1.3267	91.8213
12	12.2132	1.5158	90.3055
13	11.9971	1.7319	88.5736
14	11.7503	1.9787	86.5949
15	11.4682	2.2608	84.3341
16	11.1459	2.5831	81.7510
17	10.7777	2.9513	78.7997
18	10.3571	3.3719	75.4278
19	9.8764	3.8526	71.5752
20	9.3272	4.4018	67.1734
21	8.6998	5.0292	62.1442
22	7.9829	5.7461	56.3981
23	7.1638	6.5652	49.8330
24	6.2280	7.5010	42.3320
25	5.1588	8.5702	33.7618
26	3.9372	9.7918	23.9699
27	2.5414	11.1876	12.7823
28	.9467	12.7823	0.0000

YEARS 29	MO PAYT 1.1406	AN CONST 13.69	
#	INT	PRIN	BALANCE
1	13.3817	.3054	99.6946
2	13.3382	.3489	99.3457
3	13.2884	.3986	98.9471
4	13.2316	.4555	98.4916
5	13.1667	.5204	97.9712
6	13.0925	.5946	97.3766
7	13.0078	.6793	96.6973
8	12.9109	.7762	95.9212
9	12.8003	.8868	95.0344
10	12.6739	1.0132	94.0212
11	12.5294	1.1576	92.8635
12	12.3644	1.3226	91.5409
13	12.1759	1.5112	90.0297
14	11.9605	1.7266	88.3031
15	11.7144	1.9727	86.3304
16	11.4332	2.2539	84.0765
17	11.1119	2.5752	81.5014
18	10.7448	2.9423	78.5591
19	10.3254	3.3617	75.1975
20	9.8462	3.8408	71.3566
21	9.2988	4.3883	66.9683
22	8.6732	5.0138	61.9545
23	7.9585	5.7285	56.2259
24	7.1420	6.5451	49.6808
25	6.2090	7.4781	42.2027
26	5.1430	8.5440	33.6587
27	3.9251	9.7619	23.8967
28	2.5336	11.1534	12.7433
29	.9438	12.7433	0.0000

YEARS 30	MO PAYT 1.1375	AN CONST 13.66	
#	INT	PRIN	BALANCE
1	13.3840	.2666	99.7334
2	13.3460	.3046	99.4289
3	13.3026	.3480	99.0809
4	13.2530	.3976	98.6833
5	13.1963	.4543	98.2291
6	13.1316	.5190	97.7100
7	13.0576	.5930	97.1171
8	12.9731	.6775	96.4395
9	12.8765	.7741	95.6655
10	12.7662	.8844	94.7810
11	12.6401	1.0105	93.7705
12	12.4960	1.1545	92.6160
13	12.3315	1.3191	91.2969
14	12.1434	1.5071	89.7897
15	11.9286	1.7220	88.0677
16	11.6831	1.9674	86.1003
17	11.4027	2.2479	83.8524
18	11.0823	2.5683	81.2841
19	10.7162	2.9344	78.3497
20	10.2979	3.3527	74.9970
21	9.8200	3.8306	71.1664
22	9.2740	4.3766	66.7898
23	8.6501	5.0005	61.7893
24	7.9373	5.7133	56.0760
25	7.1229	6.5277	49.5484
26	6.1924	7.4581	42.0902
27	5.1293	8.5213	33.5690
28	3.9147	9.7359	23.8330
29	2.5269	11.1237	12.7093
30	.9413	12.7093	0.0000

#	YEARS 2 MO PAYT 4.7777 AN CONST 57.34		
#	INT	PRIN	BALANCE
1	10.6835	46.6489	53.3511
2	3.9813	53.3511	0.0000

#	YEARS 3 MO PAYT 3.3935 AN CONST 40.73		
#	INT	PRIN	BALANCE
1	11.7508	28.9715	71.0285
2	7.5884	33.1340	37.8945
3	2.8279	37.8945	0.0000

#	YEARS 4 MO PAYT 2.7076 AN CONST 32.50		
#	INT	PRIN	BALANCE
1	12.2797	20.2119	79.7881
2	9.3758	23.1158	56.6723
3	6.0546	26.4370	30.2353
4	2.2563	30.2353	0.0000

#	YEARS 5 MO PAYT 2.3010 AN CONST 27.62		
#	INT	PRIN	BALANCE
1	12.5932	15.0186	84.9814
2	10.4355	17.1764	67.8051
3	7.9677	19.6442	48.1609
4	5.1453	22.4665	25.6944
5	1.9174	25.6944	0.0000

#	YEARS 6 MO PAYT 2.0339 AN CONST 24.41		
#	INT	PRIN	BALANCE
1	12.7992	11.6076	88.3924
2	11.1315	13.2753	75.1172
3	9.2242	15.1826	59.9346
4	7.0428	17.3640	42.5706
5	4.5480	19.8587	22.7119
6	1.6949	22.7119	0.0000

#	YEARS 7 MO PAYT 1.8465 AN CONST 22.16		
#	INT	PRIN	BALANCE
1	12.9437	9.2142	90.7858
2	11.6198	10.5380	80.2478
3	10.1058	12.0521	68.1957
4	8.3742	13.7836	54.4121
5	6.3939	15.7640	38.6481
6	4.1290	18.0289	20.6192
7	1.5387	20.6192	0.0000

#	YEARS 8 MO PAYT 1.7088 AN CONST 20.51		
#	INT	PRIN	BALANCE
1	13.0498	7.4559	92.5441
2	11.9786	8.5272	84.0169
3	10.7535	9.7523	74.2646
4	9.3523	11.1535	63.1111
5	7.7498	12.7559	50.3551
6	5.9171	14.5886	35.7665
7	3.8211	16.6847	19.0818
8	1.4240	19.0818	0.0000

#	YEARS 9 MO PAYT 1.6042 AN CONST 19.26		
#	INT	PRIN	BALANCE
1	13.1305	6.1203	93.8797
2	12.2512	6.9996	86.8801
3	11.2455	8.0053	78.8748
4	10.0953	9.1554	69.7193
5	8.7799	10.4708	59.2485
6	7.2755	11.9752	47.2733

#	INT	PRIN	BALANCE
7	5.5550	13.6958	33.5775
8	3.5873	15.6635	17.9140
9	1.3368	17.9140	0.0000

#	YEARS 10 MO PAYT 1.5227 AN CONST 18.28		
#	INT	PRIN	BALANCE
1	13.1933	5.0796	94.9204
2	12.4635	5.8094	89.1110
3	11.6288	6.6441	82.4669
4	10.6743	7.5987	74.8683
5	9.5825	8.6904	66.1779
6	8.3339	9.9390	56.2389
7	6.9060	11.3669	44.8720
8	5.2728	13.0001	31.8719
9	3.4050	14.8679	17.0040
10	1.2689	17.0040	0.0000

#	YEARS 11 MO PAYT 1.4580 AN CONST 17.50		
#	INT	PRIN	BALANCE
1	13.2432	4.2526	95.7474
2	12.6323	4.8636	90.8838
3	11.9335	5.5624	85.3215
4	11.1343	6.3615	78.9599
5	10.2203	7.2755	71.6844
6	9.1750	8.3208	63.3636
7	7.9795	9.5163	53.8473
8	6.6123	10.8836	42.9637
9	5.0486	12.4472	30.5165
10	3.2602	14.2356	16.2809
11	1.2150	16.2809	0.0000

#	YEARS 12 MO PAYT 1.4057 AN CONST 16.87		
#	INT	PRIN	BALANCE
1	13.2835	3.5851	96.4149
2	12.7685	4.1001	92.3148
3	12.1794	4.6892	87.6256
4	11.5057	5.3629	82.2626
5	10.7351	6.1335	76.1292
6	9.8539	7.0147	69.1145
7	8.8461	8.0225	61.0920
8	7.6935	9.1751	51.9168
9	6.3752	10.4934	41.4235
10	4.8676	12.0010	29.4225
11	3.1434	13.7252	15.6972
12	1.1714	15.6972	0.0000

#	YEARS 13 MO PAYT 1.3630 AN CONST 16.36		
#	INT	PRIN	BALANCE
1	13.3165	3.0394	96.9606
2	12.8798	3.4761	93.4845
3	12.3804	3.9755	89.5090
4	11.8092	4.5467	84.9623
5	11.1560	5.1999	79.7623
6	10.4089	5.9470	73.8153
7	9.5544	6.8015	67.0138
8	8.5772	7.7787	59.2352
9	7.4596	8.8963	50.3389
10	6.1815	10.1744	40.1644
11	4.7197	11.6362	28.5282
12	3.0478	13.3081	15.2201
13	1.1358	15.2201	0.0000

#	YEARS 14 MO PAYT 1.3277 AN CONST 15.94		
#	INT	PRIN	BALANCE
1	13.3437	2.5888	97.4112
2	12.9718	2.9607	94.4505
3	12.5464	3.3861	91.0644

#	INT	PRIN	BALANCE
4	12.0599	3.8726	87.1918
5	11.5035	4.4290	82.7628
6	10.8672	5.0653	77.6975
7	10.1394	5.7931	71.9044
8	9.3071	6.6254	65.2790
9	8.3552	7.5773	57.7017
10	7.2665	8.6660	49.0357
11	6.0214	9.9110	39.1247
12	4.5975	11.3350	27.7897
13	2.9689	12.9636	14.8261
14	1.1064	14.8261	0.0000

#	YEARS 15 MO PAYT 1.2983 AN CONST 15.58		
#	INT	PRIN	BALANCE
1	13.3664	2.2135	97.7865
2	13.0483	2.5315	95.2551
3	12.6846	2.8952	92.3599
4	12.2687	3.3112	89.0487
5	11.7929	3.7869	85.2618
6	11.2489	4.3310	80.9309
7	10.6266	4.9532	75.9777
8	9.9150	5.6649	70.3128
9	9.1011	6.4788	63.8341
10	8.1702	7.4096	56.4245
11	7.1057	8.4742	47.9503
12	5.8882	9.6917	38.2587
13	4.4957	11.0841	27.1745
14	2.9032	12.6766	14.4979
15	1.0819	14.4979	0.0000

#	YEARS 16 MO PAYT 1.2737 AN CONST 15.29		
#	INT	PRIN	BALANCE
1	13.3854	1.8986	98.1014
2	13.1126	2.1714	95.9299
3	12.8006	2.4834	93.4465
4	12.4438	2.8402	90.6063
5	12.0357	3.2483	87.3580
6	11.5690	3.7150	83.6430
7	11.0353	4.2487	79.3943
8	10.4249	4.8592	74.5351
9	9.7267	5.5573	68.9778
10	8.9283	6.3557	62.6221
11	8.0151	7.2689	55.3532
12	6.9708	8.3133	47.0399
13	5.7764	9.5077	37.5323
14	4.4104	10.8737	26.6586
15	2.8481	12.4359	14.2227
16	1.0614	14.2227	0.0000

#	YEARS 17 MO PAYT 1.2529 AN CONST 15.04		
#	INT	PRIN	BALANCE
1	13.4014	1.6330	98.3670
2	13.1668	1.8676	96.4993
3	12.8984	2.1360	94.3634
4	12.5916	2.4429	91.9205
5	12.2406	2.7938	89.1267
6	11.8392	3.1952	85.9314
7	11.3810	3.6534	82.2771
8	10.8551	4.1793	78.0978
9	10.2546	4.7798	73.3179
10	9.5679	5.4665	67.8514
11	8.7825	6.2520	61.5994
12	7.8842	7.1502	54.4492
13	6.8569	8.1775	46.2717
14	5.6820	9.3524	36.9194
15	4.3383	10.6961	26.2233
16	2.8016	12.2329	13.9904
17	1.0440	13.9904	0.0000

#	YEARS 18 MO PAYT 1.2352 AN CONST 14.83		
#	INT	PRIN	BALANCE
1	13.4150	1.4078	98.5922
2	13.2127	1.6100	96.9822
3	12.9814	1.8414	95.1408
4	12.7169	2.1059	93.0349
5	12.4143	2.4085	90.6265
6	12.0683	2.7545	87.8720
7	11.6725	3.1503	84.7217
8	11.2199	3.6029	81.1188
9	10.7023	4.1205	76.9983
10	10.1103	4.7125	72.2858
11	9.4332	5.3896	66.8962
12	8.6588	6.1639	60.7323
13	7.7732	7.0495	53.6827
14	6.7604	8.0624	45.6203
15	5.6020	9.2207	36.3996
16	4.2773	10.5455	25.8541
17	2.7621	12.0606	13.7934
18	1.0293	13.7934	0.0000

#	YEARS 19 MO PAYT 1.2202 AN CONST 14.65		
#	INT	PRIN	BALANCE
1	13.4266	1.2160	98.7840
2	13.2519	1.3907	97.3934
3	13.0521	1.5905	95.8029
4	12.8236	1.8190	93.9840
5	12.5622	2.0803	91.9037
6	12.2634	2.3792	89.5245
7	11.9215	2.7210	86.8035
8	11.5306	3.1120	83.6915
9	11.0835	3.5591	80.1325
10	10.5721	4.0704	76.0621
11	9.9873	4.6552	71.4068
12	9.3185	5.3241	66.0828
13	8.5535	6.0890	59.9938
14	7.6787	6.9638	53.0300
15	6.6782	7.9643	45.0656
16	5.5339	9.1086	35.9570
17	4.2252	10.4173	25.5397
18	2.7285	11.9140	13.6257
19	1.0168	13.6257	0.0000

#	YEARS 20 MO PAYT 1.2074 AN CONST 14.49		
#	INT	PRIN	BALANCE
1	13.4365	1.0520	98.9480
2	13.2853	1.2032	97.7448
3	13.1125	1.3760	96.3688
4	12.9148	1.5737	94.7951
5	12.6887	1.7998	92.9953
6	12.4301	2.0584	90.9368
7	12.1343	2.3542	88.5827
8	11.7961	2.6924	85.8903
9	11.4093	3.0792	82.8111
10	10.9669	3.5216	79.2895
11	10.4609	4.0276	75.2619
12	9.8822	4.6062	70.6556
13	9.2204	5.2680	65.3876
14	8.4636	6.0249	59.3626
15	7.5979	6.8906	52.4721
16	6.6079	7.8806	44.5915
17	5.4757	9.0128	35.5787
18	4.1808	10.3077	25.2710
19	2.6998	11.7887	13.4824
20	1.0061	13.4824	0.0000

#	YEARS 21 MO PAYT 1.1964 AN CONST 14.36		
#	INT	PRIN	BALANCE
1	13.4450	.9115	99.0885
2	13.3140	1.0424	98.0461
3	13.1642	1.1922	96.8539

#	INT	PRIN	BALANCE
4	12.9930	1.3635	95.4904
5	12.7971	1.5594	93.9311
6	12.5730	1.7834	92.1476
7	12.3168	2.0397	90.1080
8	12.0237	2.3327	87.7753
9	11.6886	2.6678	85.1074
10	11.3053	3.0511	82.0563
11	10.8669	3.4895	78.5668
12	10.3656	3.9909	74.5759
13	9.7922	4.5643	70.0116
14	9.1364	5.2200	64.7916
15	8.3864	5.9700	58.8216
16	7.5287	6.8278	51.9938
17	6.5477	7.8087	44.1851
18	5.4258	8.9306	35.2544
19	4.1427	10.2137	25.0407
20	2.6752	11.6812	13.3595
21	.9969	13.3595	0.0000

YEARS 22 — MO PAYT 1.1869 — AN CONST 14.25

#	INT	PRIN	BALANCE
1	13.4523	.7907	99.2093
2	13.3387	.9043	98.3051
3	13.2087	1.0342	97.2709
4	13.0602	1.1828	96.0881
5	12.8902	1.3527	94.7354
6	12.6959	1.5470	93.1884
7	12.4736	1.7693	91.4191
8	12.2194	2.0235	89.3955
9	11.9287	2.3143	87.0813
10	11.5962	2.6468	84.4345
11	11.2159	3.0270	81.4075
12	10.7810	3.4619	77.9456
13	10.2836	3.9593	73.9862
14	9.7148	4.5282	69.4581
15	9.0642	5.1788	64.2793
16	8.3201	5.9228	58.3565
17	7.4692	6.7738	51.5827
18	6.4959	7.7470	43.8357
19	5.3829	8.8600	34.9757
20	4.1099	10.1330	24.8427
21	2.6541	11.5888	13.2539
22	.9891	13.2539	0.0000

YEARS 23 — MO PAYT 1.1788 — AN CONST 14.15

#	INT	PRIN	BALANCE
1	13.4585	.6866	99.3134
2	13.3599	.7852	98.5282
3	13.2471	.8981	97.6301
4	13.1181	1.0271	96.6030
5	12.9705	1.1746	95.4284
6	12.8017	1.3434	94.0850
7	12.6087	1.5364	92.5486
8	12.3880	1.7572	90.7914
9	12.1355	2.0096	88.7818
10	11.8468	2.2984	86.4834
11	11.5166	2.6286	83.8548
12	11.1389	3.0062	80.8486
13	10.7070	3.4382	77.4104
14	10.2130	3.9321	73.4783
15	9.6481	4.4971	68.9812
16	9.0019	5.1432	63.8380
17	8.2630	5.8821	57.9558
18	7.4179	6.7273	51.2286
19	6.4513	7.6938	43.5348
20	5.3459	8.7992	34.7356
21	4.0817	10.0634	24.6721
22	2.6359	11.5093	13.1629
23	.9823	13.1629	0.0000

YEARS 24 — MO PAYT 1.1717 — AN CONST 14.07

#	INT	PRIN	BALANCE
1	13.4640	.5968	99.4032
2	13.3782	.6825	98.7208
3	13.2802	.7805	97.9402
4	13.1680	.8927	97.0475
5	13.0398	1.0210	96.0266
6	12.8931	1.1676	94.8589
7	12.7253	1.3354	93.5235
8	12.5335	1.5273	91.9963
9	12.3140	1.7467	90.2496
10	12.0631	1.9976	88.2519
11	11.7761	2.2846	85.9673
12	11.4478	2.6129	83.3544
13	11.0724	2.9883	80.3661
14	10.6431	3.4176	76.9485
15	10.1521	3.9087	73.0398
16	9.5905	4.4702	68.5695
17	8.9482	5.1125	63.4570
18	8.2137	5.8470	57.6100
19	7.3736	6.6871	50.9229
20	6.4128	7.6479	43.2750
21	5.3140	8.7467	34.5283
22	4.0574	10.0034	24.5249
23	2.6201	11.4406	13.0843
24	.9764	13.0843	0.0000

YEARS 25 — MO PAYT 1.1656 — AN CONST 13.99

#	INT	PRIN	BALANCE
1	13.4687	.5191	99.4809
2	13.3941	.5937	98.8873
3	13.3088	.6789	98.2083
4	13.2112	.7765	97.4318
5	13.0997	.8881	96.5438
6	12.9721	1.0157	95.5281
7	12.8262	1.1616	94.3665
8	12.6593	1.3285	93.0381
9	12.4684	1.5193	91.5187
10	12.2501	1.7376	89.7811
11	12.0005	1.9873	87.7938
12	11.7149	2.2728	85.5211
13	11.3884	2.5993	82.9217
14	11.0149	2.9728	79.9489
15	10.5878	3.3999	76.5490
16	10.0994	3.8884	72.6606
17	9.5407	4.4470	68.2136
18	8.9018	5.0860	63.1276
19	8.1710	5.8167	57.3109
20	7.3353	6.6524	50.6585
21	6.3796	7.6082	43.0503
22	5.2864	8.7013	34.3491
23	4.0363	9.9514	24.3976
24	2.6065	11.3812	13.0164
25	.9713	13.0164	0.0000

YEARS 26 — MO PAYT 1.1604 — AN CONST 13.93

#	INT	PRIN	BALANCE
1	13.4727	.4518	99.5482
2	13.4078	.5167	99.0314
3	13.3336	.5910	98.4405
4	13.2487	.6759	97.7646
5	13.1516	.7730	96.9916
6	13.0405	.8840	96.1076
7	12.9135	1.0111	95.0965
8	12.7682	1.1563	93.9402
9	12.6021	1.3225	92.6177
10	12.4121	1.5125	91.1052
11	12.1948	1.7298	89.3755
12	11.9462	1.9783	87.3972
13	11.6620	2.2625	85.1347
14	11.3370	2.5876	82.5471
15	10.9652	2.9594	79.5877
16	10.5400	3.3845	76.2032
17	10.0537	3.8708	72.3324
18	9.4976	4.4270	67.9054
19	8.8615	5.0630	62.8424
20	8.1341	5.7904	57.0520
21	7.3022	6.6223	50.4296
22	6.3507	7.5738	42.8558
23	5.2626	8.6620	34.1939
24	4.0181	9.9065	24.2874
25	2.5948	11.3298	12.9576
26	.9670	12.9576	0.0000

YEARS 27 — MO PAYT 1.1558 — AN CONST 13.87

#	INT	PRIN	BALANCE
1	13.4762	.3935	99.6065
2	13.4197	.4500	99.1565
3	13.3550	.5147	98.6418
4	13.2811	.5886	98.0531
5	13.1965	.6732	97.3799
6	13.0998	.7699	96.6099
7	12.9892	.8806	95.7294
8	12.8627	1.0071	94.7223
9	12.7180	1.1518	93.5705
10	12.5525	1.3173	92.2532
11	12.3632	1.5065	90.7467
12	12.1468	1.7230	89.0238
13	11.8992	1.9705	87.0533
14	11.6161	2.2536	84.7996
15	11.2923	2.5774	82.2222
16	10.9220	2.9477	79.2745
17	10.4985	3.3712	75.9033
18	10.0142	3.8556	72.0477
19	9.4602	4.4095	67.6382
20	8.8267	5.0431	62.5951
21	8.1021	5.7676	56.8275
22	7.2735	6.5963	50.2312
23	6.3257	7.5440	42.6872
24	5.2419	8.6279	34.0593
25	4.0022	9.8675	24.1918
26	2.5845	11.2852	12.9066
27	.9631	12.9066	0.0000

YEARS 28 — MO PAYT 1.1518 — AN CONST 13.83

#	INT	PRIN	BALANCE
1	13.4793	.3429	99.6571
2	13.4300	.3922	99.2650
3	13.3737	.4485	98.8165
4	13.3093	.5129	98.3035
5	13.2356	.5866	97.7169
6	13.1513	.6709	97.0460
7	13.0549	.7673	96.2787
8	12.9446	.8775	95.4011
9	12.8186	1.0036	94.3975
10	12.6744	1.1478	93.2497
11	12.5094	1.3127	91.9369
12	12.3208	1.5013	90.4356
13	12.1051	1.7171	88.7185
14	11.8584	1.9638	86.7548
15	11.5763	2.2459	84.5089
16	11.2536	2.5686	81.9403
17	10.8846	2.9376	79.0027
18	10.4625	3.3597	75.6430
19	9.9798	3.8424	71.8007
20	9.4278	4.3944	67.4063
21	8.7964	5.0258	62.3805
22	8.0743	5.7479	56.6326
23	7.2485	6.5737	50.0590
24	6.3040	7.5181	42.5408
25	5.2239	8.5983	33.9425
26	3.9885	9.8337	24.1089
27	2.5757	11.2465	12.8623
28	.9598	12.8623	0.0000

YEARS 29 — MO PAYT 1.1484 — AN CONST 13.79

#	INT	PRIN	BALANCE
1	13.4820	.2989	99.7011
2	13.4390	.3419	99.3592
3	13.3899	.3910	98.9682
4	13.3337	.4472	98.5211
5	13.2695	.5114	98.0097
6	13.1960	.5849	97.4248
7	13.1120	.6689	96.7559
8	13.0159	.7650	95.9909
9	12.9059	.8749	95.1160
10	12.7802	1.0006	94.1153
11	12.6365	1.1444	92.9709
12	12.4721	1.3088	91.6621
13	12.2840	1.4969	90.1652
14	12.0689	1.7119	88.4533
15	11.8230	1.9579	86.4954
16	11.5417	2.2392	84.2563
17	11.2200	2.5609	81.6954
18	10.8520	2.9288	78.7665
19	10.4312	3.3496	75.4169
20	9.9500	3.8309	71.5861
21	9.3996	4.3813	67.2048
22	8.7701	5.0108	62.1940
23	8.0502	5.7307	56.4633
24	7.2268	6.5540	49.9093
25	6.2852	7.4957	42.4137
26	5.2083	8.5726	33.8411
27	3.9766	9.8043	24.0368
28	2.5680	11.2129	12.8239
29	.9570	12.8239	0.0000

YEARS 30 — MO PAYT 1.1454 — AN CONST 13.75

#	INT	PRIN	BALANCE
1	13.4843	.2607	99.7393
2	13.4468	.2981	99.4412
3	13.4040	.3410	99.1002
4	13.3550	.3900	98.7102
5	13.2990	.4460	98.2642
6	13.2349	.5101	97.7542
7	13.1616	.5834	97.1708
8	13.0778	.6672	96.5037
9	12.9819	.7630	95.7406
10	12.8723	.8726	94.8680
11	12.7469	.9980	93.8700
12	12.6035	1.1414	92.7286
13	12.4395	1.3054	91.4232
14	12.2520	1.4930	89.9302
15	12.0375	1.7075	88.2227
16	11.7922	1.9528	86.2700
17	11.5116	2.2333	84.0366
18	11.1907	2.5542	81.4824
19	10.8238	2.9212	78.5612
20	10.4041	3.3409	75.2203
21	9.9241	3.8209	71.3994
22	9.3751	4.3699	67.0296
23	8.7473	4.9977	62.0319
24	8.0292	5.7157	56.3162
25	7.2080	6.5369	49.7792
26	6.2688	7.4761	42.3031
27	5.1947	8.5503	33.7528
28	3.9662	9.7787	23.9741
29	2.5613	11.1837	12.7905
30	.9545	12.7905	0.0000

MONTHLY PAYMENT AMORTIZATION SCHEDULE PER $100   13.60 %

YEARS 2 — MO PAYT 4.7824 — AN CONST 57.39

#	INT	PRIN	BALANCE
1	10.7647	46.6243	53.3757
2	4.0132	53.3757	0.0000

YEARS 3 — MO PAYT 3.3984 — AN CONST 40.79

#	INT	PRIN	BALANCE
1	11.8401	28.9403	71.0597
2	7.6494	33.1311	37.9286
3	2.8518	37.9286	0.0000

YEARS 4 — MO PAYT 2.7126 — AN CONST 32.56

#	INT	PRIN	BALANCE
1	12.3729	20.1786	79.8214
2	9.4509	23.1006	56.7208
3	6.1058	26.4457	30.2752
4	2.2763	30.2752	0.0000

YEARS 5 — MO PAYT 2.3061 — AN CONST 27.68

#	INT	PRIN	BALANCE
1	12.6887	14.9849	85.0151
2	10.5148	17.1548	67.8602
3	8.0347	19.6390	48.2213
4	5.1909	22.4828	25.7384
5	1.9352	25.7384	0.0000

YEARS 6 — MO PAYT 2.0392 — AN CONST 24.48

#	INT	PRIN	BALANCE
1	12.8961	11.5745	88.4255
2	11.2201	13.2505	75.1750
3	9.3013	15.1693	60.0058
4	7.1047	17.3659	42.6399
5	4.5901	19.8805	22.7594
6	1.7112	22.7594	0.0000

YEARS 7 — MO PAYT 1.8520 — AN CONST 22.23

#	INT	PRIN	BALANCE
1	13.0416	9.1821	90.8179
2	11.7120	10.5117	80.3062
3	10.1899	12.0338	68.2724
4	8.4473	13.7764	54.4960
5	6.4524	15.7713	38.7247
6	4.1686	18.0551	20.6696
7	1.5541	20.6696	0.0000

YEARS 8 — MO PAYT 1.7145 — AN CONST 20.58

#	INT	PRIN	BALANCE
1	13.1485	7.4251	92.5749
2	12.0733	8.5003	84.0746
3	10.8424	9.7312	74.3434
4	9.4332	11.1403	63.2031
5	7.8201	12.7535	50.4496
6	5.9733	14.6003	35.8493
7	3.8591	16.7145	19.1348
8	1.4387	19.1348	0.0000

YEARS 9 — MO PAYT 1.6100 — AN CONST 19.33

#	INT	PRIN	BALANCE
1	13.2296	6.0909	93.9091
2	12.3476	6.9728	86.9363
3	11.3379	7.9826	78.9538
4	10.1820	9.1385	69.8153
5	8.8587	10.4618	59.3535
6	7.3438	11.9767	47.3768
7	5.6095	13.7110	33.6658
8	3.6240	15.6964	17.9694
9	1.3511	17.9694	0.0000

YEARS 10 — MO PAYT 1.5287 — AN CONST 18.35

#	INT	PRIN	BALANCE
1	13.2928	5.0517	94.9483
2	12.5613	5.7832	89.1652
3	11.7239	6.6206	82.5446
4	10.7652	7.5793	74.9653
5	9.6676	8.6768	66.2885
6	8.4112	9.9333	56.3552
7	6.9728	11.3717	44.9835
8	5.3261	13.0184	31.9651
9	3.4409	14.9035	17.0616
10	1.2828	17.0616	0.0000

YEARS 11 — MO PAYT 1.4641 — AN CONST 17.57

#	INT	PRIN	BALANCE
1	13.3430	4.2262	95.7738
2	12.7310	4.8382	90.9357
3	12.0304	5.5388	85.3969
4	11.2284	6.3408	79.0561
5	10.3102	7.2590	71.7971
6	9.2591	8.3101	63.4870
7	8.0557	9.5135	53.9735
8	6.6781	10.8911	43.0824
9	5.1010	12.4682	30.6142
10	3.2955	14.2737	16.3406
11	1.2286	16.3406	0.0000

YEARS 12 — MO PAYT 1.4120 — AN CONST 16.95

#	INT	PRIN	BALANCE
1	13.3835	3.5602	96.4398
2	12.8680	4.0757	92.3641
3	12.2778	4.6659	87.6982
4	11.6021	5.3416	82.3566
5	10.8286	6.1151	76.2416
6	9.9431	7.0006	69.2410
7	8.9294	8.0143	61.2267
8	7.7689	9.1748	52.0519
9	6.4403	10.5033	41.5486
10	4.9194	12.0243	29.5243
11	3.1782	13.7655	15.7588
12	1.1849	15.7588	0.0000

YEARS 13 — MO PAYT 1.3694 — AN CONST 16.44

#	INT	PRIN	BALANCE
1	13.4166	3.0161	96.9839
2	12.9798	3.4528	93.5311
3	12.4799	3.9528	89.5783
4	11.9075	4.5252	85.0531
5	11.2522	5.1805	79.8727
6	10.5020	5.9306	73.9421
7	9.6432	6.7894	67.1526
8	8.6601	7.7726	59.3801
9	7.5346	8.8981	50.4820
10	6.2461	10.1866	40.2955
11	4.7710	11.6616	28.6338
12	3.0823	13.3503	15.2835
13	1.1491	15.2835	0.0000

YEARS 14 — MO PAYT 1.3342 — AN CONST 16.02

#	INT	PRIN	BALANCE
1	13.4439	2.5669	97.4331
2	13.0722	2.9386	94.4944
3	12.6467	3.3642	91.1302
4	12.1595	3.8513	87.2789
5	11.6018	4.4090	82.8699
6	10.9634	5.0475	77.8224
7	10.2325	5.7784	72.0440
8	9.3957	6.6151	65.4289
9	8.4378	7.5730	57.8558
10	7.3412	8.6697	49.1862
11	6.0858	9.9251	39.2611
12	4.6485	11.3623	27.8988
13	3.0032	13.0076	14.8912
14	1.1196	14.8912	0.0000

YEARS 15 — MO PAYT 1.3050 — AN CONST 15.66

#	INT	PRIN	BALANCE
1	13.4666	2.1931	97.8069
2	13.1491	2.5106	95.2963
3	12.7855	2.8742	92.4221
4	12.3693	3.2904	89.1317
5	11.8928	3.7669	85.3648
6	11.3474	4.3123	81.0525
7	10.7229	4.9368	76.1157
8	10.0080	5.6517	70.4640
9	9.1897	6.4701	63.9940
10	8.2528	7.4070	56.5870
11	7.1802	8.4795	48.1075
12	5.9523	9.7074	38.4001
13	4.5466	11.1131	27.2870
14	2.9374	12.7223	14.5646
15	1.0951	14.5646	0.0000

YEARS 16 — MO PAYT 1.2804 — AN CONST 15.37

#	INT	PRIN	BALANCE
1	13.4857	1.8797	98.1203
2	13.2135	2.1519	95.9685
3	12.9019	2.4635	93.5050
4	12.5452	2.8202	90.6849
5	12.1368	3.2286	87.4563
6	11.6693	3.6961	83.7602
7	11.1341	4.2313	79.5290
8	10.5214	4.8440	74.6850
9	9.8199	5.5454	69.1395
10	9.0169	6.3484	62.7911
11	8.0976	7.2677	55.5234
12	7.0452	8.3201	47.2032
13	5.8404	9.5249	37.6783
14	4.4611	10.9042	26.7741
15	2.8821	12.4832	14.2909
16	1.0745	14.2909	0.0000

YEARS 17 — MO PAYT 1.2598 — AN CONST 15.12

#	INT	PRIN	BALANCE
1	13.5018	1.6154	98.3846
2	13.2678	1.8493	96.5353
3	13.0001	2.1171	94.4182
4	12.6935	2.4237	91.9946
5	12.3425	2.7746	89.2200
6	11.9408	3.1764	86.0436
7	11.4808	3.6364	82.4072
8	10.9542	4.1629	78.2443
9	10.3514	4.7657	73.4785
10	9.6613	5.4558	68.0227
11	8.8713	6.2459	61.7768
12	7.9668	7.1503	54.6265
13	6.9314	8.1857	46.4407
14	5.7461	9.3711	37.0696
15	4.3891	10.7281	26.3416
16	2.8356	12.2816	14.0600
17	1.0571	14.0600	0.0000

YEARS 18 — MO PAYT 1.2422 — AN CONST 14.91

#	INT	PRIN	BALANCE
1	13.5154	1.3914	98.6086
2	13.3139	1.5929	97.0157
3	13.0832	1.8236	95.1921
4	12.8192	2.0876	93.1045
5	12.5169	2.3899	90.7145
6	12.1708	2.7360	87.9785
7	11.7746	3.1322	84.8463
8	11.3210	3.5858	81.2606
9	10.8018	4.1050	77.1556
10	10.2074	4.6994	72.4561
11	9.5269	5.3799	67.0762
12	8.7478	6.1590	60.9172
13	7.8560	7.0508	53.8664
14	6.8350	8.0718	45.7945
15	5.6661	9.2407	36.5538
16	4.3280	10.5788	25.9750
17	2.7961	12.1107	13.8644
18	1.0424	13.8644	0.0000

YEARS 19 — MO PAYT 1.2273 — AN CONST 14.73

#	INT	PRIN	BALANCE
1	13.5270	1.2008	98.7992
2	13.3531	1.3747	97.4245
3	13.1540	1.5738	95.8507
4	12.9261	1.8017	94.0490
5	12.6652	2.0626	91.9864
6	12.3666	2.3612	89.6252
7	12.0246	2.7032	86.9221
8	11.6332	3.0946	83.8275
9	11.1851	3.5427	80.2848
10	10.6721	4.0557	76.2291
11	10.0848	4.6430	71.5861
12	9.4125	5.3153	66.2707
13	8.6428	6.0850	60.1857
14	7.7616	6.9662	53.2195
15	6.7529	7.9749	45.2446
16	5.5981	9.1297	36.1149
17	4.2760	10.4518	25.6631
18	2.7626	11.9652	13.6979
19	1.0299	13.6979	0.0000

YEARS 20 — MO PAYT 1.2146 — AN CONST 14.58

#	INT	PRIN	BALANCE
1	13.5369	1.0380	98.9620
2	13.3866	1.1884	97.7736
3	13.2145	1.3604	96.4132
4	13.0175	1.5574	94.8557
5	12.7920	1.7830	93.0727
6	12.5338	2.0412	91.0316
7	12.2382	2.3367	88.6949
8	11.8998	2.6751	86.0198
9	11.5125	3.0625	82.9573
10	11.0690	3.5059	79.4514
11	10.5613	4.0136	75.4378
12	9.9801	4.5948	70.8430
13	9.3148	5.2602	65.5828
14	8.5531	6.0219	59.5609
15	7.6811	6.8939	52.6671
16	6.6828	7.8921	44.7750
17	5.5400	9.0350	35.7400
18	4.2316	10.3433	25.3967
19	2.7339	11.8410	13.5557
20	1.0192	13.5557	0.0000

YEARS 21 — MO PAYT 1.2037 — AN CONST 14.45

#	INT	PRIN	BALANCE
1	13.5454	.8986	99.1014
2	13.4152	1.0287	98.0727
3	13.2663	1.1777	96.8950

#	INT	PRIN	BALANCE
4	13.0957	1.3482	95.5468
5	12.9005	1.5434	94.0033
6	12.6770	1.7669	92.2364
7	12.4211	2.0228	90.2136
8	12.1282	2.3157	87.8979
9	11.7929	2.6511	85.2468
10	11.4090	3.0349	82.2119
11	10.9695	3.4744	78.7374
12	10.4664	3.9775	74.7599
13	9.8904	4.5535	70.2064
14	9.2311	5.2129	64.9935
15	8.4762	5.9677	59.0257
16	7.6120	6.8319	52.1938
17	6.6227	7.8212	44.3726
18	5.4902	8.9538	35.4188
19	4.1936	10.2503	25.1685
20	2.7093	11.7346	13.4339
21	1.0101	13.4339	0.0000

YEARS 22 — MO PAYT 1.1943 — AN CONST 14.34

#	INT	PRIN	BALANCE
1	13.5526	.7788	99.2212
2	13.4399	.8916	98.3296
3	13.3108	1.0207	97.3089
4	13.1629	1.1685	96.1404
5	12.9937	1.3377	94.8027
6	12.8000	1.5314	93.2712
7	12.5783	1.7532	91.5180
8	12.3244	2.0071	89.5110
9	12.0338	2.2977	87.2133
10	11.7010	2.6304	84.5829
11	11.3201	3.0113	81.5716
12	10.8841	3.4474	78.1242
13	10.3849	3.9466	74.1776
14	9.8134	4.5180	69.6596
15	9.1592	5.1723	64.4873
16	8.4102	5.9213	58.5660
17	7.5528	6.7787	51.7873
18	6.5712	7.7603	44.0270
19	5.4474	8.8840	35.1430
20	4.1610	10.1705	24.9725
21	2.6882	11.6432	13.3293
22	1.0022	13.3293	0.0000

YEARS 23 — MO PAYT 1.1862 — AN CONST 14.24

#	INT	PRIN	BALANCE
1	13.5589	.6757	99.3243
2	13.4611	.7736	98.5507
3	13.3490	.8856	97.6652
4	13.2208	1.0138	96.6514
5	13.0740	1.1606	95.4907
6	12.9059	1.3287	94.1621
7	12.7135	1.5211	92.6410
8	12.4933	1.7413	90.8996
9	12.2411	1.9935	88.9061
10	11.9525	2.2822	86.6240
11	11.6220	2.6126	84.0113
12	11.2437	2.9910	81.0204
13	10.8105	3.4241	77.5963
14	10.3147	3.9199	73.6764
15	9.7471	4.4875	69.1889
16	9.0973	5.1373	64.0516
17	8.3534	5.8813	58.1703
18	7.5017	6.7329	51.4374
19	6.5268	7.7079	43.7295
20	5.4106	8.8240	34.9055
21	4.1328	10.1018	24.8038
22	2.6700	11.5646	13.2392
23	.9954	13.2392	0.0000

YEARS 24 — MO PAYT 1.1793 — AN CONST 14.16

#	INT	PRIN	BALANCE
1	13.5643	.5868	99.4132
2	13.4793	.6717	98.7415
3	13.3821	.7690	97.9725
4	13.2707	.8804	97.0921
5	13.1432	1.0079	96.0842
6	12.9973	1.1538	94.9304
7	12.8302	1.3209	93.6095
8	12.6389	1.5122	92.0974
9	12.4200	1.7311	90.3663
10	12.1693	1.9818	88.3845
11	11.8823	2.2688	86.1157
12	11.5538	2.5973	83.5184
13	11.1777	2.9734	80.5450
14	10.7471	3.4040	77.1410
15	10.2542	3.8969	73.2441
16	9.6899	4.4612	68.7829
17	9.0439	5.1072	63.6757
18	8.3043	5.8467	57.8290
19	7.4577	6.6934	51.1356
20	6.4885	7.6626	43.4729
21	5.3789	8.7722	34.7007
22	4.1086	10.0425	24.6582
23	2.6544	11.4967	13.1615
24	.9896	13.1615	0.0000

YEARS 25 — MO PAYT 1.1732 — AN CONST 14.08

#	INT	PRIN	BALANCE
1	13.5690	.5099	99.4901
2	13.4951	.5838	98.9063
3	13.4106	.6683	98.2380
4	13.3138	.7651	97.4729
5	13.2030	.8759	96.5970
6	13.0762	1.0027	95.5943
7	12.9310	1.1479	94.4463
8	12.7648	1.3141	93.1322
9	12.5745	1.5044	91.6277
10	12.3566	1.7223	89.9054
11	12.1072	1.9717	87.9338
12	11.8217	2.2572	85.6766
13	11.4949	2.5841	83.0925
14	11.1207	2.9582	80.1342
15	10.6923	3.3866	76.7476
16	10.2019	3.8770	72.8706
17	9.6405	4.4384	68.4322
18	8.9978	5.0812	63.3510
19	8.2620	5.8169	57.5341
20	7.4197	6.6593	50.8748
21	6.4554	7.6236	43.2513
22	5.3514	8.7275	34.5238
23	4.0876	9.9913	24.5325
24	2.6408	11.4381	13.0944
25	.9845	13.0944	0.0000

YEARS 26 — MO PAYT 1.1680 — AN CONST 14.02

#	INT	PRIN	BALANCE
1	13.5730	.4435	99.5565
2	13.5088	.5077	99.0489
3	13.4353	.5812	98.4677
4	13.3511	.6654	97.8023
5	13.2548	.7617	97.0406
6	13.1445	.8720	96.1686
7	13.0182	.9983	95.1703
8	12.8737	1.1428	94.0275
9	12.7082	1.3083	92.7192
10	12.5187	1.4978	91.2214
11	12.3018	1.7147	89.5068
12	12.0535	1.9629	87.5438
13	11.7693	2.2472	85.2966
14	11.4439	2.5726	82.7240
15	11.0714	2.9451	79.7789

#	INT	PRIN	BALANCE
16	10.6449	3.3716	76.4073
17	10.1567	3.8598	72.5474
18	9.5977	4.4188	68.1287
19	8.9579	5.0586	63.0701
20	8.2254	5.7911	57.2789
21	7.3868	6.6297	50.6492
22	6.4267	7.5898	43.0595
23	5.3277	8.6888	34.3707
24	4.0695	9.9470	24.4237
25	2.6291	11.3874	13.0363
26	.9802	13.0363	0.0000

YEARS 27 — MO PAYT 1.1635 — AN CONST 13.97

#	INT	PRIN	BALANCE
1	13.5765	.3859	99.6141
2	13.5207	.4418	99.1724
3	13.4567	.5057	98.6667
4	13.3835	.5790	98.0877
5	13.2996	.6628	97.4249
6	13.2036	.7588	96.6661
7	13.0938	.8686	95.7975
8	12.9680	.9944	94.8031
9	12.8240	1.1384	93.6647
10	12.6591	1.3033	92.3614
11	12.4704	1.4920	90.8694
12	12.2544	1.7080	89.1614
13	12.0070	1.9554	87.2060
14	11.7239	2.2385	84.9675
15	11.3997	2.5627	82.4048
16	11.0286	2.9338	79.4710
17	10.6038	3.3586	76.1124
18	10.1175	3.8449	72.2675
19	9.5607	4.4017	67.8658
20	8.9233	5.0391	62.8267
21	8.1936	5.7688	57.0579
22	7.3583	6.6041	50.4538
23	6.4019	7.5605	42.8933
24	5.3071	8.6553	34.2380
25	4.0538	9.9086	24.3294
26	2.6190	11.3434	12.9860
27	.9764	12.9860	0.0000

YEARS 28 — MO PAYT 1.1596 — AN CONST 13.92

#	INT	PRIN	BALANCE
1	13.5796	.3359	99.6641
2	13.5309	.3846	99.2795
3	13.4752	.4403	98.8392
4	13.4115	.5040	98.3352
5	13.3385	.5770	97.7582
6	13.2549	.6606	97.0976
7	13.1593	.7562	96.3414
8	13.0498	.8657	95.4757
9	12.9244	.9911	94.4846
10	12.7809	1.1346	93.3500
11	12.6166	1.2989	92.0511
12	12.4285	1.4870	90.5641
13	12.2132	1.7023	88.8618
14	11.9667	1.9488	86.9130
15	11.6845	2.2310	84.6820
16	11.3614	2.5541	82.1280
17	10.9916	2.9239	79.2041
18	10.5682	3.3473	75.8567
19	10.0835	3.8320	72.0247
20	9.5286	4.3869	67.6378
21	8.8933	5.0222	62.6156
22	8.1661	5.7494	56.8662
23	7.3335	6.5820	50.2843
24	6.3804	7.5351	42.7492
25	5.2893	8.6262	34.1230
26	4.0402	9.8753	24.2477
27	2.6102	11.3053	12.9424

#	INT	PRIN	BALANCE
28	.9731	12.9424	0.0000

YEARS 29 — MO PAYT 1.1562 — AN CONST 13.88

#	INT	PRIN	BALANCE
1	13.5822	.2926	99.7074
2	13.5398	.3350	99.3725
3	13.4913	.3835	98.9890
4	13.4358	.4390	98.5500
5	13.3722	.5025	98.0475
6	13.2995	.5753	97.4722
7	13.2162	.6586	96.8135
8	13.1208	.7540	96.0595
9	13.0116	.8632	95.1963
10	12.8866	.9882	94.2082
11	12.7435	1.1313	93.0769
12	12.5797	1.2951	91.7818
13	12.3922	1.4826	90.2992
14	12.1775	1.6973	88.6018
15	11.9317	1.9431	86.6587
16	11.6503	2.2245	84.4343
17	11.3282	2.5466	81.8877
18	10.9594	2.9154	78.9723
19	10.5373	3.3375	75.6348
20	10.0540	3.8208	71.8140
21	9.5007	4.3741	67.4399
22	8.8673	5.0075	62.4324
23	8.1422	5.7326	56.6998
24	7.3121	6.5627	50.1371
25	6.3618	7.5130	42.6241
26	5.2738	8.6009	34.0232
27	4.0284	9.8464	24.1768
28	2.6026	11.2722	12.9045
29	.9703	12.9045	0.0000

YEARS 30 — MO PAYT 1.1533 — AN CONST 13.84

#	INT	PRIN	BALANCE
1	13.5845	.2549	99.7451
2	13.5476	.2918	99.4532
3	13.5053	.3341	99.1191
4	13.4569	.3825	98.7367
5	13.4016	.4379	98.2988
6	13.3382	.5013	97.7975
7	13.2656	.5739	97.2237
8	13.1825	.6570	96.5667
9	13.0873	.7521	95.8147
10	12.9784	.8610	94.9537
11	12.8538	.9857	93.9680
12	12.7110	1.1284	92.8396
13	12.5476	1.2918	91.5478
14	12.3606	1.4788	90.0690
15	12.1464	1.6930	88.3760
16	11.9013	1.9381	86.4378
17	11.6206	2.2188	84.2190
18	11.2993	2.5401	81.6789
19	10.9315	2.9079	78.7710
20	10.5104	3.3290	75.4420
21	10.0284	3.8111	71.6309
22	9.4765	4.3629	67.2680
23	8.8447	4.9947	62.2733
24	8.1214	5.7180	56.5553
25	7.2934	6.5460	50.0093
26	6.3456	7.4939	42.5155
27	5.2604	8.5790	33.9364
28	4.0181	9.8213	24.1151
29	2.5959	11.2435	12.8716
30	.9678	12.8716	0.0000

YEARS 2 — MO PAYT 4.7836 — AN CONST 57.41

#	INT	PRIN	BALANCE
1	10.7850	46.6181	53.3819
2	4.0212	53.3819	0.0000

YEARS 3 — MO PAYT 3.3996 — AN CONST 40.80

#	INT	PRIN	BALANCE
1	11.8624	28.9325	71.0675
2	7.6646	33.1303	37.9372
3	2.8578	37.9372	0.0000

YEARS 4 — MO PAYT 2.7139 — AN CONST 32.57

#	INT	PRIN	BALANCE
1	12.3962	20.1703	79.8297
2	9.4697	23.0968	56.7330
3	6.1186	26.4478	30.2851
4	2.2814	30.2851	0.0000

YEARS 5 — MO PAYT 2.3074 — AN CONST 27.69

#	INT	PRIN	BALANCE
1	12.7126	14.9765	85.0235
2	10.5397	17.1495	67.8740
3	8.0515	19.6377	48.2363
4	5.2023	22.4869	25.7495
5	1.9397	25.7495	0.0000

YEARS 6 — MO PAYT 2.0405 — AN CONST 24.49

#	INT	PRIN	BALANCE
1	12.9204	11.5662	88.4338
2	11.2423	13.2443	75.1895
3	9.3206	15.1659	60.0236
4	7.1202	17.3663	42.6572
5	4.6006	19.8860	22.7712
6	1.7153	22.7712	0.0000

YEARS 7 — MO PAYT 1.8533 — AN CONST 22.25

#	INT	PRIN	BALANCE
1	13.0661	9.1741	90.8259
2	11.7351	10.5051	80.3208
3	10.2109	12.0293	68.2916
4	8.4656	13.7746	54.5170
5	6.4670	15.7731	38.7438
6	4.1785	18.0616	20.6822
7	1.5580	20.6822	0.0000

YEARS 8 — MO PAYT 1.7159 — AN CONST 20.60

#	INT	PRIN	BALANCE
1	13.1731	7.4174	92.5826
2	12.0969	8.4936	84.0890
3	10.8646	9.7259	74.3631
4	9.4535	11.1370	63.2261
5	7.8376	12.7529	50.4732
6	5.9873	14.6032	35.8700
7	3.8686	16.7219	19.1481
8	1.4424	19.1481	0.0000

YEARS 9 — MO PAYT 1.6115 — AN CONST 19.34

#	INT	PRIN	BALANCE
1	13.2544	6.0835	93.9165
2	12.3717	6.9662	86.9503
3	11.3610	7.9769	78.9735
4	10.2037	9.1342	69.8392
5	8.8784	10.4595	59.3797
6	7.3608	11.9771	47.4027
7	5.6231	13.7148	33.6879
8	3.6332	15.7047	17.9832
9	1.3547	17.9832	0.0000

YEARS 10 — MO PAYT 1.5302 — AN CONST 18.37

#	INT	PRIN	BALANCE
1	13.3177	5.0447	94.9553
2	12.5857	5.7766	89.1787
3	11.7476	6.6147	82.5640
4	10.7879	7.5745	74.9895
5	9.6889	8.6734	66.3161
6	8.4305	9.9319	56.3842
7	6.9895	11.3729	45.0114
8	5.3394	13.0229	31.9884
9	3.4499	14.9124	17.0760
10	1.2863	17.0760	0.0000

YEARS 11 — MO PAYT 1.4656 — AN CONST 17.59

#	INT	PRIN	BALANCE
1	13.3679	4.2196	95.7804
2	12.7557	4.8318	90.9486
3	12.0547	5.5329	85.4157
4	11.2519	6.3356	79.0801
5	10.3327	7.2548	71.8252
6	9.2801	8.3074	63.5178
7	8.0748	9.5128	54.0050
8	6.6946	10.8930	43.1121
9	5.1141	12.4734	30.6387
10	3.3044	14.2832	16.3555
11	1.2320	16.3555	0.0000

YEARS 12 — MO PAYT 1.4135 — AN CONST 16.97

#	INT	PRIN	BALANCE
1	13.4085	3.5540	96.4460
2	12.8928	4.0696	92.3764
3	12.3024	4.6601	87.7163
4	11.6263	5.3362	82.3800
5	10.8520	6.1105	76.2696
6	9.9655	6.9970	69.2726
7	8.9503	8.0122	61.2604
8	7.7878	9.1747	52.0857
9	6.4567	10.5058	41.5799
10	4.9324	12.0301	29.5498
11	3.1869	13.7755	15.7742
12	1.1883	15.7742	0.0000

YEARS 13 — MO PAYT 1.3710 — AN CONST 16.46

#	INT	PRIN	BALANCE
1	13.4416	3.0103	96.9897
2	13.0049	3.4470	93.5427
3	12.5047	3.9471	89.5956
4	11.9321	4.5198	85.0758
5	11.2763	5.1756	79.9002
6	10.5254	5.9265	73.9737
7	9.6655	6.7864	67.1873
8	8.6809	7.7710	59.4163
9	7.5534	8.8985	50.5178
10	6.2623	10.1896	40.3282
11	4.7839	11.6680	28.6602
12	3.0910	13.3609	15.2994
13	1.1525	15.2994	0.0000

YEARS 14 — MO PAYT 1.3359 — AN CONST 16.04

#	INT	PRIN	BALANCE
1	13.4690	2.5615	97.4385
2	13.0973	2.9331	94.5054
3	12.6717	3.3587	91.1466
4	12.1844	3.8460	87.3006
5	11.6264	4.4040	82.8966
6	10.9874	5.0430	77.8536
7	10.2557	5.7747	72.0788
8	9.4179	6.6126	65.4663
9	8.4585	7.5720	57.8943
10	7.3599	8.6706	49.2238
11	6.1019	9.9286	39.2952
12	4.6614	11.3691	27.9261
13	3.0118	13.0186	14.9075
14	1.1230	14.9075	0.0000

YEARS 15 — MO PAYT 1.3066 — AN CONST 15.68

#	INT	PRIN	BALANCE
1	13.4917	2.1880	97.8120
2	13.1743	2.5055	95.3065
3	12.8107	2.8690	92.4376
4	12.3945	3.2852	89.1524
5	11.9178	3.7619	85.3905
6	11.3720	4.3077	81.0828
7	10.7470	4.9327	76.1501
8	10.0314	5.6484	70.5018
9	9.2118	6.4679	64.0339
10	8.2734	7.4063	56.6276
11	7.1989	8.4809	48.1468
12	5.9684	9.7113	38.4354
13	4.5594	11.1203	27.3151
14	2.9459	12.7338	14.5813
15	1.0984	14.5813	0.0000

YEARS 16 — MO PAYT 1.2821 — AN CONST 15.39

#	INT	PRIN	BALANCE
1	13.5108	1.8749	98.1251
2	13.2387	2.1470	95.9781
3	12.9272	2.4585	93.5196
4	12.5705	2.8152	90.7044
5	12.1621	3.2236	87.4808
6	11.6944	3.6913	83.7895
7	11.1588	4.2269	79.5625
8	10.5455	4.8402	74.7223
9	9.8433	5.5425	69.1799
10	9.0391	6.3466	62.8333
11	8.1183	7.2674	55.5659
12	7.0639	8.3218	47.2440
13	5.8565	9.5293	37.7148
14	4.4739	10.9118	26.8029
15	2.8907	12.4950	14.3079
16	1.0778	14.3079	0.0000

YEARS 17 — MO PAYT 1.2615 — AN CONST 15.14

#	INT	PRIN	BALANCE
1	13.5269	1.6110	98.3890
2	13.2931	1.8447	96.5443
3	13.0255	2.1124	94.4319
4	12.7190	2.4189	92.0130
5	12.3680	2.7698	89.2432
6	11.9662	3.1717	86.0715
7	11.5060	3.6319	82.4396
8	10.9790	4.1588	78.2808
9	10.3756	4.7622	73.5186
10	9.6847	5.4532	68.0654
11	8.8935	6.2444	61.8211
12	7.9875	7.1503	54.6707
13	6.9501	8.1878	46.4829
14	5.7621	9.3757	37.1072
15	4.4018	10.7360	26.3711
16	2.8441	12.2937	14.0774
17	1.0604	14.0774	0.0000

YEARS 18 — MO PAYT 1.2440 — AN CONST 14.93

#	INT	PRIN	BALANCE
1	13.5405	1.3874	98.6126
2	13.3392	1.5886	97.0240
3	13.1087	1.8191	95.2048
4	12.8448	2.0831	93.1218
5	12.5425	2.3853	90.7364
6	12.1964	2.7314	88.0051
7	11.8001	3.1277	84.8774
8	11.3464	3.5815	81.2959
9	10.8267	4.1011	77.1948
10	10.2317	4.6961	72.4986
11	9.5503	5.3775	67.1211
12	8.7701	6.1577	60.9634
13	7.8767	7.0511	53.9122
14	6.8537	8.0742	45.8380
15	5.6822	9.2457	36.5924
16	4.3407	10.5871	26.0053
17	2.8047	12.1232	13.8821
18	1.0457	13.8821	0.0000

YEARS 19 — MO PAYT 1.2291 — AN CONST 14.75

#	INT	PRIN	BALANCE
1	13.5521	1.1971	98.8029
2	13.3784	1.3708	97.4322
3	13.1795	1.5696	95.8625
4	12.9518	1.7974	94.0652
5	12.6910	2.0581	92.0070
6	12.3924	2.3568	89.6503
7	12.0504	2.6987	86.9516
8	11.6589	3.0903	83.8613
9	11.2105	3.5386	80.3227
10	10.6971	4.0520	76.2707
11	10.1092	4.6399	71.6307
12	9.4360	5.3131	66.3176
13	8.6651	6.0840	60.2336
14	7.7824	6.9667	53.2669
15	6.7716	7.9775	45.2893
16	5.6142	9.1350	36.1543
17	4.2888	10.4604	25.6940
18	2.7711	11.9781	13.7159
19	1.0332	13.7159	0.0000

YEARS 20 — MO PAYT 1.2164 — AN CONST 14.60

#	INT	PRIN	BALANCE
1	13.5620	1.0346	98.9654
2	13.4119	1.1847	97.7807
3	13.2400	1.3566	96.4242
4	13.0432	1.5534	94.8708
5	12.8178	1.7788	93.0920
6	12.5597	2.0369	91.0551
7	12.2642	2.3324	88.7228
8	11.9258	2.6708	86.0520
9	11.5383	3.0583	82.9937
10	11.0945	3.5020	79.4917
11	10.5864	4.0101	75.4816
12	10.0046	4.5919	70.8897
13	9.3384	5.2582	65.6315
14	8.5755	6.0211	59.6104
15	7.7019	6.8947	52.7158
16	6.7016	7.8950	44.8208
17	5.5561	9.0405	35.7803
18	4.2444	10.3521	25.4282
19	2.7424	11.8541	13.5740
20	1.0225	13.5740	0.0000

YEARS 21 — MO PAYT 1.2055 — AN CONST 14.47

#	INT	PRIN	BALANCE
1	13.5705	.8954	99.1046
2	13.4405	1.0253	98.0793
3	13.2918	1.1741	96.9052

#	INT	PRIN	BALANCE
4	13.1214	1.3444	95.5608
5	12.9264	1.5395	94.0213
6	12.7030	1.7628	92.2585
7	12.4472	2.0186	90.2398
8	12.1544	2.3115	87.9283
9	11.8190	2.6469	85.2815
10	11.4350	3.0309	82.2506
11	10.9952	3.4706	78.7799
12	10.4917	3.9742	74.8057
13	9.9150	4.5508	70.2549
14	9.2548	5.2111	65.0438
15	8.4987	5.9672	59.0767
16	7.6329	6.8329	52.2438
17	6.6415	7.8243	44.4195
18	5.5063	8.9595	35.4599
19	4.2064	10.2595	25.2005
20	2.7179	11.7480	13.4525
21	1.0134	13.4525	0.0000

YEARS 22 — MO PAYT 1.1961 — AN CONST 14.36

#	INT	PRIN	BALANCE
1	13.5777	.7759	99.2241
2	13.4652	.8885	98.3357
3	13.3363	1.0174	97.3183
4	13.1886	1.1650	96.1533
5	13.0196	1.3340	94.8193
6	12.8261	1.5275	93.2918
7	12.6044	1.7492	91.5426
8	12.3507	2.0030	89.5397
9	12.0601	2.2936	87.2461
10	11.7273	2.6263	84.6198
11	11.3462	3.0074	81.6124
12	10.9099	3.4437	78.1687
13	10.4103	3.9434	74.2253
14	9.8381	4.5155	69.7098
15	9.1830	5.1707	64.5392
16	8.4328	5.9209	58.6183
17	7.5737	6.7799	51.8384
18	6.5900	7.7636	44.0748
19	5.4636	8.8900	35.1848
20	4.1738	10.1799	25.0049
21	2.6968	11.6568	13.3481
22	1.0055	13.3481	0.0000

YEARS 23 — MO PAYT 1.1881 — AN CONST 14.26

#	INT	PRIN	BALANCE
1	13.5840	.6730	99.3270
2	13.4864	.7707	98.5563
3	13.3745	.8825	97.6738
4	13.2465	1.0105	96.6633
5	13.0999	1.1571	95.5062
6	12.9320	1.3250	94.1812
7	12.7398	1.5173	92.6639
8	12.5196	1.7374	90.9265
9	12.2675	1.9895	88.9371
10	11.9789	2.2781	86.6589
11	11.6484	2.6087	84.0503
12	11.2699	2.9871	81.0631
13	10.8365	3.4205	77.6426
14	10.3402	3.9168	73.7258
15	9.7719	4.4851	69.2407
16	9.1212	5.1359	64.1048
17	8.3760	5.8810	58.2238
18	7.5227	6.7343	51.4895
19	6.5457	7.7113	43.7782
20	5.4268	8.8302	34.9480
21	4.1457	10.1113	24.8367
22	2.6786	11.5784	13.2583
23	.9987	13.2583	0.0000

YEARS 24 — MO PAYT 1.1811 — AN CONST 14.18

#	INT	PRIN	BALANCE
1	13.5894	.5843	99.4157
2	13.5046	.6691	98.7466
3	13.4076	.7662	97.9805
4	13.2964	.8773	97.1031
5	13.1691	1.0046	96.0985
6	13.0233	1.1504	94.9482
7	12.8564	1.3173	93.6309
8	12.6653	1.5084	92.1225
9	12.4465	1.7272	90.3952
10	12.1959	1.9778	88.4174
11	11.9089	2.2648	86.1526
12	11.5803	2.5934	83.5592
13	11.2040	2.9697	80.5895
14	10.7732	3.4006	77.1889
15	10.2798	3.8939	73.2950
16	9.7148	4.4589	68.8361
17	9.0679	5.1058	63.7302
18	8.3271	5.8466	57.8836
19	7.4788	6.6949	51.1887
20	6.5074	7.6663	43.5224
21	5.3951	8.7786	34.7438
22	4.1215	10.0523	24.6915
23	2.6630	11.5107	13.1808
24	.9929	13.1808	0.0000

YEARS 25 — MO PAYT 1.1751 — AN CONST 14.11

#	INT	PRIN	BALANCE
1	13.5941	.5077	99.4923
2	13.5204	.5813	98.9110
3	13.4361	.6657	98.2453
4	13.3395	.7623	97.4830
5	13.2289	.8729	96.6102
6	13.1022	.9995	95.6107
7	12.9572	1.1445	94.4661
8	12.7912	1.3106	93.1555
9	12.6010	1.5007	91.6548
10	12.3833	1.7185	89.9363
11	12.1339	1.9678	87.9685
12	11.8484	2.2533	85.7152
13	11.5215	2.5802	83.1350
14	11.1471	2.9546	80.1804
15	10.7185	3.3833	76.7971
16	10.2276	3.8742	72.9229
17	9.6655	4.4363	68.4866
18	9.0218	5.0799	63.4067
19	8.2848	5.8170	57.5897
20	7.4408	6.6609	50.9288
21	6.4744	7.6274	43.3014
22	5.3677	8.7340	34.5674
23	4.1005	10.0012	24.5662
24	2.6495	11.4523	13.1139
25	.9879	13.1139	0.0000

YEARS 26 — MO PAYT 1.1700 — AN CONST 14.04

#	INT	PRIN	BALANCE
1	13.5981	.4414	99.5586
2	13.5341	.5054	99.0532
3	13.4607	.5788	98.4744
4	13.3768	.6627	97.8116
5	13.2806	.7589	97.0527
6	13.1705	.8690	96.1837
7	13.0444	.9951	95.1886
8	12.9000	1.1395	94.0492
9	12.7347	1.3048	92.7444
10	12.5454	1.4941	91.2502
11	12.3286	1.7109	89.5394
12	12.0804	1.9591	87.5802
13	11.7961	2.2434	85.3369
14	11.4707	2.5689	82.7680
15	11.0979	2.9416	79.8264
16	10.6711	3.3684	76.4581
17	10.1824	3.8571	72.6010
18	9.6228	4.4167	68.1843
19	8.9820	5.0575	63.1268
20	8.2482	5.7913	57.3355
21	7.4080	6.6315	50.7040
22	6.4458	7.5937	43.1103
23	5.3440	8.6955	34.4148
24	4.0824	9.9571	24.4578
25	2.6378	11.4017	13.0560
26	.9835	13.0560	0.0000

YEARS 27 — MO PAYT 1.1655 — AN CONST 13.99

#	INT	PRIN	BALANCE
1	13.6016	.3840	99.6160
2	13.5459	.4397	99.1763
3	13.4821	.5035	98.6728
4	13.4090	.5766	98.0963
5	13.3254	.6602	97.4361
6	13.2296	.7560	96.6801
7	13.1199	.8657	95.8144
8	12.9943	.9913	94.8231
9	12.8505	1.1351	93.6880
10	12.6858	1.2998	92.3882
11	12.4972	1.4884	90.8999
12	12.2813	1.7043	89.1955
13	12.0340	1.9516	87.2439
14	11.7508	2.2348	85.0092
15	11.4266	2.5590	82.4502
16	11.0553	2.9303	79.5199
17	10.6302	3.3554	76.1645
18	10.1433	3.8423	72.3222
19	9.5859	4.3997	67.9225
20	8.9475	5.0381	62.8844
21	8.2165	5.7690	57.1154
22	7.3795	6.6061	50.5093
23	6.4211	7.5645	42.9448
24	5.3235	8.6621	34.2827
25	4.0668	9.9188	24.3638
26	2.6276	11.3580	13.0059
27	.9797	13.0059	0.0000

YEARS 28 — MO PAYT 1.1616 — AN CONST 13.94

#	INT	PRIN	BALANCE
1	13.6046	.3342	99.6658
2	13.5561	.3827	99.2831
3	13.5006	.4382	98.8448
4	13.4370	.5018	98.3430
5	13.3642	.5746	97.7684
6	13.2809	.6580	97.1104
7	13.1854	.7535	96.3569
8	13.0761	.8628	95.4942
9	12.9509	.9880	94.5062
10	12.8075	1.1313	93.3749
11	12.6434	1.2954	92.0795
12	12.4555	1.4834	90.5961
13	12.2402	1.6986	88.8974
14	11.9938	1.9451	86.9524
15	11.7116	2.2273	84.7251
16	11.3884	2.5504	82.1746
17	11.0184	2.9205	79.2541
18	10.5946	3.3442	75.9099
19	10.1094	3.8294	72.0805
20	9.5538	4.3850	67.6955
21	8.9176	5.0212	62.6743
22	8.1891	5.7498	56.9245
23	7.3549	6.5840	50.3405
24	6.3996	7.5393	42.8012
25	5.3057	8.6331	34.1681
26	4.0532	9.8857	24.2824
27	2.6189	11.3200	12.9624
28	.9764	12.9624	0.0000

YEARS 29 — MO PAYT 1.1582 — AN CONST 13.90

#	INT	PRIN	BALANCE
1	13.6073	.2910	99.7090
2	13.5650	.3332	99.3757
3	13.5167	.3816	98.9941
4	13.4613	.4370	98.5572
5	13.3979	.5004	98.0568
6	13.3253	.5730	97.4839
7	13.2422	.6561	96.8278
8	13.1470	.7513	96.0765
9	13.0380	.8603	95.2163
10	12.9132	.9851	94.2312
11	12.7703	1.1280	93.1032
12	12.6066	1.2917	91.8115
13	12.4192	1.4791	90.3324
14	12.2046	1.6937	88.6387
15	11.9589	1.9394	86.6993
16	11.6775	2.2208	84.4785
17	11.3553	2.5430	81.9355
18	10.9863	2.9120	79.0235
19	10.5638	3.3345	75.6890
20	10.0800	3.8183	71.8707
21	9.5260	4.3723	67.4985
22	8.8917	5.0066	62.4919
23	8.1653	5.7330	56.7588
24	7.3335	6.5648	50.1940
25	6.3810	7.5173	42.6767
26	5.2903	8.6080	34.0687
27	4.0414	9.8569	24.2117
28	2.6112	11.2871	12.9247
29	.9736	12.9247	0.0000

YEARS 30 — MO PAYT 1.1553 — AN CONST 13.87

#	INT	PRIN	BALANCE
1	13.6096	.2535	99.7465
2	13.5728	.2903	99.4562
3	13.5307	.3324	99.1238
4	13.4824	.3806	98.7432
5	13.4272	.4359	98.3073
6	13.3640	.4991	97.8083
7	13.2916	.5715	97.2368
8	13.2086	.6544	96.5823
9	13.1137	.7494	95.8330
10	13.0050	.8581	94.9749
11	12.8805	.9826	93.9923
12	12.7379	1.1252	92.8671
13	12.5747	1.2884	91.5787
14	12.3877	1.4753	90.1034
15	12.1737	1.6894	88.4140
16	11.9286	1.9345	86.4795
17	11.6479	2.2152	84.2643
18	11.3265	2.5366	81.7278
19	10.9585	2.9046	78.8232
20	10.5370	3.3260	75.4972
21	10.0545	3.8086	71.6886
22	9.5019	4.3612	67.3274
23	8.8691	4.9939	62.3334
24	8.1446	5.7185	56.6149
25	7.3149	6.5482	50.0667
26	6.3648	7.4983	42.5685
27	5.2769	8.5862	33.9823
28	4.0311	9.8319	24.1504
29	2.6046	11.2584	12.8919
30	.9711	12.8919	0.0000

YEARS 2 — MO PAYT 4.7871 — AN CONST 57.45

#	INT	PRIN	BALANCE
1	10.8459	46.5997	53.4003
2	4.0452	53.4003	0.0000

YEARS 3 — MO PAYT 3.4032 — AN CONST 40.84

#	INT	PRIN	BALANCE
1	11.9294	28.9091	71.0909
2	7.7104	33.1281	37.9628
3	2.8758	37.9628	0.0000

YEARS 4 — MO PAYT 2.7176 — AN CONST 32.62

#	INT	PRIN	BALANCE
1	12.4661	20.1453	79.8547
2	9.5262	23.0853	56.7694
3	6.1571	26.4543	30.3150
4	2.2964	30.3150	0.0000

YEARS 5 — MO PAYT 2.3113 — AN CONST 27.74

#	INT	PRIN	BALANCE
1	12.7843	14.9514	85.0486
2	10.6023	17.1333	67.9153
3	8.1019	19.6337	48.2816
4	5.2366	22.4991	25.7825
5	1.9531	25.7825	0.0000

YEARS 6 — MO PAYT 2.0445 — AN CONST 24.54

#	INT	PRIN	BALANCE
1	12.9931	11.5414	88.4586
2	11.3088	13.2258	75.2328
3	9.3786	15.1559	60.0769
4	7.1668	17.3677	42.7092
5	4.6322	19.9023	22.8069
6	1.7277	22.8069	0.0000

YEARS 7 — MO PAYT 1.8575 — AN CONST 22.29

#	INT	PRIN	BALANCE
1	13.1396	9.1500	90.8500
2	11.8042	10.4854	80.3646
3	10.2740	12.0156	68.3490
4	8.5205	13.7691	54.5799
5	6.5110	15.7786	38.8013
6	4.2083	18.0813	20.7200
7	1.5696	20.7200	0.0000

YEARS 8 — MO PAYT 1.7201 — AN CONST 20.65

#	INT	PRIN	BALANCE
1	13.2471	7.3943	92.6057
2	12.1680	8.4734	84.1322
3	10.9314	9.7101	74.4222
4	9.5143	11.1271	63.2950
5	7.8905	12.7510	50.5441
6	6.0296	14.6119	35.9322
7	3.8972	16.7443	19.1879
8	1.4535	19.1879	0.0000

YEARS 9 — MO PAYT 1.6159 — AN CONST 19.40

#	INT	PRIN	BALANCE
1	13.3287	6.0615	93.9385
2	12.4441	6.9461	86.9924
3	11.4304	7.9598	79.0325
4	10.2688	9.1215	69.9111
5	8.9376	10.4526	59.4584
6	7.4122	11.9781	47.4803
7	5.6641	13.7262	33.7542
8	3.6609	15.7293	18.0248
9	1.3654	18.0248	0.0000

YEARS 10 — MO PAYT 1.5347 — AN CONST 18.42

#	INT	PRIN	BALANCE
1	13.3923	5.0238	94.9762
2	12.6591	5.7570	89.2192
3	11.8190	6.5972	82.6220
4	10.8562	7.5599	75.0621
5	9.7529	8.6632	66.3988
6	8.4886	9.9275	56.4713
7	7.0398	11.3763	45.0950
8	5.3796	13.0366	32.0584
9	3.4770	14.9391	17.1193
10	1.2968	17.1193	0.0000

YEARS 11 — MO PAYT 1.4702 — AN CONST 17.65

#	INT	PRIN	BALANCE
1	13.4428	4.1999	95.8001
2	12.8298	4.8128	90.9873
3	12.1275	5.5152	85.4721
4	11.3226	6.3201	79.1520
5	10.4002	7.2424	71.9095
6	9.3433	8.2994	63.6102
7	8.1321	9.5106	54.0996
8	6.7441	10.8985	43.2010
9	5.1536	12.4891	30.7120
10	3.3310	14.3117	16.4003
11	1.2424	16.4003	0.0000

YEARS 12 — MO PAYT 1.4182 — AN CONST 17.02

#	INT	PRIN	BALANCE
1	13.4835	3.5355	96.4645
2	12.9675	4.0514	92.4131
3	12.3762	4.6427	87.7704
4	11.6987	5.3202	82.4502
5	10.9223	6.0966	76.3536
6	10.0325	6.9864	69.3672
7	9.0130	8.0060	61.3612
8	7.8446	9.1743	52.1869
9	6.5057	10.5132	41.6737
10	4.9714	12.0475	29.6262
11	3.2132	13.8057	15.8205
12	1.1984	15.8205	0.0000

YEARS 13 — MO PAYT 1.3758 — AN CONST 16.51

#	INT	PRIN	BALANCE
1	13.5167	2.9929	97.0071
2	13.0799	3.4296	93.5775
3	12.5794	3.9302	89.6473
4	12.0058	4.5037	85.1436
5	11.3486	5.1610	79.9826
6	10.5954	5.9142	74.0684
7	9.7323	6.7773	67.2911
8	8.7432	7.7664	59.5248
9	7.6098	8.8998	50.6250
10	6.3110	10.1986	40.4264
11	4.8226	11.6869	28.7395
12	3.1171	13.3925	15.3470
13	1.1626	15.3470	0.0000

YEARS 14 — MO PAYT 1.3408 — AN CONST 16.09

#	INT	PRIN	BALANCE
1	13.5441	2.5452	97.4548
2	13.1727	2.9167	94.5381
3	12.7470	3.3424	91.1957
4	12.2592	3.8301	87.3656
5	11.7003	4.3891	82.9765
6	11.0597	5.0296	77.9468
7	10.3257	5.7636	72.1832
8	9.4846	6.6048	65.5784
9	8.5207	7.5687	58.0097
10	7.4161	8.6732	49.3365
11	6.1504	9.9390	39.3975
12	4.6999	11.3895	28.0080
13	3.0377	13.0516	14.9564
14	1.1330	14.9564	0.0000

YEARS 15 — MO PAYT 1.3116 — AN CONST 15.74

#	INT	PRIN	BALANCE
1	13.5669	2.1728	97.8272
2	13.2498	2.4899	95.3372
3	12.8864	2.8533	92.4839
4	12.4700	3.2697	89.2142
5	11.9929	3.7469	85.4673
6	11.4460	4.2937	81.1735
7	10.8194	4.9203	76.2532
8	10.1013	5.6384	70.6148
9	9.2785	6.4613	64.1535
10	8.3355	7.4042	56.7493
11	7.2550	8.4848	48.2645
12	6.0167	9.7230	38.5415
13	4.5978	11.1420	27.3994
14	2.9717	12.7680	14.6314
15	1.1084	14.6314	0.0000

YEARS 16 — MO PAYT 1.2872 — AN CONST 15.45

#	INT	PRIN	BALANCE
1	13.5860	1.8608	98.1392
2	13.3145	2.1324	96.0068
3	13.0033	2.4436	93.5631
4	12.6466	2.8002	90.7629
5	12.2380	3.2089	87.5540
6	11.7697	3.6772	83.8768
7	11.2330	4.2138	79.6630
8	10.6181	4.8288	74.8342
9	9.9134	5.5335	69.3007
10	9.1058	6.3410	62.9597
11	8.1804	7.2664	55.6933
12	7.1200	8.3269	47.3664
13	5.9048	9.5421	37.8243
14	4.5122	10.9347	26.8896
15	2.9164	12.5305	14.3591
16	1.0877	14.3591	0.0000

YEARS 17 — MO PAYT 1.2667 — AN CONST 15.21

#	INT	PRIN	BALANCE
1	13.6021	1.5979	98.4021
2	13.3689	1.8311	96.5710
3	13.1017	2.0983	94.4727
4	12.7955	2.4046	92.0681
5	12.4446	2.7555	89.3126
6	12.0424	3.1576	86.1550
7	11.5816	3.6184	82.5366
8	11.0535	4.1465	78.3901
9	10.4484	4.7516	73.6385
10	9.7550	5.4451	68.1934
11	8.9603	6.2397	61.9537
12	8.0497	7.1503	54.8033
13	7.0062	8.1938	46.6095
14	5.8104	9.3896	37.2199
15	4.4401	10.7599	26.4599
16	2.8698	12.3302	14.1297
17	1.0704	14.1297	0.0000

YEARS 18 — MO PAYT 1.2493 — AN CONST 15.00

#	INT	PRIN	BALANCE
1	13.6158	1.3752	98.6248
2	13.4151	1.5759	97.0488
3	13.1851	1.8059	95.2429
4	12.9215	2.0695	93.1734
5	12.6195	2.3715	90.8019
6	12.2734	2.7176	88.0844
7	11.8768	3.1142	84.9702
8	11.4223	3.5687	81.4015
9	10.9015	4.0895	77.3120
10	10.3047	4.6863	72.6257
11	9.6208	5.3702	67.2556
12	8.8371	6.1539	61.1017
13	7.9390	7.0520	54.0497
14	6.9099	8.0812	45.9685
15	5.7305	9.2605	36.7080
16	4.3790	10.6120	26.0960
17	2.8303	12.1607	13.9354
18	1.0556	13.9354	0.0000

YEARS 19 — MO PAYT 1.2344 — AN CONST 14.82

#	INT	PRIN	BALANCE
1	13.6274	1.1859	98.8141
2	13.4543	1.3589	97.4552
3	13.2560	1.5572	95.8980
4	13.0287	1.7845	94.1135
5	12.7683	2.0449	92.0685
6	12.4699	2.3434	89.7251
7	12.1279	2.6854	87.0398
8	11.7360	3.0773	83.9625
9	11.2869	3.5263	80.4362
10	10.7723	4.0410	76.3952
11	10.1825	4.6307	71.7645
12	9.5067	5.3065	66.4580
13	8.7323	6.0809	60.3771
14	7.8449	6.9684	53.4087
15	6.8279	7.9853	45.4234
16	5.6625	9.1507	36.2727
17	4.3271	10.4861	25.7866
18	2.7968	12.0165	13.7701
19	1.0431	13.7701	0.0000

YEARS 20 — MO PAYT 1.2218 — AN CONST 14.67

#	INT	PRIN	BALANCE
1	13.6373	1.0242	98.9758
2	13.4878	1.1737	97.8020
3	13.3165	1.3450	96.4570
4	13.1202	1.5413	94.9157
5	12.8953	1.7662	93.1495
6	12.6375	2.0240	91.1255
7	12.3421	2.3194	88.8061
8	12.0037	2.6579	86.1483
9	11.6158	3.0457	83.1026
10	11.1713	3.4902	79.6123
11	10.6619	3.9996	75.6127
12	10.0782	4.5833	71.0295
13	9.4094	5.2522	65.7773
14	8.6429	6.0186	59.7587
15	7.7645	6.8970	52.8617
16	6.7580	7.9035	44.9581
17	5.6045	9.0570	35.9012
18	4.2828	10.3787	25.5225
19	2.7681	11.8934	13.6291
20	1.0324	13.6291	0.0000

YEARS 21 — MO PAYT 1.2110 — AN CONST 14.54

#	INT	PRIN	BALANCE
1	13.6457	.8859	99.1141
2	13.5165	1.0152	98.0989
3	13.3683	1.1633	96.9356

MONTHLY PAYMENT AMORTIZATION SCHEDULE PER $100   13.70 %

#	INT	PRIN	BALANCE
4	13.1985	1.3331	95.6025
5	13.0040	1.5276	94.0749
6	12.7810	1.7506	92.3243
7	12.5256	2.0061	90.3183
8	12.2328	2.2988	88.0194
9	11.8973	2.6343	85.3851
10	11.5129	3.0188	82.3664
11	11.0723	3.4593	78.9071
12	10.5675	3.9642	74.9429
13	9.9889	4.5427	70.4002
14	9.3260	5.2056	65.1946
15	8.5663	5.9653	59.2293
16	7.6957	6.8359	52.3934
17	6.6981	7.8335	44.5599
18	5.5549	8.9767	35.5831
19	4.2448	10.2868	25.2964
20	2.7436	11.7880	13.5083
21	1.0233	13.5083	0.0000

YEARS 22 — MO PAYT 1.2017 — AN CONST 14.43

#	INT	PRIN	BALANCE
1	13.6530	.7671	99.2329
2	13.5411	.8791	98.3538
3	13.4128	1.0074	97.3464
4	13.2658	1.1544	96.1920
5	13.0973	1.3229	94.8691
6	12.9042	1.5159	93.3532
7	12.6830	1.7372	91.6161
8	12.4295	1.9907	89.6254
9	12.1390	2.2812	87.3442
10	11.8060	2.6141	84.7301
11	11.4246	2.9956	81.7345
12	10.9874	3.4328	78.3017
13	10.4864	3.9337	74.3680
14	9.9123	4.5078	69.8602
15	9.2545	5.1657	64.6945
16	8.5006	5.9196	58.7749
17	7.6367	6.7835	51.9914
18	6.6467	7.7734	44.2180
19	5.5123	8.9079	35.3102
20	4.2123	10.2079	25.1023
21	2.7226	11.6976	13.4047
22	1.0154	13.4047	0.0000

YEARS 23 — MO PAYT 1.1937 — AN CONST 14.33

#	INT	PRIN	BALANCE
1	13.6593	.6650	99.3350
2	13.5622	.7620	98.5730
3	13.4510	.8732	97.6997
4	13.3236	1.0007	96.6991
5	13.1775	1.1467	95.5523
6	13.0102	1.3141	94.2383
7	12.8184	1.5058	92.7324
8	12.5987	1.7256	91.0068
9	12.3468	1.9774	89.0294
10	12.0582	2.2660	86.7634
11	11.7275	2.5967	84.1667
12	11.3486	2.9757	81.1910
13	10.9143	3.4099	77.7810
14	10.4167	3.9076	73.8735
15	9.8464	4.4779	69.3956
16	9.1929	5.1313	64.2643
17	8.4441	5.8802	58.3841
18	7.5859	6.7383	51.6457
19	6.6025	7.7217	43.9240
20	5.4756	8.8486	35.0754
21	4.1843	10.1400	24.9354
22	2.7045	11.6198	13.3156
23	1.0087	13.3156	0.0000

YEARS 24 — MO PAYT 1.1868 — AN CONST 14.25

#	INT	PRIN	BALANCE
1	13.6647	.5769	99.4231
2	13.5805	.6611	98.7619
3	13.4840	.7576	98.0043
4	13.3734	.8682	97.1361
5	13.2467	.9949	96.1412
6	13.1015	1.1401	95.0011
7	12.9351	1.3065	93.6946
8	12.7445	1.4972	92.1974
9	12.5260	1.7156	90.4818
10	12.2756	1.9660	88.5157
11	11.9887	2.2529	86.2628
12	11.6599	2.5817	83.6811
13	11.2831	2.9585	80.7226
14	10.8513	3.3903	77.3323
15	10.3566	3.8850	73.4472
16	9.7896	4.4520	68.9952
17	9.1399	5.1017	63.8935
18	8.3953	5.8463	58.0472
19	7.5421	6.6995	51.3477
20	6.5644	7.6772	43.6706
21	5.4440	8.7976	34.8730
22	4.1601	10.0815	24.7915
23	2.6889	11.5528	13.2387
24	1.0029	13.2387	0.0000

YEARS 25 — MO PAYT 1.1809 — AN CONST 14.18

#	INT	PRIN	BALANCE
1	13.6693	.5010	99.4990
2	13.5962	.5741	98.9250
3	13.5124	.6578	98.2672
4	13.4164	.7538	97.5133
5	13.3064	.8639	96.6495
6	13.1803	.9899	95.6595
7	13.0359	1.1344	94.5251
8	12.8703	1.2999	93.2252
9	12.6806	1.4897	91.7355
10	12.4632	1.7071	90.0285
11	12.2141	1.9562	88.0723
12	11.9286	2.2417	85.8307
13	11.6015	2.5688	83.2619
14	11.2266	2.9437	80.3182
15	10.7970	3.3733	76.9449
16	10.3047	3.8656	73.0793
17	9.7406	4.4297	68.6496
18	9.0941	5.0762	63.5734
19	8.3533	5.8170	57.7564
20	7.5044	6.6659	51.0905
21	6.5315	7.6387	43.4518
22	5.4168	8.7535	34.6983
23	4.1393	10.0310	24.6673
24	2.6754	11.4949	13.1724
25	.9978	13.1724	0.0000

YEARS 26 — MO PAYT 1.1757 — AN CONST 14.11

#	INT	PRIN	BALANCE
1	13.6733	.4353	99.5647
2	13.6098	.4988	99.0660
3	13.5370	.5716	98.4944
4	13.4536	.6550	97.8394
5	13.3580	.7506	97.0889
6	13.2485	.8601	96.2288
7	13.1230	.9856	95.2432
8	12.9791	1.1295	94.1137
9	12.8143	1.2943	92.8194
10	12.6254	1.4832	91.3363
11	12.4090	1.6996	89.6366
12	12.1609	1.9477	87.6890
13	11.8767	2.2319	85.4571
14	11.5510	2.5576	82.8995
15	11.1777	2.9309	79.9686
16	10.7500	3.3586	76.6100
17	10.2598	3.8488	72.7612
18	9.6982	4.4104	68.3508
19	9.0545	5.0541	63.2967
20	8.3169	5.7917	57.5050
21	7.4717	6.6369	50.8681
22	6.5031	7.6055	43.2627
23	5.3932	8.7154	34.5473
24	4.1213	9.9873	24.5599
25	2.6637	11.4449	13.1151
26	.9935	13.1151	0.0000

YEARS 27 — MO PAYT 1.1713 — AN CONST 14.06

#	INT	PRIN	BALANCE
1	13.6768	.3784	99.6216
2	13.6216	.4336	99.1880
3	13.5583	.4969	98.6911
4	13.4858	.5694	98.1217
5	13.4027	.6525	97.4692
6	13.3075	.7477	96.7215
7	13.1984	.8568	95.8647
8	13.0733	.9819	94.8828
9	12.9300	1.1252	93.7576
10	12.7658	1.2894	92.4682
11	12.5776	1.4776	90.9907
12	12.3620	1.6932	89.2975
13	12.1149	1.9403	87.3572
14	11.8318	2.2235	85.1337
15	11.5073	2.5479	82.5858
16	11.1354	2.9198	79.6660
17	10.7093	3.3459	76.3201
18	10.2210	3.8342	72.4859
19	9.6615	4.3937	68.0922
20	9.0202	5.0350	63.0572
21	8.2855	5.7698	57.2875
22	7.4434	6.6118	50.6757
23	6.4785	7.5767	43.0990
24	5.3728	8.6824	34.4165
25	4.1057	9.9495	24.4670
26	2.6537	11.4015	13.0655
27	.9897	13.0655	0.0000

YEARS 28 — MO PAYT 1.1674 — AN CONST 14.01

#	INT	PRIN	BALANCE
1	13.6798	.3291	99.6709
2	13.6318	.3771	99.2938
3	13.5768	.4322	98.8616
4	13.5137	.4952	98.3663
5	13.4414	.5675	97.7988
6	13.3586	.6503	97.1485
7	13.2637	.7453	96.4032
8	13.1549	.8540	95.5492
9	13.0303	.9787	94.5705
10	12.8875	1.1215	93.4490
11	12.7238	1.2851	92.1639
12	12.5363	1.4727	90.6912
13	12.3213	1.6876	89.0036
14	12.0750	1.9339	87.0697
15	11.7928	2.2161	84.8535
16	11.4694	2.5396	82.3140
17	11.0988	2.9102	79.4038
18	10.6741	3.3349	76.0689
19	10.1874	3.8216	72.2474
20	9.6297	4.3793	67.8681
21	8.9906	5.0184	62.8497
22	8.2582	5.7508	57.0989
23	7.4189	6.5900	50.5089
24	6.4572	7.5518	42.9571
25	5.3551	8.6539	34.3033
26	4.0922	9.9168	24.3865
27	2.6449	11.3640	13.0225
28	.9865	13.0225	0.0000

YEARS 29 — MO PAYT 1.1641 — AN CONST 13.97

#	INT	PRIN	BALANCE
1	13.6825	.2864	99.7136
2	13.6407	.3282	99.3855
3	13.5928	.3761	99.0094
4	13.5379	.4309	98.5785
5	13.4750	.4938	98.0846
6	13.4029	.5659	97.5187
7	13.3203	.6485	96.8703
8	13.2257	.7431	96.1271
9	13.1173	.8516	95.2756
10	12.9930	.9759	94.2997
11	12.8506	1.1183	93.1814
12	12.6874	1.2815	91.9000
13	12.5004	1.4685	90.4315
14	12.2860	1.6828	88.7487
15	12.0405	1.9284	86.8203
16	11.7590	2.2098	84.6105
17	11.4365	2.5323	82.0783
18	11.0670	2.9018	79.1764
19	10.6435	3.3253	75.8511
20	10.1582	3.8106	72.0405
21	9.6021	4.3667	67.6737
22	8.9648	5.0040	62.6697
23	8.2345	5.7343	56.9354
24	7.3977	6.5712	50.3642
25	6.4387	7.5301	42.8341
26	5.3398	8.6291	34.2050
27	4.0804	9.8884	24.3167
28	2.6374	11.3315	12.9852
29	.9837	12.9852	0.0000

YEARS 30 — MO PAYT 1.1612 — AN CONST 13.94

#	INT	PRIN	BALANCE
1	13.6847	.2493	99.7507
2	13.6484	.2857	99.4651
3	13.6067	.3273	99.1377
4	13.5589	.3751	98.7626
5	13.5041	.4299	98.3327
6	13.4414	.4926	97.8401
7	13.3695	.5645	97.2756
8	13.2871	.6469	96.6288
9	13.1927	.7413	95.8875
10	13.0846	.8495	95.0380
11	12.9606	.9734	94.0646
12	12.8185	1.1155	92.9492
13	12.6557	1.2783	91.6709
14	12.4692	1.4648	90.2061
15	12.2554	1.6786	88.5275
16	12.0105	1.9236	86.6039
17	11.7297	2.2043	84.3996
18	11.4080	2.5260	81.8737
19	11.0394	2.8946	78.9790
20	10.6170	3.3170	75.6620
21	10.1329	3.8011	71.8609
22	9.5782	4.3559	67.5050
23	8.9425	4.9915	62.5135
24	8.2140	5.7200	56.7935
25	7.3792	6.5548	50.2387
26	6.4226	7.5114	42.7273
27	5.3265	8.6076	34.1198
28	4.0703	9.8637	24.2560
29	2.6308	11.3032	12.9528
30	.9812	12.9528	0.0000

MONTHLY PAYMENT AMORTIZATION SCHEDULE PER $100

13.75 %

YEARS 2 — MO PAYT 4.7895 — AN CONST 57.48

#	INT	PRIN	BALANCE
1	10.8865	46.5874	53.4126
2	4.0612	53.4126	0.0000

YEARS 3 — MO PAYT 3.4056 — AN CONST 40.87

#	INT	PRIN	BALANCE
1	11.9740	28.8936	71.1064
2	7.7410	33.1266	37.9798
3	2.8878	37.9798	0.0000

YEARS 4 — MO PAYT 2.7201 — AN CONST 32.65

#	INT	PRIN	BALANCE
1	12.5128	20.1287	79.8713
2	9.5638	23.0777	56.7936
3	6.1828	26.4587	30.3350
4	2.3065	30.3350	0.0000

YEARS 5 — MO PAYT 2.3139 — AN CONST 27.77

#	INT	PRIN	BALANCE
1	12.8320	14.9346	85.0654
2	10.6440	17.1226	67.9429
3	8.1355	19.6531	48.3117
4	5.2594	22.5072	25.8046
5	1.9620	25.8046	0.0000

YEARS 6 — MO PAYT 2.0472 — AN CONST 24.57

#	INT	PRIN	BALANCE
1	13.0416	11.5249	88.4751
2	11.3532	13.2134	75.2617
3	9.4172	15.1492	60.1125
4	7.1979	17.3686	42.7439
5	4.6533	19.9132	22.8306
6	1.7359	22.8306	0.0000

YEARS 7 — MO PAYT 1.8602 — AN CONST 22.33

#	INT	PRIN	BALANCE
1	13.1886	9.1340	90.8660
2	11.8504	10.4722	80.3937
3	10.3162	12.0065	68.3873
4	8.5571	13.7655	54.6218
5	6.5404	15.7822	38.8396
6	4.2283	18.0943	20.7453
7	1.5774	20.7453	0.0000

YEARS 8 — MO PAYT 1.7230 — AN CONST 20.68

#	INT	PRIN	BALANCE
1	13.2964	7.3790	92.6210
2	12.2154	8.4600	84.1610
3	10.9759	9.6995	74.4615
4	9.5549	11.1205	63.3410
5	7.9257	12.7497	50.5913
6	6.0578	14.6176	35.9736
7	3.9163	16.7592	19.2145
8	1.4610	19.2145	0.0000

YEARS 9 — MO PAYT 1.6188 — AN CONST 19.43

#	INT	PRIN	BALANCE
1	13.3783	6.0469	93.9531
2	12.4924	6.9328	87.0203
3	11.4767	7.9485	79.0718
4	10.3122	9.1130	69.9589
5	8.9771	10.4481	59.5108
6	7.4465	11.9788	47.5321
7	5.6915	13.7337	33.7984
8	3.6795	15.7458	18.0526
9	1.3726	18.0526	0.0000

YEARS 10 — MO PAYT 1.5377 — AN CONST 18.46

#	INT	PRIN	BALANCE
1	13.4421	5.0100	94.9900
2	12.7081	5.7439	89.2461
3	11.8666	6.5855	82.6606
4	10.9018	7.5503	75.1104
5	9.7956	8.6564	66.4540
6	8.5274	9.9246	56.5294
7	7.0734	11.3786	45.1507
8	5.4064	13.0457	32.1051
9	3.4951	14.9569	17.1482
10	1.3038	17.1482	0.0000

YEARS 11 — MO PAYT 1.4733 — AN CONST 17.68

#	INT	PRIN	BALANCE
1	13.4927	4.1868	95.8132
2	12.8793	4.8002	91.0130
3	12.1760	5.5035	85.5095
4	11.3697	6.3097	79.1998
5	10.4453	7.2341	71.9657
6	9.3855	8.2940	63.6717
7	8.1704	9.5091	54.1626
8	6.7772	10.9022	43.2603
9	5.1800	12.4995	30.7609
10	3.3488	14.3307	16.4302
11	1.2493	16.4302	0.0000

YEARS 12 — MO PAYT 1.4214 — AN CONST 17.06

#	INT	PRIN	BALANCE
1	13.5334	3.5231	96.4769
2	13.0173	4.0393	92.4376
3	12.4255	4.6311	87.8065
4	11.7470	5.3096	82.4969
5	10.9692	6.0874	76.4095
6	10.0773	6.9793	69.4302
7	9.0548	8.0018	61.4284
8	7.8825	9.1741	52.2543
9	6.5385	10.5181	41.7362
10	4.9975	12.0591	29.6771
11	3.2308	13.8258	15.8513
12	1.2052	15.8513	0.0000

YEARS 13 — MO PAYT 1.3790 — AN CONST 16.55

#	INT	PRIN	BALANCE
1	13.5668	2.9813	97.0187
2	13.1300	3.4181	93.6006
3	12.6292	3.9189	89.6817
4	12.0551	4.4930	85.1887
5	11.3968	5.1513	80.0374
6	10.6421	5.9059	74.1315
7	9.7769	6.7712	67.3603
8	8.7849	7.7632	59.5970
9	7.6475	8.9006	50.6965
10	6.3435	10.2045	40.4919
11	4.8485	11.6996	28.7924
12	3.1345	13.4136	15.3788
13	1.1693	15.3788	0.0000

YEARS 14 — MO PAYT 1.3441 — AN CONST 16.13

#	INT	PRIN	BALANCE
1	13.5942	2.5345	97.4655
2	13.2229	2.9058	94.5598
3	12.7972	3.3315	91.2283
4	12.3091	3.8196	87.4087
5	11.7495	4.3791	83.0296
6	11.1080	5.0207	78.0089
7	10.3724	5.7563	72.2526
8	9.5291	6.5996	65.6530
9	8.5622	7.5665	58.0866
10	7.4537	8.6750	49.4116
11	6.1828	9.9459	39.4657
12	4.7256	11.4030	28.0626
13	3.0550	13.0736	14.9890
14	1.1397	14.9890	0.0000

YEARS 15 — MO PAYT 1.3150 — AN CONST 15.78

#	INT	PRIN	BALANCE
1	13.6171	2.1628	97.8372
2	13.3002	2.4796	95.3576
3	12.9369	2.8429	92.5146
4	12.5204	3.2594	89.2552
5	12.0429	3.7369	85.5183
6	11.4954	4.2844	81.2338
7	10.8677	4.9121	76.3217
8	10.1481	5.6318	70.6900
9	9.3230	6.4569	64.2331
10	8.3770	7.4028	56.8303
11	7.2925	8.4874	48.3429
12	6.0490	9.7308	38.6121
13	4.6234	11.1564	27.4557
14	2.9890	12.7909	14.6648
15	1.1150	14.6648	0.0000

YEARS 16 — MO PAYT 1.2906 — AN CONST 15.49

#	INT	PRIN	BALANCE
1	13.6362	1.8515	98.1485
2	13.3649	2.1227	96.0258
3	13.0540	2.4337	93.5920
4	12.6974	2.7903	90.8018
5	12.2886	3.1991	87.6027
6	11.8199	3.6678	83.9349
7	11.2826	4.2051	79.7298
8	10.6665	4.8212	74.9086
9	9.9602	5.5275	69.3811
10	9.1504	6.3373	63.0438
11	8.2219	7.2658	55.7781
12	7.1575	8.3302	47.4479
13	5.9370	9.5506	37.8972
14	4.5378	10.9499	26.9474
15	2.9336	12.5541	14.3933
16	1.0944	14.3933	0.0000

YEARS 17 — MO PAYT 1.2701 — AN CONST 15.25

#	INT	PRIN	BALANCE
1	13.6523	1.5892	98.4108
2	13.4195	1.8221	96.5887
3	13.1525	2.0890	94.4997
4	12.8465	2.3951	92.1046
5	12.4956	2.7459	89.3587
6	12.0933	3.1482	86.2105
7	11.6321	3.6095	82.6010
8	11.1033	4.1383	78.4627
9	10.4970	4.7446	73.7182
10	9.8019	5.4397	68.2785
11	9.0050	6.2366	62.0419
12	8.0913	7.1503	54.8916
13	7.0437	8.1978	46.6938
14	5.8427	9.3989	37.2949
15	4.4657	10.7758	26.5191
16	2.8870	12.3546	14.1646
17	1.0770	14.1646	0.0000

YEARS 18 — MO PAYT 1.2528 — AN CONST 15.04

#	INT	PRIN	BALANCE
1	13.6660	1.3672	98.6328
2	13.4657	1.5675	97.0653
3	13.2360	1.7972	95.2681
4	12.9727	2.0604	93.2077
5	12.6709	2.3623	90.8454
6	12.3248	2.7084	88.1370
7	11.9280	3.1052	85.0318
8	11.4730	3.5601	81.4717
9	10.9515	4.0817	77.3900
10	10.3535	4.6797	72.7103
11	9.6679	5.3653	67.3450
12	8.8818	6.1513	61.1937
13	7.9806	7.0525	54.1412
14	6.9474	8.0858	46.0554
15	5.7628	9.2704	36.7851
16	4.4047	10.6285	26.1565
17	2.8475	12.1856	13.9709
18	1.0623	13.9709	0.0000

YEARS 19 — MO PAYT 1.2380 — AN CONST 14.86

#	INT	PRIN	BALANCE
1	13.6776	1.1784	98.8216
2	13.5049	1.3511	97.4705
3	13.3070	1.5490	95.9214
4	13.0800	1.7760	94.1455
5	12.8198	2.0362	92.1093
6	12.5215	2.3345	89.7748
7	12.1795	2.6765	87.0983
8	11.7874	3.0686	84.0297
9	11.3378	3.5182	80.5116
10	10.8224	4.0336	76.4780
11	10.2315	4.6245	71.8534
12	9.5540	5.3021	66.5514
13	8.7772	6.0788	60.4726
14	7.8866	6.9694	53.5031
15	6.8655	7.9905	45.5127
16	5.6949	9.1611	36.3516
17	4.3527	10.5033	25.8483
18	2.8140	12.0420	13.8063
19	1.0498	13.8063	0.0000

YEARS 20 — MO PAYT 1.2254 — AN CONST 14.71

#	INT	PRIN	BALANCE
1	13.6875	1.0174	98.9826
2	13.5384	1.1665	97.8161
3	13.3675	1.3373	96.4788
4	13.1716	1.5333	94.9455
5	12.9470	1.7579	93.1876
6	12.6894	2.0154	91.1722
7	12.3941	2.3107	88.8615
8	12.0556	2.6493	86.2122
9	11.6675	3.0374	83.1748
10	11.2225	3.4824	79.6924
11	10.7123	3.9926	75.6999
12	10.1274	4.5775	71.1224
13	9.4568	5.2481	65.8743
14	8.6879	6.0170	59.8573
15	7.8064	6.8985	52.9588
16	6.7957	7.9092	45.0496
17	5.6370	9.0679	35.9817
18	4.3085	10.3964	25.5853
19	2.7853	11.9195	13.6658
20	1.0391	13.6658	0.0000

YEARS 21 — MO PAYT 1.2146 — AN CONST 14.58

#	INT	PRIN	BALANCE
1	13.6959	.8796	99.1204
2	13.5671	1.0085	98.1120
3	13.4193	1.1562	96.9558

#	INT	PRIN	BALANCE
4	13.2499	1.3256	95.6302
5	13.0557	1.5198	94.1104
6	12.8331	1.7424	92.3680
7	12.5778	1.9977	90.3702
8	12.2851	2.2904	88.0798
9	11.9496	2.6259	85.4539
10	11.5649	3.0107	82.4432
11	11.1238	3.4517	78.9915
12	10.6181	3.9574	75.0340
13	10.0383	4.5372	70.4968
14	9.3736	5.2020	65.2949
15	8.6115	5.9641	59.3308
16	7.7377	6.8378	52.4930
17	6.7359	7.8396	44.6534
18	5.5874	8.9881	35.6652
19	4.2706	10.3050	25.3603
20	2.7608	11.8147	13.5456
21	1.0299	13.5456	0.0000

YEARS 22   MO PAYT 1.2054   AN CONST 14.47

#	INT	PRIN	BALANCE
1	13.7032	.7613	99.2387
2	13.5917	.8729	98.3658
3	13.4638	1.0008	97.3650
4	13.3172	1.1474	96.2176
5	13.1491	1.3155	94.9021
6	12.9563	1.5082	93.3939
7	12.7354	1.7292	91.6647
8	12.4820	1.9825	89.6822
9	12.1916	2.2730	87.4092
10	11.8586	2.6060	84.8033
11	11.4768	2.9877	81.8155
12	11.0391	3.4255	78.3901
13	10.5372	3.9273	74.4628
14	9.9619	4.5027	69.9601
15	9.3022	5.1623	64.7977
16	8.5459	5.9187	58.8791
17	7.6788	6.7858	52.0933
18	6.6846	7.7799	44.3134
19	5.5448	8.9197	35.3937
20	4.2381	10.2265	25.1672
21	2.7398	11.7247	13.4425
22	1.0221	13.4425	0.0000

YEARS 23   MO PAYT 1.1974   AN CONST 14.37

#	INT	PRIN	BALANCE
1	13.7095	.6597	99.3403
2	13.6128	.7563	98.5840
3	13.5020	.8671	97.7169
4	13.3750	.9942	96.7227
5	13.2293	1.1398	95.5829
6	13.0623	1.3068	94.2761
7	12.8709	1.4983	92.7778
8	12.6514	1.7178	91.0600
9	12.3997	1.9694	89.0906
10	12.1112	2.2580	86.8326
11	11.7804	2.5888	84.2439
12	11.4011	2.9680	81.2758
13	10.9663	3.4029	77.8730
14	10.4677	3.9014	73.9716
15	9.8962	4.4730	69.4986
16	9.2408	5.1283	64.3703
17	8.4895	5.8796	58.4907
18	7.6281	6.7410	51.7497
19	6.6405	7.7286	44.0211
20	5.5083	8.8609	35.1602
21	4.2101	10.1590	25.0012
22	2.7217	11.6474	13.3538
23	1.0153	13.3538	0.0000

YEARS 24   MO PAYT 1.1906   AN CONST 14.29

#	INT	PRIN	BALANCE
1	13.7148	.5721	99.4279
2	13.6310	.6559	98.7720
3	13.5349	.7520	98.0200
4	13.4248	.8622	97.1578
5	13.2984	.9885	96.1693
6	13.1536	1.1333	95.0360
7	12.9876	1.2993	93.7367
8	12.7972	1.4897	92.2470
9	12.5790	1.7079	90.5391
10	12.3288	1.9582	88.5809
11	12.0419	2.2450	86.3359
12	11.7130	2.5740	83.7619
13	11.3359	2.9511	80.8109
14	10.9035	3.3834	77.4275
15	10.4078	3.8791	73.5484
16	9.8395	4.4474	69.1010
17	9.1880	5.0990	64.0020
18	8.4410	5.8460	58.1561
19	7.5845	6.7024	51.4536
20	6.6025	7.6844	43.7692
21	5.4767	8.8102	34.9591
22	4.1860	10.1009	24.8581
23	2.7062	11.5808	13.2774
24	1.0095	13.2774	0.0000

YEARS 25   MO PAYT 1.1847   AN CONST 14.22

#	INT	PRIN	BALANCE
1	13.7195	.4965	99.5035
2	13.6467	.5693	98.9342
3	13.5633	.6526	98.2816
4	13.4677	.7483	97.5333
5	13.3581	.8579	96.6754
6	13.2324	.9836	95.6919
7	13.0883	1.1277	94.5642
8	12.9231	1.2929	93.2713
9	12.7337	1.4823	91.7890
10	12.5165	1.6995	90.0895
11	12.2675	1.9484	88.1411
12	11.9821	2.2339	85.9072
13	11.6548	2.5612	83.3460
14	11.2796	2.9364	80.4096
15	10.8494	3.3666	77.0430
16	10.3562	3.8598	73.1832
17	9.7907	4.4253	68.7579
18	9.1424	5.0736	63.6843
19	8.3990	5.8169	57.8673
20	7.5468	6.6692	51.1981
21	6.5698	7.6462	43.5519
22	5.4496	8.7664	34.7855
23	4.1652	10.0508	24.7347
24	2.6927	11.5233	13.2115
25	1.0045	13.2115	0.0000

YEARS 26   MO PAYT 1.1796   AN CONST 14.16

#	INT	PRIN	BALANCE
1	13.7235	.4312	99.5688
2	13.6603	.4944	99.0744
3	13.5879	.5668	98.5076
4	13.5049	.6498	97.8578
5	13.4097	.7450	97.1128
6	13.3005	.8542	96.2586
7	13.1754	.9793	95.2792
8	13.0319	1.1228	94.1564
9	12.8674	1.2873	92.8691
10	12.6788	1.4759	91.3932
11	12.4626	1.6921	89.7011
12	12.2147	1.9400	87.7610
13	11.9304	2.2243	85.5368
14	11.6046	2.5501	82.9866
15	11.2310	2.9237	80.0629
16	10.8026	3.3521	76.7108
17	10.3115	3.8432	72.8676
18	9.7485	4.4062	68.4614
19	9.1029	5.0518	63.4097
20	8.3628	5.7919	57.6178
21	7.5143	6.6404	50.9774
22	6.5414	7.6133	43.3641
23	5.4261	8.7286	34.6355
24	4.1473	10.0074	24.6281
25	2.6811	11.4736	13.1545
26	1.0002	13.1545	0.0000

YEARS 27   MO PAYT 1.1751   AN CONST 14.11

#	INT	PRIN	BALANCE
1	13.7270	.3747	99.6253
2	13.6721	.4296	99.1957
3	13.6091	.4925	98.7032
4	13.5370	.5647	98.1385
5	13.4543	.6474	97.4911
6	13.3594	.7422	96.7489
7	13.2507	.8510	95.8979
8	13.1260	.9757	94.9222
9	12.9831	1.1186	93.8036
10	12.8192	1.2825	92.5211
11	12.6313	1.4704	91.0508
12	12.4159	1.6858	89.3650
13	12.1689	1.9328	87.4322
14	11.8857	2.2159	85.2163
15	11.5611	2.5406	82.6757
16	11.1889	2.9128	79.7629
17	10.7621	3.3395	76.4234
18	10.2729	3.8288	72.5946
19	9.7119	4.3897	68.2049
20	9.0688	5.0328	63.1721
21	8.3315	5.7702	57.4019
22	7.4861	6.6155	50.7864
23	6.5169	7.5847	43.2016
24	5.4057	8.6959	34.5057
25	4.1317	9.9699	24.5358
26	2.6711	11.4306	13.1052
27	.9964	13.1052	0.0000

YEARS 28   MO PAYT 1.1713   AN CONST 14.06

#	INT	PRIN	BALANCE
1	13.7300	.3257	99.6743
2	13.6823	.3735	99.3008
3	13.6275	.4282	98.8726
4	13.5648	.4909	98.3817
5	13.4929	.5628	97.8189
6	13.4104	.6453	97.1736
7	13.3159	.7398	96.4337
8	13.2075	.8482	95.5855
9	13.0832	.9725	94.6130
10	12.9408	1.1150	93.4981
11	12.7774	1.2783	92.2198
12	12.5901	1.4656	90.7542
13	12.3754	1.6803	89.0739
14	12.1292	1.9265	87.1474
15	11.8470	2.2087	84.9387
16	11.5234	2.5323	82.4064
17	11.1524	2.9033	79.5031
18	10.7271	3.3286	76.1744
19	10.2394	3.8163	72.3581
20	9.6803	4.3754	67.9827
21	9.0393	5.0164	62.9663
22	8.3044	5.7514	57.2149
23	7.4617	6.5940	50.6209
24	6.4957	7.5600	43.0609
25	5.3881	8.6676	34.3933
26	4.1183	9.9375	24.4559
27	2.6624	11.3933	13.0625
28	.9932	13.0625	0.0000

YEARS 29   MO PAYT 1.1680   AN CONST 14.02

#	INT	PRIN	BALANCE
1	13.7326	.2833	99.7167
2	13.6911	.3248	99.3919
3	13.6435	.3724	99.0195
4	13.5889	.4270	98.5925
5	13.5264	.4895	98.1030
6	13.4547	.5612	97.5417
7	13.3724	.6435	96.8983
8	13.2782	.7377	96.1605
9	13.1701	.8458	95.3147
10	13.0462	.9697	94.3450
11	12.9041	1.1118	93.2332
12	12.7412	1.2747	91.9585
13	12.5545	1.4614	90.4971
14	12.3404	1.6755	88.8215
15	12.0949	1.9210	86.9005
16	11.8134	2.2025	84.6980
17	11.4908	2.5251	82.1729
18	11.1208	2.8951	79.2778
19	10.6967	3.3192	75.9586
20	10.2104	3.8055	72.1531
21	9.6529	4.3630	67.7901
22	9.0137	5.0022	62.7879
23	8.2808	5.7351	57.0528
24	7.4406	6.5753	50.4775
25	6.4773	7.5386	42.9389
26	5.3729	8.6430	34.2959
27	4.1066	9.9093	24.3866
28	2.6548	11.3611	13.0255
29	.9904	13.0255	0.0000

YEARS 30   MO PAYT 1.1651   AN CONST 13.99

#	INT	PRIN	BALANCE
1	13.7348	.2465	99.7535
2	13.6987	.2826	99.4709
3	13.6573	.3240	99.1469
4	13.6099	.3715	98.7754
5	13.5554	.4259	98.3495
6	13.4930	.4883	97.8611
7	13.4215	.5599	97.3013
8	13.3395	.6419	96.6594
9	13.2454	.7359	95.9235
10	13.1376	.8437	95.0798
11	13.0140	.9673	94.1124
12	12.8723	1.1091	93.0034
13	12.7098	1.2715	91.7318
14	12.5235	1.4578	90.2740
15	12.3099	1.6714	88.6026
16	12.0651	1.9163	86.6863
17	11.7843	2.1970	84.4893
18	11.4624	2.5189	81.9704
19	11.0934	2.8879	79.0824
20	10.6703	3.3110	75.7714
21	10.1852	3.7961	71.9753
22	9.6291	4.3523	67.6230
23	8.9915	4.9899	62.6331
24	8.2604	5.7209	56.9122
25	7.4223	6.5591	50.3531
26	6.4613	7.5200	42.8331
27	5.3596	8.6217	34.2113
28	4.0965	9.8849	24.3265
29	2.6483	11.3331	12.9934
30	.9879	12.9934	0.0000

YEARS 2 — MO PAYT 4.7918 — AN CONST 57.51

#	INT	PRIN	BALANCE
1	10.9271	46.5751	53.4249
2	4.0772	53.4249	0.0000

YEARS 3 — MO PAYT 3.4081 — AN CONST 40.90

#	INT	PRIN	BALANCE
1	12.0187	28.8780	71.1220
2	7.7716	33.1251	37.9969
3	2.8998	37.9969	0.0000

YEARS 4 — MO PAYT 2.7226 — AN CONST 32.68

#	INT	PRIN	BALANCE
1	12.5594	20.1121	79.8879
2	9.6015	23.0700	56.8179
3	6.2085	26.4630	30.3549
4	2.3166	30.3549	0.0000

YEARS 5 — MO PAYT 2.3165 — AN CONST 27.80

#	INT	PRIN	BALANCE
1	12.8798	14.9178	85.0822
2	10.6858	17.1118	67.9704
3	8.1692	19.6285	48.3419
4	5.2824	22.5153	25.8266
5	1.9710	25.8266	0.0000

YEARS 6 — MO PAYT 2.0499 — AN CONST 24.60

#	INT	PRIN	BALANCE
1	13.0901	11.5084	88.4916
2	11.3976	13.2010	75.2906
3	9.4561	15.1425	60.1480
4	7.2290	17.3695	42.7785
5	4.6744	19.9241	22.8544
6	1.7442	22.8544	0.0000

YEARS 7 — MO PAYT 1.8630 — AN CONST 22.36

#	INT	PRIN	BALANCE
1	13.2376	9.1181	90.8819
2	11.8966	10.4591	80.4228
3	10.3583	11.9973	68.4255
4	8.5938	13.7618	54.6637
5	6.5699	15.7858	38.8779
6	4.2482	18.1074	20.7705
7	1.5851	20.7705	0.0000

YEARS 8 — MO PAYT 1.7258 — AN CONST 20.71

#	INT	PRIN	BALANCE
1	13.3458	7.3637	92.6363
2	12.2628	8.4467	84.1897
3	11.0205	9.6889	74.5008
4	9.5956	11.1139	63.3869
5	7.9610	12.7484	50.6385
6	6.0861	14.6234	36.0151
7	3.9354	16.7740	19.2410
8	1.4684	19.2410	0.0000

YEARS 9 — MO PAYT 1.6217 — AN CONST 19.47

#	INT	PRIN	BALANCE
1	13.4279	6.0323	93.9677
2	12.5407	6.9195	87.0482
3	11.5231	7.9371	79.1111
4	10.3557	9.1045	70.0067
5	9.0167	10.4435	59.5632
6	7.4808	11.9794	47.5838
7	5.7190	13.7412	33.8426
8	3.6980	15.7622	18.0804
9	1.3798	18.0804	0.0000

YEARS 10 — MO PAYT 1.5407 — AN CONST 18.49

#	INT	PRIN	BALANCE
1	13.4918	4.9961	95.0039
2	12.7570	5.7309	89.2730
3	11.9142	6.5738	82.6992
4	10.9474	7.5406	75.1586
5	9.8384	8.6496	66.5090
6	8.5662	9.9217	56.5874
7	7.1070	11.3809	45.2065
8	5.4332	13.0547	32.1517
9	3.5132	14.9747	17.1770
10	1.3109	17.1770	0.0000

YEARS 11 — MO PAYT 1.4764 — AN CONST 17.72

#	INT	PRIN	BALANCE
1	13.5425	4.1738	95.8262
2	12.9287	4.7876	91.0387
3	12.2246	5.4917	85.5469
4	11.4169	6.2994	79.2476
5	10.4904	7.2259	72.0217
6	9.4277	8.2886	63.7331
7	8.2087	9.5076	54.2255
8	6.8104	10.9059	43.3196
9	5.2065	12.5098	30.8098
10	3.3666	14.3497	16.4601
11	1.2562	16.4601	0.0000

YEARS 12 — MO PAYT 1.4245 — AN CONST 17.10

#	INT	PRIN	BALANCE
1	13.5834	3.5109	96.4891
2	13.0671	4.0272	92.4619
3	12.4748	4.6195	87.8424
4	11.7954	5.2989	82.5435
5	11.0161	6.0782	76.4653
6	10.1221	6.9722	69.4931
7	9.0967	7.9976	61.4955
8	7.9205	9.1738	52.3217
9	6.5713	10.5230	41.7988
10	5.0237	12.0706	29.7281
11	3.2484	13.8459	15.8822
12	1.2121	15.8822	0.0000

YEARS 13 — MO PAYT 1.3822 — AN CONST 16.59

#	INT	PRIN	BALANCE
1	13.6168	2.9698	97.0302
2	13.1800	3.4066	93.6236
3	12.6790	3.9076	89.7160
4	12.1043	4.4823	85.2336
5	11.4451	5.1415	80.0921
6	10.6889	5.8977	74.1944
7	9.8215	6.7651	67.4293
8	8.8266	7.7601	59.6692
9	7.6853	8.9013	50.7679
10	6.3761	10.2105	40.5574
11	4.8745	11.7122	28.8452
12	3.1519	13.4347	15.4106
13	1.1761	15.4106	0.0000

YEARS 14 — MO PAYT 1.3473 — AN CONST 16.17

#	INT	PRIN	BALANCE
1	13.6443	2.5237	97.4763
2	13.2732	2.8949	94.5814
3	12.8474	3.3206	91.2608
4	12.3590	3.8090	87.4518
5	11.7988	4.3692	83.0826
6	11.1563	5.0118	78.0708
7	10.4192	5.7489	72.3219
8	9.5737	6.5944	65.7276
9	8.6038	7.5642	58.1634
10	7.4913	8.6767	49.4867
11	6.2152	9.9528	39.5339
12	4.7515	11.4166	28.1173
13	3.0724	13.0956	15.0216
14	1.1464	15.0216	0.0000

YEARS 15 — MO PAYT 1.3183 — AN CONST 15.82

#	INT	PRIN	BALANCE
1	13.6672	2.1528	97.8472
2	13.3506	2.4694	95.3779
3	12.9874	2.8326	92.5453
4	12.5708	3.2491	89.2962
5	12.0930	3.7270	85.5692
6	11.5448	4.2751	81.2940
7	10.9161	4.9039	76.3901
8	10.1949	5.6251	70.7650
9	9.3676	6.4524	64.3126
10	8.4186	7.4014	56.9112
11	7.3301	8.4899	48.4213
12	6.0814	9.7385	38.6828
13	4.6492	11.1708	27.5120
14	3.0063	12.8137	14.6983
15	1.1217	14.6983	0.0000

YEARS 16 — MO PAYT 1.2940 — AN CONST 15.53

#	INT	PRIN	BALANCE
1	13.6864	1.8422	98.1578
2	13.4154	2.1131	96.0447
3	13.1047	2.4239	93.6208
4	12.7482	2.7804	90.8405
5	12.3393	3.1893	87.6512
6	11.8702	3.6583	83.9928
7	11.3322	4.1964	79.7964
8	10.7150	4.8136	74.9829
9	10.0071	5.5215	69.4614
10	9.1950	6.3335	63.1279
11	8.2635	7.2650	55.8628
12	7.1950	8.3335	47.5293
13	5.9694	9.5591	37.9702
14	4.5635	10.9650	27.0052
15	2.9509	12.5777	14.4275
16	1.1011	14.4275	0.0000

YEARS 17 — MO PAYT 1.2736 — AN CONST 15.29

#	INT	PRIN	BALANCE
1	13.7025	1.5806	98.4194
2	13.4700	1.8131	96.6063
3	13.2034	2.0797	94.5266
4	12.8975	2.3856	92.1411
5	12.5467	2.7364	89.4046
6	12.1442	3.1389	86.2658
7	11.6826	3.6005	82.6652
8	11.1530	4.1301	78.5352
9	10.5456	4.7375	73.7977
10	9.8489	5.4342	68.3635
11	9.0497	6.2334	62.1301
12	8.1329	7.1502	54.9799
13	7.0813	8.2018	46.7781
14	5.8751	9.4080	37.3700
15	4.4914	10.7917	26.5783
16	2.9042	12.3789	14.1994
17	1.0837	14.1994	0.0000

YEARS 18 — MO PAYT 1.2563 — AN CONST 15.08

#	INT	PRIN	BALANCE
1	13.7162	1.3592	98.6408
2	13.5163	1.5591	97.0817
3	13.2870	1.7884	95.2933
4	13.0239	2.0514	93.2418
5	12.7222	2.3532	90.8887
6	12.3761	2.6992	88.1894
7	11.9792	3.0962	85.0932
8	11.5238	3.5516	81.5416
9	11.0015	4.0739	77.4677
10	10.4023	4.6731	72.7947
11	9.7150	5.3604	67.4343
12	8.9267	6.1487	61.2856
13	8.0224	7.0530	54.2326
14	6.9851	8.0903	46.1423
15	5.7952	9.2802	36.8621
16	4.4303	10.6450	26.2171
17	2.8648	12.2106	14.0064
18	1.0689	14.0064	0.0000

YEARS 19 — MO PAYT 1.2416 — AN CONST 14.90

#	INT	PRIN	BALANCE
1	13.7278	1.1711	98.8289
2	13.5555	1.3433	97.4856
3	13.3580	1.5409	95.9448
4	13.1314	1.7675	94.1773
5	12.8714	2.0274	92.1499
6	12.5732	2.3256	89.8243
7	12.2312	2.6676	87.1567
8	11.8389	3.0600	84.0967
9	11.3888	3.5100	80.5867
10	10.8726	4.0262	76.5605
11	10.2805	4.6184	71.9422
12	9.6012	5.2976	66.6446
13	8.8221	6.0767	60.5679
14	7.9284	6.9704	53.5975
15	6.9033	7.9956	45.6019
16	5.7273	9.1715	36.4304
17	4.3785	10.5204	25.9100
18	2.8312	12.0676	13.8424
19	1.0564	13.8424	0.0000

YEARS 20 — MO PAYT 1.2290 — AN CONST 14.75

#	INT	PRIN	BALANCE
1	13.7377	1.0106	98.9894
2	13.5890	1.1592	97.8302
3	13.4185	1.3297	96.5005
4	13.2230	1.5253	94.9752
5	12.9987	1.7496	93.2256
6	12.7413	2.0069	91.2186
7	12.4462	2.3021	88.9165
8	12.1076	2.6407	86.2759
9	11.7192	3.0290	83.2468
10	11.2737	3.4745	79.7723
11	10.7627	3.9855	75.7868
12	10.1766	4.5717	71.2151
13	9.5042	5.2440	65.9711
14	8.7330	6.0153	59.9558
15	7.8483	6.9000	53.0558
16	6.8335	7.9148	45.1410
17	5.6695	9.0788	36.0622
18	4.3342	10.4140	25.6482
19	2.8026	11.9457	13.7025
20	1.0457	13.7025	0.0000

YEARS 21 — MO PAYT 1.2183 — AN CONST 14.62

#	INT	PRIN	BALANCE
1	13.7461	.8733	99.1267
2	13.6177	1.0018	98.1249
3	13.4704	1.1491	96.9758

MONTHLY PAYMENT AMORTIZATION SCHEDULE PER $100   13.80 %

#	INT	PRIN	BALANCE
4	13.3014	1.3181	95.6577
5	13.1075	1.5120	94.1457
6	12.8851	1.7343	92.4114
7	12.6301	1.9894	90.4220
8	12.3375	2.2820	88.1400
9	12.0019	2.6176	85.5224
10	11.6169	3.0026	82.5198
11	11.1753	3.4442	79.0757
12	10.6687	3.9507	75.1249
13	10.0877	4.5318	70.5932
14	9.4212	5.1982	65.3949
15	8.6567	5.9628	59.4322
16	7.7797	6.8397	52.5925
17	6.7738	7.8456	44.7468
18	5.6199	8.9995	35.7473
19	4.2964	10.3231	25.4242
20	2.7781	11.8413	13.5829
21	1.0366	13.5829	0.0000

YEARS 22 — MO PAYT 1.2091 — AN CONST 14.51

#	INT	PRIN	BALANCE
1	13.7534	.7556	99.2444
2	13.6423	.8667	98.3777
3	13.5148	.9942	97.3835
4	13.3686	1.1404	96.2430
5	13.2008	1.3081	94.9349
6	13.0085	1.5005	93.4344
7	12.7878	1.7212	91.7131
8	12.5346	1.9744	89.7388
9	12.2443	2.2647	87.4740
10	11.9112	2.5978	84.8762
11	11.5291	2.9799	81.8963
12	11.0908	3.4181	78.4782
13	10.5881	3.9209	74.5573
14	10.0115	4.4975	70.0598
15	9.3500	5.1590	64.9008
16	8.5913	5.9177	58.9831
17	7.7210	6.7880	52.1951
18	6.7226	7.7864	44.4087
19	5.5775	8.9315	35.4772
20	4.2639	10.2451	25.2321
21	2.7571	11.7519	13.4802
22	1.0288	13.4802	0.0000

YEARS 23 — MO PAYT 1.2012 — AN CONST 14.42

#	INT	PRIN	BALANCE
1	13.7596	.6544	99.3456
2	13.6634	.7507	98.5949
3	13.5530	.8611	97.7339
4	13.4263	.9877	96.7462
5	13.2811	1.1330	95.6132
6	13.1145	1.2996	94.3136
7	12.9233	1.4907	92.8229
8	12.7041	1.7100	91.1129
9	12.4526	1.9614	89.1515
10	12.1641	2.2499	86.9016
11	11.8332	2.5808	84.3208
12	11.4537	2.9604	81.3604
13	11.0183	3.3958	77.9646
14	10.5188	3.8952	74.0694
15	9.9460	4.4681	69.6013
16	9.2888	5.1252	64.4761
17	8.5351	5.8790	58.5971
18	7.6704	6.7436	51.8535
19	6.6786	7.7354	44.1181
20	5.5410	8.8731	35.2450
21	4.2360	10.1781	25.0670
22	2.7391	11.6750	13.3920
23	1.0220	13.3920	0.0000

YEARS 24 — MO PAYT 1.1944 — AN CONST 14.34

#	INT	PRIN	BALANCE
1	13.7650	.5673	99.4327
2	13.6816	.6507	98.7820
3	13.5859	.7464	98.0356
4	13.4761	.8562	97.1795
5	13.3502	.9821	96.1974
6	13.2057	1.1265	95.0708
7	13.0401	1.2922	93.7786
8	12.8500	1.4823	92.2964
9	12.6320	1.7003	90.5961
10	12.3820	1.9503	88.6458
11	12.0951	2.2372	86.4086
12	11.7661	2.5662	83.8424
13	11.3887	2.9436	80.8988
14	10.9558	3.3765	77.5223
15	10.4592	3.8731	73.6492
16	9.8895	4.4427	69.2065
17	9.2361	5.0961	64.1103
18	8.4866	5.8456	58.2647
19	7.6269	6.7054	51.5594
20	6.6408	7.6915	43.8678
21	5.5095	8.8227	35.0451
22	4.2120	10.1203	24.9248
23	2.7236	11.6087	13.3160
24	1.0162	13.3160	0.0000

YEARS 25 — MO PAYT 1.1885 — AN CONST 14.27

#	INT	PRIN	BALANCE
1	13.7696	.4921	99.5079
2	13.6973	.5645	98.9434
3	13.6143	.6475	98.2959
4	13.5190	.7427	97.5532
5	13.4098	.8520	96.7012
6	13.2845	.9773	95.7240
7	13.1408	1.1210	94.6030
8	12.9759	1.2859	93.3171
9	12.7868	1.4750	91.8422
10	12.5699	1.6919	90.1503
11	12.3210	1.9407	88.2095
12	12.0356	2.2262	85.9834
13	11.7082	2.5536	83.4298
14	11.3326	2.9291	80.5007
15	10.9018	3.3599	77.1408
16	10.4077	3.8540	73.2868
17	9.8409	4.4209	68.8659
18	9.1907	5.0711	63.7949
19	8.4449	5.8169	57.9780
20	7.5894	6.6724	51.3056
21	6.6081	7.6537	43.6519
22	5.4824	8.7793	34.8726
23	4.1912	10.0705	24.8021
24	2.7101	11.5516	13.2505
25	1.0112	13.2505	0.0000

YEARS 26 — MO PAYT 1.1834 — AN CONST 14.21

#	INT	PRIN	BALANCE
1	13.7737	.4272	99.5728
2	13.7108	.4900	99.0828
3	13.6388	.5621	98.5208
4	13.5561	.6447	97.8760
5	13.4613	.7396	97.1365
6	13.3525	.8483	96.2881
7	13.2277	.9731	95.3151
8	13.0846	1.1162	94.1989
9	12.9205	1.2804	92.9185
10	12.7322	1.4687	91.4498
11	12.5162	1.6847	89.7652
12	12.2684	1.9324	87.8327
13	11.9842	2.2166	85.6161
14	11.6582	2.5426	83.0734
15	11.2842	2.9166	80.1568
16	10.8553	3.3455	76.8113
17	10.3632	3.8376	72.9737
18	9.7988	4.4020	68.5717
19	9.1514	5.0494	63.5223
20	8.4088	5.7920	57.7303
21	7.5570	6.6439	51.0865
22	6.5798	7.6210	43.4655
23	5.4590	8.7418	34.7237
24	4.1733	10.0275	24.6962
25	2.6986	11.5023	13.1939
26	1.0069	13.1939	0.0000

YEARS 27 — MO PAYT 1.1790 — AN CONST 14.15

#	INT	PRIN	BALANCE
1	13.7771	.3710	99.6290
2	13.7225	.4256	99.2034
3	13.6600	.4882	98.7152
4	13.5882	.5600	98.1552
5	13.5058	.6423	97.5129
6	13.4113	.7368	96.7761
7	13.3030	.8452	95.9309
8	13.1787	.9695	94.9614
9	13.0361	1.1121	93.8494
10	12.8725	1.2756	92.5737
11	12.6849	1.4632	91.1105
12	12.4697	1.6784	89.4321
13	12.2229	1.9253	87.5068
14	11.9397	2.2084	85.2984
15	11.6149	2.5332	82.7652
16	11.2424	2.9058	79.8594
17	10.8150	3.3331	76.5263
18	10.3248	3.8233	72.7030
19	9.7625	4.3857	68.3173
20	9.1175	5.0307	63.2867
21	8.3776	5.7705	57.5161
22	7.5289	6.6192	50.8969
23	6.5554	7.5927	43.3042
24	5.4388	8.7094	34.5948
25	4.1579	9.9903	24.6045
26	2.6886	11.4596	13.1450
27	1.0032	13.1450	0.0000

YEARS 28 — MO PAYT 1.1752 — AN CONST 14.11

#	INT	PRIN	BALANCE
1	13.7801	.3224	99.6776
2	13.7327	.3698	99.3078
3	13.6783	.4242	98.8835
4	13.6159	.4866	98.3969
5	13.5443	.5582	97.8388
6	13.4623	.6403	97.1985
7	13.3681	.7344	96.4641
8	13.2601	.8424	95.6216
9	13.1362	.9664	94.6553
10	12.9941	1.1085	93.5468
11	12.8310	1.2715	92.2753
12	12.6440	1.4585	90.8168
13	12.4295	1.6730	89.1438
14	12.1835	1.9191	87.2247
15	11.9012	2.2013	85.0234
16	11.5775	2.5250	82.4984
17	11.2061	2.8964	79.6020
18	10.7801	3.3224	76.2796
19	10.2915	3.8110	72.4686
20	9.7310	4.3715	68.0970
21	9.0881	5.0144	63.0826
22	8.3506	5.7519	57.3307
23	7.5047	6.5979	50.7328
24	6.5343	7.5682	43.1646
25	5.4212	8.6813	34.4833
26	4.1444	9.9581	24.5252
27	2.6799	11.4226	13.1026
28	.9999	13.1026	0.0000

YEARS 29 — MO PAYT 1.1719 — AN CONST 14.07

#	INT	PRIN	BALANCE
1	13.7827	.2803	99.7197
2	13.7415	.3215	99.3982
3	13.6942	.3688	99.0294
4	13.6400	.4230	98.6064
5	13.5777	.4852	98.1211
6	13.5064	.5566	97.5645
7	13.4245	.6385	96.9261
8	13.3306	.7324	96.1937
9	13.2229	.8401	95.3536
10	13.0994	.9636	94.3899
11	12.9576	1.1054	93.2846
12	12.7951	1.2679	92.0166
13	12.6086	1.4544	90.5622
14	12.3947	1.6683	88.8939
15	12.1493	1.9137	86.9802
16	11.8679	2.1951	84.7851
17	11.5450	2.5180	82.2671
18	11.1747	2.8883	79.3789
19	10.7499	3.3131	76.0658
20	10.2627	3.8003	72.2654
21	9.7037	4.3593	67.9062
22	9.0626	5.0004	62.9058
23	8.3272	5.7358	57.1700
24	7.4836	6.5794	50.5906
25	6.5160	7.5470	43.0436
26	5.4060	8.6570	34.3866
27	4.1328	9.9302	24.4565
28	2.6724	11.3906	13.0659
29	.9971	13.0659	0.0000

YEARS 30 — MO PAYT 1.1691 — AN CONST 14.03

#	INT	PRIN	BALANCE
1	13.7850	.2438	99.7562
2	13.7491	.2796	99.4766
3	13.7080	.3207	99.1559
4	13.6608	.3679	98.7880
5	13.6067	.4220	98.3660
6	13.5447	.4841	97.8820
7	13.4735	.5553	97.3267
8	13.3918	.6369	96.6898
9	13.2981	.7306	95.9592
10	13.1907	.8380	95.1212
11	13.0674	.9613	94.1599
12	12.9260	1.1027	93.0572
13	12.7639	1.2648	91.7924
14	12.5778	1.4509	90.3415
15	12.3645	1.6642	88.6772
16	12.1197	1.9090	86.7682
17	11.8389	2.1898	84.5784
18	11.5169	2.5118	82.0666
19	11.1475	2.8812	79.1854
20	10.7237	3.3050	75.8804
21	10.2376	3.7911	72.0893
22	9.6801	4.3486	67.7407
23	9.0405	4.9882	62.7525
24	8.3069	5.7218	57.0306
25	7.4654	6.5633	50.4673
26	6.5001	7.5286	42.9387
27	5.3928	8.6359	34.3028
28	4.1228	9.9060	24.3969
29	2.6659	11.3629	13.0340
30	.9947	13.0340	0.0000

YEARS 2 — MO PAYT 4.7954 — AN CONST 57.55

#	INT	PRIN	BALANCE
1	10.9880	46.5566	53.4434
2	4.1012	53.4434	0.0000

YEARS 3 — MO PAYT 3.4117 — AN CONST 40.95

#	INT	PRIN	BALANCE
1	12.0857	28.8546	71.1454
2	7.8175	33.1229	38.0225
3	2.9178	38.0225	0.0000

YEARS 4 — MO PAYT 2.7264 — AN CONST 32.72

#	INT	PRIN	BALANCE
1	12.6294	20.0872	79.9128
2	9.6580	23.0585	56.8543
3	6.2472	26.4694	30.3849
4	2.3317	30.3849	0.0000

YEARS 5 — MO PAYT 2.3203 — AN CONST 27.85

#	INT	PRIN	BALANCE
1	12.9515	14.8927	85.1073
2	10.7485	17.0957	68.0116
3	8.2197	19.6245	48.3871
4	5.3168	22.5274	25.8597
5	1.9845	25.8597	0.0000

YEARS 6 — MO PAYT 2.0539 — AN CONST 24.65

#	INT	PRIN	BALANCE
1	13.1629	11.4837	88.5163
2	11.4642	13.1825	75.3338
3	9.5142	15.1324	60.2014
4	7.2758	17.3709	42.8305
5	4.7062	19.9404	22.8901
6	1.7566	22.8901	0.0000

YEARS 7 — MO PAYT 1.8671 — AN CONST 22.41

#	INT	PRIN	BALANCE
1	13.3111	9.0942	90.9058
2	11.9658	10.4394	80.4664
3	10.4216	11.9836	68.4828
4	8.6490	13.7563	54.7265
5	6.6141	15.7911	38.9354
6	4.2782	18.1270	20.8084
7	1.5968	20.8084	0.0000

YEARS 8 — MO PAYT 1.7300 — AN CONST 20.77

#	INT	PRIN	BALANCE
1	13.4198	7.3407	92.6593
2	12.3339	8.4266	84.2327
3	11.0875	9.6731	74.5596
4	9.6566	11.1039	63.4557
5	8.0141	12.7465	50.7092
6	6.1286	14.6320	36.0773
7	3.9642	16.7964	19.2809
8	1.4796	19.2809	0.0000

YEARS 9 — MO PAYT 1.6261 — AN CONST 19.52

#	INT	PRIN	BALANCE
1	13.5023	6.0104	93.9896
2	12.6132	6.8995	87.0900
3	11.5926	7.9201	79.1699
4	10.4211	9.0917	70.0783
5	9.0762	10.4365	59.6417
6	7.5324	11.9803	47.6614
7	5.7602	13.7525	33.9089
8	3.7259	15.7868	18.1220
9	1.3907	18.1220	0.0000

YEARS 10 — MO PAYT 1.5452 — AN CONST 18.55

#	INT	PRIN	BALANCE
1	13.5665	4.9754	95.0246
2	12.8305	5.7114	89.3132
3	11.9857	6.5562	82.7570
4	11.0158	7.5261	75.2309
5	9.9026	8.6393	66.5916
6	8.6246	9.9173	56.6743
7	7.1576	11.3843	45.2900
8	5.4736	13.0683	32.2218
9	3.5405	15.0014	17.2204
10	1.3215	17.2204	0.0000

YEARS 11 — MO PAYT 1.4810 — AN CONST 17.78

#	INT	PRIN	BALANCE
1	13.6174	4.1542	95.8458
2	13.0029	4.7687	91.0771
3	12.2975	5.4741	85.6029
4	11.4877	6.2839	79.3190
5	10.5582	7.2134	72.1056
6	9.4912	8.2804	63.8252
7	8.2663	9.5053	54.3199
8	6.8603	10.9113	43.4086
9	5.2462	12.5254	30.8832
10	3.3934	14.3782	16.5050
11	1.2666	16.5050	0.0000

YEARS 12 — MO PAYT 1.4292 — AN CONST 17.16

#	INT	PRIN	BALANCE
1	13.6584	3.4925	96.5075
2	13.1418	4.0091	92.4984
3	12.5488	4.6022	87.8962
4	11.8680	5.2829	82.6132
5	11.0865	6.0644	76.5488
6	10.1895	6.9615	69.5873
7	9.1597	7.9912	61.5961
8	7.9776	9.1733	52.4228
9	6.6207	10.5303	41.8925
10	5.0630	12.0879	29.8046
11	3.2749	13.8760	15.9286
12	1.2224	15.9286	0.0000

YEARS 13 — MO PAYT 1.3870 — AN CONST 16.65

#	INT	PRIN	BALANCE
1	13.6919	2.9526	97.0474
2	13.2551	3.3894	93.6580
3	12.7538	3.8908	89.7672
4	12.1782	4.4663	85.3009
5	11.5176	5.1270	80.1740
6	10.7592	5.8854	74.2886
7	9.8886	6.7559	67.5327
8	8.8893	7.7553	59.7774
9	7.7421	8.9025	50.8749
10	6.4252	10.2193	40.6556
11	4.9135	11.7310	28.9246
12	3.1782	13.4663	15.4583
13	1.1863	15.4583	0.0000

YEARS 14 — MO PAYT 1.3523 — AN CONST 16.23

#	INT	PRIN	BALANCE
1	13.7195	2.5077	97.4923
2	13.3486	2.8786	94.6138
3	12.9228	3.3044	91.3094
4	12.4340	3.7932	87.5162
5	11.8729	4.3543	83.1619
6	11.2288	4.9984	78.1635
7	10.4894	5.7378	72.4257
8	9.6406	6.5865	65.8392
9	8.6663	7.5608	58.2784
10	7.5479	8.6792	49.5992
11	6.2641	9.9631	39.6361
12	4.7903	11.4368	28.1992
13	3.0985	13.1286	15.0706
14	1.1565	15.0706	0.0000

YEARS 15 — MO PAYT 1.3234 — AN CONST 15.89

#	INT	PRIN	BALANCE
1	13.7424	2.1378	97.8622
2	13.4262	2.4540	95.4081
3	13.0632	2.8171	92.5911
4	12.6465	3.2338	89.3573
5	12.1681	3.7121	85.6452
6	11.6190	4.2612	81.3840
7	10.9887	4.8915	76.4925
8	10.2651	5.6151	70.8774
9	9.4345	6.4457	64.4317
10	8.4811	7.3992	57.0325
11	7.3866	8.4937	48.5388
12	6.1302	9.7501	38.7887
13	4.6879	11.1923	27.5964
14	3.0323	12.8479	14.7485
15	1.1318	14.7485	0.0000

YEARS 16 — MO PAYT 1.2992 — AN CONST 15.59

#	INT	PRIN	BALANCE
1	13.7616	1.8283	98.1717
2	13.4912	2.0987	96.0730
3	13.1807	2.4092	93.6638
4	12.8244	2.7655	90.8983
5	12.4153	3.1746	87.7236
6	11.9457	3.6442	84.0794
7	11.4066	4.1833	79.8961
8	10.7878	4.8021	75.0940
9	10.0775	5.5124	69.5816
10	9.2620	6.3279	63.2537
11	8.3260	7.2639	55.9898
12	7.2515	8.3384	47.6514
13	6.0181	9.5718	38.0796
14	4.6022	10.9877	27.0919
15	2.9769	12.6131	14.4788
16	1.1111	14.4788	0.0000

YEARS 17 — MO PAYT 1.2788 — AN CONST 15.35

#	INT	PRIN	BALANCE
1	13.7778	1.5677	98.4323
2	13.5459	1.7996	96.6327
3	13.2797	2.0658	94.5668
4	12.9741	2.3714	92.1954
5	12.6233	2.7222	89.4732
6	12.2206	3.1249	86.3484
7	11.7584	3.5871	82.7613
8	11.2278	4.1177	78.6436
9	10.6187	4.7268	73.9167
10	9.9195	5.4260	68.4907
11	9.1168	6.2287	62.2621
12	8.1955	7.1500	55.1120
13	7.1378	8.2077	46.9044
14	5.9237	9.4218	37.4826
15	4.5300	10.8155	26.6671
16	2.9302	12.4153	14.2518
17	1.0937	14.2518	0.0000

YEARS 18 — MO PAYT 1.2616 — AN CONST 15.14

#	INT	PRIN	BALANCE
1	13.7915	1.3473	98.6527
2	13.5922	1.5466	97.1061
3	13.3634	1.7754	95.3307
4	13.1008	2.0380	93.2927
5	12.7993	2.3395	90.9533
6	12.4532	2.6855	88.2678
7	12.0560	3.0828	85.1850
8	11.6000	3.5388	81.6462
9	11.0765	4.0622	77.5840
10	10.4756	4.6631	72.9209
11	9.7858	5.3529	67.5679
12	8.9940	6.1447	61.4232
13	8.0851	7.0537	54.3695
14	7.0417	8.0971	46.2724
15	5.8439	9.2948	36.9776
16	4.4690	10.6697	26.3079
17	2.8907	12.2480	14.0598
18	1.0789	14.0598	0.0000

YEARS 19 — MO PAYT 1.2469 — AN CONST 14.97

#	INT	PRIN	BALANCE
1	13.8031	1.1601	98.8399
2	13.6315	1.3317	97.5083
3	13.4345	1.5287	95.9796
4	13.2084	1.7548	94.2248
5	12.9488	2.0143	92.2105
6	12.6508	2.3123	89.8982
7	12.3088	2.6544	87.2438
8	11.9161	3.0470	84.1968
9	11.4654	3.4977	80.6991
10	10.9480	4.0151	76.6840
11	10.3541	4.6090	72.0749
12	9.6723	5.2908	66.7841
13	8.8897	6.0735	60.7106
14	7.9913	6.9719	53.7388
15	6.9600	8.0032	45.7356
16	5.7761	9.1870	36.5486
17	4.4172	10.5460	26.0027
18	2.8572	12.1060	13.8967
19	1.0664	13.8967	0.0000

YEARS 20 — MO PAYT 1.2345 — AN CONST 14.82

#	INT	PRIN	BALANCE
1	13.8130	1.0005	98.9995
2	13.6650	1.1485	97.8511
3	13.4951	1.3183	96.5327
4	13.3001	1.5134	95.0194
5	13.0762	1.7372	93.2821
6	12.8192	1.9942	91.2879
7	12.5242	2.2892	88.9988
8	12.1856	2.6278	86.3710
9	11.7969	3.0165	83.3544
10	11.3507	3.4627	79.8917
11	10.8385	3.9749	75.9168
12	10.2505	4.5629	71.3538
13	9.5755	5.2379	66.1159
14	8.8007	6.0127	60.1033
15	7.9113	6.9021	53.2011
16	6.8903	7.9231	45.2781
17	5.7183	9.0951	36.1830
18	4.3730	10.4405	25.7425
19	2.8286	11.9848	13.7577
20	1.0558	13.7577	0.0000

YEARS 21 — MO PAYT 1.2238 — AN CONST 14.69

#	INT	PRIN	BALANCE
1	13.8214	.8640	99.1360
2	13.6936	.9918	98.1442
3	13.5469	1.1385	97.0056

MONTHLY PAYMENT AMORTIZATION SCHEDULE PER $100

13.875%

#	INT	PRIN	BALANCE
4	13.3785	1.3070	95.6987
5	13.1852	1.5003	94.1984
6	12.9632	1.7222	92.4762
7	12.7085	1.9770	90.4992
8	12.4160	2.2694	88.2298
9	12.0803	2.6051	85.6247
10	11.6950	2.9905	82.6342
11	11.2526	3.4328	79.2014
12	10.7448	3.9406	75.2608
13	10.1619	4.5235	70.7373
14	9.4928	5.1926	65.5447
15	8.7247	5.9607	59.5839
16	7.8430	6.8425	52.7415
17	6.8308	7.8546	44.8869
18	5.6689	9.0165	35.8703
19	4.3352	10.3503	25.5201
20	2.8042	11.8813	13.6388
21	1.0466	13.6388	0.0000

YEARS 22	MO PAYT 1.2146	AN CONST 14.58	
#	INT	PRIN	BALANCE
1	13.8287	.7471	99.2529
2	13.7182	.8576	98.3954
3	13.5913	.9844	97.4110
4	13.4457	1.1300	96.2809
5	13.2785	1.2972	94.9837
6	13.0867	1.4891	93.4947
7	12.8664	1.7093	91.7853
8	12.6135	1.9622	89.8231
9	12.3233	2.2524	87.5707
10	11.9901	2.5856	84.9850
11	11.6076	2.9681	82.0169
12	11.1686	3.4072	78.6097
13	10.6646	3.9112	74.6986
14	10.0860	4.4897	70.2089
15	9.4219	5.1538	65.0550
16	8.6595	5.9162	59.1388
17	7.7844	6.7914	52.3475
18	6.7798	7.7959	44.5515
19	5.6266	8.9491	35.6024
20	4.3028	10.2729	25.3294
21	2.7832	11.7925	13.5369
22	1.0388	13.5369	0.0000

YEARS 23	MO PAYT 1.2068	AN CONST 14.49	
#	INT	PRIN	BALANCE
1	13.8349	.6466	99.3534
2	13.7393	.7422	98.6112
3	13.6295	.8520	97.7592
4	13.5034	.9781	96.7811
5	13.3588	1.1227	95.6584
6	13.1927	1.2888	94.3696
7	13.0020	1.4794	92.8901
8	12.7832	1.6983	91.1918
9	12.5320	1.9495	89.2423
10	12.2436	2.2379	87.0044
11	11.9126	2.5689	84.4355
12	11.5326	2.9489	81.4866
13	11.0964	3.3851	78.1015
14	10.5859	3.8859	74.2156
15	10.0208	4.4607	69.7549
16	9.3610	5.1205	64.6344
17	8.6035	5.8780	58.7564
18	7.7340	6.7474	52.0090
19	6.7359	7.7455	44.2635
20	5.5902	8.8913	35.3722
21	4.2750	10.2065	25.1657
22	2.7652	11.7163	13.4494
23	1.0321	13.4494	0.0000

YEARS 24	MO PAYT 1.2000	AN CONST 14.41	
#	INT	PRIN	BALANCE
1	13.8403	.5601	99.4399
2	13.7574	.6430	98.7969
3	13.6623	.7381	98.0589
4	13.5531	.8472	97.2116
5	13.4278	.9726	96.2390
6	13.2839	1.1164	95.1226
7	13.1188	1.2816	93.8410
8	12.9292	1.4712	92.3699
9	12.7116	1.6888	90.6811
10	12.4618	1.9386	88.7425
11	12.1750	2.2254	86.5171
12	11.8458	2.5545	83.9626
13	11.4680	2.9324	81.0302
14	11.0342	3.3662	77.6640
15	10.5363	3.8641	73.7999
16	9.9647	4.4357	69.3642
17	9.3085	5.0918	64.2724
18	8.5553	5.8450	58.4273
19	7.6907	6.7096	51.7177
20	6.6982	7.7022	44.0155
21	5.5589	8.8415	35.1741
22	4.2510	10.1493	25.0247
23	2.7497	11.6507	13.3741
24	1.0263	13.3741	0.0000

YEARS 25	MO PAYT 1.1942	AN CONST 14.34	
#	INT	PRIN	BALANCE
1	13.8449	.4856	99.5144
2	13.7731	.5574	98.9570
3	13.6906	.6398	98.3172
4	13.5960	.7345	97.5827
5	13.4873	.8431	96.7396
6	13.3626	.9679	95.7717
7	13.2194	1.1110	94.6607
8	13.0551	1.2754	93.3854
9	12.8664	1.4640	91.9213
10	12.6499	1.6806	90.2408
11	12.4013	1.9292	88.3116
12	12.1159	2.2145	86.0970
13	11.7883	2.5421	83.5549
14	11.4123	2.9182	80.6367
15	10.9806	3.3498	77.2869
16	10.4851	3.8453	73.4416
17	9.9163	4.4142	69.0274
18	9.2633	5.0671	63.9603
19	8.5138	5.8167	58.1436
20	7.6534	6.6771	51.4666
21	6.6657	7.6648	43.8018
22	5.5319	8.7986	35.0033
23	4.2304	10.1001	24.9032
24	2.7364	11.5941	13.3091
25	1.0213	13.3091	0.0000

YEARS 26	MO PAYT 1.1892	AN CONST 14.28	
#	INT	PRIN	BALANCE
1	13.8489	.4212	99.5788
2	13.7866	.4835	99.0953
3	13.7151	.5550	98.5402
4	13.6329	.6371	97.9031
5	13.5387	.7314	97.1717
6	13.4305	.8396	96.3321
7	13.3063	.9638	95.3683
8	13.1638	1.1063	94.2620
9	13.0001	1.2700	92.9920
10	12.8122	1.4579	91.5342
11	12.5966	1.6735	89.8607
12	12.3490	1.9211	87.9396
13	12.0649	2.2052	85.7344
14	11.7387	2.5314	83.2030
15	11.3642	2.9059	80.2971

#	INT	PRIN	BALANCE
16	10.9344	3.3357	76.9614
17	10.4409	3.8291	73.1322
18	9.8745	4.3956	68.7367
19	9.2243	5.0458	63.6909
20	8.4779	5.7922	57.8987
21	7.6211	6.6489	51.2498
22	6.6376	7.6325	43.6173
23	5.5086	8.7615	34.8558
24	4.2126	10.0575	24.7983
25	2.7248	11.5453	13.2531
26	1.0170	13.2531	0.0000

YEARS 27	MO PAYT 1.1848	AN CONST 14.22	
#	INT	PRIN	BALANCE
1	13.8523	.3656	99.6344
2	13.7983	.4197	99.2147
3	13.7362	.4817	98.7330
4	13.6649	.5530	98.1800
5	13.5831	.6348	97.5452
6	13.4892	.7287	96.8164
7	13.3814	.8365	95.9799
8	13.2577	.9603	95.0197
9	13.1156	1.1023	93.9174
10	12.9526	1.2653	92.6520
11	12.7654	1.4525	91.1995
12	12.5505	1.6674	89.5321
13	12.3039	1.9140	87.6181
14	12.0208	2.1972	85.4209
15	11.6958	2.5222	82.8988
16	11.3227	2.8953	80.0035
17	10.8944	3.3235	76.6800
18	10.4028	3.8151	72.8649
19	9.8384	4.3795	68.4854
20	9.1906	5.0273	63.4580
21	8.4469	5.7710	57.6871
22	7.5933	6.6246	51.0624
23	6.6133	7.6046	43.4579
24	5.4885	8.7295	34.7284
25	4.1972	10.0207	24.7076
26	2.7149	11.5030	13.2046
27	1.0133	13.2046	0.0000

YEARS 28	MO PAYT 1.1811	AN CONST 14.18	
#	INT	PRIN	BALANCE
1	13.8553	.3175	99.6825
2	13.8084	.3644	99.3181
3	13.7544	.4183	98.8998
4	13.6926	.4802	98.4195
5	13.6215	.5513	97.8683
6	13.5400	.6328	97.2355
7	13.4464	.7264	96.5091
8	13.3389	.8339	95.6752
9	13.2156	.9572	94.7180
10	13.0740	1.0988	93.6192
11	12.9115	1.2613	92.3579
12	12.7249	1.4479	90.9100
13	12.5107	1.6621	89.2479
14	12.2648	1.9080	87.3399
15	11.9826	2.1902	85.1498
16	11.6586	2.5142	82.6356
17	11.2867	2.8861	79.7495
18	10.8598	3.3130	76.4366
19	10.3697	3.8030	72.6335
20	9.8072	4.3656	68.2679
21	9.1614	5.0114	63.2566
22	8.4201	5.7527	57.5039
23	7.5692	6.6036	50.9003
24	6.5924	7.5804	43.3199
25	5.4710	8.7017	34.6181
26	4.1839	9.9889	24.6292
27	2.7063	11.4665	13.1627

#	INT	PRIN	BALANCE
28	1.0101	13.1627	0.0000

YEARS 29	MO PAYT 1.1778	AN CONST 14.14	
#	INT	PRIN	BALANCE
1	13.8579	.2758	99.7242
2	13.8171	.3166	99.4076
3	13.7703	.3634	99.0442
4	13.7165	.4172	98.6270
5	13.6548	.4789	98.1481
6	13.5840	.5497	97.5984
7	13.5026	.6311	96.9673
8	13.4093	.7244	96.2429
9	13.3021	.8316	95.4114
10	13.1791	.9546	94.4568
11	13.0379	1.0958	93.3610
12	12.8758	1.2579	92.1032
13	12.6898	1.4439	90.6593
14	12.4762	1.6575	89.0017
15	12.2310	1.9027	87.0991
16	11.9496	2.1841	84.9149
17	11.6265	2.5072	82.4077
18	11.2556	2.8781	79.5296
19	10.8299	3.3038	76.2258
20	10.3411	3.7925	72.4332
21	9.7801	4.3536	68.0797
22	9.1362	4.9975	63.0821
23	8.3969	5.7368	57.3453
24	7.5483	6.5854	50.7599
25	6.5742	7.5595	43.2004
26	5.4559	8.6777	34.5227
27	4.1723	9.9614	24.5613
28	2.6988	11.4349	13.1264
29	1.0073	13.1264	0.0000

YEARS 30	MO PAYT 1.1750	AN CONST 14.10	
#	INT	PRIN	BALANCE
1	13.8601	.2397	99.7603
2	13.8247	.2751	99.4852
3	13.7840	.3158	99.1693
4	13.7373	.3626	98.8068
5	13.6836	.4162	98.3906
6	13.6221	.4777	97.9129
7	13.5514	.5484	97.3644
8	13.4703	.6295	96.7349
9	13.3772	.7227	96.0122
10	13.2703	.8296	95.1827
11	13.1475	.9523	94.2304
12	13.0067	1.0931	93.1373
13	12.8450	1.2548	91.8824
14	12.6594	1.4405	90.4420
15	12.4463	1.6535	88.7884
16	12.2017	1.8981	86.8903
17	11.9209	2.1789	84.7114
18	11.5986	2.5012	82.2102
19	11.2286	2.8712	79.3390
20	10.8039	3.2959	76.0431
21	10.3164	3.7835	72.2596
22	9.7567	4.3431	67.9165
23	9.1143	4.9856	62.9309
24	8.3768	5.7230	57.2079
25	7.5302	6.5696	50.6383
26	6.5584	7.5414	43.0969
27	5.4429	8.6569	34.4399
28	4.1623	9.9375	24.5024
29	2.6923	11.4075	13.0949
30	1.0049	13.0949	0.0000

MONTHLY PAYMENT AMORTIZATION SCHEDULE PER $100

13.90 %

YEARS 2 — MO PAYT 4.7966 — AN CONST 57.56

#	INT	PRIN	BALANCE
1	11.0083	46.5505	53.4495
2	4.1092	53.4495	0.0000

YEARS 3 — MO PAYT 3.4129 — AN CONST 40.96

#	INT	PRIN	BALANCE
1	12.1081	28.8468	71.1532
2	7.8328	33.1221	38.0310
3	2.9239	38.0310	0.0000

YEARS 4 — MO PAYT 2.7276 — AN CONST 32.74

#	INT	PRIN	BALANCE
1	12.6527	20.0789	79.9211
2	9.6769	23.0547	56.8664
3	6.2600	26.4716	30.3948
4	2.3368	30.3948	0.0000

YEARS 5 — MO PAYT 2.3216 — AN CONST 27.86

#	INT	PRIN	BALANCE
1	12.9754	14.8843	85.1157
2	10.7694	17.0903	68.0254
3	8.2366	19.6232	48.4022
4	5.3283	22.5315	25.8708
5	1.9890	25.8708	0.0000

YEARS 6 — MO PAYT 2.0552 — AN CONST 24.67

#	INT	PRIN	BALANCE
1	13.1872	11.4755	88.5245
2	11.4864	13.1763	75.3482
3	9.5336	15.1291	60.2191
4	7.2914	17.3713	42.8478
5	4.7168	19.9459	22.9020
6	1.7607	22.9020	0.0000

YEARS 7 — MO PAYT 1.8685 — AN CONST 22.43

#	INT	PRIN	BALANCE
1	13.3356	9.0862	90.9138
2	11.9889	10.4328	80.4810
3	10.4427	11.9791	68.5019
4	8.6674	13.7544	54.7475
5	6.6289	15.7929	38.9546
6	4.2882	18.1335	20.8210
7	1.6007	20.8210	0.0000

YEARS 8 — MO PAYT 1.7315 — AN CONST 20.78

#	INT	PRIN	BALANCE
1	13.4445	7.3331	92.6669
2	12.3577	8.4199	84.2470
3	11.1098	9.6678	74.5792
4	9.6770	11.1006	63.4786
5	8.0318	12.7458	50.7328
6	6.1428	14.6348	36.0980
7	3.9738	16.8038	19.2942
8	1.4834	19.2942	0.0000

YEARS 9 — MO PAYT 1.6275 — AN CONST 19.54

#	INT	PRIN	BALANCE
1	13.5271	6.0032	93.9968
2	12.6374	6.8929	87.1040
3	11.6158	7.9144	79.1895
4	10.4428	9.0874	70.1021
5	9.0960	10.4342	59.6679
6	7.5496	11.9806	47.6872
7	5.7740	13.7563	33.9310
8	3.7352	15.7950	18.1359
9	1.3943	18.1359	0.0000

YEARS 10 — MO PAYT 1.5467 — AN CONST 18.56

#	INT	PRIN	BALANCE
1	13.5914	4.9685	95.0315
2	12.8550	5.7049	89.3266
3	12.0095	6.5504	82.7762
4	11.0387	7.5212	75.2550
5	9.9240	8.6359	66.6191
6	8.6441	9.9158	56.7033
7	7.1745	11.3854	45.3179
8	5.4871	13.0728	32.2451
9	3.5496	15.0102	17.2349
10	1.3250	17.2349	0.0000

YEARS 11 — MO PAYT 1.4825 — AN CONST 17.80

#	INT	PRIN	BALANCE
1	13.6423	4.1477	95.8523
2	13.0276	4.7624	91.0898
3	12.3218	5.4683	85.6216
4	11.5114	6.2787	79.3428
5	10.5808	7.2093	72.1336
6	9.5124	8.2777	63.8559
7	8.2856	9.5045	54.3514
8	6.8769	10.9132	43.4382
9	5.2595	12.5306	30.9077
10	3.4024	14.3877	16.5200
11	1.2701	16.5200	0.0000

YEARS 12 — MO PAYT 1.4308 — AN CONST 17.17

#	INT	PRIN	BALANCE
1	13.6834	3.4864	96.5136
2	13.1667	4.0031	92.5105
3	12.5734	4.5964	87.9141
4	11.8922	5.2776	82.6364
5	11.1100	6.0598	76.5766
6	10.2119	6.9579	69.6187
7	9.1807	7.9891	61.6296
8	7.9967	9.1732	52.4564
9	6.6372	10.5327	41.9238
10	5.0762	12.0937	29.8301
11	3.2838	13.8860	15.9440
12	1.2258	15.9440	0.0000

YEARS 13 — MO PAYT 1.3887 — AN CONST 16.67

#	INT	PRIN	BALANCE
1	13.7169	2.9469	97.0531
2	13.2802	3.3837	93.6694
3	12.7787	3.8852	89.7843
4	12.2029	4.4610	85.3233
5	11.5418	5.1221	80.2012
6	10.7826	5.8812	74.3200
7	9.9110	6.7529	67.5671
8	8.9102	7.7537	59.8134
9	7.7610	8.9028	50.9106
10	6.4416	10.2223	40.6883
11	4.9266	11.7373	28.9510
12	3.1870	13.4768	15.4742
13	1.1897	15.4742	0.0000

YEARS 14 — MO PAYT 1.3539 — AN CONST 16.25

#	INT	PRIN	BALANCE
1	13.7446	2.5023	97.4977
2	13.3737	2.8732	94.6245
3	12.9479	3.2990	91.3255
4	12.4589	3.7879	87.5376
5	11.8975	4.3493	83.1882
6	11.2529	4.9939	78.1943
7	10.5128	5.7341	72.4603
8	9.6630	6.5839	65.8764
9	8.6872	7.5597	58.3167
10	7.5668	8.6801	49.6367
11	6.2804	9.9665	39.6702
12	4.8033	11.4436	28.2266
13	3.1073	13.1396	15.0870
14	1.1599	15.0870	0.0000

YEARS 15 — MO PAYT 1.3250 — AN CONST 15.91

#	INT	PRIN	BALANCE
1	13.7675	2.1328	97.8672
2	13.4514	2.4489	95.4182
3	13.0885	2.8119	92.6063
4	12.6717	3.2286	89.3777
5	12.1932	3.7071	85.6705
6	11.6438	4.2566	81.4140
7	11.0129	4.8874	76.5265
8	10.2886	5.6118	70.9148
9	9.4569	6.4435	64.4713
10	8.5019	7.3984	57.0729
11	7.4054	8.4949	48.5780
12	6.1464	9.7539	38.8241
13	4.7008	11.1995	27.6245
14	3.0410	12.8594	14.7652
15	1.1352	14.7652	0.0000

YEARS 16 — MO PAYT 1.3009 — AN CONST 15.62

#	INT	PRIN	BALANCE
1	13.7867	1.8237	98.1763
2	13.5164	2.0939	96.0824
3	13.2061	2.4043	93.6781
4	12.8498	2.7606	90.9175
5	12.4406	3.1698	87.7477
6	11.9708	3.6395	84.1082
7	11.4314	4.1789	79.9292
8	10.8121	4.7983	75.1310
9	10.1010	5.5094	69.6215
10	9.2844	6.3260	63.2956
11	8.3469	7.2635	56.0321
12	7.2704	8.3400	47.6921
13	6.0343	9.5760	38.1160
14	4.6151	10.9953	27.1208
15	2.9855	12.6248	14.4959
16	1.1145	14.4959	0.0000

YEARS 17 — MO PAYT 1.2805 — AN CONST 15.37

#	INT	PRIN	BALANCE
1	13.8029	1.5634	98.4366
2	13.5712	1.7952	96.6414
3	13.3051	2.0612	94.5802
4	12.9996	2.3667	92.2135
5	12.6489	2.7175	89.4960
6	12.2461	3.1202	86.3758
7	11.7837	3.5826	82.7932
8	11.2527	4.1136	78.6796
9	10.6431	4.7233	73.9563
10	9.9430	5.4233	68.5330
11	9.1393	6.2271	62.3060
12	8.2164	7.1499	55.1560
13	7.1567	8.2096	46.9464
14	5.9400	9.4263	37.5201
15	4.5430	10.8234	26.6967
16	2.9389	12.4275	14.2693
17	1.0970	14.2693	0.0000

YEARS 18 — MO PAYT 1.2633 — AN CONST 15.16

#	INT	PRIN	BALANCE
1	13.8166	1.3433	98.6567
2	13.6175	1.5424	97.1142
3	13.3889	1.7710	95.3432
4	13.1264	2.0335	93.3096
5	12.8250	2.3349	90.9747
6	12.4790	2.6810	88.2938
7	12.0816	3.0783	85.2155
8	11.6254	3.5345	81.6810
9	11.1016	4.0583	77.6227
10	10.5001	4.6598	72.9628
11	9.8095	5.3504	67.6124
12	9.0165	6.1434	61.4690
13	8.1060	7.0539	54.4151
14	7.0606	8.0993	46.3158
15	5.8602	9.2997	37.0161
16	4.4819	10.6780	26.3381
17	2.8994	12.2605	14.0776
18	1.0823	14.0776	0.0000

YEARS 19 — MO PAYT 1.2487 — AN CONST 14.99

#	INT	PRIN	BALANCE
1	13.8282	1.1564	98.8436
2	13.6568	1.3278	97.5158
3	13.4600	1.5246	95.9912
4	13.2340	1.7506	94.2406
5	12.9746	2.0100	92.2306
6	12.6767	2.3079	89.9227
7	12.3346	2.6499	87.2727
8	11.9419	3.0427	84.2300
9	11.4910	3.4936	80.7364
10	10.9732	4.0114	76.7250
11	10.3787	4.6059	72.1191
12	9.6960	5.2886	66.8305
13	8.9122	6.0724	60.7582
14	8.0123	6.9723	53.7858
15	6.9789	8.0057	45.7802
16	5.7924	9.1922	36.5880
17	4.4301	10.5545	26.0335
18	2.8659	12.1187	13.9148
19	1.0698	13.9148	0.0000

YEARS 20 — MO PAYT 1.2363 — AN CONST 14.84

#	INT	PRIN	BALANCE
1	13.8381	.9971	99.0029
2	13.6903	1.1449	97.8580
3	13.5206	1.3146	96.5434
4	13.3258	1.5094	95.0340
5	13.1021	1.7331	93.3009
6	12.8452	1.9900	91.3109
7	12.5503	2.2849	89.0261
8	12.2117	2.6235	86.4025
9	11.8228	3.0123	83.3902
10	11.3764	3.4588	79.9314
11	10.8638	3.9714	75.9600
12	10.2752	4.5600	71.4000
13	9.5994	5.2358	66.1641
14	8.8234	6.0118	60.1523
15	7.9324	6.9028	53.2495
16	6.9093	7.9258	45.3237
17	5.7347	9.1005	36.2232
18	4.3859	10.4492	25.7740
19	2.8373	11.9979	13.7761
20	1.0591	13.7761	0.0000

YEARS 21 — MO PAYT 1.2256 — AN CONST 14.71

#	INT	PRIN	BALANCE
1	13.8465	.8609	99.1391
2	13.7189	.9885	98.1505
3	13.5724	1.1350	97.0155

MONTHLY PAYMENT AMORTIZATION SCHEDULE PER $100　　　　13.90 %

#	INT	PRIN	BALANCE
4	13.4042	1.3033	95.7122
5	13.2110	1.4964	94.2158
6	12.9893	1.7182	92.4976
7	12.7346	1.9728	90.5248
8	12.4422	2.2652	88.2596
9	12.1065	2.6009	85.6587
10	11.7210	2.9864	82.6722
11	11.2784	3.4290	79.2432
12	10.7702	3.9372	75.3060
13	10.1867	4.5207	70.7853
14	9.5167	5.1907	65.5945
15	8.7474	5.9601	59.6345
16	7.8641	6.8434	52.7911
17	6.8499	7.8576	44.9335
18	5.6853	9.0221	35.9113
19	4.3482	10.3593	25.5521
20	2.8129	11.8946	13.6575
21	1.0500	13.6575	0.0000

YEARS 22	MO PAYT 1.2165	AN CONST 14.60	
#	INT	PRIN	BALANCE
1	13.8538	.7442	99.2558
2	13.7435	.8545	98.4012
3	13.6168	.9812	97.4201
4	13.4714	1.1266	96.2935
5	13.3044	1.2936	94.9999
6	13.1127	1.4853	93.5147
7	12.8926	1.7054	91.8093
8	12.6398	1.9581	89.8511
9	12.3496	2.2484	87.6027
10	12.0164	2.5816	85.0212
11	11.6338	2.9642	82.0570
12	11.1945	3.4035	78.6535
13	10.6901	3.9079	74.7456
14	10.1109	4.4871	70.2585
15	9.4459	5.1521	65.1063
16	8.6823	5.9157	59.1906
17	7.8056	6.7924	52.3982
18	6.7989	7.7991	44.5991
19	5.6430	8.9550	35.6441
20	4.3158	10.2822	25.3619
21	2.7919	11.8061	13.5558
22	1.0422	13.5558	0.0000

YEARS 23	MO PAYT 1.2087	AN CONST 14.51	
#	INT	PRIN	BALANCE
1	13.8600	.6440	99.3560
2	13.7646	.7394	98.6166
3	13.6550	.8490	97.7675
4	13.5291	.9749	96.7927
5	13.3847	1.1193	95.6734
6	13.2188	1.2852	94.3881
7	13.0283	1.4757	92.9124
8	12.8096	1.6944	91.2180
9	12.5584	1.9455	89.2725
10	12.2701	2.2339	87.0386
11	11.9390	2.5650	84.4736
12	11.5589	2.9451	81.5285
13	11.1224	3.3816	78.1470
14	10.6212	3.8828	74.2642
15	10.0458	4.4582	69.8060
16	9.3850	5.1189	64.6871
17	8.6264	5.8776	58.8095
18	7.7553	6.7487	52.0608
19	6.7551	7.7489	44.3119
20	5.6067	8.8973	35.4145
21	4.2880	10.2160	25.1986
22	2.7739	11.7300	13.4685
23	1.0355	13.4685	0.0000

YEARS 24	MO PAYT 1.2019	AN CONST 14.43	
#	INT	PRIN	BALANCE
1	13.8654	.5577	99.4423
2	13.7827	.6404	98.8019
3	13.6878	.7353	98.0666
4	13.5788	.8443	97.2223
5	13.4537	.9694	96.2528
6	13.3100	1.1131	95.1398
7	13.1450	1.2781	93.8617
8	12.9556	1.4675	92.3942
9	12.7381	1.6850	90.7093
10	12.4884	1.9347	88.7746
11	12.2017	2.2214	86.5531
12	11.8724	2.5507	84.0025
13	11.4944	2.9287	81.0738
14	11.0604	3.3627	77.7111
15	10.5620	3.8611	73.8500
16	9.9898	4.4333	69.4167
17	9.3327	5.0904	64.3263
18	8.5783	5.8448	58.4815
19	7.7120	6.7111	51.7704
20	6.7174	7.7057	44.0647
21	5.5754	8.8477	35.2170
22	4.2641	10.1590	25.0580
23	2.7585	11.6646	13.3934
24	1.0297	13.3934	0.0000

YEARS 25	MO PAYT 1.1961	AN CONST 14.36	
#	INT	PRIN	BALANCE
1	13.8700	.4834	99.5166
2	13.7983	.5550	98.9616
3	13.7161	.6373	98.3243
4	13.6216	.7318	97.5925
5	13.5132	.8402	96.7523
6	13.3886	.9647	95.7876
7	13.2457	1.1077	94.6798
8	13.0815	1.2719	93.4080
9	12.8930	1.4604	91.9476
10	12.6766	1.6768	90.2708
11	12.4280	1.9253	88.3454
12	12.1427	2.2107	86.1347
13	11.8151	2.5383	83.5964
14	11.4389	2.9145	80.6819
15	11.0069	3.3465	77.3354
16	10.5109	3.8424	73.4930
17	9.9415	4.4119	69.0811
18	9.2876	5.0658	64.0153
19	8.5368	5.8166	58.1988
20	7.6748	6.6786	51.5201
21	6.6849	7.6684	43.8517
22	5.5484	8.8049	35.0468
23	4.2435	10.1099	24.9369
24	2.7451	11.6082	13.3287
25	1.0247	13.3287	0.0000

YEARS 26	MO PAYT 1.1911	AN CONST 14.30	
#	INT	PRIN	BALANCE
1	13.8740	.4192	99.5808
2	13.8118	.4814	99.0994
3	13.7405	.5527	98.5467
4	13.6586	.6346	97.9120
5	13.5645	.7287	97.1834
6	13.4565	.8367	96.3467
7	13.3325	.9607	95.3860
8	13.1901	1.1031	94.2829
9	13.0266	1.2665	93.0164
10	12.8389	1.4543	91.5621
11	12.6234	1.6698	89.8923
12	12.3759	1.9173	87.9750
13	12.0918	2.2014	85.7736
14	11.7655	2.5277	83.2460
15	11.3909	2.9023	80.3437
16	10.9608	3.3324	77.0112
17	10.4669	3.8263	73.1849
18	9.8998	4.3934	68.7915
19	9.2487	5.0445	63.7469
20	8.5010	5.7922	57.9548
21	7.6426	6.6506	51.3042
22	6.6569	7.6363	43.6679
23	5.5252	8.7680	34.8998
24	4.2257	10.0675	24.8323
25	2.7336	11.5596	13.2728
26	1.0204	13.2728	0.0000

YEARS 27	MO PAYT 1.1868	AN CONST 14.25	
#	INT	PRIN	BALANCE
1	13.8774	.3638	99.6362
2	13.8235	.4177	99.2185
3	13.7616	.4796	98.7389
4	13.6905	.5507	98.1882
5	13.6089	.6323	97.5558
6	13.5152	.7260	96.8298
7	13.4076	.8336	95.9962
8	13.2840	.9572	95.0390
9	13.1421	1.0991	93.9399
10	12.9793	1.2619	92.6780
11	12.7922	1.4490	91.2290
12	12.5775	1.6637	89.5653
13	12.3309	1.9103	87.6550
14	12.0478	2.1934	85.4616
15	11.7227	2.5185	82.9431
16	11.3495	2.8917	80.0514
17	10.9209	3.3203	76.7311
18	10.4288	3.8124	72.9187
19	9.8638	4.3774	68.5412
20	9.2150	5.0262	63.5150
21	8.4701	5.7711	57.7439
22	7.6148	6.6264	51.1175
23	6.6327	7.6085	43.5090
24	5.5051	8.7361	34.7729
25	4.2103	10.0309	24.7420
26	2.7237	11.5175	13.2245
27	1.0167	13.2245	0.0000

YEARS 28	MO PAYT 1.1830	AN CONST 14.20	
#	INT	PRIN	BALANCE
1	13.8804	.3158	99.6842
2	13.8336	.3626	99.3215
3	13.7798	.4164	98.9051
4	13.7181	.4781	98.4270
5	13.6473	.5490	97.8780
6	13.5659	.6303	97.2477
7	13.4725	.7237	96.5240
8	13.3652	.8310	95.6930
9	13.2421	.9542	94.7388
10	13.1006	1.0956	93.6432
11	12.9383	1.2580	92.3853
12	12.7518	1.4444	90.9409
13	12.5378	1.6585	89.2824
14	12.2920	1.9043	87.3781
15	12.0097	2.1865	85.1917
16	11.6857	2.5105	82.6811
17	11.3136	2.8826	79.7985
18	10.8864	3.3098	76.4887
19	10.3959	3.8004	72.6883
20	9.8326	4.3636	68.3247
21	9.1859	5.0103	63.3144
22	8.4433	5.7529	57.5615
23	7.5907	6.6055	50.9561
24	6.6118	7.5845	43.3716
25	5.4877	8.7085	34.6631
26	4.1970	9.9992	24.6639
27	2.7151	11.4811	13.1827
28	1.0135	13.1827	0.0000

YEARS 29	MO PAYT 1.1798	AN CONST 14.16	
#	INT	PRIN	BALANCE
1	13.8830	.2743	99.7257
2	13.8423	.3150	99.4107
3	13.7956	.3617	99.0491
4	13.7420	.4153	98.6338
5	13.6805	.4768	98.1570
6	13.6098	.5475	97.6095
7	13.5287	.6286	96.9810
8	13.4355	.7218	96.2592
9	13.3285	.8287	95.4305
10	13.2057	.9516	94.4789
11	13.0647	1.0926	93.3863
12	12.9028	1.2545	92.1318
13	12.7168	1.4404	90.6914
14	12.5034	1.6539	89.0375
15	12.2582	1.8990	87.1385
16	11.9768	2.1805	84.9580
17	11.6536	2.5036	82.4543
18	11.2826	2.8747	79.5796
19	10.8565	3.3007	76.2789
20	10.3673	3.7899	72.4889
21	9.8056	4.3516	68.1373
22	9.1607	4.9966	63.1407
23	8.4201	5.7371	57.4036
24	7.5699	6.5874	50.8163
25	6.5936	7.5637	43.2526
26	5.4726	8.6846	34.5680
27	4.1855	9.9718	24.5962
28	2.7076	11.4496	13.1466
29	1.0107	13.1466	0.0000

YEARS 30	MO PAYT 1.1770	AN CONST 14.13	
#	INT	PRIN	BALANCE
1	13.8852	.2383	99.7617
2	13.8499	.2737	99.4880
3	13.8093	.3142	99.1738
4	13.7627	.3608	98.8130
5	13.7093	.4143	98.3987
6	13.6479	.4757	97.9231
7	13.5774	.5462	97.3769
8	13.4964	.6271	96.7498
9	13.4035	.7200	96.0298
10	13.2968	.8268	95.2030
11	13.1743	.9493	94.2537
12	13.0336	1.0900	93.1638
13	12.8720	1.2515	91.9122
14	12.6865	1.4370	90.4752
15	12.4736	1.6500	88.8253
16	12.2290	1.8945	86.9308
17	11.9483	2.1753	84.7555
18	11.6259	2.4977	82.2578
19	11.2557	2.8678	79.3900
20	10.8307	3.2929	76.0971
21	10.3426	3.7809	72.3162
22	9.7823	4.3413	67.9749
23	9.1389	4.9847	62.9903
24	8.4001	5.7234	57.2668
25	7.5519	6.5717	50.6952
26	6.5779	7.5456	43.1495
27	5.4596	8.6639	34.4856
28	4.1755	9.9480	24.5376
29	2.7012	11.4224	13.1152
30	1.0083	13.1152	0.0000

YEARS 2 — MO PAYT 4.8013 — AN CONST 57.62

#	INT	PRIN	BALANCE
1	11.0896	46.5259	53.4741
2	4.1413	53.4741	0.0000

YEARS 3 — MO PAYT 3.4178 — AN CONST 41.02

#	INT	PRIN	BALANCE
1	12.1974	28.8157	71.1843
2	7.8940	33.1191	38.0652
3	2.9480	38.0652	0.0000

YEARS 4 — MO PAYT 2.7326 — AN CONST 32.80

#	INT	PRIN	BALANCE
1	12.7460	20.0457	79.9543
2	9.7524	23.0394	56.9149
3	6.3116	26.4801	30.4347
4	2.3570	30.4347	0.0000

YEARS 5 — MO PAYT 2.3268 — AN CONST 27.93

#	INT	PRIN	BALANCE
1	13.0710	14.8509	85.1491
2	10.8531	17.0688	68.0804
3	8.3041	19.6178	48.4625
4	5.3743	22.5476	25.9149
5	2.0070	25.9149	0.0000

YEARS 6 — MO PAYT 2.0606 — AN CONST 24.73

#	INT	PRIN	BALANCE
1	13.2842	11.4427	88.5573
2	11.5753	13.1516	75.4058
3	9.6113	15.1156	60.2901
4	7.3539	17.3730	42.9171
5	4.7593	19.9676	22.9496
6	1.7773	22.9496	0.0000

YEARS 7 — MO PAYT 1.8740 — AN CONST 22.49

#	INT	PRIN	BALANCE
1	13.4336	9.0544	90.9456
2	12.0814	10.4066	80.5390
3	10.5273	11.9608	68.5782
4	8.7410	13.7470	54.8312
5	6.6880	15.8000	39.0312
6	4.3284	18.1596	20.8716
7	1.6164	20.8716	0.0000

YEARS 8 — MO PAYT 1.7372 — AN CONST 20.85

#	INT	PRIN	BALANCE
1	13.5432	7.3026	92.6974
2	12.4526	8.3932	84.3042
3	11.1991	9.6467	74.6575
4	9.7585	11.0873	63.5702
5	8.1027	12.7431	50.8271
6	6.1996	14.6462	36.1809
7	4.0123	16.8335	19.3474
8	1.4984	19.3474	0.0000

YEARS 9 — MO PAYT 1.6334 — AN CONST 19.61

#	INT	PRIN	BALANCE
1	13.6263	5.9742	94.0258
2	12.7341	6.8663	87.1595
3	11.7087	7.8918	79.2677
4	10.5301	9.0704	70.1974
5	9.1755	10.4249	59.7724
6	7.6186	11.9818	47.7906
7	5.8292	13.7712	34.0194
8	3.7726	15.8278	18.1916
9	1.4089	18.1916	0.0000

YEARS 10 — MO PAYT 1.5527 — AN CONST 18.64

#	INT	PRIN	BALANCE
1	13.6909	4.9411	95.0589
2	12.9530	5.6790	89.3800
3	12.1049	6.5271	82.8529
4	11.1301	7.5018	75.3511
5	10.0098	8.6222	66.7289
6	8.7221	9.9098	56.8190
7	7.2422	11.3898	45.4293
8	5.5412	13.0908	32.3385
9	3.5862	15.0458	17.2927
10	1.3392	17.2927	0.0000

YEARS 11 — MO PAYT 1.4887 — AN CONST 17.87

#	INT	PRIN	BALANCE
1	13.7422	4.1218	95.8782
2	13.1266	4.7374	91.1408
3	12.4191	5.4449	85.6959
4	11.6060	6.2580	79.4378
5	10.6714	7.1926	72.2452
6	9.5972	8.2668	63.9784
7	8.3626	9.5014	54.4771
8	6.9437	10.9203	43.5567
9	5.3128	12.5512	31.0056
10	3.4384	14.4256	16.5800
11	1.2840	16.5800	0.0000

YEARS 12 — MO PAYT 1.4371 — AN CONST 17.25

#	INT	PRIN	BALANCE
1	13.7834	3.4621	96.5379
2	13.2664	3.9791	92.5588
3	12.6721	4.5734	87.9854
4	11.9891	5.2564	82.7290
5	11.2041	6.0414	76.6876
6	10.3019	6.9436	69.7440
7	9.2649	7.9806	61.7634
8	8.0731	9.1724	52.5910
9	6.7033	10.5422	42.0488
10	5.1289	12.1167	29.9321
11	3.3193	13.9262	16.0059
12	1.2396	16.0059	0.0000

YEARS 13 — MO PAYT 1.3951 — AN CONST 16.75

#	INT	PRIN	BALANCE
1	13.8171	2.9242	97.0758
2	13.3804	3.3609	93.7150
3	12.8785	3.8628	89.8522
4	12.3016	4.4396	85.4126
5	11.6386	5.1027	80.3099
6	10.8765	5.8647	74.4452
7	10.0007	6.7406	67.7046
8	8.9940	7.7472	59.9574
9	7.8370	8.9042	51.0532
10	6.5073	10.2340	40.8192
11	4.9789	11.7623	29.0569
12	3.2223	13.5190	15.5379
13	1.2033	15.5379	0.0000

YEARS 14 — MO PAYT 1.3605 — AN CONST 16.33

#	INT	PRIN	BALANCE
1	13.8448	2.4811	97.5189
2	13.4743	2.8516	94.6673
3	13.0484	3.2775	91.3898
4	12.5589	3.7669	87.6229
5	11.9964	4.3295	83.2934
6	11.3498	4.9761	78.3173
7	10.6067	5.7192	72.5981
8	9.7525	6.5733	66.0248
9	8.7709	7.5550	58.4698
10	7.6426	8.6833	49.7865
11	6.3458	9.9801	39.8064
12	4.8554	11.4705	28.3359
13	3.1423	13.1835	15.1524
14	1.1735	15.1524	0.0000

YEARS 15 — MO PAYT 1.3317 — AN CONST 15.99

#	INT	PRIN	BALANCE
1	13.8678	2.1131	97.8869
2	13.5522	2.4287	95.4583
3	13.1895	2.7914	92.6669
4	12.7727	3.2082	89.4587
5	12.2936	3.6873	85.7714
6	11.7429	4.2380	81.5334
7	11.1100	4.8709	76.6624
8	10.3825	5.5984	71.0641
9	9.5465	6.4344	64.6296
10	8.5855	7.3954	57.2343
11	7.4811	8.4998	48.7345
12	6.2117	9.7692	38.9653
13	4.7528	11.2281	27.7372
14	3.0759	12.9050	14.8322
15	1.1487	14.8322	0.0000

YEARS 16 — MO PAYT 1.3077 — AN CONST 15.70

#	INT	PRIN	BALANCE
1	13.8871	1.8053	98.1947
2	13.6175	2.0749	96.1197
3	13.3076	2.3848	93.7349
4	12.9514	2.7410	90.9940
5	12.5421	3.1503	87.8437
6	12.0716	3.6208	84.2229
7	11.5309	4.1615	80.0614
8	10.9094	4.7830	75.2784
9	10.1951	5.4973	69.7811
10	9.3741	6.3183	63.4629
11	8.4305	7.2619	56.2010
12	7.3460	8.3464	47.8547
13	6.0996	9.5928	38.2618
14	4.6670	11.0254	27.2364
15	3.0204	12.6720	14.5644
16	1.1279	14.5644	0.0000

YEARS 17 — MO PAYT 1.2875 — AN CONST 15.45

#	INT	PRIN	BALANCE
1	13.9033	1.5465	98.4535
2	13.6723	1.7774	96.6761
3	13.4069	2.0428	94.6333
4	13.1018	2.3479	92.2854
5	12.7511	2.6986	89.5868
6	12.3481	3.1016	86.4852
7	11.8849	3.5648	82.9204
8	11.3526	4.0971	78.8233
9	10.7407	4.7090	74.1143
10	10.0374	5.4123	68.7020
11	9.2292	6.2206	62.4814
12	8.3002	7.1496	55.3319
13	7.2324	8.2173	47.1146
14	6.0053	9.4445	37.6701
15	4.5948	10.8549	26.8152
16	2.9737	12.4760	14.3392
17	1.1105	14.3392	0.0000

YEARS 18 — MO PAYT 1.2704 — AN CONST 15.25

#	INT	PRIN	BALANCE
1	13.9169	1.3276	98.6724
2	13.7187	1.5259	97.1464
3	13.4908	1.7538	95.3926
4	13.2289	2.0157	93.3769
5	12.9278	2.3168	91.0602
6	12.5819	2.6627	88.3974
7	12.1842	3.0604	85.3370
8	11.7271	3.5174	81.8196
9	11.2018	4.0428	77.7768
10	10.5981	4.6465	73.1303
11	9.9042	5.3404	67.7899
12	9.1066	6.1380	61.6519
13	8.1900	7.0546	54.5973
14	7.1364	8.1082	46.4891
15	5.9255	9.3191	37.1700
16	4.5338	10.7108	26.4592
17	2.9342	12.3104	14.1488
18	1.0958	14.1488	0.0000

YEARS 19 — MO PAYT 1.2559 — AN CONST 15.08

#	INT	PRIN	BALANCE
1	13.9286	1.1419	98.8581
2	13.7580	1.3125	97.5456
3	13.5620	1.5085	96.0371
4	13.3367	1.7338	94.3033
5	13.0778	1.9927	92.3106
6	12.7802	2.2903	90.0203
7	12.4382	2.6323	87.3880
8	12.0451	3.0255	84.3625
9	11.5932	3.4773	80.8852
10	11.0739	3.9966	76.8886
11	10.4771	4.5934	72.2952
12	9.7911	5.2794	67.0158
13	9.0026	6.0679	60.9479
14	8.0964	6.9741	53.9738
15	7.0549	8.0156	45.9582
16	5.8579	9.2127	36.7456
17	4.4820	10.5885	26.1571
18	2.9007	12.1698	13.9873
19	1.0832	13.9873	0.0000

YEARS 20 — MO PAYT 1.2435 — AN CONST 14.93

#	INT	PRIN	BALANCE
1	13.9385	.9838	99.0162
2	13.7915	1.1307	97.8855
3	13.6227	1.2996	96.5859
4	13.4286	1.4937	95.0923
5	13.2055	1.7167	93.3755
6	12.9492	1.9731	91.4024
7	12.6545	2.2678	89.1347
8	12.3158	2.6064	86.5282
9	11.9266	2.9957	83.5326
10	11.4792	3.4431	80.0895
11	10.9650	3.9573	76.1322
12	10.3740	4.5483	71.5840
13	9.6948	5.2275	66.3565
14	8.9141	6.0082	60.3483
15	8.0168	6.9055	53.4428
16	6.9855	7.9367	45.5061
17	5.8002	9.1220	36.3841
18	4.4379	10.4843	25.8997
19	2.8722	12.0501	13.8497
20	1.0726	13.8497	0.0000

YEARS 21 — MO PAYT 1.2330 — AN CONST 14.80

#	INT	PRIN	BALANCE
1	13.9469	.8487	99.1513
2	13.8202	.9754	98.1759
3	13.6745	1.1211	97.0547

MONTHLY PAYMENT AMORTIZATION SCHEDULE PER $100 — 14.00 %

#	INT	PRIN	BALANCE
4	13.5071	1.2885	95.7662
5	13.3146	1.4810	94.2852
6	13.0935	1.7022	92.5831
7	12.8393	1.9564	90.6267
8	12.5471	2.2485	88.3782
9	12.2113	2.5843	85.7939
10	11.8253	2.9703	82.8236
11	11.3818	3.4139	79.4098
12	10.8719	3.9237	75.4861
13	10.2860	4.5097	70.9764
14	9.6125	5.1831	65.7933
15	8.8384	5.9572	59.8361
16	7.9488	6.8469	52.9892
17	6.9262	7.8694	45.1199
18	5.7510	9.0446	36.0753
19	4.4003	10.3953	25.6799
20	2.8478	11.9478	13.7321
21	1.0635	13.7321	0.0000

YEARS 22 — MO PAYT 1.2239 — AN CONST 14.69

#	INT	PRIN	BALANCE
1	13.9541	.7330	99.2670
2	13.8447	.8425	98.4245
3	13.7189	.9683	97.4562
4	13.5743	1.1129	96.3433
5	13.4081	1.2791	95.0642
6	13.2170	1.4701	93.5941
7	12.9975	1.6897	91.9044
8	12.7451	1.9420	89.9624
9	12.4551	2.2320	87.7304
10	12.1218	2.5654	85.1650
11	11.7387	2.9485	82.2165
12	11.2983	3.3888	78.8277
13	10.7922	3.8949	74.9328
14	10.2106	4.4766	70.4562
15	9.5420	5.1451	65.3110
16	8.7736	5.9135	59.3975
17	7.8905	6.7967	52.6008
18	6.8755	7.8117	44.7891
19	5.7088	8.9783	35.8108
20	4.3680	10.3191	25.4917
21	2.8269	11.8602	13.6315
22	1.0557	13.6315	0.0000

YEARS 23 — MO PAYT 1.2162 — AN CONST 14.60

#	INT	PRIN	BALANCE
1	13.9604	.6337	99.3663
2	13.8657	.7284	98.6379
3	13.7569	.8371	97.8008
4	13.6319	.9622	96.8386
5	13.4882	1.1058	95.7328
6	13.3231	1.2710	94.4618
7	13.1333	1.4608	93.0010
8	12.9151	1.6790	91.3220
9	12.6644	1.9297	89.3923
10	12.3762	2.2179	87.1744
11	12.0450	2.5491	84.6253
12	11.6643	2.9298	81.6955
13	11.2267	3.3674	78.3281
14	10.7238	3.8702	74.4579
15	10.1458	4.4482	70.0097
16	9.4815	5.1125	64.8971
17	8.7180	5.8761	59.0211
18	7.8405	6.7536	52.2675
19	6.8319	7.7622	44.5053
20	5.6727	8.9214	35.5839
21	4.3403	10.2538	25.3301
22	2.8090	11.7851	13.5451
23	1.0490	13.5451	0.0000

YEARS 24 — MO PAYT 1.2095 — AN CONST 14.52

#	INT	PRIN	BALANCE
1	13.9657	.5484	99.4516
2	13.8838	.6302	98.8214
3	13.7897	.7244	98.0970
4	13.6815	.8325	97.2645
5	13.5572	.9569	96.3076
6	13.4143	1.0998	95.2078
7	13.2500	1.2640	93.9438
8	13.0613	1.4528	92.4910
9	12.8443	1.6698	90.8213
10	12.5949	1.9191	88.9021
11	12.3083	2.2057	86.6964
12	11.9789	2.5351	84.1613
13	11.6003	2.9137	81.2475
14	11.1652	3.3489	77.8986
15	10.6650	3.8490	74.0496
16	10.0902	4.4238	69.6258
17	9.4295	5.0845	64.5413
18	8.6702	5.8438	58.6974
19	7.7975	6.7166	51.9809
20	6.7944	7.7196	44.2613
21	5.6416	8.8725	35.3888
22	4.3165	10.1975	25.1912
23	2.7936	11.7204	13.4708
24	1.0433	13.4708	0.0000

YEARS 25 — MO PAYT 1.2038 — AN CONST 14.45

#	INT	PRIN	BALANCE
1	13.9703	.4748	99.5252
2	13.8994	.5457	98.9794
3	13.8179	.6273	98.3522
4	13.7242	.7209	97.6312
5	13.6165	.8286	96.8026
6	13.4928	.9523	95.8503
7	13.3506	1.0946	94.7558
8	13.1871	1.2580	93.4977
9	12.9992	1.4459	92.0518
10	12.7833	1.6618	90.3900
11	12.5351	1.9100	88.4800
12	12.2499	2.1953	86.2847
13	11.9220	2.5231	83.7616
14	11.5452	2.8999	80.8617
15	11.1121	3.3330	77.5287
16	10.6144	3.8307	73.6980
17	10.0423	4.4028	69.2952
18	9.3848	5.0604	64.2348
19	8.6291	5.8161	58.4187
20	7.7605	6.6847	51.7341
21	6.7622	7.6830	44.0511
22	5.6148	8.8304	35.2207
23	4.2960	10.1491	25.0716
24	2.7803	11.6648	13.4068
25	1.0383	13.4068	0.0000

YEARS 26 — MO PAYT 1.1988 — AN CONST 14.39

#	INT	PRIN	BALANCE
1	13.9743	.4114	99.5886
2	13.9128	.4729	99.1157
3	13.8422	.5435	98.5722
4	13.7610	.6247	97.9475
5	13.6677	.7180	97.2295
6	13.5605	.8252	96.4044
7	13.4373	.9484	95.4559
8	13.2956	1.0901	94.3659
9	13.1329	1.2528	93.1130
10	12.9458	1.4399	91.6731
11	12.7307	1.6550	90.0181
12	12.4835	1.9022	88.1159
13	12.1995	2.1862	85.9297
14	11.8730	2.5127	83.4170
15	11.4977	2.8880	80.5290
16	11.0664	3.3193	77.2098
17	10.5707	3.8150	73.3948
18	10.0010	4.3847	69.0101
19	9.3462	5.0395	63.9705
20	8.5935	5.7922	58.1784
21	7.7285	6.6572	51.5212
22	6.7343	7.6514	43.8698
23	5.5917	8.7940	35.0758
24	4.2784	10.1073	24.9685
25	2.7689	11.6168	13.3517
26	1.0340	13.3517	0.0000

YEARS 27 — MO PAYT 1.1945 — AN CONST 14.34

#	INT	PRIN	BALANCE
1	13.9777	.3567	99.6433
2	13.9244	.4100	99.2333
3	13.8632	.4712	98.7621
4	13.7928	.5416	98.2206
5	13.7119	.6224	97.5981
6	13.6190	.7154	96.8827
7	13.5121	.8222	96.0605
8	13.3894	.9450	95.1155
9	13.2482	1.0862	94.0293
10	13.0860	1.2484	92.7809
11	12.8996	1.4348	91.3461
12	12.6853	1.6491	89.6970
13	12.4390	1.8954	87.8016
14	12.1560	2.1784	85.6232
15	11.8306	2.5038	83.1195
16	11.4567	2.8777	80.2418
17	11.0270	3.3074	76.9343
18	10.5330	3.8014	73.1330
19	9.9653	4.3691	68.7639
20	9.3128	5.0216	63.7423
21	8.5629	5.7715	57.9708
22	7.7010	6.6334	51.3374
23	6.7103	7.6241	43.7134
24	5.5717	8.7627	34.9507
25	4.2631	10.0713	24.8794
26	2.7590	11.5754	13.3040
27	1.0303	13.3040	0.0000

YEARS 28 — MO PAYT 1.1908 — AN CONST 14.30

#	INT	PRIN	BALANCE
1	13.9806	.3094	99.6906
2	13.9344	.3556	99.3350
3	13.8813	.4087	98.9263
4	13.8203	.4697	98.4566
5	13.7501	.5399	97.9167
6	13.6695	.6205	97.2962
7	13.5769	.7132	96.5830
8	13.4703	.8197	95.7633
9	13.3479	.9421	94.8212
10	13.2072	1.0828	93.7384
11	13.0455	1.2445	92.4939
12	12.8597	1.4304	91.0635
13	12.6460	1.6440	89.4195
14	12.4005	1.8895	87.5300
15	12.1183	2.1717	85.3583
16	11.7940	2.4960	82.8623
17	11.4213	2.8688	79.9935
18	10.9928	3.2972	76.6963
19	10.5004	3.7896	72.9067
20	9.9345	4.3556	68.5512
21	9.2840	5.0060	63.5451
22	8.5364	5.7536	57.7915
23	7.6771	6.6129	51.1786
24	6.6896	7.6005	43.5781
25	5.5545	8.7355	34.8426
26	4.2499	10.0401	24.8024
27	2.7505	11.5395	13.2629
28	1.0271	13.2629	0.0000

YEARS 29 — MO PAYT 1.1876 — AN CONST 14.26

#	INT	PRIN	BALANCE
1	13.9832	.2685	99.7315
2	13.9431	.3086	99.4230
3	13.8970	.3546	99.0683
4	13.8441	.4076	98.6607
5	13.7832	.4685	98.1923
6	13.7132	.5384	97.6538
7	13.6328	.6189	97.0350
8	13.5404	.7113	96.3237
9	13.4342	.8175	95.5062
10	13.3121	.9396	94.5666
11	13.1718	1.0799	93.4867
12	13.0105	1.2412	92.2455
13	12.8251	1.4265	90.8190
14	12.6121	1.6396	89.1794
15	12.3672	1.8844	87.2950
16	12.0858	2.1659	85.1291
17	11.7624	2.4893	82.6398
18	11.3906	2.8611	79.7788
19	10.9633	3.2883	76.4904
20	10.4722	3.7794	72.7110
21	9.9078	4.3439	68.3671
22	9.2591	4.9926	63.3745
23	8.5135	5.7382	57.6363
24	7.6565	6.5951	51.0412
25	6.6716	7.5801	43.4611
26	5.5396	8.7121	34.7490
27	4.2385	10.0132	24.7358
28	2.7431	11.5086	13.2273
29	1.0244	13.2273	0.0000

YEARS 30 — MO PAYT 1.1849 — AN CONST 14.22

#	INT	PRIN	BALANCE
1	13.9854	.2330	99.7670
2	13.9506	.2678	99.4991
3	13.9106	.3078	99.1913
4	13.8646	.3538	98.8375
5	13.8118	.4067	98.4308
6	13.7511	.4674	97.9634
7	13.6813	.5372	97.4262
8	13.6011	.6174	96.8088
9	13.5088	.7096	96.0992
10	13.4029	.8156	95.2836
11	13.2811	.9374	94.3462
12	13.1411	1.0774	93.2689
13	12.9802	1.2383	92.0306
14	12.7953	1.4232	90.6074
15	12.5827	1.6358	88.9716
16	12.3384	1.8800	87.0916
17	12.0577	2.1608	84.9308
18	11.7350	2.4835	82.4472
19	11.3641	2.8544	79.5928
20	10.9378	3.2807	76.3122
21	10.4478	3.7706	72.5415
22	9.8847	4.3337	68.2078
23	9.2375	4.9810	63.2268
24	8.4936	5.7248	57.5020
25	7.6387	6.5798	50.9223
26	6.6561	7.5624	43.3598
27	5.5267	8.6918	34.6680
28	4.2286	9.9898	24.6782
29	2.7367	11.4817	13.1965
30	1.0220	13.1965	0.0000

YEARS 2 — MO PAYT 4.8060 — AN CONST 57.68

#	INT	PRIN	BALANCE
1	11.1709	46.5013	53.4987
2	4.1734	53.4987	0.0000

YEARS 3 — MO PAYT 3.4226 — AN CONST 41.08

#	INT	PRIN	BALANCE
1	12.2869	28.7846	71.2154
2	7.9554	33.1161	38.0993
3	2.9721	38.0993	0.0000

YEARS 4 — MO PAYT 2.7377 — AN CONST 32.86

#	INT	PRIN	BALANCE
1	12.8394	20.0126	79.9874
2	9.8279	23.0241	56.9634
3	6.3633	26.4887	30.4747
4	2.3773	30.4747	0.0000

YEARS 5 — MO PAYT 2.3320 — AN CONST 27.99

#	INT	PRIN	BALANCE
1	13.1666	14.8175	85.1825
2	10.9369	17.0472	68.1353
3	8.3717	19.6125	48.5228
4	5.4204	22.5637	25.9591
5	2.0251	25.9591	0.0000

YEARS 6 — MO PAYT 2.0659 — AN CONST 24.80

#	INT	PRIN	BALANCE
1	13.3813	11.4099	88.5901
2	11.6643	13.1268	75.4633
3	9.6890	15.1022	60.3611
4	7.4165	17.3747	42.9864
5	4.8020	19.9892	22.9972
6	1.7940	22.9972	0.0000

YEARS 7 — MO PAYT 1.8795 — AN CONST 22.56

#	INT	PRIN	BALANCE
1	13.5317	9.0227	90.9773
2	12.1739	10.3804	80.5969
3	10.6119	11.9424	68.6544
4	8.8148	13.7395	54.9149
5	6.7473	15.8070	39.1079
6	4.3687	18.1857	20.9222
7	1.6321	20.9222	0.0000

YEARS 8 — MO PAYT 1.7428 — AN CONST 20.92

#	INT	PRIN	BALANCE
1	13.6419	7.2722	92.7278
2	12.5476	8.3665	84.3612
3	11.2886	9.6255	74.7357
4	9.8402	11.0740	63.6617
5	8.1738	12.7404	50.9214
6	6.2566	14.6575	36.2639
7	4.0510	16.8632	19.4007
8	1.5135	19.4007	0.0000

YEARS 9 — MO PAYT 1.6392 — AN CONST 19.68

#	INT	PRIN	BALANCE
1	13.7255	5.9452	94.0548
2	12.8309	6.8399	87.2149
3	11.8016	7.8691	79.3457
4	10.6175	9.0533	70.2925
5	9.2552	10.4156	59.8769
6	7.6878	11.9829	47.8940
7	5.8847	13.7861	34.1079
8	3.8102	15.8606	18.2473
9	1.4235	18.2473	0.0000

YEARS 10 — MO PAYT 1.5587 — AN CONST 18.71

#	INT	PRIN	BALANCE
1	13.7905	4.9137	95.0863
2	13.0511	5.6531	89.4332
3	12.2004	6.5038	82.9294
4	11.2217	7.4825	75.4469
5	10.0958	8.6084	66.8385
6	8.8004	9.9038	56.9347
7	7.3101	11.3941	45.5406
8	5.5955	13.1087	32.4319
9	3.6229	15.0813	17.3507
10	1.3535	17.3507	0.0000

YEARS 11 — MO PAYT 1.4948 — AN CONST 17.94

#	INT	PRIN	BALANCE
1	13.8420	4.0961	95.9039
2	13.2256	4.7124	91.1915
3	12.5165	5.4216	85.7699
4	11.7007	6.2374	79.5326
5	10.7621	7.1760	72.3566
6	9.6822	8.2558	64.1008
7	8.4399	9.4981	54.6026
8	7.0107	10.9274	43.6752
9	5.3663	12.5717	31.1035
10	3.4745	14.4635	16.6400
11	1.2981	16.6400	0.0000

YEARS 12 — MO PAYT 1.4434 — AN CONST 17.33

#	INT	PRIN	BALANCE
1	13.8834	3.4379	96.5621
2	13.3661	3.9552	92.6068
3	12.7709	4.5504	88.0564
4	12.0862	5.2352	82.8212
5	11.2984	6.0230	76.7983
6	10.3921	6.9293	69.8690
7	9.3494	7.9720	61.8970
8	8.1498	9.1716	52.7254
9	6.7696	10.5517	42.1737
10	5.1818	12.1395	30.0342
11	3.3551	13.9663	16.0679
12	1.2535	16.0679	0.0000

YEARS 13 — MO PAYT 1.4016 — AN CONST 16.82

#	INT	PRIN	BALANCE
1	13.9172	2.9015	97.0985
2	13.4806	3.3382	93.7603
3	12.9783	3.8405	89.9198
4	12.4004	4.4184	85.5014
5	11.7355	5.0833	80.4181
6	10.9706	5.8482	74.5700
7	10.0906	6.7282	67.8417
8	9.0781	7.7407	60.1011
9	7.9133	8.9055	51.1956
10	6.5732	10.2456	40.9500
11	5.0315	11.7873	29.1627
12	3.2577	13.5610	15.6017
13	1.2171	15.6017	0.0000

YEARS 14 — MO PAYT 1.3671 — AN CONST 16.41

#	INT	PRIN	BALANCE
1	13.9450	2.4600	97.5400
2	13.5749	2.8302	94.7098
3	13.1490	3.2560	91.4538
4	12.6590	3.7460	87.7078
5	12.0953	4.3097	83.3981
6	11.4468	4.9582	78.4399
7	10.7007	5.7043	72.7355
8	9.8423	6.5627	66.1728
9	8.8548	7.5503	58.6226
10	7.7186	8.6864	49.9362
11	6.4115	9.9935	39.9427
12	4.9077	11.4973	28.4453
13	3.1776	13.2274	15.2179
14	1.1871	15.2179	0.0000

YEARS 15 — MO PAYT 1.3385 — AN CONST 16.07

#	INT	PRIN	BALANCE
1	13.9681	2.0935	97.9065
2	13.6531	2.4085	95.4980
3	13.2907	2.7709	92.7271
4	12.8737	3.1879	89.5392
5	12.3940	3.6676	85.8717
6	11.8421	4.2195	81.6522
7	11.2072	4.8544	76.7978
8	10.4767	5.5849	71.2129
9	9.6363	6.4253	64.7875
10	8.6694	7.3922	57.3953
11	7.5570	8.5046	48.8908
12	6.2773	9.7843	39.1065
13	4.8050	11.2566	27.8498
14	3.1111	12.9505	14.8993
15	1.1623	14.8993	0.0000

YEARS 16 — MO PAYT 1.3145 — AN CONST 15.78

#	INT	PRIN	BALANCE
1	13.9874	1.7871	98.2129
2	13.7185	2.0561	96.1568
3	13.4091	2.3654	93.7914
4	13.0532	2.7214	91.0700
5	12.6437	3.1309	87.9391
6	12.1725	3.6020	84.3370
7	11.6305	4.1441	80.1930
8	11.0069	4.7677	75.4253
9	10.2895	5.4851	69.9402
10	9.4641	6.3105	63.6297
11	8.5145	7.2601	56.3696
12	7.4220	8.3526	48.0170
13	6.1651	9.6095	38.4076
14	4.7191	11.0555	27.3521
15	3.0555	12.7191	14.6330
16	1.1415	14.6330	0.0000

YEARS 17 — MO PAYT 1.2944 — AN CONST 15.54

#	INT	PRIN	BALANCE
1	14.0036	1.5296	98.4704
2	13.7735	1.7598	96.7106
3	13.5087	2.0246	94.6860
4	13.2040	2.3293	92.3567
5	12.8535	2.6798	89.6770
6	12.4503	3.0830	86.5939
7	11.9863	3.5469	83.0470
8	11.4526	4.0807	78.9663
9	10.8385	4.6947	74.2716
10	10.1321	5.4012	68.8704
11	9.3193	6.2140	62.6564
12	8.3842	7.1490	55.5074
13	7.3085	8.2248	47.2826
14	6.0708	9.4625	37.8201
15	4.6469	10.8864	26.9337
16	3.0087	12.5245	14.4092
17	1.1241	14.4092	0.0000

YEARS 18 — MO PAYT 1.2775 — AN CONST 15.33

#	INT	PRIN	BALANCE
1	14.0174	1.3121	98.6879
2	13.8199	1.5095	97.1783
3	13.5928	1.7367	95.4416
4	13.3314	1.9980	93.4436
5	13.0308	2.2987	91.1449
6	12.6848	2.6446	88.5003
7	12.2869	3.0426	85.4577
8	11.8291	3.5004	81.9573
9	11.3023	4.0271	77.9302
10	10.6963	4.6331	73.2970
11	9.9991	5.3303	67.9667
12	9.1970	6.1324	61.8343
13	8.2742	7.0552	54.7791
14	7.2126	8.1169	46.6622
15	5.9911	9.3383	37.3239
16	4.5859	10.7435	26.5803
17	2.9693	12.3602	14.2201
18	1.1093	14.2201	0.0000

YEARS 19 — MO PAYT 1.2630 — AN CONST 15.16

#	INT	PRIN	BALANCE
1	14.0290	1.1276	98.8724
2	13.8593	1.2973	97.5751
3	13.6641	1.4925	96.0825
4	13.4395	1.7171	94.3654
5	13.1811	1.9755	92.3899
6	12.8838	2.2728	90.1171
7	12.5418	2.6148	87.5023
8	12.1483	3.0083	84.4941
9	11.6957	3.4609	81.0332
10	11.1749	3.9817	77.0514
11	10.5757	4.5809	72.4705
12	9.8864	5.2702	67.2003
13	9.0933	6.0633	61.1370
14	8.1809	6.9757	54.1614
15	7.1312	8.0254	46.1360
16	5.9236	9.2330	36.9030
17	4.5342	10.6224	26.2806
18	2.9358	12.2208	14.0598
19	1.0968	14.0598	0.0000

YEARS 20 — MO PAYT 1.2508 — AN CONST 15.01

#	INT	PRIN	BALANCE
1	14.0389	.9706	99.0294
2	13.8928	1.1167	97.9127
3	13.7248	1.2847	96.6280
4	13.5314	1.4780	95.1499
5	13.3090	1.7005	93.4495
6	13.0531	1.9563	91.4932
7	12.7588	2.2507	89.2424
8	12.4201	2.5894	86.6530
9	12.0304	2.9791	83.6740
10	11.5821	3.4273	80.2466
11	11.0664	3.9431	76.3035
12	10.4731	4.5364	71.7671
13	9.7904	5.2191	66.5480
14	9.0051	6.0044	60.5436
15	8.1015	6.9080	53.6357
16	7.0620	7.9475	45.6882
17	5.8661	9.1434	36.5448
18	4.4902	10.5193	26.0255
19	2.9073	12.1022	13.9233
20	1.0862	13.9233	0.0000

YEARS 21 — MO PAYT 1.2403 — AN CONST 14.89

#	INT	PRIN	BALANCE
1	14.0473	.8366	99.1634
2	13.9214	.9625	98.2009
3	13.7766	1.1073	97.0935

#	INT	PRIN	BALANCE
4	13.6099	1.2740	95.8196
5	13.4182	1.4657	94.3539
6	13.1977	1.6862	92.6677
7	12.9439	1.9400	90.7277
8	12.6520	2.2319	88.4958
9	12.3162	2.5677	85.9281
10	11.9298	2.9541	82.9739
11	11.4852	3.3987	79.5753
12	10.9738	3.9101	75.6652
13	10.3854	4.4985	71.1667
14	9.7085	5.1754	65.9913
15	8.9297	5.9542	60.0371
16	8.0337	6.8502	53.1869
17	7.0029	7.8810	45.3060
18	5.8170	9.0669	36.2391
19	4.4526	10.4313	25.8078
20	2.8830	12.0010	13.8068
21	1.0771	13.8068	0.0000

YEARS 22 — MO PAYT 1.2314 — AN CONST 14.78

#	INT	PRIN	BALANCE
1	14.0545	.7219	99.2781
2	13.9459	.8306	98.4475
3	13.8209	.9556	97.4919
4	13.6771	1.0993	96.3926
5	13.5117	1.2648	95.1278
6	13.3214	1.4551	93.6727
7	13.1024	1.6741	91.9987
8	12.8505	1.9260	90.0727
9	12.5607	2.2158	87.8569
10	12.2273	2.5492	85.3077
11	11.8437	2.9328	82.3749
12	11.4023	3.3741	79.0008
13	10.8946	3.8819	75.1189
14	10.3105	4.4660	70.6529
15	9.6384	5.1380	65.5149
16	8.8653	5.9112	59.6037
17	7.9757	6.8007	52.8030
18	6.9524	7.8241	44.9789
19	5.7750	9.0014	35.9774
20	4.4205	10.3560	25.6215
21	2.8621	11.9143	13.7072
22	1.0693	13.7072	0.0000

YEARS 23 — MO PAYT 1.2237 — AN CONST 14.69

#	INT	PRIN	BALANCE
1	14.0607	.6236	99.3764
2	13.9669	.7174	98.6590
3	13.8589	.8254	97.8336
4	13.7347	.9496	96.8840
5	13.5918	1.0925	95.7915
6	13.4274	1.2569	94.5346
7	13.2383	1.4460	93.0886
8	13.0207	1.6636	91.4250
9	12.7704	1.9140	89.5110
10	12.4824	2.2020	87.3091
11	12.1510	2.5333	84.7758
12	11.7698	2.9145	81.8612
13	11.3312	3.3531	78.5082
14	10.8267	3.8577	74.6505
15	10.2462	4.4382	70.2123
16	9.5783	5.1060	65.1063
17	8.8100	5.8743	59.2320
18	7.9260	6.7583	52.4737
19	6.9090	7.7753	44.6984
20	5.7390	8.9453	35.7531
21	4.3929	10.2914	25.4617
22	2.8443	11.8400	13.6217
23	1.0626	13.6217	0.0000

YEARS 24 — MO PAYT 1.2171 — AN CONST 14.61

#	INT	PRIN	BALANCE
1	14.0660	.5391	99.4609
2	13.9849	.6202	98.8407
3	13.8916	.7136	98.1271
4	13.7842	.8209	97.3062
5	13.6607	.9445	96.3617
6	13.5186	1.0866	95.2751
7	13.3550	1.2501	94.0250
8	13.1669	1.4382	92.5867
9	12.9505	1.6546	90.9321
10	12.7015	1.9036	89.0285
11	12.4151	2.1901	86.8384
12	12.0855	2.5197	84.3187
13	11.7063	2.8988	81.4199
14	11.2701	3.3350	78.0849
15	10.7683	3.8369	74.2480
16	10.1909	4.4142	69.8338
17	9.5267	5.0785	64.7553
18	8.7625	5.8427	58.9127
19	7.8833	6.7219	52.1908
20	6.8718	7.7334	44.4574
21	5.7081	8.8971	35.5603
22	4.3692	10.2359	25.3244
23	2.8290	11.7762	13.5482
24	1.0569	13.5482	0.0000

YEARS 25 — MO PAYT 1.2114 — AN CONST 14.54

#	INT	PRIN	BALANCE
1	14.0706	.4664	99.5336
2	14.0004	.5366	98.9970
3	13.9197	.6173	98.3797
4	13.8268	.7102	97.6694
5	13.7199	.8171	96.8523
6	13.5970	.9401	95.9122
7	13.4555	1.0815	94.8307
8	13.2928	1.2443	93.5864
9	13.1055	1.4315	92.1549
10	12.8901	1.6469	90.5080
11	12.6423	1.8948	88.6132
12	12.3572	2.1799	86.4334
13	12.0291	2.5079	83.9255
14	11.6517	2.8853	81.0402
15	11.2176	3.3195	77.7207
16	10.7181	3.8190	73.9017
17	10.1434	4.3936	69.5081
18	9.4822	5.0548	64.4533
19	8.7216	5.8154	58.6379
20	7.8465	6.6905	51.9474
21	6.8397	7.6973	44.2501
22	5.6814	8.8556	35.3945
23	4.3489	10.1882	25.2063
24	2.8158	11.7213	13.4851
25	1.0520	13.4851	0.0000

YEARS 26 — MO PAYT 1.2065 — AN CONST 14.48

#	INT	PRIN	BALANCE
1	14.0746	.4038	99.5962
2	14.0138	.4645	99.1317
3	13.9439	.5344	98.5973
4	13.8635	.6148	97.9824
5	13.7710	.7074	97.2751
6	13.6645	.8138	96.4612
7	13.5421	.9363	95.5250
8	13.4012	1.0772	94.4478
9	13.2391	1.2393	93.2086
10	13.0526	1.4257	91.7828
11	12.8381	1.6403	90.1425
12	12.5912	1.8871	88.2554
13	12.3073	2.1711	86.0844
14	11.9806	2.4978	83.5866
15	11.6047	2.8736	80.7130
16	11.1723	3.3061	77.4069
17	10.6748	3.8035	73.6034
18	10.1024	4.3759	69.2275
19	9.4440	5.0344	64.1931
20	8.6864	5.7919	58.4011
21	7.8148	6.6635	51.7376
22	6.8121	7.6662	44.0714
23	5.6585	8.8198	35.2516
24	4.3313	10.1470	25.1045
25	2.8044	11.6739	13.4306
26	1.0477	13.4306	0.0000

YEARS 27 — MO PAYT 1.2023 — AN CONST 14.43

#	INT	PRIN	BALANCE
1	14.0780	.3497	99.6503
2	14.0253	.4024	99.2479
3	13.9648	.4629	98.7850
4	13.8951	.5326	98.2525
5	13.8150	.6127	97.6398
6	13.7228	.7049	96.9349
7	13.6167	.8110	96.1239
8	13.4947	.9330	95.1909
9	13.3543	1.0734	94.1175
10	13.1928	1.2349	92.8826
11	13.0070	1.4207	91.4618
12	12.7932	1.6345	89.8273
13	12.5472	1.8805	87.9468
14	12.2642	2.1635	85.7833
15	11.9387	2.4890	83.2943
16	11.5641	2.8636	80.4307
17	11.1332	3.2945	77.1362
18	10.6375	3.7902	73.3459
19	10.0671	4.3606	68.9853
20	9.4109	5.0168	63.9686
21	8.6560	5.7717	58.1969
22	7.7875	6.6402	51.5567
23	6.7883	7.6394	43.9173
24	5.6387	8.7890	35.1283
25	4.3162	10.1115	25.0167
26	2.7946	11.6331	13.3836
27	1.0441	13.3836	0.0000

YEARS 28 — MO PAYT 1.1987 — AN CONST 14.39

#	INT	PRIN	BALANCE
1	14.0809	.3031	99.6969
2	14.0353	.3487	99.3483
3	13.9828	.4011	98.9471
4	13.9225	.4615	98.4856
5	13.8530	.5309	97.9547
6	13.7731	.6108	97.3438
7	13.6812	.7028	96.6411
8	13.5755	.8085	95.8326
9	13.4538	.9302	94.9024
10	13.3138	1.0701	93.8323
11	13.1528	1.2312	92.6011
12	12.9675	1.4164	91.1846
13	12.7544	1.6296	89.5551
14	12.5092	1.8748	87.6802
15	12.2271	2.1569	85.5233
16	11.9025	2.4815	83.0418
17	11.5291	2.8549	80.1869
18	11.0995	3.2845	76.9024
19	10.6052	3.7788	73.1237
20	10.0366	4.3474	68.7763
21	9.3824	5.0016	63.7747
22	8.6298	5.7542	58.0205
23	7.7639	6.6201	51.4004
24	6.7677	7.6163	43.7842
25	5.6216	8.7623	35.0218
26	4.3031	10.0809	24.9409
27	2.7861	11.5979	13.3431
28	1.0409	13.3431	0.0000

YEARS 29 — MO PAYT 1.1955 — AN CONST 14.35

#	INT	PRIN	BALANCE
1	14.0835	.2627	99.7373
2	14.0439	.3023	99.4350
3	13.9984	.3478	99.0872
4	13.9461	.4001	98.6872
5	13.8859	.4603	98.2269
6	13.8166	.5295	97.6973
7	13.7369	.6092	97.0881
8	13.6453	.7009	96.3872
9	13.5398	.8064	95.5808
10	13.4185	.9277	94.6531
11	13.2789	1.0673	93.5857
12	13.1182	1.2279	92.3578
13	12.9335	1.4127	90.9451
14	12.7209	1.6253	89.3198
15	12.4763	1.8699	87.4499
16	12.1949	2.1513	85.2986
17	11.8712	2.4750	82.8237
18	11.4988	2.8474	79.9762
19	11.0703	3.2759	76.7004
20	10.5774	3.7688	72.9315
21	10.0102	4.3360	68.5956
22	9.3578	4.9884	63.6071
23	8.6071	5.7391	57.8681
24	7.7435	6.6027	51.2654
25	6.7499	7.5963	43.6691
26	5.6069	8.7393	34.9298
27	4.2918	10.0544	24.8754
28	2.7788	11.5574	13.3080
29	1.0382	13.3080	0.0000

YEARS 30 — MO PAYT 1.1928 — AN CONST 14.32

#	INT	PRIN	BALANCE
1	14.0856	.2278	99.7722
2	14.0514	.2621	99.5100
3	14.0119	.3016	99.2084
4	13.9665	.3470	98.8615
5	13.9143	.3992	98.4623
6	13.8543	.4592	98.0031
7	13.7852	.5283	97.4747
8	13.7056	.6078	96.8669
9	13.6142	.6993	96.1676
10	13.5089	.8045	95.3630
11	13.3879	.9256	94.4374
12	13.2486	1.0649	93.3725
13	13.0884	1.2251	92.1474
14	12.9040	1.4095	90.7379
15	12.6919	1.6216	89.1163
16	12.4479	1.8656	87.2506
17	12.1671	2.1464	85.1043
18	11.8442	2.4693	82.6349
19	11.4726	2.8409	79.7940
20	11.0451	3.2684	76.5256
21	10.5533	3.7602	72.7654
22	9.9874	4.3261	68.4393
23	9.3364	4.9771	63.4622
24	8.5875	5.7260	57.7362
25	7.7259	6.5876	51.1486
26	6.7346	7.5789	43.5696
27	5.5941	8.7194	34.8502
28	4.2820	10.0315	24.8187
29	2.7725	11.5410	13.2777
30	1.0358	13.2777	0.0000

MONTHLY PAYMENT AMORTIZATION SCHEDULE PER $100

14.125%

YEARS 2 — MO PAYT 4.8072 — AN CONST 57.69

#	INT	PRIN	BALANCE
1	11.1912	46.4951	53.5049
2	4.1815	53.5049	0.0000

YEARS 3 — MO PAYT 3.4238 — AN CONST 41.09

#	INT	PRIN	BALANCE
1	12.3092	28.7768	71.2232
2	7.9707	33.1153	38.1079
3	2.9782	38.1079	0.0000

YEARS 4 — MO PAYT 2.7389 — AN CONST 32.87

#	INT	PRIN	BALANCE
1	12.8628	20.0043	79.9957
2	9.8468	23.0202	56.9755
3	6.3762	26.4908	30.4847
4	2.3824	30.4847	0.0000

YEARS 5 — MO PAYT 2.3333 — AN CONST 28.00

#	INT	PRIN	BALANCE
1	13.1906	14.8092	85.1908
2	10.9579	17.0418	68.1490
3	8.3886	19.6111	48.5379
4	5.4320	22.5677	25.9701
5	2.0296	25.9701	0.0000

YEARS 6 — MO PAYT 2.0673 — AN CONST 24.81

#	INT	PRIN	BALANCE
1	13.4056	11.4017	88.5983
2	11.6866	13.1207	75.4776
3	9.7085	15.0988	60.3788
4	7.4322	17.3751	43.0037
5	4.8126	19.9946	23.0091
6	1.7982	23.0091	0.0000

YEARS 7 — MO PAYT 1.8809 — AN CONST 22.58

#	INT	PRIN	BALANCE
1	13.5562	9.0148	90.9852
2	12.1971	10.3739	80.6113
3	10.6331	11.9379	68.6735
4	8.8333	13.7377	54.9358
5	6.7622	15.8088	39.1270
6	4.3788	18.1922	20.9349
7	1.6361	20.9349	0.0000

YEARS 8 — MO PAYT 1.7443 — AN CONST 20.94

#	INT	PRIN	BALANCE
1	13.6666	7.2646	92.7354
2	12.5714	8.3599	84.3755
3	11.3110	9.6202	74.7552
4	9.8606	11.0706	63.6846
5	8.1916	12.7397	50.9449
6	6.2709	14.6603	36.2846
7	4.0607	16.8706	19.4140
8	1.5172	19.4140	0.0000

YEARS 9 — MO PAYT 1.6407 — AN CONST 19.69

#	INT	PRIN	BALANCE
1	13.7503	5.9380	94.0620
2	12.8551	6.8333	87.2287
3	11.8249	7.8635	79.3652
4	10.6394	9.0490	70.3162
5	9.2751	10.4132	59.9030
6	7.7052	11.9832	47.9198
7	5.8986	13.7898	34.1300
8	3.8196	15.8688	18.2612
9	1.4271	18.2612	0.0000

YEARS 10 — MO PAYT 1.5602 — AN CONST 18.73

#	INT	PRIN	BALANCE
1	13.8154	4.9069	95.0931
2	13.0756	5.6467	89.4465
3	12.2243	6.4980	82.9485
4	11.2446	7.4776	75.4709
5	10.1173	8.6050	66.8659
6	8.8200	9.9023	56.9636
7	7.3271	11.3952	45.5684
8	5.6091	13.1131	32.4553
9	3.6321	15.0901	17.3652
10	1.3571	17.3652	0.0000

YEARS 11 — MO PAYT 1.4964 — AN CONST 17.96

#	INT	PRIN	BALANCE
1	13.8669	4.0896	95.9104
2	13.2504	4.7062	91.2041
3	12.5409	5.4157	85.7884
4	11.7244	6.2322	79.5562
5	10.7848	7.1718	72.3844
6	9.7035	8.2531	64.1313
7	8.4593	9.4973	54.6340
8	7.0274	10.9292	43.7048
9	5.3797	12.5769	31.1280
10	3.4836	14.4730	16.6550
11	1.3016	16.6550	0.0000

YEARS 12 — MO PAYT 1.4450 — AN CONST 17.35

#	INT	PRIN	BALANCE
1	13.9085	3.4319	96.5681
2	13.3911	3.9493	92.6188
3	12.7956	4.5447	88.0741
4	12.1105	5.2299	82.8442
5	11.3220	6.0183	76.8259
6	10.4147	6.9257	69.9002
7	9.3705	7.9698	61.9304
8	8.1690	9.1714	52.7590
9	6.7863	10.5541	42.2049
10	5.1951	12.1452	30.0597
11	3.3640	13.9763	16.0834
12	1.2569	16.0834	0.0000

YEARS 13 — MO PAYT 1.4032 — AN CONST 16.84

#	INT	PRIN	BALANCE
1	13.9423	2.8959	97.1041
2	13.5057	3.3325	93.7716
3	13.0033	3.8349	89.9367
4	12.4251	4.4131	85.5236
5	11.7598	5.0784	80.4452
6	10.9941	5.8441	74.6011
7	10.1131	6.7251	67.8760
8	9.0992	7.7390	60.1369
9	7.9324	8.9058	51.2312
10	6.5897	10.2484	40.9827
11	5.0447	11.7935	29.1892
12	3.2666	13.5716	15.6176
13	1.2205	15.6176	0.0000

YEARS 14 — MO PAYT 1.3687 — AN CONST 16.43

#	INT	PRIN	BALANCE
1	13.9701	2.4547	97.5453
2	13.6000	2.8248	94.7204
3	13.1741	3.2507	91.4697
4	12.6841	3.7408	87.7289
5	12.1201	4.3048	83.4242
6	11.4711	4.9538	78.4704
7	10.7242	5.7006	72.7698
8	9.8648	6.5600	66.2098
9	8.8758	7.5491	58.6607
10	7.7377	8.6872	49.9736
11	6.4280	9.9969	39.9767
12	4.9208	11.5040	28.4727
13	3.1864	13.2384	15.2343
14	1.1906	15.2343	0.0000

YEARS 15 — MO PAYT 1.3402 — AN CONST 16.09

#	INT	PRIN	BALANCE
1	13.9932	2.0886	97.9114
2	13.6783	2.4035	95.5079
3	13.3160	2.7658	92.7421
4	12.8990	3.1828	89.5593
5	12.4191	3.6627	85.8967
6	11.8670	4.2149	81.6818
7	11.2315	4.8503	76.8315
8	10.5003	5.5815	71.2500
9	9.6588	6.4230	64.8269
10	8.6904	7.3914	57.4356
11	7.5761	8.5057	48.9298
12	6.2937	9.7881	39.1418
13	4.8180	11.2638	27.8780
14	3.1199	12.9619	14.9161
15	1.1657	14.9161	0.0000

YEARS 16 — MO PAYT 1.3163 — AN CONST 15.80

#	INT	PRIN	BALANCE
1	14.0125	1.7826	98.2174
2	13.7438	2.0514	96.1660
3	13.4345	2.3606	93.8054
4	13.0786	2.7165	91.0889
5	12.6691	3.1261	87.9628
6	12.1978	3.5974	84.3655
7	11.6554	4.1397	80.2257
8	11.0313	4.7638	75.4619
9	10.3131	5.4820	69.9799
10	9.4866	6.3085	63.6713
11	8.5355	7.2596	56.4117
12	7.4410	8.3541	48.0576
13	6.1815	9.6136	38.4440
14	4.7322	11.0630	27.3810
15	3.0643	12.7309	14.6502
16	1.1449	14.6502	0.0000

YEARS 17 — MO PAYT 1.2962 — AN CONST 15.56

#	INT	PRIN	BALANCE
1	14.0287	1.5254	98.4746
2	13.7988	1.7554	96.7192
3	13.5341	2.0201	94.6991
4	13.2296	2.3246	92.3745
5	12.8791	2.6751	89.6994
6	12.4758	3.0784	86.6210
7	12.0117	3.5425	83.0785
8	11.4776	4.0766	79.0019
9	10.8630	4.6912	74.3108
10	10.1558	5.3984	68.9124
11	9.3419	6.2123	62.7001
12	8.4053	7.1489	55.5512
13	7.3275	8.2267	47.3245
14	6.0872	9.4669	37.8576
15	4.6600	10.8942	26.9634
16	3.0175	12.5367	14.4267
17	1.1275	14.4267	0.0000

YEARS 18 — MO PAYT 1.2792 — AN CONST 15.36

#	INT	PRIN	BALANCE
1	14.0425	1.3082	98.6918
2	13.8452	1.5055	97.1863
3	13.6182	1.7324	95.4538
4	13.3571	1.9936	93.4602
5	13.0565	2.2942	91.1660
6	12.7106	2.6401	88.5259
7	12.3126	3.0381	85.4878
8	11.8545	3.4961	81.9916
9	11.3275	4.0232	77.9684
10	10.7209	4.6298	73.3386
11	10.0229	5.3278	68.0108
12	9.2197	6.1310	61.8798
13	8.2953	7.0554	54.8244
14	7.2317	8.1190	46.7054
15	6.0076	9.3431	37.3623
16	4.5990	10.7517	26.6106
17	2.9781	12.3726	14.2380
18	1.1127	14.2380	0.0000

YEARS 19 — MO PAYT 1.2648 — AN CONST 15.18

#	INT	PRIN	BALANCE
1	14.0541	1.1241	98.8759
2	13.8846	1.2935	97.5824
3	13.6896	1.4886	96.0938
4	13.4652	1.7130	94.3809
5	13.2069	1.9712	92.4096
6	12.9097	2.2684	90.1412
7	12.5677	2.6104	87.5308
8	12.1742	3.0040	84.5268
9	11.7213	3.4568	81.0700
10	11.2001	3.9780	77.0920
11	10.6004	4.5777	72.5142
12	9.9102	5.2679	67.2463
13	9.1160	6.0621	61.1842
14	8.2021	6.9760	54.2082
15	7.1504	8.0278	46.1804
16	5.9401	9.2381	36.9423
17	4.5473	10.6308	26.3115
18	2.9446	12.2336	14.0779
19	1.1002	14.0779	0.0000

YEARS 20 — MO PAYT 1.2526 — AN CONST 15.04

#	INT	PRIN	BALANCE
1	14.0640	.9674	99.0326
2	13.9181	1.1132	97.9194
3	13.7503	1.2810	96.6384
4	13.5572	1.4742	95.1643
5	13.3349	1.6964	93.4679
6	13.0792	1.9522	91.5157
7	12.7848	2.2465	89.2692
8	12.4462	2.5852	86.6841
9	12.0564	2.9749	83.7092
10	11.6079	3.4234	80.2858
11	11.0918	3.9395	76.3462
12	10.4979	4.5335	71.8128
13	9.8144	5.2169	66.5958
14	9.0278	6.0035	60.5924
15	8.1227	6.9086	53.6838
16	7.0812	7.9501	45.7337
17	5.8826	9.1487	36.5850
18	4.5033	10.5280	26.0570
19	2.9161	12.1152	13.9417
20	1.0896	13.9417	0.0000

YEARS 21 — MO PAYT 1.2422 — AN CONST 14.91

#	INT	PRIN	BALANCE
1	14.0724	.8336	99.1664
2	13.9467	.9593	98.2071
3	13.8021	1.1039	97.1032

MONTHLY PAYMENT AMORTIZATION SCHEDULE PER $100   14.125%

Column 1

#	INT	PRIN	BALANCE
4	13.6357	1.2703	95.8328
5	13.4441	1.4619	94.3710
6	13.2238	1.6823	92.6887
7	12.9701	1.9359	90.7528
8	12.6783	2.2277	88.5251
9	12.3424	2.5636	85.9615
10	11.9559	2.9501	83.0114
11	11.5111	3.3949	79.6165
12	10.9993	3.9067	75.7098
13	10.4103	4.4957	71.2141
14	9.7326	5.1735	66.0407
15	8.9526	5.9534	60.0873
16	8.0550	6.8510	53.2363
17	7.0222	7.8838	45.3524
18	5.8336	9.0724	36.2800
19	4.4658	10.4402	25.8398
20	2.8918	12.0142	13.8255
21	1.0805	13.8255	0.0000

YEARS 22 — MO PAYT 1.2332 — AN CONST 14.80

#	INT	PRIN	BALANCE
1	14.0796	.7192	99.2808
2	13.9712	.8276	98.4532
3	13.8464	.9524	97.5008
4	13.7028	1.0960	96.4048
5	13.5376	1.2612	95.1436
6	13.3475	1.4514	93.6923
7	13.1286	1.6702	92.0221
8	12.8768	1.9220	90.1001
9	12.5871	2.2117	87.8884
10	12.2536	2.5452	85.3432
11	11.8699	2.9289	82.4144
12	11.4284	3.3705	79.0439
13	10.9202	3.8786	75.1653
14	10.3355	4.4633	70.7020
15	9.6626	5.1362	65.5657
16	8.8882	5.9106	59.6551
17	7.9971	6.8017	52.8534
18	6.9717	7.8271	45.0263
19	5.7916	9.0072	36.0191
20	4.4337	10.3651	25.6539
21	2.8710	11.9278	13.7261
22	1.0727	13.7261	0.0000

YEARS 23 — MO PAYT 1.2256 — AN CONST 14.71

#	INT	PRIN	BALANCE
1	14.0858	.6211	99.3789
2	13.9922	.7147	98.6642
3	13.8844	.8225	97.8417
4	13.7604	.9465	96.8952
5	13.6177	1.0892	95.8061
6	13.4535	1.2534	94.5527
7	13.2646	1.4423	93.1103
8	13.0471	1.6598	91.4506
9	12.7969	1.9100	89.5405
10	12.5089	2.1980	87.3425
11	12.1775	2.5294	84.8132
12	11.7962	2.9107	81.9025
13	11.3574	3.3495	78.5530
14	10.8524	3.8545	74.6985
15	10.2713	4.4356	70.2628
16	9.6025	5.1043	65.1585
17	8.8330	5.8739	59.2846
18	7.9474	6.7595	52.5251
19	6.9284	7.7785	44.7466
20	5.7556	8.9513	35.7954
21	4.4061	10.3008	25.4946
22	2.8532	11.8537	13.6408
23	1.0661	13.6408	0.0000

Column 2

YEARS 24 — MO PAYT 1.2190 — AN CONST 14.63

#	INT	PRIN	BALANCE
1	14.0911	.5368	99.4632
2	14.0102	.6178	98.8454
3	13.9171	.7109	98.1345
4	13.8099	.8181	97.3165
5	13.6866	.9414	96.3751
6	13.5446	1.0833	95.2918
7	13.3813	1.2466	94.0451
8	13.1934	1.4346	92.6105
9	12.9771	1.6509	90.9596
10	12.7282	1.8998	89.0599
11	12.4418	2.1862	86.8737
12	12.1122	2.5158	84.3579
13	11.7329	2.8951	81.4628
14	11.2964	3.3315	78.1313
15	10.7941	3.8338	74.2975
16	10.2161	4.4118	69.8857
17	9.5510	5.0769	64.8087
18	8.7856	5.8424	58.9664
19	7.9048	6.7232	52.2432
20	6.8912	7.7368	44.5064
21	5.7247	8.9032	35.6032
22	4.3825	10.2455	25.3577
23	2.8378	11.7901	13.5676
24	1.0603	13.5676	0.0000

YEARS 25 — MO PAYT 1.2133 — AN CONST 14.57

#	INT	PRIN	BALANCE
1	14.0957	.4643	99.5357
2	14.0257	.5343	99.0013
3	13.9451	.6149	98.3865
4	13.8524	.7076	97.6789
5	13.7458	.8143	96.8646
6	13.6230	.9370	95.9276
7	13.4817	1.0783	94.8493
8	13.3192	1.2409	93.6084
9	13.1321	1.4279	92.1805
10	12.9168	1.6432	90.5373
11	12.6691	1.8910	88.6463
12	12.3840	2.1760	86.4703
13	12.0559	2.5041	83.9662
14	11.6784	2.8816	81.0846
15	11.2440	3.3161	77.7685
16	10.7440	3.8160	73.9525
17	10.1687	4.3913	69.5612
18	9.5067	5.0534	64.5078
19	8.7744	5.8152	58.6926
20	7.8681	6.6920	52.0006
21	6.8592	7.7009	44.2997
22	5.6982	8.8619	35.4379
23	4.3621	10.1979	25.2400
24	2.8247	11.7354	13.5046
25	1.0554	13.5046	0.0000

YEARS 26 — MO PAYT 1.2085 — AN CONST 14.51

#	INT	PRIN	BALANCE
1	14.0996	.4019	99.5981
2	14.0391	.4625	99.1357
3	13.9693	.5322	98.6035
4	13.8891	.6124	97.9911
5	13.7968	.7047	97.2863
6	13.6905	.8110	96.4753
7	13.5683	.9333	95.5421
8	13.4276	1.0740	94.4681
9	13.2656	1.2359	93.2323
10	13.0793	1.4222	91.8101
11	12.8649	1.6366	90.1734
12	12.6182	1.8834	88.2901
13	12.3342	2.1673	86.1228
14	12.0075	2.4940	83.6288
15	11.6315	2.8700	80.7587

Column 3

#	INT	PRIN	BALANCE
16	11.1988	3.3027	77.4560
17	10.7008	3.8007	73.6553
18	10.1278	4.3737	69.2816
19	9.4684	5.0331	64.2486
20	8.7096	5.7919	58.4567
21	7.8365	6.6651	51.7916
22	6.8316	7.6699	44.1217
23	5.6753	8.8262	35.2955
24	4.3446	10.1569	25.1386
25	2.8133	11.6882	13.4504
26	1.0512	13.4504	0.0000

YEARS 27 — MO PAYT 1.2043 — AN CONST 14.46

#	INT	PRIN	BALANCE
1	14.1030	.3480	99.6520
2	14.0506	.4005	99.2515
3	13.9902	.4608	98.7907
4	13.9207	.5303	98.2603
5	13.8408	.6103	97.6501
6	13.7488	.7023	96.9478
7	13.6429	.8082	96.1396
8	13.5210	.9300	95.2096
9	13.3808	1.0702	94.1394
10	13.2195	1.2316	92.9078
11	13.0338	1.4172	91.4905
12	12.8201	1.6309	89.8596
13	12.5742	1.8768	87.9828
14	12.2913	2.1597	85.8231
15	11.9657	2.4854	83.3377
16	11.5910	2.8601	80.4777
17	11.1598	3.2913	77.1864
18	10.6636	3.7874	73.3990
19	10.0926	4.3585	69.0405
20	9.4355	5.0155	64.0250
21	8.6793	5.7717	58.2533
22	7.8092	6.6419	51.6114
23	6.8078	7.6432	43.9682
24	5.6555	8.7955	35.1726
25	4.3295	10.1216	25.0511
26	2.8035	11.6475	13.4035
27	1.0475	13.4035	0.0000

YEARS 28 — MO PAYT 1.2006 — AN CONST 14.41

#	INT	PRIN	BALANCE
1	14.1060	.3015	99.6985
2	14.0605	.3470	99.3515
3	14.0082	.3993	98.9523
4	13.9480	.4595	98.4928
5	13.8787	.5287	97.9641
6	13.7990	.6084	97.3556
7	13.7073	.7002	96.6555
8	13.6017	.8057	95.8497
9	13.4803	.9272	94.9225
10	13.3405	1.0670	93.8555
11	13.1796	1.2279	92.6277
12	12.9945	1.4130	91.2147
13	12.7815	1.6260	89.5887
14	12.5363	1.8711	87.7176
15	12.2542	2.1532	85.5643
16	11.9296	2.4779	83.0865
17	11.5560	2.8514	80.2350
18	11.1262	3.2813	76.9537
19	10.6314	3.7760	73.1777
20	10.0622	4.3453	68.8324
21	9.4070	5.0004	63.8319
22	8.6532	5.7543	58.0776
23	7.7856	6.6218	51.4558
24	6.7873	7.6202	43.8356
25	5.6385	8.7690	35.0666
26	4.3164	10.0911	24.9755
27	2.7951	11.6124	13.3631

Column 4

#	INT	PRIN	BALANCE
28	1.0443	13.3631	0.0000

YEARS 29 — MO PAYT 1.1975 — AN CONST 14.37

#	INT	PRIN	BALANCE
1	14.1085	.2613	99.7387
2	14.0691	.3007	99.4380
3	14.0238	.3461	99.0919
4	13.9716	.3982	98.6937
5	13.9116	.4583	98.2354
6	13.8425	.5273	97.7081
7	13.7630	.6069	97.1012
8	13.6715	.6983	96.4029
9	13.5662	.8036	95.5993
10	13.4450	.9248	94.6745
11	13.3056	1.0642	93.6103
12	13.1452	1.2247	92.3856
13	12.9605	1.4093	90.9763
14	12.7481	1.6217	89.3546
15	12.5036	1.8662	87.4883
16	12.2222	2.1476	85.3407
17	11.8984	2.4714	82.8693
18	11.5258	2.8440	80.0254
19	11.0971	3.2728	76.7526
20	10.6037	3.7662	72.9864
21	10.0359	4.3340	68.6525
22	9.3825	4.9874	63.6651
23	8.6306	5.7393	57.9259
24	7.7653	6.6045	51.3213
25	6.7696	7.6003	43.7211
26	5.6237	8.7461	34.9750
27	4.3051	10.0647	24.9103
28	2.7878	11.5821	13.3282
29	1.0416	13.3282	0.0000

YEARS 30 — MO PAYT 1.1948 — AN CONST 14.34

#	INT	PRIN	BALANCE
1	14.1107	.2266	99.7734
2	14.0765	.2607	99.5127
3	14.0372	.3000	99.2127
4	13.9920	.3453	98.8674
5	13.9400	.3973	98.4701
6	13.8801	.4572	98.0129
7	13.8111	.5262	97.4867
8	13.7318	.6055	96.8812
9	13.6405	.6968	96.1845
10	13.5355	.8018	95.3827
11	13.4146	.9227	94.4600
12	13.2755	1.0618	93.3982
13	13.1154	1.2219	92.1763
14	12.9312	1.4061	90.7702
15	12.7192	1.6181	89.1521
16	12.4752	1.8620	87.2901
17	12.1945	2.1427	85.1474
18	11.8715	2.4658	82.6816
19	11.4997	2.8375	79.8440
20	11.0719	3.2653	76.5787
21	10.5796	3.7576	72.8211
22	10.0131	4.3241	68.4969
23	9.3612	4.9761	63.5209
24	8.6110	5.7263	57.7946
25	7.7477	6.5896	51.2050
26	6.7542	7.5830	43.6220
27	5.6110	8.7263	34.8957
28	4.2954	10.0419	24.8538
29	2.7814	11.5558	13.2980
30	1.0393	13.2980	0.0000

YEARS 2 — MO PAYT 4.8107 — AN CONST 57.73

#	INT	PRIN	BALANCE
1	11.2522	46.4767	53.5233
2	4.2056	53.5233	0.0000

YEARS 3 — MO PAYT 3.4275 — AN CONST 41.13

#	INT	PRIN	BALANCE
1	12.3763	28.7535	71.2465
2	8.0168	33.1130	38.1335
3	2.9963	38.1335	0.0000

YEARS 4 — MO PAYT 2.7427 — AN CONST 32.92

#	INT	PRIN	BALANCE
1	12.9328	19.9795	80.0205
2	9.9036	23.0087	57.0118
3	6.4151	26.4972	30.5146
4	2.3977	30.5146	0.0000

YEARS 5 — MO PAYT 2.3372 — AN CONST 28.05

#	INT	PRIN	BALANCE
1	13.2623	14.7842	85.2158
2	11.0208	17.0257	68.1901
3	8.4394	19.6071	48.5831
4	5.4667	22.5798	26.0033
5	2.0432	26.0033	0.0000

YEARS 6 — MO PAYT 2.0713 — AN CONST 24.86

#	INT	PRIN	BALANCE
1	13.4784	11.3772	88.6228
2	11.7534	13.1021	75.5207
3	9.7669	15.0886	60.4320
4	7.4793	17.3763	43.0557
5	4.8447	20.0109	23.0448
6	1.8107	23.0448	0.0000

YEARS 7 — MO PAYT 1.8851 — AN CONST 22.63

#	INT	PRIN	BALANCE
1	13.6297	8.9911	91.0089
2	12.2666	10.3543	80.6547
3	10.6967	11.9241	68.7306
4	8.8888	13.7320	54.9985
5	6.8068	15.8140	39.1845
6	4.4091	18.2117	20.9729
7	1.6479	20.9729	0.0000

YEARS 8 — MO PAYT 1.7486 — AN CONST 20.99

#	INT	PRIN	BALANCE
1	13.7407	7.2419	92.7581
2	12.6427	8.3399	84.4181
3	11.3782	9.6044	74.8137
4	9.9220	11.0606	63.7531
5	8.2451	12.7376	51.0156
6	6.3138	14.6688	36.3468
7	4.0898	16.8928	19.4540
8	1.5286	19.4540	0.0000

YEARS 9 — MO PAYT 1.6451 — AN CONST 19.75

#	INT	PRIN	BALANCE
1	13.8247	5.9164	94.0836
2	12.9277	6.8135	87.2701
3	11.8947	7.8465	79.4236
4	10.7050	9.0362	70.3874
5	9.3350	10.4062	59.9812
6	7.7573	11.9839	47.9973
7	5.9403	13.8009	34.1964
8	3.8478	15.8933	18.3030
9	1.4382	18.3030	0.0000

YEARS 10 — MO PAYT 1.5647 — AN CONST 18.78

#	INT	PRIN	BALANCE
1	13.8901	4.8865	95.1135
2	13.1492	5.6273	89.4862
3	12.2960	6.4805	83.0057
4	11.3135	7.4631	75.5426
5	10.1819	8.5946	66.9480
6	8.8788	9.8977	57.0503
7	7.3782	11.3983	45.6519
8	5.6500	13.1265	32.5254
9	3.6598	15.1167	17.4087
10	1.3679	17.4087	0.0000

YEARS 11 — MO PAYT 1.5010 — AN CONST 18.02

#	INT	PRIN	BALANCE
1	13.9418	4.0704	95.9296
2	13.3247	4.6876	91.2420
3	12.6140	5.3983	85.8437
4	11.7955	6.2167	79.6270
5	10.8530	7.1593	72.4677
6	9.7675	8.2448	64.2229
7	8.5174	9.4948	54.7281
8	7.0779	10.9344	43.7937
9	5.4200	12.5922	31.2015
10	3.5109	14.5014	16.7001
11	1.3122	16.7001	0.0000

YEARS 12 — MO PAYT 1.4498 — AN CONST 17.40

#	INT	PRIN	BALANCE
1	13.9835	3.4139	96.5861
2	13.4659	3.9315	92.6547
3	12.8698	4.5275	88.1271
4	12.1834	5.2140	82.9131
5	11.3928	6.0045	76.9086
6	10.4824	6.9149	69.9937
7	9.4340	7.9633	62.0304
8	8.2267	9.1707	52.8597
9	6.8362	10.5611	42.2986
10	5.2350	12.1623	30.1363
11	3.3910	14.0063	16.1299
12	1.2674	16.1299	0.0000

YEARS 13 — MO PAYT 1.4080 — AN CONST 16.90

#	INT	PRIN	BALANCE
1	14.0174	2.8791	97.1209
2	13.5809	3.3156	93.8053
3	13.0782	3.8183	89.9871
4	12.4993	4.3972	85.5899
5	11.8326	5.0639	80.5260
6	11.0648	5.8316	74.6944
7	10.1806	6.7158	67.9785
8	9.1624	7.7340	60.2445
9	7.9898	8.9066	51.3379
10	6.6394	10.2570	41.0808
11	5.0843	11.8122	29.2686
12	3.2934	13.6031	15.6655
13	1.2309	15.6655	0.0000

YEARS 14 — MO PAYT 1.3737 — AN CONST 16.49

#	INT	PRIN	BALANCE
1	14.0453	2.4390	97.5610
2	13.6755	2.8088	94.7521
3	13.2496	3.2347	91.5174
4	12.7592	3.7251	87.7922
5	12.1944	4.2899	83.5023
6	11.5440	4.9404	78.5619
7	10.7949	5.6894	72.8725
8	9.9323	6.5520	66.3205
9	8.9389	7.5454	58.7751
10	7.7949	8.6894	50.0857
11	6.4775	10.0069	40.0788
12	4.9603	11.5241	28.5548
13	3.2130	13.2713	15.2835
14	1.2009	15.2835	0.0000

YEARS 15 — MO PAYT 1.3452 — AN CONST 16.15

#	INT	PRIN	BALANCE
1	14.0685	2.0740	97.9260
2	13.7540	2.3885	95.5375
3	13.3919	2.7506	92.7869
4	12.9748	3.1676	89.6193
5	12.4946	3.6479	85.9714
6	11.9415	4.2010	81.7705
7	11.3046	4.8379	76.9326
8	10.5711	5.5714	71.3611
9	9.7263	6.4161	64.9450
10	8.7536	7.3889	57.5561
11	7.6333	8.5092	49.0469
12	6.3431	9.7993	39.2476
13	4.8574	11.2851	27.9625
14	3.1464	12.9961	14.9665
15	1.1760	14.9665	0.0000

YEARS 16 — MO PAYT 1.3214 — AN CONST 15.86

#	INT	PRIN	BALANCE
1	14.0878	1.7691	98.2309
2	13.8196	2.0373	96.1936
3	13.5107	2.3462	93.8474
4	13.1550	2.7019	91.1455
5	12.7453	3.1116	88.0339
6	12.2735	3.5834	84.4505
7	11.7302	4.1266	80.3239
8	11.1046	4.7523	75.5715
9	10.3840	5.4728	70.0987
10	9.5543	6.3026	63.7961
11	8.5987	7.2582	56.5379
12	7.4982	8.3587	48.1792
13	6.2309	9.6260	38.5533
14	4.7715	11.0854	27.4678
15	3.0907	12.7661	14.7017
16	1.1552	14.7017	0.0000

YEARS 17 — MO PAYT 1.3014 — AN CONST 15.62

#	INT	PRIN	BALANCE
1	14.1040	1.5129	98.4871
2	13.8747	1.7423	96.7447
3	13.6105	2.0065	94.7382
4	13.3063	2.3107	92.4275
5	12.9559	2.6611	89.7665
6	12.5525	3.0645	86.7020
7	12.0878	3.5291	83.1728
8	11.5528	4.0642	79.1086
9	10.9366	4.6804	74.4282
10	10.2269	5.3900	69.0381
11	9.4097	6.2073	62.8309
12	8.4686	7.1484	55.6825
13	7.3848	8.2322	47.4503
14	6.1367	9.4803	37.9700
15	4.6993	10.9177	27.0523
16	3.0440	12.5730	14.4793
17	1.1377	14.4793	0.0000

YEARS 18 — MO PAYT 1.2845 — AN CONST 15.42

#	INT	PRIN	BALANCE
1	14.1178	1.2967	98.7033
2	13.9212	1.4933	97.2100
3	13.6947	1.7197	95.4902
4	13.4340	1.9805	93.5097
5	13.1337	2.2807	91.2290
6	12.7879	2.6265	88.6025
7	12.3897	3.0248	85.5777
8	11.9311	3.4834	82.0943
9	11.4030	4.0115	78.0828
10	10.7948	4.6197	73.4631
11	10.0943	5.3201	68.1429
12	9.2877	6.1268	62.0161
13	8.3588	7.0557	54.9605
14	7.2890	8.1254	46.8350
15	6.0571	9.3574	37.4776
16	4.6383	10.7761	26.7015
17	3.0045	12.4100	14.2915
18	1.1230	14.2915	0.0000

YEARS 19 — MO PAYT 1.2702 — AN CONST 15.25

#	INT	PRIN	BALANCE
1	14.1294	1.1135	98.8865
2	13.9606	1.2823	97.6043
3	13.7661	1.4767	96.1276
4	13.5423	1.7006	94.4270
5	13.2844	1.9584	92.4686
6	12.9875	2.2554	90.2132
7	12.6455	2.5973	87.6159
8	12.2517	2.9911	84.6248
9	11.7982	3.4446	81.1802
10	11.2760	3.9668	77.2134
11	10.6746	4.5683	72.6451
12	9.9819	5.2609	67.3842
13	9.1843	6.0586	61.3256
14	8.2657	6.9771	54.3485
15	7.2079	8.0350	46.3135
16	5.9896	9.2532	37.0603
17	4.5867	10.6561	26.4042
18	2.9711	12.2718	14.1324
19	1.1105	14.1324	0.0000

YEARS 20 — MO PAYT 1.2581 — AN CONST 15.10

#	INT	PRIN	BALANCE
1	14.1393	.9576	99.0424
2	13.9941	1.1028	97.9396
3	13.8269	1.2700	96.6696
4	13.6343	1.4626	95.2070
5	13.4126	1.6843	93.5227
6	13.1572	1.9397	91.5831
7	12.8631	2.2338	89.3493
8	12.5244	2.5724	86.7769
9	12.1344	2.9624	83.8144
10	11.6853	3.4116	80.4028
11	11.1680	3.9289	76.4740
12	10.5723	4.5245	71.9494
13	9.8863	5.2105	66.7389
14	9.0963	6.0005	60.7384
15	8.1866	6.9103	53.8280
16	7.1388	7.9580	45.8700
17	5.9323	9.1646	36.7054
18	4.5428	10.5541	26.1513
19	2.9426	12.1543	13.9971
20	1.0998	13.9971	0.0000

YEARS 21 — MO PAYT 1.2477 — AN CONST 14.98

#	INT	PRIN	BALANCE
1	14.1477	.8247	99.1753
2	14.0227	.9497	98.2256
3	13.8787	1.0937	97.1319

#	INT	PRIN	BALANCE
4	13.7128	1.2595	95.8724
5	13.5219	1.4505	94.4219
6	13.3020	1.6704	92.7515
7	13.0487	1.9237	90.8278
8	12.7570	2.2153	88.6125
9	12.4212	2.5512	86.0613
10	12.0344	2.9380	83.1232
11	11.5889	3.3835	79.7398
12	11.0759	3.8965	75.8433
13	10.4851	4.4872	71.3561
14	9.8048	5.1676	66.1885
15	9.0213	5.9510	60.2375
16	8.1190	6.8533	53.3841
17	7.0800	7.8924	45.4917
18	5.8834	9.0890	36.4027
19	4.5053	10.4671	25.9357
20	2.9183	12.0540	13.8816
21	1.0907	13.8816	0.0000

YEARS 22 — MO PAYT 1.2388 — AN CONST 14.87

#	INT	PRIN	BALANCE
1	14.1549	.7110	99.2890
2	14.0471	.8188	98.4702
3	13.9230	.9430	97.5272
4	13.7800	1.0859	96.4413
5	13.6153	1.2506	95.1907
6	13.4257	1.4402	93.7505
7	13.2074	1.6585	92.0920
8	12.9559	1.9100	90.1820
9	12.6663	2.1996	87.9824
10	12.3328	2.5331	85.4493
11	11.9488	2.9171	82.5322
12	11.5065	3.3594	79.1728
13	10.9972	3.8688	75.3040
14	10.4106	4.4553	70.8487
15	9.7351	5.1308	65.7179
16	8.9572	5.9087	59.8092
17	8.0613	6.8046	53.0046
18	7.0296	7.8363	45.1683
19	5.8415	9.0244	36.1439
20	4.4733	10.3926	25.7513
21	2.8976	11.9683	13.7829
22	1.0830	13.7829	0.0000

YEARS 23 — MO PAYT 1.2312 — AN CONST 14.78

#	INT	PRIN	BALANCE
1	14.1611	.6136	99.3864
2	14.0680	.7067	98.6797
3	13.9609	.8138	97.8659
4	13.8375	.9372	96.9288
5	13.6954	1.0793	95.8495
6	13.5318	1.2429	94.6066
7	13.3434	1.4313	93.1753
8	13.1263	1.6484	91.5269
9	12.8764	1.8983	89.6286
10	12.5886	2.1861	87.4425
11	12.2572	2.5175	84.9250
12	11.8755	2.8992	82.0258
13	11.4359	3.3388	78.6870
14	10.9297	3.8450	74.8420
15	10.3467	4.4280	70.4140
16	9.6754	5.0993	65.3146
17	8.9022	5.8725	59.4422
18	8.0119	6.7628	52.6793
19	6.9865	7.7882	44.8911
20	5.8057	8.9690	35.9221
21	4.4458	10.3289	25.5932
22	2.8798	11.8949	13.6984
23	1.0763	13.6984	0.0000

YEARS 24 — MO PAYT 1.2247 — AN CONST 14.70

#	INT	PRIN	BALANCE
1	14.1664	.5300	99.4700
2	14.0860	.6104	98.8596
3	13.9935	.7029	98.1567
4	13.8869	.8095	97.3472
5	13.7642	.9322	96.4150
6	13.6228	1.0735	95.3415
7	13.4601	1.2363	94.1052
8	13.2726	1.4238	92.6814
9	13.0568	1.6396	91.0418
10	12.8082	1.8882	89.1536
11	12.5219	2.1745	86.9791
12	12.1922	2.5042	84.4749
13	11.8125	2.8839	81.5910
14	11.3753	3.3211	78.2699
15	10.8718	3.8246	74.4453
16	10.2919	4.4045	70.0408
17	9.6241	5.0723	64.9685
18	8.8550	5.8414	59.1271
19	7.9694	6.7270	52.4001
20	6.9495	7.7469	44.6532
21	5.7749	8.9215	35.7317
22	4.4223	10.2741	25.4576
23	2.8645	11.8318	13.6257
24	1.0706	13.6257	0.0000

YEARS 25 — MO PAYT 1.2191 — AN CONST 14.63

#	INT	PRIN	BALANCE
1	14.1709	.4581	99.5419
2	14.1015	.5276	99.0143
3	14.0215	.6076	98.4067
4	13.9294	.6997	97.7070
5	13.8233	.8058	96.9013
6	13.7011	.9279	95.9733
7	13.5604	1.0686	94.9047
8	13.3984	1.2306	93.6741
9	13.2118	1.4172	92.2568
10	12.9970	1.6321	90.6247
11	12.7495	1.8796	88.7452
12	12.4645	2.1645	86.5806
13	12.1363	2.4927	84.0879
14	11.7584	2.8707	81.2173
15	11.3232	3.3059	77.9114
16	10.8219	3.8071	74.1043
17	10.2447	4.3843	69.7199
18	9.5800	5.0491	64.6708
19	8.8145	5.8146	58.8562
20	7.9329	6.6962	52.1601
21	6.9176	7.7114	44.4486
22	5.7485	8.8806	35.5680
23	4.4020	10.2271	25.3410
24	2.8514	11.7776	13.5633
25	1.0657	13.5633	0.0000

YEARS 26 — MO PAYT 1.2143 — AN CONST 14.58

#	INT	PRIN	BALANCE
1	14.1749	.3962	99.6038
2	14.1148	.4563	99.1475
3	14.0456	.5255	98.6220
4	13.9659	.6052	98.0168
5	13.8742	.6969	97.3199
6	13.7685	.8026	96.5173
7	13.6468	.9243	95.5931
8	13.5067	1.0644	94.5287
9	13.3453	1.2258	93.3029
10	13.1595	1.4116	91.8913
11	12.9455	1.6256	90.2656
12	12.6990	1.8721	88.3935
13	12.4151	2.1560	86.2376
14	12.0883	2.4828	83.7547
15	11.7118	2.8593	80.8955
16	11.2783	3.2928	77.6027
17	10.7791	3.7920	73.8106
18	10.2041	4.3670	69.4437
19	9.5420	5.0291	64.4146
20	8.7795	5.7916	58.6230
21	7.9014	6.6696	51.9534
22	6.8902	7.6809	44.2725
23	5.7257	8.8454	35.4271
24	4.3846	10.1865	25.2406
25	2.8401	11.7310	13.5096
26	1.0615	13.5096	0.0000

YEARS 27 — MO PAYT 1.2101 — AN CONST 14.53

#	INT	PRIN	BALANCE
1	14.1783	.3429	99.6571
2	14.1263	.3949	99.2622
3	14.0664	.4547	98.8075
4	13.9975	.5237	98.2838
5	13.9181	.6031	97.6807
6	13.8266	.6945	96.9862
7	13.7213	.7998	96.1864
8	13.6000	.9211	95.2653
9	13.4604	1.0607	94.2046
10	13.2996	1.2216	92.9830
11	13.1144	1.4068	91.5762
12	12.9011	1.6201	89.9561
13	12.6554	1.8657	88.0904
14	12.3726	2.1486	85.9419
15	12.0468	2.4743	83.4675
16	11.6717	2.8495	80.6181
17	11.2396	3.2815	77.3366
18	10.7421	3.7790	73.5575
19	10.1691	4.3520	69.2056
20	9.5093	5.0118	64.1937
21	8.7494	5.7717	58.4220
22	7.8744	6.6468	51.7753
23	6.8666	7.6545	44.1207
24	5.7060	8.8151	35.3056
25	4.3695	10.1516	25.1540
26	2.8304	11.6908	13.4633
27	1.0579	13.4633	0.0000

YEARS 28 — MO PAYT 1.2065 — AN CONST 14.48

#	INT	PRIN	BALANCE
1	14.1812	.2969	99.7031
2	14.1362	.3419	99.3613
3	14.0843	.3937	98.9676
4	14.0246	.4534	98.5142
5	13.9559	.5221	97.9921
6	13.8767	.6013	97.3908
7	13.7856	.6925	96.6983
8	13.6806	.7974	95.9008
9	13.5597	.9184	94.9825
10	13.4204	1.0576	93.9249
11	13.2601	1.2179	92.7070
12	13.0754	1.4026	91.3044
13	12.8628	1.6153	89.6891
14	12.6179	1.8602	87.8289
15	12.3358	2.1422	85.6867
16	12.0110	2.4670	83.2198
17	11.6370	2.8410	80.3788
18	11.2063	3.2718	77.1070
19	10.7102	3.7678	73.3392
20	10.1390	4.3391	69.0001
21	9.4811	4.9969	64.0032
22	8.7235	5.7546	58.2486
23	7.8510	6.6270	51.6216
24	6.8462	7.6318	43.9897
25	5.6891	8.7889	35.2008
26	4.3566	10.1215	25.0793
27	2.8220	11.6560	13.4233
28	1.0547	13.4233	0.0000

YEARS 29 — MO PAYT 1.2034 — AN CONST 14.45

#	INT	PRIN	BALANCE
1	14.1837	.2571	99.7429
2	14.1447	.2961	99.4468
3	14.0998	.3410	99.1058
4	14.0481	.3927	98.7131
5	13.9886	.4522	98.2609
6	13.9200	.5208	97.7401
7	13.8411	.5997	97.1404
8	13.7501	.6907	96.4497
9	13.6454	.7954	95.6543
10	13.5248	.9160	94.7383
11	13.3859	1.0549	93.6834
12	13.2260	1.2148	92.4686
13	13.0418	1.3990	91.0696
14	12.8297	1.6111	89.4585
15	12.5854	1.8554	87.6031
16	12.3041	2.1367	85.4664
17	11.9802	2.4606	83.0058
18	11.6071	2.8337	80.1721
19	11.1775	3.2633	76.9087
20	10.6827	3.7581	73.1506
21	10.1129	4.3279	68.8227
22	9.4567	4.9841	63.8386
23	8.7010	5.7398	58.0988
24	7.8308	6.6100	51.4888
25	6.8286	7.6122	43.8766
26	5.6745	8.7663	35.1103
27	4.3454	10.0954	25.0149
28	2.8147	11.6261	13.3888
29	1.0520	13.3888	0.0000

YEARS 30 — MO PAYT 1.2007 — AN CONST 14.41

#	INT	PRIN	BALANCE
1	14.1859	.2228	99.7772
2	14.1521	.2565	99.5207
3	14.1132	.2954	99.2253
4	14.0684	.3402	98.8850
5	14.0168	.3918	98.4932
6	13.9574	.4512	98.0420
7	13.8890	.5196	97.5224
8	13.8102	.5984	96.9240
9	13.7195	.6891	96.2348
10	13.6150	.7936	95.4412
11	13.4947	.9140	94.5272
12	13.3561	1.0525	93.4747
13	13.1965	1.2121	92.2626
14	13.0128	1.3959	90.8667
15	12.8011	1.6075	89.2592
16	12.5574	1.8512	87.4080
17	12.2767	2.1319	85.2760
18	11.9535	2.4552	82.8209
19	11.5812	2.8274	79.9935
20	11.1526	3.2561	76.7374
21	10.6589	3.7498	72.9877
22	10.0904	4.3183	68.6694
23	9.4356	4.9730	63.6964
24	8.6817	5.7270	57.9694
25	7.8134	6.5953	51.3741
26	6.8134	7.5952	43.7789
27	5.6618	8.7468	35.0321
28	4.3357	10.0730	24.9591
29	2.8085	11.6002	13.3590
30	1.0497	13.3590	0.0000

MONTHLY PAYMENT AMORTIZATION SCHEDULE PER $100   14.25 %

YEARS 2 — MO PAYT 4.8131 — AN CONST 57.76

#	INT	PRIN	BALANCE
1	11.2929	46.4644	53.5356
2	4.2217	53.5356	0.0000

YEARS 3 — MO PAYT 3.4299 — AN CONST 41.16

#	INT	PRIN	BALANCE
1	12.4210	28.7380	71.2620
2	8.0475	33.1115	38.1506
3	3.0085	38.1506	0.0000

YEARS 4 — MO PAYT 2.7452 — AN CONST 32.95

#	INT	PRIN	BALANCE
1	12.9795	19.9630	80.0370
2	9.9414	23.0010	57.0360
3	6.4410	26.5014	30.5346
4	2.4079	30.5346	0.0000

YEARS 5 — MO PAYT 2.3398 — AN CONST 28.08

#	INT	PRIN	BALANCE
1	13.3102	14.7675	85.2325
2	11.0628	17.0149	68.2176
3	8.4733	19.6043	48.6132
4	5.4898	22.5878	26.0254
5	2.0523	26.0254	0.0000

YEARS 6 — MO PAYT 2.0740 — AN CONST 24.89

#	INT	PRIN	BALANCE
1	13.5270	11.3608	88.6392
2	11.7980	13.0898	75.5494
3	9.8059	15.0819	60.4675
4	7.5107	17.3771	43.0903
5	4.8661	20.0217	23.0687
6	1.8191	23.0687	0.0000

YEARS 7 — MO PAYT 1.8878 — AN CONST 22.66

#	INT	PRIN	BALANCE
1	13.6788	8.9753	91.0247
2	12.3129	10.3412	80.6835
3	10.7391	11.9150	68.7686
4	8.9258	13.7282	55.0403
5	6.8366	15.8175	39.2229
6	4.4294	18.2247	20.9982
7	1.6559	20.9982	0.0000

YEARS 8 — MO PAYT 1.7514 — AN CONST 21.02

#	INT	PRIN	BALANCE
1	13.7901	7.2268	92.7732
2	12.6902	8.3266	84.4465
3	11.4231	9.5938	74.8527
4	9.9630	11.0539	63.7988
5	8.2808	12.7361	51.0627
6	6.3425	14.6744	36.3883
7	4.1093	16.9076	19.4807
8	1.5362	19.4807	0.0000

YEARS 9 — MO PAYT 1.6480 — AN CONST 19.78

#	INT	PRIN	BALANCE
1	13.8744	5.9021	94.0979
2	12.9762	6.8003	87.2976
3	11.9413	7.8352	79.4624
4	10.7489	9.0276	70.4348
5	9.3750	10.4015	60.0333
6	7.7920	11.9844	48.0489
7	5.9682	13.8083	34.2406
8	3.8668	15.9097	18.3309
9	1.4455	18.3309	0.0000

YEARS 10 — MO PAYT 1.5677 — AN CONST 18.82

#	INT	PRIN	BALANCE
1	13.9399	4.8729	95.1271
2	13.1983	5.6145	89.5126
3	12.3439	6.4689	83.0437
4	11.3594	7.4534	75.5903
5	10.2251	8.5877	67.0026
6	8.9182	9.8946	57.1080
7	7.4123	11.4004	45.7075
8	5.6774	13.1354	32.5721
9	3.6783	15.1344	17.4377
10	1.3751	17.4377	0.0000

YEARS 11 — MO PAYT 1.5041 — AN CONST 18.05

#	INT	PRIN	BALANCE
1	13.9918	4.0577	95.9423
2	13.3742	4.6752	91.2672
3	12.6628	5.3867	85.8805
4	11.8430	6.2064	79.6741
5	10.8984	7.1510	72.5231
6	9.8102	8.2392	64.2839
7	8.5563	9.4931	54.7907
8	7.1116	10.9378	43.8529
9	5.4470	12.6024	31.2505
10	3.5291	14.5203	16.7301
11	1.3193	16.7301	0.0000

YEARS 12 — MO PAYT 1.4529 — AN CONST 17.44

#	INT	PRIN	BALANCE
1	14.0335	3.4019	96.5981
2	13.5158	3.9196	92.6785
3	12.9193	4.5161	88.1624
4	12.2320	5.2034	82.9589
5	11.4401	5.9953	76.9636
6	10.5277	6.9077	70.0559
7	9.4764	7.9589	62.0970
8	8.2652	9.1702	52.9268
9	6.8696	10.5658	42.3611
10	5.2617	12.1737	30.1873
11	3.4090	14.0264	16.1610
12	1.2744	16.1610	0.0000

YEARS 13 — MO PAYT 1.4113 — AN CONST 16.94

#	INT	PRIN	BALANCE
1	14.0675	2.8679	97.1321
2	13.6310	3.3043	93.8278
3	13.1282	3.8072	90.0206
4	12.5488	4.3866	85.6340
5	11.8812	5.0542	80.5798
6	11.1120	5.8234	74.7564
7	10.2258	6.7096	68.0468
8	9.2047	7.7307	60.3161
9	8.0282	8.9072	51.4089
10	6.6726	10.2627	41.1462
11	5.1108	11.8246	29.3216
12	3.3113	13.6241	15.6975
13	1.2379	15.6975	0.0000

YEARS 14 — MO PAYT 1.3770 — AN CONST 16.53

#	INT	PRIN	BALANCE
1	14.0954	2.4286	97.5714
2	13.7258	2.7982	94.7731
3	13.3000	3.2241	91.5490
4	12.8093	3.7147	87.8343
5	12.2440	4.2801	83.5542
6	11.5926	4.9314	78.6228
7	10.8421	5.6819	72.9409
8	9.9774	6.5466	66.3942
9	8.9811	7.5429	58.8513
10	7.8332	8.6909	50.1604
11	6.5106	10.0135	40.1469
12	4.9867	11.5374	28.6095
13	3.2308	13.2932	15.3163
14	1.2078	15.3163	0.0000

YEARS 15 — MO PAYT 1.3486 — AN CONST 16.19

#	INT	PRIN	BALANCE
1	14.1186	2.0643	97.9357
2	13.8045	2.3785	95.5572
3	13.4425	2.7405	92.8167
4	13.0254	3.1575	89.6592
5	12.5449	3.6381	86.0211
6	11.9912	4.1917	81.8294
7	11.3533	4.8296	76.9997
8	10.6183	5.5646	71.4351
9	9.7715	6.4115	65.0236
10	8.7957	7.3872	57.6364
11	7.6715	8.5115	49.1249
12	6.3762	9.8068	39.3181
13	4.8837	11.2992	28.0189
14	3.1641	13.0188	15.0001
15	1.1829	15.0001	0.0000

YEARS 16 — MO PAYT 1.3248 — AN CONST 15.90

#	INT	PRIN	BALANCE
1	14.1380	1.7601	98.2399
2	13.8701	2.0280	96.2119
3	13.5615	2.3366	93.8752
4	13.2059	2.6922	91.1830
5	12.7962	3.1020	88.0810
6	12.3241	3.5740	84.5070
7	11.7802	4.1179	80.3891
8	11.1535	4.7446	75.6445
9	10.4314	5.4667	70.1778
10	9.5995	6.2986	63.8791
11	8.6409	7.2572	56.6219
12	7.5365	8.3616	48.2603
13	6.2639	9.6342	38.6261
14	4.7978	11.1004	27.5257
15	3.1084	12.7897	14.7361
16	1.1620	14.7361	0.0000

YEARS 17 — MO PAYT 1.3049 — AN CONST 15.66

#	INT	PRIN	BALANCE
1	14.1542	1.5047	98.4953
2	13.9253	1.7336	96.7617
3	13.6614	1.9975	94.7642
4	13.3574	2.3015	92.4627
5	13.0072	2.6517	89.8110
6	12.6036	3.0553	86.7557
7	12.1387	3.5202	83.2355
8	11.6029	4.0560	79.1795
9	10.9857	4.6732	74.5063
10	10.2745	5.3844	69.1218
11	9.4550	6.2039	62.9179
12	8.5109	7.1480	55.7699
13	7.4231	8.2358	47.5341
14	6.1697	9.4892	38.0449
15	4.7256	10.9333	27.1116
16	3.0617	12.5972	14.5143
17	1.1446	14.5143	0.0000

YEARS 18 — MO PAYT 1.2881 — AN CONST 15.46

#	INT	PRIN	BALANCE
1	14.1680	1.2891	98.7109
2	13.9718	1.4853	97.2256
3	13.7457	1.7113	95.5143
4	13.4853	1.9717	93.5426
5	13.1852	2.2718	91.2708
6	12.8395	2.6175	88.6533
7	12.4412	3.0159	85.6374
8	11.9822	3.4749	82.1625
9	11.4534	4.0037	78.1588
10	10.8440	4.6130	73.5458
11	10.1420	5.3150	68.2308
12	9.3331	6.1239	62.1069
13	8.4012	7.0559	55.0510
14	7.3274	8.1297	46.9213
15	6.0902	9.3669	37.5545
16	4.6647	10.7924	26.7621
17	3.0222	12.4348	14.3272
18	1.1298	14.3272	0.0000

YEARS 19 — MO PAYT 1.2738 — AN CONST 15.29

#	INT	PRIN	BALANCE
1	14.1796	1.1064	98.8936
2	14.0112	1.2748	97.6187
3	13.8172	1.4688	96.1499
4	13.5937	1.6924	94.4575
5	13.3361	1.9499	92.5076
6	13.0394	2.2467	90.2609
7	12.6974	2.5886	87.6724
8	12.3035	2.9825	84.6898
9	11.8496	3.4364	81.2534
10	11.3266	3.9594	77.2940
11	10.7241	4.5620	72.7321
12	10.0298	5.2562	67.4758
13	9.2299	6.0561	61.4197
14	8.3082	6.9778	54.4419
15	7.2463	8.0397	46.4022
16	6.0228	9.2632	37.1389
17	4.6130	10.6730	26.4660
18	2.9888	12.2973	14.1687
19	1.1173	14.1687	0.0000

YEARS 20 — MO PAYT 1.2617 — AN CONST 15.15

#	INT	PRIN	BALANCE
1	14.1895	.9512	99.0488
2	14.0447	1.0959	97.9529
3	13.8779	1.2627	96.6902
4	13.6858	1.4549	95.2354
5	13.4644	1.6763	93.5591
6	13.2093	1.9314	91.6277
7	12.9153	2.2253	89.4024
8	12.5767	2.5640	86.8385
9	12.1865	2.9542	83.8843
10	11.7369	3.4037	80.4806
11	11.2189	3.9217	76.5588
12	10.6221	4.5186	72.0403
13	9.9344	5.2062	66.8340
14	9.1421	5.9985	60.8355
15	8.2292	6.9114	53.9241
16	7.1774	7.9632	45.9608
17	5.9655	9.1751	36.7857
18	4.5692	10.5715	26.2142
19	2.9603	12.1803	14.0339
20	1.1067	14.0339	0.0000

YEARS 21 — MO PAYT 1.2514 — AN CONST 15.02

#	INT	PRIN	BALANCE
1	14.1979	.8188	99.1812
2	14.0733	.9434	98.2379
3	13.9297	1.0869	97.1509

#	INT	PRIN	BALANCE
4	13.7643	1.2524	95.8986
5	13.5737	1.4429	94.4556
6	13.3541	1.6625	92.7931
7	13.1011	1.9156	90.8775
8	12.8096	2.2071	88.6704
9	12.4737	2.5430	86.1275
10	12.0867	2.9300	83.1975
11	11.6408	3.3759	79.8216
12	11.1270	3.8896	75.9320
13	10.5351	4.4816	71.4504
14	9.8531	5.1636	66.2868
15	9.0672	5.9494	60.3374
16	8.1618	6.8548	53.4826
17	7.1186	7.8980	45.5845
18	5.9166	9.1000	36.4845
19	4.5318	10.4849	25.9996
20	2.9361	12.0806	13.9190
21	1.0976	13.9190	0.0000

YEARS 22 — MO PAYT 1.2426 — AN CONST 14.92

#	INT	PRIN	BALANCE
1	14.2051	.7056	99.2944
2	14.0977	.8130	98.4814
3	13.9740	.9367	97.5447
4	13.8314	1.0793	96.4654
5	13.6672	1.2435	95.2219
6	13.4779	1.4328	93.7891
7	13.2599	1.6508	92.1383
8	13.0087	1.9020	90.2363
9	12.7192	2.1915	88.0448
10	12.3857	2.5250	85.5197
11	12.0014	2.9093	82.6104
12	11.5587	3.3520	79.2584
13	11.0485	3.8622	75.3962
14	10.4608	4.4499	70.9463
15	9.7835	5.1272	65.8191
16	9.0033	5.9074	59.9117
17	8.1042	6.8065	53.1052
18	7.0684	7.8423	45.2629
19	5.8749	9.0358	36.2271
20	4.4998	10.4109	25.8161
21	2.9154	11.9953	13.8208
22	1.0899	13.8208	0.0000

YEARS 23 — MO PAYT 1.2350 — AN CONST 14.82

#	INT	PRIN	BALANCE
1	14.2113	.6087	99.3913
2	14.1186	.7013	98.6900
3	14.0119	.8080	97.8820
4	13.8889	.9310	96.9509
5	13.7472	1.0727	95.8782
6	13.5840	1.2360	94.6423
7	13.3959	1.4240	93.2182
8	13.1792	1.6408	91.5775
9	12.9295	1.8905	89.6870
10	12.6418	2.1782	87.5088
11	12.3103	2.5097	84.9992
12	11.9284	2.8916	82.1076
13	11.4883	3.3316	78.7760
14	10.9813	3.8387	74.9373
15	10.3971	4.4229	70.5144
16	9.7240	5.0960	65.4185
17	8.9485	5.8715	59.5470
18	8.0549	6.7650	52.7819
19	7.0254	7.7946	44.9874
20	5.8391	8.9808	36.0066
21	4.4724	10.3476	25.6590
22	2.8976	11.9223	13.7367
23	1.0832	13.7367	0.0000

YEARS 24 — MO PAYT 1.2285 — AN CONST 14.75

#	INT	PRIN	BALANCE
1	14.2166	.5255	99.4745
2	14.1366	.6055	98.8690
3	14.0444	.6976	98.1714
4	13.9383	.8038	97.3676
5	13.8159	.9261	96.4415
6	13.6750	1.0671	95.3744
7	13.5126	1.2295	94.1449
8	13.3255	1.4166	92.7284
9	13.1099	1.6321	91.0962
10	12.8615	1.8805	89.2157
11	12.5753	2.1667	87.0490
12	12.2496	2.4965	84.5525
13	11.8657	2.8764	81.6761
14	11.4279	3.3141	78.3620
15	10.9236	3.8185	74.5435
16	10.3424	4.3996	70.1439
17	9.6729	5.0692	65.0747
18	8.9014	5.8406	59.2341
19	8.0126	6.7295	52.5046
20	6.9884	7.7536	44.7509
21	5.8085	8.9336	35.8173
22	4.4489	10.2932	25.5242
23	2.8824	11.8596	13.6645
24	1.0775	13.6645	0.0000

YEARS 25 — MO PAYT 1.2229 — AN CONST 14.68

#	INT	PRIN	BALANCE
1	14.2211	.4540	99.5460
2	14.1520	.5231	99.0229
3	14.0724	.6027	98.4201
4	13.9807	.6945	97.7257
5	13.8750	.8001	96.9255
6	13.7532	.9219	96.0036
7	13.6129	1.0622	94.9414
8	13.4513	1.2239	93.7175
9	13.2650	1.4101	92.3074
10	13.0504	1.6247	90.6826
11	12.8031	1.8720	88.8106
12	12.5182	2.1569	86.6538
13	12.1900	2.4851	84.1686
14	11.8118	2.8633	81.3053
15	11.3760	3.2991	78.0062
16	10.8740	3.8012	74.2050
17	10.2955	4.3796	69.8254
18	9.6290	5.0462	64.7792
19	8.8610	5.8141	58.9651
20	7.9762	6.6989	52.2662
21	6.9567	7.7184	44.5478
22	5.7821	8.8930	35.6547
23	4.4287	10.2464	25.4083
24	2.8693	11.8058	13.6025
25	1.0727	13.6025	0.0000

YEARS 26 — MO PAYT 1.2181 — AN CONST 14.62

#	INT	PRIN	BALANCE
1	14.2250	.3925	99.6075
2	14.1653	.4522	99.1552
3	14.0965	.5211	98.6342
4	14.0172	.6004	98.0338
5	13.9258	.6917	97.3421
6	13.8205	.7970	96.5451
7	13.6992	.9183	95.6268
8	13.5595	1.0581	94.5687
9	13.3985	1.2191	93.3496
10	13.2129	1.4046	91.9450
11	12.9992	1.6184	90.3267
12	12.7529	1.8646	88.4620
13	12.4691	2.1484	86.3136
14	12.1422	2.4754	83.8383
15	11.7654	2.8521	80.9862
16	11.3314	3.2861	77.7000
17	10.8313	3.7862	73.9138
18	10.2551	4.3625	69.5513
19	9.5912	5.0264	64.5250
20	8.8262	5.7913	58.7337
21	7.9449	6.6726	52.0610
22	6.9294	7.6881	44.3729
23	5.7594	8.8581	35.5148
24	4.4113	10.2062	25.3085
25	2.8581	11.7595	13.5491
26	1.0684	13.5491	0.0000

YEARS 27 — MO PAYT 1.2140 — AN CONST 14.57

#	INT	PRIN	BALANCE
1	14.2284	.3395	99.6605
2	14.1767	.3912	99.2693
3	14.1172	.4507	98.8186
4	14.0486	.5193	98.2993
5	13.9696	.5983	97.7010
6	13.8785	.6894	97.0116
7	13.7736	.7943	96.2173
8	13.6527	.9152	95.3021
9	13.5134	1.0545	94.2476
10	13.3530	1.2149	93.0327
11	13.1681	1.3998	91.6329
12	12.9550	1.6129	90.0200
13	12.7096	1.8583	88.1617
14	12.4268	2.1411	86.0206
15	12.1009	2.4670	83.5536
16	11.7255	2.8424	80.7112
17	11.2929	3.2750	77.4362
18	10.7945	3.7734	73.6628
19	10.2203	4.3476	69.3152
20	9.5586	5.0093	64.3059
21	8.7963	5.7716	58.5343
22	7.9179	6.6500	51.8843
23	6.9059	7.6620	44.2223
24	5.7398	8.8281	35.3942
25	4.3963	10.1716	25.2226
26	2.8484	11.7195	13.5031
27	1.0648	13.5031	0.0000

YEARS 28 — MO PAYT 1.2104 — AN CONST 14.53

#	INT	PRIN	BALANCE
1	14.2313	.2938	99.7062
2	14.1866	.3385	99.3677
3	14.1351	.3900	98.9777
4	14.0757	.4494	98.5283
5	14.0073	.5178	98.0105
6	13.9285	.5966	97.4139
7	13.8377	.6874	96.7266
8	13.7331	.7920	95.9346
9	13.6126	.9125	95.0221
10	13.4737	1.0514	93.9708
11	13.3137	1.2114	92.7594
12	13.1294	1.3957	91.3637
13	12.9170	1.6081	89.7555
14	12.6722	1.8529	87.9027
15	12.3903	2.1348	85.7679
16	12.0654	2.4597	83.3081
17	11.6910	2.8341	80.4741
18	11.2597	3.2654	77.2087
19	10.7628	3.7623	73.4464
20	10.1902	4.3349	69.1115
21	9.5305	4.9946	64.1170
22	8.7704	5.7547	58.3623
23	7.8946	6.6305	51.7318
24	6.8856	7.6395	44.0923
25	5.7230	8.8021	35.2902
26	4.3834	10.1417	25.1485
27	2.8400	11.6851	13.4634
28	1.0617	13.4634	0.0000

YEARS 29 — MO PAYT 1.2073 — AN CONST 14.49

#	INT	PRIN	BALANCE
1	14.2338	.2543	99.7457
2	14.1951	.2931	99.4526
3	14.1505	.3377	99.1150
4	14.0991	.3890	98.7259
5	14.0399	.4482	98.2777
6	13.9717	.5165	97.7612
7	13.8931	.5951	97.1662
8	13.8025	.6856	96.4806
9	13.6982	.7900	95.6906
10	13.5780	.9102	94.7804
11	13.4395	1.0487	93.7317
12	13.2799	1.2083	92.5235
13	13.0960	1.3922	91.1313
14	12.8841	1.6040	89.5273
15	12.6400	1.8481	87.6791
16	12.3588	2.1294	85.5497
17	12.0347	2.4535	83.0962
18	11.6613	2.8268	80.2694
19	11.2311	3.2571	77.0123
20	10.7354	3.7527	73.2596
21	10.1643	4.3238	68.9358
22	9.5063	4.9819	63.9539
23	8.7481	5.7400	58.2139
24	7.8746	6.6136	51.6003
25	6.8681	7.6201	43.9802
26	5.7084	8.7797	35.2004
27	4.3723	10.1159	25.0846
28	2.8328	11.6554	13.4292
29	1.0590	13.4292	0.0000

YEARS 30 — MO PAYT 1.2047 — AN CONST 14.46

#	INT	PRIN	BALANCE
1	14.2360	.2203	99.7797
2	14.2025	.2538	99.5260
3	14.1638	.2924	99.2335
4	14.1193	.3369	98.8966
5	14.0681	.3882	98.5085
6	14.0090	.4473	98.0612
7	13.9409	.5153	97.5459
8	13.8625	.5937	96.9521
9	13.7721	.6841	96.2680
10	13.6680	.7882	95.4798
11	13.5481	.9082	94.5717
12	13.4099	1.0464	93.5253
13	13.2506	1.2056	92.3197
14	13.0671	1.3891	90.9306
15	12.8557	1.6005	89.3301
16	12.6122	1.8441	87.4860
17	12.3315	2.1247	85.3613
18	12.0082	2.4481	82.9132
19	11.6356	2.8206	80.0926
20	11.2064	3.2499	76.8427
21	10.7118	3.7445	73.0982
22	10.1419	4.3143	68.7839
23	9.4853	4.9709	63.8130
24	8.7289	5.7274	58.0856
25	7.8572	6.5990	51.4866
26	6.8529	7.6033	43.8833
27	5.6958	8.7604	35.1229
28	4.3626	10.0936	25.0293
29	2.8265	11.6297	13.3996
30	1.0567	13.3996	0.0000

MONTHLY PAYMENT AMORTIZATION SCHEDULE PER $100   14.30 %

YEARS 2	MO PAYT 4.8155	AN CONST 57.79
# INT	PRIN	BALANCE
1 11.3336	46.4521	53.5479
2 4.2378	53.5479	0.0000

YEARS 3	MO PAYT 3.4324	AN CONST 41.19
# INT	PRIN	BALANCE
1 12.4658	28.7224	71.2776
2 8.0783	33.1099	38.1676
3 3.0206	38.1676	0.0000

YEARS 4	MO PAYT 2.7477	AN CONST 32.98
# INT	PRIN	BALANCE
1 13.0262	19.9464	80.0536
2 9.9793	22.9933	57.0602
3 6.4670	26.5057	30.5546
4 2.4181	30.5546	0.0000

YEARS 5	MO PAYT 2.3424	AN CONST 28.11
# INT	PRIN	BALANCE
1 13.3580	14.7509	85.2491
2 11.1047	17.0041	68.2450
3 8.5073	19.6016	48.6434
4 5.5130	22.5959	26.0475
5 2.0614	26.0475	0.0000

YEARS 6	MO PAYT 2.0767	AN CONST 24.93
# INT	PRIN	BALANCE
1 13.5755	11.3445	88.6555
2 11.8426	13.0775	75.5780
3 9.8450	15.0751	60.5029
4 7.5422	17.3779	43.1250
5 4.8876	20.0325	23.0925
6 1.8275	23.0925	0.0000

YEARS 7	MO PAYT 1.8906	AN CONST 22.69
# INT	PRIN	BALANCE
1 13.7278	8.9595	91.0405
2 12.3592	10.3281	80.7124
3 10.7816	11.9058	68.8066
4 8.9629	13.7245	55.0821
5 6.8664	15.8209	39.2612
6 4.4497	18.2377	21.0235
7 1.6638	21.0235	0.0000

YEARS 8	MO PAYT 1.7543	AN CONST 21.06
# INT	PRIN	BALANCE
1 13.8395	7.2117	92.7883
2 12.7378	8.3134	84.4749
3 11.4679	9.5833	74.8916
4 10.0040	11.0472	63.8444
5 8.3165	12.7347	51.1098
6 6.3712	14.6800	36.4298
7 4.1288	16.9224	19.5074
8 1.5438	19.5074	0.0000

YEARS 9	MO PAYT 1.6510	AN CONST 19.82
# INT	PRIN	BALANCE
1 13.9240	5.8877	94.1123
2 13.0246	6.7871	87.3251
3 11.9879	7.8239	79.5012
4 10.7927	9.0190	70.4822
5 9.4150	10.3967	60.0854
6 7.8269	11.9849	48.1005

#	INT	PRIN	BALANCE
7	5.9961	13.8156	34.2849
8	3.8857	15.9261	18.3588
9	1.4529	18.3588	0.0000

YEARS 10	MO PAYT 1.5708	AN CONST 18.85
# INT	PRIN	BALANCE
1 13.9897	4.8594	95.1406
2 13.2474	5.6016	89.5390
3 12.3917	6.4573	83.0817
4 11.4053	7.4437	75.6380
5 10.2683	8.5808	67.0572
6 8.9575	9.8915	57.1657
7 7.4465	11.4025	45.7632
8 5.7047	13.1443	32.6189
9 3.6969	15.1522	17.4667
10 1.3823	17.4667	0.0000

YEARS 11	MO PAYT 1.5072	AN CONST 18.09
# INT	PRIN	BALANCE
1 14.0417	4.0449	95.9551
2 13.4238	4.6628	91.2923
3 12.7115	5.3751	85.9172
4 11.8905	6.1961	79.7211
5 10.9440	7.1426	72.5785
6 9.8529	8.2337	64.3448
7 8.5952	9.4914	54.8534
8 7.1453	10.9413	43.9121
9 5.4740	12.6126	31.2995
10 3.5473	14.5393	16.7602
11 1.3264	16.7602	0.0000

YEARS 12	MO PAYT 1.4561	AN CONST 17.48
# INT	PRIN	BALANCE
1 14.0835	3.3900	96.6100
2 13.5657	3.9078	92.7022
3 12.9687	4.5047	88.1975
4 12.2806	5.1928	83.0047
5 11.4874	5.9861	77.0186
6 10.5730	6.9005	70.1181
7 9.5189	7.9546	62.1635
8 8.3038	9.1697	52.9939
9 6.9031	10.5704	42.4235
10 5.2884	12.1851	30.2384
11 3.4271	14.0464	16.1920
12 1.2814	16.1920	0.0000

YEARS 13	MO PAYT 1.4145	AN CONST 16.98
# INT	PRIN	BALANCE
1 14.1176	2.8567	97.1433
2 13.6812	3.2931	93.8501
3 13.1781	3.7962	90.0540
4 12.5983	4.3760	85.6779
5 11.9298	5.0445	80.6334
6 11.1592	5.8151	74.8184
7 10.2710	6.7034	68.1150
8 9.2470	7.7273	60.3877
9 8.0666	8.9077	51.4800
10 6.7059	10.2684	41.2116
11 5.1373	11.8370	29.3746
12 3.3292	13.6451	15.7295
13 1.2448	15.7295	0.0000

YEARS 14	MO PAYT 1.3803	AN CONST 16.57
# INT	PRIN	BALANCE
1 14.1456	2.4183	97.5817
2 13.7762	2.7877	94.7941
3 13.3503	3.2135	91.5806

#	INT	PRIN	BALANCE
4	12.8595	3.7044	87.8763
5	12.2936	4.2702	83.6060
6	11.6413	4.9225	78.6835
7	10.8894	5.6745	73.0091
8	10.0226	6.5413	66.4678
9	9.0234	7.5405	58.9274
10	7.8715	8.6923	50.2351
11	6.5437	10.0201	40.2150
12	5.0131	11.5507	28.6642
13	3.2487	13.3151	15.3491
14	1.2147	15.3491	0.0000

YEARS 15	MO PAYT 1.3520	AN CONST 16.23
# INT	PRIN	BALANCE
1 14.1688	2.0547	97.9453
2 13.8549	2.3686	95.5767
3 13.4931	2.7304	92.8464
4 13.0760	3.1475	89.6989
5 12.5952	3.6282	86.0707
6 12.0410	4.1825	81.8882
7 11.4021	4.8214	77.0668
8 10.6656	5.5579	71.5089
9 9.8166	6.4068	65.1021
10 8.8380	7.3855	57.7166
11 7.7098	8.5137	49.2029
12 6.4093	9.8142	39.3887
13 4.9101	11.3134	28.0753
14 3.1819	13.0416	15.0337
15 1.1898	15.0337	0.0000

YEARS 16	MO PAYT 1.3283	AN CONST 15.94
# INT	PRIN	BALANCE
1 14.1882	1.7512	98.2488
2 13.9207	2.0187	96.2301
3 13.6123	2.3271	93.9030
4 13.2568	2.6826	91.2204
5 12.8470	3.0923	88.1281
6 12.3747	3.5647	84.5634
7 11.8301	4.1092	80.4541
8 11.2024	4.7369	75.7172
9 10.4789	5.4605	70.2567
10 9.6447	6.2947	63.9620
11 8.6832	7.2562	56.7058
12 7.5748	8.3646	48.3412
13 6.2970	9.6423	38.6989
14 4.8241	11.1153	27.5836
15 3.1262	12.8132	14.7704
16 1.1689	14.7704	0.0000

YEARS 17	MO PAYT 1.3084	AN CONST 15.71
# INT	PRIN	BALANCE
1 14.2044	1.4964	98.5036
2 13.9759	1.7250	96.7786
3 13.7123	1.9885	94.7901
4 13.4086	2.2923	92.4978
5 13.0584	2.6424	89.8554
6 12.6548	3.0461	86.8093
7 12.1895	3.5114	83.2980
8 11.6531	4.0477	79.2502
9 11.0348	4.6661	74.5842
10 10.3220	5.3788	69.2053
11 9.5004	6.2005	63.0049
12 8.5533	7.1476	55.8573
13 7.4614	8.2394	47.6178
14 6.2028	9.4981	38.1198
15 4.7519	10.9489	27.1709
16 3.0794	12.6214	14.5494
17 1.1514	14.5494	0.0000

YEARS 18	MO PAYT 1.2916	AN CONST 15.50
# INT	PRIN	BALANCE
1 14.2182	1.2815	98.7185
2 14.0224	1.4772	97.2413
3 13.7968	1.7029	95.5384
4 13.5366	1.9630	93.5753
5 13.2368	2.2629	91.3124
6 12.8911	2.6086	88.7039
7 12.4926	3.0070	85.6969
8 12.0333	3.4664	82.2305
9 11.5038	3.9959	78.2346
10 10.8934	4.6063	73.6284
11 10.1898	5.3099	68.3185
12 9.3787	6.1210	62.1975
13 8.4436	7.0560	55.1415
14 7.3658	8.1339	47.0076
15 6.1233	9.3763	37.6313
16 4.6910	10.8086	26.8227
17 3.0400	12.4597	14.3630
18 1.1367	14.3630	0.0000

YEARS 19	MO PAYT 1.2774	AN CONST 15.33
# INT	PRIN	BALANCE
1 14.2298	1.0995	98.9005
2 14.0618	1.2674	97.6331
3 13.8682	1.4610	96.1721
4 13.6451	1.6842	94.4880
5 13.3878	1.9414	92.5465
6 13.0912	2.2380	90.3085
7 12.7494	2.5799	87.7286
8 12.3553	2.9740	84.7547
9 11.9010	3.4283	81.3264
10 11.3773	3.9519	77.3745
11 10.7736	4.5556	72.8189
12 10.0777	5.2515	67.5673
13 9.2755	6.0537	61.5136
14 8.3508	6.9784	54.5352
15 7.2848	8.0444	46.4908
16 6.0560	9.2732	37.2175
17 4.6395	10.6898	26.5278
18 3.0065	12.3227	14.2051
19 1.1242	14.2051	0.0000

YEARS 20	MO PAYT 1.2654	AN CONST 15.19
# INT	PRIN	BALANCE
1 14.2397	.9448	99.0552
2 14.0954	1.0891	97.9662
3 13.9290	1.2554	96.7108
4 13.7372	1.4472	95.2636
5 13.5162	1.6683	93.5953
6 13.2613	1.9231	91.6722
7 12.9676	2.2169	89.4553
8 12.6289	2.5555	86.8998
9 12.2386	2.9459	83.9539
10 11.7886	3.3959	80.5581
11 11.2698	3.9146	76.6435
12 10.6718	4.5126	72.1309
13 9.9825	5.2019	66.9290
14 9.1879	5.9965	60.9325
15 8.2719	6.9125	54.0200
16 7.2160	7.9684	46.0516
17 5.9988	9.1856	36.8659
18 4.5956	10.5888	26.2771
19 2.9781	12.2063	14.0709
20 1.1136	14.0709	0.0000

YEARS 21	MO PAYT 1.2551	AN CONST 15.07
# INT	PRIN	BALANCE
1 14.2481	.8129	99.1871
2 14.1239	.9371	98.2500
3 13.9808	1.0802	97.1698

MONTHLY PAYMENT AMORTIZATION SCHEDULE PER $100   14.30 %

#	INT	PRIN	BALANCE
4	13.8158	1.2452	95.9246
5	13.6256	1.4354	94.4892
6	13.4063	1.6547	92.8345
7	13.1535	1.9075	90.9270
8	12.8621	2.1988	88.7281
9	12.5263	2.5347	86.1934
10	12.1391	2.9219	83.2715
11	11.6927	3.3683	79.9032
12	11.1782	3.8828	76.0204
13	10.5851	4.4759	71.5445
14	9.9014	5.1596	66.3849
15	9.1132	5.9478	60.4372
16	8.2047	6.8563	53.5809
17	7.1573	7.9036	45.6772
18	5.9500	9.1110	36.5662
19	4.5583	10.5027	26.0635
20	2.9539	12.1071	13.9565
21	1.1045	13.9565	0.0000

YEARS 22 — MO PAYT 1.2463 — AN CONST 14.96

#	INT	PRIN	BALANCE
1	14.2553	.7002	99.2998
2	14.1483	.8072	98.4926
3	14.0250	.9305	97.5620
4	13.8829	1.0726	96.4894
5	13.7190	1.2365	95.2529
6	13.5301	1.4254	93.8275
7	13.3124	1.6431	92.1844
8	13.0614	1.8941	90.2903
9	12.7721	2.1834	88.1068
10	12.4385	2.5170	85.5898
11	12.0541	2.9015	82.6884
12	11.6108	3.3447	79.3437
13	11.0999	3.8556	75.4881
14	10.5110	4.4446	71.0436
15	9.8320	5.1235	65.9201
16	9.0494	5.9061	60.0140
17	8.1472	6.8083	53.2057
18	7.1072	7.8483	45.3574
19	5.9084	9.0472	36.3102
20	4.5264	10.4292	25.8810
21	2.9332	12.0223	13.8587
22	1.0968	13.8587	0.0000

YEARS 23 — MO PAYT 1.2388 — AN CONST 14.87

#	INT	PRIN	BALANCE
1	14.2614	.6038	99.3962
2	14.1692	.6960	98.7002
3	14.0629	.8023	97.8979
4	13.9403	.9249	96.9730
5	13.7991	1.0662	95.9068
6	13.6362	1.2290	94.6778
7	13.4484	1.4168	93.2610
8	13.2320	1.6332	91.6278
9	12.9825	1.8827	89.7451
10	12.6950	2.1703	87.5749
11	12.3634	2.5018	85.0731
12	11.9813	2.8839	82.1891
13	11.5407	3.3245	78.8646
14	11.0329	3.8323	75.0323
15	10.4475	4.4177	70.6146
16	9.7727	5.0925	65.5221
17	8.9948	5.8705	59.6516
18	8.0980	6.7672	52.8844
19	7.0643	7.8009	45.0835
20	5.8727	8.9925	36.0910
21	4.4990	10.3662	25.7248
22	2.9155	11.9497	13.7751
23	1.0902	13.7751	0.0000

YEARS 24 — MO PAYT 1.2323 — AN CONST 14.79

#	INT	PRIN	BALANCE
1	14.2667	.5210	99.4790
2	14.1871	.6006	98.8783
3	14.0954	.6924	98.1859
4	13.9896	.7982	97.3878
5	13.8677	.9201	96.4677
6	13.7272	1.0606	95.4071
7	13.5651	1.2226	94.1845
8	13.3784	1.4094	92.7751
9	13.1631	1.6247	91.1504
10	12.9149	1.8729	89.2775
11	12.6288	2.1590	87.1186
12	12.2990	2.4887	84.6298
13	11.9189	2.8689	81.7609
14	11.4806	3.3072	78.4537
15	10.9754	3.8123	74.6414
16	10.3931	4.3947	70.2467
17	9.7218	5.0660	65.1807
18	8.9479	5.8399	59.3408
19	8.0558	6.7319	52.6089
20	7.0275	7.7603	44.8486
21	5.8421	8.9457	35.9029
22	4.4756	10.3122	25.5907
23	2.9003	11.8874	13.7033
24	1.0845	13.7033	0.0000

YEARS 25 — MO PAYT 1.2268 — AN CONST 14.73

#	INT	PRIN	BALANCE
1	14.2713	.4500	99.5500
2	14.2025	.5187	99.0313
3	14.1233	.5979	98.4334
4	14.0320	.6893	97.7441
5	13.9267	.7946	96.9496
6	13.8053	.9159	96.0336
7	13.6654	1.0558	94.9778
8	13.5041	1.2171	93.7607
9	13.3182	1.4031	92.3576
10	13.1039	1.6174	90.7402
11	12.8568	1.8644	88.8758
12	12.5720	2.1492	86.7265
13	12.2437	2.4776	84.2490
14	11.8652	2.8560	81.3930
15	11.4290	3.2923	78.1007
16	10.9260	3.7952	74.3055
17	10.3463	4.3749	69.9306
18	9.6780	5.0432	64.8874
19	8.9076	5.8136	59.0738
20	8.0196	6.7016	52.3722
21	6.9959	7.7254	44.6468
22	5.8158	8.9054	35.7414
23	4.4554	10.2658	25.4756
24	2.8873	11.8339	13.6416
25	1.0796	13.6416	0.0000

YEARS 26 — MO PAYT 1.2220 — AN CONST 14.67

#	INT	PRIN	BALANCE
1	14.2752	.3888	99.6112
2	14.2158	.4482	99.1630
3	14.1473	.5167	98.6463
4	14.0684	.5956	98.0507
5	13.9774	.6866	97.3641
6	13.8725	.7915	96.5726
7	13.7516	.9124	95.6602
8	13.6123	1.0517	94.6085
9	13.4516	1.2124	93.3961
10	13.2664	1.3976	91.9985
11	13.0529	1.6111	90.3874
12	12.8068	1.8572	88.5302
13	12.5231	2.1409	86.3893
14	12.1961	2.4679	83.9214
15	11.8191	2.8449	81.0765
16	11.3845	3.2795	77.7970
17	10.8836	3.7804	74.0166
18	10.3061	4.3579	69.6587
19	9.6404	5.0236	64.6351
20	8.8730	5.7910	58.8441
21	7.9884	6.6756	52.1685
22	6.9687	7.6953	44.4732
23	5.7932	8.8708	35.6024
24	4.4381	10.2259	25.3765
25	2.8761	11.7879	13.5886
26	1.0754	13.5886	0.0000

YEARS 27 — MO PAYT 1.2179 — AN CONST 14.62

#	INT	PRIN	BALANCE
1	14.2785	.3362	99.6638
2	14.2272	.3875	99.2763
3	14.1680	.4467	98.8296
4	14.0998	.5149	98.3147
5	14.0211	.5936	97.7211
6	13.9304	.6843	97.0368
7	13.8259	.7888	96.2480
8	13.7054	.9093	95.3387
9	13.5665	1.0482	94.2905
10	13.4064	1.2083	93.0821
11	13.2218	1.3929	91.6892
12	13.0090	1.6057	90.0836
13	12.7637	1.8509	88.2326
14	12.4810	2.1337	86.0989
15	12.1551	2.4596	83.6393
16	11.7794	2.8353	80.8040
17	11.3462	3.2685	77.5355
18	10.8470	3.7677	73.7678
19	10.2714	4.3433	69.4245
20	9.6080	5.0067	64.4178
21	8.8432	5.7715	58.6463
22	7.9615	6.6531	51.9931
23	6.9452	7.6694	44.3237
24	5.7737	8.8410	35.4827
25	4.4232	10.1915	25.2912
26	2.8664	11.7483	13.5429
27	1.0718	13.5429	0.0000

YEARS 28 — MO PAYT 1.2144 — AN CONST 14.58

#	INT	PRIN	BALANCE
1	14.2814	.2908	99.7092
2	14.2370	.3352	99.3740
3	14.1858	.3864	98.9877
4	14.1268	.4454	98.5422
5	14.0588	.5134	98.0288
6	13.9803	.5919	97.4369
7	13.8899	.6823	96.7546
8	13.7857	.7865	95.9681
9	13.6655	.9067	95.0615
10	13.5270	1.0452	94.0163
11	13.3674	1.2048	92.8115
12	13.1834	1.3889	91.4226
13	12.9712	1.6010	89.8216
14	12.7266	1.8456	87.9761
15	12.4447	2.1275	85.8486
16	12.1197	2.4525	83.3961
17	11.7451	2.8271	80.5690
18	11.3133	3.2589	77.3101
19	10.8154	3.7568	73.5533
20	10.2416	4.3306	69.2227
21	9.5800	4.9922	64.2305
22	8.8175	5.7547	58.4758
23	7.9384	6.6338	51.8420
24	6.9251	7.6471	44.1948
25	5.7569	8.8153	35.3795
26	4.4103	10.1619	25.2177
27	2.8581	11.7141	13.5035
28	1.0687	13.5035	0.0000

YEARS 29 — MO PAYT 1.2113 — AN CONST 14.54

#	INT	PRIN	BALANCE
1	14.2839	.2516	99.7484
2	14.2455	.2900	99.4584
3	14.2012	.3343	99.1240
4	14.1501	.3854	98.7386
5	14.0912	.4443	98.2943
6	14.0234	.5122	97.7822
7	13.9451	.5904	97.1918
8	13.8550	.6806	96.5112
9	13.7510	.7845	95.7267
10	13.6312	.9044	94.8223
11	13.4930	1.0425	93.7797
12	13.3338	1.2018	92.5780
13	13.1502	1.3854	91.1926
14	12.9386	1.5970	89.5956
15	12.6946	1.8409	87.7547
16	12.4134	2.1221	85.6326
17	12.0892	2.4463	83.1863
18	11.7156	2.8200	80.3663
19	11.2848	3.2507	77.1155
20	10.7882	3.7473	73.3682
21	10.2158	4.3197	69.0485
22	9.5559	4.9796	64.0689
23	8.7953	5.7403	58.3286
24	7.9184	6.6171	51.7115
25	6.9076	7.6279	44.0836
26	5.7424	8.7931	35.2905
27	4.3992	10.1363	25.1542
28	2.8509	11.6847	13.4696
29	1.0660	13.4696	0.0000

YEARS 30 — MO PAYT 1.2087 — AN CONST 14.51

#	INT	PRIN	BALANCE
1	14.2861	.2178	99.7822
2	14.2528	.2511	99.5312
3	14.2145	.2894	99.2417
4	14.1703	.3336	98.9081
5	14.1193	.3846	98.5236
6	14.0606	.4433	98.0802
7	13.9928	.5110	97.5692
8	13.9148	.5891	96.9801
9	13.8248	.6791	96.3010
10	13.7211	.7828	95.5182
11	13.6015	.9024	94.6158
12	13.4636	1.0403	93.5755
13	13.3047	1.1992	92.3763
14	13.1215	1.3823	90.9940
15	12.9104	1.5935	89.4005
16	12.6670	1.8369	87.5636
17	12.3864	2.1175	85.4461
18	12.0629	2.4410	83.0051
19	11.6900	2.8138	80.1913
20	11.2602	3.2437	76.9476
21	10.7647	3.7392	73.2084
22	10.1936	4.3103	68.8981
23	9.5351	4.9688	63.9294
24	8.7761	5.7278	58.2016
25	7.9012	6.6027	51.5989
26	6.8926	7.6113	43.9876
27	5.7299	8.7740	35.2137
28	4.3897	10.1142	25.0994
29	2.8447	11.6592	13.4402
30	1.0637	13.4402	0.0000

MONTHLY PAYMENT AMORTIZATION SCHEDULE PER $100

14.375%

YEARS 2 — MO PAYT 4.8190 — AN CONST 57.83

#	INT	PRIN	BALANCE
1	11.3946	46.4337	53.5663
2	4.2619	53.5663	0.0000

YEARS 3 — MO PAYT 3.4360 — AN CONST 41.24

#	INT	PRIN	BALANCE
1	12.5329	28.6991	71.3009
2	8.1244	33.1076	38.1933
3	3.0388	38.1933	0.0000

YEARS 4 — MO PAYT 2.7515 — AN CONST 33.02

#	INT	PRIN	BALANCE
1	13.0963	19.9216	80.0784
2	10.0362	22.9818	57.0966
3	6.5059	26.5120	30.5845
4	2.4334	30.5845	0.0000

YEARS 5 — MO PAYT 2.3463 — AN CONST 28.16

#	INT	PRIN	BALANCE
1	13.4298	14.7259	85.2741
2	11.1678	16.9880	68.2861
3	8.5582	19.5975	48.6885
4	5.5479	22.6079	26.0807
5	2.0751	26.0807	0.0000

YEARS 6 — MO PAYT 2.0807 — AN CONST 24.97

#	INT	PRIN	BALANCE
1	13.6484	11.3201	88.6799
2	11.9095	13.0590	75.6210
3	9.9036	15.0649	60.5560
4	7.5894	17.3791	43.1770
5	4.9198	20.0486	23.1283
6	1.8402	23.1283	0.0000

YEARS 7 — MO PAYT 1.8948 — AN CONST 22.74

#	INT	PRIN	BALANCE
1	13.8014	8.9359	91.0641
2	12.4288	10.3085	80.7556
3	10.8453	11.8920	68.8635
4	9.0186	13.7188	55.1448
5	6.9112	15.8261	39.3187
6	4.4802	18.2571	21.0616
7	1.6757	21.0616	0.0000

YEARS 8 — MO PAYT 1.7586 — AN CONST 21.11

#	INT	PRIN	BALANCE
1	13.9136	7.1892	92.8108
2	12.8092	8.2935	84.5174
3	11.5353	9.5674	74.9499
4	10.0656	11.0371	63.9128
5	8.3702	12.7325	51.1804
6	6.4144	14.6883	36.4920
7	4.1581	16.9446	19.5474
8	1.5553	19.5474	0.0000

YEARS 9 — MO PAYT 1.6554 — AN CONST 19.87

#	INT	PRIN	BALANCE
1	13.9985	5.8663	94.1337
2	13.0973	6.7674	87.3663
3	12.0578	7.8070	79.5593
4	10.8586	9.0062	70.5531
5	9.4751	10.3896	60.1635
6	7.8792	11.9856	48.1780
7	6.0381	13.8267	34.3513
8	3.9142	15.9506	18.4007
9	1.4640	18.4007	0.0000

YEARS 10 — MO PAYT 1.5753 — AN CONST 18.91

#	INT	PRIN	BALANCE
1	14.0644	4.8391	95.1609
2	13.3211	5.5824	89.5785
3	12.4636	6.4399	83.1385
4	11.4743	7.4292	75.7094
5	10.3331	8.5704	67.1390
6	9.0166	9.8869	57.2522
7	7.4979	11.4056	45.8466
8	5.7459	13.1576	32.6890
9	3.7248	15.1787	17.5103
10	1.3932	17.5103	0.0000

YEARS 11 — MO PAYT 1.5119 — AN CONST 18.15

#	INT	PRIN	BALANCE
1	14.1166	4.0259	95.9741
2	13.4982	4.6443	91.3299
3	12.7848	5.3577	85.9722
4	11.9618	6.1807	79.7915
5	11.0124	7.1301	72.6614
6	9.9171	8.2253	64.4361
7	8.6536	9.4888	54.9473
8	7.1961	10.9464	44.0009
9	5.5146	12.6279	31.3730
10	3.5748	14.5676	16.8054
11	1.3371	16.8054	0.0000

YEARS 12 — MO PAYT 1.4609 — AN CONST 17.54

#	INT	PRIN	BALANCE
1	14.1586	3.3721	96.6279
2	13.6406	3.8901	92.7378
3	13.0430	4.4877	88.2501
4	12.3537	5.1770	83.0731
5	11.5584	5.9723	77.1008
6	10.6410	6.8896	70.2112
7	9.5827	7.9480	62.2632
8	8.3618	9.1688	53.0944
9	6.9534	10.5773	42.5171
10	5.3286	12.2020	30.3151
11	3.4543	14.0764	16.2387
12	1.2920	16.2387	0.0000

YEARS 13 — MO PAYT 1.4194 — AN CONST 17.04

#	INT	PRIN	BALANCE
1	14.1927	2.8401	97.1599
2	13.7564	3.2763	93.8836
3	13.2532	3.7796	90.1039
4	12.6726	4.3602	85.7437
5	12.0028	5.0300	80.7137
6	11.2302	5.8026	74.9111
7	10.3388	6.6940	68.2171
8	9.3106	7.7222	60.4949
9	8.1243	8.9084	51.5865
10	6.7559	10.2769	41.3096
11	5.1773	11.8555	29.4541
12	3.3562	13.6766	15.7775
13	1.2553	15.7775	0.0000

YEARS 14 — MO PAYT 1.3853 — AN CONST 16.63

#	INT	PRIN	BALANCE
1	14.2208	2.4028	97.5972
2	13.8517	2.7718	94.8254
3	13.4259	3.1976	91.6278
4	12.9347	3.6888	87.9390
5	12.3681	4.2554	83.6835
6	11.7144	4.9091	78.7744
7	10.9603	5.6632	73.1112
8	10.0904	6.5331	66.5780
9	9.0868	7.5367	59.0414
10	7.9291	8.6944	50.3470
11	6.5936	10.0299	40.3170
12	5.0529	11.5706	28.7464
13	3.2755	13.3480	15.3984
14	1.2252	15.3984	0.0000

YEARS 15 — MO PAYT 1.3570 — AN CONST 16.29

#	INT	PRIN	BALANCE
1	14.2440	2.0403	97.9597
2	13.9306	2.3537	95.6059
3	13.5691	2.7153	92.8907
4	13.1520	3.1324	89.7583
5	12.6708	3.6135	86.1447
6	12.1157	4.1686	81.9761
7	11.4754	4.8090	77.1671
8	10.7367	5.5477	71.6195
9	9.8845	6.3998	65.2196
10	8.9014	7.3829	57.8367
11	7.7674	8.5170	49.3197
12	6.4591	9.8253	39.4944
13	4.9498	11.3346	28.1599
14	3.2087	13.0757	15.0842
15	1.2002	15.0842	0.0000

YEARS 16 — MO PAYT 1.3334 — AN CONST 16.01

#	INT	PRIN	BALANCE
1	14.2635	1.7379	98.2621
2	13.9965	2.0049	96.2572
3	13.6885	2.3128	93.9444
4	13.3333	2.6681	91.2763
5	12.9234	3.0779	88.1984
6	12.4506	3.5507	84.6476
7	11.9052	4.0962	80.5514
8	11.2760	4.7254	75.8261
9	10.5501	5.4513	70.3748
10	9.7127	6.2886	64.0862
11	8.7467	7.2546	56.8316
12	7.6324	8.3690	48.4626
13	6.3468	9.6545	38.8080
14	4.8638	11.1376	27.6705
15	3.1529	12.8484	14.8221
16	1.1793	14.8221	0.0000

YEARS 17 — MO PAYT 1.3137 — AN CONST 15.77

#	INT	PRIN	BALANCE
1	14.2797	1.4841	98.5159
2	14.0518	1.7121	96.8038
3	13.7888	1.9751	94.8287
4	13.4854	2.2785	92.5501
5	13.1354	2.6285	89.9216
6	12.7316	3.0323	86.8894
7	12.2658	3.4980	83.3913
8	11.7285	4.0354	79.3560
9	11.1086	4.6553	74.7007
10	10.3935	5.3703	69.3303
11	9.5686	6.1953	63.1351
12	8.6169	7.1469	55.9881
13	7.5191	8.2448	47.7433
14	6.2526	9.5113	38.2321
15	4.7916	10.9723	27.2598
16	3.1061	12.6577	14.6021
17	1.1618	14.6021	0.0000

YEARS 18 — MO PAYT 1.2970 — AN CONST 15.57

#	INT	PRIN	BALANCE
1	14.2935	1.2702	98.7298
2	14.0984	1.4653	97.2645
3	13.8733	1.6904	95.5742
4	13.6136	1.9500	93.6242
5	13.3141	2.2496	91.3746
6	12.9685	2.5951	88.7795
7	12.5699	2.9937	85.7857
8	12.1100	3.4536	82.3321
9	11.5795	3.9841	78.3480
10	10.9675	4.5961	73.7519
11	10.2615	5.3021	68.4497
12	9.4470	6.1166	62.3331
13	8.5075	7.0562	55.2770
14	7.4236	8.1401	47.1369
15	6.1732	9.3904	37.7465
16	4.7307	10.8329	26.9136
17	3.0667	12.4970	14.4166
18	1.1470	14.4166	0.0000

YEARS 19 — MO PAYT 1.2828 — AN CONST 15.40

#	INT	PRIN	BALANCE
1	14.3051	1.0890	98.9110
2	14.1378	1.2563	97.6546
3	13.9448	1.4493	96.2053
4	13.7222	1.6720	94.5333
5	13.4654	1.9288	92.6046
6	13.1691	2.2251	90.3795
7	12.8273	2.5669	87.8126
8	12.4330	2.9611	84.8515
9	11.9781	3.4160	81.4355
10	11.4534	3.9407	77.4947
11	10.8481	4.5461	72.9487
12	10.1498	5.2444	67.7043
13	9.3442	6.0500	61.6543
14	8.4148	6.9793	54.6750
15	7.3427	8.0514	46.6236
16	6.1060	9.2882	37.3354
17	4.6792	10.7149	26.6205
18	3.0333	12.3609	14.2596
19	1.1345	14.2596	0.0000

YEARS 20 — MO PAYT 1.2708 — AN CONST 15.26

#	INT	PRIN	BALANCE
1	14.3150	.9352	99.0648
2	14.1713	1.0789	97.9859
3	14.0056	1.2446	96.7413
4	13.8144	1.4358	95.3056
5	13.5939	1.6563	93.6493
6	13.3394	1.9107	91.7385
7	13.0459	2.2043	89.5343
8	12.7073	2.5428	86.9914
9	12.3167	2.9335	84.0580
10	11.8661	3.3841	80.6739
11	11.3463	3.9039	76.7700
12	10.7466	4.5036	72.2665
13	10.0548	5.1953	67.0711
14	9.2568	5.9934	61.0777
15	8.3361	6.9140	54.1637
16	7.2741	7.9761	46.1875
17	6.0489	9.2013	36.9862
18	4.6355	10.6147	26.3715
19	3.0049	12.2453	14.1262
20	1.1239	14.1262	0.0000

YEARS 21 — MO PAYT 1.2606 — AN CONST 15.13

#	INT	PRIN	BALANCE
1	14.3234	.8042	99.1958
2	14.1999	.9277	98.2682
3	14.0574	1.0702	97.1980

#	INT	PRIN	BALANCE
4	13.8930	1.2346	95.9634
5	13.7033	1.4242	94.5392
6	13.4845	1.6430	92.8962
7	13.2322	1.8954	91.0008
8	12.9410	2.1865	88.8143
9	12.6051	2.5224	86.2919
10	12.2177	2.9099	83.3820
11	11.7707	3.3568	80.0251
12	11.2551	3.8725	76.1527
13	10.6602	4.4673	71.6853
14	9.9740	5.1536	66.5317
15	9.1823	5.9452	60.5865
16	8.2691	6.8584	53.7281
17	7.2156	7.9120	45.8161
18	6.0002	9.1273	36.6888
19	4.5982	10.5294	26.1594
20	2.9808	12.1468	14.0126
21	1.1149	14.0126	0.0000

YEARS 22 — MO PAYT 1.2519 — AN CONST 15.03

#	INT	PRIN	BALANCE
1	14.3306	.6923	99.3077
2	14.2242	.7986	98.5091
3	14.1016	.9213	97.5879
4	13.9600	1.0628	96.5251
5	13.7968	1.2260	95.2991
6	13.6085	1.4144	93.8847
7	13.3912	1.6316	92.2531
8	13.1406	1.8823	90.3708
9	12.8514	2.1714	88.1994
10	12.5179	2.5049	85.6945
11	12.1331	2.8897	82.8048
12	11.6892	3.3336	79.4712
13	11.1771	3.8457	75.6255
14	10.5864	4.4364	71.1891
15	9.9049	5.1179	66.0712
16	9.1188	5.9041	60.1671
17	8.2119	6.8110	53.3562
18	7.1656	7.8572	45.4990
19	5.9587	9.0641	36.4348
20	4.5663	10.4565	25.9783
21	2.9601	12.0627	13.9156
22	1.1072	13.9156	0.0000

YEARS 23 — MO PAYT 1.2444 — AN CONST 14.94

#	INT	PRIN	BALANCE
1	14.3367	.5965	99.4035
2	14.2451	.6881	98.7154
3	14.1394	.7938	97.9215
4	14.0174	.9158	97.0058
5	13.8768	1.0564	95.9493
6	13.7145	1.2187	94.7306
7	13.5273	1.4059	93.3247
8	13.3113	1.6219	91.7028
9	13.0622	1.8710	89.8318
10	12.7748	2.1584	87.6733
11	12.4432	2.4900	85.1833
12	12.0607	2.8725	82.3108
13	11.6195	3.3137	78.9971
14	11.1105	3.8227	75.1744
15	10.5233	4.4100	70.7644
16	9.8458	5.0874	65.6771
17	9.0644	5.8688	59.8082
18	8.1629	6.7703	53.0379
19	7.1229	7.8103	45.2276
20	5.9231	9.0101	36.2175
21	4.5391	10.3941	25.8234
22	2.9425	11.9907	13.8326
23	1.1006	13.8326	0.0000

YEARS 24 — MO PAYT 1.2380 — AN CONST 14.86

#	INT	PRIN	BALANCE
1	14.3420	.5144	99.4856
2	14.2630	.5934	98.8922
3	14.1718	.6846	98.2076
4	14.0666	.7897	97.4178
5	13.9453	.9111	96.5068
6	13.8054	1.0510	95.4558
7	13.6439	1.2125	94.2433
8	13.4577	1.3987	92.8446
9	13.2428	1.6135	91.2311
10	12.9950	1.8614	89.3697
11	12.7091	2.1473	87.2223
12	12.3792	2.4772	84.7451
13	11.9987	2.8577	81.8874
14	11.5597	3.2967	78.5907
15	11.0533	3.8031	74.7877
16	10.4691	4.3873	70.4004
17	9.7952	5.0612	65.3392
18	9.0178	5.8386	59.5006
19	8.1209	6.7355	52.7651
20	7.0862	7.7702	44.9949
21	5.8927	8.9637	36.0312
22	4.5158	10.3406	25.6905
23	2.9273	11.9291	13.7615
24	1.0949	13.7615	0.0000

YEARS 25 — MO PAYT 1.2325 — AN CONST 14.80

#	INT	PRIN	BALANCE
1	14.3465	.4439	99.5561
2	14.2783	.5121	99.0439
3	14.1996	.5908	98.4531
4	14.1089	.6815	97.7716
5	14.0042	.7862	96.9854
6	13.8834	.9070	96.0783
7	13.7441	1.0463	95.0320
8	13.5834	1.2071	93.8249
9	13.3980	1.3925	92.4324
10	13.1841	1.6064	90.8261
11	12.9373	1.8531	88.9729
12	12.6526	2.1378	86.8351
13	12.3243	2.4662	84.3689
14	11.9454	2.8450	81.5239
15	11.5084	3.2820	78.2419
16	11.0042	3.7862	74.4557
17	10.4226	4.3678	70.0879
18	9.7517	5.0387	65.0491
19	8.9777	5.8127	59.2364
20	8.0848	6.7056	52.5308
21	7.0548	7.7357	44.7952
22	5.8665	8.9239	35.8712
23	4.4957	10.2947	25.5765
24	2.9143	11.8761	13.7004
25	1.0901	13.7004	0.0000

YEARS 26 — MO PAYT 1.2278 — AN CONST 14.74

#	INT	PRIN	BALANCE
1	14.3504	.3833	99.6167
2	14.2915	.4422	99.1744
3	14.2242	.5102	98.6643
4	14.1452	.5885	98.0757
5	14.0548	.6789	97.3968
6	13.9505	.7832	96.6136
7	13.8302	.9035	95.7100
8	13.6914	1.0423	94.6677
9	13.5313	1.2024	93.4652
10	13.3466	1.3871	92.0781
11	13.1335	1.6002	90.4779
12	12.8877	1.8460	88.6318
13	12.6041	2.1296	86.5022
14	12.2770	2.4567	84.0455
15	11.8996	2.8341	81.2114
16	11.4643	3.2695	77.9419
17	10.9621	3.7717	74.1702
18	10.3827	4.3510	69.8192
19	9.7143	5.0194	64.7998
20	8.9433	5.7904	59.0093
21	8.0538	6.6799	52.3294
22	7.0277	7.7060	44.6234
23	5.8440	8.8897	35.7337
24	4.4785	10.2553	25.4784
25	2.9032	11.8306	13.6479
26	1.0859	13.6479	0.0000

YEARS 27 — MO PAYT 1.2237 — AN CONST 14.69

#	INT	PRIN	BALANCE
1	14.3537	.3312	99.6688
2	14.3029	.3821	99.2867
3	14.2442	.4408	98.8460
4	14.1765	.5085	98.3375
5	14.0984	.5866	97.7509
6	14.0083	.6767	97.0742
7	13.9043	.7806	96.2936
8	13.7844	.9005	95.3930
9	13.6461	1.0389	94.3541
10	13.4865	1.1985	93.1557
11	13.3024	1.3826	91.7731
12	13.0900	1.5949	90.1782
13	12.8450	1.8399	88.3383
14	12.5624	2.1226	86.2157
15	12.2524	2.4486	83.7671
16	11.8602	2.8247	80.9424
17	11.4263	3.2586	77.6838
18	10.9258	3.7592	73.9246
19	10.3483	4.3366	69.5879
20	9.6822	5.0028	64.5852
21	8.9137	5.7713	58.8139
22	8.0272	6.6578	52.1561
23	7.0045	7.6805	44.4756
24	5.8247	8.8603	35.6154
25	4.4636	10.2213	25.3941
26	2.8936	11.7914	13.6027
27	1.0823	13.6027	0.0000

YEARS 28 — MO PAYT 1.2202 — AN CONST 14.65

#	INT	PRIN	BALANCE
1	14.3566	.2863	99.7137
2	14.3126	.3303	99.3835
3	14.2619	.3810	99.0025
4	14.2034	.4395	98.5630
5	14.1359	.5070	98.0560
6	14.0580	.5849	97.4711
7	13.9682	.6747	96.7963
8	13.8645	.7784	96.0179
9	13.7449	.8980	95.1199
10	13.6070	1.0359	94.0840
11	13.4479	1.1950	92.8890
12	13.2643	1.3786	91.5104
13	13.0525	1.5904	89.9200
14	12.8082	1.8347	88.0854
15	12.5264	2.1165	85.9689
16	12.2013	2.4416	83.5273
17	11.8263	2.8166	80.7107
18	11.3936	3.2493	77.4614
19	10.8945	3.7484	73.7130
20	10.3187	4.3242	69.3887
21	9.6544	4.9885	64.4003
22	8.8882	5.7547	58.6455
23	8.0042	6.6387	52.0068
24	6.9844	7.6585	44.3483
25	5.8080	8.8349	35.5134
26	4.4509	10.1920	25.3214
27	2.8853	11.7576	13.5637
28	1.0792	13.5637	0.0000

YEARS 29 — MO PAYT 1.2172 — AN CONST 14.61

#	INT	PRIN	BALANCE
1	14.3591	.2475	99.7525
2	14.3211	.2856	99.4669
3	14.2772	.3294	99.1374
4	14.2266	.3800	98.7574
5	14.1682	.4384	98.3190
6	14.1009	.5058	97.8132
7	14.0232	.5835	97.2298
8	13.9336	.6731	96.5567
9	13.8302	.7765	95.7802
10	13.7109	.8957	94.8845
11	13.5733	1.0333	93.8511
12	13.4146	1.1921	92.6591
13	13.2315	1.3752	91.2839
14	13.0202	1.5864	89.6975
15	12.7765	1.8301	87.8673
16	12.4954	2.1112	85.7561
17	12.1711	2.4355	83.3206
18	11.7970	2.8097	80.5109
19	11.3654	3.2413	77.2696
20	10.8675	3.7391	73.5305
21	10.2931	4.3135	69.2170
22	9.6305	4.9761	64.2408
23	8.8662	5.7405	58.5004
24	7.9844	6.6223	51.8781
25	6.9671	7.6395	44.2385
26	5.7936	8.8130	35.4255
27	4.4398	10.1668	25.2587
28	2.8781	11.7285	13.5301
29	1.0765	13.5301	0.0000

YEARS 30 — MO PAYT 1.2146 — AN CONST 14.58

#	INT	PRIN	BALANCE
1	14.3613	.2141	99.7859
2	14.3284	.2470	99.5389
3	14.2904	.2850	99.2539
4	14.2466	.3287	98.9252
5	14.1962	.3792	98.5459
6	14.1379	.4375	98.1085
7	14.0707	.5047	97.6038
8	13.9932	.5822	97.0216
9	13.9037	.6716	96.3499
10	13.8006	.7748	95.5751
11	13.6816	.8938	94.6813
12	13.5443	1.0311	93.6502
13	13.3859	1.1895	92.4607
14	13.2031	1.3722	91.0884
15	12.9924	1.5830	89.5054
16	12.7492	1.8262	87.6792
17	12.4687	2.1067	85.5725
18	12.1451	2.4303	83.1421
19	11.7717	2.8037	80.3385
20	11.3411	3.2343	77.1042
21	10.8442	3.7311	73.3730
22	10.2711	4.3043	69.0688
23	9.6099	4.9655	64.1033
24	8.8472	5.7282	58.3751
25	7.9673	6.6081	51.7670
26	6.9522	7.6232	44.1438
27	5.7812	8.7942	35.3496
28	4.4303	10.1450	25.2046
29	2.8720	11.7034	13.5012
30	1.0742	13.5012	0.0000

MONTHLY PAYMENT AMORTIZATION SCHEDULE PER $100

14.40 %

YEARS 2 — MO PAYT 4.8202 — AN CONST 57.85

#	INT	PRIN	BALANCE
1	11.4150	46.4275	53.5725
2	4.2700	53.5725	0.0000

YEARS 3 — MO PAYT 3.4372 — AN CONST 41.25

#	INT	PRIN	BALANCE
1	12.5553	28.6914	71.3086
2	8.1398	33.1068	38.2018
3	3.0449	38.2018	0.0000

YEARS 4 — MO PAYT 2.7528 — AN CONST 33.04

#	INT	PRIN	BALANCE
1	13.1197	19.9134	80.0866
2	10.0551	22.9780	57.1087
3	6.5189	26.5141	30.5945
4	2.4385	30.5945	0.0000

YEARS 5 — MO PAYT 2.3476 — AN CONST 28.18

#	INT	PRIN	BALANCE
1	13.4537	14.7176	85.2824
2	11.1888	16.9826	68.2997
3	8.5752	19.5961	48.7036
4	5.5595	22.6119	26.0917
5	2.0796	26.0917	0.0000

YEARS 6 — MO PAYT 2.0821 — AN CONST 24.99

#	INT	PRIN	BALANCE
1	13.6727	11.3119	88.6881
2	11.9319	13.0528	75.6353
3	9.9231	15.0615	60.5737
4	7.6052	17.3794	43.1943
5	4.9306	20.0540	23.1402
6	1.8444	23.1402	0.0000

YEARS 7 — MO PAYT 1.8962 — AN CONST 22.76

#	INT	PRIN	BALANCE
1	13.8260	8.9280	91.0720
2	12.4520	10.3020	80.7700
3	10.8666	11.8874	68.8825
4	9.0372	13.7168	55.1657
5	6.9262	15.8278	39.3379
6	4.4904	18.2636	21.0743
7	1.6797	21.0743	0.0000

YEARS 8 — MO PAYT 1.7600 — AN CONST 21.12

#	INT	PRIN	BALANCE
1	13.9383	7.1816	92.8184
2	12.8330	8.2869	84.5315
3	11.5577	9.5622	74.9694
4	10.0862	11.0337	63.9356
5	8.3881	12.7318	51.2039
6	6.4288	14.6911	36.5128
7	4.1679	16.9520	19.5608
8	1.5591	19.5608	0.0000

YEARS 9 — MO PAYT 1.6569 — AN CONST 19.89

#	INT	PRIN	BALANCE
1	14.0233	5.8592	94.1408
2	13.1216	6.7609	87.3800
3	12.0811	7.8013	79.5787
4	10.8806	9.0019	70.5768
5	9.4952	10.3872	60.1895
6	7.8967	11.9858	48.2038
7	6.0521	13.8303	34.3734
8	3.9237	15.9587	18.4147
9	1.4677	18.4147	0.0000

YEARS 10 — MO PAYT 1.5768 — AN CONST 18.93

#	INT	PRIN	BALANCE
1	14.0893	4.8324	95.1676
2	13.3456	5.5760	89.5916
3	12.4875	6.4341	83.1575
4	11.4973	7.4243	75.7331
5	10.3548	8.5669	67.1663
6	9.0364	9.8853	57.2810
7	7.5151	11.4066	45.8744
8	5.7597	13.1620	32.7124
9	3.7341	15.1876	17.5248
10	1.3968	17.5248	0.0000

YEARS 11 — MO PAYT 1.5134 — AN CONST 18.17

#	INT	PRIN	BALANCE
1	14.1416	4.0195	95.9805
2	13.5230	4.6381	91.3424
3	12.8092	5.3519	85.9905
4	11.9856	6.1755	79.8149
5	11.0352	7.1259	72.6890
6	9.9386	8.2225	64.4665
7	8.6731	9.4879	54.9785
8	7.2130	10.9481	44.0305
9	5.5282	12.6329	31.3975
10	3.5840	14.5771	16.8204
11	1.3407	16.8204	0.0000

YEARS 12 — MO PAYT 1.4625 — AN CONST 17.55

#	INT	PRIN	BALANCE
1	14.1836	3.3662	96.6338
2	13.6655	3.8842	92.7496
3	13.0678	4.4820	88.2676
4	12.3780	5.1717	83.0959
5	11.5821	5.9676	77.1282
6	10.6637	6.8860	70.2422
7	9.6040	7.9458	62.2964
8	8.3812	9.1686	53.1279
9	6.9702	10.5796	42.5483
10	5.3421	12.2077	30.3406
11	3.4634	14.0864	16.2542
12	1.2955	16.2542	0.0000

YEARS 13 — MO PAYT 1.4210 — AN CONST 17.06

#	INT	PRIN	BALANCE
1	14.2178	2.8345	97.1655
2	13.7815	3.2708	93.8947
3	13.2782	3.7741	90.1206
4	12.6974	4.3549	85.7656
5	12.0272	5.0251	80.7405
6	11.2538	5.7985	74.9420
7	10.3615	6.6908	68.2511
8	9.3318	7.7205	60.5306
9	8.1436	8.9087	51.6219
10	6.7726	10.2797	41.3422
11	5.1906	11.8617	29.4806
12	3.3652	13.6871	15.7935
13	1.2588	15.7935	0.0000

YEARS 14 — MO PAYT 1.3870 — AN CONST 16.65

#	INT	PRIN	BALANCE
1	14.2458	2.3976	97.6024
2	13.8769	2.7666	94.8358
3	13.4511	3.1924	91.6435
4	12.9598	3.6836	87.9598
5	12.3929	4.2505	83.7093
6	11.7388	4.9047	78.8046
7	10.9840	5.6595	73.1452
8	10.1130	6.5304	66.6147
9	9.1080	7.5354	59.0793
10	7.9484	8.6951	50.3842
11	6.6102	10.0332	40.3510
12	5.0662	11.5773	28.7738
13	3.2845	13.3589	15.4148
14	1.2286	15.4148	0.0000

YEARS 15 — MO PAYT 1.3587 — AN CONST 16.31

#	INT	PRIN	BALANCE
1	14.2691	2.0355	97.9645
2	13.9559	2.3488	95.6157
3	13.5944	2.7103	92.9054
4	13.1773	3.1274	89.7780
5	12.6960	3.6087	86.1694
6	12.1407	4.1640	82.0053
7	11.4998	4.8048	77.2005
8	10.7604	5.5443	71.6563
9	9.9072	6.3975	65.2588
10	8.9226	7.3820	57.8767
11	7.7866	8.5181	49.3586
12	6.4757	9.8290	39.5297
13	4.9631	11.3416	28.1881
14	3.2177	13.0870	15.1010
15	1.2036	15.1010	0.0000

YEARS 16 — MO PAYT 1.3352 — AN CONST 16.03

#	INT	PRIN	BALANCE
1	14.2885	1.7335	98.2665
2	14.0218	2.0003	96.2663
3	13.7139	2.3081	93.9582
4	13.3587	2.6633	91.2949
5	12.9489	3.0732	88.2217
6	12.4759	3.5461	84.6756
7	11.9302	4.0918	80.5838
8	11.3005	4.7215	75.8623
9	10.5739	5.4482	70.4141
10	9.7354	6.2866	64.1275
11	8.7680	7.2541	56.8734
12	7.6516	8.3704	48.5030
13	6.3634	9.6586	38.8444
14	4.8770	11.1450	27.6994
15	3.1619	12.8602	14.8393
16	1.1828	14.8393	0.0000

YEARS 17 — MO PAYT 1.3154 — AN CONST 15.79

#	INT	PRIN	BALANCE
1	14.3048	1.4801	98.5199
2	14.0771	1.7078	96.8121
3	13.8142	1.9707	94.8415
4	13.5110	2.2739	92.5675
5	13.1610	2.6239	89.9437
6	12.7572	3.0277	86.9160
7	12.2913	3.4936	83.4224
8	11.7536	4.0313	79.3911
9	11.1332	4.6517	74.7395
10	10.4174	5.3675	69.3719
11	9.5913	6.1935	63.1784
12	8.6382	7.1467	56.0317
13	7.5384	8.2465	47.7851
14	6.2693	9.5156	38.2695
15	4.8048	10.9800	27.2895
16	3.1151	12.6698	14.6196
17	1.1653	14.6196	0.0000

YEARS 18 — MO PAYT 1.2987 — AN CONST 15.59

#	INT	PRIN	BALANCE
1	14.3186	1.2664	98.7336
2	14.1237	1.4613	97.2723
3	13.8988	1.6862	95.5861
4	13.6393	1.9457	93.6404
5	13.3399	2.2451	91.3952
6	12.9944	2.5906	88.8046
7	12.5957	2.9893	85.8153
8	12.1356	3.4494	82.3659
9	11.6048	3.9802	78.3857
10	10.9922	4.5927	73.7929
11	10.2855	5.2995	68.4934
12	9.4691	6.1151	62.3783
13	8.5288	7.0562	55.3221
14	7.4429	8.1421	47.1800
15	6.1899	9.3951	37.7848
16	4.7440	10.8410	26.9439
17	3.0756	12.5094	14.4345
18	1.1505	14.4345	0.0000

YEARS 19 — MO PAYT 1.2847 — AN CONST 15.42

#	INT	PRIN	BALANCE
1	14.3302	1.0856	98.9144
2	14.1631	1.2527	97.6617
3	13.9704	1.4454	96.2163
4	13.7479	1.6679	94.5484
5	13.4912	1.9246	92.6238
6	13.1950	2.2208	90.4031
7	12.8533	2.5625	87.8405
8	12.4589	2.9569	84.8837
9	12.0039	3.4119	81.4717
10	11.4788	3.9370	77.5347
11	10.8729	4.5429	72.9918
12	10.1738	5.2420	67.7498
13	9.3671	6.0487	61.7011
14	8.4362	6.9796	54.7215
15	7.3621	8.0537	46.6678
16	6.1227	9.2931	37.3747
17	4.6925	10.7233	26.6514
18	3.0422	12.3736	14.2778
19	1.1380	14.2778	0.0000

YEARS 20 — MO PAYT 1.2727 — AN CONST 15.28

#	INT	PRIN	BALANCE
1	14.3401	.9320	99.0680
2	14.1966	1.0755	97.9925
3	14.0311	1.2410	96.7515
4	13.8401	1.4320	95.3195
5	13.6198	1.6523	93.6672
6	13.3655	1.9066	91.7605
7	13.0721	2.2001	89.5605
8	12.7335	2.5386	87.0218
9	12.3428	2.9293	84.0925
10	11.8920	3.3801	80.7124
11	11.3718	3.9003	76.8121
12	10.7716	4.5005	72.3115
13	10.0790	5.1932	67.1184
14	9.2798	5.9924	61.1260
15	8.3576	6.9145	54.2115
16	7.2935	7.9787	46.2328
17	6.0656	9.2065	37.0263
18	4.6488	10.6234	26.4029
19	3.0139	12.2582	14.1447
20	1.1274	14.1447	0.0000

YEARS 21 — MO PAYT 1.2625 — AN CONST 15.15

#	INT	PRIN	BALANCE
1	14.3485	.8013	99.1987
2	14.2252	.9246	98.2742
3	14.0829	1.0669	97.2073

MONTHLY PAYMENT AMORTIZATION SCHEDULE PER $100   14.50 %

#	INT	PRIN	BALANCE
4	14.0217	1.2170	96.0273
5	13.8330	1.4057	94.6216
6	13.6150	1.6236	92.9980
7	13.3633	1.8753	91.1227
8	13.0726	2.1661	88.9566
9	12.7368	2.5019	86.4547
10	12.3489	2.8898	83.5649
11	11.9009	3.3378	80.2271
12	11.3834	3.8553	76.3718
13	10.7857	4.4530	71.9188
14	10.0953	5.1434	66.7754
15	9.2979	5.9408	60.8347
16	8.3769	6.8618	53.9729
17	7.3130	7.9256	46.0472
18	6.0843	9.1544	36.8929
19	4.6650	10.5736	26.3192
20	3.0258	12.2129	14.1063
21	1.1323	14.1063	0.0000

YEARS 22 — MO PAYT 1.2613 — AN CONST 15.14

#	INT	PRIN	BALANCE
1	14.4560	.6791	99.3209
2	14.3508	.7844	98.5364
3	14.2291	.9060	97.6304
4	14.0887	1.0465	96.5839
5	13.9264	1.2087	95.3752
6	13.7390	1.3961	93.9790
7	13.5226	1.6126	92.3664
8	13.2726	1.8626	90.5038
9	12.9838	2.1514	88.3524
10	12.6503	2.4849	85.8675
11	12.2650	2.8702	82.9974
12	11.8200	3.3151	79.6822
13	11.3061	3.8291	75.8531
14	10.7124	4.4228	71.4304
15	10.0267	5.1084	66.3219
16	9.2347	5.9004	60.4215
17	8.3200	6.8152	53.6063
18	7.2634	7.8718	45.7345
19	6.0430	9.0922	36.6423
20	4.6334	10.5018	26.1405
21	3.0052	12.1300	14.0105
22	1.1246	14.0105	0.0000

YEARS 23 — MO PAYT 1.2539 — AN CONST 15.05

#	INT	PRIN	BALANCE
1	14.4622	.5845	99.4155
2	14.3715	.6752	98.7403
3	14.2669	.7798	97.9605
4	14.1460	.9007	97.0597
5	14.0063	1.0404	96.0193
6	13.8450	1.2017	94.8177
7	13.6587	1.3880	93.4297
8	13.4435	1.6032	91.8265
9	13.1950	1.8517	89.9748
10	12.9079	2.1388	87.8360
11	12.5763	2.4704	85.3656
12	12.1933	2.8534	82.5122
13	11.7509	3.2958	79.2165
14	11.2400	3.8067	75.4097
15	10.6498	4.3969	71.0128
16	9.9681	5.0786	65.9343
17	9.1808	5.8659	60.0683
18	8.2713	6.7754	53.2930
19	7.2209	7.8258	45.4672
20	6.0076	9.0391	36.4281
21	4.6063	10.4404	25.9877
22	2.9876	12.0591	13.9286
23	1.1181	13.9286	0.0000

YEARS 24 — MO PAYT 1.2476 — AN CONST 14.98

#	INT	PRIN	BALANCE
1	14.4674	.5035	99.4965
2	14.3893	.5816	98.9149
3	14.2992	.6718	98.2431
4	14.1950	.7759	97.4672
5	14.0747	.8962	96.5710
6	13.9358	1.0351	95.5359
7	13.7753	1.1956	94.3402
8	13.5899	1.3810	92.9592
9	13.3758	1.5951	91.3641
10	13.1285	1.8424	89.5217
11	12.8429	2.1280	87.3937
12	12.5130	2.4580	84.9358
13	12.1319	2.8390	82.0967
14	11.6918	3.2792	78.8176
15	11.1834	3.7876	75.0300
16	10.5962	4.3748	70.6553
17	9.9179	5.0530	65.6023
18	9.1345	5.8364	59.7659
19	8.2297	6.7412	53.0246
20	7.1846	7.7864	45.2382
21	5.9774	8.9935	36.2447
22	4.5831	10.3879	25.8568
23	2.9726	11.9983	13.8585
24	1.1124	13.8585	0.0000

YEARS 25 — MO PAYT 1.2422 — AN CONST 14.91

#	INT	PRIN	BALANCE
1	14.4719	.4341	99.5659
2	14.4046	.5013	99.0646
3	14.3269	.5791	98.4855
4	14.2371	.6688	97.8167
5	14.1334	.7725	97.0441
6	14.0136	.8923	96.1518
7	13.8753	1.0307	95.1212
8	13.7155	1.1904	93.9307
9	13.5310	1.3750	92.5557
10	13.3178	1.5882	90.9676
11	13.0716	1.8344	89.1332
12	12.7872	2.1188	87.0144
13	12.4587	2.4473	84.5671
14	12.0793	2.8267	81.7404
15	11.6410	3.2649	78.4755
16	11.1348	3.7711	74.7043
17	10.5502	4.3558	70.3486
18	9.8749	5.0311	65.3175
19	9.0949	5.8111	59.5064
20	8.1940	6.7120	52.7945
21	7.1534	7.7526	45.0419
22	5.9515	8.9545	36.0874
23	4.5632	10.3428	25.7446
24	2.9597	11.9463	13.7984
25	1.1076	13.7984	0.0000

YEARS 26 — MO PAYT 1.2375 — AN CONST 14.86

#	INT	PRIN	BALANCE
1	14.4758	.3744	99.6256
2	14.4177	.4324	99.1932
3	14.3507	.4995	98.6937
4	14.2732	.5769	98.1168
5	14.1838	.6663	97.4505
6	14.0805	.7696	96.6808
7	13.9612	.8890	95.7919
8	13.8234	1.0268	94.7651
9	13.6642	1.1860	93.5791
10	13.4803	1.3699	92.2092
11	13.2679	1.5822	90.6270
12	13.0226	1.8275	88.7995
13	12.7393	2.1109	86.6886
14	12.4120	2.4381	84.2505
15	12.0340	2.8161	81.4344
16	11.5974	3.2527	78.1817
17	11.0932	3.7570	74.4247
18	10.5107	4.3395	70.0852
19	9.8379	5.0122	65.0730
20	9.0608	5.7893	59.2837
21	8.1633	6.6869	52.5968
22	7.1266	7.7236	44.8733
23	5.9292	8.9210	35.9523
24	4.5461	10.3040	25.6482
25	2.9486	11.9015	13.7467
26	1.1035	13.7467	0.0000

YEARS 27 — MO PAYT 1.2335 — AN CONST 14.81

#	INT	PRIN	BALANCE
1	14.4791	.3231	99.6769
2	14.4290	.3732	99.3037
3	14.3711	.4310	98.8727
4	14.3043	.4979	98.3749
5	14.2271	.5750	97.7998
6	14.1380	.6642	97.1356
7	14.0350	.7672	96.3685
8	13.9161	.8861	95.4824
9	13.7787	1.0235	94.4589
10	13.6200	1.1822	93.2767
11	13.4367	1.3654	91.9113
12	13.2251	1.5771	90.3342
13	12.9805	1.8216	88.5126
14	12.6981	2.1040	86.4085
15	12.3719	2.4302	83.9783
16	11.9952	2.8070	81.1713
17	11.5600	3.2422	77.9291
18	11.0573	3.7449	74.1842
19	10.4767	4.3254	69.8588
20	9.8061	4.9960	64.8627
21	9.0316	5.7706	59.0921
22	8.1369	6.6653	52.4269
23	7.1036	7.6986	44.7283
24	5.9100	8.8922	35.8361
25	4.5314	10.2708	25.5654
26	2.9391	11.8631	13.7023
27	1.0999	13.7023	0.0000

YEARS 28 — MO PAYT 1.2301 — AN CONST 14.77

#	INT	PRIN	BALANCE
1	14.4819	.2789	99.7211
2	14.4387	.3222	99.3989
3	14.3887	.3721	99.0267
4	14.3311	.4298	98.5969
5	14.2644	.4965	98.1005
6	14.1874	.5734	97.5270
7	14.0985	.6623	96.8647
8	13.9959	.7650	96.0997
9	13.8773	.8836	95.2160
10	13.7403	1.0206	94.1954
11	13.5820	1.1789	93.0166
12	13.3993	1.3616	91.6549
13	13.1882	1.5727	90.0822
14	12.9443	1.8165	88.2657
15	12.6627	2.0982	86.1675
16	12.3374	2.4235	83.7440
17	11.9617	2.7992	80.9449
18	11.5277	3.2332	77.7117
19	11.0265	3.7344	73.9773
20	10.4475	4.3134	69.6639
21	9.7788	4.9821	64.6818
22	9.0064	5.7545	58.9273
23	8.1142	6.6467	52.2806
24	7.0838	7.6771	44.6035
25	5.8935	8.8674	35.7362
26	4.5188	10.2421	25.4941
27	2.9309	11.8300	13.6641
28	1.0968	13.6641	0.0000

YEARS 29 — MO PAYT 1.2271 — AN CONST 14.73

#	INT	PRIN	BALANCE
1	14.4844	.2409	99.7591
2	14.4471	.2783	99.4808
3	14.4039	.3214	99.1594
4	14.3541	.3712	98.7882
5	14.2965	.4288	98.3594
6	14.2301	.4953	97.8641
7	14.1533	.5721	97.2921
8	14.0646	.6607	96.6313
9	13.9621	.7632	95.8681
10	13.8438	.8815	94.9866
11	13.7072	1.0182	93.9685
12	13.5493	1.1760	92.7925
13	13.3670	1.3583	91.4341
14	13.1564	1.5689	89.8652
15	12.9132	1.8122	88.0530
16	12.6322	2.0931	85.9599
17	12.3077	2.4176	83.5423
18	11.9329	2.7924	80.7498
19	11.5000	3.2254	77.5245
20	10.9999	3.7254	73.7991
21	10.4223	4.3030	69.4961
22	9.7552	4.9701	64.5260
23	8.9847	5.7406	58.7853
24	8.0947	6.6306	52.1547
25	7.0667	7.6586	44.4961
26	5.8793	8.8460	35.6501
27	4.5079	10.2174	25.4326
28	2.9238	11.8015	13.6311
29	1.0942	13.6311	0.0000

YEARS 30 — MO PAYT 1.2246 — AN CONST 14.70

#	INT	PRIN	BALANCE
1	14.4865	.2081	99.7919
2	14.4543	.2404	99.5514
3	14.4170	.2777	99.2738
4	14.3739	.3207	98.9530
5	14.3242	.3705	98.5826
6	14.2668	.4279	98.1547
7	14.2004	.4942	97.6604
8	14.1238	.5709	97.0896
9	14.0353	.6594	96.4302
10	13.9331	.7616	95.6686
11	13.8150	.8797	94.7889
12	13.6786	1.0160	93.7729
13	13.5211	1.1736	92.5993
14	13.3392	1.3555	91.2438
15	13.1290	1.5657	89.6782
16	12.8863	1.8084	87.8698
17	12.6059	2.0888	85.7810
18	12.2821	2.4126	83.3684
19	11.9080	2.7866	80.5818
20	11.4760	3.2187	77.3631
21	10.9770	3.7177	73.6455
22	10.4006	4.2940	69.3514
23	9.7349	4.9598	64.3917
24	8.9660	5.7287	58.6630
25	8.0778	6.6168	52.0461
26	7.0520	7.6427	44.4034
27	5.8671	8.8276	35.5759
28	4.4985	10.1962	25.3797
29	2.9177	11.7769	13.6028
30	1.0919	13.6028	0.0000

YEARS 2 — MO PAYT 4.8297 — AN CONST 57.96

#	INT	PRIN	BALANCE
1	11.5778	46.3784	53.6216
2	4.3346	53.6216	0.0000

YEARS 3 — MO PAYT 3.4470 — AN CONST 41.37

#	INT	PRIN	BALANCE
1	12.7344	28.6293	71.3707
2	8.2632	33.1006	38.2701
3	3.0936	38.2701	0.0000

YEARS 4 — MO PAYT 2.7628 — AN CONST 33.16

#	INT	PRIN	BALANCE
1	13.3067	19.8474	80.1526
2	10.2070	22.9471	57.2054
3	6.6231	26.5310	30.6745
4	2.4796	30.6745	0.0000

YEARS 5 — MO PAYT 2.3580 — AN CONST 28.30

#	INT	PRIN	BALANCE
1	13.6453	14.6513	85.3487
2	11.3571	16.9395	68.4092
3	8.7115	19.5851	48.8241
4	5.6528	22.6438	26.1803
5	2.1163	26.1803	0.0000

YEARS 6 — MO PAYT 2.0928 — AN CONST 25.12

#	INT	PRIN	BALANCE
1	13.8671	11.2470	88.7530
2	12.1106	13.0035	75.7495
3	10.0797	15.0343	60.7152
4	7.7317	17.3824	43.3329
5	5.0170	20.0971	23.2358
6	1.8783	23.2358	0.0000

YEARS 7 — MO PAYT 1.9073 — AN CONST 22.89

#	INT	PRIN	BALANCE
1	14.0223	8.8653	91.1347
2	12.6377	10.2499	80.8848
3	11.0369	11.8507	69.0341
4	9.1861	13.7015	55.3326
5	7.0463	15.8414	39.4913
6	4.5722	18.3154	21.1759
7	1.7118	21.1759	0.0000

YEARS 8 — MO PAYT 1.7715 — AN CONST 21.26

#	INT	PRIN	BALANCE
1	14.1359	7.1217	92.8783
2	13.0237	8.2340	84.6443
3	11.7377	9.5199	75.1244
4	10.2509	11.0067	64.1177
5	8.5319	12.7257	51.3920
6	6.5445	14.7132	36.6788
7	4.2466	17.0110	19.6678
8	1.5899	19.6678	0.0000

YEARS 9 — MO PAYT 1.6687 — AN CONST 20.03

#	INT	PRIN	BALANCE
1	14.2219	5.8023	94.1977
2	13.3157	6.7085	87.4892
3	12.2680	7.7562	79.7330
4	11.0567	8.9675	70.7655
5	9.6561	10.3681	60.3974
6	8.0369	11.9873	48.4101
7	6.1647	13.8595	34.5506
8	4.0002	16.0240	18.5266
9	1.4976	18.5266	0.0000

YEARS 10 — MO PAYT 1.5889 — AN CONST 19.07

#	INT	PRIN	BALANCE
1	14.2886	4.7787	95.2213
2	13.5423	5.5250	89.6963
3	12.6794	6.3879	83.3084
4	11.6817	7.3856	75.9228
5	10.5283	8.5390	67.3838
6	9.1947	9.8726	57.5112
7	7.6528	11.4145	46.0967
8	5.8701	13.1972	32.8995
9	3.8090	15.2583	17.6413
10	1.4260	17.6413	0.0000

YEARS 11 — MO PAYT 1.5259 — AN CONST 18.32

#	INT	PRIN	BALANCE
1	14.3414	3.9691	96.0309
2	13.7215	4.5890	91.4418
3	13.0048	5.3057	86.1361
4	12.1761	6.1344	80.0017
5	11.2181	7.0924	72.9093
6	10.1104	8.2001	64.7092
7	8.8297	9.4808	55.2285
8	7.3491	10.9614	44.2670
9	5.6371	12.6734	31.5937
10	3.6579	14.6526	16.9410
11	1.3694	16.9410	0.0000

YEARS 12 — MO PAYT 1.4752 — AN CONST 17.71

#	INT	PRIN	BALANCE
1	14.3837	3.3190	96.6810
2	13.8654	3.8374	92.8436
3	13.2660	4.4367	88.4068
4	12.5731	5.1296	83.2772
5	11.7720	5.9308	77.3464
6	10.8457	6.8570	70.4894
7	9.7748	7.9279	62.5615
8	8.5367	9.1661	53.3954
9	7.1051	10.5976	42.7978
10	5.4400	12.2527	30.5451
11	3.5364	14.1663	16.3788
12	1.3240	16.3788	0.0000

YEARS 13 — MO PAYT 1.4341 — AN CONST 17.21

#	INT	PRIN	BALANCE
1	14.4182	2.7906	97.2094
2	13.9823	3.2264	93.9830
3	13.4784	3.7303	90.2527
4	12.8958	4.3129	85.9398
5	12.2223	4.9865	80.9533
6	11.4435	5.7653	75.1880
7	10.5431	6.6657	68.5223
8	9.5021	7.7067	60.8157
9	8.2985	8.9103	51.9054
10	6.9069	10.3019	41.6035
11	5.2980	11.9108	29.6927
12	3.4378	13.7710	15.9217
13	1.2870	15.9217	0.0000

YEARS 14 — MO PAYT 1.4003 — AN CONST 16.81

#	INT	PRIN	BALANCE
1	14.4464	2.3568	97.6432
2	14.0784	2.7248	94.9184
3	13.6528	3.1504	91.7680
4	13.1608	3.6424	88.1256
5	12.5919	4.2113	83.9144
6	11.9342	4.8690	79.0454
7	11.1738	5.6294	73.4160
8	10.2946	6.5086	66.9074
9	9.2781	7.5251	59.3824
10	8.1029	8.7003	50.6821
11	6.7441	10.0591	40.6230
12	5.1731	11.6301	28.9929
13	3.3567	13.4464	15.5465
14	1.2567	15.5465	0.0000

YEARS 15 — MO PAYT 1.3723 — AN CONST 16.47

#	INT	PRIN	BALANCE
1	14.4698	1.9977	98.0023
2	14.1578	2.3097	95.6926
3	13.7971	2.6704	93.0222
4	13.3801	3.0875	89.9348
5	12.8979	3.5696	86.3652
6	12.3404	4.1271	82.2380
7	11.6958	4.7717	77.4663
8	10.9506	5.5169	71.9494
9	10.0890	6.3785	65.5708
10	9.0928	7.3747	58.1961
11	7.9410	8.5265	49.6696
12	6.6094	9.8581	39.8115
13	5.0698	11.3978	28.4137
14	3.2897	13.1778	15.2359
15	1.2316	15.2359	0.0000

YEARS 16 — MO PAYT 1.3490 — AN CONST 16.19

#	INT	PRIN	BALANCE
1	14.4893	1.6985	98.3015
2	14.2241	1.9638	96.3378
3	13.9174	2.2704	94.0673
4	13.5628	2.6250	91.4423
5	13.1528	3.0350	88.4073
6	12.6788	3.5090	84.8983
7	12.1308	4.0570	80.8412
8	11.4972	4.6907	76.1506
9	10.7646	5.4232	70.7273
10	9.9176	6.2702	64.4571
11	8.9383	7.2495	57.2077
12	7.8061	8.3817	48.8260
13	6.4971	9.6907	39.1353
14	4.9836	11.2042	27.9311
15	3.2338	12.9540	14.9771
16	1.2107	14.9771	0.0000

YEARS 17 — MO PAYT 1.3295 — AN CONST 15.96

#	INT	PRIN	BALANCE
1	14.5057	1.4478	98.5522
2	14.2795	1.6739	96.8783
3	14.0181	1.9353	94.9430
4	13.7159	2.2376	92.7054
5	13.3664	2.5870	90.1184
6	12.9624	2.9911	87.1273
7	12.4952	3.4582	83.6691
8	11.9551	3.9983	79.6708
9	11.3307	4.6227	75.0481
10	10.6087	5.3447	69.7034
11	9.7740	6.1794	63.5239
12	8.8089	7.1445	56.3794
13	7.6931	8.2603	48.1191
14	6.4030	9.5504	38.5687
15	4.9115	11.0420	27.5267
16	3.1870	12.7665	14.7603
17	1.1932	14.7603	0.0000

YEARS 18 — MO PAYT 1.3130 — AN CONST 15.76

#	INT	PRIN	BALANCE
1	14.5194	1.2367	98.7633
2	14.3263	1.4299	97.3334
3	14.1029	1.6532	95.6802
4	13.8448	1.9114	93.7688
5	13.5462	2.2099	91.5589
6	13.2011	2.5550	89.0039
7	12.8021	2.9541	86.0498
8	12.3407	3.4154	82.6343
9	11.8073	3.9489	78.6855
10	11.1906	4.5656	74.1199
11	10.4775	5.2786	68.8413
12	9.6531	6.1030	62.7383
13	8.7000	7.0562	55.6821
14	7.5980	8.1582	47.5240
15	6.3239	9.4323	38.0917
16	4.8507	10.9054	27.1863
17	3.1476	12.6086	14.5777
18	1.1784	14.5777	0.0000

YEARS 19 — MO PAYT 1.2991 — AN CONST 15.59

#	INT	PRIN	BALANCE
1	14.5310	1.0584	98.9416
2	14.3657	1.2236	97.7180
3	14.1746	1.4147	96.3033
4	13.9537	1.6357	94.6676
5	13.6982	1.8912	92.7764
6	13.4029	2.1865	90.5899
7	13.0614	2.5280	88.0619
8	12.6666	2.9228	85.1391
9	12.2101	3.3793	81.7598
10	11.6823	3.9071	77.8527
11	11.0721	4.5173	73.3355
12	10.3666	5.2227	68.1127
13	9.5510	6.0384	62.0743
14	8.6079	6.9815	55.0928
15	7.5176	8.0718	47.0210
16	6.2569	9.3325	37.6885
17	4.7994	10.7900	26.8986
18	3.1143	12.4751	14.4235
19	1.1659	14.4235	0.0000

YEARS 20 — MO PAYT 1.2873 — AN CONST 15.45

#	INT	PRIN	BALANCE
1	14.5409	.9071	99.0929
2	14.3992	1.0488	98.0442
3	14.2354	1.2125	96.8316
4	14.0461	1.4019	95.4297
5	13.8271	1.6209	93.8088
6	13.5740	1.8740	91.9348
7	13.2813	2.1667	89.7682
8	12.9429	2.5051	87.2631
9	12.5517	2.8963	84.3668
10	12.0993	3.3486	81.0181
11	11.5764	3.8716	77.1465
12	10.9717	4.4763	72.6703
13	10.2726	5.1754	67.4949
14	9.4643	5.9836	61.5112
15	8.5298	6.9181	54.5931
16	7.4494	7.9986	46.5945
17	6.2002	9.2478	37.3467
18	4.7559	10.6921	26.6546
19	3.0860	12.3620	14.2926
20	1.1554	14.2926	0.0000

YEARS 21 — MO PAYT 1.2773 — AN CONST 15.33

#	INT	PRIN	BALANCE
1	14.5493	.7784	99.2216
2	14.4277	.9000	98.3215
3	14.2871	1.0406	97.2809

#	INT	PRIN	BALANCE
4	14.1246	1.2031	96.0778
5	13.9367	1.3910	94.6868
6	13.7195	1.6082	93.0786
7	13.4683	1.8594	91.2192
8	13.1779	2.1498	89.0694
9	12.8422	2.4856	86.5838
10	12.4540	2.8738	83.7100
11	12.0052	3.3226	80.3875
12	11.4862	3.8415	76.5460
13	10.8863	4.4414	72.1046
14	10.1926	5.1351	66.9695
15	9.3907	5.9371	61.0324
16	8.4634	6.8643	54.1681
17	7.3914	7.9363	46.2318
18	6.1519	9.1758	37.0560
19	4.7189	10.6089	26.4471
20	3.0620	12.2657	14.1814
21	1.1464	14.1814	0.0000

YEARS 22 — MO PAYT 1.2688 — AN CONST 15.23

#	INT	PRIN	BALANCE
1	14.5564	.6688	99.3312
2	14.4520	.7732	98.5580
3	14.3312	.8940	97.6640
4	14.1916	1.0336	96.6303
5	14.0302	1.1951	95.4353
6	13.8435	1.3817	94.0536
7	13.6277	1.5975	92.4561
8	13.3782	1.8470	90.6091
9	13.0898	2.1354	88.4737
10	12.7563	2.4689	86.0047
11	12.3707	2.8545	83.1502
12	11.9249	3.3003	79.8498
13	11.4094	3.8158	76.0340
14	10.8135	4.4117	71.6223
15	10.1245	5.1007	66.5216
16	9.3279	5.8974	60.6242
17	8.4068	6.8184	53.8058
18	7.3419	7.8833	45.9226
19	6.1108	9.1144	36.8081
20	4.6873	10.5379	26.2702
21	3.0415	12.1837	14.0865
22	1.1387	14.0865	0.0000

YEARS 23 — MO PAYT 1.2615 — AN CONST 15.14

#	INT	PRIN	BALANCE
1	14.5625	.5751	99.4249
2	14.4727	.6649	98.7599
3	14.3689	.7688	97.9911
4	14.2488	.8889	97.1023
5	14.1100	1.0277	96.0746
6	13.9495	1.1882	94.8864
7	13.7639	1.3738	93.5126
8	13.5493	1.5883	91.9243
9	13.3013	1.8364	90.0880
10	13.0145	2.1232	87.9648
11	12.6829	2.4547	85.5101
12	12.2995	2.8381	82.6720
13	11.8563	3.2814	79.3906
14	11.3438	3.7938	75.5968
15	10.7513	4.3864	71.2104
16	10.0662	5.0714	66.1390
17	9.2742	5.8634	60.2756
18	8.3585	6.7792	53.4964
19	7.2997	7.8379	45.6585
20	6.0756	9.0620	36.5964
21	4.6603	10.4773	26.1191
22	3.0240	12.1136	14.0055
23	1.1321	14.0055	0.0000

YEARS 24 — MO PAYT 1.2552 — AN CONST 15.07

#	INT	PRIN	BALANCE
1	14.5677	.4950	99.5050
2	14.4904	.5723	98.9327
3	14.4011	.6617	98.2711
4	14.2977	.7650	97.5061
5	14.1783	.8845	96.6216
6	14.0401	1.0226	95.5990
7	13.8804	1.1823	94.4167
8	13.6958	1.3670	93.0498
9	13.4823	1.5804	91.4693
10	13.2355	1.8273	89.6421
11	12.9501	2.1126	87.5294
12	12.6201	2.4426	85.0868
13	12.2386	2.8241	82.2628
14	11.7976	3.2651	78.9976
15	11.2877	3.7751	75.2226
16	10.6981	4.3646	70.8579
17	10.0164	5.0463	65.8116
18	9.2283	5.8344	59.9772
19	8.3171	6.7456	53.2316
20	7.2636	7.7991	45.4325
21	6.0455	9.0172	36.4153
22	4.6373	10.4255	25.9898
23	3.0091	12.0537	13.9362
24	1.1265	13.9362	0.0000

YEARS 25 — MO PAYT 1.2499 — AN CONST 15.00

#	INT	PRIN	BALANCE
1	14.5722	.4263	99.5737
2	14.5056	.4929	99.0808
3	14.4287	.5698	98.5110
4	14.3397	.6588	97.8522
5	14.2368	.7617	97.0904
6	14.1178	.8807	96.2097
7	13.9803	1.0182	95.1915
8	13.8212	1.1773	94.0142
9	13.6374	1.3611	92.6531
10	13.4248	1.5737	91.0794
11	13.1790	1.8195	89.2599
12	12.8949	2.1036	87.1563
13	12.5663	2.4322	84.7241
14	12.1865	2.8120	81.9121
15	11.7473	3.2512	78.6609
16	11.2395	3.7590	74.9019
17	10.6525	4.3460	70.5559
18	9.9737	5.0248	65.5311
19	9.1890	5.8095	59.7215
20	8.2816	6.7169	53.0047
21	7.2326	7.7659	45.2388
22	6.0198	8.9787	36.2601
23	4.6175	10.3810	25.8791
24	2.9962	12.0023	13.8768
25	1.1217	13.8768	0.0000

YEARS 26 — MO PAYT 1.2453 — AN CONST 14.95

#	INT	PRIN	BALANCE
1	14.5761	.3674	99.6326
2	14.5187	.4247	99.2079
3	14.4524	.4911	98.7169
4	14.3757	.5677	98.1491
5	14.2870	.6564	97.4927
6	14.1845	.7589	96.7338
7	14.0660	.8775	95.8563
8	13.9289	1.0145	94.8418
9	13.7705	1.1729	93.6689
10	13.5873	1.3561	92.3128
11	13.3755	1.5679	90.7448
12	13.1306	1.8128	88.9320
13	12.8475	2.0959	86.8361
14	12.5202	2.4232	84.4129
15	12.1417	2.8017	81.6112
16	11.7041	3.2393	78.3719
17	11.1983	3.7452	74.6268
18	10.6133	4.3301	70.2967
19	9.9371	5.0063	65.2904
20	9.1552	5.7882	59.5022
21	8.2512	6.6922	52.8100
22	7.2061	7.7374	45.0726
23	5.9977	8.9458	36.1269
24	4.6005	10.3429	25.7840
25	2.9852	11.9582	13.8258
26	1.1176	13.8258	0.0000

YEARS 27 — MO PAYT 1.2413 — AN CONST 14.90

#	INT	PRIN	BALANCE
1	14.5794	.3167	99.6833
2	14.5299	.3662	99.3171
3	14.4727	.4234	98.8937
4	14.4066	.4895	98.4042
5	14.3301	.5659	97.8383
6	14.2417	.6543	97.1839
7	14.1396	.7565	96.4274
8	14.0214	.8747	95.5527
9	13.8848	1.0113	94.5414
10	13.7269	1.1692	93.3722
11	13.5443	1.3518	92.0204
12	13.3331	1.5630	90.4574
13	13.0890	1.8071	88.6504
14	12.8068	2.0893	86.5611
15	12.4805	2.4156	84.1455
16	12.1033	2.7928	81.3527
17	11.6671	3.2290	78.1237
18	11.1628	3.7333	74.3904
19	10.5797	4.3164	70.0740
20	9.9056	4.9905	65.0836
21	9.1262	5.7699	59.3137
22	8.2251	6.6710	52.6427
23	7.1832	7.7128	44.9299
24	5.9787	8.9174	36.0124
25	4.5860	10.3101	25.7023
26	2.9758	11.9203	13.7820
27	1.1141	13.7820	0.0000

YEARS 28 — MO PAYT 1.2379 — AN CONST 14.86

#	INT	PRIN	BALANCE
1	14.5822	.2732	99.7268
2	14.5395	.3159	99.4110
3	14.4902	.3652	99.0458
4	14.4332	.4222	98.6235
5	14.3672	.4882	98.1354
6	14.2910	.5644	97.5710
7	14.2028	.6525	96.9184
8	14.1009	.7545	96.1640
9	13.9831	.8723	95.2917
10	13.8469	1.0085	94.2832
11	13.6894	1.1660	93.1171
12	13.5073	1.3481	91.7690
13	13.2967	1.5587	90.2103
14	13.0533	1.8021	88.4082
15	12.7718	2.0836	86.3246
16	12.4464	2.4090	83.9156
17	12.0702	2.7852	81.1305
18	11.6352	3.2202	77.9103
19	11.1323	3.7231	74.1872
20	10.5508	4.3046	69.8826
21	9.8785	4.9768	64.9058
22	9.1013	5.7541	59.1517
23	8.2026	6.6528	52.4989
24	7.1636	7.6918	44.8071
25	5.9623	8.8931	35.9141
26	4.5734	10.2819	25.6321
27	2.9676	11.8878	13.7443
28	1.1110	13.7443	0.0000

YEARS 29 — MO PAYT 1.2350 — AN CONST 14.83

#	INT	PRIN	BALANCE
1	14.5846	.2357	99.7643
2	14.5478	.2725	99.4917
3	14.5053	.3151	99.1766
4	14.4560	.3643	98.8123
5	14.3991	.4212	98.3911
6	14.3334	.4870	97.9040
7	14.2573	.5631	97.3410
8	14.1694	.6510	96.6900
9	14.0677	.7527	95.9373
10	13.9501	.8702	95.0670
11	13.8142	1.0061	94.0609
12	13.6571	1.1633	92.8976
13	13.4754	1.3450	91.5527
14	13.2654	1.5550	89.9977
15	13.0225	1.7979	88.1998
16	12.7417	2.0787	86.1211
17	12.4171	2.4033	83.7178
18	12.0417	2.7786	80.9392
19	11.6078	3.2126	77.7266
20	11.1060	3.7143	74.0123
21	10.5260	4.2944	69.7179
22	9.8553	4.9651	64.7528
23	9.0798	5.7405	59.0122
24	8.1833	6.6371	52.3751
25	7.1467	7.6736	44.7015
26	5.9483	8.8721	35.8294
27	4.5627	10.2577	25.5717
28	2.9606	11.8597	13.7119
29	1.1084	13.7119	0.0000

YEARS 30 — MO PAYT 1.2325 — AN CONST 14.80

#	INT	PRIN	BALANCE
1	14.5867	.2035	99.7965
2	14.5550	.2353	99.5613
3	14.5182	.2720	99.2893
4	14.4757	.3145	98.9748
5	14.4266	.3636	98.6112
6	14.3698	.4204	98.1909
7	14.3042	.4860	97.7048
8	14.2283	.5619	97.1429
9	14.1405	.6497	96.4932
10	14.0391	.7512	95.7421
11	13.9218	.8685	94.8736
12	13.7861	1.0041	93.8695
13	13.6293	1.1609	92.7086
14	13.4480	1.3422	91.3664
15	13.2384	1.5518	89.8145
16	12.9960	1.7942	88.0203
17	12.7158	2.0744	85.9459
18	12.3918	2.3984	83.5475
19	12.0172	2.7730	80.7745
20	11.5842	3.2061	77.5685
21	11.0834	3.7068	73.8617
22	10.5045	4.2857	69.5760
23	9.8352	4.9550	64.6210
24	9.0614	5.7289	58.8921
25	8.1666	6.6236	52.2686
26	7.1322	7.6580	44.6105
27	5.9362	8.8540	35.7565
28	4.5534	10.2368	25.5196
29	2.9546	11.8356	13.6840
30	1.1062	13.6840	0.0000

YEARS 2 — MO PAYT 4.8309 — AN CONST 57.98

#	INT	PRIN	BALANCE
1	11.5982	46.3722	53.6278
2	4.3426	53.6278	0.0000

YEARS 3 — MO PAYT 3.4482 — AN CONST 41.38

#	INT	PRIN	BALANCE
1	12.7568	28.6216	71.3784
2	8.2786	33.0998	38.2787
3	3.0997	38.2787	0.0000

YEARS 4 — MO PAYT 2.7641 — AN CONST 33.17

#	INT	PRIN	BALANCE
1	13.3300	19.8392	80.1608
2	10.2260	22.9433	57.2175
3	6.6362	26.5330	30.6845
4	2.4848	30.6845	0.0000

YEARS 5 — MO PAYT 2.3594 — AN CONST 28.32

#	INT	PRIN	BALANCE
1	13.6692	14.6430	85.3570
2	11.3781	16.9341	68.4228
3	8.7286	19.5837	48.8391
4	5.6644	22.6478	26.1913
5	2.1209	26.1913	0.0000

YEARS 6 — MO PAYT 2.0942 — AN CONST 25.14

#	INT	PRIN	BALANCE
1	13.8914	11.2389	88.7611
2	12.1329	12.9973	75.7638
3	10.0994	15.0309	60.7329
4	7.7476	17.3827	43.3502
5	5.0278	20.1024	23.2477
6	1.8825	23.2477	0.0000

YEARS 7 — MO PAYT 1.9087 — AN CONST 22.91

#	INT	PRIN	BALANCE
1	14.0468	8.8575	91.1425
2	12.6610	10.2434	80.8991
3	11.0583	11.8461	69.0530
4	9.2048	13.6996	55.3535
5	7.0613	15.8430	39.5104
6	4.5825	18.3219	21.1886
7	1.7158	21.1886	0.0000

YEARS 8 — MO PAYT 1.7729 — AN CONST 21.28

#	INT	PRIN	BALANCE
1	14.1606	7.1143	92.8857
2	13.0475	8.2274	84.6584
3	11.7602	9.5146	75.1437
4	10.2716	11.0033	64.1404
5	8.5499	12.7249	51.4155
6	6.5590	14.7159	36.6996
7	4.2565	17.0184	19.6812
8	1.5937	19.6812	0.0000

YEARS 9 — MO PAYT 1.6702 — AN CONST 20.05

#	INT	PRIN	BALANCE
1	14.2467	5.7952	94.2048
2	13.3400	6.7020	87.5028
3	12.2914	7.7506	79.7522
4	11.0787	8.9632	70.7890
5	9.6763	10.3657	60.4233
6	8.0545	11.9875	48.4358
7	6.1789	13.8631	34.5727
8	4.0098	16.0322	18.5406
9	1.5014	18.5406	0.0000

YEARS 10 — MO PAYT 1.5905 — AN CONST 19.09

#	INT	PRIN	BALANCE
1	14.3135	4.7720	95.2280
2	13.5669	5.5187	89.7093
3	12.7034	6.3821	83.3271
4	11.7048	7.3807	75.9464
5	10.5500	8.5355	67.4109
6	9.2145	9.8710	57.5399
7	7.6701	11.4155	46.1245
8	5.8840	13.2015	32.9229
9	3.8185	15.2671	17.6558
10	1.4297	17.6558	0.0000

YEARS 11 — MO PAYT 1.5274 — AN CONST 18.33

#	INT	PRIN	BALANCE
1	14.3663	3.9629	96.0371
2	13.7463	4.5829	91.4542
3	13.0292	5.3000	86.1542
4	12.2000	6.1292	80.0250
5	11.2410	7.0882	72.9368
6	10.1319	8.1973	64.7395
7	8.8494	9.4798	55.2597
8	7.3661	10.9631	44.2966
9	5.6508	12.6784	31.6182
10	3.6671	14.6621	16.9561
11	1.3731	16.9561	0.0000

YEARS 12 — MO PAYT 1.4768 — AN CONST 17.73

#	INT	PRIN	BALANCE
1	14.4087	3.3132	96.6868
2	13.8903	3.8316	92.8552
3	13.2908	4.4311	88.4241
4	12.5976	5.1244	83.2998
5	11.7958	5.9262	77.3736
6	10.8686	6.8534	70.5202
7	9.7963	7.9257	62.5946
8	8.5562	9.1657	53.4288
9	7.1221	10.5998	42.8290
10	5.4636	12.2583	30.5707
11	3.5456	14.1763	16.3944
12	1.3276	16.3944	0.0000

YEARS 13 — MO PAYT 1.4357 — AN CONST 17.23

#	INT	PRIN	BALANCE
1	14.4432	2.7851	97.2149
2	14.0074	3.2209	93.9939
3	13.5035	3.7249	90.2691
4	12.9207	4.3077	85.9614
5	12.2467	4.9817	80.9798
6	11.4672	5.7611	75.2186
7	10.5658	6.6625	68.5562
8	9.5234	7.7049	60.8512
9	8.3179	8.9105	51.9408
10	6.9237	10.3046	41.6361
11	5.3114	11.9169	29.7192
12	3.4469	13.7815	15.9378
13	1.2906	15.9378	0.0000

YEARS 14 — MO PAYT 1.4019 — AN CONST 16.83

#	INT	PRIN	BALANCE
1	14.4715	2.3517	97.6483
2	14.1035	2.7196	94.9287
3	13.6780	3.1452	91.7835
4	13.1859	3.6373	88.1462
5	12.6168	4.2064	83.9399
6	11.9587	4.8645	79.0754
7	11.1976	5.6256	73.4497
8	10.3174	6.5058	66.9439
9	9.2995	7.5237	59.4202
10	8.1223	8.7009	50.7193
11	6.7609	10.0623	40.6570
12	5.1865	11.6367	29.0203
13	3.3658	13.4574	15.5629
14	1.2602	15.5629	0.0000

YEARS 15 — MO PAYT 1.3740 — AN CONST 16.49

#	INT	PRIN	BALANCE
1	14.4949	1.9930	98.0070
2	14.1831	2.3048	95.7022
3	13.8225	2.6654	93.0367
4	13.4054	3.0825	89.9543
5	12.9231	3.5648	86.3895
6	12.3654	4.1225	82.2669
7	11.7204	4.7676	77.4994
8	10.9744	5.5135	71.9859
9	10.1117	6.3762	65.6097
10	9.1141	7.3738	58.2359
11	7.9604	8.5275	49.7084
12	6.6262	9.8617	39.8467
13	5.0832	11.4047	28.4419
14	3.2987	13.1892	15.2528
15	1.2351	15.2528	0.0000

YEARS 16 — MO PAYT 1.3507 — AN CONST 16.21

#	INT	PRIN	BALANCE
1	14.5144	1.6942	98.3058
2	14.2493	1.9592	96.3466
3	13.9428	2.2658	94.0808
4	13.5883	2.6203	91.4606
5	13.1783	3.0303	88.4303
6	12.7042	3.5044	84.9259
7	12.1559	4.0527	80.8732
8	11.5218	4.6868	76.1864
9	10.7885	5.4201	70.7663
10	9.9404	6.2681	64.4982
11	8.9597	7.2489	57.2493
12	7.8255	8.3830	48.8663
13	6.5139	9.6947	39.1716
14	4.9970	11.2115	27.9601
15	3.2429	12.9657	14.9944
16	1.2142	14.9944	0.0000

YEARS 17 — MO PAYT 1.3312 — AN CONST 15.98

#	INT	PRIN	BALANCE
1	14.5308	1.4438	98.5562
2	14.3049	1.6697	96.8865
3	14.0436	1.9309	94.9556
4	13.7415	2.2331	92.7225
5	13.3921	2.5825	90.1400
6	12.9880	2.9865	87.1535
7	12.5208	3.4538	83.6997
8	11.9804	3.9942	79.7056
9	11.3554	4.6191	75.0865
10	10.6327	5.3418	69.7446
11	9.7969	6.1776	63.5670
12	8.8304	7.1442	56.4228
13	7.7125	8.2620	48.1608
14	6.4199	9.5547	38.6061
15	4.9249	11.0497	27.5564
16	3.1960	12.7785	14.7779
17	1.1967	14.7779	0.0000

YEARS 18 — MO PAYT 1.3148 — AN CONST 15.78

#	INT	PRIN	BALANCE
1	14.5445	1.2331	98.7669
2	14.3516	1.4260	97.3409
3	14.1285	1.6491	95.6918
4	13.8704	1.9071	93.7847
5	13.5721	2.2055	91.5792
6	13.2270	2.5506	89.0286
7	12.8279	2.9497	86.0789
8	12.3664	3.4112	82.6677
9	11.8327	3.9449	78.7227
10	11.2154	4.5622	74.1606
11	10.5016	5.2760	68.8846
12	9.6761	6.1015	62.7832
13	8.7215	7.0561	55.7270
14	7.6174	8.1601	47.5669
15	6.3407	9.4369	38.1300
16	4.8642	10.9134	27.2166
17	3.1566	12.6210	14.5957
18	1.1819	14.5957	0.0000

YEARS 19 — MO PAYT 1.3009 — AN CONST 15.62

#	INT	PRIN	BALANCE
1	14.5561	1.0550	98.9450
2	14.3911	1.2201	97.7250
3	14.2002	1.4109	96.3140
4	13.9794	1.6317	94.6823
5	13.7241	1.8870	92.7953
6	13.4289	2.1823	90.6130
7	13.0874	2.5237	88.0893
8	12.6926	2.9186	85.1708
9	12.2359	3.3752	81.7955
10	11.7078	3.9033	77.8922
11	11.0971	4.5140	73.3782
12	10.3908	5.2203	68.1579
13	9.5740	6.0371	62.1208
14	8.6295	6.9817	55.1391
15	7.5371	8.0740	47.0651
16	6.2738	9.3373	37.7278
17	4.8129	10.7983	26.9295
18	3.1233	12.4878	14.4417
19	1.1695	14.4417	0.0000

YEARS 20 — MO PAYT 1.2892 — AN CONST 15.48

#	INT	PRIN	BALANCE
1	14.5660	.9040	99.0960
2	14.4245	1.0455	98.0505
3	14.2610	1.2090	96.8415
4	14.0718	1.3982	95.4433
5	13.8530	1.6170	93.8264
6	13.6000	1.8700	91.9564
7	13.3075	2.1625	89.7939
8	12.9691	2.5009	87.2930
9	12.5778	2.8922	84.4008
10	12.1253	3.3447	81.0561
11	11.6020	3.8680	77.1881
12	10.9968	4.4732	72.7149
13	10.2969	5.1731	67.5417
14	9.4875	5.9825	61.5592
15	8.5514	6.9186	54.6407
16	7.4689	8.0011	46.6396
17	6.2171	9.2529	37.3867
18	4.7693	10.7007	26.6860
19	3.0951	12.3749	14.3111
20	1.1589	14.3111	0.0000

YEARS 21 — MO PAYT 1.2792 — AN CONST 15.36

#	INT	PRIN	BALANCE
1	14.5744	.7756	99.2244
2	14.4530	.8970	98.3274
3	14.3127	1.0373	97.2900

#	INT	PRIN	BALANCE
4	14.1504	1.1996	96.0904
5	13.9627	1.3873	94.7030
6	13.7456	1.6044	93.0986
7	13.4946	1.8554	91.2432
8	13.2043	2.1458	89.0974
9	12.8685	2.4815	86.6159
10	12.4803	2.8697	83.7462
11	12.0313	3.3188	80.4274
12	11.5120	3.8380	76.5894
13	10.9115	4.4385	72.1509
14	10.2170	5.1330	67.0179
15	9.4139	5.9361	61.0817
16	8.4851	6.8649	54.2169
17	7.4110	7.9390	46.2779
18	6.1689	9.1812	37.0967
19	4.7324	10.6177	26.4790
20	3.0711	12.2789	14.2001
21	1.1499	14.2001	0.0000

YEARS 22 — MO PAYT 1.2706 — AN CONST 15.25

#	INT	PRIN	BALANCE
1	14.5815	.6662	99.3338
2	14.4773	.7705	98.5633
3	14.3567	.8910	97.6723
4	14.2173	1.0304	96.6418
5	14.0561	1.1917	95.4502
6	13.8696	1.3781	94.0721
7	13.6540	1.5937	92.4784
8	13.4047	1.8431	90.6353
9	13.1163	2.1315	88.5038
10	12.7828	2.4650	86.0388
11	12.3971	2.8506	83.1882
12	11.9511	3.2966	79.8916
13	11.4353	3.8125	76.0791
14	10.8388	4.4090	71.6702
15	10.1489	5.0988	66.5714
16	9.3512	5.8966	60.6748
17	8.4286	6.8192	53.8556
18	7.3616	7.8861	45.9695
19	6.1278	9.1200	36.8496
20	4.7008	10.5469	26.3026
21	3.0506	12.1971	14.1055
22	1.1422	14.1055	0.0000

YEARS 23 — MO PAYT 1.2634 — AN CONST 15.17

#	INT	PRIN	BALANCE
1	14.5876	.5728	99.4272
2	14.4980	.6624	98.7648
3	14.3943	.7661	97.9987
4	14.2745	.8859	97.1128
5	14.1359	1.0245	96.0883
6	13.9756	1.1848	94.9035
7	13.7902	1.3702	93.5332
8	13.5758	1.5846	91.9486
9	13.3279	1.8325	90.1161
10	13.0412	2.1193	87.9969
11	12.7096	2.4508	85.5460
12	12.3261	2.8343	82.7117
13	11.8826	3.2778	79.4340
14	11.3698	3.7906	75.6433
15	10.7767	4.3837	71.2596
16	10.0908	5.0696	66.1900
17	9.2976	5.8628	60.3273
18	8.3803	6.7801	53.5472
19	7.3195	7.8409	45.7062
20	6.0927	9.0677	36.6385
21	4.6739	10.4865	26.1520
22	3.0331	12.1273	14.0247
23	1.1357	14.0247	0.0000

YEARS 24 — MO PAYT 1.2571 — AN CONST 15.09

#	INT	PRIN	BALANCE
1	14.5928	.4929	99.5071
2	14.5157	.5700	98.9372
3	14.4265	.6591	98.2780
4	14.3234	.7623	97.5157
5	14.2041	.8816	96.6342
6	14.0662	1.0195	95.6147
7	13.9067	1.1790	94.4357
8	13.7222	1.3635	93.0723
9	13.5089	1.5768	91.4955
10	13.2622	1.8235	89.6720
11	12.9769	2.1088	87.5632
12	12.6469	2.4388	85.1244
13	12.2654	2.8203	82.3041
14	11.8241	3.2616	79.0425
15	11.3138	3.7719	75.2705
16	10.7236	4.3621	70.9084
17	10.0411	5.0446	65.8638
18	9.2518	5.8339	60.0299
19	8.3390	6.7467	53.2832
20	7.2834	7.8023	45.4810
21	6.0626	9.0231	36.4579
22	4.6509	10.4348	26.0231
23	3.0182	12.0675	13.9556
24	1.1301	13.9556	0.0000

YEARS 25 — MO PAYT 1.2518 — AN CONST 15.03

#	INT	PRIN	BALANCE
1	14.5973	.4244	99.5756
2	14.5309	.4908	99.0849
3	14.4541	.5676	98.5173
4	14.3653	.6564	97.8610
5	14.2626	.7590	97.1019
6	14.1439	.8778	96.2241
7	14.0065	1.0152	95.2090
8	13.8477	1.1740	94.0350
9	13.6640	1.3577	92.6773
10	13.4516	1.5701	91.1072
11	13.2059	1.8158	89.2914
12	12.9218	2.0999	87.1916
13	12.5933	2.4284	84.7632
14	12.2133	2.8084	81.9548
15	11.7739	3.2478	78.7070
16	11.2657	3.7559	74.9511
17	10.6781	4.3436	70.6075
18	9.9985	5.0232	65.5843
19	9.2125	5.8091	59.7752
20	8.3036	6.7181	53.0571
21	7.2525	7.7692	45.2880
22	6.0369	8.9848	36.3032
23	4.6311	10.3905	25.9127
24	3.0054	12.0163	13.8964
25	1.1253	13.8964	0.0000

YEARS 26 — MO PAYT 1.2472 — AN CONST 14.97

#	INT	PRIN	BALANCE
1	14.6011	.3656	99.6344
2	14.5439	.4228	99.2116
3	14.4778	.4890	98.7226
4	14.4013	.5655	98.1571
5	14.3128	.6540	97.5032
6	14.2105	.7563	96.7469
7	14.0921	.8746	95.8723
8	13.9553	1.0114	94.8609
9	13.7971	1.1697	93.6912
10	13.6140	1.3527	92.3385
11	13.4024	1.5644	90.7741
12	13.1576	1.8091	88.9650
13	12.8746	2.0922	86.8728
14	12.5472	2.4195	84.4533
15	12.1687	2.7981	81.6552
16	11.7309	3.2359	78.4193
17	11.2246	3.7422	74.6771
18	10.6390	4.3277	70.3494
19	9.9619	5.0048	65.3445
20	9.1788	5.7879	59.5566
21	8.2733	6.6935	52.8631
22	7.2260	7.7408	45.1224
23	6.0148	8.9519	36.1705
24	4.6142	10.3526	25.8179
25	2.9944	11.9723	13.8456
26	1.1212	13.8456	0.0000

YEARS 27 — MO PAYT 1.2433 — AN CONST 14.92

#	INT	PRIN	BALANCE
1	14.6044	.3152	99.6848
2	14.5551	.3645	99.3204
3	14.4981	.4215	98.8989
4	14.4321	.4874	98.4115
5	14.3559	.5637	97.8478
6	14.2677	.6519	97.1959
7	14.1657	.7539	96.4420
8	14.0477	.8718	95.5702
9	13.9113	1.0083	94.5619
10	13.7536	1.1660	93.3959
11	13.5711	1.3484	92.0474
12	13.3602	1.5594	90.4880
13	13.1162	1.8034	88.6846
14	12.8340	2.0856	86.5990
15	12.5077	2.4119	84.1871
16	12.1303	2.7893	81.3978
17	11.6939	3.2257	78.1721
18	11.1892	3.7304	74.4417
19	10.6055	4.3141	70.1277
20	9.9305	4.9891	65.1386
21	9.1499	5.7697	59.3689
22	8.2472	6.6724	52.6966
23	7.2032	7.7164	44.9802
24	5.9959	8.9237	36.0565
25	4.5997	10.3199	25.7365
26	2.9850	11.9346	13.8019
27	1.1176	13.8019	0.0000

YEARS 28 — MO PAYT 1.2399 — AN CONST 14.88

#	INT	PRIN	BALANCE
1	14.6073	.2718	99.7282
2	14.5647	.3143	99.4139
3	14.5156	.3635	99.0505
4	14.4587	.4203	98.6301
5	14.3929	.4861	98.1440
6	14.3169	.5622	97.5819
7	14.2289	.6501	96.9317
8	14.1272	.7518	96.1799
9	14.0096	.8695	95.3104
10	13.8735	1.0055	94.3049
11	13.7162	1.1628	93.1421
12	13.5343	1.3448	91.7973
13	13.3238	1.5552	90.2421
14	13.0805	1.7985	88.4436
15	12.7991	2.0799	86.3637
16	12.4737	2.4054	83.9583
17	12.0973	2.7817	81.1766
18	11.6621	3.2169	77.9597
19	11.1588	3.7203	74.2394
20	10.5767	4.3023	69.9371
21	9.9035	4.9755	64.9616
22	9.1251	5.7540	59.2076
23	8.2248	6.6543	52.5533
24	7.1836	7.6954	44.8579
25	5.9796	8.8994	35.9585
26	4.5872	10.2919	25.6666
27	2.9769	11.9022	13.7644
28	1.1146	13.7644	0.0000

YEARS 29 — MO PAYT 1.2370 — AN CONST 14.85

#	INT	PRIN	BALANCE
1	14.6097	.2345	99.7655
2	14.5730	.2711	99.4944
3	14.5306	.3136	99.1809
4	14.4815	.3626	98.8182
5	14.4248	.4194	98.3989
6	14.3592	.4850	97.9139
7	14.2833	.5608	97.3531
8	14.1956	.6486	96.7045
9	14.0941	.7501	95.9544
10	13.9767	.8674	95.0870
11	13.8410	1.0032	94.0838
12	13.6840	1.1601	92.9237
13	13.5025	1.3416	91.5821
14	13.2926	1.5515	90.0305
15	13.0498	1.7943	88.2362
16	12.7691	2.0750	86.1612
17	12.4444	2.3997	83.7615
18	12.0690	2.7752	80.9863
19	11.6348	3.2094	77.7769
20	11.1326	3.7115	74.0654
21	10.5519	4.2923	69.7731
22	9.8803	4.9638	64.8093
23	9.1037	5.7405	59.0688
24	8.2055	6.6387	52.4301
25	7.1668	7.6774	44.7528
26	5.9656	8.8786	35.8742
27	4.5764	10.2678	25.6064
28	2.9699	11.8743	13.7322
29	1.1120	13.7322	0.0000

YEARS 30 — MO PAYT 1.2345 — AN CONST 14.82

#	INT	PRIN	BALANCE
1	14.6118	.2023	99.7977
2	14.5801	.2340	99.5637
3	14.5435	.2706	99.2931
4	14.5012	.3129	98.9802
5	14.4522	.3619	98.6183
6	14.3956	.4185	98.1998
7	14.3301	.4840	97.7158
8	14.2544	.5597	97.1561
9	14.1668	.6473	96.5088
10	14.0656	.7486	95.7603
11	13.9484	.8657	94.8946
12	13.8130	1.0011	93.8935
13	13.6563	1.1578	92.7357
14	13.4752	1.3389	91.3968
15	13.2657	1.5484	89.8484
16	13.0234	1.7907	88.0577
17	12.7433	2.0708	85.9869
18	12.4193	2.3949	83.5920
19	12.0446	2.7696	80.8224
20	11.6112	3.2029	77.6195
21	11.1101	3.7040	73.9155
22	10.5305	4.2836	69.6319
23	9.8603	4.9538	64.6782
24	9.0852	5.7289	58.9493
25	8.1889	6.6252	52.3240
26	7.1523	7.6618	44.6622
27	5.9535	8.8606	35.8016
28	4.5671	10.2470	25.5546
29	2.9639	11.8502	13.7044
30	1.1097	13.7044	0.0000

YEARS 2 — MO PAYT 4.8344 — AN CONST 58.02

#	INT	PRIN	BALANCE
1	11.6593	46.3538	53.6462
2	4.3669	53.6462	0.0000

YEARS 3 — MO PAYT 3.4519 — AN CONST 41.43

#	INT	PRIN	BALANCE
1	12.8240	28.5983	71.4017
2	8.3249	33.0974	38.3043
3	3.1180	38.3043	0.0000

YEARS 4 — MO PAYT 2.7679 — AN CONST 33.22

#	INT	PRIN	BALANCE
1	13.4002	19.8145	80.1855
2	10.2830	22.9317	57.2538
3	6.6754	26.5393	30.7145
4	2.5002	30.7145	0.0000

YEARS 5 — MO PAYT 2.3633 — AN CONST 28.36

#	INT	PRIN	BALANCE
1	13.7411	14.6182	85.3818
2	11.4413	16.9180	68.4638
3	8.7798	19.5795	48.8843
4	5.6996	22.6597	26.2246
5	2.1347	26.2246	0.0000

YEARS 6 — MO PAYT 2.0982 — AN CONST 25.18

#	INT	PRIN	BALANCE
1	13.9643	11.2146	88.7854
2	12.2001	12.9789	75.8066
3	10.1582	15.0207	60.7859
4	7.7952	17.3837	43.4021
5	5.0604	20.1185	23.2836
6	1.8953	23.2836	0.0000

YEARS 7 — MO PAYT 1.9129 — AN CONST 22.96

#	INT	PRIN	BALANCE
1	14.1205	8.8341	91.1659
2	12.7307	10.2239	80.9420
3	11.1223	11.8323	69.1097
4	9.2608	13.6937	55.4160
5	7.1065	15.8480	39.5680
6	4.6133	18.3413	21.2267
7	1.7279	21.2267	0.0000

YEARS 8 — MO PAYT 1.7772 — AN CONST 21.33

#	INT	PRIN	BALANCE
1	14.2348	7.0919	92.9081
2	13.1191	8.2076	84.7005
3	11.8279	9.4988	75.2017
4	10.3335	10.9932	64.2086
5	8.6041	12.7226	51.4860
6	6.6026	14.7241	36.7618
7	4.2862	17.0405	19.7213
8	1.6054	19.7213	0.0000

YEARS 9 — MO PAYT 1.6746 — AN CONST 20.10

#	INT	PRIN	BALANCE
1	14.3212	5.7740	94.2260
2	13.4129	6.6824	87.5436
3	12.3616	7.7337	79.8099
4	11.1449	8.9503	70.8595
5	9.7369	10.3584	60.5011
6	8.1073	11.9880	48.5131
7	6.2213	13.8739	34.6392
8	4.0387	16.0566	18.5826
9	1.5127	18.5826	0.0000

YEARS 10 — MO PAYT 1.5950 — AN CONST 19.15

#	INT	PRIN	BALANCE
1	14.3883	4.7521	95.2479
2	13.6407	5.4996	89.7483
3	12.7755	6.3649	83.3834
4	11.7742	7.3662	76.0173
5	10.6153	8.5250	67.4923
6	9.2742	9.8662	57.6261
7	7.7220	11.4183	46.2078
8	5.9257	13.2146	32.9931
9	3.8468	15.2936	17.6996
10	1.4408	17.6996	0.0000

YEARS 11 — MO PAYT 1.5321 — AN CONST 18.39

#	INT	PRIN	BALANCE
1	14.4413	3.9441	96.0559
2	13.8208	4.5646	91.4912
3	13.1027	5.2827	86.2085
4	12.2716	6.1138	80.0947
5	11.3098	7.0756	73.0190
6	10.1966	8.1888	64.8303
7	8.9084	9.4770	55.3532
8	7.4174	10.9680	44.3853
9	5.6920	12.6934	31.6918
10	3.6950	14.6904	17.0015
11	1.3839	17.0015	0.0000

YEARS 12 — MO PAYT 1.4816 — AN CONST 17.78

#	INT	PRIN	BALANCE
1	14.4838	3.2957	96.7043
2	13.9653	3.8142	92.8902
3	13.3653	4.4142	88.4760
4	12.6709	5.1086	83.3673
5	11.8672	5.9123	77.4550
6	10.9370	6.8424	70.6126
7	9.8606	7.9189	62.6937
8	8.6148	9.1647	53.5290
9	7.1730	10.6065	42.9225
10	5.5044	12.2751	30.6474
11	3.5733	14.2062	16.4411
12	1.3383	16.4411	0.0000

YEARS 13 — MO PAYT 1.4406 — AN CONST 17.29

#	INT	PRIN	BALANCE
1	14.5184	2.7688	97.2312
2	14.0828	3.2044	94.0267
3	13.5787	3.7085	90.3182
4	12.9952	4.2920	86.0262
5	12.3200	4.9672	81.0590
6	11.5386	5.7486	75.3104
7	10.6342	6.6530	68.6574
8	9.5876	7.6996	60.9578
9	8.3763	8.9109	52.0468
10	6.9744	10.3128	41.7340
11	5.3520	11.9352	29.7988
12	3.4743	13.8129	15.9859
13	1.3013	15.9859	0.0000

YEARS 14 — MO PAYT 1.4069 — AN CONST 16.89

#	INT	PRIN	BALANCE
1	14.5467	2.3366	97.6634
2	14.1791	2.7041	94.9593
3	13.7537	3.1296	91.8298

#	INT	PRIN	BALANCE
4	13.2614	3.6219	88.2079
5	12.6916	4.1917	84.0162
6	12.0322	4.8511	79.1651
7	11.2690	5.6143	73.5508
8	10.3857	6.4975	67.0532
9	9.3635	7.5197	59.5335
10	8.1805	8.7027	50.8307
11	6.8114	10.0719	40.7589
12	5.2269	11.6564	29.1025
13	3.3931	13.4901	15.6124
14	1.2709	15.6124	0.0000

YEARS 15 — MO PAYT 1.3791 — AN CONST 16.55

#	INT	PRIN	BALANCE
1	14.5702	1.9790	98.0210
2	14.2588	2.2903	95.7307
3	13.8985	2.6506	93.0801
4	13.4815	3.0676	90.0125
5	12.9989	3.5502	86.4623
6	12.4404	4.1087	82.3535
7	11.7940	4.7551	77.5984
8	11.0460	5.5032	72.0952
9	10.1802	6.3690	65.7262
10	9.1782	7.3709	58.3553
11	8.0186	8.5305	49.8248
12	6.6766	9.8725	39.9523
13	5.1235	11.4257	28.5266
14	3.3260	13.2232	15.3034
15	1.2457	15.3034	0.0000

YEARS 16 — MO PAYT 1.3559 — AN CONST 16.28

#	INT	PRIN	BALANCE
1	14.5897	1.6812	98.3188
2	14.3252	1.9457	96.3731
3	14.0191	2.2518	94.1213
4	13.6649	2.6061	91.5152
5	13.2549	3.0160	88.4992
6	12.7804	3.4905	85.0086
7	12.2313	4.0397	80.9690
8	11.5958	4.6752	76.2938
9	10.8603	5.4107	70.8831
10	10.0091	6.2619	64.6212
11	9.0239	7.2470	57.3742
12	7.8838	8.3871	48.9872
13	6.5644	9.7066	39.2806
14	5.0373	11.2336	28.0470
15	3.2701	13.0009	15.0462
16	1.2248	15.0462	0.0000

YEARS 17 — MO PAYT 1.3365 — AN CONST 16.04

#	INT	PRIN	BALANCE
1	14.6061	1.4319	98.5681
2	14.3808	1.6571	96.9110
3	14.1201	1.9178	94.9931
4	13.8184	2.2196	92.7736
5	13.4692	2.5687	90.2048
6	13.0651	2.9729	87.2320
7	12.5974	3.4405	83.7914
8	12.0561	3.9818	79.8096
9	11.4297	4.6082	75.2014
10	10.7048	5.3332	69.8682
11	9.8657	6.1722	63.6959
12	8.8947	7.1432	56.5527
13	7.7709	8.2670	48.2857
14	6.4704	9.5676	38.7181
15	4.9652	11.0727	27.6454
16	3.2233	12.8147	14.8307
17	1.2072	14.8307	0.0000

YEARS 18 — MO PAYT 1.3202 — AN CONST 15.85

#	INT	PRIN	BALANCE
1	14.6198	1.2221	98.7779
2	14.4276	1.4144	97.3635
3	14.2051	1.6369	95.7266
4	13.9475	1.8944	93.8322
5	13.6495	2.1924	91.6398
6	13.3046	2.5374	89.1024
7	12.9054	2.9365	86.1659
8	12.4434	3.3985	82.7674
9	11.9088	3.9332	78.8342
10	11.2900	4.5519	74.2823
11	10.5739	5.2680	69.0143
12	9.7452	6.0968	62.9175
13	8.7860	7.0559	55.8616
14	7.6760	8.1660	47.6956
15	6.3913	9.4506	38.2450
16	4.9045	10.9374	27.3075
17	3.1839	12.6581	14.6495
18	1.1925	14.6495	0.0000

YEARS 19 — MO PAYT 1.3064 — AN CONST 15.68

#	INT	PRIN	BALANCE
1	14.6315	1.0450	98.9550
2	14.4671	1.2093	97.7457
3	14.2768	1.3996	96.3461
4	14.0566	1.6198	94.7263
5	13.8018	1.8746	92.8517
6	13.5069	2.1695	90.6822
7	13.1656	2.5108	88.1713
8	12.7706	2.9058	85.2655
9	12.3134	3.3630	81.9025
10	11.7844	3.8921	78.0104
11	11.1721	4.5043	73.5061
12	10.4634	5.2130	68.2931
13	9.6433	6.0331	62.2600
14	8.6942	6.9822	55.2778
15	7.5958	8.0806	47.1972
16	6.3245	9.3519	37.8453
17	4.8533	10.8231	27.0222
18	3.1506	12.5258	14.4964
19	1.1800	14.4964	0.0000

YEARS 20 — MO PAYT 1.2947 — AN CONST 15.54

#	INT	PRIN	BALANCE
1	14.6413	.8948	99.1052
2	14.5005	1.0356	98.0696
3	14.3376	1.1985	96.8710
4	14.1491	1.3871	95.4840
5	13.9308	1.6053	93.8787
6	13.6783	1.8578	92.0208
7	13.3860	2.1501	89.8707
8	13.0478	2.4884	87.3823
9	12.6563	2.8798	84.5025
10	12.2032	3.3329	81.1696
11	11.6789	3.8572	77.3124
12	11.0721	4.4640	72.8483
13	10.3698	5.1663	67.6820
14	9.5570	5.9791	61.7029
15	8.6164	6.9197	54.7832
16	7.5278	8.0083	46.7749
17	6.2679	9.2682	37.5067
18	4.8099	10.7263	26.7804
19	3.1224	12.4137	14.3667
20	1.1695	14.3667	0.0000

YEARS 21 — MO PAYT 1.2847 — AN CONST 15.42

#	INT	PRIN	BALANCE
1	14.6497	.7673	99.2327
2	14.5290	.8880	98.3448
3	14.3893	1.0277	97.3171

#	INT	PRIN	BALANCE
4	14.2276	1.1893	96.1278
5	14.0405	1.3764	94.7514
6	13.8240	1.5930	93.1584
7	13.5733	1.8436	91.3148
8	13.2833	2.1336	89.1812
9	12.9477	2.4693	86.7119
10	12.5592	2.8577	83.8542
11	12.1096	3.3073	80.5468
12	11.5893	3.8276	76.7192
13	10.9871	4.4298	72.2894
14	10.2902	5.1267	67.1627
15	9.4837	5.9332	61.2295
16	8.5503	6.8666	54.3629
17	7.4700	7.9469	46.4160
18	6.2198	9.1971	37.2189
19	4.7730	10.6440	26.5749
20	3.0984	12.3185	14.2564
21	1.1605	14.2564	0.0000

YEARS 22 — MO PAYT 1.2763 — AN CONST 15.32

#	INT	PRIN	BALANCE
1	14.6568	.6586	99.3414
2	14.5532	.7622	98.5792
3	14.4333	.8821	97.6971
4	14.2945	1.0209	96.6762
5	14.1339	1.1815	95.4947
6	13.9480	1.3674	94.1273
7	13.7329	1.5825	92.5448
8	13.4840	1.8314	90.7134
9	13.1958	2.1196	88.5938
10	12.8624	2.4530	86.1408
11	12.4765	2.8389	83.3019
12	12.0299	3.2855	80.0164
13	11.5130	3.8024	76.2139
14	10.9148	4.4006	71.8133
15	10.2225	5.0929	66.7204
16	9.4213	5.8941	60.8262
17	8.4940	6.8214	54.0048
18	7.4208	7.8946	46.1103
19	6.1365	9.1365	36.9738
20	4.7415	10.5739	26.3999
21	3.0780	12.2374	14.1625
22	1.1529	14.1625	0.0000

YEARS 23 — MO PAYT 1.2691 — AN CONST 15.23

#	INT	PRIN	BALANCE
1	14.6629	.5658	99.4342
2	14.5739	.6549	98.7793
3	14.4708	.7579	98.0214
4	14.3516	.8771	97.1443
5	14.2136	1.0151	96.1291
6	14.0539	1.1748	94.9543
7	13.8691	1.3596	93.5947
8	13.6552	1.5735	92.0212
9	13.4077	1.8211	90.2001
10	13.1212	2.1076	88.0925
11	12.7896	2.4391	85.6534
12	12.4059	2.8229	82.8305
13	11.9618	3.2669	79.5636
14	11.4478	3.7809	75.7827
15	10.8530	4.3757	71.4070
16	10.1646	5.0641	66.3429
17	9.3679	5.8608	60.4821
18	8.4459	6.7828	53.6993
19	7.3789	7.8499	45.8494
20	6.1439	9.0848	36.7646
21	4.7147	10.5140	26.2505
22	3.0606	12.1681	14.0824
23	1.1463	14.0824	0.0000

YEARS 24 — MO PAYT 1.2629 — AN CONST 15.16

#	INT	PRIN	BALANCE
1	14.6681	.4866	99.5134
2	14.5915	.5631	98.9504
3	14.5030	.6517	98.2987
4	14.4004	.7542	97.5445
5	14.2818	.8729	96.6716
6	14.1445	1.0102	95.6614
7	13.9855	1.1691	94.4923
8	13.8016	1.3530	93.1393
9	13.5888	1.5659	91.5734
10	13.3424	1.8122	89.7612
11	13.0573	2.0973	87.6639
12	12.7274	2.4273	85.2366
13	12.3455	2.8091	82.4275
14	11.9036	3.2511	79.1765
15	11.3921	3.7625	75.4140
16	10.8002	4.3544	71.0595
17	10.1152	5.0395	66.0201
18	9.3224	5.8323	60.1878
19	8.4048	6.7498	53.4380
20	7.3430	7.8117	45.6263
21	6.1140	9.0406	36.5857
22	4.6917	10.4629	26.1228
23	3.0457	12.1089	14.0139
24	1.1408	14.0139	0.0000

YEARS 25 — MO PAYT 1.2576 — AN CONST 15.10

#	INT	PRIN	BALANCE
1	14.6725	.4187	99.5813
2	14.6067	.4845	99.0968
3	14.5305	.5607	98.5361
4	14.4422	.6490	97.8871
5	14.3401	.7510	97.1361
6	14.2220	.8692	96.2669
7	14.0852	1.0059	95.2609
8	13.9270	1.1642	94.0967
9	13.7438	1.3474	92.7494
10	13.5319	1.5593	91.1901
11	13.2866	1.8046	89.3854
12	13.0027	2.0885	87.2969
13	12.6741	2.4171	84.8798
14	12.2938	2.7974	82.0824
15	11.8537	3.2374	78.8450
16	11.3444	3.7468	75.0982
17	10.7550	4.3362	70.7620
18	10.0728	5.0184	65.7437
19	9.2833	5.8079	59.9358
20	8.3696	6.7215	53.2143
21	7.3122	7.7790	45.4353
22	6.0884	9.0028	36.4325
23	4.6917	10.4191	26.0134
24	3.0330	12.0582	13.9552
25	1.1360	13.9552	0.0000

YEARS 26 — MO PAYT 1.2531 — AN CONST 15.04

#	INT	PRIN	BALANCE
1	14.6764	.3604	99.6396
2	14.6197	.4171	99.2224
3	14.5540	.4828	98.7396
4	14.4781	.5587	98.1809
5	14.3902	.6466	97.5343
6	14.2885	.7483	96.7860
7	14.1707	.8661	95.9199
8	14.0345	1.0023	94.9176
9	13.8768	1.1600	93.7576
10	13.6943	1.3425	92.4151
11	13.4831	1.5537	90.8614
12	13.2387	1.7981	89.0633
13	12.9558	2.0810	86.9822
14	12.6284	2.4084	84.5739
15	12.2495	2.7873	81.7866
16	11.8110	3.2258	78.5608
17	11.3035	3.7333	74.8275
18	10.7162	4.3206	70.5070
19	10.0365	5.0003	65.5067
20	9.2499	5.7869	59.7198
21	8.3395	6.6973	53.0225
22	7.2859	7.7509	45.2715
23	6.0665	8.9703	36.3012
24	4.6553	10.3815	25.9197
25	3.0220	12.0148	13.9049
26	1.1319	13.9049	0.0000

YEARS 27 — MO PAYT 1.2492 — AN CONST 15.00

#	INT	PRIN	BALANCE
1	14.6796	.3105	99.6895
2	14.6308	.3593	99.3302
3	14.5743	.4158	98.9144
4	14.5088	.4813	98.4331
5	14.4331	.5570	97.8761
6	14.3455	.6446	97.2315
7	14.2441	.7460	96.4855
8	14.1267	.8634	95.6221
9	13.9909	.9992	94.6229
10	13.8337	1.1564	93.4665
11	13.6518	1.3383	92.1282
12	13.4412	1.5489	90.5793
13	13.1976	1.7925	88.7867
14	12.9156	2.0745	86.7122
15	12.5892	2.4009	84.3113
16	12.2115	2.7786	81.5326
17	11.7744	3.2158	78.3169
18	11.2684	3.7217	74.5952
19	10.6830	4.3072	70.2881
20	10.0054	4.9848	65.3033
21	9.2212	5.7690	59.5344
22	8.3136	6.6765	52.8578
23	7.2632	7.7269	45.1310
24	6.0476	8.9425	36.1885
25	4.6408	10.3493	25.8392
26	3.0127	11.9774	13.8617
27	1.1284	13.8617	0.0000

YEARS 28 — MO PAYT 1.2458 — AN CONST 14.96

#	INT	PRIN	BALANCE
1	14.6824	.2676	99.7324
2	14.6404	.3096	99.4228
3	14.5916	.3584	99.0644
4	14.5353	.4147	98.6497
5	14.4700	.4800	98.1697
6	14.3945	.5555	97.6142
7	14.3071	.6429	96.9713
8	14.2060	.7440	96.2273
9	14.0889	.8611	95.3663
10	13.9535	.9965	94.3697
11	13.7967	1.1533	93.2164
12	13.6153	1.3347	91.8817
13	13.4053	1.5447	90.3369
14	13.1623	1.7877	88.5492
15	12.8810	2.0690	86.4802
16	12.5555	2.3945	84.0857
17	12.1788	2.7712	81.3145
18	11.7428	3.2072	78.1073
19	11.2383	3.7117	74.3956
20	10.6544	4.2956	70.1000
21	9.9786	4.9714	65.1286
22	9.1965	5.7535	59.3751
23	8.2913	6.6587	52.7164
24	7.2438	7.7062	45.0102
25	6.0315	8.9185	36.0917
26	4.6284	10.3216	25.7701
27	3.0046	11.9454	13.8247
28	1.1254	13.8247	0.0000

YEARS 29 — MO PAYT 1.2430 — AN CONST 14.92

#	INT	PRIN	BALANCE
1	14.6849	.2307	99.7693
2	14.6486	.2669	99.5024
3	14.6066	.3089	99.1935
4	14.5580	.3575	98.8359
5	14.5017	.4138	98.4222
6	14.4366	.4789	97.9433
7	14.3613	.5542	97.3891
8	14.2741	.6414	96.7477
9	14.1732	.7423	96.0054
10	14.0564	.8591	95.1463
11	13.9213	.9942	94.1521
12	13.7649	1.1506	93.0014
13	13.5839	1.3317	91.6697
14	13.3744	1.5412	90.1286
15	13.1319	1.7836	88.3449
16	12.8513	2.0642	86.2807
17	12.5266	2.3890	83.8917
18	12.1507	2.7648	81.1269
19	11.7158	3.1998	77.9272
20	11.2124	3.7031	74.2240
21	10.6298	4.2857	69.9383
22	9.9556	4.9600	64.9784
23	9.1753	5.7402	59.2381
24	8.2722	6.6433	52.5948
25	7.2271	7.6884	44.9064
26	6.0175	8.8980	36.0084
27	4.6177	10.2978	25.7106
28	2.9977	11.9179	13.7928
29	1.1228	13.7928	0.0000

YEARS 30 — MO PAYT 1.2405 — AN CONST 14.89

#	INT	PRIN	BALANCE
1	14.6870	.1989	99.8011
2	14.6557	.2302	99.5709
3	14.6194	.2664	99.3045
4	14.5775	.3083	98.9962
5	14.5290	.3568	98.6394
6	14.4729	.4130	98.2264
7	14.4079	.4779	97.7485
8	14.3327	.5531	97.1954
9	14.2457	.6401	96.5552
10	14.1450	.7408	95.8144
11	14.0285	.8574	94.9570
12	13.8936	.9923	93.9648
13	13.7375	1.1484	92.8164
14	13.5568	1.3290	91.4874
15	13.3478	1.5381	89.9493
16	13.1058	1.7801	88.1692
17	12.8257	2.0601	86.1091
18	12.5016	2.3842	83.7249
19	12.1266	2.7593	80.9656
20	11.6925	3.1934	77.7722
21	11.1901	3.6958	74.0764
22	10.6087	4.2772	69.7992
23	9.9358	4.9501	64.8491
24	9.1570	5.7288	59.1203
25	8.2558	6.6301	52.4902
26	7.2127	7.6731	44.8171
27	6.0056	8.8803	35.9368
28	4.6085	10.2773	25.6595
29	2.9917	11.8941	13.7653
30	1.1205	13.7653	0.0000

YEARS 2 — MO PAYT 4.8368 — AN CONST 58.05

#	INT	PRIN	BALANCE
1	11.7000	46.3415	53.6585
2	4.3831	53.6585	0.0000

YEARS 3 — MO PAYT 3.4543 — AN CONST 41.46

#	INT	PRIN	BALANCE
1	12.8688	28.5828	71.4172
2	8.3558	33.0958	38.3214
3	3.1303	38.3214	0.0000

YEARS 4 — MO PAYT 2.7704 — AN CONST 33.25

#	INT	PRIN	BALANCE
1	13.4470	19.7980	80.2020
2	10.3210	22.9240	57.2780
3	6.7015	26.5435	30.7345
4	2.5105	30.7345	0.0000

YEARS 5 — MO PAYT 2.3659 — AN CONST 28.40

#	INT	PRIN	BALANCE
1	13.7890	14.6017	85.3983
2	11.4835	16.9072	68.4911
3	8.8140	19.5767	48.9144
4	5.7230	22.6677	26.2467
5	2.1440	26.2467	0.0000

YEARS 6 — MO PAYT 2.1009 — AN CONST 25.22

#	INT	PRIN	BALANCE
1	14.0130	11.1984	88.8016
2	12.2448	12.9665	75.8351
3	10.1975	15.0139	60.8212
4	7.8270	17.3844	43.4368
5	5.0821	20.1293	23.3075
6	1.9039	23.3075	0.0000

YEARS 7 — MO PAYT 1.9157 — AN CONST 22.99

#	INT	PRIN	BALANCE
1	14.1696	8.8185	91.1815
2	12.7772	10.2109	80.9706
3	11.1650	11.8231	69.1475
4	9.2983	13.6899	55.4577
5	7.1367	15.8514	39.6063
6	4.6339	18.3542	21.2521
7	1.7360	21.2521	0.0000

YEARS 8 — MO PAYT 1.7801 — AN CONST 21.37

#	INT	PRIN	BALANCE
1	14.2842	7.0770	92.9230
2	13.1668	8.1944	84.7286
3	11.8730	9.4882	75.2403
4	10.3749	10.9864	64.2539
5	8.6402	12.7210	51.5329
6	6.6317	14.7296	36.8034
7	4.3060	17.0552	19.7481
8	1.6131	19.7481	0.0000

YEARS 9 — MO PAYT 1.6776 — AN CONST 20.14

#	INT	PRIN	BALANCE
1	14.3709	5.7599	94.2401
2	13.4615	6.6694	87.5707
3	12.4084	7.7224	79.8483
4	11.1891	8.9417	70.9065
5	9.7773	10.3536	60.5530
6	8.1425	11.9883	48.5647

(YEARS 9 continued)

#	INT	PRIN	BALANCE
7	6.2497	13.8812	34.6835
8	4.0580	16.0729	18.6106
9	1.5202	18.6106	0.0000

YEARS 10 — MO PAYT 1.5981 — AN CONST 19.18

#	INT	PRIN	BALANCE
1	14.4381	4.7388	95.2612
2	13.6899	5.4870	89.7742
3	12.8236	6.3533	83.4209
4	11.8204	7.3565	76.0644
5	10.6589	8.5180	67.5464
6	9.3140	9.8629	57.6835
7	7.7567	11.4202	46.2633
8	5.9535	13.2234	33.0399
9	3.8657	15.3112	17.7287
10	1.4482	17.7287	0.0000

YEARS 11 — MO PAYT 1.5352 — AN CONST 18.43

#	INT	PRIN	BALANCE
1	14.4912	3.9317	96.0683
2	13.8705	4.5525	91.5159
3	13.1517	5.2713	86.2446
4	12.3194	6.1035	80.1411
5	11.3557	7.0672	73.0738
6	10.2398	8.1831	64.8907
7	8.9478	9.4751	55.4156
8	7.4517	10.9712	44.4444
9	5.7195	12.7035	31.7409
10	3.7137	14.7092	17.0317
11	1.3912	17.0317	0.0000

YEARS 12 — MO PAYT 1.4848 — AN CONST 17.82

#	INT	PRIN	BALANCE
1	14.5339	3.2840	96.7160
2	14.0153	3.8026	92.9134
3	13.4149	4.4030	88.5104
4	12.7198	5.0981	83.4123
5	11.9148	5.9031	77.5092
6	10.9827	6.8352	70.6740
7	9.9005	7.9144	62.7597
8	8.6539	9.1640	53.5957
9	7.2070	10.6109	42.9848
10	5.5316	12.2863	30.6985
11	3.5917	14.2262	16.4724
12	1.3455	16.4724	0.0000

YEARS 13 — MO PAYT 1.4439 — AN CONST 17.33

#	INT	PRIN	BALANCE
1	14.5685	2.7580	97.2420
2	14.1330	3.1935	94.0485
3	13.6288	3.6977	90.3508
4	13.0450	4.2815	86.0693
5	12.3689	4.9575	81.1118
6	11.5862	5.7403	75.3715
7	10.6798	6.6466	68.7248
8	9.6304	7.6961	61.0288
9	8.4152	8.9112	52.1175
10	7.0082	10.3182	41.7993
11	5.3791	11.9474	29.8519
12	3.4927	13.8338	16.0181
13	1.3084	16.0181	0.0000

YEARS 14 — MO PAYT 1.4103 — AN CONST 16.93

#	INT	PRIN	BALANCE
1	14.5969	2.3265	97.6735
2	14.2295	2.6938	94.9797
3	13.8042	3.1192	91.8605
4	13.3117	3.6117	88.2488
5	12.7415	4.1819	84.0669
6	12.0812	4.8422	79.2247
7	11.3166	5.6067	73.6180
8	10.4314	6.4920	67.1260
9	9.4063	7.5170	59.6089
10	8.2195	8.7039	50.9050
11	6.8452	10.0782	40.8268
12	5.2539	11.6695	29.1574
13	3.4114	13.5120	15.6454
14	1.2780	15.6454	0.0000

YEARS 15 — MO PAYT 1.3825 — AN CONST 16.60

#	INT	PRIN	BALANCE
1	14.6204	1.9697	98.0303
2	14.3094	2.2807	95.7496
3	13.9493	2.6408	93.1089
4	13.5323	3.0577	90.0511
5	13.0495	3.5405	86.5106
6	12.4905	4.0995	82.4111
7	11.8432	4.7468	77.6642
8	11.0937	5.4963	72.1679
9	10.2259	6.3641	65.8038
10	9.2211	7.3690	58.4348
11	8.0576	8.5325	49.9023
12	6.7104	9.8797	40.0227
13	5.1504	11.4396	28.5831
14	3.3442	13.2458	15.3372
15	1.2528	15.3372	0.0000

YEARS 16 — MO PAYT 1.3594 — AN CONST 16.32

#	INT	PRIN	BALANCE
1	14.6399	1.6726	98.3274
2	14.3758	1.9367	96.3906
3	14.0700	2.2425	94.1481
4	13.7159	2.5966	91.5515
5	13.3060	3.0066	88.5449
6	12.8313	3.4813	85.0636
7	12.2816	4.0310	81.0326
8	11.6451	4.6674	76.3652
9	10.9082	5.4044	70.9608
10	10.0549	6.2577	64.7031
11	9.0668	7.2457	57.4574
12	7.9228	8.3898	49.0677
13	6.5981	9.7144	39.3532
14	5.0643	11.2483	28.1050
15	3.2883	13.0243	15.0807
16	1.2319	15.0807	0.0000

YEARS 17 — MO PAYT 1.3400 — AN CONST 16.09

#	INT	PRIN	BALANCE
1	14.6563	1.4240	98.5760
2	14.4314	1.6488	96.9272
3	14.1711	1.9092	95.0180
4	13.8697	2.2106	92.8074
5	13.5206	2.5596	90.2478
6	13.1165	2.9638	87.2840
7	12.6485	3.4317	83.8523
8	12.1067	3.9736	79.8787
9	11.4793	4.6010	75.2778
10	10.7528	5.3274	69.9503
11	9.9117	6.1686	63.7818
12	8.9377	7.1425	56.6392
13	7.8100	8.2703	48.3689
14	6.5042	9.5761	38.7928
15	4.9922	11.0881	27.7048
16	3.2415	12.8388	14.8659
17	1.2143	14.8659	0.0000

YEARS 18 — MO PAYT 1.3237 — AN CONST 15.89

#	INT	PRIN	BALANCE
1	14.6700	1.2149	98.7851
2	14.4782	1.4067	97.3784
3	14.2561	1.6288	95.7497
4	13.9989	1.8860	93.8637
5	13.7012	2.1837	91.6800
6	13.3564	2.5285	89.1514
7	12.9571	2.9278	86.2237
8	12.4949	3.3900	82.8336
9	11.9596	3.9253	78.9083
10	11.3398	4.5451	74.3632
11	10.6222	5.2627	69.1005
12	9.7913	6.0936	63.0069
13	8.8291	7.0558	55.9511
14	7.7151	8.1698	47.7813
15	6.4251	9.4598	38.3216
16	4.9315	10.9534	27.3682
17	3.2021	12.6828	14.6853
18	1.1996	14.6853	0.0000

YEARS 19 — MO PAYT 1.3100 — AN CONST 15.72

#	INT	PRIN	BALANCE
1	14.6817	1.0383	98.9617
2	14.5177	1.2023	97.7594
3	14.3279	1.3921	96.3674
4	14.1081	1.6119	94.7555
5	13.8536	1.8664	92.8891
6	13.5589	2.1611	90.7280
7	13.2177	2.5023	88.2257
8	12.8226	2.8974	85.3284
9	12.3651	3.3548	81.9735
10	11.8354	3.8845	78.0890
11	11.2221	4.4979	73.5911
12	10.5119	5.2081	68.3831
13	9.6896	6.0304	62.3527
14	8.7375	6.9825	55.3702
15	7.6350	8.0850	47.2852
16	6.3584	9.3615	37.9237
17	4.8803	10.8397	27.0840
18	3.1688	12.5511	14.5329
19	1.1871	14.5329	0.0000

YEARS 20 — MO PAYT 1.2984 — AN CONST 15.59

#	INT	PRIN	BALANCE
1	14.6915	.8888	99.1112
2	14.5512	1.0291	98.0822
3	14.3887	1.1916	96.8906
4	14.2006	1.3797	95.5109
5	13.9827	1.5976	93.9133
6	13.7305	1.8498	92.0635
7	13.4384	2.1419	89.9217
8	13.1002	2.4800	87.4416
9	12.7086	2.8716	84.5700
10	12.2552	3.3250	81.2450
11	11.7302	3.8500	77.3950
12	11.1224	4.4579	72.9371
13	10.4185	5.1618	67.7753
14	9.6035	5.9768	61.7985
15	8.6598	6.9205	54.8781
16	7.5671	8.0131	46.8650
17	6.3019	9.2783	37.5866
18	4.8369	10.7433	26.8433
19	3.1407	12.4396	14.4037
20	1.1766	14.4037	0.0000

YEARS 21 — MO PAYT 1.2885 — AN CONST 15.47

#	INT	PRIN	BALANCE
1	14.6999	.7617	99.2383
2	14.5796	.8820	98.3563
3	14.4403	1.0212	97.3350

#	INT	PRIN	BALANCE
4	14.2791	1.1825	96.1526
5	14.0924	1.3692	94.7834
6	13.8762	1.5854	93.1980
7	13.6259	1.8357	91.3623
8	13.3360	2.1255	89.2367
9	13.0004	2.4612	86.7756
10	12.6118	2.8497	83.9258
11	12.1619	3.2997	80.6261
12	11.6409	3.8207	76.8054
13	11.0376	4.4239	72.3815
14	10.3391	5.1225	67.2590
15	9.5303	5.9312	61.3278
16	8.5938	6.8677	54.4601
17	7.5095	7.9521	46.5080
18	6.2539	9.2077	37.3003
19	4.8001	10.6615	26.6388
20	3.1167	12.3448	14.2940
21	1.1676	14.2940	0.0000

YEARS 22	MO PAYT 1.2800	AN CONST 15.37	
#	INT	PRIN	BALANCE
1	14.7070	.6536	99.3464
2	14.6038	.7567	98.5897
3	14.4843	.8762	97.7135
4	14.3460	1.0146	96.6989
5	14.1858	1.1748	95.5241
6	14.0003	1.3602	94.1639
7	13.7856	1.5750	92.5889
8	13.5368	1.8237	90.7652
9	13.2489	2.1117	88.6535
10	12.9155	2.4451	86.2085
11	12.5294	2.8311	83.3773
12	12.0824	3.2781	80.0992
13	11.5648	3.7957	76.3035
14	10.9655	4.3950	71.9084
15	10.2716	5.0890	66.8195
16	9.4681	5.8925	60.9270
17	8.5377	6.8229	54.1041
18	7.4604	7.9001	46.2040
19	6.2130	9.1475	37.0565
20	4.7687	10.5918	26.4647
21	3.0964	12.2642	14.2006
22	1.1600	14.2006	0.0000

YEARS 23	MO PAYT 1.2729	AN CONST 15.28	
#	INT	PRIN	BALANCE
1	14.7131	.5613	99.4387
2	14.6244	.6499	98.7889
3	14.5218	.7525	98.0364
4	14.4030	.8713	97.1651
5	14.2654	1.0089	96.1562
6	14.1062	1.1682	94.9880
7	13.9217	1.3526	93.6354
8	13.7081	1.5662	92.0692
9	13.4609	1.8135	90.2557
10	13.1745	2.0998	88.1559
11	12.8430	2.4313	85.7246
12	12.4591	2.8152	82.9094
13	12.0146	3.2597	79.6496
14	11.4999	3.7744	75.8752
15	10.9040	4.3704	71.5049
16	10.2139	5.0604	66.4444
17	9.4149	5.8594	60.5850
18	8.4898	6.7846	53.8005
19	7.4185	7.8558	45.9447
20	6.1782	9.0961	36.8485
21	4.7420	10.5324	26.3162
22	3.0790	12.1953	14.1209
23	1.1535	14.1209	0.0000

YEARS 24	MO PAYT 1.2667	AN CONST 15.21	
#	INT	PRIN	BALANCE
1	14.7183	.4824	99.5176
2	14.6421	.5586	98.9591
3	14.5539	.6467	98.3123
4	14.4518	.7489	97.5634
5	14.3335	.8671	96.6963
6	14.1966	1.0040	95.6923
7	14.0381	1.1625	94.5298
8	13.8546	1.3461	93.1837
9	13.6420	1.5586	91.6251
10	13.3959	1.8047	89.8204
11	13.1110	2.0897	87.7307
12	12.7810	2.4196	85.3111
13	12.3990	2.8017	82.5094
14	11.9566	3.2440	79.2654
15	11.4444	3.7562	75.5092
16	10.8514	4.3493	71.1599
17	10.1646	5.0360	66.1239
18	9.3695	5.8311	60.2928
19	8.4488	6.7518	53.5409
20	7.3828	7.8179	45.7231
21	6.1484	9.0523	36.6708
22	4.7191	10.4815	26.1892
23	3.0641	12.1365	14.0527
24	1.1479	14.0527	0.0000

YEARS 25	MO PAYT 1.2615	AN CONST 15.14	
#	INT	PRIN	BALANCE
1	14.7227	.4149	99.5851
2	14.6572	.4804	99.1047
3	14.5813	.5562	98.5485
4	14.4935	.6441	97.9044
5	14.3918	.7458	97.1587
6	14.2741	.8635	96.2952
7	14.1377	.9998	95.2953
8	13.9799	1.1577	94.1376
9	13.7971	1.3405	92.7971
10	13.5854	1.5522	91.2449
11	13.3403	1.7972	89.4477
12	13.0566	2.0810	87.3667
13	12.7280	2.4096	84.9571
14	12.3476	2.7900	82.1671
15	11.9070	3.2305	78.9366
16	11.3970	3.7406	75.1959
17	10.8063	4.3312	70.8647
18	10.1225	5.0151	65.8496
19	9.3306	5.8069	60.0426
20	8.4138	6.7238	53.3188
21	7.3521	7.7855	45.5334
22	6.1229	9.0147	36.5187
23	4.6995	10.4381	26.0806
24	3.0514	12.0861	13.9944
25	1.1431	13.9944	0.0000

YEARS 26	MO PAYT 1.2570	AN CONST 15.09	
#	INT	PRIN	BALANCE
1	14.7265	.3570	99.6430
2	14.6701	.4134	99.2296
3	14.6049	.4787	98.7509
4	14.5293	.5543	98.1966
5	14.4418	.6418	97.5549
6	14.3404	.7431	96.8118
7	14.2231	.8604	95.9514
8	14.0873	.9963	94.9551
9	13.9300	1.1536	93.8015
10	13.7478	1.3357	92.4658
11	13.5369	1.5466	90.9192
12	13.2927	1.7908	89.1284
13	13.0100	2.0736	87.0548
14	12.6826	2.4010	84.6538
15	12.3035	2.7801	81.8737
16	11.8645	3.2190	78.6547
17	11.3563	3.7273	74.9275
18	10.7678	4.3158	70.6117
19	10.0863	4.9972	65.6145
20	9.2973	5.7862	59.8283
21	8.3837	6.6998	53.1285
22	7.3259	7.7577	45.3708
23	6.1010	8.9825	36.3883
24	4.6827	10.4008	25.9875
25	3.0405	12.0430	13.9445
26	1.1390	13.9445	0.0000

YEARS 27	MO PAYT 1.2531	AN CONST 15.04	
#	INT	PRIN	BALANCE
1	14.7298	.3074	99.6926
2	14.6812	.3559	99.3367
3	14.6250	.4121	98.9245
4	14.5600	.4772	98.4473
5	14.4846	.5525	97.8948
6	14.3974	.6398	97.2550
7	14.2964	.7408	96.5142
8	14.1794	.8578	95.6564
9	14.0440	.9932	94.6632
10	13.8871	1.1500	93.5132
11	13.7056	1.3316	92.1816
12	13.4953	1.5419	90.6397
13	13.2519	1.7853	88.8544
14	12.9700	2.0672	86.7872
15	12.6436	2.3936	84.3936
16	12.2656	2.7715	81.6221
17	11.8280	3.2091	78.4129
18	11.3214	3.7158	74.6971
19	10.7347	4.3025	70.3946
20	10.0553	4.9818	65.4128
21	9.2687	5.7684	59.6444
22	8.3579	6.6792	52.9651
23	7.3034	7.7338	45.2313
24	6.0822	8.9549	36.2764
25	4.6683	10.3688	25.9076
26	3.0312	12.0060	13.9016
27	1.1355	13.9016	0.0000

YEARS 28	MO PAYT 1.2498	AN CONST 15.00	
#	INT	PRIN	BALANCE
1	14.7326	.2648	99.7352
2	14.6908	.3066	99.4286
3	14.6424	.3550	99.0737
4	14.5863	.4110	98.6626
5	14.5214	.4759	98.1867
6	14.4463	.5511	97.6356
7	14.3593	.6381	96.9975
8	14.2585	.7388	96.2586
9	14.1418	.8555	95.4031
10	14.0068	.9906	94.4126
11	13.8504	1.1470	93.2656
12	13.6693	1.3281	91.9375
13	13.4596	1.5378	90.3997
14	13.2168	1.7806	88.6191
15	12.9356	2.0617	86.5574
16	12.6101	2.3873	84.1701
17	12.2332	2.7642	81.4060
18	11.7967	3.2006	78.2053
19	11.2914	3.7060	74.4994
20	10.7062	4.2911	70.2082
21	10.0287	4.9686	65.2396
22	9.2442	5.7532	59.4864
23	8.3358	6.6615	52.8249
24	7.2840	7.7133	45.1116
25	6.0661	8.9312	36.1804
26	4.6560	10.3414	25.8390
27	3.0232	11.9742	13.8648

#	INT	PRIN	BALANCE
28	1.1325	13.8648	0.0000

YEARS 29	MO PAYT 1.2469	AN CONST 14.97	
#	INT	PRIN	BALANCE
1	14.7350	.2281	99.7719
2	14.6990	.2642	99.5077
3	14.6573	.3059	99.2018
4	14.6090	.3542	98.8476
5	14.5530	.4101	98.4375
6	14.4883	.4749	97.9627
7	14.4133	.5498	97.4128
8	14.3265	.6366	96.7762
9	14.2260	.7372	96.0390
10	14.1096	.8536	95.1855
11	13.9748	.9883	94.1972
12	13.8188	1.1444	93.0528
13	13.6381	1.3251	91.7277
14	13.4289	1.5343	90.1934
15	13.1866	1.7765	88.4169
16	12.9061	2.0570	86.3599
17	12.5813	2.3818	83.9781
18	12.2053	2.7579	81.2202
19	11.7698	3.1933	78.0269
20	11.2656	3.6975	74.3294
21	10.6818	4.2813	70.0481
22	10.0058	4.9573	65.0907
23	9.2231	5.7400	59.3507
24	8.3168	6.6463	52.7044
25	7.2674	7.6957	45.0086
26	6.0523	8.9108	36.0978
27	4.6454	10.3178	25.7800
28	3.0163	11.9469	13.8332
29	1.1300	13.8332	0.0000

YEARS 30	MO PAYT 1.2445	AN CONST 14.94	
#	INT	PRIN	BALANCE
1	14.7371	.1967	99.8033
2	14.7060	.2277	99.5756
3	14.6701	.2637	99.3120
4	14.6284	.3053	99.0067
5	14.5802	.3535	98.6532
6	14.5244	.4093	98.2439
7	14.4598	.4739	97.7700
8	14.3850	.5487	97.2213
9	14.2983	.6354	96.5859
10	14.1980	.7357	95.8502
11	14.0818	.8519	94.9983
12	13.9473	.9864	94.0119
13	13.7916	1.1421	92.8698
14	13.6113	1.3225	91.5473
15	13.4025	1.5313	90.0161
16	13.1607	1.7730	88.2431
17	12.8807	2.0530	86.1901
18	12.5566	2.3771	83.8130
19	12.1813	2.7525	81.0605
20	11.7467	3.1870	77.8735
21	11.2435	3.6902	74.1832
22	10.6608	4.2729	69.9103
23	9.9861	4.9476	64.9627
24	9.2050	5.7287	59.2340
25	8.3004	6.6333	52.6007
26	7.2531	7.6806	44.9201
27	6.0404	8.8933	36.0268
28	4.6362	10.2975	25.7293
29	3.0103	11.9234	13.8060
30	1.1277	13.8060	0.0000

YEARS 2 — MO PAYT 4.8392 — AN CONST 58.08

#	INT	PRIN	BALANCE
1	11.7408	46.3292	53.6708
2	4.3993	53.6708	0.0000

YEARS 3 — MO PAYT 3.4567 — AN CONST 41.49

#	INT	PRIN	BALANCE
1	12.9136	28.5673	71.4327
2	8.3867	33.0942	38.3385
3	3.1425	38.3385	0.0000

YEARS 4 — MO PAYT 2.7729 — AN CONST 33.28

#	INT	PRIN	BALANCE
1	13.4938	19.7816	80.2184
2	10.3591	22.9163	57.3021
3	6.7277	26.5477	30.7545
4	2.5209	30.7545	0.0000

YEARS 5 — MO PAYT 2.3685 — AN CONST 28.43

#	INT	PRIN	BALANCE
1	13.8369	14.5852	85.4148
2	11.5257	16.8964	68.5184
3	8.8482	19.5739	48.9445
4	5.7465	22.6756	26.2689
5	2.1532	26.2689	0.0000

YEARS 6 — MO PAYT 2.1037 — AN CONST 25.25

#	INT	PRIN	BALANCE
1	14.0616	11.1823	88.8177
2	12.2896	12.9542	75.8635
3	10.2369	15.0070	60.8565
4	7.8588	17.3851	43.4714
5	5.1039	20.1400	23.3314
6	1.9124	23.3314	0.0000

YEARS 7 — MO PAYT 1.9185 — AN CONST 23.03

#	INT	PRIN	BALANCE
1	14.2187	8.8029	91.1971
2	12.8238	10.1979	80.9992
3	11.2078	11.8139	69.1853
4	9.3357	13.6860	55.4993
5	7.1670	15.8547	39.6447
6	4.6546	18.3671	21.2776
7	1.7441	21.2776	0.0000

YEARS 8 — MO PAYT 1.7830 — AN CONST 21.40

#	INT	PRIN	BALANCE
1	14.3337	7.0622	92.9378
2	13.2146	8.1813	84.7566
3	11.9181	9.4777	75.2789
4	10.4163	10.9796	64.2993
5	8.6764	12.7194	51.5799
6	6.6608	14.7350	36.8449
7	4.3259	17.0700	19.7749
8	1.6209	19.7749	0.0000

YEARS 9 — MO PAYT 1.6805 — AN CONST 20.17

#	INT	PRIN	BALANCE
1	14.4206	5.7459	94.2541
2	13.5101	6.6564	87.5977
3	12.4553	7.7112	79.8866
4	11.2333	8.9331	70.9535
5	9.8178	10.3487	60.6048
6	8.1779	11.9886	48.6162
7	6.2781	13.8883	34.7278
8	4.0773	16.0891	18.6387
9	1.5278	18.6387	0.0000

YEARS 10 — MO PAYT 1.6011 — AN CONST 19.22

#	INT	PRIN	BALANCE
1	14.4880	4.7255	95.2745
2	13.7391	5.4743	89.8001
3	12.8717	6.3418	83.4583
4	11.8667	7.3468	76.1115
5	10.7025	8.5110	67.6005
6	9.3538	9.8597	57.7409
7	7.7914	11.4221	46.3188
8	5.9814	13.2320	33.0868
9	3.8846	15.3288	17.7579
10	1.4556	17.7579	0.0000

YEARS 11 — MO PAYT 1.5384 — AN CONST 18.47

#	INT	PRIN	BALANCE
1	14.5412	3.9193	96.0807
2	13.9201	4.5403	91.5404
3	13.2007	5.2598	86.2806
4	12.3672	6.0933	80.1874
5	11.4016	7.0588	73.1285
6	10.2830	8.1774	64.9511
7	8.9872	9.4732	55.4779
8	7.4861	10.9744	44.5035
9	5.7470	12.7134	31.7900
10	3.7324	14.7281	17.0619
11	1.3985	17.0619	0.0000

YEARS 12 — MO PAYT 1.4880 — AN CONST 17.86

#	INT	PRIN	BALANCE
1	14.5839	3.2724	96.7276
2	14.0653	3.7910	92.9366
3	13.4646	4.3917	88.5448
4	12.7687	5.0877	83.4572
5	11.9625	5.8939	77.5633
6	11.0285	6.8278	70.7354
7	9.9465	7.9098	62.8256
8	8.6931	9.1632	53.6624
9	7.2411	10.6153	43.0471
10	5.5589	12.2974	30.7497
11	3.6103	14.2461	16.5036
12	1.3528	16.5036	0.0000

YEARS 13 — MO PAYT 1.4472 — AN CONST 17.37

#	INT	PRIN	BALANCE
1	14.6186	2.7472	97.2528
2	14.1833	3.1825	94.0703
3	13.6789	3.6869	90.3834
4	13.0947	4.2711	86.1123
5	12.4179	4.9479	81.1644
6	11.6338	5.7320	75.4324
7	10.7255	6.6403	68.7922
8	9.6733	7.6925	61.0997
9	8.4543	8.9115	52.1882
10	7.0422	10.3236	41.8645
11	5.4062	11.9596	29.9049
12	3.5111	13.8547	16.0502
13	1.3156	16.0502	0.0000

YEARS 14 — MO PAYT 1.4136 — AN CONST 16.97

#	INT	PRIN	BALANCE
1	14.6470	2.3165	97.6835
2	14.2800	2.6836	94.9999
3	13.8547	3.1088	91.8911
4	13.3621	3.6014	88.2897
5	12.7914	4.1721	84.1175
6	12.1302	4.8333	79.2842
7	11.3643	5.5992	73.6851
8	10.4771	6.4865	67.1986
9	9.4492	7.5143	59.6843
10	8.2585	8.7051	50.9792
11	6.8790	10.0845	40.8947
12	5.2810	11.6825	29.2122
13	3.4297	13.5338	15.6784
14	1.2851	15.6784	0.0000

YEARS 15 — MO PAYT 1.3859 — AN CONST 16.64

#	INT	PRIN	BALANCE
1	14.6705	1.9604	98.0396
2	14.3599	2.2711	95.7685
3	14.0000	2.6310	93.1375
4	13.5831	3.0479	90.0897
5	13.1001	3.5308	86.5588
6	12.5406	4.0904	82.4685
7	11.8924	4.7385	77.7299
8	11.1416	5.4894	72.2405
9	10.2717	6.3593	65.8812
10	9.2640	7.3670	58.5142
11	8.0966	8.5344	49.9798
12	6.7442	9.8868	40.0930
13	5.1775	11.4535	28.6395
14	3.3625	13.2685	15.3710
15	1.2599	15.3710	0.0000

YEARS 16 — MO PAYT 1.3629 — AN CONST 16.36

#	INT	PRIN	BALANCE
1	14.6901	1.6641	98.3359
2	14.4264	1.9278	96.4081
3	14.1209	2.2333	94.1748
4	13.7670	2.5872	91.5876
5	13.3571	2.9972	88.5905
6	12.8821	3.4721	85.1184
7	12.3319	4.0223	81.0961
8	11.6945	4.6597	76.4364
9	10.9561	5.3981	71.0384
10	10.1007	6.2535	64.7849
11	9.1098	7.2444	57.5405
12	7.9618	8.3924	49.1481
13	6.6319	9.7223	39.4258
14	5.0913	11.2629	28.1629
15	3.3065	13.0477	15.1153
16	1.2390	15.1153	0.0000

YEARS 17 — MO PAYT 1.3436 — AN CONST 16.13

#	INT	PRIN	BALANCE
1	14.7065	1.4161	98.5839
2	14.4821	1.6405	96.9433
3	14.2221	1.9005	95.0428
4	13.9210	2.2017	92.8412
5	13.5721	2.5505	90.2907
6	13.1679	2.9547	87.3359
7	12.6997	3.4229	83.9130
8	12.1573	3.9653	79.9477
9	11.5289	4.5937	75.3540
10	10.8010	5.3216	70.0324
11	9.9577	6.1649	63.8675
12	8.9808	7.1418	56.7257
13	7.8491	8.2735	48.4521
14	6.5380	9.5846	38.8675
15	5.0192	11.1034	27.7641
16	3.2597	12.8629	14.9012
17	1.2214	14.9012	0.0000

YEARS 18 — MO PAYT 1.3273 — AN CONST 15.93

#	INT	PRIN	BALANCE
1	14.7203	1.2077	98.7923
2	14.5289	1.3990	97.3933
3	14.3072	1.6207	95.7726
4	14.0504	1.8775	93.8951
5	13.7528	2.1751	91.7200
6	13.4082	2.5197	89.2003
7	13.0089	2.9190	86.2812
8	12.5463	3.3816	82.8996
9	12.0105	3.9174	78.9822
10	11.3897	4.5382	74.4440
11	10.6706	5.2574	69.1866
12	9.8375	6.0905	63.0962
13	8.8723	7.0556	56.0406
14	7.7543	8.1736	47.8670
15	6.4591	9.4688	38.3981
16	4.9586	10.9693	27.4288
17	3.2204	12.7076	14.7212
18	1.2067	14.7212	0.0000

YEARS 19 — MO PAYT 1.3136 — AN CONST 15.77

#	INT	PRIN	BALANCE
1	14.7319	1.0317	98.9683
2	14.5684	1.1952	97.7731
3	14.3790	1.3846	96.3885
4	14.1596	1.6040	94.7845
5	13.9054	1.8582	92.9263
6	13.6110	2.1526	90.7737
7	13.2698	2.4937	88.2800
8	12.8747	2.8889	85.3911
9	12.4169	3.3467	82.0444
10	11.8866	3.8770	78.1673
11	11.2722	4.4914	73.6759
12	10.5605	5.2031	68.4728
13	9.7360	6.0276	62.4452
14	8.7808	6.9828	55.4624
15	7.6743	8.0893	47.3731
16	6.3924	9.3712	38.0020
17	4.9074	10.8561	27.1458
18	3.1871	12.5765	14.5694
19	1.1942	14.5694	0.0000

YEARS 20 — MO PAYT 1.3020 — AN CONST 15.63

#	INT	PRIN	BALANCE
1	14.7417	.8827	99.1173
2	14.6018	1.0226	98.0947
3	14.4398	1.1846	96.9100
4	14.2521	1.3724	95.5377
5	14.0346	1.5898	93.9478
6	13.7827	1.8418	92.1061
7	13.4908	2.1336	89.9724
8	13.1527	2.4717	87.5007
9	12.7610	2.8634	84.6373
10	12.3073	3.3172	81.3201
11	11.7816	3.8428	77.4773
12	11.1727	4.4517	73.0256
13	10.4672	5.1572	67.8684
14	9.6500	5.9744	61.8940
15	8.7033	6.9211	54.9728
16	7.6065	8.0179	46.9550
17	6.3360	9.2884	37.6665
18	4.8641	10.7603	26.9062
19	3.1590	12.4654	14.4408
20	1.1837	14.4408	0.0000

YEARS 21 — MO PAYT 1.2922 — AN CONST 15.51

#	INT	PRIN	BALANCE
1	14.7501	.7562	99.2438
2	14.6302	.8760	98.3677
3	14.4914	1.0149	97.3529

#	INT	PRIN	BALANCE
4	14.3306	1.1757	96.1772
5	14.1443	1.3620	94.8152
6	13.9285	1.5778	93.2374
7	13.6784	1.8278	91.4095
8	13.3888	2.1175	89.2920
9	13.0532	2.4530	86.8390
10	12.6645	2.8418	83.9973
11	12.2142	3.2921	80.7052
12	11.6925	3.8137	76.8914
13	11.0882	4.4181	72.4734
14	10.3881	5.1182	67.3552
15	9.5770	5.9292	61.4259
16	8.6375	6.8688	54.5571
17	7.5490	7.9573	46.5999
18	6.2881	9.2182	37.3817
19	4.8273	10.6789	26.7027
20	3.1351	12.3712	14.3316
21	1.1747	14.3316	0.0000

YEARS 22 — MO PAYT 1.2838 — AN CONST 15.41

#	INT	PRIN	BALANCE
1	14.7572	.6485	99.3515
2	14.6544	.7513	98.6002
3	14.5354	.8704	97.7298
4	14.3974	1.0083	96.7215
5	14.2377	1.1681	95.5534
6	14.0526	1.3532	94.2003
7	13.8381	1.5676	92.6327
8	13.5897	1.8160	90.8167
9	13.3020	2.1038	88.7129
10	12.9686	2.4371	86.2758
11	12.5824	2.8233	83.4525
12	12.1350	3.2707	80.1818
13	11.6167	3.7890	76.3928
14	11.0163	4.3894	72.0033
15	10.3207	5.0850	66.9183
16	9.5149	5.8908	61.0276
17	8.5815	6.8243	54.2033
18	7.5001	7.9057	46.2977
19	6.2473	9.1584	37.1392
20	4.7960	10.6097	26.5296
21	3.1148	12.2909	14.2386
22	1.1671	14.2386	0.0000

YEARS 23 — MO PAYT 1.2767 — AN CONST 15.32

#	INT	PRIN	BALANCE
1	14.7632	.5567	99.4433
2	14.6750	.6449	98.7984
3	14.5728	.7471	98.0512
4	14.4544	.8655	97.1857
5	14.3173	1.0027	96.1830
6	14.1584	1.1616	95.0215
7	13.9743	1.3456	93.6759
8	13.7611	1.5589	92.1170
9	13.5141	1.8059	90.3111
10	13.2279	2.0920	88.2191
11	12.8964	2.4236	85.7955
12	12.5123	2.8076	82.9879
13	12.0674	3.2525	79.7354
14	11.5520	3.7679	75.9675
15	10.9550	4.3650	71.6025
16	10.2633	5.0567	66.5458
17	9.4620	5.8580	60.6878
18	8.5337	6.7863	53.9016
19	7.4583	7.8616	46.0399
20	6.2125	9.1074	36.9325
21	4.7693	10.5506	26.3819
22	3.0974	12.2225	14.1593
23	1.1606	14.1593	0.0000

YEARS 24 — MO PAYT 1.2706 — AN CONST 15.25

#	INT	PRIN	BALANCE
1	14.7684	.4783	99.5217
2	14.6926	.5540	98.9677
3	14.6048	.6418	98.3258
4	14.5031	.7436	97.5823
5	14.3853	.8614	96.7209
6	14.2488	.9979	95.7230
7	14.0907	1.1560	94.5670
8	13.9075	1.3392	93.2278
9	13.6953	1.5514	91.6764
10	13.4494	1.7972	89.8792
11	13.1646	2.0820	87.7972
12	12.8347	2.4120	85.3852
13	12.4525	2.7942	82.5910
14	12.0097	3.2370	79.3541
15	11.4968	3.7499	75.6042
16	10.9026	4.3441	71.2600
17	10.2142	5.0325	66.2275
18	9.4167	5.8300	60.3976
19	8.4929	6.7538	53.6438
20	7.4226	7.8240	45.8197
21	6.1828	9.0639	36.7559
22	4.7465	10.5002	26.2557
23	3.0826	12.1641	14.0916
24	1.1551	14.0916	0.0000

YEARS 25 — MO PAYT 1.2653 — AN CONST 15.19

#	INT	PRIN	BALANCE
1	14.7729	.4111	99.5889
2	14.7077	.4763	99.1126
3	14.6322	.5518	98.5608
4	14.5448	.6392	97.9216
5	14.4435	.7405	97.1811
6	14.3262	.8578	96.3233
7	14.1902	.9938	95.3295
8	14.0327	1.1513	94.1782
9	13.8503	1.3337	92.8445
10	13.6390	1.5450	91.2995
11	13.3941	1.7899	89.5097
12	13.1105	2.0735	87.4362
13	12.7819	2.4021	85.0341
14	12.4013	2.7827	82.2514
15	11.9603	3.2236	79.0278
16	11.4495	3.7345	75.2933
17	10.8577	4.3263	70.9671
18	10.1722	5.0118	65.9553
19	9.3780	5.8060	60.1493
20	8.4580	6.7260	53.4232
21	7.3921	7.7919	45.6313
22	6.1574	9.0266	36.6047
23	4.7270	10.4570	26.1477
24	3.0699	12.1140	14.0337
25	1.1503	14.0337	0.0000

YEARS 26 — MO PAYT 1.2609 — AN CONST 15.14

#	INT	PRIN	BALANCE
1	14.7766	.3536	99.6464
2	14.7206	.4097	99.2367
3	14.6557	.4746	98.7621
4	14.5805	.5498	98.2122
5	14.4934	.6369	97.5753
6	14.3924	.7379	96.8374
7	14.2755	.8548	95.9826
8	14.1400	.9903	94.9923
9	13.9831	1.1472	93.8452
10	13.8013	1.3290	92.5162
11	13.5907	1.5396	90.9766
12	13.3468	1.7835	89.1931
13	13.0641	2.0661	87.1270
14	12.7367	2.3936	84.7334
15	12.3574	2.7728	81.9606
16	11.9181	3.2122	78.7483
17	11.4090	3.7213	75.0270
18	10.8193	4.3110	70.7161
19	10.1362	4.9941	65.7220
20	9.3448	5.7855	59.9365
21	8.4280	6.7023	53.2343
22	7.3660	7.7643	45.4700
23	6.1356	8.9947	36.4753
24	4.7103	10.4200	26.0553
25	3.0591	12.0712	13.9841
26	1.1462	13.9841	0.0000

YEARS 27 — MO PAYT 1.2570 — AN CONST 15.09

#	INT	PRIN	BALANCE
1	14.7799	.3043	99.6957
2	14.7317	.3526	99.3431
3	14.6758	.4084	98.9346
4	14.6111	.4732	98.4615
5	14.5361	.5481	97.9133
6	14.4492	.6350	97.2783
7	14.3486	.7356	96.5427
8	14.2320	.8522	95.6905
9	14.0970	.9872	94.7032
10	13.9406	1.1437	93.5596
11	13.7593	1.3249	92.2346
12	13.5494	1.5349	90.6998
13	13.3062	1.7781	88.9217
14	13.0244	2.0599	86.8618
15	12.6980	2.3863	84.4755
16	12.3198	2.7644	81.7111
17	11.8818	3.2025	78.5087
18	11.3743	3.7099	74.7987
19	10.7864	4.2978	70.5009
20	10.1054	4.9789	65.5220
21	9.3164	5.7679	59.7541
22	8.4024	6.6819	53.0723
23	7.3436	7.7407	45.3316
24	6.1169	8.9673	36.3643
25	4.6959	10.3883	25.9760
26	3.0498	12.0345	13.9415
27	1.1428	13.9415	0.0000

YEARS 28 — MO PAYT 1.2537 — AN CONST 15.05

#	INT	PRIN	BALANCE
1	14.7827	.2620	99.7380
2	14.7412	.3035	99.4344
3	14.6931	.3516	99.0828
4	14.6374	.4074	98.6754
5	14.5728	.4719	98.2035
6	14.4980	.5467	97.6568
7	14.4114	.6333	97.0234
8	14.3110	.7337	96.2897
9	14.1948	.8500	95.4398
10	14.0601	.9847	94.4551
11	13.9040	1.1407	93.3144
12	13.7233	1.3215	91.9930
13	13.5139	1.5309	90.4621
14	13.2713	1.7734	88.6887
15	12.9903	2.0545	86.6342
16	12.6647	2.3800	84.2542
17	12.2876	2.7572	81.4970
18	11.8506	3.1941	78.3029
19	11.3445	3.7002	74.6027
20	10.7581	4.2866	70.3161
21	10.0789	4.9658	65.3503
22	9.2920	5.7527	59.5976
23	8.3804	6.6643	52.9332
24	7.3243	7.7204	45.2128
25	6.1009	8.9438	36.2690
26	4.6836	10.3611	25.9079
27	3.0418	12.0029	13.9050
28	1.1398	13.9050	0.0000

YEARS 29 — MO PAYT 1.2509 — AN CONST 15.02

#	INT	PRIN	BALANCE
1	14.7851	.2257	99.7743
2	14.7493	.2614	99.5129
3	14.7079	.3029	99.2100
4	14.6599	.3509	98.8592
5	14.6043	.4065	98.4527
6	14.5399	.4709	97.9819
7	14.4653	.5455	97.4364
8	14.3789	.6319	96.8045
9	14.2787	.7320	96.0724
10	14.1627	.8481	95.2244
11	14.0283	.9824	94.2419
12	13.8727	1.1381	93.1038
13	13.6923	1.3185	91.7854
14	13.4834	1.5274	90.2580
15	13.2413	1.7694	88.4885
16	12.9609	2.0498	86.4387
17	12.6361	2.3746	84.0640
18	12.2598	2.7509	81.3131
19	11.8239	3.1869	78.1262
20	11.3189	3.6919	74.4344
21	10.7339	4.2769	70.1575
22	10.0561	4.9546	65.2028
23	9.2710	5.7398	59.4631
24	8.3615	6.6493	52.8137
25	7.3078	7.7030	45.1108
26	6.0871	8.9236	36.1871
27	4.6731	10.3377	25.8494
28	3.0349	11.9758	13.8736
29	1.1372	13.8736	0.0000

YEARS 30 — MO PAYT 1.2485 — AN CONST 14.99

#	INT	PRIN	BALANCE
1	14.7872	.1944	99.8056
2	14.7564	.2252	99.5803
3	14.7207	.2609	99.3194
4	14.6793	.3023	99.0171
5	14.6314	.3502	98.6670
6	14.5759	.4057	98.2613
7	14.5116	.4699	97.7914
8	14.4372	.5444	97.2469
9	14.3509	.6307	96.6163
10	14.2510	.7306	95.8856
11	14.1352	.8464	95.0392
12	14.0011	.9805	94.0587
13	13.8457	1.1359	92.9228
14	13.6657	1.3159	91.6069
15	13.4572	1.5244	90.0825
16	13.2156	1.7660	88.3165
17	12.9357	2.0458	86.2706
18	12.6116	2.3700	83.9006
19	12.2360	2.7456	81.1550
20	11.8009	3.1807	77.9743
21	11.2969	3.6847	74.2896
22	10.7130	4.2686	70.0211
23	10.0366	4.9450	65.0760
24	9.2530	5.7286	59.3474
25	8.3452	6.6364	52.7111
26	7.2936	7.6880	45.0231
27	6.0753	8.9063	36.1168
28	4.6640	10.3176	25.7992
29	3.0290	11.9526	13.8466
30	1.1350	13.8466	0.0000

YEARS 2 — MO PAYT 4.8427 — AN CONST 58.12

#	INT	PRIN	BALANCE
1	11.8019	46.3108	53.6892
2	4.4236	53.6892	0.0000

YEARS 3 — MO PAYT 3.4604 — AN CONST 41.53

#	INT	PRIN	BALANCE
1	12.9809	28.5441	71.4559
2	8.4332	33.0918	38.3641
3	3.1609	38.3641	0.0000

YEARS 4 — MO PAYT 2.7767 — AN CONST 33.33

#	INT	PRIN	BALANCE
1	13.5640	19.7569	80.2431
2	10.4162	22.9047	57.3384
3	6.7670	26.5539	30.7845
4	2.5364	30.7845	0.0000

YEARS 5 — MO PAYT 2.3724 — AN CONST 28.47

#	INT	PRIN	BALANCE
1	13.9088	14.5604	85.4396
2	11.5890	16.8802	68.5593
3	8.8996	19.5696	48.9897
4	5.7817	22.6875	26.3022
5	2.1671	26.3022	0.0000

YEARS 6 — MO PAYT 2.1077 — AN CONST 25.30

#	INT	PRIN	BALANCE
1	14.1346	11.1581	88.8419
2	12.3568	12.9358	75.9062
3	10.2959	14.9967	60.9094
4	7.9066	17.3861	43.5234
5	5.1366	20.1560	23.3673
6	1.9253	23.3673	0.0000

YEARS 7 — MO PAYT 1.9227 — AN CONST 23.08

#	INT	PRIN	BALANCE
1	14.2924	8.7796	91.2204
2	12.8936	10.1784	81.0420
3	11.2720	11.8001	69.2419
4	9.3919	13.6801	55.5618
5	7.2124	15.8596	39.7022
6	4.6856	18.3864	21.3158
7	1.7563	21.3158	0.0000

YEARS 8 — MO PAYT 1.7873 — AN CONST 21.45

#	INT	PRIN	BALANCE
1	14.4078	7.0399	92.9601
2	13.2862	8.1615	84.7985
3	11.9859	9.4619	75.3367
4	10.4784	10.9693	64.3673
5	8.7308	12.7170	51.6503
6	6.7047	14.7431	36.9072
7	4.3558	17.0920	19.8152
8	1.6326	19.8152	0.0000

YEARS 9 — MO PAYT 1.6850 — AN CONST 20.22

#	INT	PRIN	BALANCE
1	14.4951	5.7248	94.2752
2	13.5830	6.6369	87.6383
3	12.5256	7.6943	79.9440
4	11.2997	8.9202	71.0238
5	9.8786	10.3414	60.6824
6	8.2309	11.9890	48.6934
7	6.3208	13.8991	34.7943
8	4.1064	16.1135	18.6808
9	1.5391	18.6808	0.0000

YEARS 10 — MO PAYT 1.6057 — AN CONST 19.27

#	INT	PRIN	BALANCE
1	14.5627	4.7057	95.2943
2	13.8130	5.4554	89.8389
3	12.9438	6.3246	83.5143
4	11.9362	7.3322	76.1820
5	10.7680	8.5004	67.6816
6	9.4137	9.8547	57.8269
7	7.8436	11.4248	46.4020
8	6.0234	13.2450	33.1570
9	3.9132	15.3553	17.8017
10	1.4667	17.8017	0.0000

YEARS 11 — MO PAYT 1.5431 — AN CONST 18.52

#	INT	PRIN	BALANCE
1	14.6162	3.9007	96.0993
2	13.9947	4.5221	91.5772
3	13.2742	5.2426	86.3345
4	12.4389	6.0779	80.2567
5	11.4706	7.0462	73.2104
6	10.3480	8.1689	65.0416
7	9.0465	9.4703	55.5712
8	7.5377	10.9792	44.5921
9	5.7884	12.7284	31.8637
10	3.7605	14.7563	17.1073
11	1.4095	17.1073	0.0000

YEARS 12 — MO PAYT 1.4928 — AN CONST 17.92

#	INT	PRIN	BALANCE
1	14.6590	3.2551	96.7449
2	14.1404	3.7737	92.9712
3	13.5392	4.3749	88.5962
4	12.8421	5.0720	83.5243
5	12.0340	5.8800	77.6442
6	11.0972	6.8169	70.8274
7	10.0111	7.9030	62.9244
8	8.7520	9.1621	53.7623
9	7.2923	10.6218	43.1405
10	5.6000	12.3141	30.8265
11	3.6381	14.2760	16.5505
12	1.3636	16.5505	0.0000

YEARS 13 — MO PAYT 1.4521 — AN CONST 17.43

#	INT	PRIN	BALANCE
1	14.6938	2.7311	97.2689
2	14.2586	3.1662	94.1027
3	13.7542	3.6706	90.4321
4	13.1694	4.2555	86.1766
5	12.4914	4.9335	81.2432
6	11.7054	5.7195	75.5237
7	10.7942	6.6307	68.8930
8	9.7377	7.6871	61.2059
9	8.5130	8.9118	52.2940
10	7.0931	10.3317	41.9623
11	5.4471	11.9778	29.9846
12	3.5388	13.8861	16.0985
13	1.3264	16.0985	0.0000

YEARS 14 — MO PAYT 1.4187 — AN CONST 17.03

#	INT	PRIN	BALANCE
1	14.7223	2.3015	97.6985
2	14.3556	2.6682	95.0302
3	13.9305	3.0933	91.9369
4	13.4376	3.5862	88.3507
5	12.8663	4.1575	84.1932
6	12.2039	4.8199	79.3733
7	11.4360	5.5878	73.7855
8	10.5457	6.4781	67.3074
9	9.5136	7.5102	59.7972
10	8.3171	8.7067	51.0905
11	6.9299	10.0939	40.9966
12	5.3217	11.7021	29.2945
13	3.4573	13.5665	15.7280
14	1.2959	15.7280	0.0000

YEARS 15 — MO PAYT 1.3910 — AN CONST 16.70

#	INT	PRIN	BALANCE
1	14.7458	1.9466	98.0534
2	14.4357	2.2567	95.7967
3	14.0761	2.6163	93.1804
4	13.6593	3.0331	90.1473
5	13.1761	3.5164	86.6309
6	12.6158	4.0766	82.5543
7	11.9663	4.7261	77.8282
8	11.2134	5.4791	72.3492
9	10.3404	6.3520	65.9972
10	9.3284	7.3640	58.6332
11	8.1552	8.5373	50.0959
12	6.7950	9.8974	40.1985
13	5.2181	11.4743	28.7242
14	3.3900	13.3024	15.4218
15	1.2706	15.4218	0.0000

YEARS 16 — MO PAYT 1.3681 — AN CONST 16.42

#	INT	PRIN	BALANCE
1	14.7654	1.6514	98.3486
2	14.5023	1.9145	96.4342
3	14.1973	2.2195	94.2147
4	13.8437	2.5731	91.6416
5	13.4337	2.9830	88.6586
6	12.9585	3.4583	85.2003
7	12.4075	4.0093	81.1911
8	11.7687	4.6480	76.5430
9	11.0282	5.3886	71.1544
10	10.1697	6.2471	64.9074
11	9.1744	7.2424	57.6650
12	8.0205	8.3963	49.2687
13	6.6828	9.7340	39.5347
14	5.1319	11.2848	28.2499
15	3.3340	13.0827	15.1671
16	1.2497	15.1671	0.0000

YEARS 17 — MO PAYT 1.3489 — AN CONST 16.19

#	INT	PRIN	BALANCE
1	14.7818	1.4044	98.5956
2	14.5581	1.6282	96.9674
3	14.2986	1.8876	95.0799
4	13.9979	2.1883	92.8916
5	13.6493	2.5369	90.3546
6	13.2451	2.9411	87.4135
7	12.7765	3.4097	84.0038
8	12.2333	3.9530	80.0508
9	11.6035	4.5828	75.4680
10	10.8733	5.3129	70.1551
11	10.0269	6.1594	63.9958
12	9.0455	7.1407	56.8551
13	7.9079	8.2784	48.5767
14	6.5889	9.5973	38.9795
15	5.0599	11.1263	27.8531
16	3.2872	12.8990	14.9541
17	1.2321	14.9541	0.0000

YEARS 18 — MO PAYT 1.3327 — AN CONST 16.00

#	INT	PRIN	BALANCE
1	14.7956	1.1969	98.8031
2	14.6049	1.3876	97.4155
3	14.3838	1.6087	95.8068
4	14.1275	1.8650	93.9418
5	13.8304	2.1621	91.7797
6	13.4859	2.5066	89.2732
7	13.0866	2.9059	86.3672
8	12.6236	3.3689	82.9983
9	12.0868	3.9057	79.0927
10	11.4646	4.5279	74.5648
11	10.7432	5.2493	69.3155
12	9.9068	6.0856	63.2298
13	8.9373	7.0552	56.1746
14	7.8132	8.1793	47.9953
15	6.5101	9.4824	38.5129
16	4.9993	10.9932	27.5198
17	3.2479	12.7446	14.7751
18	1.2174	14.7751	0.0000

YEARS 19 — MO PAYT 1.3191 — AN CONST 15.83

#	INT	PRIN	BALANCE
1	14.8072	1.0219	98.9781
2	14.6444	1.1847	97.7935
3	14.4556	1.3734	96.4200
4	14.2368	1.5922	94.8278
5	13.9831	1.8459	92.9819
6	13.6890	2.1400	90.8419
7	13.3481	2.4810	88.3609
8	12.9528	2.8762	85.4847
9	12.4946	3.3345	82.1502
10	11.9633	3.8657	78.2844
11	11.3474	4.4816	73.8028
12	10.6334	5.1957	68.6071
13	9.8056	6.0235	62.5837
14	8.8459	6.9831	55.6006
15	7.7334	8.0957	47.5049
16	6.4435	9.3855	38.1194
17	4.9482	10.8808	27.2385
18	3.2147	12.6144	14.6241
19	1.2049	14.6241	0.0000

YEARS 20 — MO PAYT 1.3076 — AN CONST 15.70

#	INT	PRIN	BALANCE
1	14.8170	.8737	99.1263
2	14.6778	1.0129	98.1133
3	14.5164	1.1743	96.9390
4	14.3293	1.3614	95.5776
5	14.1124	1.5783	93.9993
6	13.8610	1.8298	92.1695
7	13.5694	2.1213	90.0482
8	13.2315	2.4593	87.5889
9	12.8397	2.8511	84.7378
10	12.3854	3.3053	81.4324
11	11.8588	3.8320	77.6004
12	11.2483	4.4425	73.1580
13	10.5405	5.1503	68.0077
14	9.7199	5.9708	62.0369
15	8.7686	6.9221	55.1148
16	7.6658	8.0250	47.0898
17	6.3872	9.3035	37.7863
18	4.9050	10.7858	27.0005
19	3.1866	12.5042	14.4964
20	1.1944	14.4964	0.0000

YEARS 21 — MO PAYT 1.2978 — AN CONST 15.58

#	INT	PRIN	BALANCE
1	14.8254	.7480	99.2520
2	14.7062	.8672	98.3848
3	14.5680	1.0054	97.3794

MONTHLY PAYMENT AMORTIZATION SCHEDULE PER $100 — 14.875%

#	INT	PRIN	BALANCE
4	14.4078	1.1655	96.2139
5	14.2221	1.3512	94.8626
6	14.0069	1.5665	93.2961
7	13.7573	1.8161	91.4800
8	13.4679	2.1054	89.3746
9	13.1325	2.4409	86.9337
10	12.7436	2.8298	84.1039
11	12.2928	3.2806	80.8233
12	11.7701	3.8033	77.0200
13	11.1641	4.4093	72.6107
14	10.4616	5.1117	67.4990
15	9.6472	5.9262	61.5728
16	8.7031	6.8703	54.7025
17	7.6085	7.9649	46.7376
18	6.3395	9.2339	37.5037
19	4.8683	10.7051	26.7986
20	3.1627	12.4106	14.3879
21	1.1855	14.3879	0.0000

YEARS 22 — MO PAYT 1.2895 — AN CONST 15.48

#	INT	PRIN	BALANCE
1	14.8325	.6411	99.3589
2	14.7303	.7432	98.6157
3	14.6119	.8616	97.7540
4	14.4746	.9989	96.7551
5	14.3155	1.1581	95.5971
6	14.1310	1.3426	94.2545
7	13.9171	1.5565	92.6980
8	13.6691	1.8045	90.8936
9	13.3816	2.0919	88.8016
10	13.0483	2.4252	86.3764
11	12.6619	2.8116	83.5647
12	12.2140	3.2596	80.3051
13	11.6946	3.7789	76.5262
14	11.0926	4.3810	72.1452
15	10.3946	5.0790	67.0663
16	9.5854	5.8882	61.1781
17	8.6473	6.8263	54.3518
18	7.5597	7.9139	46.4379
19	6.2988	9.1747	37.2632
20	4.8371	10.6365	26.6268
21	3.1425	12.3311	14.2957
22	1.1779	14.2957	0.0000

YEARS 23 — MO PAYT 1.2824 — AN CONST 15.39

#	INT	PRIN	BALANCE
1	14.8385	.5499	99.4501
2	14.7509	.6376	98.8125
3	14.6493	.7391	98.0734
4	14.5315	.8569	97.2165
5	14.3950	.9934	96.2230
6	14.2368	1.1517	95.0713
7	14.0533	1.3352	93.7361
8	13.8405	1.5479	92.1882
9	13.5939	1.7945	90.3937
10	13.3080	2.0804	88.3132
11	12.9765	2.4119	85.9013
12	12.5923	2.7962	83.1052
13	12.1468	3.2417	79.8635
14	11.6303	3.7581	76.1054
15	11.0316	4.3569	71.7485
16	10.3374	5.0510	66.6974
17	9.5327	5.8558	60.8416
18	8.5997	6.7887	54.0529
19	7.5181	7.8703	46.1826
20	6.2642	9.1243	37.0583
21	4.8105	10.5780	26.4803
22	3.1252	12.2633	14.2171
23	1.1714	14.2171	0.0000

YEARS 24 — MO PAYT 1.2763 — AN CONST 15.32

#	INT	PRIN	BALANCE
1	14.8437	.4721	99.5279
2	14.7685	.5473	98.9805
3	14.6812	.6346	98.3460
4	14.5801	.7356	97.6103
5	14.4629	.8529	96.7575
6	14.3271	.9887	95.7687
7	14.1695	1.1463	94.6225
8	13.9869	1.3289	93.2936
9	13.7752	1.5406	91.7530
10	13.5297	1.7861	89.9669
11	13.2452	2.0706	87.8963
12	12.9153	2.4005	85.4958
13	12.5328	2.7830	82.7128
14	12.0894	3.2264	79.4864
15	11.5754	3.7404	75.7461
16	10.9795	4.3363	71.4097
17	10.2886	5.0272	66.3825
18	9.4877	5.8281	60.5544
19	8.5591	6.7567	53.7977
20	7.4826	7.8332	45.9645
21	6.2346	9.0812	36.8833
22	4.7878	10.5280	26.3553
23	3.1104	12.2054	14.1500
24	1.1658	14.1500	0.0000

YEARS 25 — MO PAYT 1.2711 — AN CONST 15.26

#	INT	PRIN	BALANCE
1	14.8481	.4056	99.5944
2	14.7835	.4702	99.1242
3	14.7086	.5451	98.5791
4	14.6217	.6320	97.9471
5	14.5210	.7327	97.2144
6	14.4043	.8494	96.3650
7	14.2690	.9847	95.3803
8	14.1121	1.1416	94.2387
9	13.9302	1.3235	92.9152
10	13.7193	1.5344	91.3808
11	13.4749	1.7788	89.6020
12	13.1915	2.0622	87.5398
13	12.8629	2.3908	85.1490
14	12.4820	2.7717	82.3773
15	12.0404	3.2133	79.1641
16	11.5285	3.7252	75.4388
17	10.9349	4.3187	71.1201
18	10.2469	5.0068	66.1133
19	9.4492	5.8045	60.3088
20	8.5244	6.7293	53.5795
21	7.4523	7.8014	45.7781
22	6.2093	9.0444	36.7337
23	4.7684	10.4853	26.2484
24	3.0978	12.1559	14.0926
25	1.1611	14.0926	0.0000

YEARS 26 — MO PAYT 1.2667 — AN CONST 15.21

#	INT	PRIN	BALANCE
1	14.8519	.3486	99.6514
2	14.7963	.4042	99.2472
3	14.7319	.4686	98.7786
4	14.6573	.5432	98.2354
5	14.5707	.6298	97.6056
6	14.4704	.7301	96.8755
7	14.3541	.8464	96.0291
8	14.2192	.9813	95.0478
9	14.0629	1.1376	93.9101
10	13.8816	1.3189	92.5913
11	13.6715	1.5290	91.0623
12	13.4279	1.7726	89.2896
13	13.1455	2.0550	87.2346
14	12.8181	2.3824	84.8522
15	12.4385	2.7620	82.0901
16	11.9984	3.2021	78.8881
17	11.4883	3.7122	75.1758
18	10.8968	4.3037	70.8721
19	10.2111	4.9893	65.8828
20	9.4162	5.7843	60.0985
21	8.4947	6.7058	53.3927
22	7.4263	7.7742	45.6185
23	6.1877	9.0128	36.6057
24	4.7517	10.4488	26.1569
25	3.0870	12.1135	14.0434
26	1.1571	14.0434	0.0000

YEARS 27 — MO PAYT 1.2629 — AN CONST 15.16

#	INT	PRIN	BALANCE
1	14.8551	.2998	99.7002
2	14.8073	.3476	99.3526
3	14.7520	.4030	98.9496
4	14.6878	.4672	98.4825
5	14.6133	.5416	97.9409
6	14.5270	.6279	97.3130
7	14.4270	.7279	96.5851
8	14.3110	.8439	95.7412
9	14.1766	.9783	94.7628
10	14.0207	1.1342	93.6286
11	13.8400	1.3149	92.3137
12	13.6305	1.5244	90.7892
13	13.3876	1.7673	89.0219
14	13.1061	2.0489	86.9731
15	12.7796	2.3753	84.5978
16	12.4012	2.7537	81.8440
17	11.9625	3.1925	78.6515
18	11.4538	3.7011	74.9504
19	10.8642	4.2908	70.6597
20	10.1805	4.9744	65.6853
21	9.3880	5.7669	59.9183
22	8.4692	6.6857	53.2326
23	7.4040	7.7509	45.4817
24	6.1691	8.9858	36.4959
25	4.7375	10.4174	26.0785
26	3.0778	12.0772	14.0013
27	1.1536	14.0013	0.0000

YEARS 28 — MO PAYT 1.2597 — AN CONST 15.12

#	INT	PRIN	BALANCE
1	14.8579	.2579	99.7421
2	14.8168	.2990	99.4430
3	14.7691	.3467	99.0963
4	14.7139	.4019	98.6944
5	14.6499	.4660	98.2284
6	14.5756	.5402	97.6882
7	14.4896	.6263	97.0620
8	14.3898	.7260	96.3359
9	14.2741	.8417	95.4942
10	14.1400	.9758	94.5184
11	13.9845	1.1313	93.3871
12	13.8043	1.3115	92.0755
13	13.5953	1.5205	90.5550
14	13.3531	1.7627	88.7923
15	13.0722	2.0436	86.7487
16	12.7467	2.3692	84.3795
17	12.3692	2.7466	81.6329
18	11.9316	3.1842	78.4487
19	11.4243	3.6916	74.7571
20	10.8361	4.2797	70.4774
21	10.1543	4.9616	65.5158
22	9.3638	5.7520	59.7638
23	8.4474	6.6685	53.0953
24	7.3849	7.7309	45.3644
25	6.1532	8.9626	36.4018
26	4.7253	10.3906	26.0112
27	3.0698	12.0460	13.9652
28	1.1506	13.9652	0.0000

YEARS 29 — MO PAYT 1.2569 — AN CONST 15.09

#	INT	PRIN	BALANCE
1	14.8603	.2220	99.7780
2	14.8249	.2574	99.5206
3	14.7839	.2984	99.2222
4	14.7364	.3459	98.8763
5	14.6812	.4010	98.4753
6	14.6173	.4649	98.0104
7	14.5433	.5390	97.4713
8	14.4574	.6249	96.8465
9	14.3578	.7244	96.1220
10	14.2424	.8399	95.2822
11	14.1086	.9737	94.3085
12	13.9535	1.1288	93.1797
13	13.7736	1.3086	91.8711
14	13.5652	1.5171	90.3540
15	13.3234	1.7588	88.5952
16	13.0432	2.0390	86.5561
17	12.7184	2.3639	84.1922
18	12.3417	2.7405	81.4517
19	11.9051	3.1772	78.2745
20	11.3989	3.6834	74.5911
21	10.8121	4.2702	70.3209
22	10.1317	4.9505	65.3704
23	9.3430	5.7393	59.6311
24	8.4286	6.6537	52.9774
25	7.3685	7.7137	45.2637
26	6.1396	8.9427	36.3210
27	4.7148	10.3675	25.9535
28	3.0630	12.0193	13.9342
29	1.1481	13.9342	0.0000

YEARS 30 — MO PAYT 1.2545 — AN CONST 15.06

#	INT	PRIN	BALANCE
1	14.8623	.1911	99.8089
2	14.8319	.2216	99.5873
3	14.7966	.2569	99.3304
4	14.7556	.2978	99.0326
5	14.7082	.3453	98.6873
6	14.6532	.4003	98.2871
7	14.5894	.4640	97.8230
8	14.5155	.5380	97.2851
9	14.4298	.6237	96.6614
10	14.3304	.7230	95.9383
11	14.2152	.8382	95.1001
12	14.0816	.9718	94.1283
13	13.9268	1.1266	93.0016
14	13.7473	1.3061	91.6955
15	13.5392	1.5142	90.1813
16	13.2980	1.7555	88.4258
17	13.0183	2.0352	86.3907
18	12.6941	2.3594	84.0313
19	12.3181	2.7353	81.2960
20	11.8824	3.1711	78.1249
21	11.3771	3.6763	74.4486
22	10.7914	4.2620	70.1865
23	10.1124	4.9411	65.2454
24	9.3251	5.7283	59.5171
25	8.4125	6.6410	52.8762
26	7.3544	7.6990	45.1772
27	6.1278	8.9256	36.2515
28	4.7058	10.3477	25.9039
29	3.0572	11.9963	13.9076
30	1.1459	13.9076	0.0000

YEARS 2 — MO PAYT 4.8439 — AN CONST 58.13

#	INT	PRIN	BALANCE
1	11.8223	46.3047	53.6953
2	4.4317	53.6953	0.0000

YEARS 3 — MO PAYT 3.4616 — AN CONST 41.54

#	INT	PRIN	BALANCE
1	13.0033	28.5364	71.4636
2	8.4486	33.0910	38.3726
3	3.1670	38.3726	0.0000

YEARS 4 — MO PAYT 2.7780 — AN CONST 33.34

#	INT	PRIN	BALANCE
1	13.5874	19.7487	80.2513
2	10.4353	22.9008	57.3505
3	6.7801	26.5560	30.7945
4	2.5416	30.7945	0.0000

YEARS 5 — MO PAYT 2.3737 — AN CONST 28.49

#	INT	PRIN	BALANCE
1	13.9328	14.5522	85.4478
2	11.6101	16.8749	68.5729
3	8.9167	19.5682	49.0047
4	5.7935	22.6915	26.3132
5	2.1717	26.3132	0.0000

YEARS 6 — MO PAYT 2.1091 — AN CONST 25.31

#	INT	PRIN	BALANCE
1	14.1589	11.1500	88.8500
2	12.3793	12.9296	75.9204
3	10.3156	14.9933	60.9271
4	7.9225	17.3864	43.5407
5	5.1475	20.1614	23.3793
6	1.9296	23.3793	0.0000

YEARS 7 — MO PAYT 1.9241 — AN CONST 23.09

#	INT	PRIN	BALANCE
1	14.3170	8.7719	91.2281
2	12.9169	10.1719	81.0562
3	11.2934	11.7955	69.2607
4	9.4107	13.6781	55.5826
5	7.2276	15.8613	39.7214
6	4.6960	18.3929	21.3285
7	1.7603	21.3285	0.0000

YEARS 8 — MO PAYT 1.7888 — AN CONST 21.47

#	INT	PRIN	BALANCE
1	14.4326	7.0325	92.9675
2	13.3101	8.1550	84.8125
3	12.0085	9.4566	75.3559
4	10.4992	10.9659	64.3900
5	8.7489	12.7162	51.6738
6	6.7193	14.7458	36.9280
7	4.3657	17.0994	19.8286
8	1.6365	19.8286	0.0000

YEARS 9 — MO PAYT 1.6865 — AN CONST 20.24

#	INT	PRIN	BALANCE
1	14.5200	5.7178	94.2822
2	13.6073	6.6304	87.6518
3	12.5491	7.6887	79.9631
4	11.3219	8.9159	71.0472
5	9.8988	10.3389	60.7083
6	8.2487	11.9891	48.7192
7	6.3351	13.9027	34.8165
8	4.1161	16.1217	18.6948
9	1.5430	18.6948	0.0000

YEARS 10 — MO PAYT 1.6072 — AN CONST 19.29

#	INT	PRIN	BALANCE
1	14.5877	4.6991	95.3009
2	13.8376	5.4491	89.8518
3	12.9679	6.3189	83.5329
4	11.9594	7.3274	76.2055
5	10.7899	8.4969	67.7086
6	9.4337	9.8531	57.8555
7	7.8610	11.4257	46.4298
8	6.0374	13.2494	33.1804
9	3.9227	15.3641	17.8163
10	1.4704	17.8163	0.0000

YEARS 11 — MO PAYT 1.5446 — AN CONST 18.54

#	INT	PRIN	BALANCE
1	14.6411	3.8945	96.1055
2	14.0195	4.5161	91.5894
3	13.2987	5.2369	86.3525
4	12.4629	6.0728	80.2797
5	11.4936	7.0420	73.2377
6	10.3697	8.1660	65.0717
7	9.0663	9.4694	55.6023
8	7.5549	10.9808	44.6216
9	5.8023	12.7334	31.8882
10	3.7699	14.7657	17.1225
11	1.4132	17.1225	0.0000

YEARS 12 — MO PAYT 1.4944 — AN CONST 17.94

#	INT	PRIN	BALANCE
1	14.6840	3.2493	96.7507
2	14.1654	3.7680	92.9827
3	13.5640	4.3694	88.6133
4	12.8666	5.0667	83.5466
5	12.0579	5.8754	77.6712
6	11.1202	6.8132	70.8580
7	10.0327	7.9007	62.9573
8	8.7717	9.1617	53.7956
9	7.3094	10.6240	43.1717
10	5.6137	12.3196	30.8520
11	3.6474	14.2859	16.5661
12	1.3673	16.5661	0.0000

YEARS 13 — MO PAYT 1.4537 — AN CONST 17.45

#	INT	PRIN	BALANCE
1	14.7188	2.7257	97.2743
2	14.2838	3.1608	94.1135
3	13.7793	3.6653	90.4483
4	13.1943	4.2503	86.1980
5	12.5159	4.9286	81.2694
6	11.7293	5.7153	75.5541
7	10.8170	6.6275	68.9266
8	9.7592	7.6853	61.2413
9	8.5326	8.9119	52.3293
10	7.1102	10.3344	41.9949
11	5.4607	11.9838	30.0111
12	3.5480	13.8965	16.1146
13	1.3300	16.1146	0.0000

YEARS 14 — MO PAYT 1.4203 — AN CONST 17.05

#	INT	PRIN	BALANCE
1	14.7474	2.2966	97.7034
2	14.3808	2.6631	95.0403
3	13.9557	3.0882	91.9521
4	13.4628	3.5811	88.3711
5	12.8913	4.1527	84.2184
6	12.2285	4.8154	79.4030
7	11.4599	5.5840	73.8189
8	10.5686	6.4753	67.3436
9	9.5351	7.5088	59.8348
10	8.3366	8.7073	51.1275
11	6.9469	10.0970	41.0305
12	5.3353	11.7086	29.3219
13	3.4665	13.5774	15.7445
14	1.2994	15.7445	0.0000

YEARS 15 — MO PAYT 1.3927 — AN CONST 16.72

#	INT	PRIN	BALANCE
1	14.7709	1.9420	98.0580
2	14.4610	2.2520	95.8060
3	14.1015	2.6114	93.1946
4	13.6847	3.0282	90.1664
5	13.2014	3.5115	86.6549
6	12.6409	4.0720	82.5829
7	11.9910	4.7219	77.8609
8	11.2373	5.4756	72.3853
9	10.3634	6.3495	66.0358
10	9.3499	7.3630	58.6728
11	8.1747	8.5382	50.1346
12	6.8120	9.9010	40.2337
13	5.2317	11.4812	28.7524
14	3.3992	13.3137	15.4387
15	1.2742	15.4387	0.0000

YEARS 16 — MO PAYT 1.3698 — AN CONST 16.44

#	INT	PRIN	BALANCE
1	14.7905	1.6471	98.3529
2	14.5276	1.9100	96.4429
3	14.2228	2.2149	94.2280
4	13.8693	2.5684	91.6596
5	13.4593	2.9783	88.6813
6	12.9840	3.4537	85.2276
7	12.4327	4.0049	81.2226
8	11.7935	4.6442	76.5785
9	11.0522	5.3854	71.1931
10	10.1927	6.2450	64.9481
11	9.1959	7.2417	57.7064
12	8.0401	8.3975	49.3088
13	6.6998	9.7379	39.5710
14	5.1455	11.2921	28.2789
15	3.3432	13.0944	15.1844
16	1.2532	15.1844	0.0000

YEARS 17 — MO PAYT 1.3506 — AN CONST 16.21

#	INT	PRIN	BALANCE
1	14.8069	1.4005	98.5995
2	14.5834	1.6241	96.9754
3	14.3242	1.8833	95.0921
4	14.0236	2.1839	92.9083
5	13.6750	2.5324	90.3759
6	13.2708	2.9366	87.4393
7	12.8021	3.4053	84.0339
8	12.2586	3.9488	80.0851
9	11.6283	4.5791	75.5060
10	10.8975	5.3100	70.1960
11	10.0499	6.1575	64.0385
12	9.0671	7.1403	56.8982
13	7.9275	8.2799	48.6183
14	6.6059	9.6015	39.0168
15	5.0735	11.1340	27.8828
16	3.2964	12.9110	14.9718
17	1.2357	14.9718	0.0000

YEARS 18 — MO PAYT 1.3345 — AN CONST 16.02

#	INT	PRIN	BALANCE
1	14.8207	1.1933	98.8067
2	14.6302	1.3838	97.4228
3	14.4093	1.6047	95.8182
4	14.1532	1.8608	93.9574
5	13.8562	2.1578	91.7996
6	13.5118	2.5022	89.2974
7	13.1125	2.9016	86.3958
8	12.6493	3.3647	83.0311
9	12.1123	3.9017	79.1294
10	11.4896	4.5245	74.6049
11	10.7674	5.2466	69.3583
12	9.9300	6.0840	63.2743
13	8.9559	7.0551	56.2192
14	7.8329	8.1811	48.0381
15	6.5271	9.4869	38.5512
16	5.0129	11.0011	27.5501
17	3.2571	12.7570	14.7931
18	1.2209	14.7931	0.0000

YEARS 19 — MO PAYT 1.3209 — AN CONST 15.86

#	INT	PRIN	BALANCE
1	14.8323	1.0186	98.9814
2	14.6697	1.1812	97.8002
3	14.4812	1.3697	96.4305
4	14.2626	1.5883	94.8422
5	14.0091	1.8418	93.0003
6	13.7151	2.1358	90.8645
7	13.3742	2.4767	88.3878
8	12.9789	2.8720	85.5158
9	12.5205	3.3304	82.1854
10	11.9889	3.8620	78.3234
11	11.3725	4.4784	73.8450
12	10.6577	5.1932	68.6518
13	9.8289	6.0220	62.6298
14	8.8677	6.9832	55.6466
15	7.7531	8.0978	47.5488
16	6.4606	9.3903	38.1585
17	4.9619	10.8890	27.2694
18	3.2239	12.6270	14.6424
19	1.2085	14.6424	0.0000

YEARS 20 — MO PAYT 1.3094 — AN CONST 15.72

#	INT	PRIN	BALANCE
1	14.8421	.8708	99.1292
2	14.7031	1.0097	98.1195
3	14.5420	1.1709	96.9486
4	14.3551	1.3578	95.5908
5	14.1384	1.5745	94.0163
6	13.8871	1.8258	92.1905
7	13.5957	2.1172	90.0733
8	13.2577	2.4551	87.6181
9	12.8659	2.8470	84.7711
10	12.4115	3.3014	81.4697
11	11.8845	3.8283	77.6414
12	11.2735	4.4394	73.2020
13	10.5649	5.1480	68.0540
14	9.7433	5.9696	62.0844
15	8.7905	6.9224	55.1620
16	7.6856	8.0273	47.1347
17	6.4044	9.3085	37.8262
18	4.9187	10.7942	27.0320
19	3.1958	12.5171	14.5149
20	1.1980	14.5149	0.0000

YEARS 21 — MO PAYT 1.2996 — AN CONST 15.60

#	INT	PRIN	BALANCE
1	14.8505	.7453	99.2547
2	14.7315	.8643	98.3904
3	14.5936	1.0022	97.3882

#	INT	PRIN	BALANCE
4	14.4336	1.1622	96.2260
5	14.2481	1.3477	94.8784
6	14.0330	1.5628	93.3156
7	13.7836	1.8122	91.5034
8	13.4943	2.1014	89.4020
9	13.1589	2.4368	86.9651
10	12.7700	2.8258	84.1393
11	12.3190	3.2768	80.8625
12	11.7960	3.7998	77.0627
13	11.1895	4.4063	72.6564
14	10.4862	5.1096	67.5468
15	9.6707	5.9251	61.6217
16	8.7250	6.8708	54.7509
17	7.6283	7.9675	46.7834
18	6.3566	9.2391	37.5443
19	4.8820	10.7138	26.8305
20	3.1720	12.4238	14.4067
21	1.1890	14.4067	0.0000

YEARS 22 — MO PAYT 1.2913 — AN CONST 15.50

#	INT	PRIN	BALANCE
1	14.8576	.6386	99.3614
2	14.7556	.7406	98.6208
3	14.6374	.8587	97.7621
4	14.5004	.9958	96.7663
5	14.3414	1.1548	95.6115
6	14.1571	1.3391	94.2725
7	13.9434	1.5528	92.7197
8	13.6955	1.8006	90.9190
9	13.4082	2.0880	88.8310
10	13.0749	2.4213	86.4097
11	12.6884	2.8077	83.6020
12	12.2403	3.2559	80.3461
13	11.7206	3.7755	76.5706
14	11.1180	4.3782	72.1924
15	10.4192	5.0770	67.1155
16	9.6089	5.8873	61.2282
17	8.6692	6.8269	54.4012
18	7.5796	7.9166	46.4847
19	6.3160	9.1801	37.3045
20	4.8508	10.6454	26.6592
21	3.1517	12.3444	14.3147
22	1.1814	14.3147	0.0000

YEARS 23 — MO PAYT 1.2843 — AN CONST 15.42

#	INT	PRIN	BALANCE
1	14.8636	.5477	99.4523
2	14.7762	.6351	98.8172
3	14.6748	.7365	98.0807
4	14.5573	.8540	97.2266
5	14.4209	.9904	96.2363
6	14.2629	1.1484	95.0878
7	14.0796	1.3317	93.7561
8	13.8670	1.5443	92.2118
9	13.6205	1.7908	90.4211
10	13.3347	2.0766	88.3445
11	13.0033	2.4080	85.9365
12	12.6189	2.7924	83.1441
13	12.1733	3.2381	79.9061
14	11.6564	3.7549	76.1512
15	11.0571	4.3542	71.7970
16	10.3622	5.0491	66.7479
17	9.5563	5.8550	60.8928
18	8.6218	6.7895	54.1033
19	7.5381	7.8732	46.2301
20	6.2815	9.1298	37.1002
21	4.8242	10.5871	26.5132
22	3.1345	12.2768	14.2363
23	1.1750	14.2363	0.0000

YEARS 24 — MO PAYT 1.2782 — AN CONST 15.34

#	INT	PRIN	BALANCE
1	14.8688	.4701	99.5299
2	14.7937	.5451	98.9848
3	14.7067	.6321	98.3526
4	14.6058	.7330	97.6196
5	14.4888	.8500	96.7696
6	14.3532	.9857	95.7839
7	14.1958	1.1430	94.6408
8	14.0134	1.3255	93.3154
9	13.8018	1.5370	91.7784
10	13.5565	1.7823	89.9960
11	13.2720	2.0668	87.9292
12	12.9421	2.3967	85.5325
13	12.5596	2.7792	82.7532
14	12.1160	3.2228	79.5304
15	11.6016	3.7372	75.7932
16	11.0051	4.3337	71.4595
17	10.3134	5.0254	66.4341
18	9.5113	5.8275	60.6066
19	8.5812	6.7576	53.8489
20	7.5026	7.8362	46.0127
21	6.2519	9.0869	36.9258
22	4.8016	10.5373	26.3885
23	3.1197	12.2191	14.1694
24	1.1695	14.1694	0.0000

YEARS 25 — MO PAYT 1.2731 — AN CONST 15.28

#	INT	PRIN	BALANCE
1	14.8732	.4038	99.5962
2	14.8087	.4682	99.1280
3	14.7340	.5429	98.5851
4	14.6473	.6296	97.9555
5	14.5468	.7301	97.2255
6	14.4303	.8466	96.3789
7	14.2952	.9817	95.3971
8	14.1385	1.1384	94.2587
9	13.9568	1.3201	92.9386
10	13.7461	1.5308	91.4078
11	13.5018	1.7751	89.6326
12	13.2184	2.0585	87.5742
13	12.8899	2.3870	85.1871
14	12.5089	2.7680	82.4191
15	12.0671	3.2098	79.2093
16	11.5548	3.7221	75.4872
17	10.9607	4.3162	71.1710
18	10.2718	5.0051	66.1658
19	9.4729	5.8040	60.3619
20	8.5466	6.7303	53.6315
21	7.4724	7.8046	45.8270
22	6.2267	9.0502	36.7767
23	4.7822	10.4947	26.2820
24	3.1071	12.1698	14.1122
25	1.1647	14.1122	0.0000

YEARS 26 — MO PAYT 1.2687 — AN CONST 15.23

#	INT	PRIN	BALANCE
1	14.8769	.3470	99.6530
2	14.8216	.4024	99.2507
3	14.7573	.4666	98.7841
4	14.6829	.5410	98.2430
5	14.5965	.6274	97.6156
6	14.4964	.7275	96.8881
7	14.3803	.8437	96.0444
8	14.2456	.9783	95.0661
9	14.0894	1.1345	93.9317
10	13.9084	1.3155	92.6161
11	13.6984	1.5255	91.0906
12	13.4549	1.7690	89.3216
13	13.1726	2.0513	87.2703
14	12.8452	2.3787	84.8916
15	12.4655	2.7584	82.1332
16	12.0252	3.1987	78.9345
17	11.5147	3.7092	75.2253
18	10.9227	4.3012	70.9240
19	10.2362	4.9878	65.9363
20	9.4401	5.7838	60.1524
21	8.5169	6.7070	53.4454
22	7.4464	7.7775	45.6679
23	6.2051	9.0188	36.6491
24	4.7656	10.4583	26.1908
25	3.0964	12.1276	14.0632
26	1.1607	14.0632	0.0000

YEARS 27 — MO PAYT 1.2649 — AN CONST 15.18

#	INT	PRIN	BALANCE
1	14.8802	.2983	99.7017
2	14.8326	.3459	99.3557
3	14.7773	.4012	98.9546
4	14.7133	.4652	98.4894
5	14.6391	.5394	97.9500
6	14.5530	.6255	97.3244
7	14.4531	.7254	96.5991
8	14.3374	.8411	95.7579
9	14.2031	.9754	94.7825
10	14.0474	1.1311	93.6514
11	13.8669	1.3116	92.3398
12	13.6575	1.5210	90.8189
13	13.4148	1.7637	89.0552
14	13.1333	2.0452	87.0100
15	12.8068	2.3716	84.6383
16	12.4283	2.7502	81.8881
17	11.9894	3.1891	78.6990
18	11.4803	3.6981	75.0008
19	10.8901	4.2884	70.7124
20	10.2056	4.9729	65.7396
21	9.4119	5.7666	59.9730
22	8.4915	6.6870	53.2860
23	7.4242	7.7543	45.5317
24	6.1866	8.9919	36.5398
25	4.7514	10.4271	26.1127
26	3.0871	12.0914	14.0213
27	1.1572	14.0213	0.0000

YEARS 28 — MO PAYT 1.2616 — AN CONST 15.14

#	INT	PRIN	BALANCE
1	14.8829	.2566	99.7434
2	14.8420	.2976	99.4458
3	14.7945	.3451	99.1008
4	14.7394	.4001	98.7007
5	14.6756	.4640	98.2367
6	14.6015	.5380	97.6986
7	14.5156	.6239	97.0747
8	14.4160	.7235	96.3512
9	14.3006	.8390	95.5122
10	14.1667	.9729	94.5393
11	14.0114	1.1282	93.4111
12	13.8313	1.3082	92.1029
13	13.6225	1.5171	90.5858
14	13.3804	1.7592	88.8267
15	13.0996	2.0400	86.7867
16	12.7740	2.3656	84.4211
17	12.3964	2.7431	81.6780
18	11.9586	3.1810	78.4970
19	11.4509	3.6887	74.8084
20	10.8621	4.2774	70.5310
21	10.1794	4.9601	65.5709
22	9.3878	5.7518	59.8191
23	8.4697	6.6698	53.1493
24	7.4052	7.7344	45.4149
25	6.1707	8.9689	36.4460
26	4.7392	10.4004	26.0456
27	3.0792	12.0604	13.9853
28	1.1543	13.9853	0.0000

YEARS 29 — MO PAYT 1.2588 — AN CONST 15.11

#	INT	PRIN	BALANCE
1	14.8853	.2208	99.7792
2	14.8501	.2560	99.5232
3	14.8092	.2969	99.2263
4	14.7618	.3443	98.8820
5	14.7069	.3992	98.4827
6	14.6432	.4630	98.0198
7	14.5693	.5369	97.4829
8	14.4836	.6225	96.8604
9	14.3842	.7219	96.1384
10	14.2690	.8371	95.3013
11	14.1354	.9707	94.3306
12	13.9804	1.1257	93.2049
13	13.8008	1.3054	91.8995
14	13.5924	1.5137	90.3858
15	13.3508	1.7553	88.6305
16	13.0707	2.0355	86.5951
17	12.7458	2.3603	84.2347
18	12.3691	2.7371	81.4977
19	11.9322	3.1739	78.3237
20	11.4256	3.6805	74.6432
21	10.8382	4.2680	70.3753
22	10.1570	4.9492	65.4261
23	9.3670	5.7391	59.6870
24	8.4510	6.6551	53.0319
25	7.3888	7.7173	45.3146
26	6.1571	8.9491	36.3655
27	4.7287	10.3774	25.9881
28	3.0724	12.0337	13.9544
29	1.1517	13.9544	0.0000

YEARS 30 — MO PAYT 1.2565 — AN CONST 15.08

#	INT	PRIN	BALANCE
1	14.8874	.1900	99.8100
2	14.8570	.2204	99.5896
3	14.8219	.2556	99.3340
4	14.7811	.2963	99.0377
5	14.7338	.3436	98.6941
6	14.6789	.3985	98.2956
7	14.6153	.4621	97.8335
8	14.5416	.5358	97.2976
9	14.4560	.6214	96.6763
10	14.3569	.7205	95.9557
11	14.2419	.8355	95.1202
12	14.1085	.9689	94.1513
13	13.9539	1.1235	93.0278
14	13.7745	1.3029	91.7249
15	13.5666	1.5108	90.2141
16	13.3254	1.7520	88.4621
17	13.0458	2.0316	86.4305
18	12.7216	2.3559	84.0746
19	12.3455	2.7319	81.3428
20	11.9095	3.1679	78.1749
21	11.4039	3.6735	74.5014
22	10.8176	4.2598	70.2415
23	10.1377	4.9398	65.3018
24	9.3492	5.7282	59.5736
25	8.4350	6.6424	52.9311
26	7.3748	7.7026	45.2285
27	6.1454	8.9320	36.2964
28	4.7197	10.3577	25.9388
29	3.0666	12.0109	13.9279
30	1.1495	13.9279	0.0000

MONTHLY PAYMENT AMORTIZATION SCHEDULE PER $100 — 15.00 %

YEARS 2 — MO PAYT 4.8487 — AN CONST 58.19

#	INT	PRIN	BALANCE
1	11.9038	46.2801	53.7199
2	4.4641	53.7199	0.0000

YEARS 3 — MO PAYT 3.4665 — AN CONST 41.60

#	INT	PRIN	BALANCE
1	13.0930	28.5054	71.4946
2	8.5106	33.0878	38.4068
3	3.1916	38.4068	0.0000

YEARS 4 — MO PAYT 2.7831 — AN CONST 33.40

#	INT	PRIN	BALANCE
1	13.6810	19.7159	80.2841
2	10.5116	22.8853	57.3988
3	6.8327	26.5642	30.8346
4	2.5623	30.8346	0.0000

YEARS 5 — MO PAYT 2.3790 — AN CONST 28.55

#	INT	PRIN	BALANCE
1	14.0287	14.5193	85.4807
2	11.6946	16.8533	68.6274
3	8.9854	19.5625	49.0649
4	5.8406	22.7073	26.3576
5	2.1903	26.3576	0.0000

YEARS 6 — MO PAYT 2.1145 — AN CONST 25.38

#	INT	PRIN	BALANCE
1	14.2562	11.1178	88.8822
2	12.4690	12.9050	75.9772
3	10.3944	14.9796	60.9976
4	7.9864	17.3876	43.6100
5	5.1913	20.1828	23.4272
6	1.9468	23.4272	0.0000

YEARS 7 — MO PAYT 1.9297 — AN CONST 23.16

#	INT	PRIN	BALANCE
1	14.4152	8.7409	91.2591
2	13.0101	10.1460	81.1131
3	11.3791	11.7770	69.3361
4	9.4859	13.6702	55.6659
5	7.2883	15.8678	39.7981
6	4.7375	18.4186	21.3795
7	1.7766	21.3795	0.0000

YEARS 8 — MO PAYT 1.7945 — AN CONST 21.54

#	INT	PRIN	BALANCE
1	14.5315	7.0030	92.9970
2	13.4057	8.1287	84.8683
3	12.0990	9.4355	75.4328
4	10.5822	10.9523	64.4805
5	8.8216	12.7129	51.7676
6	6.7779	14.7566	37.0110
7	4.4057	17.1288	19.8823
8	1.6522	19.8823	0.0000

YEARS 9 — MO PAYT 1.6924 — AN CONST 20.31

#	INT	PRIN	BALANCE
1	14.6193	5.6899	94.3101
2	13.7047	6.6045	87.7056
3	12.6430	7.6662	80.0394
4	11.4106	8.8986	71.1408
5	9.9801	10.3291	60.8117
6	8.3196	11.9896	48.8221
7	6.3923	13.9169	34.9052
8	4.1551	16.1541	18.7510
9	1.5582	18.7510	0.0000

YEARS 10 — MO PAYT 1.6133 — AN CONST 19.37

#	INT	PRIN	BALANCE
1	14.6874	4.6728	95.3272
2	13.9362	5.4240	89.9032
3	13.0643	6.2959	83.6073
4	12.0522	7.3080	76.2993
5	10.8774	8.4828	67.8165
6	9.5137	9.8465	57.9700
7	7.9309	11.4293	46.5407
8	6.0936	13.2666	33.2741
9	3.9609	15.3993	17.8748
10	1.4854	17.8748	0.0000

YEARS 11 — MO PAYT 1.5509 — AN CONST 18.62

#	INT	PRIN	BALANCE
1	14.7411	3.8699	96.1301
2	14.1190	4.4920	91.6381
3	13.3969	5.2141	86.4241
4	12.5587	6.0523	80.3718
5	11.5858	7.0252	73.3466
6	10.4565	8.1545	65.1921
7	9.1456	9.4654	55.7267
8	7.6240	10.9870	44.7397
9	5.8578	12.7532	31.9864
10	3.8076	14.8034	17.1831
11	1.4279	17.1831	0.0000

YEARS 12 — MO PAYT 1.5009 — AN CONST 18.02

#	INT	PRIN	BALANCE
1	14.7842	3.2264	96.7736
2	14.2655	3.7450	93.0286
3	13.6635	4.3470	88.6816
4	12.9647	5.0459	83.6357
5	12.1535	5.8570	77.7787
6	11.2120	6.7985	70.9802
7	10.1191	7.8914	63.0887
8	8.8505	9.1600	53.9287
9	7.3780	10.6325	43.2962
10	5.6688	12.3418	30.9544
11	3.6848	14.3258	16.6287
12	1.3818	16.6287	0.0000

YEARS 13 — MO PAYT 1.4603 — AN CONST 17.53

#	INT	PRIN	BALANCE
1	14.8191	2.7044	97.2956
2	14.3843	3.1391	94.1565
3	13.8797	3.6437	90.5128
4	13.2940	4.2295	86.2833
5	12.6141	4.9094	81.3739
6	11.8248	5.6986	75.6753
7	10.9088	6.6147	69.0606
8	9.8454	7.6780	61.3826
9	8.6112	8.9123	52.4703
10	7.1785	10.3450	42.1253
11	5.5155	12.0080	30.1173
12	3.5851	13.9383	16.1790
13	1.3445	16.1790	0.0000

YEARS 14 — MO PAYT 1.4270 — AN CONST 17.13

#	INT	PRIN	BALANCE
1	14.8477	2.2768	97.7232
2	14.4817	2.6428	95.0804
3	14.0568	3.0676	92.0128
4	13.5637	3.5608	88.4520
5	12.9913	4.1332	84.3188
6	12.3269	4.7976	79.5212
7	11.5556	5.5689	73.9523
8	10.6604	6.4641	67.4882
9	9.6213	7.5032	59.9850
10	8.4151	8.7094	51.2757
11	7.0150	10.1095	41.1662
12	5.3899	11.7346	29.4316
13	3.5035	13.6210	15.8106
14	1.3139	15.8106	0.0000

YEARS 15 — MO PAYT 1.3996 — AN CONST 16.80

#	INT	PRIN	BALANCE
1	14.8713	1.9237	98.0763
2	14.5621	2.2330	95.8433
3	14.2031	2.5920	93.2513
4	13.7864	3.0086	90.2427
5	13.3028	3.4923	86.7504
6	12.7414	4.0537	82.6967
7	12.0897	4.7053	77.9914
8	11.3333	5.4617	72.5297
9	10.4553	6.3397	66.1899
10	9.4362	7.3589	58.8311
11	8.2532	8.5418	50.2892
12	6.8801	9.9150	40.3743
13	5.2862	11.5089	28.8654
14	3.4361	13.3590	15.5065
15	1.2886	15.5065	0.0000

YEARS 16 — MO PAYT 1.3768 — AN CONST 16.53

#	INT	PRIN	BALANCE
1	14.8909	1.6303	98.3697
2	14.6289	1.8924	96.4773
3	14.3246	2.1966	94.2807
4	13.9715	2.5497	91.7310
5	13.5617	2.9596	88.7714
6	13.0859	3.4353	85.3361
7	12.5336	3.9876	81.3485
8	11.8926	4.6286	76.7199
9	11.1486	5.3727	71.3472
10	10.2849	6.2364	65.1108
11	9.2823	7.2389	57.8719
12	8.1187	8.4026	49.4694
13	6.7679	9.7533	39.7160
14	5.2000	11.3212	28.3948
15	3.3801	13.1412	15.2537
16	1.2676	15.2537	0.0000

YEARS 17 — MO PAYT 1.3577 — AN CONST 16.30

#	INT	PRIN	BALANCE
1	14.9073	1.3851	98.6149
2	14.6847	1.6077	97.0072
3	14.4262	1.8662	95.1410
4	14.1262	2.1662	92.9749
5	13.7780	2.5144	90.4605
6	13.3738	2.9186	87.5419
7	12.9046	3.3878	84.1541
8	12.3600	3.9324	80.2218
9	11.7279	4.5645	75.6573
10	10.9941	5.2983	70.3590
11	10.1424	6.1500	64.2090
12	9.1538	7.1386	57.0704
13	8.0062	8.2862	48.7842
14	6.6742	9.6182	39.1659
15	5.1280	11.1644	28.0015
16	3.3333	12.9591	15.0424
17	1.2500	15.0424	0.0000

YEARS 18 — MO PAYT 1.3417 — AN CONST 16.11

#	INT	PRIN	BALANCE
1	14.9211	1.1792	98.8208
2	14.7316	1.3687	97.4521
3	14.5115	1.5888	95.8633
4	14.2561	1.8442	94.0192
5	13.9597	2.1406	91.8785
6	13.6156	2.4847	89.3938
7	13.2161	2.8842	86.5096
8	12.7525	3.3478	83.1618
9	12.2143	3.8860	79.2758
10	11.5896	4.5107	74.7651
11	10.8645	5.2358	69.5293
12	10.0228	6.0775	63.4519
13	9.0458	7.0545	56.3974
14	7.9118	8.1885	48.2089
15	6.5955	9.5048	38.7041
16	5.0675	11.0328	27.6713
17	3.2940	12.8063	14.8650
18	1.2353	14.8650	0.0000

YEARS 19 — MO PAYT 1.3282 — AN CONST 15.94

#	INT	PRIN	BALANCE
1	14.9327	1.0057	98.9943
2	14.7711	1.1673	97.8270
3	14.5834	1.3550	96.4721
4	14.3656	1.5728	94.8993
5	14.1128	1.8256	93.0737
6	13.8193	2.1191	90.9546
7	13.4786	2.4598	88.4948
8	13.0832	2.8552	85.6396
9	12.6242	3.3141	82.3255
10	12.0915	3.8469	78.4786
11	11.4731	4.4653	74.0133
12	10.7552	5.1831	68.8301
13	9.9220	6.0164	62.8138
14	8.9549	6.9835	55.8303
15	7.8322	8.1061	47.7241
16	6.5291	9.4092	38.3149
17	5.0166	10.9218	27.3931
18	3.2608	12.6775	14.7155
19	1.2229	14.7155	0.0000

YEARS 20 — MO PAYT 1.3168 — AN CONST 15.81

#	INT	PRIN	BALANCE
1	14.9425	.8589	99.1411
2	14.8045	.9970	98.1404
3	14.6442	1.1573	96.9868
4	14.4581	1.3433	95.6434
5	14.2422	1.5593	94.0841
6	13.9915	1.8099	92.2742
7	13.7006	2.1009	90.1733
8	13.3629	2.4386	87.7347
9	12.9708	2.8306	84.9040
10	12.5158	3.2857	81.6184
11	11.9876	3.8139	77.8045
12	11.3745	4.4270	73.3775
13	10.6629	5.1386	68.2389
14	9.8368	5.9647	62.2742
15	8.8780	6.9235	55.3507
16	7.7650	8.0365	47.3142
17	6.4731	9.3284	37.9858
18	4.9735	10.8280	27.1578
19	3.2328	12.5687	14.5891
20	1.2124	14.5891	0.0000

YEARS 21 — MO PAYT 1.3071 — AN CONST 15.69

#	INT	PRIN	BALANCE
1	14.9509	.7345	99.2655
2	14.8328	.8526	98.4128
3	14.6957	.9897	97.4231

#	INT	PRIN	BALANCE
4	14.5366	1.1488	96.2743
5	14.3519	1.3335	94.9409
6	14.1376	1.5478	93.3931
7	13.8888	1.7966	91.5964
8	13.5999	2.0855	89.5109
9	13.2647	2.4207	87.0902
10	12.8756	2.8098	84.2804
11	12.4239	3.2615	81.0188
12	11.8996	3.7859	77.2330
13	11.2910	4.3944	72.8385
14	10.5845	5.1009	67.7377
15	9.7645	5.9209	61.8168
16	8.8127	6.8727	54.9441
17	7.7079	7.9775	46.9667
18	6.4255	9.2599	37.7068
19	4.9369	10.7485	26.9583
20	3.2091	12.4763	14.4820
21	1.2034	14.4820	0.0000

YEARS 22	MO PAYT 1.2989	AN CONST 15.59	
#	INT	PRIN	BALANCE
1	14.9579	.6288	99.3712
2	14.8568	.7299	98.6412
3	14.7395	.8473	97.7940
4	14.6033	.9835	96.8105
5	14.4452	1.1416	95.6689
6	14.2617	1.3251	94.3439
7	14.0487	1.5381	92.8058
8	13.8014	1.7853	91.0204
9	13.5144	2.0723	88.9481
10	13.1813	2.4055	86.5426
11	12.7946	2.7922	83.7504
12	12.3457	3.2410	80.5094
13	11.8247	3.7620	76.7473
14	11.2200	4.3668	72.3805
15	10.5180	5.0688	67.3117
16	9.7031	5.8836	61.4281
17	8.7573	6.8295	54.5986
18	7.6595	7.9273	46.6713
19	6.3851	9.2017	37.4696
20	4.9059	10.6809	26.7888
21	3.1889	12.3979	14.3909
22	1.1959	14.3909	0.0000

YEARS 23	MO PAYT 1.2919	AN CONST 15.51	
#	INT	PRIN	BALANCE
1	14.9640	.5388	99.4612
2	14.8773	.6255	98.8357
3	14.7768	.7260	98.1097
4	14.6601	.8427	97.2670
5	14.5246	.9782	96.2889
6	14.3674	1.1354	95.1534
7	14.1848	1.3179	93.8355
8	13.9730	1.5298	92.3057
9	13.7271	1.7757	90.5300
10	13.4416	2.0612	88.4688
11	13.1103	2.3925	86.0763
12	12.7256	2.7771	83.2991
13	12.2792	3.2236	80.0756
14	11.7610	3.7418	76.3338
15	11.1595	4.3433	71.9905
16	10.4613	5.0415	66.9490
17	9.6509	5.8519	61.0971
18	8.7101	6.7927	54.3044
19	7.6182	7.8846	46.4198
20	6.3507	9.1521	37.2677
21	4.8795	10.6233	26.6444
22	3.1717	12.3311	14.3133
23	1.1894	14.3133	0.0000

YEARS 24	MO PAYT 1.2859	AN CONST 15.44	
#	INT	PRIN	BALANCE
1	14.9691	.4621	99.5379
2	14.8948	.5363	99.0016
3	14.8086	.6226	98.3790
4	14.7085	.7226	97.6564
5	14.5923	.8388	96.8176
6	14.4575	.9737	95.8439
7	14.3010	1.1302	94.7138
8	14.1193	1.3118	93.4019
9	13.9084	1.5227	91.8792
10	13.6636	1.7675	90.1117
11	13.3795	2.0517	88.0600
12	13.0497	2.3815	85.6785
13	12.6668	2.7643	82.9142
14	12.2225	3.2087	79.7056
15	11.7067	3.7245	75.9811
16	11.1079	4.3232	71.6579
17	10.4130	5.0182	66.6397
18	9.6063	5.8249	60.8148
19	8.6699	6.7613	54.0535
20	7.5830	7.8482	46.2053
21	6.3214	9.1098	37.0955
22	4.8569	10.5742	26.5213
23	3.1571	12.2741	14.2472
24	1.1839	14.2472	0.0000

YEARS 25	MO PAYT 1.2808	AN CONST 15.37	
#	INT	PRIN	BALANCE
1	14.9735	.3965	99.6035
2	14.9097	.4602	99.1433
3	14.8358	.5342	98.6091
4	14.7499	.6201	97.9890
5	14.6502	.7198	97.2692
6	14.5345	.8355	96.4337
7	14.4002	.9698	95.4639
8	14.2443	1.1257	94.3382
9	14.0633	1.3066	93.0316
10	13.8533	1.5167	91.5149
11	13.6095	1.7605	89.7544
12	13.3264	2.0435	87.7109
13	12.9979	2.3720	85.3388
14	12.6166	2.7533	82.5855
15	12.1740	3.1960	79.3895
16	11.6602	3.7097	75.6798
17	11.0639	4.3061	71.3737
18	10.3717	4.9983	66.3754
19	9.5682	5.8018	60.5736
20	8.6355	6.7345	53.8392
21	7.5529	7.8171	46.0221
22	6.2963	9.0737	36.9485
23	4.8377	10.5323	26.4162
24	3.1445	12.2254	14.1907
25	1.1792	14.1907	0.0000

YEARS 26	MO PAYT 1.2765	AN CONST 15.32	
#	INT	PRIN	BALANCE
1	14.9772	.3404	99.6596
2	14.9225	.3951	99.2644
3	14.8590	.4587	98.8058
4	14.7852	.5324	98.2734
5	14.6997	.6180	97.6554
6	14.6003	.7173	96.9381
7	14.4850	.8326	96.1054
8	14.3512	.9665	95.1389
9	14.1958	1.1219	94.0171
10	14.0154	1.3022	92.7149
11	13.8061	1.5115	91.2034
12	13.5631	1.7545	89.4488
13	13.2811	2.0366	87.4123
14	12.9537	2.3640	85.0483
15	12.5737	2.7440	82.3043
16	12.1326	3.1851	79.1193
17	11.6206	3.6971	75.4222
18	11.0262	4.2914	71.1308
19	10.3364	4.9813	66.1495
20	9.5356	5.7820	60.3674
21	8.6061	6.7115	53.6559
22	7.5272	7.7904	45.8655
23	6.2749	9.0428	36.8227
24	4.8212	10.4965	26.3262
25	3.1338	12.1838	14.1424
26	1.1752	14.1424	0.0000

YEARS 27	MO PAYT 1.2727	AN CONST 15.28	
#	INT	PRIN	BALANCE
1	14.9804	.2924	99.7076
2	14.9334	.3394	99.3682
3	14.8789	.3940	98.9742
4	14.8155	.4573	98.5168
5	14.7420	.5308	97.9860
6	14.6567	.6162	97.3698
7	14.5576	.7152	96.6546
8	14.4427	.8302	95.8244
9	14.3092	.9637	94.8607
10	14.1543	1.1186	93.7422
11	13.9745	1.2984	92.4438
12	13.7667	1.5071	90.9367
13	13.5235	1.7494	89.1873
14	13.2422	2.0306	87.1567
15	12.9158	2.3570	84.7996
16	12.5369	2.7359	82.0637
17	12.0971	3.1758	78.8879
18	11.5866	3.6863	75.2016
19	10.9940	4.2789	70.9228
20	10.3061	4.9667	65.9561
21	9.5077	5.7651	60.1909
22	8.5809	6.6919	53.4990
23	7.5052	7.7677	45.7314
24	6.2565	9.0163	36.7150
25	4.8071	10.4658	26.2492
26	3.1247	12.1482	14.1011
27	1.1718	14.1011	0.0000

YEARS 28	MO PAYT 1.2695	AN CONST 15.24	
#	INT	PRIN	BALANCE
1	14.9832	.2513	99.7487
2	14.9428	.2917	99.4570
3	14.8959	.3386	99.1185
4	14.8415	.3930	98.7255
5	14.7783	.4562	98.2693
6	14.7050	.5295	97.7398
7	14.6198	.6146	97.1252
8	14.5210	.7134	96.4117
9	14.4064	.8281	95.5836
10	14.2732	.9612	94.6224
11	14.1187	1.1158	93.5066
12	13.9393	1.2951	92.2115
13	13.7311	1.5033	90.7082
14	13.4895	1.7450	88.9632
15	13.2090	2.0255	86.9376
16	12.8834	2.3511	84.5865
17	12.5054	2.7291	81.8575
18	12.0667	3.1678	78.6897
19	11.5575	3.6770	75.0127
20	10.9664	4.2681	70.7445
21	10.2802	4.9542	65.7903
22	9.4838	5.7506	60.0397
23	8.5594	6.6751	53.3646
24	7.4863	7.7481	45.6164
25	6.2408	8.9937	36.6227
26	4.7950	10.4395	26.1833
27	3.1168	12.1177	14.0656
28	1.1688	14.0656	0.0000

YEARS 29	MO PAYT 1.2668	AN CONST 15.21	
#	INT	PRIN	BALANCE
1	14.9855	.2160	99.7840
2	14.9508	.2507	99.5332
3	14.9105	.2911	99.2422
4	14.8637	.3378	98.9043
5	14.8094	.3921	98.5122
6	14.7464	.4552	98.0570
7	14.6732	.5284	97.5286
8	14.5883	.6133	96.9154
9	14.4897	.7119	96.2035
10	14.3752	.8263	95.3771
11	14.2424	.9592	94.4180
12	14.0882	1.1134	93.3046
13	13.9092	1.2923	92.0123
14	13.7015	1.5001	90.5122
15	13.4603	1.7412	88.7710
16	13.1804	2.0211	86.7498
17	12.8555	2.3460	84.4038
18	12.4784	2.7232	81.6806
19	12.0406	3.1609	78.5197
20	11.5325	3.6691	74.8506
21	10.9427	4.2589	70.5917
22	10.2580	4.9435	65.6482
23	9.4633	5.7382	59.9100
24	8.5409	6.6607	53.2493
25	7.4702	7.7314	45.5179
26	6.2273	8.9743	36.5436
27	4.7847	10.4169	26.1267
28	3.1101	12.0915	14.0352
29	1.1663	14.0352	0.0000

YEARS 30	MO PAYT 1.2644	AN CONST 15.18	
#	INT	PRIN	BALANCE
1	14.9876	.1858	99.8142
2	14.9577	.2156	99.5986
3	14.9231	.2503	99.3484
4	14.8828	.2905	99.0578
5	14.8361	.3372	98.7206
6	14.7819	.3914	98.3292
7	14.7190	.4543	97.8749
8	14.6459	.5274	97.3475
9	14.5612	.6122	96.7353
10	14.4628	.7106	96.0248
11	14.3485	.8248	95.2000
12	14.2159	.9574	94.2426
13	14.0620	1.1113	93.1313
14	13.8834	1.2899	91.8414
15	13.6760	1.4973	90.3441
16	13.4353	1.7380	88.6061
17	13.1559	2.0174	86.5887
18	12.8316	2.3417	84.2470
19	12.4552	2.7181	81.5289
20	12.0183	3.1551	78.3738
21	11.5111	3.6623	74.7116
22	10.9223	4.2510	70.4606
23	10.2390	4.9343	65.5263
24	9.4458	5.7276	59.7987
25	8.5250	6.6483	53.1504
26	7.4563	7.7170	45.4333
27	6.2157	8.9576	36.4758
28	4.7758	10.3976	26.0782
29	3.1043	12.0690	14.0092
30	1.1642	14.0092	0.0000

YEARS 2 — MO PAYT 4.8963 — AN CONST 58.76

#	INT	PRIN	BALANCE
1	12.7210	46.0348	53.9652
2	4.7905	53.9652	0.0000

YEARS 3 — MO PAYT 3.5157 — AN CONST 42.19

#	INT	PRIN	BALANCE
1	13.9915	28.1969	71.8031
2	9.1340	33.0544	38.7487
3	3.4397	38.7487	0.0000

YEARS 4 — MO PAYT 2.8340 — AN CONST 34.01

#	INT	PRIN	BALANCE
1	14.6189	19.3894	80.6106
2	11.2787	22.7297	57.8809
3	7.3630	26.6453	31.2355
4	2.7728	31.2355	0.0000

YEARS 5 — MO PAYT 2.4318 — AN CONST 29.19

#	INT	PRIN	BALANCE
1	14.9891	14.1926	85.8074
2	12.5441	16.6376	69.1698
3	9.6779	19.5037	49.6661
4	6.3180	22.8637	26.8024
5	2.3793	26.8024	0.0000

YEARS 6 — MO PAYT 2.1692 — AN CONST 26.04

#	INT	PRIN	BALANCE
1	15.2308	10.7995	89.2005
2	13.3703	12.6599	76.5407
3	11.1894	14.8408	61.6999
4	8.6328	17.3974	44.3024
5	5.6357	20.3945	23.9079
6	2.1223	23.9079	0.0000

YEARS 7 — MO PAYT 1.9862 — AN CONST 23.84

#	INT	PRIN	BALANCE
1	15.3992	8.4353	91.5647
2	13.9460	9.8885	81.6762
3	12.2425	11.5920	70.0842
4	10.2455	13.5889	56.4953
5	7.9046	15.9299	40.5654
6	5.1603	18.6742	21.8912
7	1.9433	21.8912	0.0000

YEARS 8 — MO PAYT 1.8529 — AN CONST 22.24

#	INT	PRIN	BALANCE
1	15.5219	6.7127	93.2873
2	14.3655	7.8691	85.4182
3	13.0098	9.2247	76.1935
4	11.4207	10.8138	65.3797
5	9.5578	12.6768	52.7029
6	7.3740	14.8606	37.8423
7	4.8139	17.4206	20.4217
8	1.8128	20.4217	0.0000

YEARS 9 — MO PAYT 1.7525 — AN CONST 21.04

#	INT	PRIN	BALANCE
1	15.6142	5.4161	94.5839
2	14.6812	6.3491	88.2348
3	13.5874	7.4429	80.7919
4	12.3052	8.7251	72.0668
5	10.8021	10.2282	61.8387
6	9.0401	11.9902	49.8485
7	6.9746	14.0557	35.7928
8	4.5532	16.4771	19.3156
9	1.7147	19.3156	0.0000

YEARS 10 — MO PAYT 1.6751 — AN CONST 20.11

#	INT	PRIN	BALANCE
1	15.6854	4.4161	95.5839
2	14.9247	5.1769	90.4070
3	14.0328	6.0687	84.3382
4	12.9874	7.1142	77.2240
5	11.7618	8.3398	68.8843
6	10.3251	9.7765	59.1078
7	8.6409	11.4607	47.6471
8	6.6666	13.4350	34.2121
9	4.3521	15.7495	18.4626
10	1.6389	18.4626	0.0000

YEARS 11 — MO PAYT 1.6143 — AN CONST 19.38

#	INT	PRIN	BALANCE
1	15.7414	3.6304	96.3696
2	15.1160	4.2558	92.1138
3	14.3828	4.9890	87.1248
4	13.5234	5.8484	81.2764
5	12.5159	6.8559	74.4205
6	11.3348	8.0370	66.3835
7	9.9503	9.4215	56.9619
8	8.3272	11.0446	45.9173
9	6.4245	12.9473	32.9701
10	4.1941	15.1777	17.7924
11	1.5794	17.7924	0.0000

YEARS 12 — MO PAYT 1.5658 — AN CONST 18.79

#	INT	PRIN	BALANCE
1	15.7860	3.0039	96.9961
2	15.2686	3.5213	93.4748
3	14.6619	4.1280	89.3468
4	13.9508	4.8391	84.5077
5	13.1172	5.6727	78.8350
6	12.1399	6.6500	72.1850
7	10.9943	7.7956	64.3894
8	9.6514	9.1385	55.2509
9	8.0771	10.7128	44.5380
10	6.2316	12.5583	31.9797
11	4.0681	14.7218	17.2579
12	1.5320	17.2579	0.0000

YEARS 13 — MO PAYT 1.5267 — AN CONST 18.33

#	INT	PRIN	BALANCE
1	15.8220	2.4984	97.5016
2	15.3916	2.9288	94.5728
3	14.8871	3.4334	91.1394
4	14.2956	4.0248	87.1146
5	13.6023	4.7182	82.3964
6	12.7894	5.5310	76.8653
7	11.8366	6.4838	70.3815
8	10.7196	7.6008	62.7807
9	9.4102	8.9102	53.8705
10	7.8753	10.4452	43.4253
11	6.0759	12.2446	31.1807
12	3.9665	14.3540	16.8267
13	1.4937	16.8267	0.0000

YEARS 14 — MO PAYT 1.4948 — AN CONST 17.94

#	INT	PRIN	BALANCE
1	15.8514	2.0868	97.9132
2	15.4919	2.4463	95.4669
3	15.0704	2.8677	92.5992
4	14.5764	3.3617	89.2375
5	13.9973	3.9408	85.2967
6	13.3184	4.6197	80.6769
7	12.5226	5.4156	75.2613
8	11.5896	6.3485	68.9128
9	10.4959	7.4422	61.4706
10	9.2139	8.7243	52.7463
11	7.7109	10.2272	42.5191
12	5.9491	11.9891	30.5300
13	3.8837	14.0544	16.4756
14	1.4625	16.4756	0.0000

YEARS 15 — MO PAYT 1.4687 — AN CONST 17.63

#	INT	PRIN	BALANCE
1	15.8754	1.7490	98.2510
2	15.5741	2.0503	96.2007
3	15.2209	2.4035	93.7972
4	14.8069	2.8175	90.9797
5	14.3215	3.3029	87.6768
6	13.7525	3.8719	83.8048
7	13.0855	4.5389	79.2659
8	12.3035	5.3209	73.9450
9	11.3869	6.2375	67.7075
10	10.3124	7.3120	60.3955
11	9.0527	8.5717	51.8238
12	7.5761	10.0483	41.7754
13	5.8450	11.7794	29.9961
14	3.8158	13.8086	16.1874
15	1.4370	16.1874	0.0000

YEARS 16 — MO PAYT 1.4471 — AN CONST 17.37

#	INT	PRIN	BALANCE
1	15.8953	1.4700	98.5300
2	15.6420	1.7233	96.8067
3	15.3452	2.0201	94.7865
4	14.9972	2.3682	92.4184
5	14.5892	2.7761	89.6423
6	14.1110	3.2544	86.3879
7	13.5503	3.8150	82.5729
8	12.8931	4.4722	78.1007
9	12.1227	5.2427	72.8580
10	11.2195	6.1458	66.7122
11	10.1608	7.2046	59.5076
12	8.9196	8.4457	51.0620
13	7.4647	9.9006	41.1613
14	5.7591	11.6062	29.5551
15	3.7597	13.6056	15.9495
16	1.4158	15.9495	0.0000

YEARS 17 — MO PAYT 1.4292 — AN CONST 17.16

#	INT	PRIN	BALANCE
1	15.9118	1.2385	98.7615
2	15.6984	1.4518	97.3097
3	15.4483	1.7019	95.6078
4	15.1551	1.9951	93.6126
5	14.8114	2.3388	91.2738
6	14.4085	2.7417	88.5321
7	13.9362	3.2141	85.3180
8	13.3825	3.7678	81.5502
9	12.7334	4.4168	77.1334
10	11.9725	5.1777	71.9557
11	11.0806	6.0697	65.8860
12	10.0349	7.1153	58.7707
13	8.8092	8.3411	50.4296
14	7.3722	9.7780	40.6516
15	5.6878	11.4625	29.1891
16	3.7131	13.4371	15.7520
17	1.3983	15.7520	0.0000

YEARS 18 — MO PAYT 1.4142 — AN CONST 16.98

#	INT	PRIN	BALANCE
1	15.9255	1.0454	98.9546
2	15.7454	1.2255	97.7290
3	15.5343	1.4367	96.2924
4	15.2868	1.6841	94.6082
5	14.9967	1.9743	92.6340
6	14.6566	2.3144	90.3196
7	14.2579	2.7131	87.6065
8	13.7905	3.1805	84.4260
9	13.2426	3.7284	80.6977
10	12.6003	4.3707	76.3270
11	11.8474	5.1236	71.2034
12	10.9647	6.0062	65.1972
13	9.9300	7.0409	58.1563
14	8.7171	8.2539	49.9024
15	7.2952	9.6758	40.2266
16	5.6283	11.3426	28.8839
17	3.6743	13.2967	15.5873
18	1.3837	15.5873	0.0000

YEARS 19 — MO PAYT 1.4017 — AN CONST 16.83

#	INT	PRIN	BALANCE
1	15.9370	.8839	99.1161
2	15.7848	1.0362	98.0799
3	15.6063	1.2147	96.8652
4	15.3970	1.4240	95.4412
5	15.1517	1.6693	93.7720
6	14.8641	1.9568	91.8152
7	14.5270	2.2939	89.5212
8	14.1319	2.6891	86.8321
9	13.6686	3.1524	83.6798
10	13.1255	3.6954	79.9844
11	12.4889	4.3320	75.6524
12	11.7427	5.0783	70.5741
13	10.8678	5.9531	64.6209
14	9.8423	6.9787	57.6422
15	8.6400	8.1809	49.4613
16	7.2307	9.5903	39.8710
17	5.5786	11.2424	28.6286
18	3.6418	13.1791	15.4495
19	1.3715	15.4495	0.0000

YEARS 20 — MO PAYT 1.3913 — AN CONST 16.70

#	INT	PRIN	BALANCE
1	15.9467	.7484	99.2516
2	15.8178	.8773	98.3743
3	15.6666	1.0284	97.3459
4	15.4895	1.2056	96.1403
5	15.2818	1.4133	94.7270
6	15.0383	1.6568	93.0702
7	14.7529	1.9422	91.1280
8	14.4183	2.2768	88.8513
9	14.0261	2.6690	86.1823
10	13.5663	3.1288	83.0536
11	13.0273	3.6678	79.3858
12	12.3955	4.2996	75.0862
13	11.6548	5.0403	70.0459
14	10.7865	5.9086	64.1373
15	9.7686	6.9265	57.2108
16	8.5754	8.1197	49.0911
17	7.1766	9.5185	39.5726
18	5.5368	11.1583	28.4144
19	3.6146	13.0805	15.3339
20	1.3612	15.3339	0.0000

YEARS 21 — MO PAYT 1.3824 — AN CONST 16.59

#	INT	PRIN	BALANCE
1	15.9548	.6344	99.3656
2	15.8455	.7436	98.6220
3	15.7174	.8717	97.7503

MONTHLY PAYMENT AMORTIZATION SCHEDULE PER $100

16.00 %

#	INT	PRIN	BALANCE
4	15.5673	1.0219	96.7284
5	15.3912	1.1980	95.5304
6	15.1848	1.4043	94.1261
7	14.9429	1.6463	92.4798
8	14.6593	1.9299	90.5500
9	14.3269	2.2623	88.2877
10	13.9371	2.6520	85.6356
11	13.4803	3.1089	82.5267
12	12.9447	3.6445	78.8822
13	12.3168	4.2723	74.6099
14	11.5808	5.0083	69.6016
15	10.7181	5.8711	63.7304
16	9.7066	6.8825	56.8479
17	8.5210	8.0682	48.7797
18	7.1311	9.4581	39.3216
19	5.5017	11.0875	28.2341
20	3.5917	12.9975	15.2366
21	1.3526	15.2366	0.0000

YEARS 22 — MO PAYT 1.3750 — AN CONST 16.50

#	INT	PRIN	BALANCE
1	15.9617	.5382	99.4618
2	15.8689	.6309	98.8308
3	15.7603	.7396	98.0912
4	15.6328	.8670	97.2242
5	15.4835	1.0164	96.2078
6	15.3084	1.1915	95.0163
7	15.1031	1.3968	93.6195
8	14.8625	1.6374	91.9821
9	14.5804	1.9195	90.0626
10	14.2497	2.2501	87.8125
11	13.8621	2.6378	85.1747
12	13.4077	3.0922	82.0825
13	12.8750	3.6249	78.4577
14	12.2505	4.2493	74.2083
15	11.5185	4.9814	69.2269
16	10.6604	5.8395	63.3874
17	9.6544	6.8455	56.5419
18	8.4751	8.0248	48.5172
19	7.0927	9.4072	39.1100
20	5.4721	11.0278	28.0822
21	3.5723	12.9276	15.1546
22	1.3453	15.1546	0.0000

YEARS 23 — MO PAYT 1.3687 — AN CONST 16.43

#	INT	PRIN	BALANCE
1	15.9674	.4570	99.5430
2	15.8887	.5358	99.0072
3	15.7964	.6281	98.3792
4	15.6882	.7362	97.6429
5	15.5614	.8631	96.7798
6	15.4127	1.0118	95.7681
7	15.2384	1.1861	94.5820
8	15.0341	1.3904	93.1916
9	14.7946	1.6299	91.5617
10	14.5138	1.9107	89.6510
11	14.1846	2.2399	87.4112
12	13.7988	2.6257	84.7854
13	13.3464	3.0781	81.7074
14	12.8162	3.6083	78.0991
15	12.1946	4.2299	73.8692
16	11.4659	4.9586	68.9106
17	10.6116	5.8128	63.0977
18	9.6103	6.8142	56.2835
19	8.4364	7.9881	48.2954
20	7.0603	9.3642	38.9312
21	5.4471	10.9774	27.9538
22	3.5560	12.8685	15.0853
23	1.3391	15.0853	0.0000

YEARS 24 — MO PAYT 1.3634 — AN CONST 16.37

#	INT	PRIN	BALANCE
1	15.9723	.3883	99.6117
2	15.9054	.4553	99.1564
3	15.8270	.5337	98.6227
4	15.7351	.6256	97.9971
5	15.6273	.7334	97.2637
6	15.5010	.8597	96.4040
7	15.3529	1.0078	95.3962
8	15.1792	1.1815	94.2147
9	14.9757	1.3850	92.8297
10	14.7371	1.6236	91.2061
11	14.4574	1.9033	89.3028
12	14.1295	2.2312	87.0717
13	13.7452	2.6155	84.4562
14	13.2946	3.0661	81.3901
15	12.7664	3.5943	77.7958
16	12.1472	4.2135	73.5823
17	11.4213	4.9393	68.6429
18	10.5704	5.7903	62.8527
19	9.5729	6.7877	56.0649
20	8.4036	7.9571	48.1079
21	7.0328	9.3278	38.7800
22	5.4259	10.9348	27.8453
23	3.5422	12.8185	15.0268
24	1.3339	15.0268	0.0000

YEARS 25 — MO PAYT 1.3589 — AN CONST 16.31

#	INT	PRIN	BALANCE
1	15.9765	.3302	99.6698
2	15.9196	.3871	99.2827
3	15.8529	.4537	98.8290
4	15.7748	.5319	98.2971
5	15.6831	.6235	97.6735
6	15.5757	.7310	96.9426
7	15.4498	.8569	96.0857
8	15.3022	1.0045	95.0812
9	15.1291	1.1776	93.9036
10	14.9263	1.3804	92.5232
11	14.6884	1.6182	90.9050
12	14.4097	1.8970	89.0080
13	14.0829	2.2238	86.7842
14	13.6998	2.6069	84.1773
15	13.2507	3.0560	81.1213
16	12.7242	3.5824	77.5389
17	12.1071	4.1996	73.3393
18	11.3836	4.9230	68.4163
19	10.5355	5.7711	62.6452
20	9.5413	6.7653	55.8798
21	8.3759	7.9308	47.9490
22	7.0096	9.2970	38.6520
23	5.4080	10.8987	27.7533
24	3.5305	12.7762	14.9771
25	1.3295	14.9771	0.0000

YEARS 26 — MO PAYT 1.3551 — AN CONST 16.27

#	INT	PRIN	BALANCE
1	15.9800	.2809	99.7191
2	15.9316	.3293	99.3899
3	15.8749	.3860	99.0039
4	15.8084	.4525	98.5514
5	15.7304	.5304	98.0210
6	15.6391	.6218	97.3992
7	15.5320	.7289	96.6703
8	15.4064	.8545	95.8158
9	15.2592	1.0017	94.8141
10	15.0866	1.1742	93.6399
11	14.8843	1.3765	92.2633
12	14.6472	1.6137	90.6497
13	14.3692	1.8917	88.7580
14	14.0433	2.2175	86.5404
15	13.6613	2.5996	83.9409
16	13.2135	3.0474	80.8935
17	12.6885	3.5724	77.3211
18	12.0731	4.1878	73.1333
19	11.3517	4.9092	68.2241
20	10.5059	5.7549	62.4692
21	9.5145	6.7463	55.7229
22	8.3523	7.9085	47.8144
23	6.9899	9.2709	38.5434
24	5.3928	10.8680	27.6754
25	3.5206	12.7403	14.9351
26	1.3258	14.9351	0.0000

YEARS 27 — MO PAYT 1.3518 — AN CONST 16.23

#	INT	PRIN	BALANCE
1	15.9830	.2390	99.7610
2	15.9418	.2802	99.4808
3	15.8935	.3285	99.1523
4	15.8369	.3851	98.7672
5	15.7706	.4514	98.3159
6	15.6928	.5292	97.7867
7	15.6017	.6203	97.1664
8	15.4948	.7272	96.4392
9	15.3696	.8524	95.5868
10	15.2227	.9993	94.5875
11	15.0506	1.1714	93.4160
12	14.8488	1.3732	92.0428
13	14.6122	1.6098	90.4330
14	14.3349	1.8871	88.5458
15	14.0098	2.2122	86.3336
16	13.6287	2.5933	83.7402
17	13.1819	3.0401	80.7001
18	12.6582	3.5638	77.1363
19	12.0442	4.1778	72.9585
20	11.3245	4.8975	68.0611
21	10.4808	5.7412	62.3199
22	9.4918	6.7302	55.5897
23	8.3324	7.8896	47.7001
24	6.9732	9.2488	38.4513
25	5.3799	10.8421	27.6092
26	3.5122	12.7098	14.8994
27	1.3226	14.8994	0.0000

YEARS 28 — MO PAYT 1.3491 — AN CONST 16.19

#	INT	PRIN	BALANCE
1	15.9855	.2035	99.7965
2	15.9505	.2385	99.5580
3	15.9094	.2796	99.2783
4	15.8612	.3278	98.9505
5	15.8047	.3843	98.5663
6	15.7385	.4505	98.1158
7	15.6609	.5281	97.5877
8	15.5699	.6190	96.9687
9	15.4633	.7257	96.2430
10	15.3383	.8507	95.3923
11	15.1917	.9973	94.3950
12	15.0199	1.1691	93.2260
13	14.8185	1.3705	91.8555
14	14.5824	1.6065	90.2490
15	14.3057	1.8833	88.3657
16	13.9812	2.2077	86.1579
17	13.6009	2.5881	83.5698
18	13.1551	3.0339	80.5359
19	12.6324	3.5566	76.9794
20	12.0197	4.1693	72.8101
21	11.3015	4.8875	67.9226
22	10.4595	5.7295	62.1931
23	9.4725	6.7165	55.4766
24	8.3154	7.8736	47.6030
25	6.9590	9.2300	38.3730
26	5.3690	10.8200	27.5530
27	3.5050	12.6840	14.8691
28	1.3199	14.8691	0.0000

YEARS 29 — MO PAYT 1.3467 — AN CONST 16.17

#	INT	PRIN	BALANCE
1	15.9877	.1733	99.8267
2	15.9578	.2031	99.6236
3	15.9228	.2381	99.3855
4	15.8818	.2791	99.1063
5	15.8337	.3272	98.7791
6	15.7773	.3836	98.3955
7	15.7112	.4497	97.9458
8	15.6338	.5272	97.4186
9	15.5430	.6180	96.8006
10	15.4365	.7244	96.0762
11	15.3117	.8492	95.2270
12	15.1654	.9955	94.2314
13	14.9939	1.1670	93.0644
14	14.7929	1.3681	91.6963
15	14.5572	1.6038	90.0926
16	14.2809	1.8800	88.2125
17	13.9570	2.2039	86.0086
18	13.5774	2.5836	83.4250
19	13.1323	3.0287	80.3964
20	12.6105	3.5504	76.8460
21	11.9989	4.1620	72.6839
22	11.2819	4.8790	67.8049
23	10.4414	5.7196	62.0853
24	9.4561	6.7049	55.3804
25	8.3010	7.8599	47.5205
26	6.9470	9.2140	38.3066
27	5.3597	10.8013	27.5053
28	3.4989	12.6620	14.8433
29	1.3176	14.8433	0.0000

YEARS 30 — MO PAYT 1.3448 — AN CONST 16.14

#	INT	PRIN	BALANCE
1	15.9895	.1476	99.8524
2	15.9641	.1730	99.6794
3	15.9343	.2028	99.4765
4	15.8993	.2378	99.2388
5	15.8583	.2787	98.9600
6	15.8103	.3268	98.6333
7	15.7540	.3830	98.2502
8	15.6881	.4490	97.8012
9	15.6107	.5264	97.2748
10	15.5200	.6171	96.6578
11	15.4137	.7234	95.9344
12	15.2891	.8480	95.0864
13	15.1430	.9941	94.0924
14	14.9718	1.1653	92.9271
15	14.7710	1.3661	91.5610
16	14.5357	1.6014	89.9596
17	14.2598	1.8773	88.0823
18	13.9364	2.2007	85.8817
19	13.5573	2.5798	83.3019
20	13.1129	3.0242	80.2777
21	12.5919	3.5452	76.7325
22	11.9812	4.1559	72.5766
23	11.2652	4.8718	67.7048
24	10.4260	5.7111	61.9937
25	9.4421	6.6950	55.2987
26	8.2888	7.8483	47.4504
27	6.9367	9.2004	38.2500
28	5.3518	10.7853	27.4647
29	3.4938	12.6433	14.8214
30	1.3157	14.8214	0.0000

YEARS 2 — MO PAYT 4.9442 — AN CONST 59.34

#	INT	PRIN	BALANCE
1	13.5409	45.7898	54.2102
2	5.1205	54.2102	0.0000

YEARS 3 — MO PAYT 3.5653 — AN CONST 42.79

#	INT	PRIN	BALANCE
1	14.8931	27.8902	72.1098
2	9.7643	33.0190	39.0909
3	3.6924	39.0909	0.0000

YEARS 4 — MO PAYT 2.8855 — AN CONST 34.63

#	INT	PRIN	BALANCE
1	15.5597	19.0664	80.9336
2	12.0535	22.5725	58.3611
3	7.9026	26.7234	31.6377
4	2.9884	31.6377	0.0000

YEARS 5 — MO PAYT 2.4853 — AN CONST 29.83

#	INT	PRIN	BALANCE
1	15.9521	13.8709	86.1291
2	13.4014	16.4217	69.7074
3	10.3816	19.4415	50.2659
4	6.8064	23.0166	27.2492
5	2.5739	27.2492	0.0000

YEARS 6 — MO PAYT 2.2246 — AN CONST 26.70

#	INT	PRIN	BALANCE
1	16.2077	10.4876	89.5124
2	14.2791	12.4162	77.0962
3	11.9959	14.6994	62.3967
4	9.2928	17.4026	44.9942
5	6.0926	20.6027	24.3914
6	2.3039	24.3914	0.0000

YEARS 7 — MO PAYT 2.0436 — AN CONST 24.53

#	INT	PRIN	BALANCE
1	16.3853	8.1377	91.8623
2	14.8888	9.6342	82.2281
3	13.1172	11.4058	70.8223
4	11.0197	13.5033	57.3191
5	8.5366	15.9864	41.3327
6	5.5968	18.9262	22.4065
7	2.1165	22.4065	0.0000

YEARS 8 — MO PAYT 1.9121 — AN CONST 22.95

#	INT	PRIN	BALANCE
1	16.5141	6.4316	93.5684
2	15.3314	7.6143	85.9541
3	13.9312	9.0145	76.9395
4	12.2735	10.6722	66.2673
5	10.3110	12.6348	53.6325
6	7.9875	14.9582	38.6743
7	5.2368	17.7089	20.9654
8	1.9803	20.9654	0.0000

YEARS 9 — MO PAYT 1.8136 — AN CONST 21.77

#	INT	PRIN	BALANCE
1	16.6108	5.1527	94.8473
2	15.6632	6.1002	88.7471
3	14.5414	7.2220	81.5251
4	13.2134	8.5500	72.9751
5	11.6411	10.1223	62.8528
6	9.7797	11.9837	50.8690
7	7.5760	14.1875	36.6815
8	4.9670	16.7964	19.8851
9	1.8783	19.8851	0.0000

YEARS 10 — MO PAYT 1.7380 — AN CONST 20.86

#	INT	PRIN	BALANCE
1	16.6849	4.1708	95.8292
2	15.9180	4.9378	90.8914
3	15.0099	5.8458	85.0457
4	13.9349	6.9208	78.1249
5	12.6623	8.1934	69.9314
6	11.1556	9.7002	60.2313
7	9.3718	11.4839	48.7474
8	7.2600	13.5957	35.1516
9	4.7598	16.0959	19.0558
10	1.8000	19.0558	0.0000

YEARS 11 — MO PAYT 1.6788 — AN CONST 20.15

#	INT	PRIN	BALANCE
1	16.7429	3.4031	96.5969
2	16.1171	4.0289	92.5681
3	15.3763	4.7697	87.7983
4	14.4991	5.6468	82.1515
5	13.4607	6.6853	75.4662
6	12.2314	7.9146	67.5516
7	10.7759	9.3700	58.1816
8	9.0529	11.0931	47.0885
9	7.0129	13.1331	33.9554
10	4.5979	15.5481	18.4073
11	1.7387	18.4073	0.0000

YEARS 12 — MO PAYT 1.6319 — AN CONST 19.59

#	INT	PRIN	BALANCE
1	16.7889	2.7942	97.2058
2	16.2751	3.3080	93.8979
3	15.6668	3.9163	89.9816
4	14.9466	4.6365	85.3451
5	14.0940	5.4891	79.8561
6	13.0846	6.4985	73.3576
7	11.8896	7.6935	65.6641
8	10.4748	9.1082	56.5559
9	8.7999	10.7832	45.7727
10	6.8170	12.7661	33.0066
11	4.4694	15.1137	17.8930
12	1.6901	17.8930	0.0000

YEARS 13 — MO PAYT 1.5943 — AN CONST 19.14

#	INT	PRIN	BALANCE
1	16.8258	2.3057	97.6943
2	16.4018	2.7297	94.9645
3	15.8998	3.2317	91.7328
4	15.3056	3.8260	87.9069
5	14.6020	4.5296	83.3773
6	13.7690	5.3625	78.0148
7	12.7829	6.3486	71.6662
8	11.6155	7.5161	64.1501
9	10.2333	8.8982	55.2519
10	8.5970	10.5345	44.7173
11	6.6598	12.4717	32.2456
12	4.3663	14.7652	17.4804
13	1.6511	17.4804	0.0000

YEARS 14 — MO PAYT 1.5638 — AN CONST 18.77

#	INT	PRIN	BALANCE
1	16.8557	1.9104	98.0896
2	16.5044	2.2617	95.8279
3	16.0885	2.6776	93.1504
4	15.5961	3.1700	89.9804
5	15.0132	3.7529	86.2275
6	14.3230	4.4430	81.7845
7	13.5060	5.2601	76.5244
8	12.5387	6.2273	70.2971
9	11.3936	7.3725	62.9246
10	10.0378	8.7282	54.1964
11	8.4328	10.3333	43.8631
12	6.5326	12.2335	31.6296
13	4.2829	14.4831	17.1465
14	1.6196	17.1465	0.0000

YEARS 15 — MO PAYT 1.5390 — AN CONST 18.47

#	INT	PRIN	BALANCE
1	16.8800	1.5880	98.4120
2	16.5880	1.8800	96.5319
3	16.2423	2.2258	94.3062
4	15.8330	2.6351	91.6711
5	15.3484	3.1196	88.5515
6	14.7748	3.6933	84.8582
7	14.0956	4.3725	80.4857
8	13.2915	5.1765	75.3092
9	12.3396	6.1284	69.1808
10	11.2126	7.2554	61.9253
11	9.8784	8.5896	53.3357
12	8.2989	10.1692	43.1665
13	6.4288	12.0392	31.1273
14	4.2149	14.2531	16.8742
15	1.5939	16.8742	0.0000

YEARS 16 — MO PAYT 1.5186 — AN CONST 18.23

#	INT	PRIN	BALANCE
1	16.9000	1.3236	98.6764
2	16.6566	1.5670	97.1094
3	16.3685	1.8552	95.2543
4	16.0273	2.1963	93.0580
5	15.6234	2.6002	90.4578
6	15.1453	3.0783	87.3794
7	14.5792	3.6444	83.7350
8	13.9090	4.3146	79.4204
9	13.1156	5.1080	74.3124
10	12.1763	6.0473	68.2651
11	11.0642	7.1594	61.1057
12	9.7477	8.4759	52.6298
13	8.1890	10.0346	42.5952
14	6.3437	11.8799	30.7153
15	4.1591	14.0645	16.6508
16	1.5728	16.6508	0.0000

YEARS 17 — MO PAYT 1.5018 — AN CONST 18.03

#	INT	PRIN	BALANCE
1	16.9165	1.1056	98.8944
2	16.7132	1.3090	97.5854
3	16.4725	1.5497	96.0357
4	16.1875	1.8346	94.2011
5	15.8501	2.1720	92.0291
6	15.4507	2.5714	89.4576
7	14.9778	3.0443	86.4133
8	14.4180	3.6041	82.8092
9	13.7552	4.2669	78.5423
10	12.9706	5.0515	73.4908
11	12.0417	5.9805	67.5103
12	10.9419	7.0802	60.4301
13	9.6399	8.3822	52.0479
14	8.0985	9.9236	42.1242
15	6.2736	11.7485	30.3757
16	4.1131	13.9090	16.4667
17	1.5554	16.4667	0.0000

YEARS 18 — MO PAYT 1.4879 — AN CONST 17.86

#	INT	PRIN	BALANCE
1	16.9301	.9253	99.0747
2	16.7600	1.0954	97.9793
3	16.5585	1.2969	96.6825
4	16.3200	1.5353	95.1471
5	16.0377	1.8177	93.3295
6	15.7034	2.1519	91.1775
7	15.3077	2.5476	88.6299
8	14.8392	3.0161	85.6138
9	14.2846	3.5708	82.0430
10	13.6280	4.2274	77.8156
11	12.8506	5.0048	72.8108
12	11.9302	5.9251	66.8857
13	10.8407	7.0147	59.8710
14	9.5507	8.3047	51.5663
15	8.0235	9.8318	41.7345
16	6.2156	11.6398	30.0946
17	4.0751	13.7803	16.3144
18	1.5410	16.3144	0.0000

YEARS 19 — MO PAYT 1.4764 — AN CONST 17.72

#	INT	PRIN	BALANCE
1	16.9414	.7755	99.2245
2	16.7988	.9181	98.3064
3	16.6300	1.0869	97.2195
4	16.4301	1.2868	95.9327
5	16.1935	1.5234	94.4093
6	15.9133	1.8036	92.6057
7	15.5817	2.1352	90.4705
8	15.1890	2.5279	87.9426
9	14.7242	2.9927	84.9499
10	14.1738	3.5431	81.4068
11	13.5223	4.1946	77.2121
12	12.7509	4.9660	72.2462
13	11.8377	5.8792	66.3670
14	10.7566	6.9603	59.4067
15	9.4766	8.2403	51.1664
16	7.9613	9.7556	41.4108
17	6.1674	11.5496	29.8613
18	4.0435	13.6734	16.1878
19	1.5291	16.1878	0.0000

YEARS 20 — MO PAYT 1.4668 — AN CONST 17.61

#	INT	PRIN	BALANCE
1	16.9508	.6508	99.3492
2	16.8312	.7704	98.5788
3	16.6895	.9121	97.6667
4	16.5218	1.0798	96.5868
5	16.3232	1.2784	95.3084
6	16.0881	1.5135	93.7949
7	15.8098	1.7918	92.0031
8	15.4803	2.1213	89.8817
9	15.0902	2.5114	87.3703
10	14.6283	2.9733	84.3970
11	14.0816	3.5200	80.8770
12	13.4343	4.1673	76.7097
13	12.6679	4.9337	71.7760
14	11.7607	5.8409	65.9351
15	10.6866	6.9150	59.0201
16	9.4150	8.1866	50.8334
17	7.9095	9.6921	41.1413
18	6.1272	11.4744	29.6669
19	4.0172	13.5844	16.0825
20	1.5191	16.0825	0.0000

YEARS 21 — MO PAYT 1.4588 — AN CONST 17.51

#	INT	PRIN	BALANCE
1	16.9587	.5467	99.4533
2	16.8582	.6472	98.8061
3	16.7392	.7662	98.0399

#	INT	PRIN	BALANCE
4	16.5983	.9071	97.1328
5	16.4314	1.0739	96.0588
6	16.2340	1.2714	94.7874
7	16.0001	1.5052	93.2821
8	15.7233	1.7820	91.5001
9	15.3956	2.1097	89.3904
10	15.0077	2.4977	86.8927
11	14.5484	2.9570	83.9356
12	14.0046	3.5008	80.4349
13	13.3608	4.1445	76.2903
14	12.5987	4.9067	71.3836
15	11.6964	5.8090	65.5746
16	10.6282	6.8772	58.6974
17	9.3635	8.1419	50.5555
18	7.8663	9.6391	40.9164
19	6.0937	11.4117	29.5048
20	3.9952	13.5102	15.9946
21	1.5108	15.9946	0.0000

YEARS 22	MO PAYT 1.4521	AN CONST 17.43	
#	INT	PRIN	BALANCE
1	16.9653	.4596	99.5404
2	16.8808	.5442	98.9962
3	16.7807	.6442	98.3520
4	16.6622	.7627	97.5893
5	16.5220	.9030	96.6863
6	16.3559	1.0690	95.6173
7	16.1593	1.2656	94.3517
8	15.9266	1.4983	92.8534
9	15.6511	1.7738	91.0795
10	15.3249	2.1000	88.9795
11	14.9387	2.4862	86.4933
12	14.4815	2.9434	83.5498
13	13.9402	3.4847	80.0652
14	13.2994	4.1255	75.9397
15	12.5408	4.8841	71.0555
16	11.6426	5.7823	65.2732
17	10.5793	6.8456	58.4276
18	9.3205	8.1045	50.3232
19	7.8301	9.5948	40.7283
20	6.0657	11.3592	29.3691
21	3.9768	13.4481	15.9211
22	1.5039	15.9211	0.0000

YEARS 23	MO PAYT 1.4465	AN CONST 17.36	
#	INT	PRIN	BALANCE
1	16.9708	.3867	99.6133
2	16.8997	.4579	99.1554
3	16.8155	.5421	98.6133
4	16.7158	.6417	97.9716
5	16.5978	.7598	97.2118
6	16.4581	.8995	96.3124
7	16.2927	1.0649	95.2475
8	16.0968	1.2607	93.9868
9	15.8650	1.4925	92.4943
10	15.5905	1.7670	90.7273
11	15.2656	2.0919	88.6354
12	14.8809	2.4766	86.1588
13	14.4255	2.9320	83.2267
14	13.8863	3.4712	79.7555
15	13.2480	4.1095	75.6460
16	12.4923	4.8653	70.7807
17	11.5976	5.7599	65.0208
18	10.5384	6.8191	58.2016
19	9.2844	8.0731	50.1285
20	7.7998	9.5577	40.5708
21	6.0423	11.3153	29.2556
22	3.9615	13.3961	15.8595
23	1.4980	15.8595	0.0000

YEARS 24	MO PAYT 1.4418	AN CONST 17.31	
#	INT	PRIN	BALANCE
1	16.9754	.3256	99.6744
2	16.9155	.3855	99.2889
3	16.8446	.4564	98.8325
4	16.7607	.5403	98.2922
5	16.6614	.6397	97.6526
6	16.5437	.7573	96.8953
7	16.4045	.8965	95.9988
8	16.2396	1.0614	94.9374
9	16.0444	1.2566	93.6808
10	15.8133	1.4877	92.1931
11	15.5398	1.7612	90.4319
12	15.2159	2.0851	88.3468
13	14.8325	2.4685	85.8782
14	14.3785	2.9225	82.9557
15	13.8411	3.4599	79.4958
16	13.2049	4.0962	75.3997
17	12.4516	4.8494	70.5502
18	11.5598	5.7412	64.8091
19	10.5041	6.7969	58.0121
20	9.2542	8.0468	49.9653
21	7.7744	9.5266	40.4387
22	6.0226	11.2784	29.1603
23	3.9486	13.3524	15.8078
24	1.4932	15.8078	0.0000

YEARS 25	MO PAYT 1.4378	AN CONST 17.26	
#	INT	PRIN	BALANCE
1	16.9793	.2743	99.7257
2	16.9288	.3247	99.4010
3	16.8691	.3844	99.0166
4	16.7984	.4551	98.5615
5	16.7147	.5388	98.0226
6	16.6157	.6379	97.3847
7	16.4984	.7552	96.6295
8	16.3595	.8941	95.7355
9	16.1951	1.0585	94.6770
10	16.0004	1.2531	93.4238
11	15.7700	1.4836	91.9402
12	15.4972	1.7564	90.1838
13	15.1742	2.0794	88.1044
14	14.7918	2.4618	85.6427
15	14.3391	2.9145	82.7282
16	13.8031	3.4504	79.2778
17	13.1686	4.0849	75.1928
18	12.4175	4.8361	70.3567
19	11.5281	5.7254	64.6313
20	10.4753	6.7783	57.8530
21	9.2288	8.0248	49.8283
22	7.7531	9.5004	40.3278
23	6.0061	11.2475	29.0803
24	3.9377	13.3158	15.7645
25	1.4891	15.7645	0.0000

YEARS 26	MO PAYT 1.4345	AN CONST 17.22	
#	INT	PRIN	BALANCE
1	16.9825	.2311	99.7689
2	16.9400	.2736	99.4952
3	16.8897	.3240	99.1712
4	16.8301	.3835	98.7877
5	16.7596	.4541	98.3336
6	16.6761	.5376	97.7961
7	16.5773	.6364	97.1596
8	16.4602	.7535	96.4062
9	16.3217	.8920	95.5142
10	16.1576	1.0560	94.4581
11	15.9634	1.2502	93.2079
12	15.7335	1.4802	91.7277
13	15.4613	1.7523	89.9754
14	15.1391	2.0746	87.9008
15	14.7576	2.4561	85.4447
16	14.3059	2.9077	82.5370
17	13.7712	3.4424	79.0945
18	13.1382	4.0755	75.0190
19	12.3887	4.8249	70.1941
20	11.5015	5.7122	64.4819
21	10.4511	6.7626	57.7193
22	9.2075	8.0062	49.7131
23	7.7352	9.4785	40.2346
24	5.9922	11.2215	29.0131
25	3.9286	13.2850	15.7281
26	1.4856	15.7281	0.0000

YEARS 27	MO PAYT 1.4317	AN CONST 17.19	
#	INT	PRIN	BALANCE
1	16.9853	.1949	99.8051
2	16.9494	.2307	99.5745
3	16.9070	.2731	99.3013
4	16.8568	.3233	98.9780
5	16.7973	.3828	98.5952
6	16.7270	.4532	98.1420
7	16.6436	.5365	97.6055
8	16.5450	.6352	96.9703
9	16.4281	.7520	96.2183
10	16.2899	.8903	95.3281
11	16.1261	1.0540	94.2741
12	15.9323	1.2478	93.0263
13	15.7029	1.4773	91.5490
14	15.4312	1.7489	89.8001
15	15.1096	2.0705	87.7295
16	14.7288	2.4513	85.2782
17	14.2781	2.9021	82.3761
18	13.7444	3.4357	78.9404
19	13.1126	4.0675	74.8729
20	12.3646	4.8155	70.0573
21	11.4791	5.7011	64.3563
22	10.4307	6.7494	57.6068
23	9.1895	7.9906	49.6162
24	7.7201	9.4600	40.1562
25	5.9805	11.1996	28.9566
26	3.9210	13.2592	15.6974
27	1.4827	15.6974	0.0000

YEARS 28	MO PAYT 1.4293	AN CONST 17.16	
#	INT	PRIN	BALANCE
1	16.9876	.1643	99.8357
2	16.9574	.1945	99.6411
3	16.9216	.2303	99.4108
4	16.8792	.2727	99.1382
5	16.8291	.3228	98.8154
6	16.7697	.3822	98.4332
7	16.6995	.4524	97.9808
8	16.6163	.5356	97.4451
9	16.5178	.6341	96.8110
10	16.4012	.7508	96.0602
11	16.2631	.8888	95.1714
12	16.0996	1.0523	94.1192
13	15.9061	1.2458	92.8734
14	15.6771	1.4748	91.3986
15	15.4059	1.7461	89.6525
16	15.0848	2.0671	87.5854
17	14.7046	2.4473	85.1381
18	14.2546	2.8973	82.2408
19	13.7218	3.4301	78.8107
20	13.0910	4.0609	74.7498
21	12.3443	4.8076	69.9422
22	11.4602	5.6917	64.2505
23	10.4136	6.7384	57.5122
24	9.1744	7.9775	49.5347
25	7.7074	9.4445	40.0902
26	5.9707	11.1812	28.9090
27	3.9145	13.2374	15.6716
28	1.4803	15.6716	0.0000

YEARS 29	MO PAYT 1.4273	AN CONST 17.13	
#	INT	PRIN	BALANCE
1	16.9895	.1386	99.8614
2	16.9640	.1641	99.6973
3	16.9339	.1943	99.5030
4	16.8981	.2300	99.2730
5	16.8558	.2723	99.0008
6	16.8058	.3224	98.6784
7	16.7465	.3816	98.2968
8	16.6763	.4518	97.8450
9	16.5932	.5349	97.3101
10	16.4949	.6333	96.6768
11	16.3784	.7497	95.9271
12	16.2406	.8876	95.0395
13	16.0773	1.0508	93.9887
14	15.8841	1.2440	92.7447
15	15.6553	1.4728	91.2719
16	15.3845	1.7436	89.5282
17	15.0639	2.0643	87.4640
18	14.6843	2.4439	85.0201
19	14.2348	2.8933	82.1268
20	13.7028	3.4253	78.7015
21	13.0729	4.0552	74.6462
22	12.3272	4.8010	69.8453
23	11.4443	5.6838	64.1615
24	10.3991	6.7290	57.4325
25	9.1617	7.9664	49.4660
26	7.6968	9.4314	40.0346
27	5.9624	11.1657	28.8689
28	3.9091	13.2190	15.6499
29	1.4782	15.6499	0.0000

YEARS 30	MO PAYT 1.4257	AN CONST 17.11	
#	INT	PRIN	BALANCE
1	16.9912	.1169	99.8831
2	16.9697	.1384	99.7446
3	16.9442	.1639	99.5807
4	16.9141	.1940	99.3867
5	16.8784	.2297	99.1570
6	16.8361	.2720	98.8850
7	16.7861	.3220	98.5630
8	16.7269	.3812	98.1818
9	16.6568	.4513	97.7305
10	16.5738	.5343	97.1963
11	16.4756	.6325	96.5637
12	16.3593	.7488	95.8149
13	16.2216	.8865	94.9284
14	16.0585	1.0496	93.8788
15	15.8655	1.2426	92.6362
16	15.6370	1.4711	91.1651
17	15.3665	1.7416	89.4235
18	15.0462	2.0619	87.3617
19	14.6671	2.4410	84.9207
20	14.2182	2.8899	82.0308
21	13.6868	3.4213	78.6094
22	13.0576	4.0505	74.5589
23	12.3128	4.7953	69.7636
24	11.4309	5.6772	64.0864
25	10.3870	6.7211	57.3653
26	9.1510	7.9571	49.4082
27	7.6878	9.4204	39.9878
28	5.9554	11.1527	28.8352
29	3.9045	13.2036	15.6316
30	1.4765	15.6316	0.0000

MONTHLY PAYMENT AMORTIZATION SCHEDULE PER $100 — 18.00 %

YEARS 2 — MO PAYT 4.9924 — AN CONST 59.91

#	INT	PRIN	BALANCE
1	14.3637	45.5453	54.4547
2	5.4542	54.4547	0.0000

YEARS 3 — MO PAYT 3.6152 — AN CONST 43.39

#	INT	PRIN	BALANCE
1	15.7976	27.5853	72.4147
2	10.4014	32.9815	39.4332
3	3.9496	39.4332	0.0000

YEARS 4 — MO PAYT 2.9375 — AN CONST 35.25

#	INT	PRIN	BALANCE
1	16.5033	18.7467	81.2533
2	12.8361	22.4139	58.8393
3	8.4515	26.7985	32.0408
4	3.2092	32.0408	0.0000

YEARS 5 — MO PAYT 2.5393 — AN CONST 30.48

#	INT	PRIN	BALANCE
1	16.9178	13.5543	86.4457
2	14.2664	16.2058	70.2400
3	11.0962	19.3759	50.8641
4	7.3059	23.1662	27.6979
5	2.7742	27.6979	0.0000

YEARS 6 — MO PAYT 2.2808 — AN CONST 27.37

#	INT	PRIN	BALANCE
1	17.1870	10.1823	89.8177
2	15.1952	12.1741	77.6435
3	12.8137	14.5556	63.0879
4	9.9664	17.4030	45.6849
5	6.5620	20.8073	24.8776
6	2.4917	24.8776	0.0000

YEARS 7 — MO PAYT 2.1018 — AN CONST 25.23

#	INT	PRIN	BALANCE
1	17.3734	7.8480	92.1520
2	15.8382	9.3832	82.7688
3	14.0027	11.2187	71.5501
4	11.8081	13.4133	58.1368
5	9.1842	16.0372	42.0996
6	6.0470	19.1744	22.9252
7	2.2962	22.9252	0.0000

YEARS 8 — MO PAYT 1.9723 — AN CONST 23.67

#	INT	PRIN	BALANCE
1	17.5082	6.1596	93.8404
2	16.3033	7.3646	86.4758
3	14.8626	8.8052	77.6705
4	13.1402	10.5277	67.1429
5	11.0808	12.5871	54.5558
6	8.6185	15.0494	39.5064
7	5.6746	17.9933	21.5131
8	2.1548	21.5131	0.0000

YEARS 9 — MO PAYT 1.8757 — AN CONST 22.51

#	INT	PRIN	BALANCE
1	17.6088	4.8994	95.1006
2	16.6504	5.8579	89.2427
3	15.5045	7.0038	82.2389
4	14.1344	8.3738	73.8651
5	12.4964	10.0119	63.8532
6	10.5379	11.9704	51.8828
7	8.1962	14.3120	37.5708
8	5.3965	17.1117	20.4591
9	2.0492	20.4591	0.0000

YEARS 10 — MO PAYT 1.8019 — AN CONST 21.63

#	INT	PRIN	BALANCE
1	17.6857	3.9365	96.0635
2	16.9157	4.7066	91.3569
3	15.9950	5.6273	85.7297
4	14.8942	6.7281	79.0016
5	13.5780	8.0442	70.9574
6	12.0045	9.6178	61.3396
7	10.1230	11.4992	49.8405
8	7.8736	13.7486	36.0918
9	5.1841	16.4381	19.6537
10	1.9685	19.6537	0.0000

YEARS 11 — MO PAYT 1.7444 — AN CONST 20.94

#	INT	PRIN	BALANCE
1	17.7455	3.1875	96.8125
2	17.1220	3.8110	93.0015
3	16.3765	4.5565	88.4449
4	15.4851	5.4479	82.9970
5	14.4194	6.5136	76.4834
6	13.1452	7.7878	68.6956
7	11.6218	9.3112	59.3844
8	9.8004	11.1326	48.2518
9	7.6226	13.3104	34.9414
10	5.0189	15.9142	19.0272
11	1.9058	19.0272	0.0000

YEARS 12 — MO PAYT 1.6991 — AN CONST 20.39

#	INT	PRIN	BALANCE
1	17.7927	2.5968	97.4032
2	17.2847	3.1047	94.2985
3	16.6774	3.7121	90.5864
4	15.9512	4.4382	86.1482
5	15.0830	5.3064	80.8418
6	14.0450	6.3445	74.4973
7	12.8039	7.5855	66.9118
8	11.3200	9.0694	57.8424
9	9.5459	10.8436	46.9988
10	7.4247	12.9648	34.0341
11	4.8885	15.5009	18.5332
12	1.8563	18.5332	0.0000

YEARS 13 — MO PAYT 1.6630 — AN CONST 19.96

#	INT	PRIN	BALANCE
1	17.8303	2.1257	97.8743
2	17.4145	2.5416	95.3327
3	16.9173	3.0387	92.2940
4	16.3228	3.6332	88.6608
5	15.6121	4.3439	84.3169
6	14.7624	5.1936	79.1233
7	13.7464	6.2096	72.9137
8	12.5317	7.4243	65.4894
9	11.0794	8.8766	56.6128
10	9.3430	10.6131	45.9997
11	7.2668	12.6892	33.3106
12	4.7846	15.1714	18.1392
13	1.8168	18.1392	0.0000

YEARS 14 — MO PAYT 1.6340 — AN CONST 19.61

#	INT	PRIN	BALANCE
1	17.8605	1.7469	98.2531
2	17.5188	2.0886	96.1645
3	17.1102	2.4972	93.6674
4	16.6218	2.9857	90.6817
5	16.0377	3.5697	87.1120
6	15.3394	4.2680	82.8440
7	14.5045	5.1029	77.7411
8	13.5063	6.1011	71.6400
9	12.3128	7.2946	64.3454
10	10.8858	8.7216	55.6238
11	9.1797	10.4277	45.1962
12	7.1399	12.4675	32.7287
13	4.7010	14.9064	17.8223
14	1.7851	17.8223	0.0000

YEARS 15 — MO PAYT 1.6104 — AN CONST 19.33

#	INT	PRIN	BALANCE
1	17.8850	1.4400	98.5600
2	17.6033	1.7217	96.8383
3	17.2665	2.0585	94.7797
4	16.8639	2.4612	92.3185
5	16.3824	2.9427	89.3759
6	15.8068	3.5183	85.8576
7	15.1185	4.2065	81.6510
8	14.2956	5.0294	76.6216
9	13.3118	6.0133	70.6084
10	12.1355	7.1896	63.4188
11	10.7291	8.5960	54.8228
12	9.0476	10.2775	44.5453
13	7.0371	12.2880	32.2574
14	4.6333	14.6917	17.5657
15	1.7594	17.5657	0.0000

YEARS 16 — MO PAYT 1.5913 — AN CONST 19.10

#	INT	PRIN	BALANCE
1	17.9050	1.1901	98.8099
2	17.6722	1.4229	97.3870
3	17.3938	1.7012	95.6858
4	17.0610	2.0340	93.6518
5	16.6632	2.4319	91.2199
6	16.1874	2.9076	88.3122
7	15.6186	3.4764	84.8358
8	14.9386	4.1565	80.6793
9	14.1255	4.9696	75.7098
10	13.1534	5.9417	69.7681
11	11.9911	7.1040	62.6641
12	10.6014	8.4937	54.1704
13	8.9399	10.1552	44.0152
14	6.9533	12.1417	31.8735
15	4.5782	14.5169	17.3566
16	1.7384	17.3566	0.0000

YEARS 17 — MO PAYT 1.5756 — AN CONST 18.91

#	INT	PRIN	BALANCE
1	17.9213	.9856	99.0144
2	17.7285	1.1784	97.8361
3	17.4980	1.4089	96.4272
4	17.2224	1.6845	94.7428
5	16.8929	2.0140	92.7288
6	16.4989	2.4079	90.3208
7	16.0279	2.8790	87.4419
8	15.4647	3.4422	83.9997
9	14.7914	4.1155	79.8842
10	13.9863	4.9206	74.9636
11	13.0237	5.8831	69.0805
12	11.8729	7.0340	62.0465
13	10.4969	8.4100	53.6365
14	8.8518	10.0551	43.5814
15	6.8848	12.0221	31.5594
16	4.5331	14.3738	17.1856
17	1.7213	17.1856	0.0000

YEARS 18 — MO PAYT 1.5627 — AN CONST 18.76

#	INT	PRIN	BALANCE
1	17.9347	.8176	99.1824
2	17.7748	.9775	98.2049
3	17.5836	1.1687	97.0362
4	17.3550	1.3973	95.6389
5	17.0816	1.6707	93.9682
6	16.7548	1.9975	91.9707
7	16.3640	2.3883	89.5824
8	15.8969	2.8554	86.7270
9	15.3383	3.4140	83.3129
10	14.6704	4.0819	79.2311
11	13.8719	4.8804	74.3507
12	12.9173	5.8350	68.5157
13	11.7758	6.9765	61.5392
14	10.4111	8.3412	53.1980
15	8.7794	9.9729	43.2251
16	6.8285	11.9238	31.3013
17	4.4960	14.2563	17.0451
18	1.7072	17.0451	0.0000

YEARS 19 — MO PAYT 1.5521 — AN CONST 18.63

#	INT	PRIN	BALANCE
1	17.9458	.6792	99.3208
2	17.8129	.8120	98.5088
3	17.6541	.9709	97.5380
4	17.4642	1.1608	96.3772
5	17.2371	1.3879	94.9893
6	16.9656	1.6593	93.3300
7	16.6410	1.9839	91.3460
8	16.2529	2.3720	88.9740
9	15.7889	2.8361	86.1379
10	15.2341	3.3908	82.7471
11	14.5708	4.0541	78.6930
12	13.7777	4.8472	73.8458
13	12.8295	5.7954	68.0504
14	11.6958	6.9291	61.1213
15	10.3404	8.2846	52.8367
16	8.7198	9.9052	42.9315
17	6.7821	11.8428	31.0888
18	4.4655	14.1595	16.9293
19	1.6956	16.9293	0.0000

YEARS 20 — MO PAYT 1.5433 — AN CONST 18.52

#	INT	PRIN	BALANCE
1	17.9549	.5648	99.4352
2	17.8444	.6753	98.7598
3	17.7123	.8074	97.9524
4	17.5544	.9654	96.9870
5	17.3655	1.1542	95.8328
6	17.1397	1.3800	94.4528
7	16.8698	1.6500	92.8028
8	16.5470	1.9727	90.8301
9	16.1611	2.3586	88.4714
10	15.6997	2.8200	85.6514
11	15.1481	3.3717	82.2797
12	14.4885	4.0312	78.2485
13	13.6999	4.8198	73.4287
14	12.7571	5.7627	67.6660
15	11.6298	6.8900	60.7760
16	10.2820	8.2378	52.5383
17	8.6705	9.8492	42.6891
18	6.7438	11.7759	30.9132
19	4.4403	14.0795	16.8337
20	1.6861	16.8337	0.0000

YEARS 21 — MO PAYT 1.5361 — AN CONST 18.44

#	INT	PRIN	BALANCE
1	17.9625	.4702	99.5298
2	17.8705	.5622	98.9676
3	17.7605	.6722	98.2955

#	INT	PRIN	BALANCE
4	17.6290	.8036	97.4918
5	17.4718	.9608	96.5310
6	17.2839	1.1488	95.3822
7	17.0591	1.3735	94.0087
8	16.7904	1.6422	92.3665
9	16.4692	1.9635	90.4030
10	16.0851	2.3475	88.0554
11	15.6259	2.8068	85.2487
12	15.0768	3.3558	81.8928
13	14.4204	4.0123	77.8806
14	13.6355	4.7972	73.0834
15	12.6971	5.7356	67.3478
16	11.5751	6.8576	60.4903
17	10.2336	8.1990	52.2912
18	8.6298	9.8029	42.4883
19	6.7121	11.7205	30.7678
20	4.4194	14.0133	16.7545
21	1.6781	16.7545	0.0000

YEARS 22 — MO PAYT 1.5300 — AN CONST 18.37

#	INT	PRIN	BALANCE
1	17.9687	.3917	99.6083
2	17.8921	.4684	99.1399
3	17.8005	.5600	98.5799
4	17.6909	.6695	97.9104
5	17.5600	.8005	97.1099
6	17.4034	.9571	96.1529
7	17.2162	1.1443	95.0086
8	16.9923	1.3681	93.6404
9	16.7247	1.6358	92.0046
10	16.4047	1.9558	90.0489
11	16.0221	2.3384	87.7105
12	15.5647	2.7958	84.9147
13	15.0178	3.3427	81.5720
14	14.3639	3.9966	77.5755
15	13.5821	4.7784	72.7971
16	12.6473	5.7131	67.0840
17	11.5298	6.8307	60.2533
18	10.1935	8.1669	52.0864
19	8.5960	9.7645	42.3219
20	6.6858	11.6746	30.6473
21	4.4021	13.9584	16.6889
22	1.6716	16.6889	0.0000

YEARS 23 — MO PAYT 1.5250 — AN CONST 18.31

#	INT	PRIN	BALANCE
1	17.9739	.3266	99.6734
2	17.9100	.3904	99.2830
3	17.8337	.4668	98.8162
4	17.7423	.5581	98.2580
5	17.6332	.6673	97.5907
6	17.5026	.7979	96.7928
7	17.3465	.9540	95.8388
8	17.1599	1.1406	94.6983
9	16.9368	1.3637	93.3346
10	16.6701	1.6304	91.7042
11	16.3511	1.9494	89.7548
12	15.9698	2.3307	87.4241
13	15.5138	2.7866	84.6374
14	14.9687	3.3318	81.3057
15	14.3170	3.9835	77.3221
16	13.5377	4.7628	72.5594
17	12.6060	5.6945	66.8649
18	11.4921	6.8084	60.0565
19	10.1603	8.1402	51.9163
20	8.5679	9.7326	42.1837
21	6.6640	11.6365	30.5472
22	4.3877	13.9128	16.6344
23	1.6661	16.6344	0.0000

YEARS 24 — MO PAYT 1.5209 — AN CONST 18.26

#	INT	PRIN	BALANCE
1	17.9783	.2724	99.7276
2	17.9250	.3257	99.4019
3	17.8613	.3894	99.0125
4	17.7851	.4656	98.5470
5	17.6940	.5566	97.9904
6	17.5851	.6655	97.3248
7	17.4549	.7957	96.5291
8	17.2993	.9514	95.5778
9	17.1132	1.1375	94.4403
10	16.8907	1.3600	93.0804
11	16.6246	1.6260	91.4544
12	16.3066	1.9441	89.5103
13	15.9263	2.3244	87.1859
14	15.4716	2.7791	84.4069
15	14.9280	3.3227	81.0842
16	14.2780	3.9727	77.1115
17	13.5008	4.7498	72.3617
18	12.5717	5.6789	66.6828
19	11.4608	6.7898	59.8929
20	10.1326	8.1181	51.7749
21	8.5445	9.7061	42.0688
22	6.6459	11.6048	30.4640
23	4.3757	13.8749	16.5891
24	1.6616	16.5891	0.0000

YEARS 25 — MO PAYT 1.5174 — AN CONST 18.21

#	INT	PRIN	BALANCE
1	17.9819	.2273	99.7727
2	17.9374	.2718	99.5009
3	17.8842	.3249	99.1760
4	17.8207	.3885	98.7875
5	17.7447	.4645	98.3230
6	17.6538	.5554	97.7676
7	17.5452	.6640	97.1036
8	17.4153	.7939	96.3097
9	17.2600	.9492	95.3605
10	17.0743	1.1349	94.2257
11	16.8523	1.3569	92.8688
12	16.5869	1.6223	91.2465
13	16.2695	1.9397	89.3068
14	15.8901	2.3191	86.9878
15	15.4364	2.7727	84.2150
16	14.8940	3.3151	80.8999
17	14.2455	3.9636	76.9362
18	13.4702	4.7390	72.1972
19	12.5431	5.6660	66.5312
20	11.4347	6.7744	59.7568
21	10.1096	8.0996	51.6572
22	8.5251	9.6840	41.9732
23	6.6307	11.5784	30.3947
24	4.3658	13.8434	16.5514
25	1.6578	16.5514	0.0000

YEARS 26 — MO PAYT 1.5146 — AN CONST 18.18

#	INT	PRIN	BALANCE
1	17.9848	.1898	99.8102
2	17.9477	.2269	99.5834
3	17.9033	.2713	99.3121
4	17.8503	.3243	98.9878
5	17.7868	.3878	98.6000
6	17.7110	.4636	98.1364
7	17.6203	.5543	97.5821
8	17.5119	.6627	96.9194
9	17.3822	.7924	96.1270
10	17.2272	.9474	95.1796
11	17.0419	1.1327	94.0469
12	16.8203	1.3543	92.6926
13	16.5554	1.6192	91.0733
14	16.2386	1.9360	89.1374
15	15.8599	2.3147	86.8227
16	15.4071	2.7675	84.0552
17	14.8658	3.3088	80.7464
18	14.2185	3.9561	76.7902
19	13.4446	4.7300	72.0602
20	12.5193	5.6553	66.4050
21	11.4131	6.7616	59.6434
22	10.0904	8.0842	51.5592
23	8.5089	9.6657	41.8935
24	6.6182	11.5564	30.3371
25	4.3575	13.8171	16.5200
26	1.6546	16.5200	0.0000

YEARS 27 — MO PAYT 1.5122 — AN CONST 18.15

#	INT	PRIN	BALANCE
1	17.9873	.1585	99.8415
2	17.9564	.1895	99.6521
3	17.9193	.2265	99.4256
4	17.8750	.2708	99.1547
5	17.8220	.3238	98.8309
6	17.7587	.3871	98.4438
7	17.6829	.4629	97.9809
8	17.5924	.5534	97.4275
9	17.4841	.6617	96.7658
10	17.3547	.7911	95.9747
11	17.1999	.9459	95.0288
12	17.0149	1.1309	93.8978
13	16.7937	1.3522	92.5457
14	16.5292	1.6167	90.9290
15	16.2129	1.9329	88.9961
16	15.8348	2.3110	86.6851
17	15.3827	2.7631	83.9220
18	14.8422	3.3036	80.6184
19	14.1960	3.9498	76.6686
20	13.4233	4.7225	71.9461
21	12.4995	5.6463	66.2997
22	11.3950	6.7508	59.5489
23	10.0744	8.0714	51.4775
24	8.4955	9.6503	41.8271
25	6.6077	11.5381	30.2890
26	4.3506	13.7952	16.4938
27	1.6520	16.4938	0.0000

YEARS 28 — MO PAYT 1.5101 — AN CONST 18.13

#	INT	PRIN	BALANCE
1	17.9894	.1324	99.8676
2	17.9635	.1582	99.7094
3	17.9326	.1892	99.5202
4	17.8956	.2262	99.2940
5	17.8513	.2705	99.0235
6	17.7984	.3234	98.7001
7	17.7352	.3866	98.3135
8	17.6595	.4623	97.8512
9	17.5691	.5527	97.2985
10	17.4610	.6608	96.6377
11	17.3317	.7901	95.8476
12	17.1772	.9446	94.9030
13	16.9924	1.1294	93.7736
14	16.7714	1.3504	92.4232
15	16.5073	1.6145	90.8087
16	16.1914	1.9303	88.8783
17	15.8138	2.3080	86.5704
18	15.3624	2.7594	83.8109
19	14.8226	3.2992	80.5117
20	14.1772	3.9446	76.5671
21	13.4055	4.7163	71.8508
22	12.4829	5.6388	66.2120
23	11.3799	6.7419	59.4701
24	10.0610	8.0607	51.4093
25	8.4842	9.6376	41.7718
26	6.5989	11.5229	30.2489
27	4.3448	13.7769	16.4720
28	1.6498	16.4720	0.0000

YEARS 29 — MO PAYT 1.5085 — AN CONST 18.11

#	INT	PRIN	BALANCE
1	17.9912	.1106	99.8894
2	17.9695	.1322	99.7572
3	17.9437	.1581	99.5991
4	17.9128	.1890	99.4101
5	17.8758	.2260	99.1842
6	17.8316	.2702	98.9140
7	17.7787	.3230	98.5910
8	17.7155	.3862	98.2048
9	17.6400	.4618	97.7430
10	17.5497	.5521	97.1909
11	17.4417	.6601	96.5308
12	17.3125	.7892	95.7416
13	17.1582	.9436	94.7980
14	16.9736	1.1282	93.6699
15	16.7529	1.3489	92.3210
16	16.4890	1.6127	90.7083
17	16.1735	1.9282	88.7801
18	15.7963	2.3054	86.4746
19	15.3454	2.7564	83.7183
20	14.8062	3.2956	80.4227
21	14.1615	3.9403	76.4824
22	13.3907	4.7110	71.7714
23	12.4691	5.6326	66.1388
24	11.3673	6.7345	59.4043
25	10.0499	8.0518	51.3525
26	8.4748	9.6269	41.7256
27	6.5916	11.5101	30.2155
28	4.3400	13.7617	16.4537
29	1.6480	16.4537	0.0000

YEARS 30 — MO PAYT 1.5071 — AN CONST 18.09

#	INT	PRIN	BALANCE
1	17.9926	.0924	99.9076
2	17.9745	.1105	99.7971
3	17.9529	.1321	99.6650
4	17.9271	.1579	99.5071
5	17.8962	.1888	99.3183
6	17.8593	.2258	99.0925
7	17.8151	.2699	98.8226
8	17.7623	.3227	98.4999
9	17.6992	.3859	98.1140
10	17.6237	.4613	97.6527
11	17.5334	.5516	97.1011
12	17.4255	.6595	96.4416
13	17.2965	.7885	95.6532
14	17.1423	.9427	94.7104
15	16.9579	1.1271	93.5833
16	16.7374	1.3476	92.2357
17	16.4738	1.6112	90.6244
18	16.1586	1.9264	88.6980
19	15.7817	2.3033	86.3947
20	15.3312	2.7538	83.6409
21	14.7925	3.2925	80.3484
22	14.1484	3.9366	76.4118
23	13.3783	4.7067	71.7051
24	12.4576	5.6274	66.0777
25	11.3568	6.7282	59.3494
26	10.0406	8.0444	51.3050
27	8.4670	9.6180	41.6870
28	6.5855	11.4995	30.1875
29	4.3360	13.7490	16.4385
30	1.6465	16.4385	0.0000

MONTHLY PAYMENT AMORTIZATION SCHEDULE PER $100

19.00 %

YEARS 2 — MO PAYT 5.0409 — AN CONST 60.50

#	INT	PRIN	BALANCE
1	15.1892	45.3011	54.6989
2	5.7915	54.6989	0.0000

YEARS 3 — MO PAYT 3.6656 — AN CONST 43.99

#	INT	PRIN	BALANCE
1	16.7050	27.2822	72.7178
2	11.0453	32.9420	39.7758
3	4.2114	39.7758	0.0000

YEARS 4 — MO PAYT 2.9900 — AN CONST 35.89

#	INT	PRIN	BALANCE
1	17.4496	18.4305	81.5695
2	13.6262	22.2540	59.3155
3	9.0096	26.8706	32.4449
4	3.4352	32.4449	0.0000

YEARS 5 — MO PAYT 2.5941 — AN CONST 31.13

#	INT	PRIN	BALANCE
1	17.8860	13.2426	86.7574
2	15.1388	15.9898	70.7675
3	11.8217	19.3070	51.4605
4	7.8165	23.3122	28.1483
5	2.9803	28.1483	0.0000

YEARS 6 — MO PAYT 2.3377 — AN CONST 28.06

#	INT	PRIN	BALANCE
1	18.1686	9.8835	90.1165
2	16.1183	11.9338	78.1827
3	13.6426	14.4095	63.7732
4	10.6533	17.3988	46.3745
5	7.0439	21.0081	25.3663
6	2.6858	25.3663	0.0000

YEARS 7 — MO PAYT 2.1608 — AN CONST 25.93

#	INT	PRIN	BALANCE
1	18.3635	7.5661	92.4339
2	16.7939	9.1357	83.2982
3	14.8987	11.0309	72.2673
4	12.6104	13.3193	58.9481
5	9.8473	16.0824	42.8657
6	6.5110	19.4187	23.4471
7	2.4826	23.4471	0.0000

YEARS 8 — MO PAYT 2.0334 — AN CONST 24.41

#	INT	PRIN	BALANCE
1	18.5040	5.8967	94.1033
2	17.2807	7.1199	86.9834
3	15.8037	8.5970	78.3864
4	14.0202	10.3804	68.0060
5	11.8668	12.5339	55.4721
6	9.2666	15.1340	40.3381
7	6.1270	18.2736	22.0645
8	2.3362	22.0645	0.0000

YEARS 9 — MO PAYT 1.9387 — AN CONST 23.27

#	INT	PRIN	BALANCE
1	18.6083	4.6562	95.3438
2	17.6424	5.6221	89.7217
3	16.4761	6.7884	82.9333
4	15.0678	8.1967	74.7366
5	13.3674	9.8971	64.8395
6	11.3142	11.9503	52.8892
7	8.8351	14.4294	38.4599
8	5.8418	17.4227	21.0371
9	2.2274	21.0371	0.0000

YEARS 10 — MO PAYT 1.8667 — AN CONST 22.41

#	INT	PRIN	BALANCE
1	18.6877	3.7130	96.2870
2	17.9174	4.4833	91.8037
3	16.9873	5.4134	86.3903
4	15.8643	6.5364	79.8539
5	14.5083	7.8923	71.9616
6	12.8711	9.5296	62.4320
7	10.8941	11.5065	50.9254
8	8.5071	13.8936	37.0318
9	5.6248	16.7758	20.2560
10	2.1447	20.2560	0.0000

YEARS 11 — MO PAYT 1.8110 — AN CONST 21.74

#	INT	PRIN	BALANCE
1	18.7490	2.9834	97.0166
2	18.1301	3.6023	93.4144
3	17.3828	4.3495	89.0648
4	16.4805	5.2519	83.8130
5	15.3910	6.3414	77.4716
6	14.0755	7.6569	69.8147
7	12.4871	9.2453	60.5694
8	10.5691	11.1633	49.4061
9	8.2533	13.4791	35.9270
10	5.4570	16.2754	19.6517
11	2.0807	19.6517	0.0000

YEARS 12 — MO PAYT 1.7674 — AN CONST 21.21

#	INT	PRIN	BALANCE
1	18.7972	2.4112	97.5888
2	18.2970	2.9114	94.6774
3	17.6930	3.5154	91.1620
4	16.9637	4.2447	86.9173
5	16.0831	5.1252	81.7921
6	15.0199	6.1885	75.6036
7	13.7361	7.4723	68.1314
8	12.1860	9.0224	59.1090
9	10.3143	10.8941	48.2149
10	8.0543	13.1541	35.0608
11	5.3255	15.8829	19.1778
12	2.0305	19.1778	0.0000

YEARS 13 — MO PAYT 1.7328 — AN CONST 20.80

#	INT	PRIN	BALANCE
1	18.8353	1.9578	98.0422
2	18.4291	2.3640	95.6782
3	17.9387	2.8544	92.8237
4	17.3466	3.4466	89.3772
5	16.6316	4.1616	85.2156
6	15.7683	5.0249	80.1907
7	14.7258	6.0673	74.1234
8	13.4672	7.3260	66.7974
9	11.9474	8.8457	57.9517
10	10.1123	10.6808	47.2709
11	7.8966	12.8966	34.3743
12	5.2212	15.5720	18.8024
13	1.9908	18.8024	0.0000

YEARS 14 — MO PAYT 1.7051 — AN CONST 20.47

#	INT	PRIN	BALANCE
1	18.8658	1.5956	98.4044
2	18.5348	1.9266	96.4778
3	18.1351	2.3263	94.1515
4	17.6525	2.8089	91.3426
5	17.0698	3.3916	87.9511
6	16.3662	4.0952	83.8559
7	15.5167	4.9447	78.9112
8	14.4909	5.9705	72.9407
9	13.2523	7.2091	65.7316
10	11.7568	8.7046	57.0270
11	9.9510	10.5104	46.5166
12	7.7706	12.6908	33.8259
13	5.1379	15.3235	18.5024
14	1.9590	18.5024	0.0000

YEARS 15 — MO PAYT 1.6829 — AN CONST 20.20

#	INT	PRIN	BALANCE
1	18.8903	1.3042	98.6958
2	18.6197	1.5748	97.1210
3	18.2930	1.9015	95.2195
4	17.8986	2.2959	92.9236
5	17.4223	2.7722	90.1513
6	16.8472	3.3473	86.8040
7	16.1528	4.0418	82.7622
8	15.3143	4.8802	77.8820
9	14.3019	5.8926	71.9894
10	13.0795	7.1151	64.8743
11	11.6034	8.5911	56.2833
12	9.8212	10.3733	45.9099
13	7.6693	12.5253	33.3847
14	5.0709	15.1236	18.2611
15	1.9335	18.2611	0.0000

YEARS 16 — MO PAYT 1.6649 — AN CONST 19.98

#	INT	PRIN	BALANCE
1	18.9101	1.0686	98.9314
2	18.6884	1.2903	97.6411
3	18.4208	1.5580	96.0831
4	18.0976	1.8812	94.2020
5	17.7073	2.2714	91.9306
6	17.2361	2.7426	89.1880
7	16.6671	3.3116	85.8764
8	15.9802	3.9986	81.8778
9	15.1506	4.8281	77.0498
10	14.1491	5.8297	71.2201
11	12.9397	7.0390	64.1811
12	11.4794	8.4993	55.6818
13	9.7163	10.2625	45.4194
14	7.5873	12.3914	33.0279
15	5.0167	14.9620	18.0659
16	1.9128	18.0659	0.0000

YEARS 17 — MO PAYT 1.6503 — AN CONST 19.81

#	INT	PRIN	BALANCE
1	18.9262	.8772	99.1228
2	18.7442	1.0592	98.0635
3	18.5245	1.2790	96.7846
4	18.2592	1.5443	95.2403
5	17.9388	1.8647	93.3756
6	17.5520	2.2515	91.1241
7	17.0849	2.7186	88.4056
8	16.5209	3.2825	85.1230
9	15.8400	3.9635	81.1596
10	15.0177	4.7857	76.3738
11	14.0249	5.7785	70.5953
12	12.8262	6.9773	63.6181
13	11.3787	8.4247	55.1933
14	9.6310	10.1724	45.0209
15	7.5207	12.2827	32.7382
16	4.9727	14.8308	17.9074
17	1.8960	17.9074	0.0000

YEARS 18 — MO PAYT 1.6384 — AN CONST 19.67

#	INT	PRIN	BALANCE
1	18.9393	.7213	99.2787
2	18.7897	.8709	98.4078
3	18.6090	1.0516	97.3562
4	18.3909	1.2697	96.0865
5	18.1275	1.5332	94.5533
6	17.8094	1.8512	92.7021
7	17.4254	2.2352	90.4669
8	16.9617	2.6989	87.7679
9	16.4018	3.2588	84.5091
10	15.7257	3.9349	80.5742
11	14.9094	4.7512	75.8230
12	13.9238	5.7368	70.0861
13	12.7337	6.9269	63.1592
14	11.2967	8.3639	54.7952
15	9.5616	10.0991	44.6962
16	7.4665	12.1941	32.5021
17	4.9368	14.7238	17.7783
18	1.8823	17.7783	0.0000

YEARS 19 — MO PAYT 1.6287 — AN CONST 19.55

#	INT	PRIN	BALANCE
1	18.9500	.5938	99.4062
2	18.8269	.7170	98.6892
3	18.6781	.8657	97.8234
4	18.4985	1.0453	96.7781
5	18.2817	1.2622	95.5159
6	18.0198	1.5240	93.9918
7	17.7036	1.8402	92.1516
8	17.3219	2.2220	89.9296
9	16.8609	2.6829	87.2467
10	16.3044	3.2395	84.0072
11	15.6323	3.9115	80.0957
12	14.8209	4.7230	75.3727
13	13.8411	5.7028	69.6700
14	12.6580	6.8858	62.7841
15	11.2296	8.3143	54.4699
16	9.5048	10.0391	44.4308
17	7.4222	12.1217	32.3091
18	4.9075	14.6364	17.6727
19	1.8712	17.6727	0.0000

YEARS 20 — MO PAYT 1.6207 — AN CONST 19.45

#	INT	PRIN	BALANCE
1	18.9588	.4894	99.5106
2	18.8573	.5909	98.9197
3	18.7347	.7135	98.2062
4	18.5867	.8615	97.3447
5	18.4080	1.0402	96.3045
6	18.1922	1.2560	95.0484
7	17.9316	1.5166	93.5319
8	17.6170	1.8312	91.7006
9	17.2371	2.2111	89.4895
10	16.7784	2.6698	86.8198
11	16.2246	3.2236	83.5961
12	15.5558	3.8924	79.7037
13	14.7484	4.6999	75.0039
14	13.7734	5.6749	69.3290
15	12.5961	6.8521	62.4769
16	11.1746	8.2736	54.2033
17	9.4583	9.9900	44.2133
18	7.3858	12.0624	32.1509
19	4.8835	14.5647	17.5862
20	1.8620	17.5862	0.0000

YEARS 21 — MO PAYT 1.6141 — AN CONST 19.37

#	INT	PRIN	BALANCE
1	18.9660	.4037	99.5963
2	18.8823	.4874	99.1089
3	18.7812	.5885	98.5204

#	INT	PRIN	BALANCE
4	18.6591	.7106	97.8098
5	18.5117	.8580	96.9518
6	18.3337	1.0360	95.9157
7	18.1188	1.2510	94.6648
8	17.8592	1.5105	93.1543
9	17.5459	1.8238	91.3305
10	17.1675	2.2022	89.1283
11	16.7107	2.6590	86.4693
12	16.1591	3.2106	83.2587
13	15.4930	3.8767	79.3820
14	14.6888	4.6809	74.7011
15	13.7178	5.6520	69.0491
16	12.5453	6.8245	62.2247
17	11.1295	8.2402	53.9845
18	9.4201	9.9496	44.0349
19	7.3560	12.0137	32.0212
20	4.8638	14.5059	17.5152
21	1.8545	17.5152	0.0000

YEARS 22 — MO PAYT 1.6088 — AN CONST 19.31

#	INT	PRIN	BALANCE
1	18.9720	.3332	99.6668
2	18.9028	.4023	99.2645
3	18.8194	.4858	98.7787
4	18.7186	.5866	98.1921
5	18.5969	.7082	97.4839
6	18.4500	.8552	96.6287
7	18.2726	1.0326	95.5961
8	18.0584	1.2468	94.3493
9	17.7997	1.5054	92.8439
10	17.4874	1.8177	91.0262
11	17.1103	2.1948	88.8313
12	16.6550	2.6502	86.1812
13	16.1052	3.1999	82.9812
14	15.4414	3.8638	79.1175
15	14.6399	4.6653	74.4522
16	13.6721	5.6331	68.8191
17	12.5035	6.8017	62.0174
18	11.0924	8.2127	53.8046
19	9.3887	9.9165	43.8881
20	7.3315	11.9737	31.9145
21	4.8476	14.4576	17.4569
22	1.8483	17.4569	0.0000

YEARS 23 — MO PAYT 1.6043 — AN CONST 19.26

#	INT	PRIN	BALANCE
1	18.9769	.2752	99.7248
2	18.9198	.3323	99.3925
3	18.8508	.4012	98.9913
4	18.7676	.4844	98.5069
5	18.6671	.5849	97.9219
6	18.5457	.7063	97.2156
7	18.3992	.8528	96.3628
8	18.2223	1.0297	95.3331
9	18.0087	1.2434	94.0897
10	17.7508	1.5013	92.5884
11	17.4393	1.8127	90.7757
12	17.0633	2.1888	88.5869
13	16.6092	2.6429	85.9440
14	16.0609	3.1911	82.7529
15	15.3989	3.8531	78.8998
16	14.5996	4.6525	74.2473
17	13.6344	5.6176	68.6297
18	12.4690	6.7830	61.8467
19	11.0619	8.1901	53.6565
20	9.3629	9.8892	43.7674
21	7.3113	11.9407	31.8266
22	4.8342	14.4178	17.4088
23	1.8432	17.4088	0.0000

YEARS 24 — MO PAYT 1.6007 — AN CONST 19.21

#	INT	PRIN	BALANCE
1	18.9809	.2274	99.7726
2	18.9337	.2746	99.4980
3	18.8767	.3315	99.1665
4	18.8080	.4003	98.7662
5	18.7249	.4833	98.2829
6	18.6246	.5836	97.6992
7	18.5036	.7047	96.9945
8	18.3574	.8509	96.1437
9	18.1809	1.0274	95.1163
10	17.9677	1.2405	93.8757
11	17.7104	1.4979	92.3779
12	17.3997	1.8086	90.5692
13	17.0245	2.1838	88.3854
14	16.5714	2.6369	85.7486
15	16.0244	3.1839	82.5647
16	15.3639	3.8444	78.7203
17	14.5664	4.6419	74.0785
18	13.6034	5.6048	68.4736
19	12.4407	6.7676	61.7060
20	11.0368	8.1715	53.5345
21	9.3416	9.8667	43.6678
22	7.2947	11.9136	31.7543
23	4.8232	14.3850	17.3692
24	1.8390	17.3692	0.0000

YEARS 25 — MO PAYT 1.5977 — AN CONST 19.18

#	INT	PRIN	BALANCE
1	18.9842	.1880	99.8120
2	18.9452	.2270	99.5851
3	18.8981	.2741	99.3110
4	18.8413	.3309	98.9801
5	18.7726	.3996	98.5805
6	18.6897	.4824	98.0981
7	18.5896	.5825	97.5156
8	18.4688	.7034	96.8122
9	18.3229	.8493	95.9629
10	18.1467	1.0255	94.9375
11	17.9340	1.2382	93.6993
12	17.6771	1.4951	92.2042
13	17.3669	1.8052	90.3990
14	16.9924	2.1797	88.2193
15	16.5403	2.6319	85.5874
16	15.9943	3.1779	82.4095
17	15.3350	3.8371	78.5724
18	14.5390	4.6332	73.9392
19	13.5779	5.5943	68.3449
20	12.4173	6.7549	61.5901
21	11.0160	8.1562	53.4339
22	9.3240	9.8482	43.5857
23	7.2810	11.8912	31.6946
24	4.8142	14.3580	17.3366
25	1.8356	17.3366	0.0000

YEARS 26 — MO PAYT 1.5952 — AN CONST 19.15

#	INT	PRIN	BALANCE
1	18.9869	.1554	99.8446
2	18.9547	.1877	99.6569
3	18.9157	.2266	99.4303
4	18.8687	.2736	99.1566
5	18.8120	.3304	98.8263
6	18.7434	.3989	98.4273
7	18.6607	.4817	97.9456
8	18.5607	.5816	97.3640
9	18.4401	.7023	96.6617
10	18.2944	.8480	95.8138
11	18.1185	1.0239	94.7899
12	17.9061	1.2363	93.5536
13	17.6496	1.4927	92.0609
14	17.3399	1.8024	90.2585
15	16.9660	2.1763	88.0822
16	16.5146	2.6278	85.4544
17	15.9694	3.1729	82.2814
18	15.3112	3.8312	78.4502
19	14.5164	4.6260	73.8243
20	13.5567	5.5856	68.2387
21	12.3980	6.7444	61.4943
22	10.9989	8.1435	53.3508
23	9.3095	9.8328	43.5180
24	7.2697	11.8727	31.6453
25	4.8067	14.3357	17.3096
26	1.8327	17.3096	0.0000

YEARS 27 — MO PAYT 1.5931 — AN CONST 19.12

#	INT	PRIN	BALANCE
1	18.9892	.1286	99.8714
2	18.9625	.1552	99.7162
3	18.9303	.1874	99.5288
4	18.8914	.2263	99.3024
5	18.8445	.2733	99.0292
6	18.7878	.3300	98.6992
7	18.7193	.3984	98.3008
8	18.6367	.4811	97.8197
9	18.5369	.5809	97.2388
10	18.4164	.7014	96.5375
11	18.2709	.8469	95.6906
12	18.0952	1.0226	94.6680
13	17.8831	1.2347	93.4334
14	17.6269	1.4908	91.9425
15	17.3177	1.8001	90.1424
16	16.9442	2.1735	87.9689
17	16.4933	2.6244	85.3445
18	15.9489	3.1689	82.1756
19	15.2915	3.8262	78.3494
20	14.4977	4.6200	73.7294
21	13.5393	5.5784	68.1509
22	12.3821	6.7357	61.4153
23	10.9847	8.1330	53.2823
24	9.2975	9.8202	43.4621
25	7.2603	11.8574	31.6046
26	4.8005	14.3173	17.2874
27	1.8304	17.2874	0.0000

YEARS 28 — MO PAYT 1.5915 — AN CONST 19.10

#	INT	PRIN	BALANCE
1	18.9911	.1064	99.8936
2	18.9690	.1284	99.7652
3	18.9423	.1551	99.6101
4	18.9102	.1872	99.4229
5	18.8713	.2261	99.1968
6	18.8244	.2730	98.9238
7	18.7678	.3296	98.5942
8	18.6994	.3980	98.1962
9	18.6169	.4806	97.7157
10	18.5172	.5803	97.1354
11	18.3968	.7006	96.4348
12	18.2514	.8460	95.5888
13	18.0759	1.0215	94.5674
14	17.8640	1.2334	93.3340
15	17.6082	1.4892	91.8447
16	17.2992	1.7982	90.0466
17	16.9262	2.1712	87.8754
18	16.4758	2.6216	85.2537
19	15.9319	3.1655	82.0882
20	15.2752	3.8222	78.2661
21	14.4823	4.6151	73.6510
22	13.5249	5.5725	68.0785
23	12.3689	6.7285	61.3499
24	10.9731	8.1244	53.2256
25	9.2877	9.8098	43.4158
26	7.2526	11.8448	31.5710
27	4.7954	14.3020	17.2690
28	1.8284	17.2690	0.0000

YEARS 29 — MO PAYT 1.5901 — AN CONST 19.09

#	INT	PRIN	BALANCE
1	18.9926	.0880	99.9120
2	18.9743	.1063	99.8057
3	18.9523	.1283	99.6774
4	18.9257	.1549	99.5225
5	18.8935	.1871	99.3354
6	18.8547	.2259	99.1095
7	18.8079	.2727	98.8368
8	18.7513	.3293	98.5074
9	18.6830	.3976	98.1098
10	18.6005	.4801	97.6297
11	18.5009	.5797	97.0499
12	18.3806	.7000	96.3499
13	18.2354	.8452	95.5047
14	18.0600	1.0206	94.4841
15	17.8483	1.2323	93.2518
16	17.5927	1.4879	91.7639
17	17.2840	1.7966	89.9673
18	16.9113	2.1693	87.7980
19	16.4613	2.6193	85.1787
20	15.9179	3.1627	82.0160
21	15.2618	3.8188	78.1972
22	14.4696	4.6110	73.5861
23	13.5130	5.5676	68.0185
24	12.3580	6.7226	61.2959
25	10.9634	8.1172	53.1787
26	9.2795	9.8011	43.3776
27	7.2462	11.8344	31.5432
28	4.7912	14.2894	17.2538
29	1.8268	17.2538	0.0000

YEARS 30 — MO PAYT 1.5889 — AN CONST 19.07

#	INT	PRIN	BALANCE
1	18.9939	.0728	99.9272
2	18.9788	.0879	99.8392
3	18.9605	.1062	99.7330
4	18.9385	.1282	99.6048
5	18.9119	.1548	99.4500
6	18.8798	.1869	99.2630
7	18.8410	.2257	99.0373
8	18.7942	.2725	98.7648
9	18.7376	.3291	98.4357
10	18.6694	.3974	98.0383
11	18.5869	.4798	97.5586
12	18.4874	.5793	96.9792
13	18.3672	.6995	96.2797
14	18.2221	.8446	95.4351
15	18.0469	1.0198	94.4153
16	17.8353	1.2314	93.1839
17	17.5799	1.4868	91.6971
18	17.2714	1.7953	89.9018
19	16.8990	2.1677	87.7341
20	16.4493	2.6174	85.1166
21	15.9063	3.1604	81.9562
22	15.2507	3.8160	78.1402
23	14.4590	4.6077	73.5325
24	13.5032	5.5635	67.9690
25	12.3490	6.7177	61.2513
26	10.9554	8.1113	53.1400
27	9.2727	9.7940	43.3460
28	7.2409	11.8258	31.5203
29	4.7877	14.2790	17.2412
30	1.8255	17.2412	0.0000

YEARS 2 — MO PAYT 5.0896 — AN CONST 61.08

#	INT	PRIN	BALANCE
1	16.0176	45.0574	54.9426
2	6.1324	54.9426	0.0000

YEARS 3 — MO PAYT 3.7164 — AN CONST 44.60

#	INT	PRIN	BALANCE
1	17.6153	26.9810	73.0190
2	11.6959	32.9004	40.1185
3	4.4778	40.1185	0.0000

YEARS 4 — MO PAYT 3.0430 — AN CONST 36.52

#	INT	PRIN	BALANCE
1	18.3986	18.1178	81.8822
2	14.4238	22.0927	59.7895
3	9.5768	26.9396	32.8499
4	3.6665	32.8499	0.0000

YEARS 5 — MO PAYT 2.6494 — AN CONST 31.80

#	INT	PRIN	BALANCE
1	18.8566	12.9360	87.0640
2	16.0186	15.7741	71.2899
3	12.5579	19.2348	52.0551
4	8.3380	23.4547	28.6004
5	3.1922	28.6004	0.0000

YEARS 6 — MO PAYT 2.3953 — AN CONST 28.75

#	INT	PRIN	BALANCE
1	19.1523	9.5911	90.4089
2	17.0481	11.6953	78.7136
3	14.4822	14.2612	64.4524
4	11.3535	17.3899	47.0625
5	7.5383	21.2051	25.8573
6	2.8860	25.8573	0.0000

YEARS 7 — MO PAYT 2.2206 — AN CONST 26.65

#	INT	PRIN	BALANCE
1	19.3555	7.2919	92.7081
2	17.7557	8.8917	83.8163
3	15.8049	10.8425	72.9738
4	13.4262	13.2212	59.7526
5	10.5256	16.1219	43.6307
6	6.9886	19.6589	23.9718
7	2.6756	23.9718	0.0000

YEARS 8 — MO PAYT 2.0953 — AN CONST 25.15

#	INT	PRIN	BALANCE
1	19.5013	5.6426	94.3574
2	18.2633	6.8805	87.4769
3	16.7538	8.3900	79.0869
4	14.9131	10.2307	68.8562
5	12.6686	12.4752	56.3810
6	9.9317	15.2122	41.1688
7	6.5942	18.5496	22.6192
8	2.5246	22.6192	0.0000

YEARS 9 — MO PAYT 2.0027 — AN CONST 24.04

#	INT	PRIN	BALANCE
1	19.6091	4.4227	95.5773
2	18.6388	5.3930	90.1843
3	17.4556	6.5762	83.6081
4	16.0129	8.0189	75.5892
5	14.2536	9.7782	65.8109
6	12.1083	11.9235	53.8874
7	9.4924	14.5394	39.3480
8	6.3026	17.7292	21.6188
9	2.4130	21.6188	0.0000

YEARS 10 — MO PAYT 1.9326 — AN CONST 23.20

#	INT	PRIN	BALANCE
1	19.6906	3.5000	96.5000
2	18.9228	4.2679	92.2321
3	17.9864	5.2043	87.0278
4	16.8447	6.3460	80.6818
5	15.4524	7.7383	72.9435
6	13.7547	9.4360	63.5075
7	11.6845	11.5062	52.0014
8	9.1602	14.0305	37.9708
9	6.0820	17.1087	20.8622
10	2.3285	20.8622	0.0000

YEARS 11 — MO PAYT 1.8786 — AN CONST 22.55

#	INT	PRIN	BALANCE
1	19.7534	2.7902	97.2098
2	19.1412	3.4024	93.8074
3	18.3948	4.1488	89.6586
4	17.4846	5.0590	84.5995
5	16.3747	6.1690	78.4306
6	15.0212	7.5224	70.9082
7	13.3709	9.1727	61.7355
8	11.3585	11.1851	50.5504
9	8.9046	13.6390	36.9114
10	5.9123	16.6313	20.2801
11	2.2635	20.2801	0.0000

YEARS 12 — MO PAYT 1.8366 — AN CONST 22.04

#	INT	PRIN	BALANCE
1	19.8023	2.2370	97.7630
2	19.3115	2.7278	95.0352
3	18.7130	3.3263	91.7089
4	17.9833	4.0560	87.6529
5	17.0934	4.9459	82.7070
6	16.0084	6.0309	76.6761
7	14.6852	7.3541	69.3220
8	13.0718	8.9675	60.3545
9	11.1044	10.9349	49.4196
10	8.7054	13.3339	36.0857
11	5.7800	16.2593	19.8264
12	2.2129	19.8264	0.0000

YEARS 13 — MO PAYT 1.8035 — AN CONST 21.65

#	INT	PRIN	BALANCE
1	19.8408	1.8015	98.1985
2	19.4455	2.1967	96.0018
3	18.9636	2.6787	93.3231
4	18.3759	3.2663	90.0568
5	17.6593	3.9829	86.0738
6	16.7855	4.8568	81.2171
7	15.7200	5.9223	75.2948
8	14.4207	7.2216	68.0732
9	12.8363	8.8060	59.2672
10	10.9044	10.7379	48.5293
11	8.5486	13.0937	35.4356
12	5.6759	15.9664	19.4692
13	2.1730	19.4692	0.0000

YEARS 14 — MO PAYT 1.7773 — AN CONST 21.33

#	INT	PRIN	BALANCE
1	19.8713	1.4559	98.5441
2	19.5519	1.7753	96.7689
3	19.1624	2.1647	94.6041
4	18.6875	2.6397	91.9645
5	18.1084	3.2188	88.7457
6	17.4022	3.9250	84.8207
7	16.5411	4.7861	80.0346
8	15.4911	5.8361	74.1986
9	14.2107	7.1165	67.0821
10	12.6494	8.6778	58.4043
11	10.7456	10.5816	47.8228
12	8.4241	12.9031	34.9197
13	5.5933	15.7339	19.1858
14	2.1414	19.1858	0.0000

YEARS 15 — MO PAYT 1.7563 — AN CONST 21.08

#	INT	PRIN	BALANCE
1	19.8957	1.1798	98.8202
2	19.6369	1.4387	97.3815
3	19.3212	1.7543	95.6272
4	18.9364	2.1392	93.4880
5	18.4670	2.6085	90.8794
6	17.8947	3.1808	87.6986
7	17.1969	3.8787	83.8200
8	16.3460	4.7296	79.0904
9	15.3083	5.7672	73.3231
10	14.0431	7.0325	66.2906
11	12.5002	8.5754	57.7153
12	10.6188	10.4567	47.2585
13	8.3247	12.7508	34.5077
14	5.5273	15.5483	18.9594
15	2.1161	18.9594	0.0000

YEARS 16 — MO PAYT 1.7395 — AN CONST 20.88

#	INT	PRIN	BALANCE
1	19.9153	.9583	99.0417
2	19.7051	1.1685	97.8732
3	19.4487	1.4249	96.4483
4	19.1361	1.7375	94.7108
5	18.7549	2.1187	92.5921
6	18.2901	2.5835	90.0085
7	17.7233	3.1503	86.8582
8	17.0321	3.8415	83.0167
9	16.1893	4.6843	78.3325
10	15.1616	5.7120	72.6205
11	13.9085	6.9651	65.6554
12	12.3804	8.4932	57.1622
13	10.5171	10.3565	46.8057
14	8.2449	12.6287	34.1770
15	5.4743	15.3993	18.7777
16	2.0959	18.7777	0.0000

YEARS 17 — MO PAYT 1.7259 — AN CONST 20.72

#	INT	PRIN	BALANCE
1	19.9311	.7797	99.2203
2	19.7600	.9508	98.2694
3	19.5514	1.1594	97.1100
4	19.2970	1.4138	95.6962
5	18.9869	1.7240	93.9723
6	18.6086	2.1022	91.8701
7	18.1474	2.5634	89.3067
8	17.5851	3.1258	86.1809
9	16.8993	3.8115	82.3694
10	16.0631	4.6477	77.7217
11	15.0434	5.6674	72.0542
12	13.8000	6.9108	65.1434
13	12.2839	8.4270	56.7165
14	10.4351	10.2758	46.4407
15	8.1806	12.5302	33.9105
16	5.4316	15.2792	18.6313
17	2.0795	18.6313	0.0000

YEARS 18 — MO PAYT 1.7149 — AN CONST 20.58

#	INT	PRIN	BALANCE
1	19.9438	.6354	99.3646
2	19.8044	.7748	98.5898
3	19.6345	.9448	97.6450
4	19.4272	1.1521	96.4930
5	19.1744	1.4048	95.0882
6	18.8662	1.7130	93.3752
7	18.4904	2.0888	91.2863
8	18.0321	2.5471	88.7392
9	17.4733	3.1059	85.6333
10	16.7919	3.7873	81.8460
11	15.9610	4.6182	77.2278
12	14.9478	5.6314	71.5964
13	13.7123	6.8669	64.7295
14	12.2058	8.3734	56.3561
15	10.3688	10.2105	46.1456
16	8.1287	12.4506	33.6950
17	5.3971	15.1821	18.5129
18	2.0663	18.5129	0.0000

YEARS 19 — MO PAYT 1.7060 — AN CONST 20.48

#	INT	PRIN	BALANCE
1	19.9542	.5184	99.4816
2	19.8405	.6321	98.8495
3	19.7018	.7708	98.0787
4	19.5327	.9399	97.1389
5	19.3265	1.1461	95.9928
6	19.0750	1.3975	94.5953
7	18.7684	1.7041	92.8911
8	18.3946	2.0780	90.8131
9	17.9387	2.5339	88.2792
10	17.3828	3.0898	85.1894
11	16.7049	3.7677	81.4218
12	15.8783	4.5943	76.8275
13	14.8703	5.6022	71.2253
14	13.6413	6.8313	64.3940
15	12.1425	8.3300	56.0640
16	10.3150	10.1576	45.9064
17	8.0865	12.3860	33.5204
18	5.3691	15.1034	18.4170
19	2.0556	18.4170	0.0000

YEARS 20 — MO PAYT 1.6988 — AN CONST 20.39

#	INT	PRIN	BALANCE
1	19.9626	.4233	99.5767
2	19.8697	.5162	99.0605
3	19.7565	.6294	98.4311
4	19.6184	.7675	97.6636
5	19.4500	.9359	96.7277
6	19.2447	1.1412	95.5864
7	18.9943	1.3916	94.1948
8	18.6890	1.6969	92.4979
9	18.3167	2.0692	90.4287
10	17.8627	2.5232	87.9055
11	17.3092	3.0767	84.8288
12	16.6342	3.7517	81.0771
13	15.8111	4.5748	76.5023
14	14.8074	5.5785	70.9238
15	13.5835	6.8024	64.1214
16	12.0911	8.2948	55.8266
17	10.2713	10.1146	45.7121
18	8.0523	12.3336	33.3785
19	5.3464	15.0395	18.3390
20	2.0469	18.3390	0.0000

YEARS 21 — MO PAYT 1.6929 — AN CONST 20.32

#	INT	PRIN	BALANCE
1	19.9694	.3459	99.6541
2	19.8935	.4218	99.2322
3	19.8010	.5144	98.7178

#	INT	PRIN	BALANCE
4	19.6881	.6272	98.0906
5	19.5505	.7649	97.3257
6	19.3827	.9327	96.3930
7	19.1781	1.1373	95.2558
8	18.9286	1.3868	93.8690
9	18.6243	1.6910	92.1779
10	18.2533	2.0620	90.1159
11	17.8009	2.5144	87.6014
12	17.2493	3.0661	84.5354
13	16.5766	3.7388	80.7966
14	15.7564	4.5590	76.2376
15	14.7562	5.5592	70.6784
16	13.5365	6.7788	63.8996
17	12.0493	8.2661	55.6335
18	10.2358	10.0796	45.5539
19	8.0244	12.2909	33.2630
20	5.3279	14.9874	18.2756
21	2.0398	18.2756	0.0000

YEARS 22 — MO PAYT 1.6882 — AN CONST 20.26

#	INT	PRIN	BALANCE
1	19.9750	.2829	99.7171
2	19.9129	.3450	99.3721
3	19.8372	.4207	98.9515
4	19.7450	.5129	98.4385
5	19.6324	.6255	97.8131
6	19.4952	.7627	97.0504
7	19.3279	.9300	96.1203
8	19.1238	1.1341	94.9863
9	18.8750	1.3829	93.6034
10	18.5716	1.6863	91.9171
11	18.2017	2.0562	89.8609
12	17.7506	2.5073	87.3536
13	17.2005	3.0574	84.2962
14	16.5297	3.7282	80.5680
15	15.7118	4.5461	76.0219
16	14.7144	5.5435	70.4785
17	13.4982	6.7597	63.7188
18	12.0152	8.2427	55.4761
19	10.2069	10.0510	45.4251
20	8.0017	12.2562	33.1689
21	5.3128	14.9450	18.2239
22	2.0340	18.2239	0.0000

YEARS 23 — MO PAYT 1.6843 — AN CONST 20.22

#	INT	PRIN	BALANCE
1	19.9795	.2315	99.7685
2	19.9288	.2822	99.4863
3	19.8668	.3442	99.1421
4	19.7913	.4197	98.7224
5	19.6993	.5118	98.2107
6	19.5870	.6240	97.5867
7	19.4501	.7609	96.8257
8	19.2831	.9279	95.8979
9	19.0796	1.1314	94.7664
10	18.8313	1.3797	93.3867
11	18.5287	1.6824	91.7044
12	18.1596	2.0514	89.6529
13	17.7095	2.5015	87.1514
14	17.1607	3.0503	84.1011
15	16.4915	3.7195	80.3815
16	15.6754	4.5356	75.8460
17	14.6804	5.5306	70.3153
18	13.4670	6.7440	63.5713
19	11.9874	8.2236	55.3477
20	10.1832	10.0278	45.3199
21	7.9832	12.2278	33.0921
22	5.3006	14.9105	18.1817
23	2.0293	18.1817	0.0000

YEARS 24 — MO PAYT 1.6811 — AN CONST 20.18

#	INT	PRIN	BALANCE
1	19.9833	.1895	99.8105
2	19.9417	.2310	99.5795
3	19.8910	.2817	99.2978
4	19.8292	.3435	98.9543
5	19.7538	.4189	98.5354
6	19.6619	.5108	98.0246
7	19.5499	.6228	97.4018
8	19.4132	.7595	96.6423
9	19.2466	.9261	95.7162
10	19.0434	1.1293	94.5869
11	18.7957	1.3771	93.2098
12	18.4935	1.6792	91.5306
13	18.1252	2.0476	89.4831
14	17.6759	2.4968	86.9863
15	17.1282	3.0446	83.9418
16	16.4602	3.7125	80.2293
17	15.6457	4.5270	75.7023
18	14.6525	5.5202	70.1821
19	13.4415	6.7312	63.4509
20	11.9647	8.2080	55.2428
21	10.1639	10.0088	45.2341
22	7.9681	12.2046	33.0294
23	5.2905	14.8822	18.1472
24	2.0255	18.1472	0.0000

YEARS 25 — MO PAYT 1.6785 — AN CONST 20.15

#	INT	PRIN	BALANCE
1	19.9863	.1551	99.8449
2	19.9523	.1892	99.6557
3	19.9108	.2307	99.4250
4	19.8601	.2813	99.1438
5	19.7984	.3430	98.8008
6	19.7232	.4182	98.3825
7	19.6314	.5100	97.8725
8	19.5195	.6219	97.2507
9	19.3831	.7583	96.4924
10	19.2167	.9247	95.5677
11	19.0139	1.1275	94.4401
12	18.7665	1.3749	93.0652
13	18.4649	1.6766	91.3887
14	18.0970	2.0444	89.3443
15	17.6485	2.4929	86.8514
16	17.1016	3.0398	83.8115
17	16.4347	3.7067	80.1048
18	15.6215	4.5200	75.5848
19	14.6298	5.5116	70.0732
20	13.4206	6.7208	63.3524
21	11.9461	8.1953	55.1571
22	10.1482	9.9933	45.1639
23	7.9557	12.1857	32.9782
24	5.2823	14.8591	18.1191
25	2.0223	18.1191	0.0000

YEARS 26 — MO PAYT 1.6763 — AN CONST 20.12

#	INT	PRIN	BALANCE
1	19.9888	.1271	99.8729
2	19.9609	.1549	99.7180
3	19.9269	.1889	99.5291
4	19.8855	.2304	99.2987
5	19.8349	.2809	99.0178
6	19.7733	.3425	98.6752
7	19.6981	.4177	98.2575
8	19.6065	.5093	97.7482
9	19.4947	.6211	97.1271
10	19.3585	.7573	96.3698
11	19.1923	.9235	95.4462
12	18.9897	1.1261	94.3201
13	18.7427	1.3732	92.9470
14	18.4414	1.6744	91.2725
15	18.0740	2.0418	89.2307
16	17.6261	2.4897	86.7410
17	17.0799	3.0360	83.7050
18	16.4138	3.7020	80.0030
19	15.6016	4.5142	75.4888
20	14.6112	5.5046	69.9842
21	13.4036	6.7123	63.2719
22	11.9310	8.1849	55.0871
23	10.1353	9.9806	45.1065
24	7.9456	12.1702	32.9363
25	5.2756	14.8402	18.0961
26	2.0198	18.0961	0.0000

YEARS 27 — MO PAYT 1.6746 — AN CONST 20.10

#	INT	PRIN	BALANCE
1	19.9908	.1041	99.8959
2	19.9680	.1269	99.7690
3	19.9401	.1548	99.6142
4	19.9062	.1887	99.4255
5	19.8648	.2301	99.1953
6	19.8143	.2806	98.9147
7	19.7527	.3422	98.5725
8	19.6776	.4173	98.1553
9	19.5861	.5088	97.6464
10	19.4745	.6204	97.0260
11	19.3383	.7566	96.2694
12	19.1723	.9225	95.3469
13	18.9700	1.1249	94.2220
14	18.7231	1.3717	92.8502
15	18.4222	1.6727	91.1775
16	18.0552	2.0397	89.1379
17	17.6077	2.4871	86.6507
18	17.0621	3.0328	83.6179
19	16.3967	3.6982	79.9197
20	15.5854	4.5095	75.4102
21	14.5960	5.4989	69.9113
22	13.3896	6.7053	63.2061
23	11.9185	8.1764	55.0297
24	10.1247	9.9702	45.0595
25	7.9374	12.1575	32.9020
26	5.2701	14.8248	18.0772
27	2.0177	18.0772	0.0000

YEARS 28 — MO PAYT 1.6731 — AN CONST 20.08

#	INT	PRIN	BALANCE
1	19.9925	.0853	99.9147
2	19.9737	.1040	99.8107
3	19.9509	.1268	99.6839
4	19.9231	.1546	99.5292
5	19.8892	.1886	99.3407
6	19.8478	.2299	99.1107
7	19.7974	.2804	98.8303
8	19.7359	.3419	98.4884
9	19.6608	.4169	98.0715
10	19.5694	.5084	97.5632
11	19.4578	.6199	96.9432
12	19.3218	.7559	96.1873
13	19.1560	.9218	95.2656
14	18.9538	1.1240	94.1416
15	18.7072	1.3706	92.7710
16	18.4065	1.6713	91.0998
17	18.0398	2.0379	89.0618
18	17.5927	2.4850	86.5768
19	17.0475	3.0302	83.5466
20	16.3827	3.6950	79.8516
21	15.5721	4.5057	75.3459
22	14.5836	5.4942	69.8517
23	13.3782	6.6996	63.1522
24	11.9084	8.1694	54.9828
25	10.1161	9.9617	45.0211
26	7.9306	12.1472	32.8739
27	5.2656	14.8121	18.0618
28	2.0160	18.0618	0.0000

YEARS 29 — MO PAYT 1.6720 — AN CONST 20.07

#	INT	PRIN	BALANCE
1	19.9938	.0699	99.9301
2	19.9785	.0852	99.8449
3	19.9598	.1039	99.7409
4	19.9370	.1267	99.6142
5	19.9092	.1545	99.4597
6	19.8753	.1884	99.2712
7	19.8339	.2298	99.0415
8	19.7835	.2802	98.7613
9	19.7221	.3417	98.4196
10	19.6471	.4166	98.0030
11	19.5557	.5080	97.4950
12	19.4442	.6195	96.8755
13	19.3083	.7554	96.1201
14	19.1426	.9211	95.1990
15	18.9405	1.1232	94.0758
16	18.6941	1.3696	92.7062
17	18.3936	1.6701	91.0361
18	18.0272	2.0365	88.9996
19	17.5804	2.4833	86.5163
20	17.0356	3.0281	83.4882
21	16.3713	3.6924	79.7958
22	15.5612	4.5025	75.2932
23	14.5734	5.4903	69.8029
24	13.3688	6.6949	63.1080
25	11.9001	8.1637	54.9444
26	10.1090	9.9547	44.9896
27	7.9250	12.1387	32.8510
28	5.2619	14.8018	18.0492
29	2.0145	18.0492	0.0000

YEARS 30 — MO PAYT 1.6710 — AN CONST 20.06

#	INT	PRIN	BALANCE
1	19.9949	.0573	99.9427
2	19.9824	.0699	99.8729
3	19.9670	.0852	99.7877
4	19.9484	.1039	99.6838
5	19.9256	.1267	99.5571
6	19.8978	.1544	99.4027
7	19.8639	.1883	99.2144
8	19.8226	.2296	98.9847
9	19.7722	.2800	98.7047
10	19.7108	.3415	98.3632
11	19.6358	.4164	97.9468
12	19.5445	.5077	97.4391
13	19.4331	.6191	96.8200
14	19.2973	.7550	96.0650
15	19.1316	.9206	95.1445
16	18.9297	1.1226	94.0219
17	18.6834	1.3688	92.6531
18	18.3831	1.6691	90.9839
19	18.0169	2.0353	88.9486
20	17.5704	2.4819	86.4667
21	17.0259	3.0264	83.4404
22	16.3619	3.6903	79.7500
23	15.5523	4.4999	75.2501
24	14.5650	5.4872	69.7629
25	13.3612	6.6910	63.0719
26	11.8932	8.1590	54.9129
27	10.1032	9.9490	44.9639
28	7.9205	12.1317	32.8322
29	5.2589	14.7933	18.0388
30	2.0134	18.0388	0.0000

YEARS 2 — QTR PAYT 12.5000 — AN CONST 50.00

#	INT	PRIN	BALANCE
1	0.0000	50.0000	50.0000
2	0.0000	50.0000	0.0000

YEARS 3 — QTR PAYT 8.3333 — AN CONST 33.34

#	INT	PRIN	BALANCE
1	0.0000	33.3333	66.6667
2	0.0000	33.3333	33.3333
3	0.0000	33.3333	0.0000

YEARS 4 — QTR PAYT 6.2500 — AN CONST 25.00

#	INT	PRIN	BALANCE
1	0.0000	25.0000	75.0000
2	0.0000	25.0000	50.0000
3	0.0000	25.0000	25.0000
4	0.0000	25.0000	0.0000

YEARS 5 — QTR PAYT 5.0000 — AN CONST 20.00

#	INT	PRIN	BALANCE
1	0.0000	20.0000	80.0000
2	0.0000	20.0000	60.0000
3	0.0000	20.0000	40.0000
4	0.0000	20.0000	20.0000
5	0.0000	20.0000	0.0000

YEARS 6 — QTR PAYT 4.1667 — AN CONST 16.67

#	INT	PRIN	BALANCE
1	0.0000	16.6667	83.3333
2	0.0000	16.6667	66.6667
3	0.0000	16.6667	50.0000
4	0.0000	16.6667	33.3333
5	0.0000	16.6667	16.6667
6	0.0000	16.6667	0.0000

YEARS 7 — QTR PAYT 3.5714 — AN CONST 14.29

#	INT	PRIN	BALANCE
1	0.0000	14.2857	85.7143
2	0.0000	14.2857	71.4286
3	0.0000	14.2857	57.1429
4	0.0000	14.2857	42.8571
5	0.0000	14.2857	28.5714
6	0.0000	14.2857	14.2857
7	0.0000	14.2857	0.0000

YEARS 8 — QTR PAYT 3.1250 — AN CONST 12.50

#	INT	PRIN	BALANCE
1	0.0000	12.5000	87.5000
2	0.0000	12.5000	75.0000
3	0.0000	12.5000	62.5000
4	0.0000	12.5000	50.0000
5	0.0000	12.5000	37.5000
6	0.0000	12.5000	25.0000
7	0.0000	12.5000	12.5000
8	0.0000	12.5000	0.0000

YEARS 9 — QTR PAYT 2.7778 — AN CONST 11.12

#	INT	PRIN	BALANCE
1	0.0000	11.1111	88.8889
2	0.0000	11.1111	77.7778
3	0.0000	11.1111	66.6667
4	0.0000	11.1111	55.5556
5	0.0000	11.1111	44.4444
6	0.0000	11.1111	33.3333
7	0.0000	11.1111	22.2222
8	0.0000	11.1111	11.1111
9	0.0000	11.1111	0.0000

YEARS 10 — QTR PAYT 2.5000 — AN CONST 10.00

#	INT	PRIN	BALANCE
1	0.0000	10.0000	90.0000
2	0.0000	10.0000	80.0000
3	0.0000	10.0000	70.0000
4	0.0000	10.0000	60.0000
5	0.0000	10.0000	50.0000
6	0.0000	10.0000	40.0000
7	0.0000	10.0000	30.0000
8	0.0000	10.0000	20.0000
9	0.0000	10.0000	10.0000
10	0.0000	10.0000	0.0000

YEARS 11 — QTR PAYT 2.2727 — AN CONST 9.10

#	INT	PRIN	BALANCE
1	0.0000	9.0909	90.9091
2	0.0000	9.0909	81.8182
3	0.0000	9.0909	72.7273
4	0.0000	9.0909	63.6364
5	0.0000	9.0909	54.5455
6	0.0000	9.0909	45.4545
7	0.0000	9.0909	36.3636
8	0.0000	9.0909	27.2727
9	0.0000	9.0909	18.1818
10	0.0000	9.0909	9.0909
11	0.0000	9.0909	0.0000

YEARS 12 — QTR PAYT 2.0833 — AN CONST 8.34

#	INT	PRIN	BALANCE
1	0.0000	8.3333	91.6667
2	0.0000	8.3333	83.3333
3	0.0000	8.3333	75.0000
4	0.0000	8.3333	66.6667
5	0.0000	8.3333	58.3333
6	0.0000	8.3333	50.0000
7	0.0000	8.3333	41.6667
8	0.0000	8.3333	33.3333
9	0.0000	8.3333	25.0000
10	0.0000	8.3333	16.6667
11	0.0000	8.3333	8.3333
12	0.0000	8.3333	0.0000

YEARS 13 — QTR PAYT 1.9231 — AN CONST 7.70

#	INT	PRIN	BALANCE
1	0.0000	7.6923	92.3077
2	0.0000	7.6923	84.6154
3	0.0000	7.6923	76.9231
4	0.0000	7.6923	69.2308
5	0.0000	7.6923	61.5385
6	0.0000	7.6923	53.8462
7	0.0000	7.6923	46.1538
8	0.0000	7.6923	38.4615
9	0.0000	7.6923	30.7692
10	0.0000	7.6923	23.0769
11	0.0000	7.6923	15.3846
12	0.0000	7.6923	7.6923
13	0.0000	7.6923	0.0000

YEARS 14 — QTR PAYT 1.7857 — AN CONST 7.15

#	INT	PRIN	BALANCE
1	0.0000	7.1429	92.8571
2	0.0000	7.1429	85.7143
3	0.0000	7.1429	78.5714
4	0.0000	7.1429	71.4286
5	0.0000	7.1429	64.2857
6	0.0000	7.1429	57.1429
7	0.0000	7.1429	50.0000
8	0.0000	7.1429	42.8571
9	0.0000	7.1429	35.7143
10	0.0000	7.1429	28.5714
11	0.0000	7.1429	21.4286
12	0.0000	7.1429	14.2857
13	0.0000	7.1429	7.1429
14	0.0000	7.1429	0.0000

YEARS 15 — QTR PAYT 1.6667 — AN CONST 6.67

#	INT	PRIN	BALANCE
1	0.0000	6.6667	93.3333
2	0.0000	6.6667	86.6667
3	0.0000	6.6667	80.0000
4	0.0000	6.6667	73.3333
5	0.0000	6.6667	66.6667
6	0.0000	6.6667	60.0000
7	0.0000	6.6667	53.3333
8	0.0000	6.6667	46.6667
9	0.0000	6.6667	40.0000
10	0.0000	6.6667	33.3333
11	0.0000	6.6667	26.6667
12	0.0000	6.6667	20.0000
13	0.0000	6.6667	13.3333
14	0.0000	6.6667	6.6667
15	0.0000	6.6667	0.0000

YEARS 16 — QTR PAYT 1.5625 — AN CONST 6.25

#	INT	PRIN	BALANCE
1	0.0000	6.2500	93.7500
2	0.0000	6.2500	87.5000
3	0.0000	6.2500	81.2500
4	0.0000	6.2500	75.0000
5	0.0000	6.2500	68.7500
6	0.0000	6.2500	62.5000
7	0.0000	6.2500	56.2500
8	0.0000	6.2500	50.0000
9	0.0000	6.2500	43.7500
10	0.0000	6.2500	37.5000
11	0.0000	6.2500	31.2500
12	0.0000	6.2500	25.0000
13	0.0000	6.2500	18.7500
14	0.0000	6.2500	12.5000
15	0.0000	6.2500	6.2500
16	0.0000	6.2500	0.0000

YEARS 17 — QTR PAYT 1.4706 — AN CONST 5.89

#	INT	PRIN	BALANCE
1	0.0000	5.8824	94.1176
2	0.0000	5.8824	88.2353
3	0.0000	5.8824	82.3529
4	0.0000	5.8824	76.4706
5	0.0000	5.8824	70.5882
6	0.0000	5.8824	64.7059
7	0.0000	5.8824	58.8235
8	0.0000	5.8824	52.9412
9	0.0000	5.8824	47.0588
10	0.0000	5.8824	41.1765
11	0.0000	5.8824	35.2941
12	0.0000	5.8824	29.4118
13	0.0000	5.8824	23.5294
14	0.0000	5.8824	17.6471
15	0.0000	5.8824	11.7647
16	0.0000	5.8824	5.8824
17	0.0000	5.8824	0.0000

YEARS 18 — QTR PAYT 1.3889 — AN CONST 5.56

#	INT	PRIN	BALANCE
1	0.0000	5.5556	94.4444
2	0.0000	5.5556	88.8889
3	0.0000	5.5556	83.3333
4	0.0000	5.5556	77.7778
5	0.0000	5.5556	72.2222
6	0.0000	5.5556	66.6667
7	0.0000	5.5556	61.1111
8	0.0000	5.5556	55.5556
9	0.0000	5.5556	50.0000
10	0.0000	5.5556	44.4444
11	0.0000	5.5556	38.8889
12	0.0000	5.5556	33.3333
13	0.0000	5.5556	27.7778
14	0.0000	5.5556	22.2222
15	0.0000	5.5556	16.6667
16	0.0000	5.5556	11.1111
17	0.0000	5.5556	5.5556
18	0.0000	5.5556	0.0000

YEARS 19 — QTR PAYT 1.3158 — AN CONST 5.27

#	INT	PRIN	BALANCE
1	0.0000	5.2632	94.7368
2	0.0000	5.2632	89.4737
3	0.0000	5.2632	84.2105
4	0.0000	5.2632	78.9474
5	0.0000	5.2632	73.6842
6	0.0000	5.2632	68.4211
7	0.0000	5.2632	63.1579
8	0.0000	5.2632	57.8947
9	0.0000	5.2632	52.6316
10	0.0000	5.2632	47.3684
11	0.0000	5.2632	42.1053
12	0.0000	5.2632	36.8421
13	0.0000	5.2632	31.5789
14	0.0000	5.2632	26.3158
15	0.0000	5.2632	21.0526
16	0.0000	5.2632	15.7895
17	0.0000	5.2632	10.5263
18	0.0000	5.2632	5.2632
19	0.0000	5.2632	0.0000

YEARS 20 — QTR PAYT 1.2500 — AN CONST 5.00

#	INT	PRIN	BALANCE
1	0.0000	5.0000	95.0000
2	0.0000	5.0000	90.0000
3	0.0000	5.0000	85.0000
4	0.0000	5.0000	80.0000
5	0.0000	5.0000	75.0000
6	0.0000	5.0000	70.0000
7	0.0000	5.0000	65.0000
8	0.0000	5.0000	60.0000
9	0.0000	5.0000	55.0000
10	0.0000	5.0000	50.0000
11	0.0000	5.0000	45.0000
12	0.0000	5.0000	40.0000
13	0.0000	5.0000	35.0000
14	0.0000	5.0000	30.0000
15	0.0000	5.0000	25.0000
16	0.0000	5.0000	20.0000
17	0.0000	5.0000	15.0000
18	0.0000	5.0000	10.0000
19	0.0000	5.0000	5.0000
20	0.0000	5.0000	0.0000

YEARS 21 — QTR PAYT 1.1905 — AN CONST 4.77

#	INT	PRIN	BALANCE
1	0.0000	4.7619	95.2381
2	0.0000	4.7619	90.4762
3	0.0000	4.7619	85.7143

#	INT	PRIN	BALANCE
4	0.0000	4.7619	80.9524
5	0.0000	4.7619	76.1905
6	0.0000	4.7619	71.4286
7	0.0000	4.7619	66.6667
8	0.0000	4.7619	61.9048
9	0.0000	4.7619	57.1429
10	0.0000	4.7619	52.3810
11	0.0000	4.7619	47.6190
12	0.0000	4.7619	42.8571
13	0.0000	4.7619	38.0952
14	0.0000	4.7619	33.3333
15	0.0000	4.7619	28.5714
16	0.0000	4.7619	23.8095
17	0.0000	4.7619	19.0476
18	0.0000	4.7619	14.2857
19	0.0000	4.7619	9.5238
20	0.0000	4.7619	4.7619
21	0.0000	4.7619	0.0000

YEARS 22	QTR PAYT 1.1364	AN CONST 4.55	
#	INT	PRIN	BALANCE
1	0.0000	4.5455	95.4545
2	0.0000	4.5455	90.9091
3	0.0000	4.5455	86.3636
4	0.0000	4.5455	81.8182
5	0.0000	4.5455	77.2727
6	0.0000	4.5455	72.7273
7	0.0000	4.5455	68.1818
8	0.0000	4.5455	63.6364
9	0.0000	4.5455	59.0909
10	0.0000	4.5455	54.5455
11	0.0000	4.5455	50.0000
12	0.0000	4.5455	45.4545
13	0.0000	4.5455	40.9091
14	0.0000	4.5455	36.3636
15	0.0000	4.5455	31.8182
16	0.0000	4.5455	27.2727
17	0.0000	4.5455	22.7273
18	0.0000	4.5455	18.1818
19	0.0000	4.5455	13.6364
20	0.0000	4.5455	9.0909
21	0.0000	4.5455	4.5455
22	0.0000	4.5455	0.0000

YEARS 23	QTR PAYT 1.0870	AN CONST 4.35	
#	INT	PRIN	BALANCE
1	0.0000	4.3478	95.6522
2	0.0000	4.3478	91.3043
3	0.0000	4.3478	86.9565
4	0.0000	4.3478	82.6087
5	0.0000	4.3478	78.2609
6	0.0000	4.3478	73.9130
7	0.0000	4.3478	69.5652
8	0.0000	4.3478	65.2174
9	0.0000	4.3478	60.8696
10	0.0000	4.3478	56.5217
11	0.0000	4.3478	52.1739
12	0.0000	4.3478	47.8261
13	0.0000	4.3478	43.4783
14	0.0000	4.3478	39.1304
15	0.0000	4.3478	34.7826
16	0.0000	4.3478	30.4348
17	0.0000	4.3478	26.0870
18	0.0000	4.3478	21.7391
19	0.0000	4.3478	17.3913
20	0.0000	4.3478	13.0435
21	0.0000	4.3478	8.6957
22	0.0000	4.3478	4.3478
23	0.0000	4.3478	0.0000

YEARS 24	QTR PAYT 1.0417	AN CONST 4.17	
#	INT	PRIN	BALANCE
1	0.0000	4.1667	95.8333
2	0.0000	4.1667	91.6667
3	0.0000	4.1667	87.5000
4	0.0000	4.1667	83.3333
5	0.0000	4.1667	79.1667
6	0.0000	4.1667	75.0000
7	0.0000	4.1667	70.8333
8	0.0000	4.1667	66.6667
9	0.0000	4.1667	62.5000
10	0.0000	4.1667	58.3333
11	0.0000	4.1667	54.1667
12	0.0000	4.1667	50.0000
13	0.0000	4.1667	45.8333
14	0.0000	4.1667	41.6667
15	0.0000	4.1667	37.5000
16	0.0000	4.1667	33.3333
17	0.0000	4.1667	29.1667
18	0.0000	4.1667	25.0000
19	0.0000	4.1667	20.8333
20	0.0000	4.1667	16.6667
21	0.0000	4.1667	12.5000
22	0.0000	4.1667	8.3333
23	0.0000	4.1667	4.1667
24	0.0000	4.1667	0.0000

YEARS 25	QTR PAYT 1.0000	AN CONST 4.00	
#	INT	PRIN	BALANCE
1	0.0000	4.0000	96.0000
2	0.0000	4.0000	92.0000
3	0.0000	4.0000	88.0000
4	0.0000	4.0000	84.0000
5	0.0000	4.0000	80.0000
6	0.0000	4.0000	76.0000
7	0.0000	4.0000	72.0000
8	0.0000	4.0000	68.0000
9	0.0000	4.0000	64.0000
10	0.0000	4.0000	60.0000
11	0.0000	4.0000	56.0000
12	0.0000	4.0000	52.0000
13	0.0000	4.0000	48.0000
14	0.0000	4.0000	44.0000
15	0.0000	4.0000	40.0000
16	0.0000	4.0000	36.0000
17	0.0000	4.0000	32.0000
18	0.0000	4.0000	28.0000
19	0.0000	4.0000	24.0000
20	0.0000	4.0000	20.0000
21	0.0000	4.0000	16.0000
22	0.0000	4.0000	12.0000
23	0.0000	4.0000	8.0000
24	0.0000	4.0000	4.0000
25	0.0000	4.0000	0.0000

YEARS 26	QTR PAYT .9615	AN CONST 3.85	
#	INT	PRIN	BALANCE
1	0.0000	3.8462	96.1538
2	0.0000	3.8462	92.3077
3	0.0000	3.8462	88.4615
4	0.0000	3.8462	84.6154
5	0.0000	3.8462	80.7692
6	0.0000	3.8462	76.9231
7	0.0000	3.8462	73.0769
8	0.0000	3.8462	69.2308
9	0.0000	3.8462	65.3846
10	0.0000	3.8462	61.5385
11	0.0000	3.8462	57.6923
12	0.0000	3.8462	53.8462
13	0.0000	3.8462	50.0000
14	0.0000	3.8462	46.1538
15	0.0000	3.8462	42.3077
16	0.0000	3.8462	38.4615
17	0.0000	3.8462	34.6154
18	0.0000	3.8462	30.7692
19	0.0000	3.8462	26.9231
20	0.0000	3.8462	23.0769
21	0.0000	3.8462	19.2308
22	0.0000	3.8462	15.3846
23	0.0000	3.8462	11.5385
24	0.0000	3.8462	7.6923
25	0.0000	3.8462	3.8462
26	0.0000	3.8462	0.0000

YEARS 27	QTR PAYT .9259	AN CONST 3.71	
#	INT	PRIN	BALANCE
1	0.0000	3.7037	96.2963
2	0.0000	3.7037	92.5926
3	0.0000	3.7037	88.8889
4	0.0000	3.7037	85.1852
5	0.0000	3.7037	81.4815
6	0.0000	3.7037	77.7778
7	0.0000	3.7037	74.0741
8	0.0000	3.7037	70.3704
9	0.0000	3.7037	66.6667
10	0.0000	3.7037	62.9630
11	0.0000	3.7037	59.2593
12	0.0000	3.7037	55.5556
13	0.0000	3.7037	51.8519
14	0.0000	3.7037	48.1481
15	0.0000	3.7037	44.4444
16	0.0000	3.7037	40.7407
17	0.0000	3.7037	37.0370
18	0.0000	3.7037	33.3333
19	0.0000	3.7037	29.6296
20	0.0000	3.7037	25.9259
21	0.0000	3.7037	22.2222
22	0.0000	3.7037	18.5185
23	0.0000	3.7037	14.8148
24	0.0000	3.7037	11.1111
25	0.0000	3.7037	7.4074
26	0.0000	3.7037	3.7037
27	0.0000	3.7037	0.0000

YEARS 28	QTR PAYT .8929	AN CONST 3.58	
#	INT	PRIN	BALANCE
1	0.0000	3.5714	96.4286
2	0.0000	3.5714	92.8571
3	0.0000	3.5714	89.2857
4	0.0000	3.5714	85.7143
5	0.0000	3.5714	82.1429
6	0.0000	3.5714	78.5714
7	0.0000	3.5714	75.0000
8	0.0000	3.5714	71.4286
9	0.0000	3.5714	67.8571
10	0.0000	3.5714	64.2857
11	0.0000	3.5714	60.7143
12	0.0000	3.5714	57.1429
13	0.0000	3.5714	53.5714
14	0.0000	3.5714	50.0000
15	0.0000	3.5714	46.4286
16	0.0000	3.5714	42.8571
17	0.0000	3.5714	39.2857
18	0.0000	3.5714	35.7143
19	0.0000	3.5714	32.1429
20	0.0000	3.5714	28.5714
21	0.0000	3.5714	25.0000
22	0.0000	3.5714	21.4286
23	0.0000	3.5714	17.8571
24	0.0000	3.5714	14.2857
25	0.0000	3.5714	10.7143
26	0.0000	3.5714	7.1429
27	0.0000	3.5714	3.5714
28	0.0000	3.5714	0.0000

YEARS 29	QTR PAYT .8621	AN CONST 3.45	
#	INT	PRIN	BALANCE
1	0.0000	3.4483	96.5517
2	0.0000	3.4483	93.1034
3	0.0000	3.4483	89.6552
4	0.0000	3.4483	86.2069
5	0.0000	3.4483	82.7586
6	0.0000	3.4483	79.3103
7	0.0000	3.4483	75.8621
8	0.0000	3.4483	72.4138
9	0.0000	3.4483	68.9655
10	0.0000	3.4483	65.5172
11	0.0000	3.4483	62.0690
12	0.0000	3.4483	58.6207
13	0.0000	3.4483	55.1724
14	0.0000	3.4483	51.7241
15	0.0000	3.4483	48.2759
16	0.0000	3.4483	44.8276
17	0.0000	3.4483	41.3793
18	0.0000	3.4483	37.9310
19	0.0000	3.4483	34.4828
20	0.0000	3.4483	31.0345
21	0.0000	3.4483	27.5862
22	0.0000	3.4483	24.1379
23	0.0000	3.4483	20.6897
24	0.0000	3.4483	17.2414
25	0.0000	3.4483	13.7931
26	0.0000	3.4483	10.3448
27	0.0000	3.4483	6.8966
28	0.0000	3.4483	3.4483
29	0.0000	3.4483	0.0000

YEARS 30	QTR PAYT .8333	AN CONST 3.34	
#	INT	PRIN	BALANCE
1	0.0000	3.3333	96.6667
2	0.0000	3.3333	93.3333
3	0.0000	3.3333	90.0000
4	0.0000	3.3333	86.6667
5	0.0000	3.3333	83.3333
6	0.0000	3.3333	80.0000
7	0.0000	3.3333	76.6667
8	0.0000	3.3333	73.3333
9	0.0000	3.3333	70.0000
10	0.0000	3.3333	66.6667
11	0.0000	3.3333	63.3333
12	0.0000	3.3333	60.0000
13	0.0000	3.3333	56.6667
14	0.0000	3.3333	53.3333
15	0.0000	3.3333	50.0000
16	0.0000	3.3333	46.6667
17	0.0000	3.3333	43.3333
18	0.0000	3.3333	40.0000
19	0.0000	3.3333	36.6667
20	0.0000	3.3333	33.3333
21	0.0000	3.3333	30.0000
22	0.0000	3.3333	26.6667
23	0.0000	3.3333	23.3333
24	0.0000	3.3333	20.0000
25	0.0000	3.3333	16.6667
26	0.0000	3.3333	13.3333
27	0.0000	3.3333	10.0000
28	0.0000	3.3333	6.6667
29	0.0000	3.3333	3.3333
30	0.0000	3.3333	0.0000

YEARS 2 — QTR PAYT 12.6410 — AN CONST 50.57

#	INT	PRIN	BALANCE
1	.8138	49.7503	50.2497
2	.3145	50.2497	0.0000

YEARS 3 — QTR PAYT 8.4694 — AN CONST 33.88

#	INT	PRIN	BALANCE
1	.8765	33.0010	66.9990
2	.5453	33.3322	33.6668
3	.2107	33.6668	0.0000

YEARS 4 — QTR PAYT 6.3836 — AN CONST 25.54

#	INT	PRIN	BALANCE
1	.9078	24.6267	75.3733
2	.6606	24.8739	50.4994
3	.4110	25.1236	25.3758
4	.1588	25.3758	0.0000

YEARS 5 — QTR PAYT 5.1323 — AN CONST 20.53

#	INT	PRIN	BALANCE
1	.9266	19.6025	80.3975
2	.7299	19.7993	60.5982
3	.5311	19.9980	40.6002
4	.3304	20.1987	20.4015
5	.1277	20.4015	0.0000

YEARS 6 — QTR PAYT 4.2981 — AN CONST 17.20

#	INT	PRIN	BALANCE
1	.9392	16.2533	83.7467
2	.7760	16.4165	67.3302
3	.6113	16.5812	50.7490
4	.4448	16.7477	34.0013
5	.2767	16.9158	17.0856
6	.1069	17.0856	0.0000

YEARS 7 — QTR PAYT 3.7023 — AN CONST 14.81

#	INT	PRIN	BALANCE
1	.9481	13.8613	86.1387
2	.8090	14.0004	72.1383
3	.6685	14.1409	57.9974
4	.5265	14.2829	43.7146
5	.3832	14.4262	29.2883
6	.2384	14.5710	14.7173
7	.0921	14.7173	0.0000

YEARS 8 — QTR PAYT 3.2556 — AN CONST 13.03

#	INT	PRIN	BALANCE
1	.9548	12.0674	87.9326
2	.8337	12.1886	75.7440
3	.7114	12.3109	63.4331
4	.5878	12.4345	50.9986
5	.4630	12.5593	38.4393
6	.3369	12.6854	25.7540
7	.2096	12.8127	12.9413
8	.0810	12.9413	0.0000

YEARS 9 — QTR PAYT 2.9081 — AN CONST 11.64

#	INT	PRIN	BALANCE
1	.9601	10.6724	89.3276
2	.8529	10.7795	78.5480
3	.7447	10.8877	67.6603
4	.6354	10.9970	56.6632
5	.5251	11.1074	45.5558
6	.4136	11.2189	34.3369
7	.3010	11.3315	23.0054
8	.1872	11.4453	11.5601
9	.0723	11.5601	0.0000

YEARS 10 — QTR PAYT 2.6302 — AN CONST 10.53

#	INT	PRIN	BALANCE
1	.9642	9.5566	90.4434
2	.8683	9.6525	80.7909
3	.7714	9.7494	71.0415
4	.6736	9.8473	61.1943
5	.5747	9.9461	51.2482
6	.4749	10.0459	41.2023
7	.3741	10.1468	31.0555
8	.2722	10.2486	20.8069
9	.1693	10.3515	10.4554
10	.0654	10.4554	0.0000

YEARS 11 — QTR PAYT 2.4029 — AN CONST 9.62

#	INT	PRIN	BALANCE
1	.9677	8.6438	91.3562
2	.8809	8.7305	82.6257
3	.7933	8.8182	73.8075
4	.7047	8.9067	64.9009
5	.6153	8.9961	55.9048
6	.5250	9.0864	46.8184
7	.4338	9.1776	37.6408
8	.3417	9.2697	28.3711
9	.2487	9.3627	19.0084
10	.1547	9.4567	9.5516
11	.0598	9.5516	0.0000

YEARS 12 — QTR PAYT 2.2134 — AN CONST 8.86

#	INT	PRIN	BALANCE
1	.9705	7.8832	92.1168
2	.8914	7.9624	84.1544
3	.8114	8.0423	76.1121
4	.7307	8.1230	67.9891
5	.6492	8.2045	59.7846
6	.5668	8.2869	51.4977
7	.4837	8.3701	43.1276
8	.3996	8.4541	34.6735
9	.3148	8.5390	26.1346
10	.2291	8.6247	17.5099
11	.1425	8.7112	8.7987
12	.0551	8.7987	0.0000

YEARS 13 — QTR PAYT 2.0532 — AN CONST 8.22

#	INT	PRIN	BALANCE
1	.9729	7.2398	92.7602
2	.9002	7.3125	85.4477
3	.8268	7.3859	78.0618
4	.7527	7.4600	70.6017
5	.6778	7.5349	63.0668
6	.6022	7.6105	55.4563
7	.5258	7.6869	47.7693
8	.4486	7.7641	40.0052
9	.3707	7.8420	32.1632
10	.2920	7.9207	24.2425
11	.2125	8.0002	16.2422
12	.1322	8.0806	8.1617
13	.0511	8.1617	0.0000

YEARS 14 — QTR PAYT 1.9159 — AN CONST 7.67

#	INT	PRIN	BALANCE
1	.9750	6.6885	93.3115
2	.9078	6.7556	86.5559
3	.8400	6.8234	79.7325
4	.7715	6.8919	72.8406
5	.7024	6.9611	65.8796
6	.6325	7.0309	58.8486
7	.5619	7.1015	51.7471
8	.4906	7.1728	44.5743
9	.4186	7.2448	37.3295
10	.3459	7.3175	30.0120
11	.2725	7.3910	22.6210
12	.1983	7.4652	15.1559
13	.1233	7.5401	7.6158
14	.0477	7.6158	0.0000

YEARS 15 — QTR PAYT 1.7969 — AN CONST 7.19

#	INT	PRIN	BALANCE
1	.9768	6.2107	93.7893
2	.9144	6.2731	87.5162
3	.8515	6.3360	81.1802
4	.7879	6.3996	74.7806
5	.7236	6.4639	68.3167
6	.6587	6.5287	61.7880
7	.5932	6.5943	55.1937
8	.5270	6.6605	48.5332
9	.4602	6.7273	41.8059
10	.3926	6.7948	35.0111
11	.3244	6.8630	28.1480
12	.2555	6.9319	21.2161
13	.1860	7.0015	14.2146
14	.1157	7.0718	7.1428
15	.0447	7.1428	0.0000

YEARS 16 — QTR PAYT 1.6928 — AN CONST 6.78

#	INT	PRIN	BALANCE
1	.9783	5.7928	94.2072
2	.9202	5.8509	88.3563
3	.8614	5.9097	82.4466
4	.8021	5.9690	76.4776
5	.7422	6.0289	70.4487
6	.6817	6.0894	64.3593
7	.6206	6.1505	58.2087
8	.5588	6.2123	51.9964
9	.4965	6.2746	45.7218
10	.4335	6.3376	39.3842
11	.3699	6.4012	32.9830
12	.3056	6.4655	26.5175
13	.2407	6.5304	19.9871
14	.1752	6.5959	13.3912
15	.1090	6.6621	6.7290
16	.0421	6.7290	0.0000

YEARS 17 — QTR PAYT 1.6010 — AN CONST 6.41

#	INT	PRIN	BALANCE
1	.9797	5.4241	94.5759
2	.9253	5.4786	89.0973
3	.8703	5.5336	83.5637
4	.8147	5.5891	77.9746
5	.7586	5.6452	72.3293
6	.7020	5.7019	66.6275
7	.6447	5.7591	60.8683
8	.5869	5.8169	55.0514
9	.5285	5.8753	49.1761
10	.4696	5.9343	43.2418
11	.4100	5.9939	37.2479
12	.3498	6.0540	31.1939
13	.2891	6.1148	25.0791
14	.2277	6.1762	18.9030
15	.1657	6.2382	12.6648
16	.1031	6.3008	6.3640
17	.0398	6.3640	0.0000

YEARS 18 — QTR PAYT 1.5194 — AN CONST 6.08

#	INT	PRIN	BALANCE
1	.9809	5.0965	94.9035
2	.9298	5.1477	89.7558
3	.8781	5.1994	84.5564
4	.8259	5.2516	79.3048
5	.7732	5.3043	74.0006
6	.7200	5.3575	68.6430
7	.6662	5.4113	63.2318
8	.6119	5.4656	57.7661
9	.5570	5.5205	52.2457
10	.5016	5.5759	46.6698
11	.4456	5.6318	41.0380
12	.3891	5.6884	35.3496
13	.3320	5.7455	29.6041
14	.2743	5.8031	23.8010
15	.2161	5.8614	17.9396
16	.1572	5.9202	12.0193
17	.0978	5.9797	6.0397
18	.0378	6.0397	0.0000

YEARS 19 — QTR PAYT 1.4464 — AN CONST 5.79

#	INT	PRIN	BALANCE
1	.9820	4.8035	95.1965
2	.9338	4.8517	90.3448
3	.8851	4.9004	85.4443
4	.8359	4.9496	80.4947
5	.7862	4.9993	75.4954
6	.7361	5.0495	70.4459
7	.6854	5.1002	65.3458
8	.6342	5.1514	60.1944
9	.5825	5.2031	54.9913
10	.5302	5.2553	49.7361
11	.4775	5.3080	44.4280
12	.4242	5.3613	39.0667
13	.3704	5.4151	33.6516
14	.3160	5.4695	28.1821
15	.2611	5.5244	22.6577
16	.2057	5.5798	17.0778
17	.1497	5.6359	11.4420
18	.0931	5.6924	5.7496
19	.0360	5.7496	0.0000

YEARS 20 — QTR PAYT 1.3807 — AN CONST 5.53

#	INT	PRIN	BALANCE
1	.9830	4.5399	95.4601
2	.9374	4.5854	90.8747
3	.8914	4.6315	86.2432
4	.8449	4.6780	81.5653
5	.7980	4.7249	76.8404
6	.7505	4.7723	72.0680
7	.7026	4.8202	67.2478
8	.6543	4.8686	62.3792
9	.6054	4.9175	57.4617
10	.5560	4.9669	52.4948
11	.5062	5.0167	47.4781
12	.4558	5.0671	42.4110
13	.4050	5.1179	37.2931
14	.3536	5.1693	32.1238
15	.3017	5.2212	26.9026
16	.2493	5.2736	21.6290
17	.1964	5.3265	16.3025
18	.1429	5.3800	10.9225
19	.0889	5.4340	5.4885
20	.0343	5.4885	0.0000

YEARS 21 — QTR PAYT 1.3213 — AN CONST 5.29

#	INT	PRIN	BALANCE
1	.9839	4.3014	95.6986
2	.9407	4.3446	91.3540
3	.8971	4.3882	86.9658

#	INT	PRIN	BALANCE
4	.8531	4.4322	82.5335
5	.8086	4.4767	78.0568
6	.7636	4.5217	73.5351
7	.7183	4.5671	68.9681
8	.6724	4.6129	64.3552
9	.6261	4.6592	59.6960
10	.5793	4.7060	54.9900
11	.5321	4.7532	50.2369
12	.4844	4.8009	45.4359
13	.4362	4.8491	40.5868
14	.3875	4.8978	35.6890
15	.3384	4.9469	30.7420
16	.2887	4.9966	25.7454
17	.2386	5.0468	20.6987
18	.1879	5.0974	15.6013
19	.1367	5.1486	10.4527
20	.0851	5.2003	5.2525
21	.0329	5.2525	0.0000

YEARS 22 QTR PAYT 1.2674 AN CONST 5.07

#	INT	PRIN	BALANCE
1	.9847	4.0847	95.9153
2	.9437	4.1257	91.7896
3	.9023	4.1671	87.6224
4	.8605	4.2090	83.4135
5	.8182	4.2512	79.1623
6	.7756	4.2939	74.8684
7	.7325	4.3370	70.5314
8	.6889	4.3805	66.1509
9	.6450	4.4245	61.7264
10	.6005	4.4689	57.2576
11	.5557	4.5137	52.7438
12	.5104	4.5591	48.1848
13	.4646	4.6048	43.5799
14	.4184	4.6510	38.9289
15	.3717	4.6977	34.2312
16	.3246	4.7449	29.4863
17	.2769	4.7925	24.6938
18	.2288	4.8406	19.8532
19	.1802	4.8892	14.9640
20	.1312	4.9383	10.0257
21	.0816	4.9878	5.0379
22	.0315	5.0379	0.0000

YEARS 23 QTR PAYT 1.2181 AN CONST 4.88

#	INT	PRIN	BALANCE
1	.9855	3.8869	96.1131
2	.9464	3.9259	92.1871
3	.9070	3.9654	88.2218
4	.8672	4.0052	84.2166
5	.8270	4.0454	80.1713
6	.7864	4.0860	76.0853
7	.7454	4.1270	71.9583
8	.7040	4.1684	67.7899
9	.6621	4.2102	63.5797
10	.6199	4.2525	59.3272
11	.5772	4.2952	55.0320
12	.5341	4.3383	50.6937
13	.4905	4.3818	46.3118
14	.4466	4.4258	41.8860
15	.4021	4.4703	37.4158
16	.3573	4.5151	32.9006
17	.3119	4.5604	28.3402
18	.2662	4.6062	23.7340
19	.2199	4.6525	19.0815
20	.1732	4.6992	14.3824
21	.1261	4.7463	9.6360
22	.0784	4.7940	4.8421
23	.0303	4.8421	0.0000

YEARS 24 QTR PAYT 1.1730 AN CONST 4.70

#	INT	PRIN	BALANCE
1	.9861	3.7057	96.2943
2	.9489	3.7429	92.5514
3	.9114	3.7805	88.7709
4	.8734	3.8184	84.9525
5	.8351	3.8567	81.0958
6	.7964	3.8954	77.2004
7	.7573	3.9345	73.2658
8	.7178	3.9740	69.2918
9	.6779	4.0139	65.2778
10	.6376	4.0542	61.2236
11	.5969	4.0949	57.1287
12	.5558	4.1360	52.9927
13	.5143	4.1775	48.8151
14	.4724	4.2195	44.5957
15	.4300	4.2618	40.3339
16	.3872	4.3046	36.0293
17	.3440	4.3478	31.6814
18	.3004	4.3914	27.2900
19	.2563	4.4355	22.8545
20	.2118	4.4800	18.3744
21	.1668	4.5250	13.8494
22	.1214	4.5704	9.2790
23	.0755	4.6163	4.6627
24	.0292	4.6627	0.0000

YEARS 25 QTR PAYT 1.1314 AN CONST 4.53

#	INT	PRIN	BALANCE
1	.9868	3.5390	96.4610
2	.9512	3.5746	92.8864
3	.9154	3.6104	89.2760
4	.8791	3.6467	85.6293
5	.8425	3.6833	81.9460
6	.8055	3.7202	78.2258
7	.7682	3.7576	74.4682
8	.7305	3.7953	70.6729
9	.6924	3.8334	66.8395
10	.6539	3.8719	62.9676
11	.6150	3.9107	59.0569
12	.5758	3.9500	55.1069
13	.5361	3.9896	51.1172
14	.4961	4.0297	47.0876
15	.4556	4.0701	43.0174
16	.4148	4.1110	38.9064
17	.3735	4.1523	34.7542
18	.3318	4.1939	30.5602
19	.2898	4.2360	26.3242
20	.2472	4.2786	22.0456
21	.2043	4.3215	17.7241
22	.1609	4.3649	13.3593
23	.1171	4.4087	8.9506
24	.0728	4.4529	4.4976
25	.0281	4.4976	0.0000

YEARS 26 QTR PAYT 1.0931 AN CONST 4.38

#	INT	PRIN	BALANCE
1	.9873	3.3852	96.6148
2	.9534	3.4192	93.1955
3	.9190	3.4535	89.7420
4	.8844	3.4882	86.2538
5	.8494	3.5232	82.7306
6	.8140	3.5586	79.1720
7	.7783	3.5943	75.5777
8	.7422	3.6304	71.9473
9	.7058	3.6668	68.2805
10	.6689	3.7036	64.5768
11	.6318	3.7408	60.8360
12	.5942	3.7784	57.0577
13	.5563	3.8163	53.2414
14	.5180	3.8546	49.3868
15	.4793	3.8933	45.4935
16	.4402	3.9324	41.5612
17	.4007	3.9718	37.5893
18	.3609	4.0117	33.5777
19	.3206	4.0520	29.5257
20	.2799	4.0926	25.4331
21	.2389	4.1337	21.2993
22	.1974	4.1752	17.1241
23	.1555	4.2171	12.9070
24	.1131	4.2594	8.6476
25	.0704	4.3022	4.3454
26	.0272	4.3454	0.0000

YEARS 27 QTR PAYT 1.0577 AN CONST 4.24

#	INT	PRIN	BALANCE
1	.9879	3.2429	96.7571
2	.9553	3.2755	93.4816
3	.9224	3.3083	90.1733
4	.8892	3.3415	86.8317
5	.8557	3.3751	83.4566
6	.8218	3.4090	80.0477
7	.7876	3.4432	76.6045
8	.7530	3.4777	73.1268
9	.7181	3.5127	69.6141
10	.6829	3.5479	66.0662
11	.6473	3.5835	62.4827
12	.6113	3.6195	58.8632
13	.5750	3.6558	55.2073
14	.5383	3.6925	51.5148
15	.5012	3.7296	47.7852
16	.4638	3.7670	44.0182
17	.4259	3.8048	40.2134
18	.3878	3.8430	36.3704
19	.3492	3.8816	32.4888
20	.3102	3.9206	28.5682
21	.2709	3.9599	24.6083
22	.2311	3.9997	20.6086
23	.1910	4.0398	16.5688
24	.1504	4.0804	12.4885
25	.1095	4.1213	8.3671
26	.0681	4.1627	4.2045
27	.0263	4.2045	0.0000

YEARS 28 QTR PAYT 1.0248 AN CONST 4.10

#	INT	PRIN	BALANCE
1	.9884	3.1108	96.8892
2	.9571	3.1420	93.7472
3	.9256	3.1736	90.5736
4	.8937	3.2054	87.3682
5	.8616	3.2376	84.1306
6	.8291	3.2701	80.8605
7	.7962	3.3029	77.5576
8	.7631	3.3361	74.2215
9	.7296	3.3696	70.8519
10	.6958	3.4034	67.4485
11	.6616	3.4375	64.0110
12	.6271	3.4720	60.5389
13	.5923	3.5069	57.0320
14	.5571	3.5421	53.4899
15	.5215	3.5777	49.9123
16	.4856	3.6136	46.2987
17	.4493	3.6498	42.6489
18	.4127	3.6865	38.9624
19	.3757	3.7235	35.2389
20	.3383	3.7608	31.4781
21	.3006	3.7986	27.6795
22	.2624	3.8367	23.8428
23	.2239	3.8752	19.9675
24	.1850	3.9141	16.0534
25	.1457	3.9534	12.1000
26	.1061	3.9931	8.1069
27	.0660	4.0332	4.0737
28	.0255	4.0737	0.0000

YEARS 29 QTR PAYT .9942 AN CONST 3.98

#	INT	PRIN	BALANCE
1	.9888	2.9879	97.0121
2	.9588	3.0179	93.9943
3	.9285	3.0482	90.9461
4	.8979	3.0787	87.8674
5	.8670	3.1097	84.7577
6	.8358	3.1409	81.6169
7	.8043	3.1724	78.4445
8	.7725	3.2042	75.2402
9	.7403	3.2364	72.0038
10	.7078	3.2689	68.7350
11	.6750	3.3017	65.4333
12	.6419	3.3348	62.0984
13	.6084	3.3683	58.7301
14	.5746	3.4021	55.3280
15	.5404	3.4363	51.8917
16	.5059	3.4708	48.4210
17	.4711	3.5056	44.9154
18	.4359	3.5408	41.3746
19	.4004	3.5763	37.7983
20	.3645	3.6122	34.1861
21	.3282	3.6485	30.5376
22	.2916	3.6851	26.8525
23	.2546	3.7221	23.1304
24	.2172	3.7595	19.3709
25	.1795	3.7972	15.5737
26	.1414	3.8353	11.7384
27	.1029	3.8738	7.8646
28	.0640	3.9127	3.9520
29	.0247	3.9520	0.0000

YEARS 30 QTR PAYT .9656 AN CONST 3.87

#	INT	PRIN	BALANCE
1	.9892	2.8732	97.1268
2	.9604	2.9020	94.2248
3	.9313	2.9312	91.2936
4	.9019	2.9606	88.3331
5	.8721	2.9903	85.3428
6	.8421	3.0203	82.3225
7	.8118	3.0506	79.2719
8	.7812	3.0812	76.1906
9	.7503	3.1122	73.0784
10	.7190	3.1434	69.9350
11	.6875	3.1750	66.7601
12	.6556	3.2068	63.5532
13	.6234	3.2390	60.3142
14	.5909	3.2715	57.0427
15	.5581	3.3044	53.7383
16	.5249	3.3375	50.4008
17	.4914	3.3710	47.0298
18	.4576	3.4049	43.6249
19	.4234	3.4391	40.1858
20	.3889	3.4736	36.7123
21	.3540	3.5084	33.2038
22	.3188	3.5437	29.6602
23	.2832	3.5792	26.0810
24	.2473	3.6151	22.4658
25	.2110	3.6514	18.8144
26	.1743	3.6881	15.1263
27	.1373	3.7251	11.4012
28	.0999	3.7625	7.6387
29	.0622	3.8003	3.8384
30	.0240	3.8384	0.0000

YEARS 2 — QTR PAYT 12.7829 — AN CONST 51.14

#	INT	PRIN	BALANCE
1	1.6303	49.5013	50.4987
2	.6328	50.4987	0.0000

YEARS 3 — QTR PAYT 8.6066 — AN CONST 34.43

#	INT	PRIN	BALANCE
1	1.7560	32.6706	67.3294
2	1.0977	33.3289	34.0005
3	.4261	34.0005	0.0000

YEARS 4 — QTR PAYT 6.5189 — AN CONST 26.08

#	INT	PRIN	BALANCE
1	1.8188	24.2569	75.7431
2	1.3300	24.7457	50.9974
3	.8314	25.2443	25.7530
4	.3227	25.7530	0.0000

YEARS 5 — QTR PAYT 5.2666 — AN CONST 21.07

#	INT	PRIN	BALANCE
1	1.8565	19.2101	80.7899
2	1.4694	19.5971	61.1928
3	1.0745	19.9920	41.2008
4	.6717	20.3949	20.8059
5	.2607	20.8059	0.0000

YEARS 6 — QTR PAYT 4.4321 — AN CONST 17.73

#	INT	PRIN	BALANCE
1	1.8816	15.8466	84.1534
2	1.5623	16.1659	67.9875
3	1.2366	16.4917	51.4958
4	.9043	16.8240	34.6718
5	.5652	17.1630	17.5088
6	.2194	17.5088	0.0000

YEARS 7 — QTR PAYT 3.8362 — AN CONST 15.35

#	INT	PRIN	BALANCE
1	1.8996	13.4451	86.5549
2	1.6287	13.7160	72.8389
3	1.3523	13.9924	58.8465
4	1.0703	14.2743	44.5722
5	.7827	14.5620	30.0102
6	.4893	14.8554	15.1548
7	.1899	15.1548	0.0000

YEARS 8 — QTR PAYT 3.3895 — AN CONST 13.56

#	INT	PRIN	BALANCE
1	1.9130	11.6448	88.3552
2	1.6784	11.8794	76.4758
3	1.4390	12.1188	64.3570
4	1.1948	12.3630	51.9940
5	.9457	12.6121	39.3818
6	.6915	12.8663	26.5156
7	.4323	13.1255	13.3900
8	.1678	13.3900	0.0000

YEARS 9 — QTR PAYT 3.0422 — AN CONST 12.17

#	INT	PRIN	BALANCE
1	1.9235	10.2453	89.7547
2	1.7170	10.4517	79.3030
3	1.5064	10.6624	68.6406
4	1.2916	10.8772	57.7634
5	1.0724	11.0964	46.6670
6	.8488	11.3200	35.3470
7	.6207	11.5481	23.7990
8	.3880	11.7808	12.0182
9	.1506	12.0182	0.0000

YEARS 10 — QTR PAYT 2.7646 — AN CONST 11.06

#	INT	PRIN	BALANCE
1	1.9318	9.1264	90.8736
2	1.7479	9.3103	81.5634
3	1.5603	9.4979	72.0655
4	1.3689	9.6893	62.3762
5	1.1737	9.8845	52.4917
6	.9745	10.0837	42.4080
7	.7713	10.2869	32.1211
8	.5640	10.4942	21.6270
9	.3526	10.7056	10.9214
10	.1369	10.9214	0.0000

YEARS 11 — QTR PAYT 2.5375 — AN CONST 10.16

#	INT	PRIN	BALANCE
1	1.9387	8.2115	91.7885
2	1.7732	8.3770	83.4115
3	1.6044	8.5458	74.8658
4	1.4322	8.7180	66.1478
5	1.2565	8.8936	57.2542
6	1.0773	9.0728	48.1814
7	.8945	9.2557	38.9257
8	.7080	9.4422	29.4835
9	.5177	9.6324	19.8511
10	.3236	9.8265	10.0245
11	.1256	10.0245	0.0000

YEARS 12 — QTR PAYT 2.3485 — AN CONST 9.40

#	INT	PRIN	BALANCE
1	1.9444	7.4497	92.5503
2	1.7942	7.5998	84.9506
3	1.6411	7.7529	77.1977
4	1.4849	7.9091	69.2885
5	1.3255	8.0685	61.2200
6	1.1629	8.2311	52.9890
7	.9971	8.3969	44.5920
8	.8279	8.5662	36.0259
9	.6552	8.7388	27.2871
10	.4792	8.9149	18.3722
11	.2995	9.0945	9.2778
12	.1163	9.2778	0.0000

YEARS 13 — QTR PAYT 2.1887 — AN CONST 8.76

#	INT	PRIN	BALANCE
1	1.9492	6.8055	93.1945
2	1.8120	6.9427	86.2518
3	1.6721	7.0826	79.1692
4	1.5294	7.2253	71.9440
5	1.3838	7.3709	64.5731
6	1.2353	7.5194	57.0537
7	1.0838	7.6709	49.3828
8	.9292	7.8255	41.5573
9	.7715	7.9832	33.5741
10	.6107	8.1440	25.4301
11	.4465	8.3082	17.1219
12	.2791	8.4756	8.6464
13	.1083	8.6464	0.0000

YEARS 14 — QTR PAYT 2.0518 — AN CONST 8.21

#	INT	PRIN	BALANCE
1	1.9533	6.2539	93.7461
2	1.8273	6.3799	87.3662
3	1.6987	6.5085	80.8577
4	1.5676	6.6396	74.2181
5	1.4338	6.7734	67.4447
6	1.2973	6.9099	60.5348
7	1.1580	7.0491	53.4856
8	1.0160	7.1912	46.2944
9	.8711	7.3361	38.9583
10	.7233	7.4839	31.4744
11	.5725	7.6347	23.8397
12	.4186	7.7886	16.0511
13	.2617	7.9455	8.1056
14	.1016	8.1056	0.0000

YEARS 15 — QTR PAYT 1.9333 — AN CONST 7.74

#	INT	PRIN	BALANCE
1	1.9569	5.7763	94.2237
2	1.8405	5.8927	88.3311
3	1.7217	6.0114	82.3197
4	1.6006	6.1325	76.1872
5	1.4770	6.2561	69.9311
6	1.3510	6.3822	63.5489
7	1.2223	6.5108	57.0381
8	1.0912	6.6420	50.3961
9	.9573	6.7758	43.6203
10	.8208	6.9123	36.7080
11	.6815	7.0516	29.6564
12	.5394	7.1937	22.4627
13	.3944	7.3387	15.1240
14	.2466	7.4866	7.6374
15	.0957	7.6374	0.0000

YEARS 16 — QTR PAYT 1.8297 — AN CONST 7.32

#	INT	PRIN	BALANCE
1	1.9600	5.3587	94.6413
2	1.8520	5.4667	89.1745
3	1.7418	5.5769	83.5976
4	1.6295	5.6893	77.9084
5	1.5148	5.8039	72.1045
6	1.3979	5.9209	66.1836
7	1.2786	6.0402	60.1435
8	1.1568	6.1619	53.9816
9	1.0327	6.2860	47.6955
10	.9060	6.4127	41.2828
11	.7768	6.5419	34.7409
12	.6450	6.6737	28.0672
13	.5105	6.8082	21.2589
14	.3733	6.9454	14.3135
15	.2334	7.0854	7.2281
16	.0906	7.2281	0.0000

YEARS 17 — QTR PAYT 1.7384 — AN CONST 6.96

#	INT	PRIN	BALANCE
1	1.9627	4.9907	95.0093
2	1.8622	5.0913	89.9180
3	1.7596	5.1939	84.7241
4	1.6549	5.2986	79.4255
5	1.5481	5.4053	74.0202
6	1.4392	5.5142	68.5059
7	1.3281	5.6254	62.8806
8	1.2147	5.7387	57.1419
9	1.0991	5.8544	51.2875
10	.9811	5.9723	45.3152
11	.8608	6.0927	39.2225
12	.7380	6.2154	33.0071
13	.6128	6.3407	26.6664
14	.4850	6.4684	20.1980
15	.3547	6.5988	13.5992
16	.2217	6.7318	6.8674
17	.0861	6.8674	0.0000

YEARS 18 — QTR PAYT 1.6573 — AN CONST 6.63

#	INT	PRIN	BALANCE
1	1.9652	4.6640	95.3360
2	1.8712	4.7580	90.5780
3	1.7753	4.8538	85.7242
4	1.6775	4.9517	80.7725
5	1.5777	5.0514	75.7211
6	1.4759	5.1532	70.5679
7	1.3721	5.2571	65.3108
8	1.2662	5.3630	59.9478
9	1.1581	5.4711	54.4768
10	1.0478	5.5813	48.8955
11	.9354	5.6938	43.2017
12	.8207	5.8085	37.3932
13	.7036	5.9255	31.4676
14	.5842	6.0450	25.4227
15	.4624	6.1668	19.2559
16	.3381	6.2910	12.9649
17	.2114	6.4178	6.5471
18	.0820	6.5471	0.0000

YEARS 19 — QTR PAYT 1.5848 — AN CONST 6.34

#	INT	PRIN	BALANCE
1	1.9673	4.3720	95.6280
2	1.8792	4.4601	91.1679
3	1.7894	4.5500	86.6180
4	1.6977	4.6416	81.9763
5	1.6042	4.7352	77.2412
6	1.5087	4.8306	72.4106
7	1.4114	4.9279	67.4827
8	1.3121	5.0272	62.4554
9	1.2108	5.1285	57.3269
10	1.1075	5.2319	52.0951
11	1.0020	5.3373	46.7578
12	.8945	5.4448	41.3129
13	.7848	5.5546	35.7584
14	.6728	5.6665	30.0919
15	.5587	5.7807	24.3112
16	.4422	5.8972	18.4141
17	.3233	6.0160	12.3981
18	.2021	6.1372	6.2609
19	.0785	6.2609	0.0000

YEARS 20 — QTR PAYT 1.5197 — AN CONST 6.08

#	INT	PRIN	BALANCE
1	1.9693	4.1095	95.8905
2	1.8865	4.1923	91.6982
3	1.8020	4.2768	87.4214
4	1.7158	4.3630	83.0584
5	1.6279	4.4509	78.6075
6	1.5382	4.5406	74.0669
7	1.4467	4.6321	69.4349
8	1.3534	4.7254	64.7095
9	1.2582	4.8206	59.8888
10	1.1610	4.9178	54.9711
11	1.0620	5.0169	49.9542
12	.9609	5.1180	44.8362
13	.8577	5.2211	39.6152
14	.7525	5.3263	34.2889
15	.6452	5.4336	28.8552
16	.5357	5.5431	23.3121
17	.4240	5.6548	17.6573
18	.3101	5.7688	11.8886
19	.1938	5.8850	6.0036
20	.0752	6.0036	0.0000

YEARS 21 — QTR PAYT 1.4609 — AN CONST 5.85

#	INT	PRIN	BALANCE
1	1.9711	3.8723	96.1277
2	1.8930	3.9504	92.1773
3	1.8134	4.0300	88.1473

#	INT	PRIN	BALANCE
4	1.7322	4.1112	84.0361
5	1.6494	4.1940	79.8421
6	1.5649	4.2785	75.5636
7	1.4787	4.3648	71.1988
8	1.3907	4.4527	66.7461
9	1.3010	4.5424	62.2037
10	1.2095	4.6340	57.5697
11	1.1161	4.7273	52.8424
12	1.0208	4.8226	48.0198
13	.9237	4.9198	43.1000
14	.8245	5.0189	38.0811
15	.7234	5.1200	32.9611
16	.6202	5.2232	27.7379
17	.5150	5.3285	22.4094
18	.4076	5.4358	16.9736
19	.2981	5.5454	11.4282
20	.1863	5.6571	5.7711
21	.0723	5.7711	0.0000

YEARS 22	QTR PAYT 1.4074	AN CONST 5.63	
#	INT	PRIN	BALANCE
1	1.9727	3.6570	96.3430
2	1.8990	3.7307	92.6122
3	1.8238	3.8059	88.8063
4	1.7471	3.8826	84.9237
5	1.6689	3.9608	80.9629
6	1.5891	4.0406	76.9222
7	1.5077	4.1221	72.8002
8	1.4246	4.2051	68.5950
9	1.3399	4.2899	64.3052
10	1.2534	4.3763	59.9289
11	1.1652	4.4645	55.4644
12	1.0753	4.5545	50.9099
13	.9835	4.6462	46.2637
14	.8899	4.7399	41.5238
15	.7944	4.8354	36.6885
16	.6969	4.9328	31.7557
17	.5975	5.0322	26.7235
18	.4961	5.1336	21.5899
19	.3927	5.2370	16.3528
20	.2872	5.3426	11.0103
21	.1795	5.4502	5.5601
22	.0697	5.5601	0.0000

YEARS 23	QTR PAYT 1.3587	AN CONST 5.44	
#	INT	PRIN	BALANCE
1	1.9742	3.4607	96.5393
2	1.9044	3.5305	93.0088
3	1.8333	3.6016	89.4072
4	1.7607	3.6742	85.7330
5	1.6867	3.7482	81.9847
6	1.6111	3.8238	78.1610
7	1.5341	3.9008	74.2602
8	1.4555	3.9794	70.2808
9	1.3753	4.0596	66.2212
10	1.2935	4.1414	62.0797
11	1.2100	4.2249	57.8549
12	1.1249	4.3100	53.5449
13	1.0381	4.3968	49.1481
14	.9495	4.4854	44.6626
15	.8591	4.5758	40.0868
16	.7669	4.6680	35.4188
17	.6728	4.7621	30.6567
18	.5769	4.8580	25.7987
19	.4790	4.9559	20.8427
20	.3791	5.0558	15.7869
21	.2772	5.1577	10.6292
22	.1733	5.2616	5.3676
23	.0673	5.3676	0.0000

YEARS 24	QTR PAYT 1.3141	AN CONST 5.26	
#	INT	PRIN	BALANCE
1	1.9755	3.2811	96.7189
2	1.9094	3.3472	93.3717
3	1.8419	3.4146	89.9571
4	1.7731	3.4834	86.4736
5	1.7029	3.5536	82.9200
6	1.6313	3.6252	79.2948
7	1.5583	3.6983	75.5965
8	1.4838	3.7728	71.8236
9	1.4077	3.8488	67.9748
10	1.3302	3.9264	64.0484
11	1.2511	4.0055	60.0429
12	1.1703	4.0862	55.9566
13	1.0880	4.1686	51.7881
14	1.0040	4.2526	47.5355
15	.9183	4.3383	43.1972
16	.8309	4.4257	38.7715
17	.7417	4.5149	34.2567
18	.6507	4.6058	29.6508
19	.5579	4.6986	24.9522
20	.4632	4.7933	20.1589
21	.3667	4.8899	15.2689
22	.2681	4.9885	10.2805
23	.1676	5.0890	5.1915
24	.0651	5.1915	0.0000

YEARS 25	QTR PAYT 1.2732	AN CONST 5.10	
#	INT	PRIN	BALANCE
1	1.9767	3.1160	96.8840
2	1.9139	3.1788	93.7051
3	1.8499	3.2429	90.4622
4	1.7845	3.3082	87.1540
5	1.7179	3.3749	83.7791
6	1.6499	3.4429	80.3362
7	1.5805	3.5123	76.8239
8	1.5097	3.5831	73.2408
9	1.4375	3.6553	69.5856
10	1.3639	3.7289	65.8567
11	1.2887	3.8041	62.0526
12	1.2121	3.8807	58.1719
13	1.1339	3.9589	54.2130
14	1.0541	4.0387	50.1743
15	.9727	4.1201	46.0543
16	.8897	4.2031	41.8512
17	.8050	4.2878	37.5634
18	.7186	4.3742	33.1892
19	.6305	4.4623	28.7269
20	.5405	4.5522	24.1747
21	.4488	4.6440	19.5307
22	.3552	4.7375	14.7932
23	.2598	4.8330	9.9601
24	.1624	4.9304	5.0297
25	.0630	5.0297	0.0000

YEARS 26	QTR PAYT 1.2355	AN CONST 4.95	
#	INT	PRIN	BALANCE
1	1.9779	2.9640	97.0360
2	1.9181	3.0237	94.0123
3	1.8572	3.0846	90.9277
4	1.7951	3.1468	87.7810
5	1.7316	3.2102	84.5708
6	1.6670	3.2749	81.2959
7	1.6010	3.3409	77.9550
8	1.5336	3.4082	74.5469
9	1.4650	3.4769	71.0700
10	1.3949	3.5469	67.5231
11	1.3234	3.6184	63.9047
12	1.2505	3.6913	60.2134
13	1.1761	3.7657	56.4477
14	1.1003	3.8416	52.6061
15	1.0229	3.9190	48.6872
16	.9439	3.9979	44.6892
17	.8633	4.0785	40.6107
18	.7811	4.1607	36.4500
19	.6973	4.2445	32.2055
20	.6118	4.3301	27.8754
21	.5245	4.4173	23.4581
22	.4355	4.5063	18.9518
23	.3447	4.5971	14.3547
24	.2521	4.6898	9.6649
25	.1576	4.7843	4.8807
26	.0612	4.8807	0.0000

YEARS 27	QTR PAYT 1.2006	AN CONST 4.81	
#	INT	PRIN	BALANCE
1	1.9789	2.8234	97.1766
2	1.9220	2.8803	94.2963
3	1.8640	2.9383	91.3580
4	1.8048	2.9975	88.3605
5	1.7444	3.0579	85.3026
6	1.6828	3.1195	82.1830
7	1.6199	3.1824	79.0006
8	1.5558	3.2465	75.7541
9	1.4903	3.3120	72.4421
10	1.4236	3.3787	69.0634
11	1.3555	3.4468	65.6166
12	1.2861	3.5162	62.1004
13	1.2152	3.5871	58.5133
14	1.1429	3.6594	54.8540
15	1.0692	3.7331	51.1209
16	.9940	3.8083	47.3125
17	.9172	3.8851	43.4275
18	.8389	3.9634	39.4641
19	.7591	4.0432	35.4209
20	.6776	4.1247	31.2962
21	.5945	4.2078	27.0884
22	.5097	4.2926	22.7958
23	.4232	4.3791	18.4167
24	.3350	4.4673	13.9494
25	.2449	4.5573	9.3920
26	.1531	4.6492	4.7429
27	.0594	4.7429	0.0000

YEARS 28	QTR PAYT 1.1682	AN CONST 4.68	
#	INT	PRIN	BALANCE
1	1.9799	2.6931	97.3069
2	1.9256	2.7474	94.5596
3	1.8703	2.8027	91.7569
4	1.8138	2.8592	88.8977
5	1.7562	2.9168	85.9809
6	1.6974	2.9756	83.0053
7	1.6374	3.0355	79.9698
8	1.5763	3.0967	76.8730
9	1.5139	3.1591	73.7139
10	1.4502	3.2228	70.4912
11	1.3853	3.2877	67.2035
12	1.3190	3.3540	63.8495
13	1.2514	3.4215	60.4280
14	1.1825	3.4905	56.9375
15	1.1122	3.5608	53.3767
16	1.0404	3.6326	49.7441
17	.9672	3.7058	46.0384
18	.8925	3.7804	42.2579
19	.8164	3.8566	38.4013
20	.7386	3.9343	34.4670
21	.6594	4.0136	30.4534
22	.5785	4.0945	26.3589
23	.4960	4.1770	22.1819
24	.4118	4.2612	17.9208
25	.3259	4.3470	13.5737
26	.2384	4.4346	9.1391
27	.1490	4.5240	4.6151
28	.0578	4.6151	0.0000

YEARS 29	QTR PAYT 1.1382	AN CONST 4.56	
#	INT	PRIN	BALANCE
1	1.9808	2.5720	97.4280
2	1.9290	2.6238	94.8042
3	1.8761	2.6767	92.1275
4	1.8222	2.7306	89.3969
5	1.7671	2.7856	86.6112
6	1.7110	2.8418	83.7694
7	1.6537	2.8990	80.8704
8	1.5953	2.9575	77.9129
9	1.5357	3.0171	74.8959
10	1.4749	3.0779	71.8180
11	1.4129	3.1399	68.6782
12	1.3496	3.2031	65.4750
13	1.2851	3.2677	62.2073
14	1.2192	3.3335	58.8738
15	1.1521	3.4007	55.4731
16	1.0836	3.4692	52.0039
17	1.0136	3.5391	48.4647
18	.9423	3.6105	44.8543
19	.8696	3.6832	41.1711
20	.7954	3.7574	37.4136
21	.7196	3.8331	33.5805
22	.6424	3.9104	29.6701
23	.5636	3.9892	25.6810
24	.4832	4.0696	21.6114
25	.4012	4.1516	17.4598
26	.3176	4.2352	13.2246
27	.2322	4.3206	8.9041
28	.1452	4.4076	4.4964
29	.0563	4.4964	0.0000

YEARS 30	QTR PAYT 1.1102	AN CONST 4.45	
#	INT	PRIN	BALANCE
1	1.9816	2.4592	97.5408
2	1.9321	2.5087	95.0321
3	1.8815	2.5593	92.4728
4	1.8300	2.6109	89.8619
5	1.7773	2.6635	87.1984
6	1.7237	2.7171	84.4813
7	1.6689	2.7719	81.7094
8	1.6131	2.8278	78.8816
9	1.5561	2.8847	75.9969
10	1.4980	2.9429	73.0540
11	1.4387	3.0022	70.0519
12	1.3782	3.0627	66.9892
13	1.3164	3.1244	63.8649
14	1.2535	3.1873	60.6775
15	1.1893	3.2516	57.4260
16	1.1237	3.3171	54.1089
17	1.0569	3.3839	50.7250
18	.9887	3.4521	47.2729
19	.9192	3.5217	43.7512
20	.8482	3.5926	40.1586
21	.7758	3.6650	36.4936
22	.7019	3.7389	32.7547
23	.6266	3.8142	28.9405
24	.5497	3.8911	25.0494
25	.4713	3.9695	21.0799
26	.3914	4.0495	17.0305
27	.3098	4.1311	12.8994
28	.2265	4.2143	8.6851
29	.1416	4.2992	4.3859
30	.0550	4.3859	0.0000

QUARTERLY PAYMENT AMORTIZATION SCHEDULE PER $100 — 3.00 %

YEARS 2 — QTR PAYT 12.9256 — AN CONST 51.71

#	INT	PRIN	BALANCE
1	2.4494	49.2529	50.7471
2	.9551	50.7471	0.0000

YEARS 3 — QTR PAYT 8.7451 — AN CONST 34.99

#	INT	PRIN	BALANCE
1	2.6384	32.3422	67.6578
2	1.6572	33.3234	34.3344
3	.6462	34.3344	0.0000

YEARS 4 — QTR PAYT 6.6559 — AN CONST 26.63

#	INT	PRIN	BALANCE
1	2.7329	23.8906	76.1094
2	2.0081	24.6154	51.4940
3	1.2613	25.3622	26.1317
4	.4918	26.1317	0.0000

YEARS 5 — QTR PAYT 5.4031 — AN CONST 21.62

#	INT	PRIN	BALANCE
1	2.7896	18.8227	81.1773
2	2.2185	19.3938	61.7836
3	1.6301	19.9821	41.8014
4	1.0239	20.5884	21.2130
5	.3992	21.2130	0.0000

YEARS 6 — QTR PAYT 4.5685 — AN CONST 18.28

#	INT	PRIN	BALANCE
1	2.8273	15.4466	84.5534
2	2.3587	15.9152	68.6382
3	1.8758	16.3981	52.2401
4	1.3783	16.8956	35.3445
5	.8657	17.4082	17.9363
6	.3376	17.9363	0.0000

YEARS 7 — QTR PAYT 3.9729 — AN CONST 15.90

#	INT	PRIN	BALANCE
1	2.8542	13.0372	86.9628
2	2.4587	13.4328	73.5300
3	2.0512	13.8403	59.6897
4	1.6313	14.2602	45.4294
5	1.1986	14.6929	30.7366
6	.7528	15.1386	15.5979
7	.2936	15.5979	0.0000

YEARS 8 — QTR PAYT 3.5266 — AN CONST 14.11

#	INT	PRIN	BALANCE
1	2.8744	11.2321	88.7679
2	2.5337	11.5729	77.1950
3	2.1825	11.9240	65.2710
4	1.8208	12.2858	52.9853
5	1.4480	12.6585	40.3268
6	1.0640	13.0425	27.2842
7	.6683	13.4382	13.8460
8	.2606	13.8460	0.0000

YEARS 9 — QTR PAYT 3.1800 — AN CONST 12.72

#	INT	PRIN	BALANCE
1	2.8901	9.8298	90.1702
2	2.5919	10.1280	80.0422
3	2.2846	10.4353	69.6069
4	1.9680	10.7519	58.8550
5	1.6418	11.0781	47.7769
6	1.3057	11.4142	36.3627
7	.9594	11.7605	24.6022
8	.6026	12.1173	12.4849
9	.2350	12.4849	0.0000

YEARS 10 — QTR PAYT 2.9030 — AN CONST 11.62

#	INT	PRIN	BALANCE
1	2.9026	8.7094	91.2906
2	2.6384	8.9737	82.3169
3	2.3661	9.2459	73.0710
4	2.0856	9.5264	63.5445
5	1.7966	9.8155	53.7291
6	1.4988	10.1133	43.6158
7	1.1920	10.4201	33.1957
8	.8758	10.7362	22.4595
9	.5501	11.0619	11.3976
10	.2145	11.3976	0.0000

YEARS 11 — QTR PAYT 2.6768 — AN CONST 10.71

#	INT	PRIN	BALANCE
1	2.9129	7.7941	92.2059
2	2.6764	8.0306	84.1753
3	2.4328	8.2743	75.9010
4	2.1817	8.5253	67.3757
5	1.9231	8.7839	58.5918
6	1.6566	9.0504	49.5414
7	1.3820	9.3250	40.2163
8	1.0991	9.6079	30.6084
9	.8076	9.8994	20.7090
10	.5072	10.1998	10.5092
11	.1978	10.5092	0.0000

YEARS 12 — QTR PAYT 2.4885 — AN CONST 9.96

#	INT	PRIN	BALANCE
1	2.9214	7.0326	92.9674
2	2.7080	7.2460	85.7214
3	2.4882	7.4658	78.2555
4	2.2617	7.6924	70.5632
5	2.0283	7.9257	62.6374
6	1.7878	8.1662	54.4712
7	1.5401	8.4139	46.0573
8	1.2848	8.6692	37.3881
9	1.0218	8.9322	28.4558
10	.7508	9.2032	19.2526
11	.4716	9.4825	9.7701
12	.1839	9.7701	0.0000

YEARS 13 — QTR PAYT 2.3295 — AN CONST 9.32

#	INT	PRIN	BALANCE
1	2.9286	6.3894	93.6106
2	2.7347	6.5833	87.0273
3	2.5350	6.7830	80.2442
4	2.3292	6.9888	73.2554
5	2.1172	7.2009	66.0546
6	1.8987	7.4193	58.6352
7	1.6736	7.6444	50.9908
8	1.4417	7.8763	43.1145
9	1.2027	8.1153	34.9992
10	.9565	8.3615	26.6377
11	.7028	8.6152	18.0225
12	.4414	8.8766	9.1459
13	.1721	9.1459	0.0000

YEARS 14 — QTR PAYT 2.1935 — AN CONST 8.78

#	INT	PRIN	BALANCE
1	2.9347	5.8392	94.1608
2	2.7576	6.0164	88.1445
3	2.5750	6.1989	81.9456
4	2.3870	6.3870	75.5586
5	2.1932	6.5807	68.9779
6	1.9935	6.7804	62.1975
7	1.7878	6.9861	55.2114
8	1.5759	7.1980	48.0134
9	1.3575	7.4164	40.5969
10	1.1325	7.6414	32.9555
11	.9006	7.8733	25.0822
12	.6618	8.1121	16.9701
13	.4157	8.3583	8.6118
14	.1621	8.6118	0.0000

YEARS 15 — QTR PAYT 2.0758 — AN CONST 8.31

#	INT	PRIN	BALANCE
1	2.9400	5.3633	94.6367
2	2.7773	5.5260	89.1107
3	2.6097	5.6937	83.4170
4	2.4369	5.8664	77.5506
5	2.2589	6.0444	71.5062
6	2.0756	6.2278	65.2784
7	1.8866	6.4167	58.8617
8	1.6919	6.6114	52.2503
9	1.4914	6.8120	45.4383
10	1.2847	7.0187	38.4196
11	1.0717	7.2316	31.1880
12	.8523	7.4510	23.7370
13	.6263	7.6771	16.0599
14	.3934	7.9100	8.1500
15	.1534	8.1500	0.0000

YEARS 16 — QTR PAYT 1.9731 — AN CONST 7.90

#	INT	PRIN	BALANCE
1	2.9447	4.9478	95.0522
2	2.7946	5.0979	89.9542
3	2.6399	5.2526	84.7016
4	2.4805	5.4120	79.2897
5	2.3163	5.5762	73.7135
6	2.1472	5.7453	67.9682
7	1.9729	5.9196	62.0485
8	1.7933	6.0992	55.9493
9	1.6082	6.2843	49.6650
10	1.4176	6.4749	43.1901
11	1.2211	6.6714	36.5187
12	1.0187	6.8738	29.6449
13	.8102	7.0823	22.5625
14	.5953	7.2972	15.2653
15	.3739	7.5186	7.7467
16	.1458	7.7467	0.0000

YEARS 17 — QTR PAYT 1.8827 — AN CONST 7.54

#	INT	PRIN	BALANCE
1	2.9488	4.5821	95.4179
2	2.8098	4.7211	90.6968
3	2.6665	4.8643	85.8325
4	2.5189	5.0119	80.8205
5	2.3669	5.1640	75.6565
6	2.2102	5.3207	70.3359
7	2.0488	5.4821	64.8538
8	1.8825	5.6484	59.2054
9	1.7111	5.8198	53.3856
10	1.5345	5.9963	47.3893
11	1.3526	6.1783	41.2111
12	1.1652	6.3657	34.8454
13	.9720	6.5588	28.2865
14	.7730	6.7578	21.5287
15	.5680	6.9628	14.5658
16	.3568	7.1741	7.3918
17	.1391	7.3918	0.0000

YEARS 18 — QTR PAYT 1.8026 — AN CONST 7.22

#	INT	PRIN	BALANCE
1	2.9524	4.2578	95.7422
2	2.8232	4.3870	91.3552
3	2.6901	4.5201	86.8351
4	2.5530	4.6572	82.1779
5	2.4117	4.7985	77.3793
6	2.2661	4.9441	72.4352
7	2.1161	5.0941	67.3411
8	1.9616	5.2487	62.0925
9	1.8023	5.4079	56.6846
10	1.6382	5.5720	51.1126
11	1.4692	5.7410	45.3716
12	1.2950	5.9152	39.4564
13	1.1156	6.0947	33.3617
14	.9306	6.2796	27.0821
15	.7401	6.4701	20.6120
16	.5438	6.6664	13.9457
17	.3416	6.8686	7.0770
18	.1332	7.0770	0.0000

YEARS 19 — QTR PAYT 1.7310 — AN CONST 6.93

#	INT	PRIN	BALANCE
1	2.9556	3.9684	96.0316
2	2.8352	4.0888	91.9427
3	2.7112	4.2129	87.7298
4	2.5834	4.3407	83.3891
5	2.4517	4.4724	78.9167
6	2.3160	4.6081	74.3086
7	2.1762	4.7479	69.5607
8	2.0321	4.8920	64.6687
9	1.8837	5.0404	59.6283
10	1.7308	5.1933	54.4351
11	1.5732	5.3509	49.0842
12	1.4109	5.5132	43.5710
13	1.2436	5.6805	37.8906
14	1.0713	5.8528	32.0378
15	.8937	6.0304	26.0074
16	.7108	6.2133	19.7941
17	.5222	6.4018	13.3922
18	.3280	6.5961	6.7962
19	.1279	6.7962	0.0000

YEARS 20 — QTR PAYT 1.6668 — AN CONST 6.67

#	INT	PRIN	BALANCE
1	2.9585	3.7087	96.2913
2	2.8460	3.8213	92.4700
3	2.7301	3.9372	88.5328
4	2.6106	4.0567	84.4761
5	2.4876	4.1797	80.2964
6	2.3607	4.3065	75.9899
7	2.2301	4.4372	71.5527
8	2.0955	4.5718	66.9808
9	1.9568	4.7105	62.2703
10	1.8138	4.8534	57.4169
11	1.6666	5.0007	52.4162
12	1.5149	5.1524	47.2638
13	1.3586	5.3087	41.9551
14	1.1975	5.4698	36.4853
15	1.0316	5.6357	30.8496
16	.8606	5.8067	25.0428
17	.6844	5.9829	19.0600
18	.5029	6.1644	12.8956
19	.3159	6.3514	6.5441
20	.1232	6.5441	0.0000

YEARS 21 — QTR PAYT 1.6089 — AN CONST 6.44

#	INT	PRIN	BALANCE
1	2.9612	3.4745	96.5255
2	2.8557	3.5799	92.9456
3	2.7471	3.6885	89.2571

#	INT	PRIN	BALANCE
4	2.6352	3.8004	85.4567
5	2.5199	3.9157	81.5410
6	2.4011	4.0345	77.5065
7	2.2787	4.1569	73.3496
8	2.1526	4.2830	69.0666
9	2.0227	4.4130	64.6536
10	1.8888	4.5469	60.1068
11	1.7508	4.6848	55.4219
12	1.6087	4.8269	50.5950
13	1.4622	4.9734	45.6216
14	1.3114	5.1243	40.4974
15	1.1559	5.2797	35.2176
16	.9957	5.4399	29.7777
17	.8307	5.6050	24.1727
18	.6606	5.7750	18.3977
19	.4854	5.9502	12.4475
20	.3049	6.1307	6.3167
21	.1189	6.3167	0.0000

YEARS 22 — **QTR PAYT 1.5564** — **AN CONST 6.23**

#	INT	PRIN	BALANCE
1	2.9635	3.2622	96.7378
2	2.8646	3.3611	93.3767
3	2.7626	3.4631	89.9136
4	2.6575	3.5682	86.3454
5	2.5493	3.6764	82.6690
6	2.4377	3.7880	78.8810
7	2.3228	3.9029	74.9781
8	2.2044	4.0213	70.9568
9	2.0824	4.1433	66.8135
10	1.9567	4.2690	62.5445
11	1.8272	4.3985	58.1460
12	1.6937	4.5320	53.6140
13	1.5562	4.6695	48.9445
14	1.4145	4.8111	44.1334
15	1.2686	4.9571	39.1763
16	1.1182	5.1075	34.0688
17	.9632	5.2625	28.8063
18	.8036	5.4221	23.3842
19	.6391	5.5866	17.7976
20	.4696	5.7561	12.0414
21	.2949	5.9308	6.1107
22	.1150	6.1107	0.0000

YEARS 23 — **QTR PAYT 1.5087** — **AN CONST 6.04**

#	INT	PRIN	BALANCE
1	2.9657	3.0689	96.9311
2	2.8726	3.1620	93.7690
3	2.7766	3.2580	90.5110
4	2.6778	3.3568	87.1542
5	2.5760	3.4587	83.6955
6	2.4710	3.5636	80.1319
7	2.3629	3.6717	76.4602
8	2.2515	3.7831	72.6771
9	2.1367	3.8979	68.7792
10	2.0185	4.0162	64.7631
11	1.8966	4.1380	60.6251
12	1.7711	4.2635	56.3615
13	1.6417	4.3929	51.9686
14	1.5085	4.5262	47.4424
15	1.3711	4.6635	42.7790
16	1.2296	4.8050	37.9740
17	1.0839	4.9508	33.0232
18	.9337	5.1010	27.9223
19	.7789	5.2557	22.6665
20	.6195	5.4152	17.2514
21	.4552	5.5795	11.6719
22	.2859	5.7487	5.9232
23	.1115	5.9232	0.0000

YEARS 24 — **QTR PAYT 1.4650** — **AN CONST 5.87**

#	INT	PRIN	BALANCE
1	2.9677	2.8924	97.1076
2	2.8799	2.9802	94.1274
3	2.7895	3.0706	91.0568
4	2.6963	3.1637	87.8931
5	2.6003	3.2597	84.6333
6	2.5015	3.3586	81.2747
7	2.3996	3.4605	77.8142
8	2.2946	3.5655	74.2487
9	2.1864	3.6737	70.5750
10	2.0749	3.7851	66.7898
11	1.9601	3.9000	62.8898
12	1.8418	4.0183	58.8715
13	1.7199	4.1402	54.7313
14	1.5942	4.2658	50.4655
15	1.4648	4.3953	46.0702
16	1.3315	4.5286	41.5416
17	1.1941	4.6660	36.8756
18	1.0525	4.8076	32.0680
19	.9067	4.9534	27.1146
20	.7564	5.1037	22.0109
21	.6015	5.2585	16.7524
22	.4420	5.4181	11.3343
23	.2776	5.5825	5.7518
24	.1082	5.7518	0.0000

YEARS 25 — **QTR PAYT 1.4250** — **AN CONST 5.71**

#	INT	PRIN	BALANCE
1	2.9695	2.7306	97.2694
2	2.8866	2.8134	94.4560
3	2.8013	2.8988	91.5572
4	2.7133	2.9867	88.5704
5	2.6227	3.0774	85.4931
6	2.5293	3.1707	82.3223
7	2.4331	3.2669	79.0554
8	2.3340	3.3660	75.6894
9	2.2319	3.4682	72.2212
10	2.1267	3.5734	68.6479
11	2.0183	3.6818	64.9661
12	1.9066	3.7935	61.1726
13	1.7915	3.9086	57.2640
14	1.6729	4.0272	53.2368
15	1.5507	4.1494	49.0875
16	1.4248	4.2752	44.8122
17	1.2951	4.4049	40.4073
18	1.1615	4.5386	35.8687
19	1.0238	4.6763	31.1924
20	.8819	4.8182	26.3742
21	.7357	4.9643	21.4099
22	.5851	5.1150	16.2949
23	.4299	5.2701	11.0248
24	.2700	5.4300	5.5948
25	.1053	5.5948	0.0000

YEARS 26 — **QTR PAYT 1.3882** — **AN CONST 5.56**

#	INT	PRIN	BALANCE
1	2.9711	2.5818	97.4182
2	2.8928	2.6601	94.7581
3	2.8121	2.7408	92.0173
4	2.7289	2.8240	89.1934
5	2.6433	2.9096	86.2837
6	2.5550	2.9979	83.2858
7	2.4640	3.0889	80.1970
8	2.3703	3.1826	77.0144
9	2.2738	3.2791	73.7353
10	2.1743	3.3786	70.3567
11	2.0718	3.4811	66.8755
12	1.9662	3.5867	63.2888
13	1.8573	3.6956	59.5932
14	1.7452	3.8077	55.7856
15	1.6297	3.9232	51.8624
16	1.5107	4.0422	47.8201
17	1.3880	4.1649	43.6553
18	1.2617	4.2912	39.3640
19	1.1315	4.4214	34.9426
20	.9973	4.5556	30.3871
21	.8591	4.6938	25.6933
22	.7167	4.8362	20.8571
23	.5700	4.9829	15.8742
24	.4188	5.1341	10.7402
25	.2631	5.2898	5.4503
26	.1026	5.4503	0.0000

YEARS 27 — **QTR PAYT 1.3543** — **AN CONST 5.42**

#	INT	PRIN	BALANCE
1	2.9727	2.4445	97.5555
2	2.8985	2.5187	95.0369
3	2.8221	2.5951	92.4418
4	2.7434	2.6738	89.7680
5	2.6622	2.7549	87.0131
6	2.5787	2.8385	84.1745
7	2.4925	2.9246	81.2499
8	2.4038	3.0134	78.2366
9	2.3124	3.1048	75.1318
10	2.2182	3.1990	71.9328
11	2.1211	3.2960	68.6368
12	2.0211	3.3960	65.2408
13	1.9181	3.4991	61.7417
14	1.8119	3.6052	58.1365
15	1.7026	3.7146	54.4219
16	1.5899	3.8273	50.5946
17	1.4738	3.9434	46.6512
18	1.3541	4.0631	42.5881
19	1.2308	4.1863	38.4018
20	1.1038	4.3133	34.0885
21	.9730	4.4442	29.6443
22	.8381	4.5790	25.0652
23	.6992	4.7180	20.3473
24	.5561	4.8611	15.4862
25	.4086	5.0086	10.4776
26	.2566	5.1605	5.3171
27	.1001	5.3171	0.0000

YEARS 28 — **QTR PAYT 1.3229** — **AN CONST 5.30**

#	INT	PRIN	BALANCE
1	2.9741	2.3175	97.6825
2	2.9038	2.3878	95.2946
3	2.8313	2.4603	92.8343
4	2.7567	2.5349	90.2994
5	2.6798	2.6118	87.6876
6	2.6005	2.6911	84.9965
7	2.5189	2.7727	82.2238
8	2.4348	2.8568	79.3669
9	2.3481	2.9435	76.4234
10	2.2588	3.0328	73.3906
11	2.1668	3.1248	70.2658
12	2.0720	3.2196	67.0461
13	1.9743	3.3173	63.7288
14	1.8737	3.4180	60.3108
15	1.7700	3.5217	56.7892
16	1.6631	3.6285	53.1606
17	1.5530	3.7386	49.4220
18	1.4396	3.8520	45.5700
19	1.3227	3.9689	41.6011
20	1.2023	4.0893	37.5118
21	1.0782	4.2134	33.2985
22	.9504	4.3412	28.9573
23	.8187	4.4729	24.4843
24	.6830	4.6086	19.8757
25	.5432	4.7484	15.1273
26	.3991	4.8925	10.2348
27	.2507	5.0409	5.1939
28	.0977	5.1939	0.0000

YEARS 29 — **QTR PAYT 1.2938** — **AN CONST 5.18**

#	INT	PRIN	BALANCE
1	2.9754	2.1998	97.8002
2	2.9087	2.2665	95.5336
3	2.8399	2.3353	93.1983
4	2.7690	2.4062	90.7922
5	2.6960	2.4792	88.3130
6	2.6208	2.5544	85.7586
7	2.5433	2.6319	83.1267
8	2.4635	2.7117	80.4150
9	2.3812	2.7940	77.6210
10	2.2964	2.8788	74.7422
11	2.2091	2.9661	71.7761
12	2.1191	3.0561	68.7200
13	2.0264	3.1488	65.5712
14	1.9309	3.2443	62.3269
15	1.8324	3.3428	58.9841
16	1.7310	3.4442	55.5399
17	1.6265	3.5487	51.9912
18	1.5189	3.6564	48.3349
19	1.4079	3.7673	44.5676
20	1.2936	3.8816	40.6860
21	1.1759	3.9993	36.6866
22	1.0545	4.1207	32.5660
23	.9295	4.2457	28.3203
24	.8007	4.3745	23.9457
25	.6680	4.5072	19.4385
26	.5312	4.6440	14.7945
27	.3903	4.7849	10.0097
28	.2452	4.9300	5.0796
29	.0956	5.0796	0.0000

YEARS 30 — **QTR PAYT 1.2668** — **AN CONST 5.07**

#	INT	PRIN	BALANCE
1	2.9766	2.0904	97.9096
2	2.9132	2.1538	95.7558
3	2.8479	2.2192	93.5366
4	2.7805	2.2865	91.2501
5	2.7112	2.3559	88.8942
6	2.6397	2.4273	86.4669
7	2.5660	2.5010	83.9659
8	2.4902	2.5769	81.3891
9	2.4120	2.6550	78.7340
10	2.3314	2.7356	75.9984
11	2.2484	2.8186	73.1798
12	2.1629	2.9041	70.2757
13	2.0748	2.9922	67.2835
14	1.9840	3.0830	64.2005
15	1.8905	3.1765	61.0240
16	1.7941	3.2729	57.7511
17	1.6948	3.3722	54.3789
18	1.5925	3.4745	50.9044
19	1.4871	3.5799	47.3245
20	1.3785	3.6885	43.6359
21	1.2666	3.8004	39.8355
22	1.1513	3.9157	35.9197
23	1.0325	4.0345	31.8852
24	.9101	4.1569	27.7282
25	.7840	4.2831	23.4452
26	.6540	4.4130	19.0322
27	.5201	4.5469	14.4853
28	.3822	4.6848	9.8004
29	.2400	4.8270	4.9734
30	.0936	4.9734	0.0000

QUARTERLY PAYMENT AMORTIZATION SCHEDULE PER $100   4.00 %

YEARS 2	QTR PAYT 13.0690	AN CONST 52.28
# INT	PRIN	BALANCE
1 3.2710	49.0051	50.9949
2 1.2812	50.9949	0.0000

YEARS 3	QTR PAYT 8.8849	AN CONST 35.54
# INT	PRIN	BALANCE
1 3.5237	32.0158	67.9842
2 2.2238	33.3157	34.6685
3 .8710	34.6685	0.0000

YEARS 4	QTR PAYT 6.7945	AN CONST 27.18
# INT	PRIN	BALANCE
1 3.6500	23.5278	76.4722
2 2.6947	24.4832	51.9890
3 1.7006	25.4773	26.5117
4 .6661	26.5117	0.0000

YEARS 5	QTR PAYT 5.5415	AN CONST 22.17
# INT	PRIN	BALANCE
1 3.7257	18.4404	81.5596
2 2.9769	19.1892	62.3704
3 2.1978	19.9684	42.4020
4 1.3870	20.7791	21.6229
5 .5433	21.6229	0.0000

YEARS 6	QTR PAYT 4.7073	AN CONST 18.83
# INT	PRIN	BALANCE
1 3.7761	15.0533	84.9467
2 3.1648	15.6645	69.2821
3 2.5288	16.3006	52.9816
4 1.8669	16.9625	36.0191
5 1.1782	17.6512	18.3679
6 .4615	18.3679	0.0000

YEARS 7	QTR PAYT 4.1124	AN CONST 16.45
# INT	PRIN	BALANCE
1 3.8120	12.6378	87.3622
2 3.2989	13.1509	74.2113
3 2.7649	13.6849	60.5264
4 2.2092	14.2406	46.2859
5 1.6310	14.8188	31.4671
6 1.0293	15.4205	16.0466
7 .4032	16.0466	0.0000

YEARS 8	QTR PAYT 3.6671	AN CONST 14.67
# INT	PRIN	BALANCE
1 3.8389	10.8294	89.1706
2 3.3992	11.2692	77.9014
3 2.9416	11.7267	66.1746
4 2.4655	12.2029	53.9717
5 1.9700	12.6984	41.2734
6 1.4544	13.2140	28.0594
7 .9178	13.7505	14.3089
8 .3595	14.3089	0.0000

YEARS 9	QTR PAYT 3.3214	AN CONST 13.29
# INT	PRIN	BALANCE
1 3.8598	9.4259	90.5741
2 3.4771	9.8087	80.7654
3 3.0788	10.2069	70.5584
4 2.6643	10.6214	59.9371
5 2.2331	11.0527	48.8844
6 1.7843	11.5014	37.3830

# INT	PRIN	BALANCE
7 1.3173	11.9684	25.4145
8 .8313	12.4544	12.9601
9 .3256	12.9601	0.0000

YEARS 10	QTR PAYT 3.0456	AN CONST 12.19
# INT	PRIN	BALANCE
1 3.8764	8.3058	91.6942
2 3.5392	8.6430	83.0512
3 3.1883	8.9940	74.0572
4 2.8231	9.3592	64.6980
5 2.4430	9.7392	54.9588
6 2.0476	10.1346	44.8242
7 1.6361	10.5462	34.2780
8 1.2079	10.9744	23.3036
9 .7623	11.4200	11.8837
10 .2986	11.8837	0.0000

YEARS 11	QTR PAYT 2.8204	AN CONST 11.29
# INT	PRIN	BALANCE
1 3.8900	7.3917	92.6083
2 3.5899	7.6919	84.9164
3 3.2776	8.0042	76.9123
4 2.9526	8.3292	68.5831
5 2.6144	8.6674	59.9157
6 2.2625	9.0193	50.8964
7 1.8962	9.3855	41.5109
8 1.5152	9.7666	31.7443
9 1.1186	10.1632	21.5811
10 .7059	10.5758	11.0053
11 .2765	11.0053	0.0000

YEARS 12	QTR PAYT 2.6334	AN CONST 10.54
# INT	PRIN	BALANCE
1 3.9013	6.6322	93.3678
2 3.6320	6.9015	86.4663
3 3.3518	7.1817	79.2846
4 3.0602	7.4733	71.8113
5 2.7568	7.7768	64.0345
6 2.4410	8.0925	55.9420
7 2.1124	8.4211	47.5209
8 1.7705	8.7631	38.7578
9 1.4147	9.1189	29.6389
10 1.0444	9.4891	20.1498
11 .6591	9.8744	10.2754
12 .2582	10.2754	0.0000

YEARS 13	QTR PAYT 2.4756	AN CONST 9.91
# INT	PRIN	BALANCE
1 3.9109	5.9915	94.0085
2 3.6676	6.2348	87.7736
3 3.4144	6.4880	81.2857
4 3.1510	6.7514	74.5342
5 2.8769	7.0256	67.5087
6 2.5916	7.3108	60.1979
7 2.2947	7.6077	52.5902
8 1.9858	7.9166	44.6736
9 1.6644	8.2380	36.4356
10 1.3299	8.5725	27.8631
11 .9818	8.9206	18.9425
12 .6196	9.2828	9.6597
13 .2427	9.6597	0.0000

YEARS 14	QTR PAYT 2.3408	AN CONST 9.37
# INT	PRIN	BALANCE
1 3.9190	5.4443	94.5557
2 3.6980	5.6653	88.8904
3 3.4679	5.8954	82.9950

# INT	PRIN	BALANCE
4 3.2285	6.1348	76.8602
5 2.9794	6.3839	70.4764
6 2.7202	6.6431	63.8333
7 2.4505	6.9128	56.9205
8 2.1698	7.1935	49.7270
9 1.8777	7.4856	42.2415
10 1.5738	7.7895	34.4520
11 1.2575	8.1058	26.3462
12 .9284	8.4349	17.9112
13 .5859	8.7774	9.1338
14 .2295	9.1338	0.0000

YEARS 15	QTR PAYT 2.2244	AN CONST 8.90
# INT	PRIN	BALANCE
1 3.9260	4.9717	95.0283
2 3.7242	5.1736	89.8547
3 3.5141	5.3837	84.4710
4 3.2955	5.6023	78.8687
5 3.0680	5.8298	73.0389
6 2.8313	6.0665	66.9725
7 2.5850	6.3128	60.6597
8 2.3287	6.5691	54.0906
9 2.0619	6.8358	47.2547
10 1.7844	7.1134	40.1413
11 1.4955	7.4022	32.7391
12 1.1950	7.7028	25.0363
13 .8822	8.0156	17.0207
14 .5568	8.3410	8.6797
15 .2181	8.6797	0.0000

YEARS 16	QTR PAYT 2.1230	AN CONST 8.50
# INT	PRIN	BALANCE
1 3.9322	4.5599	95.4401
2 3.7470	4.7450	90.6951
3 3.5544	4.9377	85.7574
4 3.3539	5.1382	80.6192
5 3.1452	5.3468	75.2724
6 2.9281	5.5639	69.7085
7 2.7022	5.7898	63.9186
8 2.4671	6.0249	57.8937
9 2.2225	6.2696	51.6241
10 1.9679	6.5241	45.1000
11 1.7030	6.7890	38.3109
12 1.4273	7.0647	31.2462
13 1.1405	7.3516	23.8947
14 .8420	7.6501	16.2446
15 .5314	7.9607	8.2839
16 .2081	8.2839	0.0000

YEARS 17	QTR PAYT 2.0339	AN CONST 8.14
# INT	PRIN	BALANCE
1 3.9376	4.1980	95.8020
2 3.7671	4.3685	91.4335
3 3.5897	4.5458	86.8877
4 3.4051	4.7304	82.1573
5 3.2131	4.9225	77.2348
6 3.0132	5.1224	72.1124
7 2.8052	5.3303	66.7821
8 2.5888	5.5468	61.2353
9 2.3636	5.7720	55.4633
10 2.1292	6.0064	49.4569
11 1.8853	6.2503	43.2067
12 1.6315	6.5040	36.7026
13 1.3674	6.7681	29.9345
14 1.0926	7.0429	22.8916
15 .8066	7.3289	15.5627
16 .5091	7.6265	7.9362
17 .1994	7.9362	0.0000

YEARS 18	QTR PAYT 1.9550	AN CONST 7.83
# INT	PRIN	BALANCE
1 3.9423	3.8778	96.1222
2 3.7849	4.0352	92.0870
3 3.6210	4.1991	87.8880
4 3.4505	4.3696	83.5184
5 3.2731	4.5470	78.9714
6 3.0885	4.7316	74.2398
7 2.8963	4.9237	69.3161
8 2.6964	5.1237	64.1924
9 2.4884	5.3317	58.8608
10 2.2719	5.5482	53.3126
11 2.0466	5.7735	47.5391
12 1.8122	6.0079	41.5312
13 1.5682	6.2518	35.2794
14 1.3144	6.5057	28.7737
15 1.0502	6.7698	22.0039
16 .7754	7.0447	14.9592
17 .4893	7.3308	7.6284
18 .1917	7.6284	0.0000

YEARS 19	QTR PAYT 1.8848	AN CONST 7.54
# INT	PRIN	BALANCE
1 3.9466	3.5926	96.4074
2 3.8007	3.7384	92.6690
3 3.6489	3.8902	88.7787
4 3.4909	4.0482	84.7305
5 3.3266	4.2126	80.5179
6 3.1555	4.3836	76.1343
7 2.9775	4.5616	71.5727
8 2.7923	4.7468	66.8259
9 2.5996	4.9396	61.8863
10 2.3990	5.1401	56.7461
11 2.1903	5.3489	51.3973
12 1.9731	5.5660	45.8312
13 1.7471	5.7920	40.0392
14 1.5119	6.0272	34.0120
15 1.2672	6.2720	27.7400
16 1.0125	6.5266	21.2134
17 .7475	6.7916	14.4218
18 .4717	7.0674	7.3544
19 .1848	7.3544	0.0000

YEARS 20	QTR PAYT 1.8219	AN CONST 7.29
# INT	PRIN	BALANCE
1 3.9504	3.3372	96.6628
2 3.8149	3.4727	93.1901
3 3.6738	3.6137	89.5764
4 3.5271	3.7604	85.8160
5 3.3744	3.9131	81.9029
6 3.2155	4.0720	77.8309
7 3.0502	4.2373	73.5936
8 2.8782	4.4094	69.1842
9 2.6991	4.5884	64.5958
10 2.5128	4.7747	59.8210
11 2.3189	4.9686	54.8524
12 2.1172	5.1704	49.6821
13 1.9072	5.3803	44.3018
14 1.6888	5.5988	38.7030
15 1.4615	5.8261	32.8769
16 1.2249	6.0626	26.8143
17 .9787	6.3088	20.5055
18 .7226	6.5650	13.9405
19 .4560	6.8315	7.1089
20 .1786	7.1089	0.0000

YEARS 21	QTR PAYT 1.7653	AN CONST 7.07
# INT	PRIN	BALANCE
1 3.9538	3.1073	96.8927
2 3.8276	3.2335	93.6592
3 3.6963	3.3648	90.2944

QUARTERLY PAYMENT AMORTIZATION SCHEDULE PER $100 4.00 %

#	INT	PRIN	BALANCE
4	3.5597	3.5014	86.7930
5	3.4175	3.6436	83.1494
6	3.2696	3.7915	79.3579
7	3.1156	3.9455	75.4125
8	2.9554	4.1057	71.3068
9	2.7887	4.2724	67.0344
10	2.6152	4.4459	62.5886
11	2.4347	4.6264	57.9622
12	2.2469	4.8142	53.1480
13	2.0514	5.0097	48.1383
14	1.8480	5.2131	42.9252
15	1.6363	5.4248	37.5004
16	1.4160	5.6451	31.8553
17	1.1868	5.8743	25.9811
18	.9483	6.1128	19.8683
19	.7001	6.3610	13.5073
20	.4418	6.6193	6.8880
21	.1731	6.8880	0.0000

YEARS 22	QTR PAYT 1.7141	AN CONST 6.86	
#	INT	PRIN	BALANCE
1	3.9569	2.8995	97.1005
2	3.8391	3.0172	94.0833
3	3.7166	3.1397	90.9436
4	3.5891	3.2672	87.6763
5	3.4565	3.3999	84.2765
6	3.3184	3.5379	80.7385
7	3.1748	3.6816	77.0570
8	3.0253	3.8311	73.2259
9	2.8697	3.9866	69.2393
10	2.7079	4.1485	65.0908
11	2.5394	4.3169	60.7738
12	2.3641	4.4922	56.2816
13	2.1817	4.6746	51.6070
14	1.9919	4.8644	46.7425
15	1.7944	5.0620	41.6806
16	1.5889	5.2675	36.4131
17	1.3750	5.4814	30.9317
18	1.1524	5.7039	25.2278
19	.9208	5.9355	19.2922
20	.6798	6.1765	13.1157
21	.4290	6.4273	6.6883
22	.1680	6.6883	0.0000

YEARS 23	QTR PAYT 1.6676	AN CONST 6.68	
#	INT	PRIN	BALANCE
1	3.9597	2.7108	97.2892
2	3.8496	2.8209	94.4683
3	3.7351	2.9354	91.5329
4	3.6159	3.0546	88.4782
5	3.4918	3.1786	85.2996
6	3.3628	3.3077	81.9919
7	3.2285	3.4420	78.5499
8	3.0887	3.5818	74.9681
9	2.9433	3.7272	71.2409
10	2.7919	3.8786	67.3623
11	2.6345	4.0360	63.3263
12	2.4706	4.1999	59.1263
13	2.3000	4.3705	54.7559
14	2.1226	4.5479	50.2080
15	1.9379	4.7326	45.4754
16	1.7458	4.9247	40.5507
17	1.5458	5.1247	35.4260
18	1.3377	5.3328	30.0932
19	1.1212	5.5493	24.5439
20	.8959	5.7746	18.7692
21	.6614	6.0091	12.7601
22	.4174	6.2531	6.5070
23	.1635	6.5070	0.0000

YEARS 24	QTR PAYT 1.6253	AN CONST 6.51	
#	INT	PRIN	BALANCE
1	3.9622	2.5389	97.4611
2	3.8591	2.6420	94.8191
3	3.7519	2.7493	92.0698
4	3.6402	2.8609	89.2089
5	3.5241	2.9771	86.2319
6	3.4032	3.0979	83.1339
7	3.2774	3.2237	79.9102
8	3.1465	3.3546	76.5556
9	3.0103	3.4908	73.0647
10	2.8686	3.6326	69.4321
11	2.7211	3.7801	65.6520
12	2.5676	3.9336	61.7185
13	2.4078	4.0933	57.6252
14	2.2416	4.2595	53.3657
15	2.0687	4.4324	48.9333
16	1.8887	4.6124	44.3208
17	1.7014	4.7997	39.5211
18	1.5065	4.9946	34.5265
19	1.3037	5.1974	29.3292
20	1.0927	5.4084	23.9207
21	.8731	5.6280	18.2927
22	.6446	5.8565	12.4362
23	.4068	6.0943	6.3418
24	.1593	6.3418	0.0000

YEARS 25	QTR PAYT 1.5866	AN CONST 6.35	
#	INT	PRIN	BALANCE
1	3.9646	2.3817	97.6183
2	3.8679	2.4784	95.1398
3	3.7672	2.5791	92.5608
4	3.6625	2.6838	89.8770
5	3.5535	2.7928	87.0842
6	3.4401	2.9062	84.1781
7	3.3221	3.0242	81.1539
8	3.1993	3.1470	78.0069
9	3.0716	3.2747	74.7322
10	2.9386	3.4077	71.3245
11	2.8002	3.5461	67.7784
12	2.6562	3.6901	64.0884
13	2.5064	3.8399	60.2485
14	2.3505	3.9958	56.2527
15	2.1883	4.1580	52.0947
16	2.0194	4.3269	47.7678
17	1.8437	4.5026	43.2652
18	1.6609	4.6854	38.5798
19	1.4707	4.8756	33.7042
20	1.2727	5.0736	28.6306
21	1.0667	5.2796	23.3510
22	.8523	5.4940	17.8570
23	.6292	5.7171	12.1400
24	.3971	5.9492	6.1908
25	.1555	6.1908	0.0000

YEARS 26	QTR PAYT 1.5511	AN CONST 6.21	
#	INT	PRIN	BALANCE
1	3.9667	2.2376	97.7624
2	3.8759	2.3284	95.4340
3	3.7813	2.4230	93.0110
4	3.6829	2.5214	90.4896
5	3.5806	2.6237	87.8659
6	3.4740	2.7303	85.1356
7	3.3632	2.8411	82.2945
8	3.2478	2.9565	79.3380
9	3.1278	3.0765	76.2615
10	3.0028	3.2015	73.0600
11	2.8728	3.3315	69.7286
12	2.7376	3.4667	66.2618
13	2.5968	3.6075	62.6544
14	2.4503	3.7540	58.9004
15	2.2979	3.9064	54.9940
16	2.1393	4.0650	50.9290
17	1.9742	4.2301	46.6990
18	1.8025	4.4018	42.2971
19	1.6237	4.5805	37.7166
20	1.4378	4.7665	32.9501
21	1.2442	4.9601	27.9900
22	1.0428	5.1615	22.8285
23	.8332	5.3711	17.4575
24	.6152	5.5891	11.8683
25	.3882	5.8161	6.0522
26	.1521	6.0522	0.0000

YEARS 27	QTR PAYT 1.5184	AN CONST 6.08	
#	INT	PRIN	BALANCE
1	3.9687	2.1050	97.8950
2	3.8832	2.1905	95.7045
3	3.7943	2.2794	93.4251
4	3.7017	2.3720	91.0531
5	3.6054	2.4683	88.5848
6	3.5052	2.5685	86.0163
7	3.4009	2.6728	83.3435
8	3.2924	2.7813	80.5622
9	3.1794	2.8943	77.6679
10	3.0619	3.0118	74.6562
11	2.9396	3.1341	71.5221
12	2.8124	3.2613	68.2608
13	2.6799	3.3937	64.8670
14	2.5421	3.5315	61.3355
15	2.3988	3.6749	57.6605
16	2.2495	3.8242	53.8364
17	2.0943	3.9794	49.8570
18	1.9327	4.1410	45.7159
19	1.7645	4.3092	41.4068
20	1.5896	4.4841	36.9227
21	1.4075	4.6662	32.2565
22	1.2180	4.8557	27.4008
23	1.0209	5.0528	22.3480
24	.8157	5.2580	17.0900
25	.6022	5.4715	11.6185
26	.3800	5.6937	5.9248
27	.1489	5.9248	0.0000

YEARS 28	QTR PAYT 1.4883	AN CONST 5.96	
#	INT	PRIN	BALANCE
1	3.9705	1.9828	98.0172
2	3.8900	2.0633	95.9540
3	3.8062	2.1470	93.8069
4	3.7190	2.2342	91.5727
5	3.6283	2.3249	89.2478
6	3.5339	2.4193	86.8284
7	3.4357	2.5176	84.3108
8	3.3335	2.6198	81.6910
9	3.2271	2.7262	78.9648
10	3.1164	2.8369	76.1280
11	3.0012	2.9521	73.1759
12	2.8813	3.0719	70.1040
13	2.7566	3.1967	66.9073
14	2.6268	3.3265	63.5809
15	2.4917	3.4615	60.1193
16	2.3512	3.6021	56.5173
17	2.2049	3.7483	52.7689
18	2.0527	3.9005	48.8684
19	1.8944	4.0589	44.8095
20	1.7295	4.2237	40.5858
21	1.5580	4.3952	36.1906
22	1.3796	4.5737	31.6169
23	1.1939	4.7594	26.8575
24	1.0006	4.9526	21.9049
25	.7995	5.1537	16.7511
26	.5903	5.3630	11.3881
27	.3725	5.5808	5.8074
28	.1459	5.8074	0.0000

YEARS 29	QTR PAYT 1.4605	AN CONST 5.85	
#	INT	PRIN	BALANCE
1	3.9722	1.8698	98.1302
2	3.8963	1.9457	96.1845
3	3.8173	2.0247	94.1599
4	3.7351	2.1069	92.0530
5	3.6495	2.1924	89.8605
6	3.5605	2.2815	87.5790
7	3.4678	2.3741	85.2049
8	3.3714	2.4705	82.7344
9	3.2711	2.5708	80.1636
10	3.1667	2.6752	77.4884
11	3.0581	2.7838	74.7046
12	2.9451	2.8969	71.8077
13	2.8275	3.0145	68.7932
14	2.7051	3.1369	65.6563
15	2.5777	3.2643	62.3921
16	2.4452	3.3968	58.9953
17	2.3072	3.5347	55.4605
18	2.1637	3.6782	51.7823
19	2.0144	3.8276	47.9547
20	1.8589	3.9830	43.9717
21	1.6972	4.1447	39.8269
22	1.5289	4.3130	35.5139
23	1.3538	4.4882	31.0257
24	1.1716	4.6704	26.3553
25	.9819	4.8600	21.4953
26	.7846	5.0574	16.4379
27	.5792	5.2627	11.1752
28	.3655	5.4764	5.6988
29	.1432	5.6988	0.0000

YEARS 30	QTR PAYT 1.4347	AN CONST 5.74	
#	INT	PRIN	BALANCE
1	3.9737	1.7651	98.2349
2	3.9021	1.8368	96.3981
3	3.8275	1.9113	94.4868
4	3.7499	1.9890	92.4978
5	3.6691	2.0697	90.4281
6	3.5851	2.1538	88.2744
7	3.4976	2.2412	86.0332
8	3.4066	2.3322	83.7010
9	3.3119	2.4269	81.2741
10	3.2134	2.5254	78.7486
11	3.1109	2.6280	76.1206
12	3.0041	2.7347	73.3860
13	2.8931	2.8457	70.5402
14	2.7776	2.9613	67.5789
15	2.6573	3.0815	64.4974
16	2.5322	3.2066	61.2908
17	2.4020	3.3368	57.9539
18	2.2665	3.4723	54.4816
19	2.1255	3.6133	50.8683
20	1.9788	3.7600	47.1082
21	1.8261	3.9127	43.1955
22	1.6673	4.0716	39.1239
23	1.5019	4.2369	34.8870
24	1.3299	4.4089	30.4781
25	1.1509	4.5880	25.8901
26	.9646	4.7743	21.1159
27	.7707	4.9681	16.1478
28	.5690	5.1698	10.9779
29	.3591	5.3797	5.5982
30	.1407	5.5982	0.0000

YEARS 2 — QTR PAYT 13.1050 — AN CONST 52.43

#	INT	PRIN	BALANCE
1	3.4768	48.9433	51.0567
2	1.3634	51.0567	0.0000

YEARS 3 — QTR PAYT 8.9200 — AN CONST 35.69

#	INT	PRIN	BALANCE
1	3.7455	31.9345	68.0655
2	2.3665	33.3135	34.7520
3	.9280	34.7520	0.0000

YEARS 4 — QTR PAYT 6.8294 — AN CONST 27.32

#	INT	PRIN	BALANCE
1	3.8798	23.4377	76.5623
2	2.8677	24.4498	52.1125
3	1.8119	25.5056	26.6070
4	.7105	26.6070	0.0000

YEARS 5 — QTR PAYT 5.5765 — AN CONST 22.31

#	INT	PRIN	BALANCE
1	3.9602	18.3457	81.6543
2	3.1680	19.1379	62.5164
3	2.3416	19.9643	42.5521
4	1.4795	20.8264	21.7257
5	.5801	21.7257	0.0000

YEARS 6 — QTR PAYT 4.7424 — AN CONST 18.97

#	INT	PRIN	BALANCE
1	4.0137	14.9561	85.0439
2	3.3679	15.6019	69.4421
3	2.6942	16.2756	53.1664
4	1.9914	16.9784	36.1880
5	1.2582	17.7116	18.4764
6	.4934	18.4764	0.0000

YEARS 7 — QTR PAYT 4.1478 — AN CONST 16.60

#	INT	PRIN	BALANCE
1	4.0519	12.5392	87.4608
2	3.5104	13.0807	74.3801
3	2.9456	13.6455	60.7346
4	2.3564	14.2348	46.4998
5	1.7417	14.8495	31.6503
6	1.1004	15.4907	16.1596
7	.4315	16.1596	0.0000

YEARS 8 — QTR PAYT 3.7027 — AN CONST 14.82

#	INT	PRIN	BALANCE
1	4.0805	10.7304	89.2696
2	3.6171	11.1937	78.0759
3	3.1338	11.6771	66.3989
4	2.6295	12.1813	54.2175
5	2.1035	12.7073	41.5102
6	1.5548	13.2561	28.2541
7	.9823	13.8285	14.4256
8	.3852	14.4256	0.0000

YEARS 9 — QTR PAYT 3.3574 — AN CONST 13.43

#	INT	PRIN	BALANCE
1	4.1027	9.3268	90.6732
2	3.6999	9.7296	80.9436
3	3.2798	10.1497	70.7939
4	2.8415	10.5880	60.2060
5	2.3843	11.0452	49.1608
6	1.9073	11.5221	37.6386
7	1.4098	12.0197	25.6189
8	.8907	12.5387	13.0802
9	.3493	13.0802	0.0000

YEARS 10 — QTR PAYT 3.0818 — AN CONST 12.33

#	INT	PRIN	BALANCE
1	4.1204	8.2070	91.7930
2	3.7660	8.5614	83.2317
3	3.3963	8.9311	74.3006
4	3.0106	9.3167	64.9839
5	2.6083	9.7190	55.2649
6	2.1886	10.1387	45.1262
7	1.7508	10.5765	34.5496
8	1.2941	11.0332	23.5164
9	.8176	11.5097	12.0067
10	.3206	12.0067	0.0000

YEARS 11 — QTR PAYT 2.8571 — AN CONST 11.43

#	INT	PRIN	BALANCE
1	4.1348	7.2934	92.7066
2	3.8198	7.6084	85.0982
3	3.4913	7.9369	77.1612
4	3.1486	8.2797	68.8816
5	2.7910	8.6372	60.2444
6	2.4180	9.0102	51.2342
7	2.0290	9.3993	41.8349
8	1.6231	9.8051	32.0298
9	1.1997	10.2285	21.8012
10	.7580	10.6702	11.1310
11	.2972	11.1310	0.0000

YEARS 12 — QTR PAYT 2.6704 — AN CONST 10.69

#	INT	PRIN	BALANCE
1	4.1468	6.5347	93.4653
2	3.8646	6.8168	86.6485
3	3.5702	7.1112	79.5373
4	3.2631	7.4183	72.1190
5	2.9428	7.7386	64.3804
6	2.6086	8.0728	56.3076
7	2.2600	8.4214	47.8862
8	1.8964	8.7850	39.1011
9	1.5170	9.1644	29.9367
10	1.1213	9.5601	20.3766
11	.7085	9.9730	10.4036
12	.2778	10.4036	0.0000

YEARS 13 — QTR PAYT 2.5129 — AN CONST 10.06

#	INT	PRIN	BALANCE
1	4.1569	5.8949	94.1051
2	3.9023	6.1494	87.9557
3	3.6368	6.4150	81.5407
4	3.3598	6.6920	74.8486
5	3.0708	6.9810	67.8677
6	2.7693	7.2824	60.5852
7	2.4549	7.5969	52.9883
8	2.1268	7.9250	45.0634
9	1.7846	8.2672	36.7962
10	1.4276	8.6242	28.1720
11	1.0552	8.9966	19.1754
12	.6667	9.3851	9.7903
13	.2614	9.7903	0.0000

YEARS 14 — QTR PAYT 2.3785 — AN CONST 9.52

#	INT	PRIN	BALANCE
1	4.1655	5.3486	94.6514
2	3.9345	5.5796	89.0718
3	3.6936	5.8205	83.2512
4	3.4423	6.0719	77.1793
5	3.1801	6.3341	70.8453
6	2.9065	6.6076	64.2377
7	2.6212	6.8929	57.3447
8	2.3236	7.1906	50.1542
9	2.0131	7.5011	42.6531
10	1.6891	7.8250	34.8281
11	1.3512	8.1629	26.6652
12	.9988	8.5154	18.1498
13	.6310	8.8831	9.2667
14	.2474	9.2667	0.0000

YEARS 15 — QTR PAYT 2.2625 — AN CONST 9.06

#	INT	PRIN	BALANCE
1	4.1730	4.8772	95.1228
2	3.9623	5.0878	90.0351
3	3.7426	5.3075	84.7276
4	3.5135	5.5367	79.1909
5	3.2744	5.7757	73.4152
6	3.0250	6.0252	67.3900
7	2.7648	6.2853	61.1047
8	2.4934	6.5567	54.5479
9	2.2102	6.8399	47.7081
10	1.9149	7.1352	40.5728
11	1.6068	7.4434	33.1295
12	1.2853	7.7648	25.3647
13	.9500	8.1001	17.2646
14	.6003	8.4499	8.8147
15	.2354	8.8147	0.0000

YEARS 16 — QTR PAYT 2.1615 — AN CONST 8.65

#	INT	PRIN	BALANCE
1	4.1794	4.4665	95.5335
2	3.9866	4.6593	90.8742
3	3.7854	4.8605	86.0137
4	3.5755	5.0704	80.9433
5	3.3565	5.2894	75.6539
6	3.1281	5.5178	70.1361
7	2.8899	5.7560	64.3801
8	2.6413	6.0046	58.3755
9	2.3820	6.2639	52.1116
10	2.1115	6.5344	45.5772
11	1.8293	6.8166	38.7606
12	1.5350	7.1109	31.6497
13	1.2279	7.4180	24.2318
14	.9076	7.7383	16.4935
15	.5735	8.0724	8.4210
16	.2249	8.4210	0.0000

YEARS 17 — QTR PAYT 2.0727 — AN CONST 8.30

#	INT	PRIN	BALANCE
1	4.1851	4.1058	95.8942
2	4.0078	4.2831	91.6111
3	3.8229	4.4680	87.1431
4	3.6300	4.6610	82.4822
5	3.4287	4.8622	77.6199
6	3.2187	5.0722	72.5477
7	2.9997	5.2912	67.2565
8	2.7712	5.5197	61.7368
9	2.5329	5.7581	55.9787
10	2.2842	6.0067	49.9720
11	2.0248	6.2661	43.7059
12	1.7542	6.5367	37.1692
13	1.4720	6.8189	30.3503
14	1.1775	7.1134	23.2369
15	.8703	7.4206	15.8163
16	.5499	7.7410	8.0753
17	.2156	8.0753	0.0000

YEARS 18 — QTR PAYT 1.9942 — AN CONST 7.98

#	INT	PRIN	BALANCE
1	4.1902	3.7868	96.2132
2	4.0267	3.9503	92.2629
3	3.8561	4.1209	88.1420
4	3.6781	4.2988	83.8432
5	3.4925	4.4845	79.3587
6	3.2988	4.6781	74.6806
7	3.0968	4.8801	69.8005
8	2.8861	5.0909	64.7096
9	2.6663	5.3107	59.3989
10	2.4369	5.5400	53.8589
11	2.1977	5.7793	48.0797
12	1.9481	6.0288	42.0509
13	1.6878	6.2891	35.7617
14	1.4162	6.5607	29.2010
15	1.1329	6.8440	22.3569
16	.8374	7.1396	15.2174
17	.5291	7.4479	7.7695
18	.2075	7.7695	0.0000

YEARS 19 — QTR PAYT 1.9244 — AN CONST 7.70

#	INT	PRIN	BALANCE
1	4.1947	3.5029	96.4971
2	4.0434	3.6541	92.8430
3	3.8856	3.8119	89.0311
4	3.7210	3.9765	85.0545
5	3.5493	4.1483	80.9063
6	3.3702	4.3274	76.5789
7	3.1833	4.5142	72.0647
8	2.9884	4.7092	67.3555
9	2.7850	4.9125	62.4429
10	2.5729	5.1247	57.3183
11	2.3516	5.3460	51.9723
12	2.1207	5.5768	46.3955
13	1.8799	5.8176	40.5779
14	1.6287	6.0688	34.5090
15	1.3666	6.3309	28.1781
16	1.0932	6.6043	21.5738
17	.8081	6.8895	14.6843
18	.5105	7.1870	7.4973
19	.2002	7.4973	0.0000

YEARS 20 — QTR PAYT 1.8619 — AN CONST 7.45

#	INT	PRIN	BALANCE
1	4.1987	3.2488	96.7512
2	4.0584	3.3891	93.3621
3	3.9120	3.5354	89.8267
4	3.7594	3.6881	86.1386
5	3.6001	3.8473	82.2913
6	3.4340	4.0135	78.2778
7	3.2607	4.1868	74.0910
8	3.0799	4.3676	69.7234
9	2.8913	4.5562	65.1672
10	2.6945	4.7529	60.4143
11	2.4893	4.9582	55.4561
12	2.2752	5.1723	50.2838
13	2.0518	5.3956	44.8882
14	1.8188	5.6286	39.2596
15	1.5758	5.8717	33.3879
16	1.3222	6.1252	27.2627
17	1.0577	6.3897	20.8729
18	.7818	6.6657	14.2073
19	.4940	6.9535	7.2538
20	.1937	7.2538	0.0000

YEARS 21 — QTR PAYT 1.8056 — AN CONST 7.23

#	INT	PRIN	BALANCE
1	4.2023	3.0202	96.9798
2	4.0719	3.1507	93.8291
3	3.9358	3.2867	90.5424

#	INT	PRIN	BALANCE
4	3.7939	3.4286	87.1137
5	3.6458	3.5767	83.5370
6	3.4914	3.7311	79.8059
7	3.3303	3.8923	75.9136
8	3.1622	4.0603	71.8533
9	2.9869	4.2357	67.6176
10	2.8039	4.4186	63.1990
11	2.6131	4.6094	58.5896
12	2.4141	4.8084	53.7812
13	2.2065	5.0161	48.7651
14	1.9899	5.2327	43.5325
15	1.7639	5.4586	38.0738
16	1.5282	5.6943	32.3795
17	1.2823	5.9402	26.4393
18	1.0258	6.1968	20.2425
19	.7582	6.4643	13.7782
20	.4790	6.7435	7.0347
21	.1878	7.0347	0.0000

YEARS 22 — QTR PAYT 1.7548 — AN CONST 7.02

#	INT	PRIN	BALANCE
1	4.2056	2.8138	97.1862
2	4.0840	2.9353	94.2510
3	3.9573	3.0620	91.1890
4	3.8251	3.1942	87.9947
5	3.6871	3.3322	84.6626
6	3.5432	3.4761	81.1865
7	3.3931	3.6262	77.5604
8	3.2366	3.7827	73.7776
9	3.0732	3.9461	69.8315
10	2.9028	4.1165	65.7150
11	2.7251	4.2943	61.4208
12	2.5396	4.4797	56.9411
13	2.3462	4.6731	52.2679
14	2.1444	4.8749	47.3930
15	1.9339	5.0854	42.3076
16	1.7143	5.3050	37.0025
17	1.4852	5.5341	31.4684
18	1.2462	5.7731	25.6953
19	.9969	6.0224	19.6729
20	.7369	6.2825	13.3905
21	.4656	6.5537	6.8367
22	.1826	6.8367	0.0000

YEARS 23 — QTR PAYT 1.7087 — AN CONST 6.84

#	INT	PRIN	BALANCE
1	4.2085	2.6264	97.3736
2	4.0951	2.7399	94.6337
3	3.9768	2.8582	91.7755
4	3.8534	2.9816	88.7940
5	3.7246	3.1103	85.6836
6	3.5903	3.2447	82.4390
7	3.4502	3.3848	79.0542
8	3.3040	3.5309	75.5233
9	3.1516	3.6834	71.8399
10	2.9925	3.8425	67.9974
11	2.8266	4.0084	63.9891
12	2.6535	4.1815	59.8076
13	2.4729	4.3620	55.4456
14	2.2846	4.5504	50.8952
15	2.0881	4.7469	46.1483
16	1.8831	4.9519	41.1964
17	1.6692	5.1657	36.0307
18	1.4462	5.3888	30.6419
19	1.2135	5.6215	25.0205
20	.9707	5.8642	19.1562
21	.7175	6.1174	13.0388
22	.4533	6.3816	6.6572
23	.1778	6.6572	0.0000

YEARS 24 — QTR PAYT 1.6668 — AN CONST 6.67

#	INT	PRIN	BALANCE
1	4.2112	2.4559	97.5441
2	4.1052	2.5619	94.9822
3	3.9945	2.6726	92.3096
4	3.8791	2.7880	89.5216
5	3.7587	2.9084	86.6133
6	3.6331	3.0340	83.5793
7	3.5021	3.1650	80.4144
8	3.3655	3.3016	77.1127
9	3.2229	3.4442	73.6685
10	3.0742	3.5929	70.0756
11	2.9190	3.7481	66.3275
12	2.7572	3.9099	62.4176
13	2.5883	4.0788	58.3388
14	2.4122	4.2549	54.0839
15	2.2284	4.4386	49.6452
16	2.0368	4.6303	45.0149
17	1.8368	4.8303	40.1847
18	1.6282	5.0388	35.1458
19	1.4107	5.2564	29.8894
20	1.1837	5.4834	24.4060
21	.9469	5.7202	18.6858
22	.6999	5.9672	12.7186
23	.4422	6.2249	6.4937
24	.1734	6.4937	0.0000

YEARS 25 — QTR PAYT 1.6284 — AN CONST 6.52

#	INT	PRIN	BALANCE
1	4.2137	2.3001	97.6999
2	4.1143	2.3994	95.3005
3	4.0107	2.5030	92.7975
4	3.9026	2.6111	90.1864
5	3.7899	2.7238	87.4626
6	3.6723	2.8415	84.6211
7	3.5496	2.9642	81.6569
8	3.4216	3.0922	78.5648
9	3.2880	3.2257	75.3391
10	3.1488	3.3650	71.9741
11	3.0034	3.5103	68.4638
12	2.8519	3.6619	64.8019
13	2.6937	3.8200	60.9819
14	2.5288	3.9850	56.9969
15	2.3567	4.1570	52.8399
16	2.1772	4.3366	48.5034
17	1.9899	4.5238	43.9795
18	1.7946	4.7192	39.2604
19	1.5908	4.9229	34.3374
20	1.3782	5.1355	29.2019
21	1.1565	5.3573	23.8446
22	.9251	5.5886	18.2560
23	.6838	5.8300	12.4260
24	.4320	6.0817	6.3443
25	.1694	6.3443	0.0000

YEARS 26 — QTR PAYT 1.5933 — AN CONST 6.38

#	INT	PRIN	BALANCE
1	4.2159	2.1573	97.8427
2	4.1228	2.2505	95.5922
3	4.0256	2.3476	93.2446
4	3.9242	2.4490	90.7956
5	3.8185	2.5548	88.2408
6	3.7081	2.6651	85.5757
7	3.5931	2.7802	82.7956
8	3.4730	2.9002	79.8954
9	3.3478	3.0255	76.8699
10	3.2171	3.1561	73.7138
11	3.0808	3.2924	70.4214
12	2.9387	3.4346	66.9868
13	2.7903	3.5829	63.4039
14	2.6356	3.7376	59.6663
15	2.4742	3.8990	55.7674
16	2.3059	4.0674	51.7000
17	2.1302	4.2430	47.4570
18	1.9470	4.4262	43.0308
19	1.7559	4.6174	38.4134
20	1.5565	4.8167	33.5967
21	1.3485	5.0247	28.5719
22	1.1315	5.2417	23.3302
23	.9052	5.4681	17.8622
24	.6690	5.7042	12.1580
25	.4227	5.9505	6.2075
26	.1658	6.2075	0.0000

YEARS 27 — QTR PAYT 1.5610 — AN CONST 6.25

#	INT	PRIN	BALANCE
1	4.2180	2.0261	97.9739
2	4.1305	2.1136	95.8603
3	4.0392	2.2049	93.6555
4	3.9440	2.3001	91.3554
5	3.8447	2.3994	88.9560
6	3.7411	2.5030	86.4530
7	3.6330	2.6111	83.8419
8	3.5203	2.7238	81.1181
9	3.4026	2.8415	78.2766
10	3.2799	2.9642	75.3124
11	3.1519	3.0922	72.2203
12	3.0184	3.2257	68.9946
13	2.8791	3.3650	65.6296
14	2.7338	3.5103	62.1193
15	2.5822	3.6619	58.4574
16	2.4241	3.8200	54.6374
17	2.2591	3.9850	50.6525
18	2.0871	4.1570	46.4955
19	1.9076	4.3365	42.1589
20	1.7203	4.5238	37.6351
21	1.5249	4.7191	32.9160
22	1.3212	4.9229	27.9930
23	1.1086	5.1355	22.8575
24	.8868	5.3573	17.5003
25	.6555	5.5886	11.9116
26	.4141	5.8299	6.0817
27	.1624	6.0817	0.0000

YEARS 28 — QTR PAYT 1.5313 — AN CONST 6.13

#	INT	PRIN	BALANCE
1	4.2199	1.9052	98.0948
2	4.1376	1.9875	96.1073
3	4.0518	2.0733	94.0340
4	3.9623	2.1629	91.8711
5	3.8689	2.2562	89.6149
6	3.7714	2.3537	87.2612
7	3.6698	2.4553	84.8059
8	3.5638	2.5613	82.2445
9	3.4532	2.6719	79.5726
10	3.3378	2.7873	76.7852
11	3.2174	2.9077	73.8776
12	3.0919	3.0332	70.8443
13	2.9609	3.1642	67.6801
14	2.8243	3.3009	64.3792
15	2.6817	3.4434	60.9358
16	2.5330	3.5921	57.3437
17	2.3779	3.7472	53.5965
18	2.2161	3.9090	49.6875
19	2.0473	4.0778	45.6096
20	1.8712	4.2539	41.3557
21	1.6875	4.4376	36.9181
22	1.4959	4.6292	32.2889
23	1.2960	4.8291	27.4597
24	1.0875	5.0377	22.4220
25	.8699	5.2552	17.1668
26	.6430	5.4821	11.6847
27	.4063	5.7189	5.9658
28	.1593	5.9658	0.0000

YEARS 29 — QTR PAYT 1.5038 — AN CONST 6.02

#	INT	PRIN	BALANCE
1	4.2217	1.7936	98.2064
2	4.1442	1.8711	96.3353
3	4.0634	1.9518	94.3835
4	3.9791	2.0361	92.3474
5	3.8912	2.1241	90.2233
6	3.7995	2.2158	88.0075
7	3.7038	2.3115	85.6961
8	3.6040	2.4113	83.2848
9	3.4999	2.5154	80.7694
10	3.3912	2.6240	78.1454
11	3.2779	2.7373	75.4080
12	3.1597	2.8555	72.5525
13	3.0364	2.9788	69.5736
14	2.9078	3.1075	66.4662
15	2.7736	3.2417	63.2245
16	2.6336	3.3816	59.8429
17	2.4876	3.5277	56.3152
18	2.3353	3.6800	52.6352
19	2.1764	3.8389	48.7963
20	2.0106	4.0047	44.7916
21	1.8376	4.1776	40.6139
22	1.6572	4.3580	36.2559
23	1.4691	4.5462	31.7097
24	1.2727	4.7425	26.9672
25	1.0680	4.9473	22.0199
26	.8543	5.1610	16.8589
27	.6315	5.3838	11.4751
28	.3990	5.6163	5.8588
29	.1564	5.8588	0.0000

YEARS 30 — QTR PAYT 1.4784 — AN CONST 5.92

#	INT	PRIN	BALANCE
1	4.2233	1.6903	98.3097
2	4.1503	1.7633	96.5464
3	4.0742	1.8394	94.7070
4	3.9947	1.9189	92.7881
5	3.9119	2.0017	90.7864
6	3.8254	2.0882	88.6983
7	3.7353	2.1783	86.5199
8	3.6412	2.2724	84.2475
9	3.5431	2.3705	81.8770
10	3.4407	2.4729	79.4041
11	3.3339	2.5797	76.8245
12	3.2225	2.6911	74.1334
13	3.1063	2.8073	71.3261
14	2.9851	2.9285	68.3976
15	2.8586	3.0550	65.3427
16	2.7267	3.1869	62.1558
17	2.5891	3.3245	58.8313
18	2.4455	3.4680	55.3633
19	2.2958	3.6178	51.7455
20	2.1396	3.7740	47.9715
21	1.9766	3.9370	44.0345
22	1.8066	4.1070	39.9275
23	1.6292	4.2844	35.6431
24	1.4442	4.4694	31.1737
25	1.2512	4.6624	26.5114
26	1.0499	4.8637	21.6477
27	.8399	5.0737	16.5740
28	.6208	5.2928	11.2812
29	.3922	5.5214	5.7598
30	.1538	5.7598	0.0000

YEARS 2 — QTR PAYT 13.1411 — AN CONST 52.57

#	INT	PRIN	BALANCE
1	3.6828	48.8815	51.1185
2	1.4458	51.1185	0.0000

YEARS 3 — QTR PAYT 8.9552 — AN CONST 35.83

#	INT	PRIN	BALANCE
1	3.9675	31.8533	68.1467
2	2.5097	33.3111	34.8356
3	.9852	34.8356	0.0000

YEARS 4 — QTR PAYT 6.8644 — AN CONST 27.46

#	INT	PRIN	BALANCE
1	4.1097	23.3478	76.6522
2	3.0412	24.4163	52.2359
3	1.9238	25.5337	26.7022
4	.7552	26.7022	0.0000

YEARS 5 — QTR PAYT 5.6115 — AN CONST 22.45

#	INT	PRIN	BALANCE
1	4.1949	18.2512	81.7488
2	3.3596	19.0865	62.6622
3	2.4861	19.9600	42.7022
4	1.5726	20.8735	21.8288
5	.6174	21.8288	0.0000

YEARS 6 — QTR PAYT 4.7777 — AN CONST 19.12

#	INT	PRIN	BALANCE
1	4.2516	14.8592	85.1408
2	3.5716	15.5393	69.6015
3	2.8604	16.2504	53.3511
4	2.1167	16.9941	36.3570
5	1.3390	17.7718	18.5852
6	.5256	18.5852	0.0000

YEARS 7 — QTR PAYT 4.1833 — AN CONST 16.74

#	INT	PRIN	BALANCE
1	4.2920	12.4412	87.5588
2	3.7226	13.0106	74.5483
3	3.1272	13.6060	60.9423
4	2.5045	14.2287	46.7136
5	1.8534	14.8798	31.8338
6	1.1724	15.5608	16.2730
7	.4602	16.2730	0.0000

YEARS 8 — QTR PAYT 3.7385 — AN CONST 14.96

#	INT	PRIN	BALANCE
1	4.3223	10.6319	89.3681
2	3.8357	11.1185	78.2497
3	3.3269	11.6273	66.6224
4	2.7947	12.1594	54.4630
5	2.2383	12.7159	41.7471
6	1.6563	13.2978	28.4492
7	1.0477	13.9064	14.5428
8	.4113	14.5428	0.0000

YEARS 9 — QTR PAYT 3.3935 — AN CONST 13.58

#	INT	PRIN	BALANCE
1	4.3457	9.2284	90.7716
2	3.9234	9.6507	81.1209
3	3.4817	10.0924	71.0285
4	3.0198	10.5543	60.4742
5	2.5368	11.0373	49.4369
6	2.0317	11.5424	37.8945
7	1.5035	12.0707	25.8238
8	.9510	12.6231	13.2008
9	.3733	13.2008	0.0000

YEARS 10 — QTR PAYT 3.1183 — AN CONST 12.48

#	INT	PRIN	BALANCE
1	4.3644	8.1090	91.8910
2	3.9933	8.4801	83.4110
3	3.6052	8.8682	74.5428
4	3.1994	9.2740	65.2688
5	2.7750	9.6984	55.5704
6	2.3311	10.1423	45.4281
7	1.8669	10.6064	34.8216
8	1.3815	11.0919	23.7298
9	.8739	11.5995	12.1303
10	.3431	12.1303	0.0000

YEARS 11 — QTR PAYT 2.8939 — AN CONST 11.58

#	INT	PRIN	BALANCE
1	4.3797	7.1961	92.8039
2	4.0504	7.5254	85.2785
3	3.7060	7.8698	77.4086
4	3.3458	8.2300	69.1786
5	2.9692	8.6066	60.5720
6	2.5753	9.0005	51.5715
7	2.1634	9.4124	42.1590
8	1.7326	9.8432	32.3158
9	1.2821	10.2937	22.0222
10	.8110	10.7648	11.2574
11	.3184	11.2574	0.0000

YEARS 12 — QTR PAYT 2.7076 — AN CONST 10.84

#	INT	PRIN	BALANCE
1	4.3924	6.4382	93.5618
2	4.0977	6.7328	86.8290
3	3.7896	7.0409	79.7881
4	3.4674	7.3632	72.4249
5	3.1304	7.7001	64.7248
6	2.7780	8.0525	56.6723
7	2.4095	8.4211	48.2512
8	2.0241	8.8064	39.4448
9	1.6211	9.2095	30.2353
10	1.1996	9.6309	20.6044
11	.7588	10.0717	10.5326
12	.2979	10.5326	0.0000

YEARS 13 — QTR PAYT 2.5506 — AN CONST 10.21

#	INT	PRIN	BALANCE
1	4.4030	5.7994	94.2006
2	4.1376	6.0648	88.1358
3	3.8601	6.3423	81.7935
4	3.5698	6.6326	75.1609
5	3.2663	6.9361	68.2247
6	2.9489	7.2536	60.9712
7	2.6169	7.5855	53.3856
8	2.2697	7.9327	45.4530
9	1.9067	8.2957	37.1572
10	1.5270	8.6754	28.4818
11	1.1300	9.0724	19.4094
12	.7148	9.4876	9.9218
13	.2806	9.9218	0.0000

YEARS 14 — QTR PAYT 2.4166 — AN CONST 9.67

#	INT	PRIN	BALANCE
1	4.4122	5.2542	94.7458
2	4.1717	5.4947	89.2511
3	3.9202	5.7461	83.5050
4	3.6573	6.0091	77.4959
5	3.3823	6.2841	71.2118
6	3.0947	6.5717	64.6401
7	2.7939	6.8725	57.7676
8	2.4794	7.1870	50.5806
9	2.1505	7.5159	43.0648
10	1.8065	7.8599	35.2049
11	1.4468	8.2196	26.9853
12	1.0706	8.5957	18.3896
13	.6773	8.9891	9.4005
14	.2659	9.4005	0.0000

YEARS 15 — QTR PAYT 2.3010 — AN CONST 9.21

#	INT	PRIN	BALANCE
1	4.4200	4.7839	95.2161
2	4.2011	5.0029	90.2132
3	3.9721	5.2318	84.9814
4	3.7327	5.4712	79.5102
5	3.4823	5.7216	73.7886
6	3.2205	5.9835	67.8051
7	2.9466	6.2573	61.5478
8	2.6603	6.5437	55.0041
9	2.3608	6.8432	48.1609
10	2.0476	7.1563	41.0046
11	1.7201	7.4838	33.5207
12	1.3776	7.8263	25.6944
13	1.0194	8.1845	17.5099
14	.6449	8.5591	8.9508
15	.2531	8.9508	0.0000

YEARS 16 — QTR PAYT 2.2003 — AN CONST 8.81

#	INT	PRIN	BALANCE
1	4.4269	4.3744	95.6256
2	4.2267	4.5746	91.0509
3	4.0173	4.7840	86.2669
4	3.7984	5.0029	81.2640
5	3.5694	5.2319	76.0321
6	3.3300	5.4713	70.5607
7	3.0796	5.7217	64.8390
8	2.8177	5.9836	58.8554
9	2.5439	6.2574	52.5979
10	2.2575	6.5438	46.0541
11	1.9580	6.8433	39.2109
12	1.6448	7.1565	32.0544
13	1.3173	7.4840	24.5704
14	.9748	7.8265	16.7439
15	.6166	8.1847	8.5592
16	.2421	8.5592	0.0000

YEARS 17 — QTR PAYT 2.1120 — AN CONST 8.45

#	INT	PRIN	BALANCE
1	4.4329	4.0151	95.9849
2	4.2491	4.1988	91.7861
3	4.0570	4.3910	87.3952
4	3.8560	4.5919	82.8032
5	3.6459	4.8021	78.0012
6	3.4261	5.0218	72.9793
7	3.1963	5.2517	67.7277
8	2.9559	5.4920	62.2357
9	2.7046	5.7433	56.4923
10	2.4417	6.0062	50.4861
11	2.1669	6.2811	44.2050
12	1.8794	6.5685	37.6365
13	1.5788	6.8691	30.7674
14	1.2644	7.1835	23.5839
15	.9357	7.5123	16.0716
16	.5919	7.8561	8.2156
17	.2324	8.2156	0.0000

YEARS 18 — QTR PAYT 2.0339 — AN CONST 8.14

#	INT	PRIN	BALANCE
1	4.4382	3.6974	96.3026
2	4.2690	3.8666	92.4360
3	4.0920	4.0436	88.3924
4	3.9070	4.2286	84.1638
5	3.7134	4.4221	79.7417
6	3.5111	4.6245	75.1172
7	3.2994	4.8362	70.2810
8	3.0781	5.0575	65.2235
9	2.8466	5.2889	59.9346
10	2.6046	5.5310	54.4036
11	2.3515	5.7841	48.6194
12	2.0868	6.0488	42.5706
13	1.8099	6.3257	36.2449
14	1.5204	6.6152	29.6298
15	1.2177	6.9179	22.7119
16	.9011	7.2345	15.4774
17	.5700	7.5656	7.9118
18	.2238	7.9118	0.0000

YEARS 19 — QTR PAYT 1.9644 — AN CONST 7.86

#	INT	PRIN	BALANCE
1	4.4429	3.4149	96.5851
2	4.2866	3.5711	93.0140
3	4.1232	3.7346	89.2794
4	3.9523	3.9055	85.3740
5	3.7735	4.0842	81.2897
6	3.5866	4.2711	77.0186
7	3.3912	4.4666	72.5520
8	3.1868	4.6710	67.8810
9	2.9730	4.8848	62.9962
10	2.7494	5.1083	57.8879
11	2.5156	5.3421	52.5458
12	2.2712	5.5866	46.9592
13	2.0155	5.8423	41.1169
14	1.7481	6.1096	35.0072
15	1.4685	6.3893	28.6180
16	1.1761	6.6817	21.9363
17	.8703	6.9874	14.9489
18	.5505	7.3072	7.6416
19	.2161	7.6416	0.0000

YEARS 20 — QTR PAYT 1.9023 — AN CONST 7.61

#	INT	PRIN	BALANCE
1	4.4471	3.1622	96.8378
2	4.3024	3.3069	93.5310
3	4.1511	3.4582	90.0728
4	3.9928	3.6165	86.4563
5	3.8273	3.7820	82.6743
6	3.6542	3.9551	78.7192
7	3.4732	4.1361	74.5832
8	3.2839	4.3254	70.2578
9	3.0860	4.5233	65.7345
10	2.8790	4.7303	61.0042
11	2.6625	4.9468	56.0574
12	2.4361	5.1732	50.8842
13	2.1993	5.4099	45.4742
14	1.9518	5.6575	39.8167
15	1.6928	5.9164	33.9002
16	1.4221	6.1872	27.7130
17	1.1389	6.4704	21.2427
18	.8428	6.7665	14.4762
19	.5331	7.0762	7.4000
20	.2093	7.4000	0.0000

YEARS 21 — QTR PAYT 1.8465 — AN CONST 7.39

#	INT	PRIN	BALANCE
1	4.4509	2.9350	97.0650
2	4.3166	3.0693	93.9956
3	4.1761	3.2098	90.7858

#	INT	PRIN	BALANCE
4	4.0292	3.3567	87.4291
5	3.8756	3.5103	83.9188
6	3.7150	3.6710	80.2478
7	3.5470	3.8390	76.4088
8	3.3713	4.0147	72.3941
9	3.1875	4.1984	68.1957
10	2.9954	4.3905	63.8052
11	2.7945	4.5915	59.2137
12	2.5843	4.8016	54.4121
13	2.3646	5.0214	49.3907
14	2.1348	5.2512	44.1395
15	1.8945	5.4915	38.6481
16	1.6432	5.7428	32.9053
17	1.3803	6.0056	26.8996
18	1.1055	6.2805	20.6192
19	.8181	6.5679	14.0513
20	.5175	6.8685	7.1828
21	.2031	7.1828	0.0000

YEARS 22 — QTR PAYT 1.7961 — AN CONST 7.19

#	INT	PRIN	BALANCE
1	4.4544	2.7300	97.2700
2	4.3294	2.8549	94.4151
3	4.1988	2.9856	91.4296
4	4.0621	3.1222	88.3074
5	3.9192	3.2651	85.0423
6	3.7698	3.4145	81.6278
7	3.6136	3.5708	78.0571
8	3.4501	3.7342	74.3229
9	3.2792	3.9051	70.4178
10	3.1005	4.0838	66.3340
11	2.9136	4.2707	62.0633
12	2.7182	4.4661	57.5972
13	2.5138	4.6705	52.9266
14	2.3000	4.8843	48.0424
15	2.0765	5.1078	42.9346
16	1.8428	5.3416	37.5930
17	1.5983	5.5860	32.0070
18	1.3427	5.8417	26.1653
19	1.0753	6.1090	20.0563
20	.7957	6.3886	13.6677
21	.5034	6.6810	6.9867
22	.1976	6.9867	0.0000

YEARS 23 — QTR PAYT 1.7504 — AN CONST 7.01

#	INT	PRIN	BALANCE
1	4.4575	2.5441	97.4559
2	4.3410	2.6605	94.7954
3	4.2193	2.7823	92.0131
4	4.0919	2.9096	89.1035
5	3.9588	3.0428	86.0608
6	3.8195	3.1820	82.8788
7	3.6739	3.3276	79.5511
8	3.5216	3.4799	76.0712
9	3.3624	3.6392	72.4320
10	3.1958	3.8057	68.6263
11	3.0216	3.9799	64.6464
12	2.8395	4.1620	60.4844
13	2.6490	4.3525	56.1319
14	2.4498	4.5517	51.5801
15	2.2415	4.7600	46.8201
16	2.0237	4.9779	41.8423
17	1.7959	5.2057	36.6366
18	1.5576	5.4439	31.1927
19	1.3085	5.6931	25.4996
20	1.0480	5.9536	19.5460
21	.7755	6.2261	13.3200
22	.4905	6.5110	6.8090
23	.1926	6.8090	0.0000

YEARS 24 — QTR PAYT 1.7088 — AN CONST 6.84

#	INT	PRIN	BALANCE
1	4.4603	2.3750	97.6250
2	4.3516	2.4837	95.1414
3	4.2379	2.5973	92.5441
4	4.1191	2.7162	89.8279
5	3.9948	2.8405	86.9874
6	3.8648	2.9705	84.0169
7	3.7288	3.1064	80.9104
8	3.5867	3.2486	77.6618
9	3.4380	3.3973	74.2646
10	3.2825	3.5528	70.7118
11	3.1199	3.7153	66.9965
12	2.9499	3.8854	63.1111
13	2.7721	4.0632	59.0479
14	2.5861	4.2491	54.7987
15	2.3917	4.4436	50.3551
16	2.1883	4.6470	45.7082
17	1.9756	4.8596	40.8485
18	1.7532	5.0820	35.7665
19	1.5206	5.3146	30.4519
20	1.2774	5.5578	24.8940
21	1.0231	5.8122	19.0818
22	.7571	6.0782	13.0036
23	.4789	6.3564	6.6473
24	.1880	6.6473	0.0000

YEARS 25 — QTR PAYT 1.6709 — AN CONST 6.69

#	INT	PRIN	BALANCE
1	4.4629	2.2206	97.7794
2	4.3613	2.3222	95.4572
3	4.2550	2.4285	93.0287
4	4.1438	2.5396	90.4890
5	4.0276	2.6559	87.8331
6	3.9061	2.7774	85.0557
7	3.7790	2.9045	82.1512
8	3.6460	3.0375	79.1137
9	3.5070	3.1765	75.9373
10	3.3616	3.3218	72.6154
11	3.2096	3.4739	69.1416
12	3.0506	3.6328	65.5087
13	2.8844	3.7991	61.7096
14	2.7105	3.9730	57.7367
15	2.5287	4.1548	53.5819
16	2.3385	4.3449	49.2369
17	2.1397	4.5438	44.6932
18	1.9318	4.7517	39.9414
19	1.7143	4.9692	34.9723
20	1.4869	5.1966	29.7757
21	1.2491	5.4344	24.3412
22	1.0003	5.6831	18.6581
23	.7403	5.9432	12.7149
24	.4683	6.2152	6.4997
25	.1838	6.4997	0.0000

YEARS 26 — QTR PAYT 1.6361 — AN CONST 6.55

#	INT	PRIN	BALANCE
1	4.4652	2.0793	97.9207
2	4.3701	2.1744	95.7463
3	4.2706	2.2739	93.4724
4	4.1665	2.3780	91.0943
5	4.0577	2.4868	88.6075
6	3.9439	2.6007	86.0068
7	3.8248	2.7197	83.2872
8	3.7004	2.8441	80.4430
9	3.5702	2.9743	77.4687
10	3.4341	3.1104	74.3583
11	3.2917	3.2528	71.1056
12	3.1429	3.4016	67.7039
13	2.9872	3.5573	64.1466
14	2.8244	3.7201	60.4265
15	2.6542	3.8904	56.5362
16	2.4761	4.0684	52.4678
17	2.2899	4.2546	48.2132
18	2.0952	4.4493	43.7639
19	1.8916	4.6529	39.1110
20	1.6786	4.8659	34.2451
21	1.4560	5.0886	29.1565
22	1.2231	5.3214	23.8351
23	.9795	5.5650	18.2701
24	.7249	5.8196	12.4505
25	.4585	6.0860	6.3645
26	.1800	6.3645	0.0000

YEARS 27 — QTR PAYT 1.6042 — AN CONST 6.42

#	INT	PRIN	BALANCE
1	4.4674	1.9495	98.0505
2	4.3782	2.0387	96.0117
3	4.2849	2.1320	93.8797
4	4.1873	2.2296	91.6501
5	4.0853	2.3317	89.3184
6	3.9786	2.4384	86.8801
7	3.8670	2.5500	84.3301
8	3.7503	2.6666	81.6635
9	3.6282	2.7887	78.8748
10	3.5006	2.9163	75.9585
11	3.3671	3.0498	72.9087
12	3.2276	3.1894	69.7193
13	3.0816	3.3353	66.3840
14	2.9290	3.4880	62.8961
15	2.7693	3.6476	59.2485
16	2.6024	3.8145	55.4340
17	2.4278	3.9891	51.4449
18	2.2453	4.1716	47.2733
19	2.0544	4.3626	42.9107
20	1.8547	4.5622	38.3485
21	1.6459	4.7710	33.5775
22	1.4276	4.9893	28.5881
23	1.1992	5.2177	23.3704
24	.9604	5.4565	17.9140
25	.7107	5.7062	12.2078
26	.4496	5.9673	6.2404
27	.1765	6.2404	0.0000

YEARS 28 — QTR PAYT 1.5749 — AN CONST 6.30

#	INT	PRIN	BALANCE
1	4.4694	1.8301	98.1699
2	4.3857	1.9138	96.2561
3	4.2981	2.0014	94.2546
4	4.2065	2.0930	92.1616
5	4.1107	2.1888	89.9728
6	4.0105	2.2890	87.6838
7	3.9058	2.3937	85.2901
8	3.7962	2.5033	82.7868
9	3.6816	2.6178	80.1690
10	3.5618	2.7377	77.4313
11	3.4365	2.8629	74.5684
12	3.3055	2.9940	71.5744
13	3.1685	3.1310	68.4434
14	3.0252	3.2743	65.1691
15	2.8754	3.4241	61.7450
16	2.7187	3.5808	58.1642
17	2.5548	3.7447	54.4195
18	2.3834	3.9161	50.5034
19	2.2042	4.0953	46.4081
20	2.0168	4.2827	42.1254
21	1.8208	4.4787	37.6467
22	1.6158	4.6837	32.9630
23	1.4015	4.8980	28.0649
24	1.1773	5.1222	22.9427
25	.9429	5.3566	17.5861
26	.6977	5.6018	11.9844
27	.4414	5.8581	6.1262
28	.1733	6.1262	0.0000

YEARS 29 — QTR PAYT 1.5478 — AN CONST 6.20

#	INT	PRIN	BALANCE
1	4.4712	1.7199	98.2801
2	4.3925	1.7986	96.4815
3	4.3102	1.8809	94.6006
4	4.2241	1.9670	92.6336
5	4.1341	2.0570	90.5765
6	4.0400	2.1512	88.4254
7	3.9415	2.2496	86.1758
8	3.8386	2.3526	83.8232
9	3.7309	2.4602	81.3630
10	3.6183	2.5728	78.7901
11	3.5006	2.6906	76.0996
12	3.3774	2.8137	73.2859
13	3.2487	2.9425	70.3434
14	3.1140	3.0771	67.2663
15	2.9732	3.2180	64.0483
16	2.8259	3.3652	60.6831
17	2.6719	3.5192	57.1638
18	2.5108	3.6803	53.4835
19	2.3424	3.8487	49.6348
20	2.1663	4.0249	45.6099
21	1.9821	4.2091	41.4009
22	1.7895	4.4017	36.9992
23	1.5880	4.6031	32.3960
24	1.3773	4.8138	27.5822
25	1.1570	5.0341	22.5481
26	.9267	5.2645	17.2837
27	.6857	5.5054	11.7782
28	.4338	5.7574	6.0209
29	.1703	6.0209	0.0000

YEARS 30 — QTR PAYT 1.5227 — AN CONST 6.10

#	INT	PRIN	BALANCE
1	4.4730	1.6180	98.3820
2	4.3989	1.6921	96.6899
3	4.3215	1.7695	94.9204
4	4.2405	1.8505	93.0699
5	4.1558	1.9352	91.1347
6	4.0672	2.0237	89.1110
7	3.9746	2.1164	86.9946
8	3.8778	2.2132	84.7814
9	3.7765	2.3145	82.4669
10	3.6705	2.4204	80.0465
11	3.5598	2.5312	77.5153
12	3.4439	2.6470	74.8683
13	3.3228	2.7682	72.1001
14	3.1961	2.8949	69.2052
15	3.0636	3.0273	66.1779
16	2.9251	3.1659	63.0120
17	2.7802	3.3108	59.7012
18	2.6287	3.4623	56.2389
19	2.4702	3.6208	52.6182
20	2.3045	3.7865	48.8317
21	2.1312	3.9597	44.8720
22	1.9500	4.1410	40.7310
23	1.7605	4.3305	36.4005
24	1.5623	4.5287	31.8719
25	1.3551	4.7359	27.1360
26	1.1383	4.9527	22.1833
27	.9117	5.1793	17.0040
28	.6746	5.4163	11.5877
29	.4268	5.6642	5.9234
30	.1675	5.9234	0.0000

QUARTERLY PAYMENT AMORTIZATION SCHEDULE PER $100 — 4.75 %

YEARS 2 — QTR PAYT 13.1772 — AN CONST 52.71

#	INT	PRIN	BALANCE
1	3.8890	48.8197	51.1803
2	1.5284	51.1803	0.0000

YEARS 3 — QTR PAYT 8.9905 — AN CONST 35.97

#	INT	PRIN	BALANCE
1	4.1896	31.7723	68.2277
2	2.6533	33.3086	34.9191
3	1.0428	34.9191	0.0000

YEARS 4 — QTR PAYT 6.8995 — AN CONST 27.60

#	INT	PRIN	BALANCE
1	4.3398	23.2581	76.7419
2	3.2152	24.3827	52.3593
3	2.0362	25.5616	26.7976
4	.8002	26.7976	0.0000

YEARS 5 — QTR PAYT 5.6467 — AN CONST 22.59

#	INT	PRIN	BALANCE
1	4.4298	18.1571	81.8429
2	3.5518	19.0351	62.8078
3	2.6314	19.9555	42.8523
4	1.6665	20.9204	21.9319
5	.6549	21.9319	0.0000

YEARS 6 — QTR PAYT 4.8131 — AN CONST 19.26

#	INT	PRIN	BALANCE
1	4.4896	14.7628	85.2372
2	3.7758	15.4766	69.7606
3	3.0275	16.2250	53.5356
4	2.2429	17.0095	36.5261
5	1.4205	17.8319	18.6942
6	.5583	18.6942	0.0000

YEARS 7 — QTR PAYT 4.2190 — AN CONST 16.88

#	INT	PRIN	BALANCE
1	4.5323	12.3437	87.6563
2	3.9354	12.9405	74.7158
3	3.3097	13.5662	61.1495
4	2.6538	14.2222	46.9273
5	1.9661	14.9099	32.0174
6	1.2451	15.6308	16.3866
7	.4893	16.3866	0.0000

YEARS 8 — QTR PAYT 3.7746 — AN CONST 15.10

#	INT	PRIN	BALANCE
1	4.5642	10.5340	89.4660
2	4.0549	11.0434	78.4226
3	3.5209	11.5774	66.8452
4	2.9611	12.1372	54.7080
5	2.3742	12.7240	41.9840
6	1.7590	13.3393	28.6447
7	1.1140	13.9843	14.6604
8	.4378	14.6604	0.0000

YEARS 9 — QTR PAYT 3.4299 — AN CONST 13.72

#	INT	PRIN	BALANCE
1	4.5890	9.1307	90.8693
2	4.1475	9.5722	81.2971
3	3.6846	10.0351	71.2620
4	3.1994	10.5203	60.7418
5	2.6907	11.0290	49.7128
6	2.1574	11.5622	38.1506
7	1.5984	12.1213	26.0293
8	1.0123	12.7074	13.3218
9	.3978	13.3218	0.0000

YEARS 10 — QTR PAYT 3.1551 — AN CONST 12.63

#	INT	PRIN	BALANCE
1	4.6087	8.0118	91.9882
2	4.2213	8.3992	83.5890
3	3.8152	8.8053	74.7837
4	3.3894	9.2311	65.5527
5	2.9431	9.6774	55.8753
6	2.4751	10.1453	45.7299
7	1.9846	10.6359	35.0940
8	1.4703	11.1502	23.9438
9	.9312	11.6893	12.2545
10	.3660	12.2545	0.0000

YEARS 11 — QTR PAYT 2.9311 — AN CONST 11.73

#	INT	PRIN	BALANCE
1	4.6248	7.0997	92.9003
2	4.2815	7.4430	85.4573
3	3.9216	7.8029	77.6545
4	3.5443	8.1802	69.4743
5	3.1488	8.5757	60.8986
6	2.7341	8.9903	51.9083
7	2.2994	9.4251	42.4832
8	1.8437	9.8808	32.6025
9	1.3659	10.3585	22.2439
10	.8651	10.8594	11.3845
11	.3400	11.3845	0.0000

YEARS 12 — QTR PAYT 2.7452 — AN CONST 10.99

#	INT	PRIN	BALANCE
1	4.6381	6.3427	93.6573
2	4.3314	6.6494	87.0079
3	4.0099	6.9709	80.0370
4	3.6729	7.3080	72.7291
5	3.3195	7.6613	65.0678
6	2.9491	8.0318	57.0360
7	2.5607	8.4201	48.6159
8	2.1536	8.8273	39.7887
9	1.7267	9.2541	30.5346
10	1.2793	9.7015	20.8330
11	.8102	10.1706	10.6624
12	.3184	10.6624	0.0000

YEARS 13 — QTR PAYT 2.5886 — AN CONST 10.36

#	INT	PRIN	BALANCE
1	4.6494	5.7050	94.2950
2	4.3735	5.9808	88.3142
3	4.0843	6.2700	82.0441
4	3.7812	6.5732	75.4709
5	3.4633	6.8910	68.5799
6	3.1301	7.2242	61.3557
7	2.7808	7.5735	53.7821
8	2.4146	7.9398	45.8424
9	2.0307	8.3237	37.5187
10	1.6282	8.7261	28.7926
11	1.2063	9.1481	19.6445
12	.7640	9.5904	10.0541
13	.3002	10.0541	0.0000

YEARS 14 — QTR PAYT 2.4550 — AN CONST 9.82

#	INT	PRIN	BALANCE
1	4.6590	5.1610	94.8390
2	4.4094	5.4106	89.4284
3	4.1478	5.6722	83.7563
4	3.8735	5.9464	77.8098
5	3.5860	6.2340	71.5759
6	3.2846	6.5354	65.0405
7	2.9686	6.8514	58.1891
8	2.6373	7.1827	51.0064
9	2.2900	7.5300	43.4765
10	1.9259	7.8941	35.5824
11	1.5442	8.2758	27.3066
12	1.1440	8.6759	18.6307
13	.7245	9.0954	9.5352
14	.2847	9.5352	0.0000

YEARS 15 — QTR PAYT 2.3398 — AN CONST 9.36

#	INT	PRIN	BALANCE
1	4.6672	4.6920	95.3080
2	4.4404	4.9188	90.3892
3	4.2025	5.1567	85.2325
4	3.9532	5.4060	79.8265
5	3.6918	5.6674	74.1590
6	3.4178	5.9415	68.2176
7	3.1305	6.2287	61.9888
8	2.8293	6.5299	55.4589
9	2.5136	6.8457	48.6132
10	2.1826	7.1767	41.4365
11	1.8355	7.5237	33.9129
12	1.4717	7.8875	26.0254
13	1.0904	8.2689	17.7565
14	.6905	8.6687	9.0878
15	.2714	9.0878	0.0000

YEARS 16 — QTR PAYT 2.2396 — AN CONST 8.96

#	INT	PRIN	BALANCE
1	4.6744	4.2838	95.7162
2	4.4673	4.4910	91.2252
3	4.2502	4.7081	86.5170
4	4.0225	4.9358	81.5813
5	3.7838	5.1744	76.4068
6	3.5336	5.4246	70.9822
7	3.2714	5.6869	65.2952
8	2.9964	5.9619	59.3333
9	2.7081	6.2502	53.0831
10	2.4059	6.5524	46.5307
11	2.0891	6.8692	39.6615
12	1.7569	7.2014	32.4601
13	1.4087	7.5496	24.9105
14	1.0437	7.9146	16.9959
15	.6610	8.2973	8.6985
16	.2598	8.6985	0.0000

YEARS 17 — QTR PAYT 2.1517 — AN CONST 8.61

#	INT	PRIN	BALANCE
1	4.6808	3.9258	96.0742
2	4.4909	4.1157	91.9585
3	4.2919	4.3147	87.6438
4	4.0833	4.5233	83.1205
5	3.8646	4.7420	78.3785
6	3.6353	4.9713	73.4072
7	3.3949	5.2117	68.1955
8	3.1429	5.4637	62.7318
9	2.8787	5.7279	57.0040
10	2.6018	6.0048	50.9992
11	2.3114	6.2952	44.7040
12	2.0070	6.5996	38.1044
13	1.6879	6.9187	31.1858
14	1.3534	7.2532	23.9325
15	1.0027	7.6039	16.3286
16	.6350	7.9716	8.3570
17	.2496	8.3570	0.0000

YEARS 18 — QTR PAYT 2.0740 — AN CONST 8.30

#	INT	PRIN	BALANCE
1	4.6863	3.6096	96.3904
2	4.5118	3.7841	92.6063
3	4.3288	3.9671	88.6392
4	4.1370	4.1589	84.4802
5	3.9359	4.3600	80.1202
6	3.7251	4.5708	75.5494
7	3.5041	4.7919	70.7575
8	3.2724	5.0236	65.7339
9	3.0295	5.2665	60.4675
10	2.7748	5.5211	54.9464
11	2.5079	5.7881	49.1583
12	2.2280	6.0679	43.0903
13	1.9346	6.3613	36.7290
14	1.6270	6.6689	30.0601
15	1.3045	6.9914	23.0687
16	.9665	7.3294	15.7392
17	.6121	7.6838	8.0554
18	.2406	8.0554	0.0000

YEARS 19 — QTR PAYT 2.0050 — AN CONST 8.02

#	INT	PRIN	BALANCE
1	4.6913	3.3285	96.6715
2	4.5304	3.4895	93.1820
3	4.3616	3.6582	89.5239
4	4.1847	3.8351	85.6888
5	3.9993	4.0205	81.6683
6	3.8049	4.2149	77.4534
7	3.6011	4.4187	73.0347
8	3.3874	4.6324	68.4023
9	3.1635	4.8563	63.5460
10	2.9286	5.0912	58.4548
11	2.6825	5.3373	53.1175
12	2.4244	5.5954	47.5220
13	2.1538	5.8660	41.6561
14	1.8702	6.1496	35.5065
15	1.5729	6.4470	29.0595
16	1.2611	6.7587	22.3008
17	.9343	7.0855	15.2153
18	.5917	7.4281	7.7873
19	.2325	7.7873	0.0000

YEARS 20 — QTR PAYT 1.9433 — AN CONST 7.78

#	INT	PRIN	BALANCE
1	4.6957	3.0773	96.9227
2	4.5469	3.2261	93.6966
3	4.3909	3.3821	90.3146
4	4.2274	3.5456	86.7689
5	4.0560	3.7170	83.0519
6	3.8762	3.8968	79.1551
7	3.6878	4.0852	75.0699
8	3.4903	4.2827	70.7872
9	3.2832	4.4898	66.2974
10	3.0661	4.7069	61.5905
11	2.8385	4.9345	56.6560
12	2.5999	5.1731	51.4829
13	2.3498	5.4232	46.0597
14	2.0876	5.6855	40.3742
15	1.8126	5.9604	34.4138
16	1.5244	6.2486	28.1653
17	1.2223	6.5507	21.6146
18	.9056	6.8674	14.7471
19	.5735	7.1995	7.5476
20	.2254	7.5476	0.0000

YEARS 21 — QTR PAYT 1.8878 — AN CONST 7.56

#	INT	PRIN	BALANCE
1	4.6997	2.8517	97.1483
2	4.5618	2.9895	94.1588
3	4.4173	3.1341	91.0247

#	INT	PRIN	BALANCE
4	4.2657	3.2856	87.7391
5	4.1069	3.4445	84.2946
6	3.9403	3.6111	80.6835
7	3.7657	3.7857	76.8979
8	3.5827	3.9687	72.9292
9	3.3908	4.1606	68.7686
10	3.1896	4.3618	64.4068
11	2.9787	4.5727	59.8341
12	2.7576	4.7938	55.0403
13	2.5258	5.0256	50.0148
14	2.2828	5.2686	44.7462
15	2.0280	5.5233	39.2229
16	1.7610	5.7904	33.4325
17	1.4810	6.0704	27.3621
18	1.1875	6.3639	20.9982
19	.8797	6.6716	14.3266
20	.5572	6.9942	7.3324
21	.2190	7.3324	0.0000

YEARS 22   QTR PAYT 1.8378   AN CONST 7.36

#	INT	PRIN	BALANCE
1	4.7033	2.6481	97.3519
2	4.5753	2.7761	94.5758
3	4.4410	2.9104	91.6654
4	4.3003	3.0511	88.6143
5	4.1528	3.1986	85.4157
6	3.9981	3.3533	82.0624
7	3.8360	3.5154	78.5470
8	3.6660	3.6854	74.8616
9	3.4878	3.8636	70.9980
10	3.3010	4.0504	66.9475
11	3.1051	4.2463	62.7013
12	2.8998	4.4516	58.2497
13	2.6845	4.6668	53.5828
14	2.4589	4.8925	48.6903
15	2.2223	5.1291	43.5613
16	1.9743	5.3771	38.1842
17	1.7143	5.6371	32.5472
18	1.4418	5.9096	26.6375
19	1.1560	6.1954	20.4421
20	.8564	6.4949	13.9472
21	.5424	6.8090	7.1382
22	.2132	7.1382	0.0000

YEARS 23   QTR PAYT 1.7926   AN CONST 7.18

#	INT	PRIN	BALANCE
1	4.7065	2.4637	97.5363
2	4.5874	2.5829	94.9534
3	4.4625	2.7077	92.2457
4	4.3316	2.8387	89.4070
5	4.1943	2.9759	86.4311
6	4.0505	3.1198	83.3113
7	3.8996	3.2707	80.0406
8	3.7415	3.4288	76.6118
9	3.5757	3.5946	73.0172
10	3.4019	3.7684	69.2488
11	3.2196	3.9506	65.2981
12	3.0286	4.1417	61.1565
13	2.8284	4.3419	56.8146
14	2.6184	4.5519	52.2627
15	2.3983	4.7720	47.4907
16	2.1676	5.0027	42.4880
17	1.9257	5.2446	37.2435
18	1.6721	5.4982	31.7453
19	1.4062	5.7640	25.9812
20	1.1275	6.0427	19.9385
21	.8353	6.3349	13.6036
22	.5290	6.6412	6.9624
23	.2079	6.9624	0.0000

YEARS 24   QTR PAYT 1.7514   AN CONST 7.01

#	INT	PRIN	BALANCE
1	4.7095	2.2961	97.7039
2	4.5985	2.4072	95.2967
3	4.4821	2.5235	92.7732
4	4.3601	2.6456	90.1276
5	4.2321	2.7735	87.3541
6	4.0980	2.9076	84.4465
7	3.9574	3.0482	81.3983
8	3.8101	3.1956	78.2028
9	3.6555	3.3501	74.8527
10	3.4936	3.5121	71.3406
11	3.3237	3.6819	67.6587
12	3.1457	3.8599	63.7988
13	2.9591	4.0466	59.7522
14	2.7634	4.2422	55.5100
15	2.5583	4.4473	51.0627
16	2.3432	4.6624	46.4003
17	2.1178	4.8878	41.5125
18	1.8815	5.1242	36.3883
19	1.6337	5.3719	31.0164
20	1.3739	5.6317	25.3847
21	1.1016	5.9040	19.4807
22	.8162	6.1895	13.2912
23	.5169	6.4887	6.8025
24	.2031	6.8025	0.0000

YEARS 25   QTR PAYT 1.7139   AN CONST 6.86

#	INT	PRIN	BALANCE
1	4.7122	2.1433	97.8567
2	4.6086	2.2469	95.6098
3	4.4999	2.3556	93.2542
4	4.3860	2.4695	90.7848
5	4.2666	2.5889	88.1959
6	4.1414	2.7140	85.4819
7	4.0102	2.8453	82.6366
8	3.8726	2.9829	79.6537
9	3.7284	3.1271	76.5267
10	3.5772	3.2783	73.2484
11	3.4187	3.4368	69.8116
12	3.2525	3.6030	66.2086
13	3.0783	3.7772	62.4314
14	2.8957	3.9598	58.4716
15	2.7042	4.1513	54.3203
16	2.5035	4.3520	49.9683
17	2.2930	4.5625	45.4058
18	2.0724	4.7831	40.6227
19	1.8411	5.0143	35.6084
20	1.5987	5.2568	30.3516
21	1.3445	5.5110	24.8406
22	1.0780	5.7775	19.0632
23	.7987	6.0568	13.0064
24	.5058	6.3497	6.6567
25	.1988	6.6567	0.0000

YEARS 26   QTR PAYT 1.6795   AN CONST 6.72

#	INT	PRIN	BALANCE
1	4.7147	2.0035	97.9965
2	4.6178	2.1003	95.8962
3	4.5162	2.2019	93.6943
4	4.4098	2.3084	91.3859
5	4.2981	2.4200	88.9659
6	4.1811	2.5370	86.4289
7	4.0585	2.6597	83.7693
8	3.9299	2.7883	80.9810
9	3.7950	2.9231	78.0579
10	3.6537	3.0644	74.9935
11	3.5055	3.2126	71.7809
12	3.3502	3.3679	68.4129
13	3.1873	3.5308	64.8821
14	3.0166	3.7015	61.1806
15	2.8376	3.8805	57.3001
16	2.6500	4.0681	53.2320
17	2.4533	4.2648	48.9672
18	2.2471	4.4711	44.4961
19	2.0309	4.6872	39.8089
20	1.8043	4.9139	34.8950
21	1.5667	5.1515	29.7435
22	1.3176	5.4006	24.3429
23	1.0564	5.6617	18.6812
24	.7827	5.9355	12.7458
25	.4957	6.2225	6.5233
26	.1948	6.5233	0.0000

YEARS 27   QTR PAYT 1.6480   AN CONST 6.60

#	INT	PRIN	BALANCE
1	4.7169	1.8752	98.1248
2	4.6263	1.9659	96.1589
3	4.5312	2.0610	94.0979
4	4.4315	2.1606	91.9373
5	4.3271	2.2651	89.6722
6	4.2175	2.3746	87.2976
7	4.1027	2.4894	84.8082
8	3.9824	2.6098	82.1984
9	3.8562	2.7360	79.4624
10	3.7239	2.8683	76.5941
11	3.5852	3.0070	73.5872
12	3.4398	3.1524	70.4348
13	3.2874	3.3048	67.1300
14	3.1276	3.4646	63.6654
15	2.9600	3.6321	60.0333
16	2.7844	3.8077	56.2256
17	2.6003	3.9918	52.2338
18	2.4073	4.1849	48.0489
19	2.2049	4.3872	43.6617
20	1.9928	4.5993	39.0624
21	1.7704	4.8217	34.2406
22	1.5373	5.0549	29.1858
23	1.2929	5.2993	23.8865
24	1.0366	5.5555	18.3309
25	.7680	5.8242	12.5068
26	.4864	6.1058	6.4010
27	.1912	6.4010	0.0000

YEARS 28   QTR PAYT 1.6191   AN CONST 6.48

#	INT	PRIN	BALANCE
1	4.7190	1.7573	98.2427
2	4.6340	1.8423	96.4004
3	4.5540	1.9314	94.4691
4	4.4516	2.0247	92.4443
5	4.3537	2.1226	90.3217
6	4.2510	2.2253	88.0964
7	4.1434	2.3329	85.7635
8	4.0306	2.4457	83.3179
9	3.9124	2.5639	80.7539
10	3.7884	2.6879	78.0660
11	3.6584	2.8179	75.2482
12	3.5222	2.9541	72.2940
13	3.3793	3.0970	69.1971
14	3.2296	3.2467	65.9504
15	3.0726	3.4037	62.5467
16	2.9080	3.5683	58.9784
17	2.7355	3.7408	55.2376
18	2.5546	3.9217	51.3159
19	2.3650	4.1113	47.2046
20	2.1662	4.3101	42.8944
21	1.9578	4.5185	38.3759
22	1.7393	4.7370	33.6389
23	1.5103	4.9660	28.6729
24	1.2701	5.2062	23.4667
25	1.0184	5.4579	18.0088
26	.7545	5.7218	12.2870
27	.4778	5.9985	6.2885
28	.1878	6.2885	0.0000

YEARS 29   QTR PAYT 1.5924   AN CONST 6.37

#	INT	PRIN	BALANCE
1	4.7209	1.6486	98.3514
2	4.6412	1.7283	96.6231
3	4.5576	1.8119	94.8111
4	4.4700	1.8995	92.9116
5	4.3782	1.9914	90.9203
6	4.2819	2.0876	88.8326
7	4.1809	2.1886	86.6440
8	4.0751	2.2944	84.3496
9	3.9642	2.4054	81.9443
10	3.8479	2.5217	79.4226
11	3.7259	2.6436	76.7790
12	3.5981	2.7714	74.0076
13	3.4641	2.9054	71.1022
14	3.3236	3.0459	68.0563
15	3.1764	3.1932	64.8631
16	3.0220	3.3476	61.5155
17	2.8601	3.5095	58.0060
18	2.6904	3.6791	54.3269
19	2.5125	3.8570	50.4699
20	2.3260	4.0435	46.4263
21	2.1305	4.2391	42.1873
22	1.9255	4.4440	37.7432
23	1.7106	4.6589	33.0843
24	1.4854	4.8842	28.2002
25	1.2492	5.1203	23.0798
26	1.0016	5.3679	17.7119
27	.7421	5.6275	12.0844
28	.4700	5.8996	6.1848
29	.1847	6.1848	0.0000

YEARS 30   QTR PAYT 1.5677   AN CONST 6.28

#	INT	PRIN	BALANCE
1	4.7227	1.5482	98.4518
2	4.6478	1.6231	96.8287
3	4.5694	1.7016	95.1271
4	4.4871	1.7838	93.3433
5	4.4008	1.8701	91.4732
6	4.3104	1.9605	89.5126
7	4.2156	2.0553	87.4573
8	4.1162	2.1547	85.3026
9	4.0120	2.2589	83.0437
10	3.9028	2.3681	80.6756
11	3.7883	2.4826	78.1930
12	3.6683	2.6027	75.5903
13	3.5424	2.7285	72.8618
14	3.4105	2.8604	70.0014
15	3.2722	2.9988	67.0026
16	3.1272	3.1437	63.8589
17	2.9752	3.2958	60.5631
18	2.8158	3.4551	57.1080
19	2.6487	3.6222	53.4858
20	2.4736	3.7973	49.6885
21	2.2900	3.9809	45.7075
22	2.0975	4.1734	41.5341
23	1.8957	4.3752	37.1589
24	1.6841	4.5868	32.5721
25	1.4624	4.8086	27.7636
26	1.2299	5.0411	22.7225
27	.9861	5.2848	17.4377
28	.7306	5.5404	11.8973
29	.4627	5.8082	6.0891
30	.1818	6.0891	0.0000

QUARTERLY PAYMENT AMORTIZATION SCHEDULE PER $100   5.00 %

YEARS 2 — QTR PAYT 13.2133 — AN CONST 52.86

#	INT	PRIN	BALANCE
1	4.0953	48.7580	51.2420
2	1.6113	51.2420	0.0000

YEARS 3 — QTR PAYT 9.0258 — AN CONST 36.11

#	INT	PRIN	BALANCE
1	4.4119	31.6914	68.3086
2	2.7974	33.3059	35.0027
3	1.1006	35.0027	0.0000

YEARS 4 — QTR PAYT 6.9347 — AN CONST 27.74

#	INT	PRIN	BALANCE
1	4.5701	23.1686	76.8314
2	3.3898	24.3489	52.4825
3	2.1493	25.5894	26.8931
4	.8456	26.8931	0.0000

YEARS 5 — QTR PAYT 5.6820 — AN CONST 22.73

#	INT	PRIN	BALANCE
1	4.6648	18.0633	81.9367
2	3.7446	18.9836	62.9531
3	2.7775	19.9507	43.0024
4	1.7611	20.9671	22.0353
5	.6929	22.0353	0.0000

YEARS 6 — QTR PAYT 4.8487 — AN CONST 19.40

#	INT	PRIN	BALANCE
1	4.7278	14.6668	85.3332
2	3.9806	15.4140	69.9192
3	3.1954	16.1993	53.7199
4	2.3701	17.0246	36.6953
5	1.5028	17.8919	18.8034
6	.5913	18.8034	0.0000

YEARS 7 — QTR PAYT 4.2549 — AN CONST 17.02

#	INT	PRIN	BALANCE
1	4.7728	12.2467	87.7533
2	4.1488	12.8706	74.8827
3	3.4931	13.5263	61.3564
4	2.8040	14.2154	47.1410
5	2.0798	14.9396	32.2013
6	1.3187	15.7007	16.5006
7	.5188	16.5006	0.0000

YEARS 8 — QTR PAYT 3.8108 — AN CONST 15.25

#	INT	PRIN	BALANCE
1	4.8063	10.4368	89.5632
2	4.2746	10.9685	78.5946
3	3.7158	11.5273	67.0673
4	3.1286	12.1146	54.9527
5	2.5114	12.7318	42.2209
6	1.8628	13.3804	28.8405
7	1.1811	14.0621	14.7785
8	.4647	14.7785	0.0000

YEARS 9 — QTR PAYT 3.4665 — AN CONST 13.87

#	INT	PRIN	BALANCE
1	4.8324	9.0338	90.9662
2	4.3721	9.4940	81.4722
3	3.8885	9.9777	71.4946
4	3.3802	10.4860	61.0086
5	2.8459	11.0202	49.9884
6	2.2845	11.5816	38.4068
7	1.6945	12.1716	26.2352
8	1.0744	12.7917	13.4434
9	.4227	13.4434	0.0000

YEARS 10 — QTR PAYT 3.1921 — AN CONST 12.77

#	INT	PRIN	BALANCE
1	4.8531	7.9154	92.0846
2	4.4499	8.3187	83.7659
3	4.0261	8.7425	75.0234
4	3.5807	9.1879	65.8355
5	3.1126	9.6560	56.1795
6	2.6207	10.1479	46.0316
7	2.1037	10.6649	35.3667
8	1.5604	11.2082	24.1585
9	.9894	11.7792	12.3793
10	.3893	12.3793	0.0000

YEARS 11 — QTR PAYT 2.9686 — AN CONST 11.88

#	INT	PRIN	BALANCE
1	4.8700	7.0042	92.9958
2	4.5132	7.3610	85.6348
3	4.1382	7.7360	77.8987
4	3.7441	8.1302	69.7686
5	3.3299	8.5443	61.2242
6	2.8946	8.9796	52.2446
7	2.4371	9.4371	42.8075
8	1.9563	9.9179	32.8896
9	1.4511	10.4232	22.4664
10	.9201	10.9542	11.5122
11	.3620	11.5122	0.0000

YEARS 12 — QTR PAYT 2.7831 — AN CONST 11.14

#	INT	PRIN	BALANCE
1	4.8841	6.2482	93.7518
2	4.5657	6.5666	87.1852
3	4.2312	6.9011	80.2841
4	3.8796	7.2527	73.0314
5	3.5101	7.6222	65.4093
6	3.1218	8.0105	57.3988
7	2.7137	8.4186	48.9802
8	2.2848	8.8475	40.1328
9	1.8341	9.2982	30.8346
10	1.3604	9.7719	21.0627
11	.8626	10.2697	10.7929
12	.3394	10.7929	0.0000

YEARS 13 — QTR PAYT 2.6269 — AN CONST 10.51

#	INT	PRIN	BALANCE
1	4.8959	5.6117	94.3883
2	4.6100	5.8976	88.4907
3	4.3095	6.1981	82.2926
4	3.9938	6.5138	75.7788
5	3.6619	6.8457	68.9331
6	3.3132	7.1944	61.7387
7	2.9466	7.5610	54.1777
8	2.5614	7.9461	46.2316
9	2.1566	8.3510	37.8806
10	1.7312	8.7764	29.1042
11	1.2841	9.2235	19.8807
12	.8142	9.6934	10.1873
13	.3203	10.1873	0.0000

YEARS 14 — QTR PAYT 2.4937 — AN CONST 9.98

#	INT	PRIN	BALANCE
1	4.9059	5.0690	94.9310
2	4.6477	5.3273	89.6037
3	4.3763	5.5987	84.0051
4	4.0911	5.8839	78.1212
5	3.7913	6.1836	71.9375
6	3.4763	6.4987	65.4389
7	3.1452	6.8297	58.6091
8	2.7973	7.1777	51.4315
9	2.4316	7.5434	43.8881
10	2.0473	7.9277	35.9604
11	1.6434	8.3315	27.6289
12	1.2190	8.7560	18.8729
13	.7729	9.2021	9.6709
14	.3041	9.6709	0.0000

YEARS 15 — QTR PAYT 2.3790 — AN CONST 9.52

#	INT	PRIN	BALANCE
1	4.9146	4.6014	95.3986
2	4.6802	4.8358	90.5629
3	4.4338	5.0821	85.4807
4	4.1749	5.3410	80.1397
5	3.9028	5.6131	74.5266
6	3.6169	5.8991	68.6274
7	3.3163	6.1996	62.4278
8	3.0005	6.5155	55.9123
9	2.6686	6.8474	49.0649
10	2.3197	7.1963	41.8687
11	1.9531	7.5629	34.3058
12	1.5678	7.9482	26.3576
13	1.1629	8.3531	18.0045
14	.7373	8.7786	9.2259
15	.2901	9.2259	0.0000

YEARS 16 — QTR PAYT 2.2792 — AN CONST 9.12

#	INT	PRIN	BALANCE
1	4.9222	4.1946	95.8054
2	4.7085	4.4083	91.3970
3	4.4839	4.6329	86.7641
4	4.2479	4.8690	81.8951
5	3.9998	5.1170	76.7781
6	3.7391	5.3777	71.4004
7	3.4651	5.6517	65.7488
8	3.1772	5.9396	59.8092
9	2.8746	6.2422	53.5670
10	2.5566	6.5602	47.0068
11	2.2224	6.8944	40.1124
12	1.8712	7.2456	32.8668
13	1.5020	7.6148	25.2520
14	1.1141	8.0027	17.2493
15	.7064	8.4104	8.8389
16	.2779	8.8389	0.0000

YEARS 17 — QTR PAYT 2.1917 — AN CONST 8.77

#	INT	PRIN	BALANCE
1	4.9288	3.8381	96.1619
2	4.7332	4.0337	92.1282
3	4.5278	4.2391	87.8891
4	4.3118	4.4551	83.4340
5	4.0848	4.6821	78.7519
6	3.8463	4.9206	73.8313
7	3.5956	5.1713	68.6600
8	3.3322	5.4347	63.2253
9	3.0553	5.7116	57.5136
10	2.7643	6.0026	51.5110
11	2.4585	6.3084	45.2026
12	2.1371	6.6298	38.5728
13	1.7994	6.9675	31.6053
14	1.4444	7.3225	24.2828
15	1.0713	7.6956	16.5872
16	.6793	8.0876	8.4996
17	.2673	8.4996	0.0000

YEARS 18 — QTR PAYT 2.1145 — AN CONST 8.46

#	INT	PRIN	BALANCE
1	4.9346	3.5234	96.4766
2	4.7551	3.7029	92.7737
3	4.5665	3.8915	88.8822
4	4.3682	4.0898	84.7924
5	4.1599	4.2981	80.4943
6	3.9409	4.5171	75.9772
7	3.7108	4.7472	71.2299
8	3.4689	4.9891	66.2408
9	3.2147	5.2433	60.9976
10	2.9476	5.5104	55.4872
11	2.6669	5.7911	49.6961
12	2.3719	6.0861	43.6100
13	2.0618	6.3962	37.2138
14	1.7360	6.7221	30.4917
15	1.3935	7.0645	23.4272
16	1.0336	7.4244	16.0028
17	.6554	7.8027	8.2002
18	.2578	8.2002	0.0000

YEARS 19 — QTR PAYT 2.0459 — AN CONST 8.19

#	INT	PRIN	BALANCE
1	4.9398	3.2438	96.7562
2	4.7745	3.4091	93.3471
3	4.6009	3.5828	89.7643
4	4.4183	3.7653	85.9990
5	4.2265	3.9571	82.0419
6	4.0249	4.1587	77.8832
7	3.8131	4.3706	73.5126
8	3.5904	4.5932	68.9193
9	3.3564	4.8272	64.0921
10	3.1105	5.0732	59.0189
11	2.8520	5.3316	53.6873
12	2.5804	5.6033	48.0840
13	2.2949	5.8887	42.1953
14	1.9949	6.1887	36.0066
15	1.6796	6.5040	29.5026
16	1.3483	6.8353	22.6673
17	1.0001	7.1836	15.4837
18	.6341	7.5495	7.9342
19	.2495	7.9342	0.0000

YEARS 20 — QTR PAYT 1.9847 — AN CONST 7.94

#	INT	PRIN	BALANCE
1	4.9444	2.9942	97.0058
2	4.7919	3.1467	93.8591
3	4.6316	3.3070	90.5521
4	4.4631	3.4755	87.0766
5	4.2861	3.6526	83.4241
6	4.1000	3.8386	79.5854
7	3.9044	4.0342	75.5512
8	3.6989	4.2397	71.3115
9	3.4829	4.4557	66.8558
10	3.2559	4.6827	62.1731
11	3.0173	4.9213	57.2518
12	2.7666	5.1720	52.0798
13	2.5031	5.4355	46.6443
14	2.2262	5.7124	40.9319
15	1.9352	6.0034	34.9285
16	1.6294	6.3093	28.6193
17	1.3079	6.6307	21.9886
18	.9701	6.9685	15.0201
19	.6151	7.3235	7.6966
20	.2420	7.6966	0.0000

YEARS 21 — QTR PAYT 1.9297 — AN CONST 7.72

#	INT	PRIN	BALANCE
1	4.9486	2.7701	97.2299
2	4.8075	2.9112	94.3187
3	4.6592	3.0595	91.2591

QUARTERLY PAYMENT AMORTIZATION SCHEDULE PER $100   5.00 %

#	INT	PRIN	BALANCE
4	4.5033	3.2154	88.0437
5	4.3395	3.3792	84.6645
6	4.1673	3.5514	81.1131
7	3.9864	3.7323	77.3808
8	3.7963	3.9224	73.4584
9	3.5964	4.1223	69.3361
10	3.3864	4.3323	65.0038
11	3.1657	4.5530	60.4508
12	2.9338	4.7850	55.6659
13	2.6900	5.0287	50.6371
14	2.4338	5.2849	45.3522
15	2.1645	5.5542	39.7981
16	1.8816	5.8371	33.9610
17	1.5842	6.1345	27.8265
18	1.2717	6.4470	21.3795
19	.9432	6.7755	14.6040
20	.5981	7.1206	7.4834
21	.2353	7.4834	0.0000

YEARS 22   QTR PAYT 1.8801   AN CONST 7.53

#	INT	PRIN	BALANCE
1	4.9523	2.5681	97.4319
2	4.8215	2.6990	94.7329
3	4.6840	2.8365	91.8964
4	4.5395	2.9810	88.9155
5	4.3876	3.1328	85.7826
6	4.2280	3.2924	82.4902
7	4.0603	3.4602	79.0300
8	3.8840	3.6365	75.3936
9	3.6988	3.8217	71.5719
10	3.5041	4.0164	67.5555
11	3.2994	4.2210	63.3344
12	3.0844	4.4361	58.8984
13	2.8584	4.6621	54.2363
14	2.6209	4.8996	49.3367
15	2.3713	5.1492	44.1875
16	2.1090	5.4115	38.7760
17	1.8333	5.6872	33.0888
18	1.5435	5.9769	27.1119
19	1.2390	6.2814	20.8304
20	.9190	6.6015	14.2290
21	.5827	6.9378	7.2912
22	.2293	7.2912	0.0000

YEARS 23   QTR PAYT 1.8353   AN CONST 7.35

#	INT	PRIN	BALANCE
1	4.9557	2.3853	97.6147
2	4.8342	2.5069	95.1078
3	4.7065	2.6346	92.4732
4	4.5723	2.7688	89.7044
5	4.4312	2.9099	86.7945
6	4.2830	3.0581	83.7364
7	4.1272	3.2139	80.5225
8	3.9635	3.3776	77.1449
9	3.7914	3.5497	73.5952
10	3.6105	3.7306	69.8646
11	3.4205	3.9206	65.9440
12	3.2207	4.1203	61.8237
13	3.0108	4.3303	57.4934
14	2.7902	4.5509	52.9426
15	2.5584	4.7827	48.1599
16	2.3147	5.0264	43.1335
17	2.0587	5.2824	37.8511
18	1.7895	5.5515	32.2995
19	1.5067	5.8344	26.4652
20	1.2095	6.1316	20.3335
21	.8971	6.4440	13.8896
22	.5688	6.7723	7.1173
23	.2238	7.1173	0.0000

YEARS 24   QTR PAYT 1.7945   AN CONST 7.18

#	INT	PRIN	BALANCE
1	4.9588	2.2193	97.7807
2	4.8458	2.3324	95.4482
3	4.7269	2.4512	92.9970
4	4.6020	2.5761	90.4209
5	4.4708	2.7074	87.7135
6	4.3329	2.8453	84.8683
7	4.1879	2.9902	81.8780
8	4.0356	3.1426	78.7355
9	3.8755	3.3027	75.4328
10	3.7072	3.4709	71.9618
11	3.5304	3.6478	68.3141
12	3.3446	3.8336	64.4805
13	3.1493	4.0289	60.4516
14	2.9440	4.2342	56.2175
15	2.7283	4.4499	51.7676
16	2.5016	4.6766	47.0910
17	2.2634	4.9148	42.1762
18	2.0130	5.1652	37.0110
19	1.7498	5.4283	31.5827
20	1.4733	5.7049	25.8778
21	1.1826	5.9955	19.8823
22	.8772	6.3010	13.5813
23	.5562	6.6220	6.9593
24	.2188	6.9593	0.0000

YEARS 25   QTR PAYT 1.7574   AN CONST 7.03

#	INT	PRIN	BALANCE
1	4.9616	2.0681	97.9319
2	4.8563	2.1734	95.7585
3	4.7455	2.2842	93.4743
4	4.6292	2.4005	91.0738
5	4.5069	2.5228	88.5509
6	4.3783	2.6514	85.8996
7	4.2433	2.7864	83.1131
8	4.1013	2.9284	80.1847
9	3.9521	3.0776	77.1071
10	3.7953	3.2344	73.8728
11	3.6306	3.3991	70.4736
12	3.4574	3.5723	66.9013
13	3.2754	3.7543	63.1470
14	3.0841	3.9456	59.2014
15	2.8831	4.1466	55.0548
16	2.6719	4.3578	50.6970
17	2.4499	4.5798	46.1171
18	2.2165	4.8132	41.3040
19	1.9713	5.0584	36.2456
20	1.7136	5.3161	30.9295
21	1.4428	5.5869	25.3426
22	1.1582	5.8715	19.4711
23	.8591	6.1707	13.3004
24	.5447	6.4850	6.8154
25	.2143	6.8154	0.0000

YEARS 26   QTR PAYT 1.7235   AN CONST 6.90

#	INT	PRIN	BALANCE
1	4.9642	1.9299	98.0701
2	4.8659	2.0282	96.0420
3	4.7625	2.1315	93.9105
4	4.6540	2.2401	91.6704
5	4.5398	2.3542	89.3162
6	4.4199	2.4742	86.8420
7	4.2939	2.6002	84.2418
8	4.1614	2.7327	81.5091
9	4.0222	2.8719	78.6373
10	3.8759	3.0182	75.6191
11	3.7221	3.1720	72.4471
12	3.5605	3.3335	69.1136
13	3.3907	3.5034	65.6102
14	3.2122	3.6819	61.9283
15	3.0246	3.8694	58.0589
16	2.8275	4.0666	53.9923
17	2.6203	4.2737	49.7186
18	2.4026	4.4915	45.2272
19	2.1738	4.7203	40.5069
20	1.9333	4.9608	35.5461
21	1.6806	5.2135	30.3326
22	1.4150	5.4791	24.8535
23	1.1358	5.7582	19.0953
24	.8425	6.0516	13.0438
25	.5342	6.3599	6.6839
26	.2102	6.6839	0.0000

YEARS 27   QTR PAYT 1.6924   AN CONST 6.77

#	INT	PRIN	BALANCE
1	4.9665	1.8032	98.1968
2	4.8747	1.8951	96.3017
3	4.7781	1.9916	94.3101
4	4.6767	2.0931	92.2171
5	4.5700	2.1997	90.0174
6	4.4580	2.3118	87.7056
7	4.3402	2.4295	85.2761
8	4.2164	2.5533	82.7228
9	4.0863	2.6834	80.0394
10	3.9496	2.8201	77.2193
11	3.8060	2.9638	74.2555
12	3.6550	3.1148	71.1408
13	3.4963	3.2734	67.8673
14	3.3295	3.4402	64.4271
15	3.1543	3.6155	60.8117
16	2.9701	3.7997	57.0120
17	2.7765	3.9932	53.0188
18	2.5731	4.1967	48.8221
19	2.3593	4.4105	44.4116
20	2.1346	4.6352	39.7765
21	1.8984	4.8713	34.9052
22	1.6503	5.1195	29.7857
23	1.3894	5.3803	24.4054
24	1.1153	5.6544	18.7510
25	.8273	5.9425	12.8085
26	.5245	6.2452	6.5634
27	.2064	6.5634	0.0000

YEARS 28   QTR PAYT 1.6639   AN CONST 6.66

#	INT	PRIN	BALANCE
1	4.9687	1.6868	98.3132
2	4.8828	1.7728	96.5404
3	4.7924	1.8631	94.6773
4	4.6975	1.9580	92.7193
5	4.5978	2.0578	90.6615
6	4.4929	2.1626	88.4989
7	4.3828	2.2728	86.2262
8	4.2670	2.3886	83.8376
9	4.1453	2.5102	81.3274
10	4.0174	2.6381	78.6892
11	3.8830	2.7725	75.9167
12	3.7418	2.9138	73.0029
13	3.5933	3.0622	69.9407
14	3.4373	3.2182	66.7225
15	3.2734	3.3822	63.3403
16	3.1011	3.5545	59.7859
17	2.9200	3.7356	56.0503
18	2.7297	3.9259	52.1244
19	2.5297	4.1259	47.9985
20	2.3195	4.3361	43.6625
21	2.0986	4.5570	39.1055
22	1.8664	4.7891	34.3164
23	1.6224	5.0331	29.2832
24	1.3660	5.2895	23.9937
25	1.0965	5.5590	18.4347
26	.8133	5.8422	12.5925
27	.5157	6.1398	6.4526
28	.2029	6.4526	0.0000

YEARS 29   QTR PAYT 1.6376   AN CONST 6.56

#	INT	PRIN	BALANCE
1	4.9707	1.5797	98.4203
2	4.8902	1.6602	96.7601
3	4.8056	1.7448	95.0153
4	4.7167	1.8337	93.1817
5	4.6233	1.9271	91.2546
6	4.5251	2.0253	89.2293
7	4.4220	2.1284	87.1009
8	4.3135	2.2369	84.8640
9	4.1996	2.3508	82.5132
10	4.0798	2.4706	80.0426
11	3.9540	2.5964	77.4462
12	3.8217	2.7287	74.7174
13	3.6827	2.8677	71.8497
14	3.5366	3.0138	68.8359
15	3.3830	3.1674	65.6685
16	3.2217	3.3287	62.3397
17	3.0521	3.4983	58.8414
18	2.8738	3.6766	55.1649
19	2.6865	3.8639	51.3010
20	2.4897	4.0607	47.2403
21	2.2828	4.2676	42.9727
22	2.0654	4.4850	38.4877
23	1.8369	4.7135	33.7743
24	1.5968	4.9536	28.8206
25	1.3444	5.2060	23.6147
26	1.0792	5.4712	18.1435
27	.8005	5.7499	12.3936
28	.5075	6.0429	6.3507
29	.1997	6.3507	0.0000

YEARS 30   QTR PAYT 1.6133   AN CONST 6.46

#	INT	PRIN	BALANCE
1	4.9725	1.4809	98.5191
2	4.8971	1.5563	96.9628
3	4.8178	1.6356	95.3272
4	4.7345	1.7189	93.6083
5	4.6469	1.8065	91.8018
6	4.5549	1.8985	89.9032
7	4.4581	1.9953	87.9080
8	4.3565	2.0969	85.8110
9	4.2497	2.2037	83.6073
10	4.1374	2.3160	81.2913
11	4.0194	2.4340	78.8573
12	3.8954	2.5580	76.2993
13	3.7651	2.6883	73.6110
14	3.6281	2.8253	70.7857
15	3.4842	2.9692	67.8165
16	3.3329	3.1205	64.6960
17	3.1739	3.2795	61.4166
18	3.0069	3.4465	57.9700
19	2.8313	3.6221	54.3479
20	2.6468	3.8066	50.5413
21	2.4528	4.0006	46.5407
22	2.2490	4.2044	42.3363
23	2.0348	4.4186	37.9178
24	1.8097	4.6437	33.2741
25	1.5731	4.8803	28.3938
26	1.3245	5.1289	23.2650
27	1.0632	5.3902	17.8748
28	.7866	5.6648	12.2100
29	.5000	5.9534	6.2567
30	.1967	6.2567	0.0000

QUARTERLY PAYMENT AMORTIZATION SCHEDULE PER $100   5.25 %

YEARS 2	QTR PAYT 13.2495	AN CONST 53.00
# INT	PRIN	BALANCE
1 4.3017	48.6963	51.3037
2 1.6944	51.3037	0.0000

YEARS 3	QTR PAYT 9.0613	AN CONST 36.25
# INT	PRIN	BALANCE
1 4.6344	31.6106	68.3894
2 2.9419	33.3031	35.0863
3 1.1588	35.0863	0.0000

YEARS 4	QTR PAYT 6.9700	AN CONST 27.88
# INT	PRIN	BALANCE
1 4.8006	23.0794	76.9206
2 3.5648	24.3151	52.6056
3 2.2629	25.6170	26.9886
4 .8913	26.9886	0.0000

YEARS 5	QTR PAYT 5.7175	AN CONST 22.87
# INT	PRIN	BALANCE
1 4.9001	17.9699	82.0301
2 3.9379	18.9320	63.0981
3 2.9242	19.9457	43.1524
4 1.8563	21.0136	22.1388
5 .7312	22.1388	0.0000

YEARS 6	QTR PAYT 4.8844	AN CONST 19.54
# INT	PRIN	BALANCE
1 4.9662	14.5713	85.4287
2 4.1861	15.3514	70.0773
3 3.3641	16.1734	53.9039
4 2.4981	17.0394	36.8646
5 1.5858	17.9517	18.9129
6 .6246	18.9129	0.0000

YEARS 7	QTR PAYT 4.2909	AN CONST 17.17
# INT	PRIN	BALANCE
1 5.0134	12.1503	87.8497
2 4.3628	12.8008	75.0489
3 3.6774	13.4862	61.5627
4 2.9554	14.2083	47.3545
5 2.1946	14.9690	32.3854
6 1.3931	15.7705	16.6149
7 .5487	16.6149	0.0000

YEARS 8	QTR PAYT 3.8472	AN CONST 15.39
# INT	PRIN	BALANCE
1 5.0486	10.3402	89.6598
2 4.4950	10.8939	78.7659
3 3.9117	11.4772	67.2887
4 3.2972	12.0917	55.1970
5 2.6498	12.7391	42.4579
6 1.9677	13.4212	29.0367
7 1.2491	14.1398	14.8969
8 .4920	14.8969	0.0000

YEARS 9	QTR PAYT 3.5034	AN CONST 14.02
# INT	PRIN	BALANCE
1 5.0760	8.9375	91.0625
2 4.5974	9.4161	81.6464
3 4.0933	9.9202	71.7261
4 3.5621	10.4514	61.2747
5 3.0025	11.0110	50.2638
6 2.4129	11.6006	38.6632
7 1.7918	12.2217	26.4415
8 1.1374	12.8761	13.5655
9 .4480	13.5655	0.0000

YEARS 10	QTR PAYT 3.2294	AN CONST 12.92
# INT	PRIN	BALANCE
1 5.0977	7.8199	92.1801
2 4.6790	8.2386	83.9414
3 4.2379	8.6797	75.2617
4 3.7732	9.1445	66.1172
5 3.2835	9.6341	56.4831
6 2.7677	10.1499	46.3332
7 2.2243	10.6934	35.6398
8 1.6517	11.2659	24.3738
9 1.0485	11.8692	12.5047
10 .4130	12.5047	0.0000

YEARS 11	QTR PAYT 3.0063	AN CONST 12.03
# INT	PRIN	BALANCE
1 5.1154	6.9096	93.0904
2 4.7455	7.2796	85.8108
3 4.3557	7.6694	78.1414
4 3.9451	8.0800	70.0614
5 3.5125	8.5126	61.5487
6 3.0567	8.9684	52.5803
7 2.5765	9.4486	43.1317
8 2.0706	9.9545	33.1772
9 1.5376	10.4875	22.6897
10 .9760	11.0490	11.6406
11 .3844	11.6406	0.0000

YEARS 12	QTR PAYT 2.8212	AN CONST 11.29
# INT	PRIN	BALANCE
1 5.1301	6.1548	93.8452
2 4.8006	6.4844	87.3608
3 4.4534	6.8316	80.5293
4 4.0876	7.1973	73.3319
5 3.7023	7.5827	65.7492
6 3.2963	7.9887	57.7605
7 2.8685	8.4164	49.3441
8 2.4179	8.8671	40.4770
9 1.9431	9.3418	31.1352
10 1.4429	9.8420	21.2932
11 .9160	10.3690	10.9242
12 .3608	10.9242	0.0000

YEARS 13	QTR PAYT 2.6655	AN CONST 10.67
# INT	PRIN	BALANCE
1 5.1425	5.5196	94.4804
2 4.8470	5.8151	88.6653
3 4.5356	6.1265	82.5389
4 4.2076	6.4545	76.0844
5 3.8620	6.8001	69.2843
6 3.4979	7.1642	62.1202
7 3.1143	7.5478	54.5724
8 2.7102	7.9519	46.6205
9 2.2844	8.3776	38.2429
10 1.8359	8.8262	29.4167
11 1.3633	9.2988	20.1179
12 .8654	9.7967	10.3212
13 .3409	10.3212	0.0000

YEARS 14	QTR PAYT 2.5328	AN CONST 10.14
# INT	PRIN	BALANCE
1 5.1531	4.9782	95.0218
2 4.8865	5.2448	89.7770
3 4.6057	5.5256	84.2514
4 4.3098	5.8215	78.4299
5 3.9981	6.1332	72.2967
6 3.6697	6.4615	65.8352
7 3.3238	6.8075	59.0277
8 2.9593	7.1720	51.8557
9 2.5753	7.5560	44.2996
10 2.1707	7.9606	36.3391
11 1.7445	8.3868	27.9522
12 1.2954	8.8359	19.1164
13 .8223	9.3090	9.8074
14 .3239	9.8074	0.0000

YEARS 15	QTR PAYT 2.4185	AN CONST 9.68
# INT	PRIN	BALANCE
1 5.1621	4.5120	95.4880
2 4.9205	4.7536	90.7343
3 4.6660	5.0081	85.7262
4 4.3979	5.2763	80.4499
5 4.1154	5.5588	74.8911
6 3.8177	5.8564	69.0347
7 3.5042	6.1700	62.8647
8 3.1738	6.5004	56.3643
9 2.8258	6.8484	49.5159
10 2.4591	7.2151	42.3008
11 2.0728	7.6014	34.6994
12 1.6658	8.0084	26.6910
13 1.2370	8.4372	18.2538
14 .7852	8.8889	9.3649
15 .3093	9.3649	0.0000

YEARS 16	QTR PAYT 2.3192	AN CONST 9.28
# INT	PRIN	BALANCE
1 5.1700	4.1068	95.8932
2 4.9501	4.3267	91.5664
3 4.7185	4.5584	87.0080
4 4.4744	4.8025	82.2056
5 4.2173	5.0596	77.1460
6 3.9464	5.3305	71.8154
7 3.6609	5.6159	66.1995
8 3.3603	5.9166	60.2829
9 3.0435	6.2334	54.0495
10 2.7097	6.5672	47.4824
11 2.3581	6.9188	40.5636
12 1.9876	7.2892	33.2744
13 1.5974	7.6795	25.5949
14 1.1862	8.0907	17.5042
15 .7530	8.5239	8.9803
16 .2966	8.9803	0.0000

YEARS 17	QTR PAYT 2.2322	AN CONST 8.93
# INT	PRIN	BALANCE
1 5.1769	3.7519	96.2481
2 4.9761	3.9528	92.2954
3 4.7644	4.1644	88.1310
4 4.5414	4.3874	83.7436
5 4.3065	4.6223	79.1213
6 4.0590	4.8698	74.2515
7 3.7983	5.1305	69.1210
8 3.5236	5.4052	63.7158
9 3.2342	5.6946	58.0212
10 2.9293	5.9995	52.0217
11 2.6080	6.3208	45.7009
12 2.2696	6.6592	39.0417
13 1.9131	7.0157	32.0260
14 1.5374	7.3914	24.6346
15 1.1417	7.7871	16.8474
16 .7247	8.2041	8.6434
17 .2855	8.6434	0.0000

YEARS 18	QTR PAYT 2.1554	AN CONST 8.63
# INT	PRIN	BALANCE
1 5.1830	3.4387	96.5613
2 4.9989	3.6229	92.9384
3 4.8049	3.8168	89.1216
4 4.6006	4.0212	85.1004
5 4.3853	4.2365	80.8639
6 4.1584	4.4633	76.4005
7 3.9195	4.7023	71.6982
8 3.6677	4.9541	66.7441
9 3.4024	5.2193	61.5248
10 3.1230	5.4988	56.0260
11 2.8285	5.7932	50.2328
12 2.5184	6.1034	44.1294
13 2.1916	6.4302	37.6992
14 1.8473	6.7745	30.9247
15 1.4846	7.1372	23.7875
16 1.1024	7.5194	16.2681
17 .6998	7.9220	8.3461
18 .2756	8.3461	0.0000

YEARS 19	QTR PAYT 2.0873	AN CONST 8.35
# INT	PRIN	BALANCE
1 5.1884	3.1608	96.8392
2 5.0192	3.3300	93.5091
3 4.8409	3.5083	90.0008
4 4.6531	3.6962	86.3046
5 4.4552	3.8941	82.4105
6 4.2467	4.1026	78.3079
7 4.0270	4.3223	73.9857
8 3.7956	4.5537	69.4320
9 3.5518	4.7975	64.6345
10 3.2949	5.0544	59.5801
11 3.0243	5.3250	54.2551
12 2.7391	5.6101	48.6450
13 2.4388	5.9105	42.7345
14 2.1223	6.2270	36.5076
15 1.7889	6.5604	29.9472
16 1.4376	6.9116	23.0356
17 1.0676	7.2817	15.7539
18 .6777	7.6716	8.0823
19 .2669	8.0823	0.0000

YEARS 20	QTR PAYT 2.0265	AN CONST 8.11
# INT	PRIN	BALANCE
1 5.1933	2.9128	97.0872
2 5.0373	3.0687	94.0185
3 4.8730	3.2330	90.7854
4 4.6999	3.4062	87.3793
5 4.5175	3.5885	83.7907
6 4.3254	3.7807	80.0101
7 4.1230	3.9831	76.0270
8 3.9097	4.1964	71.8306
9 3.6850	4.4210	67.4096
10 3.4483	4.6578	62.7518
11 3.1989	4.9071	57.8447
12 2.9362	5.1699	52.6748
13 2.6594	5.4467	47.2281
14 2.3677	5.7383	41.4898
15 2.0605	6.0456	35.4442
16 1.7368	6.3693	29.0749
17 1.3958	6.7103	22.3646
18 1.0365	7.0696	15.2950
19 .6579	7.4481	7.8469
20 .2592	7.8469	0.0000

YEARS 21	QTR PAYT 1.9720	AN CONST 7.89
# INT	PRIN	BALANCE
1 5.1976	2.6904	97.3096
2 5.0536	2.8344	94.4752
3 4.9018	2.9862	91.4890

#	INT	PRIN	BALANCE
4	4.7419	3.1461	88.3430
5	4.5735	3.3145	85.0285
6	4.3960	3.4920	81.5365
7	4.2090	3.6790	77.8575
8	4.0120	3.8759	73.9816
9	3.8045	4.0835	69.8981
10	3.5859	4.3021	65.5960
11	3.3555	4.5324	61.0636
12	3.1128	4.7751	56.2884
13	2.8572	5.0308	51.2576
14	2.5878	5.3002	45.9575
15	2.3040	5.5839	40.3735
16	2.0050	5.8829	34.4906
17	1.6901	6.1979	28.2927
18	1.3582	6.5298	21.7629
19	1.0086	6.8794	14.8835
20	.6402	7.2477	7.6358
21	.2522	7.6358	0.0000

YEARS 22 — QTR PAYT 1.9229 — AN CONST 7.70

#	INT	PRIN	BALANCE
1	5.2015	2.4901	97.5099
2	5.0682	2.6234	94.8866
3	4.9277	2.7638	92.1227
4	4.7797	2.9118	89.2109
5	4.6238	3.0677	86.1432
6	4.4596	3.2320	82.9112
7	4.2865	3.4050	79.5062
8	4.1042	3.5873	75.9188
9	3.9121	3.7794	72.1394
10	3.7098	3.9818	68.1576
11	3.4966	4.1950	63.9626
12	3.2720	4.4196	59.5431
13	3.0353	4.6562	54.8868
14	2.7860	4.9055	49.9813
15	2.5234	5.1682	44.8131
16	2.2467	5.4449	39.3682
17	1.9551	5.7364	33.6318
18	1.6480	6.0436	27.5882
19	1.3244	6.3672	21.2210
20	.9835	6.7081	14.5129
21	.6243	7.0673	7.4457
22	.2459	7.4457	0.0000

YEARS 23 — QTR PAYT 1.8785 — AN CONST 7.52

#	INT	PRIN	BALANCE
1	5.2050	2.3089	97.6911
2	5.0814	2.4326	95.2585
3	4.9512	2.5628	92.6957
4	4.8139	2.7000	89.9957
5	4.6694	2.8446	87.1511
6	4.5171	2.9969	84.1542
7	4.3566	3.1574	80.9968
8	4.1876	3.3264	77.6704
9	4.0095	3.5045	74.1659
10	3.8218	3.6922	70.4738
11	3.6241	3.8898	66.5839
12	3.4158	4.0981	62.4858
13	3.1964	4.3175	58.1682
14	2.9653	4.5487	53.6195
15	2.7217	4.7923	48.8273
16	2.4651	5.0489	43.7784
17	2.1948	5.3192	38.4592
18	1.9100	5.6040	32.8552
19	1.6099	5.9040	26.9512
20	1.2938	6.2202	20.7310
21	.9608	6.5532	14.1778
22	.6099	6.9041	7.2737
23	.2402	7.2737	0.0000

YEARS 24 — QTR PAYT 1.8382 — AN CONST 7.36

#	INT	PRIN	BALANCE
1	5.2082	2.1446	97.8554
2	5.0934	2.2594	95.5960
3	4.9724	2.3804	93.2156
4	4.8450	2.5078	90.7078
5	4.7107	2.6421	88.0656
6	4.5692	2.7836	85.2821
7	4.4202	2.9326	82.3494
8	4.2632	3.0896	79.2598
9	4.0978	3.2551	76.0047
10	3.9235	3.4294	72.5754
11	3.7398	3.6130	68.9624
12	3.5464	3.8064	65.1560
13	3.3426	4.0102	61.1457
14	3.1279	4.2249	56.9208
15	2.9017	4.4512	52.4696
16	2.6633	4.6895	47.7801
17	2.4122	4.9406	42.8395
18	2.1477	5.2051	37.6344
19	1.8690	5.4838	32.1506
20	1.5754	5.7774	26.3732
21	1.2661	6.0868	20.2864
22	.9402	6.4127	13.8738
23	.5968	6.7560	7.1178
24	.2351	7.1178	0.0000

YEARS 25 — QTR PAYT 1.8015 — AN CONST 7.21

#	INT	PRIN	BALANCE
1	5.2112	1.9950	98.0050
2	5.1043	2.1018	95.9032
3	4.9918	2.2143	93.6889
4	4.8732	2.3329	91.3560
5	4.7483	2.4578	88.8982
6	4.6167	2.5894	86.3087
7	4.4781	2.7281	83.5807
8	4.3320	2.8741	80.7066
9	4.1781	3.0280	77.6786
10	4.0160	3.1901	74.4884
11	3.8452	3.3609	71.1275
12	3.6652	3.5409	67.5866
13	3.4757	3.7305	63.8561
14	3.2759	3.9302	59.9259
15	3.0655	4.1407	55.7852
16	2.8438	4.3624	51.4228
17	2.6102	4.5959	46.8269
18	2.3641	4.8420	41.9849
19	2.1049	5.1013	36.8836
20	1.8317	5.3744	31.5092
21	1.5440	5.6622	25.8471
22	1.2408	5.9653	19.8817
23	.9214	6.2847	13.5970
24	.5849	6.6212	6.9758
25	.2304	6.9758	0.0000

YEARS 26 — QTR PAYT 1.7681 — AN CONST 7.08

#	INT	PRIN	BALANCE
1	5.2138	1.8584	98.1416
2	5.1143	1.9579	96.1837
3	5.0095	2.0627	94.1209
4	4.8990	2.1732	91.9477
5	4.7827	2.2895	89.6582
6	4.6601	2.4121	87.2461
7	4.5309	2.5413	84.7048
8	4.3949	2.6774	82.0274
9	4.2515	2.8207	79.2067
10	4.1005	2.9717	76.2350
11	3.9414	3.1309	73.1041
12	3.7737	3.2985	69.8056
13	3.5971	3.4751	66.3306
14	3.4111	3.6612	62.6694
15	3.2150	3.8572	58.8122
16	3.0085	4.0637	54.7485
17	2.7909	4.2813	50.4672
18	2.5617	4.5105	45.9567
19	2.3202	4.7520	41.2046
20	2.0658	5.0065	36.1982
21	1.7977	5.2745	30.9236
22	1.5153	5.5569	25.3667
23	1.2177	5.8545	19.5122
24	.9043	6.1679	13.3443
25	.5740	6.4982	6.8461
26	.2261	6.8461	0.0000

YEARS 27 — QTR PAYT 1.7374 — AN CONST 6.95

#	INT	PRIN	BALANCE
1	5.2162	1.7334	98.2666
2	5.1234	1.8262	96.4404
3	5.0257	1.9240	94.5164
4	4.9226	2.0270	92.4895
5	4.8141	2.1355	90.3539
6	4.6998	2.2499	88.1041
7	4.5793	2.3703	85.7338
8	4.4524	2.4972	83.2365
9	4.3187	2.6309	80.6056
10	4.1778	2.7718	77.8338
11	4.0294	2.9202	74.9135
12	3.8730	3.0766	71.8370
13	3.7083	3.2413	68.5956
14	3.5348	3.4149	65.1808
15	3.3519	3.5977	61.5831
16	3.1593	3.7903	57.7928
17	2.9564	3.9933	53.7995
18	2.7425	4.2071	49.5924
19	2.5173	4.4323	45.1601
20	2.2800	4.6697	40.4904
21	2.0299	4.9197	35.5707
22	1.7665	5.1831	30.3876
23	1.4890	5.4606	24.9270
24	1.1966	5.7530	19.1740
25	.8886	6.0610	13.1130
26	.5641	6.3855	6.7274
27	.2222	6.7274	0.0000

YEARS 28 — QTR PAYT 1.7093 — AN CONST 6.84

#	INT	PRIN	BALANCE
1	5.2185	1.6187	98.3813
2	5.1318	1.7053	96.6760
3	5.0405	1.7966	94.8794
4	4.9443	1.8928	92.9865
5	4.8430	1.9942	90.9924
6	4.7362	2.1010	88.8914
7	4.6237	2.2134	86.6780
8	4.5052	2.3320	84.3460
9	4.3803	2.4568	81.8892
10	4.2488	2.5884	79.3008
11	4.1102	2.7269	76.5739
12	3.9642	2.8730	73.7009
13	3.8104	3.0268	70.6742
14	3.6483	3.1888	67.4853
15	3.4776	3.3596	64.1257
16	3.2977	3.5395	60.5863
17	3.1082	3.7290	56.8573
18	2.9085	3.9286	52.9287
19	2.6982	4.1390	48.7897
20	2.4765	4.3606	44.4291
21	2.2431	4.5941	39.8350
22	1.9971	4.8401	34.9950
23	1.7379	5.0992	29.8958
24	1.4649	5.3722	24.5235
25	1.1773	5.6599	18.8637
26	.8742	5.9629	12.9007
27	.5550	6.2822	6.6186
28	.2186	6.6186	0.0000

YEARS 29 — QTR PAYT 1.6834 — AN CONST 6.74

#	INT	PRIN	BALANCE
1	5.2205	1.5131	98.4869
2	5.1395	1.5942	96.8927
3	5.0542	1.6795	95.2132
4	4.9642	1.7694	93.4437
5	4.8695	1.8642	91.5795
6	4.7697	1.9640	89.6155
7	4.6645	2.0692	87.5464
8	4.5537	2.1799	85.3664
9	4.4370	2.2967	83.0697
10	4.3140	2.4196	80.6501
11	4.1845	2.5492	78.1009
12	4.0480	2.6857	75.4152
13	3.9042	2.8295	72.5857
14	3.7527	2.9810	69.6048
15	3.5931	3.1406	66.4642
16	3.4249	3.3087	63.1554
17	3.2478	3.4859	59.6695
18	3.0611	3.6726	55.9970
19	2.8645	3.8692	52.1278
20	2.6573	4.0764	48.0514
21	2.4391	4.2946	43.7568
22	2.2091	4.5246	39.2322
23	1.9669	4.7668	34.4654
24	1.7116	5.0220	29.4434
25	1.4427	5.2909	24.1524
26	1.1595	5.5742	18.5782
27	.8610	5.8727	12.7055
28	.5466	6.1871	6.5184
29	.2153	6.5184	0.0000

YEARS 30 — QTR PAYT 1.6596 — AN CONST 6.64

#	INT	PRIN	BALANCE
1	5.2224	1.4159	98.5841
2	5.1466	1.4917	97.0924
3	5.0667	1.5716	95.5208
4	4.9826	1.6557	93.8650
5	4.8939	1.7444	92.1206
6	4.8005	1.8378	90.2828
7	4.7021	1.9362	88.3466
8	4.5985	2.0399	86.3068
9	4.4893	2.1491	84.1577
10	4.3742	2.2642	81.8935
11	4.2530	2.3854	79.5082
12	4.1252	2.5131	76.9951
13	3.9907	2.6477	74.3474
14	3.8489	2.7894	71.5580
15	3.6996	2.9388	68.6192
16	3.5422	3.0961	65.5231
17	3.3764	3.2619	62.2612
18	3.2018	3.4365	58.8246
19	3.0178	3.6206	55.2041
20	2.8239	3.8144	51.3897
21	2.6197	4.0186	47.3711
22	2.4045	4.2338	43.1372
23	2.1778	4.4605	38.6768
24	1.9390	4.6993	33.9774
25	1.6874	4.9509	29.0265
26	1.4223	5.2160	23.8105
27	1.1430	5.4953	18.3152
28	.8488	5.7895	12.5256
29	.5388	6.0995	6.4261
30	.2122	6.4261	0.0000

QUARTERLY PAYMENT AMORTIZATION SCHEDULE PER $100   5.50 %

YEARS 2 — QTR PAYT 13.2858 — AN CONST 53.15

#	INT	PRIN	BALANCE
1	4.5083	48.6347	51.3653
2	1.7777	51.3653	0.0000

YEARS 3 — QTR PAYT 9.0968 — AN CONST 36.39

#	INT	PRIN	BALANCE
1	4.8571	31.5300	68.4700
2	3.0869	33.3002	35.1698
3	1.2172	35.1698	0.0000

YEARS 4 — QTR PAYT 7.0054 — AN CONST 28.03

#	INT	PRIN	BALANCE
1	5.0312	22.9903	77.0097
2	3.7404	24.2811	52.7286
3	2.3772	25.6444	27.0842
4	.9374	27.0842	0.0000

YEARS 5 — QTR PAYT 5.7531 — AN CONST 23.02

#	INT	PRIN	BALANCE
1	5.1355	17.8767	82.1233
2	4.1318	18.8804	63.2429
3	3.0718	19.9404	43.3024
4	1.9522	21.0600	22.2424
5	.7698	22.2424	0.0000

YEARS 6 — QTR PAYT 4.9202 — AN CONST 19.69

#	INT	PRIN	BALANCE
1	5.2048	14.4761	85.5239
2	4.3921	15.2889	70.2350
3	3.5337	16.1473	54.0878
4	2.6271	17.0538	37.0339
5	1.6696	18.0113	19.0226
6	.6584	19.0226	0.0000

YEARS 7 — QTR PAYT 4.3271 — AN CONST 17.31

#	INT	PRIN	BALANCE
1	5.2542	12.0543	87.9457
2	4.5774	12.7311	75.2146
3	3.8626	13.4459	61.7687
4	3.1077	14.2008	47.5678
5	2.3104	14.9981	32.5697
6	1.4683	15.8402	16.7295
7	.5790	16.7295	0.0000

YEARS 8 — QTR PAYT 3.8839 — AN CONST 15.54

#	INT	PRIN	BALANCE
1	5.2911	10.2443	89.7557
2	4.7160	10.8194	78.9363
3	4.1085	11.4269	67.5094
4	3.4669	12.0685	55.4409
5	2.7894	12.7460	42.6949
6	2.0737	13.4617	29.2332
7	1.3179	14.2175	15.0157
8	.5197	15.0157	0.0000

YEARS 9 — QTR PAYT 3.5404 — AN CONST 14.17

#	INT	PRIN	BALANCE
1	5.3197	8.8420	91.1580
2	4.8233	9.3385	81.8195
3	4.2990	9.8628	71.9567
4	3.7452	10.4165	61.5402
5	3.1604	11.0014	50.5388
6	2.5427	11.6190	38.9198
7	1.8904	12.2714	26.6484
8	1.2014	12.9604	13.6880
9	.4737	13.6880	0.0000

YEARS 10 — QTR PAYT 3.2669 — AN CONST 13.07

#	INT	PRIN	BALANCE
1	5.3425	7.7252	92.2748
2	4.9087	8.1590	84.1158
3	4.4507	8.6171	75.4987
4	3.9669	9.1009	66.3979
5	3.4559	9.6118	56.7860
6	2.9162	10.1515	46.6345
7	2.3463	10.7214	35.9131
8	1.7443	11.3234	24.5897
9	1.1086	11.9591	12.6306
10	.4371	12.6306	0.0000

YEARS 11 — QTR PAYT 3.0443 — AN CONST 12.18

#	INT	PRIN	BALANCE
1	5.3610	6.8160	93.1840
2	4.9783	7.1987	85.9853
3	4.5742	7.6029	78.3824
4	4.1473	8.0297	70.3527
5	3.6965	8.4805	61.8722
6	3.2203	8.9567	52.9155
7	2.7175	9.4596	43.4559
8	2.1864	9.9907	33.4653
9	1.6254	10.5516	22.9137
10	1.0330	11.1440	11.7697
11	.4073	11.7697	0.0000

YEARS 12 — QTR PAYT 2.8597 — AN CONST 11.44

#	INT	PRIN	BALANCE
1	5.3764	6.0624	93.9376
2	5.0360	6.4028	87.5348
3	4.6765	6.7623	80.7725
4	4.2969	7.1419	73.6306
5	3.8959	7.5429	66.0876
6	3.4724	7.9664	58.1212
7	3.0251	8.4137	49.7075
8	2.5527	8.8861	40.8215
9	2.0538	9.3850	31.4365
10	1.5269	9.9119	21.5246
11	.9704	10.4684	11.0562
12	.3827	11.0562	0.0000

YEARS 13 — QTR PAYT 2.7045 — AN CONST 10.82

#	INT	PRIN	BALANCE
1	5.3893	5.4285	94.5715
2	5.0845	5.7333	88.8381
3	4.7626	6.0552	82.7829
4	4.4227	6.3952	76.3878
5	4.0636	6.7542	69.6335
6	3.6844	7.1335	62.5001
7	3.2839	7.5340	54.9661
8	2.8609	7.9570	47.0091
9	2.4141	8.4037	38.6054
10	1.9423	8.8755	29.7299
11	1.4440	9.3738	20.3561
12	.9177	9.9001	10.4560
13	.3619	10.4560	0.0000

YEARS 14 — QTR PAYT 2.5722 — AN CONST 10.29

#	INT	PRIN	BALANCE
1	5.4003	4.8887	95.1113
2	5.1258	5.1632	89.9482
3	4.8360	5.4530	84.4951
4	4.5298	5.7592	78.7359
5	4.2065	6.0825	72.6534
6	3.8649	6.4240	66.2294
7	3.5043	6.7847	59.4446
8	3.1233	7.1657	52.2790
9	2.7210	7.5680	44.7110
10	2.2961	7.9929	36.7182
11	1.8474	8.4416	28.2765
12	1.3734	8.9156	19.3609
13	.8729	9.4161	9.9448
14	.3442	9.9448	0.0000

YEARS 15 — QTR PAYT 2.4585 — AN CONST 9.84

#	INT	PRIN	BALANCE
1	5.4098	4.4240	95.5760
2	5.1614	4.6724	90.9036
3	4.8991	4.9347	85.9689
4	4.6220	5.2118	80.7571
5	4.3294	5.5044	75.2527
6	4.0204	5.8135	69.4392
7	3.6940	6.1398	63.2994
8	3.3492	6.4846	56.8148
9	2.9852	6.8486	49.9662
10	2.6007	7.2332	42.7330
11	2.1945	7.6393	35.0937
12	1.7656	8.0682	27.0256
13	1.3127	8.5212	18.5044
14	.8342	8.9996	9.5048
15	.3290	9.5048	0.0000

YEARS 16 — QTR PAYT 2.3596 — AN CONST 9.44

#	INT	PRIN	BALANCE
1	5.4180	4.0204	95.9796
2	5.1923	4.2462	91.7334
3	4.9539	4.4846	87.2489
4	4.7021	4.7363	82.5125
5	4.4362	5.0023	77.5103
6	4.1553	5.2831	72.2272
7	3.8587	5.5797	66.6475
8	3.5454	5.8930	60.7545
9	3.2146	6.2239	54.5306
10	2.8652	6.5733	47.9573
11	2.4961	6.9424	41.0149
12	2.1063	7.3321	33.6828
13	1.6947	7.7438	25.9390
14	1.2599	8.1786	17.7605
15	.8007	8.6377	9.1227
16	.3157	9.1227	0.0000

YEARS 17 — QTR PAYT 2.2731 — AN CONST 9.10

#	INT	PRIN	BALANCE
1	5.4252	3.6671	96.3329
2	5.2193	3.8730	92.4599
3	5.0019	4.0904	88.3695
4	4.7722	4.3201	84.0494
5	4.5297	4.5626	79.4867
6	4.2735	4.8188	74.6679
7	4.0030	5.0894	69.5785
8	3.7172	5.3751	64.2034
9	3.4154	5.6769	58.5265
10	3.0967	5.9956	52.5309
11	2.7601	6.3322	46.1987
12	2.4046	6.6878	39.5109
13	2.0291	7.0633	32.4476
14	1.6325	7.4598	24.9878
15	1.2137	7.8786	17.1092
16	.7713	8.3210	8.7882
17	.3042	8.7882	0.0000

YEARS 18 — QTR PAYT 2.1968 — AN CONST 8.79

#	INT	PRIN	BALANCE
1	5.4316	3.3556	96.6444
2	5.2432	3.5440	93.1003
3	5.0442	3.7430	89.3573
4	4.8340	3.9532	85.4041
5	4.6121	4.1751	81.2290
6	4.3777	4.4095	76.8194
7	4.1301	4.6571	72.1623
8	3.8686	4.9186	67.2437
9	3.5925	5.1947	62.0490
10	3.3008	5.4864	56.5626
11	2.9928	5.7944	50.7682
12	2.6675	6.1198	44.6484
13	2.3239	6.4634	38.1850
14	1.9610	6.8262	31.3588
15	1.5777	7.2095	24.1493
16	1.1730	7.6143	16.5350
17	.7455	8.0418	8.4933
18	.2939	8.4933	0.0000

YEARS 19 — QTR PAYT 2.1292 — AN CONST 8.52

#	INT	PRIN	BALANCE
1	5.4372	3.0794	96.9206
2	5.2643	3.2523	93.6683
3	5.0817	3.4349	90.2334
4	4.8889	3.6278	86.6056
5	4.6852	3.8314	82.7741
6	4.4701	4.0466	78.7276
7	4.2429	4.2738	74.4538
8	4.0029	4.5137	69.9401
9	3.7495	4.7671	65.1730
10	3.4819	5.0348	60.1382
11	3.1992	5.3174	54.8208
12	2.9006	5.6160	49.2048
13	2.5853	5.9313	43.2735
14	2.2523	6.2643	37.0092
15	1.9006	6.6160	30.3931
16	1.5291	6.9875	23.4057
17	1.1368	7.3798	16.0259
18	.7225	7.7941	8.2317
19	.2849	8.2317	0.0000

YEARS 20 — QTR PAYT 2.0688 — AN CONST 8.28

#	INT	PRIN	BALANCE
1	5.4422	2.8331	97.1669
2	5.2832	2.9922	94.1747
3	5.1152	3.1602	91.0145
4	4.9377	3.3376	87.6769
5	4.7504	3.5250	84.1520
6	4.5524	3.7229	80.4291
7	4.3434	3.9319	76.4971
8	4.1227	4.1527	72.3445
9	3.8895	4.3858	67.9586
10	3.6433	4.6321	63.3266
11	3.3832	4.8921	58.4345
12	3.1085	5.1668	53.2677
13	2.8185	5.4569	47.8108
14	2.5121	5.7633	42.0475
15	2.1885	6.0868	35.9607
16	1.8468	6.4286	29.5321
17	1.4858	6.7895	22.7425
18	1.1046	7.1707	15.5718
19	.7020	7.5733	7.9985
20	.2768	7.9985	0.0000

YEARS 21 — QTR PAYT 2.0148 — AN CONST 8.06

#	INT	PRIN	BALANCE
1	5.4467	2.6124	97.3876
2	5.3001	2.7591	94.6285
3	5.1451	2.9140	91.7145

#	INT	PRIN	BALANCE
4	4.9815	3.0776	88.6369
5	4.8088	3.2504	85.3865
6	4.6263	3.4329	81.9536
7	4.4335	3.6256	78.3279
8	4.2300	3.8292	74.4987
9	4.0150	4.0442	70.4545
10	3.7879	4.2712	66.1833
11	3.5481	4.5111	61.6722
12	3.2948	4.7643	56.9079
13	3.0273	5.0318	51.8761
14	2.7448	5.3143	46.5617
15	2.4465	5.6127	40.9490
16	2.1313	5.9278	35.0212
17	1.7985	6.2606	28.7606
18	1.4470	6.6121	22.1484
19	1.0758	6.9834	15.1650
20	.6837	7.3755	7.7896
21	.2696	7.7896	0.0000

YEARS 22 — QTR PAYT 1.9662 — AN CONST 7.87

#	INT	PRIN	BALANCE
1	5.4508	2.4138	97.5862
2	5.3153	2.5494	95.0368
3	5.1721	2.6925	92.3443
4	5.0210	2.8437	89.5006
5	4.8613	3.0033	86.4973
6	4.6927	3.1719	83.3254
7	4.5146	3.3500	79.9753
8	4.3265	3.5381	76.4372
9	4.1279	3.7368	72.7004
10	3.9181	3.9466	68.7539
11	3.6965	4.1681	64.5857
12	3.4625	4.4022	60.1836
13	3.2153	4.6493	55.5342
14	2.9543	4.9104	50.6239
15	2.6786	5.1861	45.4378
16	2.3874	5.4772	39.9606
17	2.0799	5.7847	34.1759
18	1.7551	6.1095	28.0663
19	1.4121	6.4525	21.6138
20	1.0498	6.8148	14.7990
21	.6672	7.1974	7.6015
22	.2631	7.6015	0.0000

YEARS 23 — QTR PAYT 1.9222 — AN CONST 7.69

#	INT	PRIN	BALANCE
1	5.4544	2.2345	97.7655
2	5.3290	2.3599	95.4056
3	5.1965	2.4924	92.9132
4	5.0566	2.6323	90.2809
5	4.9088	2.7801	87.5008
6	4.7527	2.9362	84.5646
7	4.5878	3.1011	81.4635
8	4.4137	3.2752	78.1883
9	4.2298	3.4591	74.7293
10	4.0356	3.6533	71.0760
11	3.8305	3.8584	67.2176
12	3.6139	4.0750	63.1426
13	3.3851	4.3038	58.8388
14	3.1435	4.5454	54.2933
15	2.8882	4.8006	49.4927
16	2.6187	5.0702	44.4225
17	2.3341	5.3548	39.0677
18	2.0334	5.6555	33.4122
19	1.7159	5.9730	27.4392
20	1.3805	6.3084	21.1308
21	1.0263	6.6625	14.4683
22	.6523	7.0366	7.4317
23	.2572	7.4317	0.0000

YEARS 24 — QTR PAYT 1.8824 — AN CONST 7.53

#	INT	PRIN	BALANCE
1	5.4578	2.0718	97.9282
2	5.3414	2.1882	95.7400
3	5.2186	2.3110	93.4290
4	5.0888	2.4408	90.9882
5	4.9518	2.5778	88.4104
6	4.8071	2.7225	85.6879
7	4.6542	2.8754	82.8125
8	4.4928	3.0368	79.7757
9	4.3223	3.2073	76.5684
10	4.1422	3.3874	73.1810
11	3.9520	3.5776	69.6034
12	3.7511	3.7784	65.8250
13	3.5390	3.9906	61.8344
14	3.3150	4.2146	57.6197
15	3.0783	4.4513	53.1685
16	2.8284	4.7012	48.4673
17	2.5645	4.9651	43.5022
18	2.2857	5.2439	38.2583
19	1.9913	5.5383	32.7200
20	1.6803	5.8493	26.8707
21	1.3519	6.1777	20.6930
22	1.0051	6.5245	14.1685
23	.6388	6.8908	7.2777
24	.2519	7.2777	0.0000

YEARS 25 — QTR PAYT 1.8462 — AN CONST 7.39

#	INT	PRIN	BALANCE
1	5.4608	1.9240	98.0760
2	5.3528	2.0320	96.0441
3	5.2387	2.1461	93.8980
4	5.1182	2.2665	91.6315
5	4.9909	2.3938	89.2377
6	4.8565	2.5282	86.7095
7	4.7146	2.6701	84.0393
8	4.5647	2.8201	81.2193
9	4.4063	2.9784	78.2409
10	4.2391	3.1456	75.0952
11	4.0625	3.3222	71.7730
12	3.8760	3.5088	68.2643
13	3.6790	3.7057	64.5585
14	3.4709	3.9138	60.6447
15	3.2512	4.1335	56.5112
16	3.0191	4.3656	52.1455
17	2.7740	4.6107	47.5348
18	2.5151	4.8696	42.6652
19	2.2417	5.1430	37.5222
20	1.9530	5.4318	32.0904
21	1.6480	5.7367	26.3537
22	1.3259	6.0588	20.2949
23	.9857	6.3990	13.8959
24	.6265	6.7582	7.1377
25	.2470	7.1377	0.0000

YEARS 26 — QTR PAYT 1.8132 — AN CONST 7.26

#	INT	PRIN	BALANCE
1	5.4635	1.7891	98.2109
2	5.3631	1.8895	96.3214
3	5.2570	1.9956	94.3258
4	5.1449	2.1077	92.2181
5	5.0266	2.2260	89.9921
6	4.9016	2.3510	87.6411
7	4.7696	2.4830	85.1582
8	4.6302	2.6224	82.5358
9	4.4830	2.7696	79.7662
10	4.3275	2.9251	76.8411
11	4.1633	3.0893	73.7517
12	3.9898	3.2628	70.4889
13	3.8066	3.4460	67.0430
14	3.6132	3.6395	63.4035
15	3.4088	3.8438	59.5597
16	3.1930	4.0596	55.5001
17	2.9651	4.2875	51.2126
18	2.7244	4.5282	46.6844
19	2.4701	4.7825	41.9019
20	2.2016	5.0510	36.8509
21	1.9180	5.3346	31.5163
22	1.6185	5.6341	25.8822
23	1.3022	5.9504	19.9318
24	.9681	6.2845	13.6473
25	.6153	6.6373	7.0100
26	.2426	7.0100	0.0000

YEARS 27 — QTR PAYT 1.7829 — AN CONST 7.14

#	INT	PRIN	BALANCE
1	5.4660	1.6658	98.3342
2	5.3725	1.7593	96.5750
3	5.2737	1.8581	94.7169
4	5.1694	1.9624	92.7545
5	5.0592	2.0726	90.6820
6	4.9429	2.1889	88.4931
7	4.8200	2.3118	86.1812
8	4.6902	2.4416	83.7396
9	4.5531	2.5787	81.1609
10	4.4083	2.7235	78.4375
11	4.2554	2.8764	75.5611
12	4.0939	3.0379	72.5232
13	3.9234	3.2084	69.3148
14	3.7432	3.3886	65.9262
15	3.5530	3.5788	62.3474
16	3.3520	3.7798	58.5676
17	3.1398	3.9920	54.5756
18	2.9157	4.2161	50.3595
19	2.6790	4.4528	45.9067
20	2.4290	4.7028	41.2039
21	2.1649	4.9669	36.2371
22	1.8861	5.2457	30.9913
23	1.5916	5.5402	25.4511
24	1.2805	5.8513	19.5998
25	.9520	6.1798	13.4200
26	.6050	6.5268	6.8932
27	.2386	6.8932	0.0000

YEARS 28 — QTR PAYT 1.7553 — AN CONST 7.03

#	INT	PRIN	BALANCE
1	5.4683	1.5527	98.4473
2	5.3812	1.6399	96.8074
3	5.2891	1.7320	95.0754
4	5.1919	1.8292	93.2462
5	5.0891	1.9319	91.3143
6	4.9807	2.0404	89.2739
7	4.8661	2.1549	87.1190
8	4.7451	2.2759	84.8431
9	4.6174	2.4037	82.4394
10	4.4824	2.5387	79.9007
11	4.3399	2.6812	77.2196
12	4.1893	2.8317	74.3878
13	4.0303	2.9907	71.3971
14	3.8624	3.1586	68.2385
15	3.6851	3.3360	64.9025
16	3.4978	3.5233	61.3793
17	3.3000	3.7211	57.6582
18	3.0911	3.9300	53.7282
19	2.8704	4.1506	49.5776
20	2.6374	4.3837	45.1939
21	2.3913	4.6298	40.5641
22	2.1313	4.8897	35.6744
23	1.8568	5.1643	30.5101
24	1.5668	5.4542	25.0559
25	1.2606	5.7604	19.2955
26	.9372	6.0839	13.2116
27	.5956	6.4254	6.7862
28	.2349	6.7862	0.0000

YEARS 29 — QTR PAYT 1.7298 — AN CONST 6.92

#	INT	PRIN	BALANCE
1	5.4705	1.4489	98.5511
2	5.3891	1.5302	97.0209
3	5.3032	1.6161	95.4048
4	5.2125	1.7069	93.6979
5	5.1166	1.8027	91.8952
6	5.0154	1.9039	89.9913
7	4.9085	2.0108	87.9805
8	4.7956	2.1237	85.8568
9	4.6764	2.2429	83.6138
10	4.5505	2.3689	81.2450
11	4.4175	2.5019	78.7431
12	4.2770	2.6423	76.1007
13	4.1286	2.7907	73.3100
14	3.9720	2.9474	70.3627
15	3.8065	3.1129	67.2498
16	3.6317	3.2876	63.9622
17	3.4471	3.4722	60.4900
18	3.2522	3.6672	56.8228
19	3.0463	3.8730	52.9498
20	2.8288	4.0905	48.8593
21	2.5992	4.3202	44.5391
22	2.3566	4.5627	39.9764
23	2.1004	4.8189	35.1575
24	1.8299	5.0894	30.0681
25	1.5441	5.3752	24.6929
26	1.2424	5.6770	19.0159
27	.9236	5.9957	13.0202
28	.5870	6.3323	6.6879
29	.2315	6.6879	0.0000

YEARS 30 — QTR PAYT 1.7064 — AN CONST 6.83

#	INT	PRIN	BALANCE
1	5.4724	1.3533	98.6467
2	5.3964	1.4293	97.2174
3	5.3162	1.5095	95.7079
4	5.2314	1.5943	94.1137
5	5.1419	1.6838	92.4299
6	5.0474	1.7783	90.6516
7	4.9475	1.8782	88.7734
8	4.8421	1.9836	86.7898
9	4.7307	2.0950	84.6949
10	4.6131	2.2126	82.4823
11	4.4889	2.3368	80.1455
12	4.3577	2.4680	77.6775
13	4.2191	2.6066	75.0709
14	4.0728	2.7529	72.3180
15	3.9182	2.9075	69.4105
16	3.7550	3.0707	66.3397
17	3.5826	3.2431	63.0966
18	3.4005	3.4252	59.6714
19	3.2082	3.6175	56.0538
20	3.0051	3.8206	52.2332
21	2.7905	4.0351	48.1981
22	2.5640	4.2617	43.9364
23	2.3247	4.5010	39.4354
24	2.0720	4.7537	34.6817
25	1.8051	5.0206	29.6612
26	1.5232	5.3024	24.3587
27	1.2255	5.6002	18.7586
28	.9111	5.9146	12.8440
29	.5790	6.2466	6.5974
30	.2283	6.5974	0.0000

YEARS 2 — QTR PAYT 13.3221 — AN CONST 53.29

#	INT	PRIN	BALANCE
1	4.7151	48.5731	51.4269
2	1.8613	51.4269	0.0000

YEARS 3 — QTR PAYT 9.1323 — AN CONST 36.53

#	INT	PRIN	BALANCE
1	5.0799	31.4494	68.5506
2	3.2322	33.2971	35.2534
3	1.2760	35.2534	0.0000

YEARS 4 — QTR PAYT 7.0409 — AN CONST 28.17

#	INT	PRIN	BALANCE
1	5.2621	22.9015	77.0985
2	3.9166	24.2470	52.8514
3	2.4920	25.6716	27.1798
4	.9837	27.1798	0.0000

YEARS 5 — QTR PAYT 5.7888 — AN CONST 23.16

#	INT	PRIN	BALANCE
1	5.3711	17.7839	82.2161
2	4.3263	18.8287	63.3873
3	3.2200	19.9350	43.4524
4	2.0488	21.1062	22.3462
5	.8088	22.3462	0.0000

YEARS 6 — QTR PAYT 4.9562 — AN CONST 19.83

#	INT	PRIN	BALANCE
1	5.4436	14.3814	85.6186
2	4.5987	15.2263	70.3923
3	3.7041	16.1209	54.2714
4	2.7570	17.0680	37.2033
5	1.7542	18.0708	19.1325
6	.6925	19.1325	0.0000

YEARS 7 — QTR PAYT 4.3635 — AN CONST 17.46

#	INT	PRIN	BALANCE
1	5.4952	11.9589	88.0411
2	4.7926	12.6615	75.3795
3	4.0487	13.4054	61.9741
4	3.2611	14.1930	47.7811
5	2.4272	15.0269	32.7542
6	1.5444	15.9097	16.8445
7	.6097	16.8445	0.0000

YEARS 8 — QTR PAYT 3.9207 — AN CONST 15.69

#	INT	PRIN	BALANCE
1	5.5338	10.1490	89.8510
2	4.9375	10.7452	79.1058
3	4.3062	11.3765	67.7293
4	3.6378	12.0449	55.6844
5	2.9301	12.7526	42.9318
6	2.1809	13.5018	29.4300
7	1.3877	14.2951	15.1349
8	.5478	15.1349	0.0000

YEARS 9 — QTR PAYT 3.5777 — AN CONST 14.32

#	INT	PRIN	BALANCE
1	5.5636	8.7473	91.2527
2	5.0497	9.2612	81.9915
3	4.5056	9.8053	72.1862
4	3.9295	10.3814	61.8048
5	3.3196	10.9913	50.8135
6	2.6738	11.6371	39.1764
7	1.9901	12.3208	26.8557
8	1.2663	13.0446	13.8110
9	.4999	13.8110	0.0000

YEARS 10 — QTR PAYT 3.3047 — AN CONST 13.22

#	INT	PRIN	BALANCE
1	5.5874	7.6314	92.3686
2	5.1390	8.0797	84.2889
3	4.6643	8.5544	75.7344
4	4.1618	9.0570	66.6774
5	3.6296	9.5891	57.0883
6	3.0663	10.1525	46.9357
7	2.4698	10.7490	36.1867
8	1.8383	11.3805	24.8062
9	1.1696	12.0492	12.7571
10	.4617	12.7571	0.0000

YEARS 11 — QTR PAYT 3.0825 — AN CONST 12.34

#	INT	PRIN	BALANCE
1	5.6068	6.7233	93.2767
2	5.2117	7.1183	86.1584
3	4.7935	7.5365	78.6219
4	4.3508	7.9793	70.6426
5	3.8820	8.4481	62.1945
6	3.3856	8.9444	53.2500
7	2.8601	9.4699	43.7801
8	2.3037	10.0263	33.7538
9	1.7147	10.6154	23.1384
10	1.0910	11.2391	11.8994
11	.4307	11.8994	0.0000

YEARS 12 — QTR PAYT 2.8985 — AN CONST 11.60

#	INT	PRIN	BALANCE
1	5.6228	5.9710	94.0290
2	5.2720	6.3218	87.7071
3	4.9006	6.6933	81.0138
4	4.5073	7.0865	73.9273
5	4.0910	7.5029	66.4245
6	3.6502	7.9437	58.4808
7	3.1835	8.4104	50.0705
8	2.6893	8.9045	41.1660
9	2.1662	9.4276	31.7383
10	1.6123	9.9815	21.7568
11	1.0259	10.5680	11.1888
12	.4050	11.1888	0.0000

YEARS 13 — QTR PAYT 2.7437 — AN CONST 10.98

#	INT	PRIN	BALANCE
1	5.6363	5.3386	94.6614
2	5.3226	5.6523	89.0091
3	4.9905	5.9843	83.0248
4	4.6389	6.3359	76.6888
5	4.2667	6.7082	69.9806
6	3.8726	7.1023	62.8783
7	3.4553	7.5196	55.3588
8	3.0135	7.9614	47.3974
9	2.5458	8.4291	38.9683
10	2.0505	8.9243	30.0440
11	1.5262	9.4487	20.5953
12	.9711	10.0038	10.5915
13	.3833	10.5915	0.0000

YEARS 14 — QTR PAYT 2.6120 — AN CONST 10.45

#	INT	PRIN	BALANCE
1	5.6477	4.8003	95.1997
2	5.3657	5.0823	90.1173
3	5.0671	5.3809	84.7364
4	4.7510	5.6971	79.0393
5	4.4162	6.0318	73.0075
6	4.0619	6.3862	66.6214
7	3.6867	6.7614	59.8600
8	3.2894	7.1586	52.7014
9	2.8688	7.5792	45.1222
10	2.4236	8.0245	37.0977
11	1.9521	8.4959	28.6018
12	1.4530	8.9951	19.6067
13	.9245	9.5236	10.0831
14	.3649	10.0831	0.0000

YEARS 15 — QTR PAYT 2.4987 — AN CONST 10.00

#	INT	PRIN	BALANCE
1	5.6576	4.3373	95.6627
2	5.4028	4.5921	91.0706
3	5.1330	4.8619	86.2087
4	4.8473	5.1476	81.0611
5	4.5449	5.4500	75.6112
6	4.2247	5.7702	69.8410
7	3.8857	6.1092	63.7318
8	3.5268	6.4681	57.2637
9	3.1468	6.8481	50.4156
10	2.7444	7.2505	43.1651
11	2.3184	7.6764	35.4887
12	1.8674	8.1274	27.3612
13	1.3899	8.6049	18.7563
14	.8844	9.1105	9.6458
15	.3491	9.6458	0.0000

YEARS 16 — QTR PAYT 2.4004 — AN CONST 9.61

#	INT	PRIN	BALANCE
1	5.6662	3.9354	96.0646
2	5.4349	4.1666	91.8980
3	5.1901	4.4114	87.4866
4	4.9310	4.6706	82.8160
5	4.6566	4.9450	77.8711
6	4.3660	5.2355	72.6356
7	4.0584	5.5431	67.0925
8	3.7328	5.8688	61.2237
9	3.3880	6.2136	55.0101
10	3.0229	6.5786	48.4315
11	2.6364	6.9651	41.4664
12	2.2272	7.3743	34.0920
13	1.7939	7.8076	26.2844
14	1.3352	8.2663	18.0181
15	.8496	8.7520	9.2662
16	.3354	9.2662	0.0000

YEARS 17 — QTR PAYT 2.3144 — AN CONST 9.26

#	INT	PRIN	BALANCE
1	5.6736	3.5838	96.4162
2	5.4631	3.7944	92.6218
3	5.2402	4.0173	88.6046
4	5.0041	4.2533	84.3513
5	4.7543	4.5032	79.8481
6	4.4897	4.7678	75.0803
7	4.2096	5.0479	70.0325
8	3.9130	5.3444	64.6880
9	3.5990	5.6584	59.0296
10	3.2666	5.9909	53.0387
11	2.9146	6.3429	46.6958
12	2.5419	6.7155	39.9803
13	2.1474	7.1101	32.8702
14	1.7297	7.5278	25.3425
15	1.2874	7.9701	17.3724
16	.8191	8.4383	8.9341
17	.3234	8.9341	0.0000

YEARS 18 — QTR PAYT 2.2386 — AN CONST 8.96

#	INT	PRIN	BALANCE
1	5.6802	3.2741	96.7259
2	5.4879	3.4665	93.2594
3	5.2842	3.6701	89.5893
4	5.0686	3.8857	85.7036
5	4.8403	4.1140	81.5895
6	4.5986	4.3557	77.2338
7	4.3427	4.6117	72.6221
8	4.0717	4.8826	67.7395
9	3.7849	5.1695	62.5701
10	3.4812	5.4732	57.0969
11	3.1596	5.7947	51.3021
12	2.8192	6.1352	45.1670
13	2.4587	6.4956	38.6713
14	2.0771	6.8773	31.7940
15	1.6730	7.2813	24.5127
16	1.2452	7.7091	16.8036
17	.7923	8.1620	8.6416
18	.3128	8.6416	0.0000

YEARS 19 — QTR PAYT 2.1714 — AN CONST 8.69

#	INT	PRIN	BALANCE
1	5.6861	2.9997	97.0003
2	5.5099	3.1759	93.8245
3	5.3233	3.3625	90.4620
4	5.1257	3.5600	86.9019
5	4.9166	3.7692	83.1328
6	4.6951	3.9906	79.1421
7	4.4607	4.2251	74.9170
8	4.2124	4.4733	70.4437
9	3.9496	4.7361	65.7076
10	3.6713	5.0144	60.6932
11	3.3767	5.3090	55.3842
12	3.0648	5.6209	49.7633
13	2.7346	5.9512	43.8121
14	2.3850	6.3008	37.5113
15	2.0148	6.6710	30.8403
16	1.6228	7.0629	23.7774
17	1.2079	7.4779	16.2996
18	.7685	7.9172	8.3824
19	.3034	8.3824	0.0000

YEARS 20 — QTR PAYT 2.1116 — AN CONST 8.45

#	INT	PRIN	BALANCE
1	5.6913	2.7551	97.2449
2	5.5294	2.9170	94.3278
3	5.3580	3.0884	91.2395
4	5.1766	3.2698	87.9696
5	4.9845	3.4619	84.5077
6	4.7811	3.6653	80.8423
7	4.5658	3.8807	76.9616
8	4.3378	4.1087	72.8530
9	4.0964	4.3501	68.5029
10	3.8408	4.6057	63.8972
11	3.5702	4.8762	59.0210
12	3.2837	5.1627	53.8583
13	2.9804	5.4660	48.3922
14	2.6592	5.7872	42.6050
15	2.3192	6.1272	36.4778
16	1.9593	6.4872	29.9906
17	1.5781	6.8683	23.1223
18	1.1746	7.2718	15.8505
19	.7474	7.6991	8.1514
20	.2950	8.1514	0.0000

YEARS 21 — QTR PAYT 2.0581 — AN CONST 8.24

#	INT	PRIN	BALANCE
1	5.6960	2.5363	97.4637
2	5.5470	2.6853	94.7785
3	5.3892	2.8430	91.9355

#	INT	PRIN	BALANCE
4	5.2222	3.0101	88.9254
5	5.0453	3.1869	85.7385
6	4.8581	3.3741	82.3643
7	4.6598	3.5724	78.7920
8	4.4500	3.7823	75.0097
9	4.2277	4.0045	71.0052
10	3.9925	4.2397	66.7655
11	3.7434	4.4888	62.2766
12	3.4796	4.7526	57.5241
13	3.2004	5.0318	52.4923
14	2.9048	5.3274	47.1649
15	2.5918	5.6404	41.5244
16	2.2604	5.9718	35.5526
17	1.9096	6.3226	29.2300
18	1.5381	6.6941	22.5359
19	1.1448	7.0874	15.4485
20	.7284	7.5038	7.9447
21	.2875	7.9447	0.0000

YEARS 22 — QTR PAYT 2.0099 — AN CONST 8.04

#	INT	PRIN	BALANCE
1	5.7002	2.3395	97.6605
2	5.5627	2.4769	95.1836
3	5.4172	2.6224	92.5612
4	5.2631	2.7765	89.7847
5	5.1000	2.9396	86.8450
6	4.9273	3.1123	83.7327
7	4.7444	3.2952	80.4375
8	4.5508	3.4888	76.9486
9	4.3458	3.6938	73.2549
10	4.1288	3.9108	69.3441
11	3.8991	4.1406	65.2035
12	3.6558	4.3838	60.8197
13	3.3982	4.6414	56.1783
14	3.1256	4.9141	51.2642
15	2.8368	5.2028	46.0614
16	2.5312	5.5085	40.5530
17	2.2075	5.8321	34.7209
18	1.8649	6.1747	28.5462
19	1.5021	6.5375	22.0087
20	1.1180	6.9216	15.0871
21	.7114	7.3283	7.7588
22	.2808	7.7588	0.0000

YEARS 23 — QTR PAYT 1.9665 — AN CONST 7.87

#	INT	PRIN	BALANCE
1	5.7039	2.1619	97.8381
2	5.5769	2.2889	95.5492
3	5.4424	2.4234	93.1259
4	5.3001	2.5657	90.5601
5	5.1493	2.7165	87.8436
6	4.9897	2.8761	84.9675
7	4.8208	3.0451	81.9225
8	4.6419	3.2240	78.6985
9	4.4524	3.4134	75.2851
10	4.2519	3.6139	71.6712
11	4.0396	3.8262	67.8449
12	3.8148	4.0510	63.7939
13	3.5768	4.2891	59.5048
14	3.3248	4.5410	54.9638
15	3.0580	4.8078	50.1560
16	2.7755	5.0903	45.0657
17	2.4764	5.3894	39.6763
18	2.1598	5.7060	33.9703
19	1.8246	6.0412	27.9290
20	1.4696	6.3962	21.5329
21	1.0939	6.7720	14.7609
22	.6960	7.1698	7.5911
23	.2748	7.5911	0.0000

YEARS 24 — QTR PAYT 1.9271 — AN CONST 7.71

#	INT	PRIN	BALANCE
1	5.7074	2.0011	97.9989
2	5.5898	2.1186	95.8803
3	5.4653	2.2431	93.6372
4	5.3335	2.3749	91.2624
5	5.1940	2.5144	88.7479
6	5.0463	2.6621	86.0858
7	4.8899	2.8185	83.2673
8	4.7243	2.9841	80.2831
9	4.5490	3.1595	77.1237
10	4.3633	3.3451	73.7786
11	4.1668	3.5416	70.2370
12	3.9587	3.7497	66.4873
13	3.7384	3.9700	62.5173
14	3.5052	4.2032	58.3141
15	3.2582	4.4502	53.8639
16	2.9968	4.7116	49.1523
17	2.7200	4.9884	44.1639
18	2.4269	5.2815	38.8823
19	2.1166	5.5918	33.2905
20	1.7881	5.9204	27.3702
21	1.4402	6.2682	21.1020
22	1.0720	6.6365	14.4655
23	.6821	7.0264	7.4392
24	.2693	7.4392	0.0000

YEARS 25 — QTR PAYT 1.8914 — AN CONST 7.57

#	INT	PRIN	BALANCE
1	5.7105	1.8550	98.1450
2	5.6015	1.9639	96.1811
3	5.4861	2.0793	94.1018
4	5.3639	2.2015	91.9003
5	5.2346	2.3308	89.5695
6	5.0977	2.4678	87.1017
7	4.9527	2.6128	84.4890
8	4.7992	2.7663	81.7227
9	4.6367	2.9288	78.7939
10	4.4646	3.1008	75.6931
11	4.2824	3.2830	72.4101
12	4.0895	3.4759	68.9341
13	3.8853	3.6801	65.2540
14	3.6691	3.8963	61.3577
15	3.4402	4.1253	57.2324
16	3.1978	4.3676	52.8648
17	2.9412	4.6242	48.2406
18	2.6695	4.8959	43.3446
19	2.3819	5.1836	38.1611
20	2.0773	5.4881	32.6730
21	1.7549	5.8105	26.8625
22	1.4135	6.1519	20.7105
23	1.0521	6.5133	14.1972
24	.6694	6.8960	7.3012
25	.2643	7.3012	0.0000

YEARS 26 — QTR PAYT 1.8588 — AN CONST 7.44

#	INT	PRIN	BALANCE
1	5.7133	1.7219	98.2781
2	5.6122	1.8230	96.4551
3	5.5050	1.9301	94.5250
4	5.3916	2.0435	92.4815
5	5.2716	2.1636	90.3179
6	5.1445	2.2907	88.0272
7	5.0099	2.4253	85.6020
8	4.8674	2.5678	83.0342
9	4.7165	2.7186	80.3156
10	4.5568	2.8783	77.4372
11	4.3877	3.0475	74.3898
12	4.2087	3.2265	71.1633
13	4.0191	3.4161	67.7472
14	3.8184	3.6168	64.1304
15	3.6059	3.8293	60.3012
16	3.3809	4.0542	56.2470
17	3.1427	4.2924	51.9545
18	2.8906	4.5446	47.4099
19	2.6236	4.8116	42.5983
20	2.3409	5.0943	37.5040
21	2.0416	5.3936	32.1104
22	1.7247	5.7105	26.3999
23	1.3892	6.0460	20.3539
24	1.0340	6.4012	13.9527
25	.6579	6.7773	7.1755
26	.2597	7.1755	0.0000

YEARS 27 — QTR PAYT 1.8290 — AN CONST 7.32

#	INT	PRIN	BALANCE
1	5.7159	1.6003	98.3997
2	5.6219	1.6943	96.7054
3	5.5223	1.7938	94.9116
4	5.4170	1.8992	93.0123
5	5.3054	2.0108	91.0015
6	5.1872	2.1290	88.8726
7	5.0621	2.2540	86.6185
8	4.9297	2.3865	84.2321
9	4.7895	2.5267	81.7054
10	4.6411	2.6751	79.0303
11	4.4839	2.8323	76.1980
12	4.3175	2.9987	73.1993
13	4.1413	3.1749	70.0245
14	3.9548	3.3614	66.6631
15	3.7573	3.5589	63.1042
16	3.5482	3.7680	59.3362
17	3.3268	3.9893	55.3469
18	3.0925	4.2237	51.1231
19	2.8443	4.4719	46.6512
20	2.5816	4.7346	41.9166
21	2.3034	5.0128	36.9038
22	2.0089	5.3073	31.5966
23	1.6971	5.6191	25.9775
24	1.3669	5.9492	20.0282
25	1.0174	6.2988	13.7295
26	.6474	6.6688	7.0606
27	.2556	7.0606	0.0000

YEARS 28 — QTR PAYT 1.8018 — AN CONST 7.21

#	INT	PRIN	BALANCE
1	5.7183	1.4890	98.5110
2	5.6308	1.5765	96.9346
3	5.5382	1.6691	95.2655
4	5.4401	1.7671	93.4984
5	5.3363	1.8710	91.6274
6	5.2264	1.9809	89.6465
7	5.1100	2.0973	87.5493
8	4.9868	2.2205	85.3288
9	4.8563	2.3509	82.9779
10	4.7182	2.4891	80.4888
11	4.5720	2.6353	77.8536
12	4.4171	2.7901	75.0634
13	4.2532	2.9540	72.1094
14	4.0797	3.1276	68.9818
15	3.8959	3.3113	65.6705
16	3.7014	3.5059	62.1646
17	3.4954	3.7119	58.4527
18	3.2773	3.9299	54.5228
19	3.0464	4.1608	50.3619
20	2.8020	4.4053	45.9566
21	2.5431	4.6641	41.2925
22	2.2691	4.9381	36.3544
23	1.9790	5.2283	31.1261
24	1.6718	5.5354	25.5907
25	1.3466	5.8607	19.7300
26	1.0023	6.2050	13.5250
27	.6377	6.5695	6.9555
28	.2517	6.9555	0.0000

YEARS 29 — QTR PAYT 1.7768 — AN CONST 7.11

#	INT	PRIN	BALANCE
1	5.7205	1.3868	98.6132
2	5.6390	1.4683	97.1448
3	5.5527	1.5546	95.5902
4	5.4614	1.6459	93.9443
5	5.3647	1.7426	92.2017
6	5.2623	1.8450	90.3567
7	5.1539	1.9534	88.4033
8	5.0391	2.0682	86.3351
9	4.9176	2.1897	84.1454
10	4.7890	2.3183	81.8271
11	4.6528	2.4545	79.3726
12	4.5086	2.5987	76.7738
13	4.3559	2.7514	74.0224
14	4.1942	2.9131	71.1094
15	4.0231	3.0842	68.0251
16	3.8419	3.2654	64.7597
17	3.6500	3.4573	61.3024
18	3.4469	3.6604	57.6421
19	3.2318	3.8754	53.7666
20	3.0042	4.1031	49.6635
21	2.7631	4.3442	45.3193
22	2.5079	4.5994	40.7198
23	2.2376	4.8697	35.8502
24	1.9515	5.1558	30.6944
25	1.6486	5.4587	25.2358
26	1.3279	5.7794	19.4564
27	.9884	6.1189	13.3375
28	.6289	6.4784	6.8590
29	.2483	6.8590	0.0000

YEARS 30 — QTR PAYT 1.7539 — AN CONST 7.02

#	INT	PRIN	BALANCE
1	5.7225	1.2929	98.7071
2	5.6465	1.3689	97.3381
3	5.5661	1.4493	95.8888
4	5.4809	1.5345	94.3543
5	5.3908	1.6246	92.7297
6	5.2953	1.7201	91.0096
7	5.1942	1.8212	89.1884
8	5.0873	1.9281	87.2603
9	4.9740	2.0414	85.2189
10	4.8540	2.1614	83.0575
11	4.7270	2.2884	80.7691
12	4.5926	2.4228	78.3463
13	4.4503	2.5651	75.7812
14	4.2996	2.7158	73.0654
15	4.1400	2.8754	70.1900
16	3.9711	3.0443	67.1456
17	3.7922	3.2232	63.9224
18	3.6028	3.4126	60.5098
19	3.4023	3.6131	56.8968
20	3.1901	3.8253	53.0714
21	2.9653	4.0501	49.0213
22	2.7274	4.2880	44.7333
23	2.4754	4.5400	40.1934
24	2.2087	4.8067	35.3867
25	1.9263	5.0891	30.2976
26	1.6273	5.3881	24.9095
27	1.3108	5.7046	19.2048
28	.9756	6.0398	13.1650
29	.6207	6.3947	6.7704
30	.2450	6.7704	0.0000

YEARS 2 — QTR PAYT 13.3584 — AN CONST 53.44

#	INT	PRIN	BALANCE
1	4.9220	48.5116	51.4884
2	1.9452	51.4884	0.0000
7	2.0911	12.3698	27.0634
8	1.3321	13.1289	13.9345
9	.5264	13.9345	0.0000

YEARS 3 — QTR PAYT 9.1680 — AN CONST 36.68

#	INT	PRIN	BALANCE
1	5.3030	31.3690	68.6310
2	3.3780	33.2940	35.3370
3	1.3350	35.3370	0.0000

YEARS 4 — QTR PAYT 7.0765 — AN CONST 28.31

#	INT	PRIN	BALANCE
1	5.4931	22.8130	77.1870
2	4.0932	24.2128	52.9742
3	2.6074	25.6986	27.2756
4	1.0304	27.2756	0.0000

YEARS 5 — QTR PAYT 5.8246 — AN CONST 23.30

#	INT	PRIN	BALANCE
1	5.6069	17.6914	82.3086
2	4.5213	18.7770	63.5316
3	3.3690	19.9292	43.6023
4	2.1461	21.1522	22.4501
5	.8481	22.4501	0.0000

YEARS 6 — QTR PAYT 4.9924 — AN CONST 19.97

#	INT	PRIN	BALANCE
1	5.6825	14.2871	85.7129
2	4.8058	15.1638	70.5491
3	3.8753	16.0943	54.4547
4	2.8877	17.0819	37.3728
5	1.8395	18.1301	19.2427
6	.7270	19.2427	0.0000

YEARS 7 — QTR PAYT 4.4001 — AN CONST 17.61

#	INT	PRIN	BALANCE
1	5.7364	11.8641	88.1359
2	5.0083	12.5921	75.5439
3	4.2357	13.3648	62.1791
4	3.4155	14.1849	47.9942
5	2.5451	15.0553	32.9389
6	1.6213	15.9792	16.9597
7	.6407	16.9597	0.0000

YEARS 8 — QTR PAYT 3.9577 — AN CONST 15.84

#	INT	PRIN	BALANCE
1	5.7766	10.0543	89.9457
2	5.1596	10.6712	79.2745
3	4.5048	11.3260	67.9485
4	3.8098	12.0210	55.9274
5	3.0721	12.7587	43.1687
6	2.2892	13.5416	29.6271
7	1.4583	14.3726	15.2545
8	.5763	15.2545	0.0000

YEARS 9 — QTR PAYT 3.6152 — AN CONST 14.47

#	INT	PRIN	BALANCE
1	5.8077	8.6532	91.3468
2	5.2767	9.1842	82.1625
3	4.7131	9.7478	72.4147
4	4.1150	10.3460	62.0687
5	3.4801	10.9808	51.0879
6	2.8063	11.6547	39.4332

YEARS 10 — QTR PAYT 3.3427 — AN CONST 13.38

#	INT	PRIN	BALANCE
1	5.8325	7.5383	92.4617
2	5.3699	8.0009	84.4607
3	4.8789	8.4919	75.9688
4	4.3579	9.0130	66.9558
5	3.8048	9.5661	57.3898
6	3.2178	10.1531	47.2367
7	2.5947	10.7761	36.4606
8	1.9335	11.4374	25.0233
9	1.2317	12.1392	12.8841
10	.4867	12.8841	0.0000

YEARS 11 — QTR PAYT 3.1210 — AN CONST 12.49

#	INT	PRIN	BALANCE
1	5.8526	6.6315	93.3685
2	5.4457	7.0384	86.3300
3	5.0138	7.4703	78.8597
4	4.5554	7.9288	70.9309
5	4.0689	8.4153	62.5157
6	3.5525	8.9317	53.5840
7	3.0044	9.4798	44.1042
8	2.4227	10.0615	34.0427
9	1.8053	10.6789	23.3639
10	1.1500	11.3342	12.0297
11	.4545	12.0297	0.0000

YEARS 12 — QTR PAYT 2.9375 — AN CONST 11.75

#	INT	PRIN	BALANCE
1	5.8693	5.8807	94.1193
2	5.5085	6.2415	87.8778
3	5.1255	6.6245	81.2533
4	4.7190	7.0310	74.2222
5	4.2875	7.4625	66.7597
6	3.8296	7.9204	58.8393
7	3.3436	8.4064	50.4329
8	2.8277	8.9223	41.5106
9	2.2802	9.4698	32.0408
10	1.6991	10.0509	21.9899
11	1.0823	10.6676	11.3223
12	.4277	11.3223	0.0000

YEARS 13 — QTR PAYT 2.7833 — AN CONST 11.14

#	INT	PRIN	BALANCE
1	5.8833	5.2498	94.7502
2	5.5612	5.5719	89.1782
3	5.2193	5.9139	83.2644
4	4.8564	6.2768	76.9876
5	4.4712	6.6619	70.3257
6	4.0624	7.0707	63.2550
7	3.6285	7.5046	55.7504
8	3.1680	7.9651	47.7852
9	2.6793	8.4539	39.3314
10	2.1605	8.9726	30.3587
11	1.6099	9.5232	20.8355
12	1.0255	10.1076	10.7279
13	.4053	10.7279	0.0000

YEARS 14 — QTR PAYT 2.6521 — AN CONST 10.61

#	INT	PRIN	BALANCE
1	5.8953	4.7132	95.2868
2	5.6061	5.0024	90.2845
3	5.2991	5.3093	84.9751
4	4.9733	5.6351	79.3400
5	4.6275	5.9809	73.3591
6	4.2605	6.3479	67.0111
7	3.8710	6.7375	60.2737
8	3.4575	7.1509	53.1228
9	3.0187	7.5897	45.5331
10	2.5530	8.0554	37.4776
11	2.0587	8.5498	28.9279
12	1.5340	9.0744	19.8535
13	.9772	9.6312	10.2222
14	.3862	10.2222	0.0000

YEARS 15 — QTR PAYT 2.5393 — AN CONST 10.16

#	INT	PRIN	BALANCE
1	5.9055	4.2519	95.7481
2	5.6446	4.5128	91.2354
3	5.3677	4.7897	86.4457
4	5.0738	5.0836	81.3621
5	4.7618	5.3955	75.9666
6	4.4307	5.7266	70.2400
7	4.0793	6.0780	64.1619
8	3.7064	6.4510	57.7109
9	3.3105	6.8469	50.8641
10	2.8904	7.2670	43.5971
11	2.4444	7.7129	35.8841
12	1.9711	8.1862	27.6979
13	1.4688	8.6886	19.0093
14	.9356	9.2217	9.7876
15	.3698	9.7876	0.0000

YEARS 16 — QTR PAYT 2.4415 — AN CONST 9.77

#	INT	PRIN	BALANCE
1	5.9144	3.8517	96.1483
2	5.6781	4.0881	92.0602
3	5.4272	4.3389	87.7213
4	5.1609	4.6052	83.1161
5	4.8784	4.8878	78.2283
6	4.5784	5.1877	73.0406
7	4.2601	5.5061	67.5345
8	3.9222	5.8439	61.6906
9	3.5636	6.2025	55.4881
10	3.1830	6.5831	48.9049
11	2.7790	6.9871	41.9178
12	2.3503	7.4159	34.5020
13	1.8952	7.8709	26.6310
14	1.4122	8.3539	18.2771
15	.8996	8.8665	9.4106
16	.3555	9.4106	0.0000

YEARS 17 — QTR PAYT 2.3560 — AN CONST 9.43

#	INT	PRIN	BALANCE
1	5.9222	3.5019	96.4981
2	5.7073	3.7168	92.7812
3	5.4792	3.9449	88.8363
4	5.2371	4.1870	84.6493
5	4.9802	4.4439	80.2054
6	4.7075	4.7166	75.4888
7	4.4181	5.0060	70.4827
8	4.1109	5.3132	65.1695
9	3.7849	5.6393	59.5302
10	3.4388	5.9853	53.5449
11	3.0715	6.3526	47.1923
12	2.6817	6.7424	40.4499
13	2.2680	7.1562	33.2937
14	1.8288	7.5953	25.6984
15	1.3628	8.0614	17.6371
16	.8681	8.5560	9.0811
17	.3431	9.0811	0.0000

YEARS 18 — QTR PAYT 2.2808 — AN CONST 9.13

#	INT	PRIN	BALANCE
1	5.9290	3.1941	96.8059
2	5.7330	3.3901	93.4158
3	5.5250	3.5981	89.8177
4	5.3042	3.8189	85.9988
5	5.0699	4.0533	81.9455
6	4.8211	4.3020	77.6435
7	4.5572	4.5660	73.0776
8	4.2770	4.8461	68.2314
9	3.9796	5.1435	63.0879
10	3.6640	5.4591	57.6288
11	3.3290	5.7941	51.8346
12	2.9734	6.1497	45.6849
13	2.5961	6.5271	39.1579
14	2.1955	6.9276	32.2303
15	1.7704	7.3527	24.8776
16	1.3192	7.8039	17.0737
17	.8404	8.2827	8.7910
18	.3321	8.7910	0.0000

YEARS 19 — QTR PAYT 2.2141 — AN CONST 8.86

#	INT	PRIN	BALANCE
1	5.9351	2.9215	97.0785
2	5.7558	3.1008	93.9777
3	5.5655	3.2911	90.6867
4	5.3636	3.4930	87.1937
5	5.1492	3.7073	83.4863
6	4.9217	3.9348	79.5515
7	4.6803	4.1763	75.3752
8	4.4240	4.4326	70.9426
9	4.1520	4.7046	66.2381
10	3.8633	4.9933	61.2448
11	3.5569	5.2997	55.9451
12	3.2317	5.6249	50.3203
13	2.8866	5.9700	44.3502
14	2.5202	6.3364	38.0139
15	2.1314	6.7252	31.2887
16	1.7187	7.1379	24.1508
17	1.2807	7.5759	16.5749
18	.8158	8.0408	8.5342
19	.3224	8.5342	0.0000

YEARS 20 — QTR PAYT 2.1548 — AN CONST 8.62

#	INT	PRIN	BALANCE
1	5.9405	2.6789	97.3211
2	5.7761	2.8432	94.4779
3	5.6016	3.0177	91.4602
4	5.4164	3.2029	88.2573
5	5.2199	3.3994	84.8579
6	5.0113	3.6080	81.2498
7	4.7899	3.8294	77.4204
8	4.5549	4.0644	73.3560
9	4.3055	4.3138	69.0422
10	4.0408	4.5785	64.4636
11	3.7598	4.8595	59.6041
12	3.4616	5.1577	54.4464
13	3.1451	5.4742	48.9723
14	2.8092	5.8101	43.1622
15	2.4527	6.1666	36.9955
16	2.0743	6.5450	30.4505
17	1.6727	6.9467	23.5038
18	1.2464	7.3729	16.1309
19	.7940	7.8254	8.3056
20	.3138	8.3056	0.0000

YEARS 21 — QTR PAYT 2.1018 — AN CONST 8.41

#	INT	PRIN	BALANCE
1	5.9453	2.4618	97.5382
2	5.7942	2.6129	94.9253
3	5.6339	2.7732	92.1520

QUARTERLY PAYMENT AMORTIZATION SCHEDULE PER $100 — 6.00 %

#	INT	PRIN	BALANCE
4	5.4637	2.9434	89.2086
5	5.2831	3.1240	86.0846
6	5.0914	3.3157	82.7688
7	4.8879	3.5192	79.2496
8	4.6720	3.7352	75.5144
9	4.4428	3.9644	71.5501
10	4.1995	4.2076	67.3425
11	3.9413	4.4658	62.8766
12	3.6673	4.7399	58.1368
13	3.3764	5.0307	53.1061
14	3.0677	5.3394	47.7666
15	2.7401	5.6671	42.0996
16	2.3923	6.0148	36.0848
17	2.0232	6.3839	29.7009
18	1.6315	6.7756	22.9252
19	1.2157	7.1914	15.7338
20	.7744	7.6327	8.1011
21	.3061	8.1011	0.0000

YEARS 22 — QTR PAYT 2.0541 — AN CONST 8.22

#	INT	PRIN	BALANCE
1	5.9496	2.2669	97.7331
2	5.8105	2.4060	95.3270
3	5.6629	2.5537	92.7734
4	5.5062	2.7104	90.0630
5	5.3399	2.8767	87.1863
6	5.1633	3.0532	84.1331
7	4.9760	3.2406	80.8925
8	4.7771	3.4394	77.4531
9	4.5661	3.6505	73.8026
10	4.3421	3.8745	69.9281
11	4.1043	4.1122	65.8159
12	3.8520	4.3646	61.4513
13	3.5841	4.6324	56.8189
14	3.2999	4.9167	51.9022
15	2.9982	5.2184	46.6838
16	2.6780	5.5386	41.1452
17	2.3381	5.8785	35.2668
18	1.9774	6.2392	29.0276
19	1.5945	6.6220	22.4055
20	1.1882	7.0284	15.3771
21	.7569	7.4597	7.9174
22	.2991	7.9174	0.0000

YEARS 23 — QTR PAYT 2.0112 — AN CONST 8.05

#	INT	PRIN	BALANCE
1	5.9535	2.0912	97.9088
2	5.8252	2.2195	95.6893
3	5.6890	2.3557	93.3336
4	5.5445	2.5003	90.8333
5	5.3910	2.6537	88.1796
6	5.2282	2.8165	85.3631
7	5.0554	2.9894	82.3737
8	4.8719	3.1728	79.2009
9	4.6772	3.3675	75.8334
10	4.4706	3.5741	72.2592
11	4.2513	3.7935	68.4658
12	4.0185	4.0262	64.4395
13	3.7714	4.2733	60.1662
14	3.5092	4.5355	55.6307
15	3.2309	4.8139	50.8168
16	2.9355	5.1093	45.7076
17	2.6220	5.4228	40.2848
18	2.2892	5.7555	34.5293
19	1.9360	6.1087	28.4205
20	1.5612	6.4836	21.9370
21	1.1633	6.8814	15.0556
22	.7410	7.3037	7.7519
23	.2929	7.7519	0.0000

YEARS 24 — QTR PAYT 1.9723 — AN CONST 7.89

#	INT	PRIN	BALANCE
1	5.9571	1.9322	98.0678
2	5.8385	2.0508	96.0170
3	5.7127	2.1766	93.8404
4	5.5791	2.3102	91.5302
5	5.4373	2.4520	89.0782
6	5.2869	2.6024	86.4758
7	5.1272	2.7621	83.7137
8	4.9577	2.9316	80.7821
9	4.7778	3.1115	77.6705
10	4.5868	3.3024	74.3681
11	4.3842	3.5051	70.8630
12	4.1691	3.7202	67.1429
13	3.9408	3.9485	63.1944
14	3.6985	4.1907	59.0037
15	3.4414	4.4479	54.5558
16	3.1684	4.7208	49.8349
17	2.8788	5.0105	44.8244
18	2.5713	5.3180	39.5064
19	2.2450	5.6443	33.8621
20	1.8986	5.9907	27.8714
21	1.5310	6.3583	21.5131
22	1.1408	6.7485	14.7647
23	.7267	7.1626	7.6021
24	.2872	7.6021	0.0000

YEARS 25 — QTR PAYT 1.9371 — AN CONST 7.75

#	INT	PRIN	BALANCE
1	5.9603	1.7880	98.2120
2	5.8506	1.8977	96.3144
3	5.7341	2.0141	94.3002
4	5.6105	2.1377	92.1625
5	5.4793	2.2689	89.8936
6	5.3401	2.4081	87.4855
7	5.1923	2.5559	84.9296
8	5.0355	2.7127	82.2169
9	4.8690	2.8792	79.3377
10	4.6924	3.0559	76.2818
11	4.5048	3.2434	73.0384
12	4.3058	3.4424	69.5960
13	4.0946	3.6537	65.9424
14	3.8704	3.8779	62.0645
15	3.6324	4.1158	57.9487
16	3.3799	4.3684	53.5803
17	3.1118	4.6364	48.9439
18	2.8273	4.9209	44.0229
19	2.5253	5.2229	38.8000
20	2.2048	5.5434	33.2566
21	1.8647	5.8836	27.3731
22	1.5036	6.2446	21.1285
23	1.1204	6.6278	14.5007
24	.7137	7.0345	7.4662
25	.2821	7.4662	0.0000

YEARS 26 — QTR PAYT 1.9050 — AN CONST 7.62

#	INT	PRIN	BALANCE
1	5.9632	1.6567	98.3433
2	5.8615	1.7583	96.5850
3	5.7536	1.8662	94.7187
4	5.6391	1.9808	92.7380
5	5.5176	2.1023	90.6357
6	5.3886	2.2313	88.4044
7	5.2516	2.3682	86.0362
8	5.1063	2.5135	83.5226
9	4.9521	2.6678	80.8548
10	4.7884	2.8315	78.0233
11	4.6146	3.0052	75.0181
12	4.4302	3.1897	71.8284
13	4.2345	3.3854	68.4430
14	4.0267	3.5931	64.8499
15	3.8063	3.8136	61.0363
16	3.5722	4.0476	56.9887
17	3.3239	4.2960	52.6927
18	3.0602	4.5596	48.1330
19	2.7804	4.8394	43.2936
20	2.4835	5.1364	38.1572
21	2.1683	5.4516	32.7057
22	1.8338	5.7861	26.9196
23	1.4787	6.1412	20.7784
24	1.1019	6.5180	14.2604
25	.7019	6.9180	7.3425
26	.2774	7.3425	0.0000

YEARS 27 — QTR PAYT 1.8757 — AN CONST 7.51

#	INT	PRIN	BALANCE
1	5.9658	1.5369	98.4631
2	5.8715	1.6312	96.8319
3	5.7714	1.7313	95.1006
4	5.6652	1.8376	93.2630
5	5.5524	1.9503	91.3127
6	5.4328	2.0700	89.2427
7	5.3057	2.1970	87.0457
8	5.1709	2.3318	84.7139
9	5.0278	2.4749	82.2389
10	4.8760	2.6268	79.6122
11	4.7148	2.7880	76.8242
12	4.5437	2.9591	73.8651
13	4.3621	3.1406	70.7245
14	4.1694	3.3334	67.3911
15	3.9649	3.5379	63.8532
16	3.7478	3.7550	60.0982
17	3.5173	3.9854	56.1128
18	3.2728	4.2300	51.8828
19	3.0132	4.4895	47.3933
20	2.7377	4.7650	42.6282
21	2.4453	5.0574	37.5708
22	2.1350	5.3678	32.2030
23	1.8056	5.6972	26.5059
24	1.4560	6.0468	20.4591
25	1.0849	6.4178	14.0413
26	.6911	6.8116	7.2296
27	.2731	7.2296	0.0000

YEARS 28 — QTR PAYT 1.8489 — AN CONST 7.40

#	INT	PRIN	BALANCE
1	5.9683	1.4274	98.5726
2	5.8807	1.5150	97.0577
3	5.7877	1.6079	95.4497
4	5.6891	1.7066	93.7431
5	5.5843	1.8113	91.9318
6	5.4732	1.9225	90.0093
7	5.3552	2.0404	87.9689
8	5.2300	2.1657	85.8032
9	5.0971	2.2985	83.5047
10	4.9561	2.4396	81.0651
11	4.8064	2.5893	78.4758
12	4.6475	2.7482	75.7276
13	4.4788	2.9168	72.8108
14	4.2999	3.0958	69.7150
15	4.1099	3.2858	66.4292
16	3.9083	3.4874	62.9418
17	3.6943	3.7014	59.2404
18	3.4671	3.9285	55.3119
19	3.2261	4.1696	51.1423
20	2.9702	4.4255	46.7168
21	2.6986	4.6970	42.0198
22	2.4104	4.9853	37.0345
23	2.1045	5.2912	31.7434
24	1.7798	5.6158	26.1275
25	1.4352	5.9605	20.1671
26	1.0694	6.3262	13.8408
27	.6813	6.7144	7.1264
28	.2692	7.1264	0.0000

YEARS 29 — QTR PAYT 1.8244 — AN CONST 7.30

#	INT	PRIN	BALANCE
1	5.9705	1.3270	98.6730
2	5.8891	1.4084	97.2646
3	5.8027	1.4949	95.7697
4	5.7109	1.5866	94.1831
5	5.6136	1.6840	92.4991
6	5.5102	1.7873	90.7118
7	5.4006	1.8970	88.8149
8	5.2842	2.0134	86.8015
9	5.1606	2.1369	84.6646
10	5.0295	2.2680	82.3966
11	4.8903	2.4072	79.9893
12	4.7426	2.5549	77.4344
13	4.5858	2.7117	74.7227
14	4.4194	2.8781	71.8446
15	4.2428	3.0547	68.7899
16	4.0553	3.2422	65.5477
17	3.8564	3.4411	62.1066
18	3.6452	3.6523	58.4543
19	3.4211	3.8764	54.5779
20	3.1833	4.1143	50.4636
21	2.9308	4.3667	46.0969
22	2.6628	4.6347	41.4622
23	2.3784	4.9191	36.5431
24	2.0766	5.2210	31.3221
25	1.7562	5.5413	25.7808
26	1.4162	5.8814	19.8994
27	1.0553	6.2423	13.6572
28	.6722	6.6253	7.0319
29	.2657	7.0319	0.0000

YEARS 30 — QTR PAYT 1.8019 — AN CONST 7.21

#	INT	PRIN	BALANCE
1	5.9726	1.2348	98.7652
2	5.8968	1.3106	97.4545
3	5.8164	1.3910	96.0635
4	5.7310	1.4764	94.5871
5	5.6404	1.5670	93.0201
6	5.5442	1.6632	91.3569
7	5.4422	1.7652	89.5917
8	5.3339	1.8735	87.7182
9	5.2189	1.9885	85.7297
10	5.0969	2.1105	83.6191
11	4.9674	2.2400	81.3791
12	4.8299	2.3775	79.0016
13	4.6840	2.5234	76.4782
14	4.5292	2.6782	73.8000
15	4.3648	2.8426	70.9574
16	4.1904	3.0170	67.9404
17	4.0053	3.2021	64.7383
18	3.8088	3.3986	61.3396
19	3.6002	3.6072	57.7325
20	3.3789	3.8285	53.9039
21	3.1439	4.0635	49.8405
22	2.8946	4.3128	45.5276
23	2.6299	4.5775	40.9502
24	2.3491	4.8584	36.0918
25	2.0509	5.1565	30.9353
26	1.7345	5.4729	25.4624
27	1.3987	5.8087	19.6537
28	1.0422	6.1652	13.4885
29	.6639	6.5435	6.9450
30	.2624	6.9450	0.0000

YEARS 2 — QTR PAYT 13.3948 — AN CONST 53.58

#	INT	PRIN	BALANCE
1	5.1291	48.4501	51.5499
2	2.0293	51.5499	0.0000

YEARS 3 — QTR PAYT 9.2037 — AN CONST 36.82

#	INT	PRIN	BALANCE
1	5.5261	31.2888	68.7112
2	3.5243	33.2906	35.4206
3	1.3943	35.4206	0.0000

YEARS 4 — QTR PAYT 7.1122 — AN CONST 28.45

#	INT	PRIN	BALANCE
1	5.7243	22.7246	77.2754
2	4.2703	24.1785	53.0969
3	2.7234	25.7255	27.3714
4	1.0775	27.3714	0.0000

YEARS 5 — QTR PAYT 5.8605 — AN CONST 23.45

#	INT	PRIN	BALANCE
1	5.8428	17.5992	82.4008
2	4.7168	18.7252	63.6755
3	3.5188	19.9233	43.7522
4	2.2441	21.1980	22.5542
5	.8879	22.5542	0.0000

YEARS 6 — QTR PAYT 5.0287 — AN CONST 20.12

#	INT	PRIN	BALANCE
1	5.9216	14.1933	85.8067
2	5.0136	15.1013	70.7054
3	4.0474	16.0675	54.6379
4	3.0194	17.0955	37.5424
5	1.9256	18.1893	19.3531
6	.7618	19.3531	0.0000

YEARS 7 — QTR PAYT 4.4369 — AN CONST 17.75

#	INT	PRIN	BALANCE
1	5.9777	11.7697	88.2303
2	5.2247	12.5227	75.7075
3	4.4235	13.3240	62.3836
4	3.5710	14.1764	48.2072
5	2.6640	15.0834	33.1237
6	1.6990	16.0485	17.0753
7	.6722	17.0753	0.0000

YEARS 8 — QTR PAYT 3.9949 — AN CONST 15.98

#	INT	PRIN	BALANCE
1	6.0196	9.9602	90.0398
2	5.3823	10.5974	79.4424
3	4.7043	11.2755	68.1669
4	3.9829	11.9969	56.1701
5	3.2153	12.7644	43.4056
6	2.3987	13.5811	29.8245
7	1.5297	14.4500	15.3745
8	.6052	15.3745	0.0000

YEARS 9 — QTR PAYT 3.6530 — AN CONST 14.62

#	INT	PRIN	BALANCE
1	6.0520	8.5599	91.4401
2	5.5043	9.1076	82.3325
3	4.9216	9.6903	72.6422
4	4.3016	10.3103	62.3319
5	3.6420	10.9699	51.3619
6	2.9401	11.6718	39.6901
7	2.1933	12.4186	27.2716
8	1.3988	13.2131	14.0585
9	.5534	14.0585	0.0000

YEARS 10 — QTR PAYT 3.3810 — AN CONST 13.53

#	INT	PRIN	BALANCE
1	6.0777	7.4461	92.5539
2	5.6013	7.9225	84.6313
3	5.0944	8.4294	76.2019
4	4.5551	8.9687	67.2331
5	3.9813	9.5426	57.6906
6	3.3708	10.1531	47.5375
7	2.7212	10.8027	36.7348
8	2.0300	11.4939	25.2409
9	1.2946	12.2292	13.0117
10	.5122	13.0117	0.0000

YEARS 11 — QTR PAYT 3.1598 — AN CONST 12.64

#	INT	PRIN	BALANCE
1	6.0987	6.5406	93.4594
2	5.6802	6.9591	86.5002
3	5.2350	7.4044	79.0959
4	4.7612	7.8781	71.2178
5	4.2572	8.3821	62.8357
6	3.7209	8.9184	53.9172
7	3.1503	9.4890	44.4282
8	2.5432	10.0961	34.3321
9	1.8972	10.7421	23.5900
10	1.2100	11.4294	12.1606
11	.4787	12.1606	0.0000

YEARS 12 — QTR PAYT 2.9768 — AN CONST 11.91

#	INT	PRIN	BALANCE
1	6.1160	5.7913	94.2087
2	5.7455	6.1619	88.0468
3	5.3513	6.5561	81.4907
4	4.9318	6.9755	74.5152
5	4.4855	7.4218	67.0933
6	4.0106	7.8967	59.1966
7	3.5054	8.4019	50.7947
8	2.9679	8.9395	41.8552
9	2.3959	9.5114	32.3438
10	1.7874	10.1200	22.2238
11	1.1399	10.7675	11.4564
12	.4510	11.4564	0.0000

YEARS 13 — QTR PAYT 2.8232 — AN CONST 11.30

#	INT	PRIN	BALANCE
1	6.1306	5.1621	94.8379
2	5.8003	5.4924	89.3455
3	5.4489	5.8438	83.5018
4	5.0750	6.2177	77.2841
5	4.6772	6.6155	70.6686
6	4.2540	7.0387	63.6299
7	3.8036	7.4891	56.1409
8	3.3245	7.9682	48.1726
9	2.8147	8.4780	39.6946
10	2.2722	9.0204	30.6742
11	1.6951	9.5976	21.0766
12	1.0810	10.2116	10.8650
13	.4277	10.8650	0.0000

YEARS 14 — QTR PAYT 2.6925 — AN CONST 10.78

#	INT	PRIN	BALANCE
1	6.1430	4.6272	95.3728
2	5.8469	4.9232	90.4496
3	5.5319	5.2382	85.2113
4	5.1968	5.5734	79.6380
5	4.8402	5.9300	73.7080
6	4.4608	6.3094	67.3987
7	4.0571	6.7130	60.6856
8	3.6276	7.1425	53.5431
9	3.1706	7.5995	45.9436
10	2.6844	8.0857	37.8579
11	2.1671	8.6031	29.2548
12	1.6167	9.1535	20.1013
13	1.0310	9.7391	10.3622
14	.4079	10.3622	0.0000

YEARS 15 — QTR PAYT 2.5803 — AN CONST 10.33

#	INT	PRIN	BALANCE
1	6.1536	4.1677	95.8323
2	5.8869	4.4343	91.3980
3	5.6032	4.7181	86.6799
4	5.3014	5.0199	81.6600
5	4.9802	5.3411	76.3189
6	4.6385	5.6828	70.6361
7	4.2749	6.0464	64.5897
8	3.8880	6.4332	58.1564
9	3.4764	6.8448	51.3116
10	3.0385	7.2828	44.0288
11	2.5725	7.7487	36.2801
12	2.0768	8.2445	28.0356
13	1.5493	8.7720	19.2636
14	.9881	9.3332	9.9304
15	.3909	9.9304	0.0000

YEARS 16 — QTR PAYT 2.4831 — AN CONST 9.94

#	INT	PRIN	BALANCE
1	6.1628	3.7694	96.2306
2	5.9216	4.0106	92.2200
3	5.6650	4.2672	87.9528
4	5.3920	4.5402	83.4126
5	5.1015	4.8307	78.5819
6	4.7925	5.1398	73.4421
7	4.4636	5.4686	67.9735
8	4.1137	5.8185	62.1550
9	3.7415	6.1908	55.9643
10	3.3454	6.5868	49.3774
11	2.9240	7.0083	42.3692
12	2.4756	7.4567	34.9125
13	1.9985	7.9337	26.9788
14	1.4909	8.4413	18.5375
15	.9508	8.9814	9.5560
16	.3762	9.5560	0.0000

YEARS 17 — QTR PAYT 2.3981 — AN CONST 9.60

#	INT	PRIN	BALANCE
1	6.1708	3.4215	96.5785
2	5.9519	3.6405	92.9380
3	5.7190	3.8734	89.0646
4	5.4712	4.1212	84.9434
5	5.2075	4.3849	80.5586
6	4.9270	4.6654	75.8932
7	4.6285	4.9639	70.9293
8	4.3109	5.2815	65.6478
9	3.9730	5.6194	60.0284
10	3.6135	5.9789	54.0494
11	3.2309	6.3615	47.6880
12	2.8239	6.7685	40.9195
13	2.3909	7.2015	33.7180
14	1.9301	7.6623	26.0557
15	1.4399	8.1525	17.9032
16	.9183	8.6741	9.2291
17	.3633	9.2291	0.0000

YEARS 18 — QTR PAYT 2.3234 — AN CONST 9.30

#	INT	PRIN	BALANCE
1	6.1779	3.1156	96.8844
2	5.9786	3.3149	93.5695
3	5.7665	3.5270	90.0424
4	5.5408	3.7527	86.2897
5	5.3007	3.9928	82.2969
6	5.0453	4.2482	78.0487
7	4.7735	4.5201	73.5286
8	4.4843	4.8092	68.7194
9	4.1766	5.1169	63.6025
10	3.8492	5.4443	58.1581
11	3.5009	5.7927	52.3655
12	3.1303	6.1633	46.2022
13	2.7359	6.5576	39.6446
14	2.3164	6.9772	32.6675
15	1.8700	7.4236	25.2439
16	1.3950	7.8985	17.3454
17	.8897	8.4039	8.9415
18	.3520	8.9415	0.0000

YEARS 19 — QTR PAYT 2.2573 — AN CONST 9.03

#	INT	PRIN	BALANCE
1	6.1842	2.8449	97.1551
2	6.0022	3.0270	94.1281
3	5.8085	3.2206	90.9075
4	5.6024	3.4267	87.4808
5	5.3832	3.6459	83.8348
6	5.1499	3.8792	79.9556
7	4.9017	4.1274	75.8283
8	4.6377	4.3915	71.4368
9	4.3567	4.6724	66.7644
10	4.0578	4.9714	61.7930
11	3.7397	5.2894	56.5036
12	3.4013	5.6279	50.8757
13	3.0412	5.9879	44.8878
14	2.6581	6.3710	38.5167
15	2.2505	6.7787	31.7381
16	1.8168	7.2124	24.5257
17	1.3553	7.6738	16.8519
18	.8644	8.1648	8.6872
19	.3420	8.6872	0.0000

YEARS 20 — QTR PAYT 2.1985 — AN CONST 8.80

#	INT	PRIN	BALANCE
1	6.1898	2.6042	97.3958
2	6.0231	2.7709	94.6249
3	5.8459	2.9481	91.6768
4	5.6572	3.1368	88.5400
5	5.4565	3.3375	85.2026
6	5.2430	3.5510	81.6516
7	5.0158	3.7782	77.8734
8	4.7741	4.0199	73.8535
9	4.5169	4.2771	69.5764
10	4.2432	4.5507	65.0257
11	3.9521	4.8419	60.1838
12	3.6423	5.1517	55.0321
13	3.3127	5.4813	49.5508
14	2.9620	5.8320	43.7188
15	2.5889	6.2051	37.5137
16	2.1919	6.6021	30.9116
17	1.7695	7.0245	23.8870
18	1.3200	7.4740	16.4131
19	.8418	7.9521	8.4609
20	.3331	8.4609	0.0000

YEARS 21 — QTR PAYT 2.1460 — AN CONST 8.59

#	INT	PRIN	BALANCE
1	6.1947	2.3892	97.6108
2	6.0419	2.5420	95.0688
3	5.8792	2.7047	92.3642

#	INT	PRIN	BALANCE
4	5.7062	2.8777	89.4865
5	5.5221	3.0618	86.4246
6	5.3262	3.2577	83.1669
7	5.1177	3.4661	79.7008
8	4.8960	3.6879	76.0129
9	4.6600	3.9239	72.0890
10	4.4090	4.1749	67.9141
11	4.1419	4.4420	63.4721
12	3.8577	4.7262	58.7459
13	3.5553	5.0286	53.7173
14	3.2336	5.3503	48.3669
15	2.8912	5.6927	42.6743
16	2.5270	6.0569	36.6174
17	2.1395	6.4444	30.1730
18	1.7272	6.8567	23.3163
19	1.2885	7.2954	16.0209
20	.8217	7.7622	8.2588
21	.3251	8.2588	0.0000

YEARS 22   QTR PAYT 2.0988   AN CONST 8.40

#	INT	PRIN	BALANCE
1	6.1992	2.1962	97.8038
2	6.0587	2.3367	95.4671
3	5.9092	2.4862	92.9809
4	5.7501	2.6453	90.3357
5	5.5809	2.8145	87.5212
6	5.4008	2.9946	84.5266
7	5.2092	3.1862	81.3404
8	5.0054	3.3900	77.9504
9	4.7885	3.6069	74.3435
10	4.5577	3.8377	70.5058
11	4.3121	4.0832	66.4226
12	4.0509	4.3445	62.0781
13	3.7729	4.6224	57.4557
14	3.4772	4.9182	52.5375
15	3.1625	5.2328	47.3047
16	2.8277	5.5676	41.7371
17	2.4715	5.9238	35.8132
18	2.0925	6.3029	29.5104
19	1.6893	6.7061	22.8043
20	1.2602	7.1352	15.6691
21	.8037	7.5917	8.0774
22	.3180	8.0774	0.0000

YEARS 23   QTR PAYT 2.0564   AN CONST 8.23

#	INT	PRIN	BALANCE
1	6.2032	2.0224	97.9776
2	6.0738	2.1518	95.8259
3	5.9362	2.2894	93.5364
4	5.7897	2.4359	91.1005
5	5.6338	2.5918	88.5088
6	5.4680	2.7576	85.7512
7	5.2916	2.9340	82.8172
8	5.1039	3.1217	79.6954
9	4.9041	3.3215	76.3740
10	4.6916	3.5340	72.8400
11	4.4655	3.7601	69.0799
12	4.2249	4.0006	65.0793
13	3.9690	4.2566	60.8227
14	3.6966	4.5289	56.2937
15	3.4069	4.8187	51.4750
16	3.0986	5.1270	46.3480
17	2.7706	5.4550	40.8930
18	2.4215	5.8040	35.0890
19	2.0502	6.1754	28.9136
20	1.6551	6.5705	22.3431
21	1.2347	6.9909	15.3522
22	.7874	7.4382	7.9140
23	.3115	7.9140	0.0000

YEARS 24   QTR PAYT 2.0180   AN CONST 8.08

#	INT	PRIN	BALANCE
1	6.2068	1.8653	98.1347
2	6.0875	1.9846	96.1500
3	5.9605	2.1116	94.0384
4	5.8254	2.2467	91.7917
5	5.6817	2.3905	89.4012
6	5.5287	2.5434	86.8578
7	5.3660	2.7061	84.1517
8	5.1929	2.8793	81.2724
9	5.0087	3.0635	78.2089
10	4.8126	3.2595	74.9494
11	4.6041	3.4680	71.4813
12	4.3822	3.6899	67.7914
13	4.1461	3.9260	63.8654
14	3.8949	4.1772	59.6882
15	3.6277	4.4445	55.2437
16	3.3433	4.7288	50.5149
17	3.0408	5.0314	45.4835
18	2.7189	5.3533	40.1302
19	2.3764	5.6958	34.4344
20	2.0120	6.0602	28.3742
21	1.6242	6.4479	21.9263
22	1.2117	6.8605	15.0658
23	.7727	7.2994	7.7664
24	.3057	7.7664	0.0000

YEARS 25   QTR PAYT 1.9833   AN CONST 7.94

#	INT	PRIN	BALANCE
1	6.2101	1.7229	98.2771
2	6.0999	1.8332	96.4439
3	5.9826	1.9505	94.4934
4	5.8578	2.0752	92.4182
5	5.7251	2.2080	90.2102
6	5.5838	2.3493	87.8609
7	5.4335	2.4996	85.3613
8	5.2736	2.6595	82.7018
9	5.1034	2.8297	79.8721
10	4.9224	3.0107	76.8614
11	4.7297	3.2033	73.6580
12	4.5248	3.4083	70.2497
13	4.3067	3.6264	66.6234
14	4.0747	3.8584	62.7650
15	3.8278	4.1052	58.6598
16	3.5652	4.3679	54.2919
17	3.2857	4.6473	49.6445
18	2.9884	4.9447	44.6999
19	2.6720	5.2610	39.4388
20	2.3354	5.5976	33.8412
21	1.9773	5.9558	27.8854
22	1.5962	6.3368	21.5485
23	1.1908	6.7423	14.8063
24	.7594	7.1736	7.6326
25	.3005	7.6326	0.0000

YEARS 26   QTR PAYT 1.9517   AN CONST 7.81

#	INT	PRIN	BALANCE
1	6.2131	1.5935	98.4065
2	6.1112	1.6955	96.7110
3	6.0027	1.8040	94.9070
4	5.8873	1.9194	92.9877
5	5.7645	2.0422	90.9455
6	5.6338	2.1728	88.7727
7	5.4948	2.3119	86.4608
8	5.3469	2.4598	84.0010
9	5.1895	2.6171	81.3839
10	5.0221	2.7846	78.5993
11	4.8439	2.9627	75.6366
12	4.6544	3.1523	72.4843
13	4.4527	3.3540	69.1303
14	4.2381	3.5686	65.5617
15	4.0098	3.7969	61.7648
16	3.7668	4.0398	57.7250
17	3.5084	4.2983	53.4267
18	3.2334	4.5733	48.8534
19	2.9408	4.8659	43.9875
20	2.6294	5.1772	38.8103
21	2.2982	5.5084	33.3019
22	1.9458	5.8609	27.4410
23	1.5708	6.2359	21.2051
24	1.1718	6.6348	14.5703
25	.7473	7.0593	7.5110
26	.2957	7.5110	0.0000

YEARS 27   QTR PAYT 1.9229   AN CONST 7.70

#	INT	PRIN	BALANCE
1	6.2159	1.4756	98.5244
2	6.1215	1.5700	96.9544
3	6.0210	1.6705	95.2839
4	5.9141	1.7773	93.5066
5	5.8004	1.8911	91.6155
6	5.6794	2.0120	89.6035
7	5.5507	2.1408	87.4627
8	5.4137	2.2777	85.1850
9	5.2680	2.4235	82.7615
10	5.1129	2.5785	80.1830
11	4.9480	2.7435	77.4395
12	4.7724	2.9190	74.5205
13	4.5857	3.1058	71.4147
14	4.3870	3.3045	68.1102
15	4.1755	3.5159	64.5943
16	3.9506	3.7409	60.8534
17	3.7113	3.9802	56.8732
18	3.4566	4.2349	52.6384
19	3.1857	4.5058	48.1326
20	2.8974	4.7941	43.3385
21	2.5906	5.1008	38.2377
22	2.2643	5.4272	32.8105
23	1.9171	5.7744	27.0361
24	1.5476	6.1438	20.8922
25	1.1545	6.5369	14.3553
26	.7363	6.9552	7.4002
27	.2913	7.4002	0.0000

YEARS 28   QTR PAYT 1.8966   AN CONST 7.59

#	INT	PRIN	BALANCE
1	6.2184	1.3679	98.6321
2	6.1308	1.4554	97.1767
3	6.0377	1.5485	95.6282
4	5.9386	1.6476	93.9805
5	5.8332	1.7530	92.2275
6	5.7211	1.8652	90.3623
7	5.6017	1.9845	88.3778
8	5.4748	2.1115	86.2663
9	5.3397	2.2466	84.0197
10	5.1959	2.3903	81.6294
11	5.0430	2.5432	79.0862
12	4.8803	2.7060	76.3802
13	4.7072	2.8791	73.5011
14	4.5230	3.0633	70.4378
15	4.3270	3.2593	67.1785
16	4.1184	3.4678	63.7107
17	3.8966	3.6897	60.0210
18	3.6605	3.9258	56.0953
19	3.4093	4.1769	51.9183
20	3.1421	4.4442	47.4742
21	2.8577	4.7285	42.7456
22	2.5552	5.0310	37.7146
23	2.2333	5.3529	32.3617
24	1.8908	5.6954	26.6663
25	1.5264	6.0598	20.6065
26	1.1387	6.4475	14.1590
27	.7262	6.8600	7.2989
28	.2873	7.2989	0.0000

YEARS 29   QTR PAYT 1.8725   AN CONST 7.49

#	INT	PRIN	BALANCE
1	6.2206	1.2693	98.7307
2	6.1394	1.3505	97.3801
3	6.0530	1.4369	95.9432
4	5.9611	1.5289	94.4143
5	5.8633	1.6267	92.7876
6	5.7592	1.7308	91.0569
7	5.6485	1.8415	89.2153
8	5.5306	1.9593	87.2560
9	5.4053	2.0847	85.1713
10	5.2719	2.2181	82.9533
11	5.1300	2.3600	80.5933
12	4.9790	2.5110	78.0823
13	4.8183	2.6716	75.4107
14	4.6474	2.8426	72.5682
15	4.4655	3.0244	69.5437
16	4.2720	3.2179	66.3258
17	4.0662	3.4238	62.9020
18	3.8471	3.6429	59.2592
19	3.6140	3.8759	55.3832
20	3.3660	4.1239	51.2593
21	3.1022	4.3878	46.8716
22	2.8215	4.6685	42.2031
23	2.5228	4.9672	37.2359
24	2.2050	5.2850	31.9509
25	1.8668	5.6231	26.3278
26	1.5071	5.9829	20.3449
27	1.1243	6.3657	13.9792
28	.7170	6.7729	7.2063
29	.2837	7.2063	0.0000

YEARS 30   QTR PAYT 1.8504   AN CONST 7.41

#	INT	PRIN	BALANCE
1	6.2227	1.1789	98.8211
2	6.1473	1.2544	97.5667
3	6.0670	1.3346	96.2321
4	5.9817	1.4200	94.8121
5	5.8908	1.5109	93.3012
6	5.7941	1.6075	91.6937
7	5.6913	1.7104	89.9834
8	5.5819	1.8198	88.1636
9	5.4654	1.9362	86.2273
10	5.3415	2.0601	84.1672
11	5.2097	2.1919	81.9753
12	5.0695	2.3322	79.6432
13	4.9203	2.4814	77.1618
14	4.7615	2.6401	74.5217
15	4.5926	2.8090	71.7126
16	4.4129	2.9888	68.7239
17	4.2217	3.1800	65.5439
18	4.0182	3.3834	62.1604
19	3.8017	3.5999	58.5605
20	3.5714	3.8302	54.7303
21	3.3264	4.0753	50.6550
22	3.0656	4.3360	46.3190
23	2.7882	4.6135	41.7055
24	2.4930	4.9086	36.7969
25	2.1790	5.2227	31.5742
26	1.8448	5.5568	26.0174
27	1.4893	5.9123	20.1050
28	1.1110	6.2906	13.8144
29	.7086	6.6931	7.1213
30	.2803	7.1213	0.0000

QUARTERLY PAYMENT AMORTIZATION SCHEDULE PER $100   6.50 %

YEARS 2 — QTR PAYT 13.4312 — AN CONST 53.73

#	INT	PRIN	BALANCE
1	5.3364	48.3886	51.6114
2	2.1136	51.6114	0.0000

YEARS 3 — QTR PAYT 9.2395 — AN CONST 36.96

#	INT	PRIN	BALANCE
1	5.7495	31.2086	68.7914
2	3.6710	33.2872	35.5042
3	1.4540	35.5042	0.0000

YEARS 4 — QTR PAYT 7.1480 — AN CONST 28.60

#	INT	PRIN	BALANCE
1	5.9556	22.6365	77.3635
2	4.4480	24.1441	53.2194
3	2.8400	25.7521	27.4673
4	1.1249	27.4673	0.0000

YEARS 5 — QTR PAYT 5.8966 — AN CONST 23.59

#	INT	PRIN	BALANCE
1	6.0790	17.5074	82.4926
2	4.9130	18.6734	63.8192
3	3.6693	19.9171	43.9021
4	2.3428	21.2436	22.6585
5	.9279	22.6585	0.0000

YEARS 6 — QTR PAYT 5.0652 — AN CONST 20.27

#	INT	PRIN	BALANCE
1	6.1609	14.0998	85.9002
2	5.2219	15.0389	70.8613
3	4.2202	16.0405	54.8208
4	3.1519	17.1088	37.7120
5	2.0125	18.2483	19.4637
6	.7971	19.4637	0.0000

YEARS 7 — QTR PAYT 4.4738 — AN CONST 17.90

#	INT	PRIN	BALANCE
1	6.2192	11.6759	88.3241
2	5.4416	12.4535	75.8706
3	4.6122	13.2830	62.5876
4	3.7275	14.1676	48.4200
5	2.7839	15.1112	33.3088
6	1.7775	16.1176	17.1911
7	.7040	17.1911	0.0000

YEARS 8 — QTR PAYT 4.0324 — AN CONST 16.13

#	INT	PRIN	BALANCE
1	6.2627	9.8667	90.1333
2	5.6056	10.5239	79.6094
3	4.9047	11.2248	68.3846
4	4.1571	11.9724	56.4122
5	3.3597	12.7697	43.6425
6	2.5092	13.6202	30.0223
7	1.6021	14.5274	15.4949
8	.6346	15.4949	0.0000

YEARS 9 — QTR PAYT 3.6909 — AN CONST 14.77

#	INT	PRIN	BALANCE
1	6.2964	8.4673	91.5327
2	5.7324	9.0313	82.5014
3	5.1309	9.6328	72.8686
4	4.4894	10.2743	62.5943
5	3.8051	10.9586	51.6356
6	3.0752	11.6885	39.9471
7	2.2968	12.4670	27.4802
8	1.4664	13.2973	14.1829
9	.5808	14.1829	0.0000

YEARS 10 — QTR PAYT 3.4195 — AN CONST 13.68

#	INT	PRIN	BALANCE
1	6.3231	7.3548	92.6452
2	5.8333	7.8446	84.8007
3	5.3108	8.3671	76.4336
4	4.7536	8.9243	67.5093
5	4.1592	9.5187	57.9906
6	3.5252	10.1526	47.8380
7	2.8491	10.8288	37.0091
8	2.1278	11.5500	25.4591
9	1.3586	12.3193	13.1398
10	.5381	13.1398	0.0000

YEARS 11 — QTR PAYT 3.1989 — AN CONST 12.80

#	INT	PRIN	BALANCE
1	6.3449	6.4507	93.5493
2	5.9152	6.8803	86.6690
3	5.4570	7.3386	79.3304
4	4.9682	7.8273	71.5031
5	4.4469	8.3486	63.1545
6	3.8909	8.9047	54.2498
7	3.2978	9.4977	44.7521
8	2.6653	10.1303	34.6218
9	1.9906	10.8050	23.8168
10	1.2710	11.5246	12.2922
11	.5034	12.2922	0.0000

YEARS 12 — QTR PAYT 3.0165 — AN CONST 12.07

#	INT	PRIN	BALANCE
1	6.3629	5.7030	94.2970
2	5.9830	6.0828	88.2142
3	5.5779	6.4879	81.7263
4	5.1458	6.9200	74.8062
5	4.6849	7.3809	67.4253
6	4.1933	7.8725	59.5528
7	3.6690	8.3968	51.1559
8	3.1098	8.9561	42.1999
9	2.5133	9.5526	32.6473
10	1.8771	10.1888	22.4585
11	1.1985	10.8674	11.5912
12	.4747	11.5912	0.0000

YEARS 13 — QTR PAYT 2.8634 — AN CONST 11.46

#	INT	PRIN	BALANCE
1	6.3779	5.0755	94.9245
2	6.0399	5.4135	89.5110
3	5.6794	5.7741	83.7369
4	5.2948	6.1586	77.5783
5	4.8846	6.5688	71.0094
6	4.4471	7.0063	64.0031
7	3.9805	7.4729	56.5302
8	3.4828	7.9707	48.5595
9	2.9519	8.5015	40.0580
10	2.3857	9.0677	30.9903
11	1.7818	9.6717	21.3186
12	1.1376	10.3158	11.0028
13	.4506	11.0028	0.0000

YEARS 14 — QTR PAYT 2.7333 — AN CONST 10.94

#	INT	PRIN	BALANCE
1	6.3908	4.5424	95.4576
2	6.0882	4.8449	90.6126
3	5.7656	5.1676	85.4450
4	5.4214	5.5118	79.9332
5	5.0543	5.8789	74.0543
6	4.6627	6.2704	67.7839
7	4.2451	6.6881	61.0958
8	3.7997	7.1335	53.9624
9	3.3246	7.6086	46.3538
10	2.8178	8.1153	38.2384
11	2.2773	8.6558	29.5826
12	1.7009	9.2323	20.3503
13	1.0860	9.8472	10.5031
14	.4301	10.5031	0.0000

YEARS 15 — QTR PAYT 2.6216 — AN CONST 10.49

#	INT	PRIN	BALANCE
1	6.4018	4.0848	95.9152
2	6.1297	4.3569	91.5583
3	5.8395	4.6470	86.9113
4	5.5300	4.9565	81.9548
5	5.1999	5.2867	76.6681
6	4.8478	5.6387	71.0294
7	4.4723	6.0143	65.0151
8	4.0717	6.4149	58.6002
9	3.6445	6.8421	51.7581
10	3.1888	7.2978	44.4603
11	2.7027	7.7838	36.6765
12	2.1843	8.3023	28.3742
13	1.6314	8.8552	19.5190
14	1.0416	9.4450	10.0740
15	.4126	10.0740	0.0000

YEARS 16 — QTR PAYT 2.5249 — AN CONST 10.10

#	INT	PRIN	BALANCE
1	6.4113	3.6885	96.3115
2	6.1656	3.9341	92.3774
3	5.9036	4.1962	88.1812
4	5.6242	4.4756	83.7056
5	5.3261	4.7737	78.9319
6	5.0081	5.0917	73.8402
7	4.6690	5.4308	68.4095
8	4.3073	5.7925	62.6170
9	3.9215	6.1783	56.4387
10	3.5101	6.5897	49.8490
11	3.0712	7.0286	42.8204
12	2.6030	7.4967	35.3237
13	2.1038	7.9960	27.3276
14	1.5712	8.5286	18.7990
15	1.0032	9.0966	9.7024
16	.3973	9.7024	0.0000

YEARS 17 — QTR PAYT 2.4405 — AN CONST 9.77

#	INT	PRIN	BALANCE
1	6.4196	3.3426	96.6574
2	6.1970	3.5652	93.0922
3	5.9596	3.8026	89.2896
4	5.7063	4.0559	85.2337
5	5.4362	4.3260	80.9077
6	5.1480	4.6142	76.2935
7	4.8407	4.9215	71.3721
8	4.5130	5.2492	66.1228
9	4.1633	5.5988	60.5240
10	3.7905	5.9717	54.5522
11	3.3927	6.3695	48.1828
12	2.9685	6.7937	41.3891
13	2.5160	7.2462	34.1429
14	2.0334	7.7288	26.4142
15	1.5187	8.2435	18.1707
16	.9697	8.7925	9.3781
17	.3841	9.3781	0.0000

YEARS 18 — QTR PAYT 2.3664 — AN CONST 9.47

#	INT	PRIN	BALANCE
1	6.4269	3.0386	96.9614
2	6.2246	3.2410	93.7204
3	6.0087	3.4569	90.2635
4	5.7785	3.6871	86.5764
5	5.5329	3.9327	82.6438
6	5.2710	4.1946	78.4492
7	4.9916	4.4739	73.9752
8	4.6936	4.7719	69.2033
9	4.3758	5.0897	64.1136
10	4.0368	5.4287	58.6849
11	3.6753	5.7903	52.8946
12	3.2896	6.1759	46.7187
13	2.8783	6.5872	40.1314
14	2.4396	7.0260	33.1055
15	1.9716	7.4939	25.6115
16	1.4725	7.9930	17.6185
17	.9402	8.5254	9.0932
18	.3724	9.0932	0.0000

YEARS 19 — QTR PAYT 2.3008 — AN CONST 9.21

#	INT	PRIN	BALANCE
1	6.4334	2.7700	97.2300
2	6.2489	2.9545	94.2756
3	6.0521	3.1512	91.1243
4	5.8423	3.3611	87.7632
5	5.6184	3.5850	84.1783
6	5.3796	3.8237	80.3546
7	5.1250	4.0784	76.2762
8	4.8533	4.3500	71.9261
9	4.5636	4.6397	67.2864
10	4.2546	4.9487	62.3377
11	3.9250	5.2783	57.0593
12	3.5735	5.6299	51.4294
13	3.1985	6.0048	45.4246
14	2.7986	6.4048	39.0198
15	2.3720	6.8314	32.1884
16	1.9170	7.2863	24.9021
17	1.4317	7.7716	17.1305
18	.9141	8.2892	8.8413
19	.3621	8.8413	0.0000

YEARS 20 — QTR PAYT 2.2426 — AN CONST 8.98

#	INT	PRIN	BALANCE
1	6.4391	2.5313	97.4687
2	6.2705	2.6999	94.7689
3	6.0907	2.8797	91.8892
4	5.8989	3.0715	88.8177
5	5.6944	3.2760	85.5417
6	5.4762	3.4942	82.0475
7	5.2435	3.7269	78.3206
8	4.9952	3.9752	74.3454
9	4.7305	4.2399	70.1055
10	4.4481	4.5223	65.5832
11	4.1469	4.8235	60.7597
12	3.8257	5.1447	55.6150
13	3.4830	5.4874	50.1276
14	3.1175	5.8529	44.2748
15	2.7277	6.2427	38.0321
16	2.3120	6.6584	31.3737
17	1.8685	7.1019	24.2718
18	1.3955	7.5749	16.6969
19	.8910	8.0794	8.6175
20	.3529	8.6175	0.0000

YEARS 21 — QTR PAYT 2.1906 — AN CONST 8.77

#	INT	PRIN	BALANCE
1	6.4443	2.3182	97.6818
2	6.2899	2.4726	95.2092
3	6.1252	2.6373	92.5719

#	INT	PRIN	BALANCE
4	5.9495	2.8129	89.7590
5	5.7622	3.0003	86.7588
6	5.5624	3.2001	83.5587
7	5.3492	3.4132	80.1455
8	5.1219	3.6405	76.5049
9	4.8794	3.8830	72.6219
10	4.6208	4.1416	68.4803
11	4.3450	4.4175	64.0629
12	4.0508	4.7117	59.3512
13	3.7370	5.0255	54.3257
14	3.4023	5.3602	48.9656
15	3.0453	5.7172	43.2484
16	2.6645	6.0979	37.1504
17	2.2584	6.5041	30.6464
18	1.8252	6.9373	23.7091
19	1.3632	7.3993	16.3098
20	.8704	7.8921	8.4177
21	.3447	8.4177	0.0000

YEARS 22 — QTR PAYT 2.1440 — AN CONST 8.58

#	INT	PRIN	BALANCE
1	6.4488	2.1272	97.8728
2	6.3072	2.2689	95.6039
3	6.1561	2.4200	93.1839
4	5.9949	2.5812	90.6028
5	5.8230	2.7531	87.8497
6	5.6396	2.9364	84.9132
7	5.4440	3.1320	81.7812
8	5.2354	3.3406	78.4406
9	5.0130	3.5631	74.8775
10	4.7756	3.8004	71.0771
11	4.5225	4.0535	67.0236
12	4.2526	4.3235	62.7001
13	3.9646	4.6114	58.0887
14	3.6575	4.9186	53.1701
15	3.3299	5.2462	47.9240
16	2.9805	5.5956	42.3284
17	2.6078	5.9682	36.3602
18	2.2103	6.3657	29.9945
19	1.7864	6.7897	23.2048
20	1.3342	7.2419	15.9629
21	.8518	7.7242	8.2387
22	.3374	8.2387	0.0000

YEARS 23 — QTR PAYT 2.1021 — AN CONST 8.41

#	INT	PRIN	BALANCE
1	6.4530	1.9554	98.0446
2	6.3227	2.0856	95.9590
3	6.1838	2.2245	93.7345
4	6.0357	2.3727	91.3618
5	5.8777	2.5307	88.8311
6	5.7091	2.6992	86.1319
7	5.5293	2.8790	83.2529
8	5.3376	3.0708	80.1821
9	5.1331	3.2753	76.9068
10	4.9149	3.4934	73.4134
11	4.6823	3.7261	69.6873
12	4.4341	3.9743	65.7130
13	4.1694	4.2389	61.4741
14	3.8871	4.5213	56.9528
15	3.5860	4.8224	52.1304
16	3.2648	5.1436	46.9869
17	2.9222	5.4861	41.5007
18	2.5568	5.8515	35.6492
19	2.1671	6.2412	29.4079
20	1.7514	6.6569	22.7510
21	1.3081	7.1003	15.6507
22	.8352	7.5732	8.0776
23	.3308	8.0776	0.0000

YEARS 24 — QTR PAYT 2.0642 — AN CONST 8.26

#	INT	PRIN	BALANCE
1	6.4567	1.8003	98.1997
2	6.3368	1.9202	96.2795
3	6.2089	2.0481	94.2315
4	6.0725	2.1845	92.0470
5	5.9270	2.3300	89.7171
6	5.7718	2.4851	87.2319
7	5.6063	2.6507	84.5813
8	5.4298	2.8272	81.7541
9	5.2415	3.0155	78.7386
10	5.0407	3.2163	75.5223
11	4.8265	3.4305	72.0917
12	4.5980	3.6590	68.4327
13	4.3543	3.9027	64.5300
14	4.0944	4.1626	60.3674
15	3.8171	4.4399	55.9275
16	3.5214	4.7356	51.1919
17	3.2060	5.0510	46.1410
18	2.8696	5.3874	40.7536
19	2.5108	5.7462	35.0074
20	2.1281	6.1289	28.8785
21	1.7199	6.5371	22.3414
22	1.2845	6.9725	15.3690
23	.8201	7.4368	7.9321
24	.3248	7.9321	0.0000

YEARS 25 — QTR PAYT 2.0300 — AN CONST 8.12

#	INT	PRIN	BALANCE
1	6.4601	1.6598	98.3402
2	6.3495	1.7704	96.5698
3	6.2316	1.8883	94.6815
4	6.1059	2.0141	92.6674
5	5.9717	2.1482	90.5192
6	5.8286	2.2913	88.2279
7	5.6760	2.4439	85.7840
8	5.5133	2.6067	83.1773
9	5.3397	2.7803	80.3971
10	5.1545	2.9654	77.4317
11	4.9570	3.1629	74.2687
12	4.7463	3.3736	70.8951
13	4.5217	3.5983	67.2969
14	4.2820	3.8379	63.4589
15	4.0264	4.0935	59.3654
16	3.7538	4.3662	54.9992
17	3.4630	4.6570	50.3422
18	3.1528	4.9671	45.3751
19	2.8220	5.2980	40.0771
20	2.4691	5.6508	34.4263
21	2.0928	6.0272	28.3992
22	1.6914	6.4286	21.9706
23	1.2632	6.8567	15.1139
24	.8065	7.3134	7.8005
25	.3194	7.8005	0.0000

YEARS 26 — QTR PAYT 1.9989 — AN CONST 8.00

#	INT	PRIN	BALANCE
1	6.4632	1.5324	98.4676
2	6.3611	1.6344	96.8332
3	6.2522	1.7433	95.0900
4	6.1361	1.8594	93.2306
5	6.0123	1.9832	91.2474
6	5.8802	2.1153	89.1321
7	5.7393	2.2562	86.8759
8	5.5891	2.4064	84.4695
9	5.4288	2.5667	81.9028
10	5.2578	2.7377	79.1651
11	5.0755	2.9200	76.2451
12	4.8810	3.1145	73.1307
13	4.6736	3.3219	69.8088
14	4.4524	3.5431	66.2656
15	4.2164	3.7791	62.4865
16	3.9647	4.0308	58.4557
17	3.6962	4.2993	54.1564
18	3.4099	4.5856	49.5708
19	3.1045	4.8910	44.6798
20	2.7787	5.2168	39.4630
21	2.4313	5.5642	33.8988
22	2.0607	5.9348	27.9640
23	1.6654	6.3301	21.6339
24	1.2438	6.7517	14.8823
25	.7942	7.2013	7.6810
26	.3146	7.6810	0.0000

YEARS 27 — QTR PAYT 1.9706 — AN CONST 7.89

#	INT	PRIN	BALANCE
1	6.4659	1.4163	98.5837
2	6.3716	1.5107	97.0730
3	6.2710	1.6113	95.4618
4	6.1637	1.7186	93.7432
5	6.0492	1.8330	91.9102
6	5.9271	1.9551	89.9550
7	5.7969	2.0853	87.8697
8	5.6580	2.2242	85.6455
9	5.5099	2.3724	83.2731
10	5.3519	2.5304	80.7428
11	5.1834	2.6989	78.0439
12	5.0036	2.8786	75.1652
13	4.8119	3.0704	72.0949
14	4.6074	3.2748	68.8200
15	4.3893	3.4930	65.3271
16	4.1567	3.7256	61.6015
17	3.9085	3.9737	57.6278
18	3.6439	4.2384	53.3894
19	3.3616	4.5207	48.8687
20	3.0605	4.8217	44.0470
21	2.7394	5.1429	38.9041
22	2.3969	5.4854	33.4187
23	2.0315	5.8507	27.5679
24	1.6418	6.2404	21.3275
25	1.2262	6.6560	14.6715
26	.7829	7.0993	7.5722
27	.3101	7.5722	0.0000

YEARS 28 — QTR PAYT 1.9447 — AN CONST 7.78

#	INT	PRIN	BALANCE
1	6.4685	1.3105	98.6895
2	6.3812	1.3978	97.2918
3	6.2881	1.4909	95.8009
4	6.1888	1.5901	94.2108
5	6.0829	1.6961	92.5147
6	5.9700	1.8090	90.7057
7	5.8495	1.9295	88.7762
8	5.7210	2.0580	86.7182
9	5.5839	2.1951	84.5231
10	5.4377	2.3413	82.1818
11	5.2818	2.4972	79.6846
12	5.1155	2.6635	77.0211
13	4.9381	2.8409	74.1802
14	4.7488	3.0301	71.1501
15	4.5470	3.2319	67.9182
16	4.3318	3.4472	64.4710
17	4.1022	3.6768	60.7942
18	3.8573	3.9216	56.8726
19	3.5961	4.1828	52.6897
20	3.3175	4.4614	48.2283
21	3.0204	4.7586	43.4698
22	2.7035	5.0755	38.3943
23	2.3654	5.4135	32.9807
24	2.0049	5.7741	27.2067
25	1.6203	6.1586	21.0480
26	1.2102	6.5688	14.4792
27	.7727	7.0063	7.4729
28	.3060	7.4729	0.0000

YEARS 29 — QTR PAYT 1.9211 — AN CONST 7.69

#	INT	PRIN	BALANCE
1	6.4708	1.2137	98.7863
2	6.3900	1.2946	97.4917
3	6.3038	1.3808	96.1109
4	6.2118	1.4728	94.6381
5	6.1137	1.5708	93.0673
6	6.0091	1.6755	91.3918
7	5.8975	1.7871	89.6048
8	5.7785	1.9061	87.6987
9	5.6515	2.0330	85.6657
10	5.5161	2.1684	83.4972
11	5.3717	2.3128	81.1844
12	5.2177	2.4669	78.7175
13	5.0534	2.6312	76.0863
14	4.8781	2.8064	73.2799
15	4.6912	2.9933	70.2865
16	4.4918	3.1927	67.0938
17	4.2792	3.4053	63.6885
18	4.0524	3.6321	60.0563
19	3.8105	3.8741	56.1823
20	3.5525	4.1321	52.0502
21	3.2773	4.4073	47.6429
22	2.9837	4.7008	42.9421
23	2.6707	5.0139	37.9283
24	2.3367	5.3478	32.5804
25	1.9806	5.7040	26.8765
26	1.6007	6.0839	20.7926
27	1.1955	6.4891	14.3035
28	.7633	6.9213	7.3822
29	.3023	7.3822	0.0000

YEARS 30 — QTR PAYT 1.8995 — AN CONST 7.60

#	INT	PRIN	BALANCE
1	6.4729	1.1251	98.8749
2	6.3980	1.2001	97.6748
3	6.3181	1.2800	96.3948
4	6.2328	1.3653	95.0295
5	6.1419	1.4562	93.5733
6	6.0449	1.5532	92.0201
7	5.9415	1.6566	90.3635
8	5.8311	1.7670	88.5966
9	5.7135	1.8846	86.7119
10	5.5879	2.0102	84.7018
11	5.4541	2.1440	82.5578
12	5.3113	2.2868	80.2709
13	5.1590	2.4391	77.8318
14	4.9965	2.6016	75.2302
15	4.8232	2.7749	72.4554
16	4.6384	2.9597	69.4957
17	4.4413	3.1568	66.3389
18	4.2311	3.3670	62.9719
19	4.0068	3.5913	59.3806
20	3.7676	3.8305	55.5502
21	3.5125	4.0856	51.4646
22	3.2404	4.3577	47.1069
23	2.9502	4.6479	42.4590
24	2.6406	4.9575	37.5015
25	2.3104	5.2876	32.2139
26	1.9583	5.6398	26.5741
27	1.5827	6.0154	20.5586
28	1.1820	6.4161	14.1426
29	.7547	6.8434	7.2992
30	.2989	7.2992	0.0000

QUARTERLY PAYMENT AMORTIZATION SCHEDULE PER $100

6.75 %

YEARS 2 — QTR PAYT 13.4677 — AN CONST 53.88

#	INT	PRIN	BALANCE
1	5.5438	48.3272	51.6728
2	2.1982	51.6728	0.0000

YEARS 3 — QTR PAYT 9.2754 — AN CONST 37.11

#	INT	PRIN	BALANCE
1	5.9730	31.1286	68.8714
2	3.8181	33.2836	35.5878
3	1.5139	35.5878	0.0000

YEARS 4 — QTR PAYT 7.1839 — AN CONST 28.74

#	INT	PRIN	BALANCE
1	6.1872	22.5486	77.4514
2	4.6262	24.1096	53.3419
3	2.9572	25.7786	27.5632
4	1.1726	27.5632	0.0000

YEARS 5 — QTR PAYT 5.9328 — AN CONST 23.74

#	INT	PRIN	BALANCE
1	6.3153	17.4159	82.5841
2	5.1096	18.6215	63.9626
3	3.8205	19.9107	44.0519
4	2.4421	21.2891	22.7628
5	.9683	22.7628	0.0000

YEARS 6 — QTR PAYT 5.1018 — AN CONST 20.41

#	INT	PRIN	BALANCE
1	6.4004	14.0068	85.9932
2	5.4307	14.9765	71.0167
3	4.3939	16.0133	55.0035
4	3.2854	17.1218	37.8816
5	2.1001	18.3071	19.5745
6	.8327	19.5745	0.0000

YEARS 7 — QTR PAYT 4.5109 — AN CONST 18.05

#	INT	PRIN	BALANCE
1	6.4609	11.5826	88.4174
2	5.6591	12.3845	76.0329
3	4.8017	13.2418	62.7911
4	3.8850	14.1585	48.6326
5	2.9048	15.1387	33.4939
6	1.8568	16.1867	17.3073
7	.7363	17.3073	0.0000

YEARS 8 — QTR PAYT 4.0700 — AN CONST 16.28

#	INT	PRIN	BALANCE
1	6.5060	9.7739	90.2261
2	5.8294	10.4505	79.7755
3	5.1060	11.1740	68.6015
4	4.3324	11.9476	56.6540
5	3.5053	12.7747	43.8793
6	2.6209	13.6590	30.2203
7	1.6753	14.6046	15.6157
8	.6643	15.6157	0.0000

YEARS 9 — QTR PAYT 3.7291 — AN CONST 14.92

#	INT	PRIN	BALANCE
1	6.5410	8.3755	91.6245
2	5.9611	8.9553	82.6692
3	5.3412	9.5753	73.0940
4	4.6783	10.2381	62.8558
5	3.9695	10.9469	51.9089
6	3.2117	11.7047	40.2042
7	2.4014	12.5150	27.6892
8	1.5350	13.3814	14.3078
9	.6087	14.3078	0.0000

YEARS 10 — QTR PAYT 3.4582 — AN CONST 13.84

#	INT	PRIN	BALANCE
1	6.5687	7.2642	92.7358
2	6.0658	7.7671	84.9687
3	5.5281	8.3048	76.6640
4	4.9532	8.8797	67.7843
5	4.3385	9.4944	58.2899
6	3.6812	10.1517	48.1382
7	2.9784	10.8545	37.2837
8	2.2270	11.6059	25.6778
9	1.4235	12.4094	13.2684
10	.5644	13.2684	0.0000

YEARS 11 — QTR PAYT 3.2382 — AN CONST 12.96

#	INT	PRIN	BALANCE
1	6.5912	6.3617	93.6383
2	6.1508	6.8021	86.8363
3	5.6799	7.2730	79.5633
4	5.1764	7.7764	71.7869
5	4.6381	8.3148	63.4721
6	4.0625	8.8904	54.5817
7	3.4470	9.5059	45.0758
8	2.7889	10.1639	34.9118
9	2.0853	10.8676	24.0443
10	1.3330	11.6199	12.4243
11	.5285	12.4243	0.0000

YEARS 12 — QTR PAYT 3.0564 — AN CONST 12.23

#	INT	PRIN	BALANCE
1	6.6098	5.6157	94.3843
2	6.2211	6.0044	88.3799
3	5.8054	6.4201	81.9599
4	5.3610	6.8645	75.0953
5	4.8857	7.3398	67.7556
6	4.3776	7.8479	59.9077
7	3.8343	8.3912	51.5165
8	3.2544	8.9721	42.5445
9	2.6323	9.5932	32.9513
10	1.9682	10.2573	22.6940
11	1.2581	10.9674	11.7266
12	.4989	11.7266	0.0000

YEARS 13 — QTR PAYT 2.9039 — AN CONST 11.62

#	INT	PRIN	BALANCE
1	6.6255	4.9900	95.0100
2	6.2800	5.3354	89.6746
3	5.9106	5.7048	83.9698
4	5.5157	6.0997	77.8701
5	5.0934	6.5220	71.3481
6	4.6419	6.9735	64.3746
7	4.1592	7.4563	56.9183
8	3.6430	7.9724	48.9459
9	3.0911	8.5244	40.4215
10	2.5010	9.1145	31.3070
11	1.8700	9.7455	21.5616
12	1.1953	10.4201	11.1415
13	.4740	11.1415	0.0000

YEARS 14 — QTR PAYT 2.7744 — AN CONST 11.10

#	INT	PRIN	BALANCE
1	6.6387	4.4588	95.5412
2	6.3300	4.7675	90.7737
3	6.0000	5.0975	85.6762
4	5.6471	5.4504	80.2257
5	5.2698	5.8277	74.3980
6	4.8663	6.2312	68.1668
7	4.4350	6.6626	61.5042
8	3.9737	7.1238	54.3804
9	3.4806	7.6170	46.7635
10	2.9533	8.1443	38.6192
11	2.3894	8.7081	29.9111
12	1.7866	9.3109	20.6002
13	1.1420	9.9555	10.6447
14	.4528	10.6447	0.0000

YEARS 15 — QTR PAYT 2.6633 — AN CONST 10.66

#	INT	PRIN	BALANCE
1	6.6501	4.0032	95.9968
2	6.3729	4.2803	91.7165
3	6.0766	4.5766	87.1398
4	5.7598	4.8935	82.2464
5	5.4210	5.2322	77.0141
6	5.0588	5.5945	71.4197
7	4.6715	5.9817	65.4379
8	4.2574	6.3958	59.0421
9	3.8147	6.8386	52.2035
10	3.3412	7.3120	44.8914
11	2.8350	7.8182	37.0732
12	2.2938	8.3595	28.7137
13	1.7151	8.9382	19.7755
14	1.0963	9.5570	10.2186
15	.4347	10.2186	0.0000

YEARS 16 — QTR PAYT 2.5672 — AN CONST 10.27

#	INT	PRIN	BALANCE
1	6.6599	3.6089	96.3911
2	6.4101	3.8587	92.5324
3	6.1430	4.1259	88.4065
4	5.8573	4.4115	83.9951
5	5.5519	4.7169	79.2782
6	5.2254	5.0434	74.2348
7	4.8763	5.3926	68.8422
8	4.5029	5.7659	63.0764
9	4.1038	6.1650	56.9113
10	3.6770	6.5918	50.3195
11	3.2206	7.0482	43.2714
12	2.7327	7.5361	35.7353
13	2.2110	8.0578	27.6775
14	1.6532	8.6156	19.0619
15	1.0567	9.2121	9.8498
16	.4190	9.8498	0.0000

YEARS 17 — QTR PAYT 2.4834 — AN CONST 9.94

#	INT	PRIN	BALANCE
1	6.6685	3.2650	96.7350
2	6.4425	3.4911	93.2439
3	6.2008	3.7327	89.5112
4	5.9424	3.9911	85.5201
5	5.6661	4.2674	81.2526
6	5.3707	4.5629	76.6898
7	5.0548	4.8787	71.8110
8	4.7170	5.2165	66.5945
9	4.3559	5.5776	61.0169
10	3.9698	5.9637	55.0532
11	3.5569	6.3766	48.6766
12	3.1155	6.8180	41.8585
13	2.6435	7.2900	34.5685
14	2.1388	7.7947	26.7738
15	1.5992	8.3343	18.4395
16	1.0222	8.9113	9.5282
17	.4053	9.5282	0.0000

YEARS 18 — QTR PAYT 2.4098 — AN CONST 9.64

#	INT	PRIN	BALANCE
1	6.6760	2.9631	97.0369
2	6.4709	3.1683	93.8686
3	6.2516	3.3876	90.4810
4	6.0171	3.6221	86.8588
5	5.7663	3.8729	82.9860
6	5.4982	4.1410	78.8450
7	5.2115	4.4277	74.4173
8	4.9050	4.7342	69.6831
9	4.5773	5.0619	64.6212
10	4.2268	5.4123	59.2089
11	3.8522	5.7870	53.4219
12	3.4515	6.1876	47.2342
13	3.0232	6.6160	40.6182
14	2.5652	7.0740	33.5442
15	2.0754	7.5637	25.9805
16	1.5518	8.0874	17.8931
17	.9920	8.6472	9.2459
18	.3933	9.2459	0.0000

YEARS 19 — QTR PAYT 2.3448 — AN CONST 9.38

#	INT	PRIN	BALANCE
1	6.6827	2.6966	97.3034
2	6.4960	2.8832	94.4202
3	6.2964	3.0828	91.3374
4	6.0830	3.2963	88.0411
5	5.8548	3.5245	84.5166
6	5.6108	3.7684	80.7482
7	5.3499	4.0293	76.7189
8	5.0710	4.3083	72.4106
9	4.7727	4.6065	67.8041
10	4.4538	4.9254	62.8787
11	4.1129	5.2664	57.6123
12	3.7483	5.6310	51.9813
13	3.3585	6.0208	45.9605
14	2.9417	6.4376	39.5229
15	2.4960	6.8833	32.6397
16	2.0195	7.3598	25.2799
17	1.5100	7.8693	17.4106
18	.9652	8.4141	8.9965
19	.3827	8.9965	0.0000

YEARS 20 — QTR PAYT 2.2871 — AN CONST 9.15

#	INT	PRIN	BALANCE
1	6.6886	2.4599	97.5401
2	6.5183	2.6302	94.9098
3	6.3362	2.8123	92.0975
4	6.1415	3.0070	89.0905
5	5.9334	3.2152	85.8753
6	5.7108	3.4378	82.4376
7	5.4728	3.6757	78.7619
8	5.2183	3.9302	74.8316
9	4.9462	4.2023	70.6294
10	4.6553	4.4932	66.1362
11	4.3443	4.8043	61.3319
12	4.0117	5.1368	56.1951
13	3.6561	5.4925	50.7026
14	3.2758	5.8727	44.8299
15	2.8693	6.2792	38.5507
16	2.4346	6.7139	31.8367
17	1.9698	7.1787	24.6580
18	1.4728	7.6757	16.9823
19	.9415	8.2071	8.7752
20	.3733	8.7752	0.0000

YEARS 21 — QTR PAYT 2.2357 — AN CONST 8.95

#	INT	PRIN	BALANCE
1	6.6939	2.2489	97.7511
2	6.5382	2.4046	95.3465
3	6.3717	2.5711	92.7754

#	INT	PRIN	BALANCE
4	6.1937	2.7491	90.0263
5	6.0034	2.9394	87.0869
6	5.7999	3.1429	83.9441
7	5.5824	3.3604	80.5836
8	5.3497	3.5931	76.9906
9	5.1010	3.8418	73.1487
10	4.8350	4.1078	69.0410
11	4.5506	4.3922	64.6488
12	4.2466	4.6962	59.9526
13	3.9215	5.0213	54.9313
14	3.5739	5.3689	49.5623
15	3.2022	5.7406	43.8217
16	2.8048	6.1380	37.6837
17	2.3798	6.5629	31.1208
18	1.9255	7.0173	24.1035
19	1.4397	7.5031	16.6004
20	.9203	8.0225	8.5779
21	.3649	8.5779	0.0000

YEARS 22	QTR PAYT 2.1896	AN CONST 8.76	
#	INT	PRIN	BALANCE
1	6.6986	2.0600	97.9400
2	6.5560	2.2026	95.7374
3	6.4035	2.3551	93.3823
4	6.2405	2.5181	90.8642
5	6.0661	2.6924	88.1718
6	5.8797	2.8788	85.2930
7	5.6804	3.0781	82.2148
8	5.4674	3.2912	78.9236
9	5.2395	3.5191	75.4046
10	4.9959	3.7627	71.6419
11	4.7354	4.0232	67.6187
12	4.4569	4.3017	63.3171
13	4.1591	4.5995	58.7176
14	3.8407	4.9179	53.7997
15	3.5002	5.2583	48.5414
16	3.1362	5.6224	42.9190
17	2.7470	6.0116	36.9074
18	2.3308	6.4278	30.4797
19	1.8858	6.8727	23.6069
20	1.4101	7.3485	16.2584
21	.9013	7.8572	8.4012
22	.3574	8.4012	0.0000

YEARS 23	QTR PAYT 2.1483	AN CONST 8.60	
#	INT	PRIN	BALANCE
1	6.7028	1.8902	98.1098
2	6.5720	2.0210	96.0888
3	6.4321	2.1610	93.9278
4	6.2825	2.3106	91.6172
5	6.1225	2.4705	89.1467
6	5.9515	2.6415	86.5052
7	5.7686	2.8244	83.6808
8	5.5731	3.0199	80.6608
9	5.3640	3.2290	77.4318
10	5.1405	3.4525	73.9793
11	4.9015	3.6916	70.2877
12	4.6459	3.9471	66.3406
13	4.3727	4.2204	62.1202
14	4.0805	4.5125	57.6077
15	3.7681	4.8249	52.7828
16	3.4341	5.1589	47.6238
17	3.0769	5.5161	42.1078
18	2.6951	5.8980	36.2098
19	2.2868	6.3063	29.9035
20	1.8502	6.7428	23.1607
21	1.3834	7.2096	15.9511
22	.8843	7.7087	8.2424
23	.3506	8.2424	0.0000

YEARS 24	QTR PAYT 2.1109	AN CONST 8.45	
#	INT	PRIN	BALANCE
1	6.7066	1.7371	98.2629
2	6.5864	1.8574	96.4055
3	6.4578	1.9859	94.4196
4	6.3203	2.1234	92.2962
5	6.1733	2.2704	90.0257
6	6.0161	2.4276	87.5981
7	5.8481	2.5957	85.0025
8	5.6684	2.7754	82.2271
9	5.4763	2.9675	79.2597
10	5.2708	3.1729	76.0867
11	5.0512	3.3926	72.6942
12	4.8163	3.6274	69.0667
13	4.5652	3.8785	65.1882
14	4.2967	4.1471	61.0411
15	4.0096	4.4341	56.6070
16	3.7026	4.7411	51.8659
17	3.3744	5.0693	46.7966
18	3.0235	5.4203	41.3763
19	2.6482	5.7955	35.5808
20	2.2470	6.1967	29.3841
21	1.8181	6.6257	22.7584
22	1.3594	7.0844	15.6740
23	.8689	7.5748	8.0992
24	.3445	8.0992	0.0000

YEARS 25	QTR PAYT 2.0772	AN CONST 8.31	
#	INT	PRIN	BALANCE
1	6.7101	1.5987	98.4013
2	6.5994	1.7093	96.6920
3	6.4811	1.8277	94.8643
4	6.3546	1.9542	92.9101
5	6.2193	2.0895	90.8207
6	6.0746	2.2341	88.5865
7	5.9200	2.3888	86.1977
8	5.7546	2.5542	83.6436
9	5.5778	2.7310	80.9126
10	5.3887	2.9200	77.9926
11	5.1866	3.1222	74.8704
12	4.9704	3.3383	71.5320
13	4.7393	3.5694	67.9626
14	4.4922	3.8165	64.1461
15	4.2280	4.0808	60.0653
16	3.9455	4.3633	55.7020
17	3.6434	4.6653	51.0367
18	3.3205	4.9883	46.0484
19	2.9751	5.3336	40.7148
20	2.6059	5.7028	35.0120
21	2.2111	6.0976	28.9143
22	1.7890	6.5198	22.3946
23	1.3376	6.9711	15.4234
24	.8550	7.4537	7.9697
25	.3390	7.9697	0.0000

YEARS 26	QTR PAYT 2.0466	AN CONST 8.19	
#	INT	PRIN	BALANCE
1	6.7132	1.4731	98.5269
2	6.6112	1.5751	96.9518
3	6.5022	1.6842	95.2676
4	6.3856	1.8007	93.4669
5	6.2610	1.9254	91.5415
6	6.1277	2.0587	89.4828
7	5.9851	2.2012	87.2815
8	5.8328	2.3536	84.9279
9	5.6698	2.5165	82.4114
10	5.4956	2.6908	79.7207
11	5.3093	2.8770	76.8436
12	5.1102	3.0762	73.7674
13	4.8972	3.2892	70.4783
14	4.6695	3.5169	66.9614
15	4.4260	3.7603	63.2011
16	4.1657	4.0206	59.1805
17	3.8874	4.2990	54.8815
18	3.5898	4.5966	50.2849
19	3.2716	4.9148	45.3701
20	2.9313	5.2550	40.1150
21	2.5675	5.6188	34.4962
22	2.1785	6.0078	28.4884
23	1.7626	6.4237	22.0647
24	1.3179	6.8684	15.1962
25	.8424	7.3439	7.8523
26	.3340	7.8523	0.0000

YEARS 27	QTR PAYT 2.0188	AN CONST 8.08	
#	INT	PRIN	BALANCE
1	6.7161	1.3590	98.6410
2	6.6220	1.4531	97.1879
3	6.5214	1.5537	95.6342
4	6.4138	1.6613	93.9729
5	6.2988	1.7763	92.1966
6	6.1759	1.8992	90.2974
7	6.0444	2.0307	88.2667
8	5.9038	2.1713	86.0954
9	5.7535	2.3216	83.7738
10	5.5928	2.4823	81.2914
11	5.4209	2.6542	78.6372
12	5.2372	2.8379	75.7993
13	5.0407	3.0344	72.7649
14	4.8307	3.2445	69.5205
15	4.6060	3.4691	66.0514
16	4.3659	3.7092	62.3422
17	4.1091	3.9660	58.3762
18	3.8346	4.2406	54.1356
19	3.5410	4.5341	49.6015
20	3.2271	4.8480	44.7535
21	2.8915	5.1836	39.5699
22	2.5326	5.5425	34.0274
23	2.1489	5.9262	28.1012
24	1.7387	6.3364	21.7648
25	1.3000	6.7751	14.9897
26	.8310	7.2441	7.7456
27	.3295	7.7456	0.0000

YEARS 28	QTR PAYT 1.9934	AN CONST 7.98	
#	INT	PRIN	BALANCE
1	6.7187	1.2551	98.7449
2	6.6318	1.3420	97.4029
3	6.5389	1.4349	95.9681
4	6.4396	1.5342	94.4339
5	6.3333	1.6404	92.7935
6	6.2198	1.7540	91.0395
7	6.0984	1.8754	89.1641
8	5.9685	2.0052	87.1588
9	5.8297	2.1440	85.0148
10	5.6813	2.2925	82.7223
11	5.5226	2.4512	80.2711
12	5.3529	2.6209	77.6503
13	5.1714	2.8023	74.8480
14	4.9775	2.9963	71.8517
15	4.7700	3.2037	68.6479
16	4.5482	3.4255	65.2224
17	4.3111	3.6627	61.5597
18	4.0575	3.9162	57.6435
19	3.7864	4.1873	53.4562
20	3.4965	4.4772	48.9790
21	3.1866	4.7872	44.1918
22	2.8552	5.1186	39.0732
23	2.5008	5.4729	33.6003
24	2.1220	5.8518	27.7485
25	1.7169	6.2569	21.4916
26	1.2837	6.6901	14.8016
27	.8206	7.1532	7.6484
28	.3254	7.6484	0.0000

YEARS 29	QTR PAYT 1.9703	AN CONST 7.89	
#	INT	PRIN	BALANCE
1	6.7210	1.1602	98.8398
2	6.6407	1.2405	97.5993
3	6.5548	1.3264	96.2729
4	6.4630	1.4182	94.8547
5	6.3648	1.5164	93.3382
6	6.2599	1.6214	91.7169
7	6.1476	1.7336	89.9832
8	6.0276	1.8536	88.1296
9	5.8993	1.9820	86.1476
10	5.7621	2.1192	84.0285
11	5.6154	2.2659	81.7626
12	5.4585	2.4227	79.3398
13	5.2908	2.5905	76.7494
14	5.1114	2.7698	73.9796
15	4.9197	2.9615	71.0180
16	4.7147	3.1666	67.8515
17	4.4955	3.3858	64.4657
18	4.2611	3.6202	60.8455
19	4.0105	3.8708	56.9747
20	3.7425	4.1388	52.8360
21	3.4560	4.4253	48.4107
22	3.1496	4.7316	43.6791
23	2.8221	5.0592	38.6199
24	2.4718	5.4094	33.2105
25	2.0973	5.7839	27.4266
26	1.6969	6.1843	21.2423
27	1.2688	6.6124	14.6299
28	.8110	7.0702	7.5597
29	.3216	7.5597	0.0000

YEARS 30	QTR PAYT 1.9492	AN CONST 7.80	
#	INT	PRIN	BALANCE
1	6.7232	1.0734	98.9266
2	6.6489	1.1477	97.7788
3	6.5694	1.2272	96.5516
4	6.4845	1.3122	95.2394
5	6.3936	1.4030	93.8364
6	6.2965	1.5001	92.3363
7	6.1927	1.6040	90.7323
8	6.0816	1.7150	89.0173
9	5.9629	1.8337	87.1836
10	5.8360	1.9607	85.2229
11	5.7002	2.0964	83.1265
12	5.5551	2.2416	80.8849
13	5.3999	2.3967	78.4882
14	5.2340	2.5627	75.9255
15	5.0566	2.7401	73.1854
16	4.8669	2.9298	70.2557
17	4.6641	3.1326	67.1231
18	4.4472	3.3494	63.7737
19	4.2153	3.5813	60.1924
20	3.9674	3.8292	56.3631
21	3.7023	4.0943	52.2688
22	3.4189	4.3778	47.8911
23	3.1158	4.6808	43.2102
24	2.7918	5.0049	38.2054
25	2.4453	5.3514	32.8540
26	2.0748	5.7218	27.1322
27	1.6787	6.1179	21.0143
28	1.2552	6.5415	14.4728
29	.8023	6.9943	7.4785
30	.3181	7.4785	0.0000

YEARS 2 — QTR PAYT 13.5043 — AN CONST 54.02

#	INT	PRIN	BALANCE
1	5.7513	48.2658	51.7342
2	2.2830	51.7342	0.0000

YEARS 3 — QTR PAYT 9.3114 — AN CONST 37.25

#	INT	PRIN	BALANCE
1	6.1968	31.0488	68.9512
2	3.9656	33.2799	35.6714
3	1.5742	35.6714	0.0000

YEARS 4 — QTR PAYT 7.2200 — AN CONST 28.88

#	INT	PRIN	BALANCE
1	6.4189	22.4609	77.5391
2	4.8049	24.0749	53.4642
3	3.0749	25.8049	27.6592
4	1.2206	27.6592	0.0000

YEARS 5 — QTR PAYT 5.9691 — AN CONST 23.88

#	INT	PRIN	BALANCE
1	6.5518	17.3247	82.6753
2	5.3069	18.5696	64.1057
3	3.9725	19.9040	44.2017
4	2.5422	21.3343	22.8674
5	1.0091	22.8674	0.0000

YEARS 6 — QTR PAYT 5.1386 — AN CONST 20.56

#	INT	PRIN	BALANCE
1	6.6400	13.9142	86.0858
2	5.6402	14.9141	71.1717
3	4.5685	15.9858	55.1859
4	3.4197	17.1345	38.0513
5	2.1885	18.3658	19.6855
6	.8687	19.6855	0.0000

YEARS 7 — QTR PAYT 4.5482 — AN CONST 18.20

#	INT	PRIN	BALANCE
1	6.7028	11.4899	88.5101
2	5.8771	12.3155	76.1946
3	4.9921	13.2005	62.9942
4	4.0435	14.1491	48.8451
5	3.0268	15.1658	33.6793
6	1.9370	16.2556	17.4237
7	.7689	17.4237	0.0000

YEARS 8 — QTR PAYT 4.1078 — AN CONST 16.44

#	INT	PRIN	BALANCE
1	6.7495	9.6817	90.3183
2	6.0538	10.3774	79.9408
3	5.3081	11.1232	68.8177
4	4.5088	11.9225	56.8952
5	3.6521	12.7792	44.1161
6	2.7338	13.6975	30.4186
7	1.7495	14.6818	15.7368
8	.6945	15.7368	0.0000

YEARS 9 — QTR PAYT 3.7675 — AN CONST 15.08

#	INT	PRIN	BALANCE
1	6.7857	8.2843	91.7157
2	6.1904	8.8797	82.8360
3	5.5523	9.5177	73.3183
4	4.8684	10.2017	63.1166
5	4.1353	10.9348	52.1818
6	3.3495	11.7205	40.4613
7	2.5073	12.5627	27.8986
8	1.6045	13.4655	14.4331
9	.6369	14.4331	0.0000

YEARS 10 — QTR PAYT 3.4972 — AN CONST 13.99

#	INT	PRIN	BALANCE
1	6.8144	7.1744	92.8256
2	6.2988	7.6900	85.1356
3	5.7462	8.2426	76.8930
4	5.1539	8.8349	68.0581
5	4.5191	9.4698	58.5883
6	3.8386	10.1502	48.4381
7	3.1092	10.8796	37.5585
8	2.3274	11.6614	25.8970
9	1.4894	12.4994	13.3976
10	.5912	13.3976	0.0000

YEARS 11 — QTR PAYT 3.2778 — AN CONST 13.12

#	INT	PRIN	BALANCE
1	6.8377	6.2735	93.7265
2	6.3869	6.7244	87.0021
3	5.9037	7.2076	79.7946
4	5.3858	7.7255	72.0691
5	4.8306	8.2806	63.7884
6	4.2356	8.8757	54.9128
7	3.5978	9.5135	45.3993
8	2.9141	10.1971	35.2022
9	2.1814	10.9298	24.2724
10	1.3960	11.7153	12.5571
11	.5541	12.5571	0.0000

YEARS 12 — QTR PAYT 3.0966 — AN CONST 12.39

#	INT	PRIN	BALANCE
1	6.8570	5.5293	94.4707
2	6.4596	5.9267	88.5440
3	6.0337	6.3525	82.1915
4	5.5773	6.8090	75.3825
5	5.0880	7.2983	68.0841
6	4.5635	7.8228	60.2614
7	4.0014	8.3849	51.8765
8	3.3988	8.9874	42.8890
9	2.7530	9.6333	33.2558
10	2.0608	10.3255	22.9303
11	1.3188	11.0675	11.8628
12	.5235	11.8628	0.0000

YEARS 13 — QTR PAYT 2.9447 — AN CONST 11.78

#	INT	PRIN	BALANCE
1	6.8731	4.9056	95.0944
2	6.5206	5.2581	89.8364
3	6.1427	5.6359	84.2004
4	5.7377	6.0409	78.1595
5	5.3037	6.4750	71.6845
6	4.8384	6.9403	64.7442
7	4.3396	7.4390	57.3052
8	3.8051	7.9736	49.3316
9	3.2321	8.5466	40.7851
10	2.6180	9.1607	31.6244
11	1.9597	9.8190	21.8054
12	1.2541	10.5246	11.2808
13	.4978	11.2808	0.0000

YEARS 14 — QTR PAYT 2.8158 — AN CONST 11.27

#	INT	PRIN	BALANCE
1	6.8868	4.3764	95.6236
2	6.5723	4.6909	90.9327
3	6.2352	5.0280	85.9048
4	5.8739	5.3893	80.5155
5	5.4866	5.7765	74.7389
6	5.0715	6.1916	68.5473
7	4.6266	6.6366	61.9108
8	4.1497	7.1135	54.7973
9	3.6386	7.6246	47.1727
10	3.0907	8.1725	39.0002
11	2.5034	8.7598	30.2404
12	1.8739	9.3893	20.8511
13	1.1992	10.0640	10.7871
14	.4760	10.7871	0.0000

YEARS 15 — QTR PAYT 2.7053 — AN CONST 10.83

#	INT	PRIN	BALANCE
1	6.8985	3.9228	96.0772
2	6.6166	4.2047	91.8725
3	6.3145	4.5069	87.3656
4	5.9906	4.8307	82.5349
5	5.6435	5.1779	77.3570
6	5.2714	5.5499	71.8071
7	4.8726	5.9487	65.8583
8	4.4451	6.3762	59.4821
9	3.9869	6.8344	52.6477
10	3.4958	7.3255	45.3222
11	2.9694	7.8519	37.4702
12	2.4052	8.4162	29.0541
13	1.8004	9.0209	20.0332
14	1.1522	9.6692	10.3640
15	.4574	10.3640	0.0000

YEARS 16 — QTR PAYT 2.6098 — AN CONST 10.44

#	INT	PRIN	BALANCE
1	6.9087	3.5306	96.4694
2	6.6550	3.7843	92.6850
3	6.3830	4.0563	88.6288
4	6.0915	4.3477	84.2810
5	5.7791	4.6602	79.6209
6	5.4442	4.9950	74.6258
7	5.0853	5.3540	69.2718
8	4.7006	5.7387	63.5331
9	4.2882	6.1511	57.3820
10	3.8462	6.5931	50.7889
11	3.3724	7.0669	43.7220
12	2.8646	7.5747	36.1473
13	2.3203	8.1190	28.0283
14	1.7368	8.7024	19.3259
15	1.1115	9.3278	9.9981
16	.4412	9.9981	0.0000

YEARS 17 — QTR PAYT 2.5266 — AN CONST 10.11

#	INT	PRIN	BALANCE
1	6.9175	3.1889	96.8111
2	6.6884	3.4180	93.3931
3	6.4427	3.6637	89.7294
4	6.1795	3.9269	85.8025
5	5.8973	4.2091	81.5934
6	5.5948	4.5116	77.0818
7	5.2706	4.8358	72.2461
8	4.9231	5.1833	67.0628
9	4.5507	5.5557	61.5071
10	4.1514	5.9549	55.5522
11	3.7235	6.3829	49.1693
12	3.2649	6.8415	42.3278
13	2.7732	7.3332	34.9946
14	2.2463	7.8601	27.1345
15	1.6815	8.4249	18.7096
16	1.0761	9.0303	9.6792
17	.4271	9.6792	0.0000

YEARS 18 — QTR PAYT 2.4536 — AN CONST 9.82

#	INT	PRIN	BALANCE
1	6.9253	2.8891	97.1109
2	6.7176	3.0968	94.0141
3	6.4951	3.3193	90.6948
4	6.2566	3.5578	87.1370
5	6.0009	3.8135	83.3236
6	5.7269	4.0875	79.2361
7	5.4332	4.3812	74.8548
8	5.1183	4.6960	70.1588
9	4.7809	5.0335	65.1253
10	4.4192	5.3952	59.7301
11	4.0315	5.7829	53.9472
12	3.6159	6.1985	47.7487
13	3.1705	6.6439	41.1049
14	2.6931	7.1213	33.9836
15	2.1814	7.6330	26.3506
16	1.6329	8.1815	18.1690
17	1.0450	8.7694	9.3996
18	.4148	9.3996	0.0000

YEARS 19 — QTR PAYT 2.3892 — AN CONST 9.56

#	INT	PRIN	BALANCE
1	6.9321	2.6247	97.3753
2	6.7435	2.8133	94.5620
3	6.5413	3.0155	91.5465
4	6.3246	3.2322	88.3144
5	6.0924	3.4644	84.8499
6	5.8434	3.7134	81.1366
7	5.5766	3.9802	77.1563
8	5.2906	4.2662	72.8901
9	4.9840	4.5728	68.3173
10	4.6554	4.9014	63.4159
11	4.3032	5.2536	58.1623
12	3.9257	5.6311	52.5312
13	3.5210	6.0358	46.4955
14	3.0873	6.4695	40.0260
15	2.6224	6.9344	33.0916
16	2.1241	7.4327	25.6589
17	1.5900	7.9668	17.6922
18	1.0175	8.5393	9.1529
19	.4039	9.1529	0.0000

YEARS 20 — QTR PAYT 2.3321 — AN CONST 9.33

#	INT	PRIN	BALANCE
1	6.9382	2.3902	97.6098
2	6.7664	2.5620	95.0478
3	6.5823	2.7461	92.3018
4	6.3850	2.9434	89.3584
5	6.1735	3.1549	86.2035
6	5.9468	3.3816	82.8218
7	5.7038	3.6246	79.1972
8	5.4433	3.8851	75.3122
9	5.1641	4.1643	71.1479
10	4.8649	4.4635	66.6844
11	4.5441	4.7842	61.9002
12	4.2003	5.1280	56.7721
13	3.8319	5.4965	51.2756
14	3.4369	5.8915	45.3841
15	3.0135	6.3149	39.0693
16	2.5597	6.7686	32.3006
17	2.0734	7.2550	25.0456
18	1.5520	7.7764	17.2693
19	.9932	8.3352	8.9341
20	.3943	8.9341	0.0000

YEARS 21 — QTR PAYT 2.2812 — AN CONST 9.13

#	INT	PRIN	BALANCE
1	6.9436	2.1813	97.8187
2	6.7868	2.3381	95.4806
3	6.6188	2.5061	92.9745

#	INT	PRIN	BALANCE
4	6.4387	2.6862	90.2884
5	6.2457	2.8792	87.4092
6	6.0388	3.0861	84.3231
7	5.8170	3.3079	81.0152
8	5.5793	3.5455	77.4697
9	5.3246	3.8003	73.6694
10	5.0515	4.0734	69.5959
11	4.7588	4.3661	65.2298
12	4.4450	4.6799	60.5499
13	4.1087	5.0162	55.5338
14	3.7483	5.3766	50.1571
15	3.3619	5.7630	44.3942
16	2.9478	6.1771	38.2171
17	2.5039	6.6210	31.5961
18	2.0281	7.0968	24.4993
19	1.5182	7.6067	16.8926
20	.9715	8.1533	8.7392
21	.3857	8.7392	0.0000

YEARS 22	QTR PAYT 2.2357	AN CONST 8.95	
#	INT	PRIN	BALANCE
1	6.9484	1.9945	98.0055
2	6.8051	2.1378	95.8677
3	6.6515	2.2914	93.5763
4	6.4868	2.4561	91.1202
5	6.3103	2.6326	88.4876
6	6.1211	2.8218	85.6658
7	5.9184	3.0245	82.6413
8	5.7010	3.2419	79.3994
9	5.4681	3.4748	75.9246
10	5.2184	3.7245	72.2000
11	4.9507	3.9922	68.2078
12	4.6638	4.2790	63.9288
13	4.3564	4.5865	59.3423
14	4.0268	4.9161	54.4261
15	3.6735	5.2694	49.1568
16	3.2949	5.6480	43.5087
17	2.8890	6.0539	37.4548
18	2.4540	6.4889	30.9659
19	1.9877	6.9552	24.0107
20	1.4879	7.4550	16.5557
21	.9522	7.9907	8.5649
22	.3780	8.5649	0.0000

YEARS 23	QTR PAYT 2.1949	AN CONST 8.78	
#	INT	PRIN	BALANCE
1	6.9527	1.8268	98.1732
2	6.8215	1.9581	96.2152
3	6.6808	2.0988	94.1164
4	6.5299	2.2496	91.8668
5	6.3683	2.4112	89.4556
6	6.1950	2.5845	86.8711
7	6.0093	2.7702	84.1009
8	5.8102	2.9693	81.1316
9	5.5969	3.1827	77.9489
10	5.3682	3.4114	74.5376
11	5.1230	3.6565	70.8811
12	4.8603	3.9192	66.9618
13	4.5786	4.2009	62.7610
14	4.2768	4.5027	58.2582
15	3.9532	4.8263	53.4319
16	3.6064	5.1731	48.2588
17	3.2347	5.5449	42.7139
18	2.8362	5.9433	36.7706
19	2.4091	6.3704	30.4002
20	1.9514	6.8282	23.5720
21	1.4607	7.3188	16.2532
22	.9348	7.8448	8.4085
23	.3711	8.4085	0.0000

YEARS 24	QTR PAYT 2.1581	AN CONST 8.64	
#	INT	PRIN	BALANCE
1	6.9566	1.6758	98.3242
2	6.8362	1.7962	96.5281
3	6.7072	1.9252	94.6028
4	6.5688	2.0636	92.5392
5	6.4205	2.2119	90.3273
6	6.2616	2.3708	87.9565
7	6.0912	2.5412	85.4153
8	5.9086	2.7238	82.6915
9	5.7129	2.9195	79.7720
10	5.5031	3.1293	76.6427
11	5.2782	3.3542	73.2885
12	5.0372	3.5952	69.6933
13	4.7788	3.8536	65.8397
14	4.5019	4.1305	61.7092
15	4.2051	4.4273	57.2819
16	3.8870	4.7454	52.5365
17	3.5460	5.0864	47.4501
18	3.1805	5.4519	41.9981
19	2.7887	5.8437	36.1544
20	2.3688	6.2636	29.8908
21	1.9187	6.7137	23.1770
22	1.4362	7.1962	15.9809
23	.9191	7.7133	8.2676
24	.3648	8.2676	0.0000

YEARS 25	QTR PAYT 2.1249	AN CONST 8.50	
#	INT	PRIN	BALANCE
1	6.9602	1.5393	98.4607
2	6.8496	1.6500	96.8107
3	6.7310	1.7685	95.0422
4	6.6039	1.8956	93.1466
5	6.4677	2.0318	91.1147
6	6.3217	2.1778	88.9369
7	6.1652	2.3343	86.6026
8	5.9975	2.5021	84.1005
9	5.8177	2.6819	81.4186
10	5.6249	2.8746	78.5440
11	5.4184	3.0811	75.4629
12	5.1970	3.3026	72.1603
13	4.9596	3.5399	68.6205
14	4.7053	3.7942	64.8262
15	4.4326	4.0669	60.7593
16	4.1404	4.3591	56.4002
17	3.8271	4.6724	51.7278
18	3.4914	5.0081	46.7196
19	3.1315	5.3680	41.3516
20	2.7458	5.7538	35.5979
21	2.3323	6.1672	29.4306
22	1.8891	6.6104	22.8203
23	1.4141	7.0854	15.7349
24	.9050	7.5946	8.1403
25	.3592	8.1403	0.0000

YEARS 26	QTR PAYT 2.0948	AN CONST 8.38	
#	INT	PRIN	BALANCE
1	6.9634	1.4158	98.5842
2	6.8616	1.5176	97.0666
3	6.7526	1.6266	95.4400
4	6.6357	1.7435	93.6965
5	6.5104	1.8688	91.8278
6	6.3761	2.0031	89.8247
7	6.2322	2.1470	87.6777
8	6.0779	2.3013	85.3764
9	5.9125	2.4666	82.9098
10	5.7353	2.6439	80.2659
11	5.5453	2.8339	77.4320
12	5.3417	3.0375	74.3945
13	5.1234	3.2558	71.1387
14	4.8894	3.4898	67.6489
15	4.6387	3.7405	63.9084

#	INT	PRIN	BALANCE
16	4.3699	4.0093	59.8991
17	4.0818	4.2974	55.6017
18	3.7730	4.6062	50.9954
19	3.4420	4.9372	46.0582
20	3.0872	5.2920	40.7662
21	2.7069	5.6723	35.0939
22	2.2993	6.0799	29.0140
23	1.8624	6.5168	22.4972
24	1.3941	6.9851	15.5121
25	.8922	7.4870	8.0250
26	.3541	8.0250	0.0000

YEARS 27	QTR PAYT 2.0675	AN CONST 8.27	
#	INT	PRIN	BALANCE
1	6.9663	1.3037	98.6963
2	6.8726	1.3974	97.2990
3	6.7722	1.4978	95.8012
4	6.6646	1.6054	94.1958
5	6.5492	1.7208	92.4751
6	6.4255	1.8444	90.6306
7	6.2930	1.9769	88.6537
8	6.1509	2.1190	86.5347
9	5.9987	2.2713	84.2634
10	5.8355	2.4345	81.8289
11	5.6605	2.6094	79.2195
12	5.4730	2.7969	76.4226
13	5.2720	2.9979	73.4246
14	5.0566	3.2134	70.2113
15	4.8257	3.4443	66.7670
16	4.5782	3.6918	63.0752
17	4.3129	3.9571	59.1182
18	4.0285	4.2414	54.8768
19	3.7238	4.5462	50.3306
20	3.3971	4.8729	45.4577
21	3.0469	5.2230	40.2347
22	2.6716	5.5983	34.6364
23	2.2693	6.0006	28.6357
24	1.8381	6.4318	22.2039
25	1.3759	6.8940	15.3098
26	.8805	7.3894	7.9204
27	.3495	7.9204	0.0000

YEARS 28	QTR PAYT 2.0426	AN CONST 8.18	
#	INT	PRIN	BALANCE
1	6.9689	1.2017	98.7983
2	6.8826	1.2880	97.5103
3	6.7900	1.3806	96.1298
4	6.6908	1.4798	94.6500
5	6.5845	1.5861	93.0639
6	6.4705	1.7001	91.3638
7	6.3483	1.8222	89.5416
8	6.2174	1.9532	87.5884
9	6.0770	2.0935	85.4948
10	5.9266	2.2440	83.2509
11	5.7653	2.4052	80.8456
12	5.5925	2.5781	78.2675
13	5.4072	2.7633	75.5042
14	5.2087	2.9619	72.5423
15	4.9958	3.1747	69.3676
16	4.7677	3.4029	65.9647
17	4.5232	3.6474	62.3173
18	4.2611	3.9095	58.4078
19	3.9801	4.1904	54.2174
20	3.6790	4.4916	49.7258
21	3.3563	4.8143	44.9115
22	3.0103	5.1603	39.7512
23	2.6395	5.5311	34.2201
24	2.2420	5.9285	28.2916
25	1.8160	6.3546	21.9371
26	1.3594	6.8112	15.1259
27	.8699	7.3006	7.8252

#	INT	PRIN	BALANCE
28	.3453	7.8252	0.0000

YEARS 29	QTR PAYT 2.0200	AN CONST 8.08	
#	INT	PRIN	BALANCE
1	6.9713	1.1087	98.8913
2	6.8917	1.1883	97.7030
3	6.8063	1.2737	96.4293
4	6.7147	1.3653	95.0640
5	6.6166	1.4634	93.6006
6	6.5115	1.5685	92.0321
7	6.3988	1.6812	90.3509
8	6.2779	1.8020	88.5489
9	6.1484	1.9315	86.6173
10	6.0097	2.0703	84.5470
11	5.8609	2.2191	82.3279
12	5.7014	2.3786	79.9493
13	5.5305	2.5495	77.3998
14	5.3473	2.7327	74.6671
15	5.1509	2.9291	71.7381
16	4.9404	3.1395	68.5985
17	4.7148	3.3651	65.2334
18	4.4730	3.6070	61.6264
19	4.2138	3.8662	57.7602
20	3.9360	4.1440	53.6163
21	3.6382	4.4418	49.1745
22	3.3190	4.7609	44.4136
23	2.9769	5.1031	39.3105
24	2.6102	5.4698	33.8408
25	2.2172	5.8628	27.9780
26	1.7959	6.2841	21.6939
27	1.3443	6.7357	14.9582
28	.8603	7.2197	7.7385
29	.3415	7.7385	0.0000

YEARS 30	QTR PAYT 1.9993	AN CONST 8.00	
#	INT	PRIN	BALANCE
1	6.9735	1.0238	98.9762
2	6.8999	1.0973	97.8789
3	6.8211	1.1762	96.7028
4	6.7366	1.2607	95.4421
5	6.6460	1.3513	94.0908
6	6.5489	1.4484	92.6424
7	6.4448	1.5525	91.0899
8	6.3332	1.6640	89.4259
9	6.2137	1.7836	87.6423
10	6.0855	1.9118	85.7306
11	5.9481	2.0491	83.6814
12	5.8009	2.1964	81.4850
13	5.6430	2.3542	79.1308
14	5.4739	2.5234	76.6074
15	5.2925	2.7047	73.9027
16	5.0982	2.8991	71.0036
17	4.8899	3.1074	67.8962
18	4.6666	3.3307	64.5655
19	4.4272	3.5700	60.9955
20	4.1707	3.8266	57.1689
21	3.8957	4.1016	53.0674
22	3.6010	4.3963	48.6711
23	3.2851	4.7122	43.9589
24	2.9465	5.0508	38.9081
25	2.5835	5.4138	33.4943
26	2.1945	5.8028	27.6915
27	1.7775	6.2198	21.4718
28	1.3306	6.6667	14.8050
29	.8515	7.1458	7.6593
30	.3380	7.6593	0.0000

YEARS 2 — QTR PAYT 13.5409 — AN CONST 54.17

#	INT	PRIN	BALANCE
1	5.9591	48.2045	51.7955
2	2.3681	51.7955	0.0000

YEARS 3 — QTR PAYT 9.3474 — AN CONST 37.39

#	INT	PRIN	BALANCE
1	6.4206	30.9690	69.0310
2	4.1136	33.2760	35.7549
3	1.6347	35.7549	0.0000

YEARS 4 — QTR PAYT 7.2561 — AN CONST 29.03

#	INT	PRIN	BALANCE
1	6.6508	22.3735	77.6265
2	4.9841	24.0402	53.5864
3	3.1932	25.8310	27.7553
4	1.2690	27.7553	0.0000

YEARS 5 — QTR PAYT 6.0056 — AN CONST 24.03

#	INT	PRIN	BALANCE
1	6.7885	17.2338	82.7662
2	5.5046	18.5177	64.2485
3	4.1252	19.8971	44.3514
4	2.6429	21.3794	22.9720
5	1.0503	22.9720	0.0000

YEARS 6 — QTR PAYT 5.1755 — AN CONST 20.71

#	INT	PRIN	BALANCE
1	6.8798	13.8221	86.1779
2	5.8502	14.8518	71.3262
3	4.7438	15.9581	55.3680
4	3.5550	17.1469	38.2211
5	2.2776	18.4243	19.7968
6	.9051	19.7968	0.0000

YEARS 7 — QTR PAYT 4.5856 — AN CONST 18.35

#	INT	PRIN	BALANCE
1	6.9448	11.3976	88.6024
2	6.0957	12.2467	76.3557
3	5.1834	13.1590	63.1967
4	4.2031	14.1393	49.0574
5	3.1498	15.1926	33.8648
6	2.0180	16.3244	17.5404
7	.8019	17.5404	0.0000

YEARS 8 — QTR PAYT 4.1458 — AN CONST 16.59

#	INT	PRIN	BALANCE
1	6.9932	9.5902	90.4098
2	6.2788	10.3046	80.1053
3	5.5111	11.0722	69.0331
4	4.6863	11.8970	57.1360
5	3.8000	12.7833	44.3527
6	2.8477	13.7356	30.6171
7	1.8245	14.7588	15.8583
8	.7250	15.8583	0.0000

YEARS 9 — QTR PAYT 3.8061 — AN CONST 15.23

#	INT	PRIN	BALANCE
1	7.0306	8.1939	91.8061
2	6.4202	8.8043	83.0017
3	5.7643	9.4602	73.5415
4	5.0595	10.1650	63.3765
5	4.3023	10.9222	52.4543
6	3.4886	11.7358	40.7185
7	2.6144	12.6101	28.1084
8	1.6750	13.5495	14.5589
9	.6656	14.5589	0.0000

YEARS 10 — QTR PAYT 3.5364 — AN CONST 14.15

#	INT	PRIN	BALANCE
1	7.0602	7.0855	92.9145
2	6.5324	7.6134	85.3011
3	5.9653	8.1805	77.1206
4	5.3558	8.7899	68.3307
5	4.7010	9.4447	58.8860
6	3.9975	10.1483	48.7377
7	3.2415	10.9043	37.8334
8	2.4291	11.7166	26.1168
9	1.5563	12.5895	13.5273
10	.6185	13.5273	0.0000

YEARS 11 — QTR PAYT 3.3177 — AN CONST 13.28

#	INT	PRIN	BALANCE
1	7.0843	6.1863	93.8137
2	6.6235	6.6472	87.1665
3	6.1283	7.1424	80.0241
4	5.5962	7.6744	72.3497
5	5.0245	8.2461	64.1035
6	4.4102	8.8604	55.2431
7	3.7502	9.5205	45.7226
8	3.0409	10.2297	35.4929
9	2.2789	10.9918	24.5011
10	1.4600	11.8106	12.6905
11	.5802	12.6905	0.0000

YEARS 12 — QTR PAYT 3.1371 — AN CONST 12.55

#	INT	PRIN	BALANCE
1	7.1042	5.4440	94.5560
2	6.6987	5.8495	88.7065
3	6.2629	6.2853	82.4211
4	5.7947	6.7535	75.6676
5	5.2916	7.2566	68.4110
6	4.7510	7.7972	60.6137
7	4.1701	8.3781	52.2357
8	3.5460	9.0022	43.2335
9	2.8754	9.6728	33.5606
10	2.1548	10.3934	23.1672
11	1.3805	11.1677	11.9996
12	.5486	11.9996	0.0000

YEARS 13 — QTR PAYT 2.9858 — AN CONST 11.95

#	INT	PRIN	BALANCE
1	7.1209	4.8222	95.1778
2	6.7616	5.1815	89.9963
3	6.3756	5.5675	84.4288
4	5.9609	5.9822	78.4466
5	5.5152	6.4279	72.0187
6	5.0364	6.9067	65.1120
7	4.5219	7.4212	57.6908
8	3.9690	7.9741	49.7167
9	3.3750	8.5681	41.1486
10	2.7367	9.2064	31.9423
11	2.0509	9.8922	22.0501
12	1.3140	10.6291	11.4209
13	.5222	11.4209	0.0000

YEARS 14 — QTR PAYT 2.8575 — AN CONST 11.44

#	INT	PRIN	BALANCE
1	7.1350	4.2952	95.7048
2	6.8150	4.6151	91.0897
3	6.4712	4.9589	86.1308
4	6.1018	5.3283	80.8025
5	5.7049	5.7253	75.0772
6	5.2783	6.1518	68.9254
7	4.8201	6.6101	62.3154
8	4.3277	7.1025	55.2129
9	3.7986	7.6316	47.5813
10	3.2300	8.2001	39.3812
11	2.6192	8.8109	30.5703
12	1.9628	9.4673	21.1030
13	1.2575	10.1726	10.9304
14	.4997	10.9304	0.0000

YEARS 15 — QTR PAYT 2.7477 — AN CONST 11.00

#	INT	PRIN	BALANCE
1	7.1471	3.8437	96.1563
2	6.8607	4.1301	92.0262
3	6.5531	4.4377	87.5885
4	6.2225	4.7683	82.8202
5	5.8673	5.1235	77.6966
6	5.4856	5.5052	72.1914
7	5.0755	5.9153	66.2761
8	4.6348	6.3560	59.9201
9	4.1613	6.8295	53.0907
10	3.6526	7.3382	45.7524
11	3.1059	7.8849	37.8675
12	2.5185	8.4723	29.3953
13	1.8874	9.1034	20.2918
14	1.2092	9.7816	10.5103
15	.4805	10.5103	0.0000

YEARS 16 — QTR PAYT 2.6528 — AN CONST 10.62

#	INT	PRIN	BALANCE
1	7.1575	3.4537	96.5463
2	6.9002	3.7110	92.8353
3	6.6238	3.9874	88.8479
4	6.3267	4.2845	84.5635
5	6.0076	4.6036	79.9598
6	5.6646	4.9466	75.0132
7	5.2961	5.3151	69.6982
8	4.9002	5.7110	63.9871
9	4.4747	6.1365	57.8507
10	4.0176	6.5936	51.2571
11	3.5264	7.0848	44.1723
12	2.9986	7.6126	36.5597
13	2.4315	8.1797	28.3800
14	1.8222	8.7890	19.5910
15	1.1674	9.4438	10.1473
16	.4639	10.1473	0.0000

YEARS 17 — QTR PAYT 2.5702 — AN CONST 10.29

#	INT	PRIN	BALANCE
1	7.1666	3.1141	96.8859
2	6.9346	3.3461	93.5397
3	6.6853	3.5954	89.9443
4	6.4175	3.8632	86.0811
5	6.1297	4.1510	81.9300
6	5.8205	4.4603	77.4698
7	5.4882	4.7925	72.6772
8	5.1312	5.1496	67.5277
9	4.7476	5.5332	61.9945
10	4.3354	5.9454	56.0491
11	3.8925	6.3883	49.6609
12	3.4166	6.8642	42.7967
13	2.9052	7.3755	35.4212
14	2.3558	7.9249	27.4962
15	1.7654	8.5153	18.9809
16	1.1311	9.1497	9.8313
17	.4495	9.8313	0.0000

YEARS 18 — QTR PAYT 2.4978 — AN CONST 10.00

#	INT	PRIN	BALANCE
1	7.1746	2.8166	97.1834
2	6.9647	3.0264	94.1570
3	6.7393	3.2519	90.9051
4	6.4970	3.4941	87.4109
5	6.2367	3.7544	83.6565
6	5.9571	4.0341	79.6224
7	5.6565	4.3346	75.2877
8	5.3336	4.6575	70.6302
9	4.9867	5.0045	65.6257
10	4.6139	5.3773	60.2484
11	4.2133	5.7779	54.4704
12	3.7828	6.2083	48.2621
13	3.3204	6.6708	41.5913
14	2.8234	7.1678	34.4235
15	2.2894	7.7017	26.7218
16	1.7157	8.2755	18.4463
17	1.0992	8.8920	9.5544
18	.4368	9.5544	0.0000

YEARS 19 — QTR PAYT 2.4340 — AN CONST 9.74

#	INT	PRIN	BALANCE
1	7.1816	2.5544	97.4456
2	6.9913	2.7447	94.7010
3	6.7868	2.9491	91.7518
4	6.5671	3.1688	88.5830
5	6.3311	3.4049	85.1781
6	6.0774	3.6585	81.5196
7	5.8049	3.9311	77.5885
8	5.5120	4.2239	73.3646
9	5.1974	4.5386	68.8260
10	4.8593	4.8767	63.9494
11	4.4960	5.2400	58.7094
12	4.1056	5.6303	53.0791
13	3.6862	6.0498	47.0293
14	3.2355	6.5004	40.5289
15	2.7513	6.9847	33.5442
16	2.2310	7.5050	26.0392
17	1.6719	8.0641	17.9751
18	1.0711	8.6648	9.3103
19	.4257	9.3103	0.0000

YEARS 20 — QTR PAYT 2.3775 — AN CONST 9.51

#	INT	PRIN	BALANCE
1	7.1878	2.3221	97.6779
2	7.0148	2.4951	95.1829
3	6.8290	2.6809	92.5019
4	6.6292	2.8806	89.6213
5	6.4147	3.0952	86.5260
6	6.1841	3.3258	83.2002
7	5.9363	3.5736	79.6267
8	5.6701	3.8398	75.7869
9	5.3841	4.1258	71.6610
10	5.0767	4.4332	67.2278
11	4.7465	4.7634	62.4644
12	4.3916	5.1183	57.3461
13	4.0103	5.4996	51.8465
14	3.6006	5.9093	45.9373
15	3.1604	6.3495	39.5878
16	2.6874	6.8225	32.7653
17	2.1792	7.3307	25.4346
18	1.6331	7.8768	17.5577
19	1.0463	8.4636	9.0941
20	.4158	9.0941	0.0000

YEARS 21 — QTR PAYT 2.3272 — AN CONST 9.31

#	INT	PRIN	BALANCE
1	7.1933	2.1154	97.8846
2	7.0358	2.2730	95.6117
3	6.8664	2.4423	93.1694

#	INT	PRIN	BALANCE
4	6.6845	2.6242	90.5452
5	6.4890	2.8197	87.7255
6	6.2790	3.0298	84.6957
7	6.0533	3.2555	81.4402
8	5.8107	3.4980	77.9423
9	5.5502	3.7586	74.1837
10	5.2702	4.0386	70.1451
11	4.9693	4.3394	65.8057
12	4.6460	4.6627	61.1430
13	4.2987	5.0100	56.1330
14	3.9255	5.3832	50.7498
15	3.5245	5.7843	44.9655
16	3.0936	6.2152	38.7503
17	2.6306	6.6782	32.0722
18	2.1331	7.1757	24.8965
19	1.5985	7.7102	17.1863
20	1.0241	8.2846	8.9017
21	.4070	8.9017	0.0000

YEARS 22 — QTR PAYT 2.2822 — AN CONST 9.13

#	INT	PRIN	BALANCE
1	7.1983	1.9307	98.0693
2	7.0545	2.0745	95.9948
3	6.8999	2.2291	93.7657
4	6.7339	2.3951	91.3706
5	6.5554	2.5736	88.7970
6	6.3637	2.7653	86.0317
7	6.1577	2.9713	83.0605
8	5.9364	3.1926	79.8679
9	5.6986	3.4304	76.4374
10	5.4430	3.6860	72.7514
11	5.1684	3.9606	68.7908
12	4.8734	4.2556	64.5352
13	4.5563	4.5727	59.9626
14	4.2157	4.9133	55.0493
15	3.8497	5.2793	49.7700
16	3.4564	5.6726	44.0974
17	3.0338	6.0952	38.0022
18	2.5798	6.5492	31.4530
19	2.0919	7.0371	24.4158
20	1.5677	7.5613	16.8545
21	1.0044	8.1246	8.7299
22	.3991	8.7299	0.0000

YEARS 23 — QTR PAYT 2.2420 — AN CONST 8.97

#	INT	PRIN	BALANCE
1	7.2027	1.7651	98.2349
2	7.0712	1.8966	96.3382
3	6.9299	2.0379	94.3003
4	6.7781	2.1897	92.1106
5	6.6150	2.3529	89.7578
6	6.4397	2.5281	87.2296
7	6.2514	2.7165	84.5132
8	6.0490	2.9188	81.5944
9	5.8316	3.1363	78.4581
10	5.5980	3.3699	75.0882
11	5.3469	3.6209	71.4673
12	5.0772	3.8907	67.5766
13	4.7873	4.1805	63.3961
14	4.4759	4.4919	58.9041
15	4.1413	4.8266	54.0776
16	3.7817	5.1861	48.8914
17	3.3954	5.5725	43.3190
18	2.9803	5.9876	37.3314
19	2.5342	6.4336	30.8978
20	2.0550	6.9129	23.9849
21	1.5400	7.4279	16.5570
22	.9866	7.9812	8.5758
23	.3921	8.5758	0.0000

YEARS 24 — QTR PAYT 2.2057 — AN CONST 8.83

#	INT	PRIN	BALANCE
1	7.2067	1.6162	98.3838
2	7.0863	1.7366	96.6472
3	6.9569	1.8660	94.7812
4	6.8179	2.0050	92.7763
5	6.6686	2.1543	90.6219
6	6.5081	2.3148	88.3071
7	6.3357	2.4873	85.8198
8	6.1504	2.6726	83.1473
9	5.9513	2.8716	80.2756
10	5.7373	3.0856	77.1901
11	5.5075	3.3154	73.8746
12	5.2605	3.5624	70.3122
13	4.9951	3.8278	66.4844
14	4.7100	4.1129	62.3715
15	4.4036	4.4193	57.9521
16	4.0744	4.7486	53.2036
17	3.7206	5.1023	48.1013
18	3.3405	5.4824	42.6189
19	2.9321	5.8908	36.7281
20	2.4933	6.3296	30.3984
21	2.0217	6.8012	23.5972
22	1.5151	7.3078	16.2894
23	.9707	7.8522	8.4372
24	.3857	8.4372	0.0000

YEARS 25 — QTR PAYT 2.1730 — AN CONST 8.70

#	INT	PRIN	BALANCE
1	7.2103	1.4819	98.5181
2	7.0999	1.5923	96.9259
3	6.9813	1.7109	95.2150
4	6.8539	1.8383	93.3767
5	6.7169	1.9753	91.4014
6	6.5698	2.1224	89.2790
7	6.4117	2.2805	86.9985
8	6.2418	2.4504	84.5481
9	6.0592	2.6330	81.9151
10	5.8631	2.8291	79.0860
11	5.6523	3.0398	76.0462
12	5.4259	3.2663	72.7799
13	5.1826	3.5096	69.2703
14	4.9211	3.7711	65.4992
15	4.6402	4.0520	61.4472
16	4.3383	4.3539	57.0934
17	4.0140	4.6782	52.4152
18	3.6655	5.0267	47.3885
19	3.2910	5.4012	41.9873
20	2.8887	5.8035	36.1838
21	2.4563	6.2359	29.9479
22	1.9918	6.7004	23.2476
23	1.4926	7.1995	16.0480
24	.9563	7.7359	8.3121
25	.3800	8.3121	0.0000

YEARS 26 — QTR PAYT 2.1435 — AN CONST 8.58

#	INT	PRIN	BALANCE
1	7.2136	1.3604	98.6396
2	7.1122	1.4617	97.1779
3	7.0033	1.5706	95.6073
4	6.8863	1.6876	93.9197
5	6.7606	1.8133	92.1064
6	6.6255	1.9484	90.1580
7	6.4804	2.0935	88.0645
8	6.3244	2.2495	85.8150
9	6.1569	2.4171	83.3979
10	5.9768	2.5971	80.8008
11	5.7833	2.7906	78.0102
12	5.5754	2.9985	75.0117
13	5.3521	3.2219	71.7898
14	5.1121	3.4619	68.3280
15	4.8542	3.7198	64.6082
16	4.5771	3.9969	60.6113
17	4.2793	4.2946	56.3167
18	3.9594	4.6146	51.7021
19	3.6156	4.9583	46.7438
20	3.2462	5.3277	41.4161
21	2.8494	5.7246	35.6916
22	2.4229	6.1510	29.5405
23	1.9647	6.6092	22.9313
24	1.4723	7.1016	15.8297
25	.9433	7.6306	8.1991
26	.3749	8.1991	0.0000

YEARS 27 — QTR PAYT 2.1167 — AN CONST 8.47

#	INT	PRIN	BALANCE
1	7.2165	1.2502	98.7498
2	7.1234	1.3434	97.4064
3	7.0233	1.4434	95.9630
4	6.9158	1.5510	94.4120
5	6.8002	1.6665	92.7455
6	6.6761	1.7906	90.9549
7	6.5427	1.9240	89.0309
8	6.3994	2.0674	86.9635
9	6.2454	2.2214	84.7421
10	6.0799	2.3869	82.3553
11	5.9021	2.5647	79.7906
12	5.7110	2.7557	77.0349
13	5.5057	2.9610	74.0739
14	5.2852	3.1816	70.8923
15	5.0481	3.4186	67.4737
16	4.7935	3.6733	63.8004
17	4.5198	3.9469	59.8535
18	4.2258	4.2409	55.6126
19	3.9099	4.5569	51.0557
20	3.5704	4.8963	46.1594
21	3.2057	5.2611	40.8983
22	2.8137	5.6530	35.2453
23	2.3926	6.0741	29.1712
24	1.9401	6.5266	22.6446
25	1.4539	7.0128	15.6318
26	.9315	7.5352	8.0966
27	.3702	8.0966	0.0000

YEARS 28 — QTR PAYT 2.0923 — AN CONST 8.37

#	INT	PRIN	BALANCE
1	7.2192	1.1502	98.8498
2	7.1335	1.2358	97.6140
3	7.0415	1.3279	96.2861
4	6.9425	1.4268	94.8593
5	6.8362	1.5331	93.3262
6	6.7220	1.6473	91.6788
7	6.5993	1.7700	89.9088
8	6.4675	1.9019	88.0069
9	6.3258	2.0436	85.9633
10	6.1735	2.1958	83.7675
11	6.0100	2.3594	81.4081
12	5.8342	2.5352	78.8729
13	5.6453	2.7240	76.1489
14	5.4424	2.9269	73.2219
15	5.2244	3.1450	70.0769
16	4.9901	3.3793	66.6976
17	4.7383	3.6310	63.0666
18	4.4678	3.9015	59.1651
19	4.1772	4.1922	54.9730
20	3.8649	4.5044	50.4685
21	3.5293	4.8400	45.6285
22	3.1688	5.2006	40.4279
23	2.7814	5.5880	34.8400
24	2.3651	6.0043	28.8357
25	1.9178	6.4515	22.3842
26	1.4372	6.9322	15.4520
27	.9208	7.4486	8.0034
28	.3659	8.0034	0.0000

YEARS 29 — QTR PAYT 2.0702 — AN CONST 8.29

#	INT	PRIN	BALANCE
1	7.2216	1.0591	98.9409
2	7.1427	1.1380	97.8029
3	7.0580	1.2228	96.5802
4	6.9669	1.3138	95.2663
5	6.8690	1.4117	93.8546
6	6.7638	1.5169	92.3378
7	6.6508	1.6299	90.7079
8	6.5294	1.7513	88.9566
9	6.3990	1.8818	87.0748
10	6.2588	2.0219	85.0529
11	6.1082	2.1726	82.8803
12	5.9463	2.3344	80.5459
13	5.7724	2.5083	78.0376
14	5.5855	2.6952	75.3424
15	5.3848	2.8960	72.4464
16	5.1690	3.1117	69.3348
17	4.9372	3.3435	65.9913
18	4.6882	3.5926	62.3987
19	4.4205	3.8602	58.5385
20	4.1330	4.1478	54.3908
21	3.8240	4.4567	49.9340
22	3.4920	4.7887	45.1453
23	3.1352	5.1455	39.9998
24	2.7519	5.5288	34.4710
25	2.3401	5.9407	28.5303
26	1.8975	6.3832	22.1471
27	1.4220	6.8587	15.2884
28	.9110	7.3697	7.9187
29	.3620	7.9187	0.0000

YEARS 30 — QTR PAYT 2.0500 — AN CONST 8.20

#	INT	PRIN	BALANCE
1	7.2239	.9760	99.0240
2	7.1512	1.0487	97.9752
3	7.0730	1.1269	96.8483
4	6.9891	1.2108	95.6375
5	6.8989	1.3010	94.3365
6	6.8020	1.3979	92.9386
7	6.6978	1.5021	91.4365
8	6.5859	1.6140	89.8225
9	6.4657	1.7342	88.0883
10	6.3365	1.8634	86.2249
11	6.1977	2.0022	84.2227
12	6.0485	2.1514	82.0714
13	5.8883	2.3116	79.7597
14	5.7161	2.4838	77.2759
15	5.5310	2.6689	74.6070
16	5.3322	2.8677	71.7393
17	5.1186	3.0813	68.6580
18	4.8890	3.3109	65.3472
19	4.6424	3.5575	61.7897
20	4.3774	3.8225	57.9672
21	4.0926	4.1073	53.8599
22	3.7867	4.4132	49.4466
23	3.4579	4.7420	44.7046
24	3.1046	5.0953	39.6094
25	2.7251	5.4748	34.1345
26	2.3172	5.8827	28.2518
27	1.8790	6.3209	21.9309
28	1.4081	6.7918	15.1391
29	.9021	7.2977	7.8414
30	.3585	7.8414	0.0000

YEARS 2 — QTR PAYT 13.5775 — AN CONST 54.32

#	INT	PRIN	BALANCE
1	6.1669	48.1432	51.8568
2	2.4534	51.8568	0.0000

YEARS 3 — QTR PAYT 9.3835 — AN CONST 37.54

#	INT	PRIN	BALANCE
1	6.6447	30.8894	69.1106
2	4.2620	33.2721	35.8385
3	1.6955	35.8385	0.0000

YEARS 4 — QTR PAYT 7.2923 — AN CONST 29.17

#	INT	PRIN	BALANCE
1	6.8829	22.2862	77.7138
2	5.1638	24.0053	53.7085
3	3.3122	25.8570	27.8515
4	1.3177	27.8515	0.0000

YEARS 5 — QTR PAYT 6.0421 — AN CONST 24.17

#	INT	PRIN	BALANCE
1	7.0253	17.1433	82.8567
2	5.7029	18.4656	64.3911
3	4.2786	19.8900	44.5011
4	2.7443	21.4242	23.0768
5	1.0918	23.0768	0.0000

YEARS 6 — QTR PAYT 5.2125 — AN CONST 20.86

#	INT	PRIN	BALANCE
1	7.1198	13.7303	86.2697
2	6.0607	14.7895	71.4802
3	4.9199	15.9302	55.5500
4	3.6911	17.1590	38.3909
5	2.3675	18.4826	19.9083
6	.9419	19.9083	0.0000

YEARS 7 — QTR PAYT 4.6232 — AN CONST 18.50

#	INT	PRIN	BALANCE
1	7.1869	11.3059	88.6941
2	6.3149	12.1780	76.5161
3	5.3755	13.1174	63.3987
4	4.3637	14.1292	49.2695
5	3.2738	15.2191	34.0505
6	2.0999	16.3930	17.6575
7	.8354	17.6575	0.0000

YEARS 8 — QTR PAYT 4.1840 — AN CONST 16.74

#	INT	PRIN	BALANCE
1	7.2370	9.4992	90.5008
2	6.5042	10.2319	80.2688
3	5.7150	11.0212	69.2477
4	4.8649	11.8713	57.3763
5	3.9492	12.7870	44.5893
6	2.9628	13.7734	30.8159
7	1.9004	14.8358	15.9802
8	.7560	15.9802	0.0000

YEARS 9 — QTR PAYT 3.8450 — AN CONST 15.38

#	INT	PRIN	BALANCE
1	7.2756	8.1042	91.8958
2	6.6505	8.7294	83.1664
3	5.9771	9.4027	73.7637
4	5.2518	10.1280	63.6357
5	4.4706	10.9092	52.7264
6	3.6291	11.7507	40.9757
7	2.7227	12.6571	28.3185
8	1.7464	13.6335	14.6851
9	.6948	14.6851	0.0000

YEARS 10 — QTR PAYT 3.5759 — AN CONST 14.31

#	INT	PRIN	BALANCE
1	7.3062	6.9974	93.0026
2	6.7665	7.5372	85.4654
3	6.1851	8.1185	77.3469
4	5.5589	8.7448	68.6021
5	4.8843	9.4193	59.1828
6	4.1578	10.1459	49.0369
7	3.3752	10.9285	38.1084
8	2.5322	11.7715	26.3370
9	1.6242	12.6795	13.6575
10	.6461	13.6575	0.0000

YEARS 11 — QTR PAYT 3.3578 — AN CONST 13.44

#	INT	PRIN	BALANCE
1	7.3311	6.1000	93.9000
2	6.8606	6.5706	87.3294
3	6.3537	7.0774	80.2520
4	5.8078	7.6233	72.6287
5	5.2198	8.2113	64.4174
6	4.5864	8.8447	55.5726
7	3.9041	9.5270	46.0457
8	3.1693	10.2618	35.7838
9	2.3777	11.0534	24.7304
10	1.5251	11.9060	12.8244
11	.6067	12.8244	0.0000

YEARS 12 — QTR PAYT 3.1778 — AN CONST 12.72

#	INT	PRIN	BALANCE
1	7.3516	5.3597	94.6403
2	6.9382	5.7731	88.8672
3	6.4929	6.2184	82.6488
4	6.0132	6.6981	75.9508
5	5.4965	7.2147	68.7360
6	4.9400	7.7712	60.9648
7	4.3406	8.3707	52.5941
8	3.6949	9.0164	43.5778
9	2.9994	9.7118	33.8659
10	2.2503	10.4610	23.4049
11	1.4434	11.2679	12.1371
12	.5742	12.1371	0.0000

YEARS 13 — QTR PAYT 3.0272 — AN CONST 12.11

#	INT	PRIN	BALANCE
1	7.3688	4.7400	95.2600
2	7.0031	5.1056	90.1544
3	6.6093	5.4994	84.6549
4	6.1851	5.9237	78.7313
5	5.7282	6.3806	72.3507
6	5.2360	6.8727	65.4780
7	4.7059	7.4029	58.0751
8	4.1348	7.9739	50.1012
9	3.5198	8.5890	41.5122
10	2.8572	9.2515	32.2607
11	2.1436	9.9651	22.2956
12	1.3750	10.7338	11.5618
13	.5470	11.5618	0.0000

YEARS 14 — QTR PAYT 2.8996 — AN CONST 11.60

#	INT	PRIN	BALANCE
1	7.3833	4.2151	95.7849
2	7.0582	4.5402	91.2447
3	6.7079	4.8904	86.3543
4	6.3307	5.2676	81.0867
5	5.9244	5.6740	75.4127
6	5.4867	6.1116	69.3011
7	5.0153	6.5831	62.7180
8	4.5075	7.0908	55.6272
9	3.9605	7.6378	47.9894
10	3.3714	8.2270	39.7624
11	2.7368	8.8615	30.9009
12	2.0533	9.5451	21.3558
13	1.3170	10.2814	11.0744
14	.5239	11.0744	0.0000

YEARS 15 — QTR PAYT 2.7904 — AN CONST 11.17

#	INT	PRIN	BALANCE
1	7.3957	3.7659	96.2341
2	7.1052	4.0563	92.1778
3	6.7924	4.3692	87.8086
4	6.4553	4.7062	83.1023
5	6.0923	5.0693	78.0331
6	5.7013	5.4603	72.5728
7	5.2801	5.8815	66.6913
8	4.8264	6.3351	60.3562
9	4.3378	6.8238	53.5323
10	3.8114	7.3502	46.1822
11	3.2444	7.9171	38.2650
12	2.6337	8.5278	29.7372
13	1.9759	9.1856	20.5516
14	1.2674	9.8942	10.6574
15	.5042	10.6574	0.0000

YEARS 16 — QTR PAYT 2.6961 — AN CONST 10.79

#	INT	PRIN	BALANCE
1	7.4065	3.3781	96.6219
2	7.1459	3.6386	92.9833
3	6.8652	3.9193	89.0640
4	6.5629	4.2216	84.8424
5	6.2373	4.5473	80.2951
6	5.8865	4.8980	75.3971
7	5.5087	5.2758	70.1212
8	5.1017	5.6828	64.4384
9	4.6634	6.1211	58.3173
10	4.1912	6.5933	51.7240
11	3.6826	7.1019	44.6221
12	3.1348	7.6497	36.9724
13	2.5448	8.2398	28.7326
14	1.9092	8.8753	19.8573
15	1.2246	9.5599	10.2974
16	.4872	10.2974	0.0000

YEARS 17 — QTR PAYT 2.6141 — AN CONST 10.46

#	INT	PRIN	BALANCE
1	7.4158	3.0408	96.9592
2	7.1812	3.2753	93.6839
3	6.9286	3.5280	90.1559
4	6.6565	3.8001	86.3557
5	6.3633	4.0933	82.2625
6	6.0476	4.4090	77.8535
7	5.7075	4.7491	73.1044
8	5.3412	5.1154	67.9890
9	4.9466	5.5100	62.4790
10	4.5216	5.9350	56.5440
11	4.0638	6.3928	50.1512
12	3.5707	6.8859	43.2652
13	3.0395	7.4171	35.8481
14	2.4674	7.9892	27.8589
15	1.8511	8.6055	19.2535
16	1.1873	9.2692	9.9842
17	.4724	9.9842	0.0000

YEARS 18 — QTR PAYT 2.5424 — AN CONST 10.17

#	INT	PRIN	BALANCE
1	7.4240	2.7455	97.2545
2	7.2122	2.9573	94.2972
3	6.9841	3.1854	91.1117
4	6.7384	3.4311	87.6806
5	6.4737	3.6958	83.9848
6	6.1886	3.9809	80.0039
7	5.8816	4.2879	75.7160
8	5.5508	4.6187	71.0973
9	5.1945	4.9750	66.1223
10	4.8108	5.3587	60.7636
11	4.3974	5.7721	54.9915
12	3.9522	6.2173	48.7742
13	3.4726	6.6969	42.0774
14	2.9561	7.2134	34.8639
15	2.3996	7.7699	27.0941
16	1.8003	8.3692	18.7249
17	1.1548	9.0148	9.7101
18	.4594	9.7101	0.0000

YEARS 19 — QTR PAYT 2.4792 — AN CONST 9.92

#	INT	PRIN	BALANCE
1	7.4312	2.4856	97.5144
2	7.2394	2.6773	94.8371
3	7.0329	2.8838	91.9533
4	6.8105	3.1062	88.8471
5	6.5709	3.3459	85.5012
6	6.3128	3.6039	81.8973
7	6.0348	3.8819	78.0154
8	5.7354	4.1814	73.8340
9	5.4128	4.5039	69.3301
10	5.0654	4.8513	64.4788
11	4.6912	5.2255	59.2533
12	4.2881	5.6286	53.6247
13	3.8540	6.0628	47.5619
14	3.3863	6.5304	41.0315
15	2.8826	7.0341	33.9974
16	2.3400	7.5767	26.4206
17	1.7556	8.1612	18.2595
18	1.1260	8.7907	9.4688
19	.4480	9.4688	0.0000

YEARS 20 — QTR PAYT 2.4233 — AN CONST 9.70

#	INT	PRIN	BALANCE
1	7.4375	2.2555	97.7445
2	7.2636	2.4295	95.3150
3	7.0762	2.6169	92.6981
4	6.8743	2.8188	89.8793
5	6.6569	3.0362	86.8431
6	6.4227	3.2704	83.5727
7	6.1704	3.5226	80.0501
8	5.8987	3.7944	76.2557
9	5.6060	4.0871	72.1687
10	5.2908	4.4023	67.7664
11	4.9512	4.7419	63.0245
12	4.5854	5.1077	57.9168
13	4.1914	5.5016	52.4152
14	3.7670	5.9260	46.4892
15	3.3099	6.3831	40.1060
16	2.8176	6.8755	33.2305
17	2.2872	7.4058	25.8247
18	1.7160	7.9771	17.8476
19	1.1006	8.5924	9.2552
20	.4379	9.2552	0.0000

YEARS 21 — QTR PAYT 2.3736 — AN CONST 9.50

#	INT	PRIN	BALANCE
1	7.4432	2.0510	97.9490
2	7.2850	2.2093	95.7397
3	7.1146	2.3797	93.3600

QUARTERLY PAYMENT AMORTIZATION SCHEDULE PER $100 — 7.50 %

#	INT	PRIN	BALANCE
4	6.9310	2.5632	90.7968
5	6.7333	2.7609	88.0359
6	6.5203	2.9739	85.0619
7	6.2909	3.2033	81.8586
8	6.0439	3.4504	78.4082
9	5.7777	3.7165	74.6917
10	5.4910	4.0032	70.6885
11	5.1822	4.3120	66.3764
12	4.8496	4.6446	61.7318
13	4.4914	5.0029	56.7289
14	4.1055	5.3888	51.3401
15	3.6898	5.8045	45.5356
16	3.2421	6.2522	39.2834
17	2.7598	6.7345	32.5490
18	2.2403	7.2539	25.2950
19	1.6808	7.8135	17.4815
20	1.0781	8.4162	9.0654
21	.4289	9.0654	0.0000

YEARS 22 — QTR PAYT 2.3292 — AN CONST 9.32

#	INT	PRIN	BALANCE
1	7.4483	1.8686	98.1314
2	7.3041	2.0127	96.1187
3	7.1489	2.1680	93.9507
4	6.9816	2.3352	91.6155
5	6.8015	2.5153	89.1002
6	6.6075	2.7094	86.3908
7	6.3985	2.9183	83.4725
8	6.1734	3.1435	80.3290
9	5.9309	3.3859	76.9431
10	5.6697	3.6471	73.2960
11	5.3884	3.9284	69.3676
12	5.0854	4.2314	65.1361
13	4.7590	4.5578	60.5783
14	4.4074	4.9094	55.6689
15	4.0287	5.2881	50.3808
16	3.6208	5.6960	44.6848
17	3.1815	6.1354	38.5494
18	2.7082	6.6086	31.9408
19	2.1985	7.1184	24.8224
20	1.6494	7.6675	17.1549
21	1.0579	8.2589	8.8960
22	.4209	8.8960	0.0000

YEARS 23 — QTR PAYT 2.2895 — AN CONST 9.16

#	INT	PRIN	BALANCE
1	7.4528	1.7052	98.2948
2	7.3213	1.8367	96.4581
3	7.1796	1.9784	94.4797
4	7.0270	2.1310	92.3487
5	6.8626	2.2954	90.0533
6	6.6855	2.4724	87.5809
7	6.4948	2.6632	84.9177
8	6.2894	2.8686	82.0491
9	6.0681	3.0898	78.9593
10	5.8298	3.3282	75.6311
11	5.5731	3.5849	72.0462
12	5.2965	3.8614	68.1847
13	4.9987	4.1593	64.0254
14	4.6779	4.4801	59.5453
15	4.3323	4.8257	54.7196
16	3.9600	5.1979	49.5217
17	3.5591	5.5989	43.9228
18	3.1272	6.0308	37.8921
19	2.6620	6.4959	31.3961
20	2.1610	6.9970	24.3991
21	1.6212	7.5367	16.8624
22	1.0399	8.1181	8.7443
23	.4137	8.7443	0.0000

YEARS 24 — QTR PAYT 2.2538 — AN CONST 9.02

#	INT	PRIN	BALANCE
1	7.4568	1.5584	98.4416
2	7.3366	1.6786	96.7630
3	7.2072	1.8081	94.9549
4	7.0677	1.9476	93.0073
5	6.9175	2.0978	90.9095
6	6.7556	2.2596	88.6499
7	6.5813	2.4339	86.2160
8	6.3936	2.6217	83.5943
9	6.1914	2.8239	80.7705
10	5.9736	3.0417	77.7288
11	5.7389	3.2763	74.4524
12	5.4862	3.5290	70.9234
13	5.2140	3.8013	67.1221
14	4.9208	4.0945	63.0277
15	4.6050	4.4103	58.6174
16	4.2648	4.7505	53.8669
17	3.8983	5.1169	48.7499
18	3.5036	5.5116	43.2383
19	3.0785	5.9368	37.3015
20	2.6205	6.3947	30.9068
21	2.1273	6.8880	24.0189
22	1.5960	7.4193	16.5996
23	1.0237	7.9916	8.6080
24	.4072	8.6080	0.0000

YEARS 25 — QTR PAYT 2.2217 — AN CONST 8.89

#	INT	PRIN	BALANCE
1	7.4605	1.4262	98.5738
2	7.3505	1.5362	97.0376
3	7.2320	1.6547	95.3830
4	7.1044	1.7823	93.6006
5	6.9669	1.9198	91.6809
6	6.8188	2.0679	89.6130
7	6.6593	2.2274	87.3856
8	6.4875	2.3992	84.9864
9	6.3024	2.5843	82.4021
10	6.1031	2.7836	79.6185
11	5.8884	2.9983	76.6202
12	5.6571	3.2296	73.3906
13	5.4080	3.4787	69.9119
14	5.1396	3.7470	66.1649
15	4.8506	4.0361	62.1288
16	4.5393	4.3474	57.7814
17	4.2039	4.6827	53.0986
18	3.8427	5.0440	48.0547
19	3.4537	5.4330	42.6217
20	3.0346	5.8521	36.7696
21	2.5832	6.3035	30.4660
22	2.0969	6.7897	23.6763
23	1.5732	7.3135	16.3628
24	1.0091	7.8776	8.4852
25	.4014	8.4852	0.0000

YEARS 26 — QTR PAYT 2.1926 — AN CONST 8.78

#	INT	PRIN	BALANCE
1	7.4638	1.3067	98.6933
2	7.3630	1.4075	97.2857
3	7.2544	1.5161	95.7696
4	7.1375	1.6331	94.1366
5	7.0115	1.7590	92.3775
6	6.8759	1.8947	90.4828
7	6.7297	2.0409	88.4420
8	6.5723	2.1983	86.2437
9	6.4027	2.3678	83.8758
10	6.2201	2.5505	81.3253
11	6.0233	2.7472	78.5781
12	5.8114	2.9591	75.6190
13	5.5832	3.1874	72.4316
14	5.3373	3.4333	68.9983
15	5.0725	3.6981	65.3003
16	4.7872	3.9833	61.3169
17	4.4800	4.2906	57.0263
18	4.1490	4.6216	52.4048
19	3.7925	4.9780	47.4267
20	3.4085	5.3620	42.0647
21	2.9949	5.7756	36.2891
22	2.5494	6.2211	30.0679
23	2.0695	6.7010	23.3669
24	1.5527	7.2179	16.1490
25	.9959	7.7747	8.3744
26	.3962	8.3744	0.0000

YEARS 27 — QTR PAYT 2.1664 — AN CONST 8.67

#	INT	PRIN	BALANCE
1	7.4668	1.1986	98.8014
2	7.3744	1.2911	97.5103
3	7.2748	1.3907	96.1196
4	7.1675	1.4979	94.6217
5	7.0520	1.6135	93.0082
6	6.9275	1.7379	91.2703
7	6.7934	1.8720	89.3983
8	6.6490	2.0164	87.3819
9	6.4935	2.1719	85.2100
10	6.3260	2.3395	82.8705
11	6.1455	2.5199	80.3506
12	5.9511	2.7143	77.6363
13	5.7418	2.9237	74.7126
14	5.5162	3.1492	71.5634
15	5.2733	3.3921	68.1713
16	5.0117	3.6538	64.5176
17	4.7298	3.9356	60.5820
18	4.4263	4.2392	56.3428
19	4.0993	4.5662	51.7766
20	3.7471	4.9184	46.8583
21	3.3677	5.2978	41.5605
22	2.9590	5.7064	35.8541
23	2.5189	6.1466	29.7075
24	2.0447	6.6207	23.0868
25	1.5340	7.1314	15.9555
26	.9840	7.6815	8.2740
27	.3914	8.2740	0.0000

YEARS 28 — QTR PAYT 2.1425 — AN CONST 8.58

#	INT	PRIN	BALANCE
1	7.4695	1.1005	98.8995
2	7.3846	1.1854	97.7140
3	7.2932	1.2769	96.4372
4	7.1947	1.3754	95.0618
5	7.0886	1.4815	93.5803
6	6.9743	1.5957	91.9846
7	6.8513	1.7188	90.2658
8	6.7187	1.8514	88.4144
9	6.5759	1.9942	86.4202
10	6.4220	2.1480	84.2722
11	6.2563	2.3137	81.9585
12	6.0779	2.4922	79.4663
13	5.8856	2.6844	76.7818
14	5.6786	2.8915	73.8904
15	5.4555	3.1145	70.7758
16	5.2153	3.3548	67.4211
17	4.9565	3.6135	63.8075
18	4.6778	3.8923	59.9152
19	4.3776	4.1925	55.7227
20	4.0542	4.5159	51.2068
21	3.7058	4.8642	46.3426
22	3.3306	5.2395	41.1031
23	2.9265	5.6436	35.4595
24	2.4911	6.0789	29.3806
25	2.0222	6.5478	22.8328
26	1.5172	7.0529	15.7799
27	.9731	7.5969	8.1829
28	.3871	8.1829	0.0000

YEARS 29 — QTR PAYT 2.1208 — AN CONST 8.49

#	INT	PRIN	BALANCE
1	7.4720	1.0114	98.9886
2	7.3940	1.0894	97.8992
3	7.3099	1.1734	96.7258
4	7.2194	1.2640	95.4618
5	7.1219	1.3615	94.1003
6	7.0169	1.4665	92.6339
7	6.9038	1.5796	91.0543
8	6.7820	1.7014	89.3529
9	6.6507	1.8327	87.5202
10	6.5094	1.9740	85.5462
11	6.3571	2.1263	83.4199
12	6.1931	2.2903	81.1295
13	6.0164	2.4670	78.6626
14	5.8261	2.6573	76.0053
15	5.6211	2.8622	73.1430
16	5.4004	3.0830	70.0600
17	5.1625	3.3208	66.7392
18	4.9064	3.5770	63.1622
19	4.6305	3.8529	59.3093
20	4.3333	4.1501	55.1591
21	4.0132	4.4702	50.6889
22	3.6683	4.8150	45.8739
23	3.2969	5.1865	40.6874
24	2.8969	5.5865	35.1009
25	2.4659	6.0174	29.0834
26	2.0018	6.4816	22.6018
27	1.5018	6.9816	15.6203
28	.9633	7.5201	8.1002
29	.3832	8.1002	0.0000

YEARS 30 — QTR PAYT 2.1011 — AN CONST 8.41

#	INT	PRIN	BALANCE
1	7.4742	.9302	99.0698
2	7.4025	1.0020	98.0678
3	7.3252	1.0793	96.9885
4	7.2419	1.1625	95.8260
5	7.1523	1.2522	94.5738
6	7.0557	1.3488	93.2250
7	6.9516	1.4528	91.7722
8	6.8396	1.5649	90.2073
9	6.7189	1.6856	88.5217
10	6.5889	1.8156	86.7061
11	6.4488	1.9557	84.7504
12	6.2979	2.1065	82.6439
13	6.1355	2.2690	80.3748
14	5.9604	2.4440	77.9308
15	5.7719	2.6326	75.2983
16	5.5689	2.8356	72.4626
17	5.3501	3.0543	69.4083
18	5.1145	3.2899	66.1183
19	4.8608	3.5437	62.5746
20	4.5874	3.8171	58.7575
21	4.2930	4.1115	54.6460
22	3.9758	4.4286	50.2174
23	3.6342	4.7703	45.4471
24	3.2663	5.1382	40.3089
25	2.8699	5.5346	34.7744
26	2.4430	5.9615	28.8129
27	1.9832	6.4213	22.3916
28	1.4878	6.9166	15.4750
29	.9543	7.4501	8.0248
30	.3797	8.0248	0.0000

YEARS 2 — QTR PAYT 13.6142 — AN CONST 54.46

#	INT	PRIN	BALANCE
1	6.3750	48.0820	51.9180
2	2.5389	51.9180	0.0000

YEARS 3 — QTR PAYT 9.4197 — AN CONST 37.68

#	INT	PRIN	BALANCE
1	6.8689	30.8099	69.1901
2	4.4108	33.2680	35.9221
3	1.7567	35.9221	0.0000

YEARS 4 — QTR PAYT 7.3286 — AN CONST 29.32

#	INT	PRIN	BALANCE
1	7.1152	22.1992	77.8008
2	5.3441	23.9703	53.8304
3	3.4317	25.8827	27.9477
4	1.3667	27.9477	0.0000

YEARS 5 — QTR PAYT 6.0788 — AN CONST 24.32

#	INT	PRIN	BALANCE
1	7.2623	17.0531	82.9469
2	5.9018	18.4136	64.5333
3	4.4327	19.8827	44.6507
4	2.8465	21.4689	23.1818
5	1.1336	23.1818	0.0000

YEARS 6 — QTR PAYT 5.2498 — AN CONST 21.00

#	INT	PRIN	BALANCE
1	7.3600	13.6390	86.3610
2	6.2718	14.7272	71.6338
3	5.0968	15.9022	55.7316
4	3.8282	17.1709	38.5608
5	2.4582	18.5408	20.0200
6	.9790	20.0200	0.0000

YEARS 7 — QTR PAYT 4.6610 — AN CONST 18.65

#	INT	PRIN	BALANCE
1	7.4293	11.2147	88.7853
2	6.5346	12.1095	76.6758
3	5.5684	13.0756	63.6002
4	4.5253	14.1188	49.4815
5	3.3988	15.2452	34.2363
6	2.1825	16.4615	17.7748
7	.8692	17.7748	0.0000

YEARS 8 — QTR PAYT 4.2225 — AN CONST 16.89

#	INT	PRIN	BALANCE
1	7.4809	9.4089	90.5911
2	6.7303	10.1596	80.4315
3	5.9197	10.9701	69.4615
4	5.0445	11.8453	57.6161
5	4.0995	12.7903	44.8258
6	3.0790	13.8108	31.0150
7	1.9772	14.9126	16.1024
8	.7874	16.1024	0.0000

YEARS 9 — QTR PAYT 3.8840 — AN CONST 15.54

#	INT	PRIN	BALANCE
1	7.5208	8.0153	91.9847
2	6.8813	8.6547	83.3300
3	6.1908	9.3452	73.9847
4	5.4452	10.0908	63.8939
5	4.6402	10.8959	52.9980
6	3.7709	11.7652	41.2329
7	2.8322	12.7038	28.5291
8	1.8187	13.7173	14.8117
9	.7243	14.8117	0.0000

YEARS 10 — QTR PAYT 3.6156 — AN CONST 14.47

#	INT	PRIN	BALANCE
1	7.5524	6.9101	93.0899
2	7.0011	7.4614	85.6285
3	6.4058	8.0567	77.5718
4	5.7630	8.6995	68.8723
5	5.0690	9.3935	59.4788
6	4.3195	10.1430	49.3358
7	3.5103	10.9522	38.3836
8	2.6365	11.8260	26.5577
9	1.6930	12.7695	13.7882
10	.6743	13.7882	0.0000

YEARS 11 — QTR PAYT 3.3982 — AN CONST 13.60

#	INT	PRIN	BALANCE
1	7.5780	6.0146	93.9854
2	7.0981	6.4945	87.4909
3	6.5800	7.0126	80.4782
4	6.0205	7.5721	72.9061
5	5.4164	8.1762	64.7299
6	4.7641	8.8285	55.9013
7	4.0597	9.5329	46.3685
8	3.2992	10.2934	36.0750
9	2.4780	11.1147	24.9603
10	1.5912	12.0014	12.9589
11	.6337	12.9589	0.0000

YEARS 12 — QTR PAYT 3.2189 — AN CONST 12.88

#	INT	PRIN	BALANCE
1	7.5991	5.2763	94.7237
2	7.1782	5.6973	89.0264
3	6.7236	6.1518	82.8746
4	6.2328	6.6426	76.2319
5	5.7029	7.1726	69.0594
6	5.1306	7.7448	61.3145
7	4.5127	8.3627	52.9518
8	3.8455	9.0299	43.9219
9	3.1251	9.7503	34.1716
10	2.3472	10.5282	23.6433
11	1.5073	11.3682	12.2752
12	.6003	12.2752	0.0000

YEARS 13 — QTR PAYT 3.0689 — AN CONST 12.28

#	INT	PRIN	BALANCE
1	7.6168	4.6588	95.3412
2	7.2451	5.0305	90.3107
3	6.8437	5.4319	84.8788
4	6.4104	5.8652	79.0136
5	5.9424	6.3332	72.6804
6	5.4372	6.8384	65.8420
7	4.8916	7.3840	58.4580
8	4.3025	7.9731	50.4849
9	3.6664	8.6092	41.8757
10	2.9795	9.2961	32.5796
11	2.2379	10.0377	22.5418
12	1.4370	10.8386	11.7033
13	.5723	11.7033	0.0000

YEARS 14 — QTR PAYT 2.9420 — AN CONST 11.77

#	INT	PRIN	BALANCE
1	7.6317	4.1361	95.8639
2	7.3017	4.4661	91.3977
3	6.9454	4.8224	86.5753
4	6.5607	5.2072	81.3681
5	6.1452	5.6226	75.7455
6	5.6967	6.0712	69.6743
7	5.2123	6.5556	63.1187
8	4.6893	7.0786	56.0401
9	4.1245	7.6433	48.3967
10	3.5147	8.2531	40.1436
11	2.8563	8.9116	31.2320
12	2.1453	9.6226	21.6095
13	1.3776	10.3903	11.2192
14	.5486	11.2192	0.0000

YEARS 15 — QTR PAYT 2.8334 — AN CONST 11.34

#	INT	PRIN	BALANCE
1	7.6445	3.6892	96.3108
2	7.3502	3.9836	92.3272
3	7.0324	4.3014	88.0259
4	6.6892	4.6445	83.3813
5	6.3186	5.0151	78.3662
6	5.9185	5.4152	72.9510
7	5.4865	5.8472	67.1038
8	5.0200	6.3137	60.7901
9	4.5163	6.8174	53.9726
10	3.9724	7.3614	46.6113
11	3.3851	7.9487	38.6626
12	2.7509	8.5828	30.0798
13	2.0662	9.2676	20.8123
14	1.3268	10.0069	10.8053
15	.5284	10.8053	0.0000

YEARS 16 — QTR PAYT 2.7398 — AN CONST 10.96

#	INT	PRIN	BALANCE
1	7.6555	3.3038	96.6962
2	7.3919	3.5673	93.1289
3	7.1073	3.8519	89.2770
4	6.8000	4.1593	85.1177
5	6.4682	4.4911	80.6266
6	6.1099	4.8494	75.7772
7	5.7230	5.2363	70.5409
8	5.3052	5.6540	64.8869
9	4.8541	6.1051	58.7817
10	4.3671	6.5922	52.1895
11	3.8411	7.1182	45.0714
12	3.2732	7.6861	37.3853
13	2.6600	8.2993	29.0861
14	1.9979	8.9614	20.1247
15	1.2829	9.6763	10.4483
16	.5109	10.4483	0.0000

YEARS 17 — QTR PAYT 2.6585 — AN CONST 10.64

#	INT	PRIN	BALANCE
1	7.6651	2.9688	97.0312
2	7.4282	3.2057	93.8255
3	7.1725	3.4614	90.3641
4	6.8963	3.7376	86.6265
5	6.5981	4.0358	82.5907
6	6.2762	4.3578	78.2330
7	5.9285	4.7054	73.5275
8	5.5531	5.0808	68.4467
9	5.1477	5.4862	62.9605
10	4.7100	5.9239	57.0366
11	4.2374	6.3965	50.6401
12	3.7271	6.9068	43.7333
13	3.1761	7.4579	36.2754
14	2.5810	8.0529	28.2225
15	1.9386	8.6953	19.5272
16	1.2449	9.3891	10.1381
17	.4958	10.1381	0.0000

YEARS 18 — QTR PAYT 2.5873 — AN CONST 10.35

#	INT	PRIN	BALANCE
1	7.6735	2.6759	97.3241
2	7.4600	2.8894	94.4347
3	7.2295	3.1199	91.3148
4	6.9806	3.3688	87.9460
5	6.7118	3.6376	84.3085
6	6.4216	3.9278	80.3807
7	6.1082	4.2412	76.1395
8	5.7698	4.5795	71.5600
9	5.4045	4.9449	66.6151
10	5.0100	5.3394	61.2757
11	4.5840	5.7654	55.5104
12	4.1240	6.2253	49.2850
13	3.6274	6.7220	42.5630
14	3.0911	7.2583	35.3047
15	2.5120	7.8374	27.4673
16	1.8867	8.4627	19.0047
17	1.2115	9.1378	9.8669
18	.4825	9.8669	0.0000

YEARS 19 — QTR PAYT 2.5248 — AN CONST 10.10

#	INT	PRIN	BALANCE
1	7.6808	2.4182	97.5818
2	7.4879	2.6112	94.9706
3	7.2796	2.8195	92.1511
4	7.0546	3.0444	89.1066
5	6.8118	3.2873	85.8193
6	6.5495	3.5496	82.2697
7	6.2663	3.8328	78.4369
8	5.9605	4.1386	74.2983
9	5.6303	4.4688	69.8295
10	5.2738	4.8253	65.0042
11	4.8888	5.2103	59.7939
12	4.4731	5.6260	54.1680
13	4.0243	6.0748	48.0932
14	3.5396	6.5595	41.5337
15	3.0163	7.0828	34.4510
16	2.4512	7.6479	26.8031
17	1.8411	8.2580	18.5451
18	1.1822	8.9168	9.6282
19	.4708	9.6282	0.0000

YEARS 20 — QTR PAYT 2.4695 — AN CONST 9.88

#	INT	PRIN	BALANCE
1	7.6874	2.1905	97.8095
2	7.5126	2.3653	95.4442
3	7.3239	2.5540	92.8902
4	7.1201	2.7577	90.1325
5	6.9001	2.9778	87.1547
6	6.6625	3.2153	83.9394
7	6.4060	3.4719	80.4675
8	6.1290	3.7488	76.7187
9	5.8299	4.0479	72.6708
10	5.5070	4.3709	68.2999
11	5.1583	4.7196	63.5803
12	4.7817	5.0961	58.4842
13	4.3752	5.5027	52.9814
14	3.9361	5.9417	47.0397
15	3.4621	6.4158	40.6239
16	2.9502	6.9276	33.6963
17	2.3975	7.4803	26.2160
18	1.8008	8.0771	18.1389
19	1.1563	8.7215	9.4173
20	.4605	9.4173	0.0000

YEARS 21 — QTR PAYT 2.4204 — AN CONST 9.69

#	INT	PRIN	BALANCE
1	7.6931	1.9883	98.0117
2	7.5345	2.1470	95.8647
3	7.3632	2.3182	93.5465

QUARTERLY PAYMENT AMORTIZATION SCHEDULE PER $100   7.75 %

#	INT	PRIN	BALANCE
4	7.1783	2.5032	91.0433
5	6.9786	2.7029	88.3404
6	6.7629	2.9186	85.4218
7	6.5301	3.1514	82.2704
8	6.2786	3.4028	78.8676
9	6.0072	3.6743	75.1933
10	5.7140	3.9674	71.2258
11	5.3975	4.2840	66.9419
12	5.0557	4.6258	62.3161
13	4.6867	4.9948	57.3213
14	4.2882	5.3933	51.9280
15	3.8579	5.8236	46.1044
16	3.3933	6.2882	39.8162
17	2.8916	6.7899	33.0263
18	2.3499	7.3316	25.6947
19	1.7649	7.9165	17.7782
20	1.1334	8.5481	9.2301
21	.4514	9.2301	0.0000

YEARS 22 — QTR PAYT 2.3766 — AN CONST 9.51

#	INT	PRIN	BALANCE
1	7.6983	1.8081	98.1919
2	7.5540	1.9524	96.2395
3	7.3983	2.1081	94.1314
4	7.2301	2.2763	91.8550
5	7.0485	2.4579	89.3971
6	6.8524	2.6540	86.7431
7	6.6406	2.8658	83.8773
8	6.4120	3.0944	80.7829
9	6.1651	3.3413	77.4416
10	5.8985	3.6079	73.8337
11	5.6107	3.8957	69.9380
12	5.2999	4.2065	65.7315
13	4.9643	4.5421	61.1894
14	4.6019	4.9045	56.2849
15	4.2106	5.2958	50.9891
16	3.7881	5.7183	45.2708
17	3.3319	6.1745	39.0963
18	2.8393	6.6671	32.4292
19	2.3074	7.1990	25.2301
20	1.7330	7.7734	17.4568
21	1.1129	8.3936	9.0632
22	.4432	9.0632	0.0000

YEARS 23 — QTR PAYT 2.3375 — AN CONST 9.35

#	INT	PRIN	BALANCE
1	7.7029	1.6469	98.3531
2	7.5715	1.7783	96.5747
3	7.4296	1.9202	94.6545
4	7.2764	2.0734	92.5811
5	7.1110	2.2388	90.3422
6	6.9324	2.4175	87.9248
7	6.7395	2.6103	85.3144
8	6.5313	2.8186	82.4959
9	6.3064	3.0435	79.4524
10	6.0636	3.2863	76.1661
11	5.8014	3.5484	72.6177
12	5.5183	3.8315	68.7861
13	5.2126	4.1372	64.6489
14	4.8825	4.4673	60.1816
15	4.5261	4.8237	55.3579
16	4.1413	5.2086	50.1493
17	3.7257	5.6241	44.5252
18	3.2770	6.0728	38.4524
19	2.7925	6.5573	31.8951
20	2.2694	7.0805	24.8146
21	1.7045	7.6454	17.1693
22	1.0945	8.2553	8.9139
23	.4359	8.9139	0.0000

YEARS 24 — QTR PAYT 2.3023 — AN CONST 9.21

#	INT	PRIN	BALANCE
1	7.7070	1.5023	98.4977
2	7.5872	1.6222	96.8755
3	7.4578	1.7516	95.1238
4	7.3180	1.8914	93.2325
5	7.1671	2.0423	91.1902
6	7.0042	2.2052	88.9850
7	6.8282	2.3811	86.6038
8	6.6383	2.5711	84.0327
9	6.4331	2.7762	81.2565
10	6.2116	2.9977	78.2588
11	5.9725	3.2369	75.0219
12	5.7142	3.4951	71.5267
13	5.4354	3.7740	67.7527
14	5.1343	4.0751	63.6777
15	4.8092	4.4002	59.2775
16	4.4581	4.7513	54.5262
17	4.0791	5.1303	49.3959
18	3.6698	5.5396	43.8563
19	3.2278	5.9816	37.8747
20	2.7506	6.4588	31.4159
21	2.2353	6.9741	24.4418
22	1.6789	7.5305	16.9113
23	1.0781	8.1313	8.7800
24	.4294	8.7800	0.0000

YEARS 25 — QTR PAYT 2.2708 — AN CONST 9.09

#	INT	PRIN	BALANCE
1	7.7108	1.3722	98.6278
2	7.6013	1.4817	97.1460
3	7.4831	1.5999	95.5461
4	7.3554	1.7276	93.8185
5	7.2176	1.8654	91.9531
6	7.0688	2.0142	89.9388
7	6.9081	2.1749	87.7639
8	6.7345	2.3485	85.4154
9	6.5472	2.5358	82.8796
10	6.3449	2.7381	80.1415
11	6.1264	2.9566	77.1849
12	5.8905	3.1925	73.9924
13	5.6358	3.4472	70.5452
14	5.3608	3.7222	66.8230
15	5.0638	4.0192	62.8038
16	4.7432	4.3398	58.4640
17	4.3970	4.6861	53.7780
18	4.0231	5.0599	48.7181
19	3.6194	5.4636	43.2545
20	3.1835	5.8995	37.3550
21	2.7128	6.3702	30.9848
22	2.2046	6.8784	24.1064
23	1.6558	7.4272	16.6792
24	1.0633	8.0197	8.6595
25	.4235	8.6595	0.0000

YEARS 26 — QTR PAYT 2.2423 — AN CONST 8.97

#	INT	PRIN	BALANCE
1	7.7141	1.2549	98.7451
2	7.6140	1.3550	97.3901
3	7.5059	1.4631	95.9269
4	7.3892	1.5799	94.3471
5	7.2631	1.7059	92.6412
6	7.1270	1.8420	90.7991
7	6.9801	1.9890	88.8102
8	6.8214	2.1477	86.6625
9	6.6500	2.3190	84.3435
10	6.4650	2.5040	81.8395
11	6.2652	2.7038	79.1357
12	6.0495	2.9195	76.2163
13	5.8166	3.1524	73.0638
14	5.5651	3.4039	69.6599
15	5.2935	3.6755	65.9844
16	5.0003	3.9687	62.0157
17	4.6837	4.2854	57.7304
18	4.3418	4.6272	53.1031
19	3.9726	4.9964	48.1067
20	3.5740	5.3950	42.7117
21	3.1436	5.8255	36.8862
22	2.6788	6.2902	30.5960
23	2.1769	6.7921	23.8039
24	1.6351	7.3340	16.4699
25	1.0500	7.9191	8.5509
26	.4182	8.5509	0.0000

YEARS 27 — QTR PAYT 2.2165 — AN CONST 8.87

#	INT	PRIN	BALANCE
1	7.7171	1.1488	98.8512
2	7.6255	1.2405	97.6107
3	7.5265	1.3395	96.2712
4	7.4197	1.4463	94.8249
5	7.3043	1.5617	93.2632
6	7.1797	1.6863	91.5769
7	7.0451	1.8208	89.7560
8	6.8999	1.9661	87.7899
9	6.7430	2.1230	85.6669
10	6.5736	2.2924	83.3746
11	6.3907	2.4752	80.8993
12	6.1933	2.6727	78.2266
13	5.9800	2.8860	75.3407
14	5.7498	3.1162	72.2245
15	5.5012	3.3648	68.8596
16	5.2327	3.6333	65.2264
17	4.9429	3.9231	61.3033
18	4.6299	4.2361	57.0671
19	4.2919	4.5741	52.4930
20	3.9270	4.9390	47.5540
21	3.5329	5.3331	42.2210
22	3.1074	5.7585	36.4624
23	2.6480	6.2180	30.2445
24	2.1519	6.7140	23.5304
25	1.6163	7.2497	16.2807
26	1.0379	7.8281	8.4526
27	.4134	8.4526	0.0000

YEARS 28 — QTR PAYT 2.1932 — AN CONST 8.78

#	INT	PRIN	BALANCE
1	7.7199	1.0528	98.9472
2	7.6359	1.1367	97.8105
3	7.5452	1.2274	96.5831
4	7.4473	1.3254	95.2577
5	7.3415	1.4311	93.8266
6	7.2274	1.5453	92.2813
7	7.1041	1.6686	90.6128
8	6.9710	1.8017	88.8111
9	6.8272	1.9454	86.8657
10	6.6720	2.1006	84.7651
11	6.5044	2.2682	82.4968
12	6.3235	2.4492	80.0477
13	6.1281	2.6446	77.4031
14	5.9171	2.8556	74.5475
15	5.6893	3.0834	71.4641
16	5.4433	3.3294	68.1347
17	5.1776	3.5950	64.5397
18	4.8908	3.8818	60.6579
19	4.5811	4.1915	56.4664
20	4.2467	4.5259	51.9404
21	3.8856	4.8870	47.0534
22	3.4957	5.2769	41.7765
23	3.0747	5.6979	36.0786
24	2.6201	6.1525	29.9261
25	2.1293	6.6434	23.2827
26	1.5993	7.1734	16.1093
27	1.0270	7.7457	8.3636
28	.4090	8.3636	0.0000

YEARS 29 — QTR PAYT 2.1720 — AN CONST 8.69

#	INT	PRIN	BALANCE
1	7.7224	.9656	99.0344
2	7.6454	1.0426	97.9919
3	7.5622	1.1258	96.8661
4	7.4724	1.2156	95.6505
5	7.3754	1.3126	94.3380
6	7.2707	1.4173	92.9207
7	7.1576	1.5304	91.3903
8	7.0355	1.6524	89.7379
9	6.9037	1.7843	87.9536
10	6.7613	1.9266	86.0270
11	6.6076	2.0803	83.9466
12	6.4416	2.2463	81.7003
13	6.2624	2.4255	79.2748
14	6.0689	2.6190	76.6557
15	5.8599	2.8280	73.8277
16	5.6343	3.0536	70.7741
17	5.3907	3.2972	67.4768
18	5.1276	3.5603	63.9165
19	4.8436	3.8443	60.0722
20	4.5369	4.1511	55.9211
21	4.2057	4.4822	51.4389
22	3.8481	4.8398	46.5991
23	3.4620	5.2260	41.3731
24	3.0450	5.6429	35.7302
25	2.5948	6.0931	29.6371
26	2.1087	6.5792	23.0579
27	1.5838	7.1041	15.9538
28	1.0170	7.6709	8.2829
29	.4051	8.2829	0.0000

YEARS 30 — QTR PAYT 2.1527 — AN CONST 8.62

#	INT	PRIN	BALANCE
1	7.7247	.8863	99.1137
2	7.6539	.9570	98.1567
3	7.5776	1.0333	97.1234
4	7.4952	1.1158	96.0076
5	7.4061	1.2048	94.8028
6	7.3100	1.3009	93.5018
7	7.2062	1.4047	92.0971
8	7.0942	1.5168	90.5803
9	6.9731	1.6378	88.9425
10	6.8425	1.7685	87.1741
11	6.7014	1.9096	85.2645
12	6.5490	2.0619	83.2026
13	6.3845	2.2264	80.9762
14	6.2069	2.4040	78.5722
15	6.0151	2.5958	75.9763
16	5.8080	2.8029	73.1734
17	5.5844	3.0266	70.1468
18	5.3429	3.2680	66.8788
19	5.0822	3.5287	63.3501
20	4.8007	3.8103	59.5398
21	4.4967	4.1143	55.4255
22	4.1684	4.4425	50.9830
23	3.8140	4.7969	46.1861
24	3.4313	5.1796	41.0064
25	3.0181	5.5929	35.4135
26	2.5718	6.0391	29.3744
27	2.0900	6.5209	22.8535
28	1.5698	7.0412	15.8124
29	1.0080	7.6029	8.2095
30	.4015	8.2095	0.0000

YEARS 2 — QTR PAYT 13.6510 — AN CONST 54.61

#	INT	PRIN	BALANCE
1	6.5831	48.0208	51.9792
2	2.6247	51.9792	0.0000

YEARS 3 — QTR PAYT 9.4560 — AN CONST 37.83

#	INT	PRIN	BALANCE
1	7.0933	30.7305	69.2695
2	4.5601	33.2637	36.0057
3	1.8181	36.0057	0.0000

YEARS 4 — QTR PAYT 7.3650 — AN CONST 29.47

#	INT	PRIN	BALANCE
1	7.3476	22.1125	77.8875
2	5.5248	23.9353	53.9523
3	3.5518	25.9083	28.0440
4	1.4161	28.0440	0.0000

YEARS 5 — QTR PAYT 6.1157 — AN CONST 24.47

#	INT	PRIN	BALANCE
1	7.4995	16.9632	83.0368
2	6.1012	18.3615	64.6753
3	4.5876	19.8751	44.8002
4	2.9493	21.5134	23.2868
5	1.1759	23.2868	0.0000

YEARS 6 — QTR PAYT 5.2871 — AN CONST 21.15

#	INT	PRIN	BALANCE
1	7.6003	13.5482	86.4518
2	6.4835	14.6650	71.7868
3	5.2746	15.8738	55.9130
4	3.9661	17.1824	38.7306
5	2.5497	18.5987	20.1319
6	1.0166	20.1319	0.0000

YEARS 7 — QTR PAYT 4.6990 — AN CONST 18.80

#	INT	PRIN	BALANCE
1	7.6718	11.1241	88.8759
2	6.7548	12.0411	76.8348
3	5.7622	13.0336	63.8012
4	4.6878	14.1080	49.6932
5	3.5249	15.2710	34.4222
6	2.2661	16.5298	17.8924
7	.9035	17.8924	0.0000

YEARS 8 — QTR PAYT 4.2611 — AN CONST 17.05

#	INT	PRIN	BALANCE
1	7.7250	9.3192	90.6808
2	6.9568	10.0874	80.5934
3	6.1253	10.9189	69.6745
4	5.2252	11.8190	57.8554
5	4.2510	12.7933	45.0622
6	3.1964	13.8478	31.2143
7	2.0549	14.9894	16.2250
8	.8193	16.2250	0.0000

YEARS 9 — QTR PAYT 3.9233 — AN CONST 15.70

#	INT	PRIN	BALANCE
1	7.7661	7.9270	92.0730
2	7.1127	8.5805	83.4925
3	6.4054	9.2878	74.2047
4	5.6398	10.0534	64.1513
5	4.8110	10.8821	53.2692
6	3.9140	11.7791	41.4901
7	2.9430	12.7501	28.7400
8	1.8920	13.8011	14.9388
9	.7543	14.9388	0.0000

YEARS 10 — QTR PAYT 3.6556 — AN CONST 14.63

#	INT	PRIN	BALANCE
1	7.7987	6.8236	93.1764
2	7.2362	7.3861	85.7903
3	6.6273	7.9950	77.7953
4	5.9683	8.6540	69.1413
5	5.2549	9.3674	59.7739
6	4.4827	10.1396	49.6343
7	3.6469	10.9754	38.6590
8	2.7422	11.8801	26.7788
9	1.7629	12.8594	13.9194
10	.7029	13.9194	0.0000

YEARS 11 — QTR PAYT 3.4388 — AN CONST 13.76

#	INT	PRIN	BALANCE
1	7.8250	5.9301	94.0699
2	7.3362	6.4190	87.6509
3	6.8071	6.9481	80.7028
4	6.2343	7.5209	73.1819
5	5.6144	8.1408	65.0411
6	4.9433	8.8119	56.2292
7	4.2169	9.5383	46.6909
8	3.4307	10.3245	36.3664
9	2.5796	11.1756	25.1908
10	1.6583	12.0968	13.0940
11	.6612	13.0940	0.0000

YEARS 12 — QTR PAYT 3.2602 — AN CONST 13.05

#	INT	PRIN	BALANCE
1	7.8468	5.1940	94.8060
2	7.4186	5.6221	89.1839
3	6.9552	6.0856	83.0983
4	6.4535	6.5872	76.5111
5	5.9105	7.1302	69.3809
6	5.3227	7.7180	61.6629
7	4.6865	8.3542	53.3087
8	3.9979	9.0428	44.2658
9	3.2525	9.7883	34.4776
10	2.4456	10.5951	23.8824
11	1.5722	11.4685	12.4139
12	.6268	12.4139	0.0000

YEARS 13 — QTR PAYT 3.1109 — AN CONST 12.45

#	INT	PRIN	BALANCE
1	7.8649	4.5787	95.4213
2	7.4875	4.9562	90.4651
3	7.0789	5.3647	85.1004
4	6.6367	5.8069	79.2935
5	6.1580	6.2856	73.0078
6	5.6399	6.8038	66.2041
7	5.0790	7.3646	58.8395
8	4.4720	7.9717	50.8678
9	3.8148	8.6288	42.2390
10	3.1035	9.3401	32.8989
11	2.3336	10.1100	22.7889
12	1.5002	10.9434	11.8455
13	.5981	11.8455	0.0000

YEARS 14 — QTR PAYT 2.9847 — AN CONST 11.94

#	INT	PRIN	BALANCE
1	7.8803	4.0584	95.9416
2	7.5457	4.3929	91.5487
3	7.1836	4.7550	86.7937
4	6.7916	5.1470	81.6467
5	6.3674	5.5713	76.0754
6	5.9081	6.0305	70.0449
7	5.4110	6.5276	63.5173
8	4.8729	7.0657	56.4516
9	4.2905	7.6482	48.8034
10	3.6600	8.2786	40.5248
11	2.9776	8.9610	31.5638
12	2.2389	9.6997	21.8640
13	1.4393	10.4993	11.3648
14	.5739	11.3648	0.0000

YEARS 15 — QTR PAYT 2.8768 — AN CONST 11.51

#	INT	PRIN	BALANCE
1	7.8934	3.6138	96.3862
2	7.5955	3.9117	92.4745
3	7.2730	4.2342	88.2403
4	6.9240	4.5832	83.6571
5	6.5462	4.9610	78.6961
6	6.1373	5.3699	73.3262
7	5.6946	5.8126	67.5136
8	5.2155	6.2917	61.2219
9	4.6968	6.8104	54.4115
10	4.1354	7.3718	47.0397
11	3.5277	7.9794	39.0603
12	2.8700	8.6372	30.4231
13	2.1580	9.3492	21.0739
14	1.3873	10.1199	10.9541
15	.5531	10.9541	0.0000

YEARS 16 — QTR PAYT 2.7839 — AN CONST 11.14

#	INT	PRIN	BALANCE
1	7.9047	3.2307	96.7693
2	7.6384	3.4971	93.2722
3	7.3501	3.7853	89.4869
4	7.0381	4.0974	85.3895
5	6.7003	4.4351	80.9544
6	6.3347	4.8007	76.1537
7	5.9390	5.1964	70.9572
8	5.5106	5.6248	65.3324
9	5.0470	6.0885	59.2440
10	4.5451	6.5903	52.6536
11	4.0018	7.1336	45.5200
12	3.4138	7.7216	37.7984
13	2.7773	8.3582	29.4402
14	2.0883	9.0471	20.3931
15	1.3425	9.7929	10.6002
16	.5353	10.6002	0.0000

YEARS 17 — QTR PAYT 2.7032 — AN CONST 10.82

#	INT	PRIN	BALANCE
1	7.9145	2.8982	97.1018
2	7.6756	3.1371	93.9647
3	7.4170	3.3957	90.5690
4	7.1371	3.6756	86.8934
5	6.8341	3.9786	82.9147
6	6.5061	4.3066	78.6082
7	6.1511	4.6616	73.9466
8	5.7668	5.0458	68.9007
9	5.3509	5.4618	63.4390
10	4.9007	5.9120	57.5270
11	4.4133	6.3993	51.1276
12	3.8858	6.9269	44.2008
13	3.3148	7.4979	36.7029
14	2.6968	8.1159	28.5870
15	2.0278	8.7849	19.8020
16	1.3036	9.5091	10.2929
17	.5197	10.2929	0.0000

YEARS 18 — QTR PAYT 2.6327 — AN CONST 10.54

#	INT	PRIN	BALANCE
1	7.9231	2.6077	97.3923
2	7.7081	2.8226	94.5697
3	7.4754	3.0553	91.5144
4	7.2236	3.3072	88.2072
5	6.9510	3.5798	84.6275
6	6.6559	3.8749	80.7526
7	6.3365	4.1943	76.5583
8	5.9907	4.5400	72.0183
9	5.6165	4.9143	67.1040
10	5.2114	5.3194	61.7847
11	4.7729	5.7578	56.0268
12	4.2983	6.2325	49.7944
13	3.7845	6.7462	43.0481
14	3.2284	7.3023	35.7458
15	2.6264	7.9043	27.8415
16	1.9749	8.5559	19.2857
17	1.2696	9.2611	10.0245
18	.5062	10.0245	0.0000

YEARS 19 — QTR PAYT 2.5708 — AN CONST 10.29

#	INT	PRIN	BALANCE
1	7.9306	2.3524	97.6476
2	7.7367	2.5463	95.1013
3	7.5268	2.7562	92.3450
4	7.2996	2.9834	89.3616
5	7.0536	3.2294	86.1322
6	6.7874	3.4956	82.6367
7	6.4993	3.7837	78.8530
8	6.1874	4.0956	74.7574
9	5.8498	4.4332	70.3241
10	5.4843	4.7987	65.5255
11	5.0888	5.1942	60.3313
12	4.6606	5.6224	54.7089
13	4.1971	6.0859	48.6230
14	3.6955	6.5875	42.0355
15	3.1525	7.1306	34.9049
16	2.5647	7.7183	27.1866
17	1.9284	8.3546	18.8320
18	1.2397	9.0433	9.7887
19	.4943	9.7887	0.0000

YEARS 20 — QTR PAYT 2.5161 — AN CONST 10.07

#	INT	PRIN	BALANCE
1	7.9372	2.1270	97.8730
2	7.7619	2.3024	95.5706
3	7.5721	2.4922	93.0784
4	7.3667	2.6976	90.3808
5	7.1443	2.9200	87.4608
6	6.9036	3.1607	84.3002
7	6.6431	3.4212	80.8790
8	6.3611	3.7032	77.1757
9	6.0558	4.0085	73.1672
10	5.7254	4.3389	68.8283
11	5.3677	4.6966	64.1317
12	4.9805	5.0837	59.0480
13	4.5615	5.5028	53.5452
14	4.1079	5.9564	47.5888
15	3.6169	6.4474	41.1414
16	3.0854	6.9789	34.1625
17	2.5101	7.5542	26.6083
18	1.8874	8.1769	18.4314
19	1.2134	8.8509	9.5805
20	.4838	9.5805	0.0000

YEARS 21 — QTR PAYT 2.4676 — AN CONST 9.88

#	INT	PRIN	BALANCE
1	7.9431	1.9272	98.0728
2	7.7843	2.0860	95.9868
3	7.6123	2.2580	93.7288

#	INT	PRIN	BALANCE
4	7.4262	2.4441	91.2846
5	7.2247	2.6456	88.6390
6	7.0066	2.8637	85.7753
7	6.7706	3.0998	82.6756
8	6.5150	3.3553	79.3203
9	6.2385	3.6319	75.6884
10	5.9391	3.9312	71.7572
11	5.6150	4.2553	67.5019
12	5.2642	4.6061	62.8958
13	4.8846	4.9858	57.9100
14	4.4736	5.3968	52.5133
15	4.0287	5.8416	46.6716
16	3.5472	6.3232	40.3485
17	3.0259	6.8444	33.5041
18	2.4617	7.4086	26.0955
19	1.8510	8.0193	18.0762
20	1.1900	8.6803	9.3959
21	.4744	9.3959	0.0000

YEARS 22	QTR PAYT 2.4244	AN CONST 9.70	
#	INT	PRIN	BALANCE
1	7.9484	1.7493	98.2507
2	7.8042	1.8935	96.3572
3	7.6481	2.0496	94.3077
4	7.4792	2.2185	92.0892
5	7.2963	2.4014	89.6878
6	7.0983	2.5993	87.0885
7	6.8841	2.8136	84.2749
8	6.6521	3.0455	81.2293
9	6.4011	3.2966	77.9327
10	6.1293	3.5683	74.3644
11	5.8352	3.8625	70.5019
12	5.5168	4.1809	66.3211
13	5.1722	4.5255	61.7956
14	4.7991	4.8986	56.8970
15	4.3953	5.3023	51.5947
16	3.9582	5.7394	45.8552
17	3.4851	6.2125	39.6427
18	2.9730	6.7247	32.9180
19	2.4187	7.2790	25.6390
20	1.8187	7.8790	17.7600
21	1.1692	8.5285	9.2315
22	.4661	9.2315	0.0000

YEARS 23	QTR PAYT 2.3859	AN CONST 9.55	
#	INT	PRIN	BALANCE
1	7.9531	1.5904	98.4096
2	7.8220	1.7215	96.6882
3	7.6801	1.8634	94.8248
4	7.5265	2.0170	92.8079
5	7.3602	2.1832	90.6246
6	7.1802	2.3632	88.2614
7	6.9854	2.5580	85.7034
8	6.7746	2.7689	82.9346
9	6.5463	2.9971	79.9375
10	6.2993	3.2442	76.6933
11	6.0319	3.5116	73.1817
12	5.7424	3.8010	69.3807
13	5.4291	4.1144	65.2663
14	5.0899	4.4535	60.8128
15	4.7228	4.8206	55.9921
16	4.3254	5.2180	50.7741
17	3.8953	5.6482	45.1260
18	3.4297	6.1137	39.0122
19	2.9257	6.6177	32.3945
20	2.3802	7.1632	25.2313
21	1.7897	7.7537	17.4776
22	1.1506	8.3929	9.0847
23	.4587	9.0847	0.0000

YEARS 24	QTR PAYT 2.3513	AN CONST 9.41	
#	INT	PRIN	BALANCE
1	7.9573	1.4480	98.5520
2	7.8379	1.5673	96.9847
3	7.7087	1.6965	95.2882
4	7.5689	1.8364	93.4518
5	7.4175	1.9878	91.4640
6	7.2536	2.1516	89.3124
7	7.0763	2.3290	86.9834
8	6.8843	2.5210	84.4625
9	6.6765	2.7288	81.7337
10	6.4515	2.9537	78.7800
11	6.2081	3.1972	75.5828
12	5.9445	3.4607	72.1221
13	5.6592	3.7460	68.3761
14	5.3505	4.0548	64.3213
15	5.0162	4.3890	59.9322
16	4.6544	4.7508	55.1814
17	4.2628	5.1425	50.0389
18	3.8389	5.5664	44.4726
19	3.3800	6.0252	38.4473
20	2.8834	6.5219	31.9254
21	2.3457	7.0595	24.8659
22	1.7638	7.6414	17.2245
23	1.1339	8.2713	8.9532
24	.4521	8.9532	0.0000

YEARS 25	QTR PAYT 2.3203	AN CONST 9.29	
#	INT	PRIN	BALANCE
1	7.9611	1.3200	98.6800
2	7.8522	1.4289	97.2511
3	7.7345	1.5466	95.7045
4	7.6070	1.6741	94.0303
5	7.4690	1.8121	92.2182
6	7.3196	1.9615	90.2567
7	7.1579	2.1232	88.1334
8	6.9829	2.2982	85.8352
9	6.7934	2.4877	83.3475
10	6.5884	2.6927	80.6548
11	6.3664	2.9147	77.7401
12	6.1261	3.1550	74.5851
13	5.8660	3.4151	71.1701
14	5.5845	3.6966	67.4735
15	5.2798	4.0013	63.4722
16	4.9500	4.3311	59.1411
17	4.5930	4.6881	54.4530
18	4.2065	5.0746	49.3784
19	3.7882	5.4929	43.8855
20	3.3354	5.9457	37.9398
21	2.8453	6.4358	31.5040
22	2.3148	6.9663	24.5377
23	1.7405	7.5406	16.9971
24	1.1189	8.1622	8.8350
25	.4461	8.8350	0.0000

YEARS 26	QTR PAYT 2.2923	AN CONST 9.17	
#	INT	PRIN	BALANCE
1	7.9645	1.2048	98.7952
2	7.8651	1.3041	97.4910
3	7.7576	1.4116	96.0794
4	7.6413	1.5280	94.5514
5	7.5153	1.6540	92.8974
6	7.3790	1.7903	91.1071
7	7.2314	1.9379	89.1692
8	7.0716	2.0976	87.0716
9	6.8987	2.2705	84.8011
10	6.7116	2.4577	82.3433
11	6.5090	2.6603	79.6830
12	6.2897	2.8796	76.8034
13	6.0523	3.1170	73.6865
14	5.7954	3.3739	70.3126
15	5.5173	3.6520	66.6606
16	5.2162	3.9531	62.7075
17	4.8903	4.2789	58.4286
18	4.5376	4.6316	53.7969
19	4.1558	5.0134	48.7835
20	3.7426	5.4267	43.3568
21	3.2952	5.8740	37.4827
22	2.8110	6.3583	31.1244
23	2.2869	6.8824	24.2421
24	1.7196	7.4497	16.7923
25	1.1055	8.0638	8.7285
26	.4407	8.7285	0.0000

YEARS 27	QTR PAYT 2.2671	AN CONST 9.07	
#	INT	PRIN	BALANCE
1	7.9675	1.1008	98.8992
2	7.8768	1.1916	97.7076
3	7.7786	1.2898	96.4178
4	7.6722	1.3961	95.0217
5	7.5572	1.5112	93.5105
6	7.4326	1.6358	91.8748
7	7.2977	1.7706	90.1042
8	7.1518	1.9166	88.1876
9	6.9938	2.0745	86.1131
10	6.8228	2.2455	83.8675
11	6.6377	2.4307	81.4369
12	6.4373	2.6310	78.8059
13	6.2204	2.8479	75.9580
14	5.9857	3.0827	72.8753
15	5.7316	3.3368	69.5386
16	5.4565	3.6118	65.9267
17	5.1588	3.9096	62.0172
18	4.8365	4.2318	57.7854
19	4.4877	4.5807	53.2047
20	4.1101	4.9583	48.2464
21	3.7014	5.3670	42.8795
22	3.2590	5.8094	37.0701
23	2.7801	6.2883	30.7818
24	2.2617	6.8066	23.9752
25	1.7006	7.3677	16.6075
26	1.0933	7.9750	8.6324
27	.4359	8.6324	0.0000

YEARS 28	QTR PAYT 2.2443	AN CONST 8.98	
#	INT	PRIN	BALANCE
1	7.9703	1.0067	98.9933
2	7.8873	1.0897	97.9035
3	7.7975	1.1796	96.7239
4	7.7002	1.2768	95.4471
5	7.5950	1.3820	94.0651
6	7.4811	1.4960	92.5691
7	7.3578	1.6193	90.9498
8	7.2243	1.7528	89.1971
9	7.0798	1.8973	87.2998
10	6.9234	2.0537	85.2462
11	6.7541	2.2229	83.0232
12	6.5709	2.4062	80.6170
13	6.3725	2.6045	78.0125
14	6.1578	2.8192	75.1933
15	5.9254	3.0516	72.1417
16	5.6739	3.3032	68.8385
17	5.4016	3.5755	65.2630
18	5.1069	3.8702	61.3928
19	4.7878	4.1892	57.2036
20	4.4425	4.5345	52.6691
21	4.0687	4.9083	47.7607
22	3.6641	5.3129	42.4478
23	3.2261	5.7509	36.6969
24	2.7521	6.2250	30.4719
25	2.2389	6.7381	23.7338
26	1.6835	7.2935	16.4403
27	1.0823	7.8948	8.5455
28	.4315	8.5455	0.0000

YEARS 29	QTR PAYT 2.2236	AN CONST 8.90	
#	INT	PRIN	BALANCE
1	7.9728	.9215	99.0785
2	7.8968	.9975	98.0810
3	7.8146	1.0797	97.0013
4	7.7256	1.1687	95.8326
5	7.6293	1.2650	94.5676
6	7.5250	1.3693	93.1983
7	7.4121	1.4822	91.7161
8	7.2900	1.6044	90.1117
9	7.1577	1.7366	88.3751
10	7.0145	1.8798	86.4953
11	6.8596	2.0347	84.4606
12	6.6919	2.2025	82.2581
13	6.5103	2.3840	79.8741
14	6.3138	2.5805	77.2936
15	6.1011	2.7932	74.5004
16	5.8708	3.0235	71.4769
17	5.6216	3.2727	68.2041
18	5.3518	3.5425	64.6616
19	5.0598	3.8345	60.8271
20	4.7437	4.1506	56.6765
21	4.4016	4.4928	52.1837
22	4.0312	4.8631	47.3206
23	3.6303	5.2640	42.0566
24	3.1964	5.6979	36.3587
25	2.7267	6.1676	30.1911
26	2.2183	6.6760	23.5151
27	1.6680	7.2263	16.2888
28	1.0723	7.8220	8.4668
29	.4275	8.4668	0.0000

YEARS 30	QTR PAYT 2.2048	AN CONST 8.82	
#	INT	PRIN	BALANCE
1	7.9751	.8441	99.1559
2	7.9055	.9137	98.2421
3	7.8302	.9891	97.2531
4	7.7487	1.0706	96.1825
5	7.6604	1.1588	95.0237
6	7.5649	1.2544	93.7693
7	7.4615	1.3578	92.4116
8	7.3496	1.4697	90.9419
9	7.2284	1.5908	89.3510
10	7.0973	1.7220	87.6291
11	6.9553	1.8639	85.7652
12	6.8017	2.0176	83.7476
13	6.6354	2.1839	81.5638
14	6.4554	2.3639	79.1999
15	6.2605	2.5587	76.6411
16	6.0496	2.7697	73.8715
17	5.8213	2.9980	70.8735
18	5.5741	3.2451	67.6284
19	5.3066	3.5126	64.1158
20	5.0171	3.8022	60.3136
21	4.7037	4.1156	56.1980
22	4.3644	4.4548	51.7432
23	3.9972	4.8221	46.9212
24	3.5997	5.2195	41.7016
25	3.1694	5.6498	36.0518
26	2.7037	6.1155	29.9363
27	2.1996	6.6197	23.3166
28	1.6539	7.1653	16.1513
29	1.0633	7.7560	8.3953
30	.4239	8.3953	0.0000

QUARTERLY PAYMENT AMORTIZATION SCHEDULE PER $100

8.25 %

YEARS 2 — QTR PAYT 13.6878 — AN CONST 54.76

#	INT	PRIN	BALANCE
1	6.7915	47.9596	52.0404
2	2.7107	52.0404	0.0000

YEARS 3 — QTR PAYT 9.4923 — AN CONST 37.97

#	INT	PRIN	BALANCE
1	7.3179	30.6513	69.3487
2	4.7098	33.2594	36.0893
3	1.8798	36.0893	0.0000

YEARS 4 — QTR PAYT 7.4015 — AN CONST 29.61

#	INT	PRIN	BALANCE
1	7.5802	22.0259	77.9741
2	5.7060	23.9001	54.0740
3	3.6724	25.9337	28.1403
4	1.4658	28.1403	0.0000

YEARS 5 — QTR PAYT 6.1526 — AN CONST 24.62

#	INT	PRIN	BALANCE
1	7.7369	16.8736	83.1264
2	6.3011	18.3094	64.8170
3	4.7432	19.8673	44.9497
4	3.0528	21.5577	23.3920
5	1.2185	23.3920	0.0000

YEARS 6 — QTR PAYT 5.3246 — AN CONST 21.30

#	INT	PRIN	BALANCE
1	7.8407	13.4577	86.5423
2	6.6956	14.6028	71.9394
3	5.4531	15.8453	56.0941
4	4.1049	17.1936	38.9005
5	2.6419	18.6565	20.2440
6	1.0545	20.2440	0.0000

YEARS 7 — QTR PAYT 4.7371 — AN CONST 18.95

#	INT	PRIN	BALANCE
1	7.9144	11.0340	88.9660
2	6.9756	11.9728	76.9932
3	5.9569	12.9916	64.0017
4	4.8514	14.0970	49.9047
5	3.6520	15.2964	34.6083
6	2.3504	16.5980	18.0103
7	.9381	18.0103	0.0000

YEARS 8 — QTR PAYT 4.2999 — AN CONST 17.20

#	INT	PRIN	BALANCE
1	7.9693	9.2301	90.7699
2	7.1839	10.0155	80.7544
3	6.3317	10.8677	69.8866
4	5.4070	11.7924	58.0942
5	4.4036	12.7958	45.2984
6	3.3149	13.8846	31.4139
7	2.1335	15.0660	16.3479
8	.8515	16.3479	0.0000

YEARS 9 — QTR PAYT 3.9628 — AN CONST 15.86

#	INT	PRIN	BALANCE
1	8.0116	7.8395	92.1605
2	7.3445	8.5065	83.6540
3	6.6207	9.2303	74.4236
4	5.8354	10.0157	64.4079
5	4.9831	10.8679	53.5399
6	4.0584	11.7927	41.7473
7	3.0550	12.7961	28.9512
8	1.9662	13.8849	15.0663
9	.7848	15.0663	0.0000

YEARS 10 — QTR PAYT 3.6958 — AN CONST 14.79

#	INT	PRIN	BALANCE
1	8.0451	6.7380	93.2620
2	7.4718	7.3113	85.9508
3	6.8497	7.9334	78.0174
4	6.1746	8.6084	69.4090
5	5.4422	9.3409	60.0681
6	4.6474	10.1357	49.9324
7	3.7850	10.9981	38.9343
8	2.8492	11.9339	27.0005
9	1.8337	12.9493	14.0511
10	.7319	14.0511	0.0000

YEARS 11 — QTR PAYT 3.4797 — AN CONST 13.92

#	INT	PRIN	BALANCE
1	8.0722	5.8466	94.1534
2	7.5747	6.3440	87.8094
3	7.0349	6.8838	80.9256
4	6.4492	7.4695	73.4561
5	5.8136	8.1051	65.3510
6	5.1240	8.7948	56.5562
7	4.3757	9.5431	47.0131
8	3.5637	10.3551	36.6580
9	2.6826	11.2362	25.4219
10	1.7265	12.1922	13.2296
11	.6891	13.2296	0.0000

YEARS 12 — QTR PAYT 3.3018 — AN CONST 13.21

#	INT	PRIN	BALANCE
1	8.0945	5.1126	94.8874
2	7.6595	5.5476	89.3397
3	7.1875	6.0197	83.3201
4	6.6753	6.5319	76.7882
5	6.1195	7.0877	69.7005
6	5.5164	7.6907	62.0098
7	4.8620	8.3451	53.6647
8	4.1520	9.0552	44.6095
9	3.3815	9.8257	34.7838
10	2.5454	10.6617	24.1221
11	1.6383	11.5689	12.5533
12	.6539	12.5533	0.0000

YEARS 13 — QTR PAYT 3.1532 — AN CONST 12.62

#	INT	PRIN	BALANCE
1	8.1132	4.4997	95.5003
2	7.7303	4.8826	90.6177
3	7.3148	5.2980	85.3197
4	6.8640	5.7488	79.5709
5	6.3749	6.2380	73.3330
6	5.8441	6.7687	66.5642
7	5.2682	7.3447	59.2196
8	4.6432	7.9696	51.2499
9	3.9651	8.6477	42.6022
10	3.2293	9.3835	33.2187
11	2.4309	10.1820	23.0367
12	1.5645	11.0483	11.9884
13	.6245	11.9884	0.0000

YEARS 14 — QTR PAYT 3.0277 — AN CONST 12.12

#	INT	PRIN	BALANCE
1	8.1289	3.9817	96.0183
2	7.7901	4.3205	91.6977
3	7.4225	4.6882	87.0096
4	7.0236	5.0871	81.9225
5	6.5907	5.5199	76.4026
6	6.1211	5.9896	70.4130
7	5.6114	6.4992	63.9138
8	5.0584	7.0522	56.8616
9	4.4584	7.6523	49.2093
10	3.8073	8.3034	40.9059
11	3.1007	9.0099	31.8960
12	2.3341	9.7765	22.1195
13	1.5022	10.6084	11.5110
14	.5996	11.5110	0.0000

YEARS 15 — QTR PAYT 2.9205 — AN CONST 11.69

#	INT	PRIN	BALANCE
1	8.1424	3.5396	96.4604
2	7.8412	3.8408	92.6196
3	7.5144	4.1676	88.4520
4	7.1598	4.5222	83.9298
5	6.7750	4.9070	79.0228
6	6.3575	5.3245	73.6982
7	5.9044	5.7776	67.9207
8	5.4128	6.2692	61.6515
9	4.8794	6.8026	54.8489
10	4.3006	7.3814	47.4675
11	3.6725	8.0095	39.4580
12	2.9910	8.6910	30.7670
13	2.2515	9.4305	21.3365
14	1.4491	10.2329	11.1036
15	.5784	11.1036	0.0000

YEARS 16 — QTR PAYT 2.8282 — AN CONST 11.32

#	INT	PRIN	BALANCE
1	8.1539	3.1590	96.8410
2	7.8851	3.4278	93.4132
3	7.5935	3.7195	89.6937
4	7.2770	4.0359	85.6578
5	6.9336	4.3794	81.2784
6	6.5610	4.7520	76.5264
7	6.1566	5.1563	71.3701
8	5.7179	5.5951	65.7751
9	5.2418	6.0711	59.7039
10	4.7252	6.5877	53.1162
11	4.1647	7.1482	45.9680
12	3.5565	7.7565	38.2115
13	2.8965	8.4164	29.7951
14	2.1804	9.1326	20.6625
15	1.4033	9.9096	10.7528
16	.5601	10.7528	0.0000

YEARS 17 — QTR PAYT 2.7482 — AN CONST 11.00

#	INT	PRIN	BALANCE
1	8.1640	2.8289	97.1711
2	7.9233	3.0696	94.1014
3	7.6621	3.3308	90.7706
4	7.3787	3.6142	87.1563
5	7.0711	3.9218	83.2346
6	6.7374	4.2555	78.9791
7	6.3754	4.6176	74.3615
8	5.9825	5.0105	69.3511
9	5.5561	5.4368	63.9143
10	5.0935	5.8994	58.0149
11	4.5916	6.4013	51.6136
12	4.0469	6.9460	44.6676
13	3.4559	7.5370	37.1305
14	2.8146	8.1783	28.9522
15	2.1187	8.8742	20.0780
16	1.3636	9.6293	10.4486
17	.5443	10.4486	0.0000

YEARS 18 — QTR PAYT 2.6784 — AN CONST 10.72

#	INT	PRIN	BALANCE
1	8.1727	2.5409	97.4591
2	7.9565	2.7571	94.7021
3	7.7219	2.9916	91.7104
4	7.4674	3.2462	88.4642
5	7.1912	3.5224	84.9418
6	6.8915	3.8221	81.1197
7	6.5662	4.1473	76.9724
8	6.2134	4.5002	72.4721
9	5.8304	4.8831	67.5890
10	5.4150	5.2986	62.2903
11	4.9641	5.7495	56.5409
12	4.4749	6.2387	50.3022
13	3.9441	6.7695	43.5326
14	3.3681	7.3455	36.1871
15	2.7430	7.9705	28.2166
16	2.0648	8.6487	19.5678
17	1.3289	9.3846	10.1832
18	.5304	10.1832	0.0000

YEARS 19 — QTR PAYT 2.6171 — AN CONST 10.47

#	INT	PRIN	BALANCE
1	8.1804	2.2880	97.7120
2	7.9857	2.4827	95.2292
3	7.7745	2.6940	92.5353
4	7.5453	2.9232	89.6121
5	7.2965	3.1719	86.4401
6	7.0266	3.4418	82.9983
7	6.7338	3.7347	79.2636
8	6.4160	4.0524	75.2112
9	6.0712	4.3973	70.8139
10	5.6970	4.7714	66.0425
11	5.2911	5.1774	60.8651
12	4.8505	5.6179	55.2472
13	4.3725	6.0960	49.1512
14	3.8538	6.6146	42.5366
15	3.2910	7.1775	35.3591
16	2.6803	7.7882	27.5709
17	2.0176	8.4509	19.1201
18	1.2985	9.1699	9.9502
19	.5183	9.9502	0.0000

YEARS 20 — QTR PAYT 2.5631 — AN CONST 10.26

#	INT	PRIN	BALANCE
1	8.1872	2.0651	97.9349
2	8.0115	2.2408	95.6941
3	7.8208	2.4315	93.2627
4	7.6139	2.6383	90.6243
5	7.3894	2.8628	87.7615
6	7.1459	3.1064	84.6551
7	6.8815	3.3707	81.2843
8	6.5947	3.6575	77.6268
9	6.2835	3.9688	73.6580
10	5.9458	4.3065	69.3516
11	5.5794	4.6729	64.6787
12	5.1818	5.0705	59.6082
13	4.7504	5.5019	54.1063
14	4.2822	5.9701	48.1362
15	3.7742	6.4780	41.6582
16	3.2230	7.0292	34.6289
17	2.6249	7.6273	27.0016
18	1.9759	8.2763	18.7252
19	1.2717	8.9806	9.7447
20	.5076	9.7447	0.0000

YEARS 21 — QTR PAYT 2.5152 — AN CONST 10.07

#	INT	PRIN	BALANCE
1	8.1932	1.8676	98.1324
2	8.0343	2.0265	96.1059
3	7.8619	2.1989	93.9069

QUARTERLY PAYMENT AMORTIZATION SCHEDULE PER $100 — 8.25 %

#	INT	PRIN	BALANCE
4	7.6748	2.3860	91.5209
5	7.4717	2.5891	88.9318
6	7.2514	2.8094	86.1225
7	7.0124	3.0484	83.0741
8	6.7530	3.3078	79.7663
9	6.4716	3.5892	76.1770
10	6.1662	3.8946	72.2824
11	5.8348	4.2260	68.0564
12	5.4752	4.5856	63.4708
13	5.0850	4.9758	58.4950
14	4.6616	5.3992	53.0958
15	4.2022	5.8586	47.2372
16	3.7037	6.3571	40.8802
17	3.1628	6.8980	33.9822
18	2.5759	7.4849	26.4973
19	1.9390	8.1218	18.3755
20	1.2480	8.8128	9.5627
21	.4981	9.5627	0.0000

YEARS 22 — QTR PAYT 2.4726 — AN CONST 9.90

#	INT	PRIN	BALANCE
1	8.1985	1.6920	98.3080
2	8.0546	1.8360	96.4720
3	7.8984	1.9922	94.4797
4	7.7288	2.1617	92.3180
5	7.5449	2.3457	89.9723
6	7.3453	2.5453	87.4271
7	7.1287	2.7618	84.6652
8	6.8937	2.9968	81.6684
9	6.6388	3.2518	78.4166
10	6.3621	3.5285	74.8881
11	6.0618	3.8287	71.0593
12	5.7361	4.1545	66.9048
13	5.3826	4.5080	62.3968
14	4.9990	4.8916	57.5052
15	4.5828	5.3078	52.1974
16	4.1311	5.7594	46.4380
17	3.6411	6.2495	40.1885
18	3.1093	6.7813	33.4072
19	2.5323	7.3583	26.0490
20	1.9062	7.9843	18.0646
21	1.2269	8.6637	9.4009
22	.4897	9.4009	0.0000

YEARS 23 — QTR PAYT 2.4347 — AN CONST 9.74

#	INT	PRIN	BALANCE
1	8.2033	1.5354	98.4646
2	8.0727	1.6661	96.7985
3	7.9309	1.8078	94.9907
4	7.7771	1.9616	93.0291
5	7.6102	2.1285	90.9006
6	7.4291	2.3097	88.5909
7	7.2325	2.5062	86.0847
8	7.0193	2.7194	83.3653
9	6.7879	2.9508	80.4145
10	6.5368	3.2019	77.2126
11	6.2644	3.4743	73.7383
12	5.9688	3.7700	69.9683
13	5.6480	4.0907	65.8776
14	5.2999	4.4388	61.4388
15	4.9222	4.8165	56.6223
16	4.5124	5.2263	51.3960
17	4.0677	5.6710	45.7249
18	3.5852	6.1535	39.5714
19	3.0616	6.6771	32.8943
20	2.4934	7.2453	25.6490
21	1.8770	7.8618	17.7872
22	1.2080	8.5307	9.2566
23	.4822	9.2566	0.0000

YEARS 24 — QTR PAYT 2.4007 — AN CONST 9.61

#	INT	PRIN	BALANCE
1	8.2076	1.3953	98.6047
2	8.0888	1.5140	97.0908
3	7.9600	1.6428	95.4479
4	7.8202	1.7826	93.6654
5	7.6686	1.9343	91.7311
6	7.5040	2.0988	89.6323
7	7.3254	2.2774	87.3548
8	7.1316	2.4712	84.8836
9	6.9214	2.6815	82.2021
10	6.6932	2.9096	79.2925
11	6.4456	3.1572	76.1353
12	6.1770	3.4259	72.7094
13	5.8855	3.7174	68.9921
14	5.5692	4.0337	64.9584
15	5.2260	4.3769	60.5815
16	4.8535	4.7493	55.8322
17	4.4494	5.1534	50.6788
18	4.0109	5.5919	45.0870
19	3.5351	6.0677	39.0193
20	3.0189	6.5840	32.4353
21	2.4586	7.1442	25.2911
22	1.8508	7.7521	17.5391
23	1.1912	8.4117	9.1274
24	.4754	9.1274	0.0000

YEARS 25 — QTR PAYT 2.3702 — AN CONST 9.49

#	INT	PRIN	BALANCE
1	8.2114	1.2695	98.7305
2	8.1034	1.3776	97.3529
3	7.9862	1.4948	95.8582
4	7.8590	1.6219	94.2362
5	7.7210	1.7600	92.4763
6	7.5712	1.9097	90.5665
7	7.4087	2.0722	88.4943
8	7.2324	2.2485	86.2458
9	7.0411	2.4398	83.8060
10	6.8335	2.6474	81.1585
11	6.6082	2.8727	78.2858
12	6.3638	3.1171	75.1687
13	6.0986	3.3824	71.7863
14	5.8108	3.6702	68.1162
15	5.4985	3.9824	64.1337
16	5.1596	4.3213	59.8124
17	4.7919	4.6890	55.1234
18	4.3930	5.0880	50.0355
19	3.9600	5.5209	44.5146
20	3.4903	5.9907	38.5239
21	2.9805	6.5004	32.0235
22	2.4274	7.0535	24.9701
23	1.8273	7.6536	17.3164
24	1.1760	8.3049	9.0115
25	.4694	9.0115	0.0000

YEARS 26 — QTR PAYT 2.3428 — AN CONST 9.38

#	INT	PRIN	BALANCE
1	8.2148	1.1564	98.8436
2	8.1164	1.2548	97.5887
3	8.0097	1.3616	96.2271
4	7.8938	1.4775	94.7496
5	7.7681	1.6032	93.1464
6	7.6317	1.7396	91.4068
7	7.4837	1.8876	89.5192
8	7.3230	2.0482	87.4710
9	7.1488	2.2225	85.2484
10	6.9597	2.4116	82.8368
11	6.7545	2.6168	80.2200
12	6.5318	2.8395	77.3805
13	6.2902	3.0811	74.2994
14	6.0280	3.3432	70.9562
15	5.7436	3.6277	67.3285
16	5.4349	3.9364	63.3921
17	5.0999	4.2713	59.1207
18	4.7365	4.6348	54.4860
19	4.3421	5.0291	49.4568
20	3.9142	5.4570	43.9998
21	3.4499	5.9214	38.0784
22	2.9461	6.4252	31.6532
23	2.3994	6.9719	24.6813
24	1.8061	7.5651	17.1161
25	1.1624	8.2088	8.9073
26	.4640	8.9073	0.0000

YEARS 27 — QTR PAYT 2.3181 — AN CONST 9.28

#	INT	PRIN	BALANCE
1	8.2179	1.0545	98.9455
2	8.1282	1.1443	97.8012
3	8.0308	1.2416	96.5596
4	7.9252	1.3473	95.2123
5	7.8106	1.4619	93.7504
6	7.6862	1.5863	92.1642
7	7.5512	1.7213	90.4429
8	7.4047	1.8677	88.5752
9	7.2458	2.0266	86.5485
10	7.0734	2.1991	84.3495
11	6.8863	2.3862	81.9633
12	6.6832	2.5892	79.3740
13	6.4629	2.8095	76.5645
14	6.2239	3.0486	73.5159
15	5.9645	3.3080	70.2079
16	5.6830	3.5895	66.6185
17	5.3776	3.8949	62.7236
18	5.0462	4.2263	58.4973
19	4.6866	4.5859	53.9114
20	4.2964	4.9761	48.9353
21	3.8730	5.3995	43.5358
22	3.4135	5.8589	37.6769
23	2.9150	6.3575	31.3194
24	2.3741	6.8984	24.4210
25	1.7871	7.4854	16.9357
26	1.1502	8.1223	8.8134
27	.4591	8.8134	0.0000

YEARS 28 — QTR PAYT 2.2958 — AN CONST 9.19

#	INT	PRIN	BALANCE
1	8.2207	.9625	99.0375
2	8.1388	1.0444	97.9931
3	8.0500	1.1332	96.8599
4	7.9535	1.2297	95.6302
5	7.8489	1.3343	94.2959
6	7.7354	1.4478	92.8481
7	7.6122	1.5710	91.2771
8	7.4785	1.7047	89.5724
9	7.3335	1.8497	87.7227
10	7.1761	2.0071	85.7155
11	7.0053	2.1779	83.5376
12	6.8200	2.3632	81.1744
13	6.6189	2.5643	78.6101
14	6.4007	2.7825	75.8276
15	6.1640	3.0193	72.8083
16	5.9071	3.2762	69.5322
17	5.6283	3.5549	65.9773
18	5.3258	3.8574	62.1199
19	4.9976	4.1856	57.9343
20	4.6415	4.5418	53.3925
21	4.2550	4.9282	48.4643
22	3.8357	5.3475	43.1168
23	3.3807	5.8025	37.3142
24	2.8869	6.2963	31.0180
25	2.3512	6.8320	24.1860
26	1.7699	7.4133	16.7727
27	1.1391	8.0441	8.7286
28	.4547	8.7286	0.0000

YEARS 29 — QTR PAYT 2.2756 — AN CONST 9.11

#	INT	PRIN	BALANCE
1	8.2233	.8792	99.1208
2	8.1485	.9540	98.1668
3	8.0673	1.0352	97.1316
4	7.9792	1.1233	96.0083
5	7.8836	1.2189	94.7894
6	7.7799	1.3226	93.4669
7	7.6674	1.4351	92.0318
8	7.5453	1.5572	90.4746
9	7.4128	1.6897	88.7849
10	7.2690	1.8335	86.9514
11	7.1130	1.9895	84.9619
12	6.9437	2.1588	82.8032
13	6.7600	2.3424	80.4607
14	6.5607	2.5418	77.9189
15	6.3444	2.7580	75.1609
16	6.1098	2.9927	72.1682
17	5.8551	3.2474	68.9208
18	5.5788	3.5237	65.3972
19	5.2790	3.8235	61.5737
20	4.9537	4.1488	57.4249
21	4.6006	4.5018	52.9231
22	4.2176	4.8849	48.0382
23	3.8020	5.3005	42.7377
24	3.3509	5.7515	36.9862
25	2.8616	6.2409	30.7453
26	2.3305	6.7719	23.9733
27	1.7543	7.3481	16.6252
28	1.1291	7.9734	8.6518
29	.4507	8.6518	0.0000

YEARS 30 — QTR PAYT 2.2573 — AN CONST 9.03

#	INT	PRIN	BALANCE
1	8.2256	.8038	99.1962
2	8.1572	.8721	98.3241
3	8.0830	.9464	97.3778
4	8.0024	1.0269	96.3509
5	7.9151	1.1142	95.2366
6	7.8203	1.2091	94.0276
7	7.7174	1.3119	92.7156
8	7.6057	1.4236	91.2921
9	7.4846	1.5447	89.7474
10	7.3532	1.6761	88.0713
11	7.2106	1.8187	86.2525
12	7.0558	1.9735	84.2790
13	6.8879	2.1414	82.1376
14	6.7057	2.3236	79.8140
15	6.5080	2.5213	77.2927
16	6.2934	2.7359	74.5568
17	6.0607	2.9687	71.5881
18	5.8081	3.2213	68.3669
19	5.5340	3.4953	64.8716
20	5.2366	3.7927	61.0788
21	4.9138	4.1155	56.9633
22	4.5637	4.4656	52.4977
23	4.1837	4.8456	47.6521
24	3.7714	5.2579	42.3942
25	3.3240	5.7053	36.6889
26	2.8386	6.1907	30.4981
27	2.3118	6.7175	23.7806
28	1.7402	7.2891	16.4916
29	1.1200	7.9093	8.5823
30	.4470	8.5823	0.0000

QUARTERLY PAYMENT AMORTIZATION SCHEDULE PER $100   8.50 %

YEARS 2 — QTR PAYT 13.7246 — AN CONST 54.90

#	INT	PRIN	BALANCE
1	7.0000	47.8985	52.1015
2	2.7970	52.1015	0.0000

YEARS 3 — QTR PAYT 9.5287 — AN CONST 38.12

#	INT	PRIN	BALANCE
1	7.5426	30.5722	69.4278
2	4.8599	33.2549	36.1729
3	1.9419	36.1729	0.0000

YEARS 4 — QTR PAYT 7.4381 — AN CONST 29.76

#	INT	PRIN	BALANCE
1	7.8129	21.9396	78.0604
2	5.8878	23.8648	54.1956
3	3.7937	25.9589	28.2367
4	1.5158	28.2367	0.0000

YEARS 5 — QTR PAYT 6.1897 — AN CONST 24.76

#	INT	PRIN	BALANCE
1	7.9744	16.7844	83.2156
2	6.5016	18.2572	64.9584
3	4.8995	19.8592	45.0992
4	3.1569	21.6018	23.4973
5	1.2614	23.4973	0.0000

YEARS 6 — QTR PAYT 5.3623 — AN CONST 21.45

#	INT	PRIN	BALANCE
1	8.0814	13.3677	86.6323
2	6.9084	14.5407	72.0916
3	5.6325	15.8166	56.2750
4	4.2446	17.2045	39.0705
5	2.7349	18.7142	20.3563
6	1.0928	20.3563	0.0000

YEARS 7 — QTR PAYT 4.7754 — AN CONST 19.11

#	INT	PRIN	BALANCE
1	8.1573	10.9444	89.0556
2	7.1969	11.9047	77.1509
3	6.1523	12.9493	64.2016
4	5.0160	14.0856	50.1160
5	3.7800	15.3216	34.7944
6	2.4356	16.6660	18.1284
7	.9732	18.1284	0.0000

YEARS 8 — QTR PAYT 4.3389 — AN CONST 17.36

#	INT	PRIN	BALANCE
1	8.2137	9.1417	90.8583
2	7.4115	9.9439	80.9144
3	6.5390	10.8164	70.0980
4	5.5899	11.7655	58.3325
5	4.5575	12.7979	45.5346
6	3.4345	13.9209	31.6136
7	2.2129	15.1425	16.4712
8	.8842	16.4712	0.0000

YEARS 9 — QTR PAYT 4.0025 — AN CONST 16.01

#	INT	PRIN	BALANCE
1	8.2572	7.7527	92.2473
2	7.5769	8.4330	83.8143
3	6.8370	9.1729	74.6414
4	6.0320	9.9779	64.6636
5	5.1565	10.8534	53.8102
6	4.2041	11.8058	42.0044
7	3.1682	12.8417	29.1627
8	2.0414	13.9685	15.1942
9	.8157	15.1942	0.0000

YEARS 10 — QTR PAYT 3.7362 — AN CONST 14.95

#	INT	PRIN	BALANCE
1	8.2916	6.6531	93.3469
2	7.7079	7.2369	86.1100
3	7.0728	7.8719	78.2381
4	6.3821	8.5627	69.6754
5	5.6307	9.3140	60.3614
6	4.8134	10.1313	50.2301
7	3.9244	11.0203	39.2098
8	2.9574	11.9873	27.2225
9	1.9056	13.0392	14.1833
10	.7614	14.1833	0.0000

YEARS 11 — QTR PAYT 3.5208 — AN CONST 14.09

#	INT	PRIN	BALANCE
1	8.3195	5.7639	94.2361
2	7.8137	6.2696	87.9665
3	7.2636	6.8198	81.1468
4	6.6652	7.4182	73.7286
5	6.0142	8.0691	65.6594
6	5.3062	8.7772	56.8823
7	4.5360	9.5473	47.3349
8	3.6982	10.3851	36.9498
9	2.7870	11.2964	25.6534
10	1.7957	12.2876	13.3658
11	.7175	13.3658	0.0000

YEARS 12 — QTR PAYT 3.3437 — AN CONST 13.38

#	INT	PRIN	BALANCE
1	8.3424	5.0322	94.9678
2	7.9008	5.4738	89.4940
3	7.4205	5.9541	83.5398
4	6.8981	6.4766	77.0633
5	6.3298	7.0449	70.0184
6	5.7116	7.6631	62.3553
7	5.0392	8.3355	54.0198
8	4.3077	9.0669	44.9529
9	3.5121	9.8625	35.0904
10	2.6467	10.7279	24.3625
11	1.7054	11.6693	12.6932
12	.6814	12.6932	0.0000

YEARS 13 — QTR PAYT 3.1958 — AN CONST 12.79

#	INT	PRIN	BALANCE
1	8.3615	4.4217	95.5783
2	7.9735	4.8097	90.7685
3	7.5515	5.2318	85.5368
4	7.0924	5.6908	79.8459
5	6.5930	6.1902	73.6557
6	6.0499	6.7334	66.9223
7	5.4590	7.3242	59.5981
8	4.8163	7.9669	51.6312
9	4.1173	8.6660	42.9652
10	3.3568	9.4264	33.5388
11	2.5297	10.2536	23.2853
12	1.6300	11.1533	12.1320
13	.6513	12.1320	0.0000

YEARS 14 — QTR PAYT 3.0710 — AN CONST 12.29

#	INT	PRIN	BALANCE
1	8.3777	3.9062	96.0938
2	8.0349	4.2490	91.8448
3	7.6621	4.6218	87.2229
4	7.2565	5.0274	82.1955
5	6.8154	5.4685	76.7270
6	6.3355	5.9484	70.7786
7	5.8135	6.4704	64.3082
8	5.2458	7.0381	57.2701
9	4.6282	7.6557	49.6144
10	3.9564	8.3275	41.2869
11	3.2257	9.0582	32.2287
12	2.4309	9.8530	22.3757
13	1.5663	10.7176	11.6581
14	.6258	11.6581	0.0000

YEARS 15 — QTR PAYT 2.9645 — AN CONST 11.86

#	INT	PRIN	BALANCE
1	8.3914	3.4666	96.5334
2	8.0872	3.7708	92.7625
3	7.7564	4.1017	88.6608
4	7.3964	4.4616	84.1992
5	7.0050	4.8531	79.3461
6	6.5791	5.2790	74.0671
7	6.1159	5.7422	68.3249
8	5.6120	6.2461	62.0789
9	5.0639	6.7941	55.2847
10	4.4678	7.3903	47.8944
11	3.8193	8.0388	39.8556
12	3.1139	8.7442	31.1115
13	2.3466	9.5115	21.6000
14	1.5120	10.3461	11.2539
15	.6041	11.2539	0.0000

YEARS 16 — QTR PAYT 2.8730 — AN CONST 11.50

#	INT	PRIN	BALANCE
1	8.4033	3.0886	96.9114
2	8.1323	3.3596	93.5519
3	7.8375	3.6544	89.8975
4	7.5168	3.9750	85.9225
5	7.1680	4.3238	81.5987
6	6.7886	4.7032	76.8954
7	6.3759	5.1159	71.7795
8	5.9270	5.5648	66.2147
9	5.4387	6.0531	60.1615
10	4.9075	6.5843	53.5772
11	4.3298	7.1621	46.4152
12	3.7013	7.7905	38.6247
13	3.0177	8.4741	30.1506
14	2.2741	9.2177	20.9329
15	1.4653	10.0265	10.9063
16	.5855	10.9063	0.0000

YEARS 17 — QTR PAYT 2.7936 — AN CONST 11.18

#	INT	PRIN	BALANCE
1	8.4135	2.7610	97.2390
2	8.1713	3.0033	94.2357
3	7.9077	3.2668	90.9689
4	7.6211	3.5535	87.4154
5	7.3093	3.8653	83.5502
6	6.9701	4.2044	79.3457
7	6.6012	4.5734	74.7724
8	6.1999	4.9747	69.7977
9	5.7633	5.4112	64.3865
10	5.2885	5.8860	58.5005
11	4.7720	6.4025	52.0980
12	4.2102	6.9643	45.1337
13	3.5991	7.5754	37.5582
14	2.9344	8.2401	29.3181
15	2.2113	8.9632	20.3549
16	1.4248	9.7497	10.6052
17	.5693	10.6052	0.0000

YEARS 18 — QTR PAYT 2.7245 — AN CONST 10.90

#	INT	PRIN	BALANCE
1	8.4225	2.4754	97.5246
2	8.2053	2.6927	94.8319
3	7.9690	2.9289	91.9030
4	7.7120	3.1859	88.7170
5	7.4324	3.4655	85.2515
6	7.1283	3.7696	81.4819
7	6.7976	4.1004	77.3816
8	6.4378	4.4602	72.9214
9	6.0464	4.8515	68.0699
10	5.6207	5.2772	62.7926
11	5.1576	5.7403	57.0523
12	4.6539	6.2440	50.8083
13	4.1060	6.7919	44.0164
14	3.5100	7.3879	36.6285
15	2.8618	8.0362	28.5924
16	2.1566	8.7413	19.8510
17	1.3896	9.5083	10.3427
18	.5552	10.3427	0.0000

YEARS 19 — QTR PAYT 2.6639 — AN CONST 10.66

#	INT	PRIN	BALANCE
1	8.4303	2.2251	97.7749
2	8.2351	2.4204	95.3545
3	8.0227	2.6327	92.7218
4	7.7917	2.8638	89.8580
5	7.5404	3.1150	86.7430
6	7.2670	3.3884	83.3546
7	6.9697	3.6857	79.6689
8	6.6463	4.0091	75.6598
9	6.2945	4.3609	71.2988
10	5.9118	4.7436	66.5553
11	5.4956	5.1598	61.3954
12	5.0428	5.6126	55.7828
13	4.5504	6.1051	49.6778
14	4.0146	6.6408	43.0370
15	3.4319	7.2235	35.8135
16	2.7981	7.8573	27.9561
17	2.1086	8.5468	19.4093
18	1.3587	9.2968	10.1126
19	.5429	10.1126	0.0000

YEARS 20 — QTR PAYT 2.6105 — AN CONST 10.45

#	INT	PRIN	BALANCE
1	8.4372	2.0046	97.9954
2	8.2613	2.1805	95.8149
3	8.0700	2.3718	93.4430
4	7.8619	2.5800	90.8631
5	7.6355	2.8064	88.0567
6	7.3892	3.0526	85.0041
7	7.1214	3.3205	81.6837
8	6.8300	3.6118	78.0718
9	6.5131	3.9288	74.1431
10	6.1683	4.2735	69.8696
11	5.7933	4.6485	65.2211
12	5.3854	5.0564	60.1647
13	4.9418	5.5001	54.6646
14	4.4591	5.9827	48.6819
15	3.9342	6.5077	42.1743
16	3.3631	7.0787	35.0956
17	2.7420	7.6998	27.3957
18	2.0663	8.3755	19.0202
19	1.3314	9.1104	9.9098
20	.5320	9.9098	0.0000

YEARS 21 — QTR PAYT 2.5632 — AN CONST 10.26

#	INT	PRIN	BALANCE
1	8.4433	1.8095	98.1905
2	8.2845	1.9683	96.2221
3	8.1118	2.1410	94.0811

QUARTERLY PAYMENT AMORTIZATION SCHEDULE PER $100   8.50 %

#	INT	PRIN	BALANCE
4	7.9240	2.3289	91.7521
5	7.7196	2.5333	89.2189
6	7.4973	2.7556	86.4633
7	7.2555	2.9974	83.4659
8	6.9925	3.2604	80.2056
9	6.7064	3.5465	76.6591
10	6.3952	3.8577	72.8014
11	6.0567	4.1962	68.6052
12	5.6885	4.5644	64.0409
13	5.2880	4.9649	59.0760
14	4.8523	5.4005	53.6754
15	4.3784	5.8744	47.8010
16	3.8630	6.3899	41.4111
17	3.3023	6.9506	34.4605
18	2.6924	7.5605	26.9000
19	2.0290	8.2239	18.6761
20	1.3073	8.9456	9.7305
21	.5224	9.7305	0.0000

YEARS 22 — QTR PAYT 2.5213 — AN CONST 10.09

#	INT	PRIN	BALANCE
1	8.4488	1.6364	98.3636
2	8.3052	1.7799	96.5837
3	8.1490	1.9361	94.6476
4	7.9791	2.1060	92.5416
5	7.7943	2.2908	90.2508
6	7.5933	2.4918	87.7589
7	7.3746	2.7105	85.0485
8	7.1368	2.9483	82.1001
9	6.8781	3.2070	78.8931
10	6.5967	3.4884	75.4047
11	6.2906	3.7945	71.6101
12	5.9576	4.1275	67.4826
13	5.5954	4.4897	62.9929
14	5.2015	4.8836	58.1093
15	4.7729	5.3122	52.7971
16	4.3068	5.7783	47.0188
17	3.7998	6.2853	40.7335
18	3.2482	6.8369	33.8966
19	2.6483	7.4368	26.4598
20	1.9958	8.0894	18.3705
21	1.2859	8.7992	9.5713
22	.5138	9.5713	0.0000

YEARS 23 — QTR PAYT 2.4839 — AN CONST 9.94

#	INT	PRIN	BALANCE
1	8.4536	1.4821	98.5179
2	8.3235	1.6121	96.9058
3	8.1821	1.7536	95.1523
4	8.0282	1.9074	93.2449
5	7.8608	2.0748	91.1701
6	7.6788	2.2569	88.9132
7	7.4807	2.4549	86.4583
8	7.2653	2.6703	83.7880
9	7.0310	2.9046	80.8834
10	6.7761	3.1595	77.7239
11	6.4989	3.4367	74.2871
12	6.1973	3.7383	70.5488
13	5.8693	4.0663	66.4825
14	5.5125	4.4231	62.0594
15	5.1244	4.8113	57.2481
16	4.7022	5.2334	52.0146
17	4.2430	5.6927	46.3220
18	3.7434	6.1922	40.1298
19	3.2001	6.7355	33.3942
20	2.6091	7.3266	26.0677
21	1.9662	7.9695	18.0982
22	1.2669	8.6688	9.4294
23	.5062	9.4294	0.0000

YEARS 24 — QTR PAYT 2.4505 — AN CONST 9.81

#	INT	PRIN	BALANCE
1	8.4579	1.3442	98.6558
2	8.3400	1.4621	97.1937
3	8.2117	1.5904	95.6033
4	8.0721	1.7300	93.8733
5	7.9203	1.8818	91.9915
6	7.7552	2.0469	89.9446
7	7.5756	2.2265	87.7180
8	7.3802	2.4219	85.2961
9	7.1677	2.6344	82.6617
10	6.9365	2.8656	79.7961
11	6.6851	3.1170	76.6791
12	6.4115	3.3905	73.2886
13	6.1140	3.6881	69.6005
14	5.7904	4.0117	65.5889
15	5.4384	4.3637	61.2252
16	5.0555	4.7466	56.4786
17	4.6390	5.1631	51.3155
18	4.1859	5.6161	45.6993
19	3.6931	6.1090	39.5904
20	3.1571	6.6450	32.9454
21	2.5740	7.2281	25.7173
22	1.9397	7.8623	17.8549
23	1.2498	8.5522	9.3027
24	.4994	9.3027	0.0000

YEARS 25 — QTR PAYT 2.4206 — AN CONST 9.69

#	INT	PRIN	BALANCE
1	8.4618	1.2207	98.7793
2	8.3547	1.3278	97.4516
3	8.2382	1.4443	96.0073
4	8.1114	1.5710	94.4363
5	7.9736	1.7089	92.7274
6	7.8236	1.8588	90.8686
7	7.6605	2.0219	88.8466
8	7.4831	2.1993	86.6473
9	7.2901	2.3923	84.2550
10	7.0802	2.6023	81.6527
11	6.8518	2.8306	78.8221
12	6.6035	3.0790	75.7431
13	6.3333	3.3492	72.3940
14	6.0394	3.6430	68.7509
15	5.7197	3.9627	64.7882
16	5.3720	4.3104	60.4778
17	4.9938	4.6887	55.7892
18	4.5824	5.1001	50.6891
19	4.1348	5.5476	45.1415
20	3.6481	6.0344	39.1071
21	3.1185	6.5639	32.5432
22	2.5426	7.1399	25.4033
23	1.9161	7.7664	17.6370
24	1.2346	8.4479	9.1891
25	.4933	9.1891	0.0000

YEARS 26 — QTR PAYT 2.3937 — AN CONST 9.58

#	INT	PRIN	BALANCE
1	8.4652	1.1097	98.8903
2	8.3679	1.2071	97.6831
3	8.2619	1.3130	96.3701
4	8.1467	1.4283	94.9418
5	8.0214	1.5536	93.3883
6	7.8851	1.6899	91.6984
7	7.7368	1.8382	89.8602
8	7.5755	1.9995	87.8607
9	7.4000	2.1749	85.6857
10	7.2092	2.3658	83.3200
11	7.0016	2.5734	80.7466
12	6.7758	2.7992	77.9474
13	6.5302	3.0448	74.9026
14	6.2630	3.3120	71.5906
15	5.9724	3.6026	67.9880
16	5.6563	3.9187	64.0693
17	5.3124	4.2626	59.8067
18	4.9384	4.6366	55.1700
19	4.5315	5.0435	50.1266
20	4.0890	5.4860	44.6405
21	3.6076	5.9674	38.6731
22	3.0839	6.4910	32.1821
23	2.5144	7.0606	25.1214
24	1.8948	7.6802	17.4413
25	1.2209	8.3541	9.0872
26	.4878	9.0872	0.0000

YEARS 27 — QTR PAYT 2.3696 — AN CONST 9.48

#	INT	PRIN	BALANCE
1	8.4684	1.0099	98.9901
2	8.3798	1.0985	97.8916
3	8.2834	1.1949	96.6966
4	8.1785	1.2998	95.3968
5	8.0645	1.4138	93.9830
6	7.9404	1.5379	92.4451
7	7.8054	1.6728	90.7723
8	7.6587	1.8196	88.9527
9	7.4990	1.9793	86.9734
10	7.3253	2.1530	84.8204
11	7.1364	2.3419	82.4785
12	6.9309	2.5474	79.9311
13	6.7074	2.7709	77.1602
14	6.4642	3.0141	74.1461
15	6.1997	3.2785	70.8676
16	5.9121	3.5662	67.3014
17	5.5991	3.8792	63.4222
18	5.2587	4.2195	59.2027
19	4.8885	4.5898	54.6129
20	4.4857	4.9925	49.6203
21	4.0477	5.4306	44.1897
22	3.5711	5.9072	38.2825
23	3.0528	6.4255	31.8571
24	2.4890	6.9893	24.8677
25	1.8757	7.6026	17.2651
26	1.2086	8.2697	8.9954
27	.4829	8.9954	0.0000

YEARS 28 — QTR PAYT 2.3478 — AN CONST 9.40

#	INT	PRIN	BALANCE
1	8.4712	.9199	99.0801
2	8.3905	1.0006	98.0795
3	8.3027	1.0884	96.9910
4	8.2072	1.1839	95.8071
5	8.1033	1.2878	94.5193
6	7.9903	1.4008	93.1185
7	7.8674	1.5237	91.5947
8	7.7336	1.6575	89.9373
9	7.5882	1.8029	88.1344
10	7.4300	1.9611	86.1733
11	7.2579	2.1332	84.0401
12	7.0707	2.3204	81.7198
13	6.8671	2.5240	79.1958
14	6.6457	2.7454	76.4504
15	6.4048	2.9863	73.4641
16	6.1427	3.2484	70.2157
17	5.8577	3.5334	66.6823
18	5.5476	3.8435	62.8388
19	5.2104	4.1807	58.6581
20	4.8435	4.5476	54.1105
21	4.4445	4.9466	49.1639
22	4.0104	5.3807	43.7832
23	3.5383	5.8528	37.9304
24	3.0247	6.3664	31.5640
25	2.4661	6.9250	24.6390
26	1.8584	7.5327	17.1063
27	1.1974	8.1937	8.9126
28	.4785	8.9126	0.0000

YEARS 29 — QTR PAYT 2.3281 — AN CONST 9.32

#	INT	PRIN	BALANCE
1	8.4737	.8386	99.1614
2	8.4002	.9122	98.2492
3	8.3201	.9922	97.2570
4	8.2330	1.0793	96.1777
5	8.1383	1.1740	95.0037
6	8.0353	1.2770	93.7266
7	7.9233	1.3891	92.3376
8	7.8014	1.5110	90.8266
9	7.6688	1.6436	89.1831
10	7.5246	1.7878	87.3953
11	7.3677	1.9446	85.4506
12	7.1971	2.1153	83.3354
13	7.0114	2.3009	81.0345
14	6.8096	2.5028	78.5317
15	6.5899	2.7224	75.8093
16	6.3511	2.9613	72.8480
17	6.0912	3.2211	69.6268
18	5.8086	3.5038	66.1231
19	5.5011	3.8112	62.3118
20	5.1667	4.1457	58.1662
21	4.8029	4.5094	53.6567
22	4.4072	4.9051	48.7516
23	3.9768	5.3355	43.4160
24	3.5086	5.8037	37.6123
25	2.9993	6.3130	31.2993
26	2.4454	6.8670	24.4324
27	1.8428	7.4695	16.9628
28	1.1874	8.1249	8.8379
29	.4744	8.8379	0.0000

YEARS 30 — QTR PAYT 2.3103 — AN CONST 9.25

#	INT	PRIN	BALANCE
1	8.4760	.7651	99.2349
2	8.4089	.8322	98.4028
3	8.3359	.9052	97.4975
4	8.2565	.9846	96.5129
5	8.1701	1.0710	95.4419
6	8.0761	1.1650	94.2768
7	7.9738	1.2673	93.0096
8	7.8626	1.3785	91.6311
9	7.7417	1.4994	90.1317
10	7.6101	1.6310	88.5008
11	7.4670	1.7741	86.7267
12	7.3113	1.9298	84.7969
13	7.1420	2.0991	82.6978
14	6.9578	2.2833	80.4145
15	6.7575	2.4836	77.9309
16	6.5395	2.7016	75.2293
17	6.3025	2.9386	72.2907
18	6.0446	3.1965	69.0942
19	5.7641	3.4770	65.6172
20	5.4590	3.7821	61.8351
21	5.1271	4.1139	57.7211
22	4.7662	4.4749	53.2462
23	4.3735	4.8676	48.3786
24	3.9464	5.2947	43.0839
25	3.4818	5.7593	37.3245
26	2.9764	6.2647	31.0598
27	2.4267	6.8144	24.2454
28	1.8287	7.4124	16.8331
29	1.1783	8.0628	8.7703
30	.4708	8.7703	0.0000

YEARS 2	QTR PAYT 13.7615	AN CONST 55.05
# INT	PRIN	BALANCE
1 7.2086	47.8374	52.1626
2 2.8835	52.1626	0.0000

YEARS 3	QTR PAYT 9.5652	AN CONST 38.27
# INT	PRIN	BALANCE
1 7.7675	30.4933	69.5067
2 5.0105	33.2502	36.2565
3 2.0042	36.2565	0.0000

YEARS 4	QTR PAYT 7.4749	AN CONST 29.90
# INT	PRIN	BALANCE
1 8.0459	21.8535	78.1465
2 6.0700	23.8294	54.3171
3 3.9155	25.9839	28.3332
4 1.5662	28.3332	0.0000

YEARS 5	QTR PAYT 6.2269	AN CONST 24.91
# INT	PRIN	BALANCE
1 8.2121	16.6955	83.3045
2 6.7026	18.2050	65.0995
3 5.0566	19.8510	45.2486
4 3.2618	21.6457	23.6028
5 1.3047	23.6028	0.0000

YEARS 6	QTR PAYT 5.4001	AN CONST 21.61
# INT	PRIN	BALANCE
1 8.3222	13.2781	86.7219
2 7.1216	14.4786	72.2432
3 5.8126	15.7877	56.4555
4 4.3852	17.2151	39.2404
5 2.8287	18.7716	20.4688
6 1.1315	20.4688	0.0000

YEARS 7	QTR PAYT 4.8139	AN CONST 19.26
# INT	PRIN	BALANCE
1 8.4002	10.8553	89.1447
2 7.4188	11.8367	77.3080
3 6.3486	12.9066	64.4010
4 5.1816	14.0739	50.3271
5 3.9091	15.3464	34.9807
6 2.5216	16.7339	18.2469
7 1.0087	18.2469	0.0000

YEARS 8	QTR PAYT 4.3780	AN CONST 17.52
# INT	PRIN	BALANCE
1 8.4583	9.0539	90.9461
2 7.6397	9.8725	81.0737
3 6.7471	10.7651	70.3086
4 5.7738	11.7384	58.5702
5 4.7125	12.7997	45.7706
6 3.5552	13.9569	31.8136
7 2.2933	15.2188	16.5948
8 .9173	16.5948	0.0000

YEARS 9	QTR PAYT 4.0424	AN CONST 16.17
# INT	PRIN	BALANCE
1 8.5030	7.6666	92.3334
2 7.8098	8.3598	83.9737
3 7.0540	9.1156	74.8581
4 6.2298	9.9398	64.9183
5 5.3311	10.8384	54.0799
6 4.3512	11.8184	42.2615

#	INT	PRIN	BALANCE
7	3.2827	12.8869	29.3746
8	2.1175	14.0521	15.3225
9	.8470	15.3225	0.0000

YEARS 10	QTR PAYT 3.7768	AN CONST 15.11
# INT	PRIN	BALANCE
1 8.5383	6.5690	93.4310
2 7.9444	7.1630	86.2680
3 7.2968	7.8106	78.4574
4 6.5906	8.5168	69.9406
5 5.8206	9.2868	60.6538
6 4.9809	10.1265	50.5274
7 4.0654	11.0420	39.4853
8 3.0670	12.0404	27.4450
9 1.9784	13.1290	14.3160
10 .7914	14.3160	0.0000

YEARS 11	QTR PAYT 3.5622	AN CONST 14.25
# INT	PRIN	BALANCE
1 8.5669	5.6821	94.3179
2 8.0532	6.1958	88.1222
3 7.4930	6.7560	81.3662
4 6.8822	7.3668	73.9994
5 6.2161	8.0328	65.9666
6 5.4898	8.7591	57.2074
7 4.6979	9.5511	47.6564
8 3.8344	10.4146	37.2418
9 2.8927	11.3562	25.8855
10 1.8660	12.3830	13.5026
11 .7464	13.5026	0.0000

YEARS 12	QTR PAYT 3.3858	AN CONST 13.55
# INT	PRIN	BALANCE
1 8.5904	4.9528	95.0472
2 8.1426	5.4006	89.6465
3 7.6543	5.8889	83.7576
4 7.1219	6.4214	77.3363
5 6.5413	7.0019	70.3343
6 5.9082	7.6350	62.6993
7 5.2179	8.3253	54.3740
8 4.4652	9.0780	45.2960
9 3.6445	9.8988	35.3972
10 2.7495	10.7938	24.6035
11 1.7736	11.7697	12.8338
12 .7094	12.8338	0.0000

YEARS 13	QTR PAYT 3.2387	AN CONST 12.96
# INT	PRIN	BALANCE
1 8.6100	4.3448	95.6552
2 8.2172	4.7376	90.9176
3 7.7888	5.1660	85.7516
4 7.3218	5.6331	80.1185
5 6.8125	6.1424	73.9762
6 6.2571	6.6977	67.2784
7 5.6515	7.3033	59.9752
8 4.9912	7.9636	52.0116
9 4.2712	8.6836	43.3280
10 3.4861	9.4687	33.8593
11 2.6300	10.3248	23.5345
12 1.6965	11.2583	12.2762
13 .6786	12.2762	0.0000

YEARS 14	QTR PAYT 3.1146	AN CONST 12.46
# INT	PRIN	BALANCE
1 8.6265	3.8319	96.1681
2 8.2801	4.1783	91.9898
3 7.9023	4.5561	87.4337

#	INT	PRIN	BALANCE
4	7.4904	4.9680	82.4657
5	7.0412	5.4172	77.0485
6	6.5514	5.9070	71.1415
7	6.0173	6.4411	64.7004
8	5.4350	7.0234	57.6770
9	4.8000	7.6584	50.0186
10	4.1076	8.3508	41.6677
11	3.3525	9.1059	32.5619
12	2.5292	9.9292	22.6327
13	1.6315	10.8269	11.8058
14	.6526	11.8058	0.0000

YEARS 15	QTR PAYT 3.0089	AN CONST 12.04
# INT	PRIN	BALANCE
1 8.6406	3.3948	96.6052
2 8.3337	3.7018	92.9034
3 7.9990	4.0365	88.8669
4 7.6340	4.4014	84.4655
5 7.2361	4.7994	79.6661
6 6.8022	5.2333	74.4328
7 6.3290	5.7065	68.7263
8 5.8131	6.2224	62.5039
9 5.2505	6.7850	55.7190
10 4.6370	7.3984	48.3205
11 3.9681	8.0674	40.2532
12 3.2387	8.7967	31.4564
13 2.4434	9.5921	21.8643
14 1.5761	10.4593	11.4050
15 .6305	11.4050	0.0000

YEARS 16	QTR PAYT 2.9180	AN CONST 11.68
# INT	PRIN	BALANCE
1 8.6527	3.0194	96.9806
2 8.3797	3.2923	93.6883
3 8.0821	3.5900	90.0983
4 7.7575	3.9146	86.1837
5 7.4035	4.2685	81.9152
6 7.0176	4.6545	77.2607
7 6.5968	5.0753	72.1854
8 6.1379	5.5342	66.6513
9 5.6375	6.0345	60.6167
10 5.0919	6.5801	54.0366
11 4.4970	7.1751	46.8616
12 3.8483	7.8238	39.0378
13 3.1409	8.5311	30.5066
14 2.3696	9.3025	21.2042
15 1.5285	10.1435	11.0606
16 .6114	11.0606	0.0000

YEARS 17	QTR PAYT 2.8394	AN CONST 11.36
# INT	PRIN	BALANCE
1 8.6632	2.6944	97.3056
2 8.4196	2.9380	94.3676
3 8.1539	3.2036	91.1640
4 7.8643	3.4933	87.6707
5 7.5485	3.8091	83.8616
6 7.2041	4.1535	79.7080
7 6.8285	4.5291	75.1790
8 6.4190	4.9385	70.2405
9 5.9725	5.3850	64.8554
10 5.4856	5.8719	58.9835
11 4.9547	6.4028	52.5807
12 4.3758	6.9817	45.5989
13 3.7446	7.6130	37.9860
14 3.0563	8.3013	29.6847
15 2.3058	9.0518	20.6329
16 1.4873	9.8702	10.7626
17 .5949	10.7626	0.0000

YEARS 18	QTR PAYT 2.7709	AN CONST 11.09
# INT	PRIN	BALANCE
1 8.6723	2.4114	97.5886
2 8.4543	2.6294	94.9592
3 8.2165	2.8672	92.0920
4 7.9573	3.1264	88.9656
5 7.6747	3.4090	85.5566
6 7.3664	3.7173	81.8393
7 7.0303	4.0534	77.7860
8 6.6639	4.4198	73.3661
9 6.2642	4.8195	68.5467
10 5.8285	5.2552	63.2915
11 5.3534	5.7303	57.5612
12 4.8353	6.2484	51.3127
13 4.2703	6.8134	44.4994
14 3.6543	7.4294	37.0700
15 2.9826	8.1011	28.9689
16 2.2502	8.8335	20.1353
17 1.4515	9.6322	10.5031
18 .5806	10.5031	0.0000

YEARS 19	QTR PAYT 2.7110	AN CONST 10.85
# INT	PRIN	BALANCE
1 8.6803	2.1636	97.8364
2 8.4847	2.3592	95.4772
3 8.2714	2.5725	92.9046
4 8.0388	2.8051	90.0995
5 7.7852	3.0587	87.0408
6 7.5086	3.3353	83.7055
7 7.2070	3.6368	80.0686
8 6.8782	3.9657	76.1030
9 6.5197	4.3242	71.7788
10 6.1287	4.7152	67.0636
11 5.7024	5.1415	61.9221
12 5.2375	5.6063	56.3158
13 4.7307	6.1132	50.2025
14 4.1779	6.6660	43.5366
15 3.5752	7.2686	36.2679
16 2.9181	7.9258	28.3421
17 2.2015	8.6424	19.6997
18 1.4201	9.4238	10.2759
19 .5680	10.2759	0.0000

YEARS 20	QTR PAYT 2.6582	AN CONST 10.64
# INT	PRIN	BALANCE
1 8.6873	1.9456	98.0544
2 8.5114	2.1215	95.9329
3 8.3196	2.3133	93.6196
4 8.1104	2.5225	91.0971
5 7.8824	2.7505	88.3465
6 7.6337	2.9992	85.3473
7 7.3625	3.2704	82.0769
8 7.0668	3.5661	78.5108
9 6.7444	3.8885	74.6223
10 6.3928	4.2401	70.3822
11 6.0095	4.6234	65.7588
12 5.5915	5.0415	60.7173
13 5.1356	5.4973	55.2201
14 4.6386	5.9943	49.2258
15 4.0967	6.5363	42.6895
16 3.5057	7.1272	35.5623
17 2.8613	7.7716	27.7907
18 2.1586	8.4743	19.3164
19 1.3924	9.2405	10.0759
20 .5570	10.0759	0.0000

YEARS 21	QTR PAYT 2.6116	AN CONST 10.45
# INT	PRIN	BALANCE
1 8.6935	1.7530	98.2470
2 8.5350	1.9115	96.3355
3 8.3622	2.0843	94.2512

QUARTERLY PAYMENT AMORTIZATION SCHEDULE PER $100

#	INT	PRIN	BALANCE
4	8.1737	2.2728	91.9784
5	7.9683	2.4783	89.5002
6	7.7442	2.7023	86.7978
7	7.4999	2.9467	83.8512
8	7.2334	3.2131	80.6381
9	6.9429	3.5036	77.1345
10	6.6262	3.8203	73.3142
11	6.2808	4.1658	69.1484
12	5.9041	4.5424	64.6061
13	5.4934	4.9531	59.6530
14	5.0456	5.4009	54.2521
15	4.5573	5.8892	48.3628
16	4.0248	6.4217	41.9412
17	3.4442	7.0023	34.9389
18	2.8111	7.6354	27.3035
19	2.1208	8.3257	18.9778
20	1.3680	9.0785	9.8993
21	.5472	9.8993	0.0000

	YEARS 22	QTR PAYT 2.5703	AN CONST 10.29
#	INT	PRIN	BALANCE
1	8.6990	1.5822	98.4178
2	8.5560	1.7253	96.6925
3	8.4000	1.8813	94.8113
4	8.2299	2.0513	92.7599
5	8.0444	2.2368	90.5231
6	7.8422	2.4390	88.0841
7	7.6216	2.6596	85.4245
8	7.3812	2.9000	82.5245
9	7.1190	3.1622	79.3622
10	6.8331	3.4481	75.9141
11	6.5213	3.7599	72.1542
12	6.1814	4.0998	68.0544
13	5.8107	4.4705	63.5838
14	5.4065	4.8747	58.7091
15	4.9658	5.3155	53.3937
16	4.4852	5.7960	47.5976
17	3.9612	6.3201	41.2776
18	3.3897	6.8915	34.3861
19	2.7667	7.5146	26.8715
20	2.0872	8.1940	18.6775
21	1.3464	8.9348	9.7427
22	.5386	9.7427	0.0000

	YEARS 23	QTR PAYT 2.5335	AN CONST 10.14
#	INT	PRIN	BALANCE
1	8.7039	1.4303	98.5697
2	8.5746	1.5596	97.0102
3	8.4336	1.7006	95.3096
4	8.2798	1.8543	93.4552
5	8.1122	2.0220	91.4332
6	7.9294	2.2048	89.2284
7	7.7300	2.4042	86.8242
8	7.5127	2.6215	84.2027
9	7.2756	2.8586	81.3442
10	7.0172	3.1170	78.2271
11	6.7354	3.3988	74.8283
12	6.4281	3.7061	71.1222
13	6.0930	4.0412	67.0810
14	5.7276	4.4066	62.6744
15	5.3292	4.8050	57.8694
16	4.8948	5.2394	52.6300
17	4.4210	5.7131	46.9169
18	3.9045	6.2297	40.6872
19	3.3413	6.7929	33.8943
20	2.7271	7.4071	26.4872
21	2.0574	8.0768	18.4104
22	1.3271	8.8070	9.6033
23	.5309	9.6033	0.0000

	YEARS 24	QTR PAYT 2.5007	AN CONST 10.01
#	INT	PRIN	BALANCE
1	8.7083	1.2947	98.7053
2	8.5912	1.4117	97.2936
3	8.4636	1.5394	95.7542
4	8.3244	1.6786	94.0756
5	8.1726	1.8303	92.2453
6	8.0072	1.9958	90.2494
7	7.8267	2.1763	88.0732
8	7.6299	2.3730	85.7001
9	7.4154	2.5876	83.1125
10	7.1814	2.8215	80.2910
11	6.9263	3.0766	77.2143
12	6.6482	3.3548	73.8595
13	6.3448	3.6581	70.2014
14	6.0141	3.9889	66.2125
15	5.6534	4.3495	61.8630
16	5.2602	4.7428	57.1202
17	4.8314	5.1716	51.9486
18	4.3638	5.6392	46.3094
19	3.8539	6.1490	40.1604
20	3.2980	6.7050	33.4554
21	2.6918	7.3112	26.1442
22	2.0307	7.9722	18.1720
23	1.3100	8.6930	9.4790
24	.5240	9.4790	0.0000

	YEARS 25	QTR PAYT 2.4714	AN CONST 9.89
#	INT	PRIN	BALANCE
1	8.7122	1.1734	98.8266
2	8.6061	1.2795	97.5471
3	8.4904	1.3952	96.1519
4	8.3643	1.5213	94.6306
5	8.2267	1.6589	92.9717
6	8.0767	1.8089	91.1628
7	7.9132	1.9724	89.1904
8	7.7349	2.1507	87.0397
9	7.5404	2.3452	84.6945
10	7.3284	2.5572	82.1373
11	7.0972	2.7884	79.3489
12	6.8451	3.0405	76.3083
13	6.5702	3.3155	72.9929
14	6.2704	3.6152	69.3776
15	5.9435	3.9421	65.4356
16	5.5871	4.2985	61.1371
17	5.1985	4.6871	56.4500
18	4.7747	5.1109	51.3390
19	4.3126	5.5730	45.7660
20	3.8087	6.0769	39.6892
21	3.2593	6.6263	33.0629
22	2.6602	7.2254	25.8375
23	2.0069	7.8787	17.9588
24	1.2946	8.5910	9.3678
25	.5178	9.3678	0.0000

	YEARS 26	QTR PAYT 2.4451	AN CONST 9.79
#	INT	PRIN	BALANCE
1	8.7157	1.0647	98.9353
2	8.6194	1.1609	97.7744
3	8.5145	1.2659	96.5085
4	8.4000	1.3803	95.1282
5	8.2752	1.5051	93.6231
6	8.1391	1.6412	91.9819
7	7.9908	1.7896	90.1923
8	7.8289	1.9514	88.2409
9	7.6525	2.1278	86.1130
10	7.4601	2.3202	83.7928
11	7.2504	2.5300	81.2628
12	7.0216	2.7587	78.5041
13	6.7722	3.0082	75.4959
14	6.5002	3.2802	72.2157
15	6.2036	3.5767	68.6390

#	INT	PRIN	BALANCE
16	5.8802	3.9001	64.7389
17	5.5276	4.2527	60.4862
18	5.1431	4.6372	55.8490
19	4.7239	5.0565	50.7925
20	4.2667	5.5137	45.2788
21	3.7682	6.0122	39.2666
22	3.2246	6.5558	32.7109
23	2.6319	7.1485	25.5624
24	1.9856	7.7948	17.7676
25	1.2808	8.4996	9.2680
26	.5123	9.2680	0.0000

	YEARS 27	QTR PAYT 2.4214	AN CONST 9.69
#	INT	PRIN	BALANCE
1	8.7188	.9669	99.0331
2	8.6314	1.0544	97.9787
3	8.5361	1.1497	96.8290
4	8.4321	1.2536	95.5754
5	8.3188	1.3670	94.2084
6	8.1952	1.4906	92.7178
7	8.0604	1.6253	91.0925
8	7.9135	1.7723	89.3202
9	7.7532	1.9325	87.3876
10	7.5785	2.1073	85.2804
11	7.3880	2.2978	82.9826
12	7.1802	2.5055	80.4770
13	6.9537	2.7321	77.7450
14	6.7067	2.9791	74.7659
15	6.4373	3.2484	71.5175
16	6.1436	3.5421	67.9753
17	5.8234	3.8624	64.1129
18	5.4742	4.2116	59.9013
19	5.0934	4.5924	55.3089
20	4.6782	5.0076	50.3013
21	4.2254	5.4604	44.8410
22	3.7317	5.9540	38.8869
23	3.1934	6.4924	32.3946
24	2.6064	7.0794	25.3152
25	1.9664	7.7194	17.5958
26	1.2684	8.4174	9.1784
27	.5074	9.1784	0.0000

	YEARS 28	QTR PAYT 2.4002	AN CONST 9.61
#	INT	PRIN	BALANCE
1	8.7217	.8790	99.1210
2	8.6422	.9584	98.1626
3	8.5556	1.0451	97.1175
4	8.4611	1.1396	95.9779
5	8.3580	1.2426	94.7353
6	8.2457	1.3550	93.3803
7	8.1232	1.4775	91.9028
8	7.9896	1.6111	90.2918
9	7.8439	1.7567	88.5351
10	7.6851	1.9155	86.6195
11	7.5119	2.0887	84.5308
12	7.3231	2.2776	82.2532
13	7.1171	2.4835	79.7697
14	6.8926	2.7081	77.0616
15	6.6477	2.9529	74.1087
16	6.3808	3.2199	70.8888
17	6.0896	3.5110	67.3778
18	5.7722	3.8284	63.5494
19	5.4261	4.1746	59.3748
20	5.0486	4.5520	54.8228
21	4.6371	4.9636	49.8592
22	4.1883	5.4124	44.4468
23	3.6989	5.9017	38.5451
24	3.1653	6.4353	32.1098
25	2.5835	7.0171	25.0927
26	1.9491	7.6516	17.4411
27	1.2573	8.3434	9.0977

#	INT	PRIN	BALANCE
28	.5029	9.0977	0.0000

	YEARS 29	QTR PAYT 2.3810	AN CONST 9.53
#	INT	PRIN	BALANCE
1	8.7242	.7996	99.2004
2	8.6519	.8719	98.3284
3	8.5731	.9508	97.3776
4	8.4871	1.0367	96.3409
5	8.3934	1.1305	95.2104
6	8.2912	1.2327	93.9777
7	8.1797	1.3441	92.6336
8	8.0582	1.4657	91.1680
9	7.9257	1.5982	89.5698
10	7.7812	1.7427	87.8271
11	7.6236	1.9002	85.9269
12	7.4518	2.0720	83.8548
13	7.2645	2.2594	81.5955
14	7.0602	2.4637	79.1318
15	6.8375	2.6864	76.4454
16	6.5946	2.9293	73.5161
17	6.3297	3.1941	70.3220
18	6.0410	3.4829	66.8391
19	5.7260	3.7978	63.0412
20	5.3827	4.1412	58.9000
21	5.0083	4.5156	54.3844
22	4.6000	4.9239	49.4605
23	4.1548	5.3691	44.0914
24	3.6694	5.8545	38.2369
25	3.1400	6.3838	31.8531
26	2.5629	6.9610	24.8920
27	1.9335	7.5904	17.3016
28	1.2472	8.2767	9.0250
29	.4989	9.0250	0.0000

	YEARS 30	QTR PAYT 2.3636	AN CONST 9.46
#	INT	PRIN	BALANCE
1	8.7265	.7280	99.2720
2	8.6607	.7938	98.4782
3	8.5890	.8656	97.6126
4	8.5107	.9439	96.6687
5	8.4254	1.0292	95.6395
6	8.3323	1.1222	94.5173
7	8.2308	1.2237	93.2936
8	8.1202	1.3343	91.9592
9	7.9996	1.4550	90.5043
10	7.8680	1.5865	88.9177
11	7.7246	1.7300	87.1877
12	7.5681	1.8864	85.3013
13	7.3976	2.0570	83.2444
14	7.2116	2.2429	81.0014
15	7.0088	2.4457	78.5557
16	6.7877	2.6668	75.8889
17	6.5466	2.9080	72.9809
18	6.2837	3.1709	69.8100
19	5.9970	3.4576	66.3525
20	5.6844	3.7702	62.5823
21	5.3435	4.1111	58.4712
22	4.9718	4.4827	53.9885
23	4.5665	4.8880	49.1004
24	4.1246	5.3300	43.7704
25	3.6426	5.8119	37.9585
26	3.1172	6.3374	31.6212
27	2.5442	6.9103	24.7108
28	1.9194	7.5351	17.1757
29	1.2381	8.2164	8.9593
30	.4953	8.9593	0.0000

YEARS 2 — QTR PAYT 13.7985 — AN CONST 55.20

#	INT	PRIN	BALANCE
1	7.4174	47.7764	52.2236
2	2.9703	52.2236	0.0000

YEARS 3 — QTR PAYT 9.6017 — AN CONST 38.41

#	INT	PRIN	BALANCE
1	7.9925	30.4144	69.5856
2	5.1615	33.2455	36.3401
3	2.0669	36.3401	0.0000

YEARS 4 — QTR PAYT 7.5117 — AN CONST 30.05

#	INT	PRIN	BALANCE
1	8.2790	21.7677	78.2323
2	6.2528	23.7939	54.4384
3	4.0379	26.0087	28.4297
4	1.6170	28.4297	0.0000

YEARS 5 — QTR PAYT 6.2642 — AN CONST 25.06

#	INT	PRIN	BALANCE
1	8.4499	16.6069	83.3931
2	6.9041	18.1527	65.2403
3	5.2144	19.8425	45.3979
4	3.3674	21.6895	23.7084
5	1.3484	23.7084	0.0000

YEARS 6 — QTR PAYT 5.4380 — AN CONST 21.76

#	INT	PRIN	BALANCE
1	8.5631	13.1890	86.8110
2	7.3355	14.4166	72.3944
3	5.9935	15.7586	56.6358
4	4.5266	17.2254	39.4104
5	2.9232	18.8289	20.5815
6	1.1706	20.5815	0.0000

YEARS 7 — QTR PAYT 4.8525 — AN CONST 19.42

#	INT	PRIN	BALANCE
1	8.6434	10.7667	89.2333
2	7.6412	11.7689	77.4643
3	6.5457	12.8644	64.5999
4	5.3482	14.0619	50.5380
5	4.0393	15.3708	35.1671
6	2.6085	16.8016	18.3655
7	1.0446	18.3655	0.0000

YEARS 8 — QTR PAYT 4.4174 — AN CONST 17.67

#	INT	PRIN	BALANCE
1	8.7030	8.9667	91.0333
2	7.8683	9.8013	81.2320
3	6.9560	10.7137	70.5183
4	5.9587	11.7109	58.8074
5	4.8686	12.8010	46.0064
6	3.6771	13.9926	32.0138
7	2.3746	15.2951	16.7188
8	.9509	16.7188	0.0000

YEARS 9 — QTR PAYT 4.0825 — AN CONST 16.34

#	INT	PRIN	BALANCE
1	8.7489	7.5812	92.4188
2	8.0432	8.2869	84.1319
3	7.2718	9.0583	75.0736
4	6.4286	9.9014	65.1722
5	5.5070	10.8231	54.3491
6	4.4995	11.8305	42.5186
7	3.3983	12.9318	29.5868
8	2.1946	14.1355	15.4513
9	.8788	15.4513	0.0000

YEARS 10 — QTR PAYT 3.8177 — AN CONST 15.28

#	INT	PRIN	BALANCE
1	8.7852	6.4858	93.5142
2	8.1814	7.0895	86.4247
3	7.5215	7.7494	78.6753
4	6.8002	8.4708	70.2045
5	6.0117	9.2593	60.9453
6	5.1498	10.1211	50.8241
7	4.2077	11.0632	39.7609
8	3.1779	12.0930	27.6679
9	2.0522	13.2187	14.4491
10	.8218	14.4491	0.0000

YEARS 11 — QTR PAYT 3.6039 — AN CONST 14.42

#	INT	PRIN	BALANCE
1	8.8145	5.6011	94.3989
2	8.2931	6.1225	88.2764
3	7.7232	6.6924	81.5839
4	7.1002	7.3154	74.2686
5	6.4193	7.9963	66.2723
6	5.6750	8.7406	57.5316
7	4.8614	9.5542	47.9774
8	3.9720	10.4436	37.5338
9	2.9999	11.4157	26.1181
10	1.9373	12.4783	13.6398
11	.7758	13.6398	0.0000

YEARS 12 — QTR PAYT 3.4282 — AN CONST 13.72

#	INT	PRIN	BALANCE
1	8.8385	4.8744	95.1256
2	8.3848	5.3281	89.7975
3	7.8889	5.8241	83.9734
4	7.3467	6.3662	77.6072
5	6.7541	6.9588	70.6484
6	6.1064	7.6065	63.0419
7	5.3984	8.3146	54.7273
8	4.6244	9.0885	45.6388
9	3.7784	9.9345	35.7043
10	2.8537	10.8593	24.8450
11	1.8429	11.8701	12.9750
12	.7380	12.9750	0.0000

YEARS 13 — QTR PAYT 3.2819 — AN CONST 13.13

#	INT	PRIN	BALANCE
1	8.8586	4.2689	95.7311
2	8.4612	4.6663	91.0648
3	8.0269	5.1007	85.9641
4	7.5521	5.5754	80.3886
5	7.0331	6.0944	74.2942
6	6.4658	6.6617	67.6325
7	5.8457	7.2818	60.3507
8	5.1679	7.9596	52.3910
9	4.4270	8.7005	43.6905
10	3.6171	9.5104	34.1801
11	2.7319	10.3957	23.7844
12	1.7642	11.3633	12.4211
13	.7065	12.4211	0.0000

YEARS 14 — QTR PAYT 3.1585 — AN CONST 12.64

#	INT	PRIN	BALANCE
1	8.8755	3.7586	96.2414
2	8.5256	4.1085	92.1329
3	8.1432	4.4909	87.6420
4	7.7252	4.9089	82.7330
5	7.2682	5.3659	77.3671
6	6.7688	5.8654	71.5018
7	6.2228	6.4113	65.0904
8	5.6260	7.0081	58.0823
9	4.9737	7.6605	50.4219
10	4.2606	8.3735	42.0483
11	3.4812	9.1530	32.8954
12	2.6292	10.0049	22.8904
13	1.6979	10.9362	11.9542
14	.6799	11.9542	0.0000

YEARS 15 — QTR PAYT 3.0535 — AN CONST 12.22

#	INT	PRIN	BALANCE
1	8.8899	3.3242	96.6758
2	8.5805	3.6337	93.0421
3	8.2422	3.9719	89.0702
4	7.8725	4.3416	84.7285
5	7.4684	4.7458	79.9828
6	7.0266	5.1875	74.7953
7	6.5437	5.6704	69.1249
8	6.0159	6.1982	62.9267
9	5.4390	6.7752	56.1515
10	4.8083	7.4058	48.7457
11	4.1190	8.0952	40.6506
12	3.3654	8.8487	31.8019
13	2.5418	9.6724	22.1295
14	1.6414	10.5727	11.5568
15	.6573	11.5568	0.0000

YEARS 16 — QTR PAYT 2.9634 — AN CONST 11.86

#	INT	PRIN	BALANCE
1	8.9022	2.9514	97.0486
2	8.6275	3.2261	93.8225
3	8.3272	3.5264	90.2960
4	7.9990	3.8547	86.4413
5	7.6402	4.2135	82.2279
6	7.2479	4.6057	77.6222
7	6.8192	5.0344	72.5878
8	6.3506	5.5030	67.0847
9	5.8384	6.0153	61.0695
10	5.2785	6.5752	54.4943
11	4.6664	7.1872	47.3070
12	3.9974	7.8562	39.4508
13	3.2661	8.5875	30.8633
14	2.4668	9.3869	21.4764
15	1.5930	10.2606	11.2157
16	.6379	11.2157	0.0000

YEARS 17 — QTR PAYT 2.8855 — AN CONST 11.55

#	INT	PRIN	BALANCE
1	8.9129	2.6291	97.3709
2	8.6682	2.8738	94.4971
3	8.4007	3.1413	91.3558
4	8.1083	3.4337	87.9221
5	7.7887	3.7533	84.1687
6	7.4393	4.1027	80.0660
7	7.0054	4.4846	75.5814
8	6.6399	4.9021	70.6794
9	6.1837	5.3583	65.3210
10	5.6849	5.8571	59.4639
11	5.1397	6.4023	53.0616
12	4.5437	6.9983	46.0633
13	3.8923	7.6497	38.4136
14	3.1802	8.3618	30.0518
15	2.4019	9.1401	20.9118
16	1.5511	9.9909	10.9209
17	.6211	10.9209	0.0000

YEARS 18 — QTR PAYT 2.8177 — AN CONST 11.28

#	INT	PRIN	BALANCE
1	8.9222	2.3487	97.6513
2	8.7036	2.5673	95.0840
3	8.4646	2.8063	92.2776
4	8.2034	3.0675	89.2101
5	7.9178	3.3531	85.8570
6	7.6057	3.6652	82.1918
7	7.2646	4.0064	78.1855
8	6.8916	4.3793	73.8062
9	6.4840	4.7869	69.0193
10	6.0384	5.2325	63.7868
11	5.5514	5.7196	58.0673
12	5.0190	6.2520	51.8153
13	4.4370	6.8339	44.9814
14	3.8009	7.4700	37.5114
15	3.1056	8.1654	29.3460
16	2.3455	8.9254	20.4206
17	1.5147	9.7562	10.6644
18	.6065	10.6644	0.0000

YEARS 19 — QTR PAYT 2.7585 — AN CONST 11.04

#	INT	PRIN	BALANCE
1	8.9303	2.1035	97.8965
2	8.7345	2.2993	95.5972
3	8.5205	2.5133	93.0839
4	8.2865	2.7473	90.3366
5	8.0308	3.0030	87.3336
6	7.7513	3.2825	84.0510
7	7.4457	3.5881	80.4629
8	7.1117	3.9221	76.5409
9	6.7467	4.2872	72.2537
10	6.3476	4.6862	67.5675
11	5.9114	5.1224	62.4450
12	5.4346	5.5992	56.8458
13	4.9134	6.1204	50.7254
14	4.3437	6.6902	44.0352
15	3.7209	7.3129	36.7223
16	3.0402	7.9936	28.7287
17	2.2962	8.7377	19.9910
18	1.4828	9.5510	10.4400
19	.5938	10.4400	0.0000

YEARS 20 — QTR PAYT 2.7064 — AN CONST 10.83

#	INT	PRIN	BALANCE
1	8.9375	1.8880	98.1120
2	8.7617	2.0638	96.0482
3	8.5696	2.2559	93.7923
4	8.3596	2.4659	91.3264
5	8.1301	2.6954	88.6310
6	7.8792	2.9463	85.6847
7	7.6049	3.2206	82.4641
8	7.3052	3.5203	78.9438
9	6.9775	3.8480	75.0957
10	6.6193	4.2062	70.8895
11	6.2278	4.5977	66.2918
12	5.7998	5.0257	61.2661
13	5.3320	5.4935	55.7725
14	4.8206	6.0049	49.7676
15	4.2617	6.5638	43.2038
16	3.6507	7.1748	36.0290
17	2.9828	7.8427	28.1863
18	2.2528	8.5727	19.6136
19	1.4548	9.3707	10.2429
20	.5826	10.2429	0.0000

YEARS 21 — QTR PAYT 2.6604 — AN CONST 10.65

#	INT	PRIN	BALANCE
1	8.9438	1.6979	98.3021
2	8.7857	1.8560	96.4461
3	8.6129	2.0287	94.4173

#	INT	PRIN	BALANCE
4	8.4241	2.2176	92.1997
5	8.2177	2.4240	89.7757
6	7.9920	2.6496	87.1261
7	7.7454	2.8963	84.2298
8	7.4758	3.1659	81.0639
9	7.1811	3.4606	77.6033
10	6.8590	3.7827	73.8207
11	6.5069	4.1348	69.6859
12	6.1220	4.5197	65.1662
13	5.7013	4.9404	60.2258
14	5.2414	5.4003	54.8255
15	4.7388	5.9029	48.9226
16	4.1893	6.4524	42.4702
17	3.5887	7.0530	35.4172
18	2.9322	7.7095	27.7077
19	2.2146	8.4271	19.2806
20	1.4301	9.2116	10.0690
21	.5727	10.0690	0.0000

YEARS 22 — QTR PAYT 2.6197 — AN CONST 10.48

#	INT	PRIN	BALANCE
1	8.9493	1.5296	98.4704
2	8.8070	1.6720	96.7984
3	8.6513	1.8276	94.9709
4	8.4812	1.9977	92.9731
5	8.2952	2.1837	90.7895
6	8.0920	2.3869	88.4025
7	7.8698	2.6091	85.7934
8	7.6269	2.8520	82.9414
9	7.3615	3.1175	79.8240
10	7.0713	3.4076	76.4163
11	6.7541	3.7248	72.6915
12	6.4074	4.0716	68.6200
13	6.0284	4.4505	64.1694
14	5.6141	4.8648	59.3046
15	5.1613	5.3176	53.9869
16	4.6663	5.8126	48.1743
17	4.1252	6.3537	41.8206
18	3.5338	6.9451	34.8755
19	2.8873	7.5916	27.2839
20	2.1807	8.2982	18.9857
21	1.4083	9.0707	9.9150
22	.5639	9.9150	0.0000

YEARS 23 — QTR PAYT 2.5836 — AN CONST 10.34

#	INT	PRIN	BALANCE
1	8.9543	1.3800	98.6200
2	8.8258	1.5085	97.1115
3	8.6854	1.6489	95.4626
4	8.5319	1.8024	93.6602
5	8.3642	1.9701	91.6901
6	8.1808	2.1535	89.5366
7	7.9803	2.3540	87.1826
8	7.7612	2.5731	84.6094
9	7.5217	2.8126	81.7968
10	7.2599	3.0744	78.7224
11	6.9737	3.3606	75.3618
12	6.6609	3.6734	71.6883
13	6.3189	4.0154	67.6730
14	5.9452	4.3891	63.2839
15	5.5366	4.7977	58.4862
16	5.0900	5.2443	53.2419
17	4.6019	5.7324	47.5095
18	4.0683	6.2660	41.2435
19	3.4850	6.8493	34.3942
20	2.8475	7.4868	26.9074
21	2.1506	8.1837	18.7237
22	1.3888	8.9455	9.7782
23	.5561	9.7782	0.0000

YEARS 24 — QTR PAYT 2.5514 — AN CONST 10.21

#	INT	PRIN	BALANCE
1	8.9587	1.2468	98.7532
2	8.8426	1.3628	97.3904
3	8.7158	1.4897	95.9008
4	8.5771	1.6283	94.2724
5	8.4256	1.7799	92.4925
6	8.2599	1.9456	90.5469
7	8.0788	2.1267	88.4202
8	7.8808	2.3246	86.0956
9	7.6644	2.5410	83.5546
10	7.4279	2.7776	80.7770
11	7.1694	3.0361	77.7409
12	6.8868	3.3187	74.4222
13	6.5778	3.6276	70.7946
14	6.2402	3.9653	66.8293
15	5.8711	4.3344	62.4949
16	5.4676	4.7379	57.7570
17	5.0266	5.1789	52.5781
18	4.5445	5.6609	46.9172
19	4.0176	6.1879	40.7293
20	3.4416	6.7639	33.9654
21	2.8120	7.3935	26.5719
22	2.1238	8.0817	18.4902
23	1.3715	8.8340	9.6563
24	.5492	9.6563	0.0000

YEARS 25 — QTR PAYT 2.5226 — AN CONST 10.10

#	INT	PRIN	BALANCE
1	8.9626	1.1277	98.8723
2	8.8577	1.2327	97.6396
3	8.7429	1.3474	96.2921
4	8.6175	1.4729	94.8193
5	8.4804	1.6100	93.2093
6	8.3305	1.7598	91.4494
7	8.1667	1.9236	89.5258
8	7.9877	2.1027	87.4231
9	7.7919	2.2984	85.1247
10	7.5780	2.5124	82.6123
11	7.3441	2.7462	79.8661
12	7.0885	3.0019	76.8642
13	6.8091	3.2813	73.5829
14	6.5037	3.5867	69.9962
15	6.1698	3.9206	66.0756
16	5.8049	4.2855	61.7901
17	5.4059	4.6844	57.1057
18	4.9699	5.1205	51.9852
19	4.4933	5.5971	46.3881
20	3.9723	6.1181	40.2700
21	3.4028	6.6876	33.5824
22	2.7803	7.3101	26.2723
23	2.0998	7.9906	18.2817
24	1.3560	8.7343	9.5474
25	.5430	9.5474	0.0000

YEARS 26 — QTR PAYT 2.4968 — AN CONST 9.99

#	INT	PRIN	BALANCE
1	8.9662	1.0212	98.9788
2	8.8711	1.1162	97.8626
3	8.7672	1.2201	96.6425
4	8.6536	1.3337	95.3088
5	8.5295	1.4578	93.8510
6	8.3938	1.5935	92.2575
7	8.2455	1.7419	90.5156
8	8.0833	1.9040	88.6116
9	7.9061	2.0812	86.5304
10	7.7124	2.2750	84.2554
11	7.5006	2.4867	81.7687
12	7.2691	2.7182	79.0505
13	7.0161	2.9712	76.0793
14	6.7396	3.2478	72.8315
15	6.4372	3.5501	69.2814
16	6.1068	3.8805	65.4009
17	5.7456	4.2418	61.1591
18	5.3507	4.6366	56.5225
19	4.9191	5.0682	51.4543
20	4.4474	5.5400	45.9144
21	3.9317	6.0556	39.8587
22	3.3680	6.6193	33.2394
23	2.7519	7.2355	26.0040
24	2.0784	7.9090	18.0950
25	1.3422	8.6451	9.4499
26	.5375	9.4499	0.0000

YEARS 27 — QTR PAYT 2.4737 — AN CONST 9.90

#	INT	PRIN	BALANCE
1	8.9693	.9256	99.0744
2	8.8832	1.0117	98.0627
3	8.7890	1.1059	96.9569
4	8.6861	1.2088	95.7480
5	8.5736	1.3213	94.4267
6	8.4506	1.4443	92.9824
7	8.3161	1.5788	91.4036
8	8.1692	1.7257	89.6778
9	8.0085	1.8864	87.7915
10	7.8329	2.0620	85.7295
11	7.6410	2.2539	83.4756
12	7.4312	2.4637	81.0119
13	7.2019	2.6930	78.3188
14	6.9512	2.9437	75.3751
15	6.6772	3.2177	72.1574
16	6.3777	3.5172	68.6402
17	6.0503	3.8446	64.7956
18	5.6924	4.2025	60.5930
19	5.3012	4.5937	55.9994
20	4.8736	5.0213	50.9781
21	4.4062	5.4887	45.4894
22	3.8953	5.9996	39.4898
23	3.3369	6.5580	32.9318
24	2.7264	7.1685	25.7633
25	2.0591	7.8358	17.9275
26	1.3298	8.5651	9.3624
27	.5325	9.3624	0.0000

YEARS 28 — QTR PAYT 2.4530 — AN CONST 9.82

#	INT	PRIN	BALANCE
1	8.9722	.8396	99.1604
2	8.8940	.9178	98.2426
3	8.8086	1.0032	97.2394
4	8.7152	1.0966	96.1428
5	8.6131	1.1987	94.9441
6	8.5016	1.3102	93.6339
7	8.3796	1.4322	92.2016
8	8.2463	1.5655	90.6361
9	8.1006	1.7112	88.9249
10	7.9413	1.8705	87.0543
11	7.7672	2.0447	85.0097
12	7.5768	2.2350	82.7747
13	7.3688	2.4430	80.3317
14	7.1414	2.6704	77.6613
15	6.8928	2.9190	74.7423
16	6.6211	3.1907	71.5516
17	6.3241	3.4877	68.0639
18	5.9995	3.8124	64.2515
19	5.6446	4.1672	60.0843
20	5.2567	4.5551	55.5292
21	4.8327	4.9791	50.5501
22	4.3692	5.4426	45.1075
23	3.8626	5.9492	39.1583
24	3.3088	6.5030	32.6553
25	2.7035	7.1083	25.5470
26	2.0419	7.7700	17.7770
27	1.3186	8.4932	9.2838
28	.5280	9.2838	0.0000

YEARS 29 — QTR PAYT 2.4343 — AN CONST 9.74

#	INT	PRIN	BALANCE
1	8.9748	.7623	99.2377
2	8.9038	.8332	98.4045
3	8.8262	.9108	97.4937
4	8.7415	.9956	96.4981
5	8.6488	1.0882	95.4099
6	8.5475	1.1895	94.2204
7	8.4368	1.3003	92.9201
8	8.3157	1.4213	91.4988
9	8.1834	1.5536	89.9452
10	8.0388	1.6982	88.2470
11	7.8807	1.8563	86.3907
12	7.7080	2.0291	84.3617
13	7.5191	2.2179	82.1437
14	7.3126	2.4244	79.7193
15	7.0870	2.6501	77.0693
16	6.8403	2.8967	74.1725
17	6.5706	3.1664	71.0061
18	6.2759	3.4611	67.5450
19	5.9537	3.7833	63.7617
20	5.6016	4.1355	59.6263
21	5.2166	4.5204	55.1059
22	4.7959	4.9412	50.1647
23	4.3359	5.4011	44.7636
24	3.8332	5.9039	38.8598
25	3.2836	6.4534	32.4064
26	2.6829	7.0541	25.3522
27	2.0263	7.7107	17.6415
28	1.3085	8.4285	9.2130
29	.5240	9.2130	0.0000

YEARS 30 — QTR PAYT 2.4174 — AN CONST 9.67

#	INT	PRIN	BALANCE
1	8.9771	.6925	99.3075
2	8.9126	.7570	98.5505
3	8.8421	.8275	97.7230
4	8.7651	.9045	96.8185
5	8.6809	.9887	95.8299
6	8.5889	1.0807	94.7492
7	8.4883	1.1813	93.5679
8	8.3783	1.2913	92.2766
9	8.2581	1.4115	90.8652
10	8.1268	1.5428	89.3223
11	7.9831	1.6864	87.6359
12	7.8262	1.8434	85.7925
13	7.6546	2.0150	83.7774
14	7.4670	2.2026	81.5749
15	7.2620	2.4076	79.1673
16	7.0379	2.6317	76.5355
17	6.7929	2.8767	73.6589
18	6.5251	3.1445	70.5144
19	6.2324	3.4371	67.0773
20	5.9125	3.7571	63.3202
21	5.5628	4.1068	59.2134
22	5.1805	4.4891	54.7243
23	4.7626	4.9069	49.8173
24	4.3059	5.3637	44.4536
25	3.8066	5.8630	38.5906
26	3.2609	6.4087	32.1819
27	2.6643	7.0053	25.1767
28	2.0123	7.6573	17.5193
29	1.2995	8.3701	9.1492
30	.5204	9.1492	0.0000

YEARS 2	QTR PAYT 13.8355	AN CONST 55.35
# INT	PRIN	BALANCE
1 7.6264	47.7154	52.2846
2 3.0572	52.2846	0.0000

YEARS 3	QTR PAYT 9.6384	AN CONST 38.56
# INT	PRIN	BALANCE
1 8.2178	30.3357	69.6643
2 5.3129	33.2406	36.4237
3 2.1298	36.4237	0.0000

YEARS 4	QTR PAYT 7.5486	AN CONST 30.20
# INT	PRIN	BALANCE
1 8.5122	21.6821	78.3179
2 6.4360	23.7583	54.5596
3 4.1609	26.0334	28.5263
4 1.6680	28.5263	0.0000

YEARS 5	QTR PAYT 6.3016	AN CONST 25.21
# INT	PRIN	BALANCE
1 8.6879	16.5187	83.4813
2 7.1061	18.1005	65.3809
3 5.3729	19.8337	45.5471
4 3.4736	21.7330	23.8141
5 1.3925	23.8141	0.0000

YEARS 6	QTR PAYT 5.4761	AN CONST 21.91
# INT	PRIN	BALANCE
1 8.8042	13.1002	86.8998
2 7.5498	14.3547	72.5451
3 6.1752	15.7293	56.8158
4 4.6690	17.2355	39.5803
5 3.0186	18.8859	20.6944
6 1.2101	20.6944	0.0000

YEARS 7	QTR PAYT 4.8913	AN CONST 19.57
# INT	PRIN	BALANCE
1 8.8866	10.6787	89.3213
2 7.8641	11.7013	77.6200
3 6.7436	12.8218	64.7982
4 5.5158	14.0496	50.7486
5 4.1704	15.3950	35.3537
6 2.6962	16.8691	18.4845
7 1.0808	18.4845	0.0000

YEARS 8	QTR PAYT 4.4570	AN CONST 17.83
# INT	PRIN	BALANCE
1 8.9478	8.8801	91.1199
2 8.0975	9.7304	81.3895
3 7.1657	10.6622	70.7273
4 6.1447	11.6832	59.0441
5 5.0260	12.8020	46.2421
6 3.8001	14.0279	32.2142
7 2.4568	15.3712	16.8431
8 .9849	16.8431	0.0000

YEARS 9	QTR PAYT 4.1229	AN CONST 16.50
# INT	PRIN	BALANCE
1 8.9949	7.4965	92.5035
2 8.2771	8.2144	84.2891
3 7.4905	9.0010	75.2881
4 6.6285	9.8629	65.4252
5 5.6841	10.8074	54.6178
6 4.6492	11.8423	42.7755

#	INT	PRIN	BALANCE
7	3.5152	12.9763	29.7993
8	2.2726	14.2188	15.5804
9	.9110	15.5804	0.0000

YEARS 10	QTR PAYT 3.8589	AN CONST 15.44
# INT	PRIN	BALANCE
1 9.0321	6.4033	93.5967
2 8.4189	7.0165	86.5802
3 7.7471	7.6884	78.8918
4 7.0108	8.4246	70.4671
5 6.2041	9.2314	61.2358
6 5.3201	10.1153	51.1204
7 4.3515	11.0840	40.0365
8 3.2901	12.1453	27.8911
9 2.1271	13.3084	14.5828
10 .8527	14.5828	0.0000

YEARS 11	QTR PAYT 3.6458	AN CONST 14.59
# INT	PRIN	BALANCE
1 9.0621	5.5211	94.4789
2 8.5334	6.0498	88.4291
3 7.9541	6.6291	81.8000
4 7.3193	7.2639	74.5361
5 6.6237	7.9595	66.5766
6 5.8616	8.7217	57.8549
7 5.0264	9.5569	48.2980
8 4.1112	10.4720	37.8260
9 3.1085	11.4748	26.3512
10 2.0096	12.5736	13.7776
11 .8056	13.7776	0.0000

YEARS 12	QTR PAYT 3.4709	AN CONST 13.89
# INT	PRIN	BALANCE
1 9.0868	4.7969	95.2031
2 8.6274	5.2563	89.9468
3 8.1241	5.7596	84.1872
4 7.5726	6.3111	77.8761
5 6.9682	6.9155	70.9606
6 6.3060	7.5777	63.3829
7 5.5804	8.3033	55.0796
8 4.7853	9.0984	45.9812
9 3.9140	9.9697	36.0115
10 2.9593	10.9244	25.0872
11 1.9132	11.9705	13.1167
12 .7670	13.1167	0.0000

YEARS 13	QTR PAYT 3.3253	AN CONST 13.31
# INT	PRIN	BALANCE
1 9.1073	4.1941	95.8059
2 8.7057	4.5957	91.2102
3 8.2656	5.0358	86.1743
4 7.7834	5.5180	80.6563
5 7.2550	6.0464	74.6099
6 6.6760	6.6254	67.9844
7 6.0415	7.2599	60.7246
8 5.3463	7.9551	52.7695
9 4.5846	8.7168	44.0527
10 3.7499	9.5515	34.5012
11 2.8352	10.4662	24.0350
12 1.8330	11.4684	12.5666
13 .7348	12.5666	0.0000

YEARS 14	QTR PAYT 3.2028	AN CONST 12.82
# INT	PRIN	BALANCE
1 9.1246	3.6865	96.3135
2 8.7715	4.0395	92.2740
3 8.3847	4.4263	87.8477

#	INT	PRIN	BALANCE
4	7.9609	4.8502	82.9975
5	7.4964	5.3146	77.6829
6	6.9875	5.8235	71.8594
7	6.4299	6.3812	65.4782
8	5.8188	6.9922	58.4860
9	5.1492	7.6618	50.8242
10	4.4156	8.3955	42.4287
11	3.6116	9.1994	33.2293
12	2.7307	10.0803	23.1489
13	1.7654	11.0456	12.1033
14	.7077	12.1033	0.0000

YEARS 15	QTR PAYT 3.0985	AN CONST 12.40
# INT	PRIN	BALANCE
1 9.1392	3.2548	96.7452
2 8.8276	3.5665	93.1787
3 8.4861	3.9080	89.2707
4 8.1118	4.2822	84.9884
5 7.7018	4.6923	80.2961
6 7.2524	5.1416	75.1545
7 6.7601	5.6340	69.5205
8 6.2206	6.1735	63.3470
9 5.6294	6.7646	56.5824
10 4.9816	7.4124	49.1699
11 4.2718	8.1222	41.0477
12 3.4941	8.9000	32.1477
13 2.6418	9.7522	22.3955
14 1.7080	10.6861	11.7094
15 .6847	11.7094	0.0000

YEARS 16	QTR PAYT 3.0091	AN CONST 12.04
# INT	PRIN	BALANCE
1 9.1518	2.8847	97.1153
2 8.8756	3.1609	93.9544
3 8.5729	3.4636	90.4908
4 8.2413	3.7953	86.6955
5 7.8778	4.1587	82.5368
6 7.4796	4.5569	77.9798
7 7.0432	4.9933	72.9865
8 6.5651	5.4715	67.5150
9 6.0411	5.9954	61.5196
10 5.4670	6.5695	54.9501
11 4.8379	7.1986	47.7515
12 4.1486	7.8879	39.8636
13 3.3933	8.6433	31.2204
14 2.5656	9.4709	21.7494
15 1.6587	10.3778	11.3716
16 .6649	11.3716	0.0000

YEARS 17	QTR PAYT 2.9319	AN CONST 11.73
# INT	PRIN	BALANCE
1 9.1627	2.5651	97.4349
2 8.9171	2.8107	94.6242
3 8.6479	3.0798	91.5444
4 8.3530	3.3748	88.1696
5 8.0299	3.6979	84.4717
6 7.6758	4.0520	80.4196
7 7.2877	4.4401	75.9796
8 6.8626	4.8652	71.1144
9 6.3967	5.3311	65.7832
10 5.8862	5.8416	59.9416
11 5.3268	6.4010	53.5406
12 4.7138	7.0139	46.5267
13 4.0422	7.6856	38.8411
14 3.3062	8.4215	30.4195
15 2.4998	9.2280	21.1916
16 1.6162	10.1116	11.0799
17 .6479	11.0799	0.0000

YEARS 18	QTR PAYT 2.8649	AN CONST 11.46
# INT	PRIN	BALANCE
1 9.1722	2.2874	97.7126
2 8.9531	2.5064	95.2062
3 8.7131	2.7464	92.4598
4 8.4501	3.0094	89.4504
5 8.1620	3.2976	86.1528
6 7.8462	3.6133	82.5395
7 7.5002	3.9594	78.5801
8 7.1210	4.3385	74.2416
9 6.7056	4.7539	69.4877
10 6.2504	5.2092	64.2785
11 5.7515	5.7080	58.5705
12 5.2050	6.2546	52.3160
13 4.6060	6.8535	45.4624
14 3.9497	7.5098	37.9526
15 3.2306	8.2289	29.7237
16 2.4426	9.0169	20.7068
17 1.5792	9.8803	10.8265
18 .6331	10.8265	0.0000

YEARS 19	QTR PAYT 2.8063	AN CONST 11.23
# INT	PRIN	BALANCE
1 9.1804	2.0448	97.9552
2 8.9846	2.2406	95.7146
3 8.7701	2.4552	93.2595
4 8.5350	2.6903	90.5692
5 8.2773	2.9479	87.6214
6 7.9951	3.2301	84.3912
7 7.6857	3.5395	80.8517
8 7.3468	3.8784	76.9733
9 6.9754	4.2498	72.7236
10 6.5685	4.6567	68.0668
11 6.1226	5.1027	62.9642
12 5.6339	5.5913	57.3729
13 5.0985	6.1267	51.2462
14 4.5118	6.7134	44.5328
15 3.8690	7.3562	37.1766
16 3.1646	8.0607	29.1159
17 2.3927	8.8325	20.2834
18 1.5469	9.6783	10.6051
19 .6201	10.6051	0.0000

YEARS 20	QTR PAYT 2.7549	AN CONST 11.02
# INT	PRIN	BALANCE
1 9.1877	1.8319	98.1681
2 9.0122	2.0073	96.1608
3 8.8200	2.1995	93.9612
4 8.6094	2.4102	91.5510
5 8.3786	2.6410	88.9101
6 8.1257	2.8939	86.0162
7 7.8486	3.1710	82.8452
8 7.5450	3.4746	79.3706
9 7.2122	3.8073	75.5633
10 6.8476	4.1719	71.3913
11 6.4481	4.5714	66.8199
12 6.0104	5.0092	61.8107
13 5.5307	5.4889	56.3219
14 5.0051	6.0145	50.3074
15 4.4292	6.5904	43.7170
16 3.7981	7.2215	36.4956
17 3.1066	7.9130	28.5826
18 2.3489	8.6707	19.9118
19 1.5186	9.5010	10.4108
20 .6088	10.4108	0.0000

YEARS 21	QTR PAYT 2.7096	AN CONST 10.84
# INT	PRIN	BALANCE
1 9.1940	1.6443	98.3557
2 9.0366	1.8018	96.5539
3 8.8641	1.9743	94.5796

#	INT	PRIN	BALANCE
4	8.6750	2.1634	92.4162
5	8.4678	2.3705	90.0456
6	8.2408	2.5975	87.4481
7	7.9921	2.8463	84.6018
8	7.7195	3.1188	81.4830
9	7.4209	3.4175	78.0655
10	7.0936	3.7447	74.3208
11	6.7350	4.1033	70.2174
12	6.3421	4.4963	65.7212
13	5.9116	4.9268	60.7944
14	5.4398	5.3986	55.3958
15	4.9228	5.9156	49.4802
16	4.3564	6.4820	42.9982
17	3.7356	7.1027	35.8954
18	3.0555	7.7829	28.1126
19	2.3102	8.5281	19.5844
20	1.4936	9.3448	10.2396
21	.5987	10.2396	0.0000

YEARS 22	QTR PAYT 2.6695	AN CONST 10.68	
#	INT	PRIN	BALANCE
1	9.1997	1.4784	98.5216
2	9.0581	1.6200	96.9015
3	8.9030	1.7751	95.1264
4	8.7330	1.9451	93.1813
5	8.5467	2.1314	91.0499
6	8.3426	2.3355	88.7144
7	8.1190	2.5591	86.1552
8	7.8739	2.8042	83.3510
9	7.6054	3.0727	80.2783
10	7.3112	3.3670	76.9113
11	6.9888	3.6894	73.2220
12	6.6355	4.0427	69.1793
13	6.2484	4.4298	64.7495
14	5.8242	4.8540	59.8955
15	5.3594	5.3188	54.5768
16	4.8500	5.8281	48.7487
17	4.2919	6.3862	42.3625
18	3.6804	6.9977	35.3648
19	3.0103	7.6678	27.6969
20	2.2761	8.4021	19.2949
21	1.4715	9.2066	10.0882
22	.5899	10.0882	0.0000

YEARS 23	QTR PAYT 2.6340	AN CONST 10.54	
#	INT	PRIN	BALANCE
1	9.2047	1.3313	98.6687
2	9.0772	1.4588	97.2100
3	8.9375	1.5985	95.6115
4	8.7845	1.7515	93.8600
5	8.6167	1.9192	91.9407
6	8.4330	2.1030	89.8377
7	8.2316	2.3044	87.5333
8	8.0109	2.5251	85.0083
9	7.7691	2.7669	82.2414
10	7.5042	3.0318	79.2096
11	7.2138	3.3221	75.8874
12	6.8957	3.6403	72.2472
13	6.5471	3.9888	68.2583
14	6.1652	4.3708	63.8875
15	5.7466	4.7894	59.0982
16	5.2880	5.2480	53.8502
17	4.7855	5.7505	48.0997
18	4.2348	6.3012	41.7985
19	3.6314	6.9046	34.8939
20	2.9703	7.5657	27.3282
21	2.2458	8.2902	19.0380
22	1.4519	9.0841	9.9539
23	.5820	9.9539	0.0000

YEARS 24	QTR PAYT 2.6024	AN CONST 10.41	
#	INT	PRIN	BALANCE
1	9.2092	1.2004	98.7996
2	9.0942	1.3153	97.4843
3	8.9683	1.4413	96.0431
4	8.8302	1.5793	94.4638
5	8.6790	1.7305	92.7333
6	8.5133	1.8962	90.8371
7	8.3317	2.0778	88.7594
8	8.1328	2.2767	86.4826
9	7.9148	2.4948	83.9879
10	7.6759	2.7337	81.2542
11	7.4141	2.9954	78.2588
12	7.1273	3.2823	74.9765
13	6.8129	3.5966	71.3799
14	6.4685	3.9410	67.4390
15	6.0912	4.3183	63.1206
16	5.6776	4.7319	58.3888
17	5.2245	5.1850	53.2038
18	4.7280	5.6815	47.5223
19	4.1840	6.2255	41.2968
20	3.5878	6.8217	34.4751
21	2.9346	7.4749	27.0002
22	2.2188	8.1907	18.8095
23	1.4345	8.9750	9.8345
24	.5751	9.8345	0.0000

YEARS 25	QTR PAYT 2.5742	AN CONST 10.30	
#	INT	PRIN	BALANCE
1	9.2131	1.0836	98.9164
2	9.1094	1.1874	97.7291
3	8.9957	1.3010	96.4280
4	8.8711	1.4256	95.0024
5	8.7346	1.5622	93.4402
6	8.5850	1.7117	91.7285
7	8.4211	1.8757	89.8528
8	8.2415	2.0553	87.7976
9	8.0446	2.2521	85.5455
10	7.8290	2.4677	83.0778
11	7.5927	2.7040	80.3737
12	7.3338	2.9630	77.4108
13	7.0500	3.2467	74.1641
14	6.7391	3.5576	70.6065
15	6.3985	3.8983	66.7082
16	6.0252	4.2716	62.4367
17	5.6161	4.6806	57.7561
18	5.1679	5.1288	52.6273
19	4.6768	5.6199	47.0074
20	4.1386	6.1581	40.8493
21	3.5490	6.7478	34.1015
22	2.9028	7.3939	26.7076
23	2.1948	8.1019	18.6057
24	1.4189	8.8778	9.7279
25	.5688	9.7279	0.0000

YEARS 26	QTR PAYT 2.5490	AN CONST 10.20	
#	INT	PRIN	BALANCE
1	9.2167	.9792	99.0208
2	9.1229	1.0730	97.9478
3	9.0202	1.1757	96.7721
4	8.9076	1.2883	95.4838
5	8.7842	1.4117	94.0721
6	8.6490	1.5469	92.5253
7	8.5009	1.6950	90.8303
8	8.3386	1.8573	88.9730
9	8.1608	2.0351	86.9378
10	7.9659	2.2300	84.7078
11	7.7523	2.4436	82.2643
12	7.5183	2.6776	79.5867
13	7.2619	2.9340	76.6528
14	6.9810	3.2149	73.4379
15	6.6731	3.5228	69.9151
16	6.3358	3.8601	66.0550
17	5.9662	4.2297	61.8253
18	5.5611	4.6348	57.1905
19	5.1173	5.0786	52.1120
20	4.6310	5.5649	46.5471
21	4.0981	6.0978	40.4493
22	3.5142	6.6817	33.7676
23	2.8744	7.3215	26.4461
24	2.1733	8.0226	18.4235
25	1.4050	8.7908	9.6326
26	.5633	9.6326	0.0000

YEARS 27	QTR PAYT 2.5264	AN CONST 10.11	
#	INT	PRIN	BALANCE
1	9.2199	.8857	99.1143
2	9.1350	.9705	98.1437
3	9.0421	1.0635	97.0803
4	8.9403	1.1653	95.9150
5	8.8287	1.2769	94.6381
6	8.7064	1.3992	93.2389
7	8.5724	1.5332	91.7057
8	8.4256	1.6800	90.0258
9	8.2647	1.8408	88.1849
10	8.0885	2.0171	86.1678
11	7.8953	2.2103	83.9576
12	7.6837	2.4219	81.5356
13	7.4517	2.6538	78.8818
14	7.1976	2.9080	75.9738
15	6.9192	3.1864	72.7874
16	6.6140	3.4916	69.2958
17	6.2797	3.8259	65.4699
18	5.9133	4.1923	61.2777
19	5.5119	4.5937	56.6840
20	5.0720	5.0336	51.6504
21	4.5900	5.5156	46.1348
22	4.0618	6.0438	40.0910
23	3.4831	6.6225	33.4685
24	2.8489	7.2567	26.2119
25	2.1540	7.9516	18.2603
26	1.3926	8.7130	9.5473
27	.5583	9.5473	0.0000

YEARS 28	QTR PAYT 2.5061	AN CONST 10.03	
#	INT	PRIN	BALANCE
1	9.2227	.8018	99.1982
2	9.1459	.8786	98.3195
3	9.0618	.9628	97.3568
4	8.9696	1.0549	96.3018
5	8.8686	1.1560	95.1459
6	8.7579	1.2667	93.8792
7	8.6366	1.3880	92.4913
8	8.5037	1.5209	90.9704
9	8.3581	1.6665	89.3039
10	8.1985	1.8261	87.4778
11	8.0236	2.0009	85.4769
12	7.8320	2.1925	83.2844
13	7.6221	2.4025	80.8819
14	7.3920	2.6326	78.2493
15	7.1399	2.8846	75.3646
16	6.8637	3.1609	72.2038
17	6.5610	3.4636	68.7402
18	6.2293	3.7952	64.9450
19	5.8659	4.1586	60.7863
20	5.4677	4.5569	56.2295
21	5.0313	4.9932	51.2362
22	4.5532	5.4714	45.7649
23	4.0292	5.9953	39.7696
24	3.4551	6.5694	33.2002
25	2.8261	7.1985	26.0017
26	2.1368	7.8878	18.1139
27	1.3814	8.6431	9.4708
28	.5538	9.4708	0.0000

YEARS 29	QTR PAYT 2.4879	AN CONST 9.96	
#	INT	PRIN	BALANCE
1	9.2253	.7264	99.2736
2	9.1557	.7960	98.4775
3	9.0795	.8722	97.6053
4	8.9960	.9558	96.6495
5	8.9044	1.0473	95.6023
6	8.8042	1.1476	94.4547
7	8.6943	1.2575	93.1972
8	8.5739	1.3779	91.8194
9	8.4419	1.5098	90.3096
10	8.2973	1.6544	88.6552
11	8.1389	1.8128	86.8424
12	7.9653	1.9864	84.8560
13	7.7751	2.1766	82.6793
14	7.5667	2.3850	80.2943
15	7.3383	2.6134	77.6809
16	7.0880	2.8637	74.8172
17	6.8138	3.1379	71.6792
18	6.5133	3.4384	68.2408
19	6.1841	3.7677	64.4732
20	5.8233	4.1284	60.3448
21	5.4280	4.5238	55.8210
22	4.9948	4.9570	50.8640
23	4.5201	5.4316	45.4324
24	4.0000	5.9518	39.4807
25	3.4300	6.5217	32.9590
26	2.8055	7.1462	25.8128
27	2.1212	7.8305	17.9823
28	1.3714	8.5803	9.4020
29	.5498	9.4020	0.0000

YEARS 30	QTR PAYT 2.4715	AN CONST 9.89	
#	INT	PRIN	BALANCE
1	9.2276	.6586	99.3414
2	9.1645	.7217	98.6197
3	9.0954	.7908	97.8290
4	9.0197	.8665	96.9625
5	8.9367	.9495	96.0130
6	8.8458	1.0404	94.9726
7	8.7462	1.1400	93.8326
8	8.6370	1.2492	92.5834
9	8.5174	1.3688	91.2146
10	8.3863	1.4999	89.7148
11	8.2427	1.6435	88.0713
12	8.0853	1.8009	86.2704
13	7.9129	1.9733	84.2971
14	7.7239	2.1623	82.1348
15	7.5168	2.3693	79.7655
16	7.2900	2.5962	77.1692
17	7.0414	2.8448	74.3244
18	6.7689	3.1172	71.2072
19	6.4704	3.4158	67.7914
20	6.1433	3.7428	64.0486
21	5.7849	4.1012	59.9473
22	5.3922	4.4940	55.4534
23	4.9619	4.9243	50.5290
24	4.4903	5.3959	45.1332
25	3.9736	5.9124	39.2206
26	3.4075	6.4787	32.7419
27	2.7871	7.0991	25.6428
28	2.1073	7.7789	17.8639
29	1.3624	8.5238	9.3400
30	.5461	9.3400	0.0000

YEARS 2 — QTR PAYT 13.8725 — AN CONST 55.49

#	INT	PRIN	BALANCE
1	7.8355	47.6545	52.3455
2	3.1445	52.3455	0.0000

YEARS 3 — QTR PAYT 9.6751 — AN CONST 38.71

#	INT	PRIN	BALANCE
1	8.4432	30.2571	69.7429
2	5.4647	33.2356	36.5073
3	2.1931	36.5073	0.0000

YEARS 4 — QTR PAYT 7.5856 — AN CONST 30.35

#	INT	PRIN	BALANCE
1	8.7457	21.5967	78.4033
2	6.6197	23.7226	54.6807
3	4.2845	26.0578	28.6229
4	1.7194	28.6229	0.0000

YEARS 5 — QTR PAYT 6.3392 — AN CONST 25.36

#	INT	PRIN	BALANCE
1	8.9261	16.4308	83.5692
2	7.3087	18.0482	65.5211
3	5.5321	19.8248	45.6963
4	3.5805	21.7763	23.9199
5	1.4369	23.9199	0.0000

YEARS 6 — QTR PAYT 5.5144 — AN CONST 22.06

#	INT	PRIN	BALANCE
1	9.0455	13.0119	86.9881
2	7.7646	14.2928	72.6953
3	6.3577	15.6998	56.9955
4	4.8122	17.2452	39.7503
5	3.1146	18.9428	20.8075
6	1.2499	20.8075	0.0000

YEARS 7 — QTR PAYT 4.9303 — AN CONST 19.73

#	INT	PRIN	BALANCE
1	9.1301	10.5912	89.4088
2	8.0875	11.6338	77.7750
3	6.9423	12.7790	64.9960
4	5.6843	14.0370	50.9590
5	4.3026	15.4187	35.5403
6	2.7848	16.9365	18.6037
7	1.1176	18.6037	0.0000

YEARS 8 — QTR PAYT 4.4967 — AN CONST 17.99

#	INT	PRIN	BALANCE
1	9.1928	8.7941	91.2059
2	8.3272	9.6598	81.5460
3	7.3763	10.6107	70.9353
4	6.3318	11.6552	59.2801
5	5.1844	12.8025	46.4776
6	3.9242	14.0628	32.4148
7	2.5399	15.4471	16.9677
8	1.0193	16.9677	0.0000

YEARS 9 — QTR PAYT 4.1634 — AN CONST 16.66

#	INT	PRIN	BALANCE
1	9.2411	7.4126	92.5874
2	8.5114	8.1423	84.4452
3	7.7099	8.9438	75.5014
4	6.8295	9.8242	65.6772
5	5.8624	10.7913	54.8859
6	4.8001	11.8535	43.0324
7	3.6333	13.0204	30.0120
8	2.3516	14.3021	15.7099
9	.9437	15.7099	0.0000

YEARS 10 — QTR PAYT 3.9002 — AN CONST 15.61

#	INT	PRIN	BALANCE
1	9.2792	6.3217	93.6783
2	8.6569	6.9440	86.7343
3	7.9733	7.6275	79.1068
4	7.2225	8.3784	70.7284
5	6.3978	9.2031	61.5253
6	5.4918	10.1091	51.4162
7	4.4967	11.1042	40.3120
8	3.4036	12.1973	28.1148
9	2.2029	13.3979	14.7168
10	.8841	14.7168	0.0000

YEARS 11 — QTR PAYT 3.6880 — AN CONST 14.76

#	INT	PRIN	BALANCE
1	9.3099	5.4420	94.5580
2	8.7742	5.9777	88.5804
3	8.1858	6.5661	82.0143
4	7.5394	7.2124	74.8018
5	6.8295	7.9224	66.8794
6	6.0496	8.7023	58.1771
7	5.1929	9.5589	48.6182
8	4.2520	10.4999	38.1183
9	3.2184	11.5335	26.5848
10	2.0831	12.6688	13.9159
11	.8360	13.9159	0.0000

YEARS 12 — QTR PAYT 3.5139 — AN CONST 14.06

#	INT	PRIN	BALANCE
1	9.3351	4.7204	95.2796
2	8.8705	5.1851	90.0945
3	8.3600	5.6955	84.3990
4	7.7994	6.2561	78.1429
5	7.1835	6.8720	71.2709
6	6.5071	7.5485	63.7224
7	5.7640	8.2915	55.4309
8	4.9478	9.1077	46.3232
9	4.0513	10.0043	36.3189
10	3.0665	10.9891	25.3299
11	1.9847	12.0708	13.2590
12	.7965	13.2590	0.0000

YEARS 13 — QTR PAYT 3.3691 — AN CONST 13.48

#	INT	PRIN	BALANCE
1	9.3561	4.1203	95.8797
2	8.9505	4.5259	91.3538
3	8.5050	4.9714	86.3823
4	8.0156	5.4608	80.9215
5	7.4780	5.9984	74.9231
6	6.8876	6.5888	68.3343
7	6.2390	7.2374	61.0969
8	5.5265	7.9499	53.1470
9	4.7440	8.7325	44.4145
10	3.8843	9.5921	34.8225
11	2.9401	10.5363	24.2862
12	1.9029	11.5735	12.7127
13	.7637	12.7127	0.0000

YEARS 14 — QTR PAYT 3.2473 — AN CONST 12.99

#	INT	PRIN	BALANCE
1	9.3737	3.6155	96.3845
2	9.0178	3.9714	92.4132
3	8.6269	4.3623	88.0509
4	8.1975	4.7917	83.2592
5	7.7258	5.2634	77.9958
6	7.2077	5.7815	72.2143
7	6.6385	6.3506	65.8637
8	6.0134	6.9758	58.8879
9	5.3267	7.6625	51.2255
10	4.5724	8.4167	42.8087
11	3.7439	9.2453	33.5635
12	2.8338	10.1553	23.4081
13	1.8341	11.1550	12.2531
14	.7361	12.2531	0.0000

YEARS 15 — QTR PAYT 3.1438 — AN CONST 12.58

#	INT	PRIN	BALANCE
1	9.3887	3.1866	96.8134
2	9.0750	3.5002	93.3132
3	8.7305	3.8448	89.4684
4	8.3520	4.2233	85.2451
5	7.9363	4.6390	80.6061
6	7.4796	5.0957	75.5104
7	6.9780	5.5973	69.9132
8	6.4270	6.1483	63.7649
9	5.8218	6.7535	57.0114
10	5.1570	7.4183	49.5931
11	4.4267	8.1485	41.4446
12	3.6246	8.9507	32.4940
13	2.7435	9.8317	22.6622
14	1.7757	10.7996	11.8627
15	.7126	11.8627	0.0000

YEARS 16 — QTR PAYT 3.0552 — AN CONST 12.23

#	INT	PRIN	BALANCE
1	9.4015	2.8192	97.1808
2	9.1240	3.0967	94.0841
3	8.8192	3.4016	90.6825
4	8.4843	3.7364	86.9461
5	8.1165	4.1042	82.8419
6	7.7125	4.5082	78.3337
7	7.2687	4.9520	73.3816
8	6.7813	5.4395	67.9422
9	6.2458	5.9749	61.9672
10	5.6577	6.5631	55.4042
11	5.0116	7.2091	48.1950
12	4.3019	7.9188	40.2762
13	3.5224	8.6983	31.5779
14	2.6662	9.5546	22.0233
15	1.7256	10.4951	11.5282
16	.6925	11.5282	0.0000

YEARS 17 — QTR PAYT 2.9787 — AN CONST 11.92

#	INT	PRIN	BALANCE
1	9.4126	2.5023	97.4977
2	9.1663	2.7487	94.7490
3	8.8957	3.0192	91.7298
4	8.5985	3.3164	88.4133
5	8.2720	3.6429	84.7704
6	7.9134	4.0015	80.7689
7	7.5195	4.3954	76.3735
8	7.0868	4.8281	71.5454
9	6.6116	5.3034	66.2420
10	6.0895	5.8254	60.4166
11	5.5161	6.3989	54.0178
12	4.8862	7.0288	46.9890
13	4.1943	7.7206	39.2684
14	3.4343	8.4807	30.7877
15	2.5995	9.3155	21.4722
16	1.6825	10.2325	11.2397
17	.6752	11.2397	0.0000

YEARS 18 — QTR PAYT 2.9124 — AN CONST 11.65

#	INT	PRIN	BALANCE
1	9.4222	2.2273	97.7727
2	9.2029	2.4466	95.3261
3	8.9621	2.6874	92.6386
4	8.6976	2.9520	89.6866
5	8.4070	3.2426	86.4440
6	8.0878	3.5618	82.8823
7	7.7372	3.9124	78.9699
8	7.3520	4.2975	74.6724
9	6.9290	4.7206	69.9518
10	6.4643	5.1852	64.7666
11	5.9539	5.6957	59.0709
12	5.3932	6.2563	52.8146
13	4.7774	6.8722	45.9424
14	4.1009	7.5487	38.3937
15	3.3578	8.2918	30.1020
16	2.5416	9.1080	20.9940
17	1.6450	10.0046	10.9894
18	.6602	10.9894	0.0000

YEARS 19 — QTR PAYT 2.8545 — AN CONST 11.42

#	INT	PRIN	BALANCE
1	9.4306	1.9874	98.0126
2	9.2349	2.1831	95.8295
3	9.0200	2.3980	93.4315
4	8.7840	2.6340	90.7975
5	8.5247	2.8933	87.9042
6	8.2399	3.1781	84.7260
7	7.9270	3.4910	81.2350
8	7.5834	3.8346	77.4004
9	7.2059	4.2121	73.1883
10	6.7913	4.6267	68.5616
11	6.3358	5.0822	63.4794
12	5.8356	5.5825	57.8969
13	5.2860	6.1320	51.7649
14	4.6824	6.7356	45.0293
15	4.0194	7.3987	37.6307
16	3.2911	8.1270	29.5037
17	2.4910	8.9270	20.5767
18	1.6123	9.8057	10.7710
19	.6470	10.7710	0.0000

YEARS 20 — QTR PAYT 2.8038 — AN CONST 11.22

#	INT	PRIN	BALANCE
1	9.4379	1.7772	98.2228
2	9.2630	1.9521	96.2707
3	9.0708	2.1443	94.1264
4	8.8597	2.3554	91.7711
5	8.6279	2.5872	89.1838
6	8.3732	2.8419	86.3419
7	8.0935	3.1217	83.2203
8	7.7862	3.4289	79.7914
9	7.4486	3.7665	76.0249
10	7.0779	4.1372	71.8876
11	6.6706	4.5445	67.3431
12	6.2232	4.9919	62.3513
13	5.7318	5.4833	56.8680
14	5.1921	6.0230	50.8450
15	4.5992	6.6159	44.2291
16	3.9479	7.2672	36.9619
17	3.2326	7.9825	28.9794
18	2.4468	8.7683	20.2110
19	1.5836	9.6315	10.5796
20	.6355	10.5796	0.0000

YEARS 21 — QTR PAYT 2.7591 — AN CONST 11.04

#	INT	PRIN	BALANCE
1	9.4444	1.5922	98.4078
2	9.2877	1.7489	96.6590
3	9.1155	1.9210	94.7379

#	INT	PRIN	BALANCE
4	8.9264	2.1101	92.6278
5	8.7187	2.3179	90.3099
6	8.4905	2.5460	87.7639
7	8.2399	2.7967	84.9672
8	7.9646	3.0720	81.8953
9	7.6622	3.3743	78.5210
10	7.3300	3.7065	74.8144
11	6.9652	4.0714	70.7431
12	6.5644	4.4722	66.2709
13	6.1242	4.9124	61.3585
14	5.6406	5.3960	55.9626
15	5.1094	5.9271	50.0355
16	4.5260	6.5106	43.5249
17	3.8851	7.1515	36.3734
18	3.1811	7.8554	28.5180
19	2.4078	8.6287	19.8892
20	1.5584	9.4781	10.4111
21	.6254	10.4111	0.0000

YEARS 22 — QTR PAYT 2.7197 — AN CONST 10.88

#	INT	PRIN	BALANCE
1	9.4501	1.4288	98.5712
2	9.3095	1.5694	97.0018
3	9.1550	1.7239	95.2779
4	8.9853	1.8936	93.3844
5	8.7989	2.0800	91.3044
6	8.5941	2.2847	89.0196
7	8.3692	2.5096	86.5100
8	8.1222	2.7567	83.7533
9	7.8508	3.0281	80.7252
10	7.5527	3.3261	77.3991
11	7.2253	3.6536	73.7455
12	6.8657	4.0132	69.7323
13	6.4706	4.4083	65.3241
14	6.0367	4.8422	60.4819
15	5.5600	5.3189	55.1630
16	5.0364	5.8424	49.3206
17	4.4613	6.4176	42.9030
18	3.8296	7.0493	35.8537
19	3.1356	7.7432	28.1105
20	2.3734	8.5054	19.6051
21	1.5362	9.3427	10.2624
22	.6165	10.2624	0.0000

YEARS 23 — QTR PAYT 2.6848 — AN CONST 10.74

#	INT	PRIN	BALANCE
1	9.4552	1.2840	98.7160
2	9.3288	1.4104	97.3056
3	9.1899	1.5493	95.7563
4	9.0374	1.7018	94.0546
5	8.8699	1.8693	92.1853
6	8.6859	2.0533	90.1320
7	8.4838	2.2554	87.8766
8	8.2617	2.4774	85.3992
9	8.0179	2.7213	82.6779
10	7.7500	2.9892	79.6887
11	7.4557	3.2834	76.4053
12	7.1325	3.6066	72.7986
13	6.7775	3.9617	68.8369
14	6.3875	4.3517	64.4853
15	5.9591	4.7800	59.7053
16	5.4886	5.2506	54.4547
17	4.9718	5.7674	48.6873
18	4.4040	6.3352	42.3521
19	3.7804	6.9588	35.3934
20	3.0954	7.6438	27.7496
21	2.3429	8.3962	19.3533
22	1.5164	9.2227	10.1306
23	.6086	10.1306	0.0000

YEARS 24 — QTR PAYT 2.6538 — AN CONST 10.62

#	INT	PRIN	BALANCE
1	9.4596	1.1554	98.8446
2	9.3459	1.2692	97.5754
3	9.2210	1.3941	96.1813
4	9.0837	1.5314	94.6499
5	8.9330	1.6821	92.9678
6	8.7674	1.8477	91.1201
7	8.5855	2.0296	89.0906
8	8.3857	2.2293	86.8612
9	8.1663	2.4488	84.4124
10	7.9252	2.6899	81.7226
11	7.6604	2.9546	78.7679
12	7.3696	3.2455	75.5224
13	7.0501	3.5650	71.9575
14	6.6992	3.9159	68.0416
15	6.3137	4.3014	63.7402
16	5.8903	4.7248	59.0154
17	5.4252	5.1899	53.8255
18	4.9143	5.7008	48.1247
19	4.3531	6.2620	41.8628
20	3.7367	6.8784	34.9844
21	3.0596	7.5555	27.4289
22	2.3159	8.2992	19.1297
23	1.4989	9.1162	10.0136
24	.6015	10.0136	0.0000

YEARS 25 — QTR PAYT 2.6261 — AN CONST 10.51

#	INT	PRIN	BALANCE
1	9.4636	1.0409	98.9591
2	9.3612	1.1434	97.8156
3	9.2486	1.2560	96.5597
4	9.1250	1.3796	95.1801
5	8.9892	1.5154	93.6647
6	8.8400	1.6646	92.0001
7	8.6761	1.8284	90.1716
8	8.4962	2.0084	88.1632
9	8.2984	2.2061	85.9570
10	8.0813	2.4233	83.5337
11	7.8427	2.6619	80.8719
12	7.5807	2.9239	77.9480
13	7.2929	3.2117	74.7363
14	6.9767	3.5279	71.2084
15	6.6294	3.8751	67.3333
16	6.2480	4.2566	63.0767
17	5.8290	4.6756	58.4011
18	5.3687	5.1359	53.2652
19	4.8631	5.6414	47.6238
20	4.3078	6.1968	41.4270
21	3.6978	6.8068	34.6202
22	3.0278	7.4768	27.1434
23	2.2918	8.2128	18.9306
24	1.4833	9.0213	9.9093
25	.5953	9.9093	0.0000

YEARS 26 — QTR PAYT 2.6015 — AN CONST 10.41

#	INT	PRIN	BALANCE
1	9.4672	.9388	99.0612
2	9.3748	1.0312	98.0301
3	9.2733	1.1327	96.8974
4	9.1618	1.2442	95.6532
5	9.0393	1.3667	94.2865
6	8.9048	1.5012	92.7854
7	8.7750	1.6490	91.1364
8	8.5947	1.8113	89.3251
9	8.4164	1.9896	87.3355
10	8.2205	2.1854	85.1501
11	8.0054	2.4006	82.7496
12	7.7691	2.6369	80.1127
13	7.5095	2.8964	77.2163
14	7.2244	3.1816	74.0347
15	6.9112	3.4947	70.5400
16	6.5672	3.8388	66.7012
17	6.1893	4.2166	62.4846
18	5.7743	4.6317	57.8528
19	5.3183	5.0877	52.7652
20	4.8175	5.5885	47.1767
21	4.2674	6.1386	41.0381
22	3.6631	6.7429	34.2952
23	2.9993	7.4066	26.8886
24	2.2703	8.1357	18.7529
25	1.4694	8.9366	9.8163
26	.5897	9.8163	0.0000

YEARS 27 — QTR PAYT 2.5794 — AN CONST 10.32

#	INT	PRIN	BALANCE
1	9.4704	.8474	99.1526
2	9.3870	.9308	98.2218
3	9.2954	1.0224	97.1994
4	9.1947	1.1231	96.0763
5	9.0842	1.2336	94.8426
6	8.9627	1.3551	93.4876
7	8.8293	1.4885	91.9991
8	8.6828	1.6350	90.3641
9	8.5219	1.7959	88.5682
10	8.3451	1.9727	86.5955
11	8.1509	2.1669	84.4286
12	7.9376	2.3802	82.0483
13	7.7033	2.6145	79.4338
14	7.4459	2.8719	76.5619
15	7.1632	3.1546	73.4073
16	6.8527	3.4651	69.9422
17	6.5116	3.8062	66.1360
18	6.1369	4.1809	61.9551
19	5.7253	4.5925	57.3626
20	5.2732	5.0445	52.3181
21	4.7767	5.5411	46.7769
22	4.2312	6.0866	40.6903
23	3.6321	6.6857	34.0046
24	2.9739	7.3439	26.6608
25	2.2510	8.0668	18.5940
26	1.4569	8.8609	9.7331
27	.5847	9.7331	0.0000

YEARS 28 — QTR PAYT 2.5597 — AN CONST 10.24

#	INT	PRIN	BALANCE
1	9.4733	.7655	99.2345
2	9.3979	.8409	98.3935
3	9.3151	.9237	97.4699
4	9.2242	1.0146	96.4553
5	9.1243	1.1145	95.3408
6	9.0146	1.2242	94.1166
7	8.8941	1.3447	92.7719
8	8.7617	1.4771	91.2948
9	8.6163	1.6225	89.6723
10	8.4566	1.7822	87.8902
11	8.2812	1.9576	85.9325
12	8.0885	2.1503	83.7822
13	7.8768	2.3620	81.4202
14	7.6443	2.5945	78.8257
15	7.3889	2.8499	75.9758
16	7.1084	3.1304	72.8454
17	6.8002	3.4386	69.4068
18	6.4617	3.7771	65.6297
19	6.0899	4.1489	61.4808
20	5.6815	4.5573	56.9235
21	5.2329	5.0059	51.9175
22	4.7401	5.4987	46.4188
23	4.1988	6.0400	40.3788
24	3.6043	6.6345	33.7443
25	2.9512	7.2876	26.4567
26	2.2338	8.0050	18.4516
27	1.4458	8.7930	9.6586
28	.5802	9.6586	0.0000

YEARS 29 — QTR PAYT 2.5420 — AN CONST 10.17

#	INT	PRIN	BALANCE
1	9.4758	.6921	99.3079
2	9.4077	.7602	98.5476
3	9.3329	.8351	97.7126
4	9.2507	.9173	96.7953
5	9.1604	1.0076	95.7877
6	9.0612	1.1068	94.6809
7	8.9522	1.2157	93.4652
8	8.8325	1.3354	92.1298
9	8.7011	1.4668	90.6629
10	8.5567	1.6112	89.0517
11	8.3981	1.7698	87.2819
12	8.2239	1.9441	85.3378
13	8.0325	2.1354	83.2024
14	7.8223	2.3456	80.8567
15	7.5914	2.5766	78.2802
16	7.3378	2.8302	75.4500
17	7.0592	3.1088	72.3412
18	6.7531	3.4148	68.9264
19	6.4170	3.7509	65.1754
20	6.0478	4.1202	61.0553
21	5.6422	4.5258	56.5295
22	5.1967	4.9713	51.5582
23	4.7073	5.4606	46.0976
24	4.1698	5.9982	40.0994
25	3.5793	6.5886	33.5107
26	2.9307	7.2372	26.2735
27	2.2183	7.9496	18.3239
28	1.4358	8.7322	9.5917
29	.5762	9.5917	0.0000

YEARS 30 — QTR PAYT 2.5261 — AN CONST 10.11

#	INT	PRIN	BALANCE
1	9.4781	.6261	99.3739
2	9.4165	.6878	98.6861
3	9.3488	.7555	97.9306
4	9.2744	.8299	97.1007
5	9.1927	.9115	96.1892
6	9.1030	1.0013	95.1879
7	9.0044	1.0998	94.0881
8	8.8962	1.2081	92.8800
9	8.7772	1.3270	91.5529
10	8.6466	1.4577	90.0953
11	8.5031	1.6012	88.4941
12	8.3455	1.7588	86.7353
13	8.1724	1.9319	84.8035
14	7.9822	2.1221	82.6814
15	7.7733	2.3310	80.3504
16	7.5439	2.5604	77.7900
17	7.2918	2.8125	74.9775
18	7.0150	3.0893	71.8882
19	6.7109	3.3934	68.4948
20	6.3768	3.7275	64.7673
21	6.0099	4.0944	60.6730
22	5.6068	4.4974	56.1755
23	5.1641	4.9402	51.2354
24	4.6778	5.4265	45.8089
25	4.1437	5.9606	39.8483
26	3.5569	6.5474	33.3009
27	2.9124	7.1919	26.1090
28	2.2044	7.8998	18.2092
29	1.4268	8.6775	9.5317
30	.5726	9.5317	0.0000

YEARS 2 — QTR PAYT 13.9096 — AN CONST 55.64

#	INT	PRIN	BALANCE
1	8.0448	47.5936	52.4064
2	3.2320	52.4064	0.0000

YEARS 3 — QTR PAYT 9.7119 — AN CONST 38.85

#	INT	PRIN	BALANCE
1	8.6687	30.1787	69.8213
2	5.6170	33.2305	36.5908
3	2.2566	36.5908	0.0000

YEARS 4 — QTR PAYT 7.6227 — AN CONST 30.50

#	INT	PRIN	BALANCE
1	8.9793	21.5115	78.4885
2	6.8040	23.6868	54.8017
3	4.4087	26.0821	28.7196
4	1.7712	28.7196	0.0000

YEARS 5 — QTR PAYT 6.3769 — AN CONST 25.51

#	INT	PRIN	BALANCE
1	9.1644	16.3432	83.6568
2	7.5118	17.9958	65.6610
3	5.6920	19.8156	45.8454
4	3.6882	21.8195	24.0259
5	1.4817	24.0259	0.0000

YEARS 6 — QTR PAYT 5.5527 — AN CONST 22.22

#	INT	PRIN	BALANCE
1	9.2869	12.9240	87.0760
2	7.9800	14.2310	72.8450
3	6.5409	15.6700	57.1749
4	4.9563	17.2547	39.9203
5	3.2115	18.9995	20.9208
6	1.2902	20.9208	0.0000

YEARS 7 — QTR PAYT 4.9695 — AN CONST 19.88

#	INT	PRIN	BALANCE
1	9.3736	10.5043	89.4957
2	8.3114	11.5665	77.9293
3	7.1418	12.7361	65.1932
4	5.8539	14.0240	51.1691
5	4.4357	15.4422	35.7270
6	2.8742	17.0037	18.7232
7	1.1547	18.7232	0.0000

YEARS 8 — QTR PAYT 4.5367 — AN CONST 18.15

#	INT	PRIN	BALANCE
1	9.4380	8.7088	91.2912
2	8.5573	9.5895	81.7017
3	7.5876	10.5592	71.1426
4	6.5198	11.6269	59.5156
5	5.3441	12.8027	46.7129
6	4.0494	14.0974	32.6156
7	2.6238	15.5229	17.0926
8	1.0541	17.0926	0.0000

YEARS 9 — QTR PAYT 4.2042 — AN CONST 16.82

#	INT	PRIN	BALANCE
1	9.4874	7.3293	92.6707
2	8.7462	8.0705	84.6002
3	7.9301	8.8866	75.7136
4	7.0315	9.7853	65.9283
5	6.0420	10.7748	55.1535
6	4.9524	11.8644	43.2892
7	3.7526	13.0641	30.2251
8	2.4315	14.3852	15.8399
9	.9769	15.8399	0.0000

YEARS 10 — QTR PAYT 3.9418 — AN CONST 15.77

#	INT	PRIN	BALANCE
1	9.5264	6.2408	93.7592
2	8.8953	6.8719	86.8872
3	8.2004	7.5668	79.3204
4	7.4352	8.3320	70.9884
5	6.5927	9.1746	61.8138
6	5.6649	10.1023	51.7115
7	4.6433	11.1239	40.5876
8	3.5184	12.2488	28.3388
9	2.2798	13.4874	14.8513
10	.9159	14.8513	0.0000

YEARS 11 — QTR PAYT 3.7304 — AN CONST 14.93

#	INT	PRIN	BALANCE
1	9.5578	5.3637	94.6363
2	9.0154	5.9061	88.7302
3	8.4182	6.5033	82.2269
4	7.7606	7.1610	75.0659
5	7.0364	7.8851	67.1808
6	6.2390	8.6825	58.4983
7	5.3610	9.5605	48.9378
8	4.3943	10.5273	38.4106
9	3.3297	11.5918	26.8188
10	2.1575	12.7640	14.0547
11	.8668	14.0547	0.0000

YEARS 12 — QTR PAYT 3.5571 — AN CONST 14.23

#	INT	PRIN	BALANCE
1	9.5836	4.6449	95.3551
2	9.1139	5.1146	90.2406
3	8.5967	5.6318	84.6088
4	8.0272	6.2013	78.4076
5	7.4001	6.8284	71.5792
6	6.7096	7.5189	64.0603
7	5.9492	8.2792	55.7812
8	5.1210	9.1164	46.6647
9	4.1902	10.0383	36.6265
10	3.1750	11.0534	25.5731
11	2.0573	12.1711	13.4019
12	.8265	13.4019	0.0000

YEARS 13 — QTR PAYT 3.4131 — AN CONST 13.66

#	INT	PRIN	BALANCE
1	9.6050	4.0476	95.9524
2	9.1957	4.4569	91.4956
3	8.7450	4.9075	86.5880
4	8.2487	5.4038	81.1842
5	7.7023	5.9503	75.2340
6	7.1006	6.5520	68.6820
7	6.4380	7.2145	61.4675
8	5.7085	7.9441	53.5234
9	4.9051	8.7474	44.7760
10	4.0206	9.6320	35.1440
11	3.0465	10.6060	24.5380
12	1.9740	11.6785	12.8595
13	.7931	12.8595	0.0000

YEARS 14 — QTR PAYT 3.2921 — AN CONST 13.17

#	INT	PRIN	BALANCE
1	9.6230	3.5455	96.4545
2	9.2644	3.9040	92.5504
3	8.8696	4.2988	88.2516
4	8.4349	4.7335	83.5181
5	7.9563	5.2122	78.3058
6	7.4292	5.7393	72.5665
7	6.8488	6.3197	66.2469
8	6.2097	6.9587	59.2881
9	5.5061	7.6624	51.6257
10	4.7312	8.4373	43.1884
11	3.8780	9.2905	33.8979
12	2.9385	10.2300	23.6680
13	1.9040	11.2644	12.4035
14	.7649	12.4035	0.0000

YEARS 15 — QTR PAYT 3.1894 — AN CONST 12.76

#	INT	PRIN	BALANCE
1	9.6382	3.1195	96.8805
2	9.3228	3.4349	93.4456
3	8.9754	3.7823	89.6634
4	8.5930	4.1647	85.4986
5	8.1718	4.5859	80.9127
6	7.7081	5.0496	75.8631
7	7.1974	5.5603	70.3028
8	6.6352	6.1225	64.1803
9	6.0160	6.7417	57.4387
10	5.3343	7.4234	50.0153
11	4.5836	8.1741	41.8412
12	3.7570	9.0007	32.8405
13	2.8469	9.9108	22.9297
14	1.8446	10.9131	12.0166
15	.7411	12.0166	0.0000

YEARS 16 — QTR PAYT 3.1016 — AN CONST 12.41

#	INT	PRIN	BALANCE
1	9.6513	2.7549	97.2451
2	9.3727	3.0335	94.2115
3	9.0659	3.3403	90.8713
4	8.7282	3.6781	87.1932
5	8.3562	4.0500	83.1432
6	7.9467	4.4595	78.6836
7	7.4957	4.9105	73.7731
8	6.9992	5.4071	68.3661
9	6.4524	5.9539	62.4122
10	5.8503	6.5559	55.8563
11	5.1873	7.2189	48.6374
12	4.4573	7.9489	40.6885
13	3.6535	8.7527	31.9358
14	2.7684	9.6378	22.2980
15	1.7938	10.6124	11.6856
16	.7207	11.6856	0.0000

YEARS 17 — QTR PAYT 3.0259 — AN CONST 12.11

#	INT	PRIN	BALANCE
1	9.6625	2.4409	97.5591
2	9.4157	2.6877	94.8714
3	9.1439	2.9595	91.9120
4	8.8447	3.2588	88.6532
5	8.5151	3.5883	85.0649
6	8.1523	3.9511	81.1138
7	7.7527	4.3507	76.7631
8	7.3128	4.7907	71.9724
9	6.8283	5.2751	66.6973
10	6.2949	5.8085	60.8888
11	5.7075	6.3959	54.4929
12	5.0607	7.0427	47.4502
13	4.3485	7.7549	39.6953
14	3.5643	8.5391	31.1563
15	2.7009	9.4026	21.7537
16	1.7500	10.3534	11.4003
17	.7031	11.4003	0.0000

YEARS 18 — QTR PAYT 2.9602 — AN CONST 11.85

#	INT	PRIN	BALANCE
1	9.6723	2.1686	97.8314
2	9.4530	2.3879	95.4434
3	9.2115	2.6294	92.8140
4	8.9456	2.8953	89.9187
5	8.6529	3.1881	86.7307
6	8.3305	3.5105	83.2202
7	7.9755	3.8655	79.3547
8	7.5846	4.2563	75.0984
9	7.1542	4.6868	70.4116
10	6.6802	5.1607	65.2509
11	6.1584	5.6826	59.5683
12	5.5837	6.2572	53.3111
13	4.9510	6.8900	46.4212
14	4.2542	7.5867	38.8345
15	3.4871	8.3539	30.4806
16	2.6423	9.1987	21.2820
17	1.7121	10.1288	11.1531
18	.6878	11.1531	0.0000

YEARS 19 — QTR PAYT 2.9031 — AN CONST 11.62

#	INT	PRIN	BALANCE
1	9.6808	1.9314	98.0686
2	9.4855	2.1267	95.9418
3	9.2704	2.3418	93.6000
4	9.0336	2.5786	91.0214
5	8.7729	2.8394	88.1820
6	8.4857	3.1265	85.0555
7	8.1696	3.4427	81.6128
8	7.8214	3.7908	77.8220
9	7.4381	4.1741	73.6479
10	7.0160	4.5962	69.0517
11	6.5512	5.0610	63.9906
12	6.0394	5.5728	58.4178
13	5.4759	6.1364	52.2815
14	4.8554	6.7569	45.5246
15	4.1721	7.4402	38.0844
16	3.4197	8.1925	29.8919
17	2.5912	9.0210	20.8709
18	1.6790	9.9332	10.9377
19	.6745	10.9377	0.0000

YEARS 20 — QTR PAYT 2.8530 — AN CONST 11.42

#	INT	PRIN	BALANCE
1	9.6882	1.7238	98.2762
2	9.5139	1.8981	96.3780
3	9.3220	2.0901	94.2880
4	9.1106	2.3014	91.9865
5	8.8779	2.5342	89.4523
6	8.6216	2.7904	86.6619
7	8.3394	3.0726	83.5893
8	8.0287	3.3833	80.2060
9	7.6866	3.7255	76.4805
10	7.3099	4.1022	72.3783
11	6.8950	4.5170	67.8613
12	6.4383	4.9738	62.8875
13	5.9353	5.4767	57.4108
14	5.3815	6.0306	51.3802
15	4.7717	6.6404	44.7398
16	4.1002	7.3119	37.4279
17	3.3608	8.0513	29.3766
18	2.5466	8.8655	20.5111
19	1.6501	9.7620	10.7491
20	.6629	10.7491	0.0000

YEARS 21 — QTR PAYT 2.8090 — AN CONST 11.24

#	INT	PRIN	BALANCE
1	9.6948	1.5414	98.4586
2	9.5389	1.6973	96.7614
3	9.3673	1.8689	94.8925

#	INT	PRIN	BALANCE
4	9.1783	2.0579	92.8346
5	8.9702	2.2660	90.5687
6	8.7410	2.4951	88.0735
7	8.4887	2.7474	85.3261
8	8.2109	3.0252	82.3009
9	7.9050	3.3312	78.9697
10	7.5681	3.6680	75.3017
11	7.1972	4.0390	71.2627
12	6.7888	4.4474	66.8153
13	6.3390	4.8971	61.9182
14	5.8438	5.3923	56.5259
15	5.2985	5.9376	50.5883
16	4.6981	6.5381	44.0502
17	4.0370	7.1992	36.8510
18	3.3090	7.9272	28.9238
19	2.5073	8.7288	20.1950
20	1.6246	9.6115	10.5835
21	.6527	10.5835	0.0000

YEARS 22 — QTR PAYT 2.7703 — AN CONST 11.09

#	INT	PRIN	BALANCE
1	9.7005	1.3805	98.6195
2	9.5609	1.5201	97.0994
3	9.4072	1.6738	95.4256
4	9.2380	1.8431	93.5825
5	9.0516	2.0295	91.5530
6	8.8464	2.2347	89.3183
7	8.6204	2.4607	86.8577
8	8.3715	2.7095	84.1482
9	8.0976	2.9835	81.1647
10	7.7959	3.2852	77.8795
11	7.4636	3.6174	74.2621
12	7.0978	3.9832	70.2789
13	6.6951	4.3860	65.8929
14	6.2515	4.8295	61.0634
15	5.7632	5.3179	55.7455
16	5.2254	5.8557	49.8899
17	4.6332	6.4478	43.4421
18	3.9812	7.0998	36.3423
19	3.2633	7.8178	28.5245
20	2.4727	8.6083	19.9162
21	1.6022	9.4788	10.4374
22	.6437	10.4374	0.0000

YEARS 23 — QTR PAYT 2.7360 — AN CONST 10.95

#	INT	PRIN	BALANCE
1	9.7056	1.2382	98.7618
2	9.5804	1.3634	97.3984
3	9.4426	1.5013	95.8971
4	9.2907	1.6531	94.2440
5	9.1236	1.8203	92.4238
6	8.9395	2.0043	90.4194
7	8.7368	2.2070	88.2124
8	8.5136	2.4302	85.7822
9	8.2679	2.6759	83.1063
10	7.9973	2.9465	80.1597
11	7.6993	3.2445	76.9152
12	7.3712	3.5726	73.3426
13	7.0100	3.9339	69.4087
14	6.6122	4.3317	65.0771
15	6.1741	4.7697	60.3073
16	5.6918	5.2520	55.0553
17	5.1607	5.7831	49.2722
18	4.5759	6.3680	42.9042
19	3.9319	7.0119	35.8923
20	3.2229	7.7210	28.1713
21	2.4421	8.5017	19.6696
22	1.5824	9.3615	10.3081
23	.6357	10.3081	0.0000

YEARS 24 — QTR PAYT 2.7055 — AN CONST 10.83

#	INT	PRIN	BALANCE
1	9.7102	1.1120	98.8880
2	9.5977	1.2244	97.6636
3	9.4739	1.3482	96.3153
4	9.3376	1.4846	94.8308
5	9.1874	1.6347	93.1960
6	9.0221	1.8000	91.3960
7	8.8401	1.9820	89.4140
8	8.6397	2.1825	87.2315
9	8.4190	2.4032	84.8283
10	8.1760	2.6462	82.1821
11	7.9084	2.9138	79.2684
12	7.6137	3.2084	76.0599
13	7.2893	3.5329	72.5271
14	6.9320	3.8901	68.6369
15	6.5386	4.2835	64.3534
16	6.1055	4.7167	59.6367
17	5.6285	5.1936	54.4431
18	5.1033	5.7188	48.7243
19	4.5250	6.2971	42.4271
20	3.8882	6.9339	35.4932
21	3.1870	7.6351	27.8581
22	2.4149	8.4072	19.4509
23	1.5648	9.2574	10.1935
24	.6286	10.1935	0.0000

YEARS 25 — QTR PAYT 2.6785 — AN CONST 10.72

#	INT	PRIN	BALANCE
1	9.7142	.9998	99.0002
2	9.6131	1.1009	97.8994
3	9.5018	1.2122	96.6872
4	9.3792	1.3348	95.3524
5	9.2442	1.4697	93.8827
6	9.0956	1.6184	92.2643
7	8.9319	1.7820	90.4823
8	8.7517	1.9622	88.5200
9	8.5533	2.1607	86.3594
10	8.3348	2.3791	83.9802
11	8.0942	2.6197	81.3605
12	7.8293	2.8846	78.4759
13	7.5376	3.1764	75.2995
14	7.2164	3.4976	71.8020
15	6.8627	3.8512	67.9507
16	6.4733	4.2407	63.7100
17	6.0444	4.6695	59.0405
18	5.5722	5.1417	53.8988
19	5.0523	5.6617	48.2371
20	4.4798	6.2342	42.0029
21	3.8493	6.8646	35.1383
22	3.1552	7.5588	27.5795
23	2.3908	8.3231	19.2564
24	1.5491	9.1648	10.0916
25	.6224	10.0916	0.0000

YEARS 26 — QTR PAYT 2.6544 — AN CONST 10.62

#	INT	PRIN	BALANCE
1	9.7178	.8998	99.1002
2	9.6268	.9908	98.1094
3	9.5266	1.0910	97.0185
4	9.4163	1.2013	95.8172
5	9.2948	1.3228	94.4945
6	9.1610	1.4565	93.0379
7	9.0137	1.6038	91.4341
8	8.8516	1.7660	89.6681
9	8.6730	1.9446	87.7236
10	8.4763	2.1412	85.5823
11	8.2598	2.3577	83.2246
12	8.0214	2.5962	80.6284
13	7.7589	2.8587	77.7698
14	7.4698	3.1478	74.6220
15	7.1515	3.4661	71.1559
16	6.8010	3.8166	67.3393
17	6.4150	4.2025	63.1368
18	5.9900	4.6275	58.5093
19	5.5221	5.0955	53.4138
20	5.0068	5.6107	47.8031
21	4.4394	6.1781	41.6250
22	3.8147	6.8028	34.8222
23	3.1268	7.4908	27.3314
24	2.3693	8.2483	19.0831
25	1.5352	9.0823	10.0008
26	.6168	10.0008	0.0000

YEARS 27 — QTR PAYT 2.6329 — AN CONST 10.54

#	INT	PRIN	BALANCE
1	9.7210	.8105	99.1895
2	9.6390	.8925	98.2970
3	9.5487	.9827	97.3142
4	9.4494	1.0821	96.2321
5	9.3399	1.1915	95.0406
6	9.2194	1.3120	93.7285
7	9.0868	1.4447	92.2838
8	8.9407	1.5908	90.6930
9	8.7798	1.7517	88.9414
10	8.6027	1.9288	87.0125
11	8.4076	2.1239	84.8887
12	8.1929	2.3386	82.5501
13	7.9564	2.5751	79.9749
14	7.6960	2.8355	77.1394
15	7.4092	3.1223	74.0172
16	7.0935	3.4380	70.5792
17	6.7458	3.7857	66.7935
18	6.3630	4.1685	62.6250
19	5.9415	4.5900	58.0350
20	5.4773	5.0542	52.9809
21	4.9662	5.5652	47.4156
22	4.4035	6.1280	41.2876
23	3.7838	6.7477	34.5399
24	3.1014	7.4301	27.1099
25	2.3501	8.1814	18.9285
26	1.5228	9.0087	9.9197
27	.6118	9.9197	0.0000

YEARS 28 — QTR PAYT 2.6136 — AN CONST 10.46

#	INT	PRIN	BALANCE
1	9.7238	.7307	99.2693
2	9.6499	.8046	98.4647
3	9.5686	.8860	97.5787
4	9.4790	.9756	96.6032
5	9.3803	1.0742	95.5290
6	9.2717	1.1828	94.3461
7	9.1521	1.3024	93.0437
8	9.0204	1.4342	91.6095
9	8.8753	1.5792	90.0303
10	8.7157	1.7389	88.2914
11	8.5398	1.9147	86.3767
12	8.3462	2.1083	84.2684
13	8.1300	2.3215	81.9469
14	7.8982	2.5563	79.3905
15	7.6397	2.8148	76.5757
16	7.3551	3.0994	73.4763
17	7.0417	3.4129	70.0634
18	6.6965	3.7580	66.3054
19	6.3165	4.1380	62.1674
20	5.8981	4.5565	57.6110
21	5.4373	5.0172	52.5937
22	4.9300	5.5246	47.0692
23	4.3713	6.0832	40.9859
24	3.7561	6.6984	34.2875
25	3.0788	7.3758	26.9118
26	2.3329	8.1216	18.7901
27	1.5116	8.9429	9.8472
28	.6073	9.8472	0.0000

YEARS 29 — QTR PAYT 2.5964 — AN CONST 10.39

#	INT	PRIN	BALANCE
1	9.7264	.6592	99.3408
2	9.6597	.7259	98.6149
3	9.5863	.7993	97.8156
4	9.5055	.8801	96.9355
5	9.4165	.9691	95.9663
6	9.3185	1.0671	94.8992
7	9.2106	1.1750	93.7242
8	9.0917	1.2939	92.4303
9	8.9609	1.4247	91.0056
10	8.8168	1.5688	89.4368
11	8.6582	1.7274	87.7094
12	8.4835	1.9021	85.8073
13	8.2912	2.0944	83.7129
14	8.0794	2.3062	81.4066
15	7.8462	2.5395	78.8672
16	7.5894	2.7962	76.0709
17	7.3066	3.0790	72.9919
18	6.9952	3.3904	69.6016
19	6.6524	3.7332	65.8683
20	6.2749	4.1107	61.7576
21	5.8592	4.5264	57.2312
22	5.4015	4.9841	52.2470
23	4.8975	5.4882	46.7589
24	4.3425	6.0431	40.7157
25	3.7314	6.6542	34.0615
26	3.0585	7.3271	26.7344
27	2.3175	8.0681	18.6663
28	1.5017	8.8840	9.7823
29	.6033	9.7823	0.0000

YEARS 30 — QTR PAYT 2.5810 — AN CONST 10.33

#	INT	PRIN	BALANCE
1	9.7287	.5951	99.4049
2	9.6685	.6553	98.7496
3	9.6022	.7216	98.0280
4	9.5293	.7945	97.2335
5	9.4489	.8749	96.3586
6	9.3604	.9634	95.3952
7	9.2630	1.0608	94.3344
8	9.1558	1.1680	93.1664
9	9.0376	1.2862	91.8802
10	8.9076	1.4162	90.4640
11	8.7644	1.5594	88.9046
12	8.6067	1.7171	87.1874
13	8.4330	1.8908	85.2966
14	8.2418	2.0820	83.2147
15	8.0313	2.2925	80.9222
16	7.7995	2.5243	78.3978
17	7.5442	2.7796	75.6182
18	7.2631	3.0607	72.5575
19	6.9536	3.3702	69.1873
20	6.6128	3.7110	65.4763
21	6.2375	4.0863	61.3901
22	5.8243	4.4995	56.8906
23	5.3693	4.9545	51.9361
24	4.8683	5.4555	46.4806
25	4.3166	6.0072	40.4734
26	3.7092	6.6146	33.8588
27	3.0403	7.2835	26.5753
28	2.3037	8.0201	18.5552
29	1.4927	8.8311	9.7241
30	.5997	9.7241	0.0000

YEARS 2 — QTR PAYT 13.9467 — AN CONST 55.79

#	INT	PRIN	BALANCE
1	8.2542	47.5327	52.4673
2	3.3197	52.4673	0.0000

YEARS 3 — QTR PAYT 9.7487 — AN CONST 39.00

#	INT	PRIN	BALANCE
1	8.8945	30.1004	69.8996
2	5.7696	33.2252	36.6744
3	2.3204	36.6744	0.0000

YEARS 4 — QTR PAYT 7.6599 — AN CONST 30.64

#	INT	PRIN	BALANCE
1	9.2130	21.4266	78.5734
2	6.9887	23.6509	54.9225
3	4.5334	26.1062	28.8163
4	1.8233	28.8163	0.0000

YEARS 5 — QTR PAYT 6.4147 — AN CONST 25.66

#	INT	PRIN	BALANCE
1	9.4029	16.2559	83.7441
2	7.7154	17.9435	65.8006
3	5.8524	19.8062	45.9944
4	3.7965	21.8624	24.1320
5	1.5269	24.1320	0.0000

YEARS 6 — QTR PAYT 5.5913 — AN CONST 22.37

#	INT	PRIN	BALANCE
1	9.5285	12.8366	87.1634
2	8.1959	14.1692	72.9942
3	6.7250	15.6401	57.3541
4	5.1013	17.2638	40.0903
5	3.3091	19.0560	21.0343
6	1.3309	21.0343	0.0000

YEARS 7 — QTR PAYT 5.0088 — AN CONST 20.04

#	INT	PRIN	BALANCE
1	9.6174	10.4178	89.5822
2	8.5359	11.4993	78.0829
3	7.3421	12.6931	65.3898
4	6.0244	14.0108	51.3790
5	4.5699	15.4653	35.9137
6	2.9644	17.0708	18.8430
7	1.1922	18.8430	0.0000

YEARS 8 — QTR PAYT 4.5768 — AN CONST 18.31

#	INT	PRIN	BALANCE
1	9.6833	8.6241	91.3759
2	8.7880	9.5194	81.8566
3	7.7997	10.5076	71.3490
4	6.7089	11.5984	59.7505
5	5.5048	12.8025	46.9481
6	4.1758	14.1315	32.8165
7	2.7087	15.5986	17.2179
8	1.0894	17.2179	0.0000

YEARS 9 — QTR PAYT 4.2452 — AN CONST 16.99

#	INT	PRIN	BALANCE
1	9.7338	7.2468	92.7532
2	8.9815	7.9991	84.7541
3	8.1511	8.8295	75.9246
4	7.2345	9.7461	66.1785
5	6.2227	10.7579	55.4205
6	5.1059	11.8747	43.5458
7	3.8732	13.1075	30.4384
8	2.5124	14.4682	15.9702
9	1.0105	15.9702	0.0000

YEARS 10 — QTR PAYT 3.9836 — AN CONST 15.94

#	INT	PRIN	BALANCE
1	9.7737	6.1608	93.8392
2	9.1342	6.8003	87.0389
3	8.4282	7.5063	79.5326
4	7.6489	8.2855	71.2470
5	6.7888	9.1457	62.1014
6	5.8394	10.0951	52.0062
7	4.7914	11.1431	40.8631
8	3.6345	12.2999	28.5631
9	2.3577	13.5768	14.9863
10	.9482	14.9863	0.0000

YEARS 11 — QTR PAYT 3.7730 — AN CONST 15.10

#	INT	PRIN	BALANCE
1	9.8058	5.2863	94.7137
2	9.2571	5.8351	88.8786
3	8.6513	6.4408	82.4378
4	7.9827	7.1095	75.3283
5	7.2446	7.8475	67.4807
6	6.4299	8.6622	58.8185
7	5.5307	9.5615	49.2570
8	4.5381	10.5541	38.7029
9	3.4424	11.6497	27.0532
10	2.2330	12.8591	14.1941
11	.8981	14.1941	0.0000

YEARS 12 — QTR PAYT 3.6006 — AN CONST 14.41

#	INT	PRIN	BALANCE
1	9.8321	4.5703	95.4297
2	9.3577	5.0447	90.3850
3	8.8340	5.5684	84.8166
4	8.2559	6.1465	78.6701
5	7.6178	6.7846	71.8856
6	6.9135	7.4889	64.3967
7	6.1361	8.2663	56.1303
8	5.2779	9.1245	47.0058
9	4.3307	10.0717	36.9341
10	3.2851	11.1173	25.8168
11	2.1310	12.2714	13.5454
12	.8570	13.5454	0.0000

YEARS 13 — QTR PAYT 3.4574 — AN CONST 13.83

#	INT	PRIN	BALANCE
1	9.8540	3.9758	96.0242
2	9.4412	4.3886	91.6356
3	8.9856	4.8441	86.7915
4	8.4828	5.3470	81.4445
5	7.9277	5.9021	75.5424
6	7.3150	6.5148	69.0275
7	6.6386	7.1912	61.8364
8	5.8921	7.9377	53.8987
9	5.0681	8.7617	45.1370
10	4.1585	9.6713	35.4657
11	3.1545	10.6753	24.7904
12	2.0462	11.7835	13.0068
13	.8230	13.0068	0.0000

YEARS 14 — QTR PAYT 3.3372 — AN CONST 13.35

#	INT	PRIN	BALANCE
1	9.8723	3.4767	96.5233
2	9.5114	3.8376	92.6858
3	9.1130	4.2360	88.4498
4	8.6732	4.6757	83.7741
5	8.1878	5.1611	78.6129
6	7.6521	5.6969	72.9160
7	7.0606	6.2883	66.6277
8	6.4078	6.9411	59.6865
9	5.6873	7.6617	52.0248
10	4.8919	8.4571	43.5677
11	4.0139	9.3351	34.2326
12	3.0448	10.3042	23.9285
13	1.9751	11.3739	12.5546
14	.7943	12.5546	0.0000

YEARS 15 — QTR PAYT 3.2353 — AN CONST 12.95

#	INT	PRIN	BALANCE
1	9.8878	3.0535	96.9465
2	9.5709	3.3705	93.5760
3	9.2210	3.7204	89.8556
4	8.8347	4.1066	85.7490
5	8.4084	4.5330	81.2160
6	7.9378	5.0035	76.2125
7	7.4184	5.5230	70.6895
8	6.8450	6.0963	64.5932
9	6.2122	6.7292	57.8640
10	5.5136	7.4278	50.4362
11	4.7425	8.1989	42.2374
12	3.8913	9.0500	33.1874
13	2.9518	9.9895	23.1978
14	1.9148	11.0266	12.1713
15	.7701	12.1713	0.0000

YEARS 16 — QTR PAYT 3.1482 — AN CONST 12.60

#	INT	PRIN	BALANCE
1	9.9011	2.6919	97.3081
2	9.6217	2.9713	94.3368
3	9.3132	3.2798	91.0571
4	8.9727	3.6203	87.4368
5	8.5969	3.9961	83.4407
6	8.1821	4.4109	79.0298
7	7.7242	4.8688	74.1609
8	7.2187	5.3743	68.7866
9	6.6608	5.9322	62.8544
10	6.0449	6.5481	56.3064
11	5.3652	7.2278	49.0786
12	4.6148	7.9782	41.1004
13	3.7866	8.8064	32.2940
14	2.8724	9.7206	22.5734
15	1.8633	10.7297	11.8436
16	.7494	11.8436	0.0000

YEARS 17 — QTR PAYT 3.0733 — AN CONST 12.30

#	INT	PRIN	BALANCE
1	9.9126	2.3806	97.6194
2	9.6654	2.6278	94.9916
3	9.3926	2.9006	92.0910
4	9.0915	3.2017	88.8893
5	8.7591	3.5341	85.3552
6	8.3922	3.9010	81.4543
7	7.9873	4.3059	77.1484
8	7.5403	4.7529	72.3954
9	7.0469	5.2463	67.1491
10	6.5022	5.7910	61.3581
11	5.9010	6.3922	54.9659
12	5.2374	7.0558	47.9102
13	4.5050	7.7882	40.1219
14	3.6964	8.5968	31.5252
15	2.8040	9.4892	22.0360
16	1.8189	10.4743	11.5617
17	.7315	11.5617	0.0000

YEARS 18 — QTR PAYT 3.0084 — AN CONST 12.04

#	INT	PRIN	BALANCE
1	9.9225	2.1112	97.8888
2	9.7033	2.3304	95.5584
3	9.4614	2.5723	92.9861
4	9.1943	2.8393	90.1468
5	8.8996	3.1341	87.0127
6	8.5742	3.4595	83.5532
7	8.2151	3.8186	79.7346
8	7.8187	4.2150	75.5196
9	7.3811	4.6526	70.8670
10	6.8981	5.1356	65.7314
11	6.3649	5.6687	60.0627
12	5.7765	6.2572	53.8055
13	5.1269	6.9068	46.8987
14	4.4099	7.6238	39.2749
15	3.6184	8.4153	30.8596
16	2.7448	9.2889	21.5708
17	1.7805	10.2532	11.3176
18	.7161	11.3176	0.0000

YEARS 19 — QTR PAYT 2.9520 — AN CONST 11.81

#	INT	PRIN	BALANCE
1	9.9311	1.8768	98.1232
2	9.7362	2.0716	96.0517
3	9.5212	2.2866	93.7650
4	9.2838	2.5240	91.2410
5	9.0218	2.7861	88.4549
6	8.7325	3.0753	85.3797
7	8.4133	3.3945	81.9851
8	8.0609	3.7469	78.2382
9	7.6719	4.1359	74.1023
10	7.2426	4.5653	69.5370
11	6.7686	5.0392	64.4978
12	6.2455	5.5623	58.9355
13	5.6680	6.1398	52.7957
14	5.0307	6.7772	46.0185
15	4.3271	7.4807	38.5378
16	3.5505	8.2573	30.2805
17	2.6933	9.1145	21.1659
18	1.7471	10.0607	11.1052
19	.7026	11.1052	0.0000

YEARS 20 — QTR PAYT 2.9026 — AN CONST 11.62

#	INT	PRIN	BALANCE
1	9.9386	1.6718	98.3282
2	9.7650	1.8454	96.4828
3	9.5735	2.0370	94.4458
4	9.3620	2.2484	92.1974
5	9.1286	2.4818	89.7156
6	8.8709	2.7395	86.9761
7	8.5866	3.0239	83.9523
8	8.2726	3.3378	80.6145
9	7.9261	3.6843	76.9302
10	7.5437	4.0668	72.8634
11	7.1215	4.4889	68.3745
12	6.6555	4.9550	63.4195
13	6.1411	5.4693	57.9502
14	5.5733	6.0371	51.9130
15	4.9466	6.6639	45.2492
16	4.2548	7.3557	37.8935
17	3.4911	8.1193	29.7742
18	2.6483	8.9622	20.8121
19	1.7179	9.8925	10.9195
20	.6909	10.9195	0.0000

YEARS 21 — QTR PAYT 2.8593 — AN CONST 11.44

#	INT	PRIN	BALANCE
1	9.9452	1.4920	98.5080
2	9.7903	1.6469	96.8611
3	9.6193	1.8178	95.0433

#	INT	PRIN	BALANCE
4	9.4306	2.0066	93.0367
5	9.2223	2.2149	90.8219
6	8.9924	2.4448	88.3771
7	8.7386	2.6986	85.6785
8	8.4584	2.9788	82.6997
9	8.1492	3.2880	79.4117
10	7.8079	3.6293	75.7824
11	7.4311	4.0061	71.7763
12	7.0152	4.4220	67.3543
13	6.5562	4.8810	62.4733
14	6.0494	5.3877	57.0856
15	5.4901	5.9471	51.1385
16	4.8727	6.5644	44.5741
17	4.1913	7.2459	37.3281
18	3.4391	7.9981	29.3300
19	2.6087	8.8284	20.5016
20	1.6922	9.7450	10.7566
21	.6806	10.7566	0.0000

YEARS 22　QTR PAYT 2.8212　AN CONST 11.29

#	INT	PRIN	BALANCE
1	9.9510	1.3336	98.6664
2	9.8126	1.4721	97.1943
3	9.6597	1.6249	95.5693
4	9.4911	1.7936	93.7757
5	9.3049	1.9798	91.7959
6	9.0993	2.1853	89.6106
7	8.8725	2.4122	87.1984
8	8.6226	2.6626	84.5358
9	8.3456	2.9390	81.5968
10	8.0405	3.2441	78.3527
11	7.7037	3.5809	74.7717
12	7.3320	3.9527	70.8191
13	6.9217	4.3630	66.4561
14	6.4687	4.8159	61.6401
15	5.9688	5.3159	56.3242
16	5.4169	5.8677	50.4565
17	4.8078	6.4769	43.9796
18	4.1354	7.1493	36.8303
19	3.3932	7.8915	28.9388
20	2.5740	8.7107	20.2281
21	1.6697	9.6150	10.6132
22	.6715	10.6132	0.0000

YEARS 23　QTR PAYT 2.7875　AN CONST 11.15

#	INT	PRIN	BALANCE
1	9.9562	1.1938	98.8062
2	9.8322	1.3177	97.4885
3	9.6954	1.4545	96.0340
4	9.5444	1.6055	94.4285
5	9.3778	1.7722	92.6563
6	9.1938	1.9562	90.7001
7	8.9907	2.1592	88.5409
8	8.7665	2.3834	86.1575
9	8.5191	2.6308	83.5266
10	8.2460	2.9039	80.6227
11	7.9445	3.2054	77.4173
12	7.6118	3.5382	73.8791
13	7.2445	3.9055	69.9736
14	6.8390	4.3109	65.6627
15	6.3915	4.7584	60.9043
16	5.8975	5.2524	55.6519
17	5.3522	5.7977	49.8542
18	4.7504	6.3996	43.4546
19	4.0860	7.0639	36.3906
20	3.3527	7.7973	28.5934
21	2.5432	8.6067	19.9867
22	1.6497	9.5002	10.4865
23	.6635	10.4865	0.0000

YEARS 24　QTR PAYT 2.7577　AN CONST 11.04

#	INT	PRIN	BALANCE
1	9.9607	1.0699	98.9301
2	9.8496	1.1810	97.7490
3	9.7270	1.3036	96.4454
4	9.5917	1.4390	95.0065
5	9.4423	1.5883	93.4181
6	9.2774	1.7532	91.6649
7	9.0954	1.9352	89.7297
8	8.8945	2.1361	87.5935
9	8.6727	2.3579	85.2356
10	8.4280	2.6027	82.6329
11	8.1578	2.8729	79.7601
12	7.8595	3.1711	76.5890
13	7.5303	3.5003	73.0887
14	7.1670	3.8637	69.2250
15	6.7659	4.2648	64.9602
16	6.3231	4.7075	60.2526
17	5.8344	5.1962	55.0564
18	5.2950	5.7357	49.3207
19	4.6995	6.3311	42.9896
20	4.0423	6.9884	36.0013
21	3.3168	7.7138	28.2874
22	2.5160	8.5146	19.7728
23	1.6321	9.3986	10.3743
24	.6564	10.3743	0.0000

YEARS 25　QTR PAYT 2.7312　AN CONST 10.93

#	INT	PRIN	BALANCE
1	9.9647	.9600	99.0400
2	9.8651	1.0597	97.9803
3	9.7551	1.1697	96.8106
4	9.6336	1.2911	95.5195
5	9.4996	1.4251	94.0944
6	9.3517	1.5731	92.5213
7	9.1884	1.7364	90.7849
8	9.0081	1.9167	88.8682
9	8.8091	2.1156	86.7526
10	8.5895	2.3353	84.4173
11	8.3471	2.5777	81.8397
12	8.0795	2.8453	78.9944
13	7.7841	3.1407	75.8537
14	7.4580	3.4667	72.3870
15	7.0982	3.8266	68.5604
16	6.7009	4.2238	64.3365
17	6.2624	4.6623	59.6742
18	5.7784	5.1463	54.5279
19	5.2441	5.6806	48.8473
20	4.6544	6.2703	42.5769
21	4.0035	6.9213	35.6557
22	3.2850	7.6398	28.0159
23	2.4919	8.4329	19.5830
24	1.6164	9.3083	10.2747
25	.6501	10.2747	0.0000

YEARS 26　QTR PAYT 2.7076　AN CONST 10.84

#	INT	PRIN	BALANCE
1	9.9683	.8622	99.1378
2	9.8788	.9517	98.1860
3	9.7800	1.0505	97.1355
4	9.6710	1.1596	95.9759
5	9.5506	1.2800	94.6959
6	9.4177	1.4129	93.2831
7	9.2710	1.5595	91.7236
8	9.1091	1.7214	90.0021
9	8.9304	1.9001	88.1020
10	8.7332	2.0974	86.0046
11	8.5154	2.3151	83.6895
12	8.2751	2.5555	81.1340
13	8.0098	2.8208	78.3133
14	7.7170	3.1136	75.1997
15	7.3937	3.4368	71.7629
16	7.0370	3.7936	67.9693
17	6.6431	4.1874	63.7818
18	6.2084	4.6221	59.1597
19	5.7286	5.1020	54.0577
20	5.1989	5.6316	48.4261
21	4.6143	6.2163	42.2098
22	3.9690	6.8616	35.3482
23	3.2566	7.5739	27.7743
24	2.4704	8.3602	19.4141
25	1.6025	9.2281	10.1861
26	.6445	10.1861	0.0000

YEARS 27　QTR PAYT 2.6867　AN CONST 10.75

#	INT	PRIN	BALANCE
1	9.9715	.7751	99.2249
2	9.8911	.8555	98.3694
3	9.8023	.9444	97.4250
4	9.7042	1.0424	96.3826
5	9.5960	1.1506	95.2320
6	9.4766	1.2701	93.9620
7	9.3447	1.4019	92.5601
8	9.1992	1.5474	91.0126
9	9.0385	1.7081	89.3045
10	8.8612	1.8854	87.4191
11	8.6655	2.0811	85.3380
12	8.4494	2.2972	83.0408
13	8.2110	2.5357	80.5052
14	7.9477	2.7989	77.7063
15	7.6572	3.0895	74.6168
16	7.3364	3.4102	71.2066
17	6.9824	3.7642	67.4424
18	6.5916	4.1550	63.2875
19	6.1603	4.5863	58.7012
20	5.6842	5.0624	53.6387
21	5.1586	5.5880	48.0507
22	4.5785	6.1681	41.8827
23	3.9382	6.8084	35.0743
24	3.2314	7.5152	27.5590
25	2.4512	8.2954	19.2637
26	1.5901	9.1565	10.1071
27	.6395	10.1071	0.0000

YEARS 28　QTR PAYT 2.6679　AN CONST 10.68

#	INT	PRIN	BALANCE
1	9.9744	.6973	99.3027
2	9.9020	.7697	98.5330
3	9.8221	.8496	97.6835
4	9.7339	.9378	96.7457
5	9.6366	1.0351	95.7106
6	9.5291	1.1426	94.5680
7	9.4105	1.2612	93.3068
8	9.2795	1.3921	91.9147
9	9.1350	1.5366	90.3780
10	8.9755	1.6962	88.6818
11	8.7994	1.8723	86.8096
12	8.6051	2.0666	84.7430
13	8.3905	2.2812	82.4618
14	8.1537	2.5180	79.9438
15	7.8923	2.7794	77.1644
16	7.6038	3.0679	74.0965
17	7.2853	3.3864	70.7101
18	6.9337	3.7380	66.9722
19	6.5457	4.1260	62.8462
20	6.1173	4.5543	58.2918
21	5.6445	5.0271	53.2647
22	5.1227	5.5490	47.7157
23	4.5466	6.1251	41.5906
24	3.9107	6.7609	34.8297
25	3.2089	7.4628	27.3669
26	2.4341	8.2375	19.1293
27	1.5790	9.0927	10.0366
28	.6350	10.0366	0.0000

YEARS 29　QTR PAYT 2.6512　AN CONST 10.61

#	INT	PRIN	BALANCE
1	9.9769	.6277	99.3723
2	9.9118	.6929	98.6793
3	9.8398	.7648	97.9145
4	9.7604	.8442	97.0703
5	9.6728	.9319	96.1384
6	9.5761	1.0286	95.1098
7	9.4693	1.1354	93.9743
8	9.3514	1.2533	92.7211
9	9.2213	1.3834	91.3377
10	9.0777	1.5270	89.8107
11	8.9192	1.6855	88.1251
12	8.7442	1.8605	86.2646
13	8.5510	2.0536	84.2110
14	8.3378	2.2668	81.9441
15	8.1025	2.5022	79.4420
16	7.8428	2.7619	76.6800
17	7.5560	3.0487	73.6314
18	7.2395	3.3651	70.2662
19	6.8902	3.7145	66.5518
20	6.5046	4.1001	62.4517
21	6.0789	4.5257	57.9259
22	5.6091	4.9956	52.9303
23	5.0905	5.5142	47.4162
24	4.5181	6.0866	41.3295
25	3.8862	6.7185	34.6110
26	3.1887	7.4160	27.1951
27	2.4189	8.1858	19.0093
28	1.5691	9.0356	9.9736
29	.6310	9.9736	0.0000

YEARS 30　QTR PAYT 2.6362　AN CONST 10.55

#	INT	PRIN	BALANCE
1	9.9792	.5655	99.4345
2	9.9205	.6242	98.8103
3	9.8557	.6890	98.1213
4	9.7842	.7605	97.3608
5	9.7052	.8395	96.5213
6	9.6181	.9266	95.5947
7	9.5219	1.0228	94.5719
8	9.4157	1.1290	93.4429
9	9.2985	1.2462	92.1967
10	9.1692	1.3756	90.8212
11	9.0263	1.5184	89.3028
12	8.8687	1.6760	87.6268
13	8.6947	1.8500	85.7768
14	8.5027	2.0420	83.7348
15	8.2907	2.2540	81.4808
16	8.0567	2.4880	78.9927
17	7.7984	2.7463	76.2464
18	7.5133	3.0314	73.2150
19	7.1986	3.3461	69.8689
20	6.8512	3.6935	66.1754
21	6.4678	4.0769	62.0985
22	6.0446	4.5002	57.5984
23	5.5774	4.9673	52.6310
24	5.0617	5.4830	47.1480
25	4.4925	6.0522	41.0958
26	3.8642	6.6805	34.4153
27	3.1707	7.3740	27.0413
28	2.4052	8.1395	18.9018
29	1.5602	8.9845	9.9172
30	.6275	9.9172	0.0000

YEARS 2 — QTR PAYT 13.9839 — AN CONST 55.94

#	INT	PRIN	BALANCE
1	8.4638	47.4719	52.5281
2	3.4076	52.5281	0.0000

YEARS 3 — QTR PAYT 9.7856 — AN CONST 39.15

#	INT	PRIN	BALANCE
1	9.1203	30.0222	69.9778
2	5.9228	33.2198	36.7580
3	2.3846	36.7580	0.0000

YEARS 4 — QTR PAYT 7.6972 — AN CONST 30.79

#	INT	PRIN	BALANCE
1	9.4470	21.3419	78.6581
2	7.1739	23.6149	55.0432
3	4.6587	26.1301	28.9131
4	1.8757	28.9131	0.0000

YEARS 5 — QTR PAYT 6.4526 — AN CONST 25.82

#	INT	PRIN	BALANCE
1	9.6416	16.1690	83.8310
2	7.9195	17.8911	65.9399
3	6.0140	19.7966	46.1433
4	3.9055	21.9051	24.2382
5	1.5724	24.2382	0.0000

YEARS 6 — QTR PAYT 5.6300 — AN CONST 22.52

#	INT	PRIN	BALANCE
1	9.7703	12.7496	87.2504
2	8.4123	14.1075	73.1429
3	6.9098	15.6101	57.5329
4	5.2472	17.2726	40.2602
5	3.4075	19.1123	21.1479
6	1.3719	21.1479	0.0000

YEARS 7 — QTR PAYT 5.0483 — AN CONST 20.20

#	INT	PRIN	BALANCE
1	9.8612	10.3319	89.6681
2	8.7608	11.4323	78.2358
3	7.5432	12.6499	65.5859
4	6.1959	13.9972	51.5886
5	4.7051	15.4881	36.1006
6	3.0555	17.1377	18.9629
7	1.2302	18.9629	0.0000

YEARS 8 — QTR PAYT 4.6172 — AN CONST 18.47

#	INT	PRIN	BALANCE
1	9.9287	8.5400	91.4600
2	9.0191	9.4495	82.0105
3	8.0126	10.4560	71.5545
4	6.8990	11.5696	59.9849
5	5.6668	12.8019	47.1830
6	4.3033	14.1654	33.0176
7	2.7945	15.6741	17.3435
8	1.1251	17.3435	0.0000

YEARS 9 — QTR PAYT 4.2863 — AN CONST 17.15

#	INT	PRIN	BALANCE
1	9.9804	7.1650	92.8350
2	9.2173	7.9281	84.9070
3	8.3729	8.7725	76.1345
4	7.4385	9.7068	66.4277
5	6.4047	10.7407	55.6870
6	5.2607	11.8846	43.8023
7	3.9949	13.1504	30.6519
8	2.5943	14.5511	16.1009
9	1.0445	16.1009	0.0000

YEARS 10 — QTR PAYT 4.0257 — AN CONST 16.11

#	INT	PRIN	BALANCE
1	10.0212	6.0815	93.9185
2	9.3734	6.7292	87.1893
3	8.6567	7.4459	79.7433
4	7.8637	8.2390	71.5044
5	6.9862	9.1165	62.3879
6	6.0152	10.0875	52.3004
7	4.9408	11.1619	41.1385
8	3.7520	12.3507	28.7878
9	2.4365	13.6661	15.1217
10	.9810	15.1217	0.0000

YEARS 11 — QTR PAYT 3.8159 — AN CONST 15.27

#	INT	PRIN	BALANCE
1	10.0540	5.2098	94.7902
2	9.4991	5.7647	89.0256
3	8.8851	6.3786	82.6469
4	8.2057	7.0580	75.5889
5	7.4540	7.8098	67.7791
6	6.6222	8.6416	59.1376
7	5.7018	9.5619	49.5756
8	4.6834	10.5804	38.9953
9	3.5565	11.7072	27.2880
10	2.3096	12.9542	14.3339
11	.9299	14.3339	0.0000

YEARS 12 — QTR PAYT 3.6444 — AN CONST 14.58

#	INT	PRIN	BALANCE
1	10.0808	4.4966	95.5034
2	9.6019	4.9755	90.5279
3	9.0720	5.5055	85.0224
4	8.4856	6.0918	78.9306
5	7.8368	6.7406	72.1900
6	7.1188	7.4586	64.7314
7	6.3244	8.2530	56.4784
8	5.4454	9.1320	47.3464
9	4.4728	10.1046	37.2418
10	3.3966	11.1808	26.0610
11	2.2057	12.3717	13.6893
12	.8881	13.6893	0.0000

YEARS 13 — QTR PAYT 3.5020 — AN CONST 14.01

#	INT	PRIN	BALANCE
1	10.1031	3.9051	96.0949
2	9.6871	4.3210	91.7739
3	9.2269	4.7812	86.9927
4	8.7177	5.2905	81.7022
5	8.1542	5.8539	75.8483
6	7.5307	6.4774	69.3709
7	6.8408	7.1673	62.2036
8	6.0775	7.9307	54.2729
9	5.2328	8.7754	45.4975
10	4.2981	9.7100	35.7875
11	3.2639	10.7442	25.0433
12	2.1196	11.8885	13.1548
13	.8534	13.1548	0.0000

YEARS 14 — QTR PAYT 3.3827 — AN CONST 13.54

#	INT	PRIN	BALANCE
1	10.1217	3.4089	96.5911
2	9.7587	3.7720	92.8191
3	9.3569	4.1737	88.6454
4	8.9124	4.6182	84.0272
5	8.4205	5.1101	78.9171
6	7.8762	5.6544	73.2627
7	7.2740	6.2566	67.0061
8	6.6076	6.9230	60.0831
9	5.8703	7.6603	52.4228
10	5.0544	8.4762	43.9465
11	4.1516	9.3790	34.5675
12	3.1527	10.3779	24.1896
13	2.0474	11.4833	12.7063
14	.8243	12.7063	0.0000

YEARS 15 — QTR PAYT 3.2816 — AN CONST 13.13

#	INT	PRIN	BALANCE
1	10.1375	2.9887	97.0113
2	9.8192	3.3070	93.7043
3	9.4670	3.6592	90.0451
4	9.0773	4.0490	85.9961
5	8.6460	4.4802	81.5159
6	8.1688	4.9574	76.5585
7	7.6408	5.4854	71.0731
8	7.0566	6.0696	65.0035
9	6.4102	6.7161	58.2874
10	5.6948	7.4314	50.8560
11	4.9033	8.2229	42.6331
12	4.0275	9.0987	33.5344
13	3.0585	10.0678	23.4666
14	1.9862	11.1401	12.3266
15	.7997	12.3266	0.0000

YEARS 16 — QTR PAYT 3.1953 — AN CONST 12.79

#	INT	PRIN	BALANCE
1	10.1510	2.6300	97.3700
2	9.8709	2.9101	94.4599
3	9.5610	3.2200	91.2399
4	9.2180	3.5630	87.6769
5	8.8385	3.9425	83.7344
6	8.4186	4.3624	79.3720
7	7.9540	4.8270	74.5450
8	7.4399	5.3411	69.2039
9	6.8710	5.9100	63.2939
10	6.2416	6.5395	56.7545
11	5.5451	7.2360	49.5185
12	4.7744	8.0066	41.5119
13	3.9216	8.8594	32.6525
14	2.9780	9.8030	22.8495
15	1.9339	10.8471	12.0024
16	.7786	12.0024	0.0000

YEARS 17 — QTR PAYT 3.1211 — AN CONST 12.49

#	INT	PRIN	BALANCE
1	10.1626	2.3216	97.6784
2	9.9154	2.5689	95.1094
3	9.6418	2.8425	92.2669
4	9.3390	3.1453	89.1216
5	9.0040	3.4803	85.6414
6	8.6333	3.8509	81.7904
7	8.2232	4.2611	77.5293
8	7.7693	4.7149	72.8144
9	7.2672	5.2171	67.5972
10	6.7115	5.7728	61.8245
11	6.0967	6.3876	55.4368
12	5.4163	7.0680	48.3689
13	4.6635	7.8208	40.5481
14	3.8306	8.6537	31.8944
15	2.9089	9.5754	22.3190
16	1.8890	10.5953	11.7237
17	.7606	11.7237	0.0000

YEARS 18 — QTR PAYT 3.0569 — AN CONST 12.23

#	INT	PRIN	BALANCE
1	10.1727	2.0551	97.9449
2	9.9538	2.2739	95.6710
3	9.7116	2.5161	93.1549
4	9.4436	2.7841	90.3708
5	9.1471	3.0806	87.2901
6	8.8190	3.4088	83.8814
7	8.4559	3.7718	80.1096
8	8.0542	4.1735	75.9360
9	7.6097	4.6180	71.3180
10	7.1178	5.1099	66.2081
11	6.5736	5.6541	60.5539
12	5.9714	6.2564	54.2976
13	5.3050	6.9227	47.3749
14	4.5677	7.6600	39.7148
15	3.7518	8.4759	31.2390
16	2.8491	9.3786	21.8603
17	1.8502	10.3775	11.4828
18	.7449	11.4828	0.0000

YEARS 19 — QTR PAYT 3.0012 — AN CONST 12.01

#	INT	PRIN	BALANCE
1	10.1814	1.8234	98.1766
2	9.9872	2.0176	96.1590
3	9.7723	2.2325	93.9266
4	9.5345	2.4702	91.4563
5	9.2714	2.7333	88.7230
6	8.9803	3.0245	85.6985
7	8.6582	3.3466	82.3519
8	8.3017	3.7030	78.6489
9	7.9073	4.0974	74.5514
10	7.4709	4.5338	70.0176
11	6.9880	5.0167	65.0009
12	6.4537	5.5511	59.4498
13	5.8625	6.1423	53.3075
14	5.2083	6.7965	46.5110
15	4.4844	7.5204	38.9907
16	3.6834	8.3213	30.6694
17	2.7972	9.2076	21.4617
18	1.8165	10.1883	11.2734
19	.7313	11.2734	0.0000

YEARS 20 — QTR PAYT 2.9525 — AN CONST 11.82

#	INT	PRIN	BALANCE
1	10.1890	1.6212	98.3788
2	10.0163	1.7938	96.5850
3	9.8253	1.9849	94.6002
4	9.6139	2.1963	92.4039
5	9.3800	2.4302	89.9737
6	9.1211	2.6890	87.2846
7	8.8347	2.9754	84.3092
8	8.5178	3.2923	81.0169
9	8.1672	3.6430	77.3739
10	7.7791	4.0310	73.3428
11	7.3498	4.4603	68.8825
12	6.8748	4.9354	63.9471
13	6.3491	5.4611	58.4860
14	5.7674	6.0427	52.4433
15	5.1239	6.6863	45.7570
16	4.4117	7.3984	38.3586
17	3.6237	8.1864	30.1722
18	2.7518	9.0583	21.1138
19	1.7870	10.0231	11.0907
20	.7195	11.0907	0.0000

YEARS 21 — QTR PAYT 2.9099 — AN CONST 11.64

#	INT	PRIN	BALANCE
1	10.1957	1.4440	98.5560
2	10.0419	1.5977	96.9583
3	9.8717	1.7679	95.1904

#	INT	PRIN	BALANCE
4	9.6834	1.9562	93.2342
5	9.4751	2.1646	91.0696
6	9.2445	2.3951	88.6745
7	8.9894	2.6502	86.0243
8	8.7071	2.9325	83.0918
9	8.3948	3.2448	79.8470
10	8.0492	3.5904	76.2566
11	7.6668	3.9728	72.2838
12	7.2437	4.3959	67.8879
13	6.7755	4.8641	63.0237
14	6.2574	5.3822	57.6415
15	5.6842	5.9555	51.6861
16	5.0499	6.5898	45.0963
17	4.3480	7.2916	37.8047
18	3.5714	8.0682	29.7365
19	2.7121	8.9276	20.8089
20	1.7612	9.8784	10.9305
21	.7091	10.9305	0.0000

YEARS 22 — QTR PAYT 2.8724 — AN CONST 11.49

#	INT	PRIN	BALANCE
1	10.2015	1.2882	98.7118
2	10.0643	1.4254	97.2865
3	9.9125	1.5772	95.7093
4	9.7445	1.7451	93.9642
5	9.5587	1.9310	92.0332
6	9.3530	2.1367	89.8965
7	9.1254	2.3643	87.5322
8	8.8736	2.6161	84.9162
9	8.5950	2.8947	82.0215
10	8.2867	3.2030	78.8185
11	7.9455	3.5441	75.2743
12	7.5681	3.9216	71.3527
13	7.1504	4.3393	67.0134
14	6.6882	4.8015	62.2119
15	6.1768	5.3129	56.8990
16	5.6109	5.8787	51.0203
17	4.9848	6.5049	44.5154
18	4.2920	7.1977	37.3177
19	3.5254	7.9643	29.3534
20	2.6771	8.8126	20.5409
21	1.7385	9.7512	10.7897
22	.7000	10.7897	0.0000

YEARS 23 — QTR PAYT 2.8394 — AN CONST 11.36

#	INT	PRIN	BALANCE
1	10.2067	1.1508	98.8492
2	10.0841	1.2733	97.5759
3	9.9485	1.4090	96.1670
4	9.7985	1.5590	94.6079
5	9.6324	1.7251	92.8829
6	9.4487	1.9088	90.9741
7	9.2454	2.1121	88.8620
8	9.0204	2.3370	86.5249
9	8.7715	2.5860	83.9390
10	8.4961	2.8614	81.0776
11	8.1913	3.1661	77.9114
12	7.8541	3.5034	74.4081
13	7.4810	3.8765	70.5316
14	7.0681	4.2894	66.2422
15	6.6112	4.7462	61.4960
16	6.1057	5.2517	56.2442
17	5.5464	5.8111	50.4332
18	4.9275	6.4300	44.0031
19	4.2426	7.1149	36.8883
20	3.4848	7.8726	29.0156
21	2.6463	8.7111	20.3045
22	1.7185	9.6389	10.6656
23	.6919	10.6656	0.0000

YEARS 24 — QTR PAYT 2.8101 — AN CONST 11.25

#	INT	PRIN	BALANCE
1	10.2113	1.0293	98.9707
2	10.1016	1.1389	97.8318
3	9.9803	1.2602	96.5716
4	9.8461	1.3944	95.1771
5	9.6976	1.5430	93.6341
6	9.5333	1.7073	91.9268
7	9.3514	1.8891	90.0377
8	9.1502	2.0904	87.9473
9	8.9276	2.3130	85.6343
10	8.6812	2.5593	83.0750
11	8.4086	2.8319	80.2431
12	8.1070	3.1336	77.1095
13	7.7733	3.4673	73.6422
14	7.4040	3.8366	69.8056
15	6.9953	4.2452	65.5604
16	6.5432	4.6974	60.8630
17	6.0429	5.1977	55.6653
18	5.4893	5.7513	49.9140
19	4.8767	6.3638	43.5502
20	4.1989	7.0416	36.5086
21	3.4490	7.7916	28.7170
22	2.6191	8.6215	20.0955
23	1.7008	9.5397	10.5558
24	.6848	10.5558	0.0000

YEARS 25 — QTR PAYT 2.7842 — AN CONST 11.14

#	INT	PRIN	BALANCE
1	10.2153	.9216	99.0784
2	10.1172	1.0198	98.0585
3	10.0085	1.1284	96.9301
4	9.8884	1.2486	95.6815
5	9.7554	1.3816	94.2999
6	9.6082	1.5287	92.7712
7	9.4454	1.6916	91.0796
8	9.2652	1.8717	89.2079
9	9.0659	2.0711	87.1368
10	8.8453	2.2917	84.8451
11	8.6012	2.5358	82.3093
12	8.3311	2.8058	79.5035
13	8.0323	3.1047	76.3988
14	7.7016	3.4353	72.9635
15	7.3357	3.8012	69.1622
16	6.9309	4.2061	64.9561
17	6.4829	4.6541	60.3021
18	5.9872	5.1498	55.1523
19	5.4387	5.6983	49.4540
20	4.8318	6.3052	43.1488
21	4.1602	6.9767	36.1721
22	3.4172	7.7198	28.4523
23	2.5950	8.5420	19.9103
24	1.6852	9.4518	10.4585
25	.6785	10.4585	0.0000

YEARS 26 — QTR PAYT 2.7612 — AN CONST 11.05

#	INT	PRIN	BALANCE
1	10.2189	.8261	99.1739
2	10.1309	.9140	98.2599
3	10.0336	1.0114	97.2485
4	9.9259	1.1191	96.1294
5	9.8067	1.2383	94.8911
6	9.6748	1.3702	93.5210
7	9.5289	1.5161	92.0048
8	9.3674	1.6776	90.3272
9	9.1887	1.8563	88.4710
10	8.9910	2.0540	86.4170
11	8.7722	2.2727	84.1442
12	8.5302	2.5148	81.6294
13	8.2623	2.7827	78.8468
14	7.9659	3.0790	75.7677
15	7.6380	3.4070	72.3608
16	7.2751	3.7698	68.5909
17	6.8736	4.1714	64.4196
18	6.4293	4.6156	59.8039
19	5.9377	5.1072	54.6967
20	5.3938	5.6512	49.0455
21	4.7919	6.2531	42.7924
22	4.1259	6.9191	35.8733
23	3.3889	7.6560	28.2173
24	2.5735	8.4715	19.7458
25	1.6712	9.3737	10.3721
26	.6729	10.3721	0.0000

YEARS 27 — QTR PAYT 2.7408 — AN CONST 10.97

#	INT	PRIN	BALANCE
1	10.2221	.7410	99.2590
2	10.1432	.8199	98.4391
3	10.0559	.9073	97.5318
4	9.9592	1.0039	96.5279
5	9.8523	1.1108	95.4171
6	9.7340	1.2291	94.1880
7	9.6031	1.3600	92.8280
8	9.4582	1.5049	91.3231
9	9.2980	1.6652	89.6579
10	9.1206	1.8425	87.8154
11	8.9244	2.0388	85.7766
12	8.7072	2.2559	83.5207
13	8.4669	2.4962	81.0245
14	8.2011	2.7620	78.2625
15	7.9069	3.0562	75.2063
16	7.5814	3.3817	71.8246
17	7.2212	3.7419	68.0827
18	6.8227	4.1404	63.9422
19	6.3817	4.5814	59.3608
20	5.8937	5.0694	54.2914
21	5.3538	5.6093	48.6821
22	4.7564	6.2068	42.4753
23	4.0953	6.8678	35.6075
24	3.3638	7.5993	28.0082
25	2.5544	8.4087	19.5995
26	1.6589	9.3043	10.2952
27	.6679	10.2952	0.0000

YEARS 28 — QTR PAYT 2.7225 — AN CONST 10.90

#	INT	PRIN	BALANCE
1	10.2250	.6652	99.3348
2	10.1541	.7361	98.5987
3	10.0757	.8145	97.7842
4	9.9890	.9012	96.8830
5	9.8930	.9972	95.8858
6	9.7868	1.1034	94.7824
7	9.6693	1.2209	93.5614
8	9.5392	1.3510	92.2104
9	9.3953	1.4949	90.7156
10	9.2361	1.6541	89.0615
11	9.0599	1.8303	87.2312
12	8.8650	2.0252	85.2060
13	8.6493	2.2409	82.9651
14	8.4106	2.4796	80.4855
15	8.1465	2.7437	77.7419
16	7.8543	3.0359	74.7060
17	7.5310	3.3592	71.3468
18	7.1732	3.7170	67.6298
19	6.7773	4.1129	63.5169
20	6.3392	4.5510	58.9659
21	5.8545	5.0357	53.9302
22	5.3182	5.5720	48.3582
23	4.7247	6.1655	42.1928
24	4.0681	6.8221	35.3706
25	3.3415	7.5487	27.8219
26	2.5375	8.3527	19.4691
27	1.6478	9.2424	10.2268
28	.6634	10.2268	0.0000

YEARS 29 — QTR PAYT 2.7063 — AN CONST 10.83

#	INT	PRIN	BALANCE
1	10.2275	.5976	99.4024
2	10.1639	.6613	98.7411
3	10.0934	.7317	98.0095
4	10.0155	.8096	97.1999
5	9.9293	.8958	96.3040
6	9.8339	.9913	95.3128
7	9.7283	1.0968	94.2159
8	9.6115	1.2136	93.0023
9	9.4822	1.3429	91.6594
10	9.3392	1.4859	90.1734
11	9.1809	1.6442	88.5292
12	9.0058	1.8193	86.7099
13	8.8120	2.0131	84.6968
14	8.5976	2.2275	82.4693
15	8.3604	2.4648	80.0046
16	8.0978	2.7273	77.2773
17	7.8074	3.0177	74.2596
18	7.4860	3.3392	70.9204
19	7.1303	3.6948	67.2256
20	6.7368	4.0883	63.1373
21	6.3014	4.5238	58.6135
22	5.8195	5.0056	53.6079
23	5.2864	5.5387	48.0692
24	4.6965	6.1286	41.9406
25	4.0437	6.7814	35.1592
26	3.3215	7.5036	27.6556
27	2.5223	8.3028	19.3528
28	1.6380	9.1871	10.1656
29	.6595	10.1656	0.0000

YEARS 30 — QTR PAYT 2.6917 — AN CONST 10.77

#	INT	PRIN	BALANCE
1	10.2298	.5372	99.4628
2	10.1726	.5944	98.8684
3	10.1093	.6577	98.2107
4	10.0392	.7277	97.4830
5	9.9617	.8053	96.6777
6	9.8759	.8910	95.7867
7	9.7810	.9859	94.8008
8	9.6760	1.0909	93.7098
9	9.5598	1.2071	92.5027
10	9.4313	1.3357	91.1670
11	9.2890	1.4780	89.6891
12	9.1316	1.6354	88.0537
13	8.9574	1.8096	86.2441
14	8.7647	2.0023	84.2418
15	8.5514	2.2155	82.0263
16	8.3155	2.4515	79.5748
17	8.0543	2.7126	76.8622
18	7.7654	3.0015	73.8606
19	7.4457	3.3212	70.5394
20	7.0920	3.6750	66.8645
21	6.7006	4.0664	62.7981
22	6.2675	4.4995	58.2987
23	5.7883	4.9787	53.3200
24	5.2580	5.5090	47.8110
25	4.6713	6.0957	41.7153
26	4.0220	6.7449	34.9704
27	3.3036	7.4633	27.5071
28	2.5087	8.2582	19.2488
29	1.6292	9.1378	10.1110
30	.6559	10.1110	0.0000

YEARS 2 — QTR PAYT 14.0212 — AN CONST 56.09

#	INT	PRIN	BALANCE
1	8.6735	47.4112	52.5888
2	3.4958	52.5888	0.0000

YEARS 3 — QTR PAYT 9.8226 — AN CONST 39.30

#	INT	PRIN	BALANCE
1	9.3464	29.9442	70.0558
2	6.0763	33.2143	36.8415
3	2.4490	36.8415	0.0000

YEARS 4 — QTR PAYT 7.7346 — AN CONST 30.94

#	INT	PRIN	BALANCE
1	9.6811	21.2574	78.7426
2	7.3596	23.5788	55.1638
3	4.7846	26.1538	29.0100
4	1.9284	29.0100	0.0000

YEARS 5 — QTR PAYT 6.4907 — AN CONST 25.97

#	INT	PRIN	BALANCE
1	9.8804	16.0824	83.9176
2	8.1241	17.8387	66.0789
3	6.1760	19.7868	46.2922
4	4.0151	21.9477	24.3445
5	1.6183	24.3445	0.0000

YEARS 6 — QTR PAYT 5.6688 — AN CONST 22.68

#	INT	PRIN	BALANCE
1	10.0122	12.6630	87.3370
2	8.6293	14.0459	73.2912
3	7.0954	15.5798	57.7114
4	5.3939	17.2812	40.4302
5	3.5067	19.1684	21.2618
6	1.4134	21.2618	0.0000

YEARS 7 — QTR PAYT 5.0879 — AN CONST 20.36

#	INT	PRIN	BALANCE
1	10.1053	10.2465	89.7535
2	8.9863	11.3655	78.3881
3	7.7451	12.6067	65.7814
4	6.3683	13.9834	51.7980
5	4.8412	15.5105	36.2875
6	3.1474	17.2043	19.0832
7	1.2686	19.0832	0.0000

YEARS 8 — QTR PAYT 4.6577 — AN CONST 18.64

#	INT	PRIN	BALANCE
1	10.1742	8.4565	91.5435
2	9.2507	9.3800	82.1635
3	8.2263	10.4043	71.7592
4	7.0901	11.5406	60.2186
5	5.8298	12.8009	47.4177
6	4.4319	14.1988	33.2189
7	2.8812	15.7495	17.4694
8	1.1613	17.4694	0.0000

YEARS 9 — QTR PAYT 4.3277 — AN CONST 17.32

#	INT	PRIN	BALANCE
1	10.2271	7.0838	92.9162
2	9.4535	7.8574	85.0587
3	8.5954	8.7155	76.3432
4	7.6436	9.6673	66.6759
5	6.5879	10.7231	55.9528
6	5.4168	11.8941	44.0587
7	4.1179	13.1930	30.8657
8	2.6771	14.6338	16.2319
9	1.0790	16.2319	0.0000

YEARS 10 — QTR PAYT 4.0679 — AN CONST 16.28

#	INT	PRIN	BALANCE
1	10.2687	6.0030	93.9970
2	9.6132	6.6586	87.3384
3	8.8860	7.3858	79.9526
4	8.0794	8.1923	71.7603
5	7.1848	9.0870	62.6733
6	6.1924	10.0794	52.5940
7	5.0917	11.1801	41.4139
8	3.8707	12.4010	29.0128
9	2.5164	13.7553	15.2575
10	1.0142	15.2575	0.0000

YEARS 11 — QTR PAYT 3.8591 — AN CONST 15.44

#	INT	PRIN	BALANCE
1	10.3022	5.1341	94.8659
2	9.7415	5.6948	89.1711
3	9.1196	6.3167	82.8543
4	8.4298	7.0066	75.8478
5	7.6646	7.7717	68.0760
6	6.8159	8.6205	59.4556
7	5.8745	9.5619	49.8937
8	4.8302	10.6061	39.2876
9	3.6720	11.7644	27.5233
10	2.3872	13.0491	14.4742
11	.9622	14.4742	0.0000

YEARS 12 — QTR PAYT 3.6884 — AN CONST 14.76

#	INT	PRIN	BALANCE
1	10.3296	4.4239	95.5761
2	9.8465	4.9070	90.6691
3	9.3106	5.4429	85.2262
4	8.7162	6.0373	79.1890
5	8.0569	6.6966	72.4924
6	7.3255	7.4279	65.0644
7	6.5144	8.2391	56.8253
8	5.6146	9.1389	47.6865
9	4.6166	10.1369	37.5496
10	3.5095	11.2439	26.3057
11	2.2816	12.4718	13.8338
12	.9196	13.8338	0.0000

YEARS 13 — QTR PAYT 3.5469 — AN CONST 14.19

#	INT	PRIN	BALANCE
1	10.3522	3.8354	96.1646
2	9.9334	4.2542	91.9104
3	9.4688	4.7188	87.1916
4	8.9535	5.2341	81.9575
5	8.3819	5.8057	76.1518
6	7.7478	6.4398	69.7120
7	7.0446	7.1430	62.5690
8	6.2645	7.9231	54.6459
9	5.3992	8.7884	45.8575
10	4.4395	9.7481	36.1094
11	3.3749	10.8127	25.2968
12	2.1941	11.9935	13.3033
13	.8843	13.3033	0.0000

YEARS 14 — QTR PAYT 3.4284 — AN CONST 13.72

#	INT	PRIN	BALANCE
1	10.3712	3.3422	96.6578
2	10.0063	3.7072	92.9506
3	9.6014	4.1120	88.8386
4	9.1523	4.5611	84.2775
5	8.6542	5.0592	79.2183
6	8.1017	5.6117	73.6066
7	7.4889	6.2245	67.3821
8	6.8091	6.9043	60.4778
9	6.0551	7.6583	52.8195
10	5.2188	8.4946	44.3249
11	4.2911	9.4223	34.9026
12	3.2621	10.4513	24.4513
13	2.1208	11.5926	12.8586
14	.8548	12.8586	0.0000

YEARS 15 — QTR PAYT 3.3281 — AN CONST 13.32

#	INT	PRIN	BALANCE
1	10.3873	2.9250	97.0750
2	10.0679	3.2444	93.8306
3	9.7136	3.5987	90.2318
4	9.3206	3.9917	86.2401
5	8.8846	4.4277	81.8124
6	8.4011	4.9112	76.9012
7	7.8648	5.4476	71.4536
8	7.2698	6.0425	65.4112
9	6.6100	6.7023	58.7088
10	5.8780	7.4343	51.2746
11	5.0661	8.2462	43.0284
12	4.1656	9.1467	33.8817
13	3.1667	10.1456	23.7361
14	2.0587	11.2536	12.4825
15	.8298	12.4825	0.0000

YEARS 16 — QTR PAYT 3.2426 — AN CONST 12.98

#	INT	PRIN	BALANCE
1	10.4010	2.5693	97.4307
2	10.1204	2.8498	94.5809
3	9.8092	3.1611	91.4198
4	9.4640	3.5063	87.9135
5	9.0811	3.8892	84.0244
6	8.6564	4.3139	79.7104
7	8.1853	4.7850	74.9254
8	7.6627	5.3076	69.6178
9	7.0831	5.8872	63.7306
10	6.4401	6.5301	57.2005
11	5.7270	7.2433	49.9572
12	4.9360	8.0343	41.9229
13	4.0586	8.9117	33.0112
14	3.0854	9.8849	23.1263
15	2.0059	10.9644	12.1618
16	.8085	12.1618	0.0000

YEARS 17 — QTR PAYT 3.1692 — AN CONST 12.68

#	INT	PRIN	BALANCE
1	10.4128	2.2639	97.7361
2	10.1656	2.5111	95.2250
3	9.8913	2.7853	92.4397
4	9.5871	3.0895	89.3502
5	9.2497	3.4269	85.9233
6	8.8755	3.8011	82.1222
7	8.4604	4.2163	77.9059
8	7.9999	4.6767	73.2292
9	7.4892	5.1874	68.0418
10	6.9227	5.7539	62.2878
11	6.2943	6.3823	55.9055
12	5.5973	7.0793	48.8262
13	4.8242	7.8524	40.9738
14	3.9667	8.7100	32.2638
15	3.0155	9.6611	22.6027
16	1.9604	10.7162	11.8865
17	.7902	11.8865	0.0000

YEARS 18 — QTR PAYT 3.1058 — AN CONST 12.43

#	INT	PRIN	BALANCE
1	10.4229	2.0002	97.9998
2	10.2045	2.2186	95.7813
3	9.9622	2.4609	93.3204
4	9.6935	2.7296	90.5908
5	9.3954	3.0277	87.5631
6	9.0647	3.3584	84.2047
7	8.6980	3.7251	80.4796
8	8.2912	4.1319	76.3477
9	7.8399	4.5832	71.7645
10	7.3394	5.0837	66.6808
11	6.7842	5.6388	61.0420
12	6.1684	6.2547	54.7873
13	5.4854	6.9377	47.8496
14	4.7277	7.6954	40.1543
15	3.8874	8.5357	31.6185
16	2.9552	9.4679	22.1506
17	1.9212	10.5019	11.6487
18	.7744	11.6487	0.0000

YEARS 19 — QTR PAYT 3.0508 — AN CONST 12.21

#	INT	PRIN	BALANCE
1	10.4318	1.7713	98.2287
2	10.2383	1.9647	96.2640
3	10.0238	2.1793	94.0847
4	9.7858	2.4173	91.6674
5	9.5218	2.6813	88.9861
6	9.2290	2.9741	86.0121
7	8.9042	3.2989	82.7132
8	8.5439	3.6591	79.0541
9	8.1443	4.0587	74.9953
10	7.7011	4.5020	70.4933
11	7.2094	4.9936	65.4997
12	6.6641	5.5390	59.9607
13	6.0592	6.1439	53.8169
14	5.3882	6.8148	47.0021
15	4.6440	7.5590	39.4430
16	3.8185	8.3845	31.0585
17	2.9028	9.3002	21.7583
18	1.8872	10.3158	11.4424
19	.7606	11.4424	0.0000

YEARS 20 — QTR PAYT 3.0028 — AN CONST 12.02

#	INT	PRIN	BALANCE
1	10.4394	1.5718	98.4282
2	10.2678	1.7434	96.6848
3	10.0774	1.9338	94.7509
4	9.8662	2.1450	92.6059
5	9.6320	2.3793	90.2266
6	9.3721	2.6391	87.5875
7	9.0839	2.9273	84.6601
8	8.7642	3.2470	81.4131
9	8.4096	3.6016	77.8115
10	8.0163	3.9949	73.8165
11	7.5800	4.4312	69.3853
12	7.0961	4.9151	64.4702
13	6.5593	5.4519	59.0183
14	5.9639	6.0473	52.9710
15	5.3035	6.7077	46.2633
16	4.5710	7.4402	38.8231
17	3.7585	8.2528	30.5703
18	2.8572	9.1540	21.4163
19	1.8575	10.1537	11.2626
20	.7487	11.2626	0.0000

YEARS 21 — QTR PAYT 2.9609 — AN CONST 11.85

#	INT	PRIN	BALANCE
1	10.4462	1.3972	98.6028
2	10.2936	1.5498	97.0529
3	10.1243	1.7191	95.3338

#	INT	PRIN	BALANCE
4	9.9366	1.9068	93.4270
5	9.7284	2.1151	91.3119
6	9.4974	2.3460	88.9659
7	9.2412	2.6022	86.3637
8	8.9570	2.8864	83.4772
9	8.6418	3.2017	80.2756
10	8.2921	3.5513	76.7243
11	7.9043	3.9391	72.7851
12	7.4741	4.3693	68.4158
13	6.9970	4.8465	63.5694
14	6.4677	5.3757	58.1937
15	5.8806	5.9628	52.2309
16	5.2294	6.6140	45.6169
17	4.5071	7.3363	38.2806
18	3.7060	8.1374	30.1431
19	2.8173	9.0261	21.1170
20	1.8316	10.0118	11.1052
21	.7382	11.1052	0.0000

YEARS 22 — QTR PAYT 2.9240 — AN CONST 11.70

#	INT	PRIN	BALANCE
1	10.4521	1.2440	98.7560
2	10.3162	1.3799	97.3761
3	10.1655	1.5306	95.8456
4	9.9984	1.6977	94.1479
5	9.8130	1.8831	92.2648
6	9.6073	2.0888	90.1760
7	9.3792	2.3169	87.8592
8	9.1262	2.5699	85.2893
9	8.8456	2.8505	82.4388
10	8.5343	3.1618	79.2769
11	8.1890	3.5071	75.7698
12	7.8060	3.8901	71.8797
13	7.3811	4.3149	67.5647
14	6.9099	4.7862	62.7786
15	6.3872	5.3089	57.4697
16	5.8075	5.8886	51.5811
17	5.1644	6.5317	45.0494
18	4.4511	7.2450	37.8044
19	3.6599	8.0362	29.7682
20	2.7823	8.9138	20.8543
21	1.8088	9.8873	10.9670
22	.7290	10.9670	0.0000

YEARS 23 — QTR PAYT 2.8916 — AN CONST 11.57

#	INT	PRIN	BALANCE
1	10.4573	1.1091	98.8909
2	10.3362	1.2302	97.6607
3	10.2018	1.3646	96.2961
4	10.0528	1.5136	94.7826
5	9.8875	1.6789	93.1037
6	9.7041	1.8622	91.2415
7	9.5008	2.0656	89.1759
8	9.2752	2.2912	86.8847
9	9.0250	2.5414	84.3433
10	8.7475	2.8189	81.5244
11	8.4396	3.1268	78.3977
12	8.0981	3.4682	74.9295
13	7.7194	3.8470	71.0825
14	7.2993	4.2671	66.8154
15	6.8333	4.7331	62.0823
16	6.3164	5.2500	56.8323
17	5.7431	5.8233	51.0090
18	5.1071	6.4593	44.5498
19	4.4017	7.1647	37.3851
20	3.6193	7.9471	29.4380
21	2.7514	8.8150	20.6230
22	1.7887	9.7777	10.8454
23	.7209	10.8454	0.0000

YEARS 24 — QTR PAYT 2.8630 — AN CONST 11.46

#	INT	PRIN	BALANCE
1	10.4619	.9900	99.0100
2	10.3537	1.0981	97.9119
3	10.2338	1.2180	96.6939
4	10.1008	1.3511	95.3428
5	9.9533	1.4986	93.8442
6	9.7896	1.6623	92.1820
7	9.6081	1.8438	90.3382
8	9.4067	2.0451	88.2930
9	9.1834	2.2685	86.0246
10	8.9356	2.5162	83.5083
11	8.6609	2.7910	80.7173
12	8.3561	3.0958	77.6215
13	8.0180	3.4339	74.1877
14	7.6430	3.8089	70.3788
15	7.2270	4.2248	66.1539
16	6.7656	4.6862	61.4677
17	6.2539	5.1980	56.2697
18	5.6862	5.7657	50.5040
19	5.0565	6.3953	44.1087
20	4.3581	7.0937	37.0150
21	3.5834	7.8684	29.1466
22	2.7242	8.7277	20.4189
23	1.7710	9.6808	10.7380
24	.7138	10.7380	0.0000

YEARS 25 — QTR PAYT 2.8376 — AN CONST 11.36

#	INT	PRIN	BALANCE
1	10.4659	.8846	99.1154
2	10.3693	.9812	98.1341
3	10.2622	1.0884	97.0457
4	10.1433	1.2073	95.8385
5	10.0115	1.3391	94.4994
6	9.8652	1.4853	93.0140
7	9.7030	1.6475	91.3665
8	9.5231	1.8275	89.5390
9	9.3235	2.0270	87.5120
10	9.1021	2.2484	85.2636
11	8.8566	2.4940	82.7696
12	8.5842	2.7663	80.0033
13	8.2821	3.0684	76.9349
14	7.9470	3.4035	73.5314
15	7.5754	3.7752	69.7562
16	7.1631	4.1875	65.5687
17	6.7058	4.6448	60.9239
18	6.1985	5.1520	55.7719
19	5.6359	5.7147	50.0573
20	5.0118	6.3387	43.7185
21	4.3196	7.0310	36.6875
22	3.5517	7.7988	28.8887
23	2.7001	8.6505	20.2382
24	1.7554	9.5952	10.6431
25	.7075	10.6431	0.0000

YEARS 26 — QTR PAYT 2.8152 — AN CONST 11.27

#	INT	PRIN	BALANCE
1	10.4695	.7912	99.2088
2	10.3831	.8776	98.3311
3	10.2873	.9735	97.3577
4	10.1774	1.0798	96.2779
5	10.0630	1.1977	95.0802
6	9.9322	1.3285	93.7517
7	9.7872	1.4736	92.2781
8	9.6262	1.6345	90.6436
9	9.4477	1.8130	88.8306
10	9.2497	2.0110	86.8196
11	9.0301	2.2306	84.5889
12	8.7865	2.4742	82.1147
13	8.5163	2.7444	79.3703
14	8.2166	3.0441	76.3262
15	7.8842	3.3766	72.9496
16	7.5154	3.7453	69.2043
17	7.1064	4.1543	65.0499
18	6.6527	4.6080	60.4419
19	6.1495	5.1113	55.3306
20	5.5913	5.6694	49.6612
21	4.9722	6.2886	43.3726
22	4.2854	6.9753	36.3973
23	3.5236	7.7371	28.6602
24	2.6787	8.5820	20.0781
25	1.7415	9.5193	10.5588
26	.7019	10.5588	0.0000

YEARS 27 — QTR PAYT 2.7952 — AN CONST 11.19

#	INT	PRIN	BALANCE
1	10.4727	.7083	99.2917
2	10.3954	.7856	98.5061
3	10.3096	.8714	97.6347
4	10.2144	.9666	96.6681
5	10.1088	1.0721	95.5960
6	9.9918	1.1892	94.4068
7	9.8619	1.3191	93.0877
8	9.7178	1.4631	91.6245
9	9.5581	1.6229	90.0016
10	9.3808	1.8002	88.2014
11	9.1842	1.9968	86.2046
12	8.9662	2.2148	83.9898
13	8.7243	2.4567	81.5331
14	8.4560	2.7250	78.8081
15	8.1584	3.0226	75.7856
16	7.8283	3.3527	72.4329
17	7.4622	3.7188	68.7141
18	7.0561	4.1249	64.5892
19	6.6056	4.5754	60.0138
20	6.1059	5.0751	54.9387
21	5.5517	5.6293	49.3095
22	4.9369	6.2440	43.0654
23	4.2550	6.9259	36.1395
24	3.4987	7.6823	28.4572
25	2.6597	8.5213	19.9359
26	1.7291	9.4518	10.4841
27	.6969	10.4841	0.0000

YEARS 28 — QTR PAYT 2.7775 — AN CONST 11.12

#	INT	PRIN	BALANCE
1	10.4756	.6345	99.3655
2	10.4063	.7038	98.6617
3	10.3294	.7806	97.8811
4	10.2442	.8659	97.0152
5	10.1496	.9604	96.0548
6	10.0447	1.0653	94.9894
7	9.9284	1.1817	93.8078
8	9.7993	1.3107	92.4970
9	9.6562	1.4539	91.0432
10	9.4974	1.6126	89.4305
11	9.3213	1.7887	87.6418
12	9.1259	1.9841	85.6577
13	8.9093	2.2008	83.4569
14	8.6689	2.4411	81.0158
15	8.4023	2.7077	78.3081
16	8.1066	3.0034	75.3047
17	7.7787	3.3314	71.9733
18	7.4148	3.6952	68.2781
19	7.0113	4.0987	64.1794
20	6.5637	4.5464	59.6330
21	6.0672	5.0429	54.5902
22	5.5165	5.5936	48.9966
23	4.9056	6.2044	42.7922
24	4.2280	6.8820	35.9102
25	3.4765	7.6336	28.2766
26	2.6428	8.4672	19.8094
27	1.7182	9.3919	10.4175
28	.6925	10.4175	0.0000

YEARS 29 — QTR PAYT 2.7617 — AN CONST 11.05

#	INT	PRIN	BALANCE
1	10.4781	.5688	99.4312
2	10.4160	.6309	98.8004
3	10.3471	.6998	98.1006
4	10.2707	.7762	97.3244
5	10.1859	.8610	96.4634
6	10.0919	.9550	95.5084
7	9.9876	1.0593	94.4492
8	9.8719	1.1750	93.2742
9	9.7436	1.3033	91.9709
10	9.6013	1.4456	90.5253
11	9.4434	1.6035	88.9219
12	9.2683	1.7786	87.1433
13	9.0740	1.9728	85.1705
14	8.8586	2.1883	82.9822
15	8.6196	2.4272	80.5550
16	8.3546	2.6923	77.8627
17	8.0605	2.9863	74.8764
18	7.7344	3.3124	71.5640
19	7.3727	3.6742	67.8898
20	6.9714	4.0754	63.8143
21	6.5264	4.5205	59.2938
22	6.0327	5.0142	54.2797
23	5.4851	5.5618	48.7179
24	4.8777	6.1691	42.5488
25	4.2040	6.8429	35.7059
26	3.4567	7.5901	28.1158
27	2.6278	8.4190	19.6967
28	1.7084	9.3385	10.3583
29	.6886	10.3583	0.0000

YEARS 30 — QTR PAYT 2.7476 — AN CONST 11.00

#	INT	PRIN	BALANCE
1	10.4803	.5102	99.4898
2	10.4246	.5659	98.9240
3	10.3628	.6277	98.2963
4	10.2943	.6962	97.6001
5	10.2183	.7722	96.8279
6	10.1339	.8566	95.9713
7	10.0404	.9501	95.0212
8	9.9366	1.0539	93.9673
9	9.8215	1.1690	92.7984
10	9.6939	1.2966	91.5017
11	9.5523	1.4382	90.0635
12	9.3952	1.5953	88.4682
13	9.2210	1.7695	86.6987
14	9.0278	1.9627	84.7360
15	8.8134	2.1771	82.5589
16	8.5757	2.4148	80.1441
17	8.3319	2.6786	77.4655
18	8.0194	2.9711	74.4944
19	7.6950	3.2955	71.1989
20	7.3351	3.6554	67.5434
21	6.9359	4.0546	63.4888
22	6.4931	4.4974	58.9914
23	6.0019	4.9886	54.0028
24	5.4571	5.5334	48.4694
25	4.8528	6.1377	42.3317
26	4.1826	6.8079	35.5238
27	3.4391	7.5514	27.9724
28	2.6144	8.3761	19.5963
29	1.6997	9.2908	10.3054
30	.6851	10.3054	0.0000

YEARS 2	QTR PAYT 14.0585	AN CONST 56.24
# INT	PRIN	BALANCE
1 8.8834	47.3505	52.6495
2 3.5843	52.6495	0.0000

YEARS 3	QTR PAYT 9.8597	AN CONST 39.44
# INT	PRIN	BALANCE
1 9.5726	29.8663	70.1337
2 6.2302	33.2086	36.9251
3 2.5138	36.9251	0.0000

YEARS 4	QTR PAYT 7.7721	AN CONST 31.09
# INT	PRIN	BALANCE
1 9.9153	21.1731	78.8269
2 7.5458	23.5426	55.2842
3 4.9111	26.1773	29.1069
4 1.9815	29.1069	0.0000

YEARS 5	QTR PAYT 6.5289	AN CONST 26.12
# INT	PRIN	BALANCE
1 10.1194	15.9961	84.0039
2 8.3293	17.7862	66.2177
3 6.3388	19.7767	46.4409
4 4.1255	21.9900	24.4509
5 1.6646	24.4509	0.0000

YEARS 6	QTR PAYT 5.7078	AN CONST 22.84
# INT	PRIN	BALANCE
1 10.2542	12.5768	87.4232
2 8.8467	13.9843	73.4389
3 7.2817	15.5493	57.8896
4 5.5415	17.2895	40.6001
5 3.6067	19.2244	21.3758
6 1.4552	21.3758	0.0000

YEARS 7	QTR PAYT 5.1278	AN CONST 20.52
# INT	PRIN	BALANCE
1 10.3494	10.1616	89.8384
2 9.2122	11.2988	78.5396
3 7.9477	12.5633	65.9763
4 6.5418	13.9692	52.0071
5 4.9784	15.5326	36.4745
6 3.2402	17.2708	19.2037
7 1.3074	19.2037	0.0000

YEARS 8	QTR PAYT 4.6984	AN CONST 18.80
# INT	PRIN	BALANCE
1 10.4199	8.3736	91.6264
2 9.4828	9.3107	82.3157
3 8.4408	10.3527	71.9630
4 7.2822	11.5113	60.4517
5 5.9940	12.7995	47.6522
6 4.5616	14.2319	33.4203
7 2.9688	15.8247	17.5956
8 1.1979	17.5956	0.0000

YEARS 9	QTR PAYT 4.3693	AN CONST 17.48
# INT	PRIN	BALANCE
1 10.4739	7.0034	92.9966
2 9.6902	7.7872	85.2094
3 8.8187	8.6586	76.5508
4 7.8497	9.6276	66.9231
5 6.7722	10.7051	56.2181
6 5.5742	11.9031	44.3149
7 4.2421	13.2352	31.0797
8 2.7609	14.7164	16.3633
9 1.1140	16.3633	0.0000

YEARS 10	QTR PAYT 4.1104	AN CONST 16.45
# INT	PRIN	BALANCE
1 10.5164	5.9253	94.0747
2 9.8533	6.5884	87.4863
3 9.1160	7.3258	80.1605
4 8.2961	8.1456	72.0149
5 7.3846	9.0572	62.9577
6 6.3709	10.0708	52.8870
7 5.2439	11.1978	41.6891
8 3.9907	12.4510	29.2381
9 2.5973	13.8444	15.3938
10 1.0480	15.3938	0.0000

YEARS 11	QTR PAYT 3.9025	AN CONST 15.61
# INT	PRIN	BALANCE
1 10.5506	5.0593	94.9407
2 9.9844	5.6255	89.3151
3 9.3548	6.2551	83.0600
4 8.6548	6.9551	76.1049
5 7.8764	7.7335	68.3714
6 7.0109	8.5989	59.7725
7 6.0486	9.5613	50.2112
8 4.9786	10.6313	39.5799
9 3.7888	11.8211	27.7589
10 2.4659	13.1440	14.6149
11 .9950	14.6149	0.0000

YEARS 12	QTR PAYT 3.7326	AN CONST 14.94
# INT	PRIN	BALANCE
1 10.5784	4.3521	95.6479
2 10.0914	4.8391	90.8088
3 9.5498	5.3807	85.4280
4 8.9477	5.9829	79.4452
5 8.2781	6.6524	72.7928
6 7.5336	7.3969	65.3958
7 6.7058	8.2247	57.1711
8 5.7854	9.1452	48.0260
9 4.7619	10.1686	37.8574
10 3.6239	11.3066	26.5508
11 2.3586	12.5719	13.9789
12 .9517	13.9789	0.0000

YEARS 13	QTR PAYT 3.5920	AN CONST 14.37
# INT	PRIN	BALANCE
1 10.6015	3.7666	96.2334
2 10.1800	4.1882	92.0452
3 9.7113	4.6569	87.3883
4 9.1901	5.1780	82.2103
5 8.6106	5.7575	76.4528
6 7.9663	6.4019	70.0509
7 7.2499	7.1183	62.9326
8 6.4532	7.9149	55.0177
9 5.5675	8.8007	46.2170
10 4.5826	9.7856	36.4314
11 3.4874	10.8807	25.5507
12 2.2698	12.0984	13.4523
13 .9158	13.4523	0.0000

YEARS 14	QTR PAYT 3.4743	AN CONST 13.90
# INT	PRIN	BALANCE
1 10.6208	3.2765	96.7235
2 10.2541	3.6432	93.0802
3 9.8464	4.0509	89.0293
4 9.3931	4.5043	84.5250
5 8.8890	5.0084	79.5166
6 8.3285	5.5689	73.9478
7 7.7053	6.1921	67.7557
8 7.0123	6.8851	60.8706
9 6.2418	7.6556	53.2150
10 5.3850	8.5123	44.7027
11 4.4324	9.4650	35.2377
12 3.3732	10.5242	24.7135
13 2.1954	11.7020	13.0116
14 .8858	13.0116	0.0000

YEARS 15	QTR PAYT 3.3749	AN CONST 13.50
# INT	PRIN	BALANCE
1 10.6372	2.8624	97.1376
2 10.3168	3.1828	93.9548
3 9.9606	3.5389	90.4159
4 9.5646	3.9350	86.4809
5 9.1242	4.3754	82.1055
6 8.6346	4.8650	77.2405
7 8.0901	5.4095	71.8311
8 7.4847	6.0148	65.8162
9 6.8116	6.6880	59.1282
10 6.0631	7.4364	51.6918
11 5.2309	8.2687	43.4231
12 4.3055	9.1940	34.2291
13 3.2766	10.2230	24.0061
14 2.1326	11.3670	12.6391
15 .8604	12.6391	0.0000

YEARS 16	QTR PAYT 3.2902	AN CONST 13.17
# INT	PRIN	BALANCE
1 10.6511	2.5097	97.4903
2 10.3702	2.7906	94.6997
3 10.0579	3.1029	91.5968
4 9.7107	3.4501	88.1467
5 9.3245	3.8362	84.3105
6 8.8952	4.2656	80.0449
7 8.4179	4.7429	75.3020
8 7.8871	5.2737	70.0283
9 7.2969	5.8639	64.1644
10 6.6406	6.5201	57.6443
11 5.9110	7.2498	50.3945
12 5.0996	8.0612	42.3333
13 4.1975	8.9633	33.3700
14 3.1944	9.9664	23.4037
15 2.0790	11.0817	12.3219
16 .8389	12.3219	0.0000

YEARS 17	QTR PAYT 3.2176	AN CONST 12.88
# INT	PRIN	BALANCE
1 10.6630	2.2073	97.7927
2 10.4160	2.4543	95.3384
3 10.1413	2.7290	92.6094
4 9.8359	3.0344	89.5750
5 9.4963	3.3740	86.2011
6 9.1187	3.7516	82.4495
7 8.6989	4.1714	78.2781
8 8.2321	4.6382	73.6399
9 7.7130	5.1573	68.4826
10 7.1358	5.7345	62.7481
11 6.4941	6.3762	56.3719
12 5.7805	7.0898	49.2821
13 4.9871	7.8832	41.3989
14 4.1048	8.7654	32.6335
15 3.1239	9.7464	22.8871
16 2.0331	10.8371	12.0499
17 .8203	12.0499	0.0000

YEARS 18	QTR PAYT 3.1549	AN CONST 12.62
# INT	PRIN	BALANCE
1 10.6733	1.9465	98.0535
2 10.4554	2.1643	95.8892
3 10.2132	2.4065	93.4826
4 9.9439	2.6759	90.8068
5 9.6444	2.9753	87.8315
6 9.3115	3.3083	84.5232
7 8.9412	3.6785	80.8446
8 8.5296	4.0902	76.7544
9 8.0718	4.5479	72.2065
10 7.5628	5.0569	67.1496
11 6.9969	5.6228	61.5267
12 6.3677	6.2521	55.2746
13 5.6680	6.9518	48.3229
14 4.8900	7.7298	40.5931
15 4.0249	8.5948	31.9983
16 3.0631	9.5567	22.4416
17 1.9936	10.6262	11.8154
18 .8044	11.8154	0.0000

YEARS 19	QTR PAYT 3.1007	AN CONST 12.41
# INT	PRIN	BALANCE
1 10.6822	1.7205	98.2795
2 10.4896	1.9130	96.3665
3 10.2755	2.1271	94.2394
4 10.0375	2.3651	91.8743
5 9.7728	2.6298	89.2445
6 9.4785	2.9241	86.3204
7 9.1513	3.2514	83.0690
8 8.7874	3.6152	79.4537
9 8.3828	4.0198	75.4339
10 7.9329	4.4697	70.9642
11 7.4327	4.9699	65.9943
12 6.8765	5.5261	60.4682
13 6.2581	6.1445	54.3237
14 5.5705	6.8322	47.4915
15 4.8059	7.5968	39.8947
16 3.9557	8.4470	31.4477
17 3.0104	9.3923	22.0555
18 1.9593	10.4434	11.6121
19 .7905	11.6121	0.0000

YEARS 20	QTR PAYT 3.0534	AN CONST 12.22
# INT	PRIN	BALANCE
1 10.6899	1.5237	98.4763
2 10.5194	1.6942	96.7820
3 10.3298	1.8839	94.8982
4 10.1190	2.0947	92.8035
5 9.8846	2.3291	90.4744
6 9.6239	2.5898	87.8846
7 9.3341	2.8796	85.0051
8 9.0118	3.2018	81.8032
9 8.6535	3.5602	78.2431
10 8.2551	3.9586	74.2845
11 7.8121	4.4016	69.8829
12 7.3195	4.8942	64.9887
13 6.7718	5.4419	59.5468
14 6.1627	6.0509	53.4959
15 5.4856	6.7281	46.7678
16 4.7326	7.4810	39.2868
17 3.8954	8.3182	30.9686
18 2.9645	9.2492	21.7194
19 1.9294	10.2842	11.4352
20 .7785	11.4352	0.0000

YEARS 21	QTR PAYT 3.0121	AN CONST 12.05
# INT	PRIN	BALANCE
1 10.6967	1.3518	98.6482
2 10.5454	1.5031	97.1450
3 10.3772	1.6713	95.4737

#	INT	PRIN	BALANCE
4	10.1902	1.8584	93.6153
5	9.9822	2.0664	91.5489
6	9.7509	2.2976	89.2513
7	9.4938	2.5547	86.6966
8	9.2079	2.8406	83.8559
9	8.8900	3.1586	80.6974
10	8.5365	3.5120	77.1854
11	8.1435	3.9051	73.2803
12	7.7065	4.3421	68.9382
13	7.2205	4.8280	64.1102
14	6.6802	5.3683	58.7419
15	6.0794	5.9691	52.7727
16	5.4114	6.6371	46.1356
17	4.6686	7.3799	38.7557
18	3.8428	8.2058	30.5499
19	2.9244	9.1241	21.4258
20	1.9033	10.1452	11.2806
21	.7680	11.2806	0.0000

YEARS 22	QTR PAYT 2.9760	AN CONST 11.91	
#	INT	PRIN	BALANCE
1	10.7026	1.2012	98.7988
2	10.5682	1.3356	97.4632
3	10.4188	1.4851	95.9782
4	10.2526	1.6513	94.3269
5	10.0678	1.8361	92.4908
6	9.8623	2.0415	90.4493
7	9.6338	2.2700	88.1793
8	9.3798	2.5241	85.6552
9	9.0973	2.8065	82.8487
10	8.7832	3.1206	79.7281
11	8.4340	3.4698	76.2582
12	8.0457	3.8582	72.4001
13	7.6139	4.2899	68.1101
14	7.1338	4.7700	63.3401
15	6.6000	5.3038	58.0363
16	6.0064	5.8974	52.1388
17	5.3464	6.6574	45.5814
18	4.6126	7.2913	38.2902
19	3.7966	8.1072	30.1830
20	2.8893	9.0145	21.1684
21	1.8805	10.0234	11.1451
22	.7587	11.1451	0.0000

YEARS 23	QTR PAYT 2.9442	AN CONST 11.78	
#	INT	PRIN	BALANCE
1	10.7079	1.0687	98.9313
2	10.5883	1.1883	97.7429
3	10.4553	1.3213	96.4216
4	10.3074	1.4692	94.9524
5	10.1430	1.6336	93.3188
6	9.9602	1.8164	91.5023
7	9.7569	2.0197	89.4826
8	9.5308	2.2458	87.2369
9	9.2795	2.4971	84.7398
10	9.0001	2.7765	81.9632
11	8.6893	3.0873	78.8760
12	8.3438	3.4328	75.4432
13	7.9597	3.8169	71.6263
14	7.5325	4.2441	67.3822
15	7.0576	4.7190	62.6632
16	6.5294	5.2472	57.4160
17	5.9422	5.8344	51.5816
18	5.2893	6.4873	45.0943
19	4.5633	7.2133	37.8810
20	3.7560	8.0206	29.8604
21	2.8584	8.9182	20.9422
22	1.8604	9.9162	11.0260
23	.7506	11.0260	0.0000

YEARS 24	QTR PAYT 2.9161	AN CONST 11.67	
#	INT	PRIN	BALANCE
1	10.7125	.9520	99.0480
2	10.6059	1.0586	97.9894
3	10.4875	1.1770	96.8124
4	10.3557	1.3087	95.5036
5	10.2093	1.4552	94.0484
6	10.0464	1.6181	92.4304
7	9.8653	1.7991	90.6312
8	9.6640	2.0005	88.6307
9	9.4401	2.2244	86.4063
10	9.1912	2.4733	83.9330
11	8.9144	2.7501	81.1829
12	8.6066	3.0579	78.1251
13	8.2644	3.4001	74.7250
14	7.8839	3.7806	70.9444
15	7.4608	4.2037	66.7407
16	6.9904	4.6741	62.0666
17	6.4673	5.1972	56.8694
18	5.8856	5.7788	51.0906
19	5.2389	6.4256	44.6650
20	4.5198	7.1447	37.5203
21	3.7203	7.9442	29.5761
22	2.8312	8.8333	20.7428
23	1.8427	9.8218	10.9210
24	.7435	10.9210	0.0000

YEARS 25	QTR PAYT 2.8914	AN CONST 11.57	
#	INT	PRIN	BALANCE
1	10.7165	.8489	99.1511
2	10.6215	.9439	98.2071
3	10.5159	1.0496	97.1576
4	10.3984	1.1670	95.9905
5	10.2678	1.2976	94.6929
6	10.1226	1.4429	93.2500
7	9.9611	1.6043	91.6457
8	9.7816	1.7839	89.8618
9	9.5820	1.9835	87.8783
10	9.3600	2.2055	85.6728
11	9.1132	2.4523	83.2205
12	8.8387	2.7268	80.4938
13	8.5336	3.0319	77.4618
14	8.1942	3.3712	74.0906
15	7.8170	3.7485	70.3421
16	7.3975	4.1680	66.1741
17	6.9310	4.6344	61.5397
18	6.4124	5.1531	56.3866
19	5.8357	5.7298	50.6568
20	5.1945	6.3710	44.2858
21	4.4815	7.0840	37.2018
22	3.6887	7.8768	29.3250
23	2.8072	8.7583	20.5667
24	1.8270	9.7384	10.8283
25	.7372	10.8283	0.0000

YEARS 26	QTR PAYT 2.8695	AN CONST 11.48	
#	INT	PRIN	BALANCE
1	10.7201	.7577	99.2423
2	10.6353	.8425	98.3998
3	10.5410	.9368	97.4630
4	10.4362	1.0416	96.4214
5	10.3196	1.1582	95.2632
6	10.1900	1.2878	93.9754
7	10.0459	1.4319	92.5435
8	9.8857	1.5922	90.9513
9	9.7075	1.7704	89.1809
10	9.5093	1.9685	87.2125
11	9.2891	2.1888	85.0237
12	9.0441	2.4337	82.5899
13	8.7717	2.7061	79.8839
14	8.4689	3.0089	76.8749
15	8.1322	3.3457	73.5292

#	INT	PRIN	BALANCE
16	7.7577	3.7201	69.8092
17	7.3414	4.1364	65.6727
18	6.8785	4.5993	61.0734
19	6.3638	5.1140	55.9594
20	5.7915	5.6864	50.2730
21	5.1551	6.3227	43.9503
22	4.4475	7.0303	36.9199
23	3.6607	7.8171	29.1028
24	2.7859	8.6919	20.4109
25	1.8132	9.6647	10.7462
26	.7316	10.7462	0.0000

YEARS 27	QTR PAYT 2.8500	AN CONST 11.41	
#	INT	PRIN	BALANCE
1	10.7233	.6768	99.3232
2	10.6476	.7526	98.5706
3	10.5634	.8368	97.7338
4	10.4697	.9304	96.8034
5	10.3656	1.0346	95.7688
6	10.2498	1.1504	94.6184
7	10.1211	1.2791	93.3393
8	9.9779	1.4222	91.9171
9	9.8187	1.5814	90.3357
10	9.6418	1.7584	88.5773
11	9.4450	1.9552	86.6222
12	9.2262	2.1740	84.4482
13	8.9829	2.4173	82.0310
14	8.7124	2.6878	79.3432
15	8.4116	2.9886	76.3546
16	8.0771	3.3230	73.0316
17	7.7052	3.6949	69.3367
18	7.2917	4.1084	65.2282
19	6.8320	4.5682	60.6601
20	6.3207	5.0794	55.5806
21	5.7523	5.6479	49.9327
22	5.1202	6.2799	43.6528
23	4.4174	6.9827	36.6701
24	3.6360	7.7642	28.9059
25	2.7670	8.6331	20.2728
26	1.8009	9.5992	10.6735
27	.7266	10.6735	0.0000

YEARS 28	QTR PAYT 2.8328	AN CONST 11.34	
#	INT	PRIN	BALANCE
1	10.7261	.6050	99.3950
2	10.6584	.6727	98.7222
3	10.5832	.7480	97.9742
4	10.4994	.8317	97.1425
5	10.4064	.9248	96.2177
6	10.3029	1.0283	95.1894
7	10.1878	1.1434	94.0460
8	10.0598	1.2714	92.7746
9	9.9175	1.4136	91.3610
10	9.7593	1.5718	89.7892
11	9.5834	1.7477	88.0414
12	9.3878	1.9433	86.0981
13	9.1704	2.1608	83.9373
14	8.9285	2.4026	81.5346
15	8.6597	2.6715	78.8631
16	8.3607	2.9705	75.8926
17	8.0283	3.3029	72.5897
18	7.6586	3.6726	68.9172
19	7.2476	4.0836	64.8336
20	6.7906	4.5406	60.2930
21	6.2825	5.0487	55.2443
22	5.7175	5.6137	49.6306
23	5.0892	6.2419	43.3887
24	4.3907	6.9405	36.4482
25	3.6140	7.7172	28.7310
26	2.7503	8.5809	20.1501
27	1.7900	9.5412	10.6089

#	INT	PRIN	BALANCE
28	.7222	10.6089	0.0000

YEARS 29	QTR PAYT 2.8175	AN CONST 11.27	
#	INT	PRIN	BALANCE
1	10.7287	.5412	99.4588
2	10.6681	.6018	98.8571
3	10.6008	.6691	98.1880
4	10.5259	.7440	97.4440
5	10.4426	.8272	96.6168
6	10.3500	.9198	95.6970
7	10.2471	1.0227	94.6742
8	10.1326	1.1372	93.5370
9	10.0054	1.2645	92.2725
10	9.8639	1.4060	90.8666
11	9.7065	1.5633	89.3032
12	9.5316	1.7383	87.5650
13	9.3370	1.9328	85.6321
14	9.1207	2.1491	83.4830
15	8.8802	2.3896	81.0934
16	8.6128	2.6571	78.4363
17	8.3154	2.9544	75.4819
18	7.9848	3.2850	72.1969
19	7.6172	3.6527	68.5442
20	7.2084	4.0615	64.4827
21	6.7539	4.5160	59.9667
22	6.2485	5.0214	54.9454
23	5.6865	5.5833	49.3620
24	5.0617	6.2082	43.1539
25	4.3669	6.9029	36.2509
26	3.5944	7.6755	28.5755
27	2.7354	8.5344	20.0411
28	1.7803	9.4895	10.5515
29	.7183	10.5515	0.0000

YEARS 30	QTR PAYT 2.8038	AN CONST 11.22	
#	INT	PRIN	BALANCE
1	10.7309	.4844	99.5156
2	10.6767	.5386	98.9771
3	10.6164	.5988	98.3782
4	10.5494	.6659	97.7124
5	10.4749	.7404	96.9720
6	10.3920	.8232	96.1488
7	10.2999	.9154	95.2334
8	10.1975	1.0178	94.2156
9	10.0836	1.1317	93.0840
10	9.9569	1.2583	91.8256
11	9.8161	1.3992	90.4264
12	9.6595	1.5558	88.8707
13	9.4854	1.7299	87.1408
14	9.2918	1.9235	85.2174
15	9.0766	2.1387	83.0787
16	8.8372	2.3781	80.7006
17	8.5711	2.6442	78.0564
18	8.2752	2.9401	75.1163
19	7.9461	3.2691	71.8472
20	7.5803	3.6350	68.2122
21	7.1735	4.0418	64.1704
22	6.7212	4.4941	59.6763
23	6.2182	4.9971	54.6792
24	5.6590	5.5563	49.1230
25	5.0372	6.1781	42.9449
26	4.3458	6.8695	36.0754
27	3.5770	7.6383	28.4371
28	2.7222	8.4931	19.9440
29	1.7717	9.4436	10.5004
30	.7148	10.5004	0.0000

YEARS 2 — QTR PAYT 14.0958 — AN CONST 56.39

#	INT	PRIN	BALANCE
1	9.0934	47.2898	52.7102
2	3.6730	52.7102	0.0000

YEARS 3 — QTR PAYT 9.8969 — AN CONST 39.59

#	INT	PRIN	BALANCE
1	9.7990	29.7885	70.2115
2	6.3846	33.2029	37.0086
3	2.5788	37.0086	0.0000

YEARS 4 — QTR PAYT 7.8097 — AN CONST 31.24

#	INT	PRIN	BALANCE
1	10.1497	21.0891	78.9109
2	7.7325	23.5064	55.4045
3	5.0381	26.2007	29.2038
4	2.0350	29.2038	0.0000

YEARS 5 — QTR PAYT 6.5672 — AN CONST 26.27

#	INT	PRIN	BALANCE
1	10.3585	15.9102	84.0898
2	8.5349	17.7338	66.3561
3	6.5022	19.7665	46.5896
4	4.2366	22.0321	24.5575
5	1.7112	24.5575	0.0000

YEARS 6 — QTR PAYT 5.7469 — AN CONST 22.99

#	INT	PRIN	BALANCE
1	10.4964	12.4911	87.5089
2	9.0646	13.9228	73.5861
3	7.4688	15.5187	58.0675
4	5.6900	17.2974	40.7701
5	3.7074	19.2801	21.4900
6	1.4975	21.4900	0.0000

YEARS 7 — QTR PAYT 5.1677 — AN CONST 20.68

#	INT	PRIN	BALANCE
1	10.5937	10.0772	89.9228
2	9.4386	11.2323	78.6904
3	8.1512	12.5198	66.1707
4	6.7161	13.9548	52.2159
5	5.1166	15.5543	36.6616
6	3.3338	17.3372	19.3244
7	1.3466	19.3244	0.0000

YEARS 8 — QTR PAYT 4.7393 — AN CONST 18.96

#	INT	PRIN	BALANCE
1	10.6657	8.2913	91.7087
2	9.7153	9.2417	82.4670
3	8.6561	10.3010	72.1660
4	7.4753	11.4817	60.6842
5	6.1593	12.7978	47.8865
6	4.6924	14.2647	33.6218
7	3.0574	15.8997	17.7221
8	1.2349	17.7221	0.0000

YEARS 9 — QTR PAYT 4.4111 — AN CONST 17.65

#	INT	PRIN	BALANCE
1	10.7209	6.9237	93.0763
2	9.9273	7.7173	85.3591
3	9.0427	8.6018	76.7572
4	8.0567	9.5878	67.1694
5	6.9578	10.6868	56.4827
6	5.7328	11.9117	44.5710
7	4.3675	13.2770	31.2940
8	2.8457	14.7988	16.4951
9	1.1494	16.4951	0.0000

YEARS 10 — QTR PAYT 4.1532 — AN CONST 16.62

#	INT	PRIN	BALANCE
1	10.7642	5.8484	94.1516
2	10.0939	6.5188	87.6329
3	9.3467	7.2659	80.3669
4	8.5138	8.0988	72.2681
5	7.5855	9.0271	63.2411
6	6.5509	10.0618	53.1793
7	5.3976	11.2150	41.9643
8	4.1121	12.5005	29.4638
9	2.6793	13.9334	15.5304
10	1.0822	15.5304	0.0000

YEARS 11 — QTR PAYT 3.9461 — AN CONST 15.79

#	INT	PRIN	BALANCE
1	10.7990	4.9854	95.0146
2	10.2276	5.5568	89.4578
3	9.5906	6.1938	83.2640
4	8.8807	6.9037	76.3603
5	8.0894	7.6950	68.6653
6	7.2074	8.5770	60.0883
7	6.2243	9.5601	50.5281
8	5.1285	10.6559	39.8722
9	3.9071	11.8773	27.9949
10	2.5457	13.2387	14.7562
11	1.0282	14.7562	0.0000

YEARS 12 — QTR PAYT 3.7772 — AN CONST 15.11

#	INT	PRIN	BALANCE
1	10.8274	4.2812	95.7188
2	10.3367	4.7720	90.9468
3	9.7897	5.3189	85.6279
4	9.1800	5.9286	79.6993
5	8.5005	6.6081	73.0911
6	7.7431	7.3656	65.7256
7	6.8988	8.2098	57.5157
8	5.9578	9.1508	48.3649
9	4.9089	10.1997	38.1652
10	3.7398	11.3688	26.7963
11	2.4367	12.6719	14.1244
12	.9842	14.1244	0.0000

YEARS 13 — QTR PAYT 3.6374 — AN CONST 14.55

#	INT	PRIN	BALANCE
1	10.8509	3.6989	96.3011
2	10.4269	4.1229	92.1782
3	9.9543	4.5955	87.5828
4	9.4276	5.1222	82.4606
5	8.8405	5.7093	76.7513
6	8.1861	6.3637	70.3876
7	7.4567	7.0931	63.2944
8	6.6436	7.9061	55.3883
9	5.7374	8.8124	46.5759
10	4.7273	9.8224	36.7535
11	3.6015	10.9483	25.8052
12	2.3466	12.2032	13.6020
13	.9478	13.6020	0.0000

YEARS 14 — QTR PAYT 3.5206 — AN CONST 14.09

#	INT	PRIN	BALANCE
1	10.8705	3.2119	96.7881
2	10.5023	3.5801	93.2080
3	10.0920	3.9905	89.2175
4	9.6346	4.4478	84.7696
5	9.1248	4.9577	79.8120
6	8.5565	5.5259	74.2861
7	7.9231	6.1593	68.1267
8	7.2171	6.8653	61.2614
9	6.4302	7.6522	53.6092
10	5.5531	8.5293	45.0799
11	4.5755	9.5070	35.5730
12	3.4858	10.5967	24.9763
13	2.2712	11.8113	13.1651
14	.9174	13.1651	0.0000

YEARS 15 — QTR PAYT 3.4220 — AN CONST 13.69

#	INT	PRIN	BALANCE
1	10.8871	2.8009	97.1991
2	10.5660	3.1220	94.0771
3	10.2082	3.4798	90.5973
4	9.8093	3.8787	86.7186
5	9.3647	4.3233	82.3953
6	8.8692	4.8188	77.5765
7	8.3169	5.3711	72.2054
8	7.7012	5.9868	66.2186
9	7.0150	6.6730	59.5456
10	6.2501	7.4379	52.1077
11	5.3976	8.2904	43.8173
12	4.4473	9.2407	34.5766
13	3.3882	10.2998	24.2768
14	2.2076	11.4804	12.7963
15	.8917	12.7963	0.0000

YEARS 16 — QTR PAYT 3.3381 — AN CONST 13.36

#	INT	PRIN	BALANCE
1	10.9012	2.4513	97.5487
2	10.6202	2.7323	94.8164
3	10.3070	3.0455	91.7710
4	9.9579	3.3945	88.3764
5	9.5689	3.7836	84.5928
6	9.1352	4.2173	80.3755
7	8.6518	4.7007	75.6749
8	8.1130	5.2395	70.4354
9	7.5124	5.8400	64.5953
10	6.8430	6.5094	58.0859
11	6.0969	7.2555	50.8304
12	5.2653	8.0872	42.7432
13	4.3383	9.0142	33.7290
14	3.3051	10.0474	23.6817
15	2.1535	11.1990	12.4827
16	.8698	12.4827	0.0000

YEARS 17 — QTR PAYT 3.2663 — AN CONST 13.07

#	INT	PRIN	BALANCE
1	10.9132	2.1519	97.8481
2	10.6666	2.3986	95.4495
3	10.3917	2.6735	92.7761
4	10.0852	2.9799	89.7962
5	9.7437	3.3215	86.4747
6	9.3630	3.7022	82.7725
7	8.9386	4.1265	78.6459
8	8.4656	4.5995	74.0464
9	7.9384	5.1267	68.9197
10	7.3508	5.7144	63.2053
11	6.6958	6.3694	56.8360
12	5.9657	7.0994	49.7365
13	5.1520	7.9132	41.8234
14	4.2450	8.8202	33.0032
15	3.2340	9.8312	23.1721
16	2.1071	10.9580	12.2140
17	.8511	12.2140	0.0000

YEARS 18 — QTR PAYT 3.2044 — AN CONST 12.82

#	INT	PRIN	BALANCE
1	10.9236	1.8940	98.1060
2	10.7065	2.1111	95.9948
3	10.4646	2.3531	93.6417
4	10.1948	2.6228	91.0188
5	9.8942	2.9235	88.0954
6	9.5591	3.2586	84.8368
7	9.1856	3.6321	81.2047
8	8.7693	4.0484	77.1564
9	8.3053	4.5124	72.6439
10	7.7881	5.0296	67.6143
11	7.2115	5.6061	62.0082
12	6.5690	6.2487	55.7595
13	5.8527	6.9650	48.7945
14	5.0544	7.7633	41.0312
15	4.1646	8.6531	32.3781
16	3.1727	9.6450	22.7332
17	2.0672	10.7505	11.9827
18	.8350	11.9827	0.0000

YEARS 19 — QTR PAYT 3.1509 — AN CONST 12.61

#	INT	PRIN	BALANCE
1	10.9326	1.6709	98.3291
2	10.7411	1.8624	96.4667
3	10.5276	2.0759	94.3909
4	10.2897	2.3138	92.0771
5	10.0245	2.5790	89.4980
6	9.7289	2.8746	86.6234
7	9.3994	3.2041	83.4193
8	9.0321	3.5714	79.8479
9	8.6228	3.9807	75.8672
10	8.1665	4.4370	71.4302
11	7.6579	4.9456	66.4846
12	7.0911	5.5125	60.9721
13	6.4592	6.1443	54.8278
14	5.7549	6.8486	47.9792
15	4.9699	7.6336	40.3457
16	4.0950	8.5085	31.8371
17	3.1197	9.4838	22.3533
18	2.0327	10.5708	11.7825
19	.8210	11.7825	0.0000

YEARS 20 — QTR PAYT 3.1043 — AN CONST 12.42

#	INT	PRIN	BALANCE
1	10.9405	1.4769	98.5231
2	10.7712	1.6462	96.8769
3	10.5825	1.8349	95.0420
4	10.3722	2.0452	92.9968
5	10.1377	2.2796	90.7172
6	9.8764	2.5409	88.1762
7	9.5852	2.8322	85.3441
8	9.2606	3.1568	82.1873
9	8.8987	3.5186	78.6686
10	8.4954	3.9219	74.7467
11	8.0459	4.3715	70.3752
12	7.5448	4.8725	65.5026
13	6.9863	5.4310	60.0716
14	6.3638	6.0536	54.0180
15	5.6699	6.7474	47.2706
16	4.8965	7.5208	39.7498
17	4.0345	8.3829	31.3669
18	3.0736	9.3437	22.0232
19	2.0027	10.4147	11.6085
20	.8089	11.6085	0.0000

YEARS 21 — QTR PAYT 3.0637 — AN CONST 12.26

#	INT	PRIN	BALANCE
1	10.9473	1.3077	98.6923
2	10.7974	1.4576	97.2347
3	10.6303	1.6247	95.6100

#	INT	PRIN	BALANCE
4	10.4441	1.8109	93.7991
5	10.2365	2.0185	91.7807
6	10.0052	2.2498	89.5308
7	9.7473	2.5077	87.0231
8	9.4599	2.7951	84.2280
9	9.1395	3.1155	81.1125
10	8.7824	3.4726	77.6399
11	8.3843	3.8707	73.7692
12	7.9407	4.3143	69.4549
13	7.4462	4.8088	64.6461
14	6.8950	5.3600	59.2860
15	6.2806	5.9744	53.3116
16	5.5958	6.6592	46.6524
17	4.8325	7.4225	39.2300
18	3.9817	8.2732	30.9567
19	3.0334	9.2215	21.7352
20	1.9765	10.2785	11.4567
21	.7983	11.4567	0.0000

YEARS 22   QTR PAYT 3.0282   AN CONST 12.12

#	INT	PRIN	BALANCE
1	10.9532	1.1596	98.8404
2	10.8203	1.2925	97.5478
3	10.6722	1.4407	96.1071
4	10.5070	1.6058	94.5013
5	10.3230	1.7899	92.7114
6	10.1178	1.9951	90.7163
7	9.8891	2.2237	88.4926
8	9.6343	2.4786	86.0140
9	9.3502	2.7627	83.2513
10	9.0335	3.0794	80.1719
11	8.6805	3.4324	76.7395
12	8.2871	3.8258	72.9138
13	7.8486	4.2643	68.6495
14	7.3598	4.7531	63.8964
15	6.8150	5.2979	58.5985
16	6.2078	5.9051	52.6934
17	5.5309	6.5820	46.1114
18	4.7765	7.3364	38.7750
19	3.9356	8.1773	30.5977
20	2.9983	9.1146	21.4831
21	1.9535	10.1593	11.3238
22	.7891	11.3238	0.0000

YEARS 23   QTR PAYT 2.9970   AN CONST 11.99

#	INT	PRIN	BALANCE
1	10.9585	1.0297	98.9703
2	10.8405	1.1477	97.8226
3	10.7089	1.2792	96.5434
4	10.5623	1.4259	95.1175
5	10.3989	1.5893	93.5282
6	10.2167	1.7715	91.7568
7	10.0136	1.9745	89.7823
8	9.7873	2.2008	87.5814
9	9.5351	2.4531	85.1283
10	9.2539	2.7343	82.3941
11	8.9405	3.0477	79.3464
12	8.5911	3.3970	75.9494
13	8.2018	3.7864	72.1630
14	7.7678	4.2204	67.9426
15	7.2840	4.7041	63.2385
16	6.7448	5.2433	57.9952
17	6.1438	5.8443	52.1508
18	5.4740	6.5142	45.6367
19	4.7273	7.2609	38.3758
20	3.8950	8.0931	30.2827
21	2.9674	9.0208	21.2619
22	1.9334	10.0547	11.2072
23	.7809	11.2072	0.0000

YEARS 24   QTR PAYT 2.9696   AN CONST 11.88

#	INT	PRIN	BALANCE
1	10.9631	.9153	99.0847
2	10.8582	1.0202	98.0644
3	10.7412	1.1372	96.9273
4	10.6109	1.2675	95.6597
5	10.4656	1.4128	94.2469
6	10.3037	1.5748	92.6722
7	10.1232	1.7553	90.9169
8	9.9220	1.9564	88.9605
9	9.6977	2.1807	86.7798
10	9.4478	2.4306	84.3491
11	9.1692	2.7092	81.6399
12	8.8586	3.0198	78.6201
13	8.5125	3.3659	75.2542
14	8.1267	3.7517	71.5025
15	7.6967	4.1817	67.3207
16	7.2174	4.6611	62.6596
17	6.6831	5.1953	57.4643
18	6.0876	5.7908	51.6735
19	5.4239	6.4546	45.2189
20	4.6840	7.1944	38.0245
21	3.8594	8.0190	30.0055
22	2.9402	8.9382	21.0673
23	1.9157	9.9627	11.1046
24	.7738	11.1046	0.0000

YEARS 25   QTR PAYT 2.9454   AN CONST 11.79

#	INT	PRIN	BALANCE
1	10.9672	.8145	99.1855
2	10.8738	.9079	98.2776
3	10.7697	1.0119	97.2657
4	10.6538	1.1279	96.1378
5	10.5245	1.2572	94.8806
6	10.3804	1.4013	93.4793
7	10.2197	1.5619	91.9173
8	10.0407	1.7410	90.1764
9	9.8412	1.9405	88.2359
10	9.6187	2.1629	86.0729
11	9.3708	2.4108	83.6621
12	9.0945	2.6872	80.9749
13	8.7865	2.9952	77.9797
14	8.4432	3.3385	74.6412
15	8.0605	3.7212	70.9201
16	7.6340	4.1477	66.7724
17	7.1586	4.6231	62.1493
18	6.6287	5.1530	56.9963
19	6.0380	5.7437	51.2526
20	5.3797	6.4020	44.8506
21	4.6459	7.1358	37.7148
22	3.8280	7.9537	29.7611
23	2.9163	8.8654	20.8957
24	1.9001	9.8815	11.0142
25	.7675	11.0142	0.0000

YEARS 26   QTR PAYT 2.9241   AN CONST 11.70

#	INT	PRIN	BALANCE
1	10.9708	.7254	99.2746
2	10.8876	.8086	98.4659
3	10.7949	.9013	97.5647
4	10.6916	1.0046	96.5601
5	10.5765	1.1197	95.4403
6	10.4481	1.2481	94.1923
7	10.3051	1.3911	92.8011
8	10.1456	1.5506	91.2505
9	9.9679	1.7283	89.5222
10	9.7698	1.9264	87.5958
11	9.5490	2.1472	85.4485
12	9.3028	2.3934	83.0552
13	9.0285	2.6677	80.3875
14	8.7227	2.9735	77.4140
15	8.3819	3.3143	74.0997
16	8.0020	3.6942	70.4056
17	7.5786	4.1176	66.2880
18	7.1066	4.5896	61.6984
19	6.5806	5.1156	56.5828
20	5.9942	5.7020	50.8808
21	5.3406	6.3556	44.5252
22	4.6122	7.0840	37.4412
23	3.8002	7.8960	29.5452
24	2.8951	8.8011	20.7441
25	1.8863	9.8099	10.9343
26	.7619	10.9343	0.0000

YEARS 27   QTR PAYT 2.9051   AN CONST 11.63

#	INT	PRIN	BALANCE
1	10.9739	.6466	99.3534
2	10.8998	.7208	98.6326
3	10.8172	.8034	97.8292
4	10.7251	.8955	96.9338
5	10.6225	.9981	95.9357
6	10.5081	1.1125	94.8232
7	10.3806	1.2400	93.5832
8	10.2384	1.3821	92.2010
9	10.0800	1.5406	90.6605
10	9.9034	1.7171	88.9433
11	9.7066	1.9140	87.0293
12	9.4872	2.1334	84.8960
13	9.2427	2.3779	82.5181
14	8.9701	2.6504	79.8677
15	8.6663	2.9542	76.9134
16	8.3277	3.2929	73.6206
17	7.9503	3.6703	69.9503
18	7.5296	4.0910	65.8593
19	7.0607	4.5599	61.2994
20	6.5380	5.0825	56.2169
21	5.9555	5.6651	50.5518
22	5.3061	6.3145	44.2373
23	4.5823	7.0382	37.1991
24	3.7756	7.8450	29.3541
25	2.8764	8.7442	20.6100
26	1.8741	9.7464	10.8636
27	.7570	10.8636	0.0000

YEARS 28   QTR PAYT 2.8884   AN CONST 11.56

#	INT	PRIN	BALANCE
1	10.9767	.5768	99.4232
2	10.9106	.6429	98.7803
3	10.8369	.7166	98.0637
4	10.7548	.7987	97.2650
5	10.6633	.8903	96.3747
6	10.5612	.9923	95.3823
7	10.4475	1.1061	94.2762
8	10.3207	1.2329	93.0434
9	10.1794	1.3742	91.6692
10	10.0219	1.5317	90.1375
11	9.8463	1.7072	88.4303
12	9.6506	1.9029	86.5274
13	9.4325	2.1210	84.4063
14	9.1894	2.3642	82.0421
15	8.9184	2.6351	79.4070
16	8.6163	2.9372	76.4698
17	8.2797	3.2739	73.1959
18	7.9044	3.6491	69.5468
19	7.4862	4.0674	65.4795
20	7.0200	4.5336	60.9459
21	6.5003	5.0532	55.8926
22	5.9211	5.6324	50.2602
23	5.2755	6.2780	43.9822
24	4.5559	6.9976	36.9845
25	3.7538	7.7997	29.1848
26	2.8598	8.6937	20.4911
27	1.8633	9.6902	10.8009
28	.7526	10.8009	0.0000

YEARS 29   QTR PAYT 2.8735   AN CONST 11.50

#	INT	PRIN	BALANCE
1	10.9792	.5148	99.4852
2	10.9202	.5738	98.9114
3	10.8545	.6396	98.2718
4	10.7812	.7129	97.5588
5	10.6994	.7946	96.7642
6	10.6084	.8857	95.8785
7	10.5068	.9872	94.8913
8	10.3937	1.1004	93.7909
9	10.2675	1.2265	92.5644
10	10.1270	1.3671	91.1973
11	9.9703	1.5238	89.6735
12	9.7956	1.6985	87.9750
13	9.6009	1.8931	86.0819
14	9.3839	2.1101	83.9718
15	9.1421	2.3520	81.6198
16	8.8725	2.6216	78.9982
17	8.5720	2.9221	76.0761
18	8.2371	3.2570	72.8191
19	7.8637	3.6303	69.1888
20	7.4476	4.0464	65.1424
21	6.9838	4.5102	60.6321
22	6.4668	5.0272	55.6049
23	5.8906	5.6034	50.0015
24	5.2483	6.2457	43.7557
25	4.5325	6.9616	36.7941
26	3.7345	7.7596	29.0346
27	2.8451	8.6490	20.3856
28	1.8537	9.6403	10.7453
29	.7488	10.7453	0.0000

YEARS 30   QTR PAYT 2.8603   AN CONST 11.45

#	INT	PRIN	BALANCE
1	10.9815	.4598	99.5402
2	10.9288	.5125	99.0278
3	10.8700	.5712	98.4566
4	10.8046	.6367	97.8199
5	10.7316	.7096	97.1103
6	10.6502	.7910	96.3193
7	10.5596	.8816	95.4377
8	10.4585	.9827	94.4550
9	10.3459	1.0953	93.3597
10	10.2203	1.2209	92.1388
11	10.0804	1.3608	90.7780
12	9.9244	1.5168	89.2612
13	9.7506	1.6906	87.5706
14	9.5568	1.8844	85.6861
15	9.3408	2.1004	83.5857
16	9.1000	2.3412	81.2445
17	8.8317	2.6095	78.6350
18	8.5326	2.9086	75.7264
19	8.1992	3.2420	72.4843
20	7.8276	3.6136	68.8707
21	7.4134	4.0278	64.8429
22	6.9517	4.4895	60.3534
23	6.4371	5.0041	55.3493
24	5.8635	5.5777	49.7716
25	5.2242	6.2170	43.5546
26	4.5116	6.9296	36.6250
27	3.7173	7.7239	28.9011
28	2.8320	8.6092	20.2919
29	1.8452	9.5960	10.6959
30	.7453	10.6959	0.0000

YEARS 2 — QTR PAYT 14.1332 — AN CONST 56.54

#	INT	PRIN	BALANCE
1	9.3036	47.2292	52.7708
2	3.7619	52.7708	0.0000

YEARS 3 — QTR PAYT 9.9341 — AN CONST 39.74

#	INT	PRIN	BALANCE
1	10.0255	29.7108	70.2892
2	6.5394	33.1970	37.0922
3	2.6442	37.0922	0.0000

YEARS 4 — QTR PAYT 7.8474 — AN CONST 31.39

#	INT	PRIN	BALANCE
1	10.3843	21.0053	78.9947
2	7.9196	23.4700	55.5247
3	5.1658	26.2239	29.3008
4	2.0888	29.3008	0.0000

YEARS 5 — QTR PAYT 6.6056 — AN CONST 26.43

#	INT	PRIN	BALANCE
1	10.5978	15.8245	84.1755
2	8.7410	17.6813	66.4941
3	6.6664	19.7560	46.7382
4	4.3483	22.0741	24.6641
5	1.7582	24.6641	0.0000

YEARS 6 — QTR PAYT 5.7861 — AN CONST 23.15

#	INT	PRIN	BALANCE
1	10.7387	12.4057	87.5943
2	9.2831	13.8614	73.7329
3	7.6567	15.4878	58.2450
4	5.8394	17.3051	40.9400
5	3.8089	19.3356	21.6044
6	1.5401	21.6044	0.0000

YEARS 7 — QTR PAYT 5.2079 — AN CONST 20.84

#	INT	PRIN	BALANCE
1	10.8381	9.9934	90.0066
2	9.6656	11.1660	78.8406
3	8.3554	12.4762	66.3644
4	6.8915	13.9401	52.4244
5	5.2558	15.5757	36.8487
6	3.4282	17.4033	19.4453
7	1.3862	19.4453	0.0000

YEARS 8 — QTR PAYT 4.7803 — AN CONST 19.13

#	INT	PRIN	BALANCE
1	10.9117	8.2097	91.7903
2	9.9484	9.1730	82.6173
3	8.8720	10.2493	72.3680
4	7.6694	11.4519	60.9161
5	6.3257	12.7956	48.1205
6	4.8243	14.2970	33.8235
7	3.1468	15.9746	17.8489
8	1.2724	17.8489	0.0000

YEARS 9 — QTR PAYT 4.4531 — AN CONST 17.82

#	INT	PRIN	BALANCE
1	10.9679	6.8446	93.1554
2	10.1648	7.6478	85.5076
3	9.2674	8.5451	76.9625
4	8.2648	9.5478	67.4147
5	7.1445	10.6681	56.7466
6	5.8928	11.9198	44.8268
7	4.4941	13.3184	31.5084
8	2.9314	14.8812	16.6272
9	1.1853	16.6272	0.0000

YEARS 10 — QTR PAYT 4.1961 — AN CONST 16.79

#	INT	PRIN	BALANCE
1	11.0121	5.7723	94.2277
2	10.3348	6.4496	87.7782
3	9.5781	7.2063	80.5719
4	8.7325	8.0519	72.5200
5	7.7877	8.9966	63.5233
6	6.7321	10.0523	53.4711
7	5.5526	11.2318	42.2393
8	4.2347	12.5497	29.6897
9	2.7622	14.0222	15.6675
10	1.1169	15.6675	0.0000

YEARS 11 — QTR PAYT 3.9900 — AN CONST 15.96

#	INT	PRIN	BALANCE
1	11.0476	4.9123	95.0877
2	10.4712	5.4887	89.5990
3	9.8271	6.1327	83.4662
4	9.1076	6.8523	76.6139
5	8.3035	7.6563	68.9576
6	7.4052	8.5547	60.4029
7	6.4014	9.5585	50.8444
8	5.2798	10.6800	40.1644
9	4.0267	11.9332	28.2312
10	2.6265	13.3334	14.8978
11	1.0620	14.8978	0.0000

YEARS 12 — QTR PAYT 3.8219 — AN CONST 15.29

#	INT	PRIN	BALANCE
1	11.0764	4.2113	95.7887
2	10.5823	4.7054	91.0832
3	10.0302	5.2576	85.8257
4	9.4133	5.8745	79.9512
5	8.7240	6.5637	73.3875
6	7.9538	7.3339	66.0536
7	7.0933	8.1944	57.8591
8	6.1318	9.1559	48.7032
9	5.0575	10.2303	38.4729
10	3.8571	11.4306	27.0423
11	2.5159	12.7719	14.2704
12	1.0173	14.2704	0.0000

YEARS 13 — QTR PAYT 3.6831 — AN CONST 14.74

#	INT	PRIN	BALANCE
1	11.1003	3.6322	96.3678
2	10.6741	4.0583	92.3095
3	10.1979	4.5345	87.7750
4	9.6659	5.0666	82.7084
5	9.0714	5.6611	77.0473
6	8.4071	6.3253	70.7219
7	7.6649	7.0675	63.6544
8	6.8357	7.8968	55.7576
9	5.9091	8.8234	46.9342
10	4.8738	9.8587	37.0755
11	3.7170	11.0155	26.0601
12	2.4245	12.3080	13.7521
13	.9804	13.7521	0.0000

YEARS 14 — QTR PAYT 3.5672 — AN CONST 14.27

#	INT	PRIN	BALANCE
1	11.1202	3.1484	96.8516
2	10.7508	3.5178	93.3338
3	10.3381	3.9306	89.4032
4	9.8769	4.3918	85.0115
5	9.3616	4.9071	80.1044
6	8.7858	5.4829	74.6215
7	8.1424	6.1262	68.4953
8	7.4236	6.8450	61.6503
9	6.6205	7.6482	54.0021
10	5.7231	8.5456	45.4565
11	4.7204	9.5483	35.9082
12	3.6000	10.6686	25.2396
13	2.3482	11.9205	13.3192
14	.9495	13.3192	0.0000

YEARS 15 — QTR PAYT 3.4694 — AN CONST 13.88

#	INT	PRIN	BALANCE
1	11.1371	2.7405	97.2595
2	10.8155	3.0621	94.1973
3	10.4562	3.4214	90.7759
4	10.0547	3.8229	86.9531
5	9.6062	4.2714	82.6817
6	9.1050	4.7726	77.9091
7	8.5450	5.3326	72.5765
8	7.9193	5.9583	66.6182
9	7.2202	6.6574	59.9607
10	6.4390	7.4386	52.5222
11	5.5662	8.3114	44.2108
12	4.5910	9.2866	34.9242
13	3.5013	10.3763	24.5479
14	2.2838	11.5938	12.9541
15	.9235	12.9541	0.0000

YEARS 16 — QTR PAYT 3.3863 — AN CONST 13.55

#	INT	PRIN	BALANCE
1	11.1513	2.3940	97.6060
2	10.8704	2.6749	94.9310
3	10.5566	2.9888	91.9422
4	10.2059	3.3395	88.6027
5	9.8140	3.7313	84.8714
6	9.3762	4.1692	80.7023
7	8.8870	4.6583	76.0439
8	8.3404	5.2049	70.8390
9	7.7297	5.8157	65.0233
10	7.0473	6.4980	58.5253
11	6.2849	7.2605	51.2648
12	5.4330	8.1124	43.1524
13	4.4811	9.0643	34.0881
14	3.4175	10.1279	23.9602
15	2.2292	11.3162	12.6440
16	.9014	12.6440	0.0000

YEARS 17 — QTR PAYT 3.3153 — AN CONST 13.27

#	INT	PRIN	BALANCE
1	11.1635	2.0977	97.9023
2	10.9174	2.3438	95.5585
3	10.6424	2.6188	92.9397
4	10.3351	2.9261	90.0136
5	9.9918	3.2694	86.7441
6	9.6082	3.6531	83.0911
7	9.1795	4.0817	79.0094
8	8.7006	4.5606	74.4488
9	8.1655	5.0958	69.3530
10	7.5676	5.6937	63.6593
11	6.8995	6.3617	57.2976
12	6.1530	7.1082	50.1894
13	5.3190	7.9422	42.2472
14	4.3871	8.8741	33.3730
15	3.3458	9.9154	23.4576
16	2.1824	11.0788	12.3788
17	.8825	12.3788	0.0000

YEARS 18 — QTR PAYT 3.2542 — AN CONST 13.02

#	INT	PRIN	BALANCE
1	11.1741	1.8428	98.1572
2	10.9578	2.0590	96.0982
3	10.7162	2.3006	93.7976
4	10.4463	2.5706	91.2270
5	10.1447	2.8722	88.3548
6	9.8077	3.2092	85.1456
7	9.4311	3.5857	81.5599
8	9.0104	4.0065	77.5534
9	8.5403	4.4766	73.0768
10	8.0150	5.0018	68.0750
11	7.4281	5.5887	62.4862
12	6.7723	6.2445	56.2417
13	6.0396	6.9772	49.2645
14	5.2210	7.7959	41.4686
15	4.3062	8.7106	32.7580
16	3.2842	9.7327	23.0253
17	2.1422	10.8747	12.1507
18	.8662	12.1507	0.0000

YEARS 19 — QTR PAYT 3.2014 — AN CONST 12.81

#	INT	PRIN	BALANCE
1	11.1831	1.6225	98.3775
2	10.9928	1.8129	96.5646
3	10.7800	2.0256	94.5390
4	10.5424	2.2633	92.2757
5	10.2768	2.5289	89.7468
6	9.9801	2.8256	86.9212
7	9.6485	3.1571	83.7641
8	9.2781	3.5276	80.2366
9	8.8642	3.9415	76.2951
10	8.4017	4.4040	71.8911
11	7.8850	4.9207	66.9704
12	7.3076	5.4981	61.4724
13	6.6625	6.1432	55.3292
14	5.9417	6.8640	48.4652
15	5.1363	7.6694	40.7958
16	4.2364	8.5693	32.2265
17	3.2309	9.5748	22.6517
18	2.1074	10.6982	11.9535
19	.8521	11.9535	0.0000

YEARS 20 — QTR PAYT 3.1556 — AN CONST 12.63

#	INT	PRIN	BALANCE
1	11.1910	1.4313	98.5687
2	11.0231	1.5993	96.9694
3	10.8354	1.7869	95.1824
4	10.6257	1.9966	93.1858
5	10.3915	2.2309	90.9549
6	10.1297	2.4927	88.4622
7	9.8372	2.7851	85.6771
8	9.5104	3.1119	82.5652
9	9.1453	3.4771	79.0881
10	8.7373	3.8851	75.2030
11	8.2814	4.3409	70.8621
12	7.7721	4.8503	66.0119
13	7.2030	5.4194	60.5925
14	6.5671	6.0553	54.5372
15	5.8566	6.7658	47.7715
16	5.0627	7.5596	40.2119
17	4.1757	8.4466	31.7652
18	3.1846	9.4377	22.3275
19	2.0773	10.5451	11.7824
20	.8399	11.7824	0.0000

YEARS 21 — QTR PAYT 3.1157 — AN CONST 12.47

#	INT	PRIN	BALANCE
1	11.1979	1.2648	98.7352
2	11.0495	1.4132	97.3219
3	10.8836	1.5791	95.7429

#	INT	PRIN	BALANCE
4	10.6984	1.7643	93.9785
5	10.4913	1.9714	92.0071
6	10.2600	2.2027	89.8045
7	10.0016	2.4611	87.3433
8	9.7128	2.7499	84.5934
9	9.3901	3.0726	81.5209
10	9.0296	3.4331	78.0878
11	8.6268	3.8359	74.2518
12	8.1767	4.2860	69.9658
13	7.6738	4.7889	65.1769
14	7.1119	5.3508	59.8261
15	6.4840	5.9787	53.8474
16	5.7825	6.6802	47.1673
17	4.9987	7.4640	39.7033
18	4.1229	8.3398	31.3635
19	3.1444	9.3183	22.0451
20	2.0510	10.4117	11.6334
21	.8293	11.6334	0.0000

YEARS 22   QTR PAYT 3.0808   AN CONST 12.33

#	INT	PRIN	BALANCE
1	11.2039	1.1193	98.8807
2	11.0725	1.2507	97.6300
3	10.9258	1.3974	96.2326
4	10.7618	1.5614	94.6712
5	10.5786	1.7446	92.9266
6	10.3739	1.9493	90.9773
7	10.1452	2.1780	88.7993
8	9.8896	2.4336	86.3657
9	9.6041	2.7191	83.6465
10	9.2850	3.0382	80.6084
11	8.9285	3.3947	77.2137
12	8.5302	3.7930	73.4207
13	8.0852	4.2380	69.1827
14	7.5879	4.7353	64.4474
15	7.0323	5.2909	59.1564
16	6.4115	5.9117	53.2447
17	5.7178	6.6054	46.6393
18	4.9428	7.3805	39.2588
19	4.0768	8.2464	31.0124
20	3.1092	9.2140	21.7984
21	2.0280	10.2952	11.5032
22	.8200	11.5032	0.0000

YEARS 23   QTR PAYT 3.0502   AN CONST 12.21

#	INT	PRIN	BALANCE
1	11.2091	.9919	99.0081
2	11.0927	1.1082	97.8999
3	10.9627	1.2383	96.6616
4	10.8174	1.3836	95.2781
5	10.6551	1.5459	93.7322
6	10.4737	1.7273	92.0049
7	10.2710	1.9300	90.0749
8	10.0446	2.1564	87.9185
9	9.7915	2.4094	85.5091
10	9.5088	2.6922	82.8169
11	9.1929	3.0080	79.8088
12	8.8400	3.3610	76.4478
13	8.4456	3.7554	72.6925
14	8.0050	4.1960	68.4965
15	7.5126	4.6883	63.8081
16	6.9625	5.2385	58.5697
17	6.3479	5.8531	52.7166
18	5.6611	6.5399	46.1767
19	4.8937	7.3072	38.8695
20	4.0363	8.1646	30.7048
21	3.0783	9.1227	21.5821
22	2.0079	10.1931	11.3891
23	.8119	11.3891	0.0000

YEARS 24   QTR PAYT 3.0234   AN CONST 12.10

#	INT	PRIN	BALANCE
1	11.2137	.8799	99.1201
2	11.1105	.9831	98.1370
3	10.9951	1.0985	97.0385
4	10.8662	1.2274	95.8111
5	10.7222	1.3714	94.4397
6	10.5613	1.5323	92.9074
7	10.3815	1.7121	91.1953
8	10.1806	1.9130	89.2824
9	9.9562	2.1374	87.1449
10	9.7054	2.3882	84.7567
11	9.4252	2.6685	82.0882
12	9.1120	2.9816	79.1066
13	8.7622	3.3314	75.7752
14	8.3713	3.7223	72.0529
15	7.9345	4.1591	67.8938
16	7.4465	4.6471	63.2467
17	6.9013	5.1924	58.0543
18	6.2920	5.8016	52.2527
19	5.6113	6.4823	45.7704
20	4.8507	7.2430	38.5274
21	4.0008	8.0928	30.4346
22	3.0512	9.0424	21.3922
23	1.9902	10.1034	11.2889
24	.8048	11.2889	0.0000

YEARS 25   QTR PAYT 2.9998   AN CONST 12.00

#	INT	PRIN	BALANCE
1	11.2178	.7813	99.2187
2	11.1261	.8730	98.3457
3	11.0237	.9754	97.3702
4	10.9092	1.0899	96.2803
5	10.7813	1.2178	95.0625
6	10.6385	1.3607	93.7019
7	10.4788	1.5203	92.1815
8	10.3004	1.6987	90.4828
9	10.1011	1.8980	88.5848
10	9.8784	2.1207	86.4640
11	9.6295	2.3696	84.0944
12	9.3515	2.6476	81.4468
13	9.0408	2.9583	78.4885
14	8.6937	3.3054	75.1831
15	8.3059	3.6932	71.4899
16	7.8725	4.1266	67.3633
17	7.3884	4.6108	62.7525
18	6.8473	5.1518	57.6008
19	6.2429	5.7563	51.8445
20	5.5674	6.4317	45.4128
21	4.8128	7.1864	38.2264
22	3.9696	8.0296	30.1968
23	3.0274	8.9717	21.2251
24	1.9747	10.0244	11.2007
25	.7985	11.2007	0.0000

YEARS 26   QTR PAYT 2.9790   AN CONST 11.92

#	INT	PRIN	BALANCE
1	11.2214	.6944	99.3056
2	11.1399	.7759	98.5297
3	11.0489	.8669	97.6627
4	10.9471	.9687	96.6940
5	10.8335	1.0823	95.6117
6	10.7065	1.2093	94.4024
7	10.5646	1.3512	93.0512
8	10.4060	1.5098	91.5414
9	10.2289	1.6869	89.8545
10	10.0309	1.8849	87.9696
11	9.8098	2.1060	85.8636
12	9.5627	2.3531	83.5105
13	9.2866	2.6292	80.8812
14	8.9781	2.9377	77.9435
15	8.6334	3.2824	74.6610
16	8.2482	3.6676	70.9935
17	7.8179	4.0979	66.8955
18	7.3370	4.5788	62.3168
19	6.7998	5.1160	57.2008
20	6.1995	5.7163	51.4845
21	5.5288	6.3870	45.0974
22	4.7793	7.1365	37.9610
23	3.9420	7.9738	29.9871
24	3.0064	8.9094	21.0777
25	1.9610	9.9548	11.1229
26	.7929	11.1229	0.0000

YEARS 27   QTR PAYT 2.9606   AN CONST 11.85

#	INT	PRIN	BALANCE
1	11.2245	.6177	99.3823
2	11.1521	.6901	98.6922
3	11.0711	.7711	97.9211
4	10.9806	.8616	97.0595
5	10.8795	.9627	96.0968
6	10.7666	1.0756	95.0212
7	10.6403	1.2019	93.8193
8	10.4993	1.3429	92.4764
9	10.3418	1.5004	90.9760
10	10.1657	1.6765	89.2995
11	9.9690	1.8732	87.4263
12	9.7492	2.0930	85.3333
13	9.5036	2.3386	82.9947
14	9.2292	2.6130	80.3817
15	8.9226	2.9196	77.4621
16	8.5800	3.2622	74.1999
17	8.1973	3.6449	70.5550
18	7.7696	4.0726	66.4823
19	7.2917	4.5505	61.9319
20	6.7578	5.0844	56.8475
21	6.1612	5.6810	51.1665
22	5.4946	6.3476	44.8189
23	4.7498	7.0924	37.7265
24	3.9176	7.9246	29.8019
25	2.9878	8.8544	20.9475
26	1.9489	9.8933	11.0542
27	.7880	11.0542	0.0000

YEARS 28   QTR PAYT 2.9443   AN CONST 11.78

#	INT	PRIN	BALANCE
1	11.2273	.5498	99.4502
2	11.1628	.6143	98.8360
3	11.0908	.6863	98.1496
4	11.0102	.7669	97.3828
5	10.9202	.8569	96.5259
6	10.8197	.9574	95.5685
7	10.7074	1.0697	94.4988
8	10.5819	1.1953	93.3035
9	10.4416	1.3355	91.9680
10	10.2849	1.4922	90.4758
11	10.1098	1.6673	88.8085
12	9.9142	1.8629	86.9456
13	9.6956	2.0815	84.8641
14	9.4514	2.3257	82.5384
15	9.1785	2.5986	79.9398
16	8.8736	2.9035	77.0362
17	8.5329	3.2442	73.7920
18	8.1522	3.6249	70.1671
19	7.7269	4.0502	66.1169
20	7.2516	4.5255	61.5914
21	6.7206	5.0565	56.5349
22	6.1273	5.6498	50.8852
23	5.4644	6.3127	44.5725
24	4.7237	7.0534	37.5191
25	3.8961	7.8810	29.6381
26	2.9714	8.8057	20.8324
27	1.9382	9.8390	10.9934
28	.7837	10.9934	0.0000

YEARS 29   QTR PAYT 2.9299   AN CONST 11.72

#	INT	PRIN	BALANCE
1	11.2298	.4896	99.5104
2	11.1724	.5471	98.9633
3	11.1082	.6113	98.3521
4	11.0365	.6830	97.6691
5	10.9563	.7631	96.9060
6	10.8668	.8527	96.0533
7	10.7667	.9527	95.1006
8	10.6549	1.0645	94.0361
9	10.5300	1.1894	92.8467
10	10.3905	1.3290	91.5177
11	10.2345	1.4849	90.0328
12	10.0603	1.6591	88.3737
13	9.8656	1.8538	86.5199
14	9.6481	2.0713	84.4486
15	9.4051	2.3144	82.1343
16	9.1335	2.5859	79.5484
17	8.8301	2.8893	76.6590
18	8.4911	3.2283	73.4307
19	8.1123	3.6071	69.8235
20	7.6890	4.0304	65.7931
21	7.2161	4.5033	61.2898
22	6.6877	5.0317	56.2581
23	6.0973	5.6221	50.6360
24	5.4377	6.2818	44.3542
25	4.7006	7.0189	37.3354
26	3.8770	7.8424	29.4930
27	2.9568	8.7626	20.7304
28	1.9287	9.7908	10.9396
29	.7799	10.9396	0.0000

YEARS 30   QTR PAYT 2.9171   AN CONST 11.67

#	INT	PRIN	BALANCE
1	11.2320	.4363	99.5637
2	11.1808	.4875	99.0762
3	11.1236	.5447	98.5315
4	11.0597	.6086	97.9230
5	10.9883	.6800	97.2430
6	10.9085	.7598	96.4832
7	10.8194	.8489	95.6342
8	10.7198	.9486	94.6857
9	10.6085	1.0599	93.6258
10	10.4841	1.1842	92.4416
11	10.3452	1.3232	91.1185
12	10.1899	1.4784	89.6400
13	10.0164	1.6519	87.9882
14	9.8226	1.8457	86.1424
15	9.6060	2.0623	84.0802
16	9.3641	2.3043	81.7759
17	9.0937	2.5746	79.2013
18	8.7916	2.8767	76.3246
19	8.4540	3.2143	73.1103
20	8.0769	3.5914	69.5189
21	7.6555	4.0128	65.5061
22	7.1847	4.4837	61.0224
23	6.6586	5.0098	56.0127
24	6.0707	5.5976	50.4151
25	5.4139	6.2544	44.1607
26	4.6801	6.9882	37.1725
27	3.8601	7.8082	29.3643
28	2.9439	8.7244	20.6399
29	1.9202	9.7481	10.8919
30	.7765	10.8919	0.0000

YEARS 2 — QTR PAYT 14.1706 — AN CONST 56.69

#	INT	PRIN	BALANCE
1	9.5139	47.1686	52.8314
2	3.8511	52.8314	0.0000

YEARS 3 — QTR PAYT 9.9714 — AN CONST 39.89

#	INT	PRIN	BALANCE
1	10.2522	29.6333	70.3667
2	6.6946	33.1910	37.1757
3	2.7099	37.1757	0.0000

YEARS 4 — QTR PAYT 7.8852 — AN CONST 31.55

#	INT	PRIN	BALANCE
1	10.6191	20.9218	79.0782
2	8.1073	23.4335	55.6447
3	5.2940	26.2468	29.3979
4	2.1429	29.3979	0.0000

YEARS 5 — QTR PAYT 6.6441 — AN CONST 26.58

#	INT	PRIN	BALANCE
1	10.8373	15.7392	84.2608
2	8.9477	17.6288	66.6319
3	6.8313	19.7453	46.8867
4	4.4607	22.1158	24.7709
5	1.8056	24.7709	0.0000

YEARS 6 — QTR PAYT 5.8255 — AN CONST 23.31

#	INT	PRIN	BALANCE
1	10.9812	12.3209	87.6791
2	9.5020	13.8000	73.8791
3	7.8453	15.4568	58.4223
4	5.9896	17.3125	41.1098
5	3.9111	19.3909	21.7189
6	1.5832	21.7189	0.0000

YEARS 7 — QTR PAYT 5.2482 — AN CONST 21.00

#	INT	PRIN	BALANCE
1	11.0827	9.9101	90.0899
2	9.8930	11.0998	78.9901
3	8.5604	12.4324	66.5576
4	7.0678	13.9250	52.6326
5	5.3960	15.5968	37.0358
6	3.5235	17.4693	19.5665
7	1.4263	19.5665	0.0000

YEARS 8 — QTR PAYT 4.8216 — AN CONST 19.29

#	INT	PRIN	BALANCE
1	11.1577	8.1286	91.8714
2	10.1818	9.1045	82.7668
3	9.0888	10.1976	72.5692
4	7.8645	11.4219	61.1474
5	6.4933	12.7931	48.3543
6	4.9574	14.3290	34.0253
7	3.2371	16.0492	17.9760
8	1.3103	17.9760	0.0000

YEARS 9 — QTR PAYT 4.4954 — AN CONST 17.99

#	INT	PRIN	BALANCE
1	11.2151	6.7663	93.2337
2	10.4028	7.5786	85.6551
3	9.4929	8.4885	77.1666
4	8.4738	9.5076	67.6590
5	7.3324	10.6490	57.0100
6	6.0539	11.9275	45.0825
7	4.6220	13.3594	31.7230
8	3.0181	14.9633	16.7597
9	1.2217	16.7597	0.0000

YEARS 10 — QTR PAYT 4.2393 — AN CONST 16.96

#	INT	PRIN	BALANCE
1	11.2601	5.6969	94.3031
2	10.5762	6.3808	87.9223
3	9.8101	7.1469	80.7754
4	8.9521	8.0049	72.7705
5	7.9911	8.9659	63.8045
6	6.9147	10.0424	53.7622
7	5.7090	11.2480	42.5142
8	4.3587	12.5984	29.9158
9	2.8462	14.1109	15.8049
10	1.1521	15.8049	0.0000

YEARS 11 — QTR PAYT 4.0341 — AN CONST 16.14

#	INT	PRIN	BALANCE
1	11.2962	4.8401	95.1599
2	10.7151	5.4212	89.7388
3	10.0643	6.0720	83.6667
4	9.3353	6.8010	76.8658
5	8.5188	7.6175	69.2483
6	7.6043	8.5320	60.7163
7	6.5800	9.5563	51.1600
8	5.4327	10.7036	40.4565
9	4.1477	11.9886	28.4679
10	2.7084	13.4279	15.0400
11	1.0963	15.0400	0.0000

YEARS 12 — QTR PAYT 3.8670 — AN CONST 15.47

#	INT	PRIN	BALANCE
1	11.3256	4.1423	95.8577
2	10.8283	4.6396	91.2181
3	10.2713	5.1966	86.0215
4	9.6474	5.8205	80.2010
5	8.9486	6.5193	73.6818
6	8.1659	7.3019	66.3798
7	7.2893	8.1786	58.2013
8	6.3074	9.1604	49.0408
9	5.2077	10.2602	38.7806
10	3.9759	11.4920	27.2886
11	2.5962	12.8717	14.4170
12	1.0509	14.4170	0.0000

YEARS 13 — QTR PAYT 3.7291 — AN CONST 14.92

#	INT	PRIN	BALANCE
1	11.3498	3.5664	96.4336
2	10.9217	3.9946	92.4390
3	10.4421	4.4741	87.9649
4	9.9050	5.0113	82.9536
5	9.3033	5.6129	77.3407
6	8.6295	6.2868	71.0540
7	7.8747	7.0415	64.0125
8	7.0293	7.8869	56.1256
9	6.0825	8.8337	47.2918
10	5.0219	9.8943	37.3976
11	3.8341	11.0821	26.3154
12	2.5036	12.4126	13.9028
13	1.0134	13.9028	0.0000

YEARS 14 — QTR PAYT 3.6140 — AN CONST 14.46

#	INT	PRIN	BALANCE
1	11.3701	3.0859	96.9141
2	10.9996	3.4563	93.4578
3	10.5846	3.8713	89.5865
4	10.1199	4.3361	85.2504
5	9.5993	4.8566	80.3938
6	9.0162	5.4397	74.9541
7	8.3632	6.0928	68.8613
8	7.6317	6.8242	62.0371
9	6.8124	7.6435	54.3936
10	5.8948	8.5611	45.8325
11	4.8670	9.5890	36.2435
12	3.7158	10.7402	25.5034
13	2.4264	12.0296	13.4738
14	.9821	13.4738	0.0000

YEARS 15 — QTR PAYT 3.5171 — AN CONST 14.07

#	INT	PRIN	BALANCE
1	11.3871	2.6812	97.3188
2	11.0652	3.0031	94.3156
3	10.7047	3.3637	90.9520
4	10.3008	3.7675	87.1845
5	9.8485	4.2198	82.9647
6	9.3419	4.7264	78.2383
7	8.7745	5.2938	72.9444
8	8.1389	5.9294	67.0150
9	7.4271	6.6412	60.3738
10	6.6298	7.4386	52.9352
11	5.7367	8.3316	44.6036
12	4.7365	9.3319	35.2717
13	3.6161	10.4522	24.8196
14	2.3613	11.7070	13.1125
15	.9558	13.1125	0.0000

YEARS 16 — QTR PAYT 3.4349 — AN CONST 13.74

#	INT	PRIN	BALANCE
1	11.4016	2.3379	97.6621
2	11.1209	2.6185	95.0436
3	10.8065	2.9329	92.1107
4	10.4544	3.2850	88.8256
5	10.0600	3.6794	85.1462
6	9.6183	4.1211	81.0251
7	9.1235	4.6159	76.4091
8	8.5694	5.1701	71.2391
9	7.9487	5.7908	65.4483
10	7.2535	6.4860	58.9623
11	6.4748	7.2647	51.6976
12	5.6026	8.1368	43.5608
13	4.6257	9.1137	34.4471
14	3.5316	10.2078	24.2393
15	2.3061	11.4333	12.8060
16	.9335	12.8060	0.0000

YEARS 17 — QTR PAYT 3.3646 — AN CONST 13.46

#	INT	PRIN	BALANCE
1	11.4139	2.0446	97.9554
2	11.1684	2.2901	95.6653
3	10.8935	2.5650	93.1003
4	10.5856	2.8730	90.2274
5	10.2407	3.2179	87.0095
6	9.8543	3.6042	83.4053
7	9.4216	4.0369	79.3684
8	8.9370	4.5215	74.8469
9	8.3941	5.0644	69.7825
10	7.7861	5.6724	64.1101
11	7.1051	6.3534	57.7568
12	6.3424	7.1161	50.6406
13	5.4881	7.9705	42.6702
14	4.5312	8.9273	33.7428
15	3.4594	9.9991	23.7437
16	2.2589	11.1996	12.5441
17	.9144	12.5441	0.0000

YEARS 18 — QTR PAYT 3.3043 — AN CONST 13.22

#	INT	PRIN	BALANCE
1	11.4245	1.7927	98.2073
2	11.2093	2.0080	96.1993
3	10.9682	2.2490	93.9503
4	10.6982	2.5190	91.4313
5	10.3958	2.8214	88.6098
6	10.0571	3.1602	85.4496
7	9.6777	3.5396	81.9101
8	9.2527	3.9645	77.9455
9	8.7768	4.4405	73.5051
10	8.2437	4.9736	68.5315
11	7.6466	5.5707	62.9608
12	6.9778	6.2395	56.7213
13	6.2287	6.9886	49.7328
14	5.3897	7.8276	41.9052
15	4.4499	8.7673	33.1379
16	3.3974	9.8199	23.3180
17	2.2185	10.9988	12.3193
18	.8980	12.3193	0.0000

YEARS 19 — QTR PAYT 3.2523 — AN CONST 13.01

#	INT	PRIN	BALANCE
1	11.4337	1.5754	98.4246
2	11.2445	1.7645	96.6602
3	11.0327	1.9763	94.6838
4	10.7954	2.2136	92.4702
5	10.5297	2.4793	89.9909
6	10.2320	2.7770	87.2139
7	9.8986	3.1104	84.1035
8	9.5252	3.4838	80.6197
9	9.1070	3.9021	76.7176
10	8.6385	4.3705	72.3471
11	8.1138	4.8952	67.4519
12	7.5261	5.4829	61.9689
13	6.8678	6.1412	55.8278
14	6.1306	6.8785	48.9493
15	5.3048	7.7043	41.2451
16	4.3798	8.6292	32.6159
17	3.3439	9.6652	22.9507
18	2.1835	10.8255	12.1252
19	.8838	12.1252	0.0000

YEARS 20 — QTR PAYT 3.2071 — AN CONST 12.83

#	INT	PRIN	BALANCE
1	11.4416	1.3870	98.6130
2	11.2751	1.5535	97.0595
3	11.0886	1.7400	95.3195
4	10.8797	1.9489	93.3706
5	10.6457	2.1829	91.1877
6	10.3836	2.4450	88.7427
7	10.0901	2.7385	86.0042
8	9.7613	3.0673	82.9370
9	9.3931	3.4355	79.5015
10	8.9806	3.8479	75.6536
11	8.5187	4.3099	71.3437
12	8.0013	4.8273	66.5163
13	7.4217	5.4069	61.1094
14	6.7726	6.0560	55.0534
15	6.0455	6.7831	48.2704
16	5.2312	7.5974	40.6730
17	4.3191	8.5095	32.1635
18	3.2975	9.5311	22.6324
19	2.1532	10.6754	11.9570
20	.8716	11.9570	0.0000

YEARS 21 — QTR PAYT 3.1679 — AN CONST 12.68

#	INT	PRIN	BALANCE
1	11.4485	1.2232	98.7768
2	11.3016	1.3700	97.4068
3	11.1372	1.5345	95.8723

#	INT	PRIN	BALANCE
4	10.9529	1.7187	94.1536
5	10.7466	1.9251	92.2285
6	10.5155	2.1562	90.0723
7	10.2566	2.4150	87.6573
8	9.9667	2.7050	84.9523
9	9.6419	3.0297	81.9225
10	9.2782	3.3935	78.5291
11	8.8708	3.8009	74.7282
12	8.4145	4.2572	70.4710
13	7.9034	4.7683	65.7027
14	7.3309	5.3407	60.3620
15	6.6897	5.9819	54.3800
16	5.9716	6.7001	47.6800
17	5.1672	7.5045	40.1755
18	4.2663	8.4054	31.7701
19	3.2571	9.4145	22.3555
20	2.1269	10.5448	11.8107
21	.8609	11.8107	0.0000

YEARS 22	QTR PAYT 3.1337	AN CONST 12.54	
#	INT	PRIN	BALANCE
1	11.4545	1.0803	98.9197
2	11.3248	1.2100	97.7098
3	11.1796	1.3552	96.3545
4	11.0169	1.5179	94.8366
5	10.8346	1.7002	93.1364
6	10.6305	1.9043	91.2322
7	10.4019	2.1329	89.0993
8	10.1458	2.3890	86.7103
9	9.8590	2.6758	84.0345
10	9.5378	2.9970	81.0375
11	9.1780	3.3568	77.6807
12	8.7750	3.7598	73.9209
13	8.3236	4.2112	69.7097
14	7.8180	4.7168	64.9929
15	7.2517	5.2830	59.7099
16	6.6175	5.9173	53.7926
17	5.9071	6.6277	47.1649
18	5.1114	7.4234	39.7415
19	4.2202	8.3146	31.4269
20	3.2220	9.3128	22.1140
21	2.1039	10.4309	11.6832
22	.8516	11.6832	0.0000

YEARS 23	QTR PAYT 3.1038	AN CONST 12.42	
#	INT	PRIN	BALANCE
1	11.4598	.9553	99.0447
2	11.3451	1.0700	97.9748
3	11.2166	1.1984	96.7764
4	11.0728	1.3423	95.4341
5	10.9116	1.5034	93.9307
6	10.7311	1.6839	92.2467
7	10.5290	1.8861	90.3607
8	10.3025	2.1125	88.2481
9	10.0489	2.3661	85.8820
10	9.7648	2.6502	83.2318
11	9.4467	2.9684	80.2634
12	9.0903	3.3247	76.9387
13	8.6911	3.7239	73.2148
14	8.2441	4.1710	69.0438
15	7.7433	4.6717	64.3721
16	7.1825	5.2326	59.1395
17	6.5543	5.8608	53.2787
18	5.8506	6.5644	46.7143
19	5.0626	7.3525	39.3618
20	4.1799	8.2352	31.1267
21	3.1912	9.2239	21.9028
22	2.0838	10.3312	11.5716
23	.8435	11.5716	0.0000

YEARS 24	QTR PAYT 3.0775	AN CONST 12.32	
#	INT	PRIN	BALANCE
1	11.4644	.8457	99.1543
2	11.3629	.9472	98.2071
3	11.2492	1.0609	97.1462
4	11.1218	1.1883	95.9580
5	10.9791	1.3309	94.6270
6	10.8193	1.4907	93.1363
7	10.6404	1.6697	91.4666
8	10.4399	1.8701	89.5965
9	10.2154	2.0947	87.5019
10	9.9639	2.3461	85.1557
11	9.6823	2.6278	82.5279
12	9.3668	2.9433	79.5847
13	9.0134	3.2966	76.2880
14	8.6176	3.6924	72.5956
15	8.1744	4.1357	68.4599
16	7.6778	4.6322	63.8277
17	7.1217	5.1883	58.6394
18	6.4988	5.8112	52.8282
19	5.8012	6.5089	46.3193
20	5.0197	7.2903	39.0290
21	4.1445	8.1655	30.8634
22	3.1642	9.1459	21.7176
23	2.0662	10.2439	11.4737
24	.8364	11.4737	0.0000

YEARS 25	QTR PAYT 3.0545	AN CONST 12.22	
#	INT	PRIN	BALANCE
1	11.4684	.7494	99.2506
2	11.3785	.8393	98.4113
3	11.2777	.9401	97.4712
4	11.1649	1.0530	96.4183
5	11.0384	1.1794	95.2389
6	10.8969	1.3210	93.9179
7	10.7383	1.4795	92.4384
8	10.5606	1.6572	90.7812
9	10.3617	1.8561	88.9251
10	10.1388	2.0790	86.8462
11	9.8893	2.3285	84.5176
12	9.6097	2.6081	81.9095
13	9.2966	2.9212	78.9883
14	8.9459	3.2719	75.7164
15	8.5531	3.6647	72.0516
16	8.1131	4.1047	67.9469
17	7.6203	4.5975	63.3494
18	7.0684	5.1495	58.2000
19	6.4501	5.7677	52.4323
20	5.7577	6.4601	45.9722
21	4.9821	7.2357	38.7365
22	4.1135	8.1044	30.6322
23	3.1405	9.0773	21.5548
24	2.0507	10.1671	11.3877
25	.8301	11.3877	0.0000

YEARS 26	QTR PAYT 3.0342	AN CONST 12.14	
#	INT	PRIN	BALANCE
1	11.4720	.6646	99.3354
2	11.3922	.7444	98.5910
3	11.3029	.8337	97.7573
4	11.2028	.9338	96.8234
5	11.0907	1.0460	95.7775
6	10.9651	1.1715	94.6059
7	10.8244	1.3122	93.2938
8	10.6669	1.4697	91.8241
9	10.4905	1.6462	90.1779
10	10.2928	1.8438	88.3341
11	10.0715	2.0651	86.2690
12	9.8235	2.3131	83.9559
13	9.5458	2.5908	81.3651
14	9.2348	2.9018	78.4633
15	8.8864	3.2502	75.2132
16	8.4962	3.6404	71.5728
17	8.0592	4.0774	67.4953
18	7.5697	4.5669	62.9284
19	7.0214	5.1152	57.8132
20	6.4073	5.7293	52.0838
21	5.7194	6.4172	45.6667
22	4.9490	7.1876	38.4791
23	4.0861	8.0505	30.4286
24	3.1196	9.0170	21.4116
25	2.0371	10.0995	11.3120
26	.8246	11.3120	0.0000

YEARS 27	QTR PAYT 3.0163	AN CONST 12.07	
#	INT	PRIN	BALANCE
1	11.4752	.5899	99.4101
2	11.4043	.6607	98.7495
3	11.3250	.7400	98.0095
4	11.2362	.8288	97.1806
5	11.1367	.9283	96.2523
6	11.0252	1.0398	95.2125
7	10.9004	1.1646	94.0479
8	10.7606	1.3044	92.7435
9	10.6040	1.4610	91.2824
10	10.4286	1.6364	89.6460
11	10.2321	1.8329	87.8131
12	10.0121	2.0530	85.7601
13	9.7656	2.2994	83.4607
14	9.4895	2.5755	80.8852
15	9.1803	2.8847	78.0005
16	8.8340	3.2310	74.7695
17	8.4461	3.6189	71.1506
18	8.0116	4.0534	67.0972
19	7.5250	4.5400	62.5572
20	6.9800	5.0851	57.4722
21	6.3695	5.6955	51.7766
22	5.6857	6.3793	45.3973
23	4.9198	7.1452	38.2521
24	4.0620	8.0030	30.2491
25	3.1012	8.9638	21.2853
26	2.0251	10.0400	11.2453
27	.8197	11.2453	0.0000

YEARS 28	QTR PAYT 3.0005	AN CONST 12.01	
#	INT	PRIN	BALANCE
1	11.4779	.5239	99.4761
2	11.4150	.5868	98.8894
3	11.3446	.6572	98.2321
4	11.2657	.7361	97.4960
5	11.1773	.8245	96.6715
6	11.0783	.9235	95.7481
7	10.9675	1.0343	94.7137
8	10.8433	1.1585	93.5552
9	10.7042	1.2976	92.2576
10	10.5484	1.4534	90.8042
11	10.3739	1.6279	89.1764
12	10.1785	1.8233	87.3530
13	9.9596	2.0422	85.3108
14	9.7144	2.2874	83.0235
15	9.4398	2.5620	80.4615
16	9.1322	2.8696	77.5919
17	8.7877	3.2141	74.3778
18	8.4019	3.5999	70.7779
19	7.9697	4.0321	66.7457
20	7.4856	4.5162	62.2295
21	6.9434	5.0584	57.1711
22	6.3361	5.6657	51.5054
23	5.6559	6.3459	45.1595
24	4.8941	7.1078	38.0517
25	4.0407	7.9611	30.0906
26	3.0850	8.9169	21.1738
27	2.0144	9.9874	11.1864
28	.8154	11.1864	0.0000

YEARS 29	QTR PAYT 2.9865	AN CONST 11.95	
#	INT	PRIN	BALANCE
1	11.4804	.4655	99.5345
2	11.4245	.5214	99.0130
3	11.3619	.5840	98.4290
4	11.2918	.6542	97.7748
5	11.2133	.7327	97.0421
6	11.1253	.8206	96.2215
7	11.0268	.9192	95.3023
8	10.9164	1.0295	94.2728
9	10.7928	1.1531	93.1197
10	10.6544	1.2916	91.8281
11	10.4993	1.4466	90.3815
12	10.3256	1.6203	88.7612
13	10.1311	1.8148	86.9464
14	9.9132	2.0327	84.9137
15	9.6692	2.2767	82.6369
16	9.3959	2.5501	80.0869
17	9.0897	2.8562	77.2307
18	8.7468	3.1991	74.0315
19	8.3628	3.5832	70.4484
20	7.9326	4.0134	66.4350
21	7.4507	4.4952	61.9398
22	6.9111	5.0349	56.9049
23	6.3066	5.6393	51.2656
24	5.6296	6.3164	44.9492
25	4.8713	7.0747	37.8746
26	4.0219	7.9240	29.9505
27	3.0706	8.8753	21.0752
28	2.0051	9.9409	11.1343
29	.8116	11.1343	0.0000

YEARS 30	QTR PAYT 2.9741	AN CONST 11.90	
#	INT	PRIN	BALANCE
1	11.4826	.4139	99.5861
2	11.4329	.4636	99.1225
3	11.3772	.5193	98.6032
4	11.3149	.5816	98.0216
5	11.2450	.6514	97.3701
6	11.1668	.7297	96.6405
7	11.0792	.8173	95.8232
8	10.9811	.9154	94.9078
9	10.8712	1.0253	93.8826
10	10.7481	1.1484	92.7342
11	10.6103	1.2862	91.4480
12	10.4559	1.4406	90.0074
13	10.2829	1.6136	88.3938
14	10.0892	1.8073	86.5865
15	9.8722	2.0243	84.5622
16	9.6292	2.2673	82.2949
17	9.3570	2.5395	79.7554
18	9.0521	2.8444	76.9110
19	8.7106	3.1859	73.7251
20	8.3281	3.5684	70.1567
21	7.8997	3.9968	66.1600
22	7.4199	4.4766	61.6834
23	6.8825	5.0140	56.6694
24	6.2805	5.6160	51.0534
25	5.6063	6.2902	44.7632
26	4.8511	7.0454	37.7178
27	4.0053	7.8912	29.8266
28	3.0579	8.8386	20.9880
29	1.9968	9.8997	11.0882
30	.8083	11.0882	0.0000

YEARS 2 — QTR PAYT 14.2081 — AN CONST 56.84

#	INT	PRIN	BALANCE
1	9.7244	47.1080	52.8920
2	3.9405	52.8920	0.0000

YEARS 3 — QTR PAYT 10.0088 — AN CONST 40.04

#	INT	PRIN	BALANCE
1	10.4791	29.5560	70.4440
2	6.8502	33.1848	37.2592
3	2.7758	37.2592	0.0000

YEARS 4 — QTR PAYT 7.9231 — AN CONST 31.70

#	INT	PRIN	BALANCE
1	10.8540	20.8384	79.1616
2	8.2954	23.3970	55.7646
3	5.4228	26.2696	29.4950
4	2.1974	29.4950	0.0000

YEARS 5 — QTR PAYT 6.6828 — AN CONST 26.74

#	INT	PRIN	BALANCE
1	11.0769	15.6543	84.3457
2	9.1548	17.5763	66.7694
3	6.9968	19.7343	47.0351
4	4.5739	22.1573	24.8778
5	1.8534	24.8778	0.0000

YEARS 6 — QTR PAYT 5.8651 — AN CONST 23.47

#	INT	PRIN	BALANCE
1	11.2238	12.2364	87.7636
2	9.7215	13.7388	74.0248
3	8.0346	15.4256	58.5992
4	6.1407	17.3196	41.2797
5	4.0142	19.4460	21.8336
6	1.6266	21.8336	0.0000

YEARS 7 — QTR PAYT 5.2887 — AN CONST 21.16

#	INT	PRIN	BALANCE
1	11.3274	9.8273	90.1727
2	10.1208	11.0339	79.1388
3	8.7661	12.3886	66.7502
4	7.2450	13.9097	52.8405
5	5.5372	15.6175	37.2230
6	3.6197	17.5350	19.6880
7	1.4668	19.6880	0.0000

YEARS 8 — QTR PAYT 4.8630 — AN CONST 19.46

#	INT	PRIN	BALANCE
1	11.4039	8.0482	91.9518
2	10.4158	9.0364	82.9154
3	9.3063	10.1459	72.7696
4	8.0606	11.3916	61.3780
5	6.6619	12.7902	48.5878
6	5.0916	14.3606	34.2272
7	3.3284	16.1238	18.1034
8	1.3487	18.1034	0.0000

YEARS 9 — QTR PAYT 4.5378 — AN CONST 18.16

#	INT	PRIN	BALANCE
1	11.4624	6.6887	93.3113
2	10.6412	7.5099	85.8014
3	9.7191	8.4320	77.3695
4	8.6838	9.4672	67.9022
5	7.5214	10.6296	57.2726
6	6.2163	11.9347	45.3379
7	4.7510	13.4001	31.9379
8	3.1058	15.0453	16.8926
9	1.2585	16.8926	0.0000

YEARS 10 — QTR PAYT 4.2826 — AN CONST 17.14

#	INT	PRIN	BALANCE
1	11.5082	5.6223	94.3777
2	10.8179	6.3126	88.0651
3	10.0429	7.0877	80.9774
4	9.1727	7.9579	73.0195
5	8.1956	8.9350	64.0846
6	7.0986	10.0320	54.0526
7	5.8668	11.2637	42.7889
8	4.4839	12.6467	30.1422
9	2.9311	14.1994	15.9428
10	1.1877	15.9428	0.0000

YEARS 11 — QTR PAYT 4.0784 — AN CONST 16.32

#	INT	PRIN	BALANCE
1	11.5449	4.7687	95.2313
2	10.9594	5.3542	89.8771
3	10.3021	6.0116	83.8655
4	9.5640	6.7497	77.1158
5	8.7352	7.5784	69.5374
6	7.8048	8.5089	61.0286
7	6.7601	9.5536	51.4750
8	5.5871	10.7266	40.7484
9	4.2701	12.0436	28.7048
10	2.7914	13.5223	15.1825
11	1.1311	15.1825	0.0000

YEARS 12 — QTR PAYT 3.9122 — AN CONST 15.65

#	INT	PRIN	BALANCE
1	11.5748	4.0742	95.9258
2	11.0746	4.5744	91.3514
3	10.5129	5.1361	86.2153
4	9.8823	5.7667	80.4487
5	9.1743	6.4747	73.9740
6	8.3794	7.2696	66.7044
7	7.4868	8.1622	58.5421
8	6.4846	9.1644	49.3778
9	5.3594	10.2896	39.0882
10	4.0961	11.5529	27.5353
11	2.6776	12.9714	14.5640
12	1.0850	14.5640	0.0000

YEARS 13 — QTR PAYT 3.7753 — AN CONST 15.11

#	INT	PRIN	BALANCE
1	11.5994	3.5016	96.4984
2	11.1695	3.9315	92.5669
3	10.6868	4.4142	88.1526
4	10.1448	4.9562	83.1964
5	9.5363	5.5647	77.6317
6	8.8531	6.2480	71.3837
7	8.0859	7.0151	64.3686
8	7.2246	7.8764	56.4922
9	6.2576	8.8435	47.6488
10	5.1718	9.9293	37.7195
11	3.9527	11.1484	26.5712
12	2.5839	12.5172	14.0540
13	1.0470	14.0540	0.0000

YEARS 14 — QTR PAYT 3.6611 — AN CONST 14.65

#	INT	PRIN	BALANCE
1	11.6200	3.0244	96.9756
2	11.2486	3.3957	93.5799
3	10.8317	3.8126	89.7673
4	10.3636	4.2807	85.4866
5	9.8380	4.8063	80.6803
6	9.2479	5.3964	75.2838
7	8.5853	6.0590	69.2248
8	7.8414	6.8029	62.4219
9	7.0061	7.6382	54.7837
10	6.0683	8.5760	46.2077
11	5.0154	9.6290	36.5787
12	3.8331	10.8112	25.7675
13	2.5057	12.1386	13.6290
14	1.0154	13.6290	0.0000

YEARS 15 — QTR PAYT 3.5651 — AN CONST 14.27

#	INT	PRIN	BALANCE
1	11.6372	2.6230	97.3770
2	11.3152	2.9450	94.4320
3	10.9536	3.3066	91.1253
4	10.5476	3.7126	87.4127
5	10.0918	4.1684	83.2443
6	9.5800	4.6802	78.5640
7	9.0053	5.2549	73.3091
8	8.3601	5.9001	67.4091
9	7.6357	6.6245	60.7846
10	6.8224	7.4378	53.3467
11	5.9091	8.3511	44.9957
12	4.8838	9.3764	35.6193
13	3.7326	10.5276	25.0917
14	2.4400	11.8202	13.2715
15	.9887	13.2715	0.0000

YEARS 16 — QTR PAYT 3.4837 — AN CONST 13.94

#	INT	PRIN	BALANCE
1	11.6518	2.2828	97.7172
2	11.3716	2.5631	95.1541
3	11.0569	2.8778	92.2763
4	10.7035	3.2311	89.0451
5	10.3068	3.6279	85.4172
6	9.8614	4.0733	81.3440
7	9.3613	4.5734	76.7705
8	8.7997	5.1349	71.6356
9	8.1693	5.7654	65.8702
10	7.4614	6.4733	59.3970
11	6.6666	7.2680	52.1289
12	5.7743	8.1604	43.9685
13	4.7723	9.1623	34.8062
14	3.6474	10.2873	24.5189
15	2.3843	11.5504	12.9685
16	.9662	12.9685	0.0000

YEARS 17 — QTR PAYT 3.4142 — AN CONST 13.66

#	INT	PRIN	BALANCE
1	11.6643	1.9927	98.0073
2	11.4197	2.2373	95.7700
3	11.1450	2.5120	93.2579
4	10.8365	2.8205	90.4375
5	10.4902	3.1668	87.2707
6	10.1014	3.5556	83.7152
7	9.6649	3.9921	79.7230
8	9.1747	4.4823	75.2408
9	8.6244	5.0326	70.2082
10	8.0065	5.6505	64.5576
11	7.3127	6.3443	58.2134
12	6.5338	7.1232	51.0902
13	5.6592	7.9978	43.0924
14	4.6772	8.9798	34.1126
15	3.5747	10.0823	24.0303
16	2.3368	11.3202	12.7101
17	.9469	12.7101	0.0000

YEARS 18 — QTR PAYT 3.3547 — AN CONST 13.42

#	INT	PRIN	BALANCE
1	11.6750	1.7438	98.2562
2	11.4609	1.9579	96.2982
3	11.2205	2.1983	94.0999
4	10.9506	2.4682	91.6317
5	10.6476	2.7713	88.8604
6	10.3073	3.1115	85.7489
7	9.9253	3.4936	82.2553
8	9.4963	3.9225	78.3328
9	9.0147	4.4041	73.9287
10	8.4740	4.9448	68.9838
11	7.8669	5.5520	63.4319
12	7.1852	6.2336	57.1982
13	6.4198	6.9990	50.1992
14	5.5605	7.8583	42.3409
15	4.5957	8.8232	33.5177
16	3.5124	9.9065	23.6112
17	2.2960	11.1228	12.4884
18	.9304	12.4884	0.0000

YEARS 19 — QTR PAYT 3.3034 — AN CONST 13.22

#	INT	PRIN	BALANCE
1	11.6842	1.5294	98.4706
2	11.4965	1.7172	96.7535
3	11.2856	1.9280	94.8255
4	11.0489	2.1647	92.6608
5	10.7831	2.4305	90.2303
6	10.4847	2.7289	87.5014
7	10.1497	3.0639	84.4375
8	9.7735	3.4401	80.9973
9	9.3511	3.8625	77.1348
10	8.8769	4.3368	72.7980
11	8.3444	4.8692	67.9288
12	7.7466	5.4671	62.4618
13	7.0753	6.1383	56.3235
14	6.3217	6.8920	49.4315
15	5.4755	7.7382	41.6933
16	4.5254	8.6882	33.0051
17	3.4586	9.7550	23.2501
18	2.2609	10.9527	12.2975
19	.9162	12.2975	0.0000

YEARS 20 — QTR PAYT 3.2590 — AN CONST 13.04

#	INT	PRIN	BALANCE
1	11.6922	1.3438	98.6562
2	11.5272	1.5088	97.1473
3	11.3420	1.6941	95.4533
4	11.1340	1.9021	93.5512
5	10.9004	2.1356	91.4156
6	10.6382	2.3978	89.0178
7	10.3438	2.6922	86.3255
8	10.0133	3.0228	83.3028
9	9.6421	3.3939	79.9088
10	9.2254	3.8106	76.0982
11	8.7576	4.2785	71.8198
12	8.2323	4.8038	67.0160
13	7.6425	5.3936	61.6224
14	6.9802	6.0558	55.5666
15	6.2367	6.7993	48.7672
16	5.4019	7.6342	41.1331
17	4.4646	8.5715	32.5616
18	3.4122	9.6239	22.9377
19	2.2305	10.8055	12.1322
20	.9039	12.1322	0.0000

YEARS 21 — QTR PAYT 3.2205 — AN CONST 12.89

#	INT	PRIN	BALANCE
1	11.6991	1.1827	98.8173
2	11.5539	1.3279	97.4893
3	11.3909	1.4910	95.9984

QUARTERLY PAYMENT AMORTIZATION SCHEDULE PER $100

11.75 %

#	INT	PRIN	BALANCE
4	11.2078	1.6740	94.3243
5	11.0023	1.8796	92.4447
6	10.7715	2.1104	90.3344
7	10.5124	2.3695	87.9649
8	10.2215	2.6604	85.3045
9	9.8948	2.9870	82.3175
10	9.5281	3.3538	78.9637
11	9.1163	3.7655	75.1982
12	8.6540	4.2279	70.9703
13	8.1349	4.7470	66.2234
14	7.5521	5.3298	60.8936
15	6.8977	5.9842	54.9094
16	6.1629	6.7189	48.1904
17	5.3380	7.5439	40.6466
18	4.4118	8.4701	32.1765
19	3.3718	9.5101	22.6664
20	2.2042	10.6777	11.9887
21	.8932	11.9887	0.0000

YEARS 22	QTR PAYT 3.1869	AN CONST 12.75	
#	INT	PRIN	BALANCE
1	11.7052	1.0424	98.9576
2	11.5772	1.1704	97.7872
3	11.4335	1.3141	96.4731
4	11.2721	1.4754	94.9977
5	11.0910	1.6566	93.3411
6	10.8876	1.8600	91.4811
7	10.6592	2.0884	89.3927
8	10.4028	2.3448	87.0480
9	10.1149	2.6327	84.4153
10	9.7917	2.9559	81.4594
11	9.4288	3.3188	78.1406
12	9.0213	3.7263	74.4143
13	8.5638	4.1838	70.2305
14	8.0501	4.6975	65.5330
15	7.4733	5.2742	60.2588
16	6.8258	5.9218	54.3370
17	6.0987	6.6489	47.6881
18	5.2823	7.4652	40.2229
19	4.3658	8.3318	31.8411
20	3.3367	9.4109	22.4301
21	2.1812	10.5664	11.8637
22	.8839	11.8637	0.0000

YEARS 23	QTR PAYT 3.1576	AN CONST 12.64	
#	INT	PRIN	BALANCE
1	11.7104	.9199	99.0801
2	11.5975	1.0328	98.0473
3	11.4707	1.1596	96.8877
4	11.3283	1.3020	95.5857
5	11.1685	1.4619	94.1238
6	10.9890	1.6414	92.4825
7	10.7874	1.8429	90.6396
8	10.5612	2.0691	88.5704
9	10.3071	2.3232	86.2472
10	10.0219	2.6084	83.6388
11	9.7016	2.9287	80.7101
12	9.3420	3.2883	77.4218
13	8.9383	3.6920	73.7298
14	8.4850	4.1453	69.5845
15	7.9760	4.6543	64.9302
16	7.4046	5.2257	59.7045
17	6.7630	5.8673	53.8372
18	6.0426	6.5877	47.2494
19	5.2338	7.3966	39.8529
20	4.3256	8.3047	31.5482
21	3.3060	9.3244	22.2238
22	2.1611	10.4692	11.7546
23	.8757	11.7546	0.0000

YEARS 24	QTR PAYT 3.1319	AN CONST 12.53	
#	INT	PRIN	BALANCE
1	11.7151	.8126	99.1874
2	11.6153	.9124	98.2750
3	11.5033	1.0244	97.2505
4	11.3775	1.1502	96.1003
5	11.2363	1.2914	94.8089
6	11.0777	1.4500	93.3589
7	10.8997	1.6280	91.7309
8	10.6998	1.8279	89.9030
9	10.4754	2.0523	87.8507
10	10.2234	2.3043	85.5464
11	9.9404	2.5872	82.9591
12	9.6228	2.9049	80.0542
13	9.2661	3.2616	76.7927
14	8.8657	3.6620	73.1307
15	8.4161	4.1116	69.0190
16	7.9112	4.6165	64.4026
17	7.3444	5.1833	59.2193
18	6.7080	5.8197	53.3997
19	5.9935	6.5342	46.8655
20	5.1912	7.3365	39.5290
21	4.2905	8.2372	31.2918
22	3.2791	9.2486	22.0432
23	2.1436	10.3841	11.6591
24	.8686	11.6591	0.0000

YEARS 25	QTR PAYT 3.1094	AN CONST 12.44	
#	INT	PRIN	BALANCE
1	11.7191	.7186	99.2814
2	11.6309	.8068	98.4746
3	11.5318	.9058	97.5688
4	11.4206	1.0171	96.5517
5	11.2957	1.1419	95.4098
6	11.1555	1.2821	94.1277
7	10.9981	1.4396	92.6881
8	10.8213	1.6163	91.0718
9	10.6229	1.8148	89.2570
10	10.4001	2.0376	87.2194
11	10.1499	2.2878	84.9317
12	9.8690	2.5686	82.3630
13	9.5536	2.8840	79.4790
14	9.1995	3.2381	76.2409
15	8.8020	3.6357	72.6052
16	8.3556	4.0821	68.5231
17	7.8544	4.5833	63.9398
18	7.2917	5.1460	58.7938
19	6.6598	5.7778	53.0160
20	5.9504	6.4872	46.5287
21	5.1539	7.2837	39.2450
22	4.2596	8.1780	31.0669
23	3.2555	9.1821	21.8848
24	2.1282	10.3095	11.5753
25	.8624	11.5753	0.0000

YEARS 26	QTR PAYT 3.0896	AN CONST 12.36	
#	INT	PRIN	BALANCE
1	11.7227	.6359	99.3641
2	11.6446	.7140	98.6501
3	11.5569	.8017	97.8484
4	11.4585	.9001	96.9483
5	11.3480	1.0106	95.9377
6	11.2239	1.1347	94.8031
7	11.0846	1.2740	93.5291
8	10.9282	1.4304	92.0987
9	10.7525	1.6060	90.4926
10	10.5553	1.8032	88.6894
11	10.3339	2.0246	86.6648
12	10.0854	2.2732	84.3916
13	9.8063	2.5523	81.8393
14	9.4929	2.8657	78.9736
15	9.1410	3.2175	75.7560
16	8.7460	3.6126	72.1435
17	8.3024	4.0561	68.0873
18	7.8044	4.5541	63.5332
19	7.2453	5.1133	58.4199
20	6.6175	5.7411	52.6788
21	5.9126	6.4460	46.2328
22	5.1212	7.2374	38.9954
23	4.2325	8.1260	30.8694
24	3.2348	9.1237	21.7456
25	2.1146	10.2439	11.5017
26	.8569	11.5017	0.0000

YEARS 27	QTR PAYT 3.0722	AN CONST 12.29	
#	INT	PRIN	BALANCE
1	11.7258	.5632	99.4368
2	11.6566	.6323	98.8045
3	11.5790	.7100	98.0945
4	11.4918	.7971	97.2974
5	11.3940	.8950	96.4023
6	11.2841	1.0049	95.3974
7	11.1607	1.1283	94.2692
8	11.0222	1.2668	93.0023
9	10.8666	1.4224	91.5800
10	10.6920	1.5970	89.9830
11	10.4959	1.7931	88.1899
12	10.2757	2.0132	86.1767
13	10.0286	2.2604	83.9163
14	9.7510	2.5379	81.3783
15	9.4394	2.8495	78.5288
16	9.0896	3.1994	75.3294
17	8.6967	3.5922	71.7372
18	8.2557	4.0333	67.7039
19	7.7605	4.5285	63.1754
20	7.2045	5.0845	58.0909
21	6.5802	5.7088	52.3821
22	5.8793	6.4097	45.9725
23	5.0923	7.1967	38.7758
24	4.2087	8.0803	30.6955
25	3.2166	9.0724	21.6232
26	2.1027	10.1863	11.4369
27	.8521	11.4369	0.0000

YEARS 28	QTR PAYT 3.0569	AN CONST 12.23	
#	INT	PRIN	BALANCE
1	11.7285	.4991	99.5009
2	11.6673	.5604	98.9405
3	11.5985	.6292	98.3113
4	11.5212	.7064	97.6049
5	11.4345	.7932	96.8118
6	11.3371	.8905	95.9212
7	11.2277	.9999	94.9213
8	11.1050	1.1227	93.7987
9	10.9671	1.2605	92.5382
10	10.8124	1.4153	91.1229
11	10.6386	1.5890	89.5339
12	10.4435	1.7841	87.7498
13	10.2245	2.0032	85.7466
14	9.9785	2.2491	83.4975
15	9.7024	2.5253	80.9722
16	9.3923	2.8353	78.1369
17	9.0442	3.1834	74.9534
18	8.6533	3.5743	71.3791
19	8.2145	4.0132	67.3660
20	7.7218	4.5059	62.8601
21	7.1685	5.0591	57.8010
22	6.5474	5.6803	52.1207
23	5.8499	6.3777	45.7430
24	5.0669	7.1607	38.5823
25	4.1877	8.0399	30.5423
26	3.2006	9.0271	21.5152
27	2.0922	10.1354	11.3798
28	.8478	11.3798	0.0000

YEARS 29	QTR PAYT 3.0434	AN CONST 12.18	
#	INT	PRIN	BALANCE
1	11.7310	.4426	99.5574
2	11.6766	.4969	99.0606
3	11.6156	.5579	98.5027
4	11.5471	.6264	97.8763
5	11.4702	.7033	97.1730
6	11.3839	.7897	96.3833
7	11.2869	.8866	95.4967
8	11.1781	.9955	94.5012
9	11.0558	1.1177	93.3836
10	10.9186	1.2549	92.1286
11	10.7645	1.4090	90.7196
12	10.5915	1.5820	89.1376
13	10.3973	1.7762	87.3614
14	10.1792	1.9943	85.3671
15	9.9344	2.2392	83.1279
16	9.6594	2.5141	80.6138
17	9.3507	2.8228	77.7911
18	9.0042	3.1694	74.6217
19	8.6150	3.5585	71.0632
20	8.1781	3.9954	67.0678
21	7.6876	4.4859	62.5819
22	7.1368	5.0367	57.5452
23	6.5184	5.6551	51.8900
24	5.8241	6.3495	45.5406
25	5.0445	7.1291	38.4115
26	4.1692	8.0044	30.4072
27	3.1864	8.9871	21.4200
28	2.0830	10.0906	11.3295
29	.8440	11.3295	0.0000

YEARS 30	QTR PAYT 3.0314	AN CONST 12.13	
#	INT	PRIN	BALANCE
1	11.7331	.3926	99.6074
2	11.6849	.4408	99.1666
3	11.6308	.4949	98.6716
4	11.5700	.5557	98.1159
5	11.5018	.6239	97.4920
6	11.4252	.7005	96.7915
7	11.3392	.7866	96.0049
8	11.2426	.8831	95.1218
9	11.1342	.9916	94.1302
10	11.0124	1.1133	93.0169
11	10.8757	1.2500	91.7669
12	10.7223	1.4035	90.3635
13	10.5499	1.5758	88.7877
14	10.3565	1.7693	87.0184
15	10.1392	1.9865	85.0320
16	9.8953	2.2304	82.8016
17	9.6215	2.5042	80.2973
18	9.3140	2.8117	77.4857
19	8.9688	3.1569	74.3287
20	8.5812	3.5445	70.7842
21	8.1460	3.9797	66.8045
22	7.6574	4.4683	62.3362
23	7.1088	5.0170	57.3192
24	6.4928	5.6329	51.6863
25	5.8012	6.3245	45.3618
26	5.0247	7.1011	38.2607
27	4.1528	7.9729	30.2878
28	3.1739	8.9518	21.3359
29	2.0748	10.0509	11.2850
30	.8407	11.2850	0.0000

QUARTERLY PAYMENT AMORTIZATION SCHEDULE PER $100 — 12.00 %

YEARS 2 — QTR PAYT 14.2456 — AN CONST 56.99

#	INT	PRIN	BALANCE
1	9.9350	47.0476	52.9524
2	4.0301	52.9524	0.0000

YEARS 3 — QTR PAYT 10.0462 — AN CONST 40.19

#	INT	PRIN	BALANCE
1	10.7061	29.4787	70.5213
2	7.0063	33.1785	37.3427
3	2.8421	37.3427	0.0000

YEARS 4 — QTR PAYT 7.9611 — AN CONST 31.85

#	INT	PRIN	BALANCE
1	11.0890	20.7553	79.2447
2	8.4840	23.3603	55.8844
3	5.5521	26.2922	29.5921
4	2.2522	29.5921	0.0000

YEARS 5 — QTR PAYT 6.7216 — AN CONST 26.89

#	INT	PRIN	BALANCE
1	11.3166	15.5697	84.4303
2	9.3625	17.5238	66.9065
3	7.1631	19.7232	47.1834
4	4.6877	22.1986	24.9847
5	1.9015	24.9847	0.0000

YEARS 6 — QTR PAYT 5.9047 — AN CONST 23.62

#	INT	PRIN	BALANCE
1	11.4666	12.1524	87.8476
2	9.9414	13.6776	74.1701
3	8.2247	15.3942	58.7758
4	6.2926	17.3264	41.4495
5	4.1180	19.5010	21.9485
6	1.6705	21.9485	0.0000

YEARS 7 — QTR PAYT 5.3293 — AN CONST 21.32

#	INT	PRIN	BALANCE
1	11.5723	9.7450	90.2550
2	10.3492	10.9681	79.2869
3	8.9726	12.3447	66.9422
4	7.4232	13.8941	53.0481
5	5.6794	15.6379	37.4102
6	3.7167	17.6006	19.8096
7	1.5077	19.8096	0.0000

YEARS 8 — QTR PAYT 4.9047 — AN CONST 19.62

#	INT	PRIN	BALANCE
1	11.6503	7.9684	92.0316
2	10.6501	8.9685	83.0631
3	9.5245	10.0941	72.9690
4	8.2576	11.3610	61.6080
5	6.8317	12.7869	48.8210
6	5.2268	14.3918	34.4292
7	3.4205	16.1981	18.2311
8	1.3875	18.2311	0.0000

YEARS 9 — QTR PAYT 4.5804 — AN CONST 18.33

#	INT	PRIN	BALANCE
1	11.7098	6.6117	93.3883
2	10.8800	7.4415	85.9467
3	9.9460	8.3755	77.5712
4	8.8948	9.4267	68.1445
5	7.7117	10.6099	57.5346
6	6.3800	11.9415	45.5931
7	4.8813	13.4403	32.1529
8	3.1944	15.1271	17.0257
9	1.2958	17.0257	0.0000

YEARS 10 — QTR PAYT 4.3262 — AN CONST 17.31

#	INT	PRIN	BALANCE
1	11.7565	5.5485	94.4515
2	11.0601	6.2449	88.2066
3	10.2763	7.0287	81.1780
4	9.3941	7.9108	73.2672
5	8.4013	8.9037	64.3635
6	7.2838	10.0212	54.3423
7	6.0260	11.2789	43.0634
8	4.6104	12.6945	30.3689
9	3.0171	14.2878	16.0811
10	1.2239	16.0811	0.0000

YEARS 11 — QTR PAYT 4.1230 — AN CONST 16.50

#	INT	PRIN	BALANCE
1	11.7938	4.6981	95.3019
2	11.2041	5.2878	90.0140
3	10.5405	5.9515	84.0626
4	9.7935	6.6984	77.3641
5	8.9528	7.5392	69.8250
6	8.0066	8.4854	61.3396
7	6.9416	9.5504	51.7892
8	5.7429	10.7490	41.0402
9	4.3938	12.0981	28.9421
10	2.8754	13.6165	15.3255
11	1.1664	15.3255	0.0000

YEARS 12 — QTR PAYT 3.9578 — AN CONST 15.84

#	INT	PRIN	BALANCE
1	11.8241	4.0070	95.9930
2	11.3212	4.5099	91.4831
3	10.7552	5.0759	86.4072
4	10.1181	5.7130	80.6942
5	9.4011	6.4300	74.2642
6	8.5941	7.2371	67.0271
7	7.6857	8.1454	58.8817
8	6.6634	9.1677	49.7140
9	5.5128	10.3183	39.3957
10	4.2178	11.6134	27.7824
11	2.7602	13.0709	14.7114
12	1.1197	14.7114	0.0000

YEARS 13 — QTR PAYT 3.8217 — AN CONST 15.29

#	INT	PRIN	BALANCE
1	11.8491	3.4378	96.5622
2	11.4176	3.8692	92.6930
3	10.9320	4.3549	88.3381
4	10.3854	4.9014	83.4367
5	9.7703	5.5166	77.9201
6	9.0779	6.2090	71.7111
7	8.2986	6.9883	64.7229
8	7.4215	7.8654	56.8575
9	6.4343	8.8525	48.0050
10	5.3233	9.9636	38.0414
11	4.0728	11.2141	26.8273
12	2.6653	12.6216	14.2057
13	1.0812	14.2057	0.0000

YEARS 14 — QTR PAYT 3.7084 — AN CONST 14.84

#	INT	PRIN	BALANCE
1	11.8699	2.9639	97.0361
2	11.4979	3.3359	93.7002
3	11.0792	3.7546	89.9457
4	10.6080	4.2258	85.7199
5	10.0776	4.7562	80.9638
6	9.4807	5.3531	75.6107
7	8.8088	6.0250	69.5857
8	8.0526	6.7811	62.8046
9	7.2016	7.6322	55.1723
10	6.2436	8.5901	46.5822
11	5.1655	9.6683	36.9139
12	3.9520	10.8817	26.0322
13	2.5863	12.2475	13.7847
14	1.0491	13.7847	0.0000

YEARS 15 — QTR PAYT 3.6133 — AN CONST 14.46

#	INT	PRIN	BALANCE
1	11.8874	2.5658	97.4342
2	11.5654	2.8878	94.5464
3	11.2029	3.2503	91.2961
4	10.7950	3.6582	87.6379
5	10.3358	4.1174	83.5205
6	9.8191	4.6341	78.8864
7	9.2374	5.2157	73.6706
8	8.5828	5.8704	67.8003
9	7.8460	6.6072	61.1931
10	7.0168	7.4364	53.7567
11	6.0834	8.3697	45.3870
12	5.0330	9.4202	35.9668
13	3.8506	10.6025	25.3642
14	2.5199	11.9332	13.4310
15	1.0222	13.4310	0.0000

YEARS 16 — QTR PAYT 3.5328 — AN CONST 14.14

#	INT	PRIN	BALANCE
1	11.9022	2.2289	97.7711
2	11.6224	2.5086	95.2625
3	11.3076	2.8235	92.4391
4	10.9532	3.1778	89.2612
5	10.5544	3.5767	85.6845
6	10.1055	4.0256	81.6589
7	9.6002	4.5308	77.1281
8	9.0315	5.0995	72.0286
9	8.3915	5.7395	66.2891
10	7.6712	6.4599	59.8292
11	6.8604	7.2707	52.5586
12	5.9479	8.1832	44.3754
13	4.9208	9.2103	35.1651
14	3.7648	10.3662	24.7989
15	2.4638	11.6673	13.1316
16	.9994	13.1316	0.0000

YEARS 17 — QTR PAYT 3.4642 — AN CONST 13.86

#	INT	PRIN	BALANCE
1	11.9148	1.9419	98.0581
2	11.6710	2.1856	95.8725
3	11.3967	2.4599	93.4126
4	11.0880	2.7686	90.6440
5	10.7405	3.1161	87.5279
6	10.3494	3.5072	84.0207
7	9.9092	3.9474	80.0732
8	9.4138	4.4429	75.6304
9	8.8562	5.0005	70.6299
10	8.2286	5.6281	65.0018
11	7.5222	6.3344	58.6674
12	6.7272	7.1295	51.5379
13	5.8324	8.0243	43.5137
14	4.8252	9.0314	34.4822
15	3.6917	10.1649	24.3173
16	2.4159	11.4407	12.8766
17	.9800	12.8766	0.0000

YEARS 18 — QTR PAYT 3.4054 — AN CONST 13.63

#	INT	PRIN	BALANCE
1	11.9256	1.6961	98.3039
2	11.7127	1.9089	96.3950
3	11.4731	2.1485	94.2465
4	11.2034	2.4182	91.8283
5	10.8999	2.7217	89.1066
6	10.5583	3.0633	86.0434
7	10.1739	3.4477	82.5956
8	9.7412	3.8805	78.7151
9	9.2541	4.3675	74.3477
10	8.7060	4.9157	69.4320
11	8.0890	5.5326	63.8994
12	7.3946	6.2270	57.6724
13	6.6131	7.0086	50.6638
14	5.7334	7.8882	42.7756
15	4.7434	8.8782	33.8974
16	3.6291	9.9925	23.9049
17	2.3750	11.2467	12.6582
18	.9634	12.6582	0.0000

YEARS 19 — QTR PAYT 3.3548 — AN CONST 13.42

#	INT	PRIN	BALANCE
1	11.9348	1.4846	98.5154
2	11.7485	1.6709	96.8446
3	11.5388	1.8806	94.9640
4	11.3028	2.1166	92.8473
5	11.0371	2.3823	90.4651
6	10.7381	2.6813	87.7838
7	10.4016	3.0178	84.7660
8	10.0228	3.3966	81.3694
9	9.5965	3.8229	77.5466
10	9.1167	4.3027	73.2439
11	8.5767	4.8427	68.4012
12	7.9689	5.4505	62.9508
13	7.2848	6.1346	56.8162
14	6.5149	6.9045	49.9117
15	5.6483	7.7711	42.1406
16	4.6730	8.7464	33.3942
17	3.5752	9.8442	23.5500
18	2.3397	11.0797	12.4703
19	.9491	12.4703	0.0000

YEARS 20 — QTR PAYT 3.3112 — AN CONST 13.25

#	INT	PRIN	BALANCE
1	11.9429	1.3018	98.6982
2	11.7795	1.4652	97.2329
3	11.5956	1.6491	95.5838
4	11.3886	1.8561	93.7277
5	11.1556	2.0891	91.6386
6	10.8934	2.3513	89.2874
7	10.5983	2.6464	86.6410
8	10.2662	2.9785	83.6625
9	9.8924	3.3523	80.3101
10	9.4716	3.7731	76.5370
11	8.9981	4.2466	72.2904
12	8.4651	4.7796	67.5108
13	7.8652	5.3795	62.1312
14	7.1900	6.0547	56.0765
15	6.4301	6.8146	49.2619
16	5.5748	7.6699	41.5920
17	4.6121	8.6326	32.9594
18	3.5287	9.7160	23.2434
19	2.3092	10.9355	12.3080
20	.9367	12.3080	0.0000

YEARS 21 — QTR PAYT 3.2733 — AN CONST 13.10

#	INT	PRIN	BALANCE
1	11.9498	1.1434	98.8566
2	11.8063	1.2870	97.5696
3	11.6448	1.4485	96.1211

QUARTERLY PAYMENT AMORTIZATION SCHEDULE PER $100 — 12.00 %

#	INT	PRIN	BALANCE
4	11.4630	1.6303	94.4909
5	11.2584	1.8349	92.6560
6	11.0281	2.0652	90.5908
7	10.7689	2.3244	88.2664
8	10.4771	2.6161	85.6503
9	10.1488	2.9445	82.7058
10	9.7792	3.3140	79.3918
11	9.3633	3.7299	75.6619
12	8.8952	4.1981	71.4638
13	8.3683	4.7250	66.7388
14	7.7752	5.3180	61.4208
15	7.1078	5.9855	55.4353
16	6.3566	6.7367	48.6986
17	5.5110	7.5822	41.1164
18	4.5594	8.5338	32.5826
19	3.4883	9.6049	22.9777
20	2.2828	10.8104	12.1672
21	.9260	12.1672	0.0000

YEARS 22 — QTR PAYT 3.2404 — AN CONST 12.97

#	INT	PRIN	BALANCE
1	11.9559	1.0057	98.9943
2	11.8296	1.1319	97.8623
3	11.6876	1.2740	96.5883
4	11.5277	1.4339	95.1544
5	11.3477	1.6139	93.5405
6	11.1451	1.8164	91.7241
7	9.9172	2.0444	89.6797
8	10.6606	2.3010	87.3787
9	10.3718	2.5898	84.7889
10	10.0467	2.9148	81.8741
11	9.6809	3.2807	78.5934
12	9.2691	3.6924	74.9009
13	8.8057	4.1559	70.7451
14	8.2841	4.6775	66.0676
15	7.6970	5.2645	60.8031
16	7.0363	5.9253	54.8778
17	6.2926	6.6689	48.2089
18	5.4556	7.5060	40.7029
19	4.5135	8.4480	32.2549
20	3.4532	9.5083	22.7466
21	2.2599	10.7017	12.0449
22	.9167	12.0449	0.0000

YEARS 23 — QTR PAYT 3.2117 — AN CONST 12.85

#	INT	PRIN	BALANCE
1	11.9611	.8857	99.1143
2	11.8500	.9968	98.1175
3	11.7249	1.1219	96.9956
4	11.5841	1.2627	95.7329
5	11.4256	1.4212	94.3117
6	11.2472	1.5996	92.7121
7	11.0464	1.8003	90.9118
8	10.8205	2.0263	88.8855
9	10.5662	2.2806	86.6048
10	10.2799	2.5669	84.0380
11	9.9578	2.8890	81.1489
12	9.5952	3.2516	77.8973
13	9.1870	3.6597	74.2376
14	8.7277	4.1191	70.1185
15	8.2107	4.6360	65.4825
16	7.6289	5.2179	60.2646
17	6.9740	5.8728	54.3918
18	6.2369	6.6099	47.7819
19	5.4073	7.4395	40.3424
20	4.4736	8.3732	31.9692
21	3.4227	9.4241	22.5451
22	2.2399	10.6069	11.9382
23	.9086	11.9382	0.0000

YEARS 24 — QTR PAYT 3.1866 — AN CONST 12.75

#	INT	PRIN	BALANCE
1	11.9657	.7807	99.2193
2	11.8677	.8787	98.3405
3	11.7575	.9890	97.3515
4	11.6333	1.1132	96.2383
5	11.4936	1.2529	94.9855
6	11.3364	1.4101	93.5754
7	11.1594	1.5871	91.9883
8	10.9602	1.7863	90.2020
9	10.7360	2.0105	88.1915
10	10.4837	2.2628	85.9287
11	10.1997	2.5468	83.3818
12	9.8800	2.8665	80.5154
13	9.5202	3.2262	77.2891
14	9.1153	3.6312	73.6580
15	8.6596	4.0869	69.5711
16	8.1466	4.5998	64.9712
17	7.5693	5.1772	59.7941
18	6.9195	5.8269	53.9671
19	6.1882	6.5583	47.4088
20	5.3651	7.3814	40.0275
21	4.4386	8.3078	31.7196
22	3.3959	9.3505	22.3691
23	2.2224	10.5241	11.8450
24	.9015	11.8450	0.0000

YEARS 25 — QTR PAYT 3.1647 — AN CONST 12.66

#	INT	PRIN	BALANCE
1	11.9698	.6889	99.3111
2	11.8833	.7754	98.5357
3	11.7860	.8727	97.6630
4	11.6765	.9822	96.6808
5	11.5532	1.1055	95.5753
6	11.4144	1.2442	94.3311
7	11.2583	1.4004	92.9307
8	11.0825	1.5762	91.3545
9	10.8847	1.7740	89.5806
10	10.6620	1.9966	87.5839
11	10.4114	2.2472	85.3367
12	10.1294	2.5293	82.8074
13	9.8119	2.8467	79.9607
14	9.4547	3.2040	76.7567
15	9.0525	3.6061	73.1505
16	8.5999	4.0587	69.0918
17	8.0905	4.5682	64.5236
18	7.5172	5.1415	59.3821
19	6.8719	5.7868	53.5953
20	6.1456	6.5131	47.0822
21	5.3281	7.3305	39.7517
22	4.4081	8.2506	31.5011
23	3.3725	9.2861	22.2150
24	2.2071	10.4516	11.7634
25	.8953	11.7634	0.0000

YEARS 26 — QTR PAYT 3.1454 — AN CONST 12.59

#	INT	PRIN	BALANCE
1	11.9733	.6084	99.3916
2	11.8969	.6847	98.7069
3	11.8110	.7707	97.9363
4	11.7143	.8674	97.0689
5	11.6054	.9762	96.0927
6	11.4829	1.0988	94.9939
7	11.3450	1.2367	93.7572
8	11.1898	1.3919	92.3654
9	11.0151	1.5666	90.7988
10	10.8185	1.7632	89.0356
11	10.5972	1.9845	87.0511
12	10.3481	2.2336	84.8175
13	10.0678	2.5139	82.3037
14	9.7523	2.8294	79.4743
15	9.3971	3.1845	76.2897
16	8.9975	3.5842	72.7055
17	8.5476	4.0341	68.6715
18	8.0413	4.5404	64.1311
19	7.4714	5.1102	59.0209
20	6.8301	5.7516	53.2693
21	6.1082	6.4735	46.7958
22	5.2957	7.2860	39.5099
23	4.3813	8.2004	31.3095
24	3.3520	9.2296	22.0798
25	2.1936	10.3880	11.6918
26	.8898	11.6918	0.0000

YEARS 27 — QTR PAYT 3.1285 — AN CONST 12.52

#	INT	PRIN	BALANCE
1	11.9764	.5376	99.4624
2	11.9089	.6051	98.8573
3	11.8330	.6810	98.1763
4	11.7475	.7665	97.4098
5	11.6513	.8627	96.5471
6	11.5430	.9710	95.5761
7	11.4212	1.0929	94.4832
8	11.2840	1.2300	93.2532
9	11.1296	1.3844	91.8688
10	10.9559	1.5582	90.3106
11	10.7603	1.7537	88.5569
12	10.5402	1.9738	86.5831
13	10.2925	2.2216	84.3616
14	10.0136	2.5004	81.8612
15	9.6998	2.8142	79.0470
16	9.3466	3.1674	75.8796
17	8.9491	3.5649	72.3147
18	8.5016	4.0124	68.3023
19	7.9981	4.5160	63.7863
20	7.4313	5.0827	58.7036
21	6.7933	5.7207	52.9829
22	6.0753	6.4387	46.5442
23	5.2672	7.2468	39.2975
24	4.3577	8.1563	31.1411
25	3.3340	9.1800	21.9611
26	2.1818	10.3322	11.6290
27	.8851	11.6290	0.0000

YEARS 28 — QTR PAYT 3.1136 — AN CONST 12.46

#	INT	PRIN	BALANCE
1	11.9791	.4754	99.5246
2	11.9195	.5351	98.9896
3	11.8523	.6022	98.3873
4	11.7767	.6778	97.7095
5	11.6917	.7629	96.9467
6	11.5959	.8586	96.0881
7	11.4882	.9664	95.1217
8	11.3669	1.0877	94.0340
9	11.2304	1.2242	92.8099
10	11.0767	1.3778	91.4321
11	10.9038	1.5507	89.8813
12	10.7091	1.7454	88.1359
13	10.4901	1.9644	86.1715
14	10.2435	2.2110	83.9605
15	9.9660	2.4885	81.4720
16	9.6537	2.8008	78.6712
17	9.3022	3.1523	75.5189
18	8.9065	3.5480	71.9709
19	8.4612	3.9933	67.9776
20	7.9600	4.4945	63.4831
21	7.3959	5.0586	58.4245
22	6.7610	5.6935	52.7310
23	6.0465	6.4081	46.3230
24	5.2422	7.2123	39.1106
25	4.3370	8.1175	30.9931
26	3.3182	9.1364	21.8567
27	2.1715	10.2831	11.5737
28	.8809	11.5737	0.0000

YEARS 29 — QTR PAYT 3.1005 — AN CONST 12.41

#	INT	PRIN	BALANCE
1	11.9815	.4206	99.5794
2	11.9287	.4734	99.1060
3	11.8693	.5328	98.5732
4	11.8025	.5997	97.9735
5	11.7272	.6749	97.2986
6	11.6425	.7597	96.5389
7	11.5471	.8550	95.6839
8	11.4398	.9623	94.7216
9	11.3191	1.0831	93.6385
10	11.1831	1.2190	92.4195
11	11.0301	1.3720	91.0475
12	10.8579	1.5442	89.5033
13	10.6641	1.7380	87.7652
14	10.4460	1.9562	85.8091
15	10.2005	2.2017	83.6074
16	9.9241	2.4780	81.1294
17	9.6131	2.7890	78.3403
18	9.2631	3.1391	75.2012
19	8.8691	3.5331	71.6682
20	8.4256	3.9765	67.6917
21	7.9266	4.4756	63.2161
22	7.3648	5.0373	58.1788
23	6.7326	5.6695	52.5092
24	6.0210	6.3811	46.1281
25	5.2201	7.1820	38.9461
26	4.3187	8.0834	30.8627
27	3.3042	9.0979	21.7648
28	2.1623	10.2398	11.5250
29	.8771	11.5250	0.0000

YEARS 30 — QTR PAYT 3.0890 — AN CONST 12.36

#	INT	PRIN	BALANCE
1	11.9837	.3723	99.6277
2	11.9369	.4190	99.2087
3	11.8843	.4716	98.7370
4	11.8251	.5308	98.2062
5	11.7585	.5974	97.6088
6	11.6835	.6724	96.9363
7	11.5991	.7568	96.1795
8	11.5042	.8518	95.3277
9	11.3972	.9587	94.3690
10	11.2769	1.0791	93.2899
11	11.1415	1.2145	92.0754
12	10.9891	1.3669	90.7085
13	10.8175	1.5385	89.1700
14	10.6244	1.7316	87.4385
15	10.4071	1.9489	85.4896
16	10.1625	2.1935	83.2961
17	9.8872	2.4688	80.8273
18	9.5773	2.7787	78.0486
19	9.2286	3.1274	74.9213
20	8.8361	3.5199	71.4013
21	8.3943	3.9617	67.4396
22	7.8970	4.4589	62.9807
23	7.3374	5.0186	57.9622
24	6.7075	5.6484	52.3138
25	5.9986	6.3574	45.9564
26	5.2007	7.1553	38.8011
27	4.3027	8.0533	30.7478
28	3.2919	9.0641	21.6838
29	2.1543	10.2017	11.4821
30	.8739	11.4821	0.0000

YEARS 2	QTR PAYT 14.2832	AN CONST 57.14
# INT	PRIN	BALANCE
1	10.1458	46.9871	53.0129
2	4.1200	53.0129	0.0000

YEARS 3	QTR PAYT 10.0837	AN CONST 40.34
# INT	PRIN	BALANCE
1	10.9333	29.4016	70.5984
2	7.1628	33.1722	37.4263
3	2.9087	37.4263	0.0000

YEARS 4	QTR PAYT 7.9992	AN CONST 32.00
# INT	PRIN	BALANCE
1	11.3242	20.6725	79.3275
2	8.6731	23.3236	56.0040
3	5.6820	26.3147	29.6893
4	2.3074	29.6893	0.0000

YEARS 5	QTR PAYT 6.7605	AN CONST 27.05
# INT	PRIN	BALANCE
1	11.5565	15.4854	84.5146
2	9.5706	17.4713	67.0434
3	7.3301	19.7118	47.3316
4	4.8022	22.2397	25.0918
5	1.9501	25.0918	0.0000

YEARS 6	QTR PAYT 5.9446	AN CONST 23.78
# INT	PRIN	BALANCE
1	11.7095	12.0687	87.9313
2	10.1618	13.6165	74.3148
3	8.4156	15.3627	58.9521
4	6.4454	17.3329	41.6192
5	4.2226	19.5557	22.0636
6	1.7147	22.0636	0.0000

YEARS 7	QTR PAYT 5.3701	AN CONST 21.49
# INT	PRIN	BALANCE
1	11.8172	9.6633	90.3367
2	10.5780	10.9025	79.4342
3	9.1798	12.3007	67.1335
4	7.6024	13.8782	53.2554
5	5.8226	15.6579	37.5975
6	3.8146	17.6660	19.9315
7	1.5490	19.9315	0.0000

YEARS 8	QTR PAYT 4.9465	AN CONST 19.79
# INT	PRIN	BALANCE
1	11.8967	7.8892	92.1108
2	10.8850	8.9009	83.2099
3	9.7435	10.0424	73.1675
4	8.4556	11.3303	61.8373
5	7.0026	12.7833	49.0540
6	5.3632	14.4227	34.6313
7	3.5136	16.2723	18.3591
8	1.4268	18.3591	0.0000

YEARS 9	QTR PAYT 4.6232	AN CONST 18.50
# INT	PRIN	BALANCE
1	11.9573	6.5355	93.4645
2	11.1192	7.3736	86.0910
3	10.1736	8.3192	77.7718
4	9.1067	9.3861	68.3857
5	7.9030	10.5898	57.7959
6	6.5449	11.9478	45.8481

#	INT	PRIN	BALANCE
7	5.0127	13.4801	32.3680
8	3.2840	15.2088	17.1592
9	1.3336	17.1592	0.0000

YEARS 10	QTR PAYT 4.3701	AN CONST 17.49
# INT	PRIN	BALANCE
1	12.0048	5.4754	94.5246
2	11.3026	6.1776	88.3470
3	10.5104	6.9698	81.3771
4	9.6165	7.8637	73.5134
5	8.6081	8.8721	64.6413
6	7.4703	10.0099	54.6313
7	6.1866	11.2936	43.3377
8	4.7382	12.7420	30.5957
9	3.1042	14.3760	16.2197
10	1.2605	16.2197	0.0000

YEARS 11	QTR PAYT 4.1678	AN CONST 16.68
# INT	PRIN	BALANCE
1	12.0427	4.6284	95.3716
2	11.4492	5.2220	90.1496
3	10.7795	5.8917	84.2579
4	10.0239	6.6473	77.6106
5	9.1714	7.4997	70.1109
6	8.2097	8.4615	61.6494
7	7.1245	9.5466	52.1028
8	5.9002	10.7709	41.3318
9	4.5189	12.1522	29.1796
10	2.9605	13.7107	15.4690
11	1.2022	15.4690	0.0000

YEARS 12	QTR PAYT 4.0036	AN CONST 16.02
# INT	PRIN	BALANCE
1	12.0735	3.9407	96.0593
2	11.5682	4.4460	91.6133
3	10.9980	5.0162	86.5971
4	10.3547	5.6595	80.9375
5	9.6289	6.3853	74.5522
6	8.8100	7.2042	67.3481
7	7.8861	8.1281	59.2200
8	6.8438	9.1704	50.0496
9	5.6677	10.3465	39.7031
10	4.3409	11.6733	28.0297
11	2.8438	13.1704	14.8594
12	1.1548	14.8594	0.0000

YEARS 13	QTR PAYT 3.8684	AN CONST 15.48
# INT	PRIN	BALANCE
1	12.0989	3.3749	96.6251
2	11.6661	3.8077	92.8174
3	11.1777	4.2960	88.5214
4	10.6268	4.8469	83.6745
5	10.0052	5.4685	78.2060
6	9.3039	6.1698	72.0362
7	8.5127	6.9610	65.0751
8	7.6200	7.8538	57.2214
9	6.6128	8.8609	48.3605
10	5.4764	9.9973	38.3632
11	4.1944	11.2794	27.0838
12	2.7479	12.7259	14.3579
13	1.1159	14.3579	0.0000

YEARS 14	QTR PAYT 3.7561	AN CONST 15.03
# INT	PRIN	BALANCE
1	12.1199	2.9044	97.0956
2	11.7475	3.2769	93.8187
3	11.3272	3.6971	90.1217

#	INT	PRIN	BALANCE
4	10.8531	4.1712	85.9504
5	10.3182	4.7062	81.2443
6	9.7146	5.3097	75.9346
7	9.0337	5.9906	69.9440
8	8.2655	6.7589	63.1851
9	7.3987	7.6256	55.5595
10	6.4207	8.6036	46.9559
11	5.3174	9.7069	37.2489
12	4.0725	10.9518	26.2972
13	2.6681	12.3563	13.9409
14	1.0834	13.9409	0.0000

YEARS 15	QTR PAYT 3.6618	AN CONST 14.65
# INT	PRIN	BALANCE
1	12.1376	2.5097	97.4903
2	11.8158	2.8315	94.6588
3	11.4526	3.1946	91.4642
4	11.0430	3.6043	87.8599
5	10.5807	4.0665	83.7934
6	10.0592	4.5880	79.2053
7	9.4708	5.1764	74.0289
8	8.8070	5.8403	68.1886
9	8.0580	6.5892	61.5994
10	7.2130	7.4343	54.1651
11	6.2596	8.3877	45.7774
12	5.1839	9.4633	36.3141
13	3.9703	10.6769	25.6372
14	2.6011	12.0462	13.5910
15	1.0563	13.5910	0.0000

YEARS 16	QTR PAYT 3.5821	AN CONST 14.33
# INT	PRIN	BALANCE
1	12.1526	2.1760	97.8240
2	11.8735	2.4550	95.3690
3	11.5587	2.7699	92.5991
4	11.2034	3.1251	89.4740
5	10.8027	3.5259	85.9481
6	10.3505	3.9781	81.9700
7	9.8403	4.4882	77.4818
8	9.2648	5.0638	72.4180
9	8.6154	5.7132	66.7048
10	7.8827	6.4459	60.2590
11	7.0560	7.2725	52.9865
12	6.1234	8.2052	44.7813
13	5.0711	9.2574	35.5239
14	3.8839	10.4446	25.0793
15	2.5445	11.7841	13.2953
16	1.0333	13.2953	0.0000

YEARS 17	QTR PAYT 3.5144	AN CONST 14.06
# INT	PRIN	BALANCE
1	12.1653	1.8922	98.1078
2	11.9226	2.1348	95.9730
3	11.6488	2.4086	93.5644
4	11.3399	2.7175	90.8470
5	10.9914	3.0660	87.7810
6	10.5983	3.4592	84.3218
7	10.1546	3.9028	80.4190
8	9.6541	4.4033	76.0157
9	9.0894	4.9680	71.0478
10	8.4523	5.6051	65.4427
11	7.7335	6.3239	59.1188
12	6.9225	7.1349	51.9839
13	6.0075	8.0499	43.9340
14	4.9752	9.0822	34.8518
15	3.8104	10.2470	24.6048
16	2.4963	11.5611	13.0437
17	1.0137	13.0437	0.0000

YEARS 18	QTR PAYT 3.4564	AN CONST 13.83
# INT	PRIN	BALANCE
1	12.1761	1.6494	98.3506
2	11.9646	1.8610	96.4896
3	11.7260	2.0996	94.3900
4	11.4567	2.3689	92.0212
5	11.1529	2.6727	89.3485
6	10.8102	3.0154	86.3331
7	10.4234	3.4021	82.9310
8	9.9872	3.8384	79.0926
9	9.4949	4.3307	74.7619
10	8.9395	4.8860	69.8759
11	8.3129	5.5126	64.3633
12	7.6060	6.2196	58.1437
13	6.8083	7.0172	51.1265
14	5.9084	7.9171	43.2093
15	4.8931	8.9324	34.2769
16	3.7476	10.0780	24.1989
17	2.4552	11.3704	12.8286
18	.9970	12.8286	0.0000

YEARS 19	QTR PAYT 3.4066	AN CONST 13.63
# INT	PRIN	BALANCE
1	12.1855	1.4409	98.5591
2	12.0007	1.6257	96.9335
3	11.7922	1.8341	95.0993
4	11.5570	2.0694	93.0300
5	11.2916	2.3347	90.6952
6	10.9922	2.6341	88.0611
7	10.6544	2.9720	85.0891
8	10.2733	3.3531	81.7361
9	9.8432	3.7831	77.9530
10	9.3581	4.2683	73.6847
11	8.8107	4.8156	68.8691
12	8.1931	5.4332	63.4359
13	7.4964	6.1300	57.3059
14	6.7102	6.9161	50.3898
15	5.8233	7.8030	42.5867
16	4.8226	8.8037	33.7830
17	3.6936	9.9327	23.8503
18	2.4198	11.2066	12.6437
19	.9826	12.6437	0.0000

YEARS 20	QTR PAYT 3.3636	AN CONST 13.46
# INT	PRIN	BALANCE
1	12.1935	1.2610	98.7390
2	12.0318	1.4227	97.3163
3	11.8494	1.6052	95.7111
4	11.6435	1.8110	93.9001
5	11.4113	2.0433	91.8569
6	11.1492	2.3053	89.5516
7	10.8536	2.6009	86.9507
8	10.5200	2.9345	84.0162
9	10.1437	3.3108	80.7054
10	9.7191	3.7354	76.9700
11	9.2401	4.2144	72.7555
12	8.6996	4.7549	68.0006
13	8.0898	5.3647	62.6359
14	7.4018	6.0527	56.5833
15	6.6256	6.8289	49.7544
16	5.7499	7.7046	42.0497
17	4.7618	8.6927	33.3570
18	3.6470	9.8075	23.5495
19	2.3893	11.0652	12.4843
20	.9702	12.4843	0.0000

YEARS 21	QTR PAYT 3.3265	AN CONST 13.31
# INT	PRIN	BALANCE
1	12.2005	1.1053	98.8947
2	12.0588	1.2471	97.6476
3	11.8988	1.4070	96.2407

#	INT	PRIN	BALANCE
4	11.7184	1.5874	94.6532
5	11.5148	1.7910	92.8623
6	11.2851	2.0207	90.8416
7	11.0260	2.2798	88.5618
8	10.7336	2.5722	85.9896
9	10.4038	2.9020	83.0875
10	10.0316	3.2742	79.8133
11	9.6117	3.6941	76.1192
12	9.1380	4.1679	71.9514
13	8.6035	4.7024	67.2490
14	8.0004	5.3054	61.9436
15	7.3200	5.9858	55.9578
16	6.5524	6.7534	49.2044
17	5.6863	7.6195	41.5850
18	4.7092	8.5966	32.9883
19	3.6067	9.6991	23.2892
20	2.3629	10.9429	12.3463
21	.9595	12.3463	0.0000

YEARS 22 — QTR PAYT 3.2942 — AN CONST 13.18

#	INT	PRIN	BALANCE
1	12.2066	.9702	99.0298
2	12.0821	1.0946	97.9353
3	11.9418	1.2350	96.7003
4	11.7834	1.3933	95.3070
5	11.6047	1.5720	93.7349
6	11.4031	1.7736	91.9613
7	11.1756	2.0011	89.9603
8	10.9190	2.2577	87.7026
9	10.6295	2.5472	85.1553
10	10.3028	2.8739	82.2815
11	9.9343	3.2424	79.0390
12	9.5184	3.6583	75.3807
13	9.0493	4.1274	71.2533
14	8.5200	4.6567	66.5966
15	7.9228	5.2539	61.3427
16	7.2490	5.9277	55.4150
17	6.4888	6.6879	48.7271
18	5.6312	7.5456	41.1815
19	4.6635	8.5132	32.6683
20	3.5717	9.6050	23.0633
21	2.3399	10.8368	12.2265
22	.9502	12.2265	0.0000

YEARS 23 — QTR PAYT 3.2661 — AN CONST 13.07

#	INT	PRIN	BALANCE
1	12.2118	.8526	99.1474
2	12.1025	.9619	98.1855
3	11.9791	1.0853	97.1003
4	11.8400	1.2244	95.8759
5	11.6829	1.3815	94.4944
6	11.5058	1.5586	92.9358
7	11.3059	1.7585	91.1773
8	11.0804	1.9840	89.1933
9	10.8259	2.2384	86.9549
10	10.5389	2.5255	84.4293
11	10.2150	2.8494	81.5800
12	9.8496	3.2148	78.3652
13	9.4373	3.6271	74.7381
14	8.9722	4.0922	70.6458
15	8.4474	4.6170	66.0288
16	7.8552	5.2091	60.8197
17	7.1872	5.8772	54.9425
18	6.4335	6.6309	48.3116
19	5.5831	7.4812	40.8304
20	4.6237	8.4407	32.3898
21	3.5413	9.5231	22.8667
22	2.3200	10.7444	12.1223
23	.9421	12.1223	0.0000

YEARS 24 — QTR PAYT 3.2416 — AN CONST 12.97

#	INT	PRIN	BALANCE
1	12.2164	.7500	99.2500
2	12.1202	.8462	98.4038
3	12.0117	.9547	97.4492
4	11.8893	1.0771	96.3721
5	11.7512	1.2152	95.1568
6	11.5953	1.3711	93.7857
7	11.4195	1.5469	92.2388
8	11.2211	1.7453	90.4935
9	10.9973	1.9691	88.5244
10	10.7447	2.2217	86.3027
11	10.4598	2.5066	83.7961
12	10.1384	2.8280	80.9681
13	9.7757	3.1907	77.7774
14	9.3665	3.5999	74.1775
15	8.9049	4.0615	70.1160
16	8.3840	4.5824	65.5336
17	7.7963	5.1701	60.3635
18	7.1333	5.8331	54.5305
19	6.3853	6.5811	47.9493
20	5.5413	7.4251	40.5242
21	4.5891	8.3773	32.1468
22	3.5147	9.4517	22.6952
23	2.3026	10.6638	12.0314
24	.9350	12.0314	0.0000

YEARS 25 — QTR PAYT 3.2202 — AN CONST 12.89

#	INT	PRIN	BALANCE
1	12.2204	.6603	99.3397
2	12.1357	.7450	98.5946
3	12.0402	.8406	97.7540
4	11.9324	.9484	96.8057
5	11.8108	1.0700	95.7357
6	11.6736	1.2072	94.5284
7	11.5187	1.3620	93.1664
8	11.3441	1.5367	91.6297
9	11.1470	1.7338	89.8959
10	10.9246	1.9561	87.9398
11	10.6738	2.2070	85.7328
12	10.3908	2.4900	83.2428
13	10.0714	2.8093	80.4334
14	9.7112	3.1696	77.2638
15	9.3047	3.5761	73.6877
16	8.8461	4.0347	69.6530
17	8.3286	4.5521	65.1009
18	7.7449	5.1359	59.9649
19	7.0862	5.7946	54.1704
20	6.3431	6.5377	47.6327
21	5.5047	7.3761	40.2566
22	4.5587	8.3220	31.9346
23	3.4915	9.3893	22.5453
24	2.2874	10.5934	11.9519
25	.9289	11.9519	0.0000

YEARS 26 — QTR PAYT 3.2015 — AN CONST 12.81

#	INT	PRIN	BALANCE
1	12.2239	.5819	99.4181
2	12.1493	.6565	98.7616
3	12.0651	.7407	98.0209
4	11.9701	.8357	97.1852
5	11.8630	.9429	96.2424
6	11.7421	1.0638	95.1786
7	11.6056	1.2002	93.9784
8	11.4517	1.3541	92.6243
9	11.2781	1.5278	91.0965
10	11.0821	1.7237	89.3728
11	10.8611	1.9447	87.4281
12	10.6117	2.1941	85.2339
13	10.3303	2.4755	82.7584
14	10.0128	2.7930	79.9654
15	9.6546	3.1512	76.8142
16	9.2505	3.5553	73.2589
17	8.7946	4.0112	69.2477
18	8.2802	4.5257	64.7220
19	7.6998	5.1060	59.6160
20	7.0450	5.7609	53.8552
21	6.3062	6.4996	47.3555
22	5.4726	7.3332	40.0223
23	4.5322	8.2736	31.7487
24	3.4712	9.3346	22.4141
25	2.2741	10.5317	11.8824
26	.9235	11.8824	0.0000

YEARS 27 — QTR PAYT 3.1850 — AN CONST 12.75

#	INT	PRIN	BALANCE
1	12.2270	.5131	99.4869
2	12.1612	.5789	98.9080
3	12.0870	.6531	98.2549
4	12.0032	.7369	97.5180
5	11.9087	.8314	96.6866
6	11.8021	.9380	95.7486
7	11.6818	1.0583	94.6902
8	11.5461	1.1940	93.4962
9	11.3930	1.3472	92.1490
10	11.2202	1.5199	90.6291
11	11.0253	1.7148	88.9143
12	10.8054	1.9348	86.9795
13	10.5572	2.1829	84.7966
14	10.2773	2.4628	82.3338
15	9.9615	2.7787	79.5551
16	9.6051	3.1350	76.4201
17	9.2031	3.5371	72.8831
18	8.7495	3.9907	68.8924
19	8.2377	4.5024	64.3900
20	7.6603	5.0798	59.3101
21	7.0088	5.7313	53.5788
22	6.2738	6.4663	47.1125
23	5.4446	7.2955	39.8170
24	4.5090	8.2312	31.5858
25	3.4534	9.2867	22.2991
26	2.2624	10.4777	11.8214
27	.9187	11.8214	0.0000

YEARS 28 — QTR PAYT 3.1706 — AN CONST 12.69

#	INT	PRIN	BALANCE
1	12.2297	.4527	99.5473
2	12.1717	.5108	99.0365
3	12.1062	.5763	98.4602
4	12.0323	.6502	97.8101
5	11.9489	.7336	97.0765
6	11.8548	.8276	96.2489
7	11.7487	.9338	95.3151
8	11.6289	1.0535	94.2616
9	11.4938	1.1886	93.0729
10	11.3414	1.3411	91.7319
11	11.1694	1.5130	90.2188
12	10.9754	1.7071	88.5117
13	10.7564	1.9260	86.5857
14	10.5094	2.1730	84.4127
15	10.2308	2.4517	81.9610
16	9.9164	2.7661	79.1950
17	9.5616	3.1208	76.0741
18	9.1614	3.5210	72.5531
19	8.7099	3.9726	68.5805
20	8.2004	4.4820	64.0985
21	7.6256	5.0568	59.0416
22	6.9771	5.7053	53.3363
23	6.2454	6.4370	46.8993
24	5.4199	7.2625	39.6367
25	4.4886	8.1939	31.4428
26	3.4377	9.2447	22.1981
27	2.2522	10.4303	11.7679
28	.9146	11.7679	0.0000

YEARS 29 — QTR PAYT 3.1579 — AN CONST 12.64

#	INT	PRIN	BALANCE
1	12.2321	.3997	99.6003
2	12.1808	.4509	99.1494
3	12.1230	.5087	98.6407
4	12.0578	.5740	98.0667
5	11.9842	.6476	97.4192
6	11.9011	.7306	96.6885
7	11.8074	.8243	95.8642
8	11.7017	.9300	94.9342
9	11.5824	1.0493	93.8848
10	11.4479	1.1839	92.7010
11	11.2961	1.3357	91.3653
12	11.1248	1.5070	89.8583
13	10.9315	1.7003	88.1580
14	10.7134	1.9183	86.2397
15	10.4674	2.1643	84.0754
16	10.1899	2.4419	81.6335
17	9.8767	2.7550	78.8785
18	9.5234	3.1083	75.7701
19	9.1248	3.5070	72.2631
20	8.6750	3.9567	68.3064
21	8.1676	4.4641	63.8423
22	7.5951	5.0366	58.8057
23	6.9492	5.6825	53.1231
24	6.2205	6.4113	46.7118
25	5.3983	7.2335	39.4783
26	4.4706	8.1611	31.3172
27	3.4240	9.2078	22.1094
28	2.2432	10.3886	11.7208
29	.9109	11.7208	0.0000

YEARS 30 — QTR PAYT 3.1468 — AN CONST 12.59

#	INT	PRIN	BALANCE
1	12.2342	.3530	99.6470
2	12.1889	.3982	99.2488
3	12.1379	.4493	98.7995
4	12.0802	.5069	98.2925
5	12.0152	.5719	97.7206
6	11.9419	.6453	97.0753
7	11.8591	.7281	96.3472
8	11.7658	.8214	95.5258
9	11.6604	.9268	94.5991
10	11.5416	1.0456	93.5535
11	11.4075	1.1797	92.3737
12	11.2562	1.3310	91.0428
13	11.0855	1.5017	89.5411
14	10.8929	1.6943	87.8468
15	10.6756	1.9115	85.9353
16	10.4305	2.1567	83.7786
17	10.1539	2.4333	81.3453
18	9.8419	2.7453	78.6000
19	9.4898	3.0974	75.5027
20	9.0926	3.4946	72.0081
21	8.6444	3.9427	68.0653
22	8.1388	4.4484	63.6169
23	7.5683	5.0189	58.5981
24	6.9247	5.6625	52.9356
25	6.1985	6.3887	46.5469
26	5.3792	7.2080	39.3390
27	4.4548	8.1323	31.2066
28	3.4119	9.1753	22.0314
29	2.2353	10.3519	11.6795
30	.9077	11.6795	0.0000

QUARTERLY PAYMENT AMORTIZATION SCHEDULE PER $100

12.50 %

YEARS 2 — QTR PAYT 14.3209 — AN CONST 57.29

#	INT	PRIN	BALANCE
1	10.3567	46.9267	53.0733
2	4.2101	53.0733	0.0000

YEARS 3 — QTR PAYT 10.1213 — AN CONST 40.49

#	INT	PRIN	BALANCE
1	11.1606	29.3246	70.6754
2	7.3196	33.1656	37.5097
3	2.9755	37.5097	0.0000

YEARS 4 — QTR PAYT 8.0374 — AN CONST 32.15

#	INT	PRIN	BALANCE
1	11.5596	20.5898	79.4102
2	8.8627	23.2867	56.1234
3	5.8125	26.3369	29.7866
4	2.3629	29.7866	0.0000

YEARS 5 — QTR PAYT 6.7995 — AN CONST 27.20

#	INT	PRIN	BALANCE
1	11.7966	15.4014	84.5986
2	9.7793	17.4187	67.1799
3	7.4977	19.7003	47.4796
4	4.9173	22.2806	25.1990
5	1.9990	25.1990	0.0000

YEARS 6 — QTR PAYT 5.9845 — AN CONST 23.94

#	INT	PRIN	BALANCE
1	11.9526	11.9856	88.0144
2	10.3827	13.5555	74.4590
3	8.6072	15.3310	59.1280
4	6.5991	17.3391	41.7889
5	4.3280	19.6102	22.1788
6	1.7594	22.1788	0.0000

YEARS 7 — QTR PAYT 5.4111 — AN CONST 21.65

#	INT	PRIN	BALANCE
1	12.0624	9.5820	90.4180
2	10.8073	10.8371	79.5809
3	9.3878	12.2566	67.3243
4	7.7824	13.8620	53.4624
5	5.9667	15.6776	37.7847
6	3.9133	17.7311	20.0536
7	1.5908	20.0536	0.0000

YEARS 8 — QTR PAYT 4.9885 — AN CONST 19.96

#	INT	PRIN	BALANCE
1	12.1433	7.8106	92.1894
2	11.1202	8.8336	83.3558
3	9.9632	9.9907	73.3652
4	8.6546	11.2993	62.0659
5	7.1746	12.7793	49.2866
6	5.5007	14.4531	34.8335
7	3.6076	16.3462	18.4873
8	1.4665	18.4873	0.0000

YEARS 9 — QTR PAYT 4.6662 — AN CONST 18.67

#	INT	PRIN	BALANCE
1	12.2050	6.4599	93.5401
2	11.3588	7.3060	86.2341
3	10.4019	8.2630	77.9711
4	9.3196	9.3453	68.6259
5	8.0955	10.5693	58.0565
6	6.7111	11.9537	46.1028
7	5.1454	13.5195	32.5833
8	3.3746	15.2903	17.2930
9	1.3718	17.2930	0.0000

YEARS 10 — QTR PAYT 4.4141 — AN CONST 17.66

#	INT	PRIN	BALANCE
1	12.2532	5.4031	94.5969
2	11.5455	6.1108	88.4860
3	10.7451	6.9113	81.5748
4	9.8398	7.8165	73.7583
5	8.8160	8.8403	64.9179
6	7.6581	9.9983	54.9197
7	6.3485	11.3079	43.6118
8	4.8674	12.7890	30.8228
9	3.1922	14.4641	16.3587
10	1.2977	16.3587	0.0000

YEARS 11 — QTR PAYT 4.2128 — AN CONST 16.86

#	INT	PRIN	BALANCE
1	12.2918	4.5596	95.4404
2	11.6945	5.1568	90.2837
3	11.0191	5.8322	84.4515
4	10.2552	6.5961	77.8553
5	9.3912	7.4601	70.3952
6	8.4140	8.4373	61.9580
7	7.3089	9.5424	52.4156
8	6.0590	10.7923	41.6233
9	4.6454	12.2059	29.4174
10	3.0467	13.8046	15.6128
11	1.2385	15.6128	0.0000

YEARS 12 — QTR PAYT 4.0496 — AN CONST 16.20

#	INT	PRIN	BALANCE
1	12.3230	3.8753	96.1247
2	11.8154	4.3829	91.7419
3	11.2413	4.9569	86.7849
4	10.5921	5.6062	81.1787
5	9.8578	6.3405	74.8382
6	9.0273	7.1710	67.6672
7	8.0880	8.1103	59.5569
8	7.0257	9.1726	50.3843
9	5.8242	10.3740	40.0103
10	4.4654	11.7329	28.2774
11	2.9286	13.2697	15.0078
12	1.1905	15.0078	0.0000

YEARS 13 — QTR PAYT 3.9154 — AN CONST 15.67

#	INT	PRIN	BALANCE
1	12.3487	3.3129	96.6871
2	11.9147	3.7469	92.9402
3	11.4240	4.2377	88.7025
4	10.8689	4.7927	83.9098
5	10.2412	5.4205	78.4893
6	9.5312	6.1305	72.3589
7	8.7282	6.9334	65.4254
8	7.8200	7.8416	57.5838
9	6.7929	8.8687	48.7151
10	5.6313	10.0304	38.6848
11	4.3175	11.3442	27.3406
12	2.8316	12.8300	14.5106
13	1.1511	14.5106	0.0000

YEARS 14 — QTR PAYT 3.8040 — AN CONST 15.22

#	INT	PRIN	BALANCE
1	12.3700	2.8459	97.1541
2	11.9973	3.2187	93.9354
3	11.5757	3.6402	90.2952
4	11.0989	4.1171	86.1781
5	10.5596	4.6563	81.5218
6	9.9497	5.2662	76.2556
7	9.2599	5.9560	70.2996
8	8.4798	6.7361	63.5635
9	7.5975	7.6184	55.9451
10	6.5996	8.6163	47.3287
11	5.4710	9.7449	37.5838
12	4.1946	11.0213	26.5625
13	2.7510	12.4649	14.0976
14	1.1183	14.0976	0.0000

YEARS 15 — QTR PAYT 3.7106 — AN CONST 14.85

#	INT	PRIN	BALANCE
1	12.3879	2.4545	97.5455
2	12.0664	2.7760	94.7694
3	11.7028	3.1397	91.6298
4	11.2915	3.5509	88.0789
5	10.8264	4.0160	84.0629
6	10.3004	4.5420	79.5208
7	9.7055	5.1370	74.3839
8	9.0326	5.8098	68.5741
9	8.2717	6.5708	62.0033
10	7.4110	7.4314	54.5719
11	6.4376	8.4048	46.1670
12	5.3367	9.5057	36.6613
13	4.0916	10.7508	25.9105
14	2.6835	12.1590	13.7516
15	1.0909	13.7516	0.0000

YEARS 16 — QTR PAYT 3.6318 — AN CONST 14.53

#	INT	PRIN	BALANCE
1	12.4030	2.1242	97.8758
2	12.1248	2.4024	95.4734
3	11.8101	2.7171	92.7563
4	11.4542	3.0730	89.6834
5	11.0517	3.4755	86.2079
6	10.5965	3.9307	82.2772
7	10.0816	4.4455	77.8317
8	9.4993	5.0278	72.8038
9	8.8408	5.6864	67.1175
10	8.0959	6.4312	60.6862
11	7.2536	7.2736	53.4127
12	6.3009	8.2263	45.1864
13	5.2234	9.3038	35.8826
14	4.0047	10.5224	25.3601
15	2.6265	11.9007	13.4595
16	1.0677	13.4595	0.0000

YEARS 17 — QTR PAYT 3.5648 — AN CONST 14.26

#	INT	PRIN	BALANCE
1	12.4158	1.8435	98.1565
2	12.1743	2.0850	96.0714
3	11.9012	2.3581	93.7133
4	11.5924	2.6670	91.0463
5	11.2430	3.0163	88.0300
6	10.8479	3.4114	84.6186
7	10.4011	3.8582	80.7604
8	9.8958	4.3636	76.3968
9	9.3242	4.9351	71.4617
10	8.6778	5.5816	65.8801
11	7.9467	6.3126	59.5675
12	7.1198	7.1395	52.4280
13	6.1847	8.0746	44.3533
14	5.1271	9.1323	35.2211
15	3.9309	10.3284	24.8926
16	2.5781	11.6813	13.2113
17	1.0480	13.2113	0.0000

YEARS 18 — QTR PAYT 3.5077 — AN CONST 14.04

#	INT	PRIN	BALANCE
1	12.4267	1.6039	98.3961
2	12.2167	1.8140	96.5821
3	11.9791	2.0516	94.5306
4	11.7103	2.3203	92.2103
5	11.4064	2.6242	89.5861
6	11.0627	2.9679	86.6181
7	10.6740	3.3567	83.2614
8	10.2343	3.7963	79.4651
9	9.7370	4.2936	75.1715
10	9.1746	4.8560	70.3155
11	8.5386	5.4920	64.8235
12	7.8192	6.2114	58.6121
13	7.0057	7.0250	51.5871
14	6.0855	7.9451	43.6420
15	5.0448	8.9858	34.6562
16	3.8679	10.1628	24.4934
17	2.5367	11.4939	12.9994
18	1.0312	12.9994	0.0000

YEARS 19 — QTR PAYT 3.4586 — AN CONST 13.84

#	INT	PRIN	BALANCE
1	12.4361	1.3983	98.6017
2	12.2530	1.5815	97.0202
3	12.0458	1.7886	95.2316
4	11.8116	2.0229	93.2087
5	11.5466	2.2878	90.9209
6	11.2469	2.5875	88.3334
7	10.9080	2.9264	85.4069
8	10.5247	3.3097	82.0972
9	10.0912	3.7433	78.3539
10	9.6009	4.2336	74.1204
11	9.0464	4.7881	69.3323
12	8.4192	5.4152	63.9170
13	7.7099	6.1245	57.7925
14	6.9077	6.9268	50.8657
15	6.0004	7.8340	43.0317
16	4.9743	8.8602	34.1716
17	3.8138	10.0207	24.1509
18	2.5012	11.3332	12.8177
19	1.0168	12.8177	0.0000

YEARS 20 — QTR PAYT 3.4164 — AN CONST 13.67

#	INT	PRIN	BALANCE
1	12.4442	1.2213	98.7787
2	12.2843	1.3812	97.3975
3	12.1033	1.5622	95.8353
4	11.8987	1.7668	94.0686
5	11.6673	1.9982	92.0704
6	11.4056	2.2599	89.8105
7	11.1096	2.5559	87.2546
8	10.7748	2.8907	84.3639
9	10.3962	3.2693	81.0946
10	9.9679	3.6975	77.3970
11	9.4836	4.1819	73.2152
12	8.9359	4.7296	68.4855
13	8.3164	5.3491	63.1364
14	7.6157	6.0497	57.0867
15	6.8233	6.8422	50.2445
16	5.9271	7.7384	42.5062
17	4.9135	8.7519	33.7542
18	3.7672	9.8983	23.8559
19	2.4707	11.1948	12.6611
20	1.0044	12.6611	0.0000

YEARS 21 — QTR PAYT 3.3799 — AN CONST 13.52

#	INT	PRIN	BALANCE
1	12.4512	1.0683	98.9317
2	12.3113	1.2082	97.7235
3	12.1530	1.3665	96.3570

#	INT	PRIN	BALANCE
4	11.9740	1.5455	94.8115
5	11.7716	1.7479	93.0637
6	11.5427	1.9768	91.0868
7	11.2837	2.2358	88.8511
8	10.9909	2.5286	86.3224
9	10.6597	2.8598	83.4626
10	10.2851	3.2344	80.2282
11	9.8615	3.6580	76.5702
12	9.3823	4.1372	72.4330
13	8.8404	4.6791	67.7539
14	8.2275	5.2920	62.4620
15	7.5344	5.9851	56.4768
16	6.7504	6.7691	49.7078
17	5.8638	7.6557	42.0521
18	4.8611	8.6585	33.3936
19	3.7269	9.7926	23.6011
20	2.4443	11.0752	12.5259
21	.9936	12.5259	0.0000

YEARS 22 — QTR PAYT 3.3482 — AN CONST 13.40

#	INT	PRIN	BALANCE
1	12.4573	.9357	99.0643
2	12.3347	1.0583	98.0060
3	12.1961	1.1969	96.8091
4	12.0393	1.3537	95.4554
5	11.8620	1.5310	93.9244
6	11.6615	1.7315	92.1928
7	11.4347	1.9583	90.2345
8	11.1782	2.2148	88.0196
9	10.8880	2.5049	85.5147
10	10.5599	2.8331	82.6816
11	10.1889	3.2041	79.4775
12	9.7692	3.6238	75.8537
13	9.2945	4.0985	71.7552
14	8.7577	4.6353	67.1199
15	8.1506	5.2424	61.8775
16	7.4639	5.9291	55.9484
17	6.6873	6.7057	49.2426
18	5.8089	7.5841	41.6586
19	4.8156	8.5774	33.0812
20	3.6921	9.7009	23.3802
21	2.4214	10.9716	12.4087
22	.9843	12.4087	0.0000

YEARS 23 — QTR PAYT 3.3208 — AN CONST 13.29

#	INT	PRIN	BALANCE
1	12.4625	.8206	99.1794
2	12.3550	.9281	98.2514
3	12.2335	1.0496	97.2018
4	12.0960	1.1871	96.0147
5	11.9405	1.3426	94.6721
6	11.7647	1.5184	93.1536
7	11.5658	1.7173	91.4363
8	11.3408	1.9423	89.4940
9	11.0864	2.1967	87.2974
10	10.7987	2.4844	84.8130
11	10.4733	2.8098	82.0032
12	10.1053	3.1778	78.8253
13	9.6890	3.5941	75.2313
14	9.2183	4.0648	71.1664
15	8.6858	4.5973	66.5692
16	8.0837	5.1994	61.3697
17	7.4026	5.8805	55.4893
18	6.6324	6.6507	48.8386
19	5.7613	7.5218	41.3167
20	4.7760	8.5070	32.8097
21	3.6618	9.6213	23.1884
22	2.4016	10.8815	12.3068
23	.9763	12.3068	0.0000

YEARS 24 — QTR PAYT 3.2969 — AN CONST 13.19

#	INT	PRIN	BALANCE
1	12.4671	.7203	99.2797
2	12.3728	.8147	98.4650
3	12.2660	.9214	97.5437
4	12.1454	1.0421	96.5016
5	12.0089	1.1785	95.3231
6	11.8545	1.3329	93.9901
7	11.6799	1.5075	92.4826
8	11.4825	1.7050	90.7777
9	11.2591	1.9283	88.8494
10	11.0066	2.1808	86.6686
11	10.7209	2.4665	84.2021
12	10.3978	2.7896	81.4125
13	10.0325	3.1549	78.2576
14	9.6192	3.5682	74.6894
15	9.1519	4.0356	70.6538
16	8.6233	4.5642	66.0896
17	8.0254	5.1620	60.9277
18	7.3493	5.8381	55.0896
19	6.5846	6.6028	48.4868
20	5.7198	7.4676	41.0191
21	4.7416	8.4458	32.5734
22	3.6354	9.5520	23.0214
23	2.3843	10.8032	12.2182
24	.9692	12.2182	0.0000

YEARS 25 — QTR PAYT 3.2760 — AN CONST 13.11

#	INT	PRIN	BALANCE
1	12.4711	.6329	99.3671
2	12.3882	.7158	98.6514
3	12.2944	.8095	97.8419
4	12.1884	.9155	96.9263
5	12.0685	1.0355	95.8909
6	11.9329	1.1711	94.7198
7	11.7795	1.3245	93.3953
8	11.6060	1.4980	91.8974
9	11.4098	1.6942	90.2032
10	11.1879	1.9161	88.2871
11	10.9369	2.1670	86.1201
12	10.6531	2.4509	83.6692
13	10.3320	2.7719	80.8973
14	9.9690	3.1350	77.7623
15	9.5583	3.5456	74.2167
16	9.0939	4.0100	70.2067
17	8.5687	4.5353	65.6714
18	7.9747	5.1293	60.5421
19	7.3028	5.8012	54.7409
20	6.5430	6.5610	48.1799
21	5.6836	7.4204	40.7595
22	4.7116	8.3923	32.3672
23	3.6124	9.4916	22.8757
24	2.3692	10.7348	12.1409
25	.9631	12.1409	0.0000

YEARS 26 — QTR PAYT 3.2578 — AN CONST 13.04

#	INT	PRIN	BALANCE
1	12.4746	.5565	99.4435
2	12.4017	.6293	98.8142
3	12.3193	.7118	98.1024
4	12.2260	.8050	97.2974
5	12.1206	.9104	96.3870
6	12.0013	1.0297	95.3573
7	11.8665	1.1646	94.1927
8	11.7139	1.3171	92.8756
9	11.5414	1.4896	91.3860
10	11.3463	1.6847	89.7012
11	11.1256	1.9054	87.7958
12	10.8761	2.1550	85.6409
13	10.5938	2.4373	83.2036
14	10.2746	2.7565	80.4471
15	9.9135	3.1175	77.3296
16	9.5052	3.5259	73.8037
17	9.0433	3.9877	69.8160
18	8.5210	4.5100	65.3060
19	7.9303	5.1008	60.2052
20	7.2622	5.7689	54.4363
21	6.5065	6.5245	47.9118
22	5.6520	7.3791	40.5327
23	4.6854	8.3456	32.1871
24	3.5923	9.4387	22.7484
25	2.3560	10.6751	12.0733
26	.9577	12.0733	0.0000

YEARS 27 — QTR PAYT 3.2418 — AN CONST 12.97

#	INT	PRIN	BALANCE
1	12.4776	.4896	99.5104
2	12.4135	.5537	98.9567
3	12.3410	.6263	98.3304
4	12.2590	.7083	97.6221
5	12.1662	.8011	96.8211
6	12.0613	.9060	95.9151
7	11.9426	1.0247	94.8904
8	11.8084	1.1589	93.7315
9	11.6566	1.3107	92.4209
10	11.4849	1.4823	90.9386
11	11.2907	1.6765	89.2621
12	11.0712	1.8961	87.3660
13	10.8228	2.1444	85.2216
14	10.5419	2.4253	82.7962
15	10.2242	2.7430	80.0532
16	9.8650	3.1023	76.9510
17	9.4586	3.5086	73.4424
18	8.9991	3.9682	69.4742
19	8.4793	4.4879	64.9862
20	7.8914	5.0758	59.9104
21	7.2266	5.7406	54.1698
22	6.4747	6.4926	47.6772
23	5.6243	7.3430	40.3343
24	4.6625	8.3048	32.0295
25	3.5747	9.3925	22.6370
26	2.3444	10.6228	12.0142
27	.9530	12.0142	0.0000

YEARS 28 — QTR PAYT 3.2278 — AN CONST 12.92

#	INT	PRIN	BALANCE
1	12.4803	.4310	99.5690
2	12.4239	.4875	99.0815
3	12.3600	.5513	98.5301
4	12.2878	.6236	97.9066
5	12.2061	.7052	97.2013
6	12.1137	.7976	96.4037
7	12.0093	.9021	95.5016
8	11.8911	1.0202	94.4814
9	11.7575	1.1539	93.3275
10	11.6063	1.3050	92.0225
11	11.4354	1.4759	90.5466
12	11.2421	1.6693	88.8773
13	11.0234	1.8879	86.9894
14	10.7762	2.1352	84.8542
15	10.4965	2.4149	82.4394
16	10.1802	2.7312	79.7082
17	9.8224	3.0889	76.6193
18	9.4179	3.4935	73.1258
19	8.9603	3.9511	69.1747
20	8.4427	4.4686	64.7061
21	7.8574	5.0539	59.6522
22	7.1955	5.7159	53.9363
23	6.4468	6.4646	47.4717
24	5.6000	7.3113	40.1604
25	4.6424	8.2690	31.8915
26	3.5593	9.3521	22.5394
27	2.3343	10.5770	11.9624
28	.9489	11.9624	0.0000

YEARS 29 — QTR PAYT 3.2156 — AN CONST 12.87

#	INT	PRIN	BALANCE
1	12.4827	.3797	99.6203
2	12.4329	.4294	99.1909
3	12.3767	.4856	98.7053
4	12.3131	.5493	98.1560
5	12.2411	.6212	97.5349
6	12.1598	.7026	96.8323
7	12.0677	.7946	96.0377
8	11.9637	.8987	95.1391
9	11.8460	1.0164	94.1227
10	11.7128	1.1495	92.9732
11	11.5623	1.3001	91.6731
12	11.3920	1.4703	90.2028
13	11.1994	1.6629	88.5399
14	10.9816	1.8807	86.6591
15	10.7352	2.1271	84.5321
16	10.4566	2.4057	82.1264
17	10.1415	2.7208	79.4056
18	9.7852	3.0772	76.3284
19	9.3821	3.4802	72.8482
20	8.9262	3.9361	68.9121
21	8.4107	4.4516	64.4604
22	7.8276	5.0347	59.4257
23	7.1681	5.6942	53.7315
24	6.4223	6.4400	47.2915
25	5.5788	7.2836	40.0080
26	4.6248	8.2376	31.7704
27	3.5458	9.3165	22.4538
28	2.3255	10.5368	11.9170
29	.9453	11.9170	0.0000

YEARS 30 — QTR PAYT 3.2048 — AN CONST 12.82

#	INT	PRIN	BALANCE
1	12.4847	.3346	99.6654
2	12.4409	.3784	99.2870
3	12.3913	.4280	98.8591
4	12.3353	.4840	98.3751
5	12.2719	.5474	97.8276
6	12.2002	.6191	97.2085
7	12.1191	.7002	96.5083
8	12.0274	.7919	95.7164
9	11.9236	.8957	94.8207
10	11.8063	1.0130	93.8078
11	11.6736	1.1456	92.6621
12	11.5236	1.2957	91.3664
13	11.3539	1.4654	89.9010
14	11.1619	1.6574	88.2437
15	10.9448	1.8744	86.3692
16	10.6993	2.1200	84.2492
17	10.4216	2.3976	81.8516
18	10.1076	2.7117	79.1399
19	9.7524	3.0669	76.0730
20	9.3507	3.4686	72.6044
21	8.8964	3.9229	68.6815
22	8.3825	4.4367	64.2448
23	7.8014	5.0179	59.2269
24	7.1442	5.6751	53.5518
25	6.4008	6.4185	47.1333
26	5.5601	7.2592	39.8741
27	4.6093	8.2100	31.6641
28	3.5339	9.2854	22.3787
29	2.3177	10.5016	11.8771
30	.9422	11.8771	0.0000

YEARS 2 — QTR PAYT 14.3585 — AN CONST 57.44

#	INT	PRIN	BALANCE
1	10.5678	46.8664	53.1336
2	4.3005	53.1336	0.0000

YEARS 3 — QTR PAYT 10.1590 — AN CONST 40.64

#	INT	PRIN	BALANCE
1	11.3881	29.2478	70.7522
2	7.4769	33.1590	37.5932
3	3.0427	37.5932	0.0000

YEARS 4 — QTR PAYT 8.0756 — AN CONST 32.31

#	INT	PRIN	BALANCE
1	11.7951	20.5074	79.4926
2	9.0527	23.2498	56.2428
3	5.9436	26.3589	29.8838
4	2.4187	29.8838	0.0000

YEARS 5 — QTR PAYT 6.8386 — AN CONST 27.36

#	INT	PRIN	BALANCE
1	12.0368	15.3178	84.6822
2	9.9884	17.3661	67.3161
3	7.6661	19.6858	47.6276
4	5.0332	22.3213	25.3063
5	2.0482	25.3063	0.0000

YEARS 6 — QTR PAYT 6.0246 — AN CONST 24.10

#	INT	PRIN	BALANCE
1	12.1958	11.9028	88.0972
2	10.6041	13.4945	74.6027
3	8.7995	15.2991	59.3036
4	6.7536	17.3450	41.9586
5	4.4341	19.6645	22.2941
6	1.8044	22.2941	0.0000

YEARS 7 — QTR PAYT 5.4522 — AN CONST 21.81

#	INT	PRIN	BALANCE
1	12.3076	9.5013	90.4987
2	11.0370	10.7719	79.7268
3	9.5965	12.2124	67.5145
4	7.9634	13.8455	53.6690
5	6.1119	15.6970	37.9720
6	4.0128	17.7961	20.1759
7	1.6330	20.1759	0.0000

YEARS 8 — QTR PAYT 5.0306 — AN CONST 20.13

#	INT	PRIN	BALANCE
1	12.3900	7.7326	92.2674
2	11.3559	8.7666	83.5008
3	10.1836	9.9389	73.5619
4	8.8545	11.2680	62.2939
5	7.3476	12.7749	49.5190
6	5.6393	14.4832	35.0358
7	3.7025	16.4200	18.6158
8	1.5067	18.6158	0.0000

YEARS 9 — QTR PAYT 4.7094 — AN CONST 18.84

#	INT	PRIN	BALANCE
1	12.4527	6.3850	93.6150
2	11.5989	7.2388	86.3762
3	10.6308	8.2069	78.1693
4	9.5334	9.3043	68.8650
5	8.2891	10.5486	58.3164
6	6.8785	11.9592	46.3572
7	5.2792	13.5585	32.7988
8	3.4661	15.3716	17.4272
9	1.4105	17.4272	0.0000

YEARS 10 — QTR PAYT 4.4583 — AN CONST 17.84

#	INT	PRIN	BALANCE
1	12.5017	5.3316	94.6684
2	11.7888	6.0446	88.6238
3	10.9805	6.8529	81.7710
4	10.0640	7.7693	74.0017
5	9.0251	8.8083	65.1934
6	7.8472	9.9862	55.2072
7	6.5118	11.3216	43.8856
8	4.9978	12.8356	31.0501
9	3.2813	14.5520	16.4980
10	1.3353	16.4980	0.0000

YEARS 11 — QTR PAYT 4.2581 — AN CONST 17.04

#	INT	PRIN	BALANCE
1	12.5409	4.4915	95.5085
2	11.9402	5.0921	90.4164
3	11.2593	5.7731	84.6433
4	10.4873	6.5451	78.0982
5	9.6120	7.4203	70.6779
6	8.6197	8.4126	62.2652
7	7.4947	9.5376	52.7276
8	6.2193	10.8131	41.9145
9	4.7733	12.2591	29.6555
10	3.1339	13.8984	15.7570
11	1.2753	15.7570	0.0000

YEARS 12 — QTR PAYT 4.0958 — AN CONST 16.39

#	INT	PRIN	BALANCE
1	12.5726	3.8107	96.1893
2	12.0630	4.3203	91.8689
3	11.4852	4.8981	86.9709
4	10.8302	5.5531	81.4178
5	10.0876	6.2957	75.1221
6	9.2457	7.1376	67.9845
7	8.2912	8.0921	59.8925
8	7.2091	9.1742	50.7183
9	5.9823	10.4010	40.3173
10	4.5914	11.7919	28.5254
11	3.0145	13.3688	15.1566
12	1.2267	15.1566	0.0000

YEARS 13 — QTR PAYT 3.9626 — AN CONST 15.86

#	INT	PRIN	BALANCE
1	12.5986	3.2519	96.7481
2	12.1637	3.6868	93.0612
3	11.6707	4.1798	88.8814
4	11.1117	4.7388	84.1426
5	10.4780	5.3725	78.7701
6	9.7596	6.0909	72.6792
7	8.9451	6.9055	65.7737
8	8.0216	7.8289	57.9448
9	6.9747	8.8758	49.0690
10	5.7877	10.0628	39.0062
11	4.4421	11.4084	27.5977
12	2.9165	12.9341	14.6637
13	1.1868	14.6637	0.0000

YEARS 14 — QTR PAYT 3.8521 — AN CONST 15.41

#	INT	PRIN	BALANCE
1	12.6202	2.7884	97.2116
2	12.2473	3.1613	94.0504
3	11.8245	3.5840	90.4663
4	11.3453	4.0633	86.4031
5	10.8019	4.6067	81.7964
6	10.1859	5.2227	76.5737
7	9.4874	5.9211	70.6526
8	8.6956	6.7129	63.9397
9	7.7979	7.6106	56.3291
10	6.7802	8.6284	47.7007
11	5.6264	9.7822	37.9185
12	4.3182	11.0903	26.8282
13	2.8351	12.5734	14.2548
14	1.1537	14.2548	0.0000

YEARS 15 — QTR PAYT 3.7597 — AN CONST 15.04

#	INT	PRIN	BALANCE
1	12.6382	2.4004	97.5996
2	12.3172	2.7214	94.8781
3	11.9533	3.0854	91.7927
4	11.5407	3.4980	88.2947
5	11.0729	3.9658	84.3290
6	10.5426	4.4961	79.8329
7	9.9414	5.0973	74.7356
8	9.2597	5.7790	68.9566
9	8.4869	6.5518	62.4048
10	7.6108	7.4279	54.9769
11	6.6174	8.4212	46.5557
12	5.4913	9.5474	37.0083
13	4.2146	10.8241	26.1842
14	2.7671	12.2716	13.9126
15	1.1261	13.9126	0.0000

YEARS 16 — QTR PAYT 3.6817 — AN CONST 14.73

#	INT	PRIN	BALANCE
1	12.6535	2.0734	97.9266
2	12.3762	2.3507	95.5759
3	12.0618	2.6650	92.9109
4	11.7055	3.0214	89.8895
5	11.3014	3.4255	86.4640
6	10.8433	3.8835	82.5805
7	10.3240	4.4029	78.1777
8	9.7352	4.9916	73.1860
9	9.0677	5.6591	67.5269
10	8.3109	6.4159	61.1109
11	7.4530	7.2739	53.8370
12	6.4802	8.2466	45.5904
13	5.3774	9.3494	36.2410
14	4.1272	10.5997	25.6413
15	2.7097	12.0171	13.6242
16	1.1027	13.6242	0.0000

YEARS 17 — QTR PAYT 3.6156 — AN CONST 14.47

#	INT	PRIN	BALANCE
1	12.6664	1.7960	98.2040
2	12.4262	2.0362	96.1678
3	12.1539	2.3085	93.8594
4	11.8452	2.6172	91.2422
5	11.4952	2.9671	88.2751
6	11.0984	3.3639	84.9111
7	10.6486	3.8138	81.0974
8	10.1386	4.3238	76.7736
9	9.5604	4.9020	71.8716
10	8.9049	5.5575	66.3141
11	8.1617	6.3007	60.0134
12	7.3191	7.1433	52.8701
13	6.3639	8.0985	44.7716
14	5.2809	9.1815	35.5901
15	4.0531	10.4093	25.1808
16	2.6610	11.8013	13.3795
17	1.0829	13.3795	0.0000

YEARS 18 — QTR PAYT 3.5592 — AN CONST 14.24

#	INT	PRIN	BALANCE
1	12.6774	1.5594	98.4406
2	12.4688	1.7680	96.6726
3	12.2324	2.0044	94.6682
4	11.9644	2.2725	92.3957
5	11.6605	2.5763	89.8193
6	11.3160	2.9209	86.8985
7	10.9254	3.3115	83.5870
8	10.4825	3.7543	79.8327
9	9.9805	4.2564	75.5763
10	9.4113	4.8255	70.7508
11	8.7660	5.4708	65.2800
12	8.0344	6.2024	59.0775
13	7.2050	7.0319	52.0456
14	6.2646	7.9722	44.0734
15	5.1985	9.0383	35.0351
16	3.9898	10.2470	24.7881
17	2.6196	11.6173	13.1708
18	1.0660	13.1708	0.0000

YEARS 19 — QTR PAYT 3.5109 — AN CONST 14.05

#	INT	PRIN	BALANCE
1	12.6868	1.3568	98.6432
2	12.5054	1.5383	97.1049
3	12.2997	1.7440	95.3609
4	12.0664	1.9772	93.3837
5	11.8020	2.2416	91.1420
6	11.5023	2.5414	88.6006
7	11.1624	2.8812	85.7194
8	10.7771	3.2665	82.4529
9	10.3403	3.7034	78.7495
10	9.8451	4.1986	74.5509
11	9.2836	4.7601	69.7908
12	8.6470	5.3966	64.3942
13	7.9254	6.1183	58.2759
14	7.1072	6.9365	51.3395
15	6.1796	7.8641	43.4754
16	5.1280	8.9157	34.5597
17	3.9357	10.1080	24.4518
18	2.5840	11.4597	12.9921
19	1.0515	12.9921	0.0000

YEARS 20 — QTR PAYT 3.4694 — AN CONST 13.88

#	INT	PRIN	BALANCE
1	12.6949	1.1826	98.8174
2	12.5368	1.3408	97.4766
3	12.3575	1.5201	95.9565
4	12.1542	1.7234	94.2331
5	11.9237	1.9538	92.2793
6	11.6625	2.2151	90.0641
7	11.3662	2.5113	87.5528
8	11.0304	2.8472	84.7056
9	10.6497	3.2279	81.4777
10	10.2180	3.6596	77.8182
11	9.7286	4.1489	73.6692
12	9.1738	4.7038	68.9655
13	8.5448	5.3328	63.6327
14	7.8316	6.0459	57.5867
15	7.0231	6.8544	50.7323
16	6.1065	7.7710	42.9613
17	5.0673	8.8102	34.1510
18	3.8892	9.9884	24.1626
19	2.5534	11.3241	12.8385
20	1.0391	12.8385	0.0000

YEARS 21 — QTR PAYT 3.4336 — AN CONST 13.74

#	INT	PRIN	BALANCE
1	12.7019	1.0324	98.9676
2	12.5639	1.1704	97.7972
3	12.4074	1.3270	96.4702

#	INT	PRIN	BALANCE
4	12.2299	1.5044	94.9658
5	12.0287	1.7056	93.2602
6	11.8006	1.9337	91.3266
7	11.5421	2.1922	89.1343
8	11.2489	2.4854	86.6489
9	10.9165	2.8178	83.8312
10	10.5397	3.1946	80.6366
11	10.1125	3.6218	77.0148
12	9.6282	4.1061	72.9087
13	9.0791	4.6552	68.2535
14	8.4566	5.2777	62.9757
15	7.7508	5.9835	56.9922
16	6.9506	6.7837	50.2086
17	6.0435	7.6908	42.5177
18	5.0150	8.7193	33.7984
19	3.8490	9.8853	23.9131
20	2.5271	11.2072	12.7059
21	1.0284	12.7059	0.0000

YEARS 22	QTR PAYT 3.4026	AN CONST 13.62	
# INT	PRIN	BALANCE	
1	12.7080	.9024	99.0976
2	12.5873	1.0231	98.0745
3	12.4505	1.1599	96.9147
4	12.2954	1.3150	95.5997
5	12.1195	1.4908	94.1089
6	11.9202	1.6902	92.4187
7	11.6942	1.9162	90.5025
8	11.4379	2.1725	88.3300
9	11.1474	2.4630	85.8670
10	10.8180	2.7923	83.0747
11	10.4446	3.1658	79.9089
12	10.0213	3.5891	76.3198
13	9.5413	4.0691	72.2508
14	8.9972	4.6132	67.6376
15	8.3803	5.2301	62.4074
16	7.6809	5.9295	56.4779
17	6.8879	6.7225	49.7555
18	5.9889	7.6214	42.1341
19	4.9698	8.6406	33.4934
20	3.8143	9.7961	23.6974
21	2.5043	11.1061	12.5913
22	1.0191	12.5913	0.0000

YEARS 23	QTR PAYT 3.3757	AN CONST 13.51	
# INT	PRIN	BALANCE	
1	12.7132	.7897	99.2103
2	12.6076	.8953	98.3151
3	12.4879	1.0150	97.3001
4	12.3522	1.1507	96.1494
5	12.1983	1.3046	94.8448
6	12.0238	1.4791	93.3657
7	11.8261	1.6768	91.6889
8	11.6018	1.9011	89.7878
9	11.3476	2.1553	87.6325
10	11.0594	2.4435	85.1890
11	10.7326	2.7703	82.4187
12	10.3621	3.1408	79.2779
13	9.9421	3.5608	75.7171
14	9.4660	4.0369	71.6802
15	8.9261	4.5768	67.1034
16	8.3141	5.1888	61.9146
17	7.6202	5.8827	56.0319
18	6.8335	6.6694	49.3626
19	5.9417	7.5612	41.8013
20	4.9305	8.5724	33.2290
21	3.7842	9.7187	23.5102
22	2.4845	11.0184	12.4918
23	1.0111	12.4918	0.0000

YEARS 24	QTR PAYT 3.3524	AN CONST 13.41	
# INT	PRIN	BALANCE	
1	12.7178	.6917	99.3083
2	12.6253	.7842	98.5241
3	12.5204	.8891	97.6350
4	12.4015	1.0080	96.6271
5	12.2667	1.1428	95.4843
6	12.1139	1.2956	94.1887
7	11.9407	1.4688	92.7199
8	11.7443	1.6652	91.0547
9	11.5216	1.8879	89.1667
10	11.2691	2.1404	87.0263
11	10.9829	2.4266	84.5997
12	10.6584	2.7511	81.8486
13	10.2905	3.1190	78.7295
14	9.8734	3.5361	75.1934
15	9.4005	4.0090	71.1844
16	8.8644	4.5451	66.6393
17	8.2566	5.1529	61.4864
18	7.5675	5.8420	55.6444
19	6.7863	6.6232	49.0211
20	5.9006	7.5089	41.5122
21	4.8964	8.5131	32.9991
22	3.7580	9.6515	23.3476
23	2.4673	10.9422	12.4054
24	1.0041	12.4054	0.0000

YEARS 25	QTR PAYT 3.3320	AN CONST 13.33	
# INT	PRIN	BALANCE	
1	12.7218	.6064	99.3936
2	12.6407	.6875	98.7061
3	12.5487	.7794	97.9266
4	12.4445	.8837	97.0430
5	12.3263	1.0019	96.0411
6	12.1924	1.1358	94.9053
7	12.0405	1.2877	93.6176
8	11.8683	1.4599	92.1576
9	11.6730	1.6551	90.5025
10	11.4517	1.8765	88.6260
11	11.2008	2.1274	86.4986
12	10.9163	2.4119	84.0867
13	10.5937	2.7344	81.3522
14	10.2281	3.1001	78.2521
15	9.8135	3.5147	74.7374
16	9.3435	3.9847	70.7527
17	8.8106	4.5176	66.2352
18	8.2065	5.1217	61.1135
19	7.5216	5.8066	55.3069
20	6.7451	6.5831	48.7239
21	5.8648	7.4634	41.2605
22	4.8667	8.4615	32.7990
23	3.7352	9.5930	23.2060
24	2.4524	10.8758	12.3302
25	.9980	12.3302	0.0000

YEARS 26	QTR PAYT 3.3143	AN CONST 13.26	
# INT	PRIN	BALANCE	
1	12.7252	.5320	99.4680
2	12.6541	.6032	98.8648
3	12.5734	.6839	98.1809
4	12.4820	.7753	97.4056
5	12.3783	.8790	96.5266
6	12.2607	.9965	95.5301
7	12.1275	1.1298	94.4003
8	11.9764	1.2809	93.1195
9	11.8051	1.4521	91.6673
10	11.6109	1.6463	90.0210
11	11.3908	1.8665	88.1545
12	11.1412	2.1161	86.0384
13	10.8582	2.3991	83.6393
14	10.5374	2.7199	80.9194
15	10.1736	3.0836	77.8358

#	INT	PRIN	BALANCE
16	9.7613	3.4960	74.3398
17	9.2938	3.9635	70.3763
18	8.7637	4.4935	65.8828
19	8.1628	5.0944	60.7884
20	7.4816	5.7757	55.0127
21	6.7092	6.5480	48.4646
22	5.8336	7.4237	41.0409
23	4.8408	8.4164	32.6245
24	3.7153	9.5419	23.0826
25	2.4393	10.8180	12.2646
26	.9927	12.2646	0.0000

YEARS 27	QTR PAYT 3.2988	AN CONST 13.20	
# INT	PRIN	BALANCE	
1	12.7283	.4671	99.5329
2	12.6658	.5296	99.0034
3	12.5950	.6004	98.4030
4	12.5147	.6807	97.7223
5	12.4237	.7717	96.9506
6	12.3205	.8749	96.0758
7	12.2035	.9919	95.0839
8	12.0708	1.1245	93.9594
9	11.9205	1.2749	92.6845
10	11.7500	1.4454	91.2392
11	11.5567	1.6387	89.6005
12	11.3376	1.8578	87.7427
13	11.0891	2.1062	85.6365
14	10.8075	2.3879	83.2486
15	10.4881	2.7072	80.5414
16	10.1261	3.0692	77.4722
17	9.7157	3.4797	73.9926
18	9.2504	3.9450	70.0476
19	8.7228	4.4725	65.5750
20	8.1247	5.0706	60.5044
21	7.4466	5.7487	54.7557
22	6.6779	6.5175	48.2383
23	5.8063	7.3890	40.8492
24	4.8182	8.3771	32.4721
25	3.6980	9.4974	22.9747
26	2.4279	10.7674	12.2073
27	.9880	12.2073	0.0000

YEARS 28	QTR PAYT 3.2853	AN CONST 13.15	
# INT	PRIN	BALANCE	
1	12.7309	.4103	99.5897
2	12.6760	.4652	99.1245
3	12.6138	.5274	98.5971
4	12.5433	.5979	97.9992
5	12.4633	.6779	97.3214
6	12.3727	.7685	96.5529
7	12.2699	.8713	95.6816
8	12.1534	.9878	94.6938
9	12.0213	1.1199	93.5739
10	11.8716	1.2697	92.3042
11	11.7018	1.4394	90.8648
12	11.5093	1.6319	89.2329
13	11.2910	1.8502	87.3827
14	11.0436	2.0976	85.2851
15	10.7631	2.3781	82.9071
16	10.4451	2.6961	80.2110
17	10.0846	3.0566	77.1543
18	9.6758	3.4654	73.6890
19	9.2124	3.9288	69.7602
20	8.6870	4.4542	65.3060
21	8.0914	5.0498	60.2562
22	7.4161	5.7251	54.5310
23	6.6505	6.4907	48.0403
24	5.7825	7.3587	40.6816
25	4.7984	8.3428	32.3389
26	3.6828	9.4584	22.8805
27	2.4180	10.7232	12.1572
28	.9840	12.1572	0.0000

YEARS 29	QTR PAYT 3.2735	AN CONST 13.10	
# INT	PRIN	BALANCE	
1	12.7332	.3606	99.6394
2	12.6850	.4088	99.2306
3	12.6303	.4635	98.7671
4	12.5683	.5255	98.2416
5	12.4981	.5958	97.6458
6	12.4184	.6754	96.9704
7	12.3281	.7657	96.2047
8	12.2257	.8681	95.3365
9	12.1096	.9842	94.3523
10	11.9780	1.1159	93.2365
11	11.8287	1.2651	91.9714
12	11.6596	1.4342	90.5371
13	11.4678	1.6260	88.9111
14	11.2503	1.8435	87.0676
15	11.0038	2.0900	84.9776
16	10.7243	2.3695	82.6081
17	10.4074	2.6864	79.9217
18	10.0482	3.0456	76.8761
19	9.6409	3.4529	73.4232
20	9.1792	3.9146	69.5086
21	8.6557	4.4381	65.0705
22	8.0622	5.0316	60.0389
23	7.3893	5.7045	54.3344
24	6.6265	6.4673	47.8671
25	5.7616	7.3322	40.5349
26	4.7811	8.3127	32.2223
27	3.6695	9.4243	22.7980
28	2.4092	10.6846	12.1134
29	.9804	12.1134	0.0000

YEARS 30	QTR PAYT 3.2631	AN CONST 13.06	
# INT	PRIN	BALANCE	
1	12.7352	.3171	99.6829
2	12.6928	.3595	99.3235
3	12.6448	.4075	98.9159
4	12.5903	.4620	98.4539
5	12.5285	.5238	97.9301
6	12.4584	.5939	97.3362
7	12.3790	.6733	96.6630
8	12.2890	.7633	95.8996
9	12.1869	.8654	95.0343
10	12.0712	.9811	94.0531
11	11.9400	1.1123	92.9408
12	11.7912	1.2611	91.6798
13	11.6226	1.4297	90.2501
14	11.4314	1.6209	88.6292
15	11.2147	1.8376	86.7915
16	10.9689	2.0834	84.7082
17	10.6903	2.3620	82.3462
18	10.3744	2.6778	79.6683
19	10.0163	3.0359	76.6324
20	9.6104	3.4419	73.1904
21	9.1501	3.9022	69.2882
22	8.6283	4.4240	64.8642
23	8.0366	5.0157	59.8485
24	7.3659	5.6864	54.1621
25	6.6055	6.4468	47.7153
26	5.7434	7.3089	40.4064
27	4.7660	8.2863	32.1201
28	3.6579	9.3944	22.7257
29	2.4016	10.6507	12.0750
30	.9773	12.0750	0.0000

QUARTERLY PAYMENT AMORTIZATION SCHEDULE PER $100   13.00 %

YEARS 2	QTR PAYT 14.3963	AN CONST 57.59
# INT	PRIN	BALANCE
1 10.7790	46.8061	53.1939
2 4.3911	53.1939	0.0000

YEARS 3	QTR PAYT 10.1967	AN CONST 40.79
# INT	PRIN	BALANCE
1 11.6158	29.1711	70.8289
2 7.6347	33.1522	37.6767
3 3.1102	37.6767	0.0000

YEARS 4	QTR PAYT 8.1140	AN CONST 32.46
# INT	PRIN	BALANCE
1 12.0308	20.4253	79.5747
2 9.2432	23.2128	56.3619
3 6.0753	26.3808	29.9811
4 2.4749	29.9811	0.0000

YEARS 5	QTR PAYT 6.8779	AN CONST 27.52
# INT	PRIN	BALANCE
1 12.2771	15.2344	84.7656
2 10.1980	17.3136	67.4520
3 7.8351	19.6765	47.7755
4 5.1497	22.3618	25.4137
5 2.0979	25.4137	0.0000

YEARS 6	QTR PAYT 6.0649	AN CONST 24.26
# INT	PRIN	BALANCE
1 12.4391	11.8205	88.1795
2 10.8259	13.4337	74.7459
3 8.9925	15.2670	59.4788
4 6.9089	17.3506	42.1282
5 4.5410	19.7186	22.4097
6 1.8499	22.4097	0.0000

YEARS 7	QTR PAYT 5.4935	AN CONST 21.98
# INT	PRIN	BALANCE
1 12.5530	9.4211	90.5789
2 11.2672	10.7068	79.8721
3 9.8060	12.1681	67.7040
4 8.1453	13.8287	53.8753
5 6.2580	15.7160	38.1593
6 4.1132	17.8609	20.2984
7 1.6756	20.2984	0.0000

YEARS 8	QTR PAYT 5.0730	AN CONST 20.30
# INT	PRIN	BALANCE
1 12.6368	7.6551	92.3449
2 11.5920	8.6999	83.6450
3 10.4047	9.8872	73.7577
4 9.0553	11.2366	62.5212
5 7.5218	12.7701	49.7511
6 5.7790	14.5129	35.2381
7 3.7983	16.4936	18.7446
8 1.5473	18.7446	0.0000

YEARS 9	QTR PAYT 4.7528	AN CONST 19.02
# INT	PRIN	BALANCE
1 12.7005	6.3108	93.6892
2 11.8393	7.1720	86.5172
3 10.8605	8.1509	78.3663
4 9.7481	9.2633	69.1031
5 8.4839	10.5275	58.5756
6 7.0471	11.9642	46.6114

#	INT	PRIN	BALANCE
7	5.4143	13.5970	33.0143
8	3.5586	15.4527	17.5616
9	1.4497	17.5616	0.0000

YEARS 10	QTR PAYT 4.5028	AN CONST 18.02
# INT	PRIN	BALANCE
1 12.7504	5.2608	94.7392
2 12.0324	5.9788	88.7604
3 11.2164	6.7947	81.9657
4 10.2891	7.7221	74.2436
5 9.2352	8.7759	65.4677
6 8.0375	9.9736	55.4940
7 6.6764	11.3348	44.1592
8 5.1295	12.8817	31.2775
9 3.3714	14.6398	16.6377
10 1.3734	16.6377	0.0000

YEARS 11	QTR PAYT 4.3036	AN CONST 17.22
# INT	PRIN	BALANCE
1 12.7901	4.4243	95.5757
2 12.1863	5.0281	90.5477
3 11.5001	5.7143	84.8334
4 10.7202	6.4941	78.3393
5 9.8339	7.3804	70.9589
6 8.8267	8.3877	62.5712
7 7.6819	9.5324	53.0388
8 6.3810	10.8333	42.2055
9 4.9025	12.3118	29.8937
10 3.2222	13.9921	15.9017
11 1.3127	15.9017	0.0000

YEARS 12	QTR PAYT 4.1423	AN CONST 16.57
# INT	PRIN	BALANCE
1 12.8222	3.7471	96.2529
2 12.3108	4.2585	91.9944
3 11.7296	4.8397	87.1548
4 11.0691	5.5001	81.6546
5 10.3185	6.2508	75.4039
6 9.4654	7.1039	68.3000
7 8.4959	8.0734	60.2266
8 7.3941	9.1752	51.0514
9 6.1419	10.4274	40.6241
10 4.7188	11.8505	28.7736
11 3.1015	13.4678	15.3058
12 1.2635	15.3058	0.0000

YEARS 13	QTR PAYT 4.0101	AN CONST 16.05
# INT	PRIN	BALANCE
1 12.8485	3.1919	96.8081
2 12.4129	3.6275	93.1806
3 11.9179	4.1225	89.0581
4 11.3552	4.6852	84.3729
5 10.7158	5.3246	79.0483
6 9.9891	6.0513	72.9971
7 9.1633	6.8771	66.1200
8 8.2247	7.8157	58.3043
9 7.1581	8.8823	49.4219
10 5.9459	10.0946	39.3274
11 4.5682	11.4722	27.8552
12 3.0025	13.0379	14.8173
13 1.2231	14.8173	0.0000

YEARS 14	QTR PAYT 3.9006	AN CONST 15.61
# INT	PRIN	BALANCE
1 12.8704	2.7318	97.2682
2 12.4975	3.1047	94.1635
3 12.0738	3.5284	90.6351

#	INT	PRIN	BALANCE
4	11.5923	4.0099	86.6252
5	11.0450	4.5572	82.0680
6	10.4231	5.1791	76.8889
7	9.7163	5.8860	71.0029
8	8.9130	6.6892	64.3137
9	8.0000	7.6022	56.7115
10	6.9625	8.6397	48.0718
11	5.7834	9.8188	38.2530
12	4.4434	11.1588	27.0942
13	2.9205	12.6817	14.4125
14	1.1897	14.4125	0.0000

YEARS 15	QTR PAYT 3.8090	AN CONST 15.24
# INT	PRIN	BALANCE
1 12.8886	2.3474	97.6526
2 12.5683	2.6677	94.9849
3 12.2042	3.0318	91.9531
4 11.7904	3.4456	88.5076
5 11.3202	3.9158	84.5918
6 10.7858	4.4502	80.1416
7 10.1784	5.0576	75.0840
8 9.4882	5.7478	69.3362
9 8.7037	6.5322	62.8040
10 7.8123	7.4237	55.3803
11 6.7991	8.4369	46.9434
12 5.6477	9.5883	37.3551
13 4.3391	10.8969	26.4582
14 2.8519	12.3840	14.0742
15 1.1618	14.0742	0.0000

YEARS 16	QTR PAYT 3.7319	AN CONST 14.93
# INT	PRIN	BALANCE
1 12.9040	2.0237	97.9763
2 12.6278	2.2999	95.6765
3 12.3139	2.6137	93.0627
4 11.9572	2.9704	90.0923
5 11.5518	3.3758	86.7165
6 11.0911	3.8366	82.8799
7 10.5675	4.3602	78.5198
8 9.9724	4.9552	73.5646
9 9.2962	5.6315	67.9331
10 8.5276	6.4000	61.5330
11 7.6542	7.2735	54.2596
12 6.6615	8.2661	45.9934
13 5.5334	9.3943	36.5991
14 4.2513	10.6764	25.9228
15 2.7942	12.1334	13.7894
16 1.1383	13.7894	0.0000

YEARS 17	QTR PAYT 3.6666	AN CONST 14.67
# INT	PRIN	BALANCE
1 12.9170	1.7495	98.2505
2 12.6782	1.9883	96.2622
3 12.4069	2.2596	94.0026
4 12.0985	2.5680	91.4346
5 11.7480	2.9185	88.5161
6 11.3497	3.3168	85.1994
7 10.8971	3.7694	81.4299
8 10.3826	4.2839	77.1461
9 9.7980	4.8685	72.2775
10 9.1335	5.5330	66.7446
11 8.3784	6.2881	60.4565
12 7.5203	7.1462	53.3103
13 6.5450	8.1215	45.1888
14 5.4366	9.2299	35.9588
15 4.1769	10.4896	25.4693
16 2.7453	11.9212	13.5481
17 1.1184	13.5481	0.0000

YEARS 18	QTR PAYT 3.6110	AN CONST 14.45
# INT	PRIN	BALANCE
1 12.9281	1.5161	98.4839
2 12.7212	1.7230	96.7609
3 12.4860	1.9581	94.8028
4 12.2188	2.2254	92.5775
5 11.9151	2.5291	90.0484
6 11.5699	2.8742	87.1742
7 11.1776	3.2665	83.9077
8 10.7318	3.7123	80.1954
9 10.2252	4.2189	75.9765
10 9.6494	4.7947	71.1818
11 8.9951	5.4491	65.7327
12 8.2514	6.1927	59.5400
13 7.4062	7.0379	52.5021
14 6.4457	7.9984	44.5037
15 5.3541	9.0900	35.4137
16 4.1136	10.3306	25.0831
17 2.7037	11.7404	13.3427
18 1.1014	13.3427	0.0000

YEARS 19	QTR PAYT 3.5635	AN CONST 14.26
# INT	PRIN	BALANCE
1 12.9375	1.3164	98.6836
2 12.7579	1.4961	97.1874
3 12.5537	1.7003	95.4871
4 12.3216	1.9323	93.5548
5 12.0579	2.1961	91.3587
6 11.7582	2.4958	88.8630
7 11.4176	2.8364	86.0266
8 11.0305	3.2235	82.8031
9 10.5906	3.6634	79.1397
10 10.0906	4.1634	74.9763
11 9.5224	4.7316	70.2447
12 8.8766	5.3773	64.8674
13 8.1428	6.1112	58.7561
14 7.3087	6.9452	51.8109
15 6.3609	7.8931	43.9178
16 5.2837	8.9703	34.9475
17 4.0594	10.1946	24.7529
18 2.6681	11.5859	13.1671
19 1.0869	13.1671	0.0000

YEARS 20	QTR PAYT 3.5227	AN CONST 14.10
# INT	PRIN	BALANCE
1 12.9457	1.1451	98.8549
2 12.7894	1.3014	97.5535
3 12.6118	1.4790	96.0745
4 12.4099	1.6808	94.3937
5 12.1805	1.9102	92.4835
6 11.9198	2.1709	90.3126
7 11.6236	2.4672	87.8454
8 11.2869	2.8039	85.0415
9 10.9042	3.1866	81.8549
10 10.4693	3.6215	78.2334
11 9.9751	4.1157	74.1177
12 9.4134	4.6774	69.4403
13 8.7750	5.3158	64.1246
14 8.0495	6.0412	58.0833
15 7.2250	6.8657	51.2176
16 6.2880	7.8027	43.4149
17 5.2232	8.8676	34.5473
18 4.0129	10.0778	24.4695
19 2.6376	11.4532	13.0163
20 1.0745	13.0163	0.0000

YEARS 21	QTR PAYT 3.4876	AN CONST 13.96
# INT	PRIN	BALANCE
1 12.9527	.9975	99.0025
2 12.8165	1.1337	97.8688
3 12.6618	1.2884	96.5804

#	INT	PRIN	BALANCE
4	12.4860	1.4642	95.1162
5	12.2861	1.6641	93.4521
6	12.0590	1.8912	91.5609
7	11.8009	2.1493	89.4117
8	11.5076	2.4426	86.9691
9	11.1743	2.7759	84.1932
10	10.7954	3.1548	81.0384
11	10.3649	3.5853	77.4530
12	9.8755	4.0747	73.3784
13	9.3195	4.6307	68.7476
14	8.6875	5.2627	63.4849
15	7.9692	5.9810	57.5039
16	7.1530	6.7972	50.7067
17	6.2253	7.7249	42.9818
18	5.1711	8.7791	34.2027
19	3.9729	9.9773	24.2254
20	2.6113	11.3389	12.8864
21	1.0638	12.8864	0.0000

YEARS 22 — QTR PAYT 3.4572 — AN CONST 13.83

#	INT	PRIN	BALANCE
1	12.9587	.8701	99.1299
2	12.8400	.9889	98.1410
3	12.7050	1.1238	97.0172
4	12.5516	1.2772	95.7400
5	12.3773	1.4515	94.2886
6	12.1792	1.6496	92.6390
7	11.9541	1.8747	90.7643
8	11.6983	2.1306	88.6337
9	11.4075	2.4213	86.2124
10	11.0770	2.7518	83.4606
11	10.7015	3.1273	80.3332
12	10.2747	3.5541	76.7791
13	9.7896	4.0392	72.7399
14	9.2384	4.5905	68.1494
15	8.6119	5.2169	62.9325
16	7.8999	5.9289	57.0036
17	7.0907	6.7381	50.2655
18	6.1712	7.6577	42.6078
19	5.1261	8.7028	33.9051
20	3.9383	9.8905	24.0146
21	2.5885	11.2403	12.7743
22	1.0545	12.7743	0.0000

YEARS 23 — QTR PAYT 3.4309 — AN CONST 13.73

#	INT	PRIN	BALANCE
1	12.9639	.7598	99.2402
2	12.8603	.8635	98.3767
3	12.7424	.9813	97.3954
4	12.6085	1.1153	96.2801
5	12.4563	1.2675	95.0126
6	12.2833	1.4405	93.5722
7	12.0867	1.6370	91.9351
8	11.8633	1.8605	90.0746
9	11.6094	2.1144	87.9603
10	11.3208	2.4029	85.5573
11	10.9929	2.7309	82.8265
12	10.6202	3.1036	79.7229
13	10.1966	3.5271	76.1957
14	9.7152	4.0085	72.1872
15	9.1682	4.5556	67.6316
16	8.5464	5.1773	62.4543
17	7.8399	5.8839	56.5705
18	7.0369	6.6869	49.8836
19	6.1243	7.5995	42.2841
20	5.0871	8.6366	33.6475
21	3.9084	9.8153	23.8321
22	2.5689	11.1549	12.6773
23	1.0465	12.6773	0.0000

YEARS 24 — QTR PAYT 3.4082 — AN CONST 13.64

#	INT	PRIN	BALANCE
1	12.9685	.6641	99.3359
2	12.8779	.7548	98.5811
3	12.7748	.8578	97.7234
4	12.6558	.9748	96.7485
5	12.5247	1.1079	95.6407
6	12.3735	1.2591	94.3816
7	12.2017	1.4309	92.9507
8	12.0064	1.6262	91.3245
9	11.7845	1.8481	89.4764
10	11.5323	2.1003	87.3761
11	11.2456	2.3870	84.9891
12	10.9199	2.7127	82.2764
13	10.5496	3.0830	79.1934
14	10.1289	3.5037	75.6897
15	9.6507	3.9819	71.7078
16	9.1073	4.5253	67.1825
17	8.4897	5.1429	62.0396
18	7.7878	5.8448	56.1948
19	6.9901	6.6425	49.5523
20	6.0836	7.5490	42.0033
21	5.0533	8.5793	33.4240
22	3.8825	9.7501	23.6739
23	2.5518	11.0808	12.5931
24	1.0395	12.5931	0.0000

YEARS 25 — QTR PAYT 3.3884 — AN CONST 13.56

#	INT	PRIN	BALANCE
1	12.9724	.5810	99.4190
2	12.8931	.6603	98.7588
3	12.8030	.7504	98.0084
4	12.7006	.8528	97.1556
5	12.5842	.9692	96.1865
6	12.4520	1.1014	95.0850
7	12.3017	1.2517	93.8333
8	12.1308	1.4226	92.4107
9	11.9367	1.6167	90.7940
10	11.7160	1.8374	88.9566
11	11.4653	2.0881	86.8685
12	11.1803	2.3731	84.4954
13	10.8564	2.6970	81.7984
14	10.4883	3.0651	78.7333
15	10.0700	3.4834	75.2500
16	9.5946	3.9588	71.2912
17	9.0544	4.4990	66.7922
18	8.4404	5.1130	61.6791
19	7.7426	5.8108	55.8683
20	6.9495	6.6039	49.2644
21	6.0482	7.5052	41.7592
22	5.0240	8.5294	33.2298
23	3.8599	9.6935	23.5363
24	2.5370	11.0164	12.5199
25	1.0335	12.5199	0.0000

YEARS 26 — QTR PAYT 3.3711 — AN CONST 13.49

#	INT	PRIN	BALANCE
1	12.9759	.5086	99.4914
2	12.9065	.5780	98.9134
3	12.8276	.6569	98.2565
4	12.7379	.7466	97.5099
5	12.6360	.8484	96.6615
6	12.5202	.9642	95.6972
7	12.3886	1.0958	94.6014
8	12.2391	1.2454	93.3560
9	12.0691	1.4153	91.9407
10	11.8760	1.6085	90.3322
11	11.6564	1.8280	88.5042
12	11.4070	2.0775	86.4267
13	11.1234	2.3610	84.0656
14	10.8012	2.6833	81.3824
15	10.4350	3.0495	78.3329
16	10.0188	3.4656	74.8672
17	9.5458	3.9386	70.9286
18	9.0083	4.4761	66.4525
19	8.3974	5.0870	61.3654
20	7.7032	5.7813	55.5841
21	6.9142	6.5703	49.0138
22	6.0175	7.4670	41.5469
23	4.9984	8.4861	33.0608
24	3.8403	9.6442	23.4166
25	2.5241	10.9604	12.4562
26	1.0282	12.4562	0.0000

YEARS 27 — QTR PAYT 3.3561 — AN CONST 13.43

#	INT	PRIN	BALANCE
1	12.9789	.4455	99.5545
2	12.9181	.5063	99.0481
3	12.8490	.5754	98.4727
4	12.7704	.6540	97.8187
5	12.6812	.7432	97.0755
6	12.5797	.8447	96.2308
7	12.4645	.9599	95.2709
8	12.3334	1.0909	94.1799
9	12.1846	1.2398	92.9401
10	12.0154	1.4090	91.5311
11	11.8231	1.6013	89.9297
12	11.6045	1.8199	88.1098
13	11.3561	2.0683	86.0416
14	11.0739	2.3505	83.6911
15	10.7531	2.6713	81.0198
16	10.3885	3.0359	77.9839
17	9.9742	3.4502	74.5337
18	9.5033	3.9211	70.6126
19	8.9682	4.4562	66.1564
20	8.3600	5.0644	61.0920
21	7.6689	5.7555	55.3365
22	6.8834	6.5410	48.7955
23	5.9907	7.4337	41.3618
24	4.9761	8.4482	32.9135
25	3.8232	9.6012	23.3123
26	2.5128	10.9116	12.4007
27	1.0237	12.4007	0.0000

YEARS 28 — QTR PAYT 3.3430 — AN CONST 13.38

#	INT	PRIN	BALANCE
1	12.9815	.3905	99.6095
2	12.9282	.4438	99.1657
3	12.8676	.5044	98.6613
4	12.7988	.5732	98.0881
5	12.7205	.6514	97.4367
6	12.6316	.7403	96.6964
7	12.5306	.8414	95.8550
8	12.4158	.9562	94.8989
9	12.2853	1.0867	93.8122
10	12.1370	1.2350	92.5772
11	11.9684	1.4035	91.1736
12	11.7769	1.5951	89.5786
13	11.5592	1.8128	87.7658
14	11.3118	2.0602	85.7056
15	11.0306	2.3413	83.3643
16	10.7111	2.6609	80.7034
17	10.3479	3.0240	77.6794
18	9.9352	3.4367	74.2426
19	9.4662	3.9058	70.3369
20	8.9332	4.4388	65.8981
21	8.3274	5.0446	60.8535
22	7.6389	5.7331	55.1204
23	6.8565	6.5155	48.6049
24	5.9673	7.4047	41.2002
25	4.9567	8.4153	32.7850
26	3.8082	9.5637	23.2213
27	2.5030	10.8690	12.3523
28	1.0197	12.3523	0.0000

YEARS 29 — QTR PAYT 3.3315 — AN CONST 13.33

#	INT	PRIN	BALANCE
1	12.9838	.3424	99.6576
2	12.9370	.3892	99.2684
3	12.8839	.4423	98.8261
4	12.8235	.5026	98.3235
5	12.7549	.5712	97.7523
6	12.6770	.6492	97.1031
7	12.5884	.7378	96.3653
8	12.4877	.8385	95.5268
9	12.3733	.9529	94.5739
10	12.2432	1.0830	93.4909
11	12.0954	1.2308	92.2602
12	11.9275	1.3987	90.8614
13	11.7366	1.5896	89.2718
14	11.5196	1.8066	87.4652
15	11.2731	2.0531	85.4121
16	10.9929	2.3333	83.0788
17	10.6744	2.6518	80.4270
18	10.3125	3.0137	77.4134
19	9.9012	3.4250	73.9884
20	9.4338	3.8924	70.0960
21	8.9026	4.4236	65.6724
22	8.2989	5.0273	60.6451
23	7.6128	5.7134	54.9317
24	6.8330	6.4932	48.4385
25	5.9468	7.3793	41.0592
26	4.9397	8.3864	32.6727
27	3.7952	9.5310	23.1417
28	2.4944	10.8317	12.3100
29	1.0162	12.3100	0.0000

YEARS 30 — QTR PAYT 3.3215 — AN CONST 13.29

#	INT	PRIN	BALANCE
1	12.9857	.3004	99.6996
2	12.9447	.3414	99.3582
3	12.8982	.3880	98.9702
4	12.8452	.4409	98.5293
5	12.7850	.5011	98.0281
6	12.7166	.5695	97.4586
7	12.6389	.6472	96.8114
8	12.5506	.7356	96.0758
9	12.4502	.8360	95.2398
10	12.3361	.9501	94.2898
11	12.2064	1.0797	93.2101
12	12.0591	1.2271	91.9830
13	11.8916	1.3945	90.5885
14	11.7013	1.5848	89.0036
15	11.4850	1.8011	87.2025
16	11.2392	2.0470	85.1555
17	10.9598	2.3263	82.8292
18	10.6423	2.6438	80.1854
19	10.2815	3.0046	77.1808
20	9.8715	3.4147	73.7661
21	9.4055	3.8807	69.8854
22	8.8758	4.4103	65.4751
23	8.2739	5.0122	60.4629
24	7.5899	5.6963	54.7666
25	6.8125	6.4737	48.2930
26	5.9290	7.3572	40.9358
27	4.9249	8.3612	32.5746
28	3.7838	9.5024	23.0722
29	2.4870	10.7992	12.2730
30	1.0131	12.2730	0.0000

YEARS 2	QTR PAYT 14.4340	AN CONST 57.74
# INT	PRIN	BALANCE
1 10.9904	46.7458	53.2542
2 4.4820	53.2542	0.0000

YEARS 3	QTR PAYT 10.2345	AN CONST 40.94
# INT	PRIN	BALANCE
1 11.8436	29.0945	70.9055
2 7.7928	33.1453	37.7602
3 3.1780	37.7602	0.0000

YEARS 4	QTR PAYT 8.1525	AN CONST 32.61
# INT	PRIN	BALANCE
1 12.2666	20.3433	79.6567
2 9.4342	23.1757	56.4810
3 6.2075	26.4025	30.0785
4 2.5314	30.0785	0.0000

YEARS 5	QTR PAYT 6.9173	AN CONST 27.67
# INT	PRIN	BALANCE
1 12.5176	15.1515	84.8485
2 10.4081	17.2610	67.5875
3 8.0048	19.6643	47.9233
4 5.2669	22.4021	25.5212
5 2.1479	25.5212	0.0000

YEARS 6	QTR PAYT 6.1053	AN CONST 24.43
# INT	PRIN	BALANCE
1 12.6826	11.7385	88.2615
2 11.0482	13.3729	74.8886
3 9.1863	15.2348	59.6537
4 7.0652	17.3560	42.2978
5 4.6487	19.7724	22.5254
6 1.8958	22.5254	0.0000

YEARS 7	QTR PAYT 5.5350	AN CONST 22.14
# INT	PRIN	BALANCE
1 12.7985	9.3414	90.6586
2 11.4978	10.6420	80.0166
3 10.0162	12.1237	67.8929
4 8.3282	13.8117	54.0813
5 6.4052	15.7347	38.3466
6 4.2144	17.9254	20.4212
7 1.7187	20.4212	0.0000

YEARS 8	QTR PAYT 5.1155	AN CONST 20.47
# INT	PRIN	BALANCE
1 12.8837	7.5783	92.4217
2 11.8285	8.6335	83.7882
3 10.6265	9.8355	73.9527
4 9.2571	11.2049	62.7478
5 7.6970	12.7650	49.9828
6 5.9198	14.5422	35.4405
7 3.8950	16.5670	18.8736
8 1.5884	18.8736	0.0000

YEARS 9	QTR PAYT 4.7964	AN CONST 19.19
# INT	PRIN	BALANCE
1 12.9485	6.2372	93.7628
2 12.0801	7.1057	86.6571
3 11.0908	8.0950	78.5621
4 9.9637	9.2220	69.3401
5 8.6797	10.5060	58.8340
6 7.2170	11.9688	46.8652
7 5.5505	13.6352	33.2300
8 3.6521	15.5336	17.6964
9 1.4894	17.6964	0.0000

YEARS 10	QTR PAYT 4.5475	AN CONST 18.19
# INT	PRIN	BALANCE
1 12.9991	5.1908	94.8092
2 12.2764	5.9135	88.8957
3 11.4530	6.7368	82.1589
4 10.5151	7.6748	74.4841
5 9.4465	8.7434	65.7408
6 8.2292	9.9607	55.7801
7 6.8423	11.3475	44.4326
8 5.2624	12.9274	31.5051
9 3.4625	14.7273	16.7778
10 1.4120	16.7778	0.0000

YEARS 11	QTR PAYT 4.3493	AN CONST 17.40
# INT	PRIN	BALANCE
1 13.0393	4.3578	95.6422
2 12.4326	4.9646	90.6776
3 11.7414	5.6558	85.0218
4 10.9539	6.4432	78.5786
5 10.0568	7.3403	71.2382
6 9.0348	8.3623	62.8759
7 7.8706	9.5266	53.3493
8 6.5442	10.8530	42.4963
9 5.0331	12.3641	30.1322
10 3.3116	14.0855	16.0467
11 1.3505	16.0467	0.0000

YEARS 12	QTR PAYT 4.1891	AN CONST 16.76
# INT	PRIN	BALANCE
1 13.0719	3.6843	96.3157
2 12.5589	4.1973	92.1184
3 11.9746	4.7817	87.3368
4 11.3088	5.4474	81.8894
5 10.5504	6.2059	75.6835
6 9.6863	7.0699	68.6136
7 8.7020	8.0542	60.5594
8 7.5806	9.1756	51.3837
9 6.3031	10.4532	40.9306
10 4.8477	11.9086	29.0220
11 3.1896	13.5666	15.4555
12 1.3008	15.4555	0.0000

YEARS 13	QTR PAYT 4.0578	AN CONST 16.24
# INT	PRIN	BALANCE
1 13.0986	3.1327	96.8673
2 12.6624	3.5689	93.2984
3 12.1655	4.0658	89.2326
4 11.5994	4.6319	84.6008
5 10.9545	5.2768	79.3240
6 10.2198	6.0114	73.3126
7 9.3829	6.8484	66.4641
8 8.4294	7.8019	58.6622
9 7.3431	8.8882	49.7740
10 6.1056	10.1257	39.6483
11 4.6958	11.5355	28.1129
12 3.0897	13.1416	14.9713
13 1.2600	14.9713	0.0000

YEARS 14	QTR PAYT 3.9492	AN CONST 15.80
# INT	PRIN	BALANCE
1 13.1206	2.6763	97.3237
2 12.7480	3.0489	94.2749
3 12.3235	3.4734	90.8015
4 11.8399	3.9570	86.8445
5 11.2890	4.5079	82.3366
6 10.6614	5.1355	77.2011
7 9.9463	5.8506	71.3505
8 9.1318	6.6651	64.6854
9 8.2038	7.5931	57.0923
10 7.1466	8.6503	48.4420
11 5.9422	9.8547	38.5873
12 4.5701	11.2268	27.3605
13 3.0070	12.7899	14.5706
14 1.2263	14.5706	0.0000

YEARS 15	QTR PAYT 3.8586	AN CONST 15.44
# INT	PRIN	BALANCE
1 13.1391	2.2953	97.7047
2 12.8195	2.6148	95.0899
3 12.4554	2.9789	92.1110
4 12.0407	3.3937	88.7174
5 11.5682	3.8661	84.8512
6 11.0299	4.4044	80.4468
7 10.4167	5.0177	75.4291
8 9.7180	5.7163	69.7128
9 8.9222	6.5122	63.2007
10 8.0155	7.4188	55.7818
11 6.9825	8.4518	47.3301
12 5.8058	9.6285	37.7016
13 4.4652	10.9691	26.7325
14 2.9380	12.4963	14.2362
15 1.1981	14.2362	0.0000

YEARS 16	QTR PAYT 3.7824	AN CONST 15.13
# INT	PRIN	BALANCE
1 13.1545	1.9750	98.0250
2 12.8796	2.2499	95.7751
3 12.5663	2.5632	93.2119
4 12.2094	2.9201	90.2919
5 11.8029	3.3266	86.9652
6 11.3397	3.7898	83.1754
7 10.8120	4.3174	78.8580
8 10.2109	4.9186	73.9394
9 9.5261	5.6034	68.3360
10 8.7460	6.3835	61.9525
11 7.8572	7.2723	54.6802
12 6.8446	8.2848	46.3953
13 5.6911	9.4383	36.9570
14 4.3770	10.7525	26.2045
15 2.8800	12.2495	13.9550
16 1.1745	13.9550	0.0000

YEARS 17	QTR PAYT 3.7179	AN CONST 14.88
# INT	PRIN	BALANCE
1 13.1676	1.7040	98.2960
2 12.9304	1.9413	96.3546
3 12.6601	2.2116	94.1431
4 12.3522	2.5195	91.6235
5 12.0014	2.8703	88.7532
6 11.6017	3.2699	85.4833
7 11.1465	3.7252	81.7581
8 10.6278	4.2439	77.5142
9 10.0369	4.8348	72.6795
10 9.3638	5.5079	67.1716
11 8.5969	6.2748	60.8968
12 7.7233	7.1484	53.7484
13 6.7280	8.1437	45.6047
14 5.5942	9.2775	36.3272
15 4.3025	10.5692	25.7580
16 2.8309	12.0408	13.7172
17 1.1545	13.7172	0.0000

YEARS 18	QTR PAYT 3.6631	AN CONST 14.66
# INT	PRIN	BALANCE
1 13.1788	1.4737	98.5263
2 12.9736	1.6789	96.8473
3 12.7398	1.9127	94.9346
4 12.4735	2.1790	92.7556
5 12.1701	2.4824	90.2732
6 11.8245	2.8280	87.4452
7 11.4308	3.2217	84.2235
8 10.9822	3.6703	80.5532
9 10.4712	4.1813	76.3718
10 9.8890	4.7635	71.6083
11 9.2258	5.4267	66.1816
12 8.4702	6.1823	59.9993
13 7.6095	7.0430	52.9563
14 6.6289	8.0237	44.9326
15 5.5117	9.1408	35.7918
16 4.2390	10.4135	25.3784
17 2.7892	11.8633	13.5151
18 1.1374	13.5151	0.0000

YEARS 19	QTR PAYT 3.6163	AN CONST 14.47
# INT	PRIN	BALANCE
1 13.1883	1.2771	98.7229
2 13.0105	1.4549	97.2680
3 12.8079	1.6575	95.6105
4 12.5771	1.8883	93.7222
5 12.3142	2.1512	91.5710
6 12.0147	2.4507	89.1203
7 11.6735	2.7919	86.3285
8 11.2848	3.1806	83.1479
9 10.8419	3.6234	79.5244
10 10.3374	4.1279	75.3965
11 9.7627	4.7027	70.6938
12 9.1080	5.3574	65.3364
13 8.3620	6.1033	59.2331
14 7.5123	6.9531	52.2800
15 6.5442	7.9212	44.3588
16 5.4413	9.0240	35.3347
17 4.1849	10.2805	25.0543
18 2.7536	11.7118	13.3425
19 1.1229	13.3425	0.0000

YEARS 20	QTR PAYT 3.5763	AN CONST 14.31
# INT	PRIN	BALANCE
1 13.1964	1.1086	98.8914
2 13.0421	1.2630	97.6284
3 12.8662	1.4388	96.1896
4 12.6659	1.6391	94.5505
5 12.4377	1.8673	92.6832
6 12.1777	2.1273	90.5559
7 11.8815	2.4235	88.1324
8 11.5441	2.7609	85.3714
9 11.1597	3.1453	82.2261
10 10.7217	3.5833	78.6428
11 10.2228	4.0822	74.5606
12 9.6545	4.6505	69.9101
13 9.0070	5.2980	64.6121
14 8.2693	6.0357	58.5764
15 7.4290	6.8760	51.7004
16 6.4716	7.8334	43.8670
17 5.3810	8.9240	34.9430
18 4.1385	10.1665	24.7765
19 2.7230	11.5820	13.1945
20 1.1105	13.1945	0.0000

YEARS 21	QTR PAYT 3.5418	AN CONST 14.17
# INT	PRIN	BALANCE
1 13.2034	.9637	99.0363
2 13.0692	1.0979	97.9383
3 12.9164	1.2508	96.6876

#	INT	PRIN	BALANCE
4	12.7422	1.4249	95.2626
5	12.5438	1.6233	93.6393
6	12.3178	1.8493	91.7900
7	12.0603	2.1068	89.6831
8	11.7670	2.4002	87.2830
9	11.4328	2.7343	84.5487
10	11.0521	3.1150	81.4336
11	10.6184	3.5487	77.8849
12	10.1243	4.0428	73.8421
13	9.5614	4.6057	69.2364
14	8.9202	5.2470	63.9894
15	8.1897	5.9775	58.0119
16	7.3574	6.8098	51.2021
17	6.4093	7.7579	43.4443
18	5.3291	8.8380	34.6063
19	4.0986	10.0685	24.5377
20	2.6968	11.4704	13.0674
21	1.0998	13.0674	0.0000

YEARS 22 — QTR PAYT 3.5121 — AN CONST 14.05

#	INT	PRIN	BALANCE
1	13.2095	.8389	99.1611
2	13.0927	.9557	98.2055
3	12.9596	1.0887	97.1168
4	12.8080	1.2403	95.8765
5	12.6353	1.4130	94.4635
6	12.4386	1.6097	92.8538
7	12.2145	1.8338	91.0200
8	11.9592	2.0891	88.9308
9	11.6683	2.3800	86.5508
10	11.3369	2.7114	83.8394
11	10.9594	3.0889	80.7505
12	10.5293	3.5190	77.2316
13	10.0394	4.0089	73.2226
14	9.4812	4.5671	68.6556
15	8.8454	5.2030	63.4526
16	8.1210	5.9274	57.5253
17	7.2957	6.7526	50.7726
18	6.3555	7.6928	43.0798
19	5.2844	8.7639	34.3160
20	4.0643	9.9841	24.3319
21	2.6742	11.3741	12.9578
22	1.0905	12.9578	0.0000

YEARS 23 — QTR PAYT 3.4864 — AN CONST 13.95

#	INT	PRIN	BALANCE
1	13.2147	.7310	99.2690
2	13.1129	.8327	98.4363
3	12.9970	.9487	97.4876
4	12.8649	1.0808	96.4069
5	12.7144	1.2312	95.1757
6	12.5430	1.4026	93.7730
7	12.3477	1.5979	92.1751
8	12.1252	1.8204	90.3547
9	11.8717	2.0739	88.2808
10	11.5830	2.3626	85.9182
11	11.2540	2.6916	83.2266
12	10.8793	3.0663	80.1603
13	10.4524	3.4932	76.6670
14	9.9660	3.9796	72.6874
15	9.4119	4.5337	68.1537
16	8.7807	5.1649	62.9888
17	8.0616	5.8840	57.1048
18	7.2424	6.7033	50.4015
19	6.3091	7.6366	42.7649
20	5.2458	8.6998	34.0651
21	4.0345	9.9111	24.1541
22	2.6546	11.2910	12.8630
23	1.0826	12.8630	0.0000

YEARS 24 — QTR PAYT 3.4642 — AN CONST 13.86

#	INT	PRIN	BALANCE
1	13.2192	.6375	99.3625
2	13.1304	.7263	98.6362
3	13.0293	.8274	97.8088
4	12.9141	.9426	96.8661
5	12.7829	1.0739	95.7923
6	12.6333	1.2234	94.5689
7	12.4630	1.3937	93.1752
8	12.2690	1.5878	91.5874
9	12.0479	1.8088	89.7786
10	11.7961	2.0607	87.7180
11	11.5092	2.3476	85.3704
12	11.1823	2.6744	82.6960
13	10.8099	3.0468	79.6492
14	10.3857	3.4710	76.1782
15	9.9025	3.9542	72.2240
16	9.3519	4.5048	67.7192
17	8.7247	5.1320	62.5872
18	8.0102	5.8465	56.7407
19	7.1962	6.6605	50.0802
20	6.2688	7.5879	42.4923
21	5.2124	8.6443	33.8480
22	4.0088	9.8479	24.0001
23	2.6377	11.2190	12.7810
24	1.0757	12.7810	0.0000

YEARS 25 — QTR PAYT 3.4449 — AN CONST 13.78

#	INT	PRIN	BALANCE
1	13.2231	.5565	99.4435
2	13.1456	.6340	98.8095
3	13.0573	.7223	98.0873
4	12.9568	.8228	97.2644
5	12.8422	.9374	96.3271
6	12.7117	1.0679	95.2592
7	12.5630	1.2166	94.0426
8	12.3937	1.3859	92.6567
9	12.2007	1.5789	91.0778
10	11.9809	1.7987	89.2790
11	11.7304	2.0492	87.2298
12	11.4451	2.3345	84.8953
13	11.1201	2.6595	82.2358
14	10.7498	3.0298	79.2060
15	10.3279	3.4517	75.7543
16	9.8474	3.9322	71.8221
17	9.2999	4.4797	67.3424
18	8.6762	5.1034	62.2389
19	7.9656	5.8140	56.4249
20	7.1561	6.6235	49.8015
21	6.2339	7.5457	42.2558
22	5.1834	8.5962	33.6596
23	3.9865	9.7931	23.8665
24	2.6230	11.1566	12.7099
25	1.0697	12.7099	0.0000

YEARS 26 — QTR PAYT 3.4282 — AN CONST 13.72

#	INT	PRIN	BALANCE
1	13.2265	.4861	99.5139
2	13.1588	.5538	98.9601
3	13.0817	.6309	98.3292
4	12.9939	.7187	97.6104
5	12.8938	.8188	96.7916
6	12.7798	.9328	95.8588
7	12.6499	1.0627	94.7961
8	12.5020	1.2107	93.5855
9	12.3334	1.3792	92.2063
10	12.1414	1.5712	90.6350
11	11.9226	1.7900	88.8450
12	11.6734	2.0392	86.8058
13	11.3895	2.3231	84.4826
14	11.0660	2.6466	81.8360
15	10.6975	3.0151	78.8209
16	10.2777	3.4349	75.3861
17	9.7995	3.9131	71.4729
18	9.2547	4.4579	67.0150
19	8.6340	5.0786	61.9364
20	7.9269	5.7857	56.1507
21	7.1213	6.5913	49.5594
22	6.2036	7.5090	42.0504
23	5.1582	8.5544	33.4960
24	3.9671	9.7455	23.7505
25	2.6103	11.1023	12.6481
26	1.0645	12.6481	0.0000

YEARS 27 — QTR PAYT 3.4136 — AN CONST 13.66

#	INT	PRIN	BALANCE
1	13.2295	.4249	99.5751
2	13.1703	.4840	99.0911
3	13.1029	.5514	98.5396
4	13.0261	.6282	97.9114
5	12.9387	.7157	97.1957
6	12.8390	.8153	96.3804
7	12.7255	.9289	95.4515
8	12.5962	1.0582	94.3933
9	12.4488	1.2055	93.1878
10	12.2810	1.3734	91.8145
11	12.0898	1.5646	90.2499
12	11.8720	1.7824	88.4675
13	11.6238	2.0306	86.4369
14	11.3411	2.3133	84.1237
15	11.0190	2.6354	81.4883
16	10.6521	3.0023	78.4860
17	10.2341	3.4203	75.0657
18	9.7579	3.8965	71.1693
19	9.2154	4.4390	66.7303
20	8.5973	5.0570	61.6732
21	7.8932	5.7611	55.9121
22	7.0911	6.5633	49.3488
23	6.1773	7.4771	41.8717
24	5.1363	8.5181	33.3536
25	3.9503	9.7041	23.6496
26	2.5992	11.0552	12.5944
27	1.0600	12.5944	0.0000

YEARS 28 — QTR PAYT 3.4009 — AN CONST 13.61

#	INT	PRIN	BALANCE
1	13.2320	.3716	99.6284
2	13.1803	.4233	99.2051
3	13.1214	.4823	98.7229
4	13.0542	.5494	98.1735
5	12.9777	.6259	97.5476
6	12.8906	.7130	96.8345
7	12.7913	.8123	96.0222
8	12.6782	.9254	95.0968
9	12.5494	1.0542	94.0426
10	12.4026	1.2010	92.8416
11	12.2354	1.3682	91.4733
12	12.0449	1.5588	89.9146
13	11.8278	1.7758	88.1388
14	11.5806	2.0230	86.1158
15	11.2989	2.3047	83.8111
16	10.9781	2.6256	81.1855
17	10.6125	2.9911	78.1944
18	10.1960	3.4076	74.7868
19	9.7216	3.8820	70.9048
20	9.1811	4.4225	66.4823
21	8.5654	5.0383	61.4440
22	7.8639	5.7397	55.7043
23	7.0647	6.5389	49.1654
24	6.1543	7.4493	41.7162
25	5.1172	8.4864	33.2297
26	3.9356	9.6680	23.5617
27	2.5895	11.0141	12.5476
28	1.0560	12.5476	0.0000

YEARS 29 — QTR PAYT 3.3898 — AN CONST 13.56

#	INT	PRIN	BALANCE
1	13.2343	.3251	99.6749
2	13.1890	.3704	99.3045
3	13.1375	.4219	98.8826
4	13.0787	.4807	98.4019
5	13.0118	.5476	97.8543
6	12.9355	.6239	97.2304
7	12.8487	.7107	96.5197
8	12.7497	.8097	95.7101
9	12.6370	.9224	94.7877
10	12.5086	1.0508	93.7369
11	12.3623	1.1971	92.5397
12	12.1956	1.3638	91.1759
13	12.0057	1.5537	89.6222
14	11.7894	1.7700	87.8522
15	11.5429	2.0164	85.8358
16	11.2622	2.2972	83.5386
17	10.9424	2.6170	80.9216
18	10.5780	2.9814	77.9402
19	10.1629	3.3965	74.5437
20	9.6900	3.8694	70.6743
21	9.1513	4.4081	66.2662
22	8.5375	5.0219	61.2443
23	7.8383	5.7211	55.5232
24	7.0418	6.5176	49.0056
25	6.1343	7.4251	41.5805
26	5.1005	8.4589	33.1217
27	3.9228	9.6366	23.4851
28	2.5811	10.9783	12.5068
29	1.0526	12.5068	0.0000

YEARS 30 — QTR PAYT 3.3802 — AN CONST 13.53

#	INT	PRIN	BALANCE
1	13.2362	.2846	99.7154
2	13.1966	.3242	99.3913
3	13.1515	.3693	99.0219
4	13.1001	.4207	98.6012
5	13.0415	.4793	98.1219
6	12.9748	.5461	97.5758
7	12.8987	.6221	96.9538
8	12.8121	.7087	96.2451
9	12.7134	.8074	95.4377
10	12.6010	.9198	94.5179
11	12.4730	1.0478	93.4701
12	12.3271	1.1937	92.2764
13	12.1609	1.3599	90.9165
14	11.9715	1.5493	89.3672
15	11.7558	1.7650	87.6022
16	11.5101	2.0107	85.5915
17	11.2302	2.2907	83.3009
18	10.9112	2.6096	80.6913
19	10.5479	2.9729	77.7184
20	10.1340	3.3868	74.3316
21	9.6624	3.8584	70.4732
22	9.1252	4.3956	66.0776
23	8.5132	5.0076	61.0700
24	7.8160	5.7048	55.3652
25	7.0217	6.4991	48.8662
26	6.1169	7.4039	41.4622
27	5.0860	8.4348	33.0274
28	3.9116	9.6092	23.4183
29	2.5738	10.9471	12.4712
30	1.0496	12.4712	0.0000

QUARTERLY PAYMENT AMORTIZATION SCHEDULE PER $100   13.50 %

YEARS 2 — QTR PAYT 14.4719 — AN CONST 57.89

#	INT	PRIN	BALANCE
1	11.2019	46.6856	53.3144
2	4.5730	53.3144	0.0000

YEARS 3 — QTR PAYT 10.2724 — AN CONST 41.09

#	INT	PRIN	BALANCE
1	12.0716	29.0181	70.9819
2	7.9513	33.1383	37.8436
3	3.2460	37.8436	0.0000

YEARS 4 — QTR PAYT 8.1911 — AN CONST 32.77

#	INT	PRIN	BALANCE
1	12.5026	20.2616	79.7384
2	9.6257	23.1385	56.5999
3	6.3403	26.4240	30.1759
4	2.5883	30.1759	0.0000

YEARS 5 — QTR PAYT 6.9568 — AN CONST 27.83

#	INT	PRIN	BALANCE
1	12.7582	15.0688	84.9312
2	10.6186	17.2084	67.7228
3	8.1752	19.6518	48.0709
4	5.3849	22.4422	25.6287
5	2.1983	25.6287	0.0000

YEARS 6 — QTR PAYT 6.1458 — AN CONST 24.59

#	INT	PRIN	BALANCE
1	12.9262	11.6571	88.3429
2	11.2710	13.3122	75.0307
3	9.3808	15.2024	59.8283
4	7.2222	17.3610	42.4673
5	4.7571	19.8261	22.6412
6	1.9420	22.6412	0.0000

YEARS 7 — QTR PAYT 5.5766 — AN CONST 22.31

#	INT	PRIN	BALANCE
1	13.0441	9.2622	90.7378
2	11.7289	10.5774	80.1604
3	10.2271	12.0792	68.0812
4	8.5119	13.7943	54.2869
5	6.5533	15.7530	38.5339
6	4.3165	17.9898	20.5441
7	1.7622	20.5441	0.0000

YEARS 8 — QTR PAYT 5.1582 — AN CONST 20.64

#	INT	PRIN	BALANCE
1	13.1307	7.5021	92.4979
2	12.0655	8.5674	83.9305
3	10.8490	9.7838	74.1467
4	9.4598	11.1730	62.9737
5	7.8734	12.7595	50.2142
6	6.0616	14.5712	35.6430
7	3.9927	16.6401	19.0029
8	1.6300	19.0029	0.0000

YEARS 9 — QTR PAYT 4.8402 — AN CONST 19.37

#	INT	PRIN	BALANCE
1	13.1966	6.1644	93.8356
2	12.3213	7.0397	86.7959
3	11.3217	8.0392	78.7567
4	10.1802	9.1807	69.5760
5	8.8767	10.4843	59.0917
6	7.3880	11.9729	47.1188
7	5.6880	13.6730	33.4458
8	3.7466	15.6144	17.8315
9	1.5295	17.8315	0.0000

YEARS 10 — QTR PAYT 4.5923 — AN CONST 18.37

#	INT	PRIN	BALANCE
1	13.2479	5.1215	94.8785
2	12.5207	5.8487	89.0298
3	11.6902	6.6791	82.3507
4	10.7419	7.6275	74.7232
5	9.6589	8.7105	66.0127
6	8.4221	9.9473	56.0654
7	7.0096	11.3597	44.7056
8	5.3967	12.9727	31.7329
9	3.5547	14.8147	16.9182
10	1.4512	16.9182	0.0000

YEARS 11 — QTR PAYT 4.3952 — AN CONST 17.59

#	INT	PRIN	BALANCE
1	13.2887	4.2922	95.7078
2	12.6793	4.9017	90.8061
3	11.9833	5.5976	85.2085
4	11.1885	6.3924	78.8160
5	10.2808	7.3001	71.5159
6	9.2443	8.3366	63.1793
7	8.0606	9.5204	53.6589
8	6.7088	10.8722	42.7868
9	5.1650	12.4159	30.3709
10	3.4021	14.1788	16.1921
11	1.3889	16.1921	0.0000

YEARS 12 — QTR PAYT 4.2360 — AN CONST 16.95

#	INT	PRIN	BALANCE
1	13.3217	3.6224	96.3776
2	12.8073	4.1367	92.2409
3	12.2200	4.7241	87.5168
4	11.5492	5.3949	82.1219
5	10.7832	6.1609	75.9610
6	9.9084	7.0357	68.9253
7	8.9094	8.0347	60.8907
8	7.7686	9.1755	51.7152
9	6.4658	10.4783	41.2369
10	4.9779	11.9661	29.2707
11	3.2789	13.6652	15.6055
12	1.3386	15.6055	0.0000

YEARS 13 — QTR PAYT 4.1058 — AN CONST 16.43

#	INT	PRIN	BALANCE
1	13.3487	3.0745	96.9255
2	12.9121	3.5110	93.4145
3	12.4136	4.0095	89.4050
4	11.8443	4.5789	84.8261
5	11.1941	5.2290	79.5971
6	10.4517	5.9715	73.6256
7	9.6038	6.8194	66.8062
8	8.6355	7.7876	59.0186
9	7.5297	8.8934	50.1252
10	6.2670	10.1562	39.9690
11	4.8249	11.5982	28.3708
12	3.1781	13.2451	15.1257
13	1.2974	15.1257	0.0000

YEARS 14 — QTR PAYT 3.9981 — AN CONST 16.00

#	INT	PRIN	BALANCE
1	13.3709	2.6216	97.3784
2	12.9987	2.9939	94.3845
3	12.5736	3.4190	90.9655
4	12.0881	3.9044	87.0611
5	11.5338	4.4588	82.6023
6	10.9007	5.0919	77.5103
7	10.1777	5.8149	71.6954
8	9.3520	6.6406	65.0548
9	8.4091	7.5835	57.4714
10	7.3323	8.6602	48.8111
11	6.1027	9.8899	38.9212
12	4.6984	11.2942	27.6270
13	3.0948	12.8978	14.7292
14	1.2634	14.7292	0.0000

YEARS 15 — QTR PAYT 3.9084 — AN CONST 15.64

#	INT	PRIN	BALANCE
1	13.3895	2.2442	97.7558
2	13.0709	2.5628	95.1931
3	12.7070	2.9267	92.2664
4	12.2914	3.3422	88.9241
5	11.8169	3.8168	85.1073
6	11.2749	4.3588	80.7485
7	10.6560	4.9777	75.7709
8	9.9493	5.6844	70.0865
9	9.1421	6.4916	63.5949
10	8.2204	7.4133	56.1816
11	7.1678	8.4659	47.7157
12	5.9657	9.6680	38.0477
13	4.5930	11.0407	27.0070
14	3.0253	12.6084	14.3986
15	1.2350	14.3986	0.0000

YEARS 16 — QTR PAYT 3.8331 — AN CONST 15.34

#	INT	PRIN	BALANCE
1	13.4051	1.9273	98.0727
2	13.1315	2.2009	95.8718
3	12.8190	2.5134	93.3584
4	12.4621	2.8703	90.4882
5	12.0545	3.2778	87.2103
6	11.5891	3.7433	83.4671
7	11.0576	4.2748	79.1923
8	10.4507	4.8817	74.3106
9	9.7575	5.5749	68.7357
10	8.9659	6.3664	62.3693
11	8.0620	7.2704	55.0989
12	7.0296	8.3027	46.7961
13	5.8507	9.4816	37.3145
14	4.5044	10.8279	26.4865
15	2.9670	12.3654	14.1211
16	1.2112	14.1211	0.0000

YEARS 17 — QTR PAYT 3.7695 — AN CONST 15.08

#	INT	PRIN	BALANCE
1	13.4183	1.6596	98.3404
2	13.1827	1.8953	96.4451
3	12.9135	2.1644	94.2807
4	12.6062	2.4717	91.8090
5	12.2553	2.8226	88.9864
6	11.8545	3.2234	85.7630
7	11.3968	3.6811	82.0818
8	10.8741	4.2038	77.8780
9	10.2772	4.8007	73.0773
10	9.5956	5.4824	67.5950
11	8.8171	6.2608	61.3342
12	7.9282	7.1498	54.1844
13	6.9130	8.1649	46.0195
14	5.7536	9.3243	36.6952
15	4.4297	10.6482	26.0470
16	2.9178	12.1602	13.8868
17	1.1911	13.8868	0.0000

YEARS 18 — QTR PAYT 3.7155 — AN CONST 14.87

#	INT	PRIN	BALANCE
1	13.4295	1.4325	98.5675
2	13.2261	1.6358	96.9317
3	12.9938	1.8681	95.0636
4	12.7286	2.1334	92.9302
5	12.4257	2.4363	90.4939
6	12.0797	2.7822	87.7117
7	11.6847	3.1773	84.5345
8	11.2335	3.6284	80.9061
9	10.7183	4.1436	76.7625
10	10.1300	4.7319	72.0305
11	9.4581	5.4038	66.6267
12	8.6908	6.1711	60.4556
13	7.8146	7.0473	53.4083
14	6.8140	8.0480	45.3603
15	5.6712	9.1907	36.1695
16	4.3662	10.4957	25.6738
17	2.8760	11.9860	13.6879
18	1.1741	13.6879	0.0000

YEARS 19 — QTR PAYT 3.6695 — AN CONST 14.68

#	INT	PRIN	BALANCE
1	13.4390	1.2388	98.7612
2	13.2631	1.4147	97.3465
3	13.0622	1.6156	95.7309
4	12.8329	1.8450	93.8859
5	12.5709	2.1069	91.7790
6	12.2717	2.4061	89.3729
7	11.9301	2.7477	86.6251
8	11.5399	3.1379	83.4872
9	11.0944	3.5834	79.9038
10	10.5856	4.0923	75.8115
11	10.0045	4.6733	71.1382
12	9.3409	5.3369	65.8013
13	8.5832	6.0947	59.7067
14	7.7178	6.9600	52.7466
15	6.7295	7.9483	44.7983
16	5.6010	9.0769	35.7215
17	4.3121	10.3657	25.3558
18	2.8403	11.8375	13.5183
19	1.1595	13.5183	0.0000

YEARS 20 — QTR PAYT 3.6301 — AN CONST 14.53

#	INT	PRIN	BALANCE
1	13.4472	1.0731	98.9269
2	13.2948	1.2255	97.7013
3	13.1208	1.3995	96.3018
4	12.9221	1.5982	94.7036
5	12.6951	1.8252	92.8784
6	12.4360	2.0843	90.7941
7	12.1400	2.3803	88.4138
8	11.8021	2.7183	85.6955
9	11.4161	3.1042	82.5913
10	10.9753	3.5450	79.0463
11	10.4720	4.0483	74.9980
12	9.8971	4.6232	70.3748
13	9.2407	5.2796	65.0952
14	8.4911	6.0293	59.0659
15	7.6350	6.8853	52.1806
16	6.6573	7.8630	44.3176
17	5.5409	8.9795	35.3381
18	4.2659	10.2544	25.0837
19	2.8098	11.7105	13.3732
20	1.1471	13.3732	0.0000

YEARS 21 — QTR PAYT 3.5963 — AN CONST 14.39

#	INT	PRIN	BALANCE
1	13.4542	.9310	99.0690
2	13.3220	1.0631	98.0059
3	13.1710	1.2141	96.7918

QUARTERLY PAYMENT AMORTIZATION SCHEDULE PER $100   13.50 %

#	INT	PRIN	BALANCE
4	12.9986	1.3865	95.4053
5	12.8018	1.5834	93.8219
6	12.5770	1.8082	92.0137
7	12.3202	2.0649	89.9488
8	12.0270	2.3581	87.5907
9	11.6922	2.6930	84.8977
10	11.3098	3.0753	81.8224
11	10.8731	3.5120	78.3104
12	10.3745	4.0107	74.2998
13	9.8050	4.5801	69.7196
14	9.1547	5.2305	64.4892
15	8.4120	5.9731	58.5160
16	7.5639	6.8212	51.6948
17	6.5953	7.7898	43.9050
18	5.4893	8.8959	35.0092
19	4.2262	10.1590	24.8502
20	2.7837	11.6014	13.2487
21	1.1364	13.2487	0.0000

YEARS 22 — QTR PAYT 3.5672 — AN CONST 14.27

#	INT	PRIN	BALANCE
1	13.4602	.8086	99.1914
2	13.3454	.9234	98.2679
3	13.2143	1.0546	97.2134
4	13.0645	1.2043	96.0091
5	12.8935	1.3753	94.6338
6	12.6983	1.5706	93.0633
7	12.4753	1.7936	91.2697
8	12.2206	2.0482	89.2215
9	11.9298	2.3391	86.8824
10	11.5976	2.6712	84.2112
11	11.2184	3.0505	81.1608
12	10.7852	3.4836	77.6772
13	10.2906	3.9782	73.6990
14	9.7257	4.5431	69.1559
15	9.0807	5.1882	63.9677
16	8.3440	5.9248	58.0429
17	7.5027	6.7661	51.2768
18	6.5420	7.7268	43.5500
19	5.4449	8.8239	34.7261
20	4.1920	10.0768	24.6492
21	2.7612	11.5076	13.1416
22	1.1272	13.1416	0.0000

YEARS 23 — QTR PAYT 3.5421 — AN CONST 14.17

#	INT	PRIN	BALANCE
1	13.4654	.7031	99.2969
2	13.3656	.8029	98.4940
3	13.2515	.9169	97.5770
4	13.1214	1.0471	96.5299
5	12.9727	1.1958	95.3341
6	12.8029	1.3656	93.9684
7	12.6090	1.5595	92.4089
8	12.3875	1.7810	90.6280
9	12.1347	2.0338	88.5941
10	11.8459	2.3226	86.2715
11	11.5161	2.6524	83.6191
12	11.1395	3.0290	80.5901
13	10.7094	3.4591	77.1310
14	10.2182	3.9503	73.1808
15	9.6573	4.5111	68.6696
16	9.0168	5.1517	63.5179
17	8.2853	5.8832	57.6348
18	7.4500	6.7185	50.9163
19	6.4960	7.6725	43.2438
20	5.4046	8.7619	34.4819
21	4.1625	10.0060	24.4759
22	2.7418	11.4267	13.0492
23	1.1193	13.0492	0.0000

YEARS 24 — QTR PAYT 3.5204 — AN CONST 14.09

#	INT	PRIN	BALANCE
1	13.4699	.6119	99.3881
2	13.3830	.6988	98.6893
3	13.2838	.7980	97.8913
4	13.1705	.9113	96.9799
5	13.0411	1.0407	95.9392
6	12.8933	1.1885	94.7507
7	12.7245	1.3573	93.3934
8	12.5318	1.5500	91.8435
9	12.3117	1.7701	90.0734
10	12.0604	2.0214	88.0520
11	11.7734	2.3084	85.7436
12	11.4456	2.6362	83.1075
13	11.0713	3.0105	80.0970
14	10.6439	3.4379	76.6591
15	10.1557	3.9261	72.7330
16	9.5982	4.4835	68.2494
17	8.9616	5.1202	63.1293
18	8.2346	5.8472	57.2821
19	7.4044	6.6774	50.6047
20	6.4563	7.6255	42.9792
21	5.3735	8.7083	34.2709
22	4.1370	9.9448	24.3261
23	2.7250	11.3568	12.9693
24	1.1124	12.9693	0.0000

YEARS 25 — QTR PAYT 3.5017 — AN CONST 14.01

#	INT	PRIN	BALANCE
1	13.4738	.5330	99.4670
2	13.3981	.6087	98.8584
3	13.3117	.6951	98.1633
4	13.2130	.7938	97.3695
5	13.1003	.9065	96.4631
6	12.9716	1.0352	95.4279
7	12.8246	1.1822	94.2457
8	12.6567	1.3500	92.8957
9	12.4650	1.5417	91.3540
10	12.2461	1.7606	89.5933
11	11.9961	2.0106	87.5827
12	11.7106	2.2961	85.2866
13	11.3846	2.6221	82.6645
14	11.0123	2.9944	79.6701
15	10.5871	3.4196	76.2505
16	10.1016	3.9052	72.3453
17	9.5471	4.4596	67.8857
18	8.9139	5.0929	62.7928
19	8.1907	5.8160	56.9768
20	7.3649	6.6418	50.3350
21	6.4219	7.5849	42.7501
22	5.3449	8.6619	34.0882
23	4.1150	9.8917	24.1965
24	2.7105	11.2963	12.9002
25	1.1065	12.9002	0.0000

YEARS 26 — QTR PAYT 3.4854 — AN CONST 13.95

#	INT	PRIN	BALANCE
1	13.4771	.4645	99.5355
2	13.4112	.5305	99.0050
3	13.3358	.6058	98.3991
4	13.2498	.6918	97.7073
5	13.1516	.7901	96.9172
6	13.0394	.9023	96.0149
7	12.9113	1.0304	94.9846
8	12.7650	1.1767	93.8079
9	12.5979	1.3438	92.4641
10	12.4071	1.5346	90.9296
11	12.1892	1.7524	89.1771
12	11.9404	2.0013	87.1759
13	11.6562	2.2854	84.8904
14	11.3317	2.6099	82.2805
15	10.9612	2.9805	79.3000
16	10.5379	3.4037	75.8963
17	10.0547	3.8870	72.0093
18	9.5027	4.4389	67.5703
19	8.8725	5.0692	62.5011
20	8.1527	5.7890	56.7121
21	7.3307	6.6110	50.1012
22	6.3920	7.5496	42.5515
23	5.3201	8.6216	33.9299
24	4.0959	9.8458	24.0841
25	2.6979	11.2438	12.8403
26	1.1014	12.8403	0.0000

YEARS 27 — QTR PAYT 3.4713 — AN CONST 13.89

#	INT	PRIN	BALANCE
1	13.4801	.4051	99.5949
2	13.4225	.4627	99.1322
3	13.3568	.5284	98.6039
4	13.2818	.6034	98.0005
5	13.1961	.6890	97.3114
6	13.0983	.7869	96.5246
7	12.9866	.8986	95.6260
8	12.8590	1.0262	94.5998
9	12.7133	1.1719	93.4278
10	12.5469	1.3383	92.0895
11	12.3569	1.5283	90.5612
12	12.1398	1.7453	88.8159
13	11.8920	1.9932	86.8227
14	11.6090	2.2762	84.5465
15	11.2858	2.5994	81.9472
16	10.9167	2.9684	78.9787
17	10.4953	3.3899	75.5888
18	10.0139	3.8713	71.7175
19	9.4642	4.4209	67.2966
20	8.8365	5.0487	62.2479
21	8.1197	5.7655	56.4824
22	7.3010	6.5842	49.8982
23	6.3661	7.5191	42.3791
24	5.2985	8.5867	33.7924
25	4.0793	9.8059	23.9865
26	2.6869	11.1982	12.7883
27	1.0969	12.7883	0.0000

YEARS 28 — QTR PAYT 3.4590 — AN CONST 13.84

#	INT	PRIN	BALANCE
1	13.4826	.3535	99.6465
2	13.4324	.4037	99.2428
3	13.3751	.4610	98.7818
4	13.3096	.5265	98.2553
5	13.2349	.6012	97.6541
6	13.1495	.6866	96.9674
7	13.0520	.7841	96.1833
8	12.9407	.8954	95.2879
9	12.8135	1.0226	94.2653
10	12.6683	1.1678	93.0976
11	12.5025	1.3336	91.7640
12	12.3132	1.5229	90.2411
13	12.0969	1.7392	88.5019
14	11.8500	1.9861	86.5158
15	11.5680	2.2681	84.2476
16	11.2459	2.5902	81.6575
17	10.8782	2.9580	78.6995
18	10.4582	3.3779	75.3216
19	9.9785	3.8576	71.4640
20	9.4308	4.4053	67.0587
21	8.8053	5.0308	62.0278
22	8.0910	5.7452	56.2827
23	7.2752	6.5609	49.7218
24	6.3436	7.4925	42.2293
25	5.2798	8.5563	33.6730
26	4.0649	9.7712	23.9017
27	2.6774	11.1587	12.7431
28	1.0930	12.7431	0.0000

YEARS 29 — QTR PAYT 3.4484 — AN CONST 13.80

#	INT	PRIN	BALANCE
1	13.4848	.3086	99.6914
2	13.4410	.3524	99.3390
3	13.3910	.4025	98.9365
4	13.3338	.4596	98.4769
5	13.2685	.5249	97.9521
6	13.1940	.5994	97.3527
7	13.1089	.6845	96.6682
8	13.0117	.7817	95.8865
9	12.9007	.8927	94.9939
10	12.7740	1.0194	93.9744
11	12.6292	1.1642	92.8103
12	12.4639	1.3295	91.4808
13	12.2752	1.5182	89.9626
14	12.0596	1.7338	88.2288
15	11.8134	1.9800	86.2488
16	11.5323	2.2611	83.9877
17	11.2112	2.5822	81.4055
18	10.8446	2.9488	78.4567
19	10.4259	3.3675	75.0891
20	9.9477	3.8457	71.2435
21	9.4017	4.3917	66.8517
22	8.7781	5.0153	61.8364
23	8.0660	5.7274	56.1090
24	7.2528	6.5407	49.5683
25	6.3240	7.4694	42.0990
26	5.2635	8.5299	33.5691
27	4.0523	9.7411	23.8280
28	2.6692	11.1242	12.7037
29	1.0897	12.7037	0.0000

YEARS 30 — QTR PAYT 3.4391 — AN CONST 13.76

#	INT	PRIN	BALANCE
1	13.4867	.2695	99.7305
2	13.4485	.3078	99.4227
3	13.4048	.3515	99.0713
4	13.3549	.4014	98.6699
5	13.2979	.4584	98.2115
6	13.2328	.5234	97.6881
7	13.1585	.5978	97.0903
8	13.0736	.6826	96.4077
9	12.9767	.7796	95.6281
10	12.8660	.8903	94.7378
11	12.7396	1.0167	93.7212
12	12.5952	1.1610	92.5602
13	12.4304	1.3259	91.2343
14	12.2421	1.5141	89.7201
15	12.0271	1.7291	87.9910
16	11.7816	1.9747	86.0163
17	11.5012	2.2550	83.7613
18	11.1810	2.5752	81.1861
19	10.8154	2.9409	78.2452
20	10.3978	3.3584	74.8868
21	9.9209	3.8353	71.0515
22	9.3763	4.3799	66.6716
23	8.7544	5.0018	61.6698
24	8.0442	5.7120	55.9578
25	7.2332	6.5230	49.4348
26	6.3070	7.4492	41.9855
27	5.2493	8.5069	33.4786
28	4.0414	9.7148	23.7638
29	2.6620	11.0942	12.6695
30	1.0867	12.6695	0.0000

YEARS 2	QTR PAYT 14.5097	AN CONST 58.04
# INT	PRIN	BALANCE
1 11.4136	46.6254	53.3746
2 4.6644	53.3746	0.0000

YEARS 3	QTR PAYT 10.3104	AN CONST 41.25
# INT	PRIN	BALANCE
1 12.2997	28.9418	71.0582
2 8.1103	33.1312	37.9271
3 3.3144	37.9271	0.0000

YEARS 4	QTR PAYT 8.2297	AN CONST 32.92
# INT	PRIN	BALANCE
1 12.7388	20.1801	79.8199
2 9.8176	23.1013	56.7186
3 6.4736	26.4453	30.2733
4 2.6456	30.2733	0.0000

YEARS 5	QTR PAYT 6.9964	AN CONST 27.99
# INT	PRIN	BALANCE
1 12.9990	14.9865	85.0135
2 10.8297	17.1558	67.8577
3 8.3463	19.6392	48.2185
4 5.5034	22.4821	25.7364
5 2.2491	25.7364	0.0000

YEARS 6	QTR PAYT 6.1865	AN CONST 24.75
# INT	PRIN	BALANCE
1 13.1699	11.5760	88.4240
2 11.4943	13.2517	75.1724
3 9.5760	15.1699	60.0025
4 7.3801	17.3658	42.6367
5 4.8664	19.8795	22.7572
6 1.9887	22.7572	0.0000

YEARS 7	QTR PAYT 5.6183	AN CONST 22.48
# INT	PRIN	BALANCE
1 13.2898	9.1835	90.8165
2 11.9605	10.5129	80.3036
3 10.4387	12.0347	68.2689
4 8.6966	13.7767	54.4921
5 6.7024	15.7710	38.7211
6 4.4195	18.0539	20.6673
7 1.8061	20.6673	0.0000

YEARS 8	QTR PAYT 5.2011	AN CONST 20.81
# INT	PRIN	BALANCE
1 13.3779	7.4265	92.5735
2 12.3028	8.5015	84.0720
3 11.0722	9.7322	74.3398
4 9.6634	11.1409	63.1989
5 8.0508	12.7536	50.4453
6 6.2046	14.5997	35.8455
7 4.0913	16.7131	19.1324
8 1.6720	19.1324	0.0000

YEARS 9	QTR PAYT 4.8842	AN CONST 19.54
# INT	PRIN	BALANCE
1 13.4447	6.0922	93.9078
2 12.5628	6.9741	86.9337
3 11.5533	7.9836	78.9501
4 10.3977	9.1393	69.8109
5 9.0747	10.4622	59.3487
6 7.5603	11.9766	47.3720

# INT	PRIN	BALANCE
7 5.8266	13.7103	33.6617
8 3.8420	15.6949	17.9668
9 1.5701	17.9668	0.0000

YEARS 10	QTR PAYT 4.6374	AN CONST 18.55
# INT	PRIN	BALANCE
1 13.4968	5.0529	94.9471
2 12.7654	5.7844	89.1627
3 11.9281	6.6217	82.5410
4 10.9695	7.5802	74.9608
5 9.8723	8.6775	66.2834
6 8.6162	9.9335	56.3498
7 7.1783	11.3715	44.9784
8 5.5322	13.0175	31.9608
9 3.6479	14.9019	17.0590
10 1.4908	17.0590	0.0000

YEARS 11	QTR PAYT 4.4414	AN CONST 17.77
# INT	PRIN	BALANCE
1 13.5382	4.2274	95.7726
2 12.9262	4.8393	90.9333
3 12.2257	5.5398	85.3934
4 11.4238	6.3418	79.0517
5 10.5058	7.2597	71.7919
6 9.4549	8.3106	63.4813
7 8.2519	9.5136	53.9677
8 6.8748	10.8907	43.0769
9 5.2983	12.4672	30.6097
10 3.4937	14.2719	16.3378
11 1.4277	16.3378	0.0000

YEARS 12	QTR PAYT 4.2832	AN CONST 17.14
# INT	PRIN	BALANCE
1 13.5715	3.5613	96.4387
2 13.0560	4.0768	92.3618
3 12.4659	4.6670	87.6948
4 11.7903	5.3426	82.3523
5 11.0170	6.1159	76.2364
6 10.1317	7.0012	69.2352
7 9.1182	8.0147	61.2205
8 7.9581	9.1748	52.0457
9 6.6300	10.5029	41.5428
10 5.1096	12.0232	29.5196
11 3.3692	13.7636	15.7560
12 1.3769	15.7560	0.0000

YEARS 13	QTR PAYT 4.1540	AN CONST 16.62
# INT	PRIN	BALANCE
1 13.5988	3.0171	96.9829
2 13.1621	3.4539	93.5290
3 12.6621	3.9538	89.5751
4 12.0898	4.5262	85.0490
5 11.4346	5.1814	79.8676
6 10.6846	5.9314	73.9362
7 9.8260	6.7900	67.1463
8 8.8431	7.7728	59.3734
9 7.7180	8.8980	50.4754
10 6.4299	10.1860	40.2894
11 4.9555	11.6605	28.6290
12 3.2676	13.3484	15.2806
13 1.3354	15.2806	0.0000

YEARS 14	QTR PAYT 4.0473	AN CONST 16.19
# INT	PRIN	BALANCE
1 13.6213	2.5679	97.4321
2 13.2496	2.9397	94.4924
3 12.8241	3.3652	91.1272

# INT	PRIN	BALANCE
4 12.3369	3.8523	87.2749
5 11.7793	4.4099	82.8650
6 11.1410	5.0483	77.8166
7 10.4102	5.7791	72.0376
8 9.5737	6.6156	65.4220
9 8.6160	7.5732	57.8487
10 7.5198	8.6695	49.1792
11 6.2648	9.9244	39.2548
12 4.8282	11.3610	27.8938
13 3.1837	13.0056	14.8882
14 1.3011	14.8882	0.0000

YEARS 15	QTR PAYT 3.9585	AN CONST 15.84
# INT	PRIN	BALANCE
1 13.6401	2.1940	97.8060
2 13.3225	2.5116	95.2944
3 12.9589	2.8752	92.4192
4 12.5427	3.2914	89.1279
5 12.0663	3.7678	85.3601
6 11.5209	4.3132	81.0469
7 10.8965	4.9375	76.1093
8 10.1818	5.6523	70.4571
9 9.3636	6.4705	63.9866
10 8.4270	7.4071	56.5795
11 7.3548	8.4793	48.1002
12 6.1274	9.7067	38.3936
13 4.7223	11.1118	27.2818
14 3.1138	12.7202	14.5615
15 1.2725	14.5615	0.0000

YEARS 16	QTR PAYT 3.8841	AN CONST 15.54
# INT	PRIN	BALANCE
1 13.6558	1.8805	98.1195
2 13.3836	2.1528	95.9667
3 13.0719	2.4644	93.5023
4 12.7152	2.8211	90.6812
5 12.3068	3.2295	87.4518
6 11.8394	3.6969	83.7549
7 11.3042	4.2321	79.5228
8 10.6916	4.8447	74.6781
9 9.9903	5.5460	69.1321
10 9.1875	6.3488	62.7833
11 8.2685	7.2678	55.5155
12 7.2165	8.3198	47.1957
13 6.0121	9.5242	37.6716
14 4.6335	10.9028	26.7687
15 3.0553	12.4810	14.2877
16 1.2486	14.2877	0.0000

YEARS 17	QTR PAYT 3.8213	AN CONST 15.29
# INT	PRIN	BALANCE
1 13.6690	1.6162	98.3838
2 13.4351	1.8501	96.5337
3 13.1672	2.1180	94.4157
4 12.8607	2.4245	91.9912
5 12.5097	2.7755	89.2157
6 12.1079	3.1773	86.0384
7 11.6480	3.6372	82.4012
8 11.1215	4.1637	78.2375
9 10.5188	4.7664	73.4711
10 9.8289	5.4563	68.0148
11 9.0390	6.2462	61.7686
12 8.1349	7.1503	54.6183
13 7.0998	8.1854	46.4329
14 5.9150	9.3702	37.0627
15 4.5586	10.7266	26.3361
16 3.0059	12.2793	14.0568
17 1.2284	14.0568	0.0000

YEARS 18	QTR PAYT 3.7681	AN CONST 15.08
# INT	PRIN	BALANCE
1 13.6802	1.3922	98.6078
2 13.4787	1.5937	97.0141
3 13.2480	1.8244	95.1898
4 12.9839	2.0885	93.1013
5 12.6816	2.3908	90.7105
6 12.3355	2.7369	87.9736
7 11.9394	3.1330	84.8406
8 11.4859	3.5866	81.2540
9 10.9667	4.1057	77.1483
10 10.3724	4.7000	72.4483
11 9.6920	5.3804	67.0679
12 8.9132	6.1592	60.9087
13 8.0216	7.0508	53.8579
14 7.0010	8.0714	45.7865
15 5.8326	9.2398	36.5467
16 4.4951	10.5773	25.9695
17 2.9640	12.1084	13.8611
18 1.2113	13.8611	0.0000

YEARS 19	QTR PAYT 3.7228	AN CONST 14.90
# INT	PRIN	BALANCE
1 13.6898	1.2015	98.7985
2 13.5159	1.3754	97.4230
3 13.3168	1.5745	95.8485
4 13.0888	1.8025	94.0460
5 12.8279	2.0634	91.9826
6 12.5292	2.3621	89.6206
7 12.1873	2.7040	86.9166
8 11.7959	3.0954	83.8212
9 11.3479	3.5435	80.2778
10 10.8349	4.0564	76.2214
11 10.2477	4.6436	71.5778
12 9.5756	5.3157	66.2621
13 8.8061	6.0852	60.1769
14 7.9252	6.9661	53.2108
15 6.9169	7.9744	45.2364
16 5.7626	9.1288	36.1076
17 4.4411	10.4502	25.6574
18 2.9284	11.9629	13.6946
19 1.1968	13.6946	0.0000

YEARS 20	QTR PAYT 3.6842	AN CONST 14.74
# INT	PRIN	BALANCE
1 13.6980	1.0387	98.9613
2 13.5476	1.1890	97.7723
3 13.3755	1.3612	96.4111
4 13.1784	1.5582	94.8529
5 12.9529	1.7837	93.0692
6 12.6947	2.0419	91.0272
7 12.3991	2.3375	88.6897
8 12.0607	2.6759	86.0138
9 11.6734	3.0632	82.9506
10 11.2300	3.5067	79.4439
11 10.7224	4.0143	75.4297
12 10.1413	4.5953	70.8343
13 9.4761	5.2605	65.5738
14 8.7146	6.0220	59.5518
15 7.8429	6.8937	52.6581
16 6.8450	7.8916	44.7665
17 5.7027	9.0339	35.7326
18 4.3950	10.3416	25.3909
19 2.8980	11.8386	13.5523
20 1.1843	13.5523	0.0000

YEARS 21	QTR PAYT 3.6510	AN CONST 14.61
# INT	PRIN	BALANCE
1 13.7049	.8992	99.1008
2 13.5748	1.0293	98.0715
3 13.4258	1.1783	96.8931

#	INT	PRIN	BALANCE
4	13.2552	1.3489	95.5442
5	13.0599	1.5442	94.0000
6	12.8364	1.7677	92.2323
7	12.5805	2.0236	90.2087
8	12.2876	2.3165	87.8922
9	11.9523	2.6518	85.2404
10	11.5684	3.0357	82.2047
11	11.1290	3.4751	78.7296
12	10.6260	3.9782	74.7514
13	10.0501	4.5540	70.1974
14	9.3909	5.2132	64.9842
15	8.6363	5.9679	59.0163
16	7.7724	6.8317	52.1846
17	6.7835	7.8206	44.3640
18	5.6514	8.9527	35.4113
19	4.3555	10.2486	25.1626
20	2.8720	11.7322	13.4304
21	1.1737	13.4304	0.0000

YEARS 22   QTR PAYT 3.6226   AN CONST 14.50

#	INT	PRIN	BALANCE
1	13.7109	.7794	99.2206
2	13.5981	.8922	98.3285
3	13.4690	1.0213	97.3071
4	13.3211	1.1692	96.1380
5	13.1519	1.3384	94.7996
6	12.9582	1.5321	93.2674
7	12.7364	1.7539	91.5135
8	12.4825	2.0078	89.5057
9	12.1919	2.2985	87.2072
10	11.8591	2.6312	84.5761
11	11.4783	3.0120	81.5640
12	11.0423	3.4480	78.1160
13	10.5432	3.9472	74.1688
14	9.9718	4.5185	69.6503
15	9.3177	5.1726	64.4777
16	8.5690	5.9213	58.5564
17	7.7118	6.7785	51.7779
18	6.7306	7.7597	44.0182
19	5.6074	8.8829	35.1353
20	4.3215	10.1688	24.9665
21	2.8496	11.6407	13.3258
22	1.1645	13.3258	0.0000

YEARS 23   QTR PAYT 3.5991   AN CONST 14.40

#	INT	PRIN	BALANCE
1	13.7161	.6762	99.3238
2	13.6182	.7741	98.5497
3	13.5062	.8861	97.6636
4	13.3779	1.0144	96.6491
5	13.2311	1.1613	95.4879
6	13.0630	1.3294	94.1585
7	12.8705	1.5218	92.6367
8	12.6503	1.7421	90.8947
9	12.3981	1.9942	88.9004
10	12.1094	2.2829	86.6175
11	11.7790	2.6134	84.0042
12	11.4007	2.9917	81.0125
13	10.9676	3.4247	77.5878
14	10.4719	3.9205	73.6673
15	9.9044	4.4880	69.1793
16	9.2547	5.1376	64.0417
17	8.5110	5.8813	58.1604
18	7.6597	6.7326	51.4278
19	6.6851	7.7072	43.7206
20	5.5695	8.8229	34.8977
21	4.2923	10.1000	24.7977
22	2.8303	11.5620	13.2357
23	1.1567	13.2357	0.0000

YEARS 24   QTR PAYT 3.5770   AN CONST 14.31

#	INT	PRIN	BALANCE
1	13.7206	.5872	99.4128
2	13.6356	.6722	98.7405
3	13.5383	.7695	97.9710
4	13.4269	.8809	97.0900
5	13.2993	1.0085	96.0816
6	13.1534	1.1544	94.9271
7	12.9863	1.3215	93.6056
8	12.7950	1.5128	92.0927
9	12.5760	1.7318	90.3609
10	12.3253	1.9825	88.3784
11	12.0383	2.2695	86.1089
12	11.7098	2.5980	83.5109
13	11.3337	2.9741	80.5368
14	10.9032	3.4046	77.1321
15	10.4104	3.8974	73.2347
16	9.8462	4.4616	68.7731
17	9.2004	5.1074	63.6657
18	8.4610	5.8468	57.8189
19	7.6147	6.6931	51.1258
20	6.6458	7.6620	43.4638
21	5.5368	8.7711	34.6928
22	4.2671	10.0407	24.6521
23	2.8137	11.4941	13.1579
24	1.1499	13.1579	0.0000

YEARS 25   QTR PAYT 3.5587   AN CONST 14.24

#	INT	PRIN	BALANCE
1	13.7244	.5104	99.4896
2	13.6505	.5842	98.9054
3	13.5660	.6688	98.2366
4	13.4692	.7656	97.4710
5	13.3583	.8764	96.5945
6	13.2315	1.0033	95.5912
7	13.0862	1.1485	94.4427
8	12.9200	1.3148	93.1279
9	12.7297	1.5051	91.6227
10	12.5118	1.7230	89.8997
11	12.2624	1.9724	87.9273
12	11.9769	2.2579	85.6694
13	11.6500	2.5848	83.0846
14	11.2759	2.9589	80.1257
15	10.8476	3.3872	76.7385
16	10.3572	3.8775	72.8609
17	9.7959	4.4388	68.4221
18	9.1534	5.0814	63.3407
19	8.4719	5.8169	57.5238
20	7.5758	6.6589	50.8649
21	6.6119	7.6229	43.2420
22	5.5085	8.7263	34.5157
23	4.2453	9.9895	24.5263
24	2.7993	11.4355	13.0908
25	1.1440	13.0908	0.0000

YEARS 26   QTR PAYT 3.5429   AN CONST 14.18

#	INT	PRIN	BALANCE
1	13.7278	.4438	99.5562
2	13.6635	.5081	99.0481
3	13.5900	.5816	98.4664
4	13.5058	.6658	97.8006
5	13.4094	.7622	97.0384
6	13.2990	.8726	96.1658
7	13.1727	.9989	95.1669
8	13.0282	1.1434	94.0235
9	12.8626	1.3090	92.7145
10	12.6732	1.4984	91.2161
11	12.4563	1.7154	89.5007
12	12.2079	1.9637	87.5371
13	11.9237	2.2479	85.2892
14	11.5983	2.5733	82.7159
15	11.2258	2.9458	79.7701
16	10.7994	3.3722	76.3979
17	10.3113	3.8603	72.5376
18	9.7525	4.4191	68.1184
19	9.1128	5.0588	63.0596
20	8.3805	5.7911	57.2685
21	7.5422	6.6294	50.6391
22	6.5826	7.5890	43.0501
23	5.4840	8.6876	34.3625
24	4.2265	9.9451	24.4174
25	2.7869	11.3847	13.0327
26	1.1389	13.0327	0.0000

YEARS 27   QTR PAYT 3.5292   AN CONST 14.12

#	INT	PRIN	BALANCE
1	13.7306	.3862	99.6138
2	13.6747	.4421	99.1716
3	13.6107	.5061	98.6655
4	13.5375	.5794	98.0861
5	13.4536	.6633	97.4228
6	13.3576	.7593	96.6636
7	13.2477	.8692	95.7944
8	13.1219	.9950	94.7994
9	12.9778	1.1390	93.6604
10	12.8130	1.3039	92.3564
11	12.6242	1.4927	90.8638
12	12.4081	1.7087	89.1551
13	12.1608	1.9561	87.1990
14	11.8777	2.2392	84.9598
15	11.5535	2.5634	82.3964
16	11.1825	2.9344	79.4620
17	10.7577	3.3592	76.1028
18	10.2714	3.8454	72.2574
19	9.7148	4.4021	67.8553
20	9.0776	5.0393	62.8160
21	8.3481	5.7687	57.0473
22	7.5131	6.6038	50.4435
23	6.5572	7.5597	42.8838
24	5.4629	8.6540	34.2298
25	4.2102	9.9067	24.3231
26	2.7761	11.3407	12.9824
27	1.1345	12.9824	0.0000

YEARS 28   QTR PAYT 3.5174   AN CONST 14.07

#	INT	PRIN	BALANCE
1	13.7332	.3363	99.6637
2	13.6845	.3849	99.2788
3	13.6288	.4406	98.8382
4	13.5650	.5044	98.3337
5	13.4920	.5774	97.7563
6	13.4084	.6610	97.0953
7	13.3127	.7567	96.3385
8	13.2031	.8663	95.4723
9	13.0777	.9917	94.4806
10	12.9342	1.1352	93.3454
11	12.7699	1.2995	92.0459
12	12.5818	1.4876	90.5582
13	12.3664	1.7030	88.8553
14	12.1199	1.9495	86.9058
15	11.8377	2.2317	84.6741
16	11.5147	2.5547	82.1194
17	11.1449	2.9245	79.1948
18	10.7215	3.3479	75.8469
19	10.2369	3.8325	72.0144
20	9.6821	4.3873	67.6272
21	9.0471	5.0223	62.6048
22	8.3201	5.7493	56.8555
23	7.4878	6.5816	50.2739
24	6.5351	7.5343	42.7396
25	5.4445	8.6249	34.1147
26	4.1960	9.8734	24.2413
27	2.7668	11.3026	12.9387
28	1.1307	12.9387	0.0000

YEARS 29   QTR PAYT 3.5070   AN CONST 14.03

#	INT	PRIN	BALANCE
1	13.7353	.2929	99.7071
2	13.6929	.3353	99.3719
3	13.6444	.3838	98.9881
4	13.5888	.4394	98.5487
5	13.5252	.5030	98.0458
6	13.4524	.5758	97.4700
7	13.3691	.6591	96.8109
8	13.2737	.7545	96.0564
9	13.1645	.8637	95.1927
10	13.0394	.9888	94.2039
11	12.8963	1.1319	93.0720
12	12.7325	1.2957	91.7763
13	12.5449	1.4833	90.2930
14	12.3302	1.6980	88.5950
15	12.0844	1.9438	86.6513
16	11.8030	2.2252	84.4261
17	11.4809	2.5473	81.8788
18	11.1122	2.9160	78.9629
19	10.6901	3.3381	75.6248
20	10.2069	3.8213	71.8035
21	9.6538	4.3744	67.4291
22	9.0206	5.0076	62.4215
23	8.2957	5.7325	56.6890
24	7.4659	6.5623	50.1267
25	6.5160	7.5122	42.6144
26	5.4285	8.5996	34.0148
27	4.1837	9.8445	24.1703
28	2.7587	11.2695	12.9008
29	1.1274	12.9008	0.0000

YEARS 30   QTR PAYT 3.4981   AN CONST 14.00

#	INT	PRIN	BALANCE
1	13.7372	.2552	99.7448
2	13.7003	.2921	99.4527
3	13.6580	.3344	99.1183
4	13.6096	.3828	98.7355
5	13.5542	.4382	98.2972
6	13.4907	.5017	97.7956
7	13.4181	.5743	97.2213
8	13.3350	.6574	96.5638
9	13.2398	.7526	95.8113
10	13.1309	.8615	94.9497
11	13.0062	.9862	93.9635
12	12.8634	1.1290	92.8345
13	12.7000	1.2924	91.5421
14	12.5129	1.4795	90.0626
15	12.2987	1.6937	88.3690
16	12.0536	1.9388	86.4301
17	11.7729	2.2195	84.2107
18	11.4516	2.5408	81.6699
19	11.0839	2.9085	78.7614
20	10.6628	3.3296	75.4318
21	10.1809	3.8115	71.6203
22	9.6291	4.3633	67.2570
23	8.9975	4.9949	62.2622
24	8.2745	5.7179	56.5443
25	7.4468	6.5456	49.9987
26	6.4993	7.4931	42.5057
27	5.4147	8.5777	33.9280
28	4.1730	9.8194	24.1086
29	2.7517	11.2407	12.8679
30	1.1245	12.8679	0.0000

YEARS 2 — QTR PAYT 14.5477 — AN CONST 58.20

#	INT	PRIN	BALANCE
1	11.6254	46.5653	53.4347
2	4.7559	53.4347	0.0000

YEARS 3 — QTR PAYT 10.3484 — AN CONST 41.40

#	INT	PRIN	BALANCE
1	12.5280	28.8656	71.1344
2	8.2696	33.1239	38.0105
3	3.3831	38.0105	0.0000

YEARS 4 — QTR PAYT 8.2685 — AN CONST 33.08

#	INT	PRIN	BALANCE
1	12.9750	20.0989	79.9011
2	10.0100	23.0639	56.8372
3	6.6075	26.4664	30.3708
4	2.7031	30.3708	0.0000

YEARS 5 — QTR PAYT 7.0361 — AN CONST 28.15

#	INT	PRIN	BALANCE
1	13.2399	14.9045	85.0955
2	11.0412	17.1032	67.9923
3	8.5181	19.6264	48.3659
4	5.6227	22.5217	25.8442
5	2.3002	25.8442	0.0000

YEARS 6 — QTR PAYT 6.2273 — AN CONST 24.91

#	INT	PRIN	BALANCE
1	13.4138	11.4953	88.5047
2	11.7180	13.1912	75.3135
3	9.7720	15.1372	60.1763
4	7.5389	17.3703	42.8061
5	4.9764	19.9328	22.8733
6	2.0358	22.8733	0.0000

YEARS 7 — QTR PAYT 5.6603 — AN CONST 22.65

#	INT	PRIN	BALANCE
1	13.5357	9.1054	90.8946
2	12.1924	10.4486	80.4460
3	10.6510	11.9901	68.4559
4	8.8822	13.7589	54.6970
5	6.8524	15.7886	38.9084
6	4.5233	18.1178	20.7906
7	1.8505	20.7906	0.0000

YEARS 8 — QTR PAYT 5.2442 — AN CONST 20.98

#	INT	PRIN	BALANCE
1	13.6251	7.3515	92.6485
2	12.5406	8.4360	84.2125
3	11.2961	9.6805	74.5320
4	9.8680	11.1086	63.4234
5	8.2292	12.7474	50.6760
6	6.3487	14.6279	36.0481
7	4.1907	16.7859	19.2622
8	1.7144	19.2622	0.0000

YEARS 9 — QTR PAYT 4.9284 — AN CONST 19.72

#	INT	PRIN	BALANCE
1	13.6930	6.0207	93.9793
2	12.8048	6.9089	87.0704
3	11.7856	7.9281	79.1423
4	10.6160	9.0977	70.0446
5	9.2739	10.4398	59.6048
6	7.7338	11.9799	47.6249
7	5.9664	13.7472	33.8777
8	3.9384	15.7753	18.1025
9	1.6112	18.1025	0.0000

YEARS 10 — QTR PAYT 4.6827 — AN CONST 18.74

#	INT	PRIN	BALANCE
1	13.7458	4.9851	95.0149
2	13.0104	5.7206	89.2943
3	12.1664	6.5645	82.7298
4	11.1980	7.5329	75.1970
5	10.0868	8.6441	66.5528
6	8.8116	9.9194	56.6335
7	7.3482	11.3827	45.2508
8	5.6690	13.0619	32.1889
9	3.7421	14.9888	17.2000
10	1.5309	17.2000	0.0000

YEARS 11 — QTR PAYT 4.4878 — AN CONST 17.96

#	INT	PRIN	BALANCE
1	13.7877	4.1634	95.8366
2	13.1735	4.7776	91.0590
3	12.4687	5.4824	85.5766
4	11.6599	6.2912	79.2855
5	10.7318	7.2193	72.0662
6	9.6668	8.2843	63.7820
7	8.4447	9.5064	54.2756
8	7.0423	10.9088	43.3668
9	5.4330	12.5181	30.8487
10	3.5863	14.3648	16.4839
11	1.4671	16.4839	0.0000

YEARS 12 — QTR PAYT 4.3306 — AN CONST 17.33

#	INT	PRIN	BALANCE
1	13.8215	3.5011	96.4989
2	13.3050	4.0176	92.4813
3	12.7123	4.6103	87.8709
4	12.0321	5.2904	82.5805
5	11.2517	6.0709	76.5096
6	10.3561	6.9665	69.5431
7	9.3284	7.9942	61.5489
8	8.1490	9.1735	52.3753
9	6.7957	10.5269	41.8485
10	5.2428	12.0798	29.7687
11	3.4607	13.8619	15.9068
12	1.4158	15.9068	0.0000

YEARS 13 — QTR PAYT 4.2024 — AN CONST 16.81

#	INT	PRIN	BALANCE
1	13.8490	2.9607	97.0393
2	13.4122	3.3975	93.6418
3	12.9110	3.8987	89.7432
4	12.3359	4.4738	85.2694
5	11.6759	5.1338	80.1355
6	10.9186	5.8912	74.2444
7	10.0495	6.7602	67.4841
8	9.0522	7.7575	59.7266
9	7.9078	8.9019	50.8247
10	6.5945	10.2152	40.6095
11	5.0875	11.7222	28.8873
12	3.3583	13.4515	15.4359
13	1.3739	15.4359	0.0000

YEARS 14 — QTR PAYT 4.0967 — AN CONST 16.39

#	INT	PRIN	BALANCE
1	13.8717	2.5152	97.4848
2	13.5007	2.8862	94.5986
3	13.0749	3.3120	91.2866
4	12.5863	3.8006	87.4860
5	12.0256	4.3613	83.1247
6	11.3822	5.0047	78.1200
7	10.6439	5.7430	72.3770
8	9.7967	6.5902	65.7868
9	8.8245	7.5624	58.2244
10	7.7089	8.6780	49.5463
11	6.4287	9.9583	39.5881
12	4.9596	11.4273	28.1607
13	3.2738	13.1131	15.0476
14	1.3393	15.0476	0.0000

YEARS 15 — QTR PAYT 4.0089 — AN CONST 16.04

#	INT	PRIN	BALANCE
1	13.8906	2.1448	97.8552
2	13.5742	2.4612	95.3939
3	13.2111	2.8243	92.5696
4	12.7945	3.2410	89.3286
5	12.3164	3.7191	85.6095
6	11.7677	4.2677	81.3418
7	11.1381	4.8973	76.4445
8	10.4156	5.6198	70.8246
9	9.5866	6.4489	64.3758
10	8.6352	7.4002	56.9756
11	7.5435	8.4919	48.4836
12	6.2908	9.7447	38.7390
13	4.8532	11.1822	27.5567
14	3.2036	12.8319	14.7249
15	1.3106	14.7249	0.0000

YEARS 16 — QTR PAYT 3.9353 — AN CONST 15.75

#	INT	PRIN	BALANCE
1	13.9064	1.8348	98.1652
2	13.6358	2.1055	96.0597
3	13.3252	2.4161	93.6437
4	12.9687	2.7725	90.8712
5	12.5597	3.1815	87.6896
6	12.0904	3.6509	84.0388
7	11.5518	4.1894	79.8493
8	10.9337	4.8075	75.0419
9	10.2245	5.5167	69.5252
10	9.4107	6.3305	63.1946
11	8.4768	7.2644	55.9302
12	7.4051	8.3361	47.5941
13	6.1754	9.5659	38.0282
14	4.7642	10.9771	27.0511
15	3.1448	12.5964	14.4547
16	1.2865	14.4547	0.0000

YEARS 17 — QTR PAYT 3.8734 — AN CONST 15.50

#	INT	PRIN	BALANCE
1	13.9197	1.5738	98.4262
2	13.6876	1.8059	96.6203
3	13.4212	2.0723	94.5480
4	13.1154	2.3781	92.1699
5	12.7646	2.7289	89.4411
6	12.3621	3.1314	86.3096
7	11.9001	3.5934	82.7162
8	11.3700	4.1235	78.5927
9	10.7617	4.7318	73.8609
10	10.0636	5.4299	68.4310
11	9.2626	6.2309	62.2001
12	8.3434	7.1501	55.0500
13	7.2886	8.2049	46.8451
14	6.0782	9.4153	37.4297
15	4.6892	10.8043	26.6254
16	3.0953	12.3982	14.2272
17	1.2663	14.2272	0.0000

YEARS 18 — QTR PAYT 3.8210 — AN CONST 15.29

#	INT	PRIN	BALANCE
1	13.9310	1.3529	98.6471
2	13.7314	1.5525	97.0947
3	13.5024	1.7815	95.3132
4	13.2396	2.0443	93.2689
5	12.9380	2.3459	90.9230
6	12.5919	2.6920	88.2310
7	12.1948	3.0891	85.1419
8	11.7391	3.5448	81.5972
9	11.2162	4.0677	77.5294
10	10.6161	4.6678	72.8616
11	9.9275	5.3564	67.5052
12	9.1373	6.1466	61.3586
13	8.2305	7.0534	54.3052
14	7.1900	8.0939	46.2113
15	5.9959	9.2880	36.9233
16	4.6258	10.6581	26.2652
17	3.0534	12.2305	14.0347
18	1.2492	14.0347	0.0000

YEARS 19 — QTR PAYT 3.7765 — AN CONST 15.11

#	INT	PRIN	BALANCE
1	13.9406	1.1652	98.8348
2	13.7687	1.3371	97.4977
3	13.5714	1.5344	95.9633
4	13.3451	1.7607	94.2026
5	13.0853	2.0205	92.1821
6	12.7873	2.3185	89.8635
7	12.4452	2.6606	87.2029
8	12.0527	3.0531	84.1499
9	11.6023	3.5035	80.6464
10	11.0855	4.0203	76.6260
11	10.4924	4.6134	72.0126
12	9.8118	5.2940	66.7186
13	9.0308	6.0750	60.6436
14	8.1346	6.9712	53.6724
15	7.1062	7.9996	45.6728
16	5.9261	9.1797	36.4931
17	4.5719	10.5340	25.9592
18	3.0179	12.0880	13.8712
19	1.2346	13.8712	0.0000

YEARS 20 — QTR PAYT 3.7385 — AN CONST 14.96

#	INT	PRIN	BALANCE
1	13.9487	1.0052	98.9948
2	13.8004	1.1535	97.8413
3	13.6303	1.3237	96.5176
4	13.4350	1.5190	94.9986
5	13.2109	1.7430	93.2556
6	12.9538	2.0002	91.2554
7	12.6587	2.2952	88.9602
8	12.3201	2.6338	86.3264
9	11.9316	3.0224	83.3040
10	11.4857	3.4683	79.8357
11	10.9740	3.9799	75.8558
12	10.3869	4.5670	71.2887
13	9.7132	5.2408	66.0480
14	8.9400	6.0139	60.0340
15	8.0528	6.9011	53.1329
16	7.0348	7.9192	45.2137
17	5.8665	9.0875	36.1263
18	4.5259	10.4281	25.6982
19	2.9875	11.9664	13.7318
20	1.2222	13.7318	0.0000

YEARS 21 — QTR PAYT 3.7060 — AN CONST 14.83

#	INT	PRIN	BALANCE
1	13.9557	.8684	99.1316
2	13.8276	.9965	98.1351
3	13.6806	1.1435	96.9916

#	INT	PRIN	BALANCE
4	13.5119	1.3122	95.6795
5	13.3183	1.5058	94.1737
6	13.0962	1.7279	92.4458
7	12.8413	1.9828	90.4630
8	12.5488	2.2753	88.1877
9	12.2131	2.6110	85.5767
10	11.8280	2.9961	82.5806
11	11.3859	3.4381	79.1424
12	10.8787	3.9454	75.1971
13	10.2967	4.5274	70.6697
14	9.6288	5.1953	65.4744
15	8.8624	5.9617	59.5127
16	7.9829	6.8412	52.6715
17	6.9737	7.8504	44.8211
18	5.8156	9.0085	35.8126
19	4.4866	10.3375	25.4750
20	2.9616	11.8625	13.6125
21	1.2116	13.6125	0.0000

YEARS 22 — QTR PAYT 3.6782 — AN CONST 14.72

#	INT	PRIN	BALANCE
1	13.9617	.7511	99.2489
2	13.8509	.8619	98.3871
3	13.7238	.9890	97.3981
4	13.5779	1.1349	96.2632
5	13.4104	1.3023	94.9608
6	13.2183	1.4945	93.4664
7	12.9978	1.7149	91.7515
8	12.7449	1.9679	89.7836
9	12.4545	2.2582	87.5253
10	12.1214	2.5914	84.9340
11	11.7391	2.9736	81.9603
12	11.3004	3.4123	78.5480
13	10.7970	3.9157	74.6323
14	10.2194	4.4934	70.1389
15	9.5565	5.1563	64.9827
16	8.7958	5.9169	59.0657
17	7.9230	6.7898	52.2759
18	6.9213	7.7915	44.4845
19	5.7719	8.9409	35.5436
20	4.4529	10.2599	25.2837
21	2.9393	11.7734	13.5103
22	1.2025	13.5103	0.0000

YEARS 23 — QTR PAYT 3.6543 — AN CONST 14.62

#	INT	PRIN	BALANCE
1	13.9668	.6503	99.3497
2	13.8709	.7462	98.6036
3	13.7608	.8563	97.7473
4	13.6345	.9826	96.7647
5	13.4896	1.1275	95.6372
6	13.3232	1.2939	94.3434
7	13.1324	1.4847	92.8586
8	12.9133	1.7038	91.1549
9	12.6620	1.9551	89.1997
10	12.3736	2.2435	86.9562
11	12.0426	2.5745	84.3817
12	11.6628	2.9543	81.4274
13	11.2270	3.3901	78.0373
14	10.7268	3.8903	74.1470
15	10.1529	4.4642	69.6828
16	9.4944	5.1227	64.5601
17	8.7386	5.8785	58.6817
18	7.8714	6.7457	51.9360
19	6.8763	7.7408	44.1952
20	5.7343	8.8827	35.3125
21	4.4239	10.1932	25.1193
22	2.9202	11.6969	13.4224
23	1.1947	13.4224	0.0000

YEARS 24 — QTR PAYT 3.6337 — AN CONST 14.54

#	INT	PRIN	BALANCE
1	13.9713	.5635	99.4365
2	13.8881	.6466	98.7900
3	13.7928	.7420	98.0480
4	13.6833	.8514	97.1965
5	13.5577	.9770	96.2195
6	13.4136	1.1212	95.0983
7	13.2482	1.2866	93.8118
8	13.0584	1.4764	92.3354
9	12.8406	1.6942	90.6412
10	12.5906	1.9441	88.6971
11	12.3038	2.2309	86.4662
12	11.9747	2.5600	83.9062
13	11.5971	2.9377	80.9686
14	11.1637	3.3710	77.5975
15	10.6664	3.8683	73.7292
16	10.0957	4.4390	69.2902
17	9.4409	5.0939	64.1963
18	8.6894	5.8453	58.3510
19	7.8271	6.7076	51.6434
20	6.8375	7.6972	43.9462
21	5.7020	8.8327	35.1135
22	4.3990	10.1357	24.9778
23	2.9038	11.6310	13.3468
24	1.1879	13.3468	0.0000

YEARS 25 — QTR PAYT 3.6159 — AN CONST 14.47

#	INT	PRIN	BALANCE
1	13.9751	.4886	99.5114
2	13.9030	.5607	98.9507
3	13.8203	.6434	98.3072
4	13.7254	.7383	97.5689
5	13.6164	.8473	96.7216
6	13.4914	.9723	95.7494
7	13.3480	1.1157	94.6337
8	13.1834	1.2803	93.3534
9	12.9946	1.4692	91.8842
10	12.7778	1.6859	90.1983
11	12.5291	1.9346	88.2637
12	12.2437	2.2200	86.0437
13	11.9162	2.5475	83.4963
14	11.5404	2.9233	80.5729
15	11.1091	3.3546	77.2184
16	10.6143	3.8494	73.3689
17	10.0464	4.4173	68.9516
18	9.3947	5.0690	63.8827
19	8.6469	5.8168	58.0659
20	7.7888	6.6749	51.3910
21	6.8041	7.6596	43.7314
22	5.6742	8.7895	34.9419
23	4.3775	10.0862	24.8557
24	2.8896	11.5741	13.2816
25	1.1821	13.2816	0.0000

YEARS 26 — QTR PAYT 3.6006 — AN CONST 14.41

#	INT	PRIN	BALANCE
1	13.9784	.4240	99.5760
2	13.9158	.4866	99.0894
3	13.8440	.5583	98.5311
4	13.7617	.6407	97.8904
5	13.6672	.7352	97.1552
6	13.5587	.8437	96.3115
7	13.4342	.9681	95.3434
8	13.2914	1.1110	94.2324
9	13.1275	1.2749	92.9576
10	12.9395	1.4629	91.4946
11	12.7236	1.6787	89.8159
12	12.4760	1.9264	87.8895
13	12.1918	2.2106	85.6789
14	11.8657	2.5367	83.1422
15	11.4915	2.9109	80.2313
16	11.0620	3.3403	76.8910
17	10.5693	3.8331	73.0579
18	10.0038	4.3986	68.6593
19	9.3549	5.0475	63.6118
20	8.6103	5.7921	57.8197
21	7.7558	6.6466	51.1731
22	6.7753	7.6271	43.5460
23	5.6501	8.7523	34.7938
24	4.3590	10.0434	24.7503
25	2.8773	11.5251	13.2253
26	1.1771	13.2253	0.0000

YEARS 27 — QTR PAYT 3.5873 — AN CONST 14.35

#	INT	PRIN	BALANCE
1	13.9812	.3681	99.6319
2	13.9269	.4224	99.2094
3	13.8646	.4848	98.7247
4	13.7931	.5563	98.1684
5	13.7110	.6383	97.5300
6	13.6169	.7325	96.7975
7	13.5088	.8406	95.9570
8	13.3848	.9646	94.9924
9	13.2425	1.1069	93.8855
10	13.0792	1.2702	92.6154
11	12.8918	1.4575	91.1578
12	12.6768	1.6726	89.4853
13	12.4301	1.9193	87.5659
14	12.1469	2.2024	85.3635
15	11.8220	2.5274	82.8362
16	11.4492	2.9002	79.9360
17	11.0213	3.3280	76.6079
18	10.5304	3.8190	72.7889
19	9.9670	4.3824	68.4065
20	9.3205	5.0289	63.3776
21	8.5786	5.7708	57.6068
22	7.7273	6.6221	50.9847
23	6.7503	7.5990	43.3857
24	5.6293	8.7200	34.6657
25	4.3429	10.0065	24.6592
26	2.8667	11.4826	13.1766
27	1.1728	13.1766	0.0000

YEARS 28 — QTR PAYT 3.5759 — AN CONST 14.31

#	INT	PRIN	BALANCE
1	13.9837	.3198	99.6802
2	13.9365	.3670	99.3133
3	13.8824	.4211	98.8922
4	13.8203	.4832	98.4090
5	13.7490	.5545	97.8545
6	13.6672	.6363	97.2182
7	13.5733	.7302	96.4880
8	13.4656	.8379	95.6501
9	13.3420	.9615	94.6886
10	13.2001	1.1033	93.5853
11	13.0374	1.2661	92.3192
12	12.8506	1.4529	90.8663
13	12.6363	1.6672	89.1991
14	12.3903	1.9132	87.2859
15	12.1081	2.1954	85.0905
16	11.7842	2.5193	82.5713
17	11.4126	2.8909	79.6803
18	10.9861	3.3174	76.3629
19	10.4967	3.8068	72.5561
20	9.9351	4.3684	68.1878
21	9.2907	5.0128	63.1749
22	8.5511	5.7523	57.4226
23	7.7025	6.6009	50.8217
24	6.7288	7.5747	43.2470
25	5.6113	8.6922	34.5548
26	4.3290	9.9745	24.5804
27	2.8576	11.4459	13.1344
28	1.1690	13.1344	0.0000

YEARS 29 — QTR PAYT 3.5659 — AN CONST 14.27

#	INT	PRIN	BALANCE
1	13.9858	.2779	99.7221
2	13.9448	.3189	99.4032
3	13.8978	.3659	99.0373
4	13.8438	.4199	98.6174
5	13.7819	.4819	98.1355
6	13.7108	.5530	97.5825
7	13.6292	.6345	96.9480
8	13.5356	.7281	96.2199
9	13.4282	.8356	95.3843
10	13.3049	.9588	94.4255
11	13.1635	1.1003	93.3252
12	13.0011	1.2626	92.0626
13	12.8149	1.4488	90.6138
14	12.6011	1.6626	88.9512
15	12.3559	1.9078	87.0434
16	12.0744	2.1893	84.8541
17	11.7515	2.5123	82.3418
18	11.3808	2.8829	79.4589
19	10.9555	3.3082	76.1507
20	10.4675	3.7962	72.3545
21	9.9075	4.3562	67.9983
22	9.2648	4.9989	62.9994
23	8.5274	5.7363	57.2630
24	7.6811	6.5826	50.6805
25	6.7101	7.5537	43.1268
26	5.5957	8.6680	34.4588
27	4.3170	9.9467	24.5121
28	2.8496	11.4141	13.0979
29	1.1658	13.0979	0.0000

YEARS 30 — QTR PAYT 3.5573 — AN CONST 14.23

#	INT	PRIN	BALANCE
1	13.9877	.2416	99.7584
2	13.9520	.2772	99.4812
3	13.9111	.3181	99.1631
4	13.8642	.3651	98.7980
5	13.8104	.4189	98.3791
6	13.7486	.4807	97.8984
7	13.6776	.5516	97.3468
8	13.5963	.6330	96.7138
9	13.5029	.7264	95.9874
10	13.3957	.8335	95.1539
11	13.2728	.9565	94.1974
12	13.1317	1.0976	93.0998
13	12.9697	1.2595	91.8402
14	12.7839	1.4453	90.3949
15	12.5707	1.6586	88.7363
16	12.3260	1.9032	86.8331
17	12.0453	2.1840	84.6491
18	11.7231	2.5062	82.1429
19	11.3533	2.8759	79.2669
20	10.9291	3.3002	75.9668
21	10.4422	3.7870	72.1797
22	9.8835	4.3457	67.8340
23	9.2425	4.9868	62.8472
24	8.5068	5.7225	57.1247
25	7.6626	6.5667	50.5580
26	6.6939	7.5354	43.0226
27	5.5822	8.6471	34.3755
28	4.3066	9.9227	24.4528
29	2.8427	11.3865	13.0663
30	1.1630	13.0663	0.0000

QUARTERLY PAYMENT AMORTIZATION SCHEDULE PER $100 — 14.25 %

YEARS 2 — QTR PAYT 14.5856 — AN CONST 58.35

#	INT	PRIN	BALANCE
1	11.8373	46.5052	53.4948
2	4.8477	53.4948	0.0000

YEARS 3 — QTR PAYT 10.3865 — AN CONST 41.55

#	INT	PRIN	BALANCE
1	12.7564	28.7896	71.2104
2	8.4294	33.1166	38.0939
3	3.4521	38.0939	0.0000

YEARS 4 — QTR PAYT 8.3073 — AN CONST 33.23

#	INT	PRIN	BALANCE
1	13.2115	20.0179	79.9821
2	10.2029	23.0265	56.9556
3	6.7420	26.4873	30.4683
4	2.7611	30.4683	0.0000

YEARS 5 — QTR PAYT 7.0760 — AN CONST 28.31

#	INT	PRIN	BALANCE
1	13.4810	14.8228	85.1772
2	11.2532	17.0507	68.1265
3	8.6905	19.6133	48.5132
4	5.7427	22.5612	25.9520
5	2.3518	25.9520	0.0000

YEARS 6 — QTR PAYT 6.2682 — AN CONST 25.08

#	INT	PRIN	BALANCE
1	13.6578	11.4151	88.5849
2	11.9421	13.1308	75.4541
3	9.9686	15.1043	60.3498
4	7.6985	17.3744	42.9754
5	5.0871	19.9858	22.9896
6	2.0833	22.9896	0.0000

YEARS 7 — QTR PAYT 5.7023 — AN CONST 22.81

#	INT	PRIN	BALANCE
1	13.7816	9.0277	90.9723
2	12.4248	10.3846	80.5877
3	10.8640	11.9454	68.6423
4	9.0687	13.7407	54.9016
5	7.0035	15.8059	39.0956
6	4.6279	18.1815	20.9141
7	1.8953	20.9141	0.0000

YEARS 8 — QTR PAYT 5.2874 — AN CONST 21.15

#	INT	PRIN	BALANCE
1	13.8725	7.2771	92.7229
2	12.7787	8.3708	84.3521
3	11.5206	9.6289	74.7232
4	10.0734	11.0761	63.6471
5	8.4087	12.7408	50.9063
6	6.4938	14.6557	36.2506
7	4.2911	16.8584	19.3922
8	1.7573	19.3922	0.0000

YEARS 9 — QTR PAYT 4.9728 — AN CONST 19.90

#	INT	PRIN	BALANCE
1	13.9413	5.9498	94.0502
2	13.0471	6.8441	87.2061
3	12.0184	7.8727	79.3333
4	10.8352	9.0560	70.2773
5	9.4741	10.4171	59.8602
6	7.9084	11.9827	47.8775
7	6.1075	13.7837	34.0938
8	4.0358	15.8554	18.2384
9	1.6528	18.2384	0.0000

YEARS 10 — QTR PAYT 4.7282 — AN CONST 18.92

#	INT	PRIN	BALANCE
1	13.9949	4.9181	95.0819
2	13.2557	5.6572	89.4247
3	12.4054	6.5075	82.9172
4	11.4274	7.4856	75.4317
5	10.3023	8.6106	66.8210
6	9.0081	9.9048	56.9163
7	7.5195	11.3934	45.5228
8	5.8071	13.1058	32.4170
9	3.8373	15.0756	17.3414
10	1.5715	17.3414	0.0000

YEARS 11 — QTR PAYT 4.5344 — AN CONST 18.14

#	INT	PRIN	BALANCE
1	14.0373	4.1002	95.8998
2	13.4210	4.7164	91.1834
3	12.7122	5.4253	85.7581
4	11.8968	6.2407	79.5175
5	10.9588	7.1786	72.3388
6	9.8799	8.2576	64.0813
7	8.6388	9.4987	54.5826
8	7.2112	10.9263	43.6563
9	5.5690	12.5685	31.0879
10	3.6800	14.4575	16.6304
11	1.5071	16.6304	0.0000

YEARS 12 — QTR PAYT 4.3783 — AN CONST 17.52

#	INT	PRIN	BALANCE
1	14.0714	3.4418	96.5582
2	13.5542	3.9590	92.5992
3	12.9591	4.5541	88.0451
4	12.2747	5.2385	82.8066
5	11.4873	6.0259	76.7807
6	10.5816	6.9316	69.8491
7	9.5398	7.9734	61.8757
8	8.3415	9.1717	52.7040
9	6.9630	10.5502	42.1538
10	5.3773	12.1359	30.0179
11	3.5533	13.9599	16.0580
12	1.4552	16.0580	0.0000

YEARS 13 — QTR PAYT 4.2511 — AN CONST 17.01

#	INT	PRIN	BALANCE
1	14.0993	2.9051	97.0949
2	13.6626	3.3418	93.7531
3	13.1604	3.8440	89.9091
4	12.5826	4.4218	85.4873
5	11.9181	5.0864	80.4009
6	11.1536	5.8508	74.5501
7	10.2742	6.7302	67.8199
8	9.2627	7.7417	60.0782
9	8.0991	8.9053	51.1729
10	6.7607	10.2437	40.9292
11	5.2211	11.7833	29.1458
12	3.4501	13.5543	15.5915
13	1.4129	15.5915	0.0000

YEARS 14 — QTR PAYT 4.1464 — AN CONST 16.59

#	INT	PRIN	BALANCE
1	14.1222	2.4633	97.5367
2	13.7520	2.8336	94.7031
3	13.3261	3.2595	91.4436
4	12.8362	3.7493	87.6943
5	12.2727	4.3129	83.3814
6	11.6245	4.9611	78.4204
7	10.8788	5.7067	72.7137
8	10.0211	6.5644	66.1493
9	9.0345	7.5510	58.5982
10	7.8996	8.6859	49.9123
11	6.5942	9.9914	39.9209
12	5.0925	11.4931	28.4279
13	3.3651	13.2204	15.2074
14	1.3781	15.2074	0.0000

YEARS 15 — QTR PAYT 4.0595 — AN CONST 16.24

#	INT	PRIN	BALANCE
1	14.1412	2.0966	97.9034
2	13.8261	2.4117	95.4917
3	13.4636	2.7742	92.7176
4	13.0467	3.1911	89.5264
5	12.5671	3.6707	85.8557
6	12.0154	4.2224	81.6333
7	11.3808	4.8571	76.7762
8	10.6508	5.5871	71.1892
9	9.8110	6.4268	64.7624
10	8.8451	7.3927	57.3697
11	7.7340	8.5038	48.8659
12	6.4559	9.7819	39.0840
13	4.9857	11.2521	27.8319
14	3.2946	12.9433	14.8886
15	1.3492	14.8886	0.0000

YEARS 16 — QTR PAYT 3.9868 — AN CONST 15.95

#	INT	PRIN	BALANCE
1	14.1571	1.7900	98.2100
2	13.8881	2.0591	96.1509
3	13.5786	2.3685	93.7824
4	13.2226	2.7245	91.0579
5	12.8132	3.1340	87.9239
6	12.3421	3.6050	84.3189
7	11.8003	4.1469	80.1720
8	11.1770	4.7701	75.4019
9	10.4601	5.4870	69.9149
10	9.6354	6.3117	63.6031
11	8.6868	7.2604	56.3427
12	7.5956	8.3516	47.9912
13	6.3403	9.6068	38.3844
14	4.8965	11.0507	27.3337
15	3.2356	12.7116	14.6221
16	1.3251	14.6221	0.0000

YEARS 17 — QTR PAYT 3.9257 — AN CONST 15.71

#	INT	PRIN	BALANCE
1	14.1705	1.5323	98.4677
2	13.9402	1.7626	96.7051
3	13.6753	2.0275	94.6776
4	13.3706	2.3322	92.3454
5	13.0200	2.6828	89.6626
6	12.6168	3.0860	86.5766
7	12.1530	3.5498	83.0269
8	11.6195	4.0833	78.9435
9	11.0058	4.6970	74.2465
10	10.2998	5.4030	68.8436
11	9.4878	6.2150	62.6285
12	8.5537	7.1491	55.4794
13	7.4792	8.2236	47.2558
14	6.2432	9.4596	37.7962
15	4.8214	10.8814	26.9148
16	3.1860	12.5168	14.3980
17	1.3048	14.3980	0.0000

YEARS 18 — QTR PAYT 3.8741 — AN CONST 15.50

#	INT	PRIN	BALANCE
1	14.1818	1.3146	98.6854
2	13.9842	1.5121	97.1733
3	13.7570	1.7394	95.4339
4	13.4955	2.0009	93.4330
5	13.1948	2.3016	91.1314
6	12.8489	2.6475	88.4839
7	12.4510	3.0454	85.4385
8	11.9933	3.5031	81.9354
9	11.4667	4.0296	77.9058
10	10.8611	4.6353	73.2705
11	10.1644	5.3319	67.9386
12	9.3631	6.1333	61.8052
13	8.4412	7.0551	54.7501
14	7.3809	8.1155	46.6346
15	6.1611	9.3353	37.2993
16	4.7581	10.7383	26.5610
17	3.1441	12.3523	14.2088
18	1.2876	14.2088	0.0000

YEARS 19 — QTR PAYT 3.8303 — AN CONST 15.33

#	INT	PRIN	BALANCE
1	14.1914	1.1299	98.8701
2	14.0216	1.2997	97.5704
3	13.8262	1.4951	96.0753
4	13.6015	1.7198	94.3556
5	13.3430	1.9782	92.3773
6	13.0457	2.2756	90.1017
7	12.7037	2.6176	87.4842
8	12.3103	3.0110	84.4732
9	11.8577	3.4635	81.0096
10	11.3372	3.9841	77.0255
11	10.7384	4.5829	72.4426
12	10.0496	5.2717	67.1709
13	9.2573	6.0640	61.1069
14	8.3459	6.9754	54.1315
15	7.2975	8.0238	46.1077
16	6.0915	9.2298	36.8779
17	4.7043	10.6170	26.2609
18	3.1086	12.2127	14.0482
19	1.2731	14.0482	0.0000

YEARS 20 — QTR PAYT 3.7931 — AN CONST 15.18

#	INT	PRIN	BALANCE
1	14.1995	.9727	99.0273
2	14.0533	1.1189	97.9084
3	13.8852	1.2871	96.6213
4	13.6917	1.4805	95.1408
5	13.4692	1.7030	93.4377
6	13.2132	1.9590	91.4787
7	12.9188	2.2534	89.2253
8	12.5801	2.5921	86.6332
9	12.1905	2.9817	83.6515
10	11.7424	3.4299	80.2216
11	11.2269	3.9453	76.2763
12	10.6339	4.5383	71.7380
13	9.9518	5.2204	66.5175
14	9.1672	6.0050	60.5125
15	8.2647	6.9076	53.6049
16	7.2265	7.9458	45.6592
17	6.0323	9.1400	36.5192
18	4.6585	10.5137	26.0055
19	3.0784	12.0939	13.9116
20	1.2607	13.9116	0.0000

YEARS 21 — QTR PAYT 3.7613 — AN CONST 15.05

#	INT	PRIN	BALANCE
1	14.2065	.8385	99.1615
2	14.0805	.9646	98.1969
3	13.9355	1.1095	97.0874

#	INT	PRIN	BALANCE
4	13.7687	1.2763	95.8111
5	13.5769	1.4681	94.3430
6	13.3563	1.6888	92.6542
7	13.1025	1.9426	90.7117
8	12.8105	2.2345	88.4771
9	12.4746	2.5704	85.9067
10	12.0883	2.9567	82.9500
11	11.6439	3.4011	79.5490
12	11.1328	3.9123	75.6367
13	10.5448	4.5003	71.1364
14	9.8684	5.1766	65.9598
15	9.0903	5.9547	60.0051
16	8.1954	6.8497	53.1554
17	7.1659	7.8791	45.2763
18	5.9817	9.0634	36.2129
19	4.6195	10.4255	25.7874
20	3.0525	11.9925	13.7949
21	1.2501	13.7949	0.0000

YEARS 22	QTR PAYT 3.7340	AN CONST 14.94	
#	INT	PRIN	BALANCE
1	14.2125	.7237	99.2763
2	14.1037	.8325	98.4439
3	13.9786	.9576	97.4863
4	13.8346	1.1015	96.3848
5	13.6691	1.2670	95.1177
6	13.4787	1.4575	93.6603
7	13.2596	1.6765	91.9837
8	13.0076	1.9285	90.0552
9	12.7178	2.2184	87.8368
10	12.3844	2.5518	85.2850
11	12.0008	2.9353	82.3497
12	11.5597	3.3765	78.9733
13	11.0522	3.8840	75.0893
14	10.4684	4.4677	70.6216
15	9.7970	5.1392	65.4824
16	9.0246	5.9116	59.5708
17	8.1361	6.8001	52.7708
18	7.1140	7.8221	44.9486
19	5.9384	8.9978	35.9509
20	4.5860	10.3501	25.6008
21	3.0305	11.9057	13.6951
22	1.2411	13.6951	0.0000

YEARS 23	QTR PAYT 3.7107	AN CONST 14.85	
#	INT	PRIN	BALANCE
1	14.2176	.6252	99.3748
2	14.1236	.7192	98.6556
3	14.0155	.8273	97.8284
4	13.8912	.9516	96.8768
5	13.7482	1.0946	95.7822
6	13.5836	1.2591	94.5231
7	13.3944	1.4484	93.0747
8	13.1767	1.6661	91.4086
9	12.9263	1.9165	89.4922
10	12.6383	2.2045	87.2877
11	12.3069	2.5358	84.7518
12	11.9258	2.9170	81.8349
13	11.4874	3.3554	78.4795
14	10.9831	3.8597	74.6199
15	10.4030	4.4398	70.1801
16	9.7357	5.1071	65.0730
17	8.9681	5.8746	59.1984
18	8.0852	6.7576	52.4408
19	7.0696	7.7732	44.6676
20	5.9013	8.9415	35.7261
21	4.5574	10.2854	25.4407
22	3.0115	11.8313	13.6095
23	1.2333	13.6095	0.0000

YEARS 24	QTR PAYT 3.6906	AN CONST 14.77	
#	INT	PRIN	BALANCE
1	14.2220	.5406	99.4594
2	14.1407	.6218	98.8376
3	14.0473	.7153	98.1223
4	13.9397	.8228	97.2995
5	13.8161	.9464	96.3531
6	13.6738	1.0887	95.2644
7	13.5102	1.2523	94.0121
8	13.3220	1.4405	92.5716
9	13.1055	1.6570	90.9145
10	12.8564	1.9061	89.0084
11	12.5699	2.1926	86.8158
12	12.2404	2.5221	84.2937
13	11.8613	2.9012	81.3925
14	11.4253	3.3372	78.0553
15	10.9237	3.8388	74.2165
16	10.3468	4.4158	69.8007
17	9.6831	5.0794	64.7213
18	8.9197	5.8429	58.8784
19	8.0415	6.7210	52.1574
20	7.0313	7.7312	44.4262
21	5.8694	8.8932	35.5330
22	4.5327	10.2298	25.3032
23	2.9952	11.7673	13.5359
24	1.2266	13.5359	0.0000

YEARS 25	QTR PAYT 3.6734	AN CONST 14.70	
#	INT	PRIN	BALANCE
1	14.2257	.4677	99.5323
2	14.1554	.5380	98.9942
3	14.0746	.6189	98.3753
4	13.9815	.7119	97.6634
5	13.8745	.8189	96.8444
6	13.7515	.9420	95.9024
7	13.6099	1.0836	94.8188
8	13.4470	1.2465	93.5724
9	13.2597	1.4338	92.1386
10	13.0442	1.6493	90.4893
11	12.7963	1.8972	88.5921
12	12.5112	2.1823	86.4097
13	12.1832	2.5103	83.8994
14	11.8059	2.8876	81.0118
15	11.3719	3.3216	77.6902
16	10.8726	3.8208	73.8693
17	10.2984	4.3951	69.4742
18	9.6378	5.0557	64.4185
19	8.8779	5.8155	58.6030
20	8.0039	6.6896	51.9134
21	6.9984	7.6950	44.2184
22	5.8419	8.8516	35.3668
23	4.5115	10.1819	25.1848
24	2.9812	11.7123	13.4726
25	1.2209	13.4726	0.0000

YEARS 26	QTR PAYT 3.6585	AN CONST 14.64	
#	INT	PRIN	BALANCE
1	14.2290	.4050	99.5950
2	14.1681	.4658	99.1292
3	14.0981	.5359	98.5933
4	14.0176	.6164	97.9769
5	13.9249	.7090	97.2678
6	13.8184	.8156	96.4522
7	13.6958	.9382	95.5140
8	13.5548	1.0792	94.4348
9	13.3926	1.2414	93.1934
10	13.2060	1.4280	91.7654
11	12.9914	1.6426	90.1228
12	12.7445	1.8895	88.2333
13	12.4605	2.1735	86.0598
14	12.1338	2.5002	83.5596
15	11.7580	2.8759	80.6837

#	INT	PRIN	BALANCE
16	11.3258	3.3082	77.3756
17	10.8286	3.8054	73.5702
18	10.2567	4.3773	69.1929
19	9.5988	5.0352	64.1577
20	8.8420	5.7920	58.3657
21	7.9715	6.6625	51.7032
22	6.9701	7.6639	44.0393
23	5.8182	8.8157	35.2236
24	4.4933	10.1407	25.0828
25	2.9691	11.6648	13.4180
26	1.2160	13.4180	0.0000

YEARS 27	QTR PAYT 3.6457	AN CONST 14.59	
#	INT	PRIN	BALANCE
1	14.2318	.3508	99.6492
2	14.1791	.4036	99.2456
3	14.1184	.4642	98.7814
4	14.0486	.5340	98.2474
5	13.9684	.6142	97.6332
6	13.8761	.7066	96.9266
7	13.7699	.8128	96.1138
8	13.6477	.9349	95.1789
9	13.5072	1.0754	94.1035
10	13.3456	1.2371	92.8665
11	13.1596	1.4230	91.4435
12	12.9458	1.6369	89.8066
13	12.6998	1.8829	87.9237
14	12.4168	2.1659	85.7579
15	12.0912	2.4914	83.2665
16	11.7168	2.8658	80.4007
17	11.2861	3.2966	77.1041
18	10.7906	3.7920	73.3121
19	10.2207	4.3620	68.9501
20	9.5651	5.0175	63.9326
21	8.8110	5.7717	58.1609
22	7.9435	6.6391	51.5218
23	6.9457	7.6370	43.8848
24	5.7978	8.7848	35.1000
25	4.4775	10.1051	24.9949
26	2.9587	11.6239	13.3709
27	1.2117	13.3709	0.0000

YEARS 28	QTR PAYT 3.6346	AN CONST 14.54	
#	INT	PRIN	BALANCE
1	14.2342	.3041	99.6959
2	14.1885	.3498	99.3462
3	14.1360	.4023	98.9438
4	14.0755	.4628	98.4810
5	14.0059	.5324	97.9487
6	13.9259	.6124	97.3363
7	13.8339	.7044	96.6319
8	13.7280	.8103	95.8216
9	13.6062	.9321	94.8895
10	13.4661	1.0722	93.8174
11	13.3050	1.2333	92.5841
12	13.1196	1.4187	91.1654
13	12.9064	1.6319	89.5335
14	12.6611	1.8771	87.6564
15	12.3790	2.1593	85.4971
16	12.0545	2.4838	83.0133
17	11.6812	2.8571	80.1562
18	11.2518	3.2865	76.8696
19	10.7578	3.7805	73.0892
20	10.1896	4.3487	68.7405
21	9.5360	5.0023	63.7382
22	8.7842	5.7541	57.9840
23	7.9193	6.6189	51.3651
24	6.9245	7.6138	43.7513
25	5.7802	8.7581	34.9933
26	4.4639	10.0744	24.9188
27	2.9497	11.5886	13.3303
28	1.2080	13.3303	0.0000

YEARS 29	QTR PAYT 3.6250	AN CONST 14.50	
#	INT	PRIN	BALANCE
1	14.2363	.2636	99.7364
2	14.1967	.3033	99.4331
3	14.1511	.3488	99.0843
4	14.0987	.4013	98.6830
5	14.0384	.4616	98.2214
6	13.9690	.5310	97.6904
7	13.8892	.6108	97.0797
8	13.7974	.7026	96.3771
9	13.6918	.8081	95.5690
10	13.5704	.9296	94.6394
11	13.4306	1.0693	93.5700
12	13.2699	1.2300	92.3400
13	13.0850	1.4149	90.9251
14	12.8724	1.6276	89.2975
15	12.6278	1.8722	87.4253
16	12.3464	2.1536	85.2717
17	12.0227	2.4773	82.7944
18	11.6504	2.8496	79.9449
19	11.2221	3.2779	76.6670
20	10.7294	3.7705	72.8965
21	10.1627	4.3372	68.5592
22	9.5109	4.9891	63.5701
23	8.7610	5.7390	57.8312
24	7.8985	6.6015	51.2297
25	6.9063	7.5937	43.6360
26	5.7650	8.7350	34.9010
27	4.4521	10.0478	24.8532
28	2.9420	11.5580	13.2951
29	1.2048	13.2951	0.0000

YEARS 30	QTR PAYT 3.6167	AN CONST 14.47	
#	INT	PRIN	BALANCE
1	14.2381	.2287	99.7713
2	14.2038	.2630	99.5083
3	14.1642	.3026	99.2057
4	14.1188	.3480	98.8577
5	14.0664	.4004	98.4573
6	14.0063	.4605	97.9968
7	13.9371	.5297	97.4671
8	13.8574	.6094	96.8577
9	13.7659	.7009	96.1567
10	13.6605	.8063	95.3504
11	13.5393	.9275	94.4230
12	13.3999	1.0669	93.3561
13	13.2396	1.2272	92.1288
14	13.0551	1.4117	90.7172
15	12.8429	1.6239	89.0933
16	12.5989	1.8679	87.2254
17	12.3181	2.1487	85.0767
18	11.9952	2.4716	82.6051
19	11.6237	2.8431	79.7621
20	11.1964	3.2704	76.4917
21	10.7049	3.7619	72.7298
22	10.1395	4.3273	68.4025
23	9.4891	4.9777	63.4248
24	8.7410	5.7258	57.6989
25	7.8804	6.5864	51.1125
26	6.8905	7.5763	43.5362
27	5.7518	8.7150	34.8212
28	4.4419	10.0249	24.7963
29	2.9352	11.5316	13.2647
30	1.2021	13.2647	0.0000

YEARS 2 — QTR PAYT 14.6237 — AN CONST 58.50

#	INT	PRIN	BALANCE
1	12.0495	46.4452	53.5548
2	4.9398	53.5548	0.0000

YEARS 3 — QTR PAYT 10.4247 — AN CONST 41.70

#	INT	PRIN	BALANCE
1	12.9850	28.7137	71.2863
2	8.5896	33.1091	38.1773
3	3.5214	38.1773	0.0000

YEARS 4 — QTR PAYT 8.3463 — AN CONST 33.39

#	INT	PRIN	BALANCE
1	13.4481	19.9371	80.0629
2	10.3962	22.9890	57.0739
3	6.8771	26.5081	30.5658
4	2.8193	30.5658	0.0000

YEARS 5 — QTR PAYT 7.1159 — AN CONST 28.47

#	INT	PRIN	BALANCE
1	13.7222	14.7415	85.2585
2	11.4656	16.9981	68.2604
3	8.8636	19.6001	48.6604
4	5.8633	22.6004	26.0600
5	2.4037	26.0600	0.0000

YEARS 6 — QTR PAYT 6.3093 — AN CONST 25.24

#	INT	PRIN	BALANCE
1	13.9019	11.3353	88.6647
2	12.1668	13.0705	75.5942
3	10.1660	15.0713	60.5229
4	7.8589	17.3783	43.1446
5	5.1987	20.0386	23.1060
6	2.1312	23.1060	0.0000

YEARS 7 — QTR PAYT 5.7446 — AN CONST 22.98

#	INT	PRIN	BALANCE
1	14.0277	8.9506	91.0494
2	12.6576	10.3207	80.7286
3	11.0778	11.9006	68.8280
4	9.2560	13.7223	55.1057
5	7.1555	15.8229	39.2829
6	4.7334	18.2450	21.0379
7	1.9405	21.0379	0.0000

YEARS 8 — QTR PAYT 5.3308 — AN CONST 21.33

#	INT	PRIN	BALANCE
1	14.1199	7.2032	92.7968
2	13.0173	8.3059	84.4909
3	11.7459	9.5773	74.9136
4	10.2798	11.0434	63.8702
5	8.5893	12.7339	51.1363
6	6.6401	14.6831	36.4532
7	4.3924	16.9308	19.5225
8	1.8007	19.5225	0.0000

YEARS 9 — QTR PAYT 5.0174 — AN CONST 20.07

#	INT	PRIN	BALANCE
1	14.1898	5.8797	94.1203
2	13.2897	6.7797	87.3406
3	12.2519	7.8175	79.5231
4	11.0552	9.0142	70.5089
5	9.6754	10.3941	60.1148
6	8.0843	11.9852	48.1297
7	6.2496	13.8198	34.3099
8	4.1342	15.9353	18.3746
9	1.6948	18.3746	0.0000

YEARS 10 — QTR PAYT 4.7739 — AN CONST 19.10

#	INT	PRIN	BALANCE
1	14.2440	4.8517	95.1483
2	13.5013	5.5944	89.5539
3	12.6450	6.4508	83.1031
4	11.6575	7.4382	75.6649
5	10.5189	8.5769	67.0880
6	9.2060	9.8898	57.1982
7	7.6921	11.4037	45.7946
8	5.9464	13.1493	32.6453
9	3.9336	15.1622	17.4831
10	1.6126	17.4831	0.0000

YEARS 11 — QTR PAYT 4.5812 — AN CONST 18.33

#	INT	PRIN	BALANCE
1	14.2870	4.0377	95.9623
2	13.6689	4.6558	91.3064
3	12.9562	5.3685	85.9379
4	12.1344	6.1903	79.7476
5	11.1868	7.1379	72.6097
6	10.0941	8.2305	64.3792
7	8.8342	9.4905	54.8887
8	7.3815	10.9432	43.9455
9	5.7063	12.6184	31.3271
10	3.7748	14.5499	16.7772
11	1.5475	16.7772	0.0000

YEARS 12 — QTR PAYT 4.4262 — AN CONST 17.71

#	INT	PRIN	BALANCE
1	14.3215	3.3832	96.6168
2	13.8036	3.9011	92.7156
3	13.2064	4.4983	88.2173
4	12.5178	5.1869	83.0305
5	11.7239	5.9809	77.0496
6	10.8083	6.8964	70.1532
7	9.7526	7.9521	62.2011
8	8.5354	9.1694	53.0317
9	7.1317	10.5730	42.4587
10	5.5133	12.1915	30.2673
11	3.6470	14.0577	16.2096
12	1.4951	16.2096	0.0000

YEARS 13 — QTR PAYT 4.3000 — AN CONST 17.21

#	INT	PRIN	BALANCE
1	14.3496	2.8505	97.1495
2	13.9133	3.2868	93.8627
3	13.4101	3.7899	90.0728
4	12.8300	4.3701	85.7027
5	12.1610	5.0390	80.6637
6	11.3897	5.8104	74.8533
7	10.5002	6.6998	68.1535
8	9.4746	7.7254	60.4281
9	8.2921	8.9080	51.5201
10	6.9285	10.2716	41.2485
11	5.3561	11.8439	29.4045
12	3.5431	13.6570	15.7475
13	1.4525	15.7475	0.0000

YEARS 14 — QTR PAYT 4.1963 — AN CONST 16.79

#	INT	PRIN	BALANCE
1	14.3727	2.4124	97.5876
2	14.0034	2.7817	94.8059
3	13.5776	3.2075	91.5984
4	13.0866	3.6985	87.8999
5	12.5205	4.2647	83.6352
6	11.8677	4.9175	78.7178
7	11.1149	5.6702	73.0475
8	10.2469	6.5382	66.5093
9	9.2461	7.5390	58.9703
10	8.0920	8.6931	50.2772
11	6.7613	10.0238	40.2534
12	5.2269	11.5582	28.6952
13	3.4576	13.3275	15.3676
14	1.4175	15.3676	0.0000

YEARS 15 — QTR PAYT 4.1103 — AN CONST 16.45

#	INT	PRIN	BALANCE
1	14.3919	2.0493	97.9507
2	14.0782	2.3630	95.5878
3	13.7165	2.7247	92.8631
4	13.2994	3.1418	89.7213
5	12.8184	3.6227	86.0986
6	12.2639	4.1773	81.9213
7	11.6245	4.8167	77.1046
8	10.8871	5.5540	71.5506
9	10.0369	6.4042	65.1464
10	9.0566	7.3846	57.7618
11	7.9262	8.5150	49.2469
12	6.6228	9.8184	39.4285
13	5.1198	11.3214	28.1071
14	3.3868	13.0544	15.0527
15	1.3884	15.0527	0.0000

YEARS 16 — QTR PAYT 4.0385 — AN CONST 16.16

#	INT	PRIN	BALANCE
1	14.4079	1.7462	98.2538
2	14.1406	2.0135	96.2403
3	13.8323	2.3217	93.9186
4	13.4769	2.6771	91.2415
5	13.0671	3.0869	88.1546
6	12.5946	3.5594	84.5951
7	12.0497	4.1043	80.4908
8	11.4215	4.7326	75.7582
9	10.6970	5.4570	70.3012
10	9.8617	6.2924	64.0088
11	8.8985	7.2556	56.7532
12	7.7878	8.3663	48.3869
13	6.5071	9.6469	38.7400
14	5.0304	11.1237	27.6163
15	3.3276	12.8264	14.7899
16	1.3642	14.7899	0.0000

YEARS 17 — QTR PAYT 3.9783 — AN CONST 15.92

#	INT	PRIN	BALANCE
1	14.4213	1.4918	98.5082
2	14.1929	1.7201	96.7881
3	13.9296	1.9835	94.8046
4	13.6260	2.2871	92.5175
5	13.2759	2.6372	89.8804
6	12.8722	3.0409	86.8395
7	12.4067	3.5063	83.3332
8	11.8700	4.0431	79.2901
9	11.2511	4.6620	74.6281
10	10.5374	5.3756	69.2524
11	9.7146	6.1985	63.0539
12	8.7657	7.1474	55.9066
13	7.6716	8.2415	47.6651
14	6.4100	9.5030	38.1621
15	4.9553	10.9577	27.2043
16	3.2780	12.6351	14.5692
17	1.3438	14.5692	0.0000

YEARS 18 — QTR PAYT 3.9275 — AN CONST 15.71

#	INT	PRIN	BALANCE
1	14.4326	1.2772	98.7228
2	14.2371	1.4727	97.2501
3	14.0117	1.6982	95.5519
4	13.7517	1.9581	93.5938
5	13.4520	2.2579	91.3359
6	13.1063	2.6035	88.7324
7	12.7078	3.0020	85.7304
8	12.2483	3.4616	82.2688
9	11.7184	3.9914	78.2774
10	11.1074	4.6024	73.6749
11	10.4029	5.3070	68.3679
12	9.5905	6.1193	62.2486
13	8.6538	7.0561	55.1925
14	7.5736	8.1362	47.0563
15	6.3282	9.3817	37.6747
16	4.8921	10.8178	26.8569
17	3.2361	12.4737	14.3832
18	1.3267	14.3832	0.0000

YEARS 19 — QTR PAYT 3.8844 — AN CONST 15.54

#	INT	PRIN	BALANCE
1	14.4422	1.0955	98.9045
2	14.2745	1.2632	97.6412
3	14.0811	1.4566	96.1846
4	13.8582	1.6796	94.5051
5	13.6011	1.9367	92.5684
6	13.3046	2.2331	90.3353
7	12.9628	2.5750	87.7603
8	12.5686	2.9691	84.7912
9	12.1141	3.4236	81.3675
10	11.5900	3.9477	77.4198
11	10.9857	4.5520	72.8678
12	10.2889	5.2488	67.6189
13	9.4854	6.0523	61.5666
14	8.5589	6.9788	54.5879
15	7.4907	8.0471	46.5408
16	6.2588	9.2789	37.2619
17	4.8385	10.6993	26.5627
18	3.2007	12.3371	14.2256
19	1.3121	14.2256	0.0000

YEARS 20 — QTR PAYT 3.8479 — AN CONST 15.40

#	INT	PRIN	BALANCE
1	14.4503	.9411	99.0589
2	14.3063	1.0852	97.9736
3	14.1402	1.2513	96.7223
4	13.9486	1.4429	95.2794
5	13.7277	1.6638	93.6156
6	13.4730	1.9184	91.6972
7	13.1794	2.2121	89.4851
8	12.8408	2.5507	86.9344
9	12.4503	2.9412	83.9932
10	12.0001	3.3914	80.6017
11	11.4809	3.9106	76.6912
12	10.8823	4.5092	72.1820
13	10.1921	5.1994	66.9826
14	9.3961	5.9953	60.9872
15	8.4784	6.9131	54.0741
16	7.4202	7.9713	46.1028
17	6.1999	9.1916	36.9112
18	4.7929	10.5986	26.3127
19	3.1705	12.2210	14.0917
20	1.2998	14.0917	0.0000

YEARS 21 — QTR PAYT 3.8167 — AN CONST 15.27

#	INT	PRIN	BALANCE
1	14.4573	.8096	99.1904
2	14.3334	.9335	98.2569
3	14.1905	1.0764	97.1804

QUARTERLY PAYMENT AMORTIZATION SCHEDULE PER $100   14.50 %

#	INT	PRIN	BALANCE
4	14.0257	1.2412	95.9392
5	13.8357	1.4312	94.5080
6	13.6166	1.6503	92.8577
7	13.3640	1.9029	90.9548
8	13.0727	2.1942	88.7606
9	12.7368	2.5301	86.2305
10	12.3495	2.9174	83.3132
11	11.9029	3.3640	79.9492
12	11.3880	3.8789	76.0703
13	10.7942	4.4727	71.5976
14	10.1095	5.1573	66.4403
15	9.3201	5.9468	60.4935
16	8.4098	6.8571	53.6363
17	7.3601	7.9068	45.7295
18	6.1497	9.1171	36.6124
19	4.7541	10.5128	26.0996
20	3.1449	12.1220	13.9776
21	1.2893	13.9776	0.0000

YEARS 22	QTR PAYT 3.7901	AN CONST 15.17	
#	INT	PRIN	BALANCE
1	14.4632	.6972	99.3028
2	14.3565	.8040	98.4988
3	14.2334	.9270	97.5718
4	14.0915	1.0689	96.5029
5	13.9279	1.2326	95.2703
6	13.7392	1.4212	93.8491
7	13.5217	1.6388	92.2103
8	13.2708	1.8896	90.3207
9	12.9815	2.1789	88.1418
10	12.6480	2.5124	85.6293
11	12.2634	2.8970	82.7323
12	11.8199	3.3405	79.3918
13	11.3086	3.8519	75.5399
14	10.7189	4.4415	71.0984
15	10.0391	5.1214	65.9770
16	9.2551	5.9053	60.0717
17	8.3511	6.8093	53.2624
18	7.3088	7.8517	45.4107
19	6.1069	9.0536	36.3571
20	4.7210	10.4395	25.9177
21	3.1229	12.0375	13.8802
22	1.2803	13.8802	0.0000

YEARS 23	QTR PAYT 3.7673	AN CONST 15.07	
#	INT	PRIN	BALANCE
1	14.4683	.6010	99.3990
2	14.3763	.6930	98.7059
3	14.2702	.7991	97.9068
4	14.1479	.9214	96.9854
5	14.0068	1.0625	95.9229
6	13.8442	1.2251	94.6977
7	13.6566	1.4127	93.2850
8	13.4404	1.6289	91.6561
9	13.1910	1.8783	89.7778
10	12.9035	2.1658	87.6120
11	12.5720	2.4973	85.1147
12	12.1897	2.8796	82.2350
13	11.7489	3.3204	78.9146
14	11.2406	3.8287	75.0859
15	10.6545	4.4148	70.6711
16	9.9787	5.0906	65.5805
17	9.1995	5.8699	59.7106
18	8.3009	6.7684	52.9422
19	7.2648	7.8045	45.1378
20	6.0702	8.9992	36.1386
21	4.6926	10.3767	25.7619
22	3.1042	11.9652	13.7967
23	1.2726	13.7967	0.0000

YEARS 24	QTR PAYT 3.7478	AN CONST 15.00	
#	INT	PRIN	BALANCE
1	14.4726	.5185	99.4815
2	14.3933	.5979	98.8835
3	14.3017	.6894	98.1941
4	14.1962	.7950	97.3991
5	14.0745	.9167	96.4825
6	13.9342	1.0570	95.4255
7	13.7724	1.2188	94.2067
8	13.5858	1.4054	92.8013
9	13.3707	1.6205	91.1808
10	13.1226	1.8685	89.3123
11	12.8366	2.1546	87.1577
12	12.5068	2.4844	84.6733
13	12.1265	2.8647	81.8086
14	11.6880	3.3032	78.5054
15	11.1823	3.8089	74.6965
16	10.5993	4.3919	70.3046
17	9.9270	5.0642	65.2404
18	9.1518	5.8394	59.4010
19	8.2579	6.7333	52.6677
20	7.2272	7.7640	44.9037
21	6.0387	8.9525	35.9512
22	4.6683	10.3229	25.6283
23	3.0881	11.9031	13.7252
24	1.2660	13.7252	0.0000

YEARS 25	QTR PAYT 3.7310	AN CONST 14.93	
#	INT	PRIN	BALANCE
1	14.4764	.4477	99.5523
2	14.4078	.5162	99.0361
3	14.3288	.5952	98.4409
4	14.2377	.6864	97.7545
5	14.1326	.7914	96.9631
6	14.0115	.9126	96.0505
7	13.8718	1.0523	94.9983
8	13.7107	1.2133	93.7849
9	13.5250	1.3991	92.3859
10	13.3108	1.6132	90.7726
11	13.0639	1.8602	88.9124
12	12.7791	2.1449	86.7675
13	12.4508	2.4733	84.2942
14	12.0722	2.8519	81.4424
15	11.6356	3.2884	78.1539
16	11.1323	3.7918	74.3621
17	10.5518	4.3722	69.9899
18	9.8825	5.0415	64.9484
19	9.1108	5.8133	59.1351
20	8.2209	6.7032	52.4319
21	7.1948	7.7292	44.7027
22	6.0117	8.9124	35.7903
23	4.6474	10.2767	25.5136
24	3.0742	11.8498	13.6637
25	1.2603	13.6637	0.0000

YEARS 26	QTR PAYT 3.7166	AN CONST 14.87	
#	INT	PRIN	BALANCE
1	14.4796	.3868	99.6132
2	14.4204	.4460	99.1673
3	14.3521	.5142	98.6531
4	14.2734	.5929	98.0601
5	14.1826	.6837	97.3764
6	14.0780	.7884	96.5881
7	13.9573	.9090	95.6790
8	13.8182	1.0482	94.6309
9	13.6577	1.2086	93.4222
10	13.4727	1.3937	92.0286
11	13.2594	1.6070	90.4216
12	13.0134	1.8530	88.5686
13	12.7297	2.1366	86.4319
14	12.4026	2.4637	83.9682
15	12.0255	2.8408	81.1274

#	INT	PRIN	BALANCE
16	11.5906	3.2757	77.8517
17	11.0892	3.7771	74.0745
18	10.5110	4.3553	69.7192
19	9.8443	5.0220	64.6972
20	9.0756	5.7908	58.9064
21	8.1891	6.6772	52.2291
22	7.1670	7.6994	44.5298
23	5.9884	8.8779	35.6518
24	4.6294	10.2370	25.4149
25	3.0624	11.8040	13.6109
26	1.2554	13.6109	0.0000

YEARS 27	QTR PAYT 3.7042	AN CONST 14.82	
#	INT	PRIN	BALANCE
1	14.4824	.3343	99.6657
2	14.4312	.3855	99.2803
3	14.3722	.4445	98.8358
4	14.3041	.5125	98.3233
5	14.2257	.5910	97.7323
6	14.1352	.6814	97.0509
7	14.0309	.7857	96.2652
8	13.9107	.9060	95.3592
9	13.7720	1.0447	94.3145
10	13.6120	1.2046	93.1099
11	13.4277	1.3890	91.7209
12	13.2150	1.6016	90.1193
13	12.9699	1.8468	88.2725
14	12.6872	2.1295	86.1430
15	12.3612	2.4555	83.6875
16	11.9853	2.8313	80.8562
17	11.5519	3.2648	77.5914
18	11.0521	3.7645	73.8269
19	10.4759	4.3408	69.4861
20	9.8114	5.0052	64.4809
21	9.0452	5.7714	58.7095
22	8.1617	6.6549	52.0545
23	7.1430	7.6736	44.3809
24	5.9684	8.8483	35.5327
25	4.6139	10.2027	25.3299
26	3.0521	11.7645	13.5654
27	1.2512	13.5654	0.0000

YEARS 28	QTR PAYT 3.6935	AN CONST 14.78	
#	INT	PRIN	BALANCE
1	14.4847	.2891	99.7109
2	14.4405	.3333	99.3776
3	14.3895	.3843	98.9933
4	14.3306	.4432	98.5501
5	14.2628	.5110	98.0391
6	14.1846	.5892	97.4498
7	14.0944	.6794	96.7704
8	13.9904	.7835	95.9869
9	13.8704	.9034	95.0835
10	13.7322	1.0417	94.0419
11	13.5727	1.2011	92.8408
12	13.3888	1.3850	91.4558
13	13.1768	1.5970	89.8588
14	12.9324	1.8415	88.0173
15	12.6505	2.1233	85.8940
16	12.3254	2.4484	83.4456
17	11.9507	2.8232	80.6225
18	11.5185	3.2553	77.3671
19	11.0202	3.7536	73.6135
20	10.4456	4.3282	69.2853
21	9.7830	4.9908	64.2945
22	9.0191	5.7548	58.5397
23	8.1382	6.6357	51.9041
24	7.1224	7.6514	44.2526
25	5.9511	8.8227	35.4300
26	4.6006	10.1732	25.2567
27	3.0433	11.7305	13.5262

#	INT	PRIN	BALANCE
28	1.2476	13.5262	0.0000

YEARS 29	QTR PAYT 3.6842	AN CONST 14.74	
#	INT	PRIN	BALANCE
1	14.4868	.2501	99.7499
2	14.4485	.2883	99.4616
3	14.4044	.3325	99.1291
4	14.3535	.3834	98.7457
5	14.2948	.4421	98.3036
6	14.2271	.5097	97.7939
7	14.1491	.5878	97.2061
8	14.0591	.6777	96.5284
9	13.9554	.7815	95.7469
10	13.8358	.9011	94.8458
11	13.6978	1.0391	93.8067
12	13.5388	1.1981	92.6086
13	13.3554	1.3815	91.2271
14	13.1439	1.5930	89.6341
15	12.9000	1.8369	87.7972
16	12.6188	2.1180	85.6792
17	12.2946	2.4422	83.2369
18	11.9208	2.8161	80.4208
19	11.4897	3.2472	77.1737
20	10.9926	3.7442	73.4294
21	10.4195	4.3174	69.1120
22	9.7586	4.9783	64.1337
23	8.9965	5.7404	58.3934
24	8.1178	6.6191	51.7743
25	7.1046	7.6323	44.1420
26	5.9362	8.8006	35.3414
27	4.5891	10.1478	25.1936
28	3.0357	11.7012	13.4924
29	1.2445	13.4924	0.0000

YEARS 30	QTR PAYT 3.6762	AN CONST 14.71	
#	INT	PRIN	BALANCE
1	14.4886	.2164	99.7836
2	14.4555	.2495	99.5341
3	14.4173	.2877	99.2463
4	14.3732	.3318	98.9146
5	14.3224	.3826	98.5320
6	14.2639	.4411	98.0909
7	14.1963	.5086	97.5823
8	14.1185	.5865	96.9958
9	14.0287	.6763	96.3195
10	13.9252	.7798	95.5397
11	13.8058	.8992	94.6405
12	13.6682	1.0368	93.6037
13	13.5095	1.1955	92.4082
14	13.3265	1.3785	91.0297
15	13.1154	1.5896	89.4401
16	12.8721	1.8329	87.6072
17	12.5915	2.1134	85.4938
18	12.2680	2.4370	83.0568
19	11.8950	2.8100	80.2468
20	11.4648	3.2402	77.0067
21	10.9688	3.7361	73.2705
22	10.3969	4.3081	68.9625
23	9.7375	4.9675	63.9949
24	8.9770	5.7279	58.2670
25	8.1002	6.6048	51.6622
26	7.0892	7.6158	44.0465
27	5.9234	8.7816	35.2649
28	4.5791	10.1258	25.1390
29	3.0291	11.6759	13.4632
30	1.2418	13.4632	0.0000

QUARTERLY PAYMENT AMORTIZATION SCHEDULE PER $100   14.75 %

YEARS 2 — QTR PAYT 14.6617 — AN CONST 58.65

#	INT	PRIN	BALANCE
1	12.2617	46.3852	53.6148
2	5.0321	53.6148	0.0000

YEARS 3 — QTR PAYT 10.4629 — AN CONST 41.86

#	INT	PRIN	BALANCE
1	13.2137	28.6379	71.3621
2	8.7502	33.1014	38.2607
3	3.5910	38.2607	0.0000

YEARS 4 — QTR PAYT 8.3853 — AN CONST 33.55

#	INT	PRIN	BALANCE
1	13.6848	19.8565	80.1435
2	10.5900	22.9514	57.1920
3	7.0127	26.5286	30.6634
4	2.8779	30.6634	0.0000

YEARS 5 — QTR PAYT 7.1560 — AN CONST 28.63

#	INT	PRIN	BALANCE
1	13.9636	14.6605	85.3395
2	11.6786	16.9455	68.3940
3	9.0374	19.5866	48.8074
4	5.9846	22.6394	26.1680
5	2.4560	26.1680	0.0000

YEARS 6 — QTR PAYT 6.3505 — AN CONST 25.41

#	INT	PRIN	BALANCE
1	14.1462	11.2559	88.7441
2	12.3918	13.0103	75.7337
3	10.3640	15.0381	60.6956
4	8.0202	17.3820	43.3137
5	5.3110	20.0911	23.2226
6	2.1796	23.2226	0.0000

YEARS 7 — QTR PAYT 5.7870 — AN CONST 23.15

#	INT	PRIN	BALANCE
1	14.2740	8.8740	91.1260
2	12.8909	10.2571	80.8689
3	11.2922	11.8558	69.0131
4	9.4443	13.7036	55.3095
5	7.3085	15.8395	39.4700
6	4.8397	18.3082	21.1618
7	1.9862	21.1618	0.0000

YEARS 8 — QTR PAYT 5.3744 — AN CONST 21.50

#	INT	PRIN	BALANCE
1	14.3675	7.1300	92.8700
2	13.2562	8.2413	84.6287
3	11.9717	9.5258	75.1030
4	10.4807	11.0105	64.0925
5	8.7709	12.7266	51.3660
6	6.7874	14.7101	36.6558
7	4.4946	17.0029	19.6530
8	1.8445	19.6530	0.0000

YEARS 9 — QTR PAYT 5.0621 — AN CONST 20.25

#	INT	PRIN	BALANCE
1	14.4383	5.8101	94.1899
2	13.5327	6.7157	87.4741
3	12.4860	7.7624	79.7117
4	11.2762	8.9723	70.7394
5	9.8777	10.3707	60.3687
6	8.2613	11.9871	48.3815
7	6.3930	13.8555	34.5261
8	4.2335	16.0150	18.5111
9	1.7374	18.5111	0.0000

YEARS 10 — QTR PAYT 4.8198 — AN CONST 19.28

#	INT	PRIN	BALANCE
1	14.4933	4.7861	95.2139
2	13.7473	5.5321	89.6818
3	12.8851	6.3943	83.2875
4	11.8884	7.3909	75.8966
5	10.7365	8.5429	67.3537
6	9.4050	9.8744	57.4793
7	7.8659	11.4134	46.0659
8	6.0870	13.1923	32.8736
9	4.0309	15.2485	17.6251
10	1.6542	17.6251	0.0000

YEARS 11 — QTR PAYT 4.6282 — AN CONST 18.52

#	INT	PRIN	BALANCE
1	14.5367	3.9761	96.0239
2	13.9170	4.5958	91.4281
3	13.2007	5.3121	86.1160
4	12.3727	6.1401	79.9759
5	11.4157	7.0971	72.8789
6	10.3096	8.2032	64.6757
7	9.0310	9.4818	55.1939
8	7.5532	10.9596	44.2343
9	5.8450	12.6678	31.5665
10	3.8706	14.6422	16.9243
11	1.5885	16.9243	0.0000

YEARS 12 — QTR PAYT 4.4743 — AN CONST 17.90

#	INT	PRIN	BALANCE
1	14.5716	3.3255	96.6745
2	14.0533	3.8439	92.8306
3	13.4542	4.4430	88.3876
4	12.7617	5.1355	83.2522
5	11.9613	5.9359	77.3163
6	11.0361	6.8610	70.4553
7	9.9667	7.9304	62.5249
8	8.7307	9.1664	53.3584
9	7.3020	10.5951	42.7633
10	5.6506	12.2465	30.5168
11	3.7419	14.1553	16.3615
12	1.5356	16.3615	0.0000

YEARS 13 — QTR PAYT 4.3492 — AN CONST 17.40

#	INT	PRIN	BALANCE
1	14.6000	2.7966	97.2034
2	14.1641	3.2325	93.9708
3	13.6603	3.7364	90.2345
4	13.0779	4.3187	85.9157
5	12.4048	4.9918	80.9239
6	11.6268	5.7699	75.1541
7	10.7275	6.6692	68.4849
8	9.6880	7.7086	60.7763
9	8.4865	8.9101	51.8662
10	7.0978	10.2988	41.5673
11	5.4926	11.9040	29.6633
12	3.6372	13.7594	15.9039
13	1.4927	15.9039	0.0000

YEARS 14 — QTR PAYT 4.2464 — AN CONST 16.99

#	INT	PRIN	BALANCE
1	14.6233	2.3624	97.6376
2	14.2551	2.7306	94.9070
3	13.8295	3.1562	91.7509
4	13.3376	3.6481	88.1028
5	12.7690	4.2167	83.8861
6	12.1117	4.8739	79.0122
7	11.3521	5.6336	73.3786
8	10.4740	6.5116	66.8670
9	9.4591	7.5265	59.3405
10	8.2860	8.6996	50.6409
11	6.9301	10.0555	40.5854
12	5.3628	11.6228	28.9626
13	3.5513	13.4343	15.5282
14	1.4574	15.5282	0.0000

YEARS 15 — QTR PAYT 4.1614 — AN CONST 16.65

#	INT	PRIN	BALANCE
1	14.6426	2.0029	97.9971
2	14.3304	2.3151	95.6821
3	13.9696	2.6759	93.0062
4	13.5525	3.0930	89.9132
5	13.0704	3.5750	86.3382
6	12.5132	4.1322	82.2060
7	11.8692	4.7763	77.4297
8	11.1247	5.5207	71.9089
9	10.2643	6.3812	65.5278
10	9.2697	7.3758	58.1520
11	8.1201	8.5254	49.6266
12	6.7913	9.8541	39.7725
13	5.2554	11.3900	28.3825
14	3.4802	13.1653	15.2172
15	1.4282	15.2172	0.0000

YEARS 16 — QTR PAYT 4.0905 — AN CONST 16.37

#	INT	PRIN	BALANCE
1	14.6586	1.7033	98.2967
2	14.3932	1.9688	96.3279
3	14.0863	2.2756	94.0523
4	13.7316	2.6303	91.4220
5	13.3217	3.0403	88.3817
6	12.8478	3.5141	84.8676
7	12.3001	4.0618	80.8057
8	11.6670	4.6949	76.1108
9	10.9352	5.4267	70.6841
10	10.0894	6.2725	64.4116
11	9.1118	7.2501	57.1615
12	7.9818	8.3801	48.7813
13	6.6756	9.6863	39.0950
14	5.1659	11.1960	27.8990
15	3.4209	12.9410	14.9580
16	1.4039	14.9580	0.0000

YEARS 17 — QTR PAYT 4.0311 — AN CONST 16.13

#	INT	PRIN	BALANCE
1	14.6721	1.4522	98.5478
2	14.4458	1.6786	96.8692
3	14.1841	1.9402	94.9290
4	13.8817	2.2426	92.6865
5	13.5322	2.5921	90.0943
6	13.1282	2.9961	87.0982
7	12.6612	3.4631	83.6351
8	12.1215	4.0029	79.6323
9	11.4976	4.6268	75.0055
10	10.7764	5.3479	69.6576
11	9.9429	6.1814	63.4762
12	8.9795	7.1448	56.3314
13	7.8659	8.2585	48.0729
14	6.5787	9.5456	38.5273
15	5.0909	11.0334	27.4939
16	3.3712	12.7531	14.7408
17	1.3835	14.7408	0.0000

YEARS 18 — QTR PAYT 3.9811 — AN CONST 15.93

#	INT	PRIN	BALANCE
1	14.6834	1.2408	98.7592
2	14.4900	1.4342	97.3250
3	14.2665	1.6577	95.6673
4	14.0081	1.9161	93.7512
5	13.7095	2.2148	91.5364
6	13.3643	2.5599	88.9765
7	12.9653	2.9589	86.0175
8	12.5041	3.4201	82.5974
9	11.9710	3.9532	78.6442
10	11.3549	4.5693	74.0748
11	10.6427	5.2815	68.7933
12	9.8195	6.1047	62.6886
13	8.8680	7.0562	55.6324
14	7.7683	8.1560	47.4764
15	6.4971	9.4272	38.0493
16	5.0277	10.8965	27.1527
17	3.3294	12.5949	14.5579
18	1.3663	14.5579	0.0000

YEARS 19 — QTR PAYT 3.9388 — AN CONST 15.76

#	INT	PRIN	BALANCE
1	14.6930	1.0621	98.9379
2	14.5275	1.2276	97.7103
3	14.3361	1.4190	96.2913
4	14.1150	1.6401	94.6512
5	13.8594	1.8958	92.7554
6	13.5639	2.1912	90.5642
7	13.2224	2.5328	88.0314
8	12.8276	2.9275	85.1039
9	12.3713	3.3838	81.7201
10	11.8439	3.9112	77.8089
11	11.2343	4.5208	73.2881
12	10.5297	5.2254	68.0627
13	9.7152	6.0399	62.0228
14	8.7739	6.9813	55.0416
15	7.6858	8.0694	46.9722
16	6.4281	9.3271	37.6451
17	4.9743	10.7808	26.8644
18	3.2940	12.4611	14.4033
19	1.3518	14.4033	0.0000

YEARS 20 — QTR PAYT 3.9029 — AN CONST 15.62

#	INT	PRIN	BALANCE
1	14.7012	.9105	99.0895
2	14.5592	1.0524	98.0371
3	14.3952	1.2164	96.8206
4	14.2056	1.4060	95.4146
5	13.9865	1.6252	93.7894
6	13.7332	1.8785	91.9109
7	13.4404	2.1713	89.7396
8	13.1020	2.5097	87.2299
9	12.7108	2.9009	84.3291
10	12.2587	3.3530	80.9761
11	11.7361	3.8756	77.1005
12	11.1320	4.4796	72.6208
13	10.4338	5.1779	67.4430
14	9.6268	5.9849	61.4581
15	8.6940	6.9177	54.5404
16	7.6158	7.9959	46.5445
17	6.3695	9.2421	37.3024
18	4.9290	10.6826	26.6198
19	3.2640	12.3476	14.2721
20	1.3395	14.2721	0.0000

YEARS 21 — QTR PAYT 3.8724 — AN CONST 15.49

#	INT	PRIN	BALANCE
1	14.7081	.7816	99.2184
2	14.5863	.9034	98.3150
3	14.4455	1.0442	97.2708

#	INT	PRIN	BALANCE
4	14.2827	1.2069	96.0639
5	14.0946	1.3951	94.6689
6	13.8772	1.6125	93.0564
7	13.6258	1.8638	91.1925
8	13.3353	2.1543	89.0382
9	12.9996	2.4901	86.5482
10	12.6115	2.8782	83.6700
11	12.1629	3.3268	80.3432
12	11.6443	3.8453	76.4979
13	11.0450	4.4446	72.0532
14	10.3523	5.1374	66.9158
15	9.5515	5.9381	60.9777
16	8.6260	6.8636	54.1141
17	7.5563	7.9334	46.1807
18	6.3197	9.1699	37.0108
19	4.8905	10.5991	26.4117
20	3.2385	12.2511	14.1606
21	1.3291	14.1606	0.0000

YEARS 22 — QTR PAYT 3.8464 — AN CONST 15.39

#	INT	PRIN	BALANCE
1	14.7140	.6716	99.3284
2	14.6093	.7763	98.5520
3	14.4883	.8973	97.6547
4	14.3484	1.0372	96.6175
5	14.1868	1.1988	95.4187
6	13.9999	1.3857	94.0330
7	13.7840	1.6017	92.4314
8	13.5343	1.8513	90.5801
9	13.2458	2.1398	88.4402
10	12.9123	2.4734	85.9669
11	12.5268	2.8589	83.1080
12	12.0812	3.3044	79.8036
13	11.5661	3.8195	75.9841
14	10.9708	4.4148	71.5693
15	10.2827	5.1029	66.4664
16	9.4874	5.8982	60.5682
17	8.5681	6.8175	53.7507
18	7.5055	7.8801	45.8706
19	6.2773	9.1083	36.7623
20	4.8577	10.5279	26.2343
21	3.2168	12.1688	14.0655
22	1.3201	14.0655	0.0000

YEARS 23 — QTR PAYT 3.8242 — AN CONST 15.30

#	INT	PRIN	BALANCE
1	14.7190	.5777	99.4223
2	14.6290	.6678	98.7545
3	14.5249	.7718	97.9827
4	14.4046	.8921	97.0905
5	14.2655	1.0312	96.0594
6	14.1048	1.1919	94.8675
7	13.9190	1.3777	93.4898
8	13.7043	1.5924	91.8974
9	13.4561	1.8406	90.0568
10	13.1692	2.1275	87.9293
11	12.8377	2.4591	85.4702
12	12.4544	2.8423	82.6279
13	12.0114	3.2854	79.3425
14	11.4993	3.7974	75.5451
15	10.9074	4.3893	71.1558
16	10.2233	5.0734	66.0824
17	9.4326	5.8641	60.2183
18	8.5186	6.7781	53.4401
19	7.4621	7.8346	45.6056
20	6.2410	9.0557	36.5499
21	4.8296	10.4671	26.0828
22	3.1982	12.0985	13.9842
23	1.3125	13.9842	0.0000

YEARS 24 — QTR PAYT 3.8052 — AN CONST 15.23

#	INT	PRIN	BALANCE
1	14.7233	.4973	99.5027
2	14.6458	.5748	98.9278
3	14.5562	.6644	98.2634
4	14.4527	.7680	97.4954
5	14.3330	.8877	96.6077
6	14.1946	1.0261	95.5816
7	14.0347	1.1860	94.3956
8	13.8498	1.3708	93.0248
9	13.6362	1.5845	91.4403
10	13.3892	1.8314	89.6089
11	13.1038	2.1169	87.4920
12	12.7738	2.4468	85.0451
13	12.3924	2.8282	82.2169
14	11.9516	3.2690	78.9479
15	11.4421	3.7785	75.1694
16	10.8532	4.3675	70.8019
17	10.1725	5.0482	65.7538
18	9.3857	5.8350	59.9188
19	8.4762	6.7444	53.1744
20	7.4250	7.7956	45.3788
21	6.2100	9.0107	36.3681
22	4.8056	10.4151	25.9530
23	3.1823	12.0384	13.9147
24	1.3060	13.9147	0.0000

YEARS 25 — QTR PAYT 3.7889 — AN CONST 15.16

#	INT	PRIN	BALANCE
1	14.7270	.4284	99.5716
2	14.6602	.4952	99.0764
3	14.5831	.5724	98.5040
4	14.4938	.6616	97.8424
5	14.3907	.7647	97.0777
6	14.2715	.8839	96.1938
7	14.1338	1.0217	95.1721
8	13.9745	1.1809	93.9912
9	13.7905	1.3650	92.6263
10	13.5777	1.5777	91.0486
11	13.3318	1.8236	89.2250
12	13.0476	2.1078	87.1172
13	12.7191	2.4364	84.6808
14	12.3394	2.8161	81.8647
15	11.9004	3.2550	78.6097
16	11.3931	3.7623	74.8474
17	10.8067	4.3487	70.4986
18	10.1289	5.0265	65.4721
19	9.3455	5.8100	59.6621
20	8.4399	6.7155	52.9466
21	7.3932	7.7622	45.1843
22	6.1834	8.9720	36.2123
23	4.7850	10.3704	25.8418
24	3.1687	11.9868	13.8551
25	1.3004	13.8551	0.0000

YEARS 26 — QTR PAYT 3.7749 — AN CONST 15.10

#	INT	PRIN	BALANCE
1	14.7302	.3693	99.6307
2	14.6726	.4268	99.2039
3	14.6061	.4934	98.7105
4	14.5292	.5703	98.1402
5	14.4403	.6591	97.4811
6	14.3376	.7619	96.7192
7	14.2188	.8806	95.8386
8	14.0816	1.0179	94.8207
9	13.9229	1.1765	93.6441
10	13.7396	1.3599	92.2842
11	13.5276	1.5719	90.7124
12	13.2826	1.8169	88.8955
13	12.9994	2.1000	86.7954
14	12.6721	2.4274	84.3681
15	12.2938	2.8057	81.5624
16	11.8565	3.2430	78.3194
17	11.3510	3.7484	74.5710
18	10.7668	4.3327	70.2383
19	10.0915	5.0080	65.2303
20	9.3109	5.7885	59.4418
21	8.4087	6.6907	52.7510
22	7.3659	7.7336	45.0175
23	6.1606	8.9389	36.0786
24	4.7673	10.3321	25.7464
25	3.1570	11.9425	13.8039
26	1.2956	13.8039	0.0000

YEARS 27 — QTR PAYT 3.7628 — AN CONST 15.06

#	INT	PRIN	BALANCE
1	14.7329	.3185	99.6815
2	14.6833	.3681	99.3134
3	14.6259	.4255	98.8879
4	14.5596	.4918	98.3961
5	14.4829	.5685	97.8277
6	14.3943	.6571	97.1706
7	14.2919	.7595	96.4112
8	14.1736	.8778	95.5334
9	14.0367	1.0146	94.5187
10	13.8786	1.1728	93.3459
11	13.6958	1.3556	91.9903
12	13.4845	1.5669	90.4235
13	13.2403	1.8111	88.6124
14	12.9580	2.0934	86.5190
15	12.6318	2.4196	84.0994
16	12.2546	2.7968	81.3026
17	11.8187	3.2327	78.0700
18	11.3149	3.7365	74.3335
19	10.7325	4.3189	70.0146
20	10.0594	4.9920	65.0226
21	9.2813	5.7701	59.2525
22	8.3820	6.6694	52.5830
23	7.3425	7.7089	44.8741
24	6.1409	8.9104	35.9637
25	4.7521	10.2992	25.6644
26	3.1469	11.9045	13.7599
27	1.2915	13.7599	0.0000

YEARS 28 — QTR PAYT 3.7525 — AN CONST 15.02

#	INT	PRIN	BALANCE
1	14.7353	.2748	99.7252
2	14.6924	.3176	99.4076
3	14.6429	.3671	99.0405
4	14.5857	.4243	98.6162
5	14.5196	.4904	98.1258
6	14.4431	.5669	97.5589
7	14.3548	.6552	96.9036
8	14.2527	.7574	96.1463
9	14.1346	.8754	95.2709
10	13.9982	1.0119	94.2590
11	13.8405	1.1696	93.0894
12	13.6582	1.3519	91.7376
13	13.4475	1.5626	90.1750
14	13.2039	1.8061	88.3689
15	12.9224	2.0876	86.2813
16	12.5970	2.4130	83.8683
17	12.2210	2.7891	81.0792
18	11.7863	3.2238	77.8555
19	11.2838	3.7262	74.1292
20	10.7030	4.3070	69.8222
21	10.0317	4.9783	64.8439
22	9.2558	5.7542	59.0897
23	8.3589	6.6511	52.4386
24	7.3223	7.6877	44.7508
25	6.1241	8.8860	35.8648
26	4.7391	10.2709	25.5939
27	3.1383	11.8718	13.7221
28	1.2879	13.7221	0.0000

YEARS 29 — QTR PAYT 3.7436 — AN CONST 14.98

#	INT	PRIN	BALANCE
1	14.7373	.2372	99.7628
2	14.7003	.2741	99.4887
3	14.6576	.3168	99.1719
4	14.6082	.3662	98.8057
5	14.5511	.4233	98.3823
6	14.4851	.4893	97.8931
7	14.4089	.5655	97.3275
8	14.3207	.6537	96.6738
9	14.2189	.7556	95.9183
10	14.1011	.8733	95.0449
11	13.9650	1.0095	94.0355
12	13.8076	1.1668	92.8687
13	13.6258	1.3487	91.5200
14	13.4156	1.5589	89.9611
15	13.1726	1.8018	88.1593
16	12.8918	2.0827	86.0767
17	12.5672	2.4073	83.6694
18	12.1920	2.7825	80.8870
19	11.7583	3.2161	77.6708
20	11.2570	3.7174	73.9534
21	10.6776	4.2968	69.6566
22	10.0079	4.9665	64.6901
23	9.2338	5.7406	58.9495
24	8.3391	6.6353	52.3142
25	7.3049	7.6695	44.6447
26	6.1095	8.8649	35.7798
27	4.7279	10.2466	25.5332
28	3.1308	11.8436	13.6896
29	1.2848	13.6896	0.0000

YEARS 30 — QTR PAYT 3.7359 — AN CONST 14.95

#	INT	PRIN	BALANCE
1	14.7390	.2048	99.7952
2	14.7071	.2367	99.5586
3	14.6702	.2736	99.2850
4	14.6276	.3162	98.9688
5	14.5783	.3655	98.6033
6	14.5213	.4224	98.1809
7	14.4555	.4883	97.6926
8	14.3794	.5644	97.1282
9	14.2914	.6524	96.4759
10	14.1897	.7540	95.7219
11	14.0722	.8716	94.8503
12	13.9364	1.0074	93.8429
13	13.7794	1.1644	92.6785
14	13.5979	1.3459	91.3326
15	13.3881	1.5557	89.7769
16	13.1456	1.7981	87.9788
17	12.8654	2.0784	85.9004
18	12.5414	2.4023	83.4981
19	12.1670	2.7768	80.7213
20	11.7342	3.2095	77.5118
21	11.2340	3.7098	73.8020
22	10.6558	4.2880	69.5140
23	9.9874	4.9563	64.5577
24	9.2149	5.7288	58.8288
25	8.3220	6.6217	52.2071
26	7.2900	7.6538	44.5533
27	6.0970	8.8467	35.7065
28	4.7182	10.2256	25.4809
29	3.1244	11.8194	13.6616
30	1.2822	13.6616	0.0000

QUARTERLY PAYMENT AMORTIZATION SCHEDULE PER $100 — 15.00 %

YEARS 2 — QTR PAYT 14.6998 — AN CONST 58.80

#	INT	PRIN	BALANCE
1	12.4741	46.3252	53.6748
2	5.1246	53.6748	0.0000

YEARS 3 — QTR PAYT 10.5012 — AN CONST 42.01

#	INT	PRIN	BALANCE
1	13.4426	28.5623	71.4377
2	8.9112	33.0937	38.3440
3	3.6609	38.3440	0.0000

YEARS 4 — QTR PAYT 8.4245 — AN CONST 33.70

#	INT	PRIN	BALANCE
1	13.9217	19.7762	80.2238
2	10.7842	22.9137	57.3100
3	7.1489	26.5490	30.7610
4	2.9369	30.7610	0.0000

YEARS 5 — QTR PAYT 7.1962 — AN CONST 28.79

#	INT	PRIN	BALANCE
1	14.2050	14.5798	85.4202
2	11.8919	16.8929	68.5273
3	9.2119	19.5730	48.9543
4	6.1066	22.6782	26.2761
5	2.5087	26.2761	0.0000

YEARS 6 — QTR PAYT 6.3919 — AN CONST 25.57

#	INT	PRIN	BALANCE
1	14.3906	11.1770	88.8230
2	12.6173	12.9502	75.8728
3	10.5628	15.0048	60.8680
4	8.1823	17.3853	43.4827
5	5.4241	20.1435	23.3392
6	2.2283	23.3392	0.0000

YEARS 7 — QTR PAYT 5.8295 — AN CONST 23.32

#	INT	PRIN	BALANCE
1	14.5203	8.7979	91.2021
2	13.1245	10.1937	81.0085
3	11.5073	11.8109	69.1976
4	9.6335	13.6847	55.5129
5	7.4624	15.8558	39.6572
6	4.9469	18.3713	21.2859
7	2.0323	21.2859	0.0000

YEARS 8 — QTR PAYT 5.4181 — AN CONST 21.68

#	INT	PRIN	BALANCE
1	14.6152	7.0573	92.9427
2	13.4956	8.1770	84.7657
3	12.1983	9.4743	75.2915
4	10.6952	10.9773	64.3141
5	8.9536	12.7189	51.5952
6	6.9358	14.7368	36.8584
7	4.5978	17.0748	19.7837
8	1.8888	19.7837	0.0000

YEARS 9 — QTR PAYT 5.1071 — AN CONST 20.43

#	INT	PRIN	BALANCE
1	14.6870	5.7413	94.2587
2	13.7761	6.6521	87.6066
3	12.7207	7.7075	79.8991
4	11.4979	8.9303	70.9688
5	10.0811	10.3471	60.6217
6	8.4396	11.9887	48.6330
7	6.5376	13.8907	34.7423
8	4.3338	16.0944	18.6478
9	1.7804	18.6478	0.0000

YEARS 10 — QTR PAYT 4.8659 — AN CONST 19.47

#	INT	PRIN	BALANCE
1	14.7426	4.7212	95.2788
2	13.9936	5.4702	89.8086
3	13.1257	6.3381	83.4705
4	12.1202	7.3436	76.1269
5	10.9551	8.5087	67.6182
6	9.6052	9.8586	57.7596
7	8.0411	11.4227	46.3369
8	6.2289	13.2349	33.1020
9	4.1292	15.3346	17.7674
10	1.6963	17.7674	0.0000

YEARS 11 — QTR PAYT 4.6754 — AN CONST 18.71

#	INT	PRIN	BALANCE
1	14.7865	3.9152	96.0848
2	14.1654	4.5364	91.5484
3	13.4457	5.2561	86.2924
4	12.6118	6.0899	80.2024
5	11.6456	7.0561	73.1463
6	10.5262	8.1756	64.9708
7	9.2291	9.4726	55.4982
8	7.7263	10.9754	44.5227
9	5.9850	12.7167	31.8060
10	3.9675	14.7342	17.0718
11	1.6299	17.0718	0.0000

YEARS 12 — QTR PAYT 4.5226 — AN CONST 18.10

#	INT	PRIN	BALANCE
1	14.8218	3.2687	96.7313
2	14.3032	3.7872	92.9441
3	13.7024	4.3881	88.5560
4	13.0062	5.0843	83.4718
5	12.1996	5.8909	77.5809
6	11.2650	6.8255	70.7554
7	10.1821	7.9083	62.8471
8	8.9275	9.1630	53.6841
9	7.4737	10.6167	43.0674
10	5.7894	12.3010	30.7664
11	3.8378	14.2526	16.5138
12	1.5767	16.5138	0.0000

YEARS 13 — QTR PAYT 4.3985 — AN CONST 17.60

#	INT	PRIN	BALANCE
1	14.8504	2.7437	97.2563
2	14.4151	3.1790	94.0773
3	13.9108	3.6833	90.3940
4	13.3264	4.2677	86.1263
5	12.6493	4.9448	81.1816
6	11.8648	5.7292	75.4523
7	10.9559	6.6382	68.8141
8	9.9027	7.6913	61.1228
9	8.6825	8.9116	52.2112
10	7.2687	10.3254	41.8858
11	5.6306	11.9635	29.9223
12	3.7325	13.8616	16.0607
13	1.5334	16.0607	0.0000

YEARS 14 — QTR PAYT 4.2968 — AN CONST 17.19

#	INT	PRIN	BALANCE
1	14.8739	2.3132	97.6868
2	14.5069	2.6802	95.0065
3	14.0817	3.1054	91.9011
4	13.5890	3.5981	88.3030
5	13.0181	4.1690	84.1340
6	12.3567	4.8304	79.3036
7	11.5904	5.5967	73.7069
8	10.7025	6.4846	67.2223
9	9.6737	7.5134	59.7089
10	8.4817	8.7054	51.0034
11	7.1005	10.0866	40.9169
12	5.5003	11.6868	29.2301
13	3.6462	13.5409	15.6892
14	1.4979	15.6892	0.0000

YEARS 15 — QTR PAYT 4.2127 — AN CONST 16.86

#	INT	PRIN	BALANCE
1	14.8933	1.9574	98.0426
2	14.5827	2.2679	95.7746
3	14.2229	2.6278	93.1469
4	13.8060	3.0447	90.1022
5	13.3230	3.5277	86.5745
6	12.7633	4.0874	82.4872
7	12.1149	4.7358	77.7513
8	11.3635	5.4872	72.2642
9	10.4930	6.3577	65.9065
10	9.4843	7.3664	58.5401
11	8.3156	8.5350	50.0051
12	6.9616	9.8891	40.1160
13	5.3926	11.4580	28.6579
14	3.5748	13.2759	15.3821
15	1.4686	15.3821	0.0000

YEARS 16 — QTR PAYT 4.1427 — AN CONST 16.58

#	INT	PRIN	BALANCE
1	14.9094	1.6613	98.3387
2	14.6458	1.9249	96.4138
3	14.3405	2.2303	94.1835
4	13.9866	2.5841	91.5994
5	13.5767	2.9941	88.6053
6	13.1016	3.4691	85.1363
7	12.5513	4.0195	81.1168
8	11.9136	4.6571	76.4596
9	11.1747	5.3960	71.0636
10	10.3187	6.2521	64.8116
11	9.3268	7.2440	57.5676
12	8.1775	8.3932	49.1743
13	6.8459	9.7248	39.4495
14	5.3031	11.2677	28.1818
15	3.5154	13.0553	15.1265
16	1.4442	15.1265	0.0000

YEARS 17 — QTR PAYT 4.0841 — AN CONST 16.34

#	INT	PRIN	BALANCE
1	14.9229	1.4136	98.5864
2	14.6987	1.6378	96.9486
3	14.4388	1.8977	95.0509
4	14.1378	2.1987	92.8522
5	13.7889	2.5476	90.3046
6	13.3847	2.9518	87.3528
7	12.9164	3.4200	83.9328
8	12.3739	3.9626	79.9702
9	11.7452	4.5913	75.3788
10	11.0168	5.3197	70.0591
11	10.1728	6.1637	63.8954
12	9.1949	7.1416	56.7538
13	8.0619	8.2746	48.4792
14	6.7491	9.5874	38.8919
15	5.2281	11.1084	27.7835
16	3.4657	12.8708	14.9127
17	1.4238	14.9127	0.0000

YEARS 18 — QTR PAYT 4.0349 — AN CONST 16.14

#	INT	PRIN	BALANCE
1	14.9343	1.2053	98.7947
2	14.7431	1.3965	97.3982
3	14.5215	1.6181	95.7801
4	14.2648	1.8748	93.9053
5	13.9673	2.1722	91.7330
6	13.6227	2.5169	89.2161
7	13.2234	2.9162	86.3000
8	12.7608	3.3788	82.9211
9	12.2247	3.9149	79.0063
10	11.6036	4.5360	74.4703
11	10.8840	5.2556	69.2147
12	10.0502	6.0894	63.1253
13	9.0841	7.0555	56.0698
14	7.9647	8.1749	47.8949
15	6.6678	9.4718	38.4231
16	5.1651	10.9745	27.4486
17	3.4240	12.7156	14.7330
18	1.4066	14.7330	0.0000

YEARS 19 — QTR PAYT 3.9934 — AN CONST 15.98

#	INT	PRIN	BALANCE
1	14.9439	1.0296	98.9704
2	14.7805	1.1929	97.7775
3	14.5913	1.3822	96.3954
4	14.3720	1.6014	94.7939
5	14.1179	1.8555	92.9384
6	13.8235	2.1499	90.7886
7	13.4825	2.4910	88.2976
8	13.0873	2.8862	85.4115
9	12.6294	3.3440	82.0674
10	12.0989	3.8746	78.1928
11	11.4841	4.4893	73.7036
12	10.7719	5.2015	68.5021
13	9.9467	6.0267	62.4754
14	8.9906	6.9829	55.4925
15	7.8827	8.0907	47.4018
16	6.5991	9.3743	38.0275
17	5.1119	10.8615	27.1660
18	3.3887	12.5847	14.5813
19	1.3921	14.5813	0.0000

YEARS 20 — QTR PAYT 3.9582 — AN CONST 15.84

#	INT	PRIN	BALANCE
1	14.9520	.8808	99.1192
2	14.8122	1.0205	98.0987
3	14.6503	1.1824	96.9164
4	14.4628	1.3700	95.5464
5	14.2454	1.5873	93.9590
6	13.9936	1.8392	92.1199
7	13.7018	2.1309	89.9889
8	13.3637	2.4690	87.5199
9	12.9720	2.8607	84.6592
10	12.5182	3.3146	81.3446
11	11.9923	3.8404	77.5042
12	11.3830	4.4497	73.0544
13	10.6770	5.1557	67.8987
14	9.8591	5.9736	61.9251
15	8.9114	6.9214	55.0037
16	7.8133	8.0194	46.9843
17	6.5410	9.2917	37.6926
18	5.0669	10.7659	26.9267
19	3.3589	12.4739	14.4529
20	1.3799	14.4529	0.0000

YEARS 21 — QTR PAYT 3.9283 — AN CONST 15.72

#	INT	PRIN	BALANCE
1	14.9589	.7544	99.2456
2	14.8392	.8741	98.3715
3	14.7005	1.0128	97.3587

QUARTERLY PAYMENT AMORTIZATION SCHEDULE PER $100   15.00 %

#	INT	PRIN	BALANCE
4	14.5398	1.1735	96.1852
5	14.3536	1.3596	94.8255
6	14.1379	1.5754	93.2502
7	13.8880	1.8253	91.4249
8	13.5984	2.1149	89.3100
9	13.2629	2.4504	86.8596
10	12.8741	2.8391	84.0205
11	12.4237	3.2896	80.7309
12	11.9018	3.8115	76.9194
13	11.2971	4.4162	72.5033
14	10.5965	5.1168	67.3865
15	9.7847	5.9286	61.4579
16	8.8441	6.8691	54.5888
17	7.7544	7.9589	46.6298
18	6.4917	9.2216	37.4082
19	5.0287	10.6846	26.7236
20	3.3335	12.3798	14.3438
21	1.3695	14.3438	0.0000

YEARS 22 — QTR PAYT 3.9029 — AN CONST 15.62

#	INT	PRIN	BALANCE
1	14.9647	.6469	99.3531
2	14.8621	.7495	98.6035
3	14.7432	.8685	97.7351
4	14.6054	1.0062	96.7288
5	14.4458	1.1659	95.5630
6	14.2608	1.3509	94.2121
7	14.0465	1.5652	92.6469
8	13.7982	1.8135	90.8335
9	13.5105	2.1012	88.7323
10	13.1771	2.4345	86.2977
11	12.7909	2.8208	83.4770
12	12.3433	3.2683	80.2087
13	11.8248	3.7868	76.4218
14	11.2240	4.3876	72.0342
15	10.5279	5.0837	66.9506
16	9.7214	5.8902	61.0603
17	8.7869	6.8247	54.2356
18	7.7042	7.9074	46.3282
19	6.4497	9.1620	37.1662
20	4.9961	10.6155	26.5507
21	3.3120	12.2997	14.2510
22	1.3606	14.2510	0.0000

YEARS 23 — QTR PAYT 3.8812 — AN CONST 15.53

#	INT	PRIN	BALANCE
1	14.9697	.5552	99.4448
2	14.8816	.6433	98.8014
3	14.7796	.7454	98.0561
4	14.6613	.8636	97.1924
5	14.5243	1.0007	96.1918
6	14.3655	1.1594	95.0324
7	14.1816	1.3434	93.6890
8	13.9685	1.5565	92.1325
9	13.7215	1.8034	90.3291
10	13.4354	2.0895	88.2396
11	13.1039	2.4210	85.8186
12	12.7198	2.8051	83.0135
13	12.2748	3.2502	79.7633
14	11.7592	3.7658	75.9975
15	11.1617	4.3632	71.6343
16	10.4695	5.0555	66.5788
17	9.6674	5.8575	60.7213
18	8.7381	6.7868	53.9345
19	7.6614	7.8635	46.0710
20	6.4139	9.1111	36.9599
21	4.9684	10.5566	26.4033
22	3.2936	12.2314	14.1719
23	1.3531	14.1719	0.0000

YEARS 24 — QTR PAYT 3.8627 — AN CONST 15.46

#	INT	PRIN	BALANCE
1	14.9740	.4769	99.5231
2	14.8983	.5526	98.9705
3	14.8107	.6403	98.3302
4	14.7091	.7418	97.5884
5	14.5914	.8595	96.7289
6	14.4550	.9959	95.7330
7	14.2970	1.1539	94.5791
8	14.1140	1.3369	93.2422
9	13.9019	1.5491	91.6931
10	13.6561	1.7948	89.8983
11	13.3714	2.0796	87.8188
12	13.0414	2.4095	85.4093
13	12.6592	2.7917	82.6176
14	12.2163	3.2347	79.3829
15	11.7031	3.7478	75.6351
16	11.1085	4.3424	71.2927
17	10.4196	5.0314	66.2613
18	9.6213	5.8296	60.4317
19	8.6965	6.7544	53.6773
20	7.6249	7.8260	45.8512
21	6.3833	9.0676	36.7836
22	4.9447	10.5062	26.2774
23	3.2779	12.1730	14.1043
24	1.3466	14.1043	0.0000

YEARS 25 — QTR PAYT 3.8469 — AN CONST 15.39

#	INT	PRIN	BALANCE
1	14.9776	.4099	99.5901
2	14.9126	.4750	99.1151
3	14.8373	.5503	98.5648
4	14.7500	.6376	97.9272
5	14.6488	.7388	97.1884
6	14.5316	.8560	96.3324
7	14.3958	.9918	95.3406
8	14.2384	1.1491	94.1914
9	14.0561	1.3315	92.8600
10	13.8449	1.5427	91.3173
11	13.6001	1.7875	89.5298
12	13.3165	2.0710	87.4588
13	12.9880	2.3996	85.0592
14	12.6073	2.7803	82.2789
15	12.1662	3.2214	79.0575
16	11.6551	3.7325	75.3250
17	11.0630	4.3246	71.0004
18	10.3769	5.0107	65.9897
19	9.5819	5.8057	60.1840
20	8.6608	6.7268	53.4572
21	7.5936	7.7940	45.6633
22	6.3571	9.0305	36.6328
23	4.9244	10.4632	26.1696
24	3.2644	12.1231	14.0465
25	1.3411	14.0465	0.0000

YEARS 26 — QTR PAYT 3.8333 — AN CONST 15.34

#	INT	PRIN	BALANCE
1	14.9808	.3526	99.6474
2	14.9248	.4085	99.2390
3	14.8600	.4733	98.7657
4	14.7850	.5484	98.2173
5	14.6979	.6354	97.5819
6	14.5971	.7362	96.8457
7	14.4804	.8530	95.9928
8	14.3450	.9883	95.0044
9	14.1882	1.1451	93.8594
10	14.0066	1.3268	92.5326
11	13.7961	1.5373	90.9953
12	13.5522	1.7811	89.2142
13	13.2696	2.0637	87.1504
14	12.9422	2.3911	84.7593
15	12.5628	2.7705	81.9888
16	12.1233	3.2100	78.7788
17	11.6140	3.7193	75.0595
18	11.0240	4.3094	70.7501
19	10.3403	4.9931	65.7570
20	9.5481	5.7852	59.9718
21	8.6303	6.7030	53.2688
22	7.5668	7.7665	45.5023
23	6.3347	8.9986	36.5037
24	4.9071	10.4263	26.0774
25	3.2529	12.0804	13.9970
26	1.3364	13.9970	0.0000

YEARS 27 — QTR PAYT 3.8217 — AN CONST 15.29

#	INT	PRIN	BALANCE
1	14.9835	.3034	99.6966
2	14.9353	.3515	99.3452
3	14.8796	.4072	98.9379
4	14.8150	.4719	98.4661
5	14.7401	.5467	97.9193
6	14.6534	.6335	97.2859
7	14.5529	.7339	96.5519
8	14.4364	.8504	95.7016
9	14.3015	.9853	94.7162
10	14.1452	1.1416	93.5746
11	13.9641	1.3227	92.2519
12	13.7542	1.5326	90.7193
13	13.5111	1.7757	88.9435
14	13.2293	2.0575	86.8861
15	12.9029	2.3839	84.5022
16	12.5247	2.7621	81.7401
17	12.0865	3.2003	78.5398
18	11.5788	3.7080	74.8318
19	10.9905	4.2963	70.5355
20	10.3089	4.9779	65.5575
21	9.5192	5.7677	59.7899
22	8.6041	6.6827	53.1072
23	7.5439	7.7429	45.3643
24	6.3155	8.9713	36.3929
25	4.8922	10.3946	25.9983
26	3.2431	12.0438	13.9545
27	1.3323	13.9545	0.0000

YEARS 28 — QTR PAYT 3.8117 — AN CONST 15.25

#	INT	PRIN	BALANCE
1	14.9858	.2611	99.7389
2	14.9443	.3026	99.4363
3	14.8963	.3506	99.0857
4	14.8407	.4062	98.6796
5	14.7763	.4706	98.2089
6	14.7016	.5453	97.6636
7	14.6151	.6318	97.0318
8	14.5149	.7320	96.2998
9	14.3987	.8482	95.4516
10	14.2642	.9827	94.4689
11	14.1083	1.1386	93.3303
12	13.9276	1.3193	92.0110
13	13.7183	1.5286	90.4824
14	13.4758	1.7711	88.7113
15	13.1948	2.0521	86.6592
16	12.8692	2.3777	84.2815
17	12.4920	2.7549	81.5266
18	12.0550	3.1919	78.3347
19	11.5486	3.6983	74.6364
20	10.9618	4.2851	70.3513
21	10.2820	4.9649	65.3864
22	9.4943	5.7526	59.6338
23	8.5816	6.6653	52.9685
24	7.5242	7.7227	45.2458
25	6.2990	8.9479	36.2979
26	4.8794	10.3675	25.9304
27	3.2346	12.0123	13.9181
28	1.3288	13.9181	0.0000

YEARS 29 — QTR PAYT 3.8032 — AN CONST 15.22

#	INT	PRIN	BALANCE
1	14.9877	.2249	99.7751
2	14.9521	.2605	99.5146
3	14.9107	.3019	99.2127
4	14.8628	.3498	98.8629
5	14.8073	.4053	98.4577
6	14.7430	.4696	97.9881
7	14.6685	.5441	97.4440
8	14.5822	.6304	96.8137
9	14.4822	.7304	96.0833
10	14.3663	.8463	95.2370
11	14.2321	.9805	94.2565
12	14.0765	1.1361	93.1204
13	13.8963	1.3163	91.8041
14	13.6875	1.5252	90.2789
15	13.4455	1.7671	88.5118
16	13.1651	2.0475	86.4643
17	12.8403	2.3723	84.0920
18	12.4639	2.7487	81.3433
19	12.0278	3.1848	78.1585
20	11.5226	3.6900	74.4685
21	10.9372	4.2755	70.1931
22	10.2589	4.9538	65.2393
23	9.4729	5.7397	59.4997
24	8.5623	6.6503	52.8494
25	7.5073	7.7053	45.1440
26	6.2848	8.9278	36.2163
27	4.8684	10.3442	25.8721
28	3.2273	11.9853	13.8868
29	1.3258	13.8868	0.0000

YEARS 30 — QTR PAYT 3.7958 — AN CONST 15.19

#	INT	PRIN	BALANCE
1	14.9894	.1937	99.8063
2	14.9587	.2244	99.5819
3	14.9231	.2600	99.3218
4	14.8818	.3013	99.0205
5	14.8340	.3491	98.6714
6	14.7787	.4045	98.2669
7	14.7145	.4687	97.7983
8	14.6401	.5430	97.2553
9	14.5540	.6292	96.6261
10	14.4542	.7290	95.8971
11	14.3385	.8446	95.0525
12	14.2045	.9786	94.0739
13	14.0493	1.1339	92.9400
14	13.8694	1.3138	91.6262
15	13.6609	1.5222	90.1040
16	13.4194	1.7637	88.3403
17	13.1396	2.0435	86.2968
18	12.8154	2.3677	83.9291
19	12.4398	2.7434	81.1857
20	12.0045	3.1786	78.0072
21	11.5003	3.6829	74.3243
22	10.9160	4.2672	70.0571
23	10.2390	4.9442	65.1129
24	9.4546	5.7285	59.3844
25	8.5458	6.6374	52.7470
26	7.4927	7.6904	45.0566
27	6.2726	8.9105	36.1461
28	4.8590	10.3242	25.8220
29	3.2211	11.9621	13.8599
30	1.3233	13.8599	0.0000

QUARTERLY PAYMENT AMORTIZATION SCHEDULE PER $100   16.00 %

YEARS 2 — QTR PAYT 14.8528 — AN CONST 59.42

#	INT	PRIN	BALANCE
1	13.3252	46.0860	53.9140
2	5.4971	53.9140	0.0000

YEARS 3 — QTR PAYT 10.6552 — AN CONST 42.63

#	INT	PRIN	BALANCE
1	14.3597	28.2611	71.7389
2	9.5593	33.0615	38.6773
3	3.9435	38.6773	0.0000

YEARS 4 — QTR PAYT 8.5820 — AN CONST 34.33

#	INT	PRIN	BALANCE
1	14.8707	19.4573	80.5427
2	11.5657	22.7623	57.7804
3	7.6993	26.6287	31.1518
4	3.1762	31.1518	0.0000

YEARS 5 — QTR PAYT 7.3582 — AN CONST 29.44

#	INT	PRIN	BALANCE
1	15.1723	14.2604	85.7396
2	12.7501	16.6826	69.0570
3	9.9164	19.5163	49.5407
4	6.6014	22.8313	26.7094
5	2.7233	26.7094	0.0000

YEARS 6 — QTR PAYT 6.5587 — AN CONST 26.24

#	INT	PRIN	BALANCE
1	15.3694	10.8654	89.1346
2	13.5238	12.7109	76.4237
3	11.3647	14.8700	61.5537
4	8.8389	17.3958	44.1579
5	5.8841	20.3506	23.8073
6	2.4274	23.8073	0.0000

YEARS 7 — QTR PAYT 6.0013 — AN CONST 24.01

#	INT	PRIN	BALANCE
1	15.5068	8.4984	91.5016
2	14.0632	9.9420	81.5596
3	12.3745	11.6307	69.9289
4	10.3989	13.6063	56.3226
5	8.0878	15.9174	40.4052
6	5.3841	18.6211	21.7841
7	2.2211	21.7841	0.0000

YEARS 8 — QTR PAYT 5.5949 — AN CONST 22.38

#	INT	PRIN	BALANCE
1	15.6069	6.7725	93.2275
2	14.4566	7.9229	85.3046
3	13.1108	9.2686	76.0360
4	11.5364	10.8430	65.1930
5	9.6946	12.6848	52.5082
6	7.5400	14.8394	37.6688
7	5.0194	17.3600	20.3088
8	2.0707	20.3088	0.0000

YEARS 9 — QTR PAYT 5.2887 — AN CONST 21.16

#	INT	PRIN	BALANCE
1	15.6824	5.4724	94.5276
2	14.7529	6.4019	88.1257
3	13.6654	7.4893	80.6364
4	12.3933	8.7614	71.8750
5	10.9051	10.2496	61.6254
6	9.1641	11.9906	49.6347
7	7.1274	14.0273	35.6074
8	4.7447	16.4100	19.1974
9	1.9574	19.1974	0.0000

YEARS 10 — QTR PAYT 5.0523 — AN CONST 20.21

#	INT	PRIN	BALANCE
1	15.7406	4.4688	95.5312
2	14.9816	5.2278	90.3034
3	14.0936	6.1158	84.1876
4	13.0548	7.1546	77.0330
5	11.8395	8.3699	68.6631
6	10.4178	9.7916	58.8715
7	8.7546	11.4548	47.4167
8	6.8089	13.4005	34.0162
9	4.5327	15.6767	18.3395
10	1.8699	18.3395	0.0000

YEARS 11 — QTR PAYT 4.8665 — AN CONST 19.47

#	INT	PRIN	BALANCE
1	15.7865	3.6794	96.3206
2	15.1615	4.3043	92.0163
3	14.4303	5.0355	86.9808
4	13.5750	5.8908	81.0900
5	12.5744	6.8914	74.1987
6	11.4039	8.0619	66.1367
7	10.0345	9.4313	56.7054
8	8.4325	11.0333	45.6720
9	6.5584	12.9074	32.7646
10	4.3659	15.0999	17.6647
11	1.8011	17.6647	0.0000

YEARS 12 — QTR PAYT 4.7181 — AN CONST 18.88

#	INT	PRIN	BALANCE
1	15.8230	3.0492	96.9508
2	15.3051	3.5672	93.3836
3	14.6992	4.1731	89.2105
4	13.9903	4.8819	84.3286
5	13.1611	5.7112	78.6174
6	12.1910	6.6813	71.9362
7	11.0561	7.8161	64.1200
8	9.7285	9.1438	54.9763
9	8.1754	10.6969	44.2794
10	6.3584	12.5139	31.7655
11	4.2328	14.6394	17.1261
12	1.7462	17.1261	0.0000

YEARS 13 — QTR PAYT 4.5982 — AN CONST 18.40

#	INT	PRIN	BALANCE
1	15.8526	2.5403	97.4597
2	15.4211	2.9718	94.4879
3	14.9163	3.4766	91.0114
4	14.3258	4.0671	86.9443
5	13.6349	4.7579	82.1864
6	12.8268	5.5661	76.6203
7	11.8813	6.5115	70.1088
8	10.7753	7.6176	62.4912
9	9.4814	8.9115	53.5797
10	7.9677	10.4252	43.1546
11	6.1969	12.1960	30.9586
12	4.1253	14.2676	16.6910
13	1.7018	16.6910	0.0000

YEARS 14 — QTR PAYT 4.5005 — AN CONST 18.01

#	INT	PRIN	BALANCE
1	15.8766	2.1253	97.8747
2	15.5156	2.4863	95.3884
3	15.0933	2.9086	92.4798
4	14.5993	3.4027	89.0771
5	14.0213	3.9806	85.0965
6	13.3452	4.6568	80.4397
7	12.5542	5.4478	74.9919
8	11.6288	6.3731	68.6188
9	10.5463	7.4557	61.1631
10	9.2799	8.7221	52.4410
11	7.7983	10.2036	42.2374
12	6.0652	11.9368	30.3006
13	4.0376	13.9643	16.3363
14	1.6657	16.3363	0.0000

YEARS 15 — QTR PAYT 4.4202 — AN CONST 17.69

#	INT	PRIN	BALANCE
1	15.8964	1.7843	98.2157
2	15.5934	2.0874	96.1283
3	15.2388	2.4419	93.6864
4	14.8240	2.8567	90.8297
5	14.3388	3.3420	87.4877
6	13.7711	3.9096	83.5781
7	13.1070	4.5737	79.0044
8	12.3302	5.3506	73.6538
9	11.4213	6.2594	67.3944
10	10.3581	7.3226	60.0718
11	9.1143	8.5665	51.5053
12	7.6592	10.0215	41.4838
13	5.9570	11.7238	29.7600
14	3.9656	13.7152	16.0448
15	1.6359	16.0448	0.0000

YEARS 16 — QTR PAYT 4.3538 — AN CONST 17.42

#	INT	PRIN	BALANCE
1	15.9128	1.5023	98.4977
2	15.6576	1.7575	96.7402
3	15.3591	2.0560	94.6842
4	15.0099	2.4053	92.2789
5	14.6013	2.8138	89.4651
6	14.1234	3.2918	86.1734
7	13.5642	3.8509	82.3225
8	12.9101	4.5050	77.8175
9	12.1449	5.2702	72.5473
10	11.2497	6.1654	66.3819
11	10.2025	7.2126	59.1693
12	8.9774	8.4378	50.7315
13	7.5441	9.8710	40.8605
14	5.8675	11.5477	29.3129
15	3.9060	13.5091	15.8038
16	1.6114	15.8038	0.0000

YEARS 17 — QTR PAYT 4.2986 — AN CONST 17.20

#	INT	PRIN	BALANCE
1	15.9264	1.2679	98.7321
2	15.7110	1.4833	97.2488
3	15.4591	1.7352	95.5136
4	15.1644	2.0299	93.4837
5	14.8196	2.3748	91.1089
6	14.4162	2.7781	88.3308
7	13.9443	3.2500	85.0808
8	13.3923	3.8021	81.2787
9	12.7464	4.4479	76.8309
10	11.9909	5.2034	71.6275
11	11.1071	6.0872	65.5403
12	10.0731	7.1212	58.4191
13	8.8635	8.3308	50.0883
14	7.4485	9.7458	40.3425
15	5.7931	11.4012	28.9412
16	3.8565	13.3378	15.6034
17	1.5909	15.6034	0.0000

YEARS 18 — QTR PAYT 4.2525 — AN CONST 17.01

#	INT	PRIN	BALANCE
1	15.9378	1.0722	98.9278
2	15.7557	1.2543	97.6735
3	15.5426	1.4674	96.2061
4	15.2934	1.7166	94.4895
5	15.0018	2.0082	92.4814
6	14.6607	2.3493	90.1321
7	14.2616	2.7483	87.3837
8	13.7948	3.2152	84.1686
9	13.2487	3.7613	80.4073
10	12.6098	4.4002	76.0071
11	11.8624	5.1476	70.8595
12	10.9880	6.0220	64.8375
13	9.9651	7.0448	57.7927
14	8.7685	8.2415	49.5513
15	7.3686	9.6413	39.9099
16	5.7310	11.2790	28.6309
17	3.8151	13.1948	15.4361
18	1.5739	15.4361	0.0000

YEARS 19 — QTR PAYT 4.2139 — AN CONST 16.86

#	INT	PRIN	BALANCE
1	15.9473	.9082	99.0918
2	15.7930	1.0624	98.0294
3	15.6126	1.2429	96.7865
4	15.4014	1.4540	95.3324
5	15.1545	1.7010	93.6314
6	14.8655	1.9899	91.6415
7	14.5275	2.3280	89.3135
8	14.1321	2.7234	86.5901
9	13.6695	3.1860	83.4042
10	13.1283	3.7271	79.6770
11	12.4953	4.3602	75.3168
12	11.7546	5.1008	70.2160
13	10.8882	5.9673	64.2487
14	9.8746	6.9808	57.2679
15	8.6889	8.1666	49.1012
16	7.3017	9.5538	39.5475
17	5.6789	11.1766	28.3709
18	3.7805	13.0750	15.2959
19	1.5596	15.2959	0.0000

YEARS 20 — QTR PAYT 4.1814 — AN CONST 16.73

#	INT	PRIN	BALANCE
1	15.9553	.7703	99.2297
2	15.8244	.9012	98.3285
3	15.6714	1.0543	97.2742
4	15.4923	1.2333	96.0409
5	15.2828	1.4428	94.5980
6	15.0377	1.6879	92.9101
7	14.7510	1.9746	90.9355
8	14.4156	2.3100	88.6255
9	14.0232	2.7024	85.9231
10	13.5642	3.1614	82.7617
11	13.0272	3.6984	79.0632
12	12.3990	4.3266	74.7366
13	11.6641	5.0615	69.6751
14	10.8043	5.9213	63.7538
15	9.7986	6.9271	56.8267
16	8.6219	8.1037	48.7230
17	7.2455	9.4802	39.2428
18	5.6352	11.0905	28.1524
19	3.7514	12.9743	15.1781
20	1.5476	15.1781	0.0000

YEARS 21 — QTR PAYT 4.1541 — AN CONST 16.62

#	INT	PRIN	BALANCE
1	15.9620	.6542	99.3458
2	15.8509	.7653	98.5805
3	15.7209	.8953	97.6852

QUARTERLY PAYMENT AMORTIZATION SCHEDULE PER $100 — 16.00 %

#	INT	PRIN	BALANCE
4	15.5688	1.0474	96.6379
5	15.3909	1.2253	95.4126
6	15.1828	1.4334	93.9792
7	14.9393	1.6769	92.3023
8	14.6545	1.9617	90.3406
9	14.3213	2.2949	88.0457
10	13.9315	2.6847	85.3610
11	13.4755	3.1407	82.2202
12	12.9420	3.6742	78.5460
13	12.3179	4.2983	74.2477
14	11.5878	5.0284	69.2193
15	10.7337	5.8826	63.3367
16	9.7345	6.8818	56.4549
17	8.5655	8.0507	48.4043
18	7.1981	9.4182	38.9861
19	5.5983	11.0179	27.9682
20	3.7268	12.8894	15.0788
21	1.5374	15.0788	0.0000

YEARS 22 — QTR PAYT 4.1310 — AN CONST 16.53

#	INT	PRIN	BALANCE
1	15.9677	.5561	99.4439
2	15.8733	.6505	98.7934
3	15.7628	.7610	98.0323
4	15.6335	.8903	97.1420
5	15.4823	1.0415	96.1005
6	15.3054	1.2185	94.8820
7	15.0984	1.4254	93.4566
8	14.8563	1.6675	91.7890
9	14.5730	1.9508	89.8382
10	14.2417	2.2821	87.5561
11	13.8540	2.6698	84.8863
12	13.4005	3.1233	81.7630
13	12.8700	3.6538	78.1092
14	12.2494	4.2744	73.8348
15	11.5233	5.0005	68.8343
16	10.6740	5.8498	62.9845
17	9.6803	6.8435	56.1410
18	8.5179	8.0059	48.1351
19	7.1580	9.3658	38.7693
20	5.5672	10.9566	27.8127
21	3.7061	12.8177	14.9949
22	1.5289	14.9949	0.0000

YEARS 23 — QTR PAYT 4.1114 — AN CONST 16.45

#	INT	PRIN	BALANCE
1	15.9725	.4731	99.5269
2	15.8922	.5535	98.9734
3	15.7982	.6475	98.3260
4	15.6882	.7574	97.5685
5	15.5595	.8861	96.6824
6	15.4090	1.0366	95.6458
7	15.2329	1.2127	94.4331
8	15.0270	1.4187	93.0144
9	14.7860	1.6597	91.3548
10	14.5041	1.9416	89.4132
11	14.1743	2.2714	87.1419
12	13.7885	2.6572	84.4847
13	13.3371	3.1085	81.3762
14	12.8091	3.6365	77.7397
15	12.1914	4.2542	73.4855
16	11.4688	4.9768	68.5087
17	10.6235	5.8222	62.6865
18	9.6345	6.8111	55.8754
19	8.4776	7.9680	47.9074
20	7.1242	9.3215	38.5859
21	5.5408	10.9048	27.6811
22	3.6886	12.7571	14.9240
23	1.5217	14.9240	0.0000

YEARS 24 — QTR PAYT 4.0949 — AN CONST 16.38

#	INT	PRIN	BALANCE
1	15.9766	.4028	99.5972
2	15.9082	.4712	99.1260
3	15.8282	.5512	98.5748
4	15.7345	.6449	97.9299
5	15.6250	.7544	97.1755
6	15.4969	.8825	96.2930
7	15.3470	1.0324	95.2606
8	15.1716	1.2078	94.0528
9	14.9664	1.4130	92.6398
10	14.7264	1.6530	90.9868
11	14.4457	1.9337	89.0531
12	14.1172	2.2622	86.7909
13	13.7329	2.6465	84.1444
14	13.2834	3.0960	81.0484
15	12.7575	3.6219	77.4266
16	12.1423	4.2371	73.1895
17	11.4226	4.9568	68.2327
18	10.5807	5.7987	62.4340
19	9.5957	6.7837	55.6503
20	8.4435	7.9359	47.7144
21	7.0955	9.2839	38.4305
22	5.5185	10.8609	27.5696
23	3.6737	12.7057	14.8639
24	1.5155	14.8639	0.0000

YEARS 25 — QTR PAYT 4.0808 — AN CONST 16.33

#	INT	PRIN	BALANCE
1	15.9801	.3431	99.6569
2	15.9218	.4014	99.2555
3	15.8536	.4696	98.7859
4	15.7739	.5493	98.2366
5	15.6806	.6426	97.5939
6	15.5714	.7518	96.8421
7	15.4437	.8795	95.9626
8	15.2943	1.0289	94.9337
9	15.1195	1.2037	93.7301
10	14.9151	1.4081	92.3219
11	14.6759	1.6473	90.6746
12	14.3961	1.9271	88.7475
13	14.0688	2.2544	86.4931
14	13.6858	2.6374	83.8557
15	13.2378	3.0854	80.7704
16	12.7138	3.6094	77.1609
17	12.1007	4.2225	72.9384
18	11.3834	4.9398	67.9986
19	10.5444	5.7788	62.2198
20	9.5628	6.7604	55.4594
21	8.4145	7.9087	47.5507
22	7.0711	9.2521	38.2986
23	5.4996	10.8236	27.4750
24	3.6611	12.6621	14.8129
25	1.5103	14.8129	0.0000

YEARS 26 — QTR PAYT 4.0689 — AN CONST 16.28

#	INT	PRIN	BALANCE
1	15.9830	.2924	99.7076
2	15.9334	.3421	99.3655
3	15.8752	.4002	98.9652
4	15.8073	.4682	98.4970
5	15.7277	.5477	97.9493
6	15.6347	.6408	97.3085
7	15.5259	.7496	96.5589
8	15.3985	.8769	95.6820
9	15.2496	1.0259	94.6561
10	15.0753	1.2001	93.4560
11	14.8715	1.4040	92.0520
12	14.6330	1.6425	90.4095
13	14.3540	1.9215	88.4880
14	14.0276	2.2478	86.2402
15	13.6458	2.6297	83.6105
16	13.1991	3.0763	80.5341
17	12.6766	3.5989	76.9353
18	12.0653	4.2102	72.7251
19	11.3501	4.9253	67.7998
20	10.5135	5.7619	62.0379
21	9.5348	6.7406	55.2972
22	8.3899	7.8856	47.4116
23	7.0504	9.2250	38.1866
24	5.4835	10.7920	27.3946
25	3.6504	12.6251	14.7696
26	1.5059	14.7696	0.0000

YEARS 27 — QTR PAYT 4.0587 — AN CONST 16.24

#	INT	PRIN	BALANCE
1	15.9855	.2494	99.7506
2	15.9432	.2917	99.4589
3	15.8936	.3413	99.1177
4	15.8357	.3992	98.7185
5	15.7678	.4670	98.2514
6	15.6885	.5464	97.7051
7	15.5957	.6392	97.0659
8	15.4871	.7477	96.3181
9	15.3601	.8747	95.4434
10	15.2116	1.0233	94.4201
11	15.0377	1.1972	93.2229
12	14.8344	1.4005	91.8224
13	14.5965	1.6384	90.1840
14	14.3182	1.9167	88.2674
15	13.9926	2.2422	86.0251
16	13.6118	2.6231	83.4020
17	13.1662	3.0687	80.3333
18	12.6450	3.5899	76.7434
19	12.0352	4.1997	72.5437
20	11.3218	4.9130	67.6307
21	10.4873	5.7476	61.8832
22	9.5111	6.7238	55.1593
23	8.3690	7.8659	47.2934
24	7.0329	9.2020	38.0914
25	5.4698	10.7651	27.3263
26	3.6413	12.5936	14.7327
27	1.5022	14.7327	0.0000

YEARS 28 — QTR PAYT 4.0501 — AN CONST 16.21

#	INT	PRIN	BALANCE
1	15.9877	.2127	99.7873
2	15.9515	.2488	99.5385
3	15.9093	.2911	99.2474
4	15.8598	.3405	98.9069
5	15.8020	.3984	98.5085
6	15.7343	.4660	98.0424
7	15.6551	.5452	97.4972
8	15.5625	.6378	96.8594
9	15.4542	.7461	96.1133
10	15.3275	.8729	95.2404
11	15.1792	1.0212	94.2192
12	15.0057	1.1946	93.0246
13	14.8028	1.3975	91.6271
14	14.5654	1.6349	89.9922
15	14.2877	1.9126	88.0796
16	13.9629	2.2375	85.8421
17	13.5828	2.6175	83.2246
18	13.1382	3.0621	80.1625
19	12.6181	3.5823	76.5802
20	12.0096	4.1907	72.3894
21	11.2978	4.9026	67.4869
22	10.4650	5.7353	61.7515
23	9.4908	6.7095	55.0420
24	8.3512	7.8492	47.1928
25	7.0179	9.1824	38.0104
26	5.4582	10.7422	27.2682
27	3.6335	12.5668	14.7014
28	1.4990	14.7014	0.0000

YEARS 29 — QTR PAYT 4.0427 — AN CONST 16.18

#	INT	PRIN	BALANCE
1	15.9895	.1815	99.8185
2	15.9586	.2123	99.6062
3	15.9226	.2484	99.3578
4	15.8804	.2906	99.0673
5	15.8310	.3399	98.7274
6	15.7733	.3977	98.3297
7	15.7058	.4652	97.8645
8	15.6267	.5442	97.3203
9	15.5343	.6367	96.6836
10	15.4262	.7448	95.9389
11	15.2996	.8713	95.0676
12	15.1516	1.0193	94.0483
13	14.9785	1.1924	92.8558
14	14.7760	1.3950	91.4608
15	14.5390	1.6319	89.8289
16	14.2618	1.9091	87.9198
17	13.9375	2.2334	85.6863
18	13.5582	2.6128	83.0736
19	13.1144	3.0566	80.0170
20	12.5952	3.5758	76.4412
21	11.9878	4.1831	72.2581
22	11.2773	4.8937	67.3644
23	10.4460	5.7249	61.6395
24	9.4736	6.6973	54.9421
25	8.3360	7.8349	47.1072
26	7.0052	9.1658	37.9414
27	5.4483	10.7227	27.2187
28	3.6269	12.5440	14.6747
29	1.4962	14.6747	0.0000

YEARS 30 — QTR PAYT 4.0365 — AN CONST 16.15

#	INT	PRIN	BALANCE
1	15.9910	.1549	99.8451
2	15.9647	.1812	99.6639
3	15.9339	.2120	99.4519
4	15.8979	.2480	99.2039
5	15.8558	.2901	98.9138
6	15.8065	.3394	98.5744
7	15.7489	.3970	98.1774
8	15.6814	.4645	97.7129
9	15.6025	.5434	97.1696
10	15.5102	.6357	96.5339
11	15.4023	.7436	95.7903
12	15.2759	.8700	94.9203
13	15.1282	1.0177	93.9026
14	14.9553	1.1906	92.7120
15	14.7531	1.3928	91.3192
16	14.5165	1.6294	89.6898
17	14.2397	1.9062	87.7836
18	13.9159	2.2300	85.5536
19	13.5372	2.6087	82.9449
20	13.0941	3.0518	79.8930
21	12.5757	3.5702	76.3228
22	11.9692	4.1767	72.1462
23	11.2598	4.8861	67.2600
24	10.4298	5.7161	61.5440
25	9.4589	6.6870	54.8570
26	8.3231	7.8228	47.0342
27	6.9943	9.1516	37.8826
28	5.4398	10.7061	27.1766
29	3.6213	12.5246	14.6520
30	1.4939	14.6520	0.0000

QUARTERLY PAYMENT AMORTIZATION SCHEDULE PER $100   17.00 %

YEARS 2 — QTR PAYT 15.0065 — AN CONST 60.03

#	INT	PRIN	BALANCE
1	14.1786	45.8474	54.1526
2	5.8734	54.1526	0.0000

YEARS 3 — QTR PAYT 10.8103 — AN CONST 43.25

#	INT	PRIN	BALANCE
1	15.2792	27.9622	72.0378
2	10.2139	33.0275	39.0103
3	4.2311	39.0103	0.0000

YEARS 4 — QTR PAYT 8.7410 — AN CONST 34.97

#	INT	PRIN	BALANCE
1	15.8220	19.1421	80.8579
2	12.3544	22.6096	58.2483
3	8.2588	26.7053	31.5429
4	3.4211	31.5429	0.0000

YEARS 5 — QTR PAYT 7.5220 — AN CONST 30.09

#	INT	PRIN	BALANCE
1	16.1418	13.9462	86.0538
2	13.6154	16.4725	69.5813
3	10.6315	19.4565	50.1249
4	7.1070	22.9810	27.1439
5	2.9440	27.1439	0.0000

YEARS 6 — QTR PAYT 6.7276 — AN CONST 26.92

#	INT	PRIN	BALANCE
1	16.3501	10.5604	89.4396
2	14.4371	12.4734	76.9662
3	12.1776	14.7329	62.2332
4	9.5087	17.4018	44.8315
5	6.3565	20.5541	24.2774
6	2.6331	24.2774	0.0000

YEARS 7 — QTR PAYT 6.1755 — AN CONST 24.71

#	INT	PRIN	BALANCE
1	16.4949	8.2070	91.7930
2	15.0083	9.6937	82.0993
3	13.2523	11.4497	70.6495
4	11.1782	13.5238	57.1257
5	8.7284	15.9736	41.1521
6	5.8348	18.8672	22.2849
7	2.4170	22.2849	0.0000

YEARS 8 — QTR PAYT 5.7743 — AN CONST 23.10

#	INT	PRIN	BALANCE
1	16.6002	6.4969	93.5031
2	15.4233	7.6738	85.8293
3	14.0332	9.0639	76.7653
4	12.3913	10.7058	66.0595
5	10.4519	12.6452	53.4143
6	8.1613	14.9358	38.4785
7	5.4557	17.6414	20.8371
8	2.2600	20.8371	0.0000

YEARS 9 — QTR PAYT 5.4732 — AN CONST 21.90

#	INT	PRIN	BALANCE
1	16.6791	5.2137	94.7863
2	15.7347	6.1582	88.6281
3	14.6191	7.2737	81.3543
4	13.3015	8.5914	72.7630
5	11.7452	10.1477	62.6153
6	9.9070	11.9859	50.6294
7	7.7358	14.1571	36.4723
8	5.1713	16.7216	19.7507
9	2.1422	19.7507	0.0000

YEARS 10 — QTR PAYT 5.2418 — AN CONST 20.97

#	INT	PRIN	BALANCE
1	16.7398	4.2275	95.7725
2	15.9740	4.9933	90.7792
3	15.0695	5.8979	84.8813
4	14.0011	6.9662	77.9151
5	12.7392	8.2282	69.6869
6	11.2487	9.7187	59.9683
7	9.4882	11.4792	48.4891
8	7.4087	13.5586	34.9305
9	4.9526	16.0147	18.9158
10	2.0516	18.9158	0.0000

YEARS 11 — QTR PAYT 5.0607 — AN CONST 20.25

#	INT	PRIN	BALANCE
1	16.7873	3.4555	96.5445
2	16.1614	4.0814	92.4631
3	15.4221	4.8208	87.6423
4	14.5488	5.6941	81.9483
5	13.5173	6.7255	75.2227
6	12.2990	7.9438	67.2789
7	10.8600	9.3828	57.8961
8	9.1603	11.0825	46.8135
9	7.1527	13.0901	33.7235
10	4.7815	15.4613	18.2621
11	1.9807	18.2621	0.0000

YEARS 12 — QTR PAYT 4.9169 — AN CONST 19.67

#	INT	PRIN	BALANCE
1	16.8251	2.8424	97.1576
2	16.3102	3.3573	93.8004
3	15.7020	3.9654	89.8349
4	14.9837	4.6838	85.1512
5	14.1352	5.5322	79.6190
6	13.1331	6.5344	73.0846
7	11.9494	7.7180	65.3666
8	10.5513	9.1161	56.2504
9	8.8999	10.7675	45.4829
10	6.9494	12.7180	32.7649
11	4.6456	15.0219	17.7430
12	1.9244	17.7430	0.0000

YEARS 13 — QTR PAYT 4.8013 — AN CONST 19.21

#	INT	PRIN	BALANCE
1	16.8554	2.3499	97.6501
2	16.4297	2.7756	94.8745
3	15.9269	3.2784	91.5961
4	15.3330	3.8722	87.7239
5	14.6316	4.5737	83.1502
6	13.8031	5.4022	77.7480
7	12.8245	6.3808	71.3672
8	11.6686	7.5367	63.8305
9	10.3034	8.9019	54.9286
10	8.6908	10.5145	44.4141
11	6.7861	12.4192	31.9950
12	4.5364	14.6689	17.3261
13	1.8792	17.3261	0.0000

YEARS 14 — QTR PAYT 4.7077 — AN CONST 18.84

#	INT	PRIN	BALANCE
1	16.8800	1.9507	98.0493
2	16.5266	2.3041	95.7452
3	16.1092	2.7214	93.0238
4	15.6162	3.2144	89.8094
5	15.0339	3.7967	86.0127
6	14.3462	4.4845	81.5282
7	13.5338	5.2968	76.2314
8	12.5743	6.2563	69.9750
9	11.4410	7.3897	62.5854
10	10.1024	8.7283	53.8571
11	8.5213	10.3094	43.5477
12	6.6538	12.1769	31.3708
13	4.4479	14.3827	16.9881
14	1.8425	16.9881	0.0000

YEARS 15 — QTR PAYT 4.6312 — AN CONST 18.53

#	INT	PRIN	BALANCE
1	16.9000	1.6247	98.3753
2	16.6057	1.9190	96.4563
3	16.2581	2.2666	94.1897
4	15.8475	2.6772	91.5124
5	15.3625	3.1622	88.3503
6	14.7897	3.7350	84.6152
7	14.1131	4.4116	80.2036
8	13.3139	5.2108	74.9929
9	12.3700	6.1547	68.8382
10	11.2551	7.2696	61.5686
11	9.9382	8.5865	52.9821
12	8.3828	10.1419	42.8402
13	6.5456	11.9791	30.8612
14	4.3757	14.1490	16.7121
15	1.8126	16.7121	0.0000

YEARS 16 — QTR PAYT 4.5683 — AN CONST 18.28

#	INT	PRIN	BALANCE
1	16.9165	1.3569	98.6431
2	16.6707	1.6027	97.0405
3	16.3804	1.8930	95.1475
4	16.0375	2.2359	92.9117
5	15.6325	2.6409	90.2708
6	15.1541	3.1193	87.1515
7	14.5890	3.6843	83.4671
8	13.9216	4.3518	79.1154
9	13.1333	5.1401	73.9753
10	12.2022	6.0712	67.9041
11	11.1024	7.1710	60.7332
12	9.8034	8.4700	52.2632
13	8.2691	10.0043	42.2589
14	6.4568	11.8165	30.4424
15	4.3163	13.9571	16.4854
16	1.7880	16.4854	0.0000

YEARS 17 — QTR PAYT 4.5165 — AN CONST 18.07

#	INT	PRIN	BALANCE
1	16.9301	1.1357	98.8643
2	16.7244	1.3414	97.5228
3	16.4814	1.5844	95.9384
4	16.1944	1.8715	94.0669
5	15.8553	2.2105	91.8564
6	15.4549	2.6109	89.2455
7	14.9820	3.0839	86.1617
8	14.4233	3.6425	82.5192
9	13.7635	4.3023	78.2168
10	12.9841	5.0817	73.1352
11	12.0636	6.0022	67.1329
12	10.9763	7.0895	60.0434
13	9.6921	8.3738	51.6697
14	8.1752	9.8907	41.7790
15	6.3835	11.6823	30.0967
16	4.2673	13.7986	16.2981
17	1.7677	16.2981	0.0000

YEARS 18 — QTR PAYT 4.4734 — AN CONST 17.90

#	INT	PRIN	BALANCE
1	16.9414	.9524	99.0476
2	16.7689	1.1249	97.9227
3	16.5651	1.3287	96.5940
4	16.3244	1.5694	95.0247
5	16.0401	1.8536	93.1710
6	15.7043	2.1894	90.9816
7	15.3077	2.5860	88.3956
8	14.8393	3.0545	85.3411
9	14.2860	3.6078	81.7333
10	13.6324	4.2614	77.4719
11	12.8605	5.0333	72.4386
12	11.9487	5.9451	66.4936
13	10.8718	7.0220	59.4716
14	9.5998	8.2940	51.1776
15	8.0973	9.7965	41.3811
16	6.3227	11.5711	29.8100
17	4.2266	13.6671	16.1429
18	1.7509	16.1429	0.0000

YEARS 19 — QTR PAYT 4.4377 — AN CONST 17.76

#	INT	PRIN	BALANCE
1	16.9508	.7999	99.2001
2	16.8059	.9448	98.2554
3	16.6347	1.1159	97.1395
4	16.4326	1.3180	95.8214
5	16.1938	1.5568	94.2646
6	15.9118	1.8388	92.4258
7	15.5787	2.1719	90.2539
8	15.1853	2.5654	87.6885
9	14.7206	3.0301	84.6585
10	14.1717	3.5790	81.0795
11	13.5234	4.2273	76.8523
12	12.7576	4.9930	71.8592
13	11.8531	5.8975	65.9617
14	10.7848	6.9658	58.9959
15	9.5230	8.2277	50.7682
16	8.0325	9.7181	41.0501
17	6.2721	11.4785	29.5716
18	4.1928	13.5578	16.0138
19	1.7369	16.0138	0.0000

YEARS 20 — QTR PAYT 4.4078 — AN CONST 17.64

#	INT	PRIN	BALANCE
1	16.9586	.6726	99.3274
2	16.8368	.7945	98.5329
3	16.6928	.9384	97.5945
4	16.5228	1.1084	96.4861
5	16.3221	1.3092	95.1769
6	16.0849	1.5463	93.6306
7	15.8048	1.8264	91.8041
8	15.4739	2.1573	89.6468
9	15.0831	2.5481	87.0987
10	14.6216	3.0097	84.0890
11	14.0764	3.5549	80.5341
12	13.4324	4.1988	76.3353
13	12.6718	4.9594	71.3759
14	11.7734	5.8578	65.5180
15	10.7123	6.9190	58.5991
16	9.4589	8.1723	50.4267
17	7.9785	9.6527	40.7740
18	6.2299	11.4013	29.3727
19	4.1646	13.4666	15.9061
20	1.7252	15.9061	0.0000

YEARS 21 — QTR PAYT 4.3829 — AN CONST 17.54

#	INT	PRIN	BALANCE
1	16.9652	.5663	99.4337
2	16.8626	.6688	98.7649
3	16.7414	.7900	97.9749

#	INT	PRIN	BALANCE
4	16.5983	.9331	97.0418
5	16.4293	1.1021	95.9397
6	16.2296	1.3018	94.6380
7	15.9938	1.5376	93.1004
8	15.7153	1.8161	91.2843
9	15.3863	2.1451	89.1392
10	14.9977	2.5337	86.6055
11	14.5388	2.9926	83.6129
12	13.9967	3.5347	80.0781
13	13.3563	4.1751	75.9031
14	12.6000	4.9314	70.9717
15	11.7067	5.8247	65.1470
16	10.6516	6.8798	58.2672
17	9.4054	8.1261	50.1412
18	7.9333	9.5981	40.5431
19	6.1947	11.3367	29.2064
20	4.1410	13.3904	15.8160
21	1.7154	15.8160	0.0000

YEARS 22   QTR PAYT 4.3619   AN CONST 17.45

#	INT	PRIN	BALANCE
1	16.9706	.4771	99.5229
2	16.8842	.5636	98.9593
3	16.7821	.6656	98.2937
4	16.6615	.7862	97.5075
5	16.5191	.9286	96.5788
6	16.3509	1.0969	95.4820
7	16.1522	1.2956	94.1864
8	15.9175	1.5302	92.6562
9	15.6403	1.8074	90.8487
10	15.3129	2.1349	88.7139
11	14.9262	2.5216	86.1923
12	14.4694	2.9784	83.2139
13	13.9299	3.5179	79.6960
14	13.2926	4.1551	75.5409
15	12.5399	4.9078	70.6331
16	11.6509	5.7969	64.8362
17	10.6008	6.8470	57.9892
18	9.3605	8.0873	49.9019
19	7.8955	9.5523	40.3497
20	6.1651	11.2827	29.0670
21	4.1213	13.3265	15.7405
22	1.7072	15.7405	0.0000

YEARS 23   QTR PAYT 4.3444   AN CONST 17.38

#	INT	PRIN	BALANCE
1	16.9752	.4023	99.5977
2	16.9024	.4752	99.1225
3	16.8163	.5613	98.5612
4	16.7146	.6630	97.8982
5	16.5945	.7831	97.1152
6	16.4527	.9249	96.1903
7	16.2851	1.0924	95.0978
8	16.0872	1.2903	93.8075
9	15.8535	1.5241	92.2834
10	15.5774	1.8002	90.4832
11	15.2513	2.1263	88.3570
12	14.8661	2.5114	85.8455
13	14.4112	2.9664	82.8791
14	13.8738	3.5037	79.3754
15	13.2391	4.1384	75.2370
16	12.4895	4.8881	70.3489
17	11.6040	5.7736	64.5753
18	10.5581	6.8194	57.7559
19	9.3228	8.0547	49.7012
20	7.8637	9.5138	40.1873
21	6.1403	11.2373	28.9501
22	4.1047	13.2729	15.6772
23	1.7004	15.6772	0.0000

YEARS 24   QTR PAYT 4.3296   AN CONST 17.32

#	INT	PRIN	BALANCE
1	16.9791	.3395	99.6605
2	16.9176	.4010	99.2596
3	16.8450	.4736	98.7860
4	16.7592	.5594	98.2266
5	16.6579	.6607	97.5659
6	16.5382	.7804	96.7855
7	16.3968	.9218	95.8637
8	16.2298	1.0887	94.7750
9	16.0326	1.2860	93.4890
10	15.7997	1.5189	91.9701
11	15.5245	1.7941	90.1761
12	15.1995	2.1190	88.0570
13	14.8157	2.5029	85.5541
14	14.3623	2.9563	82.5978
15	13.8267	3.4918	79.1060
16	13.1942	4.1244	74.9816
17	12.4471	4.8715	70.1101
18	11.5646	5.7540	64.3561
19	10.5223	6.7963	57.5599
20	9.2912	8.0274	49.5325
21	7.8370	9.4815	40.0509
22	6.1195	11.1991	28.8518
23	4.0908	13.2278	15.6240
24	1.6946	15.6240	0.0000

YEARS 25   QTR PAYT 4.3172   AN CONST 17.27

#	INT	PRIN	BALANCE
1	16.9824	.2866	99.7134
2	16.9305	.3385	99.3749
3	16.8691	.3998	98.9751
4	16.7967	.4722	98.5029
5	16.7112	.5578	97.9451
6	16.6101	.6588	97.2863
7	16.4908	.7782	96.5081
8	16.3498	.9191	95.5890
9	16.1833	1.0856	94.5034
10	15.9867	1.2823	93.2211
11	15.7544	1.5146	91.7066
12	15.4800	1.7889	89.9176
13	15.1560	2.1130	87.8047
14	14.7732	2.4957	85.3089
15	14.3211	2.9478	82.3611
16	13.7871	3.4818	78.8793
17	13.1564	4.1126	74.7667
18	12.4114	4.8575	69.9092
19	11.5315	5.7375	64.1717
20	10.4921	6.7768	57.3949
21	9.2645	8.0044	49.3905
22	7.8146	9.4544	39.9361
23	6.1019	11.1670	28.7691
24	4.0790	13.1899	15.5792
25	1.6897	15.5792	0.0000

YEARS 26   QTR PAYT 4.3068   AN CONST 17.23

#	INT	PRIN	BALANCE
1	16.9851	.2420	99.7580
2	16.9413	.2859	99.4721
3	16.8895	.3377	99.1344
4	16.8283	.3988	98.7356
5	16.7561	.4711	98.2645
6	16.6707	.5564	97.7080
7	16.5699	.6572	97.0508
8	16.4509	.7763	96.2745
9	16.3102	.9169	95.3576
10	16.1442	1.0830	94.2747
11	15.9480	1.2792	92.9955
12	15.7163	1.5109	91.4846
13	15.4426	1.7846	89.7000
14	15.1193	2.1079	87.5921
15	14.7374	2.4897	85.1024
16	14.2864	2.9407	82.1617
17	13.7537	3.4734	78.6883
18	13.1245	4.1026	74.5857
19	12.3814	4.8458	69.7400
20	11.5036	5.7236	64.0164
21	10.4668	6.7604	57.2560
22	9.2421	7.9850	49.2710
23	7.7957	9.4315	39.8395
24	6.0872	11.1400	28.6995
25	4.0692	13.1580	15.5415
26	1.6856	15.5415	0.0000

YEARS 27   QTR PAYT 4.2980   AN CONST 17.20

#	INT	PRIN	BALANCE
1	16.9874	.2045	99.7955
2	16.9504	.2415	99.5540
3	16.9066	.2853	99.2687
4	16.8549	.3370	98.9317
5	16.7939	.3980	98.5336
6	16.7218	.4701	98.0635
7	16.6366	.5553	97.5082
8	16.5360	.6559	96.8524
9	16.4172	.7747	96.0777
10	16.2769	.9150	95.1626
11	16.1111	1.0808	94.0819
12	15.9154	1.2766	92.8053
13	15.6841	1.5078	91.2975
14	15.4110	1.7809	89.5166
15	15.0884	2.1036	87.4130
16	14.7073	2.4846	84.9284
17	14.2572	2.9347	81.9937
18	13.7256	3.4663	78.5274
19	13.0977	4.0942	74.4332
20	12.3560	4.8359	69.5973
21	11.4800	5.7119	63.8855
22	10.4453	6.7466	57.1389
23	9.2232	7.9687	49.1702
24	7.7797	9.4122	39.7580
25	6.0747	11.1172	28.6408
26	4.0609	13.1311	15.5097
27	1.6822	15.5097	0.0000

YEARS 28   QTR PAYT 4.2906   AN CONST 17.17

#	INT	PRIN	BALANCE
1	16.9894	.1728	99.8272
2	16.9581	.2041	99.6230
3	16.9211	.2411	99.3819
4	16.8774	.2848	99.0971
5	16.8258	.3364	98.7607
6	16.7649	.3973	98.3633
7	16.6929	.4693	97.8940
8	16.6079	.5543	97.3397
9	16.5075	.6547	96.6850
10	16.3889	.7734	95.9116
11	16.2488	.9134	94.9982
12	16.0833	1.0789	93.9193
13	15.8878	1.2744	92.6449
14	15.6570	1.5052	91.1397
15	15.3843	1.7779	89.3618
16	15.0623	2.0999	87.2619
17	14.6819	2.4803	84.7816
18	14.2326	2.9296	81.8520
19	13.7019	3.4603	78.3917
20	13.0751	4.0871	74.3046
21	12.3347	4.8275	69.4771
22	11.4602	5.7020	63.7751
23	10.4273	6.7349	57.0401
24	9.2073	7.9549	49.0852
25	7.7663	9.3959	39.6893
26	6.0642	11.0980	28.5913
27	4.0538	13.1084	15.4829
28	1.6793	15.4829	0.0000

YEARS 29   QTR PAYT 4.2843   AN CONST 17.14

#	INT	PRIN	BALANCE
1	16.9910	.1461	99.8539
2	16.9645	.1726	99.6813
3	16.9333	.2038	99.4775
4	16.8963	.2408	99.2367
5	16.8527	.2844	98.9523
6	16.8012	.3359	98.6164
7	16.7404	.3968	98.2196
8	16.6685	.4686	97.7510
9	16.5836	.5535	97.1975
10	16.4833	.6538	96.5437
11	16.3649	.7722	95.7715
12	16.2250	.9121	94.8594
13	16.0598	1.0773	93.7820
14	15.8646	1.2725	92.5095
15	15.6341	1.5030	91.0065
16	15.3619	1.7753	89.2313
17	15.0403	2.0968	87.1344
18	14.6604	2.4767	84.6577
19	14.2118	2.9253	81.7324
20	13.6819	3.4553	78.2772
21	13.0560	4.0812	74.1960
22	12.3167	4.8205	69.3755
23	11.4435	5.6937	63.6819
24	10.4121	6.7251	56.9568
25	9.1938	7.9433	49.0135
26	7.7549	9.3822	39.6313
27	6.0553	11.0818	28.5495
28	4.0479	13.0892	15.4603
29	1.6768	15.4603	0.0000

YEARS 30   QTR PAYT 4.2790   AN CONST 17.12

#	INT	PRIN	BALANCE
1	16.9924	.1236	99.8764
2	16.9700	.1459	99.7305
3	16.9436	.1724	99.5581
4	16.9124	.2036	99.3545
5	16.8755	.2405	99.1141
6	16.8319	.2840	98.8300
7	16.7805	.3355	98.4945
8	16.7197	.3963	98.0983
9	16.6479	.4680	97.6302
10	16.5631	.5528	97.0774
11	16.4630	.6530	96.4244
12	16.3447	.7713	95.6531
13	16.2050	.9110	94.7422
14	16.0399	1.0760	93.6662
15	15.8450	1.2709	92.3952
16	15.6148	1.5011	90.8941
17	15.3429	1.7731	89.1210
18	15.0217	2.0943	87.0268
19	14.6423	2.4736	84.5531
20	14.1942	2.9217	81.6314
21	13.6650	3.4510	78.1804
22	13.0398	4.0761	74.1043
23	12.3015	4.8145	69.2898
24	11.4293	5.6866	63.6032
25	10.3992	6.7168	56.8864
26	9.1825	7.9335	48.9529
27	7.7453	9.3706	39.5823
28	6.0479	11.0681	28.5142
29	4.0429	13.0730	15.4412
30	1.6748	15.4412	0.0000

YEARS 2 — QTR PAYT 15.1610 — AN CONST 60.65

#	INT	PRIN	BALANCE
1	15.0342	45.6096	54.3904
2	6.2535	54.3904	0.0000

YEARS 3 — QTR PAYT 10.9666 — AN CONST 43.87

#	INT	PRIN	BALANCE
1	16.2010	27.6654	72.3346
2	10.8749	32.9915	39.3430
3	4.5234	39.3430	0.0000

YEARS 4 — QTR PAYT 8.9015 — AN CONST 35.61

#	INT	PRIN	BALANCE
1	16.7755	18.8306	81.1694
2	13.1503	22.4559	58.7135
3	8.8271	26.7790	31.9345
4	3.6717	31.9345	0.0000

YEARS 5 — QTR PAYT 7.6876 — AN CONST 30.76

#	INT	PRIN	BALANCE
1	17.1132	13.6372	86.3628
2	14.4878	16.2626	70.1001
3	11.3570	19.3935	50.7066
4	7.6233	23.1271	27.5795
5	3.1709	27.5795	0.0000

YEARS 6 — QTR PAYT 6.8987 — AN CONST 27.60

#	INT	PRIN	BALANCE
1	17.3327	10.2621	89.7379
2	15.3571	12.2378	77.5001
3	13.0011	14.5938	62.9064
4	10.1915	17.4033	45.5031
5	6.8410	20.7538	24.7493
6	2.8455	24.7493	0.0000

YEARS 7 — QTR PAYT 6.3521 — AN CONST 25.41

#	INT	PRIN	BALANCE
1	17.4848	7.9236	92.0764
2	15.9593	9.4490	82.6275
3	14.1402	11.2681	71.3594
4	11.9709	13.4374	57.9220
5	9.3840	16.0244	41.8976
6	6.2990	19.1093	22.7883
7	2.6201	22.7883	0.0000

YEARS 8 — QTR PAYT 5.9563 — AN CONST 23.83

#	INT	PRIN	BALANCE
1	17.5949	6.2304	93.7696
2	16.3954	7.4299	86.3397
3	14.9650	8.8603	77.4794
4	13.2592	10.5660	66.9134
5	11.2251	12.6002	54.3132
6	8.7993	15.0260	39.2872
7	5.9065	17.9188	21.3684
8	2.4568	21.3684	0.0000

YEARS 9 — QTR PAYT 5.6606 — AN CONST 22.65

#	INT	PRIN	BALANCE
1	17.6771	4.9652	95.0348
2	16.7212	5.9211	89.1138
3	15.5813	7.0610	82.0528
4	14.2220	8.4203	73.6324
5	12.6009	10.0414	63.5910
6	10.6677	11.9746	51.6164
7	8.3624	14.2799	37.3365
8	5.6133	17.0291	20.3075
9	2.3348	20.3075	0.0000

YEARS 10 — QTR PAYT 5.4343 — AN CONST 21.74

#	INT	PRIN	BALANCE
1	17.7401	3.9972	96.0028
2	16.9706	4.7667	91.2361
3	16.0529	5.6844	85.5517
4	14.9585	6.7787	78.7730
5	13.6535	8.0838	70.6892
6	12.0972	9.6400	61.0492
7	10.2413	11.4959	49.5532
8	8.0281	13.7091	35.8441
9	5.3889	16.3484	19.4957
10	2.2415	19.4957	0.0000

YEARS 11 — QTR PAYT 5.2581 — AN CONST 21.04

#	INT	PRIN	BALANCE
1	17.7891	3.2432	96.7568
2	17.1647	3.8675	92.8893
3	16.4202	4.6121	88.2772
4	15.5322	5.5000	82.7771
5	14.4734	6.5589	76.2182
6	13.2107	7.8216	68.3966
7	11.7049	9.3274	59.0692
8	9.9092	11.1231	47.9461
9	7.7678	13.2645	34.6816
10	5.2141	15.8182	18.8635
11	2.1688	18.8635	0.0000

YEARS 12 — QTR PAYT 5.1189 — AN CONST 20.48

#	INT	PRIN	BALANCE
1	17.8278	2.6476	97.3524
2	17.3181	3.1573	94.1951
3	16.7103	3.7651	90.4300
4	15.9854	4.4900	85.9400
5	15.1210	5.3544	80.5855
6	14.0902	6.3852	74.2003
7	12.8609	7.6145	66.5858
8	11.3950	9.0805	57.5053
9	9.6468	10.8286	46.6767
10	7.5621	12.9133	33.7634
11	5.0761	15.3994	18.3640
12	2.1114	18.3640	0.0000

YEARS 13 — QTR PAYT 5.0077 — AN CONST 20.04

#	INT	PRIN	BALANCE
1	17.8588	2.1719	97.8281
2	17.4406	2.5901	95.2380
3	16.9420	3.0887	92.1492
4	16.3473	3.6834	88.4659
5	15.6382	4.3925	84.0734
6	14.7926	5.2381	78.8353
7	13.7842	6.2466	72.5887
8	12.5816	7.4491	65.1396
9	11.1475	8.8832	56.2563
10	9.4373	10.5934	45.6629
11	7.3979	12.6328	33.0301
12	4.9658	15.0649	17.9652
13	2.0655	17.9652	0.0000

YEARS 14 — QTR PAYT 4.9181 — AN CONST 19.68

#	INT	PRIN	BALANCE
1	17.8837	1.7887	98.2113
2	17.5393	2.1331	96.0782
3	17.1287	2.5438	93.5344
4	16.6389	3.0335	90.5009
5	16.0549	3.6175	86.8834
6	15.3585	4.3139	82.5695
7	14.5280	5.1444	77.4251
8	13.5376	6.1348	71.2903
9	12.3565	7.3159	63.9744
10	10.9481	8.7243	55.2501
11	9.2685	10.4039	44.8461
12	7.2655	12.4069	32.4393
13	4.8770	14.7954	17.6438
14	2.0286	17.6438	0.0000

YEARS 15 — QTR PAYT 4.8454 — AN CONST 19.39

#	INT	PRIN	BALANCE
1	17.9039	1.4778	98.5222
2	17.6194	1.7623	96.7599
3	17.2801	2.1016	94.6583
4	16.8755	2.5062	92.1522
5	16.3931	2.9887	89.1635
6	15.8177	3.5640	85.5995
7	15.1315	4.2502	81.3493
8	14.3133	5.0684	76.2809
9	13.3375	6.0442	70.2368
10	12.1739	7.2078	63.0290
11	10.7863	8.5954	54.4336
12	9.1315	10.2502	44.1834
13	7.1582	12.2235	31.9599
14	4.8049	14.5768	17.3831
15	1.9986	17.3831	0.0000

YEARS 16 — QTR PAYT 4.7861 — AN CONST 19.15

#	INT	PRIN	BALANCE
1	17.9204	1.2241	98.7759
2	17.6848	1.4597	97.3162
3	17.4037	1.7407	95.5755
4	17.0686	2.0759	93.4997
5	16.6690	2.4755	91.0242
6	16.1924	2.9521	88.0721
7	15.6241	3.5204	84.5517
8	14.9463	4.1981	80.3536
9	14.1381	5.0064	75.3472
10	13.1743	5.9702	69.3770
11	12.0249	7.1195	62.2575
12	10.6543	8.4902	53.7673
13	9.0197	10.1247	43.6426
14	7.0706	12.0739	31.5687
15	4.7461	14.3984	17.1703
16	1.9741	17.1703	0.0000

YEARS 17 — QTR PAYT 4.7375 — AN CONST 18.95

#	INT	PRIN	BALANCE
1	17.9339	1.0160	98.9840
2	17.7383	1.2116	97.7724
3	17.5051	1.4449	96.3275
4	17.2269	1.7230	94.6044
5	16.8952	2.0548	92.5497
6	16.4996	2.4503	90.0993
7	16.0279	2.9221	87.1773
8	15.4653	3.4846	83.6926
9	14.7945	4.1555	79.5372
10	13.9945	4.9555	74.5817
11	13.0404	5.9095	68.6721
12	11.9027	7.0472	61.6249
13	10.5460	8.4039	53.2210
14	8.9281	10.0218	43.1992
15	6.9987	11.9512	31.2479
16	4.6979	14.2521	16.9959
17	1.9541	16.9959	0.0000

YEARS 18 — QTR PAYT 4.6975 — AN CONST 18.79

#	INT	PRIN	BALANCE
1	17.9451	.8448	99.1552
2	17.7824	1.0074	98.1478
3	17.5885	1.2014	96.9464
4	17.3572	1.4327	95.5137
5	17.0814	1.7085	93.8052
6	16.7525	2.0374	91.7678
7	16.3602	2.4296	89.3382
8	15.8925	2.8974	86.4408
9	15.3347	3.4552	82.9856
10	14.6695	4.1204	78.8652
11	13.8762	4.9136	73.9516
12	12.9303	5.8596	68.0920
13	11.8022	6.9877	61.1043
14	10.4569	8.3329	52.7714
15	8.8527	9.9372	42.8342
16	6.9396	11.8503	30.9839
17	4.6582	14.1317	16.8523
18	1.9376	16.8523	0.0000

YEARS 19 — QTR PAYT 4.6644 — AN CONST 18.66

#	INT	PRIN	BALANCE
1	17.9543	.7034	99.2966
2	17.8188	.8389	98.4577
3	17.6573	1.0003	97.4574
4	17.4648	1.1929	96.2644
5	17.2351	1.4226	94.8418
6	16.9612	1.6965	93.1454
7	16.6346	2.0231	91.1223
8	16.2451	2.4125	88.7098
9	15.7807	2.8770	85.8328
10	15.2268	3.4309	82.4019
11	14.5663	4.0914	78.3105
12	13.7786	4.8791	73.4314
13	12.8393	5.8184	67.6130
14	11.7192	6.9385	60.6745
15	10.3834	8.2743	52.4002
16	8.7904	9.8673	42.5329
17	6.8908	11.7669	30.7660
18	4.6254	14.0323	16.7337
19	1.9240	16.7337	0.0000

YEARS 20 — QTR PAYT 4.6371 — AN CONST 18.55

#	INT	PRIN	BALANCE
1	17.9619	.5864	99.4136
2	17.8490	.6993	98.7143
3	17.7143	.8339	97.8804
4	17.5538	.9945	96.8859
5	17.3623	1.1859	95.6999
6	17.1340	1.4143	94.2857
7	16.8618	1.6865	92.5992
8	16.5371	2.0112	90.5880
9	16.1499	2.3984	88.1896
10	15.6881	2.8601	85.3294
11	15.1375	3.4108	81.9187
12	14.4809	4.0674	77.8513
13	13.6978	4.8505	73.0008
14	12.7640	5.7843	67.2165
15	11.6504	6.8978	60.3187
16	10.3225	8.2258	52.0929
17	8.7389	9.8094	42.2835
18	6.8504	11.6979	30.5856
19	4.5983	13.9500	16.6356
20	1.9127	16.6356	0.0000

YEARS 21 — QTR PAYT 4.6144 — AN CONST 18.46

#	INT	PRIN	BALANCE
1	17.9682	.4893	99.5107
2	17.8740	.5835	98.9271
3	17.7616	.6959	98.2312

QUARTERLY PAYMENT AMORTIZATION SCHEDULE PER $100   18.00 %

#	INT	PRIN	BALANCE
4	17.6277	.8299	97.4014
5	17.4679	.9896	96.4118
6	17.2774	1.1801	95.2316
7	17.0502	1.4073	93.8243
8	16.7792	1.6783	92.1461
9	16.4561	2.0014	90.1447
10	16.0708	2.3867	87.7580
11	15.6114	2.8461	84.9119
12	15.0634	3.3941	81.5178
13	14.4100	4.0475	77.4703
14	13.6308	4.8267	72.6436
15	12.7016	5.7560	66.8876
16	11.5934	6.8641	60.0235
17	10.2720	8.1855	51.8380
18	8.6961	9.7614	42.0766
19	6.8168	11.6407	30.4359
20	4.5758	13.8817	16.5542
21	1.9033	16.5542	0.0000

YEARS 22	QTR PAYT 4.5955	AN CONST 18.39	
#	INT	PRIN	BALANCE
1	17.9734	.4087	99.5913
2	17.8948	.4873	99.1040
3	17.8009	.5812	98.5229
4	17.6890	.6930	97.8298
5	17.5556	.8265	97.0034
6	17.3965	.9856	96.0178
7	17.2068	1.1753	94.8425
8	16.9805	1.4016	93.4409
9	16.7107	1.6714	91.7695
10	16.3889	1.9932	89.7763
11	16.0052	2.3769	87.3994
12	15.5476	2.8345	84.5649
13	15.0019	3.3802	81.1847
14	14.3511	4.0310	77.1537
15	13.5751	4.8070	72.3467
16	12.6497	5.7324	66.6143
17	11.5461	6.8360	59.7783
18	10.2300	8.1521	51.6262
19	8.6606	9.7215	41.9046
20	6.7890	11.5931	30.3115
21	4.5571	13.8250	16.4866
22	1.8955	16.4866	0.0000

YEARS 23	QTR PAYT 4.5798	AN CONST 18.32	
#	INT	PRIN	BALANCE
1	17.9778	.3415	99.6585
2	17.9120	.4073	99.2512
3	17.8336	.4857	98.7656
4	17.7401	.5792	98.1864
5	17.6286	.6907	97.4957
6	17.4957	.8236	96.6721
7	17.3371	.9822	95.6899
8	17.1480	1.1713	94.5186
9	16.9225	1.3968	93.1218
10	16.6536	1.6657	91.4561
11	16.3329	1.9864	89.4697
12	15.9505	2.3688	87.1009
13	15.4945	2.8248	84.2761
14	14.9506	3.3687	80.9074
15	14.3021	4.0172	76.8902
16	13.5287	4.7906	72.0996
17	12.6065	5.7129	66.3868
18	11.5066	6.8127	59.5741
19	10.1951	8.1243	51.4498
20	8.6310	9.6883	41.7615
21	6.7658	11.5535	30.2080
22	4.5415	13.7778	16.4302
23	1.8891	16.4302	0.0000

YEARS 24	QTR PAYT 4.5667	AN CONST 18.27	
#	INT	PRIN	BALANCE
1	17.9814	.2856	99.7144
2	17.9265	.3405	99.3739
3	17.8609	.4061	98.9678
4	17.7827	.4843	98.4835
5	17.6895	.5775	97.9060
6	17.5783	.6887	97.2173
7	17.4457	.8213	96.3960
8	17.2876	.9794	95.4166
9	17.0990	1.1680	94.2487
10	16.8742	1.3928	92.8559
11	16.6061	1.6609	91.1949
12	16.2863	1.9807	89.2142
13	15.9050	2.3620	86.8522
14	15.4502	2.8168	84.0354
15	14.9080	3.3590	80.6764
16	14.2613	4.0057	76.6706
17	13.4901	4.7769	71.8937
18	12.5705	5.6965	66.1972
19	11.4738	6.7932	59.4040
20	10.1659	8.1011	51.3029
21	8.6063	9.6607	41.6423
22	6.7465	11.5205	30.1218
23	4.5286	13.7384	16.3833
24	1.8837	16.3833	0.0000

YEARS 25	QTR PAYT 4.5558	AN CONST 18.23	
#	INT	PRIN	BALANCE
1	17.9845	.2389	99.7611
2	17.9385	.2849	99.4762
3	17.8836	.3397	99.1365
4	17.8182	.4051	98.7314
5	17.7402	.4831	98.2482
6	17.6472	.5761	97.6721
7	17.5363	.6871	96.9851
8	17.4040	.8193	96.1657
9	17.2463	.9771	95.1887
10	17.0582	1.1652	94.0235
11	16.8339	1.3895	92.6340
12	16.5664	1.6570	90.9771
13	16.2474	1.9760	89.0011
14	15.8670	2.3564	86.6447
15	15.4133	2.8100	83.8347
16	14.8723	3.3510	80.4836
17	14.2272	3.9962	76.4875
18	13.4579	4.7655	71.7220
19	12.5404	5.6829	66.0391
20	11.4464	6.7770	59.2621
21	10.1417	8.0817	51.1804
22	8.5858	9.6376	41.5428
23	6.7304	11.4930	30.0498
24	4.5178	13.7056	16.3442
25	1.8792	16.3442	0.0000

YEARS 26	QTR PAYT 4.5467	AN CONST 18.19	
#	INT	PRIN	BALANCE
1	17.9870	.1999	99.8001
2	17.9485	.2384	99.5617
3	17.9026	.2843	99.2774
4	17.8479	.3390	98.9383
5	17.7826	.4043	98.5340
6	17.7048	.4822	98.0518
7	17.6119	.5750	97.4768
8	17.5012	.6857	96.7912
9	17.3692	.8177	95.9735
10	17.2118	.9751	94.9984
11	17.0241	1.1628	93.8355
12	16.8002	1.3867	92.4488
13	16.5333	1.6537	90.7952
14	16.2149	1.9720	88.8231
15	15.8352	2.3517	86.4715
16	15.3825	2.8044	83.6671
17	14.8426	3.3443	80.3227
18	14.1988	3.9882	76.3346
19	13.4310	4.7560	71.5786
20	12.5154	5.6716	65.9070
21	11.4235	6.7635	59.1436
22	10.1214	8.0655	51.0780
23	8.5686	9.6183	41.4597
24	6.7169	11.4700	29.9897
25	4.5087	13.6782	16.3115
26	1.8754	16.3115	0.0000

YEARS 27	QTR PAYT 4.5391	AN CONST 18.16	
#	INT	PRIN	BALANCE
1	17.9891	.1674	99.8326
2	17.9569	.1996	99.6330
3	17.9185	.2380	99.3950
4	17.8726	.2838	99.1112
5	17.8180	.3385	98.7727
6	17.7528	.4036	98.3691
7	17.6751	.4814	97.8877
8	17.5825	.5740	97.3137
9	17.4720	.6845	96.6292
10	17.3402	.8163	95.8128
11	17.1830	.9735	94.8394
12	16.9956	1.1609	93.6785
13	16.7721	1.3844	92.2941
14	16.5056	1.6509	90.6432
15	16.1878	1.9687	88.6745
16	15.8087	2.3477	86.3267
17	15.3568	2.7997	83.5270
18	14.8178	3.3387	80.1883
19	14.1750	3.9815	76.2068
20	13.4085	4.7480	71.4588
21	12.4944	5.6621	65.7967
22	11.4044	6.7521	59.0446
23	10.1044	8.0520	50.9926
24	8.5543	9.6022	41.3903
25	6.7057	11.4508	29.9395
26	4.5012	13.6553	16.2842
27	1.8723	16.2842	0.0000

YEARS 28	QTR PAYT 4.5328	AN CONST 18.14	
#	INT	PRIN	BALANCE
1	17.9909	.1402	99.8598
2	17.9639	.1671	99.6927
3	17.9317	.1993	99.4934
4	17.8934	.2377	99.2557
5	17.8476	.2834	98.9723
6	17.7930	.3380	98.6343
7	17.7280	.4031	98.2312
8	17.6504	.4807	97.7505
9	17.5578	.5732	97.1773
10	17.4475	.6836	96.4937
11	17.3159	.8152	95.6786
12	17.1589	.9721	94.7065
13	16.9718	1.1593	93.5472
14	16.7486	1.3824	92.1648
15	16.4825	1.6486	90.5162
16	16.1651	1.9660	88.5502
17	15.7866	2.3444	86.2058
18	15.3352	2.7958	83.4100
19	14.7970	3.3340	80.0759
20	14.1551	3.9759	76.1000
21	13.3897	4.7413	71.3587
22	12.4769	5.6541	65.7045
23	11.3884	6.7427	58.9618
24	10.0903	8.0408	50.9211
25	8.5423	9.5888	41.3323
26	6.6963	11.4348	29.8976
27	4.4949	13.6362	16.2614
28	1.8696	16.2614	0.0000

YEARS 29	QTR PAYT 4.5274	AN CONST 18.11	
#	INT	PRIN	BALANCE
1	17.9924	.1174	99.8826
2	17.9698	.1400	99.7426
3	17.9428	.1669	99.5757
4	17.9107	.1991	99.3766
5	17.8724	.2374	99.1392
6	17.8266	.2831	98.8561
7	17.7721	.3376	98.5185
8	17.7071	.4026	98.1159
9	17.6296	.4801	97.6358
10	17.5372	.5725	97.0632
11	17.4270	.6828	96.3805
12	17.2955	.8142	95.5662
13	17.1388	.9710	94.5953
14	16.9519	1.1579	93.4374
15	16.7289	1.3808	92.0566
16	16.4631	1.6466	90.4099
17	16.1461	1.9637	88.4463
18	15.7681	2.3417	86.1046
19	15.3172	2.7925	83.3120
20	14.7796	3.3301	79.9819
21	14.1385	3.9712	76.0107
22	13.3740	4.7358	71.2749
23	12.4622	5.6475	65.6274
24	11.3750	6.7348	58.8926
25	10.0784	8.0313	50.8613
26	8.5323	9.5775	41.2838
27	6.6884	11.4213	29.8625
28	4.4896	13.6202	16.2423
29	1.8675	16.2423	0.0000

YEARS 30	QTR PAYT 4.5230	AN CONST 18.10	
#	INT	PRIN	BALANCE
1	17.9936	.0983	99.9017
2	17.9747	.1173	99.7844
3	17.9521	.1398	99.6445
4	17.9252	.1668	99.4778
5	17.8931	.1989	99.2789
6	17.8548	.2372	99.0417
7	17.8091	.2828	98.7589
8	17.7547	.3373	98.4216
9	17.6897	.4022	98.0194
10	17.6123	.4796	97.5398
11	17.5200	.5720	96.9678
12	17.4098	.6821	96.2857
13	17.2785	.8134	95.4723
14	17.1219	.9700	94.5023
15	16.9352	1.1568	93.3455
16	16.7125	1.3795	91.9660
17	16.4469	1.6450	90.3210
18	16.1302	1.9617	88.3593
19	15.7526	2.3394	86.0199
20	15.3022	2.7898	83.2301
21	14.7651	3.3269	79.9033
22	14.1246	3.9673	75.9359
23	13.3608	4.7311	71.2048
24	12.4500	5.6420	65.5629
25	11.3638	6.7281	58.8347
26	10.0685	8.0234	50.8113
27	8.5239	9.5681	41.2432
28	6.6818	11.4101	29.8331
29	4.4852	13.6068	16.2263
30	1.8656	16.2263	0.0000

YEARS 2 — QTR PAYT 15.3162 — AN CONST 61.27

#	INT	PRIN	BALANCE
1	15.8921	45.3726	54.6274
2	6.6374	54.6274	0.0000

YEARS 3 — QTR PAYT 11.1240 — AN CONST 44.50

#	INT	PRIN	BALANCE
1	17.1252	27.3709	72.6291
2	11.5423	32.9538	39.6754
3	4.8207	39.6754	0.0000

YEARS 4 — QTR PAYT 9.0635 — AN CONST 36.26

#	INT	PRIN	BALANCE
1	17.7313	18.5229	81.4771
2	13.9531	22.3010	59.1761
3	9.4044	26.8498	32.3264
4	3.9278	32.3264	0.0000

YEARS 5 — QTR PAYT 7.8550 — AN CONST 31.43

#	INT	PRIN	BALANCE
1	18.0867	13.3335	86.6665
2	15.3671	16.0531	70.6134
3	12.0927	19.3275	51.2859
4	8.1504	23.2698	28.0161
5	3.4041	28.0161	0.0000

YEARS 6 — QTR PAYT 7.0719 — AN CONST 28.29

#	INT	PRIN	BALANCE
1	18.3171	9.9704	90.0296
2	16.2834	12.0041	78.0255
3	13.8349	14.4526	63.5730
4	10.8870	17.4005	46.1725
5	7.3378	20.9497	25.2228
6	3.0647	25.2228	0.0000

YEARS 7 — QTR PAYT 6.5310 — AN CONST 26.13

#	INT	PRIN	BALANCE
1	18.4761	7.6479	92.3521
2	16.9162	9.2079	83.1442
3	15.0380	11.0860	72.0582
4	12.7768	13.3472	58.7109
5	10.0544	16.0697	42.6412
6	6.7766	19.3475	23.2938
7	2.8303	23.2938	0.0000

YEARS 8 — QTR PAYT 6.1409 — AN CONST 24.57

#	INT	PRIN	BALANCE
1	18.5909	5.9728	94.0272
2	17.3726	7.1911	86.8360
3	15.9058	8.6579	78.1781
4	14.1399	10.4239	67.7543
5	12.0137	12.5500	55.2042
6	9.4538	15.1099	40.0944
7	6.3719	18.1919	21.9025
8	2.6612	21.9025	0.0000

YEARS 9 — QTR PAYT 5.8507 — AN CONST 23.41

#	INT	PRIN	BALANCE
1	18.6763	4.7265	95.2735
2	17.7122	5.6905	89.5830
3	16.5515	6.8512	82.7318
4	15.1540	8.2487	74.4831
5	13.4715	9.9312	64.5519
6	11.4459	11.9569	52.5950
7	9.0070	14.3957	38.1993
8	6.0707	17.3320	20.8673
9	2.5355	20.8673	0.0000

YEARS 10 — QTR PAYT 5.6297 — AN CONST 22.52

#	INT	PRIN	BALANCE
1	18.7413	3.7774	96.2226
2	17.9708	4.5479	91.6746
3	17.0431	5.4756	86.1991
4	15.9263	6.5924	79.6066
5	14.5816	7.9371	71.6695
6	12.9627	9.5560	62.1135
7	11.0135	11.5052	50.6083
8	8.6668	13.8519	36.7563
9	5.8414	16.6773	20.0790
10	2.4397	20.0790	0.0000

YEARS 11 — QTR PAYT 5.4584 — AN CONST 21.84

#	INT	PRIN	BALANCE
1	18.7916	3.0420	96.9580
2	18.1711	3.6625	93.2954
3	17.4241	4.4096	88.8859
4	16.5247	5.3090	83.5769
5	15.4418	6.3919	77.1850
6	14.1380	7.6957	69.4893
7	12.5683	9.2653	60.2240
8	10.6785	11.1552	49.0688
9	8.4031	13.4305	35.6382
10	5.6637	16.1700	19.4682
11	2.3655	19.4682	0.0000

YEARS 12 — QTR PAYT 5.3239 — AN CONST 21.30

#	INT	PRIN	BALANCE
1	18.8312	2.4644	97.5356
2	18.3285	2.9671	94.5685
3	17.7233	3.5723	90.9963
4	16.9947	4.3009	86.6953
5	16.1174	5.1782	81.5172
6	15.0612	6.2344	75.2828
7	13.7896	7.5060	67.7768
8	12.2586	9.0370	58.7398
9	10.4153	10.8803	47.8595
10	8.1960	13.0996	34.7599
11	5.5241	15.7715	18.9884
12	2.3072	18.9884	0.0000

YEARS 13 — QTR PAYT 5.2171 — AN CONST 20.87

#	INT	PRIN	BALANCE
1	18.8626	2.0058	97.9942
2	18.4535	2.4150	95.5792
3	17.9609	2.9076	92.6716
4	17.3678	3.5006	89.1710
5	16.6538	4.2146	84.9564
6	15.7941	5.0743	79.8821
7	14.7591	6.1093	73.7728
8	13.5130	7.3554	66.4173
9	12.0127	8.8557	57.5616
10	10.2064	10.6621	46.8995
11	8.0316	12.8368	34.0627
12	5.4133	15.4552	18.6076
13	2.2609	18.6076	0.0000

YEARS 14 — QTR PAYT 5.1316 — AN CONST 20.53

#	INT	PRIN	BALANCE
1	18.8878	1.6387	98.3613
2	18.5535	1.9730	96.3883
3	18.1511	2.3754	94.0129
4	17.6666	2.8599	91.1530
5	17.0832	3.4432	87.7098
6	16.3809	4.1456	83.5642
7	15.5353	4.9912	78.5730
8	14.5173	6.0092	72.5638
9	13.2916	7.2349	65.3289
10	11.8159	8.7106	56.6183
11	10.0391	10.4873	46.1310
12	7.9000	12.6265	33.5045
13	5.3246	15.2019	18.3026
14	2.2238	18.3026	0.0000

YEARS 15 — QTR PAYT 5.0627 — AN CONST 20.26

#	INT	PRIN	BALANCE
1	18.9080	1.3428	98.6572
2	18.6341	1.6167	97.0405
3	18.3044	1.9465	95.0940
4	17.9073	2.3435	92.7505
5	17.4293	2.8215	89.9290
6	16.8538	3.3970	86.5320
7	16.1609	4.0899	82.4421
8	15.3267	4.9241	77.5179
9	14.3223	5.9285	71.5894
10	13.1131	7.1378	64.4517
11	11.6572	8.5937	55.8580
12	9.9043	10.3465	45.5115
13	7.7939	12.4569	33.0546
14	5.2531	14.9978	18.0569
15	2.1940	18.0569	0.0000

YEARS 16 — QTR PAYT 5.0069 — AN CONST 20.03

#	INT	PRIN	BALANCE
1	18.9244	1.1030	98.8970
2	18.6995	1.3280	97.5690
3	18.4286	1.5989	95.9701
4	18.1025	1.9250	94.0451
5	17.7098	2.3177	91.7274
6	17.2371	2.7904	88.9371
7	16.6679	3.3595	85.5775
8	15.9827	4.0448	81.5327
9	15.1577	4.8698	76.6629
10	14.1644	5.8631	70.7998
11	12.9684	7.0590	63.7408
12	11.5286	8.4989	55.2419
13	9.7951	10.2324	45.0095
14	7.7080	12.3195	32.6900
15	5.1951	14.8323	17.8577
16	2.1698	17.8577	0.0000

YEARS 17 — QTR PAYT 4.9614 — AN CONST 19.85

#	INT	PRIN	BALANCE
1	18.9378	.9078	99.0922
2	18.7526	1.0930	97.9992
3	18.5297	1.3159	96.6832
4	18.2613	1.5844	95.0988
5	17.9381	1.9075	93.1913
6	17.5490	2.2966	90.8947
7	17.0806	2.7651	88.1297
8	16.5166	3.3290	84.8006
9	15.8376	4.0081	80.7925
10	15.0200	4.8256	75.9669
11	14.0358	5.8099	70.1570
12	12.8507	6.9949	63.1621
13	11.4239	8.4217	54.7404
14	9.7062	10.1395	44.6009
15	7.6380	12.2077	32.3932
16	5.1480	14.6977	17.6956
17	2.1501	17.6956	0.0000

YEARS 18 — QTR PAYT 4.9243 — AN CONST 19.70

#	INT	PRIN	BALANCE
1	18.9487	.7484	99.2516
2	18.7961	.9010	98.3506
3	18.6123	1.0848	97.2657
4	18.3910	1.3061	95.9596
5	18.1246	1.5725	94.3871
6	17.8039	1.8933	92.4939
7	17.4177	2.2794	90.2145
8	16.9528	2.7444	87.4701
9	16.3930	3.3041	84.1660
10	15.7191	3.9781	80.1879
11	14.9076	4.7895	75.3984
12	13.9307	5.7664	69.6320
13	12.7545	6.9426	62.6894
14	11.3384	8.3587	54.3307
15	9.6335	10.0636	44.2671
16	7.5808	12.1163	32.1508
17	5.1095	14.5877	17.5631
18	2.1340	17.5631	0.0000

YEARS 19 — QTR PAYT 4.8939 — AN CONST 19.58

#	INT	PRIN	BALANCE
1	18.9577	.6178	99.3822
2	18.8317	.7438	98.6385
3	18.6800	.8955	97.7430
4	18.4973	1.0781	96.6649
5	18.2774	1.2980	95.3668
6	18.0127	1.5628	93.8040
7	17.6939	1.8816	91.9225
8	17.3101	2.2653	89.6572
9	16.8480	2.7274	86.9297
10	16.2917	3.2837	83.6460
11	15.6219	3.9535	79.6925
12	14.8155	4.7599	74.9326
13	13.8447	5.7308	69.2018
14	12.6757	6.8997	62.3021
15	11.2684	8.3070	53.9951
16	9.5740	10.0014	43.9936
17	7.5340	12.0414	31.9522
18	5.0779	14.4976	17.4546
19	2.1208	17.4546	0.0000

YEARS 20 — QTR PAYT 4.8689 — AN CONST 19.48

#	INT	PRIN	BALANCE
1	18.9650	.5105	99.4895
2	18.8609	.6146	98.8749
3	18.7355	.7400	98.1349
4	18.5846	.8909	97.2440
5	18.4029	1.0726	96.1714
6	18.1841	1.2914	94.8800
7	17.9207	1.5548	93.3252
8	17.6036	1.8720	91.4532
9	17.2217	2.2538	89.1995
10	16.7620	2.7135	86.4860
11	16.2086	3.2670	83.2190
12	15.5422	3.9333	79.2857
13	14.7399	4.7356	74.5501
14	13.7740	5.7015	68.8486
15	12.6110	6.8645	61.9841
16	11.2109	8.2646	53.7195
17	9.5251	9.9504	43.7691
18	7.4955	11.9800	31.7891
19	5.0520	14.4236	17.3655
20	2.1100	17.3655	0.0000

YEARS 21 — QTR PAYT 4.8483 — AN CONST 19.40

#	INT	PRIN	BALANCE
1	18.9711	.4222	99.5778
2	18.8850	.5083	99.0695
3	18.7813	.6120	98.4574

#	INT	PRIN	BALANCE
4	18.6564	.7368	97.7206
5	18.5061	.8871	96.8335
6	18.3252	1.0681	95.7654
7	18.1073	1.2860	94.4794
8	17.8450	1.5483	92.9312
9	17.5292	1.8640	91.0671
10	17.1490	2.2443	88.8229
11	16.6913	2.7020	86.1208
12	16.1401	3.2532	82.8677
13	15.4766	3.9167	78.9510
14	14.6777	4.7156	74.2353
15	13.7158	5.6775	68.5579
16	12.5578	6.8355	61.7224
17	11.1635	8.2297	53.4926
18	9.4849	9.9084	43.5843
19	7.4639	11.9294	31.6549
20	5.0306	14.3627	17.2922
21	2.1011	17.2922	0.0000

YEARS 22	QTR PAYT 4.8314	AN CONST 19.33	
#	INT	PRIN	BALANCE
1	18.9761	.3495	99.6505
2	18.9048	.4207	99.2298
3	18.8190	.5066	98.7233
4	18.7156	.6099	98.1134
5	18.5912	.7343	97.3791
6	18.4415	.8840	96.4951
7	18.2612	1.0644	95.4307
8	18.0441	1.2815	94.1493
9	17.7827	1.5428	92.6064
10	17.4680	1.8575	90.7489
11	17.0891	2.2364	88.5125
12	16.6329	2.6926	85.8199
13	16.0837	3.2418	82.5781
14	15.4225	3.9030	78.6751
15	14.6264	4.6991	73.9759
16	13.6679	5.6576	68.3183
17	12.5139	6.8116	61.5067
18	11.1245	8.2010	53.3057
19	9.4518	9.8737	43.4320
20	7.4378	11.8877	31.5443
21	5.0131	14.3125	17.2318
22	2.0937	17.2318	0.0000

YEARS 23	QTR PAYT 4.8174	AN CONST 19.27	
#	INT	PRIN	BALANCE
1	18.9802	.2894	99.7106
2	18.9211	.3484	99.3621
3	18.8501	.4195	98.9426
4	18.7645	.5051	98.4375
5	18.6615	.6081	97.8294
6	18.5374	.7321	97.0973
7	18.3881	.8815	96.2158
8	18.2083	1.0613	95.1545
9	17.9918	1.2778	93.8768
10	17.7312	1.5384	92.3384
11	17.4174	1.8522	90.4862
12	17.0396	2.2299	88.2563
13	16.5848	2.6848	85.5715
14	16.0372	3.2324	82.3391
15	15.3779	3.8917	78.4474
16	14.5841	4.6855	73.7618
17	13.6283	5.6412	68.1206
18	12.4777	6.7919	61.3287
19	11.0923	8.1772	53.1514
20	9.4244	9.8452	43.3063
21	7.4163	11.8533	31.4530
22	4.9985	14.2710	17.1819
23	2.0877	17.1819	0.0000

YEARS 24	QTR PAYT 4.8058	AN CONST 19.23	
#	INT	PRIN	BALANCE
1	18.9836	.2398	99.7602
2	18.9347	.2887	99.4715
3	18.8758	.3476	99.1239
4	18.8049	.4185	98.7054
5	18.7195	.5039	98.2015
6	18.6167	.6067	97.5948
7	18.4930	.7304	96.8644
8	18.3440	.8794	95.9851
9	18.1646	1.0587	94.9263
10	17.9487	1.2747	93.6517
11	17.6887	1.5347	92.1170
12	17.3757	1.8477	90.2692
13	16.9988	2.2246	88.0447
14	16.5450	2.6784	85.3663
15	15.9987	3.2247	82.1416
16	15.3410	3.8824	78.2592
17	14.5491	4.6743	73.5849
18	13.5957	5.6277	67.9572
19	12.4478	6.7756	61.1816
20	11.0657	8.1576	53.0240
21	9.4018	9.8216	43.2024
22	7.3985	11.8249	31.3775
23	4.9866	14.2368	17.1407
24	2.0827	17.1407	0.0000

YEARS 25	QTR PAYT 4.7963	AN CONST 19.19	
#	INT	PRIN	BALANCE
1	18.9864	.1988	99.8012
2	18.9458	.2393	99.5619
3	18.8970	.2881	99.2737
4	18.8382	.3469	98.9268
5	18.7675	.4177	98.5091
6	18.6823	.5029	98.0063
7	18.5797	.6054	97.4008
8	18.4562	.7289	96.6719
9	18.3075	.8776	95.7943
10	18.1285	1.0566	94.7376
11	17.9130	1.2722	93.4655
12	17.6535	1.5316	91.9339
13	17.3411	1.8440	90.0898
14	16.9650	2.2202	87.8696
15	16.5121	2.6730	85.1966
16	15.9669	3.2182	81.9784
17	15.3105	3.8747	78.1037
18	14.5202	4.6650	73.4387
19	13.5686	5.6165	67.8221
20	12.4230	6.7621	61.0600
21	11.0437	8.1414	52.9186
22	9.3831	9.8020	43.1165
23	7.3838	11.8014	31.3152
24	4.9767	14.2085	17.1066
25	2.0785	17.1066	0.0000

YEARS 26	QTR PAYT 4.7884	AN CONST 19.16	
#	INT	PRIN	BALANCE
1	18.9887	.1648	99.8352
2	18.9551	.1985	99.6367
3	18.9146	.2389	99.3978
4	18.8659	.2877	99.1101
5	18.8072	.3463	98.7638
6	18.7366	.4170	98.3468
7	18.6515	.5020	97.8447
8	18.5491	.6044	97.2403
9	18.4258	.7277	96.5125
10	18.2774	.8762	95.6364
11	18.0987	1.0549	94.5815
12	17.8835	1.2701	93.3114
13	17.6244	1.5291	91.7823
14	17.3125	1.8410	89.9413
15	16.9370	2.2165	87.7248

#	INT	PRIN	BALANCE
16	16.4849	2.6686	85.0562
17	15.9406	3.2129	81.8432
18	15.2852	3.8683	77.9749
19	14.4962	4.6573	73.3176
20	13.5463	5.6073	67.7103
21	12.4025	6.7510	60.9594
22	11.0255	8.1280	52.8314
23	9.3677	9.7859	43.0455
24	7.3716	11.7819	31.2635
25	4.9684	14.1851	17.0784
26	2.0751	17.0784	0.0000

YEARS 27	QTR PAYT 4.7818	AN CONST 19.13	
#	INT	PRIN	BALANCE
1	18.9906	.1367	99.8633
2	18.9627	.1646	99.6987
3	18.9292	.1982	99.5005
4	18.8887	.2386	99.2619
5	18.8401	.2873	98.9746
6	18.7815	.3459	98.6287
7	18.7109	.4164	98.2123
8	18.6260	.5014	97.7110
9	18.5237	.6036	97.1073
10	18.4006	.7267	96.3806
11	18.2524	.8750	95.5056
12	18.0739	1.0534	94.4522
13	17.8594	1.2683	93.1839
14	17.6003	1.5270	91.6568
15	17.2889	1.8385	89.8183
16	16.9139	2.2135	87.6049
17	16.4624	2.6650	84.9399
18	15.9188	3.2086	81.7313
19	15.2644	3.8630	77.8683
20	14.4764	4.6509	73.2174
21	13.5278	5.5996	67.6178
22	12.3856	6.7418	60.8760
23	11.0105	8.1169	52.7591
24	9.3549	9.7725	42.9866
25	7.3615	11.7658	31.2208
26	4.9617	14.1657	17.0551
27	2.0723	17.0551	0.0000

YEARS 28	QTR PAYT 4.7764	AN CONST 19.11	
#	INT	PRIN	BALANCE
1	18.9922	.1134	99.8866
2	18.9691	.1366	99.7500
3	18.9412	.1644	99.5856
4	18.9077	.1980	99.3876
5	18.8673	.2383	99.1493
6	18.8187	.2870	98.8623
7	18.7602	.3455	98.5169
8	18.6897	.4159	98.1009
9	18.6049	.5008	97.6001
10	18.5027	.6029	96.9972
11	18.3797	.7259	96.2713
12	18.2317	.8740	95.3973
13	18.0534	1.0523	94.3450
14	17.8388	1.2669	93.0782
15	17.5804	1.5253	91.5529
16	17.2693	1.8364	89.7165
17	16.8947	2.2110	87.5055
18	16.4437	2.6620	84.8435
19	15.9007	3.2049	81.6386
20	15.2470	3.8586	77.7800
21	14.4600	4.6457	73.1343
22	13.5124	5.5933	67.5411
23	12.3715	6.7341	60.8070
24	10.9980	8.1077	52.6993
25	9.3442	9.7614	42.9379
26	7.3532	11.7525	31.1854
27	4.9560	14.1496	17.0358

#	INT	PRIN	BALANCE
28	2.0699	17.0358	0.0000

YEARS 29	QTR PAYT 4.7719	AN CONST 19.09	
#	INT	PRIN	BALANCE
1	18.9936	.0941	99.9059
2	18.9744	.1133	99.7926
3	18.9512	.1364	99.6561
4	18.9234	.1643	99.4918
5	18.8899	.1978	99.2941
6	18.8496	.2381	99.0560
7	18.8010	.2867	98.7693
8	18.7425	.3452	98.4241
9	18.6721	.4156	98.0086
10	18.5874	.5003	97.5083
11	18.4853	.6024	96.9059
12	18.3624	.7252	96.1807
13	18.2145	.8732	95.3075
14	18.0364	1.0513	94.2562
15	17.8220	1.2657	92.9905
16	17.5638	1.5239	91.4667
17	17.2530	1.8347	89.6320
18	16.8788	2.2089	87.4231
19	16.4282	2.6594	84.7637
20	15.8858	3.2019	81.5618
21	15.2327	3.8550	77.7068
22	14.4464	4.6413	73.0655
23	13.4997	5.5880	67.4775
24	12.3599	6.7278	60.7497
25	10.9876	8.1001	52.6497
26	9.3354	9.7522	42.8974
27	7.3463	11.7414	31.1560
28	4.9514	14.1363	17.0197
29	2.0680	17.0197	0.0000

YEARS 30	QTR PAYT 4.7682	AN CONST 19.08	
#	INT	PRIN	BALANCE
1	18.9946	.0781	99.9219
2	18.9787	.0941	99.8278
3	18.9595	.1132	99.7146
4	18.9364	.1363	99.5783
5	18.9086	.1641	99.4141
6	18.8751	.1976	99.2165
7	18.8348	.2379	98.9786
8	18.7863	.2865	98.6921
9	18.7279	.3449	98.3472
10	18.6575	.4152	97.9320
11	18.5728	.4999	97.4321
12	18.4709	.6019	96.8302
13	18.3481	.7247	96.1055
14	18.2003	.8725	95.2330
15	18.0223	1.0504	94.1826
16	17.8081	1.2647	92.9179
17	17.5501	1.5227	91.3952
18	17.2395	1.8332	89.5620
19	16.8656	2.2072	87.3548
20	16.4154	2.6574	84.6975
21	15.8734	3.1994	81.4981
22	15.2208	3.8520	77.6461
23	14.4351	4.6377	73.0084
24	13.4891	5.5836	67.4248
25	12.3502	6.7225	60.7023
26	10.9790	8.0937	52.6085
27	9.3282	9.7446	42.8639
28	7.3405	11.7322	31.1317
29	4.9475	14.1253	17.0064
30	2.0663	17.0064	0.0000

QUARTERLY PAYMENT AMORTIZATION SCHEDULE PER $100   20.00 %

YEARS 2 — QTR PAYT 15.4722 — AN CONST 61.89

#	INT	PRIN	BALANCE
1	16.7523	45.1364	54.8636
2	7.0251	54.8636	0.0000

YEARS 3 — QTR PAYT 11.2825 — AN CONST 45.14

#	INT	PRIN	BALANCE
1	18.0516	27.0785	72.9215
2	12.2160	32.9141	40.0073
3	5.1228	40.0073	0.0000

YEARS 4 — QTR PAYT 9.2270 — AN CONST 36.91

#	INT	PRIN	BALANCE
1	18.6891	18.2189	81.7811
2	14.7628	22.1451	59.6360
3	9.9904	26.9176	32.7185
4	4.1895	32.7185	0.0000

YEARS 5 — QTR PAYT 8.0243 — AN CONST 32.10

#	INT	PRIN	BALANCE
1	19.0621	13.0349	86.9651
2	16.2530	15.8440	71.1210
3	12.8385	19.2585	51.8625
4	8.6882	23.4089	28.4536
5	3.6434	28.4536	0.0000

YEARS 6 — QTR PAYT 7.2471 — AN CONST 28.99

#	INT	PRIN	BALANCE
1	19.3031	9.6852	90.3148
2	17.2159	11.7725	78.5423
3	14.6789	14.3095	64.2328
4	11.5951	17.3933	46.8395
5	7.8467	21.1417	25.6978
6	3.2905	25.6978	0.0000

YEARS 7 — QTR PAYT 6.7123 — AN CONST 26.85

#	INT	PRIN	BALANCE
1	19.4690	7.3800	92.6200
2	17.8785	8.9705	83.6495
3	15.9454	10.9037	72.7459
4	13.5955	13.2535	59.4924
5	10.7393	16.1097	43.3827
6	7.2676	19.5814	23.8013
7	3.0477	23.8013	0.0000

YEARS 8 — QTR PAYT 6.3280 — AN CONST 25.32

#	INT	PRIN	BALANCE
1	19.5881	5.7240	94.2760
2	18.3546	6.9516	87.3184
3	16.8552	8.4570	78.8614
4	15.0326	10.2795	68.5819
5	12.8173	12.4948	56.0870
6	10.1246	15.1875	40.8995
7	6.8516	18.4606	22.4389
8	2.8732	22.4389	0.0000

YEARS 9 — QTR PAYT 6.0434 — AN CONST 24.18

#	INT	PRIN	BALANCE
1	19.6764	4.4974	95.5026
2	18.7072	5.4666	90.0360
3	17.5291	6.6447	83.3913
4	16.0971	8.0767	75.3147
5	14.3566	9.8172	65.4975
6	12.2409	11.9329	53.5646
7	9.6693	14.5045	39.0601
8	6.5435	17.6303	21.4298
9	2.7440	21.4298	0.0000

YEARS 10 — QTR PAYT 5.8278 — AN CONST 23.32

#	INT	PRIN	BALANCE
1	19.7433	3.5680	96.4320
2	18.9743	4.3369	92.0951
3	18.0397	5.2715	86.8235
4	16.9037	6.4076	80.4159
5	15.5228	7.7885	72.6275
6	13.8443	9.4669	63.1605
7	11.8041	11.5071	51.6534
8	9.3243	13.9870	37.6664
9	6.3100	17.0013	20.6651
10	2.6461	20.6651	0.0000

YEARS 11 — QTR PAYT 5.6616 — AN CONST 22.65

#	INT	PRIN	BALANCE
1	19.7948	2.8517	97.1483
2	19.1803	3.4662	93.6821
3	18.4333	4.2132	89.4688
4	17.5253	5.1212	84.3476
5	16.4216	6.2249	78.1227
6	15.0801	7.5664	70.5564
7	13.4495	9.1970	61.3594
8	11.4675	11.1790	50.1804
9	9.0584	13.5881	36.5923
10	6.1301	16.5164	20.0758
11	2.5707	20.0758	0.0000

YEARS 12 — QTR PAYT 5.5318 — AN CONST 22.13

#	INT	PRIN	BALANCE
1	19.8351	2.2923	97.7077
2	19.3411	2.7863	94.9214
3	18.7406	3.3868	91.5346
4	18.0107	4.1167	87.4179
5	17.1235	5.0038	82.4141
6	16.0452	6.0822	76.3319
7	14.7344	7.3929	68.9390
8	13.1412	8.9862	59.9528
9	11.2046	10.9227	49.0301
10	8.8507	13.2766	35.7535
11	5.9895	16.1378	19.6156
12	2.5117	19.6156	0.0000

YEARS 13 — QTR PAYT 5.4294 — AN CONST 21.72

#	INT	PRIN	BALANCE
1	19.8668	1.8510	98.1490
2	19.4679	2.2499	95.8991
3	18.9831	2.7347	93.1644
4	18.3937	3.3241	89.8403
5	17.6773	4.0405	85.7998
6	16.8066	4.9112	80.8886
7	15.7482	5.9696	74.9190
8	14.4617	7.2561	67.6629
9	12.8980	8.8198	58.8431
10	10.9973	10.7205	48.1226
11	8.6869	13.0309	35.0917
12	5.8787	15.8391	19.2526
13	2.4652	19.2526	0.0000

YEARS 14 — QTR PAYT 5.3480 — AN CONST 21.40

#	INT	PRIN	BALANCE
1	19.8921	1.5000	98.5000
2	19.5688	1.8232	96.6768
3	19.1759	2.2161	94.4607
4	18.6983	2.6937	91.7670
5	18.1178	3.2742	88.4927
6	17.4122	3.9799	84.5129
7	16.5545	4.8375	79.6753
8	15.5120	5.8801	73.7953
9	14.2448	7.1472	66.6480
10	12.7045	8.6875	57.9605
11	10.8323	10.5597	47.4008
12	8.5566	12.8354	34.5653
13	5.7905	15.6015	18.9638
14	2.4283	18.9638	0.0000

YEARS 15 — QTR PAYT 5.2828 — AN CONST 21.14

#	INT	PRIN	BALANCE
1	19.9123	1.2190	98.7810
2	19.6496	1.4817	97.2993
3	19.3303	1.8010	95.4983
4	18.9422	2.1891	93.3092
5	18.4704	2.6609	90.6483
6	17.8969	3.2343	87.4140
7	17.1999	3.9313	83.4827
8	16.3527	4.7786	78.7041
9	15.3229	5.8084	72.8957
10	14.0711	7.0601	65.8356
11	12.5496	8.5816	57.2540
12	10.7003	10.4310	46.8229
13	8.4523	12.6790	34.1440
14	5.7199	15.4114	18.7326
15	2.3987	18.7326	0.0000

YEARS 16 — QTR PAYT 5.2304 — AN CONST 20.93

#	INT	PRIN	BALANCE
1	19.9286	.9929	99.0071
2	19.7146	1.2069	97.8002
3	19.4545	1.4670	96.3332
4	19.1384	1.7831	94.5501
5	18.7541	2.1674	92.3828
6	18.2870	2.6345	89.7483
7	17.7193	3.2022	86.5461
8	17.0292	3.8923	82.6538
9	16.1903	4.7311	77.9226
10	15.1708	5.7507	72.1719
11	13.9314	6.9900	65.1819
12	12.4250	8.4964	56.6855
13	10.5940	10.3274	46.3580
14	8.3684	12.5531	33.8050
15	5.6631	15.2583	18.5466
16	2.3748	18.5466	0.0000

YEARS 17 — QTR PAYT 5.1880 — AN CONST 20.76

#	INT	PRIN	BALANCE
1	19.9417	.8102	99.1898
2	19.7671	.9849	98.2049
3	19.5548	1.1971	97.0078
4	19.2969	1.4551	95.5527
5	18.9833	1.7687	93.7840
6	18.6021	2.1498	91.6342
7	18.1388	2.6131	89.0211
8	17.5757	3.1763	85.8448
9	16.8912	3.8608	81.9841
10	16.0592	4.6928	77.2913
11	15.0478	5.7041	71.5872
12	13.8186	6.9334	64.6538
13	12.3244	8.4276	56.2262
14	10.5082	10.2438	45.9824
15	8.3006	12.4514	33.5311
16	5.6172	15.1347	18.3963
17	2.3556	18.3963	0.0000

YEARS 18 — QTR PAYT 5.1536 — AN CONST 20.62

#	INT	PRIN	BALANCE
1	19.9524	.6622	99.3378
2	19.8097	.8049	98.5329
3	19.6362	.9783	97.5546
4	19.4254	1.1892	96.3654
5	19.1691	1.4454	94.9200
6	18.8576	1.7570	93.1630
7	18.4789	2.1356	91.0274
8	18.0187	2.5958	88.4316
9	17.4593	3.1552	85.2764
10	16.7793	3.8352	81.4412
11	15.9528	4.6617	76.7795
12	14.9482	5.6663	71.1131
13	13.7271	6.8875	64.2257
14	12.2428	8.3718	55.8539
15	10.4386	10.1759	45.6779
16	8.2456	12.3689	33.3090
17	5.5800	15.0345	18.2745
18	2.3400	18.2745	0.0000

YEARS 19 — QTR PAYT 5.1257 — AN CONST 20.51

#	INT	PRIN	BALANCE
1	19.9610	.5418	99.4582
2	19.8442	.6586	98.7996
3	19.7023	.8005	97.9991
4	19.5298	.9730	97.0260
5	19.3201	1.1827	95.8433
6	19.0652	1.4376	94.4057
7	18.7554	1.7474	92.6583
8	18.3788	2.1240	90.5342
9	17.9211	2.5818	87.9525
10	17.3647	3.1381	84.8144
11	16.6884	3.8144	80.9999
12	15.8664	4.6365	76.3635
13	14.8672	5.6356	70.7278
14	13.6527	6.8502	63.8777
15	12.1764	8.3264	55.5513
16	10.3820	10.1208	45.4305
17	8.2009	12.3019	33.1285
18	5.5498	14.9530	18.1755
19	2.3273	18.1755	0.0000

YEARS 20 — QTR PAYT 5.1030 — AN CONST 20.42

#	INT	PRIN	BALANCE
1	19.9681	.4438	99.5562
2	19.8724	.5394	99.0168
3	19.7562	.6557	98.3611
4	19.6149	.7970	97.5642
5	19.4431	.9687	96.5955
6	19.2344	1.1775	95.4180
7	18.9806	1.4312	93.9867
8	18.6722	1.7397	92.2471
9	18.2973	2.1146	90.1325
10	17.8416	2.5703	87.5622
11	17.2876	3.1242	84.4380
12	16.6144	3.7975	80.6405
13	15.7960	4.6159	76.0246
14	14.8012	5.6106	70.4139
15	13.5921	6.8198	63.5942
16	12.1224	8.2895	55.3047
17	10.3360	10.0759	45.2288
18	8.1645	12.2473	32.9815
19	5.5252	14.8867	18.0949
20	2.3170	18.0949	0.0000

YEARS 21 — QTR PAYT 5.0844 — AN CONST 20.34

#	INT	PRIN	BALANCE
1	19.9738	.3638	99.6362
2	19.8954	.4422	99.1941
3	19.8001	.5375	98.6566

#	INT	PRIN	BALANCE
4	19.6843	.6533	98.0033
5	19.5435	.7941	97.2093
6	19.3724	.9652	96.2441
7	19.1644	1.1732	95.0709
8	18.9116	1.4260	93.6448
9	18.6042	1.7333	91.9115
10	18.2307	2.1069	89.8046
11	17.7767	2.5609	87.2436
12	17.2248	3.1128	84.1308
13	16.5539	3.7837	80.3471
14	15.7385	4.5991	75.7480
15	14.7474	5.5902	70.1578
16	13.5426	6.7950	63.3629
17	12.0783	8.2593	55.1035
18	10.2984	10.0392	45.0643
19	8.1348	12.2028	32.8616
20	5.5051	14.8325	18.0290
21	2.3086	18.0290	0.0000

	YEARS 22	QTR PAYT 5.0692	AN CONST 20.28
#	INT	PRIN	BALANCE
1	19.9785	.2984	99.7016
2	19.9142	.3627	99.3389
3	19.8361	.4408	98.8981
4	19.7411	.5359	98.3622
5	19.6256	.6513	97.7109
6	19.4852	.7917	96.9192
7	19.3146	.9623	95.9569
8	19.1072	1.1697	94.7872
9	18.8551	1.4218	93.3654
10	18.5487	1.7282	91.6372
11	18.1763	2.1006	89.5366
12	17.7236	2.5533	86.9833
13	17.1734	3.1036	83.8798
14	16.5045	3.7724	80.1074
15	15.6915	4.5854	75.5220
16	14.7034	5.5735	69.9485
17	13.5022	6.7747	63.1738
18	12.0423	8.2347	54.9391
19	10.2676	10.0093	44.9298
20	8.1106	12.1663	32.7635
21	5.4886	14.7883	17.9752
22	2.3017	17.9752	0.0000

	YEARS 23	QTR PAYT 5.0568	AN CONST 20.23
#	INT	PRIN	BALANCE
1	19.9824	.2449	99.7551
2	19.9296	.2977	99.4575
3	19.8655	.3618	99.0957
4	19.7875	.4398	98.6559
5	19.6927	.5345	98.1214
6	19.5775	.6497	97.4716
7	19.4375	.7898	96.6819
8	19.2673	.9600	95.7219
9	19.0604	1.1668	94.5551
10	18.8090	1.4183	93.1368
11	18.5033	1.7239	91.4128
12	18.1318	2.0955	89.3174
13	17.6802	2.5471	86.7703
14	17.1313	3.0960	83.6744
15	16.4641	3.7632	79.9112
16	15.6531	4.5741	75.3371
17	14.6674	5.5599	69.7772
18	13.4692	6.7581	63.0191
19	12.0128	8.2145	54.8046
20	10.2425	9.9848	44.8198
21	8.0907	12.1366	32.6833
22	5.4752	14.7521	17.9312
23	2.2960	17.9312	0.0000

	YEARS 24	QTR PAYT 5.0466	AN CONST 20.19
#	INT	PRIN	BALANCE
1	19.9855	.2011	99.7989
2	19.9422	.2444	99.5546
3	19.8895	.2971	99.2575
4	19.8255	.3611	98.8964
5	19.7477	.4389	98.4575
6	19.6531	.5335	97.9241
7	19.5382	.6484	97.2757
8	19.3984	.7882	96.4875
9	19.2286	.9580	95.5295
10	19.0221	1.1645	94.3650
11	18.7711	1.4154	92.9495
12	18.4661	1.7205	91.2290
13	18.0953	2.0913	89.1378
14	17.6447	2.5419	86.5959
15	17.0969	3.0897	83.5061
16	16.4310	3.7556	79.7505
17	15.6216	4.5649	75.1856
18	14.6379	5.5487	69.6369
19	13.4421	6.7445	62.8924
20	11.9886	8.1980	54.6944
21	10.2219	9.9647	44.7297
22	8.0744	12.1122	32.6176
23	5.4642	14.7224	17.8952
24	2.2914	17.8952	0.0000

	YEARS 25	QTR PAYT 5.0383	AN CONST 20.16
#	INT	PRIN	BALANCE
1	19.9881	.1651	99.8349
2	19.9525	.2007	99.6341
3	19.9093	.2440	99.3902
4	19.8567	.2966	99.0936
5	19.7928	.3605	98.7331
6	19.7151	.4382	98.2950
7	19.6207	.5326	97.7624
8	19.5059	.6474	97.1150
9	19.3664	.7869	96.3281
10	19.1968	.9564	95.3717
11	18.9907	1.1626	94.2091
12	18.7402	1.4131	92.7960
13	18.4356	1.7176	91.0784
14	18.0655	2.0878	88.9906
15	17.6155	2.5377	86.4529
16	17.0686	3.0846	83.3682
17	16.4039	3.7494	79.6188
18	15.5959	4.5574	75.0614
19	14.6137	5.5396	69.5219
20	13.4199	6.7334	62.7885
21	11.9688	8.1844	54.6041
22	10.2050	9.9482	44.6558
23	8.0611	12.0921	32.5637
24	5.4552	14.6981	17.8656
25	2.2876	17.8656	0.0000

	YEARS 26	QTR PAYT 5.0315	AN CONST 20.13
#	INT	PRIN	BALANCE
1	19.9902	.1357	99.8643
2	19.9610	.1649	99.6994
3	19.9255	.2005	99.4990
4	19.8823	.2437	99.2553
5	19.8298	.2962	98.9591
6	19.7659	.3600	98.5992
7	19.6883	.4376	98.1616
8	19.5941	.5319	97.6297
9	19.4794	.6465	96.9833
10	19.3401	.7858	96.1975
11	19.1708	.9551	95.2423
12	18.9649	1.1610	94.0813
13	18.7147	1.4112	92.6701
14	18.4106	1.7153	90.9548
15	18.0409	2.0850	88.8699

#	INT	PRIN	BALANCE
16	17.5916	2.5343	86.3356
17	17.0455	3.0804	83.2551
18	16.3816	3.7443	79.5108
19	15.5747	4.5512	74.9596
20	14.5939	5.5320	69.4276
21	13.4017	6.7242	62.7033
22	11.9526	8.1733	54.5300
23	10.1912	9.9347	44.5953
24	8.0502	12.0757	32.5195
25	5.4478	14.6781	17.8414
26	2.2845	17.8414	0.0000

	YEARS 27	QTR PAYT 5.0259	AN CONST 20.11
#	INT	PRIN	BALANCE
1	19.9920	.1115	99.8885
2	19.9679	.1355	99.7530
3	19.9387	.1647	99.5883
4	19.9032	.2002	99.3880
5	19.8601	.2434	99.1446
6	19.8076	.2958	98.8488
7	19.7439	.3596	98.4892
8	19.6664	.4371	98.0522
9	19.5722	.5313	97.5209
10	19.4577	.6458	96.8751
11	19.3185	.7849	96.0902
12	19.1494	.9541	95.1361
13	18.9438	1.1597	93.9764
14	18.6939	1.4096	92.5668
15	18.3901	1.7134	90.8534
16	18.0208	2.0826	88.7708
17	17.5720	2.5315	86.2393
18	17.0265	3.0770	83.1623
19	16.3633	3.7401	79.4222
20	15.5573	4.5461	74.8760
21	14.5776	5.5259	69.3502
22	13.3867	6.7167	62.6334
23	11.9392	8.1642	54.4692
24	10.1798	9.9237	44.5455
25	8.0412	12.0623	32.4833
26	5.4417	14.6618	17.8215
27	2.2820	17.8215	0.0000

	YEARS 28	QTR PAYT 5.0213	AN CONST 20.09
#	INT	PRIN	BALANCE
1	19.9934	.0916	99.9084
2	19.9737	.1114	99.7970
3	19.9497	.1354	99.6616
4	19.9205	.1646	99.4970
5	19.8850	.2000	99.2969
6	19.8419	.2432	99.0538
7	19.7895	.2956	98.7582
8	19.7258	.3593	98.3990
9	19.6484	.4367	97.9623
10	19.5543	.5308	97.4315
11	19.4399	.6452	96.7863
12	19.3008	.7842	96.0021
13	19.1318	.9532	95.0489
14	18.9264	1.1586	93.8903
15	18.6767	1.4083	92.4820
16	18.3732	1.7118	90.7702
17	18.0043	2.0807	88.6894
18	17.5559	2.5291	86.1603
19	17.0109	3.0742	83.0861
20	16.3484	3.7367	79.3494
21	15.5431	4.5420	74.8074
22	14.5642	5.5208	69.2866
23	13.3745	6.7106	62.5760
24	11.9283	8.1567	54.4193
25	10.1705	9.9146	44.5047
26	8.0338	12.0512	32.4535
27	5.4367	14.6483	17.8051

#	INT	PRIN	BALANCE
28	2.2799	17.8051	0.0000

	YEARS 29	QTR PAYT 5.0175	AN CONST 20.07
#	INT	PRIN	BALANCE
1	19.9946	.0753	99.9247
2	19.9783	.0916	99.8331
3	19.9586	.1113	99.7218
4	19.9346	.1353	99.5865
5	19.9055	.1645	99.4220
6	19.8700	.1999	99.2221
7	19.8269	.2430	98.9792
8	19.7746	.2953	98.6838
9	19.7109	.3590	98.3248
10	19.6336	.4363	97.8885
11	19.5395	.5304	97.3581
12	19.4252	.6447	96.7134
13	19.2863	.7836	95.9298
14	19.1174	.9525	94.9773
15	18.9122	1.1578	93.8196
16	18.6627	1.4073	92.4123
17	18.3594	1.7105	90.7018
18	17.9908	2.0792	88.6226
19	17.5427	2.5272	86.0954
20	16.9980	3.0719	83.0235
21	16.3360	3.7339	79.2896
22	15.5314	4.5386	74.7510
23	14.5533	5.5166	69.2344
24	13.3644	6.7055	62.5289
25	11.9193	8.1506	54.3783
26	10.1628	9.9071	44.4712
27	8.0278	12.0421	32.4290
28	5.4326	14.6373	17.7917
29	2.2782	17.7917	0.0000

	YEARS 30	QTR PAYT 5.0144	AN CONST 20.06
#	INT	PRIN	BALANCE
1	19.9955	.0619	99.9381
2	19.9822	.0753	99.8628
3	19.9660	.0915	99.7712
4	19.9462	.1112	99.6600
5	19.9223	.1352	99.5248
6	19.8931	.1644	99.3604
7	19.8577	.1998	99.1607
8	19.8147	.2428	98.9178
9	19.7623	.2952	98.6227
10	19.6987	.3588	98.2639
11	19.6214	.4361	97.8279
12	19.5274	.5301	97.2978
13	19.4132	.6443	96.6535
14	19.2744	.7831	95.8704
15	19.1056	.9519	94.9185
16	18.9004	1.1570	93.7614
17	18.6511	1.4064	92.3551
18	18.3480	1.7095	90.6456
19	17.9796	2.0779	88.5677
20	17.5318	2.5257	86.0420
21	16.9875	3.0700	82.9721
22	16.3259	3.7316	79.2405
23	15.5217	4.5357	74.7047
24	14.5443	5.5132	69.1915
25	13.3561	6.7014	62.4902
26	11.9119	8.1455	54.3446
27	10.1565	9.9010	44.4436
28	8.0228	12.0347	32.4089
29	5.4292	14.6282	17.7807
30	2.2768	17.7807	0.0000

TABLE **6**

Points on Monthly Payment Loan

Interest Rates:	0, 1, 2, 3%; 4 to 19% by .25%; 20, 25, 30%.
Terms:	1 to 30 years, each year.
Payment:	Monthly.
Points:	1, 2, 3, 4, 5.

This table shows the Annual Percentage Rate (APR) for a monthly payment loan when points are paid from the loan amount at closing. The Truth in Lending Act of 1969 requires that all credit costs be expressed as a single rate on the proceeds the borrower receives. This single rate is called the APR.

Points. Points are an additional finance charge paid to the lender at closing for making the loan. A mortgage point is 1% of the loan. Points usually come out of the loan amount along with other closing costs.

Example: For a loan of $100,000 at 8% for 30 years, 2 points are paid at closing. The lender receives an additional finance charge of $2,000. The proceeds to the borrower are therefore $98,000. The mortgage loan payment is based on the higher amount, while the borrower gets the lower amount. Therefore, the rate on the lower amount is higher than the interest rate at which the loan was written. In this case, the rate is 8.21% rather than 8%. The 8.21% is the APR.

The APR is computed from a formula that expresses the relationship between the loan and the payments. The formula states that the loan is the present worth of the payments at the interest rate. The formula is written:

$$\text{Loan} = \text{Payment} \times A_{\overline{n}|}$$

When points are paid from the loan amount, however, and the interest rate on the proceeds is higher than the contract rate on the loan, the APR formula must account for this difference: proceeds = loan − points. Now the formula becomes:

$$\text{Loan} - \text{Points} = \text{Payment} \times A_{\overline{n}|}$$

The rate is determined by iteration, a process that is neither simple nor direct. A description of computing an interest rate by iteration is found in the Appendix. The rate that solves this equation is the APR.

POINTS ON MONTHLY PAYMENT LOAN

Description: This table shows the Annual Percentage Rate for a monthly payment loan when points are subtracted from the proceeds at closing.

Example: The interest rate on a 1 year loan is 8 %. At closing two points are paid to the lender. To maturity, the Annual Percentage Rate is 11.82 %.

	1 YEAR POINTS PAID						2 YEARS POINTS PAID						3 YEARS POINTS PAID				
RATE	1	2	3	4	5	RATE	1	2	3	4	5	RATE	1	2	3	4	5
0.00	1.87	3.75	5.66	7.61	9.58	0.00	.98	1.95	2.95	3.95	4.98	0.00	.66	1.32	1.99	2.67	3.36
1.00	2.87	4.76	6.68	8.62	10.60	1.00	1.98	2.96	3.96	4.97	6.00	1.00	1.66	2.33	3.00	3.69	4.38
2.00	3.87	5.77	7.69	9.64	11.62	2.00	2.98	3.97	4.97	5.98	7.02	2.00	2.66	3.33	4.01	4.70	5.40
3.00	4.88	6.78	8.70	10.66	12.65	3.00	3.98	4.97	5.98	7.00	8.04	3.00	3.67	4.34	5.02	5.72	6.42
4.00	5.88	7.78	9.72	11.68	13.67	4.00	4.98	5.98	6.99	8.02	9.06	4.00	4.67	5.35	6.03	6.73	7.44
4.25	6.13	8.04	9.97	11.93	13.93	4.25	5.24	6.23	7.24	8.27	9.31	4.25	4.92	5.60	6.29	6.99	7.69
4.50	6.38	8.29	10.22	12.19	14.18	4.50	5.49	6.48	7.50	8.52	9.57	4.50	5.17	5.85	6.54	7.24	7.95
4.75	6.63	8.54	10.48	12.44	14.44	4.75	5.74	6.74	7.75	8.78	9.82	4.75	5.42	6.10	6.79	7.49	8.20
5.00	6.88	8.79	10.73	12.70	14.69	5.00	5.99	6.99	8.00	9.03	10.08	5.00	5.67	6.35	7.05	7.75	8.46
5.25	7.14	9.05	10.98	12.95	14.95	5.25	6.24	7.24	8.26	9.29	10.33	5.25	5.92	6.61	7.30	8.00	8.71
5.50	7.39	9.30	11.24	13.21	15.21	5.50	6.49	7.49	8.51	9.54	10.59	5.50	6.18	6.86	7.55	8.26	8.97
5.75	7.64	9.55	11.49	13.46	15.46	5.75	6.74	7.74	8.76	9.80	10.84	5.75	6.43	7.11	7.81	8.51	9.22
6.00	7.89	9.80	11.74	13.72	15.72	6.00	6.99	8.00	9.02	10.05	11.10	6.00	6.68	7.36	8.06	8.76	9.48
6.25	8.14	10.05	12.00	13.97	15.97	6.25	7.24	8.25	9.27	10.30	11.35	6.25	6.93	7.61	8.31	9.02	9.73
6.50	8.39	10.31	12.25	14.22	16.23	6.50	7.49	8.50	9.52	10.56	11.61	6.50	7.18	7.87	8.56	9.27	9.99
6.75	8.64	10.56	12.50	14.48	16.48	6.75	7.74	8.75	9.77	10.81	11.86	6.75	7.43	8.12	8.82	9.53	10.24
7.00	8.89	10.81	12.76	14.73	16.74	7.00	8.00	9.00	10.03	11.07	12.12	7.00	7.68	8.37	9.07	9.78	10.50
7.25	9.14	11.06	13.01	14.99	17.00	7.25	8.25	9.26	10.28	11.32	12.38	7.25	7.93	8.62	9.32	10.03	10.76
7.50	9.40	11.32	13.26	15.24	17.25	7.50	8.50	9.51	10.53	11.57	12.63	7.50	8.18	8.87	9.58	10.29	11.01
7.75	9.65	11.57	13.52	15.50	17.51	7.75	8.75	9.76	10.79	11.83	12.89	7.75	8.43	9.13	9.83	10.54	11.27
8.00	9.90	11.82	13.77	15.75	17.76	8.00	9.00	10.01	11.04	12.08	13.14	8.00	8.68	9.38	10.08	10.80	11.52
8.25	10.15	12.07	14.02	16.01	18.02	8.25	9.25	10.26	11.29	12.34	13.40	8.25	8.94	9.63	10.34	11.05	11.78
8.50	10.40	12.32	14.28	16.26	18.27	8.50	9.50	10.52	11.55	12.59	13.65	8.50	9.19	9.88	10.59	11.30	12.03
8.75	10.65	12.58	14.53	16.52	18.53	8.75	9.75	10.77	11.80	12.85	13.91	8.75	9.44	10.13	10.84	11.56	12.29
9.00	10.90	12.83	14.78	16.77	18.79	9.00	10.00	11.02	12.05	13.10	14.16	9.00	9.69	10.39	11.09	11.81	12.54
9.25	11.15	13.08	15.04	17.03	19.04	9.25	10.25	11.27	12.31	13.35	14.42	9.25	9.94	10.64	11.35	12.07	12.80
9.50	11.40	13.33	15.29	17.28	19.30	9.50	10.51	11.52	12.56	13.61	14.67	9.50	10.19	10.89	11.60	12.32	13.05
9.75	11.65	13.59	15.55	17.53	19.55	9.75	10.76	11.78	12.81	13.86	14.93	9.75	10.44	11.14	11.85	12.58	13.31
10.00	11.91	13.84	15.80	17.79	19.81	10.00	11.01	12.03	13.07	14.12	15.18	10.00	10.69	11.39	12.11	12.83	13.56
10.25	12.16	14.09	16.05	18.04	20.07	10.25	11.26	12.28	13.32	14.37	15.44	10.25	10.94	11.65	12.36	13.08	13.82
10.50	12.41	14.34	16.31	18.30	20.32	10.50	11.51	12.53	13.57	14.63	15.69	10.50	11.19	11.90	12.61	13.34	14.07
10.75	12.66	14.59	16.56	18.55	20.58	10.75	11.76	12.79	13.82	14.88	15.95	10.75	11.45	12.15	12.87	13.34	14.07
11.00	12.91	14.85	16.81	18.81	20.83	11.00	12.01	13.04	14.08	15.13	16.21	11.00	11.70	12.40	13.12	13.85	14.58
11.25	13.16	15.10	17.07	19.06	21.09	11.25	12.26	13.29	14.33	15.39	16.46	11.25	11.95	12.65	13.37	14.10	14.84
11.50	13.41	15.35	17.32	19.32	21.35	11.50	12.51	13.54	14.58	15.64	16.72	11.50	12.20	12.91	13.63	14.35	15.09
11.75	13.66	15.60	17.57	19.57	21.60	11.75	12.76	13.79	14.84	15.90	16.97	11.75	12.45	13.16	13.88	14.61	15.35
12.00	13.91	15.86	17.83	19.83	21.86	12.00	13.02	14.05	15.09	16.15	17.23	12.00	12.70	13.41	14.13	14.86	15.61
12.25	14.17	16.11	18.08	20.08	22.11	12.25	13.27	14.30	15.34	16.40	17.48	12.25	12.95	13.66	14.39	15.12	15.86
12.50	14.42	16.36	18.33	20.34	22.37	12.50	13.52	14.55	15.60	16.66	17.74	12.50	13.20	13.92	14.64	15.37	16.12
12.75	14.67	16.61	18.59	20.59	22.62	12.75	13.77	14.80	15.85	16.91	17.99	12.75	13.45	14.17	14.89	15.63	16.37
13.00	14.92	16.86	18.84	20.84	22.88	13.00	14.02	15.05	16.10	17.17	18.25	13.00	13.71	14.42	15.14	15.88	16.63
13.25	15.17	17.12	19.09	21.10	23.14	13.25	14.27	15.31	16.36	17.42	18.50	13.25	13.96	14.67	15.40	16.13	16.88
13.50	15.42	17.37	19.35	21.35	23.39	13.50	14.52	15.56	16.61	17.68	18.76	13.50	14.21	14.92	15.65	16.39	17.14
13.75	15.67	17.62	19.60	21.61	23.65	13.75	14.77	15.81	16.86	17.93	19.01	13.75	14.46	15.18	15.90	16.64	17.39
14.00	15.92	17.87	19.85	21.86	23.90	14.00	15.02	16.06	17.12	18.19	19.27	14.00	14.71	15.43	16.16	16.90	17.65
14.25	16.17	18.13	20.11	22.12	24.16	14.25	15.28	16.31	17.37	18.44	19.53	14.25	14.96	15.68	16.41	17.15	17.90
14.50	16.43	18.38	20.36	22.37	24.42	14.50	15.53	16.57	17.62	18.69	19.78	14.50	15.21	15.93	16.66	17.41	18.16
14.75	16.68	18.63	20.61	22.63	24.67	14.75	15.78	16.82	17.88	18.95	20.04	14.75	15.46	16.18	16.92	17.66	18.42
15.00	16.93	18.88	20.87	22.88	24.93	15.00	16.03	17.07	18.13	19.20	20.29	15.00	15.71	16.44	17.17	17.92	18.67
15.25	17.18	19.14	21.12	23.14	25.18	15.25	16.28	17.32	18.38	19.46	20.55	15.25	15.96	16.69	17.42	18.17	18.93
15.50	17.43	19.39	21.37	23.39	25.44	15.50	16.53	17.58	18.64	19.71	20.80	15.50	16.22	16.94	17.68	18.42	19.18
15.75	17.68	19.64	21.63	23.65	25.70	15.75	16.78	17.83	18.89	19.97	21.06	15.75	16.47	17.19	17.93	18.68	19.44
16.00	17.93	19.89	21.88	23.90	25.95	16.00	17.03	18.08	19.14	20.22	21.31	16.00	16.72	17.45	18.18	18.93	19.69
16.25	18.18	20.14	22.14	24.16	26.21	16.25	17.28	18.33	19.40	20.47	21.57	16.25	16.97	17.70	18.44	19.19	19.95
16.50	18.43	20.40	22.39	24.41	26.46	16.50	17.53	18.58	19.65	20.73	21.83	16.50	17.22	17.95	18.69	19.44	20.20
16.75	18.69	20.65	22.64	24.67	26.72	16.75	17.79	18.84	19.90	20.98	22.08	16.75	17.47	18.20	18.94	19.70	20.46
17.00	18.94	20.90	22.90	24.92	26.98	17.00	18.04	19.09	20.16	21.24	22.34	17.00	17.72	18.45	19.20	19.95	20.72
17.25	19.19	21.15	23.15	25.17	27.23	17.25	18.29	19.34	20.41	21.49	22.59	17.25	17.97	18.71	19.45	20.20	20.97
17.50	19.44	21.41	23.40	25.43	27.49	17.50	18.54	19.59	20.66	21.75	22.85	17.50	18.22	18.96	19.70	20.46	21.23
17.75	19.69	21.66	23.66	25.68	27.74	17.75	18.79	19.84	20.92	22.00	23.10	17.75	18.48	19.21	19.96	20.71	21.48
18.00	19.94	21.91	23.91	25.94	28.00	18.00	19.04	20.10	21.17	22.26	23.36	18.00	18.73	19.46	20.21	20.97	21.74
18.25	20.19	22.16	24.16	26.19	28.26	18.25	19.29	20.35	21.42	22.51	23.61	18.25	18.98	19.71	20.46	21.22	21.99
18.50	20.44	22.42	24.42	26.45	28.51	18.50	19.54	20.60	21.67	22.76	23.87	18.50	19.23	19.97	20.72	21.48	22.25
18.75	20.69	22.67	24.67	26.70	28.77	18.75	19.79	20.85	21.93	23.02	24.13	18.75	19.48	20.22	20.97	21.73	22.51
19.00	20.95	22.92	24.92	26.96	29.02	19.00	20.05	21.11	22.18	23.27	24.38	19.00	19.73	20.47	21.22	21.99	22.76
20.00	21.95	23.93	25.94	27.98	30.05	20.00	21.05	22.11	23.19	24.29	25.40	20.00	20.73	21.48	22.24	23.00	22.76
25.00	26.97	28.98	31.01	33.07	35.17	25.00	26.07	27.16	28.26	29.38	30.52	25.00	25.76	26.53	27.31	28.10	28.90
30.00	32.00	34.02	36.08	38.17	40.29	30.00	31.09	32.20	33.33	34.48	35.64	30.00	30.78	31.57	32.38	33.20	34.03

POINTS ON MONTHLY PAYMENT LOAN

Description: This table shows the Annual Percentage Rate for a monthly payment loan when points are subtracted from the proceeds at closing.

Example: The interest rate on a 4 year loan is 8 %. At closing two points are paid to the lender. To maturity, the Annual Percentage Rate is 9.06 %.

4 YEARS

RATE	POINTS PAID 1	2	3	4	5
0.00	.50	1.00	1.50	2.02	2.54
1.00	1.50	2.00	2.51	3.03	3.56
2.00	2.50	3.01	3.52	4.05	4.58
3.00	3.51	4.02	4.54	5.06	5.59
4.00	4.51	5.02	5.55	6.08	6.61
4.25	4.76	5.28	5.80	6.33	6.87
4.50	5.01	5.53	6.05	6.58	7.12
4.75	5.26	5.78	6.31	6.84	7.38
5.00	5.51	6.03	6.56	7.09	7.63
5.25	5.76	6.28	6.81	7.35	7.89
5.50	6.01	6.54	7.06	7.60	8.14
5.75	6.27	6.79	7.32	7.85	8.40
6.00	6.52	7.04	7.57	8.11	8.65
6.25	6.77	7.29	7.82	8.36	8.91
6.50	7.02	7.54	8.08	8.62	9.16
6.75	7.27	7.80	8.33	8.87	9.42
7.00	7.52	8.05	8.58	9.12	9.67
7.25	7.77	8.30	8.84	9.38	9.93
7.50	8.02	8.55	9.09	9.63	10.19
7.75	8.27	8.80	9.34	9.89	10.44
8.00	8.52	9.06	9.59	10.14	10.70
8.25	8.78	9.31	9.85	10.40	10.95
8.50	9.03	9.56	10.10	10.65	11.21
8.75	9.28	9.81	10.35	10.90	11.46
9.00	9.53	10.06	10.61	11.16	11.72
9.25	9.78	10.32	10.86	11.41	11.97
9.50	10.03	10.57	11.11	11.67	12.23
9.75	10.28	10.82	11.37	11.92	12.48
10.00	10.53	11.07	11.62	12.17	12.74
10.25	10.78	11.32	11.87	12.43	12.99
10.50	11.03	11.58	12.13	12.68	13.25
10.75	11.29	11.83	12.38	12.94	13.50
11.00	11.54	12.08	12.63	13.19	13.76
11.25	11.79	12.33	12.88	13.45	14.01
11.50	12.04	12.58	13.14	13.70	14.27
11.75	12.29	12.84	13.39	13.95	14.53
12.00	12.54	13.09	13.64	14.21	14.78
12.25	12.79	13.34	13.90	14.46	15.04
12.50	13.04	13.59	14.15	14.72	15.29
12.75	13.29	13.84	14.40	14.97	15.55
13.00	13.54	14.10	14.66	15.23	15.80
13.25	13.80	14.35	14.91	15.48	16.06
13.50	14.05	14.60	15.16	15.73	16.31
13.75	14.30	14.85	15.42	15.99	16.57
14.00	14.55	15.11	15.67	16.24	16.83
14.25	14.80	15.36	15.92	16.50	17.08
14.50	15.05	15.61	16.18	16.75	17.34
14.75	15.30	15.86	16.43	17.01	17.59
15.00	15.55	16.11	16.68	17.26	17.85
15.25	15.80	16.37	16.94	17.52	18.10
15.50	16.06	16.62	17.19	17.77	18.36
15.75	16.31	16.87	17.44	18.02	18.62
16.00	16.56	17.12	17.70	18.28	18.87
16.25	16.81	17.38	17.95	18.53	19.13
16.50	17.06	17.63	18.20	18.79	19.38
16.75	17.31	17.88	18.46	19.04	19.64
17.00	17.56	18.13	18.71	19.30	19.89
17.25	17.81	18.38	18.96	19.55	20.15
17.50	18.06	18.64	19.22	19.81	20.41
17.75	18.32	18.89	19.47	20.06	20.66
18.00	18.57	19.14	19.72	20.32	20.92
18.25	18.82	19.39	19.98	20.57	21.17
18.50	19.07	19.65	20.23	20.83	21.43
18.75	19.32	19.90	20.48	21.08	21.68
19.00	19.57	20.15	20.74	21.33	21.94
20.00	20.58	21.16	21.75	22.35	22.96
25.00	25.60	26.21	26.82	27.45	28.09
30.00	30.62	31.26	31.90	32.55	33.22

5 YEARS

RATE	POINTS PAID 1	2	3	4	5
0.00	.41	.80	1.21	1.62	2.04
1.00	1.40	1.81	2.22	2.63	3.06
2.00	2.41	2.81	3.23	3.65	4.08
3.00	3.41	3.82	4.24	4.66	5.09
4.00	4.41	4.83	5.25	5.68	6.11
4.25	4.66	5.08	5.50	5.93	6.37
4.50	4.91	5.33	5.76	6.19	6.62
4.75	5.16	5.58	6.01	6.44	6.88
5.00	5.42	5.84	6.26	6.70	7.13
5.25	5.67	6.09	6.52	6.95	7.39
5.50	5.92	6.34	6.77	7.20	7.64
5.75	6.17	6.59	7.02	7.46	7.90
6.00	6.42	6.84	7.27	7.71	8.15
6.25	6.67	7.10	7.53	7.97	8.41
6.50	6.92	7.35	7.78	8.22	8.67
6.75	7.17	7.60	8.03	8.47	8.92
7.00	7.42	7.85	8.29	8.73	9.18
7.25	7.67	8.10	8.54	8.98	9.43
7.50	7.93	8.36	8.79	9.24	9.69
7.75	8.18	8.61	9.05	9.49	9.94
8.00	8.43	8.86	9.30	9.74	10.20
8.25	8.68	9.11	9.55	10.00	10.45
8.50	8.93	9.36	9.81	10.25	10.71
8.75	9.18	9.62	10.06	10.51	10.96
9.00	9.43	9.87	10.31	10.76	11.22
9.25	9.68	10.12	10.56	11.02	11.47
9.50	9.93	10.37	10.82	11.27	11.73
9.75	10.18	10.62	11.07	11.52	11.98
10.00	10.44	10.88	11.32	11.78	12.24
10.25	10.69	11.13	11.58	12.03	12.49
10.50	10.94	11.38	11.83	12.29	12.75
10.75	11.19	11.63	12.08	12.54	13.01
11.00	11.44	11.88	12.34	12.80	13.26
11.25	11.69	12.14	12.59	13.05	13.52
11.50	11.94	12.39	12.84	13.30	13.77
11.75	12.19	12.64	13.10	13.56	14.03
12.00	12.44	12.89	13.35	13.81	14.28
12.25	12.69	13.15	13.60	14.07	14.54
12.50	12.95	13.40	13.86	14.32	14.79
12.75	13.20	13.65	14.11	14.58	15.05
13.00	13.45	13.90	14.36	14.83	15.31
13.25	13.70	14.15	14.62	15.09	15.56
13.50	13.95	14.41	14.87	15.34	15.82
13.75	14.20	14.66	15.12	15.59	16.07
14.00	14.45	14.91	15.38	15.85	16.33
14.25	14.70	15.16	15.63	16.10	16.58
14.50	14.95	15.42	15.88	16.36	16.84
14.75	15.21	15.67	16.14	16.61	17.10
15.00	15.46	15.92	16.39	16.87	17.35
15.25	15.71	16.17	16.64	17.12	17.61
15.50	15.96	16.42	16.90	17.38	17.86
15.75	16.21	16.68	17.15	17.63	18.12
16.00	16.46	16.93	17.40	17.89	18.38
16.25	16.71	17.18	17.66	18.14	18.63
16.50	16.96	17.43	17.91	18.40	18.89
16.75	17.21	17.69	18.16	18.65	19.14
17.00	17.47	17.94	18.42	18.90	19.40
17.25	17.72	18.19	18.67	19.16	19.66
17.50	17.97	18.44	18.92	19.41	19.91
17.75	18.22	18.70	19.18	19.67	20.17
18.00	18.47	18.95	19.43	19.92	20.42
18.25	18.72	19.20	19.69	20.18	20.68
18.50	18.97	19.45	19.94	20.43	20.94
18.75	19.22	19.70	20.19	20.69	21.19
19.00	19.48	19.96	20.45	20.94	21.45
20.00	20.48	20.97	21.46	21.96	22.47
25.00	25.50	26.02	26.54	27.07	27.60
30.00	30.53	31.07	31.62	32.17	32.74

6 YEARS

RATE	POINTS PAID 1	2	3	4	5
0.00	.34	.67	1.01	1.35	1.70
1.00	1.34	1.68	2.02	2.37	2.72
2.00	2.34	2.68	3.03	3.38	3.74
3.00	3.34	3.69	4.04	4.40	4.76
4.00	4.35	4.70	5.05	5.41	5.78
4.25	4.60	4.95	5.31	5.67	6.03
4.50	4.85	5.20	5.56	5.92	6.29
4.75	5.10	5.45	5.81	6.18	6.54
5.00	5.35	5.70	6.06	6.43	6.80
5.25	5.60	5.96	6.32	6.68	7.05
5.50	5.85	6.21	6.57	6.94	7.31
5.75	6.10	6.46	6.82	7.19	7.56
6.00	6.35	6.71	7.08	7.45	7.82
6.25	6.61	6.96	7.33	7.70	8.07
6.50	6.86	7.22	7.58	7.95	8.33
6.75	7.11	7.47	7.84	8.21	8.59
7.00	7.36	7.72	8.09	8.46	8.84
7.25	7.61	7.97	8.34	8.72	9.10
7.50	7.86	8.22	8.59	8.97	9.35
7.75	8.11	8.48	8.85	9.22	9.61
8.00	8.36	8.73	9.10	9.48	9.86
8.25	8.61	8.98	9.35	9.73	10.12
8.50	8.86	9.23	9.61	9.99	10.37
8.75	9.12	9.49	9.86	10.24	10.63
9.00	9.37	9.74	10.11	10.50	10.88
9.25	9.62	9.99	10.37	10.75	11.14
9.50	9.87	10.24	10.62	11.00	11.39
9.75	10.12	10.49	10.87	11.26	11.65
10.00	10.37	10.75	11.13	11.51	11.91
10.25	10.62	11.00	11.38	11.77	12.16
10.50	10.87	11.25	11.63	12.02	12.42
10.75	11.12	11.50	11.89	12.28	12.67
11.00	11.37	11.75	12.14	12.53	12.93
11.25	11.63	12.01	12.39	12.79	13.18
11.50	11.88	12.26	12.65	13.04	13.44
11.75	12.13	12.51	12.90	13.29	13.69
12.00	12.38	12.76	13.15	13.55	13.95
12.25	12.63	13.02	13.41	13.80	14.21
12.50	12.88	13.27	13.66	14.06	14.46
12.75	13.13	13.52	13.91	14.31	14.72
13.00	13.38	13.77	14.17	14.57	14.97
13.25	13.63	14.02	14.42	14.82	15.23
13.50	13.89	14.28	14.67	15.08	15.49
13.75	14.14	14.53	14.93	15.33	15.74
14.00	14.39	14.78	15.18	15.59	16.00
14.25	14.64	15.03	15.43	15.84	16.25
14.50	14.89	15.29	15.69	16.10	16.51
14.75	15.14	15.54	15.94	16.35	16.77
15.00	15.39	15.79	16.19	16.60	17.02
15.25	15.64	16.04	16.45	16.86	17.28
15.50	15.89	16.30	16.70	17.11	17.53
15.75	16.15	16.55	16.96	17.37	17.79
16.00	16.40	16.80	17.21	17.62	18.05
16.25	16.65	17.05	17.46	17.88	18.30
16.50	16.90	17.30	17.72	18.13	18.56
16.75	17.15	17.56	17.97	18.39	18.81
17.00	17.40	17.81	18.22	18.64	19.07
17.25	17.65	18.06	18.48	18.90	19.33
17.50	17.90	18.31	18.73	19.15	19.58
17.75	18.16	18.57	18.98	19.41	19.84
18.00	18.41	18.82	19.24	19.66	20.10
18.25	18.66	19.07	19.49	19.92	20.35
18.50	18.91	19.32	19.75	20.17	20.61
18.75	19.16	19.58	20.00	20.43	20.86
19.00	19.41	19.83	20.25	20.68	21.12
20.00	20.42	20.84	21.27	21.70	22.15
25.00	25.44	25.89	26.35	26.81	27.28
30.00	30.47	30.95	31.43	31.93	32.43

POINTS ON MONTHLY PAYMENT LOAN

Description: This table shows the Annual Percentage Rate for a monthly payment loan when points are subtracted from the proceeds at closing.

Example: The interest rate on a 7 year loan is 8 %. At closing two points are paid to the lender. To maturity, the Annual Percentage Rate is 8.63 %.

7 YEARS

RATE	1	2	3	4	5
0.00	.30	.58	.87	1.16	1.46
1.00	1.29	1.58	1.88	2.18	2.48
2.00	2.29	2.59	2.89	3.19	3.50
3.00	3.30	3.60	3.90	4.21	4.52
4.00	4.30	4.60	4.91	5.22	5.54
4.25	4.55	4.85	5.16	5.48	5.79
4.50	4.80	5.11	5.42	5.73	6.05
4.75	5.05	5.36	5.67	5.98	6.30
5.00	5.30	5.61	5.92	6.24	6.56
5.25	5.55	5.86	6.18	6.49	6.81
5.50	5.81	6.11	6.43	6.75	7.07
5.75	6.06	6.37	6.68	7.00	7.32
6.00	6.31	6.62	6.93	7.25	7.58
6.25	6.56	6.87	7.19	7.51	7.83
6.50	6.81	7.12	7.44	7.76	8.09
6.75	7.06	7.37	7.69	8.02	8.35
7.00	7.31	7.63	7.95	8.27	8.60
7.25	7.56	7.88	8.20	8.53	8.86
7.50	7.81	8.13	8.45	8.78	9.11
7.75	8.06	8.38	8.71	9.03	9.37
8.00	8.32	8.63	8.96	9.29	9.62
8.25	8.57	8.89	9.21	9.54	9.88
8.50	8.82	9.14	9.47	9.80	10.13
8.75	9.07	9.39	9.72	10.05	10.39
9.00	9.32	9.64	9.97	10.31	10.64
9.25	9.57	9.90	10.23	10.56	10.90
9.50	9.82	10.15	10.48	10.81	11.16
9.75	10.07	10.40	10.73	11.07	11.41
10.00	10.32	10.65	10.99	11.32	11.67
10.25	10.57	10.90	11.24	11.58	11.92
10.50	10.83	11.16	11.49	11.83	12.18
10.75	11.08	11.41	11.75	12.09	12.43
11.00	11.33	11.66	12.00	12.34	12.69
11.25	11.58	11.91	12.25	12.60	12.95
11.50	11.83	12.17	12.51	12.85	13.20
11.75	12.08	12.42	12.76	13.11	13.46
12.00	12.33	12.67	13.01	13.36	13.71
12.25	12.58	12.92	13.27	13.61	13.97
12.50	12.83	13.17	13.52	13.87	14.23
12.75	13.09	13.43	13.77	14.12	14.48
13.00	13.34	13.68	14.03	14.38	14.74
13.25	13.59	13.93	14.28	14.63	14.99
13.50	13.84	14.18	14.53	14.89	15.25
13.75	14.09	14.44	14.79	15.14	15.51
14.00	14.34	14.69	15.04	15.40	15.76
14.25	14.59	14.94	15.29	15.65	16.02
14.50	14.84	15.19	15.55	15.91	16.27
14.75	15.10	15.45	15.80	16.16	16.53
15.00	15.35	15.70	16.06	16.42	16.79
15.25	15.60	15.95	16.31	16.67	17.04
15.50	15.85	16.20	16.56	16.93	17.30
15.75	16.10	16.46	16.82	17.18	17.56
16.00	16.35	16.71	17.07	17.44	17.81
16.25	16.60	16.96	17.32	17.69	18.07
16.50	16.85	17.21	17.58	17.95	18.32
16.75	17.11	17.47	17.83	18.20	18.58
17.00	17.36	17.72	18.09	18.46	18.84
17.25	17.61	17.97	18.34	18.71	19.09
17.50	17.86	18.22	18.59	18.97	19.35
17.75	18.11	18.48	18.85	19.22	19.61
18.00	18.36	18.73	19.10	19.48	19.86
18.25	18.61	18.98	19.35	19.73	20.12
18.50	18.86	19.23	19.61	19.99	20.38
18.75	19.12	19.49	19.86	20.24	20.63
19.00	19.37	19.74	20.12	20.50	20.89
20.00	20.37	20.75	21.13	21.52	21.92
25.00	25.40	25.80	26.22	26.64	27.06
30.00	30.43	30.86	31.31	31.76	32.22

8 YEARS

RATE	1	2	3	4	5
0.00	.26	.51	.76	1.02	1.28
1.00	1.25	1.51	1.77	2.03	2.30
2.00	2.26	2.52	2.78	3.05	3.32
3.00	3.26	3.52	3.79	4.06	4.34
4.00	4.26	4.53	4.80	5.08	5.36
4.25	4.52	4.78	5.06	5.33	5.61
4.50	4.77	5.04	5.31	5.59	5.87
4.75	5.02	5.29	5.56	5.84	6.12
5.00	5.27	5.54	5.82	6.09	6.38
5.25	5.52	5.79	6.07	6.35	6.63
5.50	5.77	6.04	6.32	6.60	6.89
5.75	6.02	6.30	6.57	6.86	7.14
6.00	6.27	6.55	6.83	7.11	7.40
6.25	6.52	6.80	7.08	7.37	7.65
6.50	6.77	7.05	7.33	7.62	7.91
6.75	7.03	7.30	7.59	7.87	8.17
7.00	7.28	7.56	7.84	8.13	8.42
7.25	7.53	7.81	8.09	8.38	8.68
7.50	7.78	8.06	8.35	8.64	8.93
7.75	8.03	8.31	8.60	8.89	9.19
8.00	8.28	8.56	8.85	9.15	9.44
8.25	8.53	8.82	9.11	9.40	9.70
8.50	8.78	9.07	9.36	9.65	9.95
8.75	9.03	9.32	9.61	9.91	10.21
9.00	9.28	9.57	9.87	10.16	10.47
9.25	9.54	9.83	10.12	10.42	10.72
9.50	9.79	10.08	10.37	10.67	10.98
9.75	10.04	10.33	10.63	10.93	11.23
10.00	10.29	10.58	10.88	11.18	11.49
10.25	10.54	10.83	11.13	11.44	11.74
10.50	10.79	11.09	11.39	11.69	12.00
10.75	11.04	11.34	11.64	11.95	12.26
11.00	11.29	11.59	11.89	12.20	12.51
11.25	11.54	11.84	12.15	12.45	12.77
11.50	11.80	12.10	12.40	12.71	13.02
11.75	12.05	12.35	12.65	12.96	13.28
12.00	12.30	12.60	12.91	13.22	13.54
12.25	12.55	12.85	13.16	13.47	13.79
12.50	12.80	13.11	13.41	13.73	14.05
12.75	13.05	13.36	13.67	13.98	14.30
13.00	13.30	13.61	13.92	14.24	14.56
13.25	13.55	13.86	14.18	14.49	14.82
13.50	13.81	14.11	14.43	14.75	15.07
13.75	14.06	14.37	14.68	15.00	15.33
14.00	14.31	14.62	14.94	15.26	15.59
14.25	14.56	14.87	15.19	15.51	15.84
14.50	14.81	15.12	15.44	15.77	16.10
14.75	15.06	15.38	15.70	16.02	16.35
15.00	15.31	15.63	15.95	16.28	16.61
15.25	15.56	15.88	16.21	16.53	16.87
15.50	15.82	16.13	16.46	16.79	17.12
15.75	16.07	16.39	16.71	17.04	17.38
16.00	16.32	16.64	16.97	17.30	17.64
16.25	16.57	16.89	17.22	17.55	17.89
16.50	16.82	17.15	17.48	17.81	18.15
16.75	17.07	17.40	17.73	18.07	18.41
17.00	17.32	17.65	17.98	18.32	18.66
17.25	17.57	17.90	18.24	18.58	18.92
17.50	17.83	18.16	18.49	18.83	19.18
17.75	18.08	18.41	18.74	19.09	19.43
18.00	18.33	18.66	19.00	19.34	19.69
18.25	18.58	18.91	19.25	19.60	19.95
18.50	18.83	19.17	19.51	19.85	20.21
18.75	19.08	19.42	19.76	20.11	20.46
19.00	19.33	19.67	20.02	20.36	20.72
20.00	20.34	20.68	21.03	21.39	21.75
25.00	25.37	25.74	26.12	26.51	26.90
30.00	30.40	30.80	31.22	31.64	32.06

9 YEARS

RATE	1	2	3	4	5
0.00	.23	.45	.68	.91	1.14
1.00	1.23	1.46	1.69	1.92	2.16
2.00	2.23	2.46	2.70	2.94	3.18
3.00	3.23	3.47	3.71	3.95	4.20
4.00	4.24	4.48	4.72	4.97	5.22
4.25	4.49	4.73	4.97	5.22	5.47
4.50	4.74	4.98	5.23	5.47	5.73
4.75	4.99	5.23	5.48	5.73	5.98
5.00	5.24	5.48	5.73	5.98	6.24
5.25	5.49	5.74	5.99	6.24	6.49
5.50	5.74	5.99	6.24	6.49	6.75
5.75	5.99	6.24	6.49	6.75	7.00
6.00	6.24	6.49	6.74	7.00	7.26
6.25	6.50	6.74	7.00	7.25	7.51
6.50	6.75	7.00	7.25	7.51	7.77
6.75	7.00	7.25	7.50	7.76	8.03
7.00	7.25	7.50	7.76	8.02	8.28
7.25	7.50	7.75	8.01	8.27	8.54
7.50	7.75	8.01	8.26	8.53	8.79
7.75	8.00	8.26	8.52	8.78	9.05
8.00	8.25	8.51	8.77	9.03	9.30
8.25	8.50	8.76	9.02	9.29	9.56
8.50	8.76	9.01	9.28	9.54	9.81
8.75	9.01	9.27	9.53	9.80	10.07
9.00	9.26	9.52	9.78	10.05	10.33
9.25	9.51	9.77	10.04	10.31	10.58
9.50	9.76	10.02	10.29	10.56	10.84
9.75	10.01	10.28	10.54	10.82	11.09
10.00	10.26	10.53	10.80	11.07	11.35
10.25	10.51	10.78	11.05	11.33	11.61
10.50	10.76	11.03	11.30	11.58	11.86
10.75	11.02	11.28	11.56	11.84	12.12
11.00	11.27	11.54	11.81	12.09	12.37
11.25	11.52	11.79	12.07	12.35	12.63
11.50	11.77	12.04	12.32	12.60	12.89
11.75	12.02	12.29	12.57	12.86	13.14
12.00	12.27	12.55	12.83	13.11	13.40
12.25	12.52	12.80	13.08	13.37	13.65
12.50	12.77	13.05	13.33	13.62	13.91
12.75	13.03	13.30	13.59	13.88	14.17
13.00	13.28	13.56	13.84	14.13	14.42
13.25	13.53	13.81	14.09	14.39	14.68
13.50	13.78	14.06	14.35	14.64	14.94
13.75	14.03	14.31	14.60	14.90	15.19
14.00	14.28	14.57	14.86	15.15	15.45
14.25	14.53	14.82	15.11	15.41	15.71
14.50	14.78	15.07	15.36	15.66	15.96
14.75	15.04	15.32	15.62	15.92	16.22
15.00	15.29	15.58	15.87	16.17	16.48
15.25	15.54	15.83	16.13	16.43	16.73
15.50	15.79	16.08	16.38	16.68	16.99
15.75	16.04	16.33	16.63	16.94	17.25
16.00	16.29	16.59	16.89	17.19	17.50
16.25	16.54	16.84	17.14	17.45	17.76
16.50	16.79	17.09	17.40	17.70	18.02
16.75	17.05	17.35	17.65	17.96	18.27
17.00	17.30	17.60	17.90	18.22	18.53
17.25	17.55	17.85	18.16	18.47	18.79
17.50	17.80	18.10	18.41	18.73	19.05
17.75	18.05	18.36	18.67	18.98	19.30
18.00	18.30	18.61	18.92	19.24	19.56
18.25	18.55	18.86	19.18	19.49	19.82
18.50	18.81	19.11	19.43	19.75	20.07
18.75	19.06	19.37	19.68	20.01	20.33
19.00	19.31	19.62	19.94	20.26	20.59
20.00	20.31	20.63	20.94	21.28	21.62
25.00	25.34	25.69	26.05	26.41	26.78
30.00	30.38	30.76	31.15	31.55	31.95

Description: This table shows the Annual Percentage Rate for a monthly payment loan when points are subtracted from the proceeds at closing.

Example: The interest rate on a 10 year loan is 8 %. At closing two points are paid to the lender. To maturity, the Annual Percentage Rate is 8.47 %.

10 YEARS — POINTS PAID

RATE	1	2	3	4	5
0.00	.21	.41	.61	.82	1.03
1.00	1.21	1.41	1.62	1.83	2.05
2.00	2.21	2.42	2.63	2.85	3.06
3.00	3.21	3.42	3.64	3.86	4.08
4.00	4.22	4.43	4.65	4.88	5.10
4.25	4.47	4.68	4.91	5.13	5.36
4.50	4.72	4.94	5.16	5.39	5.61
4.75	4.97	5.19	5.41	5.64	5.87
5.00	5.22	5.44	5.67	5.89	6.12
5.25	5.47	5.69	5.92	6.15	6.38
5.50	5.72	5.94	6.17	6.40	6.64
5.75	5.97	6.20	6.42	6.66	6.89
6.00	6.22	6.45	6.68	6.91	7.15
6.25	6.47	6.70	6.93	7.16	7.40
6.50	6.72	6.95	7.18	7.42	7.66
6.75	6.98	7.21	7.44	7.67	7.91
7.00	7.23	7.46	7.69	7.93	8.17
7.25	7.48	7.71	7.94	8.18	8.42
7.50	7.73	7.96	8.20	8.44	8.68
7.75	7.98	8.21	8.45	8.69	8.94
8.00	8.23	8.47	8.70	8.95	9.19
8.25	8.48	8.72	8.96	9.20	9.45
8.50	8.73	8.97	9.21	9.46	9.70
8.75	8.98	9.22	9.46	9.71	9.96
9.00	9.24	9.48	9.72	9.96	10.21
9.25	9.49	9.73	9.97	10.22	10.47
9.50	9.74	9.98	10.23	10.47	10.73
9.75	9.99	10.23	10.48	10.73	10.98
10.00	10.24	10.48	10.73	10.98	11.24
10.25	10.49	10.74	10.99	11.24	11.50
10.50	10.74	10.99	11.24	11.49	11.75
10.75	10.99	11.24	11.49	11.75	12.01
11.00	11.25	11.49	11.75	12.00	12.26
11.25	11.50	11.75	12.00	12.26	12.52
11.50	11.75	12.00	12.25	12.51	12.78
11.75	12.00	12.25	12.51	12.77	13.03
12.00	12.25	12.50	12.76	13.02	13.29
12.25	12.50	12.76	13.02	13.28	13.55
12.50	12.75	13.01	13.27	13.53	13.80
12.75	13.00	13.26	13.52	13.79	14.06
13.00	13.26	13.51	13.78	14.04	14.32
13.25	13.51	13.77	14.03	14.30	14.57
13.50	13.76	14.02	14.28	14.55	14.83
13.75	14.01	14.27	14.54	14.81	15.09
14.00	14.26	14.52	14.79	15.07	15.34
14.25	14.51	14.78	15.05	15.32	15.60
14.50	14.76	15.03	15.30	15.58	15.86
14.75	15.01	15.28	15.55	15.83	16.11
15.00	15.27	15.54	15.81	16.09	16.37
15.25	15.52	15.79	16.06	16.34	16.63
15.50	15.77	16.04	16.32	16.60	16.88
15.75	16.02	16.29	16.57	16.85	17.14
16.00	16.27	16.55	16.83	17.11	17.40
16.25	16.52	16.80	17.08	17.37	17.66
16.50	16.77	17.05	17.33	17.62	17.91
16.75	17.03	17.30	17.59	17.88	18.17
17.00	17.28	17.56	17.84	18.13	18.43
17.25	17.53	17.81	18.10	18.39	18.68
17.50	17.78	18.06	18.35	18.64	18.94
17.75	18.03	18.32	18.61	18.90	19.20
18.00	18.28	18.57	18.86	19.16	19.46
18.25	18.53	18.82	19.11	19.41	19.71
18.50	18.79	19.07	19.37	19.67	19.97
18.75	19.04	19.33	19.62	19.92	20.23
19.00	19.29	19.58	19.88	20.18	20.49
20.00	20.29	20.59	20.90	21.20	21.52
25.00	25.33	25.66	25.99	26.34	26.68
30.00	30.36	30.73	31.10	31.48	31.86

11 YEARS — POINTS PAID

RATE	1	2	3	4	5
0.00	.19	.37	.56	.74	.94
1.00	1.19	1.37	1.56	1.76	1.95
2.00	2.19	2.38	2.58	2.77	2.97
3.00	3.19	3.39	3.59	3.79	3.99
4.00	4.20	4.40	4.60	4.80	5.01
4.25	4.45	4.65	4.85	5.06	5.27
4.50	4.70	4.90	5.10	5.31	5.52
4.75	4.95	5.15	5.36	5.57	5.78
5.00	5.20	5.40	5.61	5.82	6.03
5.25	5.45	5.66	5.86	6.07	6.29
5.50	5.70	5.91	6.12	6.33	6.54
5.75	5.95	6.16	6.37	6.58	6.80
6.00	6.21	6.41	6.62	6.84	7.05
6.25	6.46	6.66	6.88	7.09	7.31
6.50	6.71	6.92	7.13	7.35	7.57
6.75	6.96	7.17	7.38	7.60	7.82
7.00	7.21	7.42	7.64	7.86	8.08
7.25	7.46	7.67	7.89	8.11	8.33
7.50	7.71	7.93	8.14	8.36	8.59
7.75	7.96	8.18	8.40	8.62	8.84
8.00	8.21	8.43	8.65	8.87	9.10
8.25	8.46	8.68	8.90	9.13	9.36
8.50	8.72	8.94	9.16	9.38	9.61
8.75	8.97	9.19	9.41	9.64	9.87
9.00	9.22	9.44	9.66	9.89	10.12
9.25	9.47	9.69	9.92	10.15	10.38
9.50	9.72	9.94	10.17	10.40	10.64
9.75	9.97	10.20	10.43	10.66	10.89
10.00	10.22	10.45	10.68	10.91	11.15
10.25	10.47	10.70	10.93	11.17	11.41
10.50	10.73	10.95	11.19	11.42	11.66
10.75	10.98	11.21	11.44	11.68	11.92
11.00	11.23	11.46	11.69	11.93	12.17
11.25	11.48	11.71	11.95	12.19	12.43
11.50	11.73	11.96	12.20	12.44	12.69
11.75	11.98	12.22	12.46	12.70	12.94
12.00	12.23	12.47	12.71	12.95	13.20
12.25	12.48	12.72	12.96	13.21	13.46
12.50	12.74	12.97	13.22	13.46	13.71
12.75	12.99	13.23	13.47	13.72	13.97
13.00	13.24	13.48	13.73	13.97	14.23
13.25	13.49	13.73	13.98	14.23	14.48
13.50	13.74	13.99	14.23	14.49	14.74
13.75	13.99	14.24	14.49	14.74	15.00
14.00	14.24	14.49	14.74	15.00	15.26
14.25	14.49	14.74	15.00	15.25	15.51
14.50	14.75	15.00	15.25	15.51	15.77
14.75	15.00	15.25	15.50	15.76	16.03
15.00	15.25	15.50	15.76	16.02	16.28
15.25	15.50	15.75	16.01	16.27	16.54
15.50	15.75	16.01	16.27	16.53	16.80
15.75	16.00	16.26	16.52	16.79	17.06
16.00	16.25	16.51	16.78	17.04	17.31
16.25	16.51	16.77	17.03	17.30	17.57
16.50	16.76	17.02	17.28	17.55	17.83
16.75	17.01	17.27	17.54	17.81	18.09
17.00	17.26	17.52	17.79	18.07	18.34
17.25	17.51	17.78	18.05	18.32	18.60
17.50	17.76	18.03	18.30	18.58	18.86
17.75	18.01	18.28	18.56	18.83	19.12
18.00	18.27	18.54	18.81	19.09	19.37
18.25	18.52	18.79	19.07	19.35	19.63
18.50	18.77	19.04	19.32	19.60	19.89
18.75	19.02	19.30	19.57	19.86	20.15
19.00	19.27	19.55	19.83	20.12	20.41
20.00	20.28	20.56	20.85	21.14	21.44
25.00	25.31	25.63	25.95	26.28	26.61
30.00	30.35	30.70	31.06	31.43	31.80

12 YEARS — POINTS PAID

RATE	1	2	3	4	5
0.00	.18	.34	.51	.68	.86
1.00	1.17	1.34	1.52	1.70	1.88
2.00	2.17	2.35	2.53	2.71	2.89
3.00	3.18	3.36	3.54	3.73	3.91
4.00	4.18	4.37	4.55	4.74	4.93
4.25	4.43	4.62	4.81	5.00	5.19
4.50	4.68	4.87	5.06	5.25	5.45
4.75	4.93	5.12	5.31	5.50	5.70
5.00	5.19	5.37	5.57	5.76	5.96
5.25	5.44	5.63	5.82	6.01	6.21
5.50	5.69	5.88	6.07	6.27	6.47
5.75	5.94	6.13	6.33	6.52	6.72
6.00	6.19	6.38	6.58	6.78	6.98
6.25	6.44	6.63	6.83	7.03	7.23
6.50	6.69	6.89	7.09	7.29	7.49
6.75	6.94	7.14	7.34	7.54	7.75
7.00	7.19	7.39	7.59	7.79	8.00
7.25	7.45	7.64	7.85	8.05	8.26
7.50	7.70	7.90	8.10	8.30	8.51
7.75	7.95	8.15	8.35	8.56	8.77
8.00	8.20	8.40	8.61	8.81	9.02
8.25	8.45	8.65	8.86	9.07	9.28
8.50	8.70	8.91	9.11	9.32	9.54
8.75	8.95	9.16	9.37	9.58	9.79
9.00	9.20	9.41	9.62	9.83	10.05
9.25	9.45	9.66	9.87	10.09	10.31
9.50	9.71	9.92	10.13	10.34	10.56
9.75	9.96	10.17	10.38	10.60	10.82
10.00	10.21	10.42	10.63	10.85	11.07
10.25	10.46	10.67	10.89	11.11	11.33
10.50	10.71	10.93	11.14	11.36	11.59
10.75	10.96	11.18	11.40	11.62	11.84
11.00	11.21	11.43	11.65	11.87	12.10
11.25	11.46	11.68	11.90	12.13	12.36
11.50	11.72	11.94	12.16	12.38	12.61
11.75	11.97	12.19	12.41	12.64	12.87
12.00	12.22	12.44	12.67	12.90	13.13
12.25	12.47	12.69	12.92	13.15	13.38
12.50	12.72	12.95	13.17	13.41	13.64
12.75	12.97	13.20	13.43	13.66	13.90
13.00	13.22	13.45	13.68	13.92	14.16
13.25	13.48	13.70	13.94	14.17	14.41
13.50	13.73	13.96	14.19	14.43	14.67
13.75	13.98	14.21	14.45	14.68	14.93
14.00	14.23	14.46	14.70	14.94	15.18
14.25	14.48	14.72	14.95	15.20	15.44
14.50	14.73	14.97	15.21	15.45	15.70
14.75	14.98	15.22	15.46	15.71	15.96
15.00	15.24	15.47	15.72	15.96	16.21
15.25	15.49	15.73	15.97	16.22	16.47
15.50	15.74	15.98	16.23	16.48	16.73
15.75	15.99	16.23	16.48	16.73	16.99
16.00	16.24	16.49	16.73	16.99	17.24
16.25	16.49	16.74	16.99	17.24	17.50
16.50	16.74	16.99	17.24	17.50	17.76
16.75	17.00	17.24	17.50	17.76	18.02
17.00	17.25	17.50	17.75	18.01	18.28
17.25	17.50	17.75	18.01	18.27	18.53
17.50	17.75	18.00	18.26	18.52	18.79
17.75	18.00	18.26	18.52	18.78	19.05
18.00	18.25	18.51	18.77	19.04	19.31
18.25	18.50	18.76	19.03	19.29	19.57
18.50	18.76	19.02	19.28	19.55	19.82
18.75	19.01	19.27	19.54	19.81	20.08
19.00	19.26	19.52	19.79	20.06	20.34
20.00	20.27	20.54	20.81	21.09	21.37
25.00	25.30	25.60	25.92	26.23	26.55
30.00	30.34	30.68	31.03	31.39	31.75

Description: This table shows the Annual Percentage Rate for a monthly payment loan when points are subtracted from the proceeds at closing.

Example: The interest rate on a 13 year loan is 8 %. At closing two points are paid to the lender. To maturity, the Annual Percentage Rate is 8.38 %.

13 YEARS POINTS PAID						14 YEARS POINTS PAID						15 YEARS POINTS PAID				
RATE	1	2	3	4	5	RATE	1	2	3	4	5	RATE	1	2	3	4	5
0.00	.16	.32	.47	.63	.79	0.00	.15	.29	.44	.59	.74	0.00	.14	.27	.41	.55	.69
1.00	1.16	1.32	1.48	1.64	1.81	1.00	1.15	1.30	1.45	1.60	1.75	1.00	1.14	1.28	1.42	1.56	1.71
2.00	2.16	2.33	2.49	2.66	2.83	2.00	2.15	2.30	2.46	2.61	2.77	2.00	2.14	2.28	2.43	2.58	2.72
3.00	3.17	3.33	3.50	3.67	3.85	3.00	3.15	3.31	3.47	3.63	3.79	3.00	3.15	3.29	3.44	3.59	3.74
4.00	4.17	4.34	4.51	4.69	4.87	4.00	4.16	4.32	4.48	4.65	4.81	4.00	4.15	4.30	4.45	4.61	4.77
4.25	4.42	4.59	4.77	4.94	5.12	4.25	4.41	4.57	4.73	4.90	5.07	4.25	4.40	4.55	4.71	4.86	5.02
4.50	4.67	4.84	5.02	5.20	5.38	4.50	4.66	4.82	4.99	5.15	5.32	4.50	4.65	4.80	4.96	5.12	5.28
4.75	4.92	5.10	5.27	5.45	5.64	4.75	4.91	5.07	5.24	5.41	5.58	4.75	4.90	5.06	5.21	5.37	5.53
5.00	5.17	5.35	5.53	5.71	5.89	5.00	5.16	5.33	5.49	5.66	5.84	5.00	5.15	5.31	5.47	5.63	5.79
5.25	5.42	5.60	5.78	5.96	6.15	5.25	5.41	5.58	5.75	5.92	6.09	5.25	5.40	5.56	5.72	5.88	6.04
5.50	5.68	5.85	6.03	6.22	6.40	5.50	5.66	5.83	6.00	6.17	6.35	5.50	5.66	5.81	5.97	6.13	6.30
5.75	5.93	6.11	6.29	6.47	6.66	5.75	5.92	6.08	6.25	6.43	6.60	5.75	5.91	6.06	6.23	6.39	6.55
6.00	6.18	6.36	6.54	6.73	6.91	6.00	6.17	6.34	6.51	6.68	6.86	6.00	6.16	6.32	6.48	6.64	6.81
6.25	6.43	6.61	6.79	6.98	7.17	6.25	6.42	6.59	6.76	6.94	7.11	6.25	6.41	6.57	6.73	6.90	7.07
6.50	6.68	6.86	7.05	7.23	7.43	6.50	6.67	6.84	7.01	7.19	7.37	6.50	6.66	6.82	6.99	7.15	7.32
6.75	6.93	7.11	7.30	7.49	7.68	6.75	6.92	7.09	7.27	7.45	7.63	6.75	6.91	7.07	7.24	7.41	7.58
7.00	7.18	7.37	7.55	7.74	7.94	7.00	7.17	7.34	7.52	7.70	7.88	7.00	7.16	7.33	7.49	7.66	7.83
7.25	7.43	7.62	7.81	8.00	8.19	7.25	7.42	7.60	7.77	7.96	8.14	7.25	7.41	7.58	7.75	7.92	8.09
7.50	7.68	7.87	8.06	8.25	8.45	7.50	7.67	7.85	8.03	8.21	8.39	7.50	7.66	7.83	8.00	8.17	8.35
7.75	7.94	8.12	8.31	8.51	8.71	7.75	7.92	8.10	8.28	8.46	8.65	7.75	7.92	8.08	8.25	8.43	8.60
8.00	8.19	8.38	8.57	8.76	8.96	8.00	8.18	8.35	8.54	8.72	8.91	8.00	8.17	8.34	8.51	8.68	8.86
8.25	8.44	8.63	8.82	9.02	9.22	8.25	8.43	8.61	8.79	8.97	9.16	8.25	8.42	8.59	8.76	8.94	9.12
8.50	8.69	8.88	9.08	9.27	9.47	8.50	8.68	8.86	9.04	9.23	9.42	8.50	8.67	8.84	9.02	9.19	9.37
8.75	8.94	9.13	9.33	9.53	9.73	8.75	8.93	9.11	9.30	9.49	9.68	8.75	8.92	9.09	9.27	9.45	9.63
9.00	9.19	9.39	9.58	9.78	9.99	9.00	9.18	9.36	9.55	9.74	9.93	9.00	9.17	9.35	9.52	9.70	9.89
9.25	9.44	9.64	9.84	10.04	10.24	9.25	9.43	9.62	9.80	10.00	10.19	9.25	9.42	9.60	9.78	9.96	10.14
9.50	9.69	9.89	10.09	10.29	10.50	9.50	9.68	9.87	10.06	10.25	10.45	9.50	9.67	9.85	10.03	10.21	10.40
9.75	9.95	10.14	10.34	10.55	10.76	9.75	9.93	10.12	10.31	10.51	10.70	9.75	9.93	10.10	10.29	10.47	10.66
10.00	10.20	10.40	10.60	10.80	11.01	10.00	10.19	10.37	10.57	10.76	10.96	10.00	10.18	10.36	10.54	10.72	10.91
10.25	10.45	10.65	10.85	11.06	11.27	10.25	10.44	10.63	10.82	11.02	11.22	10.25	10.43	10.61	10.79	10.98	11.17
10.50	10.70	10.90	11.11	11.31	11.53	10.50	10.69	10.88	11.07	11.27	11.47	10.50	10.68	10.86	11.05	11.24	11.43
10.75	10.95	11.15	11.36	11.57	11.78	10.75	10.94	11.13	11.33	11.53	11.73	10.75	10.93	11.11	11.30	11.49	11.68
11.00	11.20	11.41	11.61	11.82	12.04	11.00	11.19	11.39	11.58	11.78	11.99	11.00	11.18	11.37	11.56	11.75	11.94
11.25	11.45	11.66	11.87	12.08	12.30	11.25	11.44	11.64	11.84	12.04	12.24	11.25	11.43	11.62	11.81	12.00	12.20
11.50	11.70	11.91	12.12	12.34	12.55	11.50	11.69	11.89	12.09	12.29	12.50	11.50	11.69	11.87	12.06	12.26	12.46
11.75	11.96	12.16	12.38	12.59	12.81	11.75	11.95	12.14	12.35	12.55	12.76	11.75	11.94	12.13	12.32	12.51	12.71
12.00	12.21	12.42	12.63	12.85	13.07	12.00	12.20	12.40	12.60	12.81	13.02	12.00	12.19	12.38	12.57	12.77	12.97
12.25	12.46	12.67	12.88	13.10	13.32	12.25	12.45	12.65	12.85	13.06	13.27	12.25	12.44	12.63	12.83	13.03	13.23
12.50	12.71	12.92	13.14	13.36	13.58	12.50	12.70	12.90	13.11	13.32	13.53	12.50	12.69	12.88	13.08	13.28	13.49
12.75	12.96	13.17	13.39	13.61	13.84	12.75	12.95	13.15	13.36	13.57	13.79	12.75	12.94	13.14	13.34	13.54	13.74
13.00	13.21	13.43	13.65	13.87	14.10	13.00	13.20	13.41	13.62	13.83	14.04	13.00	13.19	13.39	13.59	13.79	14.00
13.25	13.46	13.68	13.90	14.13	14.35	13.25	13.45	13.66	13.87	14.08	14.30	13.25	13.45	13.64	13.85	14.05	14.26
13.50	13.72	13.93	14.16	14.38	14.61	13.50	13.71	13.91	14.13	14.34	14.56	13.50	13.70	13.90	14.10	14.31	14.52
13.75	13.97	14.19	14.41	14.64	14.87	13.75	13.96	14.17	14.38	14.60	14.82	13.75	13.95	14.15	14.35	14.56	14.77
14.00	14.22	14.44	14.66	14.89	15.13	14.00	14.21	14.42	14.63	14.85	15.08	14.00	14.20	14.40	14.61	14.82	15.03
14.25	14.47	14.69	14.92	15.15	15.38	14.25	14.46	14.67	14.89	15.11	15.33	14.25	14.45	14.66	14.86	15.08	15.29
14.50	14.72	14.95	15.17	15.40	15.64	14.50	14.71	14.93	15.14	15.37	15.59	14.50	14.70	14.91	15.12	15.33	15.55
14.75	14.97	15.20	15.43	15.66	15.90	14.75	14.96	15.18	15.40	15.62	15.85	14.75	14.95	15.16	15.37	15.59	15.81
15.00	15.22	15.45	15.68	15.92	16.16	15.00	15.21	15.43	15.65	15.88	16.11	15.00	15.21	15.42	15.63	15.84	16.07
15.25	15.48	15.70	15.94	16.17	16.41	15.25	15.47	15.68	15.91	16.13	16.36	15.25	15.46	15.67	15.88	16.10	16.32
15.50	15.73	15.96	16.19	16.43	16.67	15.50	15.72	15.94	16.16	16.39	16.62	15.50	15.71	15.92	16.14	16.36	16.58
15.75	15.98	16.21	16.45	16.69	16.93	15.75	15.97	16.19	16.42	16.65	16.88	15.75	15.96	16.18	16.39	16.61	16.84
16.00	16.23	16.46	16.70	16.94	17.19	16.00	16.22	16.44	16.67	16.90	17.14	16.00	16.21	16.43	16.65	16.87	17.10
16.25	16.48	16.72	16.96	17.20	17.44	16.25	16.47	16.70	16.93	17.16	17.40	16.25	16.46	16.68	16.90	17.13	17.36
16.50	16.73	16.97	17.21	17.45	17.70	16.50	16.72	16.95	17.18	17.42	17.66	16.50	16.72	16.93	17.16	17.38	17.62
16.75	16.98	17.22	17.46	17.71	17.96	16.75	16.98	17.20	17.44	17.67	17.91	16.75	16.97	17.19	17.41	17.64	17.87
17.00	17.24	17.48	17.72	17.97	18.22	17.00	17.23	17.46	17.69	17.93	18.17	17.00	17.22	17.44	17.67	17.90	18.13
17.25	17.49	17.73	17.97	18.22	18.48	17.25	17.48	17.71	17.95	18.19	18.43	17.25	17.47	17.70	17.92	18.16	18.39
17.50	17.74	17.98	18.23	18.48	18.74	17.50	17.73	17.96	18.20	18.44	18.69	17.50	17.72	17.95	18.18	18.41	18.65
17.75	17.99	18.24	18.48	18.74	18.99	17.75	17.98	18.22	18.46	18.70	18.95	17.75	17.97	18.20	18.43	18.67	18.91
18.00	18.24	18.49	18.74	18.99	19.25	18.00	18.23	18.47	18.71	18.96	19.21	18.00	18.23	18.46	18.69	18.93	19.17
18.25	18.49	18.74	18.99	19.25	19.51	18.25	18.48	18.72	18.97	19.21	19.47	18.25	18.48	18.71	18.94	19.18	19.43
18.50	18.75	18.99	19.25	19.51	19.77	18.50	18.74	18.98	19.22	19.47	19.72	18.50	18.73	18.96	19.20	19.44	19.69
18.75	19.00	19.25	19.50	19.76	20.03	18.75	18.99	19.23	19.48	19.73	19.98	18.75	18.98	19.22	19.45	19.70	19.94
19.00	19.25	19.50	19.76	20.02	20.29	19.00	19.24	19.48	19.73	19.98	20.24	19.00	19.23	19.47	19.71	19.96	20.20
20.00	20.26	20.51	20.78	21.05	21.32	20.00	20.25	20.50	20.75	21.01	21.28	20.00	20.24	20.48	20.73	20.98	21.24
25.00	25.29	25.59	25.89	26.20	26.51	25.00	25.28	25.57	25.87	26.17	26.47	25.00	25.28	25.56	25.85	26.14	26.44
30.00	30.33	30.67	31.01	31.36	31.71	30.00	30.32	30.65	30.99	31.33	31.68	30.00	30.32	30.64	30.98	31.31	31.66

POINTS ON MONTHLY PAYMENT LOAN

Description: This table shows the Annual Percentage Rate for a monthly payment loan when points are subtracted from the proceeds at closing.

Example: The interest rate on a 16 year loan is 8 %. At closing two points are paid to the lender. To maturity, the Annual Percentage Rate is 8.32 %.

16 YEARS POINTS PAID						17 YEARS POINTS PAID						18 YEARS POINTS PAID				
RATE	1	2	3	4	5	**RATE**	1	2	3	4	5	**RATE**	1	2	3	4	5
0.00	.14	.26	.38	.51	.65	**0.00**	.13	.24	.36	.48	.61	**0.00**	.12	.23	.34	.46	.57
1.00	1.13	1.26	1.39	1.53	1.66	**1.00**	1.12	1.25	1.37	1.50	1.62	**1.00**	1.12	1.23	1.35	1.47	1.59
2.00	2.13	2.27	2.40	2.54	2.68	**2.00**	2.13	2.25	2.38	2.51	2.64	**2.00**	2.12	2.24	2.36	2.49	2.61
3.00	3.14	3.27	3.42	3.56	3.70	**3.00**	3.13	3.26	3.39	3.53	3.66	**3.00**	3.12	3.25	3.37	3.50	3.63
4.00	4.14	4.28	4.43	4.57	4.72	**4.00**	4.13	4.27	4.41	4.54	4.69	**4.00**	4.13	4.26	4.39	4.52	4.65
4.25	4.39	4.54	4.68	4.83	4.98	**4.25**	4.38	4.52	4.66	4.80	4.94	**4.25**	4.38	4.51	4.64	4.77	4.91
4.50	4.64	4.79	4.93	5.08	5.23	**4.50**	4.64	4.77	4.91	5.05	5.20	**4.50**	4.63	4.76	4.89	5.03	5.16
4.75	4.89	5.04	5.19	5.34	5.49	**4.75**	4.89	5.03	5.17	5.31	5.45	**4.75**	4.88	5.01	5.15	5.28	5.42
5.00	5.14	5.29	5.44	5.59	5.75	**5.00**	5.14	5.28	5.42	5.56	5.71	**5.00**	5.13	5.26	5.40	5.54	5.68
5.25	5.40	5.54	5.69	5.85	6.00	**5.25**	5.39	5.53	5.67	5.82	5.96	**5.25**	5.38	5.52	5.65	5.79	5.93
5.50	5.65	5.80	5.95	6.10	6.26	**5.50**	5.64	5.78	5.93	6.07	6.22	**5.50**	5.63	5.77	5.91	6.05	6.19
5.75	5.90	6.05	6.20	6.36	6.51	**5.75**	5.89	6.03	6.18	6.33	6.48	**5.75**	5.88	6.02	6.16	6.30	6.44
6.00	6.15	6.30	6.45	6.61	6.77	**6.00**	6.14	6.29	6.43	6.58	6.73	**6.00**	6.14	6.27	6.41	6.56	6.70
6.25	6.40	6.55	6.71	6.87	7.03	**6.25**	6.39	6.54	6.69	6.84	6.99	**6.25**	6.39	6.53	6.67	6.81	6.96
6.50	6.65	6.81	6.96	7.12	7.28	**6.50**	6.64	6.79	6.94	7.09	7.24	**6.50**	6.64	6.78	6.92	7.07	7.21
6.75	6.90	7.06	7.22	7.38	7.54	**6.75**	6.90	7.04	7.19	7.35	7.50	**6.75**	6.89	7.03	7.17	7.32	7.47
7.00	7.15	7.31	7.47	7.63	7.79	**7.00**	7.15	7.30	7.45	7.60	7.76	**7.00**	7.14	7.28	7.43	7.58	7.73
7.25	7.41	7.56	7.72	7.89	8.05	**7.25**	7.40	7.55	7.70	7.86	8.01	**7.25**	7.39	7.54	7.68	7.83	7.98
7.50	7.66	7.82	7.98	8.14	8.31	**7.50**	7.65	7.80	7.96	8.11	8.27	**7.50**	7.64	7.79	7.94	8.09	8.24
7.75	7.91	8.07	8.23	8.40	8.56	**7.75**	7.90	8.05	8.21	8.37	8.53	**7.75**	7.89	8.04	8.19	8.34	8.50
8.00	8.16	8.32	8.48	8.65	8.82	**8.00**	8.15	8.31	8.46	8.62	8.78	**8.00**	8.15	8.29	8.44	8.60	8.75
8.25	8.41	8.57	8.74	8.91	9.08	**8.25**	8.40	8.56	8.72	8.88	9.04	**8.25**	8.40	8.55	8.70	8.85	9.01
8.50	8.66	8.83	8.99	9.16	9.33	**8.50**	8.65	8.81	8.97	9.13	9.30	**8.50**	8.65	8.80	8.95	9.11	9.27
8.75	8.91	9.08	9.25	9.42	9.59	**8.75**	8.91	9.06	9.22	9.39	9.55	**8.75**	8.90	9.05	9.21	9.36	9.52
9.00	9.16	9.33	9.50	9.67	9.85	**9.00**	9.16	9.32	9.48	9.64	9.81	**9.00**	9.15	9.30	9.46	9.62	9.78
9.25	9.42	9.58	9.75	9.93	10.10	**9.25**	9.41	9.57	9.73	9.90	10.07	**9.25**	9.40	9.56	9.71	9.87	10.04
9.50	9.67	9.84	10.01	10.18	10.36	**9.50**	9.66	9.82	9.99	10.15	10.32	**9.50**	9.65	9.81	9.97	10.13	10.29
9.75	9.92	10.09	10.26	10.44	10.62	**9.75**	9.91	10.07	10.24	10.41	10.58	**9.75**	9.91	10.06	10.22	10.39	10.55
10.00	10.17	10.34	10.52	10.69	10.87	**10.00**	10.16	10.33	10.50	10.67	10.84	**10.00**	10.16	10.32	10.48	10.64	10.81
10.25	10.42	10.59	10.77	10.95	11.13	**10.25**	10.41	10.58	10.75	10.92	11.10	**10.25**	10.41	10.57	10.73	10.90	11.07
10.50	10.67	10.85	11.02	11.20	11.39	**10.50**	10.67	10.83	11.00	11.18	11.35	**10.50**	10.66	10.82	10.99	11.15	11.32
10.75	10.92	11.10	11.28	11.46	11.65	**10.75**	10.92	11.09	11.26	11.43	11.61	**10.75**	10.91	11.07	11.24	11.41	11.58
11.00	11.17	11.35	11.53	11.72	11.90	**11.00**	11.17	11.34	11.51	11.69	11.87	**11.00**	11.16	11.33	11.50	11.67	11.84
11.25	11.43	11.61	11.79	11.97	12.16	**11.25**	11.42	11.59	11.77	11.95	12.13	**11.25**	11.41	11.58	11.75	11.92	12.10
11.50	11.68	11.86	12.04	12.23	12.42	**11.50**	11.67	11.85	12.02	12.20	12.38	**11.50**	11.67	11.83	12.00	12.18	12.36
11.75	11.93	12.11	12.30	12.48	12.68	**11.75**	11.92	12.10	12.28	12.46	12.64	**11.75**	11.92	12.09	12.26	12.43	12.61
12.00	12.18	12.36	12.55	12.74	12.93	**12.00**	12.17	12.35	12.53	12.71	12.90	**12.00**	12.17	12.34	12.51	12.69	12.87
12.25	12.43	12.62	12.81	13.00	13.19	**12.25**	12.43	12.60	12.79	12.97	13.16	**12.25**	12.42	12.59	12.77	12.95	13.13
12.50	12.68	12.87	13.06	13.25	13.45	**12.50**	12.68	12.86	13.04	13.23	13.42	**12.50**	12.67	12.85	13.02	13.20	13.39
12.75	12.94	13.12	13.31	13.51	13.71	**12.75**	12.93	13.11	13.30	13.48	13.67	**12.75**	12.92	13.10	13.28	13.46	13.65
13.00	13.19	13.38	13.57	13.76	13.96	**13.00**	13.18	13.36	13.55	13.74	13.93	**13.00**	13.17	13.35	13.53	13.72	13.90
13.25	13.44	13.63	13.82	14.02	14.22	**13.25**	13.43	13.62	13.80	14.00	14.19	**13.25**	13.43	13.61	13.79	13.97	14.16
13.50	13.69	13.88	14.08	14.28	14.48	**13.50**	13.68	13.87	14.06	14.25	14.45	**13.50**	13.68	13.86	14.04	14.23	14.42
13.75	13.94	14.14	14.33	14.53	14.74	**13.75**	13.94	14.12	14.31	14.51	14.71	**13.75**	13.93	14.11	14.30	14.49	14.68
14.00	14.19	14.39	14.59	14.79	15.00	**14.00**	14.19	14.38	14.57	14.77	14.97	**14.00**	14.18	14.37	14.55	14.74	14.94
14.25	14.44	14.64	14.84	15.05	15.25	**14.25**	14.44	14.63	14.82	15.02	15.22	**14.25**	14.43	14.62	14.81	15.00	15.20
14.50	14.70	14.90	15.10	15.30	15.51	**14.50**	14.69	14.88	15.08	15.28	15.48	**14.50**	14.68	14.87	15.06	15.26	15.46
14.75	14.95	15.15	15.35	15.56	15.77	**14.75**	14.94	15.14	15.33	15.54	15.74	**14.75**	14.94	15.13	15.32	15.51	15.71
15.00	15.20	15.40	15.61	15.82	16.03	**15.00**	15.19	15.39	15.59	15.79	16.00	**15.00**	15.19	15.38	15.57	15.77	15.97
15.25	15.45	15.65	15.86	16.07	16.29	**15.25**	15.44	15.64	15.84	16.05	16.26	**15.25**	15.44	15.63	15.83	16.03	16.23
15.50	15.70	15.91	16.12	16.33	16.55	**15.50**	15.70	15.90	16.10	16.31	16.52	**15.50**	15.69	15.89	16.08	16.29	16.49
15.75	15.95	16.16	16.37	16.59	16.81	**15.75**	15.95	16.15	16.35	16.56	16.78	**15.75**	15.94	16.14	16.34	16.54	16.75
16.00	16.21	16.41	16.63	16.84	17.06	**16.00**	16.20	16.40	16.61	16.82	17.04	**16.00**	16.20	16.39	16.60	16.80	17.01
16.25	16.46	16.67	16.88	17.10	17.32	**16.25**	16.45	16.66	16.87	17.08	17.29	**16.25**	16.45	16.65	16.85	17.06	17.27
16.50	16.71	16.92	17.14	17.36	17.58	**16.50**	16.70	16.91	17.12	17.34	17.55	**16.50**	16.70	16.90	17.11	17.32	17.53
16.75	16.96	17.18	17.39	17.62	17.84	**16.75**	16.96	17.16	17.38	17.59	17.81	**16.75**	16.95	17.15	17.36	17.57	17.79
17.00	17.21	17.43	17.65	17.87	18.10	**17.00**	17.21	17.42	17.63	17.85	18.07	**17.00**	17.20	17.41	17.62	17.83	18.05
17.25	17.46	17.68	17.90	18.13	18.36	**17.25**	17.46	17.67	17.89	18.11	18.33	**17.25**	17.45	17.66	17.87	18.09	18.31
17.50	17.72	17.94	18.16	18.39	18.62	**17.50**	17.71	17.92	18.14	18.36	18.59	**17.50**	17.71	17.92	18.13	18.38	18.57
17.75	17.97	18.19	18.41	18.64	18.88	**17.75**	17.96	18.18	18.40	18.62	18.85	**17.75**	17.96	18.17	18.38	18.60	18.83
18.00	18.22	18.44	18.67	18.90	19.14	**18.00**	18.21	18.43	18.65	18.88	19.11	**18.00**	18.21	18.42	18.64	18.86	19.09
18.25	18.47	18.70	18.93	19.16	19.40	**18.25**	18.47	18.69	18.91	19.14	19.37	**18.25**	18.46	18.68	18.90	19.12	19.35
18.50	18.72	18.95	19.18	19.42	19.65	**18.50**	18.72	18.94	19.16	19.39	19.63	**18.50**	18.71	18.93	19.15	19.38	19.61
18.75	18.97	19.20	19.44	19.67	19.91	**18.75**	18.97	19.19	19.42	19.65	19.89	**18.75**	18.97	19.18	19.41	19.63	19.87
19.00	19.23	19.46	19.69	19.93	20.17	**19.00**	19.22	19.45	19.68	19.91	20.15	**19.00**	19.22	19.44	19.66	19.89	20.13
20.00	20.23	20.47	20.71	20.96	21.21	**20.00**	20.23	20.46	20.70	20.94	21.19	**20.00**	20.22	20.45	20.69	20.92	21.17
25.00	25.27	25.55	25.83	26.12	26.42	**25.00**	25.27	25.54	25.82	26.11	26.40	**25.00**	25.27	25.54	25.81	26.10	26.38
30.00	30.32	30.64	30.97	31.30	31.64	**30.00**	30.31	30.63	30.96	31.29	31.63	**30.00**	30.31	30.63	30.95	31.28	31.62

Description: This table shows the Annual Percentage Rate for a monthly payment loan when points are subtracted from the proceeds at closing.

Example: The interest rate on a 19 year loan is 8 %. At closing two points are paid to the lender. To maturity, the Annual Percentage Rate is 8.28 %.

19 YEARS

RATE	POINTS PAID 1	2	3	4	5
0.00	.12	.22	.32	.43	.54
1.00	1.11	1.22	1.33	1.45	1.56
2.00	2.11	2.23	2.34	2.46	2.58
3.00	3.12	3.24	3.36	3.48	3.60
4.00	4.12	4.24	4.37	4.49	4.62
4.25	4.37	4.50	4.62	4.75	4.88
4.50	4.62	4.75	4.88	5.00	5.13
4.75	4.87	5.00	5.13	5.26	5.39
5.00	5.13	5.25	5.38	5.51	5.65
5.25	5.38	5.51	5.64	5.77	5.90
5.50	5.63	5.76	5.89	6.02	6.16
5.75	5.88	6.01	6.14	6.28	6.41
6.00	6.13	6.26	6.40	6.53	6.67
6.25	6.38	6.51	6.65	6.79	6.93
6.50	6.63	6.77	6.90	7.04	7.18
6.75	6.88	7.02	7.16	7.30	7.44
7.00	7.14	7.27	7.41	7.55	7.70
7.25	7.39	7.52	7.67	7.81	7.95
7.50	7.64	7.78	7.92	8.06	8.21
7.75	7.89	8.03	8.17	8.32	8.47
8.00	8.14	8.28	8.43	8.57	8.72
8.25	8.39	8.54	8.68	8.83	8.98
8.50	8.64	8.79	8.94	9.09	9.24
8.75	8.89	9.04	9.19	9.34	9.50
9.00	9.15	9.29	9.44	9.60	9.75
9.25	9.40	9.55	9.70	9.85	10.01
9.50	9.65	9.80	9.95	10.11	10.27
9.75	9.90	10.05	10.21	10.36	10.52
10.00	10.15	10.31	10.46	10.62	10.78
10.25	10.40	10.56	10.72	10.88	11.04
10.50	10.65	10.81	10.97	11.13	11.30
10.75	10.91	11.06	11.23	11.39	11.56
11.00	11.16	11.32	11.48	11.65	11.81
11.25	11.41	11.57	11.73	11.90	12.07
11.50	11.66	11.82	11.99	12.16	12.33
11.75	11.91	12.08	12.24	12.41	12.59
12.00	12.16	12.33	12.50	12.67	12.85
12.25	12.42	12.58	12.75	12.93	13.10
12.50	12.67	12.84	13.01	13.18	13.36
12.75	12.92	13.09	13.26	13.44	13.62
13.00	13.17	13.34	13.52	13.70	13.88
13.25	13.42	13.60	13.77	13.95	14.14
13.50	13.67	13.85	14.03	14.21	14.40
13.75	13.93	14.10	14.28	14.47	14.66
14.00	14.18	14.36	14.54	14.73	14.91
14.25	14.43	14.61	14.79	14.98	15.17
14.50	14.68	14.86	15.05	15.24	15.43
14.75	14.93	15.12	15.31	15.50	15.69
15.00	15.18	15.37	15.56	15.75	15.95
15.25	15.44	15.62	15.82	16.01	16.21
15.50	15.69	15.88	16.07	16.27	16.47
15.75	15.94	16.13	16.33	16.53	16.73
16.00	16.19	16.38	16.58	16.78	16.99
16.25	16.44	16.64	16.84	17.04	17.25
16.50	16.69	16.89	17.09	17.30	17.51
16.75	16.95	17.15	17.35	17.56	17.77
17.00	17.20	17.40	17.60	17.81	18.03
17.25	17.45	17.65	17.86	18.07	18.29
17.50	17.70	17.91	18.12	18.33	18.55
17.75	17.95	18.16	18.37	18.59	18.81
18.00	18.21	18.42	18.63	18.85	19.07
18.25	18.46	18.67	18.88	19.10	19.33
18.50	18.71	18.92	19.14	19.36	19.59
18.75	18.96	19.18	19.40	19.62	19.85
19.00	19.21	19.43	19.65	19.88	20.11
20.00	20.22	20.45	20.68	20.91	21.15
25.00	25.26	25.53	25.81	26.09	26.37
30.00	30.31	30.62	30.95	31.27	31.61

20 YEARS

RATE	POINTS PAID 1	2	3	4	5
0.00	.11	.21	.31	.41	.52
1.00	1.10	1.21	1.32	1.42	1.53
2.00	2.11	2.22	2.33	2.44	2.55
3.00	3.11	3.22	3.34	3.46	3.57
4.00	4.12	4.23	4.35	4.47	4.60
4.25	4.37	4.49	4.61	4.73	4.85
4.50	4.62	4.74	4.86	4.98	5.11
4.75	4.87	4.99	5.11	5.24	5.36
5.00	5.12	5.24	5.37	5.49	5.62
5.25	5.37	5.49	5.62	5.75	5.88
5.50	5.62	5.75	5.87	6.00	6.13
5.75	5.87	6.00	6.13	6.26	6.39
6.00	6.13	6.25	6.38	6.51	6.65
6.25	6.38	6.50	6.63	6.77	6.90
6.50	6.63	6.76	6.89	7.02	7.16
6.75	6.88	7.01	7.14	7.28	7.41
7.00	7.13	7.26	7.40	7.53	7.67
7.25	7.38	7.51	7.65	7.79	7.93
7.50	7.63	7.77	7.90	8.04	8.19
7.75	7.88	8.02	8.16	8.30	8.44
8.00	8.14	8.27	8.41	8.55	8.70
8.25	8.39	8.53	8.67	8.81	8.96
8.50	8.64	8.78	8.92	9.07	9.21
8.75	8.89	9.03	9.18	9.32	9.47
9.00	9.14	9.28	9.43	9.58	9.73
9.25	9.39	9.54	9.68	9.83	9.99
9.50	9.64	9.79	9.94	10.09	10.24
9.75	9.90	10.04	10.19	10.35	10.50
10.00	10.15	10.30	10.45	10.60	10.76
10.25	10.40	10.55	10.70	10.86	11.02
10.50	10.65	10.80	10.96	11.11	11.27
10.75	10.90	11.06	11.21	11.37	11.53
11.00	11.15	11.31	11.47	11.63	11.79
11.25	11.40	11.56	11.72	11.88	12.05
11.50	11.66	11.81	11.98	12.14	12.31
11.75	11.91	12.07	12.23	12.40	12.57
12.00	12.16	12.32	12.49	12.65	12.82
12.25	12.41	12.57	12.74	12.91	13.08
12.50	12.66	12.83	13.00	13.17	13.34
12.75	12.91	13.08	13.25	13.42	13.60
13.00	13.17	13.33	13.51	13.68	13.86
13.25	13.42	13.59	13.76	13.94	14.12
13.50	13.67	13.84	14.02	14.19	14.38
13.75	13.92	14.09	14.27	14.45	14.64
14.00	14.17	14.35	14.53	14.71	14.89
14.25	14.42	14.60	14.78	14.97	15.15
14.50	14.68	14.86	15.04	15.22	15.41
14.75	14.93	15.11	15.29	15.48	15.67
15.00	15.18	15.36	15.55	15.74	15.93
15.25	15.43	15.62	15.80	16.00	16.19
15.50	15.68	15.87	16.06	16.25	16.45
15.75	15.94	16.12	16.32	16.51	16.71
16.00	16.19	16.38	16.57	16.77	16.97
16.25	16.44	16.63	16.83	17.03	17.23
16.50	16.69	16.89	17.08	17.28	17.49
16.75	16.94	17.14	17.34	17.54	17.75
17.00	17.19	17.39	17.59	17.80	18.01
17.25	17.45	17.65	17.85	18.06	18.27
17.50	17.70	17.90	18.11	18.32	18.53
17.75	17.95	18.15	18.36	18.57	18.79
18.00	18.20	18.41	18.62	18.83	19.05
18.25	18.45	18.66	18.87	19.09	19.31
18.50	18.71	18.92	19.13	19.35	19.57
18.75	18.96	19.17	19.39	19.61	19.83
19.00	19.21	19.42	19.64	19.86	20.09
20.00	20.22	20.44	20.67	20.90	21.13
25.00	25.26	25.53	25.80	26.08	26.36
30.00	30.31	30.62	30.94	31.27	31.60

21 YEARS

RATE	POINTS PAID 1	2	3	4	5
0.00	.11	.20	.29	.39	.49
1.00	1.10	1.20	1.30	1.41	1.51
2.00	2.10	2.21	2.31	2.42	2.53
3.00	3.11	3.22	3.33	3.44	3.55
4.00	4.11	4.22	4.34	4.45	4.57
4.25	4.36	4.48	4.59	4.71	4.83
4.50	4.61	4.73	4.85	4.96	5.08
4.75	4.86	4.98	5.10	5.22	5.34
5.00	5.12	5.23	5.35	5.47	5.60
5.25	5.37	5.49	5.61	5.73	5.85
5.50	5.62	5.74	5.86	5.98	6.11
5.75	5.87	5.99	6.11	6.24	6.37
6.00	6.12	6.24	6.37	6.49	6.62
6.25	6.37	6.50	6.62	6.75	6.88
6.50	6.62	6.75	6.88	7.00	7.13
6.75	6.87	7.00	7.13	7.26	7.39
7.00	7.13	7.25	7.38	7.51	7.65
7.25	7.38	7.51	7.64	7.77	7.91
7.50	7.63	7.76	7.89	8.03	8.16
7.75	7.88	8.01	8.15	8.28	8.42
8.00	8.13	8.26	8.40	8.54	8.68
8.25	8.38	8.52	8.65	8.79	8.93
8.50	8.63	8.77	8.91	9.05	9.19
8.75	8.89	9.02	9.16	9.30	9.45
9.00	9.14	9.28	9.42	9.56	9.71
9.25	9.39	9.53	9.67	9.82	9.96
9.50	9.64	9.78	9.93	10.07	10.22
9.75	9.89	10.03	10.18	10.33	10.48
10.00	10.14	10.29	10.44	10.59	10.74
10.25	10.39	10.54	10.69	10.84	11.00
10.50	10.65	10.79	10.94	11.10	11.25
10.75	10.90	11.05	11.20	11.35	11.51
11.00	11.15	11.30	11.45	11.61	11.77
11.25	11.40	11.55	11.71	11.87	12.03
11.50	11.65	11.81	11.96	12.12	12.29
11.75	11.90	12.06	12.22	12.38	12.55
12.00	12.16	12.31	12.47	12.64	12.80
12.25	12.41	12.57	12.73	12.89	13.06
12.50	12.66	12.82	12.98	13.15	13.32
12.75	12.91	13.07	13.24	13.41	13.58
13.00	13.16	13.33	13.49	13.67	13.84
13.25	13.41	13.58	13.75	13.92	14.10
13.50	13.67	13.83	14.01	14.18	14.36
13.75	13.92	14.09	14.26	14.44	14.62
14.00	14.17	14.34	14.52	14.69	14.88
14.25	14.42	14.59	14.77	14.95	15.14
14.50	14.67	14.85	15.03	15.21	15.39
14.75	14.92	15.10	15.28	15.47	15.65
15.00	15.18	15.36	15.54	15.72	15.91
15.25	15.43	15.61	15.79	15.98	16.17
15.50	15.68	15.86	16.05	16.24	16.43
15.75	15.93	16.12	16.31	16.50	16.69
16.00	16.18	16.37	16.56	16.76	16.95
16.25	16.44	16.62	16.82	17.01	17.21
16.50	16.69	16.88	17.07	17.27	17.47
16.75	16.94	17.13	17.33	17.53	17.73
17.00	17.19	17.39	17.59	17.79	17.99
17.25	17.44	17.64	17.84	18.05	18.25
17.50	17.70	17.89	18.10	18.30	18.51
17.75	17.95	18.15	18.35	18.56	18.77
18.00	18.20	18.40	18.61	18.82	19.04
18.25	18.45	18.66	18.87	19.08	19.30
18.50	18.70	18.91	19.12	19.34	19.56
18.75	18.96	19.16	19.38	19.60	19.82
19.00	19.21	19.42	19.63	19.85	20.08
20.00	20.22	20.44	20.66	20.89	21.12
25.00	25.26	25.52	25.79	26.07	26.35
30.00	30.31	30.62	30.94	31.26	31.60

Description: This table shows the Annual Percentage Rate for a monthly payment loan when points are subtracted from the proceeds at closing.

Example: The interest rate on a 22 year loan is 8 %. At closing two points are paid to the lender. To maturity, the Annual Percentage Rate is 8.26 %.

22 YEARS — POINTS PAID

RATE	1	2	3	4	5
0.00	.10	.19	.28	.38	.47
1.00	1.10	1.19	1.29	1.39	1.49
2.00	2.10	2.20	2.30	2.40	2.51
3.00	3.10	3.21	3.31	3.42	3.53
4.00	4.11	4.22	4.33	4.44	4.55
4.25	4.36	4.47	4.58	4.69	4.81
4.50	4.61	4.72	4.83	4.95	5.06
4.75	4.86	4.97	5.09	5.20	5.32
5.00	5.11	5.22	5.34	5.46	5.58
5.25	5.36	5.48	5.59	5.71	5.83
5.50	5.61	5.73	5.85	5.97	6.09
5.75	5.87	5.98	6.10	6.22	6.34
6.00	6.12	6.23	6.35	6.48	6.60
6.25	6.37	6.49	6.61	6.73	6.86
6.50	6.62	6.74	6.86	6.99	7.11
6.75	6.87	6.99	7.12	7.24	7.37
7.00	7.12	7.25	7.37	7.50	7.63
7.25	7.37	7.50	7.62	7.75	7.88
7.50	7.62	7.75	7.88	8.01	8.14
7.75	7.88	8.00	8.13	8.27	8.40
8.00	8.13	8.26	8.39	8.52	8.66
8.25	8.38	8.51	8.64	8.78	8.91
8.50	8.63	8.76	8.90	9.03	9.17
8.75	8.88	9.02	9.15	9.29	9.43
9.00	9.13	9.27	9.41	9.54	9.69
9.25	9.38	9.52	9.66	9.80	9.94
9.50	9.64	9.77	9.91	10.06	10.20
9.75	9.89	10.03	10.17	10.31	10.46
10.00	10.14	10.28	10.42	10.57	10.72
10.25	10.39	10.53	10.68	10.83	10.98
10.50	10.64	10.79	10.93	11.08	11.24
10.75	10.89	11.04	11.19	11.34	11.49
11.00	11.15	11.29	11.44	11.60	11.75
11.25	11.40	11.55	11.70	11.85	12.01
11.50	11.65	11.80	11.95	12.11	12.27
11.75	11.90	12.05	12.21	12.37	12.53
12.00	12.15	12.31	12.46	12.62	12.79
12.25	12.40	12.56	12.72	12.88	13.05
12.50	12.66	12.81	12.97	13.14	13.30
12.75	12.91	13.07	13.23	13.40	13.56
13.00	13.16	13.32	13.48	13.65	13.82
13.25	13.41	13.57	13.74	13.91	14.08
13.50	13.66	13.83	14.00	14.17	14.34
13.75	13.91	14.08	14.25	14.42	14.60
14.00	14.17	14.33	14.51	14.68	14.86
14.25	14.42	14.59	14.76	14.94	15.12
14.50	14.67	14.84	15.02	15.20	15.38
14.75	14.92	15.10	15.27	15.45	15.64
15.00	15.17	15.35	15.53	15.71	15.90
15.25	15.43	15.60	15.79	15.97	16.16
15.50	15.68	15.86	16.04	16.23	16.42
15.75	15.93	16.11	16.30	16.49	16.68
16.00	16.18	16.37	16.55	16.74	16.94
16.25	16.43	16.62	16.81	17.00	17.20
16.50	16.68	16.87	17.07	17.26	17.46
16.75	16.94	17.13	17.32	17.52	17.72
17.00	17.19	17.38	17.58	17.78	17.98
17.25	17.44	17.64	17.83	18.04	18.24
17.50	17.69	17.89	18.09	18.29	18.50
17.75	17.94	18.14	18.35	18.55	18.76
18.00	18.20	18.40	18.60	18.81	19.02
18.25	18.45	18.65	18.86	19.07	19.28
18.50	18.70	18.91	19.11	19.33	19.54
18.75	18.95	19.16	19.37	19.59	19.81
19.00	19.21	19.41	19.63	19.84	20.07
20.00	20.21	20.43	20.65	20.88	21.11
25.00	25.26	25.52	25.79	26.06	26.34
30.00	30.31	30.62	30.94	31.26	31.59

23 YEARS — POINTS PAID

RATE	1	2	3	4	5
0.00	.10	.18	.27	.36	.45
1.00	1.09	1.18	1.28	1.37	1.47
2.00	2.09	2.19	2.29	2.39	2.49
3.00	3.10	3.20	3.30	3.40	3.51
4.00	4.10	4.21	4.31	4.42	4.53
4.25	4.35	4.46	4.57	4.68	4.79
4.50	4.61	4.71	4.82	4.93	5.04
4.75	4.86	4.96	5.07	5.19	5.30
5.00	5.11	5.22	5.33	5.44	5.56
5.25	5.36	5.47	5.58	5.70	5.81
5.50	5.61	5.72	5.84	5.95	6.07
5.75	5.86	5.97	6.09	6.21	6.32
6.00	6.11	6.23	6.34	6.46	6.58
6.25	6.36	6.48	6.60	6.72	6.84
6.50	6.62	6.73	6.85	6.97	7.10
6.75	6.87	6.99	7.11	7.23	7.35
7.00	7.12	7.24	7.36	7.48	7.61
7.25	7.37	7.49	7.61	7.74	7.87
7.50	7.62	7.74	7.87	7.99	8.12
7.75	7.87	8.00	8.12	8.25	8.38
8.00	8.12	8.25	8.38	8.51	8.64
8.25	8.38	8.50	8.63	8.76	8.90
8.50	8.63	8.76	8.89	9.02	9.15
8.75	8.88	9.01	9.14	9.27	9.41
9.00	9.13	9.26	9.39	9.53	9.67
9.25	9.38	9.51	9.65	9.79	9.93
9.50	9.63	9.77	9.90	10.04	10.19
9.75	9.88	10.02	10.16	10.30	10.44
10.00	10.14	10.27	10.41	10.56	10.70
10.25	10.39	10.53	10.67	10.81	10.96
10.50	10.64	10.78	10.92	11.07	11.22
10.75	10.89	11.03	11.18	11.33	11.48
11.00	11.14	11.29	11.43	11.58	11.74
11.25	11.39	11.54	11.69	11.84	11.99
11.50	11.65	11.79	11.94	12.10	12.25
11.75	11.90	12.05	12.20	12.35	12.51
12.00	12.15	12.30	12.45	12.61	12.77
12.25	12.40	12.55	12.71	12.87	13.03
12.50	12.65	12.81	12.97	13.13	13.29
12.75	12.90	13.06	13.22	13.38	13.55
13.00	13.16	13.31	13.48	13.64	13.81
13.25	13.41	13.57	13.73	13.90	14.07
13.50	13.66	13.83	13.99	14.16	14.33
13.75	13.91	14.08	14.24	14.41	14.59
14.00	14.16	14.33	14.50	14.67	14.85
14.25	14.42	14.58	14.75	14.93	15.11
14.50	14.67	14.84	15.01	15.19	15.37
14.75	14.92	15.09	15.27	15.44	15.63
15.00	15.17	15.34	15.52	15.70	15.89
15.25	15.42	15.60	15.78	15.96	16.15
15.50	15.67	15.85	16.03	16.22	16.41
15.75	15.93	16.11	16.29	16.48	16.67
16.00	16.18	16.36	16.55	16.73	16.93
16.25	16.43	16.61	16.80	16.99	17.19
16.50	16.68	16.87	17.06	17.25	17.45
16.75	16.93	17.12	17.31	17.51	17.71
17.00	17.19	17.38	17.57	17.77	17.97
17.25	17.44	17.63	17.83	18.03	18.23
17.50	17.69	17.89	18.08	18.28	18.49
17.75	17.94	18.14	18.34	18.54	18.75
18.00	18.19	18.39	18.60	18.80	19.01
18.25	18.45	18.65	18.85	19.06	19.27
18.50	18.70	18.90	19.11	19.32	19.53
18.75	18.95	19.16	19.37	19.58	19.80
19.00	19.20	19.41	19.62	19.84	20.06
20.00	20.21	20.43	20.65	20.87	21.10
25.00	25.26	25.52	25.79	26.06	26.34
30.00	30.31	30.62	30.93	31.26	31.59

24 YEARS — POINTS PAID

RATE	1	2	3	4	5
0.00	.09	.17	.26	.34	.43
1.00	1.09	1.18	1.27	1.36	1.45
2.00	2.09	2.18	2.28	2.37	2.47
3.00	3.10	3.19	3.29	3.39	3.49
4.00	4.10	4.20	4.30	4.41	4.51
4.25	4.35	4.45	4.56	4.66	4.77
4.50	4.60	4.71	4.81	4.92	5.03
4.75	4.85	4.96	5.06	5.17	5.28
5.00	5.10	5.21	5.32	5.43	5.54
5.25	5.36	5.46	5.57	5.68	5.79
5.50	5.61	5.72	5.83	5.94	6.05
5.75	5.86	5.97	6.08	6.19	6.31
6.00	6.11	6.22	6.33	6.45	6.56
6.25	6.36	6.47	6.59	6.70	6.82
6.50	6.61	6.73	6.84	6.96	7.08
6.75	6.86	6.98	7.10	7.21	7.33
7.00	7.11	7.23	7.35	7.47	7.59
7.25	7.37	7.48	7.60	7.73	7.85
7.50	7.62	7.74	7.86	7.98	8.11
7.75	7.87	7.99	8.11	8.24	8.36
8.00	8.12	8.24	8.37	8.49	8.62
8.25	8.37	8.50	8.62	8.75	8.88
8.50	8.62	8.75	8.88	9.01	9.14
8.75	8.87	9.00	9.13	9.26	9.40
9.00	9.13	9.25	9.39	9.52	9.65
9.25	9.38	9.51	9.64	9.77	9.91
9.50	9.63	9.76	9.89	10.03	10.17
9.75	9.88	10.01	10.15	10.29	10.43
10.00	10.13	10.27	10.40	10.54	10.69
10.25	10.38	10.52	10.66	10.80	10.94
10.50	10.64	10.77	10.91	11.06	11.20
10.75	10.89	11.03	11.17	11.31	11.46
11.00	11.14	11.28	11.43	11.57	11.72
11.25	11.39	11.53	11.68	11.83	11.98
11.50	11.64	11.79	11.94	12.09	12.24
11.75	11.89	12.04	12.19	12.34	12.50
12.00	12.15	12.29	12.45	12.60	12.76
12.25	12.40	12.55	12.70	12.86	13.02
12.50	12.65	12.80	12.96	13.12	13.28
12.75	12.90	13.06	13.21	13.37	13.54
13.00	13.15	13.31	13.47	13.63	13.79
13.25	13.41	13.57	13.72	13.89	14.05
13.50	13.66	13.82	13.98	14.15	14.31
13.75	13.91	14.07	14.24	14.40	14.57
14.00	14.16	14.32	14.49	14.66	14.83
14.25	14.41	14.58	14.75	14.92	15.09
14.50	14.66	14.83	15.00	15.18	15.35
14.75	14.92	15.09	15.26	15.43	15.61
15.00	15.17	15.34	15.51	15.69	15.87
15.25	15.42	15.59	15.77	15.95	16.13
15.50	15.67	15.85	16.03	16.21	16.40
15.75	15.92	16.10	16.28	16.47	16.66
16.00	16.18	16.36	16.54	16.73	16.92
16.25	16.43	16.61	16.80	16.98	17.18
16.50	16.68	16.86	17.05	17.24	17.44
16.75	16.93	17.12	17.31	17.50	17.70
17.00	17.18	17.37	17.56	17.76	17.96
17.25	17.44	17.63	17.82	18.02	18.22
17.50	17.69	17.88	18.08	18.28	18.48
17.75	17.94	18.14	18.33	18.54	18.74
18.00	18.19	18.39	18.59	18.79	19.00
18.25	18.45	18.64	18.85	19.05	19.26
18.50	18.70	18.90	19.10	19.31	19.53
18.75	18.95	19.15	19.36	19.57	19.79
19.00	19.20	19.41	19.62	19.83	20.05
20.00	20.21	20.42	20.64	20.87	21.09
25.00	25.26	25.52	25.79	26.06	26.33
30.00	30.30	30.62	30.93	31.26	31.59

Description: This table shows the Annual Percentage Rate for a monthly payment loan when points are subtracted from the proceeds at closing.

Example: The interest rate on a 25 year loan is 8 %. At closing two points are paid to the lender. To maturity, the Annual Percentage Rate is 8.24 %.

RATE	25 YEARS POINTS PAID 1	2	3	4	5	RATE	26 YEARS POINTS PAID 1	2	3	4	5	RATE	27 YEARS POINTS PAID 1	2	3	4	5
0.00	.09	.17	.25	.33	.41	0.00	.09	.16	.24	.32	.40	0.00	.08	.16	.23	.31	.38
1.00	1.08	1.17	1.26	1.34	1.43	1.00	1.08	1.16	1.25	1.33	1.42	1.00	1.08	1.16	1.24	1.32	1.40
2.00	2.09	2.18	2.27	2.36	2.45	2.00	2.08	2.17	2.26	2.35	2.44	2.00	2.08	2.17	2.25	2.33	2.42
3.00	3.09	3.19	3.28	3.38	3.47	3.00	3.09	3.18	3.27	3.36	3.46	3.00	3.09	3.17	3.26	3.35	3.44
4.00	4.10	4.19	4.29	4.39	4.50	4.00	4.09	4.19	4.28	4.38	4.48	4.00	4.09	4.18	4.28	4.37	4.47
4.25	4.35	4.45	4.55	4.65	4.75	4.25	4.34	4.44	4.54	4.64	4.74	4.25	4.34	4.44	4.53	4.63	4.72
4.50	4.60	4.70	4.80	4.90	5.01	4.50	4.60	4.69	4.79	4.89	4.99	4.50	4.59	4.69	4.78	4.88	4.98
4.75	4.85	4.95	5.05	5.16	5.26	4.75	4.85	4.95	5.05	5.15	5.25	4.75	4.84	4.94	5.04	5.14	5.24
5.00	5.10	5.20	5.31	5.41	5.52	5.00	5.10	5.20	5.30	5.40	5.51	5.00	5.10	5.19	5.29	5.39	5.49
5.25	5.35	5.46	5.56	5.67	5.78	5.25	5.35	5.45	5.55	5.66	5.76	5.25	5.35	5.45	5.54	5.65	5.75
5.50	5.60	5.71	5.82	5.92	6.03	5.50	5.60	5.70	5.81	5.91	6.02	5.50	5.60	5.70	5.80	5.90	6.01
5.75	5.85	5.96	6.07	6.18	6.29	5.75	5.85	5.96	6.06	6.17	6.28	5.75	5.85	5.95	6.05	6.16	6.26
6.00	6.11	6.21	6.32	6.43	6.55	6.00	6.10	6.21	6.31	6.42	6.53	6.00	6.10	6.20	6.31	6.41	6.52
6.25	6.36	6.47	6.58	6.69	6.81	6.25	6.35	6.46	6.57	6.68	6.79	6.25	6.35	6.46	6.56	6.67	6.78
6.50	6.61	6.72	6.83	6.95	7.06	6.50	6.61	6.71	6.82	6.93	7.05	6.50	6.60	6.71	6.82	6.92	7.03
6.75	6.86	6.97	7.09	7.20	7.32	6.75	6.86	6.97	7.08	7.19	7.30	6.75	6.85	6.96	7.07	7.18	7.29
7.00	7.11	7.23	7.34	7.46	7.58	7.00	7.11	7.22	7.33	7.45	7.56	7.00	7.11	7.21	7.32	7.44	7.55
7.25	7.36	7.48	7.59	7.71	7.83	7.25	7.36	7.47	7.59	7.70	7.82	7.25	7.36	7.47	7.58	7.69	7.81
7.50	7.61	7.73	7.85	7.97	8.09	7.50	7.61	7.73	7.84	7.96	8.08	7.50	7.61	7.72	7.83	7.95	8.06
7.75	7.87	7.98	8.10	8.23	8.35	7.75	7.86	7.98	8.10	8.21	8.34	7.75	7.86	7.97	8.09	8.20	8.32
8.00	8.12	8.24	8.36	8.48	8.61	8.00	8.11	8.23	8.35	8.47	8.59	8.00	8.11	8.23	8.34	8.46	8.58
8.25	8.37	8.49	8.61	8.74	8.86	8.25	8.37	8.48	8.60	8.73	8.85	8.25	8.36	8.48	8.60	8.72	8.84
8.50	8.62	8.74	8.87	8.99	9.12	8.50	8.62	8.74	8.86	8.98	9.11	8.50	8.62	8.73	8.85	8.97	9.10
8.75	8.87	9.00	9.12	9.25	9.38	8.75	8.87	8.99	9.11	9.24	9.37	8.75	8.87	8.99	9.11	9.23	9.36
9.00	9.12	9.25	9.38	9.51	9.64	9.00	9.12	9.24	9.37	9.50	9.63	9.00	9.12	9.24	9.36	9.49	9.61
9.25	9.38	9.50	9.63	9.76	9.90	9.25	9.37	9.50	9.62	9.75	9.88	9.25	9.37	9.49	9.62	9.74	9.87
9.50	9.63	9.76	9.89	10.02	10.16	9.50	9.62	9.75	9.88	10.01	10.14	9.50	9.62	9.75	9.87	10.00	10.13
9.75	9.88	10.01	10.14	10.28	10.41	9.75	9.88	10.00	10.13	10.27	10.40	9.75	9.87	10.00	10.13	10.26	10.39
10.00	10.13	10.26	10.40	10.53	10.67	10.00	10.13	10.26	10.39	10.52	10.66	10.00	10.13	10.25	10.38	10.51	10.65
10.25	10.38	10.52	10.65	10.79	10.93	10.25	10.38	10.51	10.64	10.78	10.92	10.25	10.38	10.51	10.64	10.77	10.91
10.50	10.63	10.77	10.91	11.05	11.19	10.50	10.63	10.76	10.90	11.04	11.18	10.50	10.63	10.76	10.90	11.03	11.17
10.75	10.89	11.02	11.16	11.30	11.45	10.75	10.88	11.02	11.15	11.29	11.44	10.75	10.88	11.01	11.15	11.29	11.43
11.00	11.14	11.28	11.42	11.56	11.71	11.00	11.13	11.27	11.41	11.55	11.70	11.00	11.13	11.27	11.40	11.54	11.69
11.25	11.39	11.53	11.67	11.82	11.97	11.25	11.39	11.52	11.67	11.81	11.96	11.25	11.38	11.52	11.66	11.80	11.94
11.50	11.64	11.78	11.93	12.08	12.23	11.50	11.64	11.78	11.92	12.07	12.21	11.50	11.64	11.77	11.92	12.06	12.20
11.75	11.89	12.04	12.18	12.33	12.49	11.75	11.89	12.03	12.18	12.32	12.47	11.75	11.89	12.03	12.17	12.32	12.46
12.00	12.14	12.29	12.44	12.59	12.74	12.00	12.14	12.29	12.43	12.58	12.73	12.00	12.14	12.28	12.43	12.57	12.72
12.25	12.40	12.54	12.69	12.85	13.00	12.25	12.39	12.54	12.69	12.84	12.99	12.25	12.39	12.54	12.68	12.83	12.98
12.50	12.65	12.80	12.95	13.11	13.26	12.50	12.65	12.79	12.94	13.10	13.25	12.50	12.64	12.79	12.94	13.09	13.24
12.75	12.90	13.05	13.21	13.36	13.52	12.75	12.90	13.05	13.20	13.35	13.51	12.75	12.90	13.04	13.19	13.35	13.50
13.00	13.15	13.30	13.46	13.62	13.78	13.00	13.15	13.30	13.46	13.61	13.77	13.00	13.15	13.30	13.45	13.61	13.76
13.25	13.40	13.56	13.72	13.88	14.04	13.25	13.40	13.55	13.71	13.87	14.03	13.25	13.40	13.55	13.71	13.86	14.02
13.50	13.65	13.81	13.97	14.14	14.30	13.50	13.65	13.81	13.97	14.13	14.29	13.50	13.65	13.81	13.96	14.12	14.28
13.75	13.91	14.07	14.23	14.39	14.56	13.75	13.90	14.06	14.22	14.39	14.55	13.75	13.90	14.06	14.22	14.38	14.54
14.00	14.16	14.32	14.48	14.65	14.82	14.00	14.16	14.32	14.48	14.64	14.81	14.00	14.16	14.31	14.47	14.64	14.80
14.25	14.41	14.57	14.74	14.91	15.08	14.25	14.41	14.57	14.74	14.90	15.07	14.25	14.41	14.57	14.73	14.90	15.07
14.50	14.66	14.83	15.00	15.17	15.34	14.50	14.66	14.82	14.99	15.16	15.33	14.50	14.66	14.82	14.99	15.15	15.33
14.75	14.91	15.08	15.25	15.43	15.60	14.75	14.91	15.08	15.25	15.42	15.59	14.75	14.91	15.08	15.24	15.41	15.59
15.00	15.17	15.34	15.51	15.68	15.86	15.00	15.16	15.33	15.50	15.69	15.86	15.00	15.16	15.33	15.50	15.67	15.85
15.25	15.42	15.59	15.77	15.94	16.12	15.25	15.42	15.59	15.76	15.94	16.12	15.25	15.42	15.58	15.76	15.93	16.11
15.50	15.67	15.84	16.02	16.20	16.39	15.50	15.67	15.84	16.02	16.19	16.38	15.50	15.67	15.84	16.01	16.19	16.37
15.75	15.92	16.10	16.28	16.46	16.65	15.75	15.92	16.10	16.27	16.45	16.64	15.75	15.92	16.09	16.27	16.45	16.63
16.00	16.17	16.35	16.53	16.72	16.91	16.00	16.17	16.35	16.53	16.71	16.90	16.00	16.17	16.35	16.52	16.71	16.89
16.25	16.43	16.61	16.79	16.98	17.17	16.25	16.43	16.61	16.79	16.97	17.16	16.25	16.42	16.60	16.78	16.97	17.15
16.50	16.68	16.86	17.05	17.24	17.43	16.50	16.68	16.86	17.04	17.23	17.42	16.50	16.68	16.86	17.04	17.22	17.41
16.75	16.93	17.12	17.30	17.49	17.69	16.75	16.93	17.11	17.30	17.49	17.68	16.75	16.93	17.11	17.29	17.48	17.68
17.00	17.18	17.37	17.56	17.75	17.95	17.00	17.18	17.37	17.55	17.75	17.94	17.00	17.18	17.36	17.55	17.74	17.94
17.25	17.44	17.62	17.82	18.01	18.21	17.25	17.43	17.62	17.81	18.01	18.20	17.25	17.43	17.62	17.81	18.00	18.20
17.50	17.69	17.88	18.07	18.27	18.47	17.50	17.69	17.88	18.07	18.26	18.47	17.50	17.68	17.87	18.06	18.26	18.46
17.75	17.94	18.13	18.33	18.53	18.73	17.75	17.94	18.13	18.32	18.52	18.73	17.75	17.94	18.13	18.32	18.52	18.72
18.00	18.19	18.39	18.59	18.79	19.00	18.00	18.19	18.38	18.58	18.78	18.99	18.00	18.19	18.38	18.58	18.78	18.98
18.25	18.44	18.64	18.84	19.05	19.26	18.25	18.44	18.64	18.84	19.04	19.25	18.25	18.44	18.64	18.83	19.04	19.24
18.50	18.70	18.90	19.10	19.31	19.52	18.50	18.69	18.89	19.10	19.30	19.51	18.50	18.69	18.89	19.09	19.30	19.51
18.75	18.95	19.15	19.36	19.57	19.78	18.75	18.95	19.15	19.35	19.56	19.77	18.75	18.95	19.15	19.35	19.56	19.77
19.00	19.20	19.40	19.61	19.82	20.04	19.00	19.20	19.40	19.61	19.82	20.03	19.00	19.20	19.40	19.61	19.82	20.03
20.00	20.21	20.42	20.64	20.86	21.09	20.00	20.21	20.42	20.64	20.86	21.08	20.00	20.21	20.42	20.63	20.85	21.08
25.00	25.26	25.52	25.78	26.05	26.33	25.00	25.26	25.52	25.78	26.05	26.33	25.00	25.25	25.51	25.78	26.05	26.33
30.00	30.30	30.61	30.93	31.25	31.59	30.00	30.30	30.61	30.93	31.25	31.58	30.00	30.30	30.61	30.93	31.25	31.58

POINTS ON MONTHLY PAYMENT LOAN

Description: This table shows the Annual Percentage Rate for a monthly payment loan when points are subtracted from the proceeds at closing.

Example: The interest rate on a 28 year loan is 8 %. At closing two points are paid to the lender. To maturity, the Annual Percentage Rate is 8.22 %.

28 YEARS — POINTS PAID

RATE	1	2	3	4	5
0.00	.08	.15	.22	.30	.37
1.00	1.08	1.15	1.23	1.31	1.39
2.00	2.08	2.16	2.24	2.32	2.41
3.00	3.08	3.17	3.25	3.34	3.43
4.00	4.09	4.18	4.27	4.36	4.45
4.25	4.34	4.43	4.52	4.62	4.71
4.50	4.59	4.68	4.78	4.87	4.97
4.75	4.84	4.93	5.03	5.13	5.22
5.00	5.09	5.19	5.28	5.38	5.48
5.25	5.34	5.44	5.54	5.64	5.74
5.50	5.60	5.69	5.79	5.89	5.99
5.75	5.85	5.95	6.05	6.15	6.25
6.00	6.10	6.20	6.30	6.40	6.51
6.25	6.35	6.45	6.55	6.66	6.76
6.50	6.60	6.70	6.81	6.91	7.02
6.75	6.85	6.96	7.06	7.17	7.28
7.00	7.10	7.21	7.32	7.43	7.54
7.25	7.36	7.46	7.57	7.68	7.80
7.50	7.61	7.72	7.83	7.94	8.05
7.75	7.86	7.97	8.08	8.20	8.31
8.00	8.11	8.22	8.34	8.45	8.57
8.25	8.36	8.48	8.59	8.71	8.83
8.50	8.61	8.73	8.85	8.96	9.09
8.75	8.86	8.98	9.10	9.22	9.34
9.00	9.12	9.24	9.36	9.48	9.60
9.25	9.37	9.49	9.61	9.73	9.86
9.50	9.62	9.74	9.87	9.99	10.12
9.75	9.87	10.00	10.12	10.25	10.38
10.00	10.12	10.25	10.38	10.51	10.64
10.25	10.38	10.50	10.63	10.76	10.90
10.50	10.63	10.76	10.89	11.02	11.16
10.75	10.88	11.01	11.14	11.28	11.42
11.00	11.13	11.26	11.40	11.54	11.68
11.25	11.38	11.52	11.65	11.79	11.94
11.50	11.63	11.77	11.91	12.05	12.19
11.75	11.89	12.02	12.17	12.31	12.45
12.00	12.14	12.28	12.42	12.57	12.71
12.25	12.39	12.53	12.68	12.82	12.97
12.50	12.64	12.79	12.93	13.08	13.23
12.75	12.89	13.04	13.19	13.34	13.49
13.00	13.15	13.29	13.44	13.60	13.76
13.25	13.40	13.55	13.70	13.86	14.02
13.50	13.65	13.80	13.96	14.12	14.28
13.75	13.90	14.06	14.21	14.37	14.54
14.00	14.15	14.31	14.47	14.63	14.80
14.25	14.41	14.56	14.73	14.89	15.06
14.50	14.66	14.82	14.98	15.15	15.32
14.75	14.91	15.07	15.24	15.41	15.58
15.00	15.16	15.33	15.49	15.67	15.84
15.25	15.41	15.58	15.75	15.92	16.10
15.50	15.67	15.84	16.01	16.18	16.36
15.75	15.92	16.09	16.26	16.44	16.62
16.00	16.17	16.34	16.52	16.70	16.89
16.25	16.42	16.60	16.78	16.96	17.15
16.50	16.67	16.85	17.03	17.22	17.41
16.75	16.93	17.11	17.29	17.48	17.67
17.00	17.18	17.36	17.55	17.74	17.93
17.25	17.43	17.62	17.80	18.00	18.19
17.50	17.68	17.87	18.06	18.26	18.45
17.75	17.94	18.13	18.32	18.52	18.72
18.00	18.19	18.38	18.58	18.77	18.98
18.25	18.44	18.63	18.83	19.03	19.24
18.50	18.69	18.89	19.09	19.29	19.50
18.75	18.94	19.14	19.35	19.55	19.76
19.00	19.20	19.40	19.60	19.81	20.03
20.00	20.21	20.42	20.63	20.85	21.07
25.00	25.25	25.51	25.78	26.05	26.32
30.00	30.30	30.61	30.93	31.25	31.58

29 YEARS — POINTS PAID

RATE	1	2	3	4	5
0.00	.08	.14	.21	.29	.36
1.00	1.07	1.15	1.22	1.30	1.37
2.00	2.08	2.15	2.23	2.31	2.40
3.00	3.08	3.16	3.25	3.33	3.42
4.00	4.09	4.17	4.26	4.35	4.44
4.25	4.34	4.43	4.51	4.61	4.70
4.50	4.59	4.68	4.77	4.86	4.95
4.75	4.84	4.93	5.02	5.12	5.21
5.00	5.09	5.18	5.28	5.37	5.47
5.25	5.34	5.44	5.53	5.63	5.72
5.50	5.59	5.69	5.78	5.88	5.98
5.75	5.84	5.94	6.04	6.14	6.24
6.00	6.10	6.19	6.29	6.39	6.50
6.25	6.35	6.45	6.55	6.65	6.75
6.50	6.60	6.70	6.80	6.91	7.01
6.75	6.85	6.95	7.06	7.16	7.27
7.00	7.10	7.21	7.31	7.42	7.53
7.25	7.35	7.46	7.57	7.67	7.78
7.50	7.60	7.71	7.82	7.93	8.04
7.75	7.86	7.96	8.07	8.19	8.30
8.00	8.11	8.22	8.33	8.44	8.56
8.25	8.36	8.47	8.58	8.70	8.82
8.50	8.61	8.72	8.84	8.96	9.08
8.75	8.86	8.98	9.09	9.21	9.33
9.00	9.11	9.23	9.35	9.47	9.59
9.25	9.37	9.48	9.60	9.73	9.85
9.50	9.62	9.74	9.86	9.98	10.11
9.75	9.87	9.99	10.12	10.24	10.37
10.00	10.12	10.25	10.37	10.50	10.63
10.25	10.37	10.50	10.63	10.76	10.89
10.50	10.63	10.75	10.88	11.01	11.15
10.75	10.88	11.01	11.14	11.27	11.41
11.00	11.13	11.26	11.39	11.53	11.67
11.25	11.38	11.51	11.65	11.79	11.93
11.50	11.63	11.77	11.90	12.04	12.19
11.75	11.88	12.02	12.16	12.30	12.45
12.00	12.14	12.27	12.42	12.56	12.71
12.25	12.39	12.53	12.67	12.82	12.97
12.50	12.64	12.78	12.93	13.08	13.23
12.75	12.89	13.04	13.18	13.33	13.49
13.00	13.14	13.29	13.44	13.59	13.75
13.25	13.40	13.54	13.70	13.85	14.01
13.50	13.65	13.80	13.95	14.11	14.27
13.75	13.90	14.05	14.21	14.37	14.53
14.00	14.15	14.31	14.47	14.63	14.79
14.25	14.40	14.56	14.72	14.89	15.05
14.50	14.66	14.82	14.98	15.14	15.31
14.75	14.91	15.07	15.23	15.40	15.57
15.00	15.16	15.32	15.49	15.66	15.83
15.25	15.41	15.58	15.75	15.92	16.10
15.50	15.66	15.83	16.00	16.18	16.36
15.75	15.92	16.09	16.26	16.44	16.62
16.00	16.17	16.34	16.52	16.70	16.88
16.25	16.42	16.60	16.77	16.96	17.14
16.50	16.67	16.85	17.03	17.22	17.40
16.75	16.93	17.11	17.29	17.47	17.66
17.00	17.18	17.36	17.54	17.73	17.93
17.25	17.43	17.61	17.80	17.99	18.19
17.50	17.68	17.87	18.06	18.26	18.45
17.75	17.93	18.12	18.32	18.51	18.71
18.00	18.19	18.38	18.57	18.77	18.97
18.25	18.44	18.63	18.83	19.03	19.24
18.50	18.69	18.89	19.09	19.29	19.50
18.75	18.94	19.14	19.34	19.55	19.76
19.00	19.20	19.40	19.60	19.81	20.02
20.00	20.21	20.42	20.63	20.85	21.07
25.00	25.25	25.51	25.78	26.05	26.32
30.00	30.30	30.61	30.93	31.25	31.58

30 YEARS — POINTS PAID

RATE	1	2	3	4	5
0.00	.08	.14	.21	.28	.35
1.00	1.07	1.14	1.22	1.29	1.36
2.00	2.07	2.15	2.23	2.30	2.38
3.00	3.08	3.16	3.24	3.32	3.41
4.00	4.08	4.17	4.25	4.34	4.43
4.25	4.33	4.42	4.51	4.60	4.69
4.50	4.59	4.68	4.77	4.86	4.94
4.75	4.84	4.93	5.02	5.11	5.20
5.00	5.09	5.18	5.27	5.36	5.46
5.25	5.34	5.43	5.52	5.62	5.71
5.50	5.59	5.68	5.78	5.87	5.97
5.75	5.84	5.94	6.03	6.13	6.23
6.00	6.09	6.19	6.29	6.39	6.49
6.25	6.35	6.44	6.54	6.64	6.74
6.50	6.60	6.70	6.80	6.90	7.00
6.75	6.85	6.95	7.05	7.15	7.26
7.00	7.10	7.20	7.30	7.41	7.52
7.25	7.35	7.45	7.56	7.67	7.77
7.50	7.60	7.71	7.81	7.92	8.03
7.75	7.85	7.96	8.07	8.18	8.29
8.00	8.11	8.21	8.32	8.44	8.55
8.25	8.36	8.47	8.58	8.69	8.81
8.50	8.61	8.72	8.83	8.95	9.07
8.75	8.86	8.97	9.09	9.21	9.32
9.00	9.11	9.23	9.34	9.46	9.58
9.25	9.36	9.48	9.60	9.72	9.84
9.50	9.62	9.73	9.85	9.98	10.10
9.75	9.87	9.99	10.11	10.23	10.36
10.00	10.12	10.24	10.37	10.49	10.62
10.25	10.37	10.50	10.62	10.75	10.88
10.50	10.62	10.75	10.88	11.01	11.14
10.75	10.88	11.00	11.13	11.26	11.40
11.00	11.13	11.26	11.39	11.52	11.66
11.25	11.38	11.51	11.64	11.78	11.92
11.50	11.63	11.76	11.90	12.04	12.18
11.75	11.88	12.02	12.16	12.30	12.44
12.00	12.13	12.27	12.41	12.55	12.70
12.25	12.39	12.53	12.67	12.81	12.96
12.50	12.64	12.78	12.92	13.07	13.22
12.75	12.89	13.03	13.18	13.33	13.48
13.00	13.14	13.29	13.44	13.59	13.74
13.25	13.39	13.54	13.69	13.85	14.00
13.50	13.65	13.80	13.95	14.10	14.26
13.75	13.90	14.05	14.21	14.36	14.52
14.00	14.15	14.30	14.46	14.62	14.78
14.25	14.40	14.56	14.72	14.88	15.05
14.50	14.66	14.81	14.97	15.14	15.31
14.75	14.91	15.07	15.23	15.40	15.57
15.00	15.16	15.32	15.49	15.66	15.83
15.25	15.41	15.58	15.74	15.92	16.09
15.50	15.66	15.83	16.00	16.17	16.35
15.75	15.92	16.09	16.26	16.43	16.61
16.00	16.17	16.34	16.51	16.69	16.88
16.25	16.42	16.59	16.77	16.95	17.14
16.50	16.67	16.85	17.03	17.21	17.40
16.75	16.93	17.10	17.29	17.47	17.66
17.00	17.18	17.36	17.54	17.73	17.92
17.25	17.43	17.61	17.80	17.99	18.18
17.50	17.68	17.87	18.06	18.25	18.45
17.75	17.93	18.12	18.31	18.51	18.71
18.00	18.19	18.38	18.57	18.77	18.97
18.25	18.44	18.63	18.83	19.03	19.23
18.50	18.69	18.89	19.08	19.29	19.49
18.75	18.94	19.14	19.34	19.55	19.76
19.00	19.20	19.40	19.60	19.81	20.02
20.00	20.21	20.41	20.63	20.85	21.07
25.00	25.25	25.51	25.78	26.05	26.32
30.00	30.30	30.61	30.93	31.25	31.58

TABLE **7**

Scan Table

Interest Rates: 4 to 15% by 1%.

Terms: 1 to 30 years, each year.

Compound Periods: Monthly, quarterly, semiannual, annual.

This table simplifies the search for a rate, term, payment, or value by showing the range of interest rates that are covered in Table 8. The 4 compound periods in the Scan Table are shown on facing pages to show the effect of more or less frequent payments.

Description: This table shows what a single $ 1 deposit will grow to in the future. The deposit is made at the beginning of the first period.

Example: At 8 % one dollar will grow to $ 1.49 by the end of the fifth year.

MONTHLY COMPOUNDING

YEAR	4 %	5 %	6 %	7 %	8 %	9 %	10 %	11 %	12 %	13 %	14 %	15 %
1	1.04	1.05	1.06	1.07	1.08	1.09	1.10	1.12	1.13	1.14	1.15	1.16
2	1.08	1.10	1.13	1.15	1.17	1.20	1.22	1.24	1.27	1.30	1.32	1.35
3	1.13	1.16	1.20	1.23	1.27	1.31	1.35	1.39	1.43	1.47	1.52	1.56
4	1.17	1.22	1.27	1.32	1.38	1.43	1.49	1.55	1.61	1.68	1.75	1.82
5	1.22	1.28	1.35	1.42	1.49	1.57	1.65	1.73	1.82	1.91	2.01	2.11
6	1.27	1.35	1.43	1.52	1.61	1.71	1.82	1.93	2.05	2.17	2.31	2.45
7	1.32	1.42	1.52	1.63	1.75	1.87	2.01	2.15	2.31	2.47	2.65	2.84
8	1.38	1.49	1.61	1.75	1.89	2.05	2.22	2.40	2.60	2.81	3.05	3.30
9	1.43	1.57	1.71	1.87	2.05	2.24	2.45	2.68	2.93	3.20	3.50	3.83
10	1.49	1.65	1.82	2.01	2.22	2.45	2.71	2.99	3.30	3.64	4.02	4.44
11	1.55	1.73	1.93	2.15	2.40	2.68	2.99	3.34	3.72	4.15	4.62	5.15
12	1.61	1.82	2.05	2.31	2.60	2.93	3.30	3.72	4.19	4.72	5.31	5.98
13	1.68	1.91	2.18	2.48	2.82	3.21	3.65	4.15	4.72	5.37	6.11	6.94
14	1.75	2.01	2.31	2.66	3.05	3.51	4.03	4.63	5.32	6.11	7.02	8.06
15	1.82	2.11	2.45	2.85	3.31	3.84	4.45	5.17	6.00	6.96	8.07	9.36
16	1.89	2.22	2.61	3.05	3.58	4.20	4.92	5.77	6.76	7.92	9.27	10.86
17	1.97	2.34	2.77	3.28	3.88	4.59	5.44	6.43	7.61	9.01	10.66	12.61
18	2.05	2.46	2.94	3.51	4.20	5.02	6.00	7.18	8.58	10.25	12.25	14.63
19	2.14	2.58	3.12	3.77	4.55	5.49	6.63	8.01	9.67	11.67	14.08	16.99
20	2.22	2.71	3.31	4.04	4.93	6.01	7.33	8.94	10.89	13.28	16.18	19.72
21	2.31	2.85	3.51	4.33	5.34	6.57	8.10	9.97	12.27	15.11	18.60	22.88
22	2.41	3.00	3.73	4.64	5.78	7.19	8.94	11.12	13.83	17.20	21.37	26.56
23	2.51	3.15	3.96	4.98	6.26	7.86	9.88	12.41	15.58	19.57	24.57	30.83
24	2.61	3.31	4.21	5.34	6.78	8.60	10.91	13.85	17.56	22.27	28.23	35.79
25	2.71	3.48	4.46	5.73	7.34	9.41	12.06	15.45	19.79	25.34	32.45	41.54
26	2.82	3.66	4.74	6.14	7.95	10.29	13.32	17.24	22.30	28.84	37.30	48.22
27	2.94	3.85	5.03	6.58	8.61	11.26	14.71	19.23	25.13	32.82	42.87	55.97
28	3.06	4.04	5.34	7.06	9.32	12.31	16.25	21.46	28.31	37.35	49.27	64.97
29	3.18	4.25	5.67	7.57	10.10	13.47	17.96	23.94	31.90	42.51	56.63	75.42
30	3.31	4.47	6.02	8.12	10.94	14.73	19.84	26.71	35.95	48.38	65.08	87.54

QUARTERLY COMPOUNDING

YEAR	4 %	5 %	6 %	7 %	8 %	9 %	10 %	11 %	12 %	13 %	14 %	15 %
1	1.04	1.05	1.06	1.07	1.08	1.09	1.10	1.11	1.13	1.14	1.15	1.16
2	1.08	1.10	1.13	1.15	1.17	1.19	1.22	1.24	1.27	1.29	1.32	1.34
3	1.13	1.16	1.20	1.23	1.27	1.31	1.34	1.38	1.43	1.47	1.51	1.56
4	1.17	1.22	1.27	1.32	1.37	1.43	1.48	1.54	1.60	1.67	1.73	1.80
5	1.22	1.28	1.35	1.41	1.49	1.56	1.64	1.72	1.81	1.90	1.99	2.09
6	1.27	1.35	1.43	1.52	1.61	1.71	1.81	1.92	2.03	2.15	2.28	2.42
7	1.32	1.42	1.52	1.63	1.74	1.86	2.00	2.14	2.29	2.45	2.62	2.80
8	1.37	1.49	1.61	1.74	1.88	2.04	2.20	2.38	2.58	2.78	3.01	3.25
9	1.43	1.56	1.71	1.87	2.04	2.23	2.43	2.66	2.90	3.16	3.45	3.76
10	1.49	1.64	1.81	2.00	2.21	2.44	2.69	2.96	3.26	3.59	3.96	4.36
11	1.55	1.73	1.93	2.15	2.39	2.66	2.96	3.30	3.67	4.08	4.54	5.05
12	1.61	1.82	2.04	2.30	2.59	2.91	3.27	3.68	4.13	4.64	5.21	5.85
13	1.68	1.91	2.17	2.46	2.80	3.18	3.61	4.10	4.65	5.28	5.98	6.78
14	1.75	2.01	2.30	2.64	3.03	3.48	3.99	4.57	5.23	6.00	6.87	7.86
15	1.82	2.11	2.44	2.83	3.28	3.80	4.40	5.09	5.89	6.81	7.88	9.11
16	1.89	2.21	2.59	3.04	3.55	4.15	4.86	5.68	6.63	7.74	9.04	10.55
17	1.97	2.33	2.75	3.25	3.84	4.54	5.36	6.33	7.46	8.80	10.37	12.22
18	2.05	2.45	2.92	3.49	4.16	4.96	5.92	7.05	8.40	10.00	11.90	14.16
19	2.13	2.57	3.10	3.74	4.50	5.43	6.53	7.86	9.45	11.37	13.66	16.41
20	2.22	2.70	3.29	4.01	4.88	5.93	7.21	8.76	10.64	12.92	15.68	19.01
21	2.31	2.84	3.49	4.29	5.28	6.48	7.96	9.77	11.98	14.68	17.99	22.03
22	2.40	2.98	3.71	4.60	5.71	7.09	8.78	10.88	13.48	16.68	20.64	25.52
23	2.50	3.14	3.93	4.93	6.18	7.75	9.70	12.13	15.17	18.96	23.69	29.57
24	2.60	3.30	4.18	5.29	6.69	8.47	10.70	13.52	17.08	21.55	27.18	34.27
25	2.70	3.46	4.43	5.67	7.24	9.25	11.81	15.07	19.22	24.49	31.19	39.70
26	2.81	3.64	4.70	6.08	7.84	10.12	13.04	16.80	21.63	27.83	35.79	46.00
27	2.93	3.83	4.99	6.51	8.49	11.06	14.39	18.73	24.35	31.63	41.07	53.30
28	3.05	4.02	5.30	6.98	9.19	12.09	15.89	20.87	27.40	35.95	47.13	61.75
29	3.17	4.22	5.62	7.48	9.95	13.21	17.54	23.26	30.84	40.86	54.09	71.55
30	3.30	4.44	5.97	8.02	10.77	14.44	19.36	25.93	34.71	46.43	62.06	82.90

Description: This table shows what a single $ 1 deposit will grow to in the future. The deposit is made at the beginning of the first period.

Example: At 8 % one dollar will grow to $ 1.48 by the end of the fifth year.

SEMIANNUAL COMPOUNDING

YEAR	4 %	5 %	6 %	7 %	8 %	9 %	10 %	11 %	12 %	13 %	14 %	15 %
1	1.04	1.05	1.06	1.07	1.08	1.09	1.10	1.11	1.12	1.13	1.14	1.16
2	1.08	1.10	1.13	1.15	1.17	1.19	1.22	1.24	1.26	1.29	1.31	1.34
3	1.13	1.16	1.19	1.23	1.27	1.30	1.34	1.38	1.42	1.46	1.50	1.54
4	1.17	1.22	1.27	1.32	1.37	1.42	1.48	1.53	1.59	1.65	1.72	1.78
5	1.22	1.28	1.34	1.41	1.48	1.55	1.63	1.71	1.79	1.88	1.97	2.06
6	1.27	1.34	1.43	1.51	1.60	1.70	1.80	1.90	2.01	2.13	2.25	2.38
7	1.32	1.41	1.51	1.62	1.73	1.85	1.98	2.12	2.26	2.41	2.58	2.75
8	1.37	1.48	1.60	1.73	1.87	2.02	2.18	2.36	2.54	2.74	2.95	3.18
9	1.43	1.56	1.70	1.86	2.03	2.21	2.41	2.62	2.85	3.11	3.38	3.68
10	1.49	1.64	1.81	1.99	2.19	2.41	2.65	2.92	3.21	3.52	3.87	4.25
11	1.55	1.72	1.92	2.13	2.37	2.63	2.93	3.25	3.60	4.00	4.43	4.91
12	1.61	1.81	2.03	2.28	2.56	2.88	3.23	3.61	4.05	4.53	5.07	5.67
13	1.67	1.90	2.16	2.45	2.77	3.14	3.56	4.02	4.55	5.14	5.81	6.56
14	1.74	2.00	2.29	2.62	3.00	3.43	3.92	4.48	5.11	5.83	6.65	7.58
15	1.81	2.10	2.43	2.81	3.24	3.75	4.32	4.98	5.74	6.61	7.61	8.75
16	1.88	2.20	2.58	3.01	3.51	4.09	4.76	5.55	6.45	7.50	8.72	10.12
17	1.96	2.32	2.73	3.22	3.79	4.47	5.25	6.17	7.25	8.51	9.98	11.69
18	2.04	2.43	2.90	3.45	4.10	4.88	5.79	6.87	8.15	9.65	11.42	13.51
19	2.12	2.56	3.07	3.70	4.44	5.33	6.39	7.65	9.15	10.95	13.08	15.61
20	2.21	2.69	3.26	3.96	4.80	5.82	7.04	8.51	10.29	12.42	14.97	18.04
21	2.30	2.82	3.46	4.24	5.19	6.35	7.76	9.48	11.56	14.08	17.14	20.85
22	2.39	2.96	3.67	4.54	5.62	6.94	8.56	10.55	12.99	15.97	19.63	24.10
23	2.49	3.11	3.90	4.87	6.07	7.57	9.43	11.74	14.59	18.12	22.47	27.85
24	2.59	3.27	4.13	5.21	6.57	8.27	10.40	13.07	16.39	20.55	25.73	32.18
25	2.69	3.44	4.38	5.58	7.11	9.03	11.47	14.54	18.42	23.31	29.46	37.19
26	2.80	3.61	4.65	5.98	7.69	9.86	12.64	16.19	20.70	26.44	33.73	42.98
27	2.91	3.79	4.93	6.41	8.31	10.77	13.94	18.01	23.26	29.98	38.61	49.67
28	3.03	3.99	5.23	6.87	8.99	11.76	15.37	20.05	26.13	34.01	44.21	57.39
29	3.15	4.19	5.55	7.35	9.73	12.85	16.94	22.32	29.36	38.57	50.61	66.33
30	3.28	4.40	5.89	7.88	10.52	14.03	18.68	24.84	32.99	43.75	57.95	76.65

ANNUAL COMPOUNDING

YEAR	4 %	5 %	6 %	7 %	8 %	9 %	10 %	11 %	12 %	13 %	14 %	15 %
1	1.04	1.05	1.06	1.07	1.08	1.09	1.10	1.11	1.12	1.13	1.14	1.15
2	1.08	1.10	1.12	1.14	1.17	1.19	1.21	1.23	1.25	1.28	1.30	1.32
3	1.12	1.16	1.19	1.23	1.26	1.30	1.33	1.37	1.40	1.44	1.48	1.52
4	1.17	1.22	1.26	1.31	1.36	1.41	1.46	1.52	1.57	1.63	1.69	1.75
5	1.22	1.28	1.34	1.40	1.47	1.54	1.61	1.69	1.76	1.84	1.93	2.01
6	1.27	1.34	1.42	1.50	1.59	1.68	1.77	1.87	1.97	2.08	2.19	2.31
7	1.32	1.41	1.50	1.61	1.71	1.83	1.95	2.08	2.21	2.35	2.50	2.66
8	1.37	1.48	1.59	1.72	1.85	1.99	2.14	2.30	2.48	2.66	2.85	3.06
9	1.42	1.55	1.69	1.84	2.00	2.17	2.36	2.56	2.77	3.00	3.25	3.52
10	1.48	1.63	1.79	1.97	2.16	2.37	2.59	2.84	3.11	3.39	3.71	4.05
11	1.54	1.71	1.90	2.10	2.33	2.58	2.85	3.15	3.48	3.84	4.23	4.65
12	1.60	1.80	2.01	2.25	2.52	2.81	3.14	3.50	3.90	4.33	4.82	5.35
13	1.67	1.89	2.13	2.41	2.72	3.07	3.45	3.88	4.36	4.90	5.49	6.15
14	1.73	1.98	2.26	2.58	2.94	3.34	3.80	4.31	4.89	5.53	6.26	7.08
15	1.80	2.08	2.40	2.76	3.17	3.64	4.18	4.78	5.47	6.25	7.14	8.14
16	1.87	2.18	2.54	2.95	3.43	3.97	4.59	5.31	6.13	7.07	8.14	9.36
17	1.95	2.29	2.69	3.16	3.70	4.33	5.05	5.90	6.87	7.99	9.28	10.76
18	2.03	2.41	2.85	3.38	4.00	4.72	5.56	6.54	7.69	9.02	10.58	12.38
19	2.11	2.53	3.03	3.62	4.32	5.14	6.12	7.26	8.61	10.20	12.06	14.23
20	2.19	2.65	3.21	3.87	4.66	5.60	6.73	8.06	9.65	11.52	13.74	16.37
21	2.28	2.79	3.40	4.14	5.03	6.11	7.40	8.95	10.80	13.02	15.67	18.82
22	2.37	2.93	3.60	4.43	5.44	6.66	8.14	9.93	12.10	14.71	17.86	21.64
23	2.46	3.07	3.82	4.74	5.87	7.26	8.95	11.03	13.55	16.63	20.36	24.89
24	2.56	3.23	4.05	5.07	6.34	7.91	9.85	12.24	15.18	18.79	23.21	28.63
25	2.67	3.39	4.29	5.43	6.85	8.62	10.83	13.59	17.00	21.23	26.46	32.92
26	2.77	3.56	4.55	5.81	7.40	9.40	11.92	15.08	19.04	23.99	30.17	37.86
27	2.88	3.73	4.82	6.21	7.99	10.25	13.11	16.74	21.32	27.11	34.39	43.54
28	3.00	3.92	5.11	6.65	8.63	11.17	14.42	18.58	23.88	30.63	39.20	50.07
29	3.12	4.12	5.42	7.11	9.32	12.17	15.86	20.62	26.75	34.62	44.69	57.58
30	3.24	4.32	5.74	7.61	10.06	13.27	17.45	22.89	29.96	39.12	50.95	66.21

SCAN TABLE

AMOUNT OF 1 PER PERIOD

Description: This table shows what a series of $ 1 deposits will grow to in the future. A deposit is made at the end of each period.

Example: At 8 % a regular one dollar deposit will grow to $ 73.48 by the end of the fifth year.

MONTHLY COMPOUNDING

YEAR	4 %	5 %	6 %	7 %	8 %	9 %	10 %	11 %	12 %	13 %	14 %	15 %
1	12.22	12.28	12.34	12.39	12.45	12.51	12.57	12.62	12.68	12.74	12.80	12.86
2	24.94	25.19	25.43	25.68	25.93	26.19	26.45	26.71	26.97	27.24	27.51	27.79
3	38.18	38.75	39.34	39.93	40.54	41.15	41.78	42.42	43.08	43.74	44.42	45.12
4	51.96	53.01	54.10	55.21	56.35	57.52	58.72	59.96	61.22	62.52	63.86	65.23
5	66.30	68.01	69.77	71.59	73.48	75.42	77.44	79.52	81.67	83.89	86.20	88.57
6	81.22	83.76	86.41	89.16	92.03	95.01	98.11	101.34	104.71	108.22	111.87	115.67
7	96.75	100.33	104.07	108.00	112.11	116.43	120.95	125.69	130.67	135.89	141.38	147.13
8	112.92	117.74	122.83	128.20	133.87	139.86	146.18	152.86	159.93	167.39	175.29	183.64
9	129.74	136.04	142.74	149.86	157.43	165.48	174.05	183.18	192.89	203.24	214.27	226.02
10	147.25	155.28	163.88	173.08	182.95	193.51	204.84	217.00	230.04	244.04	259.07	275.22
11	165.47	175.51	186.32	197.99	210.58	224.17	238.86	254.73	271.90	290.46	310.56	332.32
12	184.44	196.76	210.15	224.69	240.51	257.71	276.44	296.83	319.06	343.30	369.74	398.60
13	204.17	219.11	235.45	253.33	272.92	294.39	317.95	343.81	372.21	403.43	437.76	475.54
14	224.71	242.60	262.30	284.04	308.02	334.52	363.81	396.22	432.10	471.85	515.93	564.85
15	246.09	267.29	290.82	316.96	346.04	378.41	414.47	454.69	499.58	549.73	605.79	668.51
16	268.34	293.24	321.09	352.27	387.21	426.41	470.44	519.93	575.62	638.35	709.06	788.83
17	291.49	320.52	353.23	390.13	431.80	478.92	532.26	592.72	661.31	739.20	827.75	928.50
18	315.59	349.20	387.35	430.72	480.09	536.35	600.56	673.93	757.86	853.98	964.17	1090.62
19	340.67	379.35	423.58	474.25	532.38	599.17	676.02	764.54	866.60	984.59	1120.96	1278.81
20	366.77	411.03	462.04	520.93	589.02	667.89	759.37	865.64	989.26	1133.24	1301.17	1497.24
21	393.94	444.34	502.87	570.98	650.36	743.05	851.45	978.43	1127.40	1302.41	1508.29	1750.79
22	422.21	479.35	546.23	624.65	716.79	825.26	953.17	1104.28	1283.07	1494.92	1746.34	2045.10
23	451.64	516.16	592.25	682.19	788.73	915.18	1065.55	1244.69	1458.47	1714.01	2019.94	2386.71
24	482.26	554.84	641.12	743.90	866.65	1013.54	1189.69	1401.35	1656.13	1963.34	2334.40	2783.25
25	514.13	595.51	692.99	810.07	951.03	1121.12	1326.83	1576.13	1878.85	2247.09	2695.83	3243.53
26	547.30	638.26	748.02	881.02	1042.41	1238.80	1478.34	1771.15	2129.81	2570.00	3111.23	3777.80
27	581.82	683.19	806.55	957.11	1141.38	1367.51	1645.70	1988.72	2412.61	2937.49	3588.67	4397.96
28	617.75	730.42	868.63	1038.69	1248.56	1508.30	1830.59	2231.48	2731.27	3355.70	4137.40	5117.81
29	655.14	780.07	934.54	1126.17	1364.64	1662.30	2034.85	2502.33	3090.35	3831.64	4768.09	5953.39
30	694.05	832.26	1004.52	1219.97	1490.36	1830.74	2260.49	2804.52	3494.96	4373.27	5492.97	6923.28

QUARTERLY COMPOUNDING

YEAR	4 %	5 %	6 %	7 %	8 %	9 %	10 %	11 %	12 %	13 %	14 %	15 %
1	4.06	4.08	4.09	4.11	4.12	4.14	4.15	4.17	4.18	4.20	4.21	4.23
2	8.29	8.36	8.43	8.51	8.58	8.66	8.74	8.81	8.89	8.97	9.05	9.13
3	12.68	12.86	13.04	13.23	13.41	13.60	13.80	13.99	14.19	14.40	14.60	14.81
4	17.26	17.59	17.93	18.28	18.64	19.01	19.38	19.76	20.16	20.56	20.97	21.39
5	22.02	22.56	23.12	23.70	24.30	24.91	25.54	26.20	26.87	27.56	28.28	29.02
6	26.97	27.79	28.63	29.51	30.42	31.37	32.35	33.37	34.43	35.53	36.67	37.85
7	32.13	33.28	34.48	35.74	37.05	38.42	39.86	41.36	42.93	44.57	46.29	48.09
8	37.49	39.05	40.69	42.41	44.23	46.14	48.15	50.27	52.50	54.86	57.33	59.95
9	43.08	45.12	47.28	49.57	51.99	54.57	57.30	60.20	63.28	66.54	70.01	73.69
10	48.89	51.49	54.27	57.23	60.40	63.79	67.40	71.27	75.40	79.82	84.55	89.61
11	54.93	58.19	61.69	65.45	69.50	73.86	78.55	83.61	89.05	94.91	101.24	108.06
12	61.22	65.23	69.57	74.26	79.35	84.87	90.86	97.36	104.41	112.07	120.39	129.43
13	67.77	72.63	77.92	83.71	90.02	96.91	104.44	112.68	121.70	131.56	142.36	154.20
14	74.58	80.40	86.80	93.83	101.56	110.07	119.44	129.77	141.15	153.72	167.58	182.89
15	81.67	88.57	96.21	104.68	114.05	124.45	135.99	148.81	163.05	178.89	196.52	216.14
16	89.05	97.16	106.21	116.30	127.57	140.17	154.26	170.03	187.70	207.51	229.72	254.66
17	96.72	106.19	116.82	128.77	142.21	157.36	174.43	193.69	215.44	240.03	267.83	299.29
18	104.71	115.67	128.08	142.13	158.06	176.14	196.69	220.06	246.67	276.98	311.55	351.00
19	113.02	125.64	140.03	156.45	175.21	196.67	221.26	249.45	281.81	318.98	361.73	410.92
20	121.67	136.12	152.71	171.79	193.77	219.12	248.38	282.21	321.36	366.72	419.31	480.34
21	130.67	147.13	166.17	188.24	213.87	243.65	278.32	318.73	365.88	420.96	485.38	560.78
22	140.04	158.70	180.46	205.88	235.62	270.47	311.37	359.43	415.99	482.61	561.20	653.98
23	149.79	170.86	195.63	224.78	259.16	299.78	347.84	404.80	472.38	552.68	648.20	761.97
24	159.93	183.64	211.72	245.04	284.65	331.82	388.11	455.36	535.85	632.31	748.04	887.08
25	170.48	197.07	228.80	266.75	312.23	366.85	432.55	511.72	607.29	722.80	862.61	1032.05
26	181.46	211.19	246.93	290.03	342.09	405.13	481.61	574.55	687.69	825.64	994.08	1200.01
27	192.89	226.02	266.18	314.97	374.41	446.98	535.75	644.57	778.19	942.52	1144.95	1394.63
28	204.79	241.61	286.60	341.71	409.40	492.72	595.53	722.62	880.04	1075.35	1318.07	1620.12
29	217.16	258.00	308.28	370.38	447.27	542.72	661.50	809.62	994.68	1226.31	1516.73	1881.38
30	230.04	275.22	331.29	401.10	488.26	597.38	734.33	906.58	1123.70	1397.87	1744.69	2184.09

Description: This table shows what a series of $ 1 deposits will grow to in the future. A deposit is made at the end of each period.

Example: At 8 % a regular one dollar deposit will grow to $ 12.01 by the end of the fifth year.

SEMIANNUAL COMPOUNDING

YEAR	4 %	5 %	6 %	7 %	8 %	9 %	10 %	11 %	12 %	13 %	14 %	15 %
1	2.02	2.03	2.03	2.04	2.04	2.05	2.05	2.06	2.06	2.07	2.07	2.08
2	4.12	4.15	4.18	4.21	4.25	4.28	4.31	4.34	4.37	4.41	4.44	4.47
3	6.31	6.39	6.47	6.55	6.63	6.72	6.80	6.89	6.98	7.06	7.15	7.24
4	8.58	8.74	8.89	9.05	9.21	9.38	9.55	9.72	9.90	10.08	10.26	10.45
5	10.95	11.20	11.46	11.73	12.01	12.29	12.58	12.88	13.18	13.49	13.82	14.15
6	13.41	13.80	14.19	14.60	15.03	15.46	15.92	16.39	16.87	17.37	17.89	18.42
7	15.97	16.52	17.09	17.68	18.29	18.93	19.60	20.29	21.02	21.77	22.55	23.37
8	18.64	19.38	20.16	20.97	21.82	22.72	23.66	24.64	25.67	26.75	27.89	29.08
9	21.41	22.39	23.41	24.50	25.65	26.86	28.13	29.48	30.91	32.41	34.00	35.68
10	24.30	25.54	26.87	28.28	29.78	31.37	33.07	34.87	36.79	38.83	41.00	43.30
11	27.30	28.86	30.54	32.33	34.25	36.30	38.51	40.86	43.39	46.10	49.01	52.12
12	30.42	32.35	34.43	36.67	39.08	41.69	44.50	47.54	50.82	54.35	58.18	62.30
13	33.67	36.01	38.55	41.31	44.31	47.57	51.11	54.97	59.16	63.72	68.68	74.08
14	37.05	39.86	42.93	46.29	49.97	53.99	58.40	63.23	68.53	74.33	80.70	87.68
15	40.57	43.90	47.58	51.62	56.08	61.01	66.44	72.44	79.06	86.37	94.46	103.40
16	44.23	48.15	52.50	57.33	62.70	68.67	75.30	82.68	90.89	100.03	110.22	121.57
17	48.03	52.61	57.73	63.45	69.86	77.03	85.07	94.08	104.18	115.53	128.26	142.56
18	51.99	57.30	63.28	70.01	77.60	86.16	95.84	106.77	119.12	133.10	148.91	166.82
19	56.11	62.23	69.16	77.03	85.97	96.14	107.71	120.89	135.90	153.03	172.56	194.86
20	60.40	67.40	75.40	84.55	95.03	107.03	120.80	136.61	154.76	175.63	199.64	227.26
21	64.86	72.84	82.02	92.61	104.82	118.92	135.23	154.10	175.95	201.27	230.63	264.70
22	69.50	78.55	89.05	101.24	115.41	131.91	151.14	173.57	199.76	230.35	266.12	307.97
23	74.33	84.55	96.50	110.48	126.87	146.10	168.69	195.25	226.51	263.34	306.75	357.97
24	79.35	90.86	104.41	120.39	139.26	161.59	188.03	219.37	256.56	300.75	353.27	415.75
25	84.58	97.48	112.80	131.00	152.67	178.50	209.35	246.22	290.34	343.18	406.53	482.53
26	90.02	104.44	121.70	142.36	167.16	196.97	232.86	276.10	328.28	391.31	467.50	559.70
27	95.67	111.76	131.14	154.54	182.85	217.15	258.77	309.36	370.92	445.90	537.32	648.88
28	101.56	119.44	141.15	167.58	199.81	239.17	287.35	346.38	418.82	507.81	617.24	751.93
29	107.68	127.51	151.78	181.55	218.15	263.23	318.85	387.59	472.65	578.04	708.75	871.03
30	114.05	135.99	163.05	196.52	237.99	289.50	353.58	433.45	533.13	657.69	813.52	1008.66

ANNUAL COMPOUNDING

YEAR	4 %	5 %	6 %	7 %	8 %	9 %	10 %	11 %	12 %	13 %	14 %	15 %
1	1.00	1.00	1.00	1.00	1.00	1.00	1.00	1.00	1.00	1.00	1.00	1.00
2	2.04	2.05	2.06	2.07	2.08	2.09	2.10	2.11	2.12	2.13	2.14	2.15
3	3.12	3.15	3.18	3.21	3.25	3.28	3.31	3.34	3.37	3.41	3.44	3.47
4	4.25	4.31	4.37	4.44	4.51	4.57	4.64	4.71	4.78	4.85	4.92	4.99
5	5.42	5.53	5.64	5.75	5.87	5.98	6.11	6.23	6.35	6.48	6.61	6.74
6	6.63	6.80	6.98	7.15	7.34	7.52	7.72	7.91	8.12	8.32	8.54	8.75
7	7.90	8.14	8.39	8.65	8.92	9.20	9.49	9.78	10.09	10.40	10.73	11.07
8	9.21	9.55	9.90	10.26	10.64	11.03	11.44	11.86	12.30	12.76	13.23	13.73
9	10.58	11.03	11.49	11.98	12.49	13.02	13.58	14.16	14.78	15.42	16.09	16.79
10	12.01	12.58	13.18	13.82	14.49	15.19	15.94	16.72	17.55	18.42	19.34	20.30
11	13.49	14.21	14.97	15.78	16.65	17.56	18.53	19.56	20.65	21.81	23.04	24.35
12	15.03	15.92	16.87	17.89	18.98	20.14	21.38	22.71	24.13	25.65	27.27	29.00
13	16.63	17.71	18.88	20.14	21.50	22.95	24.52	26.21	28.03	29.98	32.09	34.35
14	18.29	19.60	21.02	22.55	24.21	26.02	27.97	30.09	32.39	34.88	37.58	40.50
15	20.02	21.58	23.28	25.13	27.15	29.36	31.77	34.41	37.28	40.42	43.84	47.58
16	21.82	23.66	25.67	27.89	30.32	33.00	35.95	39.19	42.75	46.67	50.98	55.72
17	23.70	25.84	28.21	30.84	33.75	36.97	40.54	44.50	48.88	53.74	59.12	65.08
18	25.65	28.13	30.91	34.00	37.45	41.30	45.60	50.40	55.75	61.73	68.39	75.84
19	27.67	30.54	33.76	37.38	41.45	46.02	51.16	56.94	63.44	70.75	78.97	88.21
20	29.78	33.07	36.79	41.00	45.76	51.16	57.27	64.20	72.05	80.95	91.02	102.44
21	31.97	35.72	39.99	44.87	50.42	56.76	64.00	72.27	81.70	92.47	104.77	118.81
22	34.25	38.51	43.39	49.01	55.46	62.87	71.40	81.21	92.50	105.49	120.44	137.63
23	36.62	41.43	47.00	53.44	60.89	69.53	79.54	91.15	104.60	120.20	138.30	159.28
24	39.08	44.50	50.82	58.18	66.76	76.79	88.50	102.17	118.16	136.83	158.66	184.17
25	41.65	47.73	54.86	63.25	73.11	84.70	98.35	114.41	133.33	155.62	181.87	212.79
26	44.31	51.11	59.16	68.68	79.95	93.32	109.18	128.00	150.33	176.85	208.33	245.71
27	47.08	54.67	63.71	74.48	87.35	102.72	121.10	143.08	169.37	200.84	238.50	283.57
28	49.97	58.40	68.53	80.70	95.34	112.97	134.21	159.82	190.70	227.95	272.89	327.10
29	52.97	62.32	73.64	87.35	103.97	124.14	148.63	178.40	214.58	258.58	312.09	377.17
30	56.08	66.44	79.06	94.46	113.28	136.31	164.49	199.02	241.33	293.20	356.79	434.75

SCAN TABLE

SINKING FUND PAYMENT

Description: This table shows the amount to be deposited at the end of each period that will grow to $ 1 in the future.

Example: At 8 % a regular deposit of $ 136.10 will grow to $ 10,000 by the end of the fifth year.

MONTHLY COMPOUNDING

YEAR	4 %	5 %	6 %	7 %	8 %	9 %	10 %	11 %	12 %	13 %	14 %	15 %
1	.0818	.0814	.0811	.0807	.0803	.0800	.0796	.0792	.0788	.0785	.0781	.0778
2	.0401	.0397	.0393	.0389	.0386	.0382	.0378	.0374	.0371	.0367	.0363	.0360
3	.0262	.0258	.0254	.0250	.0247	.0243	.0239	.0236	.0232	.0229	.0225	.0222
4	.0192	.0189	.0185	.0181	.0177	.0174	.0170	.0167	.0163	.0160	.0157	.0153
5	.0151	.0147	.0143	.0140	.0136	.0133	.0129	.0126	.0122	.0119	.0116	.0113
6	.0123	.0119	.0116	.0112	.0109	.0105	.0102	.0099	.0096	.0092	.0089	.0086
7	.0103	.0100	.0096	.0093	.0089	.0086	.0083	.0080	.0077	.0074	.0071	.0068
8	.0089	.0085	.0081	.0078	.0075	.0072	.0068	.0065	.0063	.0060	.0057	.0054
9	.0077	.0074	.0070	.0067	.0064	.0060	.0057	.0055	.0052	.0049	.0047	.0044
10	.0068	.0064	.0061	.0058	.0055	.0052	.0049	.0046	.0043	.0041	.0039	.0036
11	.0060	.0057	.0054	.0051	.0047	.0045	.0042	.0039	.0037	.0034	.0032	.0030
12	.0054	.0051	.0048	.0045	.0042	.0039	.0036	.0034	.0031	.0029	.0027	.0025
13	.0049	.0046	.0042	.0039	.0037	.0034	.0031	.0029	.0027	.0025	.0023	.0021
14	.0045	.0041	.0038	.0035	.0032	.0030	.0027	.0025	.0023	.0021	.0019	.0018
15	.0041	.0037	.0034	.0032	.0029	.0026	.0024	.0022	.0020	.0018	.0017	.0015
16	.0037	.0034	.0031	.0028	.0026	.0023	.0021	.0019	.0017	.0016	.0014	.0013
17	.0034	.0031	.0028	.0026	.0023	.0021	.0019	.0017	.0015	.0014	.0012	.0011
18	.0032	.0029	.0026	.0023	.0021	.0019	.0017	.0015	.0013	.0012	.0010	.0009
19	.0029	.0026	.0024	.0021	.0019	.0017	.0015	.0013	.0012	.0010	.0009	.0008
20	.0027	.0024	.0022	.0019	.0017	.0015	.0013	.0012	.0010	.0009	.0008	.0007
21	.0025	.0023	.0020	.0018	.0015	.0013	.0012	.0010	.0009	.0008	.0007	.0006
22	.0024	.0021	.0018	.0016	.0014	.0012	.0010	.0009	.0008	.0007	.0006	.0005
23	.0022	.0019	.0017	.0015	.0013	.0011	.0009	.0008	.0007	.0006	.0005	.0004
24	.0021	.0018	.0016	.0013	.0012	.0010	.0008	.0007	.0006	.0005	.0005	.0004
25	.0019	.0017	.0014	.0012	.0011	.0009	.0008	.0006	.0005	.0004	.0004	.0003
26	.0018	.0016	.0013	.0011	.0010	.0008	.0007	.0006	.0005	.0004	.0003	.0003
27	.0017	.0015	.0012	.0010	.0009	.0007	.0006	.0005	.0004	.0003	.0003	.0002
28	.0016	.0014	.0012	.0010	.0008	.0007	.0005	.0004	.0004	.0003	.0002	.0002
29	.0015	.0013	.0011	.0009	.0007	.0006	.0005	.0004	.0003	.0003	.0002	.0002
30	.0014	.0012	.0010	.0008	.0007	.0005	.0004	.0004	.0003	.0002	.0002	.0001

QUARTERLY COMPOUNDING

YEAR	4 %	5 %	6 %	7 %	8 %	9 %	10 %	11 %	12 %	13 %	14 %	15 %
1	.2463	.2454	.2444	.2435	.2426	.2417	.2408	.2399	.2390	.2381	.2373	.2364
2	.1207	.1196	.1186	.1175	.1165	.1155	.1145	.1135	.1125	.1115	.1105	.1095
3	.0788	.0778	.0767	.0756	.0746	.0735	.0725	.0715	.0705	.0695	.0685	.0675
4	.0579	.0568	.0558	.0547	.0537	.0526	.0516	.0506	.0496	.0486	.0477	.0467
5	.0454	.0443	.0432	.0422	.0412	.0401	.0391	.0382	.0372	.0363	.0354	.0345
6	.0371	.0360	.0349	.0339	.0329	.0319	.0309	.0300	.0290	.0281	.0273	.0264
7	.0311	.0300	.0290	.0280	.0270	.0260	.0251	.0242	.0233	.0224	.0216	.0208
8	.0267	.0256	.0246	.0236	.0226	.0217	.0208	.0199	.0190	.0182	.0174	.0167
9	.0232	.0222	.0212	.0202	.0192	.0183	.0175	.0166	.0158	.0150	.0143	.0136
10	.0205	.0194	.0184	.0175	.0166	.0157	.0148	.0140	.0133	.0125	.0118	.0112
11	.0182	.0172	.0162	.0153	.0144	.0135	.0127	.0120	.0112	.0105	.0099	.0093
12	.0163	.0153	.0144	.0135	.0126	.0118	.0110	.0103	.0096	.0089	.0083	.0077
13	.0148	.0138	.0128	.0119	.0111	.0103	.0096	.0089	.0082	.0076	.0070	.0065
14	.0134	.0124	.0115	.0107	.0098	.0091	.0084	.0077	.0071	.0065	.0060	.0055
15	.0122	.0113	.0104	.0096	.0088	.0080	.0074	.0067	.0061	.0056	.0051	.0046
16	.0112	.0103	.0094	.0086	.0078	.0071	.0065	.0059	.0053	.0048	.0044	.0039
17	.0103	.0094	.0086	.0078	.0070	.0064	.0057	.0052	.0046	.0042	.0037	.0033
18	.0096	.0086	.0078	.0070	.0063	.0057	.0051	.0045	.0041	.0036	.0032	.0028
19	.0088	.0080	.0071	.0064	.0057	.0051	.0045	.0040	.0035	.0031	.0028	.0024
20	.0082	.0073	.0065	.0058	.0052	.0046	.0040	.0035	.0031	.0027	.0024	.0021
21	.0077	.0068	.0060	.0053	.0047	.0041	.0036	.0031	.0027	.0024	.0021	.0018
22	.0071	.0063	.0055	.0049	.0042	.0037	.0032	.0028	.0024	.0021	.0018	.0015
23	.0067	.0059	.0051	.0044	.0039	.0033	.0029	.0025	.0021	.0018	.0015	.0013
24	.0063	.0054	.0047	.0041	.0035	.0030	.0026	.0022	.0019	.0016	.0013	.0011
25	.0059	.0051	.0044	.0037	.0032	.0027	.0023	.0020	.0016	.0014	.0012	.0010
26	.0055	.0047	.0040	.0034	.0029	.0025	.0021	.0017	.0015	.0012	.0010	.0008
27	.0052	.0044	.0038	.0032	.0027	.0022	.0019	.0016	.0013	.0011	.0009	.0007
28	.0049	.0041	.0035	.0029	.0024	.0020	.0017	.0014	.0011	.0009	.0008	.0006
29	.0046	.0039	.0032	.0027	.0022	.0018	.0015	.0012	.0010	.0008	.0007	.0005
30	.0043	.0036	.0030	.0025	.0020	.0017	.0014	.0011	.0009	.0007	.0006	.0005

Description: This table shows the amount to be deposited at the end of each period that will grow to $ 1 in the future.

Example: At 8 % a regular deposit of $ 832.91 will grow to $ 10,000 by the end of the fifth year.

SEMIANNUAL COMPOUNDING

YEAR	4 %	5 %	6 %	7 %	8 %	9 %	10 %	11 %	12 %	13 %	14 %	15 %
1	.4950	.4938	.4926	.4914	.4902	.4890	.4878	.4866	.4854	.4843	.4831	.4819
2	.2426	.2408	.2390	.2373	.2355	.2337	.2320	.2303	.2286	.2269	.2252	.2236
3	.1585	.1565	.1546	.1527	.1508	.1489	.1470	.1452	.1434	.1416	.1398	.1380
4	.1165	.1145	.1125	.1105	.1085	.1066	.1047	.1029	.1010	.0992	.0975	.0957
5	.0913	.0893	.0872	.0852	.0833	.0814	.0795	.0777	.0759	.0741	.0724	.0707
6	.0746	.0725	.0705	.0685	.0666	.0647	.0628	.0610	.0593	.0576	.0559	.0543
7	.0626	.0605	.0585	.0566	.0547	.0528	.0510	.0493	.0476	.0459	.0443	.0428
8	.0537	.0516	.0496	.0477	.0458	.0440	.0423	.0406	.0390	.0374	.0359	.0344
9	.0467	.0447	.0427	.0408	.0390	.0372	.0355	.0339	.0324	.0309	.0294	.0280
10	.0412	.0391	.0372	.0354	.0336	.0319	.0302	.0287	.0272	.0258	.0244	.0231
11	.0366	.0346	.0327	.0309	.0292	.0275	.0260	.0245	.0230	.0217	.0204	.0192
12	.0329	.0309	.0290	.0273	.0256	.0240	.0225	.0210	.0197	.0184	.0172	.0161
13	.0297	.0278	.0259	.0242	.0226	.0210	.0196	.0182	.0169	.0157	.0146	.0135
14	.0270	.0251	.0233	.0216	.0200	.0185	.0171	.0158	.0146	.0135	.0124	.0114
15	.0246	.0228	.0210	.0194	.0178	.0164	.0151	.0138	.0126	.0116	.0106	.0097
16	.0226	.0208	.0190	.0174	.0159	.0146	.0133	.0121	.0110	.0100	.0091	.0082
17	.0208	.0190	.0173	.0158	.0143	.0130	.0118	.0106	.0096	.0087	.0078	.0070
18	.0192	.0175	.0158	.0143	.0129	.0116	.0104	.0093	.0083	.0074	.0065	.0051
19	.0178	.0161	.0145	.0130	.0116	.0104	.0093	.0083	.0074	.0065	.0058	.0044
20	.0166	.0148	.0133	.0118	.0105	.0093	.0083	.0073	.0065	.0057	.0050	.0044
21	.0154	.0137	.0122	.0108	.0095	.0084	.0074	.0065	.0057	.0050	.0043	.0038
22	.0144	.0127	.0112	.0099	.0087	.0076	.0066	.0058	.0050	.0043	.0038	.0032
23	.0135	.0118	.0104	.0091	.0079	.0068	.0059	.0051	.0044	.0038	.0033	.0028
24	.0126	.0110	.0096	.0083	.0072	.0062	.0053	.0046	.0039	.0033	.0028	.0024
25	.0118	.0103	.0089	.0076	.0066	.0056	.0048	.0041	.0034	.0029	.0025	.0021
26	.0111	.0096	.0082	.0070	.0060	.0051	.0043	.0036	.0030	.0026	.0021	.0018
27	.0105	.0089	.0076	.0065	.0055	.0046	.0039	.0032	.0027	.0022	.0019	.0015
28	.0098	.0084	.0071	.0060	.0050	.0042	.0035	.0029	.0024	.0020	.0016	.0013
29	.0093	.0078	.0066	.0055	.0046	.0038	.0031	.0026	.0021	.0017	.0014	.0011
30	.0088	.0074	.0061	.0051	.0042	.0035	.0028	.0023	.0019	.0015	.0012	.0010

ANNUAL COMPOUNDING

YEAR	4 %	5 %	6 %	7 %	8 %	9 %	10 %	11 %	12 %	13 %	14 %	15 %
1	1.0000	1.0000	1.0000	1.0000	1.0000	1.0000	1.0000	1.0000	1.0000	1.0000	1.0000	1.0000
2	.4902	.4878	.4854	.4831	.4808	.4785	.4762	.4739	.4717	.4695	.4673	.4651
3	.3203	.3172	.3141	.3111	.3080	.3051	.3021	.2992	.2963	.2935	.2907	.2880
4	.2355	.2320	.2286	.2252	.2219	.2187	.2155	.2123	.2092	.2062	.2032	.2003
5	.1846	.1810	.1774	.1739	.1705	.1671	.1638	.1606	.1574	.1543	.1513	.1483
6	.1508	.1470	.1434	.1398	.1363	.1329	.1296	.1264	.1232	.1202	.1172	.1142
7	.1266	.1228	.1191	.1156	.1121	.1087	.1054	.1022	.0991	.0961	.0932	.0904
8	.1085	.1047	.1010	.0975	.0940	.0907	.0874	.0843	.0813	.0784	.0756	.0729
9	.0945	.0907	.0870	.0835	.0801	.0768	.0736	.0706	.0677	.0649	.0622	.0596
10	.0833	.0795	.0759	.0724	.0690	.0658	.0627	.0598	.0570	.0543	.0517	.0493
11	.0741	.0704	.0668	.0634	.0601	.0569	.0540	.0511	.0484	.0458	.0434	.0411
12	.0666	.0628	.0593	.0559	.0527	.0497	.0468	.0440	.0414	.0390	.0367	.0345
13	.0601	.0565	.0530	.0497	.0465	.0436	.0408	.0382	.0357	.0334	.0312	.0291
14	.0547	.0510	.0476	.0443	.0413	.0384	.0357	.0332	.0309	.0287	.0266	.0247
15	.0499	.0463	.0430	.0398	.0368	.0341	.0315	.0291	.0268	.0247	.0228	.0210
16	.0458	.0423	.0390	.0359	.0330	.0303	.0278	.0255	.0234	.0214	.0196	.0179
17	.0422	.0387	.0354	.0324	.0296	.0270	.0247	.0225	.0205	.0186	.0169	.0154
18	.0390	.0355	.0324	.0294	.0267	.0242	.0219	.0198	.0179	.0162	.0146	.0132
19	.0361	.0327	.0296	.0268	.0241	.0217	.0195	.0176	.0158	.0141	.0127	.0113
20	.0336	.0302	.0272	.0244	.0219	.0195	.0175	.0156	.0139	.0124	.0110	.0098
21	.0313	.0280	.0250	.0223	.0198	.0176	.0156	.0138	.0122	.0108	.0095	.0084
22	.0292	.0260	.0230	.0204	.0180	.0159	.0140	.0123	.0108	.0095	.0083	.0073
23	.0273	.0241	.0213	.0187	.0164	.0144	.0126	.0110	.0096	.0083	.0072	.0063
24	.0256	.0225	.0197	.0172	.0150	.0130	.0113	.0098	.0085	.0073	.0063	.0054
25	.0240	.0210	.0182	.0158	.0137	.0118	.0102	.0087	.0075	.0064	.0055	.0047
26	.0226	.0196	.0169	.0146	.0125	.0107	.0092	.0078	.0067	.0057	.0048	.0041
27	.0212	.0183	.0157	.0134	.0114	.0097	.0083	.0070	.0059	.0050	.0042	.0035
28	.0200	.0171	.0146	.0124	.0105	.0089	.0075	.0063	.0052	.0044	.0037	.0031
29	.0189	.0160	.0136	.0114	.0096	.0081	.0067	.0056	.0047	.0039	.0032	.0027
30	.0178	.0151	.0126	.0106	.0088	.0073	.0061	.0050	.0041	.0034	.0028	.0023

Description: This table shows what $ 1, to be paid in the future, is worth today.

Example: At 8 % one dollar, to be paid in five years, is worth $ .67 today.

MONTHLY COMPOUNDING

YEAR	4%	5%	6%	7%	8%	9%	10%	11%	12%	13%	14%	15%
1	.9609	.9513	.9419	.9326	.9234	.9142	.9052	.8963	.8874	.8787	.8701	.8615
2	.9232	.9050	.8872	.8697	.8526	.8358	.8194	.8033	.7876	.7721	.7570	.7422
3	.8871	.8610	.8356	.8111	.7873	.7641	.7417	.7200	.6989	.6785	.6586	.6394
4	.8524	.8191	.7871	.7564	.7269	.6986	.6714	.6453	.6203	.5962	.5731	.5509
5	.8190	.7792	.7414	.7054	.6712	.6387	.6078	.5784	.5504	.5239	.4986	.4746
6	.7869	.7413	.6983	.6578	.6198	.5839	.5502	.5184	.4885	.4603	.4338	.4088
7	.7561	.7052	.6577	.6135	.5723	.5338	.4980	.4646	.4335	.4045	.3774	.3522
8	.7265	.6709	.6195	.5721	.5284	.4881	.4508	.4164	.3847	.3554	.3284	.3034
9	.6981	.6382	.5835	.5336	.4879	.4462	.4081	.3733	.3414	.3123	.2857	.2614
10	.6708	.6072	.5496	.4976	.4505	.4079	.3694	.3345	.3030	.2744	.2486	.2252
11	.6445	.5776	.5177	.4641	.4160	.3730	.3344	.2998	.2689	.2412	.2163	.1940
12	.6193	.5495	.4876	.4328	.3841	.3410	.3027	.2687	.2386	.2119	.1882	.1672
13	.5950	.5228	.4593	.4036	.3547	.3117	.2740	.2409	.2118	.1862	.1637	.1440
14	.5717	.4973	.4326	.3764	.3275	.2850	.2480	.2159	.1879	.1636	.1425	.1241
15	.5494	.4731	.4075	.3510	.3024	.2605	.2245	.1935	.1668	.1438	.1240	.1069
16	.5279	.4501	.3838	.3273	.2792	.2382	.2032	.1734	.1480	.1263	.1078	.0921
17	.5072	.4282	.3615	.3053	.2578	.2178	.1840	.1554	.1314	.1110	.0938	.0793
18	.4873	.4073	.3405	.2847	.2381	.1991	.1665	.1393	.1166	.0975	.0816	.0683
19	.4683	.3875	.3207	.2655	.2198	.1820	.1508	.1249	.1034	.0857	.0710	.0589
20	.4499	.3686	.3021	.2476	.2030	.1664	.1365	.1119	.0918	.0753	.0618	.0507
21	.4323	.3507	.2845	.2309	.1874	.1521	.1235	.1003	.0815	.0662	.0538	.0437
22	.4154	.3336	.2680	.2153	.1731	.1391	.1118	.0899	.0723	.0582	.0468	.0376
23	.3991	.3174	.2524	.2008	.1598	.1272	.1012	.0806	.0642	.0511	.0407	.0324
24	.3835	.3019	.2378	.1873	.1475	.1163	.0916	.0722	.0569	.0449	.0354	.0279
25	.3685	.2872	.2240	.1747	.1362	.1063	.0829	.0647	.0505	.0395	.0308	.0241
26	.3541	.2733	.2110	.1629	.1258	.0972	.0751	.0580	.0448	.0347	.0268	.0207
27	.3402	.2600	.1987	.1519	.1162	.0888	.0680	.0520	.0398	.0305	.0233	.0179
28	.3269	.2473	.1872	.1417	.1073	.0812	.0615	.0466	.0353	.0268	.0203	.0154
29	.3141	.2353	.1763	.1321	.0990	.0743	.0557	.0418	.0313	.0235	.0177	.0133
30	.3018	.2238	.1660	.1232	.0914	.0679	.0504	.0374	.0278	.0207	.0154	.0114

QUARTERLY COMPOUNDING

YEAR	4%	5%	6%	7%	8%	9%	10%	11%	12%	13%	14%	15%
1	.9610	.9515	.9422	.9330	.9238	.9148	.9060	.8972	.8885	.8799	.8714	.8631
2	.9235	.9054	.8877	.8704	.8535	.8369	.8207	.8049	.7894	.7742	.7594	.7449
3	.8874	.8615	.8364	.8121	.7885	.7657	.7436	.7221	.7014	.6813	.6618	.6429
4	.8528	.8197	.7880	.7576	.7284	.7005	.6736	.6479	.6232	.5995	.5767	.5549
5	.8195	.7800	.7425	.7068	.6730	.6408	.6103	.5813	.5537	.5275	.5026	.4789
6	.7876	.7422	.6995	.6594	.6217	.5862	.5529	.5215	.4919	.4641	.4380	.4133
7	.7568	.7062	.6591	.6152	.5744	.5363	.5009	.4679	.4371	.4084	.3817	.3567
8	.7273	.6720	.6210	.5740	.5306	.4907	.4538	.4197	.3883	.3594	.3326	.3079
9	.6989	.6394	.5851	.5355	.4902	.4489	.4111	.3766	.3450	.3162	.2898	.2657
10	.6717	.6084	.5513	.4996	.4529	.4106	.3724	.3379	.3066	.2782	.2526	.2293
11	.6454	.5789	.5194	.4661	.4184	.3757	.3374	.3031	.2724	.2448	.2201	.1979
12	.6203	.5509	.4894	.4349	.3865	.3437	.3057	.2719	.2420	.2154	.1918	.1708
13	.5961	.5242	.4611	.4057	.3571	.3144	.2769	.2440	.2150	.1895	.1671	.1474
14	.5728	.4987	.4344	.3785	.3299	.2876	.2509	.2189	.1910	.1668	.1457	.1273
15	.5504	.4746	.4093	.3531	.3048	.2631	.2273	.1964	.1697	.1468	.1269	.1098
16	.5290	.4516	.3856	.3295	.2816	.2407	.2059	.1762	.1508	.1291	.1106	.0948
17	.5083	.4297	.3633	.3074	.2601	.2202	.1865	.1581	.1340	.1136	.0964	.0818
18	.4885	.4088	.3423	.2868	.2403	.2015	.1690	.1418	.1190	.1000	.0840	.0706
19	.4694	.3890	.3225	.2675	.2220	.1843	.1531	.1272	.1058	.0880	.0732	.0609
20	.4511	.3702	.3039	.2496	.2051	.1686	.1387	.1141	.0940	.0774	.0638	.0526
21	.4335	.3522	.2863	.2329	.1895	.1543	.1257	.1024	.0835	.0681	.0556	.0454
22	.4166	.3351	.2698	.2173	.1751	.1411	.1138	.0919	.0742	.0599	.0484	.0392
23	.4003	.3189	.2542	.2027	.1617	.1291	.1031	.0824	.0659	.0527	.0422	.0338
24	.3847	.3034	.2395	.1891	.1494	.1181	.0934	.0740	.0586	.0464	.0368	.0292
25	.3697	.2887	.2256	.1764	.1380	.1081	.0846	.0663	.0520	.0408	.0321	.0252
26	.3553	.2747	.2126	.1646	.1275	.0989	.0767	.0595	.0462	.0359	.0279	.0217
27	.3414	.2614	.2003	.1536	.1178	.0904	.0695	.0534	.0411	.0316	.0243	.0188
28	.3281	.2487	.1887	.1433	.1088	.0827	.0629	.0479	.0365	.0278	.0212	.0162
29	.3153	.2367	.1778	.1337	.1005	.0757	.0570	.0430	.0324	.0245	.0185	.0140
30	.3030	.2252	.1675	.1247	.0929	.0692	.0517	.0386	.0288	.0215	.0161	.0121

Description: This table shows what $ 1, to be paid in the future, is worth today.

Example: At 8 % one dollar, to be paid in five years, is worth $ .68 today.

SEMIANNUAL COMPOUNDING

YEAR	4 %	5 %	6 %	7 %	8 %	9 %	10 %	11 %	12 %	13 %	14 %	15 %
1	.9612	.9518	.9426	.9335	.9246	.9157	.9070	.8985	.8900	.8817	.8734	.8653
2	.9238	.9060	.8885	.8714	.8548	.8386	.8227	.8072	.7921	.7773	.7629	.7488
3	.8880	.8623	.8375	.8135	.7903	.7679	.7462	.7252	.7050	.6853	.6663	.6480
4	.8535	.8207	.7894	.7594	.7307	.7032	.6768	.6516	.6274	.6042	.5820	.5607
5	.8203	.7812	.7441	.7089	.6756	.6439	.6139	.5854	.5584	.5327	.5083	.4852
6	.7885	.7436	.7014	.6618	.6246	.5897	.5568	.5260	.4970	.4697	.4440	.4199
7	.7579	.7077	.6611	.6178	.5775	.5400	.5051	.4726	.4423	.4141	.3878	.3633
8	.7284	.6736	.6232	.5767	.5339	.4945	.4581	.4246	.3936	.3651	.3387	.3144
9	.7002	.6412	.5874	.5384	.4936	.4528	.4155	.3815	.3503	.3219	.2959	.2720
10	.6730	.6103	.5537	.5026	.4564	.4146	.3769	.3427	.3118	.2838	.2584	.2354
11	.6468	.5809	.5219	.4692	.4220	.3797	.3418	.3079	.2775	.2502	.2257	.2037
12	.6217	.5529	.4919	.4380	.3901	.3477	.3101	.2767	.2470	.2206	.1971	.1763
13	.5976	.5262	.4637	.4088	.3607	.3184	.2812	.2486	.2198	.1945	.1722	.1525
14	.5744	.5009	.4371	.3817	.3335	.2916	.2551	.2233	.1956	.1715	.1504	.1320
15	.5521	.4767	.4120	.3563	.3083	.2670	.2314	.2006	.1741	.1512	.1314	.1142
16	.5306	.4538	.3883	.3326	.2851	.2445	.2099	.1803	.1550	.1333	.1147	.0988
17	.5100	.4319	.3660	.3105	.2636	.2239	.1904	.1620	.1379	.1175	.1002	.0855
18	.4902	.4111	.3450	.2898	.2437	.2050	.1727	.1455	.1227	.1036	.0875	.0740
19	.4712	.3913	.3252	.2706	.2253	.1878	.1566	.1307	.1092	.0914	.0765	.0640
20	.4529	.3724	.3066	.2526	.2083	.1719	.1420	.1175	.0972	.0805	.0668	.0554
21	.4353	.3545	.2890	.2358	.1926	.1574	.1288	.1055	.0865	.0710	.0583	.0480
22	.4184	.3374	.2724	.2201	.1780	.1442	.1169	.0948	.0770	.0626	.0509	.0415
23	.4022	.3211	.2567	.2055	.1646	.1320	.1060	.0852	.0685	.0552	.0445	.0359
24	.3865	.3057	.2420	.1918	.1522	.1209	.0961	.0765	.0610	.0487	.0389	.0311
25	.3715	.2909	.2281	.1791	.1407	.1107	.0872	.0688	.0543	.0429	.0339	.0269
26	.3571	.2769	.2150	.1671	.1301	.1014	.0791	.0618	.0483	.0378	.0297	.0233
27	.3432	.2636	.2027	.1560	.1203	.0928	.0717	.0555	.0430	.0334	.0259	.0201
28	.3299	.2509	.1910	.1457	.1112	.0850	.0651	.0499	.0383	.0294	.0226	.0174
29	.3171	.2388	.1801	.1360	.1028	.0778	.0590	.0448	.0341	.0303	.0259	.0198	.0151
30	.3048	.2273	.1697	.1269	.0951	.0713	.0535	.0403	.0303	.0229	.0173	.0130

ANNUAL COMPOUNDING

YEAR	4 %	5 %	6 %	7 %	8 %	9 %	10 %	11 %	12 %	13 %	14 %	15 %
1	.9615	.9524	.9434	.9346	.9259	.9174	.9091	.9009	.8929	.8850	.8772	.8696
2	.9246	.9070	.8900	.8734	.8573	.8417	.8264	.8116	.7972	.7831	.7695	.7561
3	.8890	.8638	.8396	.8163	.7938	.7722	.7513	.7312	.7118	.6931	.6750	.6575
4	.8548	.8227	.7921	.7629	.7350	.7084	.6830	.6587	.6355	.6133	.5921	.5718
5	.8219	.7835	.7473	.7130	.6806	.6499	.6209	.5935	.5674	.5428	.5194	.4972
6	.7903	.7462	.7050	.6663	.6302	.5963	.5645	.5346	.5066	.4803	.4556	.4323
7	.7599	.7107	.6651	.6227	.5835	.5470	.5132	.4817	.4523	.4251	.3996	.3759
8	.7307	.6768	.6274	.5820	.5403	.5019	.4665	.4339	.4039	.3762	.3506	.3269
9	.7026	.6446	.5919	.5439	.5002	.4604	.4241	.3909	.3606	.3329	.3075	.2843
10	.6756	.6139	.5584	.5083	.4632	.4224	.3855	.3522	.3220	.2946	.2697	.2472
11	.6496	.5847	.5268	.4751	.4289	.3875	.3505	.3173	.2875	.2607	.2366	.2149
12	.6246	.5568	.4970	.4440	.3971	.3555	.3186	.2858	.2567	.2307	.2076	.1869
13	.6006	.5303	.4688	.4150	.3677	.3262	.2897	.2575	.2292	.2042	.1821	.1625
14	.5775	.5051	.4423	.3878	.3405	.2992	.2633	.2320	.2046	.1807	.1597	.1413
15	.5553	.4810	.4173	.3624	.3152	.2745	.2394	.2090	.1827	.1599	.1401	.1229
16	.5339	.4581	.3936	.3387	.2919	.2519	.2176	.1883	.1631	.1415	.1229	.1069
17	.5134	.4363	.3714	.3166	.2703	.2311	.1978	.1696	.1456	.1252	.1078	.0929
18	.4936	.4155	.3503	.2959	.2502	.2120	.1799	.1528	.1300	.1108	.0946	.0808
19	.4746	.3957	.3305	.2765	.2317	.1945	.1635	.1377	.1161	.0981	.0829	.0703
20	.4564	.3769	.3118	.2584	.2145	.1784	.1486	.1240	.1037	.0868	.0728	.0611
21	.4388	.3589	.2942	.2415	.1987	.1637	.1351	.1117	.0926	.0768	.0638	.0531
22	.4220	.3418	.2775	.2257	.1839	.1502	.1228	.1007	.0826	.0680	.0560	.0462
23	.4057	.3256	.2618	.2109	.1703	.1378	.1117	.0907	.0738	.0601	.0491	.0402
24	.3901	.3101	.2470	.1971	.1577	.1264	.1015	.0817	.0659	.0532	.0431	.0349
25	.3751	.2953	.2330	.1842	.1460	.1160	.0923	.0736	.0588	.0471	.0378	.0304
26	.3607	.2812	.2198	.1722	.1352	.1064	.0839	.0663	.0525	.0417	.0331	.0264
27	.3468	.2678	.2074	.1609	.1252	.0976	.0763	.0597	.0469	.0369	.0291	.0230
28	.3335	.2551	.1956	.1504	.1159	.0895	.0693	.0538	.0419	.0326	.0255	.0200
29	.3207	.2429	.1846	.1406	.1073	.0822	.0630	.0485	.0374	.0289	.0224	.0174
30	.3083	.2314	.1741	.1314	.0994	.0754	.0573	.0437	.0334	.0256	.0196	.0151

Description: This table shows what $ 1, to be paid in end of each period, is worth today.

Example: At 8 % a payment of $ 1, made at the end of each period for five years, is worth $ 49.32 today.

MONTHLY COMPOUNDING

YEAR	4 %	5 %	6 %	7 %	8 %	9 %	10 %	11 %	12 %	13 %	14 %	15 %
1	11.74	11.68	11.62	11.56	11.50	11.43	11.37	11.31	11.26	11.20	11.14	11.08
2	23.03	22.79	22.56	22.34	22.11	21.89	21.67	21.46	21.24	21.03	20.83	20.62
3	33.87	33.37	32.87	32.39	31.91	31.45	30.99	30.54	30.11	29.68	29.26	28.85
4	44.29	43.42	42.58	41.76	40.96	40.18	39.43	38.69	37.97	37.28	36.59	35.93
5	54.30	52.99	51.73	50.50	49.32	48.17	47.07	45.99	44.96	43.95	42.98	42.03
6	63.92	62.09	60.34	58.65	57.03	55.48	53.98	52.54	51.15	49.82	48.53	47.29
7	73.16	70.75	68.45	66.26	64.16	62.15	60.24	58.40	56.65	54.97	53.36	51.82
8	82.04	78.99	76.10	73.35	70.74	68.26	65.90	63.66	61.53	59.50	57.57	55.72
9	90.57	86.83	83.29	79.96	76.81	73.84	71.03	68.37	65.86	63.48	61.22	59.09
10	98.77	94.28	90.07	86.13	82.42	78.94	75.67	72.60	69.70	66.97	64.41	61.98
11	106.65	101.37	96.46	91.88	87.60	83.61	79.87	76.38	73.11	70.05	67.17	64.48
12	114.22	108.12	102.47	97.24	92.38	87.87	83.68	79.77	76.14	72.75	69.58	66.63
13	121.49	114.54	108.14	102.24	96.80	91.77	87.12	82.81	78.82	75.12	71.68	68.48
14	128.48	120.65	113.48	106.91	100.88	95.33	90.24	85.54	81.21	77.20	73.50	70.08
15	135.19	126.46	118.50	111.26	104.64	98.59	93.06	87.98	83.32	79.04	75.09	71.45
16	141.64	131.98	123.24	115.31	108.12	101.57	95.61	90.17	85.20	80.65	76.47	72.63
17	147.84	137.24	127.70	119.10	111.33	104.30	97.92	92.13	86.86	82.06	77.67	73.65
18	153.80	142.24	131.90	122.62	114.29	106.79	100.02	93.89	88.34	83.30	78.72	74.53
19	159.52	147.00	135.85	125.91	117.03	109.06	101.91	95.47	89.66	84.40	79.63	75.29
20	165.02	151.53	139.58	128.98	119.55	111.14	103.62	96.88	90.82	85.36	80.42	75.94
21	170.31	155.83	143.09	131.84	121.89	113.05	105.18	98.15	91.85	86.20	81.11	76.50
22	175.38	159.93	146.40	134.51	124.04	114.79	106.58	99.28	92.77	86.94	81.70	76.99
23	180.26	163.83	149.51	137.00	126.03	116.38	107.85	100.30	93.58	87.59	82.23	77.41
24	184.95	167.53	152.44	139.32	127.87	117.83	109.01	101.21	94.31	88.16	82.68	77.76
25	189.45	171.06	155.21	141.49	129.56	119.16	110.05	102.03	94.95	88.67	83.07	78.07
26	193.78	174.42	157.81	143.51	131.13	120.38	110.99	102.76	95.52	89.11	83.42	78.34
27	197.94	177.61	160.26	145.39	132.58	121.49	111.84	103.42	96.02	89.50	83.71	78.57
28	201.93	180.64	162.57	147.14	133.91	122.50	112.62	104.01	96.47	89.84	83.97	78.77
29	205.77	183.53	164.74	148.78	135.15	123.43	113.32	104.53	96.87	90.14	84.20	78.94
30	209.46	186.28	166.79	150.31	136.28	124.28	113.95	105.01	97.22	90.40	84.40	79.09

QUARTERLY COMPOUNDING

YEAR	4 %	5 %	6 %	7 %	8 %	9 %	10 %	11 %	12 %	13 %	14 %	15 %
1	3.90	3.88	3.85	3.83	3.81	3.78	3.76	3.74	3.72	3.69	3.67	3.65
2	7.65	7.57	7.49	7.41	7.33	7.25	7.17	7.09	7.02	6.95	6.87	6.80
3	11.26	11.08	10.91	10.74	10.58	10.41	10.26	10.10	9.95	9.81	9.66	9.52
4	14.72	14.42	14.13	13.85	13.58	13.31	13.06	12.80	12.56	12.32	12.09	11.87
5	18.05	17.60	17.17	16.75	16.35	15.96	15.59	15.23	14.88	14.54	14.21	13.90
6	21.24	20.62	20.03	19.46	18.91	18.39	17.88	17.40	16.94	16.49	16.06	15.64
7	24.32	23.50	22.73	21.99	21.28	20.61	19.96	19.35	18.76	18.20	17.67	17.15
8	27.27	26.24	25.27	24.34	23.47	22.64	21.85	21.10	20.39	19.71	19.07	18.46
9	30.11	28.85	27.66	26.54	25.49	24.49	23.56	22.67	21.83	21.04	20.29	19.58
10	32.83	31.33	29.92	28.59	27.36	26.19	25.10	24.08	23.11	22.21	21.36	20.55
11	35.46	33.69	32.04	30.51	29.08	27.75	26.50	25.34	24.25	23.24	22.28	21.39
12	37.97	35.93	34.04	32.29	30.67	29.17	27.77	26.47	25.27	24.14	23.09	22.11
13	40.39	38.07	35.93	33.96	32.14	30.47	28.92	27.49	26.17	24.94	23.80	22.73
14	42.72	40.10	37.71	35.51	33.50	31.66	29.96	28.40	26.97	25.64	24.41	23.27
15	44.96	42.03	39.38	36.96	34.76	32.75	30.91	29.22	27.68	26.25	24.94	23.74
16	47.10	43.87	40.96	38.32	35.92	33.74	31.76	29.96	28.31	26.80	25.41	24.14
17	49.17	45.63	42.44	39.58	36.99	34.66	32.54	30.62	28.87	27.27	25.82	24.49
18	51.15	47.29	43.84	40.76	37.98	35.49	33.24	31.21	29.37	27.69	26.17	24.78
19	53.06	48.88	45.16	41.86	38.90	36.25	33.88	31.74	29.81	28.06	26.48	25.04
20	54.89	50.39	46.41	42.88	39.74	36.95	34.45	32.21	30.20	28.39	26.75	25.26
21	56.65	51.82	47.58	43.84	40.53	37.59	34.97	32.64	30.55	28.67	26.98	25.46
22	58.34	53.19	48.68	44.73	41.25	38.17	35.45	33.02	30.86	28.93	27.19	25.62
23	59.97	54.49	49.72	45.56	41.91	38.71	35.87	33.37	31.14	29.15	27.37	25.76
24	61.53	55.72	50.70	46.34	42.53	39.19	36.26	33.67	31.38	29.34	27.52	25.89
25	63.03	56.90	51.62	47.06	43.10	39.64	36.61	33.95	31.60	29.51	27.66	25.99
26	64.47	58.02	52.49	47.74	43.62	40.05	36.93	34.20	31.79	29.66	27.77	26.09
27	65.86	59.09	53.31	48.37	44.11	40.42	37.22	34.42	31.96	29.80	27.88	26.17
28	67.19	60.10	54.09	48.96	44.56	40.77	37.48	34.62	32.12	29.91	27.97	26.23
29	68.47	61.06	54.81	49.51	44.97	41.08	37.72	34.80	32.25	30.02	28.04	26.29
30	69.70	61.98	55.50	50.02	45.36	41.37	37.93	34.96	32.37	30.11	28.11	26.35

Description: This table shows what $ 1, to be paid in end of each period, is worth today.

Example: At 8 % a payment of $ 1, made at the end of each period for five years, is worth $ 8.11 today.

SEMIANNUAL COMPOUNDING

YEAR	4 %	5 %	6 %	7 %	8 %	9 %	10 %	11 %	12 %	13 %	14 %	15 %
1	1.94	1.93	1.91	1.90	1.89	1.87	1.86	1.85	1.83	1.82	1.81	1.80
2	3.81	3.76	3.72	3.67	3.63	3.59	3.55	3.51	3.47	3.43	3.39	3.35
3	5.60	5.51	5.42	5.33	5.24	5.16	5.08	5.00	4.92	4.84	4.77	4.69
4	7.33	7.17	7.02	6.87	6.73	6.60	6.46	6.33	6.21	6.09	5.97	5.86
5	8.98	8.75	8.53	8.32	8.11	7.91	7.72	7.54	7.36	7.19	7.02	6.86
6	10.58	10.26	9.95	9.66	9.39	9.12	8.86	8.62	8.38	8.16	7.94	7.74
7	12.11	11.69	11.30	10.92	10.56	10.22	9.90	9.59	9.29	9.01	8.75	8.49
8	13.58	13.06	12.56	12.09	11.65	11.23	10.84	10.46	10.11	9.77	9.45	9.14
9	14.99	14.35	13.75	13.19	12.66	12.16	11.69	11.25	10.83	10.43	10.06	9.71
10	16.35	15.59	14.88	14.21	13.59	13.01	12.46	11.95	11.47	11.02	10.59	10.19
11	17.66	16.77	15.94	15.17	14.45	13.78	13.16	12.58	12.04	11.54	11.06	10.62
12	18.91	17.88	16.94	16.06	15.25	14.50	13.80	13.15	12.55	11.99	11.47	10.98
13	20.12	18.95	17.88	16.89	15.98	15.15	14.38	13.66	13.00	12.39	11.83	11.30
14	21.28	19.96	18.76	17.67	16.66	15.74	14.90	14.12	13.41	12.75	12.14	11.57
15	22.40	20.93	19.60	18.39	17.29	16.29	15.37	14.53	13.76	13.06	12.41	11.81
16	23.47	21.85	20.39	19.07	17.87	16.79	15.80	14.90	14.08	13.33	12.65	12.02
17	24.50	22.72	21.13	19.70	18.41	17.25	16.19	15.24	14.37	13.58	12.85	12.19
18	25.49	23.56	21.83	20.29	18.91	17.67	16.55	15.54	14.62	13.79	13.04	12.35
19	26.44	24.35	22.49	20.84	19.37	18.05	16.87	15.80	14.85	13.98	13.19	12.48
20	27.36	25.10	23.11	21.36	19.79	18.40	17.16	16.05	15.05	14.15	13.33	12.59
21	28.23	25.82	23.70	21.83	20.19	18.72	17.42	16.26	15.22	14.29	13.45	12.69
22	29.08	26.50	24.25	22.28	20.55	19.02	17.66	16.46	15.38	14.42	13.56	12.78
23	29.89	27.15	24.78	22.70	20.88	19.29	17.88	16.63	15.52	14.54	13.65	12.85
24	30.67	27.77	25.27	23.09	21.20	19.54	18.08	16.79	15.65	14.64	13.73	12.92
25	31.42	28.36	25.73	23.46	21.48	19.76	18.26	16.93	15.76	14.72	13.80	12.97
26	32.14	28.92	26.17	23.80	21.75	19.97	18.42	17.06	15.86	14.80	13.86	13.02
27	32.84	29.46	26.58	24.11	21.99	20.16	18.57	17.17	15.95	14.87	13.92	13.06
28	33.50	29.96	26.97	24.41	22.22	20.33	18.70	17.28	16.03	14.93	13.96	13.10
29	34.15	30.45	27.33	24.69	22.43	20.49	18.82	17.37	16.10	14.99	14.00	13.13
30	34.76	30.91	27.68	24.94	22.62	20.64	18.93	17.45	16.16	15.03	14.04	13.16

ANNUAL COMPOUNDING

YEAR	4 %	5 %	6 %	7 %	8 %	9 %	10 %	11 %	12 %	13 %	14 %	15 %
1	.96	.95	.94	.93	.93	.92	.91	.90	.89	.88	.88	.87
2	1.89	1.86	1.83	1.81	1.78	1.76	1.74	1.71	1.69	1.67	1.65	1.63
3	2.78	2.72	2.67	2.62	2.58	2.53	2.49	2.44	2.40	2.36	2.32	2.28
4	3.63	3.55	3.47	3.39	3.31	3.24	3.17	3.10	3.04	2.97	2.91	2.85
5	4.45	4.33	4.21	4.10	3.99	3.89	3.79	3.70	3.60	3.52	3.43	3.35
6	5.24	5.08	4.92	4.77	4.62	4.49	4.36	4.23	4.11	4.00	3.89	3.78
7	6.00	5.79	5.58	5.39	5.21	5.03	4.87	4.71	4.56	4.42	4.29	4.16
8	6.73	6.46	6.21	5.97	5.75	5.53	5.33	5.15	4.97	4.80	4.64	4.49
9	7.44	7.11	6.80	6.52	6.25	6.00	5.76	5.54	5.33	5.13	4.95	4.77
10	8.11	7.72	7.36	7.02	6.71	6.42	6.14	5.89	5.65	5.43	5.22	5.02
11	8.76	8.31	7.89	7.50	7.14	6.81	6.50	6.21	5.94	5.69	5.45	5.23
12	9.39	8.86	8.38	7.94	7.54	7.16	6.81	6.49	6.19	5.92	5.66	5.42
13	9.99	9.39	8.85	8.36	7.90	7.49	7.10	6.75	6.42	6.12	5.84	5.58
14	10.56	9.90	9.29	8.75	8.24	7.79	7.37	6.98	6.63	6.30	6.00	5.72
15	11.12	10.38	9.71	9.11	8.56	8.06	7.61	7.19	6.81	6.46	6.14	5.85
16	11.65	10.84	10.11	9.45	8.85	8.31	7.82	7.38	6.97	6.60	6.27	5.95
17	12.17	11.27	10.48	9.76	9.12	8.54	8.02	7.55	7.12	6.73	6.37	6.05
18	12.66	11.69	10.83	10.06	9.37	8.76	8.20	7.70	7.25	6.84	6.47	6.13
19	13.13	12.09	11.16	10.34	9.60	8.95	8.36	7.84	7.37	6.94	6.55	6.20
20	13.59	12.46	11.47	10.59	9.82	9.13	8.51	7.96	7.47	7.02	6.62	6.26
21	14.03	12.82	11.76	10.84	10.02	9.29	8.65	8.08	7.56	7.10	6.69	6.31
22	14.45	13.16	12.04	11.06	10.20	9.44	8.77	8.18	7.64	7.17	6.74	6.36
23	14.86	13.49	12.30	11.27	10.37	9.58	8.88	8.27	7.72	7.23	6.79	6.40
24	15.25	13.80	12.55	11.47	10.53	9.71	8.98	8.35	7.78	7.28	6.84	6.43
25	15.62	14.09	12.78	11.65	10.67	9.82	9.08	8.42	7.84	7.33	6.87	6.46
26	15.98	14.38	13.00	11.83	10.81	9.93	9.16	8.49	7.90	7.37	6.91	6.49
27	16.33	14.64	13.21	11.99	10.94	10.03	9.24	8.55	7.94	7.41	6.94	6.51
28	16.66	14.90	13.41	12.14	11.05	10.12	9.31	8.60	7.98	7.44	6.96	6.53
29	16.98	15.14	13.59	12.28	11.16	10.20	9.37	8.65	8.02	7.47	6.98	6.55
30	17.29	15.37	13.76	12.41	11.26	10.27	9.43	8.69	8.06	7.50	7.00	6.57

Description: This table shows the regular, periodic payment needed to amortize a loan of $ 1.

Example: At 8 % a loan of $ 10,000 is amortized over five years by a payment of $ 202.77.

MONTHLY COMPOUNDING

YEAR	4 %	5 %	6 %	7 %	8 %	9 %	10 %	11 %	12 %	13 %	14 %	15 %
1	.0851	.0856	.0861	.0865	.0870	.0875	.0879	.0884	.0888	.0893	.0898	.0903
2	.0434	.0439	.0443	.0448	.0452	.0457	.0461	.0466	.0471	.0475	.0480	.0485
3	.0295	.0300	.0304	.0309	.0313	.0318	.0323	.0327	.0332	.0337	.0342	.0347
4	.0226	.0230	.0235	.0239	.0244	.0249	.0254	.0258	.0263	.0268	.0273	.0278
5	.0184	.0189	.0193	.0198	.0203	.0208	.0212	.0217	.0222	.0228	.0233	.0238
6	.0156	.0161	.0166	.0170	.0175	.0180	.0185	.0190	.0196	.0201	.0206	.0211
7	.0137	.0141	.0146	.0151	.0156	.0161	.0166	.0171	.0177	.0182	.0187	.0193
8	.0122	.0127	.0131	.0136	.0141	.0147	.0152	.0157	.0163	.0168	.0174	.0179
9	.0110	.0115	.0120	.0125	.0130	.0135	.0141	.0146	.0152	.0158	.0163	.0169
10	.0101	.0106	.0111	.0116	.0121	.0127	.0132	.0138	.0143	.0149	.0155	.0161
11	.0094	.0099	.0104	.0109	.0114	.0120	.0125	.0131	.0137	.0143	.0149	.0155
12	.0088	.0092	.0098	.0103	.0108	.0114	.0120	.0125	.0131	.0137	.0144	.0150
13	.0082	.0087	.0092	.0098	.0103	.0109	.0115	.0121	.0127	.0133	.0140	.0146
14	.0078	.0083	.0088	.0094	.0099	.0105	.0111	.0117	.0123	.0130	.0136	.0143
15	.0074	.0079	.0084	.0090	.0096	.0101	.0107	.0114	.0120	.0127	.0133	.0140
16	.0071	.0076	.0081	.0087	.0092	.0098	.0105	.0111	.0117	.0124	.0131	.0138
17	.0068	.0073	.0078	.0084	.0090	.0096	.0102	.0109	.0115	.0122	.0129	.0136
18	.0065	.0070	.0076	.0082	.0087	.0094	.0100	.0107	.0113	.0120	.0127	.0134
19	.0063	.0068	.0074	.0079	.0085	.0092	.0098	.0105	.0112	.0118	.0126	.0133
20	.0061	.0066	.0072	.0078	.0084	.0090	.0097	.0103	.0110	.0117	.0124	.0132
21	.0059	.0064	.0070	.0076	.0082	.0088	.0095	.0102	.0109	.0116	.0123	.0131
22	.0057	.0063	.0068	.0074	.0081	.0087	.0094	.0101	.0108	.0115	.0122	.0130
23	.0055	.0061	.0067	.0073	.0079	.0086	.0093	.0100	.0107	.0114	.0122	.0129
24	.0054	.0060	.0066	.0072	.0078	.0085	.0092	.0099	.0106	.0113	.0121	.0129
25	.0053	.0058	.0064	.0071	.0077	.0084	.0091	.0098	.0105	.0113	.0120	.0128
26	.0052	.0057	.0063	.0070	.0076	.0083	.0090	.0097	.0105	.0112	.0120	.0128
27	.0051	.0056	.0062	.0069	.0075	.0082	.0089	.0097	.0104	.0112	.0119	.0127
28	.0050	.0055	.0062	.0068	.0075	.0082	.0089	.0096	.0104	.0111	.0119	.0127
29	.0049	.0054	.0061	.0067	.0074	.0081	.0088	.0096	.0103	.0111	.0119	.0127
30	.0048	.0054	.0060	.0067	.0073	.0080	.0088	.0095	.0103	.0111	.0118	.0126

QUARTERLY COMPOUNDING

YEAR	4 %	5 %	6 %	7 %	8 %	9 %	10 %	11 %	12 %	13 %	14 %	15 %
1	.2563	.2579	.2594	.2610	.2626	.2642	.2658	.2674	.2690	.2706	.2723	.2739
2	.1307	.1321	.1336	.1350	.1365	.1380	.1395	.1410	.1425	.1440	.1455	.1470
3	.0888	.0903	.0917	.0931	.0946	.0960	.0975	.0990	.1005	.1020	.1035	.1050
4	.0679	.0693	.0708	.0722	.0737	.0751	.0766	.0781	.0796	.0811	.0827	.0842
5	.0554	.0568	.0582	.0597	.0612	.0626	.0641	.0657	.0672	.0688	.0704	.0720
6	.0471	.0485	.0499	.0514	.0529	.0544	.0559	.0575	.0590	.0606	.0623	.0639
7	.0411	.0425	.0440	.0455	.0470	.0485	.0501	.0517	.0533	.0549	.0566	.0583
8	.0367	.0381	.0396	.0411	.0426	.0442	.0458	.0474	.0490	.0507	.0524	.0542
9	.0332	.0347	.0362	.0377	.0392	.0408	.0425	.0441	.0458	.0475	.0493	.0511
10	.0305	.0319	.0334	.0350	.0366	.0382	.0398	.0415	.0433	.0450	.0468	.0487
11	.0282	.0297	.0312	.0328	.0344	.0360	.0377	.0395	.0412	.0430	.0449	.0468
12	.0263	.0278	.0294	.0310	.0326	.0343	.0360	.0378	.0396	.0414	.0433	.0452
13	.0248	.0263	.0278	.0294	.0311	.0328	.0346	.0364	.0382	.0401	.0420	.0440
14	.0234	.0249	.0265	.0282	.0298	.0316	.0334	.0352	.0371	.0390	.0410	.0430
15	.0222	.0238	.0254	.0271	.0288	.0305	.0324	.0342	.0361	.0381	.0401	.0421
16	.0212	.0228	.0244	.0261	.0278	.0296	.0315	.0334	.0353	.0373	.0394	.0414
17	.0203	.0219	.0236	.0253	.0270	.0289	.0307	.0327	.0346	.0367	.0387	.0408
18	.0196	.0211	.0228	.0245	.0263	.0282	.0301	.0320	.0341	.0361	.0382	.0403
19	.0188	.0205	.0221	.0239	.0257	.0276	.0295	.0315	.0335	.0356	.0378	.0399
20	.0182	.0198	.0215	.0233	.0252	.0271	.0290	.0310	.0331	.0352	.0374	.0396
21	.0177	.0193	.0210	.0228	.0247	.0266	.0286	.0306	.0327	.0349	.0371	.0393
22	.0171	.0188	.0205	.0224	.0242	.0262	.0282	.0303	.0324	.0346	.0368	.0390
23	.0167	.0184	.0201	.0219	.0239	.0258	.0279	.0300	.0321	.0343	.0365	.0388
24	.0163	.0179	.0197	.0216	.0235	.0255	.0276	.0297	.0319	.0341	.0363	.0386
25	.0159	.0176	.0194	.0212	.0232	.0252	.0273	.0295	.0316	.0339	.0362	.0385
26	.0155	.0172	.0190	.0209	.0229	.0250	.0271	.0292	.0315	.0337	.0360	.0383
27	.0152	.0169	.0188	.0207	.0227	.0247	.0269	.0291	.0313	.0336	.0359	.0382
28	.0149	.0166	.0185	.0204	.0224	.0245	.0267	.0289	.0311	.0334	.0358	.0381
29	.0146	.0164	.0182	.0202	.0222	.0243	.0265	.0287	.0310	.0333	.0357	.0380
30	.0143	.0161	.0180	.0200	.0220	.0242	.0264	.0286	.0309	.0332	.0356	.0380

PERIODIC PAYMENT TO AMORTIZE 1

Description: This table shows the regular, periodic payment needed to amortize a loan of $ 1.

Example: At 8 % a loan of $ 10,000 is amortized over five years by a payment of $ 1232.91.

SEMIANNUAL COMPOUNDING

YEAR	4 %	5 %	6 %	7 %	8 %	9 %	10 %	11 %	12 %	13 %	14 %	15 %
1	.5150	.5188	.5226	.5264	.5302	.5340	.5378	.5416	.5454	.5493	.5531	.5569
2	.2626	.2658	.2690	.2723	.2755	.2787	.2820	.2853	.2886	.2919	.2952	.2986
3	.1785	.1815	.1846	.1877	.1908	.1939	.1970	.2002	.2034	.2066	.2098	.2130
4	.1365	.1395	.1425	.1455	.1485	.1516	.1547	.1579	.1610	.1642	.1675	.1707
5	.1113	.1143	.1172	.1202	.1233	.1264	.1295	.1327	.1359	.1391	.1424	.1457
6	.0946	.0975	.1005	.1035	.1066	.1097	.1128	.1160	.1193	.1226	.1259	.1293
7	.0826	.0855	.0885	.0916	.0947	.0978	.1010	.1043	.1076	.1109	.1143	.1178
8	.0737	.0766	.0796	.0827	.0858	.0890	.0923	.0956	.0990	.1024	.1059	.1094
9	.0667	.0697	.0727	.0758	.0790	.0822	.0855	.0889	.0924	.0959	.0994	.1030
10	.0612	.0641	.0672	.0704	.0736	.0769	.0802	.0837	.0872	.0908	.0944	.0981
11	.0566	.0596	.0627	.0659	.0692	.0725	.0760	.0795	.0830	.0867	.0904	.0942
12	.0529	.0559	.0590	.0623	.0656	.0690	.0725	.0760	.0797	.0834	.0872	.0911
13	.0497	.0528	.0559	.0592	.0626	.0660	.0696	.0732	.0769	.0807	.0846	.0885
14	.0470	.0501	.0533	.0566	.0600	.0635	.0671	.0708	.0746	.0785	.0824	.0864
15	.0446	.0478	.0510	.0544	.0578	.0614	.0651	.0688	.0726	.0766	.0806	.0847
16	.0426	.0458	.0490	.0524	.0559	.0596	.0633	.0671	.0710	.0750	.0791	.0832
17	.0408	.0440	.0473	.0508	.0543	.0580	.0618	.0656	.0696	.0737	.0778	.0820
18	.0392	.0425	.0458	.0493	.0529	.0566	.0604	.0644	.0684	.0725	.0767	.0810
19	.0378	.0411	.0445	.0480	.0516	.0554	.0593	.0633	.0674	.0715	.0758	.0801
20	.0366	.0398	.0433	.0468	.0505	.0543	.0583	.0623	.0665	.0707	.0750	.0794
21	.0354	.0387	.0422	.0458	.0495	.0534	.0574	.0615	.0657	.0700	.0743	.0788
22	.0344	.0377	.0412	.0449	.0487	.0526	.0566	.0608	.0650	.0693	.0738	.0782
23	.0335	.0368	.0404	.0441	.0479	.0518	.0559	.0601	.0644	.0688	.0733	.0778
24	.0326	.0360	.0396	.0433	.0472	.0512	.0553	.0596	.0639	.0683	.0728	.0774
25	.0318	.0353	.0389	.0426	.0466	.0506	.0548	.0591	.0634	.0679	.0725	.0771
26	.0311	.0346	.0382	.0420	.0460	.0501	.0543	.0586	.0630	.0676	.0721	.0768
27	.0305	.0339	.0376	.0415	.0455	.0496	.0539	.0582	.0627	.0672	.0719	.0765
28	.0298	.0334	.0371	.0410	.0450	.0492	.0535	.0579	.0624	.0670	.0716	.0763
29	.0293	.0328	.0366	.0405	.0446	.0488	.0531	.0576	.0621	.0667	.0714	.0761
30	.0288	.0324	.0361	.0401	.0442	.0485	.0528	.0573	.0619	.0665	.0712	.0760

ANNUAL COMPOUNDING

YEAR	4 %	5 %	6 %	7 %	8 %	9 %	10 %	11 %	12 %	13 %	14 %	15 %
1	1.0400	1.0500	1.0600	1.0700	1.0800	1.0900	1.1000	1.1100	1.1200	1.1300	1.1400	1.1500
2	.5302	.5378	.5454	.5531	.5608	.5685	.5762	.5839	.5917	.5995	.6073	.6151
3	.3603	.3672	.3741	.3811	.3880	.3951	.4021	.4092	.4163	.4235	.4307	.4380
4	.2755	.2820	.2886	.2952	.3019	.3087	.3155	.3223	.3292	.3362	.3432	.3503
5	.2246	.2310	.2374	.2439	.2505	.2571	.2638	.2706	.2774	.2843	.2913	.2983
6	.1908	.1970	.2034	.2098	.2163	.2229	.2296	.2364	.2432	.2502	.2572	.2642
7	.1666	.1728	.1791	.1856	.1921	.1987	.2054	.2122	.2191	.2261	.2332	.2404
8	.1485	.1547	.1610	.1675	.1740	.1807	.1874	.1943	.2013	.2084	.2156	.2229
9	.1345	.1407	.1470	.1535	.1601	.1668	.1736	.1806	.1877	.1949	.2022	.2096
10	.1233	.1295	.1359	.1424	.1490	.1558	.1627	.1698	.1770	.1843	.1917	.1993
11	.1141	.1204	.1268	.1334	.1401	.1469	.1540	.1611	.1684	.1758	.1834	.1911
12	.1066	.1128	.1193	.1259	.1327	.1397	.1468	.1540	.1614	.1690	.1767	.1845
13	.1001	.1065	.1130	.1197	.1265	.1336	.1408	.1482	.1557	.1634	.1712	.1791
14	.0947	.1010	.1076	.1143	.1213	.1284	.1357	.1432	.1509	.1587	.1666	.1747
15	.0899	.0963	.1030	.1098	.1168	.1241	.1315	.1391	.1468	.1547	.1628	.1710
16	.0858	.0923	.0990	.1059	.1130	.1203	.1278	.1355	.1434	.1514	.1596	.1679
17	.0822	.0887	.0954	.1024	.1096	.1170	.1247	.1325	.1405	.1486	.1569	.1654
18	.0790	.0855	.0924	.0994	.1067	.1142	.1219	.1298	.1379	.1462	.1546	.1632
19	.0761	.0827	.0896	.0968	.1041	.1117	.1195	.1276	.1358	.1441	.1527	.1613
20	.0736	.0802	.0872	.0944	.1019	.1095	.1175	.1256	.1339	.1424	.1510	.1598
21	.0713	.0780	.0850	.0923	.0998	.1076	.1156	.1238	.1322	.1408	.1495	.1584
22	.0692	.0760	.0830	.0904	.0980	.1059	.1140	.1223	.1308	.1395	.1483	.1573
23	.0673	.0741	.0813	.0887	.0964	.1044	.1126	.1210	.1296	.1383	.1472	.1563
24	.0656	.0725	.0797	.0872	.0950	.1030	.1113	.1198	.1285	.1373	.1463	.1554
25	.0640	.0710	.0782	.0858	.0937	.1018	.1102	.1187	.1275	.1364	.1455	.1547
26	.0626	.0696	.0769	.0846	.0925	.1007	.1092	.1178	.1267	.1357	.1448	.1541
27	.0612	.0683	.0757	.0834	.0914	.0997	.1083	.1170	.1259	.1350	.1442	.1535
28	.0600	.0671	.0746	.0824	.0905	.0989	.1075	.1163	.1252	.1344	.1437	.1531
29	.0589	.0660	.0736	.0814	.0896	.0981	.1067	.1156	.1247	.1339	.1432	.1527
30	.0578	.0651	.0726	.0806	.0888	.0973	.1061	.1150	.1241	.1334	.1428	.1523

Description: This table shows the total annual payment of interest and principal needed to amortize a loan of $ 100.

Example: At 8 % a loan is amortized over thirty years by a constant of 8.81 %.

MONTHLY COMPOUNDING

YEAR	4 %	5 %	6 %	7 %	8 %	9 %	10 %	11 %	12 %	13 %	14 %	15 %
1	102.18	102.73	103.28	103.84	104.39	104.95	105.50	106.06	106.62	107.19	107.75	108.31
2	52.11	52.65	53.19	53.73	54.28	54.83	55.38	55.93	56.49	57.06	57.62	58.19
3	35.43	35.97	36.51	37.06	37.61	38.16	38.73	39.29	39.86	40.44	41.02	41.60
4	27.10	27.64	28.19	28.74	29.30	29.87	30.44	31.02	31.61	32.20	32.80	33.40
5	22.10	22.65	23.20	23.77	24.34	24.92	25.50	26.10	26.70	27.31	27.93	28.55
6	18.78	19.33	19.89	20.46	21.04	21.64	22.24	22.85	23.47	24.09	24.73	25.38
7	16.41	16.97	17.54	18.12	18.71	19.31	19.93	20.55	21.19	21.84	22.49	23.16
8	14.63	15.20	15.77	16.37	16.97	17.59	18.21	18.86	19.51	20.17	20.85	21.54
9	13.25	13.83	14.41	15.01	15.63	16.26	16.90	17.56	18.23	18.91	19.61	20.31
10	12.15	12.73	13.33	13.94	14.56	15.21	15.86	16.54	17.22	17.92	18.64	19.37
11	11.26	11.84	12.45	13.07	13.70	14.36	15.03	15.72	16.42	17.14	17.87	18.62
12	10.51	11.10	11.72	12.35	12.99	13.66	14.35	15.05	15.77	16.50	17.25	18.02
13	9.88	10.48	11.10	11.74	12.40	13.08	13.78	14.50	15.23	15.98	16.75	17.53
14	9.35	9.95	10.58	11.23	11.90	12.59	13.30	14.03	14.78	15.55	16.33	17.13
15	8.88	9.49	10.13	10.79	11.47	12.18	12.90	13.64	14.41	15.19	15.99	16.80
16	8.48	9.10	9.74	10.41	11.10	11.82	12.56	13.31	14.09	14.88	15.70	16.53
17	8.12	8.75	9.40	10.08	10.78	11.51	12.26	13.03	13.82	14.63	15.45	16.30
18	7.81	8.44	9.10	9.79	10.50	11.24	12.00	12.79	13.59	14.41	15.25	16.11
19	7.53	8.17	8.84	9.54	10.26	11.01	11.78	12.57	13.39	14.22	15.08	15.94
20	7.28	7.92	8.60	9.31	10.04	10.80	11.59	12.39	13.22	14.06	14.93	15.81
21	7.05	7.71	8.39	9.11	9.85	10.62	11.41	12.23	13.07	13.93	14.80	15.69
22	6.85	7.51	8.20	8.93	9.68	10.46	11.26	12.09	12.94	13.81	14.69	15.59
23	6.66	7.33	8.03	8.76	9.53	10.32	11.13	11.97	12.83	13.71	14.60	15.51
24	6.49	7.17	7.88	8.62	9.39	10.19	11.01	11.86	12.73	13.62	14.52	15.44
25	6.34	7.02	7.74	8.49	9.27	10.08	10.91	11.77	12.64	13.54	14.45	15.37
26	6.20	6.89	7.61	8.37	9.16	9.97	10.82	11.68	12.57	13.47	14.39	15.32
27	6.07	6.76	7.49	8.26	9.06	9.88	10.73	11.61	12.50	13.41	14.34	15.28
28	5.95	6.65	7.39	8.16	8.97	9.80	10.66	11.54	12.44	13.36	14.30	15.24
29	5.84	6.54	7.29	8.07	8.88	9.73	10.59	11.48	12.39	13.32	14.26	15.21
30	5.73	6.45	7.20	7.99	8.81	9.66	10.54	11.43	12.35	13.28	14.22	15.18

QUARTERLY COMPOUNDING

YEAR	4 %	5 %	6 %	7 %	8 %	9 %	10 %	11 %	12 %	13 %	14 %	15 %
1	102.52	103.15	103.78	104.42	105.05	105.69	106.33	106.97	107.62	108.26	108.91	109.55
2	52.28	52.86	53.44	54.02	54.61	55.20	55.79	56.39	56.99	57.59	58.20	58.80
3	35.54	36.11	36.68	37.25	37.83	38.41	39.00	39.59	40.19	40.79	41.40	42.01
4	27.18	27.74	28.31	28.88	29.47	30.05	30.64	31.24	31.85	32.46	33.08	33.70
5	22.17	22.73	23.30	23.88	24.47	25.06	25.66	26.27	26.89	27.52	28.15	28.79
6	18.83	19.40	19.97	20.56	21.15	21.76	22.37	22.99	23.62	24.26	24.91	25.57
7	16.45	17.02	17.61	18.20	18.80	19.42	20.04	20.68	21.32	21.98	22.65	23.32
8	14.67	15.25	15.84	16.44	17.05	17.67	18.31	18.96	19.62	20.30	20.98	21.68
9	13.29	13.87	14.47	15.08	15.70	16.34	16.99	17.65	18.33	19.02	19.72	20.43
10	12.19	12.77	13.38	13.99	14.63	15.28	15.94	16.62	17.31	18.02	18.74	19.47
11	11.29	11.88	12.49	13.12	13.76	14.42	15.10	15.79	16.50	17.22	17.96	18.71
12	10.54	11.14	11.75	12.39	13.05	13.72	14.41	15.11	15.84	16.57	17.33	18.10
13	9.91	10.51	11.14	11.78	12.45	13.13	13.83	14.55	15.29	16.05	16.81	17.60
14	9.37	9.98	10.61	11.27	11.94	12.64	13.35	14.09	14.84	15.61	16.39	17.19
15	8.90	9.52	10.16	10.83	11.51	12.22	12.95	13.69	14.46	15.24	16.04	16.86
16	8.50	9.12	9.77	10.44	11.14	11.86	12.60	13.36	14.14	14.93	15.75	16.58
17	8.14	8.77	9.43	10.11	10.82	11.55	12.30	13.07	13.86	14.67	15.50	16.34
18	7.83	8.46	9.13	9.82	10.54	11.28	12.04	12.82	13.63	14.45	15.29	16.14
19	7.54	8.19	8.86	9.56	10.29	11.04	11.81	12.61	13.42	14.26	15.11	15.98
20	7.29	7.94	8.62	9.33	10.07	10.83	11.62	12.42	13.25	14.10	14.96	15.84
21	7.07	7.72	8.41	9.13	9.88	10.65	11.44	12.26	13.10	13.96	14.83	15.72
22	6.86	7.53	8.22	8.95	9.70	10.48	11.29	12.12	12.97	13.83	14.72	15.62
23	6.68	7.35	8.05	8.78	9.55	10.34	11.15	11.99	12.85	13.73	14.62	15.53
24	6.51	7.18	7.89	8.64	9.41	10.21	11.04	11.88	12.75	13.64	14.54	15.46
25	6.35	7.03	7.75	8.50	9.29	10.10	10.93	11.79	12.66	13.56	14.47	15.39
26	6.21	6.90	7.62	8.38	9.17	9.99	10.84	11.70	12.59	13.49	14.41	15.34
27	6.08	6.77	7.51	8.27	9.07	9.90	10.75	11.63	12.52	13.43	14.35	15.29
28	5.96	6.66	7.40	8.18	8.98	9.82	10.68	11.56	12.46	13.38	14.31	15.25
29	5.85	6.56	7.30	8.08	8.90	9.74	10.61	11.50	12.41	13.33	14.27	15.22
30	5.74	6.46	7.21	8.00	8.82	9.67	10.55	11.45	12.36	13.29	14.23	15.19

Description: This table shows the total annual payment of interest and principal needed to amortize a loan of $ 100.

Example: At 8 % a loan is amortized over thirty years by a constant of 8.85 %.

SEMIANNUAL COMPOUNDING

YEAR	4 %	5 %	6 %	7 %	8 %	9 %	10 %	11 %	12 %	13 %	14 %	15 %
1	103.01	103.77	104.53	105.29	106.04	106.80	107.57	108.33	109.09	109.86	110.62	111.39
2	52.53	53.17	53.81	54.46	55.10	55.75	56.41	57.06	57.72	58.39	59.05	59.72
3	35.71	36.31	36.92	37.54	38.16	38.78	39.41	40.04	40.68	41.32	41.96	42.61
4	27.31	27.90	28.50	29.10	29.71	30.33	30.95	31.58	32.21	32.85	33.50	34.15
5	22.27	22.86	23.45	24.05	24.66	25.28	25.91	26.54	27.18	27.83	28.48	29.14
6	18.92	19.50	20.10	20.70	21.32	21.94	22.57	23.21	23.86	24.52	25.19	25.86
7	16.53	17.11	17.71	18.32	18.94	19.57	20.21	20.86	21.52	22.19	22.87	23.56
8	14.74	15.32	15.93	16.54	17.17	17.81	18.46	19.12	19.80	20.48	21.18	21.88
9	13.35	13.94	14.55	15.17	15.80	16.45	17.11	17.79	18.48	19.18	19.89	20.61
10	12.24	12.83	13.45	14.08	14.72	15.38	16.05	16.74	17.44	18.16	18.88	19.62
11	11.33	11.93	12.55	13.19	13.84	14.51	15.20	15.90	16.61	17.34	18.09	18.84
12	10.58	11.19	11.81	12.46	13.12	13.80	14.50	15.21	15.94	16.68	17.44	18.22
13	9.94	10.56	11.19	11.85	12.52	13.21	13.92	14.64	15.39	16.14	16.92	17.70
14	9.40	10.02	10.66	11.33	12.01	12.71	13.43	14.17	14.92	15.70	16.48	17.29
15	8.93	9.56	10.21	10.88	11.57	12.28	13.02	13.77	14.53	15.32	16.12	16.94
16	8.53	9.16	9.81	10.49	11.19	11.92	12.66	13.42	14.21	15.00	15.82	16.65
17	8.17	8.81	9.47	10.16	10.87	11.60	12.36	13.13	13.92	14.74	15.56	16.41
18	7.85	8.50	9.17	9.86	10.58	11.33	12.09	12.88	13.68	14.51	15.35	16.20
19	7.57	8.22	8.90	9.60	10.33	11.09	11.86	12.66	13.48	14.31	15.16	16.03
20	7.32	7.97	8.66	9.37	10.11	10.87	11.66	12.47	13.30	14.14	15.01	15.89
21	7.09	7.75	8.44	9.16	9.91	10.69	11.48	12.30	13.14	14.00	14.87	15.76
22	6.88	7.55	8.25	8.98	9.74	10.52	11.33	12.16	13.01	13.87	14.76	15.65
23	6.70	7.37	8.08	8.82	9.58	10.37	11.19	12.03	12.89	13.76	14.66	15.56
24	6.53	7.21	7.92	8.67	9.44	10.24	11.07	11.92	12.78	13.67	14.57	15.49
25	6.37	7.06	7.78	8.53	9.32	10.13	10.96	11.82	12.69	13.59	14.50	15.42
26	6.23	6.92	7.65	8.41	9.20	10.02	10.86	11.73	12.61	13.52	14.43	15.36
27	6.10	6.79	7.53	8.30	9.10	9.93	10.78	11.65	12.54	13.45	14.38	15.31
28	5.97	6.68	7.42	8.20	9.01	9.84	10.70	11.58	12.48	13.40	14.33	15.27
29	5.86	6.57	7.32	8.11	8.92	9.76	10.63	11.52	12.43	13.35	14.29	15.23
30	5.76	6.48	7.23	8.02	8.85	9.70	10.57	11.47	12.38	13.31	14.25	15.20

ANNUAL COMPOUNDING

YEAR	4 %	5 %	6 %	7 %	8 %	9 %	10 %	11 %	12 %	13 %	14 %	15 %
1	104.00	105.00	106.00	107.00	108.00	109.00	110.00	111.00	112.00	113.00	114.00	115.00
2	53.02	53.79	54.55	55.31	56.08	56.85	57.62	58.40	59.17	59.95	60.73	61.52
3	36.04	36.73	37.42	38.11	38.81	39.51	40.22	40.93	41.64	42.36	43.08	43.80
4	27.55	28.21	28.86	29.53	30.20	30.87	31.55	32.24	32.93	33.62	34.33	35.03
5	22.47	23.10	23.74	24.39	25.05	25.71	26.38	27.06	27.75	28.44	29.13	29.84
6	19.08	19.71	20.34	20.98	21.64	22.30	22.97	23.64	24.33	25.02	25.72	26.43
7	16.67	17.29	17.92	18.56	19.21	19.87	20.55	21.23	21.92	22.62	23.32	24.04
8	14.86	15.48	16.11	16.75	17.41	18.07	18.75	19.44	20.14	20.84	21.56	22.29
9	13.45	14.07	14.71	15.35	16.01	16.68	17.37	18.07	18.77	19.49	20.22	20.96
10	12.33	12.96	13.59	14.24	14.91	15.59	16.28	16.99	17.70	18.43	19.18	19.93
11	11.42	12.04	12.68	13.34	14.01	14.70	15.40	16.12	16.85	17.59	18.34	19.11
12	10.66	11.29	11.93	12.60	13.27	13.97	14.68	15.41	16.15	16.90	17.67	18.45
13	10.02	10.65	11.30	11.97	12.66	13.36	14.08	14.82	15.57	16.34	17.12	17.92
14	9.47	10.11	10.76	11.44	12.13	12.85	13.58	14.33	15.09	15.87	16.67	17.47
15	9.00	9.64	10.30	10.98	11.69	12.41	13.15	13.91	14.69	15.48	16.29	17.11
16	8.59	9.23	9.90	10.59	11.30	12.03	12.79	13.56	14.34	15.15	15.97	16.80
17	8.22	8.87	9.55	10.25	10.97	11.71	12.47	13.25	14.05	14.87	15.70	16.54
18	7.90	8.56	9.24	9.95	10.68	11.43	12.20	12.99	13.80	14.63	15.47	16.32
19	7.62	8.28	8.97	9.68	10.42	11.18	11.96	12.76	13.58	14.42	15.27	16.14
20	7.36	8.03	8.72	9.44	10.19	10.96	11.75	12.56	13.39	14.24	15.10	15.98
21	7.13	7.80	8.51	9.23	9.99	10.77	11.57	12.39	13.23	14.09	14.96	15.85
22	6.92	7.60	8.31	9.05	9.81	10.60	11.41	12.24	13.09	13.95	14.84	15.73
23	6.74	7.42	8.13	8.88	9.65	10.44	11.26	12.10	12.96	13.84	14.73	15.63
24	6.56	7.25	7.97	8.72	9.50	10.31	11.13	11.98	12.85	13.74	14.64	15.55
25	6.41	7.10	7.83	8.59	9.37	10.19	11.02	11.88	12.75	13.65	14.55	15.47
26	6.26	6.96	7.70	8.46	9.26	10.08	10.92	11.79	12.67	13.57	14.49	15.41
27	6.13	6.83	7.57	8.35	9.15	9.98	10.83	11.70	12.60	13.50	14.42	15.36
28	6.01	6.72	7.46	8.24	9.05	9.89	10.75	11.63	12.53	13.44	14.37	15.31
29	5.89	6.61	7.36	8.15	8.97	9.81	10.68	11.57	12.47	13.39	14.33	15.27
30	5.79	6.51	7.27	8.06	8.89	9.74	10.61	11.51	12.42	13.35	14.29	15.24

Description: This table shows the total interest paid over the term on a loan of $ 1.

Example: At 8 % the total interest paid on a $ 10,000 loan amortized over thirty years is $ 16415.52.

MONTHLY COMPOUNDING

YEAR	4 %	5 %	6 %	7 %	8 %	9 %	10 %	11 %	12 %	13 %	14 %	15 %
1	.02	.03	.03	.04	.04	.05	.05	.06	.07	.07	.08	.08
2	.04	.05	.06	.07	.09	.10	.11	.12	.13	.14	.15	.16
3	.06	.08	.10	.11	.13	.14	.16	.18	.20	.21	.23	.25
4	.08	.11	.13	.15	.17	.19	.22	.24	.26	.29	.31	.34
5	.10	.13	.16	.19	.22	.25	.27	.30	.33	.37	.40	.43
6	.13	.16	.19	.23	.26	.30	.33	.37	.41	.45	.48	.52
7	.15	.19	.23	.27	.31	.35	.39	.44	.48	.53	.57	.62
8	.17	.22	.26	.31	.36	.41	.46	.51	.56	.61	.67	.72
9	.19	.24	.30	.35	.41	.46	.52	.58	.64	.70	.76	.83
10	.21	.27	.33	.39	.46	.52	.59	.65	.72	.79	.86	.94
11	.24	.30	.37	.44	.51	.58	.65	.73	.81	.88	.97	1.05
12	.26	.33	.41	.48	.56	.64	.72	.81	.89	.98	1.07	1.16
13	.28	.36	.44	.53	.61	.70	.79	.88	.98	1.08	1.18	1.28
14	.31	.39	.48	.57	.67	.76	.86	.96	1.07	1.18	1.29	1.40
15	.33	.42	.52	.62	.72	.83	.93	1.05	1.16	1.28	1.40	1.52
16	.36	.45	.56	.67	.78	.89	1.01	1.13	1.25	1.38	1.51	1.64
17	.38	.49	.60	.71	.83	.96	1.08	1.21	1.35	1.49	1.63	1.77
18	.40	.52	.64	.76	.89	1.02	1.16	1.30	1.45	1.59	1.74	1.90
19	.43	.55	.68	.81	.95	1.09	1.24	1.39	1.54	1.70	1.86	2.03
20	.45	.58	.72	.86	1.01	1.16	1.32	1.48	1.64	1.81	1.98	2.16
21	.48	.62	.76	.91	1.07	1.23	1.40	1.57	1.74	1.92	2.11	2.29
22	.51	.65	.80	.96	1.13	1.30	1.48	1.66	1.85	2.04	2.23	2.43
23	.53	.68	.85	1.01	1.19	1.37	1.56	1.75	1.95	2.15	2.36	2.57
24	.56	.72	.89	1.07	1.25	1.44	1.64	1.85	2.05	2.27	2.48	2.70
25	.58	.75	.93	1.12	1.32	1.52	1.73	1.94	2.16	2.38	2.61	2.84
26	.61	.79	.98	1.17	1.38	1.59	1.81	2.04	2.27	2.50	2.74	2.98
27	.64	.82	1.02	1.23	1.44	1.67	1.90	2.13	2.37	2.62	2.87	3.12
28	.66	.86	1.07	1.28	1.51	1.74	1.98	2.23	2.48	2.74	3.00	3.27
29	.69	.90	1.11	1.34	1.58	1.82	2.07	2.33	2.59	2.86	3.13	3.41
30	.72	.93	1.16	1.40	1.64	1.90	2.16	2.43	2.70	2.98	3.27	3.55

QUARTERLY COMPOUNDING

YEAR	4 %	5 %	6 %	7 %	8 %	9 %	10 %	11 %	12 %	13 %	14 %	15 %
1	.03	.03	.04	.04	.05	.06	.06	.07	.08	.08	.09	.10
2	.05	.06	.07	.08	.09	.10	.12	.13	.14	.15	.16	.18
3	.07	.08	.10	.12	.13	.15	.17	.19	.21	.22	.24	.26
4	.09	.11	.13	.16	.18	.20	.23	.25	.27	.30	.32	.35
5	.11	.14	.16	.19	.22	.25	.28	.31	.34	.38	.41	.44
6	.13	.16	.20	.23	.27	.31	.34	.38	.42	.46	.49	.53
7	.15	.19	.23	.27	.32	.36	.40	.45	.49	.54	.58	.63
8	.17	.22	.27	.31	.36	.41	.46	.52	.57	.62	.68	.73
9	.20	.25	.30	.36	.41	.47	.53	.59	.65	.71	.77	.84
10	.22	.28	.34	.40	.46	.53	.59	.66	.73	.80	.87	.95
11	.24	.31	.37	.44	.51	.59	.66	.74	.81	.89	.97	1.06
12	.26	.34	.41	.49	.56	.65	.73	.81	.90	.99	1.08	1.17
13	.29	.37	.45	.53	.62	.71	.80	.89	.99	1.09	1.19	1.29
14	.31	.40	.49	.58	.67	.77	.87	.97	1.08	1.18	1.29	1.41
15	.33	.43	.52	.62	.73	.83	.94	1.05	1.17	1.29	1.41	1.53
16	.36	.46	.56	.67	.78	.90	1.01	1.14	1.26	1.39	1.52	1.65
17	.38	.49	.60	.72	.84	.96	1.09	1.22	1.36	1.49	1.63	1.78
18	.41	.52	.64	.77	.90	1.03	1.17	1.31	1.45	1.60	1.75	1.91
19	.43	.55	.68	.82	.95	1.10	1.24	1.39	1.55	1.71	1.87	2.03
20	.46	.59	.72	.87	1.01	1.17	1.32	1.48	1.65	1.82	1.99	2.17
21	.48	.62	.77	.92	1.07	1.23	1.40	1.57	1.75	1.93	2.11	2.30
22	.51	.65	.81	.97	1.13	1.31	1.48	1.66	1.85	2.04	2.24	2.43
23	.53	.69	.85	1.02	1.19	1.38	1.56	1.76	1.95	2.16	2.36	2.57
24	.56	.72	.89	1.07	1.26	1.45	1.65	1.85	2.06	2.27	2.49	2.71
25	.59	.76	.94	1.12	1.32	1.52	1.73	1.95	2.16	2.39	2.62	2.85
26	.61	.79	.98	1.18	1.38	1.60	1.82	2.04	2.27	2.51	2.74	2.99
27	.64	.83	1.03	1.23	1.45	1.67	1.90	2.14	2.38	2.62	2.87	3.13
28	.67	.86	1.07	1.29	1.51	1.75	1.99	2.23	2.49	2.74	3.00	3.27
29	.69	.90	1.12	1.34	1.58	1.82	2.08	2.33	2.60	2.86	3.14	3.41
30	.72	.94	1.16	1.40	1.65	1.90	2.16	2.43	2.71	2.99	3.27	3.55

Description: This table shows the total interest paid over the term on a loan of $ 1.

Example: At 8 % the total interest paid on a $ 10,000 loan amortized over thirty years is $ 16521.11.

SEMIANNUAL COMPOUNDING

YEAR	4 %	5 %	6 %	7 %	8 %	9 %	10 %	11 %	12 %	13 %	14 %	15 %
1	.03	.04	.05	.05	.06	.07	.08	.08	.09	.10	.11	.11
2	.05	.06	.08	.09	.10	.11	.13	.14	.15	.17	.18	.19
3	.07	.09	.11	.13	.14	.16	.18	.20	.22	.24	.26	.28
4	.09	.12	.14	.16	.19	.21	.24	.26	.29	.31	.34	.37
5	.11	.14	.17	.20	.23	.26	.30	.33	.36	.39	.42	.46
6	.13	.17	.21	.24	.28	.32	.35	.39	.43	.47	.51	.55
7	.16	.20	.24	.28	.33	.37	.41	.46	.51	.55	.60	.65
8	.18	.23	.27	.32	.37	.42	.48	.53	.58	.64	.69	.75
9	.20	.25	.31	.36	.42	.48	.54	.60	.66	.73	.79	.85
10	.22	.28	.34	.41	.47	.54	.60	.67	.74	.82	.89	.96
11	.25	.31	.38	.45	.52	.60	.67	.75	.83	.91	.99	1.07
12	.27	.34	.42	.49	.57	.66	.74	.82	.91	1.00	1.09	1.19
13	.29	.37	.45	.54	.63	.72	.81	.90	1.00	1.10	1.20	1.30
14	.32	.40	.49	.58	.68	.78	.88	.98	1.09	1.20	1.31	1.42
15	.34	.43	.53	.63	.73	.84	.95	1.06	1.18	1.30	1.42	1.54
16	.36	.46	.57	.68	.79	.91	1.02	1.15	1.27	1.40	1.53	1.66
17	.39	.50	.61	.73	.85	.97	1.10	1.23	1.37	1.50	1.65	1.79
18	.41	.53	.65	.77	.90	1.04	1.18	1.32	1.46	1.61	1.76	1.92
19	.44	.56	.69	.82	.96	1.11	1.25	1.40	1.56	1.72	1.88	2.05
20	.46	.59	.73	.87	1.02	1.17	1.33	1.49	1.66	1.83	2.00	2.18
21	.49	.63	.77	.92	1.08	1.24	1.41	1.58	1.76	1.94	2.12	2.31
22	.51	.66	.81	.97	1.14	1.31	1.49	1.67	1.86	2.05	2.25	2.44
23	.54	.69	.86	1.03	1.20	1.38	1.57	1.77	1.96	2.16	2.37	2.58
24	.56	.73	.90	1.08	1.26	1.46	1.66	1.86	2.07	2.28	2.50	2.72
25	.59	.76	.94	1.13	1.33	1.53	1.74	1.95	2.17	2.40	2.62	2.85
26	.62	.80	.99	1.19	1.39	1.60	1.82	2.05	2.28	2.51	2.75	2.99
27	.64	.83	1.03	1.24	1.46	1.68	1.91	2.14	2.39	2.63	2.88	3.13
28	.67	.87	1.08	1.29	1.52	1.75	1.99	2.24	2.49	2.75	3.01	3.27
29	.70	.90	1.12	1.35	1.59	1.83	2.08	2.34	2.60	2.87	3.14	3.42
30	.73	.94	1.17	1.41	1.65	1.91	2.17	2.44	2.71	2.99	3.27	3.56

ANNUAL COMPOUNDING

YEAR	4 %	5 %	6 %	7 %	8 %	9 %	10 %	11 %	12 %	13 %	14 %	15 %
1	.04	.05	.06	.07	.08	.09	.10	.11	.12	.13	.14	.15
2	.06	.08	.09	.11	.12	.14	.15	.17	.18	.20	.21	.23
3	.08	.10	.12	.14	.16	.19	.21	.23	.25	.27	.29	.31
4	.10	.13	.15	.18	.21	.23	.26	.29	.32	.34	.37	.40
5	.12	.15	.19	.22	.25	.29	.32	.35	.39	.42	.46	.49
6	.14	.18	.22	.26	.30	.34	.38	.42	.46	.50	.54	.59
7	.17	.21	.25	.30	.34	.39	.44	.49	.53	.58	.63	.68
8	.19	.24	.29	.34	.39	.45	.50	.55	.61	.67	.72	.78
9	.21	.27	.32	.38	.44	.50	.56	.63	.69	.75	.82	.89
10	.23	.30	.36	.42	.49	.56	.63	.70	.77	.84	.92	.99
11	.26	.32	.39	.47	.54	.62	.69	.77	.85	.93	1.02	1.10
12	.28	.35	.43	.51	.59	.68	.76	.85	.94	1.03	1.12	1.21
13	.30	.38	.47	.56	.64	.74	.83	.93	1.02	1.12	1.23	1.33
14	.33	.41	.51	.60	.70	.80	.90	1.01	1.11	1.22	1.33	1.45
15	.35	.45	.54	.65	.75	.86	.97	1.09	1.20	1.32	1.44	1.57
16	.37	.48	.58	.69	.81	.92	1.05	1.17	1.29	1.42	1.55	1.69
17	.40	.51	.62	.74	.86	.99	1.12	1.25	1.39	1.53	1.67	1.81
18	.42	.54	.66	.79	.92	1.06	1.19	1.34	1.48	1.63	1.78	1.94
19	.45	.57	.70	.84	.98	1.12	1.27	1.42	1.58	1.74	1.90	2.07
20	.47	.60	.74	.89	1.04	1.19	1.35	1.51	1.68	1.85	2.02	2.20
21	.50	.64	.79	.94	1.10	1.26	1.43	1.60	1.78	1.96	2.14	2.33
22	.52	.67	.83	.99	1.16	1.33	1.51	1.69	1.88	2.07	2.26	2.46
23	.55	.71	.87	1.04	1.22	1.40	1.59	1.78	1.98	2.18	2.39	2.59
24	.57	.74	.91	1.09	1.28	1.47	1.67	1.87	2.08	2.30	2.51	2.73
25	.60	.77	.96	1.15	1.34	1.55	1.75	1.97	2.19	2.41	2.64	2.87
26	.63	.81	1.00	1.20	1.41	1.62	1.84	2.06	2.29	2.53	2.76	3.01
27	.65	.84	1.04	1.25	1.47	1.69	1.92	2.16	2.40	2.64	2.89	3.15
28	.68	.88	1.09	1.31	1.53	1.77	2.01	2.26	2.51	2.76	3.02	3.29
29	.71	.92	1.13	1.36	1.60	1.84	2.10	2.35	2.62	2.88	3.15	3.43
30	.73	.95	1.18	1.42	1.66	1.92	2.18	2.45	2.72	3.00	3.28	3.57

Description: This table shows the average annual interest rate on a loan that is amortized over the term.

Example: At 8 % the average interest rate on a five year amortized loan is 4.33 %.

MONTHLY COMPOUNDING

YEAR	4 %	5 %	6 %	7 %	8 %	9 %	10 %	11 %	12 %	13 %	14 %	15 %
1	2.18	2.73	3.28	3.83	4.39	4.94	5.50	6.06	6.62	7.18	7.74	8.31
2	2.11	2.65	3.18	3.73	4.27	4.82	5.37	5.93	6.49	7.05	7.62	8.18
3	2.10	2.63	3.17	3.72	4.27	4.83	5.39	5.95	6.52	7.10	7.68	8.27
4	2.09	2.64	3.18	3.74	4.30	4.86	5.44	6.01	6.60	7.19	7.79	8.40
5	2.10	2.65	3.20	3.76	4.33	4.91	5.50	6.09	6.69	7.30	7.92	8.55
6	2.11	2.66	3.22	3.79	4.37	4.96	5.56	6.17	6.79	7.42	8.06	8.71
7	2.12	2.67	3.24	3.83	4.42	5.02	5.64	6.26	6.90	7.54	8.20	8.87
8	2.13	2.69	3.27	3.86	4.46	5.08	5.71	6.35	7.00	7.67	8.35	9.03
9	2.14	2.71	3.30	3.90	4.51	5.14	5.78	6.44	7.11	7.79	8.49	9.20
10	2.15	2.73	3.32	3.93	4.56	5.20	5.86	6.53	7.22	7.92	8.63	9.36
11	2.16	2.75	3.35	3.97	4.61	5.26	5.93	6.62	7.32	8.04	8.77	9.52
12	2.17	2.77	3.38	4.01	4.66	5.32	6.01	6.71	7.43	8.16	8.91	9.68
13	2.19	2.78	3.40	4.04	4.70	5.38	6.08	6.80	7.53	8.28	9.05	9.83
14	2.20	2.80	3.43	4.08	4.75	5.44	6.16	6.89	7.63	8.40	9.18	9.98
15	2.21	2.82	3.46	4.12	4.80	5.50	6.23	6.97	7.74	8.52	9.31	10.13
16	2.22	2.84	3.49	4.16	4.85	5.56	6.30	7.06	7.83	8.63	9.44	10.27
17	2.23	2.86	3.51	4.19	4.90	5.62	6.37	7.14	7.93	8.74	9.57	10.41
18	2.25	2.88	3.54	4.23	4.94	5.68	6.44	7.23	8.03	8.85	9.69	10.54
19	2.26	2.90	3.57	4.27	4.99	5.74	6.51	7.31	8.12	8.96	9.81	10.68
20	2.27	2.92	3.60	4.30	5.04	5.80	6.58	7.39	8.21	9.06	9.92	10.80
21	2.28	2.94	3.62	4.34	5.08	5.85	6.65	7.46	8.30	9.16	10.03	10.92
22	2.30	2.96	3.65	4.38	5.13	5.91	6.71	7.54	8.39	9.26	10.14	11.04
23	2.31	2.98	3.68	4.41	5.17	5.96	6.78	7.62	8.47	9.35	10.25	11.15
24	2.32	3.00	3.71	4.45	5.22	6.02	6.84	7.69	8.56	9.44	10.35	11.26
25	2.33	3.02	3.73	4.48	5.26	6.07	6.90	7.76	8.64	9.53	10.45	11.37
26	2.35	3.03	3.76	4.52	5.31	6.12	6.97	7.83	8.72	9.62	10.54	11.47
27	2.36	3.05	3.78	4.55	5.35	6.17	7.03	7.90	8.79	9.70	10.63	11.57
28	2.37	3.07	3.81	4.58	5.39	6.22	7.08	7.97	8.87	9.79	10.72	11.66
29	2.38	3.09	3.84	4.62	5.43	6.27	7.14	8.03	8.94	9.86	10.80	11.75
30	2.40	3.11	3.86	4.65	5.47	6.32	7.20	8.09	9.01	9.94	10.89	11.84

QUARTERLY COMPOUNDING

YEAR	4 %	5 %	6 %	7 %	8 %	9 %	10 %	11 %	12 %	13 %	14 %	15 %
1	2.51	3.14	3.78	4.41	5.05	5.69	6.33	6.97	7.61	8.25	8.90	9.55
2	2.28	2.85	3.43	4.02	4.60	5.19	5.79	6.38	6.98	7.59	8.19	8.80
3	2.21	2.77	3.34	3.91	4.49	5.07	5.66	6.25	6.85	7.45	8.06	8.67
4	2.18	2.74	3.31	3.88	4.46	5.05	5.64	6.24	6.84	7.46	8.06	8.67
5	2.17	2.73	3.30	3.88	4.46	5.06	5.66	6.27	6.89	7.51	8.07	8.70
6	2.16	2.73	3.30	3.89	4.48	5.09	5.70	6.32	6.95	7.59	8.14	8.78
7	2.16	2.73	3.31	3.91	4.51	5.12	5.75	6.39	7.03	7.69	8.24	8.90
8	2.17	2.74	3.33	3.93	4.54	5.17	5.81	6.46	7.12	7.79	8.36	9.03
9	2.17	2.76	3.35	3.96	4.58	5.22	5.87	6.53	7.21	7.90	8.48	9.17
10	2.18	2.77	3.37	3.99	4.62	5.27	5.93	6.61	7.30	8.01	8.60	9.32
11	2.19	2.78	3.39	4.02	4.66	5.32	6.00	6.69	7.40	8.12	8.73	9.46
12	2.20	2.80	3.42	4.05	4.71	5.38	6.07	6.78	7.50	8.24	8.86	9.61
13	2.21	2.82	3.44	4.09	4.75	5.44	6.14	6.86	7.59	8.35	8.99	9.76
14	2.22	2.83	3.47	4.12	4.80	5.49	6.21	6.94	7.69	8.46	9.12	9.90
15	2.23	2.85	3.49	4.15	4.84	5.55	6.27	7.02	7.79	8.57	9.24	10.04
16	2.24	2.87	3.52	4.19	4.89	5.60	6.34	7.10	7.88	8.68	9.37	10.18
17	2.25	2.88	3.54	4.22	4.93	5.66	6.41	7.18	7.97	8.78	9.49	10.32
18	2.26	2.90	3.57	4.26	4.98	5.72	6.48	7.26	8.07	8.89	9.61	10.45
19	2.28	2.92	3.59	4.29	5.02	5.77	6.54	7.34	8.16	8.99	9.73	10.58
20	2.29	2.94	3.62	4.33	5.06	5.83	6.61	7.42	8.24	9.09	9.84	10.71
21	2.30	2.96	3.65	4.36	5.11	5.88	6.68	7.49	8.33	9.19	9.95	10.83
22	2.31	2.98	3.67	4.40	5.15	5.93	6.74	7.57	8.42	9.28	10.06	10.95
23	2.32	2.99	3.70	4.43	5.20	5.99	6.80	7.64	8.50	9.38	10.17	11.07
24	2.33	3.01	3.72	4.47	5.24	6.04	6.86	7.71	8.58	9.47	10.27	11.18
25	2.35	3.03	3.75	4.50	5.28	6.09	6.92	7.78	8.66	9.55	10.37	11.28
26	2.36	3.05	3.77	4.53	5.32	6.14	6.98	7.85	8.74	9.64	10.46	11.39
27	2.37	3.07	3.80	4.57	5.36	6.19	7.04	7.92	8.81	9.72	10.56	11.49
28	2.38	3.08	3.82	4.60	5.41	6.24	7.10	7.98	8.88	9.80	10.65	11.58
29	2.39	3.10	3.85	4.63	5.45	6.29	7.16	8.05	8.95	9.88	10.73	11.68
30	2.41	3.12	3.87	4.66	5.49	6.34	7.21	8.11	9.02	9.95	10.82	11.76

SCAN TABLE

Description: This table shows the average annual interest rate on a loan that is amortized over the term.

Example: At 8 % the average interest rate on a five year amortized loan is 4.66 %.

SEMIANNUAL COMPOUNDING

YEAR	4 %	5 %	6 %	7 %	8 %	9 %	10 %	11 %	12 %	13 %	14 %	15 %
1	3.01	3.77	4.52	5.28	6.04	6.80	7.56	8.32	9.09	9.85	10.62	11.39
2	2.52	3.16	3.81	4.45	5.10	5.75	6.40	7.06	7.72	8.38	9.05	9.71
3	2.37	2.98	3.59	4.20	4.82	5.44	6.07	6.70	7.34	7.98	8.63	9.28
4	2.30	2.89	3.49	4.10	4.71	5.32	5.94	6.57	7.21	7.85	8.49	9.15
5	2.27	2.85	3.45	4.05	4.66	5.28	5.90	6.53	7.17	7.82	8.48	9.14
6	2.25	2.83	3.43	4.03	4.64	5.27	5.90	6.54	7.19	7.85	8.51	9.19
7	2.23	2.82	3.42	4.03	4.65	5.28	5.92	6.57	7.23	7.90	8.58	9.27
8	2.23	2.82	3.42	4.04	4.66	5.30	5.95	6.62	7.29	7.98	8.67	9.38
9	2.23	2.82	3.43	4.05	4.69	5.34	6.00	6.67	7.36	8.06	8.77	9.49
10	2.23	2.83	3.44	4.07	4.72	5.38	6.05	6.74	7.44	8.15	8.88	9.62
11	2.24	2.84	3.46	4.10	4.75	5.42	6.10	6.80	7.52	8.25	8.99	9.75
12	2.24	2.85	3.48	4.12	4.78	5.46	6.16	6.87	7.60	8.35	9.10	9.88
13	2.25	2.86	3.50	4.15	4.82	5.51	6.22	6.95	7.69	8.45	9.22	10.01
14	2.26	2.87	3.52	4.18	4.86	5.56	6.28	7.02	7.78	8.55	9.34	10.14
15	2.26	2.89	3.54	4.21	4.90	5.61	6.34	7.09	7.86	8.65	9.45	10.27
16	2.27	2.90	3.56	4.24	4.94	5.66	6.41	7.17	7.95	8.75	9.56	10.40
17	2.28	2.92	3.58	4.27	4.98	5.71	6.47	7.24	8.04	8.85	9.68	10.52
18	2.29	2.93	3.61	4.30	5.02	5.77	6.53	7.32	8.12	8.95	9.79	10.64
19	2.30	2.95	3.63	4.33	5.06	5.82	6.59	7.39	8.21	9.04	9.90	10.76
20	2.31	2.97	3.65	4.37	5.10	5.87	6.66	7.46	8.29	9.14	10.00	10.88
21	2.32	2.98	3.68	4.40	5.15	5.92	6.72	7.54	8.37	9.23	10.11	10.99
22	2.33	3.00	3.70	4.43	5.19	5.97	6.78	7.61	8.46	9.32	10.21	11.10
23	2.34	3.02	3.72	4.46	5.23	6.02	6.84	7.68	8.54	9.41	10.30	11.21
24	2.35	3.03	3.75	4.49	5.27	6.07	6.90	7.75	8.61	9.50	10.40	11.31
25	2.36	3.05	3.77	4.53	5.31	6.12	6.96	7.81	8.69	9.58	10.49	11.41
26	2.38	3.07	3.80	4.56	5.35	6.17	7.01	7.88	8.76	9.66	10.58	11.51
27	2.39	3.09	3.82	4.59	5.39	6.22	7.07	7.94	8.84	9.74	10.67	11.60
28	2.40	3.10	3.85	4.62	5.43	6.26	7.12	8.01	8.91	9.82	10.75	11.69
29	2.41	3.12	3.87	4.65	5.47	6.31	7.18	8.07	8.97	9.90	10.83	11.78
30	2.42	3.14	3.89	4.68	5.51	6.36	7.23	8.13	9.04	9.97	10.91	11.86

ANNUAL COMPOUNDING

YEAR	4 %	5 %	6 %	7 %	8 %	9 %	10 %	11 %	12 %	13 %	14 %	15 %
1	4.00	5.00	6.00	7.00	8.00	9.00	10.00	11.00	12.00	13.00	14.00	15.00
2	3.02	3.78	4.54	5.31	6.08	6.85	7.62	8.39	9.17	9.95	10.73	11.51
3	2.70	3.39	4.08	4.77	5.47	6.17	6.88	7.59	8.30	9.02	9.74	10.46
4	2.55	3.20	3.86	4.52	5.19	5.87	6.55	7.23	7.92	8.62	9.32	10.03
5	2.46	3.10	3.74	4.39	5.05	5.71	6.38	7.06	7.74	8.43	9.13	9.83
6	2.41	3.04	3.67	4.31	4.96	5.63	6.29	6.97	7.66	8.35	9.05	9.76
7	2.38	3.00	3.63	4.27	4.92	5.58	6.25	6.94	7.63	8.33	9.03	9.75
8	2.35	2.97	3.60	4.25	4.90	5.57	6.24	6.93	7.63	8.34	9.06	9.79
9	2.34	2.96	3.59	4.24	4.90	5.57	6.25	6.95	7.66	8.38	9.11	9.85
10	2.33	2.95	3.59	4.24	4.90	5.58	6.27	6.98	7.70	8.43	9.17	9.93
11	2.32	2.95	3.59	4.24	4.92	5.60	6.31	7.02	7.75	8.49	9.25	10.02
12	2.32	2.95	3.59	4.26	4.94	5.63	6.34	7.07	7.81	8.57	9.33	10.11
13	2.32	2.95	3.60	4.27	4.96	5.66	6.39	7.12	7.88	8.64	9.42	10.22
14	2.32	2.96	3.62	4.29	4.99	5.70	6.43	7.18	7.94	8.72	9.52	10.33
15	2.33	2.97	3.63	4.31	5.02	5.74	6.48	7.24	8.02	8.81	9.61	10.44
16	2.33	2.98	3.65	4.34	5.05	5.78	6.53	7.30	8.09	8.89	9.71	10.54
17	2.34	2.99	3.66	4.36	5.08	5.82	6.58	7.36	8.16	8.98	9.81	10.65
18	2.34	3.00	3.68	4.39	5.11	5.87	6.64	7.43	8.24	9.06	9.91	10.76
19	2.35	3.01	3.70	4.41	5.15	5.91	6.69	7.49	8.31	9.15	10.00	10.87
20	2.36	3.02	3.72	4.44	5.19	5.95	6.75	7.56	8.39	9.24	10.10	10.98
21	2.37	3.04	3.74	4.47	5.22	6.00	6.80	7.62	8.46	9.32	10.19	11.08
22	2.37	3.05	3.76	4.50	5.26	6.05	6.86	7.69	8.54	9.40	10.28	11.18
23	2.38	3.07	3.78	4.52	5.29	6.09	6.91	7.75	8.61	9.48	10.38	11.28
24	2.39	3.08	3.80	4.55	5.33	6.14	6.96	7.81	8.68	9.56	10.46	11.38
25	2.40	3.10	3.82	4.58	5.37	6.18	7.02	7.87	8.75	9.64	10.55	11.47
26	2.41	3.11	3.84	4.61	5.40	6.23	7.07	7.94	8.82	9.72	10.63	11.56
27	2.42	3.13	3.87	4.64	5.44	6.27	7.12	8.00	8.89	9.79	10.72	11.65
28	2.43	3.14	3.89	4.67	5.48	6.31	7.17	8.05	8.95	9.87	10.80	11.73
29	2.44	3.16	3.91	4.70	5.51	6.36	7.22	8.11	9.02	9.94	10.87	11.82
30	2.45	3.17	3.93	4.73	5.55	6.40	7.27	8.17	9.08	10.01	10.95	11.90

TABLE **8**

Compound Interest and Annuity

Interest Rates:

Monthly: 0, 1%;
2 to 4.75% by .25%;
5 to 15% by .25%, .125%, .10%, .05%;
16 to 20% by 1%.

Quarterly: 0, 1%;
2 to 4.75% by .25%;
5 to 15% by .25%, .125%;
16 to 20% by 1%.

Semiannual: 0, 1%;
2 to 4.75% by .25%;
5 to 15% by .25%;
16 to 20% by 1%.

Annual: 0, 1%;
2 to 4.75% by .25%;
5 to 15% by .25%;
16 to 20% by 1%.

Terms: 1 to 50 years, each year.

Compound Periods: Monthly, quarterly, semiannual, annual.

This table shows the 3 compound interest functions that relate to savings and deposits, the 3 annuity functions that relate to payments and loans, and the 3 functions for measuring loans. These functions are:

Compound interest functions:
- Amount of 1
- Amount of 1 Per Period
- Sinking Fund

Annuity functions:
- Present Worth of 1
- Present Worth of 1 Per Period
- Periodic Payment to Amortize 1

Loan measurements:
- Constant Annual Percent
- Total Interest
- Annual Add On Rate

The Compound Interest and Annuity tables apply to fixed-rate transactions. Every transaction that includes an interest rate is at inception a fixed-rate transaction. Over time, the rate may change, as it does with a variable-rate mortgage, but even then, if the change in rate causes a change in payment, the new rate is computed as though it were fixed for the remainder of the term.

Elements of a Financial Transaction. The 4 elements in a financial transaction are:

- Amount
- Rate
- Term
- Payment

When 3 are known, then the fourth can be computed from this table. An additional 2 elements may be part of the transaction:

- Balance
- Yield

When the transaction is a loan, the table is used to compute a payment for the amount, at the interest rate, over the term. The amount is the present value of the loan, i.e., the value today, or the dollars borrowed and to be repaid. The rate is the stated

annual rate. The pages in this table are indexed by the annual rate. The term is usually computed in years; the term years are given in the left-hand index that runs down each page of the table. The payment per $1 can be read directly from the Periodic Payment to Amortize 1 column. If the term is in periods rather than years, use the index on the right-hand side of the table.

Within Table 8, there are separate tables for monthly, quarterly, semiannual, and annual payment periods. The tables are identified by an **M, Q, S,** or **A** in the right corner of each page. The first question to answer is how frequently the payment is to be made. Since most loans require monthly payments, the first set of tables beginning on page 8-2 are for these payments.

When a balance is part of the transaction, this is usually understood as a balance in the future, or future value (e.g., the balance in 10 years on a loan that amortizes in 30 years). In the calculation of a bond value, the balance, or future value, is the face amount of the bond, which is the amount that is paid at maturity.

The word "balloon" is often used in describing a loan balance in the future, although the term is ambiguous. For example, "a 10% balloon at the end of 20 years" might mean, on the one hand, 10% of the principal amount of the loan, or, on the other, that the 10% balloon includes the final interest payment plus the remaining balance. The distinction must be made when calculating a payment or a yield.

"Yield" refers to a rate of return to an investor. A loan, such as a mortgage, becomes a negotiable security once it is signed, sealed, and delivered. The lender may sell the security for more or less than the loan amount. The corresponding return, or yield, to the purchaser-investor will be less or more than the interest rate on the loan. In computing the present worth of an existing loan, it is necessary to know the yield rate, the term, and the payments. The calculated amount is the price at the yield rate.

Savings and Deposits. "Amount," "rate," "term," and "payment" also apply with respect to savings and deposits. "Amount" is the amount that is put on deposit, or at interest, in a savings account. "Rate" is the annual rate, or nominal rate, as differentiated from the effective rate. "Term" is the number of years of saving. "Payment" is the deposit that is made at regular intervals into a savings account. The term "balance" is used to refer to an amount in the future, i.e., the future value, or value to which the savings will grow. Here, as with loans, it is necessary to know how frequently deposits are made and interest is computed.

Period. The period determines the table to be used. The period is an interval of time; it is the time between 2 calculations of interest or between 2 payments on a loan. A period may be a month, a quarter, or a year, and it may be referred to as a compounding period, a payment period, or an interest period.

When the period is a month, there are 12 periods per year, 12 calculations of interest, and, if the loan is a mortgage, 12

payments of interest and principal. The interest rate is divided by 12 to compute the monthly interest factor.

If payments or deposits are made more or less frequently than the compounding period—for example, if deposits are made weekly and interest is computed monthly—then an equivalent monthly amount must be computed before the monthly tables are used.

The tables for monthly, quarterly, semiannual, and annual periods are clearly marked.

Periodic Interest Factor, _i._ The periodic interest factor, whose symbol is a lowercase _i_, is computed by the following formula:

$$i = \frac{\text{Annual interest rate} \div 100}{\text{Periods per year}}$$

The periodic interest factor can also be read directly from each page on Table 8 as the decimal portion of the Amount of 1 Per Period column.

Nominal Rate. The "nominal" rate is the named annual interest rate (e.g., a 6% bond, an 8% mortgage, a 5% interest rate on savings, an 18% rate on revolving credit). The nominal rate is the index rate shown in the upper right-hand corner of each page of the table; it is also the APR on the bottom line.

Effective Rate. When interest on savings is compounded more frequently than once a year (e.g., monthly or quarterly), then, by the end of a year, interest has been computed on interest. When interest is compounded, there is more money in the account at the end of the year than there would be if simple interest had been paid for the same period. This greater amount, when expressed as a rate per year, is known as the effective rate. For example, a nominal rate of 6% with interest compounded monthly produces an effective rate of 6.17%. Compounded quarterly, the rate is 6.13%.

Amount of 1, S

$$S = (1 + i)^n$$

This formula computes what a single $1 deposit will grow to in the future. The deposit is made at the beginning of the period. The symbol for the Amount of 1 is S,

where:

n = number of periods
i = periodic interest factor per period

Example: A deposit of $100 in a savings institution that pays 5% interest compounded annually grows in 5 years to $127.63. The periodic interest factor per $1 is found on page

8-436. The following table shows how the $100 grows year by year:

Year	Amount at Beginning of Year		Amount at End of Year
1	$100.00 × 1.05 =		$105.00
2	105.00 × 1.05 =		110.25
3	110.25 × 1.05 =		115.76
4	115.76 × 1.05 =		121.55
5	121.55 × 1.05 =		127.63

The amount at the end of the year equals the amount at the beginning of the year plus the interest for the year on the amount. When the $5 of interest at the end of year 1 is added to the principal amount, the interest is said to convert to principal. In the amount of $105, then, there is no distinction between interest and principal; it is all of a piece, all principal.

The symbol S^n is also used for the Amount of 1 where n indicates the number of periods. For the rate of 5% and a term of 5 years, n and i vary with the interest period, as follows:

Interest Period	5 Years (n)	Periodic Interest Factor (i)
Annual	5	.05
Semiannual	10	.025
Quarterly	20	.0125
Monthly	60	.0041666667

The Amount of 1 is the fundamental building block of Table 8. The formula for Amount of 1 expresses the underlying concept of compound interest. All of the functions shown in the table and discussed within are constructed on this concept.

The effective rate is the decimal portion of the Amount of 1 for 1 year, multiplied by 100, as shown in the following table for a 5% nominal rate.

Interest Period	Amount of 1 for 1 Year	Effective Rate
Annual	1.050000	5.00%
Semiannual	1.050625	5.06
Quarterly	1.050945	5.09
Monthly	1.051162	5.12

Simple and Compound Interest. Simple interest is interest on principal. Compound interest is interest on principal and on the interest that has been converted to principal. Interest is converted to principal after it has been computed and then added to the principal balance.

Example: If the $24 paid for the island of Manhattan were put at 4% simple interest for 356 years, the total amount would be $341.76.

$$24 \times .04 = .96$$

$$.96 \times 356 = 341.76$$

In contrast, if the $24 were put at 4% compound interest for 356 years, the total would be $27,802,255.63.

$$24 \times (1.04)^{356} = 27,802,255.63$$

Compound interest is the subject matter of this table. It underlies most of the tables in this book.

Amount of 1 Per Period, $S_{\overline{n}|}$

$$S_{\overline{n}|} = \frac{(1 + i)^n - 1}{i}$$

This formula computes what a series of $1 deposits will grow to in the future. A deposit is made at the end of each period. The symbol for the Amount of 1 Per Period, $S_{\overline{n}|}$, is read "S angle n."

Example: A regular deposit of $100 at the end of each year in a savings institution that pays 5% interest compounded annually grows to $552.56 in 5 years. The Amount of 1 Per Period factor is found on page 8-436.

The $100 deposits grow year by year in the following manner:

Year	Amount at Beginning of Year		Amount at End of Year	Amount Plus Deposit
1				$100.00
2	$100.00 × 1.05 =		$105.00	205.00
3	205.00 × 1.05 =		215.25	315.25
4	315.25 × 1.05 =		331.01	431.01
5	431.01 × 1.05 =		452.56	552.56

The Amount of 1 Per Period is a sum. The equation is:

$$S_{\overline{n}|} = 1 + S^1 + S^2 + S^3 + S^4 + \cdots + S^{n-1}$$

The right-hand side of the preceding equation is a series that transforms into a simpler expression, so the equation becomes:

$$S_{\overline{n}|} = \frac{S^n - 1}{i} = \frac{(1 + i)^n - 1}{i}$$

Example: A regular quarterly deposit of $25 in a savings institution that pays 5% interest compounded quarterly grows to $564.07 in 5 years. The Amount of 1 Per Period factor is found on page 8-276.

A regular monthly deposit of $8.33 in a savings institution that pays 5% interest compounded monthly grows to $566.49 in 5 years. The factor per $1 is found on page 8-16.

Sinking Fund, $1/S_{\overline{n}|}$

$$\frac{1}{S_{\overline{n}|}} = \frac{i}{(1 + i)^n - 1}$$

This formula computes the amount to be deposited at the end of each period that will grow to $1 in the future. The symbol for the Sinking Fund, $1/S_{\overline{n}|}$, is read "one over S angle n." The Sinking Fund is the reciprocal of the Amount of 1 Per Period.

Example: The amount of $500 will be needed in 5 years. A regular deposit of $90.49 in a savings institution that pays 5% compounded annually grows to $500 in 5 years. The deposits grow year by year in the following manner:

Year	Amount at Beginning of Year	Amount at End of Year	Amount Plus Deposit
1			$ 90.49
2	$ 90.49 × 1.05 =	$ 95.01	185.50
3	185.50 × 1.05 =	194.78	285.27
4	285.27 × 1.05 =	299.53	390.02
5	390.02 × 1.05 =	409.52	500.01

Another way of illustrating the concept of Sinking Fund is to view each deposit as an independent entity, allowing each to grow at compound interest period by period to maturity, when the total of all of the payments plus interest will equal the required amount.

Year of Deposit	Deposit	Year 5
1	$90.49 × (1.05)^4 =	$109.99
2	90.49 × (1.05)^3 =	104.75
3	90.49 × (1.05)^2 =	99.77
4	90.49 × (1.05)^1 =	95.01
5	90.49 × (1.05)^0 =	90.49
	Total	$500.01

Present Worth of 1, V^n

$$V^n = \frac{1}{(1 + i)^n}$$

This formula computes what $1 to be paid in the future is worth today, or the value today of a single payment tomorrow. The symbol for the Present Worth of 1, V^n, is read "V to the nth." The Present Worth of 1 is the reciprocal of the Amount of 1.

Example: An amount of $500 is due in 5 years. A deposit of $391.77 in a savings institution that pays 5% interest compounded annually grows to $500 in 5 years. The Present Worth of 1 factor can be found on page 8-436.

The $391.77 grows year by year in the following manner:

Year	Amount at Beginning of Year	Amount at End of Year
1	$391.77 × 1.05 =	$411.36
2	441.36 × 1.05 =	431.92
3	431.92 × 1.05 =	453.52
4	453.52 × 1.05 =	476.20
5	476.20 × 1.05 =	500.01

The 2 amounts are equivalent, that is, the $500 due in 5 years is equivalent to $391.77 today, assuming 5% interest compounded annually.

Present Worth of 1 Per Period, $A_{\overline{n}|}$

$$A_{\overline{n}|} = \frac{1 - V^n}{i}$$

This formula computes what $1 to be paid at the end of each period is worth today. It is the value today of a series of payments tomorrow. The symbol for the Present Worth of 1 Per Period, $A_{\overline{n}|}$, is read "A angle n."

Example: An amount of $100 is to be received at the end of each year for 5 years. A deposit of $432.95 in a savings institution that pays 5% compounded annually will provide $100 each year for 5 years. The deposits and withdrawals proceed in the following manner:

Year	Amount at Beginning of Year	Amount at End of Year	Amount Less $100 Withdrawal
1	$432.95 × 1.05 =	$454.60	$354.60
2	354.60 × 1.05 =	372.33	272.33
3	272.33 × 1.05 =	285.94	185.94
4	185.94 × 1.05 =	195.24	95.24
5	95.24 × 1.05 =	100.00	.00

The Present Worth of 1 Per Period is the sum of the present worths of all the individual payments, as follows:

$$A_{\overline{n}|} = V^1 + V^2 + V^3 + \cdots + V^n$$

The right-hand side of the preceding equation is a series that transforms into a simpler expression, where i is the periodic interest factor:

$$A_{\overline{n}|} = \frac{1 - V^n}{i}$$

Periodic Payment to Amortize 1, $1/A_{\overline{n}|}$

$$\frac{1}{A_{\overline{n}|}} = \frac{i}{1 - V^n}$$

This formula computes the payment to amortize a loan of $1. The payment is an annuity certain worth $1 today. The symbol for the Periodic Payment to Amortize 1, $1/A_{\overline{n}|}$, is read "one over A angle n." The Periodic Payment to Amortize 1 is the reciprocal of the Present Worth of 1 Per Period.

Example: The annual payment to amortize a loan of $500 at 5% for 5 years is $115.49. The process is shown by an amortization schedule:

| | Amount: $500 | | Term: 5 years | |
| | Rate: 5% | | Payment: 115.49 annual | |

Year	Interest	Principal	Balance
1	$25.00	$ 90.49	$409.51
2	20.48	95.01	314.50
3	15.73	99.76	214.74
4	10.74	104.75	109.99
5	5.50	109.99	.00

Constant Annual Percent

The Constant Annual Percent (Constant) shows the percent of a loan required each year to amortize the loan. The Constant is the periodic payment times the number of periods per year times 100.

Example: The Constant needed to amortize an 8% monthly payment loan for 30 years is 8.81%. An amortization schedule for this loan is shown on page 5-115.

Total Interest

This function shows the total interest paid over the life of an amortized loan of $1. The total interest is the periodic payment times the number of periods less the loan amount.

Example: The total interest paid on an 8%, 30 year monthly payment loan is 1.641552 per $1 of loan.

Annual Add On Rate

This function shows the average annual interest rate on a loan that is amortized over the term by level periodic payments. The annual add on rate is computed by dividing the total interest by the number of years and then multiplying by 100.

Example: The annual add on rate for an 8%, 30 year monthly payment loan is 5.47%.

Applications

Extension of Tables. Table 8 shows the values of the compound interest and annuity functions for each year. Values of functions for terms between years can be computed. Both S and V^n are exponential functions. When exponentials are multiplied, the exponents add. The formulas are:

$$S^n \times S^m = S^{n + m}$$

$$V^n \times V^m = V^{n + m}$$

To compute a new value, first compute the new value for S or V^n, and then substitute the value into the formula.

Example: Compute the monthly payment to amortize a loan of $1 at 6% for 20 years and 6 months (a total of 246 periods).

$$V^{246} = V^{240} \times V^6$$

$$= .302096 \times .970518$$

$$= .293190$$

The formula for the payment is $i \div (1 - V^n)$.

$$\text{Payment} = \frac{.005}{1 - .293190}$$

$$= .00707403$$

Two Accounts Method. The two accounts method is the process for finding the balance of a loan using the Amount of 1 and the Amount of 1 Per Period. The name comes from the process. The principal amount is put into an account to grow at compound interest for the term, and the monthly payments are deposited into another account, also to grow at compound interest for the term. At the end of the term, the difference between the principal account and the payment account is the balance. The formula is:

$$\text{Balance} = (\text{Amount} \times V^n) - (\text{Payment} \times S_{\overline{n}|})$$

Example: Compute the balance at the end of year 1 on a loan of $10,000 at 4% for 20 years where the monthly payment is $60.60.

$$\text{Balance} = (10,000 \times 1.040742) - (60.60 \times 12.222463)$$

$$= 9,666.74$$

COMPOUND INTEREST AND ANNUITY

Makeham's Formula. Makeham's formula is used to find the present worth of a loan. The formula is particularly useful in finding the present worth of a loan that is repaid by equal payments of principal plus interest. The formula is:

$$A = K + \frac{j}{i}(C - K)$$

where:

A = present worth
K = present worth of C at yield rate i
j = nominal interest rate on loan
i = yield rate
C = capital repayable

Example: A loan of $5,000 at 8% for 5 years is amortized annually by principal payments of $1,000 per year, according to the following schedule:

Year	Payment	Interest	Principal	Balance
1	$1,400	$400	$1,000	$4,000
2	1,320	320	1,000	3,000
3	1,240	240	1,000	2,000
4	1,160	160	1,000	1,000
5	1,080	80	1,000	0

Using Makeham's formula, compute the present worth of the loan to yield 10%.

where:

$K = 1,000 \times A_{\overline{5}|}$
    $= 1,000 \times 3.790787$
    $= 3,790.787$
$j = .08$
$i = .10$
$C = 5,000$

$$A = 3,790.787 + \frac{.08}{.10}(5,000 - 3,790.787)$$

$$= 4,758.15$$

The yield schedule proves the calculation, as follows:

Loan: $4,758.15   Term: 5 years
Yield rate: 10%   Payment: As shown

Year	Payment	Interest	Principal	Balance
1	$1,400	$475.82	$924.18	$3,833.97
2	1,320	383.40	936.60	2,897.37
3	1,240	289.74	950.26	1,947.11
4	1,160	194.71	955.29	981.82
5	1,080	98.18	981.82	.00

Discounted Cash Flow (DCF). Discounting the cash flow from an investment is a convenient means of measuring the return on an investment. The interest rate used to equate the cash flow to the investment is called the internal rate of return (IRR). It is the same as the 10% yield rate in the previous example. Discounting the cash flow is another name for computing the present worth of future payments. When a variety of choices for investment are presented, each with a different investment schedule and payback period, discounting the cash flow puts the evaluation of pro forma projections on an even footing.

Net Present Value (NPV). The NPV method of measuring investments is similar to the DCF method in that it can be used to measure and evaluate the differing cash flows of alternative investment proposals. A single interest rate is used to compute the present value of each alternative. The initial cash investment is then subtracted from present worth, and the resulting amount is the NPV.

When the NPV method is used to compare and evaluate several alternative investments, the instruments are ranked in order of their NPVs.

Example: An investment of $1,000 will return $1,250 in 3 years. The NPV, at a 6% interest rate, is $49.52. The NPV is computed as follows:

$$NPV = \text{Present value} - \text{Investment}$$
$$= (1,250 \times V^3) - 1,000$$
$$= (1,250 \times .839619) - 1,000$$
$$= 49.52$$

Example: Each of 2 projected cash flows requires a payment of $1 million today for a return of varying future payments over 8 years, as shown in the following schedule:

Investment = $1,000,000

Year	Cash Flows Projection 1	Projection 2
1	$300,000	0
2	250,000	0
3	200,000	0
4	200,000	0
5	200,000	$500,000
6	150,000	500,000
7	100,000	500,000
8	100,000	500,000
DCF/IRR	12.41%	11.38%
NPV/12%	$ 11,718	$ −34,855

Using the DCF method, the rates are 12.41% for projection 1 and 11.38% for projection 2. Using the NPV method, calculated at a rate of 12%, the amounts are $11,718 and $−34,855. If more is better, then projection 1 is a better deal.

Irregular Payments. Most loans are amortized by a level payment for the term of the loan. There are times, however, when the amount of the payment will change in the future. When the schedule of payments is known, then a loan amount can be computed.

Example: A loan at 8% for 25 years is amortized by a payment of $240 for the first 10 years and a payment of $300 for the balance of the term. The loan amount is computed to be $33,924.05. There are 2 ways to compute this amount, as shown here:

1. Amount $= (240 \times A_{\overline{120}}) + (300 \times A_{\overline{180}} \times V^{120})$

$\qquad = 240 \times 82.421481$
$\qquad\quad + 300 \times 104.640592 \times .450523$
$\qquad = 33,924.05$

2. Amount $= (300 \times A_{\overline{300}}) - (60 \times A_{\overline{120}})$

$\qquad = 300 \times 129.564523 - 60 \times 82.421481$
$\qquad = 33,924.07$

A schedule should be prepared to prove these calculations.

Payment in Advance, With a Balance Outstanding. A loan, with payments in advance, may have a balance outstanding at the end of the term. The special formula required to compute the payment is:

$$\text{Payment in advance} = \frac{\text{Amount} - (\text{Balance} \times V^{n-1})}{1 + A_{\overline{n-1}}}$$

Example: An 8%, 20 year loan of $100,000, quarterly in advance, has a balance outstanding of $10,000 at the end of 80 payments. The payment is $2,415.13, computed by the preceding formula, as follows:

$$P = \frac{100,000 - (10,000 \times V^{79})}{1 + A_{\overline{79}}}$$

$$= \frac{100,000 - (10,000 \times .209212)}{40.539404}$$

$$= 2,415.13$$

Payment in Advance. A loan may call for payments in advance. The Periodic Payment to Amortize 1 is computed in arrears; to change from payment in arrears to payment in advance, divide the payment by 1 plus the periodic interest factor $(1 + i)$. The formula is:

$$\text{Payment in advance} = \frac{\text{Payment in arrears}}{(1 + i)}$$

At 6% for 20 years, the payment in arrears is .00716431, and in advance, .00712866.

	Amount Of 1	Amount Of 1 Per Period	Sinking Fund Payment	Present Worth Of 1	Present Worth of 1 Per Period	Periodic Payment To Amortize 1	Constant Annual Percent	Total Interest	Annual Add On Rate	
	What a single $ 1 deposit grows to in the future. The deposit is made at the beginning of the first period.	What a series of $ 1 deposits grow to in the future. A deposit is made at the end of each period.	The amount to be deposited at the end of each period that grows to $ 1 in the future.	What $ 1 to be paid in the future is worth today. Value today of a single $ 1 payment tomorrow.	What $ 1 to be paid at the end of each period is worth today. Value today of a series of $ 1 payments tomorrow.	The mortgage payment to amortize a loan of $ 1. An annuity certain, payable at the end of each period, worth $ 1 today.	The annual payment, including interest and principal, to amortize completely a loan of $ 100.	The total interest paid over the term on a loan of $1. The loan is amortized by regular periodic payments.	The average annual interest rate on a loan that is completely amortized by regular periodic payments.	
	$S = (1+i)^n$	$S\overline{n} = \dfrac{(1+i)^n - 1}{i}$	$\dfrac{1}{S\overline{n}} = \dfrac{i}{(1+i)^n - 1}$	$V^n = \dfrac{1}{(1+i)^n}$	$A\overline{n} = \dfrac{1-V^n}{i}$	$\dfrac{1}{A\overline{n}} = \dfrac{i}{1-V^n}$				

YEAR										PERIODS
	1.000 000	1.000 000	1.000 000 0000	1.000 000	1.000 000	1.000 000 0000	1200.00	0.000 000	0.00	1
	1.000 000	2.000 000	.500 000 0000	1.000 000	2.000 000	.500 000 0000	600.00	0.000 000	0.00	2
	1.000 000	3.000 000	.333 333 3333	1.000 000	3.000 000	.333 333 3333	400.00	0.000 000	0.00	3
	1.000 000	4.000 000	.250 000 0000	1.000 000	4.000 000	.250 000 0000	300.00	0.000 000	0.00	4
	1.000 000	5.000 000	.200 000 0000	1.000 000	5.000 000	.200 000 0000	240.00	0.000 000	0.00	5
	1.000 000	6.000 000	.166 666 6667	1.000 000	6.000 000	.166 666 6667	200.00	0.000 000	0.00	6
	1.000 000	7.000 000	.142 857 1429	1.000 000	7.000 000	.142 857 1429	171.43	0.000 000	0.00	7
	1.000 000	8.000 000	.125 000 0000	1.000 000	8.000 000	.125 000 0000	150.00	0.000 000	0.00	8
	1.000 000	9.000 000	.111 111 1111	1.000 000	9.000 000	.111 111 1111	133.34	0.000 000	0.00	9
	1.000 000	10.000 000	.100 000 0000	1.000 000	10.000 000	.100 000 0000	120.00	0.000 000	0.00	10
	1.000 000	11.000 000	.090 909 0909	1.000 000	11.000 000	.090 909 0909	109.10	0.000 000	0.00	11
	1.000 000	12.000 000	.083 333 3333	1.000 000	12.000 000	.083 333 3333	100.00	0.000 000	0.00	12
1	1.000 000	12.000 000	.083 333 3333	1.000 000	12.000 000	.083 333 3333	100.00	0.000 000	0.00	12
2	1.000 000	24.000 000	.041 666 6667	1.000 000	24.000 000	.041 666 6667	50.00	0.000 000	0.00	24
3	1.000 000	36.000 000	.027 777 7778	1.000 000	36.000 000	.027 777 7778	33.34	0.000 000	0.00	36
4	1.000 000	48.000 000	.020 833 3333	1.000 000	48.000 000	.020 833 3333	25.00	0.000 000	0.00	48
5	1.000 000	60.000 000	.016 666 6667	1.000 000	60.000 000	.016 666 6667	20.00	0.000 000	0.00	60
6	1.000 000	72.000 000	.013 888 8889	1.000 000	72.000 000	.013 888 8889	16.67	0.000 000	0.00	72
7	1.000 000	84.000 000	.011 904 7619	1.000 000	84.000 000	.011 904 7619	14.29	0.000 000	0.00	84
8	1.000 000	96.000 000	.010 416 6667	1.000 000	96.000 000	.010 416 6667	12.50	0.000 000	0.00	96
9	1.000 000	108.000 000	.009 259 2593	1.000 000	108.000 000	.009 259 2593	11.12	0.000 000	0.00	108
10	1.000 000	120.000 000	.008 333 3333	1.000 000	120.000 000	.008 333 3333	10.00	0.000 000	0.00	120
11	1.000 000	132.000 000	.007 575 7576	1.000 000	132.000 000	.007 575 7576	9.10	0.000 000	0.00	132
12	1.000 000	144.000 000	.006 944 4444	1.000 000	144.000 000	.006 944 4444	8.34	0.000 000	0.00	144
13	1.000 000	156.000 000	.006 410 2564	1.000 000	156.000 000	.006 410 2564	7.70	0.000 000	0.00	156
14	1.000 000	168.000 000	.005 952 3810	1.000 000	168.000 000	.005 952 3810	7.15	0.000 000	0.00	168
15	1.000 000	180.000 000	.005 555 5556	1.000 000	180.000 000	.005 555 5556	6.67	0.000 000	0.00	180
16	1.000 000	192.000 000	.005 208 3333	1.000 000	192.000 000	.005 208 3333	6.25	0.000 000	0.00	192
17	1.000 000	204.000 000	.004 901 9608	1.000 000	204.000 000	.004 901 9608	5.89	0.000 000	0.00	204
18	1.000 000	216.000 000	.004 629 6296	1.000 000	216.000 000	.004 629 6296	5.56	0.000 000	0.00	216
19	1.000 000	228.000 000	.004 385 9649	1.000 000	228.000 000	.004 385 9649	5.27	0.000 000	0.00	228
20	1.000 000	240.000 000	.004 166 6667	1.000 000	240.000 000	.004 166 6667	5.00	0.000 000	0.00	240
21	1.000 000	252.000 000	.003 968 2540	1.000 000	252.000 000	.003 968 2540	4.77	0.000 000	0.00	252
22	1.000 000	264.000 000	.003 787 8788	1.000 000	264.000 000	.003 787 8788	4.55	0.000 000	0.00	264
23	1.000 000	276.000 000	.003 623 1884	1.000 000	276.000 000	.003 623 1884	4.35	0.000 000	0.00	276
24	1.000 000	288.000 000	.003 472 2222	1.000 000	288.000 000	.003 472 2222	4.17	0.000 000	0.00	288
25	1.000 000	300.000 000	.003 333 3333	1.000 000	300.000 000	.003 333 3333	4.00	0.000 000	0.00	300
26	1.000 000	312.000 000	.003 205 1282	1.000 000	312.000 000	.003 205 1282	3.85	0.000 000	0.00	312
27	1.000 000	324.000 000	.003 086 4198	1.000 000	324.000 000	.003 086 4198	3.71	0.000 000	0.00	324
28	1.000 000	336.000 000	.002 976 1905	1.000 000	336.000 000	.002 976 1905	3.58	0.000 000	0.00	336
29	1.000 000	348.000 000	.002 873 5632	1.000 000	348.000 000	.002 873 5632	3.45	0.000 000	0.00	348
30	1.000 000	360.000 000	.002 777 7778	1.000 000	360.000 000	.002 777 7778	3.34	0.000 000	0.00	360
31	1.000 000	372.000 000	.002 688 1720	1.000 000	372.000 000	.002 688 1720	3.23	0.000 000	0.00	372
32	1.000 000	384.000 000	.002 604 1667	1.000 000	384.000 000	.002 604 1667	3.13	0.000 000	0.00	384
33	1.000 000	396.000 000	.002 525 2525	1.000 000	396.000 000	.002 525 2525	3.04	0.000 000	0.00	396
34	1.000 000	408.000 000	.002 450 9804	1.000 000	408.000 000	.002 450 9804	2.95	0.000 000	0.00	408
35	1.000 000	420.000 000	.002 380 9524	1.000 000	420.000 000	.002 380 9524	2.86	0.000 000	0.00	420
36	1.000 000	432.000 000	.002 314 8148	1.000 000	432.000 000	.002 314 8148	2.78	0.000 000	0.00	432
37	1.000 000	444.000 000	.002 252 2523	1.000 000	444.000 000	.002 252 2523	2.71	0.000 000	0.00	444
38	1.000 000	456.000 000	.002 192 9825	1.000 000	456.000 000	.002 192 9825	2.64	0.000 000	0.00	456
39	1.000 000	468.000 000	.002 136 7521	1.000 000	468.000 000	.002 136 7521	2.57	0.000 000	0.00	468
40	1.000 000	480.000 000	.002 083 3333	1.000 000	480.000 000	.002 083 3333	2.50	0.000 000	0.00	480
41	1.000 000	492.000 000	.002 032 5203	1.000 000	492.000 000	.002 032 5203	2.44	0.000 000	0.00	492
42	1.000 000	504.000 000	.001 984 1270	1.000 000	504.000 000	.001 984 1270	2.39	0.000 000	0.00	504
43	1.000 000	516.000 000	.001 937 9845	1.000 000	516.000 000	.001 937 9845	2.33	0.000 000	0.00	516
44	1.000 000	528.000 000	.001 893 9394	1.000 000	528.000 000	.001 893 9394	2.28	0.000 000	0.00	528
45	1.000 000	540.000 000	.001 851 8519	1.000 000	540.000 000	.001 851 8519	2.23	0.000 000	0.00	540
46	1.000 000	552.000 000	.001 811 5942	1.000 000	552.000 000	.001 811 5942	2.18	0.000 000	0.00	552
47	1.000 000	564.000 000	.001 773 0496	1.000 000	564.000 000	.001 773 0496	2.13	0.000 000	0.00	564
48	1.000 000	576.000 000	.001 736 1111	1.000 000	576.000 000	.001 736 1111	2.09	0.000 000	0.00	576
49	1.000 000	588.000 000	.001 700 6803	1.000 000	588.000 000	.001 700 6803	2.05	0.000 000	0.00	588
50	1.000 000	600.000 000	.001 666 6667	1.000 000	600.000 000	.001 666 6667	2.00	0.000 000	0.00	600

Effective Rate is 0.00 %

Annual Percentage Rate is 0.00 %

	Amount Of 1	Amount Of 1 Per Period	Sinking Fund Payment	Present Worth Of 1	Present Worth of 1 Per Period	Periodic Payment To Amortize 1	Constant Annual Percent	Total Interest	Annual Add On Rate	
	What a single $ 1 deposit grows to in the future. The deposit is made at the beginning of the first period.	What a series of $ 1 deposits grow to in the future. A deposit is made at the end of each period.	The amount to be deposited at the end of each period that grows to $ 1 in the future.	What $ 1 to be paid in the future is worth today. Value today of a single $ 1 payment tomorrow.	What $ 1 to be paid at the end of each period is worth today. Value today of a series of $ 1 payments tomorrow.	The mortgage payment to amortize a loan of $ 1. An annuity certain, payable at the end of each period, worth $ 1 today.	The annual payment, including interest and principal, to amortize completely a loan of $ 100.	The total interest paid over the term on a loan of $1. The loan is amortized by regular periodic payments.	The average annual interest rate on a loan that is completely amortized by regular periodic payments.	
	$S = (1+i)^n$	$S\overline{n}| = \dfrac{(1+i)^n - 1}{i}$	$\dfrac{1}{S\overline{n}|} = \dfrac{i}{(1+i)^n - 1}$	$V^n = \dfrac{1}{(1+i)^n}$	$A\overline{n}| = \dfrac{1-V^n}{i}$	$\dfrac{1}{A\overline{n}|} = \dfrac{i}{1-V^n}$				**PERIODS**
YEAR										
	1.000 833	1.000 000	1.000 000 0000	.999 167	.999 167	1.000 833 3333	1201.00	.000 833	1.00	1
	1.001 667	2.000 833	.499 791 7534	.998 335	1.997 503	.500 625 0868	600.76	.001 250	.75	2
	1.002 502	3.002 501	.333 055 7098	.997 504	2.995 007	.333 889 0431	400.67	.001 667	.67	3
	1.003 338	4.005 003	.249 687 7169	.996 674	3.991 681	.250 521 0503	300.63	.002 084	.63	4
	1.004 174	5.008 340	.199 666 9443	.995 844	4.987 524	.200 500 2777	240.61	.002 501	.60	5
	1.005 010	6.012 514	.166 319 7819	.995 015	5.982 539	.167 153 1152	200.59	.002 919	.58	6
	1.005 848	7.017 524	.142 500 3967	.994 186	6.976 725	.143 333 7300	172.01	.003 336	.57	7
	1.006 686	8.023 372	.124 635 8722	.993 358	7.970 083	.125 469 2055	150.57	.003 754	.56	8
	1.007 525	9.030 058	.110 741 2549	.992 531	8.962 614	.111 574 5883	133.89	.004 171	.56	9
	1.008 365	10.037 583	.099 625 5727	.991 705	9.954 319	.100 458 9060	120.56	.004 589	.55	10
	1.009 205	11.045 948	.090 530 9341	.990 879	10.945 198	.091 364 2674	109.64	.005 007	.55	11
	1.010 046	12.055 153	.082 952 0782	.990 054	11.935 252	.083 785 4116	100.55	.005 425	.54	12
1	1.010 046	12.055 153	.082 952 0782	.990 054	11.935 252	.083 785 4116	100.55	.005 425	.54	12
2	1.020 193	24.231 412	.041 268 7470	.980 207	23.751 795	.042 102 0803	50.53	.010 450	.52	24
3	1.030 442	36.529 993	.027 374 7660	.970 458	35.450 811	.028 208 0993	33.85	.015 492	.52	36
4	1.040 793	48.952 125	.020 428 1226	.960 805	47.033 468	.021 261 4559	25.52	.020 550	.51	48
5	1.051 249	61.499 049	.016 260 4141	.951 249	58.500 923	.017 093 7474	20.52	.025 625	.51	60
6	1.061 810	74.172 019	.013 482 1731	.941 788	69.854 322	.014 315 5065	17.18	.030 716	.51	72
7	1.072 477	86.972 301	.011 497 9136	.932 421	81.094 800	.012 331 2469	14.80	.035 825	.51	84
8	1.083 251	99.901 175	.010 009 8923	.923 147	92.223 480	.010 843 2257	13.02	.040 950	.51	96
9	1.094 133	112.959 931	.008 852 6966	.913 965	103.241 473	.009 686 0300	11.63	.046 091	.51	108
10	1.105 125	126.149 875	.007 927 0788	.904 875	114.149 881	.008 760 4121	10.52	.051 249	.51	120
11	1.116 227	139.472 325	.007 169 8812	.895 875	124.949 793	.008 003 2145	9.61	.056 424	.51	132
12	1.127 441	152.928 611	.006 538 9988	.886 965	135.642 289	.007 372 3321	8.85	.061 616	.51	144
13	1.138 767	166.520 079	.006 005 2818	.878 143	146.228 437	.006 838 6151	8.21	.066 824	.51	156
14	1.150 207	180.248 087	.005 547 9091	.869 409	156.709 294	.006 381 2424	7.66	.072 049	.51	168
15	1.161 762	194.114 005	.005 151 6118	.860 762	167.085 909	.005 984 9451	7.19	.077 290	.52	180
16	1.173 433	208.119 220	.004 804 9383	.852 201	177.359 317	.005 638 2716	6.77	.082 548	.52	192
17	1.185 221	222.265 130	.004 499 1313	.843 725	187.530 546	.005 332 4646	6.40	.087 823	.52	204
18	1.197 128	236.553 150	.004 227 3798	.835 333	197.600 611	.005 060 7131	6.08	.093 114	.52	216
19	1.209 154	250.984 707	.003 984 3065	.827 025	207.570 519	.004 817 6398	5.79	.098 422	.52	228
20	1.221 301	265.561 242	.003 765 6097	.818 799	217.441 265	.004 598 9431	5.52	.103 746	.52	240
21	1.233 570	280.284 213	.003 567 8071	.810 655	227.213 837	.004 401 1404	5.29	.109 087	.52	252
22	1.245 963	295.155 091	.003 388 0493	.802 592	236.889 210	.004 221 3826	5.07	.114 445	.52	264
23	1.258 479	310.175 360	.003 223 9827	.794 610	246.468 352	.004 057 3160	4.87	.119 819	.52	276
24	1.271 122	325.346 523	.003 073 6459	.786 706	255.952 219	.003 906 9792	4.69	.125 210	.52	288
25	1.283 892	340.670 094	.002 935 3912	.778 882	265.341 759	.003 768 7245	4.53	.130 617	.52	300
26	1.296 790	356.147 606	.002 807 8246	.771 135	274.637 911	.003 641 1579	4.37	.136 041	.52	312
27	1.309 817	371.780 604	.002 689 7584	.763 465	283.841 602	.003 523 0917	4.23	.141 482	.52	324
28	1.322 976	387.570 650	.002 580 1747	.755 872	292.953 753	.003 413 5081	4.10	.146 939	.52	336
29	1.336 266	403.519 323	.002 478 1961	.748 354	301.975 274	.003 311 5294	3.98	.152 412	.53	348
30	1.349 690	419.628 215	.002 383 0619	.740 911	310.907 067	.003 216 3952	3.86	.157 902	.53	360
31	1.363 249	435.898 937	.002 294 1097	.733 542	319.750 024	.003 127 4431	3.76	.163 409	.53	372
32	1.376 944	452.333 114	.002 210 7601	.726 246	328.505 028	.003 044 0934	3.66	.168 932	.53	384
33	1.390 777	468.932 388	.002 132 5036	.719 023	337.172 955	.002 965 8369	3.56	.174 471	.53	396
34	1.404 749	485.698 417	.002 058 8908	.711 871	345.754 670	.002 892 2241	3.48	.180 027	.53	408
35	1.418 861	502.632 877	.001 989 5237	.704 791	354.251 031	.002 822 8570	3.39	.185 600	.53	420
36	1.433 115	519.737 461	.001 924 0483	.697 781	362.662 887	.002 757 3817	3.31	.191 189	.53	432
37	1.447 512	537.013 876	.001 862 1493	.690 841	370.991 078	.002 695 4826	3.24	.196 794	.53	444
38	1.462 053	554.463 849	.001 803 5441	.683 970	379.236 437	.002 636 8774	3.17	.202 416	.53	456
39	1.476 741	572.089 125	.001 747 9794	.677 167	387.399 787	.002 581 3127	3.10	.208 054	.53	468
40	1.491 576	589.891 463	.001 695 2271	.670 432	395.481 944	.002 528 5604	3.04	.213 709	.53	480
41	1.506 561	607.872 642	.001 645 0814	.663 764	403.483 715	.002 478 4148	2.98	.219 380	.54	492
42	1.521 695	626.034 460	.001 597 3562	.657 162	411.405 901	.002 430 6895	2.92	.225 068	.54	504
43	1.536 982	644.378 731	.001 551 8824	.650 626	419.249 292	.002 385 2157	2.87	.230 771	.54	516
44	1.552 423	662.907 288	.001 508 5066	.644 154	427.014 672	.002 341 8399	2.82	.236 491	.54	528
45	1.568 018	681.621 981	.001 467 0888	.637 748	434.702 818	.002 300 4222	2.77	.242 228	.54	540
46	1.583 771	700.524 682	.001 427 5015	.631 405	442.314 497	.002 260 8348	2.72	.247 981	.54	552
47	1.599 681	719.617 279	.001 389 6276	.625 125	449.850 470	.002 222 9609	2.67	.253 750	.54	564
48	1.615 751	738.901 679	.001 353 3600	.618 907	457.311 489	.002 186 6934	2.63	.259 535	.54	576
49	1.631 983	758.379 809	.001 318 6005	.612 751	464.698 302	.002 151 9338	2.59	.265 337	.54	588
50	1.648 378	778.053 616	.001 285 2585	.606 657	472.011 644	.002 118 5918	2.55	.271 155	.54	600

Effective Rate is 1.00 %   8 - 3   Annual Percentage Rate is 1.00 %

	Amount Of 1	Amount Of 1 Per Period	Sinking Fund Payment	Present Worth Of 1	Present Worth of 1 Per Period	Periodic Payment To Amortize 1	Constant Annual Percent	Total Interest	Annual Add On Rate	
	What a single $ 1 deposit grows to in the future. The deposit is made at the beginning of the first period.	What a series of $ 1 deposits grow to in the future. A deposit is made at the end of each period.	The amount to be deposited at the end of each period that grows to $ 1 in the future.	What $ 1 to be paid in the future is worth today. Value today of a single $ 1 payment tomorrow.	What $ 1 to be paid at the end of each period is worth today. Value today of a series of $ 1 payments tomorrow.	The mortgage payment to amortize a loan of $ 1. An annuity certain, payable at the end of each period, worth $ 1 today.	The annual payment, including interest and principal, to amortize completely a loan of $ 100.	The total interest paid over the term on a loan of $1. The loan is amortized by regular periodic payments.	The average annual interest rate on a loan that is completely amortized by regular periodic payments.	
	$S = (1+i)^n$	$S\overline{n}| = \dfrac{(1+i)^n - 1}{i}$	$\dfrac{1}{S\overline{n}|} = \dfrac{i}{(1+i)^n - 1}$	$V^n = \dfrac{1}{(1+i)^n}$	$A\overline{n}| = \dfrac{1 - V^n}{i}$	$\dfrac{1}{A\overline{n}|} = \dfrac{i}{1 - V^n}$				

YEAR										PERIODS
	1.001 667	1.000 000	1.000 000 0000	.998 336	.998 336	1.001 666 6667	1202.00	.001 667	2.00	1
	1.003 336	2.001 667	.499 583 6803	.996 675	1.995 011	.501 250 3469	601.51	.002 501	1.50	2
	1.005 008	3.005 003	.332 778 3945	.995 017	2.990 028	.334 445 0612	401.34	.003 335	1.33	3
	1.006 683	4.010 011	.249 375 8673	.993 361	3.983 389	.251 042 5340	301.26	.004 170	1.25	4
	1.008 361	5.016 694	.199 334 4435	.991 708	4.975 097	.201 001 1102	241.21	.005 006	1.20	5
	1.010 042	6.025 056	.165 973 5714	.990 058	5.965 155	.167 640 2381	201.17	.005 841	1.17	6
	1.011 725	7.035 097	.142 144 4431	.988 411	6.953 566	.143 811 1098	172.58	.006 678	1.14	7
	1.013 411	8.046 823	.124 272 6547	.986 766	7.940 332	.125 939 3214	151.13	.007 515	1.13	8
	1.015 100	9.060 234	.110 372 4263	.985 124	8.925 456	.112 039 0929	134.45	.008 352	1.11	9
	1.016 792	10.075 334	.099 252 2897	.983 485	9.908 941	.100 918 9564	121.11	.009 190	1.10	10
	1.018 487	11.092 127	.090 154 0383	.981 849	10.890 790	.091 820 7050	110.19	.010 028	1.09	11
	1.020 184	12.110 613	.082 572 2006	.980 215	11.871 005	.084 238 8673	101.09	.010 866	1.09	12
1	1.020 184	12.110 613	.082 572 2006	.980 215	11.871 005	.084 238 8673	101.09	.010 866	1.09	12
2	1.040 776	24.465 672	.040 873 5967	.960 821	23.507 142	.042 540 2634	51.05	.020 966	1.05	24
3	1.061 784	37.070 109	.026 975 9121	.941 812	34.913 058	.028 642 5787	34.38	.031 133	1.04	36
4	1.083 215	49.928 959	.020 028 4570	.923 178	46.093 307	.021 695 1236	26.04	.041 366	1.03	48
5	1.105 079	63.047 356	.015 861 0934	.904 913	57.052 356	.017 527 7601	21.04	.051 666	1.03	60
6	1.127 384	76.430 540	.013 083 7752	.887 009	67.794 579	.014 750 4419	17.71	.062 032	1.03	72
7	1.150 140	90.083 854	.011 100 7684	.869 460	78.324 268	.012 767 4350	15.33	.072 465	1.04	84
8	1.173 355	104.012 752	.009 614 2058	.852 257	88.645 626	.011 280 8724	13.54	.082 964	1.04	96
9	1.197 038	118.222 796	.008 458 6056	.835 395	98.762 777	.010 125 2722	12.16	.093 529	1.04	108
10	1.221 199	132.719 660	.007 534 6787	.818 867	108.679 759	.009 201 3454	11.05	.104 161	1.04	120
11	1.245 849	147.509 135	.006 779 2412	.802 666	118.400 534	.008 445 9079	10.14	.114 860	1.04	132
12	1.270 995	162.597 125	.006 150 1703	.786 785	127.928 983	.007 816 8369	9.39	.125 625	1.05	144
13	1.296 649	177.989 656	.005 618 3040	.771 218	137.268 912	.007 284 9707	8.75	.136 455	1.05	156
14	1.322 821	193.692 876	.005 162 8125	.755 960	146.424 051	.006 829 4792	8.20	.147 352	1.05	168
15	1.349 522	209.713 056	.004 768 4203	.741 003	155.398 054	.006 435 0870	7.73	.158 316	1.06	180
16	1.376 761	226.056 592	.004 423 6710	.726 342	164.194 507	.006 090 3377	7.31	.169 345	1.06	192
17	1.404 550	242.730 012	.004 119 8037	.711 972	172.816 923	.005 786 4704	6.95	.180 440	1.06	204
18	1.432 900	259.739 974	.003 850 0042	.697 885	181.268 743	.005 516 6709	6.63	.191 601	1.06	216
19	1.461 822	277.093 272	.003 608 8931	.684 078	189.553 344	.005 275 5598	6.34	.202 828	1.07	228
20	1.491 328	294.796 834	.003 392 1667	.670 543	197.674 035	.005 058 8334	6.08	.214 120	1.07	240
21	1.521 430	312.857 732	.003 196 3410	.657 277	205.634 057	.004 863 0077	5.84	.225 478	1.07	252
22	1.552 139	331.283 177	.003 018 5656	.644 272	213.436 591	.004 685 2323	5.63	.236 901	1.08	264
23	1.583 468	350.080 528	.002 856 4856	.631 525	221.084 751	.004 523 1523	5.43	.248 390	1.08	276
24	1.615 429	369.257 291	.002 708 1388	.619 031	228.581 592	.004 374 8055	5.25	.259 944	1.08	288
25	1.648 035	388.821 125	.002 571 8767	.606 783	235.930 108	.004 238 5434	5.09	.271 563	1.09	300
26	1.681 300	408.779 842	.002 446 3046	.594 778	243.133 234	.004 112 9712	4.94	.283 247	1.09	312
27	1.715 236	429.141 414	.002 330 2342	.583 010	250.193 846	.003 996 9009	4.80	.294 996	1.09	324
28	1.749 857	449.913 970	.002 222 6471	.571 475	257.114 763	.003 889 3138	4.67	.306 809	1.10	336
29	1.785 176	471.105 807	.002 122 6654	.560 169	263.898 751	.003 789 3321	4.55	.318 688	1.10	348
30	1.821 209	492.725 388	.002 029 5281	.549 086	270.548 516	.003 696 1947	4.44	.330 630	1.10	360
31	1.857 969	514.781 345	.001 942 5723	.538 222	277.066 717	.003 609 2390	4.34	.342 637	1.11	372
32	1.895 471	537.282 489	.001 861 2183	.527 573	283.455 954	.003 527 8850	4.24	.354 708	1.11	384
33	1.933 730	560.237 803	.001 784 9563	.517 135	289.718 781	.003 451 6230	4.15	.366 843	1.11	396
34	1.972 761	583.656 455	.001 713 3367	.506 904	295.857 697	.003 380 0033	4.06	.379 041	1.11	408
35	2.012 580	607.547 798	.001 645 9610	.496 875	301.875 155	.003 312 6277	3.98	.391 304	1.12	420
36	2.053 202	631.921 373	.001 582 4754	.487 044	307.773 558	.003 249 1420	3.90	.403 629	1.12	432
37	2.094 645	656.786 912	.001 522 5638	.477 408	313.555 260	.003 189 2305	3.83	.416 018	1.12	444
38	2.136 924	682.154 346	.001 465 9439	.467 962	319.222 572	.003 132 6106	3.76	.428 470	1.13	456
39	2.180 056	708.033 805	.001 412 3619	.458 704	324.777 755	.003 079 0286	3.70	.440 985	1.13	468
40	2.224 059	734.435 625	.001 361 5897	.449 628	330.223 030	.003 028 2564	3.64	.453 563	1.13	480
41	2.268 951	761.370 348	.001 313 4213	.440 732	335.560 569	.002 980 0879	3.58	.466 203	1.14	492
42	2.314 748	788.848 731	.001 267 6702	.432 012	340.792 505	.002 934 3368	3.53	.478 906	1.14	504
43	2.361 470	816.881 748	.001 224 1674	.423 465	345.920 928	.002 890 8341	3.47	.491 670	1.14	516
44	2.409 134	845.480 593	.001 182 7593	.415 087	350.947 884	.002 849 4259	3.42	.504 497	1.15	528
45	2.457 761	874.656 688	.001 143 3057	.406 874	355.875 382	.002 809 9724	3.38	.517 385	1.15	540
46	2.507 369	904.421 683	.001 105 6789	.398 824	360.705 390	.002 772 3456	3.33	.530 335	1.15	552
47	2.557 979	934.787 465	.001 069 7619	.390 934	365.439 693	.002 736 4286	3.29	.543 346	1.16	564
48	2.609 610	965.766 161	.001 035 4473	.383 199	370.080 610	.002 702 1140	3.25	.556 418	1.16	576
49	2.662 284	997.370 142	.001 002 6368	.375 617	374.629 567	.002 669 3035	3.21	.569 550	1.16	588
50	2.716 020	1029.612 029	.000 971 2396	.368 186	379.088 523	.002 637 9063	3.17	.582 744	1.17	600

MONTHLY COMPOUND INTEREST AND ANNUITY

2.25 % M

	Amount Of 1	Amount Of 1 Per Period	Sinking Fund Payment	Present Worth Of 1	Present Worth of 1 Per Period	Periodic Payment To Amortize 1	Constant Annual Percent	Total Interest	Annual Add On Rate	
	What a single $ 1 deposit grows to in the future. The deposit is made at the beginning of the first period.	What a series of $ 1 deposits grow to in the future. A deposit is made at the end of each period.	The amount to be deposited at the end of each period that grows to $ 1 in the future.	What $ 1 to be paid in the future is worth today. Value today of a single $ 1 payment tomorrow.	What $ 1 to be paid at the end of each period is worth today. Value today of a series of $ 1 payments tomorrow.	The mortgage payment to amortize a loan of $ 1. An annuity certain, payable at the end of each period, worth $ 1 today.	The annual payment, including interest and principal, to amortize completely a loan of $ 100.	The total interest paid over the term on a loan of $1. The loan is amortized by regular periodic payments.	The average annual interest rate on a loan that is completely amortized by regular periodic payments.	

$$S = (1+i)^n \qquad S\overline{n}| = \frac{(1+i)^n - 1}{i} \qquad \frac{1}{S\overline{n}|} = \frac{i}{(1+i)^n - 1} \qquad V^n = \frac{1}{(1+i)^n} \qquad A\overline{n}| = \frac{1-V^n}{i} \qquad \frac{1}{A\overline{n}|} = \frac{i}{1-V^n}$$

YEAR										PERIODS
	1.001 875	1.000 000	1.000 000 0000	.998 129	.998 129	1.001 875 0000	1202.25	.001 875	2.25	1
	1.003 754	2.001 875	.499 531 6890	.996 261	1.994 389	.501 406 6890	601.69	.002 813	1.69	2
	1.005 636	3.005 629	.332 709 1139	.994 396	2.988 785	.334 584 1139	401.51	.003 752	1.50	3
	1.007 521	4.011 264	.249 297 9726	.992 535	3.981 320	.251 172 9726	301.41	.004 692	1.41	4
	1.009 410	5.018 785	.199 251 4049	.990 678	4.971 998	.201 126 4049	241.36	.005 632	1.35	5
	1.011 303	6.028 195	.165 887 1240	.988 823	5.960 821	.167 762 1240	201.32	.006 573	1.31	6
	1.013 199	7.039 498	.142 055 5785	.986 973	6.947 794	.143 930 5785	172.72	.007 514	1.29	7
	1.015 099	8.052 697	.124 181 9925	.985 126	7.932 920	.126 056 9925	151.27	.008 456	1.27	8
	1.017 002	9.067 796	.110 280 3795	.983 282	8.916 202	.112 155 3795	134.59	.009 398	1.25	9
	1.018 909	10.084 798	.099 159 1477	.981 442	9.897 644	.101 034 1477	121.25	.010 341	1.24	10
	1.020 819	11.103 707	.090 060 0112	.979 605	10.877 249	.091 935 0112	110.33	.011 285	1.23	11
	1.022 733	12.124 527	.082 477 4462	.977 772	11.855 021	.084 352 4462	101.23	.012 229	1.22	12
1	1.022 733	12.124 527	.082 477 4462	.977 772	11.855 021	.084 352 4462	101.23	.012 229	1.22	12
2	1.045 984	24.524 686	.040 775 2414	.956 038	23.446 526	.042 650 2414	51.19	.023 606	1.18	24
3	1.069 763	37.206 745	.026 876 8475	.934 787	34.780 374	.028 751 8475	34.51	.035 067	1.17	36
4	1.094 082	50.177 110	.019 929 4059	.914 008	45.862 291	.021 804 4059	26.17	.046 611	1.17	48
5	1.118 954	63.442 338	.015 762 3448	.893 691	56.697 877	.017 637 3448	21.17	.058 241	1.16	60
6	1.144 392	77.009 130	.012 985 4733	.873 826	67.292 608	.014 860 4733	17.84	.069 954	1.17	72
7	1.170 408	90.884 343	.011 002 9953	.854 403	77.651 837	.012 877 9953	15.46	.081 752	1.17	84
8	1.197 016	105.074 988	.009 517 0128	.835 411	87.780 800	.011 392 0128	13.68	.093 633	1.17	96
9	1.224 228	119.588 235	.008 362 0266	.816 841	97.684 615	.010 237 0266	12.29	.105 599	1.17	108
10	1.252 059	134.431 420	.007 438 7372	.798 684	107.368 286	.009 313 7372	11.18	.117 648	1.18	120
11	1.280 523	149.612 041	.006 683 9540	.780 931	116.836 707	.008 558 9540	10.28	.129 782	1.18	132
12	1.309 633	165.137 772	.006 055 5498	.763 573	126.094 662	.007 930 5498	9.52	.141 999	1.18	144
13	1.339 406	181.016 456	.005 524 3596	.746 600	135.146 830	.007 399 3596	8.88	.154 300	1.19	156
14	1.369 855	197.256 118	.005 069 5513	.730 004	143.997 785	.006 944 5513	8.34	.166 685	1.19	168
15	1.400 997	213.864 964	.004 675 8477	.713 778	152.652 000	.006 550 8477	7.87	.179 153	1.19	180
16	1.432 846	230.851 387	.004 331 7912	.697 912	161.113 847	.006 206 7912	7.45	.191 704	1.20	192
17	1.465 420	248.223 971	.004 028 6198	.682 398	169.387 602	.005 903 6198	7.09	.204 338	1.20	204
18	1.498 734	265.991 494	.003 759 5187	.667 230	177.477 448	.005 634 5187	6.77	.217 056	1.21	216
19	1.532 806	284.162 935	.003 519 1078	.652 398	185.387 471	.005 394 1078	6.48	.229 857	1.21	228
20	1.567 652	302.747 477	.003 303 0829	.637 897	193.121 668	.005 178 0829	6.22	.242 740	1.21	240
21	1.603 290	321.754 509	.003 107 9595	.623 718	200.683 949	.004 982 9595	5.98	.255 706	1.22	252
22	1.639 738	341.193 638	.002 930 8870	.609 853	208.078 134	.004 805 8870	5.77	.268 754	1.22	264
23	1.677 015	361.074 686	.002 769 5101	.596 298	215.307 960	.004 644 5101	5.58	.281 885	1.23	276
24	1.715 139	381.407 700	.002 621 8663	.583 043	222.377 080	.004 496 8663	5.40	.295 097	1.23	288
25	1.754 131	402.202 954	.002 486 3070	.570 083	229.289 067	.004 361 3070	5.24	.308 392	1.23	300
26	1.794 008	423.470 956	.002 361 4370	.557 411	236.047 412	.004 236 4370	5.09	.321 768	1.24	312
27	1.834 792	445.222 455	.002 246 0682	.545 021	242.655 533	.004 121 0682	4.95	.335 226	1.24	324
28	1.876 503	467.468 441	.002 139 1818	.532 906	249.116 766	.004 014 1818	4.82	.348 765	1.25	336
29	1.919 163	490.220 155	.002 039 8998	.521 061	255.434 379	.003 914 8998	4.70	.362 385	1.25	348
30	1.962 792	513.489 096	.001 947 4610	.509 478	261.611 562	.003 822 4610	4.59	.376 086	1.25	360
31	2.007 413	537.287 021	.001 861 2026	.498 154	267.651 438	.003 736 2026	4.49	.389 867	1.26	372
32	2.053 049	561.625 955	.001 780 5445	.487 081	273.557 059	.003 655 5445	4.39	.403 729	1.26	384
33	2.099 722	586.518 199	.001 704 9769	.476 254	279.331 409	.003 579 9769	4.30	.417 671	1.27	396
34	2.147 456	611.976 329	.001 634 0501	.465 667	284.977 405	.003 509 0501	4.22	.431 692	1.27	408
35	2.196 275	638.013 212	.001 567 3657	.455 316	290.497 901	.003 442 3657	4.14	.445 794	1.27	420
36	2.246 204	664.642 005	.001 504 5694	.445 196	295.895 687	.003 379 5694	4.06	.459 974	1.28	432
37	2.297 268	691.876 162	.001 445 3454	.435 300	301.173 490	.003 320 3454	3.99	.474 233	1.28	444
38	2.349 493	719.729 447	.001 389 4110	.425 624	306.333 977	.003 264 4110	3.92	.488 571	1.29	456
39	2.402 905	748.215 934	.001 336 5126	.416 163	311.379 756	.003 211 5126	3.86	.502 988	1.29	468
40	2.457 531	777.350 018	.001 286 4218	.406 912	316.313 376	.003 161 4218	3.80	.517 482	1.29	480
41	2.513 400	807.146 422	.001 238 9326	.397 868	321.137 332	.003 113 9326	3.74	.532 055	1.30	492
42	2.570 538	837.620 202	.001 193 8585	.389 024	325.854 059	.003 068 8585	3.69	.546 705	1.30	504
43	2.628 975	868.786 757	.001 151 0304	.380 376	330.465 942	.003 026 0304	3.64	.561 432	1.31	516
44	2.688 741	900.661 837	.001 110 2946	.371 921	334.975 312	.002 985 2946	3.59	.576 236	1.31	528
45	2.749 865	933.261 548	.001 071 5110	.363 654	339.384 447	.002 946 5110	3.54	.591 116	1.31	540
46	2.812 379	966.602 365	.001 034 5516	.355 571	343.695 574	.002 909 5516	3.50	.606 072	1.32	552
47	2.876 315	1000.701 134	.000 999 2994	.347 667	347.910 874	.002 874 2994	3.45	.621 105	1.32	564
48	2.941 703	1035.575 088	.000 965 6470	.339 939	352.032 474	.002 840 6470	3.41	.636 213	1.33	576
49	3.008 578	1071.241 848	.000 933 4960	.332 383	356.062 460	.002 808 4960	3.38	.651 396	1.33	588
50	3.076 974	1107.719 438	.000 902 7557	.324 995	360.002 866	.002 777 7557	3.34	.666 653	1.33	600

MONTHLY COMPOUND INTEREST AND ANNUITY

2.50 % M

Amount Of 1	Amount Of 1 Per Period	Sinking Fund Payment	Present Worth Of 1	Present Worth of 1 Per Period	Periodic Payment To Amortize 1	Constant Annual Percent	Total Interest	Annual Add On Rate	
What a single $ 1 deposit grows to in the future. The deposit is made at the beginning of the first period.	What a series of $ 1 deposits grow to in the future. A deposit is made at the end of each period.	The amount to be deposited at the end of each period that grows to $ 1 in the future.	What $ 1 to be paid in the future is worth today. Value today of a single $ 1 payment tomorrow.	What $ 1 to be paid at the end of each period is worth today. Value today of a series of $ 1 payments tomorrow.	The mortgage payment to amortize a loan of $ 1. An annuity certain, payable at the end of each period, worth $ 1 today.	The annual interest payment, including interest and principal, to amortize completely a loan of $ 100.	The total interest paid over the term on a loan of $1. The loan is amortized by regular periodic payments.	The average annual interest rate on a loan that is completely amortized by regular periodic payments.	
$S = (1+i)^n$	$S\overline{n}| = \dfrac{(1+i)^n - 1}{i}$	$\dfrac{1}{S\overline{n}|} = \dfrac{i}{(1+i)^n - 1}$	$V^n = \dfrac{1}{(1+i)^n}$	$A\overline{n}| = \dfrac{1-V^n}{i}$	$\dfrac{1}{A\overline{n}|} = \dfrac{i}{1-V^n}$				

YEAR									PERIODS
	1.002 083	1.000 000	1.000 000 0000	.997 921	.997 921	1.002 083 3333	1202.50	.002 083	2.50	1
	1.004 171	2.002 083	.499 479 7086	.995 846	1.993 767	.501 563 0420	601.88	.003 126	1.88	2
	1.006 263	3.006 254	.332 639 8524	.993 776	2.987 543	.334 723 1857	401.67	.004 170	1.67	3
	1.008 359	4.012 517	.249 220 1049	.991 710	3.979 253	.251 303 4383	301.57	.005 214	1.56	4
	1.010 460	5.020 877	.199 168 4010	.989 648	4.968 901	.201 251 7343	241.51	.006 259	1.50	5
	1.012 565	6.031 337	.165 800 7188	.987 591	5.956 492	.167 884 0521	201.47	.007 304	1.46	6
	1.014 675	7.043 902	.141 966 7633	.985 537	6.942 029	.144 050 0966	172.87	.008 351	1.43	7
	1.016 789	8.058 577	.124 091 3870	.983 489	7.925 518	.126 174 7203	151.41	.009 398	1.41	8
	1.018 907	9.075 366	.110 188 3968	.981 444	8.906 962	.112 271 7302	134.73	.010 446	1.39	9
	1.021 030	10.094 273	.099 066 0770	.979 403	9.886 365	.101 149 4103	121.38	.011 494	1.38	10
	1.023 157	11.115 302	.089 966 0628	.977 367	10.863 732	.092 049 3961	110.46	.012 543	1.37	11
	1.025 288	12.138 459	.082 382 7778	.975 335	11.839 068	.084 466 1112	101.36	.013 593	1.36	12
1	1.025 288	12.138 459	.082 382 7778	.975 335	11.839 068	.084 466 1112	101.36	.013 593	1.36	12
2	1.051 216	24.583 882	.040 677 0589	.951 279	23.386 128	.042 760 3922	51.32	.026 249	1.31	24
3	1.077 800	37.344 029	.026 778 0423	.927 816	34.648 383	.028 861 3757	34.64	.039 010	1.30	36
4	1.105 056	50.426 862	.019 830 7007	.904 932	45.632 858	.021 914 0340	26.30	.051 874	1.30	48
5	1.133 001	63.840 539	.015 664 0283	.882 612	56.346 404	.017 747 3616	21.30	.064 842	1.30	60
6	1.161 653	77.593 427	.012 887 6896	.860 842	66.795 703	.014 971 0230	17.97	.077 914	1.30	72
7	1.191 029	91.694 104	.010 905 8266	.839 610	76.987 273	.012 989 1600	15.59	.091 089	1.30	84
8	1.221 149	106.151 366	.009 420 5100	.818 901	86.927 470	.011 503 8433	13.81	.104 369	1.30	96
9	1.252 030	120.974 229	.008 266 2234	.798 703	96.622 496	.010 349 5567	12.42	.117 752	1.31	108
10	1.283 692	136.171 940	.007 343 6568	.779 003	106.078 396	.009 426 9902	11.32	.131 239	1.31	120
11	1.316 154	151.753 978	.006 589 6131	.759 789	115.301 070	.008 672 9464	10.41	.144 829	1.32	132
12	1.349 438	167.730 061	.005 961 9605	.741 049	124.296 268	.008 045 2938	9.66	.158 522	1.32	144
13	1.383 563	184.110 155	.005 431 5309	.722 772	133.069 603	.007 514 8643	9.02	.172 319	1.33	156
14	1.418 551	200.904 476	.004 977 4899	.704 945	141.626 545	.007 060 8232	8.48	.186 218	1.33	168
15	1.454 424	218.123 500	.004 584 5588	.687 557	149.972 433	.006 667 8921	8.01	.200 221	1.33	180
16	1.491 204	235.777 966	.004 241 2784	.670 599	158.112 472	.006 324 6118	7.59	.214 325	1.34	192
17	1.528 914	253.878 886	.003 938 8860	.654 059	166.051 739	.006 022 2194	7.23	.228 533	1.34	204
18	1.567 578	272.437 551	.003 670 5660	.637 927	173.795 186	.005 753 8993	6.91	.242 842	1.35	216
19	1.607 220	291.465 535	.003 430 9374	.622 192	181.347 644	.005 514 2707	6.62	.257 254	1.35	228
20	1.647 864	310.974 708	.003 215 6956	.606 846	188.713 822	.005 299 0289	6.36	.271 767	1.36	240
21	1.689 536	330.977 238	.003 021 3558	.591 879	195.898 315	.005 104 6891	6.13	.286 382	1.36	252
22	1.732 262	351.485 601	.002 845 0668	.577 280	202.905 605	.004 928 4001	5.92	.301 098	1.37	264
23	1.776 068	372.512 589	.002 684 4730	.563 042	209.740 061	.004 767 8064	5.73	.315 915	1.37	276
24	1.820 982	394.071 317	.002 537 6117	.549 154	216.405 948	.004 620 9451	5.55	.330 832	1.38	288
25	1.867 032	416.175 232	.002 402 8340	.535 610	222.907 423	.004 486 1673	5.39	.345 850	1.38	300
26	1.914 246	438.838 121	.002 278 7446	.522 399	229.248 540	.004 362 0779	5.24	.360 968	1.39	312
27	1.962 654	462.074 119	.002 164 1550	.509 514	235.433 256	.004 247 4883	5.10	.376 186	1.39	324
28	2.012 287	485.897 720	.002 058 0463	.496 947	241.465 427	.004 141 3796	4.97	.391 504	1.40	336
29	2.063 175	510.323 783	.001 959 5403	.484 690	247.348 817	.004 042 8736	4.86	.406 920	1.40	348
30	2.115 349	535.367 543	.001 867 8757	.472 735	253.087 094	.003 951 2090	4.75	.422 435	1.41	360
31	2.168 843	561.044 621	.001 782 3894	.461 075	258.683 838	.003 865 7228	4.64	.438 049	1.41	372
32	2.223 690	587.371 034	.001 702 5014	.449 703	264.142 540	.003 785 8347	4.55	.453 761	1.42	384
33	2.279 923	614.363 200	.001 627 7017	.438 611	269.466 605	.003 711 0350	4.46	.469 570	1.42	396
34	2.337 579	642.037 957	.001 557 5403	.427 793	274.659 353	.003 640 8736	4.37	.485 476	1.43	408
35	2.396 693	670.412 565	.001 491 6188	.417 242	279.724 023	.003 574 9522	4.29	.501 480	1.43	420
36	2.457 302	699.504 724	.001 429 5829	.406 950	284.663 775	.003 512 9162	4.22	.517 580	1.44	432
37	2.519 443	729.332 579	.001 371 1166	.396 913	289.481 689	.003 454 4499	4.15	.533 776	1.44	444
38	2.583 156	759.914 733	.001 315 9371	.387 123	294.180 771	.003 399 2704	4.08	.550 067	1.45	456
39	2.648 480	791.270 264	.001 263 7907	.377 575	298.763 951	.003 347 1240	4.02	.566 454	1.45	468
40	2.715 456	823.418 727	.001 214 4489	.368 262	303.234 088	.003 297 7823	3.96	.582 935	1.46	480
41	2.784 125	856.380 176	.001 167 7057	.359 179	307.593 970	.003 251 0390	3.91	.599 511	1.46	492
42	2.854 532	890.175 168	.001 123 3744	.350 320	311.846 318	.003 206 7077	3.85	.616 181	1.47	504
43	2.926 718	924.824 784	.001 081 2859	.341 680	315.993 782	.003 164 6192	3.80	.632 944	1.47	516
44	3.000 730	960.350 635	.001 041 2863	.333 252	320.038 950	.003 124 6197	3.75	.649 799	1.48	528
45	3.076 614	996.774 880	.001 003 2356	.325 033	323.984 345	.003 086 5689	3.71	.666 747	1.48	540
46	3.154 417	1034.120 238	.000 967 0055	.317 016	327.832 428	.003 050 3389	3.67	.683 787	1.49	552
47	3.234 188	1072.410 003	.000 932 4792	.309 197	331.585 599	.003 015 8125	3.62	.700 918	1.49	564
48	3.315 975	1111.668 056	.000 899 5491	.301 570	335.246 200	.002 982 8824	3.58	.718 140	1.50	576
49	3.399 831	1151.918 885	.000 868 1167	.294 132	338.816 512	.002 951 4500	3.55	.735 453	1.50	588
50	3.485 807	1193.187 596	.000 838 0912	.286 878	342.298 764	.002 921 4245	3.51	.752 855	1.51	600

Effective Rate is 2.53 %   8 - 6   Annual Percentage Rate is 2.50 %

MONTHLY COMPOUND INTEREST AND ANNUITY

2.75 % M

	Amount Of 1	Amount Of 1 Per Period	Sinking Fund Payment	Present Worth Of 1	Present Worth of 1 Per Period	Periodic Payment To Amortize 1	Constant Annual Percent	Total Interest	Annual Add On Rate	
	What a single $ 1 deposit grows to in the future. The deposit is made at the beginning of the first period.	What a series of $ 1 deposits grow to in the future. A deposit is made at the end of each period.	The amount to be deposited at the end of each period that grows to $ 1 in the future.	What $ 1 to be paid in the future is worth today. Value today of a single $ 1 payment tomorrow.	What $ 1 to be paid at the end of each period is worth today. Value today of a series of $ 1 payments tomorrow.	The mortgage payment to amortize a loan of $ 1. An annuity certain, payable at the end of each period, worth $ 1 today.	The annual payment, including interest and principal, to amortize completely a loan of $ 100.	The total interest paid over the term on a loan of $ 1. The loan is amortized by regular periodic payments.	The average annual interest rate on a loan that is completely amortized by regular periodic payments.	
	$S = (1+i)^n$	$S\overline{n} = \dfrac{(1+i)^n - 1}{i}$	$\dfrac{1}{S\overline{n}} = \dfrac{i}{(1+i)^n - 1}$	$V^n = \dfrac{1}{(1+i)^n}$	$A\overline{n} = \dfrac{1 - V^n}{i}$	$\dfrac{1}{A\overline{n}} = \dfrac{i}{1 - V^n}$				

YEAR										PERIODS
	1.002 292	1.000 000	1.000 000 0000	.997 714	.997 714	1.002 291 6667	1202.75	.002 292	2.75	1
	1.004 589	2.002 292	.499 427 7390	.995 432	1.993 146	.501 719 4057	602.07	.003 439	2.06	2
	1.006 891	3.006 880	.332 570 6102	.993 156	2.986 302	.334 862 2768	401.84	.004 587	1.83	3
	1.009 198	4.013 771	.249 142 2643	.990 886	3.977 188	.251 433 9310	301.73	.005 736	1.72	4
	1.011 511	5.022 969	.199 085 4316	.988 620	4.965 808	.201 377 0983	241.66	.006 885	1.65	5
	1.013 829	6.034 480	.165 714 3556	.986 360	5.952 168	.168 006 0222	201.61	.008 036	1.61	6
	1.016 152	7.048 309	.141 877 9975	.984 104	6.936 272	.144 169 6642	173.01	.009 188	1.58	7
	1.018 481	8.064 462	.124 000 8383	.981 854	7.918 126	.126 292 5050	151.56	.010 340	1.55	8
	1.020 815	9.082 943	.110 096 4783	.979 609	8.897 736	.112 388 1450	134.87	.011 493	1.53	9
	1.023 154	10.103 758	.098 973 0777	.977 370	9.875 105	.101 264 7444	121.52	.012 647	1.52	10
	1.025 499	11.126 912	.089 872 1930	.975 135	10.850 240	.092 163 8597	110.60	.013 802	1.51	11
	1.027 849	12.152 411	.082 288 1953	.972 905	11.823 145	.084 579 8620	101.50	.014 958	1.50	12
1	1.027 849	12.152 411	.082 288 1953	.972 905	11.823 145	.084 579 8620	101.50	.014 958	1.50	12
2	1.056 474	24.643 259	.040 579 0491	.946 545	23.325 946	.042 870 7158	51.45	.028 897	1.44	24
3	1.085 896	37.481 967	.026 679 4964	.920 898	34.517 082	.028 971 1631	34.77	.042 962	1.43	36
4	1.116 138	50.678 224	.019 732 3411	.895 947	45.404 997	.022 024 0078	26.43	.057 152	1.43	48
5	1.147 221	64.241 987	.015 566 1437	.871 671	55.997 907	.017 857 8103	21.43	.071 469	1.43	60
6	1.179 171	78.183 491	.012 790 4240	.848 054	66.303 805	.015 082 0906	18.10	.085 911	1.43	72
7	1.212 010	92.513 256	.010 809 2617	.825 076	76.330 468	.013 100 9284	15.73	.100 478	1.44	84
8	1.245 763	107.242 095	.009 324 6966	.802 721	86.085 462	.011 616 3633	13.94	.115 171	1.44	96
9	1.280 457	122.381 121	.008 171 1950	.780 971	95.576 147	.010 462 8616	12.56	.129 989	1.44	108
10	1.316 117	137.941 758	.007 249 4364	.759 811	104.809 684	.009 541 1031	11.45	.144 932	1.45	120
11	1.352 769	153.935 747	.006 496 2169	.739 224	113.793 042	.008 787 8835	10.55	.160 001	1.45	132
12	1.390 443	170.375 158	.005 869 4003	.719 195	122.532 998	.008 161 0670	9.80	.175 194	1.46	144
13	1.429 166	187.272 394	.005 339 8153	.699 709	131.036 147	.007 631 4820	9.16	.190 511	1.47	156
14	1.468 967	204.640 206	.004 886 6253	.680 750	139.308 907	.007 178 2919	8.62	.205 953	1.47	168
15	1.509 877	222.491 699	.004 494 5497	.662 306	147.357 518	.006 786 2164	8.15	.221 519	1.48	180
16	1.551 926	240.840 343	.004 152 1283	.644 361	155.188 054	.006 443 7950	7.74	.237 209	1.48	192
17	1.595 146	259.699 983	.003 850 5971	.626 902	162.806 424	.006 142 2638	7.38	.253 022	1.49	204
18	1.639 569	279.084 851	.003 583 1397	.609 916	170.218 377	.005 874 8063	7.05	.268 958	1.49	216
19	1.685 230	299.009 574	.003 344 3745	.593 391	177.429 505	.005 636 0412	6.77	.285 017	1.50	228
20	1.732 163	319.489 185	.003 129 9964	.577 313	184.445 250	.005 421 6631	6.51	.301 199	1.51	240
21	1.780 402	340.539 139	.002 936 5200	.561 671	191.270 905	.005 228 1867	6.28	.317 503	1.51	252
22	1.829 985	362.175 319	.002 761 0937	.546 453	197.911 621	.005 052 7604	6.07	.333 929	1.52	264
23	1.880 949	384.414 051	.002 601 3617	.531 647	204.372 409	.004 893 0284	5.88	.350 476	1.52	276
24	1.933 332	407.272 115	.002 455 3608	.517 242	210.658 143	.004 747 0275	5.70	.367 144	1.53	288
25	1.987 174	430.766 760	.002 321 4419	.503 227	216.773 568	.004 613 1086	5.54	.383 933	1.54	300
26	2.042 515	454.915 714	.002 198 2094	.489 592	222.723 297	.004 489 8761	5.39	.400 841	1.54	312
27	2.099 398	479.737 199	.002 084 4746	.476 327	228.511 819	.004 376 1413	5.26	.417 870	1.55	324
28	2.157 864	505.249 944	.001 979 2184	.463 421	234.143 504	.004 270 8851	5.13	.435 017	1.55	336
29	2.217 959	531.473 200	.001 881 5624	.450 865	239.622 599	.004 173 2291	5.01	.452 284	1.56	348
30	2.279 728	558.426 755	.001 790 7451	.438 649	244.953 240	.004 082 4118	4.90	.469 668	1.57	360
31	2.343 217	586.130 948	.001 706 1034	.426 764	250.139 449	.003 997 7701	4.80	.487 170	1.57	372
32	2.408 474	614.606 681	.001 627 0568	.415 201	255.185 139	.003 918 7235	4.71	.504 790	1.58	384
33	2.475 548	643.875 444	.001 553 0954	.403 951	260.094 117	.003 844 7621	4.62	.522 526	1.58	396
34	2.544 490	673.959 320	.001 483 7691	.393 006	264.870 088	.003 775 4357	4.54	.540 378	1.59	408
35	2.615 352	704.881 011	.001 418 6792	.382 358	269.516 656	.003 710 3458	4.46	.558 345	1.60	420
36	2.688 188	736.663 848	.001 357 4713	.371 998	274.037 326	.003 649 1379	4.38	.576 428	1.60	432
37	2.763 052	769.331 814	.001 299 8293	.361 919	278.435 510	.003 591 4959	4.31	.594 624	1.61	444
38	2.840 001	802.909 560	.001 245 4703	.352 113	282.714 527	.003 537 1370	4.25	.612 934	1.61	456
39	2.919 093	837.422 421	.001 194 1405	.342 572	286.877 605	.003 485 8071	4.19	.631 358	1.62	468
40	3.000 388	872.896 440	.001 145 6113	.333 290	290.927 885	.003 437 2779	4.13	.649 893	1.62	480
41	3.083 946	909.358 386	.001 099 6764	.324 260	294.868 424	.003 391 3431	4.07	.668 541	1.63	492
42	3.169 832	946.835 770	.001 056 1494	.315 474	298.702 196	.003 347 8160	4.02	.687 299	1.64	504
43	3.258 109	985.356 872	.001 014 8607	.306 926	302.432 092	.003 306 5274	3.97	.706 168	1.64	516
44	3.348 845	1024.950 759	.000 975 6566	.298 610	306.060 928	.003 267 3233	3.93	.725 147	1.65	528
45	3.442 108	1065.647 307	.000 938 3968	.290 520	309.591 442	.003 230 0634	3.88	.744 234	1.65	540
46	3.537 969	1107.477 224	.000 902 9531	.282 648	313.026 298	.003 194 6198	3.84	.763 430	1.66	552
47	3.636 499	1150.472 074	.000 869 2084	.274 990	316.368 087	.003 160 8751	3.80	.782 734	1.67	564
48	3.737 772	1194.664 300	.000 837 0552	.267 539	319.619 331	.003 128 7219	3.76	.802 144	1.67	576
49	3.841 867	1240.087 247	.000 806 3949	.260 290	322.782 484	.003 098 0615	3.72	.821 660	1.68	588
50	3.948 860	1286.775 191	.000 777 1365	.253 238	325.859 932	.003 068 8032	3.69	.841 282	1.68	600

Effective Rate is 2.78 %

Annual Percentage Rate is 2.75 %

Amount Of 1	Amount Of 1 Per Period	Sinking Fund Payment	Present Worth Of 1	Present Worth of 1 Per Period	Periodic Payment To Amortize 1	Constant Annual Percent	Total Interest	Annual Add On Rate
What a single $ 1 deposit grows to in the future. The deposit is made at the beginning of the first period.	What a series of $ 1 deposits grow to in the future. A deposit is made at the end of each period.	The amount to be deposited at the end of each period that grows to $ 1 in the future.	What $ 1 to be paid in the future is worth today. Value today of a single $ 1 payment tomorrow.	What $ 1 to be paid at the end of each period is worth today. Value today of a series of $ 1 payments tomorrow.	The mortgage payment to amortize a loan of $ 1. An annuity certain, payable at the end of each period, worth $ 1 today.	The annual payment, including interest and principal, to amortize completely a loan of $ 100.	The total interest paid over the term on a loan of $1. The loan is amortized by regular periodic payments.	The average annual interest rate on a loan that is completely amortized by regular periodic payments.

$$S = (1+i)^n \qquad S\overline{n}| = \frac{(1+i)^n - 1}{i} \qquad \frac{1}{S\overline{n}|} = \frac{i}{(1+i)^n - 1} \qquad V^n = \frac{1}{(1+i)^n} \qquad A\overline{n}| = \frac{1 - V^n}{i} \qquad \frac{1}{A\overline{n}|} = \frac{i}{1 - V^n}$$

YEAR	Amount Of 1	Amount Of 1 Per Period	Sinking Fund Payment	Present Worth Of 1	Present Worth of 1 Per Period	Periodic Payment To Amortize 1	Constant Annual Percent	Total Interest	Annual Add On Rate	PERIODS
	1.002 500	1.000 000	1.000 000 0000	.997 506	.997 506	1.002 500 0000	1203.00	.002 500	3.00	1
	1.005 006	2.002 500	.499 375 7803	.995 019	1.992 525	.501 875 7803	602.26	.003 752	2.25	2
	1.007 519	3.007 506	.332 501 3872	.992 537	2.985 062	.335 001 3872	402.01	.005 004	2.00	3
	1.010 038	4.015 025	.249 064 4507	.990 062	3.975 124	.251 564 4507	301.88	.006 258	1.88	4
	1.012 563	5.025 063	.199 002 4969	.987 593	4.962 718	.201 502 4969	241.81	.007 512	1.80	5
	1.015 094	6.037 625	.165 628 0344	.985 130	5.947 848	.168 128 0344	201.76	.008 768	1.75	6
	1.017 632	7.052 719	.141 789 2812	.982 674	6.930 522	.144 289 2812	173.15	.010 025	1.72	7
	1.020 176	8.070 351	.123 910 3464	.980 223	7.910 745	.126 410 3464	151.70	.011 283	1.69	8
	1.022 726	9.090 527	.110 004 6238	.977 779	8.888 524	.112 504 6238	135.01	.012 542	1.67	9
	1.025 283	10.113 253	.098 880 1498	.975 340	9.863 864	.101 380 1498	121.66	.013 801	1.66	10
	1.027 846	11.138 536	.089 778 4019	.972 908	10.836 772	.092 278 4019	110.74	.015 062	1.64	11
	1.030 416	12.166 383	.082 193 6988	.970 482	11.807 254	.084 693 6988	101.64	.016 324	1.63	12
1	1.030 416	12.166 383	.082 193 6988	.970 482	11.807 254	.084 693 6988	101.64	.016 324	1.63	12
2	1.061 757	24.702 818	.040 481 2120	.941 835	23.265 980	.042 981 2120	51.58	.031 549	1.58	24
3	1.094 051	37.620 560	.026 581 2096	.914 034	34.386 465	.029 081 2096	34.90	.046 924	1.56	36
4	1.127 328	50.931 208	.019 634 3270	.887 053	45.178 695	.022 134 3270	26.57	.062 448	1.56	48
5	1.161 617	64.646 713	.015 468 6907	.860 869	55.652 358	.017 968 6907	21.57	.078 121	1.56	60
6	1.196 948	78.779 387	.012 693 6758	.835 458	65.816 858	.015 193 6758	18.24	.093 945	1.57	72
7	1.233 355	93.341 920	.010 713 3001	.810 797	75.681 321	.013 213 3001	15.86	.109 917	1.57	84
8	1.270 868	108.347 387	.009 229 5719	.786 863	85.254 603	.011 729 5719	14.08	.126 039	1.58	96
9	1.309 523	123.809 259	.008 076 9404	.763 637	94.545 300	.010 576 9404	12.70	.142 310	1.58	108
10	1.349 354	139.741 419	.007 156 0745	.741 096	103.561 753	.009 656 0745	11.59	.158 729	1.59	120
11	1.390 395	156.158 171	.006 403 7635	.719 220	112.312 057	.008 903 7635	10.69	.175 297	1.59	132
12	1.432 686	173.074 254	.005 777 8669	.697 990	120.804 069	.008 277 8669	9.94	.192 013	1.60	144
13	1.476 262	190.504 855	.005 249 2100	.677 386	129.045 412	.007 749 2100	9.30	.208 877	1.61	156
14	1.521 164	208.465 626	.004 796 9539	.657 391	137.043 486	.007 296 9539	8.76	.225 888	1.61	168
15	1.567 432	226.972 690	.004 405 8164	.637 986	144.805 471	.006 905 8164	8.29	.243 047	1.62	180
16	1.615 107	246.042 664	.004 064 3358	.619 154	152.338 338	.006 564 3358	7.88	.260 352	1.63	192
17	1.664 232	265.692 670	.003 763 7470	.600 878	159.648 848	.006 263 7470	7.52	.277 804	1.63	204
18	1.714 851	285.940 350	.003 497 2329	.583 141	166.743 566	.005 997 2329	7.20	.295 402	1.64	216
19	1.767 010	306.803 882	.003 259 4112	.565 928	173.628 861	.005 759 4112	6.92	.313 146	1.65	228
20	1.820 755	328.301 998	.003 045 9760	.549 223	180.310 914	.005 545 9760	6.66	.331 034	1.66	240
21	1.876 135	350.454 000	.002 853 4415	.533 011	186.795 726	.005 353 4415	6.43	.349 067	1.66	252
22	1.933 199	373.279 777	.002 678 9557	.517 277	193.089 119	.005 178 9557	6.22	.367 244	1.67	264
23	1.992 000	396.799 821	.002 520 1624	.502 008	199.196 742	.005 020 1624	6.03	.385 565	1.68	276
24	2.052 588	421.035 250	.002 375 0980	.487 190	205.124 080	.004 875 0980	5.86	.404 028	1.68	288
25	2.115 020	446.007 823	.002 242 1131	.472 809	210.876 453	.004 742 1131	5.70	.422 634	1.69	300
26	2.179 350	471.739 961	.002 119 8119	.458 852	216.459 028	.004 619 8119	5.55	.441 381	1.70	312
27	2.245 637	498.254 766	.002 007 0054	.445 308	221.876 815	.004 507 0054	5.41	.460 270	1.70	324
28	2.313 940	525.576 044	.001 902 6742	.432 163	227.134 679	.004 402 6742	5.29	.479 299	1.71	336
29	2.384 321	553.728 325	.001 805 9398	.419 407	232.237 341	.004 305 9398	5.17	.498 467	1.72	348
30	2.456 842	582.736 885	.001 716 0403	.407 027	237.189 382	.004 216 0403	5.06	.517 775	1.73	360
31	2.531 569	612.627 767	.001 632 3126	.395 012	241.995 247	.004 132 3126	4.96	.537 220	1.73	372
32	2.608 570	643.427 810	.001 554 1759	.383 352	246.659 253	.004 054 1759	4.87	.556 804	1.74	384
33	2.687 912	675.164 665	.001 481 1202	.372 036	251.185 586	.003 981 1202	4.78	.576 524	1.75	396
34	2.769 667	707.866 827	.001 412 6951	.361 054	255.578 310	.003 912 6951	4.70	.596 380	1.75	408
35	2.853 909	741.563 657	.001 348 5019	.350 397	259.841 368	.003 848 5019	4.62	.616 371	1.76	420
36	2.940 714	776.285 408	.001 288 1860	.340 054	263.978 590	.003 788 1860	4.55	.636 496	1.77	432
37	3.030 158	812.063 254	.001 231 4312	.330 016	267.993 688	.003 731 4312	4.48	.656 755	1.78	444
38	3.122 323	848.929 318	.001 177 9544	.320 274	271.890 268	.003 677 9544	4.42	.677 147	1.78	456
39	3.217 292	886.916 698	.001 127 5016	.310 820	275.671 828	.003 627 5016	4.36	.697 671	1.79	468
40	3.315 149	926.059 501	.001 079 8442	.301 646	279.341 764	.003 579 8442	4.30	.718 325	1.80	480
41	3.415 982	966.392 870	.001 034 7758	.292 742	282.903 370	.003 534 7758	4.25	.739 110	1.80	492
42	3.519 883	1007.953 016	.000 992 1097	.284 100	286.359 844	.003 492 1097	4.20	.760 023	1.81	504
43	3.626 943	1050.777 255	.000 951 6765	.275 714	289.714 290	.003 451 6765	4.15	.781 065	1.82	516
44	3.737 260	1094.904 033	.000 913 3221	.267 576	292.969 718	.003 413 3221	4.10	.802 234	1.82	528
45	3.850 932	1140.372 970	.000 876 9061	.259 677	296.129 052	.003 376 9061	4.06	.823 529	1.83	540
46	3.968 062	1187.224 888	.000 842 3004	.252 012	299.195 129	.003 342 3004	4.02	.844 950	1.84	552
47	4.088 755	1235.501 852	.000 809 3877	.244 573	302.170 701	.003 309 3877	3.98	.866 495	1.84	564
48	4.213 118	1285.247 205	.000 778 0604	.237 354	305.058 439	.003 278 0604	3.94	.888 163	1.85	576
49	4.341 264	1336.505 612	.000 748 2198	.230 348	307.860 937	.003 248 2198	3.90	.909 953	1.86	588
50	4.473 308	1389.323 092	.000 719 7750	.223 548	310.580 710	.003 219 7750	3.87	.931 865	1.86	600

Effective Rate is 3.04 %

Annual Percentage Rate is 3.00 %

MONTHLY COMPOUND INTEREST AND ANNUITY

	Amount Of 1	Amount Of 1 Per Period	Sinking Fund Payment	Present Worth Of 1	Present Worth of 1 Per Period	Periodic Payment To Amortize 1	Constant Annual Percent	Total Interest	Annual Add On Rate	
	What a single $ 1 deposit grows to in the future. The deposit is made at the beginning of the first period.	What a series of $ 1 deposits grow to in the future. A deposit is made at the end of each period.	The amount to be deposited at the end of each period that grows to $ 1 in the future.	What $ 1 to be paid in the future is worth today. Value today of a single $ 1 payment tomorrow.	What $ 1 to be paid at the end of each period is worth today. Value today of a series of $ 1 payments tomorrow.	The mortgage payment to amortize a loan of $ 1. An annuity certain, payable at the end of each period, worth $ 1 today.	The annual payment, including interest and principal, to amortize completely a loan of $ 100.	The total interest paid over the term on a loan of $ 1. The loan is amortized completely by regular periodic payments.	The average annual interest rate on a loan that is completely amortized by regular periodic payments.	
	$S = (1+i)^n$	$S\overline{n} = \dfrac{(1+i)^n - 1}{i}$	$\dfrac{1}{S\overline{n}} = \dfrac{i}{(1+i)^n - 1}$	$V^n = \dfrac{1}{(1+i)^n}$	$A\overline{n} = \dfrac{1 - V^n}{i}$	$\dfrac{1}{A\overline{n}} = \dfrac{i}{1 - V^n}$				PERIODS

YEAR										
	1.002 708	1.000 000	1.000 000 0000	.997 299	.997 299	1.002 708 3333	1203.25	.002 708	3.25	1
	1.005 424	2.002 708	.499 323 8323	.994 605	1.991 904	.502 032 1656	602.44	.004 064	2.44	2
	1.008 147	3.008 132	.332 432 1834	.991 919	2.983 823	.335 140 5167	402.17	.005 422	2.17	3
	1.010 877	4.016 279	.248 986 6641	.989 240	3.973 063	.251 694 9974	302.04	.006 780	2.03	4
	1.013 615	5.027 157	.198 919 5967	.986 568	4.959 630	.201 627 9301	241.96	.008 140	1.95	5
	1.016 360	6.040 772	.165 541 7553	.983 903	5.943 533	.168 250 0886	201.91	.009 501	1.90	6
	1.019 113	7.057 132	.141 700 6143	.981 245	6.924 779	.144 408 9477	173.30	.010 863	1.86	7
	1.021 873	8.076 245	.123 819 9113	.978 595	7.903 374	.126 528 2446	151.84	.012 226	1.83	8
	1.024 641	9.098 119	.109 912 8334	.975 952	8.879 326	.112 621 1667	135.15	.013 591	1.81	9
	1.027 416	10.122 759	.098 787 2932	.973 316	9.852 641	.101 495 6265	121.80	.014 956	1.79	10
	1.030 198	11.150 175	.089 684 6894	.970 687	10.823 328	.092 393 0228	110.88	.016 323	1.78	11
	1.032 989	12.180 374	.082 099 2880	.968 065	11.791 393	.084 807 6214	101.77	.017 691	1.77	12
1	1.032 989	12.180 374	.082 099 2880	.968 065	11.791 393	.084 807 6214	101.77	.017 691	1.77	12
2	1.067 065	24.762 560	.040 383 5475	.937 150	23.206 228	.043 091 8808	51.72	.034 205	1.71	24
3	1.102 266	37.759 813	.026 483 1819	.907 222	34.256 529	.029 191 5152	35.03	.050 895	1.70	36
4	1.138 628	51.185 827	.019 536 6581	.878 250	44.953 939	.022 244 9915	26.70	.067 760	1.69	48
5	1.176 190	65.054 745	.015 371 6690	.850 203	55.309 727	.018 080 0023	21.70	.084 800	1.70	60
6	1.214 991	79.381 177	.012 597 4448	.823 052	65.334 803	.015 305 7781	18.37	.102 016	1.70	72
7	1.255 071	94.180 218	.010 617 9410	.796 767	75.039 728	.013 326 2744	16.00	.119 407	1.71	84
8	1.296 474	109.467 457	.009 135 1350	.771 323	84.434 725	.011 843 4684	14.22	.136 973	1.71	96
9	1.339 243	125.258 999	.007 983 4583	.746 690	93.529 694	.010 691 7917	12.84	.154 714	1.72	108
10	1.383 423	141.571 480	.007 063 5696	.722 845	102.334 214	.009 771 9029	11.73	.172 628	1.73	120
11	1.429 060	158.422 086	.006 312 2512	.699 761	110.857 561	.009 020 5845	10.83	.190 717	1.73	132
12	1.476 202	175.828 569	.005 687 3579	.677 414	119.108 716	.008 395 6912	10.08	.208 980	1.74	144
13	1.524 900	193.809 265	.005 159 7120	.655 781	127.096 369	.007 868 0454	9.45	.227 415	1.75	156
14	1.575 204	212.383 118	.004 708 4722	.634 838	134.828 937	.007 416 8055	8.91	.246 023	1.76	168
15	1.627 168	231.569 695	.004 318 3544	.614 565	142.314 565	.007 026 6877	8.44	.264 804	1.77	180
16	1.680 846	251.389 208	.003 977 8955	.594 939	149.561 139	.006 686 2288	8.03	.283 756	1.77	192
17	1.736 294	271.862 537	.003 678 3295	.575 939	156.576 294	.006 386 6629	7.67	.302 879	1.78	204
18	1.793 572	293.011 252	.003 412 8382	.557 547	163.367 419	.006 121 1716	7.35	.322 173	1.79	216
19	1.852 739	314.857 630	.003 176 0386	.539 741	169.941 670	.005 884 3720	7.07	.341 637	1.80	228
20	1.913 859	337.424 688	.002 963 6243	.522 505	176.305 972	.005 671 9576	6.81	.361 270	1.81	240
21	1.976 994	360.736 200	.002 772 1088	.505 818	182.467 030	.005 480 4421	6.58	.381 071	1.81	252
22	2.042 212	384.816 724	.002 598 6397	.489 665	188.431 334	.005 306 9730	6.37	.401 041	1.82	264
23	2.109 581	409.691 629	.002 440 8602	.474 028	194.205 168	.005 149 1936	6.18	.421 177	1.83	276
24	2.179 173	435.387 120	.002 296 8066	.458 890	199.794 615	.005 005 1399	6.01	.441 480	1.84	288
25	2.251 061	461.930 267	.002 164 8289	.444 235	205.205 562	.004 873 1623	5.85	.461 949	1.85	300
26	2.325 320	489.349 032	.002 043 5312	.430 048	210.443 711	.004 751 8645	5.71	.482 582	1.86	312
27	2.402 029	517.672 302	.001 931 7240	.416 315	215.514 579	.004 640 0573	5.57	.503 379	1.86	324
28	2.481 269	546.929 915	.001 828 3878	.403 020	220.423 509	.004 536 7212	5.45	.524 338	1.87	336
29	2.563 122	577.152 692	.001 732 6437	.390 149	225.175 673	.004 440 9771	5.33	.545 460	1.88	348
30	2.647 675	608.372 474	.001 643 7299	.377 690	229.776 075	.004 352 0632	5.23	.566 743	1.89	360
31	2.735 018	640.622 150	.001 560 9826	.365 628	234.229 564	.004 269 3159	5.13	.588 186	1.90	372
32	2.825 243	673.935 695	.001 483 8211	.353 952	238.540 831	.004 192 1544	5.04	.609 787	1.91	384
33	2.918 443	708.348 204	.001 411 7351	.342 648	242.714 417	.004 120 0684	4.95	.631 547	1.91	396
34	3.014 718	743.895 931	.001 344 2741	.331 706	246.754 720	.004 052 6074	4.87	.653 464	1.92	408
35	3.114 169	780.616 324	.001 281 0391	.321 113	250.665 995	.003 989 3724	4.79	.675 536	1.93	420
36	3.216 901	818.548 069	.001 221 6754	.310 858	254.452 364	.003 930 0087	4.72	.697 764	1.94	432
37	3.323 022	857.731 125	.001 165 8665	.300 931	258.117 815	.003 874 1999	4.65	.720 145	1.95	444
38	3.432 643	898.206 772	.001 113 3294	.291 321	261.666 210	.003 821 6627	4.59	.742 678	1.95	456
39	3.545 881	940.017 650	.001 063 8098	.282 017	265.101 286	.003 772 1431	4.53	.765 363	1.96	468
40	3.662 854	983.207 807	.001 017 0790	.273 011	268.426 664	.003 725 4123	4.48	.788 198	1.97	480
41	3.783 687	1027.822 743	.000 972 9304	.264 293	271.645 845	.003 681 2637	4.42	.811 182	1.98	492
42	3.908 505	1073.909 459	.000 931 1772	.255 852	274.762 222	.003 639 5105	4.37	.834 313	1.99	504
43	4.037 441	1121.516 508	.000 891 6498	.247 682	277.779 077	.003 599 9832	4.32	.857 591	1.99	516
44	4.170 630	1170.694 042	.000 854 1941	.239 772	280.699 589	.003 562 5275	4.28	.881 015	2.00	528
45	4.308 213	1221.493 870	.000 818 6697	.232 115	283.526 834	.003 527 0030	4.24	.904 582	2.01	540
46	4.450 334	1273.969 508	.000 784 9481	.224 702	286.263 791	.003 493 2815	4.20	.928 291	2.02	552
47	4.597 144	1328.176 240	.000 752 9121	.217 526	288.913 344	.003 461 2455	4.16	.952 142	2.03	564
48	4.748 797	1384.171 171	.000 722 4540	.210 580	291.478 283	.003 430 7873	4.12	.976 134	2.03	576
49	4.905 453	1442.013 292	.000 693 4749	.203 855	293.961 310	.003 401 8082	4.09	1.000 263	2.04	588
50	5.067 276	1501.763 538	.000 665 8838	.197 345	296.365 042	.003 374 2171	4.05	1.024 530	2.05	600

Effective Rate is 3.30 %

8 - 9

Annual Percentage Rate is 3.25 %

MONTHLY COMPOUND INTEREST AND ANNUITY

3.50 % M

	Amount Of 1	Amount Of 1 Per Period	Sinking Fund Payment	Present Worth Of 1	Present Worth of 1 Per Period	Periodic Payment To Amortize 1	Constant Annual Percent	Total Interest	Annual Add On Rate	
	What a single $ 1 deposit grows to in the future. The deposit is made at the beginning of the first period.	What a series of $ 1 deposits grow to in the future. A deposit is made at the end of each period.	The amount to be deposited at the end of each period that grows to $ 1 in the future.	What $ 1 to be paid in the future is worth today. Value today of a single $ 1 payment tomorrow.	What $ 1 to be paid at the end of each period is worth today. Value today of a series of $ 1 payments tomorrow.	The mortgage payment to amortize a loan of $ 1. An annuity certain, payable at the end of each period, worth $ 1 today.	The annual payment, including interest and principal, to amortize completely a loan of $ 100.	The total interest paid over the term on a loan of $1. The loan is amortized by regular periodic payments.	The average annual interest rate on a loan that is completely amortized by regular periodic payments.	
	$S = (1+i)^n$	$S\overline{n}| = \dfrac{(1+i)^n - 1}{i}$	$\dfrac{1}{S\overline{n}|} = \dfrac{i}{(1+i)^n - 1}$	$V^n = \dfrac{1}{(1+i)^n}$	$A\overline{n}| = \dfrac{1 - V^n}{i}$	$\dfrac{1}{A\overline{n}|} = \dfrac{i}{1 - V^n}$				

YEAR										PERIODS
	1.002 917	1.000 000	1.000 000 0000	.997 092	.997 092	1.002 916 6667	1203.50	.002 917	3.50	1
	1.005 842	2.002 917	.499 271 8952	.994 192	1.991 284	.502 188 5618	602.63	.004 377	2.63	2
	1.008 776	3.008 759	.332 362 9988	.991 301	2.982 585	.335 279 6655	402.34	.005 839	2.34	3
	1.011 718	4.017 534	.248 908 9045	.988 418	3.971 003	.251 825 5712	302.20	.007 302	2.19	4
	1.014 669	5.029 252	.198 836 7311	.985 543	4.956 546	.201 753 3978	242.11	.008 767	2.10	5
	1.017 628	6.043 921	.165 455 5182	.982 677	5.939 223	.168 372 1848	202.05	.010 233	2.05	6
	1.020 596	7.061 549	.141 611 9969	.979 819	6.919 043	.144 528 6635	173.44	.011 701	2.01	7
	1.023 573	8.082 145	.123 729 5328	.976 970	7.896 013	.126 646 1995	151.98	.013 170	1.98	8
	1.026 558	9.105 718	.109 821 1070	.974 129	8.870 141	.112 737 7737	135.29	.014 640	1.95	9
	1.029 552	10.132 276	.098 694 5079	.971 296	9.841 437	.101 611 1746	121.94	.016 112	1.93	10
	1.032 555	11.161 829	.089 591 0555	.968 471	10.809 908	.092 507 7222	111.01	.017 585	1.92	11
	1.035 567	12.194 384	.082 004 9632	.965 655	11.775 563	.084 921 6298	101.91	.019 060	1.91	12
1	1.035 567	12.194 384	.082 004 9632	.965 655	11.775 563	.084 921 6298	101.91	.019 060	1.91	12
2	1.072 399	24.822 485	.040 286 0555	.932 489	23.146 690	.043 202 7221	51.85	.036 865	1.84	24
3	1.110 541	37.899 729	.026 385 4131	.900 462	34.127 270	.029 302 0797	35.17	.054 875	1.83	36
4	1.150 039	51.442 091	.019 439 3344	.869 535	44.730 719	.022 356 0011	26.83	.073 088	1.83	48
5	1.190 943	65.466 113	.015 275 0783	.839 671	54.969 988	.018 191 7450	21.84	.091 505	1.83	60
6	1.233 301	79.988 927	.012 501 7304	.810 832	64.857 585	.015 418 3971	18.51	.110 125	1.84	72
7	1.277 166	95.028 273	.010 523 1840	.782 984	74.405 589	.013 439 8506	16.13	.128 947	1.84	84
8	1.322 591	110.602 523	.009 041 3851	.756 092	83.625 663	.011 958 0517	14.35	.147 973	1.85	96
9	1.369 631	126.730 702	.007 890 7478	.730 124	92.529 069	.010 807 4144	12.97	.167 201	1.86	108
10	1.418 345	143.432 510	.006 971 9201	.705 047	101.126 685	.009 888 5867	11.87	.186 630	1.87	120
11	1.468 791	160.728 352	.006 221 6777	.680 832	109.429 013	.009 138 3444	10.97	.206 261	1.88	132
12	1.521 031	178.639 353	.005 597 8707	.657 449	117.446 193	.008 514 5374	10.22	.226 093	1.88	144
13	1.575 130	197.187 395	.005 071 3181	.634 868	125.188 021	.007 987 9847	9.59	.246 126	1.89	156
14	1.631 152	216.395 133	.004 621 1760	.613 063	132.663 952	.007 537 8427	9.05	.266 358	1.90	168
15	1.689 168	236.286 033	.004 232 1587	.592 008	139.883 120	.007 148 8254	8.58	.286 789	1.91	180
16	1.749 246	256.884 391	.003 892 8017	.571 675	146.854 342	.006 809 4684	8.18	.307 418	1.92	192
17	1.811 461	278.215 370	.003 594 3377	.552 040	153.586 135	.006 511 0044	7.82	.328 245	1.93	204
18	1.875 890	300.305 027	.003 329 9476	.533 080	160.086 722	.006 246 6143	7.50	.349 269	1.94	216
19	1.942 609	323.180 345	.003 094 2476	.514 772	166.364 044	.006 010 9142	7.22	.370 488	1.95	228
20	2.011 702	346.869 269	.002 882 9305	.497 092	172.425 768	.005 799 5972	6.96	.391 903	1.96	240
21	2.083 252	371.400 736	.002 692 5095	.480 019	178.279 301	.005 609 1761	6.74	.413 512	1.97	252
22	2.157 347	396.804 712	.002 520 1314	.463 532	183.931 791	.005 436 7980	6.53	.435 315	1.98	264
23	2.234 077	423.112 231	.002 363 4391	.447 612	189.390 145	.005 280 1058	6.34	.457 309	1.99	276
24	2.313 537	450.355 427	.002 220 4684	.432 239	194.661 029	.005 137 1351	6.17	.479 495	2.00	288
25	2.395 822	478.567 582	.002 089 5690	.417 393	199.750 883	.005 006 2357	6.01	.501 871	2.01	300
26	2.481 034	507.783 156	.001 969 3446	.403 058	204.665 923	.004 886 0112	5.87	.524 436	2.02	312
27	2.569 277	538.037 840	.001 858 6053	.389 215	209.412 155	.004 775 2720	5.74	.547 188	2.03	324
28	2.660 658	569.368 590	.001 756 3315	.375 847	213.995 375	.004 672 9982	5.61	.570 127	2.04	336
29	2.755 290	601.813 680	.001 661 6439	.362 938	218.421 183	.004 578 3105	5.50	.593 252	2.05	348
30	2.853 287	635.412 742	.001 573 7802	.350 473	222.694 985	.004 490 4469	5.39	.616 561	2.06	360
31	2.954 770	670.206 821	.001 492 0767	.338 436	226.822 001	.004 408 7434	5.30	.640 053	2.06	372
32	3.059 862	706.238 420	.001 415 9524	.326 812	230.807 274	.004 332 6191	5.20	.663 726	2.07	384
33	3.168 692	743.551 552	.001 344 8967	.315 588	234.655 670	.004 261 5633	5.12	.687 579	2.08	396
34	3.281 393	782.191 799	.001 278 4588	.304 749	238.371 892	.004 195 1255	5.04	.711 611	2.09	408
35	3.398 102	822.206 362	.001 216 2397	.294 282	241.960 479	.004 132 9063	4.96	.735 821	2.10	420
36	3.518 962	863.644 121	.001 157 8843	.284 175	245.425 815	.004 074 5510	4.89	.760 206	2.11	432
37	3.644 121	906.555 694	.001 103 0762	.274 415	248.772 132	.004 019 7429	4.83	.784 766	2.12	444
38	3.773 731	950.993 502	.001 051 5319	.264 990	252.003 519	.003 968 1986	4.77	.809 499	2.13	456
39	3.907 951	997.011 827	.001 002 9971	.255 889	255.123 922	.003 919 6638	4.71	.834 403	2.14	468
40	4.046 945	1044.666 884	.000 957 2429	.247 100	258.137 154	.003 873 9096	4.65	.859 477	2.15	480
41	4.190 883	1094.016 885	.000 914 0627	.238 613	261.046 895	.003 830 7293	4.60	.884 719	2.16	492
42	4.339 940	1145.122 116	.000 873 2693	.230 418	263.856 700	.003 789 9360	4.55	.910 128	2.17	504
43	4.494 298	1198.045 005	.000 834 6932	.222 504	266.570 001	.003 751 3599	4.51	.935 702	2.18	516
44	4.654 146	1252.850 199	.000 798 1800	.214 862	269.190 113	.003 714 8467	4.46	.961 439	2.19	528
45	4.819 680	1309.604 647	.000 763 5892	.207 483	271.720 236	.003 680 2559	4.42	.987 338	2.19	540
46	4.991 102	1368.377 677	.000 730 7924	.200 357	274.163 461	.003 647 4591	4.38	1.013 397	2.20	552
47	5.168 620	1429.241 086	.000 699 6720	.193 475	276.522 772	.003 616 3387	4.34	1.039 615	2.21	564
48	5.352 452	1492.269 220	.000 670 1204	.186 830	278.801 052	.003 586 7870	4.31	1.065 989	2.22	576
49	5.542 822	1557.539 073	.000 642 0385	.180 414	281.001 084	.003 558 7051	4.28	1.092 519	2.23	588
50	5.739 964	1625.130 376	.000 615 3352	.174 217	283.125 554	.003 532 0019	4.24	1.119 201	2.24	600

Effective Rate is 3.56 %

Annual Percentage Rate is 3.50 %

	Amount Of 1	Amount Of 1 Per Period	Sinking Fund Payment	Present Worth Of 1	Present Worth of 1 Per Period	Periodic Payment To Amortize 1	Constant Annual Percent	Total Interest	Annual Add On Rate	
	What a single $ 1 deposit grows to in the future. The deposit is made at the beginning of the first period.	What a series of $ 1 deposits grow to in the future. A deposit is made at the end of each period.	The amount to be deposited at the end of each period that grows to $ 1 in the future.	What $ 1 to be paid in the future is worth today. Value today of a single $ 1 payment tomorrow.	What $ 1 to be paid at the end of each period is worth today. Value today of a series of $ 1 payments tomorrow.	The mortgage payment to amortize a loan of $ 1. An annuity certain, payable at the end of each period, worth $ 1 today.	The annual payment, including interest and principal, to amortize completely a loan of $ 100.	The total interest paid over the term on a loan of $1. The loan is amortized by regular periodic payments.	The average annual interest rate on a loan that is completely amortized by regular periodic payments.	
	$S = (1+i)^n$	$S\overline{n} = \dfrac{(1+i)^n - 1}{i}$	$\dfrac{1}{S\overline{n}} = \dfrac{i}{(1+i)^n - 1}$	$V^n = \dfrac{1}{(1+i)^n}$	$A\overline{n} = \dfrac{1-V^n}{i}$	$\dfrac{1}{A\overline{n}} = \dfrac{i}{1-V^n}$				**PERIODS**

YEAR

	Amount Of 1	Amount Of 1 Per Period	Sinking Fund Payment	Present Worth Of 1	Present Worth of 1 Per Period	Periodic Payment To Amortize 1	Constant Annual Percent	Total Interest	Annual Add On Rate	PERIODS
	1.003 125	1.000 000	1.000 000 0000	.996 885	.996 885	1.003 125 0000	1203.75	.003 125	3.75	1
	1.006 260	2.003 125	.499 219 9688	.993 779	1.990 664	.502 344 9688	602.82	.004 690	2.81	2
	1.009 404	3.009 385	.332 293 8334	.990 683	2.981 347	.335 418 8334	402.51	.006 257	2.50	3
	1.012 559	4.018 789	.248 831 1720	.987 597	3.968 944	.251 956 1720	302.35	.007 825	2.35	4
	1.015 723	5.031 348	.198 753 9001	.984 520	4.953 465	.201 878 9001	242.26	.009 395	2.25	5
	1.018 897	6.047 071	.165 369 3231	.981 453	5.934 918	.168 494 3231	202.20	.010 966	2.19	6
	1.022 081	7.065 968	.141 523 4288	.978 396	6.913 314	.144 648 4288	173.58	.012 539	2.15	7
	1.025 275	8.088 049	.123 639 2111	.975 348	7.888 662	.126 764 2111	152.12	.014 114	2.12	8
	1.028 479	9.113 324	.109 729 4446	.972 309	8.860 971	.112 854 4446	135.43	.015 690	2.09	9
	1.031 693	10.141 803	.098 601 7939	.969 280	9.830 252	.101 726 7939	122.08	.017 268	2.07	10
	1.034 917	11.173 496	.089 497 5002	.966 261	10.796 513	.092 622 5002	111.15	.018 848	2.06	11
	1.038 151	12.208 414	.081 910 7241	.963 251	11.759 763	.085 035 7241	102.05	.020 429	2.04	12
1	1.038 151	12.208 414	.081 910 7241	.963 251	11.759 763	.085 035 7241	102.05	.020 429	2.04	12
2	1.077 758	24.882 594	.040 188 7360	.927 852	23.087 364	.043 313 7360	51.98	.039 530	1.98	24
3	1.118 876	38.040 311	.026 287 9030	.893 754	33.998 684	.029 412 9030	35.30	.058 865	1.96	36
4	1.161 563	51.700 011	.019 342 3555	.860 909	44.509 021	.022 467 3555	26.97	.078 433	1.96	48
5	1.205 878	65.880 847	.015 178 9183	.829 272	54.633 111	.018 303 9183	21.97	.098 235	1.96	60
6	1.251 883	80.602 700	.012 406 5322	.798 796	64.385 148	.015 531 5322	18.64	.118 270	1.97	72
7	1.299 644	95.886 211	.010 429 0282	.769 441	73.778 805	.013 554 0282	16.27	.138 538	1.98	84
8	1.349 228	111.752 808	.008 948 3210	.741 165	82.827 252	.012 073 3210	14.49	.159 039	1.99	96
9	1.400 702	128.224 735	.007 798 8073	.713 928	91.543 175	.010 923 8073	13.11	.179 771	2.00	108
10	1.454 141	145.325 088	.006 881 1243	.687 691	99.938 794	.010 006 1243	12.01	.200 735	2.01	120
11	1.509 618	163.077 842	.006 132 0409	.662 419	108.025 881	.009 257 0409	11.11	.221 929	2.02	132
12	1.567 212	181.507 886	.005 509 4025	.638 076	115.815 773	.008 634 4025	10.37	.243 354	2.03	144
13	1.627 003	200.641 060	.004 984 0247	.614 627	123.319 392	.008 109 0247	9.74	.265 008	2.04	156
14	1.689 076	220.504 190	.004 535 0612	.592 040	130.547 259	.007 660 0612	9.20	.286 890	2.05	168
15	1.753 516	241.125 123	.004 147 2244	.570 283	137.509 508	.007 272 2244	8.73	.309 000	2.06	180
16	1.820 415	262.532 772	.003 809 0483	.549 325	144.215 898	.006 934 0483	8.33	.331 337	2.07	192
17	1.889 866	284.757 150	.003 511 7643	.529 138	150.675 834	.006 636 7643	7.97	.353 900	2.08	204
18	1.961 967	307.829 417	.003 248 5524	.509 693	156.898 372	.006 373 5524	7.65	.376 687	2.09	216
19	2.036 819	331.781 921	.003 014 0280	.490 962	162.892 236	.006 139 0280	7.37	.399 698	2.10	228
20	2.114 526	356.648 243	.002 803 8831	.472 919	168.665 830	.005 928 8831	7.12	.422 932	2.11	240
21	2.195 198	382.463 248	.002 614 6303	.455 540	174.227 249	.005 739 6303	6.89	.446 387	2.13	252
22	2.278 947	409.263 129	.002 443 4158	.438 799	179.584 290	.005 568 4158	6.69	.470 062	2.14	264
23	2.365 892	437.085 460	.002 287 8821	.422 674	184.744 464	.005 412 8821	6.50	.493 955	2.15	276
24	2.456 154	465.969 249	.002 146 0644	.407 141	189.715 005	.005 271 0644	6.33	.518 067	2.16	288
25	2.549 859	495.954 992	.002 016 3120	.392 178	194.502 882	.005 141 3120	6.17	.542 394	2.17	300
26	2.647 140	527.084 730	.001 897 2282	.377 766	199.114 808	.005 022 2282	6.03	.566 935	2.18	312
27	2.748 132	559.402 107	.001 787 6229	.363 884	203.557 250	.004 912 6229	5.90	.591 690	2.19	324
28	2.852 976	592.952 434	.001 686 4759	.350 511	207.836 435	.004 811 4759	5.78	.616 656	2.20	336
29	2.961 821	627.782 750	.001 592 9077	.337 630	211.958 363	.004 717 9077	5.67	.641 832	2.21	348
30	3.074 818	663.941 886	.001 506 1559	.325 222	215.928 813	.004 631 1559	5.56	.667 216	2.22	360
31	3.192 127	701.480 541	.001 425 5563	.313 271	219.753 352	.004 550 5563	5.47	.692 807	2.23	372
32	3.313 910	740.451 344	.001 350 5276	.301 758	223.437 342	.004 475 5276	5.38	.718 603	2.25	384
33	3.440 340	780.908 934	.001 280 5590	.290 669	226.985 949	.004 405 5590	5.29	.744 601	2.26	396
34	3.571 594	822.910 033	.001 215 1997	.279 987	230.404 146	.004 340 1997	5.21	.770 801	2.27	408
35	3.707 855	866.513 528	.001 154 0501	.269 698	233.696 728	.004 279 0501	5.14	.797 201	2.28	420
36	3.849 314	911.780 552	.001 096 7551	.259 787	236.868 309	.004 221 7551	5.07	.823 798	2.29	432
37	3.996 171	958.774 572	.001 042 9980	.250 240	239.923 337	.004 167 9980	5.01	.850 591	2.30	444
38	4.148 630	1007.561 475	.000 992 4953	.241 043	242.866 096	.004 117 4953	4.95	.877 578	2.31	456
39	4.306 905	1058.209 662	.000 944 9923	.232 185	245.700 710	.004 069 9923	4.89	.904 756	2.32	468
40	4.471 219	1110.790 142	.000 900 2601	.223 653	248.431 154	.004 025 2601	4.84	.932 125	2.33	480
41	4.641 802	1165.376 635	.000 858 0917	.215 434	251.061 256	.003 983 0917	4.78	.959 681	2.34	492
42	4.818 893	1222.045 673	.000 818 3000	.207 517	253.594 704	.003 943 3000	4.74	.987 423	2.35	504
43	5.002 740	1280.876 709	.000 780 7153	.199 890	256.035 049	.003 905 7153	4.69	1.015 349	2.36	516
44	5.193 601	1341.952 225	.000 745 1830	.192 545	258.385 714	.003 870 1830	4.65	1.043 457	2.37	528
45	5.391 743	1405.357 850	.000 711 5625	.185 469	260.649 993	.003 836 5625	4.61	1.071 744	2.38	540
46	5.597 445	1471.182 482	.000 679 7253	.178 653	262.831 062	.003 804 7253	4.57	1.100 208	2.39	552
47	5.810 995	1539.518 409	.000 649 5538	.172 088	264.931 978	.003 774 5538	4.53	1.128 848	2.40	564
48	6.032 692	1610.461 440	.000 620 9400	.165 763	266.955 687	.003 745 9400	4.50	1.157 661	2.41	576
49	6.262 847	1684.111 039	.000 593 7851	.159 672	268.905 027	.003 718 7851	4.47	1.186 646	2.42	588
50	6.501 783	1760.570 466	.000 567 9977	.153 804	270.782 729	.003 692 9977	4.44	1.215 799	2.43	600

Effective Rate is 3.82 %

Annual Percentage Rate is 3.75 %

Amount Of 1	Amount Of 1 Per Period	Sinking Fund Payment	Present Worth Of 1	Present Worth of 1 Per Period	Periodic Payment To Amortize 1	Constant Annual Percent	Total Interest	Annual Add On Rate
What a single $ 1 deposit grows to in the future. The deposit is made at the beginning of the first period.	What a series of $ 1 deposits grow to in the future. A deposit is made at the end of each period.	The amount to be deposited at the end of each period that grows to $ 1 in the future.	What $ 1 to be paid in the future is worth today. Value today of a single $ 1 payment tomorrow.	What $ 1 to be paid at the end of each period is worth today. Value today of a series of $ 1 payments tomorrow.	The mortgage payment to amortize a loan of $ 1. An annuity certain, payable at the end of each period, worth $ 1 today.	The annual interest payment, including interest and principal, to amortize completely a loan of $ 100.	The total interest paid over the term on a loan of $1. The loan is amortized by regular periodic payments.	The average annual interest rate on a loan that is completely amortized by regular periodic payments.
$S = (1+i)^n$	$S\overline{n} = \dfrac{(1+i)^n - 1}{i}$	$\dfrac{1}{S\overline{n}} = \dfrac{i}{(1+i)^n - 1}$	$V^n = \dfrac{1}{(1+i)^n}$	$A\overline{n} = \dfrac{1-V^n}{i}$	$\dfrac{1}{A\overline{n}} = \dfrac{i}{1-V^n}$			

YEAR									PERIODS
	1.003 333	1.000 000	1.000 000 0000	.996 678	.996 678	1.003 333 3333	1204.00	.003 333	4.00	1
	1.006 678	2.003 333	.499 168 0532	.993 367	1.990 044	.502 501 3866	603.01	.005 003	3.00	2
	1.010 033	3.010 011	.332 224 6872	.990 066	2.980 111	.335 558 0206	402.67	.006 674	2.67	3
	1.013 400	4.020 044	.248 753 4664	.986 777	3.966 888	.252 086 7998	302.51	.008 347	2.50	4
	1.016 778	5.033 445	.198 671 1037	.983 499	4.950 386	.202 004 4370	242.41	.010 022	2.41	5
	1.020 167	6.050 223	.165 283 1700	.980 231	5.930 618	.168 616 5033	202.34	.011 699	2.34	6
	1.023 568	7.070 390	.141 434 9100	.976 975	6.907 592	.144 768 2434	173.73	.013 378	2.29	7
	1.026 980	8.093 958	.123 548 9461	.973 729	7.881 321	.126 882 2795	152.26	.015 058	2.26	8
	1.030 403	9.120 938	.109 637 8463	.970 494	8.851 815	.112 971 1796	135.57	.016 741	2.23	9
	1.033 838	10.151 341	.098 509 1513	.967 270	9.819 085	.101 842 4846	122.22	.018 425	2.21	10
	1.037 284	11.185 179	.089 404 0234	.964 056	10.783 141	.092 737 3567	111.29	.020 111	2.19	11
	1.040 742	12.222 463	.081 816 5709	.960 853	11.743 994	.085 149 9042	102.18	.021 799	2.18	12
1	1.040 742	12.222 463	.081 816 5709	.960 853	11.743 994	.085 149 9042	102.18	.021 799	2.18	12
2	1.083 143	24.942 888	.040 091 5888	.923 239	23.028 251	.043 424 9222	52.11	.042 198	2.11	24
3	1.127 272	38.181 562	.026 190 6517	.887 097	33.870 766	.029 523 9850	35.43	.062 863	2.10	36
4	1.173 199	51.959 601	.019 245 7213	.852 371	44.288 834	.022 579 0546	27.10	.083 795	2.09	48
5	1.220 997	66.298 978	.015 083 1887	.819 003	54.299 069	.018 416 5221	22.10	.104 991	2.10	60
6	1.270 742	81.222 564	.012 311 8497	.786 942	63.917 437	.015 645 1831	18.78	.126 453	2.11	72
7	1.322 514	96.754 159	.010 335 4730	.756 136	73.159 278	.013 668 8063	16.41	.148 180	2.12	84
8	1.376 395	112.918 536	.008 855 9420	.726 536	82.039 332	.012 189 2753	14.63	.170 170	2.13	96
9	1.432 472	129.741 474	.007 707 6356	.698 094	90.571 761	.011 040 9689	13.25	.192 425	2.14	108
10	1.490 833	147.249 805	.006 791 1805	.670 766	98.770 175	.010 124 5138	12.15	.214 942	2.15	120
11	1.551 572	165.471 452	.006 043 3385	.644 508	106.647 648	.009 376 6719	11.26	.237 721	2.16	132
12	1.614 785	184.435 477	.005 421 9504	.619 278	114.216 744	.008 755 2837	10.51	.260 761	2.17	144
13	1.680 574	204.172 126	.004 897 8282	.595 035	121.489 536	.008 231 1616	9.88	.284 061	2.19	156
14	1.749 043	224.712 876	.004 450 1233	.571 741	128.477 623	.007 783 4566	9.35	.307 621	2.20	168
15	1.820 302	246.090 488	.004 063 5459	.549 360	135.192 149	.007 396 8793	8.88	.331 438	2.21	180
16	1.894 464	268.339 057	.003 726 6286	.527 854	141.643 824	.007 059 9619	8.48	.355 513	2.22	192
17	1.971 647	291.494 067	.003 430 6016	.507 190	147.842 937	.006 763 9349	8.12	.379 843	2.23	204
18	2.051 975	315.592 448	.003 168 6436	.487 335	153.799 376	.006 501 9770	7.81	.404 427	2.25	216
19	2.135 575	340.672 634	.002 935 3693	.468 258	159.522 640	.006 268 7027	7.53	.429 264	2.26	228
20	2.222 582	366.774 626	.002 726 4700	.449 927	165.021 858	.006 059 8033	7.28	.454 353	2.27	240
21	2.313 134	393.940 053	.002 538 4573	.432 314	170.305 800	.005 871 7906	7.05	.479 691	2.28	252
22	2.407 374	422.212 242	.002 368 4770	.415 390	175.382 893	.005 701 8104	6.85	.505 278	2.30	264
23	2.505 454	451.636 283	.002 214 1711	.399 129	180.261 235	.005 547 5044	6.66	.531 111	2.31	276
24	2.607 530	482.259 105	.002 073 5741	.383 505	184.948 607	.005 406 9075	6.49	.557 189	2.32	288
25	2.713 765	514.129 547	.001 945 0351	.368 492	189.452 483	.005 278 3684	6.34	.583 511	2.33	300
26	2.824 328	547.298 441	.001 827 1567	.354 067	193.780 048	.005 160 4900	6.20	.610 073	2.35	312
27	2.939 396	581.818 687	.001 718 7485	.340 206	197.938 203	.005 052 0818	6.07	.636 875	2.36	324
28	3.059 151	617.745 341	.001 618 7900	.326 888	201.933 580	.004 952 1234	5.95	.663 913	2.37	336
29	3.183 786	655.135 702	.001 526 4013	.314 091	205.772 552	.004 859 7347	5.84	.691 188	2.38	348
30	3.313 498	694.049 404	.001 440 8196	.301 796	209.461 240	.004 774 1530	5.73	.718 695	2.40	360
31	3.448 495	734.548 511	.001 361 3805	.289 982	213.005 529	.004 694 7138	5.64	.746 434	2.41	372
32	3.588 992	776.697 613	.001 287 5023	.278 630	216.411 071	.004 620 8357	5.55	.774 401	2.42	384
33	3.735 213	820.563 935	.001 218 6741	.267 722	219.683 298	.004 552 0074	5.47	.802 595	2.43	396
34	3.887 391	866.217 439	.001 154 4445	.257 242	222.827 427	.004 487 7779	5.39	.831 013	2.44	408
35	4.045 770	913.730 937	.001 094 4141	.247 172	225.848 475	.004 427 7474	5.32	.859 654	2.46	420
36	4.210 601	963.180 208	.001 038 2273	.237 496	228.751 259	.004 371 5606	5.25	.888 514	2.47	432
37	4.382 147	1014.644 119	.000 985 5672	.228 199	231.540 408	.004 318 9006	5.19	.917 592	2.48	444
38	4.560 682	1068.204 748	.000 936 1501	.219 265	234.220 372	.004 269 4835	5.13	.946 884	2.49	456
39	4.746 492	1123.947 521	.000 889 7213	.210 682	236.795 424	.004 223 0546	5.07	.976 390	2.50	468
40	4.939 871	1181.961 340	.000 846 0514	.202 434	239.269 671	.004 179 3847	5.02	1.006 105	2.52	480
41	5.141 129	1242.338 732	.000 804 9334	.194 510	241.647 060	.004 138 2668	4.97	1.036 027	2.53	492
42	5.350 587	1305.175 991	.000 766 1802	.186 895	243.931 382	.004 099 5135	4.92	1.066 155	2.54	504
43	5.568 578	1370.573 338	.000 729 6217	.179 579	246.126 280	.004 062 9550	4.88	1.096 485	2.55	516
44	5.795 450	1438.635 073	.000 695 1033	.172 549	248.235 256	.004 028 4366	4.84	1.127 015	2.56	528
45	6.031 566	1509.469 748	.000 662 4843	.165 794	250.261 672	.003 995 8176	4.80	1.157 742	2.57	540
46	6.277 301	1583.190 338	.000 631 6360	.159 304	252.208 761	.003 964 9693	4.76	1.188 663	2.58	552
47	6.533 048	1659.914 418	.000 602 4407	.153 068	254.079 628	.003 935 7740	4.73	1.219 777	2.60	564
48	6.799 215	1739.764 355	.000 574 7905	.147 076	255.877 256	.003 908 1238	4.69	1.251 079	2.61	576
49	7.076 225	1822.867 502	.000 548 5862	.141 318	257.604 514	.003 881 9196	4.66	1.282 569	2.62	588
50	7.364 521	1909.356 400	.000 523 7367	.135 786	259.264 155	.003 857 0700	4.63	1.314 242	2.63	600

Effective Rate is 4.07 %

Annual Percentage Rate is 4.00 %

Amount Of 1	Amount Of 1 Per Period	Sinking Fund Payment	Present Worth Of 1	Present Worth of 1 Per Period	Periodic Payment To Amortize 1	Constant Annual Percent	Total Interest	Annual Add On Rate
What a single $ 1 deposit grows to in the future. The deposit is made at the beginning of the first period.	What a series of $ 1 deposits grow to in the future. A deposit is made at the end of each period.	The amount to be deposited at the end of each period that grows to $ 1 in the future.	What $ 1 to be paid in the future is worth today. Value today of a single $ 1 payment tomorrow.	What $ 1 to be paid at the end of each period is worth today. Value today of a series of $ 1 payments tomorrow.	The mortgage payment to amortize a loan of $ 1. An annuity certain, payable at the end of each period, worth $ 1 today.	The annual payment, including interest and principal, to amortize completely a loan of $ 100.	The total interest paid over the term on a loan of $1. The loan is amortized by regular periodic payments.	The average annual interest rate on a loan that is completely amortized by regular periodic payments.

$$S = (1+i)^n \qquad S\overline{n}| = \frac{(1+i)^n - 1}{i} \qquad \frac{1}{S\overline{n}|} = \frac{i}{(1+i)^n - 1} \qquad V^n = \frac{1}{(1+i)^n} \qquad A\overline{n}| = \frac{1-V^n}{i} \qquad \frac{1}{A\overline{n}|} = \frac{i}{1-V^n}$$

YEAR									PERIODS
	1.003 542	1.000 000	1.000 000 0000	.996 471	.996 471	1.003 541 6667	1204.25	.003 542	4.25	1
	1.007 096	2.003 542	.499 116 1485	.992 954	1.989 425	.502 657 8152	603.19	.005 316	3.19	2
	1.010 663	3.010 638	.332 155 5603	.989 450	2.978 875	.335 697 2269	402.84	.007 092	2.84	3
	1.014 242	4.021 300	.248 675 7879	.985 958	3.964 833	.252 217 4545	302.67	.008 870	2.66	4
	1.017 834	5.035 542	.198 588 3418	.982 478	4.947 311	.202 130 0085	242.56	.010 650	2.56	5
	1.021 439	6.053 377	.165 197 0589	.979 011	5.926 322	.168 738 7256	202.49	.012 432	2.49	6
	1.025 057	7.074 816	.141 346 4406	.975 556	6.901 878	.144 888 1073	173.87	.014 217	2.44	7
	1.028 687	8.099 872	.123 458 7378	.972 113	7.873 991	.127 000 4045	152.41	.016 003	2.40	8
	1.032 330	9.128 559	.109 546 3119	.968 682	8.842 673	.113 087 9785	135.71	.017 792	2.37	9
	1.035 986	10.160 890	.098 416 5798	.965 264	9.807 936	.101 958 2465	122.35	.019 582	2.35	10
	1.039 656	11.196 876	.089 310 6251	.961 857	10.769 793	.092 852 2917	111.43	.021 375	2.33	11
	1.043 338	12.236 532	.081 722 5034	.958 462	11.728 256	.085 264 1700	102.32	.023 170	2.32	12
1	1.043 338	12.236 532	.081 722 5034	.958 462	11.728 256	.085 264 1700	102.32	.023 170	2.32	12
2	1.088 554	25.003 367	.039 994 6141	.918 650	22.969 348	.043 536 2807	52.25	.044 871	2.24	24
3	1.135 729	38.323 487	.026 093 6589	.880 492	33.743 513	.029 635 3255	35.57	.066 872	2.23	36
4	1.184 949	52.220 871	.019 149 4316	.843 918	44.070 145	.022 691 0982	27.23	.089 173	2.23	48
5	1.236 302	66.720 536	.014 987 8891	.808 864	53.967 834	.018 529 5558	22.24	.111 773	2.24	60
6	1.289 880	81.848 584	.012 217 6824	.775 266	63.454 397	.015 759 3491	18.92	.134 673	2.24	72
7	1.345 781	97.632 246	.010 242 5176	.743 063	72.546 912	.013 784 1843	16.55	.157 871	2.26	84
8	1.404 104	114.099 936	.008 764 2468	.712 198	81.261 745	.012 305 9135	14.77	.181 368	2.27	96
9	1.464 955	131.281 298	.007 617 2312	.682 615	89.614 585	.011 158 8978	13.40	.205 161	2.28	108
10	1.528 442	149.207 262	.006 702 0867	.654 261	97.620 469	.010 243 7533	12.30	.229 250	2.29	120
11	1.594 682	167.910 095	.005 955 5681	.627 084	105.293 807	.009 497 2347	11.40	.253 635	2.31	132
12	1.663 791	187.423 467	.005 335 5112	.601 037	112.648 414	.008 877 1778	10.66	.278 314	2.32	144
13	1.735 896	207.782 504	.004 812 7248	.576 071	119.697 528	.008 354 3914	10.03	.303 285	2.33	156
14	1.811 126	229.023 855	.004 366 3574	.552 143	126.453 839	.007 908 0241	9.49	.328 548	2.35	168
15	1.889 616	251.185 757	.003 981 1174	.529 208	132.929 509	.007 522 7841	9.03	.354 101	2.36	180
16	1.971 508	274.308 106	.003 645 5357	.507 226	139.136 196	.007 187 2024	8.63	.379 943	2.37	192
17	2.056 949	298.432 525	.003 350 8412	.486 157	145.085 072	.006 892 5079	8.28	.406 072	2.39	204
18	2.146 092	323.602 440	.003 090 2116	.465 963	150.786 846	.006 631 8782	7.96	.432 486	2.40	216
19	2.239 099	349.863 163	.002 858 2603	.446 608	156.251 782	.006 399 9270	7.68	.459 183	2.42	228
20	2.336 136	377.261 965	.002 650 6780	.428 057	161.489 718	.006 192 3447	7.44	.486 163	2.43	240
21	2.437 379	405.848 169	.002 463 9756	.410 277	166.510 083	.006 005 6423	7.21	.513 422	2.44	252
22	2.543 009	435.673 233	.002 295 2982	.393 235	171.321 914	.005 836 9649	7.01	.540 959	2.46	264
23	2.653 218	466.790 848	.002 142 2871	.376 901	175.933 874	.005 683 9537	6.83	.568 771	2.47	276
24	2.768 202	499.257 029	.002 002 9763	.361 245	180.354 263	.005 544 6430	6.66	.596 857	2.49	288
25	2.888 170	533.130 220	.001 875 7143	.346 240	184.591 041	.005 417 3810	6.51	.625 214	2.50	300
26	3.013 336	568.471 398	.001 759 1035	.331 858	188.651 833	.005 300 7701	6.37	.653 840	2.51	312
27	3.143 927	605.344 181	.001 651 9528	.318 074	192.543 950	.005 193 6194	6.24	.682 733	2.53	324
28	3.280 178	643.814 948	.001 553 2414	.304 862	196.274 397	.005 094 9080	6.12	.711 889	2.54	336
29	3.422 333	683.952 949	.001 462 0889	.292 198	199.849 891	.005 003 7555	6.01	.741 307	2.56	348
30	3.570 649	725.830 439	.001 377 7322	.280 061	203.276 867	.004 919 3989	5.91	.770 984	2.57	360
31	3.725 393	769.522 805	.001 299 5066	.268 428	206.561 496	.004 841 1733	5.81	.800 916	2.58	372
32	3.886 843	815.108 697	.001 226 8302	.257 278	209.709 688	.004 768 4969	5.73	.831 103	2.60	384
33	4.055 290	862.670 178	.001 159 1916	.246 591	212.727 113	.004 700 8582	5.65	.861 540	2.61	396
34	4.231 037	912.292 866	.001 096 1392	.236 349	215.619 201	.004 637 8059	5.57	.892 225	2.62	408
35	4.414 401	964.066 087	.001 037 2733	.226 531	218.391 158	.004 578 9400	5.50	.923 155	2.64	420
36	4.605 711	1018.083 041	.000 982 2381	.217 122	221.047 975	.004 523 9048	5.43	.954 327	2.65	432
37	4.805 312	1074.440 967	.000 930 7166	.208 103	223.594 435	.004 472 3832	5.37	.985 738	2.66	444
38	5.013 563	1133.241 316	.000 882 4246	.199 459	226.035 121	.004 424 0913	5.31	1.017 386	2.68	456
39	5.230 839	1194.589 938	.000 837 1073	.191 174	228.374 426	.004 378 7740	5.26	1.049 266	2.69	468
40	5.457 532	1258.597 270	.000 794 5353	.183 233	230.616 563	.004 336 2020	5.21	1.081 377	2.70	480
41	5.694 049	1325.378 533	.000 754 5014	.175 622	232.765 566	.004 296 1681	5.16	1.113 715	2.72	492
42	5.940 816	1395.053 943	.000 716 8182	.168 327	234.825 305	.004 258 4848	5.12	1.146 276	2.73	504
43	6.198 277	1467.748 927	.000 681 3154	.161 335	236.799 488	.004 222 9821	5.07	1.179 059	2.74	516
44	6.466 897	1543.594 345	.000 647 8386	.154 634	238.691 668	.004 189 5053	5.03	1.212 059	2.75	528
45	6.747 157	1622.726 731	.000 616 2467	.148 211	240.505 251	.004 157 9134	4.99	1.245 273	2.77	540
46	7.039 564	1705.288 533	.000 586 4110	.142 054	242.243 503	.004 128 0777	4.96	1.278 699	2.78	552
47	7.344 642	1791.428 376	.000 558 2138	.136 154	243.909 551	.004 099 8804	4.92	1.312 333	2.79	564
48	7.662 942	1881.301 322	.000 531 5470	.130 498	245.506 397	.004 073 2136	4.89	1.346 171	2.80	576
49	7.995 037	1975.069 157	.000 506 3114	.125 078	247.036 913	.004 047 9781	4.86	1.380 211	2.82	588
50	8.341 523	2072.900 675	.000 482 4158	.119 882	248.503 855	.004 024 0824	4.83	1.414 449	2.83	600

MONTHLY COMPOUND INTEREST AND ANNUITY

Amount Of 1	Amount Of 1 Per Period	Sinking Fund Payment	Present Worth Of 1	Present Worth of 1 Per Period	Periodic Payment To Amortize 1	Constant Annual Percent	Total Interest	Annual Add On Rate	
What a single $ 1 deposit grows to in the future. The deposit is made at the beginning of the first period.	What a series of $ 1 deposits grow to in the future. A deposit is made at the end of each period.	The amount to be deposited at the end of each period that grows to $ 1 in the future.	What $ 1 to be paid in the future is worth today. Value today of a single $ 1 payment tomorrow.	What $ 1 to be paid at the end of each period is worth today. Value today of a series of $ 1 payments tomorrow.	The mortgage payment to amortize a loan of $ 1. An annuity certain, payable at the end of each period, worth $ 1 today.	The annual payment, including interest and principal, to amortize completely a loan of $ 100.	The total interest paid over the term on a loan of $1. The loan is amortized by regular periodic payments.	The average annual interest rate on a loan that is completely amortized by regular periodic payments.	
$S = (1+i)^n$	$S\overline{n}] = \dfrac{(1+i)^n - 1}{i}$	$\dfrac{1}{S\overline{n}]} = \dfrac{i}{(1+i)^n - 1}$	$V^n = \dfrac{1}{(1+i)^n}$	$A\overline{n}] = \dfrac{1 - V^n}{i}$	$\dfrac{1}{A\overline{n}]} = \dfrac{i}{1 - V^n}$				

YEAR / **PERIODS**

YEAR	Amount Of 1	Amount Of 1 Per Period	Sinking Fund Payment	Present Worth Of 1	Present Worth of 1 Per Period	Periodic Payment To Amortize 1	Constant Annual Percent	Total Interest	Annual Add On Rate	PERIODS
	1.003 750	1.000 000	1.000 000 0000	.996 264	.996 264	1.003 750 0000	1204.50	.003 750	4.50	1
	1.007 514	2.003 750	.499 064 2545	.992 542	1.988 806	.502 814 2545	603.38	.005 629	3.38	2
	1.011 292	3.011 264	.332 086 4525	.988 834	2.977 640	.335 836 4525	403.01	.007 509	3.00	3
	1.015 085	4.022 556	.248 598 1363	.985 140	3.962 779	.252 348 1363	302.82	.009 393	2.82	4
	1.018 891	5.037 641	.198 505 6144	.981 459	4.944 239	.202 255 6144	242.71	.011 278	2.71	5
	1.022 712	6.056 532	.165 110 9898	.977 792	5.922 031	.168 860 9898	202.64	.013 166	2.63	6
	1.026 547	7.079 244	.141 258 0206	.974 139	6.896 170	.145 008 0206	174.01	.015 056	2.58	7
	1.030 397	8.105 791	.123 368 5861	.970 500	7.866 670	.127 118 5861	152.55	.016 949	2.54	8
	1.034 261	9.136 188	.109 454 8414	.966 874	8.833 544	.113 204 8414	135.85	.018 844	2.51	9
	1.038 139	10.170 449	.098 324 0796	.963 262	9.796 806	.102 074 0796	122.49	.020 741	2.49	10
	1.042 032	11.208 588	.089 217 3053	.959 663	10.756 470	.092 967 3053	111.57	.022 640	2.47	11
	1.045 940	12.250 620	.081 628 5216	.956 078	11.712 548	.085 378 5216	102.46	.024 542	2.45	12
1	1.045 940	12.250 620	.081 628 5216	.956 078	11.712 548	.085 378 5216	102.46	.024 542	2.45	12
2	1.093 990	25.064 031	.039 897 8116	.914 085	22.910 656	.043 647 8116	52.38	.047 547	2.38	24
3	1.144 248	38.466 089	.025 996 9245	.873 937	33.616 921	.029 746 9245	35.70	.070 889	2.36	36
4	1.196 814	52.483 834	.019 053 4861	.835 551	43.852 944	.022 803 4861	27.37	.094 567	2.36	48
5	1.251 796	67.145 552	.014 893 0192	.798 852	53.639 380	.018 643 0192	22.38	.118 581	2.37	60
6	1.309 303	82.480 827	.012 124 0297	.763 765	62.995 976	.015 874 0297	19.05	.142 930	2.38	72
7	1.369 452	98.520 602	.010 150 1613	.730 219	71.941 611	.013 900 1613	16.69	.167 614	2.39	84
8	1.432 365	115.297 241	.008 673 2344	.698 146	80.494 336	.012 423 2344	14.91	.192 631	2.41	96
9	1.498 167	132.844 596	.007 527 5926	.667 482	88.671 407	.011 277 5926	13.54	.217 980	2.42	108
10	1.566 993	151.198 074	.006 613 8409	.638 165	96.489 324	.010 363 8409	12.44	.243 661	2.44	120
11	1.638 980	170.394 707	.005 868 7269	.610 136	103.963 862	.009 618 7269	11.55	.269 672	2.45	132
12	1.714 275	190.473 230	.005 250 0816	.583 337	111.110 104	.009 000 0816	10.81	.296 012	2.47	144
13	1.793 028	211.474 157	.004 728 7102	.557 716	117.942 467	.008 478 7102	10.18	.322 679	2.48	156
14	1.875 399	233.439 862	.004 283 7585	.533 220	124.474 740	.008 033 7585	9.65	.349 671	2.50	168
15	1.961 555	256.414 669	.003 899 9329	.509 800	130.720 101	.007 649 9329	9.18	.376 988	2.51	180
16	2.051 669	280.444 934	.003 565 7624	.487 408	136.691 153	.007 315 7624	8.78	.404 626	2.53	192
17	2.145 922	305.579 145	.003 272 4746	.466 000	142.399 945	.007 022 4746	8.43	.432 585	2.54	204
18	2.244 505	331.868 018	.003 013 2461	.445 533	147.857 994	.006 763 2461	8.12	.460 861	2.56	216
19	2.347 617	359.364 596	.002 782 6893	.425 964	153.076 315	.006 532 6893	7.84	.489 453	2.58	228
20	2.455 466	388.124 363	.002 576 4938	.407 255	158.065 437	.006 326 4938	7.60	.518 359	2.59	240
21	2.568 270	418.205 348	.002 391 1698	.389 367	162.835 426	.006 141 1698	7.37	.547 575	2.61	252
22	2.686 256	449.668 249	.002 223 8617	.372 265	167.395 907	.005 973 8617	7.17	.577 099	2.62	264
23	2.809 662	482.576 549	.002 072 2101	.355 915	171.756 083	.005 822 2101	6.99	.606 930	2.64	276
24	2.938 737	516.996 652	.001 934 2485	.340 282	175.924 751	.005 684 2485	6.83	.637 064	2.65	288
25	3.073 743	552.998 007	.001 808 3248	.325 336	179.910 322	.005 558 3248	6.67	.667 497	2.67	300
26	3.214 950	590.653 259	.001 693 0407	.311 047	183.720 839	.005 443 0407	6.54	.698 229	2.69	312
27	3.362 644	630.038 387	.001 587 2049	.297 385	187.363 990	.005 337 2049	6.41	.729 254	2.70	324
28	3.517 123	671.232 860	.001 489 7960	.284 323	190.847 126	.005 239 7960	6.29	.760 571	2.72	336
29	3.678 699	714.319 800	.001 399 9332	.271 835	194.177 276	.005 149 9332	6.18	.792 177	2.73	348
30	3.847 698	759.386 147	.001 316 8531	.259 896	197.361 159	.005 066 8531	6.09	.824 067	2.75	360
31	4.024 461	806.522 833	.001 239 8905	.248 481	200.405 199	.004 989 8905	5.99	.856 239	2.76	372
32	4.209 344	855.824 971	.001 168 4632	.237 567	203.315 539	.004 918 4632	5.91	.888 690	2.78	384
33	4.402 720	907.392 041	.001 102 0595	.227 132	206.098 051	.004 852 0595	5.83	.921 416	2.79	396
34	4.604 980	961.328 092	.001 040 2276	.217 156	208.758 349	.004 790 2276	5.75	.954 413	2.81	408
35	4.816 532	1017.741 957	.000 982 5673	.207 618	211.301 801	.004 732 5673	5.68	.987 678	2.82	420
36	5.037 803	1076.747 464	.000 928 7229	.198 499	213.733 539	.004 678 7229	5.62	1.021 208	2.84	432
37	5.269 239	1138.463 674	.000 878 3767	.189 781	216.058 471	.004 628 3767	5.56	1.054 999	2.85	444
38	5.511 307	1203.015 116	.000 831 2448	.181 445	218.281 287	.004 581 2448	5.50	1.089 048	2.87	456
39	5.764 495	1270.532 040	.000 787 0718	.173 476	220.406 472	.004 537 0718	5.45	1.123 350	2.88	468
40	6.029 315	1341.150 680	.000 745 6284	.165 856	222.438 315	.004 495 6284	5.40	1.157 902	2.89	480
41	6.306 301	1415.013 527	.000 706 7070	.158 572	224.380 915	.004 456 7070	5.35	1.192 700	2.91	492
42	6.596 011	1492.269 621	.000 670 1202	.151 607	226.238 192	.004 420 1202	5.31	1.227 741	2.92	504
43	6.899 031	1573.074 847	.000 635 6977	.144 948	228.013 894	.004 385 6977	5.27	1.263 020	2.94	516
44	7.215 971	1657.592 250	.000 603 2847	.138 581	229.711 603	.004 353 2847	5.23	1.298 534	2.95	528
45	7.547 471	1745.992 368	.000 572 7402	.132 495	231.334 745	.004 322 7402	5.19	1.334 280	2.97	540
46	7.894 201	1838.453 572	.000 543 9354	.126 675	232.886 596	.004 293 9354	5.16	1.370 252	2.98	552
47	8.256 859	1935.162 427	.000 516 7525	.121 111	234.370 286	.004 266 7525	5.13	1.406 448	2.99	564
48	8.636 178	2036.314 071	.000 491 0834	.115 792	235.788 809	.004 241 0834	5.09	1.442 864	3.01	576
49	9.032 922	2142.112 603	.000 466 8289	.110 706	237.145 028	.004 216 8289	5.07	1.479 495	3.02	588
50	9.447 893	2252.771 501	.000 443 8977	.105 844	238.441 679	.004 193 8977	5.04	1.516 339	3.03	600

Effective Rate is 4.59 %

Annual Percentage Rate is 4.50 %

Amount Of 1	Amount Of 1 Per Period	Sinking Fund Payment	Present Worth Of 1	Present Worth of 1 Per Period	Periodic Payment To Amortize 1	Constant Annual Percent	Total Interest	Annual Add On Rate	
What a single $ 1 deposit grows to in the future. The deposit is made at the beginning of the first period.	What a series of $ 1 deposits grow to in the future. A deposit is made at the end of each period.	The amount to be deposited at the end of each period that grows to $ 1 in the future.	What $ 1 to be paid in the future is worth today. Value today of a single $ 1 payment tomorrow.	What $ 1 to be paid at the end of each period is worth today. Value today of a series of $ 1 payments tomorrow.	The mortgage payment to amortize a loan of $ 1. An annuity certain, payable at the end of each period, worth $ 1 today.	The annual payment, including interest and principal, to amortize completely a loan of $ 100.	The total interest paid over the term on a loan of $1. The loan is amortized by regular periodic payments.	The average annual interest rate on a loan that is completely amortized by regular periodic payments.	
$S = (1+i)^n$	$S\overline{n}| = \dfrac{(1+i)^n - 1}{i}$	$\dfrac{1}{S\overline{n}|} = \dfrac{i}{(1+i)^n - 1}$	$V^n = \dfrac{1}{(1+i)^n}$	$A\overline{n}| = \dfrac{1 - V^n}{i}$	$\dfrac{1}{A\overline{n}|} = \dfrac{i}{1 - V^n}$				**PERIODS**

YEAR

	Amount Of 1	Amount Of 1 Per Period	Sinking Fund Payment	Present Worth Of 1	Present Worth of 1 Per Period	Periodic Payment To Amortize 1	Constant Annual Percent	Total Interest	Annual Add On Rate	PERIODS
	1.003 958	1.000 000	1.000 000 0000	.996 057	.996 057	1.003 958 3333	1204.75	.003 958	4.75	1
	1.007 932	2.003 958	.499 012 3713	.992 130	1.988 187	.502 970 7047	603.57	.005 941	3.56	2
	1.011 922	3.011 891	.332 017 3639	.988 218	2.976 406	.335 975 6972	403.18	.007 927	3.17	3
	1.015 928	4.023 813	.248 520 5117	.984 322	3.960 728	.252 478 8450	302.98	.009 915	2.97	4
	1.019 949	5.039 740	.198 422 9216	.980 441	4.941 169	.202 381 2549	242.86	.011 906	2.86	5
	1.023 986	6.059 689	.165 024 9626	.976 576	5.917 745	.168 983 2959	202.78	.013 900	2.78	6
	1.028 040	7.083 676	.141 169 6499	.972 725	6.890 470	.145 127 9832	174.16	.015 896	2.73	7
	1.032 109	8.111 715	.123 278 4911	.968 890	7.859 360	.127 236 8244	152.69	.017 895	2.68	8
	1.036 194	9.143 824	.109 363 4349	.965 070	8.824 430	.113 321 7683	135.99	.019 896	2.65	9
	1.040 296	10.180 018	.098 231 6506	.961 265	9.785 695	.102 189 9839	122.63	.021 900	2.63	10
	1.044 414	11.220 314	.089 124 0639	.957 475	10.743 170	.093 082 3973	111.70	.023 906	2.61	11
	1.048 548	12.264 728	.081 534 6255	.953 700	11.696 870	.085 492 9589	102.60	.025 916	2.59	12
1	1.048 548	12.264 728	.081 534 6255	.953 700	11.696 870	.085 492 9589	102.60	.025 916	2.59	12
2	1.099 453	25.124 882	.039 801 1812	.909 543	22.852 173	.043 759 5146	52.52	.050 228	2.51	24
3	1.152 829	38.609 370	.025 900 4484	.867 432	33.490 985	.029 858 7817	35.84	.074 916	2.50	36
4	1.208 796	52.748 501	.018 957 8846	.827 269	43.637 218	.022 916 2179	27.50	.099 978	2.50	48
5	1.267 481	67.574 057	.014 798 5786	.788 967	53.313 680	.018 756 9120	22.51	.125 415	2.51	60
6	1.329 014	83.119 362	.012 030 8911	.752 437	62.542 120	.015 989 2245	19.19	.151 224	2.52	72
7	1.393 535	99.419 359	.010 058 4032	.717 600	71.343 283	.014 016 7365	16.83	.177 406	2.53	84
8	1.461 188	116.510 687	.008 582 9037	.684 375	79.736 951	.012 541 2370	15.05	.203 959	2.55	96
9	1.532 126	134.431 762	.007 438 7183	.652 688	87.741 991	.011 397 0516	13.68	.230 882	2.57	108
10	1.606 507	153.222 867	.006 526 4410	.622 468	95.376 397	.010 484 7743	12.59	.258 173	2.58	120
11	1.684 500	172.926 240	.005 782 8124	.593 648	102.657 329	.009 741 1457	11.69	.285 831	2.60	132
12	1.766 279	193.586 171	.005 165 6582	.566 162	109.601 153	.009 123 9916	10.95	.313 855	2.62	144
13	1.852 028	215.249 097	.004 645 7802	.539 949	116.223 478	.008 604 1136	10.33	.342 242	2.63	156
14	1.941 940	237.963 713	.004 202 3214	.514 949	122.539 188	.008 160 6547	9.80	.370 990	2.65	168
15	2.036 217	261.781 075	.003 819 9858	.491 107	128.562 480	.007 778 3192	9.34	.400 097	2.67	180
16	2.135 071	286.754 719	.003 487 3009	.468 369	134.306 892	.007 445 6343	8.94	.429 562	2.68	192
17	2.238 724	312.940 781	.003 195 4928	.446 683	139.785 338	.007 153 8261	8.59	.459 381	2.70	204
18	2.347 409	340.398 121	.002 937 7365	.426 002	145.010 132	.006 896 0699	8.28	.489 551	2.72	216
19	2.461 371	369.188 457	.002 708 6437	.406 278	149.993 016	.006 666 9771	8.01	.520 071	2.74	228
20	2.580 865	399.376 502	.002 503 9029	.387 467	154.745 193	.006 462 2363	7.76	.550 937	2.75	240
21	2.706 161	431.030 113	.002 320 0235	.369 527	159.277 343	.006 278 3569	7.54	.582 146	2.77	252
22	2.837 539	464.220 440	.002 154 1490	.352 418	163.599 655	.006 112 4823	7.34	.613 695	2.79	264
23	2.975 296	499.022 087	.002 003 9193	.336 101	167.721 842	.005 962 2527	7.16	.645 582	2.81	276
24	3.119 740	535.513 280	.001 867 3673	.320 540	171.653 173	.005 825 7007	7.00	.677 802	2.82	288
25	3.271 197	573.776 043	.001 742 8403	.305 699	175.402 482	.005 701 1736	6.85	.710 352	2.84	300
26	3.430 007	613.896 382	.001 628 9394	.291 545	178.978 197	.005 587 2727	6.71	.743 229	2.86	312
27	3.596 526	655.964 479	.001 524 4728	.278 046	182.388 357	.005 482 8061	6.58	.776 429	2.88	324
28	3.771 130	700.074 893	.001 428 4186	.265 173	185.640 626	.005 386 7519	6.47	.809 949	2.89	336
29	3.954 210	746.326 774	.001 339 8957	.252 895	188.742 314	.005 298 2290	6.36	.843 784	2.91	348
30	4.146 179	794.824 085	.001 258 1400	.241 186	191.700 394	.005 216 4734	6.26	.877 930	2.93	360
31	4.347 467	845.675 839	.001 182 4862	.230 019	194.521 515	.005 140 8195	6.17	.912 385	2.94	372
32	4.558 527	898.996 337	.001 112 3516	.219 369	197.212 017	.005 070 6849	6.09	.947 143	2.96	384
33	4.779 834	954.905 433	.001 047 2241	.209 212	199.777 949	.005 005 5575	6.01	.982 201	2.98	396
34	5.011 885	1013.528 796	.000 986 6518	.199 526	202.225 078	.004 944 9851	5.94	1.017 554	2.99	408
35	5.255 201	1074.998 200	.000 930 2341	.190 288	204.558 904	.004 888 5674	5.87	1.053 198	3.01	420
36	5.510 330	1139.451 813	.000 877 6150	.181 477	206.784 674	.004 835 9483	5.81	1.089 130	3.03	432
37	5.777 845	1207.034 513	.000 828 4767	.173 075	208.907 391	.004 786 8101	5.75	1.125 344	3.04	444
38	6.058 347	1277.898 209	.000 782 5349	.165 062	210.931 826	.004 740 8683	5.69	1.161 836	3.06	456
39	6.352 467	1352.202 188	.000 739 5344	.157 419	212.862 529	.004 697 8677	5.64	1.198 602	3.07	468
40	6.660 866	1430.113 467	.000 699 2452	.150 131	214.703 840	.004 657 5785	5.59	1.235 638	3.09	480
41	6.984 237	1511.807 174	.000 661 4600	.143 180	216.459 899	.004 619 7934	5.55	1.272 938	3.10	492
42	7.323 307	1597.466 938	.000 625 9910	.136 550	218.134 651	.004 584 3244	5.51	1.310 499	3.12	504
43	7.678 838	1687.285 301	.000 592 6680	.130 228	219.731 863	.004 551 0013	5.47	1.348 317	3.14	516
44	8.051 629	1781.464 156	.000 561 3360	.124 198	221.255 123	.004 519 6694	5.43	1.386 385	3.15	528
45	8.442 518	1880.215 194	.000 531 8540	.118 448	222.707 857	.004 490 1873	5.39	1.424 701	3.17	540
46	8.852 385	1983.760 387	.000 504 0931	.112 964	224.093 328	.004 462 4265	5.36	1.463 259	3.18	552
47	9.282 149	2092.332 479	.000 477 9355	.107 734	225.414 652	.004 436 2688	5.33	1.502 056	3.20	564
48	9.732 778	2206.175 516	.000 453 2731	.102 746	226.674 799	.004 411 6064	5.30	1.541 085	3.21	576
49	10.205 284	2325.545 391	.000 430 0067	.097 988	227.876 601	.004 388 3400	5.27	1.580 344	3.23	588
50	10.700 729	2450.710 421	.000 408 0449	.093 452	229.022 759	.004 366 3783	5.24	1.619 827	3.24	600

Effective Rate is 4.85 %　　　　8-15　　　　Annual Percentage Rate is 4.75 %

MONTHLY COMPOUND INTEREST AND ANNUITY

5.00 % M

	Amount Of 1	Amount Of 1 Per Period	Sinking Fund Payment	Present Worth Of 1	Present Worth of 1 Per Period	Periodic Payment To Amortize 1	Constant Annual Percent	Total Interest	Annual Add On Rate	
	What a single $1 deposit grows to in the future. The deposit is made at the beginning of the first period.	What a series of $1 deposits grow to in the future. A deposit is made at the end of each period.	The amount to be deposited at the end of each period that grows to $1 in the future.	What $1 to be paid in the future is worth today. Value today of a single $1 payment tomorrow.	What $1 to be paid at the end of each period is worth today. Value today of a series of $1 payments tomorrow.	The mortgage payment to amortize a loan of $1. An annuity certain, payable at the end of each period, worth $1 today.	The annual payment, including interest and principal, to amortize completely a loan of $100.	The total interest paid over the term on a loan of $1. The loan is amortized by regular periodic payments.	The average annual interest rate on a loan that is completely amortized by regular periodic payments.	
	$S = (1+i)^n$	$S\overline{n}| = \frac{(1+i)^n - 1}{i}$	$\frac{1}{S\overline{n}|} = \frac{i}{(1+i)^n - 1}$	$V^n = \frac{1}{(1+i)^n}$	$A\overline{n}| = \frac{1-V^n}{i}$	$\frac{1}{A\overline{n}|} = \frac{i}{1-V^n}$				

YEAR ... **PERIODS**

YEAR	Amount Of 1	Amount Of 1 Per Period	Sinking Fund Payment	Present Worth Of 1	Present Worth of 1 Per Period	Periodic Payment To Amortize 1	Constant Annual Percent	Total Interest	Annual Add On Rate	PERIODS
	1.004 167	1.000 000	1.000 000 0000	.995 851	.995 851	1.004 166 6667	1205.00	.004 167	5.00	1
	1.008 351	2.004 167	.498 960 4990	.991 718	1.987 569	.503 127 1656	603.76	.006 254	3.75	2
	1.012 552	3.012 517	.331 948 2944	.987 603	2.975 173	.336 114 9611	403.34	.008 345	3.34	3
	1.016 771	4.025 070	.248 442 9140	.983 506	3.958 678	.252 609 5807	303.14	.010 438	3.13	4
	1.021 008	5.041 841	.198 340 2633	.979 425	4.938 103	.202 506 9300	243.01	.012 535	3.01	5
	1.025 262	6.062 848	.164 938 9774	.975 361	5.913 463	.169 105 6440	202.93	.014 634	2.93	6
	1.029 534	7.088 110	.141 081 3285	.971 313	6.884 777	.145 247 9951	174.30	.016 736	2.87	7
	1.033 824	8.117 644	.123 188 4527	.967 283	7.852 060	.127 355 1193	152.83	.018 841	2.83	8
	1.038 131	9.151 467	.109 272 0923	.963 269	8.815 329	.113 438 7590	136.13	.020 949	2.79	9
	1.042 457	10.189 599	.098 139 2927	.959 272	9.774 602	.102 305 9594	122.77	.023 060	2.77	10
	1.046 800	11.232 055	.089 030 9010	.955 292	10.729 894	.093 197 5677	111.84	.025 173	2.75	11
	1.051 162	12.278 855	.081 440 8151	.951 328	11.681 222	.085 607 4818	102.73	.027 290	2.73	12
1	1.051 162	12.278 855	.081 440 8151	.951 328	11.681 222	.085 607 4818	102.73	.027 290	2.73	12
2	1.104 941	25.185 921	.039 704 7231	.905 025	22.793 898	.043 871 3897	52.65	.052 913	2.65	24
3	1.161 472	38.753 336	.025 804 2304	.860 976	33.365 701	.029 970 8971	35.97	.078 952	2.63	36
4	1.220 895	53.014 885	.018 862 6269	.819 071	43.422 956	.023 029 2936	27.64	.105 406	2.64	48
5	1.283 359	68.006 083	.014 704 5670	.779 205	52.990 706	.018 871 2336	22.65	.132 274	2.65	60
6	1.349 018	83.764 259	.011 938 2660	.741 280	62.092 777	.016 104 9327	19.33	.159 555	2.66	72
7	1.418 036	100.328 653	.009 967 2424	.705 201	70.751 835	.014 133 9091	16.97	.187 248	2.67	84
8	1.490 585	117.740 512	.008 493 2533	.670 877	78.989 441	.012 659 9200	15.20	.215 352	2.69	96
9	1.566 847	136.043 196	.007 350 6065	.638 225	86.826 108	.011 517 2732	13.83	.243 866	2.71	108
10	1.647 009	155.282 279	.006 439 8849	.607 161	94.281 350	.010 606 5515	12.73	.272 786	2.73	120
11	1.731 274	175.505 671	.005 697 8216	.577 609	101.373 733	.009 864 4882	11.84	.302 112	2.75	132
12	1.819 849	196.763 730	.005 082 2375	.549 496	108.120 917	.009 248 9041	11.10	.331 842	2.77	144
13	1.912 956	219.109 391	.004 563 9303	.522 751	114.539 704	.008 730 5970	10.48	.361 973	2.78	156
14	2.010 826	242.598 299	.004 122 0404	.497 308	120.646 077	.008 288 7071	9.95	.392 503	2.80	168
15	2.113 704	267.288 944	.003 741 2696	.473 103	126.455 243	.007 907 9363	9.49	.423 429	2.82	180
16	2.221 845	293.242 809	.003 410 1433	.450 076	131.981 666	.007 576 8100	9.10	.454 748	2.84	192
17	2.335 519	320.524 523	.003 119 8861	.428 170	137.239 108	.007 286 5528	8.75	.486 457	2.86	204
18	2.455 008	349.202 021	.002 863 6719	.407 331	142.240 661	.007 030 3385	8.44	.518 553	2.88	216
19	2.580 611	379.346 715	.002 636 1109	.387 505	146.998 780	.006 802 7775	8.17	.551 033	2.90	228
20	2.712 640	411.033 669	.002 432 8907	.368 645	151.525 313	.006 599 5574	7.92	.583 894	2.92	240
21	2.851 424	444.341 787	.002 250 5198	.350 702	155.831 532	.006 417 1865	7.71	.617 131	2.94	252
22	2.997 308	479.354 011	.002 086 1409	.333 633	159.928 159	.006 252 8075	7.51	.650 741	2.96	264
23	3.150 656	516.157 528	.001 937 3930	.317 394	163.825 396	.006 104 0597	7.33	.684 720	2.98	276
24	3.311 850	554.843 982	.001 802 3085	.301 946	167.532 948	.005 968 9751	7.17	.719 065	3.00	288
25	3.481 290	595.509 708	.001 679 2337	.287 250	171.060 047	.005 845 9004	7.02	.753 770	3.02	300
26	3.659 400	638.255 971	.001 566 7695	.273 269	174.415 476	.005 733 4362	6.89	.788 832	3.03	312
27	3.846 622	683.189 213	.001 463 7233	.259 968	177.607 590	.005 630 3900	6.76	.824 246	3.05	324
28	4.043 422	730.421 325	.001 369 0728	.247 315	180.644 338	.005 535 7395	6.65	.860 008	3.07	336
29	4.250 291	780.069 922	.001 281 9364	.235 278	183.533 283	.005 448 6030	6.54	.896 114	3.09	348
30	4.467 744	832.258 635	.001 201 5496	.223 827	186.281 617	.005 368 2162	6.45	.932 558	3.11	360
31	4.696 323	887.117 422	.001 127 2465	.212 933	188.896 185	.005 293 9132	6.36	.969 336	3.13	372
32	4.936 595	944.782 889	.001 058 4442	.202 569	191.383 498	.005 225 1109	6.28	1.006 443	3.15	384
33	5.189 161	1005.398 630	.000 994 6304	.192 709	193.749 748	.005 161 2970	6.20	1.043 874	3.16	396
34	5.454 648	1069.115 587	.000 935 3526	.183 330	196.000 829	.005 102 0192	6.13	1.081 624	3.18	408
35	5.733 718	1136.092 425	.000 880 2101	.174 407	198.142 346	.005 046 8767	6.06	1.119 688	3.20	420
36	6.027 066	1206.495 925	.000 828 8466	.165 918	200.179 632	.004 995 5132	6.00	1.158 062	3.22	432
37	6.335 423	1280.501 402	.000 780 9441	.157 843	202.117 759	.004 947 6108	5.94	1.196 739	3.23	444
38	6.659 555	1358.293 140	.000 736 2181	.150 160	203.961 555	.004 902 8848	5.89	1.235 715	3.25	456
39	7.000 270	1440.064 850	.000 694 4132	.142 852	205.715 609	.004 861 0798	5.84	1.274 985	3.27	468
40	7.358 417	1526.020 156	.000 655 2993	.135 899	207.384 291	.004 821 9660	5.79	1.314 544	3.29	480
41	7.734 888	1616.373 099	.000 618 6690	.129 284	208.971 755	.004 785 3357	5.75	1.354 385	3.30	492
42	8.130 619	1711.348 670	.000 584 3345	.122 992	210.481 954	.004 751 0011	5.71	1.394 505	3.32	504
43	8.546 597	1811.183 372	.000 552 1252	.117 006	211.918 649	.004 718 7919	5.67	1.434 897	3.34	516
44	8.983 858	1916.125 806	.000 521 8864	.111 311	213.285 418	.004 688 5531	5.63	1.475 556	3.35	528
45	9.443 489	2026.437 294	.000 493 4769	.105 893	214.585 664	.004 660 1436	5.60	1.516 478	3.37	540
46	9.926 636	2142.392 528	.000 466 7679	.100 739	215.822 624	.004 633 4345	5.57	1.557 656	3.39	552
47	10.434 501	2264.280 251	.000 441 6414	.095 836	216.999 379	.004 608 3081	5.53	1.599 086	3.40	564
48	10.968 350	2392.403 981	.000 417 9896	.091 171	218.118 860	.004 584 6563	5.51	1.640 762	3.42	576
49	11.529 512	2527.082 765	.000 395 7132	.086 734	219.183 854	.004 562 3799	5.48	1.682 679	3.43	588
50	12.119 383	2668.651 971	.000 374 7210	.082 512	220.197 012	.004 541 3877	5.45	1.724 833	3.45	600

Effective Rate is 5.12 %

8 - 16

Annual Percentage Rate is 5.00 %

	Amount Of 1	Amount Of 1 Per Period	Sinking Fund Payment	Present Worth Of 1	Present Worth of 1 Per Period	Periodic Payment To Amortize 1	Constant Annual Percent	Total Interest	Annual Add On Rate	
	What a single $ 1 deposit grows to in the future. The deposit is made at the beginning of the first period.	What a series of $ 1 deposits grow to in the future. A deposit is made at the end of each period.	The amount to be deposited at the end of each period that grows to $ 1 in the future.	What $ 1 to be paid in the future is worth today. Value today of a single $ 1 payment tomorrow.	What $ 1 to be paid at the end of each period is worth today. Value today of a series of $ 1 payments tomorrow.	The mortgage payment to amortize a loan of $ 1. An annuity certain, payable at the end of each period, worth $ 1 today.	The annual payment, including interest and principal, to amortize completely a loan of $ 100.	The total interest paid over the term on a loan of $1. The loan is amortized by regular periodic payments.	The average annual interest rate on a loan that is completely amortized by regular periodic payments.	
	$S = (1+i)^n$	$S\overline{n} = \dfrac{(1+i)^n - 1}{i}$	$\dfrac{1}{S\overline{n}} = \dfrac{i}{(1+i)^n - 1}$	$V^n = \dfrac{1}{(1+i)^n}$	$A\overline{n} = \dfrac{1 - V^n}{i}$	$\dfrac{1}{A\overline{n}} = \dfrac{i}{1 - V^n}$				
YEAR										**PERIODS**
	1.004 208	1.000 000	1.000 000 0000	.995 809	.995 809	1.004 208 3333	1205.05	.004 208	5.05	1
	1.008 434	2.004 208	.498 950 1258	.991 636	1.987 445	.503 158 4591	603.80	.006 317	3.79	2
	1.012 678	3.012 643	.331 934 4829	.987 481	2.974 926	.336 142 8162	403.38	.008 428	3.37	3
	1.016 940	4.025 321	.248 427 3978	.983 342	3.958 268	.252 635 7311	303.17	.010 543	3.16	4
	1.021 220	5.042 261	.198 323 7358	.979 221	4.937 490	.202 532 0691	243.04	.012 660	3.04	5
	1.025 517	6.063 480	.164 921 7853	.975 118	5.912 607	.169 130 1187	202.96	.014 781	2.96	6
	1.029 833	7.088 997	.141 063 6701	.971 031	6.883 639	.145 272 0034	174.33	.016 904	2.90	7
	1.034 167	8.118 830	.123 170 4518	.966 962	7.850 601	.127 378 7851	152.86	.019 030	2.85	8
	1.038 519	9.152 997	.109 253 8315	.962 910	8.813 511	.113 462 1648	136.16	.021 159	2.82	9
	1.042 889	10.191 516	.098 120 8297	.958 875	9.772 385	.102 329 1631	122.80	.023 292	2.79	10
	1.047 278	11.234 405	.089 012 2778	.954 856	10.727 241	.093 220 6112	111.87	.025 427	2.77	11
	1.051 685	12.281 683	.081 422 0633	.950 855	11.678 096	.085 630 3967	102.76	.027 565	2.76	12
1	1.051 685	12.281 683	.081 422 0633	.950 855	11.678 096	.085 630 3967	102.76	.027 565	2.76	12
2	1.106 042	25.198 151	.039 685 4521	.904 125	22.782 268	.043 893 7854	52.68	.053 451	2.67	24
3	1.163 208	38.782 211	.025 785 0178	.859 691	33.340 723	.029 993 3511	36.00	.079 761	2.66	36
4	1.223 329	53.068 369	.018 843 6166	.817 441	43.380 278	.023 051 9499	27.67	.106 494	2.66	48
5	1.286 558	68.092 913	.014 685 8161	.777 268	52.926 437	.018 894 1494	22.68	.133 649	2.67	60
6	1.353 054	83.894 007	.011 919 8025	.739 069	62.003 446	.016 128 1359	19.36	.161 226	2.69	72
7	1.422 987	100.511 787	.009 949 0819	.702 747	70.634 363	.014 157 4152	16.99	.189 223	2.70	84
8	1.496 535	117.988 464	.008 475 4048	.668 210	78.841 110	.012 683 7382	15.23	.217 639	2.72	96
9	1.573 884	136.368 431	.007 333 0755	.635 371	86.644 535	.011 541 4088	13.85	.246 472	2.74	108
10	1.655 231	155.698 373	.006 422 6747	.604 145	94.064 457	.010 631 0080	12.76	.275 721	2.76	120
11	1.740 782	176.027 392	.005 680 9340	.574 454	101.119 726	.009 889 2673	11.87	.305 383	2.78	132
12	1.830 755	197.407 125	.005 065 6733	.546 223	107.828 260	.009 274 0066	11.13	.335 457	2.80	144
13	1.925 378	219.891 878	.004 547 6896	.519 378	114.207 102	.008 756 0229	10.51	.365 940	2.81	156
14	2.024 892	243.538 765	.004 106 1225	.493 853	120.272 453	.008 314 4558	9.98	.396 829	2.83	168
15	2.129 550	268.407 851	.003 725 6734	.469 583	126.039 721	.007 934 0068	9.53	.428 121	2.85	180
16	2.239 616	294.562 306	.003 394 8675	.446 505	131.523 555	.007 603 2008	9.13	.459 815	2.87	192
17	2.355 372	322.068 565	.003 104 9289	.424 561	136.737 883	.007 313 2622	8.78	.491 905	2.89	204
18	2.477 110	350.996 497	.002 849 0313	.403 696	141.695 952	.007 057 3646	8.47	.524 391	2.91	216
19	2.605 141	381.419 580	.002 621 7846	.383 856	146.410 355	.006 830 1180	8.20	.557 267	2.93	228
20	2.739 789	413.415 094	.002 418 8764	.364 992	150.893 067	.006 627 2097	7.96	.590 530	2.95	240
21	2.881 396	447.064 309	.002 236 8147	.347 054	155.155 475	.006 445 1480	7.74	.624 177	2.97	252
22	3.030 322	482.452 698	.002 072 7421	.329 998	159.208 406	.006 281 0754	7.54	.658 204	2.99	264
23	3.186 945	519.670 150	.001 924 2976	.313 780	163.062 154	.006 132 6309	7.36	.692 606	3.01	276
24	3.351 664	558.811 202	.001 789 5132	.298 359	166.726 508	.005 997 8465	7.20	.727 380	3.03	288
25	3.524 896	599.975 276	.001 666 7353	.283 696	170.210 776	.005 875 0687	7.06	.762 521	3.05	300
26	3.707 082	643.266 932	.001 554 5646	.269 754	173.523 809	.005 762 8979	6.92	.798 024	3.07	312
27	3.898 684	688.796 135	.001 451 8084	.256 497	176.674 022	.005 660 1417	6.80	.833 886	3.09	324
28	4.100 189	736.678 535	.001 357 4442	.243 891	179.669 416	.005 565 7775	6.68	.870 101	3.11	336
29	4.312 109	787.035 755	.001 270 5903	.231 905	182.517 601	.005 478 9236	6.58	.906 665	3.13	348
30	4.534 982	839.995 710	.001 190 4823	.220 508	185.225 811	.005 398 8156	6.48	.943 574	3.15	360
31	4.769 374	895.692 923	.001 116 4541	.209 671	187.800 925	.005 324 7874	6.39	.980 821	3.16	372
32	5.015 881	954.268 869	.001 047 9227	.199 367	190.249 485	.005 256 2560	6.31	1.018 402	3.18	384
33	5.275 129	1015.872 337	.000 984 3715	.189 569	192.577 709	.005 192 7090	6.24	1.056 313	3.20	396
34	5.547 777	1080.659 806	.000 925 3606	.180 252	194.791 512	.005 133 6939	6.17	1.094 547	3.22	408
35	5.834 516	1148.795 843	.000 870 4767	.171 394	196.896 516	.005 078 8100	6.10	1.133 100	3.24	420
36	6.136 075	1220.453 519	.000 819 3675	.162 971	198.898 070	.005 027 7009	6.04	1.171 967	3.26	432
37	6.453 221	1295.814 852	.000 771 7152	.154 961	200.801 256	.004 980 0485	5.98	1.211 142	3.27	444
38	6.786 758	1375.071 267	.000 727 2350	.147 346	202.610 910	.004 935 5684	5.93	1.250 619	3.29	456
39	7.137 535	1458.424 082	.000 685 6716	.140 104	204.331 628	.004 894 0050	5.88	1.290 394	3.31	468
40	7.506 441	1546.085 023	.000 646 7950	.133 219	205.967 781	.004 855 1283	5.83	1.330 462	3.33	480
41	7.894 415	1638.276 757	.000 610 3975	.126 672	207.523 524	.004 818 7308	5.79	1.370 816	3.34	492
42	8.302 441	1735.233 458	.000 576 2913	.120 447	209.002 810	.004 784 6247	5.75	1.411 451	3.36	504
43	8.731 556	1837.201 407	.000 544 3061	.114 527	210.409 396	.004 752 6395	5.71	1.452 362	3.38	516
44	9.182 850	1944.439 612	.000 514 2870	.108 899	211.746 855	.004 722 6203	5.67	1.493 544	3.39	528
45	9.657 469	2057.220 468	.000 486 0928	.103 547	213.018 584	.004 694 4261	5.64	1.534 990	3.41	540
46	10.156 620	2175.830 451	.000 459 5946	.098 458	214.227 813	.004 667 9280	5.61	1.576 696	3.43	552
47	10.681 569	2300.570 839	.000 434 6747	.093 619	215.377 614	.004 643 0081	5.58	1.618 657	3.44	564
48	11.233 650	2431.758 487	.000 411 2260	.089 018	216.470 909	.004 619 5584	5.55	1.660 866	3.46	576
49	11.814 266	2569.726 623	.000 389 1465	.084 643	217.510 472	.004 597 4798	5.52	1.703 318	3.48	588
50	12.424 891	2714.825 699	.000 368 3478	.080 484	218.498 946	.004 576 6811	5.50	1.746 009	3.49	600

Amount Of 1	Amount Of 1 Per Period	Sinking Fund Payment	Present Worth Of 1	Present Worth of 1 Per Period	Periodic Payment To Amortize 1	Constant Annual Percent	Total Interest	Annual Add On Rate
What a single $ 1 deposit grows to in the future. The deposit is made at the beginning of the first period.	What a series of $ 1 deposits grow to in the future. A deposit is made at the end of each period.	The amount to be deposited at the end of each period that grows to $ 1 in the future.	What $ 1 to be paid in the future is worth today. Value today of a single $ 1 payment tomorrow.	What $ 1 to be paid at the end of each period is worth today. Value today of a series of $ 1 payments tomorrow.	The mortgage payment to amortize a loan of $ 1. An annuity certain, payable at the end of each period, worth $ 1 today.	The annual payment, including interest and principal, to amortize completely a loan of $ 100.	The total interest paid over the term on a loan of $1. The loan is amortized by regular periodic payments.	The average annual interest rate on a loan that is completely amortized by regular periodic payments.
$S = (1+i)^n$	$S\overline{n}| = \dfrac{(1+i)^n - 1}{i}$	$\dfrac{1}{S\overline{n}|} = \dfrac{i}{(1+i)^n - 1}$	$V^n = \dfrac{1}{(1+i)^n}$	$A\overline{n}| = \dfrac{1 - V^n}{i}$	$\dfrac{1}{A\overline{n}|} = \dfrac{i}{1 - V^n}$			

YEAR / **PERIODS**

YEAR	Amount Of 1	Amount Of 1 Per Period	Sinking Fund Payment	Present Worth Of 1	Present Worth of 1 Per Period	Periodic Payment To Amortize 1	Constant Annual Percent	Total Interest	Annual Add On Rate	PERIODS
	1.004 250	1.000 000	1.000 000 0000	.995 768	.995 768	1.004 250 0000	1205.10	.004 250	5.10	1
	1.008 518	2.004 250	.498 939 7530	.991 554	1.987 322	.503 189 7530	603.83	.006 380	3.83	2
	1.012 804	3.012 768	.331 920 6720	.987 358	2.974 679	.336 170 6720	403.41	.008 512	3.40	3
	1.017 109	4.025 572	.248 411 8825	.983 179	3.957 859	.252 661 8825	303.20	.010 648	3.19	4
	1.021 431	5.042 681	.198 307 2096	.979 018	4.936 877	.202 557 2096	243.07	.012 786	3.07	5
	1.025 772	6.064 112	.164 904 5950	.974 875	5.911 752	.169 154 5950	202.99	.014 928	2.99	6
	1.030 132	7.089 885	.141 046 0137	.970 749	6.882 501	.145 296 0137	174.36	.017 072	2.93	7
	1.034 510	8.120 017	.123 152 4532	.966 641	7.849 142	.127 402 4532	152.89	.019 220	2.88	8
	1.038 907	9.154 527	.109 235 5732	.962 550	8.811 693	.113 485 5732	136.19	.021 370	2.85	9
	1.043 322	10.193 434	.098 102 3695	.958 477	9.770 170	.102 352 3695	122.83	.023 524	2.82	10
	1.047 756	11.236 756	.088 993 6578	.954 420	10.724 590	.093 243 6578	111.90	.025 680	2.80	11
	1.052 209	12.284 512	.081 403 3149	.950 381	11.674 971	.085 653 3149	102.79	.027 840	2.78	12
1	1.052 209	12.284 512	.081 403 3149	.950 381	11.674 971	.085 653 3149	102.79	.027 840	2.78	12
2	1.107 144	25.210 388	.039 666 1880	.903 225	22.770 647	.043 916 1880	52.70	.053 989	2.70	24
3	1.164 947	38.811 114	.025 765 8155	.858 408	33.315 770	.030 015 8155	36.02	.080 569	2.69	36
4	1.225 768	53.121 922	.018 824 6200	.815 815	43.337 658	.023 074 6200	27.69	.107 582	2.69	48
5	1.289 765	68.179 886	.014 667 0823	.775 335	52.862 275	.018 917 0823	22.71	.135 025	2.70	60
6	1.357 102	84.024 014	.011 901 3596	.736 864	61.914 292	.016 151 3596	19.39	.162 898	2.71	72
7	1.427 955	100.695 350	.009 930 9452	.700 302	70.517 162	.014 180 9452	17.02	.191 199	2.73	84
8	1.502 508	118.237 083	.008 457 5835	.665 554	78.693 168	.012 707 5835	15.25	.219 928	2.75	96
9	1.580 952	136.694 656	.007 315 5749	.632 530	86.463 492	.011 565 5749	13.88	.249 082	2.77	108
10	1.663 493	156.115 884	.006 405 4981	.601 145	93.848 264	.010 655 4981	12.79	.278 660	2.79	120
11	1.750 342	176.551 077	.005 664 0833	.571 317	100.866 613	.009 914 0833	11.90	.308 659	2.81	132
12	1.841 726	198.053 175	.005 049 1490	.542 969	107.536 721	.009 299 1490	11.16	.339 077	2.83	144
13	1.937 881	220.677 881	.004 531 4918	.516 028	113.875 868	.008 781 4918	10.54	.369 913	2.85	156
14	2.039 056	244.483 803	.004 090 2505	.490 423	119.900 475	.008 340 2505	10.01	.401 162	2.87	168
15	2.145 514	269.532 613	.003 710 1262	.466 089	125.626 149	.007 960 1262	9.56	.432 823	2.89	180
16	2.257 529	295.889 200	.003 379 6435	.442 962	131.067 724	.007 629 6435	9.16	.464 892	2.91	192
17	2.375 393	323.621 844	.003 090 0263	.420 983	136.239 294	.007 340 0263	8.81	.497 365	2.93	204
18	2.499 410	352.802 386	.002 834 4480	.400 094	141.154 259	.007 084 4480	8.51	.530 241	2.95	216
19	2.629 902	383.506 419	.002 607 5183	.380 242	145.825 349	.006 857 5183	8.23	.563 514	2.97	228
20	2.767 207	415.813 486	.002 404 9244	.361 375	150.264 667	.006 654 9244	7.99	.597 182	2.99	240
21	2.911 681	449.807 277	.002 223 1743	.343 444	154.483 712	.006 473 1743	7.77	.631 240	3.01	252
22	3.063 697	485.575 856	.002 059 4105	.326 403	158.493 413	.006 309 4105	7.58	.665 684	3.03	264
23	3.223 651	523.211 884	.001 911 2716	.310 207	162.304 159	.006 161 2716	7.40	.700 511	3.05	276
24	3.391 955	562.812 857	.001 776 7895	.294 815	165.925 820	.006 026 7895	7.24	.735 715	3.07	288
25	3.569 046	604.481 365	.001 654 3107	.280 187	169.367 780	.005 904 3107	7.09	.771 293	3.09	300
26	3.755 383	648.325 351	.001 542 4354	.266 284	172.638 955	.005 792 4354	6.96	.807 240	3.10	312
27	3.951 448	694.458 395	.001 439 9711	.253 072	175.747 818	.005 689 9711	6.83	.843 551	3.12	324
28	4.157 750	743.000 008	.001 345 8950	.240 515	178.702 424	.005 595 8950	6.72	.880 221	3.14	336
29	4.374 823	794.075 938	.001 259 3254	.228 581	181.510 426	.005 509 3254	6.62	.917 245	3.16	348
30	4.603 229	847.818 500	.001 179 4977	.217 239	184.179 099	.005 429 4977	6.52	.954 619	3.18	360
31	4.843 559	904.366 918	.001 105 7459	.206 460	186.715 356	.005 355 7459	6.43	.992 337	3.20	372
32	5.096 438	963.867 681	.001 037 4868	.196 215	189.125 768	.005 287 4868	6.35	1.030 395	3.22	384
33	5.362 518	1026.474 931	.000 974 2079	.186 480	191.416 578	.005 224 2079	6.27	1.068 786	3.24	396
34	5.642 491	1092.350 853	.000 915 4568	.177 227	193.593 721	.005 165 4568	6.20	1.107 506	3.26	408
35	5.937 081	1161.666 103	.000 860 8326	.168 433	195.662 838	.005 110 8326	6.14	1.146 550	3.28	420
36	6.247 051	1234.600 245	.000 809 9788	.160 076	197.629 287	.005 059 9788	6.08	1.185 911	3.29	432
37	6.573 204	1311.342 219	.000 762 5774	.152 133	199.498 165	.005 012 5774	6.02	1.225 584	3.31	444
38	6.916 386	1392.090 827	.000 718 3439	.144 584	201.274 311	.004 968 3439	5.97	1.265 565	3.33	456
39	7.277 485	1477.055 255	.000 677 0227	.137 410	202.962 327	.004 927 0227	5.92	1.305 847	3.35	468
40	7.657 436	1566.455 604	.000 638 3839	.130 592	204.566 586	.004 888 3839	5.87	1.346 424	3.37	480
41	8.057 225	1660.523 473	.000 602 2197	.124 112	206.091 244	.004 852 2197	5.83	1.387 292	3.38	492
42	8.477 886	1759.502 547	.000 568 3425	.117 954	207.540 250	.004 818 3425	5.79	1.428 445	3.40	504
43	8.920 509	1863.649 237	.000 536 5817	.112 101	208.917 359	.004 786 5817	5.75	1.469 876	3.42	516
44	9.386 242	1973.233 340	.000 506 7824	.106 539	210.226 138	.004 756 7824	5.71	1.511 581	3.44	528
45	9.876 290	2088.538 739	.000 478 8037	.101 253	211.469 977	.004 728 8037	5.68	1.553 554	3.45	540
46	10.391 923	2209.864 138	.000 452 5165	.096 229	212.652 098	.004 702 5165	5.65	1.595 789	3.47	552
47	10.934 476	2337.523 836	.000 427 8031	.091 454	213.775 564	.004 677 8031	5.62	1.638 281	3.49	564
48	11.505 356	2471.848 541	.000 404 5555	.086 916	214.843 285	.004 654 5555	5.59	1.681 024	3.50	576
49	12.106 041	2613.186 229	.000 382 6746	.082 603	215.858 027	.004 632 6746	5.56	1.724 013	3.52	588
50	12.738 088	2761.903 041	.000 362 0692	.078 505	216.822 419	.004 612 0692	5.54	1.767 242	3.53	600

Effective Rate is 5.22 %

Annual Percentage Rate is 5.10 %

MONTHLY COMPOUND INTEREST AND ANNUITY

5.125% M

	Amount Of 1	Amount Of 1 Per Period	Sinking Fund Payment	Present Worth Of 1	Present Worth of 1 Per Period	Periodic Payment To Amortize 1	Constant Annual Percent	Total Interest	Annual Add On Rate
	What a single $ 1 deposit grows to in the future. The deposit is made at the beginning of the first period.	What a series of $ 1 deposits grow to in the future. A deposit is made at the end of each period.	The amount to be deposited at the end of each period that grows to $ 1 in the future.	What $ 1 to be paid in the future is worth today. Value today of a single $ 1 payment tomorrow.	What $ 1 to be paid at the end of each period is worth today. Value today of a series of $ 1 payments tomorrow.	The mortgage payment to amortize a loan of $ 1. An annuity certain, payable at the end of each period, worth $ 1 today.	The annual payment, including interest and principal, to amortize completely a loan of $ 100.	The total interest paid over the term on a loan of $1. The loan is amortized completely by regular periodic payments.	The average annual interest rate on a loan that is completely amortized by regular periodic payments.
	$S = (1+i)^n$	$S_{\overline{n}} = \dfrac{(1+i)^n - 1}{i}$	$\dfrac{1}{S_{\overline{n}}} = \dfrac{i}{(1+i)^n - 1}$	$V^n = \dfrac{1}{(1+i)^n}$	$A_{\overline{n}} = \dfrac{1 - V^n}{i}$	$\dfrac{1}{A_{\overline{n}}} = \dfrac{i}{1 - V^n}$			

PERIODS

YEAR	Amount Of 1	Amount Of 1 Per Period	Sinking Fund Payment	Present Worth Of 1	Present Worth of 1 Per Period	Periodic Payment To Amortize 1	Constant Annual Percent	Total Interest	Annual Add On Rate	PERIODS
	1.004 271	1.000 000	1.000 000 0000	.995 747	.995 747	1.004 270 8333	1205.13	.004 271	5.13	1
	1.008 560	2.004 271	.498 934 5668	.991 513	1.987 260	.503 205 4001	603.85	.006 411	3.85	2
	1.012 867	3.012 831	.331 913 7669	.987 296	2.974 556	.336 184 6002	403.43	.008 554	3.42	3
	1.017 193	4.025 698	.248 404 1253	.983 098	3.957 654	.252 674 9587	303.21	.010 700	3.21	4
	1.021 537	5.042 891	.198 298 9471	.978 917	4.936 570	.202 569 7804	243.09	.012 849	3.08	5
	1.025 900	6.064 428	.164 896 0005	.974 754	5.911 324	.169 166 8338	203.01	.015 001	3.00	6
	1.030 282	7.090 329	.141 037 1862	.970 608	6.881 933	.145 308 0196	174.37	.017 156	2.94	7
	1.034 682	8.120 610	.123 143 4547	.966 481	7.848 413	.127 414 2880	152.90	.019 314	2.90	8
	1.039 101	9.155 292	.109 226 4450	.962 371	8.810 784	.113 497 2783	136.20	.021 476	2.86	9
	1.043 539	10.194 393	.098 093 1405	.958 278	9.769 062	.102 363 9738	122.84	.023 640	2.84	10
	1.047 995	11.237 931	.088 984 3489	.954 203	10.723 265	.093 255 1823	111.91	.025 807	2.82	11
	1.052 471	12.285 927	.081 393 9420	.950 145	11.673 409	.085 664 7754	102.80	.027 977	2.80	12
1	1.052 471	12.285 927	.081 393 9420	.950 145	11.673 409	.085 664 7754	102.80	.027 977	2.80	12
2	1.107 696	25.216 510	.039 656 5585	.902 775	22.764 839	.043 927 3918	52.72	.054 257	2.71	24
3	1.165 818	38.825 576	.025 756 2182	.857 767	33.303 303	.030 027 0516	36.04	.080 974	2.70	36
4	1.226 989	53.148 725	.018 815 1269	.815 003	43.316 370	.023 085 9602	27.71	.108 126	2.70	48
5	1.291 371	68.223 426	.014 657 7219	.774 371	52.830 234	.018 928 5552	22.72	.135 713	2.71	60
6	1.359 131	84.089 114	.011 892 1458	.735 764	61.869 782	.016 162 9791	19.40	.163 734	2.73	72
7	1.430 446	100.787 292	.009 921 8857	.699 083	70.458 662	.014 192 7191	17.04	.192 188	2.75	84
8	1.505 503	118.361 644	.008 448 6829	.664 230	78.619 342	.012 719 5163	15.27	.221 074	2.76	96
9	1.584 498	136.858 141	.007 306 8360	.631 115	86.373 169	.011 577 6694	13.90	.250 388	2.78	108
10	1.667 639	156.325 171	.006 396 9225	.599 650	93.740 429	.010 667 7558	12.81	.280 131	2.80	120
11	1.755 142	176.813 659	.005 655 6717	.569 755	100.740 391	.009 926 5050	11.92	.310 299	2.82	132
12	1.847 236	198.377 200	.005 040 9019	.541 349	107.391 370	.009 311 7352	11.18	.340 890	2.84	144
13	1.944 163	221.072 206	.004 523 4090	.514 360	113.710 763	.008 794 2423	10.56	.371 902	2.86	156
14	2.046 175	244.958 044	.004 082 3317	.488 717	119.715 101	.008 353 1651	10.03	.403 332	2.88	168
15	2.153 540	270.097 200	.003 702 3709	.464 352	125.420 092	.007 973 2042	9.57	.435 177	2.90	180
16	2.266 539	296.555 436	.003 372 0508	.441 201	130.840 659	.007 642 8842	9.18	.467 434	2.92	192
17	2.385 467	324.401 966	.003 082 5954	.419 205	135.990 983	.007 353 4287	8.83	.500 099	2.94	204
18	2.510 635	353.709 635	.002 827 1777	.398 306	140.884 537	.007 098 0111	8.52	.533 170	2.96	216
19	2.642 371	384.555 111	.002 600 4075	.378 448	145.534 121	.006 871 2408	8.25	.566 643	2.98	228
20	2.781 019	417.019 085	.002 397 9718	.359 580	149.951 900	.006 668 8051	8.01	.600 513	3.00	240
21	2.926 942	451.186 480	.002 216 3785	.341 653	154.149 430	.006 487 2118	7.79	.634 777	3.02	252
22	3.080 522	487.146 678	.002 052 7698	.324 620	158.137 691	.006 323 6032	7.59	.669 431	3.04	264
23	3.242 161	524.993 744	.001 904 7846	.308 436	161.927 116	.006 175 6179	7.42	.704 471	3.06	276
24	3.412 281	564.826 698	.001 770 4546	.293 059	165.527 619	.006 041 2879	7.25	.739 891	3.08	288
25	3.591 327	606.749 729	.001 648 1260	.278 449	168.948 618	.005 918 9593	7.11	.775 688	3.10	300
26	3.779 768	650.872 508	.001 536 3992	.264 567	172.199 063	.005 807 2325	6.97	.811 857	3.12	312
27	3.978 097	697.310 461	.001 434 0815	.251 376	175.287 456	.005 704 9148	6.85	.848 392	3.14	324
28	4.186 832	746.185 065	.001 340 1501	.238 844	178.221 877	.005 610 9834	6.74	.885 290	3.16	336
29	4.406 520	797.624 177	.001 253 7233	.226 936	181.010 001	.005 524 5566	6.63	.922 546	3.18	348
30	4.637 735	851.762 357	.001 174 0364	.215 622	183.659 123	.005 444 8697	6.54	.960 153	3.20	360
31	4.881 082	908.741 230	.001 100 4233	.204 873	186.176 173	.005 371 2566	6.45	.998 107	3.22	372
32	5.137 198	968.709 849	.001 032 3008	.194 659	188.567 735	.005 303 1342	6.37	1.036 404	3.24	384
33	5.406 753	1031.825 091	.000 969 1565	.184 954	190.840 065	.005 239 9898	6.29	1.075 036	3.26	396
34	5.690 452	1098.252 062	.000 910 5378	.175 733	192.999 107	.005 181 3711	6.22	1.113 999	3.28	408
35	5.989 036	1168.164 531	.000 856 0438	.166 972	195.050 510	.005 126 8771	6.16	1.153 288	3.30	420
36	6.303 288	1241.745 389	.000 805 3181	.158 647	196.999 640	.005 076 1514	6.10	1.192 897	3.31	432
37	6.634 028	1319.187 117	.000 758 0426	.150 738	198.851 596	.005 028 8759	6.04	1.232 821	3.33	444
38	6.982 123	1400.692 303	.000 713 9327	.143 223	200.611 222	.004 984 7660	5.99	1.273 053	3.35	456
39	7.348 483	1486.474 158	.000 672 7329	.136 083	202.283 122	.004 943 5662	5.94	1.313 589	3.37	468
40	7.734 067	1576.757 086	.000 634 2131	.129 298	203.871 668	.004 905 0464	5.89	1.354 422	3.39	480
41	8.139 882	1671.777 262	.000 598 1658	.122 852	205.381 018	.004 868 9991	5.85	1.395 548	3.40	492
42	8.566 991	1771.783 256	.000 564 4031	.116 727	206.815 118	.004 835 2365	5.81	1.436 959	3.42	504
43	9.016 511	1877.036 678	.000 532 7546	.110 908	208.177 722	.004 803 5880	5.77	1.478 651	3.44	516
44	9.489 617	1987.812 869	.000 503 0655	.105 378	209.472 392	.004 773 8988	5.73	1.520 619	3.46	528
45	9.987 549	2104.401 613	.000 475 1945	.100 125	210.702 516	.004 746 0278	5.70	1.562 855	3.47	540
46	10.511 607	2227.107 901	.000 449 0128	.095 133	211.871 313	.004 719 8462	5.67	1.605 355	3.49	552
47	11.063 163	2356.252 730	.000 424 4027	.090 390	212.981 838	.004 695 2360	5.64	1.648 113	3.51	564
48	11.643 660	2492.173 935	.000 401 2561	.085 884	214.036 999	.004 672 0894	5.61	1.691 124	3.52	576
49	12.254 616	2635.227 081	.000 379 4739	.081 602	215.039 554	.004 650 3073	5.59	1.734 381	3.54	588
50	12.897 629	2785.786 390	.000 358 9651	.077 534	215.992 126	.004 629 7984	5.56	1.777 879	3.56	600

Effective Rate is 5.25 %

Annual Percentage Rate is 5.125%

MONTHLY COMPOUND INTEREST AND ANNUITY

Amount Of 1	Amount Of 1 Per Period	Sinking Fund Payment	Present Worth Of 1	Present Worth of 1 Per Period	Periodic Payment To Amortize 1	Constant Annual Percent	Total Interest	Annual Add On Rate	
What a single $ 1 deposit grows to in the future. The deposit is made at the beginning of the first period.	What a series of $ 1 deposits grow to in the future. A deposit is made at the end of each period.	The amount to be deposited at the end of each period that grows to $ 1 in the future.	What $ 1 to be paid in the future is worth today. Value today of a single $ 1 payment tomorrow.	What $ 1 to be paid at the end of each period is worth today. Value today of a series of $ 1 payments tomorrow.	The mortgage payment to amortize a loan of $ 1. An annuity certain, payable at the end of each period, worth $ 1 today.	The annual payment, including interest and principal, to amortize completely a loan of $ 100.	The total interest paid over the term on a loan of $1. The loan is amortized by regular periodic payments.	The average annual interest rate on a loan that is completely amortized by regular periodic payments.	
$S = (1 + i)^n$	$S\overline{n} = \dfrac{(1+i)^n - 1}{i}$	$\dfrac{1}{S\overline{n}} = \dfrac{i}{(1+i)^n - 1}$	$V^n = \dfrac{1}{(1+i)^n}$	$A\overline{n} = \dfrac{1 - V^n}{i}$	$\dfrac{1}{A\overline{n}} = \dfrac{i}{1 - V^n}$				

YEAR									PERIODS
	1.004 292	1.000 000	1.000 000 0000	.995 727	.995 727	1.004 291 6667	1205.15	.004 292	5.15	1
	1.008 602	2.004 292	.498 929 3807	.991 472	1.987 198	.503 221 0474	603.87	.006 442	3.87	2
	1.012 930	3.012 893	.331 906 8620	.987 235	2.974 433	.336 198 5287	403.44	.008 596	3.44	3
	1.017 277	4.025 824	.248 396 3684	.983 016	3.957 449	.252 688 0351	303.23	.010 752	3.23	4
	1.021 643	5.043 101	.198 290 6849	.978 815	4.936 264	.202 582 3515	243.10	.012 912	3.10	5
	1.026 028	6.064 745	.164 887 4064	.974 632	5.910 897	.169 179 0730	203.02	.015 074	3.01	6
	1.030 431	7.090 772	.141 028 3593	.970 467	6.881 364	.145 320 0259	174.39	.017 240	2.96	7
	1.034 853	8.121 204	.123 134 4568	.966 320	7.847 684	.127 426 1235	152.92	.019 409	2.91	8
	1.039 295	9.156 057	.109 217 3174	.962 191	8.809 875	.113 508 9841	136.22	.021 581	2.88	9
	1.043 755	10.195 352	.098 083 9122	.958 079	9.767 955	.102 375 5789	122.86	.023 756	2.85	10
	1.048 235	11.239 107	.088 975 0409	.953 985	10.721 940	.093 266 7076	111.93	.025 934	2.83	11
	1.052 733	12.287 341	.081 384 5700	.949 908	11.671 848	.085 676 2367	102.82	.028 115	2.81	12
1	1.052 733	12.287 341	.081 384 5700	.949 908	11.671 848	.085 676 2367	102.82	.028 115	2.81	12
2	1.108 247	25.222 633	.039 646 9308	.902 326	22.759 033	.043 938 5974	52.73	.054 526	2.73	24
3	1.166 689	38.840 044	.025 746 6235	.857 127	33.290 843	.030 038 2902	36.05	.081 378	2.71	36
4	1.228 212	53.175 545	.018 805 6372	.814 192	43.295 097	.023 097 3039	27.72	.108 671	2.72	48
5	1.292 979	68.267 001	.014 648 3657	.773 408	52.798 220	.018 940 0324	22.73	.136 402	2.73	60
6	1.361 162	84.154 278	.011 882 9371	.734 666	61.825 317	.016 174 6038	19.41	.164 571	2.74	72
7	1.432 941	100.879 342	.009 912 8323	.697 866	70.400 230	.014 204 4990	17.05	.193 178	2.76	84
8	1.508 504	118.486 371	.008 439 7892	.662 908	78.545 612	.012 731 4559	15.28	.222 220	2.78	96
9	1.588 052	137.021 875	.007 298 1048	.629 702	86.282 979	.011 589 7714	13.91	.251 695	2.80	108
10	1.671 795	156.534 815	.006 388 3552	.598 159	93.632 767	.010 680 0219	12.82	.281 603	2.82	120
11	1.759 954	177.076 734	.005 647 2693	.568 197	100.614 392	.009 938 9359	11.93	.311 940	2.84	132
12	1.852 762	198.701 894	.005 032 6647	.539 735	107.246 296	.009 324 3313	11.19	.342 704	2.86	144
13	1.950 464	221.467 417	.004 515 3369	.512 698	113.545 997	.008 807 0036	10.57	.373 893	2.88	156
14	2.053 319	245.433 438	.004 074 4245	.487 017	119.530 135	.008 366 0911	10.04	.405 503	2.90	168
15	2.161 597	270.663 263	.003 694 6277	.462 621	125.214 517	.007 986 2944	9.59	.437 533	2.92	180
16	2.275 584	297.223 538	.003 364 4711	.439 448	130.614 160	.007 656 1378	9.19	.469 978	2.94	192
17	2.395 583	325.184 419	.003 075 1781	.417 435	135.743 325	.007 366 8448	8.85	.502 836	2.96	204
18	2.521 910	354.619 767	.002 819 9218	.396 525	140.615 561	.007 111 5884	8.54	.536 103	2.98	216
19	2.654 898	385.607 335	.002 593 3117	.376 662	145.243 740	.006 884 9783	8.27	.569 775	3.00	228
20	2.794 899	418.228 975	.002 391 0347	.357 795	149.640 084	.006 682 7014	8.02	.603 848	3.02	240
21	2.942 283	452.570 857	.002 209 5987	.339 872	153.816 209	.006 501 2654	7.81	.638 319	3.04	252
22	3.097 439	488.723 696	.002 046 1459	.322 847	157.783 144	.006 337 8126	7.61	.673 183	3.06	264
23	3.260 777	526.782 989	.001 898 3149	.306 675	161.551 370	.006 189 9816	7.43	.708 435	3.08	276
24	3.432 728	566.849 270	.001 764 1374	.291 313	165.130 838	.006 055 8041	7.27	.744 072	3.10	288
25	3.613 747	609.028 372	.001 641 9596	.276 721	168.531 005	.005 933 6263	7.13	.780 088	3.12	300
26	3.804 311	653.431 713	.001 530 3818	.262 860	171.760 851	.005 822 0485	6.99	.816 479	3.14	312
27	4.004 924	700.176 582	.001 428 2111	.249 693	174.828 909	.005 719 8778	6.87	.853 240	3.16	324
28	4.216 117	749.386 457	.001 334 4250	.237 185	177.743 283	.005 626 0916	6.76	.890 367	3.18	336
29	4.438 446	801.191 324	.001 248 1413	.225 304	180.511 671	.005 539 8080	6.65	.927 853	3.20	348
30	4.672 499	855.728 027	.001 168 5956	.214 018	183.141 386	.005 460 2623	6.56	.965 694	3.22	360
31	4.918 895	913.140 623	.001 095 1216	.203 298	185.639 374	.005 386 7882	6.47	1.003 885	3.24	372
32	5.178 284	973.580 768	.001 027 1361	.193 114	188.012 234	.005 318 8028	6.39	1.042 420	3.26	384
33	5.451 351	1037.208 113	.000 964 1267	.183 441	190.266 233	.005 255 7933	6.31	1.081 294	3.28	396
34	5.738 819	1104.190 730	.000 905 6406	.174 252	192.407 326	.005 197 3073	6.24	1.120 501	3.30	408
35	6.041 445	1174.705 553	.000 851 2772	.165 523	194.441 167	.005 142 9438	6.18	1.160 036	3.31	420
36	6.360 029	1248.938 846	.000 800 6797	.157 232	196.373 130	.005 092 3464	6.12	1.199 894	3.33	432
37	6.695 414	1327.086 697	.000 753 5303	.149 356	198.208 318	.005 045 1969	6.06	1.240 067	3.35	444
38	7.048 484	1409.355 532	.000 709 5442	.141 874	199.951 578	.005 001 2108	6.01	1.280 552	3.37	456
39	7.420 173	1495.962 663	.000 668 4659	.134 768	201.607 516	.004 960 1325	5.96	1.321 342	3.39	468
40	7.811 462	1587.136 864	.000 630 0654	.128 017	203.180 504	.004 921 7321	5.91	1.362 431	3.41	480
41	8.223 386	1683.118 969	.000 594 1351	.121 604	204.674 699	.004 885 8017	5.87	1.403 814	3.42	492
42	8.657 031	1784.162 516	.000 560 4871	.115 513	206.094 047	.004 852 1537	5.83	1.445 485	3.44	504
43	9.113 544	1890.534 409	.000 528 9510	.109 727	207.442 298	.004 820 6176	5.79	1.487 439	3.46	516
44	9.594 130	2002.515 630	.000 499 3719	.104 230	208.723 013	.004 791 0385	5.75	1.529 668	3.48	528
45	10.100 058	2120.401 976	.000 471 6087	.099 009	209.939 574	.004 763 2754	5.72	1.572 169	3.49	540
46	10.632 667	2244.504 843	.000 445 5326	.094 050	211.095 196	.004 737 1992	5.69	1.614 934	3.51	552
47	11.193 361	2375.152 048	.000 421 0257	.089 339	212.192 931	.004 712 6923	5.66	1.657 958	3.53	564
48	11.783 622	2512.688 695	.000 397 9801	.084 864	213.235 678	.004 689 6467	5.63	1.701 237	3.54	576
49	12.405 010	2657.478 086	.000 376 2966	.080 613	214.226 193	.004 667 9633	5.61	1.744 762	3.56	588
50	13.059 166	2809.902 681	.000 355 8842	.076 575	215.167 090	.004 647 5509	5.58	1.788 531	3.58	600

Effective Rate is 5.27 %

Annual Percentage Rate is 5.15 %

MONTHLY COMPOUND INTEREST AND ANNUITY

5.20 % M

Amount Of 1	Amount Of 1 Per Period	Sinking Fund Payment	Present Worth Of 1	Present Worth of 1 Per Period	Periodic Payment To Amortize 1	Constant Annual Percent	Total Interest	Annual Add On Rate
What a single $ 1 deposit grows to in the future. The deposit is made at the beginning of the first period.	What a series of $ 1 deposits grow to in the future. A deposit is made at the end of each period.	The amount to be deposited at the end of each period that grows to $ 1 in the future.	What $ 1 to be paid in the future is worth today. Value today of a single $ 1 payment tomorrow.	What $ 1 to be paid at the end of each period is worth today. Value today of a series of $ 1 payments tomorrow.	The mortgage payment to amortize a loan of $ 1. An annuity certain, payable at the end of each period, worth $ 1 today.	The annual payment, including interest and principal, to amortize completely a loan of $ 100.	The total interest paid over the term on a loan of $1. The loan is amortized completely by regular periodic payments.	The average annual interest rate on a loan that is completely amortized by regular periodic payments.

$$S = (1+i)^n \qquad S\overline{n|} = \frac{(1+i)^n - 1}{i} \qquad \frac{1}{S\overline{n|}} = \frac{i}{(1+i)^n - 1} \qquad V^n = \frac{1}{(1+i)^n} \qquad A\overline{n|} = \frac{1-V^n}{i} \qquad \frac{1}{A\overline{n|}} = \frac{i}{1-V^n}$$

YEAR / **PERIODS**

Year	Amount Of 1	Amount Of 1 Per Period	Sinking Fund Payment	Present Worth Of 1	Present Worth of 1 Per Period	Periodic Payment To Amortize 1	Constant Annual Percent	Total Interest	Annual Add On Rate	Periods
	1.004 333	1.000 000	1.000 000 0000	.995 685	.995 685	1.004 333 3333	1205.20	.004 333	5.20	1
	1.008 685	2.004 333	.498 919 0088	.991 389	1.987 075	.503 252 3421	603.91	.006 505	3.90	2
	1.013 056	3.013 019	.331 893 0527	.987 112	2.974 187	.336 226 3860	403.48	.008 679	3.47	3
	1.017 446	4.026 075	.248 380 8553	.982 853	3.957 039	.252 714 1887	303.26	.010 857	3.26	4
	1.021 855	5.043 522	.198 274 1615	.978 612	4.935 652	.202 607 4948	243.13	.013 037	3.13	5
	1.026 283	6.065 377	.164 870 2194	.974 390	5.910 041	.169 203 5527	203.05	.015 221	3.04	6
	1.030 731	7.091 660	.141 010 7068	.970 186	6.880 227	.145 344 0401	174.42	.017 408	2.98	7
	1.035 197	8.122 391	.123 116 4627	.966 000	7.846 227	.127 449 7960	152.94	.019 598	2.94	8
	1.039 683	9.157 588	.109 199 0642	.961 832	8.808 059	.113 532 3976	136.24	.021 792	2.91	9
	1.044 188	10.197 271	.098 065 4577	.957 682	9.765 740	.102 398 7910	122.88	.023 988	2.88	10
	1.048 713	11.241 459	.088 956 4271	.953 550	10.719 290	.093 289 7605	111.95	.026 187	2.86	11
	1.053 257	12.290 172	.081 365 8285	.949 436	11.668 726	.085 699 1618	102.84	.028 390	2.84	12
1	1.053 257	12.290 172	.081 365 8285	.949 436	11.668 726	.085 699 1618	102.84	.028 390	2.84	12
2	1.109 351	25.234 886	.039 627 6804	.901 428	22.747 428	.043 961 0137	52.76	.055 064	2.75	24
3	1.168 432	38.869 002	.025 727 4419	.855 848	33.265 942	.030 060 7752	36.08	.082 188	2.74	36
4	1.230 660	53.229 237	.018 786 6681	.812 572	43.252 592	.023 120 0014	27.75	.109 760	2.74	48
5	1.296 202	68.354 259	.014 629 6662	.771 485	52.734 273	.018 962 9995	22.76	.137 780	2.76	60
6	1.365 234	84.284 802	.011 864 5352	.732 475	61.736 518	.016 197 8685	19.44	.166 247	2.77	72
7	1.437 943	101.063 764	.009 894 7433	.695 438	70.283 569	.014 228 0766	17.08	.195 158	2.79	84
8	1.514 524	118.736 330	.008 422 0221	.660 273	78.398 442	.012 755 3555	15.31	.224 514	2.81	96
9	1.595 184	137.350 091	.007 280 6650	.626 887	86.102 992	.011 613 9983	13.94	.254 312	2.83	108
10	1.680 139	156.955 173	.006 371 2459	.595 189	93.417 964	.010 704 5792	12.85	.284 550	2.85	120
11	1.769 619	177.604 371	.005 630 4921	.565 093	100.363 059	.009 963 8254	11.96	.315 225	2.87	132
12	1.863 864	199.353 291	.005 016 2202	.536 520	106.956 979	.009 349 5535	11.22	.346 336	2.89	144
13	1.963 129	222.260 503	.004 499 2249	.509 391	113.217 481	.008 832 5583	10.60	.377 879	2.91	156
14	2.067 680	246.387 694	.004 058 6443	.483 634	119.161 424	.008 391 9776	10.08	.409 852	2.93	168
15	2.177 799	271.799 836	.003 679 1781	.459 179	124.804 814	.008 012 5114	9.62	.442 252	2.95	180
16	2.293 783	298.565 363	.003 349 3503	.435 961	130.162 850	.007 682 6837	9.22	.475 075	2.97	192
17	2.415 944	326.756 353	.003 060 3843	.413 917	135.249 959	.007 393 7176	8.88	.508 318	2.99	204
18	2.544 611	356.448 722	.002 805 4526	.392 987	140.079 841	.007 138 7860	8.57	.541 978	3.01	216
19	2.680 131	387.722 429	.002 579 1647	.373 116	144.665 502	.006 912 4980	8.30	.576 050	3.03	228
20	2.822 867	420.661 694	.002 377 2072	.354 250	149.019 292	.006 710 5405	8.06	.610 530	3.05	240
21	2.973 206	455.355 218	.002 196 0877	.336 337	153.152 935	.006 529 4210	7.84	.645 414	3.07	252
22	3.131 551	491.896 429	.002 032 9483	.319 331	157.077 563	.006 366 2816	7.64	.680 698	3.09	264
23	3.298 330	530.383 731	.001 885 4274	.303 184	160.803 743	.006 218 7607	7.47	.716 378	3.11	276
24	3.473 990	570.920 767	.001 751 5565	.287 853	164.341 512	.006 084 8899	7.31	.752 448	3.14	288
25	3.659 006	613.616 700	.001 629 6819	.273 298	167.700 395	.005 963 0152	7.16	.788 905	3.16	300
26	3.853 875	658.586 508	.001 518 4034	.259 479	170.889 437	.005 851 7367	7.03	.825 742	3.18	312
27	4.059 122	705.951 292	.001 416 5283	.246 359	173.917 228	.005 749 8617	6.90	.862 955	3.20	324
28	4.275 301	755.838 602	.001 323 0338	.233 902	176.791 920	.005 656 3671	6.79	.900 539	3.22	336
29	4.502 992	808.382 780	.001 237 0377	.222 075	179.521 254	.005 570 3711	6.69	.938 489	3.24	348
30	4.742 810	863.725 325	.001 157 7755	.210 845	182.112 581	.005 491 1088	6.59	.976 799	3.26	360
31	4.995 400	922.015 271	.001 084 5807	.200 184	184.572 879	.005 417 9141	6.51	1.015 464	3.28	372
32	5.261 442	983.409 589	.001 016 8703	.190 062	186.908 774	.005 350 2036	6.43	1.054 478	3.30	384
33	5.541 652	1048.073 609	.000 954 1315	.180 452	189.126 555	.005 287 4648	6.35	1.093 836	3.31	396
34	5.836 786	1116.181 467	.000 895 9117	.171 327	191.232 195	.005 229 2450	6.28	1.133 532	3.33	408
35	6.147 638	1187.916 573	.000 841 8100	.162 664	193.231 365	.005 175 1433	6.22	1.173 560	3.35	420
36	6.475 046	1263.472 105	.000 791 4698	.154 439	195.129 447	.005 124 8031	6.15	1.213 915	3.37	432
37	6.819 890	1343.051 530	.000 744 5731	.146 630	196.931 554	.005 077 9064	6.10	1.254 590	3.39	444
38	7.183 100	1426.869 148	.000 700 8351	.139 216	198.642 539	.005 034 1684	6.05	1.295 581	3.41	456
39	7.565 653	1515.150 676	.000 660 0004	.132 176	200.267 008	.004 993 3337	6.00	1.336 880	3.43	468
40	7.968 580	1608.133 849	.000 621 8388	.125 493	201.809 337	.004 955 1721	5.95	1.378 483	3.45	480
41	8.392 966	1706.069 065	.000 586 1427	.119 147	203.273 679	.004 919 4761	5.91	1.420 382	3.46	492
42	8.839 954	1809.220 058	.000 552 7244	.113 123	204.663 977	.004 886 0577	5.87	1.462 573	3.48	504
43	9.310 747	1917.864 605	.000 521 4132	.107 403	205.983 976	.004 854 7466	5.83	1.505 049	3.50	516
44	9.806 613	2032.295 279	.000 492 0545	.101 972	207.237 229	.004 825 3878	5.80	1.547 805	3.52	528
45	10.328 888	2152.820 235	.000 464 5070	.096 816	208.427 112	.004 797 8403	5.76	1.590 834	3.54	540
46	10.878 977	2279.764 038	.000 438 6419	.091 920	209.556 830	.004 771 9752	5.73	1.634 130	3.55	552
47	11.458 364	2413.468 539	.000 414 3414	.087 272	210.629 424	.004 747 6748	5.70	1.677 689	3.57	564
48	12.068 606	2554.293 795	.000 391 4976	.082 860	211.647 783	.004 724 8310	5.67	1.721 503	3.59	576
49	12.711 349	2702.619 040	.000 370 0115	.078 670	212.614 649	.004 703 3448	5.65	1.765 567	3.60	588
50	13.388 323	2858.843 704	.000 349 7918	.074 692	213.532 626	.004 683 1251	5.62	1.809 875	3.62	600

	Amount Of 1	Amount Of 1 Per Period	Sinking Fund Payment	Present Worth Of 1	Present Worth of 1 Per Period	Periodic Payment To Amortize 1	Constant Annual Percent	Total Interest	Annual Add On Rate	
	What a single $ 1 deposit grows to in the future. The deposit is made at the beginning of the first period.	What a series of $ 1 deposits grow to in the future. A deposit is made at the end of each period.	The amount to be deposited at the end of each period that grows to $ 1 in the future.	What $ 1 to be paid in the future is worth today. Value today of a single $ 1 payment tomorrow.	What $ 1 to be paid at the end of each period is worth today. Value today of a series of $ 1 payments tomorrow.	The mortgage payment to amortize a loan of $ 1. An annuity certain, payable at the end of each period, worth $ 1 today.	The annual payment, including interest and principal, to amortize completely a loan of $ 100.	The total interest paid over the term on a loan of $1. The loan is amortized by regular periodic payments.	The average annual interest rate on a loan that is completely amortized by regular periodic payments.	
	$S = (1+i)^n$	$S\overline{n}| = \dfrac{(1+i)^n - 1}{i}$	$\dfrac{1}{S\overline{n}|} = \dfrac{i}{(1+i)^n - 1}$	$V^n = \dfrac{1}{(1+i)^n}$	$A\overline{n}| = \dfrac{1-V^n}{i}$	$\dfrac{1}{A\overline{n}|} = \dfrac{i}{1-V^n}$				

YEAR									PERIODS	
	1.004 375	1.000 000	1.000 000 0000	.995 644	.995 644	1.004 375 0000	1205.25	.004 375	5.25	1
	1.008 769	2.004 375	.498 908 6374	.991 307	1.986 951	.503 283 6374	603.95	.006 567	3.94	2
	1.013 183	3.013 144	.331 879 2442	.986 989	2.973 940	.336 254 2442	403.51	.008 763	3.51	3
	1.017 615	4.026 327	.248 365 3434	.982 690	3.956 630	.252 740 3434	303.29	.010 961	3.29	4
	1.022 067	5.043 942	.198 257 6395	.978 409	4.935 039	.202 632 6395	243.16	.013 163	3.16	5
	1.026 539	6.066 009	.164 853 0341	.974 147	5.909 186	.169 228 0341	203.08	.015 368	3.07	6
	1.031 030	7.092 548	.140 993 0563	.969 904	6.879 090	.145 368 0563	174.45	.017 576	3.01	7
	1.035 541	8.123 578	.123 098 4709	.965 679	7.844 770	.127 473 4709	152.97	.019 788	2.97	8
	1.040 071	9.159 118	.109 180 8136	.961 473	8.806 242	.113 555 8136	136.27	.022 002	2.93	9
	1.044 621	10.199 190	.098 047 0061	.957 285	9.763 527	.102 422 0061	122.91	.024 220	2.91	10
	1.049 192	11.243 811	.088 937 8165	.953 115	10.716 641	.093 312 8165	111.98	.026 441	2.88	11
	1.053 782	12.293 003	.081 347 0904	.948 963	11.665 604	.085 722 0904	102.87	.028 665	2.87	12
1	1.053 782	12.293 003	.081 347 0904	.948 963	11.665 604	.085 722 0904	102.87	.028 665	2.87	12
2	1.110 456	25.247 146	.039 608 4370	.900 531	22.735 831	.043 983 4370	52.79	.055 602	2.78	24
3	1.170 179	38.897 988	.025 708 2705	.854 570	33.241 067	.030 083 2705	36.10	.082 998	2.77	36
4	1.233 113	53.282 998	.018 767 7128	.810 956	43.210 146	.023 142 7128	27.78	.110 850	2.77	48
5	1.299 432	68.441 661	.014 610 9838	.769 567	52.670 434	.018 985 9838	22.79	.139 159	2.78	60
6	1.369 318	84.415 585	.011 846 1537	.730 290	61.647 896	.016 221 1537	19.47	.167 923	2.80	72
7	1.442 963	101.248 617	.009 876 6781	.693 019	70.167 176	.014 251 6781	17.11	.197 141	2.82	84
8	1.520 568	118.986 962	.008 404 2822	.657 649	78.251 657	.012 779 2822	15.34	.226 811	2.84	96
9	1.602 347	137.679 308	.007 263 2556	.624 085	85.923 530	.011 638 2556	13.97	.256 932	2.85	108
10	1.688 524	157.376 963	.006 354 1701	.592 233	93.203 853	.010 729 1701	12.88	.287 500	2.88	120
11	1.779 336	178.133 996	.005 613 7516	.562 007	100.112 611	.009 988 7516	11.99	.318 515	2.90	132
12	1.875 032	200.007 381	.004 999 8155	.533 324	106.668 766	.009 374 8155	11.25	.349 973	2.92	144
13	1.975 875	223.057 158	.004 483 1558	.506 105	112.890 315	.008 858 1558	10.63	.381 872	2.94	156
14	2.082 141	247.346 595	.004 042 9099	.480 275	118.794 334	.008 417 9099	10.11	.414 209	2.96	168
15	2.194 123	272.942 365	.003 663 7772	.455 763	124.397 030	.008 038 7772	9.65	.446 980	2.98	180
16	2.312 127	299.914 723	.003 334 2811	.432 502	129.713 780	.007 709 2811	9.26	.480 182	3.00	192
17	2.436 477	328.337 705	.003 045 6447	.410 429	134.759 180	.007 420 6447	8.91	.513 812	3.02	204
18	2.567 516	358.289 329	.002 791 0404	.389 482	139.547 078	.007 166 0404	8.60	.547 865	3.04	216
19	2.705 602	389.851 808	.002 565 0772	.369 604	144.090 615	.006 940 0772	8.33	.582 338	3.06	228
20	2.851 114	423.111 776	.002 363 4417	.350 740	148.402 264	.006 738 4417	8.09	.617 226	3.09	240
21	3.004 452	458.160 528	.002 182 6411	.332 839	152.493 859	.006 557 6411	7.87	.652 526	3.11	252
22	3.166 037	495.094 269	.002 019 8174	.315 852	156.376 632	.006 394 8174	7.68	.688 232	3.13	264
23	3.336 313	534.014 375	.001 872 6088	.299 732	160.061 239	.006 247 6088	7.50	.724 340	3.15	276
24	3.515 746	575.027 679	.001 739 0467	.284 435	163.557 795	.006 114 0467	7.34	.760 845	3.17	288
25	3.704 830	618.246 755	.001 617 4772	.269 918	166.875 897	.005 992 4772	7.20	.797 743	3.19	300
26	3.904 082	663.790 234	.001 506 5000	.256 142	170.024 653	.005 881 5000	7.06	.835 028	3.21	312
27	4.114 051	711.783 128	.001 404 9223	.243 069	173.012 706	.005 779 9223	6.94	.872 695	3.23	324
28	4.335 313	762.357 171	.001 311 7211	.230 664	175.848 258	.005 686 7211	6.83	.910 738	3.25	336
29	4.568 474	815.651 180	.001 226 0143	.218 891	178.539 091	.005 601 0143	6.73	.949 153	3.27	348
30	4.814 175	871.811 442	.001 147 0370	.207 720	181.092 592	.005 522 0370	6.63	.987 933	3.29	360
31	5.073 090	930.992 109	.001 074 1230	.197 119	183.515 771	.005 449 1230	6.54	1.027 074	3.31	372
32	5.345 931	993.355 624	.001 006 6888	.187 058	185.815 277	.005 381 6888	6.46	1.066 569	3.33	384
33	5.633 445	1059.073 166	.000 944 2218	.177 511	187.997 424	.005 319 2218	6.39	1.106 412	3.35	396
34	5.936 422	1128.325 122	.000 886 2694	.168 452	190.068 200	.005 261 2694	6.32	1.146 598	3.37	408
35	6.255 694	1201.301 579	.000 832 4304	.159 854	192.033 290	.005 207 4304	6.25	1.187 121	3.39	420
36	6.592 137	1278.202 847	.000 782 3484	.151 696	193.898 088	.005 157 3484	6.19	1.227 975	3.41	432
37	6.946 675	1359.240 010	.000 735 7052	.143 954	195.667 712	.005 110 7052	6.14	1.269 153	3.43	444
38	7.320 280	1444.635 505	.000 692 2161	.136 607	197.347 019	.005 067 2161	6.09	1.310 651	3.45	456
39	7.713 979	1534.623 731	.000 651 6255	.129 635	198.940 620	.005 026 6255	6.04	1.352 461	3.47	468
40	8.128 851	1629.451 693	.000 613 7034	.123 019	200.452 888	.004 988 7034	5.99	1.394 578	3.49	480
41	8.566 036	1729.379 682	.000 578 2420	.116 740	201.887 975	.004 953 2420	5.95	1.436 995	3.50	492
42	9.026 734	1834.681 987	.000 545 0536	.110 782	203.249 819	.004 920 0536	5.91	1.479 707	3.52	504
43	9.512 208	1945.647 649	.000 513 9677	.105 128	204.542 158	.004 888 9677	5.87	1.522 707	3.54	516
44	10.023 793	2062.581 253	.000 484 8294	.099 763	205.768 541	.004 859 8294	5.84	1.565 990	3.56	528
45	10.562 891	2185.803 767	.000 457 4976	.094 671	206.932 332	.004 832 4976	5.80	1.609 549	3.58	540
46	11.130 984	2315.653 420	.000 431 8436	.089 839	208.036 727	.004 806 8436	5.77	1.653 378	3.59	552
47	11.729 629	2452.486 633	.000 407 7494	.085 254	209.084 757	.004 782 7494	5.74	1.697 471	3.61	564
48	12.360 471	2596.678 994	.000 385 1073	.080 903	210.079 299	.004 760 1073	5.72	1.741 822	3.63	576
49	13.025 240	2748.626 292	.000 363 8181	.076 774	211.023 082	.004 738 8181	5.69	1.786 425	3.65	588
50	13.725 762	2908.745 603	.000 343 7908	.072 856	211.918 697	.004 718 7908	5.67	1.831 274	3.66	600

Effective Rate is 5.38 %

Annual Percentage Rate is 5.25 %

MONTHLY COMPOUND INTEREST AND ANNUITY

	Amount Of 1	Amount Of 1 Per Period	Sinking Fund Payment	Present Worth Of 1	Present Worth of 1 Per Period	Periodic Payment To Amortize 1	Constant Annual Percent	Total Interest	Annual Add On Rate	
	What a single $ 1 deposit grows to in the future. The deposit is made at the beginning of the first period.	What a series of $ 1 deposits grow to in the future. A deposit is made at the end of each period.	The amount to be deposited at the end of each period that grows to $ 1 in the future.	What $ 1 to be paid in the future is worth today. Value today of a single $ 1 payment tomorrow.	What $ 1 to be paid at the end of each period is worth today. Value today of a series of $ 1 payments tomorrow.	The mortgage payment to amortize a loan of $ 1. An annuity certain, payable at the end of each period, worth $ 1 today.	The annual payment, including interest and principal, to amortize completely a loan of $ 100.	The total interest paid over the term on a loan of $1. The loan is amortized by regular periodic payments.	The average annual interest rate on a loan that is completely amortized by regular periodic payments.	
	$S = (1+i)^n$	$S\overline{n}| = \dfrac{(1+i)^n - 1}{i}$	$\dfrac{1}{S\overline{n}|} = \dfrac{i}{(1+i)^n - 1}$	$V^n = \dfrac{1}{(1+i)^n}$	$A\overline{n}| = \dfrac{1 - V^n}{i}$	$\dfrac{1}{A\overline{n}|} = \dfrac{i}{1 - V^n}$				

YEAR										PERIODS
	1.004 417	1.000 000	1.000 000 0000	.995 603	.995 603	1.004 416 6667	1205.30	.004 417	5.30	1
	1.008 853	2.004 417	.498 898 2663	.991 225	1.986 828	.503 314 9330	603.98	.006 630	3.98	2
	1.013 309	3.013 270	.331 865 4364	.986 866	2.973 694	.336 282 1031	403.54	.008 846	3.54	3
	1.017 784	4.026 578	.248 349 8325	.982 527	3.956 220	.252 766 4991	303.32	.011 066	3.32	4
	1.022 279	5.044 362	.198 241 1189	.978 206	4.934 427	.202 657 7855	243.19	.013 289	3.19	5
	1.026 794	6.066 641	.164 835 8504	.973 905	5.908 332	.169 252 5171	203.11	.015 515	3.10	6
	1.031 329	7.093 436	.140 975 4078	.969 622	6.877 954	.145 392 0745	174.48	.017 745	3.04	7
	1.035 884	8.124 765	.123 080 4813	.965 359	7.843 313	.127 497 1480	153.00	.019 977	3.00	8
	1.040 460	9.160 649	.109 162 5655	.961 114	8.804 426	.113 579 2322	136.30	.022 213	2.96	9
	1.045 055	10.201 109	.098 028 5573	.956 888	9.761 314	.102 445 2239	122.94	.024 452	2.93	10
	1.049 671	11.246 164	.088 919 2090	.952 680	10.713 994	.093 335 8757	112.01	.026 695	2.91	11
	1.054 307	12.295 834	.081 328 3557	.948 491	11.662 485	.085 745 0224	102.90	.028 940	2.89	12
1	1.054 307	12.295 834	.081 328 3557	.948 491	11.662 485	.085 745 0224	102.90	.028 940	2.89	12
2	1.111 562	25.259 414	.039 589 2004	.899 635	22.724 243	.044 005 8670	52.81	.056 141	2.81	24
3	1.171 928	38.927 001	.025 689 1095	.853 295	33.216 217	.030 105 7761	36.13	.083 808	2.79	36
4	1.235 571	53.336 829	.018 748 7711	.809 342	43.167 757	.023 165 4378	27.80	.111 941	2.80	48
5	1.302 671	68.529 205	.014 592 3186	.767 654	52.606 701	.019 008 9853	22.82	.140 539	2.81	60
6	1.373 414	84.546 628	.011 827 7928	.728 112	61.559 451	.016 244 4595	19.50	.169 601	2.83	72
7	1.448 000	101.433 903	.009 858 6367	.690 608	70.051 051	.014 275 3034	17.14	.199 125	2.84	84
8	1.526 636	119.238 268	.008 386 5693	.655 035	78.105 254	.012 803 2360	15.37	.229 111	2.86	96
9	1.609 542	138.009 528	.007 245 8766	.621 295	85.744 591	.011 662 5432	14.00	.259 555	2.88	108
10	1.696 951	157.800 191	.006 337 1280	.589 292	92.990 431	.010 753 7946	12.91	.290 455	2.90	120
11	1.789 106	178.665 617	.005 597 0478	.558 938	99.863 043	.010 013 7145	12.02	.321 810	2.93	132
12	1.886 267	200.664 174	.004 983 4506	.530 148	106.381 652	.009 400 1173	11.29	.353 617	2.95	144
13	1.988 704	223.857 398	.004 467 1296	.502 840	112.564 491	.008 883 7962	10.67	.385 872	2.97	156
14	2.096 703	248.310 168	.004 027 2213	.476 939	118.428 857	.008 443 8880	10.14	.418 573	2.99	168
15	2.210 568	274.090 884	.003 648 4249	.452 372	123.991 153	.008 065 0916	9.68	.451 716	3.01	180
16	2.330 617	301.271 663	.003 319 2634	.429 071	129.266 939	.007 735 9301	9.29	.485 299	3.03	192
17	2.457 184	329.928 537	.003 030 9594	.406 970	134.270 973	.007 447 6261	8.94	.519 316	3.05	204
18	2.590 626	360.141 670	.002 776 6851	.386 007	139.017 253	.007 193 3517	8.64	.553 764	3.08	216
19	2.731 314	391.995 575	.002 551 0492	.366 124	143.519 055	.006 967 7159	8.37	.588 639	3.10	228
20	2.879 642	425.579 357	.002 349 7380	.347 265	147.788 973	.006 766 4047	8.12	.623 937	3.12	240
21	3.036 026	460.986 960	.002 169 2588	.329 378	151.838 950	.006 585 9254	7.91	.659 653	3.14	252
22	3.200 902	498.317 430	.002 006 7530	.312 412	155.680 315	.006 423 4197	7.71	.695 783	3.16	264
23	3.374 732	537.675 191	.001 859 8589	.296 320	159.323 815	.006 276 5256	7.54	.732 321	3.18	276
24	3.558 002	579.170 338	.001 726 6078	.281 057	162.779 640	.006 143 2744	7.38	.769 263	3.21	288
25	3.751 225	622.918 946	.001 605 3453	.266 580	166.057 458	.006 022 0120	7.23	.806 604	3.23	300
26	3.954 942	669.043 392	.001 494 6714	.252 848	169.166 438	.005 911 3380	7.10	.844 337	3.25	312
27	4.169 721	717.672 700	.001 393 3928	.239 824	172.115 277	.005 810 0595	6.98	.882 459	3.27	324
28	4.396 164	768.942 900	.001 300 4867	.227 471	174.912 223	.005 717 1533	6.87	.920 964	3.29	336
29	4.634 905	822.997 411	.001 215 0707	.215 754	177.565 100	.005 631 7373	6.76	.959 845	3.31	348
30	4.886 611	879.987 439	.001 136 3799	.204 641	180.081 329	.005 553 0465	6.67	.999 097	3.33	360
31	5.151 986	940.072 401	.001 063 7479	.194 100	182.467 949	.005 480 4145	6.58	1.038 714	3.35	372
32	5.431 773	1003.420 373	.000 996 5913	.184 102	184.731 636	.005 413 2580	6.50	1.078 691	3.37	384
33	5.726 754	1070.208 559	.000 934 3973	.174 619	186.878 722	.005 351 0640	6.43	1.119 021	3.39	396
34	6.037 755	1140.623 784	.000 876 7133	.165 624	188.915 214	.005 293 3799	6.36	1.159 699	3.41	408
35	6.365 645	1214.863 021	.000 823 1381	.157 093	190.846 806	.005 239 8047	6.29	1.200 718	3.43	420
36	6.711 342	1293.133 938	.000 773 3151	.149 002	192.678 904	.005 189 9818	6.23	1.242 072	3.45	432
37	7.075 812	1375.655 483	.000 726 9262	.141 327	194.416 632	.005 143 5929	6.18	1.283 755	3.47	444
38	7.460 075	1462.658 493	.000 683 6866	.134 047	196.064 851	.005 100 3533	6.13	1.325 761	3.49	456
39	7.865 206	1554.386 340	.000 643 3407	.127 142	197.628 171	.005 060 0074	6.08	1.368 083	3.51	468
40	8.292 339	1651.095 616	.000 605 6584	.120 593	199.110 965	.005 022 3251	6.03	1.410 716	3.53	480
41	8.742 668	1753.056 843	.000 570 4322	.114 382	200.517 382	.004 987 0988	5.99	1.453 653	3.55	492
42	9.217 452	1860.555 238	.000 537 4740	.108 490	201.851 355	.004 954 1406	5.95	1.496 887	3.56	504
43	9.718 021	1973.891 506	.000 506 6135	.102 902	203.116 616	.004 923 2801	5.91	1.540 413	3.58	516
44	10.245 774	2093.382 681	.000 477 6957	.097 601	204.316 705	.004 894 3624	5.88	1.584 223	3.60	528
45	10.802 187	2219.363 017	.000 450 5797	.092 574	205.454 978	.004 867 2464	5.85	1.628 313	3.62	540
46	11.388 817	2352.184 916	.000 425 1366	.087 805	206.534 619	.004 841 8033	5.82	1.672 675	3.64	552
47	12.007 305	2492.219 921	.000 401 2487	.083 283	207.558 648	.004 817 9154	5.79	1.717 304	3.65	564
48	12.659 381	2639.859 751	.000 378 8080	.078 993	208.529 931	.004 795 4747	5.76	1.762 193	3.67	576
49	13.346 869	2795.517 399	.000 357 7155	.074 924	209.451 183	.004 774 3822	5.73	1.807 337	3.69	588
50	14.071 692	2959.628 285	.000 337 8803	.071 065	210.324 982	.004 754 5469	5.71	1.852 728	3.71	600

Effective Rate is 5.43 %

8 - 23

Annual Percentage Rate is 5.30 %

MONTHLY COMPOUND INTEREST AND ANNUITY

5.35 % M

Amount Of 1	Amount Of 1 Per Period	Sinking Fund Payment	Present Worth Of 1	Present Worth of 1 Per Period	Periodic Payment To Amortize 1	Constant Annual Percent	Total Interest	Annual Add On Rate
What a single $ 1 deposit grows to in the future. The deposit is made at the beginning of the first period.	What a series of $ 1 deposits grow to in the future. A deposit is made at the end of each period.	The amount to be deposited at the end of each period that grows to $ 1 in the future.	What $ 1 to be paid in the future is worth today. Value today of a single $ 1 payment tomorrow.	What $ 1 to be paid at the end of each period is worth today. Value today of a series of $ 1 payments tomorrow.	The mortgage payment to amortize a loan of $ 1. An annuity certain, payable at the end of each period, worth $ 1 today.	The annual payment, including interest and principal, to amortize completely a loan of $ 100.	The total interest paid over the term of a loan of $1. The loan is amortized by regular periodic payments.	The average annual interest rate on a loan that is completely amortized by regular periodic payments.
$S = (1+i)^n$	$S\overline{n}| = \dfrac{(1+i)^n - 1}{i}$	$\dfrac{1}{S\overline{n}|} = \dfrac{i}{(1+i)^n - 1}$	$V^n = \dfrac{1}{(1+i)^n}$	$A\overline{n}| = \dfrac{1 - V^n}{i}$	$\dfrac{1}{A\overline{n}|} = \dfrac{i}{1 - V^n}$			

YEAR									PERIODS
	1.004 458	1.000 000	1.000 000 0000	.995 561	.995 561	1.004 458 3333	1205.35	.004 458	5.35	1
	1.008 937	2.004 458	.498 887 8957	.991 143	1.986 704	.503 346 2291	604.02	.006 692	4.02	2
	1.013 435	3.013 395	.331 851 6294	.986 743	2.973 447	.336 309 9628	403.58	.008 930	3.57	3
	1.017 953	4.026 830	.248 334 3226	.982 364	3.955 811	.252 792 6560	303.36	.011 171	3.35	4
	1.022 491	5.044 783	.198 224 5996	.978 003	4.933 815	.202 682 9330	243.22	.013 415	3.22	5
	1.027 050	6.067 274	.164 818 6685	.973 662	5.907 477	.169 277 0018	203.14	.015 662	3.13	6
	1.031 629	7.094 324	.140 957 7613	.969 341	6.876 818	.145 416 0946	174.50	.017 913	3.07	7
	1.036 228	8.125 953	.123 062 4940	.965 038	7.841 856	.127 520 8273	153.03	.020 167	3.02	8
	1.040 848	9.162 181	.109 144 3200	.960 755	8.802 611	.113 602 6533	136.33	.022 424	2.99	9
	1.045 489	10.203 029	.098 010 1113	.956 491	9.759 102	.102 468 4446	122.97	.024 684	2.96	10
	1.050 150	11.248 517	.088 900 6046	.952 245	10.711 347	.093 358 9380	112.04	.026 948	2.94	11
	1.054 832	12.298 667	.081 309 6244	.948 019	11.659 366	.085 767 9578	102.93	.029 215	2.92	12
1	1.054 832	12.298 667	.081 309 6244	.948 019	11.659 366	.085 767 9578	102.93	.029 215	2.92	12
2	1.112 670	25.271 689	.039 569 9707	.898 739	22.712 662	.044 028 3040	52.84	.056 679	2.83	24
3	1.173 679	38.956 042	.025 669 9588	.852 022	33.191 394	.030 128 2921	36.16	.084 619	2.82	36
4	1.238 034	53.390 730	.018 729 8432	.807 732	43.125 426	.023 188 1766	27.83	.113 032	2.83	48
5	1.305 917	68.616 894	.014 573 6705	.765 745	52.543 075	.019 032 0038	22.84	.141 920	2.84	60
6	1.377 522	84.677 932	.011 809 4523	.725 941	61.471 181	.016 267 7856	19.53	.171 281	2.85	72
7	1.453 054	101.619 622	.009 840 6192	.688 206	69.935 193	.014 298 9525	17.16	.201 112	2.87	84
8	1.532 727	119.490 251	.008 368 8836	.652 432	77.959 234	.012 827 2169	15.40	.231 413	2.89	96
9	1.616 769	138.340 755	.007 228 5279	.618 517	85.566 174	.011 686 8612	14.03	.262 181	2.91	108
10	1.705 419	158.224 861	.006 320 1193	.586 366	92.777 696	.010 778 4527	12.94	.293 414	2.93	120
11	1.798 930	179.199 243	.005 580 3807	.555 886	99.614 353	.010 038 7140	12.05	.325 110	2.96	132
12	1.897 568	201.323 684	.004 967 1255	.526 990	106.095 631	.009 425 4588	11.32	.357 266	2.98	144
13	2.001 615	224.661 242	.004 451 1460	.499 597	112.240 004	.008 909 4794	10.70	.389 879	3.00	156
14	2.111 366	249.278 435	.004 011 5785	.473 627	118.064 984	.008 469 9118	10.17	.422 945	3.02	168
15	2.227 136	275.245 427	.003 633 1212	.449 007	123.587 174	.008 091 4545	9.71	.456 462	3.04	180
16	2.349 253	302.636 229	.003 304 2970	.425 667	128.822 313	.007 762 6304	9.32	.490 425	3.07	192
17	2.478 066	331.528 912	.003 016 3282	.403 540	133.785 322	.007 474 6615	8.97	.524 831	3.09	204
18	2.613 943	362.005 826	.002 762 3865	.382 564	138.490 348	.007 220 7198	8.67	.559 675	3.11	216
19	2.757 269	394.153 836	.002 537 0805	.362 678	142.950 800	.006 995 4138	8.40	.594 954	3.13	228
20	2.908 455	428.064 572	.002 336 0962	.343 825	147.179 392	.006 794 4295	8.16	.630 663	3.15	240
21	3.067 930	463.834 686	.002 155 9405	.325 953	151.188 176	.006 614 2739	7.94	.666 797	3.18	252
22	3.236 149	501.566 131	.001 993 7550	.309 009	154.988 578	.006 452 0884	7.75	.703 351	3.20	264
23	3.413 592	541.366 450	.001 847 1776	.292 947	158.591 430	.006 305 5110	7.57	.740 321	3.22	276
24	3.600 765	583.349 083	.001 714 2394	.277 719	162.007 001	.006 172 5728	7.41	.777 701	3.24	288
25	3.798 200	627.633 689	.001 593 2860	.263 283	165.245 026	.006 051 6194	7.27	.815 486	3.26	300
26	4.006 461	674.346 488	.001 482 9172	.249 597	168.314 734	.005 941 2505	7.13	.853 670	3.28	312
27	4.226 142	723.620 624	.001 381 9396	.236 622	171.224 874	.005 840 2729	7.01	.892 248	3.30	324
28	4.457 868	775.596 536	.001 289 3302	.224 322	173.983 742	.005 747 6635	6.90	.931 215	3.33	336
29	4.702 300	830.422 369	.001 204 2065	.212 662	176.599 200	.005 662 5398	6.80	.970 564	3.35	348
30	4.960 134	888.254 388	.001 125 8036	.201 607	179.078 703	.005 584 1369	6.71	1.010 289	3.37	360
31	5.232 106	949.257 427	.001 053 4550	.191 128	181.429 318	.005 511 7884	6.62	1.050 385	3.39	372
32	5.518 991	1013.605 357	.000 986 5773	.181 193	183.657 745	.005 444 9106	6.54	1.090 846	3.41	384
33	5.821 605	1081.481 584	.000 924 6574	.171 774	185.770 335	.005 382 9908	6.46	1.131 664	3.43	396
34	6.140 813	1153.079 570	.000 867 2428	.162 845	187.773 110	.005 325 5762	6.40	1.172 835	3.45	408
35	6.477 523	1228.603 386	.000 813 9323	.154 380	189.671 778	.005 272 2656	6.33	1.214 352	3.47	420
36	6.832 696	1308.268 290	.000 764 3692	.146 355	191.471 751	.005 222 7025	6.27	1.256 207	3.49	432
37	7.207 343	1392.301 345	.000 718 2353	.138 747	193.178 159	.005 176 5687	6.22	1.298 396	3.51	444
38	7.602 533	1480.942 063	.000 675 2459	.131 535	194.795 865	.005 133 5792	6.17	1.340 912	3.53	456
39	8.019 392	1574.443 090	.000 635 1452	.124 698	196.329 481	.005 093 4786	6.12	1.383 748	3.55	468
40	8.459 108	1673.070 923	.000 597 7033	.118 216	197.783 377	.005 056 0366	6.07	1.426 898	3.57	480
41	8.922 934	1777.106 674	.000 562 7124	.112 071	199.161 698	.005 021 0458	6.03	1.470 355	3.59	492
42	9.412 192	1886.846 868	.000 529 9847	.106 245	200.468 372	.004 988 3180	5.99	1.514 112	3.61	504
43	9.928 277	2002.604 287	.000 499 3498	.100 722	201.707 124	.004 957 6831	5.95	1.558 164	3.62	516
44	10.472 660	2124.708 866	.000 470 6527	.095 487	202.881 483	.004 928 9861	5.92	1.602 505	3.64	528
45	11.046 893	2253.508 629	.000 443 7525	.090 523	203.994 798	.004 902 0858	5.89	1.647 126	3.66	540
46	11.652 611	2389.370 684	.000 418 5202	.085 818	205.050 241	.004 876 8536	5.86	1.692 023	3.68	552
47	12.291 542	2532.682 266	.000 394 8303	.081 357	206.050 820	.004 853 1716	5.83	1.737 189	3.70	564
48	12.965 506	2683.851 846	.000 372 5988	.077 128	206.999 389	.004 830 9321	5.80	1.782 617	3.71	576
49	13.676 425	2843.310 290	.000 351 7027	.073 119	207.898 649	.004 810 0361	5.78	1.828 301	3.73	588
50	14.426 325	3011.512 088	.000 332 0591	.069 318	208.751 165	.004 790 3924	5.75	1.874 235	3.75	600

Effective Rate is 5.48 %

Annual Percentage Rate is 5.35 %

	Amount Of 1	Amount Of 1 Per Period	Sinking Fund Payment	Present Worth Of 1	Present Worth of 1 Per Period	Periodic Payment To Amortize 1	Constant Annual Percent	Total Interest	Annual Add On Rate
	What a single $ 1 deposit grows to in the future. The deposit is made at the beginning of the first period.	What a series of $ 1 deposits grow to in the future. A deposit is made at the end of each period.	The amount to be deposited at the end of each period that grows to $ 1 in the future.	What $ 1 to be paid in the future is worth today. Value today of a single $ 1 payment tomorrow.	What $ 1 to be paid at the end of each period is worth today. Value today of a series of $ 1 payments tomorrow.	The mortgage payment to amortize a loan of $ 1. An annuity certain, payable at the end of each period, worth $ 1 today.	The annual payment, including interest and principal, to amortize completely a loan of $ 100.	The total interest paid over the term on a loan of $1. The loan is amortized by regular periodic payments.	The average annual interest rate on a loan that is completely amortized by regular periodic payments.
	$S = (1+i)^n$	$S\overline{n}| = \dfrac{(1+i)^n - 1}{i}$	$\dfrac{1}{S\overline{n}|} = \dfrac{i}{(1+i)^n - 1}$	$V^n = \dfrac{1}{(1+i)^n}$	$A\overline{n}| = \dfrac{1 - V^n}{i}$	$\dfrac{1}{A\overline{n}|} = \dfrac{i}{1 - V^n}$			

YEAR									PERIODS
	1.004 479	1.000 000	1.000 000 0000	.995 541	.995 541	1.004 479 1667	1205.38	.004 479	5.38	1
	1.008 978	2.004 479	.498 882 7106	.991 101	1.986 642	.503 361 8773	604.04	.006 724	4.03	2
	1.013 498	3.013 458	.331 844 7262	.986 682	2.973 324	.336 323 8929	403.59	.008 972	3.59	3
	1.018 037	4.026 955	.248 326 5681	.982 282	3.955 606	.252 805 7348	303.37	.011 223	3.37	4
	1.022 597	5.044 993	.198 216 3405	.977 902	4.933 508	.202 695 5072	243.24	.013 478	3.23	5
	1.027 178	6.067 590	.164 810 0781	.973 541	5.907 050	.169 289 2448	203.15	.015 735	3.15	6
	1.031 779	7.094 768	.140 948 9387	.969 200	6.876 250	.145 428 1054	174.52	.017 997	3.09	7
	1.036 400	8.126 547	.123 053 5012	.964 878	7.841 128	.127 532 6679	153.04	.020 261	3.04	8
	1.041 042	9.162 947	.109 135 1982	.960 576	8.801 704	.113 614 3649	136.34	.022 529	3.00	9
	1.045 705	10.203 989	.098 000 8894	.956 292	9.757 996	.102 480 0561	122.98	.024 801	2.98	10
	1.050 389	11.249 694	.088 891 3036	.952 028	10.710 024	.093 370 4703	112.05	.027 075	2.95	11
	1.055 094	12.300 084	.081 300 2601	.947 783	11.657 807	.085 779 4268	102.94	.029 353	2.94	12
1	1.055 094	12.300 084	.081 300 2601	.947 783	11.657 807	.085 779 4268	102.94	.029 353	2.94	12
2	1.113 224	25.277 830	.039 560 3584	.898 292	22.706 875	.044 039 5251	52.85	.056 949	2.85	24
3	1.174 556	38.970 573	.025 660 3873	.851 386	33.178 991	.030 139 5539	36.17	.085 024	2.83	36
4	1.239 267	53.417 706	.018 720 3844	.806 929	43.104 282	.023 199 5511	27.84	.113 578	2.84	48
5	1.307 543	68.660 792	.014 564 3529	.764 793	52.511 302	.019 043 5195	22.86	.142 611	2.85	60
6	1.379 581	84.743 682	.011 800 2898	.724 858	61.427 112	.016 279 4564	19.54	.172 121	2.87	72
7	1.455 588	101.712 644	.009 831 6193	.687 008	69.877 364	.014 310 7860	17.18	.202 106	2.89	84
8	1.535 782	119.616 497	.008 360 0509	.651 134	77.886 366	.012 839 2175	15.41	.232 565	2.91	96
9	1.620 395	138.506 747	.007 219 8649	.617 134	85.477 161	.011 699 0316	14.04	.263 495	2.93	108
10	1.709 669	158.437 739	.006 311 6276	.584 909	92.671 584	.010 790 7942	12.95	.294 895	2.95	120
11	1.803 862	179.466 811	.005 572 0609	.554 366	99.490 335	.010 051 2276	12.07	.326 762	2.97	132
12	1.903 244	201.654 461	.004 958 9778	.525 419	105.953 029	.009 438 1445	11.33	.359 093	2.99	144
13	2.008 102	225.064 521	.004 443 1703	.497 983	112.078 259	.008 922 3370	10.71	.391 885	3.01	156
14	2.118 736	249.764 337	.004 003 7742	.471 979	117.883 647	.008 482 9408	10.18	.425 134	3.04	168
15	2.235 466	275.824 969	.003 625 4876	.447 334	123.385 893	.008 104 6543	9.73	.458 838	3.06	180
16	2.358 627	303.321 387	.003 296 8331	.423 975	128.600 826	.007 775 9998	9.34	.492 992	3.08	192
17	2.488 574	332.332 697	.003 009 0328	.401 837	133.543 451	.007 488 1995	8.99	.527 593	3.10	204
18	2.625 679	362.942 360	.002 755 2584	.380 854	138.227 984	.007 234 4251	8.69	.562 636	3.13	216
19	2.770 339	395.238 435	.002 530 1183	.360 967	142.667 905	.007 009 2850	8.42	.598 117	3.15	228
20	2.922 968	429.313 835	.002 329 2983	.342 118	146.875 985	.006 808 4650	8.18	.634 032	3.17	240
21	3.084 007	465.266 588	.002 149 3054	.324 254	150.864 330	.006 628 4721	7.96	.670 375	3.19	252
22	3.253 917	503.200 127	.001 987 2809	.307 322	154.644 415	.006 466 4476	7.76	.707 142	3.21	264
23	3.433 189	543.223 582	.001 840 8626	.291 274	158.227 114	.006 320 0293	7.59	.744 328	3.24	276
24	3.622 338	585.452 093	.001 708 0817	.276 065	161.622 735	.006 187 2484	7.43	.781 928	3.26	288
25	3.821 907	630.007 147	.001 587 2836	.261 649	164.841 045	.006 066 4502	7.28	.819 935	3.28	300
26	4.032 472	677.016 923	.001 477 0680	.247 987	167.891 305	.005 956 2346	7.15	.858 345	3.30	312
27	4.254 637	726.616 662	.001 376 2415	.235 038	170.782 288	.005 855 4082	7.03	.897 152	3.32	324
28	4.489 043	778.949 054	.001 283 7810	.222 765	173.522 311	.005 762 9477	6.92	.936 350	3.34	336
29	4.736 363	834.164 654	.001 198 8041	.211 132	176.119 259	.005 677 9708	6.82	.975 934	3.37	348
30	4.997 308	892.422 309	.001 120 5457	.200 108	178.580 600	.005 599 7124	6.72	1.015 896	3.39	360
31	5.272 631	953.889 619	.001 048 3393	.189 659	180.913 418	.005 527 5060	6.64	1.056 232	3.41	372
32	5.563 122	1018.743 416	.000 981 6014	.179 755	183.124 422	.005 460 7681	6.56	1.096 935	3.43	384
33	5.869 617	1087.170 277	.000 919 8191	.170 369	185.219 973	.005 398 9858	6.48	1.137 998	3.45	396
34	6.192 998	1159.367 055	.000 862 5396	.161 473	187.206 100	.005 341 7063	6.42	1.179 416	3.47	408
35	6.534 196	1235.541 452	.000 809 3618	.153 041	189.088 518	.005 288 5284	6.35	1.221 182	3.49	420
36	6.894 192	1315.912 610	.000 759 9289	.145 050	190.872 640	.005 239 0955	6.29	1.263 289	3.51	432
37	7.274 021	1400.711 747	.000 713 9228	.137 476	192.563 601	.005 193 0894	6.24	1.305 732	3.53	444
38	7.674 777	1490.182 819	.000 671 0586	.130 297	194.166 264	.005 150 2253	6.19	1.348 503	3.55	456
39	8.097 612	1584.583 220	.000 631 0808	.123 493	195.685 241	.005 110 2474	6.14	1.391 596	3.57	468
40	8.543 743	1684.184 529	.000 593 7592	.117 045	197.124 901	.005 072 9258	6.09	1.435 004	3.59	480
41	9.014 453	1789.273 286	.000 558 8861	.110 933	198.489 385	.005 038 0528	6.05	1.478 722	3.61	492
42	9.511 097	1900.151 815	.000 526 2737	.105 140	199.782 620	.005 005 4404	6.01	1.522 742	3.63	504
43	10.035 102	2017.139 099	.000 495 7516	.099 650	201.008 326	.004 974 9183	5.97	1.567 058	3.64	516
44	10.587 977	2140.571 696	.000 467 1649	.094 447	202.170 029	.004 946 3316	5.94	1.611 663	3.66	528
45	11.171 313	2270.804 704	.000 440 3725	.089 515	203.271 071	.004 919 5392	5.91	1.656 551	3.68	540
46	11.786 786	2408.212 785	.000 415 2457	.084 841	204.314 619	.004 894 4124	5.88	1.701 716	3.70	552
47	12.436 169	2553.191 244	.000 391 6667	.080 411	205.303 677	.004 870 8334	5.85	1.747 150	3.72	564
48	13.121 329	2706.157 164	.000 369 5277	.076 212	206.241 088	.004 848 6944	5.82	1.792 848	3.74	576
49	13.844 237	2867.550 608	.000 348 7297	.072 232	207.129 551	.004 827 8963	5.80	1.838 803	3.75	588
50	14.606 973	3037.835 882	.000 329 1817	.068 460	207.971 620	.004 808 3484	5.78	1.885 009	3.77	600

Effective Rate is 5.51 %

Annual Percentage Rate is 5.375%

MONTHLY COMPOUND INTEREST AND ANNUITY

5.40 % M

	Amount Of 1	Amount Of 1 Per Period	Sinking Fund Payment	Present Worth Of 1	Present Worth of 1 Per Period	Periodic Payment To Amortize 1	Constant Annual Percent	Total Interest	Annual Add On Rate	
	What a single $1 deposit grows to in the future. The deposit is made at the beginning of the first period.	What a series of $1 deposits grow to in the future. A deposit is made at the end of each period.	The amount to be deposited at the end of each period that grows to $1 in the future.	What $1 to be paid in the future is worth today. Value today of a single $1 payment tomorrow.	What $1 to be paid at the end of each period is worth today. Value today of a series of $1 payments tomorrow.	The mortgage payment to amortize a loan of $1. An annuity certain, payable at the end of each period, worth $1 today.	The annual payment, including interest and principal, to amortize completely a loan of $100.	The total interest paid over the term on a loan of $1. The loan is amortized by regular periodic payments.	The average annual interest rate on a loan that is completely amortized by regular periodic payments.	
	$S = (1+i)^n$	$S\overline{n}| = \dfrac{(1+i)^n - 1}{i}$	$\dfrac{1}{S\overline{n}|} = \dfrac{i}{(1+i)^n - 1}$	$V^n = \dfrac{1}{(1+i)^n}$	$A\overline{n}| = \dfrac{1-V^n}{i}$	$\dfrac{1}{A\overline{n}|} = \dfrac{i}{1-V^n}$				

YEAR / **PERIODS**

YEAR	Amount Of 1	Amount Of 1 Per Period	Sinking Fund Payment	Present Worth Of 1	Present Worth of 1 Per Period	Periodic Payment To Amortize 1	Constant Annual Percent	Total Interest	Annual Add On Rate	PERIODS
	1.004 500	1.000 000	1.000 000 0000	.995 520	.995 520	1.004 500 0000	1205.40	.004 500	5.40	1
	1.009 020	2.004 500	.498 877 5256	.991 060	1.986 581	.503 377 5256	604.06	.006 755	4.05	2
	1.013 561	3.013 520	.331 837 8232	.986 621	2.973 201	.336 337 8232	403.61	.009 013	3.61	3
	1.018 122	4.027 081	.248 318 8139	.982 201	3.955 402	.252 818 8139	303.39	.011 275	3.38	4
	1.022 703	5.045 203	.198 208 0818	.977 801	4.933 202	.202 708 0818	243.25	.013 540	3.25	5
	1.027 306	6.067 906	.164 801 4882	.973 420	5.906 623	.169 301 4882	203.17	.015 809	3.16	6
	1.031 928	7.095 212	.140 940 1167	.969 059	6.875 682	.145 440 1167	174.53	.018 081	3.10	7
	1.036 572	8.127 140	.123 044 5090	.964 718	7.840 400	.127 544 5090	153.06	.020 356	3.05	8
	1.041 237	9.163 713	.109 126 0770	.960 396	8.800 797	.113 626 0770	136.36	.022 635	3.02	9
	1.045 922	10.204 949	.097 991 6682	.956 094	9.756 891	.102 491 6682	123.00	.024 917	2.99	10
	1.050 629	11.250 872	.088 882 0034	.951 811	10.708 702	.093 382 0034	112.06	.027 202	2.97	11
	1.055 357	12.301 500	.081 290 8966	.947 547	11.656 248	.085 790 8966	102.95	.029 491	2.95	12
1	1.055 357	12.301 500	.081 290 8966	.947 547	11.656 248	.085 790 8966	102.95	.029 491	2.95	12
2	1.113 778	25.283 972	.039 550 7478	.897 845	22.701 090	.044 050 7478	52.87	.057 218	2.86	24
3	1.175 433	38.985 111	.025 650 8184	.850 750	33.166 596	.030 150 8184	36.19	.085 429	2.85	36
4	1.240 501	53.444 701	.018 710 9291	.806 126	43.083 153	.023 210 9291	27.86	.114 125	2.85	48
5	1.309 171	68.704 726	.014 555 0395	.763 842	52.479 555	.019 055 0395	22.87	.143 302	2.87	60
6	1.381 643	84.809 497	.011 791 1323	.723 776	61.383 087	.016 291 1323	19.55	.172 962	2.88	72
7	1.458 126	101.805 776	.009 822 6254	.685 812	69.819 602	.014 322 6254	17.19	.203 101	2.90	84
8	1.538 843	119.742 913	.008 351 2249	.649 839	77.813 594	.012 851 2249	15.43	.233 718	2.92	96
9	1.624 028	138.672 992	.007 211 2095	.615 753	85.388 277	.011 711 2095	14.06	.264 811	2.94	108
10	1.713 929	158.650 979	.006 303 1442	.583 455	92.565 644	.010 803 1442	12.97	.296 377	2.96	120
11	1.808 807	179.734 882	.005 563 7503	.552 851	99.366 536	.010 063 7503	12.08	.328 415	2.99	132
12	1.908 937	201.985 922	.004 950 8401	.523 852	105.810 699	.009 450 8401	11.35	.360 921	3.01	144
13	2.014 609	225.468 707	.004 435 2053	.496 374	111.916 847	.008 935 2053	10.73	.393 892	3.03	156
14	2.126 131	250.251 423	.003 995 9813	.470 338	117.702 708	.008 495 9813	10.20	.427 325	3.05	168
15	2.243 827	276.406 029	.003 617 8661	.445 667	123.185 082	.008 117 8661	9.75	.461 216	3.07	180
16	2.368 038	304.008 470	.003 289 3820	.422 291	128.379 889	.007 789 3820	9.35	.495 561	3.10	192
17	2.499 125	333.138 892	.003 001 7510	.400 140	133.302 212	.007 501 7510	9.01	.530 357	3.12	204
18	2.637 468	363.881 879	.002 748 1445	.379 151	137.966 344	.007 248 1445	8.70	.565 599	3.14	216
19	2.783 470	396.326 698	.002 523 1709	.359 264	142.385 827	.007 023 1709	8.43	.601 283	3.16	228
20	2.937 554	430.567 558	.002 322 5159	.340 419	146.573 495	.006 822 5159	8.19	.637 404	3.19	240
21	3.100 167	466.703 880	.002 142 6863	.322 563	150.541 507	.006 642 6863	7.98	.673 957	3.21	252
22	3.271 783	504.840 591	.001 980 8233	.305 644	154.301 384	.006 480 8233	7.78	.710 937	3.23	264
23	3.452 898	545.088 427	.001 834 5647	.289 612	157.864 043	.006 334 5647	7.61	.748 340	3.25	276
24	3.644 039	587.564 252	.001 701 9415	.274 421	161.239 830	.006 201 9415	7.45	.786 159	3.28	288
25	3.845 761	632.391 401	.001 581 2992	.260 027	164.438 547	.006 081 2992	7.30	.824 390	3.30	300
26	4.058 650	679.700 035	.001 471 2372	.246 387	167.469 481	.005 971 2372	7.17	.863 026	3.32	312
27	4.283 324	729.627 522	.001 370 5623	.233 464	170.341 433	.005 870 5623	7.05	.902 062	3.34	324
28	4.520 435	782.318 832	.001 278 2512	.221 218	173.062 742	.005 778 2512	6.94	.941 492	3.36	336
29	4.770 671	837.926 962	.001 193 4214	.209 614	175.641 310	.005 693 4214	6.84	.981 311	3.38	348
30	5.034 760	896.613 378	.001 115 3079	.198 619	178.084 624	.005 615 3079	6.74	1.021 511	3.41	360
31	5.313 468	958.548 482	.001 043 2440	.188 201	180.399 779	.005 543 2440	6.66	1.062 087	3.43	372
32	5.607 605	1023.912 113	.000 976 6463	.178 329	182.593 496	.005 476 6463	6.58	1.103 032	3.45	384
33	5.918 023	1092.894 063	.000 915 0018	.168 975	184.672 147	.005 415 0018	6.50	1.144 341	3.47	396
34	6.245 626	1165.694 629	.000 857 8576	.160 112	186.641 765	.005 357 8576	6.43	1.186 006	3.49	408
35	6.591 363	1242.525 197	.000 804 8127	.151 714	188.508 071	.005 304 8127	6.37	1.228 021	3.51	420
36	6.956 240	1323.608 857	.000 755 5102	.143 756	190.276 483	.005 255 5102	6.31	1.270 380	3.53	432
37	7.341 315	1409.181 045	.000 709 6320	.136 215	191.952 137	.005 209 6320	6.26	1.313 077	3.55	444
38	7.747 706	1499.490 231	.000 666 8933	.129 070	193.539 897	.005 166 8933	6.21	1.356 103	3.57	456
39	8.176 594	1594.798 640	.000 627 0384	.122 300	195.044 375	.005 127 0384	6.16	1.399 454	3.59	468
40	8.629 224	1695.383 013	.000 589 8372	.115 885	196.469 937	.005 089 8372	6.11	1.443 122	3.61	480
41	9.106 909	1801.535 410	.000 555 0821	.109 807	197.820 725	.005 055 0821	6.07	1.487 100	3.63	492
42	9.611 038	1913.564 060	.000 522 5851	.104 047	199.100 660	.005 022 5851	6.03	1.531 383	3.65	504
43	10.143 074	2031.794 251	.000 492 1758	.098 589	200.313 458	.004 992 1758	6.00	1.575 963	3.67	516
44	10.704 562	2156.569 282	.000 463 6995	.093 418	201.462 641	.004 963 6995	5.96	1.620 833	3.68	528
45	11.297 132	2288.251 453	.000 437 0149	.088 518	202.551 546	.004 937 0149	5.93	1.665 988	3.70	540
46	11.922 504	2427.223 122	.000 411 9934	.083 875	203.583 334	.004 911 9934	5.90	1.711 420	3.72	552
47	12.582 495	2573.887 810	.000 388 5173	.079 475	204.561 002	.004 888 5173	5.87	1.757 124	3.74	564
48	13.279 021	2728.671 380	.000 366 4787	.075 307	205.487 388	.004 866 4787	5.84	1.803 092	3.76	576
49	14.014 105	2892.023 265	.000 345 7787	.071 357	206.365 182	.004 845 7787	5.82	1.849 318	3.77	588
50	14.789 880	3064.417 780	.000 326 3263	.067 614	207.196 933	.004 826 3263	5.80	1.895 796	3.79	600

Effective Rate is 5.54 %

Annual Percentage Rate is 5.40 %

	Amount Of 1	Amount Of 1 Per Period	Sinking Fund Payment	Present Worth Of 1	Present Worth of 1 Per Period	Periodic Payment To Amortize 1	Constant Annual Percent	Total Interest	Annual Add On Rate
	What a single $ 1 deposit grows to in the future. The deposit is made at the beginning of the first period.	What a series of $ 1 deposits grow to in the future. A deposit is made at the end of each period.	The amount to be deposited at the end of each period that grows to $ 1 in the future.	What $ 1 to be paid in the future is worth today. Value today of a single $ 1 payment tomorrow.	What $ 1 to be paid at the end of each period is worth today. Value today of a series of $ 1 payments tomorrow.	The mortgage payment to amortize a loan of $ 1. An annuity certain, payable at the end of each period, worth $ 1 today.	The annual payment, including interest and principal, to amortize completely a loan of $ 100.	The total interest paid over the term on a loan of $1. The loan is amortized by regular periodic payments.	The average annual interest rate on a loan that is completely amortized by regular periodic payments.
	$S = (1+i)^n$	$S\overline{n} = \dfrac{(1+i)^n - 1}{i}$	$\dfrac{1}{S\overline{n}} = \dfrac{i}{(1+i)^n - 1}$	$V^n = \dfrac{1}{(1+i)^n}$	$A\overline{n} = \dfrac{1 - V^n}{i}$	$\dfrac{1}{A\overline{n}} = \dfrac{i}{1 - V^n}$			

YEAR									PERIODS
	1.004 542	1.000 000	1.000 000 0000	.995 479	.995 479	1.004 541 6667	1205.45	.004 542	5.45	1
	1.009 104	2.004 542	.498 867 1558	.990 978	1.986 457	.503 408 8225	604.10	.006 818	4.09	2
	1.013 687	3.013 646	.331 824 0178	.986 498	2.972 955	.336 365 6844	403.64	.009 097	3.64	3
	1.018 291	4.027 333	.248 303 3062	.982 038	3.954 993	.252 844 9729	303.42	.011 380	3.41	4
	1.022 916	5.045 623	.198 191 5653	.977 598	4.932 590	.202 733 2319	243.28	.013 666	3.28	5
	1.027 561	6.068 539	.164 784 3096	.973 178	5.905 768	.169 325 9763	203.20	.015 956	3.19	6
	1.032 228	7.096 100	.140 922 4741	.968 778	6.874 547	.145 464 1408	174.56	.018 249	3.13	7
	1.036 916	8.128 328	.123 026 5262	.964 398	7.838 945	.127 568 1928	153.09	.020 546	3.08	8
	1.041 625	9.165 245	.109 107 8366	.960 038	8.798 983	.113 649 5033	136.38	.022 846	3.05	9
	1.046 356	10.206 870	.097 973 2279	.955 697	9.754 680	.102 514 8946	123.02	.025 149	3.02	10
	1.051 108	11.253 226	.088 863 4053	.951 377	10.706 057	.093 405 0720	112.09	.027 456	3.00	11
	1.055 882	12.304 335	.081 272 1722	.947 075	11.653 132	.085 813 8389	102.98	.029 766	2.98	12
1	1.055 882	12.304 335	.081 272 1722	.947 075	11.653 132	.085 813 8389	102.98	.029 766	2.98	12
2	1.114 887	25.296 262	.039 531 5319	.896 952	22.689 526	.044 073 1986	52.89	.057 757	2.89	24
3	1.177 190	39.014 207	.025 631 6883	.849 481	33.141 823	.030 173 3549	36.21	.086 241	2.87	36
4	1.242 973	53.498 741	.018 692 0286	.804 522	43.040 936	.023 233 6953	27.89	.115 217	2.88	48
5	1.312 434	68.792 702	.014 536 4256	.761 943	52.416 142	.019 078 0923	22.90	.144 686	2.89	60
6	1.385 775	84.941 324	.011 772 8328	.721 618	61.295 169	.016 314 4995	19.58	.174 644	2.91	72
7	1.463 215	101.992 365	.009 804 6555	.683 426	69.704 276	.014 346 3221	17.22	.205 091	2.93	84
8	1.544 983	119.996 256	.008 333 5933	.647 256	77.668 334	.012 875 2600	15.46	.236 025	2.95	96
9	1.631 320	139.006 244	.007 193 9215	.613 001	85.210 898	.011 735 5881	14.09	.267 444	2.97	108
10	1.722 482	159.078 551	.006 286 2026	.580 558	92.354 274	.010 827 8693	13.00	.299 344	2.99	120
11	1.818 738	180.272 543	.005 547 1565	.549 832	99.119 589	.010 088 8231	12.11	.331 725	3.02	132
12	1.920 373	202.650 901	.004 934 5944	.520 732	105.526 852	.009 476 2611	11.38	.364 582	3.04	144
13	2.027 687	226.279 811	.004 419 3072	.493 173	111.595 013	.008 960 9739	10.76	.397 912	3.06	156
14	2.140 999	251.229 156	.003 980 4297	.467 072	117.342 019	.008 522 0964	10.23	.431 712	3.08	168
15	2.260 643	277.572 726	.003 602 6594	.442 352	122.784 867	.008 144 3261	9.78	.465 979	3.11	180
16	2.386 972	305.388 431	.003 274 5183	.418 941	127.939 654	.007 816 1849	9.38	.500 708	3.13	192
17	2.520 362	334.758 539	.002 987 2278	.396 768	132.821 626	.007 528 8944	9.04	.535 894	3.15	204
18	2.661 205	365.769 912	.002 733 9592	.375 770	137.445 221	.007 275 6258	8.74	.571 535	3.18	216
19	2.809 919	398.514 269	.002 509 3204	.355 882	141.824 114	.007 050 9871	8.47	.607 625	3.20	228
20	2.966 943	433.088 452	.002 308 9971	.337 047	145.971 256	.006 850 6638	8.23	.644 159	3.22	240
21	3.132 743	469.594 717	.002 129 4958	.319 209	149.898 912	.006 671 1625	8.01	.681 133	3.24	252
22	3.307 807	508.141 031	.001 967 9576	.302 315	153.618 697	.006 509 6243	7.82	.718 541	3.27	264
23	3.492 655	548.841 397	.001 822 0200	.286 315	157.141 615	.006 363 6867	7.64	.756 378	3.29	276
24	3.687 832	591.816 189	.001 689 7138	.271 162	160.478 084	.006 231 3805	7.48	.794 638	3.31	288
25	3.893 916	637.192 506	.001 569 3844	.256 811	163.637 971	.006 111 0511	7.34	.833 315	3.33	300
26	4.111 517	685.104 551	.001 459 6312	.243 219	166.630 622	.006 001 2979	7.21	.872 405	3.36	312
27	4.341 277	735.694 025	.001 359 2607	.230 347	169.464 888	.005 900 9274	7.09	.911 900	3.38	324
28	4.583 877	789.110 551	.001 267 2496	.218 156	172.149 152	.005 808 9162	6.98	.951 796	3.40	336
29	4.840 034	845.512 108	.001 182 7152	.206 610	174.691 351	.005 724 3818	6.87	.992 085	3.42	348
30	5.110 506	905.065 508	.001 104 8924	.195 675	177.099 006	.005 646 5591	6.78	1.032 761	3.44	360
31	5.396 092	967.946 881	.001 033 1145	.185 319	179.379 237	.005 574 7812	6.69	1.073 819	3.46	372
32	5.697 638	1034.342 204	.000 966 7980	.175 511	181.538 787	.005 508 4647	6.62	1.115 250	3.49	384
33	6.016 034	1104.447 842	.000 905 4208	.166 222	183.584 044	.005 447 0965	6.54	1.157 050	3.51	396
34	6.352 223	1178.471 137	.000 848 5571	.157 425	185.521 056	.005 390 2237	6.47	1.199 211	3.53	408
35	6.707 199	1256.631 015	.000 795 7785	.149 094	187.355 553	.005 337 4452	6.41	1.241 727	3.55	420
36	7.082 012	1339.158 638	.000 746 7375	.141 203	189.092 960	.005 288 4042	6.35	1.284 591	3.57	432
37	7.477 770	1426.298 085	.000 701 1157	.133 730	190.738 415	.005 242 7824	6.30	1.327 795	3.59	444
38	7.895 645	1518.307 075	.000 658 6283	.126 652	192.296 785	.005 200 2950	6.25	1.371 335	3.61	456
39	8.336 871	1615.457 729	.000 619 0196	.119 949	193.772 678	.005 160 6863	6.20	1.415 201	3.63	468
40	8.802 753	1718.037 373	.000 582 0595	.113 601	195.170 461	.005 123 7262	6.15	1.459 389	3.65	480
41	9.294 670	1826.349 392	.000 547 5404	.107 589	196.494 266	.005 089 2070	6.11	1.503 890	3.67	492
42	9.814 077	1940.714 123	.000 515 2742	.101 894	197.748 010	.005 056 9409	6.07	1.548 698	3.69	504
43	10.362 509	2061.469 806	.000 485 0908	.096 502	198.935 399	.005 026 7574	6.04	1.593 807	3.71	516
44	10.941 588	2188.973 580	.000 456 8351	.091 394	200.059 947	.004 998 5018	6.00	1.639 209	3.73	528
45	11.553 028	2323.602 544	.000 430 3662	.086 557	201.124 978	.004 972 0329	5.97	1.684 898	3.74	540
46	12.198 637	2465.754 869	.000 405 5553	.081 976	202.133 642	.004 947 2220	5.94	1.730 867	3.76	552
47	12.880 323	2615.850 977	.000 382 2848	.077 638	203.088 924	.004 923 9514	5.91	1.777 109	3.78	564
48	13.600 104	2774.334 783	.000 360 4468	.073 529	203.993 648	.004 902 1134	5.89	1.823 617	3.80	576
49	14.360 107	2941.675 011	.000 339 9424	.069 637	204.850 489	.004 881 6090	5.86	1.870 386	3.82	588
50	15.162 582	3118.366 576	.000 320 6807	.065 952	205.661 982	.004 862 3474	5.84	1.917 408	3.83	600

	Amount Of 1	Amount Of 1 Per Period	Sinking Fund Payment	Present Worth Of 1	Present Worth of 1 Per Period	Periodic Payment To Amortize 1	Constant Annual Percent	Total Interest	Annual Add On Rate	
	What a single $ 1 deposit grows to in the future. The deposit is made at the beginning of the first period.	What a series of $ 1 deposits grow to in the future. A deposit is made at the end of each period.	The amount to be deposited at the end of each period that grows to $ 1 in the future.	What $ 1 to be paid in the future is worth today. Value today of a single $ 1 payment tomorrow.	What $ 1 to be paid at the end of each period is worth today. Value today of a series of $ 1 payments tomorrow.	The mortgage payment to amortize a loan of $ 1. An annuity certain, payable at the end of each period, worth $ 1 today.	The annual payment, including interest and principal, to amortize completely a loan of $ 100.	The total interest paid over the term on a loan of $1. The loan is amortized by regular periodic payments.	The average annual interest rate on a loan that is completely amortized by regular periodic payments.	
	$S = (1+i)^n$	$S\overline{n} = \dfrac{(1+i)^n - 1}{i}$	$\dfrac{1}{S\overline{n}} = \dfrac{i}{(1+i)^n - 1}$	$V^n = \dfrac{1}{(1+i)^n}$	$A\overline{n} = \dfrac{1-V^n}{i}$	$\dfrac{1}{A\overline{n}} = \dfrac{i}{1-V^n}$				

YEAR   **PERIODS**

YEAR	Amount Of 1	Amount Of 1 Per Period	Sinking Fund Payment	Present Worth Of 1	Present Worth of 1 Per Period	Periodic Payment To Amortize 1	Constant Annual Percent	Total Interest	Annual Add On Rate	PERIODS
	1.004 583	1.000 000	1.000 000 0000	.995 438	.995 438	1.004 583 3333	1205.50	.004 583	5.50	1
	1.009 188	2.004 583	.498 856 7865	.990 896	1.986 334	.503 440 1199	604.13	.006 880	4.13	2
	1.013 813	3.013 771	.331 810 2131	.986 375	2.972 709	.336 393 5464	403.68	.009 181	3.67	3
	1.018 460	4.027 584	.248 287 7996	.981 875	3.954 583	.252 871 1330	303.45	.011 485	3.45	4
	1.023 128	5.046 044	.198 175 0502	.977 395	4.931 979	.202 758 3835	243.32	.013 792	3.31	5
	1.027 817	6.069 172	.164 767 1327	.972 936	5.904 914	.169 350 4660	203.23	.016 103	3.22	6
	1.032 528	7.096 989	.140 904 8335	.968 497	6.873 411	.145 488 1668	174.59	.018 417	3.16	7
	1.037 260	8.129 516	.123 008 5457	.964 078	7.837 489	.127 591 8790	153.12	.020 735	3.11	8
	1.042 014	9.166 777	.109 089 5988	.959 680	8.797 169	.113 672 9321	136.41	.023 056	3.07	9
	1.046 790	10.208 791	.097 954 7905	.955 301	9.752 470	.102 538 1239	123.05	.025 381	3.05	10
	1.051 588	11.255 581	.088 844 8104	.950 943	10.703 413	.093 428 1437	112.12	.027 710	3.02	11
	1.056 408	12.307 170	.081 253 4512	.946 604	11.650 017	.085 836 7846	103.01	.030 041	3.00	12
1	1.056 408	12.307 170	.081 253 4512	.946 604	11.650 017	.085 836 7846	103.01	.030 041	3.00	12
2	1.115 998	25.308 560	.039 512 3228	.896 059	22.677 971	.044 095 6562	52.92	.058 296	2.91	24
3	1.178 949	39.043 331	.025 612 5685	.848 213	33.117 077	.030 195 9018	36.24	.087 052	2.90	36
4	1.245 451	53.552 852	.018 673 1419	.802 922	42.998 777	.023 256 4752	27.91	.116 311	2.91	48
5	1.315 704	68.880 823	.014 517 8288	.760 050	52.352 835	.019 101 1622	22.93	.146 070	2.92	60
6	1.389 920	85.073 412	.011 754 5538	.719 466	61.207 425	.016 337 8871	19.61	.176 328	2.94	72
7	1.468 322	102.179 391	.009 786 7093	.681 049	69.589 216	.014 370 0427	17.25	.207 084	2.96	84
8	1.551 147	120.250 282	.008 315 9888	.644 684	77.523 453	.012 899 3222	15.48	.238 335	2.98	96
9	1.638 644	139.340 512	.007 176 6637	.610 261	85.034 035	.011 759 9971	14.12	.270 080	3.00	108
10	1.731 076	159.507 582	.006 269 2945	.577 675	92.143 582	.010 852 6278	13.03	.302 315	3.02	120
11	1.828 723	180.812 233	.005 530 5993	.546 830	98.873 509	.010 113 9326	12.14	.335 039	3.05	132
12	1.931 877	203.318 634	.004 918 3884	.517 631	105.244 084	.009 501 7217	11.41	.368 248	3.07	144
13	2.040 850	227.094 572	.004 403 4518	.489 992	111.274 498	.008 986 7851	10.79	.401 938	3.09	156
14	2.155 970	252.211 661	.003 964 9237	.463 828	116.982 911	.008 548 2571	10.26	.436 107	3.12	168
15	2.277 584	278.745 550	.003 587 5012	.439 062	122.386 519	.008 170 8345	9.81	.470 750	3.14	180
16	2.406 057	306.776 160	.003 259 7057	.415 618	127.501 597	.007 843 0390	9.42	.505 863	3.16	192
17	2.541 778	336.387 916	.002 972 7584	.393 425	132.343 550	.007 556 0917	9.07	.541 443	3.18	204
18	2.685 154	367.670 008	.002 719 8302	.372 418	136.926 962	.007 303 1636	8.77	.577 483	3.21	216
19	2.836 618	400.716 657	.002 495 5289	.352 532	141.265 639	.007 078 8622	8.50	.613 981	3.23	228
20	2.996 626	435.627 395	.002 295 5397	.333 709	145.372 649	.006 878 8731	8.26	.650 930	3.25	240
21	3.165 659	472.507 374	.002 116 3691	.315 890	149.260 361	.006 699 7024	8.04	.688 325	3.28	252
22	3.344 227	511.467 674	.001 955 1578	.299 023	152.940 485	.006 538 4911	7.85	.726 162	3.30	264
23	3.532 868	552.625 640	.001 809 5433	.283 056	156.424 105	.006 392 8766	7.68	.764 434	3.32	276
24	3.732 149	596.105 240	.001 677 5561	.267 942	159.721 715	.006 260 8895	7.52	.803 136	3.35	288
25	3.942 672	642.037 430	.001 557 5416	.253 635	162.843 245	.006 140 8749	7.37	.842 262	3.37	300
26	4.165 069	690.560 558	.001 448 0989	.240 092	165.798 099	.006 031 4323	7.24	.881 807	3.39	312
27	4.400 012	741.820 771	.001 348 0345	.227 272	168.595 175	.005 931 3678	7.12	.921 763	3.41	324
28	4.648 207	795.972 463	.001 256 3249	.215 137	171.242 899	.005 839 6582	7.01	.962 125	3.44	336
29	4.910 403	853.178 736	.001 172 0873	.203 649	173.749 245	.005 755 4207	6.91	1.002 886	3.46	348
30	5.187 388	913.611 893	.001 094 5567	.192 775	176.121 763	.005 677 8900	6.82	1.044 040	3.48	360
31	5.479 997	977.453 954	.001 023 0661	.182 482	178.367 598	.005 606 3994	6.73	1.085 581	3.50	372
32	5.789 112	1044.897 210	.000 957 0319	.172 738	180.493 515	.005 540 3653	6.65	1.127 500	3.52	384
33	6.115 664	1116.144 795	.000 895 9411	.163 515	182.505 916	.005 479 2744	6.58	1.169 793	3.54	396
34	6.460 635	1191.411 305	.000 839 3407	.154 784	184.410 863	.005 422 6740	6.51	1.212 451	3.57	408
35	6.825 066	1270.923 437	.000 786 8295	.146 519	186.214 094	.005 370 1628	6.45	1.255 468	3.59	420
36	7.210 053	1354.920 678	.000 738 0506	.138 695	187.921 040	.005 321 3839	6.39	1.298 838	3.61	432
37	7.616 757	1443.656 024	.000 692 6858	.131 289	189.536 842	.005 276 0191	6.34	1.342 552	3.63	444
38	8.046 402	1537.396 741	.000 650 4502	.124 279	191.066 366	.005 233 7835	6.29	1.386 605	3.65	456
39	8.500 282	1636.425 171	.000 611 0881	.117 643	192.514 221	.005 194 4215	6.24	1.430 989	3.67	468
40	8.979 765	1741.039 583	.000 574 3695	.111 361	193.884 765	.005 157 7028	6.19	1.475 697	3.69	480
41	9.486 294	1851.555 071	.000 540 0866	.105 415	195.182 129	.005 123 4199	6.15	1.520 723	3.71	492
42	10.021 396	1968.304 500	.000 508 0515	.099 787	196.410 218	.005 091 3848	6.11	1.566 058	3.73	504
43	10.586 681	2091.639 515	.000 478 0939	.094 458	197.572 732	.005 061 4272	6.08	1.611 696	3.75	516
44	11.183 853	2221.931 594	.000 450 0589	.089 415	198.673 173	.005 033 3922	6.05	1.657 631	3.77	528
45	11.814 710	2359.573 171	.000 423 8055	.084 640	199.714 855	.005 007 1388	6.01	1.703 855	3.79	540
46	12.481 153	2504.978 815	.000 399 2050	.080 121	200.700 916	.004 982 5383	5.98	1.750 361	3.81	552
47	13.185 188	2658.586 479	.000 376 1397	.075 843	201.634 324	.004 959 4731	5.96	1.797 143	3.82	564
48	13.928 936	2820.858 824	.000 354 5020	.071 792	202.517 893	.004 937 8353	5.93	1.844 193	3.84	576
49	14.714 638	2992.284 604	.000 334 1928	.067 960	203.354 282	.004 917 5261	5.91	1.891 505	3.86	588
50	15.544 659	3173.380 146	.000 315 1214	.064 331	204.146 012	.004 898 4547	5.88	1.939 073	3.88	600

Effective Rate is 5.64 %   8 - 28   Annual Percentage Rate is 5.50 %

MONTHLY COMPOUND INTEREST AND ANNUITY

5.55 % M

	Amount Of 1	Amount Of 1 Per Period	Sinking Fund Payment	Present Worth Of 1	Present Worth of 1 Per Period	Periodic Payment To Amortize 1	Constant Annual Percent	Total Interest	Annual Add On Rate	
	What a single $ 1 deposit grows to in the future. The deposit is made at the beginning of the first period.	What a series of $ 1 deposits grow to in the future. A deposit is made at the end of each period.	The amount to be deposited at the end of each period that grows to $ 1 in the future.	What $ 1 to be paid in the future is worth today. Value today of a single $ 1 payment tomorrow.	What $ 1 to be paid at the end of each period is worth today. Value today of a series of $ 1 payments tomorrow.	The mortgage payment to amortize a loan of $ 1. An annuity certain, payable at the end of each period, worth $ 1 today.	The annual payment, including interest and principal, to amortize completely a loan of $ 100.	The total interest paid over the term on a loan of $1. The loan is amortized by regular periodic payments.	The average annual interest rate on a loan that is completely amortized by regular periodic payments.	
	$S = (1+i)^n$	$S\overline{n}| = \dfrac{(1+i)^n - 1}{i}$	$\dfrac{1}{S\overline{n}|} = \dfrac{i}{(1+i)^n - 1}$	$V^n = \dfrac{1}{(1+i)^n}$	$A\overline{n}| = \dfrac{1 - V^n}{i}$	$\dfrac{1}{A\overline{n}|} = \dfrac{i}{1 - V^n}$				

YEAR										PERIODS
	1.004 625	1.000 000	1.000 000 0000	.995 396	.995 396	1.004 625 0000	1205.55	.004 625	5.55	1
	1.009 271	2.004 625	.498 846 4177	.990 814	1.986 210	.503 471 4177	604.17	.006 943	4.17	2
	1.013 939	3.013 896	.331 796 4092	.986 252	2.972 462	.336 421 4092	403.71	.009 264	3.71	3
	1.018 629	4.027 836	.248 272 2941	.981 712	3.954 174	.252 897 2941	303.48	.011 589	3.48	4
	1.023 340	5.046 464	.198 158 5364	.977 192	4.931 367	.202 783 5364	243.35	.013 918	3.34	5
	1.028 073	6.069 804	.164 749 9574	.972 694	5.904 061	.169 374 9574	203.25	.016 250	3.25	6
	1.032 828	7.097 877	.140 887 1948	.968 216	6.872 276	.145 512 1948	174.62	.018 585	3.19	7
	1.037 605	8.130 705	.122 990 5674	.963 758	7.836 035	.127 615 5674	153.14	.020 925	3.14	8
	1.042 403	9.168 309	.109 071 3635	.959 321	8.795 356	.113 696 3635	136.44	.023 267	3.10	9
	1.047 225	10.210 713	.097 936 3560	.954 905	9.750 261	.102 561 3560	123.08	.025 614	3.07	10
	1.052 068	11.257 937	.088 826 2185	.950 509	10.700 770	.093 451 2185	112.15	.027 963	3.05	11
	1.056 934	12.310 005	.081 234 7337	.946 133	11.646 903	.085 859 7337	103.04	.030 317	3.03	12
1	1.056 934	12.310 005	.081 234 7337	.946 133	11.646 903	.085 859 7337	103.04	.030 317	3.03	12
2	1.117 109	25.320 866	.039 493 1206	.895 168	22.666 423	.044 118 1206	52.95	.058 835	2.94	24
3	1.180 710	39.072 483	.025 593 4590	.846 948	33.092 356	.030 218 4590	36.27	.087 865	2.93	36
4	1.247 933	53.607 033	.018 654 2689	.801 325	42.956 676	.023 279 2689	27.94	.117 405	2.94	48
5	1.318 982	68.969 089	.014 499 2492	.758 160	52.289 635	.019 124 2492	22.95	.147 455	2.95	60
6	1.394 077	85.205 764	.011 736 2952	.717 321	61.119 856	.016 361 2952	19.64	.178 013	2.97	72
7	1.473 447	102.366 855	.009 768 7869	.678 681	69.474 420	.014 393 7869	17.28	.209 078	2.99	84
8	1.557 336	120.504 992	.008 298 4114	.642 122	77.378 950	.012 923 4114	15.51	.240 647	3.01	96
9	1.646 001	139.675 801	.007 159 4363	.607 533	84.857 687	.011 784 4363	14.15	.272 719	3.03	108
10	1.739 714	159.938 077	.006 252 4198	.574 807	91.933 567	.010 877 4198	13.06	.305 290	3.05	120
11	1.838 762	181.353 961	.005 514 0786	.543 844	98.628 291	.010 139 0786	12.17	.338 358	3.08	132
12	1.943 450	203.989 132	.004 902 2220	.514 549	104.962 391	.009 527 2220	11.44	.371 920	3.10	144
13	2.054 098	227.913 008	.004 387 6390	.486 832	110.955 293	.009 012 6390	10.82	.405 972	3.12	156
14	2.171 045	253.198 961	.003 949 4633	.460 608	116.625 376	.008 574 4633	10.29	.440 510	3.15	168
15	2.294 651	279.924 539	.003 572 3913	.435 796	121.990 028	.008 197 3913	9.84	.475 530	3.17	180
16	2.425 294	308.171 705	.003 244 9442	.412 321	127.065 703	.007 869 9442	9.45	.511 029	3.19	192
17	2.563 375	338.027 088	.002 958 3428	.390 111	131.867 967	.007 583 3428	9.11	.547 002	3.22	204
18	2.709 318	369.582 252	.002 705 7576	.369 097	136.411 548	.007 330 7576	8.80	.583 444	3.24	216
19	2.863 570	402.933 969	.002 481 7962	.349 214	140.710 381	.007 106 7962	8.53	.620 350	3.26	228
20	3.026 603	438.184 526	.002 282 1436	.330 403	144.777 648	.006 907 1436	8.29	.657 714	3.29	240
21	3.198 919	475.442 031	.002 103 3058	.312 606	148.625 824	.006 728 3058	8.08	.695 533	3.31	252
22	3.381 046	514.820 745	.001 942 4237	.295 766	152.266 711	.006 567 4237	7.89	.733 800	3.34	264
23	3.573 542	556.441 439	.001 797 1343	.279 834	155.711 474	.006 422 1343	7.71	.772 509	3.36	276
24	3.776 997	600.431 755	.001 665 4682	.264 761	158.970 679	.006 290 4682	7.55	.811 655	3.38	288
25	3.992 036	646.926 607	.001 545 7704	.250 499	162.054 320	.006 170 7704	7.41	.851 231	3.40	300
26	4.219 317	696.068 585	.001 436 6400	.237 005	164.971 855	.006 061 6400	7.28	.891 232	3.43	312
27	4.459 539	748.008 403	.001 336 8834	.224 238	167.732 231	.005 961 8834	7.16	.931 650	3.45	324
28	4.713 437	802.905 349	.001 245 4768	.212 159	170.343 914	.005 870 4768	7.05	.972 480	3.47	336
29	4.981 791	860.927 787	.001 161 5376	.200 731	172.814 914	.005 786 5376	6.95	1.013 715	3.50	348
30	5.265 423	922.253 660	.001 084 3004	.189 918	175.152 805	.005 709 3004	6.86	1.055 348	3.52	360
31	5.565 204	987.071 047	.001 013 0983	.179 688	177.364 769	.005 638 0983	6.77	1.097 373	3.54	372
32	5.882 052	1055.578 733	.000 947 3476	.170 009	179.457 577	.005 572 3476	6.69	1.139 781	3.56	384
33	6.216 939	1127.986 820	.000 886 5352	.160 851	181.437 652	.005 511 5352	6.62	1.182 568	3.58	396
34	6.570 893	1204.517 372	.000 830 2080	.152 186	183.311 066	.005 455 2080	6.55	1.225 725	3.61	408
35	6.944 999	1285.405 098	.000 777 9649	.143 989	185.083 565	.005 402 9649	6.49	1.269 245	3.63	420
36	7.340 404	1370.898 067	.000 729 4488	.136 232	186.760 586	.005 354 4488	6.43	1.313 122	3.65	432
37	7.758 320	1461.258 473	.000 684 3416	.128 894	188.347 270	.005 309 3416	6.38	1.357 348	3.67	444
38	8.200 031	1556.763 439	.000 642 3584	.121 951	189.848 486	.005 267 3584	6.33	1.401 915	3.69	456
39	8.666 890	1657.705 863	.000 603 2433	.115 382	191.268 833	.005 228 2433	6.28	1.446 818	3.71	468
40	9.160 328	1764.395 319	.000 566 7664	.109 166	192.612 672	.005 191 7664	6.24	1.492 048	3.73	480
41	9.681 860	1877.159 010	.000 532 7199	.103 286	193.884 122	.005 157 7199	6.19	1.537 598	3.75	492
42	10.233 085	1996.342 763	.000 500 9160	.097 722	195.087 084	.005 125 9160	6.16	1.583 462	3.77	504
43	10.815 693	2122.312 096	.000 471 1842	.092 458	196.225 245	.005 096 1842	6.12	1.629 631	3.79	516
44	11.431 472	2255.453 340	.000 443 3698	.087 478	197.302 097	.005 068 3698	6.09	1.676 099	3.81	528
45	12.082 309	2396.174 816	.000 417 3318	.082 766	198.320 943	.005 042 3318	6.06	1.722 859	3.83	540
46	12.770 200	2544.908 098	.000 392 9415	.078 307	199.284 906	.005 017 9415	6.03	1.769 904	3.85	552
47	13.497 256	2702.109 327	.000 370 0813	.074 089	200.196 944	.004 995 0813	6.00	1.817 226	3.87	564
48	14.265 705	2868.260 615	.000 348 6434	.070 098	201.059 853	.004 973 6434	5.97	1.864 819	3.89	576
49	15.077 906	3043.871 523	.000 328 5290	.066 322	201.876 279	.004 953 5290	5.95	1.912 675	3.90	588
50	15.936 348	3229.480 623	.000 309 6473	.062 750	202.648 728	.004 934 6473	5.93	1.960 788	3.92	600

MONTHLY COMPOUND INTEREST AND ANNUITY

5.60 % M

	Amount Of 1	Amount Of 1 Per Period	Sinking Fund Payment	Present Worth Of 1	Present Worth of 1 Per Period	Periodic Payment To Amortize 1	Constant Annual Percent	Total Interest	Annual Add On Rate
	What a single $ 1 deposit grows to in the future. The deposit is made at the beginning of the first period.	What a series of $ 1 deposits grow to in the future. A deposit is made at the end of each period.	The amount to be deposited at the end of each period that grows to $ 1 in the future.	What $ 1 to be paid in the future is worth today. Value today of a single $ 1 payment tomorrow.	What $ 1 to be paid at the end of each period is worth today. Value today of a series of $ 1 payments tomorrow.	The mortgage payment to amortize a loan of $ 1. An annuity certain, payable at the end of each period, worth $ 1 today.	The annual payment, including interest and principal, to amortize completely a loan of $ 100.	The total interest paid over the term on a loan of $1. The loan is amortized by regular periodic payments.	The average annual interest rate on a loan that is completely amortized by regular periodic payments.

$$S = (1+i)^n \qquad S\overline{n}| = \frac{(1+i)^n - 1}{i} \qquad \frac{1}{S\overline{n}|} = \frac{i}{(1+i)^n - 1} \qquad V^n = \frac{1}{(1+i)^n} \qquad A\overline{n}| = \frac{1-V^n}{i} \qquad \frac{1}{A\overline{n}|} = \frac{i}{1-V^n}$$

YEAR									PERIODS
	1.004 667	1.000 000	1.000 000 0000	.995 355	.995 355	1.004 666 6667	1205.60	.004 667	5.60	1
	1.009 355	2.004 667	.498 836 0492	.990 732	1.986 087	.503 502 7159	604.21	.007 005	4.20	2
	1.014 065	3.014 022	.331 782 6060	.986 130	2.972 216	.336 449 2727	403.74	.009 348	3.74	3
	1.018 798	4.028 087	.248 256 7897	.981 549	3.953 765	.252 923 4564	303.51	.011 694	3.51	4
	1.023 552	5.046 885	.198 142 0241	.976 990	4.930 755	.202 808 6908	243.38	.014 043	3.37	5
	1.028 329	6.070 437	.164 732 7839	.972 452	5.903 207	.169 399 4505	203.28	.016 397	3.28	6
	1.033 128	7.098 766	.140 869 5581	.967 935	6.871 142	.145 536 2248	174.65	.018 754	3.21	7
	1.037 949	8.131 893	.122 972 5914	.963 439	7.834 580	.127 639 2581	153.17	.021 114	3.17	8
	1.042 793	9.169 842	.109 053 1307	.958 963	8.793 544	.113 719 7974	136.47	.023 478	3.13	9
	1.047 659	10.212 635	.097 917 9242	.954 509	9.748 053	.102 584 5909	123.11	.025 846	3.10	10
	1.052 548	11.260 294	.088 807 6298	.950 075	10.698 128	.093 474 2965	112.17	.028 217	3.08	11
	1.057 460	12.312 842	.081 216 0196	.945 662	11.643 790	.085 882 6862	103.06	.030 592	3.06	12
1	1.057 460	12.312 842	.081 216 0196	.945 662	11.643 790	.085 882 6862	103.06	.030 592	3.06	12
2	1.118 222	25.333 179	.039 473 9253	.894 277	22.654 884	.044 140 5920	52.97	.059 374	2.97	24
3	1.182 474	39.101 663	.025 574 3598	.845 684	33.067 661	.030 241 0265	36.29	.088 677	2.96	36
4	1.250 419	53.661 284	.018 635 4096	.799 732	42.914 631	.023 302 0763	27.97	.118 500	2.96	48
5	1.322 268	69.057 499	.014 480 6866	.756 276	52.226 539	.019 147 3533	22.98	.148 841	2.98	60
6	1.398 246	85.338 380	.011 718 0570	.715 182	61.032 460	.016 384 7237	19.67	.179 700	3.00	72
7	1.478 589	102.554 759	.009 750 8883	.676 321	69.359 888	.014 417 5550	17.31	.211 075	3.02	84
8	1.563 548	120.760 389	.008 280 8610	.639 571	77.234 822	.012 947 5277	15.54	.242 963	3.04	96
9	1.653 390	140.012 115	.007 142 2391	.604 818	84.681 851	.011 808 9058	14.18	.275 362	3.06	108
10	1.748 394	160.370 042	.006 235 5786	.571 954	91.724 225	.010 902 2452	13.09	.308 269	3.08	120
11	1.848 856	181.897 735	.005 497 5946	.540 875	98.383 933	.010 164 2612	12.20	.341 682	3.11	132
12	1.955 091	204.662 408	.004 886 0952	.511 485	104.681 768	.009 552 7618	11.47	.375 598	3.13	144
13	2.067 431	228.735 137	.004 371 8688	.483 692	110.637 393	.009 038 5354	10.85	.410 012	3.15	156
14	2.186 225	254.191 084	.003 934 0483	.457 409	116.269 404	.008 600 7150	10.33	.444 920	3.18	168
15	2.311 845	281.109 727	.003 557 3298	.432 555	121.595 383	.008 223 9964	9.87	.480 319	3.20	180
16	2.444 684	309.575 113	.003 230 2338	.409 051	126.631 962	.007 896 9005	9.48	.516 205	3.23	192
17	2.585 155	339.676 119	.002 943 9809	.386 824	131.394 864	.007 610 6475	9.14	.552 572	3.25	204
18	2.733 698	371.506 726	.002 691 7413	.365 805	135.898 961	.007 358 4080	8.84	.589 416	3.27	216
19	2.890 776	405.166 318	.002 468 1222	.345 928	140.158 316	.007 134 7889	8.57	.626 732	3.30	228
20	3.056 880	440.759 987	.002 268 8085	.327 131	144.186 228	.006 935 4752	8.33	.664 514	3.32	240
21	3.232 528	478.398 866	.002 090 3060	.309 355	147.995 272	.006 756 9726	8.11	.702 757	3.35	252
22	3.418 269	518.200 473	.001 929 7551	.292 546	151.597 341	.006 596 4218	7.92	.741 455	3.37	264
23	3.614 682	560.289 077	.001 784 7930	.276 649	155.003 683	.006 451 4596	7.75	.780 603	3.39	276
24	3.822 382	604.796 089	.001 653 4498	.261 617	158.224 931	.006 320 1165	7.59	.820 194	3.42	288
25	4.042 016	651.860 470	.001 534 0706	.247 401	161.271 145	.006 200 7373	7.45	.860 221	3.44	300
26	4.274 269	701.629 168	.001 425 2543	.233 958	164.151 834	.006 091 9210	7.32	.900 679	3.46	312
27	4.519 869	754.257 572	.001 325 8070	.221 245	166.875 993	.005 992 4737	7.20	.941 561	3.49	324
28	4.779 580	809.910 000	.001 234 7051	.209 223	169.452 128	.005 901 3718	7.09	.982 861	3.51	336
29	5.054 214	868.760 212	.001 151 0656	.197 855	171.888 281	.005 817 7323	6.99	1.024 571	3.53	348
30	5.344 629	930.991 953	.001 074 1231	.187 104	174.192 060	.005 740 7898	6.89	1.066 684	3.56	360
31	5.651 731	996.799 526	.001 003 2107	.176 937	176.370 656	.005 669 8774	6.81	1.109 194	3.58	372
32	5.976 479	1066.388 397	.000 937 7446	.167 323	178.430 873	.005 604 4113	6.73	1.152 094	3.60	384
33	6.319 887	1139.975 840	.000 877 2116	.158 231	180.379 142	.005 543 8782	6.66	1.195 376	3.62	396
34	6.683 028	1217.791 612	.000 821 1586	.149 633	182.221 547	.005 487 8252	6.59	1.239 033	3.64	408
35	7.067 034	1300.078 673	.000 769 1842	.141 502	183.963 839	.005 435 8509	6.53	1.283 057	3.67	420
36	7.473 105	1387.093 942	.000 720 9317	.133 813	185.611 460	.005 387 5984	6.47	1.327 442	3.69	432
37	7.902 509	1479.109 102	.000 676 0826	.126 542	187.169 553	.005 342 7493	6.42	1.372 181	3.71	444
38	8.356 587	1576.411 447	.000 634 3522	.119 666	188.642 982	.005 301 0188	6.37	1.417 265	3.73	456
39	8.836 756	1679.304 778	.000 595 4845	.113 164	190.036 349	.005 262 1512	6.32	1.462 687	3.75	468
40	9.344 515	1788.110 352	.000 559 2496	.107 015	191.354 004	.005 225 9163	6.28	1.508 440	3.77	480
41	9.881 450	1903.167 886	.000 525 4397	.101 200	192.600 060	.005 192 1064	6.24	1.554 516	3.79	492
42	10.449 238	2024.836 618	.000 493 8670	.095 701	193.778 408	.005 160 5337	6.20	1.600 909	3.81	504
43	11.049 650	2153.496 427	.000 464 3611	.090 501	194.892 728	.005 131 0278	6.16	1.647 610	3.83	516
44	11.684 562	2289.549 019	.000 436 7672	.085 583	195.946 498	.005 103 4339	6.13	1.694 613	3.85	528
45	12.355 956	2433.419 184	.000 410 9444	.080 933	196.943 008	.005 077 6111	6.10	1.741 910	3.87	540
46	13.065 929	2585.556 118	.000 386 7640	.076 535	197.885 371	.005 053 4307	6.07	1.789 494	3.89	552
47	13.816 696	2746.434 829	.000 364 1084	.072 376	198.776 528	.005 030 7751	6.04	1.837 357	3.91	564
48	14.610 602	2916.557 619	.000 342 8700	.068 442	199.619 261	.005 009 5366	6.02	1.885 493	3.93	576
49	15.450 126	3096.455 653	.000 322 9499	.064 724	200.416 202	.004 989 6166	5.99	1.933 895	3.95	588
50	16.337 890	3286.690 615	.000 304 2574	.061 207	201.169 839	.004 970 9241	5.97	1.982 554	3.97	600

Effective Rate is 5.75 %

Annual Percentage Rate is 5.60 %

MONTHLY COMPOUND INTEREST AND ANNUITY

	Amount Of 1	Amount Of 1 Per Period	Sinking Fund Payment	Present Worth Of 1	Present Worth of 1 Per Period	Periodic Payment To Amortize 1	Constant Annual Percent	Total Interest	Annual Add On Rate	
	What a single $ 1 deposit grows to in the future. The deposit is made at the beginning of the first period.	What a series of $ 1 deposits grow to in the future. A deposit is made at the end of each period.	The amount to be deposited at the end of each period that grows to $ 1 in the future.	What $ 1 to be paid in the future is worth today. Value today of a single $ 1 payment tomorrow.	What $ 1 to be paid at the end of each period is worth today. Value today of a series of $ 1 payments tomorrow.	The mortgage payment to amortize a loan of $ 1. An annuity certain, payable at the end of each period, worth $ 1 today.	The annual payment, including interest and principal, to amortize completely a loan of $ 100.	The total interest paid over the term on a loan of $1. The loan is amortized by regular periodic payments.	The average annual interest rate on a loan that is completely amortized by regular periodic payments.	
	$S = (1+i)^n$	$S\overline{n} = \dfrac{(1+i)^n - 1}{i}$	$\dfrac{1}{S\overline{n}} = \dfrac{i}{(1+i)^n - 1}$	$V^n = \dfrac{1}{(1+i)^n}$	$A\overline{n} = \dfrac{1 - V^n}{i}$	$\dfrac{1}{A\overline{n}} = \dfrac{i}{1 - V^n}$				

YEAR / **PERIODS**

YEAR	Amount Of 1	Amount Of 1 Per Period	Sinking Fund Payment	Present Worth Of 1	Present Worth of 1 Per Period	Periodic Payment To Amortize 1	Constant Annual Percent	Total Interest	Annual Add On Rate	PERIODS
	1.004 687	1.000 000	1.000 000 0000	.995 334	.995 334	1.004 687 5000	1205.63	.004 688	5.63	1
	1.009 397	2.004 687	.498 830 8652	.990 691	1.986 025	.503 518 3652	604.23	.007 037	4.22	2
	1.014 129	3.014 084	.331 775 7047	.986 068	2.972 093	.336 463 2047	403.76	.009 390	3.76	3
	1.018 882	4.028 213	.248 249 0379	.981 468	3.953 561	.252 936 5379	303.53	.011 746	3.52	4
	1.023 658	5.047 095	.198 133 7684	.976 889	4.930 449	.202 821 2684	243.39	.014 106	3.39	5
	1.028 457	6.070 754	.164 724 1977	.972 331	5.902 780	.169 411 6977	203.30	.016 470	3.29	6
	1.033 278	7.099 210	.140 860 7405	.967 794	6.870 574	.145 548 2405	174.66	.018 838	3.23	7
	1.038 121	8.132 488	.122 963 6043	.963 279	7.833 853	.127 651 1043	153.19	.021 209	3.18	8
	1.042 987	9.170 609	.109 044 0153	.958 785	8.792 638	.113 731 5153	136.48	.023 584	3.14	9
	1.047 876	10.213 596	.097 908 7094	.954 311	9.746 949	.102 596 2094	123.12	.025 962	3.12	10
	1.052 788	11.261 472	.088 798 3367	.949 859	10.696 808	.093 485 8367	112.19	.028 344	3.09	11
	1.057 723	12.314 260	.081 206 6638	.945 427	11.642 235	.085 894 1638	103.08	.030 730	3.07	12
1	1.057 723	12.314 260	.081 206 6638	.945 427	11.642 235	.085 894 1638	103.08	.030 730	3.07	12
2	1.118 778	25.339 338	.039 464 3302	.893 832	22.649 118	.044 151 8302	52.99	.059 644	2.98	24
3	1.183 357	39.116 263	.025 564 8141	.845 053	33.055 323	.030 252 3141	36.31	.089 083	2.97	36
4	1.251 665	53.688 435	.018 625 9851	.798 936	42.893 630	.023 313 4851	27.98	.119 047	2.98	48
5	1.323 914	69.101 758	.014 471 4118	.755 336	52.195 031	.019 158 9118	23.00	.149 535	2.99	60
6	1.400 335	85.404 786	.011 708 9456	.714 115	60.988 828	.016 396 4456	19.68	.180 544	3.01	72
7	1.481 167	102.648 875	.009 741 9480	.675 143	69.302 721	.014 429 4480	17.32	.212 074	3.03	84
8	1.566 664	120.888 346	.008 272 0959	.638 299	77.162 900	.012 959 5959	15.56	.244 121	3.05	96
9	1.657 097	140.180 656	.007 133 6519	.603 465	84.594 125	.011 821 1519	14.19	.276 684	3.07	108
10	1.752 750	160.586 578	.006 227 1705	.570 532	91.619 807	.010 914 6705	13.10	.309 760	3.10	120
11	1.853 924	182.170 393	.005 489 3662	.539 397	98.262 076	.010 176 8662	12.22	.343 346	3.12	132
12	1.960 938	205.000 092	.004 878 0466	.509 960	104.541 857	.009 565 5466	11.48	.377 439	3.15	144
13	2.074 129	229.147 592	.004 363 9996	.482 130	110.478 931	.009 051 4996	10.87	.412 034	3.17	156
14	2.193 855	254.688 961	.003 926 3578	.455 819	116.092 002	.008 613 8578	10.34	.447 128	3.19	168
15	2.320 491	281.704 657	.003 549 8171	.430 943	121.398 750	.008 237 3171	9.89	.482 717	3.22	180
16	2.454 436	310.279 782	.003 222 8977	.407 425	126.415 894	.007 910 3977	9.50	.518 796	3.24	192
17	2.596 114	340.504 351	.002 936 8200	.385 191	131.159 237	.007 624 3200	9.15	.555 361	3.27	204
18	2.745 970	372.473 577	.002 684 7542	.364 170	135.643 722	.007 372 2542	8.85	.592 407	3.29	216
19	2.904 476	406.288 165	.002 461 3072	.344 296	139.883 475	.007 148 8072	8.58	.629 928	3.32	228
20	3.072 131	442.054 636	.002 262 1638	.325 507	143.891 852	.006 949 6638	8.34	.667 919	3.34	240
21	3.249 464	479.885 658	.002 083 8297	.307 743	147.681 481	.006 771 3297	8.13	.706 375	3.36	252
22	3.437 033	519.900 404	.001 923 4453	.290 949	151.264 298	.006 610 9453	7.94	.745 290	3.39	264
23	3.635 429	562.224 925	.001 778 6476	.275 071	154.651 589	.006 466 1476	7.76	.784 657	3.41	276
24	3.845 278	606.992 549	.001 647 4667	.260 059	157.854 027	.006 334 9667	7.61	.824 470	3.44	288
25	4.067 239	654.344 298	.001 528 2474	.245 867	160.881 698	.006 215 7474	7.46	.864 724	3.46	300
26	4.302 013	704.429 336	.001 419 5888	.232 449	163.744 139	.006 107 0888	7.33	.905 412	3.48	312
27	4.550 338	757.405 439	.001 320 2968	.219 764	166.450 369	.006 007 7968	7.21	.946 526	3.51	324
28	4.812 998	813.439 485	.001 229 3477	.207 771	169.008 912	.005 916 8477	7.11	.988 061	3.53	336
29	5.090 819	872.707 991	.001 145 8587	.196 432	171.427 827	.005 833 3587	7.01	1.030 009	3.55	348
30	5.384 677	935.397 658	.001 069 0640	.185 712	173.714 736	.005 756 5640	6.91	1.072 363	3.57	360
31	5.695 497	1001.705 966	.000 998 2969	.175 577	175.876 840	.005 685 7969	6.83	1.115 116	3.60	372
32	6.024 258	1071.841 796	.000 932 9735	.165 996	177.920 952	.005 620 4735	6.75	1.158 262	3.62	384
33	6.371 997	1146.026 082	.000 872 5805	.156 937	179.853 511	.005 560 0805	6.68	1.201 792	3.64	396
34	6.739 809	1224.492 515	.000 816 6649	.148 372	181.680 605	.005 504 1649	6.61	1.245 699	3.66	408
35	7.128 851	1307.488 274	.000 764 8252	.140 275	183.407 988	.005 452 3252	6.55	1.289 977	3.69	420
36	7.540 351	1395.274 805	.000 716 7047	.132 620	185.041 104	.005 404 2047	6.49	1.334 616	3.71	432
37	7.975 603	1488.128 646	.000 671 9849	.125 382	186.585 095	.005 359 4849	6.44	1.379 611	3.73	444
38	8.435 980	1586.342 298	.000 630 3810	.118 540	188.044 826	.005 317 8810	6.39	1.424 954	3.75	456
39	8.922 930	1690.225 146	.000 591 6372	.112 071	189.424 895	.005 279 1372	6.34	1.470 636	3.77	468
40	9.437 990	1800.104 434	.000 555 5233	.105 955	190.729 649	.005 243 0233	6.30	1.516 651	3.79	480
41	9.982 780	1916.326 294	.000 521 8318	.100 173	191.963 200	.005 209 3318	6.26	1.562 991	3.81	492
42	10.559 016	2039.256 840	.000 490 3747	.094 706	193.129 431	.005 177 8747	6.22	1.609 649	3.83	504
43	11.168 516	2169.283 317	.000 460 9817	.089 537	194.232 018	.005 148 4817	6.18	1.656 617	3.85	516
44	11.813 197	2306.815 326	.000 433 4981	.084 651	195.274 434	.005 120 9981	6.15	1.703 887	3.87	528
45	12.495 091	2452.286 107	.000 407 7828	.080 031	196.259 962	.005 095 2828	6.12	1.751 453	3.89	540
46	13.216 346	2606.153 912	.000 383 7072	.075 664	197.191 706	.005 071 2072	6.09	1.799 306	3.91	552
47	13.979 235	2768.903 444	.000 361 1538	.071 535	198.072 603	.005 048 6538	6.06	1.847 441	3.93	564
48	14.786 160	2941.047 382	.000 340 0149	.067 631	198.905 426	.005 027 5149	6.04	1.895 849	3.95	576
49	15.639 663	3123.128 000	.000 320 1918	.063 940	199.692 800	.005 007 6918	6.01	1.944 523	3.97	588
50	16.542 432	3315.718 876	.000 301 5937	.060 451	200.437 205	.004 989 0937	5.99	1.993 456	3.99	600

Effective Rate is 5.77 %

Annual Percentage Rate is 5.625%

Amount Of 1	Amount Of 1 Per Period	Sinking Fund Payment	Present Worth Of 1	Present Worth of 1 Per Period	Periodic Payment To Amortize 1	Constant Annual Percent	Total Interest	Annual Add On Rate
What a single $1 deposit grows to in the future. The deposit is made at the beginning of the first period.	What a series of $1 deposits grow to in the future. A deposit is made at the end of each period.	The amount to be deposited at the end of each period that grows to $1 in the future.	What $1 to be paid in the future is worth today. Value today of a single $1 payment tomorrow.	What $1 to be paid at the end of each period is worth today. Value today of a series of $1 payments tomorrow.	The mortgage payment to amortize a loan of $1. An annuity certain, payable at the end of each period, worth $1 today.	The annual payment, including interest and principal, to amortize completely a loan of $100.	The total interest paid over the term on a loan of $1. The loan is amortized by regular periodic payments.	The average annual interest rate on a loan that is completely amortized by regular periodic payments.
$S = (1+i)^n$	$S\overline{n}| = \dfrac{(1+i)^n - 1}{i}$	$\dfrac{1}{S\overline{n}|} = \dfrac{i}{(1+i)^n - 1}$	$V^n = \dfrac{1}{(1+i)^n}$	$A\overline{n}| = \dfrac{1 - V^n}{i}$	$\dfrac{1}{A\overline{n}|} = \dfrac{i}{1 - V^n}$			

YEAR / **PERIODS**

Year	Amount Of 1	Amount Of 1 Per Period	Sinking Fund Payment	Present Worth Of 1	Present Worth of 1 Per Period	Periodic Payment To Amortize 1	Constant Annual Percent	Total Interest	Annual Add On Rate	Periods
	1.004 708	1.000 000	1.000 000 0000	.995 314	.995 314	1.004 708 3333	1205.65	.004 708	5.65	1
	1.009 439	2.004 708	.498 825 6812	.990 649	1.985 963	.503 534 0145	604.25	.007 068	4.24	2
	1.014 192	3.014 147	.331 768 8036	.986 007	2.971 970	.336 477 1370	403.78	.009 431	3.77	3
	1.018 967	4.028 339	.248 241 2863	.981 386	3.953 356	.252 949 6197	303.54	.011 798	3.54	4
	1.023 764	5.047 306	.198 125 5131	.976 787	4.930 144	.202 833 8465	243.41	.014 169	3.40	5
	1.028 585	6.071 070	.164 715 6120	.972 210	5.902 353	.169 423 9453	203.31	.016 544	3.31	6
	1.033 428	7.099 655	.140 851 9234	.967 654	6.870 007	.145 560 2567	174.68	.018 922	3.24	7
	1.038 293	8.133 082	.122 954 6177	.963 119	7.833 126	.127 662 9510	153.20	.021 304	3.20	8
	1.043 182	9.171 375	.109 034 9005	.958 606	8.791 732	.113 743 2339	136.50	.023 689	3.16	9
	1.048 094	10.214 557	.097 899 4953	.954 113	9.745 845	.102 607 8287	123.13	.026 078	3.13	10
	1.053 028	11.262 651	.088 789 0443	.949 642	10.695 487	.093 497 3776	112.20	.028 471	3.11	11
	1.057 986	12.315 679	.081 197 3088	.945 192	11.640 679	.085 905 6422	103.09	.030 868	3.09	12
1	1.057 986	12.315 679	.081 197 3088	.945 192	11.640 679	.085 905 6422	103.09	.030 868	3.09	12
2	1.119 335	25.345 499	.039 454 7369	.893 388	22.643 353	.044 163 0702	53.00	.059 914	3.00	24
3	1.184 241	39.130 871	.025 555 2710	.844 423	33.042 991	.030 263 6043	36.32	.089 490	2.98	36
4	1.252 911	53.715 605	.018 616 5641	.798 141	42.872 643	.023 324 8974	27.99	.119 595	2.99	48
5	1.325 563	69.146 054	.014 462 1412	.754 397	52.163 550	.019 170 4745	23.01	.150 228	3.00	60
6	1.402 427	85.471 259	.011 699 8394	.713 050	60.945 239	.016 408 1727	19.69	.181 388	3.02	72
7	1.483 749	102.743 102	.009 733 0135	.673 969	69.245 619	.014 441 3468	17.33	.213 073	3.04	84
8	1.569 786	121.016 476	.008 263 3376	.637 030	77.091 070	.012 971 6710	15.57	.245 280	3.07	96
9	1.660 812	140.349 455	.007 125 0722	.602 115	84.506 527	.011 833 4055	14.21	.278 008	3.09	108
10	1.757 116	160.803 483	.006 218 7708	.569 114	91.515 555	.010 927 1041	13.12	.311 252	3.11	120
11	1.859 005	182.443 565	.005 481 1470	.537 922	98.140 432	.010 189 4803	12.23	.345 011	3.14	132
12	1.966 802	205.338 475	.004 870 0079	.508 440	104.402 211	.009 578 3412	11.50	.379 281	3.16	144
13	2.080 850	229.560 978	.004 356 1411	.480 573	110.320 793	.009 064 4744	10.88	.414 058	3.19	156
14	2.201 510	255.188 053	.003 918 6787	.454 234	115.914 988	.008 627 0121	10.36	.449 338	3.21	168
15	2.329 168	282.301 149	.003 542 3164	.429 338	121.202 575	.008 250 6498	9.91	.485 117	3.23	180
16	2.464 228	310.986 434	.003 215 5743	.405 807	126.200 360	.007 923 9077	9.51	.521 390	3.26	192
17	2.607 119	341.335 073	.002 929 6726	.383 565	130.924 225	.007 638 0059	9.17	.558 153	3.28	204
18	2.758 297	373.443 517	.002 677 7811	.362 543	135.389 183	.007 386 1145	8.87	.595 401	3.31	216
19	2.918 240	407.413 813	.002 454 5069	.342 672	139.609 425	.007 162 8402	8.60	.633 128	3.33	228
20	3.087 458	443.353 921	.002 255 5344	.323 891	143.598 363	.006 963 8677	8.36	.671 328	3.36	240
21	3.266 488	481.378 063	.002 077 3693	.306 139	147.368 675	.006 785 7026	8.15	.709 997	3.38	252
22	3.455 900	521.607 086	.001 917 1519	.289 360	150.932 342	.006 625 4852	7.96	.749 128	3.41	264
23	3.656 295	564.168 842	.001 772 5190	.273 501	154.300 692	.006 480 8523	7.78	.788 715	3.43	276
24	3.868 310	609.198 597	.001 641 5008	.258 511	157.484 428	.006 349 8342	7.62	.828 752	3.45	288
25	4.092 619	656.839 462	.001 522 4420	.244 342	160.493 669	.006 230 7754	7.48	.869 233	3.48	300
26	4.329 935	707.242 846	.001 413 9415	.230 950	163.337 980	.006 122 2748	7.35	.910 150	3.50	312
27	4.581 012	760.568 937	.001 314 8052	.218 292	166.026 399	.006 023 1385	7.23	.951 497	3.52	324
28	4.846 648	816.987 212	.001 224 0094	.206 328	168.567 470	.005 932 3427	7.12	.993 267	3.55	336
29	5.127 687	876.676 975	.001 140 6710	.195 020	170.969 270	.005 849 0043	7.02	1.035 454	3.57	348
30	5.425 023	939.827 928	.001 064 0246	.184 331	173.239 431	.005 772 3579	6.93	1.078 049	3.59	360
31	5.739 600	1006.640 772	.000 993 4030	.174 228	175.385 170	.005 701 7364	6.85	1.121 046	3.62	372
32	6.072 419	1077.327 848	.000 928 2225	.164 679	177.413 304	.005 636 5559	6.77	1.164 437	3.64	384
33	6.424 536	1152.113 807	.000 867 9698	.155 653	179.330 279	.005 576 3031	6.70	1.208 216	3.66	396
34	6.797 071	1231.236 329	.000 812 1918	.147 122	181.142 189	.005 520 5251	6.63	1.252 374	3.68	408
35	7.191 208	1314.946 875	.000 760 4870	.139 059	182.854 791	.005 468 8203	6.57	1.296 905	3.71	420
36	7.608 200	1403.511 487	.000 712 4986	.131 437	184.473 529	.005 420 8320	6.51	1.341 799	3.73	432
37	8.049 371	1497.211 636	.000 667 9082	.124 233	186.003 546	.005 376 2416	6.46	1.387 051	3.75	444
38	8.516 125	1596.345 112	.000 626 4310	.117 424	187.449 706	.005 334 7643	6.41	1.432 653	3.77	456
39	9.009 944	1701.226 973	.000 587 8110	.110 988	188.816 605	.005 296 1444	6.36	1.478 596	3.79	468
40	9.532 397	1812.190 548	.000 551 8184	.104 905	190.108 586	.005 260 1517	6.32	1.524 873	3.81	480
41	10.085 146	1929.588 493	.000 518 2452	.099 156	191.329 756	.005 226 5785	6.28	1.571 477	3.83	492
42	10.669 946	2053.793 912	.000 486 9038	.093 721	192.483 996	.005 195 2371	6.24	1.618 400	3.85	504
43	11.288 657	2185.201 548	.000 457 6237	.088 584	193.574 975	.005 165 9570	6.20	1.665 634	3.87	516
44	11.943 245	2324.229 028	.000 430 2502	.083 729	194.606 158	.005 138 5835	6.17	1.713 172	3.89	528
45	12.635 790	2471.318 201	.000 404 6423	.079 140	195.580 825	.005 112 9757	6.14	1.761 007	3.91	540
46	13.368 493	2626.936 534	.000 380 6715	.074 803	196.502 071	.005 089 0049	6.11	1.809 131	3.93	552
47	14.143 683	2791.578 603	.000 358 2203	.070 703	197.372 826	.005 066 5536	6.08	1.857 536	3.95	564
48	14.963 823	2965.767 659	.000 337 1808	.066 828	198.195 856	.005 045 5142	6.06	1.906 216	3.97	576
49	15.831 520	3150.057 298	.000 317 4545	.063 165	198.973 778	.005 025 7879	6.04	1.955 163	3.99	588
50	16.749 531	3345.033 215	.000 298 9507	.059 703	199.709 063	.005 007 2840	6.01	2.004 370	4.01	600

Amount Of 1	Amount Of 1 Per Period	Sinking Fund Payment	Present Worth Of 1	Present Worth of 1 Per Period	Periodic Payment To Amortize 1	Constant Annual Percent	Total Interest	Annual Add On Rate
What a single $ 1 deposit grows to in the future. The deposit is made at the beginning of the first period.	What a series of $ 1 deposits grow to in the future. A deposit is made at the end of each period.	The amount to be deposited at the end of each period that grows to $ 1 in the future.	What $ 1 to be paid in the future is worth today. Value today of a single $ 1 payment tomorrow.	What $ 1 to be paid at the end of each period is worth today. Value today of a series of $ 1 payments tomorrow.	The mortgage payment to amortize a loan of $ 1. An annuity certain, payable at the end of each period, worth $ 1 today.	The annual payment, including interest and principal, to amortize completely a loan of $ 100.	The total interest paid over the term on a loan of $ 1. The loan is amortized by regular periodic payments.	The average annual interest rate on a loan that is completely amortized by regular periodic payments.
$S = (1+i)^n$	$S\overline{n}| = \dfrac{(1+i)^n - 1}{i}$	$\dfrac{1}{S\overline{n}|} = \dfrac{i}{(1+i)^n - 1}$	$V^n = \dfrac{1}{(1+i)^n}$	$A\overline{n}| = \dfrac{1 - V^n}{i}$	$\dfrac{1}{A\overline{n}|} = \dfrac{i}{1 - V^n}$			

YEAR									PERIODS
	1.004 750	1.000 000	1.000 000 0000	.995 272	.995 272	1.004 750 0000	1205.70	.004 750	5.70	1
	1.009 523	2.004 750	.498 815 3136	.990 567	1.985 840	.503 565 3136	604.28	.007 131	4.28	2
	1.014 318	3.014 273	.331 755 0020	.985 884	2.971 724	.336 505 0020	403.81	.009 515	3.81	3
	1.019 136	4.028 590	.248 225 7840	.981 223	3.952 948	.252 975 7840	303.58	.011 903	3.57	4
	1.023 977	5.047 726	.198 109 0035	.976 585	4.929 532	.202 859 0035	243.44	.014 295	3.43	5
	1.028 841	6.071 703	.164 698 4418	.971 968	5.901 500	.169 448 4418	203.34	.016 691	3.34	6
	1.033 728	7.100 543	.140 834 2907	.967 373	6.868 873	.145 584 2907	174.71	.019 090	3.27	7
	1.038 638	8.134 271	.122 936 6462	.962 800	7.831 673	.127 686 6462	153.23	.021 493	3.22	8
	1.043 571	9.172 909	.109 016 6729	.958 248	8.789 920	.113 766 6729	136.53	.023 900	3.19	9
	1.048 528	10.216 480	.097 881 0693	.953 718	9.743 638	.102 631 0693	123.16	.026 311	3.16	10
	1.053 509	11.265 008	.088 770 4619	.949 209	10.692 847	.093 520 4619	112.23	.028 725	3.13	11
	1.058 513	12.318 517	.081 178 6016	.944 722	11.637 569	.085 928 6016	103.12	.031 143	3.11	12
1	1.058 513	12.318 517	.081 178 6016	.944 722	11.637 569	.085 928 6016	103.12	.031 143	3.11	12
2	1.120 450	25.357 827	.039 435 5553	.892 499	22.631 831	.044 185 5553	53.03	.060 453	3.02	24
3	1.186 011	39.160 106	.025 536 1924	.843 163	33.018 347	.030 286 1924	36.35	.090 303	3.01	36
4	1.255 407	53.769 997	.018 597 7322	.796 554	42.830 712	.023 347 7322	28.02	.120 691	3.02	48
5	1.328 865	69.234 755	.014 443 6128	.752 522	52.100 665	.019 193 6128	23.04	.151 617	3.03	60
6	1.406 621	85.604 403	.011 681 6421	.710 924	60.858 190	.016 431 6421	19.72	.183 078	3.05	72
7	1.488 926	102.931 887	.009 715 1624	.671 625	69.131 612	.014 465 1624	17.36	.215 074	3.07	84
8	1.576 048	121.273 253	.008 245 8413	.634 498	76.947 692	.012 995 8413	15.60	.247 601	3.10	96
9	1.668 267	140.687 827	.007 107 9355	.599 424	84.331 712	.011 857 9355	14.23	.280 657	3.12	108
10	1.765 882	161.238 405	.006 201 9964	.566 289	91.307 554	.010 951 9964	13.15	.314 240	3.14	120
11	1.869 209	182.991 458	.005 464 7360	.534 986	97.897 783	.010 214 7360	12.26	.348 345	3.17	132
12	1.978 582	206.017 346	.004 853 9602	.505 412	104.123 713	.009 603 9602	11.53	.382 970	3.19	144
13	2.094 355	230.390 548	.004 340 4559	.477 474	110.005 484	.009 090 4559	10.91	.418 111	3.22	156
14	2.216 902	256.189 897	.003 903 3546	.451 080	115.562 120	.008 653 3546	10.39	.453 764	3.24	168
15	2.346 620	283.498 842	.003 527 3513	.426 145	120.811 594	.008 277 3513	9.94	.489 923	3.27	180
16	2.483 927	312.405 715	.003 200 9658	.402 588	125.770 885	.007 950 9658	9.55	.526 585	3.29	192
17	2.629 269	343.004 014	.002 915 4178	.380 334	130.456 034	.007 665 4178	9.20	.563 745	3.32	204
18	2.783 115	375.392 711	.002 663 8770	.359 310	134.882 195	.007 413 8770	8.90	.601 397	3.34	216
19	2.945 964	409.676 565	.002 440 9500	.339 447	139.063 685	.007 190 9500	8.63	.639 537	3.37	228
20	3.118 341	445.966 470	.002 242 3210	.320 683	143.014 028	.006 992 3210	8.40	.678 157	3.39	240
21	3.300 804	484.379 804	.002 064 4957	.302 956	146.746 003	.006 814 4957	8.18	.717 253	3.42	252
22	3.493 944	525.040 815	.001 904 6138	.286 210	150.271 680	.006 654 6138	7.99	.756 818	3.44	264
23	3.698 385	568.081 023	.001 760 3123	.270 388	153.602 463	.006 510 3123	7.82	.796 846	3.46	276
24	3.914 788	613.639 641	.001 629 6209	.255 442	156.749 125	.006 379 6209	7.66	.837 331	3.49	288
25	4.143 854	661.864 027	.001 510 8843	.241 321	159.721 845	.006 260 8843	7.52	.878 265	3.51	300
26	4.386 323	712.910 166	.001 402 7013	.227 981	162.530 238	.006 152 7013	7.39	.919 643	3.54	312
27	4.642 980	766.943 165	.001 303 8776	.215 379	165.183 386	.006 053 8776	7.27	.961 456	3.56	324
28	4.914 655	824.137 794	.001 213 3893	.203 473	167.689 873	.005 963 3893	7.16	1.003 699	3.58	336
29	5.202 225	884.679 050	.001 130 3534	.192 225	170.057 805	.005 880 3534	7.06	1.046 363	3.61	348
30	5.506 623	948.762 755	.001 054 0043	.181 600	172.294 842	.005 804 0043	6.97	1.089 442	3.63	360
31	5.828 832	1016.596 186	.000 983 6748	.171 561	174.408 219	.005 733 6748	6.89	1.132 927	3.65	372
32	6.169 894	1088.398 752	.000 918 7809	.162 077	176.404 771	.005 668 7809	6.81	1.176 812	3.68	384
33	6.530 913	1164.402 698	.000 858 8094	.153 118	178.290 957	.005 608 8094	6.74	1.221 089	3.70	396
34	6.913 056	1244.853 860	.000 803 3071	.144 654	180.072 878	.005 553 3071	6.67	1.265 749	3.72	408
35	7.317 559	1330.012 457	.000 751 8727	.136 658	181.756 297	.005 501 8727	6.61	1.310 787	3.75	420
36	7.745 731	1420.153 936	.000 704 1490	.129 103	183.346 659	.005 454 1490	6.55	1.356 192	3.77	432
37	8.198 957	1515.569 859	.000 659 8178	.121 967	184.849 108	.005 409 8178	6.50	1.401 959	3.79	444
38	8.678 702	1616.568 849	.000 618 5941	.115 225	186.268 505	.005 368 5941	6.45	1.448 079	3.81	456
39	9.186 519	1723.477 590	.000 580 2222	.108 855	187.609 439	.005 330 2222	6.40	1.494 544	3.83	468
40	9.724 049	1836.641 877	.000 544 4720	.102 838	188.876 248	.005 294 4720	6.36	1.541 347	3.85	480
41	10.293 032	1956.427 740	.000 511 1357	.097 153	190.073 030	.005 261 1357	6.32	1.588 479	3.87	492
42	10.895 307	2083.222 629	.000 480 0255	.091 783	191.203 656	.005 230 0255	6.28	1.635 933	3.90	504
43	11.532 824	2217.436 662	.000 450 9712	.086 709	192.271 783	.005 200 9712	6.25	1.683 701	3.92	516
44	12.207 644	2359.503 955	.000 423 8179	.081 916	193.280 865	.005 173 8179	6.21	1.731 776	3.94	528
45	12.921 949	2509.884 025	.000 398 4248	.077 388	194.234 167	.005 148 4248	6.18	1.780 149	3.96	540
46	13.678 051	2669.063 277	.000 374 6633	.073 110	195.134 772	.005 124 6633	6.15	1.828 814	3.98	552
47	14.478 394	2837.556 579	.000 352 4159	.069 068	195.985 593	.005 102 4159	6.13	1.877 763	4.00	564
48	15.325 567	3015.908 921	.000 331 5750	.065 250	196.789 381	.005 081 5750	6.10	1.926 987	4.01	576
49	16.222 312	3204.697 186	.000 312 0420	.061 643	197.548 738	.005 062 0420	6.08	1.976 481	4.03	588
50	17.171 527	3404.532 011	.000 293 7261	.058 236	198.266 118	.005 043 7261	6.06	2.026 236	4.05	600

MONTHLY COMPOUND INTEREST AND ANNUITY

5.75 % M

	Amount Of 1	Amount Of 1 Per Period	Sinking Fund Payment	Present Worth Of 1	Present Worth of 1 Per Period	Periodic Payment To Amortize 1	Constant Annual Percent	Total Interest	Annual Add On Rate	
	What a single $ 1 deposit grows to in the future. The deposit is made at the beginning of the first period.	What a series of $ 1 deposits grow to in the future. A deposit is made at the end of each period.	The amount to be deposited at the end of each period that grows to $ 1 in the future.	What $ 1 to be paid in the future is worth today. Value today of a single $ 1 payment tomorrow.	What $ 1 to be paid at the end of each period is worth today. Value today of a series of $ 1 payments tomorrow.	The mortgage payment to amortize a loan of $ 1. An annuity certain, payable at the end of each period, worth $ 1 today.	The annual payment, including interest and principal, to amortize completely a loan of $ 100.	The total interest paid over the term on a loan of $1. The loan is amortized by regular periodic payments.	The average annual interest rate on a loan that is completely amortized by regular periodic payments.	

$$S = (1+i)^n \qquad S\overline{n}| = \frac{(1+i)^n - 1}{i} \qquad \frac{1}{S\overline{n}|} = \frac{i}{(1+i)^n - 1} \qquad V^n = \frac{1}{(1+i)^n} \qquad A\overline{n}| = \frac{1-V^n}{i} \qquad \frac{1}{A\overline{n}|} = \frac{i}{1-V^n}$$

YEAR	Amount Of 1	Amount Of 1 Per Period	Sinking Fund Payment	Present Worth Of 1	Present Worth of 1 Per Period	Periodic Payment To Amortize 1	Constant Annual Percent	Total Interest	Annual Add On Rate	PERIODS
	1.004 792	1.000 000	1.000 000 0000	.995 231	.995 231	1.004 791 6667	1205.75	.004 792	5.75	1
	1.009 606	2.004 792	.498 804 9465	.990 485	1.985 716	.503 596 6131	604.32	.007 193	4.32	2
	1.014 444	3.014 398	.331 741 2011	.985 762	2.971 478	.336 532 8678	403.84	.009 599	3.84	3
	1.019 305	4.028 842	.248 210 2828	.981 061	3.952 539	.253 001 9495	303.61	.012 008	3.60	4
	1.024 189	5.048 147	.198 092 4953	.976 382	4.928 921	.202 884 1620	243.47	.014 421	3.46	5
	1.029 097	6.072 336	.164 681 2732	.971 726	5.900 647	.169 472 9399	203.37	.016 838	3.37	6
	1.034 028	7.101 432	.140 816 6599	.967 092	6.867 739	.145 608 3266	174.73	.019 258	3.30	7
	1.038 982	8.135 460	.122 918 6770	.962 480	7.830 219	.127 710 3437	153.26	.021 683	3.25	8
	1.043 961	9.174 443	.108 998 4478	.957 890	8.788 110	.113 790 1145	136.55	.024 111	3.21	9
	1.048 963	10.218 403	.097 862 6461	.953 322	9.741 432	.102 654 3128	123.19	.026 543	3.19	10
	1.053 989	11.267 367	.088 751 8826	.948 776	10.690 208	.093 543 5492	112.26	.028 979	3.16	11
	1.059 040	12.321 356	.081 159 8977	.944 252	11.634 460	.085 951 5644	103.15	.031 419	3.14	12
1	1.059 040	12.321 356	.081 159 8977	.944 252	11.634 460	.085 951 5644	103.15	.031 419	3.14	12
2	1.121 565	25.370 163	.039 416 3806	.891 611	22.620 316	.044 208 0473	53.05	.060 993	3.05	24
3	1.187 782	39.189 369	.025 517 1242	.841 905	32.993 728	.030 308 7908	36.38	.091 116	3.04	36
4	1.257 909	53.824 459	.018 578 9141	.794 970	42.788 838	.023 370 5807	28.05	.121 788	3.04	48
5	1.332 176	69.323 602	.014 425 1015	.750 652	52.037 886	.019 216 7682	23.07	.153 006	3.06	60
6	1.410 827	85.737 812	.011 663 4654	.708 804	60.771 314	.016 455 1320	19.75	.184 770	3.08	72
7	1.494 122	103.121 114	.009 697 3351	.669 289	69.017 867	.014 489 0018	17.39	.217 076	3.10	84
8	1.582 335	121.530 723	.008 228 3720	.631 978	76.804 687	.013 020 0387	15.63	.249 924	3.12	96
9	1.675 755	141.027 233	.007 090 8291	.596 746	84.157 405	.011 882 4957	14.26	.283 310	3.15	108
10	1.774 692	161.674 813	.006 185 2553	.563 478	91.100 219	.010 976 9220	13.18	.317 231	3.17	120
11	1.879 469	183.541 423	.005 448 3614	.532 065	97.655 982	.010 240 0281	12.29	.351 684	3.20	132
12	1.990 433	206.699 033	.004 837 9520	.502 403	103.846 272	.009 629 6187	11.56	.386 665	3.22	144
13	2.107 948	231.223 866	.004 324 8131	.474 395	109.691 463	.009 116 4798	10.94	.422 171	3.25	156
14	2.232 401	257.196 640	.003 888 0757	.447 948	115.210 793	.008 679 7423	10.42	.458 197	3.27	168
15	2.364 201	284.702 842	.003 512 4342	.422 976	120.422 429	.008 304 1009	9.97	.494 738	3.30	180
16	2.503 783	313.833 006	.003 186 4080	.399 396	125.343 525	.007 978 0747	9.58	.531 790	3.32	192
17	2.651 606	344.683 010	.002 901 2164	.377 130	129.990 277	.007 692 8831	9.24	.569 348	3.35	204
18	2.808 156	377.354 392	.002 650 0288	.356 106	134.377 980	.007 441 6954	8.94	.607 406	3.37	216
19	2.973 950	411.954 688	.002 427 4514	.336 253	138.521 075	.007 219 1181	8.67	.645 959	3.40	228
20	3.149 531	448.597 780	.002 229 1684	.317 508	142.433 199	.007 020 8351	8.43	.685 000	3.43	240
21	3.335 479	487.404 273	.002 051 6849	.299 807	146.127 228	.006 843 3516	8.22	.724 525	3.45	252
22	3.532 405	528.501 895	.001 892 1408	.283 093	149.615 321	.006 683 8075	8.03	.764 525	3.48	264
23	3.740 958	572.025 914	.001 748 1725	.267 311	152.908 958	.006 539 8392	7.85	.804 996	3.50	276
24	3.961 823	618.119 583	.001 617 8099	.252 409	156.018 980	.006 409 4766	7.70	.845 929	3.52	288
25	4.195 728	666.934 615	.001 499 3974	.238 338	158.955 623	.006 291 0640	7.55	.887 319	3.55	300
26	4.443 443	718.631 679	.001 391 5334	.225 051	161.728 552	.006 183 2001	7.42	.929 158	3.57	312
27	4.705 784	773.380 928	.001 293 0239	.212 504	164.346 896	.006 084 6905	7.31	.971 440	3.60	324
28	4.983 612	831.362 563	.001 202 8446	.200 658	166.819 270	.005 994 5113	7.20	1.014 156	3.62	336
29	5.277 844	892.767 425	.001 120 1126	.189 471	169.153 814	.005 911 7792	7.10	1.057 299	3.65	348
30	5.589 447	957.797 619	.001 044 0619	.178 907	171.358 210	.005 835 7286	7.01	1.100 862	3.67	360
31	5.919 447	1026.667 185	.000 974 0255	.168 935	173.439 714	.005 765 6921	6.92	1.144 837	3.69	372
32	6.268 930	1099.602 799	.000 909 4193	.159 517	175.405 178	.005 701 0860	6.85	1.189 217	3.72	384
33	6.639 047	1176.844 518	.000 849 7299	.150 624	177.261 071	.005 641 3966	6.77	1.233 993	3.74	396
34	7.031 015	1258.646 576	.000 794 5042	.142 227	179.013 500	.005 586 1709	6.71	1.279 158	3.76	408
35	7.446 125	1345.278 214	.000 743 3407	.134 298	180.668 234	.005 535 0073	6.65	1.324 703	3.78	420
36	7.885 743	1437.024 569	.000 695 8823	.126 811	182.230 719	.005 487 5490	6.59	1.370 621	3.81	432
37	8.351 316	1534.187 613	.000 651 8108	.119 742	183.706 098	.005 443 4774	6.54	1.416 904	3.83	444
38	8.844 376	1637.087 147	.000 610 8410	.113 066	185.099 227	.005 402 5077	6.49	1.463 544	3.85	456
39	9.366 546	1746.061 852	.000 572 7174	.106 763	186.414 691	.005 364 3841	6.44	1.510 532	3.87	468
40	9.919 546	1861.470 405	.000 537 2097	.100 811	187.656 820	.005 328 8764	6.40	1.557 861	3.89	480
41	10.505 194	1983.692 660	.000 504 1103	.095 191	188.829 703	.005 295 7770	6.36	1.605 522	3.92	492
42	11.125 419	2113.130 896	.000 473 2315	.089 884	189.937 199	.005 264 8981	6.32	1.653 509	3.94	504
43	11.782 262	2250.211 144	.000 444 4027	.084 873	190.982 953	.005 236 0694	6.29	1.701 812	3.96	516
44	12.477 884	2395.384 586	.000 417 4695	.080 142	191.970 409	.005 209 1362	6.26	1.750 424	3.98	528
45	13.214 577	2549.129 044	.000 392 2909	.075 674	192.902 815	.005 183 9575	6.23	1.799 337	4.00	540
46	13.994 763	2711.950 549	.000 368 7383	.071 455	193.783 242	.005 160 4050	6.20	1.848 544	4.02	552
47	14.821 011	2884.385 008	.000 346 6944	.067 472	194.614 585	.005 138 3610	6.17	1.898 036	4.04	564
48	15.696 042	3066.999 968	.000 326 0515	.063 710	195.399 583	.005 117 7182	6.15	1.947 806	4.06	576
49	16.622 733	3260.396 485	.000 306 7112	.060 159	196.140 818	.005 098 3778	6.12	1.997 846	4.08	588
50	17.604 137	3465.211 099	.000 288 5827	.056 805	196.840 731	.005 080 2494	6.10	2.048 150	4.10	600

Effective Rate is 5.90 %

Annual Percentage Rate is 5.75 %

	Amount Of 1	Amount Of 1 Per Period	Sinking Fund Payment	Present Worth Of 1	Present Worth of 1 Per Period	Periodic Payment To Amortize 1	Constant Annual Percent	Total Interest	Annual Add On Rate	
	What a single $ 1 deposit grows to in the future. The deposit is made at the beginning of the first period.	What a series of $ 1 deposits grow to in the future. A deposit is made at the end of each period.	The amount to be deposited at the end of each period that grows to $ 1 in the future.	What $ 1 to be paid in the future is worth today. Value today of a single $ 1 payment tomorrow.	What $ 1 to be paid at the end of each period is worth today. Value today of a series of $ 1 payments tomorrow.	The mortgage payment to amortize a loan of $ 1. An annuity certain, payable at the end of each period, worth $ 1 today.	The annual payment, including interest and principal, to amortize completely a loan of $ 100.	The total interest paid over the term on a loan of $1. The loan is amortized by regular periodic payments.	The average annual interest rate on a loan that is completely amortized by regular periodic payments.	
	$S = (1+i)^n$	$S\overline{n} = \dfrac{(1+i)^n - 1}{i}$	$\dfrac{1}{S\overline{n}} = \dfrac{i}{(1+i)^n - 1}$	$V^n = \dfrac{1}{(1+i)^n}$	$A\overline{n} = \dfrac{1-V^n}{i}$	$\dfrac{1}{A\overline{n}} = \dfrac{i}{1-V^n}$				

YEAR / **PERIODS**

YEAR	Amount Of 1	Amount Of 1 Per Period	Sinking Fund Payment	Present Worth Of 1	Present Worth of 1 Per Period	Periodic Payment To Amortize 1	Constant Annual Percent	Total Interest	Annual Add On Rate	PERIODS
	1.004 833	1.000 000	1.000 000 0000	.995 190	.995 190	1.004 833 3333	1205.80	.004 833	5.80	1
	1.009 690	2.004 833	.498 794 5798	.990 403	1.985 593	.503 627 9131	604.36	.007 256	4.35	2
	1.014 570	3.014 523	.331 727 4011	.985 639	2.971 232	.336 560 7344	403.88	.009 682	3.87	3
	1.019 474	4.029 094	.248 194 7827	.980 898	3.952 130	.253 028 1160	303.64	.012 112	3.63	4
	1.024 401	5.048 568	.198 075 9885	.976 180	4.928 310	.202 909 3218	243.50	.014 547	3.49	5
	1.029 353	6.072 969	.164 664 1064	.971 484	5.899 794	.169 497 4397	203.40	.016 985	3.40	6
	1.034 328	7.102 322	.140 799 0311	.966 811	6.866 606	.145 632 3644	174.76	.019 427	3.33	7
	1.039 327	8.136 649	.122 900 7101	.962 161	7.828 767	.127 734 0434	153.29	.021 872	3.28	8
	1.044 351	9.175 977	.108 980 2253	.957 533	8.786 299	.113 813 5586	136.58	.024 322	3.24	9
	1.049 398	10.220 327	.097 844 2257	.952 927	9.739 226	.102 677 5591	123.22	.026 776	3.21	10
	1.054 470	11.269 725	.088 733 3064	.948 343	10.687 570	.093 566 6398	112.28	.029 233	3.19	11
	1.059 567	12.324 196	.081 141 1973	.943 782	11.631 352	.085 974 5306	103.17	.031 694	3.17	12
1	1.059 567	12.324 196	.081 141 1973	.943 782	11.631 352	.085 974 5306	103.17	.031 694	3.17	12
2	1.122 682	25.382 506	.039 397 2128	.890 724	22.608 810	.044 230 5461	53.08	.061 533	3.08	24
3	1.189 557	39.218 660	.025 498 0662	.840 649	32.969 135	.030 331 3996	36.40	.091 930	3.06	36
4	1.260 415	53.878 992	.018 560 1097	.793 389	42.747 021	.023 393 4430	28.08	.122 885	3.07	48
5	1.335 494	69.412 595	.014 406 6074	.748 786	51.975 212	.019 239 9407	23.09	.154 396	3.09	60
6	1.415 046	85.871 487	.011 645 3090	.706 691	60.684 611	.016 478 6423	19.78	.186 462	3.11	72
7	1.499 335	103.310 785	.009 679 5315	.666 962	68.904 383	.014 512 8649	17.42	.219 081	3.13	84
8	1.588 646	121.788 889	.008 210 9297	.629 467	76.662 054	.013 044 2630	15.66	.252 249	3.15	96
9	1.683 277	141.367 677	.007 073 7528	.594 079	83.983 603	.011 907 0861	14.29	.285 965	3.18	108
10	1.783 545	162.112 713	.006 168 5477	.560 681	90.893 548	.011 001 8810	13.21	.320 226	3.20	120
11	1.889 785	184.093 468	.005 432 0233	.529 161	97.415 028	.010 265 3566	12.32	.355 027	3.23	132
12	2.002 354	207.383 550	.004 821 9832	.499 412	103.569 882	.009 655 3166	11.59	.390 366	3.25	144
13	2.121 628	232.060 950	.004 309 2127	.471 336	109.378 722	.009 142 5461	10.98	.426 237	3.28	156
14	2.248 007	258.208 308	.003 872 8421	.444 839	114.860 998	.008 706 1754	10.45	.462 637	3.30	168
15	2.381 914	285.913 184	.003 497 5652	.419 830	120.035 072	.008 330 8985	10.00	.499 562	3.33	180
16	2.523 797	315.268 355	.003 171 9010	.396 228	124.918 268	.008 005 2343	9.61	.537 005	3.36	192
17	2.674 132	346.372 124	.002 887 0684	.373 953	129.526 939	.007 720 4017	9.27	.574 962	3.38	204
18	2.833 422	379.328 650	.002 636 2364	.352 930	133.876 519	.007 469 5697	8.97	.613 427	3.41	216
19	3.002 200	414.248 295	.002 414 0111	.333 089	137.981 574	.007 247 3445	8.70	.652 395	3.43	228
20	3.181 032	451.247 996	.002 216 0763	.314 363	141.855 850	.007 049 4097	8.46	.691 858	3.46	240
21	3.370 516	490.451 657	.002 038 9369	.296 690	145.512 321	.006 872 2703	8.25	.731 812	3.48	252
22	3.571 288	531.990 561	.001 879 7326	.280 011	148.963 232	.006 713 0659	8.06	.772 249	3.51	264
23	3.784 018	576.003 809	.001 736 0996	.264 269	152.220 139	.006 569 4330	7.89	.813 163	3.54	276
24	4.009 421	622.638 793	.001 606 0676	.249 413	155.293 949	.006 439 4009	7.73	.854 547	3.56	288
25	4.248 250	672.051 680	.001 487 9808	.235 391	158.194 954	.006 321 3141	7.59	.896 394	3.59	300
26	4.501 305	724.407 943	.001 380 4377	.222 158	160.932 870	.006 213 7710	7.46	.938 697	3.61	312
27	4.769 434	779.882 907	.001 282 2438	.209 668	163.516 866	.006 115 5771	7.34	.981 447	3.63	324
28	5.053 535	838.662 346	.001 192 3750	.197 881	165.955 594	.006 025 7083	7.24	1.024 638	3.66	336
29	5.354 558	900.943 097	.001 109 9480	.186 757	168.257 221	.005 943 2813	7.14	1.068 262	3.68	348
30	5.673 513	966.933 722	.001 034 1970	.176 258	170.429 454	.005 867 5304	7.05	1.112 311	3.71	360
31	6.011 467	1036.855 206	.000 964 4548	.166 349	172.479 569	.005 797 7882	6.96	1.156 777	3.73	372
32	6.369 552	1110.941 701	.000 900 1372	.156 997	174.414 430	.005 733 4706	6.89	1.201 653	3.76	384
33	6.748 966	1189.441 301	.000 840 7309	.148 171	176.240 516	.005 674 0642	6.81	1.246 929	3.78	396
34	7.150 982	1272.616 883	.000 785 7824	.139 841	177.963 943	.005 619 1158	6.75	1.292 599	3.80	408
35	7.576 944	1360.746 980	.000 734 8905	.131 979	179.590 482	.005 568 2238	6.69	1.338 654	3.82	420
36	8.028 279	1454.126 718	.000 687 6980	.124 560	181.125 580	.005 521 0313	6.63	1.385 086	3.85	432
37	8.506 499	1553.068 802	.000 643 8865	.117 557	182.574 378	.005 477 2198	6.58	1.431 886	3.87	444
38	9.013 205	1657.904 563	.000 603 1710	.110 948	183.941 727	.005 436 5044	6.53	1.479 046	3.89	456
39	9.550 095	1768.985 071	.000 565 2959	.104 711	185.232 206	.005 398 6292	6.48	1.526 558	3.91	468
40	10.118 964	1886.682 305	.000 530 0309	.098 824	186.450 136	.005 363 3643	6.44	1.574 415	3.94	480
41	10.721 720	2011.390 404	.000 497 1685	.093 269	187.599 597	.005 330 5019	6.40	1.622 607	3.96	492
42	11.360 380	2143.526 984	.000 466 5208	.088 025	188.684 437	.005 299 8542	6.36	1.671 127	3.98	504
43	12.037 084	2283.534 537	.000 437 9176	.083 077	189.708 289	.005 271 2509	6.33	1.719 965	4.00	516
44	12.754 096	2431.881 911	.000 411 2042	.078 406	190.674 582	.005 244 5375	6.30	1.769 116	4.02	528
45	13.513 818	2589.065 886	.000 386 2397	.073 998	191.586 552	.005 219 5730	6.27	1.818 569	4.04	540
46	14.318 795	2755.612 830	.000 362 8957	.069 838	192.447 253	.005 196 2290	6.24	1.868 318	4.06	552
47	15.171 722	2932.080 467	.000 341 0548	.065 912	193.259 567	.005 174 3881	6.21	1.918 355	4.08	564
48	16.075 455	3119.059 743	.000 320 6094	.062 207	194.026 213	.005 153 9428	6.19	1.968 671	4.10	576
49	17.033 021	3317.176 802	.000 301 4612	.058 709	194.749 761	.005 134 7945	6.17	2.019 259	4.12	588
50	18.047 626	3527.095 090	.000 283 5194	.055 409	195.432 631	.005 116 8528	6.15	2.070 112	4.14	600

Effective Rate is 5.96 %

Annual Percentage Rate is 5.80 %

MONTHLY COMPOUND INTEREST AND ANNUITY

	Amount Of 1	Amount Of 1 Per Period	Sinking Fund Payment	Present Worth Of 1	Present Worth of 1 Per Period	Periodic Payment To Amortize 1	Constant Annual Percent	Total Interest	Annual Add On Rate	
	What a single $ 1 deposit grows to in the future. The deposit is made at the beginning of the first period.	What a series of $ 1 deposits grow to in the future. A deposit is made at the end of each period.	The amount to be deposited at the end of each period that grows to $ 1 in the future.	What $ 1 to be paid in the future is worth today. Value today of a single $ 1 payment tomorrow.	What $ 1 to be paid at the end of each period is worth today. Value today of a series of $ 1 payments tomorrow.	The mortgage payment to amortize a loan of $ 1. An annuity certain, payable at the end of each period, worth $ 1 today.	The annual payment, including interest and principal, to amortize completely a loan of $ 100.	The total interest paid over the term on a loan of $1. The loan is amortized by regular periodic payments.	The average annual interest rate on a loan that is completely amortized by regular periodic payments.	
	$S = (1+i)^n$	$S\overline{n}| = \frac{(1+i)^n - 1}{i}$	$\frac{1}{S\overline{n}|} = \frac{i}{(1+i)^n - 1}$	$V^n = \frac{1}{(1+i)^n}$	$A\overline{n}| = \frac{1-V^n}{i}$	$\frac{1}{A\overline{n}|} = \frac{i}{1-V^n}$				

YEAR										PERIODS
	1.004 875	1.000 000	1.000 000 0000	.995 149	.995 149	1.004 875 0000	1205.85	.004 875	5.85	1
	1.009 774	2.004 875	.498 784 2135	.990 321	1.985 469	.503 659 2135	604.40	.007 318	4.39	2
	1.014 696	3.014 649	.331 713 6017	.985 516	2.970 986	.336 588 6017	403.91	.009 766	3.91	3
	1.019 643	4.029 345	.248 179 2837	.980 735	3.951 721	.253 054 2837	303.67	.012 217	3.67	4
	1.024 614	5.048 988	.198 059 4831	.975 977	4.927 699	.202 934 4831	243.53	.014 672	3.52	5
	1.029 609	6.073 602	.164 646 9412	.971 243	5.898 941	.169 521 9412	203.43	.017 132	3.43	6
	1.034 628	7.103 211	.140 781 4042	.966 531	6.865 472	.145 656 4042	174.79	.019 595	3.36	7
	1.039 672	8.137 839	.122 882 7454	.961 842	7.827 314	.127 757 7454	153.31	.022 062	3.31	8
	1.044 740	9.177 511	.108 962 0053	.957 176	8.784 490	.113 837 0053	136.61	.024 533	3.27	9
	1.049 833	10.222 251	.097 825 8082	.952 532	9.737 022	.102 700 8082	123.25	.027 008	3.24	10
	1.054 951	11.272 085	.088 714 7334	.947 911	10.684 933	.093 589 7334	112.31	.029 487	3.22	11
	1.060 094	12.327 036	.081 122 5002	.943 312	11.628 245	.085 997 5002	103.20	.031 970	3.20	12
1	1.060 094	12.327 036	.081 122 5002	.943 312	11.628 245	.085 997 5002	103.20	.031 970	3.20	12
2	1.123 800	25.394 857	.039 378 0519	.889 838	22.597 312	.044 253 0519	53.11	.062 073	3.10	24
3	1.191 334	39.247 980	.025 479 0186	.839 395	32.944 567	.030 354 0186	36.43	.092 745	3.09	36
4	1.262 926	53.933 596	.018 541 3189	.791 812	42.705 260	.023 416 3189	28.10	.123 983	3.10	48
5	1.338 821	69.501 734	.014 388 1303	.746 926	51.912 643	.019 263 1303	23.12	.155 788	3.12	60
6	1.419 276	86.005 428	.011 627 1731	.704 584	60.598 080	.016 502 1731	19.81	.188 156	3.14	72
7	1.504 567	103.500 900	.009 661 7517	.664 643	68.791 159	.014 536 7517	17.45	.221 087	3.16	84
8	1.594 983	122.047 751	.008 193 5144	.626 966	76.519 792	.013 068 5144	15.69	.254 577	3.18	96
9	1.690 832	141.709 162	.007 056 7068	.591 425	83.810 306	.011 931 7068	14.32	.288 624	3.21	108
10	1.792 442	162.552 111	.006 151 8734	.557 898	90.687 538	.011 026 8734	13.24	.323 225	3.23	120
11	1.900 157	184.647 603	.005 415 7215	.526 272	97.174 916	.010 290 7215	12.35	.358 375	3.26	132
12	2.014 346	208.070 908	.004 806 0539	.496 439	103.294 539	.009 681 0539	11.62	.394 072	3.28	144
13	2.135 396	232.901 820	.004 293 6547	.468 297	109.067 255	.009 168 6547	11.01	.430 310	3.31	156
14	2.263 722	259.224 928	.003 857 6537	.441 750	114.512 728	.008 732 6537	10.48	.467 086	3.34	168
15	2.399 758	287.129 906	.003 482 7442	.416 709	119.649 511	.008 357 7442	10.03	.504 394	3.36	180
16	2.543 970	316.711 813	.003 157 4446	.393 086	124.495 101	.008 032 4446	9.64	.542 229	3.39	192
17	2.696 848	348.071 425	.002 872 9736	.370 803	129.066 006	.007 747 9736	9.30	.580 587	3.42	204
18	2.858 913	381.315 570	.002 622 4998	.349 783	133.377 796	.007 497 4998	9.00	.619 460	3.44	216
19	3.030 718	416.557 499	.002 400 6290	.329 955	137.445 162	.007 275 6290	8.74	.658 843	3.47	228
20	3.212 847	453.917 267	.002 203 0446	.311 250	141.281 957	.007 078 0446	8.50	.698 731	3.49	240
21	3.405 920	493.522 145	.002 026 2515	.293 606	144.901 254	.006 901 2515	8.29	.739 115	3.52	252
22	3.610 597	535.507 050	.001 867 3890	.276 963	148.315 381	.006 742 3890	8.10	.779 991	3.55	264
23	3.827 573	580.015 008	.001 724 0933	.261 262	151.535 969	.006 599 0933	7.92	.821 350	3.57	276
24	4.057 589	627.197 641	.001 594 3938	.246 452	154.573 989	.006 469 3938	7.77	.863 185	3.60	288
25	4.301 426	677.215 682	.001 476 6344	.232 481	157.439 791	.006 351 6344	7.63	.905 490	3.62	300
26	4.559 918	730.239 521	.001 369 4137	.219 302	160.143 137	.006 244 4137	7.50	.948 257	3.65	312
27	4.833 943	786.449 792	.001 271 5370	.206 870	162.693 237	.006 146 5370	7.38	.991 478	3.67	324
28	5.124 435	846.037 979	.001 181 9800	.195 143	165.098 778	.006 056 9800	7.27	1.035 145	3.70	336
29	5.432 384	909.207 077	.001 099 8595	.184 081	167.367 954	.005 974 8595	7.17	1.079 251	3.72	348
30	5.758 840	976.172 277	.001 024 4093	.173 646	169.508 495	.005 899 4093	7.08	1.123 787	3.75	360
31	6.104 913	1047.161 705	.000 954 9623	.163 802	171.527 694	.005 829 9623	7.00	1.168 746	3.77	372
32	6.471 784	1122.417 192	.000 890 9343	.154 517	173.432 430	.005 765 9343	6.92	1.214 119	3.79	384
33	6.860 701	1202.195 106	.000 831 8117	.145 758	175.229 190	.005 706 8117	6.85	1.259 897	3.82	396
34	7.272 990	1286.767 218	.000 777 1413	.137 495	176.924 097	.005 652 1413	6.79	1.306 074	3.84	408
35	7.710 055	1376.421 631	.000 726 5216	.129 701	178.522 922	.005 601 5216	6.73	1.352 639	3.86	420
36	8.173 386	1471.463 764	.000 679 5954	.122 348	180.031 115	.005 554 5954	6.67	1.399 585	3.89	432
37	8.664 560	1572.217 388	.000 636 0444	.115 413	181.453 811	.005 511 0444	6.62	1.446 904	3.91	444
38	9.185 250	1679.025 730	.000 595 5835	.108 870	182.795 858	.005 470 5835	6.57	1.494 586	3.93	456
39	9.737 232	1792.252 645	.000 557 9571	.102 699	184.061 827	.005 432 9571	6.52	1.542 624	3.96	468
40	10.322 384	1912.283 852	.000 522 9349	.096 877	185.256 031	.005 397 9349	6.48	1.591 009	3.98	480
41	10.942 700	2039.528 251	.000 490 3095	.091 385	186.382 539	.005 365 3095	6.44	1.639 732	4.00	492
42	11.600 294	2174.419 313	.000 459 8929	.086 205	187.445 188	.005 334 8929	6.41	1.688 786	4.02	504
43	12.297 406	2317.416 559	.000 431 5150	.081 318	188.447 597	.005 306 5150	6.37	1.738 162	4.04	516
44	13.036 410	2469.007 125	.000 405 0211	.076 708	189.393 182	.005 280 0211	6.34	1.787 851	4.06	528
45	13.819 824	2629.707 421	.000 380 2704	.072 360	190.285 164	.005 255 2704	6.31	1.837 846	4.08	540
46	14.650 316	2800.064 888	.000 357 1346	.068 258	191.126 582	.005 232 1346	6.28	1.888 138	4.10	552
47	15.530 717	2980.659 868	.000 335 4962	.064 389	191.920 302	.005 210 4962	6.26	1.938 720	4.12	564
48	16.464 024	3172.107 578	.000 315 2478	.060 738	192.669 027	.005 190 2478	6.23	1.989 583	4.14	576
49	17.453 418	3375.060 204	.000 296 2910	.057 295	193.375 310	.005 171 2910	6.21	2.040 719	4.16	588
50	18.502 269	3590.209 126	.000 278 5353	.054 047	194.041 554	.005 153 5353	6.19	2.092 121	4.18	600

Effective Rate is 6.01 %   8 - 36   Annual Percentage Rate is 5.85 %

MONTHLY COMPOUND INTEREST AND ANNUITY

	Amount Of 1	Amount Of 1 Per Period	Sinking Fund Payment	Present Worth Of 1	Present Worth of 1 Per Period	Periodic Payment To Amortize 1	Constant Annual Percent	Total Interest	Annual Add On Rate	
	What a single $ 1 deposit grows to in the future. The deposit is made at the beginning of the first period.	What a series of $ 1 deposits grow to in the future. A deposit is made at the end of each period.	The amount to be deposited at the end of each period that grows to $ 1 in the future.	What $ 1 to be paid in the future is worth today. Value today of a single $ 1 payment tomorrow.	What $ 1 to be paid at the end of each period is worth today. Value today of a series of $ 1 payments tomorrow.	The mortgage payment to amortize a loan of $ 1. An annuity certain, payable at the end of each period, worth $ 1 today.	The annual payment, including interest and principal, to amortize completely a loan of $ 100.	The total interest paid over the term on a loan of $1. The loan is amortized by regular periodic payments.	The average annual interest rate on a loan that is completely amortized by regular periodic payments.	
	$S = (1+i)^n$	$S\overline{n} = \dfrac{(1+i)^n - 1}{i}$	$\dfrac{1}{S\overline{n}} = \dfrac{i}{(1+i)^n - 1}$	$V^n = \dfrac{1}{(1+i)^n}$	$A\overline{n} = \dfrac{1 - V^n}{i}$	$\dfrac{1}{A\overline{n}} = \dfrac{i}{1 - V^n}$				

YEAR										PERIODS
	1.004 896	1.000 000	1.000 000 0000	.995 128	.995 128	1.004 895 8333	1205.88	.004 896	5.88	1
	1.009 816	2.004 896	.498 779 0305	.990 280	1.985 408	.503 674 8638	604.41	.007 350	4.41	2
	1.014 760	3.014 711	.331 706 7024	.985 455	2.970 863	.336 602 5357	403.93	.009 808	3.92	3
	1.019 728	4.029 471	.248 171 5345	.980 654	3.951 517	.253 067 3679	303.69	.012 269	3.68	4
	1.024 720	5.049 199	.198 051 2308	.975 876	4.927 393	.202 947 0642	243.54	.014 735	3.54	5
	1.029 737	6.073 919	.164 638 3592	.971 122	5.898 515	.169 534 1925	203.45	.017 205	3.44	6
	1.034 778	7.103 656	.140 772 5916	.966 391	6.864 906	.145 668 4249	174.81	.019 679	3.37	7
	1.039 844	8.138 434	.122 873 7639	.961 682	7.826 588	.127 769 5972	153.33	.022 157	3.32	8
	1.044 935	9.178 278	.108 952 8962	.956 997	8.783 585	.113 848 7296	136.62	.024 639	3.29	9
	1.050 051	10.223 214	.097 816 6005	.952 335	9.735 920	.102 712 4339	123.26	.027 124	3.25	10
	1.055 192	11.273 265	.088 705 4481	.947 695	10.683 614	.093 601 2814	112.33	.029 614	3.23	11
	1.060 358	12.328 457	.081 113 1530	.943 078	11.626 692	.086 008 9863	103.22	.032 108	3.21	12
1	1.060 358	12.328 457	.081 113 1530	.943 078	11.626 692	.086 008 9863	103.22	.032 108	3.21	12
2	1.124 359	25.401 035	.039 368 4740	.889 395	22.591 566	.044 264 3073	53.12	.062 343	3.12	24
3	1.192 223	39.262 650	.025 469 4986	.838 769	32.932 293	.030 365 3320	36.44	.093 152	3.11	36
4	1.264 184	53.960 924	.018 531 9287	.791 024	42.684 401	.023 427 7621	28.12	.124 533	3.11	48
5	1.340 487	69.546 358	.014 378 8982	.745 997	51.881 397	.019 274 7315	23.13	.156 484	3.13	60
6	1.421 397	86.072 499	.011 618 1128	.703 533	60.554 878	.016 513 9461	19.82	.189 004	3.15	72
7	1.507 189	103.596 125	.009 652 8707	.663 487	68.734 645	.014 548 7040	17.46	.222 091	3.17	84
8	1.598 160	122.177 444	.008 184 8168	.625 719	76.448 799	.013 080 6501	15.70	.255 742	3.20	96
9	1.694 622	141.880 296	.007 048 1951	.590 102	83.723 847	.011 944 0284	14.34	.289 955	3.22	108
10	1.796 906	162.772 373	.006 143 5487	.556 512	90.584 781	.011 039 3820	13.25	.324 726	3.25	120
11	1.905 364	184.925 456	.005 407 5843	.524 834	97.055 175	.010 303 4177	12.37	.360 051	3.27	132
12	2.020 368	208.415 657	.004 798 1040	.494 959	103.157 258	.009 693 9374	11.64	.395 927	3.30	144
13	2.142 314	233.323 680	.004 285 8916	.466 785	108.911 997	.009 181 7249	11.02	.432 349	3.33	156
14	2.271 620	259.735 104	.003 850 0764	.440 215	114.339 163	.008 745 9098	10.50	.469 313	3.35	168
15	2.408 730	287.740 670	.003 475 3516	.415 156	119.457 401	.008 371 1849	10.05	.506 813	3.38	180
16	2.554 117	317.436 598	.003 150 2354	.391 525	124.284 298	.008 046 0687	9.66	.544 845	3.41	192
17	2.708 278	348.924 915	.002 865 9461	.369 238	128.836 436	.007 761 7794	9.32	.583 403	3.43	204
18	2.871 745	382.313 806	.002 615 6523	.348 220	133.129 456	.007 511 4857	9.02	.622 481	3.46	216
19	3.045 078	417.717 986	.002 393 9596	.328 399	137.178 107	.007 289 7930	8.75	.662 073	3.48	228
20	3.228 873	455.259 094	.002 196 5514	.309 706	140.996 299	.007 092 3847	8.52	.702 172	3.51	240
21	3.423 761	495.066 111	.002 019 9322	.292 076	144.597 151	.006 915 7656	8.30	.742 773	3.54	252
22	3.630 413	537.275 803	.001 861 2415	.275 451	147.993 034	.006 757 0748	8.11	.783 868	3.56	264
23	3.849 537	582.033 190	.001 718 1151	.259 771	151.195 615	.006 613 9484	7.94	.825 450	3.59	276
24	4.081 888	629.492 046	.001 588 5824	.244 985	154.215 898	.006 484 4158	7.79	.867 512	3.61	288
25	4.328 263	679.815 428	.001 470 9875	.231 040	157.064 259	.006 366 8208	7.65	.910 046	3.64	300
26	4.589 509	733.176 232	.001 363 9286	.217 888	159.750 485	.006 259 7619	7.52	.953 046	3.67	312
27	4.866 523	789.757 790	.001 266 2110	.205 486	162.283 805	.006 162 0443	7.40	.996 502	3.69	324
28	5.160 256	849.754 503	.001 176 8105	.193 789	164.672 922	.006 072 6438	7.29	1.040 408	3.72	336
29	5.471 720	913.372 501	.001 094 8436	.182 758	166.926 045	.005 990 6769	7.19	1.084 756	3.74	348
30	5.801 982	980.830 359	.001 019 5443	.172 355	169.050 915	.005 915 3776	7.10	1.129 536	3.77	360
31	6.152 178	1052.359 843	.000 950 2453	.162 544	171.054 832	.005 846 0786	7.02	1.174 741	3.79	372
32	6.523 512	1128.206 708	.000 886 3624	.153 292	172.944 682	.005 782 1957	6.94	1.220 363	3.81	384
33	6.917 259	1208.631 544	.000 827 3820	.144 566	174.726 957	.005 723 2153	6.87	1.266 393	3.84	396
34	7.334 771	1293.910 667	.000 772 8509	.136 337	176.407 780	.005 668 6842	6.81	1.312 823	3.86	408
35	7.777 484	1384.337 074	.000 722 3674	.128 576	177.992 928	.005 618 2008	6.75	1.359 644	3.88	420
36	8.246 917	1480.221 444	.000 675 5746	.121 257	179.487 845	.005 571 4079	6.69	1.406 848	3.91	432
37	8.744 686	1581.893 210	.000 632 1539	.114 355	180.897 667	.005 527 9873	6.64	1.454 426	3.93	444
38	9.272 498	1689.701 687	.000 591 8204	.107 846	182.227 240	.005 487 6538	6.59	1.502 370	3.95	456
39	9.832 168	1804.017 276	.000 554 3184	.101 707	183.481 130	.005 450 1517	6.55	1.550 671	3.98	468
40	10.425 619	1925.232 733	.000 519 4177	.095 918	184.663 645	.005 415 2511	6.50	1.599 321	4.00	480
41	11.054 889	2053.764 521	.000 486 9107	.090 458	185.778 849	.005 382 7441	6.46	1.648 310	4.02	492
42	11.722 141	2190.054 240	.000 456 6097	.085 309	186.830 573	.005 352 4430	6.43	1.697 631	4.04	504
43	12.429 666	2334.570 143	.000 428 3444	.080 453	187.822 431	.005 324 1777	6.39	1.747 276	4.06	516
44	13.179 897	2487.808 747	.000 401 9602	.075 873	188.757 829	.005 297 7935	6.36	1.797 235	4.08	528
45	13.975 410	2650.296 537	.000 377 3163	.071 554	189.639 983	.005 273 1496	6.33	1.847 501	4.11	540
46	14.818 939	2822.591 776	.000 354 2843	.067 481	190.471 922	.005 250 1177	6.31	1.898 065	4.13	552
47	15.713 381	3005.286 424	.000 332 7470	.063 640	191.256 505	.005 228 5803	6.28	1.948 919	4.15	564
48	16.661 811	3199.008 168	.000 312 5969	.060 017	191.996 428	.005 208 4302	6.26	2.000 056	4.17	576
49	17.667 486	3404.422 582	.000 293 7356	.056 601	192.694 233	.005 189 5689	6.23	2.051 467	4.19	588
50	18.733 861	3622.235 414	.000 276 0726	.053 379	193.352 317	.005 171 9059	6.21	2.103 144	4.21	600

	Amount Of 1	Amount Of 1 Per Period	Sinking Fund Payment	Present Worth Of 1	Present Worth of 1 Per Period	Periodic Payment To Amortize 1	Constant Annual Percent	Total Interest	Annual Add On Rate
	What a single $ 1 deposit grows to in the future. The deposit is made at the beginning of the first period.	What a series of $ 1 deposits grow to in the future. A deposit is made at the end of each period.	The amount to be deposited at the end of each period that grows to $ 1 in the future.	What $ 1 to be paid in the future is worth today. Value today of a single $ 1 payment tomorrow.	What $ 1 to be paid at the end of each period is worth today. Value today of a series of $ 1 payments tomorrow.	The mortgage payment to amortize a loan of $ 1. An annuity certain, payable at the end of each period, worth $ 1 today.	The annual payment, including interest and principal, to amortize completely a loan of $ 100.	The total interest paid over the term on a loan of $1. The loan is amortized by regular periodic payments.	The average annual interest rate on a loan that is completely amortized by regular periodic payments.
	$S = (1+i)^n$	$S\overline{n}| = \dfrac{(1+i)^n - 1}{i}$	$\dfrac{1}{S\overline{n}|} = \dfrac{i}{(1+i)^n - 1}$	$V^n = \dfrac{1}{(1+i)^n}$	$A\overline{n}| = \dfrac{1-V^n}{i}$	$\dfrac{1}{A\overline{n}|} = \dfrac{i}{1-V^n}$			

YEAR									PERIODS
	1.004 917	1.000 000	1.000 000 0000	.995 107	.995 107	1.004 916 6667	1205.90	.004 917	5.90	1
	1.009 858	2.004 917	.498 773 8476	.990 239	1.985 346	.503 690 5143	604.43	.007 381	4.43	2
	1.014 823	3.014 774	.331 699 8032	.985 394	2.970 740	.336 616 4698	403.94	.009 849	3.94	3
	1.019 812	4.029 597	.248 163 7857	.980 573	3.951 313	.253 080 4524	303.70	.012 322	3.70	4
	1.024 826	5.049 409	.198 042 9790	.975 775	4.927 088	.202 959 6457	243.56	.014 798	3.55	5
	1.029 865	6.074 235	.164 629 7776	.971 001	5.898 089	.169 546 4443	203.46	.017 279	3.46	6
	1.034 928	7.104 100	.140 763 7794	.966 250	6.864 339	.145 680 4460	174.82	.019 763	3.39	7
	1.040 017	8.139 029	.122 864 7830	.961 523	7.825 862	.127 781 4496	153.34	.022 252	3.34	8
	1.045 130	9.179 046	.108 943 7878	.956 818	8.782 681	.113 860 4545	136.64	.024 744	3.30	9
	1.050 269	10.224 176	.097 807 3936	.952 137	9.734 818	.102 724 0602	123.27	.027 241	3.27	10
	1.055 433	11.274 445	.088 696 1635	.947 479	10.682 296	.093 612 8302	112.34	.029 741	3.24	11
	1.060 622	12.329 877	.081 103 8066	.942 843	11.625 139	.086 020 4733	103.23	.032 246	3.22	12
1	1.060 622	12.329 877	.081 103 8066	.942 843	11.625 139	.086 020 4733	103.23	.032 246	3.22	12
2	1.124 919	25.407 216	.039 358 8978	.888 953	22.585 822	.044 275 5644	53.14	.062 614	3.13	24
3	1.193 114	39.277 327	.025 459 9812	.838 143	32.920 025	.030 376 6479	36.46	.093 559	3.12	36
4	1.265 442	53.988 210	.018 522 5419	.790 238	42.663 556	.023 439 2086	28.13	.125 082	3.13	48
5	1.342 156	69.591 019	.014 369 6703	.745 070	51.850 178	.019 286 3370	23.15	.157 180	3.14	60
6	1.423 520	86.139 636	.011 609 0576	.702 484	60.511 720	.016 525 7243	19.84	.189 852	3.16	72
7	1.509 816	103.691 462	.009 643 9956	.662 332	68.678 195	.014 560 6622	17.48	.223 096	3.19	84
8	1.601 344	122.307 313	.008 176 1260	.624 475	76.377 899	.013 092 7927	15.72	.256 908	3.21	96
9	1.698 421	142.051 692	.007 039 6909	.588 782	83.637 512	.011 956 3576	14.35	.291 287	3.24	108
10	1.801 382	162.993 012	.006 135 2323	.555 129	90.482 188	.011 051 8990	13.27	.326 228	3.26	120
11	1.910 586	185.203 835	.005 399 4562	.523 400	96.935 643	.010 316 1229	12.38	.361 728	3.29	132
12	2.026 409	208.761 121	.004 790 1640	.493 484	103.020 238	.009 706 8306	11.65	.397 784	3.31	144
13	2.149 254	233.746 494	.004 278 1390	.465 278	108.757 056	.009 194 8057	11.04	.434 390	3.34	156
14	2.279 545	260.246 527	.003 842 5105	.438 684	114.165 975	.008 759 1771	10.52	.471 542	3.37	168
15	2.417 736	288.353 043	.003 467 9710	.413 610	119.265 738	.008 384 6377	10.07	.509 235	3.39	180
16	2.564 304	318.163 429	.003 143 0388	.389 969	124.074 013	.008 059 7055	9.68	.547 463	3.42	192
17	2.719 756	349.780 977	.002 858 9319	.367 680	128.607 462	.007 775 5986	9.34	.586 222	3.45	204
18	2.884 633	383.315 242	.002 608 8188	.346 665	132.881 793	.007 525 4854	9.04	.625 505	3.48	216
19	3.059 505	418.882 416	.002 387 3048	.326 850	136.911 816	.007 303 9715	8.77	.665 305	3.50	228
20	3.244 978	456.605 741	.002 190 0732	.308 168	140.711 496	.007 106 7399	8.53	.705 618	3.53	240
21	3.441 695	496.615 925	.002 013 6285	.290 555	144.293 998	.006 930 2952	8.32	.746 434	3.55	252
22	3.650 337	539.051 602	.001 855 1100	.273 947	147.671 734	.006 771 7766	8.13	.787 749	3.58	264
23	3.871 627	584.059 811	.001 712 1534	.258 289	150.856 410	.006 628 8201	7.96	.829 554	3.61	276
24	4.106 333	631.796 502	.001 582 7881	.243 526	153.859 059	.006 499 4548	7.80	.871 843	3.63	288
25	4.355 266	682.427 083	.001 465 3580	.229 607	156.690 086	.006 382 0247	7.66	.914 607	3.66	300
26	4.619 291	736.126 985	.001 358 4613	.216 483	159.359 301	.006 275 1279	7.54	.957 840	3.68	312
27	4.899 321	793.082 277	.001 260 9032	.204 110	161.875 951	.006 177 5699	7.42	1.001 533	3.71	324
28	5.196 327	853.490 307	.001 171 6595	.192 444	164.248 757	.006 088 3261	7.31	1.045 678	3.73	336
29	5.511 339	917.560 387	.001 089 8465	.181 444	166.485 941	.006 006 5132	7.21	1.090 267	3.76	348
30	5.845 446	985.514 516	.001 014 6984	.171 073	168.595 254	.005 931 3651	7.12	1.135 291	3.78	360
31	6.199 808	1057.588 154	.000 945 5477	.161 295	170.584 005	.005 862 2143	7.04	1.180 744	3.81	372
32	6.575 653	1134.031 032	.000 881 8101	.152 076	172.459 086	.005 798 4768	6.96	1.226 615	3.83	384
33	6.974 281	1215.108 023	.000 822 9721	.143 384	174.226 992	.005 739 6388	6.89	1.272 897	3.86	396
34	7.397 075	1301.100 055	.000 768 5804	.135 189	175.893 851	.005 685 2471	6.83	1.319 581	3.88	408
35	7.845 500	1392.305 086	.000 718 2334	.127 462	177.465 437	.005 634 9001	6.77	1.366 658	3.90	420
36	8.321 109	1489.039 140	.000 671 5740	.120 176	178.947 196	.005 588 2407	6.71	1.414 120	3.93	432
37	8.825 551	1591.637 396	.000 628 2838	.113 307	180.344 262	.005 544 9505	6.66	1.461 958	3.95	444
38	9.360 572	1700.455 353	.000 588 0778	.106 831	181.661 476	.005 504 7444	6.61	1.510 163	3.97	456
39	9.928 028	1815.870 061	.000 550 7002	.100 725	182.903 402	.005 467 3669	6.57	1.558 728	4.00	468
40	10.529 884	1938.281 428	.000 515 9210	.094 968	184.074 344	.005 432 5876	6.52	1.607 642	4.02	480
41	11.168 225	2068.113 603	.000 483 5324	.089 540	185.178 358	.005 400 1991	6.49	1.656 898	4.04	492
42	11.845 264	2205.816 452	.000 453 3469	.084 422	186.219 270	.005 370 0135	6.45	1.706 487	4.06	504
43	12.563 347	2351.867 109	.000 425 1941	.079 597	187.200 686	.005 341 8608	6.42	1.756 400	4.08	516
44	13.324 961	2506.771 634	.000 398 9195	.075 047	188.126 008	.005 315 5861	6.38	1.806 629	4.11	528
45	14.132 745	2671.066 764	.000 374 3823	.070 758	188.998 441	.005 291 0489	6.35	1.857 166	4.13	540
46	14.989 499	2845.321 778	.000 351 4541	.066 713	189.821 009	.005 268 1208	6.33	1.908 003	4.15	552
47	15.898 191	3030.140 461	.000 330 0177	.062 900	190.596 561	.005 246 6844	6.30	1.959 130	4.17	564
48	16.861 969	3226.163 204	.000 309 9657	.059 305	191.327 785	.005 226 6324	6.28	2.010 540	4.19	576
49	17.884 174	3434.069 217	.000 291 1997	.055 915	192.017 215	.005 207 8664	6.25	2.062 225	4.21	588
50	18.968 346	3654.578 887	.000 273 6293	.052 719	192.667 239	.005 190 2960	6.23	2.114 178	4.23	600

MONTHLY COMPOUND INTEREST AND ANNUITY

5.95 % M

Amount Of 1	Amount Of 1 Per Period	Sinking Fund Payment	Present Worth Of 1	Present Worth of 1 Per Period	Periodic Payment To Amortize 1	Constant Annual Percent	Total Interest	Annual Add On Rate
What a single $ 1 deposit grows to in the future. The deposit is made at the beginning of the first period.	What a series of $ 1 deposits grow to in the future. A deposit is made at the end of each period.	The amount to be deposited at the end of each period that grows to $ 1 in the future.	What $ 1 to be paid in the future is worth today. Value today of a single $ 1 payment tomorrow.	What $ 1 to be paid at the end of each period is worth today. Value today of a series of $ 1 payments tomorrow.	The mortgage payment to amortize a loan of $ 1. An annuity certain, payable at the end of each period, worth $ 1 today.	The annual payment, including interest and principal, to amortize completely a loan of $ 100.	The total interest paid over the term on a loan of $1. The loan is amortized by regular periodic payments.	The average annual interest rate on a loan that is completely amortized by regular periodic payments.

$$S = (1+i)^n \qquad S\overline{n}| = \frac{(1+i)^n - 1}{i} \qquad \frac{1}{S\overline{n}|} = \frac{i}{(1+i)^n - 1} \qquad V^n = \frac{1}{(1+i)^n} \qquad A\overline{n}| = \frac{1 - V^n}{i} \qquad \frac{1}{A\overline{n}|} = \frac{i}{1 - V^n}$$

YEAR / **PERIODS**

YEAR	Amount Of 1	Amount Of 1 Per Period	Sinking Fund Payment	Present Worth Of 1	Present Worth of 1 Per Period	Periodic Payment To Amortize 1	Constant Annual Percent	Total Interest	Annual Add On Rate	PERIODS
	1.004 958	1.000 000	1.000 000 0000	.995 066	.995 066	1.004 958 3333	1205.95	.004 958	5.95	1
	1.009 941	2.004 958	.498 763 4822	.990 157	1.985 223	.503 721 8155	604.47	.007 444	4.47	2
	1.014 949	3.014 900	.331 686 0054	.985 271	2.970 494	.336 644 3387	403.98	.009 933	3.97	3
	1.019 981	4.029 848	.248 148 2888	.980 410	3.950 904	.253 106 6221	303.73	.012 426	3.73	4
	1.025 039	5.049 830	.198 026 4763	.975 573	4.926 477	.202 984 8096	243.59	.014 924	3.58	5
	1.030 121	6.074 869	.164 612 6158	.970 760	5.897 237	.169 570 9491	203.49	.017 426	3.49	6
	1.035 229	7.104 990	.140 746 1565	.965 970	6.863 206	.145 704 4898	174.85	.019 931	3.42	7
	1.040 362	8.140 219	.122 846 8228	.961 204	7.824 410	.127 805 1562	153.37	.022 441	3.37	8
	1.045 520	9.180 581	.108 925 5730	.956 462	8.780 872	.113 883 9063	136.67	.024 955	3.33	9
	1.050 704	10.226 101	.097 788 9817	.951 742	9.732 614	.102 747 3151	123.30	.027 473	3.30	10
	1.055 914	11.276 805	.088 677 5968	.947 047	10.679 661	.093 635 9301	112.37	.029 995	3.27	11
	1.061 150	12.332 720	.081 085 1165	.942 374	11.622 035	.086 043 4498	103.26	.032 521	3.25	12
1	1.061 150	12.332 720	.081 085 1165	.942 374	11.622 035	.086 043 4498	103.26	.032 521	3.25	12
2	1.126 039	25.419 582	.039 339 7506	.888 069	22.574 340	.044 298 0839	53.16	.063 154	3.16	24
3	1.194 896	39.306 702	.025 440 9542	.836 893	32.895 508	.030 399 2875	36.48	.094 374	3.15	36
4	1.267 963	54.043 016	.018 503 7786	.788 666	42.621 909	.023 462 1120	28.16	.126 181	3.15	48
5	1.345 499	69.680 451	.014 351 2274	.743 219	51.787 817	.019 309 5607	23.18	.158 574	3.17	60
6	1.427 776	86.274 112	.011 590 9625	.700 390	60.425 532	.016 549 2959	19.86	.191 549	3.19	72
7	1.515 084	103.882 470	.009 626 2632	.660 029	68.565 490	.014 584 5965	17.51	.225 106	3.22	84
8	1.607 731	122.567 576	.008 158 7646	.621 995	76.236 375	.013 117 0980	15.75	.259 241	3.24	96
9	1.706 043	142.395 270	.007 022 7052	.586 152	83.465 219	.011 981 0385	14.38	.293 952	3.27	108
10	1.810 367	163.435 422	.006 118 6246	.552 374	90.277 493	.011 076 9580	13.30	.329 235	3.29	120
11	1.921 071	185.762 174	.005 383 2273	.520 543	96.697 205	.010 341 5606	12.41	.365 086	3.32	132
12	2.038 544	209.454 202	.004 774 3134	.490 546	102.746 974	.009 732 6467	11.68	.401 501	3.35	144
13	2.163 200	234.594 990	.004 262 6656	.462 278	108.448 120	.009 220 9990	11.07	.438 476	3.37	156
14	2.295 479	261.273 131	.003 827 4123	.435 639	113.820 732	.008 785 7457	10.55	.476 005	3.40	168
15	2.435 847	289.582 633	.003 453 2458	.410 535	118.883 742	.008 411 5791	10.10	.514 084	3.43	180
16	2.584 799	319.623 253	.003 128 6835	.386 877	123.654 992	.008 087 0168	9.71	.552 707	3.45	192
17	2.742 858	351.500 850	.002 844 9433	.364 583	128.151 294	.007 803 2767	9.37	.591 868	3.48	204
18	2.910 583	385.327 753	.002 595 1933	.343 574	132.388 492	.007 553 5266	9.07	.631 562	3.51	216
19	3.088 565	421.223 162	.002 374 0385	.323 775	136.381 518	.007 332 3718	8.80	.671 781	3.54	228
20	3.277 430	459.313 566	.002 177 1619	.305 117	140.144 442	.007 135 4952	8.57	.712 519	3.56	240
21	3.477 844	499.733 189	.002 001 0678	.287 534	143.690 524	.006 959 4011	8.36	.753 769	3.59	252
22	3.690 513	542.624 460	.001 842 8952	.270 965	147.032 260	.006 801 2285	8.17	.795 524	3.62	264
23	3.916 187	588.138 521	.001 700 2797	.255 350	150.181 425	.006 658 6131	8.00	.837 777	3.64	276
24	4.155 661	636.435 755	.001 571 2505	.240 636	153.149 117	.006 529 5838	7.84	.880 520	3.67	288
25	4.409 778	687.686 352	.001 454 1513	.226 769	155.945 793	.006 412 4846	7.70	.923 745	3.69	300
26	4.679 435	742.070 909	.001 347 5801	.213 701	158.581 308	.006 305 9134	7.57	.967 445	3.72	312
27	4.965 581	799.781 068	.001 250 3422	.201 386	161.064 948	.006 208 6755	7.46	1.011 611	3.75	324
28	5.269 225	861.020 187	.001 161 4130	.189 781	163.405 467	.006 119 7463	7.35	1.056 235	3.77	336
29	5.591 437	926.004 062	.001 079 9089	.178 845	165.611 111	.006 038 2422	7.25	1.101 308	3.80	348
30	5.933 352	994.961 684	.001 005 0638	.168 539	167.689 653	.005 963 3972	7.16	1.146 823	3.82	360
31	6.296 175	1068.136 046	.000 936 2103	.158 827	169.648 417	.005 894 5437	7.08	1.192 770	3.85	372
32	6.681 184	1145.785 001	.000 872 7641	.149 674	171.494 305	.005 831 0974	7.00	1.239 141	3.87	384
33	7.089 737	1228.182 169	.000 814 2115	.141 049	173.233 822	.005 772 5448	6.93	1.285 928	3.90	396
34	7.523 272	1315.617 902	.000 760 0991	.132 921	174.873 098	.005 718 4324	6.87	1.333 120	3.92	408
35	7.983 318	1408.400 307	.000 710 0254	.125 261	176.417 910	.005 668 3587	6.81	1.380 711	3.94	420
36	8.471 496	1506.856 331	.000 663 6333	.118 043	177.873 700	.005 621 9666	6.75	1.428 690	3.97	432
37	8.989 526	1611.332 915	.000 620 6042	.111 241	179.245 599	.005 578 9375	6.70	1.477 048	3.99	444
38	9.539 233	1722.198 215	.000 580 6533	.104 830	180.538 440	.005 538 9866	6.65	1.525 778	4.02	456
39	10.122 554	1839.842 898	.000 543 5247	.098 789	181.756 781	.005 501 8580	6.61	1.574 870	4.04	468
40	10.741 546	1964.681 522	.000 508 9883	.093 096	182.904 914	.005 467 3217	6.57	1.624 314	4.06	480
41	11.398 389	2097.153 994	.000 476 8367	.087 732	183.986 884	.005 435 1700	6.53	1.674 104	4.08	492
42	12.095 397	2237.727 124	.000 446 8820	.082 676	185.006 505	.005 405 2153	6.49	1.724 229	4.11	504
43	12.835 027	2386.896 262	.000 418 9541	.077 912	185.967 369	.005 377 2874	6.46	1.774 680	4.13	516
44	13.619 886	2545.187 054	.000 392 8984	.073 422	186.872 863	.005 351 2318	6.43	1.825 450	4.15	528
45	14.452 738	2713.157 286	.000 368 5743	.069 191	187.726 177	.005 326 9076	6.40	1.876 530	4.17	540
46	15.336 519	2891.398 853	.000 345 8534	.065 204	188.530 317	.005 304 1867	6.37	1.927 611	4.19	552
47	16.274 343	3080.539 844	.000 324 6184	.061 446	189.288 119	.005 282 9518	6.34	1.979 585	4.21	564
48	17.269 515	3281.246 757	.000 304 7622	.057 906	190.002 251	.005 263 0955	6.32	2.031 543	4.23	576
49	18.325 541	3494.226 844	.000 286 1863	.054 569	190.675 231	.005 244 5197	6.30	2.083 778	4.25	588
50	19.446 143	3720.230 607	.000 268 8005	.051 424	191.309 430	.005 227 1339	6.28	2.136 280	4.27	600

Effective Rate is 6.11 %

Annual Percentage Rate is 5.95 %

Amount Of 1	Amount Of 1 Per Period	Sinking Fund Payment	Present Worth Of 1	Present Worth of 1 Per Period	Periodic Payment To Amortize 1	Constant Annual Percent	Total Interest	Annual Add On Rate	
What a single $ 1 deposit grows to in the future. The deposit is made at the beginning of the first period.	What a series of $ 1 deposits grow to in the future. A deposit is made at the end of each period.	The amount to be deposited at the end of each period that grows to $ 1 in the future.	What $ 1 to be paid in the future is worth today. Value today of a single $ 1 payment tomorrow.	What $ 1 to be paid at the end of each period is worth today. Value today of a series of $ 1 payments tomorrow.	The mortgage payment to amortize a loan of $ 1. An annuity certain, payable at the end of each period, worth $ 1 today.	The annual payment, including interest and principal, to amortize completely a loan of $ 100.	The total interest paid over the term on a loan of $1. The loan is amortized by regular periodic payments.	The average annual interest rate on a loan that is completely amortized by regular periodic payments.	
$S = (1+i)^n$	$S\overline{n}| = \dfrac{(1+i)^n - 1}{i}$	$\dfrac{1}{S\overline{n}|} = \dfrac{i}{(1+i)^n - 1}$	$V^n = \dfrac{1}{(1+i)^n}$	$A\overline{n}| = \dfrac{1 - V^n}{i}$	$\dfrac{1}{A\overline{n}|} = \dfrac{i}{1 - V^n}$				

YEAR									PERIODS
	1.005 000	1.000 000	1.000 000 0000	.995 025	.995 025	1.005 000 0000	1206.00	.005 000	6.00	1
	1.010 025	2.005 000	.498 753 1172	.990 075	1.985 099	.503 753 1172	604.51	.007 506	4.50	2
	1.015 075	3.015 025	.331 672 2084	.985 149	2.970 248	.336 672 2084	404.01	.010 017	4.01	3
	1.020 151	4.030 100	.248 132 7930	.980 248	3.950 496	.253 132 7930	303.76	.012 531	3.76	4
	1.025 251	5.050 251	.198 009 9750	.975 371	4.925 866	.203 009 9750	243.62	.015 050	3.61	5
	1.030 378	6.075 502	.164 595 4556	.970 518	5.896 384	.169 595 4556	203.52	.017 573	3.51	6
	1.035 529	7.105 879	.140 728 5355	.965 690	6.862 074	.145 728 5355	174.88	.020 100	3.45	7
	1.040 707	8.141 409	.122 828 8649	.960 885	7.822 959	.127 828 8649	153.40	.022 631	3.39	8
	1.045 911	9.182 116	.108 907 3606	.956 105	8.779 064	.113 907 3606	136.69	.025 166	3.36	9
	1.051 140	10.228 026	.097 770 5727	.951 348	9.730 412	.102 770 5727	123.33	.027 706	3.32	10
	1.056 396	11.279 167	.088 659 0331	.946 615	10.677 027	.093 659 0331	112.40	.030 249	3.30	11
	1.061 678	12.335 562	.081 066 4297	.941 905	11.618 932	.086 066 4297	103.28	.032 797	3.28	12
1	1.061 678	12.335 562	.081 066 4297	.941 905	11.618 932	.086 066 4297	103.28	.032 797	3.28	12
2	1.127 160	25.431 955	.039 320 6103	.887 186	22.562 866	.044 320 6103	53.19	.063 695	3.18	24
3	1.196 681	39.336 105	.025 421 9375	.835 645	32.871 016	.030 421 9375	36.51	.095 190	3.17	36
4	1.270 489	54.097 832	.018 485 0290	.787 098	42.580 318	.023 485 0290	28.19	.127 281	3.18	48
5	1.348 850	69.770 031	.014 332 8015	.741 372	51.725 561	.019 332 8015	23.20	.159 968	3.20	60
6	1.432 044	86.408 856	.011 572 8879	.698 302	60.339 514	.016 572 8879	19.89	.193 248	3.22	72
7	1.520 370	104.073 927	.009 608 5545	.657 735	68.453 042	.014 608 5545	17.54	.227 119	3.24	84
8	1.614 143	122.828 542	.008 141 4302	.619 524	76.095 218	.013 141 4302	15.77	.261 577	3.27	96
9	1.713 699	142.739 900	.007 005 7496	.583 533	83.293 424	.012 005 7496	14.41	.296 621	3.30	108
10	1.819 397	163.879 347	.006 102 0502	.549 633	90.073 453	.011 102 0502	13.33	.332 246	3.32	120
11	1.931 613	186.322 629	.005 367 0346	.517 702	96.459 599	.010 367 0346	12.45	.368 449	3.35	132
12	2.050 751	210.150 163	.004 758 5021	.487 626	102.474 743	.009 758 5021	11.72	.405 224	3.38	144
13	2.177 237	235.447 328	.004 247 2344	.459 298	108.140 440	.009 247 2344	11.10	.442 569	3.40	156
14	2.311 524	262.304 766	.003 812 3592	.432 615	113.476 990	.008 812 3592	10.58	.480 476	3.43	168
15	2.454 094	290.818 712	.003 438 5683	.407 482	118.503 515	.008 438 5683	10.13	.518 942	3.46	180
16	2.605 457	321.091 337	.003 114 3786	.383 810	123.238 025	.008 114 3786	9.74	.557 961	3.49	192
17	2.766 156	353.231 110	.002 831 0077	.361 513	127.697 486	.007 831 0077	9.40	.597 526	3.51	204
18	2.936 766	387.353 194	.002 581 6232	.340 511	131.897 876	.007 581 6232	9.10	.637 631	3.54	216
19	3.117 899	423.579 854	.002 360 8299	.320 729	135.854 246	.007 360 8299	8.84	.678 269	3.57	228
20	3.310 204	462.040 895	.002 164 3106	.302 096	139.580 772	.007 164 3106	8.60	.719 435	3.60	240
21	3.514 371	502.874 129	.001 988 5692	.284 546	143.090 806	.006 988 5692	8.39	.761 119	3.62	252
22	3.731 129	546.225 867	.001 830 7445	.268 015	146.396 927	.006 830 7445	8.20	.803 317	3.65	264
23	3.961 257	592.251 446	.001 688 4720	.252 445	149.510 979	.006 688 4720	8.03	.846 018	3.68	276
24	4.205 579	641.115 782	.001 559 7807	.237 779	152.444 121	.006 559 7807	7.88	.889 217	3.71	288
25	4.464 970	692.993 962	.001 443 0140	.223 966	155.206 864	.006 443 0140	7.74	.932 904	3.73	300
26	4.740 359	748.071 876	.001 336 7699	.210 954	157.809 106	.006 336 7699	7.61	.977 072	3.76	312
27	5.032 734	806.546 875	.001 239 8535	.198 699	160.260 172	.006 239 8535	7.49	1.021 713	3.78	324
28	5.343 142	868.628 484	.001 151 2402	.187 156	162.568 844	.006 151 2402	7.39	1.066 817	3.81	336
29	5.672 696	934.539 150	.001 070 0461	.176 283	164.743 394	.006 070 0461	7.29	1.112 376	3.84	348
30	6.022 575	1004.515 042	.000 995 5053	.166 042	166.791 614	.005 995 5053	7.20	1.158 382	3.86	360
31	6.394 034	1078.806 895	.000 926 9500	.156 396	168.720 844	.005 926 9500	7.12	1.204 825	3.89	372
32	6.788 405	1157.680 906	.000 863 7959	.147 310	170.537 996	.005 863 7959	7.04	1.251 698	3.91	384
33	7.207 098	1241.419 693	.000 805 5294	.138 752	172.249 581	.005 805 5294	6.97	1.298 990	3.94	396
34	7.651 617	1330.323 306	.000 751 6970	.130 691	173.861 732	.005 751 6970	6.91	1.346 692	3.96	408
35	8.123 551	1424.710 299	.000 701 8971	.123 099	175.380 226	.005 701 8971	6.85	1.394 797	3.99	420
36	8.624 594	1524.918 875	.000 655 7726	.115 947	176.810 504	.005 655 7726	6.79	1.443 294	4.01	432
37	9.156 540	1631.308 097	.000 613 0050	.109 212	178.157 690	.005 613 0050	6.74	1.492 174	4.03	444
38	9.721 296	1744.259 173	.000 573 3093	.102 867	179.426 611	.005 573 3093	6.69	1.541 429	4.06	456
39	10.320 884	1864.176 824	.000 536 4298	.096 891	180.621 815	.005 536 4298	6.65	1.591 049	4.08	468
40	10.957 454	1991.490 734	.000 502 1364	.091 262	181.747 584	.005 502 1364	6.61	1.641 025	4.10	480
41	11.633 285	2126.657 088	.000 470 2216	.085 960	182.807 952	.005 470 2216	6.57	1.691 349	4.13	492
42	12.350 801	2270.160 206	.000 440 4975	.080 966	183.806 718	.005 440 4975	6.53	1.742 011	4.15	504
43	13.112 571	2422.514 282	.000 412 7943	.076 263	184.747 462	.005 412 7943	6.50	1.793 002	4.17	516
44	13.921 326	2584.265 225	.000 386 9572	.071 832	185.633 553	.005 386 9572	6.47	1.844 313	4.19	528
45	14.779 963	2755.992 611	.000 362 8457	.067 659	186.468 166	.005 362 8457	6.44	1.895 937	4.21	540
46	15.691 559	2938.311 767	.000 340 3315	.063 729	187.254 294	.005 340 3315	6.41	1.947 863	4.23	552
47	16.659 380	3131.875 970	.000 319 2974	.060 026	187.994 751	.005 319 2974	6.39	2.000 084	4.26	564
48	17.686 894	3337.378 789	.000 299 6364	.056 539	188.692 192	.005 299 6364	6.36	2.052 591	4.28	576
49	18.777 783	3555.556 573	.000 281 2499	.053 254	189.349 115	.005 281 2499	6.34	2.105 375	4.30	588
50	19.935 955	3787.191 085	.000 264 0479	.050 161	189.967 875	.005 264 0479	6.32	2.158 429	4.32	600

Effective Rate is 6.17 %

Annual Percentage Rate is 6.00 %

MONTHLY COMPOUND INTEREST AND ANNUITY

	Amount Of 1	Amount Of 1 Per Period	Sinking Fund Payment	Present Worth Of 1	Present Worth of 1 Per Period	Periodic Payment To Amortize 1	Constant Annual Percent	Total Interest	Annual Add On Rate	
	What a single $ 1 deposit grows to in the future. The deposit is made at the beginning of the first period.	What a series of $ 1 deposits grow to in the future. A deposit is made at the end of each period.	The amount to be deposited at the end of each period that grows to $ 1 in the future.	What $ 1 to be paid in the future is worth today. Value today of a single $ 1 payment tomorrow.	What $ 1 to be paid at the end of each period is worth today. Value today of a series of $ 1 payments tomorrow.	The mortgage payment to amortize a loan of $ 1. An annuity certain, payable at the end of each period, worth $ 1 today.	The annual payment, including interest and principal, to amortize completely a loan of $ 100.	The total interest paid over the term on a loan of $1. The loan is amortized by regular periodic payments.	The average annual interest rate on a loan that is completely amortized by regular periodic payments.	
	$S = (1+i)^n$	$S\overline{n} = \frac{(1+i)^n - 1}{i}$	$\frac{1}{S\overline{n}} = \frac{i}{(1+i)^n - 1}$	$V^n = \frac{1}{(1+i)^n}$	$A\overline{n} = \frac{1-V^n}{i}$	$\frac{1}{A\overline{n}} = \frac{i}{1-V^n}$			**PERIODS**	

YEAR

	1.005 042	1.000 000	1.000 000 0000	.994 984	.994 984	1.005 041 6667	1206.05	.005 042	6.05	1
	1.010 109	2.005 042	.498 742 7526	.989 992	1.984 976	.503 784 4193	604.55	.007 569	4.54	2
	1.015 201	3.015 150	.331 658 4121	.985 026	2.970 002	.336 700 0788	404.05	.010 100	4.04	3
	1.020 320	4.030 352	.248 117 2982	.980 085	3.950 087	.253 158 9649	303.80	.012 636	3.79	4
	1.025 464	5.050 671	.197 993 4750	.975 169	4.925 256	.203 035 1417	243.65	.015 176	3.64	5
	1.030 634	6.076 135	.164 578 2972	.970 277	5.895 532	.169 619 9638	203.55	.017 720	3.54	6
	1.035 830	7.106 769	.140 710 9166	.965 409	6.860 942	.145 752 5832	174.91	.020 268	3.47	7
	1.041 052	8.142 599	.122 810 9093	.960 567	7.821 508	.127 852 5760	153.43	.022 821	3.42	8
	1.046 301	9.183 651	.108 889 1509	.955 748	8.777 256	.113 930 8175	136.72	.025 377	3.38	9
	1.051 576	10.229 952	.097 752 1666	.950 954	9.728 210	.102 793 8333	123.36	.027 938	3.35	10
	1.056 878	11.281 528	.088 640 4726	.946 183	10.674 393	.093 682 1393	112.42	.030 504	3.33	11
	1.062 206	12.338 406	.081 047 7464	.941 437	11.615 830	.086 089 4130	103.31	.033 073	3.31	12
1	1.062 206	12.338 406	.081 047 7464	.941 437	11.615 830	.086 089 4130	103.31	.033 073	3.31	12
2	1.128 282	25.444 336	.039 301 4768	.886 303	22.551 401	.044 343 1435	53.22	.064 235	3.21	24
3	1.198 468	39.365 536	.025 402 9310	.834 399	32.846 550	.030 444 5977	36.54	.096 006	3.20	36
4	1.273 020	54.152 720	.018 466 2932	.785 534	42.538 783	.023 507 9598	28.21	.128 382	3.21	48
5	1.352 210	69.859 757	.014 314 3928	.739 530	51.663 408	.019 356 0594	23.23	.161 364	3.23	60
6	1.436 325	86.543 868	.011 554 8337	.696 221	60.253 667	.016 596 5003	19.92	.194 948	3.25	72
7	1.525 674	104.265 833	.009 590 8695	.655 448	68.340 853	.014 632 5362	17.56	.229 133	3.27	84
8	1.620 580	123.090 213	.008 124 1227	.617 063	75.954 428	.013 165 7894	15.80	.263 916	3.30	96
9	1.721 390	143.085 585	.006 988 8242	.580 926	83.122 128	.012 030 4909	14.44	.299 293	3.33	108
10	1.828 471	164.324 792	.006 085 5090	.546 905	89.870 065	.011 127 1757	13.36	.335 261	3.35	120
11	1.942 213	186.885 207	.005 350 8783	.514 877	96.222 822	.010 392 5450	12.48	.371 816	3.38	132
12	2.063 030	210.849 019	.004 742 7302	.484 724	102.203 541	.009 784 3968	11.75	.408 953	3.41	144
13	2.191 364	236.303 526	.004 231 8454	.456 337	107.834 010	.009 273 5121	11.13	.446 668	3.44	156
14	2.327 680	263.341 460	.003 797 3512	.429 612	113.134 742	.008 839 0178	10.61	.484 955	3.46	168
15	2.472 476	292.061 319	.003 423 9385	.404 453	118.125 046	.008 465 6052	10.16	.523 809	3.49	180
16	2.626 279	322.567 730	.003 100 1241	.380 767	122.823 102	.008 141 7908	9.78	.563 224	3.52	192
17	2.789 650	354.971 826	.002 817 1250	.358 468	127.246 025	.007 858 7917	9.44	.603 193	3.55	204
18	2.963 183	389.391 655	.002 568 1084	.337 475	131.409 928	.007 609 7751	9.14	.643 711	3.58	216
19	3.147 511	425.952 609	.002 347 6790	.317 711	135.329 980	.007 389 3457	8.87	.684 771	3.60	228
20	3.343 306	464.787 879	.002 151 5191	.299 105	139.020 461	.007 193 1858	8.64	.726 365	3.63	240
21	3.551 280	506.038 940	.001 976 1325	.281 589	142.494 816	.007 017 7992	8.43	.768 485	3.66	252
22	3.772 191	549.856 071	.001 818 6577	.265 098	145.765 701	.006 860 3244	8.24	.811 126	3.69	264
23	4.006 844	596.398 895	.001 676 7301	.249 573	148.845 034	.006 718 3968	8.07	.854 278	3.71	276
24	4.256 095	645.836 968	.001 548 3784	.234 957	151.744 031	.006 590 0450	7.91	.897 933	3.74	288
25	4.520 850	698.350 393	.001 431 9459	.221 197	154.473 254	.006 473 6126	7.77	.942 084	3.77	300
26	4.802 074	754.130 474	.001 326 0305	.208 243	157.042 644	.006 367 6972	7.65	.986 722	3.80	312
27	5.100 793	813.380 419	.001 229 4370	.196 048	159.461 564	.006 271 1037	7.53	1.031 838	3.82	324
28	5.418 094	876.316 073	.001 141 1408	.184 567	161.738 823	.006 182 8074	7.42	1.077 423	3.85	336
29	5.755 132	943.166 711	.001 060 2579	.173 758	163.882 720	.006 101 9246	7.33	1.123 470	3.87	348
30	6.113 137	1014.175 868	.000 986 0223	.163 582	165.901 062	.006 027 6889	7.24	1.169 968	3.90	360
31	6.493 411	1089.602 230	.000 917 7661	.154 002	167.801 205	.005 959 4328	7.16	1.216 909	3.93	372
32	6.897 341	1169.720 574	.000 854 9050	.144 983	169.590 069	.005 896 5717	7.08	1.264 284	3.95	384
33	7.326 398	1254.822 771	.000 796 9253	.136 493	171.274 171	.005 838 5920	7.01	1.312 082	3.98	396
34	7.782 145	1345.218 845	.000 743 3735	.128 499	172.859 648	.005 785 0401	6.95	1.360 296	4.00	408
35	8.266 242	1441.238 110	.000 693 8479	.120 974	174.352 273	.005 735 5145	6.89	1.408 916	4.03	420
36	8.780 453	1543.230 362	.000 647 9914	.113 889	175.757 486	.005 689 6581	6.83	1.457 932	4.05	432
37	9.326 651	1651.567 157	.000 605 4855	.107 220	177.080 406	.005 647 1522	6.78	1.507 336	4.07	444
38	9.906 826	1766.643 164	.000 566 0453	.100 941	178.325 851	.005 607 7119	6.73	1.557 117	4.10	456
39	10.523 091	1888.877 605	.000 529 4149	.095 029	179.498 358	.005 571 0816	6.69	1.607 266	4.12	468
40	11.177 692	2018.715 777	.000 495 3644	.089 464	180.602 200	.005 537 0311	6.65	1.657 775	4.14	480
41	11.873 013	2156.630 680	.000 463 6863	.084 225	181.641 398	.005 505 3529	6.61	1.708 634	4.17	492
42	12.611 587	2303.124 735	.000 434 1927	.079 292	182.619 737	.005 475 8594	6.58	1.759 833	4.19	504
43	13.396 105	2458.731 618	.000 406 7138	.074 649	183.540 781	.005 448 3804	6.54	1.811 364	4.21	516
44	14.229 425	2624.018 203	.000 381 0949	.070 277	184.407 886	.005 422 7616	6.51	1.863 218	4.23	528
45	15.114 583	2799.586 627	.000 357 1956	.066 161	185.224 211	.005 398 8623	6.48	1.915 386	4.26	540
46	16.054 802	2986.076 484	.000 334 8876	.062 287	185.992 729	.005 376 5543	6.46	1.967 858	4.28	552
47	17.053 509	3184.167 152	.000 314 0539	.058 639	186.716 240	.005 355 7205	6.43	2.020 626	4.30	564
48	18.114 342	3394.580 275	.000 294 5872	.055 205	187.397 380	.005 336 2539	6.41	2.073 682	4.32	576
49	19.241 165	3618.082 384	.000 276 3895	.051 972	188.038 631	.005 318 0562	6.39	2.127 017	4.34	588
50	20.438 084	3855.487 694	.000 259 3706	.048 928	188.642 327	.005 301 0372	6.37	2.180 622	4.36	600

Amount Of 1	Amount Of 1 Per Period	Sinking Fund Payment	Present Worth Of 1	Present Worth of 1 Per Period	Periodic Payment To Amortize 1	Constant Annual Percent	Total Interest	Annual Add On Rate
What a single $1 deposit grows to in the future. The deposit is made at the beginning of the first period.	What a series of $1 deposits grow to in the future. A deposit is made at the end of each period.	The amount to be deposited at the end of each period that grows to $1 in the future.	What $1 to be paid in the future is worth today. Value today of a single $1 payment tomorrow.	What $1 to be paid at the end of each period is worth today. Value today of a series of $1 payments tomorrow.	The mortgage payment to amortize a loan of $1. An annuity certain, payable at the end of each period, worth $1 today.	The annual payment, including interest and principal, to amortize completely a loan of $100.	The total interest paid over the term on a loan of $1. The loan is amortized by regular periodic payments.	The average annual interest rate on a loan that is completely amortized by regular periodic payments.
$S = (1+i)^n$	$S\overline{n}\rvert = \dfrac{(1+i)^n - 1}{i}$	$\dfrac{1}{S\overline{n}\rvert} = \dfrac{i}{(1+i)^n - 1}$	$V^n = \dfrac{1}{(1+i)^n}$	$A\overline{n}\rvert = \dfrac{1-V^n}{i}$	$\dfrac{1}{A\overline{n}\rvert} = \dfrac{i}{1-V^n}$			

YEAR									PERIODS
	1.005 083	1.000 000	1.000 000 0000	.994 942	.994 942	1.005 083 3333	1206.10	.005 083	6.10	1
	1.010 193	2.005 083	.498 732 3885	.989 910	1.984 853	.503 815 7218	604.58	.007 631	4.58	2
	1.015 328	3.015 276	.331 644 6166	.984 904	2.969 756	.336 727 9499	404.08	.010 184	4.07	3
	1.020 489	4.030 603	.248 101 8046	.979 922	3.949 679	.253 185 1379	303.83	.012 741	3.82	4
	1.025 676	5.051 092	.197 976 9765	.974 966	4.924 645	.203 060 3098	243.68	.015 302	3.67	5
	1.030 890	6.076 769	.164 561 1403	.970 035	5.894 681	.169 644 4737	203.58	.017 867	3.57	6
	1.036 131	7.107 659	.140 693 2996	.965 129	6.859 810	.145 776 6329	174.94	.020 436	3.50	7
	1.041 398	8.143 790	.122 792 9559	.960 248	7.820 058	.127 876 2893	153.46	.023 010	3.45	8
	1.046 691	9.185 187	.108 870 9436	.955 391	8.775 449	.113 954 2770	136.75	.025 588	3.41	9
	1.052 012	10.231 879	.097 733 7633	.950 559	9.726 009	.102 817 0966	123.39	.028 171	3.38	10
	1.057 360	11.283 891	.088 621 9153	.945 752	10.671 761	.093 705 2486	112.45	.030 758	3.36	11
	1.062 735	12.341 250	.081 029 0665	.940 969	11.612 729	.086 112 3998	103.34	.033 349	3.33	12
1	1.062 735	12.341 250	.081 029 0665	.940 969	11.612 729	.086 112 3998	103.34	.033 349	3.33	12
2	1.129 405	25.456 725	.039 282 3502	.885 422	22.539 943	.044 365 6835	53.24	.064 776	3.24	24
3	1.200 258	39.394 996	.025 383 9349	.833 154	32.822 109	.030 467 2682	36.57	.096 822	3.23	36
4	1.275 556	54.207 679	.018 447 5710	.783 972	42.497 304	.023 530 9043	28.24	.129 483	3.24	48
5	1.355 577	69.949 631	.014 296 0011	.737 693	51.601 359	.019 379 3344	23.26	.162 760	3.26	60
6	1.440 619	86.679 150	.011 536 7998	.694 146	60.167 990	.016 620 1331	19.95	.196 650	3.28	72
7	1.530 996	104.458 190	.009 573 2082	.653 170	68.228 920	.014 656 5415	17.59	.231 149	3.30	84
8	1.627 042	123.352 592	.008 106 8422	.614 612	75.814 002	.013 190 1755	15.83	.266 257	3.33	96
9	1.729 114	143.432 329	.006 971 9289	.578 331	82.951 327	.012 055 2622	14.47	.301 968	3.36	108
10	1.837 590	164.771 762	.006 069 0011	.544 191	89.667 326	.011 152 3344	13.39	.338 280	3.38	120
11	1.952 870	187.449 918	.005 334 7583	.512 067	95.986 870	.010 418 0916	12.51	.375 188	3.41	132
12	2.075 383	211.550 781	.004 726 9974	.481 839	101.933 362	.009 810 3308	11.78	.412 688	3.44	144
13	2.205 582	237.163 604	.004 216 4986	.453 395	107.528 825	.009 299 8319	11.16	.450 774	3.47	156
14	2.343 948	264.383 240	.003 782 3880	.426 631	112.793 980	.008 865 7214	10.64	.489 441	3.50	168
15	2.490 995	293.310 490	.003 409 3564	.401 446	117.748 326	.008 492 6897	10.20	.528 684	3.52	180
16	2.647 267	324.052 483	.003 085 9199	.377 748	122.410 210	.008 169 2532	9.81	.568 497	3.55	192
17	2.813 342	356.723 066	.002 803 2950	.355 449	126.796 896	.007 886 6284	9.47	.608 872	3.58	204
18	2.989 836	391.443 227	.002 554 6489	.334 466	130.924 631	.007 637 9822	9.17	.649 804	3.61	216
19	3.177 403	428.341 547	.002 334 5856	.314 722	134.808 699	.007 417 9189	8.91	.691 286	3.64	228
20	3.376 736	467.554 671	.002 138 7873	.296 144	138.463 486	.007 222 1206	8.67	.733 309	3.67	240
21	3.588 575	509.227 819	.001 963 7576	.278 662	141.902 525	.007 047 0909	8.46	.775 867	3.69	252
22	3.813 703	553.515 318	.001 806 6347	.262 212	145.138 554	.006 889 9681	8.27	.818 952	3.72	264
23	4.052 954	600.581 180	.001 665 0538	.246 734	148.183 555	.006 748 3872	8.10	.862 555	3.75	276
24	4.307 215	650.599 705	.001 537 0434	.232 169	151.048 805	.006 620 3768	7.95	.906 669	3.78	288
25	4.577 427	703.756 126	.001 420 9468	.218 463	153.744 916	.006 504 2801	7.81	.951 284	3.81	300
26	4.864 590	760.247 298	.001 315 3615	.205 567	156.281 872	.006 398 6948	7.68	.996 393	3.83	312
27	5.169 769	820.282 427	.001 219 0923	.193 432	158.669 067	.006 302 4256	7.57	1.041 986	3.86	324
28	5.494 093	884.083 841	.001 131 1144	.182 014	160.915 344	.006 214 4478	7.46	1.088 054	3.89	336
29	5.838 763	951.887 817	.001 050 5440	.171 269	163.029 019	.006 133 8773	7.37	1.134 589	3.91	348
30	6.205 056	1023.945 454	.000 976 6145	.161 159	165.017 922	.006 059 9479	7.28	1.181 581	3.94	360
31	6.594 328	1100.523 604	.000 908 6584	.151 645	166.889 416	.005 991 9917	7.20	1.229 021	3.96	372
32	7.008 021	1181.905 862	.000 846 0911	.142 694	168.650 434	.005 929 4244	7.12	1.276 899	3.99	384
33	7.447 668	1268.393 609	.000 788 3988	.134 270	170.307 497	.005 871 7321	7.05	1.325 206	4.02	396
34	7.914 895	1360.307 139	.000 735 1281	.126 344	171.866 740	.005 818 4614	6.99	1.373 932	4.04	408
35	8.411 433	1457.986 836	.000 685 8772	.118 886	173.333 940	.005 769 2106	6.93	1.423 068	4.07	420
36	8.939 122	1561.794 438	.000 640 2891	.111 868	174.714 529	.005 723 6225	6.87	1.472 605	4.09	432
37	9.499 915	1672.114 377	.000 598 0452	.105 264	176.013 619	.005 681 3785	6.82	1.522 532	4.11	444
38	10.095 889	1789.355 204	.000 558 8605	.099 050	177.236 023	.005 642 1939	6.78	1.572 840	4.14	456
39	10.729 251	1913.951 098	.000 522 4794	.093 203	178.386 266	.005 605 8127	6.73	1.623 520	4.16	468
40	11.402 348	2046.363 076	.000 488 6717	.087 701	179.468 609	.005 572 0051	6.69	1.674 562	4.19	480
41	12.117 670	2187.082 704	.000 457 2301	.082 524	180.487 060	.005 540 5634	6.65	1.725 957	4.21	492
42	12.877 869	2336.629 909	.000 427 9668	.077 653	181.445 390	.005 511 3001	6.62	1.777 695	4.23	504
43	13.685 758	2495.558 912	.000 400 7118	.073 069	182.347 149	.005 484 0452	6.59	1.829 767	4.26	516
44	14.544 330	2664.458 276	.000 375 3108	.068 755	183.195 675	.005 458 6441	6.56	1.882 164	4.28	528
45	15.456 764	2843.953 489	.000 351 6232	.064 697	183.994 112	.005 434 9565	6.53	1.934 877	4.30	540
46	16.426 439	3034.709 279	.000 329 5209	.060 877	184.745 416	.005 412 8542	6.50	1.987 896	4.32	552
47	17.456 946	3237.432 074	.000 308 8868	.057 284	185.452 370	.005 392 2201	6.48	2.041 212	4.34	564
48	18.552 102	3452.872 621	.000 289 6139	.053 902	186.117 591	.005 372 9473	6.45	2.094 818	4.36	576
49	19.715 963	3681.828 763	.000 271 6042	.050 720	186.743 543	.005 354 9375	6.43	2.148 703	4.39	588
50	20.952 838	3925.148 398	.000 254 7674	.047 726	187.332 544	.005 338 1008	6.41	2.202 860	4.41	600

Effective Rate is 6.27 %

Annual Percentage Rate is 6.10 %

Amount Of 1	Amount Of 1 Per Period	Sinking Fund Payment	Present Worth Of 1	Present Worth of 1 Per Period	Periodic Payment To Amortize 1	Constant Annual Percent	Total Interest	Annual Add On Rate
What a single $ 1 deposit grows to in the future. The deposit is made at the beginning of the first period.	What a series of $ 1 deposits grow to in the future. A deposit is made at the end of each period.	The amount to be deposited at the end of each period that grows to $ 1 in the future.	What $ 1 to be paid in the future is worth today. Value today of a single $ 1 payment tomorrow.	What $ 1 to be paid at the end of each period is worth today. Value today of a series of $ 1 payments tomorrow.	The mortgage payment to amortize a loan of $ 1. An annuity certain, payable at the end of each period, worth $ 1 today.	The annual payment, including interest and principal, to amortize completely a loan of $ 100.	The total interest paid over the term on a loan of $1. The loan is amortized by regular periodic payments.	The average annual interest rate on a loan that is completely amortized by regular periodic payments.
$S = (1+i)^n$	$S_{\overline{n}} = \dfrac{(1+i)^n - 1}{i}$	$\dfrac{1}{S_{\overline{n}}} = \dfrac{i}{(1+i)^n - 1}$	$V^n = \dfrac{1}{(1+i)^n}$	$A_{\overline{n}} = \dfrac{1-V^n}{i}$	$\dfrac{1}{A_{\overline{n}}} = \dfrac{i}{1-V^n}$			**PERIODS**

YEAR

Amount Of 1	Amount Of 1 Per Period	Sinking Fund Payment	Present Worth Of 1	Present Worth of 1 Per Period	Periodic Payment To Amortize 1	Constant Annual Percent	Total Interest	Annual Add On Rate	PERIODS
1.005 104	1.000 000	1.000 000 0000	.994 922	.994 922	1.005 104 1667	1206.13	.005 104	6.12	1
1.010 234	2.005 104	.498 727 2066	.989 869	1.984 791	.503 831 3733	604.60	.007 663	4.60	2
1.015 391	3.015 339	.331 637 7191	.984 842	2.969 634	.336 741 8858	404.10	.010 226	4.09	3
1.020 574	4.030 729	.248 094 0581	.979 841	3.949 475	.253 198 2248	303.84	.012 793	3.84	4
1.025 783	5.051 303	.197 968 7277	.974 865	4.924 340	.203 072 8944	243.69	.015 364	3.69	5
1.031 018	6.077 086	.164 552 5626	.969 915	5.894 255	.169 656 7292	203.59	.017 940	3.59	6
1.036 281	7.108 104	.140 684 4918	.964 989	6.859 244	.145 788 6585	174.95	.020 521	3.52	7
1.041 570	8.144 385	.122 783 9801	.960 089	7.819 333	.127 888 1468	153.47	.023 105	3.47	8
1.046 887	9.185 955	.108 861 8410	.955 213	8.774 546	.113 966 0077	136.76	.025 694	3.43	9
1.052 230	10.232 842	.097 724 5627	.950 362	9.724 909	.102 828 7294	123.40	.028 287	3.39	10
1.057 601	11.285 072	.088 612 6378	.945 536	10.670 445	.093 716 8044	112.47	.030 885	3.37	11
1.062 999	12.342 673	.081 019 7278	.940 735	11.611 180	.086 123 8945	103.35	.033 487	3.35	12

YEAR	Amount Of 1	Amount Of 1 Per Period	Sinking Fund Payment	Present Worth Of 1	Present Worth of 1 Per Period	Periodic Payment To Amortize 1	Constant Annual Percent	Total Interest	Annual Add On Rate	PERIODS
1	1.062 999	12.342 673	.081 019 7278	.940 735	11.611 180	.086 123 8945	103.35	.033 487	3.35	12
2	1.129 967	25.462 923	.039 272 7895	.884 982	22.534 218	.044 376 9562	53.26	.065 047	3.25	24
3	1.201 154	39.409 736	.025 374 4406	.832 533	32.809 898	.030 478 6073	36.58	.097 230	3.24	36
4	1.276 825	54.235 185	.018 438 2150	.783 192	42.476 586	.023 542 3817	28.26	.130 034	3.25	48
5	1.357 264	69.994 624	.014 286 8116	.736 776	51.570 374	.019 390 9783	23.27	.163 459	3.27	60
6	1.442 771	86.746 892	.011 527 7905	.693 111	60.125 215	.016 631 9572	19.96	.197 501	3.29	72
7	1.533 664	104.554 537	.009 564 3864	.652 033	68.173 050	.014 668 5531	17.61	.232 158	3.32	84
8	1.630 283	123.484 048	.008 098 2120	.613 390	75.743 926	.013 202 3787	15.85	.267 428	3.34	96
9	1.732 989	143.606 100	.006 963 4925	.577 038	82.866 112	.012 067 6592	14.49	.303 307	3.37	108
10	1.842 166	164.995 822	.006 060 7595	.542 839	89.566 199	.011 164 9262	13.40	.339 791	3.40	120
11	1.958 221	187.733 076	.005 326 7118	.510 668	95.869 202	.010 430 8785	12.52	.376 876	3.43	132
12	2.081 587	211.902 757	.004 719 1458	.480 403	101.798 656	.009 823 3124	11.79	.414 557	3.45	144
13	2.212 725	237.595 104	.004 208 8409	.451 931	107.376 697	.009 313 0076	11.18	.452 829	3.48	156
14	2.352 125	264.906 045	.003 774 9233	.425 148	112.624 155	.008 879 0900	10.66	.491 687	3.51	168
15	2.500 306	293.937 550	.003 402 0832	.399 951	117.560 619	.008 506 2499	10.21	.531 125	3.54	180
16	2.657 823	324.798 012	.003 078 8366	.376 248	122.204 522	.008 183 0032	9.82	.571 137	3.57	192
17	2.825 264	357.602 654	.002 796 3998	.353 949	126.573 202	.007 900 5665	9.49	.611 716	3.60	204
18	3.003 252	392.473 958	.002 547 9398	.332 972	130.682 971	.007 652 1064	9.19	.652 855	3.63	216
19	3.192 455	429.542 121	.002 328 0604	.313 239	134.549 172	.007 432 2271	8.92	.694 548	3.66	228
20	3.393 576	468.945 544	.002 132 4438	.294 674	138.186 242	.007 236 6104	8.69	.736 787	3.68	240
21	3.607 368	510.831 345	.001 957 5933	.277 210	141.607 759	.007 061 7599	8.48	.779 564	3.71	252
22	3.834 629	555.355 912	.001 800 6471	.260 781	144.826 499	.006 904 8137	8.29	.822 871	3.74	264
23	4.076 207	602.685 486	.001 659 2402	.245 326	147.854 479	.006 763 4069	8.12	.866 700	3.77	276
24	4.333 004	652.996 777	.001 531 4011	.230 787	150.703 004	.006 635 5678	7.97	.911 044	3.80	288
25	4.605 980	706.477 633	.001 415 4730	.217 109	153.382 710	.006 519 6396	7.83	.955 892	3.82	300
26	4.896 152	763.327 733	.001 310 0533	.204 242	155.903 603	.006 414 2199	7.70	1.001 237	3.85	312
27	5.204 605	823.759 335	.001 213 9468	.192 138	158.275 094	.006 318 1135	7.59	1.047 069	3.88	324
28	5.532 490	887.998 071	.001 126 1286	.180 750	160.506 037	.006 230 2952	7.48	1.093 379	3.90	336
29	5.881 032	956.283 788	.001 045 7147	.170 038	162.604 763	.006 149 8814	7.38	1.140 159	3.93	348
30	6.251 531	1028.871 440	.000 971 9387	.159 961	164.579 107	.006 076 1054	7.30	1.187 398	3.96	360
31	6.645 372	1106.032 046	.000 904 1329	.150 481	166.436 441	.006 008 2996	7.21	1.235 087	3.98	372
32	7.064 024	1188.053 698	.000 841 7128	.141 562	168.183 699	.005 945 8795	7.14	1.283 218	4.01	384
33	7.509 051	1275.242 637	.000 784 1645	.133 173	169.827 405	.005 888 3312	7.07	1.331 779	4.04	396
34	7.982 114	1367.924 397	.000 731 0346	.125 280	171.373 696	.005 835 2012	7.01	1.380 762	4.06	408
35	8.484 980	1466.445 020	.000 681 9212	.117 855	172.828 346	.005 786 0879	6.95	1.430 157	4.09	420
36	9.019 526	1571.172 351	.000 636 4674	.110 871	174.196 785	.005 740 6341	6.89	1.479 954	4.11	432
37	9.587 747	1682.497 404	.000 594 3546	.104 300	175.484 123	.005 698 5212	6.84	1.530 143	4.14	444
38	10.191 766	1800.835 832	.000 555 2977	.098 118	176.695 167	.005 659 4644	6.80	1.580 716	4.16	456
39	10.833 838	1926.629 469	.000 519 0412	.092 303	177.834 437	.005 623 2078	6.75	1.631 661	4.18	468
40	11.516 360	2060.347 986	.000 485 3549	.086 833	178.906 189	.005 589 5216	6.71	1.682 970	4.21	480
41	12.241 879	2202.490 645	.000 454 0314	.081 687	179.914 422	.005 558 1981	6.67	1.734 633	4.23	492
42	13.013 106	2353.588 158	.000 424 8832	.076 846	180.862 902	.005 529 0498	6.64	1.786 641	4.25	504
43	13.832 920	2514.204 671	.000 397 7401	.072 291	181.755 170	.005 501 9068	6.61	1.838 984	4.28	516
44	14.704 381	2684.939 875	.000 372 4478	.068 007	182.594 558	.005 476 6145	6.58	1.891 652	4.30	528
45	15.630 743	2866.431 235	.000 348 8659	.063 976	183.384 199	.005 453 0325	6.55	1.944 638	4.32	540
46	16.615 465	3059.356 380	.000 326 8661	.060 185	184.127 041	.005 431 0328	6.52	1.997 930	4.34	552
47	17.662 224	3264.435 628	.000 306 3317	.056 618	184.825 859	.005 410 4983	6.50	2.051 521	4.36	564
48	18.774 927	3482.434 676	.000 287 1554	.053 263	185.483 261	.005 391 3221	6.47	2.105 402	4.39	576
49	19.957 730	3714.167 459	.000 269 2393	.050 106	186.101 701	.005 373 4060	6.45	2.159 563	4.41	588
50	21.215 048	3960.499 189	.000 252 4934	.047 136	186.683 490	.005 356 6601	6.43	2.213 996	4.43	600

Effective Rate is 6.30 %

Annual Percentage Rate is 6.125%

	Amount Of 1	Amount Of 1 Per Period	Sinking Fund Payment	Present Worth Of 1	Present Worth of 1 Per Period	Periodic Payment To Amortize 1	Constant Annual Percent	Total Interest	Annual Add On Rate	
	What a single $ 1 deposit grows to in the future. The deposit is made at the beginning of the first period.	What a series of $ 1 deposits grow to in the future. A deposit is made at the end of each period.	The amount to be deposited at the end of each period that grows to $ 1 in the future.	What $ 1 to be paid in the future is worth today. Value today of a single $ 1 payment tomorrow.	What $ 1 to be paid at the end of each period is worth today. Value today of a series of $ 1 payments tomorrow.	The mortgage payment to amortize a loan of $ 1. An annuity certain, payable at the end of each period, worth $ 1 today.	The annual payment, including interest and principal, to amortize completely a loan of $ 100.	The total interest paid over the term on a loan of $1. The loan is amortized by regular periodic payments.	The average annual interest rate on a loan that is completely amortized by regular periodic payments.	
	$S = (1+i)^n$	$S\overline{n}| = \dfrac{(1+i)^n - 1}{i}$	$\dfrac{1}{S\overline{n}|} = \dfrac{i}{(1+i)^n - 1}$	$V^n = \dfrac{1}{(1+i)^n}$	$A\overline{n}| = \dfrac{1-V^n}{i}$	$\dfrac{1}{A\overline{n}|} = \dfrac{i}{1-V^n}$				

YEAR										PERIODS
	1.005 125	1.000 000	1.000 000 0000	.994 901	.994 901	1.005 125 0000	1206.15	.005 125	6.15	1
	1.010 276	2.005 125	.498 722 0248	.989 828	1.984 729	.503 847 0248	604.62	.007 694	4.62	2
	1.015 454	3.015 401	.331 630 8219	.984 781	2.969 511	.336 755 8219	404.11	.010 267	4.11	3
	1.020 658	4.030 855	.248 086 3120	.979 760	3.949 271	.253 211 3120	303.86	.012 845	3.85	4
	1.025 889	5.051 513	.197 960 4793	.974 764	4.924 035	.203 085 4793	243.71	.015 427	3.70	5
	1.031 147	6.077 402	.164 543 9852	.969 794	5.893 829	.169 668 9852	203.61	.018 014	3.60	6
	1.036 431	7.108 549	.140 675 6846	.964 849	6.858 678	.145 800 6846	174.97	.020 605	3.53	7
	1.041 743	8.144 980	.122 775 0048	.959 930	7.818 608	.127 900 0048	153.49	.023 200	3.48	8
	1.047 082	9.186 723	.108 852 7390	.955 035	8.773 643	.113 977 7390	136.78	.025 800	3.44	9
	1.052 448	10.233 805	.097 715 3629	.950 165	9.723 809	.102 840 3629	123.41	.028 404	3.41	10
	1.057 842	11.286 254	.088 603 3611	.945 321	10.669 129	.093 728 3611	112.48	.031 012	3.38	11
	1.063 263	12.344 096	.081 010 3900	.940 501	11.609 630	.086 135 3900	103.37	.033 625	3.36	12
1	1.063 263	12.344 096	.081 010 3900	.940 501	11.609 630	.086 135 3900	103.37	.033 625	3.36	12
2	1.130 529	25.469 122	.039 263 2305	.884 541	22.528 494	.044 388 2305	53.27	.065 318	3.27	24
3	1.202 050	39.424 483	.025 364 9490	.831 912	32.797 693	.030 489 9490	36.59	.097 638	3.25	36
4	1.278 096	54.262 709	.018 428 8625	.782 414	42.455 882	.023 553 8625	28.27	.130 585	3.26	48
5	1.358 953	70.039 653	.014 277 6264	.735 861	51.539 414	.019 402 6264	23.29	.164 158	3.28	60
6	1.444 925	86.814 701	.011 518 7864	.692 077	60.082 482	.016 643 7864	19.98	.198 353	3.31	72
7	1.536 336	104.650 998	.009 555 5706	.650 899	68.117 243	.014 680 5706	17.62	.233 168	3.33	84
8	1.633 530	123.615 681	.008 089 5886	.612 171	75.673 941	.013 214 5886	15.86	.268 601	3.36	96
9	1.736 873	143.780 136	.006 955 0637	.575 747	82.781 021	.012 080 0637	14.50	.304 647	3.38	108
10	1.846 754	165.220 265	.006 052 5263	.541 491	89.465 233	.011 177 5263	13.42	.341 303	3.41	120
11	1.963 586	188.016 771	.005 318 6745	.509 272	95.751 740	.010 443 6745	12.54	.378 565	3.44	132
12	2.087 809	212.255 464	.004 711 3039	.478 971	101.664 203	.009 836 3039	11.81	.416 428	3.47	144
13	2.219 891	238.027 581	.004 201 1938	.450 472	107.224 879	.009 326 1938	11.20	.454 886	3.50	156
14	2.360 329	265.430 132	.003 767 4698	.423 670	112.454 698	.008 892 4698	10.68	.493 935	3.53	168
15	2.509 652	294.566 264	.003 394 8219	.398 462	117.373 346	.008 519 8219	10.23	.533 568	3.56	180
16	2.668 421	325.545 650	.003 071 7658	.374 753	121.999 338	.008 196 7658	9.84	.573 779	3.59	192
17	2.837 235	358.484 899	.002 789 5178	.352 456	126.350 086	.007 914 5178	9.50	.614 562	3.62	204
18	3.016 729	393.508 001	.002 541 2444	.331 485	130.441 967	.007 666 2444	9.20	.655 909	3.64	216
19	3.207 577	430.746 786	.002 321 5495	.311 762	134.290 384	.007 446 5495	8.94	.697 813	3.67	228
20	3.410 500	470.341 427	.002 126 1151	.293 212	137.909 823	.007 251 1151	8.71	.740 268	3.70	240
21	3.626 260	512.440 962	.001 951 4443	.275 766	141.313 908	.007 076 4443	8.50	.783 264	3.73	252
22	3.855 670	557.203 862	.001 794 6753	.259 358	144.515 452	.006 919 6753	8.31	.826 794	3.76	264
23	4.099 593	604.798 618	.001 653 4429	.243 927	147.526 506	.006 778 4429	8.14	.870 850	3.79	276
24	4.358 947	655.404 385	.001 525 7756	.229 413	150.358 404	.006 650 7756	7.99	.915 423	3.81	288
25	4.634 710	709.211 650	.001 410 0163	.215 763	153.021 806	.006 535 0163	7.85	.960 505	3.84	300
26	4.927 918	766.422 949	.001 304 7626	.202 925	155.526 737	.006 429 7626	7.72	1.006 086	3.87	312
27	5.239 675	827.253 636	.001 208 8191	.190 852	157.882 627	.006 333 8191	7.61	1.052 157	3.90	324
28	5.571 155	891.932 683	.001 121 1608	.179 496	160.098 343	.006 246 1608	7.50	1.098 710	3.92	336
29	5.923 606	960.703 553	.001 040 9038	.168 816	162.182 225	.006 165 9038	7.40	1.145 735	3.95	348
30	6.298 354	1033.825 109	.000 967 2816	.158 772	164.142 117	.006 092 2816	7.32	1.193 221	3.98	360
31	6.696 810	1111.572 589	.000 899 6264	.149 325	165.985 397	.006 024 6264	7.23	1.241 161	4.00	372
32	7.120 473	1194.238 646	.000 837 3536	.140 440	167.719 003	.005 962 3536	7.16	1.289 544	4.03	384
33	7.570 939	1282.134 446	.000 779 9494	.132 084	169.349 461	.005 904 9494	7.09	1.338 360	4.06	396
34	8.049 903	1375.590 842	.000 726 9604	.124 225	170.882 908	.005 851 9604	7.03	1.387 600	4.08	408
35	8.559 168	1474.959 615	.000 677 9847	.116 834	172.325 115	.005 802 9847	6.97	1.437 254	4.11	420
36	9.100 651	1580.614 803	.000 632 6652	.109 882	173.681 512	.005 757 6652	6.91	1.487 311	4.13	432
37	9.676 390	1692.954 108	.000 590 6835	.103 344	174.957 204	.005 715 6835	6.86	1.537 763	4.16	444
38	10.288 552	1812.400 389	.000 551 7545	.097 195	176.156 994	.005 676 7545	6.82	1.588 600	4.18	456
39	10.939 442	1939.403 258	.000 515 6225	.091 412	177.285 396	.005 640 6225	6.77	1.639 811	4.20	468
40	11.631 509	2074.440 773	.000 482 0576	.085 973	178.346 660	.005 607 0576	6.73	1.691 388	4.23	480
41	12.367 359	2218.021 232	.000 450 8523	.080 858	179.344 779	.005 575 8523	6.70	1.743 319	4.25	492
42	13.149 761	2370.685 091	.000 421 8190	.076 047	180.283 510	.005 546 8190	6.66	1.795 597	4.28	504
43	13.981 661	2533.007 000	.000 394 7877	.071 522	181.166 388	.005 519 7877	6.63	1.848 210	4.30	516
44	14.866 190	2705.597 958	.000 369 6041	.067 267	181.996 735	.005 494 6041	6.60	1.901 151	4.32	528
45	15.806 658	2889.107 624	.000 346 1276	.063 264	182.777 677	.005 471 1276	6.57	1.954 409	4.34	540
46	16.806 662	3084.226 751	.000 324 2304	.059 500	183.512 153	.005 449 2304	6.54	2.007 975	4.37	552
47	17.869 910	3291.689 795	.000 303 7953	.055 960	184.202 929	.005 428 7953	6.52	2.061 841	4.39	564
48	19.000 423	3512.277 675	.000 284 7155	.052 630	184.852 604	.005 409 7155	6.50	2.115 996	4.41	576
49	20.202 456	3746.820 714	.000 266 8929	.049 499	185.463 623	.005 391 8929	6.48	2.170 433	4.43	588
50	21.480 534	3996.201 765	.000 250 2376	.046 554	186.038 287	.005 375 2376	6.46	2.225 143	4.45	600

Effective Rate is 6.33 %   8 - 44   Annual Percentage Rate is 6.15 %

MONTHLY COMPOUND INTEREST AND ANNUITY

Amount Of 1	Amount Of 1 Per Period	Sinking Fund Payment	Present Worth Of 1	Present Worth of 1 Per Period	Periodic Payment To Amortize 1	Constant Annual Percent	Total Interest	Annual Add On Rate
What a single $ 1 deposit grows to in the future. The deposit is made at the beginning of the first period.	What a series of $ 1 deposits grow to in the future. A deposit is made at the end of each period.	The amount to be deposited at the end of each period that grows to $ 1 in the future.	What $ 1 to be paid in the future is worth today. Value today of a single $ 1 payment tomorrow.	What $ 1 to be paid at the end of each period is worth today. Value today of a series of $ 1 payments tomorrow.	The mortgage payment to amortize a loan of $ 1. An annuity certain, payable at the end of each period, worth $ 1 today.	The annual payment, including interest and principal, to amortize completely a loan of $ 100.	The total interest paid over the term on a loan of $ 1. The loan is amortized by regular periodic payments.	The average annual interest rate on a loan that is completely amortized by regular periodic payments.
$S = (1+i)^n$	$S\overline{n} = \dfrac{(1+i)^n - 1}{i}$	$\dfrac{1}{S\overline{n}} = \dfrac{i}{(1+i)^n - 1}$	$V^n = \dfrac{1}{(1+i)^n}$	$A\overline{n} = \dfrac{1-V^n}{i}$	$\dfrac{1}{A\overline{n}} = \dfrac{i}{1-V^n}$			PERIODS

YEAR	Amount Of 1	Amount Of 1 Per Period	Sinking Fund Payment	Present Worth Of 1	Present Worth of 1 Per Period	Periodic Payment To Amortize 1	Constant Annual Percent	Total Interest	Annual Add On Rate	PERIODS
	1.005 167	1.000 000	1.000 000 0000	.994 860	.994 860	1.005 166 6667	1206.20	.005 167	6.20	1
	1.010 360	2.005 167	.498 711 6615	.989 746	1.984 606	.503 878 3282	604.66	.007 757	4.65	2
	1.015 580	3.015 527	.331 617 0279	.984 659	2.969 265	.336 783 6946	404.15	.010 351	4.14	3
	1.020 827	4.031 107	.248 070 8205	.979 598	3.948 862	.253 237 4871	303.89	.012 950	3.88	4
	1.026 102	5.051 934	.197 943 9835	.974 562	4.923 425	.203 110 6502	243.74	.015 553	3.73	5
	1.031 403	6.078 036	.164 526 8317	.969 553	5.892 978	.169 693 4984	203.64	.018 161	3.63	6
	1.036 732	7.109 439	.140 658 0715	.964 569	6.857 547	.145 824 7382	174.99	.020 773	3.56	7
	1.042 089	8.146 171	.122 757 0560	.959 611	7.817 158	.127 923 7226	153.51	.023 390	3.51	8
	1.047 473	9.188 260	.108 834 5369	.954 679	8.771 837	.114 001 2035	136.81	.026 011	3.47	9
	1.052 885	10.235 732	.097 696 9652	.949 772	9.721 609	.102 863 6319	123.44	.028 636	3.44	10
	1.058 325	11.288 617	.088 584 8100	.944 890	10.666 499	.093 751 4766	112.51	.031 266	3.41	11
	1.063 793	12.346 942	.080 991 7169	.940 033	11.606 532	.086 158 3836	103.40	.033 901	3.39	12
1	1.063 793	12.346 942	.080 991 7169	.940 033	11.606 532	.086 158 3836	103.40	.033 901	3.39	12
2	1.131 655	25.481 526	.039 244 1176	.883 662	22.517 053	.044 410 7843	53.30	.065 859	3.29	24
3	1.203 846	39.453 999	.025 345 9734	.830 671	32.773 303	.030 512 6401	36.62	.098 455	3.28	36
4	1.280 642	54.317 811	.018 410 1676	.780 858	42.414 515	.023 576 8343	28.30	.131 688	3.29	48
5	1.362 337	70.129 823	.014 259 2689	.734 033	51.477 572	.019 425 9355	23.32	.165 556	3.31	60
6	1.449 244	86.950 523	.011 500 7933	.690 015	59.997 144	.016 667 4600	20.01	.200 057	3.33	72
7	1.541 695	104.844 259	.009 537 9567	.648 637	68.005 822	.014 704 6233	17.65	.235 188	3.36	84
8	1.640 044	123.879 481	.008 072 3618	.609 740	75.534 243	.013 239 0285	15.89	.270 947	3.39	96
9	1.744 667	144.129 009	.006 938 2285	.573 175	82.611 207	.012 104 8952	14.53	.307 329	3.41	108
10	1.855 963	165.670 305	.006 036 0847	.538 804	89.263 786	.011 202 7514	13.45	.344 330	3.44	120
11	1.974 360	188.585 775	.005 302 6269	.506 493	95.517 429	.010 469 2936	12.57	.381 947	3.47	132
12	2.100 309	212.963 080	.004 695 6496	.476 120	101.396 059	.009 862 3163	11.84	.420 174	3.50	144
13	2.234 293	238.895 476	.004 185 9311	.447 569	106.922 165	.009 352 5978	11.23	.459 005	3.53	156
14	2.376 825	266.482 165	.003 752 5964	.420 729	112.116 887	.008 919 2630	10.71	.498 436	3.56	168
15	2.528 448	295.828 678	.003 380 3349	.395 500	117.000 096	.008 547 0015	10.26	.538 460	3.59	180
16	2.689 744	327.047 280	.003 057 6619	.371 783	121.590 473	.008 224 3285	9.87	.579 071	3.62	192
17	2.861 330	360.257 396	.002 775 7931	.349 488	125.905 579	.007 942 4598	9.54	.620 262	3.65	204
18	3.043 861	395.586 069	.002 527 8949	.328 530	129.961 921	.007 694 5616	9.24	.662 025	3.68	216
19	3.238 037	433.168 447	.002 308 5707	.308 829	133.775 016	.007 475 2374	8.98	.704 354	3.71	228
20	3.444 600	473.148 301	.002 113 5023	.290 310	137.359 450	.007 280 1689	8.74	.747 241	3.74	240
21	3.664 339	515.678 570	.001 939 1925	.272 900	140.728 937	.007 105 8591	8.53	.790 677	3.77	252
22	3.898 097	560.921 953	.001 782 7792	.256 535	143.896 365	.006 949 4459	8.34	.834 654	3.79	264
23	4.146 766	609.051 527	.001 641 8972	.241 152	146.873 852	.006 808 5639	8.18	.879 164	3.82	276
24	4.411 299	660.251 407	.001 514 5746	.226 691	149.672 787	.006 681 2413	8.02	.924 197	3.85	288
25	4.692 707	714.717 457	.001 399 1543	.213 097	152.303 879	.006 565 8210	7.88	.969 746	3.88	300
26	4.992 067	772.658 035	.001 294 2336	.200 318	154.777 192	.006 460 9003	7.76	1.015 801	3.91	312
27	5.310 523	834.294 789	.001 198 6171	.188 305	157.102 187	.006 365 2838	7.64	1.062 352	3.93	324
28	5.649 295	899.863 507	.001 111 2796	.177 013	159.287 759	.006 277 9463	7.54	1.109 390	3.96	336
29	6.009 678	969.615 020	.001 031 3372	.166 398	161.342 269	.006 198 0038	7.44	1.156 905	3.99	348
30	6.393 050	1043.816 159	.000 958 0231	.156 420	163.273 576	.006 124 6898	7.35	1.204 888	4.02	360
31	6.800 879	1122.750 776	.000 890 6696	.147 040	165.089 068	.006 057 3363	7.27	1.253 329	4.04	372
32	7.234 724	1206.720 832	.000 828 6921	.138 222	166.795 690	.005 995 3588	7.20	1.302 218	4.07	384
33	7.696 246	1296.047 550	.000 771 5766	.129 933	168.399 971	.005 938 2433	7.13	1.351 544	4.10	396
34	8.187 209	1391.072 646	.000 718 8697	.122 142	169.908 048	.005 885 5364	7.07	1.401 299	4.12	408
35	8.709 491	1492.159 634	.000 670 1696	.114 817	171.325 690	.005 836 8363	7.01	1.451 471	4.15	420
36	9.265 092	1599.695 216	.000 625 1191	.107 932	172.658 321	.005 791 7857	6.96	1.502 051	4.17	432
37	9.856 136	1714.090 765	.000 583 3997	.101 460	173.911 037	.005 750 0663	6.91	1.553 029	4.20	444
38	10.484 883	1835.783 896	.000 544 7264	.095 375	175.088 831	.005 711 3931	6.86	1.604 395	4.22	456
39	11.153 741	1965.240 140	.000 508 8437	.089 656	176.195 609	.005 675 5103	6.82	1.656 139	4.25	468
40	11.865 266	2102.954 726	.000 475 5214	.084 280	177.236 204	.005 642 1881	6.78	1.708 250	4.27	480
41	12.622 181	2249.454 474	.000 444 5522	.079 226	178.214 398	.005 611 2189	6.74	1.760 720	4.29	492
42	13.427 382	2405.299 811	.000 415 7486	.074 475	179.133 933	.005 582 4153	6.70	1.813 537	4.32	504
43	14.283 949	2571.086 917	.000 388 9406	.070 009	179.998 326	.005 555 6072	6.67	1.866 693	4.34	516
44	15.195 158	2747.450 002	.000 363 9739	.065 810	180.810 883	.005 530 6405	6.64	1.920 178	4.36	528
45	16.164 496	2935.063 735	.000 340 7081	.061 864	181.574 714	.005 507 3748	6.61	1.973 982	4.39	540
46	17.195 670	3134.645 823	.000 319 0153	.058 154	182.292 740	.005 485 6820	6.59	2.028 096	4.41	552
47	18.292 625	3346.959 758	.000 298 7786	.054 667	182.967 709	.005 465 4453	6.56	2.082 511	4.43	564
48	19.459 558	3572.817 736	.000 279 8911	.051 389	183.602 201	.005 446 5578	6.54	2.137 217	4.45	576
49	20.700 933	3813.083 766	.000 262 2549	.048 307	184.198 645	.005 428 9216	6.52	2.192 206	4.47	588
50	22.021 498	4068.676 974	.000 245 7801	.045 410	184.759 322	.005 412 4468	6.50	2.247 468	4.49	600

Effective Rate is 6.38 %

Annual Percentage Rate is 6.20 %

MONTHLY COMPOUND INTEREST AND ANNUITY

6.25 % M

Amount Of 1	Amount Of 1 Per Period	Sinking Fund Payment	Present Worth Of 1	Present Worth of 1 Per Period	Periodic Payment To Amortize 1	Constant Annual Percent	Total Interest	Annual Add On Rate	
What a single $ 1 deposit grows to in the future. The deposit is made at the beginning of the first period.	What a series of $ 1 deposits grow to in the future. A deposit is made at the end of each period.	The amount to be deposited at the end of each period that grows to $ 1 in the future.	What $ 1 to be paid in the future is worth today. Value today of a single $ 1 payment tomorrow.	What $ 1 to be paid at the end of each period is worth today. Value today of a series of $ 1 payments tomorrow.	The mortgage payment to amortize a loan of $ 1. An annuity certain, payable at the end of each period, worth $ 1 today.	The annual payment, including interest and principal, to amortize completely a loan of $ 100.	The total interest paid over the term on a loan of $1. The loan is amortized by regular periodic payments.	The average annual interest rate on a loan that is completely amortized by regular periodic payments.	
$S = (1+i)^n$	$S\overline{n}| = \dfrac{(1+i)^n - 1}{i}$	$\dfrac{1}{S\overline{n}|} = \dfrac{i}{(1+i)^n - 1}$	$V^n = \dfrac{1}{(1+i)^n}$	$A\overline{n}| = \dfrac{1-V^n}{i}$	$\dfrac{1}{A\overline{n}|} = \dfrac{i}{1-V^n}$				

YEAR										PERIODS
	1.005 208	1.000 000	1.000 000 0000	.994 819	.994 819	1.005 208 3333	1206.25	.005 208	6.25	1
	1.010 444	2.005 208	.498 701 2987	.989 664	1.984 483	.503 909 6320	604.70	.007 819	4.69	2
	1.015 707	3.015 652	.331 603 2347	.984 536	2.969 019	.336 811 5680	404.18	.010 435	4.17	3
	1.020 997	4.031 359	.248 055 3300	.979 435	3.948 454	.253 263 6634	303.92	.013 055	3.92	4
	1.026 314	5.052 355	.197 927 4891	.974 360	4.922 815	.203 135 8224	243.77	.015 679	3.76	5
	1.031 660	6.078 670	.164 509 6799	.969 312	5.892 126	.169 718 0133	203.67	.018 308	3.66	6
	1.037 033	7.110 329	.140 640 4604	.964 290	6.856 416	.145 848 7938	175.02	.020 942	3.59	7
	1.042 434	8.147 362	.122 739 1094	.959 293	7.815 709	.127 947 4427	153.54	.023 580	3.54	8
	1.047 864	9.189 797	.108 816 3373	.954 323	8.770 032	.114 024 6706	136.83	.026 222	3.50	9
	1.053 321	10.237 660	.097 678 5705	.949 378	9.719 410	.102 886 9038	123.47	.028 869	3.46	10
	1.058 807	11.290 981	.088 566 2620	.944 459	10.663 869	.093 774 5953	112.53	.031 521	3.44	11
	1.064 322	12.349 788	.080 973 0473	.939 565	11.603 434	.086 181 3806	103.42	.034 177	3.42	12
1	1.064 322	12.349 788	.080 973 0473	.939 565	11.603 434	.086 181 3806	103.42	.034 177	3.42	12
2	1.132 781	25.493 938	.039 225 0117	.882 783	22.505 621	.044 433 3450	53.33	.066 400	3.32	24
3	1.205 643	39.483 542	.025 327 0082	.829 433	32.748 938	.030 535 3415	36.65	.099 272	3.31	36
4	1.283 193	54.372 984	.018 391 4865	.779 306	42.373 205	.023 599 8199	28.32	.132 791	3.32	48
5	1.365 730	70.220 141	.014 240 9284	.732 209	51.415 833	.019 449 2617	23.34	.166 956	3.34	60
6	1.453 576	87.086 617	.011 482 8207	.687 958	59.911 975	.016 691 1540	20.03	.201 763	3.36	72
7	1.547 073	105.037 974	.009 520 3664	.646 382	67.894 656	.014 728 6997	17.68	.237 211	3.39	84
8	1.646 583	124.143 996	.008 055 1620	.607 318	75.394 907	.013 263 4954	15.92	.273 296	3.42	96
9	1.752 495	144.478 951	.006 921 4234	.570 615	82.441 884	.012 129 7568	14.56	.310 014	3.44	108
10	1.865 218	166.121 888	.006 019 6764	.536 130	89.062 980	.011 228 0097	13.48	.347 361	3.47	120
11	1.985 192	189.156 938	.005 286 6155	.503 730	95.283 933	.010 494 9488	12.60	.385 333	3.50	132
12	2.112 884	213.673 643	.004 680 0344	.473 287	101.128 925	.009 888 3677	11.87	.423 925	3.53	144
13	2.248 788	239.767 308	.004 170 7104	.444 684	106.620 678	.009 379 0437	11.26	.463 131	3.56	156
14	2.393 434	267.539 365	.003 737 7677	.417 810	111.780 539	.008 946 1010	10.74	.502 945	3.59	168
15	2.547 384	297.097 771	.003 365 8953	.392 560	116.628 567	.008 574 2287	10.29	.543 361	3.62	180
16	2.711 237	328.557 427	.003 043 6080	.368 835	121.183 606	.008 251 9413	9.91	.584 373	3.65	192
17	2.885 628	362.040 625	.002 762 1210	.346 545	125.463 363	.007 970 4543	9.57	.625 973	3.68	204
18	3.071 237	397.677 524	.002 514 6002	.325 602	129.484 475	.007 722 9336	9.27	.668 154	3.71	216
19	3.268 785	435.606 652	.002 295 6491	.305 924	133.262 573	.007 503 9824	9.01	.710 908	3.74	228
20	3.479 039	475.975 451	.002 100 9487	.287 436	136.812 343	.007 309 2820	8.78	.754 228	3.77	240
21	3.702 817	518.940 844	.001 927 0019	.270 065	140.147 585	.007 135 3352	8.57	.798 104	3.80	252
22	3.940 989	564.669 849	.001 770 9463	.253 743	143.281 262	.006 979 2797	8.38	.842 530	3.83	264
23	4.194 480	613.340 227	.001 630 4165	.238 409	146.225 557	.006 838 7498	8.21	.887 495	3.86	276
24	4.464 277	665.141 172	.001 503 6402	.224 000	148.991 915	.006 711 7736	8.06	.932 991	3.89	288
25	4.751 427	720.274 047	.001 388 3604	.210 463	151.591 090	.006 596 6938	7.92	.979 008	3.92	300
26	5.057 048	778.953 169	.001 283 7742	.197 744	154.033 184	.006 492 1076	7.80	1.025 538	3.94	312
27	5.382 326	841.406 639	.001 188 4860	.185 793	156.327 692	.006 396 8193	7.68	1.072 569	3.97	324
28	5.728 527	907.877 229	.001 101 4705	.174 565	158.483 532	.006 309 8038	7.58	1.120 094	4.00	336
29	6.096 997	978.623 328	.001 021 8436	.164 015	160.509 085	.006 230 1769	7.48	1.168 102	4.03	348
30	6.489 166	1053.919 945	.000 948 8387	.154 103	162.412 224	.006 157 1720	7.39	1.216 582	4.06	360
31	6.906 561	1134.059 777	.000 881 7877	.144 790	164.200 348	.006 090 1211	7.31	1.265 525	4.08	372
32	7.350 804	1219.354 348	.000 820 1062	.136 040	165.880 408	.006 028 4395	7.24	1.314 921	4.11	384
33	7.823 621	1310.135 221	.000 763 2800	.127 818	167.458 934	.005 971 6133	7.17	1.364 759	4.14	396
34	8.326 850	1406.755 284	.000 710 8557	.120 093	168.942 062	.005 919 1890	7.11	1.415 029	4.16	408
35	8.862 449	1509.590 125	.000 662 4315	.112 836	170.335 558	.005 870 7648	7.05	1.465 721	4.19	420
36	9.432 497	1619.039 489	.000 617 6502	.106 016	171.644 839	.005 825 9835	7.00	1.516 825	4.21	432
37	10.039 213	1735.528 836	.000 576 1932	.099 609	172.874 994	.005 784 5266	6.95	1.568 330	4.24	444
38	10.684 953	1859.510 988	.000 537 7758	.093 590	174.030 805	.005 746 1091	6.90	1.620 226	4.26	456
39	11.372 229	1991.467 898	.000 502 1422	.087 934	175.116 766	.005 710 4755	6.86	1.672 503	4.29	468
40	12.103 711	2131.912 515	.000 469 0624	.082 619	176.137 096	.005 677 3957	6.82	1.725 150	4.31	480
41	12.882 244	2281.390 785	.000 438 3291	.077 626	177.095 764	.005 646 6624	6.78	1.778 158	4.34	492
42	13.710 853	2440.483 768	.000 409 7548	.072 935	177.996 495	.005 618 0882	6.75	1.831 516	4.36	504
43	14.592 760	2609.809 901	.000 383 1697	.068 527	178.842 790	.005 591 5030	6.71	1.885 216	4.38	516
44	15.531 393	2790.027 398	.000 358 4194	.064 386	179.637 941	.005 566 7528	6.69	1.939 245	4.41	528
45	16.530 400	2981.836 812	.000 335 3638	.060 495	180.385 036	.005 543 6971	6.66	1.993 596	4.43	540
46	17.593 665	3185.983 755	.000 313 8748	.056 839	181.086 981	.005 522 2081	6.63	2.048 259	4.45	552
47	18.725 322	3403.261 799	.000 293 8358	.053 404	181.746 505	.005 502 1691	6.61	2.103 223	4.47	564
48	19.929 769	3634.515 562	.000 275 1398	.050 176	182.366 170	.005 483 4732	6.59	2.158 481	4.50	576
49	21.211 687	3880.643 987	.000 257 6892	.047 144	182.948 386	.005 466 0225	6.56	2.214 021	4.52	588
50	22.576 062	4142.603 838	.000 241 3941	.044 295	183.495 417	.005 449 7274	6.54	2.269 836	4.54	600

Effective Rate is 6.43 %

Annual Percentage Rate is 6.25 %

MONTHLY COMPOUND INTEREST AND ANNUITY

6.30 % M

	Amount Of 1	Amount Of 1 Per Period	Sinking Fund Payment	Present Worth Of 1	Present Worth of 1 Per Period	Periodic Payment To Amortize 1	Constant Annual Percent	Total Interest	Annual Add On Rate
	What a single $ 1 deposit grows to in the future. The deposit is made at the beginning of the first period.	What a series of $ 1 deposits grow to in the future. A deposit is made at the end of each period.	The amount to be deposited at the end of each period that grows to $ 1 in the future.	What $ 1 to be paid in the future is worth today. Value today of a single $ 1 payment tomorrow.	What $ 1 to be paid at the end of each period is worth today. Value today of a series of $ 1 payments tomorrow.	The mortgage payment to amortize a loan of $ 1. An annuity certain, payable at the end of each period, worth $ 1 today.	The annual payment, including interest and principal, to amortize completely a loan of $ 100.	The total interest paid over the term on a loan of $1. The loan is amortized by regular periodic payments.	The average annual interest rate on a loan that is completely amortized by regular periodic payments.
	$S = (1+i)^n$	$Sn\rceil = \dfrac{(1+i)^n - 1}{i}$	$\dfrac{1}{Sn\rceil} = \dfrac{i}{(1+i)^n - 1}$	$V^n = \dfrac{1}{(1+i)^n}$	$An\rceil = \dfrac{1 - V^n}{i}$	$\dfrac{1}{An\rceil} = \dfrac{i}{1 - V^n}$			

YEAR / **PERIODS**

YEAR	Amount Of 1	Amount Of 1 Per Period	Sinking Fund Payment	Present Worth Of 1	Present Worth of 1 Per Period	Periodic Payment To Amortize 1	Constant Annual Percent	Total Interest	Annual Add On Rate	PERIODS
	1.005 250	1.000 000	1.000 000 0000	.994 777	.994 777	1.005 250 0000	1206.30	.005 250	6.30	1
	1.010 528	2.005 250	.498 690 9363	.989 582	1.984 360	.503 940 9363	604.73	.007 882	4.73	2
	1.015 833	3.015 778	.331 589 4423	.984 414	2.968 773	.336 839 4423	404.21	.010 518	4.21	3
	1.021 166	4.031 610	.248 039 8407	.979 273	3.948 046	.253 289 8407	303.95	.013 159	3.95	4
	1.026 527	5.052 776	.197 910 9960	.974 158	4.922 205	.203 160 9960	243.80	.015 805	3.79	5
	1.031 916	6.079 303	.164 492 5298	.969 071	5.891 275	.169 742 5298	203.70	.018 455	3.69	6
	1.037 334	7.111 220	.140 622 8513	.964 010	6.855 285	.145 872 8513	175.05	.021 110	3.62	7
	1.042 780	8.148 554	.122 721 1650	.958 975	7.814 260	.127 971 1650	153.57	.023 769	3.57	8
	1.048 255	9.191 334	.108 798 1403	.953 967	8.768 227	.114 048 1403	136.86	.026 433	3.52	9
	1.053 758	10.239 588	.097 660 1785	.948 985	9.717 212	.102 910 1785	123.50	.029 102	3.49	10
	1.059 290	11.293 346	.088 547 7172	.944 028	10.661 240	.093 797 7172	112.56	.031 775	3.47	11
	1.064 851	12.352 636	.080 954 3810	.939 098	11.600 338	.086 204 3810	103.45	.034 453	3.45	12
1	1.064 851	12.352 636	.080 954 3810	.939 098	11.600 338	.086 204 3810	103.45	.034 453	3.45	12
2	1.133 908	25.506 357	.039 205 9125	.881 905	22.494 196	.044 455 9125	53.35	.066 942	3.35	24
3	1.207 444	39.513 114	.025 308 0532	.828 196	32.724 598	.030 558 0532	36.67	.100 090	3.34	36
4	1.285 748	54.428 229	.018 372 8191	.777 757	42.331 950	.023 622 8191	28.35	.133 895	3.35	48
5	1.369 131	70.310 608	.014 222 6049	.730 390	51.354 198	.019 472 6049	23.37	.168 356	3.37	60
6	1.457 921	87.222 981	.011 464 8684	.685 908	59.826 974	.016 714 8684	20.06	.203 471	3.39	72
7	1.552 469	105.232 144	.009 502 7998	.644 135	67.783 744	.014 752 7998	17.71	.239 235	3.42	84
8	1.653 148	124.409 226	.008 037 9891	.604 906	75.255 932	.013 287 9891	15.95	.275 647	3.45	96
9	1.760 357	144.829 967	.006 904 6484	.568 066	82.273 050	.012 154 6484	14.59	.312 702	3.47	108
10	1.874 519	166.575 020	.006 003 3011	.533 470	88.862 814	.011 253 3011	13.51	.350 396	3.50	120
11	1.996 084	189.730 269	.005 270 6403	.500 981	95.051 249	.010 520 6403	12.63	.388 725	3.53	132
12	2.125 533	214.387 167	.004 664 4583	.470 470	100.862 798	.009 914 4583	11.90	.427 682	3.56	144
13	2.263 376	240.643 098	.004 155 5316	.441 818	106.320 412	.009 405 5316	11.29	.467 263	3.59	156
14	2.410 159	268.601 761	.003 722 9838	.414 910	111.445 649	.008 972 9838	10.77	.507 461	3.62	168
15	2.566 461	298.373 581	.003 351 5032	.389 642	116.258 749	.008 601 5032	10.33	.548 271	3.66	180
16	2.732 900	330.076 143	.003 029 6040	.365 912	120.778 723	.008 279 6040	9.94	.589 684	3.69	192
17	2.910 132	363.834 658	.002 748 5012	.343 627	125.023 423	.007 998 5012	9.60	.631 694	3.72	204
18	3.098 858	399.782 459	.002 501 3604	.322 700	129.009 613	.007 751 3604	9.31	.674 294	3.75	216
19	3.299 823	438.061 523	.002 282 7844	.303 047	132.753 037	.007 532 7844	9.04	.717 475	3.78	228
20	3.513 821	478.823 035	.002 088 4542	.284 590	136.268 479	.007 338 4542	8.81	.761 229	3.81	240
21	3.741 697	522.227 986	.001 914 8725	.267 258	139.569 825	.007 164 8725	8.60	.805 548	3.84	252
22	3.984 351	568.447 806	.001 759 1765	.250 982	142.670 113	.007 009 1765	8.42	.850 423	3.87	264
23	4.242 741	617.665 044	.001 619 0005	.235 697	145.581 588	.006 869 0005	8.25	.895 844	3.89	276
24	4.517 889	670.074 085	.001 492 3723	.221 342	148.315 749	.006 742 3723	8.10	.941 803	3.92	288
25	4.810 880	725.881 922	.001 377 6345	.207 862	150.883 395	.006 627 6345	7.96	.988 290	3.95	300
26	5.122 872	785.308 973	.001 273 3842	.195 203	153.294 667	.006 523 3842	7.83	1.035 296	3.98	312
27	5.455 097	848.589 947	.001 178 4255	.183 315	155.559 088	.006 428 4255	7.72	1.082 810	4.01	324
28	5.808 868	915.974 777	.001 091 7331	.172 151	157.685 601	.006 341 7331	7.62	1.130 822	4.04	336
29	6.185 580	987.729 604	.001 012 4228	.161 666	159.682 606	.006 262 4228	7.52	1.179 323	4.07	348
30	6.586 724	1064.137 827	.000 939 7279	.151 821	161.557 990	.006 189 7279	7.43	1.228 302	4.09	360
31	7.013 881	1145.501 226	.000 872 9803	.142 574	163.319 160	.006 122 9803	7.35	1.277 749	4.12	372
32	7.468 741	1232.141 150	.000 811 5953	.133 891	164.973 072	.006 061 5953	7.28	1.327 653	4.15	384
33	7.953 099	1324.399 790	.000 755 0590	.125 737	166.526 257	.006 005 0590	7.21	1.378 003	4.18	396
34	8.468 868	1422.641 525	.000 702 9178	.118 080	167.984 850	.005 952 9178	7.15	1.428 790	4.20	408
35	9.018 085	1527.254 369	.000 654 7698	.110 888	169.354 613	.005 904 7698	7.09	1.480 003	4.23	420
36	9.602 920	1638.651 496	.000 610 2579	.104 135	170.640 955	.005 860 2579	7.04	1.531 631	4.25	432
37	10.225 683	1757.272 875	.000 569 0636	.097 793	171.848 956	.005 819 0636	6.99	1.583 664	4.28	444
38	10.888 832	1883.587 010	.000 530 9019	.091 837	172.983 387	.005 780 9019	6.94	1.636 091	4.31	456
39	11.594 987	2018.092 785	.000 495 5174	.086 244	174.048 730	.005 745 5174	6.90	1.688 902	4.33	468
40	12.346 938	2161.321 441	.000 462 6799	.080 992	175.049 192	.005 712 6799	6.86	1.742 086	4.36	480
41	13.147 653	2313.838 666	.000 432 1822	.076 059	175.988 723	.005 682 1822	6.82	1.795 634	4.38	492
42	14.000 296	2476.246 837	.000 403 8370	.071 427	176.871 036	.005 653 8370	6.79	1.849 534	4.40	504
43	14.908 234	2649.187 396	.000 377 4742	.067 077	177.699 614	.005 627 4742	6.76	1.903 777	4.43	516
44	15.875 053	2833.343 382	.000 352 9399	.062 992	178.477 730	.005 602 9399	6.73	1.958 352	4.45	528
45	16.904 571	3029.442 130	.000 330 0938	.059 156	179.208 458	.005 580 0938	6.70	2.013 251	4.47	540
46	18.000 855	3238.258 144	.000 308 8080	.055 553	179.894 683	.005 558 8080	6.68	2.068 462	4.50	552
47	19.168 235	3460.616 156	.000 288 9659	.052 170	180.539 115	.005 538 9659	6.65	2.123 977	4.52	564
48	20.411 321	3697.394 384	.000 270 4607	.048 992	181.144 301	.005 520 4607	6.63	2.179 785	4.54	576
49	21.735 022	3949.527 996	.000 253 1948	.046 009	181.712 629	.005 503 1948	6.61	2.235 879	4.56	588
50	23.144 567	4218.012 810	.000 237 0785	.043 207	182.246 346	.005 487 0785	6.59	2.292 247	4.58	600

Effective Rate is 6.49 %

8 - 47

Annual Percentage Rate is 6.30 %

MONTHLY COMPOUND INTEREST AND ANNUITY

	Amount Of 1	Amount Of 1 Per Period	Sinking Fund Payment	Present Worth Of 1	Present Worth of 1 Per Period	Periodic Payment To Amortize 1	Constant Annual Percent	Total Interest	Annual Add On Rate	
	What a single $ 1 deposit grows to in the future. The deposit is made at the beginning of the first period.	What a series of $ 1 deposits grow to in the future. A deposit is made at the end of each period.	The amount to be deposited at the end of each period that grows to $ 1 in the future.	What $ 1 to be paid in the future is worth today. Value today of a single $ 1 payment tomorrow.	What $ 1 to be paid at the end of each period is worth today. Value today of a series of $ 1 payments tomorrow.	The mortgage payment to amortize a loan of $ 1. An annuity certain, payable at the end of each period, worth $ 1 today.	The annual payment, including interest and principal, to amortize completely a loan of $ 100.	The total interest paid over the term of a loan of $1. The loan is amortized by regular periodic payments.	The average annual interest rate on a loan that is completely amortized by regular periodic payments.	
	$S = (1+i)^n$	$S\overline{n}| = \dfrac{(1+i)^n - 1}{i}$	$\dfrac{1}{S\overline{n}|} = \dfrac{i}{(1+i)^n - 1}$	$V^n = \dfrac{1}{(1+i)^n}$	$A\overline{n}| = \dfrac{1-V^n}{i}$	$\dfrac{1}{A\overline{n}|} = \dfrac{i}{1-V^n}$				

YEAR / **PERIODS**

YEAR	Amount Of 1	Amount Of 1 Per Period	Sinking Fund Payment	Present Worth Of 1	Present Worth of 1 Per Period	Periodic Payment To Amortize 1	Constant Annual Percent	Total Interest	Annual Add On Rate	PERIODS
	1.005 292	1.000 000	1.000 000 0000	.994 736	.994 736	1.005 291 6667	1206.35	.005 292	6.35	1
	1.010 611	2.005 292	.498 680 5743	.989 500	1.984 236	.503 972 2410	604.77	.007 944	4.77	2
	1.015 959	3.015 903	.331 575 6506	.984 292	2.968 528	.336 867 3173	404.25	.010 602	4.24	3
	1.021 335	4.031 862	.248 024 3524	.979 110	3.947 638	.253 316 0191	303.98	.013 264	3.98	4
	1.026 740	5.053 197	.197 894 5044	.973 957	4.921 595	.203 186 1710	243.83	.015 931	3.82	5
	1.032 173	6.079 937	.164 475 3814	.968 830	5.890 425	.169 767 0481	203.73	.018 602	3.72	6
	1.037 635	7.112 110	.140 605 2441	.963 730	6.854 155	.145 896 9108	175.08	.021 278	3.65	7
	1.043 126	8.149 745	.122 703 2230	.958 657	7.812 812	.127 994 8896	153.60	.023 959	3.59	8
	1.048 646	9.192 871	.108 779 9458	.953 611	8.766 423	.114 071 6125	136.89	.026 645	3.55	9
	1.054 195	10.241 517	.097 641 7894	.948 591	9.715 014	.102 933 4561	123.53	.029 335	3.52	10
	1.059 773	11.295 711	.088 529 1754	.943 598	10.658 612	.093 820 8421	112.59	.032 029	3.49	11
	1.065 381	12.355 484	.080 935 7182	.938 631	11.597 244	.086 227 3849	103.48	.034 729	3.47	12
1	1.065 381	12.355 484	.080 935 7182	.938 631	11.597 244	.086 227 3849	103.48	.034 729	3.47	12
2	1.135 037	25.518 784	.039 186 8203	.881 029	22.482 779	.044 478 4870	53.38	.067 484	3.37	24
3	1.209 247	39.542 715	.025 289 1085	.826 961	32.700 283	.030 580 7752	36.70	.100 908	3.36	36
4	1.288 309	54.483 545	.018 354 1654	.776 211	42.290 751	.023 645 8320	28.38	.135 000	3.37	48
5	1.372 540	70.401 230	.014 204 2985	.728 576	51.292 665	.019 495 9652	23.40	.169 758	3.40	60
6	1.462 278	87.359 618	.011 446 9365	.683 865	59.742 142	.016 738 6031	20.09	.205 179	3.42	72
7	1.557 883	105.426 771	.009 485 2568	.641 897	67.673 085	.014 776 9235	17.74	.241 262	3.45	84
8	1.659 739	124.675 174	.008 020 8430	.602 504	75.117 316	.013 312 5097	15.98	.278 001	3.48	96
9	1.768 255	145.182 059	.006 887 9034	.565 529	82.104 704	.012 179 5701	14.62	.315 394	3.50	108
10	1.883 866	167.029 707	.005 986 9590	.530 823	88.663 285	.011 278 6256	13.54	.353 435	3.53	120
11	2.007 035	190.305 778	.005 254 7012	.498 247	94.819 374	.010 546 3679	12.66	.392 121	3.56	132
12	2.138 257	215.103 664	.004 648 9213	.467 671	100.597 671	.009 940 5879	11.93	.431 445	3.60	144
13	2.278 058	241.522 864	.004 140 3948	.438 970	106.021 362	.009 432 0614	11.32	.471 402	3.63	156
14	2.427 000	269.669 380	.003 708 2445	.412 031	111.112 208	.008 999 9112	10.80	.511 985	3.66	168
15	2.585 680	299.656 146	.003 337 1583	.386 745	115.890 634	.008 628 8250	10.36	.553 188	3.69	180
16	2.754 735	331.603 480	.003 015 6499	.363 011	120.375 815	.008 307 3166	9.97	.595 005	3.72	192
17	2.934 843	365.639 566	.002 734 9338	.340 734	124.585 745	.008 026 6004	9.64	.637 426	3.75	204
18	3.126 726	401.900 969	.002 488 1751	.319 823	128.537 318	.007 779 8418	9.34	.680 446	3.78	216
19	3.331 155	440.533 183	.002 269 9766	.300 196	132.246 387	.007 561 6432	9.08	.724 055	3.81	228
20	3.548 949	481.691 214	.002 076 0188	.281 774	135.727 836	.007 367 6854	8.85	.768 245	3.84	240
21	3.780 984	525.540 202	.001 902 8040	.264 481	138.995 632	.007 194 4707	8.64	.813 007	3.87	252
22	4.028 188	572.256 085	.001 747 4694	.248 251	142.062 888	.007 039 1361	8.45	.858 332	3.90	264
23	4.291 556	622.026 304	.001 607 6491	.233 016	144.941 910	.006 899 3157	8.28	.904 211	3.93	276
24	4.572 143	675.050 556	.001 481 3705	.218 716	147.644 250	.006 773 0372	8.13	.950 635	3.96	288
25	4.871 074	731.541 591	.001 366 9763	.205 294	150.180 751	.006 658 6429	8.00	.997 593	3.99	300
26	5.189 550	791.726 073	.001 263 0631	.192 695	152.561 590	.006 554 7298	7.87	1.045 076	4.02	312
27	5.528 849	855.845 482	.001 168 4352	.180 869	154.796 320	.006 460 1019	7.76	1.093 073	4.05	324
28	5.890 331	924.157 090	.001 082 0671	.169 770	156.893 908	.006 373 7338	7.65	1.141 575	4.08	336
29	6.275 448	996.934 986	.001 003 0744	.159 351	158.862 769	.006 294 7411	7.56	1.190 570	4.11	348
30	6.685 743	1074.471 181	.000 930 8740	.149 572	160.710 803	.006 222 3571	7.47	1.240 049	4.13	360
31	7.122 865	1157.076 778	.000 864 2469	.140 393	162.445 426	.006 155 9136	7.39	1.290 000	4.16	372
32	7.588 565	1245.083 220	.000 803 1592	.131 777	164.073 597	.006 094 8258	7.32	1.340 413	4.19	384
33	8.084 714	1338.843 621	.000 746 9132	.123 690	165.601 850	.006 038 5799	7.25	1.391 278	4.22	396
34	8.613 302	1438.734 180	.000 695 0554	.116 099	167.036 315	.005 986 7221	7.19	1.442 583	4.24	408
35	9.176 449	1545.155 695	.000 647 1840	.108 975	168.382 750	.005 938 8506	7.13	1.494 317	4.27	420
36	9.776 415	1658.535 165	.000 602 9417	.102 287	169.646 555	.005 894 6084	7.08	1.546 471	4.30	432
37	10.415 608	1779.327 511	.000 562 0101	.096 010	170.832 802	.005 853 6767	7.03	1.599 032	4.32	444
38	11.096 592	1908.017 394	.000 524 1042	.090 118	171.946 250	.005 815 7709	6.98	1.651 992	4.35	456
39	11.822 099	2045.121 163	.000 488 9686	.084 587	172.991 368	.005 780 6353	6.94	1.705 337	4.37	468
40	12.595 041	2191.188 928	.000 456 3732	.079 396	173.972 348	.005 748 0399	6.90	1.759 059	4.40	480
41	13.418 519	2346.806 765	.000 426 1109	.074 524	174.893 127	.005 717 7776	6.87	1.813 147	4.42	492
42	14.295 837	2512.599 069	.000 397 9943	.069 950	175.757 398	.005 689 6609	6.83	1.867 589	4.45	504
43	15.230 514	2689.231 056	.000 371 8535	.065 658	176.568 630	.005 663 5202	6.80	1.922 376	4.47	516
44	16.226 302	2877.411 437	.000 347 5346	.061 628	177.330 078	.005 639 2013	6.77	1.977 498	4.49	528
45	17.287 196	3077.895 260	.000 324 8973	.057 846	178.044 797	.005 616 5640	6.74	2.032 945	4.52	540
46	18.417 452	3291.486 937	.000 303 8141	.054 296	178.715 655	.005 595 4807	6.72	2.088 705	4.54	552
47	19.621 605	3519.043 473	.000 284 1681	.050 964	179.345 342	.005 575 8348	6.70	2.144 771	4.56	564
48	20.904 487	3761.477 907	.000 265 8530	.047 837	179.936 387	.005 557 5196	6.67	2.201 131	4.59	576
49	22.271 246	4019.762 973	.000 248 7709	.044 901	180.491 160	.005 540 4376	6.65	2.257 777	4.61	588
50	23.727 364	4294.935 001	.000 232 8324	.042 145	181.011 887	.005 524 4991	6.63	2.314 699	4.63	600

Effective Rate is 6.54 %

Annual Percentage Rate is 6.35 %

Amount Of 1	Amount Of 1 Per Period	Sinking Fund Payment	Present Worth Of 1	Present Worth of 1 Per Period	Periodic Payment To Amortize 1	Constant Annual Percent	Total Interest	Annual Add On Rate	
What a single $ 1 deposit grows to in the future. The deposit is made at the beginning of the first period.	What a series of $ 1 deposits grow to in the future. A deposit is made at the end of each period.	The amount to be deposited at the end of each period that grows to $ 1 in the future.	What $ 1 to be paid in the future is worth today. Value today of a single $ 1 payment tomorrow.	What $ 1 to be paid at the end of each period is worth today. Value today of a series of $ 1 payments tomorrow.	The mortgage payment to amortize a loan of $ 1. An annuity certain, payable at the end of each period, worth $ 1 today.	The annual payment, including interest and principal, to amortize completely a loan of $ 100.	The total interest paid over the term on a loan of $1. The loan is amortized by regular periodic payments.	The average annual interest rate on a loan that is completely amortized by regular periodic payments.	
$S = (1+i)^n$	$S\overline{n} = \dfrac{(1+i)^n - 1}{i}$	$\dfrac{1}{S\overline{n}} = \dfrac{i}{(1+i)^n - 1}$	$V^n = \dfrac{1}{(1+i)^n}$	$A\overline{n} = \dfrac{1 - V^n}{i}$	$\dfrac{1}{A\overline{n}} = \dfrac{i}{1 - V^n}$				

YEAR / **PERIODS**

	Amount Of 1	Amount Of 1 Per Period	Sinking Fund Payment	Present Worth Of 1	Present Worth of 1 Per Period	Periodic Payment To Amortize 1	Constant Annual Percent	Total Interest	Annual Add On Rate	PERIODS
	1.005 313	1.000 000	1.000 000 0000	.994 716	.994 716	1.005 312 5000	1206.38	.005 312	6.37	1
	1.010 653	2.005 313	.498 675 3935	.989 459	1.984 175	.503 987 8935	604.79	.007 976	4.79	2
	1.016 022	3.015 966	.331 568 7551	.984 230	2.968 405	.336 881 2551	404.26	.010 644	4.26	3
	1.021 420	4.031 988	.248 016 6087	.979 029	3.947 434	.253 329 1087	304.00	.013 316	3.99	4
	1.026 846	5.053 408	.197 886 2569	.973 856	4.921 290	.203 198 7590	243.84	.015 994	3.84	5
	1.032 301	6.080 254	.164 466 8078	.968 709	5.889 999	.169 779 3078	203.74	.018 676	3.74	6
	1.037 785	7.112 556	.140 596 4413	.963 590	6.853 590	.145 908 9413	175.10	.021 363	3.66	7
	1.043 299	8.150 341	.122 694 2528	.958 498	7.812 088	.128 006 7528	153.61	.024 054	3.61	8
	1.048 841	9.193 640	.108 770 8495	.953 433	8.765 521	.114 083 3495	136.91	.026 750	3.57	9
	1.054 413	10.242 481	.097 632 5960	.948 395	9.713 916	.102 945 0960	123.54	.029 451	3.53	10
	1.060 015	11.296 894	.088 519 9058	.943 383	10.657 299	.093 832 4058	112.60	.032 156	3.51	11
	1.065 646	12.356 909	.080 926 3881	.938 398	11.595 697	.086 238 8881	103.49	.034 867	3.49	12
1	1.065 646	12.356 909	.080 926 3881	.938 398	11.595 697	.086 238 8881	103.49	.034 867	3.49	12
2	1.135 602	25.525 000	.039 177 2768	.880 591	22.477 074	.044 489 7768	53.39	.067 755	3.39	24
3	1.210 149	39.557 525	.025 279 6400	.826 344	32.688 135	.030 592 1400	36.72	.101 317	3.38	36
4	1.289 591	54.511 231	.018 344 8436	.775 440	42.270 173	.023 657 3436	28.39	.135 552	3.39	48
5	1.374 247	70.446 588	.014 195 1517	.727 671	51.261 936	.019 507 6517	23.41	.170 459	3.41	60
6	1.464 461	87.428 039	.011 437 9782	.682 845	59.699 788	.016 750 4782	20.11	.206 034	3.43	72
7	1.560 598	105.524 256	.009 476 4942	.640 780	67.617 850	.014 788 9942	17.75	.242 276	3.46	84
8	1.663 045	124.808 418	.008 012 2801	.601 307	75.048 143	.013 324 7801	15.99	.279 179	3.49	96
9	1.772 217	145.358 510	.006 879 5422	.564 265	82.020 714	.012 192 0422	14.64	.316 741	3.52	108
10	1.888 556	167.257 635	.005 978 8003	.529 505	88.563 759	.011 291 3003	13.55	.354 956	3.55	120
11	2.012 532	190.594 352	.005 246 7452	.496 886	94.703 739	.010 559 2452	12.68	.393 820	3.58	132
12	2.144 647	215.463 032	.004 641 1674	.466 277	100.465 483	.009 953 6674	11.95	.433 328	3.61	144
13	2.285 435	241.964 244	.004 132 8420	.437 553	105.872 291	.009 445 3420	11.34	.473 473	3.64	156
14	2.435 465	270.205 156	.003 700 8916	.410 599	110.946 028	.009 013 3916	10.82	.514 250	3.67	168
15	2.595 344	300.299 974	.003 330 0036	.385 305	115.707 212	.008 642 5036	10.38	.555 651	3.70	180
16	2.765 718	332.370 399	.003 008 6915	.361 570	120.175 097	.008 321 1915	9.99	.597 669	3.74	192
17	2.947 276	366.546 121	.002 728 1696	.339 296	124.367 751	.008 040 6696	9.65	.640 297	3.77	204
18	3.140 753	402.965 345	.002 481 6030	.318 395	128.302 128	.007 794 1030	9.36	.683 526	3.80	216
19	3.346 932	441.775 348	.002 263 5939	.298 781	131.994 139	.007 576 0939	9.10	.727 349	3.83	228
20	3.566 644	483.133 076	.002 069 8231	.280 376	135.458 715	.007 382 3231	8.86	.771 758	3.86	240
21	3.800 781	527.205 776	.001 896 7926	.263 104	138.709 865	.007 209 2926	8.66	.816 742	3.89	252
22	4.050 287	574.171 677	.001 741 6394	.246 896	141.760 737	.007 054 1394	8.47	.862 293	3.92	264
23	4.316 172	624.220 705	.001 601 9975	.231 687	144.623 670	.006 914 4975	8.30	.908 401	3.95	276
24	4.599 512	677.555 255	.001 475 8944	.217 414	147.310 239	.006 788 3944	8.15	.955 058	3.98	288
25	4.901 452	734.391 009	.001 361 6724	.204 021	149.831 310	.006 674 1724	8.01	1.002 252	4.01	300
26	5.223 213	794.957 807	.001 257 9284	.191 453	152.197 078	.006 570 4284	7.89	1.049 974	4.04	312
27	5.566 097	859.500 578	.001 163 4663	.179 659	154.417 109	.006 475 9663	7.78	1.098 213	4.07	324
28	5.931 489	928.280 329	.001 077 2608	.168 592	156.500 381	.006 389 7608	7.67	1.146 960	4.10	336
29	6.320 868	1001.575 201	.000 998 4273	.158 206	158.455 320	.006 310 9273	7.58	1.196 203	4.12	348
30	6.735 808	1079.681 594	.000 926 1990	.148 460	160.289 830	.006 238 6990	7.49	1.245 932	4.15	360
31	7.177 988	1162.915 365	.000 859 9078	.139 315	162.011 330	.006 172 4078	7.41	1.296 136	4.18	372
32	7.649 195	1251.613 107	.000 798 9689	.130 733	163.626 783	.006 111 4689	7.34	1.346 804	4.21	384
33	8.151 334	1346.133 508	.000 742 8684	.122 679	165.142 720	.006 055 3684	7.27	1.397 926	4.24	396
34	8.686 437	1446.858 802	.000 691 1524	.115 122	166.565 272	.006 003 6524	7.21	1.449 490	4.26	408
35	9.256 668	1554.196 317	.000 643 4194	.108 030	167.900 191	.005 955 9194	7.15	1.501 486	4.29	420
36	9.864 332	1668.580 119	.000 599 3119	.101 375	169.152 877	.005 911 8119	7.10	1.553 903	4.32	432
37	10.511 887	1790.472 768	.000 558 5117	.095 130	170.328 395	.005 871 0117	7.05	1.606 729	4.34	444
38	11.201 951	1920.367 193	.000 520 7337	.089 270	171.431 498	.005 833 2337	7.00	1.659 955	4.37	456
39	11.937 315	2058.788 676	.000 485 7225	.083 771	172.466 648	.005 798 2225	6.96	1.713 568	4.39	468
40	12.720 953	2206.296 988	.000 453 2481	.078 610	173.438 030	.005 765 7481	6.92	1.767 559	4.42	480
41	13.556 033	2363.488 641	.000 423 1034	.073 768	174.349 573	.005 735 6034	6.89	1.821 917	4.44	492
42	14.445 934	2530.999 310	.000 395 1009	.069 224	175.204 963	.005 707 6009	6.85	1.876 631	4.47	504
43	15.394 253	2709.506 397	.000 369 0709	.064 959	176.007 660	.005 681 5709	6.82	1.931 691	4.49	516
44	16.404 825	2899.731 775	.000 344 8595	.060 958	176.760 908	.005 657 3595	6.79	1.987 086	4.52	528
45	17.481 737	3102.444 703	.000 322 3265	.057 203	177.467 755	.005 634 8265	6.77	2.042 806	4.54	540
46	18.629 345	3318.464 939	.000 301 3442	.053 679	178.131 058	.005 613 8442	6.74	2.098 842	4.56	552
47	19.852 288	3548.666 057	.000 281 7960	.050 372	178.753 501	.005 594 2960	6.72	2.155 183	4.59	564
48	21.155 513	3793.978 975	.000 263 5755	.047 269	179.337 600	.005 576 0755	6.70	2.211 820	4.61	576
49	22.544 290	4055.395 724	.000 246 5851	.044 357	179.885 717	.005 559 0851	6.68	2.268 742	4.63	588
50	24.024 234	4333.973 458	.000 230 7351	.041 625	180.400 068	.005 543 2351	6.66	2.325 941	4.65	600

Effective Rate is 6.56 %

Annual Percentage Rate is 6.375%

Amount Of 1	Amount Of 1 Per Period	Sinking Fund Payment	Present Worth Of 1	Present Worth of 1 Per Period	Periodic Payment To Amortize 1	Constant Annual Percent	Total Interest	Annual Add On Rate
What a single $ 1 deposit grows to in the future. The deposit is made at the beginning of the first period.	What a series of $ 1 deposits grow to in the future. A deposit is made at the end of each period.	The amount to be deposited at the end of each period that grows to $ 1 in the future.	What $ 1 to be paid in the future is worth today. Value today of a single $ 1 payment tomorrow.	What $ 1 to be paid at the end of each period is worth today. Value today of a series of $ 1 payments tomorrow.	The mortgage payment to amortize a loan of $ 1. An annuity certain, payable at the end of each period, worth $ 1 today.	The annual payment, including interest and principal, to amortize completely a loan of $ 100.	The total interest paid over the term on a loan of $1. The loan is amortized by regular periodic payments.	The average annual interest rate on a loan that is completely amortized by regular periodic payments.
$S = (1+i)^n$	$S\overline{n}| = \dfrac{(1+i)^n - 1}{i}$	$\dfrac{1}{S\overline{n}|} = \dfrac{i}{(1+i)^n - 1}$	$V^n = \dfrac{1}{(1+i)^n}$	$A\overline{n}| = \dfrac{1-V^n}{i}$	$\dfrac{1}{A\overline{n}|} = \dfrac{i}{1-V^n}$			

YEAR   **PERIODS**

Amount Of 1	Amount Of 1 Per Period	Sinking Fund Payment	Present Worth Of 1	Present Worth of 1 Per Period	Periodic Payment To Amortize 1	Constant Annual Percent	Total Interest	Annual Add On Rate	PERIODS
1.005 333	1.000 000	1.000 000 0000	.994 695	.994 695	1.005 333 3333	1206.40	.005 333	6.40	1
1.010 695	2.005 333	.498 670 2128	.989 418	1.984 113	.504 003 5461	604.81	.008 007	4.80	2
1.016 085	3.016 028	.331 561 8597	.984 169	2.968 282	.336 895 1931	404.28	.010 686	4.27	3
1.021 505	4.032 114	.248 008 8652	.978 948	3.947 230	.253 342 1985	304.02	.013 369	4.01	4
1.026 953	5.053 619	.197 878 0141	.973 755	4.920 985	.203 211 3474	243.86	.016 057	3.85	5
1.032 430	6.080 571	.164 458 2346	.968 589	5.889 574	.169 791 5680	203.75	.018 749	3.75	6
1.037 936	7.113 001	.140 587 6390	.963 451	6.853 025	.145 920 9723	175.11	.021 447	3.68	7
1.043 472	8.150 937	.122 685 2832	.958 339	7.811 364	.128 018 6165	153.63	.024 149	3.62	8
1.049 037	9.194 409	.108 761 7539	.953 255	8.764 619	.114 095 0872	136.92	.026 856	3.58	9
1.054 632	10.243 445	.097 623 4032	.948 198	9.712 818	.102 956 7365	123.55	.029 567	3.55	10
1.060 256	11.298 077	.088 510 6369	.943 168	10.655 986	.093 843 9702	112.62	.032 284	3.52	11
1.065 911	12.358 334	.080 917 0588	.938 165	11.594 150	.086 250 3922	103.51	.035 005	3.50	12

YEAR	Amount Of 1	Amount Of 1 Per Period	Sinking Fund Payment	Present Worth Of 1	Present Worth of 1 Per Period	Periodic Payment To Amortize 1	Constant Annual Percent	Total Interest	Annual Add On Rate	PERIODS
1	1.065 911	12.358 334	.080 917 0588	.938 165	11.594 150	.086 250 3922	103.51	.035 005	3.50	12
2	1.136 166	25.531 219	.039 167 7349	.880 153	22.471 371	.044 501 0683	53.41	.068 026	3.40	24
3	1.211 052	39.572 343	.025 270 1741	.825 728	32.675 993	.030 603 5075	36.73	.101 726	3.39	36
4	1.290 874	54.538 934	.018 335 5253	.774 669	42.249 608	.023 668 8587	28.41	.136 105	3.40	48
5	1.375 957	70.491 989	.014 186 0091	.726 767	51.231 234	.019 519 3425	23.43	.171 161	3.42	60
6	1.466 648	87.496 528	.011 429 0249	.681 827	59.657 477	.016 762 3583	20.12	.206 890	3.45	72
7	1.563 317	105.621 855	.009 467 7375	.639 666	67.562 679	.014 801 0709	17.77	.243 290	3.48	84
8	1.666 356	124.941 842	.008 003 7238	.600 112	74.979 059	.013 337 0572	16.01	.280 357	3.50	96
9	1.776 188	145.535 232	.006 871 1884	.563 003	81.936 844	.012 204 5218	14.65	.318 088	3.53	108
10	1.893 258	167.485 954	.005 970 6499	.528 190	88.464 391	.011 303 9833	13.57	.356 478	3.56	120
11	2.018 045	190.883 473	.005 238 7982	.495 529	94.588 305	.010 572 1316	12.69	.395 521	3.60	132
12	2.151 057	215.823 149	.004 633 4233	.464 888	100.333 543	.009 966 7566	11.97	.435 213	3.63	144
13	2.292 835	242.406 626	.004 125 2998	.436 141	105.723 521	.009 458 6331	11.36	.475 547	3.66	156
14	2.443 959	270.742 250	.003 693 5499	.409 172	110.780 208	.009 026 8832	10.84	.516 516	3.69	168
15	2.605 043	300.945 506	.003 322 8607	.383 871	115.524 212	.008 656 1941	10.39	.558 115	3.72	180
16	2.776 744	333.139 492	.003 001 7456	.360 134	119.974 869	.008 335 0789	10.01	.600 335	3.75	192
17	2.959 762	367.455 420	.002 721 4186	.337 865	124.150 317	.008 054 7519	9.67	.643 169	3.78	204
18	3.154 843	404.033 149	.002 475 0444	.316 973	128.067 574	.007 808 3778	9.38	.686 610	3.81	216
19	3.362 783	443.021 757	.002 257 2255	.297 373	131.742 606	.007 590 5588	9.11	.730 647	3.85	228
20	3.584 427	484.580 147	.002 063 6421	.278 985	135.190 391	.007 396 9754	8.88	.775 274	3.88	240
21	3.820 681	528.877 697	.001 890 7963	.261 733	138.424 980	.007 224 1296	8.67	.820 481	3.91	252
22	4.072 506	576.094 948	.001 735 8250	.245 549	141.459 557	.007 069 1583	8.49	.866 258	3.94	264
23	4.340 930	626.424 340	.001 596 3620	.230 365	144.306 489	.006 929 6953	8.32	.912 596	3.97	276
24	4.627 045	680.070 998	.001 470 4347	.216 121	146.977 380	.006 803 7680	8.17	.959 485	4.00	288
25	4.932 019	737.253 568	.001 356 3854	.202 757	149.483 115	.006 689 7188	8.03	1.006 916	4.03	300
26	5.257 094	798.205 104	.001 252 8108	.190 219	151.833 907	.006 586 1442	7.91	1.054 877	4.06	312
27	5.603 595	863.174 023	.001 158 5149	.178 457	154.039 336	.006 491 8483	7.80	1.103 359	4.09	324
28	5.972 934	932.425 117	.001 072 4722	.167 422	156.108 392	.006 405 8055	7.69	1.152 351	4.12	336
29	6.366 617	1006.240 626	.000 993 7981	.157 069	158.049 507	.006 327 1314	7.60	1.201 842	4.14	348
30	6.786 247	1084.921 399	.000 921 7258	.147 357	159.870 592	.006 255 0591	7.51	1.251 821	4.17	360
31	7.233 537	1168.788 108	.000 855 5871	.138 245	161.579 069	.006 188 9204	7.43	1.302 278	4.20	372
32	7.710 307	1258.182 566	.000 794 7972	.129 697	163.181 902	.006 128 1305	7.36	1.353 202	4.23	384
33	8.218 502	1353.469 111	.000 738 8421	.121 677	164.685 623	.006 072 1755	7.29	1.404 581	4.26	396
34	8.760 193	1455.036 099	.000 687 2682	.114 153	166.096 361	.006 020 6015	7.23	1.456 405	4.28	408
35	9.337 587	1563.297 480	.000 639 6735	.107 094	167.419 865	.005 973 0069	7.17	1.508 663	4.31	420
36	9.953 037	1678.694 489	.000 595 7010	.100 472	168.661 529	.005 929 0343	7.12	1.561 343	4.34	432
37	10.609 053	1801.697 443	.000 555 0321	.094 259	169.826 415	.005 888 3655	7.07	1.614 434	4.36	444
38	11.308 308	1932.807 659	.000 517 3821	.088 431	170.919 269	.005 850 7154	7.03	1.667 926	4.39	456
39	12.053 651	2072.559 495	.000 482 4952	.082 962	171.944 547	.005 815 8285	6.98	1.721 808	4.41	468
40	12.848 120	2221.522 529	.000 450 1417	.077 832	172.906 425	.005 783 4751	6.95	1.776 068	4.44	480
41	13.694 954	2380.303 883	.000 420 1144	.073 020	173.808 826	.005 753 4478	6.91	1.830 696	4.47	492
42	14.597 604	2549.550 693	.000 392 2260	.068 504	174.655 426	.005 725 5593	6.88	1.885 682	4.49	504
43	15.559 748	2729.952 748	.000 366 3067	.064 268	175.449 676	.005 699 6400	6.84	1.941 014	4.51	516
44	16.585 308	2922.245 303	.000 342 2026	.060 294	176.194 814	.005 675 5360	6.82	1.996 683	4.54	528
45	17.678 464	3127.212 074	.000 319 7736	.056 566	176.893 875	.005 653 1070	6.79	2.052 678	4.56	540
46	18.843 672	3345.688 433	.000 298 8921	.053 068	177.549 710	.005 632 2255	6.76	2.108 988	4.58	552
47	20.085 679	3578.564 812	.000 279 4416	.049 787	178.164 991	.005 612 7750	6.74	2.165 605	4.61	564
48	21.409 045	3826.790 332	.000 261 3156	.046 708	178.742 225	.005 594 6489	6.72	2.222 518	4.63	576
49	22.820 676	4091.376 672	.000 244 4165	.043 820	179.283 766	.005 577 7498	6.70	2.279 717	4.65	588
50	24.324 812	4373.402 192	.000 228 6549	.041 110	179.791 821	.005 561 9883	6.68	2.337 193	4.67	600

Effective Rate is 6.59 %   Annual Percentage Rate is 6.40 %

MONTHLY COMPOUND INTEREST AND ANNUITY

	Amount Of 1	Amount Of 1 Per Period	Sinking Fund Payment	Present Worth Of 1	Present Worth of 1 Per Period	Periodic Payment To Amortize 1	Constant Annual Percent	Total Interest	Annual Add On Rate	
	What a single $1 deposit grows to in the future. The deposit is made at the beginning of the first period.	What a series of $1 deposits grow to in the future. A deposit is made at the end of each period.	The amount to be deposited at the end of each period that grows to $1 in the future.	What $1 to be paid in the future is worth today. Value today of a single $1 payment tomorrow.	What $1 to be paid at the end of each period is worth today. Value today of a series of $1 payments tomorrow.	The mortgage payment to amortize a loan of $1. An annuity certain, payable at the end of each period, worth $1 today.	The annual payment, including interest and principal, to amortize completely a loan of $100.	The total interest paid over the term on a loan of $1. The loan is amortized by regular periodic payments.	The average annual interest rate on a loan that is completely amortized by regular periodic payments.	
	$S = (1+i)^n$	$S\overline{n} = \dfrac{(1+i)^n - 1}{i}$	$\dfrac{1}{S\overline{n}} = \dfrac{i}{(1+i)^n - 1}$	$V^n = \dfrac{1}{(1+i)^n}$	$A\overline{n} = \dfrac{1-V^n}{i}$	$\dfrac{1}{A\overline{n}} = \dfrac{i}{1-V^n}$				

YEAR — **PERIODS**

YEAR	Amount Of 1	Amount Of 1 Per Period	Sinking Fund Payment	Present Worth Of 1	Present Worth of 1 Per Period	Periodic Payment To Amortize 1	Constant Annual Percent	Total Interest	Annual Add On Rate	PERIODS
	1.005 375	1.000 000	1.000 000 0000	.994 654	.994 654	1.005 375 0000	1206.45	.005 375	6.45	1
	1.010 779	2.005 375	.498 659 8516	.989 336	1.983 990	.504 034 8516	604.85	.008 070	4.84	2
	1.016 212	3.016 154	.331 548 0696	.984 047	2.968 037	.336 923 0696	404.31	.010 769	4.31	3
	1.021 674	4.032 366	.247 993 3791	.978 786	3.946 822	.253 368 3791	304.05	.013 474	4.04	4
	1.027 165	5.054 040	.197 861 5252	.973 553	4.920 375	.203 236 5252	243.89	.016 183	3.88	5
	1.032 686	6.081 205	.164 441 0895	.968 348	5.888 724	.169 816 0895	203.78	.018 897	3.78	6
	1.038 237	7.113 892	.140 570 0358	.963 171	6.851 895	.145 945 0358	175.14	.021 615	3.71	7
	1.043 818	8.152 129	.122 667 3456	.958 022	7.809 916	.128 042 3456	153.66	.024 339	3.65	8
	1.049 428	9.195 946	.108 743 5645	.952 900	8.762 816	.114 118 5645	136.95	.027 067	3.61	9
	1.055 069	10.245 375	.097 605 0198	.947 805	9.710 622	.102 980 0198	123.58	.029 800	3.58	10
	1.060 740	11.300 444	.088 492 1014	.942 738	10.653 360	.093 867 1014	112.65	.032 538	3.55	11
	1.066 441	12.361 183	.080 898 4028	.937 698	11.591 058	.086 273 4028	103.53	.035 281	3.53	12
1	1.066 441	12.361 183	.080 898 4028	.937 698	11.591 058	.086 273 4028	103.53	.035 281	3.53	12
2	1.137 297	25.543 661	.039 148 6564	.879 278	22.459 970	.044 523 6564	53.43	.068 568	3.43	24
3	1.212 861	39.602 000	.025 251 2500	.824 497	32.651 728	.030 626 2500	36.76	.102 545	3.42	36
4	1.293 445	54.594 394	.018 316 8990	.773 129	42.208 520	.023 691 8990	28.44	.137 211	3.43	48
5	1.379 383	70.582 903	.014 167 7368	.724 962	51.169 906	.019 542 7368	23.46	.172 564	3.45	60
6	1.471 031	87.633 711	.011 411 1338	.679 795	59.572 979	.016 786 1338	20.15	.208 602	3.48	72
7	1.568 769	105.817 398	.009 450 2419	.637 443	67.452 525	.014 825 2419	17.80	.245 320	3.50	84
8	1.673 000	125.209 233	.007 986 6315	.597 729	74.841 160	.013 361 6315	16.04	.282 717	3.53	96
9	1.784 156	145.889 488	.006 854 5034	.560 489	81.769 469	.012 229 5034	14.68	.320 786	3.56	108
10	1.902 698	167.943 768	.005 954 3740	.525 570	88.266 130	.011 329 3740	13.60	.359 525	3.60	120
11	2.029 116	191.463 364	.005 222 9313	.492 826	94.358 037	.010 597 9313	12.72	.398 927	3.63	132
12	2.163 933	216.545 634	.004 617 9643	.462 122	100.070 407	.009 992 9643	12.00	.438 987	3.66	144
13	2.307 707	243.294 404	.004 110 2466	.433 330	105.426 885	.009 485 2466	11.39	.479 698	3.69	156
14	2.461 035	271.820 399	.003 678 8998	.406 333	110.449 643	.009 053 8998	10.87	.521 055	3.72	168
15	2.624 549	302.241 700	.003 308 6103	.381 018	115.159 475	.008 683 6103	10.43	.563 050	3.75	180
16	2.798 928	334.684 233	.002 987 8910	.357 280	119.575 874	.008 362 8910	10.04	.605 675	3.79	192
17	2.984 892	369.282 293	.002 707 9555	.335 020	123.717 124	.008 082 9555	9.70	.648 923	3.82	204
18	3.183 213	406.179 094	.002 461 9682	.314 148	127.600 365	.007 836 9682	9.41	.692 785	3.85	216
19	3.394 710	445.527 370	.002 244 5310	.294 576	131.241 673	.007 619 5310	9.15	.737 253	3.88	228
20	3.620 259	487.489 998	.002 051 3241	.276 223	134.656 121	.007 426 3241	8.92	.782 318	3.91	240
21	3.860 794	532.240 680	.001 878 8492	.259 014	137.857 842	.007 253 8492	8.71	.827 970	3.94	252
22	4.117 310	579.964 659	.001 724 2430	.242 877	140.860 089	.007 099 2430	8.52	.874 200	3.97	264
23	4.390 870	630.859 484	.001 585 1390	.227 745	143.675 291	.006 960 1390	8.36	.920 998	4.00	276
24	4.682 605	685.135 830	.001 459 5646	.213 556	146.315 100	.006 834 5646	8.21	.968 355	4.03	288
25	4.993 724	743.018 371	.001 345 8617	.200 251	148.790 444	.006 720 8617	8.07	1.016 259	4.07	300
26	5.325 514	804.746 706	.001 242 6270	.187 775	151.111 569	.006 617 6270	7.95	1.064 700	4.09	312
27	5.679 348	870.576 356	.001 148 6643	.176 077	152.288 083	.006 523 6643	7.83	1.113 667	4.12	324
28	6.056 692	940.779 818	.001 062 9480	.165 107	155.328 997	.006 437 9480	7.73	1.163 151	4.15	336
29	6.459 106	1015.647 693	.000 984 5934	.154 820	157.242 757	.006 359 5934	7.64	1.213 138	4.18	348
30	6.888 258	1095.489 892	.000 912 8336	.145 175	159.037 287	.006 287 8336	7.55	1.263 620	4.21	360
31	7.345 923	1180.636 915	.000 847 0005	.136 130	160.720 014	.006 222 0005	7.47	1.314 584	4.24	372
32	7.833 997	1271.441 222	.000 786 5090	.127 649	162.297 904	.006 161 5090	7.40	1.366 019	4.27	384
33	8.354 498	1368.278 691	.000 730 8453	.119 696	163.777 488	.006 105 8453	7.33	1.417 915	4.30	396
34	8.909 582	1471.550 173	.000 679 5555	.112 239	165.164 891	.006 054 5555	7.27	1.470 259	4.32	408
35	9.501 547	1581.683 153	.000 632 2379	.105 246	166.465 857	.006 007 2379	7.21	1.523 040	4.35	420
36	10.132 843	1699.133 518	.000 588 5353	.098 689	167.685 769	.005 963 5353	7.16	1.576 247	4.38	432
37	10.806 083	1824.387 445	.000 548 1292	.092 540	168.829 679	.005 923 1292	7.11	1.629 869	4.41	444
38	11.524 053	1957.963 413	.000 510 7348	.086 775	169.902 321	.005 885 7348	7.07	1.683 895	4.43	456
39	12.289 727	2100.414 351	.000 476 0965	.081 369	170.908 136	.005 851 0965	7.03	1.738 313	4.46	468
40	13.106 273	2252.329 923	.000 443 9847	.076 299	171.851 286	.005 818 9847	6.99	1.793 113	4.48	480
41	13.977 072	2414.338 972	.000 414 1920	.071 546	172.735 676	.005 789 1920	6.95	1.848 282	4.51	492
42	14.905 728	2587.112 123	.000 386 5314	.067 088	173.564 967	.005 761 5314	6.92	1.903 812	4.53	504
43	15.896 084	2771.364 558	.000 360 8331	.062 909	174.342 591	.005 735 8331	6.89	1.959 690	4.56	516
44	16.952 242	2967.858 975	.000 336 9432	.058 989	175.071 768	.005 711 9432	6.86	2.015 906	4.58	528
45	18.078 572	3177.408 748	.000 314 7219	.055 314	175.755 516	.005 689 7219	6.83	2.072 450	4.61	540
46	19.279 737	3400.881 294	.000 294 0414	.051 868	176.396 665	.005 669 0414	6.81	2.129 311	4.63	552
47	20.560 709	3639.201 660	.000 274 7855	.048 636	176.997 869	.005 649 7855	6.78	2.186 479	4.65	564
48	21.926 790	3893.356 355	.000 256 8478	.045 606	177.561 617	.005 631 8478	6.76	2.243 944	4.67	576
49	23.383 636	4164.397 434	.000 240 1308	.042 765	178.090 242	.005 615 1308	6.74	2.301 697	4.70	588
50	24.937 277	4453.446 851	.000 224 5452	.040 101	178.585 933	.005 599 5452	6.72	2.359 727	4.72	600

Effective Rate is 6.64 %   8 - 51   Annual Percentage Rate is 6.45 %

MONTHLY COMPOUND INTEREST AND ANNUITY

	Amount Of 1	Amount Of 1 Per Period	Sinking Fund Payment	Present Worth Of 1	Present Worth of 1 Per Period	Periodic Payment To Amortize 1	Constant Annual Percent	Total Interest	Annual Add On Rate	
	What a single $ 1 deposit grows to in the future. The deposit is made at the beginning of the first period.	What a series of $ 1 deposits grow to in the future. A deposit is made at the end of each period.	The amount to be deposited at the end of each period that grows to $ 1 in the future.	What $ 1 to be paid in the future is worth today. Value today of a single $ 1 payment tomorrow.	What $ 1 to be paid at the end of each period is worth today. Value today of a series of $ 1 payments tomorrow.	The mortgage payment to amortize a loan of $ 1. An annuity certain, payable at the end of each period, worth $ 1 today.	The annual payment, including interest and principal, to amortize completely a loan of $ 100.	The total interest paid over the term on a loan of $1. The loan is amortized by regular periodic payments.	The average annual interest rate on a loan that is completely amortized by regular periodic payments.	
	$S = (1+i)^n$	$S\overline{n]} = \dfrac{(1+i)^n - 1}{i}$	$\dfrac{1}{S\overline{n]}} = \dfrac{i}{(1+i)^n - 1}$	$V^n = \dfrac{1}{(1+i)^n}$	$A\overline{n]} = \dfrac{1-V^n}{i}$	$\dfrac{1}{A\overline{n]}} = \dfrac{i}{1-V^n}$				

YEAR ... **PERIODS**

YEAR	Amount Of 1	Amount Of 1 Per Period	Sinking Fund Payment	Present Worth Of 1	Present Worth of 1 Per Period	Periodic Payment To Amortize 1	Constant Annual Percent	Total Interest	Annual Add On Rate	PERIODS
	1.005 417	1.000 000	1.000 000 0000	.994 613	.994 613	1.005 416 6667	1206.50	.005 417	6.50	1
	1.010 863	2.005 417	.498 649 4910	.989 254	1.983 867	.504 066 1576	604.88	.008 132	4.88	2
	1.016 338	3.016 279	.331 534 2802	.983 924	2.967 791	.336 950 9469	404.35	.010 853	4.34	3
	1.021 843	4.032 618	.247 977 8940	.978 624	3.946 415	.253 394 5607	304.08	.013 578	4.07	4
	1.027 378	5.054 461	.197 845 0376	.973 351	4.919 766	.203 261 7043	243.92	.016 309	3.91	5
	1.032 943	6.081 839	.164 423 9461	.968 107	5.887 873	.169 840 6128	203.81	.019 044	3.81	6
	1.038 538	7.114 782	.140 552 4345	.962 892	6.850 765	.145 969 1012	175.17	.021 784	3.73	7
	1.044 164	8.153 321	.122 649 4103	.957 704	7.808 469	.128 066 0770	153.68	.024 529	3.68	8
	1.049 820	9.197 485	.108 725 3777	.952 545	8.761 014	.114 142 0444	136.98	.027 278	3.64	9
	1.055 506	10.247 304	.097 586 6392	.947 413	9.708 426	.103 003 3059	123.61	.030 033	3.60	10
	1.061 224	11.302 811	.088 473 5691	.942 309	10.650 735	.093 890 2358	112.67	.032 793	3.58	11
	1.066 972	12.364 034	.080 879 7503	.937 232	11.587 967	.086 296 4170	103.56	.035 557	3.56	12
1	1.066 972	12.364 034	.080 879 7503	.937 232	11.587 967	.086 296 4170	103.56	.035 557	3.56	12
2	1.138 429	25.556 111	.039 129 5848	.878 404	22.448 578	.044 546 2514	53.46	.069 110	3.46	24
3	1.214 672	39.631 685	.025 232 3362	.823 268	32.627 489	.030 649 0029	36.78	.103 364	3.45	36
4	1.296 020	54.649 927	.018 298 2863	.771 593	42.167 488	.023 714 9529	28.46	.138 318	3.46	48
5	1.382 817	70.673 968	.014 149 4816	.723 161	51.108 680	.019 566 1482	23.48	.173 969	3.48	60
6	1.475 427	87.771 168	.011 393 2630	.677 770	59.488 649	.016 809 9296	20.18	.210 315	3.51	72
7	1.574 239	106.013 400	.009 432 7698	.635 227	67.342 623	.014 849 4365	17.82	.247 353	3.53	84
8	1.679 669	125.477 348	.007 969 5659	.595 355	74.703 617	.013 386 2326	16.07	.285 078	3.56	96
9	1.792 160	146.244 833	.006 837 8484	.557 986	81.602 576	.012 254 5151	14.71	.323 488	3.59	108
10	1.912 184	168.403 154	.005 938 1311	.522 962	88.068 500	.011 354 7977	13.63	.362 576	3.63	120
11	2.040 246	192.045 460	.005 207 1005	.490 137	94.128 569	.010 623 7671	12.75	.402 337	3.66	132
12	2.176 885	217.271 134	.004 602 5442	.459 372	99.808 260	.010 019 2109	12.03	.442 766	3.69	144
13	2.322 675	244.186 218	.004 095 2352	.430 538	105.131 446	.009 511 9019	11.42	.483 857	3.72	156
14	2.478 229	272.903 856	.003 664 2941	.403 514	110.120 506	.009 080 9608	10.90	.525 601	3.75	168
15	2.644 201	303.544 767	.003 294 4070	.378 186	114.796 412	.008 711 0737	10.46	.567 993	3.79	180
16	2.821 288	336.237 756	.002 974 0860	.354 448	119.178 820	.008 390 7527	10.07	.611 025	3.82	192
17	3.010 235	371.120 256	.002 694 5444	.332 200	123.286 152	.008 111 2110	9.74	.654 687	3.85	204
18	3.211 836	408.338 901	.002 448 9462	.311 348	127.135 675	.007 865 6129	9.44	.698 972	3.88	216
19	3.426 938	448.050 147	.002 231 8930	.291 806	130.743 570	.007 648 5597	9.18	.743 872	3.92	228
20	3.656 447	490.420 930	.002 039 0647	.273 490	134.125 004	.007 455 7314	8.95	.789 376	3.95	240
21	3.901 326	535.629 362	.001 866 9626	.256 323	137.294 192	.007 283 6293	8.75	.835 475	3.98	252
22	4.162 605	583.865 486	.001 712 7233	.240 234	140.264 456	.007 129 3899	8.56	.882 159	4.01	264
23	4.441 382	635.332 073	.001 573 9800	.225 155	143.048 282	.006 990 6467	8.39	.929 418	4.04	276
24	4.738 830	690.245 473	.001 448 7600	.211 023	145.657 372	.006 865 4266	8.24	.977 243	4.07	288
25	5.056 198	748.836 525	.001 335 4049	.197 777	148.102 695	.006 752 0716	8.11	1.025 621	4.10	300
26	5.394 821	811.351 528	.001 232 5114	.185 363	150.394 529	.006 649 1781	7.98	1.074 544	4.13	312
27	5.756 122	878.053 277	.001 138 8831	.173 728	152.542 509	.006 555 5497	7.87	1.123 998	4.16	324
28	6.141 620	949.222 165	.001 053 4942	.162 823	154.555 664	.006 470 1608	7.77	1.173 974	4.19	336
29	6.552 936	1025.157 366	.000 975 4600	.152 603	156.442 457	.006 392 1267	7.68	1.224 460	4.22	348
30	6.991 798	1106.178 087	.000 904 0136	.143 025	158.210 820	.006 320 6802	7.59	1.275 445	4.25	360
31	7.460 052	1192.624 917	.000 838 4866	.134 047	159.868 185	.006 255 1533	7.51	1.326 917	4.28	372
32	7.959 665	1284.861 251	.000 778 2942	.125 633	161.421 521	.006 194 9608	7.44	1.378 865	4.31	384
33	8.492 739	1383.274 822	.000 722 9221	.117 748	162.877 357	.006 139 5888	7.37	1.431 277	4.34	396
34	9.061 513	1488.279 333	.000 671 9169	.110 357	164.241 813	.006 088 5835	7.31	1.484 142	4.37	408
35	9.668 379	1600.316 191	.000 624 8765	.103 430	165.520 625	.006 041 5432	7.25	1.537 448	4.39	420
36	10.315 889	1719.856 364	.000 581 4439	.096 938	166.719 167	.005 998 1106	7.20	1.591 184	4.42	432
37	11.006 763	1847.402 364	.000 541 3006	.090 853	167.842 480	.005 957 9673	7.15	1.645 337	4.45	444
38	11.743 906	1983.490 356	.000 504 1618	.085 151	168.895 284	.005 920 8284	7.11	1.699 898	4.47	456
39	12.530 417	2128.692 413	.000 469 7720	.079 806	169.882 006	.005 886 4386	7.07	1.754 853	4.50	468
40	13.369 602	2283.618 920	.000 437 9014	.074 797	170.806 793	.005 854 5681	7.03	1.810 193	4.53	480
41	14.264 990	2448.921 143	.000 408 3431	.070 102	171.673 533	.005 825 0097	7.00	1.865 905	4.55	492
42	15.220 342	2625.293 961	.000 380 9097	.065 702	172.485 869	.005 797 5764	6.96	1.921 979	4.58	504
43	16.239 677	2813.478 794	.000 355 4319	.061 578	173.247 216	.005 772 0985	6.93	1.978 403	4.60	516
44	17.327 278	3014.266 714	.000 331 7556	.057 712	173.960 775	.005 748 4223	6.90	2.035 167	4.63	528
45	18.487 718	3228.501 772	.000 309 7412	.054 090	174.629 545	.005 726 4079	6.88	2.092 260	4.65	540
46	19.725 875	3457.084 549	.000 289 2611	.050 695	175.256 338	.005 705 9277	6.85	2.149 672	4.67	552
47	21.046 953	3700.975 938	.000 270 1990	.047 513	175.843 788	.005 686 8657	6.83	2.207 392	4.70	564
48	22.456 506	3961.201 185	.000 252 4487	.044 531	176.394 365	.005 669 1153	6.81	2.265 410	4.72	576
49	23.960 460	4238.854 199	.000 235 9128	.041 735	176.910 383	.005 652 5795	6.79	2.323 717	4.74	588
50	25.565 137	4535.102 149	.000 220 5022	.039 116	177.394 012	.005 637 1689	6.77	2.382 301	4.76	600

	Amount Of 1	Amount Of 1 Per Period	Sinking Fund Payment	Present Worth Of 1	Present Worth of 1 Per Period	Periodic Payment To Amortize 1	Constant Annual Percent	Total Interest	Annual Add On Rate	
	What a single $ 1 deposit grows to in the future. The deposit is made at the beginning of the first period.	What a series of $ 1 deposits grow to in the future. A deposit is made at the end of each.	The amount to be deposited at the end of each period that grows to $ 1 in the future.	What $ 1 to be paid in the future is worth today. Value today of a single $ 1 payment tomorrow.	What $ 1 to be paid at the end of each period is worth today. Value today of a series of $ 1 payments tomorrow.	The mortgage payment to amortize a loan of $ 1. An annuity certain, payable at the end of each period, worth $ 1 today.	The annual payment, including interest and principal, to amortize completely a loan of $ 100.	The total interest paid over the term on a loan of $1. The loan is amortized by regular periodic payments.	The average annual interest rate on a loan that is completely amortized by regular periodic payments.	
	$S = (1+i)^n$	$S\overline{n} = \frac{(1+i)^n - 1}{i}$	$\frac{1}{S\overline{n}} = \frac{i}{(1+i)^n - 1}$	$V^n = \frac{1}{(1+i)^n}$	$A\overline{n} = \frac{1-V^n}{i}$	$\frac{1}{A\overline{n}} = \frac{i}{1-V^n}$				

YEAR   **PERIODS**

YEAR	Amount Of 1	Amount Of 1 Per Period	Sinking Fund Payment	Present Worth Of 1	Present Worth of 1 Per Period	Periodic Payment To Amortize 1	Constant Annual Percent	Total Interest	Annual Add On Rate	PERIODS
	1.005 458	1.000 000	1.000 000 0000	.994 571	.994 571	1.005 458 3333	1206.55	.005 458	6.55	1
	1.010 946	2.005 458	.498 639 1307	.989 172	1.983 743	.504 097 4640	604.92	.008 195	4.92	2
	1.016 465	3.016 405	.331 520 4916	.983 802	2.967 546	.336 978 8249	404.38	.010 936	4.37	3
	1.022 013	4.032 869	.247 962 4100	.978 461	3.946 007	.253 420 7434	304.11	.013 683	4.10	4
	1.027 591	5.054 882	.197 828 5515	.973 150	4.919 156	.203 286 8848	243.95	.016 434	3.94	5
	1.033 200	6.082 473	.164 406 8044	.967 867	5.887 023	.169 865 1377	203.84	.019 191	3.84	6
	1.038 840	7.115 673	.140 534 8352	.962 612	6.849 636	.145 993 1686	175.20	.021 952	3.76	7
	1.044 510	8.154 513	.122 631 4773	.957 387	7.807 022	.128 089 8106	153.71	.024 718	3.71	8
	1.050 211	9.199 023	.108 707 1935	.952 189	8.759 212	.114 165 5268	137.00	.027 490	3.67	9
	1.055 944	10.249 235	.097 568 2615	.947 020	9.706 232	.103 026 5948	123.64	.030 266	3.63	10
	1.061 707	11.305 178	.088 455 0399	.941 879	10.648 111	.093 913 3733	112.70	.033 047	3.61	11
	1.067 503	12.366 886	.080 861 1012	.936 766	11.584 877	.086 319 4345	103.59	.035 833	3.58	12
1	1.067 503	12.366 886	.080 861 1012	.936 766	11.584 877	.086 319 4345	103.59	.035 833	3.58	12
2	1.139 562	25.568 568	.039 110 5200	.877 530	22.437 194	.044 568 8533	53.49	.069 652	3.48	24
3	1.216 485	39.661 398	.025 213 4327	.822 040	32.603 274	.030 671 7660	36.81	.104 184	3.47	36
4	1.298 601	54.705 531	.018 279 6873	.770 059	42.126 512	.023 738 0206	28.49	.139 425	3.49	48
5	1.386 260	70.765 182	.014 131 2433	.721 365	51.047 555	.019 589 5767	23.51	.175 375	3.51	60
6	1.479 836	87.908 900	.011 375 4125	.675 751	59.404 485	.016 833 7458	20.21	.212 030	3.53	72
7	1.579 729	106.209 864	.009 415 3214	.633 020	67.232 971	.014 873 6547	17.85	.249 387	3.56	84
8	1.686 365	125.746 190	.007 952 5272	.592 992	74.566 430	.013 410 8606	16.10	.287 443	3.59	96
9	1.800 199	146.601 268	.006 821 2234	.555 494	81.436 164	.012 279 5567	14.74	.326 192	3.62	108
10	1.921 717	168.864 119	.005 921 9212	.520 368	87.871 497	.011 380 2545	13.66	.365 631	3.66	120
11	2.051 437	192.629 769	.005 191 3056	.487 463	93.899 897	.010 649 6389	12.78	.405 752	3.69	132
12	2.189 915	217.999 662	.004 587 1631	.456 639	99.547 096	.010 045 4964	12.06	.446 551	3.72	144
13	2.337 740	245.082 088	.004 080 2655	.427 764	104.837 200	.009 538 5989	11.45	.488 021	3.75	156
14	2.495 543	273.992 649	.003 649 7330	.400 714	109.792 789	.009 108 0663	10.93	.530 155	3.79	168
15	2.663 999	304.854 746	.003 280 2507	.375 376	114.435 015	.008 738 5840	10.49	.572 945	3.82	180
16	2.843 826	337.800 116	.002 960 3305	.351 639	118.783 695	.008 418 6639	10.11	.616 383	3.85	192
17	3.035 791	372.969 382	.002 681 1852	.329 403	122.857 389	.008 139 5186	9.77	.660 462	3.89	204
18	3.240 715	410.512 665	.002 435 9784	.308 574	126.673 487	.007 894 3118	9.48	.705 171	3.92	216
19	3.459 472	450.590 217	.002 219 3114	.289 061	130.248 277	.007 677 6447	9.22	.750 503	3.95	228
20	3.692 995	493.373 107	.002 026 8636	.270 783	133.597 019	.007 485 1969	8.99	.796 447	3.98	240
21	3.942 282	539.043 953	.001 855 1363	.253 660	136.734 006	.007 313 4696	8.78	.842 994	4.01	252
22	4.208 396	587.797 699	.001 701 2656	.237 620	139.672 628	.007 159 5989	8.60	.890 134	4.05	264
23	4.492 473	639.842 448	.001 562 8847	.222 595	142.425 429	.007 021 2181	8.43	.937 856	4.08	276
24	4.795 727	695.400 353	.001 438 0206	.208 519	145.004 160	.006 896 3539	8.28	.986 150	4.11	288
25	5.119 451	754.708 560	.001 325 0148	.195 333	147.419 826	.006 783 3481	8.15	1.035 004	4.14	300
26	5.465 027	818.020 225	.001 222 4637	.182 982	149.682 740	.006 680 7970	8.02	1.084 409	4.17	312
27	5.833 931	885.605 590	.001 129 1708	.171 411	151.802 561	.006 587 5042	7.91	1.134 351	4.20	324
28	6.227 736	957.753 142	.001 044 1104	.160 572	153.788 336	.006 502 4437	7.81	1.184 821	4.23	336
29	6.648 124	1034.770 840	.000 966 3975	.150 418	155.648 543	.006 424 7309	7.71	1.235 806	4.26	348
30	7.096 890	1116.987 432	.000 895 2652	.140 907	157.391 121	.006 353 5986	7.63	1.287 295	4.29	360
31	7.575 948	1204.753 857	.000 830 0451	.131 997	159.023 509	.006 288 3784	7.55	1.339 277	4.32	372
32	8.087 344	1298.444 742	.000 770 1521	.123 650	160.552 674	.006 228 4855	7.48	1.391 738	4.35	384
33	8.633 261	1398.460 004	.000 715 0723	.115 831	161.985 144	.006 173 4056	7.41	1.444 669	4.38	396
34	9.216 028	1505.226 555	.000 664 3518	.108 507	163.327 033	.006 122 6852	7.35	1.498 056	4.41	408
35	9.838 134	1619.200 124	.000 617 5889	.101 645	164.584 069	.006 075 9222	7.30	1.551 887	4.43	420
36	10.502 233	1740.867 203	.000 574 4264	.095 218	165.761 617	.006 032 7597	7.24	1.606 152	4.46	432
37	11.211 161	1870.747 125	.000 534 5458	.089 197	166.864 704	.005 992 8791	7.20	1.660 838	4.49	444
38	11.967 944	2009.394 277	.000 497 6624	.083 557	167.898 038	.005 955 9957	7.15	1.715 934	4.52	456
39	12.775 811	2157.400 470	.000 463 5208	.078 273	168.866 030	.005 921 8541	7.11	1.771 428	4.54	468
40	13.638 211	2315.397 464	.000 431 8913	.073 323	169.772 812	.005 890 2246	7.07	1.827 308	4.57	480
41	14.558 826	2484.059 663	.000 402 5668	.068 687	170.622 255	.005 860 9002	7.04	1.883 563	4.59	492
42	15.541 584	2664.106 996	.000 375 3603	.064 344	171.417 984	.005 833 6936	7.01	1.940 182	4.62	504
43	16.590 681	2856.307 991	.000 350 1023	.060 275	172.163 395	.005 808 4356	6.98	1.997 153	4.64	516
44	17.710 595	3061.483 048	.000 326 6391	.056 463	172.861 671	.005 784 9724	6.95	2.054 465	4.67	528
45	18.906 106	3280.507 953	.000 304 8308	.052 893	173.515 793	.005 763 1642	6.92	2.112 109	4.69	540
46	20.182 317	3514.317 605	.000 284 5503	.049 548	174.128 551	.005 742 8836	6.90	2.170 072	4.72	552
47	21.544 675	3763.910 013	.000 265 6812	.046 415	174.702 562	.005 724 0145	6.87	2.228 344	4.74	564
48	22.998 997	4030.350 553	.000 248 1174	.043 480	175.240 277	.005 706 4507	6.85	2.286 916	4.76	576
49	24.551 488	4314.776 519	.000 231 7617	.040 731	175.743 989	.005 690 0950	6.83	2.345 776	4.79	588
50	26.208 777	4618.401 972	.000 216 5251	.038 155	176.215 849	.005 674 8584	6.81	2.404 915	4.81	600

Effective Rate is 6.75 %   Annual Percentage Rate is 6.55

	Amount Of 1	Amount Of 1 Per Period	Sinking Fund Payment	Present Worth Of 1	Present Worth of 1 Per Period	Periodic Payment To Amortize 1	Constant Annual Percent	Total Interest	Annual Add On Rate	
	What a single $ 1 deposit grows to in the future. The deposit is made at the beginning of the first period.	What a series of $ 1 deposits grow to in the future. A deposit is made at the end of each period.	The amount to be deposited at the end of each period that grows to $ 1 in the future.	What $ 1 to be paid in the future is worth today. Value today of a single $ 1 payment tomorrow.	What $ 1 to be paid at the end of each period is worth today. Value today of a series of $ 1 payments tomorrow.	The mortgage payment to amortize a loan of $ 1. An annuity certain, payable at the end of each period, worth $ 1 today.	The annual payment, including interest and principal, to amortize completely a loan of $ 100.	The total interest paid over the term of a loan of $1. The loan is amortized by regular periodic payments.	The average annual interest rate on a loan that is completely amortized by regular periodic payments.	
	$S = (1+i)^n$	$S\overline{n} = \dfrac{(1+i)^n - 1}{i}$	$\dfrac{1}{S\overline{n}} = \dfrac{i}{(1+i)^n - 1}$	$V^n = \dfrac{1}{(1+i)^n}$	$A\overline{n} = \dfrac{1-V^n}{i}$	$\dfrac{1}{A\overline{n}} = \dfrac{i}{1-V^n}$				

YEAR										PERIODS
	1.005 500	1.000 000	1.000 000 0000	.994 530	.994 530	1.005 500 0000	1206.60	.005 500	6.60	1
	1.011 030	2.005 500	.498 628 7709	.989 090	1.983 620	.504 128 7709	604.96	.008 258	4.95	2
	1.016 591	3.016 530	.331 506 7038	.983 680	2.967 300	.337 006 7038	404.41	.011 020	4.41	3
	1.022 182	4.033 121	.247 946 9271	.978 299	3.945 599	.253 446 9271	304.14	.013 788	4.14	4
	1.027 804	5.055 303	.197 812 0667	.972 948	4.918 547	.203 312 0667	243.98	.016 560	3.97	5
	1.033 457	6.083 108	.164 389 6643	.967 626	5.886 173	.169 889 6643	203.87	.019 338	3.87	6
	1.039 141	7.116 565	.140 517 2379	.962 333	6.848 506	.146 017 2379	175.23	.022 121	3.79	7
	1.044 856	8.155 706	.122 613 5465	.957 069	7.805 576	.128 113 5465	153.74	.024 908	3.74	8
	1.050 603	9.200 562	.108 689 0118	.951 834	8.757 410	.114 189 0118	137.03	.027 701	3.69	9
	1.056 381	10.251 165	.097 549 8866	.946 628	9.704 038	.103 049 8866	123.66	.030 499	3.66	10
	1.062 192	11.307 547	.088 436 5139	.941 450	10.645 488	.093 936 5139	112.73	.033 302	3.63	11
	1.068 034	12.369 738	.080 842 4554	.936 300	11.581 788	.086 342 4554	103.62	.036 109	3.61	12
1	1.068 034	12.369 738	.080 842 4554	.936 300	11.581 788	.086 342 4554	103.62	.036 109	3.61	12
2	1.140 696	25.581 033	.039 091 4621	.876 658	22.425 818	.044 591 4621	53.51	.070 195	3.51	24
3	1.218 301	39.691 140	.025 194 5394	.820 815	32.579 085	.030 694 5394	36.84	.105 003	3.50	36
4	1.301 187	54.761 208	.018 261 1019	.768 529	42.085 590	.023 761 1019	28.52	.140 533	3.51	48
5	1.389 711	70.856 546	.014 113 0221	.719 574	50.986 533	.019 613 0221	23.54	.176 781	3.54	60
6	1.484 258	88.046 907	.011 357 5824	.673 737	59.320 487	.016 857 5824	20.23	.213 746	3.56	72
7	1.585 237	106.406 790	.009 397 8965	.630 820	67.123 570	.014 897 8965	17.88	.251 423	3.59	84
8	1.693 087	126.015 760	.007 935 5153	.590 637	74.429 598	.013 435 5153	16.13	.289 809	3.62	96
9	1.808 273	146.958 799	.006 804 6283	.553 014	81.270 232	.012 304 6283	14.77	.328 900	3.65	108
10	1.931 297	169.326 667	.005 905 7443	.517 787	87.675 120	.011 405 7443	13.69	.368 689	3.69	120
11	2.062 690	193.216 301	.005 175 5467	.484 804	93.672 017	.010 675 5467	12.82	.409 172	3.72	132
12	2.203 022	218.731 232	.004 571 8208	.453 922	99.286 913	.010 071 8208	12.09	.450 342	3.75	144
13	2.352 901	245.982 035	.004 065 3375	.425 007	104.544 141	.009 565 3375	11.48	.492 193	3.79	156
14	2.512 977	275.086 806	.003 635 2161	.397 934	109.466 485	.009 135 2161	10.97	.534 716	3.82	168
15	2.683 944	306.171 679	.003 266 1414	.372 586	114.075 276	.008 766 1414	10.52	.577 905	3.85	180
16	2.866 543	339.371 366	.002 946 6246	.348 852	118.390 488	.008 446 6246	10.14	.621 752	3.89	192
17	3.061 564	374.829 746	.002 667 8779	.326 630	122.430 821	.008 167 8779	9.81	.666 247	3.92	204
18	3.269 853	412.700 486	.002 423 0648	.305 824	126.213 786	.007 923 0648	9.51	.711 382	3.95	216
19	3.492 312	453.147 707	.002 206 7860	.286 343	129.755 777	.007 706 7860	9.25	.757 147	3.98	228
20	3.729 907	496.346 697	.002 014 7208	.268 103	133.072 143	.007 514 7208	9.02	.803 533	4.02	240
21	3.983 666	542.484 667	.001 843 3701	.251 025	136.177 258	.007 343 3701	8.82	.850 529	4.05	252
22	4.254 689	591.761 568	.001 689 8698	.235 035	139.084 577	.007 189 8698	8.63	.898 126	4.08	264
23	4.544 150	644.390 952	.001 551 8529	.220 063	141.806 701	.007 051 8529	8.47	.946 311	4.11	276
24	4.853 305	700.600 900	.001 427 3462	.206 045	144.355 425	.006 927 3462	8.32	.995 076	4.15	288
25	5.183 493	760.635 012	.001 314 6910	.192 920	146.741 797	.006 814 6910	8.18	1.044 407	4.18	300
26	5.536 144	824.753 457	.001 212 4836	.180 631	148.976 157	.006 712 4836	8.06	1.094 295	4.21	312
27	5.912 788	893.234 108	.001 119 5273	.169 125	151.068 188	.006 619 5273	7.95	1.144 727	4.24	324
28	6.315 056	966.373 742	.001 034 7963	.158 352	153.026 958	.006 534 7963	7.85	1.195 692	4.27	336
29	6.744 691	1044.489 326	.000 957 4057	.148 265	154.860 954	.006 457 4057	7.75	1.247 177	4.30	348
30	7.203 557	1127.919 391	.000 886 5882	.138 820	156.578 125	.006 386 5882	7.67	1.299 172	4.33	360
31	7.693 640	1217.025 500	.000 821 6755	.129 977	158.185 912	.006 321 6755	7.59	1.351 663	4.36	372
32	8.217 066	1312.193 814	.000 762 0825	.121 698	159.691 284	.006 262 0825	7.52	1.404 640	4.39	384
33	8.776 102	1413.836 768	.000 707 2952	.113 946	161.100 763	.006 207 2952	7.45	1.458 089	4.42	396
34	9.373 172	1522.394 854	.000 656 8598	.106 687	162.420 460	.006 156 8598	7.39	1.511 999	4.45	408
35	10.010 862	1638.338 533	.000 610 3745	.099 891	163.656 091	.006 110 3745	7.34	1.566 357	4.48	420
36	10.691 937	1762.170 273	.000 567 4821	.093 528	164.813 013	.006 067 4821	7.29	1.621 152	4.50	432
37	11.419 347	1894.426 728	.000 527 8642	.087 571	165.896 240	.006 027 8642	7.24	1.676 372	4.53	444
38	12.196 246	2035.681 059	.000 491 2361	.081 992	166.910 465	.005 991 2361	7.19	1.732 004	4.56	456
39	13.026 000	2186.545 426	.000 457 3424	.076 770	167.860 084	.005 957 3424	7.15	1.788 036	4.58	468
40	13.912 205	2347.673 632	.000 425 9536	.071 879	168.749 212	.005 925 9536	7.12	1.844 465	4.61	480
41	14.858 702	2519.763 964	.000 396 8626	.067 301	169.581 704	.005 896 8626	7.08	1.901 256	4.64	492
42	15.869 592	2703.562 213	.000 369 8824	.063 014	170.361 165	.005 869 8824	7.05	1.958 421	4.66	504
43	16.949 257	2899.864 912	.000 344 8436	.059 000	171.090 975	.005 844 8436	7.02	2.015 939	4.69	516
44	18.102 375	3109.522 782	.000 321 5928	.055 241	171.774 296	.005 821 5928	6.99	2.073 801	4.71	528
45	19.333 944	3333.444 423	.000 299 9900	.051 723	172.414 090	.005 799 9900	6.96	2.131 995	4.74	540
46	20.649 301	3572.600 251	.000 279 9082	.048 428	173.013 129	.005 779 9082	6.94	2.190 509	4.76	552
47	22.054 147	3828.026 700	.000 261 2312	.045 343	173.574 010	.005 761 2312	6.92	2.249 334	4.79	564
48	23.554 569	4100.830 721	.000 243 8530	.042 455	174.099 162	.005 743 8530	6.90	2.308 459	4.81	576
49	25.157 070	4392.194 569	.000 227 6766	.039 750	174.590 862	.005 727 6766	6.88	2.367 874	4.83	588
50	26.868 595	4703.380 938	.000 212 6130	.037 218	175.051 241	.005 712 6130	6.86	2.427 568	4.86	600

Effective Rate is 6.80 %

Annual Percentage Rate is 6.60 %

	Amount Of 1	Amount Of 1 Per Period	Sinking Fund Payment	Present Worth Of 1	Present Worth of 1 Per Period	Periodic Payment To Amortize 1	Constant Annual Percent	Total Interest	Annual Add On Rate	
	What a single $ 1 deposit grows to in the future. The deposit is made at the beginning of the first period.	What a series of $ 1 deposits grow to in the future. A deposit is made at the end of each period.	The amount to be deposited at the end of each period that grows to $ 1 in the future.	What $ 1 to be paid in the future is worth today. Value today of a single $ 1 payment tomorrow.	What $ 1 to be paid at the end of each period is worth today. Value today of a series of $ 1 payments tomorrow.	The mortgage payment to amortize a loan of $ 1. An annuity certain, payable at the end of each period, worth $ 1 today.	The annual payment, including interest and principal, to amortize completely a loan of $ 100.	The total interest paid over the term on a loan of $1. The loan is amortized by regular periodic payments.	The average annual interest rate on a loan that is completely amortized by regular periodic payments.	
	$S = (1+i)^n$	$S\overline{n} = \dfrac{(1+i)^n - 1}{i}$	$\dfrac{1}{S\overline{n}} = \dfrac{i}{(1+i)^n - 1}$	$V^n = \dfrac{1}{(1+i)^n}$	$A\overline{n} = \dfrac{1 - V^n}{i}$	$\dfrac{1}{A\overline{n}} = \dfrac{i}{1 - V^n}$				

YEAR									PERIODS	
	1.005 521	1.000 000	1.000 000 0000	.994 509	.994 509	1.005 520 8333	1206.63	.005 521	6.62	1
	1.011 072	2.005 521	.498 623 5911	.989 049	1.983 559	.504 144 4245	604.98	.008 289	4.97	2
	1.016 654	3.016 593	.331 499 8101	.983 619	2.967 177	.337 020 6435	404.43	.011 062	4.42	3
	1.022 267	4.033 247	.247 939 1861	.978 218	3.945 395	.253 460 0194	304.16	.013 840	4.15	4
	1.027 911	5.055 514	.197 803 8248	.972 847	4.918 243	.203 324 6581	243.99	.016 623	3.99	5
	1.033 586	6.083 425	.164 381 0949	.967 506	5.885 748	.169 901 9282	203.89	.019 412	3.88	6
	1.039 292	7.117 010	.140 508 4400	.962 194	6.847 942	.146 029 2733	175.24	.022 205	3.81	7
	1.045 030	8.156 302	.122 604 5820	.956 911	7.804 853	.128 125 4153	153.76	.025 003	3.75	8
	1.050 799	9.201 332	.108 679 9219	.951 657	8.756 510	.114 200 7552	137.05	.027 807	3.71	9
	1.056 600	10.252 131	.097 540 7002	.946 432	9.702 941	.103 061 5336	123.68	.030 615	3.67	10
	1.062 434	11.308 731	.088 427 2520	.941 235	10.644 176	.093 948 0854	112.74	.033 429	3.65	11
	1.068 299	12.371 165	.080 833 1339	.936 067	11.580 244	.086 353 9672	103.63	.036 248	3.62	12
1	1.068 299	12.371 165	.080 833 1339	.936 067	11.580 244	.086 353 9672	103.63	.036 248	3.62	12
2	1.141 263	25.587 269	.039 081 9357	.876 222	22.420 133	.044 602 7690	53.53	.070 466	3.52	24
3	1.219 210	39.706 022	.025 185 0967	.820 203	32.566 999	.030 705 9300	36.85	.105 413	3.51	36
4	1.302 481	54.789 074	.018 251 8144	.767 765	42.065 150	.023 772 6477	28.53	.141 087	3.53	48
5	1.391 440	70.902 285	.014 103 9179	.718 680	50.956 060	.019 624 7512	23.55	.177 485	3.55	60
6	1.486 474	88.116 014	.011 348 6749	.672 733	59.278 551	.016 869 5083	20.25	.214 605	3.58	72
7	1.587 999	106.505 426	.009 389 1930	.629 723	67.068 963	.014 910 0263	17.90	.252 442	3.61	84
8	1.696 458	126.150 820	.007 927 0194	.589 464	74.361 314	.013 447 8528	16.14	.290 994	3.64	96
9	1.812 324	147.137 976	.006 796 3419	.551 778	81.187 446	.012 317 1753	14.79	.330 255	3.67	108
10	1.936 104	169.558 538	.005 897 6682	.516 501	87.577 165	.011 418 5016	13.71	.370 220	3.70	120
11	2.068 339	193.510 404	.005 167 6808	.483 480	93.558 374	.010 688 5141	12.83	.410 884	3.74	132
12	2.209 604	219.098 163	.004 564 1642	.452 570	99.157 188	.010 084 9976	12.11	.452 240	3.77	144
13	2.360 519	246.433 543	.004 057 8892	.423 636	104.398 055	.009 578 7225	11.50	.494 281	3.80	156
14	2.521 740	275.635 906	.003 627 9744	.396 552	109.303 860	.009 148 8077	10.98	.537 000	3.84	168
15	2.693 973	306.832 765	.003 259 1044	.371 199	113.896 025	.008 779 9377	10.54	.580 389	3.87	180
16	2.877 969	340.160 343	.002 939 7901	.347 467	118.194 600	.008 460 6234	10.16	.624 440	3.90	192
17	3.074 531	375.764 165	.002 661 2437	.325 253	122.218 356	.008 182 0770	9.82	.669 144	3.94	204
18	3.284 519	413.799 698	.002 416 6282	.304 459	125.984 863	.007 937 4615	9.53	.714 492	3.97	216
19	3.508 849	454.433 025	.002 200 5443	.284 994	129.510 568	.007 721 3776	9.27	.760 474	4.00	228
20	3.748 500	497.841 573	.002 008 6711	.266 773	132.810 865	.007 529 5045	9.04	.807 081	4.04	240
21	4.004 520	544.214 888	.001 837 5095	.249 718	135.900 165	.007 358 3428	8.84	.854 302	4.07	252
22	4.278 025	593.755 460	.001 684 1950	.233 753	138.791 959	.007 205 0284	8.65	.902 127	4.10	264
23	4.570 210	646.679 611	.001 546 3608	.218 808	141.498 872	.007 067 1941	8.49	.950 546	4.13	276
24	4.882 352	703.218 435	.001 422 0333	.204 819	144.032 726	.006 942 8666	8.34	.999 546	4.16	288
25	5.215 812	763.618 812	.001 309 5539	.191 725	146.404 584	.006 830 3872	8.20	1.049 116	4.20	300
26	5.572 048	828.144 483	.001 207 5188	.179 467	148.624 802	.006 728 3521	8.08	1.099 246	4.23	312
27	5.952 614	897.077 202	.001 114 7313	.167 993	150.703 077	.006 635 5646	7.97	1.149 923	4.26	324
28	6.359 172	970.717 965	.001 030 1653	.157 253	152.648 482	.006 550 9987	7.87	1.201 136	4.29	336
29	6.793 498	1049.388 330	.000 952 9361	.147 200	154.469 512	.006 473 7694	7.77	1.252 872	4.32	348
30	7.257 488	1133.431 812	.000 882 2763	.137 789	156.174 119	.006 403 1096	7.69	1.305 119	4.35	360
31	7.753 168	1223.215 392	.000 817 5175	.128 980	157.769 746	.006 338 3508	7.61	1.357 867	4.38	372
32	8.282 703	1319.131 113	.000 758 0748	.120 734	159.263 360	.006 278 9081	7.54	1.411 101	4.41	384
33	8.848 404	1421.597 795	.000 703 4338	.113 015	160.661 484	.006 224 2672	7.47	1.464 810	4.44	396
34	9.452 743	1531.062 863	.000 653 1410	.105 789	161.970 222	.006 173 9744	7.41	1.518 982	4.47	408
35	10.098 357	1648.004 301	.000 606 7945	.099 026	163.195 289	.006 127 6279	7.36	1.573 604	4.50	420
36	10.788 066	1772.932 738	.000 564 0372	.092 695	164.342 034	.006 084 8705	7.31	1.628 664	4.52	432
37	11.524 882	1906.393 679	.000 524 5506	.086 769	165.415 465	.006 045 3840	7.26	1.684 150	4.55	444
38	12.312 021	2048.969 888	.000 488 0501	.081 221	166.420 269	.006 008 8835	7.22	1.740 051	4.58	456
39	13.152 922	2201.283 929	.000 454 2803	.076 029	167.360 833	.005 975 1137	7.18	1.796 353	4.61	468
40	14.051 255	2364.000 887	.000 423 0117	.071 168	168.241 264	.005 943 8450	7.14	1.853 046	4.63	480
41	15.010 943	2537.831 274	.000 394 0372	.066 618	169.065 407	.005 914 8706	7.10	1.910 116	4.66	492
42	16.036 178	2723.534 126	.000 367 1700	.062 359	169.836 861	.005 888 0033	7.07	1.967 554	4.68	504
43	17.131 435	2921.920 322	.000 342 2407	.058 372	170.558 993	.005 863 0740	7.04	2.025 346	4.71	516
44	18.301 497	3133.856 125	.000 319 0957	.054 640	171.234 958	.005 839 9290	7.01	2.083 483	4.74	528
45	19.551 474	3360.266 960	.000 297 5954	.051 147	171.867 706	.005 818 4287	6.99	2.141 952	4.76	540
46	20.886 823	3602.141 461	.000 277 6126	.047 877	172.460 001	.005 798 4460	6.96	2.200 742	4.78	552
47	22.313 375	3860.535 780	.000 259 0314	.044 816	173.014 430	.005 779 8647	6.94	2.259 844	4.81	564
48	23.837 359	4136.518 209	.000 241 7457	.041 951	173.533 412	.005 762 5790	6.92	2.319 246	4.83	576
49	25.465 430	4431.474 098	.000 225 6585	.039 269	174.019 214	.005 746 4919	6.90	2.378 937	4.85	588
50	27.204 697	4746.511 122	.000 210 6811	.036 758	174.473 958	.005 731 5144	6.88	2.438 909	4.88	600

	Amount Of 1	Amount Of 1 Per Period	Sinking Fund Payment	Present Worth Of 1	Present Worth of 1 Per Period	Periodic Payment To Amortize 1	Constant Annual Percent	Total Interest	Annual Add On Rate	
	What a single $ 1 deposit grows to in the future. The deposit is made at the beginning of the first period.	What a series of $ 1 deposits grow to in the future. A deposit is made at the end of each period.	The amount to be deposited at the end of each period that grows to $ 1 in the future.	What $ 1 to be paid in the future is worth today. Value today of a single $ 1 payment tomorrow.	What $ 1 to be paid at the end of each period is worth today. Value today of a series of $ 1 payments tomorrow.	The mortgage payment to amortize a loan of $ 1. An annuity certain, payable at the end of each period, worth $ 1 today.	The annual payment, including interest and principal, to amortize completely a loan of $ 100.	The total interest paid over the term on a loan of $1. The loan is amortized by regular periodic payments.	The average annual interest rate on a loan that is completely amortized by regular periodic payments.	
	$S = (1+i)^n$	$S\overline{n}| = \dfrac{(1+i)^n - 1}{i}$	$\dfrac{1}{S\overline{n}|} = \dfrac{i}{(1+i)^n - 1}$	$V^n = \dfrac{1}{(1+i)^n}$	$A\overline{n}| = \dfrac{1-V^n}{i}$	$\dfrac{1}{A\overline{n}|} = \dfrac{i}{1-V^n}$				

YEAR										PERIODS
	1.005 542	1.000 000	1.000 000 0000	.994 489	.994 489	1.005 541 6667	1206.65	.005 542	6.65	1
	1.011 114	2.005 542	.498 618 4115	.989 008	1.983 497	.504 160 0782	605.00	.008 320	4.99	2
	1.016 717	3.016 656	.33 492 9167	.983 558	2.967 055	.337 034 5834	404.45	.011 104	4.44	3
	1.022 352	4.033 373	.247 931 4453	.978 137	3.945 192	.253 473 1120	304.17	.013 892	4.17	4
	1.028 017	5.055 725	.197 795 5833	.972 746	4.917 938	.203 337 2500	244.01	.016 686	4.00	5
	1.033 714	6.083 742	.164 372 5259	.967 385	5.885 324	.169 914 1926	203.90	.019 485	3.90	6
	1.039 443	7.117 456	.140 499 6426	.962 054	6.847 378	.146 041 3092	175.25	.022 289	3.82	7
	1.045 203	8.156 898	.122 595 6180	.956 752	7.804 130	.128 137 2847	153.77	.025 098	3.76	8
	1.050 995	9.202 101	.108 670 8326	.951 479	8.755 609	.114 212 4993	137.06	.027 912	3.72	9
	1.056 819	10.253 096	.097 531 5146	.946 236	9.701 845	.103 073 1812	123.69	.030 732	3.69	10
	1.062 676	11.309 915	.088 417 9910	.941 021	10.642 866	.093 959 6576	112.76	.033 556	3.66	11
	1.068 565	12.372 591	.080 823 8131	.935 835	11.578 700	.086 365 4798	103.64	.036 386	3.64	12
1	1.068 565	12.372 591	.080 823 8131	.935 835	11.578 700	.086 365 4798	103.64	.036 386	3.64	12
2	1.141 831	25.593 506	.039 072 4110	.875 787	22.414 450	.044 614 0777	53.54	.070 738	3.54	24
3	1.220 120	39.720 911	.025 175 6565	.819 591	32.554 920	.030 717 3231	36.87	.105 824	3.54	36
4	1.303 777	54.816 957	.018 242 5303	.767 002	42.044 724	.023 784 1969	28.55	.141 641	3.54	48
5	1.393 171	70.948 061	.014 094 8179	.717 787	50.925 612	.019 636 4846	23.57	.178 189	3.56	60
6	1.488 693	88.185 190	.011 339 7726	.671 730	59.236 655	.016 881 4393	20.26	.215 464	3.59	72
7	1.590 765	106.604 179	.009 380 4953	.628 628	67.014 418	.014 922 1620	17.91	.253 462	3.62	84
8	1.699 835	126.286 062	.007 918 5302	.588 292	74.293 118	.013 460 1969	16.16	.292 179	3.65	96
9	1.816 384	147.317 429	.006 788 0631	.550 544	81.104 778	.012 329 7298	14.80	.331 611	3.68	108
10	1.940 924	169.790 806	.005 889 6004	.515 219	87.479 366	.011 431 2671	13.72	.371 752	3.72	120
11	2.074 003	193.805 066	.005 159 8238	.482 159	93.444 927	.010 701 4905	12.85	.412 597	3.75	132
12	2.216 207	219.465 858	.004 556 5174	.451 221	99.027 706	.010 098 1841	12.12	.454 139	3.78	144
13	2.368 160	246.886 077	.004 050 4512	.422 269	104.252 264	.009 592 1178	11.52	.496 370	3.82	156
14	2.530 533	276.186 357	.003 620 7437	.395 174	109.141 587	.009 162 4103	11.00	.539 285	3.85	168
15	2.704 038	307.495 604	.003 252 0790	.369 817	113.717 185	.008 793 7457	10.56	.582 874	3.89	180
16	2.889 440	340.951 562	.002 932 9679	.346 088	117.999 188	.008 474 6346	10.17	.627 130	3.92	192
17	3.087 554	376.701 421	.002 654 6223	.323 881	122.006 435	.008 196 2890	9.84	.672 043	3.95	204
18	3.299 251	414.902 461	.002 410 2050	.303 099	125.756 556	.007 951 8717	9.55	.717 604	3.99	216
19	3.525 464	455.722 747	.002 194 3166	.283 651	129.266 050	.007 735 9833	9.29	.763 804	4.02	228
20	3.767 186	499.341 866	.002 002 6360	.265 450	132.550 355	.007 544 3027	9.06	.810 633	4.05	240
21	4.025 482	545.951 721	.001 831 6638	.248 417	135.623 923	.007 373 3305	8.85	.858 079	4.09	252
22	4.301 489	595.757 370	.001 678 5357	.232 478	138.500 274	.007 220 2023	8.67	.906 133	4.12	264
23	4.596 419	648.977 932	.001 540 8844	.217 561	141.192 063	.007 082 5511	8.50	.954 784	4.15	276
24	4.911 572	705.847 549	.001 416 7365	.203 601	143.711 132	.006 958 4032	8.36	1.004 020	4.18	288
25	5.248 333	766.616 420	.001 304 4333	.190 537	146.068 565	.006 846 1000	8.22	1.053 830	4.22	300
26	5.608 183	831.551 894	.001 202 5708	.178 311	148.274 732	.006 744 2374	8.10	1.104 202	4.25	312
27	5.992 707	900.939 655	.001 109 9523	.166 869	150.339 340	.006 651 6189	7.99	1.155 125	4.28	324
28	6.403 596	975.084 972	.001 025 5516	.156 162	152.271 472	.006 567 2183	7.89	1.206 585	4.31	336
29	6.842 657	1054.314 047	.000 948 4840	.146 142	154.079 628	.006 490 1507	7.79	1.258 572	4.34	348
30	7.311 822	1138.975 445	.000 877 9821	.136 765	155.771 763	.006 419 6487	7.71	1.311 074	4.37	360
31	7.813 156	1229.441 632	.000 813 3774	.127 989	157.355 322	.006 355 0440	7.63	1.364 076	4.40	372
32	8.348 863	1326.110 614	.000 754 0849	.119 777	158.837 271	.006 295 7516	7.56	1.417 569	4.43	384
33	8.921 301	1429.407 683	.000 699 5905	.112 091	160.224 131	.006 241 2571	7.49	1.471 538	4.46	396
34	9.532 988	1539.787 292	.000 649 4404	.104 899	161.522 002	.006 191 1070	7.43	1.525 972	4.49	408
35	10.186 615	1657.735 054	.000 603 2327	.098 168	162.736 595	.006 144 8994	7.38	1.580 858	4.52	420
36	10.885 058	1783.769 879	.000 560 6104	.091 869	163.873 253	.006 102 2771	7.33	1.636 184	4.54	432
37	11.631 390	1918.446 253	.000 521 2552	.085 974	164.936 977	.006 062 9218	7.28	1.691 937	4.57	444
38	12.428 893	2062.356 682	.000 484 8822	.080 458	165.932 448	.006 026 5488	7.24	1.748 106	4.60	456
39	13.281 078	2216.134 298	.000 451 2362	.075 295	166.864 043	.005 992 9029	7.20	1.804 679	4.63	468
40	14.191 692	2380.455 641	.000 420 0876	.070 464	167.735 862	.005 961 7543	7.16	1.861 642	4.65	480
41	15.164 742	2556.043 641	.000 391 2296	.065 942	168.551 741	.005 932 8963	7.12	1.918 985	4.68	492
42	16.204 509	2743.670 792	.000 364 4752	.061 711	169.315 269	.005 906 1419	7.09	1.976 696	4.71	504
43	17.315 568	2944.162 558	.000 339 6552	.057 752	170.029 804	.005 881 3218	7.06	2.034 762	4.73	516
44	18.502 806	3158.400 996	.000 316 6159	.054 046	170.698 492	.005 858 2826	7.03	2.093 173	4.76	528
45	19.771 446	3387.328 645	.000 295 2179	.050 578	171.324 273	.005 836 8846	7.01	2.151 918	4.78	540
46	21.127 071	3631.952 667	.000 275 3340	.047 333	171.909 900	.005 817 0007	6.99	2.210 984	4.81	552
47	22.575 644	3893.349 288	.000 256 8483	.044 296	172.457 950	.005 798 5149	6.96	2.270 362	4.83	564
48	24.123 538	4172.668 494	.000 239 6648	.041 453	172.970 835	.005 781 3215	6.94	2.330 041	4.85	576
49	25.777 563	4471.139 167	.000 223 6566	.038 793	173.450 810	.005 765 3233	6.92	2.390 010	4.88	588
50	27.544 996	4790.074 415	.000 208 7650	.036 304	173.899 988	.005 750 4317	6.91	2.450 259	4.90	600

Effective Rate is 6.86 %

Annual Percentage Rate is 6.65 %

Amount Of 1	Amount Of 1 Per Period	Sinking Fund Payment	Present Worth Of 1	Present Worth of 1 Per Period	Periodic Payment To Amortize 1	Constant Annual Percent	Total Interest	Annual Add On Rate	
What a single $ 1 deposit grows to in the future. The deposit is made at the beginning of the first period.	What a series of $ 1 deposits grow to in the future. A deposit is made at the end of each period.	The amount to be deposited at the end of each period that grows to $ 1 in the future.	What $ 1 to be paid in the future is worth today. Value today of a single $ 1 payment tomorrow.	What $ 1 to be paid at the end of each period is worth today. Value today of a series of $ 1 payments tomorrow.	The mortgage payment to amortize a loan of $ 1. An annuity certain, payable at the end of each period, worth $ 1 today.	The annual payment, including interest and principal, to amortize completely a loan of $ 100.	The total interest paid over the term on a loan of $1. The loan is amortized completely by regular periodic payments.	The average annual interest rate on a loan that is completely amortized by regular periodic payments.	
$S = (1+i)^n$	$S\overline{n}| = \dfrac{(1+i)^n - 1}{i}$	$\dfrac{1}{S\overline{n}|} = \dfrac{i}{(1+i)^n - 1}$	$V^n = \dfrac{1}{(1+i)^n}$	$A\overline{n}| = \dfrac{1 - V^n}{i}$	$\dfrac{1}{A\overline{n}|} = \dfrac{i}{1 - V^n}$				

YEAR									PERIODS
	1.005 583	1.000 000	1.000 000 0000	.994 448	.994 448	1.005 583 3333	1206.70	.005 583	6.70	1
	1.011 198	2.005 583	.498 608 0525	.988 926	1.983 374	.504 191 3859	605.03	.008 383	5.03	2
	1.016 844	3.016 781	.331 479 1304	.983 435	2.966 809	.337 062 4637	404.48	.011 187	4.47	3
	1.022 521	4.033 625	.247 915 9646	.977 975	3.944 784	.253 499 2979	304.20	.013 997	4.20	4
	1.028 230	5.056 146	.197 779 1013	.972 545	4.917 329	.203 362 4346	244.04	.016 812	4.03	5
	1.033 971	6.084 376	.164 355 3892	.967 145	5.884 474	.169 938 7225	203.93	.019 632	3.93	6
	1.039 744	7.118 347	.140 482 0492	.961 775	6.846 249	.146 065 3825	175.28	.022 458	3.85	7
	1.045 549	8.158 091	.122 577 6918	.956 435	7.802 684	.128 161 0251	153.80	.025 288	3.79	8
	1.051 387	9.203 641	.108 652 6560	.951 125	8.753 809	.114 235 9893	137.09	.028 124	3.75	9
	1.057 257	10.255 028	.097 513 1454	.945 844	9.699 652	.103 096 4787	123.72	.030 965	3.72	10
	1.063 160	11.312 285	.088 399 4712	.940 592	10.640 244	.093 982 8045	112.78	.033 811	3.69	11
	1.069 096	12.375 445	.080 805 1743	.935 369	11.575 614	.086 388 5076	103.67	.036 662	3.67	12
1	1.069 096	12.375 445	.080 805 1743	.935 369	11.575 614	.086 388 5076	103.67	.036 662	3.67	12
2	1.142 967	25.605 987	.039 053 3668	.874 916	22.403 090	.044 636 7002	53.57	.071 281	3.56	24
3	1.221 941	39.750 709	.025 156 7838	.818 370	32.530 780	.030 740 1171	36.89	.106 644	3.55	36
4	1.306 373	54.872 779	.018 223 9723	.765 478	42.003 913	.023 807 3056	28.57	.142 751	3.57	48
5	1.396 638	71.039 726	.014 076 6308	.716 005	50.864 793	.019 659 9641	23.60	.179 598	3.59	60
6	1.493 141	88.323 749	.011 321 9832	.669 729	59.152 989	.016 905 3165	20.29	.217 183	3.62	72
7	1.596 311	106.802 033	.009 363 1177	.626 444	66.905 515	.014 946 4510	17.94	.255 502	3.65	84
8	1.706 610	126.557 096	.007 901 5719	.585 957	74.156 991	.013 484 9053	16.19	.294 551	3.68	96
9	1.824 531	147.677 160	.006 771 5278	.548 086	80.939 801	.012 354 8612	14.83	.334 325	3.71	108
10	1.950 599	170.256 541	.005 873 4895	.512 663	87.284 234	.011 456 8228	13.75	.374 819	3.75	120
11	2.085 378	194.396 073	.005 144 1368	.479 529	93.218 623	.010 727 4702	12.88	.416 026	3.78	132
12	2.229 470	220.203 554	.004 541 2528	.448 537	98.769 470	.010 124 5861	12.15	.457 940	3.82	144
13	2.383 518	247.794 236	.004 035 6064	.419 548	103.961 562	.009 618 9397	11.55	.500 555	3.85	156
14	2.548 210	277.291 330	.003 606 3154	.392 432	108.818 087	.009 189 6488	11.03	.543 861	3.88	168
15	2.724 282	308.826 562	.003 238 0634	.367 069	113.360 733	.008 821 3968	10.59	.587 851	3.92	180
16	2.912 519	342.540 760	.002 919 3606	.343 345	117.609 784	.008 502 6939	10.21	.632 517	3.95	192
17	3.113 763	378.584 482	.002 641 4184	.321 155	121.584 218	.008 224 7517	9.87	.677 849	3.99	204
18	3.328 913	417.118 690	.002 397 3992	.300 398	125.301 781	.007 980 7325	9.58	.723 838	4.02	216
19	3.558 928	458.315 466	.002 181 9032	.280 983	128.779 077	.007 765 2366	9.32	.770 474	4.06	228
20	3.804 837	502.358 784	.001 990 6092	.262 823	132.031 634	.007 573 9425	9.09	.817 746	4.09	240
21	4.067 736	549.445 330	.001 820 0173	.245 837	135.073 975	.007 403 3506	8.89	.865 644	4.12	252
22	4.348 802	599.785 379	.001 667 2630	.229 948	137.919 689	.007 250 5964	8.71	.914 157	4.16	264
23	4.649 236	653.603 736	.001 529 9790	.215 087	140.581 483	.007 113 3123	8.54	.963 274	4.19	276
24	4.970 536	711.140 739	.001 406 1914	.201 186	143.071 244	.006 989 5247	8.39	1.012 983	4.22	288
25	5.313 981	772.653 332	.001 294 2415	.188 183	145.400 090	.006 877 5748	8.26	1.063 272	4.25	300
26	5.681 157	838.416 213	.001 192 7250	.176 020	147.578 422	.006 776 0584	8.14	1.114 130	4.29	312
27	6.073 704	908.723 062	.001 100 4453	.164 644	149.615 967	.006 683 7786	8.03	1.165 544	4.32	324
28	6.493 374	983.887 850	.001 016 3760	.154 003	151.521 825	.006 599 7093	7.92	1.217 502	4.35	336
29	6.942 042	1064.246 241	.000 939 6322	.144 050	153.304 505	.006 522 9655	7.83	1.269 992	4.38	348
30	7.421 710	1150.157 095	.000 869 4464	.134 740	154.971 971	.006 452 7798	7.75	1.323 001	4.41	360
31	7.934 523	1242.004 066	.000 805 1503	.126 032	156.531 667	.006 388 4837	7.67	1.376 516	4.44	372
32	8.482 768	1340.197 316	.000 746 1588	.117 886	157.990 559	.006 329 4921	7.60	1.430 525	4.47	384
33	9.068 896	1445.175 350	.000 691 9576	.110 267	159.355 163	.006 275 2909	7.54	1.485 015	4.50	396
34	9.695 522	1557.406 971	.000 642 0929	.103 140	160.631 571	.006 225 4263	7.48	1.539 974	4.53	408
35	10.365 446	1677.393 375	.000 596 1631	.096 474	161.825 484	.006 179 4964	7.42	1.595 388	4.56	420
36	11.081 660	1805.670 387	.000 553 8109	.090 239	162.942 234	.006 137 1443	7.37	1.651 246	4.59	432
37	11.847 361	1942.810 858	.000 514 7181	.084 407	163.986 809	.006 098 0515	7.32	1.707 535	4.61	444
38	12.665 969	2089.427 220	.000 478 6001	.078 952	164.963 871	.006 061 9334	7.28	1.764 242	4.64	456
39	13.541 139	2246.174 219	.000 445 2014	.073 849	165.877 786	.006 028 5348	7.24	1.821 354	4.67	468
40	14.476 781	2413.751 847	.000 414 2928	.069 076	166.732 634	.005 997 6261	7.20	1.878 861	4.70	480
41	15.477 072	2592.908 458	.000 385 6673	.064 612	167.532 232	.005 969 0006	7.17	1.936 748	4.72	492
42	16.546 480	2784.444 116	.000 359 1381	.060 436	168.280 152	.005 942 4714	7.14	1.995 006	4.75	504
43	17.689 779	2989.214 166	.000 334 5361	.056 530	168.979 734	.005 917 8694	7.11	2.053 621	4.78	516
44	18.912 076	3208.133 057	.000 311 7078	.052 876	169.634 101	.005 895 0411	7.08	2.112 582	4.80	528
45	20.218 830	3442.178 419	.000 290 5137	.049 459	170.246 177	.005 873 8470	7.05	2.171 877	4.83	540
46	21.615 875	3692.395 434	.000 270 8269	.046 262	170.818 693	.005 854 1602	7.03	2.231 496	4.85	552
47	23.109 450	3959.901 502	.000 252 5315	.043 272	171.354 208	.005 835 8649	7.01	2.291 428	4.88	564
48	24.706 226	4245.861 233	.000 235 5218	.040 476	171.855 112	.005 818 8551	6.99	2.351 661	4.90	576
49	26.413 333	4551.641 778	.000 219 7009	.037 860	172.323 642	.005 803 0343	6.97	2.412 184	4.92	588
50	28.238 395	4878.518 534	.000 204 9803	.035 413	172.761 891	.005 788 3136	6.95	2.472 988	4.95	600

	Amount Of 1	Amount Of 1 Per Period	Sinking Fund Payment	Present Worth Of 1	Present Worth of 1 Per Period	Periodic Payment To Amortize 1	Constant Annual Percent	Total Interest	Annual Add On Rate	
	What a single $ 1 deposit grows to in the future. The deposit is made at the beginning of the first period.	What a series of $ 1 deposits grow to in the future. A deposit is made at the end of each period.	The amount to be deposited at the end of each period that grows to $ 1 in the future.	What $ 1 to be paid in the future is worth today. Value today of a single $ 1 payment tomorrow.	What $ 1 to be paid at the end of each period is worth today. Value today of a series of $ 1 payments tomorrow.	The mortgage payment to amortize a loan of $ 1. An annuity certain, payable at the end of each period, worth $ 1 today.	The annual payment, including interest and principal, to amortize completely a loan of $ 100.	The total interest paid over the term on a loan of $1. The loan is amortized by regular periodic payments.	The average annual interest rate on a loan that is completely amortized by regular periodic payments.	
	$S = (1+i)^n$	$S\overline{n}| = \dfrac{(1+i)^n - 1}{i}$	$\dfrac{1}{S\overline{n}|} = \dfrac{i}{(1+i)^n - 1}$	$V^n = \dfrac{1}{(1+i)^n}$	$A\overline{n}| = \dfrac{1-V^n}{i}$	$\dfrac{1}{A\overline{n}|} = \dfrac{i}{1-V^n}$				

YEAR										PERIODS
	1.005 625	1.000 000	1.000 000 0000	.994 406	.994 406	1.005 625 0000	1206.75	.005 625	6.75	1
	1.011 282	2.005 625	.498 597 6940	.988 844	1.983 251	.504 222 6940	605.07	.008 445	5.07	2
	1.016 970	3.016 907	.331 465 3448	.983 313	2.966 564	.337 090 3448	404.51	.011 271	4.51	3
	1.022 691	4.033 877	.247 900 4849	.977 813	3.944 377	.253 525 4849	304.24	.014 102	4.23	4
	1.028 443	5.056 567	.197 762 6206	.972 343	4.916 720	.203 387 6206	244.07	.016 938	4.07	5
	1.034 228	6.085 010	.164 338 2541	.966 905	5.883 625	.169 963 2541	203.96	.019 780	3.96	6
	1.040 046	7.119 239	.140 464 4578	.961 496	6.845 121	.146 089 4578	175.31	.022 626	3.88	7
	1.045 896	8.159 284	.122 559 7678	.956 118	7.801 239	.128 184 7678	153.83	.025 478	3.82	8
	1.051 779	9.205 180	.108 634 4819	.950 770	8.752 009	.114 259 4819	137.12	.028 335	3.78	9
	1.057 695	10.256 960	.097 494 7790	.945 452	9.697 461	.103 119 7790	123.75	.031 198	3.74	10
	1.063 645	11.314 655	.088 380 9545	.940 163	10.637 624	.094 005 9545	112.81	.034 065	3.72	11
	1.069 628	12.378 300	.080 786 5388	.934 905	11.572 529	.086 411 5388	103.70	.036 938	3.69	12
1	1.069 628	12.378 300	.080 786 5388	.934 905	11.572 529	.086 411 5388	103.70	.036 938	3.69	12
2	1.144 104	25.618 475	.039 034 3295	.874 046	22.391 738	.044 659 3295	53.60	.071 824	3.59	24
3	1.223 766	39.780 537	.025 137 9214	.817 150	32.506 666	.030 762 9214	36.92	.107 465	3.58	36
4	1.308 974	54.928 673	.018 205 4280	.763 957	41.963 157	.023 830 4280	28.60	.143 861	3.60	48
5	1.400 115	71.131 543	.014 058 4607	.714 227	50.804 074	.019 683 4607	23.63	.181 008	3.62	60
6	1.497 602	88.462 585	.011 304 2140	.667 734	59.069 488	.016 929 2140	20.32	.218 903	3.65	72
7	1.601 877	107.000 353	.009 345 7636	.624 268	66.796 860	.014 970 7636	17.97	.257 544	3.68	84
8	1.713 412	126.828 866	.007 884 6404	.583 631	74.021 215	.013 509 6404	16.22	.296 925	3.71	96
9	1.832 714	148.037 998	.006 755 0224	.545 639	80.775 298	.012 380 0224	14.86	.337 042	3.74	108
10	1.960 322	170.723 878	.005 857 4114	.510 120	87.089 720	.011 482 4114	13.78	.377 889	3.78	120
11	2.096 815	194.989 330	.005 128 4858	.476 914	92.993 102	.010 753 4858	12.91	.419 460	3.81	132
12	2.242 812	220.944 334	.004 526 0269	.445 869	98.512 201	.010 151 0269	12.19	.461 748	3.85	144
13	2.398 974	248.706 532	.004 020 8031	.416 845	103.672 031	.009 645 8031	11.58	.504 745	3.88	156
14	2.566 010	278.401 755	.003 591 9314	.389 710	108.495 980	.009 216 9314	11.07	.548 444	3.92	168
15	2.744 676	310.164 594	.003 224 0946	.364 342	113.005 911	.008 849 0946	10.62	.592 837	3.95	180
16	2.935 782	344.139 015	.002 905 8025	.340 625	117.222 266	.008 530 8025	10.24	.637 914	3.99	192
17	3.140 194	380.479 004	.002 628 2659	.318 452	121.164 156	.008 253 2659	9.91	.683 666	4.02	204
18	3.358 840	419.349 272	.002 384 6470	.297 722	124.849 447	.008 009 6470	9.62	.730 084	4.06	216
19	3.592 709	460.925 996	.002 169 5457	.278 342	128.294 841	.007 794 5457	9.36	.777 156	4.09	228
20	3.842 862	505.397 622	.001 978 6401	.260 223	131.515 956	.007 603 6401	9.13	.824 874	4.12	240
21	4.110 432	552.965 715	.001 808 4304	.243 283	134.527 392	.007 433 4304	8.93	.873 224	4.16	252
22	4.396 633	603.845 877	.001 656 0517	.227 447	137.342 796	.007 281 0517	8.74	.922 198	4.19	264
23	4.702 762	658.268 719	.001 519 1364	.212 641	139.974 930	.007 144 1364	8.58	.971 782	4.23	276
24	5.030 205	716.480 912	.001 395 7106	.198 799	142.435 724	.007 020 7106	8.43	1.021 965	4.26	288
25	5.380 448	778.746 299	.001 284 1153	.185 858	144.736 332	.006 909 1153	8.30	1.072 735	4.29	300
26	5.755 077	845.347 097	.001 182 9460	.173 760	146.887 181	.006 807 9460	8.17	1.124 079	4.32	312
27	6.155 792	916.585 171	.001 091 0061	.162 449	148.898 019	.006 716 0061	8.06	1.175 986	4.36	324
28	6.584 407	992.783 404	.001 007 2691	.151 874	150.777 960	.006 632 2691	7.96	1.228 442	4.39	336
29	7.042 865	1074.287 164	.000 930 8498	.141 988	152.535 526	.006 555 8498	7.87	1.281 436	4.42	348
30	7.533 245	1161.465 863	.000 860 9810	.132 745	154.178 682	.006 485 9810	7.79	1.334 953	4.45	360
31	8.057 770	1254.714 634	.000 796 9940	.124 104	155.714 877	.006 421 9940	7.71	1.388 982	4.48	372
32	8.618 816	1354.456 125	.000 738 3037	.116 025	157.151 072	.006 363 3037	7.64	1.443 509	4.51	384
33	9.218 926	1461.142 410	.000 684 3960	.108 473	158.493 777	.006 309 3960	7.58	1.498 521	4.54	396
34	9.860 821	1575.257 040	.000 634 8170	.101 411	159.749 078	.006 259 8170	7.52	1.554 005	4.57	408
35	10.547 409	1697.317 238	.000 589 1651	.094 810	160.922 665	.006 214 1651	7.46	1.609 949	4.60	420
36	11.281 804	1827.876 234	.000 547 0830	.088 638	162.019 856	.006 172 0830	7.41	1.666 340	4.63	432
37	12.067 333	1967.525 785	.000 508 2526	.082 868	163.045 626	.006 133 2526	7.36	1.723 164	4.66	444
38	12.907 556	2116.898 845	.000 472 3891	.077 474	164.004 622	.006 097 3891	7.32	1.780 409	4.69	456
39	13.806 282	2276.672 443	.000 439 2375	.072 431	164.901 192	.006 064 2375	7.28	1.838 063	4.71	468
40	14.767 585	2447.570 748	.000 408 5684	.067 716	165.739 400	.006 033 5684	7.25	1.896 113	4.74	480
41	15.795 822	2630.368 348	.000 380 1749	.063 308	166.523 044	.006 005 1749	7.21	1.954 546	4.77	492
42	16.895 652	2825.893 769	.000 353 8703	.059 187	167.255 676	.005 978 8703	7.18	2.013 351	4.79	504
43	18.072 062	3035.033 221	.000 329 4857	.055 334	167.940 617	.005 954 4857	7.15	2.072 515	4.82	516
44	19.330 382	3258.734 621	.000 306 8676	.051 732	168.580 972	.005 931 8676	7.12	2.132 026	4.85	528
45	20.676 317	3498.011 888	.000 285 8767	.048 365	169.179 642	.005 910 8767	7.10	2.191 873	4.87	540
46	22.115 966	3753.949 538	.000 266 3861	.045 216	169.739 342	.005 891 3861	7.07	2.252 045	4.90	552
47	23.655 855	4027.707 598	.000 248 2802	.042 273	170.262 608	.005 873 2802	7.05	2.312 530	4.92	564
48	25.302 964	4320.526 867	.000 231 4533	.039 521	170.751 811	.005 856 4533	7.03	2.373 317	4.94	576
49	27.064 757	4633.734 538	.000 215 8087	.036 948	171.209 170	.005 840 8087	7.01	2.434 395	4.97	588
50	28.949 220	4968.750 212	.000 201 2579	.034 543	171.636 756	.005 826 2579	7.00	2.495 755	4.99	600

	Amount Of 1	Amount Of 1 Per Period	Sinking Fund Payment	Present Worth Of 1	Present Worth of 1 Per Period	Periodic Payment To Amortize 1	Constant Annual Percent	Total Interest	Annual Add On Rate	
	What a single $ 1 deposit grows to in the future. The deposit is made at the beginning of the first period.	What a series of $ 1 deposits grow to in the future. A deposit is made at the end of each period.	The amount to be deposited at the end of each period that grows to $ 1 in the future.	What $ 1 to be paid in the future is worth today. Value today of a single $ 1 payment tomorrow.	What $ 1 to be paid at the end of each period is worth today. Value today of a series of $ 1 payments tomorrow.	The mortgage payment to amortize a loan of $ 1. An annuity certain, payable at the end of each period, worth $ 1 today.	The annual payment, including interest and principal, to amortize completely a loan of $ 100.	The total interest paid over the term on a loan of $1. The loan is amortized by regular periodic payments.	The average annual interest rate on a loan that is completely amortized by regular periodic payments.	
	$S = (1+i)^n$	$S\overline{n}| = \dfrac{(1+i)^n - 1}{i}$	$\dfrac{1}{S\overline{n}|} = \dfrac{i}{(1+i)^n - 1}$	$V^n = \dfrac{1}{(1+i)^n}$	$A\overline{n}| = \dfrac{1-V^n}{i}$	$\dfrac{1}{A\overline{n}|} = \dfrac{i}{1-V^n}$				

YEAR										PERIODS
	1.005 667	1.000 000	1.000 000 0000	.994 365	.994 365	1.005 666 6667	1206.80	.005 667	6.80	1
	1.011 365	2.005 667	.498 587 3359	.988 762	1.983 128	.504 254 0025	605.11	.008 508	5.10	2
	1.017 097	3.017 032	.331 451 5601	.983 191	2.966 318	.337 118 2267	404.55	.011 355	4.54	3
	1.022 860	4.034 129	.247 885 0063	.977 651	3.943 969	.253 551 6730	304.27	.014 207	4.26	4
	1.028 656	5.056 989	.197 746 1413	.972 142	4.916 111	.203 412 8080	244.10	.017 064	4.10	5
	1.034 485	6.085 645	.164 321 1208	.966 664	5.882 776	.169 987 7874	203.99	.019 927	3.99	6
	1.040 347	7.120 130	.140 446 8684	.961 217	6.843 993	.146 113 5350	175.34	.022 795	3.91	7
	1.046 243	8.160 478	.122 541 8460	.955 801	7.799 794	.128 208 5127	153.86	.025 668	3.85	8
	1.052 171	9.206 720	.108 616 3104	.950 415	8.750 210	.114 282 9771	137.14	.028 547	3.81	9
	1.058 134	10.258 892	.097 476 4155	.945 060	9.695 270	.103 143 0821	123.78	.031 431	3.77	10
	1.064 130	11.317 026	.088 362 4410	.939 730	10.635 005	.094 029 1076	112.84	.034 320	3.74	11
	1.070 160	12.381 155	.080 767 9068	.934 440	11.569 444	.086 434 5734	103.73	.037 215	3.72	12
1	1.070 160	12.381 155	.080 767 9068	.934 440	11.569 444	.086 434 5734	103.73	.037 215	3.72	12
2	1.145 242	25.630 971	.039 015 2990	.873 178	22.380 394	.044 681 9657	53.62	.072 367	3.62	24
3	1.225 592	39.810 392	.025 119 0693	.815 932	32.482 576	.030 785 7359	36.95	.108 286	3.61	36
4	1.311 580	54.984 640	.018 186 8973	.762 439	41.922 457	.023 853 5640	28.63	.144 971	3.62	48
5	1.403 600	71.223 511	.014 040 3076	.712 454	50.743 457	.019 706 9742	23.65	.182 418	3.65	60
6	1.502 076	88.601 699	.011 286 4652	.665 745	58.986 151	.016 953 1319	20.35	.220 625	3.68	72
7	1.607 462	107.199 139	.009 328 4331	.622 099	66.688 453	.014 995 0998	18.00	.259 588	3.71	84
8	1.720 241	127.101 373	.007 867 7356	.581 314	73.885 790	.013 534 4023	16.25	.299 303	3.74	96
9	1.840 933	148.399 946	.006 738 5469	.543 203	80.611 268	.012 405 2136	14.89	.339 763	3.78	108
10	1.970 093	171.192 824	.005 841 3664	.507 590	86.895 823	.011 508 0330	13.81	.380 964	3.81	120
11	2.108 314	195.584 847	.005 112 8705	.474 313	92.768 361	.010 779 5372	12.94	.422 899	3.84	132
12	2.256 233	221.688 212	.004 510 8398	.443 217	98.255 895	.010 177 5064	12.22	.465 561	3.88	144
13	2.414 530	249.622 986	.004 006 0413	.414 159	103.383 665	.009 672 7080	11.61	.508 942	3.91	156
14	2.583 933	279.517 660	.003 577 5915	.387 007	108.175 257	.009 244 2582	11.10	.553 035	3.95	168
15	2.765 222	311.509 741	.003 210 1725	.361 635	112.652 711	.008 876 8392	10.66	.597 831	3.99	180
16	2.959 229	345.746 382	.002 892 2935	.337 926	116.836 623	.008 558 9601	10.28	.643 320	4.02	192
17	3.166 845	382.385 062	.002 615 1649	.315 771	120.746 237	.008 281 8316	9.94	.689 494	4.06	204
18	3.389 034	421.594 308	.002 371 9485	.295 069	124.399 536	.008 038 6152	9.65	.736 341	4.09	216
19	3.626 809	463.554 469	.002 157 2438	.275 724	127.813 324	.007 823 9105	9.39	.783 852	4.13	228
20	3.881 265	508.458 550	.001 966 7287	.257 648	131.003 303	.007 633 3953	9.17	.832 015	4.16	240
21	4.153 574	556.513 097	.001 796 9029	.240 757	133.984 147	.007 463 5696	8.96	.880 820	4.19	252
22	4.444 988	607.939 144	.001 644 9015	.224 972	136.769 566	.007 311 5681	8.78	.930 254	4.23	264
23	4.756 848	662.973 237	.001 508 3565	.210 223	139.372 372	.007 175 0232	8.62	.980 306	4.26	276
24	5.090 588	721.868 516	.001 385 2938	.196 441	141.804 538	.007 051 9605	8.47	1.030 965	4.30	288
25	5.447 743	784.895 879	.001 274 0543	.183 562	144.077 251	.006 940 7210	8.33	1.082 216	4.33	300
26	5.829 956	852.345 236	.001 173 2335	.171 528	146.200 964	.006 839 9002	8.21	1.134 049	4.36	312
27	6.238 985	924.526 831	.001 081 6344	.160 282	148.185 446	.006 748 3010	8.10	1.186 450	4.39	324
28	6.676 712	1001.772 678	.000 998 2305	.149 774	150.039 825	.006 664 8971	8.00	1.239 405	4.43	336
29	7.145 149	1084.438 084	.000 922 1366	.139 955	151.772 631	.006 588 8032	7.91	1.292 904	4.46	348
30	7.646 452	1172.903 286	.000 852 5852	.130 780	153.391 834	.006 519 2519	7.83	1.346 931	4.49	360
31	8.182 926	1267.575 195	.000 788 9078	.122 206	154.904 881	.006 455 5745	7.75	1.401 474	4.52	372
32	8.757 039	1368.889 274	.000 730 5193	.114 194	156.318 733	.006 397 1859	7.68	1.456 519	4.55	384
33	9.371 432	1477.311 537	.000 676 9053	.106 707	157.639 892	.006 343 5720	7.62	1.512 054	4.58	396
34	10.028 931	1593.340 693	.000 627 6122	.099 712	158.874 436	.006 294 2788	7.56	1.568 066	4.61	408
35	10.732 559	1717.510 441	.000 582 2381	.093 174	160.028 043	.006 248 9048	7.50	1.624 540	4.64	420
36	11.485 554	1850.391 923	.000 540 4261	.087 066	161.106 019	.006 207 0927	7.45	1.681 464	4.67	432
37	12.291 379	1992.596 354	.000 501 8578	.081 358	162.113 323	.006 168 5245	7.41	1.738 825	4.70	444
38	13.153 741	2144.777 831	.000 466 2488	.076 024	163.054 588	.006 132 9154	7.36	1.796 609	4.73	456
39	14.076 606	2307.636 342	.000 433 3438	.071 040	163.934 144	.006 100 0105	7.33	1.854 805	4.76	468
40	15.064 219	2481.920 987	.000 402 9137	.066 382	164.756 035	.006 069 5804	7.29	1.913 399	4.78	480
41	16.121 123	2668.433 421	.000 374 7517	.062 030	165.524 044	.006 041 4184	7.25	1.972 378	4.81	492
42	17.252 179	2868.031 546	.000 348 6712	.057 964	166.241 701	.006 015 3379	7.22	2.031 730	4.84	504
43	18.462 590	3081.633 451	.000 324 5032	.054 164	166.912 309	.005 991 1699	7.19	2.091 444	4.86	516
44	19.757 923	3310.221 640	.000 302 0946	.050 613	167.538 951	.005 968 7612	7.17	2.151 506	4.89	528
45	21.144 136	3554.847 550	.000 281 3060	.047 294	168.124 511	.005 947 9727	7.14	2.211 905	4.92	540
46	22.627 606	3816.636 383	.000 262 0108	.044 194	168.671 682	.005 928 6775	7.12	2.272 630	4.94	552
47	24.215 156	4096.792 290	.000 244 0934	.041 296	169.182 979	.005 910 7601	7.10	2.333 669	4.97	564
48	25.914 089	4396.603 902	.000 227 4483	.038 589	169.660 756	.005 894 1149	7.08	2.395 010	4.99	576
49	27.732 218	4717.450 261	.000 211 9789	.036 059	170.107 210	.005 878 6456	7.06	2.456 644	5.01	588
50	29.677 907	5060.807 161	.000 197 5969	.033 695	170.524 394	.005 864 2636	7.04	2.518 558	5.04	600

Amount Of 1	Amount Of 1 Per Period	Sinking Fund Payment	Present Worth Of 1	Present Worth of 1 Per Period	Periodic Payment To Amortize 1	Constant Annual Percent	Total Interest	Annual Add On Rate
What a single $ 1 deposit grows to in the future. The deposit is made at the beginning of the first period.	What a series of $ 1 deposits grow to in the future. A deposit is made at the end of each period.	The amount to be deposited at the end of each period that grows to $ 1 in the future.	What $ 1 to be paid in the future is worth today. Value today of a single $ 1 payment tomorrow.	What $ 1 to be paid at the end of each period is worth today. Value today of a series of $ 1 payments tomorrow.	The mortgage payment to amortize a loan of $ 1. An annuity certain, payable at the end of each period, worth $ 1 today.	The annual payment, including interest and principal, to amortize completely a loan of $ 100.	The total interest paid over the term on a loan of $1. The loan is amortized by regular periodic payments.	The average annual interest rate on a loan that is completely amortized by regular periodic payments.
$S = (1+i)^n$	$S\overline{n}| = \dfrac{(1+i)^n - 1}{i}$	$\dfrac{1}{S\overline{n}|} = \dfrac{i}{(1+i)^n - 1}$	$V^n = \dfrac{1}{(1+i)^n}$	$A\overline{n}| = \dfrac{1 - V^n}{i}$	$\dfrac{1}{A\overline{n}|} = \dfrac{i}{1 - V^n}$			

YEAR									PERIODS
	1.005 708	1.000 000	1.000 000 0000	.994 324	.994 324	1.005 708 3333	1206.85	.005 708	6.85	1
	1.011 449	2.005 708	.498 576 9782	.988 680	1.983 004	.504 285 3115	605.15	.008 571	5.14	2
	1.017 223	3.017 158	.331 437 7761	.983 069	2.966 073	.337 146 1094	404.58	.011 438	4.58	3
	1.023 030	4.034 381	.247 869 5288	.977 489	3.943 562	.253 577 8621	304.30	.014 311	4.29	4
	1.028 869	5.057 410	.197 729 6635	.971 941	4.915 503	.203 437 9968	244.13	.017 190	4.13	5
	1.034 743	6.086 279	.164 303 9891	.966 424	5.881 927	.170 012 3224	204.02	.020 074	4.01	6
	1.040 649	7.121 022	.140 429 2809	.960 939	6.842 865	.146 137 6142	175.37	.022 963	3.94	7
	1.046 590	8.161 671	.122 523 9266	.955 484	7.798 350	.128 232 2599	153.88	.025 858	3.88	8
	1.052 564	9.208 261	.108 598 1415	.950 061	8.748 411	.114 306 4748	137.17	.028 758	3.83	9
	1.058 572	10.260 825	.097 458 0548	.944 669	9.693 079	.103 166 3881	123.80	.031 664	3.80	10
	1.064 615	11.319 397	.088 343 9306	.939 307	10.632 386	.094 052 2639	112.87	.034 575	3.77	11
	1.070 692	12.384 012	.080 749 2781	.933 975	11.566 362	.086 457 6115	103.75	.037 491	3.75	12
1	1.070 692	12.384 012	.080 749 2781	.933 975	11.566 362	.086 457 6115	103.75	.037 491	3.75	12
2	1.146 382	25.643 475	.038 996 2754	.872 310	22.369 058	.044 704 6088	53.65	.072 911	3.65	24
3	1.227 422	39.840 276	.025 100 2274	.814 716	32.458 511	.030 808 5607	36.98	.109 108	3.64	36
4	1.314 191	55.040 680	.018 168 3803	.760 925	41.881 811	.023 876 7137	28.66	.146 082	3.65	48
5	1.407 093	71.315 631	.014 022 1715	.710 685	50.682 940	.019 730 5048	23.68	.183 830	3.68	60
6	1.506 564	88.741 092	.011 268 7368	.663 762	58.902 979	.016 977 0701	20.38	.222 349	3.71	72
7	1.613 066	107.398 394	.009 311 1262	.619 937	66.580 292	.015 019 4595	18.03	.261 635	3.74	84
8	1.727 097	127.374 620	.007 850 8575	.579 006	73.750 713	.013 559 1909	16.28	.301 682	3.77	96
9	1.849 189	148.763 007	.006 722 1013	.540 777	80.447 710	.012 430 4346	14.92	.342 487	3.81	108
10	1.979 912	171.663 383	.005 825 3541	.505 073	86.702 540	.011 533 6875	13.85	.384 042	3.84	120
11	2.119 876	196.182 634	.005 097 2911	.471 726	92.544 397	.010 805 6245	12.97	.426 342	3.88	132
12	2.269 734	222.435 201	.004 495 6913	.440 580	98.000 547	.010 204 0246	12.25	.469 380	3.91	144
13	2.430 186	250.543 617	.003 991 3210	.411 491	103.096 457	.009 699 6543	11.64	.513 146	3.95	156
14	2.601 981	280.639 075	.003 563 2957	.384 323	107.855 912	.009 271 6290	11.13	.557 634	3.98	168
15	2.785 921	312.862 043	.003 196 2970	.358 948	112.301 125	.008 904 6303	10.69	.602 833	4.02	180
16	2.982 863	347.362 919	.002 878 8335	.335 248	116.452 844	.008 587 1668	10.31	.648 736	4.05	192
17	3.193 728	384.302 733	.002 602 1152	.313 114	120.330 448	.008 310 4486	9.98	.695 332	4.09	204
18	3.419 499	423.853 899	.002 359 3035	.292 440	123.952 034	.008 067 6369	9.69	.742 610	4.13	216
19	3.661 231	466.201 018	.002 144 9975	.273 132	127.334 506	.007 853 3308	9.43	.790 559	4.16	228
20	3.920 051	511.541 743	.001 954 8747	.255 099	130.493 652	.007 663 2080	9.20	.839 170	4.20	240
21	4.197 167	560.087 698	.001 785 4347	.238 256	133.444 216	.007 493 7680	9.00	.888 430	4.23	252
22	4.493 874	612.065 466	.001 633 8122	.222 525	136.199 971	.007 342 1455	8.82	.938 326	4.27	264
23	4.811 555	667.717 650	.001 497 6390	.207 833	138.773 777	.007 205 9723	8.65	.988 848	4.30	276
24	5.151 694	727.304 002	.001 374 9409	.194 111	141.177 649	.007 083 2742	8.50	1.039 983	4.33	288
25	5.515 878	791.102 637	.001 264 0585	.181 295	143.422 806	.006 972 3918	8.37	1.091 718	4.37	300
26	5.905 806	859.411 329	.001 163 5872	.169 325	145.519 728	.006 871 9205	8.25	1.144 039	4.40	312
27	6.323 300	932.548 903	.001 072 3298	.158 145	147.478 200	.006 780 6632	8.14	1.196 935	4.43	324
28	6.770 307	1010.856 724	.000 989 2599	.147 704	149.307 366	.006 697 5932	8.04	1.250 391	4.47	336
29	7.248 914	1094.700 286	.000 913 4920	.137 952	151.015 761	.006 621 8254	7.95	1.304 395	4.50	348
30	7.761 355	1184.470 923	.000 844 2588	.128 843	152.611 360	.006 552 5921	7.87	1.358 933	4.53	360
31	8.310 021	1280.587 632	.000 780 8915	.120 337	154.101 611	.006 489 2248	7.79	1.413 992	4.56	372
32	8.897 474	1383.499 029	.000 722 8050	.112 391	155.493 468	.006 431 1383	7.72	1.469 557	4.59	384
33	9.526 454	1493.685 446	.000 669 4850	.104 971	156.793 428	.006 377 8183	7.66	1.525 616	4.62	396
34	10.199 899	1611.661 168	.000 620 4778	.098 040	158.007 559	.006 328 8111	7.60	1.582 155	4.65	408
35	10.920 951	1737.976 838	.000 575 3817	.091 567	159.141 527	.006 283 7150	7.55	1.639 160	4.68	420
36	11.692 976	1873.222 024	.000 533 8395	.085 521	160.200 625	.006 242 1729	7.50	1.696 619	4.71	432
37	12.519 576	2018.027 971	.000 495 5333	.079 875	161.189 797	.006 203 8666	7.45	1.754 517	4.74	444
38	13.404 611	2173.070 550	.000 460 1783	.074 601	162.113 659	.006 168 5117	7.41	1.812 841	4.77	456
39	14.352 211	2339.073 410	.000 427 5197	.069 676	162.976 524	.006 135 8530	7.37	1.871 579	4.80	468
40	15.366 798	2516.811 354	.000 397 3282	.065 075	163.782 418	.006 105 6615	7.33	1.930 718	4.83	480
41	16.453 109	2707.113 961	.000 369 3971	.060 779	164.535 103	.006 077 7304	7.30	1.990 243	4.85	492
42	17.616 213	2910.869 453	.000 343 5400	.056 766	165.238 092	.006 051 8733	7.27	2.050 144	4.88	504
43	18.861 540	3129.028 841	.000 319 5880	.053 018	165.894 667	.006 027 9213	7.24	2.110 407	4.91	516
44	20.194 901	3362.610 368	.000 297 3880	.049 517	166.507 892	.006 005 7213	7.21	2.171 021	4.93	528
45	21.622 520	3612.704 255	.000 276 8010	.046 248	167.080 629	.005 985 1343	7.19	2.231 973	4.96	540
46	23.151 061	3880.477 795	.000 257 7002	.043 195	167.615 551	.005 966 0336	7.16	2.293 251	4.99	552
47	24.787 657	4167.180 801	.000 239 9704	.040 343	168.115 155	.005 948 3037	7.14	2.354 843	5.01	564
48	26.539 948	4474.151 435	.000 223 5061	.037 679	168.581 772	.005 931 8394	7.12	2.416 739	5.03	576
49	28.416 112	4802.822 457	.000 208 2109	.035 191	169.017 582	.005 916 5442	7.10	2.478 928	5.06	588
50	30.424 905	5154.727 912	.000 193 9967	.032 868	169.424 617	.005 902 3300	7.09	2.541 398	5.08	600

Amount Of 1	Amount Of 1 Per Period	Sinking Fund Payment	Present Worth Of 1	Present Worth of 1 Per Period	Periodic Payment To Amortize 1	Constant Annual Percent	Total Interest	Annual Add On Rate	
What a single $ 1 deposit grows to in the future. The deposit is made at the beginning of the first period.	What a series of $ 1 deposits grow to in the future. A deposit is made at the end of each period.	The amount to be deposited at the end of each period that grows to $ 1 in the future.	What $ 1 to be paid in the future is worth today. Value today of a single $ 1 payment tomorrow.	What $ 1 to be paid at the end of each period is worth today. Value today of a series of $ 1 payments tomorrow.	The mortgage payment to amortize a loan of $ 1. An annuity certain, payable at the end of each period, worth $ 1 today.	The annual payment, including interest and principal, to amortize completely a loan of $ 100.	The total interest paid over the term on a loan of $1. The loan is amortized by regular periodic payments.	The average annual interest rate on a loan that is completely amortized by regular periodic payments.	
$S = (1+i)^n$	$S\overline{n} = \dfrac{(1+i)^n - 1}{i}$	$\dfrac{1}{S\overline{n}} = \dfrac{i}{(1+i)^n - 1}$	$V^n = \dfrac{1}{(1+i)^n}$	$A\overline{n} = \dfrac{1-V^n}{i}$	$\dfrac{1}{A\overline{n}} = \dfrac{i}{1-V^n}$				

YEAR									PERIODS
	1.005 729	1.000 000	1.000 000 0000	.994 303	.994 303	1.005 729 1667	1206.88	.005 729	6.88	1
	1.011 491	2.005 729	.498 571 7995	.988 639	1.982 943	.504 300 9662	605.17	.008 602	5.16	2
	1.017 286	3.017 220	.331 430 8843	.983 008	2.965 950	.337 160 0510	404.60	.011 480	4.59	3
	1.023 114	4.034 506	.247 861 7904	.977 408	3.943 358	.253 590 9571	304.31	.014 364	4.31	4
	1.028 976	5.057 621	.197 721 4250	.971 840	4.915 198	.203 450 5917	244.15	.017 253	4.14	5
	1.034 871	6.086 597	.164 295 4238	.966 304	5.881 502	.170 024 5905	204.03	.020 148	4.03	6
	1.040 800	7.121 468	.140 420 4879	.960 799	6.842 301	.146 149 6545	175.38	.023 048	3.95	7
	1.046 763	8.162 268	.122 514 9677	.955 326	7.797 628	.128 244 1343	153.90	.025 953	3.89	8
	1.052 760	9.209 031	.108 589 0579	.949 884	8.747 512	.114 318 2246	137.19	.028 864	3.85	9
	1.058 792	10.261 791	.097 448 8755	.944 473	9.691 985	.103 178 0422	123.82	.031 780	3.81	10
	1.064 858	11.320 583	.088 334 6765	.939 093	10.631 077	.094 063 8432	112.88	.034 702	3.79	11
	1.070 958	12.385 440	.080 739 9651	.933 743	11.564 821	.086 469 1318	103.77	.037 630	3.76	12
1	1.070 958	12.385 440	.080 739 9651	.933 743	11.564 821	.086 469 1318	103.77	.037 630	3.76	12
2	1.146 952	25.649 729	.038 986 7662	.871 876	22.363 393	.044 715 9329	53.66	.073 182	3.66	24
3	1.228 337	39.855 229	.025 090 8103	.814 109	32.446 488	.030 819 9770	36.99	.109 519	3.65	36
4	1.315 498	55.068 727	.018 159 1270	.760 168	41.861 508	.023 888 2936	28.67	.146 638	3.67	48
5	1.408 843	71.361 747	.014 013 1098	.709 802	50.652 720	.019 742 2765	23.70	.184 537	3.69	60
6	1.508 812	88.810 892	.011 259 8801	.662 773	58.861 454	.016 989 0468	20.39	.223 211	3.72	72
7	1.615 875	107.498 198	.009 302 4815	.618 860	66.526 304	.015 031 6482	18.04	.262 658	3.75	84
8	1.730 535	127.511 522	.007 842 4286	.577 856	73.683 306	.013 571 5952	16.29	.302 873	3.79	96
9	1.853 330	148.944 956	.006 713 8896	.539 569	80.366 107	.012 443 0563	14.94	.343 850	3.82	108
10	1.984 840	171.899 270	.005 817 3604	.503 819	86.606 128	.011 546 5270	13.86	.385 583	3.86	120
11	2.125 680	196.482 382	.005 089 5149	.470 438	92.432 705	.010 818 6815	12.99	.428 066	3.89	132
12	2.276 515	222.809 868	.004 488 1316	.439 268	97.873 232	.010 217 2982	12.27	.471 291	3.93	144
13	2.438 052	251.005 506	.003 983 9763	.410 163	102.953 287	.009 713 1430	11.66	.515 250	3.96	156
14	2.611 052	281.201 858	.003 556 1643	.382 987	107.696 754	.009 285 3309	11.15	.559 936	4.00	168
15	2.796 328	313.540 890	.003 189 3767	.357 612	112.125 934	.008 918 5433	10.71	.605 338	4.04	180
16	2.994 751	348.174 643	.002 872 1219	.333 918	116.261 651	.008 601 2885	10.33	.651 447	4.07	192
17	3.207 253	385.265 947	.002 595 6096	.311 793	120.123 348	.008 324 7763	9.99	.698 254	4.11	204
18	3.434 834	424.989 184	.002 353 0011	.291 135	123.729 182	.008 082 1677	9.70	.745 748	4.14	216
19	3.678 564	467.531 113	.002 138 8951	.271 845	127.096 105	.007 868 0618	9.45	.793 918	4.18	228
20	3.939 588	513.091 743	.001 948 9692	.253 834	130.239 946	.007 678 1359	9.22	.842 753	4.21	240
21	4.219 134	561.885 276	.001 779 7227	.237 015	133.175 487	.007 508 8894	9.02	.892 240	4.25	252
22	4.518 517	614.141 112	.001 628 2903	.221 312	135.916 528	.007 357 4569	8.83	.942 369	4.28	264
23	4.839 143	670.104 931	.001 492 3036	.206 648	138.475 956	.007 221 4703	8.67	.993 126	4.32	276
24	5.182 520	730.039 844	.001 369 7882	.192 956	140.865 805	.007 098 9549	8.52	1.044 499	4.35	288
25	5.550 262	794.227 634	.001 259 0849	.180 172	143.097 310	.006 988 2515	8.39	1.096 475	4.39	300
26	5.944 099	862.970 078	.001 158 7887	.168 234	145.180 963	.006 887 9554	8.27	1.149 042	4.42	312
27	6.365 882	936.590 365	.001 067 7026	.157 087	147.126 560	.006 796 8693	8.16	1.202 186	4.45	324
28	6.817 594	1015.434 619	.000 984 8000	.146 679	148.943 248	.006 713 9667	8.06	1.255 893	4.49	336
29	7.301 359	1099.873 523	.000 909 1954	.136 961	150.639 568	.006 638 3621	7.97	1.310 150	4.52	348
30	7.819 450	1190.304 064	.000 840 1215	.127 886	152.223 495	.006 569 2881	7.89	1.364 944	4.55	360
31	8.374 305	1287.151 398	.000 776 9094	.119 413	153.702 476	.006 506 0761	7.81	1.420 260	4.58	372
32	8.968 531	1390.870 849	.000 718 9740	.111 501	155.083 465	.006 448 1407	7.74	1.476 086	4.61	384
33	9.604 922	1501.950 051	.000 665 8011	.104 113	156.372 954	.006 394 9678	7.68	1.532 407	4.64	396
34	10.286 471	1620.911 239	.000 616 9369	.097 215	157.577 005	.006 346 1036	7.62	1.589 210	4.67	408
35	11.016 381	1748.313 705	.000 571 9797	.090 774	158.701 280	.006 301 1464	7.57	1.646 481	4.70	420
36	11.798 084	1884.756 427	.000 530 5725	.084 760	159.751 064	.006 259 7392	7.52	1.704 207	4.73	432
37	12.635 255	2030.880 886	.000 492 3972	.079 144	160.731 293	.006 221 5638	7.47	1.762 374	4.76	444
38	13.531 831	2187.374 080	.000 457 1692	.073 900	161.646 575	.006 186 3358	7.43	1.820 969	4.79	456
39	14.492 026	2354.971 758	.000 424 6335	.069 003	162.501 213	.006 153 8002	7.39	1.879 978	4.82	468
40	15.520 354	2534.461 874	.000 394 5611	.064 432	163.299 226	.006 123 7277	7.35	1.939 389	4.85	480
41	16.621 652	2726.688 295	.000 366 7453	.060 162	164.044 365	.006 095 9119	7.32	1.999 189	4.88	492
42	17.801 095	2932.554 766	.000 340 9996	.056 176	164.740 133	.006 070 1663	7.29	2.059 364	4.90	504
43	19.064 230	3153.029 162	.000 317 1553	.052 454	165.389 802	.006 046 3220	7.26	2.119 902	4.93	516
44	20.416 994	3389.148 035	.000 295 0594	.048 979	165.996 426	.006 024 2261	7.23	2.180 791	4.96	528
45	21.865 748	3642.021 490	.000 274 5728	.045 734	166.562 858	.006 003 7395	7.21	2.242 019	4.98	540
46	23.417 303	3912.838 403	.000 255 5689	.042 703	167.091 759	.005 984 7356	7.19	2.303 574	5.01	552
47	25.078 954	4202.872 010	.000 237 9325	.039 874	167.585 617	.005 967 0992	7.17	2.365 444	5.03	564
48	26.858 513	4513.485 895	.000 221 5582	.037 232	168.046 753	.005 950 7249	7.15	2.427 618	5.06	576
49	28.764 346	4846.140 398	.000 206 3498	.034 765	168.477 336	.005 935 5164	7.13	2.490 084	5.08	588
50	30.805 414	5202.399 482	.000 192 2190	.032 462	168.879 390	.005 921 3857	7.11	2.552 831	5.11	600

Effective Rate is 7.10 %

Annual Percentage Rate is 6.875%

Amount Of 1	Amount Of 1 Per Period	Sinking Fund Payment	Present Worth Of 1	Present Worth of 1 Per Period	Periodic Payment To Amortize 1	Constant Annual Percent	Total Interest	Annual Add On Rate
What a single $ 1 deposit grows to in the future. The deposit is made at the beginning of the first period.	What a series of $ 1 deposits grow to in the future. A deposit is made at the end of each period.	The amount to be deposited at the end of each period that grows to $ 1 in the future.	What $ 1 to be paid in the future is worth today. Value today of a single $ 1 payment tomorrow.	What $ 1 to be paid at the end of each period is worth today. Value today of a series of $ 1 payments tomorrow.	The mortgage payment to amortize a loan of $ 1. An annuity certain, payable at the end of each period, worth $ 1 today.	The annual payment, including interest and principal, to amortize completely a loan of $ 100.	The total interest paid over the term on a loan of $1. The loan is amortized by regular periodic payments.	The average annual interest rate on a loan that is completely amortized by regular periodic payments.
$S = (1+i)^n$	$S\overline{n}| = \dfrac{(1+i)^n - 1}{i}$	$\dfrac{1}{S\overline{n}|} = \dfrac{i}{(1+i)^n - 1}$	$V^n = \dfrac{1}{(1+i)^n}$	$A\overline{n}| = \dfrac{1-V^n}{i}$	$\dfrac{1}{A\overline{n}|} = \dfrac{i}{1-V^n}$			

YEAR								PERIODS
	1.005 750	1.000 000	1.000 000 0000	.994 283	.994 283	1.005 750 0000	1206.90	.005 750	6.90	1
	1.011 533	2.005 750	.498 566 6210	.988 598	1.982 881	.504 316 6210	605.18	.008 633	5.18	2
	1.017 349	3.017 283	.331 423 9928	.982 946	2.965 828	.337 173 9928	404.61	.011 522	4.61	3
	1.023 199	4.034 632	.247 854 0523	.977 327	3.943 155	.253 604 0523	304.33	.014 416	4.32	4
	1.029 083	5.057 832	.197 713 1869	.971 739	4.914 894	.203 463 1869	244.16	.017 316	4.16	5
	1.035 000	6.086 914	.164 286 8590	.966 184	5.881 078	.170 036 8590	204.05	.020 221	4.04	6
	1.040 951	7.121 914	.140 411 6954	.960 660	6.841 738	.146 161 6954	175.40	.023 132	3.97	7
	1.046 936	8.162 865	.122 506 0094	.955 168	7.796 906	.128 256 0094	153.91	.026 048	3.91	8
	1.052 956	9.209 801	.108 579 9751	.949 707	8.746 613	.114 329 9751	137.20	.028 970	3.86	9
	1.059 011	10.262 758	.097 439 6969	.944 277	9.690 890	.103 189 6969	123.83	.031 897	3.83	10
	1.065 100	11.321 769	.088 325 4233	.938 879	10.629 769	.094 075 4233	112.90	.034 830	3.80	11
	1.071 224	12.386 869	.080 730 6529	.933 511	11.563 280	.086 480 6529	103.78	.037 768	3.78	12
1	1.071 224	12.386 869	.080 730 6529	.933 511	11.563 280	.086 480 6529	103.78	.037 768	3.78	12
2	1.147 522	25.655 986	.038 977 2587	.871 443	22.357 731	.044 727 2587	53.68	.073 454	3.67	24
3	1.229 254	39.870 189	.025 081 3958	.813 502	32.434 471	.030 831 3958	37.00	.109 930	3.66	36
4	1.316 807	55.096 792	.018 149 8770	.759 413	41.841 220	.023 899 8770	28.68	.147 194	3.68	48
5	1.410 595	71.407 902	.014 004 0524	.708 920	50.622 524	.019 754 0524	23.71	.185 243	3.70	60
6	1.511 064	88.880 763	.011 251 0286	.661 785	58.819 971	.017 001 0286	20.41	.224 074	3.73	72
7	1.618 689	107.598 119	.009 293 8428	.617 784	66.472 378	.015 043 8428	18.06	.263 683	3.77	84
8	1.733 980	127.648 609	.007 834 0062	.576 708	73.615 985	.013 584 0062	16.31	.304 065	3.80	96
9	1.857 481	149.127 186	.006 705 6855	.538 363	80.284 622	.012 455 6855	14.95	.345 214	3.84	108
10	1.989 779	172.135 563	.005 809 3748	.502 568	86.509 869	.011 559 3748	13.88	.387 125	3.87	120
11	2.131 501	196.782 700	.005 081 7475	.469 153	92.321 206	.010 831 7475	13.00	.429 791	3.91	132
12	2.283 316	223.185 317	.004 480 5815	.437 960	97.746 155	.010 230 5815	12.28	.473 204	3.94	144
13	2.445 944	251.468 448	.003 976 6420	.408 840	102.810 404	.009 726 6420	11.68	.517 356	3.98	156
14	2.620 155	281.766 030	.003 549 0439	.381 657	107.537 938	.009 299 0439	11.16	.562 239	4.02	168
15	2.806 774	314.221 542	.003 182 4680	.356 281	111.951 143	.008 932 4680	10.72	.607 844	4.05	180
16	3.006 685	348.988 681	.002 865 4224	.332 592	116.070 919	.008 615 4224	10.34	.654 161	4.09	192
17	3.220 835	386.232 092	.002 589 1168	.310 479	119.916 776	.008 339 1168	10.01	.701 180	4.12	204
18	3.450 237	426.128 147	.002 346 7119	.289 835	123.506 926	.008 096 7119	9.72	.748 890	4.16	216
19	3.695 978	468.865 778	.002 132 8065	.270 564	126.858 371	.007 882 8065	9.46	.797 280	4.20	228
20	3.959 222	514.647 375	.001 943 0780	.252 575	129.986 983	.007 693 0780	9.24	.846 339	4.23	240
21	4.241 216	563.689 743	.001 774 0255	.235 781	132.907 577	.007 524 0255	9.03	.896 054	4.27	252
22	4.543 294	616.225 129	.001 622 7835	.220 105	135.633 983	.007 372 7835	8.85	.946 415	4.30	264
23	4.866 888	672.502 321	.001 486 9837	.205 470	138.179 114	.007 236 9837	8.69	.997 408	4.34	276
24	5.213 530	732.787 828	.001 364 6515	.191 809	140.555 023	.007 114 6515	8.54	1.049 020	4.37	288
25	5.584 861	797.367 140	.001 254 1274	.179 055	142.772 959	.007 004 1274	8.41	1.101 238	4.40	300
26	5.982 640	866.546 081	.001 154 0067	.167 150	144.843 428	.006 904 0067	8.29	1.154 050	4.44	312
27	6.408 750	940.652 257	.001 063 0921	.156 037	146.776 234	.006 813 0921	8.18	1.207 442	4.47	324
28	6.865 210	1020.036 608	.000 980 3570	.145 662	148.580 529	.006 730 3570	8.08	1.261 400	4.50	336
29	7.354 182	1105.075 069	.000 904 9159	.135 977	150.264 859	.006 654 9159	7.99	1.315 911	4.54	348
30	7.877 980	1196.170 352	.000 836 0013	.126 936	151.837 200	.006 586 0013	7.91	1.370 960	4.57	360
31	8.439 085	1293.753 850	.000 772 9446	.118 496	153.304 998	.006 522 9446	7.83	1.426 535	4.60	372
32	9.040 154	1398.287 683	.000 715 1604	.110 618	154.675 203	.006 465 1604	7.76	1.482 622	4.63	384
33	9.684 035	1510.266 887	.000 662 1346	.103 263	155.954 305	.006 412 1346	7.70	1.539 205	4.66	396
34	10.373 775	1630.221 752	.000 613 4135	.096 397	157.148 361	.006 363 4135	7.64	1.596 273	4.69	408
35	11.112 642	1758.720 342	.000 568 5952	.089 988	158.263 026	.006 318 5952	7.59	1.653 810	4.73	420
36	11.904 134	1896.371 179	.000 527 3229	.084 004	159.303 578	.006 277 3229	7.54	1.711 804	4.76	432
37	12.752 000	2043.826 128	.000 489 2784	.078 419	160.274 944	.006 239 2784	7.49	1.770 240	4.78	444
38	13.660 255	2201.783 481	.000 454 1773	.073 205	161.181 726	.006 204 1773	7.45	1.829 105	4.81	456
39	14.633 200	2370.991 266	.000 421 7645	.068 338	162.028 217	.006 171 7645	7.41	1.888 386	4.84	468
40	15.675 442	2552.250 791	.000 391 8110	.063 794	162.818 425	.006 141 8110	7.38	1.948 069	4.87	480
41	16.791 917	2746.420 434	.000 364 1103	.059 552	163.556 094	.006 114 1103	7.34	2.008 142	4.90	492
42	17.987 913	2954.419 711	.000 338 4799	.055 593	164.244 716	.006 088 4799	7.31	2.068 592	4.93	504
43	19.269 093	3177.233 633	.000 314 7392	.051 897	164.887 552	.006 064 7392	7.28	2.129 405	4.95	516
44	20.641 525	3415.917 363	.000 292 7471	.048 446	165.487 646	.006 042 7471	7.26	2.190 570	4.98	528
45	22.111 707	3671.601 221	.000 272 3607	.045 225	166.047 841	.006 022 3607	7.23	2.252 075	5.00	540
46	23.686 602	3945.496 033	.000 253 4536	.042 218	166.570 790	.006 003 4536	7.21	2.313 906	5.03	552
47	25.373 668	4238.898 865	.000 235 9103	.039 411	167.058 968	.005 985 9103	7.19	2.376 053	5.06	564
48	27.180 895	4553.199 166	.000 219 6258	.036 791	167.514 687	.005 969 6258	7.17	2.438 504	5.08	576
49	29.116 841	4889.885 347	.000 204 5038	.034 344	167.940 107	.005 954 5038	7.15	2.501 248	5.10	588
50	31.190 673	5250.551 831	.000 190 4562	.032 061	168.337 241	.005 940 4562	7.13	2.564 274	5.13	600

Amount Of 1	Amount Of 1 Per Period	Sinking Fund Payment	Present Worth Of 1	Present Worth of 1 Per Period	Periodic Payment To Amortize 1	Constant Annual Percent	Total Interest	Annual Add On Rate
What a single $ 1 deposit grows to in the future. The deposit is made at the beginning of the first period.	What a series of $ 1 deposits grow to in the future. A deposit is made at the end of each period.	The amount to be deposited at the end of each period that grows to $ 1 in the future.	What $ 1 to be paid in the future is worth today. Value today of a single $ 1 payment tomorrow.	What $ 1 to be paid at the end of each period is worth today. Value today of a series of $ 1 payments tomorrow.	The mortgage payment to amortize a loan of $ 1. An annuity certain, payable at the end of each period, worth $ 1 today.	The annual payment, including interest and principal, to amortize completely a loan of $ 100.	The total interest paid over the term on a loan of $1. The loan is amortized by regular periodic payments.	The average annual interest rate on a loan that is completely amortized by regular periodic payments.

$$S = (1+i)^n \qquad S\overline{n}| = \frac{(1+i)^n - 1}{i} \qquad \frac{1}{S\overline{n}|} = \frac{i}{(1+i)^n - 1} \qquad V^n = \frac{1}{(1+i)^n} \qquad A\overline{n}| = \frac{1-V^n}{i} \qquad \frac{1}{A\overline{n}|} = \frac{i}{1-V^n}$$

YEAR	Amount Of 1	Amount Of 1 Per Period	Sinking Fund Payment	Present Worth Of 1	Present Worth of 1 Per Period	Periodic Payment To Amortize 1	Constant Annual Percent	Total Interest	Annual Add On Rate	PERIODS
	1.005 792	1.000 000	1.000 000 0000	.994 242	.994 242	1.005 791 6667	1206.95	.005 792	6.95	1
	1.011 617	2.005 792	.498 556 2642	.988 517	1.982 758	.504 347 9308	605.22	.008 696	5.22	2
	1.017 476	3.017 409	.331 410 2103	.982 824	2.965 583	.337 201 8770	404.65	.011 606	4.64	3
	1.023 369	4.034 884	.247 838 5770	.977 165	3.942 747	.253 630 2436	304.36	.014 521	4.36	4
	1.029 296	5.058 253	.197 696 7118	.971 538	4.914 286	.203 488 3785	244.19	.017 442	4.19	5
	1.035 257	6.087 549	.164 269 7307	.965 944	5.880 229	.170 061 3973	204.08	.020 368	4.07	6
	1.041 253	7.122 806	.140 394 1118	.960 381	6.840 611	.146 185 7785	175.43	.023 300	3.99	7
	1.047 284	8.164 059	.122 488 0944	.954 851	7.795 462	.128 279 7611	153.94	.026 238	3.94	8
	1.053 349	9.211 342	.108 561 8112	.949 353	8.744 815	.114 353 4779	137.23	.029 181	3.89	9
	1.059 450	10.264 691	.097 421 3419	.943 886	9.688 701	.103 213 0086	123.86	.032 130	3.86	10
	1.065 586	11.324 141	.088 306 9191	.938 451	10.627 152	.094 098 5858	112.92	.035 084	3.83	11
	1.071 757	12.389 727	.080 712 0311	.933 047	11.560 199	.086 503 6978	103.81	.038 044	3.80	12
1	1.071 757	12.389 727	.080 712 0311	.933 047	11.560 199	.086 503 6978	103.81	.038 044	3.80	12
2	1.148 663	25.668 505	.038 958 2488	.870 577	22.346 411	.044 749 9155	53.70	.073 998	3.70	24
3	1.231 088	39.900 131	.025 062 5745	.812 289	32.410 455	.030 854 2412	37.03	.110 753	3.69	36
4	1.319 428	55.152 978	.018 131 3873	.757 904	41.800 683	.023 923 0540	28.71	.148 307	3.71	48
5	1.414 106	71.500 326	.013 985 9503	.707 161	50.562 209	.019 777 6170	23.74	.186 657	3.73	60
6	1.515 578	89.020 713	.011 233 3407	.659 814	58.737 126	.017 025 0074	20.44	.225 801	3.76	72
7	1.624 332	107.798 314	.009 276 5830	.615 638	66.364 709	.015 068 2496	18.09	.265 733	3.80	84
8	1.740 889	127.923 342	.007 817 1816	.574 419	73.481 604	.013 608 8483	16.34	.306 449	3.83	96
9	1.865 811	149.492 485	.006 689 2995	.535 960	80.122 003	.012 480 9661	14.98	.347 944	3.87	108
10	1.999 696	172.609 369	.005 793 4283	.500 076	86.317 808	.011 585 0950	13.91	.390 211	3.90	120
11	2.143 188	197.385 055	.005 066 2397	.466 595	92.098 786	.010 857 9064	13.03	.433 244	3.94	132
12	2.296 978	223.938 574	.004 465 5103	.435 355	97.492 712	.010 257 1769	12.31	.477 033	3.98	144
13	2.461 802	252.397 498	.003 962 0044	.406 206	102.525 500	.009 753 6711	11.71	.521 573	4.01	156
14	2.638 454	282.898 554	.003 534 8360	.379 010	107.221 328	.009 326 5027	11.20	.566 852	4.05	168
15	2.827 782	315.588 279	.003 168 6855	.353 634	111.602 757	.008 960 3522	10.76	.612 863	4.09	180
16	3.030 696	350.623 726	.002 852 0603	.329 957	115.690 837	.008 643 7269	10.38	.659 596	4.12	192
17	3.248 170	388.173 218	.002 576 1695	.307 866	119.505 208	.008 367 8362	10.05	.707 039	4.16	204
18	3.481 249	428.417 155	.002 334 1736	.287 253	123.064 197	.008 125 8402	9.76	.755 181	4.20	216
19	3.731 054	471.548 883	.002 120 6709	.268 021	126.384 901	.007 912 3376	9.50	.804 013	4.23	228
20	3.998 784	517.775 621	.001 931 3385	.250 076	129.483 274	.007 723 0052	9.27	.853 521	4.27	240
21	4.285 725	567.319 459	.001 762 6753	.233 333	132.374 203	.007 554 3420	9.07	.903 694	4.30	252
22	4.593 257	620.418 423	.001 611 8155	.217 710	135.071 576	.007 403 4821	8.89	.954 519	4.34	264
23	4.922 856	677.327 618	.001 476 3904	.203 134	137.588 353	.007 268 0571	8.73	1.005 984	4.37	276
24	5.276 106	738.320 455	.001 354 4254	.189 534	139.936 624	.007 146 0921	8.58	1.058 075	4.41	288
25	5.654 704	803.689 965	.001 244 2609	.176 844	142.127 671	.007 035 9276	8.45	1.110 778	4.44	300
26	6.060 470	873.750 207	.001 144 4919	.165 004	144.172 022	.006 936 1585	8.33	1.164 081	4.48	312
27	6.495 352	948.883 772	.001 053 9209	.153 956	146.079 498	.006 845 5876	8.22	1.217 970	4.51	324
28	6.961 440	1029.313 409	.000 971 5214	.143 648	147.859 263	.006 763 1881	8.12	1.272 431	4.54	336
29	7.460 973	1115.563 750	.000 896 4078	.134 031	149.519 867	.006 688 0744	8.03	1.327 450	4.58	348
30	7.996 352	1208.003 170	.000 827 8124	.125 057	151.069 290	.006 619 4791	7.95	1.383 012	4.61	360
31	8.570 147	1307.075 781	.000 765 0666	.116 684	152.514 974	.006 556 7332	7.87	1.439 105	4.64	372
32	9.185 117	1413.257 563	.000 707 5851	.108 872	153.863 865	.006 499 2518	7.80	1.495 713	4.67	384
33	9.844 215	1527.058 648	.000 654 8537	.101 583	155.122 445	.006 446 5204	7.74	1.552 822	4.71	396
34	10.550 608	1649.625 776	.000 606 4187	.094 781	156.296 759	.006 398 0853	7.68	1.610 419	4.74	408
35	11.307 689	1779.744 920	.000 561 8783	.088 435	157.392 449	.006 353 5449	7.63	1.668 489	4.77	420
36	12.119 097	1919.844 100	.000 520 8756	.082 514	158.414 780	.006 312 5423	7.58	1.727 018	4.80	432
37	12.988 729	2069.996 399	.000 483 0926	.076 990	159.368 663	.006 274 7593	7.53	1.785 993	4.83	444
38	13.920 764	2230.923 202	.000 448 2449	.071 835	160.258 681	.006 239 9116	7.49	1.845 400	4.86	456
39	14.919 678	2403.397 657	.000 416 0776	.067 026	161.089 109	.006 207 7443	7.45	1.905 224	4.89	468
40	15.990 272	2588.248 390	.000 386 3617	.062 538	161.863 938	.006 178 0283	7.42	1.965 454	4.91	480
41	17.137 689	2786.363 487	.000 358 8907	.058 351	162.586 890	.006 150 5574	7.39	2.026 074	4.94	492
42	18.367 441	2998.694 763	.000 333 4784	.054 444	163.261 439	.006 125 1451	7.36	2.087 073	4.97	504
43	19.685 436	3226.262 329	.000 309 9562	.050 799	163.890 824	.006 101 6229	7.33	2.148 437	5.00	516
44	21.098 007	3470.159 499	.000 288 1712	.047 398	164.478 071	.006 079 8379	7.30	2.210 154	5.02	528
45	22.611 940	3731.558 039	.000 267 9846	.044 224	165.025 999	.006 059 6512	7.28	2.272 212	5.05	540
46	24.234 509	4011.713 798	.000 249 2700	.041 263	165.537 242	.006 040 9367	7.25	2.334 597	5.08	552
47	25.973 509	4311.972 740	.000 231 9124	.038 501	166.014 256	.006 023 5791	7.23	2.397 299	5.10	564
48	27.837 294	4633.777 413	.000 215 8067	.035 923	166.459 333	.006 007 4733	7.21	2.460 305	5.13	576
49	29.834 820	4978.673 877	.000 200 8567	.033 518	166.874 610	.005 992 5234	7.20	2.523 604	5.15	588
50	31.975 682	5348.319 135	.000 186 9746	.031 274	167.262 083	.005 978 6413	7.18	2.587 185	5.17	600

Amount Of 1	Amount Of 1 Per Period	Sinking Fund Payment	Present Worth Of 1	Present Worth of 1 Per Period	Periodic Payment To Amortize 1	Constant Annual Percent	Total Interest	Annual Add On Rate	
What a single $ 1 deposit grows to in the future. The deposit is made at the beginning of the first period.	What a series of $ 1 deposits grow to in the future. A deposit is made at the end of each period.	The amount to be deposited at the end of each period that grows to $ 1 in the future.	What $ 1 to be paid in the future is worth today. Value today of a single $ 1 payment tomorrow.	What $ 1 to be paid at the end of each period is worth today. Value today of a series of $ 1 payments tomorrow.	The mortgage payment to amortize a loan of $ 1. An annuity certain, payable at the end of each period, worth $ 1 today.	The annual payment, including interest and principal, to amortize completely a loan of $ 100.	The total interest paid over the term on a loan of $1. The loan is amortized by regular periodic payments.	The average annual interest rate on a loan that is completely amortized by regular periodic payments.	
$S = (1+i)^n$	$S\overline{n}] = \dfrac{(1+i)^n - 1}{i}$	$\dfrac{1}{S\overline{n}]} = \dfrac{i}{(1+i)^n - 1}$	$V^n = \dfrac{1}{(1+i)^n}$	$A\overline{n}] = \dfrac{1-V^n}{i}$	$\dfrac{1}{A\overline{n}]} = \dfrac{i}{1-V^n}$				

YEAR									PERIODS
	1.005 833	1.000 000	1.000 000 0000	.994 200	.994 200	1.005 833 3333	1207.00	.005 833	7.00	1
	1.011 701	2.005 833	.498 545 9078	.988 435	1.982 635	.504 379 2411	605.26	.008 758	5.26	2
	1.017 602	3.017 534	.331 396 4286	.982 702	2.965 337	.337 229 7619	404.68	.011 689	4.68	3
	1.023 538	4.035 136	.247 823 1027	.977 003	3.942 340	.253 656 4360	304.39	.014 626	4.39	4
	1.029 509	5.058 675	.197 680 2380	.971 337	4.913 677	.203 513 5714	244.22	.017 568	4.22	5
	1.035 514	6.088 184	.164 252 6040	.965 704	5.879 381	.170 085 9373	204.11	.020 516	4.10	6
	1.041 555	7.123 698	.140 376 5303	.960 103	6.839 484	.146 209 8636	175.46	.023 469	4.02	7
	1.047 631	8.165 253	.122 470 1817	.954 535	7.794 019	.128 303 5150	153.97	.026 428	3.96	8
	1.053 742	9.212 883	.108 543 6499	.948 999	8.743 018	.114 376 9832	137.26	.029 393	3.92	9
	1.059 889	10.266 625	.097 402 9898	.943 495	9.686 513	.103 236 3231	123.89	.032 363	3.88	10
	1.066 071	11.326 514	.088 288 4181	.938 024	10.624 537	.094 121 7514	112.95	.035 339	3.86	11
	1.072 290	12.392 585	.080 693 4128	.932 583	11.557 120	.086 526 7461	103.84	.038 321	3.83	12
1	1.072 290	12.392 585	.080 693 4128	.932 583	11.557 120	.086 526 7461	103.84	.038 321	3.83	12
2	1.149 806	25.681 032	.038 939 2458	.869 712	22.335 099	.044 772 5791	53.73	.074 542	3.73	24
3	1.232 926	39.930 101	.025 043 7635	.811 079	32.386 464	.030 877 0969	37.06	.111 575	3.72	36
4	1.322 054	55.209 236	.018 112 9113	.756 399	41.760 201	.023 946 2447	28.74	.149 420	3.74	48
5	1.417 625	71.592 902	.013 967 8652	.705 405	50.501 994	.019 801 1985	23.77	.188 072	3.76	60
6	1.520 106	89.160 944	.011 215 6731	.657 849	58.654 444	.017 049 0065	20.46	.227 528	3.79	72
7	1.629 994	107.998 981	.009 259 3466	.613 499	66.257 285	.015 092 6800	18.12	.267 785	3.83	84
8	1.747 826	128.198 821	.007 800 3837	.572 139	73.347 569	.013 633 7171	16.37	.308 837	3.86	96
9	1.874 177	149.858 909	.006 672 9433	.533 568	79.959 850	.012 506 2766	15.01	.350 678	3.90	108
10	2.009 661	173.084 807	.005 777 5146	.497 596	86.126 354	.011 610 8479	13.94	.393 302	3.93	120
11	2.154 940	197.989 707	.005 050 7676	.464 050	91.877 134	.010 884 1009	13.07	.436 701	3.97	132
12	2.310 721	224.694 985	.004 450 4776	.432 765	97.240 216	.010 283 8110	12.35	.480 869	4.01	144
13	2.477 763	253.330 789	.003 947 4081	.403 590	102.241 738	.009 780 7414	11.74	.525 796	4.04	156
14	2.656 881	284.036 677	.003 520 6721	.376 381	106.906 074	.009 354 0054	11.23	.571 473	4.08	168
15	2.848 947	316.962 297	.003 154 9494	.351 007	111.255 958	.008 988 2827	10.79	.617 891	4.12	180
16	3.054 897	352.268 112	.002 838 7469	.327 343	115.312 587	.008 672 0802	10.41	.665 039	4.16	192
17	3.275 736	390.126 188	.002 563 2732	.305 275	119.095 732	.008 396 6065	10.08	.712 908	4.19	204
18	3.512 539	430.721 027	.002 321 6884	.284 694	122.623 831	.008 155 0217	9.79	.761 485	4.23	216
19	3.766 461	474.250 470	.002 108 5904	.265 501	125.914 077	.007 941 9238	9.54	.810 759	4.27	228
20	4.038 739	520.926 660	.001 919 6560	.247 602	128.982 506	.007 752 9894	9.31	.860 717	4.30	240
21	4.330 700	570.977 075	.001 751 3838	.230 910	131.844 073	.007 584 7171	9.11	.911 349	4.34	252
22	4.643 766	624.645 640	.001 600 9077	.215 342	134.512 723	.007 434 2410	8.93	.962 640	4.38	264
23	4.979 464	682.193 909	.001 465 8589	.200 825	137.001 461	.007 299 1922	8.76	1.014 577	4.41	276
24	5.339 430	743.902 347	.001 344 2625	.187 286	139.322 418	.007 177 5958	8.62	1.067 148	4.45	288
25	5.725 418	810.071 693	.001 234 4586	.174 660	141.486 903	.007 067 7920	8.49	1.120 338	4.48	300
26	6.139 309	881.024 427	.001 135 0423	.162 885	143.505 467	.006 968 3756	8.37	1.174 133	4.52	312
27	6.583 120	957.106 339	.001 044 8160	.151 904	145.387 946	.006 878 1493	8.26	1.228 520	4.55	324
28	7.059 015	1038.688 219	.000 962 7528	.141 663	147.143 515	.006 796 0861	8.16	1.283 485	4.58	336
29	7.569 311	1126.167 659	.000 887 9673	.132 112	148.780 729	.006 721 3006	8.07	1.339 013	4.62	348
30	8.116 497	1219.970 996	.000 819 6916	.123 206	150.307 568	.006 653 0250	7.99	1.395 089	4.65	360
31	8.703 240	1320.555 383	.000 757 2571	.114 900	151.731 473	.006 590 5905	7.91	1.451 700	4.68	372
32	9.332 398	1428.411 024	.000 700 0786	.107 154	153.059 383	.006 533 4119	7.85	1.508 830	4.72	384
33	10.007 037	1544.063 557	.000 647 6417	.099 930	154.297 770	.006 480 9751	7.78	1.566 466	4.75	396
34	10.730 447	1668.076 622	.000 599 4928	.093 193	155.452 669	.006 432 8262	7.72	1.624 593	4.78	408
35	11.506 152	1801.054 601	.000 555 2303	.086 910	156.529 709	.006 388 5636	7.67	1.683 197	4.81	420
36	12.337 932	1943.645 569	.000 514 4971	.081 051	157.534 139	.006 347 8304	7.62	1.742 263	4.84	432
37	13.229 843	2096.544 450	.000 476 9753	.075 587	158.470 853	.006 310 3087	7.58	1.801 777	4.87	444
38	14.186 229	2260.496 403	.000 442 3807	.070 491	159.344 418	.006 275 7140	7.54	1.861 726	4.90	456
39	15.211 753	2436.300 456	.000 410 4584	.065 739	160.159 090	.006 243 7917	7.50	1.922 095	4.93	468
40	16.311 411	2624.813 398	.000 380 9795	.061 307	160.918 839	.006 214 3128	7.46	1.982 870	4.96	480
41	17.490 565	2826.953 956	.000 353 7376	.057 174	161.627 369	.006 187 0710	7.43	2.044 039	4.99	492
42	18.754 959	3043.707 272	.000 328 5467	.053 319	162.288 132	.006 161 8800	7.40	2.105 588	5.01	504
43	20.110 757	3276.129 702	.000 305 2382	.049 725	162.904 349	.006 138 5716	7.37	2.167 503	5.04	516
44	21.564 565	3525.353 968	.000 283 6595	.046 372	163.479 022	.006 116 9928	7.35	2.229 772	5.07	528
45	23.123 469	3792.594 677	.000 263 6717	.043 246	164.014 953	.006 097 0051	7.32	2.292 383	5.09	540
46	24.795 066	4079.154 238	.000 245 1489	.040 331	164.514 754	.006 078 4822	7.30	2.355 322	5.12	552
47	26.587 504	4386.429 213	.000 227 9759	.037 612	164.980 859	.006 061 3092	7.28	2.418 578	5.15	564
48	28.509 517	4715.917 121	.000 212 0478	.035 076	165.415 542	.006 045 3812	7.26	2.482 140	5.17	576
49	30.570 472	5069.223 736	.000 197 2689	.032 711	165.820 919	.006 030 6022	7.24	2.545 994	5.20	588
50	32.780 414	5448.070 915	.000 183 5512	.030 506	166.198 968	.006 016 8845	7.23	2.610 131	5.22	600

Effective Rate is 7.23 %

Annual Percentage Rate is 7.00 %

MONTHLY COMPOUND INTEREST AND ANNUITY

7.05 % M

	Amount Of 1	Amount Of 1 Per Period	Sinking Fund Payment	Present Worth Of 1	Present Worth of 1 Per Period	Periodic Payment To Amortize 1	Constant Annual Percent	Total Interest	Annual Add On Rate	
	What a single $ 1 deposit grows to in the future. The deposit is made at the beginning of the first period.	What a series of $ 1 deposits grow to in the future. A deposit is made at the end of each period.	The amount to be deposited at the end of each period that grows to $ 1 in the future.	What $ 1 to be paid in the future is worth today. Value today of a single $ 1 payment tomorrow.	What $ 1 to be paid at the end of each period is worth today. Value today of a series of $ 1 payments tomorrow.	The mortgage payment to amortize a loan of $ 1. An annuity certain, payable at the end of each period, worth $ 1 today.	The annual payment, including interest and principal, to amortize completely a loan of $ 100.	The total interest paid over the term on a loan of $1. The loan is amortized by regular periodic payments.	The average annual interest rate on a loan that is completely amortized by regular periodic payments.	
	$S = (1+i)^n$	$S\overline{n}| = \dfrac{(1+i)^n - 1}{i}$	$\dfrac{1}{S\overline{n}|} = \dfrac{i}{(1+i)^n - 1}$	$V^n = \dfrac{1}{(1+i)^n}$	$A\overline{n}| = \dfrac{1 - V^n}{i}$	$\dfrac{1}{A\overline{n}|} = \dfrac{i}{1 - V^n}$				

YEAR										PERIODS
	1.005 875	1.000 000	1.000 000 0000	.994 159	.994 159	1.005 875 0000	1207.05	.005 875	7.05	1
	1.011 785	2.005 875	.498 535 5518	.988 353	1.982 512	.504 410 5518	605.30	.008 821	5.29	2
	1.017 729	3.017 660	.331 382 6477	.982 580	2.965 092	.337 257 6477	404.71	.011 773	4.71	3
	1.023 708	4.035 388	.247 807 6295	.976 841	3.941 933	.253 682 6295	304.42	.014 731	4.42	4
	1.029 722	5.059 096	.197 663 7656	.971 136	4.913 069	.203 538 7656	244.25	.017 694	4.25	5
	1.035 772	6.088 818	.164 235 4790	.965 464	5.878 533	.170 110 4790	204.14	.020 663	4.13	6
	1.041 857	7.124 590	.140 358 9507	.959 825	6.838 357	.146 233 9507	175.49	.023 638	4.05	7
	1.047 978	8.166 447	.122 452 2713	.954 219	7.792 576	.128 327 2713	154.00	.026 618	3.99	8
	1.054 135	9.214 425	.108 525 4911	.948 645	8.741 221	.114 400 4911	137.29	.029 604	3.95	9
	1.060 328	10.268 560	.097 384 6404	.943 105	9.684 326	.103 259 6404	123.92	.032 596	3.91	10
	1.066 557	11.328 888	.088 269 9202	.937 596	10.621 922	.094 144 9202	112.98	.035 594	3.88	11
	1.072 823	12.395 445	.080 674 7978	.932 120	11.554 042	.086 549 7978	103.86	.038 598	3.86	12
1	1.072 823	12.395 445	.080 674 7978	.932 120	11.554 042	.086 549 7978	103.86	.038 598	3.86	12
2	1.150 950	25.693 566	.038 920 2496	.868 848	22.323 796	.044 795 2496	53.76	.075 086	3.75	24
3	1.234 766	39.960 099	.025 024 9628	.809 870	32.362 499	.030 899 9628	37.08	.112 399	3.75	36
4	1.324 685	55.265 568	.018 094 4490	.754 896	41.719 774	.023 969 4490	28.77	.150 534	3.76	48
5	1.421 153	71.685 630	.013 949 7971	.703 654	50.441 878	.019 824 7971	23.79	.189 488	3.79	60
6	1.524 646	89.301 455	.011 198 0259	.655 890	58.571 926	.017 073 0259	20.49	.229 258	3.82	72
7	1.635 676	108.200 121	.009 242 1339	.611 368	66.150 105	.015 117 1339	18.15	.269 839	3.85	84
8	1.754 791	128.475 049	.007 783 6125	.569 868	73.213 879	.013 658 6125	16.40	.311 227	3.89	96
9	1.882 580	150.226 462	.006 656 6168	.531 186	79.798 163	.012 531 6168	15.04	.353 415	3.93	108
10	2.019 676	173.561 885	.005 761 6337	.495 129	85.935 506	.011 636 6337	13.97	.396 396	3.96	120
11	2.166 755	198.596 668	.005 035 3312	.461 520	91.656 246	.010 910 3312	13.10	.440 164	4.00	132
12	2.324 546	225.454 565	.004 435 4835	.430 192	96.988 662	.010 310 4835	12.38	.484 710	4.04	144
13	2.493 827	254.268 341	.003 932 8530	.400 990	101.959 114	.009 807 8530	11.77	.530 025	4.08	156
14	2.675 435	285.180 430	.003 506 5520	.373 771	106.592 172	.009 381 5520	11.26	.576 101	4.12	168
15	2.870 269	318.343 637	.003 141 2596	.348 399	110.910 738	.009 016 2596	10.82	.622 927	4.15	180
16	3.079 291	353.921 896	.002 825 4822	.324 750	114.936 159	.008 700 4822	10.45	.670 493	4.19	192
17	3.303 535	392.091 079	.002 550 4278	.302 706	118.688 335	.008 425 4278	10.12	.718 787	4.23	204
18	3.544 109	433.039 866	.002 309 2562	.282 158	122.185 813	.008 184 2562	9.83	.767 799	4.27	216
19	3.802 203	476.970 676	.002 096 5649	.263 005	125.445 883	.007 971 5649	9.57	.817 517	4.30	228
20	4.079 091	524.100 670	.001 908 0304	.245 153	128.484 658	.007 783 0304	9.34	.867 927	4.34	240
21	4.376 144	574.662 822	.001 740 1509	.228 512	131.317 162	.007 615 1509	9.14	.919 018	4.38	252
22	4.694 829	628.907 075	.001 590 0600	.213 000	133.957 396	.007 465 0600	8.96	.970 776	4.41	264
23	5.036 722	687.101 569	.001 455 3889	.198 542	136.418 410	.007 330 3889	8.80	1.023 187	4.45	276
24	5.403 512	749.533 975	.001 334 1623	.185 065	138.712 371	.007 209 1623	8.66	1.076 239	4.48	288
25	5.797 013	816.512 911	.001 224 7204	.172 503	140.850 618	.007 099 7204	8.52	1.129 916	4.52	300
26	6.219 171	888.369 469	.001 125 6578	.160 793	142.843 720	.007 000 6578	8.41	1.184 205	4.55	312
27	6.672 071	965.458 855	.001 035 7769	.149 879	144.701 531	.006 910 7769	8.30	1.239 092	4.59	324
28	7.157 953	1048.162 140	.000 954 0509	.139 705	146.433 233	.006 829 0509	8.20	1.294 561	4.62	336
29	7.679 218	1136.888 146	.000 879 5940	.130 222	148.047 388	.006 754 5940	8.11	1.350 599	4.66	348
30	8.238 443	1232.075 467	.000 811 6386	.121 382	149.551 974	.006 686 6386	8.03	1.407 190	4.69	360
31	8.838 393	1334.194 636	.000 749 5158	.113 143	150.954 428	.006 624 5158	7.95	1.464 320	4.72	372
32	9.482 034	1443.750 455	.000 692 6405	.105 463	152.261 684	.006 567 6405	7.89	1.521 974	4.76	384
33	10.172 546	1561.284 482	.000 640 4983	.098 304	153.480 204	.006 515 4983	7.82	1.580 137	4.79	396
34	10.913 344	1687.377 719	.000 592 6355	.091 631	154.616 010	.006 467 6355	7.77	1.638 795	4.82	408
35	11.708 089	1822.653 473	.000 548 6506	.085 411	155.674 718	.006 423 6506	7.71	1.697 933	4.85	420
36	12.560 710	1967.780 445	.000 508 1868	.079 613	156.661 560	.006 383 1868	7.66	1.757 537	4.88	432
37	13.475 422	2123.476 033	.000 470 9260	.074 209	157.581 416	.006 345 9260	7.62	1.817 591	4.91	444
38	14.456 746	2290.509 879	.000 436 5840	.069 172	158.438 832	.006 311 5840	7.58	1.878 082	4.94	456
39	15.509 533	2469.707 669	.000 404 9062	.064 476	159.238 047	.006 279 9062	7.54	1.938 996	4.97	468
40	16.638 987	2661.955 223	.000 375 6637	.060 100	159.983 011	.006 250 6637	7.51	2.000 319	5.00	480
41	17.850 692	2868.202 867	.000 348 6504	.056 020	160.677 406	.006 223 6504	7.47	2.062 036	5.03	492
42	19.150 637	3089.470 132	.000 323 6801	.052 218	161.324 667	.006 198 6801	7.44	2.124 135	5.06	504
43	20.545 248	3326.850 795	.000 300 5846	.048 673	161.927 991	.006 175 5846	7.42	2.186 602	5.09	516
44	22.041 420	3581.518 287	.000 279 2112	.045 369	162.490 361	.006 154 2112	7.39	2.249 424	5.11	528
45	23.646 548	3854.731 490	.000 259 4214	.042 289	163.014 558	.006 134 4214	7.37	2.312 588	5.14	540
46	25.368 566	4147.840 964	.000 241 0893	.039 419	163.503 172	.006 116 0893	7.34	2.376 081	5.17	552
47	27.215 987	4462.295 618	.000 224 0999	.036 743	163.958 620	.006 099 0999	7.32	2.439 892	5.19	564
48	29.197 943	4799.649 879	.000 208 3485	.034 249	164.383 151	.006 083 3485	7.31	2.504 009	5.22	576
49	31.324 232	5161.571 369	.000 193 7395	.031 924	164.778 865	.006 068 7395	7.29	2.568 419	5.24	588
50	33.605 364	5549.849 154	.000 180 1851	.029 757	165.147 718	.006 055 1851	7.27	2.633 111	5.27	600

MONTHLY COMPOUND INTEREST AND ANNUITY

Amount Of 1	Amount Of 1 Per Period	Sinking Fund Payment	Present Worth Of 1	Present Worth of 1 Per Period	Periodic Payment To Amortize 1	Constant Annual Percent	Total Interest	Annual Add On Rate	
What a single $ 1 deposit grows to in the future. The deposit is made at the beginning of the first period.	What a series of $ 1 deposits grow to in the future. A deposit is made at the end of each period.	The amount to be deposited at the end of each period that grows to $ 1 in the future.	What $ 1 to be paid in the future is worth today. Value today of a single $ 1 payment tomorrow.	What $ 1 to be paid at the end of each period is worth today. Value today of a series of $ 1 payments tomorrow.	The mortgage payment to amortize a loan of $ 1. An annuity certain, payable at the end of each period, worth $ 1 today.	The annual payment, including interest and principal, to amortize completely a loan of $ 100.	The total interest paid over the term on a loan of $1. The loan is amortized by regular periodic payments.	The average annual interest rate on a loan that is completely amortized by regular periodic payments.	
$S = (1+i)^n$	$S\overline{n}| = \dfrac{(1+i)^n - 1}{i}$	$\dfrac{1}{S\overline{n}|} = \dfrac{i}{(1+i)^n - 1}$	$V^n = \dfrac{1}{(1+i)^n}$	$A\overline{n}| = \dfrac{1-V^n}{i}$	$\dfrac{1}{A\overline{n}|} = \dfrac{i}{1-V^n}$				

YEAR   **PERIODS**

YEAR	Amount Of 1	Amount Of 1 Per Period	Sinking Fund Payment	Present Worth Of 1	Present Worth of 1 Per Period	Periodic Payment To Amortize 1	Constant Annual Percent	Total Interest	Annual Add On Rate	PERIODS
	1.005 917	1.000 000	1.000 000 0000	.994 118	.994 118	1.005 916 6667	1207.10	.005 917	7.10	1
	1.011 868	2.005 917	.498 525 1963	.988 271	1.982 389	.504 441 8630	605.34	.008 884	5.33	2
	1.017 855	3.017 785	.331 368 8675	.982 458	2.964 847	.337 285 5341	404.75	.011 857	4.74	3
	1.023 878	4.035 640	.247 792 1573	.976 679	3.941 526	.253 708 8240	304.46	.014 835	4.45	4
	1.029 935	5.059 518	.197 647 2946	.970 935	4.912 461	.203 563 9613	244.28	.017 820	4.28	5
	1.036 029	6.089 453	.164 218 3556	.965 224	5.877 685	.170 135 0223	204.17	.020 810	4.16	6
	1.042 159	7.125 483	.140 341 3730	.959 546	6.837 231	.146 258 0397	175.51	.023 806*	4.08	7
	1.048 325	8.167 642	.122 434 3631	.953 902	7.791 133	.128 351 0297	154.03	.026 808	4.02	8
	1.054 528	9.215 967	.108 507 3349	.948 292	8.739 425	.114 424 0016	137.31	.029 816	3.98	9
	1.060 767	10.270 495	.097 366 2939	.942 714	9.682 139	.103 282 9606	123.94	.032 830	3.94	10
	1.067 043	11.331 262	.088 251 4254	.937 169	10.619 308	.094 168 0921	113.01	.035 849	3.91	11
	1.073 357	12.398 305	.080 656 1863	.931 657	11.550 965	.086 572 8529	103.89	.038 874	3.89	12
1	1.073 357	12.398 305	.080 656 1863	.931 657	11.550 965	.086 572 8529	103.89	.038 874	3.89	12
2	1.152 094	25.706 108	.038 901 2603	.867 984	22.312 500	.044 817 9270	53.79	.075 630	3.78	24
3	1.236 608	39.990 127	.025 006 1723	.808 664	32.338 557	.030 922 8390	37.11	.113 222	3.77	36
4	1.327 322	55.321 973	.018 076 0003	.753 397	41.679 402	.023 992 6669	28.80	.151 648	3.79	48
5	1.424 690	71.778 512	.013 931 7460	.701 907	50.381 863	.019 848 4127	23.82	.190 905	3.82	60
6	1.529 200	89.442 247	.011 180 3989	.653 937	58.489 569	.017 097 0655	20.52	.230 989	3.85	72
7	1.641 377	108.401 735	.009 224 9446	.609 245	66.043 170	.015 141 6113	18.17	.271 895	3.88	84
8	1.761 783	128.752 027	.007 766 8680	.567 607	73.080 532	.013 683 5347	16.43	.313 619	3.92	96
9	1.891 021	150.595 148	.006 640 3202	.528 815	79.636 939	.012 556 9869	15.07	.356 155	3.96	108
10	2.029 740	174.040 606	.005 745 7855	.492 674	85.745 260	.011 662 4522	14.00	.399 494	3.99	120
11	2.178 635	199.205 945	.005 019 9305	.459 003	91.436 119	.010 936 5972	13.13	.443 631	4.03	132
12	2.338 453	226.217 329	.004 420 5278	.427 633	96.738 046	.010 337 1945	12.41	.488 556	4.07	144
13	2.509 994	255.210 177	.003 918 3390	.398 407	101.677 623	.009 835 0057	11.81	.534 261	4.11	156
14	2.694 118	286.329 842	.003 492 4756	.371 179	106.279 613	.009 409 1423	11.30	.580 736	4.15	168
15	2.891 750	319.732 342	.003 127 6160	.345 811	110.567 088	.009 044 2827	10.86	.627 971	4.19	180
16	3.103 879	355.585 136	.002 812 2660	.322 178	114.561 543	.008 728 9327	10.48	.675 955	4.22	192
17	3.331 569	394.067 972	.002 537 6333	.300 159	118.283 005	.008 454 2999	10.15	.724 677	4.26	204
18	3.575 962	435.373 778	.002 296 8770	.279 645	121.750 129	.008 213 5436	9.86	.774 125	4.30	216
19	3.838 282	479.709 640	.002 084 5943	.260 533	124.980 300	.008 001 2610	9.61	.824 288	4.34	228
20	4.119 846	527.297 832	.001 896 4614	.242 728	127.989 710	.007 813 1281	9.38	.875 151	4.38	240
21	4.422 064	578.376 933	.001 728 9763	.226 139	130.793 448	.007 645 6430	9.18	.926 702	4.41	252
22	4.746 451	633.203 025	.001 579 2723	.210 684	133.405 569	.007 495 9390	9.00	.978 928	4.45	264
23	5.094 635	692.050 975	.001 444 9803	.196 285	135.839 169	.007 361 6469	8.84	1.031 815	4.49	276
24	5.468 360	755.215 813	.001 324 1248	.182 870	138.106 449	.007 240 7915	8.69	1.085 348	4.52	288
25	5.869 501	823.014 211	.001 215 0458	.170 372	140.218 776	.007 131 7125	8.56	1.139 514	4.56	300
26	6.300 068	895.786 072	.001 116 3380	.158 728	142.186 740	.007 033 0046	8.44	1.194 297	4.59	312
27	6.762 219	973.896 232	.001 026 8034	.147 880	144.020 207	.006 943 4701	8.34	1.249 684	4.63	324
28	7.258 273	1057.736 290	.000 945 4152	.137 774	145.728 369	.006 862 0819	8.24	1.305 660	4.66	336
29	7.790 716	1147.726 574	.000 871 2877	.128 358	147.319 789	.006 787 9543	8.15	1.362 208	4.70	348
30	8.362 216	1244.318 242	.000 803 6529	.119 586	148.802 447	.006 720 3196	8.07	1.419 315	4.73	360
31	8.975 640	1347.995 550	.000 741 8422	.111 413	150.183 775	.006 658 5089	8.00	1.476 965	4.76	372
32	9.634 063	1459.278 276	.000 685 2703	.103 798	151.470 699	.006 601 9369	7.93	1.535 144	4.80	384
33	10.340 786	1578.724 330	.000 633 4228	.096 704	152.669 670	.006 550 0895	7.87	1.593 835	4.83	396
34	11.099 351	1706.932 544	.000 585 8462	.090 095	153.786 700	.006 502 5129	7.81	1.653 025	4.86	408
35	11.913 562	1844.545 682	.000 542 1389	.083 938	154.827 388	.006 458 8056	7.76	1.712 698	4.89	420
36	12.787 501	1992.253 657	.000 501 9441	.078 201	155.796 953	.006 418 6108	7.71	1.772 840	4.92	432
37	13.725 549	2150.796 993	.000 464 9439	.072 857	156.700 254	.006 381 6106	7.66	1.833 435	4.96	444
38	14.732 409	2320.970 534	.000 430 8542	.067 878	157.541 821	.006 347 5209	7.62	1.894 470	4.99	456
39	15.813 129	2503.627 435	.000 399 4205	.063 239	158.325 872	.006 316 0871	7.58	1.955 929	5.02	468
40	16.973 127	2699.683 432	.000 370 4138	.058 917	159.056 339	.006 287 0805	7.55	2.017 799	5.04	480
41	18.218 219	2910.121 437	.000 343 6283	.054 890	159.736 883	.006 260 2949	7.52	2.080 065	5.07	492
42	19.554 646	3135.996 467	.000 318 8779	.051 139	160.370 917	.006 235 5446	7.49	2.142 714	5.10	504
43	20.989 109	3378.440 930	.000 295 9945	.047 644	160.961 619	.006 212 6612	7.46	2.205 733	5.13	516
44	22.528 799	3638.670 304	.000 274 8257	.044 388	161.511 950	.006 191 4923	7.43	2.269 108	5.16	528
45	24.181 436	3917.989 230	.000 255 2330	.041 354	162.024 670	.006 171 8996	7.41	2.332 826	5.18	540
46	25.955 305	4217.798 053	.000 237 0905	.038 528	162.502 349	.006 153 7572	7.39	2.396 874	5.21	552
47	27.859 299	4539.599 843	.000 220 2837	.035 895	162.947 382	.006 136 9504	7.37	2.461 240	5.24	564
48	29.902 964	4885.007 931	.000 204 7080	.033 442	163.362 000	.006 121 3746	7.35	2.525 912	5.26	576
49	32.096 544	5255.753 995	.000 190 2677	.031 156	163.748 281	.006 106 9343	7.33	2.590 877	5.29	588
50	34.451 039	5653.696 744	.000 176 8754	.029 027	164.108 163	.006 093 5421	7.32	2.656 125	5.31	600

Effective Rate is 7.34 %

Annual Percentage Rate is 7.10 %

MONTHLY COMPOUND INTEREST AND ANNUITY

7.125% M

Amount Of 1	Amount Of 1 Per Period	Sinking Fund Payment	Present Worth Of 1	Present Worth of 1 Per Period	Periodic Payment To Amortize 1	Constant Annual Percent	Total Interest	Annual Add On Rate
What a single $ 1 deposit grows to in the future. The deposit is made at the beginning of the first period.	What a series of $ 1 deposits grow to in the future. A deposit is made at the end of each period.	The amount to be deposited at the end of each period that grows to $ 1 in the future.	What $ 1 to be paid in the future is worth today. Value today of a single $ 1 payment tomorrow.	What $ 1 to be paid at the end of each period is worth today. Value today of a series of $ 1 payments tomorrow.	The mortgage payment to amortize a loan of $ 1. An annuity certain, payable at the end of each period, worth $ 1 today.	The annual payment, including interest and principal, to amortize completely a loan of $ 100.	The total interest paid over the term on a loan that is amortized by regular periodic payments.	The average annual interest rate on a loan that is completely amortized by regular periodic payments.
$S = (1+i)^n$	$S\overline{n} = \dfrac{(1+i)^n - 1}{i}$	$\dfrac{1}{S\overline{n}} = \dfrac{i}{(1+i)^n - 1}$	$V^n = \dfrac{1}{(1+i)^n}$	$A\overline{n} = \dfrac{1 - V^n}{i}$	$\dfrac{1}{A\overline{n}} = \dfrac{i}{1 - V^n}$			

YEAR									PERIODS
	1.005 937	1.000 000	1.000 000 0000	.994 098	.994 098	1.005 937 5000	1207.13	.005 938	7.13	1
	1.011 910	2.005 937	.498 520 0187	.988 230	1.982 327	.504 457 5187	605.35	.008 915	5.35	2
	1.017 918	3.017 848	.331 361 9777	.982 397	2.964 724	.337 299 4777	404.76	.011 898	4.76	3
	1.023 962	4.035 766	.247 784 4217	.976 598	3.941 323	.253 721 9217	304.47	.014 888	4.47	4
	1.030 042	5.059 729	.197 639 0596	.970 834	4.912 157	.203 576 5596	244.30	.017 883	4.29	5
	1.036 158	6.089 771	.164 209 7946	.965 104	5.877 261	.170 147 2946	204.18	.020 884	4.18	6
	1.042 310	7.125 929	.140 332 5849	.959 407	6.836 668	.146 270 0849	175.53	.023 891	4.10	7
	1.048 499	8.168 239	.122 425 4098	.953 744	7.790 412	.128 362 9098	154.04	.026 903	4.04	8
	1.054 724	9.216 738	.108 498 2578	.948 115	8.738 527	.114 435 7578	137.33	.029 922	3.99	9
	1.060 987	10.271 462	.097 357 1218	.942 519	9.681 046	.103 294 6218	123.96	.032 946	3.95	10
	1.067 286	11.332 449	.088 242 1792	.936 956	10.618 002	.094 179 6792	113.02	.035 976	3.92	11
	1.073 623	12.399 735	.080 646 8818	.931 425	11.549 427	.086 584 3818	103.91	.039 013	3.90	12
1	1.073 623	12.399 735	.080 646 8818	.931 425	11.549 427	.086 584 3818	103.91	.039 013	3.90	12
2	1.152 667	25.712 382	.038 891 7682	.867 553	22.306 855	.044 829 2682	53.80	.075 902	3.80	24
3	1.237 531	40.005 151	.024 996 7809	.808 061	32.326 596	.030 934 2809	37.13	.113 634	3.79	36
4	1.328 642	55.350 203	.018 066 7811	.752 648	41.659 236	.024 004 2811	28.81	.152 205	3.81	48
5	1.426 461	71.825 010	.013 922 7269	.701 036	50.351 892	.019 860 2269	23.84	.191 614	3.83	60
6	1.531 482	89.512 749	.011 171 5930	.652 962	58.448 452	.017 109 0930	20.54	.231 855	3.86	72
7	1.644 235	108.502 720	.009 216 3588	.608 186	65.989 793	.015 153 8588	18.19	.272 924	3.90	84
8	1.765 289	128.890 798	.007 758 5058	.566 479	73.013 988	.013 696 0058	16.44	.314 817	3.94	96
9	1.895 256	150.779 916	.006 632 1830	.527 633	79.556 501	.012 569 6830	15.09	.357 526	3.97	108
10	2.034 791	174.280 586	.005 737 8737	.491 451	85.650 363	.011 675 3737	14.02	.401 045	4.01	120
11	2.184 599	199.511 456	.005 012 2435	.457 750	91.326 340	.010 949 7435	13.14	.445 366	4.05	132
12	2.345 437	226.599 909	.004 413 0644	.426 360	96.613 089	.010 350 5644	12.43	.490 481	4.09	144
13	2.518 116	255.682 707	.003 911 0975	.397 122	101.537 300	.009 848 5975	11.82	.536 381	4.13	156
14	2.703 508	286.906 680	.003 485 4539	.369 890	106.123 835	.009 422 9539	11.31	.583 056	4.16	168
15	2.902 550	320.429 469	.003 120 8116	.344 525	110.395 849	.009 058 3116	10.87	.630 496	4.20	180
16	3.116 246	356.420 321	.002 805 6762	.320 899	114.374 911	.008 743 1762	10.50	.678 690	4.24	192
17	3.345 674	395.060 943	.002 531 2550	.298 893	118.081 111	.008 468 7550	10.17	.727 626	4.28	204
18	3.591 994	436.546 420	.002 290 7071	.278 397	121.533 158	.008 228 2071	9.88	.777 293	4.32	216
19	3.856 449	481.086 200	.002 078 6296	.259 306	124.748 483	.008 016 1296	9.62	.827 678	4.36	228
20	4.140 374	528.905 151	.001 890 6982	.241 524	127.743 317	.007 828 1982	9.40	.878 768	4.39	240
21	4.445 203	580.244 697	.001 723 4108	.224 962	130.532 781	.007 660 9108	9.20	.930 550	4.43	252
22	4.772 474	635.364 037	.001 573 9009	.209 535	133.130 959	.007 511 4009	9.02	.983 010	4.47	264
23	5.123 840	694.541 452	.001 439 7989	.195 166	135.550 968	.007 377 2989	8.86	1.036 134	4.50	276
24	5.501 075	758.075 711	.001 319 1295	.181 783	137.805 025	.007 256 6295	8.71	1.089 909	4.54	288
25	5.906 083	826.287 580	.001 210 2324	.169 317	139.904 510	.007 147 7324	8.58	1.144 320	4.58	300
26	6.340 909	899.521 441	.001 111 7022	.157 706	141.860 024	.007 049 2022	8.46	1.199 351	4.61	312
27	6.807 748	978.147 030	.001 022 3412	.146 891	143.681 439	.006 959 8412	8.36	1.254 989	4.65	324
28	7.308 958	1062.561 304	.000 941 1222	.136 818	145.377 951	.006 878 6222	8.26	1.311 217	4.68	336
29	7.847 068	1153.190 446	.000 867 1595	.127 436	146.958 126	.006 804 6595	8.17	1.368 021	4.72	348
30	8.424 796	1250.492 017	.000 799 6852	.118 697	148.429 940	.006 737 1852	8.09	1.425 387	4.75	360
31	9.045 059	1354.957 263	.000 738 0307	.110 558	149.800 825	.006 675 5307	8.02	1.483 297	4.78	372
32	9.710 987	1467.113 599	.000 681 6105	.102 976	151.077 702	.006 619 1105	7.95	1.541 738	4.82	384
33	10.425 943	1587.527 269	.000 629 9104	.095 915	152.267 017	.006 567 4104	7.89	1.600 695	4.85	396
34	11.193 537	1716.806 206	.000 582 4769	.089 337	153.374 776	.006 519 9769	7.83	1.660 151	4.88	408
35	12.017 643	1855.603 102	.000 538 9083	.083 211	154.406 570	.006 476 4083	7.78	1.720 092	4.91	420
36	12.902 424	2004.618 701	.000 498 8480	.077 505	155.367 609	.006 436 3480	7.73	1.780 502	4.95	432
37	13.852 344	2164.605 340	.000 461 9780	.072 190	156.262 746	.006 399 4780	7.68	1.841 368	4.98	444
38	14.872 201	2336.370 743	.000 428 0143	.067 240	157.096 498	.006 365 5143	7.64	1.902 675	5.01	456
39	15.967 144	2520.782 105	.000 396 7023	.062 629	157.873 076	.006 334 2023	7.61	1.964 407	5.04	468
40	17.142 700	2718.770 464	.000 367 8133	.058 334	158.596 401	.006 305 3133	7.57	2.026 550	5.07	480
41	18.404 804	2931.335 404	.000 341 1414	.054 334	159.270 124	.006 278 6414	7.54	2.089 092	5.10	492
42	19.759 829	3159.550 104	.000 316 5008	.050 608	159.897 646	.006 254 0008	7.51	2.152 016	5.12	504
43	21.214 615	3404.566 754	.000 293 7231	.047 137	160.482 136	.006 231 2231	7.48	2.215 311	5.15	516
44	22.776 508	3667.622 369	.000 272 6562	.043 905	161.026 545	.006 210 1562	7.46	2.278 962	5.18	528
45	24.453 392	3950.045 041	.000 253 1617	.040 894	161.533 622	.006 190 6617	7.43	2.342 957	5.21	540
46	26.253 735	4253.260 638	.000 235 1137	.038 090	162.005 925	.006 172 6137	7.41	2.407 283	5.23	552
47	28.186 625	4578.800 007	.000 218 3978	.035 478	162.445 841	.006 155 8978	7.39	2.471 926	5.26	564
48	30.261 821	4928.306 702	.000 202 9094	.033 045	162.855 589	.006 140 4094	7.37	2.536 876	5.29	576
49	32.489 800	5303.545 277	.000 188 5531	.030 779	163.237 239	.006 126 0531	7.36	2.602 119	5.31	588
50	34.881 811	5706.410 203	.000 175 2415	.028 668	163.592 718	.006 112 7415	7.34	2.667 645	5.34	600

Amount Of 1	Amount Of 1 Per Period	Sinking Fund Payment	Present Worth Of 1	Present Worth of 1 Per Period	Periodic Payment To Amortize 1	Constant Annual Percent	Total Interest	Annual Add On Rate	
What a single $1 deposit grows to in the future. The deposit is made at the beginning of the first period.	What a series of $1 deposits grow to in the future. A deposit is made at the end of each period.	The amount to be deposited at the end of each period that grows to $1 in the future.	What $1 to be paid in the future is worth today. Value today of a single $1 payment tomorrow.	What $1 to be paid at the end of each period is worth today. Value today of a series of $1 payments tomorrow.	The mortgage payment to amortize a loan of $1. An annuity certain, payable at the end of each period, worth $1 today.	The annual payment, including interest and principal, to amortize completely a loan of $100.	The total interest paid over the term on a loan of $1. The loan is amortized by regular periodic payments.	The average annual interest rate on a loan that is completely amortized by regular periodic payments.	
$S = (1+i)^n$	$S_{\overline{n}} = \dfrac{(1+i)^n - 1}{i}$	$\dfrac{1}{S_{\overline{n}}} = \dfrac{i}{(1+i)^n - 1}$	$V^n = \dfrac{1}{(1+i)^n}$	$A_{\overline{n}} = \dfrac{1 - V^n}{i}$	$\dfrac{1}{A_{\overline{n}}} = \dfrac{i}{1 - V^n}$				

YEAR / **PERIODS**

YEAR	Amount Of 1	Amount Of 1 Per Period	Sinking Fund Payment	Present Worth Of 1	Present Worth of 1 Per Period	Periodic Payment To Amortize 1	Constant Annual Percent	Total Interest	Annual Add On Rate	PERIODS
	1.005 958	1.000 000	1.000 000 0000	.994 077	.994 077	1.005 958 3333	1207.15	.005 958	7.15	1
	1.011 952	2.005 958	.498 514 8412	.988 189	1.982 266	.504 473 1745	605.37	.008 946	5.37	2
	1.017 982	3.017 911	.331 355 0880	.982 336	2.964 602	.337 313 4214	404.78	.011 940	4.78	3
	1.024 047	4.035 892	.247 776 6863	.976 517	3.941 119	.253 735 0196	304.49	.014 940	4.48	4
	1.030 149	5.059 939	.197 630 8250	.970 734	4.911 853	.203 589 1583	244.31	.017 946	4.31	5
	1.036 287	6.090 088	.164 201 2340	.964 984	5.876 837	.170 159 5673	204.20	.020 957	4.19	6
	1.042 461	7.126 375	.140 323 7973	.959 268	6.836 105	.146 282 1307	175.54	.023 975	4.11	7
	1.048 673	8.168 836	.122 416 4572	.953 586	7.789 691	.128 374 7905	154.05	.026 998	4.05	8
	1.054 921	9.217 509	.108 489 1812	.947 938	8.737 630	.114 447 5146	137.34	.030 028	4.00	9
	1.061 207	10.272 430	.097 347 9503	.942 324	9.679 953	.103 306 2836	123.97	.033 063	3.97	10
	1.067 530	11.333 637	.088 232 9338	.936 742	10.616 695	.094 191 2671	113.03	.036 104	3.94	11
	1.073 890	12.401 166	.080 637 5781	.931 194	11.547 889	.086 595 9115	103.92	.039 151	3.92	12
1	1.073 890	12.401 166	.080 637 5781	.931 194	11.547 889	.086 595 9115	103.92	.039 151	3.92	12
2	1.153 240	25.718 658	.038 882 2778	.867 122	22.301 213	.044 840 6112	53.81	.076 175	3.81	24
3	1.238 454	40.020 183	.024 987 3921	.807 459	32.314 641	.030 945 7254	37.14	.114 046	3.80	36
4	1.329 963	55.378 451	.018 057 5652	.751 900	41.639 083	.024 015 8986	28.82	.152 763	3.82	48
5	1.428 235	71.871 547	.013 913 7119	.700 165	50.321 947	.019 872 0453	23.85	.192 323	3.85	60
6	1.533 767	89.583 322	.011 162 7921	.651 989	58.407 375	.017 121 1255	20.55	.232 721	3.88	72
7	1.647 098	108.603 825	.009 207 7788	.607 128	65.936 477	.015 166 1122	18.20	.273 953	3.91	84
8	1.768 802	129.029 758	.007 750 1502	.565 354	72.947 529	.013 708 4835	16.46	.316 014	3.95	96
9	1.899 500	150.964 969	.006 624 0533	.526 454	79.476 178	.012 582 3866	15.10	.358 898	3.99	108
10	2.039 854	174.520 979	.005 729 9701	.490 231	85.555 616	.011 688 3035	14.03	.402 596	4.03	120
11	2.190 580	199.817 550	.005 004 5654	.456 500	91.216 750	.010 962 8988	13.16	.447 103	4.06	132
12	2.352 442	226.983 291	.004 405 6106	.425 090	96.488 364	.010 363 9440	12.44	.492 408	4.10	144
13	2.526 265	256.156 316	.003 903 8663	.395 841	101.397 258	.009 862 1996	11.84	.538 503	4.14	156
14	2.712 931	287.484 944	.003 478 4430	.368 605	105.968 390	.009 436 7764	11.33	.585 378	4.18	168
15	2.913 390	321.128 454	.003 114 0187	.343 243	110.225 000	.009 072 3520	10.89	.633 023	4.22	180
16	3.128 662	357.257 892	.002 799 0984	.319 625	114.188 729	.008 757 4318	10.51	.681 427	4.26	192
17	3.359 839	396.056 944	.002 524 8895	.297 633	117.879 729	.008 483 2228	10.18	.730 577	4.30	204
18	3.608 099	437.722 869	.002 284 5505	.277 154	121.316 765	.008 242 8838	9.90	.780 463	4.34	216
19	3.874 702	482.467 501	.002 072 6785	.258 084	124.517 312	.008 031 0118	9.64	.831 071	4.37	228
20	4.161 005	530.518 327	.001 884 9490	.240 327	127.497 641	.007 843 2824	9.42	.882 388	4.41	240
21	4.468 463	582.119 641	.001 717 8599	.223 791	130.272 906	.007 676 1933	9.22	.934 401	4.45	252
22	4.798 639	637.533 791	.001 568 5443	.208 392	132.857 215	.007 526 8776	9.04	.987 096	4.49	264
23	5.153 212	697.042 509	.001 434 6327	.194 054	135.263 708	.007 392 9661	8.88	1.040 459	4.52	276
24	5.533 984	760.948 342	.001 314 1497	.180 702	137.504 619	.007 272 4830	8.73	1.094 475	4.56	288
25	5.942 891	829.576 195	.001 205 4348	.168 268	139.591 341	.007 163 7681	8.60	1.149 130	4.60	300
26	6.382 013	903.274 979	.001 107 0826	.156 690	141.534 485	.007 065 4159	8.48	1.204 410	4.63	312
27	6.853 582	982.419 388	.001 017 8952	.145 909	143.343 927	.006 976 2286	8.38	1.260 298	4.67	324
28	7.359 995	1067.411 799	.000 936 8456	.135 870	145.028 870	.006 895 1789	8.28	1.316 780	4.70	336
29	7.903 827	1158.684 323	.000 863 0478	.126 521	146.597 877	.006 821 3812	8.19	1.373 841	4.74	348
30	8.487 843	1256.701 000	.000 795 7342	.117 816	148.058 928	.006 754 0676	8.11	1.431 464	4.77	360
31	9.115 013	1361.960 156	.000 734 2359	.109 709	149.419 449	.006 692 5692	8.04	1.489 636	4.81	372
32	9.788 523	1474.996 942	.000 677 9675	.102 160	150.686 357	.006 636 3008	7.97	1.548 340	4.84	384
33	10.511 800	1596.386 047	.000 626 4149	.095 131	151.866 095	.006 584 7482	7.91	1.607 560	4.87	396
34	11.288 520	1726.744 627	.000 579 1244	.088 586	152.964 659	.006 537 4578	7.85	1.667 283	4.90	408
35	12.122 632	1866.735 439	.000 535 6945	.082 490	153.987 636	.006 494 0279	7.80	1.727 492	4.94	420
36	13.018 377	2017.070 212	.000 495 7686	.076 814	154.940 225	.006 454 1019	7.75	1.788 172	4.97	432
37	13.980 308	2178.513 263	.000 459 0286	.071 529	155.827 270	.006 417 3620	7.71	1.849 309	5.00	444
38	15.013 317	2351.885 387	.000 425 1908	.066 608	156.653 281	.006 383 5241	7.67	1.910 887	5.03	456
39	16.122 655	2538.068 026	.000 394 0005	.062 025	157.422 458	.006 352 3338	7.63	1.972 892	5.06	468
40	17.313 963	2738.007 753	.000 365 2291	.057 757	158.138 710	.006 323 5624	7.59	2.035 310	5.09	480
41	18.593 296	2952.721 082	.000 338 6707	.053 783	158.805 680	.006 297 0040	7.56	2.098 126	5.12	492
42	19.967 160	3183.299 640	.000 314 1395	.050 082	159.426 758	.006 272 4728	7.53	2.161 326	5.15	504
43	21.442 539	3430.915 712	.000 291 4674	.046 636	160.005 102	.006 249 8007	7.50	2.224 897	5.17	516
44	23.026 935	3696.828 205	.000 270 5022	.043 427	160.543 652	.006 228 8355	7.48	2.288 825	5.20	528
45	24.728 401	3982.389 047	.000 251 1056	.040 439	161.045 147	.006 209 4389	7.46	2.353 097	5.23	540
46	26.555 590	4289.050 060	.000 233 1519	.037 657	161.512 136	.006 191 4852	7.43	2.417 700	5.26	552
47	28.517 790	4618.370 342	.000 216 5266	.035 066	161.946 993	.006 174 8599	7.41	2.482 621	5.28	564
48	30.624 977	4972.024 192	.000 201 1253	.032 653	162.351 930	.006 159 4587	7.40	2.547 848	5.31	576
49	32.887 866	5351.809 624	.000 186 8527	.030 406	162.729 004	.006 145 1860	7.38	2.613 369	5.33	588
50	35.317 959	5759.657 509	.000 173 6214	.028 314	163.080 133	.006 131 9548	7.36	2.679 173	5.36	600

MONTHLY COMPOUND INTEREST AND ANNUITY

7.20 % M

	Amount Of 1	Amount Of 1 Per Period	Sinking Fund Payment	Present Worth Of 1	Present Worth of 1 Per Period	Periodic Payment To Amortize 1	Constant Annual Percent	Total Interest	Annual Add On Rate	
	What a single $ 1 deposit grows to in the future. The deposit is made at the beginning of the first period.	What a series of $ 1 deposits grow to in the future. A deposit is made at the end of each period.	The amount to be deposited at the end of each period that grows to $ 1 in the future.	What $ 1 to be paid in the future is worth today. Value today of a single $ 1 payment tomorrow.	What $ 1 to be paid at the end of each period is worth today. Value today of a series of $ 1 payments tomorrow.	The mortgage payment to amortize a loan of $ 1. An annuity certain, payable at the end of each period, worth $ 1 today.	The annual payment, including interest and principal, to amortize completely a loan of $ 100.	The total interest paid over the term on a loan of $1. The loan is amortized by regular periodic payments.	The average annual interest rate on a loan that is completely amortized by regular periodic payments.	
	$S = (1+i)^n$	$Sn = \dfrac{(1+i)^n - 1}{i}$	$\dfrac{1}{Sn} = \dfrac{i}{(1+i)^n - 1}$	$V^n = \dfrac{1}{(1+i)^n}$	$An = \dfrac{1 - V^n}{i}$	$\dfrac{1}{An} = \dfrac{i}{1 - V^n}$				

PERIODS

YEAR										
	1.006 000	1.000 000	1.000 000 0000	.994 036	.994 036	1.006 000 0000	1207.20	.006 000	7.20	1
	1.012 036	2.006 000	.498 504 4865	.988 107	1.982 143	.504 504 4865	605.41	.009 009	5.41	2
	1.018 108	3.018 036	.331 341 3094	.982 214	2.964 357	.337 341 3094	404.81	.012 024	4.81	3
	1.024 217	4.036 144	.247 761 2163	.976 356	3.940 713	.253 761 2163	304.52	.015 045	4.51	4
	1.030 362	5.060 361	.197 614 3567	.970 533	4.911 245	.203 614 3567	244.34	.018 072	4.34	5
	1.036 544	6.090 723	.164 184 1140	.964 744	5.875 989	.170 184 1140	204.23	.021 105	4.22	6
	1.042 764	7.127 268	.140 306 2236	.958 990	6.834 979	.146 306 2236	175.57	.024 144	4.14	7
	1.049 020	8.170 031	.122 398 5535	.953 271	7.788 250	.128 398 5535	154.08	.027 188	4.08	8
	1.055 314	9.219 051	.108 471 0301	.947 585	8.735 835	.114 471 0301	137.37	.030 239	4.03	9
	1.061 646	10.274 366	.097 329 6095	.941 933	9.677 768	.103 329 6095	124.00	.033 296	4.00	10
	1.068 016	11.336 012	.088 214 4453	.936 315	10.614 084	.094 214 4453	113.06	.036 359	3.97	11
	1.074 424	12.404 028	.080 618 9734	.930 731	11.544 815	.086 618 9734	103.95	.039 428	3.94	12
1	1.074 424	12.404 028	.080 618 9734	.930 731	11.544 815	.086 618 9734	103.95	.039 428	3.94	12
2	1.154 387	25.731 215	.038 863 3023	.866 260	22.289 933	.044 863 3023	53.84	.076 719	3.84	24
3	1.240 302	40.050 268	.024 968 6222	.806 256	32.290 749	.030 968 6222	37.17	.114 870	3.83	36
4	1.332 610	55.435 003	.018 039 1438	.750 407	41.598 819	.024 039 1438	28.85	.153 879	3.85	48
5	1.431 788	71.964 735	.013 895 6948	.698 427	50.262 130	.019 895 6948	23.88	.193 742	3.87	60
6	1.538 348	89.724 679	.011 145 2057	.650 048	58.325 343	.017 145 2057	20.58	.234 455	3.91	72
7	1.652 838	108.806 391	.009 190 6366	.605 020	65.830 026	.015 190 6366	18.23	.276 013	3.94	84
8	1.775 849	129.308 244	.007 733 4590	.563 111	72.814 868	.013 733 4590	16.49	.318 412	3.98	96
9	1.908 016	151.335 931	.006 607 8161	.524 105	79.315 878	.012 607 8161	15.13	.361 644	4.02	108
10	2.050 018	175.003 009	.005 714 1874	.487 801	85.366 570	.011 714 1874	14.06	.405 702	4.06	120
11	2.202 589	200.431 491	.004 989 2360	.454 011	90.998 137	.010 989 2360	13.19	.450 579	4.10	132
12	2.366 515	227.752 466	.004 390 7318	.422 562	96.239 612	.010 390 7318	12.47	.496 265	4.14	144
13	2.542 641	257.106 781	.003 889 4346	.393 292	101.118 016	.009 889 4346	11.87	.542 752	4.18	156
14	2.731 875	288.645 767	.003 464 4541	.366 049	105.658 498	.009 464 4541	11.36	.590 028	4.21	168
15	2.935 192	322.532 016	.003 100 4674	.340 693	109.884 466	.009 100 4674	10.93	.638 084	4.25	180
16	3.153 641	358.940 221	.002 785 9792	.317 094	113.817 706	.008 785 9792	10.55	.686 908	4.29	192
17	3.388 348	398.058 076	.002 512 1962	.295 129	117.478 495	.008 512 1962	10.22	.736 488	4.33	204
18	3.640 523	440.087 245	.002 272 2767	.274 686	120.885 705	.008 272 2767	9.93	.786 812	4.37	216
19	3.911 466	485.244 400	.002 060 8172	.255 659	124.056 901	.008 060 8172	9.68	.837 866	4.41	228
20	4.202 574	533.762 339	.001 873 4930	.237 949	127.008 432	.007 873 4930	9.45	.889 638	4.45	240
21	4.515 347	585.891 185	.001 706 8016	.221 467	129.755 514	.007 706 8016	9.25	.942 114	4.49	252
22	4.851 398	641.899 676	.001 557 8758	.206 126	132.312 308	.007 557 8758	9.07	.995 279	4.52	264
23	5.212 459	702.076 554	.001 424 3461	.191 848	134.691 997	.007 424 3461	8.91	1.049 120	4.56	276
24	5.600 392	766.732 045	.001 304 2366	.178 559	136.906 847	.007 304 2366	8.77	1.103 620	4.60	288
25	6.017 197	836.199 467	.001 195 8869	.166 190	138.968 276	.007 195 8869	8.64	1.158 766	4.64	300
26	6.465 022	910.836 944	.001 097 8913	.154 679	140.886 913	.007 097 8913	8.52	1.214 542	4.67	312
27	6.946 176	991.029 254	.001 009 0519	.143 964	142.672 648	.007 009 0519	8.42	1.270 933	4.71	324
28	7.463 139	1077.189 809	.000 928 3415	.133 992	144.334 687	.006 928 3415	8.32	1.327 923	4.74	336
29	8.018 577	1169.762 792	.000 854 8742	.124 710	145.881 598	.006 854 8742	8.23	1.385 496	4.78	348
30	8.615 353	1269.225 442	.000 787 8821	.116 072	147.321 357	.006 787 8821	8.15	1.443 638	4.81	360
31	9.256 543	1376.090 517	.000 726 6964	.108 032	148.661 385	.006 726 6964	8.08	1.502 331	4.85	372
32	9.945 454	1490.908 937	.000 670 7318	.100 548	149.908 591	.006 670 7318	8.01	1.561 561	4.88	384
33	10.685 636	1614.272 621	.000 619 4741	.093 584	151.069 404	.006 619 4741	7.95	1.621 312	4.91	396
34	11.480 905	1746.817 546	.000 572 4696	.087 101	152.149 809	.006 572 4696	7.89	1.681 568	4.95	408
35	12.335 362	1889.227 016	.000 529 3170	.081 068	153.155 376	.006 529 3170	7.84	1.742 313	4.98	420
36	13.253 411	2042.235 192	.000 489 6596	.075 452	154.091 288	.006 489 6596	7.79	1.803 533	5.01	432
37	14.239 785	2206.630 874	.000 453 1796	.070 226	154.962 370	.006 453 1796	7.75	1.865 212	5.04	444
38	15.299 569	2383.261 569	.000 419 5931	.065 361	155.773 114	.006 419 5931	7.71	1.927 334	5.07	456
39	16.438 227	2573.037 855	.000 388 6457	.060 834	156.527 698	.006 388 6457	7.67	1.989 886	5.10	468
40	17.661 629	2776.938 084	.000 360 1089	.056 620	157.230 013	.006 360 1089	7.64	2.052 852	5.13	480
41	18.976 081	2996.013 418	.000 333 7769	.052 698	157.883 680	.006 333 7769	7.61	2.116 218	5.16	492
42	20.388 360	3231.393 251	.000 309 4640	.049 048	158.492 067	.006 309 4640	7.58	2.179 970	5.19	504
43	21.905 746	3484.291 032	.000 287 0024	.045 650	159.058 313	.006 287 0024	7.55	2.244 093	5.22	516
44	23.536 063	3756.010 520	.000 266 2399	.042 488	159.585 335	.006 266 2399	7.52	2.308 575	5.25	528
45	25.287 715	4047.952 505	.000 247 0385	.039 545	160.075 851	.006 247 0385	7.50	2.373 401	5.27	540
46	27.169 732	4361.622 029	.000 229 2725	.036 806	160.532 390	.006 229 2725	7.48	2.438 558	5.30	552
47	29.191 817	4698.636 147	.000 212 8277	.034 256	160.957 304	.006 212 8277	7.46	2.504 035	5.33	564
48	31.364 394	5060.732 259	.000 197 5999	.031 883	161.352 785	.006 197 5999	7.44	2.569 818	5.35	576
49	33.698 662	5449.777 074	.000 183 4937	.029 675	161.720 872	.006 183 4937	7.43	2.635 894	5.38	588
50	36.206 657	5867.776 224	.000 170 4223	.027 619	162.063 462	.006 170 4223	7.41	2.702 253	5.40	600

Effective Rate is 7.44 %

Annual Percentage Rate is 7.20 %

MONTHLY COMPOUND INTEREST AND ANNUITY

Amount Of 1	Amount Of 1 Per Period	Sinking Fund Payment	Present Worth Of 1	Present Worth of 1 Per Period	Periodic Payment To Amortize 1	Constant Annual Percent	Total Interest	Annual Add On Rate
What a single $ 1 deposit grows to in the future. The deposit is made at the beginning of the first period.	What a series of $ 1 deposits grow to in the future. A deposit is made at the end of each period.	The amount to be deposited at the end of each period that grows to $ 1 in the future.	What $ 1 to be paid in the future is worth today. Value today of a single $ 1 payment tomorrow.	What $ 1 to be paid at the end of each period is worth today. Value today of a series of $ 1 payments tomorrow.	The mortgage payment to amortize a loan of $ 1. An annuity certain, payable at the end of each period, worth $ 1 today.	The annual payment, including interest and principal, to amortize completely a loan of $ 100.	The total interest paid over the term on a loan of $1. The loan is amortized by regular periodic payments.	The average annual interest rate on a loan that is completely amortized by regular periodic payments.
$S = (1+i)^n$	$S\overline{n}| = \dfrac{(1+i)^n - 1}{i}$	$\dfrac{1}{S\overline{n}|} = \dfrac{i}{(1+i)^n - 1}$	$V^n = \dfrac{1}{(1+i)^n}$	$A\overline{n}| = \dfrac{1 - V^n}{i}$	$\dfrac{1}{A\overline{n}|} = \dfrac{i}{1 - V^n}$			

YEAR	Amount Of 1	Amount Of 1 Per Period	Sinking Fund Payment	Present Worth Of 1	Present Worth of 1 Per Period	Periodic Payment To Amortize 1	Constant Annual Percent	Total Interest	Annual Add On Rate	PERIODS
	1.006 042	1.000 000	1.000 000 0000	.993 995	.993 995	1.006 041 6667	1207.25	.006 042	7.25	1
	1.012 120	2.006 042	.498 494 1323	.988 025	1.982 020	.504 535 7990	605.45	.009 072	5.44	2
	1.018 235	3.018 162	.331 327 5315	.982 092	2.964 112	.337 369 1982	404.85	.012 108	4.84	3
	1.024 387	4.036 396	.247 745 7474	.976 194	3.940 306	.253 787 4140	304.55	.015 150	4.54	4
	1.030 576	5.060 783	.197 597 8899	.970 332	4.910 637	.203 639 5565	244.37	.018 198	4.37	5
	1.036 802	6.091 358	.164 166 9957	.964 504	5.875 142	.170 208 6623	204.26	.021 252	4.25	6
	1.043 066	7.128 160	.140 288 6519	.958 712	6.833 854	.146 330 3186	175.60	.024 312	4.17	7
	1.049 368	8.171 226	.122 380 6521	.952 955	7.786 808	.128 422 3188	154.11	.027 379	4.11	8
	1.055 708	9.220 594	.108 452 8816	.947 232	8.734 040	.114 494 5482	137.40	.030 451	4.06	9
	1.062 086	10.276 302	.097 311 2715	.941 543	9.675 584	.103 352 9382	124.03	.033 529	4.02	10
	1.068 503	11.338 388	.088 195 9599	.935 889	10.611 473	.094 237 6266	113.09	.036 614	3.99	11
	1.074 958	12.406 891	.080 600 3721	.930 269	11.541 741	.086 642 0388	103.98	.039 704	3.97	12
1	1.074 958	12.406 891	.080 600 3721	.930 269	11.541 741	.086 642 0388	103.98	.039 704	3.97	12
2	1.155 535	25.743 781	.038 844 3335	.865 400	22.278 661	.044 886 0002	53.87	.077 264	3.86	24
3	1.242 152	40.080 381	.024 949 8625	.805 054	32.266 882	.030 991 5292	37.19	.115 695	3.86	36
4	1.335 262	55.491 629	.018 020 7361	.748 917	41.558 610	.024 062 4028	28.88	.154 995	3.87	48
5	1.435 351	72.058 078	.013 877 6947	.696 694	50.202 413	.019 919 3614	23.91	.195 162	3.90	60
6	1.542 942	89.866 319	.011 127 6395	.648 112	58.243 472	.017 169 3062	20.61	.236 190	3.94	72
7	1.658 599	109.009 436	.009 173 5178	.602 919	65.723 817	.015 215 1845	18.26	.278 075	3.97	84
8	1.782 924	129.587 488	.007 716 7944	.560 876	72.682 548	.013 758 4610	16.52	.320 812	4.01	96
9	1.916 569	151.708 036	.006 591 6086	.521 766	79.156 037	.012 633 2753	15.16	.364 394	4.05	108
10	2.060 232	175.486 703	.005 698 4374	.485 382	85.178 120	.011 740 1041	14.09	.408 812	4.09	120
11	2.214 664	201.047 778	.004 973 9421	.451 536	90.780 276	.011 015 6087	13.22	.454 060	4.13	132
12	2.380 671	228.524 868	.004 375 8914	.420 050	95.991 786	.010 417 5581	12.51	.500 128	4.17	144
13	2.559 122	258.061 593	.003 875 0439	.390 759	100.839 890	.009 916 7106	11.91	.547 007	4.21	156
14	2.750 950	289.812 342	.003 450 5087	.363 511	105.349 929	.009 492 1753	11.40	.594 685	4.25	168
15	2.957 156	323.943 072	.003 086 9621	.338 163	109.545 477	.009 128 6288	10.96	.643 153	4.29	180
16	3.178 819	360.632 184	.002 772 9084	.314 582	113.448 464	.008 814 5750	10.58	.692 398	4.33	192
17	3.417 098	400.071 449	.002 499 5535	.292 646	117.079 291	.008 541 2202	10.25	.742 409	4.37	204
18	3.673 238	442.467 014	.002 260 0555	.272 239	120.456 934	.008 301 7221	9.97	.793 172	4.41	216
19	3.948 578	488.040 479	.002 049 0104	.253 256	123.599 051	.008 090 6770	9.71	.844 674	4.45	228
20	4.244 557	537.030 053	.001 862 0932	.235 596	126.522 063	.007 903 7598	9.49	.896 902	4.48	240
21	4.562 721	589.691 802	.001 695 8011	.219 167	129.241 249	.007 737 4678	9.29	.949 842	4.52	252
22	4.904 735	646.300 986	.001 547 2667	.203 885	131.770 823	.007 588 9334	9.11	1.003 478	4.56	264
23	5.272 386	707.153 498	.001 414 1201	.189 667	134.124 007	.007 455 7868	8.95	1.057 797	4.60	276
24	5.667 595	772.567 411	.001 294 3854	.176 442	136.313 100	.007 336 0521	8.81	1.112 783	4.64	288
25	6.092 428	842.884 639	.001 186 4020	.164 138	138.349 544	.007 228 0686	8.68	1.168 421	4.67	300
26	6.549 106	918.472 727	.001 088 7640	.152 693	140.243 984	.007 130 4306	8.56	1.224 694	4.71	312
27	7.040 016	999.726 770	.001 000 2733	.142 045	142.006 323	.007 041 9400	8.46	1.281 589	4.75	324
28	7.567 724	1087.071 477	.000 919 9027	.132 140	143.645 771	.006 961 5694	8.36	1.339 087	4.78	336
29	8.134 987	1180.963 395	.000 846 7663	.122 926	145.170 898	.006 888 4330	8.27	1.397 175	4.82	348
30	8.744 772	1281.893 291	.000 780 0961	.114 354	146.589 676	.006 821 7628	8.19	1.455 835	4.85	360
31	9.400 265	1390.388 720	.000 719 2233	.106 380	147.909 521	.006 760 8900	8.12	1.515 051	4.89	372
32	10.104 893	1507.016 781	.000 663 5626	.098 962	149.137 331	.006 705 2293	8.05	1.574 808	4.92	384
33	10.862 339	1632.387 084	.000 612 5998	.092 061	150.279 524	.006 654 2665	7.99	1.635 090	4.95	396
34	11.676 561	1767.154 931	.000 565 8813	.085 642	151.342 071	.006 607 5480	7.93	1.695 880	4.99	408
35	12.551 816	1912.024 747	.000 523 0058	.079 670	152.330 525	.006 564 6724	7.88	1.757 162	5.02	420
36	13.492 679	2067.753 757	.000 483 6166	.074 114	153.250 052	.006 525 2832	7.84	1.818 922	5.05	432
37	14.504 067	2235.155 949	.000 447 3961	.068 946	154.105 460	.006 489 0627	7.79	1.881 144	5.08	444
38	15.591 267	2415.106 324	.000 414 0604	.064 138	154.901 219	.006 455 7271	7.75	1.943 812	5.12	456
39	16.759 962	2608.545 473	.000 383 3554	.059 666	155.641 489	.006 425 0221	7.72	2.006 910	5.15	468
40	18.016 260	2816.484 491	.000 355 0525	.055 505	156.330 138	.006 396 7192	7.68	2.070 425	5.18	480
41	19.366 729	3040.010 263	.000 328 9463	.051 635	156.970 767	.006 370 6129	7.65	2.134 342	5.21	492
42	20.818 426	3280.291 147	.000 304 8510	.048 034	157.566 725	.006 346 5177	7.62	2.198 645	5.23	504
43	22.378 939	3538.583 078	.000 282 5990	.044 685	158.121 125	.006 324 2657	7.59	2.263 321	5.26	516
44	24.056 427	3816.236 131	.000 262 0383	.041 569	158.636 866	.006 303 7050	7.57	2.328 356	5.29	528
45	25.859 655	4114.701 584	.000 243 0310	.038 670	159.116 644	.006 284 6977	7.55	2.393 737	5.32	540
46	27.798 051	4435.539 500	.000 225 4517	.035 974	159.562 966	.006 267 1184	7.53	2.459 449	5.35	552
47	29.881 746	4780.426 880	.000 209 1863	.033 465	159.978 166	.006 250 8530	7.51	2.525 481	5.37	564
48	32.121 631	5151.166 430	.000 194 1308	.031 132	160.364 413	.006 235 7975	7.49	2.591 819	5.40	576
49	34.529 413	5549.695 986	.000 180 1901	.028 961	160.723 727	.006 221 8567	7.47	2.658 452	5.43	588
50	37.117 679	5978.098 639	.000 167 2773	.026 941	161.057 985	.006 208 9439	7.46	2.725 366	5.45	600

Effective Rate is 7.50 %

Annual Percentage Rate is 7.25 %

Amount Of 1	Amount Of 1 Per Period	Sinking Fund Payment	Present Worth Of 1	Present Worth of 1 Per Period	Periodic Payment To Amortize 1	Constant Annual Percent	Total Interest	Annual Add On Rate
What a single $ 1 deposit grows to in the future. The deposit is made at the beginning of the first period.	What a series of $ 1 deposits grow to in the future. A deposit is made at the end of each period.	The amount to be deposited at the end of each period that grows to $ 1 in the future.	What $ 1 to be paid in the future is worth today. Value today of a single $ 1 payment tomorrow.	What $ 1 to be paid at the end of each period is worth today. Value today of a series of $ 1 payments tomorrow.	The mortgage payment to amortize a loan of $ 1. An annuity certain, payable at the end of each period, worth $ 1 today.	The annual payment, including interest and principal, to amortize completely a loan of $ 100.	The total interest paid over the term on a loan of $1. The loan is amortized by regular periodic payments.	The average annual interest rate on a loan that is completely amortized by regular periodic payments.
$S = (1+i)^n$	$S\overline{n} = \frac{(1+i)^n - 1}{i}$	$\frac{1}{S\overline{n}} = \frac{i}{(1+i)^n - 1}$	$V^n = \frac{1}{(1+i)^n}$	$A\overline{n} = \frac{1-V^n}{i}$	$\frac{1}{A\overline{n}} = \frac{i}{1-V^n}$			**PERIODS**

YEAR

1.006 083	1.000 000	1.000 000 0000	.993 953	.993 953	1.006 083 3333	1207.30	.006 083	7.30 1
1.012 204	2.006 083	.498 483 7785	.987 943	1.981 897	.504 567 1118	605.49	.009 134	5.48 2
1.018 287	3.018 287	.331 313 7544	.981 970	2.963 867	.337 397 0877	404.88	.012 191	4.88 3
1.024 556	4.036 648	.247 730 2795	.976 032	3.939 899	.253 813 6128	304.58	.015 254	4.58 4
1.030 789	5.061 205	.197 581 4244	.970 131	4.910 030	.203 664 7577	244.40	.018 324	4.40 5
1.037 060	6.091 994	.164 149 8790	.964 265	5.874 294	.170 233 2124	204.28	.021 399	4.28 6
1.043 368	7.129 053	.140 271 0821	.958 434	6.832 729	.146 354 4155	175.63	.024 481	4.20 7
1.049 716	8.172 422	.122 362 7529	.952 639	7.785 368	.128 446 0863	154.14	.027 569	4.14 8
1.056 101	9.222 137	.108 434 7355	.946 879	8.732 246	.114 518 0689	137.43	.030 663	4.09 9
1.062 526	10.278 238	.097 292 9364	.941 153	9.673 400	.103 376 2697	124.06	.033 763	4.05 10
1.068 990	11.340 764	.088 177 4776	.935 463	10.608 863	.094 260 8110	113.12	.036 869	4.02 11
1.075 493	12.409 754	.080 581 7743	.929 806	11.538 669	.086 665 1076	104.00	.039 981	4.00 12

YEAR									
1	1.075 493	12.409 754	.080 581 7743	.929 806	11.538 669	.086 665 1076	104.00	.039 981	4.00 12
2	1.156 684	25.756 354	.038 825 3716	.864 540	22.267 398	.044 908 7050	53.90	.077 809	3.89 24
3	1.244 006	40.110 524	.024 931 1131	.803 855	32.243 039	.031 014 4464	37.22	.116 520	3.88 36
4	1.337 919	55.548 328	.018 002 3420	.747 429	41.518 454	.024 085 6753	28.91	.156 112	3.90 48
5	1.438 922	72.151 574	.013 859 7115	.694 965	50.142 794	.019 943 0449	23.94	.196 583	3.93 60
6	1.547 550	90.008 243	.011 110 0936	.646 183	58.161 762	.017 193 4269	20.64	.237 927	3.97 72
7	1.664 379	109.212 960	.009 156 4225	.600 825	65.617 849	.015 239 7558	18.29	.280 139	4.00 84
8	1.790 027	129.867 492	.007 700 1564	.558 651	72.550 567	.013 783 4898	16.55	.323 215	4.04 96
9	1.925 161	152.081 289	.006 575 4308	.519 437	78.996 653	.012 658 7642	15.20	.367 147	4.08 108
10	2.070 497	175.972 066	.005 682 7201	.482 976	84.990 265	.011 766 0534	14.12	.411 926	4.12 120
11	2.226 804	201.666 421	.004 958 6837	.449 074	90.563 164	.011 042 0170	13.26	.457 546	4.16 132
12	2.394 911	229.300 512	.004 361 0893	.417 552	95.744 881	.010 444 4226	12.54	.503 997	4.20 144
13	2.575 710	259.020 774	.003 860 6942	.388 243	100.562 875	.009 944 0275	11.94	.551 268	4.24 156
14	2.770 157	290.984 698	.003 436 6068	.360 990	105.042 677	.009 519 9402	11.43	.599 350	4.28 168
15	2.979 283	325.361 664	.003 073 5028	.335 651	109.208 026	.009 156 8362	10.99	.648 231	4.32 180
16	3.204 198	362.333 839	.002 759 8858	.312 091	113.080 994	.008 843 2191	10.62	.697 898	4.36 192
17	3.446 091	402.097 142	.002 486 9612	.290 184	116.682 104	.008 570 2946	10.29	.748 340	4.40 204
18	3.706 246	444.862 284	.002 247 8867	.269 815	120.030 440	.008 331 2200	10.00	.799 547	4.44 216
19	3.986 040	490.855 879	.002 037 2579	.250 876	123.143 744	.008 120 5912	9.75	.851 495	4.48 228
20	4.286 957	540.321 655	.001 850 7494	.233 266	126.038 514	.007 934 0828	9.53	.904 180	4.52 240
21	4.610 591	593.521 733	.001 684 8583	.216 892	128.730 089	.007 768 1916	9.33	.957 584	4.56 252
22	4.958 656	650.738 028	.001 536 7167	.201 668	131.232 734	.007 620 0500	9.15	1.011 693	4.60 264
23	5.332 999	712.273 734	.001 403 9546	.187 512	133.559 709	.007 487 2880	8.99	1.066 491	4.64 276
24	5.735 601	778.454 934	.001 284 5959	.174 350	135.723 345	.007 367 9292	8.85	1.121 964	4.67 288
25	6.168 597	849.632 330	.001 176 9797	.162 111	137.735 108	.007 260 3130	8.72	1.178 094	4.71 300
26	6.634 281	926.183 098	.001 079 7001	.150 732	139.605 658	.007 163 0335	8.60	1.234 866	4.75 312
27	7.135 120	1008.512 887	.000 991 5590	.140 152	141.344 908	.007 074 8923	8.49	1.292 265	4.79 324
28	7.673 769	1097.057 972	.000 911 5289	.130 314	142.962 073	.006 994 8622	8.40	1.350 274	4.82 336
29	8.253 083	1192.287 562	.000 838 7238	.121 167	144.465 724	.006 922 0572	8.31	1.408 876	4.86 348
30	8.876 130	1294.706 289	.000 772 3760	.112 662	145.863 828	.006 855 7093	8.23	1.468 055	4.89 360
31	9.546 213	1404.856 878	.000 711 8163	.104 754	147.163 794	.006 795 1496	8.16	1.527 796	4.93 372
32	10.266 882	1523.323 029	.000 656 4596	.097 401	148.372 511	.006 739 7929	8.09	1.588 080	4.96 384
33	11.041 956	1650.732 507	.000 605 7917	.090 564	149.496 384	.006 689 1250	8.03	1.648 894	5.00 396
34	11.875 543	1787.760 466	.000 559 3591	.084 207	150.541 368	.006 642 6924	7.98	1.710 218	5.03 408
35	12.772 059	1935.133 032	.000 516 7603	.078 296	151.513 001	.006 600 0937	7.93	1.772 039	5.06 420
36	13.736 256	2093.631 147	.000 477 6391	.072 800	152.416 432	.006 560 9724	7.88	1.834 340	5.10 432
37	14.773 243	2264.094 707	.000 441 6776	.067 690	153.256 447	.006 525 0110	7.84	1.897 105	5.13 444
38	15.888 514	2447.427 017	.000 408 5924	.062 939	154.037 499	.006 491 9257	7.80	1.960 318	5.16 456
39	17.087 981	2644.599 572	.000 378 1291	.058 521	154.763 726	.006 461 4624	7.76	2.023 964	5.19 468
40	18.377 998	2856.657 210	.000 350 0595	.054 413	155.438 977	.006 433 3928	7.73	2.088 029	5.22 480
41	19.765 402	3084.723 646	.000 324 1781	.050 593	156.066 829	.006 407 5115	7.69	2.152 496	5.25 492
42	21.257 545	3330.007 426	.000 300 2996	.047 042	156.650 610	.006 383 6330	7.67	2.217 351	5.28 504
43	22.862 334	3593.808 333	.000 278 2564	.043 740	157.193 414	.006 361 5897	7.64	2.282 580	5.31 516
44	24.588 273	3877.524 276	.000 257 8965	.040 670	157.698 116	.006 341 2298	7.61	2.348 169	5.34 528
45	26.444 507	4182.658 692	.000 239 0824	.037 815	158.167 391	.006 322 4157	7.59	2.414 104	5.36 540
46	28.440 874	4510.828 521	.000 221 6888	.035 161	158.603 726	.006 305 0221	7.57	2.480 372	5.39 552
47	30.587 951	4863.772 766	.000 205 6017	.032 693	159.009 434	.006 288 9350	7.55	2.546 959	5.42 564
48	32.897 117	5243.361 715	.000 190 7173	.030 398	159.386 663	.006 274 0507	7.53	2.613 853	5.45 576
49	35.380 608	5651.606 848	.000 176 9408	.028 264	159.737 413	.006 260 2742	7.52	2.681 041	5.47 588
50	38.051 585	6090.671 496	.000 164 1855	.026 280	160.063 543	.006 247 5188	7.50	2.748 511	5.50 600

Effective Rate is 7.55 %

Annual Percentage Rate is 7.30

MONTHLY COMPOUND INTEREST AND ANNUITY

	Amount Of 1	Amount Of 1 Per Period	Sinking Fund Payment	Present Worth Of 1	Present Worth of 1 Per Period	Periodic Payment To Amortize 1	Constant Annual Percent	Total Interest	Annual Add On Rate	
	What a single $ 1 deposit grows to in the future. The deposit is made at the beginning of the first period.	What a series of $ 1 deposits grow to in the future. A deposit is made at the end of each period.	The amount to be deposited at the end of each period that grows to $ 1 in the future.	What $ 1 to be paid in the future is worth today. Value today of a single $ 1 payment tomorrow.	What $ 1 to be paid at the end of each period is worth today. Value today of a series of $ 1 payments tomorrow.	The mortgage payment to amortize a loan of $ 1. An annuity certain, payable at the end of each period, worth $ 1 today.	The annual payment, including interest and principal, to amortize completely a loan of $ 100.	The total interest paid over the term on a loan of $1. The loan is amortized by regular periodic payments.	The average annual interest rate on a loan that is completely amortized by regular periodic payments.	
	$S = (1+i)^n$	$S\overline{n|} = \dfrac{(1+i)^n - 1}{i}$	$\dfrac{1}{S\overline{n|}} = \dfrac{i}{(1+i)^n - 1}$	$V^n = \dfrac{1}{(1+i)^n}$	$A\overline{n|} = \dfrac{1 - V^n}{i}$	$\dfrac{1}{A\overline{n|}} = \dfrac{i}{1 - V^n}$				

YEAR / **PERIODS**

YEAR	Amount Of 1	Amount Of 1 Per Period	Sinking Fund Payment	Present Worth Of 1	Present Worth of 1 Per Period	Periodic Payment To Amortize 1	Constant Annual Percent	Total Interest	Annual Add On Rate	PERIODS
	1.006 125	1.000 000	1.000 000 0000	.993 912	.993 912	1.006 125 0000	1207.35	.006 125	7.35	1
	1.012 288	2.006 125	.498 473 4251	.987 862	1.981 774	.504 598 4251	605.52	.009 197	5.52	2
	1.018 488	3.018 413	.331 299 9780	.981 848	2.963 622	.337 424 9780	404.91	.012 275	4.91	3
	1.024 726	4.036 900	.247 714 8128	.975 871	3.939 492	.253 839 8128	304.61	.015 359	4.61	4
	1.031 002	5.061 626	.197 564 9602	.969 930	4.909 422	.203 689 9602	244.43	.018 450	4.43	5
	1.037 317	6.092 629	.164 132 7641	.964 025	5.873 447	.170 257 7641	204.31	.021 547	4.31	6
	1.043 671	7.129 946	.140 253 5143	.958 156	6.831 604	.146 378 5143	175.66	.024 650	4.23	7
	1.050 063	8.173 617	.122 344 8560	.952 323	7.783 927	.128 469 8560	154.17	.027 759	4.16	8
	1.056 495	9.223 680	.108 416 5921	.946 526	8.730 453	.114 541 5921	137.45	.030 874	4.12	9
	1.062 966	10.280 175	.097 274 6041	.940 764	9.671 217	.103 399 6041	124.08	.033 996	4.08	10
	1.069 477	11.343 142	.088 158 9985	.935 037	10.606 254	.094 283 9985	113.15	.037 124	4.05	11
	1.076 027	12.412 618	.080 563 1798	.929 344	11.535 598	.086 688 1798	104.03	.040 258	4.03	12
1	1.076 027	12.412 618	.080 563 1798	.929 344	11.535 598	.086 688 1798	104.03	.040 258	4.03	12
2	1.157 835	25.768 934	.038 806 4166	.863 681	22.256 142	.044 931 4166	53.92	.078 354	3.92	24
3	1.245 862	40.140 695	.024 912 3740	.802 657	32.219 221	.031 037 3740	37.25	.117 345	3.91	36
4	1.340 581	55.605 101	.017 983 9615	.745 945	41.478 352	.024 108 9615	28.94	.157 230	3.93	48
5	1.442 502	72.245 224	.013 841 7453	.693 240	50.083 275	.019 966 7453	23.97	.198 005	3.96	60
6	1.552 172	90.150 451	.011 092 5679	.644 259	58.080 212	.017 217 5679	20.67	.239 665	3.99	72
7	1.670 179	109.416 964	.009 139 3507	.598 738	65.512 122	.015 264 3507	18.32	.282 205	4.03	84
8	1.797 158	130.148 257	.007 683 5451	.556 434	72.418 926	.013 808 5451	16.58	.325 620	4.07	96
9	1.933 791	152.455 694	.006 559 2827	.517 119	78.837 726	.012 684 2827	15.23	.369 903	4.11	108
10	2.080 812	176.459 105	.005 667 0354	.480 582	84.803 002	.011 792 0354	14.16	.415 044	4.15	120
11	2.239 011	202.287 431	.004 943 4609	.446 626	90.346 798	.011 068 4609	13.29	.461 037	4.19	132
12	2.409 236	230.079 414	.004 346 3254	.415 069	95.498 895	.010 471 3254	12.57	.507 871	4.23	144
13	2.592 404	259.984 345	.003 846 3854	.385 742	100.286 967	.009 971 3854	11.97	.555 536	4.27	156
14	2.789 498	292.162 868	.003 422 7484	.358 487	104.736 735	.009 547 7484	11.46	.604 022	4.31	168
15	3.001 576	326.787 837	.003 060 0894	.333 158	108.872 103	.009 185 0894	11.03	.653 316	4.36	180
16	3.229 777	364.045 248	.002 746 9113	.309 619	112.715 284	.008 871 9113	10.65	.703 407	4.40	192
17	3.475 328	404.135 239	.002 474 4192	.287 743	116.286 923	.008 599 4192	10.32	.754 282	4.44	204
18	3.739 548	447.273 163	.002 235 7702	.267 412	119.606 206	.008 360 7702	10.04	.805 926	4.48	216
19	4.023 856	493.690 746	.002 025 5595	.248 518	122.690 963	.008 150 5595	9.79	.858 328	4.52	228
20	4.329 779	543.637 333	.001 839 4616	.230 959	125.557 765	.007 964 4616	9.56	.911 471	4.56	240
21	4.658 960	597.381 223	.001 673 9729	.214 640	128.222 012	.007 798 9729	9.36	.965 341	4.60	252
22	5.013 168	655.211 115	.001 526 2256	.199 475	130.698 015	.007 651 2256	9.19	1.019 924	4.64	264
23	5.394 306	717.437 656	.001 393 8493	.185 381	132.999 074	.007 518 8493	9.03	1.075 202	4.67	276
24	5.804 420	784.395 113	.001 274 8677	.172 282	135.137 551	.007 399 8677	8.88	1.131 162	4.71	288
25	6.245 714	856.443 164	.001 167 6198	.160 110	137.124 933	.007 292 6198	8.76	1.187 786	4.75	300
26	6.720 559	933.968 833	.001 070 6995	.148 797	138.971 895	.007 195 6995	8.64	1.245 058	4.79	312
27	7.231 505	1017.388 568	.000 982 9086	.138 284	140.688 359	.007 107 9086	8.53	1.302 962	4.83	324
28	7.781 297	1107.150 479	.000 903 2196	.128 513	142.283 545	.007 028 2196	8.44	1.361 482	4.86	336
29	8.372 888	1203.736 744	.000 830 7464	.119 433	143.766 023	.006 955 7464	8.35	1.420 600	4.90	348
30	9.009 455	1307.666 202	.000 764 7211	.110 994	145.143 755	.006 889 7211	8.27	1.480 300	4.93	360
31	9.694 420	1419.497 134	.000 704 4748	.103 152	146.424 143	.006 829 4748	8.20	1.540 565	4.97	372
32	10.431 460	1539.830 268	.000 649 4222	.095 864	147.614 065	.006 774 4222	8.13	1.601 378	5.00	384
33	11.224 536	1669.312 005	.000 599 0492	.089 091	148.719 911	.006 724 0492	8.07	1.601 378	5.04	396
34	12.077 907	1808.637 886	.000 552 9023	.082 796	149.747 624	.006 677 9023	8.02	1.724 584	5.07	408
35	12.996 158	1958.556 336	.000 510 5802	.076 946	150.702 723	.006 635 5802	7.97	1.786 944	5.11	420
36	13.984 220	2119.872 679	.000 471 7264	.071 509	151.590 339	.006 596 7264	7.92	1.849 786	5.14	432
37	15.047 402	2293.453 466	.000 436 0237	.066 457	152.415 240	.006 561 0237	7.88	1.913 095	5.17	444
38	16.191 416	2480.231 130	.000 403 1882	.061 761	153.181 858	.006 528 1882	7.84	1.976 854	5.20	456
39	17.422 405	2681.208 992	.000 372 9661	.057 397	153.894 309	.006 497 9661	7.80	2.041 048	5.23	468
40	18.746 983	2897.466 656	.000 345 1291	.053 342	154.556 422	.006 470 1291	7.77	2.105 662	5.26	480
41	20.172 266	3130.165 804	.000 319 4719	.049 573	155.171 753	.006 444 4719	7.74	2.170 680	5.29	492
42	21.705 908	3380.556 437	.000 295 8093	.046 070	155.743 607	.006 420 8093	7.71	2.236 088	5.32	504
43	23.356 149	3649.983 590	.000 273 9738	.042 815	156.275 057	.006 398 9738	7.68	2.301 870	5.35	516
44	25.131 854	3939.894 558	.000 253 8139	.039 790	156.768 957	.006 378 8139	7.66	2.368 014	5.38	528
45	27.042 561	4251.846 671	.000 235 1919	.036 979	157.227 960	.006 360 1919	7.64	2.434 504	5.41	540
46	29.098 533	4587.515 657	.000 217 9829	.034 366	157.654 532	.006 342 9829	7.62	2.501 327	5.44	552
47	31.310 816	4948.704 646	.000 202 0731	.031 938	158.050 964	.006 327 0731	7.60	2.568 469	5.46	564
48	33.691 292	5337.353 853	.000 187 3588	.029 681	158.419 386	.006 312 3588	7.58	2.635 919	5.49	576
49	36.252 750	5755.551 005	.000 173 7453	.027 584	158.761 777	.006 298 7453	7.56	2.703 662	5.52	588
50	39.008 948	6205.542 552	.000 161 1463	.025 635	159.079 977	.006 286 1463	7.55	2.771 688	5.54	600

Effective Rate is 7.60 %

Annual Percentage Rate is 7.35 %

MONTHLY COMPOUND INTEREST AND ANNUITY

	Amount Of 1	Amount Of 1 Per Period	Sinking Fund Payment	Present Worth Of 1	Present Worth of 1 Per Period	Periodic Payment To Amortize 1	Constant Annual Percent	Total Interest	Annual Add On Rate	
	What a single $ 1 deposit grows to in the future. The deposit is made at the beginning of the first period.	What a series of $ 1 deposits grow to in the future. A deposit is made at the end of each period.	The amount to be deposited at the end of each period that grows to $ 1 in the future.	What $ 1 to be paid in the future is worth today. Value today of a single $ 1 payment tomorrow.	What $ 1 to be paid at the end of each period is worth today. Value today of a series of $ 1 payments tomorrow.	The mortgage payment to amortize a loan of $ 1. An annuity certain, payable at the end of each period, worth $ 1 today.	The annual payment, including interest and principal, to amortize completely a loan of $ 100.	The total interest paid over the term on a loan of $1. The loan is amortized by regular periodic payments.	The average annual interest rate on a loan that is completely amortized by regular periodic payments.	
	$S = (1+i)^n$	$S\overline{n}| = \dfrac{(1+i)^n - 1}{i}$	$\dfrac{1}{S\overline{n}|} = \dfrac{i}{(1+i)^n - 1}$	$V^n = \dfrac{1}{(1+i)^n}$	$A\overline{n}| = \dfrac{1-V^n}{i}$	$\dfrac{1}{A\overline{n}|} = \dfrac{i}{1-V^n}$				PERIODS

YEAR										
	1.006 146	1.000 000	1.000 000 0000	.993 892	.993 892	1.006 145 8333	1207.38	.006 146	7.37	1
	1.012 329	2.006 146	.498 468 2486	.987 821	1.981 712	.504 614 0819	605.54	.009 228	5.54	2
	1.018 551	3.018 475	.331 293 0901	.981 787	2.963 499	.337 438 9234	404.93	.012 317	4.93	3
	1.024 811	4.037 026	.247 707 0798	.975 790	3.939 289	.253 852 9131	304.63	.015 412	4.62	4
	1.031 109	5.061 837	.197 556 7287	.969 829	4.909 118	.203 702 5620	244.45	.018 513	4.44	5
	1.037 446	6.092 946	.164 124 2072	.963 905	5.873 024	.170 270 0405	204.33	.021 620	4.32	6
	1.043 822	7.130 393	.140 244 7311	.958 018	6.831 041	.146 390 5645	175.67	.024 734	4.24	7
	1.050 237	8.174 215	.122 335 9084	.952 166	7.783 207	.128 481 7418	154.18	.027 854	4.18	8
	1.056 692	9.224 452	.108 407 5213	.946 350	8.729 557	.114 553 3546	137.47	.030 980	4.13	9
	1.063 186	10.281 144	.097 265 4390	.940 569	9.670 126	.103 411 2723	124.10	.034 113	4.09	10
	1.069 720	11.344 330	.088 149 7601	.934 824	10.604 949	.094 295 5935	113.16	.037 252	4.06	11
	1.076 295	12.414 051	.080 553 8838	.929 114	11.534 063	.086 699 7172	104.04	.040 397	4.04	12
1	1.076 295	12.414 051	.080 553 8838	.929 114	11.534 063	.086 699 7172	104.04	.040 397	4.04	12
2	1.158 410	25.775 228	.038 796 9417	.863 252	22.250 517	.044 942 7750	53.94	.078 627	3.93	24
3	1.246 791	40.155 791	.024 903 0083	.802 059	32.207 321	.031 048 8416	37.26	.117 758	3.93	36
4	1.341 914	55.633 515	.017 974 7764	.745 204	41.458 322	.024 120 6097	28.95	.157 789	3.94	48
5	1.444 295	72.292 108	.013 832 7686	.692 379	50.053 552	.019 978 6020	23.98	.198 716	3.97	60
6	1.554 487	90.221 662	.011 083 8126	.643 299	58.039 498	.017 229 6460	20.68	.240 535	4.01	72
7	1.673 086	109.519 146	.009 130 8235	.597 698	65.459 348	.015 276 6569	18.34	.283 239	4.05	84
8	1.800 734	130.288 926	.007 675 2494	.555 329	72.353 232	.013 821 0827	16.59	.326 824	4.09	96
9	1.938 120	152.643 330	.006 551 2198	.515 964	78.758 432	.012 697 0531	15.24	.371 282	4.13	108
10	2.085 989	176.703 255	.005 659 2053	.479 389	84.709 591	.011 805 0386	14.17	.416 605	4.17	120
11	2.245 139	202.598 826	.004 935 8628	.445 407	90.238 894	.011 081 6961	13.30	.462 784	4.21	132
12	2.416 431	230.470 090	.004 338 9578	.413 833	95.376 244	.010 484 7912	12.59	.509 810	4.25	144
13	2.600 792	260.467 784	.003 839 2464	.384 498	100.149 426	.009 985 0797	11.99	.557 672	4.29	156
14	2.799 218	292.754 143	.003 415 8355	.357 243	104.584 254	.009 561 6689	11.48	.606 360	4.33	168
15	3.012 784	327.503 779	.003 053 3999	.331 919	108.704 712	.009 199 2332	11.04	.655 862	4.37	180
16	3.242 643	364.904 628	.002 740 4421	.308 390	112.533 086	.008 886 2754	10.67	.706 165	4.41	192
17	3.490 039	405.158 963	.002 468 1670	.286 530	116.090 081	.008 614 0004	10.34	.757 256	4.45	204
18	3.756 311	448.484 490	.002 229 7315	.266 219	119.394 933	.008 375 5648	10.06	.809 122	4.50	216
19	4.042 897	495.115 525	.002 019 7306	.247 347	122.465 515	.008 165 5640	9.80	.861 749	4.54	228
20	4.351 349	545.304 259	.001 833 8386	.229 814	125.318 435	.007 979 6719	9.58	.915 121	4.58	240
21	4.683 334	599.322 128	.001 668 5518	.213 523	127.969 122	.007 814 3851	9.38	.969 225	4.62	252
22	5.040 647	657.461 272	.001 521 0021	.198 387	130.431 911	.007 666 8355	9.21	1.024 045	4.65	264
23	5.425 222	720.036 125	.001 388 8192	.184 324	132.720 121	.007 534 6525	9.05	1.079 564	4.69	276
24	5.839 138	787.385 106	.001 270 0266	.171 258	134.846 129	.007 415 8599	8.90	1.135 768	4.73	288
25	6.284 633	859.872 457	.001 162 9632	.159 118	136.821 431	.007 308 7965	8.78	1.192 639	4.77	300
26	6.764 117	937.890 208	.001 066 2229	.147 839	138.656 712	.007 212 0562	8.66	1.250 162	4.81	312
27	7.280 183	1021.860 298	.000 978 6074	.137 359	140.361 896	.007 124 4407	8.55	1.308 319	4.85	324
28	7.835 622	1112.236 860	.000 899 0891	.127 622	141.946 205	.007 044 9224	8.46	1.367 094	4.88	336
29	8.433 439	1209.508 673	.000 826 7820	.118 576	143.418 209	.006 972 6153	8.37	1.426 470	4.92	348
30	9.076 865	1314.201 810	.000 760 9181	.110 170	144.785 867	.006 906 7515	8.29	1.486 431	4.95	360
31	9.769 382	1426.882 476	.000 700 8286	.102 361	146.056 577	.006 846 6619	8.22	1.546 958	4.99	372
32	10.514 734	1548.160 078	.000 645 9280	.095 105	147.237 211	.006 791 7614	8.16	1.608 036	5.03	384
33	11.316 952	1678.690 517	.000 595 7024	.088 363	148.334 154	.006 741 5358	8.09	1.669 648	5.06	396
34	12.180 375	1819.179 735	.000 549 6983	.082 099	149.353 338	.006 695 5316	8.04	1.731 777	5.09	408
35	13.109 673	1970.387 533	.000 507 5144	.076 280	150.300 276	.006 653 3477	7.99	1.794 406	5.13	420
36	14.109 872	2133.131 684	.000 468 7943	.070 872	151.180 090	.006 614 6276	7.94	1.857 519	5.16	432
37	15.186 380	2308.292 348	.000 433 2207	.065 845	151.997 536	.006 579 0540	7.90	1.921 100	5.19	444
38	16.345 020	2496.816 840	.000 400 5100	.061 181	152.757 036	.006 546 3433	7.86	1.985 133	5.22	456
39	17.592 058	2699.724 750	.000 370 4081	.056 844	153.462 699	.006 516 2415	7.82	2.049 601	5.26	468
40	18.934 239	2918.113 455	.000 342 6872	.052 814	154.118 339	.006 488 5205	7.79	2.114 490	5.29	480
41	20.378 821	3153.164 057	.000 317 1418	.049 071	154.727 503	.006 462 9751	7.76	2.179 784	5.32	492
42	21.933 617	3406.147 772	.000 293 5868	.045 592	155.293 486	.006 439 4201	7.73	2.245 468	5.35	504
43	23.607 035	3678.432 800	.000 271 8549	.042 360	155.819 348	.006 417 6882	7.71	2.311 527	5.38	516
44	25.408 126	3971.491 729	.000 251 7946	.039 357	156.307 934	.006 397 6279	7.68	2.377 948	5.40	528
45	27.346 631	4286.909 497	.000 233 2683	.036 568	156.761 886	.006 379 1016	7.66	2.444 715	5.43	540
46	29.433 034	4626.391 965	.000 216 1512	.033 975	157.183 659	.006 361 9845	7.64	2.511 815	5.46	552
47	31.678 045	4991.775 141	.000 200 3295	.031 567	157.575 534	.006 346 1629	7.62	2.579 236	5.49	564
48	34.095 528	5385.035 112	.000 185 6998	.029 329	157.939 630	.006 331 5331	7.60	2.646 963	5.51	576
49	36.696 836	5808.298 730	.000 172 1675	.027 250	158.277 916	.006 318 0008	7.59	2.714 984	5.54	588
50	39.496 610	6263.855 113	.000 159 6461	.025 319	158.592 223	.006 305 4794	7.57	2.783 288	5.57	600

Effective Rate is 7.63 %

Annual Percentage Rate is 7.375%

MONTHLY COMPOUND INTEREST AND ANNUITY

7.40 % M

	Amount Of 1	Amount Of 1 Per Period	Sinking Fund Payment	Present Worth Of 1	Present Worth of 1 Per Period	Periodic Payment To Amortize 1	Constant Annual Percent	Total Interest	Annual Add On Rate	
	What a single $ 1 deposit grows to in the future. The deposit is made at the beginning of the first period.	What a series of $ 1 deposits grow to in the future. A deposit is made at the end of each period.	The amount to be deposited at the end of each period that grows to $ 1 in the future.	What $ 1 to be paid in the future is worth today. Value today of a single $ 1 payment tomorrow.	What $ 1 to be paid at the end of each period is worth today. Value today of a series of $ 1 payments tomorrow.	The mortgage payment to amortize a loan of $ 1. An annuity certain, payable at the end of each period, worth $ 1 today.	The annual payment, including interest and principal, to amortize completely a loan of $ 100.	The total interest paid over the term on a loan of $1. The loan is amortized by regular periodic payments.	The average annual interest rate on a loan that is completely amortized by regular periodic payments.	
	$S = (1+i)^n$	$S\overline{n}\| = \dfrac{(1+i)^n - 1}{i}$	$\dfrac{1}{S\overline{n}\|} = \dfrac{i}{(1+i)^n - 1}$	$V^n = \dfrac{1}{(1+i)^n}$	$A\overline{n}\| = \dfrac{1 - V^n}{i}$	$\dfrac{1}{A\overline{n}\|} = \dfrac{i}{1 - V^n}$				

YEAR

PERIODS

Amount Of 1	Amount Of 1 Per Period	Sinking Fund Payment	Present Worth Of 1	Present Worth of 1 Per Period	Periodic Payment To Amortize 1	Constant Annual Percent	Total Interest	Annual Add On Rate	PERIODS
1.006 167	1.000 000	1.000 000 0000	.993 871	.993 871	1.006 166 6667	1207.40	.006 167	7.40	1
1.012 371	2.006 167	.498 463 0722	.987 780	1.981 651	.504 629 7389	605.56	.009 259	5.56	2
1.018 614	3.018 538	.331 286 2024	.981 726	2.963 377	.337 452 8691	404.95	.012 359	4.94	3
1.024 896	4.037 152	.247 699 3471	.975 709	3.939 086	.253 866 0137	304.64	.015 464	4.64	4
1.031 216	5.062 048	.197 548 4975	.969 729	4.908 815	.203 715 1642	244.46	.018 576	4.46	5
1.037 575	6.093 264	.164 115 6508	.963 786	5.872 600	.170 282 3174	204.34	.021 694	4.34	6
1.043 974	7.130 839	.140 235 9485	.957 879	6.830 479	.146 402 6151	175.69	.024 818	4.25	7
1.050 411	8.174 813	.122 326 9614	.952 008	7.782 487	.128 493 6281	154.20	.027 949	4.19	8
1.056 889	9.225 224	.108 398 4511	.946 173	8.728 660	.114 565 1178	137.48	.031 086	4.14	9
1.063 406	10.282 113	.097 256 2746	.940 374	9.669 035	.103 422 9413	124.11	.034 229	4.11	10
1.069 964	11.345 519	.088 140 5225	.934 611	10.603 645	.094 307 1892	113.17	.037 379	4.08	11
1.076 562	12.415 483	.080 544 5887	.928 883	11.532 528	.086 711 2554	104.06	.040 535	4.05	12

Year	Amount Of 1	Amount Of 1 Per Period	Sinking Fund Payment	Present Worth Of 1	Present Worth of 1 Per Period	Periodic Payment To Amortize 1	Constant Annual Percent	Total Interest	Annual Add On Rate	PERIODS
1	1.076 562	12.415 483	.080 544 5887	.928 883	11.532 528	.086 711 2554	104.06	.040 535	4.05	12
2	1.158 986	25.781 523	.038 787 4684	.862 823	22.244 895	.044 954 1351	53.95	.078 899	3.94	24
3	1.247 721	40.170 895	.024 893 6451	.801 462	32.195 427	.031 060 3118	37.28	.118 171	3.94	36
4	1.343 249	55.661 948	.017 965 5947	.744 464	41.438 305	.024 132 2614	28.96	.158 349	3.96	48
5	1.446 091	72.339 030	.013 823 7961	.691 520	50.023 854	.019 990 4628	23.99	.199 428	3.99	60
6	1.556 806	90.292 945	.011 075 0625	.642 341	57.998 823	.017 241 7291	20.70	.241 404	4.02	72
7	1.675 999	109.621 450	.009 122 3023	.596 659	65.406 634	.015 288 9689	18.35	.284 273	4.06	84
8	1.804 317	130.429 787	.007 666 9603	.554 226	72.287 622	.013 833 6270	16.61	.328 028	4.10	96
9	1.942 459	152.831 254	.006 543 1642	.514 811	78.679 253	.012 709 8309	15.26	.372 662	4.14	108
10	2.091 178	176.947 827	.005 651 3833	.478 199	84.616 328	.011 818 0500	14.19	.418 166	4.18	120
11	2.251 283	202.910 816	.004 928 2735	.444 191	90.131 175	.011 094 9402	13.32	.464 532	4.22	132
12	2.423 646	230.861 587	.004 331 5998	.412 601	95.253 822	.010 498 2665	12.60	.511 750	4.26	144
13	2.609 206	260.952 329	.003 832 1176	.383 258	100.012 159	.009 998 7842	12.00	.559 810	4.31	156
14	2.808 972	293.346 883	.003 408 9334	.356 002	104.432 097	.009 575 6001	11.50	.608 701	4.35	168
15	3.024 033	328.221 634	.003 046 7218	.330 684	108.537 701	.009 213 3884	11.06	.658 410	4.39	180
16	3.255 560	365.766 470	.002 733 9849	.307 167	112.351 326	.008 900 6516	10.69	.708 925	4.43	192
17	3.504 813	406.185 820	.002 461 9274	.285 322	115.893 736	.008 628 5941	10.36	.760 233	4.47	204
18	3.773 149	449.699 762	.002 223 7059	.265 031	119.184 219	.008 390 3725	10.07	.812 320	4.51	216
19	4.062 029	496.545 224	.002 013 9153	.246 182	122.240 693	.008 180 5819	9.82	.865 173	4.55	228
20	4.373 027	546.977 276	.001 828 2295	.228 675	125.079 798	.007 994 8962	9.60	.918 775	4.59	240
21	4.707 835	601.270 514	.001 663 1449	.212 412	127.716 994	.007 829 8116	9.40	.973 113	4.63	252
22	5.068 277	659.720 559	.001 515 7933	.197 306	130.166 640	.007 682 4600	9.22	1.028 169	4.67	264
23	5.456 315	722.645 665	.001 383 8041	.183 274	132.442 074	.007 550 4707	9.07	1.083 930	4.71	276
24	5.874 062	790.388 453	.001 265 2007	.170 240	134.555 685	.007 431 8673	8.92	1.140 378	4.75	288
25	6.323 793	863.317 773	.001 158 3220	.158 133	136.518 982	.007 324 9887	8.79	1.197 497	4.79	300
26	6.807 956	941.830 719	.001 061 7619	.146 887	138.342 655	.007 228 4286	8.68	1.255 270	4.83	312
27	7.329 188	1026.354 784	.000 974 3220	.136 441	140.036 633	.007 140 9886	8.57	1.313 680	4.87	324
28	7.890 326	1117.350 194	.000 894 9746	.126 737	141.610 140	.007 061 6412	8.48	1.372 711	4.90	336
29	8.494 427	1215.312 407	.000 822 8337	.117 724	143.071 743	.006 989 5004	8.39	1.432 346	4.94	348
30	9.144 778	1320.774 818	.000 757 1313	.109 352	144.429 401	.006 923 7980	8.31	1.492 567	4.98	360
31	9.844 922	1434.311 658	.000 697 1985	.101 575	145.690 507	.006 863 8652	8.24	1.553 358	5.01	372
32	10.598 670	1556.541 122	.000 642 4501	.094 351	146.861 926	.006 809 1168	8.18	1.614 701	5.05	384
33	11.410 127	1688.128 736	.000 592 3719	.087 641	147.950 036	.006 759 0386	8.12	1.676 579	5.08	396
34	12.283 711	1829.790 980	.000 546 5105	.081 409	148.960 764	.006 713 1772	8.06	1.738 976	5.11	408
35	13.224 178	1982.299 190	.000 504 4647	.075 619	149.899 611	.006 671 1314	8.01	1.801 875	5.15	420
36	14.236 650	2146.483 756	.000 465 8782	.070 241	150.771 690	.006 632 5449	7.96	1.865 259	5.18	432
37	15.326 638	2323.428 644	.000 430 4336	.065 246	151.581 749	.006 597 1003	7.92	1.929 113	5.21	444
38	16.500 079	2513.526 267	.000 397 8474	.060 606	152.334 199	.006 564 5141	7.88	1.993 418	5.25	456
39	17.763 360	2718.382 719	.000 367 8658	.056 296	153.033 137	.006 534 5325	7.85	2.058 161	5.28	468
40	19.123 361	2938.923 420	.000 340 2607	.052 292	153.682 368	.006 506 9273	7.81	2.123 325	5.31	480
41	20.587 487	3176.349 191	.000 314 8268	.048 573	154.285 428	.006 481 4935	7.78	2.188 895	5.34	492
42	22.163 709	3431.952 789	.000 291 3793	.045 119	154.845 600	.006 458 0460	7.75	2.254 855	5.37	504
43	23.860 610	3707.125 947	.000 269 7507	.041 910	155.365 933	.006 436 4174	7.73	2.321 191	5.40	516
44	25.687 430	4003.366 953	.000 249 7897	.038 930	155.849 263	.006 416 4564	7.70	2.387 889	5.43	528
45	27.654 114	4322.288 807	.000 231 3589	.036 161	156.298 219	.006 398 0256	7.68	2.454 934	5.46	540
46	29.771 373	4665.628 003	.000 214 3334	.033 589	156.715 246	.006 381 0001	7.66	2.522 312	5.48	552
47	32.050 733	5035.253 984	.000 198 5997	.031 201	157.102 616	.006 365 2664	7.64	2.590 010	5.51	564
48	34.504 606	5433.179 325	.000 184 0543	.028 982	157.462 437	.006 350 7210	7.63	2.658 015	5.54	576
49	37.146 353	5861.570 684	.000 170 6027	.026 921	157.796 669	.006 337 2694	7.61	2.726 314	5.56	588
50	39.990 357	6322.760 606	.000 158 1588	.025 006	158.107 131	.006 324 8254	7.59	2.794 895	5.59	600

Effective Rate is 7.66 %

Annual Percentage Rate is 7.40 %

MONTHLY COMPOUND INTEREST AND ANNUITY

7.45 % M

Amount Of 1	Amount Of 1 Per Period	Sinking Fund Payment	Present Worth Of 1	Present Worth of 1 Per Period	Periodic Payment To Amortize 1	Constant Annual Percent	Total Interest	Annual Add On Rate	
What a single $ 1 deposit grows to in the future. The deposit is made at the beginning of the first period.	What a series of $ 1 deposits grow to in the future. A deposit is made at the end of each period.	The amount to be deposited at the end of each period that grows to $ 1 in the future.	What $ 1 to be paid in the future is worth today. Value today of a single $ 1 payment tomorrow.	What $ 1 to be paid at the end of each period is worth today. Value today of a series of $ 1 payments tomorrow.	The mortgage payment to amortize a loan of $ 1. An annuity certain, payable at the end of each period, worth $ 1 today.	The annual payment, including interest and principal, to amortize completely a loan of $ 100.	The total interest paid over the term on a loan of $1. The loan is amortized by regular periodic payments.	The average annual interest rate on a loan that is completely amortized by regular periodic payments.	

$$S = (1+i)^n \qquad S\overline{n}| = \frac{(1+i)^n - 1}{i} \qquad \frac{1}{S\overline{n}|} = \frac{i}{(1+i)^n - 1} \qquad V^n = \frac{1}{(1+i)^n} \qquad A\overline{n}| = \frac{1-V^n}{i} \qquad \frac{1}{A\overline{n}|} = \frac{i}{1-V^n}$$

PERIODS

YEAR

Amount Of 1	Amount Of 1 Per Period	Sinking Fund Payment	Present Worth Of 1	Present Worth of 1 Per Period	Periodic Payment To Amortize 1	Constant Annual Percent	Total Interest	Annual Add On Rate	Periods
1.006 208	1.000 000	1.000 000 0000	.993 830	.993 830	1.006 208 3333	1207.45	.006 208	7.45	1
1.012 455	2.006 208	.498 452 7197	.987 698	1.981 528	.504 661 0530	605.60	.009 322	5.59	2
1.018 741	3.018 664	.331 272 4276	.981 604	2.963 132	.337 480 7609	404.98	.012 442	4.98	3
1.025 066	4.037 404	.247 683 8824	.975 547	3.938 679	.253 892 2158	304.68	.015 569	4.67	4
1.031 430	5.062 470	.197 532 0361	.969 528	4.908 207	.203 740 3694	244.49	.018 702	4.49	5
1.037 833	6.093 899	.164 098 5391	.963 546	5.871 754	.170 306 8725	204.37	.021 841	4.37	6
1.044 276	7.131 732	.140 218 3846	.957 601	6.829 355	.146 426 7179	175.72	.024 987	4.28	7
1.050 759	8.176 009	.122 309 0690	.951 693	7.781 047	.128 517 4024	154.23	.028 139	4.22	8
1.057 283	9.226 768	.108 380 3128	.945 821	8.726 868	.114 588 6461	137.51	.031 298	4.17	9
1.063 847	10.284 051	.097 237 9480	.939 985	9.666 853	.103 446 2813	124.14	.034 463	4.14	10
1.070 452	11.347 898	.088 122 0496	.934 185	10.601 038	.094 330 3830	113.20	.037 634	4.11	11
1.077 097	12.418 349	.080 526 0011	.928 421	11.529 460	.086 734 3344	104.09	.040 812	4.08	12

YEAR	Amount Of 1	Amount Of 1 Per Period	Sinking Fund Payment	Present Worth Of 1	Present Worth of 1 Per Period	Periodic Payment To Amortize 1	Constant Annual Percent	Total Interest	Annual Add On Rate	Periods
1	1.077 097	12.418 349	.080 526 0011	.928 421	11.529 460	.086 734 3344	104.09	.040 812	4.08	12
2	1.160 138	25.794 119	.038 768 5271	.861 966	22.233 655	.044 976 8604	53.98	.079 445	3.97	24
3	1.249 582	40.201 124	.024 874 9265	.800 268	32.171 658	.031 083 2598	37.30	.118 997	3.97	36
4	1.345 921	55.718 869	.017 947 2415	.742 985	41.398 311	.024 155 5748	28.99	.159 468	3.99	48
5	1.449 688	72.432 990	.013 805 8639	.689 804	49.964 532	.020 014 1972	24.02	.200 852	4.02	60
6	1.561 455	90.435 724	.011 057 5773	.640 428	57.917 594	.017 265 9106	20.72	.243 146	4.05	72
7	1.681 839	109.826 418	.009 105 2773	.594 587	65.301 386	.015 313 6107	18.38	.286 343	4.09	84
8	1.811 504	130.712 083	.007 650 4022	.552 027	72.156 655	.013 858 7355	16.64	.330 439	4.13	96
9	1.951 166	153.207 974	.006 527 0754	.512 514	78.521 233	.012 735 4087	15.29	.375 424	4.17	108
10	2.101 596	177.438 237	.005 635 7638	.475 829	84.430 243	.011 844 0972	14.22	.421 292	4.21	120
11	2.263 623	203.536 586	.004 913 1216	.441 770	89.916 293	.011 121 4549	13.35	.468 032	4.25	132
12	2.438 142	231.647 047	.004 316 9124	.410 148	95.009 659	.010 525 2457	12.64	.515 635	4.30	144
13	2.626 116	261.924 747	.003 817 8905	.380 790	99.738 448	.010 026 2238	12.04	.564 091	4.34	156
14	2.828 582	294.536 774	.003 395 1618	.353 534	104.128 756	.009 603 4951	11.53	.613 387	4.38	168
15	3.046 658	329.663 099	.003 033 3999	.328 228	108.204 812	.009 241 7332	11.10	.663 512	4.42	180
16	3.281 547	367.497 566	.002 721 1065	.304 734	111.989 108	.008 929 4398	10.72	.714 452	4.47	192
17	3.534 546	408.248 968	.002 449 4857	.282 922	115.502 530	.008 657 8190	10.39	.766 195	4.51	204
18	3.807 049	452.142 190	.002 211 6936	.262 671	118.764 465	.008 420 0270	10.11	.818 726	4.55	216
19	4.100 562	499.419 459	.002 002 3249	.243 869	121.792 916	.008 210 6582	9.86	.872 030	4.59	228
20	4.416 705	550.341 676	.001 817 0530	.226 413	124.604 593	.008 025 3863	9.64	.926 093	4.63	240
21	4.757 220	605.189 856	.001 652 3740	.210 207	127.215 014	.007 860 7074	9.44	.980 898	4.67	252
22	5.123 989	664.266 679	.001 505 4195	.195 160	129.638 585	.007 713 7528	9.26	1.036 431	4.71	264
23	5.519 034	727.898 163	.001 373 8186	.181 191	131.888 680	.007 582 1519	9.10	1.092 674	4.75	276
24	5.944 537	796.435 460	.001 255 5945	.168 222	133.977 715	.007 463 9279	8.96	1.149 611	4.79	288
25	6.402 844	870.256 794	.001 149 0861	.156 181	135.917 220	.007 357 4195	8.83	1.207 226	4.83	300
26	6.896 486	949.769 550	.001 052 8870	.145 001	137.717 898	.007 261 2203	8.72	1.265 501	4.87	312
27	7.428 186	1035.412 521	.000 965 7986	.134 622	139.389 686	.007 174 1320	8.61	1.324 419	4.91	324
28	8.000 879	1127.658 329	.000 886 7934	.124 986	140.941 809	.007 095 1268	8.52	1.383 963	4.94	336
29	8.617 725	1227.016 036	.000 814 9853	.116 040	142.382 833	.007 023 3186	8.43	1.444 115	4.98	348
30	9.282 127	1334.033 948	.000 749 6061	.107 734	143.720 710	.006 957 9394	8.35	1.504 858	5.02	360
31	9.997 754	1449.302 648	.000 689 9870	.100 022	144.962 824	.006 898 3203	8.28	1.566 175	5.05	372
32	10.768 553	1573.458 247	.000 635 5428	.092 863	146.116 029	.006 843 8761	8.22	1.628 048	5.09	384
33	11.598 779	1707.185 902	.000 585 7593	.086 216	147.186 689	.006 794 0926	8.16	1.690 461	5.12	396
34	12.493 013	1851.223 592	.000 540 1833	.080 045	148.180 713	.006 748 5166	8.10	1.753 395	5.16	408
35	13.456 190	2006.366 191	.000 498 4135	.074 315	149.103 585	.006 706 7468	8.05	1.816 834	5.19	420
36	14.493 625	2173.469 858	.000 460 0938	.068 996	149.960 400	.006 668 4271	8.01	1.880 761	5.22	432
37	15.611 044	2353.456 759	.000 424 9069	.064 057	150.755 885	.006 633 2402	7.96	1.945 159	5.26	444
38	16.814 613	2547.320 155	.000 392 5694	.059 472	151.494 430	.006 600 9028	7.93	2.010 012	5.29	456
39	18.110 973	2756.129 886	.000 362 8276	.055 215	152.180 111	.006 571 1609	7.89	2.075 303	5.32	468
40	19.507 279	2981.038 274	.000 335 4536	.051 263	152.816 712	.006 543 7869	7.86	2.141 018	5.35	480
41	21.011 237	3223.286 479	.000 310 2424	.047 594	153.407 745	.006 518 5757	7.83	2.207 139	5.38	492
42	22.631 145	3484.211 356	.000 287 0090	.044 187	153.956 474	.006 495 3423	7.80	2.273 653	5.41	504
43	24.375 945	3765.252 823	.000 265 5864	.041 024	154.465 925	.006 473 9197	7.77	2.340 543	5.44	516
44	26.255 263	4067.961 815	.000 245 8233	.038 088	154.938 910	.006 454 1567	7.75	2.407 795	5.47	528
45	28.279 472	4394.008 838	.000 227 5826	.035 361	155.378 030	.006 435 9159	7.73	2.475 395	5.50	540
46	30.459 741	4745.193 190	.000 210 7396	.032 830	155.785 736	.006 419 0729	7.71	2.543 328	5.53	552
47	32.808 103	5123.452 890	.000 195 1809	.030 480	156.164 251	.006 403 5142	7.69	2.611 582	5.56	564
48	35.337 518	5530.875 374	.000 180 8032	.028 299	156.515 672	.006 389 1365	7.67	2.680 143	5.58	576
49	38.061 943	5969.709 011	.000 167 5124	.026 273	156.841 939	.006 375 8457	7.66	2.748 997	5.61	588
50	40.996 415	6442.375 515	.000 155 2222	.024 392	157.144 852	.006 363 5556	7.64	2.818 133	5.64	600

Effective Rate is 7.71 %

Annual Percentage Rate is 7.45 %

MONTHLY COMPOUND INTEREST AND ANNUITY

7.50 % M

Amount Of 1	Amount Of 1 Per Period	Sinking Fund Payment	Present Worth Of 1	Present Worth of 1 Per Period	Periodic Payment To Amortize 1	Constant Annual Percent	Total Interest	Annual Add On Rate
What a single $ 1 deposit grows to in the future. The deposit is made at the beginning of the first period.	What a series of $ 1 deposits grow to in the future. A deposit is made at the end of each period.	The amount to be deposited at the end of each period that grows to $ 1 in the future.	What $ 1 to be paid in the future is worth today. Value today of a single $ 1 payment tomorrow.	What $ 1 to be paid at the end of each period is worth today. Value today of a series of $ 1 payments tomorrow.	The mortgage payment to amortize a loan of $ 1. An annuity certain, payable at the end of each period, worth $ 1 today.	The annual payment, including interest and principal, to amortize completely a loan of $ 100.	The total interest paid over the term of a loan of $ 1. The loan is amortized by regular periodic payments.	The average annual interest rate on a loan that is completely amortized by regular periodic payments.
$S = (1+i)^n$	$S\overline{n}| = \dfrac{(1+i)^n - 1}{i}$	$\dfrac{1}{S\overline{n}|} = \dfrac{i}{(1+i)^n - 1}$	$V^n = \dfrac{1}{(1+i)^n}$	$A\overline{n}| = \dfrac{1-V^n}{i}$	$\dfrac{1}{A\overline{n}|} = \dfrac{i}{1-V^n}$			

YEAR									PERIODS
	1.006 250	1.000 000	1.000 000 0000	.993 789	.993 789	1.006 250 0000	1207.50	.006 250	7.50	1
	1.012 539	2.006 250	.498 442 3676	.987 616	1.981 405	.504 692 3676	605.64	.009 385	5.63	2
	1.018 867	3.018 789	.331 258 6535	.981 482	2.962 887	.337 508 6535	405.02	.012 526	5.01	3
	1.025 235	4.037 656	.247 668 4189	.975 386	3.938 273	.253 918 4189	304.71	.015 674	4.70	4
	1.031 643	5.062 892	.197 515 5761	.969 327	4.907 600	.203 765 5761	244.52	.018 828	4.52	5
	1.038 091	6.094 535	.164 081 4292	.963 307	5.870 907	.170 331 4292	204.40	.021 989	4.40	6
	1.044 579	7.132 626	.140 200 8227	.957 324	6.828 231	.146 450 8227	175.75	.025 156	4.31	7
	1.051 108	8.177 205	.122 291 1789	.951 377	7.779 608	.128 541 1789	154.25	.028 329	4.25	8
	1.057 677	9.228 312	.108 362 1769	.945 468	8.725 076	.114 612 1769	137.54	.031 510	4.20	9
	1.064 287	10.285 989	.097 219 6242	.939 596	9.664 672	.103 469 6242	124.17	.034 696	4.16	10
	1.070 939	11.350 277	.088 103 5799	.933 760	10.598 432	.094 353 5799	113.23	.037 889	4.13	11
	1.077 633	12.421 216	.080 507 4169	.927 960	11.526 392	.086 757 4169	104.11	.041 089	4.11	12
1	1.077 633	12.421 216	.080 507 4169	.927 960	11.526 392	.086 757 4169	104.11	.041 089	4.11	12
2	1.161 292	25.806 723	.038 749 5927	.861 110	22.222 423	.044 999 5927	54.00	.079 990	4.00	24
3	1.251 446	40.231 382	.024 856 2182	.799 076	32.147 913	.031 106 2182	37.33	.119 824	3.99	36
4	1.348 599	55.775 864	.017 928 9019	.741 510	41.358 371	.024 178 9019	29.02	.160 587	4.01	48
5	1.453 294	72.527 105	.013 787 9486	.688 092	49.905 308	.020 037 9486	24.05	.202 277	4.05	60
6	1.566 117	90.578 789	.011 040 1123	.638 522	57.836 524	.017 290 1123	20.75	.244 888	4.08	72
7	1.687 699	110.031 871	.009 088 2759	.592 523	65.196 376	.015 338 2759	18.41	.288 415	4.12	84
8	1.818 720	130.995 147	.007 633 8706	.549 837	72.026 024	.013 883 8706	16.67	.332 852	4.16	96
9	1.959 912	153.585 857	.006 511 0162	.510 227	78.363 665	.012 761 0162	15.32	.378 190	4.20	108
10	2.112 065	177.930 342	.005 620 1769	.473 470	84.244 743	.011 870 1769	14.25	.424 421	4.24	120
11	2.276 030	204.164 753	.004 898 0051	.439 362	89.702 148	.011 148 0051	13.38	.471 537	4.29	132
12	2.452 724	232.435 809	.004 302 2631	.407 710	94.766 401	.010 552 2631	12.67	.519 526	4.33	144
13	2.643 135	262.901 620	.003 803 7042	.378 339	99.465 827	.010 053 7042	12.07	.568 378	4.37	156
14	2.848 329	295.732 572	.003 381 4334	.351 083	103.826 706	.009 631 4334	11.56	.618 081	4.41	168
15	3.069 452	331.112 276	.003 020 1236	.325 791	107.873 427	.009 270 1236	11.13	.668 622	4.46	180
16	3.307 741	369.238 599	.002 708 2759	.302 321	111.628 623	.008 958 2759	10.75	.719 989	4.50	192
17	3.564 530	410.324 767	.002 437 0939	.280 542	115.113 294	.008 687 0939	10.43	.772 167	4.54	204
18	3.841 254	454.600 560	.002 199 7333	.260 332	118.346 930	.008 449 7333	10.14	.825 142	4.58	216
19	4.139 460	502.313 599	.001 990 7882	.241 577	121.347 615	.008 240 7882	9.89	.878 900	4.63	228
20	4.460 817	553.730 725	.001 805 9319	.224 174	124.132 131	.008 055 9319	9.67	.933 424	4.67	240
21	4.807 122	609.139 496	.001 641 6601	.208 025	126.716 051	.007 891 6601	9.47	.988 698	4.71	252
22	5.180 311	668.849 794	.001 495 1040	.193 039	129.113 825	.007 745 1040	9.30	1.044 707	4.75	264
23	5.582 472	733.195 558	.001 363 8926	.179 132	131.338 863	.007 613 8926	9.14	1.101 434	4.79	276
24	6.015 854	802.536 650	.001 246 0490	.166 227	133.403 610	.007 496 0490	9.00	1.158 862	4.83	288
25	6.482 880	877.260 872	.001 139 9118	.154 252	135.319 613	.007 389 9118	8.87	1.216 974	4.87	300
26	6.986 163	957.786 129	.001 044 0744	.143 140	137.097 587	.007 294 0744	8.76	1.275 751	4.91	312
27	7.528 517	1044.562 771	.000 957 3384	.132 828	138.747 475	.007 207 3384	8.65	1.335 178	4.95	324
28	8.112 976	1138.076 109	.000 878 6759	.123 259	140.278 506	.007 128 6759	8.56	1.395 235	4.98	336
29	8.742 807	1238.849 131	.000 807 2008	.114 380	141.699 242	.007 057 2008	8.47	1.455 906	5.02	348
30	9.421 534	1347.445 425	.000 742 1451	.106 140	143.017 627	.006 992 1451	8.40	1.517 172	5.06	360
31	10.152 952	1464.472 331	.000 682 8398	.098 494	144.241 037	.006 932 8398	8.32	1.579 016	5.09	372
32	10.941 152	1590.584 340	.000 628 6998	.091 398	145.376 312	.006 878 6998	8.26	1.641 421	5.13	384
33	11.790 542	1726.486 751	.000 579 2109	.084 814	146.429 801	.006 829 2109	8.20	1.704 368	5.16	396
34	12.705 873	1872.939 621	.000 533 9200	.078 704	147.407 398	.006 783 9200	8.15	1.767 839	5.20	408
35	13.692 263	2030.762 007	.000 492 4260	.073 034	148.314 568	.006 742 4260	8.10	1.831 819	5.23	420
36	14.755 228	2200.836 555	.000 454 3727	.067 773	149.156 386	.006 704 3727	8.05	1.896 289	5.27	432
37	15.900 715	2384.114 432	.000 419 4430	.062 890	149.937 560	.006 669 4430	8.01	1.961 233	5.30	444
38	17.135 129	2581.620 647	.000 387 3536	.058 360	150.662 457	.006 637 3536	7.97	2.026 633	5.33	456
39	18.465 374	2794.459 783	.000 357 8509	.054 155	151.335 133	.006 607 8509	7.93	2.092 474	5.37	468
40	19.898 889	3023.822 174	.000 330 7073	.050 254	151.959 350	.006 580 7073	7.90	2.158 739	5.40	480
41	21.443 691	3270.990 564	.000 305 7178	.046 634	152.538 598	.006 555 7178	7.87	2.225 413	5.43	492
42	23.108 420	3537.347 278	.000 282 6977	.043 274	153.076 117	.006 532 6977	7.84	2.292 480	5.46	504
43	24.902 387	3824.381 956	.000 261 4802	.040 157	153.574 913	.006 511 4802	7.82	2.359 924	5.49	516
44	26.835 624	4133.699 882	.000 241 9140	.037 264	154.037 776	.006 491 9140	7.80	2.427 731	5.52	528
45	28.918 944	4467.030 962	.000 223 8623	.034 579	154.467 294	.006 473 8623	7.77	2.495 886	5.55	540
46	31.163 996	4826.239 401	.000 207 2007	.032 088	154.865 870	.006 457 2007	7.75	2.564 375	5.57	552
47	33.583 338	5213.334 124	.000 191 8158	.029 777	155.235 733	.006 441 8158	7.74	2.633 184	5.60	564
48	36.190 500	5630.480 017	.000 177 6048	.027 632	155.578 950	.006 427 6048	7.72	2.702 300	5.63	576
49	39.000 063	6080.010 029	.000 164 4734	.025 641	155.897 442	.006 414 4734	7.70	2.771 710	5.66	588
50	42.027 739	6564.438 225	.000 152 3360	.023 794	156.192 991	.006 402 3360	7.69	2.841 402	5.68	600

Effective Rate is 7.76 %

Annual Percentage Rate is 7.50 %

MONTHLY COMPOUND INTEREST AND ANNUITY

7.55 % M

Amount Of 1	Amount Of 1 Per Period	Sinking Fund Payment	Present Worth Of 1	Present Worth of 1 Per Period	Periodic Payment To Amortize 1	Constant Annual Percent	Total Interest	Annual Add On Rate
What a single $ 1 deposit grows to in the future. The deposit is made at the beginning of the first period.	What a series of $ 1 deposits grow to in the future. A deposit is made at the end of each period.	The amount to be deposited at the end of each period that grows to $ 1 in the future.	What $ 1 to be paid in the future is worth today. Value today of a single $ 1 payment tomorrow.	What $ 1 to be paid at the end of each period is worth today. Value today of a series of $ 1 payments tomorrow.	The mortgage payment to amortize a loan of $ 1. An annuity certain, payable at the end of each period, worth $ 1 today.	The annual payment, including interest and principal, to amortize completely a loan of $ 100.	The total interest paid over the term on a loan of $1. The loan is amortized by regular periodic payments.	The average annual interest rate on a loan that is completely amortized by regular periodic payments.

$$S = (1+i)^n \qquad S\overline{n|} = \frac{(1+i)^n - 1}{i} \qquad \frac{1}{S\overline{n|}} = \frac{i}{(1+i)^n - 1} \qquad V^n = \frac{1}{(1+i)^n} \qquad A\overline{n|} = \frac{1 - V^n}{i} \qquad \frac{1}{A\overline{n|}} = \frac{i}{1 - V^n}$$

PERIODS

YEAR	Amount Of 1	Amount Of 1 Per Period	Sinking Fund Payment	Present Worth Of 1	Present Worth of 1 Per Period	Periodic Payment To Amortize 1	Constant Annual Percent	Total Interest	Annual Add On Rate	PERIODS
	1.006 292	1.000 000	1.000 000 0000	.993 748	.993 748	1.006 291 6667	1207.55	.006 292	7.55	1
	1.012 623	2.006 292	.498 432 0159	.987 534	1.981 282	.504 723 6826	605.67	.009 447	5.67	2
	1.018 994	3.018 915	.331 244 8802	.981 360	2.962 642	.337 536 5468	405.05	.012 610	5.04	3
	1.025 405	4.037 909	.247 652 9564	.975 224	3.937 866	.253 944 6231	304.74	.015 778	4.73	4
	1.031 857	5.063 314	.197 499 1175	.969 127	4.906 993	.203 790 7842	244.55	.018 954	4.55	5
	1.038 349	6.095 170	.164 064 3209	.963 068	5.870 061	.170 355 9876	204.43	.022 136	4.43	6
	1.044 882	7.133 519	.140 183 2627	.957 046	6.827 107	.146 474 9294	175.77	.025 325	4.34	7
	1.051 456	8.178 401	.122 273 2911	.951 062	7.778 169	.128 564 9577	154.28	.028 520	4.28	8
	1.058 071	9.229 857	.108 344 0437	.945 116	8.723 285	.114 635 7103	137.57	.031 721	4.23	9
	1.064 728	10.287 928	.097 201 3032	.939 207	9.662 492	.103 492 9699	124.20	.034 930	4.19	10
	1.071 427	11.352 656	.088 085 1032	.933 335	10.595 827	.094 376 7799	113.26	.038 145	4.16	11
	1.078 168	12.424 083	.080 488 8361	.927 499	11.523 326	.086 780 5027	104.14	.041 366	4.14	12
1	1.078 168	12.424 083	.080 488 8361	.927 499	11.523 326	.086 780 5027	104.14	.041 366	4.14	12
2	1.162 447	25.819 335	.038 730 6650	.860 255	22.211 200	.045 022 3317	54.03	.080 536	4.03	24
3	1.253 313	40.261 669	.024 837 5201	.797 885	32.124 193	.031 129 1867	37.36	.120 651	4.02	36
4	1.351 282	55.832 934	.017 910 5760	.740 038	41.318 485	.024 202 2427	29.05	.161 708	4.04	48
5	1.456 909	72.621 376	.013 770 0503	.686 384	49.846 182	.020 061 7169	24.08	.203 703	4.07	60
6	1.570 793	90.722 141	.011 022 6676	.636 621	57.755 614	.017 314 3342	20.78	.246 632	4.11	72
7	1.693 580	110.237 810	.009 071 2978	.590 465	65.091 604	.015 362 9645	18.44	.290 489	4.15	84
8	1.825 964	131.278 983	.007 617 3655	.547 656	71.895 728	.013 909 0322	16.70	.335 267	4.19	96
9	1.968 696	153.964 907	.006 494 9866	.507 950	78.206 547	.012 786 6532	15.35	.380 959	4.23	108
10	2.122 585	178.424 148	.005 604 6225	.471 124	84.059 826	.011 896 2892	14.28	.427 555	4.28	120
11	2.288 504	204.795 324	.004 882 9240	.436 967	89.488 737	.011 174 5906	13.41	.475 046	4.32	132
12	2.467 392	233.227 888	.004 287 6519	.405 286	94.524 046	.010 579 3186	12.70	.523 422	4.36	144
13	2.660 264	263.882 973	.003 789 5586	.375 903	99.194 291	.010 081 2253	12.10	.572 671	4.41	156
14	2.868 212	296.934 311	.003 367 7482	.348 649	103.525 939	.009 659 4149	11.60	.622 782	4.45	168
15	3.092 415	332.569 212	.003 006 8929	.323 372	107.543 539	.009 298 5596	11.16	.673 741	4.49	180
16	3.334 143	370.989 628	.002 695 4931	.299 927	111.269 858	.008 987 1598	10.79	.725 535	4.53	192
17	3.594 767	412.413 299	.002 424 7521	.278 182	114.726 017	.008 716 4187	10.46	.778 149	4.58	204
18	3.875 763	457.074 984	.002 187 8248	.258 014	117.931 600	.008 479 4915	10.18	.831 570	4.62	216
19	4.178 725	505.227 792	.001 979 3052	.239 307	120.904 776	.008 270 9719	9.93	.885 782	4.66	228
20	4.505 368	557.144 617	.001 794 8661	.221 957	123.662 393	.008 086 5328	9.71	.940 768	4.70	240
21	4.857 545	613.119 687	.001 631 0029	.205 865	126.220 081	.007 922 6696	9.51	.996 513	4.75	252
22	5.237 250	673.470 227	.001 484 8466	.190 940	128.592 335	.007 776 5133	9.34	1.053 000	4.79	264
23	5.646 637	738.538 259	.001 354 0260	.177 097	130.792 597	.007 645 6927	9.18	1.110 211	4.83	276
24	6.088 024	808.692 541	.001 236 5639	.164 257	132.833 339	.007 528 2306	9.04	1.168 130	4.87	288
25	6.563 914	884.330 657	.001 130 7987	.152 348	134.726 125	.007 422 4654	8.91	1.226 740	4.91	300
26	7.077 003	965.881 267	.001 035 3239	.141 303	136.481 682	.007 326 9906	8.80	1.286 021	4.95	312
27	7.630 199	1053.806 542	.000 948 9408	.131 058	138.109 959	.007 240 6074	8.69	1.345 957	4.99	324
28	8.226 638	1148.604 775	.000 870 6215	.121 556	139.620 185	.007 162 2882	8.60	1.406 529	5.02	336
29	8.869 700	1250.813 215	.000 799 4799	.112 743	141.020 919	.007 091 1465	8.51	1.467 719	5.06	348
30	9.563 028	1361.011 104	.000 734 7479	.104 569	142.320 097	.007 026 4145	8.44	1.529 509	5.10	360
31	10.310 553	1479.822 963	.000 675 7565	.096 988	143.525 084	.006 967 4232	8.37	1.591 881	5.14	372
32	11.116 510	1607.922 129	.000 621 9207	.089 956	144.642 709	.006 913 5873	8.30	1.654 818	5.17	384
33	11.985 468	1746.034 575	.000 572 7263	.083 434	145.679 305	.006 864 3930	8.24	1.718 300	5.21	396
34	12.922 350	1894.943 022	.000 527 7204	.077 385	146.640 746	.006 819 3870	8.19	1.782 310	5.24	408
35	13.932 467	2055.491 372	.000 486 5017	.071 775	147.532 482	.006 778 1683	8.14	1.846 831	5.28	420
36	15.021 542	2228.589 496	.000 448 7143	.066 571	148.359 567	.006 740 3810	8.09	1.911 845	5.31	432
37	16.195 749	2415.218 388	.000 414 0412	.061 745	149.126 687	.006 705 7079	8.05	1.977 334	5.34	444
38	17.461 741	2616.435 722	.000 382 1993	.057 268	149.838 190	.006 673 8660	8.01	2.043 283	5.38	456
39	18.826 694	2833.381 851	.000 352 9351	.053 116	150.498 108	.006 644 6018	7.98	2.109 674	5.41	468
40	20.298 343	3067.286 266	.000 326 0211	.049 265	151.110 182	.006 617 6878	7.95	2.176 490	5.44	480
41	21.885 027	3319.474 567	.000 301 2525	.045 693	151.677 880	.006 592 9192	7.92	2.243 716	5.47	492
42	23.595 740	3591.375 970	.000 278 4448	.042 381	152.204 419	.006 570 1115	7.89	2.311 336	5.50	504
43	25.440 177	3884.531 414	.000 257 4313	.039 308	152.692 784	.006 549 0980	7.86	2.379 335	5.53	516
44	27.428 789	4200.602 288	.000 238 0611	.036 458	153.145 741	.006 529 7278	7.84	2.447 696	5.56	528
45	29.572 848	4541.379 851	.000 220 1974	.033 815	153.565 859	.006 511 8641	7.82	2.516 407	5.59	540
46	31.884 504	4908.795 380	.000 203 7160	.031 363	153.955 518	.006 495 3826	7.80	2.585 451	5.62	552
47	34.376 858	5304.931 115	.000 188 5039	.029 089	154.316 927	.006 480 1705	7.78	2.654 816	5.65	564
48	37.064 035	5732.032 064	.000 174 4582	.026 980	154.652 133	.006 466 1249	7.76	2.724 488	5.68	576
49	39.961 264	6192.518 721	.000 161 4852	.025 024	154.963 036	.006 453 1518	7.75	2.794 453	5.70	588
50	43.084 963	6689.000 787	.000 149 4992	.023 210	155.251 398	.006 441 1658	7.73	2.864 699	5.73	600

MONTHLY COMPOUND INTEREST AND ANNUITY

Amount Of 1	Amount Of 1 Per Period	Sinking Fund Payment	Present Worth Of 1	Present Worth of 1 Per Period	Periodic Payment To Amortize 1	Constant Annual Percent	Total Interest	Annual Add On Rate	
What a single $1 deposit grows to in the future. The deposit is made at the beginning of the first period.	What a series of $1 deposits grow to in the future. A deposit is made at the end of each period.	The amount to be deposited at the end of each period that grows to $1 in the future.	What $1 to be paid in the future is worth today. Value today of a single $1 payment tomorrow.	What $1 to be paid at the end of each period is worth today. Value today of a series of $1 payments tomorrow.	The mortgage payment to amortize a loan of $1. An annuity certain, payable at the end of each period, worth $1 today.	The annual payment, including interest and principal, to amortize completely a loan of $100.	The total interest paid over the term on a loan of $1. The loan is amortized by regular periodic payments.	The average annual interest rate on a loan that is completely amortized by regular periodic payments.	
$S = (1+i)^n$	$S\overline{n}| = \dfrac{(1+i)^n - 1}{i}$	$\dfrac{1}{S\overline{n}|} = \dfrac{i}{(1+i)^n - 1}$	$V^n = \dfrac{1}{(1+i)^n}$	$A\overline{n}| = \dfrac{1-V^n}{i}$	$\dfrac{1}{A\overline{n}|} = \dfrac{i}{1-V^n}$				

YEAR	Amount Of 1	Amount Of 1 Per Period	Sinking Fund Payment	Present Worth Of 1	Present Worth of 1 Per Period	Periodic Payment To Amortize 1	Constant Annual Percent	Total Interest	Annual Add On Rate	PERIODS
	1.006 333	1.000 000	1.000 000 0000	.993 707	.993 707	1.006 333 3333	1207.60	.006 333	7.60	1
	1.012 707	2.006 333	.498 421 6647	.987 453	1.981 159	.504 754 9981	605.71	.009 510	5.71	2
	1.019 121	3.019 040	.331 231 1076	.981 238	2.962 397	.337 564 4410	405.08	.012 693	5.08	3
	1.025 575	4.038 161	.247 637 4951	.975 063	3.937 460	.253 970 8284	304.77	.015 883	4.76	4
	1.032 070	5.063 736	.197 482 6602	.968 926	4.906 386	.203 815 9936	244.58	.019 080	4.58	5
	1.038 607	6.095 806	.164 047 2143	.962 828	5.869 215	.170 380 5476	204.46	.022 283	4.46	6
	1.045 185	7.134 413	.140 165 7047	.956 769	6.825 983	.146 499 0381	175.80	.025 493	4.37	7
	1.051 804	8.179 597	.122 255 4054	.950 747	7.776 731	.128 588 7388	154.31	.028 710	4.31	8
	1.058 466	9.231 402	.108 325 9129	.944 764	8.721 495	.114 659 2463	137.60	.031 933	4.26	9
	1.065 169	10.289 867	.097 182 9851	.938 818	9.660 313	.103 516 3184	124.22	.035 163	4.22	10
	1.071 915	11.355 036	.088 066 6497	.932 910	10.593 222	.094 399 9831	113.28	.038 400	4.19	11
	1.078 704	12.426 951	.080 470 2587	.927 038	11.520 261	.086 803 5920	104.17	.041 643	4.16	12
1	1.078 704	12.426 951	.080 470 2587	.927 038	11.520 261	.086 803 5920	104.17	.041 643	4.16	12
2	1.163 602	25.831 954	.038 711 7443	.859 400	22.199 984	.045 045 0776	54.06	.081 082	4.05	24
3	1.255 183	40.291 984	.024 818 8322	.796 697	32.100 497	.031 152 1656	37.39	.121 478	4.05	36
4	1.353 970	55.890 077	.017 892 2637	.738 569	41.278 652	.024 225 5970	29.08	.162 829	4.07	48
5	1.460 533	72.715 803	.013 752 1689	.684 681	49.787 154	.020 085 5022	24.11	.205 130	4.10	60
6	1.575 483	90.865 781	.011 005 2430	.634 726	57.674 862	.017 338 5764	20.81	.248 377	4.14	72
7	1.699 480	110.444 235	.009 054 3431	.588 415	64.987 069	.015 387 6765	18.47	.292 565	4.18	84
8	1.833 236	131.563 592	.007 600 8870	.545 483	71.765 766	.013 934 2203	16.73	.337 685	4.22	96
9	1.977 519	154.345 128	.006 478 9865	.505 684	78.049 878	.012 812 3198	15.38	.383 731	4.26	108
10	2.133 158	178.919 663	.005 589 1006	.468 789	83.875 491	.011 922 4340	14.31	.430 692	4.31	120
11	2.301 046	205.428 312	.004 867 8782	.434 585	89.276 057	.011 201 2115	13.45	.478 560	4.35	132
12	2.482 148	234.023 299	.004 273 0788	.402 877	94.282 589	.010 606 4122	12.73	.527 323	4.39	144
13	2.677 503	264.868 826	.003 775 4537	.373 482	98.923 837	.010 108 7871	12.14	.576 971	4.44	156
14	2.888 233	298.142 020	.003 354 1062	.346 232	103.226 451	.009 687 4395	11.63	.627 490	4.48	168
15	3.115 548	334.033 949	.002 993 7077	.320 971	107.215 139	.009 327 0410	11.20	.678 867	4.53	180
16	3.360 755	372.750 717	.002 682 7581	.297 552	110.912 806	.009 016 0914	10.82	.731 090	4.57	192
17	3.625 259	414.514 651	.002 412 4600	.275 842	114.340 685	.008 745 7933	10.50	.784 142	4.61	204
18	3.910 582	459.565 574	.002 175 9680	.255 716	117.518 461	.008 509 3014	10.22	.838 009	4.66	216
19	4.218 361	508.162 187	.001 967 8757	.237 059	120.464 381	.008 301 2090	9.97	.892 676	4.70	228
20	4.550 362	560.583 548	.001 783 8554	.219 763	123.195 361	.008 117 1888	9.75	.948 125	4.74	240
21	4.908 494	617.130 682	.001 620 4023	.203 728	125.727 085	.007 953 7357	9.55	1.004 341	4.78	252
22	5.294 813	678.128 302	.001 474 6472	.188 864	128.074 090	.007 807 9805	9.37	1.061 307	4.82	264
23	5.711 536	743.926 681	.001 344 2185	.175 084	130.249 853	.007 677 5518	9.22	1.119 004	4.87	276
24	6.161 056	814.903 658	.001 227 1389	.162 310	132.266 870	.007 560 4723	9.08	1.177 416	4.91	288
25	6.645 956	891.466 808	.001 121 7468	.150 467	134.136 721	.007 455 0801	8.95	1.236 524	4.95	300
26	7.169 020	974.055 786	.001 026 6352	.139 489	135.870 145	.007 359 9686	8.84	1.296 310	4.99	312
27	7.733 251	1063.144 849	.000 940 6056	.129 312	137.477 096	.007 273 9389	8.73	1.356 756	5.03	324
28	8.341 889	1159.245 581	.000 862 6300	.119 877	138.966 801	.007 195 9633	8.64	1.417 844	5.06	336
29	8.998 429	1262.909 827	.000 791 8222	.111 131	140.347 814	.007 125 1555	8.56	1.479 554	5.10	348
30	9.706 641	1374.732 866	.000 727 4140	.103 022	141.628 067	.007 060 7474	8.48	1.541 869	5.14	360
31	10.470 593	1495.356 829	.000 668 7367	.095 506	142.814 910	.007 002 0700	8.41	1.604 770	5.18	372
32	11.294 671	1625.474 383	.000 615 2050	.088 537	143.915 159	.006 948 5384	8.34	1.668 239	5.21	384
33	12.183 607	1765.832 713	.000 566 3051	.082 077	144.935 132	.006 899 6384	8.28	1.732 257	5.25	396
34	13.142 506	1917.237 808	.000 521 5837	.076 089	145.880 686	.006 854 9170	8.23	1.796 806	5.28	408
35	14.176 874	2080.559 094	.000 480 6400	.070 537	146.757 251	.006 813 9734	8.18	1.861 869	5.32	420
36	15.292 651	2256.734 422	.000 443 1182	.065 391	147.569 860	.006 776 4515	8.14	1.927 427	5.35	432
37	16.496 245	2446.775 458	.000 408 7012	.060 620	148.323 180	.006 742 0345	8.10	1.993 463	5.39	444
38	17.794 565	2651.773 489	.000 377 1061	.056 197	149.021 537	.006 710 4394	8.06	2.059 960	5.42	456
39	19.195 069	2872.905 690	.000 348 0796	.052 097	149.668 940	.006 681 4130	8.02	2.126 901	5.45	468
40	20.705 799	3111.441 886	.000 321 3944	.048 296	150.269 108	.006 654 7277	7.99	2.194 269	5.49	480
41	22.335 428	3368.751 841	.000 296 8458	.044 772	150.825 486	.006 630 1792	7.96	2.262 048	5.52	492
42	24.093 316	3646.313 124	.000 274 2496	.041 505	151.341 271	.006 607 5830	7.93	2.330 222	5.55	504
43	25.989 557	3945.719 599	.000 253 4392	.038 477	151.819 422	.006 586 7725	7.91	2.398 775	5.58	516
44	28.035 040	4268.690 568	.000 234 2639	.035 670	152.262 687	.006 567 5972	7.89	2.467 691	5.61	528
45	30.241 511	4617.080 653	.000 216 5871	.033 067	152.673 611	.006 549 9204	7.86	2.536 957	5.64	540
46	32.621 639	4992.890 441	.000 200 2848	.030 654	153.054 553	.006 533 6181	7.85	2.606 557	5.67	552
47	35.189 094	5398.277 971	.000 185 2443	.028 418	153.407 701	.006 518 5776	7.83	2.676 478	5.69	564
48	37.958 617	5835.571 133	.000 171 3628	.026 344	153.735 082	.006 504 6962	7.81	2.746 705	5.72	576
49	40.946 113	6307.281 027	.000 158 5469	.024 422	154.038 577	.006 491 8803	7.80	2.817 226	5.75	588
50	44.168 737	6816.116 388	.000 146 7111	.022 640	154.319 929	.006 480 0444	7.78	2.888 027	5.78	600

Effective Rate is 7.87 %

Annual Percentage Rate is 7.60 %

MONTHLY COMPOUND INTEREST AND ANNUITY

	Amount Of 1	Amount Of 1 Per Period	Sinking Fund Payment	Present Worth Of 1	Present Worth of 1 Per Period	Periodic Payment To Amortize 1	Constant Annual Percent	Total Interest	Annual Add On Rate	
	What a single $1 deposit grows to in the future. The deposit is made at the beginning of the first period.	What a series of $1 deposits grow to in the future. A deposit is made at the end of each period.	The amount to be deposited at the end of each period that grows to $1 in the future.	What $1 to be paid in the future is worth today. Value today of a single $1 payment tomorrow.	What $1 to be paid at the end of each period is worth today. Value today of a series of $1 payments tomorrow.	The mortgage payment to amortize a loan of $1. An annuity certain, payable at the end of each period, worth $1 today.	The annual payment, including interest and principal, to amortize completely a loan of $100.	The total interest paid over the term on a loan of $1. The loan is amortized by regular periodic payments.	The average annual interest rate on a loan that is completely amortized by regular periodic payments.	
	$S = (1+i)^n$	$S\overline{n}] = \dfrac{(1+i)^n - 1}{i}$	$\dfrac{1}{S\overline{n}]} = \dfrac{i}{(1+i)^n - 1}$	$V^n = \dfrac{1}{(1+i)^n}$	$A\overline{n}] = \dfrac{1 - V^n}{i}$	$\dfrac{1}{A\overline{n}]} = \dfrac{i}{1 - V^n}$				PERIODS

YEAR										
	1.006 354	1.000 000	1.000 000 0000	.993 686	.993 686	1.006 354 1667	1207.63	.006 354	7.62	1
	1.012 749	2.006 354	.498 416 4893	.987 412	1.981 098	.504 770 6559	605.73	.009 541	5.72	2
	1.019 184	3.019 103	.331 224 2217	.981 177	2.962 275	.337 578 3883	405.10	.012 735	5.09	3
	1.025 660	4.038 287	.247 629 7648	.974 982	3.937 257	.253 983 9314	304.79	.015 936	4.78	4
	1.032 177	5.063 947	.197 474 4321	.968 826	4.906 083	.203 828 5988	244.60	.019 143	4.59	5
	1.038 736	6.096 124	.164 038 6616	.962 709	5.868 792	.170 392 8283	204.48	.022 357	4.47	6
	1.045 336	7.134 860	.140 156 9265	.956 630	6.825 422	.146 511 0932	175.82	.025 578	4.38	7
	1.051 978	8.180 196	.122 246 4635	.950 590	7.776 012	.128 600 6302	154.33	.028 805	4.32	8
	1.058 663	9.232 174	.108 316 8485	.944 588	8.720 600	.114 671 0152	137.61	.032 039	4.27	9
	1.065 390	10.290 837	.097 173 8271	.938 624	9.659 223	.103 527 9938	124.24	.035 280	4.23	10
	1.072 159	11.356 227	.088 057 4192	.932 697	10.591 920	.094 411 5858	113.30	.038 527	4.20	11
	1.078 972	12.428 386	.080 460 9713	.926 808	11.518 728	.086 815 1379	104.18	.041 782	4.18	12
1	1.078 972	12.428 386	.080 460 9713	.926 808	11.518 728	.086 815 1379	104.18	.041 782	4.18	12
2	1.164 181	25.838 267	.038 702 2865	.858 973	22.194 379	.045 056 4531	54.07	.081 355	4.07	24
3	1.256 118	40.307 153	.024 809 4922	.796 103	32.088 658	.031 163 6588	37.40	.121 892	4.06	36
4	1.355 317	55.918 677	.017 883 1127	.737 835	41.258 756	.024 237 2793	29.09	.163 389	4.08	48
5	1.462 349	72.763 075	.013 743 2346	.683 831	49.757 677	.020 097 4012	24.12	.205 844	4.12	60
6	1.577 833	90.937 709	.010 996 5384	.633 780	57.634 546	.017 350 7050	20.83	.249 251	4.15	72
7	1.702 438	110.547 630	.009 045 8746	.587 393	64.934 891	.015 400 0413	18.49	.293 603	4.19	84
8	1.836 883	131.706 188	.007 592 6577	.544 400	71.700 910	.013 946 8244	16.74	.338 895	4.24	96
9	1.981 945	154.535 679	.006 470 9975	.504 555	77.971 711	.012 825 1642	15.40	.385 118	4.28	108
10	2.138 464	179.168 062	.005 581 3519	.467 625	83.783 540	.011 935 5185	14.33	.432 262	4.32	120
11	2.307 343	205.745 715	.004 860 3685	.433 399	89.169 991	.011 214 5352	13.46	.480 319	4.37	132
12	2.489 558	234.422 258	.004 265 8065	.401 678	94.162 196	.010 619 9732	12.75	.529 276	4.41	144
13	2.686 164	265.363 447	.003 768 4165	.372 278	98.789 013	.010 122 5832	12.15	.579 123	4.45	156
14	2.898 295	298.748 125	.003 347 3013	.345 030	103.077 184	.009 701 4680	11.65	.629 847	4.50	168
15	3.127 180	334.769 258	.002 987 1321	.319 777	107.051 495	.009 341 2988	11.21	.681 434	4.54	180
16	3.374 139	373.635 053	.002 676 4084	.296 372	110.734 919	.009 030 5751	10.84	.733 870	4.59	192
17	3.640 602	415.570 160	.002 406 3325	.274 680	114.148 746	.008 760 4992	10.52	.787 142	4.63	204
18	3.928 108	460.816 967	.002 170 0590	.254 575	117.312 709	.008 524 2257	10.23	.841 233	4.67	216
19	4.238 318	509.637 007	.001 962 1809	.235 943	120.245 095	.008 316 3476	9.98	.896 127	4.72	228
20	4.573 027	562.312 465	.001 778 3707	.218 674	122.962 854	.008 132 5373	9.76	.951 809	4.76	240
21	4.934 168	619.147 810	.001 615 1232	.202 668	125.481 695	.007 969 2899	9.57	1.008 261	4.80	252
22	5.323 830	680.471 559	.001 469 5691	.187 835	127.816 177	.007 823 7358	9.39	1.065 466	4.84	264
23	5.744 263	746.638 169	.001 339 3368	.174 087	129.979 794	.007 693 5035	9.24	1.123 407	4.88	276
24	6.197 900	818.030 091	.001 222 4489	.161 345	131.985 052	.007 576 6156	9.10	1.182 065	4.93	288
25	6.687 360	895.059 978	.001 117 2436	.149 536	133.843 541	.007 471 4102	8.97	1.241 423	4.97	300
26	7.215 475	978.173 072	.001 022 3140	.138 591	135.566 003	.007 376 4806	8.86	1.301 462	5.01	312
27	7.785 295	1067.849 776	.000 936 4613	.128 447	137.162 396	.007 290 6280	8.75	1.362 163	5.05	324
28	8.400 116	1164.608 432	.000 858 6577	.119 046	138.641 945	.007 212 8244	8.66	1.423 509	5.08	336
29	9.063 490	1269.008 316	.000 788 0169	.110 333	140.013 203	.007 142 1836	8.58	1.485 480	5.12	348
30	9.779 253	1381.652 872	.000 723 7708	.102 257	141.284 097	.007 077 9375	8.50	1.548 057	5.16	360
31	10.551 540	1503.193 197	.000 665 2505	.094 773	142.461 971	.007 019 4171	8.43	1.611 223	5.20	372
32	11.384 817	1634.331 809	.000 611 8709	.087 836	143.553 634	.006 966 0375	8.36	1.674 958	5.23	384
33	12.283 899	1775.826 705	.000 563 1180	.081 407	144.565 396	.006 917 2847	8.31	1.739 245	5.27	396
34	13.253 983	1928.495 740	.000 518 5389	.075 449	145.503 106	.006 872 7055	8.25	1.804 064	5.31	408
35	14.300 677	2093.221 359	.000 477 7326	.069 927	146.372 182	.006 831 8992	8.20	1.869 398	5.34	420
36	15.430 031	2270.955 696	.000 440 3432	.064 809	147.177 650	.006 794 5099	8.16	1.935 228	5.38	432
37	16.648 572	2462.726 076	.000 406 0541	.060 065	147.924 163	.006 760 2208	8.12	2.001 538	5.41	444
38	17.963 344	2669.640 952	.000 374 5822	.055 669	148.616 038	.006 728 7489	8.08	2.068 309	5.44	456
39	19.381 945	2892.896 318	.000 345 6743	.051 594	149.257 273	.006 699 8410	8.04	2.135 526	5.48	468
40	20.912 577	3133.782 614	.000 319 1032	.047 818	149.851 575	.006 673 2698	8.01	2.203 170	5.51	480
41	22.564 086	3393.692 191	.000 294 6643	.044 318	150.402 379	.006 648 8310	7.98	2.271 225	5.54	492
42	24.346 018	3674.127 357	.000 272 1735	.041 074	150.912 869	.006 626 3401	7.96	2.339 675	5.57	504
43	26.268 672	3976.709 058	.000 251 4642	.038 068	151.385 995	.006 605 6309	7.93	2.408 506	5.60	516
44	28.343 163	4303.186 252	.000 232 3859	.035 282	151.824 491	.006 586 5526	7.91	2.477 700	5.63	528
45	30.581 480	4655.446 015	.000 214 8022	.032 700	152.230 894	.006 568 9689	7.89	2.547 243	5.66	540
46	32.996 562	5035.524 448	.000 198 5890	.030 306	152.607 551	.006 552 7557	7.87	2.617 121	5.69	552
47	35.602 367	5445.618 449	.000 183 6339	.028 088	152.956 639	.006 537 8005	7.85	2.687 320	5.72	564
48	38.413 959	5888.098 407	.000 169 8341	.026 032	153.280 178	.006 524 0008	7.83	2.757 824	5.75	576
49	41.447 587	6365.521 908	.000 157 0963	.024 127	153.580 036	.006 511 2630	7.82	2.828 623	5.77	588
50	44.720 787	6880.648 515	.000 145 3351	.022 361	153.857 946	.006 499 5018	7.80	2.899 701	5.80	600

Effective Rate is 7.90 %

8 - 79

Annual Percentage Rate is 7.625%

MONTHLY COMPOUND INTEREST AND ANNUITY

	Amount Of 1	Amount Of 1 Per Period	Sinking Fund Payment	Present Worth Of 1	Present Worth of 1 Per Period	Periodic Payment To Amortize 1	Constant Annual Percent	Total Interest	Annual Add On Rate	
	What a single $ 1 deposit grows to in the future. The deposit is made at the beginning of the first period.	What a series of $ 1 deposits grow to in the future. A deposit is made at the end of each period.	The amount to be deposited at the end of each period that grows to $ 1 in the future.	What $ 1 to be paid in the future is worth today. Value today of a single $ 1 payment tomorrow.	What $ 1 to be paid at the end of each period is worth today. Value today of a series of $ 1 payments tomorrow.	The mortgage payment to amortize a loan of $ 1. An annuity certain, payable at the end of each period, worth $ 1 today.	The annual payment, including interest and principal, to amortize completely a loan of $ 100.	The total interest paid over the term on a loan of $ 1. The loan is amortized by regular periodic payments.	The average annual interest rate on a loan that is completely amortized by regular periodic payments.	
	$S = (1+i)^n$	$S\overline{n|} = \dfrac{(1+i)^n - 1}{i}$	$\dfrac{1}{S\overline{n|}} = \dfrac{i}{(1+i)^n - 1}$	$V^n = \dfrac{1}{(1+i)^n}$	$A\overline{n|} = \dfrac{1 - V^n}{i}$	$\dfrac{1}{A\overline{n|}} = \dfrac{i}{1 - V^n}$				

YEAR										PERIODS
	1.006 375	1.000 000	1.000 000 0000	.993 665	.993 665	1.006 375 0000	1207.65	.006 375	7.65	1
	1.012 791	2.006 375	.498 411 3139	.987 371	1.981 036	.504 786 3139	605.75	.009 573	5.74	2
	1.019 247	3.019 166	.331 217 3359	.981 116	2.962 153	.337 592 3359	405.12	.012 777	5.11	3
	1.025 745	4.038 413	.247 622 0347	.974 901	3.937 054	.253 997 0347	304.80	.015 988	4.80	4
	1.032 284	5.064 158	.197 466 2044	.968 726	4.905 779	.203 841 2044	244.61	.019 206	4.61	5
	1.038 865	6.096 442	.164 030 1093	.962 589	5.868 369	.170 405 1093	204.49	.022 431	4.49	6
	1.045 488	7.135 307	.140 148 1487	.956 492	6.824 860	.146 523 1487	175.83	.025 662	4.40	7
	1.052 153	8.180 794	.122 237 5221	.950 433	7.775 293	.128 612 5221	154.34	.028 900	4.34	8
	1.058 860	9.232 947	.108 307 7847	.944 412	8.719 705	.114 682 7847	137.62	.032 145	4.29	9
	1.065 610	10.291 807	.097 164 6698	.938 429	9.658 134	.103 539 6698	124.25	.035 397	4.25	10
	1.072 404	11.357 417	.088 048 1894	.932 485	10.590 619	.094 423 1894	113.31	.038 655	4.22	11
	1.079 240	12.429 821	.080 451 6847	.926 578	11.517 197	.086 826 6847	104.20	.041 920	4.19	12
1	1.079 240	12.429 821	.080 451 6847	.926 578	11.517 197	.086 826 6847	104.20	.041 920	4.19	12
2	1.164 759	25.844 581	.038 692 8304	.858 547	22.188 776	.045 067 8304	54.09	.081 628	4.08	24
3	1.257 055	40.322 329	.024 800 1547	.795 510	32.076 826	.031 175 1547	37.42	.122 306	4.08	36
4	1.356 664	55.947 295	.017 873 9650	.737 102	41.238 873	.024 248 9650	29.10	.163 950	4.10	48
5	1.464 166	72.810 385	.013 734 3045	.682 983	49.728 224	.020 109 3045	24.14	.206 558	4.13	60
6	1.580 187	91.009 709	.010 987 8387	.632 837	57.594 269	.017 362 8387	20.84	.250 124	4.17	72
7	1.705 401	110.651 148	.009 037 4119	.586 372	64.882 772	.015 412 4119	18.50	.294 643	4.21	84
8	1.840 537	131.848 977	.007 584 4350	.543 320	71.636 137	.013 959 4350	16.76	.340 106	4.25	96
9	1.986 382	154.726 524	.006 463 0160	.503 428	77.893 656	.012 838 0160	15.41	.386 506	4.29	108
10	2.143 783	179.416 891	.005 573 6112	.466 465	83.691 735	.011 948 6112	14.34	.433 833	4.34	120
11	2.313 656	206.063 725	.004 852 8677	.432 216	89.064 106	.011 227 8677	13.48	.482 079	4.38	132
12	2.496 991	234.822 057	.004 258 5437	.400 482	94.042 026	.010 633 5437	12.77	.531 230	4.43	144
13	2.694 852	265.859 202	.003 761 3895	.371 078	98.654 457	.010 136 3895	12.17	.581 277	4.47	156
14	2.908 393	299.355 734	.003 340 5073	.343 833	102.928 234	.009 715 5073	11.66	.632 205	4.52	168
15	3.138 854	335.506 534	.002 980 5679	.318 588	106.888 220	.009 355 5679	11.23	.684 002	4.56	180
16	3.387 577	374.521 928	.002 670 0706	.295 196	110.557 456	.009 045 0706	10.86	.736 654	4.60	192
17	3.656 009	416.628 906	.002 400 2175	.273 522	113.957 289	.008 775 2175	10.54	.790 144	4.65	204
18	3.945 712	462.072 445	.002 164 1628	.253 440	117.107 499	.008 539 1628	10.25	.844 459	4.69	216
19	4.258 370	511.116 935	.001 956 4994	.234 832	120.026 414	.008 331 4994	10.00	.899 582	4.73	228
20	4.595 804	564.047 715	.001 772 8997	.217 590	122.731 016	.008 147 8997	9.78	.955 496	4.78	240
21	4.959 976	621.172 736	.001 609 8582	.201 614	125.237 040	.007 984 8582	9.59	1.012 184	4.82	252
22	5.353 005	682.824 350	.001 464 5055	.186 811	127.559 066	.007 839 5055	9.41	1.069 629	4.86	264
23	5.777 178	749.361 244	.001 334 4699	.173 095	129.710 605	.007 709 4699	9.26	1.127 814	4.90	276
24	6.234 962	821.170 529	.001 217 7739	.160 386	131.704 173	.007 592 7739	9.12	1.186 719	4.94	288
25	6.729 021	898.669 989	.001 112 7555	.148 610	133.551 369	.007 487 7555	8.99	1.246 327	4.99	300
26	7.262 230	982.310 514	.001 018 0080	.137 699	135.262 940	.007 393 0080	8.88	1.306 619	5.03	312
27	7.837 689	1072.578 723	.000 932 3325	.127 589	136.848 843	.007 307 3325	8.77	1.367 576	5.07	324
28	8.458 749	1169.999 795	.000 854 7010	.118 221	138.318 307	.007 229 7010	8.68	1.429 180	5.10	336
29	9.129 021	1275.140 523	.000 784 2273	.109 541	139.679 879	.007 159 2273	8.60	1.491 411	5.14	348
30	9.852 405	1388.612 614	.000 720 1432	.101 498	140.941 481	.007 095 1432	8.52	1.554 252	5.18	360
31	10.633 111	1511.076 245	.000 661 7800	.094 046	142.110 454	.007 036 7800	8.45	1.617 682	5.22	372
32	11.475 680	1643.243 906	.000 608 5524	.087 141	143.193 599	.006 983 5524	8.39	1.681 684	5.26	384
33	12.385 014	1785.884 548	.000 559 9466	.080 743	144.197 217	.006 934 9466	8.33	1.746 239	5.29	396
34	13.366 404	1939.828 049	.000 515 5096	.074 814	145.127 147	.006 890 5096	8.27	1.811 328	5.33	408
35	14.425 559	2105.970 049	.000 474 8406	.069 321	145.988 799	.006 849 8406	8.22	1.876 933	5.36	420
36	15.568 642	2285.277 158	.000 437 5837	.064 232	146.787 188	.006 812 5837	8.18	1.943 036	5.40	432
37	16.802 303	2478.792 582	.000 403 4222	.059 516	147.526 957	.006 778 4222	8.14	2.009 619	5.43	444
38	18.133 719	2687.642 189	.000 372 0733	.055 146	148.212 410	.006 747 0733	8.10	2.076 665	5.46	456
39	19.570 637	2913.041 061	.000 343 2839	.051 097	148.847 536	.006 718 2839	8.07	2.144 157	5.50	468
40	21.121 416	3156.300 563	.000 316 8266	.047 345	149.436 030	.006 691 8266	8.04	2.212 077	5.53	480
41	22.795 079	3418.835 974	.000 292 4972	.043 869	149.981 315	.006 667 4972	8.01	2.280 409	5.56	492
42	24.601 364	3702.174 718	.000 270 1115	.040 648	150.486 564	.006 645 1115	7.98	2.349 136	5.59	504
43	26.550 778	4007.965 255	.000 249 5032	.037 664	150.954 717	.006 624 5032	7.95	2.418 244	5.62	516
44	28.654 665	4337.986 665	.000 230 5217	.034 898	151.388 497	.006 605 5217	7.93	2.487 715	5.65	528
45	30.925 264	4694.159 008	.000 213 0307	.032 336	151.790 428	.006 588 0307	7.91	2.557 537	5.68	540
46	33.375 785	5078.554 484	.000 196 9064	.029 962	152.162 848	.006 571 9064	7.89	2.627 692	5.71	552
47	36.020 486	5493.409 499	.000 182 0363	.027 762	152.507 925	.006 557 0363	7.87	2.698 168	5.74	564
48	38.874 753	5941.137 669	.000 168 3179	.025 724	152.827 665	.006 543 3179	7.86	2.768 951	5.77	576
49	41.955 192	6424.343 866	.000 155 6579	.023 835	153.123 929	.006 530 6579	7.84	2.840 027	5.80	588
50	45.279 726	6945.839 374	.000 143 9711	.022 085	153.398 441	.006 518 9711	7.83	2.911 383	5.82	600

Effective Rate is 7.92 %

Annual Percentage Rate is 7.65 %

MONTHLY COMPOUND INTEREST AND ANNUITY

Amount Of 1	Amount Of 1 Per Period	Sinking Fund Payment	Present Worth Of 1	Present Worth of 1 Per Period	Periodic Payment To Amortize 1	Constant Annual Percent	Total Interest	Annual Add On Rate
What a single $ 1 deposit grows to in the future. The deposit is made at the beginning of the first period.	What a series of $ 1 deposits grow to in the future. A deposit is made at the end of each period.	The amount to be deposited at the end of each period that grows to $ 1 in the future.	What $ 1 to be paid in the future is worth today. Value today of a single $ 1 payment tomorrow.	What $ 1 to be paid at the end of each period is worth today. Value today of a series of $ 1 payments tomorrow.	The mortgage payment to amortize a loan of $ 1. An annuity certain, payable at the end of each period, worth $ 1 today.	The annual payment, including interest and principal, to amortize completely a loan of $ 100.	The total interest paid over the term on a loan of $1. The loan is amortized by regular periodic payments.	The average annual interest rate on a loan that is completely amortized by regular periodic payments.

$$S = (1+i)^n \qquad S\overline{n}| = \frac{(1+i)^n - 1}{i} \qquad \frac{1}{S\overline{n}|} = \frac{i}{(1+i)^n - 1} \qquad V^n = \frac{1}{(1+i)^n} \qquad A\overline{n}| = \frac{1-V^n}{i} \qquad \frac{1}{A\overline{n}|} = \frac{i}{1-V^n}$$

YEAR	Amount Of 1	Amount Of 1 Per Period	Sinking Fund Payment	Present Worth Of 1	Present Worth of 1 Per Period	Periodic Payment To Amortize 1	Constant Annual Percent	Total Interest	Annual Add On Rate	PERIODS
	1.006 417	1.000 000	1.000 000 0000	.993 624	.993 624	1.006 416 6667	1207.70	.006 417	7.70	1
	1.012 875	2.006 417	.498 400 9636	.987 289	1.980 913	.504 817 6302	605.79	.009 635	5.78	2
	1.019 374	3.019 291	.331 203 5648	.980 994	2.961 908	.337 620 2315	405.15	.012 861	5.14	3
	1.025 915	4.038 665	.247 606 5755	.974 740	3.936 648	.254 023 2422	304.83	.016 093	4.83	4
	1.032 498	5.064 580	.197 449 7499	.968 525	4.905 173	.203 866 4165	244.64	.019 332	4.64	5
	1.039 123	6.097 077	.164 013 0061	.962 350	5.867 523	.170 429 6727	204.52	.022 578	4.52	6
	1.045 791	7.136 200	.140 130 5947	.956 214	6.823 737	.146 547 2613	175.86	.025 831	4.43	7
	1.052 501	8.181 991	.122 219 6410	.950 118	7.773 855	.128 636 3077	154.37	.029 090	4.36	8
	1.059 255	9.234 492	.108 289 6591	.944 060	8.717 915	.114 706 3258	137.65	.032 357	4.31	9
	1.066 052	10.293 747	.097 146 3574	.938 041	9.655 956	.103 563 0240	124.28	.035 630	4.28	10
	1.072 892	11.359 798	.088 029 7321	.932 060	10.588 016	.094 446 3988	113.34	.038 910	4.24	11
	1.079 776	12.432 690	.080 433 1141	.926 118	11.514 134	.086 849 7808	104.22	.042 197	4.22	12
1	1.079 776	12.432 690	.080 433 1141	.926 118	11.514 134	.086 849 7808	104.22	.042 197	4.11	12
2	1.165 917	25.857 216	.038 673 9233	.857 694	22.177 576	.045 090 5900	54.11	.082 174	4.11	24
3	1.258 930	40.352 703	.024 781 4874	.794 325	32.053 178	.031 198 1540	37.44	.123 134	4.10	36
4	1.359 363	56.004 588	.017 855 6800	.735 639	41.199 148	.024 272 3467	29.13	.165 073	4.13	48
5	1.467 808	72.905 124	.013 716 4570	.681 288	49.669 392	.020 133 1236	24.16	.207 987	4.16	60
6	1.584 904	91.153 925	.010 970 4546	.630 953	57.513 834	.017 387 1213	20.87	.251 873	4.20	72
7	1.711 342	110.858 550	.009 020 5040	.584 337	64.778 710	.015 437 1707	18.53	.296 722	4.24	84
8	1.847 867	132.135 140	.007 568 0096	.541 164	71.506 840	.013 984 6762	16.79	.342 529	4.28	96
9	1.995 283	155.109 100	.006 447 0750	.501 182	77.737 880	.012 863 7417	15.44	.389 284	4.33	108
10	2.154 460	179.915 840	.005 558 1543	.464 153	83.508 555	.011 974 8210	14.37	.436 979	4.37	120
11	2.326 335	206.701 574	.004 837 8925	.429 861	88.852 880	.011 254 5592	13.51	.485 602	4.41	132
12	2.511 922	235.624 178	.004 244 0466	.398 102	93.802 354	.010 660 7133	12.80	.535 143	4.46	144
13	2.712 314	266.854 124	.003 747 3657	.368 689	98.386 148	.010 164 0324	12.20	.585 589	4.50	156
14	2.928 693	300.575 483	.003 326 9513	.341 449	102.631 281	.009 743 6180	11.70	.636 928	4.55	168
15	3.162 333	336.987 013	.002 967 4734	.316 222	106.562 774	.009 384 1401	11.27	.689 145	4.59	180
16	3.414 613	376.303 324	.002 657 4307	.292 859	110.203 799	.009 074 0974	10.89	.742 227	4.64	192
17	3.687 019	418.756 150	.002 388 0246	.271 222	113.575 816	.008 804 6913	10.57	.796 157	4.68	204
18	3.981 156	464.595 710	.002 152 4090	.251 183	116.698 701	.008 569 0757	10.29	.850 920	4.73	216
19	4.298 758	514.092 188	.001 945 1764	.232 625	119.590 859	.008 361 8431	10.04	.906 500	4.77	228
20	4.641 698	567.537 317	.001 761 9987	.215 438	122.269 338	.008 178 6653	9.82	.962 880	4.81	240
21	5.011 996	625.246 108	.001 599 3702	.199 521	124.749 925	.008 016 0369	9.62	1.020 041	4.86	252
22	5.411 835	687.558 701	.001 454 4213	.184 780	127.047 240	.007 871 0879	9.45	1.077 967	4.90	264
23	5.843 572	754.842 369	.001 324 7799	.171 128	129.174 824	.007 741 4466	9.29	1.196 039	4.94	276
24	6.309 751	827.493 689	.001 208 4684	.158 485	131.145 217	.007 625 1351	9.16	1.196 039	4.98	288
25	6.813 121	905.940 871	.001 103 8248	.146 776	132.970 033	.007 520 4915	9.03	1.256 147	5.02	300
26	7.356 647	990.646 290	.001 009 4420	.135 931	134.660 027	.007 426 1087	8.92	1.316 946	5.07	312
27	7.943 534	1082.109 204	.000 924 1211	.125 889	136.225 161	.007 340 7878	8.81	1.378 415	5.11	324
28	8.577 241	1180.868 703	.000 846 8342	.116 588	137.674 658	.007 263 5009	8.72	1.440 536	5.14	336
29	9.261 502	1287.506 882	.000 776 6949	.107 974	139.017 064	.007 193 3615	8.64	1.503 290	5.18	348
30	10.000 352	1402.652 275	.000 712 9351	.099 996	140.260 289	.007 129 6017	8.56	1.566 657	5.22	360
31	10.798 144	1526.983 555	.000 654 8859	.092 609	141.411 662	.007 071 5526	8.49	1.630 618	5.26	372
32	11.659 582	1661.233 542	.000 601 9623	.085 766	142.477 969	.007 018 6290	8.43	1.695 154	5.30	384
33	12.589 742	1806.193 513	.000 553 6505	.079 430	143.465 494	.006 970 3172	8.37	1.760 246	5.33	396
34	13.594 106	1962.717 873	.000 509 4976	.073 561	144.380 059	.006 926 1642	8.32	1.825 875	5.37	408
35	14.678 596	2131.729 187	.000 469 1027	.068 126	145.227 053	.006 885 7694	8.27	1.892 023	5.41	420
36	15.849 602	2314.223 621	.000 432 1104	.063 093	146.011 470	.006 848 7770	8.22	1.958 672	5.44	432
37	17.114 026	2511.276 809	.000 398 2038	.058 432	146.737 932	.006 814 8705	8.18	2.025 802	5.48	444
38	18.479 322	2724.050 197	.000 367 1004	.054 115	147.410 721	.006 783 7671	8.15	2.093 398	5.51	456
39	19.953 536	2953.797 886	.000 338 5472	.050 116	148.033 803	.006 755 2139	8.11	2.161 440	5.54	468
40	21.545 358	3201.874 025	.000 312 3171	.046 414	148.610 850	.006 728 9838	8.08	2.229 912	5.57	480
41	23.264 170	3469.740 793	.000 288 2060	.042 985	149.145 264	.006 704 8726	8.05	2.298 797	5.61	492
42	25.120 103	3758.977 015	.000 266 0298	.039 809	149.640 194	.006 682 6965	8.02	2.368 079	5.64	504
43	27.124 095	4071.287 471	.000 245 6225	.036 868	150.098 557	.006 662 2892	8.00	2.437 741	5.67	516
44	29.287 958	4408.512 940	.000 226 8339	.034 144	150.523 056	.006 643 5005	7.98	2.507 768	5.70	528
45	31.624 447	4772.641 052	.000 209 5276	.031 621	150.916 191	.006 626 1943	7.96	2.578 145	5.73	540
46	34.147 332	5165.818 005	.000 193 5802	.029 285	151.280 281	.006 610 2469	7.94	2.648 856	5.76	552
47	36.871 484	5590.361 212	.000 178 8793	.027 121	151.617 471	.006 595 5460	7.92	2.719 888	5.79	564
48	39.812 960	6048.772 960	.000 165 3228	.025 117	151.929 748	.006 581 9895	7.90	2.791 226	5.82	576
49	42.989 096	6543.755 160	.000 152 8175	.023 262	152.218 954	.006 569 4841	7.89	2.862 857	5.84	588
50	46.418 612	7078.225 273	.000 141 2784	.021 543	152.486 792	.006 557 9450	7.87	2.934 767	5.87	600

Effective Rate is 7.98 %

Annual Percentage Rate is 7.70 %

	Amount Of 1	Amount Of 1 Per Period	Sinking Fund Payment	Present Worth Of 1	Present Worth of 1 Per Period	Periodic Payment To Amortize 1	Constant Annual Percent	Total Interest	Annual Add On Rate	
	What a single $ 1 deposit grows to in the future. The deposit is made at the beginning of the first period.	What a series of $ 1 deposits grow to in the future. A deposit is made at the end of each period.	The amount to be deposited at the end of each period that grows to $ 1 in the future.	What $ 1 to be paid in the future is worth today. Value today of a single $ 1 payment tomorrow.	What $ 1 to be paid at the end of each period is worth today. Value today of a series of $ 1 payments tomorrow.	The mortgage payment to amortize a loan of $ 1. An annuity certain, payable at the end of each period, worth $ 1 today.	The annual payment, including interest and principal, to amortize completely a loan of $ 100.	The total interest paid over the term on a loan of $1. The loan is amortized by regular periodic payments.	The average annual interest rate on a loan that is completely amortized by regular periodic payments.	
	$S = (1+i)^n$	$S\overline{n}| = \dfrac{(1+i)^n - 1}{i}$	$\dfrac{1}{S\overline{n}|} = \dfrac{i}{(1+i)^n - 1}$	$V^n = \dfrac{1}{(1+i)^n}$	$A\overline{n}| = \dfrac{1-V^n}{i}$	$\dfrac{1}{A\overline{n}|} = \dfrac{i}{1-V^n}$				

YEAR										PERIODS
	1.006 458	1.000 000	1.000 000 0000	.993 583	.993 583	1.006 458 3333	1207.75	.006 458	7.75	1
	1.012 958	2.006 458	.498 390 6136	.987 207	1.980 791	.504 848 9470	605.82	.009 698	5.82	2
	1.019 500	3.019 417	.331 189 7946	.980 873	2.961 663	.337 648 1279	405.18	.012 944	5.18	3
	1.026 085	4.038 917	.247 591 1173	.974 578	3.936 242	.254 049 4507	304.86	.016 198	4.86	4
	1.032 711	5.065 002	.197 433 2968	.968 325	4.904 566	.203 891 6301	244.67	.019 458	4.67	5
	1.039 381	6.097 713	.163 995 9045	.962 111	5.866 677	.170 454 2378	204.55	.022 725	4.55	6
	1.046 094	7.137 094	.140 113 0426	.955 937	6.822 615	.146 571 3759	175.89	.026 000	4.46	7
	1.052 850	8.183 188	.122 201 7622	.949 803	7.772 418	.128 660 0955	154.40	.029 281	4.39	8
	1.059 649	9.236 038	.108 271 5360	.943 708	8.716 126	.114 729 8693	137.68	.032 569	4.34	9
	1.066 493	10.295 687	.097 128 0478	.937 653	9.653 779	.103 586 3811	124.31	.035 864	4.30	10
	1.073 381	11.362 180	.088 011 2780	.931 636	10.585 415	.094 469 6113	113.37	.039 166	4.27	11
	1.080 313	12.435 561	.080 414 5470	.925 658	11.511 072	.086 872 8803	104.25	.042 475	4.25	12
1	1.080 313	12.435 561	.080 414 5470	.925 658	11.511 072	.086 872 8803	104.25	.042 475	4.25	12
2	1.167 076	25.869 859	.038 655 0231	.856 842	22.166 384	.045 113 3564	54.14	.082 721	4.14	24
3	1.260 808	40.383 106	.024 762 8303	.793 142	32.029 556	.031 221 1636	37.47	.123 962	4.13	36
4	1.362 067	56.061 955	.017 837 4086	.734 178	41.159 476	.024 295 7419	29.16	.166 196	4.15	48
5	1.471 458	73.000 020	.013 698 6264	.679 598	49.610 656	.020 156 9598	24.19	.209 418	4.19	60
6	1.589 636	91.298 431	.010 953 0907	.629 075	57.433 556	.017 411 4241	20.90	.253 623	4.23	72
7	1.717 304	111.066 443	.009 003 6196	.582 308	64.674 883	.015 461 9529	18.56	.298 804	4.27	84
8	1.855 226	132.422 083	.007 551 6106	.539 018	71.377 873	.014 009 9439	16.82	.344 955	4.31	96
9	2.004 225	155.492 858	.006 431 1635	.498 946	77.582 547	.012 889 4969	15.47	.392 066	4.36	108
10	2.165 190	180.416 517	.005 542 7298	.461 853	83.325 951	.012 001 0631	14.41	.440 128	4.40	120
11	2.339 083	207.341 869	.004 822 9526	.427 518	88.642 377	.011 281 2859	13.54	.489 130	4.45	132
12	2.526 942	236.429 677	.004 229 5875	.395 735	93.563 568	.010 687 9208	12.83	.539 061	4.49	144
13	2.729 888	267.853 614	.003 733 3825	.366 315	98.118 905	.010 191 7159	12.24	.589 908	4.54	156
14	2.949 133	301.801 302	.003 313 4383	.339 083	102.335 588	.009 771 7717	11.73	.641 658	4.58	168
15	3.185 987	338.475 430	.002 954 4242	.313 874	106.238 793	.009 412 7575	11.30	.694 296	4.63	180
16	3.441 863	378.094 967	.002 644 8382	.290 540	109.851 825	.009 103 1715	10.93	.747 809	4.67	192
17	3.718 290	420.896 468	.002 375 8812	.268 941	113.196 255	.008 834 2145	10.61	.802 180	4.72	204
18	4.016 917	467.135 486	.002 140 7066	.248 947	116.292 053	.008 599 0399	10.32	.857 393	4.76	216
19	4.339 527	517.088 099	.001 933 9064	.230 440	119.157 701	.008 392 2398	10.08	.913 431	4.81	228
20	4.688 048	571.052 555	.001 751 1523	.213 308	121.810 311	.008 209 4856	9.86	.970 277	4.85	240
21	5.064 559	629.351 059	.001 588 9383	.197 451	124.265 720	.008 047 2716	9.66	1.027 912	4.89	252
22	5.471 309	692.331 690	.001 444 3944	.182 772	126.538 587	.007 902 7277	9.49	1.086 320	4.94	264
23	5.910 726	760.370 484	.001 315 1484	.169 184	128.642 485	.007 773 4817	9.33	1.145 481	4.98	276
24	6.385 434	833.873 678	.001 199 2224	.156 606	130.589 973	.007 657 5557	9.19	1.205 376	5.02	288
25	6.898 268	913.280 134	.001 094 9543	.144 964	132.392 681	.007 553 2876	9.07	1.265 986	5.06	300
26	7.452 288	999.063 960	.001 000 9369	.134 187	134.061 371	.007 459 2703	8.96	1.327 292	5.10	312
27	8.050 804	1091.737 343	.000 915 9712	.124 211	135.606 007	.007 374 3046	8.85	1.389 275	5.15	324
28	8.697 388	1191.853 602	.000 839 0292	.114 977	137.035 812	.007 297 3626	8.76	1.451 914	5.19	336
29	9.395 901	1300.010 499	.000 769 2246	.106 429	138.359 321	.007 227 5579	8.68	1.515 190	5.22	348
30	10.150 514	1416.853 800	.000 705 7891	.098 517	139.584 437	.007 164 1225	8.60	1.579 084	5.26	360
31	10.965 732	1543.081 137	.000 648 0541	.091 193	140.718 475	.007 106 3874	8.53	1.643 576	5.30	372
32	11.846 423	1679.446 170	.000 595 4344	.084 414	141.768 207	.007 053 7677	8.47	1.708 647	5.34	384
33	12.797 845	1826.763 088	.000 547 4164	.078 138	142.739 898	.007 005 7497	8.41	1.774 277	5.38	396
34	13.825 678	1985.911 468	.000 503 5471	.072 329	143.639 352	.006 961 8805	8.36	1.840 447	5.41	408
35	14.936 060	2157.841 533	.000 463 4261	.066 952	144.471 939	.006 921 7594	8.31	1.907 139	5.45	420
36	16.135 620	2343.579 816	.000 426 6977	.061 975	145.242 629	.006 885 0310	8.27	1.974 333	5.48	432
37	17.431 520	2544.235 297	.000 393 0454	.057 367	145.956 024	.006 851 3787	8.23	2.042 012	5.52	444
38	18.831 497	2761.006 022	.000 362 1868	.053 103	146.616 384	.006 820 5202	8.19	2.110 157	5.55	456
39	20.343 911	2995.186 253	.000 333 8691	.049 155	147.227 651	.006 792 2024	8.16	2.178 751	5.59	468
40	21.977 792	3248.174 201	.000 307 8653	.045 500	147.793 475	.006 766 1986	8.12	2.247 775	5.62	480
41	23.742 894	3521.480 370	.000 283 9715	.042 118	148.317 234	.006 742 3048	8.10	2.317 214	5.65	492
42	25.649 757	3816.736 576	.000 262 0039	.038 987	148.802 056	.006 720 3373	8.07	2.387 050	5.68	504
43	27.709 766	4135.705 693	.000 241 7967	.036 088	149.250 835	.006 700 1300	8.05	2.457 267	5.71	516
44	29.935 220	4480.292 176	.000 223 1997	.033 405	149.666 250	.006 681 5331	8.02	2.527 849	5.75	528
45	32.339 408	4852.553 432	.000 206 0771	.030 922	150.050 783	.006 664 4104	8.00	2.598 782	5.78	540
46	34.936 682	5254.712 106	.000 190 3054	.028 623	150.406 729	.006 648 6387	7.98	2.670 049	5.80	552
47	37.742 552	5689.169 349	.000 175 7726	.026 495	150.736 213	.006 634 1059	7.97	2.741 636	5.83	564
48	40.773 770	6158.519 155	.000 162 3767	.024 526	151.041 202	.006 620 7100	7.95	2.813 529	5.86	576
49	44.048 433	6665.563 851	.000 150 0248	.022 702	151.323 517	.006 608 3582	7.95	2.885 715	5.89	588
50	47.586 095	7213.330 826	.000 138 6322	.021 015	151.584 845	.006 596 9655	7.92	2.958 179	5.92	600

MONTHLY COMPOUND INTEREST AND ANNUITY

	Amount Of 1	Amount Of 1 Per Period	Sinking Fund Payment	Present Worth Of 1	Present Worth of 1 Per Period	Periodic Payment To Amortize 1	Constant Annual Percent	Total Interest	Annual Add On Rate	
	What a single $ 1 deposit grows to in the future. The deposit is made at the beginning of the first period.	What a series of $ 1 deposits grow to in the future. A deposit is made at the end of each period.	The amount to be deposited at the end of each period that grows to $ 1 in the future.	What $ 1 to be paid in the future is worth today. Value today of a single $ 1 payment tomorrow.	What $ 1 to be paid at the end of each period is worth today. Value today of a series of $ 1 payments tomorrow.	The mortgage payment to amortize a loan of $ 1. An annuity certain, payable at the end of each period, worth $ 1 today.	The annual payment, including interest and principal, to amortize completely a loan of $ 100.	The total interest paid over the term on a loan of $1. The loan is amortized by regular periodic payments.	The average annual interest rate on a loan that is completely amortized by regular periodic payments.	

$$S = (1+i)^n \qquad S\overline{n}| = \frac{(1+i)^n - 1}{i} \qquad \frac{1}{S\overline{n}|} = \frac{i}{(1+i)^n - 1} \qquad V^n = \frac{1}{(1+i)^n} \qquad A\overline{n}| = \frac{1-V^n}{i} \qquad \frac{1}{A\overline{n}|} = \frac{i}{1-V^n}$$

PERIODS

YEAR	Amount Of 1	Amount Of 1 Per Period	Sinking Fund Payment	Present Worth Of 1	Present Worth of 1 Per Period	Periodic Payment To Amortize 1	Constant Annual Percent	Total Interest	Annual Add On Rate	Periods
	1.006 500	1.000 000	1.000 000 0000	.993 542	.993 542	1.006 500 0000	1207.80	.006 500	7.80	1
	1.013 042	2.006 500	.498 380 2641	.987 126	1.980 668	.504 880 2641	605.86	.009 761	5.86	2
	1.019 627	3.019 542	.331 176 0251	.980 751	2.961 418	.337 676 0251	405.22	.013 028	5.21	3
	1.026 255	4.039 169	.247 575 6602	.974 417	3.935 835	.254 075 6602	304.90	.016 303	4.89	4
	1.032 925	5.065 424	.197 416 8450	.968 124	4.903 960	.203 916 8450	244.71	.019 584	4.70	5
	1.039 639	6.098 349	.163 978 8045	.961 872	5.865 832	.170 478 8045	204.58	.022 873	4.57	6
	1.046 397	7.137 988	.140 095 4925	.955 660	6.821 492	.146 595 4925	175.92	.026 168	4.49	7
	1.053 199	8.184 385	.122 183 8856	.949 489	7.770 981	.128 683 8856	154.43	.029 471	4.42	8
	1.060 044	9.237 584	.108 253 4155	.943 357	8.714 338	.114 753 4155	137.71	.032 781	4.37	9
	1.066 935	10.297 628	.097 109 7410	.937 265	9.651 602	.103 609 7410	124.34	.036 097	4.33	10
	1.073 870	11.364 563	.087 992 8270	.931 212	10.582 814	.094 492 8270	113.40	.039 421	4.30	11
	1.080 850	12.438 432	.080 395 9833	.925 198	11.508 012	.086 895 9833	104.28	.042 752	4.28	12
1	1.080 850	12.438 432	.080 395 9833	.925 198	11.508 012	.086 895 9833	104.28	.042 752	4.28	12
2	1.168 236	25.882 510	.038 636 1297	.855 991	22.155 200	.045 136 1297	54.17	.083 267	4.16	24
3	1.262 688	40.413 538	.024 744 1835	.791 961	32.005 957	.031 244 1835	37.50	.124 791	4.16	36
4	1.364 776	56.119 397	.017 819 1508	.732 721	41.119 857	.024 319 1508	29.19	.167 319	4.18	48
5	1.475 118	73.095 072	.013 680 8128	.677 912	49.552 018	.020 180 8128	24.22	.210 849	4.22	60
6	1.594 381	91.443 227	.010 935 7470	.627 203	57.353 436	.017 435 7470	20.93	.255 374	4.26	72
7	1.723 286	111.274 827	.008 986 7585	.580 287	64.571 292	.015 486 7585	18.59	.300 888	4.30	84
8	1.862 614	132.709 808	.007 535 2381	.536 880	71.249 237	.014 035 2381	16.85	.347 383	4.34	96
9	2.013 206	155.877 804	.006 415 2816	.496 720	77.427 658	.012 915 2816	15.50	.394 850	4.39	108
10	2.175 973	180.918 927	.005 527 3377	.459 565	83.143 920	.012 027 3377	14.44	.443 281	4.43	120
11	2.351 900	207.984 620	.004 808 0478	.425 188	88.432 594	.011 308 0478	13.57	.492 662	4.48	132
12	2.542 051	237.238 569	.004 215 1662	.393 383	93.325 664	.010 715 1662	12.86	.542 984	4.52	144
13	2.747 575	268.857 695	.003 719 4398	.363 957	97.852 722	.010 219 4398	12.27	.594 233	4.57	156
14	2.969 716	303.033 221	.003 299 9682	.336 733	102.041 147	.009 799 9682	11.76	.646 395	4.62	168
15	3.209 817	339.971 832	.002 941 4202	.311 544	105.916 269	.009 441 4202	11.33	.699 456	4.66	180
16	3.469 330	379.896 923	.002 632 2930	.288 240	109.501 524	.009 132 2930	10.96	.753 400	4.71	192
17	3.749 825	423.049 949	.002 363 7871	.266 679	112.818 595	.008 863 7871	10.64	.808 213	4.75	204
18	4.052 997	469.691 890	.002 129 0553	.246 731	115.887 541	.008 629 0553	10.36	.863 876	4.80	216
19	4.380 681	520.104 822	.001 922 6893	.228 275	118.726 924	.008 422 6893	10.11	.920 373	4.84	228
20	4.734 859	574.593 631	.001 740 3604	.211 304	121.353 916	.008 240 3604	9.89	.977 686	4.89	240
21	5.117 671	633.487 849	.001 578 5622	.195 401	123.784 402	.008 078 5622	9.70	1.035 798	4.93	252
22	5.531 434	697.143 654	.001 434 4246	.180 785	126.033 084	.007 934 4246	9.53	1.094 688	4.98	264
23	5.978 649	765.946 019	.001 305 5750	.167 262	128.113 559	.007 805 5750	9.37	1.154 339	5.02	276
24	6.462 022	840.311 041	.001 190 0355	.154 750	130.038 411	.007 690 0355	9.23	1.214 730	5.06	288
25	6.984 475	920.688 462	.001 086 1437	.143 175	131.819 279	.007 586 1437	9.11	1.275 843	5.10	300
26	7.549 168	1007.564 382	.000 992 4924	.132 465	133.466 935	.007 492 4924	9.00	1.337 658	5.14	312
27	8.159 517	1101.464 204	.000 907 8824	.122 556	134.991 343	.007 407 8824	8.89	1.400 154	5.19	324
28	8.819 213	1202.955 808	.000 831 2857	.113 389	136.401 722	.007 331 2857	8.80	1.463 312	5.23	336
29	9.532 244	1312.652 989	.000 761 8160	.104 907	137.706 602	.007 261 8160	8.72	1.527 112	5.27	348
30	10.302 925	1431.219 167	.000 698 7050	.097 060	138.913 874	.007 198 7050	8.64	1.591 534	5.31	360
31	11.135 914	1559.371 397	.000 641 2840	.089 800	140.030 839	.007 141 2840	8.57	1.656 558	5.34	372
32	12.036 251	1697.884 712	.000 588 9681	.083 082	141.064 254	.007 088 9681	8.51	1.722 164	5.38	384
33	13.009 379	1847.596 801	.000 541 2436	.076 868	142.020 366	.007 041 2436	8.45	1.788 332	5.42	396
34	14.061 185	2009.413 084	.000 497 6578	.071 118	142.904 960	.006 997 6578	8.40	1.855 044	5.46	408
35	15.198 029	2184.312 183	.000 457 8100	.065 798	143.723 384	.006 957 8100	8.35	1.922 280	5.49	420
36	16.426 787	2373.351 842	.000 421 3450	.060 876	144.480 588	.006 921 3450	8.31	1.990 021	5.53	432
37	17.754 890	2577.675 320	.000 387 9465	.056 323	145.181 152	.006 887 9465	8.27	2.058 248	5.56	444
38	19.190 369	2798.518 313	.000 357 3319	.052 109	145.829 312	.006 857 3319	8.23	2.126 943	5.60	456
39	20.741 907	3037.216 421	.000 329 2488	.048 212	146.428 988	.006 829 2488	8.20	2.196 088	5.63	468
40	22.418 886	3295.213 225	.000 303 4705	.044 605	146.983 808	.006 803 4705	8.17	2.265 666	5.66	480
41	24.231 449	3574.069 022	.000 279 7931	.041 269	147.497 126	.006 779 7931	8.14	2.335 658	5.70	492
42	26.190 557	3875.470 256	.000 258 0332	.038 182	147.972 046	.006 758 0332	8.11	2.406 049	5.73	504
43	28.308 058	4201.239 724	.000 238 0250	.035 326	148.411 441	.006 738 0250	8.09	2.476 821	5.76	516
44	30.596 759	4553.347 592	.000 219 6186	.032 683	148.817 969	.006 719 6186	8.07	2.547 959	5.79	528
45	33.070 502	4933.923 313	.000 202 6785	.030 238	149.194 088	.006 702 6785	8.05	2.619 446	5.82	540
46	35.744 245	5345.268 510	.000 187 0813	.027 977	149.542 072	.006 687 0813	8.03	2.691 269	5.85	552
47	38.634 161	5789.870 888	.000 172 7154	.025 884	149.864 026	.006 672 7154	8.01	2.763 411	5.88	564
48	41.757 725	6270.419 283	.000 159 4790	.023 948	150.161 898	.006 659 4790	8.00	2.835 860	5.91	576
49	45.133 830	6789.819 926	.000 147 2793	.022 156	150.437 488	.006 647 2793	7.98	2.908 600	5.94	588
50	48.782 891	7351.214 011	.000 136 0320	.020 499	150.692 463	.006 636 0320	7.97	2.981 619	5.96	600

Effective Rate is 8.08 %

Annual Percentage Rate is 7.80 %

	Amount Of 1	Amount Of 1 Per Period	Sinking Fund Payment	Present Worth Of 1	Present Worth of 1 Per Period	Periodic Payment To Amortize 1	Constant Annual Percent	Total Interest	Annual Add On Rate	
	What a single $1 deposit grows to in the future. The deposit is made at the beginning of the first period.	What a series of $1 deposits grow to in the future. A deposit is made at the end of each period.	The amount to be deposited at the end of each period that grows to $1 in the future.	What $1 to be paid in the future is worth today. Value today of a single $1 payment tomorrow.	What $1 to be paid at the end of each period is worth today. Value today of a series of $1 payments tomorrow.	The mortgage payment to amortize a loan of $1. An annuity certain, payable at the end of each period, worth $1 today.	The annual payment, including interest and principal, to amortize completely a loan of $100.	The total interest paid over the term on a loan of $1. The loan is amortized by regular periodic payments.	The average annual interest rate on a loan that is completely amortized by regular periodic payments.	
	$S = (1+i)^n$	$S\overline{n} = \dfrac{(1+i)^n - 1}{i}$	$\dfrac{1}{S\overline{n}} = \dfrac{i}{(1+i)^n - 1}$	$V^n = \dfrac{1}{(1+i)^n}$	$A\overline{n} = \dfrac{1-V^n}{i}$	$\dfrac{1}{A\overline{n}} = \dfrac{i}{1-V^n}$				

YEAR / **PERIODS**

YEAR	Amount Of 1	Amount Of 1 Per Period	Sinking Fund Payment	Present Worth Of 1	Present Worth of 1 Per Period	Periodic Payment To Amortize 1	Constant Annual Percent	Total Interest	Annual Add On Rate	PERIODS
	1.006 542	1.000 000	1.000 000 0000	.993 501	.993 501	1.006 541 6667	1207.85	.006 542	7.85	1
	1.013 126	2.006 542	.498 369 9151	.987 044	1.980 545	.504 911 5817	605.90	.009 823	5.89	2
	1.019 754	3.019 668	.331 162 2564	.980 629	2.961 174	.337 703 9231	405.25	.013 112	5.24	3
	1.026 425	4.039 421	.247 560 2042	.974 256	3.935 430	.254 101 8709	304.93	.016 407	4.92	4
	1.033 139	5.065 846	.197 400 3946	.967 924	4.903 353	.203 942 0613	244.74	.019 710	4.73	5
	1.039 898	6.098 985	.163 961 7063	.961 633	5.864 987	.170 503 3729	204.61	.023 020	4.60	6
	1.046 700	7.138 883	.140 077 9443	.955 383	6.820 370	.146 619 6110	175.95	.026 337	4.51	7
	1.053 547	8.185 583	.122 166 0113	.949 174	7.769 544	.128 707 6779	154.45	.029 661	4.45	8
	1.060 439	9.239 130	.108 235 2975	.943 005	8.712 550	.114 776 9641	137.74	.032 993	4.40	9
	1.067 376	10.299 569	.097 091 4371	.936 877	9.649 426	.103 633 1037	124.36	.036 331	4.36	10
	1.074 359	11.366 946	.087 974 3791	.930 788	10.580 214	.094 516 0458	113.42	.039 677	4.33	11
	1.081 387	12.441 305	.080 377 4229	.924 738	11.504 953	.086 919 0896	104.31	.043 029	4.30	12
1	1.081 387	12.441 305	.080 377 4229	.924 738	11.504 953	.086 919 0896	104.31	.043 029	4.30	12
2	1.169 398	25.895 168	.038 617 2432	.855 141	22.144 024	.045 158 9099	54.20	.083 814	4.19	24
3	1.264 571	40.443 999	.024 725 5470	.790 782	31.982 383	.031 267 2136	37.53	.125 620	4.19	36
4	1.367 491	56.176 914	.017 800 9066	.731 266	41.080 291	.024 342 5732	29.22	.168 444	4.21	48
5	1.478 786	73.190 282	.013 663 0161	.676 230	49.493 477	.020 204 6828	24.25	.212 281	4.25	60
6	1.599 140	91.588 314	.010 918 4235	.625 336	57.273 473	.017 460 0902	20.96	.257 126	4.29	72
7	1.729 289	111.483 705	.008 969 9208	.578 272	64.467 934	.015 511 5875	18.62	.302 973	4.33	84
8	1.870 031	132.998 319	.007 518 8920	.534 751	71.120 929	.014 060 5587	16.88	.349 814	4.37	96
9	2.022 227	156.263 940	.006 399 4291	.494 504	77.273 209	.012 941 0957	15.53	.397 638	4.42	108
10	2.186 809	181.423 077	.005 511 9779	.457 287	82.962 459	.012 053 6446	14.47	.446 437	4.46	120
11	2.364 787	208.629 838	.004 793 1783	.422 871	88.223 527	.011 334 8449	13.61	.496 200	4.51	132
12	2.557 249	238.050 871	.004 200 7828	.391 045	93.088 639	.010 742 4494	12.90	.546 913	4.56	144
13	2.765 376	269.866 390	.003 705 5374	.361 614	97.587 595	.010 247 2041	12.30	.598 564	4.60	156
14	2.990 441	304.271 275	.003 286 5409	.334 399	101.747 953	.009 828 2076	11.80	.651 139	4.65	168
15	3.233 824	341.476 266	.002 928 4612	.309 231	105.595 195	.009 470 1279	11.37	.704 623	4.70	180
16	3.497 015	381.709 254	.002 619 7950	.285 958	109.152 888	.009 161 4617	11.00	.759 001	4.74	192
17	3.781 626	425.216 679	.002 351 7422	.264 437	112.442 823	.008 893 4088	10.68	.814 255	4.79	204
18	4.089 400	472.265 037	.002 117 4551	.244 535	115.485 153	.008 659 1217	10.40	.870 370	4.84	216
19	4.422 224	523.142 513	.001 911 5250	.226 131	118.298 512	.008 453 1917	10.15	.927 328	4.88	228
20	4.782 135	578.160 748	.001 729 6228	.209 112	120.900 134	.008 271 2894	9.93	.985 109	4.93	240
21	5.171 338	637.656 745	.001 568 2419	.193 374	123.305 953	.008 109 9085	9.74	1.043 697	4.97	252
22	5.592 217	701.994 935	.001 424 5117	.178 820	125.530 707	.007 966 1784	9.56	1.103 071	5.01	264
23	6.047 350	771.569 408	.001 296 0597	.165 362	127.588 022	.007 837 7263	9.41	1.163 212	5.06	276
24	6.539 525	846.806 330	.001 180 9076	.152 916	129.490 500	.007 722 5742	9.27	1.224 101	5.10	288
25	7.071 756	928.166 549	.001 077 3928	.141 408	131.249 795	.007 619 0595	9.15	1.285 718	5.14	300
26	7.647 304	1016.148 421	.000 984 1082	.130 765	132.876 683	.007 525 7749	9.04	1.348 042	5.18	312
27	8.269 694	1111.290 863	.000 899 8544	.120 923	134.381 128	.007 441 5211	8.93	1.411 053	5.23	324
28	8.942 739	1214.176 649	.000 823 6034	.111 823	135.772 347	.007 365 2701	8.84	1.474 731	5.27	336
29	9.670 560	1325.435 988	.000 754 4687	.103 407	137.058 860	.007 296 1354	8.76	1.539 055	5.31	348
30	10.457 617	1445.750 376	.000 691 6823	.095 624	138.248 548	.007 233 3490	8.69	1.604 006	5.35	360
31	11.308 730	1575.856 775	.000 634 5754	.088 427	139.348 699	.007 176 2421	8.62	1.669 562	5.39	372
32	12.229 112	1716.552 126	.000 582 5631	.081 772	140.366 050	.007 124 2298	8.55	1.735 704	5.42	384
33	13.224 401	1868.698 230	.000 535 1319	.075 618	141.306 834	.007 076 7985	8.50	1.802 412	5.46	396
34	14.300 693	2033.227 030	.000 491 8290	.069 927	142.176 813	.007 033 4957	8.45	1.869 666	5.50	408
35	15.464 582	2211.146 314	.000 452 2541	.064 664	142.981 317	.006 993 9208	8.40	1.937 447	5.54	420
36	16.723 196	2403.545 890	.000 416 0520	.059 797	143.725 272	.006 957 7186	8.35	2.005 734	5.57	432
37	18.084 245	2611.604 266	.000 382 9064	.055 297	144.413 235	.006 924 5731	8.31	2.074 510	5.61	444
38	19.556 065	2836.595 860	.000 352 5352	.051 135	145.049 422	.006 894 2019	8.28	2.143 756	5.64	456
39	21.147 671	3079.898 816	.000 324 6860	.047 287	145.637 728	.006 866 3527	8.24	2.213 453	5.68	468
40	22.868 814	3343.003 438	.000 299 1322	.043 728	146.181 757	.006 840 7989	8.21	2.283 583	5.71	480
41	24.730 035	3627.521 320	.000 275 6703	.040 437	146.684 842	.006 817 3370	8.19	2.354 130	5.74	492
42	26.742 735	3935.195 222	.000 254 1170	.037 393	147.150 064	.006 795 7837	8.16	2.425 075	5.77	504
43	28.919 243	4267.909 738	.000 234 3067	.034 579	147.580 272	.006 775 9734	8.14	2.496 402	5.81	516
44	31.272 889	4627.702 847	.000 216 0899	.031 977	147.978 103	.006 757 7566	8.11	2.568 095	5.84	528
45	33.818 092	5016.778 390	.000 199 3311	.029 570	148.345 992	.006 740 9978	8.09	2.640 139	5.87	540
46	36.570 441	5437.519 572	.000 183 9074	.027 344	148.686 193	.006 725 5741	8.08	2.712 517	5.90	552
47	39.546 794	5892.503 561	.000 169 7072	.025 286	149.000 790	.006 711 3738	8.06	2.785 215	5.93	564
48	42.765 384	6384.517 272	.000 156 6289	.023 383	149.291 710	.006 698 2956	8.04	2.858 218	5.95	576
49	46.245 924	6916.574 438	.000 144 5802	.021 624	149.560 735	.006 686 2469	8.03	2.931 513	5.98	588
50	50.009 735	7491.934 070	.000 133 4769	.019 996	149.809 512	.006 675 1435	8.02	3.005 086	6.01	600

Effective Rate is 8.14 %

Annual Percentage Rate is 7.85 %

MONTHLY COMPOUND INTEREST AND ANNUITY

7.875% M

Amount Of 1	Amount Of 1 Per Period	Sinking Fund Payment	Present Worth Of 1	Present Worth of 1 Per Period	Periodic Payment To Amortize 1	Constant Annual Percent	Total Interest	Annual Add On Rate	
What a single $ 1 deposit grows to in the future. The deposit is made at the beginning of the first period.	What a series of $ 1 deposits grow to in the future. A deposit is made at the end of each period.	The amount to be deposited at the end of each period that grows to $ 1 in the future.	What $ 1 to be paid in the future is worth today. Value today of a single $ 1 payment tomorrow.	What $ 1 to be paid at the end of each period is worth today. Value today of a series of $ 1 payments tomorrow.	The mortgage payment to amortize a loan of $ 1. An annuity certain, payable at the end of each period, worth $ 1 today.	The annual interest payment, including interest and principal, to amortize completely a loan of $ 100.	The total interest paid over the term on a loan of $1. The loan is amortized by regular periodic payments.	The average annual interest rate on a loan that is completely amortized by regular periodic payments.	

$$S = (1 + i)^n \qquad S\overline{n}| = \frac{(1+i)^n - 1}{i} \qquad \frac{1}{S\overline{n}|} = \frac{i}{(1+i)^n - 1} \qquad V^n = \frac{1}{(1+i)^n} \qquad A\overline{n}| = \frac{1 - V^n}{i} \qquad \frac{1}{A\overline{n}|} = \frac{i}{1 - V^n}$$

PERIODS

YEAR										
	1.006 563	1.000 000	1.000 000 0000	.993 480	.993 480	1.006 562 5000	1207.88	.006 562	7.87	1
	1.013 168	2.006 563	.498 364 7407	.987 003	1.980 483	.504 927 2407	605.92	.009 854	5.91	2
	1.019 817	3.019 731	.331 155 3723	.980 568	2.961 051	.337 717 8723	405.27	.013 154	5.26	3
	1.026 510	4.039 548	.247 552 4766	.974 175	3.935 227	.254 114 9766	304.94	.016 460	4.94	4
	1.033 246	5.066 057	.197 392 1700	.967 824	4.903 050	.203 954 6700	244.75	.019 773	4.75	5
	1.040 027	6.099 303	.163 953 1578	.961 514	5.864 564	.170 515 6578	204.62	.023 094	4.62	6
	1.046 852	7.139 330	.140 069 1710	.955 245	6.819 809	.146 631 6710	175.96	.026 422	4.53	7
	1.053 722	8.186 182	.122 157 0749	.949 017	7.768 826	.128 719 5749	154.47	.029 757	4.46	8
	1.060 637	9.239 903	.108 226 2394	.942 830	8.711 656	.114 788 7394	137.75	.033 099	4.41	9
	1.067 597	10.300 540	.097 082 2862	.936 683	9.648 339	.103 644 7862	124.38	.036 448	4.37	10
	1.074 603	11.368 138	.087 965 1563	.930 576	10.578 915	.094 527 6563	113.44	.039 804	4.34	11
	1.081 655	12.442 741	.080 368 1440	.924 509	11.503 423	.086 930 6440	104.32	.043 168	4.32	12
1	1.081 655	12.442 741	.080 368 1440	.924 509	11.503 423	.086 930 6440	104.32	.043 168	4.32	12
2	1.169 979	25.901 500	.038 607 8025	.854 716	22.138 439	.045 170 3025	54.21	.084 087	4.20	24
3	1.265 514	40.459 241	.024 716 2325	.790 193	31.970 605	.031 278 7325	37.54	.126 034	4.20	36
4	1.368 850	56.205 701	.017 791 7896	.730 540	41.060 528	.024 354 2896	29.23	.169 006	4.23	48
5	1.480 624	73.237 946	.013 654 1241	.675 391	49.464 243	.020 216 6241	24.26	.212 997	4.26	60
6	1.601 525	91.660 967	.010 909 7693	.624 405	57.233 550	.017 472 2693	20.97	.258 003	4.30	72
7	1.732 298	111.588 329	.008 961 5107	.577 268	64.416 343	.015 524 0107	18.63	.304 017	4.34	84
8	1.873 750	133.142 869	.007 510 7289	.533 689	71.056 898	.014 073 2289	16.89	.351 030	4.39	96
9	2.026 752	156.457 456	.006 391 5139	.493 400	77.196 150	.012 954 0139	15.55	.399 033	4.43	108
10	2.192 247	181.675 807	.005 504 3102	.456 153	82.871 942	.012 066 8102	14.49	.448 017	4.48	120
11	2.371 257	208.953 374	.004 785 7566	.421 717	88.119 262	.011 348 2566	13.62	.497 970	4.53	132
12	2.564 883	238.458 305	.004 193 6052	.389 881	92.970 455	.010 756 1052	12.91	.548 879	4.57	144
13	2.774 319	270.372 475	.003 698 6013	.360 449	97.455 426	.010 261 1013	12.32	.600 732	4.62	156
14	3.000 858	304.892 613	.003 279 8433	.333 238	101.601 821	.009 842 3433	11.82	.653 514	4.67	168
15	3.245 894	342.231 509	.002 921 9986	.308 082	105.435 199	.009 484 4986	11.39	.707 210	4.71	180
16	3.510 939	382.619 330	.002 613 5637	.284 824	108.979 191	.009 176 0637	11.02	.761 804	4.76	192
17	3.797 627	426.305 039	.002 345 7382	.263 322	112.255 643	.008 908 2382	10.69	.817 281	4.81	204
18	4.107 724	473.557 926	.002 111 6741	.243 444	115.284 751	.008 674 1741	10.41	.873 622	4.85	216
19	4.443 142	524.669 271	.001 905 9626	.225 066	118.085 188	.008 468 4626	10.17	.930 809	4.90	228
20	4.805 949	579.954 137	.001 724 2743	.208 075	120.674 217	.008 286 7743	9.95	.988 826	4.94	240
21	5.198 381	639.753 316	.001 563 1025	.192 368	123.067 797	.008 125 6025	9.76	1.047 652	4.99	252
22	5.622 857	704.435 426	.001 419 5765	.177 846	125.280 683	.007 982 0765	9.58	1.107 268	5.03	264
23	6.081 995	774.399 185	.001 291 3237	.164 420	127.326 515	.007 853 8237	9.43	1.167 655	5.08	276
24	6.578 623	850.075 869	.001 176 3656	.152 007	129.217 905	.007 738 8656	9.29	1.228 793	5.12	288
25	7.115 804	931.931 970	.001 073 0397	.140 532	130.966 512	.007 635 5397	9.17	1.290 662	5.16	300
26	7.696 848	1020.472 070	.000 979 9386	.129 923	132.583 114	.007 542 4386	9.06	1.353 241	5.20	312
27	8.325 338	1116.241 956	.000 895 8631	.120 115	134.077 677	.007 458 3631	8.96	1.416 510	5.25	324
28	9.005 147	1219.831 978	.000 819 7850	.111 048	135.459 413	.007 382 2850	8.86	1.480 448	5.29	336
29	9.740 467	1331.880 695	.000 750 8180	.102 664	136.736 841	.007 313 3180	8.78	1.545 035	5.33	348
30	10.535 830	1453.078 803	.000 688 1939	.094 914	137.917 834	.007 250 6939	8.71	1.610 250	5.37	360
31	11.396 138	1584.173 403	.000 631 2440	.087 749	139.009 672	.007 193 7440	8.64	1.676 073	5.41	372
32	12.326 695	1725.972 596	.000 579 3835	.081 125	140.019 086	.007 141 8835	8.58	1.742 483	5.45	384
33	13.333 237	1879.350 471	.000 532 0987	.075 001	140.952 299	.007 094 5987	8.52	1.809 461	5.48	396
34	14.421 969	2045.252 491	.000 488 9372	.069 339	141.815 062	.007 051 4372	8.47	1.876 986	5.52	408
35	15.599 602	2224.701 322	.000 449 4985	.064 104	142.612 694	.007 011 9985	8.42	1.945 039	5.56	420
36	16.873 396	2418.803 134	.000 413 4276	.059 265	143.350 111	.006 975 9276	8.38	2.013 601	5.59	432
37	18.251 201	2628.754 425	.000 380 4083	.054 791	144.031 861	.006 942 9083	8.34	2.082 651	5.63	444
38	19.741 512	2855.649 390	.000 350 1585	.050 655	144.662 144	.006 912 6585	8.30	2.152 172	5.66	456
39	21.353 514	3101.487 906	.000 322 4259	.046 831	145.244 846	.006 884 9259	8.27	2.222 145	5.70	468
40	23.097 146	3367.184 155	.000 296 9841	.043 295	145.783 559	.006 859 4841	8.24	2.292 552	5.73	480
41	24.983 155	3654.575 960	.000 273 6296	.040 027	146.281 604	.006 836 1296	8.21	2.363 376	5.76	492
42	27.023 166	3965.434 884	.000 252 1792	.037 005	146.742 052	.006 814 6792	8.18	2.434 598	5.80	504
43	29.229 756	4301.677 144	.000 232 4675	.034 212	147.167 739	.006 794 9675	8.16	2.506 203	5.83	516
44	31.616 526	4665.375 431	.000 214 3450	.031 629	147.561 291	.006 776 8450	8.14	2.578 174	5.86	528
45	34.198 189	5058.771 678	.000 197 6764	.029 241	147.925 503	.006 760 1764	8.12	2.650 495	5.89	540
46	36.990 659	5484.290 888	.000 182 3390	.027 034	148.261 508	.006 744 8390	8.10	2.723 151	5.92	552
47	40.011 149	5944.556 076	.000 168 2211	.024 993	148.572 490	.006 730 7211	8.08	2.796 127	5.95	564
48	43.278 279	6442.404 443	.000 155 2215	.023 106	148.859 996	.006 717 7215	8.07	2.869 408	5.98	576
49	46.812 188	6980.904 860	.000 143 2479	.021 362	149.125 797	.006 705 7479	8.05	2.942 980	6.01	588
50	50.634 660	7563.376 793	.000 132 2161	.019 749	149.371 533	.006 694 7161	8.04	3.016 830	6.03	600

Effective Rate is 8.17 %   8 - 85   Annual Percentage Rate is 7.875%

MONTHLY COMPOUND INTEREST AND ANNUITY

Amount Of 1	Amount Of 1 Per Period	Sinking Fund Payment	Present Worth Of 1	Present Worth of 1 Per Period	Periodic Payment To Amortize 1	Constant Annual Percent	Total Interest	Annual Add On Rate
What a single $ 1 deposit grows to in the future. The deposit is made at the beginning of the first period.	What a series of $ 1 deposits grow to in the future. A deposit is made at the end of each period.	The amount to be deposited at the end of each period that grows to $ 1 in the future.	What $ 1 to be paid in the future is worth today. Value today of a single $ 1 payment tomorrow.	What $ 1 to be paid at the end of each period is worth today. Value today of a series of $ 1 payments tomorrow.	The mortgage payment to amortize a loan of $ 1. An annuity certain, payable at the end of each period, worth $ 1 today.	The annual payment, including interest and principal, to amortize completely a loan of $ 100.	The total interest paid over the term on a loan of $ 1. The loan is amortized by regular periodic payments.	The average annual interest rate on a loan that is completely amortized by regular periodic payments.
$S = (1+i)^n$	$S\overline{n}\rceil = \dfrac{(1+i)^n - 1}{i}$	$\dfrac{1}{S\overline{n}\rceil} = \dfrac{i}{(1+i)^n - 1}$	$V^n = \dfrac{1}{(1+i)^n}$	$A\overline{n}\rceil = \dfrac{1 - V^n}{i}$	$\dfrac{1}{A\overline{n}\rceil} = \dfrac{i}{1 - V^n}$			

YEAR / **PERIODS**

YEAR	Amount Of 1	Amount Of 1 Per Period	Sinking Fund Payment	Present Worth Of 1	Present Worth of 1 Per Period	Periodic Payment To Amortize 1	Constant Annual Percent	Total Interest	Annual Add On Rate	PERIODS
	1.006 583	1.000 000	1.000 000 0000	.993 460	.993 460	1.006 583 3333	1207.90	.006 583	7.90	1
	1.013 210	2.006 583	.498 359 5664	.986 962	1.980 422	.504 942 8998	605.94	.009 886	5.93	2
	1.019 880	3.019 793	.331 148 4884	.980 507	2.960 929	.337 731 8218	405.28	.013 195	5.28	3
	1.026 595	4.039 674	.247 544 7493	.974 094	3.935 024	.254 128 0826	304.96	.016 512	4.95	4
	1.033 353	5.066 268	.197 383 9456	.967 724	4.902 747	.203 967 2790	244.77	.019 836	4.76	5
	1.040 156	6.099 621	.163 944 6097	.961 394	5.864 142	.170 527 9430	204.64	.023 168	4.63	6
	1.047 004	7.139 777	.140 060 3981	.955 107	6.819 248	.146 643 7314	175.98	.026 506	4.54	7
	1.053 896	8.186 780	.122 148 1392	.948 860	7.768 108	.128 731 4725	154.48	.029 852	4.48	8
	1.060 834	9.240 677	.108 217 1820	.942 654	8.710 762	.114 800 5153	137.77	.033 205	4.43	9
	1.067 818	10.301 511	.097 073 1360	.936 489	9.647 251	.103 656 4693	124.39	.036 565	4.39	10
	1.074 848	11.369 330	.087 955 9344	.930 364	10.577 615	.094 539 2677	113.45	.039 932	4.36	11
	1.081 924	12.444 178	.080 358 8660	.924 279	11.501 894	.086 942 1993	104.34	.043 306	4.33	12
1	1.081 924	12.444 178	.080 358 8660	.924 279	11.501 894	.086 942 1993	104.34	.043 306	4.33	12
2	1.170 560	25.907 834	.038 598 3636	.854 292	22.132 856	.045 181 6969	54.22	.084 361	4.22	24
3	1.266 457	40.474 489	.024 706 9207	.789 604	31.958 833	.031 290 2540	37.55	.126 449	4.21	36
4	1.370 210	56.234 506	.017 782 6760	.729 815	41.040 779	.024 366 0093	29.24	.169 568	4.24	48
5	1.482 464	73.285 649	.013 645 2364	.674 553	49.435 032	.020 228 5697	24.28	.213 714	4.27	60
6	1.603 913	91.733 692	.010 901 1201	.623 475	57.193 666	.017 484 4535	20.99	.258 881	4.31	72
7	1.735 313	111.693 076	.008 953 1064	.576 265	64.364 810	.015 536 4398	18.65	.305 061	4.36	84
8	1.877 477	133.287 616	.007 502 5725	.532 630	70.992 950	.014 085 9058	16.91	.352 247	4.40	96
9	2.031 288	156.651 271	.006 383 6060	.492 299	77.119 201	.012 966 9394	15.57	.400 429	4.45	108
10	2.197 699	181.928 974	.005 496 6506	.455 021	82.781 567	.012 079 9839	14.50	.449 598	4.50	120
11	2.377 744	209.277 532	.004 778 3438	.420 567	88.015 175	.011 361 6772	13.64	.499 741	4.54	132
12	2.572 538	238.866 597	.004 186 4372	.388 721	92.852 489	.010 769 7705	12.93	.550 847	4.59	144
13	2.783 292	270.879 722	.003 691 6754	.359 287	97.323 519	.010 275 0087	12.34	.602 901	4.64	156
14	3.011 310	305.515 496	.003 273 1564	.332 081	101.455 998	.009 856 4897	11.83	.655 890	4.68	168
15	3.258 009	342.988 777	.002 915 5473	.306 936	105.275 562	.009 498 8806	11.40	.709 799	4.73	180
16	3.524 919	383.532 025	.002 607 3442	.283 694	108.805 907	.009 190 6775	11.03	.764 610	4.78	192
17	3.813 695	427.396 745	.002 339 7464	.262 213	112.068 930	.008 923 0797	10.71	.820 308	4.83	204
18	4.126 129	474.855 046	.002 105 9058	.242 358	115.084 875	.008 689 2391	10.43	.876 876	4.87	216
19	4.464 159	526.201 329	.001 900 4133	.224 006	117.872 450	.008 483 7466	10.19	.934 294	4.92	228
20	4.829 881	581.754 113	.001 718 9393	.207 044	120.448 948	.008 302 2726	9.97	.992 545	4.96	240
21	5.225 565	641.858 013	.001 557 9770	.191 367	122.830 351	.008 141 3103	9.77	1.051 610	5.01	252
22	5.653 665	706.885 875	.001 414 6555	.176 876	125.031 432	.007 997 9888	9.60	1.111 469	5.05	264
23	6.116 837	777.241 091	.001 286 6021	.163 483	127.065 846	.007 869 9354	9.45	1.172 102	5.10	276
24	6.617 954	853.360 099	.001 171 8382	.151 104	128.946 212	.007 755 1716	9.31	1.233 489	5.14	288
25	7.160 124	935.715 094	.001 068 7014	.139 662	130.684 196	.007 652 0347	9.19	1.295 610	5.18	300
26	7.746 712	1024.816 953	.000 975 7840	.129 087	132.290 578	.007 559 1173	9.08	1.358 445	5.22	312
27	8.381 355	1121.218 408	.000 891 8869	.119 312	133.775 323	.007 475 2202	8.98	1.421 971	5.27	324
28	9.067 990	1225.517 472	.000 815 9818	.110 278	135.147 642	.007 399 3152	8.88	1.486 170	5.31	336
29	9.810 878	1338.361 150	.000 747 1825	.101 928	136.416 048	.007 330 5158	8.80	1.551 020	5.35	348
30	10.614 626	1460.449 453	.000 684 7207	.094 210	137.588 410	.007 268 0541	8.73	1.616 499	5.39	360
31	11.484 220	1592.539 739	.000 627 9278	.087 076	138.671 999	.007 211 2611	8.66	1.682 589	5.43	372
32	12.425 055	1735.451 412	.000 576 2190	.080 483	139.673 538	.007 159 5523	8.60	1.749 268	5.47	384
33	13.442 967	1890.071 004	.000 529 0807	.074 388	140.599 240	.007 112 4140	8.54	1.816 516	5.50	396
34	14.544 271	2057.357 678	.000 486 0604	.068 756	141.454 847	.007 069 3937	8.49	1.884 313	5.54	408
35	15.735 799	2238.349 175	.000 446 7578	.063 549	142.245 666	.007 030 0912	8.44	1.952 638	5.58	420
36	17.024 941	2434.168 249	.000 410 8179	.058 737	142.976 604	.006 994 1513	8.40	2.021 473	5.62	432
37	18.419 695	2646.029 638	.000 377 9247	.054 290	143.652 195	.006 961 2580	8.36	2.090 799	5.65	444
38	19.928 713	2875.247 595	.000 347 7961	.050 179	144.276 630	.006 931 1295	8.32	2.160 595	5.69	456
39	21.561 357	3123.244 043	.000 320 1799	.046 379	144.853 782	.006 903 5132	8.29	2.230 844	5.72	468
40	23.327 753	3391.557 394	.000 294 8498	.042 867	145.387 231	.006 878 1831	8.26	2.301 528	5.75	480
41	25.238 860	3681.852 093	.000 271 6024	.039 621	145.880 287	.006 854 9358	8.23	2.372 628	5.79	492
42	27.306 532	3995.928 944	.000 250 2547	.036 621	146.336 009	.006 833 5880	8.21	2.444 128	5.82	504
43	29.543 597	4335.736 281	.000 230 6413	.033 848	146.757 223	.006 813 9747	8.18	2.516 011	5.85	516
44	31.963 932	4703.382 051	.000 212 6130	.031 285	147.146 542	.006 795 9463	8.16	2.588 260	5.88	528
45	34.582 550	5101.146 895	.000 196 0343	.028 916	147.506 382	.006 779 3677	8.14	2.660 859	5.91	540
46	37.415 697	5531.498 254	.000 180 7828	.026 727	147.838 975	.006 764 1162	8.12	2.733 792	5.94	552
47	40.480 947	5997.105 874	.000 166 7471	.024 703	148.146 383	.006 750 0804	8.11	2.807 045	5.97	564
48	43.797 315	6500.857 967	.000 153 8258	.022 832	148.430 514	.006 737 1592	8.09	2.880 604	6.00	576
49	47.385 374	7045.879 533	.000 141 9269	.021 104	148.693 130	.006 725 2603	8.08	2.954 453	6.03	588
50	51.267 381	7635.551 537	.000 130 9663	.019 506	148.935 861	.006 714 2996	8.06	3.028 580	6.06	600

Effective Rate is 8.19 %

Annual Percentage Rate is 7.90 %

	Amount Of 1	Amount Of 1 Per Period	Sinking Fund Payment	Present Worth Of 1	Present Worth of 1 Per Period	Periodic Payment To Amortize 1	Constant Annual Percent	Total Interest	Annual Add On Rate	
	What a single $ 1 deposit grows to in the future. The deposit is made at the beginning of the first period.	What a series of $ 1 deposits grow to in the future. A deposit is made at the end of each period.	The amount to be deposited at the end of each period that grows to $ 1 in the future.	What $ 1 to be paid in the future is worth today. Value today of a single $ 1 payment tomorrow.	What $ 1 to be paid at the end of each period is worth today. Value today of a series of $ 1 payments tomorrow.	The mortgage payment to amortize a loan of $ 1. An annuity certain, payable at the end of each period, worth $ 1 today.	The annual payment, including interest and principal, to amortize completely a loan of $ 100.	The total interest paid over the term on a loan of $1. The loan is amortized by regular periodic payments.	The average annual interest rate on a loan that is completely amortized by regular periodic payments.	
	$S = (1+i)^n$	$S\overline{n}| = \dfrac{(1+i)^n - 1}{i}$	$\dfrac{1}{S\overline{n}|} = \dfrac{i}{(1+i)^n - 1}$	$V^n = \dfrac{1}{(1+i)^n}$	$A\overline{n}| = \dfrac{1-V^n}{i}$	$\dfrac{1}{A\overline{n}|} = \dfrac{i}{1-V^n}$				

YEAR										PERIODS
	1.006 625	1.000 000	1.000 000 0000	.993 419	.993 419	1.006 625 0000	1207.95	.006 625	7.95	1
	1.013 294	2.006 625	.498 349 2182	.986 881	1.980 299	.504 974 2182	605.97	.009 948	5.97	2
	1.020 007	3.019 919	.331 134 7212	.980 385	2.960 685	.337 759 7212	405.32	.013 279	5.31	3
	1.026 765	4.039 926	.247 529 2954	.973 943	3.934 618	.254 154 2954	304.99	.016 617	4.99	4
	1.033 567	5.066 690	.197 367 4980	.967 523	4.902 141	.203 992 4980	244.80	.019 962	4.79	5
	1.040 414	6.100 257	.163 927 5148	.961 156	5.863 297	.170 552 5148	204.67	.023 315	4.66	6
	1.047 307	7.140 671	.140 042 8539	.954 830	6.818 127	.146 667 8539	176.01	.026 675	4.57	7
	1.054 245	8.187 978	.122 130 2694	.948 546	7.766 672	.128 755 2694	154.51	.030 042	4.51	8
	1.061 230	9.242 224	.108 199 0691	.942 303	8.708 975	.114 824 0691	137.79	.033 417	4.46	9
	1.068 260	10.303 453	.097 054 8377	.936 101	9.645 077	.103 679 8377	124.42	.036 798	4.42	10
	1.075 338	11.371 714	.087 937 4927	.929 941	10.575 017	.094 562 4927	113.48	.040 187	4.38	11
	1.082 462	12.447 051	.080 340 3125	.923 820	11.498 838	.086 965 3125	104.36	.043 584	4.36	12
1	1.082 462	12.447 051	.080 340 3125	.923 820	11.498 838	.086 965 3125	104.36	.043 584	4.36	12
2	1.171 723	25.920 508	.038 579 4908	.853 444	22.121 696	.045 204 4908	54.25	.084 908	4.25	24
3	1.268 346	40.505 009	.024 688 3046	.788 429	31.935 307	.031 313 3046	37.58	.127 279	4.24	36
4	1.372 936	56.292 173	.017 764 4590	.728 366	41.001 319	.024 389 4590	29.27	.170 694	4.27	48
5	1.486 150	73.381 174	.013 627 4735	.672 879	49.376 685	.020 252 4735	24.31	.215 148	4.30	60
6	1.608 701	91.879 362	.010 883 8370	.621 620	57.114 016	.017 508 8370	21.02	.260 636	4.34	72
7	1.741 357	111.902 944	.008 936 3154	.574 265	64.261 920	.015 561 3154	18.68	.307 150	4.39	84
8	1.884 952	133.577 704	.007 486 2793	.530 517	70.865 297	.014 111 2793	16.94	.354 683	4.43	96
9	2.040 389	157.039 802	.006 367 8124	.490 103	76.965 631	.012 992 8124	15.60	.403 224	4.48	108
10	2.208 643	182.436 625	.005 481 3555	.452 767	82.601 242	.012 106 3555	14.53	.452 763	4.53	120
11	2.390 771	209.927 713	.004 763 5445	.418 275	87.807 533	.011 388 5445	13.67	.503 288	4.58	132
12	2.587 918	239.685 764	.004 172 1293	.386 411	92.617 211	.010 797 1293	12.96	.554 787	4.62	144
13	2.801 322	271.897 715	.003 677 8536	.356 974	97.060 488	.010 302 8536	12.37	.607 245	4.67	156
14	3.032 324	306.765 918	.003 259 8145	.329 780	101.165 277	.009 884 8145	11.87	.660 649	4.72	168
15	3.282 375	344.509 413	.002 902 6783	.304 657	104.957 364	.009 527 6783	11.44	.714 982	4.77	180
16	3.553 045	385.365 302	.002 594 9404	.281 449	108.460 571	.009 219 9404	11.07	.770 229	4.81	192
17	3.846 035	429.590 237	.002 327 7996	.260 008	111.696 904	.008 952 7996	10.75	.826 371	4.86	204
18	4.163 186	477.462 037	.002 094 4074	.240 201	114.686 694	.008 719 4074	10.47	.883 392	4.91	216
19	4.506 489	529.281 427	.001 889 3540	.221 902	117.448 722	.008 514 3540	10.22	.941 273	4.95	228
20	4.878 102	585.373 933	.001 708 3098	.204 998	120.000 340	.008 333 3098	10.00	.999 994	5.00	240
21	5.280 359	646.091 923	.001 547 7674	.189 381	122.357 575	.008 172 7674	9.81	1.059 537	5.05	252
22	5.715 786	711.816 823	.001 404 8558	.174 954	124.535 237	.008 029 8558	9.64	1.119 882	5.09	264
23	6.187 120	782.961 510	.001 277 2020	.161 626	126.547 006	.007 902 2020	9.49	1.181 008	5.13	276
24	6.697 321	859.972 911	.001 162 8273	.149 313	128.405 518	.007 787 8273	9.35	1.242 894	5.18	288
25	7.249 593	943.334 804	.001 060 0690	.137 939	130.122 449	.007 685 0690	9.23	1.305 521	5.22	300
26	7.847 407	1033.570 862	.000 967 5195	.127 431	131.708 584	.007 592 5195	9.12	1.368 866	5.26	312
27	8.494 518	1131.247 940	.000 883 9795	.117 723	133.173 888	.007 508 9795	9.02	1.432 909	5.31	324
28	9.194 990	1236.979 637	.000 808 4207	.108 755	134.527 566	.007 433 4207	8.93	1.497 629	5.35	336
29	9.953 225	1351.430 151	.000 739 9569	.100 470	135.778 121	.007 364 9569	8.84	1.563 005	5.39	348
30	10.773 985	1475.318 452	.000 677 8198	.092 816	136.933 408	.007 302 8198	8.77	1.629 015	5.43	360
31	11.662 426	1609.422 794	.000 621 3408	.085 745	138.000 686	.007 246 3408	8.70	1.695 639	5.47	372
32	12.624 130	1754.585 610	.000 569 9351	.079 213	138.986 659	.007 194 9351	8.64	1.762 855	5.51	384
33	13.665 137	1911.718 801	.000 523 0895	.073 179	139.897 521	.007 148 0895	8.58	1.830 643	5.55	396
34	14.791 988	2081.809 464	.000 480 3514	.067 604	140.738 994	.007 105 3514	8.53	1.898 983	5.59	408
35	16.011 760	2265.926 095	.000 441 3207	.062 454	141.516 363	.007 066 3207	8.48	1.967 855	5.62	420
36	17.332 118	2465.225 300	.000 405 6424	.057 696	142.234 513	.007 030 6424	8.44	2.037 238	5.66	432
37	18.761 354	2680.959 059	.000 373 0008	.053 301	142.897 954	.006 998 0008	8.40	2.107 112	5.69	444
38	20.308 447	2914.482 594	.000 343 1141	.049 241	143.510 854	.006 968 1141	8.37	2.177 460	5.73	456
39	21.983 117	3167.262 880	.000 315 7300	.045 489	144.077 063	.006 940 7300	8.33	2.248 262	5.76	468
40	23.795 882	3440.887 862	.000 290 6227	.042 024	144.600 139	.006 915 6227	8.30	2.319 499	5.80	480
41	25.758 131	3737.076 430	.000 267 5889	.038 823	145.083 367	.006 892 5889	8.28	2.391 154	5.83	492
42	27.882 191	4057.689 215	.000 246 4457	.035 865	145.529 783	.006 871 4457	8.25	2.463 209	5.86	504
43	30.181 404	4404.740 280	.000 227 0281	.033 133	145.942 191	.006 852 0281	8.23	2.535 647	5.90	516
44	32.670 215	4780.409 772	.000 209 1871	.030 609	146.323 182	.006 834 1871	8.21	2.608 451	5.93	528
45	35.364 257	5187.057 614	.000 192 7875	.028 277	146.675 149	.006 817 7875	8.19	2.681 605	5.96	540
46	38.280 454	5627.238 335	.000 177 7071	.026 123	147.000 303	.006 802 7071	8.17	2.755 094	5.99	552
47	41.437 126	6103.717 114	.000 163 8346	.024 133	147.300 687	.006 788 8346	8.15	2.828 903	6.02	564
48	44.854 102	6619.487 150	.000 151 0691	.022 295	147.578 188	.006 776 0691	8.14	2.903 016	6.05	576
49	48.552 849	7177.788 468	.000 139 3187	.020 596	147.834 549	.006 764 3187	8.12	2.977 419	6.08	588
50	52.556 600	7782.128 270	.000 128 4996	.019 027	148.071 380	.006 753 4996	8.11	3.052 100	6.10	600

MONTHLY COMPOUND INTEREST AND ANNUITY

8.00 % M

Amount Of 1	Amount Of 1 Per Period	Sinking Fund Payment	Present Worth Of 1	Present Worth of 1 Per Period	Periodic Payment To Amortize 1	Constant Annual Percent	Total Interest	Annual Add On Rate
What a single $ 1 deposit grows to in the future. The deposit is made at the beginning of the first period.	What a series of $ 1 deposits grow to in the future. A deposit is made at the end of each period.	The amount to be deposited at the end of each period that grows to $ 1 in the future.	What $ 1 to be paid in the future is worth today. Value today of a single $ 1 payment tomorrow.	What $ 1 to be paid at the end of each period is worth today. Value today of a series of $ 1 payments tomorrow.	The mortgage payment to amortize a loan of $ 1. An annuity certain, payable at the end of each period, worth $ 1 today.	The annual payment, including interest and principal, to amortize completely a loan of $ 100.	The total interest paid over the term on a loan of $1. The loan is amortized by regular periodic payments.	The average annual interest rate on a loan that is completely amortized by regular periodic payments.
$S = (1+i)^n$	$S\overline{n}| = \dfrac{(1+i)^n - 1}{i}$	$\dfrac{1}{S\overline{n}|} = \dfrac{i}{(1+i)^n - 1}$	$V^n = \dfrac{1}{(1+i)^n}$	$A\overline{n}| = \dfrac{1-V^n}{i}$	$\dfrac{1}{A\overline{n}|} = \dfrac{i}{1-V^n}$			

YEAR / **PERIODS**

YEAR	Amount Of 1	Amount Of 1 Per Period	Sinking Fund Payment	Present Worth Of 1	Present Worth of 1 Per Period	Periodic Payment To Amortize 1	Constant Annual Percent	Total Interest	Annual Add On Rate	PERIODS
	1.006 667	1.000 000	1.000 000 0000	.993 377	.993 377	1.006 666 6667	1208.00	.006 667	8.00	1
	1.013 378	2.006 667	.498 338 8704	.986 799	1.980 176	.505 005 5371	606.01	.010 011	6.01	2
	1.020 134	3.020 044	.331 120 9548	.980 264	2.960 440	.337 787 6215	405.35	.013 363	5.35	3
	1.026 935	4.040 178	.247 513 8426	.973 772	3.934 212	.254 180 5093	305.02	.016 722	5.02	4
	1.033 781	5.067 113	.197 351 0518	.967 323	4.901 535	.204 017 7184	244.83	.020 089	4.82	5
	1.040 673	6.100 893	.163 910 4215	.960 917	5.862 452	.170 577 0882	204.70	.023 463	4.69	6
	1.047 610	7.141 566	.140 025 3116	.954 553	6.817 005	.146 691 9783	176.04	.026 844	4.60	7
	1.054 595	8.189 176	.122 112 4018	.948 232	7.765 237	.128 779 0685	154.54	.030 233	4.53	8
	1.061 625	9.243 771	.108 180 9587	.941 952	8.707 189	.114 847 6254	137.82	.033 629	4.48	9
	1.068 703	10.305 396	.097 036 5423	.935 714	9.642 903	.103 703 2089	124.45	.037 032	4.44	10
	1.075 827	11.374 099	.087 919 0542	.929 517	10.572 420	.094 585 7209	113.51	.040 443	4.41	11
	1.083 000	12.449 926	.080 321 7624	.923 361	11.495 782	.086 988 4291	104.39	.043 861	4.39	12
1	1.083 000	12.449 926	.080 321 7624	.923 361	11.495 782	.086 988 4291	104.39	.043 861	4.39	12
2	1.172 888	25.933 190	.038 560 6248	.852 596	22.110 544	.045 227 2915	54.28	.085 455	4.27	24
3	1.270 237	40.535 558	.024 669 6988	.787 255	31.911 806	.031 336 3655	37.61	.128 109	4.27	36
4	1.375 666	56.349 915	.017 746 2557	.726 921	40.961 913	.024 412 9223	29.30	.171 820	4.30	48
5	1.489 846	73.476 856	.013 609 7276	.671 210	49.318 433	.020 276 3943	24.34	.216 584	4.33	60
6	1.613 502	92.025 325	.010 866 5739	.619 770	57.034 522	.017 533 2406	21.04	.262 393	4.37	72
7	1.747 422	112.113 308	.008 919 5477	.572 272	64.159 261	.015 586 2144	18.71	.309 242	4.42	84
8	1.892 457	133.868 583	.007 470 0126	.528 414	70.737 970	.014 136 6793	16.97	.357 121	4.46	96
9	2.049 530	157.429 535	.006 352 0482	.487 917	76.812 497	.013 018 7149	15.63	.406 021	4.51	108
10	2.219 640	182.946 035	.005 466 0928	.450 523	82.421 481	.012 132 7594	14.56	.455 931	4.56	120
11	2.403 869	210.580 392	.004 748 7802	.415 996	87.600 600	.011 415 4469	13.70	.506 839	4.61	132
12	2.603 389	240.508 387	.004 157 8592	.384 115	92.382 800	.010 824 5258	12.99	.558 732	4.66	144
13	2.819 469	272.920 390	.003 664 0721	.354 677	96.798 498	.010 330 7388	12.40	.611 595	4.70	156
14	3.053 484	308.022 574	.003 246 5153	.327 495	100.875 784	.009 913 1820	11.90	.665 415	4.75	168
15	3.306 921	346.038 222	.002 889 8542	.302 396	104.640 592	.009 556 5208	11.47	.720 174	4.80	180
16	3.581 394	387.209 149	.002 582 5836	.279 221	108.116 871	.009 249 2503	11.10	.775 856	4.85	192
17	3.878 648	431.797 244	.002 315 9018	.257 822	111.326 733	.008 982 5684	10.78	.832 444	4.90	204
18	4.200 574	480.086 128	.002 082 9596	.238 063	114.290 596	.008 749 6262	10.50	.889 919	4.94	216
19	4.549 220	532.382 966	.001 878 3471	.219 818	117.027 313	.008 545 0138	10.26	.948 263	4.99	228
20	4.926 803	589.020 416	.001 697 7340	.202 971	119.554 292	.008 364 4007	10.04	1.007 456	5.04	240
21	5.335 725	650.358 746	.001 537 6129	.187 416	121.887 606	.008 204 2796	9.85	1.067 478	5.08	252
22	5.778 588	716.788 127	.001 395 1124	.173 053	124.042 099	.008 061 7791	9.68	1.128 310	5.13	264
23	6.258 207	788.731 114	.001 267 8592	.159 790	126.031 475	.007 934 5259	9.53	1.189 929	5.17	276
24	6.777 636	866.645 333	.001 153 8746	.147 544	127.868 388	.007 820 5412	9.39	1.252 316	5.22	288
25	7.340 176	951.026 395	.001 051 4955	.136 237	129.564 523	.007 718 1622	9.27	1.315 449	5.26	300
26	7.949 407	1042.411 042	.000 959 3145	.125 796	131.130 668	.007 625 9811	9.16	1.379 306	5.31	312
27	8.609 204	1141.380 571	.000 876 1320	.116 155	132.576 786	.007 542 7986	9.06	1.443 867	5.35	324
28	9.323 763	1248.564 521	.000 800 9198	.107 253	133.912 076	.007 467 5864	8.97	1.509 109	5.39	336
29	10.097 631	1364.644 687	.000 732 7915	.099 033	135.145 031	.007 399 4581	8.88	1.575 011	5.43	348
30	10.935 730	1490.359 449	.000 670 9791	.091 443	136.283 494	.007 337 6457	8.81	1.641 552	5.47	360
31	11.843 390	1626.508 474	.000 614 8139	.084 435	137.334 707	.007 281 4806	8.74	1.708 711	5.51	372
32	12.826 385	1773.957 801	.000 563 7113	.077 964	138.305 357	.007 230 3779	8.68	1.776 465	5.55	384
33	13.890 969	1933.645 350	.000 517 1579	.071 989	139.201 617	.007 183 8246	8.63	1.844 795	5.59	396
34	15.043 913	2106.586 886	.000 474 7015	.066 472	140.029 190	.007 141 3682	8.57	1.913 678	5.63	408
35	16.292 550	2293.882 485	.000 435 9421	.061 378	140.793 338	.007 102 6088	8.53	1.983 096	5.67	420
36	17.644 824	2496.723 526	.000 400 5249	.056 674	141.498 923	.007 067 1916	8.49	2.053 027	5.70	432
37	19.109 335	2716.400 273	.000 368 1343	.052 330	142.150 433	.007 034 8009	8.45	2.123 452	5.74	444
38	20.695 401	2954.310 082	.000 338 4885	.048 320	142.752 013	.007 005 1552	8.41	2.194 351	5.77	456
39	22.413 109	3211.966 288	.000 311 3358	.044 617	143.307 488	.006 978 0024	8.38	2.265 705	5.81	468
40	24.273 386	3491.007 831	.000 286 4502	.041 197	143.820 392	.006 953 1169	8.35	2.337 496	5.84	480
41	26.288 065	3793.209 686	.000 263 6290	.038 040	144.293 988	.006 930 2956	8.32	2.409 705	5.88	492
42	28.469 961	4120.494 145	.000 242 6893	.035 125	144.731 289	.006 909 3560	8.30	2.482 315	5.91	504
43	30.832 954	4474.943 053	.000 223 4665	.032 433	145.135 075	.006 890 1332	8.27	2.555 309	5.94	516
44	33.392 074	4858.811 045	.000 205 8117	.029 947	145.507 916	.006 872 4783	8.25	2.628 669	5.97	528
45	36.163 599	5274.539 891	.000 189 5900	.027 652	145.852 183	.006 856 2567	8.23	2.702 379	6.01	540
46	39.165 160	5724.774 027	.000 174 6794	.025 533	146.170 065	.006 841 3461	8.21	2.776 423	6.04	552
47	42.415 849	6212.377 374	.000 160 9690	.023 576	146.463 586	.006 827 6356	8.20	2.850 787	6.07	564
48	45.936 344	6740.451 558	.000 148 3580	.021 769	146.734 612	.006 815 0247	8.18	2.925 454	6.09	576
49	49.749 038	7312.355 639	.000 136 7548	.020 101	146.984 866	.006 803 4215	8.17	3.000 412	6.12	588
50	53.878 183	7931.727 477	.000 126 0759	.018 560	147.215 942	.006 792 7426	8.16	3.075 646	6.15	600

Effective Rate is 8.30 %

Annual Percentage Rate is 8.00 %

Amount Of 1	Amount Of 1 Per Period	Sinking Fund Payment	Present Worth Of 1	Present Worth of 1 Per Period	Periodic Payment To Amortize 1	Constant Annual Percent	Total Interest	Annual Add On Rate
What a single $ 1 deposit grows to in the future. The deposit is made at the beginning of the first period.	What a series of $ 1 deposits grow to in the future. A deposit is made at the end of each period.	The amount to be deposited at the end of each period that grows to $ 1 in the future.	What $ 1 to be paid in the future is worth today. Value today of a single $ 1 payment tomorrow.	What $ 1 to be paid at the end of each period is worth today. Value today of a series of $ 1 payments tomorrow.	The mortgage payment to amortize a loan of $ 1. An annuity certain, payable at the end of each period, worth $ 1 today.	The annual payment, including interest and principal, to amortize completely a loan of $ 100.	The total interest paid over the term on a loan of $1. The loan is amortized by regular periodic payments.	The average annual interest rate on a loan that is completely amortized by regular periodic payments.

$$S = (1+i)^n \qquad S\overline{n}| = \frac{(1+i)^n - 1}{i} \qquad \frac{1}{S\overline{n}|} = \frac{i}{(1+i)^n - 1} \qquad V^n = \frac{1}{(1+i)^n} \qquad A\overline{n}| = \frac{1 - V^n}{i} \qquad \frac{1}{A\overline{n}|} = \frac{i}{1 - V^n}$$

YEAR									PERIODS
	1.006 708	1.000 000	1.000 000 0000	.993 336	.993 336	1.006 708 3333	1208.05	.006 708	8.05 1
	1.013 462	2.006 708	.498 328 5231	.986 717	1.980 054	.505 036 8564	606.05	.010 074	6.04 2
	1.020 260	3.020 170	.331 107 1891	.980 142	2.960 196	.337 815 5225	405.38	.013 447	5.38 3
	1.027 105	4.040 430	.247 498 3909	.973 611	3.933 806	.254 206 7242	305.05	.016 827	5.05 4
	1.033 995	5.067 535	.197 334 6069	.967 123	4.900 929	.204 042 9402	244.86	.020 215	4.85 5
	1.040 931	6.101 530	.163 893 3300	.960 678	5.861 608	.170 601 6633	204.73	.023 610	4.72 6
	1.047 914	7.142 461	.140 007 7713	.954 277	6.815 884	.146 716 1046	176.06	.027 013	4.63 7
	1.054 944	8.190 375	.122 094 5365	.947 918	7.763 802	.128 802 8698	154.57	.030 423	4.56 8
	1.062 021	9.245 318	.108 162 8509	.941 601	8.705 403	.114 871 1842	137.85	.033 841	4.51 9
	1.069 145	10.307 339	.097 018 2497	.935 327	9.640 730	.103 726 5830	124.48	.037 266	4.47 10
	1.076 317	11.376 484	.087 900 6188	.929 094	10.569 824	.094 608 9522	113.54	.040 698	4.44 11
	1.083 538	12.452 801	.080 303 2157	.922 903	11.492 727	.087 011 5491	104.42	.044 139	4.41 12
1	1.083 538	12.452 801	.080 303 2157	.922 903	11.492 727	.087 011 5491	104.42	.044 139	4.41 12
2	1.174 054	25.945 879	.038 541 7657	.851 750	22.099 399	.045 250 0990	54.31	.086 002	4.30 24
3	1.272 131	40.566 136	.024 651 1032	.786 082	31.888 328	.031 359 4366	37.64	.128 940	4.30 36
4	1.378 402	56.407 732	.017 728 0659	.725 478	40.922 559	.024 436 3993	29.33	.172 947	4.32 48
5	1.493 550	73.572 697	.013 591 9986	.669 546	49.260 278	.020 300 3320	24.37	.218 020	4.36 60
6	1.618 318	92.171 581	.010 849 3311	.617 926	56.955 184	.017 557 6644	21.07	.264 152	4.40 72
7	1.753 508	112.324 170	.008 902 8034	.570 285	64.056 834	.015 611 1367	18.74	.311 335	4.45 84
8	1.899 992	134.160 257	.007 453 7723	.526 318	70.610 969	.014 162 1056	17.00	.359 562	4.49 96
9	2.058 712	157.820 476	.006 336 3134	.485 741	76.659 799	.013 044 6467	15.66	.408 822	4.54 108
10	2.230 692	183.457 212	.005 450 8623	.448 291	82.242 282	.012 159 1956	14.60	.459 103	4.59 120
11	2.417 039	211.235 579	.004 734 0510	.413 729	87.394 373	.011 442 3843	13.74	.510 395	4.64 132
12	2.618 952	241.334 481	.004 143 6267	.381 832	92.149 252	.010 851 9600	13.03	.562 682	4.69 144
13	2.837 733	273.947 772	.003 650 3308	.352 394	96.537 544	.010 358 6642	12.44	.615 952	4.74 156
14	3.074 790	309.285 497	.003 233 2586	.325 225	100.587 512	.009 941 5920	11.93	.670 187	4.79 168
15	3.331 651	347.575 249	.002 877 0748	.300 152	104.325 239	.009 585 4082	11.51	.725 373	4.84 180
16	3.609 969	389.063 633	.002 570 2736	.277 011	107.774 799	.009 278 6070	11.14	.781 493	4.88 192
17	3.911 536	434.017 855	.002 304 0527	.255 654	110.958 408	.009 012 3860	10.82	.838 527	4.93 204
18	4.238 297	482.727 441	.002 071 5624	.235 944	113.896 569	.008 779 8957	10.54	.896 457	4.98 216
19	4.592 353	535.506 107	.001 867 3923	.217 753	116.608 208	.008 575 7257	10.30	.955 265	5.03 228
20	4.975 987	592.693 773	.001 687 2119	.200 965	119.110 787	.008 395 5453	10.08	1.014 931	5.07 240
21	5.391 669	654.658 756	.001 527 5134	.185 471	121.420 424	.008 235 8467	9.89	1.075 433	5.12 252
22	5.842 076	721.800 141	.001 385 4251	.171 172	123.551 996	.008 093 7584	9.72	1.136 752	5.17 264
23	6.330 109	794.550 353	.001 258 5735	.157 975	125.519 229	.007 966 9068	9.57	1.198 866	5.21 276
24	6.858 910	873.377 938	.001 144 9797	.145 796	127.334 795	.007 853 3130	9.43	1.261 754	5.26 288
25	7.431 887	958.790 587	.001 042 9806	.134 555	129.010 385	.007 751 3140	9.31	1.325 394	5.30 300
26	8.052 728	1051.338 398	.000 951 1685	.124 182	130.556 793	.007 659 5019	9.20	1.389 765	5.35 312
27	8.725 434	1151.617 426	.000 868 3439	.114 607	131.983 977	.007 576 6773	9.10	1.454 843	5.39 324
28	9.454 335	1260.273 518	.000 793 4785	.105 772	133.301 130	.007 501 8119	9.01	1.520 609	5.43 336
29	10.244 127	1378.006 472	.000 725 6860	.097 617	134.516 734	.007 434 0193	8.93	1.587 039	5.47 348
30	11.099 896	1505.574 549	.000 664 1983	.090 091	135.638 618	.007 372 5316	8.85	1.654 111	5.51 360
31	12.027 154	1643.799 349	.000 608 3468	.083 145	136.674 009	.007 316 6801	8.79	1.721 805	5.55 372
32	13.031 873	1793.571 109	.000 557 5469	.076 735	137.629 574	.007 265 8802	8.72	1.790 098	5.59 384
33	14.120 523	1955.854 434	.000 511 2855	.070 819	138.511 468	.007 219 6188	8.67	1.858 969	5.63 396
34	15.300 117	2131.694 509	.000 469 1104	.065 359	139.325 370	.007 177 4437	8.62	1.928 397	5.67 408
35	16.578 252	2322.223 832	.000 430 6217	.060 320	140.076 523	.007 138 9550	8.57	1.998 361	5.71 420
36	17.963 158	2528.669 506	.000 395 4649	.055 669	140.769 764	.007 103 7982	8.53	2.068 841	5.75 432
37	19.463 756	2752.361 145	.000 363 3244	.051 378	141.409 559	.007 071 6577	8.49	2.139 816	5.78 444
38	21.089 710	2994.739 434	.000 333 9189	.047 416	142.000 027	.007 042 2522	8.46	2.211 267	5.82 456
39	22.851 493	3257.365 409	.000 306 9966	.043 761	142.544 971	.007 015 3299	8.42	2.283 174	5.85 468
40	24.760 451	3541.930 514	.000 282 3319	.040 387	143.047 903	.006 990 6652	8.39	2.355 519	5.89 480
41	26.828 878	3850.267 487	.000 259 7222	.037 273	143.512 059	.006 968 0555	8.37	2.428 283	5.92 492
42	29.070 096	4184.362 174	.000 238 9850	.034 400	143.940 431	.006 947 3184	8.34	2.501 448	5.96 504
43	31.498 541	4546.366 311	.000 219 9559	.031 748	144.335 776	.006 928 2892	8.32	2.574 997	5.99 516
44	34.129 851	4938.611 383	.000 202 4861	.029 300	144.700 641	.006 910 8194	8.30	2.648 913	6.02 528
45	36.980 975	5363.623 645	.000 186 4411	.027 041	145.037 377	.006 894 7745	8.28	2.723 178	6.05 540
46	40.070 275	5824.140 387	.000 171 6992	.024 956	145.348 151	.006 880 0325	8.26	2.797 778	6.08 552
47	43.417 647	6323.127 566	.000 158 1496	.023 032	145.634 965	.006 866 4829	8.24	2.872 696	6.11 564
48	47.044 651	6863.798 908	.000 145 6919	.021 256	145.899 667	.006 854 0252	8.23	2.947 919	6.14 576
49	50.974 646	7449.636 605	.000 134 2347	.019 618	146.143 961	.006 842 5681	8.22	3.023 430	6.17 588
50	55.232 942	8084.413 745	.000 123 6948	.018 105	146.369 421	.006 832 0281	8.20	3.099 217	6.20 600

Effective Rate is 8.35 %   Annual Percentage Rate is 8.05 %

	Amount Of 1	Amount Of 1 Per Period	Sinking Fund Payment	Present Worth Of 1	Present Worth of 1 Per Period	Periodic Payment To Amortize 1	Constant Annual Percent	Total Interest	Annual Add On Rate	
	What a single $ 1 deposit grows to in the future. The deposit is made at the beginning of the first period.	What a series of $ 1 deposits grow to in the future. A deposit is made at the end of each period.	The amount to be deposited at the end of each period that grows to $ 1 in the future.	What $ 1 to be paid in the future is worth today. Value today of a single $ 1 payment tomorrow.	What $ 1 to be paid at the end of each period is worth today. Value today of a series of $ 1 payments tomorrow.	The mortgage payment to amortize a loan of $ 1. An annuity certain, payable at the end of each period, worth $ 1 today.	The annual payment, including interest and principal, to amortize completely a loan of $ 100.	The total interest paid over the term on a loan of $1. The loan is amortized by regular periodic payments.	The average annual interest rate on a loan that is completely amortized by regular periodic payments.	
	$S = (1+i)^n$	$S\overline{n} = \dfrac{(1+i)^n - 1}{i}$	$\dfrac{1}{S\overline{n}} = \dfrac{i}{(1+i)^n - 1}$	$V^n = \dfrac{1}{(1+i)^n}$	$A\overline{n} = \dfrac{1-V^n}{i}$	$\dfrac{1}{A\overline{n}} = \dfrac{i}{1-V^n}$				

YEAR										PERIODS
	1.006 750	1.000 000	1.000 000 0000	.993 295	.993 295	1.006 750 0000	1208.10	.006 750	8.10	1
	1.013 546	2.006 750	.498 318 1762	.986 635	1.979 931	.505 068 1762	606.09	.010 136	6.08	2
	1.020 387	3.020 296	.331 093 4242	.980 020	2.959 951	.337 843 4242	405.42	.013 530	5.41	3
	1.027 275	4.040 683	.247 482 9403	.973 450	3.933 401	.254 232 9403	305.08	.016 932	5.08	4
	1.034 209	5.067 957	.197 318 1634	.966 923	4.900 323	.204 068 1634	244.89	.020 341	4.88	5
	1.041 190	6.102 166	.163 876 2401	.960 440	5.860 763	.170 626 2401	204.76	.023 757	4.75	6
	1.048 218	7.143 355	.139 990 2330	.954 000	6.814 764	.146 740 2330	176.09	.027 182	4.66	7
	1.055 293	8.191 573	.122 076 6735	.947 604	7.762 368	.128 826 6735	154.60	.030 613	4.59	8
	1.062 416	9.246 866	.108 144 7456	.941 251	8.703 618	.114 894 7456	137.88	.034 053	4.54	9
	1.069 588	10.309 283	.096 999 9599	.934 940	9.638 558	.103 749 9599	124.50	.037 500	4.50	10
	1.076 807	11.378 870	.087 882 1866	.928 671	10.567 229	.094 632 1866	113.56	.040 954	4.47	11
	1.084 076	12.455 678	.080 284 6725	.922 445	11.489 674	.087 034 6725	104.45	.044 416	4.44	12
1	1.084 076	12.455 678	.080 284 6725	.922 445	11.489 674	.087 034 6725	104.45	.044 416	4.44	12
2	1.175 220	25.958 577	.038 522 9134	.850 904	22.088 263	.045 272 9134	54.33	.086 550	4.33	24
3	1.274 028	40.596 743	.024 632 5179	.784 912	31.864 875	.031 382 5179	37.66	.129 771	4.33	36
4	1.381 143	56.465 625	.017 709 8898	.724 038	40.883 259	.024 459 8898	29.36	.174 075	4.35	48
5	1.497 264	73.668 697	.013 574 2865	.667 885	49.202 219	.020 324 2865	24.39	.219 457	4.39	60
6	1.623 147	92.318 131	.010 832 1084	.616 087	56.876 000	.017 582 1084	21.10	.265 912	4.43	72
7	1.759 615	112.535 532	.008 886 0823	.568 306	63.954 639	.015 636 0823	18.77	.313 431	4.48	84
8	1.907 556	134.452 727	.007 437 5583	.524 231	70.484 292	.014 187 5583	17.03	.362 006	4.53	96
9	2.067 935	158.212 628	.006 320 6080	.483 574	76.507 535	.013 070 6080	15.69	.411 626	4.57	108
10	2.241 799	183.970 163	.005 435 6640	.446 070	82.063 644	.012 185 6640	14.63	.462 280	4.62	120
11	2.430 280	211.893 284	.004 719 3568	.411 475	87.188 848	.011 469 3568	13.77	.513 955	4.67	132
12	2.634 607	242.164 064	.004 129 4319	.379 563	91.916 564	.010 879 4319	13.06	.566 638	4.72	144
13	2.856 114	274.979 885	.003 636 6296	.350 126	96.277 622	.010 386 6296	12.47	.620 314	4.77	156
14	3.096 244	310.554 723	.003 220 0444	.322 972	100.300 456	.009 970 0444	11.97	.674 967	4.82	168
15	3.356 564	349.120 544	.002 864 3402	.297 924	104.011 298	.009 614 3402	11.54	.730 581	4.87	180
16	3.638 770	390.928 820	.002 558 0104	.274 818	107.434 345	.009 308 0104	11.17	.787 138	4.92	192
17	3.944 702	436.252 160	.002 292 2523	.253 505	110.591 916	.009 042 2523	10.86	.844 619	4.97	204
18	4.276 356	485.386 097	.002 060 2156	.233 844	113.504 601	.008 810 2156	10.58	.903 007	5.02	216
19	4.635 894	538.651 011	.001 856 4896	.215 708	116.191 391	.008 606 4896	10.33	.962 280	5.06	228
20	5.025 661	596.394 216	.001 676 7433	.198 979	118.669 807	.008 426 7433	10.12	1.022 418	5.11	240
21	5.448 198	658.992 229	.001 517 4686	.183 547	120.956 009	.008 267 4686	9.93	1.083 402	5.16	252
22	5.906 259	726.853 222	.001 375 7936	.169 312	123.064 903	.008 125 7936	9.76	1.145 210	5.21	264
23	6.402 833	800.419 683	.001 249 3446	.156 181	125.010 242	.007 999 3446	9.60	1.207 819	5.25	276
24	6.941 156	880.171 305	.001 136 1425	.144 068	126.804 709	.007 886 1425	9.47	1.271 209	5.30	288
25	7.524 740	966.628 111	.001 034 5240	.132 895	128.460 006	.007 784 5240	9.35	1.335 357	5.34	300
26	8.157 388	1060.353 843	.000 943 0814	.122 588	129.986 925	.007 693 0814	9.24	1.400 241	5.39	312
27	8.843 228	1161.959 644	.000 860 6151	.113 081	131.395 424	.007 610 6151	9.14	1.465 839	5.43	324
28	9.586 729	1272.108 036	.000 786 0968	.104 311	132.694 687	.007 536 0968	9.05	1.532 129	5.47	336
29	10.392 741	1391.517 245	.000 718 6400	.096 221	133.893 185	.007 468 6400	8.97	1.599 087	5.51	348
30	11.266 520	1520.965 882	.000 657 4769	.088 759	134.998 733	.007 407 4769	8.89	1.666 692	5.56	360
31	12.213 762	1661.298 020	.000 601 9390	.081 875	136.018 540	.007 351 9390	8.83	1.734 921	5.60	372
32	13.240 644	1813.428 698	.000 551 4416	.075 525	136.959 255	.007 301 4416	8.77	1.803 754	5.64	384
33	14.353 862	1978.349 887	.000 505 4718	.069 668	137.827 013	.007 255 4718	8.71	1.873 167	5.68	396
34	15.560 674	2157.136 962	.000 463 5774	.064 265	138.627 472	.007 213 5774	8.66	1.943 140	5.72	408
35	16.868 951	2350.955 708	.000 425 3589	.059 281	139.365 851	.007 175 3589	8.62	2.013 651	5.75	420
36	18.287 222	2561.069 924	.000 390 4618	.054 683	140.046 964	.007 140 4618	8.57	2.084 680	5.79	432
37	19.824 735	2788.849 666	.000 358 5708	.050 442	140.675 254	.007 108 5708	8.54	2.156 205	5.83	444
38	21.491 516	3035.780 177	.000 329 4046	.046 530	141.254 817	.007 079 4046	8.50	2.228 209	5.86	456
39	23.298 433	3303.471 575	.000 302 7119	.042 921	141.789 431	.007 052 7119	8.47	2.300 669	5.90	468
40	25.257 268	3593.669 348	.000 278 2671	.039 593	142.282 583	.007 028 2671	8.44	2.373 568	5.93	480
41	27.380 794	3908.265 737	.000 255 8680	.036 522	142.737 489	.007 005 8680	8.41	2.446 887	5.97	492
42	29.682 857	4249.312 078	.000 235 3322	.033 689	143.157 114	.006 985 3322	8.39	2.520 607	6.00	504
43	32.178 467	4619.032 170	.000 216 4956	.031 077	143.544 195	.006 966 4956	8.36	2.594 712	6.03	516
44	34.883 898	5019.836 784	.000 199 2097	.028 667	143.901 256	.006 949 2097	8.34	2.669 183	6.07	528
45	37.816 791	5454.339 376	.000 183 3403	.026 443	144.230 625	.006 933 3403	8.33	2.744 004	6.10	540
46	40.996 269	5925.373 131	.000 168 7657	.024 392	144.534 450	.006 918 7657	8.31	2.819 159	6.13	552
47	44.443 090	6436.009 438	.000 155 3758	.022 501	144.814 711	.006 905 3758	8.29	2.894 632	6.16	564
48	48.179 651	6989.577 913	.000 143 0702	.020 756	145.073 237	.006 893 0702	8.28	2.970 408	6.19	576
49	52.230 395	7589.688 114	.000 131 7577	.019 146	145.311 713	.006 881 7577	8.26	3.046 474	6.22	588
50	56.621 708	8240.253 074	.000 121 3555	.017 661	145.531 693	.006 871 3555	8.25	3.122 813	6.25	600

MONTHLY COMPOUND INTEREST AND ANNUITY

	Amount Of 1	Amount Of 1 Per Period	Sinking Fund Payment	Present Worth Of 1	Present Worth of 1 Per Period	Periodic Payment To Amortize 1	Constant Annual Percent	Total Interest	Annual Add On Rate	
	What a single $ 1 deposit grows to in the future. The deposit is made at the beginning of the first period.	What a series of $ 1 deposits grow to in the future. A deposit is made at the end of each period.	The amount to be deposited at the end of each period that grows to $ 1 in the future.	What $ 1 to be paid in the future is worth today. Value today of a single $ 1 payment tomorrow.	What $ 1 to be paid at the end of each period is worth today. Value today of a series of $ 1 payments tomorrow.	The mortgage payment to amortize a loan of $ 1. An annuity certain, payable at the end of each period, worth $ 1 today.	The annual payment, including interest and principal, to amortize completely a loan of $ 100.	The total interest paid over the term on a loan of $1. The loan is amortized by regular periodic payments.	The average annual interest rate on a loan that is completely amortized by regular periodic payments.	

$$S = (1+i)^n \qquad S\overline{n}| = \frac{(1+i)^n - 1}{i} \qquad \frac{1}{S\overline{n}|} = \frac{i}{(1+i)^n - 1} \qquad V^n = \frac{1}{(1+i)^n} \qquad A\overline{n}| = \frac{1 - V^n}{i} \qquad \frac{1}{A\overline{n}|} = \frac{i}{1 - V^n}$$

YEAR / **PERIODS**

YEAR	Amount Of 1	Amount Of 1 Per Period	Sinking Fund Payment	Present Worth Of 1	Present Worth of 1 Per Period	Periodic Payment To Amortize 1	Constant Annual Percent	Total Interest	Annual Add On Rate	PERIODS
	1.006 771	1.000 000	1.000 000 0000	.993 275	.993 275	1.006 770 8333	1208.13	.006 771	8.12	1
	1.013 588	2.006 771	.498 313 0029	.986 595	1.979 869	.505 083 8362	606.11	.010 168	6.10	2
	1.020 450	3.020 358	.331 086 5421	.979 959	2.959 829	.337 857 3754	405.43	.013 572	5.43	3
	1.027 360	4.040 809	.247 475 2153	.973 369	3.933 198	.254 246 0487	305.10	.016 984	5.10	4
	1.034 316	5.068 168	.197 309 9422	.966 823	4.900 021	.204 080 7755	244.90	.020 404	4.90	5
	1.041 319	6.102 484	.163 867 6957	.960 321	5.860 341	.170 638 5291	204.77	.023 831	4.77	6
	1.048 369	7.143 803	.139 981 4645	.953 862	6.814 203	.146 752 2979	176.11	.027 266	4.67	7
	1.055 468	8.192 172	.122 067 7428	.947 447	7.761 651	.128 838 5761	154.61	.030 709	4.61	8
	1.062 614	9.247 640	.108 135 6940	.941 075	8.702 726	.114 906 5273	137.89	.034 159	4.55	9
	1.069 809	10.310 255	.096 990 8161	.934 746	9.637 472	.103 761 6494	124.52	.037 616	4.51	10
	1.077 053	11.380 064	.087 872 9716	.928 460	10.565 932	.094 643 8050	113.58	.041 082	4.48	11
	1.084 345	12.457 116	.080 275 4021	.922 216	11.488 148	.087 046 2355	104.46	.044 555	4.46	12
1	1.084 345	12.457 116	.080 275 4021	.922 216	11.488 148	.087 046 2355	104.46	.044 555	4.46	12
2	1.175 804	25.964 928	.038 513 4898	.850 482	22.082 697	.045 284 3232	54.35	.086 824	4.34	24
3	1.274 977	40.612 058	.024 623 2291	.784 328	31.853 157	.031 394 0624	37.68	.130 186	4.34	36
4	1.382 516	56.494 600	.017 700 8068	.723 319	40.863 628	.024 471 6401	29.37	.174 639	4.37	48
5	1.499 124	73.716 756	.013 565 4368	.667 056	49.173 226	.020 336 2702	24.41	.220 110	4.40	60
6	1.625 568	92.391 516	.010 823 5046	.615 170	56.836 467	.017 594 3379	21.12	.266 792	4.45	72
7	1.762 676	112.641 400	.008 877 7306	.567 319	63.903 628	.015 648 5639	18.78	.314 479	4.49	84
8	1.911 349	134.599 261	.007 429 4613	.523 191	70.421 074	.014 200 2946	17.05	.363 228	4.54	96
9	2.072 562	158.409 160	.006 312 7663	.482 495	76.431 565	.013 083 5996	15.71	.413 029	4.59	108
10	2.247 372	184.227 305	.005 428 0770	.444 964	81.974 535	.012 198 9103	14.64	.463 869	4.64	120
11	2.436 927	212.223 084	.004 712 0228	.410 353	87.086 348	.011 482 8561	13.78	.515 737	4.69	132
12	2.642 470	242.580 168	.004 122 3485	.378 434	91.800 542	.010 893 1819	13.08	.568 618	4.74	144
13	2.865 349	275.497 722	.003 629 7941	.348 998	96.148 046	.010 400 6274	12.49	.622 498	4.79	156
14	3.107 027	311.191 709	.003 213 4532	.321 851	100.157 382	.009 984 2866	11.99	.677 360	4.84	168
15	3.369 090	349.896 307	.002 857 9896	.296 816	103.854 854	.009 628 8229	11.56	.733 188	4.89	180
16	3.653 256	391.865 447	.002 551 8963	.273 728	107.264 721	.009 322 7297	11.19	.789 964	4.94	192
17	3.961 390	437.374 476	.002 286 3703	.252 437	110.409 354	.009 057 2036	10.87	.847 670	4.99	204
18	4.295 513	486.721 967	.002 054 5611	.232 801	113.309 384	.008 825 3944	10.60	.906 285	5.03	216
19	4.657 819	540.231 675	.001 851 0577	.214 693	115.983 837	.008 621 8910	10.35	.965 791	5.08	228
20	5.050 683	598.254 663	.001 671 5290	.197 993	118.450 259	.008 442 3623	10.14	1.026 167	5.13	240
21	5.476 683	661.171 602	.001 512 4667	.182 592	120.724 832	.008 283 3000	9.94	1.087 392	5.18	252
22	5.938 614	729.395 274	.001 370 9987	.168 389	122.822 479	.008 141 8321	9.78	1.149 444	5.22	264
23	6.439 507	803.373 276	.001 244 7514	.155 291	124.756 962	.008 015 5847	9.62	1.212 301	5.27	276
24	6.982 647	883.590 956	.001 131 7454	.143 212	126.540 973	.007 902 5787	9.49	1.275 943	5.32	288
25	7.571 599	970.574 602	.001 030 3175	.132 073	128.186 215	.007 801 1508	9.37	1.340 345	5.36	300
26	8.210 226	1064.894 887	.000 939 0598	.121 799	129.703 484	.007 709 8932	9.26	1.405 487	5.41	312
27	8.902 718	1167.170 623	.000 856 7728	.112 325	131.102 732	.007 627 6061	9.16	1.471 344	5.45	324
28	9.653 618	1278.072 811	.000 782 4280	.103 588	132.393 141	.007 553 2614	9.07	1.537 896	5.49	336
29	10.467 853	1398.329 051	.000 715 1393	.095 531	133.583 177	.007 485 9726	8.99	1.605 118	5.53	348
30	11.350 765	1528.728 310	.000 654 1385	.088 100	134.680 646	.007 424 9718	8.91	1.672 990	5.58	360
31	12.308 145	1670.126 102	.000 598 7572	.081 247	135.692 750	.007 369 5905	8.85	1.741 488	5.62	372
32	13.346 277	1823.450 098	.000 548 4109	.074 927	136.626 127	.007 319 2443	8.79	1.810 590	5.66	384
33	14.471 969	1989.706 216	.000 502 5868	.069 099	137.486 903	.007 273 4201	8.73	1.880 274	5.70	396
34	15.692 608	2169.985 215	.000 460 8326	.063 724	138.280 723	.007 231 6660	8.68	1.950 520	5.74	408
35	17.016 202	2365.469 857	.000 422 7490	.058 768	139.012 797	.007 193 5823	8.64	2.021 305	5.78	420
36	18.451 435	2577.442 662	.000 387 9815	.054 196	139.687 927	.007 158 8148	8.60	2.092 608	5.81	432
37	20.007 722	2807.294 325	.000 356 2149	.049 981	140.310 542	.007 127 0482	8.56	2.164 409	5.85	444
38	21.695 274	3056.532 840	.000 327 1681	.046 093	140.884 728	.007 098 0014	8.52	2.236 689	5.89	456
39	23.525 164	3326.793 392	.000 300 5898	.042 508	141.414 251	.007 071 4231	8.49	2.309 426	5.92	468
40	25.509 395	3619.849 084	.000 276 2546	.039 201	141.902 586	.007 047 0879	8.46	2.382 602	5.96	480
41	27.660 986	3937.622 576	.000 253 9603	.036 152	142.352 935	.007 024 7937	8.43	2.456 198	5.99	492
42	29.994 054	4282.198 691	.000 233 5249	.033 340	142.768 255	.007 004 3582	8.41	2.530 197	6.02	504
43	32.523 904	4655.838 098	.000 214 7841	.030 747	143.151 269	.006 985 6174	8.39	2.604 579	6.06	516
44	35.267 134	5060.992 142	.000 197 5897	.028 355	143.504 491	.006 968 4230	8.37	2.679 327	6.09	528
45	38.241 743	5500.318 927	.000 181 8076	.026 149	143.830 237	.006 952 6410	8.35	2.754 426	6.12	540
46	41.467 245	5976.700 754	.000 167 3164	.024 115	144.130 646	.006 938 1497	8.33	2.829 859	6.15	552
47	44.964 802	6493.263 033	.000 154 0058	.022 240	144.407 687	.006 924 8391	8.31	2.905 609	6.18	564
48	48.757 361	7053.394 787	.000 141 7757	.020 510	144.663 179	.006 912 6090	8.30	2.981 663	6.21	576
49	52.869 803	7660.770 885	.000 130 5352	.018 914	144.898 798	.006 901 3685	8.29	3.058 005	6.24	588
50	57.329 109	8319.376 155	.000 120 2013	.017 443	145.116 089	.006 891 0347	8.27	3.134 621	6.27	600

Effective Rate is 8.43 %

Annual Percentage Rate is 8.125%

MONTHLY COMPOUND INTEREST AND ANNUITY

8.15 % M

Amount Of 1	Amount Of 1 Per Period	Sinking Fund Payment	Present Worth Of 1	Present Worth of 1 Per Period	Periodic Payment To Amortize 1	Constant Annual Percent	Total Interest	Annual Add On Rate
What a single $ 1 deposit grows to in the future. The deposit is made at the beginning of the first period.	What a series of $ 1 deposits grow to in the future. A deposit is made at the end of each period.	The amount to be deposited at the end of each period that grows to $ 1 in the future.	What $ 1 to be paid in the future is worth today. Value today of a single $ 1 payment tomorrow.	What $ 1 to be paid at the end of each period is worth today. Value today of a series of $ 1 payments tomorrow.	The mortgage payment to amortize a loan of $ 1. An annuity certain, payable at the end of each period, worth $ 1 today.	The annual payment, including interest and principal, to amortize completely a loan of $ 100.	The total interest paid over the term on a loan of $1. The loan is amortized by regular periodic payments.	The average annual interest rate on a loan that is completely amortized by regular periodic payments.

$$S = (1+i)^n \qquad S\overline{n}| = \frac{(1+i)^n - 1}{i} \qquad \frac{1}{S\overline{n}|} = \frac{i}{(1+i)^n - 1} \qquad V^n = \frac{1}{(1+i)^n} \qquad A\overline{n}| = \frac{1-V^n}{i} \qquad \frac{1}{A\overline{n}|} = \frac{i}{1-V^n}$$

YEAR	Amount Of 1	Amount Of 1 Per Period	Sinking Fund Payment	Present Worth Of 1	Present Worth of 1 Per Period	Periodic Payment To Amortize 1	Constant Annual Percent	Total Interest	Annual Add On Rate	PERIODS
	1.006 792	1.000 000	1.000 000 0000	.993 254	.993 254	1.006 791 6667	1208.15	.006 792	8.15	1
	1.013 629	2.006 792	.498 307 8297	.986 554	1.979 808	.505 099 4963	606.12	.010 199	6.12	2
	1.020 514	3.020 421	.331 079 6601	.979 899	2.959 707	.337 871 3268	405.45	.013 614	5.45	3
	1.027 445	4.040 935	.247 467 4907	.973 288	3.932 995	.254 259 1574	305.12	.017 037	5.11	4
	1.034 423	5.068 380	.197 301 7213	.966 723	4.899 718	.204 093 3880	244.92	.020 467	4.91	5
	1.041 448	6.102 802	.163 859 1518	.960 201	5.859 919	.170 650 8185	204.79	.023 905	4.78	6
	1.048 521	7.144 250	.139 972 6966	.953 724	6.813 643	.146 764 3633	176.12	.027 351	4.69	7
	1.055 643	8.192 772	.122 058 8127	.947 290	7.760 933	.128 850 4793	154.63	.030 804	4.62	8
	1.062 812	9.248 414	.108 126 6429	.940 900	8.701 834	.114 918 3096	137.91	.034 265	4.57	9
	1.070 030	10.311 227	.096 981 6730	.934 553	9.636 386	.103 773 3397	124.53	.037 733	4.53	10
	1.077 298	11.381 257	.087 863 7574	.928 249	10.564 635	.094 655 4241	113.59	.041 210	4.50	11
	1.084 614	12.458 555	.080 266 1326	.921 987	11.486 622	.087 057 7993	104.47	.044 694	4.47	12
1	1.084 614	12.458 555	.080 266 1326	.921 987	11.486 622	.087 057 7993	104.47	.044 694	4.47	12
2	1.176 388	25.971 282	.038 504 0680	.850 059	22.077 134	.045 295 7346	54.36	.087 098	4.35	24
3	1.275 928	40.627 380	.024 613 9429	.783 744	31.841 445	.031 405 6095	37.69	.130 602	4.35	36
4	1.383 889	56.523 594	.017 691 7272	.722 601	40.844 011	.024 483 3939	29.39	.175 203	4.38	48
5	1.500 986	73.764 855	.013 556 5913	.666 229	49.144 256	.020 348 2580	24.42	.220 895	4.42	60
6	1.627 991	92.464 975	.010 814 9058	.614 254	56.796 972	.017 606 5725	21.13	.267 673	4.46	72
7	1.765 743	112.747 394	.008 869 3846	.566 334	63.852 674	.015 661 0513	18.80	.315 528	4.51	84
8	1.915 150	134.745 996	.007 421 3708	.522 152	70.357 937	.014 213 0375	17.06	.364 452	4.56	96
9	2.077 199	158.605 996	.006 304 9319	.481 418	76.355 704	.013 096 5986	15.72	.414 433	4.60	108
10	2.252 960	184.484 893	.005 420 4980	.443 861	81.885 565	.012 212 1647	14.66	.465 460	4.65	120
11	2.443 593	212.553 518	.004 704 6975	.409 234	86.984 023	.011 496 3642	13.80	.517 520	4.70	132
12	2.650 356	242.997 150	.004 115 2746	.377 308	91.684 733	.010 906 9413	13.09	.570 600	4.75	144
13	2.874 614	276.016 751	.003 622 9685	.347 873	96.018 726	.010 414 6352	12.50	.624 683	4.81	156
14	3.117 847	311.830 283	.003 206 8726	.320 734	100.014 609	.009 998 5393	12.00	.679 755	4.86	168
15	3.381 662	350.674 155	.002 851 6501	.295 713	103.698 761	.009 643 3168	11.58	.735 797	4.91	180
16	3.667 799	392.804 775	.002 545 7939	.272 643	107.095 499	.009 337 4606	11.21	.792 792	4.95	192
17	3.978 148	438.500 251	.002 280 5004	.251 373	110.227 247	.009 072 1671	10.89	.850 722	5.00	204
18	4.314 756	488.062 219	.002 048 9191	.231 763	113.114 677	.008 840 5858	10.61	.909 567	5.05	216
19	4.679 846	541.817 842	.001 845 6387	.213 682	115.776 849	.008 637 3054	10.37	.969 306	5.10	228
20	5.075 828	600.121 961	.001 666 3280	.197 012	118.231 336	.008 457 9946	10.15	1.029 919	5.15	240
21	5.505 316	663.359 445	.001 507 4783	.181 643	120.494 340	.008 299 1450	9.96	1.091 385	5.20	252
22	5.971 145	731.947 729	.001 366 2178	.167 472	122.580 800	.008 157 8844	9.79	1.153 681	5.24	264
23	6.476 390	806.339 565	.001 240 1723	.154 407	124.504 488	.008 031 8390	9.64	1.216 788	5.29	276
24	7.024 385	887.026 018	.001 127 3626	.142 361	126.278 103	.007 919 0293	9.51	1.280 680	5.34	288
25	7.618 749	974.539 703	.001 026 1255	.131 255	127.913 353	.007 817 7921	9.39	1.345 338	5.38	300
26	8.263 404	1069.458 301	.000 935 0528	.121 015	129.421 031	.007 726 7195	9.28	1.410 736	5.43	312
27	8.962 607	1172.408 375	.000 852 9451	.111 575	130.811 090	.007 644 6118	9.18	1.476 854	5.47	324
28	9.720 972	1284.069 503	.000 778 7740	.102 870	132.092 706	.007 570 4407	9.09	1.543 668	5.51	336
29	10.543 506	1405.178 764	.000 711 6532	.094 845	133.274 339	.007 503 3199	9.01	1.611 155	5.56	348
30	11.435 638	1536.535 607	.000 650 8147	.087 446	134.363 789	.007 442 4814	8.94	1.679 293	5.60	360
31	12.403 257	1679.007 124	.000 595 5901	.080 624	135.368 247	.007 387 2568	8.87	1.748 060	5.64	372
32	13.452 750	1833.533 776	.000 545 3949	.074 334	136.294 345	.007 337 0616	8.81	1.817 432	5.68	384
33	14.591 046	2001.135 600	.000 499 7163	.068 535	137.148 194	.007 291 3829	8.75	1.887 388	5.72	396
34	15.825 658	2182.918 943	.000 458 1022	.063 189	137.935 432	.007 249 7689	8.70	1.957 906	5.76	408
35	17.164 736	2380.083 766	.000 420 1533	.058 259	138.661 254	.007 211 8199	8.66	2.028 964	5.80	420
36	18.617 119	2593.931 562	.000 385 5152	.053 714	139.330 453	.007 177 1818	8.62	2.100 543	5.83	432
37	20.192 394	2825.873 951	.000 353 8728	.049 524	139.947 446	.007 145 5395	8.58	2.172 620	5.87	444
38	21.900 960	3077.441 994	.000 324 9452	.045 660	140.516 305	.007 116 6119	8.54	2.245 175	5.91	456
39	23.754 096	3350.296 304	.000 298 4811	.042 098	141.040 785	.007 090 1477	8.51	2.318 189	5.94	468
40	25.764 033	3646.238 004	.000 274 2553	.038 814	141.524 349	.007 065 9219	8.48	2.391 643	5.98	480
41	27.944 040	3967.220 618	.000 252 0656	.035 786	141.970 188	.007 043 7323	8.46	2.465 516	6.01	492
42	30.308 507	4315.362 968	.000 231 7302	.032 994	142.381 246	.007 023 3969	8.43	2.539 792	6.05	504
43	32.873 041	4692.963 157	.000 213 0850	.030 420	142.760 236	.007 004 7517	8.41	2.614 452	6.08	516
44	35.654 572	5102.513 740	.000 195 9818	.028 047	143.109 660	.006 987 6485	8.39	2.689 478	6.11	528
45	38.671 461	5546.718 180	.000 180 2868	.025 859	143.431 824	.006 971 9535	8.37	2.764 855	6.14	540
46	41.943 622	6028.508 691	.000 165 8785	.023 842	143.728 855	.006 957 5452	8.35	2.840 565	6.18	552
47	45.492 654	6551.065 592	.000 152 6469	.021 982	144.002 713	.006 944 3136	8.34	2.916 593	6.21	564
48	49.341 985	7117.838 305	.000 140 4921	.020 267	144.255 207	.006 932 1588	8.32	2.992 923	6.24	576
49	53.517 025	7732.568 124	.000 129 3231	.018 686	144.488 004	.006 920 9898	8.31	3.069 542	6.26	588
50	58.045 333	8399.312 907	.000 119 0574	.017 228	144.702 638	.006 910 7240	8.30	3.146 434	6.29	600

Effective Rate is 8.46 %

8 - 92

Annual Percentage Rate is 8.15 %

	Amount Of 1	Amount Of 1 Per Period	Sinking Fund Payment	Present Worth Of 1	Present Worth of 1 Per Period	Periodic Payment To Amortize 1	Constant Annual Percent	Total Interest	Annual Add On Rate	
	What a single $ 1 deposit grows to in the future. The deposit is made at the beginning of the first period.	What a series of $ 1 deposits grow to in the future. A deposit is made at the end of each period.	The amount to be deposited at the end of each period that grows to $ 1 in the future.	What $ 1 to be paid in the future is worth today. Value today of a single $ 1 payment tomorrow.	What $ 1 to be paid at the end of each period is worth today. Value today of a series of $ 1 payments tomorrow.	The mortgage payment to amortize a loan of $ 1. An annuity certain, payable at the end of each period, worth $ 1 today.	The annual payment, including interest and principal, to amortize completely a loan of $ 100.	The total interest paid over the term on a loan. The loan is amortized by regular periodic payments.	The average annual interest rate on a loan that is completely amortized by regular periodic payments.	
	$S = (1+i)^n$	$S\overline{n}| = \dfrac{(1+i)^n - 1}{i}$	$\dfrac{1}{S\overline{n}|} = \dfrac{i}{(1+i)^n - 1}$	$V^n = \dfrac{1}{(1+i)^n}$	$A\overline{n}| = \dfrac{1-V^n}{i}$	$\dfrac{1}{A\overline{n}|} = \dfrac{i}{1-V^n}$				

YEAR										PERIODS
	1.006 833	1.000 000	1.000 000 0000	.993 213	.993 213	1.006 833 3333	1208.20	.006 833	8.20	1
	1.013 713	2.006 833	.498 297 4836	.986 472	1.979 685	.505 130 8169	606.16	.010 262	6.16	2
	1.020 640	3.020 547	.331 065 8967	.979 777	2.959 462	.337 899 2301	405.48	.013 698	5.48	3
	1.027 615	4.041 187	.247 452 0422	.973 127	3.932 590	.254 285 3755	305.15	.017 142	5.14	4
	1.034 637	5.068 802	.197 285 2805	.966 523	4.899 112	.204 118 6139	244.95	.020 593	4.94	5
	1.041 707	6.103 439	.163 842 0653	.959 963	5.859 075	.170 675 3986	204.82	.024 052	4.81	6
	1.048 825	7.145 146	.139 955 1622	.953 448	6.812 523	.146 788 4955	176.15	.027 519	4.72	7
	1.055 992	8.193 971	.122 040 9541	.946 977	7.759 500	.128 874 2875	154.65	.030 994	4.65	8
	1.063 208	9.249 963	.108 108 5427	.940 550	8.700 049	.114 941 8761	137.94	.034 477	4.60	9
	1.070 473	10.313 171	.096 963 3889	.934 166	9.634 216	.103 796 7222	124.56	.037 967	4.56	10
	1.077 788	11.383 644	.087 845 3314	.927 826	10.562 042	.094 678 6648	113.62	.041 465	4.52	11
	1.085 153	12.461 432	.080 247 5962	.921 529	11.483 571	.087 080 9295	104.50	.044 971	4.50	12
1	1.085 153	12.461 432	.080 247 5962	.921 529	11.483 571	.087 080 9295	104.50	.044 971	4.50	12
2	1.177 557	25.983 995	.038 485 2294	.849 216	22.066 013	.045 318 5627	54.39	.087 646	4.38	24
3	1.277 830	40.658 046	.024 595 3780	.782 577	31.818 040	.031 428 7114	37.72	.131 434	4.38	36
4	1.386 641	56.581 638	.017 673 5783	.721 167	40.804 815	.024 506 9116	29.41	.176 332	4.41	48
5	1.504 718	73.861 173	.013 538 9131	.664 576	49.086 388	.020 372 2464	24.45	.222 335	4.45	60
6	1.632 849	92.612 115	.010 797 7234	.612 426	56.718 098	.017 631 0567	21.16	.269 436	4.49	72
7	1.771 892	112.959 758	.008 852 7102	.564 369	63.750 939	.015 686 0435	18.83	.317 628	4.54	84
8	1.922 774	135.040 067	.007 405 2096	.520 082	70.231 905	.014 238 5429	17.09	.366 900	4.59	96
9	2.086 504	159.000 582	.006 289 2851	.479 271	76.204 303	.013 122 6185	15.75	.417 243	4.64	108
10	2.264 176	185.001 411	.005 405 3642	.441 662	81.708 041	.012 238 6975	14.69	.468 644	4.69	120
11	2.456 978	213.216 291	.004 690 0731	.407 004	86.779 895	.011 523 4065	13.83	.521 090	4.74	132
12	2.666 197	243.833 756	.004 101 1549	.375 066	91.453 754	.010 934 4882	13.13	.574 566	4.79	144
13	2.893 232	277.058 394	.003 609 3474	.345 634	95.760 851	.010 442 6808	12.54	.629 058	4.84	156
14	3.139 600	313.112 214	.003 193 7432	.318 512	99.729 966	.010 027 0765	12.04	.684 549	4.89	168
15	3.406 947	352.236 129	.002 839 0046	.293 518	103.387 620	.009 672 3380	11.61	.741 021	4.94	180
16	3.697 059	394.691 567	.002 533 6239	.270 485	106.758 254	.009 366 9573	11.25	.798 456	4.99	192
17	4.011 875	440.762 219	.002 268 7970	.249 260	109.864 390	.009 102 1303	10.93	.856 835	5.04	204
18	4.353 499	490.755 930	.002 037 6728	.229 700	112.726 785	.008 871 0061	10.65	.916 137	5.09	216
19	4.724 213	545.006 762	.001 834 8396	.211 675	115.364 565	.008 668 1730	10.41	.976 343	5.14	228
20	5.126 494	603.877 222	.001 655 9658	.195 065	117.795 355	.008 489 2991	10.19	1.037 432	5.19	240
21	5.563 031	667.760 685	.001 497 5425	.179 758	120.035 399	.008 330 8758	10.00	1.099 381	5.24	252
22	6.036 741	737.084 024	.001 356 6974	.165 652	122.099 663	.008 190 0308	9.83	1.162 168	5.28	264
23	6.550 788	812.310 463	.001 231 0564	.152 653	124.001 943	.008 064 3897	9.68	1.225 772	5.33	276
24	7.108 608	893.942 667	.001 118 6400	.140 675	125.754 949	.007 951 9733	9.55	1.290 168	5.38	288
25	7.713 928	982.526 108	.001 017 7847	.129 636	127.370 395	.007 851 1180	9.43	1.355 335	5.42	300
26	8.370 793	1078.652 706	.000 927 0825	.119 463	128.859 075	.007 760 4158	9.32	1.421 250	5.47	312
27	9.083 593	1182.964 784	.000 845 3337	.110 089	130.230 937	.007 678 6670	9.22	1.487 888	5.51	324
28	9.857 089	1296.159 360	.000 771 5101	.101 450	131.495 147	.007 604 8434	9.13	1.555 227	5.55	336
29	10.696 451	1418.992 809	.000 704 7252	.093 489	132.660 153	.007 538 0585	9.05	1.623 244	5.60	348
30	11.607 287	1552.285 909	.000 644 2112	.086 153	133.733 740	.007 477 5446	8.98	1.691 916	5.64	360
31	12.595 684	1696.929 332	.000 589 2997	.079 392	134.723 082	.007 422 6331	8.91	1.761 220	5.68	372
32	13.668 246	1853.889 595	.000 539 4064	.073 162	135.634 788	.007 372 7398	8.85	1.831 132	5.72	384
33	14.832 139	2024.215 514	.000 494 0185	.067 421	136.474 953	.007 327 3519	8.80	1.901 631	5.76	396
34	16.095 142	2209.045 217	.000 452 6843	.062 131	137.249 188	.007 286 0176	8.75	1.972 695	5.80	408
35	17.465 694	2409.613 746	.000 415 0043	.057 255	137.962 669	.007 248 3376	8.70	2.044 302	5.84	420
36	18.952 952	2627.261 311	.000 380 6245	.052 762	138.620 162	.007 213 9578	8.66	2.116 430	5.88	432
37	20.566 855	2863.442 246	.000 349 2300	.048 622	139.226 060	.007 182 5634	8.62	2.189 058	5.92	444
38	22.318 187	3119.734 725	.000 320 5401	.044 807	139.784 414	.007 153 8734	8.59	2.262 166	5.95	456
39	24.218 651	3397.851 308	.000 294 3036	.041 290	140.298 952	.007 127 6370	8.56	2.335 734	5.99	468
40	26.280 944	3699.650 387	.000 270 2958	.038 050	140.773 115	.007 103 6291	8.53	2.409 742	6.02	480
41	28.518 849	4027.148 600	.000 248 3147	.035 065	141.210 069	.007 081 6480	8.50	2.484 171	6.06	492
42	30.947 318	4382.534 308	.000 228 1785	.032 313	141.612 735	.007 061 5118	8.48	2.559 002	6.09	504
43	33.582 578	4768.182 218	.000 209 7235	.029 777	141.983 803	.007 043 0569	8.46	2.634 217	6.13	516
44	36.442 240	5186.669 252	.000 192 8020	.027 441	142.325 754	.007 026 1353	8.44	2.709 799	6.16	528
45	39.545 410	5640.791 763	.000 177 2801	.025 287	142.640 871	.007 010 6134	8.42	2.785 731	6.19	540
46	42.912 826	6133.584 223	.000 163 0368	.023 303	142.931 260	.006 996 3701	8.40	2.861 996	6.22	552
47	46.566 987	6668.339 500	.000 149 9624	.021 474	143.198 862	.006 983 2957	8.38	2.938 579	6.25	564
48	50.532 311	7248.630 859	.000 137 9571	.019 789	143.445 466	.006 971 2904	8.37	3.015 463	6.28	576
49	54.835 295	7878.335 838	.000 126 9304	.018 236	143.672 718	.006 960 2637	8.36	3.092 635	6.31	588
50	59.504 691	8561.662 162	.000 116 7997	.016 805	143.882 137	.006 950 1331	8.35	3.170 080	6.34	600

MONTHLY COMPOUND INTEREST AND ANNUITY

8.25 % M

	Amount Of 1	Amount Of 1 Per Period	Sinking Fund Payment	Present Worth Of 1	Present Worth of 1 Per Period	Periodic Payment To Amortize 1	Constant Annual Percent	Total Interest	Annual Add On Rate	
	What a single $ 1 deposit grows to in the future. The deposit is made at the beginning of the first period.	What a series of $ 1 deposits grow to in the future. A deposit is made at the end of each period.	The amount to be deposited at the end of each period that grows to $ 1 in the future.	What $ 1 to be paid in the future is worth today. Value today of a single $ 1 payment tomorrow.	What $ 1 to be paid at the end of each period is worth today. Value today of a series of $ 1 payments tomorrow.	The mortgage payment to amortize a loan of $ 1. An annuity certain, payable at the end of each period, worth $ 1 today.	The annual payment, including interest and principal, to amortize completely a loan of $ 100.	The total interest paid over the term on a loan of $1. The loan is amortized by regular periodic payments.	The average annual interest rate on a loan that is completely amortized by regular periodic payments.	

$$S = (1+i)^n \qquad S\overline{n}| = \frac{(1+i)^n - 1}{i} \qquad \frac{1}{S\overline{n}|} = \frac{i}{(1+i)^n - 1} \qquad V^n = \frac{1}{(1+i)^n} \qquad A\overline{n}| = \frac{1-V^n}{i} \qquad \frac{1}{A\overline{n}|} = \frac{i}{1-V^n}$$

YEAR / **PERIODS**

YEAR	Amount Of 1	Amount Of 1 Per Period	Sinking Fund Payment	Present Worth Of 1	Present Worth of 1 Per Period	Periodic Payment To Amortize 1	Constant Annual Percent	Total Interest	Annual Add On Rate	PERIODS
	1.006 875	1.000 000	1.000 000 0000	.993 172	.993 172	1.006 875 0000	1208.25	.006 875	8.25	1
	1.013 797	2.006 875	.498 287 1380	.986 391	1.979 562	.505 162 1380	606.20	.010 324	6.19	2
	1.020 767	3.020 672	.331 052 1341	.979 655	2.959 218	.337 927 1341	405.52	.013 781	5.51	3
	1.027 785	4.041 439	.247 436 5948	.972 966	3.932 184	.254 311 5948	305.18	.017 246	5.17	4
	1.034 851	5.069 224	.197 268 8412	.966 323	4.898 507	.204 143 8412	244.98	.020 719	4.97	5
	1.041 966	6.104 075	.163 824 9804	.959 725	5.858 231	.170 699 9804	204.84	.024 200	4.84	6
	1.049 129	7.146 041	.139 937 6297	.953 172	6.811 403	.146 812 6297	176.18	.027 688	4.75	7
	1.056 342	8.195 170	.122 023 0979	.946 663	7.758 066	.128 898 0979	154.68	.031 185	4.68	8
	1.063 604	9.251 512	.108 090 4451	.940 199	8.698 266	.114 965 4451	137.96	.034 689	4.63	9
	1.070 916	10.315 116	.096 945 1076	.933 780	9.632 045	.103 820 1076	124.59	.038 201	4.58	10
	1.078 279	11.386 032	.087 826 9085	.927 404	10.559 449	.094 701 9085	113.65	.041 721	4.55	11
	1.085 692	12.464 311	.080 229 0631	.921 071	11.480 521	.087 104 0631	104.53	.045 249	4.52	12
1	1.085 692	12.464 311	.080 229 0631	.921 071	11.480 521	.087 104 0631	104.53	.045 249	4.52	12
2	1.178 727	25.996 716	.038 466 3976	.848 373	22.054 900	.045 341 3976	54.41	.088 194	4.41	24
3	1.279 735	40.688 741	.024 576 8234	.781 412	31.794 659	.031 451 8234	37.75	.132 266	4.41	36
4	1.389 398	56.639 757	.017 655 4429	.719 736	40.765 672	.024 530 4429	29.44	.177 461	4.44	48
5	1.508 459	73.957 650	.013 521 2517	.662 928	49.028 616	.020 396 2517	24.48	.223 775	4.48	60
6	1.637 722	92.759 550	.010 780 5611	.610 604	56.639 378	.017 655 5611	21.19	.271 200	4.52	72
7	1.778 062	113.172 626	.008 836 0590	.562 410	63.649 433	.015 711 0590	18.86	.319 729	4.57	84
8	1.930 428	135.334 941	.007 389 0748	.518 020	70.106 194	.014 264 0748	17.12	.369 351	4.62	96
9	2.095 850	159.396 393	.006 273 6677	.477 133	76.053 333	.013 148 6677	15.78	.420 056	4.67	108
10	2.275 448	185.519 722	.005 390 2625	.439 474	81.531 072	.012 265 2625	14.72	.471 832	4.72	120
11	2.470 436	213.881 614	.004 675 4837	.404 787	86.576 461	.011 550 4837	13.87	.524 664	4.77	132
12	2.682 133	244.673 898	.004 087 0727	.372 838	91.223 625	.010 962 0727	13.16	.578 538	4.82	144
13	2.911 971	278.104 839	.003 595 7663	.343 410	95.503 994	.010 470 7663	12.57	.633 440	4.87	156
14	3.161 504	314.400 549	.003 180 6560	.316 305	99.446 520	.010 055 6560	12.07	.689 350	4.92	168
15	3.432 420	353.806 515	.002 826 4036	.291 340	103.077 868	.009 701 4036	11.65	.746 253	4.98	180
16	3.726 551	396.589 263	.002 521 5004	.268 345	106.422 599	.009 396 5004	11.28	.804 128	5.03	192
17	4.045 887	443.038 156	.002 257 1419	.247 165	109.503 335	.009 132 1419	10.96	.862 957	5.08	204
18	4.392 588	493.467 354	.002 026 4765	.227 656	112.340 913	.008 901 4765	10.69	.922 719	5.13	216
19	4.768 998	548.217 938	.001 824 0921	.209 688	114.954 525	.008 699 0921	10.44	.983 393	5.18	228
20	5.177 664	607.660 217	.001 645 6565	.193 137	117.361 849	.008 520 6565	10.23	1.044 958	5.22	240
21	5.621 349	672.196 232	.001 487 6608	.177 893	119.579 165	.008 362 6608	10.04	1.107 391	5.27	252
22	6.103 055	742.262 475	.001 347 2323	.163 852	121.621 472	.008 222 2323	9.87	1.170 669	5.32	264
23	6.626 038	818.332 845	.001 221 9967	.150 920	123.502 583	.008 096 9967	9.72	1.234 771	5.37	276
24	7.193 838	900.921 848	.001 109 9742	.139 008	125.235 220	.007 984 9742	9.59	1.299 673	5.42	288
25	7.810 293	990.588 079	.001 009 5013	.128 036	126.831 103	.007 884 5013	9.47	1.365 350	5.46	300
26	8.479 574	1087.938 001	.000 919 1700	.117 930	128.301 025	.007 794 1700	9.36	1.431 781	5.51	312
27	9.206 207	1193.630 046	.000 837 7805	.108 622	129.654 928	.007 712 7805	9.26	1.498 941	5.55	324
28	9.995 106	1308.379 069	.000 764 3045	.100 049	130.901 969	.007 639 3045	9.17	1.566 806	5.60	336
29	10.851 608	1432.961 180	.000 697 8556	.092 152	132.050 583	.007 572 8556	9.09	1.635 354	5.64	348
30	11.781 906	1568.218 999	.000 637 6660	.084 878	133.108 539	.007 512 6660	9.02	1.704 560	5.68	360
31	12.791 088	1715.067 350	.000 583 0675	.078 179	134.082 992	.007 458 0675	8.95	1.774 401	5.72	372
32	13.887 184	1874.499 451	.000 533 4757	.072 009	134.980 532	.007 408 4757	8.90	1.844 855	5.77	384
33	15.077 206	2047.593 628	.000 488 3782	.066 325	135.807 231	.007 363 3782	8.84	1.915 898	5.81	396
34	16.369 204	2235.520 617	.000 447 3231	.061 090	136.568 680	.007 322 3231	8.79	1.987 508	5.85	408
35	17.771 916	2439.551 470	.000 409 9114	.056 269	137.270 029	.007 284 9114	8.75	2.059 663	5.88	420
36	19.294 830	2661.066 164	.000 375 7892	.051 827	137.916 021	.007 250 7892	8.71	2.132 341	5.92	432
37	20.948 245	2901.562 926	.000 344 6418	.047 737	138.511 026	.007 219 6418	8.67	2.205 521	5.96	444
38	22.743 345	3162.668 369	.000 316 1887	.043 969	139.059 068	.007 191 1887	8.63	2.279 182	6.00	456
39	24.692 271	3446.148 496	.000 290 1790	.040 499	139.563 854	.007 165 1790	8.60	2.353 304	6.03	468
40	26.808 204	3753.920 642	.000 266 3882	.037 302	140.028 798	.007 141 3882	8.57	2.427 866	6.07	480
41	29.105 457	4088.066 441	.000 244 6144	.034 358	140.457 045	.007 119 6144	8.55	2.502 850	6.10	492
42	31.599 566	4450.845 909	.000 224 6764	.031 646	140.851 490	.007 099 6764	8.52	2.578 237	6.14	504
43	34.307 400	4844.712 724	.000 206 4106	.029 148	141.214 803	.007 081 4106	8.50	2.654 008	6.17	516
44	37.247 274	5272.330 830	.000 189 6694	.026 848	141.549 440	.007 064 6694	8.48	2.730 145	6.20	528
45	40.439 073	5736.592 445	.000 174 3195	.024 729	141.857 664	.007 049 3195	8.46	2.806 633	6.24	540
46	43.904 384	6240.637 631	.000 160 2400	.022 777	142.141 561	.007 035 2400	8.45	2.883 452	6.27	552
47	47.666 644	6787.875 527	.000 147 3215	.020 979	142.403 050	.007 022 3215	8.43	2.960 589	6.30	564
48	51.751 301	7382.007 409	.000 135 4645	.019 323	142.643 900	.007 010 4645	8.42	3.038 028	6.33	576
49	56.185 981	8027.051 722	.000 124 5787	.017 798	142.865 740	.006 999 5787	8.40	3.115 752	6.36	588
50	61.000 677	8727.371 262	.000 114 5820	.016 393	143.070 071	.006 989 5820	8.39	3.193 749	6.39	600

Effective Rate is 8.57 %

Annual Percentage Rate is 8.25 %

MONTHLY COMPOUND INTEREST AND ANNUITY

8.30 % M

	Amount Of 1	Amount Of 1 Per Period	Sinking Fund Payment	Present Worth Of 1	Present Worth of 1 Per Period	Periodic Payment To Amortize 1	Constant Annual Percent	Total Interest	Annual Add On Rate	
	What a single $1 deposit grows to in the future. The deposit is made at the beginning of the first period.	What a series of $1 deposits grow to in the future. A deposit is made at the end of each period.	The amount to be deposited at the end of each period that grows to $1 in the future.	What $1 to be paid in the future is worth today. Value today of a single $1 payment tomorrow.	What $1 to be paid at the end of each period is worth today. Value today of a series of $1 payments tomorrow.	The mortgage payment to amortize a loan of $1. An annuity certain, payable at the end of each period, worth $1 today.	The annual payment, including interest and principal, to amortize completely a loan of $100.	The total interest paid over the term on a loan of $1. The loan is amortized by regular periodic payments.	The average annual interest rate on a loan that is completely amortized by regular periodic payments.	
	$S = (1+i)^n$	$S\overline{n} = \dfrac{(1+i)^n - 1}{i}$	$\dfrac{1}{S\overline{n}} = \dfrac{i}{(1+i)^n - 1}$	$V^n = \dfrac{1}{(1+i)^n}$	$A\overline{n} = \dfrac{1-V^n}{i}$	$\dfrac{1}{A\overline{n}} = \dfrac{i}{1-V^n}$				

YEAR									**PERIODS**	
	1.006 917	1.000 000	1.000 000 0000	.993 131	.993 131	1.006 916 6667	1208.30	.006 917	8.30	1
	1.013 881	2.006 917	.498 276 7928	.986 309	1.979 440	.505 193 4594	606.24	.010 387	6.23	2
	1.020 894	3.020 798	.331 038 3723	.979 534	2.958 973	.337 955 0389	405.55	.013 865	5.55	3
	1.027 955	4.041 692	.247 421 1484	.972 805	3.931 779	.254 337 8151	305.21	.017 351	5.21	4
	1.035 065	5.069 647	.197 252 4032	.966 123	4.897 902	.204 169 0698	245.01	.020 845	5.00	5
	1.042 224	6.104 712	.163 807 8972	.959 486	5.857 388	.170 724 5638	204.87	.024 347	4.87	6
	1.049 433	7.146 936	.139 920 0993	.952 896	6.810 283	.146 836 7659	176.21	.027 857	4.78	7
	1.056 692	8.196 369	.122 005 2438	.946 350	7.756 633	.128 921 9105	154.71	.031 375	4.71	8
	1.064 000	9.253 061	.108 072 3500	.939 849	8.696 483	.114 989 0167	137.99	.034 901	4.65	9
	1.071 360	10.317 061	.096 926 8292	.933 393	9.629 876	.103 843 4959	124.62	.038 435	4.61	10
	1.078 770	11.388 421	.087 808 4888	.926 982	10.556 858	.094 725 1554	113.68	.041 977	4.58	11
	1.086 231	12.467 190	.080 210 5335	.920 614	11.477 472	.087 127 2002	104.56	.045 526	4.55	12
1	1.086 231	12.467 190	.080 210 5335	.920 614	11.477 472	.087 127 2002	104.56	.045 526	4.55	12
2	1.179 899	26.009 444	.038 447 5727	.847 530	22.043 795	.045 364 2394	54.44	.088 742	4.44	24
3	1.281 643	40.719 466	.024 558 2791	.780 248	31.771 302	.031 474 9458	37.77	.133 098	4.44	36
4	1.392 161	56.697 953	.017 637 3212	.718 308	40.726 582	.024 553 9878	29.47	.178 591	4.46	48
5	1.512 209	74.054 287	.013 503 6072	.661 284	48.970 940	.020 420 2738	24.51	.225 216	4.50	60
6	1.642 609	92.907 282	.010 763 4189	.608 788	56.560 812	.017 680 0856	21.22	.272 966	4.55	72
7	1.784 253	113.385 998	.008 819 4311	.560 459	63.548 156	.015 736 0978	18.89	.321 832	4.60	84
8	1.938 112	135.630 622	.007 372 9663	.515 966	69.980 804	.014 289 6329	17.15	.371 805	4.65	96
9	2.105 238	159.793 431	.006 258 0795	.475 006	75.902 790	.013 174 7462	15.81	.422 873	4.70	108
10	2.286 776	186.039 833	.005 375 1930	.437 297	81.354 655	.012 291 8596	14.76	.475 023	4.75	120
11	2.483 967	214.549 499	.004 660 9291	.402 582	86.373 719	.011 577 5958	13.90	.528 243	4.80	132
12	2.698 163	245.517 593	.004 073 0279	.370 622	90.994 340	.010 989 6945	13.19	.582 516	4.85	144
13	2.930 830	279.156 109	.003 582 2250	.341 200	95.248 149	.010 498 8917	12.60	.637 827	4.91	156
14	3.183 559	315.695 322	.003 167 6111	.314 114	99.164 266	.010 084 2777	12.11	.694 159	4.96	168
15	3.458 082	355.385 362	.002 813 8469	.289 178	102.769 499	.009 730 5136	11.68	.751 492	5.01	180
16	3.756 277	398.497 931	.002 509 4233	.266 221	106.088 527	.009 426 0900	11.32	.809 809	5.06	192
17	4.080 186	445.326 176	.002 245 5351	.245 087	109.144 071	.009 162 2018	11.00	.869 089	5.11	204
18	4.432 027	496.196 617	.002 015 3301	.225 630	111.957 048	.008 931 9968	10.72	.929 311	5.16	216
19	4.814 206	551.451 537	.001 813 3960	.207 719	114.546 715	.008 730 0626	10.48	.990 454	5.21	228
20	5.229 342	611.471 166	.001 635 4001	.191 229	116.930 799	.008 552 0668	10.27	1.052 496	5.26	240
21	5.680 276	676.666 372	.001 477 8332	.176 048	119.125 620	.008 394 4998	10.08	1.115 414	5.31	252
22	6.170 094	747.483 451	.001 337 8223	.162 072	121.146 204	.008 254 4889	9.91	1.179 185	5.36	264
23	6.702 150	824.407 187	.001 212 9928	.149 206	123.006 382	.008 129 6595	9.76	1.243 786	5.41	276
24	7.280 085	907.964 164	.001 101 3651	.137 361	124.718 888	.008 018 0317	9.63	1.309 193	5.45	288
25	7.907 857	998.726 376	.001 001 2752	.126 457	126.295 445	.007 917 9419	9.51	1.375 383	5.50	300
26	8.589 763	1097.315 141	.000 911 3152	.116 418	127.746 846	.007 827 9819	9.40	1.442 330	5.55	312
27	9.330 470	1204.405 353	.000 830 2853	.107 176	129.083 027	.007 746 9519	9.30	1.510 012	5.59	324
28	10.135 050	1320.730 105	.000 757 1570	.098 667	130.313 133	.007 673 8236	9.21	1.578 405	5.64	336
29	11.009 009	1447.085 702	.000 691 0441	.090 835	131.445 586	.007 607 7107	9.13	1.647 483	5.68	348
30	11.958 332	1584.337 120	.000 631 1788	.083 624	132.488 139	.007 547 8455	9.06	1.717 224	5.72	360
31	12.989 515	1733.423 919	.000 576 8929	.076 985	133.447 928	.007 493 5596	9.00	1.787 604	5.77	372
32	14.109 620	1895.366 683	.000 527 6024	.070 874	134.331 523	.007 444 2691	8.94	1.858 599	5.81	384
33	15.326 312	2071.273 997	.000 482 7946	.065 247	135.144 973	.007 399 4613	8.88	1.930 187	5.85	396
34	16.647 921	2262.350 046	.000 442 0182	.060 068	135.893 847	.007 358 6849	8.84	2.002 343	5.89	408
35	18.083 495	2469.902 850	.000 404 8742	.055 299	136.583 271	.007 321 5409	8.79	2.075 047	5.93	420
36	19.642 860	2695.353 223	.000 371 0089	.050 909	137.217 964	.007 287 6756	8.75	2.148 276	5.97	432
37	21.336 691	2940.244 498	.000 340 1078	.046 868	137.802 271	.007 256 7744	8.71	2.222 008	6.01	444
38	23.176 584	3206.253 090	.000 311 8905	.043 147	138.340 193	.007 228 5572	8.68	2.296 222	6.04	456
39	25.175 133	3495.199 976	.000 286 1067	.039 722	138.835 412	.007 202 7733	8.65	2.370 898	6.08	468
40	27.346 020	3809.063 157	.000 262 5317	.036 568	139.291 317	.007 179 1984	8.62	2.446 015	6.12	480
41	29.704 106	4149.991 199	.000 240 9644	.033 665	139.711 029	.007 157 6310	8.59	2.521 554	6.15	492
42	32.265 532	4520.317 944	.000 221 2234	.030 993	140.097 423	.007 137 8900	8.57	2.597 497	6.18	504
43	35.047 835	4922.578 483	.000 203 1456	.028 532	140.453 142	.007 119 8122	8.55	2.673 823	6.22	516
44	38.070 058	5359.526 512	.000 186 5836	.026 267	140.780 622	.007 103 2503	8.53	2.750 516	6.25	528
45	41.352 893	5834.153 182	.000 171 4045	.024 182	141.082 105	.007 088 0711	8.51	2.827 558	6.28	540
46	44.918 811	6349.707 574	.000 157 4876	.022 262	141.359 655	.007 074 1542	8.49	2.904 933	6.32	552
47	48.792 223	6909.718 943	.000 144 7237	.020 495	141.615 171	.007 061 3904	8.48	2.982 624	6.35	564
48	52.999 644	7518.020 877	.000 133 0137	.018 868	141.850 402	.007 049 6804	8.46	3.060 616	6.38	576
49	57.569 878	8178.777 540	.000 122 2677	.017 370	142.066 960	.007 038 9343	8.45	3.138 893	6.41	588
50	62.534 209	8896.512 174	.000 112 4036	.015 991	142.266 326	.007 029 0703	8.44	3.217 442	6.43	600

Effective Rate is 8.62 %

8 - 95

Annual Percentage Rate is 8.30 %

Amount Of 1	Amount Of 1 Per Period	Sinking Fund Payment	Present Worth Of 1	Present Worth of 1 Per Period	Periodic Payment To Amortize 1	Constant Annual Percent	Total Interest	Annual Add On Rate
What a single $ 1 deposit grows to in the future. The deposit is made at the beginning of the first period.	What a series of $ 1 deposits grow to in the future. A deposit is made at the end of each period.	The amount to be deposited at the end of each period that grows to $ 1 in the future.	What $ 1 to be paid in the future is worth today. Value today of a single $ 1 payment tomorrow.	What $ 1 to be paid at the end of each period is worth today. Value today of a series of $ 1 payments tomorrow.	The mortgage payment to amortize a loan of $ 1. An annuity certain, payable at the end of each period, worth $ 1 today.	The annual payment, including interest and principal, to amortize completely a loan of $ 100.	The total interest paid over the term on a loan of $1. The loan is amortized by regular periodic payments.	The average annual interest rate on a loan that is completely amortized by regular periodic payments.
$S = (1+i)^n$	$S\overline{n}| = \dfrac{(1+i)^n - 1}{i}$	$\dfrac{1}{S\overline{n}|} = \dfrac{i}{(1+i)^n - 1}$	$V^n = \dfrac{1}{(1+i)^n}$	$A\overline{n}| = \dfrac{1-V^n}{i}$	$\dfrac{1}{A\overline{n}|} = \dfrac{i}{1-V^n}$			

YEAR									PERIODS
	1.006 958	1.000 000	1.000 000 0000	.993 090	.993 090	1.006 958 3333	1208.35	.006 958	8.35	1
	1.013 965	2.006 958	.498 266 4480	.986 227	1.979 317	.505 224 7813	606.27	.010 450	6.27	2
	1.021 021	3.020 923	.331 024 6112	.979 412	2.958 729	.337 982 9445	405.58	.013 949	5.58	3
	1.028 125	4.041 944	.247 405 7031	.972 644	3.931 373	.254 364 0365	305.24	.017 456	5.24	4
	1.035 279	5.070 069	.197 235 9666	.965 923	4.897 296	.204 194 2999	245.04	.020 971	5.03	5
	1.042 483	6.105 348	.163 790 8156	.959 248	5.856 545	.170 749 1490	204.90	.024 495	4.90	6
	1.049 737	7.147 831	.139 902 5707	.952 620	6.809 164	.146 860 9041	176.24	.028 026	4.80	7
	1.057 041	8.197 568	.121 987 3921	.946 037	7.755 201	.128 945 7254	154.74	.031 566	4.73	8
	1.064 397	9.254 610	.108 054 2574	.939 499	8.694 700	.115 012 5908	138.02	.035 113	4.68	9
	1.071 803	10.319 007	.096 908 5536	.933 007	9.627 707	.103 866 8870	124.65	.038 669	4.64	10
	1.079 261	11.390 810	.087 790 0721	.926 560	10.554 267	.094 748 4055	113.70	.042 232	4.61	11
	1.086 771	12.470 071	.080 192 0073	.920 157	11.474 424	.087 150 3406	104.59	.045 804	4.58	12
1	1.086 771	12.470 071	.080 192 0073	.920 157	11.474 424	.087 150 3406	104.59	.045 804	4.58	12
2	1.181 071	26.022 181	.038 428 7547	.846 689	22.032 698	.045 387 0880	54.47	.089 290	4.46	24
3	1.283 554	40.750 220	.024 539 7450	.779 087	31.747 969	.031 498 0783	37.80	.133 931	4.46	36
4	1.394 929	56.756 224	.017 619 2130	.716 883	40.687 544	.024 577 5463	29.50	.179 722	4.49	48
5	1.515 968	74.151 084	.013 485 9796	.659 645	48.913 358	.020 444 3129	24.54	.226 659	4.53	60
6	1.647 510	93.055 311	.010 746 2969	.606 977	56.482 400	.017 704 6302	21.25	.274 733	4.58	72
7	1.790 466	113.599 876	.008 802 8265	.558 514	63.447 107	.015 761 1598	18.92	.323 937	4.63	84
8	1.945 826	135.927 111	.007 356 8841	.513 921	69.855 733	.014 315 2174	17.18	.374 261	4.68	96
9	2.114 667	160.191 701	.006 242 5206	.472 888	75.752 675	.013 200 8540	15.85	.425 692	4.73	108
10	2.298 159	186.561 751	.005 360 1555	.435 131	81.178 788	.012 318 4889	14.79	.478 219	4.78	120
11	2.497 572	215.219 954	.004 646 4093	.400 389	86.171 665	.011 604 7426	13.93	.531 826	4.83	132
12	2.714 289	246.364 856	.004 059 0205	.368 421	90.765 897	.011 017 3538	13.23	.586 499	4.89	144
13	2.949 810	280.212 229	.003 568 7236	.339 005	94.993 311	.010 527 0570	12.64	.642 221	4.94	156
14	3.205 768	316.996 569	.003 154 6083	.311 938	98.883 197	.010 112 9416	12.14	.698 974	4.99	168
15	3.483 935	356.972 720	.002 801 3345	.287 032	102.462 503	.009 759 6678	11.72	.756 740	5.04	180
16	3.786 239	400.417 638	.002 497 3925	.264 114	105.756 028	.009 455 7258	11.35	.815 499	5.10	192
17	4.114 775	447.632 311	.002 233 9764	.243 027	108.786 587	.009 192 3097	11.04	.875 231	5.15	204
18	4.471 818	498.943 844	.002 004 2336	.223 623	111.575 178	.008 962 5669	10.76	.935 914	5.20	216
19	4.859 841	554.707 726	.001 802 7512	.205 768	114.141 120	.008 761 0845	10.52	.997 527	5.25	228
20	5.281 534	615.310 290	.001 625 1963	.189 339	116.502 190	.008 583 5296	10.31	1.060 047	5.30	240
21	5.739 818	681.171 393	.001 468 0593	.174 222	118.674 745	.008 426 3926	10.12	1.123 451	5.35	252
22	6.237 867	752.747 325	.001 328 4670	.160 311	120.673 838	.008 286 8004	9.95	1.187 715	5.40	264
23	6.779 132	830.533 965	.001 204 0447	.147 512	122.513 316	.008 162 3780	9.80	1.252 816	5.45	276
24	7.367 364	915.070 222	.001 092 8123	.135 734	124.205 926	.008 051 1456	9.67	1.318 730	5.49	288
25	8.006 636	1006.941 767	.000 993 1061	.124 896	125.763 393	.007 951 4394	9.55	1.385 432	5.54	300
26	8.701 380	1106.785 090	.000 903 5178	.114 924	127.196 507	.007 861 8511	9.44	1.452 898	5.59	312
27	9.456 406	1215.291 909	.000 822 8476	.105 748	128.515 197	.007 781 1809	9.34	1.521 103	5.63	324
28	10.276 947	1333.213 962	.000 750 0672	.097 305	129.728 600	.007 708 4005	9.26	1.590 023	5.68	336
29	11.168 687	1461.368 220	.000 684 2902	.089 536	130.845 120	.007 642 6236	9.18	1.659 633	5.72	348
30	12.137 804	1600.642 539	.000 624 7491	.082 387	131.872 495	.007 583 0824	9.10	1.729 910	5.77	360
31	13.191 013	1752.001 817	.000 570 7757	.075 809	132.817 841	.007 529 1090	9.04	1.800 829	5.81	372
32	14.335 609	1916.494 677	.000 521 7860	.069 756	133.687 708	.007 480 1193	8.98	1.872 366	5.85	384
33	15.579 523	2095.260 732	.000 477 2676	.064 187	134.488 122	.007 435 6009	8.93	1.944 498	5.89	396
34	16.931 372	2289.538 480	.000 436 7692	.059 062	135.224 629	.007 395 1026	8.88	2.017 202	5.93	408
35	18.400 522	2500.673 885	.000 399 8922	.054 346	135.902 331	.007 358 2255	8.83	2.090 455	5.97	420
36	19.997 153	2730.129 701	.000 366 2830	.050 007	136.525 923	.007 324 6163	8.79	2.164 234	6.01	432
37	21.732 324	2979.495 606	.000 335 6273	.046 014	137.099 726	.007 293 9606	8.76	2.238 519	6.05	444
38	23.618 057	3250.499 217	.000 307 6451	.042 340	137.627 715	.007 265 9784	8.72	2.313 286	6.09	456
39	25.667 417	3545.018 059	.000 282 0860	.038 960	138.113 547	.007 240 4193	8.69	2.388 516	6.12	468
40	27.894 602	3865.092 567	.000 258 7260	.035 849	138.560 590	.007 217 0593	8.67	2.464 188	6.16	480
41	30.315 042	4212.940 231	.000 237 3639	.032 987	138.971 939	.007 195 6973	8.64	2.540 283	6.20	492
42	32.945 506	4590.970 954	.000 217 8188	.030 353	139.350 445	.007 176 1522	8.62	2.616 781	6.23	504
43	35.804 218	5001.803 745	.000 199 9279	.027 930	139.698 730	.007 158 2612	8.59	2.693 663	6.26	516
44	38.910 982	5448.284 871	.000 183 5440	.025 700	140.019 207	.007 141 8773	8.58	2.770 911	6.30	528
45	42.287 324	5933.507 571	.000 168 5344	.023 648	140.314 096	.007 126 8677	8.56	2.848 509	6.33	540
46	45.956 633	6460.833 484	.000 154 7788	.021 760	140.585 440	.007 113 1121	8.54	2.926 438	6.36	552
47	49.944 332	7033.915 946	.000 142 1683	.020 022	140.835 120	.007 100 5017	8.53	3.004 683	6.39	564
48	54.278 047	7656.725 294	.000 130 6041	.018 424	141.064 864	.007 088 9375	8.51	3.083 228	6.42	576
49	58.987 802	8333.576 375	.000 119 9965	.016 953	141.276 265	.007 078 3298	8.50	3.162 058	6.45	588
50	64.106 227	9069.158 440	.000 110 2638	.015 599	141.470 787	.007 068 5971	8.49	3.241 158	6.48	600

MONTHLY COMPOUND INTEREST AND ANNUITY

8.375% M

	Amount Of 1	Amount Of 1 Per Period	Sinking Fund Payment	Present Worth Of 1	Present Worth of 1 Per Period	Periodic Payment To Amortize 1	Constant Annual Percent	Total Interest	Annual Add On Rate	
	What a single $ 1 deposit grows to in the future. The deposit is made at the beginning of the first period.	What a series of $ 1 deposits grow to in the future. A deposit is made at the end of each period.	The amount to be deposited at the end of each period that grows to $ 1 in the future.	What $ 1 to be paid in the future is worth today. Value today of a single $ 1 payment tomorrow.	What $ 1 to be paid at the end of each period is worth today. Value today of a series of $ 1 payments tomorrow.	The mortgage payment to amortize a loan of $ 1. An annuity certain, payable at the end of each period, worth $ 1 today.	The annual payment, including interest and principal, to amortize completely a loan of $ 100.	The total interest paid over the term on a loan of $1. The loan is amortized by regular periodic payments.	The average annual interest rate on a loan that is completely amortized by regular periodic payments.	

$$S = (1+i)^n \qquad S\overline{n}| = \frac{(1+i)^n - 1}{i} \qquad \frac{1}{S\overline{n}|} = \frac{i}{(1+i)^n - 1} \qquad V^n = \frac{1}{(1+i)^n} \qquad A\overline{n}| = \frac{1 - V^n}{i} \qquad \frac{1}{A\overline{n}|} = \frac{i}{1 - V^n}$$

YEAR										PERIODS
	1.006 979	1.000 000	1.000 000 0000	.993 069	.993 069	1.006 979 1667	1208.38	.006 979	8.37	1
	1.014 007	2.006 979	.498 261 2758	.986 186	1.979 256	.505 240 4424	606.29	.010 481	6.29	2
	1.021 084	3.020 986	.331 017 7309	.979 351	2.958 607	.337 996 8976	405.60	.013 991	5.60	3
	1.028 210	4.042 070	.247 397 9809	.972 564	3.931 171	.254 377 1476	305.26	.017 509	5.25	4
	1.035 386	5.070 280	.197 227 7488	.965 823	4.896 994	.204 206 9154	245.05	.021 035	5.05	5
	1.042 612	6.105 667	.163 782 2755	.959 129	5.856 123	.170 761 4421	204.92	.024 569	4.91	6
	1.049 889	7.148 279	.139 893 8072	.952 482	6.808 605	.146 872 9739	176.25	.028 111	4.82	7
	1.057 216	8.198 168	.121 978 4670	.945 880	7.754 485	.128 957 6337	154.75	.031 661	4.75	8
	1.064 595	9.255 385	.108 045 2121	.939 324	8.693 809	.115 024 3788	138.03	.035 219	4.70	9
	1.072 025	10.319 980	.096 899 4169	.932 814	9.626 623	.103 878 5836	124.66	.038 786	4.65	10
	1.079 507	11.392 004	.087 780 8650	.926 349	10.552 972	.094 760 0316	113.72	.042 360	4.62	11
	1.087 041	12.471 511	.080 182 7455	.919 929	11.472 901	.087 161 9121	104.60	.045 943	4.59	12
1	1.087 041	12.471 511	.080 182 7455	.919 929	11.472 901	.087 161 9121	104.60	.045 943	4.59	12
2	1.181 658	26.028 552	.038 419 3482	.846 269	22.027 152	.045 398 5149	54.48	.089 564	4.48	24
3	1.284 510	40.765 608	.024 530 4818	.778 507	31.736 311	.031 509 6484	37.82	.134 347	4.48	36
4	1.396 315	56.785 388	.017 610 1640	.716 171	40.668 045	.024 589 3307	29.51	.180 288	4.51	48
5	1.517 851	74.199 542	.013 477 1721	.658 826	48.884 603	.020 456 3387	24.55	.227 380	4.55	60
6	1.649 966	93.129 438	.010 737 7434	.606 073	56.443 251	.017 716 9100	21.27	.275 618	4.59	72
7	1.793 580	113.707 005	.008 794 5329	.557 544	63.396 668	.015 773 6996	18.93	.324 991	4.64	84
8	1.949 695	136.075 660	.007 348 8528	.512 901	69.793 316	.014 328 0195	17.20	.375 490	4.69	96
9	2.119 398	160.391 299	.006 234 7522	.471 832	75.677 777	.013 213 9188	15.86	.427 103	4.75	108
10	2.303 872	186.823 390	.005 352 6488	.434 052	81.091 061	.012 331 8155	14.80	.479 818	4.80	120
11	2.504 402	215.556 150	.004 639 1625	.399 297	86.070 896	.011 618 3291	13.95	.533 619	4.85	132
12	2.722 387	246.789 831	.004 052 0308	.367 325	90.651 990	.011 031 1975	13.24	.588 492	4.90	144
13	2.959 346	280.742 115	.003 561 9878	.337 912	94.866 269	.010 541 1545	12.65	.644 420	4.96	156
14	3.216 930	317.649 631	.003 148 1227	.310 855	98.743 106	.010 127 2893	12.16	.701 385	5.01	168
15	3.496 934	357.769 606	.002 795 0949	.285 965	102.309 519	.009 774 2616	11.73	.759 967	5.06	180
16	3.801 309	401.381 654	.002 491 3944	.263 067	105.590 365	.009 470 5611	11.37	.818 348	5.11	192
17	4.132 178	448.789 727	.002 228 2150	.242 003	108.608 510	.009 207 3817	11.05	.878 306	5.17	204
18	4.491 846	500.324 234	.001 998 7039	.222 626	111.384 987	.008 977 8706	10.78	.939 220	5.22	216
19	4.882 820	556.344 344	.001 797 4479	.204 800	113.939 149	.008 776 6146	10.54	1.001 068	5.27	228
20	5.307 824	617.240 487	.001 620 1141	.188 401	116.288 796	.008 599 2807	10.32	1.063 827	5.32	240
21	5.769 821	683.437 076	.001 463 1925	.173 316	118.450 303	.008 442 3592	10.14	1.127 475	5.37	252
22	6.272 031	755.395 466	.001 323 8099	.159 438	120.438 736	.008 302 9766	9.97	1.191 986	5.42	264
23	6.817 953	833.617 168	.001 199 5914	.146 672	122.267 952	.008 178 7581	9.82	1.257 337	5.47	276
24	7.411 393	918.647 346	.001 088 5570	.134 927	123.950 700	.008 067 7237	9.69	1.323 504	5.51	288
25	8.056 486	1011.078 616	.000 989 0428	.124 124	125.498 709	.007 968 2094	9.57	1.390 463	5.56	300
26	8.757 729	1111.555 172	.000 899 6405	.114 185	126.922 767	.007 878 8071	9.46	1.458 188	5.61	312
27	9.520 008	1220.777 284	.000 819 1502	.105 042	128.232 799	.007 798 3169	9.36	1.526 655	5.65	324
28	10.348 637	1339.506 171	.000 746 5438	.096 631	129.437 934	.007 725 7104	9.28	1.595 839	5.70	336
29	11.249 390	1468.569 310	.000 680 9348	.088 894	130.546 573	.007 660 1015	9.20	1.665 715	5.74	348
30	12.228 545	1608.866 202	.000 621 5557	.081 776	131.566 442	.007 600 7224	9.13	1.736 260	5.79	360
31	13.292 927	1761.374 642	.000 567 7384	.075 228	132.504 648	.007 546 9051	9.06	1.807 449	5.83	372
32	14.449 954	1927.157 530	.000 518 8498	.069 204	133.367 731	.007 498 0656	9.00	1.879 257	5.87	384
33	15.707 688	2107.370 287	.000 474 5251	.063 663	134.161 706	.007 453 6917	8.95	1.951 662	5.91	396
34	17.074 898	2303.268 898	.000 434 1655	.058 566	134.892 107	.007 413 3322	8.90	2.024 640	5.95	408
35	18.561 109	2516.218 672	.000 397 4217	.053 876	135.564 023	.007 376 5884	8.86	2.098 167	5.99	420
36	20.176 682	2747.703 755	.000 363 9403	.049 562	136.182 138	.007 343 1069	8.82	2.172 222	6.03	432
37	21.932 876	2999.337 474	.000 333 4070	.045 594	136.750 760	.007 312 5736	8.78	2.246 783	6.07	444
38	23.841 930	3272.873 582	.000 305 5419	.041 943	137.273 851	.007 284 7086	8.75	2.321 827	6.11	456
39	25.917 150	3570.218 479	.000 280 0949	.038 584	137.755 058	.007 259 2616	8.72	2.397 334	6.15	468
40	28.172 998	3893.444 500	.000 256 8420	.035 495	138.197 734	.007 236 0086	8.69	2.473 284	6.18	480
41	30.625 197	4244.804 358	.000 235 5821	.032 653	138.604 965	.007 214 7488	8.66	2.549 656	6.22	492
42	33.290 837	4626.746 844	.000 216 1346	.030 038	138.979 588	.007 195 3012	8.64	2.626 432	6.25	504
43	36.188 497	5041.933 891	.000 198 3366	.027 633	139.324 214	.007 177 5033	8.62	2.703 592	6.29	516
44	39.338 371	5493.259 132	.000 182 0413	.025 420	139.641 246	.007 161 2080	8.60	2.781 118	6.32	528
45	42.762 413	5983.868 063	.000 167 1160	.023 385	139.932 892	.007 146 2827	8.58	2.858 993	6.35	540
46	46.484 485	6517.179 966	.000 153 4406	.021 513	140.201 186	.007 132 6073	8.56	2.937 199	6.39	552
47	50.530 530	7096.911 738	.000 140 9064	.019 790	140.447 998	.007 120 0730	8.55	3.015 721	6.42	564
48	54.928 745	7727.103 802	.000 129 4146	.018 205	140.675 047	.007 108 5813	8.54	3.094 543	6.45	576
49	59.709 785	8412.148 258	.000 118 8757	.016 748	140.883 915	.007 098 0424	8.52	3.173 649	6.48	588
50	64.906 969	9156.819 501	.000 109 2082	.015 407	141.076 060	.007 088 3749	8.51	3.253 025	6.51	600

MONTHLY COMPOUND INTEREST AND ANNUITY

8.40 % M

	Amount Of 1	Amount Of 1 Per Period	Sinking Fund Payment	Present Worth Of 1	Present Worth of 1 Per Period	Periodic Payment To Amortize 1	Constant Annual Percent	Total Interest	Annual Add On Rate	
	What a single $ 1 deposit grows to in the future. The deposit is made at the beginning of the first period.	What a series of $ 1 deposits grow to in the future. A deposit is made at the end of each period.	The amount to be deposited at the end of each period that grows to $ 1 in the future.	What $ 1 to be paid in the future is worth today. Value today of a single $ 1 payment tomorrow.	What $ 1 to be paid at the end of each period is worth today. Value today of a series of $ 1 payments tomorrow.	The mortgage payment to amortize a loan of $ 1. An annuity certain, payable at the end of each period, worth $ 1 today.	The annual payment, including interest and principal, to amortize completely a loan of $ 100.	The total interest paid over the term on a loan of $1. The loan is amortized by regular periodic payments.	The average annual interest rate on a loan that is completely amortized by regular periodic payments.	

$$S = (1+i)^n \qquad S\overline{n}| = \frac{(1+i)^n - 1}{i} \qquad \frac{1}{S\overline{n}|} = \frac{i}{(1+i)^n - 1} \qquad V^n = \frac{1}{(1+i)^n} \qquad A\overline{n}| = \frac{1 - V^n}{i} \qquad \frac{1}{A\overline{n}|} = \frac{i}{1 - V^n}$$

YEAR										PERIODS
	1.007 000	1.000 000	1.000 000 0000	.993 049	.993 049	1.007 000 0000	1208.40	.007 000	8.40	1
	1.014 049	2.007 000	.498 256 1036	.986 146	1.979 194	.505 256 1036	606.31	.010 512	6.31	2
	1.021 147	3.021 049	.331 010 8509	.979 291	2.958 485	.338 010 8509	405.62	.014 033	5.61	3
	1.028 295	4.042 196	.247 390 2589	.972 483	3.930 968	.254 390 2589	305.27	.017 561	5.27	4
	1.035 493	5.070 492	.197 219 5313	.965 723	4.896 691	.204 219 5313	245.07	.021 098	5.06	5
	1.042 742	6.105 985	.163 773 7358	.959 010	5.855 701	.170 773 7358	204.93	.024 642	4.93	6
	1.050 041	7.148 727	.139 885 0442	.952 344	6.808 045	.146 885 0442	176.27	.028 195	4.83	7
	1.057 391	8.198 768	.121 969 5425	.945 724	7.753 769	.128 969 5425	154.77	.031 756	4.76	8
	1.064 793	9.256 160	.108 036 1674	.939 150	8.692 918	.115 036 1674	138.05	.035 326	4.71	9
	1.072 247	10.320 953	.096 890 2809	.932 621	9.625 539	.103 890 2809	124.67	.038 903	4.67	10
	1.079 752	11.393 199	.087 771 6586	.926 138	10.551 678	.094 771 6586	113.73	.042 488	4.64	11
	1.087 311	12.472 952	.080 173 4845	.919 700	11.471 378	.087 173 4845	104.61	.046 082	4.61	12
1	1.087 311	12.472 952	.080 173 4845	.919 700	11.471 378	.087 173 4845	104.61	.046 082	4.61	12
2	1.182 244	26.034 925	.038 409 9435	.845 849	22.021 609	.045 409 9435	54.50	.089 839	4.49	24
3	1.285 467	40.781 003	.024 521 2211	.777 927	31.724 659	.031 521 2211	37.83	.134 764	4.49	36
4	1.397 702	56.814 571	.017 601 1184	.715 460	40.648 558	.024 601 1184	29.53	.180 854	4.52	48
5	1.519 736	74.248 041	.013 468 3688	.658 009	48.855 872	.020 468 3688	24.57	.228 102	4.56	60
6	1.652 425	93.203 638	.010 729 1949	.605 171	56.404 141	.017 729 1949	21.28	.276 502	4.61	72
7	1.796 700	113.814 261	.008 786 2451	.556 576	63.346 286	.015 786 2451	18.95	.326 045	4.66	84
8	1.953 571	136.224 411	.007 340 8282	.511 883	69.730 980	.014 340 8282	17.21	.376 720	4.71	96
9	2.124 138	160.591 207	.006 226 9910	.470 779	75.602 985	.013 226 9910	15.88	.428 515	4.76	108
10	2.309 598	187.085 483	.005 345 1502	.432 976	81.003 470	.012 345 1502	14.82	.481 418	4.81	120
11	2.511 251	215.892 992	.004 631 9243	.398 208	85.970 298	.011 631 9243	13.96	.535 414	4.87	132
12	2.730 510	247.215 704	.004 045 0505	.366 232	90.538 292	.011 045 0505	13.26	.590 487	4.92	144
13	2.968 913	281.273 222	.003 555 2620	.336 824	94.739 477	.010 555 2620	12.67	.646 621	4.97	156
14	3.228 130	318.304 325	.003 141 6475	.309 777	98.603 308	.010 141 6475	12.17	.703 797	5.03	168
15	3.509 980	358.568 638	.002 788 8663	.284 902	102.156 876	.009 788 8663	11.75	.761 996	5.08	180
16	3.816 439	402.348 455	.002 485 4078	.262 024	105.425 093	.009 485 4078	11.39	.821 198	5.13	192
17	4.149 655	449.950 717	.002 222 4656	.240 984	108.430 873	.009 222 4656	11.07	.881 383	5.18	204
18	4.511 964	501.709 163	.001 993 1866	.221 633	111.195 290	.008 993 1866	10.80	.942 528	5.24	216
19	4.905 907	557.986 674	.001 792 1575	.203 836	113.737 726	.008 792 1575	10.56	1.004 612	5.29	228
20	5.334 245	619.177 812	.001 615 0450	.187 468	116.076 005	.008 615 0450	10.34	1.067 611	5.34	240
21	5.799 981	685.711 588	.001 458 3391	.172 414	118.226 521	.008 458 3391	10.16	1.131 501	5.39	252
22	6.306 381	758.054 472	.001 319 1664	.158 570	120.204 351	.008 319 1664	9.99	1.196 260	5.44	264
23	6.856 996	836.713 662	.001 195 1520	.145 836	122.023 362	.008 195 1520	9.84	1.261 862	5.49	276
24	7.455 684	922.240 637	.001 084 3157	.134 126	123.696 307	.008 084 3157	9.71	1.328 283	5.53	288
25	8.106 645	1015.235 029	.000 984 9936	.123 356	125.234 916	.007 984 9936	9.59	1.395 498	5.58	300
26	8.814 442	1116.348 823	.000 895 7774	.113 450	126.649 974	.007 895 7774	9.48	1.463 483	5.63	312
27	9.584 037	1226.290 930	.000 815 4672	.104 340	127.951 404	.007 815 4672	9.38	1.532 211	5.67	324
28	10.420 825	1345.832 154	.000 743 0347	.095 962	129.148 330	.007 743 0347	9.30	1.601 660	5.72	336
29	11.330 674	1475.810 602	.000 677 5937	.088 256	130.249 143	.007 677 5937	9.22	1.671 803	5.76	348
30	12.319 963	1617.137 554	.000 618 3766	.081 169	131.261 561	.007 618 3766	9.15	1.742 616	5.81	360
31	13.395 627	1770.803 856	.000 564 7153	.074 651	132.192 682	.007 564 7153	9.08	1.814 074	5.85	372
32	14.565 208	1937.886 865	.000 516 0260	.068 657	133.049 034	.007 516 0260	9.02	1.886 154	5.89	384
33	15.836 906	2119.558 001	.000 471 7965	.063 144	133.836 622	.007 471 7965	8.97	1.958 831	5.94	396
34	17.219 637	2317.090 965	.000 431 5756	.058 073	134.560 967	.007 431 5756	8.92	2.032 083	5.98	408
35	18.723 095	2531.870 663	.000 394 9649	.053 410	135.227 147	.007 394 9649	8.88	2.105 885	6.02	420
36	20.357 820	2765.402 918	.000 361 6110	.049 121	135.839 833	.007 361 6110	8.84	2.180 216	6.06	432
37	22.135 275	3019.325 029	.000 331 1999	.045 177	136.403 320	.007 331 1999	8.80	2.255 053	6.09	444
38	24.067 921	3295.417 247	.000 303 4517	.041 549	136.921 560	.007 303 4517	8.77	2.330 374	6.13	456
39	26.169 307	3595.615 260	.000 278 1165	.038 213	137.398 185	.007 278 1165	8.74	2.406 159	6.17	468
40	28.454 166	3922.023 760	.000 254 9704	.035 144	137.836 537	.007 254 9704	8.71	2.482 386	6.21	480
41	30.938 518	4276.931 202	.000 233 8125	.032 322	138.239 690	.007 233 8125	8.69	2.559 036	6.24	492
42	33.639 781	4662.825 848	.000 214 4622	.029 727	138.610 470	.007 214 4622	8.66	2.636 089	6.28	504
43	36.576 892	5082.413 211	.000 196 7569	.027 340	138.951 476	.007 196 7569	8.64	2.713 527	6.31	516
44	39.770 445	5538.635 025	.000 180 5499	.025 144	139.265 100	.007 180 5499	8.62	2.791 330	6.34	528
45	43.242 829	6034.689 866	.000 165 7086	.023 125	139.553 540	.007 165 7086	8.60	2.869 483	6.38	540
46	47.018 389	6574.055 585	.000 152 1131	.021 268	139.818 818	.007 152 1131	8.59	2.947 966	6.41	552
47	51.123 596	7160.513 681	.000 139 6548	.019 560	140.062 794	.007 139 6548	8.57	3.026 765	6.44	564
48	55.587 231	7798.175 822	.000 128 2351	.017 990	140.287 180	.007 128 2351	8.56	3.105 863	6.47	576
49	60.440 589	8491.512 666	.000 117 7646	.016 545	140.493 547	.007 117 7646	8.55	3.185 246	6.50	588
50	65.717 696	9245.385 210	.000 108 1621	.015 217	140.683 343	.007 108 1621	8.53	3.264 897	6.53	600

MONTHLY COMPOUND INTEREST AND ANNUITY

8.45 % M

	Amount Of 1	Amount Of 1 Per Period	Sinking Fund Payment	Present Worth Of 1	Present Worth of 1 Per Period	Periodic Payment To Amortize 1	Constant Annual Percent	Total Interest	Annual Add On Rate	
	What a single $ 1 deposit grows to in the future. The deposit is made at the beginning of the first period.	What a series of $ 1 deposits grow to in the future. A deposit is made at the end of each period.	The amount to be deposited at the end of each period that grows to $ 1 in the future.	What $ 1 to be paid in the future is worth today. Value today of a single $ 1 payment tomorrow.	What $ 1 to be paid at the end of each period is worth today. Value today of a series of $ 1 payments tomorrow.	The mortgage payment to amortize a loan of $ 1. An annuity certain, payable at the end of each period, worth $ 1 today.	The annual payment, including interest and principal, to amortize completely a loan of $ 100.	The total interest paid over the term on a loan of $1. The loan is amortized by regular periodic payments.	The average annual interest rate on a loan that is completely amortized by regular periodic payments.	
	$S = (1+i)^n$	$S\overline{n} = \dfrac{(1+i)^n - 1}{i}$	$\dfrac{1}{S\overline{n}} = \dfrac{i}{(1+i)^n - 1}$	$V^n = \dfrac{1}{(1+i)^n}$	$A\overline{n} = \dfrac{1 - V^n}{i}$	$\dfrac{1}{A\overline{n}} = \dfrac{i}{1 - V^n}$				

YEAR										PERIODS
	1.007 042	1.000 000	1.000 000 0000	.993 008	.993 008	1.007 041 6667	1208.45	.007 042	8.45	1
	1.014 133	2.007 042	.498 245 7597	.986 064	1.979 072	.505 287 4264	606.35	.010 575	6.34	2
	1.021 274	3.021 175	.330 997 0913	.979 169	2.958 241	.338 038 7580	405.65	.014 116	5.65	3
	1.028 466	4.042 449	.247 374 8158	.972 322	3.930 563	.254 416 4825	305.30	.017 666	5.30	4
	1.035 708	5.070 914	.197 203 0974	.965 523	4.896 086	.204 244 7641	245.10	.021 224	5.09	5
	1.043 001	6.106 622	.163 756 6575	.958 772	5.854 858	.170 798 3242	204.96	.024 790	4.96	6
	1.050 345	7.149 623	.139 867 5196	.952 068	6.806 926	.146 909 1863	176.30	.028 364	4.86	7
	1.057 741	8.199 968	.121 951 6953	.945 411	7.752 337	.128 993 3619	154.80	.031 947	4.79	8
	1.065 190	9.257 709	.108 018 0800	.938 800	8.691 137	.115 059 7467	138.08	.035 538	4.74	9
	1.072 690	10.322 899	.096 872 0109	.932 235	9.623 372	.103 913 6776	124.70	.039 137	4.70	10
	1.080 244	11.395 590	.087 753 2482	.925 717	10.549 089	.094 794 9149	113.76	.042 744	4.66	11
	1.087 851	12.475 834	.080 154 9651	.919 244	11.468 333	.087 196 6318	104.64	.046 360	4.64	12
1	1.087 851	12.475 834	.080 154 9651	.919 244	11.468 333	.087 196 6318	104.64	.046 360	4.64	12
2	1.183 419	26.047 677	.038 391 1391	.845 009	22.010 527	.045 432 8057	54.52	.090 387	4.52	24
3	1.287 383	40.811 816	.024 502 7075	.776 769	31.701 374	.031 544 3742	37.86	.135 597	4.52	36
4	1.400 481	56.872 995	.017 583 0374	.714 041	40.609 625	.024 624 7041	29.55	.181 986	4.55	48
5	1.523 514	74.345 159	.013 450 7750	.656 377	48.798 480	.020 492 4416	24.60	.229 546	4.59	60
6	1.657 356	93.352 264	.010 712 1130	.603 371	56.326 034	.017 753 7797	21.31	.278 272	4.64	72
7	1.802 955	114.029 155	.008 769 6870	.554 645	63.245 692	.015 811 3537	18.98	.328 154	4.69	84
8	1.961 346	136.522 525	.007 324 7986	.509 854	69.606 544	.014 366 4653	17.24	.379 181	4.74	96
9	2.133 652	160.991 953	.006 211 4906	.468 680	75.453 719	.013 253 1573	15.91	.431 341	4.79	108
10	2.321 094	187.611 036	.005 330 1768	.430 831	80.828 698	.012 371 8435	14.85	.484 621	4.85	120
11	2.525 004	216.568 623	.004 617 4741	.396 039	85.769 614	.011 659 1407	14.00	.539 007	4.90	132
12	2.746 827	248.070 153	.004 031 1178	.364 056	90.311 521	.011 072 7844	13.29	.594 481	4.95	144
13	2.988 138	282.339 114	.003 541 8401	.334 657	94.486 640	.010 583 5068	12.71	.651 027	5.01	156
14	3.250 648	319.618 625	.003 128 7288	.307 631	98.324 593	.010 170 3955	12.21	.708 626	5.06	168
15	3.536 219	360.173 166	.002 776 4423	.282 788	101.852 608	.009 818 1089	11.79	.767 260	5.12	180
16	3.846 879	404.290 450	.002 473 4693	.259 951	105.095 714	.009 515 1359	11.42	.826 906	5.17	192
17	4.184 829	452.283 467	.002 211 0028	.238 958	108.076 918	.009 252 6694	11.11	.887 545	5.22	204
18	4.552 469	504.492 702	.001 982 1892	.219 661	110.817 372	.009 023 8559	10.83	.949 153	5.27	216
19	4.952 407	561.288 553	.001 781 6148	.201 922	113.336 518	.008 823 2815	10.59	1.011 708	5.32	228
20	5.387 479	623.073 956	.001 604 9459	.185 616	115.652 227	.008 646 6126	10.38	1.075 187	5.38	240
21	5.860 773	690.287 249	.001 448 6723	.170 626	117.780 928	.008 490 3389	10.19	1.139 565	5.43	252
22	6.375 645	763.405 273	.001 309 9202	.156 847	119.737 723	.008 351 5869	10.03	1.204 819	5.48	264
23	6.935 750	842.946 765	.001 186 3145	.144 181	121.536 495	.008 227 9812	9.88	1.270 923	5.53	276
24	7.545 060	929.476 029	.001 075 8750	.132 537	123.190 006	.008 117 5416	9.75	1.337 852	5.57	288
25	8.207 899	1023.606 946	.000 976 9375	.121 834	124.709 984	.008 018 6042	9.63	1.405 581	5.62	300
26	8.928 968	1126.007 326	.000 888 0937	.111 995	126.107 216	.007 929 7604	9.52	1.474 085	5.67	312
27	9.713 384	1237.403 648	.000 808 1437	.102 951	127.391 612	.007 849 8104	9.42	1.543 339	5.72	324
28	10.566 711	1358.586 209	.000 736 0593	.094 637	128.572 285	.007 777 7260	9.34	1.613 316	5.76	336
29	11.495 004	1490.414 739	.000 670 9542	.086 994	129.657 612	.007 712 6208	9.26	1.683 992	5.81	348
30	12.504 847	1633.828 493	.000 612 0608	.079 969	130.655 292	.007 653 7275	9.19	1.755 342	5.85	360
31	13.603 407	1789.832 888	.000 558 7114	.073 511	131.572 403	.007 600 3780	9.13	1.827 341	5.89	372
32	14.798 475	1959.546 724	.000 510 3221	.067 575	132.415 451	.007 551 9888	9.07	1.899 964	5.94	384
33	16.098 531	2144.170 032	.000 466 3809	.062 117	133.190 418	.007 508 0476	9.01	1.973 187	5.98	396
34	17.512 797	2345.012 621	.000 426 4369	.057 101	133.902 802	.007 468 1036	8.97	2.046 986	6.02	408
35	19.051 308	2563.499 363	.000 390 0918	.052 490	134.557 657	.007 431 7584	8.92	2.121 339	6.06	420
36	20.724 978	2801.180 310	.000 356 9924	.048 251	135.159 628	.007 398 6590	8.88	2.196 221	6.10	432
37	22.545 681	3059.741 685	.000 326 8250	.044 354	135.712 986	.007 368 4916	8.85	2.271 610	6.14	444
38	24.526 334	3341.017 848	.000 299 3100	.040 773	136.221 657	.007 340 9767	8.81	2.347 485	6.18	456
39	26.680 989	3647.004 308	.000 274 1976	.037 480	136.689 249	.007 315 8643	8.78	2.423 824	6.21	468
40	29.024 931	3979.871 881	.000 251 2644	.034 453	137.119 081	.007 292 9310	8.76	2.500 607	6.25	480
41	31.574 791	4341.982 089	.000 230 3096	.031 671	137.514 201	.007 271 9762	8.73	2.577 812	6.29	492
42	34.348 657	4735.903 919	.000 211 1529	.029 113	137.877 413	.007 252 8196	8.71	2.655 421	6.32	504
43	37.366 209	5164.432 043	.000 193 6321	.026 762	138.211 293	.007 235 2988	8.69	2.733 414	6.36	516
44	40.648 855	5630.606 645	.000 177 6008	.024 601	138.518 210	.007 219 2674	8.67	2.811 773	6.39	528
45	44.219 884	6137.734 994	.000 162 9266	.022 614	138.800 342	.007 204 5932	8.65	2.890 480	6.42	540
46	48.104 630	6689.414 904	.000 149 4899	.020 788	139.059 689	.007 191 1566	8.63	2.969 518	6.46	552
47	52.330 653	7289.560 258	.000 137 1825	.019 109	139.298 093	.007 178 8492	8.62	3.048 871	6.49	564
48	56.927 936	7942.428 779	.000 125 9061	.017 566	139.517 245	.007 167 5727	8.61	3.128 522	6.52	576
49	61.929 093	8652.652 230	.000 115 5715	.016 147	139.718 698	.007 157 2382	8.59	3.208 456	6.55	588
50	67.369 605	9425.269 281	.000 106 0978	.014 843	139.903 883	.007 147 7644	8.58	3.288 659	6.58	600

Effective Rate is 8.79 %

Annual Percentage Rate is 8.45 %

	Amount Of 1	Amount Of 1 Per Period	Sinking Fund Payment	Present Worth Of 1	Present Worth of 1 Per Period	Periodic Payment To Amortize 1	Constant Annual Percent	Total Interest	Annual Add On Rate	
	What a single $ 1 deposit grows to in the future. The deposit is made at the beginning of the first period.	What a series of $ 1 deposits grow to in the future. A deposit is made at the end of each period.	The amount to be deposited at the end of each period that grows to $ 1 in the future.	What $ 1 to be paid in the future is worth today. Value today of a single $ 1 payment tomorrow.	What $ 1 to be paid at the end of each period is worth today. Value today of a series of $ 1 payments tomorrow.	The mortgage payment to amortize a loan of $ 1. An annuity certain, payable at the end of each period, worth $ 1 today.	The annual payment, including interest and principal, to amortize completely a loan of $ 100.	The total interest paid over the term on a loan of $ 1. The loan is amortized by regular periodic payments.	The average annual interest rate on a loan that is completely amortized by regular periodic payments.	
	$S = (1+i)^n$	$S\overline{n} = \dfrac{(1+i)^n - 1}{i}$	$\dfrac{1}{S\overline{n}} = \dfrac{i}{(1+i)^n - 1}$	$V^n = \dfrac{1}{(1+i)^n}$	$A\overline{n} = \dfrac{1-V^n}{i}$	$\dfrac{1}{A\overline{n}} = \dfrac{i}{1-V^n}$				

YEAR										PERIODS
	1.007 083	1.000 000	1.000 000 0000	.992 966	.992 966	1.007 083 3333	1208.50	.007 083	8.50	1
	1.014 217	2.007 083	.498 235 4162	.985 982	1.978 949	.505 318 7496	606.39	.010 637	6.38	2
	1.021 401	3.021 300	.330 983 3325	.979 048	2.957 996	.338 066 6659	405.68	.014 200	5.68	3
	1.028 636	4.042 701	.247 359 3738	.972 161	3.930 158	.254 442 7071	305.34	.017 771	5.33	4
	1.035 922	5.071 337	.197 186 6649	.965 324	4.895 482	.204 269 9983	245.13	.021 350	5.12	5
	1.043 260	6.107 259	.163 739 5810	.958 534	5.854 016	.170 822 9143	204.99	.024 937	4.99	6
	1.050 650	7.150 519	.139 849 9970	.951 792	6.805 808	.146 933 3303	176.32	.028 533	4.89	7
	1.058 092	8.201 168	.121 933 8503	.945 098	7.750 906	.129 017 1836	154.83	.032 137	4.82	8
	1.065 586	9.259 260	.107 999 9951	.938 450	8.689 356	.115 083 3284	138.10	.035 750	4.77	9
	1.073 134	10.324 846	.096 853 7439	.931 850	9.621 206	.103 937 0772	124.73	.039 371	4.72	10
	1.080 736	11.397 980	.087 734 8409	.925 296	10.546 501	.094 818 1743	113.79	.043 000	4.69	11
	1.088 391	12.478 716	.080 136 4491	.918 788	11.465 289	.087 219 7825	104.67	.046 637	4.66	12
1	1.088 391	12.478 716	.080 136 4491	.918 788	11.465 289	.087 219 7825	104.67	.046 637	4.66	12
2	1.184 595	26.060 437	.038 372 3415	.844 171	21.999 453	.045 455 6749	54.55	.090 936	4.55	24
3	1.289 302	40.842 659	.024 484 2041	.775 613	31.678 112	.031 567 5374	37.89	.136 431	4.55	36
4	1.403 265	56.931 495	.017 564 9700	.712 624	40.570 744	.024 648 3034	29.58	.183 119	4.58	48
5	1.527 301	74.442 437	.013 433 1980	.654 750	48.741 183	.020 516 5313	24.62	.230 992	4.62	60
6	1.662 300	93.501 188	.010 695 0513	.601 576	56.248 080	.017 778 3846	21.34	.280 044	4.67	72
7	1.809 232	114.244 559	.008 753 1521	.552 721	63.145 324	.015 836 4854	19.01	.330 265	4.72	84
8	1.969 152	136.821 455	.007 308 7952	.507 833	69.482 425	.014 392 1286	17.28	.381 644	4.77	96
9	2.143 207	161.393 943	.006 196 0194	.466 590	75.304 875	.013 279 3527	15.94	.434 170	4.82	108
10	2.332 647	188.138 416	.005 315 2356	.428 698	80.654 470	.012 398 5689	14.88	.487 828	4.88	120
11	2.538 832	217.246 858	.004 603 0585	.393 882	85.569 611	.011 686 3919	14.03	.542 604	4.93	132
12	2.763 242	248.928 220	.004 017 2223	.361 894	90.085 581	.011 100 5556	13.33	.598 480	4.99	144
13	3.007 487	283.409 927	.003 528 4579	.332 504	94.234 798	.010 611 7912	12.74	.655 439	5.04	156
14	3.273 321	320.939 504	.003 115 8520	.305 500	98.047 046	.010 199 1854	12.24	.713 463	5.10	168
15	3.562 653	361.786 353	.002 764 0622	.280 690	101.549 693	.009 847 3956	11.82	.772 531	5.15	180
16	3.877 559	406.243 693	.002 461 5767	.257 894	104.767 881	.009 544 9100	11.46	.832 623	5.20	192
17	4.220 300	454.630 657	.002 199 5877	.236 950	107.724 713	.009 282 9210	11.14	.893 716	5.26	204
18	4.593 337	507.294 589	.001 971 2412	.217 707	110.441 412	.009 054 5745	10.87	.955 788	5.31	216
19	4.999 346	564.613 533	.001 771 1230	.200 026	112.937 482	.008 854 4563	10.63	1.018 816	5.36	228
20	5.441 243	626.998 951	.001 594 8990	.183 782	115.230 840	.008 678 2323	10.42	1.082 776	5.41	240
21	5.922 199	694.898 672	.001 439 0587	.168 856	117.337 948	.008 522 3921	10.23	1.147 643	5.46	252
22	6.445 667	768.800 112	.001 300 7282	.155 143	119.273 933	.008 384 0616	10.07	1.213 392	5.52	264
23	7.015 406	849.233 766	.001 177 5321	.142 543	121.052 692	.008 260 8654	9.92	1.279 999	5.57	276
24	7.635 504	936.777 024	.001 067 4899	.130 967	122.686 994	.008 150 8232	9.79	1.347 437	5.61	288
25	8.310 413	1032.058 310	.000 968 9375	.120 331	124.188 570	.008 052 2708	9.67	1.415 681	5.66	300
26	9.044 978	1135.761 595	.000 880 4665	.110 559	125.568 199	.007 963 7998	9.56	1.484 706	5.71	312
27	9.844 472	1248.631 307	.000 800 8769	.101 580	126.835 785	.007 884 2103	9.47	1.554 484	5.76	324
28	10.714 634	1371.477 676	.000 729 1406	.093 330	128.000 428	.007 812 4739	9.38	1.624 991	5.80	336
29	11.661 710	1505.182 546	.000 664 3712	.085 751	129.070 487	.007 747 7046	9.30	1.696 201	5.85	348
30	12.692 499	1650.705 711	.000 605 8015	.078 787	130.053 643	.007 689 1348	9.23	1.768 089	5.89	360
31	13.814 400	1809.091 800	.000 552 7635	.072 388	130.956 956	.007 636 0969	9.17	1.840 628	5.94	372
32	15.035 468	1981.477 780	.000 504 6738	.066 509	131.786 908	.007 588 0072	9.11	1.913 795	5.98	384
33	16.364 466	2169.101 112	.000 461 0205	.061 108	132.549 457	.007 544 3538	9.06	1.987 564	6.02	396
34	17.810 936	2373.308 640	.000 421 3527	.056 145	133.250 078	.007 504 6860	9.01	2.061 912	6.06	408
35	19.385 261	2595.566 257	.000 385 2724	.051 586	133.893 800	.007 468 6057	8.97	2.136 814	6.11	420
36	21.098 742	2837.469 426	.000 352 4267	.047 396	134.485 244	.007 435 7600	8.93	2.212 248	6.15	432
37	22.963 679	3100.754 635	.000 322 5021	.043 547	135.028 655	.007 405 8355	8.89	2.288 191	6.18	444
38	24.993 459	3387.311 862	.000 295 2193	.040 010	135.527 934	.007 378 5527	8.86	2.364 620	6.22	456
39	27.202 654	3699.198 142	.000 270 3289	.036 761	135.986 665	.007 353 6622	8.83	2.441 514	6.26	468
40	29.607 121	4038.652 333	.000 247 6073	.033 776	136.408 142	.007 330 9407	8.80	2.518 852	6.30	480
41	32.224 121	4408.111 188	.000 226 8545	.031 033	136.795 390	.007 310 1879	8.78	2.596 612	6.33	492
42	35.072 440	4810.226 845	.000 207 8904	.028 512	137.151 188	.007 291 2237	8.75	2.674 777	6.37	504
43	38.172 525	5247.885 869	.000 190 5529	.026 197	137.478 091	.007 273 8863	8.73	2.753 325	6.40	516
44	41.546 629	5724.229 972	.000 174 6960	.024 069	137.778 446	.007 258 0293	8.71	2.832 239	6.44	528
45	45.218 973	6242.678 560	.000 160 1876	.022 115	138.054 408	.007 243 5210	8.70	2.911 501	6.47	540
46	49.215 919	6806.953 290	.000 146 9086	.020 319	138.307 958	.007 230 2419	8.68	2.991 094	6.50	552
47	53.566 159	7421.104 774	.000 134 7508	.018 669	138.540 917	.007 218 0842	8.67	3.070 999	6.53	564
48	58.300 920	8089.541 663	.000 123 6164	.017 152	138.754 957	.007 206 9497	8.65	3.151 203	6.57	576
49	63.454 191	8817.062 295	.000 113 4165	.015 759	138.951 614	.007 196 7498	8.64	3.231 689	6.60	588
50	69.062 965	9608.889 135	.000 104 0703	.014 480	139.132 300	.007 187 4036	8.63	3.312 442	6.62	600

Effective Rate is 8.84 %   Annual Percentage Rate is 8.50 %

	Amount Of 1	Amount Of 1 Per Period	Sinking Fund Payment	Present Worth Of 1	Present Worth of 1 Per Period	Periodic Payment To Amortize 1	Constant Annual Percent	Total Interest	Annual Add On Rate	
	What a single $ 1 deposit grows to in the future. The deposit is made at the beginning of the first period.	What a series of $ 1 deposits grow to in the future. A deposit is made at the end of each period.	The amount to be deposited at the end of each period that grows to $ 1 in the future.	What $ 1 to be paid in the future is worth today. Value today of a single $ 1 payment tomorrow.	What $ 1 to be paid at the end of each period is worth today. Value today of a series of $ 1 payments tomorrow.	The mortgage payment to amortize a loan of $ 1. An annuity certain, payable at the end of each period, worth $ 1 today.	The annual payment, including interest and principal, to amortize completely a loan of $ 100.	The total interest paid over the term on a loan of $1. The loan is amortized by regular periodic payments.	The average annual interest rate on a loan that is completely amortized by regular periodic payments.	
	$S = (1+i)^n$	$S\overline{n}| = \dfrac{(1+i)^n - 1}{i}$	$\dfrac{1}{S\overline{n}|} = \dfrac{i}{(1+i)^n - 1}$	$V^n = \dfrac{1}{(1+i)^n}$	$A\overline{n}| = \dfrac{1 - V^n}{i}$	$\dfrac{1}{A\overline{n}|} = \dfrac{i}{1 - V^n}$				

YEAR										PERIODS
	1.007 125	1.000 000	1.000 000 0000	.992 925	.992 925	1.007 125 0000	1208.55	.007 125	8.55	1
	1.014 301	2.007 125	.498 225 0732	.985 901	1.978 826	.505 350 0732	606.43	.010 700	6.42	2
	1.021 528	3.021 426	.330 969 5745	.978 926	2.957 752	.338 094 5745	405.72	.014 284	5.71	3
	1.028 806	4.042 953	.247 343 9328	.972 001	3.929 753	.254 468 9328	305.37	.017 876	5.36	4
	1.036 136	5.071 759	.197 170 2338	.965 124	4.894 877	.204 295 2338	245.16	.021 476	5.15	5
	1.043 519	6.107 896	.163 722 5061	.958 296	5.853 173	.170 847 5061	205.02	.025 085	5.02	6
	1.050 954	7.151 415	.139 832 4763	.951 517	6.804 690	.146 957 4763	176.35	.028 702	4.92	7
	1.058 442	8.202 368	.121 916 0075	.944 785	7.749 475	.129 041 0075	154.85	.032 328	4.85	8
	1.065 983	9.260 810	.107 981 9127	.938 101	8.687 576	.115 106 9127	138.13	.035 962	4.79	9
	1.073 578	10.326 793	.096 835 4796	.931 464	9.619 040	.103 960 4796	124.76	.039 605	4.75	10
	1.081 228	11.400 372	.087 716 4368	.924 875	10.543 914	.094 841 4368	113.81	.043 256	4.72	11
	1.088 931	12.481 600	.080 117 9366	.918 331	11.462 246	.087 242 9366	104.70	.046 915	4.69	12
1	1.088 931	12.481 600	.080 117 9366	.918 331	11.462 246	.087 242 9366	104.70	.046 915	4.69	12
2	1.185 772	26.073 205	.038 353 5509	.843 333	21.988 388	.045 478 5509	54.58	.091 485	4.57	24
3	1.291 224	40.873 531	.024 465 7109	.774 459	31.654 875	.031 590 7109	37.91	.137 266	4.58	36
4	1.406 054	56.990 071	.017 546 9162	.711 210	40.531 915	.024 671 9162	29.61	.184 252	4.61	48
5	1.531 097	74.539 877	.013 415 6379	.653 127	48.683 980	.020 540 6379	24.65	.232 438	4.65	60
6	1.667 259	93.650 412	.010 678 0096	.599 787	56.170 278	.017 803 0096	21.37	.281 817	4.70	72
7	1.815 531	114.460 474	.008 736 6404	.550 803	63.045 182	.015 861 6404	19.04	.332 378	4.75	84
8	1.976 989	137.121 203	.007 292 8182	.505 820	69.358 622	.014 417 8182	17.31	.384 111	4.80	96
9	2.152 805	161.797 183	.006 180 5773	.464 510	75.156 453	.013 305 5773	15.97	.437 002	4.86	108
10	2.344 257	188.667 632	.005 300 3263	.426 574	80.480 784	.012 425 3263	14.92	.491 039	4.91	120
11	2.552 735	217.927 707	.004 588 6777	.391 737	85.370 285	.011 713 6777	14.06	.546 205	4.97	132
12	2.779 753	249.789 922	.004 003 3641	.359 744	89.860 468	.011 128 3641	13.36	.602 484	5.02	144
13	3.026 961	284.485 688	.003 515 1153	.330 364	93.983 944	.010 640 1153	12.77	.659 858	5.08	156
14	3.296 152	322.266 997	.003 103 0171	.303 384	97.770 662	.010 228 0171	12.28	.718 307	5.13	168
15	3.589 284	363.408 251	.002 751 7262	.278 607	101.248 124	.009 876 7262	11.86	.777 811	5.19	180
16	3.908 484	408.208 254	.002 449 7300	.255 854	104.441 588	.009 574 7300	11.49	.838 348	5.24	192
17	4.256 071	456.992 384	.002 188 2203	.234 959	107.374 245	.009 313 2203	11.18	.899 897	5.29	204
18	4.634 569	510.114 954	.001 960 3425	.215 770	110.067 398	.009 085 3425	10.91	.962 434	5.35	216
19	5.046 728	567.961 789	.001 760 6818	.198 148	112.540 604	.008 885 6818	10.67	1.025 935	5.40	228
20	5.495 540	630.953 024	.001 584 9040	.181 966	114.811 827	.008 709 9040	10.46	1.090 377	5.45	240
21	5.984 266	699.546 157	.001 429 4982	.167 105	116.897 563	.008 554 4982	10.27	1.155 734	5.50	252
22	6.516 456	774.239 373	.001 291 5902	.153 458	118.812 960	.008 416 5902	10.10	1.221 980	5.55	264
23	7.095 973	855.575 162	.001 168 8044	.140 925	120.571 930	.008 293 8044	9.96	1.289 090	5.60	276
24	7.727 028	944.144 255	.001 059 1602	.129 416	122.187 247	.008 184 1602	9.83	1.357 038	5.65	288
25	8.414 203	1040.589 922	.000 960 9934	.118 847	123.670 643	.008 085 9934	9.71	1.425 798	5.70	300
26	9.162 490	1145.612 637	.000 872 8954	.109 141	125.032 893	.007 997 8954	9.60	1.495 343	5.75	312
27	9.977 323	1259.975 168	.000 793 6664	.100 227	126.283 890	.007 918 6664	9.51	1.565 648	5.80	324
28	10.864 620	1384.508 119	.000 722 2782	.092 042	127.432 720	.007 847 2782	9.42	1.636 685	5.85	336
29	11.830 826	1520.115 960	.000 657 8446	.084 525	128.487 726	.007 782 8446	9.34	1.708 430	5.89	348
30	12.882 958	1667.783 595	.000 599 5982	.077 622	129.456 572	.007 724 5982	9.27	1.780 855	5.94	360
31	14.028 658	1828.583 519	.000 546 8714	.071 283	130.346 294	.007 671 8714	9.21	1.853 936	5.98	372
32	15.276 246	2003.683 605	.000 499 0808	.065 461	131.163 353	.007 624 0808	9.15	1.927 647	6.02	384
33	16.634 784	2194.355 586	.000 455 7147	.060 115	131.913 684	.007 580 7147	9.10	2.001 963	6.07	396
34	18.114 138	2401.984 293	.000 416 3225	.055 205	132.602 737	.007 541 3225	9.05	2.076 860	6.11	408
35	19.725 054	2628.077 710	.000 380 5063	.050 697	133.235 516	.007 505 5063	9.01	2.152 313	6.15	420
36	21.479 230	2874.277 931	.000 347 9135	.046 557	133.816 617	.007 472 9135	8.97	2.228 299	6.19	432
37	23.389 408	3142.373 082	.000 318 2308	.042 754	134.350 260	.007 443 2308	8.94	2.304 794	6.23	444
38	25.469 461	3434.310 308	.000 291 1793	.039 263	134.840 322	.007 416 1793	8.90	2.381 778	6.27	456
39	27.734 496	3752.209 920	.000 266 5096	.036 056	135.290 361	.007 391 5096	8.87	2.459 226	6.31	468
40	30.200 963	4098.380 789	.000 243 9988	.033 112	135.703 645	.007 368 9988	8.85	2.537 119	6.34	480
41	32.886 777	4475.337 116	.000 223 4469	.030 407	136.083 178	.007 348 4469	8.82	2.615 436	6.38	492
42	35.811 444	4885.816 696	.000 204 6741	.027 924	136.431 714	.007 329 6741	8.80	2.694 156	6.41	504
43	38.996 206	5332.800 799	.000 187 5187	.025 644	136.751 787	.007 312 5187	8.78	2.773 260	6.45	516
44	42.464 193	5819.535 822	.000 171 8350	.023 549	137.045 719	.007 296 8350	8.76	2.852 729	6.48	528
45	46.240 593	6349.556 870	.000 157 4913	.021 626	137.315 646	.007 282 4913	8.74	2.932 545	6.52	540
46	50.352 833	6926.713 431	.000 144 3686	.019 860	137.563 529	.007 269 3686	8.73	3.012 691	6.55	552
47	54.830 781	7555.197 331	.000 132 3592	.018 238	137.791 168	.007 257 3592	8.71	3.093 151	6.58	564
48	59.706 959	8239.573 181	.000 121 3655	.016 748	138.000 215	.007 246 3655	8.70	3.173 907	6.61	576
49	65.016 782	8984.811 532	.000 111 2989	.015 381	138.192 190	.007 236 2989	8.69	3.254 944	6.64	588
50	70.798 815	9796.324 971	.000 102 0791	.014 125	138.368 487	.007 227 0791	8.68	3.336 247	6.67	600

Amount Of 1	Amount Of 1 Per Period	Sinking Fund Payment	Present Worth Of 1	Present Worth of 1 Per Period	Periodic Payment To Amortize 1	Constant Annual Percent	Total Interest	Annual Add On Rate
What a single $ 1 deposit grows to in the future. The deposit is made at the beginning of the first period.	What a series of $ 1 deposits grow to in the future. A deposit is made at the end of each period.	The amount to be deposited at the end of each period that grows to $ 1 in the future.	What $ 1 to be paid in the future is worth today. Value today of a single $ 1 payment tomorrow.	What $ 1 to be paid at the end of each period is worth today. Value today of a series of $ 1 payments tomorrow.	The mortgage payment to amortize a loan of $ 1. An annuity certain, payable at the end of each period, worth $ 1 today.	The annual payment, including interest and principal, to amortize completely a loan of $ 100.	The total interest paid over the term on a loan of $1. The loan is amortized by regular periodic payments.	The average annual interest rate on a loan that is completely amortized by regular periodic payments.

$$S = (1+i)^n \qquad S\overline{n}| = \frac{(1+i)^n - 1}{i} \qquad \frac{1}{S\overline{n}|} = \frac{i}{(1+i)^n - 1} \qquad V^n = \frac{1}{(1+i)^n} \qquad A\overline{n}| = \frac{1 - V^n}{i} \qquad \frac{1}{A\overline{n}|} = \frac{i}{1 - V^n}$$

YEAR									PERIODS
	1.007 167	1.000 000	1.000 000 0000	.992 884	.992 884	1.007 166 6667	1208.60	.007 167	8.60	1
	1.014 385	2.007 167	.498 214 7305	.985 819	1.978 704	.505 381 3972	606.46	.010 763	6.46	2
	1.021 654	3.021 551	.330 955 8172	.978 805	2.957 508	.338 122 4839	405.75	.014 367	5.75	3
	1.028 976	4.043 206	.247 328 4929	.971 840	3.929 348	.254 495 1595	305.40	.017 981	5.39	4
	1.036 351	5.072 182	.197 153 8041	.964 924	4.894 272	.204 320 4707	245.19	.021 602	5.18	5
	1.043 778	6.108 533	.163 705 4329	.958 058	5.852 330	.170 872 0996	205.05	.025 233	5.05	6
	1.051 258	7.152 311	.139 814 9576	.951 241	6.803 572	.146 981 6242	176.38	.028 871	4.95	7
	1.058 792	8.203 569	.121 898 1670	.944 472	7.748 044	.129 064 8337	154.88	.032 519	4.88	8
	1.066 380	9.262 361	.107 963 8329	.937 752	8.685 796	.115 130 4995	138.16	.036 174	4.82	9
	1.074 023	10.328 741	.096 817 2182	.931 079	9.616 875	.103 983 8848	124.79	.039 839	4.78	10
	1.081 720	11.402 764	.087 698 0357	.924 454	10.541 329	.094 864 7024	113.84	.043 512	4.75	11
	1.089 472	12.484 484	.080 099 4274	.917 876	11.459 204	.087 266 0941	104.72	.047 193	4.72	12
1	1.089 472	12.484 484	.080 099 4274	.917 876	11.459 204	.087 266 0941	104.72	.047 193	4.72	12
2	1.186 950	26.085 981	.038 334 7670	.842 496	21.977 329	.045 501 4337	54.61	.092 034	4.60	24
3	1.293 148	40.904 433	.024 447 2280	.773 306	31.631 661	.031 613 8947	37.94	.138 100	4.60	36
4	1.408 849	57.048 724	.017 528 8759	.709 799	40.493 137	.024 695 5426	29.64	.185 386	4.63	48
5	1.534 902	74.637 478	.013 398 0946	.651 507	48.626 871	.020 564 7613	24.68	.233 886	4.68	60
6	1.672 233	93.799 937	.010 660 9880	.598 003	56.092 628	.017 827 6547	21.40	.283 591	4.73	72
7	1.821 851	114.676 901	.008 720 1519	.548 892	62.945 265	.015 886 8186	19.07	.334 493	4.78	84
8	1.984 856	137.421 772	.007 276 8673	.503 815	69.235 133	.014 443 5340	17.34	.386 579	4.83	96
9	2.162 445	162.201 674	.006 165 1645	.462 439	75.008 451	.013 331 8311	16.00	.439 838	4.89	108
10	2.355 924	189.198 688	.005 285 4489	.424 462	80.307 639	.012 452 1156	14.95	.494 254	4.94	120
11	2.566 713	218.611 182	.004 574 3314	.389 603	85.171 635	.011 740 9981	14.09	.549 812	5.00	132
12	2.796 363	250.655 275	.003 989 5430	.357 607	89.636 178	.011 156 2097	13.39	.606 494	5.05	144
13	3.046 559	285.566 421	.003 501 8123	.328 239	93.734 074	.010 668 4789	12.81	.664 283	5.11	156
14	3.319 142	323.601 142	.003 090 2240	.301 283	97.495 434	.010 256 8906	12.31	.723 158	5.17	168
15	3.616 112	365.038 910	.002 739 4340	.276 540	100.947 894	.009 906 1007	11.89	.783 098	5.22	180
16	3.939 653	410.184 204	.002 437 9291	.253 829	104.116 823	.009 604 5958	11.53	.844 082	5.28	192
17	4.292 143	459.368 743	.002 176 9004	.232 984	107.025 507	.009 343 5671	11.22	.906 088	5.33	204
18	4.676 170	512.953 929	.001 949 4928	.213 850	109.695 317	.009 116 1595	10.94	.969 090	5.38	216
19	5.094 557	571.333 495	.001 750 2912	.196 288	112.145 870	.008 916 9579	10.71	1.033 066	5.44	228
20	5.550 378	634.936 405	.001 574 9609	.180 168	114.395 174	.008 741 6275	10.49	1.097 991	5.49	240
21	6.046 982	704.230 004	.001 419 9906	.165 372	116.459 755	.008 586 6573	10.31	1.163 838	5.54	252
22	6.588 018	779.723 449	.001 282 5060	.151 791	118.354 783	.008 449 1727	10.14	1.230 582	5.59	264
23	7.177 462	861.971 453	.001 160 1312	.139 325	120.094 184	.008 326 7979	10.00	1.298 196	5.64	276
24	7.819 645	951.578 362	.001 050 8856	.127 883	121.690 738	.008 217 5523	9.87	1.366 655	5.69	288
25	8.519 285	1049.202 592	.000 953 1048	.117 381	123.156 176	.008 119 7714	9.75	1.435 931	5.74	300
26	9.281 524	1155.561 470	.000 865 3802	.107 741	124.501 266	.008 032 0469	9.64	1.505 999	5.79	312
27	10.111 962	1271.436 504	.000 786 5119	.098 893	125.735 891	.007 953 1786	9.55	1.576 830	5.84	324
28	11.016 700	1397.679 124	.000 715 4718	.090 771	126.869 124	.007 882 1385	9.46	1.648 399	5.89	336
29	12.002 388	1535.216 941	.000 651 3737	.083 317	127.909 290	.007 818 0404	9.39	1.720 678	5.93	348
30	13.076 267	1685.060 560	.000 593 4505	.076 474	128.864 034	.007 760 1171	9.32	1.793 642	5.98	360
31	14.246 229	1848.311 008	.000 541 0345	.070 194	129.740 370	.007 707 7012	9.25	1.867 265	6.02	372
32	15.520 869	2026.167 821	.000 493 5425	.064 429	130.544 738	.007 660 2092	9.20	1.941 520	6.07	384
33	16.909 555	2219.937 863	.000 450 4631	.059 138	131.283 047	.007 617 1297	9.15	2.016 383	6.11	396
34	18.422 489	2431.044 923	.000 411 3458	.054 281	131.960 723	.007 578 0124	9.10	2.091 829	6.15	408
35	20.070 788	2661.040 183	.000 375 7929	.049 824	132.582 746	.007 542 4596	9.06	2.167 833	6.19	420
36	21.866 564	2911.613 610	.000 343 4522	.045 732	133.153 685	.007 510 1188	9.02	2.244 371	6.23	432
37	23.823 012	3184.606 375	.000 314 0106	.041 976	133.677 737	.007 480 6772	8.98	2.321 421	6.27	444
38	25.954 508	3482.024 386	.000 287 1893	.038 529	134.158 751	.007 453 8559	8.95	2.398 958	6.31	456
39	28.276 713	3806.053 021	.000 262 7394	.035 365	134.600 262	.007 429 4060	8.92	2.476 962	6.35	468
40	30.806 691	4159.073 189	.000 240 4382	.032 460	135.005 514	.007 407 1048	8.89	2.555 410	6.39	480
41	33.563 032	4543.678 824	.000 220 0860	.029 795	135.377 486	.007 386 7526	8.87	2.634 282	6.43	492
42	36.565 988	4962.695 947	.000 201 5034	.027 348	135.718 909	.007 368 1700	8.85	2.713 558	6.46	504
43	39.837 625	5419.203 425	.000 184 5290	.025 102	136.032 293	.007 351 1956	8.83	2.793 217	6.50	516
44	43.401 982	5916.555 602	.000 169 0173	.023 040	136.319 941	.007 335 6839	8.81	2.873 241	6.53	528
45	47.285 250	6458.406 938	.000 154 8369	.021 148	136.583 966	.007 321 5036	8.79	2.953 612	6.56	540
46	51.515 962	7048.738 870	.000 141 8693	.019 411	136.826 308	.007 308 5360	8.78	3.034 312	6.60	552
47	56.125 205	7691.889 060	.000 130 0071	.017 817	137.048 748	.007 296 6737	8.76	3.115 324	6.63	564
48	61.146 847	8392.583 269	.000 119 1528	.016 354	137.252 920	.007 285 8195	8.75	3.196 632	6.66	576
49	66.617 786	9155.970 084	.000 109 2184	.015 011	137.440 325	.007 275 8850	8.74	3.278 220	6.69	588
50	72.578 221	9987.658 746	.000 100 1236	.013 778	137.612 339	.007 266 7902	8.73	3.360 074	6.72	600

MONTHLY COMPOUND INTEREST AND ANNUITY

8.625% M

Amount Of 1	Amount Of 1 Per Period	Sinking Fund Payment	Present Worth Of 1	Present Worth of 1 Per Period	Periodic Payment To Amortize 1	Constant Annual Percent	Total Interest	Annual Add On Rate
What a single $ 1 deposit grows to in the future. The deposit is made at the beginning of the first period.	What a series of $ 1 deposits grow to in the future. A deposit is made at the end of each period.	The amount to be deposited at the end of each period that grows to $ 1 in the future.	What $ 1 to be paid in the future is worth today. Value today of a single $ 1 payment tomorrow.	What $ 1 to be paid at the end of each period is worth today. Value today of a series of $ 1 payments tomorrow.	The mortgage payment to amortize a loan of $ 1. An annuity certain, payable at the end of each period, worth $ 1 today.	The annual payment, including interest and principal, to amortize completely a loan of $ 100.	The total interest paid over the term on a loan of $1. The loan is amortized by regular periodic payments.	The average annual interest rate on a loan that is completely amortized by regular periodic payments.

$$S = (1+i)^n \qquad S\overline{n|} = \frac{(1+i)^n - 1}{i} \qquad \frac{1}{S\overline{n|}} = \frac{i}{(1+i)^n - 1} \qquad V^n = \frac{1}{(1+i)^n} \qquad A\overline{n|} = \frac{1-V^n}{i} \qquad \frac{1}{A\overline{n|}} = \frac{i}{1-V^n}$$

YEAR									**PERIODS**
	1.007 187	1.000 000	1.000 000 0000	.992 864	.992 864	1.007 187 5000	1208.63	.007 188	8.63	1
	1.014 427	2.007 187	.498 209 5594	.985 779	1.978 642	.505 397 0594	606.48	.010 794	6.48	2
	1.021 718	3.021 614	.330 948 9389	.978 744	2.957 386	.338 136 4389	405.77	.014 409	5.76	3
	1.029 061	4.043 332	.247 320 7733	.971 759	3.929 145	.254 508 2733	305.41	.018 033	5.41	4
	1.036 458	5.072 393	.197 145 5897	.964 825	4.893 970	.204 333 0897	245.20	.021 665	5.20	5
	1.043 907	6.108 851	.163 696 8970	.957 939	5.851 909	.170 884 3970	205.07	.025 306	5.06	6
	1.051 410	7.152 759	.139 806 1990	.951 103	6.803 013	.146 993 6990	176.40	.028 956	4.96	7
	1.058 967	8.204 169	.121 889 2476	.944 316	7.747 329	.129 076 7476	154.90	.032 614	4.89	8
	1.066 579	9.263 137	.107 954 7939	.937 577	8.684 906	.115 142 2939	138.18	.036 281	4.84	9
	1.074 245	10.329 715	.096 808 0885	.930 886	9.615 792	.103 995 5885	124.80	.039 956	4.79	10
	1.081 966	11.403 960	.087 688 8364	.924 243	10.540 036	.094 876 3364	113.86	.043 640	4.76	11
	1.089 743	12.485 926	.080 090 1741	.917 648	11.457 684	.087 277 6741	104.74	.047 332	4.73	12
1	1.089 743	12.485 926	.080 090 1741	.917 648	11.457 684	.087 277 6741	104.74	.047 332	4.73	12
2	1.187 539	26.092 372	.038 325 3776	.842 078	21.971 803	.045 512 8776	54.62	.092 309	4.62	24
3	1.294 112	40.919 895	.024 437 9904	.772 731	31.620 063	.031 625 4904	37.96	.138 518	4.62	36
4	1.410 249	57.078 079	.017 519 8609	.709 095	40.473 768	.024 707 3609	29.65	.185 953	4.65	48
5	1.536 808	74.686 340	.013 389 3293	.650 699	48.598 352	.020 576 8293	24.70	.234 610	4.69	60
6	1.674 725	93.874 812	.010 652 4847	.597 113	56.053 860	.017 839 9847	21.41	.284 479	4.74	72
7	1.825 019	114.785 307	.008 711 9164	.547 939	62.895 390	.015 899 4164	19.08	.335 551	4.79	84
8	1.988 801	137.572 365	.007 268 9017	.502 815	69.173 507	.014 456 4017	17.35	.387 815	4.85	96
9	2.167 282	162.404 392	.006 157 4690	.461 408	74.934 607	.013 344 9690	16.02	.441 257	4.90	108
10	2.361 779	189.464 909	.005 278 0222	.423 410	80.221 268	.012 465 5222	14.96	.495 863	4.96	120
11	2.573 731	218.953 908	.004 567 1713	.388 541	85.072 562	.011 754 6713	14.11	.551 617	5.01	132
12	2.804 705	251.089 326	.003 982 6464	.356 544	89.524 341	.011 170 1464	13.41	.608 501	5.07	144
13	3.056 406	286.108 659	.003 495 1756	.327 182	93.609 507	.010 682 6756	12.82	.666 497	5.13	156
14	3.330 696	324.270 719	.003 083 8430	.300 238	97.358 252	.010 271 3430	12.33	.725 586	5.18	168
15	3.629 601	365.857 541	.002 733 3043	.275 512	100.798 279	.009 920 8043	11.91	.785 745	5.24	180
16	3.955 331	411.176 472	.002 432 0458	.252 823	103.955 012	.009 619 5458	11.55	.846 953	5.29	192
17	4.310 293	460.562 441	.002 171 2583	.232 003	106.851 782	.009 358 7583	11.24	.909 187	5.35	204
18	4.697 109	514.380 435	.001 944 0864	.212 897	109.509 997	.009 131 5864	10.96	.972 423	5.40	216
19	5.118 640	573.028 196	.001 745 1148	.195 364	111.949 303	.008 932 6148	10.72	1.036 636	5.46	228
20	5.578 000	636.939 159	.001 570 0087	.179 276	114.187 726	.008 757 5087	10.51	1.101 802	5.51	240
21	6.078 584	706.585 658	.001 415 2566	.164 512	116.241 811	.008 602 7566	10.33	1.167 895	5.56	252
22	6.624 092	782.482 414	.001 277 9840	.150 964	118.126 737	.008 465 4840	10.16	1.234 888	5.61	264
23	7.218 556	865.190 342	.001 155 8150	.138 532	119.856 436	.008 343 3150	10.02	1.302 725	5.66	276
24	7.866 367	955.320 695	.001 046 7689	.127 123	121.443 690	.008 234 2689	9.89	1.371 469	5.71	288
25	8.572 316	1053.539 578	.000 949 1812	.116 655	122.900 231	.008 136 6812	9.77	1.441 004	5.76	300
26	9.341 618	1160.572 879	.000 861 6434	.107 048	124.236 822	.008 049 1434	9.66	1.511 333	5.81	312
27	10.179 959	1277.211 627	.000 782 9556	.098 232	125.463 342	.007 970 4556	9.57	1.582 428	5.86	324
28	11.093 534	1404.317 838	.000 712 0895	.090 143	126.588 856	.007 899 5895	9.48	1.654 262	5.91	336
29	12.089 097	1542.830 890	.000 648 1592	.082 719	127.621 682	.007 835 6592	9.41	1.726 809	5.95	348
30	13.174 004	1693.774 462	.000 590 3974	.075 907	128.569 452	.007 777 8974	9.34	1.800 043	6.00	360
31	14.356 273	1858.264 103	.000 538 1366	.069 656	129.439 171	.007 725 6366	9.28	1.873 937	6.04	372
32	15.644 642	2037.515 471	.000 490 7938	.063 920	130.237 267	.007 678 2938	9.22	1.948 465	6.09	384
33	17.048 633	2232.853 321	.000 447 8575	.058 656	130.969 638	.007 635 3575	9.17	2.023 602	6.13	396
34	18.578 622	2445.721 297	.000 408 8773	.053 825	131.641 697	.007 596 3773	9.12	2.099 322	6.17	408
35	20.245 916	2677.692 597	.000 373 4559	.049 393	132.258 410	.007 560 9559	9.08	2.175 601	6.22	420
36	22.062 837	2930.481 604	.000 341 2408	.045 325	132.824 336	.007 528 7408	9.04	2.252 416	6.26	432
37	24.042 813	3205.956 552	.000 311 9194	.041 592	133.343 656	.007 499 4194	9.00	2.329 742	6.30	444
38	26.200 477	3506.153 336	.000 285 2129	.038 167	133.820 210	.007 472 7129	8.97	2.407 557	6.34	456
39	28.551 776	3833.290 558	.000 260 8725	.035 024	134.257 518	.007 448 3725	8.94	2.485 858	6.37	468
40	31.114 086	4189.785 924	.000 238 6757	.032 140	134.658 813	.007 426 1757	8.92	2.564 564	6.41	480
41	33.906 345	4578.274 109	.000 218 4229	.029 493	135.027 060	.007 405 9229	8.89	2.643 714	6.45	492
42	36.949 189	5001.626 231	.000 199 9350	.027 064	135.364 982	.007 387 4350	8.87	2.723 267	6.48	504
43	40.265 105	5462.971 070	.000 183 0506	.024 835	135.675 075	.007 370 5506	8.85	2.803 204	6.52	516
44	43.878 600	5965.718 193	.000 167 6244	.022 790	135.959 631	.007 355 1244	8.83	2.883 506	6.55	528
45	47.816 379	6513.583 147	.000 153 5253	.020 913	136.220 753	.007 341 0253	8.81	2.964 154	6.59	540
46	52.107 545	7110.614 923	.000 140 6348	.019 191	136.460 372	.007 328 1348	8.80	3.045 130	6.62	552
47	56.783 811	7761.225 879	.000 128 8456	.017 611	136.680 257	.007 316 3456	8.78	3.126 419	6.65	564
48	61.879 738	8470.224 350	.000 118 0606	.016 160	136.882 034	.007 305 5606	8.77	3.208 003	6.68	576
49	67.432 986	9242.850 184	.000 108 1917	.014 830	137.067 195	.007 295 6917	8.76	3.289 867	6.71	588
50	73.484 597	10084.813 464	.000 099 1590	.013 608	137.237 107	.007 286 6590	8.75	3.371 995	6.74	600

Effective Rate is 8.97 %   8 - 103   Annual Percentage Rate is 8.625

	Amount Of 1	Amount Of 1 Per Period	Sinking Fund Payment	Present Worth Of 1	Present Worth of 1 Per Period	Periodic Payment To Amortize 1	Constant Annual Percent	Total Interest	Annual Add On Rate	
	What a single $1 deposit grows to in the future. The deposit is made at the beginning of the first period.	What a series of $1 deposits grow to in the future. A deposit is made at the end of each period.	The amount to be deposited at the end of each period that grows to $1 in the future.	What $1 to be paid in the future is worth today. Value today of a single $1 payment tomorrow.	What $1 to be paid at the end of each period is worth today. Value today of a series of $1 payments tomorrow.	The mortgage payment to amortize a loan of $1. An annuity certain, payable at the end of each period, worth $1 today.	The annual payment, including interest and principal, to amortize completely a loan of $100.	The total interest paid over the term on a loan of $1. The loan is amortized by regular periodic payments.	The average annual interest rate on a loan that is completely amortized by regular periodic payments.	
	$S = (1+i)^n$	$S\overline{n}| = \dfrac{(1+i)^n - 1}{i}$	$\dfrac{1}{S\overline{n}|} = \dfrac{i}{(1+i)^n - 1}$	$V^n = \dfrac{1}{(1+i)^n}$	$A\overline{n}| = \dfrac{1 - V^n}{i}$	$\dfrac{1}{A\overline{n}|} = \dfrac{i}{1 - V^n}$				

YEAR										PERIODS
	1.007 208	1.000 000	1.000 000 0000	.992 843	.992 843	1.007 208 3333	1208.65	.007 208	8.65	1
	1.014 469	2.007 208	.498 204 3884	.985 738	1.978 581	.505 412 7217	606.50	.010 825	6.50	2
	1.021 781	3.021 677	.330 942 0607	.978 683	2.957 264	.338 150 3941	405.79	.014 451	5.78	3
	1.029 147	4.043 458	.247 313 0540	.971 679	3.928 943	.254 521 3874	305.43	.018 086	5.43	4
	1.036 565	5.072 605	.197 137 3757	.964 725	4.893 668	.204 345 7090	245.22	.021 729	5.21	5
	1.044 037	6.109 170	.163 688 3614	.957 821	5.851 488	.170 896 6947	205.08	.025 380	5.08	6
	1.051 563	7.153 207	.139 797 4408	.950 966	6.802 454	.147 005 7742	176.41	.029 040	4.98	7
	1.059 143	8.204 769	.121 880 3288	.944 160	7.746 614	.129 088 6621	154.91	.032 709	4.91	8
	1.066 777	9.263 912	.107 945 7556	.937 403	8.684 016	.115 154 0889	138.19	.036 387	4.85	9
	1.074 467	10.330 690	.096 798 9596	.930 694	9.614 710	.104 007 2929	124.81	.040 073	4.81	10
	1.082 212	11.405 157	.087 679 6378	.924 033	10.538 744	.094 887 9711	113.87	.043 768	4.77	11
	1.090 013	12.487 369	.080 080 9216	.917 420	11.456 164	.087 289 2550	104.75	.047 471	4.75	12
1	1.090 013	12.487 369	.080 080 9216	.917 420	11.456 164	.087 289 2550	104.75	.047 471	4.75	12
2	1.188 129	26.098 765	.038 315 9900	.841 660	21.966 279	.045 524 3233	54.63	.092 584	4.63	24
3	1.295 076	40.935 364	.024 428 7553	.772 156	31.608 471	.031 637 0886	37.97	.138 935	4.63	36
4	1.411 650	57.107 453	.017 510 8493	.708 391	40.454 412	.024 719 1826	29.67	.186 521	4.66	48
5	1.538 717	74.735 242	.013 380 5683	.649 892	48.569 857	.020 588 9016	24.71	.235 334	4.71	60
6	1.677 221	93.949 762	.010 643 9865	.596 224	56.015 129	.017 852 3198	21.43	.285 367	4.76	72
7	1.828 193	114.893 842	.008 703 6867	.546 988	62.845 572	.015 912 0200	19.10	.336 610	4.81	84
8	1.992 754	137.723 164	.007 260 9427	.501 818	69.111 958	.014 469 2760	17.37	.389 050	4.86	96
9	2.172 129	162.607 423	.006 149 7807	.460 378	74.860 867	.013 358 1141	16.03	.442 676	4.92	108
10	2.367 649	189.731 593	.005 270 6035	.422 360	80.135 032	.012 478 9368	14.98	.497 472	4.97	120
11	2.580 768	219.297 294	.004 560 0198	.387 482	84.973 657	.011 768 3531	14.13	.553 423	5.03	132
12	2.813 071	251.524 296	.003 975 7591	.355 483	89.412 709	.011 184 0924	13.43	.610 509	5.09	144
13	3.066 284	286.652 150	.003 488 5487	.326 128	93.485 185	.010 696 8821	12.84	.668 714	5.14	156
14	3.342 290	324.941 972	.003 077 4725	.299 196	97.221 356	.010 285 8059	12.35	.728 015	5.20	168
15	3.643 140	366.678 381	.002 727 1856	.274 488	100.648 995	.009 935 5189	11.93	.788 393	5.26	180
16	3.971 070	412.171 613	.002 426 1739	.251 821	103.793 581	.009 634 5072	11.57	.849 825	5.31	192
17	4.328 519	461.759 834	.002 165 6279	.231 026	106.678 486	.009 373 9613	11.25	.912 288	5.37	204
18	4.718 142	515.811 644	.001 938 6922	.211 948	109.325 157	.009 147 0255	10.98	.975 758	5.42	216
19	5.142 837	574.728 827	.001 739 9510	.194 445	111.753 266	.008 948 2843	10.74	1.040 209	5.47	228
20	5.605 760	638.949 328	.001 565 0693	.178 388	113.980 862	.008 773 4027	10.53	1.105 617	5.53	240
21	6.110 352	708.950 517	.001 410 5357	.163 657	116.024 504	.008 618 8690	10.35	1.171 955	5.58	252
22	6.660 363	785.252 732	.001 273 4754	.150 142	117.899 382	.008 481 8087	10.18	1.239 197	5.63	264
23	7.259 884	868.423 146	.001 151 5124	.137 743	119.619 433	.008 359 8457	10.04	1.307 317	5.68	276
24	7.913 368	959.079 989	.001 042 6659	.126 368	121.197 442	.008 250 9992	9.91	1.376 288	5.73	288
25	8.625 675	1057.897 136	.000 945 2715	.115 933	122.645 139	.008 153 6048	9.79	1.446 081	5.78	300
26	9.402 099	1165.609 123	.000 857 9205	.106 359	123.973 286	.008 066 2539	9.68	1.516 671	5.83	312
27	10.248 411	1283.016 602	.000 779 4131	.097 576	125.191 755	.007 987 7465	9.59	1.588 030	5.88	324
28	11.170 903	1410.992 294	.000 708 7211	.089 518	126.309 603	.007 917 0544	9.51	1.660 130	5.93	336
29	12.176 431	1550.487 476	.000 644 9585	.082 126	127.335 139	.007 853 2918	9.43	1.732 946	5.98	348
30	13.272 469	1702.539 055	.000 587 3580	.075 344	128.275 986	.007 795 6914	9.36	1.806 449	6.02	360
31	14.467 165	1868.277 270	.000 535 2525	.069 122	129.139 139	.007 743 5858	9.30	1.880 614	6.07	372
32	15.769 400	2048.934 098	.000 488 0586	.063 414	129.931 012	.007 696 3920	9.24	1.955 415	6.11	384
33	17.188 853	2245.852 411	.000 445 2652	.058 177	130.657 493	.007 653 5986	9.19	2.030 825	6.15	396
34	18.736 075	2460.495 955	.000 406 4221	.053 373	131.323 981	.007 614 7555	9.14	2.106 820	6.20	408
35	20.422 568	2694.460 233	.000 371 1318	.048 965	131.935 430	.007 579 4652	9.10	2.183 375	6.24	420
36	22.260 866	2949.484 364	.000 339 0423	.044 922	132.496 386	.007 547 3756	9.06	2.260 466	6.28	432
37	24.264 636	3227.464 013	.000 309 8408	.041 212	133.011 019	.007 518 1741	9.03	2.338 069	6.32	444
38	26.448 772	3530.465 476	.000 283 2488	.037 809	133.483 153	.007 491 5821	8.99	2.416 161	6.36	456
39	28.829 508	3860.741 046	.000 259 0176	.034 687	133.916 298	.007 467 3510	8.97	2.494 720	6.40	468
40	31.424 542	4220.745 748	.000 236 9250	.031 822	134.313 675	.007 445 2583	8.94	2.573 724	6.43	480
41	34.253 163	4613.155 596	.000 216 7714	.029 194	134.678 236	.007 425 1047	8.92	2.653 152	6.47	492
42	37.336 397	5040.887 477	.000 198 3778	.026 784	135.012 691	.007 406 7111	8.89	2.732 982	6.51	504
43	40.697 163	5507.120 838	.000 181 5831	.024 572	135.319 528	.007 389 9164	8.87	2.813 197	6.54	516
44	44.360 441	6015.321 316	.000 166 2422	.022 543	135.601 026	.007 374 5755	8.85	2.893 776	6.58	528
45	48.353 463	6569.266 504	.000 152 2240	.020 681	135.859 277	.007 360 5573	8.84	2.974 701	6.61	540
46	52.705 909	7173.074 024	.000 139 4102	.018 973	136.096 203	.007 347 7436	8.82	3.055 954	6.64	552
47	57.450 132	7831.232 141	.000 127 6938	.017 406	136.313 563	.007 336 0272	8.81	3.137 519	6.68	564
48	62.621 397	8548.633 122	.000 116 9778	.015 969	136.512 974	.007 325 3111	8.80	3.219 379	6.71	576
49	68.258 144	9330.609 600	.000 107 1741	.014 650	136.695 917	.007 315 5075	8.78	3.301 518	6.74	588
50	74.402 272	10182.974 218	.000 098 2031	.013 440	136.863 753	.007 306 5365	8.77	3.383 922	6.77	600

Effective Rate is 9.00 %   8 - 104   Annual Percentage Rate is 8.65 %

MONTHLY COMPOUND INTEREST AND ANNUITY

8.70 % M

Amount Of 1	Amount Of 1 Per Period	Sinking Fund Payment	Present Worth Of 1	Present Worth of 1 Per Period	Periodic Payment To Amortize 1	Constant Annual Percent	Total Interest	Annual Add On Rate	
What a single $ 1 deposit grows to in the future. The deposit is made at the beginning of the first period.	What a series of $ 1 deposits grow to in the future. A deposit is made at the end of each period.	The amount to be deposited at the end of each period that grows to $ 1 in the future.	What $ 1 to be paid in the future is worth today. Value today of a single $ 1 payment tomorrow.	What $ 1 to be paid at the end of each period is worth today. Value today of a series of $ 1 payments tomorrow.	The mortgage payment to amortize a loan of $ 1. An annuity certain, payable at the end of each period, worth $ 1 today.	The annual payment, including interest and principal, to amortize completely a loan of $ 100.	The total interest paid over the term on a loan of $1. The loan is amortized by regular periodic payments.	The average annual interest rate on a loan that is completely amortized by regular periodic payments.	

$$S = (1+i)^n \qquad S\overline{n}| = \frac{(1+i)^n - 1}{i} \qquad \frac{1}{S\overline{n}|} = \frac{i}{(1+i)^n - 1} \qquad V^n = \frac{1}{(1+i)^n} \qquad A\overline{n}| = \frac{1-V^n}{i} \qquad \frac{1}{A\overline{n}|} = \frac{i}{1-V^n}$$

YEAR / **PERIODS**

Amount Of 1	Amount Of 1 Per Period	Sinking Fund Payment	Present Worth Of 1	Present Worth of 1 Per Period	Periodic Payment To Amortize 1	Constant Annual Percent	Total Interest	Annual Add On Rate	PERIODS
1.007 250	1.000 000	1.000 000 0000	.992 802	.992 802	1.007 250 0000	1208.70	.007 250	8.70	1
1.014 553	2.007 250	.498 194 0466	.985 656	1.978 458	.505 444 0466	606.54	.010 888	6.53	2
1.021 908	3.021 803	.330 928 3050	.978 562	2.957 020	.338 178 3050	405.82	.014 535	5.81	3
1.029 317	4.043 711	.247 297 6163	.971 518	3.928 538	.254 547 6163	305.46	.018 190	5.46	4
1.036 779	5.073 028	.197 120 9487	.964 525	4.893 063	.204 370 9487	245.25	.021 855	5.25	5
1.044 296	6.109 807	.163 671 2916	.957 583	5.850 646	.170 921 2916	205.11	.025 528	5.11	6
1.051 867	7.154 103	.139 779 9261	.950 690	6.801 336	.147 029 9261	176.44	.029 209	5.01	7
1.059 493	8.205 970	.121 862 4928	.943 847	7.745 184	.129 112 4928	154.94	.032 900	4.93	8
1.067 175	9.265 464	.107 927 6808	.937 054	8.682 238	.115 177 6808	138.22	.036 599	4.88	9
1.074 912	10.332 638	.096 780 7038	.930 309	9.612 547	.104 030 7038	124.84	.040 307	4.84	10
1.082 705	11.407 550	.087 661 2430	.923 613	10.536 160	.094 911 2430	113.90	.044 024	4.80	11
1.090 554	12.490 255	.080 062 4193	.916 965	11.453 124	.087 312 4193	104.78	.047 749	4.77	12

YEAR	Amount Of 1	Amount Of 1 Per Period	Sinking Fund Payment	Present Worth Of 1	Present Worth of 1 Per Period	Periodic Payment To Amortize 1	Constant Annual Percent	Total Interest	Annual Add On Rate	PERIODS
1	1.090 554	12.490 255	.080 062 4193	.916 965	11.453 124	.087 312 4193	104.78	.047 749	4.77	12
2	1.189 309	26.111 556	.038 297 2198	.840 825	21.955 237	.045 547 2198	54.66	.093 133	4.66	24
3	1.297 006	40.966 325	.024 410 2928	.771 007	31.585 305	.031 660 2928	38.00	.139 771	4.66	36
4	1.414 455	57.166 259	.017 492 8362	.706 986	40.415 739	.024 742 8362	29.70	.187 656	4.69	48
5	1.542 540	74.833 167	.013 363 0587	.648 281	48.512 936	.020 613 0587	24.74	.236 784	4.74	60
6	1.682 224	94.099 890	.010 627 0050	.594 451	55.937 781	.017 877 0050	21.46	.287 144	4.79	72
7	1.834 557	115.111 298	.008 687 2446	.545 091	62.746 104	.015 937 2446	19.13	.338 729	4.84	84
8	2.000 684	138.025 381	.007 245 0443	.499 829	68.989 096	.014 495 0443	17.40	.391 524	4.89	96
9	2.181 855	163.014 434	.006 134 4261	.458 326	74.713 700	.013 384 4261	16.07	.445 518	4.95	108
10	2.379 431	190.266 354	.005 255 7900	.420 269	79.962 961	.012 505 7900	15.01	.500 695	5.01	120
11	2.594 899	219.986 054	.004 545 7427	.385 371	84.776 349	.011 795 7427	14.16	.557 038	5.06	132
12	2.829 878	252.397 001	.003 962 0122	.353 372	89.190 056	.011 212 0122	13.46	.614 530	5.12	144
13	3.086 136	287.742 901	.003 475 3247	.324 030	93.237 271	.010 725 3247	12.88	.673 151	5.18	156
14	3.365 599	326.289 526	.003 064 7628	.297 124	96.948 424	.010 314 7628	12.38	.732 880	5.23	168
15	3.670 369	368.326 715	.002 714 9809	.272 452	100.351 422	.009 964 9809	11.96	.793 697	5.29	180
16	4.002 737	414.170 554	.002 414 4643	.249 829	103.471 850	.009 664 4643	11.60	.855 577	5.35	192
17	4.365 202	464.165 753	.002 154 4028	.229 084	106.333 174	.009 404 4028	11.29	.918 498	5.40	204
18	4.760 490	518.688 233	.001 927 9404	.210 062	108.956 907	.009 177 9404	11.02	.982 435	5.46	216
19	5.191 573	578.147 962	.001 729 6610	.192 620	111.362 778	.008 979 6610	10.78	1.047 363	5.51	228
20	5.661 692	642.992 027	.001 555 2292	.176 626	113.568 877	.008 805 2292	10.57	1.113 255	5.57	240
21	6.174 383	713.708 003	.001 401 1332	.161 960	115.591 793	.008 651 1332	10.39	1.180 086	5.62	252
22	6.733 500	790.827 619	.001 264 4981	.148 511	117.446 735	.008 514 4981	10.22	1.247 827	5.67	264
23	7.343 248	874.930 752	.001 142 9476	.136 180	119.147 652	.008 392 9476	10.08	1.316 454	5.72	276
24	8.008 211	966.649 788	.001 034 5008	.124 872	120.707 333	.008 284 5008	9.95	1.385 936	5.77	288
25	8.733 389	1066.674 382	.000 937 4932	.114 503	122.137 506	.008 187 4932	9.83	1.456 248	5.82	300
26	9.524 236	1175.756 637	.000 850 5161	.104 995	123.448 924	.008 100 5161	9.73	1.527 361	5.87	312
27	10.386 697	1294.716 765	.000 772 3697	.096 277	124.651 448	.008 022 3697	9.63	1.599 248	5.92	324
28	11.327 257	1424.449 249	.000 702 0257	.088 283	125.754 121	.007 952 0257	9.55	1.671 881	5.97	336
29	12.352 989	1565.929 573	.000 638 5983	.080 952	126.765 232	.007 888 5983	9.47	1.745 232	6.02	348
30	13.471 606	1720.221 556	.000 581 3205	.074 230	127.692 387	.007 831 3205	9.40	1.819 275	6.06	360
31	14.691 519	1888.485 348	.000 529 5249	.068 066	128.542 554	.007 779 5249	9.34	1.893 983	6.11	372
32	16.021 900	2071.986 158	.000 482 6287	.062 415	129.322 128	.007 732 6287	9.28	1.969 329	6.15	384
33	17.472 752	2272.103 764	.000 440 1207	.057 232	130.036 970	.007 690 1207	9.23	2.045 288	6.20	396
34	19.054 986	2490.342 888	.000 401 5511	.052 480	130.692 455	.007 651 5511	9.19	2.121 833	6.24	408
35	20.780 498	2728.344 514	.000 366 5226	.048 122	131.293 511	.007 616 5226	9.14	2.198 940	6.28	420
36	22.662 262	2987.898 221	.000 334 6834	.044 126	131.844 659	.007 584 6834	9.11	2.276 583	6.32	432
37	24.714 428	3270.955 644	.000 305 7211	.040 462	132.350 042	.007 555 7211	9.07	2.354 740	6.36	444
38	26.952 427	3579.645 147	.000 279 3573	.037 102	132.813 461	.007 529 3573	9.04	2.433 387	6.40	456
39	29.393 087	3916.287 826	.000 255 3438	.034 022	133.238 399	.007 505 3438	9.01	2.512 501	6.44	468
40	32.054 758	4283.414 963	.000 233 4586	.031 197	133.628 053	.007 483 4586	8.99	2.592 060	6.48	480
41	34.957 456	4683.787 057	.000 213 5024	.028 606	133.985 352	.007 463 5024	8.96	2.672 043	6.52	492
42	38.123 006	5120.414 584	.000 195 2967	.026 231	134.312 982	.007 445 2967	8.94	2.752 430	6.55	504
43	41.575 210	5596.580 632	.000 178 6805	.024 053	134.613 408	.007 428 6805	8.92	2.833 199	6.59	516
44	45.340 025	6115.865 584	.000 163 5092	.022 056	134.888 887	.007 413 5092	8.90	2.914 333	6.62	528
45	49.445 762	6682.174 046	.000 149 6519	.020 224	135.141 492	.007 399 6519	8.88	2.995 812	6.66	540
46	53.923 290	7299.764 199	.000 136 9907	.018 545	135.373 122	.007 386 9907	8.87	3.077 619	6.69	552
47	58.806 279	7973.279 825	.000 125 4189	.017 005	135.585 519	.007 375 4189	8.86	3.159 736	6.72	564
48	64.131 443	8707.785 218	.000 114 8398	.015 593	135.780 279	.007 364 8398	8.84	3.242 148	6.75	576
49	69.938 824	9508.803 266	.000 105 1657	.014 298	135.958 868	.007 355 1657	8.83	3.324 837	6.79	588
50	76.272 088	10382.356 980	.000 096 3172	.013 111	136.122 627	.007 346 3172	8.82	3.407 790	6.82	600

Effective Rate is 9.06 %

Annual Percentage Rate is 8.70 %

	Amount Of 1	Amount Of 1 Per Period	Sinking Fund Payment	Present Worth Of 1	Present Worth of 1 Per Period	Periodic Payment To Amortize 1	Constant Annual Percent	Total Interest	Annual Add On Rate	
	What a single $ 1 deposit grows to in the future. The deposit is made at the beginning of the first period.	What a series of $ 1 deposits grow to in the future. A deposit is made at the end of each period.	The amount to be deposited at the end of each period that grows to $ 1 in the future.	What $ 1 to be paid in the future is worth today. Value today of a single $ 1 payment tomorrow.	What $ 1 to be paid at the end of each period is worth today. Value today of a series of $ 1 payments tomorrow.	The mortgage payment to amortize a loan of $ 1. An annuity certain, payable at the end of each period, worth $ 1 today.	The annual payment, including interest and principal, to amortize completely a loan of $ 100.	The total interest paid over the term on a loan of $1. The loan is amortized by regular periodic payments.	The average annual interest rate on a loan that is completely amortized by regular periodic payments.	
	$S = (1+i)^n$	$S\overline{n}| = \dfrac{(1+i)^n - 1}{i}$	$\dfrac{1}{S\overline{n}|} = \dfrac{i}{(1+i)^n - 1}$	$V^n = \dfrac{1}{(1+i)^n}$	$A\overline{n}| = \dfrac{1 - V^n}{i}$	$\dfrac{1}{A\overline{n}|} = \dfrac{i}{1 - V^n}$				

YEAR										PERIODS
	1.007 292	1.000 000	1.000 000 0000	.992 761	.992 761	1.007 291 6667	1208.75	.007 292	8.75	1
	1.014 637	2.007 292	.498 183 7052	.985 575	1.978 336	.505 475 3719	606.58	.010 951	6.57	2
	1.022 035	3.021 929	.330 914 5500	.978 440	2.956 776	.338 206 2167	405.85	.014 619	5.85	3
	1.029 487	4.043 963	.247 282 1796	.971 357	3.928 133	.254 573 8463	305.49	.018 295	5.49	4
	1.036 994	5.073 450	.197 104 5230	.964 326	4.892 459	.204 396 1897	245.28	.021 981	5.28	5
	1.044 555	6.110 444	.163 654 2234	.957 345	5.849 804	.170 945 8900	205.14	.025 675	5.14	6
	1.052 172	7.155 000	.139 762 4132	.950 415	6.800 219	.147 054 0799	176.47	.029 379	5.04	7
	1.059 844	8.207 171	.121 844 6590	.943 535	7.743 754	.129 136 3257	154.97	.033 091	4.96	8
	1.067 572	9.267 015	.107 909 6086	.936 705	8.680 459	.115 201 2753	138.25	.036 811	4.91	9
	1.075 356	10.334 587	.096 762 4509	.929 924	9.610 384	.104 054 1176	124.87	.040 541	4.86	10
	1.083 198	11.409 944	.087 642 8513	.923 193	10.533 576	.094 934 5180	113.93	.044 280	4.83	11
	1.091 096	12.493 141	.080 043 9203	.916 510	11.450 086	.087 335 5870	104.81	.048 027	4.80	12
1	1.091 096	12.493 141	.080 043 9203	.916 510	11.450 086	.087 335 5870	104.81	.048 027	4.80	12
2	1.190 490	26.124 355	.038 278 4565	.839 990	21.944 202	.045 570 1231	54.69	.093 683	4.68	24
3	1.298 939	40.997 316	.024 391 8406	.769 859	31.562 162	.031 683 5072	38.03	.140 606	4.69	36
4	1.417 267	57.225 142	.017 474 8366	.705 584	40.377 117	.024 766 5033	29.72	.188 792	4.72	48
5	1.546 374	74.931 254	.013 345 5660	.646 674	48.456 109	.020 637 2327	24.77	.238 234	4.76	60
6	1.687 242	94.250 319	.010 610 0436	.592 683	55.860 585	.017 901 7103	21.49	.288 923	4.82	72
7	1.840 943	115.329 271	.008 670 8256	.543 200	62.646 859	.015 962 4923	19.16	.340 849	4.87	84
8	2.008 645	138.328 427	.007 229 1721	.497 848	68.866 545	.014 520 8387	17.43	.394 001	4.93	96
9	2.191 624	163.422 710	.006 119 1006	.456 283	74.566 949	.013 410 7673	16.10	.448 363	4.98	108
10	2.391 272	190.802 977	.005 241 0084	.418 188	79.791 425	.012 532 6750	15.04	.503 921	5.04	120
11	2.609 107	220.677 472	.004 531 5002	.383 273	84.579 708	.011 823 1668	14.19	.560 658	5.10	132
12	2.846 785	253.273 409	.003 948 3024	.351 273	88.968 217	.011 239 9690	13.49	.618 556	5.15	144
13	3.106 116	288.838 969	.003 462 1400	.321 946	92.990 328	.010 753 8066	12.91	.677 594	5.21	156
14	3.389 070	327.643 839	.003 052 0946	.295 066	96.676 632	.010 343 7613	12.42	.737 752	5.27	168
15	3.697 800	369.983 965	.002 702 8198	.270 431	100.055 165	.009 994 4865	12.00	.799 008	5.33	180
16	4.034 654	416.181 099	.002 402 8001	.247 853	103.151 625	.009 694 4668	11.64	.861 338	5.38	192
17	4.402 194	466.586 599	.002 143 2249	.227 159	105.989 560	.009 434 8915	11.33	.924 718	5.44	204
18	4.803 215	521.583 830	.001 917 2374	.208 194	108.590 555	.009 208 9040	11.06	.989 123	5.50	216
19	5.240 768	581.591 078	.001 719 4211	.190 812	110.974 393	.009 011 0878	10.82	1.054 528	5.55	228
20	5.718 180	647.064 737	.001 545 4404	.174 881	113.159 204	.008 837 1071	10.61	1.120 906	5.60	240
21	6.239 083	718.502 772	.001 391 7831	.160 280	115.161 604	.008 683 4497	10.43	1.188 229	5.66	252
22	6.807 437	796.448 513	.001 255 5739	.146 898	116.996 823	.008 547 2406	10.26	1.256 472	5.71	264
23	7.427 566	881.494 785	.001 134 4367	.134 634	118.678 820	.008 426 1033	10.12	1.325 605	5.76	276
24	8.104 186	974.288 418	.001 026 3901	.123 393	120.220 386	.008 318 0568	9.99	1.395 600	5.82	288
25	8.842 444	1075.535 163	.000 929 7697	.113 091	121.633 247	.008 221 4364	9.87	1.466 431	5.87	300
26	9.647 954	1186.005 063	.000 843 1667	.103 649	122.928 148	.008 134 8334	9.77	1.538 068	5.92	312
27	10.526 842	1306.538 310	.000 765 3813	.094 995	124.114 937	.008 057 0480	9.67	1.610 484	5.96	324
28	11.485 793	1438.051 632	.000 695 3853	.087 064	125.202 641	.007 987 0520	9.59	1.683 649	6.01	336
29	12.532 101	1581.545 261	.000 632 2930	.079 795	126.199 532	.007 923 9597	9.51	1.757 538	6.06	348
30	13.673 723	1738.110 574	.000 575 3374	.073 133	127.113 192	.007 867 0041	9.45	1.832 121	6.11	360
31	14.919 342	1908.938 325	.000 523 8514	.067 027	127.950 571	.007 815 5181	9.38	1.907 373	6.15	372
32	16.278 432	2095.327 771	.000 477 2523	.061 431	128.718 037	.007 768 9190	9.33	1.983 265	6.20	384
33	17.761 329	2298.696 516	.000 435 0292	.056 302	129.421 427	.007 726 6958	9.28	2.059 772	6.24	396
34	19.379 312	2520.591 305	.000 396 7323	.051 601	130.066 091	.007 688 3990	9.23	2.136 867	6.28	408
35	21.144 686	2762.699 781	.000 361 9648	.047 293	130.656 932	.007 653 6314	9.19	2.214 525	6.33	420
36	23.070 878	3026.863 328	.000 330 3750	.043 345	131.198 443	.007 622 0417	9.15	2.292 722	6.37	432
37	25.172 530	3315.091 070	.000 301 6508	.039 726	131.694 743	.007 593 3175	9.12	2.371 433	6.41	444
38	27.465 652	3629.575 155	.000 275 5143	.036 409	132.149 608	.007 567 1810	9.09	2.450 635	6.45	456
39	29.967 658	3972.707 426	.000 251 7175	.033 369	132.566 495	.007 543 3842	9.06	2.530 304	6.49	468
40	32.697 587	4347.097 613	.000 230 0385	.030 583	132.948 576	.007 521 7052	9.03	2.610 419	6.53	480
41	35.676 200	4755.593 182	.000 210 2787	.028 030	133.298 758	.007 501 9454	9.01	2.690 957	6.56	492
42	38.926 153	5201.300 990	.000 192 2596	.025 690	133.619 702	.007 483 9263	8.99	2.771 899	6.60	504
43	42.472 163	5687.610 917	.000 175 8207	.023 545	133.913 851	.007 467 4874	8.97	2.853 224	6.64	516
44	46.341 200	6218.221 646	.000 160 8177	.021 579	134.183 442	.007 452 4844	8.95	2.934 912	6.67	528
45	50.562 689	6797.168 795	.000 147 1201	.019 777	134.430 524	.007 438 7867	8.93	3.016 945	6.70	540
46	55.168 739	7428.855 611	.000 134 6102	.018 126	134.656 977	.007 426 2769	8.92	3.099 305	6.74	552
47	60.194 380	8118.086 455	.000 123 1817	.016 613	134.864 524	.007 414 8484	8.90	3.181 975	6.77	564
48	65.677 837	8870.103 350	.000 112 7383	.015 226	135.054 742	.007 404 4049	8.89	3.264 937	6.80	576
49	71.660 813	9690.625 841	.000 103 1925	.013 955	135.229 080	.007 394 8592	8.88	3.348 177	6.83	588
50	78.188 814	10585.894 502	.000 094 4653	.012 790	135.388 861	.007 386 1320	8.87	3.431 679	6.86	600

Effective Rate is 9.11 %

Annual Percentage Rate is 8.75 %

	Amount Of 1	Amount Of 1 Per Period	Sinking Fund Payment	Present Worth Of 1	Present Worth of 1 Per Period	Periodic Payment To Amortize 1	Constant Annual Percent	Total Interest	Annual Add On Rate	
	What a single $ 1 deposit grows to in the future. The deposit is made at the beginning of the first period.	What a series of $ 1 deposits grow to in the future. A deposit is made at the end of each period.	The amount to be deposited at the end of each period that grows to $ 1 in the future.	What $ 1 to be paid in the future is worth today. Value today of a single $ 1 payment tomorrow.	What $ 1 to be paid at the end of each period is worth today. Value today of a series of $ 1 payments tomorrow.	The mortgage payment to amortize a loan of $ 1. An annuity certain, payable at the end of each period, worth $ 1 today.	The annual payment, including interest and principal, to amortize completely a loan of $ 100.	The total interest paid over the term on a loan of $1. The loan is amortized by regular periodic payments.	The average annual interest rate on a loan that is completely amortized by regular periodic payments.	

$$S = (1+i)^n \qquad S\overline{n}| = \frac{(1+i)^n - 1}{i} \qquad \frac{1}{S\overline{n}|} = \frac{i}{(1+i)^n - 1} \qquad V^n = \frac{1}{(1+i)^n} \qquad A\overline{n}| = \frac{1-V^n}{i} \qquad \frac{1}{A\overline{n}|} = \frac{i}{1-V^n}$$

YEAR									**PERIODS**	
	1.007 333	1.000 000	1.000 000 0000	.992 720	.992 720	1.007 333 3333	1208.80	.007 333	8.80	1
	1.014 720	2.007 333	.498 173 3643	.985 493	1.978 213	.505 506 6977	606.61	.011 013	6.61	2
	1.022 162	3.022 054	.330 900 7958	.978 319	2.956 532	.338 234 1291	405.89	.014 702	5.88	3
	1.029 658	4.044 216	.247 266 7440	.971 197	3.927 729	.254 600 0773	305.53	.018 400	5.52	4
	1.037 208	5.073 873	.197 088 0988	.964 126	4.891 855	.204 421 4321	245.31	.022 107	5.31	5
	1.044 815	6.111 081	.163 637 1568	.957 108	5.848 963	.170 970 4902	205.17	.025 823	5.16	6
	1.052 477	7.155 896	.139 744 9024	.950 140	6.799 102	.147 078 2357	176.50	.029 548	5.07	7
	1.060 195	8.208 373	.121 826 8275	.943 223	7.742 325	.129 160 1609	155.00	.033 281	4.99	8
	1.067 969	9.268 567	.107 891 5390	.936 356	8.678 682	.115 224 8723	138.27	.037 024	4.94	9
	1.075 801	10.336 537	.096 744 2008	.929 540	9.608 221	.104 077 5341	124.90	.040 775	4.89	10
	1.083 690	11.412 338	.087 624 4628	.922 773	10.530 994	.094 957 7961	113.95	.044 536	4.86	11
	1.091 638	12.496 029	.080 025 4248	.916 055	11.447 049	.087 358 7581	104.84	.048 305	4.83	12
1	1.091 638	12.496 029	.080 025 4248	.916 055	11.447 049	.087 358 7581	104.84	.048 305	4.83	12
2	1.191 673	26.137 163	.038 259 7000	.839 157	21.933 175	.045 593 0333	54.72	.094 233	4.71	24
3	1.300 874	41.028 337	.024 373 3985	.768 714	31.539 044	.031 706 7319	38.05	.141 442	4.71	36
4	1.420 083	57.284 101	.017 456 8506	.704 184	40.338 547	.024 790 1840	29.75	.189 929	4.75	48
5	1.550 216	75.029 504	.013 328 0902	.645 071	48.399 376	.020 661 4235	24.80	.239 685	4.79	60
6	1.692 274	94.401 052	.010 593 1023	.590 921	55.783 538	.017 926 4356	21.52	.290 703	4.85	72
7	1.847 350	115.547 761	.008 654 4299	.541 316	62.547 837	.015 987 7632	19.19	.342 972	4.90	84
8	2.016 637	138.632 303	.007 213 3260	.495 875	68.744 306	.014 546 6594	17.46	.396 479	4.96	96
9	2.201 437	163.832 255	.006 103 8041	.454 249	74.420 612	.013 437 1375	16.13	.451 211	5.01	108
10	2.403 171	191.341 469	.005 226 2586	.416 117	79.620 421	.012 559 5919	15.08	.507 151	5.07	120
11	2.623 391	221.371 560	.004 517 2921	.381 186	84.383 732	.011 850 6254	14.23	.564 283	5.13	132
12	2.863 793	254.153 535	.003 934 6295	.349 187	88.747 186	.011 267 9629	13.53	.622 587	5.19	144
13	3.126 224	289.939 569	.003 448 9946	.319 875	92.744 351	.010 782 3279	12.94	.682 043	5.25	156
14	3.412 703	329.004 947	.003 039 4680	.293 023	96.405 973	.010 372 8013	12.45	.742 631	5.30	168
15	3.725 435	371.650 181	.002 690 7023	.268 425	99.760 220	.010 024 0356	12.03	.804 326	5.36	180
16	4.066 824	418.203 319	.002 391 1814	.245 892	102.832 895	.009 724 5147	11.67	.867 107	5.42	192
17	4.439 498	469.022 473	.002 132 0940	.225 251	105.647 634	.009 465 4273	11.36	.930 947	5.48	204
18	4.846 323	524.498 569	.001 906 5829	.206 342	108.226 089	.009 239 9162	11.09	.995 822	5.53	216
19	5.290 428	585.058 358	.001 709 2312	.189 021	110.588 097	.009 042 5645	10.86	1.061 705	5.59	228
20	5.775 230	651.167 697	.001 535 7027	.173 153	112.751 825	.008 869 0360	10.65	1.128 569	5.64	240
21	6.304 458	723.335 133	.001 382 4850	.158 618	114.733 919	.008 715 8184	10.46	1.196 386	5.70	252
22	6.882 183	802.115 817	.001 246 7028	.145 303	116.549 626	.008 580 0361	10.30	1.265 130	5.75	264
23	7.512 849	888.115 768	.001 125 9793	.133 105	118.212 914	.008 459 3127	10.16	1.334 770	5.80	276
24	8.201 308	981.996 544	.001 018 3335	.121 932	119.736 577	.008 351 6669	10.03	1.405 280	5.86	288
25	8.952 856	1084.480 324	.000 922 1006	.111 696	121.132 336	.008 255 4340	9.91	1.476 630	5.91	300
26	9.773 273	1196.355 465	.000 835 8720	.102 320	122.410 928	.008 169 2053	9.81	1.548 792	5.96	312
27	10.668 872	1318.482 569	.000 758 4476	.093 731	123.582 188	.008 091 7810	9.72	1.621 737	6.01	324
28	11.646 541	1451.801 101	.000 688 7996	.085 862	124.655 127	.008 022 1329	9.63	1.695 437	6.06	336
29	12.713 802	1597.336 616	.000 626 0421	.078 655	125.637 998	.007 959 3755	9.56	1.769 863	6.10	348
30	13.878 863	1756.208 648	.000 569 4084	.072 052	126.538 362	.007 902 7418	9.49	1.844 987	6.15	360
31	15.150 688	1929.639 323	.000 518 2316	.066 004	127.363 145	.007 851 5649	9.43	1.920 782	6.20	372
32	16.539 060	2118.962 759	.000 471 9290	.060 463	128.118 692	.007 805 2623	9.37	1.997 221	6.24	384
33	18.054 659	2325.635 329	.000 429 9900	.055 387	128.810 814	.007 763 3234	9.32	2.074 276	6.29	396
34	19.709 144	2551.246 866	.000 391 9652	.050 738	129.444 836	.007 725 2985	9.28	2.151 922	6.33	408
35	21.515 241	2797.532 890	.000 357 4578	.046 479	130.025 635	.007 690 7912	9.23	2.230 132	6.37	420
36	23.486 845	3066.387 960	.000 326 1166	.042 577	130.557 678	.007 659 4499	9.20	2.308 882	6.41	432
37	25.639 122	3359.880 248	.000 297 6297	.039 003	131.045 060	.007 630 9630	9.16	2.388 148	6.45	444
38	27.988 628	3680.267 448	.000 271 7194	.035 729	131.491 528	.007 605 0527	9.13	2.467 904	6.49	456
39	30.553 437	4030.014 145	.000 248 1381	.032 730	131.900 517	.007 581 4714	9.10	2.548 129	6.53	468
40	33.353 279	4411.810 769	.000 226 6643	.029 982	132.275 174	.007 559 9976	9.08	2.628 799	6.57	480
41	36.409 692	4828.594 298	.000 207 0996	.027 465	132.618 380	.007 540 4329	9.05	2.709 893	6.61	492
42	39.746 186	5283.570 846	.000 189 2659	.025 160	132.932 775	.007 522 5993	9.03	2.791 390	6.65	504
43	43.388 429	5780.240 327	.000 173 0032	.023 048	133.220 779	.007 506 3365	9.01	2.873 270	6.68	516
44	47.364 438	6322.423 379	.000 158 1672	.021 113	133.484 606	.007 491 5005	8.99	2.955 512	6.72	528
45	51.704 799	6914.290 754	.000 144 6280	.019 341	133.726 287	.007 477 9613	8.98	3.038 099	6.75	540
46	56.442 900	7560.395 401	.000 132 2682	.017 717	133.947 679	.007 465 6015	8.96	3.121 012	6.78	552
47	61.615 188	8265.707 491	.000 120 9818	.016 230	134.150 487	.007 454 3151	8.95	3.204 234	6.82	564
48	67.261 453	9035.652 648	.000 110 6727	.014 867	134.336 270	.007 444 0060	8.94	3.287 747	6.85	576
49	73.425 127	9876.153 687	.000 101 2540	.013 619	134.506 457	.007 434 5873	8.93	3.371 537	6.88	588
50	80.153 625	10793.676 177	.000 092 6468	.012 476	134.662 358	.007 425 9802	8.92	3.455 588	6.91	600

	Amount Of 1	Amount Of 1 Per Period	Sinking Fund Payment	Present Worth Of 1	Present Worth of 1 Per Period	Periodic Payment To Amortize 1	Constant Annual Percent	Total Interest	Annual Add On Rate	
	What a single $ 1 deposit grows to in the future. The deposit is made at the beginning of the first period.	What a series of $ 1 deposits grow to in the future. A deposit is made at the end of each period.	The amount to be deposited at the end of each period that grows to $ 1 in the future.	What $ 1 to be paid in the future is worth today. Value today of a single $ 1 payment tomorrow.	What $ 1 to be paid at the end of each period is worth today. Value today of a series of $ 1 payments tomorrow.	The mortgage payment to amortize a loan of $ 1. An annuity certain, payable at the end of each period, worth $ 1 today.	The annual payment, including interest and principal, to amortize completely a loan of $ 100.	The total interest paid over the term on a loan of $1. The loan is amortized by regular periodic payments.	The average annual interest rate on a loan that is completely amortized by regular periodic payments.	
	$S = (1+i)^n$	$S\overline{n}| = \dfrac{(1+i)^n - 1}{i}$	$\dfrac{1}{S\overline{n}|} = \dfrac{i}{(1+i)^n - 1}$	$V^n = \dfrac{1}{(1+i)^n}$	$A\overline{n}| = \dfrac{1 - V^n}{i}$	$\dfrac{1}{A\overline{n}|} = \dfrac{i}{1 - V^n}$				

YEAR										PERIODS
	1.007 375	1.000 000	1.000 000 0000	.992 679	.992 679	1.007 375 0000	1208.85	.007 375	8.85	1
	1.014 804	2.007 375	.498 163 0238	.985 412	1.978 091	.505 538 0238	606.65	.011 076	6.65	2
	1.022 289	3.022 179	.330 887 0423	.978 197	2.956 288	.338 262 0423	405.92	.014 786	5.91	3
	1.029 828	4.044 468	.247 251 3094	.971 036	3.927 324	.254 626 3094	305.56	.018 505	5.55	4
	1.037 423	5.074 296	.197 071 6759	.963 927	4.891 251	.204 446 6759	245.34	.022 233	5.34	5
	1.045 074	6.111 719	.163 620 0920	.956 870	5.848 121	.170 995 0920	205.20	.025 971	5.19	6
	1.052 781	7.156 793	.139 727 3935	.949 865	6.797 986	.147 102 3935	176.53	.029 717	5.09	7
	1.060 546	8.209 574	.121 808 9983	.942 911	7.740 897	.129 183 9983	155.03	.033 472	5.02	8
	1.068 367	9.270 120	.107 873 4719	.936 008	8.676 905	.115 248 4719	138.30	.037 236	4.96	9
	1.076 246	10.338 487	.096 725 9535	.929 155	9.606 060	.104 100 9535	124.93	.041 010	4.92	10
	1.084 184	11.414 733	.087 606 0774	.922 353	10.528 413	.094 981 0774	113.98	.044 792	4.89	11
	1.092 180	12.498 917	.080 006 9327	.915 600	11.444 013	.087 381 9327	104.86	.048 583	4.86	12
1	1.092 180	12.498 917	.080 006 9327	.915 600	11.444 013	.087 381 9327	104.86	.048 583	4.86	12
2	1.192 856	26.149 978	.038 240 9503	.838 324	21.922 156	.045 615 9503	54.74	.094 783	4.74	24
3	1.302 813	41.059 387	.024 354 9667	.767 570	31.515 949	.031 729 9667	38.08	.142 279	4.74	36
4	1.422 906	57.343 138	.017 438 8782	.702 787	40.300 028	.024 813 8782	29.78	.191 066	4.78	48
5	1.554 068	75.127 917	.013 310 6312	.643 472	48.342 736	.020 685 6312	24.83	.241 138	4.82	60
6	1.697 322	94.552 089	.010 576 1809	.589 164	55.706 641	.017 951 1809	21.55	.292 485	4.87	72
7	1.853 780	115.766 771	.008 638 0573	.539 438	62.449 037	.016 013 0573	19.22	.345 097	4.93	84
8	2.024 660	138.937 012	.007 197 5061	.493 910	68.622 376	.014 572 5061	17.49	.398 961	4.99	96
9	2.211 293	164.243 075	.006 088 5368	.452 224	74.274 689	.013 463 5368	16.16	.454 062	5.05	108
10	2.415 129	191.881 839	.005 211 5406	.414 057	79.449 948	.012 586 5406	15.11	.510 385	5.10	120
11	2.637 754	222.068 330	.004 503 1185	.379 110	84.188 418	.011 878 1185	14.26	.567 912	5.16	132
12	2.880 901	255.037 397	.003 920 9936	.347 114	88.526 962	.011 295 9936	13.56	.626 623	5.22	144
13	3.146 461	291.045 536	.003 435 8885	.317 817	92.499 336	.010 810 8885	12.98	.686 499	5.28	156
14	3.436 500	330.372 889	.003 026 8828	.290 994	96.136 442	.010 401 8828	12.49	.747 516	5.34	168
15	3.753 275	373.325 417	.002 678 6282	.266 434	99.466 578	.010 053 6282	12.07	.809 653	5.40	180
16	4.099 250	420.237 289	.002 379 6080	.243 947	102.515 652	.009 754 6080	11.71	.872 885	5.46	192
17	4.477 117	471.473 474	.002 121 0101	.223 358	105.307 386	.009 496 0101	11.40	.937 186	5.51	204
18	4.889 815	527.432 585	.001 895 9769	.204 507	107.863 498	.009 270 9769	11.13	1.002 531	5.57	216
19	5.340 556	588.549 980	.001 699 0910	.187 246	110.203 876	.009 074 0910	10.89	1.068 893	5.63	228
20	5.832 846	655.301 147	.001 526 0159	.171 443	112.346 726	.008 901 0159	10.69	1.136 244	5.68	240
21	6.370 515	728.205 404	.001 373 2389	.156 973	114.308 721	.008 748 2389	10.50	1.204 556	5.74	252
22	6.957 746	807.829 939	.001 237 8843	.143 725	116.105 124	.008 612 8843	10.34	1.273 801	5.79	264
23	7.599 107	894.794 226	.001 117 5754	.131 594	117.749 912	.008 492 5754	10.20	1.343 951	5.84	276
24	8.299 589	989.774 837	.001 010 3308	.120 488	119.255 880	.008 385 3308	10.07	1.414 975	5.90	288
25	9.064 642	1093.510 716	.000 914 4858	.110 319	120.634 745	.008 289 4858	9.95	1.486 846	5.95	300
26	9.900 216	1206.808 916	.000 828 6316	.101 008	121.897 234	.008 203 6316	9.85	1.559 533	6.00	312
27	10.812 813	1330.550 890	.000 751 5684	.092 483	123.053 170	.008 126 5684	9.76	1.633 008	6.05	324
28	11.809 533	1465.699 339	.000 682 2682	.084 677	124.111 545	.008 057 2682	9.67	1.707 242	6.10	336
29	12.898 130	1613.305 705	.000 619 8453	.077 531	125.080 594	.007 994 8453	9.60	1.782 206	6.15	348
30	14.087 073	1774.518 354	.000 563 5332	.070 987	125.967 855	.007 938 5332	9.53	1.857 872	6.19	360
31	15.385 612	1950.591 507	.000 512 6650	.064 996	126.780 232	.007 887 6650	9.47	1.934 211	6.24	372
32	16.803 851	2142.894 996	.000 466 6584	.059 510	127.524 045	.007 841 6584	9.41	2.011 197	6.28	384
33	18.352 821	2352.924 928	.000 425 0029	.054 488	128.205 080	.007 800 0029	9.37	2.088 801	6.33	396
34	20.044 575	2582.315 316	.000 387 2494	.049 889	128.828 636	.007 762 2494	9.32	2.166 998	6.37	408
35	21.892 275	2832.850 798	.000 353 0013	.045 678	129.399 564	.007 728 0013	9.28	2.245 761	6.42	420
36	23.910 294	3106.480 519	.000 321 9077	.041 823	129.922 306	.007 696 9077	9.24	2.325 064	6.46	432
37	26.114 333	3405.333 293	.000 293 6570	.038 293	130.400 929	.007 668 6570	9.21	2.404 884	6.50	444
38	28.521 540	3731.734 171	.000 267 9719	.035 061	130.839 156	.007 642 9719	9.18	2.485 195	6.54	456
39	31.150 641	4088.222 522	.000 244 6051	.032 102	131.240 398	.007 619 6051	9.15	2.565 975	6.58	468
40	34.022 092	4477.571 795	.000 223 3353	.029 393	131.607 774	.007 598 3353	9.12	2.647 201	6.62	480
41	37.158 232	4902.811 094	.000 203 9646	.026 912	131.944 144	.007 578 9646	9.10	2.728 851	6.66	492
42	40.583 459	5367.248 745	.000 186 3152	.024 641	132.252 125	.007 561 3152	9.08	2.810 903	6.69	504
43	44.324 423	5874.498 031	.000 170 2273	.022 561	132.534 112	.007 545 2273	9.06	2.893 337	6.73	516
44	48.410 227	6428.505 308	.000 155 5572	.020 657	132.792 299	.007 530 5572	9.04	2.976 134	6.76	528
45	52.872 658	7033.580 707	.000 142 1751	.018 913	133.028 696	.007 517 1751	9.03	3.059 275	6.80	540
46	57.746 433	7694.431 659	.000 129 9641	.017 317	133.245 141	.007 504 9641	9.01	3.142 740	6.83	552
47	63.069 472	8416.199 531	.000 118 8185	.015 856	133.443 318	.007 493 8185	9.00	3.226 514	6.86	564
48	68.883 185	9204.499 612	.000 108 6425	.014 517	133.624 769	.007 483 6425	8.99	3.310 578	6.90	576
49	75.232 803	10065.464 810	.000 099 3496	.013 292	133.790 905	.007 474 3496	8.97	3.394 918	6.93	588
50	82.167 726	11005.793 359	.000 090 8612	.012 170	133.943 020	.007 465 8612	8.96	3.479 517	6.96	600

Effective Rate is 9.22 %

Annual Percentage Rate is 8.85 %

MONTHLY COMPOUND INTEREST AND ANNUITY

	Amount Of 1	Amount Of 1 Per Period	Sinking Fund Payment	Present Worth Of 1	Present Worth of 1 Per Period	Periodic Payment To Amortize 1	Constant Annual Percent	Total Interest	Annual Add On Rate	
	What a single $ 1 deposit grows to in the future. The deposit is made at the beginning of the first period.	What a series of $ 1 deposits grow to in the future. A deposit is made at the end of each period.	The amount to be deposited at the end of each period that grows to $ 1 in the future.	What $ 1 to be paid in the future is worth today. Value today of a single $ 1 payment tomorrow.	What $ 1 to be paid at the end of each period is worth today. Value today of a series of $ 1 payments tomorrow.	The mortgage payment to amortize a loan of $ 1. An annuity certain, payable at the end of each period, worth $ 1 today.	The annual payment, including interest and principal, to amortize completely a loan of $ 100.	The total interest paid over the term on a loan of $1. The loan is amortized by regular periodic payments.	The average annual interest rate on a loan that is completely amortized by regular periodic payments.	

$$S = (1+i)^n \qquad S\overline{n}| = \frac{(1+i)^n - 1}{i} \qquad \frac{1}{S\overline{n}|} = \frac{i}{(1+i)^n - 1} \qquad V^n = \frac{1}{(1+i)^n} \qquad A\overline{n}| = \frac{1-V^n}{i} \qquad \frac{1}{A\overline{n}|} = \frac{i}{1-V^n}$$

YEAR										PERIODS
	1.007 396	1.000 000	1.000 000 0000	.992 658	.992 658	1.007 395 8333	1208.88	.007 396	8.88	1
	1.014 846	2.007 396	.498 157 8538	.985 371	1.978 029	.505 553 6871	606.67	.011 107	6.66	2
	1.022 352	3.022 242	.330 880 1659	.978 137	2.956 166	.338 275 9992	405.94	.014 828	5.93	3
	1.029 913	4.044 594	.247 243 5926	.970 956	3.927 122	.254 639 4259	305.57	.018 558	5.57	4
	1.037 530	5.074 507	.197 063 4650	.963 827	4.890 949	.204 459 2983	245.36	.022 296	5.35	5
	1.045 204	6.112 038	.163 611 5602	.956 751	5.847 700	.171 007 3935	205.21	.026 044	5.21	6
	1.052 934	7.157 241	.139 718 6398	.949 727	6.797 428	.147 114 4731	176.54	.029 801	5.11	7
	1.060 721	8.210 175	.121 800 0845	.942 755	7.740 183	.129 195 9179	155.04	.033 567	5.04	8
	1.068 566	9.270 896	.107 864 4393	.935 834	8.676 016	.115 260 2726	138.32	.037 342	4.98	9
	1.076 469	10.339 462	.096 716 8310	.928 963	9.604 979	.104 112 6643	124.94	.041 127	4.94	10
	1.084 430	11.415 931	.087 596 8858	.922 143	10.527 123	.094 992 7191	114.00	.044 920	4.90	11
	1.092 451	12.500 361	.079 997 6879	.915 373	11.442 496	.087 393 5212	104.88	.048 722	4.87	12
1	1.092 451	12.500 361	.079 997 6879	.915 373	11.442 496	.087 393 5212	104.88	.048 722	4.87	12
2	1.193 448	26.156 388	.038 231 5780	.837 908	21.916 650	.045 627 4113	54.76	.095 058	4.75	24
3	1.303 783	41.074 923	.024 345 7547	.766 999	31.504 410	.031 741 5880	38.09	.142 697	4.76	36
4	1.424 319	57.372 685	.017 429 8971	.702 090	40.280 789	.024 825 7305	29.80	.191 635	4.79	48
5	1.555 998	75.177 185	.013 301 9080	.642 674	48.314 450	.020 697 7414	24.84	.241 864	4.84	60
6	1.699 851	94.627 721	.010 567 7278	.588 287	55.668 249	.017 963 5611	21.56	.293 376	4.89	72
7	1.857 003	115.876 471	.008 629 8797	.538 502	62.399 720	.016 025 7130	19.24	.346 160	4.95	84
8	2.028 684	139.089 680	.007 189 6060	.492 930	68.561 527	.014 585 4393	17.51	.400 202	5.00	96
9	2.216 237	164.448 964	.006 080 9139	.451 215	74.201 881	.013 476 7473	16.18	.455 489	5.06	108
10	2.421 130	192.152 729	.005 204 1936	.413 030	79.364 910	.012 600 0269	15.13	.512 003	5.12	120
11	2.644 964	222.417 723	.004 496 0446	.378 077	84.091 008	.011 891 8779	14.28	.569 728	5.18	132
12	2.889 493	255.480 734	.003 914 1895	.346 081	88.417 151	.011 310 0228	13.58	.628 643	5.24	144
13	3.156 628	291.600 440	.003 429 3501	.316 794	92.377 187	.010 825 1834	13.00	.688 729	5.30	156
14	3.448 460	331.059 433	.003 020 6057	.289 984	96.002 098	.010 416 4390	12.50	.749 962	5.36	168
15	3.767 273	374.166 434	.002 672 6075	.265 444	99.320 244	.010 068 4408	12.09	.812 319	5.42	180
16	4.115 559	421.258 702	.002 373 8382	.242 980	102.357 587	.009 769 6715	11.73	.875 777	5.47	192
17	4.496 045	472.704 678	.002 115 4857	.222 418	105.137 888	.009 511 3191	11.42	.940 309	5.53	204
18	4.911 707	528.906 865	.001 890 6920	.203 595	107.682 902	.009 286 5254	11.15	1.005 889	5.59	216
19	5.365 797	590.304 978	.001 694 0396	.186 366	110.012 539	.009 089 8729	10.91	1.072 491	5.64	228
20	5.861 868	657.379 382	.001 521 1916	.170 594	112.145 027	.008 917 0249	10.71	1.140 086	5.70	240
21	6.403 802	730.654 854	.001 368 6353	.156 157	114.097 049	.008 764 4686	10.52	1.208 646	5.76	252
22	6.995 837	810.704 686	.001 233 4948	.142 942	115.883 877	.008 629 3281	10.36	1.278 143	5.81	264
23	7.642 606	898.155 173	.001 113 3934	.130 845	117.519 492	.008 509 2267	10.22	1.348 547	5.86	276
24	8.349 169	993.690 509	.001 006 3496	.119 772	119.016 690	.008 402 1829	10.09	1.419 829	5.92	288
25	9.121 055	1098.058 142	.000 910 6986	.109 636	120.387 186	.008 306 5319	9.97	1.491 960	5.97	300
26	9.964 302	1212.074 625	.000 825 0317	.100 358	121.641 700	.008 220 8650	9.87	1.564 910	6.02	312
27	10.885 507	1336.631 999	.000 748 1491	.091 865	122.790 049	.008 143 9824	9.78	1.638 650	6.07	324
28	11.891 879	1472.704 775	.000 679 0227	.084 091	123.841 217	.008 074 8561	9.69	1.713 152	6.12	336
29	12.991 290	1621.357 560	.000 616 7671	.076 975	124.803 428	.008 012 6004	9.62	1.788 385	6.17	348
30	14.192 343	1783.753 382	.000 560 6156	.070 461	125.684 210	.007 956 4489	9.55	1.864 925	6.21	360
31	15.504 433	1961.162 793	.000 509 9016	.064 498	126.490 454	.007 905 7349	9.49	1.940 933	6.26	372
32	16.937 827	2154.973 809	.000 464 0428	.059 039	127.228 469	.007 859 8761	9.44	2.018 192	6.31	384
33	18.503 739	2366.702 767	.000 422 5288	.054 043	127.904 027	.007 818 3621	9.39	2.096 071	6.35	396
34	20.214 421	2598.006 192	.000 384 9106	.049 470	128.522 416	.007 780 7439	9.34	2.174 544	6.40	408
35	22.083 256	2850.693 755	.000 350 7918	.045 283	129.088 472	.007 746 6251	9.30	2.253 583	6.44	420
36	24.124 866	3126.742 432	.000 319 8217	.041 451	129.606 624	.007 715 6550	9.26	2.333 163	6.48	432
37	26.355 224	3428.311 971	.000 291 6887	.037 943	130.080 927	.007 687 5221	9.23	2.413 260	6.52	444
38	28.791 780	3757.761 792	.000 266 1159	.034 732	130.515 092	.007 661 9492	9.20	2.493 849	6.56	456
39	31.453 597	4117.669 443	.000 242 8558	.031 793	130.912 514	.007 638 6892	9.17	2.574 907	6.60	468
40	34.361 500	4510.850 768	.000 221 6877	.029 102	131.276 304	.007 617 5210	9.15	2.656 410	6.64	480
41	37.538 241	4940.381 938	.000 202 4135	.026 640	131.609 307	.007 598 2468	9.12	2.738 337	6.68	492
42	41.008 674	5409.623 517	.000 184 8557	.024 385	131.914 129	.007 580 6891	9.10	2.820 667	6.72	504
43	44.799 950	5922.246 757	.000 168 8548	.022 321	132.193 156	.007 564 6882	9.08	2.903 379	6.75	516
44	48.941 732	6482.262 316	.000 154 2671	.020 432	132.448 569	.007 550 1005	9.07	2.986 453	6.79	528
45	53.466 424	7094.051 644	.000 140 9632	.018 703	132.682 367	.007 536 7965	9.05	3.069 870	6.82	540
46	58.409 426	7762.401 255	.000 128 8261	.017 121	132.896 380	.007 524 6594	9.03	3.153 612	6.86	552
47	63.809 412	8492.540 182	.000 117 7504	.015 672	133.092 281	.007 513 5837	9.02	3.237 661	6.89	564
48	69.708 629	9290.180 881	.000 107 6405	.014 345	133.271 604	.007 503 4739	9.01	3.322 001	6.92	576
49	76.153 233	10161.563 933	.000 098 4100	.013 131	133.435 752	.007 494 2434	9.00	3.406 615	6.95	588
50	83.193 644	11113.506 861	.000 089 9806	.012 020	133.586 008	.007 485 8139	8.99	3.491 488	6.98	600

	Amount Of 1	Amount Of 1 Per Period	Sinking Fund Payment	Present Worth Of 1	Present Worth of 1 Per Period	Periodic Payment To Amortize 1	Constant Annual Percent	Total Interest	Annual Add On Rate	
	What a single $ 1 deposit grows to in the future. The deposit is made at the beginning of the first period.	What a series of $ 1 deposits grow to in the future. A deposit is made at the end of each period.	The amount to be deposited at the end of each period that grows to $ 1 in the future.	What $ 1 to be paid in the future is worth today. Value today of a single $ 1 payment tomorrow.	What $ 1 to be paid at the end of each period is worth today. Value today of a series of $ 1 payments tomorrow.	The mortgage payment to amortize a loan of $ 1. An annuity certain, payable at the end of each period, worth $ 1 today.	The annual payment, including interest and principal, to amortize completely a loan of $ 100.	The total interest paid over the term on a loan of $1. The loan is amortized by regular periodic payments.	The average annual interest rate on a loan that is completely amortized by regular periodic payments.	
	$S = (1+i)^n$	$S\overline{n} = \dfrac{(1+i)^n - 1}{i}$	$\dfrac{1}{S\overline{n}} = \dfrac{i}{(1+i)^n - 1}$	$V^n = \dfrac{1}{(1+i)^n}$	$A\overline{n} = \dfrac{1-V^n}{i}$	$\dfrac{1}{A\overline{n}} = \dfrac{i}{1-V^n}$				

YEAR										PERIODS
	1.007 417	1.000 000	1.000 000 0000	.992 638	.992 638	1.007 416 6667	1208.90	.007 417	8.90	1
	1.014 888	2.007 417	.498 152 6838	.985 330	1.977 968	.505 569 3505	606.69	.011 139	6.68	2
	1.022 415	3.022 305	.330 873 2897	.978 076	2.956 044	.338 289 9563	405.95	.014 870	5.95	3
	1.029 998	4.044 720	.247 235 8760	.970 875	3.926 919	.254 652 5426	305.59	.018 610	5.58	4
	1.037 637	5.074 719	.197 055 2544	.963 728	4.890 647	.204 471 9211	245.37	.022 360	5.37	5
	1.045 333	6.112 356	.163 603 0288	.956 633	5.847 280	.171 019 6955	205.23	.026 118	5.22	6
	1.053 086	7.157 690	.139 709 8866	.949 590	6.796 870	.147 126 5532	176.56	.029 886	5.12	7
	1.060 897	8.210 776	.121 791 1713	.942 599	7.739 469	.129 207 8380	155.05	.033 663	5.05	8
	1.068 765	9.271 672	.107 855 4073	.935 659	8.675 128	.115 272 0740	138.33	.037 449	4.99	9
	1.076 692	10.340 437	.096 707 7091	.928 771	9.603 899	.104 124 3758	124.95	.041 244	4.95	10
	1.084 677	11.417 129	.087 587 6950	.921 933	10.525 833	.095 004 3617	114.01	.045 048	4.91	11
	1.092 722	12.501 806	.079 988 4440	.915 146	11.440 979	.087 405 1106	104.89	.048 861	4.89	12
1	1.092 722	12.501 806	.079 988 4440	.915 146	11.440 979	.087 405 1106	104.89	.048 861	4.89	12
2	1.194 041	26.162 801	.038 222 2074	.837 492	21.911 145	.045 638 8741	54.77	.095 333	4.77	24
3	1.304 754	41.090 467	.024 336 5452	.766 428	31.492 877	.031 753 2118	38.11	.143 116	4.77	36
4	1.425 733	57.402 252	.017 420 9194	.701 393	40.261 562	.024 837 5861	29.81	.192 204	4.81	48
5	1.557 930	75.226 494	.013 293 1891	.641 877	48.286 189	.020 709 8557	24.86	.242 591	4.85	60
6	1.702 384	94.703 430	.010 559 2797	.587 412	55.629 895	.017 975 9463	21.58	.294 268	4.90	72
7	1.860 232	115.986 301	.008 621 7078	.537 567	62.350 458	.016 038 3745	19.25	.347 223	4.96	84
8	2.032 716	139.242 557	.007 181 7124	.491 953	68.500 756	.014 598 3791	17.52	.401 444	5.02	96
9	2.221 193	164.655 174	.006 073 2984	.450 209	74.129 176	.013 489 9651	16.19	.456 916	5.08	108
10	2.427 145	192.424 092	.005 196 8545	.412 007	79.280 004	.012 613 5211	15.14	.513 623	5.14	120
11	2.652 194	222.767 791	.004 488 9793	.377 046	83.993 763	.011 905 6459	14.29	.571 545	5.20	132
12	2.898 111	255.925 012	.003 907 3946	.345 052	88.307 541	.011 324 0612	13.59	.630 665	5.26	144
13	3.166 828	292.156 627	.003 422 8216	.315 773	92.255 278	.010 839 4882	13.01	.690 960	5.32	156
14	3.460 462	331.747 700	.003 014 3389	.288 979	95.868 034	.010 431 0056	12.52	.752 409	5.37	168
15	3.781 322	375.009 725	.002 666 5975	.264 458	99.174 234	.010 083 2642	12.10	.814 988	5.43	180
16	4.131 933	422.283 080	.002 368 0797	.242 017	102.199 890	.009 784 7464	11.75	.878 671	5.49	192
17	4.515 053	473.939 703	.002 109 9730	.221 481	104.968 806	.009 526 6397	11.44	.943 435	5.55	204
18	4.933 696	530.386 016	.001 885 4192	.202 688	107.502 770	.009 302 0859	11.17	1.009 251	5.61	216
19	5.391 157	592.066 130	.001 689 0005	.185 489	109.821 716	.009 105 6672	10.93	1.076 092	5.66	228
20	5.891 035	659.465 330	.001 516 3799	.169 749	111.943 891	.008 933 0466	10.72	1.143 931	5.72	240
21	6.437 261	733.113 900	.001 364 0445	.155 346	113.885 992	.008 780 7112	10.54	1.212 739	5.77	252
22	7.034 135	813.591 293	.001 229 1184	.142 164	115.663 297	.008 645 7850	10.38	1.282 487	5.83	264
23	7.686 353	901.530 688	.001 109 2246	.130 101	117.289 791	.008 525 8912	10.24	1.353 146	5.88	276
24	8.399 044	997.623 976	.001 002 3817	.119 061	118.778 270	.008 419 0483	10.11	1.424 686	5.94	288
25	9.177 818	1102.627 200	.000 906 9248	.108 958	120.140 446	.008 323 5915	9.99	1.497 077	5.99	300
26	10.028 802	1217.366 504	.000 821 4453	.099 713	121.387 037	.008 238 1120	9.89	1.570 291	6.04	312
27	10.958 689	1342.744 635	.000 744 7432	.091 252	122.527 849	.008 161 4099	9.80	1.644 297	6.09	324
28	11.974 798	1479.748 042	.000 675 7907	.083 509	123.571 859	.008 092 4574	9.72	1.719 066	6.14	336
29	13.085 122	1629.454 642	.000 613 7023	.076 423	124.527 280	.008 030 3689	9.64	1.794 568	6.19	348
30	14.298 397	1793.042 297	.000 557 7113	.069 938	125.401 630	.007 974 3780	9.57	1.870 776	6.24	360
31	15.624 169	1971.798 081	.000 507 1513	.064 003	126.201 788	.007 923 8180	9.51	1.947 660	6.28	372
32	17.072 869	2167.128 410	.000 461 4401	.058 572	126.934 050	.007 878 1068	9.46	2.025 193	6.33	384
33	18.655 895	2380.570 105	.000 420 0674	.053 602	127.604 176	.007 836 7341	9.41	2.103 347	6.37	396
34	20.385 702	2613.802 482	.000 382 5844	.049 054	128.217 440	.007 799 2510	9.36	2.182 094	6.42	408
35	22.275 899	2868.660 568	.000 348 5947	.044 892	128.778 665	.007 765 2614	9.32	2.261 410	6.46	420
36	24.341 359	3147.149 536	.000 317 7479	.041 082	129.292 269	.007 734 4145	9.29	2.341 267	6.50	432
37	26.598 332	3451.460 483	.000 289 7324	.037 596	129.762 291	.007 706 3991	9.25	2.421 641	6.54	444
38	29.064 575	3783.987 665	.000 264 2715	.034 406	130.192 430	.007 680 9381	9.22	2.502 508	6.59	456
39	31.759 493	4147.347 342	.000 241 1180	.031 487	130.586 070	.007 657 7846	9.19	2.583 843	6.63	468
40	34.704 288	4544.398 356	.000 220 0511	.028 815	130.946 308	.007 636 7178	9.17	2.665 625	6.66	480
41	37.922 129	4978.264 626	.000 200 8732	.026 370	131.275 978	.007 617 5399	9.15	2.747 830	6.70	492
42	41.438 335	5452.359 725	.000 183 4068	.024 132	131.577 675	.007 600 0735	9.13	2.830 437	6.74	504
43	45.280 569	5970.413 741	.000 167 4926	.022 085	131.853 771	.007 584 1592	9.11	2.913 426	6.78	516
44	49.479 061	6536.502 620	.000 152 9870	.020 211	132.106 440	.007 569 6537	9.09	2.996 777	6.81	528
45	54.066 845	7155.080 238	.000 139 7608	.018 496	132.337 669	.007 556 4275	9.07	3.080 471	6.85	540
46	59.080 016	7831.013 440	.000 127 6974	.016 926	132.549 277	.007 544 3641	9.06	3.164 489	6.88	552
47	64.558 017	8569.620 337	.000 116 6913	.015 490	132.742 929	.007 533 3580	9.05	3.248 814	6.91	564
48	70.543 948	9371.712 140	.000 106 6472	.014 176	132.920 149	.007 523 3139	9.03	3.333 429	6.94	576
49	77.084 905	10258.638 889	.000 097 4788	.012 973	133.082 331	.007 514 1455	9.02	3.418 318	6.98	588
50	84.232 351	11222.339 410	.000 089 1080	.011 872	133.230 752	.007 505 7746	9.01	3.503 465	7.01	600

MONTHLY COMPOUND INTEREST AND ANNUITY

8.95 % M

	Amount Of 1	Amount Of 1 Per Period	Sinking Fund Payment	Present Worth Of 1	Present Worth of 1 Per Period	Periodic Payment To Amortize 1	Constant Annual Percent	Total Interest	Annual Add On Rate	

| | What a single $1 deposit grows to in the future. The deposit is made at the beginning of the first period. | What a series of $1 deposits grow to in the future. A deposit is made at the end of each period. | The amount to be deposited at the end of each period that grows to $1 in the future. | What $1 to be paid in the future is worth today. Value today of a single $1 payment tomorrow. | What $1 to be paid at the end of each period is worth today. Value today of a series of $1 payments tomorrow. | The mortgage payment to amortize a loan of $1. An annuity certain, payable at the end of each period, worth $1 today. | The annual payment, including interest and principal, to amortize completely a loan of $100. | The total interest paid over the term on a loan of $1. The loan is amortized by regular periodic payments. | The average annual interest rate on a loan that is completely amortized by regular periodic payments. | |

$$S = (1+i)^n \qquad S\overline{n}| = \frac{(1+i)^n - 1}{i} \qquad \frac{1}{S\overline{n}|} = \frac{i}{(1+i)^n - 1} \qquad V^n = \frac{1}{(1+i)^n} \qquad A\overline{n}| = \frac{1-V^n}{i} \qquad \frac{1}{A\overline{n}|} = \frac{i}{1-V^n}$$

YEAR ... **PERIODS**

YEAR	Amount Of 1	Amount Of 1 Per Period	Sinking Fund Payment	Present Worth Of 1	Present Worth of 1 Per Period	Periodic Payment To Amortize 1	Constant Annual Percent	Total Interest	Annual Add On Rate	PERIODS
	1.007 458	1.000 000	1.000 000 0000	.992 597	.992 597	1.007 458 3333	1208.95	.007 458	8.95	1
	1.014 972	2.007 458	.498 142 3442	.985 249	1.977 845	.505 600 6775	606.73	.011 201	6.72	2
	1.022 542	3.022 431	.330 859 5377	.977 955	2.955 800	.338 317 8711	405.99	.014 954	5.98	3
	1.030 169	4.044 973	.247 220 4436	.970 715	3.926 515	.254 678 7769	305.62	.018 715	5.61	4
	1.037 852	5.075 142	.197 038 8343	.963 528	4.890 043	.204 497 1676	245.40	.022 486	5.40	5
	1.045 593	6.112 994	.163 585 9673	.956 395	5.846 439	.171 044 3006	205.26	.026 266	5.25	6
	1.053 391	7.158 587	.139 692 3816	.949 315	6.795 754	.147 150 7149	176.59	.030 055	5.15	7
	1.061 248	8.211 978	.121 773 3466	.942 287	7.738 041	.129 231 6799	155.08	.033 853	5.08	8
	1.069 163	9.273 225	.107 837 3453	.935 311	8.673 352	.115 295 6786	138.36	.037 661	5.02	9
	1.077 137	10.342 388	.096 689 4675	.928 387	9.601 739	.104 147 8008	124.98	.041 478	4.98	10
	1.085 171	11.419 525	.087 569 3158	.921 514	10.523 253	.095 027 6492	114.04	.045 304	4.94	11
	1.093 264	12.504 696	.079 969 9587	.914 692	11.437 945	.087 428 2920	104.92	.049 140	4.91	12
1	1.093 264	12.504 696	.079 969 9587	.914 692	11.437 945	.087 428 2920	104.92	.049 140	4.91	12
2	1.195 227	26.175 632	.038 203 4714	.836 661	21.900 142	.045 661 8048	54.80	.095 883	4.79	24
3	1.306 698	41.121 577	.024 318 1338	.765 288	31.469 829	.031 776 4671	38.14	.143 953	4.80	36
4	1.428 567	57.461 443	.017 402 9741	.700 002	40.223 146	.024 861 3074	29.84	.193 343	4.83	48
5	1.561 801	75.325 233	.013 275 7637	.640 287	48.229 735	.020 734 0971	24.89	.244 046	4.88	60
6	1.707 461	94.855 076	.010 542 3984	.585 665	55.553 297	.018 000 7317	21.61	.296 053	4.93	72
7	1.866 706	116.206 353	.008 605 3815	.535 703	62.252 101	.016 063 7148	19.28	.349 352	4.99	84
8	2.040 803	139.548 940	.007 165 9448	.490 003	68.379 444	.014 624 2781	17.55	.403 931	5.05	96
9	2.231 136	165.068 555	.006 058 0890	.448 202	73.984 075	.013 516 4224	16.22	.459 774	5.11	108
10	2.439 221	192.968 235	.005 182 2001	.409 967	79.110 586	.012 640 5334	15.17	.516 864	5.17	120
11	2.666 713	223.469 957	.004 474 8744	.374 993	83.799 764	.011 933 2078	14.32	.575 183	5.23	132
12	2.915 422	256.816 397	.003 893 8324	.343 003	88.088 919	.011 352 1657	13.63	.634 712	5.29	144
13	3.187 327	293.272 866	.003 409 7938	.313 743	92.012 174	.010 868 1271	13.05	.695 428	5.35	156
14	3.484 590	333.129 417	.003 001 8364	.286 978	95.600 743	.010 460 1697	12.56	.757 309	5.41	168
15	3.809 578	376.703 158	.002 654 6101	.262 496	98.883 180	.010 112 9434	12.14	.820 330	5.47	180
16	4.164 875	424.340 768	.002 356 5966	.240 103	101.885 598	.009 814 9299	11.78	.884 467	5.53	192
17	4.553 309	476.421 261	.002 098 9827	.219 621	104.631 885	.009 557 3161	11.47	.949 692	5.59	204
18	4.977 969	533.359 000	.001 874 9098	.200 885	107.143 893	.009 333 2431	11.20	1.015 981	5.64	216
19	5.442 235	595.606 990	.001 678 9595	.183 748	109.441 606	.009 137 2928	10.97	1.083 303	5.70	228
20	5.949 801	663.660 489	.001 506 7945	.168 073	111.543 306	.008 965 1279	10.76	1.151 631	5.76	240
21	6.504 705	738.060 941	.001 354 9017	.153 735	113.465 714	.008 813 2350	10.58	1.220 935	5.81	252
22	7.111 361	819.400 292	.001 220 4047	.140 620	115.224 125	.008 678 7381	10.42	1.291 187	5.87	264
23	7.774 596	908.325 692	.001 100 9267	.128 624	116.832 530	.008 559 2600	10.28	1.362 356	5.92	276
24	8.499 687	1005.544 646	.000 994 4859	.117 651	118.303 724	.008 452 8193	10.15	1.434 412	5.98	288
25	9.292 404	1111.830 648	.000 899 4176	.107 615	119.649 414	.008 357 7509	10.03	1.507 325	6.03	300
26	10.159 052	1228.029 327	.000 814 3128	.098 434	120.880 306	.008 272 6461	9.93	1.581 066	6.08	312
27	11.106 528	1355.065 182	.000 737 9719	.090 037	122.006 194	.008 196 3052	9.84	1.655 603	6.13	324
28	12.142 369	1493.948 933	.000 669 3669	.082 356	123.036 033	.008 127 7003	9.76	1.730 907	6.18	336
29	13.274 817	1645.785 564	.000 607 6126	.075 331	123.978 020	.008 065 9459	9.68	1.806 949	6.23	348
30	14.512 882	1811.783 116	.000 551 9424	.068 904	124.839 647	.008 010 2758	9.62	1.883 699	6.28	360
31	15.866 415	1993.262 294	.000 501 6901	.063 026	125.627 771	.007 960 0235	9.56	1.961 129	6.33	372
32	17.346 183	2191.666 981	.000 456 2737	.057 650	126.348 661	.007 914 6070	9.50	2.039 209	6.37	384
33	18.963 961	2408.575 720	.000 415 1831	.052 732	127.008 054	.007 873 5165	9.45	2.117 913	6.42	396
34	20.732 619	2645.714 277	.000 377 9698	.048 233	127.611 195	.007 836 3031	9.41	2.197 212	6.46	408
35	22.666 230	2904.969 368	.000 344 2377	.044 118	128.162 883	.007 802 5710	9.37	2.277 080	6.51	420
36	24.780 177	3188.403 676	.000 313 6366	.040 355	128.667 508	.007 771 9699	9.33	2.357 491	6.55	432
37	27.091 281	3498.272 255	.000 285 8554	.036 912	129.129 084	.007 744 1887	9.30	2.438 420	6.59	444
38	29.617 927	3837.040 475	.000 260 6175	.033 763	129.551 285	.007 718 9509	9.27	2.519 842	6.63	456
39	32.380 219	4207.403 638	.000 237 6763	.030 883	129.937 468	.007 696 0096	9.24	2.601 732	6.67	468
40	35.400 134	4612.308 422	.000 216 8112	.028 248	130.290 706	.007 675 1445	9.22	2.684 069	6.71	480
41	38.701 698	5054.976 322	.000 197 8249	.025 839	130.613 811	.007 656 1582	9.19	2.766 830	6.75	492
42	42.311 181	5538.929 284	.000 180 5403	.023 634	130.909 352	.007 638 8736	9.17	2.849 992	6.79	504
43	46.257 299	6068.017 727	.000 164 7985	.021 618	131.179 681	.007 623 1318	9.15	2.933 536	6.82	516
44	50.571 448	6646.451 174	.000 150 4562	.019 774	131.426 949	.007 608 7896	9.14	3.017 441	6.86	528
45	55.287 953	7278.831 748	.000 137 3847	.018 087	131.653 123	.007 595 7180	9.12	3.101 688	6.89	540
46	60.444 340	7970.190 783	.000 125 4675	.016 544	131.860 003	.007 583 8008	9.11	3.186 258	6.93	552
47	66.081 632	8726.028 857	.000 114 5997	.015 133	132.049 234	.007 572 9330	9.09	3.271 134	6.96	564
48	72.244 552	9552.359 557	.000 104 6862	.013 842	132.222 322	.007 563 0195	9.08	3.356 299	6.99	576
49	78.982 523	10455.757 319	.000 095 6411	.012 661	132.380 644	.007 553 9744	9.07	3.441 737	7.02	588
50	86.348 764	11443.409 741	.000 087 3865	.011 581	132.525 460	.007 545 7199	9.06	3.527 432	7.05	600

Effective Rate is 9.33 %   8 - 111   Annual Percentage Rate is 8.95 %

	Amount Of 1	Amount Of 1 Per Period	Sinking Fund Payment	Present Worth Of 1	Present Worth of 1 Per Period	Periodic Payment To Amortize 1	Constant Annual Percent	Total Interest	Annual Add On Rate	
	What a single $1 deposit grows to in the future. The deposit is made at the beginning of the first period.	What a series of $1 deposits grow to in the future. A deposit is made at the end of each period.	The amount to be deposited at the end of each period that grows to $1 in the future.	What $1 to be paid in the future is worth today. Value today of a single $1 payment tomorrow.	What $1 to be paid at the end of each period is worth today. Value today of a series of $1 payments tomorrow.	The mortgage payment to amortize a loan of $1. An annuity certain, payable at the end of each period, worth $1 today.	The annual payment, including interest and principal, to amortize completely a loan of $100.	The total interest paid over the term on a loan of $1. The loan is amortized by regular periodic payments.	The average annual interest rate on a loan that is completely amortized by regular periodic payments.	
	$S = (1+i)^n$	$S\overline{n}| = \dfrac{(1+i)^n - 1}{i}$	$\dfrac{1}{S\overline{n}|} = \dfrac{i}{(1+i)^n - 1}$	$V^n = \dfrac{1}{(1+i)^n}$	$A\overline{n}| = \dfrac{1 - V^n}{i}$	$\dfrac{1}{A\overline{n}|} = \dfrac{i}{1 - V}$				
YEAR										**PERIODS**
	1.007 500	1.000 000	1.000 000 0000	.992 556	.992 556	1.007 500 0000	1209.00	.007 500	9.00	1
	1.015 056	2.007 500	.498 132 0050	.985 167	1.977 723	.505 632 0050	606.76	.011 264	6.76	2
	1.022 669	3.022 556	.330 845 7866	.977 833	2.955 556	.338 345 7866	406.02	.015 037	6.01	3
	1.030 339	4.045 225	.247 205 0123	.970 554	3.926 110	.254 705 0123	305.65	.018 820	5.65	4
	1.038 067	5.075 565	.197 022 4155	.963 329	4.889 440	.204 522 4155	245.43	.022 612	5.43	5
	1.045 852	6.113 631	.163 568 9074	.956 158	5.845 598	.171 068 9074	205.29	.026 413	5.28	6
	1.053 696	7.159 484	.139 674 8786	.949 040	6.794 638	.147 174 8786	176.61	.030 224	5.18	7
	1.061 599	8.213 180	.121 755 5241	.941 975	7.736 613	.129 255 5241	155.11	.034 044	5.11	8
	1.069 561	9.274 779	.107 819 2858	.934 963	8.671 576	.115 319 2858	138.39	.037 874	5.05	9
	1.077 583	10.344 339	.096 671 2287	.928 003	9.599 580	.104 171 2287	125.01	.041 712	5.01	10
	1.085 664	11.421 922	.087 550 9398	.921 095	10.520 675	.095 050 9398	114.07	.045 560	4.97	11
	1.093 807	12.507 586	.079 951 4768	.914 238	11.434 913	.087 451 4768	104.95	.049 418	4.94	12
1	1.093 807	12.507 586	.079 951 4768	.914 238	11.434 913	.087 451 4768	104.95	.049 418	4.94	12
2	1.196 414	26.188 471	.038 184 7423	.835 831	21.889 146	.045 684 7423	54.83	.096 434	4.82	24
3	1.308 645	41.152 716	.024 299 7327	.764 149	31.446 805	.031 799 7327	38.16	.144 790	4.83	36
4	1.431 405	57.520 711	.017 385 0424	.698 614	40.184 782	.024 885 0424	29.87	.194 482	4.86	48
5	1.565 681	75.424 137	.013 258 3552	.638 700	48.173 374	.020 758 3552	24.92	.245 501	4.91	60
6	1.712 553	95.007 028	.010 525 5372	.583 924	55.476 849	.018 025 5372	21.64	.297 839	4.96	72
7	1.873 202	116.426 928	.008 589 0783	.533 845	62.153 965	.016 089 0783	19.31	.351 483	5.02	84
8	2.048 921	139.856 164	.007 150 2033	.488 062	68.258 439	.014 650 2033	17.59	.406 420	5.08	96
9	2.241 124	165.483 223	.006 042 9087	.446 205	73.839 382	.013 542 9087	16.26	.462 634	5.14	108
10	2.451 357	193.514 277	.005 167 5774	.407 937	78.941 693	.012 667 5774	15.21	.520 109	5.20	120
11	2.681 311	224.174 837	.004 460 8039	.372 952	83.606 420	.011 960 8039	14.36	.578 826	5.26	132
12	2.932 837	257.711 570	.003 880 3070	.340 967	87.871 092	.011 380 3070	13.66	.638 764	5.32	144
13	3.207 957	294.394 279	.003 396 8051	.311 725	91.770 018	.010 896 8051	13.08	.699 902	5.38	156
14	3.508 886	334.518 079	.002 989 3750	.284 991	95.334 564	.010 489 3750	12.59	.762 215	5.44	168
15	3.838 043	378.405 769	.002 642 6658	.260 549	98.593 409	.010 142 6658	12.18	.825 680	5.50	180
16	4.198 078	426.410 427	.002 345 1584	.238 204	101.572 769	.009 845 1584	11.82	.890 270	5.56	192
17	4.591 887	478.918 252	.002 088 0390	.217 775	104.296 613	.009 588 0390	11.51	.955 960	5.62	204
18	5.022 638	536.351 674	.001 864 4484	.199 099	106.786 856	.009 364 4484	11.24	1.022 721	5.68	216
19	5.493 796	599.172 747	.001 668 9678	.182 024	109.063 531	.009 168 9678	11.01	1.090 525	5.74	228
20	6.009 152	667.886 870	.001 497 2596	.166 413	111.144 954	.008 997 2596	10.80	1.159 342	5.80	240
21	6.572 851	743.046 852	.001 345 8102	.152 141	113.047 870	.008 845 8102	10.62	1.229 144	5.85	252
22	7.189 430	825.257 358	.001 211 7432	.139 093	114.787 589	.008 711 7432	10.46	1.299 900	5.91	264
23	7.863 848	915.179 777	.001 092 6815	.127 164	116.378 106	.008 592 6815	10.32	1.371 580	5.96	276
24	8.601 532	1013.537 539	.000 986 6433	.116 258	117.832 218	.008 486 6433	10.19	1.444 153	6.02	288
25	9.408 415	1121.121 937	.000 891 9636	.106 288	119.161 622	.008 391 9636	10.08	1.517 589	6.07	300
26	10.290 989	1238.798 495	.000 807 2338	.097 172	120.377 014	.008 307 2338	9.97	1.591 857	6.12	312
27	11.256 354	1367.513 924	.000 731 2540	.088 839	121.488 172	.008 231 2540	9.88	1.666 926	6.17	324
28	12.312 278	1508.303 750	.000 662 9964	.081 220	122.504 035	.008 162 9964	9.80	1.742 767	6.22	336
29	13.467 255	1662.300 631	.000 601 5759	.074 254	123.432 776	.008 101 5759	9.73	1.819 348	6.27	348
30	14.730 576	1830.743 483	.000 546 2262	.067 886	124.281 866	.008 046 2262	9.66	1.896 641	6.32	360
31	16.112 406	2014.987 436	.000 496 2810	.062 064	125.058 136	.007 996 2810	9.60	1.974 617	6.37	372
32	17.623 861	2216.514 743	.000 451 1587	.056 741	125.767 832	.007 951 1587	9.55	2.053 245	6.42	384
33	19.277 100	2436.946 701	.000 410 3496	.051 875	126.416 664	.007 910 3496	9.50	2.132 498	6.46	396
34	21.085 425	2678.056 697	.000 373 4051	.047 426	127.009 850	.007 873 4051	9.45	2.212 349	6.51	408
35	23.063 384	2941.784 474	.000 339 9297	.043 359	127.552 164	.007 839 9297	9.41	2.292 770	6.55	420
36	25.226 888	3230.251 735	.000 309 5734	.039 640	128.047 967	.007 809 5734	9.38	2.373 736	6.59	432
37	27.593 344	3545.779 215	.000 282 0255	.036 241	128.501 250	.007 782 0255	9.34	2.455 219	6.64	444
38	30.181 790	3890.905 350	.000 257 0096	.033 133	128.915 659	.007 757 0096	9.31	2.537 196	6.68	456
39	33.013 050	4268.406 696	.000 234 2795	.030 291	129.294 526	.007 734 2795	9.29	2.619 643	6.72	468
40	36.109 902	4681.320 273	.000 213 6150	.027 693	129.640 902	.007 713 6150	9.26	2.702 535	6.76	480
41	39.497 260	5132.967 991	.000 194 8191	.025 318	129.957 572	.007 694 8191	9.24	2.785 851	6.79	492
42	43.202 375	5626.983 380	.000 177 7151	.023 147	130.247 083	.007 677 7151	9.22	2.869 568	6.83	504
43	47.255 056	6167.340 821	.000 162 1444	.021 162	130.511 766	.007 662 1444	9.20	2.953 667	6.87	516
44	51.687 906	6758.387 516	.000 147 9643	.019 347	130.753 749	.007 647 9643	9.18	3.038 125	6.90	528
45	56.536 589	7404.878 469	.000 135 0461	.017 688	130.974 979	.007 635 0461	9.17	3.122 925	6.94	540
46	61.840 110	8112.014 732	.000 123 2739	.016 171	131.177 235	.007 623 2739	9.15	3.208 047	6.97	552
47	67.641 139	8885.485 254	.000 112 5431	.014 784	131.362 146	.007 612 5431	9.14	3.293 474	7.01	564
48	73.986 345	9731.512 646	.000 102 7589	.013 516	131.531 199	.007 602 7589	9.13	3.379 189	7.04	576
49	80.926 774	10656.903 244	.000 093 8359	.012 357	131.685 753	.007 593 8359	9.12	3.465 176	7.07	588
50	88.518 264	11669.101 862	.000 085 6964	.011 297	131.827 053	.007 585 6964	9.11	3.551 418	7.10	600

Effective Rate is 9.38 %

Annual Percentage Rate is 9.00 %

Amount Of 1	Amount Of 1 Per Period	Sinking Fund Payment	Present Worth Of 1	Present Worth of 1 Per Period	Periodic Payment To Amortize 1	Constant Annual Percent	Total Interest	Annual Add On Rate
What a single $ 1 deposit grows to in the future. The deposit is made at the beginning of the first period.	What a series of $ 1 deposits grow to in the future. A deposit is made at the end of each period.	The amount to be deposited at the end of each period that grows to $ 1 in the future.	What $ 1 to be paid in the future is worth today. Value today of a single $ 1 payment tomorrow.	What $ 1 to be paid at the end of each period is worth today. Value today of a series of $ 1 payments tomorrow.	The mortgage payment to amortize a loan of $ 1. An annuity certain, payable at the end of each period, worth $ 1 today.	The annual payment, including interest and principal, to amortize completely a loan of $ 100.	The total interest paid over the term on a loan of $1. The loan is amortized by regular periodic payments.	The average annual interest rate on a loan that is completely amortized by regular periodic payments.
$S = (1+i)^n$	$S\overline{n}| = \dfrac{(1+i)^n - 1}{i}$	$\dfrac{1}{S\overline{n}|} = \dfrac{i}{(1+i)^n - 1}$	$V^n = \dfrac{1}{(1+i)^n}$	$A\overline{n}| = \dfrac{1-V^n}{i}$	$\dfrac{1}{A\overline{n}|} = \dfrac{i}{1-V^n}$			

PERIODS

YEAR									
	1.007 542	1.000 000	1.000 000 0000	.992 515	.992 515	1.007 541 6667	1209.05	.007 542	9.05	1
	1.015 140	2.007 542	.498 121 6662	.985 086	1.977 600	.505 663 3329	606.80	.011 327	6.80	2
	1.022 796	3.022 682	.330 832 0362	.977 712	2.955 312	.338 373 7028	406.05	.015 121	6.05	3
	1.030 510	4.045 478	.247 189 5820	.970 394	3.925 706	.254 731 2487	305.68	.018 925	5.68	4
	1.038 281	5.075 988	.197 005 9981	.963 130	4.888 836	.204 547 6648	245.46	.022 738	5.46	5
	1.046 112	6.114 269	.163 551 8493	.955 921	5.844 757	.171 093 5159	205.32	.026 561	5.31	6
	1.054 001	7.160 381	.139 657 3775	.948 766	6.793 522	.147 199 0442	176.64	.030 393	5.21	7
	1.061 950	8.214 382	.121 737 7039	.941 664	7.735 186	.129 279 3705	155.14	.034 235	5.14	8
	1.069 959	9.276 332	.107 801 2289	.934 615	8.669 801	.115 342 8955	138.42	.038 086	5.08	9
	1.078 028	10.346 291	.096 652 9928	.927 619	9.597 421	.104 194 6595	125.04	.041 947	5.03	10
	1.086 158	11.424 319	.087 532 5668	.920 676	10.518 097	.095 074 2335	114.09	.045 817	5.00	11
	1.094 350	12.510 478	.079 932 9983	.913 785	11.431 881	.087 474 6649	104.97	.049 696	4.97	12
1	1.094 350	12.510 478	.079 932 9983	.913 785	11.431 881	.087 474 6649	104.97	.049 696	4.97	12
2	1.197 602	26.201 317	.038 166 0199	.835 002	21.878 158	.045 707 6866	54.85	.096 984	4.85	24
3	1.310 595	41.183 886	.024 281 3417	.763 012	31.423 805	.031 823 0084	38.19	.145 628	4.85	36
4	1.434 250	57.580 057	.017 367 1242	.697 229	40.146 469	.024 908 7909	29.90	.195 622	4.89	48
5	1.569 571	75.523 205	.013 240 9635	.637 117	48.117 105	.020 782 6302	24.94	.246 958	4.94	60
6	1.717 660	95.159 286	.010 508 6959	.582 188	55.400 549	.018 050 3626	21.67	.299 626	4.99	72
7	1.879 721	116.648 028	.008 572 7981	.531 994	62.056 048	.016 114 4648	19.34	.353 615	5.05	84
8	2.057 072	140.164 230	.007 134 4879	.486 128	68.137 740	.014 676 1545	17.62	.408 911	5.11	96
9	2.251 156	165.899 183	.006 027 7572	.444 216	73.695 096	.013 569 4239	16.29	.465 498	5.17	108
10	2.463 553	194.062 224	.005 152 9864	.405 918	78.773 323	.012 694 6531	15.24	.523 358	5.23	120
11	2.695 988	224.882 444	.004 446 7677	.370 921	83.413 727	.011 988 4344	14.39	.582 473	5.30	132
12	2.950 355	258.610 548	.003 866 8183	.338 942	87.654 058	.011 408 4850	13.70	.642 822	5.36	144
13	3.228 720	295.520 893	.003 383 8555	.309 720	91.528 806	.010 925 5222	13.12	.704 381	5.42	156
14	3.533 349	335.913 723	.002 976 9549	.283 018	95.069 491	.010 518 6216	12.63	.767 128	5.48	168
15	3.866 720	380.117 612	.002 630 7647	.258 617	98.304 915	.010 172 4314	12.21	.831 038	5.54	180
16	4.231 545	428.492 131	.002 333 7651	.236 320	101.261 395	.009 875 4318	11.86	.896 083	5.60	192
17	4.630 790	481.430 778	.002 077 1418	.215 946	103.962 981	.009 618 8085	11.55	.962 237	5.66	204
18	5.067 705	539.364 179	.001 854 0349	.197 328	106.431 648	.009 395 7015	11.28	1.029 472	5.72	216
19	5.545 842	602.763 588	.001 659 0252	.180 315	108.687 478	.009 200 6919	11.05	1.097 758	5.78	228
20	6.069 091	672.144 722	.001 487 7748	.164 769	110.748 821	.009 029 4415	10.84	1.167 066	5.84	240
21	6.641 709	748.071 956	.001 336 7698	.150 564	112.632 444	.008 878 4365	10.66	1.237 366	5.89	252
22	7.268 354	831.162 913	.001 203 1336	.137 583	114.353 670	.008 744 8002	10.50	1.308 627	5.95	264
23	7.954 122	922.093 490	.001 084 4887	.125 721	115.926 500	.008 626 1554	10.36	1.380 819	6.00	276
24	8.704 592	1021.603 353	.000 978 8535	.114 882	117.363 727	.008 520 5201	10.23	1.453 910	6.06	288
25	9.525 869	1130.501 957	.000 884 5628	.104 977	118.677 043	.008 426 2295	10.12	1.527 869	6.11	300
26	10.424 633	1249.675 129	.000 800 2080	.095 927	119.877 131	.008 341 8746	10.02	1.602 665	6.16	312
27	11.408 196	1380.092 272	.000 724 5892	.087 656	120.973 753	.008 266 2559	9.92	1.678 267	6.22	324
28	12.484 557	1522.814 253	.000 656 6789	.080 099	121.975 829	.008 198 3456	9.84	1.754 644	6.27	336
29	13.662 474	1679.002 033	.000 595 5919	.073 193	122.891 511	.008 137 2586	9.77	1.831 766	6.32	348
30	14.951 526	1849.926 106	.000 540 5621	.066 883	123.728 247	.008 082 2288	9.70	1.909 602	6.37	360
31	16.362 200	2036.976 841	.000 490 9236	.061 116	124.492 843	.008 032 5903	9.64	1.988 124	6.41	372
32	17.905 972	2241.675 785	.000 446 0948	.055 847	125.191 519	.007 987 7615	9.59	2.067 300	6.46	384
33	19.595 397	2465.688 044	.000 405 5663	.051 032	125.829 959	.007 947 2330	9.54	2.147 104	6.51	396
34	21.444 220	2710.835 827	.000 368 8899	.046 633	126.413 355	.007 910 5566	9.50	2.227 507	6.55	408
35	23.467 479	2979.113 268	.000 335 6704	.042 612	126.946 454	.007 877 3370	9.46	2.308 482	6.60	420
36	25.681 632	3272.702 646	.000 305 5579	.038 938	127.433 591	.007 847 2245	9.42	2.390 001	6.64	432
37	28.104 691	3593.992 138	.000 278 2421	.035 581	127.878 729	.007 819 9088	9.39	2.472 040	6.68	444
38	30.756 364	3945.595 247	.000 253 4472	.032 514	128.285 490	.007 795 1138	9.36	2.554 572	6.72	456
39	33.658 223	4330.372 058	.000 230 9270	.029 710	128.657 182	.007 772 5937	9.33	2.637 574	6.76	468
40	36.833 871	4751.452 505	.000 210 4620	.027 149	128.996 828	.007 752 1286	9.31	2.721 022	6.80	480
41	40.309 141	5212.261 830	.000 191 8553	.024 808	129.307 191	.007 733 5220	9.29	2.804 893	6.84	492
42	44.112 303	5716.548 447	.000 174 9307	.022 669	129.590 796	.007 716 5974	9.26	2.889 165	6.88	504
43	48.274 292	6268.414 432	.000 159 5300	.020 715	129.849 950	.007 701 1966	9.25	2.973 817	6.92	516
44	52.828 965	6872.348 893	.000 145 5107	.018 929	130.086 761	.007 687 1773	9.23	3.058 830	6.95	528
45	57.813 370	7533.264 481	.000 132 7446	.017 297	130.303 155	.007 674 4112	9.21	3.144 182	6.99	540
46	63.268 053	8256.537 358	.000 121 1161	.015 806	130.500 893	.007 662 7828	9.20	3.229 856	7.02	552
47	69.237 384	9048.050 924	.000 110 5210	.014 443	130.681 583	.007 652 1877	9.19	3.315 834	7.05	564
48	75.769 921	9914.243 680	.000 100 8650	.013 198	130.846 694	.007 642 5316	9.18	3.402 098	7.09	576
49	82.918 802	10862.161 595	.000 092 0627	.012 060	130.997 570	.007 633 7294	9.17	3.488 633	7.12	588
50	90.742 179	11899.515 427	.000 084 0370	.011 020	131.135 439	.007 625 7037	9.16	3.575 422	7.15	600

MONTHLY COMPOUND INTEREST AND ANNUITY

9.10 % M

	Amount Of 1	Amount Of 1 Per Period	Sinking Fund Payment	Present Worth Of 1	Present Worth of 1 Per Period	Periodic Payment To Amortize 1	Constant Annual Percent	Total Interest	Annual Add On Rate	

Descriptions:

Amount Of 1	Amount Of 1 Per Period	Sinking Fund Payment	Present Worth Of 1	Present Worth of 1 Per Period	Periodic Payment To Amortize 1	Constant Annual Percent	Total Interest	Annual Add On Rate
What a single $ 1 deposit grows to in the future. The deposit is made at the beginning of the first period.	What a series of $ 1 deposits grow to in the future. A deposit is made at the end of each period.	The amount to be deposited at the end of each period that grows to $ 1 in the future.	What $ 1 to be paid in the future is worth today. Value today of a single $ 1 payment tomorrow.	What $ 1 to be paid at the end of each period is worth today. Value today of a series of $ 1 payments tomorrow.	The mortgage payment to amortize a loan of $ 1. An annuity certain, payable at the end of each period, worth $ 1 today.	The annual payment, including interest and principal, to amortize completely a loan of $ 100.	The total interest paid over the term on a loan of $1. The loan is amortized by regular periodic payments.	The average annual interest rate on a loan that is completely amortized by regular periodic payments.

$$S = (1+i)^n \qquad S\overline{n}| = \frac{(1+i)^n - 1}{i} \qquad \frac{1}{S\overline{n}|} = \frac{i}{(1+i)^n - 1} \qquad V^n = \frac{1}{(1+i)^n} \qquad A\overline{n}| = \frac{1-V^n}{i} \qquad \frac{1}{A\overline{n}|} = \frac{i}{1-V^n}$$

YEAR ... **PERIODS**

YEAR	Amount Of 1	Amount Of 1 Per Period	Sinking Fund Payment	Present Worth Of 1	Present Worth of 1 Per Period	Periodic Payment To Amortize 1	Constant Annual Percent	Total Interest	Annual Add On Rate	PERIODS
	1.007 583	1.000 000	1.000 000 0000	.992 474	.992 474	1.007 583 3333	1209.10	.007 583	9.10	1
	1.015 224	2.007 583	.498 111 3279	.985 004	1.977 478	.505 694 6612	606.84	.011 389	6.83	2
	1.022 923	3.022 808	.330 818 2865	.977 591	2.955 069	.338 401 6199	406.09	.015 205	6.08	3
	1.030 680	4.045 730	.247 174 1528	.970 233	3.925 302	.254 757 4862	305.71	.019 030	5.71	4
	1.038 496	5.076 411	.196 989 5821	.962 931	4.888 233	.204 572 9154	245.49	.022 865	5.49	5
	1.046 371	6.114 907	.163 534 7928	.955 684	5.843 916	.171 118 1261	205.35	.026 709	5.34	6
	1.054 306	7.161 278	.139 639 8784	.948 491	6.792 407	.147 223 2118	176.67	.030 562	5.24	7
	1.062 302	8.215 584	.121 719 8859	.941 352	7.733 759	.129 303 2192	155.17	.034 426	5.16	8
	1.070 357	9.277 886	.107 783 1745	.934 267	8.668 027	.115 366 5078	138.44	.038 299	5.11	9
	1.078 474	10.348 243	.096 634 7597	.927 236	9.595 263	.104 218 0930	125.07	.042 181	5.06	10
	1.086 653	11.426 717	.087 514 1970	.920 257	10.515 520	.095 097 5303	114.12	.046 073	5.03	11
	1.094 893	12.513 370	.079 914 5232	.913 331	11.428 851	.087 497 8565	105.00	.049 974	5.00	12
1	1.094 893	12.513 370	.079 914 5232	.913 331	11.428 851	.087 497 8565	105.00	.049 974	5.00	12
2	1.198 791	26.214 172	.038 147 3044	.834 174	21.867 178	.045 730 6378	54.88	.097 535	4.88	24
3	1.312 548	41.215 085	.024 262 9610	.761 877	31.400 828	.031 846 2944	38.22	.146 467	4.88	36
4	1.437 099	57.639 480	.017 349 2196	.695 846	40.108 207	.024 932 5529	29.92	.196 763	4.92	48
5	1.573 470	75.622 437	.013 223 5887	.635 538	48.060 929	.020 806 9220	24.97	.248 415	4.97	60
6	1.722 782	95.311 851	.010 491 8747	.580 457	55.324 398	.018 075 2081	21.70	.301 415	5.02	72
7	1.886 262	116.869 654	.008 556 5411	.530 149	61.958 351	.016 139 8745	19.37	.355 749	5.08	84
8	2.065 255	140.473 143	.007 118 7985	.484 202	68.017 347	.014 702 1319	17.65	.411 405	5.14	96
9	2.261 233	166.316 438	.006 012 6348	.442 237	73.551 217	.013 595 9681	16.32	.468 365	5.20	108
10	2.475 808	194.612 083	.005 138 4271	.403 908	78.605 473	.012 721 7604	15.27	.526 611	5.27	120
11	2.710 745	225.592 789	.004 432 7658	.368 902	83.221 684	.012 016 0991	14.42	.586 125	5.33	132
12	2.967 976	259.513 348	.003 853 3663	.336 930	87.437 812	.011 436 6997	13.73	.646 885	5.39	144
13	3.249 617	296.652 733	.003 370 9448	.307 729	91.288 534	.010 954 2782	13.15	.708 867	5.45	156
14	3.557 983	337.316 387	.002 964 5758	.281 058	94.805 519	.010 547 9091	12.66	.772 049	5.51	168
15	3.895 610	381.838 740	.002 618 9066	.256 699	98.017 691	.010 202 2399	12.25	.836 403	5.58	180
16	4.265 277	430.585 955	.002 322 4167	.234 451	100.951 468	.009 905 7500	11.89	.901 904	5.64	192
17	4.670 022	483.958 942	.002 066 2910	.214 132	103.630 977	.009 649 6243	11.58	.968 523	5.70	204
18	5.113 175	542.396 656	.001 843 6692	.195 573	106.078 257	.009 427 0025	11.32	1.036 233	5.76	216
19	5.598 379	606.379 702	.001 649 1317	.178 623	108.313 435	.009 232 4651	11.08	1.105 002	5.82	228
20	6.129 627	676.434 295	.001 478 3402	.163 142	110.354 892	.009 061 6735	10.88	1.174 802	5.87	240
21	6.711 286	753.136 583	.001 327 7804	.149 003	112.219 418	.008 911 1137	10.70	1.245 601	5.93	252
22	7.348 140	837.117 385	.001 194 5756	.136 089	113.922 348	.008 777 9089	10.54	1.317 368	5.99	264
23	8.045 428	929.067 382	.001 076 3482	.124 294	115.477 688	.008 659 6815	10.40	1.390 072	6.04	276
24	8.808 883	1029.742 795	.000 971 1163	.113 522	116.898 228	.008 554 4496	10.27	1.463 681	6.10	288
25	9.644 785	1139.971 606	.000 877 2148	.103 683	118.195 651	.008 460 5482	10.16	1.538 164	6.15	300
26	10.560 008	1260.660 365	.000 793 2351	.094 697	119.380 629	.008 376 5684	10.06	1.613 489	6.21	312
27	11.562 079	1392.801 650	.000 717 9773	.086 490	120.462 905	.008 301 3107	9.97	1.689 625	6.26	324
28	12.659 240	1537.482 225	.000 650 4140	.078 994	121.451 383	.008 233 7474	9.89	1.766 539	6.31	336
29	13.860 514	1695.891 982	.000 589 6602	.072 147	122.354 190	.008 172 9935	9.81	1.844 202	6.36	348
30	15.175 781	1869.333 725	.000 534 9500	.065 894	123.178 751	.008 118 2833	9.75	1.922 582	6.41	360
31	16.615 857	2059.233 886	.000 485 6175	.060 183	123.931 850	.008 068 9508	9.69	2.001 650	6.46	372
32	18.192 586	2267.154 252	.000 441 0816	.054 967	124.619 678	.008 024 4149	9.63	2.081 375	6.50	384
33	19.918 937	2494.804 818	.000 400 8330	.050 203	125.247 892	.007 984 1663	9.59	2.161 730	6.55	396
34	21.809 105	2744.057 842	.000 364 4238	.045 852	125.821 660	.007 947 7571	9.54	2.242 685	6.60	408
35	23.878 638	3016.963 246	.000 331 4591	.041 878	126.345 701	.007 914 7925	9.50	2.324 213	6.64	420
36	26.144 555	3315.765 479	.000 301 5895	.038 249	126.824 323	.007 884 9228	9.47	2.406 287	6.68	432
37	28.625 492	3642.921 969	.000 274 5049	.034 934	127.261 464	.007 857 8383	9.43	2.488 880	6.73	444
38	31.341 852	4001.123 338	.000 249 9298	.031 906	127.660 718	.007 833 2631	9.40	2.571 968	6.77	456
39	34.315 976	4393.315 529	.000 227 6185	.029 141	128.025 370	.007 810 9519	9.38	2.655 525	6.81	468
40	37.572 324	4822.724 036	.000 207 3517	.026 615	128.358 417	.007 790 6850	9.35	2.739 529	6.85	480
41	41.137 677	5292.880 429	.000 188 9330	.024 309	128.662 600	.007 772 2664	9.33	2.823 955	6.89	492
42	45.041 356	5807.651 398	.000 172 1866	.022 202	128.940 420	.007 755 5200	9.31	2.908 782	6.93	504
43	49.315 468	6371.270 558	.000 156 9546	.020 278	129.194 161	.007 740 2879	9.29	2.993 989	6.96	516
44	53.995 164	6988.373 263	.000 143 0948	.018 520	129.425 911	.007 726 4282	9.28	3.079 554	7.00	528
45	59.118 930	7664.034 729	.000 130 4796	.016 915	129.637 575	.007 713 8129	9.26	3.165 459	7.03	540
46	64.728 906	8403.811 777	.000 118 9936	.015 449	129.830 895	.007 702 3270	9.25	3.251 684	7.07	552
47	70.871 230	9213.788 530	.000 108 5330	.014 110	130.007 460	.007 691 8663	9.24	3.338 213	7.10	564
48	77.596 417	10100.626 452	.000 099 0038	.012 887	130.168 722	.007 682 3371	9.22	3.425 026	7.14	576
49	84.959 778	11071.619 134	.000 090 3210	.011 770	130.316 008	.007 673 6544	9.21	3.512 109	7.17	588
50	93.021 871	12134.752 280	.000 082 4079	.010 750	130.450 528	.007 665 7413	9.20	3.599 445	7.20	600

Effective Rate is 9.49 %

8 - 114

Annual Percentage Rate is 9.10 %

	Amount Of 1	Amount Of 1 Per Period	Sinking Fund Payment	Present Worth Of 1	Present Worth of 1 Per Period	Periodic Payment To Amortize 1	Constant Annual Percent	Total Interest	Annual Add On Rate	
	What a single $ 1 deposit grows to in the future. The deposit is made at the beginning of the first period.	What a series of $ 1 deposits grow to in the future. A deposit is made at the end of each period.	The amount to be deposited at the end of each period that grows to $ 1 in the future.	What $ 1 to be paid in the future is worth today. Value today of a single $ 1 payment tomorrow.	What $ 1 to be paid at the end of each period is worth today. Value today of a series of $ 1 payments tomorrow.	The mortgage payment to amortize a loan of $ 1. An annuity certain, payable at the end of each period, worth $ 1 today.	The annual payment, including interest and principal, to amortize completely a loan of $ 100.	The total interest paid over the term on a loan of $1. The loan is amortized by regular periodic payments.	The average annual interest rate on a loan that is completely amortized by regular periodic payments.	
	$S = (1+i)^n$	$S\overline{n}| = \dfrac{(1+i)^n - 1}{i}$	$\dfrac{1}{S\overline{n}|} = \dfrac{i}{(1+i)^n - 1}$	$V^n = \dfrac{1}{(1+i)^n}$	$A\overline{n}| = \dfrac{1-V^n}{i}$	$\dfrac{1}{A\overline{n}|} = \dfrac{i}{1-V^n}$				

YEAR										PERIODS
	1.007 604	1.000 000	1.000 000 0000	.992 453	.992 453	1.007 604 1667	1209.13	.007 604	9.12	1
	1.015 266	2.007 604	.498 106 1589	.984 963	1.977 417	.505 710 3255	606.86	.011 421	6.85	2
	1.022 986	3.022 870	.330 811 4120	.977 530	2.954 947	.338 415 5787	406.10	.015 247	6.10	3
	1.030 765	4.045 857	.247 166 4386	.970 153	3.925 100	.254 770 6053	305.73	.019 082	5.72	4
	1.038 603	5.076 622	.196 981 3746	.962 831	4.887 931	.204 585 5413	245.51	.022 928	5.50	5
	1.046 501	6.115 226	.163 526 2651	.955 565	5.843 496	.171 130 4318	205.36	.026 783	5.36	6
	1.054 459	7.161 727	.139 631 1296	.948 354	6.791 850	.147 235 2963	176.69	.030 647	5.25	7
	1.062 477	8.216 186	.121 710 9778	.941 197	7.733 046	.129 315 1444	155.18	.034 521	5.18	8
	1.070 556	9.278 663	.107 774 1482	.934 094	8.667 140	.115 378 3149	138.46	.038 405	5.12	9
	1.078 697	10.349 219	.096 625 6442	.927 044	9.594 184	.104 229 8109	125.08	.042 298	5.08	10
	1.086 900	11.427 917	.087 505 0132	.920 048	10.514 232	.095 109 1799	114.14	.046 201	5.04	11
	1.095 165	12.514 816	.079 905 2869	.913 105	11.427 337	.087 509 4536	105.02	.050 113	5.01	12
1	1.095 165	12.514 816	.079 905 2869	.913 105	11.427 337	.087 509 4536	105.02	.050 113	5.01	12
2	1.199 386	26.220 602	.038 137 9493	.833 760	21.861 691	.045 742 1159	54.90	.097 811	4.89	24
3	1.313 525	41.230 696	.024 253 7745	.761 310	31.389 348	.031 857 9412	38.23	.146 886	4.90	36
4	1.438 526	57.669 221	.017 340 2723	.695 156	40.089 096	.024 944 4390	29.94	.197 333	4.93	48
5	1.575 423	75.672 115	.013 214 9076	.634 750	48.032 875	.020 819 0742	24.99	.249 144	4.98	60
6	1.725 348	95.388 249	.010 483 4716	.579 593	55.286 378	.018 087 6383	21.71	.302 310	5.04	72
7	1.889 540	116.980 664	.008 548 4213	.529 229	61.909 584	.016 152 5879	19.39	.356 817	5.10	84
8	2.069 358	140.627 916	.007 110 9636	.483 242	67.957 264	.014 715 1303	17.66	.412 653	5.16	96
9	2.266 288	166.525 553	.006 005 0844	.441 250	73.479 429	.013 609 2510	16.34	.469 799	5.22	108
10	2.481 959	194.887 733	.005 131 1593	.402 908	78.521 744	.012 735 3260	15.29	.528 239	5.28	120
11	2.718 154	225.948 991	.004 425 7777	.367 897	83.125 904	.012 029 9443	14.44	.587 953	5.35	132
12	2.976 826	259.966 187	.003 846 6541	.335 928	87.329 984	.011 450 8208	13.75	.648 918	5.41	144
13	3.260 115	297.220 621	.003 364 5041	.306 738	91.168 750	.010 968 6708	13.17	.711 113	5.47	156
14	3.570 363	338.020 364	.002 958 4016	.280 084	94.673 944	.010 562 5683	12.68	.774 511	5.53	168
15	3.910 136	382.702 803	.002 612 9937	.255 746	97.874 553	.010 217 1603	12.27	.839 089	5.59	180
16	4.282 243	431.637 437	.002 316 7592	.233 522	100.797 044	.009 920 9259	11.91	.904 818	5.66	192
17	4.689 762	485.228 922	.002 060 8829	.213 230	103.465 584	.009 665 0496	11.60	.971 670	5.72	204
18	5.136 062	543.920 427	.001 838 5042	.194 702	105.902 240	.009 442 6709	11.34	1.039 617	5.78	216
19	5.624 834	608.197 296	.001 644 2033	.177 783	108.127 162	.009 248 3700	11.10	1.108 628	5.83	228
20	6.160 119	678.591 056	.001 473 6416	.162 335	110.158 749	.009 077 8083	10.90	1.178 674	5.89	240
21	6.746 346	755.683 820	.001 323 3048	.148 228	112.013 800	.008 927 4714	10.72	1.249 723	5.95	252
22	7.388 360	840.113 099	.001 190 3159	.135 348	113.707 656	.008 794 4826	10.56	1.321 743	6.01	264
23	8.091 471	932.577 068	.001 072 2974	.123 587	115.254 323	.008 676 4641	10.42	1.394 704	6.06	276
24	8.861 494	1033.840 349	.000 967 2673	.112 848	116.666 593	.008 571 4340	10.29	1.468 573	6.12	288
25	9.704 796	1144.740 324	.000 873 5606	.103 042	117.956 142	.008 477 7272	10.18	1.543 318	6.17	300
26	10.628 351	1266.194 067	.000 789 7684	.094 088	119.133 636	.008 393 9350	10.08	1.618 908	6.23	312
27	11.639 795	1399.205 925	.000 714 6911	.085 912	120.208 811	.008 318 8578	9.99	1.695 310	6.28	324
28	12.747 493	1544.875 824	.000 647 3012	.078 447	121.190 558	.008 251 4679	9.91	1.772 493	6.33	336
29	13.960 605	1704.408 362	.000 586 7139	.071 630	122.086 996	.008 190 8805	9.83	1.850 426	6.38	348
30	15.289 163	1879.122 775	.000 532 1632	.065 406	122.905 538	.008 136 3299	9.77	1.929 070	6.43	360
31	16.744 152	2070.463 841	.000 482 9836	.059 722	123.652 952	.008 087 1502	9.71	2.008 420	6.48	372
32	18.337 605	2280.013 831	.000 438 5938	.054 533	124.335 419	.008 042 7605	9.66	2.088 420	6.53	384
33	20.082 699	2509.505 594	.000 398 4849	.049 794	124.958 584	.008 002 6515	9.61	2.169 050	6.57	396
34	21.993 864	2760.836 884	.000 362 2090	.045 467	125.527 598	.007 966 3757	9.56	2.250 281	6.62	408
35	24.086 904	3036.086 053	.000 329 3714	.041 516	126.047 167	.007 933 5381	9.53	2.332 086	6.66	420
36	26.379 129	3337.529 240	.000 299 6228	.037 909	126.521 588	.007 903 7895	9.49	2.414 437	6.71	432
37	28.889 492	3667.659 192	.000 272 6535	.034 615	126.954 784	.007 876 8201	9.46	2.497 308	6.75	444
38	31.638 753	4029.205 880	.000 248 1879	.031 607	127.350 338	.007 852 3545	9.43	2.580 674	6.79	456
39	34.649 647	4425.159 067	.000 225 9806	.028 860	127.711 519	.007 830 1472	9.40	2.664 509	6.83	468
40	37.947 072	4858.793 040	.000 205 8124	.026 352	128.041 316	.007 809 9791	9.38	2.748 790	6.87	480
41	41.558 296	5333.693 683	.000 187 4873	.024 063	128.342 455	.007 791 6540	9.35	2.833 494	6.91	492
42	45.513 181	5853.788 126	.000 170 8296	.021 972	128.617 426	.007 774 9962	9.33	2.918 598	6.95	504
43	49.844 431	6423.377 227	.000 155 6813	.020 062	128.868 503	.007 759 8480	9.32	3.004 082	6.99	516
44	54.587 864	7047.171 132	.000 141 9009	.018 319	129.097 763	.007 746 0676	9.30	3.089 924	7.02	528
45	59.782 704	7730.328 229	.000 129 3606	.016 727	129.307 102	.007 733 5273	9.29	3.176 105	7.06	540
46	65.471 910	8478.497 800	.000 117 9454	.015 274	129.498 250	.007 722 1121	9.27	3.262 606	7.09	552
47	71.702 528	9297.866 741	.000 107 5516	.013 947	129.672 788	.007 711 7182	9.26	3.349 409	7.13	564
48	78.526 082	10195.210 723	.000 098 0853	.012 735	129.832 159	.007 702 2519	9.25	3.436 497	7.16	576
49	85.998 996	11177.950 221	.000 089 4618	.011 628	129.977 682	.007 693 6285	9.24	3.523 854	7.19	588
50	94.183 069	12254.211 877	.000 081 6046	.010 618	130.110 560	.007 685 7713	9.23	3.611 463	7.22	600

Effective Rate is 9.52 %

8 - 115

Annual Percentage Rate is 9.125%

MONTHLY COMPOUND INTEREST AND ANNUITY

9.15 % M

Amount Of 1	Amount Of 1 Per Period	Sinking Fund Payment	Present Worth Of 1	Present Worth of 1 Per Period	Periodic Payment To Amortize 1	Constant Annual Percent	Total Interest	Annual Add On Rate
What a single $ 1 deposit grows to in the future. The deposit is made at the beginning of the first period.	What a series of $ 1 deposits grow to in the future. A deposit is made at the end of each period.	The amount to be deposited at the end of each period that grows to $ 1 in the future.	What $ 1 to be paid in the future is worth today. Value today of a single $ 1 payment tomorrow.	What $ 1 to be paid at the end of each period is worth today. Value today of a series of $ 1 payments tomorrow.	The mortgage payment to amortize a loan of $ 1. An annuity certain, payable at the end of each period, worth $ 1 today.	The annual payment, including interest and principal, to amortize completely a loan of $ 100.	The total interest paid over the term on a loan of $1. The loan is amortized by regular periodic payments.	The average annual interest rate on a loan that is completely amortized by regular periodic payments.

$$S = (1+i)^n \qquad S\overline{n}| = \frac{(1+i)^n - 1}{i} \qquad \frac{1}{S\overline{n}|} = \frac{i}{(1+i)^n - 1} \qquad V^n = \frac{1}{(1+i)^n} \qquad A\overline{n}| = \frac{1-V^n}{i} \qquad \frac{1}{A\overline{n}|} = \frac{i}{1-V^n}$$

YEAR ... **PERIODS**

YEAR	Amount Of 1	Amount Of 1 Per Period	Sinking Fund Payment	Present Worth Of 1	Present Worth of 1 Per Period	Periodic Payment To Amortize 1	Constant Annual Percent	Total Interest	Annual Add On Rate	PERIODS
	1.007 625	1.000 000	1.000 000 0000	.992 433	.992 433	1.007 625 0000	1209.15	.007 625	9.15	1
	1.015 308	2.007 625	.498 100 9900	.984 923	1.977 355	.505 725 9900	606.88	.011 452	6.87	2
	1.023 050	3.022 933	.330 804 5377	.977 469	2.954 825	.338 429 5377	406.12	.015 289	6.12	3
	1.030 851	4.045 983	.247 158 7247	.970 073	3.924 897	.254 783 7247	305.75	.019 135	5.74	4
	1.038 711	5.076 834	.196 973 1675	.962 732	4.887 629	.204 598 1675	245.52	.022 991	5.52	5
	1.046 631	6.115 544	.163 517 7379	.955 447	5.843 076	.171 142 7379	205.38	.026 856	5.37	6
	1.054 612	7.162 176	.139 622 3813	.948 216	6.791 292	.147 247 3813	176.70	.030 732	5.27	7
	1.062 653	8.216 787	.121 702 0702	.941 041	7.732 333	.129 327 0702	155.20	.034 617	5.19	8
	1.070 756	9.279 440	.107 765 1226	.933 920	8.666 253	.115 390 1226	138.47	.038 511	5.13	9
	1.078 920	10.350 196	.096 616 5294	.926 853	9.593 106	.104 241 5294	125.09	.042 415	5.09	10
	1.087 147	11.429 116	.087 495 8303	.919 839	10.512 944	.095 120 8303	114.15	.046 329	5.05	11
	1.095 437	12.516 263	.079 896 0515	.912 878	11.425 823	.087 521 0515	105.03	.050 253	5.03	12
1	1.095 437	12.516 263	.079 896 0515	.912 878	11.425 823	.087 521 0515	105.03	.050 253	5.03	12
2	1.199 981	26.227 035	.038 128 5958	.833 346	21.856 206	.045 753 5958	54.91	.098 086	4.90	24
3	1.314 503	41.246 314	.024 244 5906	.760 744	31.377 874	.031 869 5906	38.25	.147 305	4.91	36
4	1.439 955	57.698 981	.017 331 3285	.694 466	40.069 997	.024 956 3285	29.95	.197 904	4.95	48
5	1.577 379	75.721 834	.013 206 2306	.633 963	48.004 845	.020 831 2306	25.00	.249 874	5.00	60
6	1.727 919	95.464 724	.010 475 0735	.578 731	55.248 394	.018 100 0735	21.73	.303 205	5.05	72
7	1.892 825	117.091 807	.008 540 3072	.528 311	61.860 872	.016 165 3072	19.40	.357 886	5.11	84
8	2.073 470	140.782 903	.007 103 1353	.482 283	67.897 258	.014 728 1353	17.68	.413 901	5.17	96
9	2.271 354	166.734 994	.005 997 5412	.440 266	73.407 743	.013 622 5412	16.35	.471 234	5.24	108
10	2.488 124	195.163 863	.005 123 8994	.401 909	78.438 143	.012 748 8994	15.30	.529 868	5.30	120
11	2.725 582	226.305 883	.004 418 7981	.366 894	83.030 286	.012 043 7981	14.46	.589 781	5.36	132
12	2.985 702	260.419 989	.003 839 9510	.334 930	87.222 353	.011 464 9510	13.76	.650 953	5.42	144
13	3.270 647	297.789 826	.003 358 0731	.305 750	91.049 198	.010 983 0731	13.18	.713 359	5.49	156
14	3.582 787	338.726 109	.002 952 2377	.279 112	94.542 642	.010 577 2377	12.70	.776 976	5.55	168
15	3.924 715	383.569 209	.002 607 0914	.254 796	97.731 730	.010 232 0914	12.28	.841 776	5.61	180
16	4.299 276	432.691 977	.002 311 1129	.232 597	100.642 979	.009 936 1129	11.93	.907 734	5.67	192
17	4.709 584	486.502 850	.002 055 4864	.212 333	103.300 594	.009 680 4864	11.62	.974 819	5.73	204
18	5.159 050	545.449 245	.001 833 3511	.193 834	105.726 673	.009 458 3511	11.36	1.043 004	5.79	216
19	5.651 412	610.021 279	.001 639 2871	.176 947	107.941 387	.009 264 2871	11.12	1.112 257	5.85	228
20	6.190 763	680.755 841	.001 468 9554	.161 531	109.963 151	.009 093 9554	10.92	1.182 549	5.91	240
21	6.781 588	758.241 063	.001 318 8418	.147 458	111.808 776	.008 943 8418	10.74	1.253 848	5.97	252
22	7.428 799	843.121 204	.001 186 0691	.134 611	113.493 606	.008 811 0691	10.58	1.326 122	6.03	264
23	8.137 778	936.102 009	.001 068 2596	.122 884	115.031 650	.008 693 2596	10.44	1.399 340	6.08	276
24	8.914 419	1037.956 577	.000 963 4314	.112 178	116.435 697	.008 588 4314	10.31	1.473 468	6.14	288
25	9.765 180	1149.531 789	.000 869 9194	.102 405	117.717 421	.008 494 9194	10.20	1.548 476	6.19	300
26	10.697 135	1271.755 350	.000 786 3148	.093 483	118.887 478	.008 411 3148	10.10	1.624 330	6.25	312
27	11.718 032	1405.643 500	.000 711 4179	.085 339	119.955 598	.008 336 4179	10.01	1.700 999	6.30	324
28	12.836 360	1552.309 468	.000 644 2014	.077 904	120.930 661	.008 269 2014	9.93	1.778 452	6.35	336
29	14.061 417	1712.972 723	.000 583 7805	.071 117	121.820 775	.008 208 7805	9.86	1.856 656	6.40	348
30	15.403 390	1888.969 117	.000 529 3893	.064 921	122.633 341	.008 154 3893	9.79	1.935 580	6.45	360
31	16.873 435	2081.761 993	.000 480 3623	.059 265	123.375 114	.008 105 3623	9.73	2.015 195	6.50	372
32	18.483 777	2292.954 347	.000 436 1186	.054 101	124.052 263	.008 061 1186	9.68	2.095 470	6.55	384
33	20.247 804	2524.302 161	.000 396 1491	.049 388	124.670 417	.008 021 1491	9.63	2.176 375	6.60	396
34	22.180 184	2777.729 003	.000 360 0063	.045 085	125.234 716	.007 985 0063	9.59	2.257 883	6.64	408
35	24.296 983	3055.342 016	.000 327 2956	.041 157	125.749 853	.007 952 2956	9.55	2.339 964	6.69	420
36	26.615 802	3359.449 446	.000 297 6678	.037 572	126.220 109	.007 922 6678	9.51	2.422 592	6.73	432
37	29.155 921	3692.579 826	.000 270 8134	.034 298	126.649 397	.007 895 8134	9.48	2.505 741	6.77	444
38	31.938 460	4057.503 006	.000 246 4570	.031 310	127.041 284	.007 871 4570	9.45	2.589 384	6.81	456
39	34.986 555	4457.253 179	.000 224 3534	.028 582	127.399 028	.007 849 3534	9.42	2.673 497	6.86	468
40	38.325 550	4895.154 112	.000 204 2837	.026 092	127.725 606	.007 829 2837	9.40	2.758 056	6.90	480
41	41.983 207	5374.846 780	.000 186 0518	.023 819	128.023 731	.007 811 0518	9.38	2.843 037	6.93	492
42	45.989 937	5900.319 640	.000 169 4823	.021 744	128.295 884	.007 794 4823	9.36	2.928 419	6.97	504
43	50.379 056	6475.941 794	.000 154 4177	.019 850	128.544 325	.007 779 4177	9.34	3.014 180	7.01	516
44	55.187 057	7106.499 315	.000 140 7163	.018 120	128.771 123	.007 765 7163	9.32	3.100 298	7.05	528
45	60.453 917	7797.235 043	.000 128 2506	.016 542	128.978 161	.007 753 2506	9.31	3.186 755	7.08	540
46	66.223 428	8553.892 175	.000 116 9058	.015 100	129.167 161	.007 741 9058	9.30	3.273 532	7.12	552
47	72.543 560	9382.762 020	.000 106 5784	.013 785	129.339 696	.007 731 5784	9.28	3.360 610	7.15	564
48	79.466 864	10290.736 307	.000 097 1748	.012 584	129.497 199	.007 722 1748	9.27	3.447 973	7.18	576
49	87.050 904	11285.364 488	.000 088 6103	.011 488	129.640 979	.007 713 6103	9.26	3.535 603	7.22	588
50	95.358 738	12374.916 507	.000 080 8086	.010 487	129.772 234	.007 705 8086	9.25	3.623 485	7.25	600

Effective Rate is 9.54 %

Annual Percentage Rate is 9.15 %

MONTHLY COMPOUND INTEREST AND ANNUITY

	Amount Of 1	Amount Of 1 Per Period	Sinking Fund Payment	Present Worth Of 1	Present Worth of 1 Per Period	Periodic Payment To Amortize 1	Constant Annual Percent	Total Interest	Annual Add On Rate
	What a single $ 1 deposit grows to in the future. The deposit is made at the beginning of the first period.	What a series of $ 1 deposits grow to in the future. A deposit is made at the end of each period.	The amount to be deposited at the end of each period that grows to $ 1 in the future.	What $ 1 to be paid in the future is worth today. Value today of a single $ 1 payment tomorrow.	What $ 1 to be paid at the end of each period is worth today. Value today of a series of $ 1 payments tomorrow.	The mortgage payment to amortize a loan of $ 1. An annuity certain, payable at the end of each period, worth $ 1 today.	The annual payment, including interest and principal, to amortize completely a loan of $ 100.	The total interest paid over the term on a loan of $1. The loan is amortized by regular periodic payments.	The average annual interest rate on a loan that is completely amortized by regular periodic payments.

$$S = (1+i)^n \qquad S\overline{n}] = \frac{(1+i)^n - 1}{i} \qquad \frac{1}{S\overline{n}]} = \frac{i}{(1+i)^n - 1} \qquad V^n = \frac{1}{(1+i)^n} \qquad A\overline{n}] = \frac{1 - V^n}{i} \qquad \frac{1}{A\overline{n}]} = \frac{i}{1 - V^n}$$

YEAR									PERIODS
	1.007 667	1.000 000	1.000 000 0000	.992 392	.992 392	1.007 666 6667	1209.20	.007 667	9.20	1
	1.015 392	2.007 667	.498 090 6525	.984 841	1.977 233	.505 757 3192	606.91	.011 515	6.91	2
	1.023 177	3.023 059	.330 790 7896	.977 348	2.954 581	.338 457 4562	406.15	.015 372	6.15	3
	1.031 021	4.046 236	.247 143 2977	.969 912	3.924 493	.254 809 9644	305.78	.019 240	5.77	4
	1.038 926	5.077 257	.196 956 7542	.962 533	4.887 026	.204 623 4209	245.55	.023 117	5.55	5
	1.046 891	6.116 182	.163 500 6848	.955 210	5.842 236	.171 167 3514	205.41	.027 004	5.40	6
	1.054 917	7.163 073	.139 604 8861	.947 942	6.790 178	.147 271 5528	176.73	.030 901	5.30	7
	1.063 005	8.217 990	.121 684 2567	.940 730	7.730 907	.129 350 9234	155.23	.034 807	5.22	8
	1.071 154	9.280 995	.107 747 0733	.933 572	8.664 480	.115 413 7400	138.50	.038 724	5.16	9
	1.079 366	10.352 149	.096 598 3020	.926 469	9.590 949	.104 264 9687	125.12	.042 650	5.12	10
	1.087 642	11.431 515	.087 477 4667	.919 421	10.510 370	.095 144 1333	114.18	.046 585	5.08	11
	1.095 980	12.519 157	.079 877 5832	.912 425	11.422 795	.087 544 2499	105.06	.050 531	5.05	12
1	1.095 980	12.519 157	.079 877 5832	.912 425	11.422 795	.087 544 2499	105.06	.050 531	5.05	12
2	1.201 173	26.239 905	.038 109 8939	.832 520	21.845 241	.045 776 5606	54.94	.098 637	4.93	24
3	1.316 461	41.277 573	.024 226 2303	.759 612	31.354 944	.031 892 8970	38.28	.148 144	4.94	36
4	1.442 816	57.758 560	.017 313 4509	.693 089	40.031 837	.024 980 1176	29.98	.199 046	4.98	48
5	1.581 297	75.821 396	.013 188 8894	.632 392	47.948 853	.020 855 5561	25.03	.251 333	5.03	60
6	1.733 071	95.617 905	.010 458 2923	.577 011	55.172 539	.018 124 9589	21.75	.304 997	5.08	72
7	1.899 411	117.314 488	.008 524 0963	.526 479	61.763 612	.016 190 7630	19.43	.360 024	5.14	84
8	2.081 717	141.093 514	.007 087 4980	.480 373	67.777 473	.014 754 1647	17.71	.416 400	5.20	96
9	2.281 521	167.154 855	.005 982 4766	.438 304	73.264 672	.013 649 1432	16.38	.474 107	5.27	108
10	2.500 501	195.717 569	.005 109 4033	.399 920	78.271 331	.012 776 0700	15.34	.533 128	5.33	120
11	2.740 500	227.021 738	.004 404 8645	.364 897	82.839 532	.012 071 5312	14.49	.593 442	5.39	132
12	3.003 534	261.330 487	.003 826 5723	.332 941	87.007 675	.011 493 2390	13.80	.655 026	5.46	144
13	3.291 814	298.932 197	.003 345 2402	.303 784	90.810 794	.011 011 9069	13.22	.717 857	5.52	156
14	3.607 762	340.142 927	.002 939 9406	.277 180	94.280 855	.010 606 6073	12.73	.781 910	5.59	168
15	3.954 036	385.309 071	.002 595 3191	.252 906	97.447 026	.010 261 9858	12.32	.847 157	5.65	180
16	4.333 545	434.810 271	.002 299 8537	.230 758	100.335 921	.009 966 5203	11.96	.913 572	5.71	192
17	4.749 480	489.062 606	.002 044 7280	.210 549	102.971 822	.009 711 3947	11.66	.981 125	5.77	204
18	5.205 336	548.522 091	.001 823 0806	.192 111	105.376 884	.009 489 7473	11.39	1.049 785	5.83	216
19	5.704 945	613.688 510	.001 629 4912	.175 287	107.571 323	.009 296 1578	11.16	1.119 524	5.89	228
20	6.252 507	685.109 615	.001 459 6204	.159 936	109.573 585	.009 126 2871	10.96	1.190 309	5.95	240
21	6.852 624	763.385 732	.001 309 9537	.145 930	111.400 500	.008 976 6204	10.78	1.262 108	6.01	252
22	7.510 340	849.174 807	.001 177 6138	.133 150	113.067 422	.008 844 2805	10.62	1.334 890	6.07	264
23	8.231 184	943.197 934	.001 060 2228	.121 489	114.588 365	.008 726 8895	10.48	1.408 622	6.12	276
24	9.021 215	1046.245 420	.000 955 7987	.110 850	115.976 111	.008 622 4654	10.35	1.483 270	6.18	288
25	9.887 073	1159.183 425	.000 862 6762	.101 142	117.242 326	.008 529 3429	10.24	1.558 803	6.24	300
26	10.836 036	1282.961 243	.000 779 4468	.092 285	118.397 652	.008 446 1134	10.14	1.635 187	6.29	312
27	11.876 081	1418.619 280	.000 704 9108	.084 203	119.451 801	.008 371 5774	10.05	1.712 391	6.34	324
28	13.015 950	1567.297 804	.000 638 0408	.076 829	120.413 633	.008 304 7075	9.97	1.790 382	6.39	336
29	14.265 223	1730.246 522	.000 577 9523	.070 101	121.291 233	.008 244 6190	9.90	1.869 127	6.45	348
30	15.634 402	1908.835 092	.000 523 8797	.063 962	122.091 977	.008 190 5464	9.83	1.948 597	6.50	360
31	17.134 995	2104.564 629	.000 475 1577	.058 360	122.822 596	.008 141 8243	9.78	2.028 759	6.54	372
32	18.779 616	2319.080 327	.000 431 2054	.053 249	123.489 231	.008 097 8721	9.72	2.109 583	6.59	384
33	20.582 087	2554.185 284	.000 391 5143	.048 586	124.097 486	.008 058 1809	9.67	2.191 040	6.64	396
34	22.557 560	2811.855 664	.000 355 6370	.044 331	124.652 474	.008 022 3037	9.63	2.273 100	6.69	408
35	24.722 639	3094.257 299	.000 323 1793	.040 449	125.158 858	.007 989 8460	9.59	2.355 735	6.73	420
36	27.095 523	3403.763 900	.000 293 7924	.036 906	125.620 896	.007 960 4591	9.56	2.438 918	6.77	432
37	29.696 157	3742.977 007	.000 267 1670	.033 674	126.042 471	.007 933 8337	9.53	2.522 622	6.82	444
38	32.546 400	4114.747 858	.000 243 0283	.030 725	126.427 126	.007 909 6949	9.50	2.606 821	6.86	456
39	35.670 210	4522.201 350	.000 221 1312	.028 035	126.778 096	.007 887 7979	9.47	2.691 489	6.90	468
40	39.093 844	4968.762 311	.000 201 2574	.025 579	127.098 329	.007 867 9240	9.45	2.776 604	6.94	480
41	42.846 080	5458.184 284	.000 183 2111	.023 339	127.390 518	.007 849 8778	9.42	2.862 140	6.98	492
42	46.958 455	5994.581 078	.000 166 8173	.021 295	127.657 119	.007 833 4840	9.41	2.948 076	7.02	504
43	51.465 537	6582.461 344	.000 151 9189	.019 430	127.900 372	.007 818 5855	9.39	3.034 390	7.06	516
44	56.405 210	7226.766 478	.000 138 3745	.017 729	128.122 323	.007 805 0411	9.37	3.121 062	7.09	528
45	61.818 993	7932.912 150	.000 126 0571	.016 176	128.324 836	.007 792 7238	9.36	3.208 071	7.13	540
46	67.752 393	8706.833 827	.000 114 8523	.014 760	128.509 614	.007 781 5190	9.34	3.295 398	7.16	552
47	74.255 281	9555.036 663	.000 104 6568	.013 467	128.678 210	.007 771 3235	9.33	3.383 026	7.20	564
48	81.382 318	10484.650 180	.000 095 3775	.012 288	128.832 042	.007 762 0442	9.32	3.470 937	7.23	576
49	89.193 409	11503.488 192	.000 086 9302	.011 212	128.972 401	.007 753 5968	9.31	3.559 115	7.26	588
50	97.754 211	12620.114 482	.000 079 2386	.010 230	129.100 469	.007 745 9053	9.30	3.647 543	7.30	600

Amount Of 1	Amount Of 1 Per Period	Sinking Fund Payment	Present Worth Of 1	Present Worth of 1 Per Period	Periodic Payment To Amortize 1	Constant Annual Percent	Total Interest	Annual Add On Rate	
What a single $ 1 deposit grows to in the future. The deposit is made at the beginning of the first period.	What a series of $ 1 deposits grow to in the future. A deposit is made at the end of each period.	The amount to be deposited at the end of each period that grows to $ 1 in the future.	What $ 1 to be paid in the future is worth today. Value today of a single $ 1 payment tomorrow.	What $ 1 to be paid at the end of each period is worth today. Value today of a series of $ 1 payments tomorrow.	The mortgage payment to amortize a loan of $ 1. An annuity certain, payable at the end of each period, worth $ 1 today.	The annual payment, including interest and principal, to amortize completely a loan of $ 100.	The total interest paid over the term on a loan of $1. The loan is amortized by regular periodic payments.	The average annual interest rate on a loan that is completely amortized by regular periodic payments.	
$S = (1+i)^n$	$S\overline{n} = \dfrac{(1+i)^n - 1}{i}$	$\dfrac{1}{S\overline{n}} = \dfrac{i}{(1+i)^n - 1}$	$V^n = \dfrac{1}{(1+i)^n}$	$A\overline{n} = \dfrac{1-V^n}{i}$	$\dfrac{1}{A\overline{n}} = \dfrac{i}{1-V^n}$				

YEAR									PERIODS
	1.007 708	1.000 000	1.000 000 0000	.992 351	.992 351	1.007 708 3333	1209.25	.007 708	9.25 1
	1.015 476	2.007 708	.498 080 3155	.984 760	1.977 110	.505 788 6488	606.95	.011 577	6.95 2
	1.023 304	3.023 184	.330 777 0422	.977 227	2.954 337	.338 485 3756	406.19	.015 456	6.18 3
	1.031 192	4.046 488	.247 127 8717	.969 752	3.924 089	.254 836 2051	305.81	.019 345	5.80 4
	1.039 140	5.077 680	.196 940 3423	.962 334	4.886 423	.204 648 6756	245.58	.023 243	5.58 5
	1.047 150	6.116 820	.163 483 6333	.954 973	5.841 396	.171 191 9666	205.44	.027 152	5.43 6
	1.055 222	7.163 971	.139 587 3929	.947 668	6.789 063	.147 295 7263	176.76	.031 070	5.33 7
	1.063 356	8.219 193	.121 666 4455	.940 419	7.729 482	.129 374 7788	155.25	.034 998	5.25 8
	1.071 553	9.282 549	.107 729 0265	.933 225	8.662 707	.115 437 3598	138.53	.038 936	5.19 9
	1.079 813	10.354 102	.096 580 0774	.926 086	9.588 793	.104 288 4107	125.15	.042 884	5.15 10
	1.088 136	11.433 915	.087 459 1062	.919 002	10.507 796	.095 167 4395	114.21	.046 842	5.11 11
	1.096 524	12.522 052	.079 859 1184	.911 973	11.419 768	.087 567 4517	105.09	.050 809	5.08 12
1	1.096 524	12.522 052	.079 859 1184	.911 973	11.419 768	.087 567 4517	105.09	.050 809	5.08 12
2	1.202 365	26.252 784	.038 091 1989	.831 694	21.834 284	.045 799 5323	54.96	.099 189	4.96 24
3	1.318 422	41.308 863	.024 207 8802	.758 482	31.332 037	.031 916 2136	38.30	.148 984	4.97 36
4	1.445 682	57.818 217	.017 295 5870	.691 715	39.993 729	.025 003 9203	30.01	.200 188	5.00 48
5	1.585 225	75.921 123	.013 171 5650	.630 825	47.892 954	.020 879 8983	25.06	.252 794	5.06 60
6	1.738 238	95.771 396	.010 441 5310	.575 295	55.096 831	.018 149 8643	21.78	.306 790	5.11 72
7	1.906 020	117.537 700	.008 507 9068	.524 654	61.666 569	.016 216 2419	19.46	.362 164	5.17 84
8	2.089 997	141.404 978	.007 071 8868	.478 470	67.657 991	.014 780 2202	17.74	.418 901	5.24 96
9	2.291 732	167.576 024	.005 967 4408	.436 351	73.122 003	.013 675 7741	16.42	.476 984	5.30 108
10	2.512 939	196.273 209	.005 094 9389	.397 940	78.105 033	.012 803 2722	15.37	.536 393	5.36 120
11	2.755 499	227.740 365	.004 390 9651	.362 911	82.649 420	.012 099 2985	14.52	.597 107	5.43 132
12	3.021 471	262.244 861	.003 813 2301	.330 965	86.793 776	.011 521 5634	13.83	.659 105	5.49 144
13	3.313 116	300.079 874	.003 332 4461	.301 831	90.573 316	.011 040 7794	13.25	.722 362	5.56 156
14	3.632 911	341.566 880	.002 927 6843	.275 261	94.020 152	.010 636 0177	12.77	.786 851	5.62 168
15	3.983 575	387.058 383	.002 583 5896	.251 031	97.163 573	.010 291 9229	12.36	.852 546	5.68 180
16	4.368 086	436.940 915	.002 288 6390	.228 933	100.030 286	.009 996 9723	12.00	.919 419	5.75 192
17	4.789 712	491.638 316	.002 034 0156	.208 781	102.644 650	.009 742 3489	11.70	.987 439	5.81 204
18	5.252 035	551.615 338	.001 812 8575	.190 402	105.028 879	.009 521 1908	11.43	1.056 577	5.87 216
19	5.758 983	617.381 589	.001 619 7438	.173 642	107.203 230	.009 328 0771	11.20	1.126 802	5.93 228
20	6.314 864	689.495 873	.001 450 3350	.158 357	109.186 179	.009 158 6683	11.00	1.198 080	5.99 240
21	6.924 401	768.570 926	.001 301 1161	.144 417	110.994 574	.009 009 4494	10.82	1.270 381	6.05 252
22	7.592 773	855.278 631	.001 169 2096	.131 704	112.643 781	.008 877 5429	10.66	1.343 671	6.11 264
23	8.325 659	950.355 723	.001 052 2376	.120 111	114.147 812	.008 760 5709	10.52	1.417 918	6.16 276
24	9.129 286	1054.610 051	.000 948 2178	.109 538	115.519 447	.008 656 5511	10.39	1.493 087	6.22 288
25	10.010 482	1168.927 439	.000 855 4851	.099 895	116.770 341	.008 563 8184	10.28	1.569 146	6.28 300
26	10.976 736	1294.279 215	.000 772 6308	.091 102	117.911 122	.008 480 9641	10.18	1.646 061	6.33 312
27	12.036 256	1431.730 465	.000 698 4555	.083 082	118.951 483	.008 406 7888	10.09	1.723 800	6.38 324
28	13.198 045	1582.449 079	.000 631 9319	.075 769	119.900 264	.008 340 2652	10.01	1.802 329	6.44 336
29	14.471 975	1747.715 679	.000 572 1754	.069 099	120.765 526	.008 280 5088	9.94	1.881 617	6.49 348
30	15.868 870	1928.934 497	.000 518 4209	.063 016	121.554 622	.008 226 7543	9.88	1.961 632	6.54 360
31	17.400 599	2127.645 307	.000 470 0032	.057 469	122.274 255	.008 178 3365	9.82	2.042 341	6.59 372
32	19.080 177	2345.536 509	.000 426 3417	.052 410	122.930 541	.008 134 6750	9.77	2.123 715	6.64 384
33	20.921 875	2584.459 472	.000 386 9281	.047 797	123.529 056	.008 095 2614	9.72	2.205 724	6.68 396
34	22.941 341	2846.444 272	.000 351 3155	.043 589	124.074 885	.008 059 6488	9.68	2.288 337	6.73 408
35	25.155 735	3133.716 930	.000 319 1099	.039 752	124.572 666	.008 027 4432	9.64	2.371 526	6.78 420
36	27.583 871	3448.718 338	.000 289 9628	.036 253	125.026 629	.007 998 2961	9.60	2.455 264	6.82 432
37	30.246 380	3794.124 987	.000 263 5654	.033 062	125.440 630	.007 971 8987	9.57	2.539 523	6.86 444
38	33.165 886	4172.871 720	.000 239 6431	.030 151	125.818 189	.007 947 9765	9.54	2.624 277	6.91 456
39	36.367 195	4588.176 657	.000 217 9515	.027 497	126.162 511	.007 926 2848	9.52	2.709 501	6.95 468
40	39.877 508	5043.568 550	.000 198 2723	.025 077	126.476 524	.007 906 6056	9.49	2.795 171	6.99 480
41	43.726 650	5542.916 757	.000 180 4104	.022 869	126.762 895	.007 888 7438	9.47	2.881 262	7.03 492
42	47.947 328	6090.464 124	.000 164 1911	.020 856	127.024 058	.007 872 5244	9.45	2.967 752	7.07 504
43	52.575 403	6690.863 034	.000 149 4576	.019 020	127.262 231	.007 857 7909	9.43	3.054 620	7.10 516
44	57.650 198	7349.214 937	.000 136 0690	.017 346	127.479 439	.007 844 4023	9.42	3.141 844	7.14 528
45	63.214 835	8071.113 697	.000 123 8986	.015 819	127.677 526	.007 832 2320	9.40	3.229 405	7.18 540
46	69.316 593	8862.693 118	.000 112 8325	.014 427	127.858 176	.007 821 1659	9.39	3.317 284	7.21 552
47	76.007 318	9730.679 069	.000 102 7678	.013 157	128.022 924	.007 811 1011	9.38	3.405 461	7.25 564
48	83.343 859	10682.446 624	.000 093 6115	.011 998	128.173 170	.007 801 9448	9.37	3.493 920	7.28 576
49	91.388 554	11726.082 731	.000 085 2800	.010 942	128.310 189	.007 793 6133	9.36	3.582 645	7.31 588
50	100.209 757	12870.454 924	.000 077 6973	.009 979	128.435 148	.007 786 0307	9.35	3.671 618	7.34 600

Effective Rate is 9.65 %

Annual Percentage Rate is 9.25 %

MONTHLY COMPOUND INTEREST AND ANNUITY

	Amount Of 1	Amount Of 1 Per Period	Sinking Fund Payment	Present Worth Of 1	Present Worth of 1 Per Period	Periodic Payment To Amortize 1	Constant Annual Percent	Total Interest	Annual Add On Rate	
	What a single $ 1 deposit grows to in the future. The deposit is made at the beginning of the first period.	What a series of $ 1 deposits grow to in the future. A deposit is made at the end of each period.	The amount to be deposited at the end of each period that grows to $ 1 in the future.	What $ 1 to be paid in the future is worth today. Value today of a single $ 1 payment tomorrow.	What $ 1 to be paid at the end of each period is worth today. Value today of a series of $ 1 payments tomorrow.	The mortgage payment to amortize a loan of $ 1. An annuity certain, payable at the end of each period, worth $ 1 today.	The annual payment, including interest and principal, to amortize completely a loan of $ 100.	The total interest paid over the term on a loan of $1. The loan is amortized by regular periodic payments.	The average annual interest rate on a loan that is completely amortized by regular periodic payments.	
	$S = (1+i)^n$	$S\overline{n}| = \dfrac{(1+i)^n - 1}{i}$	$\dfrac{1}{S\overline{n}|} = \dfrac{i}{(1+i)^n - 1}$	$V^n = \dfrac{1}{(1+i)^n}$	$A\overline{n}| = \dfrac{1-V^n}{i}$	$\dfrac{1}{A\overline{n}|} = \dfrac{i}{1-V}$				

YEAR										PERIODS
	1.007 750	1.000 000	1.000 000 0000	.992 310	.992 310	1.007 750 0000	1209.30	.007 750	9.30	1
	1.015 560	2.007 750	.498 069 9788	.984 678	1.976 988	.505 819 9788	606.99	.011 640	6.98	2
	1.023 431	3.023 310	.330 763 2956	.977 106	2.954 094	.338 513 2956	406.22	.015 540	6.22	3
	1.031 362	4.046 741	.247 112 4469	.969 591	3.923 685	.254 862 4469	305.84	.019 450	5.83	4
	1.039 355	5.078 103	.196 923 9318	.962 135	4.885 819	.204 673 9318	245.61	.023 370	5.61	5
	1.047 410	6.117 458	.163 466 5834	.954 736	5.840 556	.171 216 5834	205.46	.027 300	5.46	6
	1.055 528	7.164 869	.139 569 9017	.947 393	6.787 949	.147 319 9017	176.79	.031 239	5.36	7
	1.063 708	8.220 396	.121 648 6365	.940 108	7.728 057	.129 398 6365	155.28	.035 189	5.28	8
	1.071 952	9.284 104	.107 710 9823	.932 878	8.660 934	.115 460 9823	138.56	.039 149	5.22	9
	1.080 259	10.356 056	.096 561 8556	.925 704	9.586 638	.104 311 8556	125.18	.043 119	5.17	10
	1.088 631	11.436 316	.087 440 7488	.918 585	10.505 223	.095 190 7488	114.23	.047 098	5.14	11
	1.097 068	12.524 947	.079 840 6569	.911 520	11.416 743	.087 590 6569	105.11	.051 088	5.11	12
1	1.097 068	12.524 947	.079 840 6569	.911 520	11.416 743	.087 590 6569	105.11	.051 088	5.11	12
2	1.203 559	26.265 670	.038 072 5108	.830 869	21.823 335	.045 822 5108	54.99	.099 740	4.99	24
3	1.320 386	41.340 182	.024 189 5404	.757 354	31.309 154	.031 939 5404	38.33	.149 823	4.99	36
4	1.448 554	57.877 952	.017 277 7365	.690 344	39.955 671	.025 027 7365	30.04	.201 331	5.03	48
5	1.589 163	76.021 016	.013 154 2573	.629 262	47.837 146	.020 904 2573	25.09	.254 255	5.09	60
6	1.743 420	95.925 196	.010 424 7897	.573 585	55.021 269	.018 174 7897	21.81	.308 585	5.14	72
7	1.912 651	117.761 443	.008 491 7438	.522 834	61.569 744	.016 241 7438	19.50	.364 306	5.20	84
8	2.098 309	141.717 298	.007 056 3016	.476 574	67.538 810	.014 806 3016	17.77	.421 405	5.27	96
9	2.301 988	167.998 508	.005 952 4338	.434 407	72.979 736	.013 702 4338	16.45	.479 863	5.33	108
10	2.525 439	196.830 791	.005 080 5059	.395 971	77.939 249	.012 830 5059	15.40	.539 661	5.40	120
11	2.770 579	228.461 776	.004 377 0998	.360 935	82.459 946	.012 127 0998	14.56	.600 777	5.46	132
12	3.039 514	263.163 128	.003 799 9244	.329 000	86.580 653	.011 549 9244	13.86	.663 189	5.53	144
13	3.334 555	301.232 883	.003 319 6907	.299 890	90.336 761	.011 069 6907	13.29	.726 872	5.59	156
14	3.658 235	342.998 006	.002 915 4688	.273 356	93.760 529	.010 665 4688	12.80	.791 799	5.66	168
15	4.013 333	388.817 200	.002 571 9027	.249 169	96.881 363	.010 321 9027	12.39	.857 942	5.72	180
16	4.402 901	439.083 987	.002 277 4686	.227 123	99.726 066	.010 027 4686	12.04	.925 274	5.78	192
17	4.830 283	494.230 088	.002 023 3491	.207 027	102.319 071	.009 773 3491	11.73	.993 763	5.85	204
18	5.299 151	554.729 129	.001 802 6816	.188 709	104.682 647	.009 552 6816	11.47	1.063 379	5.91	216
19	5.813 531	621.100 711	.001 610 0448	.172 013	106.837 095	.009 360 0448	11.24	1.134 090	5.97	228
20	6.377 840	693.914 873	.001 441 0990	.156 793	108.800 918	.009 191 0990	11.03	1.205 864	6.03	240
21	6.996 927	773.796 985	.001 292 3286	.142 920	110.590 982	.009 042 3286	10.86	1.278 667	6.09	252
22	7.676 107	861.433 120	.001 160 8562	.130 274	112.222 661	.008 910 8562	10.70	1.352 466	6.15	264
23	8.421 214	957.575 950	.001 044 3036	.118 748	113.709 970	.008 794 3036	10.56	1.427 228	6.21	276
24	9.238 647	1063.051 204	.000 940 6885	.108 241	115.065 683	.008 690 6885	10.43	1.502 918	6.26	288
25	10.135 427	1178.764 767	.000 848 3457	.098 664	116.301 442	.008 598 3457	10.32	1.579 504	6.32	300
26	11.119 256	1305.710 452	.000 765 8666	.089 934	117.427 861	.008 515 8666	10.22	1.656 950	6.37	312
27	12.198 584	1444.978 545	.000 692 0518	.081 977	118.454 616	.008 442 0518	10.14	1.735 225	6.43	324
28	13.382 680	1597.765 160	.000 625 8742	.074 723	119.390 523	.008 375 8742	10.06	1.814 294	6.48	336
29	14.681 715	1765.382 519	.000 566 4495	.068 112	120.243 621	.008 316 4495	9.98	1.894 124	6.53	348
30	16.106 844	1949.270 216	.000 513 0125	.062 085	121.021 238	.008 263 0125	9.92	1.974 685	6.58	360
31	17.670 309	2151.007 586	.000 464 8984	.056 592	121.730 051	.008 214 8984	9.86	2.055 942	6.63	372
32	19.385 536	2372.327 268	.000 421 5270	.051 585	122.376 148	.008 171 5270	9.81	2.137 866	6.68	384
33	21.267 258	2615.130 084	.000 382 3902	.047 021	122.965 079	.008 132 3902	9.76	2.220 427	6.73	396
34	23.331 636	2881.501 366	.000 347 0413	.042 860	123.501 902	.008 097 0413	9.72	2.303 593	6.78	408
35	25.596 399	3173.728 866	.000 315 0868	.039 068	123.991 226	.008 065 0868	9.68	2.387 336	6.82	420
36	28.080 999	3494.322 405	.000 286 1785	.035 611	124.437 256	.008 036 1785	9.65	2.471 629	6.87	432
37	30.806 775	3846.035 426	.000 260 0080	.032 460	124.843 820	.008 010 0080	9.62	2.556 444	6.91	444
38	33.797 137	4231.888 646	.000 236 3011	.029 588	125.214 412	.007 986 3011	9.59	2.641 753	6.95	456
39	37.077 769	4655.195 997	.000 214 8137	.026 970	125.552 214	.007 964 8137	9.56	2.727 533	6.99	468
40	40.676 846	5119.593 090	.000 195 3280	.024 584	125.860 128	.007 945 3280	9.54	2.813 757	7.03	480
41	44.625 280	5629.068 438	.000 177 6493	.022 409	126.140 797	.007 927 6493	9.52	2.900 403	7.07	492
42	48.956 982	6187.997 712	.000 161 6032	.020 426	126.396 633	.007 911 6032	9.50	2.987 448	7.11	504
43	53.709 155	6801.181 323	.000 147 0333	.018 619	126.629 832	.007 897 0333	9.48	3.074 869	7.15	516
44	58.922 614	7473.885 648	.000 133 7992	.016 971	126.842 398	.007 883 7992	9.47	3.162 646	7.19	528
45	64.642 134	8211.888 266	.000 121 7747	.015 470	127.036 157	.007 871 7747	9.45	3.250 758	7.22	540
46	70.916 839	9021.527 572	.000 110 8460	.014 101	127.212 771	.007 860 8460	9.44	3.339 187	7.26	552
47	77.800 618	9909.757 221	.000 100 9106	.012 853	127.373 759	.007 850 9106	9.43	3.427 914	7.29	564
48	85.352 595	10884.206 847	.000 091 8762	.011 716	127.520 503	.007 841 8762	9.42	3.516 921	7.33	576
49	93.637 630	11953.242 584	.000 083 6593	.010 679	127.654 262	.007 833 6593	9.41	3.606 192	7.36	588
50	102.726 879	13126.048 942	.000 076 1844	.009 735	127.776 187	.007 826 1844	9.40	3.695 711	7.39	600

Effective Rate is 9.71 %   8 - 119   Annual Percentage Rate is 9.30 %

Amount Of 1	Amount Of 1 Per Period	Sinking Fund Payment	Present Worth Of 1	Present Worth of 1 Per Period	Periodic Payment To Amortize 1	Constant Annual Percent	Total Interest	Annual Add On Rate
What a single $ 1 deposit grows to in the future. The deposit is made at the beginning of the first period.	What a series of $ 1 deposits grow to in the future. A deposit is made at the end of each period.	The amount to be deposited at the end of each period that grows to $ 1 in the future.	What $ 1 to be paid in the future is worth today. Value today of a single $ 1 payment tomorrow.	What $ 1 to be paid at the end of each period is worth today. Value today of a series of $ 1 payments tomorrow.	The mortgage payment to amortize a loan of $ 1. An annuity certain, payable at the end of each period, worth $ 1 today.	The annual payment, including interest and principal, to amortize completely a loan of $ 100.	The total interest paid over the term on a loan of $1. The loan is amortized by regular periodic payments.	The average annual interest rate on a loan that is completely amortized by regular periodic payments.
$S = (1+i)^n$	$S\overline{n} = \dfrac{(1+i)^n - 1}{i}$	$\dfrac{1}{S\overline{n}} = \dfrac{i}{(1+i)^n - 1}$	$V^n = \dfrac{1}{(1+i)^n}$	$A\overline{n} = \dfrac{1 - V^n}{i}$	$\dfrac{1}{A\overline{n}} = \dfrac{i}{1 - V^n}$			

YEAR									PERIODS
	1.007 792	1.000 000	1.000 000 0000	.992 269	.992 269	1.007 791 6667	1209.35	.007 792	9.35	1
	1.015 644	2.007 792	.498 059 6426	.984 597	1.976 865	.505 851 3093	607.03	.011 703	7.02	2
	1.023 558	3.023 436	.330 749 5498	.976 985	2.953 850	.338 541 2165	406.25	.015 624	6.25	3
	1.031 533	4.046 993	.247 097 0230	.969 431	3.923 281	.254 888 6897	305.87	.019 555	5.87	4
	1.039 570	5.078 526	.196 907 5226	.961 936	4.885 217	.204 699 1893	245.64	.023 496	5.64	5
	1.047 670	6.118 096	.163 449 5353	.954 499	5.839 716	.171 241 2019	205.49	.027 447	5.49	6
	1.055 833	7.165 766	.139 552 4124	.947 119	6.786 835	.147 344 0791	176.82	.031 409	5.38	7
	1.064 060	8.221 600	.121 630 8298	.939 797	7.726 632	.129 422 4965	155.31	.035 380	5.31	8
	1.072 351	9.285 660	.107 692 9406	.932 531	8.659 163	.115 484 6073	138.59	.039 361	5.25	9
	1.080 706	10.358 010	.096 543 6366	.925 321	9.584 484	.104 335 3033	125.21	.043 353	5.20	10
	1.089 127	11.438 717	.087 422 3946	.918 167	10.502 650	.095 214 0612	114.26	.047 355	5.17	11
	1.097 613	12.527 843	.079 822 1988	.911 068	11.413 719	.087 613 8655	105.14	.051 366	5.14	12
1	1.097 613	12.527 843	.079 822 1988	.911 068	11.413 719	.087 613 8655	105.14	.051 366	5.14	12
2	1.204 754	26.278 564	.038 053 8294	.830 045	21.812 393	.045 845 4961	55.02	.100 292	5.01	24
3	1.322 353	41.371 531	.024 171 2107	.756 228	31.286 295	.031 962 8774	38.36	.150 664	5.02	36
4	1.451 432	57.937 765	.017 259 8996	.688 975	39.917 664	.025 051 5662	30.07	.202 475	5.06	48
5	1.593 110	76.121 074	.013 136 9665	.627 703	47.781 429	.020 928 6331	25.12	.255 718	5.11	60
6	1.748 618	96.079 307	.010 408 0684	.571 880	54.945 855	.018 199 7351	21.84	.310 381	5.17	72
7	1.919 305	117.985 719	.008 475 6021	.521 022	61.473 135	.016 267 2687	19.53	.366 451	5.24	84
8	2.106 654	142.030 476	.007 040 7424	.474 686	67.419 931	.014 832 4091	17.80	.423 911	5.30	96
9	2.312 290	168.422 309	.005 937 4557	.432 472	72.837 868	.013 729 1224	16.48	.482 745	5.36	108
10	2.538 000	197.390 322	.005 066 1045	.394 011	77.773 977	.012 857 7712	15.43	.542 933	5.43	120
11	2.785 741	229.185 983	.004 363 2686	.358 971	82.271 109	.012 154 9353	14.59	.604 451	5.50	132
12	3.057 665	264.085 307	.003 786 6552	.327 047	86.368 302	.011 578 3219	13.90	.667 278	5.56	144
13	3.356 132	302.391 251	.003 306 9740	.297 962	90.101 124	.011 098 6407	13.32	.731 388	5.63	156
14	3.683 733	344.436 344	.002 903 2941	.271 464	93.501 979	.010 694 9607	12.84	.796 753	5.69	168
15	4.043 313	390.585 577	.002 560 2584	.247 322	96.600 390	.010 351 9251	12.43	.863 347	5.76	180
16	4.437 992	441.239 564	.002 266 3426	.225 327	99.423 253	.010 058 0092	12.07	.931 138	5.82	192
17	4.871 196	496.838 027	.002 012 7284	.205 288	101.995 074	.009 804 3951	11.77	1.000 097	5.88	204
18	5.346 687	557.863 611	.001 792 5528	.187 032	104.338 178	.009 584 2195	11.51	1.070 191	5.95	216
19	5.868 592	624.846 072	.001 600 3942	.170 399	106.472 905	.009 392 0608	11.28	1.141 390	6.01	228
20	6.441 442	698.366 876	.001 431 9121	.155 245	108.417 787	.009 223 5788	11.07	1.213 659	6.07	240
21	7.070 209	779.064 251	.001 283 5912	.141 439	110.189 707	.009 075 2578	10.90	1.286 965	6.13	252
22	7.760 352	867.638 721	.001 152 5534	.128 860	111.804 046	.008 944 2201	10.74	1.361 274	6.19	264
23	8.517 861	964.859 192	.001 036 4207	.117 400	113.274 820	.008 828 0873	10.60	1.436 552	6.25	276
24	9.349 313	1071.569 622	.000 933 2105	.106 960	114.614 794	.008 724 8771	10.47	1.512 765	6.30	288
25	10.261 926	1188.696 354	.000 841 2577	.097 448	115.835 603	.008 632 9244	10.36	1.589 877	6.36	300
26	11.263 621	1317.256 152	.000 759 1538	.088 781	116.947 842	.008 550 8205	10.27	1.667 856	6.41	312
27	12.363 094	1458.365 030	.000 685 6994	.080 886	117.961 168	.008 477 3660	10.18	1.746 667	6.47	324
28	13.569 890	1613.247 936	.000 619 8675	.073 693	118.884 377	.008 411 5342	10.10	1.826 275	6.52	336
29	14.894 485	1783.249 394	.000 560 7741	.067 139	119.725 483	.008 352 4407	10.03	1.906 649	6.57	348
30	16.348 377	1969.845 167	.000 507 6541	.061 168	120.491 788	.008 299 3208	9.96	1.987 755	6.63	360
31	17.944 187	2174.655 071	.000 459 8430	.055 728	121.189 944	.008 251 5097	9.91	2.069 562	6.68	372
32	19.695 769	2399.457 040	.000 416 7610	.050 772	121.826 012	.008 208 4276	9.86	2.152 036	6.73	384
33	21.618 328	2646.202 553	.000 377 9000	.046 257	122.405 513	.008 169 5667	9.81	2.235 148	6.77	396
34	23.728 553	2917.033 582	.000 342 8140	.042 143	122.933 478	.008 134 4807	9.77	2.318 868	6.82	408
35	26.044 763	3214.301 180	.000 311 1096	.038 395	123.414 490	.008 102 7763	9.73	2.403 166	6.87	420
36	28.587 065	3540.585 895	.000 282 4391	.034 981	123.852 724	.008 074 1058	9.69	2.488 014	6.91	432
37	31.377 528	3898.720 167	.000 256 4944	.031 870	124.251 986	.008 048 1611	9.66	2.573 384	6.96	444
38	34.440 376	4291.812 921	.000 233 0018	.029 036	124.615 741	.008 024 6684	9.63	2.659 249	7.00	456
39	37.802 196	4723.276 551	.000 211 7174	.026 453	124.947 146	.008 003 3841	9.61	2.745 584	7.04	468
40	41.492 174	5196.856 545	.000 192 4240	.024 101	125.249 078	.007 984 0907	9.59	2.832 364	7.08	480
41	45.542 340	5716.663 998	.000 174 9272	.021 958	125.524 160	.007 966 5939	9.56	2.919 564	7.12	492
42	49.987 855	6287.211 302	.000 159 0530	.020 005	125.774 777	.007 950 7197	9.55	3.007 163	7.16	504
43	54.867 308	6913.451 313	.000 144 6456	.018 226	126.003 107	.007 936 3122	9.53	3.095 137	7.20	516
44	60.223 059	7600.820 353	.000 131 5647	.016 605	126.211 131	.007 923 2314	9.51	3.183 466	7.24	528
45	66.101 599	8355.285 395	.000 119 6847	.015 128	126.400 655	.007 911 3514	9.50	3.272 130	7.27	540
46	72.553 959	9183.395 866	.000 108 8922	.013 783	126.573 325	.007 900 5588	9.49	3.361 108	7.31	552
47	79.636 153	10092.340 501	.000 099 0850	.012 557	126.730 638	.007 890 7517	9.47	3.450 384	7.34	564
48	87.409 659	11090.009 749	.000 090 1712	.011 440	126.873 962	.007 881 8379	9.46	3.539 939	7.37	576
49	95.941 959	12185.064 265	.000 082 0677	.010 423	127.004 539	.007 873 7344	9.45	3.629 756	7.41	588
50	105.307 120	13387.010 095	.000 074 6993	.009 496	127.123 504	.007 866 3659	9.44	3.719 820	7.44	600

MONTHLY COMPOUND INTEREST AND ANNUITY

9.375% M

	Amount Of 1	Amount Of 1 Per Period	Sinking Fund Payment	Present Worth Of 1	Present Worth of 1 Per Period	Periodic Payment To Amortize 1	Constant Annual Percent	Total Interest	Annual Add On Rate
	What a single $ 1 deposit grows to in the future. The deposit is made at the beginning of the first period.	What a series of $ 1 deposits grow to in the future. A deposit is made at the end of each period.	The amount to be deposited at the end of each period that grows to $ 1 in the future.	What $ 1 to be paid in the future is worth today. Value today of a single $ 1 payment tomorrow.	What $ 1 to be paid at the end of each period is worth today. Value today of a series of $ 1 payments tomorrow.	The mortgage payment to amortize a loan of $ 1. An annuity certain, payable at the end of each period, worth $ 1 today.	The annual payment, including interest and principal, to amortize completely a loan of $ 100.	The total interest paid over the term on a loan of $1. The loan is amortized by regular periodic payments.	The average annual interest rate on a loan that is completely amortized by regular periodic payments.

$$S = (1+i)^n \qquad S\overline{n}| = \frac{(1+i)^n - 1}{i} \qquad \frac{1}{S\overline{n}|} = \frac{i}{(1+i)^n - 1} \qquad V^n = \frac{1}{(1+i)^n} \qquad A\overline{n}| = \frac{1 - V^n}{i} \qquad \frac{1}{A\overline{n}|} = \frac{i}{1 - V^n}$$

YEAR   **PERIODS**

YEAR	Amount Of 1	Amount Of 1 Per Period	Sinking Fund Payment	Present Worth Of 1	Present Worth of 1 Per Period	Periodic Payment To Amortize 1	Constant Annual Percent	Total Interest	Annual Add On Rate	PERIODS
	1.007 813	1.000 000	1.000 000 0000	.992 248	.992 248	1.007 812 5000	1209.38	.007 812	9.37	1
	1.015 686	2.007 813	.498 054 4747	.984 556	1.976 804	.505 866 9747	607.05	.011 734	7.04	2
	1.023 621	3.023 499	.330 742 6772	.976 924	2.953 728	.338 555 1772	406.27	.015 666	6.27	3
	1.031 618	4.047 120	.247 089 3115	.969 351	3.923 079	.254 901 8115	305.89	.019 607	5.88	4
	1.039 678	5.078 738	.196 899 3186	.961 837	4.884 916	.204 711 8186	245.66	.023 559	5.65	5
	1.047 800	6.118 415	.163 441 0118	.954 380	5.839 296	.171 253 5118	205.51	.027 521	5.50	6
	1.055 986	7.166 215	.139 543 6685	.946 982	6.786 279	.147 356 1685	176.83	.031 493	5.40	7
	1.064 236	8.222 202	.121 621 9273	.939 641	7.725 920	.129 434 4273	155.33	.035 475	5.32	8
	1.072 550	9.286 438	.107 683 9207	.932 357	8.658 277	.115 496 4207	138.60	.039 468	5.26	9
	1.080 930	10.358 988	.096 534 5282	.925 130	9.583 407	.104 347 0282	125.22	.043 470	5.22	10
	1.089 374	11.439 917	.087 413 2186	.917 958	10.501 365	.095 225 7186	114.28	.047 483	5.18	11
	1.097 885	12.529 292	.079 812 9711	.910 842	11.412 207	.087 625 4711	105.16	.051 506	5.15	12
1	1.097 885	12.529 292	.079 812 9711	.910 842	11.412 207	.087 625 4711	105.16	.051 506	5.15	12
2	1.205 352	26.285 014	.038 044 4913	.829 633	21.806 926	.045 856 9913	55.03	.100 568	5.03	24
3	1.323 338	41.387 217	.024 162 0498	.755 665	31.274 874	.031 974 5498	38.37	.151 084	5.04	36
4	1.452 873	57.967 700	.017 250 9862	.688 292	39.898 679	.025 063 4862	30.08	.203 047	5.08	48
5	1.595 087	76.171 166	.013 128 3273	.626 925	47.753 605	.020 940 8273	25.13	.256 450	5.13	60
6	1.751 222	96.156 479	.010 399 7152	.571 030	54.908 202	.018 212 2152	21.86	.311 279	5.19	72
7	1.922 641	118.098 057	.008 467 5398	.520 118	61.424 911	.016 280 0398	19.54	.367 523	5.25	84
8	2.110 839	142.187 388	.007 032 9726	.473 745	67.360 604	.014 845 4726	17.82	.425 165	5.31	96
9	2.317 459	168.634 705	.005 929 9775	.431 507	72.767 083	.013 742 4775	16.50	.484 188	5.38	108
10	2.544 303	197.670 820	.005 058 9156	.393 035	77.691 532	.012 871 4156	15.45	.544 570	5.45	120
11	2.793 353	229.549 138	.004 356 3657	.357 993	82.176 928	.012 168 8657	14.61	.606 290	5.51	132
12	3.066 780	264.547 868	.003 780 0342	.326 075	86.262 415	.011 592 5342	13.92	.669 325	5.58	144
13	3.366 972	302.972 453	.003 300 6301	.297 003	89.983 649	.011 113 1301	13.34	.733 648	5.64	156
14	3.696 549	345.158 231	.002 897 2219	.270 523	93.373 106	.010 709 7219	12.86	.799 233	5.71	168
15	4.058 386	391.473 367	.002 554 4522	.246 403	96.460 366	.010 366 9522	12.45	.866 051	5.77	180
16	4.455 641	442.322 066	.002 260 7961	.224 435	99.272 372	.010 073 2961	12.09	.934 073	5.84	192
17	4.891 782	498.148 093	.002 007 4352	.204 424	101.833 666	.009 819 9352	11.79	1.003 267	5.90	204
18	5.370 615	559.438 657	.001 787 5061	.186 198	104.166 601	.009 600 0061	11.53	1.073 601	5.96	216
19	5.896 318	626.728 653	.001 595 5869	.169 597	106.291 536	.009 408 0869	11.29	1.145 044	6.03	228
20	6.473 479	700.605 337	.001 427 3371	.154 476	108.227 016	.009 239 8371	11.09	1.217 561	6.09	240
21	7.107 136	781.713 446	.001 279 2411	.140 704	109.989 933	.009 091 7411	10.92	1.291 119	6.15	252
22	7.802 819	870.760 830	.001 148 4210	.128 159	111.595 672	.008 960 9210	10.76	1.365 683	6.21	264
23	8.566 599	968.524 626	.001 032 4983	.116 732	113.058 247	.008 844 9983	10.62	1.441 220	6.27	276
24	9.405 141	1075.858 039	.000 929 4907	.106 325	114.390 422	.008 741 9907	10.50	1.517 693	6.32	288
25	10.325 764	1193.697 794	.000 837 7330	.096 845	115.603 823	.008 650 2330	10.39	1.595 070	6.38	300
26	11.336 502	1323.072 304	.000 755 8166	.088 211	116.709 040	.008 568 3166	10.29	1.673 315	6.44	312
27	12.446 177	1465.110 649	.000 682 5423	.080 346	117.715 717	.008 495 0423	10.20	1.752 394	6.49	324
28	13.664 472	1621.052 431	.000 616 8832	.073 182	118.632 642	.008 429 3832	10.12	1.832 273	6.54	336
29	15.002 020	1792.258 589	.000 557 9552	.066 658	119.467 816	.008 370 4552	10.05	1.912 918	6.60	348
30	16.470 494	1980.223 277	.000 504 9936	.060 715	120.228 527	.008 317 4936	9.99	1.994 298	6.65	360
31	18.082 710	2186.586 906	.000 457 3338	.055 301	120.921 415	.008 269 8338	9.93	2.076 378	6.70	372
32	19.852 738	2413.150 458	.000 414 3960	.050 371	121.552 527	.008 226 8960	9.88	2.159 128	6.75	384
33	21.796 025	2661.891 204	.000 375 6728	.045 880	122.127 370	.008 188 1728	9.83	2.242 516	6.80	396
34	23.929 531	2934.979 960	.000 340 7178	.041 789	122.650 961	.008 153 2178	9.79	2.326 513	6.84	408
35	26.271 875	3234.800 035	.000 309 1381	.038 064	123.127 870	.008 121 6381	9.75	2.411 088	6.89	420
36	28.843 500	3563.968 025	.000 280 5861	.034 670	123.562 258	.008 093 0861	9.72	2.496 213	6.93	432
37	31.666 849	3925.356 654	.000 254 7539	.031 579	123.957 918	.008 067 2539	9.69	2.581 861	6.98	444
38	34.766 561	4322.119 842	.000 231 3679	.028 763	124.318 301	.008 043 8679	9.66	2.668 004	7.02	456
39	38.169 689	4757.720 231	.000 210 1847	.026 199	124.646 554	.008 022 6847	9.63	2.754 616	7.06	468
40	41.905 933	5235.959 404	.000 190 9870	.023 863	124.945 540	.008 003 4870	9.61	2.841 674	7.10	480
41	46.007 899	5761.011 062	.000 173 5806	.021 735	125.217 869	.007 986 0806	9.59	2.929 152	7.14	492
42	50.511 386	6337.457 451	.000 157 7920	.019 798	125.465 918	.007 970 2920	9.57	3.017 027	7.18	504
43	55.455 698	6970.329 346	.000 143 4652	.018 032	125.691 851	.007 955 9652	9.55	3.105 278	7.22	516
44	60.883 984	7665.149 966	.000 130 4606	.016 425	125.897 641	.007 942 9606	9.54	3.193 883	7.26	528
45	66.843 618	8427.983 165	.000 118 6523	.014 960	126.085 083	.007 931 1523	9.52	3.282 822	7.30	540
46	73.386 612	9265.486 363	.000 107 9274	.013 626	126.255 813	.007 920 4274	9.51	3.372 076	7.33	552
47	80.570 067	10184.968 637	.000 098 1839	.012 412	126.411 321	.007 910 6839	9.50	3.461 626	7.37	564
48	88.456 676	11194.454 519	.000 089 3299	.011 305	126.552 964	.007 901 8299	9.49	3.551 454	7.40	576
49	97.115 266	12302.754 019	.000 081 2826	.010 297	126.681 979	.007 893 7826	9.48	3.641 544	7.43	588
50	106.621 402	13519.539 516	.000 073 9670	.009 379	126.799 491	.007 886 4670	9.47	3.731 880	7.46	600

Effective Rate is 9.79 %   Annual Percentage Rate is 9.375%

MONTHLY COMPOUND INTEREST AND ANNUITY

	Amount Of 1	Amount Of 1 Per Period	Sinking Fund Payment	Present Worth Of 1	Present Worth of 1 Per Period	Periodic Payment To Amortize 1	Constant Annual Percent	Total Interest	Annual Add On Rate	
	What a single $ 1 deposit grows to in the future. The deposit is made at the beginning of the first period.	What a series of $ 1 deposits grow to in the future. A deposit is made at the end of each period.	The amount to be deposited at the end of each period that grows to $ 1 in the future.	What $ 1 to be paid in the future is worth today. Value today of a single $ 1 payment tomorrow.	What $ 1 to be paid at the end of each period is worth today. Value today of a series of $ 1 payments tomorrow.	The mortgage payment to amortize a loan of $ 1. An annuity certain, payable at the end of each period, worth $ 1 today.	The annual payment, including interest and principal, to amortize completely a loan of $ 100.	The total interest paid over the term on a loan of $1. The loan is amortized by regular periodic payments.	The average annual interest rate on a loan that is completely amortized by regular periodic payments.	
	$S = (1+i)^n$	$S\overline{n} = \dfrac{(1+i)^n - 1}{i}$	$\dfrac{1}{S\overline{n}} = \dfrac{i}{(1+i)^n - 1}$	$V^n = \dfrac{1}{(1+i)^n}$	$A\overline{n} = \dfrac{1 - V^n}{i}$	$\dfrac{1}{A\overline{n}} = \dfrac{i}{1 - V^n}$				

YEAR										PERIODS
	1.007 833	1.000 000	1.000 000 0000	.992 228	.992 228	1.007 833 3333	1209.40	.007 833	9.40	1
	1.015 728	2.007 833	.498 049 3069	.984 516	1.976 743	.505 882 6402	607.06	.011 765	7.06	2
	1.023 685	3.023 561	.330 735 8048	.976 863	2.953 606	.338 569 1381	406.29	.015 707	6.28	3
	1.031 703	4.047 246	.247 081 6003	.969 271	3.922 877	.254 914 9336	305.90	.019 660	5.90	4
	1.039 785	5.078 949	.196 891 1148	.961 737	4.884 614	.204 724 4482	245.67	.023 622	5.67	5
	1.047 930	6.118 734	.163 432 4888	.954 262	5.838 877	.171 265 8221	205.52	.027 595	5.52	6
	1.056 139	7.166 665	.139 534 9251	.946 845	6.785 722	.147 368 2584	176.85	.031 578	5.41	7
	1.064 412	8.222 803	.121 613 0254	.939 486	7.725 208	.129 446 3587	155.34	.035 571	5.34	8
	1.072 750	9.287 215	.107 674 9014	.932 184	8.657 391	.115 508 2348	138.61	.039 574	5.28	9
	1.081 153	10.359 965	.096 525 4205	.924 938	9.582 330	.104 358 7538	125.24	.043 588	5.23	10
	1.089 622	11.441 118	.087 404 0435	.917 749	10.500 079	.095 237 3768	114.29	.047 611	5.19	11
	1.098 157	12.530 740	.079 803 7442	.910 616	11.410 695	.087 637 0775	105.17	.051 645	5.16	12
1	1.098 157	12.530 740	.079 803 7442	.910 616	11.410 695	.087 637 0775	105.17	.051 645	5.16	12
2	1.205 950	26.291 466	.038 035 1549	.829 222	21.801 460	.045 868 4882	55.05	.100 844	5.04	24
3	1.324 323	41.402 911	.024 152 8913	.755 103	31.263 458	.031 986 2246	38.39	.151 504	5.05	36
4	1.454 315	57.997 656	.017 242 0762	.687 609	39.879 708	.025 075 4095	30.10	.203 620	5.09	48
5	1.597 067	76.221 299	.013 119 6924	.626 148	47.725 804	.020 953 0257	25.15	.257 182	5.14	60
6	1.753 831	96.233 729	.010 391 3670	.570 180	54.870 587	.018 224 7004	21.87	.312 178	5.20	72
7	1.925 982	118.210 529	.008 459 4834	.519 216	61.376 742	.016 292 8167	19.56	.368 597	5.27	84
8	2.115 032	142.344 515	.007 025 2092	.472 806	67.301 352	.014 858 5426	17.84	.426 420	5.33	96
9	2.322 638	168.847 432	.005 922 5064	.430 545	72.696 398	.013 755 8397	16.51	.485 631	5.40	108
10	2.550 623	197.951 809	.005 051 7346	.392 061	77.609 214	.012 885 0679	15.47	.546 208	5.46	120
11	2.800 985	229.912 997	.004 349 4714	.357 017	82.082 905	.012 182 8047	14.62	.608 130	5.53	132
12	3.075 923	265.011 415	.003 773 4224	.325 106	86.156 720	.011 606 7557	13.93	.671 373	5.59	144
13	3.377 848	303.555 004	.003 294 2959	.296 047	89.866 402	.011 127 6292	13.36	.735 910	5.66	156
14	3.709 408	345.881 935	.002 891 1600	.269 585	93.244 499	.010 724 4933	12.87	.801 715	5.73	168
15	4.073 515	392.363 569	.002 548 6566	.245 488	96.320 648	.010 381 9899	12.46	.868 758	5.79	180
16	4.473 361	443.407 724	.002 255 2607	.223 546	99.121 840	.010 088 5940	12.11	.937 010	5.86	192
17	4.912 454	499.462 243	.002 002 1533	.203 564	101.672 651	.009 835 4867	11.81	1.006 439	5.92	204
18	5.394 648	561.018 931	.001 782 4710	.185 369	103.995 460	.009 615 8044	11.54	1.077 014	5.98	216
19	5.924 173	628.617 868	.001 590 7916	.168 800	106.110 648	.009 424 1249	11.31	1.148 700	6.05	228
20	6.505 675	702.852 146	.001 422 7743	.153 712	108.036 773	.009 256 1077	11.11	1.221 466	6.11	240
21	7.144 256	784.373 072	.001 274 9035	.139 973	109.790 733	.009 108 2369	10.93	1.295 276	6.17	252
22	7.845 518	873.895 886	.001 144 3011	.127 461	111.387 917	.008 977 6344	10.78	1.370 095	6.23	264
23	8.615 614	972.206 033	.001 028 5886	.116 068	112.842 340	.008 861 9219	10.64	1.445 890	6.29	276
24	9.461 301	1080.166 054	.000 925 7836	.105 694	114.166 760	.008 759 1169	10.52	1.522 626	6.34	288
25	10.389 998	1198.723 157	.000 834 2210	.096 246	115.372 799	.008 667 5543	10.41	1.600 266	6.40	300
26	11.409 854	1328.917 526	.000 752 4921	.087 644	116.471 037	.008 585 8255	10.31	1.678 778	6.46	312
27	12.529 816	1471.891 443	.000 679 3979	.079 810	117.471 111	.008 512 7313	10.22	1.758 125	6.51	324
28	13.759 711	1628.899 318	.000 613 9115	.072 676	118.381 794	.008 447 2448	10.14	1.838 274	6.57	336
29	15.110 330	1801.318 689	.000 555 1489	.066 180	119.211 078	.008 388 4822	10.07	1.919 192	6.62	348
30	16.593 521	1990.662 308	.000 502 3454	.060 264	119.966 236	.008 335 6787	10.01	2.000 844	6.67	360
31	18.222 299	2198.591 416	.000 454 8367	.054 878	120.653 896	.008 288 1700	9.95	2.083 199	6.72	372
32	20.010 954	2426.930 320	.000 412 0431	.049 973	121.280 090	.008 245 3765	9.90	2.166 225	6.77	384
33	21.975 179	2677.682 391	.000 373 4573	.045 506	121.850 312	.008 206 7906	9.85	2.249 889	6.82	396
34	24.132 207	2953.047 651	.000 338 6332	.041 438	122.369 566	.008 171 9665	9.81	2.334 162	6.87	408
35	26.500 963	3255.442 067	.000 307 1779	.037 734	122.842 407	.008 140 5113	9.77	2.419 015	6.91	420
36	29.102 230	3587.518 752	.000 278 7442	.034 362	123.272 984	.008 112 0775	9.74	2.504 417	6.96	432
37	31.958 831	3952.191 243	.000 253 0242	.031 290	123.665 074	.008 086 3575	9.71	2.590 343	7.00	444
38	35.095 829	4352.659 063	.000 229 7446	.028 493	124.022 117	.008 063 0780	9.68	2.676 764	7.04	456
39	38.540 747	4792.435 788	.000 208 6622	.025 947	124.347 247	.008 041 9955	9.66	2.763 654	7.09	468
40	42.323 809	5275.379 883	.000 189 5598	.023 627	124.643 315	.008 022 8931	9.63	2.850 989	7.13	480
41	46.478 207	5805.728 547	.000 172 2437	.021 515	124.912 920	.008 005 5770	9.61	2.938 744	7.17	492
42	51.040 390	6388.134 892	.000 156 5402	.019 592	125.158 426	.007 989 8735	9.59	3.026 896	7.21	504
43	56.050 385	7027.708 767	.000 142 2939	.017 841	125.381 988	.007 975 6272	9.58	3.115 424	7.25	516
44	61.552 149	7730.061 595	.000 129 3651	.016 246	125.585 568	.007 962 6984	9.56	3.204 305	7.28	528
45	67.593 952	8501.355 596	.000 117 6283	.014 794	125.770 950	.007 950 9616	9.55	3.293 519	7.32	540
46	74.228 803	9348.357 861	.000 106 9707	.013 472	125.939 763	.007 940 3040	9.53	3.383 048	7.35	552
47	81.514 915	10278.499 724	.000 097 2905	.012 268	126.093 486	.007 930 6238	9.52	3.472 872	7.39	564
48	89.516 212	11299.941 955	.000 088 4960	.011 171	126.233 469	.007 921 8294	9.51	3.562 974	7.42	576
49	98.302 897	12421.646 367	.000 080 5046	.010 173	126.360 940	.007 913 8380	9.50	3.653 337	7.46	588
50	107.952 060	13653.454 442	.000 073 2415	.009 263	126.477 016	.007 906 5749	9.49	3.743 945	7.49	600

Effective Rate is 9.82 %

Annual Percentage Rate is 9.40 %

MONTHLY COMPOUND INTEREST AND ANNUITY

Amount Of 1	Amount Of 1 Per Period	Sinking Fund Payment	Present Worth Of 1	Present Worth of 1 Per Period	Periodic Payment To Amortize 1	Constant Annual Percent	Total Interest	Annual Add On Rate	
What a single $ 1 deposit grows to in the future. The deposit is made at the beginning of the first period.	What a series of $ 1 deposits grow to in the future. A deposit is made at the end of each.	The amount to be deposited at the end of each period that grows to $ 1 in the future.	What $ 1 to be paid in the future is worth today. Value today of a single $ 1 payment tomorrow.	What $ 1 to be paid at the end of each period is worth today. Value today of a series of $ 1 payments tomorrow.	The mortgage payment to amortize a loan of $ 1. An annuity certain, payable at the end of each period, worth $ 1 today.	The annual payment, including interest and principal, to amortize completely a loan of $ 100.	The total interest paid over the term on a loan of $1. The loan is amortized by regular periodic payments.	The average annual interest rate on a loan that is completely amortized by regular periodic payments.	
$S = (1+i)^n$	$S\overline{n} = \dfrac{(1+i)^n - 1}{i}$	$\dfrac{1}{S\overline{n}} = \dfrac{i}{(1+i)^n - 1}$	$V^n = \dfrac{1}{(1+i)^n}$	$A\overline{n} = \dfrac{1-V^n}{i}$	$\dfrac{1}{A\overline{n}} = \dfrac{i}{1-V^n}$			**PERIODS**	

YEAR

1.007 875	1.000 000	1.000 000 0000	.992 187	.992 187	1.007 875 0000	1209.45	.007 875	9.45	1
1.015 812	2.007 875	.498 038 9715	.984 434	1.976 621	.505 913 9715	607.10	.011 828	7.10	2
1.023 812	3.023 687	.330 722 0605	.976 742	2.953 363	.338 597 0605	406.32	.015 791	6.32	3
1.031 874	4.047 499	.247 066 1786	.969 111	3.922 473	.254 941 1786	305.93	.019 765	5.93	4
1.040 000	5.079 373	.196 874 7084	.961 538	4.884 012	.204 749 7084	245.70	.023 749	5.70	5
1.048 190	6.119 373	.163 415 4439	.954 025	5.838 037	.171 290 4439	205.55	.027 743	5.55	6
1.056 445	7.167 563	.139 517 4397	.946 571	6.784 609	.147 392 4397	176.88	.031 747	5.44	7
1.064 764	8.224 007	.121 595 2231	.939 175	7.723 784	.129 470 2231	155.37	.035 762	5.36	8
1.073 149	9.288 771	.107 656 8648	.931 837	8.655 621	.115 531 8648	138.64	.039 787	5.30	9
1.081 600	10.361 920	.096 507 2072	.924 556	9.580 177	.104 382 2072	125.26	.043 822	5.26	10
1.090 118	11.443 521	.087 385 6954	.917 332	10.497 509	.095 260 6954	114.32	.047 868	5.22	11
1.098 702	12.533 638	.079 785 2929	.910 165	11.407 673	.087 660 2929	105.20	.051 924	5.19	12

YEAR									
1	1.098 702	12.533 638	.079 785 2929	.910 165	11.407 673	.087 660 2929	105.20	.051 924	5.19	12
2	1.207 147	26.304 377	.038 016 4872	.828 400	21.790 534	.045 891 4872	55.07	.101 396	5.07	24
3	1.326 295	41.434 320	.024 134 5821	.753 980	31.240 645	.032 009 5821	38.42	.152 345	5.08	36
4	1.457 204	58.057 625	.017 224 2663	.686 246	39.841 802	.025 099 2663	30.12	.204 765	5.12	48
5	1.601 033	76.321 691	.013 102 4351	.624 597	47.670 270	.020 977 4351	25.18	.258 646	5.17	60
6	1.759 059	96.388 463	.010 374 6856	.568 486	54.795 464	.018 249 6856	21.90	.313 977	5.23	72
7	1.932 683	118.435 874	.008 443 3877	.517 416	61.280 564	.016 318 3877	19.59	.370 745	5.30	84
8	2.123 443	142.659 417	.007 009 7020	.470 933	67.183 072	.014 884 7020	17.87	.428 931	5.36	96
9	2.333 032	169.273 883	.005 907 5859	.428 627	72.555 325	.013 782 5859	16.54	.488 519	5.43	108
10	2.563 308	198.515 260	.005 037 3961	.390 121	77.444 960	.012 912 3961	15.50	.549 488	5.49	120
11	2.816 312	230.642 831	.004 335 7081	.355 074	81.895 332	.012 210 7081	14.66	.611 813	5.56	132
12	3.094 289	265.941 470	.003 760 2259	.323 176	85.945 903	.011 635 2259	13.97	.675 473	5.63	144
13	3.399 703	304.724 170	.003 281 6563	.294 143	89.632 590	.011 156 6563	13.39	.740 438	5.70	156
14	3.735 262	347.334 816	.002 879 0664	.267 719	92.988 081	.010 754 0664	12.91	.806 683	5.76	168
15	4.103 941	394.151 234	.002 537 0972	.243 668	96.042 131	.010 412 0972	12.50	.874 177	5.83	180
16	4.509 010	445.588 546	.002 244 2229	.221 778	98.821 818	.010 119 2229	12.15	.942 891	5.89	192
17	4.954 060	502.102 843	.001 991 6239	.201 855	101.351 791	.009 866 6239	11.84	1.012 791	5.96	204
18	5.443 037	564.195 238	.001 772 4361	.183 721	103.654 483	.009 647 4361	11.58	1.083 846	6.02	216
19	5.980 278	632.416 301	.001 581 2369	.167 216	105.750 312	.009 456 2369	11.35	1.156 022	6.08	228
20	6.570 546	707.370 947	.001 413 6854	.152 194	107.657 860	.009 288 6854	11.15	1.229 285	6.15	240
21	7.219 075	789.723 796	.001 266 2655	.138 522	109.394 044	.009 141 2655	10.97	1.303 599	6.21	252
22	7.931 615	880.205 069	.001 136 0989	.126 078	110.974 257	.009 011 0989	10.82	1.378 930	6.27	264
23	8.714 484	979.617 062	.001 020 8070	.114 751	112.412 510	.008 895 8070	10.68	1.455 243	6.33	276
24	9.574 625	1088.841 256	.000 918 4075	.104 443	113.721 558	.008 793 4075	10.56	1.532 501	6.39	288
25	10.519 663	1208.846 141	.000 827 2351	.095 060	114.913 006	.008 702 2351	10.45	1.610 671	6.44	300
26	11.557 979	1340.695 796	.000 745 8814	.086 520	115.997 421	.008 620 8814	10.35	1.689 715	6.50	312
27	12.698 780	1485.559 329	.000 673 1471	.078 748	116.984 416	.008 548 1471	10.26	1.769 600	6.55	324
28	13.952 180	1644.721 240	.000 608 0058	.071 673	117.882 744	.008 483 0058	10.18	1.850 290	6.61	336
29	15.329 293	1819.592 814	.000 549 5735	.065 235	118.700 371	.008 424 5735	10.11	1.931 752	6.66	348
30	16.842 331	2011.724 633	.000 497 0859	.059 374	119.444 546	.008 372 0859	10.05	2.013 951	6.71	360
31	18.504 710	2222.820 323	.000 449 8789	.054 040	120.121 867	.008 324 8789	9.99	2.096 855	6.76	372
32	20.331 169	2454.751 665	.000 407 3732	.049 186	120.738 341	.008 282 3732	9.94	2.180 431	6.81	384
33	22.337 905	2709.575 187	.000 369 0615	.044 767	121.299 434	.008 244 0615	9.90	2.264 648	6.86	396
34	24.542 709	2989.550 402	.000 334 4985	.040 745	121.810 121	.008 209 4985	9.86	2.349 475	6.91	408
35	26.965 134	3297.159 844	.000 303 2913	.037 085	122.274 930	.008 178 2913	9.82	2.434 882	6.96	420
36	29.626 657	3635.131 076	.000 275 0932	.033 753	122.697 983	.008 150 0932	9.79	2.520 840	7.00	432
37	32.550 879	4006.460 881	.000 249 5968	.030 721	123.083 030	.008 124 5968	9.75	2.607 321	7.05	444
38	35.763 729	4414.441 828	.000 226 5292	.027 961	123.433 487	.008 101 5292	9.73	2.694 297	7.09	456
39	39.293 695	4862.691 475	.000 205 6474	.025 449	123.752 460	.008 080 6474	9.70	2.781 743	7.13	468
40	43.172 077	5355.184 439	.000 186 7349	.023 163	124.042 778	.008 061 7349	9.68	2.869 633	7.17	480
41	47.433 265	5896.287 640	.000 169 5982	.021 082	124.307 016	.008 044 5982	9.66	2.957 942	7.21	492
42	52.115 042	6490.799 027	.000 154 0642	.019 188	124.547 515	.008 029 0642	9.64	3.046 648	7.25	504
43	57.258 922	7143.990 116	.000 139 9778	.017 465	124.766 409	.008 014 9778	9.62	3.135 729	7.29	516
44	62.910 515	7861.652 733	.000 127 1997	.015 896	124.965 639	.008 002 1997	9.61	3.225 161	7.33	528
45	69.119 934	8650.150 374	.000 115 6049	.014 468	125.146 971	.007 990 6049	9.59	3.314 927	7.37	540
46	75.942 238	9516.474 625	.000 105 0809	.013 168	125.312 012	.007 980 0809	9.58	3.405 050	7.40	552
47	83.437 919	10468.307 161	.000 095 5264	.011 985	125.462 227	.007 970 5264	9.57	3.495 377	7.44	564
48	91.673 442	11514.087 853	.000 086 8501	.010 908	125.598 948	.007 961 8501	9.56	3.586 026	7.47	576
49	100.721 831	12663.089 611	.000 078 9697	.009 928	125.723 386	.007 953 9697	9.55	3.676 934	7.50	588
50	110.663 317	13925.500 601	.000 071 8107	.009 036	125.836 645	.007 946 8107	9.54	3.768 086	7.54	600

Effective Rate is 9.87 %

Annual Percentage Rate is 9.45 %

MONTHLY COMPOUND INTEREST AND ANNUITY

	Amount Of 1	Amount Of 1 Per Period	Sinking Fund Payment	Present Worth Of 1	Present Worth of 1 Per Period	Periodic Payment To Amortize 1	Constant Annual Percent	Total Interest	Annual Add On Rate	
	What a single $ 1 deposit grows to in the future. The deposit is made at the beginning of the first period.	What a series of $ 1 deposits grow to in the future. A deposit is made at the end of each period.	The amount to be deposited at the end of each period that grows to $ 1 in the future.	What $ 1 to be paid in the future is worth today. Value today of a single $ 1 payment tomorrow.	What $ 1 to be paid at the end of each period is worth today. Value today of a series of $ 1 payments tomorrow.	The mortgage payment to amortize a loan of $ 1. An annuity certain, payable at the end of each period, worth $ 1 today.	The annual payment, including interest and principal, to amortize completely a loan of $ 100.	The total interest paid over the term on a loan of $1. The loan is amortized by regular periodic payments.	The average annual interest rate on a loan that is completely amortized by regular periodic payments.	
	$S = (1+i)^n$	$S\overline{n|} = \dfrac{(1+i)^n - 1}{i}$	$\dfrac{1}{S\overline{n|}} = \dfrac{i}{(1+i)^n - 1}$	$V^n = \dfrac{1}{(1+i)^n}$	$A\overline{n|} = \dfrac{1-V^n}{i}$	$\dfrac{1}{A\overline{n|}} = \dfrac{i}{1-V^n}$				

YEAR										PERIODS
	1.007 917	1.000 000	1.000 000 0000	.992 146	.992 146	1.007 916 6667	1209.50	.007 917	9.50	1
	1.015 896	2.007 917	.498 028 6366	.984 353	1.976 498	.505 945 3033	607.14	.011 891	7.13	2
	1.023 939	3.023 813	.330 708 3169	.976 621	2.953 119	.338 624 9836	406.35	.015 875	6.35	3
	1.032 045	4.047 751	.247 050 7580	.968 950	3.922 070	.254 967 4247	305.97	.019 870	5.96	4
	1.040 215	5.079 796	.196 858 3034	.961 340	4.883 409	.204 774 9701	245.73	.023 875	5.73	5
	1.048 450	6.120 011	.163 398 4008	.953 789	5.837 198	.171 315 0674	205.58	.027 890	5.58	6
	1.056 750	7.168 461	.139 499 9563	.946 297	6.783 496	.147 416 6230	176.90	.031 916	5.47	7
	1.065 116	8.225 211	.121 577 4232	.938 865	7.722 360	.129 494 0898	155.40	.035 953	5.39	8
	1.073 548	9.290 328	.107 638 8308	.931 490	8.653 851	.115 555 4974	138.67	.039 999	5.33	9
	1.082 047	10.363 876	.096 488 9967	.924 174	9.578 024	.104 405 6634	125.29	.044 057	5.29	10
	1.090 614	11.445 923	.087 367 3505	.916 915	10.494 940	.095 284 0172	114.35	.048 124	5.25	11
	1.099 248	12.536 537	.079 766 8451	.909 713	11.404 653	.087 683 5118	105.23	.052 202	5.22	12
1	1.099 248	12.536 537	.079 766 8451	.909 713	11.404 653	.087 683 5118	105.23	.052 202	5.22	12
2	1.208 345	26.317 295	.037 997 8263	.827 578	21.779 615	.045 914 4930	55.10	.101 948	5.10	24
3	1.328 271	41.465 760	.024 116 2831	.752 859	31.217 856	.032 032 9497	38.44	.153 186	5.11	36
4	1.460 098	58.117 673	.017 206 4700	.684 885	39.803 947	.025 123 1367	30.15	.205 911	5.15	48
5	1.605 009	76.422 249	.013 085 1946	.623 049	47.614 827	.021 001 8613	25.21	.260 112	5.20	60
6	1.764 303	96.543 509	.010 358 0241	.566 796	54.720 488	.018 274 6908	21.93	.315 778	5.26	72
7	1.939 406	118.661 756	.008 427 3150	.515 622	61.184 601	.016 343 9817	19.62	.372 894	5.33	84
8	2.131 887	142.975 186	.006 994 2207	.469 068	67.065 090	.014 910 8873	17.90	.431 445	5.39	96
9	2.343 472	169.701 665	.005 892 6941	.426 717	72.414 648	.013 809 3608	16.58	.491 411	5.46	108
10	2.576 055	199.080 682	.005 023 0891	.388 190	77.281 211	.012 939 7558	15.53	.552 771	5.53	120
11	2.831 723	231.375 495	.004 321 9789	.353 142	81.708 388	.012 238 6455	14.69	.615 501	5.60	132
12	3.112 764	266.875 491	.003 747 0657	.321 258	85.735 849	.011 663 7324	14.00	.679 577	5.66	144
13	3.421 699	305.898 776	.003 269 0553	.292 253	89.399 684	.011 185 7219	13.43	.744 973	5.73	156
14	3.761 294	348.795 027	.002 867 0134	.265 866	92.732 722	.010 783 6800	12.95	.811 658	5.80	168
15	4.134 593	395.948 628	.002 525 5802	.241 862	95.764 831	.010 442 2468	12.54	.879 604	5.86	180
16	4.544 942	447.782 110	.002 233 2290	.220 025	98.523 180	.010 149 8957	12.18	.948 780	5.93	192
17	4.996 016	504.759 939	.001 981 1398	.200 159	101.032 487	.009 897 8065	11.88	1.019 153	6.00	204
18	5.491 859	567.392 681	.001 762 4478	.182 088	103.315 236	.009 679 1145	11.62	1.090 689	6.06	216
19	6.036 912	636.241 570	.001 571 7301	.165 648	105.391 883	.009 488 3967	11.39	1.163 354	6.12	228
20	6.636 061	711.923 546	.001 404 6452	.150 692	107.281 037	.009 321 3119	11.19	1.237 115	6.19	240
21	7.294 674	795.116 775	.001 257 6769	.137 086	108.999 624	.009 174 3436	11.01	1.311 935	6.25	252
22	8.018 653	886.566 731	.001 127 9467	.124 709	110.563 046	.009 044 6133	10.86	1.387 778	6.31	264
23	8.814 485	987.092 874	.001 013 0759	.113 450	111.985 311	.008 929 7426	10.72	1.464 609	6.37	276
24	9.689 302	1097.595 994	.000 911 0820	.103 207	113.279 165	.008 827 7487	10.60	1.542 392	6.43	288
25	10.650 941	1219.066 282	.000 820 2999	.093 888	114.456 200	.008 736 9666	10.49	1.621 090	6.48	300
26	11.708 022	1352.592 202	.000 739 3211	.085 412	115.526 965	.008 655 9878	10.39	1.700 668	6.54	312
27	12.870 014	1499.370 247	.000 666 9467	.077 700	116.501 054	.008 583 6133	10.31	1.781 091	6.60	324
28	14.147 332	1660.715 659	.000 602 1500	.070 685	117.387 195	.008 518 8167	10.23	1.862 322	6.65	336
29	15.551 421	1838.074 212	.000 544 0477	.064 303	118.193 330	.008 460 7143	10.16	1.944 329	6.70	348
30	17.094 862	2033.035 174	.000 491 8754	.058 497	118.926 681	.008 408 5421	10.10	2.027 075	6.76	360
31	18.791 486	2247.345 541	.000 444 9694	.053 216	119.593 820	.008 361 6361	10.04	2.110 529	6.81	372
32	20.656 495	2482.925 693	.000 402 7507	.048 411	120.200 725	.008 319 4173	9.99	2.194 656	6.86	384
33	22.706 602	2741.886 607	.000 364 7124	.044 040	120.752 835	.008 281 3791	9.94	2.279 426	6.91	396
34	24.960 178	3026.548 765	.000 330 4093	.040 064	121.255 097	.008 247 0760	9.90	2.364 807	6.96	408
35	27.437 415	3339.462 955	.000 299 4493	.036 447	121.712 011	.008 216 1160	9.86	2.450 769	7.00	420
36	30.160 512	3683.433 122	.000 271 4859	.033 156	122.127 671	.008 188 1525	9.83	2.537 282	7.05	432
37	33.153 870	4061.541 498	.000 246 2119	.030 162	122.505 803	.008 162 8786	9.80	2.624 318	7.09	444
38	36.444 312	4477.176 216	.000 223 3551	.027 439	122.849 795	.008 140 0217	9.77	2.711 850	7.14	456
39	40.061 322	4934.061 676	.000 202 6728	.024 962	123.162 729	.008 119 3394	9.75	2.799 851	7.18	468
40	44.037 311	5436.291 914	.000 183 9489	.022 708	123.447 408	.008 100 6156	9.73	2.888 295	7.22	480
41	48.407 908	5988.367 290	.000 166 9904	.020 658	123.706 385	.008 083 6571	9.71	2.977 159	7.26	492
42	53.212 276	6595.234 813	.000 151 6246	.018 793	123.941 980	.008 068 2913	9.69	3.066 419	7.30	504
43	58.493 465	7262.332 471	.000 137 6968	.017 096	124.156 304	.008 054 3635	9.67	3.156 052	7.34	516
44	64.298 801	7995.637 961	.000 125 0682	.015 552	124.351 277	.008 041 7349	9.66	3.246 036	7.38	528
45	70.680 301	8801.722 248	.000 113 6141	.014 148	124.528 647	.008 030 2808	9.64	3.336 352	7.41	540
46	77.695 150	9687.808 454	.000 103 2225	.012 871	124.690 002	.008 019 8892	9.63	3.426 979	7.45	552
47	85.406 206	10661.836 575	.000 093 7925	.011 709	124.836 789	.008 010 4591	9.62	3.517 899	7.48	564
48	93.882 566	11732.534 634	.000 085 2331	.010 652	124.970 324	.008 001 8997	9.61	3.609 094	7.52	576
49	103.200 184	12909.496 889	.000 077 4624	.009 690	125.091 801	.007 994 1290	9.60	3.700 548	7.55	588
50	113.442 553	14203.269 804	.000 070 4063	.008 815	125.202 311	.007 987 0730	9.59	3.792 244	7.58	600

Effective Rate is 9.92 %

Annual Percentage Rate is 9.50 %

MONTHLY COMPOUND INTEREST AND ANNUITY

9.55 % M

	Amount Of 1	Amount Of 1 Per Period	Sinking Fund Payment	Present Worth Of 1	Present Worth of 1 Per Period	Periodic Payment To Amortize 1	Constant Annual Percent	Total Interest	Annual Add On Rate	
	What a single $ 1 deposit grows to in the future. The deposit is made at the beginning of the first period.	What a series of $ 1 deposits grow to in the future. A deposit is made at the end of each period.	The amount to be deposited at the end of each period that grows to $ 1 in the future.	What $ 1 to be paid in the future is worth today. Value today of a single $ 1 payment tomorrow.	What $ 1 to be paid at the end of each period is worth today. Value today of a series of $ 1 payments tomorrow.	The mortgage payment to amortize a loan of $ 1. An annuity certain, payable at the end of each period, worth $ 1 today.	The annual payment, including interest and principal, to amortize completely a loan of $ 100.	The total interest paid over the term on a loan of $1. The loan is amortized by regular periodic payments.	The average annual interest rate on a loan that is completely amortized by regular periodic payments.	
	$S = (1+i)^n$	$S\overline{n} = \dfrac{(1+i)^n - 1}{i}$	$\dfrac{1}{S\overline{n}} = \dfrac{i}{(1+i)^n - 1}$	$V^n = \dfrac{1}{(1+i)^n}$	$A\overline{n} = \dfrac{1-V^n}{i}$	$\dfrac{1}{A\overline{n}} = \dfrac{i}{1-V^n}$				

YEAR										PERIODS
	1.007 958	1.000 000	1.000 000 0000	.992 105	.992 105	1.007 958 3333	1209.55	.007 958	9.55	1
	1.015 980	2.007 958	.498 018 3022	.984 271	1.976 376	.505 976 6355	607.18	.011 953	7.17	2
	1.024 066	3.023 938	.330 694 5742	.976 500	2.952 876	.338 652 9075	406.39	.015 959	6.38	3
	1.032 215	4.048 004	.247 035 3385	.968 790	3.921 666	.254 993 6719	306.00	.019 975	5.99	4
	1.040 430	5.080 219	.196 841 8997	.961 141	4.882 807	.204 800 2331	245.77	.024 001	5.76	5
	1.048 710	6.120 649	.163 381 3593	.953 552	5.836 359	.171 339 6926	205.61	.028 038	5.61	6
	1.057 056	7.169 359	.139 482 4749	.946 024	6.782 383	.147 440 8082	176.93	.032 086	5.50	7
	1.065 469	8.226 416	.121 559 6255	.938 554	7.720 937	.129 517 9588	155.43	.036 144	5.42	8
	1.073 948	9.291 884	.107 620 7992	.931 144	8.652 081	.115 579 1326	138.70	.040 212	5.36	9
	1.082 495	10.365 832	.096 470 7891	.923 792	9.575 873	.104 429 1224	125.32	.044 291	5.31	10
	1.091 110	11.448 327	.087 349 0088	.916 498	10.492 371	.095 307 3421	114.37	.048 381	5.28	11
	1.099 793	12.539 436	.079 748 4007	.909 262	11.401 633	.087 706 7340	105.25	.052 481	5.25	12
1	1.099 793	12.539 436	.079 748 4007	.909 262	11.401 633	.087 706 7340	105.25	.052 481	5.25	12
2	1.209 545	26.330 221	.037 979 1723	.826 757	21.768 705	.045 937 5056	55.13	.102 500	5.13	24
3	1.330 249	41.497 230	.024 097 9943	.751 739	31.195 089	.032 056 3276	38.47	.154 028	5.13	36
4	1.462 998	58.177 800	.017 188 6872	.683 528	39.766 142	.025 147 0205	30.18	.207 057	5.18	48
5	1.608 995	76.522 974	.013 067 9709	.621 506	47.559 475	.021 026 3043	25.24	.261 578	5.23	60
6	1.769 562	96.698 869	.010 341 3826	.565 112	54.645 657	.018 299 7159	21.96	.317 580	5.29	72
7	1.946 152	118.888 177	.008 411 2653	.513 835	61.088 853	.016 369 5987	19.65	.375 046	5.36	84
8	2.140 364	143.291 823	.006 978 7653	.467 210	66.947 406	.014 937 0986	17.93	.433 961	5.42	96
9	2.353 957	170.130 782	.005 877 8311	.424 817	72.274 365	.013 836 1644	16.61	.494 306	5.49	108
10	2.588 866	199.648 082	.005 008 8134	.386 270	77.117 967	.012 967 1468	15.57	.556 058	5.56	120
11	2.847 217	232.111 003	.004 308 2835	.351 220	81.522 070	.012 266 6168	14.72	.619 193	5.63	132
12	3.131 349	267.813 496	.003 733 9418	.319 351	85.526 554	.011 692 2751	14.04	.683 688	5.70	144
13	3.443 836	307.078 849	.003 256 4926	.290 374	89.167 679	.011 214 8259	13.46	.749 513	5.77	156
14	3.787 507	350.262 609	.002 855 0007	.264 026	92.478 416	.010 813 3340	12.98	.816 640	5.83	168
15	4.165 473	397.755 807	.002 514 1053	.240 069	95.488 743	.010 472 4387	12.57	.885 039	5.90	180
16	4.581 158	449.988 495	.002 222 2790	.218 285	98.225 918	.010 180 6124	12.22	.954 678	5.97	192
17	5.038 326	507.433 640	.001 970 7010	.198 479	100.714 728	.009 929 0344	11.92	1.025 523	6.03	204
18	5.541 116	570.611 409	.001 752 5061	.180 469	102.977 709	.009 710 8395	11.66	1.097 541	6.10	216
19	6.094 080	640.093 879	.001 562 2708	.164 094	105.035 351	.009 520 6042	11.43	1.170 698	6.16	228
20	6.702 227	716.510 213	.001 395 6535	.149 204	106.906 287	.009 353 9869	11.23	1.244 957	6.22	240
21	7.371 063	800.552 364	.001 249 1375	.135 666	108.607 457	.009 207 4709	11.05	1.320 283	6.29	252
22	8.106 643	892.981 334	.001 119 8442	.123 356	110.154 267	.009 078 1776	10.90	1.396 639	6.35	264
23	8.915 629	994.634 070	.001 005 3949	.112 163	111.560 723	.008 963 7282	10.76	1.473 989	6.41	276
24	9.805 347	1106.431 039	.000 903 8069	.101 985	112.839 560	.008 862 1402	10.64	1.552 296	6.47	288
25	10.783 852	1229.384 564	.000 813 4151	.092 731	114.002 357	.008 771 7485	10.53	1.631 525	6.53	300
26	11.860 005	1364.607 993	.000 732 8112	.084 317	115.059 645	.008 691 1445	10.43	1.711 637	6.58	312
27	13.043 551	1513.325 775	.000 660 7963	.076 666	116.020 996	.008 619 1296	10.35	1.792 598	6.64	324
28	14.345 206	1676.884 553	.000 596 3440	.069 710	116.895 116	.008 554 6773	10.27	1.874 372	6.69	336
29	15.776 758	1856.765 355	.000 538 5710	.063 384	117.689 921	.008 496 9043	10.20	1.956 923	6.75	348
30	17.351 168	2054.597 004	.000 486 7135	.057 633	118.412 606	.008 445 0468	10.14	2.040 217	6.80	360
31	19.082 693	2272.170 870	.000 440 1077	.052 404	119.069 717	.008 398 4411	10.08	2.124 220	6.85	372
32	20.987 013	2511.457 087	.000 398 1752	.047 649	119.667 202	.008 356 5086	10.03	2.208 899	6.90	384
33	23.081 370	2774.622 398	.000 360 4094	.043 325	120.210 473	.008 318 7427	9.99	2.294 222	6.95	396
34	25.384 729	3064.049 769	.000 326 3655	.039 394	120.704 449	.008 284 6988	9.95	2.380 157	7.00	408
35	27.917 948	3382.359 969	.000 295 6516	.035 819	121.153 602	.008 253 9849	9.91	2.466 674	7.05	420
36	30.703 964	3732.435 305	.000 267 9216	.032 569	121.562 000	.008 226 2549	9.88	2.553 742	7.09	432
37	33.768 005	4117.445 713	.000 242 8690	.029 614	121.933 341	.008 201 2024	9.85	2.641 334	7.14	444
38	37.137 817	4540.877 470	.000 220 2218	.026 927	122.270 987	.008 178 5551	9.82	2.729 421	7.18	456
39	40.843 911	5006.564 760	.000 199 7378	.024 483	122.577 995	.008 158 0711	9.79	2.817 977	7.23	468
40	44.919 848	5518.724 388	.000 181 2013	.022 262	122.857 147	.008 139 5346	9.77	2.906 977	7.27	480
41	49.402 535	6081.993 969	.000 164 4198	.020 242	123.110 968	.008 122 7531	9.75	2.996 395	7.31	492
42	54.332 563	6701.473 920	.000 149 2209	.018 405	123.341 759	.008 107 5542	9.73	3.086 207	7.35	504
43	59.754 574	7382.773 643	.000 135 4504	.016 735	123.551 608	.008 093 7838	9.72	3.176 392	7.39	516
44	65.717 663	8132.062 319	.000 122 9700	.015 217	123.742 416	.008 081 3034	9.70	3.266 928	7.42	528
45	72.275 826	8956.124 771	.000 111 6554	.013 836	123.915 910	.008 069 9888	9.69	3.357 794	7.46	540
46	79.488 449	9862.422 900	.000 101 3950	.012 580	124.073 661	.008 059 7283	9.68	3.448 970	7.50	552
47	87.420 841	10859.163 252	.000 092 0881	.011 439	124.217 099	.008 050 4215	9.67	3.540 438	7.53	564
48	96.144 830	11955.377 328	.000 083 6444	.010 401	124.347 521	.008 041 9777	9.66	3.632 179	7.57	576
49	105.739 413	13160.973 313	.000 075 9822	.009 457	124.466 110	.008 034 3156	9.65	3.724 178	7.60	588
50	116.291 467	14486.885 955	.000 069 0279	.008 599	124.573 937	.008 027 3613	9.64	3.816 417	7.63	600

MONTHLY COMPOUND INTEREST AND ANNUITY

9.60 % M

	Amount Of 1	Amount Of 1 Per Period	Sinking Fund Payment	Present Worth Of 1	Present Worth of 1 Per Period	Periodic Payment To Amortize 1	Constant Annual Percent	Total Interest	Annual Add On Rate	
	What a single $ 1 deposit grows to in the future. The deposit is made at the beginning of the first period.	What a series of $ 1 deposits grow to in the future. A deposit is made at the end of each period.	The amount to be deposited at the end of each period that grows to $ 1 in the future.	What $ 1 to be paid in the future is worth today. Value today of a single $ 1 payment tomorrow.	What $ 1 to be paid at the end of each period is worth today. Value today of a series of $ 1 payments tomorrow.	The mortgage payment to amortize a loan of $ 1. An annuity certain, payable at the end of each period, worth $ 1 today.	The annual payment, including interest and principal, to amortize completely a loan of $ 100.	The total interest paid over the term on a loan of $1. The loan is amortized by regular periodic payments.	The average annual interest rate on a loan that is completely amortized by regular periodic payments.	
	$S = (1+i)^n$	$S\overline{n}| = \dfrac{(1+i)^n - 1}{i}$	$\dfrac{1}{S\overline{n}|} = \dfrac{i}{(1+i)^n - 1}$	$V^n = \dfrac{1}{(1+i)^n}$	$A\overline{n}| = \dfrac{1-V^n}{i}$	$\dfrac{1}{A\overline{n}|} = \dfrac{i}{1-V^n}$				

YEAR										PERIODS
	1.008 000	1.000 000	1.000 000 0000	.992 063	.992 063	1.008 000 0000	1209.60	.008 000	9.60	1
	1.016 064	2.008 000	.498 007 9681	.984 190	1.976 253	.506 007 9681	607.21	.012 016	7.21	2
	1.024 193	3.024 064	.330 680 8322	.976 379	2.952 632	.338 680 8322	406.42	.016 042	6.42	3
	1.032 386	4.048 257	.247 019 9201	.968 630	3.921 262	.255 019 9201	306.03	.020 080	6.02	4
	1.040 645	5.080 643	.196 825 4974	.960 942	4.882 205	.204 825 4974	245.80	.024 127	5.79	5
	1.048 970	6.121 288	.163 364 3194	.953 316	5.835 521	.171 364 3194	205.64	.028 186	5.64	6
	1.057 362	7.170 258	.139 464 9954	.945 750	6.781 270	.147 464 9954	176.96	.032 255	5.53	7
	1.065 821	8.227 620	.121 541 8300	.938 244	7.719 514	.129 541 8300	155.46	.036 335	5.45	8
	1.074 348	9.293 441	.107 602 7702	.930 798	8.650 312	.115 602 7702	138.73	.040 425	5.39	9
	1.082 942	10.367 789	.096 452 5843	.923 410	9.573 722	.104 452 5843	125.35	.044 526	5.34	10
	1.091 606	11.450 731	.087 330 6701	.916 082	10.489 804	.095 330 6701	114.40	.048 637	5.31	11
	1.100 339	12.542 337	.079 729 9596	.908 811	11.398 615	.087 729 9596	105.28	.052 760	5.28	12
1	1.100 339	12.542 337	.079 729 9596	.908 811	11.398 615	.087 729 9596	105.28	.052 760	5.28	12
2	1.210 745	26.343 155	.037 960 5251	.825 938	21.757 802	.045 960 5251	55.16	.103 053	5.15	24
3	1.332 230	41.528 730	.024 079 7156	.750 621	31.172 346	.032 079 7156	38.50	.154 870	5.16	36
4	1.465 904	58.238 005	.017 170 9179	.682 173	39.728 388	.025 170 9179	30.21	.208 204	5.21	48
5	1.612 991	76.623 687	.013 050 7640	.619 966	47.504 214	.021 050 7640	25.27	.263 046	5.26	60
6	1.774 836	96.854 542	.010 324 7610	.563 432	54.570 971	.018 324 7610	21.99	.319 383	5.32	72
7	1.952 921	119.115 137	.008 395 2386	.512 053	60.993 318	.016 395 2386	19.68	.377 200	5.39	84
8	2.148 875	143.609 331	.006 963 3358	.465 360	66.830 018	.014 963 3358	17.96	.436 480	5.46	96
9	2.364 490	170.561 241	.005 862 9968	.422 924	72.134 476	.013 862 9968	16.64	.497 204	5.52	108
10	2.601 740	200.217 469	.004 994 5692	.384 358	76.955 225	.012 994 5692	15.60	.559 348	5.59	120
11	2.862 795	232.849 365	.004 294 6220	.349 309	81.336 376	.012 294 6220	14.76	.622 890	5.66	132
12	3.150 044	268.755 503	.003 720 8540	.317 456	85.318 015	.011 720 8540	14.07	.687 803	5.73	144
13	3.466 115	308.264 416	.003 243 9683	.288 507	88.936 572	.011 243 9683	13.50	.754 059	5.80	156
14	3.813 901	351.737 602	.002 843 0284	.262 199	92.225 157	.010 843 0284	13.02	.821 629	5.87	168
15	4.196 583	399.572 830	.002 502 6727	.238 289	95.213 860	.010 502 6727	12.61	.890 481	5.94	180
16	4.617 662	452.207 782	.002 211 3728	.216 560	97.930 025	.010 211 3728	12.26	.960 584	6.00	192
17	5.080 992	510.124 057	.001 960 3075	.196 812	100.398 507	.009 960 3075	11.96	1.031 903	6.07	204
18	5.590 813	573.851 576	.001 742 6109	.178 865	102.641 891	.009 742 6109	11.70	1.104 404	6.14	216
19	6.151 787	643.973 430	.001 552 8591	.162 554	104.680 702	.009 552 8591	11.47	1.178 052	6.20	228
20	6.769 050	721.131 219	.001 386 7102	.147 731	106.533 597	.009 386 7102	11.27	1.252 810	6.26	240
21	7.448 247	806.030 921	.001 240 6472	.134 260	108.217 528	.009 240 6472	11.09	1.328 643	6.33	252
22	8.195 595	899.449 347	.001 111 7913	.122 017	109.747 904	.009 111 7913	10.94	1.405 513	6.39	264
23	9.017 930	1002.241 256	.000 997 7638	.110 890	111.138 726	.008 997 7638	10.80	1.483 383	6.45	276
24	9.922 777	1115.347 171	.000 896 5818	.100 778	112.402 720	.008 896 5818	10.68	1.562 216	6.51	288
25	10.918 416	1239.801 986	.000 806 5804	.091 588	113.551 453	.008 806 5804	10.57	1.641 974	6.57	300
26	12.013 955	1376.744 435	.000 726 3512	.083 237	114.595 433	.008 726 3512	10.48	1.722 622	6.63	312
27	13.219 420	1527.427 510	.000 654 6956	.075 646	115.544 215	.008 654 6956	10.39	1.804 121	6.68	324
28	14.545 839	1693.229 927	.000 590 5872	.068 748	116.406 477	.008 590 5872	10.31	1.886 437	6.74	336
29	16.005 350	1875.668 743	.000 533 1432	.062 479	117.190 111	.008 533 1432	10.24	1.969 534	6.79	348
30	17.611 306	2076.413 231	.000 481 5997	.056 782	117.902 287	.008 481 5997	10.18	2.053 376	6.84	360
31	19.378 401	2297.300 159	.000 435 2936	.051 604	118.549 519	.008 435 2936	10.13	2.137 929	6.90	372
32	21.322 805	2540.350 593	.000 393 6465	.046 898	119.137 732	.008 393 6465	10.08	2.223 160	6.95	384
33	23.462 307	2807.788 390	.000 356 1522	.042 622	119.672 306	.008 356 1522	10.03	2.309 036	7.00	396
34	25.816 484	3102.060 546	.000 322 3664	.038 735	120.158 132	.008 322 3664	9.99	2.395 525	7.05	408
35	28.406 877	3425.859 586	.000 291 8975	.035 203	120.599 657	.008 291 8975	9.96	2.482 597	7.09	420
36	31.257 186	3782.148 198	.000 264 4000	.031 993	121.000 920	.008 264 4000	9.92	2.570 221	7.14	432
37	34.393 491	4174.186 344	.000 239 5676	.029 075	121.365 591	.008 239 5676	9.89	2.658 368	7.18	444
38	37.844 489	4605.561 086	.000 217 1288	.026 424	121.697 009	.008 217 1288	9.87	2.747 011	7.23	456
39	41.641 755	5080.219 406	.000 196 8419	.024 014	121.998 205	.008 196 8419	9.84	2.836 122	7.27	468
40	45.820 035	5602.504 322	.000 178 4916	.021 825	122.271 936	.008 178 4916	9.82	2.925 676	7.31	480
41	50.417 557	6177.194 624	.000 161 8858	.019 834	122.520 705	.008 161 8858	9.80	3.015 648	7.36	492
42	55.476 389	6809.548 600	.000 146 8526	.018 026	122.746 789	.008 146 8526	9.78	3.106 014	7.40	504
43	61.042 817	7505.352 148	.000 133 2383	.016 382	122.952 257	.008 133 2383	9.76	3.196 751	7.43	516
44	67.167 774	8270.971 715	.000 120 9048	.014 888	123.138 988	.008 120 9048	9.75	3.287 838	7.47	528
45	73.907 300	9113.412 549	.000 109 7284	.013 530	123.308 692	.008 109 7284	9.74	3.379 253	7.51	540
46	81.323 062	10040.382 797	.000 099 5978	.012 297	123.462 921	.008 099 5978	9.72	3.470 978	7.55	552
47	89.482 912	11060.364 027	.000 090 4129	.011 175	123.603 085	.008 090 4129	9.71	3.562 993	7.58	564
48	98.461 511	12182.688 843	.000 082 0837	.010 156	123.730 468	.008 082 0837	9.70	3.655 280	7.62	576
49	108.341 010	13417.626 264	.000 074 5288	.009 230	123.846 236	.008 074 5288	9.70	3.747 823	7.65	588
50	119.211 806	14776.475 693	.000 067 6751	.008 388	123.951 446	.008 067 6751	9.69	3.840 605	7.68	600

Effective Rate is 10.03 %

Annual Percentage Rate is 9.60 %

	Amount Of 1	Amount Of 1 Per Period	Sinking Fund Payment	Present Worth Of 1	Present Worth of 1 Per Period	Periodic Payment To Amortize 1	Constant Annual Percent	Total Interest	Annual Add On Rate	
	What a single $ 1 deposit grows to in the future. The deposit is made at the beginning of the first period.	What a series of $ 1 deposits grow to in the future. A deposit is made at the end of each period.	The amount to be deposited at the end of each period that grows to $ 1 in the future.	What $ 1 to be paid in the future is worth today. Value today of a single $ 1 payment tomorrow.	What $ 1 to be paid at the end of each period is worth today. Value today of a series of $ 1 payments tomorrow.	The mortgage payment to amortize a loan of $ 1. An annuity certain, payable at the end of each period, worth $ 1 today.	The annual payment, including interest and principal, to amortize completely a loan of $ 100.	The total interest paid over the term of a loan of $ 1. The loan is amortized by regular periodic payments.	The average annual interest rate on a loan that is completely amortized by regular periodic payments.	
	$S = (1+i)^n$	$S\overline{n} = \dfrac{(1+i)^n - 1}{i}$	$\dfrac{1}{S\overline{n}} = \dfrac{i}{(1+i)^n - 1}$	$V^n = \dfrac{1}{(1+i)^n}$	$A\overline{n} = \dfrac{1 - V^n}{i}$	$\dfrac{1}{A\overline{n}} = \dfrac{i}{1 - V^n}$				

YEAR										PERIODS
	1.008 021	1.000 000	1.000 000 0000	.992 043	.992 043	1.008 020 8333	1209.63	.008 021	9.62	1
	1.016 106	2.008 021	.498 002 8013	.984 149	1.976 192	.506 023 6346	607.23	.012 047	7.23	2
	1.024 256	3.024 127	.330 673 9614	.976 318	2.952 511	.338 694 7948	406.44	.016 084	6.43	3
	1.032 471	4.048 383	.247 012 2112	.968 550	3.921 061	.255 033 0446	306.04	.020 132	6.04	4
	1.040 753	5.080 854	.196 817 2968	.960 843	4.881 904	.204 838 1301	245.81	.024 191	5.81	5
	1.049 100	6.121 607	.163 355 8002	.953 198	5.835 101	.171 376 6335	205.66	.028 260	5.65	6
	1.057 515	7.170 707	.139 456 2564	.945 613	6.780 714	.147 477 0897	176.98	.032 340	5.54	7
	1.065 997	8.228 222	.121 532 9331	.938 089	7.718 803	.129 553 7665	155.47	.036 430	5.46	8
	1.074 547	9.294 220	.107 593 7567	.930 624	8.649 427	.115 614 5900	138.74	.040 531	5.40	9
	1.083 166	10.368 767	.096 443 4830	.923 219	9.572 647	.104 464 3163	125.36	.044 643	5.36	10
	1.091 854	11.451 933	.087 321 5020	.915 873	10.488 520	.095 342 3353	114.42	.048 766	5.32	11
	1.100 612	12.543 787	.079 720 7404	.908 586	11.397 106	.087 741 5737	105.29	.052 899	5.29	12
1	1.100 612	12.543 787	.079 720 7404	.908 586	11.397 106	.087 741 5737	105.29	.052 899	5.29	12
2	1.211 346	26.349 625	.037 951 2040	.825 528	21.752 353	.045 972 0374	55.17	.103 329	5.17	24
3	1.333 221	41.544 491	.024 070 5802	.750 063	31.160 983	.032 091 4135	38.51	.155 291	5.18	36
4	1.467 359	58.268 137	.017 162 0383	.681 496	39.709 530	.025 182 8717	30.22	.208 778	5.22	48
5	1.614 992	76.674 376	.013 042 1668	.619 198	47.476 618	.021 063 0001	25.28	.263 780	5.28	60
6	1.777 479	96.932 497	.010 316 4577	.562 594	54.533 682	.018 337 2910	22.01	.320 285	5.34	72
7	1.956 314	119.228 820	.008 387 2339	.511 165	60.945 630	.016 408 0672	19.69	.378 278	5.40	84
8	2.153 142	143.768 413	.006 955 6308	.464 437	66.771 435	.014 976 4641	17.98	.437 741	5.47	96
9	2.369 774	170.776 974	.005 855 5903	.421 981	72.064 678	.013 876 4237	16.66	.498 654	5.54	108
10	2.608 200	200.502 910	.004 987 4588	.383 406	76.874 042	.013 008 2921	15.61	.560 995	5.61	120
11	2.870 616	233.219 621	.004 287 8039	.348 357	81.243 763	.012 308 6372	14.78	.624 740	5.68	132
12	3.159 433	269.228 014	.003 714 3237	.316 512	85.214 028	.011 735 1571	14.09	.689 863	5.75	144
13	3.477 309	308.859 269	.003 237 7205	.287 579	88.821 354	.011 258 5539	13.52	.756 334	5.82	156
14	3.827 166	352.477 889	.002 837 0574	.261 290	92.098 919	.010 857 8907	13.03	.824 126	5.89	168
15	4.212 224	400.485 050	.002 496 9721	.237 404	95.076 868	.010 517 8054	12.63	.893 205	5.95	180
16	4.636 023	453.322 290	.002 205 9361	.215 702	97.782 590	.010 226 7694	12.28	.963 540	6.02	192
17	5.102 460	511.475 570	.001 955 1276	.195 984	100.240 970	.009 975 9609	11.98	1.035 096	6.09	204
18	5.615 827	575.479 746	.001 737 6806	.178 068	102.474 619	.009 758 5140	11.72	1.107 839	6.15	216
19	6.180 845	645.923 486	.001 548 1710	.161 790	104.504 081	.009 569 0043	11.49	1.181 733	6.22	228
20	6.802 709	723.454 685	.001 382 2566	.147 000	106.348 021	.009 403 0899	11.29	1.256 742	6.28	240
21	7.487 141	808.786 425	.001 236 4204	.133 562	108.023 398	.009 257 2537	11.11	1.332 828	6.35	252
22	8.240 435	902.703 529	.001 107 7834	.121 353	109.545 622	.009 128 6168	10.96	1.409 955	6.41	264
23	9.069 518	1006.069 787	.000 993 9668	.110 259	110.928 693	.009 014 8002	10.82	1.488 085	6.47	276
24	9.982 017	1119.835 891	.000 892 9880	.100 180	112.185 332	.008 913 8213	10.70	1.567 181	6.53	288
25	10.986 324	1245.048 188	.000 803 1818	.091 022	113.327 095	.008 824 0151	10.59	1.647 205	6.59	300
26	12.091 676	1382.858 298	.000 723 1399	.082 702	114.364 486	.008 743 9732	10.50	1.728 120	6.65	312
27	13.308 239	1534.533 708	.000 651 6638	.075 141	115.307 044	.008 672 4971	10.41	1.809 889	6.70	324
28	14.647 203	1701.469 427	.000 587 7273	.068 272	116.163 438	.008 608 5606	10.34	1.892 476	6.76	336
29	16.120 882	1885.200 820	.000 530 4475	.062 031	116.941 546	.008 551 2808	10.27	1.975 846	6.81	348
30	17.742 830	2087.417 727	.000 479 0608	.056 361	117.648 524	.008 499 8941	10.20	2.059 962	6.87	360
31	19.527 965	2309.980 006	.000 432 9042	.051 209	118.290 874	.008 453 7375	10.15	2.144 790	6.92	372
32	21.492 705	2554.934 639	.000 391 3994	.046 527	118.874 504	.008 412 2328	10.10	2.230 297	6.97	384
33	23.655 121	2824.534 555	.000 354 0406	.042 274	119.404 782	.008 374 8740	10.05	2.316 450	7.02	396
34	26.035 101	3121.259 357	.000 320 3835	.038 410	119.886 585	.008 341 2168	10.01	2.403 216	7.07	408
35	28.654 535	3447.838 123	.000 290 0368	.034 898	120.324 344	.008 310 8702	9.98	2.490 565	7.12	420
36	31.537 514	3807.274 511	.000 262 6551	.031 708	120.722 086	.008 283 4884	9.95	2.578 467	7.16	432
37	34.710 555	4202.874 378	.000 237 9324	.028 810	121.083 468	.008 258 7657	9.92	2.666 892	7.21	444
38	38.202 840	4638.276 191	.000 215 5973	.026 176	121.411 815	.008 236 4307	9.89	2.755 812	7.25	456
39	42.046 490	5117.484 489	.000 195 4085	.023 783	121.710 147	.008 216 2418	9.86	2.845 201	7.30	468
40	46.276 856	5644.906 712	.000 177 1508	.021 609	121.981 206	.008 197 9842	9.84	2.935 032	7.34	480
41	50.932 846	6225.393 744	.000 160 6324	.019 634	122.227 487	.008 181 4657	9.82	3.025 281	7.38	492
42	56.057 282	6864.284 519	.000 145 6816	.017 839	122.451 255	.008 166 5149	9.80	3.115 924	7.42	504
43	61.697 296	7567.455 134	.000 132 1448	.016 208	122.654 566	.008 152 9782	9.79	3.206 937	7.46	516
44	67.904 762	8341.372 889	.000 119 8843	.014 727	122.839 293	.008 140 7177	9.77	3.298 299	7.50	528
45	74.736 770	9193.155 767	.000 108 7766	.013 380	123.007 132	.008 129 6099	9.76	3.389 989	7.53	540
46	82.256 158	10130.637 906	.000 098 7105	.012 157	123.159 629	.008 119 5438	9.75	3.481 988	7.57	552
47	90.532 084	11162.441 647	.000 089 5861	.011 046	123.298 185	.008 110 4195	9.74	3.574 277	7.60	564
48	99.640 664	12298.056 841	.000 081 3137	.010 036	123.424 075	.008 102 1470	9.73	3.666 837	7.64	576
49	109.665 674	13547.928 126	.000 073 8120	.009 119	123.538 457	.008 094 6454	9.72	3.759 651	7.67	588
50	120.699 315	14923.550 993	.000 067 0082	.008 285	123.642 383	.008 087 8415	9.71	3.852 705	7.71	600

Effective Rate is 10.06 %

Annual Percentage Rate is 9.625%

MONTHLY COMPOUND INTEREST AND ANNUITY

9.65 % M

	Amount Of 1	Amount Of 1 Per Period	Sinking Fund Payment	Present Worth Of 1	Present Worth of 1 Per Period	Periodic Payment To Amortize 1	Constant Annual Percent	Total Interest	Annual Add On Rate	
	What a single $ 1 deposit grows to in the future. The deposit is made at the beginning of the first period.	What a series of $ 1 deposits grow to in the future. A deposit is made at the end of each period.	The amount to be deposited at the end of each period that grows to $ 1 in the future.	What $ 1 to be paid in the future is worth today. Value today of a single $ 1 payment tomorrow.	What $ 1 to be paid at the end of each period is worth today. Value today of a series of $ 1 payments tomorrow.	The mortgage payment to amortize a loan of $ 1. An annuity certain, payable at the end of each period, worth $ 1 today.	The annual payment, including interest and principal, to amortize completely a loan of $ 100.	The total interest paid over the term on a loan of $1. The loan is amortized by regular periodic payments.	The average annual interest rate on a loan that is completely amortized by regular periodic payments.	

$$S = (1+i)^n \qquad S\overline{n}| = \frac{(1+i)^n - 1}{i} \qquad \frac{1}{S\overline{n}|} = \frac{i}{(1+i)^n - 1} \qquad V^n = \frac{1}{(1+i)^n} \qquad A\overline{n}| = \frac{1-V^n}{i} \qquad \frac{1}{A\overline{n}|} = \frac{i}{1-V^n}$$

YEAR										PERIODS
	1.008 042	1.000 000	1.000 000 0000	.992 022	.992 022	1.008 041 6667	1209.65	.008 042	9.65	1
	1.016 148	2.008 042	.497 997 6345	.984 109	1.976 131	.506 039 3012	607.25	.012 079	7.25	2
	1.024 320	3.024 190	.330 667 0909	.976 258	2.952 389	.338 708 7576	406.46	.016 126	6.45	3
	1.032 557	4.048 509	.247 004 5027	.968 470	3.920 859	.255 046 1694	306.06	.020 185	6.06	4
	1.040 860	5.081 066	.196 809 0965	.960 744	4.881 603	.204 850 7632	245.83	.024 254	5.82	5
	1.049 230	6.121 926	.163 347 2813	.953 079	5.834 682	.171 388 9480	205.67	.028 334	5.67	6
	1.057 668	7.171 157	.139 447 5179	.945 476	6.780 158	.147 489 1846	176.99	.032 424	5.56	7
	1.066 173	8.228 825	.121 524 0368	.937 934	7.718 092	.129 565 7035	155.48	.036 526	5.48	8
	1.074 747	9.294 998	.107 584 7438	.930 451	8.648 543	.115 626 4105	138.76	.040 638	5.42	9
	1.083 390	10.369 745	.096 434 3823	.923 029	9.571 572	.104 476 0490	125.38	.044 760	5.37	10
	1.092 102	11.453 136	.087 312 3346	.915 665	10.487 237	.095 354 0012	114.43	.048 894	5.33	11
	1.100 885	12.545 238	.079 711 5220	.908 360	11.395 597	.087 753 1887	105.31	.053 038	5.30	12
1	1.100 885	12.545 238	.079 711 5220	.908 360	11.395 597	.087 753 1887	105.31	.053 038	5.30	12
2	1.211 947	26.356 097	.037 941 8847	.825 119	21.746 907	.045 983 5513	55.19	.103 605	5.18	24
3	1.334 214	41.560 260	.024 061 4472	.749 505	31.149 626	.032 103 1139	38.53	.155 712	5.19	36
4	1.468 815	58.298 289	.017 153 1622	.680 821	39.690 684	.025 194 8288	30.24	.209 352	5.23	48
5	1.616 996	76.724 927	.013 033 5738	.618 431	47.449 043	.021 075 2404	25.30	.264 514	5.29	60
6	1.780 126	97.010 530	.010 308 1593	.561 758	54.496 430	.018 349 8260	22.02	.321 187	5.35	72
7	1.959 714	119.342 639	.008 379 2349	.510 279	60.897 996	.016 420 9015	19.71	.379 356	5.42	84
8	2.157 419	143.927 713	.006 947 9322	.463 517	66.712 926	.014 989 5989	17.99	.439 001	5.49	96
9	2.375 069	170.993 044	.005 848 1911	.421 040	71.994 978	.013 889 8578	16.67	.500 105	5.56	108
10	2.614 677	200.788 850	.004 980 3562	.382 456	76.792 984	.013 022 0229	15.63	.562 643	5.63	120
11	2.878 458	233.590 595	.004 280 9943	.347 408	81.151 304	.012 322 6609	14.79	.626 591	5.70	132
12	3.168 850	269.701 531	.003 707 8025	.315 572	85.110 228	.011 749 4691	14.10	.691 924	5.77	144
13	3.488 538	309.455 506	.003 231 4823	.286 653	88.706 359	.011 273 1490	13.53	.758 611	5.84	156
14	3.840 478	353.220 045	.002 831 0964	.260 384	91.972 941	.010 872 7631	13.05	.826 624	5.90	168
15	4.227 923	401.399 753	.002 491 2821	.236 523	94.940 176	.010 532 9487	12.64	.895 931	5.97	180
16	4.654 455	454.440 053	.002 200 5103	.214 848	97.635 494	.010 242 1769	12.30	.966 498	6.04	192
17	5.124 018	512.831 303	.001 949 9590	.195 159	100.083 814	.009 991 6256	11.99	1.038 292	6.11	204
18	5.640 953	577.113 332	.001 732 7619	.177 275	102.307 771	.009 774 4286	11.73	1.111 277	6.17	216
19	6.210 038	647.880 430	.001 543 4947	.161 030	104.327 926	.009 585 1614	11.51	1.185 417	6.24	228
20	6.836 536	725.786 839	.001 377 8150	.146 273	106.162 954	.009 419 4817	11.31	1.260 676	6.30	240
21	7.526 237	811.552 807	.001 232 2057	.132 869	107.829 821	.009 273 8724	11.13	1.337 016	6.37	252
22	8.285 519	905.971 242	.001 103 7878	.120 693	109.343 937	.009 145 4545	10.98	1.414 400	6.43	264
23	9.121 400	1009.915 045	.000 990 1823	.109 632	110.719 301	.009 031 8490	10.84	1.492 790	6.49	276
24	10.041 609	1124.345 179	.000 889 4066	.099 586	111.968 626	.008 931 0732	10.72	1.572 149	6.55	288
25	11.054 653	1250.319 553	.000 799 7955	.090 460	113.103 464	.008 841 4622	10.61	1.652 439	6.61	300
26	12.169 898	1389.002 805	.000 719 9410	.082 170	114.134 305	.008 761 6076	10.52	1.733 622	6.67	312
27	13.397 653	1541.677 064	.000 648 6443	.074 640	115.070 681	.008 690 3109	10.43	1.815 661	6.72	324
28	14.749 270	1709.753 808	.000 584 8795	.067 800	115.921 248	.008 626 5462	10.36	1.898 520	6.78	336
29	16.237 245	1894.786 910	.000 527 7638	.061 587	116.693 869	.008 569 4305	10.29	1.982 162	6.84	348
30	17.875 333	2098.487 007	.000 476 5338	.055 943	117.395 687	.008 518 2005	10.23	2.066 552	6.89	360
31	19.678 679	2322.737 310	.000 430 5265	.050 816	118.033 191	.008 472 1932	10.17	2.151 656	6.94	372
32	21.663 955	2569.611 021	.000 389 1640	.046 160	118.612 275	.008 430 8306	10.12	2.237 439	6.99	384
33	23.849 515	2841.390 492	.000 351 9404	.041 930	119.138 291	.008 393 6070	10.08	2.323 868	7.04	396
34	26.255 565	3140.588 332	.000 318 4117	.038 087	119.616 104	.008 360 0783	10.04	2.410 912	7.09	408
35	28.904 347	3469.970 633	.000 288 1869	.034 597	120.050 130	.008 329 8535	10.00	2.498 538	7.14	420
36	31.820 351	3832.582 542	.000 260 9207	.031 426	120.444 382	.008 302 5873	9.97	2.586 718	7.19	432
37	35.030 535	4231.776 416	.000 236 3074	.028 547	120.802 505	.008 277 9740	9.94	2.675 420	7.23	444
38	38.564 578	4671.242 812	.000 214 0758	.025 931	121.127 810	.008 255 7425	9.91	2.764 619	7.28	456
39	42.455 150	5155.044 610	.000 193 9847	.023 554	121.423 303	.008 235 6514	9.89	2.854 285	7.32	468
40	46.738 222	5687.654 568	.000 175 8194	.021 396	121.691 718	.008 217 4861	9.87	2.944 393	7.36	480
41	51.453 390	6273.996 680	.000 159 3880	.019 435	121.935 536	.008 201 0547	9.85	3.034 919	7.40	492
42	56.644 246	6919.491 693	.000 144 5193	.017 654	122.157 010	.008 186 1860	9.83	3.125 838	7.44	504
43	62.358 779	7630.107 226	.000 131 0598	.016 036	122.358 188	.008 172 7264	9.81	3.217 127	7.48	516
44	68.649 821	8412.412 938	.000 118 8720	.014 567	122.540 931	.008 160 5386	9.80	3.308 764	7.52	528
45	75.575 532	9273.641 264	.000 107 8325	.013 232	122.706 927	.008 149 4992	9.78	3.400 730	7.56	540
46	83.199 941	10221.754 284	.000 097 8306	.012 019	122.857 711	.008 139 4972	9.77	3.493 002	7.59	552
47	91.593 535	11265.517 326	.000 088 7665	.010 918	122.994 678	.008 130 4331	9.76	3.585 564	7.63	564
48	100.833 914	12414.580 007	.000 080 5504	.009 917	123.119 092	.008 122 2171	9.75	3.678 397	7.66	576
49	111.006 505	13679.565 440	.000 073 1017	.009 008	123.232 106	.008 114 7684	9.74	3.771 484	7.70	588
50	122.205 355	15072.168 449	.000 066 3475	.008 183	123.334 763	.008 108 0141	9.73	3.864 808	7.73	600

MONTHLY COMPOUND INTEREST AND ANNUITY

9.70 % M

Amount Of 1	Amount Of 1 Per Period	Sinking Fund Payment	Present Worth Of 1	Present Worth of 1 Per Period	Periodic Payment To Amortize 1	Constant Annual Percent	Total Interest	Annual Add On Rate
What a single $1 deposit grows to in the future. The deposit is made at the beginning of the first period.	What a series of $1 deposits grow to in the future. A deposit is made at the end of each.	The amount to be deposited at the end of each period that grows to $1 in the future.	What $1 to be paid in the future is worth today. Value today of a single $1 payment tomorrow.	What $1 to be paid at the end of each period is worth today. Value today of a series of $1 payments tomorrow.	The mortgage payment to amortize a loan of $1. An annuity certain, payable at the end of each period, worth $1 today.	The annual payment, including interest and principal, to amortize completely a loan of $100.	The total interest paid over the term on a loan of $1. The loan is amortized by regular periodic payments.	The average annual interest rate on a loan that is completely amortized by regular periodic payments.

Formulas:

$$S = (1+i)^n \qquad S\overline{n}| = \frac{(1+i)^n - 1}{i} \qquad \frac{1}{S\overline{n}|} = \frac{i}{(1+i)^n - 1} \qquad V^n = \frac{1}{(1+i)^n} \qquad A\overline{n}| = \frac{1 - V^n}{i} \qquad \frac{1}{A\overline{n}|} = \frac{i}{1 - V^n}$$

YEAR / **PERIODS**

Amount Of 1	Amount Of 1 Per Period	Sinking Fund Payment	Present Worth Of 1	Present Worth of 1 Per Period	Periodic Payment To Amortize 1	Constant Annual Percent	Total Interest	Annual Add On Rate	PERIODS
1.008 083	1.000 000	1.000 000 0000	.991 981	.991 981	1.008 083 3333	1209.70	.008 083	9.70	1
1.016 232	2.008 083	.497 987 3013	.984 027	1.976 009	.506 070 6347	607.29	.012 141	7.28	2
1.024 447	3.024 315	.330 653 3504	.976 137	2.952 146	.338 736 6838	406.49	.016 210	6.48	3
1.032 727	4.048 762	.246 989 0864	.968 310	3.920 455	.255 072 4197	306.09	.020 290	6.09	4
1.041 075	5.081 489	.196 792 6970	.960 545	4.881 000	.204 876 0303	245.86	.024 380	5.85	5
1.049 491	6.122 565	.163 330 2448	.952 843	5.833 844	.171 413 5781	205.70	.028 481	5.70	6
1.057 974	7.172 055	.139 430 0423	.945 203	6.779 046	.147 513 3757	177.02	.032 594	5.59	7
1.066 526	8.230 030	.121 506 2458	.937 624	7.716 670	.129 589 5792	155.51	.036 717	5.51	8
1.075 147	9.296 556	.107 566 7199	.930 105	8.646 775	.115 650 0532	138.79	.040 850	5.45	9
1.083 838	10.371 703	.096 416 1832	.922 647	9.569 422	.104 499 5165	125.40	.044 995	5.40	10
1.092 599	11.455 541	.087 294 0022	.915 249	10.484 671	.095 377 3355	114.46	.049 151	5.36	11
1.101 431	12.548 140	.079 693 0878	.907 910	11.392 581	.087 776 4211	105.34	.053 317	5.33	12
1.101 431	12.548 140	.079 693 0878	.907 910	11.392 581	.087 776 4211	105.34	.053 317	5.33	**1** 12
1.213 150	26.369 047	.037 923 2511	.824 301	21.736 019	.046 006 5844	55.21	.104 158	5.21	**2** 24
1.336 201	41.591 820	.024 043 1890	.748 391	31.126 930	.032 126 5224	38.56	.156 555	5.22	**3** 36
1.471 732	58.358 652	.017 135 4199	.679 471	39.653 031	.025 218 7532	30.27	.210 500	5.26	**4** 48
1.621 011	76.826 156	.013 016 4003	.616 899	47.393 963	.021 099 7337	25.32	.265 984	5.32	**5** 60
1.785 432	97.166 834	.010 291 5775	.560 089	54.422 033	.018 374 9108	22.05	.322 994	5.38	**6** 72
1.966 530	119.570 683	.008 363 2541	.508 510	60.802 887	.016 446 5874	19.74	.381 513	5.45	**7** 84
2.165 996	144.246 972	.006 932 5545	.461 681	66.596 129	.015 015 8879	18.02	.441 525	5.52	**8** 96
2.385 695	171.426 197	.005 833 4141	.419 165	71.855 870	.013 916 7475	16.71	.503 009	5.59	**9** 108
2.627 678	201.362 232	.004 966 1746	.380 564	76.631 242	.013 049 5079	15.66	.565 941	5.66	**10** 120
2.894 206	234.334 703	.004 267 4004	.345 518	80.966 850	.012 350 7337	14.83	.630 297	5.73	**11** 132
3.187 767	270.651 599	.003 694 7870	.313 699	84.903 191	.011 778 1203	14.14	.696 049	5.80	**12** 144
3.511 105	310.652 145	.003 219 0346	.284 811	88.477 035	.011 302 3679	13.57	.763 169	5.87	**13** 156
3.867 239	354.709 979	.002 819 2046	.258 582	91.721 763	.010 902 5379	13.09	.831 626	5.94	**14** 168
4.259 496	403.236 635	.002 479 9334	.234 770	94.667 684	.010 563 2667	12.68	.901 388	6.01	**15** 180
4.691 540	456.685 387	.002 189 6913	.213 150	97.342 315	.010 273 0246	12.33	.972 421	6.08	**16** 192
5.167 407	515.555 489	.001 939 6554	.193 521	99.770 640	.010 022 9888	12.03	1.044 690	6.15	**17** 204
5.691 541	580.396 833	.001 722 9591	.175 699	101.975 340	.009 806 2924	11.77	1.118 159	6.21	**18** 216
6.268 839	651.815 085	.001 534 1774	.159 519	103.977 009	.009 617 5108	11.55	1.192 792	6.28	**19** 228
6.904 692	730.477 348	.001 368 9678	.144 829	105.794 344	.009 452 3012	11.35	1.268 552	6.34	**20** 240
7.605 040	817.118 387	.001 223 8129	.131 492	107.444 321	.009 307 1462	11.17	1.345 401	6.41	**21** 252
8.376 426	912.547 495	.001 095 8334	.119 383	108.942 351	.009 179 1667	11.02	1.423 300	6.47	**22** 264
9.226 053	1017.656 053	.000 982 6503	.108 389	110.302 428	.009 065 9836	10.88	1.502 211	6.53	**23** 276
10.161 859	1133.425 857	.000 882 2809	.098 407	111.537 255	.008 965 6142	10.76	1.582 097	6.59	**24** 288
11.192 584	1260.938 283	.000 793 0602	.089 345	112.658 367	.008 876 3936	10.66	1.662 918	6.65	**25** 300
12.327 857	1401.384 397	.000 713 5801	.081 117	113.676 235	.008 796 9134	10.56	1.744 637	6.71	**26** 312
13.578 282	1556.076 071	.000 642 6421	.073 647	114.600 368	.008 725 9754	10.48	1.827 216	6.77	**27** 324
14.955 537	1726.458 246	.000 579 2205	.066 865	115.439 398	.008 662 5538	10.40	1.910 618	6.82	**28** 336
16.472 490	1914.122 420	.000 522 4326	.060 707	116.201 162	.008 605 7660	10.33	1.994 807	6.88	**29** 348
18.143 307	2120.821 520	.000 471 5154	.055 117	116.892 774	.008 554 8487	10.27	2.079 746	6.93	**30** 360
19.983 597	2348.486 275	.000 425 8062	.050 041	117.520 696	.008 509 1395	10.22	2.165 400	6.99	**31** 372
22.010 550	2599.243 247	.000 384 7274	.045 433	118.090 793	.008 468 0607	10.17	2.251 735	7.04	**32** 384
24.243 097	2875.434 699	.000 347 7735	.041 249	118.608 389	.008 431 1068	10.12	2.338 718	7.09	**33** 396
26.702 094	3179.640 469	.000 314 5010	.037 450	119.078 320	.008 397 8343	10.08	2.426 316	7.14	**34** 408
29.410 508	3514.702 072	.000 284 5191	.034 001	119.504 975	.008 367 8525	10.05	2.514 498	7.18	**35** 420
32.393 640	3883.749 241	.000 257 4832	.030 870	119.892 339	.008 340 8165	10.01	2.603 233	7.23	**36** 432
35.679 352	4290.229 158	.000 233 0878	.028 027	120.244 031	.008 316 4211	9.98	2.692 491	7.28	**37** 444
39.298 337	4737.938 657	.000 211 0623	.025 446	120.563 336	.008 294 3956	9.96	2.782 244	7.32	**38** 456
43.284 399	5231.059 686	.000 191 1659	.023 103	120.853 236	.008 274 4992	9.93	2.872 466	7.37	**39** 468
47.674 770	5774.198 374	.000 173 1842	.020 975	121.116 439	.008 256 5175	9.91	2.963 128	7.41	**40** 480
52.510 460	6372.428 051	.000 156 9261	.019 044	121.355 403	.008 240 2594	9.89	3.054 208	7.45	**41** 492
57.836 638	7031.336 641	.000 142 2205	.017 290	121.572 361	.008 225 5538	9.88	3.145 679	7.49	**42** 504
63.703 054	7757.078 853	.000 128 9145	.015 698	121.769 340	.008 212 2478	9.86	3.237 520	7.53	**43** 516
70.164 506	8556.433 676	.000 116 8711	.014 252	121.948 179	.008 200 2045	9.85	3.329 708	7.57	**44** 528
77.281 347	9436.867 695	.000 105 9674	.012 940	122.110 548	.008 189 3007	9.83	3.422 222	7.60	**45** 540
85.120 056	10406.604 837	.000 096 0928	.011 748	122.257 965	.008 179 4262	9.82	3.515 043	7.64	**46** 552
93.753 851	11474.703 189	.000 087 1482	.010 666	122.391 807	.008 170 4816	9.81	3.608 152	7.68	**47** 564
103.263 378	12651.139 608	.000 079 0443	.009 684	122.513 323	.008 162 3776	9.80	3.701 529	7.71	**48** 576
113.737 465	13946.902 909	.000 071 7005	.008 792	122.623 648	.008 155 0338	9.79	3.795 160	7.75	**49** 588
125.273 947	15374.096 513	.000 065 0445	.007 983	122.723 814	.008 148 3778	9.78	3.889 027	7.78	**50** 600

Effective Rate is 10.14 %

Annual Percentage Rate is 9.70 %

MONTHLY COMPOUND INTEREST AND ANNUITY

9.75 % M

Amount Of 1	Amount Of 1 Per Period	Sinking Fund Payment	Present Worth Of 1	Present Worth of 1 Per Period	Periodic Payment To Amortize 1	Constant Annual Percent	Total Interest	Annual Add On Rate
What a single $ 1 deposit grows to in the future. The deposit is made at the beginning of the first period.	What a series of $ 1 deposits grow to in the future. A deposit is made at the end of each period.	The amount to be deposited at the end of each period that grows to $ 1 in the future.	What $ 1 to be paid in the future is worth today. Value today of a single $ 1 payment tomorrow.	What $ 1 to be paid at the end of each period is worth today. Value today of a series of $ 1 payments tomorrow.	The mortgage payment to amortize a loan of $ 1. An annuity certain, payable at the end of each period, worth $ 1 today.	The annual payment, including interest and principal, to amortize completely a loan of $ 100.	The total interest paid over the term on a loan of $1. The loan is amortized by regular periodic payments.	The average annual interest rate on a loan that is completely amortized by regular periodic payments.
$S = (1+i)^n$	$S\overline{n}| = \dfrac{(1+i)^n - 1}{i}$	$\dfrac{1}{S\overline{n}|} = \dfrac{i}{(1+i)^n - 1}$	$V^n = \dfrac{1}{(1+i)^n}$	$A\overline{n}| = \dfrac{1 - V^n}{i}$	$\dfrac{1}{A\overline{n}|} = \dfrac{i}{1 - V^n}$			

YEAR	Amount Of 1	Amount Of 1 Per Period	Sinking Fund Payment	Present Worth Of 1	Present Worth of 1 Per Period	Periodic Payment To Amortize 1	Constant Annual Percent	Total Interest	Annual Add On Rate	PERIODS
	1.008 125	1.000 000	1.000 000 0000	.991 940	.991 940	1.008 125 0000	1209.75	.008 125	9.75	1
	1.016 316	2.008 125	.497 976 9686	.983 946	1.975 886	.506 101 9686	607.33	.012 204	7.32	2
	1.024 574	3.024 441	.330 639 6107	.976 016	2.951 902	.338 764 6107	406.52	.016 294	6.52	3
	1.032 898	4.049 015	.246 973 6711	.968 150	3.920 052	.255 098 6711	306.12	.020 395	6.12	4
	1.041 291	5.081 913	.196 776 2988	.960 347	4.880 399	.204 901 2988	245.89	.024 506	5.88	5
	1.049 751	6.123 203	.163 313 2100	.952 607	5.833 005	.171 438 2100	205.73	.028 629	5.73	6
	1.058 280	7.172 954	.139 412 5687	.944 929	6.777 935	.147 537 5687	177.05	.032 763	5.62	7
	1.066 879	8.231 235	.121 488 4571	.937 314	7.715 248	.129 613 4571	155.54	.036 908	5.54	8
	1.075 547	9.298 113	.107 548 6985	.929 759	8.645 008	.115 673 6985	138.81	.041 063	5.48	9
	1.084 286	10.373 661	.096 397 9868	.922 266	9.567 273	.104 522 9868	125.43	.045 230	5.43	10
	1.093 096	11.457 947	.087 275 6728	.914 833	10.482 106	.095 400 6728	114.49	.049 407	5.39	11
	1.101 977	12.551 042	.079 674 6570	.907 460	11.389 566	.087 799 6570	105.36	.053 596	5.36	12
1	1.101 977	12.551 042	.079 674 6570	.907 460	11.389 566	.087 799 6570	105.36	.053 596	5.36	12
2	1.214 354	26.382 005	.037 904 6244	.823 483	21.725 139	.046 029 6244	55.24	.104 711	5.24	24
3	1.338 190	41.623 411	.024 024 9410	.747 278	31.104 256	.032 149 9410	38.58	.157 398	5.25	36
4	1.474 655	58.419 093	.017 117 6912	.678 125	39.615 427	.025 242 6912	30.30	.211 649	5.29	48
5	1.625 036	76.927 553	.012 999 2437	.615 371	47.338 973	.021 124 2437	25.35	.267 455	5.35	60
6	1.790 753	97.323 453	.010 275 0156	.558 424	54.347 780	.018 400 0156	22.09	.324 801	5.41	72
7	1.973 369	119.799 271	.008 347 2962	.506 748	60.707 990	.016 472 2962	19.77	.383 673	5.48	84
8	2.174 608	144.567 109	.006 917 2027	.459 853	66.479 625	.015 042 2027	18.06	.444 051	5.55	96
9	2.396 368	171.860 704	.005 818 6658	.417 298	71.717 152	.013 943 6658	16.74	.505 916	5.62	108
10	2.640 743	201.937 623	.004 952 0242	.378 681	76.469 997	.013 077 0242	15.70	.569 243	5.69	120
11	2.910 039	235.081 703	.004 253 8402	.343 638	80.783 012	.012 378 8402	14.86	.634 007	5.76	132
12	3.206 797	271.605 724	.003 681 8075	.311 838	84.696 900	.011 806 8075	14.17	.700 180	5.83	144
13	3.533 817	311.854 363	.003 206 6250	.282 980	88.248 596	.011 331 6250	13.60	.767 734	5.91	156
14	3.894 185	356.207 446	.002 807 3529	.256 793	91.471 617	.010 932 3529	13.12	.836 635	5.98	168
15	4.291 304	405.083 533	.002 468 6266	.233 029	94.396 379	.010 593 6266	12.72	.906 853	6.05	180
16	4.728 919	458.943 868	.002 178 9157	.211 465	97.050 483	.010 303 9157	12.37	.978 352	6.11	192
17	5.211 161	518.296 730	.001 929 3967	.191 896	99.458 976	.010 054 3967	12.07	1.051 097	6.18	204
18	5.742 581	583.702 232	.001 713 2023	.174 138	101.644 586	.009 838 2023	11.81	1.125 052	6.25	216
19	6.328 193	655.777 606	.001 524 9072	.158 023	103.627 939	.009 649 9072	11.58	1.200 179	6.32	228
20	6.973 525	735.203 025	.001 360 1685	.143 400	105.427 753	.009 485 1685	11.39	1.276 440	6.38	240
21	7.684 665	822.728 028	.001 215 4685	.130 129	107.061 011	.009 340 4685	11.21	1.353 798	6.45	252
22	8.468 326	919.178 587	.001 087 9279	.118 087	108.543 127	.009 212 9279	11.06	1.432 213	6.51	264
23	9.331 902	1025.464 906	.000 975 1675	.107 159	109.888 088	.009 100 1675	10.93	1.511 646	6.57	276
24	10.283 544	1142.590 009	.000 875 2046	.097 243	111.108 586	.009 000 2046	10.81	1.592 059	6.63	288
25	11.332 231	1271.659 204	.000 786 3742	.088 244	112.216 138	.008 911 3742	10.70	1.673 412	6.69	300
26	12.487 860	1413.890 516	.000 707 2683	.080 078	113.221 198	.008 832 2683	10.60	1.755 668	6.75	312
27	13.761 338	1570.626 183	.000 636 6887	.072 667	114.133 249	.008 761 6887	10.52	1.838 787	6.81	324
28	15.164 681	1743.345 316	.000 573 6098	.065 943	114.960 898	.008 698 6098	10.44	1.922 733	6.87	336
29	16.711 133	1933.677 867	.000 517 1492	.059 840	115.711 957	.008 642 1492	10.38	2.007 468	6.92	348
30	18.415 288	2143.420 002	.000 466 5441	.054 303	116.393 513	.008 591 5441	10.31	2.092 956	6.98	360
31	20.293 227	2374.551 057	.000 421 1322	.049 278	117.011 997	.008 546 1322	10.26	2.179 161	7.03	372
32	22.362 674	2629.252 215	.000 380 3363	.044 717	117.573 247	.008 505 3363	10.21	2.266 049	7.08	384
33	24.643 158	2909.927 088	.000 343 6512	.040 579	118.082 558	.008 468 6512	10.17	2.353 586	7.13	396
34	27.156 198	3219.224 404	.000 310 6338	.036 824	118.544 738	.008 435 6338	10.13	2.441 739	7.18	408
35	29.925 512	3560.063 001	.000 280 8939	.033 416	118.964 147	.008 405 8939	10.09	2.530 475	7.23	420
36	32.977 232	3935.659 371	.000 254 0870	.030 324	119.344 744	.008 379 0870	10.06	2.619 766	7.28	432
37	36.340 159	4349.558 013	.000 229 9084	.027 518	119.690 121	.008 354 9084	10.03	2.709 579	7.32	444
38	40.046 027	4805.664 889	.000 208 0878	.024 971	120.003 536	.008 333 0878	10.00	2.799 888	7.37	456
39	44.129 810	5308.284 276	.000 188 3848	.022 660	120.287 948	.008 313 3848	9.98	2.890 664	7.41	468
40	48.630 045	5862.159 390	.000 170 5856	.020 563	120.546 041	.008 295 5856	9.96	2.981 881	7.45	480
41	53.589 202	6472.517 149	.000 154 4994	.018 660	120.780 249	.008 279 4994	9.94	3.073 514	7.50	492
42	59.054 080	7145.117 495	.000 139 9557	.016 934	120.992 784	.008 264 9557	9.92	3.165 538	7.54	504
43	65.076 251	7886.307 754	.000 126 8021	.015 367	121.185 651	.008 251 8021	9.91	3.257 930	7.58	516
44	71.712 546	8703.082 535	.000 114 9018	.013 945	121.360 669	.008 239 9018	9.89	3.350 668	7.62	528
45	79.025 592	9603.149 738	.000 104 1325	.012 654	121.519 492	.008 229 1325	9.88	3.443 732	7.65	540
46	87.084 402	10595.003 291	.000 094 3841	.011 483	121.663 617	.008 219 3841	9.87	3.537 100	7.69	552
47	95.965 027	11688.003 312	.000 085 5578	.010 420	121.794 405	.008 210 5578	9.86	3.630 755	7.73	564
48	105.751 274	12892.464 437	.000 077 5647	.009 456	121.913 089	.008 202 5647	9.85	3.724 677	7.76	576
49	116.535 494	14219.753 158	.000 070 3247	.008 581	122.020 791	.008 195 3247	9.84	3.818 851	7.79	588
50	128.419 460	15682.395 093	.000 063 7658	.007 787	122.118 525	.008 188 7658	9.83	3.913 259	7.83	600

Effective Rate is 10.20 %

Annual Percentage Rate is 9.75 %

MONTHLY COMPOUND INTEREST AND ANNUITY

Amount Of 1	Amount Of 1 Per Period	Sinking Fund Payment	Present Worth Of 1	Present Worth of 1 Per Period	Periodic Payment To Amortize 1	Constant Annual Percent	Total Interest	Annual Add On Rate
What a single $ 1 deposit grows to in the future. The deposit is made at the beginning of the first period.	What a series of $ 1 deposits grow to in the future. A deposit is made at the end of each period.	The amount to be deposited at the end of each period that grows to $ 1 in the future.	What $ 1 to be paid in the future is worth today. Value today of a single $ 1 payment tomorrow.	What $ 1 to be paid at the end of each period is worth today. Value today of a series of $ 1 payments tomorrow.	The mortgage payment to amortize a loan of $ 1. An annuity certain, payable at the end of each period, worth $ 1 today.	The annual payment, including interest and principal, to amortize completely a loan of $ 100.	The total interest paid over the term on a loan of $ 1. The loan is amortized by regular periodic payments.	The average annual interest rate on a loan that is completely amortized by regular periodic payments.

$$S = (1+i)^n \qquad S\overline{n}| = \frac{(1+i)^n - 1}{i} \qquad \frac{1}{S\overline{n}|} = \frac{i}{(1+i)^n - 1} \qquad V^n = \frac{1}{(1+i)^n} \qquad A\overline{n}| = \frac{1 - V^n}{i} \qquad \frac{1}{A\overline{n}|} = \frac{i}{1 - V^n}$$

YEAR | | | | | | | | **PERIODS**

YEAR	Amount Of 1	Amount Of 1 Per Period	Sinking Fund Payment	Present Worth Of 1	Present Worth of 1 Per Period	Periodic Payment To Amortize 1	Constant Annual Percent	Total Interest	Annual Add On Rate	PERIODS
	1.008 167	1.000 000	1.000 000 0000	.991 899	.991 899	1.008 166 6667	1209.80	.008 167	9.80	1
	1.016 400	2.008 167	.497 966 6362	.983 865	1.975 764	.506 133 3029	607.36	.012 267	7.36	2
	1.024 701	3.024 567	.330 625 8717	.975 895	2.951 659	.338 792 5384	406.56	.016 378	6.55	3
	1.033 069	4.049 267	.246 958 2570	.967 990	3.919 648	.255 124 9236	306.15	.020 500	6.15	4
	1.041 506	5.082 336	.196 759 9020	.960 148	4.879 797	.204 926 5687	245.92	.024 633	5.91	5
	1.050 011	6.123 842	.163 296 1768	.952 371	5.832 167	.171 462 8435	205.76	.028 777	5.76	6
	1.058 586	7.173 853	.139 395 0971	.944 656	6.776 823	.147 561 7638	177.08	.032 932	5.65	7
	1.067 232	8.232 440	.121 470 6707	.937 004	7.713 827	.129 637 3374	155.57	.037 099	5.56	8
	1.075 947	9.299 672	.107 530 6797	.929 414	8.643 241	.115 697 3464	138.84	.041 276	5.50	9
	1.084 734	10.375 619	.096 379 7934	.921 885	9.565 125	.104 546 4600	125.46	.045 465	5.46	10
	1.093 593	11.460 353	.087 257 3467	.914 417	10.479 542	.095 424 0133	114.51	.049 664	5.42	11
	1.102 524	12.553 946	.079 656 2295	.907 010	11.386 552	.087 822 8962	105.39	.053 875	5.39	12
1	1.102 524	12.553 946	.079 656 2295	.907 010	11.386 552	.087 822 8962	105.39	.053 875	5.39	12
2	1.215 559	26.394 971	.037 886 0045	.822 667	21.714 267	.046 052 6711	55.27	.105 264	5.26	24
3	1.340 183	41.655 032	.024 006 7032	.746 167	31.081 606	.032 173 3699	38.61	.158 241	5.27	36
4	1.477 584	58.479 614	.017 099 9760	.676 781	39.577 874	.025 266 6426	30.32	.212 799	5.32	48
5	1.629 071	77.029 118	.012 982 1037	.613 847	47.284 073	.021 148 7704	25.38	.268 926	5.38	60
6	1.796 090	97.480 389	.010 258 4736	.556 765	54.273 671	.018 425 1403	22.12	.326 610	5.44	72
7	1.980 232	120.028 404	.008 331 3613	.504 991	60.613 305	.016 498 0280	19.80	.385 834	5.51	84
8	2.183 253	144.888 129	.006 901 8767	.458 032	66.363 415	.015 068 5434	18.09	.446 580	5.58	96
9	2.407 089	172.296 570	.005 803 9461	.415 440	71.578 822	.013 970 6127	16.77	.508 826	5.65	108
10	2.653 873	202.515 030	.004 937 9051	.376 808	76.309 247	.013 104 5718	15.73	.572 549	5.73	120
11	2.925 958	235.831 605	.004 240 3138	.341 768	80.599 789	.012 406 9804	14.89	.637 721	5.80	132
12	3.225 939	272.563 925	.003 668 8641	.309 987	84.491 352	.011 835 5308	14.21	.704 316	5.87	144
13	3.556 675	313.062 186	.003 194 2536	.281 162	88.021 039	.011 360 9202	13.64	.772 304	5.94	156
14	3.921 319	357.712 485	.002 795 5412	.255 016	91.222 499	.010 962 2079	13.16	.841 651	6.01	168
15	4.323 347	406.940 508	.002 457 3617	.231 302	94.126 255	.010 624 0283	12.75	.912 325	6.08	180
16	4.766 594	461.215 578	.002 168 1835	.209 793	96.759 990	.010 334 8502	12.41	.984 291	6.15	192
17	5.255 284	521.055 140	.001 919 1827	.190 285	99.148 814	.010 085 8493	12.11	1.057 513	6.22	204
18	5.794 076	587.029 687	.001 703 4914	.172 590	101.315 500	.009 870 1580	11.85	1.131 954	6.29	216
19	6.388 107	659.768 201	.001 515 6838	.156 541	103.280 706	.009 682 3505	11.62	1.207 576	6.36	228
20	7.043 041	739.964 151	.001 351 4168	.141 984	105.063 168	.009 518 0835	11.43	1.284 340	6.42	240
21	7.765 120	828.382 101	.001 207 1724	.128 781	106.679 877	.009 373 8391	11.25	1.362 207	6.49	252
22	8.561 231	925.865 004	.001 080 0711	.116 806	108.146 249	.009 246 7377	11.10	1.441 139	6.55	264
23	9.438 962	1033.342 234	.000 967 7336	.105 944	109.476 262	.009 134 4003	10.97	1.521 094	6.61	276
24	10.406 681	1151.838 447	.000 868 1773	.096 092	110.682 598	.009 034 8440	10.85	1.602 035	6.68	288
25	11.473 614	1282.483 354	.000 779 7372	.087 156	111.776 756	.008 946 4039	10.74	1.683 921	6.74	300
26	12.649 934	1426.522 484	.000 701 0054	.079 052	112.769 168	.008 867 6721	10.65	1.766 714	6.80	312
27	13.946 854	1585.329 067	.000 630 7839	.071 701	113.669 295	.008 797 4505	10.56	1.850 374	6.85	324
28	15.376 740	1760.417 119	.000 568 0472	.065 033	114.485 719	.008 734 7139	10.49	1.934 864	6.91	336
29	16.953 223	1953.455 879	.000 511 9133	.058 986	115.226 224	.008 678 5799	10.42	2.020 146	6.97	348
30	18.691 333	2166.285 725	.000 461 6196	.053 501	115.897 870	.008 628 2863	10.36	2.106 150	7.02	360
31	20.607 642	2400.935 714	.000 416 5043	.048 526	116.507 059	.008 583 1709	10.30	2.192 940	7.07	372
32	22.720 417	2659.642 934	.000 375 9903	.044 013	117.059 599	.008 542 6570	10.26	2.280 380	7.13	384
33	25.049 803	2944.873 824	.000 339 5731	.039 920	117.560 758	.008 506 2398	10.21	2.368 471	7.18	396
34	27.618 006	3259.347 696	.000 306 8099	.036 208	118.015 315	.008 473 4765	10.17	2.457 178	7.23	408
35	30.449 512	3606.062 652	.000 277 3108	.032 841	118.427 602	.008 443 9774	10.14	2.546 471	7.28	420
36	33.571 314	3988.324 176	.000 250 7319	.029 787	118.801 551	.008 417 3985	10.11	2.636 316	7.32	432
37	37.013 176	4409.776 638	.000 226 7689	.027 017	119.140 726	.008 393 4355	10.08	2.726 685	7.37	444
38	40.807 911	4874.438 048	.000 205 1519	.024 505	119.448 361	.008 371 8185	10.05	2.817 594	7.41	456
39	44.991 697	5386.738 353	.000 185 6411	.022 226	119.727 389	.008 352 3078	10.03	2.908 880	7.46	468
40	49.604 420	5951.561 680	.000 168 0231	.020 159	119.980 470	.008 334 6898	10.01	3.000 651	7.50	480
41	54.690 059	6574.292 892	.000 152 1076	.018 285	120.210 017	.008 318 7743	9.99	3.092 837	7.54	492
42	60.297 096	7260.868 932	.000 137 7246	.016 585	120.418 219	.008 304 3912	9.97	3.185 413	7.58	504
43	66.478 989	8017.835 419	.000 124 7219	.015 042	120.607 060	.008 291 3886	9.95	3.278 357	7.62	516
44	73.294 674	8852.409 057	.000 112 9636	.013 644	120.778 340	.008 279 6303	9.94	3.371 645	7.66	528
45	80.809 129	9772.546 432	.000 102 3275	.012 375	120.933 693	.008 268 9941	9.93	3.465 257	7.70	540
46	89.093 996	10787.019 872	.000 092 7040	.011 224	121.074 600	.008 259 3707	9.92	3.559 173	7.74	552
47	98.228 259	11905.501 077	.000 083 9948	.010 180	121.202 404	.008 250 6615	9.91	3.653 373	7.77	564
48	108.299 002	13138.653 329	.000 076 1113	.009 234	121.318 323	.008 242 7780	9.90	3.747 840	7.81	576
49	119.402 237	14498.233 148	.000 068 9739	.008 375	121.423 463	.008 235 6406	9.89	3.842 557	7.84	588
50	131.643 819	15997.202 382	.000 062 5109	.007 596	121.518 826	.008 229 1776	9.88	3.937 507	7.88	600

Effective Rate is 10.25 %

Annual Percentage Rate is 9.80 %

MONTHLY COMPOUND INTEREST AND ANNUITY

9.85 % M

	Amount Of 1	Amount Of 1 Per Period	Sinking Fund Payment	Present Worth Of 1	Present Worth of 1 Per Period	Periodic Payment To Amortize 1	Constant Annual Percent	Total Interest	Annual Add On Rate	
	What a single $1 deposit grows to in the future. The deposit is made at the beginning of the first period.	What a series of $1 deposits grow to in the future. A deposit is made at the end of each period.	The amount to be deposited at the end of each period that grows to $1 in the future.	What $1 to be paid in the future is worth today. Value today of a single $1 payment tomorrow.	What $1 to be paid at the end of each period is worth today. Value today of a series of $1 payments tomorrow.	The mortgage payment to amortize a loan of $1. An annuity certain, payable at the end of each period, worth $1 today.	The annual payment, including interest and principal, to amortize completely a loan of $100.	The total interest paid over the term on a loan of $1. The loan is amortized by regular periodic payments.	The average annual interest rate on a loan that is completely amortized by regular periodic payments.	
	$S = (1+i)^n$	$S\overline{n}| = \dfrac{(1+i)^n - 1}{i}$	$\dfrac{1}{S\overline{n}|} = \dfrac{i}{(1+i)^n - 1}$	$V^n = \dfrac{1}{(1+i)^n}$	$A\overline{n}| = \dfrac{1-V^n}{i}$	$\dfrac{1}{A\overline{n}|} = \dfrac{i}{1-V^n}$				

YEAR   **PERIODS**

	Amount Of 1	Amount Of 1 Per Period	Sinking Fund Payment	Present Worth Of 1	Present Worth of 1 Per Period	Periodic Payment To Amortize 1	Constant Annual Percent	Total Interest	Annual Add On Rate	
	1.008 208	1.000 000	1.000 000 0000	.991 858	.991 858	1.008 208 3333	1209.85	.008 208	9.85	1
	1.016 484	2.008 208	.497 956 3043	.983 783	1.975 642	.506 164 6377	607.40	.012 329	7.40	2
	1.024 828	3.024 692	.330 612 1335	.975 774	2.951 416	.338 820 4669	406.59	.016 461	6.58	3
	1.033 240	4.049 520	.246 942 8439	.967 830	3.919 245	.255 151 1772	306.19	.020 605	6.18	4
	1.041 721	5.082 760	.196 743 5066	.959 950	4.879 195	.204 951 8399	245.95	.024 759	5.94	5
	1.050 272	6.124 481	.163 279 1453	.952 135	5.831 330	.171 487 4787	205.79	.028 925	5.78	6
	1.058 893	7.174 753	.139 377 6274	.944 383	6.775 712	.147 585 9607	177.11	.033 102	5.67	7
	1.067 585	8.233 645	.121 452 8865	.936 694	7.712 406	.129 661 2198	155.60	.037 290	5.59	8
	1.076 348	9.301 230	.107 512 6634	.929 068	8.641 474	.115 720 9967	138.87	.041 489	5.53	9
	1.085 183	10.377 578	.096 361 6027	.921 504	9.562 978	.104 569 9360	125.49	.045 699	5.48	10
	1.094 090	11.462 760	.087 239 0236	.914 001	10.476 979	.095 447 3569	114.54	.049 921	5.45	11
	1.103 071	12.556 850	.079 637 8055	.906 560	11.383 540	.087 846 1389	105.42	.054 154	5.42	12
1	1.103 071	12.556 850	.079 637 8055	.906 560	11.383 540	.087 846 1389	105.42	.054 154	5.42	12
2	1.216 765	26.407 945	.037 867 3914	.821 851	21.703 403	.046 075 7247	55.30	.105 817	5.29	24
3	1.342 178	41.686 684	.023 988 4756	.745 058	31.058 979	.032 196 8089	38.64	.159 085	5.30	36
4	1.480 518	58.540 215	.017 082 2742	.675 439	39.540 371	.025 290 6076	30.35	.213 949	5.35	48
5	1.633 116	77.130 852	.012 964 9805	.612 326	47.229 263	.021 173 3139	25.41	.270 399	5.41	60
6	1.801 442	97.637 642	.010 241 9515	.555 111	54.199 705	.018 450 2849	22.15	.328 421	5.47	72
7	1.987 118	120.258 084	.008 315 4493	.503 241	60.518 830	.016 523 7826	19.83	.387 998	5.54	84
8	2.191 932	145.210 032	.006 886 5765	.456 218	66.247 497	.015 094 9099	18.12	.449 111	5.61	96
9	2.417 857	172.733 799	.005 789 2550	.413 589	71.440 878	.013 997 5883	16.80	.511 740	5.69	108
10	2.667 067	203.094 462	.004 923 8172	.374 944	76.148 990	.013 132 1505	15.76	.575 858	5.76	120
11	2.941 964	236.584 424	.004 226 8210	.339 909	80.417 177	.012 435 1543	14.93	.641 440	5.83	132
12	3.245 194	273.526 223	.003 655 9566	.308 148	84.286 544	.011 864 2899	14.24	.708 458	5.90	144
13	3.579 679	314.275 643	.003 181 9201	.279 355	87.794 359	.011 390 2535	13.67	.776 880	5.98	156
14	3.948 640	359.225 139	.002 783 7695	.253 252	90.974 403	.010 992 1029	13.20	.846 673	6.05	168
15	4.355 629	408.807 616	.002 446 1384	.229 588	93.857 305	.010 654 4717	12.79	.917 805	6.12	180
16	4.804 567	463.500 600	.002 157 4945	.208 135	96.470 828	.010 365 8278	12.44	.990 239	6.19	192
17	5.299 778	523.830 834	.001 909 0132	.188 687	98.840 145	.010 117 3466	12.15	1.063 939	6.26	204
18	5.846 031	590.379 354	.001 693 8262	.171 056	100.988 072	.009 902 1595	11.89	1.138 866	6.33	216
19	6.448 586	663.787 084	.001 506 5072	.155 073	102.935 298	.009 714 8405	11.66	1.214 984	6.39	228
20	7.113 247	744.761 008	.001 342 7126	.140 583	104.700 575	.009 551 0459	11.47	1.292 251	6.46	240
21	7.846 415	834.080 981	.001 198 9244	.127 447	106.300 904	.009 407 2577	11.29	1.370 629	6.53	252
22	8.655 151	932.607 235	.001 072 2628	.115 538	107.751 699	.009 280 5961	11.14	1.450 077	6.59	264
23	9.547 245	1041.288 671	.000 960 3485	.104 742	109.066 932	.009 168 6818	11.01	1.530 556	6.65	276
24	10.531 287	1161.171 991	.000 861 1989	.094 955	110.259 270	.009 069 5322	10.89	1.612 025	6.72	288
25	11.616 755	1293.411 782	.000 773 1490	.086 083	111.340 196	.008 981 4823	10.78	1.694 445	6.78	300
26	12.814 103	1439.281 636	.000 694 7911	.078 039	112.320 120	.008 903 1244	10.69	1.777 775	6.84	312
27	14.134 863	1600.186 414	.000 624 9272	.070 747	113.208 480	.008 833 2605	10.60	1.861 976	6.90	324
28	15.591 755	1777.675 778	.000 562 5323	.064 136	114.013 832	.008 770 8656	10.53	1.947 011	6.95	336
29	17.198 810	1973.459 116	.000 506 7245	.058 144	114.743 932	.008 715 0578	10.46	2.032 840	7.01	348
30	18.971 506	2189.422 001	.000 456 7416	.052 711	115.405 812	.008 665 0749	10.40	2.119 427	7.06	360
31	20.926 914	2427.644 356	.000 411 9220	.047 785	116.005 845	.008 620 2553	10.35	2.206 735	7.12	372
32	23.083 868	2690.420 483	.000 371 6891	.043 320	116.549 812	.008 580 0224	10.30	2.294 729	7.17	384
33	25.463 141	2980.281 159	.000 335 5388	.039 272	117.042 950	.008 543 8721	10.26	2.383 373	7.22	396
34	28.087 648	3300.018 010	.000 303 0286	.035 603	117.490 009	.008 511 3620	10.22	2.472 636	7.27	408
35	30.982 665	3652.710 398	.000 273 7693	.032 276	117.895 296	.008 482 1026	10.18	2.562 483	7.32	420
36	34.176 073	4041.755 077	.000 247 4173	.029 260	118.262 712	.008 455 7506	10.15	2.652 884	7.37	432
37	37.698 629	4470.898 908	.000 223 6687	.026 526	118.595 797	.008 432 0020	10.12	2.743 809	7.42	444
38	41.584 257	4944.274 942	.000 202 2541	.024 048	118.897 759	.008 410 5875	10.10	2.835 228	7.46	456
39	45.870 380	5466.442 229	.000 182 9343	.021 801	119.171 505	.008 391 2677	10.07	2.927 113	7.51	468
40	50.598 277	6042.429 722	.000 165 4963	.019 764	119.419 673	.008 373 8297	10.05	3.019 438	7.55	480
41	55.813 483	6677.784 714	.000 149 7503	.017 917	119.644 652	.008 358 0836	10.03	3.112 177	7.59	492
42	61.566 224	7378.626 261	.000 135 5266	.016 243	119.848 608	.008 343 8599	10.02	3.205 305	7.63	504
43	67.911 905	8151.704 116	.000 122 6737	.014 725	120.033 508	.008 331 0071	10.00	3.298 800	7.67	516
44	74.911 640	9004.463 735	.000 111 0560	.013 349	120.201 130	.008 319 3894	9.99	3.392 638	7.71	528
45	82.632 843	9945.117 979	.000 100 5518	.012 102	120.353 089	.008 308 8852	9.98	3.486 798	7.75	540
46	91.149 878	10982.726 222	.000 091 0521	.010 971	120.490 850	.008 299 3854	9.96	3.581 261	7.79	552
47	100.544 770	12127.281 589	.000 082 4587	.009 946	120.615 738	.008 290 7920	9.95	3.676 007	7.82	564
48	110.908 001	13389.807 208	.000 074 6837	.009 016	120.728 957	.008 283 0170	9.94	3.771 018	7.86	576
49	122.339 379	14782.462 368	.000 067 6477	.008 174	120.831 596	.008 275 9811	9.94	3.866 277	7.86	588
50	134.948 998	16318.659 628	.000 061 2795	.007 410	120.924 645	.008 269 6129	9.93	3.961 768	7.92	600

Effective Rate is 10.31 %   8 - 132   Annual Percentage Rate is 9.85 %

Amount Of 1	Amount Of 1 Per Period	Sinking Fund Payment	Present Worth Of 1	Present Worth of 1 Per Period	Periodic Payment To Amortize 1	Constant Annual Percent	Total Interest	Annual Add On Rate
What a single $ 1 deposit grows to in the future. The deposit is made at the beginning of the first period.	What a series of $ 1 deposits grow to in the future. A deposit is made at the end of each period.	The amount to be deposited at the end of each period that grows to $ 1 in the future.	What $ 1 to be paid in the future is worth today. Value today of a single $ 1 payment tomorrow.	What $ 1 to be paid at the end of each period is worth today. Value today of a series of $ 1 payments tomorrow.	The mortgage payment to amortize a loan of $ 1. An annuity certain, payable at the end of each period, worth $ 1 today.	The annual payment, including interest and principal, to amortize completely a loan of $ 100.	The total interest paid over the term on a loan of $1. The loan is amortized by regular periodic payments.	The average annual interest rate on a loan that is completely amortized by regular periodic payments.
$S = (1+i)^n$	$S\overline{n}| = \dfrac{(1+i)^n - 1}{i}$	$\dfrac{1}{S\overline{n}|} = \dfrac{i}{(1+i)^n - 1}$	$V^n = \dfrac{1}{(1+i)^n}$	$A\overline{n}| = \dfrac{1 - V^n}{i}$	$\dfrac{1}{A\overline{n}|} = \dfrac{i}{1 - V^n}$			

YEAR									PERIODS
	1.008 229	1.000 000	1.000 000 0000	.991 838	.991 838	1.008 229 1667	1209.88	.008 229	9.87	1
	1.016 526	2.008 229	.497 951 1385	.983 743	1.975 581	.506 180 3052	607.42	.012 361	7.42	2
	1.024 891	3.024 755	.330 605 2647	.975 713	2.951 294	.338 834 4314	406.61	.016 503	6.60	3
	1.033 325	4.049 646	.246 935 1377	.967 750	3.919 043	.255 164 3044	306.20	.020 657	6.20	4
	1.041 829	5.082 972	.196 735 3094	.959 851	4.878 894	.204 964 4760	245.96	.024 822	5.96	5
	1.050 402	6.124 800	.163 270 6302	.952 016	5.830 911	.171 499 7969	205.80	.028 999	5.80	6
	1.059 046	7.175 202	.139 368 8933	.944 246	6.775 157	.147 598 0600	177.12	.033 186	5.69	7
	1.067 761	8.234 248	.121 443 9952	.936 539	7.711 696	.129 673 1619	155.61	.037 385	5.61	8
	1.076 548	9.302 009	.107 503 6562	.928 895	8.640 591	.115 732 8229	138.88	.041 595	5.55	9
	1.085 407	10.378 557	.096 352 5084	.921 313	9.561 905	.104 581 6751	125.50	.045 817	5.50	10
	1.094 339	11.463 964	.087 229 8632	.913 794	10.475 698	.095 459 0299	114.56	.050 049	5.46	11
	1.103 344	12.558 303	.079 628 5948	.906 335	11.382 034	.087 857 7615	105.43	.054 293	5.43	12
1	1.103 344	12.558 303	.079 628 5948	.906 335	11.382 034	.087 857 7615	105.43	.054 293	5.43	12
2	1.217 369	26.414 435	.037 858 0874	.821 444	21.697 973	.046 087 2540	55.31	.106 094	5.30	24
3	1.343 177	41.702 521	.023 979 3656	.744 504	31.047 674	.032 208 5323	38.66	.159 507	5.32	36
4	1.481 987	58.570 544	.017 073 4284	.674 770	39.521 638	.025 302 5951	30.37	.214 525	5.36	48
5	1.635 142	77.181 783	.012 956 4252	.611 568	47.201 891	.021 185 5919	25.43	.271 136	5.42	60
6	1.804 124	97.716 388	.010 233 6979	.554 285	54.162 776	.018 462 8646	22.16	.329 326	5.49	72
7	1.990 571	120.373 129	.008 307 5019	.502 369	60.471 672	.016 536 6686	19.85	.389 080	5.56	84
8	2.196 285	145.371 317	.006 878 9361	.455 314	66.189 648	.015 108 1028	18.13	.450 378	5.63	96
9	2.423 258	172.952 926	.005 781 9201	.412 667	71.372 051	.014 011 0868	16.82	.513 197	5.70	108
10	2.673 689	203.384 939	.004 916 7849	.374 015	76.069 046	.013 145 9516	15.78	.577 514	5.78	120
11	2.949 999	236.961 930	.004 220 0872	.338 983	80.326 099	.012 449 2538	14.94	.643 302	5.85	132
12	3.254 865	274.008 913	.003 649 5163	.307 232	84.184 417	.011 878 6830	14.26	.710 530	5.92	144
13	3.591 237	314.884 493	.003 175 7677	.278 456	87.681 346	.011 404 9344	13.69	.779 170	5.99	156
14	3.962 371	359.984 334	.002 777 8987	.252 374	90.850 737	.011 007 0653	13.21	.849 187	6.07	168
15	4.371 860	409.744 990	.002 440 5423	.228 736	93.723 268	.010 669 7090	12.81	.920 548	6.14	180
16	4.823 667	464.648 129	.002 152 1662	.207 311	96.326 745	.010 381 3329	12.46	.993 216	6.21	192
17	5.322 166	525.225 198	.001 903 9641	.187 893	98.686 367	.010 133 1119	12.16	1.067 155	6.28	204
18	5.872 182	592.062 566	.001 689 0107	.170 294	100.824 977	.009 918 1774	11.91	1.142 326	6.35	216
19	6.479 038	665.807 199	.001 501 9363	.154 344	102.763 274	.009 731 1030	11.68	1.218 691	6.41	228
20	7.148 611	747.172 925	.001 338 3783	.139 887	104.520 021	.009 567 5449	11.49	1.296 211	6.48	240
21	7.887 379	836.947 340	.001 194 8183	.126 785	106.112 224	.009 423 9850	11.31	1.374 844	6.55	252
22	8.702 495	935.999 436	.001 068 3767	.114 910	107.555 293	.009 297 5434	11.16	1.454 551	6.61	264
23	9.601 849	1045.288 007	.000 956 6741	.104 147	108.863 197	.009 185 8408	11.03	1.535 292	6.68	276
24	10.594 146	1165.870 936	.000 857 7279	.094 392	110.048 598	.009 086 8945	10.91	1.617 026	6.74	288
25	11.688 992	1298.915 432	.000 769 8731	.085 551	111.122 968	.008 999 0397	10.80	1.699 712	6.80	300
26	12.896 983	1445.709 327	.000 691 7020	.077 538	112.096 707	.008 920 8686	10.71	1.783 311	6.86	312
27	14.229 814	1607.673 544	.000 622 0168	.070 275	112.979 242	.008 851 1835	10.63	1.867 783	6.92	324
28	15.700 385	1786.375 850	.000 559 7926	.063 693	113.779 114	.008 788 9593	10.55	1.953 090	6.98	336
29	17.322 931	1983.546 033	.000 504 1476	.057 727	114.504 067	.008 733 3143	10.48	2.039 193	7.03	348
30	19.113 158	2201.092 644	.000 454 3198	.052 320	115.161 117	.008 683 4865	10.43	2.126 055	7.09	360
31	21.088 395	2441.121 471	.000 409 6478	.047 419	115.756 624	.008 638 8145	10.37	2.213 639	7.14	372
32	23.267 762	2705.955 925	.000 369 5552	.042 978	116.296 354	.008 598 7218	10.32	2.301 909	7.19	384
33	25.672 354	2998.159 528	.000 333 5380	.038 952	116.785 530	.008 562 7046	10.28	2.390 831	7.24	396
34	28.325 448	3320.560 727	.000 301 1540	.035 304	117.228 888	.008 530 3206	10.24	2.480 371	7.30	408
35	31.252 723	3676.280 274	.000 272 0141	.031 997	117.630 719	.008 501 1807	10.21	2.570 496	7.34	420
36	34.482 516	4068.761 432	.000 245 7750	.029 000	117.994 912	.008 474 9417	10.17	2.661 175	7.39	432
37	38.046 090	4501.803 306	.000 222 1332	.026 284	118.324 993	.008 451 2999	10.15	2.752 377	7.44	444
38	41.977 939	4979.597 619	.000 200 8194	.023 822	118.624 158	.008 429 9861	10.12	2.844 074	7.48	456
39	46.316 122	5506.769 281	.000 181 5947	.021 591	118.895 301	.008 410 7613	10.10	2.936 236	7.53	468
40	51.102 633	6088.421 166	.000 164 2462	.019 568	119.141 047	.008 393 4129	10.08	3.028 838	7.57	480
41	56.383 802	6730.183 496	.000 148 5844	.017 736	119.363 776	.008 377 7510	10.06	3.121 854	7.61	492
42	62.210 750	7438.268 347	.000 134 4399	.016 074	119.565 643	.008 363 6066	10.04	3.215 258	7.66	504
43	68.639 880	8219.529 778	.000 121 6615	.014 569	119.748 603	.008 350 8281	10.03	3.309 027	7.70	516
44	75.733 425	9081.530 176	.000 110 1136	.013 204	119.914 425	.008 339 2803	10.01	3.403 140	7.73	528
45	83.560 048	10032.613 460	.000 099 6749	.011 967	120.064 716	.008 328 8416	10.00	3.497 574	7.77	540
46	92.195 508	11081.985 843	.000 090 2365	.010 847	120.200 930	.008 319 4032	9.99	3.592 311	7.81	552
47	101.723 395	12239.804 950	.000 081 7006	.009 831	120.324 385	.008 310 8673	9.98	3.687 329	7.85	564
48	112.235 935	13517.278 138	.000 073 9794	.008 910	120.436 277	.008 303 1461	9.97	3.782 612	7.88	576
49	123.834 886	14926.770 984	.000 066 9937	.008 075	120.537 689	.008 296 1604	9.96	3.878 142	7.91	588
50	136.632 524	16481.926 975	.000 060 6725	.007 319	120.629 602	.008 289 8392	9.95	3.973 904	7.95	600

	Amount Of 1	Amount Of 1 Per Period	Sinking Fund Payment	Present Worth Of 1	Present Worth of 1 Per Period	Periodic Payment To Amortize 1	Constant Annual Percent	Total Interest	Annual Add On Rate	
	What a single $ 1 deposit grows to in the future. The deposit is made at the beginning of the first period.	What a series of $ 1 deposits grow to in the future. A deposit is made at the end of each period.	The amount to be deposited at the end of each period that grows to $ 1 in the future.	What $ 1 to be paid in the future is worth today. Value today of a single $ 1 payment tomorrow.	What $ 1 to be paid at the end of each period is worth today. Value today of a series of $ 1 payments tomorrow.	The mortgage payment to amortize a loan of $ 1. An annuity certain, payable at the end of each period, worth $ 1 today.	The annual payment, including interest and principal, to amortize completely a loan of $ 100.	The total interest paid over the term on a loan of $1. The loan is amortized by regular periodic payments.	The average annual interest rate on a loan that is completely amortized by regular periodic payments.	
	$S = (1+i)^n$	$S\overline{n}\rceil = \dfrac{(1+i)^n - 1}{i}$	$\dfrac{1}{S\overline{n}\rceil} = \dfrac{i}{(1+i)^n - 1}$	$V^n = \dfrac{1}{(1+i)^n}$	$A\overline{n}\rceil = \dfrac{1 - V^n}{i}$	$\dfrac{1}{A\overline{n}\rceil} = \dfrac{i}{1 - V^n}$				
YEAR										**PERIODS**
	1.008 250	1.000 000	1.000 000 0000	.991 818	.991 818	1.008 250 0000	1209.90	.008 250	9.90	1
	1.016 568	2.008 250	.497 945 9729	.983 702	1.975 519	.506 195 9729	607.44	.012 392	7.44	2
	1.024 955	3.024 818	.330 598 3961	.975 653	2.951 172	.338 848 3961	406.62	.016 545	6.62	3
	1.033 411	4.049 773	.246 927 4319	.967 670	3.918 842	.255 177 4319	306.22	.020 710	6.21	4
	1.041 936	5.083 183	.196 727 1125	.959 752	4.878 593	.204 977 1125	245.98	.024 886	5.97	5
	1.050 532	6.125 120	.163 262 1155	.951 898	5.830 492	.171 512 1155	205.82	.029 073	5.81	6
	1.059 199	7.175 652	.139 360 1597	.944 110	6.774 601	.147 610 1597	177.14	.033 271	5.70	7
	1.067 938	8.234 851	.121 435 1045	.936 384	7.710 986	.129 685 1045	155.63	.037 481	5.62	8
	1.076 748	9.302 789	.107 494 6496	.928 722	8.639 708	.115 744 6496	138.90	.041 702	5.56	9
	1.085 631	10.379 537	.096 343 4148	.921 123	9.560 831	.104 593 4148	125.52	.045 934	5.51	10
	1.094 588	11.465 168	.087 220 7036	.913 586	10.474 417	.095 470 7036	114.57	.050 178	5.47	11
	1.103 618	12.559 755	.079 619 3849	.906 111	11.380 528	.087 869 3849	105.45	.054 433	5.44	12
1	1.103 618	12.559 755	.079 619 3849	.906 111	11.380 528	.087 869 3849	105.45	.054 433	5.44	12
2	1.217 973	26.420 927	.037 848 7851	.821 036	21.692 546	.046 098 7851	55.32	.106 371	5.32	24
3	1.344 177	41.718 366	.023 970 2581	.743 950	31.036 375	.032 220 2581	38.67	.159 929	5.33	36
4	1.483 457	58.600 894	.017 064 5860	.674 101	39.502 917	.025 314 5860	30.38	.215 100	5.38	48
5	1.637 170	77.232 756	.012 947 8741	.610 810	47.174 542	.021 197 8741	25.44	.271 872	5.44	60
6	1.806 811	97.795 214	.010 225 4493	.553 461	54.125 883	.018 475 4493	22.18	.330 232	5.50	72
7	1.994 029	120.488 312	.008 299 5602	.501 497	60.424 566	.016 549 5602	19.86	.390 163	5.57	84
8	2.200 646	145.532 823	.006 871 3022	.454 412	66.131 871	.015 121 3022	18.15	.451 645	5.65	96
9	2.428 672	173.172 396	.005 774 5924	.411 748	71.303 320	.014 024 5924	16.83	.514 656	5.72	108
10	2.680 326	203.675 925	.004 909 7604	.373 089	75.989 225	.013 159 7604	15.80	.579 171	5.79	120
11	2.958 056	237.340 169	.004 213 3618	.338 060	80.235 174	.012 463 3618	14.96	.645 164	5.87	132
12	3.264 564	274.492 634	.003 643 0850	.306 320	84.082 473	.011 893 0850	14.28	.712 604	5.94	144
13	3.602 832	315.494 762	.003 169 6247	.277 559	87.568 552	.011 419 6247	13.71	.781 461	6.01	156
14	3.976 150	360.745 448	.002 772 0377	.251 500	90.727 325	.011 022 0377	13.23	.851 702	6.08	168
15	4.388 151	410.684 919	.002 434 9567	.227 886	93.589 523	.010 684 9567	12.83	.923 292	6.16	180
16	4.842 842	465.799 017	.002 146 8487	.206 490	96.182 991	.010 396 8487	12.48	.996 195	6.23	192
17	5.344 647	526.623 927	.001 898 8883	.187 103	98.532 960	.010 148 8883	12.18	1.070 373	6.30	204
18	5.898 449	593.751 391	.001 684 2066	.169 536	100.662 292	.009 934 2066	11.93	1.145 789	6.37	216
19	6.509 634	667.834 467	.001 497 3770	.153 618	102.591 702	.009 747 3770	11.70	1.222 402	6.43	228
20	7.184 150	749.593 882	.001 334 0557	.139 195	104.339 961	.009 584 0557	11.51	1.300 173	6.50	240
21	7.928 557	839.825 043	.001 190 7242	.126 126	105.924 077	.009 440 7242	11.33	1.379 062	6.57	252
22	8.750 098	939.405 775	.001 064 5027	.114 284	107.359 462	.009 314 5027	11.18	1.459 029	6.63	264
23	9.656 765	1049.304 861	.000 953 0119	.103 554	108.660 079	.009 203 0119	11.05	1.540 031	6.70	276
24	10.657 380	1170.591 469	.000 854 2690	.093 832	109.838 582	.009 104 2690	10.93	1.622 029	6.76	288
25	11.761 676	1304.445 550	.000 766 6092	.085 022	110.906 437	.009 016 6092	10.82	1.704 983	6.82	300
26	12.980 397	1452.169 321	.000 688 6249	.077 039	111.874 031	.008 938 6249	10.73	1.788 851	6.88	312
27	14.325 399	1615.199 931	.000 619 1184	.069 806	112.750 778	.008 869 1184	10.65	1.873 594	6.94	324
28	15.809 768	1795.123 444	.000 557 0648	.063 252	113.545 208	.008 807 0648	10.57	1.959 174	7.00	336
29	17.447 945	1993.690 269	.000 501 5824	.057 313	114.265 050	.008 751 5824	10.51	2.045 551	7.05	348
30	19.255 866	2212.832 187	.000 451 9096	.051 932	114.917 306	.008 701 9096	10.45	2.132 687	7.11	360
31	21.251 119	2454.681 148	.000 407 3849	.047 056	115.508 322	.008 657 3849	10.39	2.220 547	7.16	372
32	23.453 118	2721.590 011	.000 367 4323	.042 638	116.043 848	.008 617 4323	10.35	2.309 094	7.22	384
33	25.883 282	3016.155 431	.000 331 5479	.038 635	116.529 094	.008 581 5479	10.30	2.398 293	7.27	396
34	28.565 256	3341.243 126	.000 299 2898	.035 008	116.968 780	.008 549 2898	10.26	2.488 110	7.32	408
35	31.525 130	3700.015 751	.000 270 2691	.031 721	117.367 185	.008 520 2691	10.23	2.578 513	7.37	420
36	34.791 700	4095.963 673	.000 244 1428	.028 742	117.728 183	.008 494 1428	10.20	2.669 470	7.42	432
37	38.396 746	4532.938 919	.000 220 6074	.026 044	118.055 288	.008 470 6074	10.17	2.760 950	7.46	444
38	42.375 339	5015.192 658	.000 199 3941	.023 599	118.351 681	.008 449 3941	10.14	2.852 924	7.51	456
39	46.766 187	5547.416 556	.000 180 2641	.021 383	118.620 246	.008 430 2641	10.12	2.945 364	7.55	468
40	51.612 004	6134.788 421	.000 163 0048	.019 375	118.863 595	.008 413 0048	10.10	3.038 242	7.60	480
41	56.959 936	6783.022 573	.000 147 4269	.017 556	119.084 097	.008 397 4269	10.08	3.131 534	7.64	492
42	62.862 010	7498.425 440	.000 133 3613	.015 908	119.283 896	.008 383 3613	10.07	3.225 214	7.68	504
43	69.375 644	8287.956 908	.000 120 6570	.014 414	119.464 936	.008 370 6570	10.05	3.319 259	7.72	516
44	76.564 209	9159.298 034	.000 109 1787	.013 061	119.628 978	.008 359 1787	10.04	3.413 646	7.76	528
45	84.497 638	10120.925 769	.000 098 8052	.011 835	119.777 618	.008 348 8052	10.02	3.508 355	7.80	540
46	93.253 112	11182.195 430	.000 089 4279	.010 724	119.912 303	.008 339 4279	10.01	3.603 364	7.83	552
47	102.915 812	12353.431 711	.000 080 9492	.009 717	120.034 342	.008 330 9492	10.00	3.698 655	7.87	564
48	113.579 740	13646.029 132	.000 073 2814	.008 804	120.144 923	.008 323 2814	9.99	3.794 210	7.90	576
49	125.348 644	15072.562 890	.000 066 3457	.007 978	120.245 121	.008 316 3457	9.98	3.890 011	7.94	588
50	138.337 017	16646.911 196	.000 060 0712	.007 229	120.335 912	.008 310 0712	9.98	3.986 043	7.97	600

MONTHLY COMPOUND INTEREST AND ANNUITY

9.95 % M

Amount Of 1	Amount Of 1 Per Period	Sinking Fund Payment	Present Worth Of 1	Present Worth of 1 Per Period	Periodic Payment To Amortize 1	Constant Annual Percent	Total Interest	Annual Add On Rate
What a single $ 1 deposit grows to in the future. The deposit is made at the beginning of the first period.	What a series of $ 1 deposits grow to in the future. A deposit is made at the end of each period.	The amount to be deposited at the end of each period that grows to $ 1 in the future.	What $ 1 to be paid in the future is worth today. Value today of a single $ 1 payment tomorrow.	What $ 1 to be paid at the end of each period is worth today. Value today of a series of $ 1 payments tomorrow.	The mortgage payment to amortize a loan of $ 1. An annuity certain, payable at the end of each period, worth $ 1 today.	The annual payment, including interest and principal, to amortize completely a loan of $ 100.	The total interest paid over the term on a loan of $1. The loan is amortized by regular periodic payments.	The average annual interest rate on a loan that is completely amortized by regular periodic payments.

$$S = (1+i)^n \qquad S\overline{n}| = \frac{(1+i)^n - 1}{i} \qquad \frac{1}{S\overline{n}|} = \frac{i}{(1+i)^n - 1} \qquad V^n = \frac{1}{(1+i)^n} \qquad A\overline{n}| = \frac{1-V^n}{i} \qquad \frac{1}{A\overline{n}|} = \frac{i}{1-V^n}$$

PERIODS

YEAR	Amount Of 1	Amount Of 1 Per Period	Sinking Fund Payment	Present Worth Of 1	Present Worth of 1 Per Period	Periodic Payment To Amortize 1	Constant Annual Percent	Total Interest	Annual Add On Rate	PERIODS
	1.008 292	1.000 000	1.000 000 0000	.991 777	.991 777	1.008 291 6667	1209.95	.008 292	9.95	1
	1.016 652	2.008 292	.497 935 6418	.983 621	1.975 397	.506 227 3085	607.48	.012 455	7.47	2
	1.025 082	3.024 944	.330 584 6594	.975 532	2.950 929	.338 876 3261	406.66	.016 629	6.65	3
	1.033 581	4.050 026	.246 912 0209	.967 510	3.918 439	.255 203 6876	306.25	.020 815	6.24	4
	1.042 152	5.083 607	.196 710 7198	.959 553	4.877 992	.205 002 3865	246.01	.025 012	6.00	5
	1.050 793	6.125 759	.163 245 0873	.951 662	5.829 654	.171 536 7540	205.85	.029 221	5.84	6
	1.059 506	7.176 551	.139 342 6939	.943 836	6.773 491	.147 634 3606	177.17	.033 441	5.73	7
	1.068 291	8.236 057	.121 417 3248	.936 075	7.709 566	.129 708 9915	155.66	.037 672	5.65	8
	1.077 149	9.304 348	.107 476 6384	.928 377	8.637 943	.115 768 3051	138.93	.041 915	5.59	9
	1.086 080	10.381 496	.096 325 2298	.920 743	9.558 685	.104 616 8965	125.55	.046 169	5.54	10
	1.095 085	11.467 576	.087 202 3868	.913 171	10.471 856	.095 494 0534	114.60	.050 435	5.50	11
	1.104 165	12.562 661	.079 600 9677	.905 661	11.377 518	.087 892 6344	105.48	.054 712	5.47	12
1	1.104 165	12.562 661	.079 600 9677	.905 661	11.377 518	.087 892 6344	105.48	.054 712	5.47	12
2	1.219 181	26.433 917	.037 830 1856	.820 223	21.681 696	.046 121 8523	55.35	.106 924	5.35	24
3	1.346 178	41.750 078	.023 952 0509	.742 844	31.013 794	.032 243 7176	38.70	.160 774	5.36	36
4	1.486 403	58.661 653	.017 046 9113	.672 765	39.465 514	.025 338 5780	30.41	.216 252	5.41	48
5	1.641 235	77.334 829	.012 930 7844	.609 297	47.119 911	.021 222 4510	25.47	.273 347	5.47	60
6	1.812 194	97.953 104	.010 208 9669	.551 817	54.052 203	.018 500 6336	22.21	.332 046	5.53	72
7	2.000 962	120.719 090	.008 283 6940	.499 760	60.330 512	.016 575 3607	19.90	.392 330	5.60	84
8	2.209 394	145.856 503	.006 856 0536	.452 613	66.016 535	.015 147 7202	18.18	.454 181	5.68	96
9	2.439 536	173.612 366	.005 759 9584	.409 914	71.166 146	.014 051 6250	16.87	.517 576	5.75	108
10	2.693 651	204.259 429	.004 895 7348	.371 243	75.829 950	.013 187 4015	15.83	.582 488	5.82	120
11	2.974 236	238.098 855	.004 199 9362	.336 221	80.053 778	.012 491 6029	14.99	.648 892	5.90	132
12	3.284 049	275.463 179	.003 630 2493	.304 502	83.879 135	.011 921 9159	14.31	.716 756	5.97	144
13	3.626 133	316.719 573	.003 157 3672	.275 776	87.343 614	.011 449 0339	13.74	.786 049	6.05	156
14	4.003 851	362.273 455	.002 760 3458	.249 760	90.481 259	.011 052 0124	13.27	.856 738	6.12	168
15	4.420 913	412.572 476	.002 423 8166	.226 198	93.322 903	.010 715 4832	12.86	.928 787	6.19	180
16	4.881 420	468.110 914	.002 136 2459	.204 858	95.896 470	.010 427 9125	12.52	1.002 159	6.26	192
17	5.389 895	529.434 536	.001 888 8076	.185 532	98.227 250	.010 180 4743	12.22	1.076 817	6.33	204
18	5.951 335	597.145 958	.001 674 6325	.168 030	100.338 148	.009 966 2991	11.96	1.152 721	6.40	216
19	6.571 258	671.910 567	.001 488 2933	.152 178	102.249 907	.009 779 9600	11.74	1.229 831	6.47	228
20	7.255 756	754.463 062	.001 325 4459	.137 822	103.981 313	.009 617 1126	11.55	1.308 107	6.54	240
21	8.011 555	845.614 670	.001 182 5717	.124 820	105.549 381	.009 474 2384	11.37	1.387 508	6.61	252
22	8.846 082	946.261 122	.001 056 7907	.113 044	106.969 520	.009 348 4574	11.22	1.467 993	6.67	264
23	9.767 537	1057.391 452	.000 945 7236	.102 380	108.255 684	.009 237 3902	11.09	1.549 520	6.74	276
24	10.784 977	1180.097 717	.000 847 3875	.092 722	109.420 514	.009 139 0541	10.97	1.632 048	6.80	288
25	11.908 398	1315.585 729	.000 760 1177	.083 974	110.475 455	.009 051 7844	10.87	1.715 535	6.86	300
26	13.148 841	1465.186 905	.000 682 5068	.076 052	111.430 875	.008 974 1734	10.77	1.799 942	6.92	312
27	14.518 496	1630.371 347	.000 613 3572	.068 878	112.296 162	.008 905 0239	10.69	1.885 228	6.98	324
28	16.030 821	1812.762 292	.000 551 6443	.062 380	113.079 819	.008 843 3110	10.62	1.971 352	7.04	336
29	17.700 678	2014.152 063	.000 496 4868	.056 495	113.789 546	.008 788 1535	10.55	2.058 277	7.10	348
30	19.544 476	2236.519 681	.000 447 1233	.051 165	114.432 319	.008 738 7899	10.49	2.145 964	7.15	360
31	21.580 334	2482.050 310	.000 402 8927	.046 338	115.014 454	.008 694 5594	10.44	2.234 376	7.21	372
32	23.828 258	2753.156 735	.000 363 2194	.041 967	115.541 671	.008 654 8861	10.39	2.323 476	7.26	384
33	26.310 338	3052.503 070	.000 327 6000	.038 008	116.019 151	.008 619 2667	10.35	2.413 230	7.31	396
34	29.050 965	3383.030 936	.000 295 5929	.034 422	116.451 586	.008 587 2596	10.31	2.503 602	7.36	408
35	32.077 070	3747.988 369	.000 266 8098	.031 175	116.843 226	.008 558 4765	10.28	2.594 560	7.41	420
36	35.418 391	4150.961 739	.000 240 9080	.028 234	117.197 919	.008 532 5747	10.24	2.686 072	7.46	432
37	39.107 762	4595.910 992	.000 217 5847	.025 570	117.519 151	.008 509 2514	10.22	2.778 108	7.51	444
38	43.181 438	5087.208 561	.000 196 5715	.023 158	117.810 079	.008 488 2381	10.19	2.870 637	7.55	456
39	47.679 449	5629.682 339	.000 177 6299	.020 973	118.073 560	.008 469 2966	10.17	2.963 631	7.60	468
40	52.645 998	6228.663 115	.000 160 5481	.018 995	118.312 185	.008 452 2148	10.15	3.057 063	7.64	480
41	58.129 890	6890.036 963	.000 145 1371	.017 203	118.528 299	.008 436 8038	10.13	3.150 907	7.69	492
42	64.185 013	7620.303 083	.000 131 2284	.015 580	118.724 025	.008 422 8950	10.11	3.245 139	7.73	504
43	70.870 871	8426.637 665	.000 118 6713	.014 110	118.901 286	.008 410 3380	10.10	3.339 734	7.77	516
44	78.253 163	9316.964 412	.000 107 3311	.012 779	119.061 825	.008 398 9978	10.08	3.434 671	7.81	528
45	86.404 435	10300.032 401	.000 097 0871	.011 573	119.207 218	.008 388 7537	10.07	3.529 927	7.84	540
46	95.404 788	11385.502 061	.000 087 8310	.010 482	119.338 896	.008 379 4977	10.06	3.625 483	7.88	552
47	105.342 666	12584.040 102	.000 079 4657	.009 493	119.458 151	.008 371 1324	10.05	3.721 319	7.92	564
48	116.315 727	13907.424 339	.000 071 9040	.008 597	119.566 156	.008 363 5707	10.04	3.817 417	7.95	576
49	128.431 801	15368.659 424	.000 065 0675	.007 786	119.663 972	.008 356 7342	10.03	3.913 760	7.99	588
50	141.809 951	16982.104 646	.000 058 8855	.007 052	119.752 560	.008 350 5522	10.03	4.010 331	8.02	600

Effective Rate is 10.42 %

Annual Percentage Rate is 9.95 %

MONTHLY COMPOUND INTEREST AND ANNUITY

	Amount Of 1	Amount Of 1 Per Period	Sinking Fund Payment	Present Worth Of 1	Present Worth of 1 Per Period	Periodic Payment To Amortize 1	Constant Annual Percent	Total Interest	Annual Add On Rate	
	What a single $ 1 deposit grows to in the future. The deposit is made at the beginning of the first period.	What a series of $ 1 deposits grow to in the future. A deposit is made at the end of each period.	The amount to be deposited at the end of each period that grows to $ 1 in the future.	What $ 1 to be paid in the future is worth today. Value today of a single $ 1 payment tomorrow.	What $ 1 to be paid at the end of each period is worth today. Value today of a series of $ 1 payments tomorrow.	The mortgage payment to amortize a loan of $ 1. An annuity certain, payable at the end of each period, worth $ 1 today.	The annual payment, including interest and principal, to amortize completely a loan of $ 100.	The total interest paid over the term on a loan of $1. The loan is amortized by regular periodic payments.	The average annual interest rate on a loan that is completely amortized by regular periodic payments.	
	$S = (1+i)^n$	$S\overline{n}| = \dfrac{(1+i)^n - 1}{i}$	$\dfrac{1}{S\overline{n}|} = \dfrac{i}{(1+i)^n - 1}$	$V^n = \dfrac{1}{(1+i)^n}$	$A\overline{n}| = \dfrac{1-V^n}{i}$	$\dfrac{1}{A\overline{n}|} = \dfrac{i}{1-V^n}$				

YEAR										PERIODS
	1.008 333	1.000 000	1.000 000 0000	.991 736	.991 736	1.008 333 3333	1210.00	.008 333	10.00	1
	1.016 736	2.008 333	.497 925 3112	.983 539	1.975 275	.506 258 6445	607.52	.012 517	7.51	2
	1.025 209	3.025 069	.330 570 9235	.975 411	2.950 686	.338 904 2569	406.69	.016 713	6.69	3
	1.033 752	4.050 278	.246 896 6110	.967 350	3.918 036	.255 229 9444	306.28	.020 920	6.28	4
	1.042 367	5.084 031	.196 694 3285	.959 355	4.877 391	.205 027 6619	246.04	.025 138	6.03	5
	1.051 053	6.126 398	.163 228 0609	.951 427	5.828 817	.171 561 3942	205.88	.029 368	5.87	6
	1.059 812	7.177 451	.139 325 2301	.943 563	6.772 381	.147 658 5635	177.20	.033 610	5.76	7
	1.068 644	8.237 263	.121 399 5474	.935 765	7.708 146	.129 732 8807	155.68	.037 863	5.68	8
	1.077 549	9.305 907	.107 458 6298	.928 032	8.636 178	.115 791 9631	138.96	.042 128	5.62	9
	1.086 529	10.383 456	.096 307 0477	.920 362	9.556 540	.104 640 3810	125.57	.046 404	5.57	10
	1.095 583	11.469 985	.087 184 0730	.912 756	10.469 296	.095 517 4064	114.63	.050 691	5.53	11
	1.104 713	12.565 568	.079 582 5539	.905 212	11.374 508	.087 915 8872	105.50	.054 991	5.50	12
1	1.104 713	12.565 568	.079 582 5539	.905 212	11.374 508	.087 915 8872	105.50	.054 991	5.50	12
2	1.220 391	26.446 915	.037 811 5930	.819 410	21.670 855	.046 144 9263	55.38	.107 478	5.37	24
3	1.348 182	41.781 821	.023 933 8539	.741 740	30.991 236	.032 267 1872	38.73	.161 619	5.39	36
4	1.489 354	58.722 492	.017 029 2501	.671 432	39.428 160	.025 362 5834	30.44	.217 404	5.44	48
5	1.645 309	77.437 072	.012 913 7114	.607 789	47.065 369	.021 247 0447	25.50	.274 823	5.50	60
6	1.817 594	98.111 314	.010 192 5044	.550 178	53.978 665	.018 525 8378	22.24	.333 860	5.56	72
7	2.007 920	120.950 418	.008 267 8507	.498 028	60.236 667	.016 601 1840	19.93	.394 499	5.64	84
8	2.218 176	146.181 076	.006 840 8308	.450 821	65.901 488	.015 174 1641	18.21	.456 720	5.71	96
9	2.450 448	174.053 713	.005 745 3529	.408 089	71.029 355	.014 078 6862	16.90	.520 498	5.78	108
10	2.707 041	204.844 979	.004 881 7404	.369 407	75.671 163	.013 215 0737	15.86	.585 809	5.86	120
11	2.990 504	238.860 493	.004 186 5441	.334 392	79.872 986	.012 519 8775	15.03	.652 624	5.93	132
12	3.303 649	276.437 876	.003 617 4493	.302 696	83.676 528	.011 950 7826	14.35	.720 913	6.01	144
13	3.649 584	317.950 102	.003 145 1476	.274 004	87.119 542	.011 478 4809	13.78	.790 643	6.08	156
14	4.031 743	363.809 201	.002 748 6935	.248 032	90.236 201	.011 082 0269	13.30	.861 781	6.16	168
15	4.453 920	414.470 346	.002 412 7178	.224 521	93.057 439	.010 746 0512	12.90	.934 289	6.23	180
16	4.920 303	470.436 376	.002 125 6860	.203 240	95.611 259	.010 459 0193	12.56	1.008 132	6.30	192
17	5.435 523	532.262 780	.001 878 7712	.183 975	97.923 008	.010 212 1046	12.26	1.083 269	6.37	204
18	6.004 693	600.563 216	.001 665 1036	.166 536	100.015 633	.009 998 4370	12.00	1.159 662	6.44	216
19	6.633 463	676.015 601	.001 479 2558	.150 751	101.909 902	.009 812 5891	11.78	1.237 270	6.51	228
20	7.328 074	759.368 836	.001 316 8831	.136 462	103.624 619	.009 650 2165	11.59	1.316 052	6.58	240
21	8.095 419	851.450 244	.001 174 4667	.123 527	105.176 801	.009 507 8001	11.41	1.395 966	6.65	252
22	8.943 115	953.173 779	.001 049 1266	.111 818	106.581 856	.009 382 4600	11.26	1.476 969	6.71	264
23	9.879 576	1065.549 097	.000 938 4833	.101 219	107.853 730	.009 271 8166	11.13	1.559 021	6.78	276
24	10.914 097	1189.691 580	.000 840 5540	.091 625	109.005 045	.009 173 8873	11.01	1.642 080	6.84	288
25	12.056 945	1326.833 403	.000 753 6741	.082 940	110.047 230	.009 087 0075	10.91	1.726 102	6.90	300
26	13.319 465	1478.335 767	.000 676 4363	.075 078	110.990 629	.009 009 7696	10.82	1.811 048	6.97	312
27	14.714 187	1645.702 407	.000 607 6433	.067 962	111.844 605	.008 940 9766	10.73	1.896 876	7.03	324
28	16.254 954	1830.594 523	.000 546 2706	.061 520	112.617 635	.008 879 6040	10.66	1.983 547	7.08	336
29	17.957 060	2034.847 258	.000 491 4374	.055 688	113.317 392	.008 824 7707	10.59	2.071 020	7.14	348
30	19.837 399	2260.487 925	.000 442 3824	.050 410	113.950 820	.008 775 7157	10.54	2.159 258	7.20	360
31	21.914 634	2509.756 117	.000 398 4451	.045 632	114.524 207	.008 731 7784	10.48	2.248 222	7.25	372
32	24.209 383	2785.125 947	.000 359 0502	.041 306	115.043 244	.008 692 3835	10.44	2.337 875	7.31	384
33	26.744 422	3089.330 596	.000 323 6947	.037 391	115.513 083	.008 657 0281	10.39	2.428 183	7.36	396
34	29.544 912	3425.389 447	.000 291 9376	.033 847	115.938 387	.008 625 2709	10.36	2.519 111	7.41	408
35	32.638 650	3796.638 052	.000 263 3909	.030 639	116.323 377	.008 596 7243	10.32	2.610 624	7.46	420
36	36.056 344	4206.761 236	.000 237 7126	.027 734	116.671 876	.008 571 0459	10.29	2.702 692	7.51	432
37	39.831 914	4659.829 677	.000 214 6001	.025 105	116.987 340	.008 547 9335	10.26	2.795 282	7.55	444
38	44.002 836	5160.340 305	.000 193 7857	.022 726	117.272 903	.008 527 1190	10.24	2.888 366	7.60	456
39	48.610 508	5713.260 935	.000 175 0314	.020 572	117.531 398	.008 508 3647	10.22	2.981 915	7.65	468
40	53.700 663	6324.079 581	.000 158 1258	.018 622	117.765 391	.008 491 4591	10.19	3.075 900	7.69	480
41	59.323 824	6998.858 921	.000 142 8804	.016 857	117.977 204	.008 476 2138	10.18	3.170 297	7.73	492
42	65.535 804	7744.296 475	.000 129 1273	.015 259	118.168 940	.008 462 4606	10.16	3.265 080	7.77	504
43	72.398 259	8567.791 082	.000 116 7162	.013 812	118.342 502	.008 450 0495	10.15	3.360 226	7.81	516
44	79.979 303	9477.516 336	.000 105 5129	.012 503	118.499 612	.008 438 8462	10.13	3.455 711	7.85	528
45	88.354 181	10482.501 711	.000 095 3971	.011 318	118.641 830	.008 428 7304	10.12	3.551 514	7.89	540
46	97.606 018	11592.722 188	.000 086 2610	.010 245	118.770 568	.008 419 5943	10.11	3.647 616	7.93	552
47	107.826 644	12819.197 256	.000 078 0080	.009 274	118.887 103	.008 411 3413	10.10	3.743 997	7.97	564
48	119.117 502	14174.100 291	.000 070 5512	.008 395	118.992 591	.008 403 8845	10.09	3.840 637	8.00	576
49	131.590 661	15670.879 379	.000 063 8126	.007 599	119.088 081	.008 397 1460	10.08	3.937 522	8.04	588
50	145.369 923	17324.390 796	.000 057 7221	.006 879	119.174 520	.008 391 0554	10.07	4.034 633	8.07	600

Effective Rate is 10.47 %

Annual Percentage Rate is 10.00 %

MONTHLY COMPOUND INTEREST AND ANNUITY

10.05 % M

	Amount Of 1	Amount Of 1 Per Period	Sinking Fund Payment	Present Worth Of 1	Present Worth of 1 Per Period	Periodic Payment To Amortize 1	Constant Annual Percent	Total Interest	Annual Add On Rate
	What a single $ 1 deposit grows to in the future. The deposit is made at the beginning of the first period.	What a series of $ 1 deposits grow to in the future. A deposit is made at the end of each period.	The amount to be deposited at the end of each period that grows to $ 1 in the future.	What $ 1 to be paid in the future is worth today. Value today of a single $ 1 payment tomorrow.	What $ 1 to be paid at the end of each period is worth today. Value today of a series of $ 1 payments tomorrow.	The mortgage payment to amortize a loan of $ 1. An annuity certain, payable at the end of each period, worth $ 1 today.	The annual payment, including interest and principal, to amortize completely a loan of $ 100.	The total interest paid over the term on a loan of $1. The loan is amortized by regular periodic payments.	The average annual interest rate on a loan that is completely amortized by regular periodic payments.
	$S = (1+i)^n$	$S\overline{n}| = \dfrac{(1+i)^n - 1}{i}$	$\dfrac{1}{S\overline{n}|} = \dfrac{i}{(1+i)^n - 1}$	$V^n = \dfrac{1}{(1+i)^n}$	$A\overline{n}| = \dfrac{1 - V^n}{i}$	$\dfrac{1}{A\overline{n}|} = \dfrac{i}{1 - V^n}$			

YEAR									**PERIODS**
	1.008 375	1.000 000	1.000 000 0000	.991 695	.991 695	1.008 375 0000	1210.05	.008 375	10.05 1
	1.016 820	2.008 375	.497 914 9810	.983 458	1.975 153	.506 289 9810	607.55	.012 580	7.55 2
	1.025 336	3.025 195	.330 557 1884	.975 290	2.950 443	.338 932 1884	406.72	.016 797	6.72 3
	1.033 923	4.050 531	.246 881 2022	.967 190	3.917 633	.255 256 2022	306.31	.021 025	6.31 4
	1.042 582	5.084 454	.196 677 9386	.959 157	4.876 789	.205 052 9386	246.07	.025 265	6.06 5
	1.051 314	6.127 037	.163 211 0360	.951 191	5.827 980	.171 586 0360	205.91	.029 516	5.90 6
	1.060 119	7.178 351	.139 307 7683	.943 291	6.771 271	.147 682 7683	177.22	.033 779	5.79 7
	1.068 997	8.238 469	.121 381 7722	.935 456	7.706 727	.129 756 7722	155.71	.038 054	5.71 8
	1.077 950	9.307 466	.107 440 6236	.927 687	8.634 414	.115 815 6236	138.98	.042 341	5.65 9
	1.086 978	10.385 416	.096 288 8683	.919 982	9.554 396	.104 663 8683	125.60	.046 639	5.60 10
	1.096 081	11.472 394	.087 165 7624	.912 341	10.466 737	.095 540 7624	114.65	.050 948	5.56 11
	1.105 261	12.568 476	.079 564 1435	.904 764	11.371 500	.087 939 1435	105.53	.055 270	5.53 12
1	1.105 261	12.568 476	.079 564 1435	.904 764	11.371 500	.087 939 1435	105.53	.055 270	5.53 12
2	1.221 602	26.459 921	.037 793 0072	.818 597	21.660 021	.046 168 0072	55.41	.108 032	5.40 24
3	1.350 189	41.813 594	.023 915 6670	.740 637	30.968 701	.032 290 6670	38.75	.162 464	5.42 36
4	1.492 311	58.783 410	.017 011 6024	.670 102	39.390 856	.025 386 6024	30.47	.218 557	5.46 48
5	1.649 393	77.539 485	.012 896 6551	.606 284	47.010 916	.021 271 6551	25.53	.276 299	5.53 60
6	1.823 010	98.269 843	.010 176 0618	.548 543	53.905 270	.018 551 0618	22.27	.335 676	5.59 72
7	2.014 902	121.182 300	.008 252 0302	.496 302	60.143 031	.016 627 0302	19.96	.396 671	5.67 84
8	2.226 992	146.506 543	.006 825 6337	.449 036	65.786 731	.015 200 6337	18.25	.459 261	5.74 96
9	2.461 408	174.496 442	.005 730 7759	.406 272	70.892 945	.014 105 7759	16.93	.523 424	5.82 108
10	2.720 498	205.432 584	.004 867 7770	.367 580	75.512 863	.013 242 7770	15.90	.589 133	5.89 120
11	3.006 860	239.625 096	.004 173 1856	.332 573	79.692 796	.012 548 1856	15.06	.656 360	5.97 132
12	3.323 365	277.416 745	.003 604 6851	.300 900	83.474 648	.011 979 6851	14.38	.725 075	6.04 144
13	3.673 186	319.186 380	.003 132 9658	.272 243	86.896 331	.011 507 9658	13.81	.795 243	6.12 156
14	4.059 829	365.352 728	.002 737 0810	.246 316	89.992 145	.011 112 0810	13.34	.866 830	6.19 168
15	4.487 171	416.378 591	.002 401 6605	.222 858	92.793 125	.010 776 6605	12.94	.939 799	6.27 180
16	4.959 495	472.775 487	.002 115 1689	.201 633	95.327 350	.010 490 1689	12.59	1.014 112	6.34 192
17	5.481 536	535.108 775	.001 868 7789	.182 431	97.620 225	.010 243 7789	12.30	1.089 731	6.41 204
18	6.058 528	604.003 327	.001 655 6200	.165 057	99.694 735	.010 030 6200	12.04	1.166 614	6.48 216
19	6.696 254	680.149 787	.001 470 2644	.149 337	101.571 676	.009 845 2644	11.82	1.244 720	6.55 228
20	7.401 109	764.311 498	.001 308 3671	.135 115	103.269 864	.009 683 3671	11.63	1.324 008	6.62 240
21	8.180 157	857.332 153	.001 166 4091	.122 247	104.806 323	.009 541 4091	11.45	1.404 435	6.69 252
22	9.041 208	960.144 255	.001 041 5102	.110 605	106.196 455	.009 416 5102	11.30	1.485 959	6.75 264
23	9.992 895	1073.778 459	.000 931 2908	.100 071	107.454 196	.009 306 2908	11.17	1.568 536	6.82 276
24	11.044 757	1199.373 911	.000 833 7683	.090 541	108.592 155	.009 208 7683	11.06	1.652 125	6.88 288
25	12.207 338	1338.189 665	.000 747 2782	.081 918	109.621 739	.009 122 2782	10.95	1.736 683	6.95 300
26	13.492 295	1491.617 301	.000 670 4132	.074 116	110.553 269	.009 045 4132	10.86	1.822 169	7.01 312
27	14.912 507	1661.194 880	.000 601 9763	.067 058	111.396 083	.008 976 9763	10.78	1.908 540	7.07 324
28	16.482 212	1848.622 363	.000 540 9434	.060 671	112.158 631	.008 915 9434	10.70	1.995 757	7.13 336
29	18.217 146	2055.778 647	.000 486 4337	.054 893	112.848 556	.008 861 4337	10.64	2.083 779	7.19 348
30	20.134 701	2284.740 405	.000 437 6865	.049 666	113.472 776	.008 812 6865	10.58	2.172 567	7.24 360
31	22.254 099	2537.802 903	.000 394 0416	.044 936	114.037 547	.008 769 0416	10.53	2.262 083	7.30 372
32	24.596 588	2817.503 008	.000 354 9242	.040 656	114.548 532	.008 729 9242	10.48	2.352 291	7.35 384
33	27.185 649	3126.644 621	.000 319 8317	.036 784	115.010 852	.008 694 8317	10.44	2.443 153	7.40 396
34	30.047 237	3468.326 785	.000 288 3235	.033 281	115.429 143	.008 663 3235	10.40	2.534 636	7.45 408
35	33.210 039	3845.974 750	.000 260 0121	.030 111	115.807 597	.008 635 0121	10.37	2.626 705	7.50 420
36	36.705 760	4263.374 310	.000 234 5560	.027 244	116.150 008	.008 609 5560	10.34	2.719 328	7.55 432
37	40.569 444	4724.709 759	.000 211 6532	.024 649	116.459 810	.008 586 6532	10.31	2.812 474	7.60 444
38	44.839 824	5234.605 831	.000 191 0364	.022 302	116.740 107	.008 566 0364	10.28	2.906 113	7.65 456
39	49.559 708	5798.174 065	.000 172 4681	.020 178	116.993 710	.008 547 4681	10.26	3.000 215	7.69 468
40	54.776 411	6421.064 045	.000 155 7374	.018 256	117.223 160	.008 530 7374	10.24	3.094 754	7.74 480
41	60.542 230	7109.520 038	.000 140 6565	.016 517	117.430 759	.008 515 6565	10.22	3.189 703	7.78 492
42	66.914 965	7870.443 585	.000 127 0576	.014 944	117.618 586	.008 502 0576	10.21	3.285 037	7.82 504
43	73.958 500	8711.462 694	.000 114 7913	.013 521	117.788 526	.008 489 7913	10.19	3.380 732	7.86 516
44	81.743 445	9641.008 301	.000 103 7236	.012 233	117.942 281	.008 478 7236	10.18	3.476 766	7.90 528
45	90.347 840	10668.398 793	.000 093 7348	.011 068	118.081 393	.008 468 7348	10.17	3.573 117	7.94 540
46	99.857 942	11803.933 418	.000 084 7175	.010 014	118.207 257	.008 459 7175	10.16	3.669 764	7.98 552
47	110.369 088	13058.995 536	.000 076 5756	.009 061	118.321 133	.008 451 5756	10.15	3.766 689	8.01 564
48	121.986 646	14446.166 726	.000 069 2225	.008 198	118.424 165	.008 444 2225	10.14	3.863 872	8.05 576
49	134.827 081	15979.352 919	.000 062 5808	.007 417	118.517 384	.008 437 5808	10.13	3.961 297	8.08 588
50	149.019 112	17673.923 800	.000 056 5805	.006 711	118.601 726	.008 431 5805	10.12	4.058 948	8.12 600

Effective Rate is 10.53 %

Annual Percentage Rate is 10.05 %

Amount Of 1	Amount Of 1 Per Period	Sinking Fund Payment	Present Worth Of 1	Present Worth of 1 Per Period	Periodic Payment To Amortize 1	Constant Annual Percent	Total Interest	Annual Add On Rate
What a single $ 1 deposit grows to in the future. The deposit is made at the beginning of the first period.	What a series of $ 1 deposits grow to in the future. A deposit is made at the end of each period.	The amount to be deposited at the end of each period that grows to $ 1 in the future.	What $ 1 to be paid in the future is worth today. Value today of a single $ 1 payment tomorrow.	What $ 1 to be paid at the end of each period is worth today. Value today of a series of $ 1 payments tomorrow.	The mortgage payment to amortize a loan of $ 1. An annuity certain, payable at the end of each period, worth $ 1 today.	The annual payment, including interest and principal, to amortize completely a loan of $ 100.	The total interest paid over the term on a loan of $1. The loan is amortized by regular periodic payments.	The average annual interest rate on a loan that is completely amortized by regular periodic payments.
$S = (1+i)^n$	$S\overline{n} = \dfrac{(1+i)^n - 1}{i}$	$\dfrac{1}{S\overline{n}} = \dfrac{i}{(1+i)^n - 1}$	$V^n = \dfrac{1}{(1+i)^n}$	$A\overline{n} = \dfrac{1 - V^n}{i}$	$\dfrac{1}{A\overline{n}} = \dfrac{i}{1 - V^n}$			

YEAR									PERIODS
	1.008 417	1.000 000	1.000 000 0000	.991 654	.991 654	1.008 416 6667	1210.10	.008 417	10.10	1
	1.016 904	2.008 417	.497 904 6513	.983 377	1.975 030	.506 321 3179	607.59	.012 643	7.59	2
	1.025 463	3.025 321	.330 543 4540	.975 169	2.950 200	.338 960 1207	406.76	.016 880	6.75	3
	1.034 094	4.050 784	.246 865 7945	.967 030	3.917 230	.255 282 4612	306.34	.021 130	6.34	4
	1.042 798	5.084 878	.196 661 5500	.958 959	4.876 188	.205 078 2167	246.10	.025 391	6.09	5
	1.051 575	6.127 676	.163 194 0129	.950 955	5.827 143	.171 610 6795	205.94	.029 664	5.93	6
	1.060 425	7.179 250	.139 290 3084	.943 018	6.770 161	.147 706 9751	177.25	.033 949	5.82	7
	1.069 351	8.239 676	.121 363 9992	.935 147	7.705 308	.129 780 6659	155.74	.038 245	5.74	8
	1.078 351	9.309 026	.107 422 6200	.927 342	8.632 650	.115 839 2867	139.01	.042 554	5.67	9
	1.087 427	10.387 377	.096 270 6918	.919 602	9.552 252	.104 687 3584	125.63	.046 874	5.62	10
	1.096 580	11.474 804	.087 147 4549	.911 926	10.464 178	.095 564 1216	114.68	.051 205	5.59	11
	1.105 809	12.571 384	.079 545 7365	.904 315	11.368 493	.087 962 4032	105.56	.055 549	5.55	12
1	1.105 809	12.571 384	.079 545 7365	.904 315	11.368 493	.087 962 4032	105.56	.055 549	5.55	12
2	1.222 814	26.472 935	.037 774 4282	.817 786	21.649 195	.046 191 0949	55.43	.108 586	5.43	24
3	1.352 199	41.845 398	.023 897 4903	.739 536	30.946 189	.032 314 1570	38.78	.163 310	5.44	36
4	1.495 274	58.844 408	.016 993 9682	.668 774	39.353 602	.025 410 6348	30.50	.219 710	5.49	48
5	1.653 487	77.642 069	.012 879 6156	.604 782	46.956 553	.021 296 2822	25.56	.277 777	5.56	60
6	1.828 442	98.428 694	.010 159 6390	.546 914	53.832 017	.018 576 3057	22.30	.337 494	5.62	72
7	2.021 907	121.414 735	.008 236 2326	.494 583	60.049 603	.016 652 8993	19.99	.398 844	5.70	84
8	2.235 844	146.832 908	.006 810 4624	.447 258	65.672 261	.015 227 1291	18.28	.461 804	5.77	96
9	2.472 416	174.940 557	.005 716 2274	.404 463	70.756 916	.014 132 8940	16.96	.526 353	5.85	108
10	2.734 021	206.022 253	.004 853 8446	.365 762	75.355 047	.013 270 5113	15.93	.592 461	5.92	120
11	3.023 305	240.392 676	.004 159 8605	.330 764	79.513 206	.012 576 5272	15.10	.660 102	6.00	132
12	3.343 198	278.399 805	.003 591 9565	.299 115	83.273 493	.012 008 6232	14.42	.729 242	6.08	144
13	3.696 939	320.428 435	.003 120 8217	.270 494	86.673 977	.011 537 4883	13.85	.799 848	6.15	156
14	4.088 109	366.904 079	.002 725 5080	.244 612	89.749 087	.011 142 1747	13.38	.871 885	6.23	168
15	4.520 669	418.297 271	.002 390 6443	.221 206	92.529 955	.010 807 3110	12.97	.945 316	6.30	180
16	4.998 997	475.128 333	.002 104 6945	.200 040	95.044 736	.010 521 3612	12.63	1.020 101	6.38	192
17	5.527 936	537.972 642	.001 858 8306	.180 899	97.318 891	.010 275 4973	12.34	1.096 201	6.45	204
18	6.112 843	607.466 453	.001 646 1814	.163 590	99.375 444	.010 062 8481	12.08	1.173 575	6.52	216
19	6.759 637	684.313 345	.001 461 3189	.147 937	101.235 216	.009 877 9855	11.86	1.252 181	6.59	228
20	7.474 869	769.291 342	.001 299 8976	.133 782	102.917 036	.009 716 5643	11.66	1.331 975	6.66	240
21	8.265 778	863.260 788	.001 158 3985	.120 981	104.437 932	.009 575 0652	11.50	1.412 916	6.73	252
22	9.140 373	967.173 061	.001 033 9411	.109 405	105.813 300	.009 450 6078	11.35	1.494 960	6.80	264
23	10.107 508	1082.080 204	.000 924 1459	.098 936	107.057 067	.009 340 8126	11.21	1.578 064	6.86	276
24	11.176 975	1209.145 573	.000 827 0303	.089 470	108.181 824	.009 243 6969	11.10	1.662 185	6.93	288
25	12.359 601	1349.655 621	.000 740 9297	.080 909	109.198 959	.009 157 5964	10.99	1.747 279	6.99	300
26	13.667 360	1505.032 917	.000 664 4373	.073 167	110.118 770	.009 081 1040	10.90	1.833 304	7.05	312
27	15.113 492	1676.850 553	.000 596 3561	.066 166	110.950 569	.009 013 0227	10.82	1.920 219	7.11	324
28	16.712 638	1866.848 067	.000 535 6622	.059 835	111.702 777	.008 952 3289	10.75	2.007 983	7.17	336
29	18.480 988	2076.949 056	.000 481 4755	.054 110	112.383 011	.008 898 1421	10.68	2.096 553	7.23	348
30	20.436 445	2309.280 651	.000 433 0353	.048 932	112.998 156	.008 849 7019	10.62	2.185 893	7.29	360
31	22.598 808	2566.195 055	.000 389 6820	.044 250	113.554 441	.008 806 3487	10.57	2.275 962	7.34	372
32	24.989 969	2850.293 354	.000 350 8411	.040 016	114.057 498	.008 767 5077	10.53	2.366 723	7.40	384
33	27.634 136	3164.451 851	.000 316 0105	.036 187	114.512 421	.008 732 6772	10.48	2.458 140	7.45	396
34	30.558 081	3511.851 192	.000 284 7501	.032 725	114.923 814	.008 701 4168	10.45	2.550 178	7.50	408
35	33.791 405	3896.008 561	.000 256 6729	.029 593	115.295 843	.008 673 3396	10.41	2.642 803	7.55	420
36	37.366 845	4320.813 295	.000 231 4379	.026 762	115.632 274	.008 648 1046	10.38	2.735 981	7.60	432
37	41.320 599	4790.566 255	.000 208 7436	.024 201	115.936 514	.008 625 4103	10.36	2.829 682	7.65	444
38	45.692 697	5310.023 377	.000 188 3231	.021 885	116.211 643	.008 604 9898	10.33	2.923 875	7.69	456
39	50.527 402	5884.443 814	.000 169 9396	.019 791	116.460 447	.008 586 6063	10.31	3.018 532	7.74	468
40	55.873 664	6519.643 190	.000 153 3826	.017 898	116.685 443	.008 570 0493	10.29	3.113 624	7.78	480
41	61.785 608	7222.052 470	.000 138 4648	.016 185	116.888 911	.008 555 1315	10.27	3.209 125	7.83	492
42	68.323 091	7998.783 078	.000 125 0190	.014 636	117.072 910	.008 541 6857	10.26	3.305 010	7.87	504
43	75.552 299	8857.698 891	.000 112 8961	.013 236	117.239 303	.008 529 5628	10.24	3.401 254	7.91	516
44	83.546 423	9807.495 855	.000 101 9628	.011 969	117.389 775	.008 518 6295	10.23	3.497 836	7.95	528
45	92.386 399	10857.790 027	.000 092 0998	.010 824	117.525 849	.008 508 7664	10.22	3.594 734	7.99	540
46	102.161 726	12019.214 931	.000 083 2001	.009 788	117.648 903	.008 499 8668	10.20	3.691 926	8.03	552
47	112.971 371	13303.529 216	.000 075 1680	.008 852	117.760 182	.008 491 8347	10.20	3.789 395	8.06	564
48	124.924 775	14723.735 702	.000 067 9175	.008 005	117.860 814	.008 484 5842	10.19	3.887 121	8.10	576
49	138.142 960	16294.213 027	.000 061 3715	.007 239	117.951 817	.008 478 0381	10.18	3.985 086	8.13	588
50	152.759 749	18030.861 222	.000 055 4605	.006 546	118.034 112	.008 472 1271	10.17	4.083 276	8.17	600

Effective Rate is 10.58 %

Annual Percentage Rate is 10.10 %

MONTHLY COMPOUND INTEREST AND ANNUITY

	Amount Of 1	Amount Of 1 Per Period	Sinking Fund Payment	Present Worth Of 1	Present Worth of 1 Per Period	Periodic Payment To Amortize 1	Constant Annual Percent	Total Interest	Annual Add On Rate
	What a single $ 1 deposit grows to in the future. The deposit is made at the beginning of the first period.	What a series of $ 1 deposits grow to in the future. A deposit is made at the end of each period.	The amount to be deposited at the end of each period that grows to $ 1 in the future.	What $ 1 to be paid in the future is worth today. Value today of a single $ 1 payment tomorrow.	What $ 1 to be paid at the end of each period is worth today. Value today of a series of $ 1 payments tomorrow.	The mortgage payment to amortize a loan of $ 1. An annuity certain, payable at the end of each period, worth $ 1 today.	The annual payment, including interest and principal, to amortize completely a loan of $ 100.	The total interest paid over the term on a loan of $1. The loan is amortized by regular periodic payments.	The average annual interest rate on a loan that is completely amortized by regular periodic payments.
	$S = (1+i)^n$	$S\overline{n|} = \dfrac{(1+i)^n - 1}{i}$	$\dfrac{1}{S\overline{n|}} = \dfrac{i}{(1+i)^n - 1}$	$V^n = \dfrac{1}{(1+i)^n}$	$A\overline{n|} = \dfrac{1 - V^n}{i}$	$\dfrac{1}{A\overline{n|}} = \dfrac{i}{1 - V^n}$			

PERIODS

YEAR										
	1.008 438	1.000 000	1.000 000 0000	.991 633	.991 633	1.008 437 5000	1210.13	.008 437	10.12	1
	1.016 946	2.008 438	.497 899 4865	.983 336	1.974 969	.506 336 9865	607.61	.012 674	7.60	2
	1.025 527	3.025 384	.330 536 5871	.975 109	2.950 078	.338 974 0871	406.77	.016 922	6.77	3
	1.034 180	4.050 910	.246 858 0910	.966 950	3.917 028	.255 295 5910	306.36	.021 182	6.35	4
	1.042 905	5.085 090	.196 653 3562	.958 860	4.875 888	.205 090 8562	246.11	.025 454	6.11	5
	1.051 705	6.127 995	.163 185 5019	.950 837	5.826 725	.171 623 0019	205.95	.029 738	5.95	6
	1.060 579	7.179 700	.139 281 5792	.942 881	6.769 606	.147 719 0792	177.27	.034 034	5.83	7
	1.069 527	8.240 279	.121 355 1136	.934 992	7.704 599	.129 792 6136	155.76	.038 341	5.75	8
	1.078 551	9.309 806	.107 413 6192	.927 169	8.631 768	.115 851 1192	139.03	.042 660	5.69	9
	1.087 652	10.388 358	.096 261 6046	.919 412	9.551 180	.104 699 1046	125.64	.046 991	5.64	10
	1.096 829	11.476 010	.087 138 3023	.911 719	10.462 899	.095 575 8023	114.70	.051 334	5.60	11
	1.106 083	12.572 838	.079 536 5343	.904 091	11.366 990	.087 974 0343	105.57	.055 688	5.57	12
1	1.106 083	12.572 838	.079 536 5343	.904 091	11.366 990	.087 974 0343	105.57	.055 688	5.57	12
2	1.223 420	26.479 446	.037 765 1413	.817 381	21.643 784	.046 202 6413	55.45	.108 863	5.44	24
3	1.353 205	41.861 312	.023 888 4058	.738 986	30.934 941	.032 325 9058	38.80	.163 733	5.46	36
4	1.496 757	58.874 937	.016 985 1561	.668 111	39.334 993	.025 422 6561	30.51	.220 287	5.51	48
5	1.655 538	77.693 425	.012 871 1021	.604 033	46.929 404	.021 308 6021	25.58	.278 516	5.57	60
6	1.831 163	98.508 240	.010 151 4350	.546 101	53.795 443	.018 588 9350	22.31	.338 403	5.64	72
7	2.025 419	121.531 160	.008 228 3424	.493 725	60.002 967	.016 665 8424	20.00	.399 931	5.71	84
8	2.240 282	146.996 428	.006 802 8864	.446 372	65.615 134	.015 240 3864	18.29	.463 077	5.79	96
9	2.477 939	175.163 137	.005 708 9638	.403 561	70.689 044	.014 146 4638	16.98	.527 818	5.86	108
10	2.740 807	206.317 863	.004 846 8901	.364 856	75.276 320	.013 284 3901	15.95	.594 127	5.94	120
11	3.031 561	240.777 587	.004 153 2105	.329 863	79.423 635	.012 590 7105	15.11	.661 974	6.02	132
12	3.353 159	278.892 912	.003 585 6056	.298 226	83.173 186	.012 023 1056	14.43	.731 327	6.09	144
13	3.708 873	321.051 638	.003 114 7637	.269 624	86.563 121	.011 552 2637	13.87	.802 153	6.17	156
14	4.102 323	367.682 701	.002 719 7363	.243 764	89.627 930	.011 157 2363	13.39	.874 416	6.25	168
15	4.537 511	419.260 543	.002 385 1517	.220 385	92.398 797	.010 822 6517	12.99	.948 077	6.32	180
16	5.018 865	476.309 934	.002 099 4733	.199 248	94.903 913	.010 536 9733	12.65	1.023 099	6.39	192
17	5.551 283	539.411 314	.001 853 8729	.180 139	97.168 766	.010 291 3729	12.35	1.099 440	6.47	204
18	6.140 182	609.206 699	.001 641 4790	.162 862	99.216 399	.010 078 9790	12.10	1.177 059	6.54	216
19	6.791 552	686.406 209	.001 456 8633	.147 242	101.067 645	.009 894 3633	11.88	1.255 915	6.61	228
20	7.512 023	771.795 300	.001 295 6803	.133 120	102.741 341	.009 733 1803	11.68	1.335 963	6.68	240
21	8.308 923	866.242 751	.001 154 4108	.120 353	104.254 514	.009 591 9108	11.52	1.417 162	6.75	252
22	9.190 361	970.709 500	.001 030 1743	.108 810	105.622 560	.009 467 6743	11.37	1.499 466	6.82	264
23	10.165 306	1086.258 430	.000 920 5912	.098 374	106.859 398	.009 358 0912	11.23	1.582 833	6.88	276
24	11.243 675	1214.065 174	.000 823 6790	.088 939	107.977 613	.009 261 1790	11.12	1.667 220	6.95	288
25	12.436 441	1355.430 083	.000 737 7732	.080 409	108.988 580	.009 175 2732	11.02	1.752 582	7.01	300
26	13.755 740	1511.791 451	.000 661 4669	.072 697	109.902 587	.009 098 9669	10.92	1.838 878	7.07	312
27	15.214 995	1684.740 153	.000 593 5633	.065 725	110.728 932	.009 031 0633	10.84	1.926 065	7.13	324
28	16.829 052	1876.035 829	.000 533 0389	.059 421	111.476 023	.008 970 5389	10.77	2.014 101	7.19	336
29	18.614 334	2087.624 785	.000 479 0133	.053 722	112.151 462	.008 916 5133	10.70	2.102 947	7.25	348
30	20.589 005	2321.659 802	.000 430 7263	.048 570	112.762 560	.008 868 2263	10.65	2.192 561	7.31	360
31	22.773 155	2580.522 032	.000 387 5185	.043 911	113.314 210	.008 825 0185	10.60	2.282 907	7.36	372
32	25.189 007	2866.845 227	.000 348 8155	.039 700	113.813 350	.008 786 3155	10.55	2.373 945	7.42	384
33	27.861 140	3183.542 539	.000 314 1155	.035 892	114.264 618	.008 751 6155	10.51	2.465 640	7.47	396
34	30.816 743	3533.836 155	.000 282 9786	.032 450	114.672 605	.008 720 4786	10.47	2.557 955	7.52	408
35	34.085 885	3921.290 082	.000 255 0181	.029 338	115.041 463	.008 692 5181	10.44	2.650 858	7.57	420
36	37.701 829	4349.846 410	.000 229 8932	.026 524	115.374 944	.008 667 3932	10.41	2.744 314	7.62	432
37	41.701 364	4823.865 418	.000 207 3026	.023 980	115.676 441	.008 644 8026	10.38	2.838 292	7.67	444
38	46.125 184	5348.169 939	.000 186 9798	.021 680	115.949 022	.008 624 4798	10.35	2.932 763	7.72	456
39	51.018 297	5928.094 426	.000 168 6883	.019 601	116.195 459	.008 606 1883	10.33	3.027 696	7.76	468
40	56.430 487	6569.539 231	.000 152 2177	.017 721	116.418 262	.008 589 7177	10.31	3.123 064	7.81	480
41	62.416 821	7279.030 634	.000 137 3809	.016 021	116.619 695	.008 574 8809	10.29	3.218 841	7.85	492
42	69.038 205	8063.787 244	.000 124 0112	.014 485	116.801 809	.008 561 5112	10.28	3.315 002	7.89	504
43	76.362 007	8931.793 444	.000 111 9596	.013 096	116.966 457	.008 549 4596	10.26	3.411 521	7.93	516
44	84.462 743	9891.880 628	.000 101 0930	.011 840	117.115 314	.008 538 5930	10.25	3.508 377	7.97	528
45	93.422 831	10953.817 052	.000 091 2924	.010 704	117.249 894	.008 528 7924	10.24	3.605 660	8.01	540
46	103.333 436	12128.407 223	.000 082 4511	.009 677	117.371 566	.008 519 9511	10.23	3.703 013	8.05	552
47	114.295 390	13427.601 824	.000 074 4735	.008 749	117.481 569	.008 511 9735	10.22	3.800 753	8.09	564
48	126.420 225	14864.619 309	.000 067 2738	.007 910	117.581 022	.008 504 7738	10.21	3.898 750	8.12	576
49	139.831 303	16454.080 386	.000 060 7752	.007 151	117.670 936	.008 498 2752	10.20	3.996 986	8.16	588
50	154.665 073	18212.156 779	.000 054 9084	.006 466	117.752 227	.008 492 4084	10.20	4.095 445	8.19	600

Effective Rate is 10.61 %

8 - 139

Annual Percentage Rate is 10.125%

MONTHLY COMPOUND INTEREST AND ANNUITY

	Amount Of 1	Amount Of 1 Per Period	Sinking Fund Payment	Present Worth Of 1	Present Worth of 1 Per Period	Periodic Payment To Amortize 1	Constant Annual Percent	Total Interest	Annual Add On Rate	
	What a single $ 1 deposit grows to in the future. The deposit is made at the beginning of the first period.	What a series of $ 1 deposits grow to in the future. A deposit is made at the end of each period.	The amount to be deposited at the end of each period that grows to $ 1 in the future.	What $ 1 to be paid in the future is worth today. Value today of a single $ 1 payment tomorrow.	What $ 1 to be paid at the end of each period is worth today. Value today of a series of $ 1 payments tomorrow.	The mortgage payment to amortize a loan of $ 1. An annuity certain, payable at the end of each period, worth $ 1 today.	The annual payment, including interest and principal, to amortize completely a loan of $ 100.	The total interest paid over the term on a loan of $1. The loan is amortized by regular periodic payments.	The average annual interest rate on a loan that is completely amortized by regular periodic payments.	
	$S = (1+i)^n$	$S\overline{n}| = \dfrac{(1+i)^n - 1}{i}$	$\dfrac{1}{S\overline{n}|} = \dfrac{i}{(1+i)^n - 1}$	$V^n = \dfrac{1}{(1+i)^n}$	$A\overline{n}| = \dfrac{1-V^n}{i}$	$\dfrac{1}{A\overline{n}|} = \dfrac{i}{1-V^n}$				

YEAR										PERIODS
	1.008 458	1.000 000	1.000 000 0000	.991 613	.991 613	1.008 458 3333	1210.15	.008 458	10.15	1
	1.016 988	2.008 458	.497 894 3219	.983 296	1.974 908	.506 352 6553	607.63	.012 705	7.62	2
	1.025 590	3.025 447	.330 529 7204	.975 048	2.949 956	.338 988 0537	406.79	.016 964	6.79	3
	1.034 265	4.051 037	.246 850 3878	.966 870	3.916 827	.255 308 7212	306.38	.021 235	6.37	4
	1.043 013	5.085 302	.196 645 1628	.958 761	4.875 587	.205 103 4961	246.13	.025 517	6.12	5
	1.051 835	6.128 315	.163 176 9914	.950 719	5.826 306	.171 635 3247	205.97	.029 812	5.96	6
	1.060 732	7.180 150	.139 272 8505	.942 745	6.769 052	.147 731 1838	177.28	.034 118	5.85	7
	1.069 704	8.240 882	.121 346 2285	.934 838	7.703 889	.129 804 5618	155.77	.038 436	5.77	8
	1.078 752	9.310 587	.107 404 6190	.926 997	8.630 887	.115 862 9523	139.04	.042 767	5.70	9
	1.087 876	10.389 339	.096 252 5181	.919 222	9.550 109	.104 710 8514	125.66	.047 109	5.65	10
	1.097 078	11.477 215	.087 129 1505	.911 512	10.461 621	.095 587 4839	114.71	.051 462	5.61	11
	1.106 358	12.574 293	.079 527 3329	.903 867	11.365 488	.087 985 6662	105.59	.055 828	5.58	12
1	1.106 358	12.574 293	.079 527 3329	.903 867	11.365 488	.087 985 6662	105.59	.055 828	5.58	12
2	1.224 027	26.485 958	.037 755 8560	.816 975	21.638 376	.046 214 1894	55.46	.109 141	5.46	24
3	1.354 212	41.877 233	.023 879 3238	.738 437	30.923 700	.032 337 6572	38.81	.164 156	5.47	36
4	1.498 242	58.905 486	.016 976 3474	.667 449	39.316 397	.025 434 6808	30.53	.220 865	5.52	48
5	1.657 592	77.744 823	.012 862 5927	.603 285	46.902 278	.021 320 9261	25.59	.279 256	5.59	60
6	1.833 889	98.587 867	.010 143 2360	.545 289	53.758 905	.018 601 5694	22.33	.339 313	5.66	72
7	2.028 937	121.647 725	.008 220 4579	.492 869	59.956 383	.016 678 7912	20.02	.401 018	5.73	84
8	2.244 730	147.160 174	.006 795 3168	.445 488	65.558 079	.015 253 6501	18.31	.464 350	5.80	96
9	2.483 474	175.386 064	.005 701 7073	.402 662	70.621 266	.014 160 0406	17.00	.529 284	5.88	108
10	2.747 610	206.613 992	.004 839 9433	.363 953	75.197 714	.013 298 2766	15.96	.595 793	5.96	120
11	3.039 839	241.163 246	.004 146 5688	.328 965	79.334 214	.012 604 9022	15.13	.663 847	6.03	132
12	3.363 149	279.387 074	.003 579 2637	.297 340	83.073 059	.012 037 5970	14.45	.733 414	6.11	144
13	3.720 845	321.676 296	.003 108 7152	.268 756	86.452 477	.011 567 0486	13.89	.804 460	6.19	156
14	4.116 585	368.463 296	.002 713 9745	.242 920	89.507 022	.011 172 3079	13.41	.876 948	6.26	168
15	4.554 415	420.226 448	.002 379 6694	.219 567	92.267 923	.010 838 0027	13.01	.950 840	6.34	180
16	5.038 812	477.495 002	.002 094 2628	.198 459	94.763 411	.010 552 5961	12.67	1.026 098	6.41	192
17	5.574 728	540.854 500	.001 848 9261	.179 381	97.019 000	.010 307 2594	12.37	1.102 681	6.49	204
18	6.167 642	610.952 760	.001 636 7878	.162 137	99.057 752	.010 095 1211	12.12	1.180 546	6.56	216
19	6.823 617	688.506 499	.001 452 4191	.146 550	100.900 512	.009 910 7524	11.90	1.259 652	6.63	228
20	7.549 361	774.308 666	.001 291 4746	.132 462	102.566 123	.009 749 8080	11.70	1.339 954	6.70	240
21	8.352 292	869.236 542	.001 150 4348	.119 728	104.071 613	.009 608 7682	11.54	1.421 410	6.77	252
22	9.240 622	974.260 716	.001 026 4193	.108 218	105.432 375	.009 484 7526	11.39	1.503 975	6.84	264
23	10.223 432	1090.455 005	.000 917 0484	.097 815	106.662 324	.009 375 3817	11.26	1.587 605	6.90	276
24	11.310 771	1219.007 435	.000 820 3395	.088 411	107.774 033	.009 278 6729	11.14	1.672 258	6.97	288
25	12.513 757	1361.232 389	.000 734 6284	.079 912	108.778 871	.009 192 9618	11.04	1.757 889	7.03	300
26	13.844 690	1518.584 042	.000 658 5082	.072 230	109.687 110	.009 116 8415	10.95	1.844 455	7.09	312
27	15.317 178	1692.671 233	.000 590 7822	.065 286	110.508 038	.009 049 1155	10.86	1.931 913	7.16	324
28	16.946 275	1885.273 914	.000 530 4269	.059 010	111.250 047	.008 988 7602	10.79	2.020 223	7.22	336
29	18.748 640	2098.361 346	.000 476 5623	.053 337	111.920 725	.008 934 8957	10.73	2.109 344	7.27	348
30	20.742 699	2334.112 239	.000 428 4284	.048 210	112.526 928	.008 886 7617	10.67	2.199 234	7.33	360
31	22.948 842	2594.937 022	.000 385 3658	.043 575	113.074 855	.008 843 6991	10.62	2.289 856	7.39	372
32	25.389 625	2883.502 494	.000 346 8005	.039 386	113.570 108	.008 805 1338	10.57	2.381 171	7.44	384
33	28.090 004	3202.759 086	.000 312 2308	.035 600	114.017 751	.008 770 5641	10.53	2.473 143	7.49	396
34	31.077 588	3555.971 031	.000 281 2171	.032 178	114.422 361	.008 739 5505	10.49	2.565 737	7.55	408
35	34.382 925	3946.749 738	.000 253 3730	.029 084	114.788 074	.008 711 7064	10.46	2.658 917	7.60	420
36	38.039 809	4379.090 715	.000 228 3579	.026 288	115.118 631	.008 686 6912	10.43	2.752 651	7.65	432
37	42.085 630	4857.414 426	.000 205 8708	.023 761	115.417 409	.008 664 2042	10.40	2.846 907	7.69	444
38	46.561 755	5386.611 481	.000 185 6455	.021 477	115.687 466	.008 643 9788	10.38	2.941 654	7.74	456
39	51.513 950	5972.092 645	.000 167 4455	.019 412	115.931 561	.008 625 7788	10.36	3.036 864	7.79	468
40	56.992 849	6619.844 159	.000 151 0610	.017 546	116.152 190	.008 609 3943	10.34	3.132 509	7.83	480
41	63.054 469	7336.488 946	.000 136 3050	.015 859	116.351 609	.008 594 6383	10.32	3.228 562	7.87	492
42	69.760 789	8129.354 326	.000 123 0110	.014 335	116.531 858	.008 581 3443	10.30	3.324 998	7.92	504
43	77.180 376	9006.546 936	.000 111 0303	.012 957	116.694 779	.008 569 3637	10.29	3.421 792	7.96	516
44	85.389 093	9977.035 614	.000 100 2302	.011 711	116.842 038	.008 558 5635	10.28	3.518 922	8.00	528
45	94.470 869	11050.743 103	.000 090 4917	.010 585	116.975 140	.008 548 8250	10.26	3.616 365	8.04	540
46	104.518 560	12238.647 504	.000 081 7084	.009 568	117.095 447	.008 540 0417	10.25	3.714 103	8.07	552
47	115.634 900	13552.694 523	.000 073 7800	.008 648	117.204 188	.008 532 1183	10.24	3.812 115	8.11	564
48	127.933 546	15006.921 652	.000 066 6359	.007 817	117.302 476	.008 524 9693	10.23	3.910 382	8.15	576
49	141.540 246	16615.595 563	.000 060 1844	.007 065	117.391 315	.008 518 5178	10.23	4.008 888	8.18	588
50	156.594 121	18395.364 111	.000 054 3615	.006 386	117.471 614	.008 512 6949	10.22	4.107 617	8.22	600

Effective Rate is 10.64 %

Annual Percentage Rate is 10.15 %

	Amount Of 1	Amount Of 1 Per Period	Sinking Fund Payment	Present Worth Of 1	Present Worth of 1 Per Period	Periodic Payment To Amortize 1	Constant Annual Percent	Total Interest	Annual Add On Rate	
	What a single $ 1 deposit grows to in the future. The deposit is made at the beginning of the first period.	What a series of $ 1 deposits grow to in the future. A deposit is made at the end of each period.	The amount to be deposited at the end of each period that grows to $ 1 in the future.	What $ 1 to be paid in the future is worth today. Value today of a single $ 1 payment tomorrow.	What $ 1 to be paid at the end of each period is worth today. Value today of a series of $ 1 payments tomorrow.	The mortgage payment to amortize a loan of $ 1. An annuity certain, payable at the end of each period, worth $ 1 today.	The annual payment, including interest and principal, to amortize completely a loan of $ 100.	The total interest paid over the term on a loan of $1. The loan is amortized by regular periodic payments.	The average annual interest rate on a loan that is completely amortized by regular periodic payments.	
	$S = (1 + i)^n$	$S\overline{n}| = \dfrac{(1+i)^n - 1}{i}$	$\dfrac{1}{S\overline{n}|} = \dfrac{i}{(1+i)^n - 1}$	$V^n = \dfrac{1}{(1+i)^n}$	$A\overline{n}| = \dfrac{1 - V^n}{i}$	$\dfrac{1}{A\overline{n}|} = \dfrac{i}{1 - V^n}$				PERIODS

YEAR										
	1.008 500	1.000 000	1.000 000 0000	.991 572	.991 572	1.008 500 0000	1210.20	.008 500	10.20	1
	1.017 072	2.008 500	.497 883 9930	.983 214	1.974 786	.506 383 9930	607.67	.012 768	7.66	2
	1.025 717	3.025 572	.330 515 9875	.974 927	2.949 713	.339 015 9875	406.82	.017 048	6.82	3
	1.034 436	4.051 290	.246 834 9823	.966 710	3.916 424	.255 334 9823	306.41	.021 340	6.40	4
	1.043 229	5.085 726	.196 628 7770	.958 563	4.874 986	.205 128 7770	246.16	.025 644	6.15	5
	1.052 096	6.128 954	.163 159 9716	.950 484	5.825 470	.171 659 9716	206.00	.029 960	5.99	6
	1.061 039	7.181 050	.139 255 3945	.942 472	6.767 942	.147 755 3945	177.31	.034 288	5.88	7
	1.070 058	8.242 089	.121 328 4600	.934 529	7.702 471	.129 828 4600	155.80	.038 628	5.79	8
	1.079 153	9.312 147	.107 386 6205	.926 652	8.629 124	.115 886 6205	139.07	.042 980	5.73	9
	1.088 326	10.391 300	.096 234 3472	.918 842	9.547 966	.104 734 3472	125.69	.047 343	5.68	10
	1.097 577	11.479 626	.087 110 8493	.911 098	10.459 064	.095 610 8493	114.74	.051 719	5.64	11
	1.106 906	12.577 203	.079 508 9327	.903 419	11.362 483	.088 008 9327	105.62	.056 107	5.61	12
1	1.106 906	12.577 203	.079 508 9327	.903 419	11.362 483	.088 008 9327	105.62	.056 107	5.61	12
2	1.225 241	26.498 988	.037 737 2907	.816 166	21.627 565	.046 237 2907	55.49	.109 695	5.48	24
3	1.356 227	41.909 098	.023 861 1675	.737 340	30.901 234	.032 361 1675	38.84	.165 002	5.50	36
4	1.501 216	58.966 644	.016 958 7402	.666 126	39.279 241	.025 458 7402	30.56	.222 020	5.55	48
5	1.661 706	77.847 749	.012 845 5866	.601 791	46.848 092	.021 345 5866	25.62	.280 735	5.61	60
6	1.839 353	98.747 361	.010 126 8529	.543 670	53.685 934	.018 626 8529	22.36	.341 133	5.69	72
7	2.035 991	121.881 272	.008 204 7060	.491 161	59.863 370	.016 704 7060	20.05	.403 195	5.76	84
8	2.253 651	147.488 342	.006 780 1969	.443 724	65.444 183	.015 280 1969	18.34	.466 899	5.84	96
9	2.494 580	175.832 968	.005 687 2156	.400 869	70.485 994	.014 187 2156	17.03	.532 219	5.91	108
10	2.761 266	207.207 810	.004 826 0729	.362 153	75.040 862	.013 326 0729	16.00	.599 129	5.99	120
11	3.056 463	241.936 818	.004 133 3105	.327 176	79.155 816	.012 633 3105	15.16	.667 597	6.07	132
12	3.383 218	280.378 574	.003 566 6063	.295 577	82.873 342	.012 066 6063	14.48	.737 591	6.15	144
13	3.744 905	322.929 992	.003 096 6464	.267 029	86.231 826	.011 596 6464	13.92	.809 077	6.22	156
14	4.145 259	370.030 423	.002 702 4805	.241 239	89.265 944	.011 202 4805	13.45	.882 017	6.30	168
15	4.588 413	422.166 182	.002 368 7354	.217 940	92.007 024	.010 868 7354	13.05	.956 372	6.38	180
16	5.078 942	479.875 579	.002 083 8735	.196 891	94.483 367	.010 583 8735	12.71	1.032 104	6.45	192
17	5.621 913	543.754 470	.001 839 0653	.177 875	96.720 542	.010 339 0653	12.41	1.109 169	6.52	204
18	6.222 930	614.462 412	.001 627 4388	.160 696	98.741 648	.010 127 4388	12.16	1.187 527	6.60	216
19	6.888 201	692.729 473	.001 443 5650	.145 176	100.567 553	.009 943 5650	11.94	1.267 133	6.67	228
20	7.624 592	779.363 770	.001 283 0979	.131 155	102.217 111	.009 783 0979	11.74	1.347 943	6.74	240
21	8.439 708	875.259 813	.001 142 5179	.118 488	103.707 352	.009 642 5179	11.58	1.429 915	6.81	252
22	9.341 966	981.407 741	.001 018 9445	.107 044	105.053 665	.009 518 9445	11.43	1.513 001	6.88	264
23	10.340 680	1098.903 543	.000 909 9980	.096 705	106.269 948	.009 409 9980	11.30	1.597 159	6.94	276
24	11.446 163	1228.960 377	.000 813 6959	.087 366	107.368 762	.009 313 6959	11.18	1.682 344	7.01	288
25	12.669 829	1372.921 097	.000 728 3740	.078 928	108.361 452	.009 228 3740	11.08	1.768 512	7.07	300
26	14.024 313	1532.272 115	.000 652 6256	.071 305	109.258 266	.009 152 6256	10.99	1.855 619	7.14	312
27	15.523 599	1708.658 748	.000 585 2544	.064 418	110.068 465	.009 085 2544	10.91	1.943 622	7.20	324
28	17.183 169	1903.902 212	.000 525 2371	.058 196	110.800 414	.009 025 2371	10.84	2.032 480	7.26	336
29	19.020 157	2120.018 417	.000 471 6940	.052 576	111.461 670	.008 971 6940	10.77	2.122 150	7.32	348
30	21.053 530	2359.238 790	.000 423 8655	.047 498	112.059 062	.008 923 8655	10.71	2.212 592	7.38	360
31	23.304 283	2624.033 310	.000 381 0927	.042 911	112.598 757	.008 881 0927	10.66	2.303 766	7.43	372
32	25.795 656	2917.136 014	.000 342 8020	.038 766	113.086 327	.008 842 8020	10.62	2.395 636	7.49	384
33	28.553 372	3241.573 222	.000 308 4922	.035 022	113.526 808	.008 808 4922	10.58	2.488 163	7.54	396
34	31.605 906	3600.694 787	.000 277 7242	.031 640	113.924 746	.008 777 7242	10.54	2.581 311	7.59	408
35	34.984 774	3998.208 685	.000 250 1120	.028 584	114.284 251	.008 750 1120	10.51	2.675 047	7.64	420
36	38.724 864	4438.219 293	.000 225 3156	.025 823	114.609 035	.008 725 3156	10.48	2.769 336	7.69	432
37	42.864 793	4925.269 775	.000 203 0346	.023 329	114.902 451	.008 703 0346	10.45	2.864 147	7.74	444
38	47.447 306	5464.388 986	.000 183 0031	.021 076	115.167 528	.008 683 0031	10.42	2.959 449	7.79	456
39	52.519 719	6061.143 398	.000 164 9854	.019 040	115.407 004	.008 664 9854	10.40	3.055 213	7.83	468
40	58.134 404	6721.694 573	.000 148 7720	.017 202	115.623 351	.008 648 7720	10.38	3.151 411	7.88	480
41	64.349 334	7452.862 781	.000 134 1766	.015 540	115.818 803	.008 634 1766	10.37	3.248 015	7.92	492
42	71.228 678	8262.197 424	.000 121 0332	.014 039	115.995 378	.008 621 0332	10.35	3.345 001	7.96	504
43	78.843 467	9158.054 980	.000 109 1935	.012 683	116.154 899	.008 609 1935	10.34	3.442 344	8.01	516
44	87.272 325	10149.685 287	.000 098 5252	.011 458	116.299 013	.008 598 5252	10.32	3.540 021	8.05	528
45	96.602 280	11247.327 049	.000 088 9100	.010 352	116.429 209	.008 588 9100	10.31	3.638 011	8.08	540
46	106.929 665	12462.313 550	.000 080 2419	.009 352	116.546 830	.008 580 2419	10.30	3.736 294	8.12	552
47	118.361 112	13807.189 673	.000 072 4260	.008 449	116.653 092	.008 572 4260	10.29	3.834 848	8.16	564
48	131.014 652	15295.841 429	.000 065 3772	.007 633	116.749 090	.008 565 3772	10.28	3.933 657	8.20	576
49	145.020 934	16943.639 327	.000 059 0192	.006 896	116.835 817	.008 559 0192	10.28	4.032 703	8.23	588
50	160.524 575	18767.597 081	.000 053 2833	.006 230	116.914 168	.008 553 2833	10.27	4.131 970	8.26	600

Effective Rate is 10.69 %

Annual Percentage Rate is 10.20

MONTHLY COMPOUND INTEREST AND ANNUITY

10.25 % M

Amount Of 1	Amount Of 1 Per Period	Sinking Fund Payment	Present Worth Of 1	Present Worth of 1 Per Period	Periodic Payment To Amortize 1	Constant Annual Percent	Total Interest	Annual Add On Rate
What a single $ 1 deposit grows to in the future. The deposit is made at the beginning of the first period.	What a series of $ 1 deposits grow to in the future. A deposit is made at the end of each period.	The amount to be deposited at the end of each period that grows to $ 1 in the future.	What $ 1 to be paid in the future is worth today. Value today of a single $ 1 payment tomorrow.	What $ 1 to be paid at the end of each period is worth today. Value today of a series of $ 1 payments tomorrow.	The mortgage payment to amortize a loan of $ 1. An annuity certain, payable at the end of each period, worth $ 1 today.	The annual payment, including interest and principal, to amortize completely a loan of $ 100.	The total interest paid over the term on a loan of $1. The loan is amortized by regular periodic payments.	The average annual interest rate on a loan that is completely amortized by regular periodic payments.
$S = (1+i)^n$	$S\overline{n}| = \dfrac{(1+i)^n - 1}{i}$	$\dfrac{1}{S\overline{n}|} = \dfrac{i}{(1+i)^n - 1}$	$V^n = \dfrac{1}{(1+i)^n}$	$A\overline{n}| = \dfrac{1 - V^n}{i}$	$\dfrac{1}{A\overline{n}|} = \dfrac{i}{1 - V^n}$			

YEAR / **PERIODS**

YEAR	Amount Of 1	Amount Of 1 Per Period	Sinking Fund Payment	Present Worth Of 1	Present Worth of 1 Per Period	Periodic Payment To Amortize 1	Constant Annual Percent	Total Interest	Annual Add On Rate	PERIODS
	1.008 542	1.000 000	1.000 000 0000	.991 531	.991 531	1.008 541 6667	1210.25	.008 542	10.25	1
	1.017 156	2.008 542	.497 873 6646	.983 133	1.974 664	.506 415 3312	607.70	.012 831	7.70	2
	1.025 845	3.025 698	.330 502 2554	.974 807	2.949 470	.339 043 9221	406.86	.017 132	6.85	3
	1.034 607	4.051 542	.246 819 5777	.966 551	3.916 021	.255 361 2444	306.44	.021 445	6.43	4
	1.043 444	5.086 149	.196 612 3925	.958 365	4.874 386	.205 154 0592	246.19	.025 770	6.18	5
	1.052 357	6.129 594	.163 142 9534	.950 248	5.824 634	.171 684 6201	206.03	.030 108	6.02	6
	1.061 346	7.181 951	.139 237 9405	.942 200	6.766 834	.147 779 6072	177.34	.034 457	5.91	7
	1.070 411	8.243 296	.121 310 6938	.934 220	7.701 054	.129 852 3605	155.83	.038 819	5.82	8
	1.079 555	9.313 708	.107 368 6245	.926 308	8.627 362	.115 910 2911	139.10	.043 193	5.76	9
	1.088 776	10.393 262	.096 216 1791	.918 463	9.545 824	.104 757 8458	125.71	.047 578	5.71	10
	1.098 076	11.482 038	.087 092 5511	.910 684	10.456 508	.095 634 2178	114.77	.051 976	5.67	11
	1.107 455	12.580 114	.079 490 5359	.902 971	11.359 479	.088 032 2026	105.64	.056 386	5.64	12
1	1.107 455	12.580 114	.079 490 5359	.902 971	11.359 479	.088 032 2026	105.64	.056 386	5.64	12
2	1.226 457	26.512 026	.037 718 7321	.815 357	21.616 761	.046 260 3988	55.52	.110 250	5.51	24
3	1.358 246	41.940 993	.023 843 0214	.736 244	30.878 791	.032 384 6881	38.87	.165 849	5.53	36
4	1.504 196	59.027 882	.016 941 1464	.664 807	39.242 135	.025 482 8131	30.58	.223 175	5.58	48
5	1.665 830	77.950 846	.012 828 5972	.600 301	46.793 994	.021 370 2638	25.65	.282 216	5.64	60
6	1.844 832	98.907 179	.010 110 4896	.542 055	53.613 104	.018 652 1562	22.39	.342 955	5.72	72
7	2.043 069	122.115 378	.008 188 9769	.489 460	59.770 564	.016 730 6435	20.08	.405 374	5.79	84
8	2.262 607	147.817 417	.006 765 1027	.441 968	65.330 572	.015 306 7693	18.37	.469 450	5.87	96
9	2.505 736	176.281 272	.005 672 7524	.399 084	70.351 099	.014 214 4190	17.06	.535 157	5.95	108
10	2.774 990	207.803 714	.004 812 2335	.360 362	74.884 490	.013 353 9002	16.03	.602 468	6.02	120
11	3.073 177	242.713 406	.004 120 0856	.325 396	78.978 010	.012 661 7522	15.20	.671 351	6.10	132
12	3.403 406	281.374 322	.003 553 9846	.293 823	82.674 341	.012 095 6512	14.52	.741 774	6.18	144
13	3.769 119	324.189 554	.003 084 6151	.265 314	86.012 022	.011 626 2818	13.96	.813 700	6.26	156
14	4.174 130	371.605 502	.002 691 0258	.239 571	89.025 850	.011 232 6925	13.48	.887 092	6.34	168
15	4.622 662	424.116 537	.002 357 8425	.216 326	91.747 251	.010 899 5092	13.08	.961 912	6.41	180
16	5.119 391	482.270 153	.002 073 5266	.195 336	94.204 596	.010 615 1933	12.74	1.038 117	6.49	192
17	5.669 496	546.672 673	.001 829 2482	.176 383	96.423 509	.010 370 9149	12.45	1.115 667	6.56	204
18	6.278 712	617.995 576	.001 618 1346	.159 268	98.427 122	.010 159 8012	12.20	1.194 517	6.64	216
19	6.953 392	696.982 491	.001 434 7563	.143 815	100.236 328	.009 976 4229	11.98	1.274 624	6.71	228
20	7.700 570	784.456 956	.001 274 7672	.129 861	101.869 988	.009 816 4339	11.78	1.355 944	6.78	240
21	8.528 036	881.331 002	.001 134 6475	.117 260	103.345 136	.009 676 3141	11.62	1.438 431	6.85	252
22	9.444 417	988.614 662	.001 011 5165	.105 883	104.677 152	.009 553 1831	11.47	1.522 040	6.92	264
23	10.459 268	1107.426 503	.000 902 9945	.095 609	105.879 924	.009 444 6611	11.34	1.606 726	6.99	276
24	11.583 170	1239.005 287	.000 807 0991	.086 332	106.965 992	.009 348 7657	11.22	1.692 445	7.05	288
25	12.827 841	1384.722 888	.000 722 1662	.077 955	107.946 680	.009 263 8328	11.12	1.779 150	7.12	300
26	14.206 259	1546.098 594	.000 646 7893	.070 392	108.832 214	.009 188 4559	11.03	1.866 798	7.18	312
27	15.732 794	1724.814 949	.000 579 7723	.063 561	109.631 824	.009 121 4390	10.95	1.955 346	7.24	324
28	17.423 364	1922.735 295	.000 520 0924	.057 394	110.353 850	.009 061 7591	10.88	2.044 751	7.30	336
29	19.295 594	2141.923 199	.000 466 8701	.051 825	111.005 818	.009 008 5368	10.82	2.134 971	7.36	348
30	21.369 005	2384.663 970	.000 419 3463	.046 797	111.594 527	.008 961 0130	10.76	2.225 965	7.42	360
31	23.665 214	2653.488 485	.000 376 8624	.042 256	112.126 113	.008 918 5291	10.71	2.317 693	7.48	372
32	26.208 163	2951.199 576	.000 338 8453	.038 156	112.606 121	.008 880 5119	10.66	2.410 117	7.53	384
33	29.024 365	3280.901 254	.000 304 7943	.034 454	113.039 554	.008 846 4610	10.62	2.503 199	7.59	396
34	32.143 182	3646.031 071	.000 274 2708	.031 111	113.430 931	.008 815 9375	10.58	2.596 903	7.64	408
35	35.597 132	4050.395 965	.000 246 8894	.028 092	113.784 334	.008 788 5561	10.55	2.691 194	7.69	420
36	39.422 227	4498.211 944	.000 222 3106	.025 366	114.103 446	.008 763 9772	10.52	2.786 038	7.74	432
37	43.658 348	4994.148 053	.000 200 2344	.022 905	114.391 595	.008 741 9010	10.50	2.881 404	7.79	444
38	48.349 662	5543.375 045	.000 180 3955	.020 683	114.651 785	.008 722 0622	10.47	2.977 260	7.83	456
39	53.545 082	6151.619 301	.000 162 5588	.018 676	114.886 730	.008 704 2255	10.45	3.073 578	7.88	468
40	59.298 776	6825.222 528	.000 146 5154	.016 864	115.098 878	.008 688 1820	10.43	3.170 327	7.93	480
41	65.670 734	7571.207 885	.000 132 0793	.015 227	115.290 441	.008 673 7460	10.41	3.267 483	7.97	492
42	72.727 392	8397.353 203	.000 119 0851	.013 750	115.463 417	.008 660 7518	10.40	3.365 019	8.01	504
43	80.542 324	9312.272 081	.000 107 3852	.012 416	115.619 610	.008 649 0518	10.38	3.462 911	8.05	516
44	89.197 011	10325.503 696	.000 096 8476	.011 211	115.760 647	.008 638 5142	10.37	3.561 136	8.09	528
45	98.781 688	11447.612 255	.000 087 3545	.010 123	115.888 000	.008 629 0211	10.36	3.659 671	8.13	540
46	109.396 288	12690.297 148	.000 078 8004	.009 141	116.002 996	.008 620 4670	10.35	3.758 498	8.17	552
47	121.151 482	14066.514 919	.000 071 0908	.008 254	116.106 834	.008 612 7575	10.34	3.857 595	8.21	564
48	134.169 831	15590.614 364	.000 064 1412	.007 453	116.200 596	.008 605 8078	10.33	3.956 945	8.24	576
49	148.587 069	17278.486 128	.000 057 8754	.006 730	116.285 261	.008 599 5421	10.32	4.056 531	8.28	588
50	164.553 513	19147.728 388	.000 052 2255	.006 077	116.361 711	.008 593 8922	10.32	4.156 335	8.31	600

Effective Rate is 10.75 %

Annual Percentage Rate is 10.25 %

MONTHLY COMPOUND INTEREST AND ANNUITY

10.30 % M

Amount Of 1	Amount Of 1 Per Period	Sinking Fund Payment	Present Worth Of 1	Present Worth of 1 Per Period	Periodic Payment To Amortize 1	Constant Annual Percent	Total Interest	Annual Add On Rate	
What a single $ 1 deposit grows to in the future. The deposit is made at the beginning of the first period.	What a series of $ 1 deposits grow to in the future. A deposit is made at the end of each period.	The amount to be deposited at the end of each period that grows to $ 1 in the future.	What $ 1 to be paid in the future is worth today. Value today of a single $ 1 payment tomorrow.	What $ 1 to be paid at the end of each period is worth today. Value today of a series of $ 1 payments tomorrow.	The mortgage payment to amortize a loan of $ 1. An annuity certain, payable at the end of each period, worth $ 1 today.	The annual payment, including interest and principal, to amortize completely a loan of $ 100.	The total interest paid over the term on a loan of $1. The loan is amortized by regular periodic payments.	The average annual interest rate on a loan that is completely amortized by regular periodic payments.	
$S = (1+i)^n$	$S\overline{n}| = \dfrac{(1+i)^n - 1}{i}$	$\dfrac{1}{S\overline{n}|} = \dfrac{i}{(1+i)^n - 1}$	$V^n = \dfrac{1}{(1+i)^n}$	$A\overline{n}| = \dfrac{1-V^n}{i}$	$\dfrac{1}{A\overline{n}|} = \dfrac{i}{1-V^n}$				**PERIODS**

YEAR										
	1.008 583	1.000 000	1.000 000 0000	.991 490	.991 490	1.008 583 3333	1210.30	.008 583	10.30	1
	1.017 240	2.008 583	.497 863 3365	.983 052	1.974 542	.506 446 6698	607.74	.012 893	7.74	2
	1.025 972	3.025 824	.330 488 5241	.974 686	2.949 227	.339 071 8574	406.89	.017 216	6.89	3
	1.034 778	4.051 795	.246 804 1743	.966 391	3.915 618	.255 387 5076	306.47	.021 550	6.47	4
	1.043 660	5.086 573	.196 596 0094	.958 167	4.873 785	.205 179 3428	246.22	.025 897	6.22	5
	1.052 618	6.130 233	.163 125 9369	.950 012	5.823 797	.171 709 2702	206.06	.030 256	6.05	6
	1.061 653	7.182 851	.139 220 4884	.941 928	6.765 725	.147 803 8218	177.37	.034 627	5.94	7
	1.070 765	8.244 504	.121 292 9298	.933 911	7.699 636	.129 876 2632	155.86	.039 010	5.85	8
	1.079 956	9.315 269	.107 350 6310	.925 964	8.625 600	.115 933 9644	139.13	.043 406	5.79	9
	1.089 226	10.395 225	.096 198 0139	.918 083	9.543 683	.104 781 3473	125.74	.047 813	5.74	10
	1.098 575	11.484 451	.087 074 2561	.910 270	10.453 954	.095 657 5894	114.79	.052 233	5.70	11
	1.108 004	12.583 026	.079 472 1425	.902 524	11.356 477	.088 055 4758	105.67	.056 666	5.67	12
1	1.108 004	12.583 026	.079 472 1425	.902 524	11.356 477	.088 055 4758	105.67	.056 666	5.67	12
2	1.227 674	26.525 072	.037 700 1804	.814 549	21.605 965	.046 283 5137	55.55	.110 804	5.54	24
3	1.360 268	41.972 919	.023 824 8855	.735 149	30.856 370	.032 408 2188	38.89	.166 696	5.56	36
4	1.507 182	59.089 201	.016 923 5661	.663 490	39.205 079	.025 506 8995	30.61	.224 331	5.61	48
5	1.669 964	78.054 114	.012 811 6244	.598 815	46.739 985	.021 394 9578	25.68	.283 697	5.67	60
6	1.850 328	99.067 320	.010 094 1461	.540 445	53.540 415	.018 677 4794	22.42	.344 779	5.75	72
7	2.050 171	122.350 043	.008 173 2706	.487 764	59.677 964	.016 756 6039	20.11	.407 555	5.82	84
8	2.271 599	148.147 399	.006 750 0341	.440 219	65.217 246	.015 333 3675	18.41	.472 003	5.90	96
9	2.516 941	176.730 981	.005 658 3175	.397 308	70.216 579	.014 241 6508	17.09	.538 098	5.98	108
10	2.788 781	208.401 713	.004 798 4250	.358 580	74.728 595	.013 381 7584	16.06	.605 811	6.06	120
11	3.089 982	243.493 021	.004 106 8939	.323 627	78.800 795	.012 690 2272	15.23	.675 110	6.14	132
12	3.423 713	282.374 340	.003 541 3983	.292 081	82.476 052	.012 124 7316	14.55	.745 961	6.22	144
13	3.793 489	325.455 009	.003 072 6213	.263 610	85.793 059	.011 655 9547	13.99	.818 329	6.29	156
14	4.203 202	373.188 576	.002 679 6104	.237 914	88.786 735	.011 262 9438	13.52	.892 175	6.37	168
15	4.657 166	426.077 574	.002 346 9905	.214 723	91.488 598	.010 930 3238	13.12	.967 458	6.45	180
16	5.160 160	484.678 810	.002 063 2220	.193 792	93.927 093	.010 646 5554	12.78	1.044 139	6.53	192
17	5.717 479	549.609 233	.001 819 4745	.174 902	96.127 893	.010 402 8079	12.49	1.122 173	6.60	204
18	6.334 992	621.552 420	.001 608 8748	.157 853	98.114 166	.010 192 2081	12.24	1.201 517	6.68	216
19	7.019 198	701.265 782	.001 425 9929	.142 466	99.906 825	.010 009 3262	12.02	1.282 126	6.75	228
20	7.777 302	789.588 529	.001 266 4824	.128 579	101.524 742	.009 849 8158	11.82	1.363 956	6.82	240
21	8.617 284	887.450 513	.001 126 8234	.116 046	102.984 949	.009 710 1567	11.66	1.446 959	6.89	252
22	9.547 987	995.882 013	.001 004 1350	.104 734	104.302 822	.009 587 4683	11.51	1.531 092	6.96	264
23	10.579 211	1116.024 580	.000 896 0376	.094 525	105.492 232	.009 479 3709	11.38	1.616 306	7.03	276
24	11.721 811	1249.143 063	.000 800 5488	.085 311	106.565 703	.009 383 8821	11.27	1.702 558	7.09	288
25	12.987 817	1396.638 914	.000 716 0047	.076 995	107.534 536	.009 299 3380	11.16	1.789 801	7.16	300
26	14.390 557	1560.064 951	.000 640 9990	.069 490	108.408 931	.009 224 3323	11.07	1.877 992	7.22	312
27	15.944 800	1741.141 704	.000 574 3358	.062 716	109.198 092	.009 157 6691	10.99	1.967 085	7.29	324
28	17.666 907	1941.775 525	.000 514 9926	.056 603	109.910 330	.009 098 3259	10.92	2.057 038	7.35	336
29	19.575 009	2164.078 662	.000 462 0904	.051 086	110.553 140	.009 045 4237	10.86	2.147 807	7.41	348
30	21.689 194	2410.391 495	.000 414 8704	.046 106	111.133 292	.008 998 2037	10.80	2.239 353	7.46	360
31	24.031 720	2683.307 173	.000 372 6744	.041 612	111.656 893	.008 956 0078	10.75	2.331 635	7.52	372
32	26.627 249	2985.698 919	.000 334 9300	.037 556	112.129 455	.008 918 2633	10.71	2.424 613	7.58	384
33	29.503 107	3320.750 274	.000 301 1368	.033 895	112.555 953	.008 884 4701	10.67	2.518 250	7.63	396
34	32.689 569	3691.988 617	.000 270 8567	.030 591	112.940 878	.008 854 1901	10.63	2.612 510	7.68	408
35	36.220 183	4103.322 299	.000 243 7050	.027 609	113.288 282	.008 827 0383	10.60	2.707 356	7.74	420
36	40.132 119	4559.081 788	.000 219 3424	.024 918	113.601 822	.008 802 6757	10.57	2.802 756	7.79	432
37	44.466 560	5064.065 263	.000 197 4698	.022 489	113.884 799	.008 780 8031	10.54	2.898 677	7.83	444
38	49.269 011	5623.589 127	.000 177 8224	.020 297	114.140 193	.008 761 1557	10.52	2.995 087	7.88	456
39	54.590 419	6243.543 974	.000 160 1654	.018 318	114.370 691	.008 743 4988	10.50	3.091 957	7.93	468
40	60.486 419	6930.456 613	.000 144 2906	.016 533	114.578 722	.008 727 6240	10.48	3.189 260	7.97	480
41	67.019 213	7691.558 773	.000 130 0127	.014 921	114.766 474	.008 713 3460	10.46	3.286 966	8.02	492
42	74.257 576	8534.863 240	.000 117 1665	.013 467	114.935 926	.008 700 4998	10.45	3.385 052	8.06	504
43	82.277 714	9469.248 219	.000 105 6050	.012 154	115.088 859	.008 688 9383	10.43	3.483 492	8.10	516
44	91.164 061	10504.550 795	.000 095 1968	.010 969	115.226 885	.008 678 5302	10.42	3.582 264	8.14	528
45	101.010 172	11651.670 505	.000 085 8246	.009 900	115.351 470	.008 669 1579	10.41	3.681 345	8.18	540
46	111.919 705	12922.684 078	.000 077 3833	.008 935	115.463 886	.008 660 7166	10.40	3.780 716	8.22	552
47	124.007 515	14330.972 587	.000 069 7789	.008 064	115.565 356	.008 653 1123	10.39	3.880 355	8.26	564
48	137.400 860	15891.362 314	.000 062 9273	.007 278	115.656 935	.008 646 2606	10.38	3.980 246	8.29	576
49	152.240 744	17620.280 845	.000 056 7528	.006 569	115.739 587	.008 640 0861	10.37	4.080 371	8.33	588
50	168.683 399	19535.930 016	.000 051 1877	.005 928	115.814 183	.008 634 5211	10.37	4.180 713	8.36	600

Effective Rate is 10.80 %

Annual Percentage Rate is 10.30 %

MONTHLY COMPOUND INTEREST AND ANNUITY

	Amount Of 1	Amount Of 1 Per Period	Sinking Fund Payment	Present Worth Of 1	Present Worth of 1 Per Period	Periodic Payment To Amortize 1	Constant Annual Percent	Total Interest	Annual Add On Rate	

The single/series deposit descriptions:

- **Amount Of 1**: What a single $1 deposit grows to in the future. The deposit is made at the beginning of the first period. $S = (1+i)^n$
- **Amount Of 1 Per Period**: What a series of $1 deposits grow to in the future. A deposit is made at the end of each period. $S\overline{n}| = \frac{(1+i)^n - 1}{i}$
- **Sinking Fund Payment**: The amount to be deposited at the end of each period that grows to $1 in the future. $\frac{1}{S\overline{n}|} = \frac{i}{(1+i)^n - 1}$
- **Present Worth Of 1**: What $1 to be paid in the future is worth today. Value today of a single $1 payment tomorrow. $V^n = \frac{1}{(1+i)^n}$
- **Present Worth of 1 Per Period**: What $1 to be paid at the end of each period is worth today. Value today of a series of $1 payments tomorrow. $A\overline{n}| = \frac{1 - V^n}{i}$
- **Periodic Payment To Amortize 1**: The mortgage payment to amortize a loan of $1. An annuity certain, payable at the end of each period, worth $1 today. $\frac{1}{A\overline{n}|} = \frac{i}{1 - V^n}$
- **Constant Annual Percent**: The annual payment, including interest and principal, to amortize completely a loan of $100.
- **Total Interest**: The total interest paid over the term on a loan of $1. The loan is amortized by regular periodic payments.
- **Annual Add On Rate**: The average annual interest rate on a loan that is completely amortized by regular periodic payments.

YEAR / PERIODS

Year	Amount Of 1	Amount Of 1 Per Period	Sinking Fund Payment	Present Worth Of 1	Present Worth of 1 Per Period	Periodic Payment To Amortize 1	Constant Annual Percent	Total Interest	Annual Add On Rate	Periods
	1.008 625	1.000 000	1.000 000 0000	.991 449	.991 449	1.008 625 0000	1210.35	.008 625	10.35	1
	1.017 324	2.008 625	.497 853 0089	.982 971	1.974 419	.506 478 0089	607.78	.012 956	7.77	2
	1.026 099	3.025 949	.330 474 7935	.974 565	2.948 984	.339 099 7935	406.92	.017 299	6.92	3
	1.034 949	4.052 048	.246 788 7719	.966 231	3.915 216	.255 413 7719	306.50	.021 655	6.50	4
	1.043 875	5.086 997	.196 579 6277	.957 969	4.873 184	.205 204 6277	246.25	.026 023	6.25	5
	1.052 879	6.130 872	.163 108 9221	.949 777	5.822 961	.171 733 9221	206.09	.030 404	6.08	6
	1.061 960	7.183 751	.139 203 0383	.941 655	6.764 617	.147 828 0383	177.40	.034 796	5.97	7
	1.071 119	8.245 711	.121 275 1681	.933 603	7.698 219	.129 900 1681	155.89	.039 201	5.88	8
	1.080 358	9.316 830	.107 332 6401	.925 619	8.623 839	.115 957 6401	139.15	.043 619	5.82	9
	1.089 676	10.397 188	.096 179 8515	.917 704	9.541 543	.104 804 8515	125.77	.048 049	5.77	10
	1.099 074	11.486 864	.087 055 9641	.909 857	10.451 400	.095 680 9641	114.82	.052 491	5.73	11
	1.108 554	12.585 938	.079 453 7525	.902 076	11.353 476	.088 078 7525	105.70	.056 945	5.69	12
1	1.108 554	12.585 938	.079 453 7525	.902 076	11.353 476	.088 078 7525	105.70	.056 945	5.69	12
2	1.228 891	26.538 126	.037 681 6355	.813 742	21.595 177	.046 306 6355	55.57	.111 359	5.57	24
3	1.362 292	42.004 876	.023 806 7597	.734 057	30.833 973	.032 431 7597	38.92	.167 543	5.58	36
4	1.510 174	59.150 600	.016 905 9993	.662 175	39.168 071	.025 530 9993	30.64	.225 488	5.64	48
5	1.674 109	78.157 555	.012 794 6684	.597 333	46.686 064	.021 419 6684	25.71	.285 180	5.70	60
6	1.855 840	99.227 786	.010 077 8224	.538 840	53.467 866	.018 702 8224	22.45	.346 603	5.78	72
7	2.057 298	122.585 269	.008 157 5870	.486 074	59.585 569	.016 782 5870	20.14	.409 737	5.85	84
8	2.280 625	148.478 293	.006 734 9912	.438 476	65.104 204	.015 359 9912	18.44	.474 559	5.93	96
9	2.528 196	177.182 101	.005 643 9109	.395 539	70.082 433	.014 268 9109	17.13	.541 042	6.01	108
10	2.802 641	209.001 815	.004 784 6475	.356 806	74.573 176	.013 409 6475	16.10	.609 158	6.09	120
11	3.106 878	244.275 676	.004 093 7355	.321 867	78.624 168	.012 718 7355	15.27	.678 873	6.17	132
12	3.444 141	283.378 646	.003 528 8474	.290 348	82.278 473	.012 153 8474	14.59	.750 154	6.25	144
13	3.818 015	326.726 389	.003 060 6649	.261 916	85.574 934	.011 685 6649	14.03	.822 964	6.33	156
14	4.232 475	374.779 690	.002 668 2342	.236 268	88.548 593	.011 293 2342	13.56	.897 263	6.41	168
15	4.691 926	428.049 356	.002 336 1792	.213 132	91.231 060	.010 961 1792	13.16	.973 012	6.49	180
16	5.201 252	487.101 641	.002 052 9596	.192 261	93.650 851	.010 677 9596	12.82	1.050 168	6.56	192
17	5.765 867	552.564 272	.001 809 7442	.173 434	95.833 686	.010 434 7442	12.53	1.128 688	6.64	204
18	6.391 773	625.133 114	.001 599 6593	.156 451	97.802 770	.010 224 6593	12.27	1.208 526	6.71	216
19	7.085 624	705.579 574	.001 417 2746	.141 131	99.579 034	.010 042 2746	12.06	1.289 639	6.79	228
20	7.854 795	794.758 796	.001 258 2434	.127 311	101.181 359	.009 883 2434	11.86	1.371 978	6.86	240
21	8.707 462	893.618 754	.001 119 0454	.114 844	102.626 779	.009 744 0454	11.70	1.455 499	6.93	252
22	9.652 689	1003.210 328	.000 996 7999	.103 598	103.930 658	.009 621 7999	11.55	1.540 155	7.00	264
23	10.700 524	1124.698 474	.000 889 1272	.093 453	105.106 856	.009 514 1272	11.42	1.625 899	7.07	276
24	11.862 106	1259.374 609	.000 794 0449	.084 302	106.167 877	.009 419 0449	11.31	1.712 685	7.14	288
25	13.149 782	1408.670 339	.000 709 8893	.076 047	107.124 998	.009 334 8893	11.21	1.800 467	7.20	300
26	14.577 239	1574.172 676	.000 635 2543	.068 600	107.988 395	.009 260 2543	11.12	1.889 199	7.27	312
27	16.159 653	1757.640 906	.000 568 9444	.061 883	108.767 244	.009 193 9444	11.04	1.978 838	7.33	324
28	17.913 843	1961.025 294	.000 509 9373	.055 823	109.469 826	.009 134 9373	10.97	2.069 339	7.39	336
29	19.858 457	2186.487 812	.000 457 3545	.050 356	110.103 608	.009 082 3545	10.90	2.160 659	7.45	348
30	22.014 167	2436.425 125	.000 410 4374	.045 425	110.675 328	.009 035 4374	10.85	2.252 757	7.51	360
31	24.403 886	2713.494 061	.000 368 5285	.040 977	111.191 063	.008 993 5285	10.80	2.345 593	7.57	372
32	27.053 019	3020.639 860	.000 331 0557	.036 964	111.656 295	.008 956 0557	10.75	2.439 125	7.62	384
33	29.989 724	3361.127 477	.000 297 5192	.033 345	112.075 970	.008 922 5192	10.71	2.533 318	7.68	396
34	33.245 220	3738.576 289	.000 267 4815	.030 080	112.454 549	.008 892 4815	10.68	2.628 132	7.73	408
35	36.854 113	4156.998 571	.000 240 5582	.027 134	112.796 056	.008 865 5582	10.64	2.723 534	7.78	420
36	40.854 764	4620.842 147	.000 216 4108	.024 477	113.104 122	.008 841 4108	10.61	2.819 489	7.83	432
37	45.289 700	5135.037 667	.000 194 7405	.022 080	113.382 020	.008 819 7405	10.59	2.915 965	7.88	444
38	50.206 065	5705.051 020	.000 175 2833	.019 918	113.632 706	.008 800 2833	10.57	3.012 929	7.93	456
39	55.656 120	6336.941 440	.000 157 8048	.017 967	113.858 843	.008 782 8048	10.54	3.110 353	7.98	468
40	61.697 798	7037.425 913	.000 142 0974	.016 208	114.062 837	.008 767 0974	10.53	3.208 207	8.02	480
41	68.395 324	7813.950 577	.000 127 9762	.014 621	114.246 854	.008 752 9762	10.51	3.306 464	8.06	492
42	75.819 890	8674.769 879	.000 115 2768	.013 189	114.412 852	.008 740 2768	10.49	3.405 100	8.11	504
43	84.050 421	9629.034 314	.000 103 8526	.011 898	114.562 595	.008 728 8526	10.48	3.504 088	8.15	516
44	93.174 406	10686.887 698	.000 093 5726	.010 733	114.697 674	.008 718 5726	10.47	3.603 406	8.19	528
45	103.288 834	11859.574 997	.000 084 3201	.009 682	114.819 526	.008 709 3201	10.46	3.703 033	8.23	540
46	114.501 221	13159.561 859	.000 075 9904	.008 734	114.929 446	.008 700 9904	10.45	3.802 947	8.27	552
47	126.930 754	14600.667 124	.000 068 4900	.007 878	115.028 602	.008 693 4900	10.44	3.903 128	8.30	564
48	140.709 559	16198.209 719	.000 061 7352	.007 107	115.118 048	.008 686 7352	10.43	4.003 559	8.34	576
49	155.984 104	17969.171 497	.000 055 6509	.006 411	115.198 735	.008 680 6509	10.42	4.104 223	8.38	588
50	172.916 758	19932.377 756	.000 050 1696	.005 783	115.271 521	.008 675 1696	10.42	4.205 102	8.41	600

Effective Rate is 10.86 %

Annual Percentage Rate is 10.35 %

MONTHLY COMPOUND INTEREST AND ANNUITY

	Amount Of 1	Amount Of 1 Per Period	Sinking Fund Payment	Present Worth Of 1	Present Worth of 1 Per Period	Periodic Payment To Amortize 1	Constant Annual Percent	Total Interest	Annual Add On Rate	

What a single $ 1 deposit grows to in the future. The deposit is made at the beginning of the first period.

What a series of $ 1 deposits grow to in the future. A deposit is made at the end of each period.

The amount to be deposited at the end of each period that grows to $ 1 in the future.

What $ 1 to be paid in the future is worth today. Value today of a single $ 1 payment tomorrow.

What $ 1 to be paid at the end of each period is worth today. Value today of a series of $ 1 payments tomorrow.

The mortgage payment to amortize a loan of $ 1. An annuity certain, payable at the end of each period, worth $ 1 today.

The annual payment, including interest and principal, to amortize completely a loan of $ 100.

The total interest paid over the term on a loan of $1. The loan is amortized by regular periodic payments.

The average annual interest rate on a loan that is completely amortized by regular periodic payments.

$S = (1+i)^n$

$S\overline{n|} = \dfrac{(1+i)^n - 1}{i}$

$\dfrac{1}{S\overline{n|}} = \dfrac{i}{(1+i)^n - 1}$

$V^n = \dfrac{1}{(1+i)^n}$

$A\overline{n|} = \dfrac{1 - V^n}{i}$

$\dfrac{1}{A\overline{n|}} = \dfrac{i}{1 - V^n}$

PERIODS

YEAR	Amount Of 1	Amount Of 1 Per Period	Sinking Fund Payment	Present Worth Of 1	Present Worth of 1 Per Period	Periodic Payment To Amortize 1	Constant Annual Percent	Total Interest	Annual Add On Rate	Periods
	1.008 646	1.000 000	1.000 000 0000	.991 428	.991 428	1.008 645 8333	1210.38	.008 646	10.38	1
	1.017 366	2.008 646	.497 847 8453	.982 930	1.974 358	.506 493 6786	607.80	.012 987	7.79	2
	1.026 162	3.026 012	.330 467 9285	.974 505	2.948 863	.339 113 7618	406.94	.017 341	6.94	3
	1.035 034	4.052 175	.246 781 0711	.966 151	3.915 014	.255 426 9045	306.52	.021 708	6.51	4
	1.043 983	5.087 209	.196 571 4374	.957 870	4.872 884	.205 217 2707	246.27	.026 086	6.26	5
	1.053 009	6.131 192	.163 100 4153	.949 659	5.822 543	.171 746 2486	206.10	.030 477	6.10	6
	1.062 113	7.184 202	.139 194 3140	.941 519	6.764 063	.147 840 1474	177.41	.034 881	5.98	7
	1.071 296	8.246 315	.121 266 2881	.933 449	7.697 511	.129 912 1215	155.90	.039 297	5.89	8
	1.080 559	9.317 611	.107 323 6456	.925 447	8.622 958	.115 969 4790	139.17	.043 725	5.83	9
	1.089 901	10.398 170	.096 170 7714	.917 515	9.540 473	.104 816 6047	125.78	.048 166	5.78	10
	1.099 324	11.488 071	.087 046 8193	.909 650	10.450 123	.095 692 6527	114.84	.052 619	5.74	11
	1.108 829	12.587 394	.079 444 5588	.901 853	11.351 976	.088 090 3921	105.71	.057 085	5.71	12
1	1.108 829	12.587 394	.079 444 5588	.901 853	11.351 976	.088 090 3921	105.71	.057 085	5.71	12
2	1.229 501	26.544 656	.037 672 3656	.813 338	21.589 786	.046 318 1989	55.59	.111 637	5.58	24
3	1.363 305	42.020 866	.023 797 7007	.733 511	30.822 783	.032 443 5340	38.94	.167 967	5.60	36
4	1.511 672	59.181 329	.016 897 2210	.661 519	39.149 586	.025 543 0543	30.66	.226 067	5.65	48
5	1.676 185	78.209 340	.012 786 1966	.596 593	46.659 136	.021 432 0300	25.72	.285 922	5.72	60
6	1.858 602	99.308 141	.010 069 6679	.538 039	53.431 644	.018 715 5013	22.46	.347 516	5.79	72
7	2.060 870	122.703 093	.008 149 7538	.485 232	59.539 449	.016 795 5872	20.16	.410 829	5.87	84
8	2.285 152	148.644 083	.006 727 4794	.437 608	65.047 789	.015 373 3127	18.45	.475 838	5.95	96
9	2.533 842	177.408 192	.005 636 7183	.394 658	70.015 500	.014 282 5516	17.14	.542 516	6.03	108
10	2.809 596	209.302 656	.004 777 7702	.355 923	74.495 645	.013 423 6036	16.11	.610 832	6.11	120
11	3.115 360	244.668 148	.004 087 1687	.320 990	78.536 075	.012 733 0021	15.28	.680 756	6.19	132
12	3.454 400	283.882 413	.003 522 5852	.289 486	82.179 948	.012 168 4186	14.61	.752 252	6.27	144
13	3.830 337	327.364 309	.003 054 7007	.261 074	85.466 184	.011 700 5341	14.05	.825 283	6.35	156
14	4.247 187	375.578 275	.002 662 5608	.235 450	88.429 886	.011 308 3942	13.58	.899 810	6.43	168
15	4.709 402	429.039 296	.002 330 7888	.212 341	91.102 708	.010 976 6222	13.18	.975 792	6.51	180
16	5.221 919	488.318 400	.002 047 8442	.191 500	93.513 199	.010 693 6775	12.84	1.053 186	6.58	192
17	5.790 213	554.048 760	.001 804 8953	.172 705	95.687 108	.010 450 7286	12.55	1.131 949	6.66	204
18	6.420 354	626.932 458	.001 595 0682	.155 755	97.647 653	.010 240 9015	12.29	1.212 035	6.73	216
19	7.119 071	707.747 981	.001 412 9323	.140 468	99.415 777	.010 058 7657	12.08	1.293 399	6.81	228
20	7.893 829	797.358 537	.001 254 1410	.126 681	101.010 363	.009 899 9743	11.88	1.375 994	6.88	240
21	8.752 903	896.721 277	.001 115 1737	.114 248	102.448 446	.009 761 0071	11.72	1.459 774	6.95	252
22	9.705 468	1006.897 516	.000 993 1497	.103 035	103.745 384	.009 638 9831	11.57	1.544 692	7.02	264
23	10.761 700	1129.064 072	.000 885 6893	.092 922	104.915 031	.009 531 5227	11.44	1.630 700	7.09	276
24	11.932 880	1264.525 832	.000 790 8103	.083 802	105.969 881	.009 436 6436	11.33	1.717 753	7.16	288
25	13.231 517	1414.729 695	.000 706 8488	.075 577	106.921 200	.009 352 6821	11.23	1.805 805	7.22	300
26	14.671 484	1581.280 021	.000 632 3991	.068 159	107.779 150	.009 278 2324	11.14	1.894 809	7.29	312
27	16.268 159	1765.955 771	.000 566 2656	.061 470	108.552 894	.009 212 0989	11.06	1.984 720	7.35	324
28	18.038 599	1970.729 509	.000 507 4263	.055 437	109.250 697	.009 153 2596	10.99	2.075 495	7.41	336
29	20.001 713	2197.788 469	.000 455 0028	.049 996	109.880 013	.009 100 8362	10.93	2.167 091	7.47	348
30	22.178 470	2449.557 918	.000 408 2369	.045 089	110.447 563	.009 054 0703	10.87	2.259 465	7.53	360
31	24.592 119	2728.727 063	.000 366 4712	.040 663	110.959 410	.009 012 3046	10.82	2.352 577	7.59	372
32	27.268 443	3038.277 771	.000 329 1338	.036 672	111.421 020	.008 974 9672	10.77	2.446 387	7.64	384
33	30.236 027	3381.516 422	.000 295 7253	.033 073	111.837 325	.008 941 5586	10.73	2.540 857	7.70	396
34	33.526 569	3762.109 226	.000 265 8083	.029 827	112.212 770	.008 911 6417	10.70	2.635 950	7.75	408
35	37.175 216	4184.121 380	.000 238 9988	.026 900	112.551 367	.008 884 8321	10.67	2.731 629	7.80	420
36	41.220 940	4652.060 490	.000 214 9585	.024 260	112.856 731	.008 860 7918	10.64	2.827 862	7.86	432
37	45.706 953	5170.924 718	.000 193 3890	.021 879	113.132 124	.008 839 2223	10.61	2.924 615	7.90	444
38	50.681 173	5746.256 169	.000 174 0264	.019 731	113.380 489	.008 819 8597	10.59	3.021 856	7.95	456
39	56.196 730	6384.200 088	.000 156 6367	.017 795	113.604 477	.008 802 4700	10.57	3.119 556	8.00	468
40	62.312 537	7091.570 495	.000 141 0125	.016 048	113.806 481	.008 786 8458	10.55	3.217 686	8.04	480
41	69.093 917	7875.922 974	.000 126 9692	.014 473	113.988 659	.008 772 8026	10.53	3.316 219	8.09	492
42	76.613 306	8745.635 368	.000 114 3428	.013 053	114.152 957	.008 760 1761	10.52	3.415 129	8.13	504
43	84.951 018	9709.997 270	.000 102 9866	.011 771	114.301 129	.008 748 8200	10.50	3.514 391	8.17	516
44	94.196 111	10779.309 245	.000 092 7703	.010 616	114.434 759	.008 738 6037	10.49	3.613 983	8.21	528
45	104.447 334	11964.992 855	.000 083 5771	.009 574	114.555 273	.008 729 4105	10.48	3.713 882	8.25	540
46	115.814 182	13279.712 650	.000 075 3028	.008 635	114.663 959	.008 721 1362	10.47	3.814 067	8.29	552
47	128.418 068	14737.511 448	.000 067 8541	.007 787	114.761 978	.008 713 6874	10.46	3.914 520	8.33	564
48	142.393 615	16353.960 324	.000 061 1473	.007 023	114.850 376	.008 706 9806	10.45	4.015 221	8.37	576
49	157.890 101	18146.324 931	.000 055 1076	.006 334	114.930 099	.008 700 9409	10.45	4.116 153	8.40	588
50	175.073 046	20133.749 915	.000 049 6678	.005 712	115.001 997	.008 695 5012	10.44	4.217 301	8.43	600

Effective Rate is 10.88 %

8 - 145

Annual Percentage Rate is 10.375%

MONTHLY COMPOUND INTEREST AND ANNUITY

10.40 % M

Amount Of 1	Amount Of 1 Per Period	Sinking Fund Payment	Present Worth Of 1	Present Worth of 1 Per Period	Periodic Payment To Amortize 1	Constant Annual Percent	Total Interest	Annual Add On Rate	
What a single $ 1 deposit grows to in the future. The deposit is made at the beginning of the first period.	What a series of $ 1 deposits grow to in the future. A deposit is made at the end of each period.	The amount to be deposited at the end of each period that grows to $ 1 in the future.	What $ 1 to be paid in the future is worth today. Value today of a single $ 1 payment tomorrow.	What $ 1 to be paid at the end of each period is worth today. Value today of a series of $ 1 payments tomorrow.	The mortgage payment to amortize a loan of $ 1. An annuity certain, payable at the end of each period, worth $ 1 today.	The annual payment, including interest and principal, to amortize completely a loan of $ 100.	The total interest paid over the term on a loan of $ 1. The loan is amortized by regular periodic payments.	The average annual interest rate on a loan that is completely amortized by regular periodic payments.	
$S = (1+i)^n$	$S\overline{n} = \dfrac{(1+i)^n - 1}{i}$	$\dfrac{1}{S\overline{n}} = \dfrac{i}{(1+i)^n - 1}$	$V^n = \dfrac{1}{(1+i)^n}$	$A\overline{n} = \dfrac{1-V^n}{i}$	$\dfrac{1}{A\overline{n}} = \dfrac{i}{1-V^n}$				

YEAR ... **PERIODS**

YEAR	Amount Of 1	Amount Of 1 Per Period	Sinking Fund Payment	Present Worth Of 1	Present Worth of 1 Per Period	Periodic Payment To Amortize 1	Constant Annual Percent	Total Interest	Annual Add On Rate	PERIODS
	1.008 667	1.000 000	1.000 000 0000	.991 408	.991 408	1.008 666 6667	1210.40	.008 667	10.40	1
	1.017 408	2.008 667	.497 842 6817	.982 889	1.974 297	.506 509 3484	607.82	.013 019	7.81	2
	1.026 226	3.026 075	.330 461 0637	.974 444	2.948 741	.339 127 7303	406.96	.017 383	6.95	3
	1.035 120	4.052 301	.246 773 3706	.966 072	3.914 813	.255 440 0373	306.53	.021 760	6.53	4
	1.044 091	5.087 421	.196 563 2474	.957 771	4.872 584	.205 229 9140	246.28	.026 150	6.28	5
	1.053 140	6.131 512	.163 091 9089	.949 542	5.822 126	.171 758 5756	206.12	.030 551	6.11	6
	1.062 267	7.184 652	.139 185 5902	.941 383	6.763 509	.147 852 2569	177.43	.034 966	5.99	7
	1.071 473	8.246 919	.121 257 4087	.933 294	7.696 803	.129 924 0753	155.91	.039 393	5.91	8
	1.080 759	9.318 392	.107 314 6518	.925 275	8.622 078	.115 981 3184	139.18	.043 832	5.84	9
	1.090 126	10.399 151	.096 161 6920	.917 325	9.539 403	.104 828 3586	125.80	.048 284	5.79	10
	1.099 574	11.489 277	.087 037 6753	.909 443	10.448 847	.095 704 3420	114.85	.052 748	5.75	11
	1.109 103	12.588 851	.079 435 3659	.901 629	11.350 476	.088 102 0326	105.73	.057 224	5.72	12
1	1.109 103	12.588 851	.079 435 3659	.901 629	11.350 476	.088 102 0326	105.73	.057 224	5.72	12
2	1.230 110	26.551 189	.037 663 0974	.812 935	21.584 397	.046 329 7641	55.60	.111 914	5.60	24
3	1.364 319	42.036 864	.023 788 6441	.732 966	30.811 598	.032 455 3108	38.95	.168 391	5.61	36
4	1.513 171	59.212 079	.016 888 4460	.660 864	39.131 113	.025 555 1127	30.67	.226 645	5.67	48
5	1.678 263	78.261 168	.012 777 7290	.595 854	46.632 230	.021 444 3957	25.74	.286 664	5.73	60
6	1.861 368	99.388 577	.010 061 5184	.537 239	53.395 457	.018 728 1851	22.48	.348 429	5.81	72
7	2.064 449	122.821 057	.008 141 9263	.484 391	59.493 379	.016 808 5930	20.18	.411 922	5.88	84
8	2.289 688	148.810 101	.006 719 9739	.436 741	64.991 445	.015 386 6406	18.47	.477 117	5.96	96
9	2.539 500	177.634 637	.005 629 5327	.393 778	69.948 661	.014 296 1994	17.16	.543 990	6.04	108
10	2.816 568	209.604 026	.004 770 9007	.355 042	74.418 231	.013 437 5674	16.13	.612 508	6.13	120
11	3.123 865	245.061 385	.004 080 6103	.320 116	78.448 127	.012 747 2769	15.30	.682 641	6.21	132
12	3.464 690	284.387 261	.003 516 3319	.288 626	82.081 599	.012 182 9986	14.62	.754 352	6.29	144
13	3.842 699	328.003 722	.003 048 7459	.260 234	85.357 643	.011 715 4126	14.06	.827 604	6.37	156
14	4.261 950	376.378 887	.002 656 8972	.234 634	88.311 420	.011 323 5638	13.59	.902 359	6.45	168
15	4.726 944	430.031 946	.002 325 4086	.211 553	90.974 632	.010 992 0753	13.20	.978 574	6.52	180
16	5.242 669	489.538 735	.002 042 7393	.190 743	93.375 861	.010 709 4059	12.86	1.056 206	6.60	192
17	5.814 662	555.537 915	.001 800 0572	.171 979	95.540 880	.010 466 7238	12.57	1.135 212	6.68	204
18	6.449 061	628.737 829	.001 590 4880	.155 061	97.492 924	.010 257 1547	12.31	1.215 545	6.75	216
19	7.152 676	709.924 100	.001 408 6013	.139 808	99.252 943	.010 075 2680	12.10	1.297 161	6.83	228
20	7.933 057	799.968 068	.001 250 0499	.126 055	100.839 829	.009 916 7166	11.91	1.380 012	6.90	240
21	8.798 580	899.836 137	.001 111 3134	.113 655	102.270 611	.009 777 9801	11.74	1.464 051	6.97	252
22	9.758 535	1010.600 149	.000 989 5110	.102 474	103.560 646	.009 656 1777	11.59	1.549 231	7.04	264
23	10.823 224	1133.448 889	.000 882 2630	.092 394	104.723 779	.009 548 9297	11.46	1.635 505	7.11	276
24	12.004 074	1269.700 842	.000 787 5871	.083 305	105.772 494	.009 454 2538	11.35	1.722 825	7.18	288
25	13.313 759	1420.818 343	.000 703 8197	.075 110	106.718 046	.009 370 4864	11.25	1.811 146	7.24	300
26	14.766 335	1588.423 273	.000 629 5551	.067 722	107.570 583	.009 296 2218	11.16	1.900 421	7.31	312
27	16.377 392	1774.314 467	.000 563 5980	.061 060	108.339 256	.009 230 2646	11.08	1.990 606	7.37	324
28	18.164 221	1980.487 018	.000 504 9263	.055 053	109.032 313	.009 171 5930	11.01	2.081 655	7.43	336
29	20.145 999	2209.153 691	.000 452 6620	.049 638	109.657 194	.009 119 3287	10.95	2.173 526	7.49	348
30	22.343 995	2462.768 670	.000 406 0471	.044 755	110.220 605	.009 072 7137	10.89	2.266 177	7.55	360
31	24.781 800	2744.053 900	.000 364 4243	.040 352	110.728 593	.009 031 0910	10.84	2.359 566	7.61	372
32	27.485 579	3056.028 298	.000 327 2221	.036 383	111.186 610	.008 993 8888	10.80	2.453 653	7.67	384
33	30.484 348	3402.040 157	.000 293 9413	.032 804	111.599 571	.008 960 6079	10.76	2.548 401	7.72	396
34	33.810 293	3785.803 078	.000 264 1447	.029 577	111.971 909	.008 930 8114	10.72	2.643 771	7.78	408
35	37.499 111	4211.435 829	.000 237 4487	.026 667	112.307 619	.008 904 1154	10.69	2.739 728	7.83	420
36	41.590 390	4683.506 551	.000 213 5152	.024 044	112.610 306	.008 880 1819	10.66	2.836 239	7.88	432
37	46.128 042	5207.081 783	.000 192 0461	.021 679	112.883 217	.008 858 7128	10.64	2.933 268	7.93	444
38	51.160 767	5787.780 840	.000 172 7778	.019 546	113.129 281	.008 839 4445	10.61	3.030 787	7.98	456
39	56.742 580	6431.836 126	.000 155 4766	.017 623	113.351 140	.008 822 1433	10.59	3.128 763	8.02	468
40	62.933 387	7146.160 019	.000 139 9353	.015 890	113.551 175	.008 806 6020	10.57	3.227 169	8.07	480
41	69.799 632	7938.419 060	.000 125 9697	.014 327	113.731 532	.008 792 6363	10.56	3.325 977	8.11	492
42	77.415 007	8817.116 238	.000 113 4158	.012 917	113.894 147	.008 780 0824	10.54	3.425 162	8.16	504
43	85.861 246	9791.682 246	.000 102 1275	.011 647	114.040 766	.008 768 7942	10.53	3.524 698	8.20	516
44	95.228 998	10872.576 696	.000 091 9745	.010 501	114.172 961	.008 758 6412	10.52	3.624 563	8.24	528
45	105.618 803	12071.400 380	.000 082 8404	.009 468	114.292 153	.008 749 5071	10.50	3.724 734	8.28	540
46	117.142 171	13401.019 777	.000 074 6212	.008 537	114.399 619	.008 741 2879	10.49	3.825 191	8.32	552
47	129.922 778	14875.705 141	.000 067 2237	.007 697	114.496 514	.008 733 8904	10.49	3.925 914	8.35	564
48	144.097 792	16511.283 657	.000 060 5646	.006 940	114.583 877	.008 727 2313	10.48	4.026 885	8.39	576
49	159.819 347	18325.309 313	.000 054 5693	.006 257	114.662 646	.008 721 2360	10.47	4.128 087	8.42	588
50	177.256 178	20337.251 293	.000 049 1709	.005 642	114.733 667	.008 715 8375	10.46	4.229 503	8.46	600

Effective Rate is 10.91 %

Annual Percentage Rate is 10.40 %

	Amount Of 1	Amount Of 1 Per Period	Sinking Fund Payment	Present Worth Of 1	Present Worth of 1 Per Period	Periodic Payment To Amortize 1	Constant Annual Percent	Total Interest	Annual Add On Rate	
	What a single $ 1 deposit grows to in the future. The deposit is made at the beginning of the first period.	What a series of $ 1 deposits grow to in the future. A deposit is made at the end of each period.	The amount to be deposited at the end of each period that grows to $ 1 in the future.	What $ 1 to be paid in the future is worth today. Value today of a single $ 1 payment tomorrow.	What $ 1 to be paid at the end of each period is worth today. Value today of a series of $ 1 payments tomorrow.	The mortgage payment to amortize a loan of $ 1. An annuity certain, payable at the end of each period, worth $ 1 today.	The annual payment, including interest and principal, to amortize completely a loan of $ 100.	The total interest paid over the term on a loan of $1. The loan is amortized by regular periodic payments.	The average annual interest rate on a loan that is completely amortized by regular periodic payments.	

$$S = (1+i)^n \qquad S\overline{n}| = \frac{(1+i)^n - 1}{i} \qquad \frac{1}{S\overline{n}|} = \frac{i}{(1+i)^n - 1} \qquad V^n = \frac{1}{(1+i)^n} \qquad A\overline{n}| = \frac{1-V^n}{i} \qquad \frac{1}{A\overline{n}|} = \frac{i}{1-V^n}$$

PERIODS

YEAR										PERIODS
	1.008 708	1.000 000	1.000 000 0000	.991 367	.991 367	1.008 708 3333	1210.45	.008 708	10.45	1
	1.017 493	2.008 708	.497 832 3550	.982 808	1.974 175	.506 540 6883	607.85	.013 081	7.85	2
	1.026 353	3.026 201	.330 447 3346	.974 323	2.948 499	.339 155 6680	406.99	.017 467	6.99	3
	1.035 291	4.052 554	.246 757 9704	.965 912	3.914 411	.255 466 3037	306.56	.021 865	6.56	4
	1.044 307	5.087 845	.196 546 8684	.957 573	4.871 984	.205 255 2017	246.31	.026 276	6.31	5
	1.053 401	6.132 152	.163 074 8974	.949 306	5.821 290	.171 783 2308	206.14	.030 699	6.14	6
	1.062 574	7.185 552	.139 168 1440	.941 111	6.762 401	.147 876 4774	177.46	.035 135	6.02	7
	1.071 827	8.248 127	.121 239 6515	.932 986	7.695 387	.129 947 9848	155.94	.039 584	5.94	8
	1.081 161	9.319 954	.107 296 6659	.924 931	8.620 318	.116 004 9993	139.21	.044 045	5.87	9
	1.090 576	10.401 115	.096 143 5352	.916 946	9.537 264	.104 851 8685	125.83	.048 519	5.82	10
	1.100 073	11.491 692	.087 019 3896	.909 030	10.446 295	.095 727 7229	114.88	.053 005	5.78	11
	1.109 653	12.591 765	.079 416 9827	.901 182	11.347 477	.088 125 3160	105.76	.057 504	5.75	12
1	1.109 653	12.591 765	.079 416 9827	.901 182	11.347 477	.088 125 3160	105.76	.057 504	5.75	12
2	1.231 330	26.564 259	.037 644 5661	.812 130	21.573 623	.046 352 8994	55.63	.112 470	5.62	24
3	1.366 350	42.068 882	.023 770 5387	.731 877	30.789 247	.032 478 8721	38.98	.169 239	5.64	36
4	1.516 175	59.273 639	.016 870 9061	.659 555	39.094 204	.025 579 2395	30.70	.227 803	5.70	48
5	1.682 428	78.364 954	.012 760 8064	.594 379	46.578 485	.021 469 1397	25.77	.288 148	5.76	60
6	1.866 912	99.549 694	.010 045 2343	.535 644	53.323 187	.018 753 5677	22.51	.350 257	5.84	72
7	2.071 625	123.057 410	.008 126 2884	.482 713	59.401 394	.016 834 6217	20.21	.414 108	5.92	84
8	2.298 785	149.142 825	.006 704 9823	.435 012	64.878 967	.015 413 3156	18.50	.479 678	6.00	96
9	2.550 855	178.088 592	.005 615 1828	.392 025	69.815 260	.014 323 5161	17.19	.546 940	6.08	108
10	2.830 564	210.208 357	.004 757 1848	.353 286	74.263 759	.013 465 5181	16.16	.615 862	6.16	120
11	3.140 945	245.850 160	.004 067 5182	.318 376	78.272 669	.012 775 8515	15.34	.686 412	6.24	132
12	3.485 360	285.400 203	.003 503 8517	.286 914	81.885 428	.012 212 1851	14.66	.758 555	6.32	144
13	3.867 541	329.287 039	.003 036 8641	.258 562	85.141 182	.011 745 1975	14.10	.832 251	6.40	156
14	4.291 630	377.586 211	.002 645 5992	.233 012	88.075 211	.011 353 9325	13.63	.907 461	6.48	168
15	4.762 221	432.025 408	.002 314 6787	.209 986	90.719 306	.011 023 0120	13.23	.984 142	6.56	180
16	5.284 414	491.990 180	.002 032 5609	.189 236	93.102 118	.010 740 8942	12.89	1.062 252	6.64	192
17	5.863 868	558.530 286	.001 790 4132	.170 536	95.249 466	.010 498 7465	12.60	1.141 744	6.72	204
18	6.506 860	632.366 734	.001 581 3609	.153 684	97.184 618	.010 289 6942	12.35	1.222 574	6.79	216
19	7.220 359	714.299 592	.001 399 9728	.138 497	98.928 543	.010 108 3061	12.13	1.304 694	6.87	228
20	8.012 095	805.216 656	.001 241 9018	.124 811	100.500 138	.009 950 2351	11.95	1.388 056	6.94	240
21	8.890 648	906.103 076	.001 103 6272	.112 478	101.916 431	.009 811 9605	11.78	1.472 614	7.01	252
22	9.865 536	1018.052 023	.000 982 2681	.101 363	103.192 770	.009 690 6014	11.63	1.558 319	7.08	264
23	10.947 325	1142.276 541	.000 875 4447	.091 347	104.342 984	.009 583 7781	11.51	1.645 123	7.15	276
24	12.147 735	1280.122 685	.000 781 1751	.082 320	105.379 536	.009 489 5085	11.39	1.732 978	7.22	288
25	13.479 774	1433.084 113	.000 697 7957	.074 185	106.313 659	.009 406 1291	11.29	1.821 839	7.29	300
26	14.957 876	1602.818 264	.000 623 9011	.066 854	107.155 474	.009 332 2344	11.20	1.911 657	7.35	312
27	16.598 056	1791.164 323	.000 558 2961	.060 248	107.914 103	.009 266 6294	11.12	2.002 388	7.42	324
28	18.418 087	2000.163 147	.000 499 9592	.054 294	108.597 766	.009 208 2925	11.05	2.093 986	7.48	336
29	20.437 691	2232.079 380	.000 448 0127	.048 929	109.213 871	.009 156 3461	10.99	2.186 408	7.54	348
30	22.678 751	2489.425 990	.000 401 6990	.044 094	109.769 094	.009 110 0324	10.94	2.279 612	7.60	360
31	25.165 551	2774.991 502	.000 360 3615	.039 737	110.269 451	.009 068 6948	10.89	2.373 554	7.66	372
32	27.925 036	3091.870 211	.000 323 4288	.035 810	110.720 364	.009 031 7622	10.84	2.468 197	7.71	384
33	30.987 109	3443.495 713	.000 290 4026	.032 271	111.126 719	.008 998 7359	10.80	2.563 499	7.77	396
34	34.384 947	3833.678 108	.000 260 8461	.029 082	111.492 919	.008 969 1794	10.77	2.659 425	7.82	408
35	38.155 369	4266.645 286	.000 234 3762	.026 209	111.822 932	.008 942 7095	10.74	2.755 938	7.87	420
36	42.339 231	4747.088 739	.000 210 6554	.023 619	112.120 334	.008 918 9888	10.71	2.853 003	7.93	432
37	46.981 867	5280.214 396	.000 189 3862	.021 285	112.388 347	.008 897 7196	10.68	2.950 587	7.97	444
38	52.133 583	5871.799 035	.000 170 3056	.019 181	112.629 876	.008 878 6389	10.66	3.048 659	8.02	456
39	57.850 202	6528.252 875	.000 153 1803	.017 286	112.847 538	.008 861 5137	10.64	3.147 188	8.07	468
40	64.193 667	7256.689 038	.000 137 8039	.015 578	113.043 691	.008 846 1372	10.62	3.246 146	8.12	480
41	71.232 714	8065.000 621	.000 123 9926	.014 038	113.220 460	.008 832 3259	10.60	3.345 504	8.16	492
42	79.043 615	8961.946 228	.000 111 5829	.012 651	113.379 762	.008 819 9162	10.59	3.445 238	8.20	504
43	87.711 007	9957.244 871	.000 100 4294	.011 401	113.523 321	.008 808 7627	10.58	3.545 322	8.24	516
44	97.328 808	11061.681 282	.000 090 4022	.010 274	113.652 695	.008 798 7355	10.56	3.645 732	8.29	528
45	108.001 232	12287.222 779	.000 081 3854	.009 259	113.769 284	.008 789 7187	10.55	3.746 448	8.33	540
46	119.843 922	13647.148 932	.000 073 2754	.008 344	113.874 352	.008 781 6087	10.54	3.847 448	8.36	552
47	132.985 202	15156.195 459	.000 065 9796	.007 520	113.969 037	.008 774 3130	10.53	3.948 713	8.40	564
48	147.567 467	16830.713 901	.000 059 4152	.006 777	114.054 366	.008 767 7485	10.53	4.050 223	8.44	576
49	163.748 725	18688.848 797	.000 053 5078	.006 107	114.131 263	.008 761 8412	10.52	4.151 963	8.47	588
50	181.704 311	20750.734 295	.000 048 1911	.005 503	114.200 561	.008 756 5244	10.51	4.253 915	8.51	600

Effective Rate is 10.97 %

Annual Percentage Rate is 10.45 %

	Amount Of 1	Amount Of 1 Per Period	Sinking Fund Payment	Present Worth Of 1	Present Worth of 1 Per Period	Periodic Payment To Amortize 1	Constant Annual Percent	Total Interest	Annual Add On Rate
	What a single $ 1 deposit grows to in the future. The deposit is made at the beginning of the first period.	What a series of $ 1 deposits grow to in the future. A deposit is made at the end of each period.	The amount to be deposited at the end of each period that grows to $ 1 in the future.	What $ 1 to be paid in the future is worth today. Value today of a single $ 1 payment tomorrow.	What $ 1 to be paid at the end of each period is worth today. Value today of a series of $ 1 payments tomorrow.	The mortgage payment to amortize a loan of $ 1. An annuity certain, payable at the end of each period, worth $ 1 today.	The annual payment, including interest and principal, to amortize completely a loan of $ 100.	The total interest paid over the term on a loan of $1. The loan is amortized by regular periodic payments.	The average annual interest rate on a loan that is completely amortized by regular periodic payments.
	$S = (1+i)^n$	$S\overline{n}| = \dfrac{(1+i)^n - 1}{i}$	$\dfrac{1}{S\overline{n}|} = \dfrac{i}{(1+i)^n - 1}$	$V^n = \dfrac{1}{(1+i)^n}$	$A\overline{n}| = \dfrac{1-V^n}{i}$	$\dfrac{1}{A\overline{n}|} = \dfrac{i}{1-V^n}$			

YEAR / **PERIODS**

YEAR	Amount Of 1	Amount Of 1 Per Period	Sinking Fund Payment	Present Worth Of 1	Present Worth of 1 Per Period	Periodic Payment To Amortize 1	Constant Annual Percent	Total Interest	Annual Add On Rate	PERIODS
	1.008 750	1.000 000	1.000 000 0000	.991 326	.991 326	1.008 750 0000	1210.50	.008 750	10.50	1
	1.017 577	2.008 750	.497 822 0286	.982 727	1.974 053	.506 572 0286	607.89	.013 144	7.89	2
	1.026 480	3.026 327	.330 433 6063	.974 203	2.948 256	.339 183 6063	407.03	.017 551	7.02	3
	1.035 462	4.052 807	.246 742 5712	.965 752	3.914 008	.255 492 5712	306.60	.021 970	6.59	4
	1.044 522	5.088 269	.196 530 4908	.957 375	4.871 384	.205 280 4908	246.34	.026 402	6.34	5
	1.053 662	6.132 791	.163 057 8876	.949 071	5.820 455	.171 807 8876	206.17	.030 847	6.17	6
	1.062 881	7.186 453	.139 150 6998	.940 839	6.761 293	.147 900 6998	177.49	.035 305	6.05	7
	1.072 182	8.249 335	.121 221 8965	.932 678	7.693 971	.129 971 8965	155.97	.039 775	5.97	8
	1.081 563	9.321 516	.107 278 6826	.924 588	8.618 559	.116 028 6826	139.24	.044 258	5.90	9
	1.091 027	10.403 080	.096 125 3813	.916 568	9.535 126	.104 875 3813	125.86	.048 754	5.85	10
	1.100 573	11.494 107	.087 001 1070	.908 617	10.443 743	.095 751 1070	114.91	.053 262	5.81	11
	1.110 203	12.594 680	.079 398 6029	.900 736	11.344 479	.088 148 6029	105.78	.057 783	5.78	12
1	1.110 203	12.594 680	.079 398 6029	.900 736	11.344 479	.088 148 6029	105.78	.057 783	5.78	12
2	1.232 552	26.577 337	.037 626 0416	.811 325	21.562 858	.046 376 0416	55.66	.113 025	5.65	24
3	1.368 383	42.100 932	.023 752 4435	.730 789	30.766 918	.032 502 4435	39.01	.170 088	5.67	36
4	1.519 184	59.335 280	.016 853 3798	.658 248	39.057 344	.025 603 3798	30.73	.228 962	5.72	48
5	1.686 603	78.468 912	.012 743 9004	.592 908	46.524 827	.021 493 9004	25.80	.289 634	5.79	60
6	1.872 472	99.711 137	.010 028 9700	.534 053	53.251 057	.018 778 9700	22.54	.352 086	5.87	72
7	2.078 825	123.294 329	.008 110 6731	.481 041	59.309 613	.016 860 6731	20.24	.416 297	5.95	84
8	2.307 919	149.476 469	.006 690 0162	.433 291	64.766 771	.015 440 0162	18.53	.482 242	6.03	96
9	2.562 260	178.543 972	.005 600 8612	.390 280	69.682 229	.014 350 8612	17.23	.549 893	6.11	108
10	2.844 630	210.814 814	.004 743 4997	.351 540	74.109 758	.013 493 4997	16.20	.619 220	6.19	120
11	3.158 118	246.642 013	.004 054 4593	.316 644	78.097 792	.012 804 4593	15.37	.690 189	6.27	132
12	3.506 153	286.417 494	.003 491 4068	.285 213	81.689 957	.012 241 4068	14.69	.762 763	6.36	144
13	3.892 543	330.576 371	.003 025 0196	.256 901	84.925 549	.011 775 0196	14.14	.836 903	6.44	156
14	4.321 515	379.601 707	.002 634 3401	.231 400	87.839 962	.011 384 3401	13.67	.912 569	6.52	168
15	4.797 761	434.029 805	.002 303 9892	.208 431	90.465 078	.011 053 9892	13.27	.989 718	6.60	180
16	5.326 491	494.456 068	.002 022 4244	.187 741	92.829 614	.010 772 4244	12.93	1.068 305	6.68	192
17	5.913 488	561.541 512	.001 780 8122	.169 105	94.959 437	.010 530 8122	12.64	1.148 286	6.75	204
18	6.565 175	636.020 005	.001 572 2776	.152 319	96.877 844	.010 322 2776	12.39	1.229 612	6.83	216
19	7.288 680	718.706 284	.001 391 3890	.137 199	98.605 822	.010 141 3890	12.17	1.312 237	6.91	228
20	8.091 918	810.504 876	.001 233 7989	.123 580	100.162 274	.009 983 7989	11.99	1.396 112	6.98	240
21	8.983 675	912.419 990	.001 095 9865	.111 313	101.564 226	.009 845 9865	11.82	1.481 189	7.05	252
22	9.973 707	1025.566 501	.000 975 0708	.100 264	102.827 014	.009 725 0708	11.68	1.567 419	7.12	264
23	11.072 844	1151.182 148	.000 868 6723	.090 311	103.964 453	.009 618 6723	11.55	1.654 754	7.19	276
24	12.293 109	1290.641 073	.000 774 8088	.081 346	104.988 985	.009 524 8088	11.43	1.743 145	7.26	288
25	13.647 852	1445.468 853	.000 691 8171	.073 272	105.911 817	.009 441 8171	11.34	1.832 545	7.33	300
26	15.151 893	1617.359 188	.000 618 2918	.065 998	106.743 045	.009 368 2918	11.25	1.922 907	7.40	312
27	16.821 684	1808.192 431	.000 553 0385	.059 447	107.491 762	.009 303 0385	11.17	2.014 184	7.46	324
28	18.675 491	2020.056 156	.000 495 0357	.053 546	108.166 158	.009 245 0357	11.10	2.106 332	7.52	336
29	20.733 595	2255.267 995	.000 443 4063	.048 231	108.773 611	.009 193 4063	11.04	2.199 305	7.58	348
30	23.018 509	2516.400 990	.000 397 3929	.043 443	109.320 766	.009 147 3929	10.98	2.293 061	7.64	360
31	25.555 228	2806.311 742	.000 356 3396	.039 131	109.813 607	.009 106 3396	10.93	2.387 558	7.70	372
32	28.371 502	3128.171 659	.000 319 6756	.035 247	110.257 527	.009 069 6756	10.89	2.482 755	7.76	384
33	31.498 139	3485.501 649	.000 286 9027	.031 748	110.657 382	.009 036 9027	10.85	2.578 613	7.81	396
34	34.969 343	3882.210 638	.000 257 5852	.028 596	111.017 546	.009 007 5852	10.81	2.675 095	7.87	408
35	38.823 085	4322.638 325	.000 231 3402	.025 758	111.341 958	.008 981 3402	10.78	2.772 163	7.92	420
36	43.101 523	4811.602 664	.000 207 8310	.023 201	111.634 167	.008 957 8310	10.75	2.869 783	7.97	432
37	47.851 460	5354.452 560	.000 186 7605	.020 898	111.897 371	.008 936 7605	10.73	2.967 922	8.02	444
38	53.124 856	5957.126 387	.000 167 8662	.018 824	112.134 448	.008 917 8662	10.71	3.066 547	8.07	456
39	58.979 398	6626.216 950	.000 150 9157	.016 955	112.347 992	.008 900 9157	10.69	3.165 629	8.12	468
40	65.479 132	7369.043 601	.000 135 7028	.015 272	112.540 338	.008 885 7028	10.67	3.265 137	8.16	480
41	72.695 158	8193.732 313	.000 122 0445	.013 756	112.713 591	.008 872 0445	10.65	3.365 046	8.21	492
42	80.706 415	9109.304 565	.000 109 7779	.012 391	112.869 647	.008 859 7779	10.64	3.465 328	8.25	504
43	89.600 540	10125.776 040	.000 098 7579	.011 161	113.010 212	.008 848 7579	10.62	3.565 959	8.29	516
44	99.474 829	11254.266 178	.000 088 8552	.010 053	113.136 824	.008 838 8552	10.61	3.666 916	8.33	528
45	110.437 298	12507.119 823	.000 079 9545	.009 055	113.250 867	.008 829 9545	10.60	3.768 175	8.37	540
46	122.607 870	13898.042 263	.000 071 9526	.008 156	113.353 590	.008 821 9526	10.59	3.869 718	8.41	552
47	136.119 680	15442.249 155	.000 064 7574	.007 346	113.446 117	.008 814 7574	10.58	3.971 523	8.45	564
48	151.120 539	17156.632 975	.000 058 2865	.006 617	113.529 459	.008 808 2865	10.57	4.073 573	8.49	576
49	167.774 543	19059.947 807	.000 052 4660	.005 960	113.604 528	.008 802 4660	10.57	4.175 850	8.52	588
50	186.263 877	21173.014 500	.000 047 2299	.005 369	113.672 145	.008 797 2299	10.56	4.278 338	8.56	600

Effective Rate is 11.02 %

Annual Percentage Rate is 10.50 %

MONTHLY COMPOUND INTEREST AND ANNUITY

10.55 % M

	Amount Of 1	Amount Of 1 Per Period	Sinking Fund Payment	Present Worth Of 1	Present Worth of 1 Per Period	Periodic Payment To Amortize 1	Constant Annual Percent	Total Interest	Annual Add On Rate	
	What a single $ 1 deposit grows to in the future. The deposit is made at the beginning of the first period.	What a series of $ 1 deposits grow to in the future. A deposit is made at the end of each period.	The amount to be deposited at the end of each period that grows to $ 1 in the future.	What $ 1 to be paid in the future is worth today. Value today of a single $ 1 payment tomorrow.	What $ 1 to be paid at the end of each period is worth today. Value today of a series of $ 1 payments tomorrow.	The mortgage payment to amortize a loan of $ 1. An annuity certain, payable at the end of each period, worth $ 1 today.	The annual payment, including interest and principal, to amortize completely a loan of $ 100.	The total interest paid over the term on a loan of $1. The loan is amortized by regular periodic payments.	The average annual interest rate on a loan that is completely amortized by regular periodic payments.	
	$S = (1+i)^n$	$S\overline{n}| = \dfrac{(1+i)^n - 1}{i}$	$\dfrac{1}{S\overline{n}|} = \dfrac{i}{(1+i)^n - 1}$	$V^n = \dfrac{1}{(1+i)^n}$	$A\overline{n}| = \dfrac{1-V^n}{i}$	$\dfrac{1}{A\overline{n}|} = \dfrac{i}{1-V^n}$				

YEAR / **PERIODS**

YEAR	Amount Of 1	Amount Of 1 Per Period	Sinking Fund Payment	Present Worth Of 1	Present Worth of 1 Per Period	Periodic Payment To Amortize 1	Constant Annual Percent	Total Interest	Annual Add On Rate	PERIODS
	1.008 792	1.000 000	1.000 000 0000	.991 285	.991 285	1.008 791 6667	1210.55	.008 792	10.55	1
	1.017 661	2.008 792	.497 811 7027	.982 646	1.973 931	.506 603 3694	607.93	.013 207	7.92	2
	1.026 608	3.026 452	.330 419 8788	.974 082	2.948 013	.339 211 5455	407.06	.017 635	7.05	3
	1.035 633	4.053 060	.246 727 1731	.965 593	3.913 606	.255 518 8398	306.63	.022 077	6.62	4
	1.044 738	5.088 693	.196 514 1146	.957 178	4.870 783	.205 305 7812	246.37	.026 529	6.37	5
	1.053 923	6.133 431	.163 040 8794	.948 836	5.819 619	.171 832 5461	206.20	.030 995	6.20	6
	1.063 189	7.187 354	.139 133 2575	.940 567	6.760 186	.147 924 9242	177.51	.035 474	6.08	7
	1.072 536	8.250 543	.121 204 1438	.932 370	7.692 556	.129 995 8104	156.00	.039 966	5.99	8
	1.081 965	9.323 079	.107 260 7019	.924 244	8.616 800	.116 052 3686	139.27	.044 471	5.93	9
	1.091 478	10.405 044	.096 107 2302	.916 189	9.532 989	.104 898 8969	125.88	.048 989	5.88	10
	1.101 074	11.496 522	.086 982 8275	.908 205	10.441 193	.095 774 4942	114.93	.053 519	5.84	11
	1.110 754	12.597 596	.079 380 2265	.900 289	11.341 483	.088 171 8932	105.81	.058 063	5.81	12
1	1.110 754	12.597 596	.079 380 2265	.900 289	11.341 483	.088 171 8932	105.81	.058 063	5.81	12
2	1.233 774	26.590 424	.037 607 5240	.810 521	21.552 100	.046 399 1907	55.68	.113 581	5.68	24
3	1.370 419	42.133 012	.023 734 3584	.729 704	30.744 611	.032 526 0251	39.04	.170 937	5.70	36
4	1.522 199	59.397 001	.016 835 8668	.656 944	39.020 532	.025 627 5335	30.76	.230 122	5.75	48
5	1.690 788	78.573 044	.012 727 0111	.591 440	46.471 257	.021 518 6777	25.83	.291 121	5.82	60
6	1.878 049	99.872 908	.010 012 7254	.532 467	53.179 066	.018 804 3921	22.57	.353 916	5.90	72
7	2.086 051	123.531 814	.008 095 0807	.479 375	59.218 035	.016 886 7474	20.27	.418 487	5.98	84
8	2.317 089	149.811 035	.006 675 0757	.431 576	64.654 856	.015 466 7424	18.57	.484 807	6.06	96
9	2.573 715	179.000 781	.005 586 5678	.388 543	69.549 568	.014 378 2345	17.26	.552 849	6.14	108
10	2.858 764	211.423 405	.004 729 8453	.349 802	73.956 226	.013 521 5120	16.23	.622 581	6.23	120
11	3.175 383	247.436 959	.004 041 4334	.314 923	77.923 494	.012 833 1001	15.40	.693 969	6.31	132
12	3.527 069	287.439 154	.003 478 9972	.283 522	81.495 183	.012 270 6638	14.73	.766 976	6.39	144
13	3.917 706	331.871 746	.003 013 2122	.255 251	84.710 738	.011 804 8789	14.17	.841 561	6.47	156
14	4.351 607	381.225 419	.002 623 1199	.229 800	87.605 667	.011 414 7866	13.70	.917 684	6.55	168
15	4.833 564	436.045 203	.002 293 3402	.206 887	90.211 942	.011 085 0069	13.31	.995 301	6.64	180
16	5.368 900	496.936 489	.002 012 3296	.186 258	92.558 344	.010 803 9963	12.97	1.074 367	6.71	192
17	5.963 526	564.571 720	.001 771 2541	.167 686	94.670 784	.010 562 9208	12.68	1.154 836	6.79	204
18	6.624 010	639.697 814	.001 563 2381	.150 966	96.572 535	.010 354 9048	12.43	1.236 659	6.87	216
19	7.357 645	723.144 413	.001 382 8497	.135 913	98.284 770	.010 174 5163	12.21	1.319 790	6.95	228
20	8.172 532	815.833 046	.001 225 7410	.122 361	99.826 226	.010 017 4077	12.03	1.404 178	7.02	240
21	9.077 672	918.787 302	.001 088 3912	.110 160	101.213 982	.009 880 0579	11.86	1.489 775	7.09	252
22	10.083 059	1033.144 140	.000 967 9192	.099 176	102.463 365	.009 759 5858	11.72	1.576 531	7.17	264
23	11.199 797	1160.166 439	.000 861 9453	.089 287	103.588 170	.009 653 6120	11.59	1.664 397	7.24	276
24	12.440 217	1301.256 949	.000 768 4877	.080 384	104.600 821	.009 560 1544	11.48	1.753 324	7.31	288
25	13.818 019	1457.973 778	.000 685 8834	.072 369	105.512 500	.009 477 5501	11.38	1.843 265	7.37	300
26	15.348 418	1632.047 600	.000 612 7272	.065 153	106.333 275	.009 404 3939	11.29	1.934 171	7.44	312
27	17.048 315	1825.400 771	.000 547 8249	.058 657	107.072 210	.009 339 4916	11.21	2.025 995	7.50	324
28	18.936 482	2040.168 552	.000 490 1556	.052 808	107.737 465	.009 281 8222	11.14	2.118 692	7.57	336
29	21.033 770	2278.722 694	.000 438 8423	.047 543	108.336 387	.009 230 5090	11.08	2.212 217	7.63	348
30	23.363 342	2543.697 629	.000 393 1285	.042 802	108.875 591	.009 184 7952	11.03	2.306 526	7.69	360
31	25.950 922	2838.019 562	.000 352 3584	.038 534	109.361 030	.009 144 0251	10.98	2.401 577	7.75	372
32	28.825 087	3164.938 785	.000 315 9619	.034 692	109.798 066	.009 107 6285	10.93	2.497 329	7.80	384
33	32.017 577	3528.065 575	.000 283 4414	.031 233	110.191 525	.009 075 1081	10.90	2.593 743	7.86	396
34	35.563 647	3931.410 059	.000 254 3617	.028 119	110.545 752	.009 046 0283	10.86	2.690 780	7.91	408
35	39.502 458	4379.426 502	.000 228 3404	.025 315	110.864 658	.009 020 0071	10.83	2.788 403	7.97	420
36	43.877 508	4877.062 497	.000 205 0415	.022 791	111.151 766	.008 996 7081	10.80	2.886 578	8.02	432
37	48.737 111	5429.813 601	.000 184 1684	.020 518	111.410 247	.008 975 8351	10.78	2.985 271	8.07	444
38	54.134 935	6043.784 024	.000 165 4593	.018 472	111.642 954	.008 957 1259	10.75	3.084 449	8.12	456
39	60.130 588	6725.754 042	.000 148 6822	.016 630	111.852 458	.008 940 3489	10.73	3.184 083	8.16	468
40	66.790 282	7483.254 874	.000 133 6317	.014 972	112.041 072	.008 925 2984	10.72	3.284 143	8.21	480
41	74.187 564	8324.651 849	.000 120 1251	.013 479	112.210 880	.008 911 7918	10.70	3.384 602	8.26	492
42	82.404 123	9259.236 789	.000 108 0003	.012 135	112.363 756	.008 899 6669	10.68	3.485 432	8.30	504
43	91.530 698	10297.330 620	.000 097 1125	.010 925	112.501 388	.008 888 7792	10.67	3.586 610	8.34	516
44	101.668 077	11450.397 352	.000 087 3332	.009 836	112.625 297	.008 878 9999	10.66	3.688 112	8.38	528
45	112.928 209	12731.170 678	.000 078 5474	.008 855	112.736 851	.008 870 2140	10.65	3.789 916	8.42	540
46	125.435 444	14153.794 597	.000 070 6524	.007 972	112.837 282	.008 862 3191	10.64	3.892 000	8.46	552
47	139.327 904	15733.979 609	.000 063 5567	.007 177	112.927 699	.008 855 2234	10.63	3.994 346	8.50	564
48	154.759 008	17499.176 214	.000 057 1782	.006 462	113.009 100	.008 848 8449	10.62	4.096 935	8.54	576
49	171.899 165	19438.767 622	.000 051 4436	.005 817	113.082 385	.008 843 1103	10.62	4.199 749	8.57	588
50	190.937 662	21604.283 809	.000 046 2871	.005 237	113.148 363	.008 837 9538	10.61	4.302 772	8.61	600

Effective Rate is 11.08 %

Annual Percentage Rate is 10.55 %

Amount Of 1	Amount Of 1 Per Period	Sinking Fund Payment	Present Worth Of 1	Present Worth of 1 Per Period	Periodic Payment To Amortize 1	Constant Annual Percent	Total Interest	Annual Add On Rate
What a single $ 1 deposit grows to in the future. The deposit is made at the beginning of the first period.	What a series of $ 1 deposits grow to in the future. A deposit is made at the end of each period.	The amount to be deposited at the end of each period that grows to $ 1 in the future.	What $ 1 to be paid in the future is worth today. Value today of a single $ 1 payment tomorrow.	What $ 1 to be paid at the end of each period is worth today. Value today of a series of $ 1 payments tomorrow.	The mortgage payment to amortize a loan of $ 1. An annuity certain, payable at the end of each period, worth $ 1 today.	The annual interest payment, including interest and principal, to amortize completely a loan of $ 100.	The total interest paid over the term on a loan of $1. The loan is amortized by regular periodic payments.	The average annual interest rate on a loan that is completely amortized by regular periodic payments.

$$S = (1+i)^n \qquad S_{\overline{n}|} = \frac{(1+i)^n - 1}{i} \qquad \frac{1}{S_{\overline{n}|}} = \frac{i}{(1+i)^n - 1} \qquad V^n = \frac{1}{(1+i)^n} \qquad A_{\overline{n}|} = \frac{1-V^n}{i} \qquad \frac{1}{A_{\overline{n}|}} = \frac{i}{1-V^n}$$

YEAR / **PERIODS**

YEAR	Amount Of 1	Amount Of 1 Per Period	Sinking Fund Payment	Present Worth Of 1	Present Worth of 1 Per Period	Periodic Payment To Amortize 1	Constant Annual Percent	Total Interest	Annual Add On Rate	PERIODS
	1.008 833	1.000 000	1.000 000 0000	.991 244	.991 244	1.008 833 3333	1210.60	.008 833	10.60	1
	1.017 745	2.008 833	.497 801 3773	.982 565	1.973 809	.506 634 7106	607.97	.013 269	7.96	2
	1.026 735	3.026 578	.330 406 1520	.973 961	2.947 770	.339 239 4854	407.09	.017 718	7.09	3
	1.035 804	4.053 313	.246 711 7761	.965 433	3.913 203	.255 545 1094	306.66	.022 180	6.65	4
	1.044 954	5.089 117	.196 497 7397	.956 980	4.870 183	.205 331 0730	246.40	.026 655	6.40	5
	1.054 184	6.134 071	.163 023 8729	.948 601	5.818 784	.171 857 2063	206.23	.031 143	6.23	6
	1.063 496	7.188 255	.139 115 8172	.940 295	6.759 079	.147 949 1506	177.54	.035 644	6.11	7
	1.072 890	8.251 751	.121 186 3933	.932 062	7.691 141	.130 019 7266	156.03	.040 158	6.02	8
	1.082 368	9.324 642	.107 242 7237	.923 900	8.615 041	.116 076 0570	139.30	.044 685	5.96	9
	1.091 929	10.407 010	.096 089 0819	.915 811	9.530 852	.104 922 4153	125.91	.049 224	5.91	10
	1.101 574	11.498 938	.086 964 5512	.907 792	10.438 644	.095 797 8845	114.96	.053 777	5.87	11
	1.111 305	12.600 512	.079 361 8535	.899 843	11.338 487	.088 195 1868	105.84	.058 342	5.83	12
1	1.111 305	12.600 512	.079 361 8535	.899 843	11.338 487	.088 195 1868	105.84	.058 342	5.83	12
2	1.234 998	26.603 518	.037 589 0131	.809 718	21.541 350	.046 422 3465	55.71	.114 136	5.71	24
3	1.372 459	42.165 122	.023 716 2836	.728 619	30.722 328	.032 549 6169	39.06	.171 786	5.73	36
4	1.525 219	59.458 803	.016 818 3674	.655 643	38.983 770	.025 651 7007	30.79	.231 282	5.78	48
5	1.694 983	78.677 349	.012 710 1384	.589 976	46.417 774	.021 543 4717	25.86	.292 608	5.85	60
6	1.883 643	100.035 007	.009 996 5006	.530 886	53.107 213	.018 829 8339	22.60	.355 748	5.93	72
7	2.093 300	123.769 868	.008 079 5110	.477 715	59.126 660	.016 912 8443	20.30	.420 679	6.01	84
8	2.326 294	150.146 526	.006 660 1608	.429 868	64.543 220	.015 493 4941	18.60	.487 375	6.09	96
9	2.585 221	179.459 026	.005 572 3026	.386 814	69.417 275	.014 405 6360	17.29	.555 809	6.18	108
10	2.872 968	212.034 139	.004 716 2217	.348 072	73.803 162	.013 549 5550	16.26	.625 947	6.26	120
11	3.192 743	248.235 010	.004 028 4406	.313 210	77.749 773	.012 861 7740	15.44	.697 754	6.34	132
12	3.548 109	288.465 202	.003 466 6226	.281 840	81.301 104	.012 299 9560	14.76	.771 194	6.43	144
13	3.943 030	333.173 196	.003 001 4419	.253 612	84.496 746	.011 834 7753	14.21	.846 225	6.51	156
14	4.381 907	382.857 393	.002 611 9386	.228 211	87.372 323	.011 445 2719	13.74	.922 806	6.59	168
15	4.869 633	438.071 665	.002 282 7315	.205 354	89.959 893	.011 116 0649	13.34	1.000 892	6.67	180
16	5.411 645	499.431 535	.002 002 2764	.184 787	92.288 299	.010 835 6098	13.01	1.080 437	6.75	192
17	6.013 986	567.621 036	.001 761 7388	.166 279	94.383 501	.010 595 0721	12.72	1.161 395	6.83	204
18	6.683 370	643.400 338	.001 554 2423	.149 625	96.268 854	.010 387 5756	12.47	1.243 716	6.91	216
19	7.427 259	727.614 218	.001 374 3547	.134 639	97.965 377	.010 207 6880	12.25	1.327 353	6.99	228
20	8.253 946	821.201 485	.001 217 7279	.121 154	99.491 981	.010 051 0613	12.07	1.412 255	7.06	240
21	9.172 648	925.205 438	.001 080 8410	.109 020	100.865 686	.009 914 1744	11.90	1.498 372	7.14	252
22	10.193 605	1040.785 501	.000 960 8128	.098 101	102.101 805	.009 794 1461	11.76	1.585 655	7.21	264
23	11.328 200	1169.230 148	.000 855 2636	.088 275	103.214 119	.009 688 5969	11.63	1.674 053	7.28	276
24	12.589 080	1311.971 265	.000 762 2118	.079 434	104.215 027	.009 595 5451	11.52	1.763 517	7.35	288
25	13.990 301	1470.600 114	.000 679 9945	.071 478	105.115 688	.009 513 3278	11.42	1.853 998	7.42	300
26	15.547 485	1646.885 072	.000 607 2069	.064 319	105.926 141	.009 440 5402	11.33	1.945 449	7.48	312
27	17.277 990	1842.791 344	.000 542 6550	.057 877	106.655 422	.009 375 9884	11.26	2.037 820	7.55	324
28	19.201 109	2060.502 869	.000 485 3184	.052 080	107.311 661	.009 318 6518	11.19	2.131 067	7.61	336
29	21.338 279	2302.446 673	.000 434 3206	.046 864	107.902 173	.009 267 6539	11.13	2.225 144	7.67	348
30	23.713 326	2571.319 916	.000 388 9053	.042 170	108.433 542	.009 222 2387	11.07	2.320 006	7.73	360
31	26.352 726	2870.119 967	.000 348 4175	.037 947	108.911 690	.009 181 7508	11.02	2.415 611	7.79	372
32	29.285 904	3202.177 817	.000 312 2875	.034 146	109.341 949	.009 145 6208	10.98	2.511 918	7.85	384
33	32.545 558	3571.195 207	.000 280 0183	.030 726	109.729 114	.009 113 3516	10.94	2.608 887	7.91	396
34	36.168 025	3981.285 902	.000 251 1751	.027 649	110.077 502	.009 084 5085	10.91	2.706 479	7.96	408
35	40.193 690	4437.021 546	.000 225 3764	.024 880	110.390 997	.009 058 7097	10.88	2.804 658	8.01	420
36	44.667 430	4943.482 630	.000 202 2865	.022 388	110.673 093	.009 035 6199	10.85	2.903 388	8.06	432
37	49.639 117	5506.315 124	.000 181 6097	.020 145	110.926 936	.009 014 9430	10.82	3.002 635	8.12	444
38	55.164 175	6131.793 420	.000 163 0844	.018 128	111.155 354	.008 996 4178	10.80	3.102 366	8.16	456
39	61.304 197	6826.890 280	.000 146 4796	.016 312	111.360 895	.008 979 8129	10.78	3.202 552	8.21	468
40	68.127 632	7599.354 566	.000 131 5901	.014 678	111.545 849	.008 964 9235	10.76	3.303 163	8.26	480
41	75.710 546	8457.797 622	.000 118 2341	.013 208	111.712 279	.008 951 5674	10.75	3.404 171	8.30	492
42	84.137 472	9411.789 273	.000 106 2497	.011 885	111.862 040	.008 939 5831	10.73	3.505 550	8.35	504
43	93.502 353	10471.964 511	.000 095 4931	.010 695	111.996 802	.008 928 8264	10.72	3.607 274	8.39	516
44	103.909 588	11650.142 049	.000 085 8359	.009 624	112.118 066	.008 919 1692	10.71	3.709 321	8.43	528
45	115.475 195	12959.456 077	.000 077 1637	.008 660	112.227 185	.008 910 4971	10.70	3.811 668	8.47	540
46	128.328 107	14414.502 680	.000 069 3746	.007 793	112.325 375	.008 902 7079	10.69	3.914 295	8.51	552
47	142.611 606	16031.502 553	.000 062 3772	.007 012	112.413 730	.008 895 7105	10.68	4.017 181	8.55	564
48	158.484 923	17828.481 827	.000 056 0900	.006 310	112.493 236	.008 889 4234	10.67	4.120 308	8.58	576
49	176.125 012	19825.473 024	.000 050 4402	.005 678	112.564 779	.008 883 7735	10.67	4.223 659	8.62	588
50	195.728 522	22044.738 376	.000 045 3623	.005 109	112.629 157	.008 878 6956	10.66	4.327 217	8.65	600

MONTHLY COMPOUND INTEREST AND ANNUITY

10.625% M

Amount Of 1	Amount Of 1 Per Period	Sinking Fund Payment	Present Worth Of 1	Present Worth of 1 Per Period	Periodic Payment To Amortize 1	Constant Annual Percent	Total Interest	Annual Add On Rate
What a single $ 1 deposit grows to in the future. The deposit is made at the beginning of the first period.	What a series of $ 1 deposits grow to in the future. A deposit is made at the end of each period.	The amount to be deposited at the end of each period that grows to $ 1 in the future.	What $ 1 to be paid in the future is worth today. Value today of a single $ 1 payment tomorrow.	What $ 1 to be paid at the end of each period is worth today. Value today of a series of $ 1 payments tomorrow.	The mortgage payment to amortize a loan of $ 1. An annuity certain, payable at the end of each period, worth $ 1 today.	The annual payment, including interest and principal, to amortize completely a loan of $ 100.	The total interest paid over the term on a loan of $1. The loan is amortized by regular periodic payments.	The average annual interest rate on a loan that is completely amortized by regular periodic payments.

$$S = (1+i)^n \qquad S\overline{n}| = \frac{(1+i)^n - 1}{i} \qquad \frac{1}{S\overline{n}|} = \frac{i}{(1+i)^n - 1} \qquad V^n = \frac{1}{(1+i)^n} \qquad A\overline{n}| = \frac{1-V^n}{i} \qquad \frac{1}{A\overline{n}|} = \frac{i}{1-V^n}$$

YEAR / **PERIODS**

YEAR	Amount Of 1	Amount Of 1 Per Period	Sinking Fund Payment	Present Worth Of 1	Present Worth of 1 Per Period	Periodic Payment To Amortize 1	Constant Annual Percent	Total Interest	Annual Add On Rate	PERIODS
	1.008 854	1.000 000	1.000 000 0000	.991 224	.991 224	1.008 854 1667	1210.63	.008 854	10.63	1
	1.017 787	2.008 854	.497 796 2147	.982 524	1.973 748	.506 650 3813	607.99	.013 301	7.98	2
	1.026 798	3.026 641	.330 399 2889	.973 901	2.947 649	.339 253 4556	407.11	.017 760	7.10	3
	1.035 890	4.053 439	.246 704 0780	.965 354	3.913 002	.255 558 2446	306.67	.022 233	6.67	4
	1.045 062	5.089 329	.196 489 5528	.956 881	4.869 884	.205 343 7194	246.42	.026 719	6.41	5
	1.054 315	6.134 391	.163 015 3703	.948 483	5.818 367	.171 869 5370	206.25	.031 217	6.24	6
	1.063 650	7.188 706	.139 107 0978	.940 159	6.758 526	.147 961 2645	177.56	.035 729	6.12	7
	1.073 068	8.252 356	.121 177 5189	.931 908	7.690 433	.130 031 6856	156.04	.040 253	6.04	8
	1.082 569	9.325 424	.107 233 7355	.923 729	8.614 162	.116 087 9022	139.31	.044 791	5.97	9
	1.092 154	10.407 992	.096 080 0088	.915 622	9.529 784	.104 934 1755	125.93	.049 342	5.92	10
	1.101 824	11.500 146	.086 955 4142	.907 586	10.437 370	.095 809 5808	114.98	.053 905	5.88	11
	1.111 580	12.601 971	.079 352 6683	.899 620	11.336 990	.088 206 8349	105.85	.058 482	5.85	12
1	1.111 580	12.601 971	.079 352 6683	.899 620	11.336 990	.088 206 8349	105.85	.058 482	5.85	12
2	1.235 610	26.610 069	.037 579 7603	.809 317	21.535 977	.046 433 9269	55.73	.114 414	5.72	24
3	1.373 479	42.181 189	.023 707 2499	.728 078	30.711 195	.032 561 4166	39.08	.172 211	5.74	36
4	1.526 732	59.489 735	.016 809 6227	.654 994	38.965 407	.025 663 7893	30.80	.231 862	5.80	48
5	1.697 085	78.729 567	.012 701 7083	.589 246	46.391 065	.021 555 8750	25.87	.293 352	5.87	60
6	1.886 445	100.116 179	.009 988 3956	.530 098	53.071 339	.018 842 5622	22.62	.356 664	5.94	72
7	2.096 935	123.889 108	.008 071 7346	.476 887	59.081 049	.016 925 9013	20.32	.421 776	6.03	84
8	2.330 911	150.314 619	.006 652 7129	.429 017	64.487 507	.015 506 8795	18.61	.488 660	6.11	96
9	2.590 994	179.688 687	.005 565 1806	.385 952	69.351 267	.014 419 3473	17.31	.557 290	6.19	108
10	2.880 097	212.340 312	.004 709 4213	.347 211	73.726 804	.013 563 5880	16.28	.627 631	6.28	120
11	3.201 458	248.635 204	.004 021 9566	.312 358	77.663 127	.012 876 1233	15.46	.699 648	6.36	132
12	3.558 676	288.979 878	.003 460 4485	.281 003	81.204 324	.012 314 6152	14.78	.773 305	6.44	144
13	3.955 753	333.826 209	.002 995 5707	.252 796	84.390 056	.011 849 7373	14.22	.848 559	6.53	156
14	4.397 136	383.676 491	.002 606 3625	.227 421	87.256 006	.011 460 5291	13.76	.925 369	6.61	168
15	4.887 768	439.089 065	.002 277 4423	.204 592	89.834 273	.011 131 6089	13.36	1.003 690	6.69	180
16	5.433 145	500.684 571	.001 997 2655	.184 055	92.153 735	.010 851 4321	13.03	1.083 475	6.77	192
17	6.039 375	569.152 901	.001 756 9971	.165 580	94.240 370	.010 611 1638	12.74	1.164 677	6.85	204
18	6.713 248	645.260 923	.001 549 7607	.148 959	96.117 549	.010 403 9273	12.49	1.247 248	6.93	216
19	7.462 312	729.861 075	.001 370 1238	.134 007	97.806 298	.010 224 2904	12.27	1.331 138	7.01	228
20	8.294 956	823.900 907	.001 213 7382	.120 555	99.325 531	.010 067 9049	12.09	1.416 297	7.08	240
21	9.220 507	928.433 698	.001 077 0828	.108 454	100.692 264	.009 931 2495	11.92	1.502 675	7.16	252
22	10.249 330	1044.630 254	.000 957 2765	.097 567	101.921 805	.009 811 4432	11.78	1.590 221	7.23	264
23	11.392 950	1173.792 014	.000 851 9397	.087 774	103.027 925	.009 706 1064	11.65	1.678 885	7.30	276
24	12.664 175	1317.365 638	.000 759 0907	.078 963	104.023 013	.009 613 2574	11.54	1.768 618	7.37	288
25	14.077 243	1476.959 199	.000 677 0668	.071 037	104.918 215	.009 531 2334	11.44	1.859 370	7.44	300
26	15.647 981	1654.360 202	.000 604 4633	.063 906	105.723 557	.009 458 6300	11.36	1.951 093	7.50	312
27	17.393 982	1851.555 599	.000 540 0864	.057 491	106.448 058	.009 394 2531	11.28	2.043 738	7.57	324
28	19.334 801	2070.754 049	.000 482 9159	.051 720	107.099 835	.009 337 0825	11.21	2.137 260	7.63	336
29	21.492 178	2314.410 651	.000 432 0754	.046 529	107.686 187	.009 286 2421	11.15	2.231 612	7.70	348
30	23.890 274	2585.254 443	.000 386 8091	.041 858	108.213 680	.009 240 9758	11.09	2.326 751	7.76	360
31	26.555 949	2886.318 973	.000 346 4621	.037 656	108.688 225	.009 200 6287	11.05	2.422 634	7.81	372
32	29.519 061	3220.976 267	.000 310 4649	.033 876	109.115 134	.009 164 6315	11.00	2.519 219	7.87	384
33	32.812 796	3592.974 604	.000 278 3209	.030 476	109.499 191	.009 132 4876	10.96	2.616 465	7.93	396
34	36.474 046	4006.480 498	.000 249 5956	.027 417	109.844 696	.009 103 7623	10.93	2.714 335	7.98	408
35	40.543 818	4466.125 357	.000 223 9077	.024 665	110.155 519	.009 078 0744	10.90	2.812 791	8.04	420
36	45.067 695	4977.057 367	.000 200 9219	.022 189	110.435 142	.009 055 0886	10.87	2.911 798	8.09	432
37	50.096 347	5544.999 144	.000 180 3427	.019 962	110.686 697	.009 034 5093	10.85	3.011 322	8.14	444
38	55.686 094	6176.311 835	.000 161 9089	.017 958	110.913 001	.009 016 0756	10.82	3.111 330	8.19	456
39	61.899 546	6878.066 365	.000 145 3897	.016 155	111.116 588	.008 999 5564	10.80	3.211 792	8.24	468
40	68.806 294	7658.122 629	.000 130 5803	.014 534	111.299 740	.008 984 7470	10.79	3.312 679	8.28	480
41	76.483 697	8525.217 531	.000 117 2991	.013 075	111.464 507	.008 971 4657	10.77	3.413 961	8.33	492
42	85.017 744	9489.062 837	.000 105 3845	.011 762	111.612 734	.008 959 5512	10.76	3.515 614	8.37	504
43	94.504 019	10560.453 954	.000 094 6929	.010 582	111.746 083	.008 948 8596	10.74	3.617 612	8.41	516
44	105.048 773	11751.390 836	.000 085 0963	.009 519	111.866 046	.008 939 2630	10.73	3.719 931	8.45	528
45	116.770 110	13075.212 396	.000 076 4806	.008 564	111.973 967	.008 930 6473	10.72	3.822 550	8.49	540
46	129.799 313	14546.745 897	.000 068 7439	.007 704	112.071 055	.008 922 9106	10.71	3.925 447	8.53	552
47	144.282 313	16182.473 030	.000 061 7953	.006 931	112.158 397	.008 915 9619	10.70	4.028 603	8.57	564
48	160.381 326	18000.714 514	.000 055 5534	.006 235	112.236 972	.008 909 7200	10.70	4.131 999	8.61	576
49	178.276 667	20021.835 289	.000 049 9455	.005 609	112.307 660	.008 904 1121	10.69	4.235 618	8.64	588
50	198.168 768	22268.472 617	.000 044 9065	.005 046	112.371 252	.008 899 0732	10.68	4.339 444	8.68	600

Effective Rate is 11.16 %

Annual Percentage Rate is 10.625%

Amount Of 1	Amount Of 1 Per Period	Sinking Fund Payment	Present Worth Of 1	Present Worth of 1 Per Period	Periodic Payment To Amortize 1	Constant Annual Percent	Total Interest	Annual Add On Rate
What a single $ 1 deposit grows to in the future. The deposit is made at the beginning of the first period.	What a series of $ 1 deposits grow to in the future. A deposit is made at the end of each period.	The amount to be deposited at the end of each period that grows to $ 1 in the future.	What $ 1 to be paid in the future is worth today. Value today of a single $ 1 payment tomorrow.	What $ 1 to be paid at the end of each period is worth today. Value today of a series of $ 1 payments tomorrow.	The mortgage payment to amortize a loan of $ 1. An annuity certain, payable at the end of each period, worth $ 1 today.	The annual payment, including interest and principal, to amortize completely a loan of $ 100.	The total interest paid over the term on a loan of $1. The loan is amortized by regular periodic payments.	The average annual interest rate on a loan that is completely amortized by regular periodic payments.
$S = (1+i)^n$	$S\overline{n}| = \dfrac{(1+i)^n - 1}{i}$	$\dfrac{1}{S\overline{n}|} = \dfrac{i}{(1+i)^n - 1}$	$V^n = \dfrac{1}{(1+i)^n}$	$A\overline{n}| = \dfrac{1-V^n}{i}$	$\dfrac{1}{A\overline{n}|} = \dfrac{i}{1-V^n}$			

YEAR … **PERIODS**

Amount Of 1	Amount Of 1 Per Period	Sinking Fund Payment	Present Worth Of 1	Present Worth of 1 Per Period	Periodic Payment To Amortize 1	Constant Annual Percent	Total Interest	Annual Add On Rate	PERIODS
1.008 875	1.000 000	1.000 000 0000	.991 203	.991 203	1.008 875 0000	1210.65	.008 875	10.65	1
1.017 829	2.008 875	.497 791 0522	.982 484	1.973 687	.506 666 0522	608.00	.013 332	8.00	2
1.026 862	3.026 704	.330 392 4260	.973 841	2.947 527	.339 267 4260	407.13	.017 802	7.12	3
1.035 975	4.053 566	.246 696 3801	.965 274	3.912 801	.255 571 3801	306.69	.022 286	6.69	4
1.045 170	5.089 541	.196 481 3662	.956 782	4.869 584	.205 356 3662	246.43	.026 782	6.43	5
1.054 446	6.134 711	.163 006 8681	.948 366	5.817 949	.171 881 8681	206.26	.031 291	6.26	6
1.063 804	7.189 156	.139 098 3789	.940 023	6.757 972	.147 973 3789	177.57	.035 814	6.14	7
1.073 245	8.252 960	.121 168 6451	.931 754	7.689 726	.130 043 6451	156.06	.040 349	6.05	8
1.082 770	9.326 205	.107 224 7480	.923 557	8.613 283	.116 099 7480	139.32	.044 898	5.99	9
1.092 380	10.408 975	.096 070 9365	.915 433	9.528 716	.104 945 9365	125.94	.049 459	5.94	10
1.102 075	11.501 355	.086 946 2779	.907 380	10.436 095	.095 821 2779	114.99	.054 034	5.89	11
1.111 855	12.603 429	.079 343 4839	.899 398	11.335 493	.088 218 4839	105.87	.058 622	5.86	12
1 1.111 855	12.603 429	.079 343 4839	.899 398	11.335 493	.088 218 4839	105.87	.058 622	5.86	12
2 1.236 223	26.616 621	.037 570 5091	.808 916	21.530 607	.046 445 5091	55.74	.114 692	5.73	24
3 1.374 501	42.197 264	.023 698 2188	.727 537	30.700 067	.032 573 2188	39.09	.172 636	5.75	36
4 1.528 246	59.520 687	.016 800 8814	.654 345	38.947 056	.025 675 8814	30.82	.232 442	5.81	48
5 1.699 189	78.781 829	.012 693 2824	.588 516	46.364 378	.021 568 2824	25.89	.294 097	5.88	60
6 1.889 252	100.197 434	.009 980 2955	.529 310	53.035 499	.018 855 2955	22.63	.357 581	5.96	72
7 2.100 575	124.008 491	.008 063 9639	.476 060	59.035 488	.016 938 9639	20.33	.422 873	6.04	84
8 2.335 536	150.482 944	.006 645 2714	.428 167	64.431 863	.015 520 2714	18.63	.489 946	6.12	96
9 2.596 779	179.918 709	.005 558 0657	.385 093	69.285 350	.014 433 0657	17.32	.558 771	6.21	108
10 2.887 242	212.647 024	.004 702 6287	.346 351	73.650 563	.013 577 6287	16.30	.629 315	6.29	120
11 3.210 196	249.036 179	.004 015 4808	.311 507	77.576 625	.012 890 4808	15.47	.701 543	6.38	132
12 3.569 274	289.495 659	.003 454 2832	.280 169	81.107 716	.012 329 2832	14.80	.775 417	6.46	144
13 3.968 517	334.480 752	.002 989 7087	.251 983	84.283 570	.011 864 7087	14.24	.850 895	6.55	156
14 4.412 417	384.497 672	.002 600 7960	.226 633	87.139 925	.011 475 7960	13.78	.927 934	6.63	168
15 4.905 970	440.109 256	.002 272 1631	.203 833	89.708 924	.011 147 1631	13.38	1.006 489	6.71	180
16 5.454 729	501.941 298	.001 992 2648	.183 327	92.019 475	.010 867 2648	13.05	1.086 515	6.79	192
17 6.064 870	570.689 591	.001 752 2661	.164 884	94.097 578	.010 627 2661	12.76	1.167 962	6.87	204
18 6.743 259	647.127 753	.001 545 2899	.148 296	95.966 620	.010 420 2899	12.51	1.250 783	6.95	216
19 7.497 529	732.115 940	.001 365 9039	.133 377	97.647 631	.010 240 9039	12.29	1.334 926	7.03	228
20 8.336 168	826.610 517	.001 209 7596	.119 959	99.159 528	.010 084 7596	12.11	1.420 342	7.10	240
21 9.268 614	931.674 826	.001 073 3359	.107 891	100.519 324	.009 948 3359	11.94	1.506 981	7.18	252
22 10.305 359	1048.491 150	.000 953 7515	.097 037	101.742 322	.009 828 7515	11.80	1.594 790	7.25	264
23 11.458 069	1178.374 014	.000 848 6270	.087 275	102.842 283	.009 723 6270	11.67	1.683 721	7.32	276
24 12.739 717	1322.784 983	.000 755 9808	.078 495	103.831 585	.009 630 9808	11.56	1.773 722	7.39	288
25 14.164 723	1483.349 104	.000 674 1501	.070 598	104.721 361	.009 549 1501	11.46	1.864 745	7.46	300
26 15.749 125	1661.873 194	.000 601 7306	.063 496	105.521 623	.009 476 7306	11.38	1.956 740	7.53	312
27 17.510 750	1860.366 175	.000 537 5286	.057 108	106.241 377	.009 412 5286	11.30	2.049 659	7.59	324
28 19.469 422	2081.061 674	.000 480 5240	.051 363	106.888 722	.009 355 5240	11.23	2.143 456	7.66	336
29 21.647 183	2326.443 165	.000 429 8407	.046 195	107.470 942	.009 304 8407	11.17	2.238 085	7.72	348
30 24.068 538	2599.271 909	.000 384 7231	.041 548	107.994 590	.009 259 7231	11.12	2.333 500	7.78	360
31 26.760 735	2902.618 032	.000 344 5166	.037 368	108.465 557	.009 219 5166	11.07	2.429 660	7.84	372
32 29.754 069	3239.895 067	.000 308 6520	.033 609	108.889 144	.009 183 6520	11.03	2.526 522	7.90	384
33 33.082 223	3614.898 372	.000 276 6329	.030 228	109.270 117	.009 151 6329	10.99	2.624 047	7.95	396
34 36.782 650	4031.847 836	.000 248 0252	.027 187	109.612 763	.009 123 0252	10.95	2.722 194	8.01	408
35 40.896 989	4495.435 364	.000 222 4479	.024 452	109.920 938	.009 097 4479	10.92	2.820 928	8.06	420
36 45.471 539	5010.877 677	.000 199 5658	.021 992	110.198 110	.009 074 5658	10.89	2.920 212	8.11	432
37 50.557 778	5583.975 014	.000 179 0839	.019 779	110.447 397	.009 054 0839	10.87	3.020 013	8.16	444
38 56.212 941	6221.176 405	.000 160 7413	.017 789	110.671 606	.009 035 7413	10.85	3.120 298	8.21	456
39 62.500 664	6929.652 235	.000 144 3074	.016 000	110.873 259	.009 019 3074	10.83	3.221 036	8.26	468
40 69.491 703	7717.374 937	.000 129 5777	.014 390	111.054 625	.009 004 5777	10.81	3.322 197	8.31	480
41 77.264 727	8593.208 707	.000 116 3710	.012 943	111.217 745	.008 991 3710	10.79	3.423 755	8.35	492
42 85.907 207	9567.009 244	.000 104 5259	.011 640	111.364 454	.008 979 5259	10.78	3.525 681	8.39	504
43 95.516 395	10649.734 666	.000 093 8991	.010 469	111.496 405	.008 968 8991	10.77	3.627 952	8.44	516
44 106.200 423	11853.568 811	.000 084 3628	.009 416	111.615 081	.008 959 3628	10.76	3.730 544	8.48	528
45 118.079 518	13192.058 351	.000 075 8032	.008 469	111.721 818	.008 950 8032	10.75	3.833 434	8.52	540
46 131.287 354	14680.265 221	.000 068 1187	.007 617	111.817 816	.008 943 1187	10.74	3.936 602	8.56	552
47 145.972 420	16334.936 120	.000 061 2185	.006 851	111.904 157	.008 936 2185	10.73	4.040 027	8.60	564
48 162.300 382	18174.690 954	.000 055 0216	.006 161	111.981 812	.008 930 0216	10.72	4.143 692	8.63	576
49 180.454 562	20220.232 368	.000 049 4554	.005 542	112.051 655	.008 924 4554	10.71	4.247 580	8.67	588
50 200.639 386	22494.578 709	.000 044 4552	.004 984	112.114 471	.008 919 4552	10.71	4.351 673	8.70	600

	Amount Of 1	Amount Of 1 Per Period	Sinking Fund Payment	Present Worth Of 1	Present Worth of 1 Per Period	Periodic Payment To Amortize 1	Constant Annual Percent	Total Interest	Annual Add On Rate	
	What a single $ 1 deposit grows to in the future. The deposit is made at the beginning of the first period.	What a series of $ 1 deposits grow to in the future. A deposit is made at the end of each period.	The amount to be deposited at the end of each period that grows to $ 1 in the future.	What $ 1 to be paid in the future is worth today. Value today of a single $ 1 payment tomorrow.	What $ 1 to be paid at the end of each period is worth today. Value today of a series of $ 1 payments tomorrow.	The mortgage payment to amortize a loan of $ 1. An annuity certain, payable at the end of each period, worth $ 1 today.	The annual payment, including interest and principal, to amortize completely a loan of $ 100.	The total interest paid over the term on a loan of $1. The loan is amortized by regular periodic payments.	The average annual interest rate on a loan that is completely amortized by regular periodic payments.	

$$S = (1+i)^n \qquad S\overline{n}| = \frac{(1+i)^n - 1}{i} \qquad \frac{1}{S\overline{n}|} = \frac{i}{(1+i)^n - 1} \qquad V^n = \frac{1}{(1+i)^n} \qquad A\overline{n}| = \frac{1-V^n}{i} \qquad \frac{1}{A\overline{n}|} = \frac{i}{1-V^n}$$

YEAR										PERIODS
	1.008 917	1.000 000	1.000 000 0000	.991 162	.991 162	1.008 916 6667	1210.70	.008 917	10.70	1
	1.017 913	2.008 917	.497 780 7276	.982 402	1.973 565	.506 697 3943	608.04	.013 395	8.04	2
	1.026 989	3.026 830	.330 378 7008	.973 720	2.947 285	.339 295 3675	407.16	.017 886	7.15	3
	1.036 147	4.053 819	.246 680 9853	.965 114	3.912 399	.255 597 6519	306.72	.022 391	6.72	4
	1.045 386	5.089 965	.196 464 9941	.956 585	4.868 984	.205 381 6607	246.46	.026 908	6.46	5
	1.054 707	6.135 351	.162 989 8649	.948 131	5.817 115	.171 906 5316	206.29	.031 439	6.29	6
	1.064 111	7.190 058	.139 080 9425	.939 751	6.756 866	.147 997 6092	177.60	.035 983	6.17	7
	1.073 600	8.254 169	.121 150 8991	.931 446	7.688 312	.130 067 5658	156.09	.040 541	6.08	8
	1.083 173	9.327 769	.107 206 7748	.923 214	8.611 526	.116 123 4415	139.35	.045 111	6.01	9
	1.092 831	10.410 941	.096 052 7939	.915 055	9.526 580	.104 969 4605	125.97	.049 695	5.96	10
	1.102 575	11.503 772	.086 928 0078	.906 968	10.433 548	.095 844 6744	115.02	.054 291	5.92	11
	1.112 407	12.606 348	.079 325 1177	.898 952	11.332 500	.088 241 7844	105.90	.058 901	5.89	12
1	1.112 407	12.606 348	.079 325 1177	.898 952	11.332 500	.088 241 7844	105.90	.058 901	5.89	12
2	1.237 448	26.629 732	.037 552 0119	.808 114	21.519 872	.046 468 6786	55.77	.115 248	5.76	24
3	1.376 546	42.229 437	.023 680 1643	.726 456	30.677 829	.032 596 8310	39.12	.173 486	5.78	36
4	1.531 279	59.582 652	.016 783 4088	.653 049	38.910 392	.025 700 0755	30.85	.233 604	5.84	48
5	1.703 404	78.886 482	.012 676 4430	.587 060	46.311 069	.021 593 1097	25.92	.295 587	5.91	60
6	1.894 878	100.360 191	.009 964 1102	.527 738	52.963 922	.018 880 7768	22.66	.359 416	5.99	72
7	2.107 875	124.247 686	.008 048 4396	.474 411	58.944 517	.016 965 1063	20.36	.425 069	6.07	84
8	2.344 814	150.820 293	.006 630 4075	.426 473	64.320 784	.015 547 0741	18.66	.492 519	6.16	96
9	2.608 387	180.379 837	.005 543 8569	.383 379	69.153 789	.014 460 5235	17.36	.561 737	6.24	108
10	2.901 587	213.262 069	.004 689 0664	.344 639	73.498 429	.013 605 7331	16.33	.632 688	6.33	120
11	3.227 744	249.840 480	.004 002 5540	.309 814	77.404 050	.012 919 2206	15.51	.705 337	6.41	132
12	3.590 564	290.530 546	.003 441 9789	.278 508	80.915 016	.012 358 6455	14.84	.779 645	6.50	144
13	3.994 167	335.794 444	.002 978 0123	.250 365	84.071 205	.011 894 6790	14.28	.855 570	6.58	156
14	4.443 138	386.146 303	.002 589 6920	.225 066	86.908 467	.011 506 3587	13.81	.933 068	6.66	168
15	4.942 576	442.158 043	.002 261 6348	.202 324	89.459 030	.011 178 3014	13.42	1.012 094	6.75	180
16	5.498 154	504.465 872	.001 982 2947	.181 879	91.751 862	.010 898 9613	13.08	1.092 601	6.83	192
17	6.116 183	573.777 512	.001 742 8358	.163 501	93.813 009	.010 659 5025	12.80	1.174 539	6.91	204
18	6.803 682	650.880 238	.001 536 3810	.146 979	95.665 880	.010 453 0476	12.55	1.257 858	6.99	216
19	7.568 461	736.649 819	.001 357 4971	.132 127	97.331 522	.010 274 1638	12.33	1.342 509	7.07	228
20	8.419 206	832.060 468	.001 201 8357	.118 776	98.828 854	.010 118 5024	12.15	1.428 441	7.14	240
21	9.365 580	938.195 902	.001 065 8755	.106 774	100.174 884	.009 982 5421	11.98	1.515 601	7.22	252
22	10.418 333	1056.261 660	.000 946 7351	.095 985	101.384 900	.009 863 4018	11.84	1.603 938	7.29	264
23	11.589 423	1187.598 788	.000 842 0352	.086 286	102.472 646	.009 758 7019	11.72	1.693 402	7.36	276
24	12.892 150	1333.699 076	.000 749 7943	.077 567	103.450 477	.009 666 4610	11.60	1.783 941	7.43	288
25	14.341 313	1496.222 000	.000 668 3500	.069 729	104.329 500	.009 585 0167	11.51	1.875 505	7.50	300
26	15.953 371	1677.013 573	.000 596 2981	.062 683	105.119 700	.009 512 9648	11.42	1.968 045	7.57	312
27	17.746 635	1878.127 312	.000 532 4453	.056 349	105.830 051	.009 449 1119	11.34	2.061 512	7.64	324
28	19.741 474	2101.847 563	.000 475 7719	.050 655	106.468 623	.009 392 4386	11.28	2.155 859	7.70	336
29	21.960 546	2350.715 446	.000 425 4024	.045 536	107.042 668	.009 342 0691	11.22	2.251 040	7.76	348
30	24.429 056	2627.557 721	.000 380 5816	.040 935	107.558 707	.009 297 2482	11.16	2.347 009	7.82	360
31	27.175 043	2935.518 894	.000 340 6553	.036 798	108.022 602	.009 257 3219	11.11	2.443 724	7.88	372
32	30.229 698	3278.096 936	.000 305 0550	.033 080	108.439 620	.009 221 7217	11.07	2.541 141	7.94	384
33	33.627 715	3659.183 010	.000 273 2850	.029 737	108.814 500	.009 189 9517	11.03	2.639 221	8.00	396
34	37.407 692	4083.105 673	.000 244 9116	.026 732	109.151 499	.009 161 5783	11.00	2.737 924	8.05	408
35	41.612 564	4554.680 042	.000 219 5544	.024 031	109.454 444	.009 136 2211	10.97	2.837 213	8.11	420
36	46.290 090	5079.262 480	.000 196 8790	.021 603	109.726 778	.009 113 5456	10.94	2.937 052	8.16	432
37	51.493 402	5662.811 447	.000 176 5907	.019 420	109.971 593	.009 093 2574	10.92	3.037 406	8.21	444
38	57.281 600	6311.955 168	.000 158 4295	.017 458	110.191 670	.009 075 0962	10.90	3.138 244	8.26	456
39	63.720 430	7034.066 927	.000 142 1653	.015 694	110.389 508	.009 058 8319	10.88	3.239 533	8.31	468
40	70.883 027	7837.348 812	.000 127 5942	.014 108	110.567 355	.009 044 2608	10.86	3.341 245	8.35	480
41	78.850 747	8730.924 882	.000 114 5354	.012 682	110.727 231	.009 031 2021	10.84	3.443 351	8.40	492
42	87.714 091	9724.944 798	.000 102 8283	.011 401	110.870 952	.009 019 4950	10.83	3.545 825	8.44	504
43	97.573 734	10830.699 112	.000 092 3301	.010 249	111.000 150	.009 008 9968	10.82	3.648 642	8.49	516
44	108.541 665	12060.747 508	.000 082 9136	.009 213	111.116 293	.008 999 5803	10.80	3.751 778	8.53	528
45	120.742 465	13429.061 460	.000 074 4654	.008 282	111.220 700	.008 991 1320	10.79	3.855 211	8.57	540
46	134.314 714	14951.182 929	.000 066 8843	.007 445	111.314 557	.008 983 5510	10.79	3.958 920	8.61	552
47	149.412 575	16644.400 896	.000 060 0803	.006 693	111.398 930	.008 976 7469	10.78	4.062 885	8.64	564
48	166.207 534	18527.947 733	.000 053 9725	.006 017	111.474 777	.008 970 6392	10.77	4.167 088	8.68	576
49	184.890 358	20623.217 665	.000 048 4890	.005 409	111.542 960	.008 965 1557	10.76	4.271 512	8.72	588
50	205.673 254	22954.009 764	.000 043 5654	.004 862	111.604 253	.008 960 2320	10.76	4.376 139	8.75	600

Amount Of 1	Amount Of 1 Per Period	Sinking Fund Payment	Present Worth Of 1	Present Worth of 1 Per Period	Periodic Payment To Amortize 1	Constant Annual Percent	Total Interest	Annual Add On Rate
What a single $ 1 deposit grows to in the future. The deposit is made at the beginning of the first period.	What a series of $ 1 deposits grow to in the future. A deposit is made at the end of each period.	The amount to be deposited at the end of each period that grows to $ 1 in the future.	What $ 1 to be paid in the future is worth today. Value today of a single $ 1 payment tomorrow.	What $ 1 to be paid at the end of each period is worth today. Value today of a series of $ 1 payments tomorrow.	The mortgage payment to amortize a loan of $ 1. An annuity certain, payable at the end of each period, worth $ 1 today.	The annual payment, including interest and principal, to amortize completely a loan of $ 100.	The total interest paid over the term on a loan of $1. The loan is amortized by regular periodic payments.	The average annual interest rate on a loan that is completely amortized by regular periodic payments.

$$S = (1+i)^n \qquad S\overline{n]} = \frac{(1+i)^n - 1}{i} \qquad \frac{1}{S\overline{n]}} = \frac{i}{(1+i)^n - 1} \qquad V^n = \frac{1}{(1+i)^n} \qquad A\overline{n]} = \frac{1-V^n}{i} \qquad \frac{1}{A\overline{n]}} = \frac{i}{1-V^n}$$

YEAR									PERIODS
	1.008 958	1.000 000	1.000 000 0000	.991 121	.991 121	1.008 958 3333	1210.75	.008 958	10.75	1
	1.017 997	2.008 958	.497 770 4034	.982 321	1.973 442	.506 728 7367	608.08	.013 457	8.07	2
	1.027 116	3.026 955	.330 364 9763	.973 599	2.947 042	.339 323 3096	407.19	.017 970	7.19	3
	1.036 318	4.054 072	.246 665 5914	.964 955	3.911 997	.255 623 9248	306.75	.022 496	6.75	4
	1.045 601	5.090 389	.196 448 6233	.956 387	4.868 384	.205 406 9567	246.49	.027 035	6.49	5
	1.054 968	6.135 991	.162 972 8634	.947 896	5.816 280	.171 931 1968	206.32	.031 587	6.32	6
	1.064 419	7.190 959	.139 063 5081	.939 480	6.755 760	.148 021 8414	177.63	.036 153	6.20	7
	1.073 954	8.255 378	.121 133 1554	.931 138	7.686 898	.130 091 4887	156.11	.040 732	6.11	8
	1.083 575	9.329 333	.107 188 8042	.922 871	8.609 769	.116 147 1376	139.38	.045 324	6.04	9
	1.093 282	10.412 908	.096 034 6541	.914 677	9.524 446	.104 992 9874	126.00	.049 930	5.99	10
	1.103 076	11.506 190	.086 909 7407	.906 556	10.431 001	.095 868 0741	115.05	.054 549	5.95	11
	1.112 958	12.609 266	.079 306 7549	.898 506	11.329 508	.088 265 0882	105.92	.059 181	5.92	12
1	1.112 958	12.609 266	.079 306 7549	.898 506	11.329 508	.088 265 0882	105.92	.059 181	5.92	12
2	1.238 676	26.642 850	.037 533 5215	.807 314	21.509 144	.046 491 8548	55.80	.115 805	5.79	24
3	1.378 594	42.261 640	.023 662 1199	.725 377	30.655 613	.032 620 4532	39.15	.174 336	5.81	36
4	1.534 317	59.644 698	.016 765 9497	.651 756	38.873 775	.025 724 2831	30.87	.234 766	5.87	48
5	1.707 630	78.991 310	.012 659 6203	.585 607	46.257 847	.021 617 9537	25.95	.297 077	5.94	60
6	1.900 521	100.523 278	.009 947 9446	.526 171	52.892 484	.018 906 2779	22.69	.361 252	6.02	72
7	2.115 200	124.487 454	.008 032 9380	.472 769	58.853 748	.016 991 2713	20.39	.427 267	6.10	84
8	2.354 129	151.158 576	.006 615 5691	.424 786	64.209 982	.015 573 9024	18.69	.495 095	6.19	96
9	2.620 047	180.842 414	.005 529 6762	.381 673	69.022 594	.014 488 0096	17.39	.564 705	6.27	108
10	2.916 002	213.879 280	.004 675 5347	.342 935	73.346 757	.013 633 8680	16.37	.636 064	6.36	120
11	3.245 388	250.647 925	.003 989 6600	.308 130	77.232 045	.012 947 9933	15.54	.709 135	6.45	132
12	3.611 980	291.569 882	.003 429 7095	.276 856	80.723 001	.012 388 0428	14.87	.783 878	6.53	144
13	4.019 982	337.114 303	.002 966 3529	.248 757	83.859 649	.011 924 6863	14.31	.860 251	6.62	156
14	4.474 072	387.803 331	.002 578 6266	.223 510	86.677 947	.011 536 9600	13.85	.938 209	6.70	168
15	4.979 454	444.218 090	.002 251 1465	.200 825	89.210 206	.011 209 4798	13.46	1.017 706	6.78	180
16	5.541 923	507.005 349	.001 972 3658	.180 443	91.485 457	.010 930 6991	13.12	1.098 694	6.87	192
17	6.167 928	576.884 931	.001 733 4479	.162 129	93.529 785	.010 691 7813	12.84	1.181 123	6.95	204
18	6.864 644	654.657 972	.001 527 5152	.145 674	95.366 626	.010 485 8485	12.59	1.264 943	7.03	216
19	7.640 061	741.216 102	.001 349 1342	.130 889	97.017 041	.010 307 4675	12.37	1.350 103	7.11	228
20	8.503 067	837.551 665	.001 193 9562	.117 605	98.499 949	.010 152 2895	12.19	1.436 549	7.18	240
21	9.463 557	944.769 102	.001 058 4597	.105 669	99.832 351	.010 016 7930	12.03	1.524 232	7.26	252
22	10.532 541	1064.097 607	.000 939 7634	.094 944	101.029 524	.009 898 0967	11.88	1.613 098	7.33	264
23	11.722 276	1196.905 224	.000 835 4880	.085 308	102.105 191	.009 793 8214	11.76	1.703 095	7.40	276
24	13.046 401	1344.714 524	.000 743 6523	.076 649	103.071 685	.009 701 9856	11.65	1.794 172	7.48	288
25	14.520 096	1509.220 069	.000 662 5939	.068 870	103.940 086	.009 620 9272	11.55	1.886 278	7.55	300
26	16.160 258	1692.307 834	.000 590 9090	.061 880	104.720 350	.009 549 2424	11.46	1.979 364	7.61	312
27	17.985 688	1896.076 828	.000 527 4048	.055 600	105.421 422	.009 485 7381	11.39	2.073 379	7.68	324
28	20.017 316	2122.863 162	.000 471 0619	.049 957	106.051 340	.009 429 3953	11.32	2.168 277	7.74	336
29	22.278 432	2375.266 830	.000 421 0053	.044 886	106.617 325	.009 379 3387	11.26	2.264 010	7.81	348
30	24.794 959	2656.181 515	.000 376 4803	.040 331	107.125 867	.009 334 8136	11.21	2.360 533	7.87	360
31	27.595 749	2968.827 763	.000 336 8333	.036 237	107.582 795	.009 295 1666	11.16	2.457 802	7.93	372
32	30.712 910	3316.789 910	.000 301 4963	.032 560	107.993 347	.009 259 8297	11.12	2.555 775	7.99	384
33	34.182 179	3704.057 170	.000 269 9742	.029 255	108.362 231	.009 228 3076	11.08	2.654 410	8.04	396
34	38.043 330	4135.069 369	.000 241 8339	.026 286	108.693 676	.009 200 1672	11.05	2.753 668	8.10	408
35	42.340 629	4614.767 848	.000 216 6956	.023 618	108.991 482	.009 175 0290	11.02	2.853 512	8.15	420
36	47.123 342	5148.652 114	.000 194 2256	.021 221	109.259 062	.009 152 5589	10.99	2.953 905	8.21	432
37	52.446 301	5742.842 886	.000 174 1298	.019 067	109.499 484	.009 132 4631	10.96	3.054 814	8.26	444
38	58.370 531	6404.152 265	.000 156 1487	.017 132	109.715 505	.009 114 4820	10.94	3.156 204	8.31	456
39	64.963 950	7140.161 837	.000 140 0528	.015 393	109.909 602	.009 098 3862	10.92	3.258 045	8.35	468
40	72.302 148	7959.309 586	.000 125 6390	.013 831	110.083 998	.009 083 9724	10.91	3.360 307	8.40	480
41	80.469 255	8870.986 637	.000 112 7270	.012 427	110.240 695	.009 071 0604	10.89	3.462 962	8.45	492
42	89.558 902	9885.644 914	.000 101 1568	.011 166	110.381 488	.009 059 4901	10.88	3.565 983	8.49	504
43	99.675 298	11014.916 972	.000 090 7860	.010 033	110.507 992	.009 049 1193	10.86	3.669 346	8.53	516
44	110.934 421	12271.749 357	.000 081 4880	.009 014	110.621 656	.009 039 8213	10.85	3.773 026	8.58	528
45	123.465 353	13670.551 029	.000 073 1499	.008 099	110.723 784	.009 031 4833	10.84	3.877 001	8.62	540
46	137.411 754	15227.358 556	.000 065 6713	.007 277	110.815 546	.009 024 0046	10.83	3.981 251	8.65	552
47	152.933 512	16960.019 965	.000 058 9622	.006 539	110.897 996	.009 017 2955	10.83	4.085 755	8.69	564
48	170.208 578	18888.399 362	.000 052 9425	.005 875	110.972 077	.009 011 2759	10.82	4.190 495	8.73	576
49	189.435 000	21034.604 662	.000 047 5407	.005 279	111.038 639	.009 005 8740	10.81	4.295 454	8.77	588
50	210.833 201	23423.241 044	.000 042 6926	.004 743	111.098 446	.009 001 0260	10.81	4.400 616	8.80	600

MONTHLY COMPOUND INTEREST AND ANNUITY

Amount Of 1	Amount Of 1 Per Period	Sinking Fund Payment	Present Worth Of 1	Present Worth of 1 Per Period	Periodic Payment To Amortize 1	Constant Annual Percent	Total Interest	Annual Add On Rate
What a single $ 1 deposit grows to in the future. The deposit is made at the beginning of the first period.	What a series of $ 1 deposits grow to in the future. A deposit is made at the end of each period.	The amount to be deposited at the end of each period that grows to $ 1 in the future.	What $ 1 to be paid in the future is worth today. Value today of a single $ 1 payment tomorrow.	What $ 1 to be paid at the end of each period is worth today. Value today of a series of $ 1 payments tomorrow.	The mortgage payment to amortize a loan of $ 1. An annuity certain, payable at the end of each period, worth $ 1 today.	The annual payment, including interest and principal, to amortize completely a loan of $ 100.	The total interest paid over the term of a loan of $1. The loan is amortized by regular periodic payments.	The average annual interest rate on a loan that is completely amortized by regular periodic payments.
$S = (1+i)^n$	$S\overline{n}| = \dfrac{(1+i)^n - 1}{i}$	$\dfrac{1}{S\overline{n}|} = \dfrac{i}{(1+i)^n - 1}$	$V^n = \dfrac{1}{(1+i)^n}$	$A\overline{n}| = \dfrac{1-V^n}{i}$	$\dfrac{1}{A\overline{n}|} = \dfrac{i}{1-V^n}$			

YEAR									PERIODS
	1.009 000	1.000 000	1.000 000 0000	.991 080	.991 080	1.009 000 0000	1210.80	.009 000	10.80	1
	1.018 081	2.009 000	.497 760 0796	.982 240	1.973 320	.506 760 0796	608.12	.013 520	8.11	2
	1.027 244	3.027 081	.330 351 2526	.973 479	2.946 799	.339 351 2526	407.23	.018 054	7.22	3
	1.036 489	4.054 325	.246 650 1987	.964 796	3.911 595	.255 650 1987	306.79	.022 601	6.78	4
	1.045 817	5.090 814	.196 432 2539	.956 190	4.867 785	.205 432 2539	246.52	.027 161	6.52	5
	1.055 230	6.136 631	.162 955 8636	.947 661	5.815 446	.171 955 8636	206.35	.031 735	6.35	6
	1.064 727	7.191 861	.139 046 0756	.939 208	6.754 654	.148 046 0756	177.66	.036 323	6.23	7
	1.074 309	8.256 587	.121 115 4139	.930 831	7.685 485	.130 115 4139	156.14	.040 923	6.14	8
	1.083 978	9.330 897	.107 170 8362	.922 528	8.608 012	.116 170 8362	139.41	.045 538	6.07	9
	1.093 734	10.414 875	.096 016 5171	.914 299	9.522 312	.105 016 5171	126.02	.050 165	6.02	10
	1.103 577	11.508 609	.086 891 4768	.906 144	10.428 456	.095 891 4768	115.07	.054 806	5.98	11
	1.113 510	12.612 186	.079 288 3955	.898 061	11.326 517	.088 288 3955	105.95	.059 461	5.95	12
1	1.113 510	12.612 186	.079 288 3955	.898 061	11.326 517	.088 288 3955	105.95	.059 461	5.95	12
2	1.239 904	26.655 977	.037 515 0379	.806 514	21.498 424	.046 515 0379	55.82	.116 361	5.82	24
3	1.380 645	42.293 875	.023 644 0857	.724 299	30.633 420	.032 644 0857	39.18	.175 187	5.84	36
4	1.537 361	59.706 825	.016 748 5041	.650 465	38.837 208	.025 748 5041	30.90	.235 928	5.90	48
5	1.711 867	79.096 313	.012 642 8143	.584 158	46.204 712	.021 642 8143	25.98	.298 569	5.97	60
6	1.906 180	100.686 696	.009 931 7987	.524 609	52.821 183	.018 931 7987	22.72	.363 090	6.05	72
7	2.122 550	124.727 796	.008 017 4590	.471 131	58.763 179	.017 017 4590	20.43	.429 467	6.14	84
8	2.363 480	151.497 794	.006 600 7562	.423 105	64.099 457	.015 600 7562	18.73	.497 673	6.22	96
9	2.631 758	181.306 446	.005 515 5237	.379 974	68.891 762	.014 515 5237	17.42	.567 677	6.31	108
10	2.930 488	214.498 667	.004 662 0336	.341 240	73.195 545	.013 662 0336	16.40	.639 444	6.39	120
11	3.263 127	251.458 528	.003 976 7989	.306 455	77.060 607	.012 976 7989	15.58	.712 937	6.48	132
12	3.633 523	292.613 689	.003 417 4751	.275 215	80.531 669	.012 417 4751	14.91	.788 116	6.57	144
13	4.045 963	338.440 360	.002 954 7303	.247 160	83.648 896	.011 954 7303	14.35	.864 938	6.65	156
14	4.505 219	389.468 802	.002 567 5998	.221 965	86.448 358	.011 567 5998	13.89	.943 357	6.74	168
15	5.016 605	446.289 465	.002 240 6982	.199 338	88.962 445	.011 240 6982	13.49	1.023 326	6.82	180
16	5.586 038	509.559 823	.001 962 4781	.179 018	91.220 251	.010 962 4781	13.16	1.104 796	6.90	192
17	6.220 108	580.011 979	.001 724 1023	.160 769	93.247 898	.010 724 1023	12.87	1.187 717	6.99	204
18	6.926 150	658.461 136	.001 518 6925	.144 380	95.068 850	.010 518 6925	12.63	1.272 038	7.07	216
19	7.712 335	745.815 032	.001 340 8150	.129 662	96.704 176	.010 340 8150	12.41	1.357 706	7.15	228
20	8.587 760	843.084 440	.001 186 1208	.116 445	98.172 800	.010 186 1208	12.23	1.444 669	7.22	240
21	9.562 554	951.394 867	.001 051 0883	.104 575	99.491 714	.010 051 0883	12.07	1.532 874	7.30	252
22	10.647 996	1071.999 575	.000 932 8362	.093 914	100.676 180	.009 932 8362	11.92	1.622 269	7.37	264
23	11.856 647	1206.294 085	.000 828 9852	.084 341	101.739 902	.009 828 9852	11.80	1.712 800	7.45	276
24	13.202 491	1355.832 320	.000 737 5543	.075 743	102.695 191	.009 737 5543	11.69	1.804 416	7.52	288
25	14.701 101	1522.344 592	.000 656 8815	.068 022	103.553 098	.009 656 8815	11.59	1.897 064	7.59	300
26	16.369 819	1707.757 618	.000 585 5632	.061 088	104.323 552	.009 585 5632	11.51	1.990 696	7.66	312
27	18.227 951	1914.216 817	.000 522 4069	.054 861	105.015 467	.009 522 4069	11.43	2.085 260	7.72	324
28	20.297 000	2144.111 131	.000 466 3937	.049 268	105.636 848	.009 466 3937	11.36	2.180 708	7.79	336
29	22.600 906	2400.100 675	.000 416 6492	.044 246	106.194 887	.009 416 6492	11.30	2.276 994	7.85	348
30	25.166 328	2685.147 509	.000 372 4190	.039 736	106.696 041	.009 372 4190	11.25	2.374 071	7.91	360
31	28.022 949	3002.549 916	.000 333 0502	.035 685	107.146 107	.009 333 0502	11.20	2.471 895	7.97	372
32	31.203 825	3355.980 567	.000 297 9755	.032 047	107.550 294	.009 297 9755	11.16	2.570 423	8.03	384
33	34.745 761	3749.529 016	.000 266 7002	.028 780	107.913 279	.009 266 7002	11.13	2.669 613	8.09	396
34	38.689 741	4187.749 022	.000 238 7918	.025 847	108.239 262	.009 238 7918	11.09	2.769 427	8.15	408
35	43.081 401	4675.711 238	.000 213 8712	.023 212	108.532 014	.009 213 8712	11.06	2.869 826	8.20	420
36	47.971 557	5219.061 887	.000 191 6053	.020 846	108.794 924	.009 191 6053	11.03	2.970 773	8.25	432
37	53.416 793	5824.088 092	.000 171 7007	.018 721	109.031 033	.009 171 7007	11.01	3.072 235	8.30	444
38	59.480 116	6497.790 624	.000 153 8985	.016 812	109.243 073	.009 153 8985	10.99	3.174 178	8.35	456
39	66.231 684	7247.964 912	.000 137 9698	.015 099	109.433 498	.009 137 9698	10.97	3.276 570	8.40	468
40	73.749 621	8083.291 239	.000 123 7120	.013 559	109.604 512	.009 123 7120	10.95	3.379 382	8.45	480
41	82.120 917	9013.435 187	.000 110 9455	.012 177	109.758 093	.009 110 9455	10.94	3.482 585	8.49	492
42	91.442 435	10049.159 471	.000 099 5108	.010 936	109.896 018	.009 099 5108	10.92	3.586 153	8.54	504
43	101.822 036	11202.448 482	.000 089 2662	.009 821	110.019 883	.009 089 2662	10.91	3.690 061	8.58	516
44	113.379 823	12486.646 954	.000 080 0856	.008 820	110.131 121	.009 080 0856	10.90	3.794 285	8.62	528
45	126.249 529	13916.614 377	.000 071 8566	.007 921	110.231 020	.009 071 8566	10.89	3.898 803	8.66	540
46	140.580 072	15508.896 938	.000 064 4791	.007 113	110.320 735	.009 064 4791	10.88	4.003 592	8.70	552
47	156.537 271	17281.918 974	.000 057 8639	.006 388	110.401 305	.009 057 8639	10.87	4.108 635	8.74	564
48	174.305 765	19256.196 166	.000 051 9313	.005 737	110.473 662	.009 051 9313	10.87	4.213 912	8.78	576
49	194.091 156	21454.572 920	.000 046 6101	.005 152	110.538 642	.009 046 6101	10.86	4.319 407	8.82	588
50	216.122 380	23902.486 704	.000 041 8367	.004 627	110.596 999	.009 041 8367	10.86	4.425 102	8.85	600

Amount Of 1	Amount Of 1 Per Period	Sinking Fund Payment	Present Worth Of 1	Present Worth of 1 Per Period	Periodic Payment To Amortize 1	Constant Annual Percent	Total Interest	Annual Add On Rate
What a single $ 1 deposit grows to in the future. The deposit is made at the beginning of the first period.	What a series of $ 1 deposits grow to in the future. A deposit is made at the end of each period.	The amount to be deposited at the end of each period that grows to $ 1 in the future.	What $ 1 to be paid in the future is worth today. Value today of a single $ 1 payment tomorrow.	What $ 1 to be paid at the end of each period is worth today. Value today of a series of $ 1 payments tomorrow.	The mortgage payment to amortize a loan of $ 1. An annuity certain, payable at the end of each period, worth $ 1 today.	The annual payment, including interest and principal, to amortize completely a loan of $ 100.	The total interest paid over the term on a loan of $1. The loan is amortized by regular periodic payments.	The average annual interest rate on a loan that is completely amortized by regular periodic payments.

$$S = (1+i)^n \qquad S\overline{n}| = \frac{(1+i)^n - 1}{i} \qquad \frac{1}{S\overline{n}|} = \frac{i}{(1+i)^n - 1} \qquad V^n = \frac{1}{(1+i)^n} \qquad A\overline{n}| = \frac{1-V^n}{i} \qquad \frac{1}{A\overline{n}|} = \frac{i}{1-V^n}$$

YEAR									PERIODS
	1.009 042	1.000 000	1.000 000 0000	.991 039	.991 039	1.009 041 6667	1210.85	.009 042	10.85	1
	1.018 165	2.009 042	.497 749 7563	.982 159	1.973 198	.506 791 4230	608.15	.013 583	8.15	2
	1.027 371	3.027 207	.330 337 5296	.973 358	2.946 557	.339 379 1963	407.26	.018 138	7.26	3
	1.036 660	4.054 578	.246 634 8070	.964 636	3.911 193	.255 676 4737	306.82	.022 706	6.81	4
	1.046 033	5.091 238	.196 415 8859	.955 993	4.867 185	.205 457 5526	246.55	.027 288	6.55	5
	1.055 491	6.137 271	.162 938 8654	.947 426	5.814 612	.171 980 5321	206.38	.031 883	6.38	6
	1.065 035	7.192 762	.139 028 6451	.938 937	6.753 548	.148 070 3117	177.69	.036 492	6.26	7
	1.074 664	8.257 797	.121 097 6746	.930 523	7.684 071	.130 139 3413	156.17	.041 115	6.17	8
	1.084 381	9.332 461	.107 152 8706	.922 185	8.606 257	.116 194 5373	139.44	.045 751	6.10	9
	1.094 186	10.416 842	.095 998 3829	.913 922	9.520 178	.105 040 0496	126.05	.050 400	6.05	10
	1.104 079	11.511 028	.086 873 2160	.905 732	10.425 911	.095 914 8827	115.10	.055 064	6.01	11
	1.114 062	12.615 107	.079 270 0395	.897 616	11.323 527	.088 311 7062	105.98	.059 740	5.97	12
1	1.114 062	12.615 107	.079 270 0395	.897 616	11.323 527	.088 311 7062	105.98	.059 740	5.97	12
2	1.241 133	26.669 112	.037 496 5611	.805 715	21.487 711	.046 538 2277	55.85	.116 917	5.85	24
3	1.382 699	42.326 140	.023 626 0616	.723 223	30.611 250	.032 667 7283	39.21	.176 038	5.87	36
4	1.540 412	59.769 034	.016 731 0719	.649 177	38.800 688	.025 772 7385	30.93	.237 091	5.93	48
5	1.716 113	79.201 491	.012 626 0249	.582 712	46.151 663	.021 667 6915	26.01	.300 061	6.00	60
6	1.911 856	100.850 446	.009 915 6726	.523 052	52.750 019	.018 957 3392	22.75	.364 928	6.08	72
7	2.129 925	124.968 715	.008 002 0028	.469 500	58.672 811	.017 043 6694	20.46	.431 668	6.17	84
8	2.372 868	151.837 951	.006 585 9687	.421 431	63.989 207	.015 627 6354	18.76	.500 253	6.25	96
9	2.643 521	181.771 936	.005 501 3993	.378 283	68.761 292	.014 543 0660	17.46	.570 651	6.34	108
10	2.945 045	215.120 239	.004 648 5631	.339 553	73.044 793	.013 690 2298	16.43	.642 828	6.43	120
11	3.280 962	252.272 301	.003 963 9707	.304 789	76.889 734	.013 005 6373	15.61	.716 744	6.52	132
12	3.655 194	293.661 988	.003 405 2756	.273 583	80.341 017	.012 446 9423	14.94	.792 360	6.60	144
13	4.072 111	339.772 647	.002 943 1445	.245 573	83.438 945	.011 984 8112	14.39	.869 631	6.69	156
14	4.536 582	391.142 762	.002 556 6113	.220 430	86.219 696	.011 598 2780	13.92	.948 511	6.78	168
15	5.054 032	448.372 233	.002 230 2898	.197 862	88.715 744	.011 271 9564	13.53	1.028 952	6.86	180
16	5.630 503	512.129 390	.001 952 6315	.177 604	90.956 238	.010 994 2982	13.20	1.110 905	6.94	192
17	6.272 727	583.158 788	.001 714 7988	.159 420	92.967 342	.010 756 4655	12.91	1.194 319	7.03	204
18	6.988 205	662.289 913	.001 509 9128	.143 098	94.772 541	.010 551 5794	12.67	1.279 141	7.11	216
19	7.785 290	750.446 859	.001 332 5394	.128 447	96.392 919	.010 374 2061	12.45	1.365 319	7.19	228
20	8.673 293	848.659 127	.001 178 3294	.115 296	97.847 396	.010 219 9961	12.27	1.452 799	7.26	240
21	9.662 583	958.073 642	.001 043 7611	.103 492	99.152 958	.010 085 4278	12.11	1.541 528	7.34	252
22	10.764 712	1079.968 151	.000 925 9532	.092 896	100.324 853	.009 967 6199	11.97	1.631 452	7.42	264
23	11.992 552	1215.766 141	.000 822 5266	.083 385	101.376 765	.009 864 1933	11.84	1.722 517	7.49	276
24	13.360 442	1367.053 466	.000 731 5003	.074 848	102.320 978	.009 773 1670	11.73	1.814 672	7.56	288
25	14.884 355	1535.596 863	.000 651 2126	.067 185	103.168 519	.009 692 8793	11.64	1.907 864	7.63	300
26	16.582 088	1723.364 588	.000 580 2603	.060 306	103.929 286	.009 621 9269	11.55	2.002 041	7.70	312
27	18.473 467	1932.549 398	.000 517 4512	.054 132	104.612 163	.009 559 1179	11.48	2.097 154	7.77	324
28	20.580 581	2165.594 159	.000 461 7670	.048 589	105.225 125	.009 503 4337	11.41	2.193 154	7.83	336
29	22.928 034	2425.220 377	.000 412 3337	.043 615	105.775 330	.009 454 0003	11.35	2.289 992	7.90	348
30	25.543 242	2714.459 974	.000 368 3974	.039 149	106.269 202	.009 410 0641	11.30	2.387 623	7.96	360
31	28.456 745	3036.690 698	.000 329 3058	.035 141	106.712 510	.009 370 9725	11.25	2.486 002	8.02	372
32	31.702 567	3395.675 571	.000 294 4922	.031 543	107.110 431	.009 336 1589	11.21	2.585 085	8.08	384
33	35.318 612	3795.606 830	.000 263 4625	.028 314	107.467 611	.009 305 1291	11.17	2.684 831	8.14	396
34	39.347 109	4241.154 882	.000 235 7848	.025 415	107.788 222	.009 277 4515	11.14	2.785 200	8.19	408
35	43.835 102	4737.522 854	.000 211 0808	.022 813	108.076 007	.009 252 7474	11.11	2.886 154	8.25	420
36	48.835 004	5290.507 346	.000 189 0178	.020 477	108.334 328	.009 230 6845	11.08	2.987 656	8.30	432
37	54.405 202	5906.566 127	.000 169 3031	.018 381	108.566 201	.009 210 9698	11.06	3.089 671	8.35	444
38	60.610 746	6592.893 552	.000 151 6785	.016 499	108.774 335	.009 193 3451	11.04	3.192 165	8.40	456
39	67.524 104	7357.504 573	.000 135 9156	.014 810	108.961 158	.009 177 5823	11.02	3.295 109	8.45	468
40	75.226 010	8209.328 343	.000 121 8126	.013 293	109.128 854	.009 163 4793	11.00	3.398 470	8.50	480
41	83.806 409	9158.312 485	.000 109 1904	.011 932	109.279 381	.009 150 8571	10.99	3.502 222	8.54	492
42	93.365 501	10215.539 267	.000 097 8901	.010 711	109.414 496	.009 139 5568	10.97	3.606 337	8.59	504
43	104.014 918	11393.355 015	.000 087 7705	.009 614	109.535 778	.009 129 4371	10.96	3.710 790	8.63	516
44	115.879 025	12705.514 299	.000 078 7060	.008 630	109.644 643	.009 120 3727	10.95	3.815 557	8.67	528
45	129.096 371	14167.340 557	.000 070 5849	.007 746	109.742 361	.009 112 2515	10.94	3.920 616	8.71	540
46	143.821 308	15795.905 040	.000 063 3075	.006 953	109.830 075	.009 104 9742	10.93	4.025 946	8.75	552
47	160.225 795	17610.226 175	.000 056 7852	.006 241	109.908 808	.009 098 4519	10.92	4.131 527	8.79	564
48	178.501 404	19631.461 663	.000 050 9386	.005 602	109.979 481	.009 092 6052	10.92	4.237 341	8.83	576
49	198.861 558	21883.305 903	.000 045 6969	.005 029	110.042 917	.009 087 3636	10.91	4.343 370	8.86	588
50	221.544 023	24391.965 655	.000 040 9971	.004 514	110.099 859	.009 082 6638	10.90	4.449 598	8.90	600

Amount Of 1	Amount Of 1 Per Period	Sinking Fund Payment	Present Worth Of 1	Present Worth of 1 Per Period	Periodic Payment To Amortize 1	Constant Annual Percent	Total Interest	Annual Add On Rate
What a single $ 1 deposit grows to in the future. The deposit is made at the beginning of the first period.	What a series of $ 1 deposits grow to in the future. A deposit is made at the end of each period.	The amount to be deposited at the end of each period that grows to $ 1 in the future.	What $ 1 to be paid in the future is worth today. Value today of a single $ 1 payment tomorrow.	What $ 1 to be paid at the end of each period is worth today. Value today of a series of $ 1 payments tomorrow.	The mortgage payment to amortize a loan of $ 1. An annuity certain, payable at the end of each period, worth $ 1 today.	The annual payment, including interest and principal, to amortize completely a loan of $ 100.	The total interest paid over the term on a loan of $1. The loan is amortized by regular periodic payments.	The average annual interest rate on a loan that is completely amortized by regular periodic payments.
$S = (1+i)^n$	$S\overline{n}| = \dfrac{(1+i)^n - 1}{i}$	$\dfrac{1}{S\overline{n}|} = \dfrac{i}{(1+i)^n - 1}$	$V^n = \dfrac{1}{(1+i)^n}$	$A\overline{n}| = \dfrac{1 - V^n}{i}$	$\dfrac{1}{A\overline{n}|} = \dfrac{i}{1 - V^n}$			

YEAR									PERIODS
	1.009 063	1.000 000	1.000 000 0000	.991 019	.991 019	1.009 062 5000	1210.88	.009 062	10.87	1
	1.018 207	2.009 062	.497 744 5948	.982 118	1.973 137	.506 807 0948	608.17	.013 614	8.17	2
	1.027 435	3.027 270	.330 330 6684	.973 298	2.946 435	.339 393 1684	407.28	.018 180	7.27	3
	1.036 746	4.054 704	.246 627 1116	.964 557	3.910 992	.255 689 6116	306.83	.022 758	6.83	4
	1.046 141	5.091 450	.196 407 7024	.955 894	4.866 886	.205 470 2024	246.57	.027 351	6.56	5
	1.055 622	6.137 591	.162 930 3670	.947 309	5.814 195	.171 992 8670	206.40	.031 957	6.39	6
	1.065 188	7.193 213	.139 019 9305	.938 801	6.752 996	.148 082 4305	177.70	.036 577	6.27	7
	1.074 842	8.258 402	.121 088 8059	.930 370	7.683 365	.130 151 3059	156.19	.041 210	6.18	8
	1.084 583	9.333 243	.107 143 8888	.922 014	8.605 379	.116 206 3888	139.45	.045 857	6.11	9
	1.094 412	10.417 826	.095 989 3169	.913 733	9.519 112	.105 051 8169	126.07	.050 518	6.06	10
	1.104 330	11.512 238	.086 864 0868	.905 527	10.424 639	.095 926 5868	115.12	.055 192	6.02	11
	1.114 338	12.616 567	.079 260 8628	.897 394	11.322 033	.088 323 3628	105.99	.059 880	5.99	12
1	1.114 338	12.616 567	.079 260 8628	.897 394	11.322 033	.088 323 3628	105.99	.059 880	5.99	12
2	1.241 748	26.675 683	.037 487 3252	.805 316	21.482 358	.046 549 8252	55.86	.117 196	5.86	24
3	1.383 727	42.342 285	.023 617 0534	.722 686	30.600 173	.032 679 5534	39.22	.176 464	5.88	36
4	1.541 939	59.800 169	.016 722 3608	.648 534	38.782 447	.025 784 8608	30.95	.237 673	5.94	48
5	1.718 241	79.254 146	.012 617 6364	.581 991	46.125 171	.021 680 1364	26.02	.300 808	6.02	60
6	1.914 700	100.932 445	.009 907 6169	.522 275	52.714 488	.018 970 1169	22.77	.365 848	6.10	72
7	2.133 623	125.089 390	.007 994 2831	.468 686	58.627 702	.017 056 7831	20.47	.432 770	6.18	84
8	2.377 576	152.008 383	.006 578 5845	.420 596	63.934 185	.015 641 0845	18.77	.501 544	6.27	96
9	2.649 422	182.005 230	.005 494 3476	.377 441	68.696 192	.014 556 8476	17.47	.572 140	6.36	108
10	2.952 351	215.431 846	.004 641 8393	.338 713	72.969 589	.013 704 3393	16.45	.644 521	6.45	120
11	3.289 916	252.680 382	.003 957 5688	.303 959	76.804 510	.013 020 0688	15.63	.718 649	6.53	132
12	3.666 077	294.187 827	.003 399 1889	.272 771	80.245 945	.012 461 6889	14.96	.794 483	6.62	144
13	4.085 248	340.441 137	.002 937 3654	.244 783	83.334 268	.011 999 8654	14.40	.871 979	6.71	156
14	4.552 345	391.982 940	.002 551 1314	.219 667	86.105 712	.011 613 6314	13.94	.951 090	6.79	168
15	5.072 850	449.417 911	.002 225 1005	.197 128	88.592 789	.011 287 6005	13.55	1.031 768	6.88	180
16	5.652 867	513.419 862	.001 947 7236	.176 901	90.824 677	.011 010 2236	13.22	1.113 963	6.96	192
17	6.299 203	584.739 645	.001 710 1628	.158 750	92.827 560	.010 772 6628	12.93	1.197 623	7.04	204
18	7.019 439	664.213 963	.001 505 5390	.142 462	94.624 935	.010 568 0390	12.69	1.282 696	7.13	216
19	7.822 025	752.775 187	.001 328 4179	.127 844	96.237 889	.010 390 9179	12.47	1.369 129	7.21	228
20	8.716 377	851.462 293	.001 174 4501	.114 727	97.685 344	.010 236 9501	12.29	1.456 868	7.28	240
21	9.712 987	961.433 049	.001 040 1140	.102 955	98.984 282	.010 102 6140	12.13	1.545 859	7.36	252
22	10.823 547	1083.977 602	.000 922 5283	.092 391	100.149 942	.009 985 0283	11.99	1.636 047	7.44	264
23	12.061 086	1220.533 610	.000 819 3138	.082 911	101.195 997	.009 881 8138	11.86	1.727 381	7.51	276
24	13.440 122	1372.703 110	.000 728 4896	.074 404	102.134 721	.009 790 9896	11.75	1.819 805	7.58	288
25	14.976 834	1542.271 311	.000 648 3943	.066 770	102.977 127	.009 710 8943	11.66	1.913 268	7.65	300
26	16.689 250	1731.227 541	.000 577 6248	.059 919	103.733 097	.009 640 1248	11.57	2.007 719	7.72	312
27	18.597 459	1941.788 579	.000 514 9891	.053 771	104.411 499	.009 577 4891	11.50	2.103 106	7.79	324
28	20.723 849	2176.424 670	.000 459 4692	.048 254	105.020 294	.009 521 9692	11.43	2.199 382	7.85	336
29	23.093 365	2437.888 498	.000 410 1910	.043 302	105.566 623	.009 472 6910	11.37	2.296 496	7.92	348
30	25.733 805	2729.247 483	.000 366 4014	.038 859	106.056 895	.009 428 9014	11.32	2.394 404	7.98	360
31	28.676 148	3053.919 766	.000 327 4480	.034 872	106.496 862	.009 389 9480	11.27	2.493 061	8.04	372
32	31.954 911	3415.714 313	.000 292 7645	.031 294	106.891 686	.009 355 2645	11.23	2.592 422	8.10	384
33	35.608 560	3818.875 594	.000 261 8572	.028 083	107.245 999	.009 324 3572	11.19	2.692 445	8.16	396
34	39.679 959	4268.133 384	.000 234 2945	.025 202	107.563 957	.009 296 7945	11.16	2.793 092	8.21	408
35	44.216 872	4768.758 250	.000 209 6982	.022 616	107.849 291	.009 272 1982	11.13	2.894 323	8.27	420
36	49.272 524	5326.623 382	.000 187 7362	.020 295	108.105 348	.009 250 2362	11.11	2.996 102	8.32	432
37	54.906 229	5948.273 496	.000 168 1160	.018 213	108.335 132	.009 230 6160	11.08	3.098 394	8.37	444
38	61.184 077	6641.001 618	.000 150 5797	.016 344	108.541 338	.009 213 0797	11.06	3.201 164	8.42	456
39	68.179 720	7412.934 638	.000 134 8993	.014 667	108.726 387	.009 197 3993	11.04	3.304 383	8.47	468
40	75.975 228	8273.128 657	.000 120 8733	.013 162	108.892 449	.009 183 3733	11.03	3.408 019	8.52	480
41	84.662 057	9231.675 232	.000 108 3227	.011 812	109.041 471	.009 170 8227	11.01	3.512 045	8.57	492
42	94.342 117	10299.819 759	.000 097 0891	.010 600	109.175 203	.009 159 5891	11.00	3.616 433	8.61	504
43	105.128 972	11490.093 411	.000 087 0315	.009 512	109.295 214	.009 149 5315	10.98	3.721 158	8.65	516
44	117.149 170	12816.460 143	.000 078 0247	.008 536	109.402 910	.009 140 5247	10.97	3.826 197	8.70	528
45	130.543 730	14294.480 518	.000 069 9571	.007 660	109.499 557	.009 132 4571	10.96	3.931 527	8.74	540
46	145.469 792	15941.494 254	.000 062 7294	.006 874	109.586 286	.009 125 2294	10.96	4.037 127	8.78	552
47	162.102 464	17776.823 653	.000 056 2530	.006 169	109.664 117	.009 118 7530	10.95	4.142 977	8.81	564
48	180.636 878	19822.000 286	.000 050 4490	.005 536	109.733 962	.009 112 9490	10.94	4.249 059	8.85	576
49	201.290 472	22101.017 588	.000 045 2468	.004 968	109.796 641	.009 107 7468	10.93	4.355 355	8.89	588
50	224.305 549	24640.612 350	.000 040 5834	.004 458	109.852 888	.009 103 0834	10.93	4.461 850	8.92	600

Amount Of 1	Amount Of 1 Per Period	Sinking Fund Payment	Present Worth Of 1	Present Worth of 1 Per Period	Periodic Payment To Amortize 1	Constant Annual Percent	Total Interest	Annual Add On Rate
What a single $1 deposit grows to in the future. The deposit is made at the beginning of the first period.	What a series of $1 deposits grow to in the future. A deposit is made at the end of each period.	The amount to be deposited at the end of each period that grows to $1 in the future.	What $1 to be paid in the future is worth today. Value today of a single $1 payment tomorrow.	What $1 to be paid at the end of each period is worth today. Value today of a series of $1 payments tomorrow.	The mortgage payment to amortize a loan of $1. An annuity certain, payable at the end of each period, worth $1 today.	The annual payment, including interest and principal, to amortize completely a loan of $100.	The total interest paid over the term on a loan of $1. The loan is amortized by regular periodic payments.	The average annual interest rate on a loan that is completely amortized by regular periodic payments.
$S = (1+i)^n$	$S\overline{n}| = \dfrac{(1+i)^n - 1}{i}$	$\dfrac{1}{S\overline{n}|} = \dfrac{i}{(1+i)^n - 1}$	$V^n = \dfrac{1}{(1+i)^n}$	$A\overline{n}| = \dfrac{1 - V^n}{i}$	$\dfrac{1}{A\overline{n}|} = \dfrac{i}{1 - V^n}$			

YEAR   **PERIODS**

	Amount Of 1	Amount Of 1 Per Period	Sinking Fund Payment	Present Worth Of 1	Present Worth of 1 Per Period	Periodic Payment To Amortize 1	Constant Annual Percent	Total Interest	Annual Add On Rate	
	1.009 083	1.000 000	1.000 000 0000	.990 998	.990 998	1.009 083 3333	1210.90	.009 083	10.90	1
	1.018 249	2.009 083	.497 739 4334	.982 078	1.973 076	.506 822 7667	608.19	.013 646	8.19	2
	1.027 498	3.027 333	.330 323 8074	.973 238	2.946 314	.339 407 1407	407.29	.018 221	7.29	3
	1.036 831	4.054 831	.246 619 4164	.964 477	3.910 791	.255 702 7498	306.85	.022 811	6.84	4
	1.046 249	5.091 662	.196 399 5193	.955 795	4.866 586	.205 482 8526	246.58	.027 414	6.58	5
	1.055 753	6.137 911	.162 921 8689	.947 192	5.813 778	.172 005 2022	206.41	.032 031	6.41	6
	1.065 342	7.193 664	.139 011 2165	.938 665	6.752 443	.148 094 5498	177.72	.036 662	6.28	7
	1.075 019	8.259 007	.121 079 9376	.930 216	7.682 659	.130 163 2710	156.20	.041 306	6.20	8
	1.084 784	9.334 026	.107 134 9076	.921 842	8.604 501	.116 218 2410	139.47	.045 964	6.13	9
	1.094 638	10.418 810	.095 980 2516	.913 544	9.518 046	.105 063 5850	126.08	.050 636	6.08	10
	1.104 580	11.513 447	.086 854 9583	.905 321	10.423 367	.095 938 2917	115.13	.055 321	6.04	11
	1.114 614	12.618 028	.079 251 6869	.897 172	11.320 539	.088 335 0202	106.01	.060 020	6.00	12
1	1.114 614	12.618 028	.079 251 6869	.897 172	11.320 539	.088 335 0202	106.01	.060 020	6.00	12
2	1.242 364	26.682 255	.037 478 0911	.804 917	21.477 006	.046 561 4244	55.88	.117 474	5.87	24
3	1.384 756	42.358 437	.023 608 0478	.722 149	30.589 102	.032 691 3811	39.23	.176 890	5.90	36
4	1.543 468	59.831 324	.016 713 6531	.647 892	38.764 218	.025 796 9865	30.96	.238 255	5.96	48
5	1.720 371	79.306 845	.012 609 2521	.581 270	46.098 701	.021 692 5854	26.04	.301 555	6.03	60
6	1.917 549	101.014 528	.009 899 5661	.521 499	52.678 992	.018 982 8995	22.78	.366 769	6.11	72
7	2.137 326	125.210 210	.007 986 5691	.467 874	58.582 643	.017 069 9025	20.49	.433 872	6.20	84
8	2.382 293	152.179 050	.006 571 2067	.419 764	63.879 232	.015 654 5401	18.79	.502 836	6.29	96
9	2.655 337	182.238 891	.005 487 3029	.376 600	68.631 183	.014 570 6363	17.49	.573 629	6.37	108
10	2.959 675	215.744 002	.004 635 1231	.337 875	72.894 499	.013 718 4564	16.47	.646 215	6.46	120
11	3.298 894	253.089 260	.003 951 1752	.303 132	76.719 425	.013 034 5085	15.65	.720 555	6.55	132
12	3.676 993	294.714 798	.003 393 1109	.271 961	80.151 041	.012 476 4443	14.98	.796 608	6.64	144
13	4.098 427	341.111 195	.002 931 5954	.243 996	83.229 791	.012 014 9287	14.42	.874 329	6.73	156
14	4.568 163	392.825 258	.002 545 6612	.218 906	85.991 957	.011 628 9945	13.96	.953 671	6.81	168
15	5.091 737	450.466 463	.002 219 9211	.196 397	88.470 096	.011 303 2544	13.57	1.034 586	6.90	180
16	5.675 320	514.714 143	.001 942 8260	.176 202	90.693 411	.011 026 1593	13.24	1.117 023	6.98	192
17	6.325 790	586.325 491	.001 705 5373	.158 083	92.688 107	.010 788 8706	12.95	1.200 930	7.06	204
18	7.050 812	666.144 485	.001 501 1758	.141 828	94.477 692	.010 584 5092	12.71	1.286 254	7.15	216
19	7.858 932	755.111 833	.001 324 3072	.127 244	96.083 257	.010 407 6405	12.49	1.372 942	7.23	228
20	8.759 674	854.276 062	.001 170 5818	.114 159	97.523 725	.010 253 9151	12.31	1.460 940	7.30	240
21	9.763 653	964.805 877	.001 036 4779	.102 421	98.816 072	.010 119 8113	12.15	1.550 192	7.38	252
22	10.882 702	1088.003 928	.000 919 1143	.091 889	99.975 529	.010 002 4477	12.01	1.640 646	7.46	264
23	12.130 010	1225.322 170	.000 816 1119	.082 440	101.015 762	.009 899 4452	11.88	1.732 247	7.53	276
24	13.520 276	1378.378 972	.000 725 4899	.073 963	101.949 029	.009 808 8232	11.78	1.824 941	7.60	288
25	15.069 885	1548.978 188	.000 645 5869	.066 358	102.786 330	.009 728 9202	11.68	1.918 676	7.67	300
26	16.797 101	1739.130 421	.000 575 0000	.059 534	103.537 532	.009 658 3333	11.59	2.013 400	7.74	312
27	18.722 280	1951.076 715	.000 512 5375	.053 412	104.211 490	.009 595 8708	11.52	2.109 062	7.81	324
28	20.868 111	2187.314 969	.000 457 1815	.047 920	104.816 146	.009 540 5149	11.45	2.205 613	7.88	336
29	23.259 884	2450.629 376	.000 408 0584	.042 992	105.358 626	.009 491 3918	11.39	2.303 004	7.94	348
30	25.925 786	2744.123 236	.000 364 4151	.038 572	105.845 324	.009 447 7485	11.34	2.401 189	8.00	360
31	28.897 238	3071.255 529	.000 325 5997	.034 605	106.281 976	.009 408 9331	11.30	2.500 123	8.06	372
32	32.209 259	3435.881 683	.000 291 0461	.031 047	106.673 728	.009 374 3794	11.25	2.599 762	8.12	384
33	35.900 883	3842.299 008	.000 260 2608	.027 854	107.025 196	.009 343 5942	11.22	2.700 063	8.18	396
34	40.015 618	4295.297 349	.000 232 8128	.024 990	107.340 524	.009 316 1461	11.18	2.800 988	8.24	408
35	44.601 958	4800.215 530	.000 208 3240	.022 421	107.623 427	.009 291 6573	11.15	2.902 496	8.29	420
36	49.713 956	5363.004 279	.000 186 4627	.020 115	107.877 239	.009 269 7960	11.13	3.004 552	8.35	432
37	55.411 859	5990.296 360	.000 166 9366	.018 047	108.104 953	.009 250 2700	11.11	3.107 120	8.40	444
38	61.762 820	6689.484 740	.000 149 4883	.016 191	108.309 251	.009 232 8217	11.08	3.210 167	8.45	456
39	68.841 688	7468.809 726	.000 133 8901	.014 526	108.492 541	.009 217 2235	11.07	3.313 661	8.50	468
40	76.731 893	8337.456 073	.000 119 9407	.013 032	108.656 985	.009 203 2740	11.05	3.417 572	8.54	480
41	85.526 423	9305.661 239	.000 107 4615	.011 692	108.804 518	.009 190 7948	11.03	3.521 871	8.59	492
42	95.328 927	10384.836 034	.000 096 2943	.010 490	108.936 881	.009 179 6276	11.02	3.626 532	8.63	504
43	106.254 934	11587.699 103	.000 086 2984	.009 411	109.055 634	.009 169 6317	11.01	3.731 530	8.68	516
44	118.433 210	12928.426 824	.000 077 3489	.008 444	109.162 175	.009 160 6823	11.00	3.836 840	8.72	528
45	132.007 285	14422.820 382	.000 069 3346	.007 575	109.257 761	.009 152 6679	10.99	3.942 441	8.76	540
46	147.137 136	16088.491 995	.000 062 1562	.006 796	109.343 518	.009 145 4896	10.98	4.048 310	8.80	552
47	164.001 075	17945.072 485	.000 055 7256	.006 098	109.420 456	.009 139 0589	10.97	4.154 429	8.84	564
48	182.797 854	20014.442 634	.000 049 9639	.005 471	109.489 484	.009 133 2973	10.96	4.260 779	8.88	576
49	203.749 002	22320.991 063	.000 044 8009	.004 908	109.551 413	.009 128 1342	10.96	4.367 343	8.91	588
50	227.101 440	24891.901 667	.000 040 1737	.004 403	109.606 974	.009 123 5070	10.95	4.474 104	8.95	600

Effective Rate is 11.46 %

Annual Percentage Rate is 10.90 %

MONTHLY COMPOUND INTEREST AND ANNUITY

	Amount Of 1	Amount Of 1 Per Period	Sinking Fund Payment	Present Worth Of 1	Present Worth of 1 Per Period	Periodic Payment To Amortize 1	Constant Annual Percent	Total Interest	Annual Add On Rate	
	What a single $ 1 deposit grows to in the future. The deposit is made at the beginning of the first period.	What a series of $ 1 deposits grow to in the future. A deposit is made at the end of each period.	The amount to be deposited at the end of each period that grows to $ 1 in the future.	What $ 1 to be paid in the future is worth today. Value today of a single $ 1 payment tomorrow.	What $ 1 to be paid at the end of each period is worth today. Value today of a series of $ 1 payments tomorrow.	The mortgage payment to amortize a loan of $ 1. An annuity certain, payable at the end of each period, worth $ 1 today.	The annual payment, including interest and principal, to amortize completely a loan of $ 100.	The total interest paid over the term on a loan of $1. The loan is amortized by regular periodic payments.	The average annual interest rate on a loan that is completely amortized by regular periodic payments.	
	$S = (1+i)^n$	$S\overline{n}| = \dfrac{(1+i)^n - 1}{i}$	$\dfrac{1}{S\overline{n}|} = \dfrac{i}{(1+i)^n - 1}$	$V^n = \dfrac{1}{(1+i)^n}$	$A\overline{n}| = \dfrac{1 - V^n}{i}$	$\dfrac{1}{A\overline{n}|} = \dfrac{i}{1 - V^n}$				

YEAR										PERIODS
	1.009 125	1.000 000	1.000 000 0000	.990 958	.990 958	1.009 125 0000	1210.95	.009 125	10.95	1
	1.018 333	2.009 125	.497 729 1109	.981 997	1.972 954	.506 854 1109	608.23	.013 708	8.22	2
	1.027 626	3.027 458	.330 310 0860	.973 117	2.946 071	.339 435 0860	407.33	.018 305	7.32	3
	1.037 003	4.055 084	.246 604 0269	.964 318	3.910 389	.255 729 0269	306.88	.022 916	6.87	4
	1.046 465	5.092 086	.196 383 1540	.955 598	4.865 987	.205 508 1540	246.61	.027 541	6.61	5
	1.056 014	6.138 552	.162 904 8741	.946 957	5.812 944	.172 029 8741	206.44	.032 179	6.44	6
	1.065 650	7.194 566	.138 993 7899	.938 394	6.751 338	.148 118 7899	177.75	.036 832	6.31	7
	1.075 374	8.260 216	.121 062 2029	.929 909	7.681 247	.130 187 2029	156.23	.041 498	6.22	8
	1.085 187	9.335 591	.107 116 9472	.921 500	8.602 746	.116 241 9472	139.50	.046 178	6.16	9
	1.095 090	10.420 778	.095 962 1231	.913 167	9.515 914	.105 087 1231	126.11	.050 871	6.10	10
	1.105 082	11.515 868	.086 836 7037	.904 910	10.420 824	.095 961 7037	115.16	.055 579	6.06	11
	1.115 166	12.620 950	.079 233 3377	.896 727	11.317 551	.088 358 3377	106.04	.060 300	6.03	12
1	1.115 166	12.620 950	.079 233 3377	.896 727	11.317 551	.088 358 3377	106.04	.060 300	6.03	12
2	1.243 596	26.695 407	.037 459 6279	.804 120	21.466 309	.046 584 6279	55.91	.118 031	5.90	24
3	1.386 816	42.390 764	.023 590 0440	.721 076	30.566 977	.032 715 0440	39.26	.177 742	5.92	36
4	1.546 530	59.893 697	.016 696 2478	.646 609	38.727 795	.025 821 2478	30.99	.239 420	5.99	48
5	1.724 638	79.412 374	.012 592 4959	.579 832	46.045 824	.021 717 4959	26.07	.303 050	6.06	60
6	1.923 258	101.178 943	.009 883 4794	.519 951	52.608 101	.019 008 4794	22.82	.368 611	6.14	72
7	2.144 752	125.452 285	.007 971 1581	.466 254	58.492 674	.017 096 1581	20.52	.436 077	6.23	84
8	2.391 755	152.521 094	.006 556 4702	.418 103	63.769 531	.015 681 4702	18.82	.505 421	6.32	96
9	2.667 204	182.707 314	.005 473 2346	.374 924	68.501 434	.014 598 2346	17.52	.576 609	6.41	108
10	2.974 376	216.369 966	.004 621 7135	.336 205	72.744 660	.013 746 7135	16.50	.649 606	6.50	120
11	3.316 923	253.909 416	.003 938 4124	.301 484	76.549 677	.013 063 4124	15.68	.724 370	6.59	132
12	3.698 921	295.772 141	.003 380 9810	.270 349	79.961 740	.012 505 9810	15.01	.800 861	6.67	144
13	4.124 911	342.456 036	.002 920 0829	.242 429	83.021 430	.012 045 0829	14.46	.879 033	6.76	156
14	4.599 962	394.516 335	.002 534 7493	.217 393	85.765 137	.011 659 7493	14.00	.958 838	6.85	168
15	5.129 722	452.572 221	.002 209 5921	.194 942	88.225 495	.011 334 5921	13.61	1.040 227	6.93	180
16	5.720 492	517.314 180	.001 933 0613	.174 810	90.431 765	.011 058 0613	13.27	1.123 148	7.02	192
17	6.379 299	589.512 223	.001 696 3177	.156 757	92.410 188	.010 821 3177	12.99	1.207 549	7.10	204
18	7.113 978	670.025 037	.001 492 4815	.140 568	94.184 294	.010 617 4815	12.75	1.293 376	7.19	216
19	7.933 268	759.810 204	.001 316 1181	.126 051	95.775 183	.010 441 1181	12.53	1.380 575	7.27	228
20	8.846 912	859.935 585	.001 162 8778	.113 034	97.201 777	.010 287 8778	12.35	1.469 091	7.35	240
21	9.865 777	971.592 023	.001 029 2386	.101 360	98.481 042	.010 154 2386	12.19	1.558 868	7.42	252
22	11.001 981	1096.107 504	.000 912 3193	.090 893	99.628 195	.010 037 3193	12.05	1.649 852	7.50	264
23	12.269 037	1234.962 957	.000 809 7409	.081 506	100.656 878	.009 934 7409	11.93	1.741 988	7.57	276
24	13.682 015	1389.809 861	.000 719 5229	.073 089	101.579 326	.009 844 5229	11.82	1.835 223	7.65	288
25	15.257 720	1562.489 889	.000 640 0041	.065 541	102.406 511	.009 765 0041	11.72	1.929 501	7.72	300
26	17.014 893	1755.056 814	.000 569 7821	.058 772	103.148 270	.009 694 7821	11.64	2.024 772	7.79	312
27	18.974 434	1969.800 935	.000 507 6655	.052 702	103.813 425	.009 632 6655	11.56	2.120 984	7.86	324
28	21.159 646	2209.276 314	.000 452 6369	.047 260	104.409 888	.009 577 6369	11.50	2.218 086	7.92	336
29	23.596 522	2476.331 154	.000 403 8232	.042 379	104.944 753	.009 528 8232	11.44	2.316 030	7.99	348
30	26.314 043	2774.141 678	.000 360 4719	.038 003	105.424 381	.009 485 4719	11.39	2.414 770	8.05	360
31	29.344 530	3106.249 899	.000 321 9316	.034 078	105.854 477	.009 446 9316	11.34	2.514 259	8.11	372
32	32.724 027	3476.605 752	.000 287 6369	.030 559	106.240 155	.009 412 6369	11.30	2.614 453	8.17	384
33	36.492 728	3889.614 069	.000 257 0949	.027 403	106.586 003	.009 382 0949	11.26	2.715 310	8.23	396
34	40.695 456	4350.186 973	.000 229 8752	.024 573	106.896 135	.009 354 8752	11.23	2.816 789	8.28	408
35	45.382 196	4863.802 293	.000 205 6005	.022 035	107.174 239	.009 330 6005	11.20	2.918 852	8.34	420
36	50.608 690	5436.568 723	.000 183 9395	.019 759	107.423 622	.009 308 9395	11.18	3.021 462	8.39	432
37	56.437 099	6075.298 468	.000 164 6010	.017 719	107.647 250	.009 289 6010	11.15	3.124 583	8.44	444
38	62.936 743	6787.588 272	.000 147 3277	.015 889	107.847 784	.009 272 3277	11.13	3.228 181	8.50	456
39	70.184 927	7581.909 764	.000 131 8929	.014 248	108.027 608	.009 256 8929	11.11	3.332 226	8.54	468
40	78.267 856	8467.710 219	.000 118 0957	.012 777	108.188 862	.009 243 0957	11.10	3.436 686	8.59	480
41	87.281 665	9455.524 920	.000 105 7583	.011 457	108.333 462	.009 230 7583	11.08	3.541 533	8.64	492
42	97.333 560	10557.102 456	.000 094 7230	.010 274	108.463 129	.009 219 7230	11.07	3.646 740	8.68	504
43	108.543 093	11785.544 458	.000 084 8497	.009 213	108.579 405	.009 209 8497	11.06	3.752 282	8.73	516
44	121.043 585	13155.461 419	.000 076 0141	.008 261	108.683 673	.009 201 0141	11.05	3.858 135	8.77	528
45	134.983 712	14683.146 469	.000 068 1053	.007 408	108.777 172	.009 193 1053	11.04	3.964 277	8.81	540
46	150.529 269	16386.769 155	.000 061 0248	.006 643	108.861 016	.009 186 0248	11.03	4.070 686	8.85	552
47	167.865 148	18286.591 540	.000 054 6849	.005 957	108.936 201	.009 179 6849	11.02	4.177 342	8.89	564
48	187.197 345	20405.209 192	.000 049 0071	.005 342	109.003 622	.009 174 0071	11.01	4.284 228	8.93	576
49	208.756 357	22767.819 924	.000 043 9216	.004 790	109.064 080	.009 168 9216	11.01	4.391 326	8.96	588
50	232.798 027	25402.523 484	.000 039 3662	.004 296	109.118 294	.009 164 3662	11.00	4.498 620	9.00	600

	Amount Of 1	Amount Of 1 Per Period	Sinking Fund Payment	Present Worth Of 1	Present Worth of 1 Per Period	Periodic Payment To Amortize 1	Constant Annual Percent	Total Interest	Annual Add On Rate	
	What a single $ 1 deposit grows to in the future. The deposit is made at the beginning of the first period.	What a series of $ 1 deposits grow to in the future. A deposit is made at the end of each period.	The amount to be deposited at the end of each period that grows to $ 1 in the future.	What $ 1 to be paid in the future is worth today. Value today of a single $ 1 payment tomorrow.	What $ 1 to be paid at the end of each period is worth today. Value today of a series of $ 1 payments tomorrow.	The mortgage payment to amortize a loan of $ 1. An annuity certain, payable at the end of each period, worth $ 1 today.	The annual payment, including interest and principal, to amortize completely a loan of $ 100.	The total interest paid over the term on a loan of $1. The loan is amortized by regular periodic payments.	The average annual interest rate on a loan that is completely amortized by regular periodic payments.	
	$S = (1+i)^n$	$S\overline{n} = \dfrac{(1+i)^n - 1}{i}$	$\dfrac{1}{S\overline{n}} = \dfrac{i}{(1+i)^n - 1}$	$V^n = \dfrac{1}{(1+i)^n}$	$A\overline{n} = \dfrac{1-V^n}{i}$	$\dfrac{1}{A\overline{n}} = \dfrac{i}{1-V^n}$				

YEAR										PERIODS
	1.009 167	1.000 000	1.000 000 0000	.990 917	.990 917	1.009 166 6667	1211.00	.009 167	11.00	1
	1.018 417	2.009 167	.497 718 7889	.981 916	1.972 832	.506 885 4556	608.27	.013 771	8.26	2
	1.027 753	3.027 584	.330 296 3653	.972 997	2.945 829	.339 463 0320	407.36	.018 389	7.36	3
	1.037 174	4.055 337	.246 588 6384	.964 158	3.909 987	.255 755 3051	306.91	.023 021	6.91	4
	1.046 681	5.092 511	.196 366 7901	.955 401	4.865 388	.205 533 4568	246.65	.027 667	6.64	5
	1.056 276	6.139 192	.162 887 8809	.946 722	5.812 110	.172 054 5476	206.47	.032 327	6.47	6
	1.065 958	7.195 468	.138 976 3652	.938 123	6.750 233	.148 143 0319	177.78	.037 001	6.34	7
	1.075 730	8.261 427	.121 044 4704	.929 602	7.679 835	.130 211 1371	156.26	.041 689	6.25	8
	1.085 591	9.337 156	.107 098 9892	.921 158	8.600 992	.116 265 6559	139.52	.046 391	6.19	9
	1.095 542	10.422 747	.095 943 9974	.912 790	9.513 783	.105 110 6641	126.14	.051 107	6.13	10
	1.105 584	11.518 289	.086 818 4523	.904 499	10.418 282	.095 985 1189	115.19	.055 836	6.09	11
	1.115 719	12.623 873	.079 214 9919	.896 283	11.314 565	.088 381 6585	106.06	.060 580	6.06	12
1	1.115 719	12.623 873	.079 214 9919	.896 283	11.314 565	.088 381 6585	106.06	.060 580	6.06	12
2	1.244 829	26.730 566	.037 441 1715	.803 323	21.455 619	.046 607 8382	55.93	.118 588	5.93	24
3	1.388 879	42.423 123	.023 572 0505	.720 005	30.544 874	.032 738 7171	39.29	.178 594	5.95	36
4	1.549 598	59.956 151	.016 678 8559	.645 329	38.691 421	.025 845 5226	31.02	.240 585	6.01	48
5	1.728 916	79.518 080	.012 575 7564	.578 397	45.993 034	.021 742 4231	26.10	.304 545	6.09	60
6	1.928 984	101.343 692	.009 867 4123	.518 408	52.537 346	.019 034 0790	22.85	.370 454	6.17	72
7	2.152 204	125.694 940	.007 955 7698	.464 640	58.402 903	.017 122 4364	20.55	.438 285	6.26	84
8	2.401 254	152.864 085	.006 541 7590	.416 449	63.660 103	.015 708 4257	18.86	.508 009	6.35	96
9	2.679 124	183.177 212	.005 459 1944	.373 256	68.372 043	.014 625 8610	17.56	.579 593	6.44	108
10	2.989 150	216.998 139	.004 608 3345	.334 543	72.595 275	.013 775 0011	16.54	.653 000	6.53	120
11	3.335 051	254.732 784	.003 925 6824	.299 846	76.380 487	.013 092 3490	15.72	.728 190	6.62	132
12	3.720 979	296.834 038	.003 368 8859	.268 747	79.773 109	.012 535 5526	15.05	.805 120	6.71	144
13	4.151 566	343.807 200	.002 908 6069	.240 873	82.813 859	.012 075 2736	14.50	.883 743	6.80	156
14	4.631 980	396.216 042	.002 523 8756	.215 890	85.539 231	.011 690 5423	14.03	.964 011	6.89	168
15	5.167 988	454.689 575	.002 199 3027	.193 499	87.981 937	.011 365 9693	13.64	1.045 874	6.97	180
16	5.766 021	519.929 596	.001 923 3373	.173 430	90.171 293	.011 090 0040	13.31	1.129 281	7.06	192
17	6.433 259	592.719 117	.001 687 1398	.155 442	92.133 576	.010 853 8064	13.03	1.214 177	7.14	204
18	7.177 708	673.931 757	.001 483 8298	.139 320	93.892 337	.010 650 4964	12.79	1.300 507	7.23	216
19	8.008 304	764.542 228	.001 307 9722	.124 870	95.468 685	.010 474 6389	12.57	1.388 218	7.31	228
20	8.935 015	865.638 038	.001 155 2173	.111 919	96.881 539	.010 321 8839	12.39	1.477 252	7.39	240
21	9.968 965	978.432 537	.001 022 0429	.100 311	98.147 856	.010 188 7095	12.23	1.567 555	7.46	252
22	11.122 562	1104.279 485	.000 905 5679	.089 907	99.282 835	.010 072 2345	12.09	1.659 070	7.54	264
23	12.409 652	1244.689 295	.000 803 4134	.080 582	100.300 098	.009 970 0800	11.97	1.751 742	7.62	276
24	13.845 682	1401.347 165	.000 713 5990	.072 225	101.211 853	.009 880 2657	11.86	1.845 517	7.69	288
25	15.447 889	1576.133 301	.000 634 4641	.064 734	102.029 044	.009 801 1308	11.77	1.940 339	7.76	300
26	17.235 500	1771.145 485	.000 564 6064	.058 020	102.761 478	.009 731 2730	11.68	2.036 157	7.83	312
27	19.229 972	1988.724 252	.000 502 8349	.052 002	103.417 947	.009 669 5016	11.61	2.132 919	7.90	324
28	21.455 242	2231.480 981	.000 448 1329	.046 609	104.006 328	.009 614 7995	11.54	2.230 573	7.97	336
29	23.938 018	2502.329 236	.000 399 6277	.041 775	104.533 685	.009 566 2943	11.48	2.329 070	8.03	348
30	26.708 098	2804.519 736	.000 356 5673	.037 442	105.006 346	.009 523 2340	11.43	2.428 364	8.09	360
31	29.798 728	3141.679 369	.000 318 3011	.033 558	105.429 984	.009 484 9678	11.39	2.528 408	8.16	372
32	33.247 002	3517.854 723	.000 284 2642	.030 078	105.809 684	.009 450 9308	11.35	2.629 157	8.22	384
33	37.094 306	3937.560 650	.000 253 9643	.026 958	106.150 002	.009 420 6310	11.31	2.730 570	8.27	396
34	41.386 816	4405.834 459	.000 226 9718	.024 162	106.455 024	.009 393 6384	11.28	2.832 604	8.33	408
35	46.176 050	4928.296 368	.000 202 9099	.021 656	106.728 409	.009 369 5765	11.25	2.935 222	8.39	420
36	51.519 489	5511.216 962	.000 181 4481	.019 410	106.973 440	.009 348 1148	11.22	3.038 386	8.44	432
37	57.481 264	6161.592 447	.000 162 2957	.017 397	107.193 057	.009 328 9624	11.20	3.142 059	8.49	444
38	64.132 929	6887.228 628	.000 145 1963	.015 593	107.389 897	.009 311 8630	11.18	3.246 210	8.54	456
39	71.554 317	7696.834 582	.000 129 9235	.013 975	107.566 320	.009 296 5902	11.16	3.350 804	8.59	468
40	79.834 499	8600.127 195	.000 116 2774	.012 526	107.724 446	.009 282 9440	11.14	3.455 813	8.64	480
41	89.072 855	9607.947 778	.000 104 0805	.011 227	107.866 171	.009 270 7472	11.13	3.561 208	8.69	492
42	99.380 262	10732.392 187	.000 093 1759	.010 062	107.993 197	.009 259 8425	11.12	3.666 961	8.73	504
43	110.880 430	11986.955 993	.000 083 4240	.009 019	108.107 048	.009 250 0907	11.11	3.773 047	8.77	516
44	123.711 384	13386.696 463	.000 074 7010	.008 083	108.209 091	.009 241 3677	11.09	3.879 442	8.82	528
45	138.027 122	14948.413 271	.000 066 8967	.007 245	108.300 551	.009 233 5634	11.09	3.986 124	8.86	540
46	153.999 460	16690.850 131	.000 059 9131	.006 494	108.382 524	.009 226 5797	11.08	4.093 072	8.90	552
47	171.820 098	18634.919 757	.000 053 6627	.005 820	108.455 996	.009 220 3294	11.07	4.200 266	8.94	564
48	191.702 920	20803.954 856	.000 048 0678	.005 216	108.521 847	.009 214 7345	11.06	4.307 687	8.97	576
49	213.886 558	23223.988 174	.000 043 0589	.004 675	108.580 868	.009 209 7256	11.06	4.415 319	9.01	588
50	238.637 262	25924.064 930	.000 038 5742	.004 190	108.633 768	.009 205 2409	11.05	4.523 145	9.05	600

Effective Rate is 11.57 %

Annual Percentage Rate is 11.00 %

	Amount Of 1	Amount Of 1 Per Period	Sinking Fund Payment	Present Worth Of 1	Present Worth of 1 Per Period	Periodic Payment To Amortize 1	Constant Annual Percent	Total Interest	Annual Add On Rate	
	What a single $ 1 deposit grows to in the future. The deposit is made at the beginning of the first period.	What a series of $ 1 deposits grow to in the future. A deposit is made at the end of each period.	The amount to be deposited at the end of each period that grows to $ 1 in the future.	What $ 1 to be paid in the future is worth today. Value today of a single $ 1 payment tomorrow.	What $ 1 to be paid at the end of each period is worth today. Value today of a series of $ 1 payments tomorrow.	The mortgage payment to amortize a loan of $ 1. An annuity certain, payable at the end of each period, worth $ 1 today.	The annual payment, including interest and principal, to amortize completely a loan of $ 100.	The total interest paid over the term on a loan of $1. The loan is amortized by regular periodic payments.	The average annual interest rate on a loan that is completely amortized by regular periodic payments.	
	$S = (1+i)^n$	$S\overline{n}| = \dfrac{(1+i)^n - 1}{i}$	$\dfrac{1}{S\overline{n}|} = \dfrac{i}{(1+i)^n - 1}$	$V^n = \dfrac{1}{(1+i)^n}$	$A\overline{n}| = \dfrac{1-V^n}{i}$	$\dfrac{1}{A\overline{n}|} = \dfrac{i}{1-V^n}$				

YEAR										PERIODS
	1.009 208	1.000 000	1.000 000 0000	.990 876	.990 876	1.009 208 3333	1211.05	.009 208	11.05	1
	1.018 501	2.009 208	.497 708 4673	.981 835	1.972 710	.506 916 8006	608.31	.013 834	8.30	2
	1.027 880	3.027 710	.330 282 6454	.972 876	2.945 586	.339 490 9787	407.39	.018 473	7.39	3
	1.037 345	4.055 590	.246 573 2511	.963 999	3.909 586	.255 781 5844	306.94	.023 126	6.94	4
	1.046 897	5.092 935	.196 350 4276	.955 203	4.864 789	.205 558 7609	246.68	.027 794	6.67	5
	1.056 538	6.139 833	.162 870 8894	.946 488	5.811 277	.172 079 2227	206.50	.032 475	6.50	6
	1.066 267	7.196 370	.138 958 9426	.937 852	6.749 129	.148 167 2759	177.81	.037 171	6.37	7
	1.076 085	8.262 637	.121 026 7402	.929 295	7.678 423	.130 235 0735	156.29	.041 881	6.28	8
	1.085 994	9.338 722	.107 081 0338	.920 815	8.599 238	.116 289 3672	139.55	.046 604	6.21	9
	1.095 994	10.424 716	.095 925 8746	.912 414	9.511 652	.105 134 2079	126.17	.051 342	6.16	10
	1.106 087	11.520 710	.086 800 2039	.904 088	10.415 740	.096 008 5372	115.22	.056 094	6.12	11
	1.116 272	12.626 797	.079 196 6494	.895 839	11.311 580	.088 404 9828	106.09	.060 860	6.09	12
1	1.116 272	12.626 797	.079 196 6494	.895 839	11.311 580	.088 404 9828	106.09	.060 860	6.09	12
2	1.246 063	26.721 733	.037 422 7220	.802 528	21.444 936	.046 631 0553	55.96	.119 145	5.96	24
3	1.390 945	42.455 513	.023 554 0670	.718 936	30.522 794	.032 762 4004	39.32	.179 446	5.98	36
4	1.552 672	60.018 687	.016 661 4775	.644 051	38.655 095	.025 869 8108	31.05	.241 751	6.04	48
5	1.733 204	79.623 962	.012 559 0335	.576 966	45.940 329	.021 767 3668	26.13	.306 042	6.12	60
6	1.934 727	101.508 776	.009 851 3650	.516 869	52.466 728	.019 059 6983	22.88	.372 298	6.20	72
7	2.159 681	125.938 176	.007 940 4040	.463 031	58.313 331	.017 148 7373	20.58	.440 494	6.29	84
8	2.410 791	153.208 026	.006 527 0732	.414 802	63.550 948	.015 735 4065	18.89	.510 599	6.38	96
9	2.691 097	183.648 588	.005 445 1821	.371 596	68.243 010	.014 653 5154	17.59	.582 580	6.47	108
10	3.003 996	217.628 529	.004 594 9858	.332 890	72.446 344	.013 803 3191	16.57	.656 398	6.56	120
11	3.353 276	255.559 376	.003 912 9850	.298 216	76.211 854	.013 121 3183	15.75	.732 014	6.65	132
12	3.743 167	297.900 510	.003 356 8254	.267 153	79.585 147	.012 565 1587	15.08	.809 383	6.74	144
13	4.178 392	345.164 721	.002 897 1675	.239 327	82.607 074	.012 105 5008	14.53	.888 458	6.83	156
14	4.664 221	397.924 426	.002 513 0400	.214 398	85.314 235	.011 721 3733	14.07	.969 191	6.92	168
15	5.206 538	456.818 594	.002 189 0528	.192 066	87.739 416	.011 397 3861	13.68	1.051 529	7.01	180
16	5.811 911	522.560 489	.001 913 6541	.172 060	89.911 988	.011 121 9874	13.35	1.135 422	7.10	192
17	6.487 672	595.946 311	.001 678 0035	.154 138	91.858 264	.010 886 3368	13.07	1.220 813	7.18	204
18	7.242 005	677.864 830	.001 475 2204	.138 083	93.601 813	.010 683 5537	12.83	1.307 648	7.26	216
19	8.084 046	769.308 160	.001 299 8692	.123 700	95.163 754	.010 508 2026	12.61	1.395 870	7.35	228
20	9.023 992	871.383 766	.001 147 6000	.110 816	96.563 001	.010 355 9333	12.43	1.485 424	7.43	240
21	10.073 228	985.327 881	.001 014 8906	.099 273	97.816 502	.010 223 2239	12.27	1.576 252	7.51	252
22	11.244 459	1112.520 479	.000 898 8599	.088 933	98.939 437	.010 107 1932	12.13	1.668 299	7.58	264
23	12.551 872	1254.501 983	.000 797 1291	.079 669	99.945 406	.010 005 4624	12.01	1.761 508	7.66	276
24	14.011 301	1412.991 926	.000 707 7181	.071 371	100.846 592	.009 916 0515	11.90	1.855 823	7.73	288
25	15.640 419	1589.909 772	.000 628 9665	.063 937	101.653 911	.009 837 2998	11.81	1.951 190	7.80	300
26	17.458 958	1787.398 167	.000 559 4724	.057 277	102.377 138	.009 767 8058	11.73	2.047 555	7.88	312
27	19.488 942	2007.848 884	.000 498 0454	.051 311	103.025 034	.009 706 3788	11.65	2.144 867	7.94	324
28	21.754 955	2253.931 792	.000 443 6691	.045 967	103.605 444	.009 652 0025	11.59	2.243 073	8.01	336
29	24.284 442	2528.627 191	.000 395 4715	.041 179	104.125 398	.009 603 8048	11.53	2.342 124	8.08	348
30	27.108 037	2835.261 906	.000 352 7011	.036 889	104.591 193	.009 561 0344	11.48	2.441 972	8.14	360
31	30.259 936	3177.549 578	.000 314 7079	.033 047	105.008 471	.009 523 0412	11.43	2.542 571	8.20	372
32	33.778 311	3559.635 637	.000 280 9276	.029 605	105.382 285	.009 489 2610	11.39	2.643 876	8.26	384
33	37.705 775	3986.147 512	.000 250 8688	.026 521	105.717 182	.009 459 2021	11.36	2.745 844	8.32	396
34	42.089 892	4462.250 672	.000 224 1022	.023 759	106.017 158	.009 432 4355	11.32	2.848 434	8.38	408
35	46.983 757	4993.711 181	.000 200 2519	.021 284	106.285 906	.009 408 5852	11.30	2.951 606	8.43	420
36	52.446 641	5586.965 535	.000 178 9880	.019 067	106.526 661	.009 387 3214	11.27	3.055 323	8.49	432
37	58.544 704	6249.198 613	.000 160 0205	.017 081	106.742 339	.009 368 3539	11.25	3.159 549	8.54	444
38	65.351 799	6988.430 693	.000 143 0936	.015 302	106.935 551	.009 351 4270	11.23	3.264 251	8.59	456
39	72.950 368	7813.614 584	.000 127 9817	.013 708	107.108 639	.009 336 3151	11.21	3.369 395	8.64	468
40	81.432 435	8734.744 053	.000 114 4853	.012 280	107.263 697	.009 322 8187	11.19	3.474 953	8.69	480
41	90.900 727	9762.974 860	.000 102 4278	.011 001	107.402 605	.009 310 7611	11.18	3.580 894	8.73	492
42	101.469 914	10910.759 868	.000 091 6526	.009 855	107.527 044	.009 299 9860	11.16	3.687 193	8.78	504
43	113.267 999	12191.999 851	.000 082 0210	.008 829	107.638 521	.009 290 3543	11.15	3.793 823	8.82	516
44	126.437 867	13622.211 854	.000 073 4095	.007 909	107.738 387	.009 281 7429	11.14	3.900 760	8.87	528
45	141.139 020	15218.717 115	.000 065 7086	.007 085	107.827 850	.009 274 0419	11.13	4.007 983	8.91	540
46	157.549 502	17000.850 842	.000 058 8206	.006 347	107.907 995	.009 267 1539	11.13	4.115 469	8.95	552
47	175.868 058	18990.196 384	.000 052 6587	.005 686	107.979 792	.009 260 9921	11.12	4.223 200	8.99	564
48	196.316 546	21210.846 622	.000 047 1457	.005 094	108.044 111	.009 255 4790	11.11	4.331 156	9.02	576
49	219.142 615	23689.695 757	.000 042 2124	.004 563	108.101 730	.009 250 5458	11.11	4.439 321	9.06	588
50	244.622 711	26456.765 029	.000 037 7975	.004 088	108.153 347	.009 246 1308	11.10	4.547 679	9.10	600

Effective Rate is 11.63 %   8 - 161   Annual Percentage Rate is 11.05 %

Amount Of 1	Amount Of 1 Per Period	Sinking Fund Payment	Present Worth Of 1	Present Worth of 1 Per Period	Periodic Payment To Amortize 1	Constant Annual Percent	Total Interest	Annual Add On Rate
What a single $ 1 deposit grows to in the future. The deposit is made at the beginning of the first period.	What a series of $ 1 deposits grow to in the future. A deposit is made at the end of each period.	The amount to be deposited at the end of each period that grows to $ 1 in the future.	What $ ·1 to be paid in the future is worth today. Value today of a single $ 1 payment tomorrow.	What $ 1 to be paid at the end of each period is worth today. Value today of a series of $ 1 payments tomorrow.	The mortgage payment to amortize a loan of $ 1. An annuity certain, payable at the end of each period, worth $ 1 today.	The annual payment, including interest and principal, to amortize completely a loan of $ 100.	The total interest paid over the term on a loan of $1. The loan is amortized by regular periodic payments.	The average annual interest rate on a loan that is completely amortized by regular periodic payments.
$S = (1+i)^n$	$S\overline{n} = \dfrac{(1+i)^n - 1}{i}$	$\dfrac{1}{S\overline{n}} = \dfrac{i}{(1+i)^n - 1}$	$V^n = \dfrac{1}{(1+i)^n}$	$A\overline{n} = \dfrac{1-V^n}{i}$	$\dfrac{1}{A\overline{n}} = \dfrac{i}{1-V^n}$			

YEAR									PERIODS
	1.009 250	1.000 000	1.000 000 0000	.990 835	.990 835	1.009 250 0000	1211.10	.009 250	11.10	1
	1.018 586	2.009 250	.497 698 1461	.981 754	1.972 588	.506 948 1461	608.34	.013 896	8.34	2
	1.028 007	3.027 836	.330 268 9262	.972 756	2.945 344	.339 518 9262	407.43	.018 557	7.42	3
	1.037 517	4.055 843	.246 557 8647	.963 840	3.909 184	.255 807 8647	306.97	.023 231	6.97	4
	1.047 114	5.093 360	.196 334 0664	.955 006	4.864 190	.205 584 0664	246.71	.027 920	6.70	5
	1.056 799	6.140 473	.162 853 8995	.946 253	5.810 444	.172 103 8995	206.53	.032 623	6.52	6
	1.066 575	7.197 273	.138 941 5218	.937 581	6.748 024	.148 191 5218	177.83	.037 341	6.40	7
	1.076 441	8.263 847	.121 009 0122	.928 988	7.677 012	.130 259 0122	156.32	.042 072	6.31	8
	1.086 398	9.340 288	.107 063 0810	.920 473	8.597 485	.116 313 0810	139.58	.046 818	6.24	9
	1.096 447	10.426 686	.095 907 7546	.912 037	9.509 522	.105 157 7546	126.19	.051 578	6.19	10
	1.106 589	11.523 132	.086 781 9587	.903 678	10.413 200	.096 031 9587	115.24	.056 352	6.15	11
	1.116 825	12.629 721	.079 178 3104	.895 395	11.308 596	.088 428 3104	106.12	.061 140	6.11	12
1	1.116 825	12.629 721	.079 178 3104	.895 395	11.308 596	.088 428 3104	106.12	.061 140	6.11	12
2	1.247 298	26.734 909	.037 404 2792	.801 733	21.434 261	.046 654 2792	55.99	.119 703	5.99	24
3	1.393 013	42.487 934	.023 536 0938	.717 868	30.500 736	.032 786 0938	39.35	.180 299	6.01	36
4	1.555 752	60.081 305	.016 644 1125	.642 776	38.618 817	.025 894 1125	31.08	.242 917	6.07	48
5	1.737 503	79.730 020	.012 542 3272	.575 539	45.887 710	.021 792 3272	26.16	.307 540	6.15	60
6	1.940 486	101.674 195	.009 835 3373	.515 335	52.396 245	.019 085 3373	22.91	.374 144	6.24	72
7	2.167 183	126.181 996	.007 925 0608	.461 428	58.223 957	.017 175 0608	20.62	.442 705	6.32	84
8	2.420 365	153.552 920	.006 512 4128	.413 161	63.442 064	.015 762 4128	18.92	.513 192	6.41	96
9	2.703 123	184.121 449	.005 431 1977	.369 942	68.114 334	.014 681 1977	17.62	.585 569	6.51	108
10	3.018 916	218.261 145	.004 581 6675	.331 245	72.297 863	.013 831 6675	16.60	.659 800	6.60	120
11	3.371 600	256.389 207	.003 900 3202	.296 595	76.043 776	.013 150 3202	15.79	.735 842	6.69	132
12	3.765 487	298.971 578	.003 344 7995	.265 570	79.397 850	.012 594 7995	15.12	.813 651	6.78	144
13	4.205 390	346.528 631	.002 885 7644	.237 790	82.401 072	.012 135 7644	14.57	.893 179	6.87	156
14	4.696 684	399.641 533	.002 502 2424	.212 916	85.090 144	.011 752 2424	14.11	.974 377	6.96	168
15	5.245 374	458.959 346	.002 178 8422	.190 644	87.497 927	.011 428 8422	13.72	1.057 192	7.05	180
16	5.858 164	525.206 957	.001 904 0113	.170 702	89.653 845	.011 154 0113	13.39	1.141 570	7.13	192
17	6.542 544	599.193 941	.001 668 9087	.152 846	91.584 244	.010 918 9087	13.11	1.227 457	7.22	204
18	7.306 876	681.824 448	.001 466 6532	.136 857	93.312 715	.010 716 6532	12.86	1.314 797	7.30	216
19	8.160 501	774.108 258	.001 291 8090	.122 541	94.860 379	.010 541 8090	12.66	1.403 532	7.39	228
20	9.113 851	877.173 117	.001 140 0258	.109 723	96.246 152	.010 390 0258	12.47	1.493 606	7.47	240
21	10.178 576	992.278 520	.001 007 7816	.098 246	97.486 966	.010 257 7816	12.31	1.584 961	7.55	252
22	11.367 688	1120.831 102	.000 892 1951	.087 969	98.597 985	.010 142 1951	12.18	1.677 540	7.63	264
23	12.695 717	1264.401 831	.000 790 8878	.078 767	99.592 787	.010 040 8878	12.05	1.771 285	7.70	276
24	14.178 893	1424.745 198	.000 701 8799	.070 527	100.483 528	.009 951 8799	11.95	1.866 141	7.78	288
25	15.835 341	1603.820 667	.000 623 5111	.063 150	101.281 093	.009 873 5111	11.85	1.962 053	7.85	300
26	17.685 304	1803.816 614	.000 554 3801	.056 544	101.995 230	.009 804 3801	11.77	2.058 967	7.92	312
27	19.751 388	2027.177 072	.000 493 2968	.050 629	102.634 664	.009 743 2968	11.70	2.156 828	7.99	324
28	22.058 842	2276.631 599	.000 439 2454	.045 333	103.207 211	.009 689 2454	11.63	2.255 586	8.06	336
29	24.635 865	2555.228 631	.000 391 3544	.040 591	103.719 867	.009 641 3544	11.57	2.355 191	8.12	348
30	27.513 948	2866.372 740	.000 348 8730	.036 345	104.178 897	.009 598 8730	11.52	2.455 594	8.19	360
31	30.728 263	3213.866 235	.000 311 1517	.032 543	104.589 910	.009 561 1517	11.48	2.556 748	8.25	372
32	34.318 090	3601.955 631	.000 277 6270	.029 139	104.957 930	.009 527 6270	11.44	2.658 609	8.31	384
33	38.327 298	4035.383 541	.000 247 8079	.026 091	105.287 452	.009 497 8079	11.40	2.761 132	8.37	396
34	42.804 881	4519.446 633	.000 221 2660	.023 362	105.582 506	.009 471 2660	11.37	2.864 277	8.42	408
35	47.805 558	5060.060 358	.000 197 6261	.020 918	105.846 695	.009 447 6261	11.34	2.968 003	8.48	420
36	53.390 439	5663.831 240	.000 176 5589	.018 730	106.083 249	.009 426 5589	11.32	3.072 273	8.53	432
37	59.627 773	6338.137 608	.000 157 7751	.016 771	106.295 059	.009 407 7751	11.29	3.177 052	8.59	444
38	66.593 783	7091.219 766	.000 141 0195	.015 016	106.484 712	.009 391 0195	11.27	3.282 305	8.64	456
39	74.373 596	7932.280 689	.000 126 0671	.013 446	106.654 526	.009 376 0671	11.26	3.387 999	8.69	468
40	83.062 286	8871.598 490	.000 112 7193	.012 039	106.806 577	.009 362 7193	11.24	3.494 105	8.74	480
41	92.766 031	9920.652 019	.000 100 7998	.010 780	106.942 723	.009 350 7998	11.23	3.600 594	8.78	492
42	103.603 416	11092.261 147	.000 090 1529	.009 652	107.064 628	.009 340 1529	11.21	3.707 437	8.83	504
43	115.706 877	12400.743 420	.000 080 6403	.008 643	107.173 781	.009 330 6403	11.20	3.814 610	8.87	516
44	129.224 324	13862.089 034	.000 072 1392	.007 738	107.271 516	.009 322 1392	11.19	3.922 089	8.91	528
45	144.320 945	15494.156 236	.000 064 5405	.006 929	107.359 027	.009 314 5405	11.18	4.029 852	8.96	540
46	161.181 228	17316.889 563	.000 057 7471	.006 204	107.437 384	.009 307 7471	11.17	4.137 876	9.00	552
47	180.011 213	19352.563 570	.000 051 6727	.005 555	107.507 545	.009 301 6727	11.17	4.246 143	9.03	564
48	201.041 009	21626.055 036	.000 046 2405	.004 974	107.570 367	.009 296 2405	11.16	4.354 635	9.07	576
49	224.527 609	24165.146 967	.000 041 3819	.004 454	107.626 617	.009 291 3819	11.15	4.463 333	9.11	588
50	250.758 030	27000.868 116	.000 037 0358	.003 988	107.676 983	.009 287 0358	11.15	4.572 222	9.14	600

Effective Rate is 11.68 %

Annual Percentage Rate is 11.10 %

MONTHLY COMPOUND INTEREST AND ANNUITY

	Amount Of 1	Amount Of 1 Per Period	Sinking Fund Payment	Present Worth Of 1	Present Worth of 1 Per Period	Periodic Payment To Amortize 1	Constant Annual Percent	Total Interest	Annual Add On Rate
	What a single $1 deposit grows to in the future. The deposit is made at the beginning of the first period.	What a series of $1 deposits grow to in the future. A deposit is made at the end of each period.	The amount to be deposited at the end of each period that grows to $1 in the future.	What $1 to be paid in the future is worth today. Value today of a single $1 payment tomorrow.	What $1 to be paid at the end of each period is worth today. Value today of a series of $1 payments tomorrow.	The mortgage payment to amortize a loan of $1. An annuity certain, payable at the end of each period, worth $1 today.	The annual payment, including interest and principal, to amortize completely a loan of $100.	The total interest paid over the term on a loan of $1. The loan is amortized by regular periodic payments.	The average annual interest rate on a loan that is completely amortized by regular periodic payments.

$$S = (1+i)^n \qquad S\overline{n}| = \frac{(1+i)^n - 1}{i} \qquad \frac{1}{S\overline{n}|} = \frac{i}{(1+i)^n - 1} \qquad V^n = \frac{1}{(1+i)^n} \qquad A\overline{n}| = \frac{1-V^n}{i} \qquad \frac{1}{A\overline{n}|} = \frac{i}{1-V^n}$$

YEAR									**PERIODS**	
	1.009 271	1.000 000	1.000 000 0000	.990 814	.990 814	1.009 270 8333	1211.13	.009 271	11.13	1
	1.018 628	2.009 271	.497 692 9856	.981 713	1.972 527	.506 963 8190	608.36	.013 928	8.36	2
	1.028 071	3.027 898	.330 262 0669	.972 695	2.945 223	.339 532 9003	407.44	.018 599	7.44	3
	1.037 602	4.055 970	.246 550 1720	.963 760	3.908 983	.255 821 0053	306.99	.023 284	6.99	4
	1.047 222	5.093 572	.196 325 8864	.954 908	4.863 891	.205 596 7197	246.72	.027 984	6.72	5
	1.056 930	6.140 793	.162 845 4052	.946 136	5.810 027	.172 116 2386	206.54	.032 697	6.54	6
	1.066 729	7.197 724	.138 932 8122	.937 445	6.747 472	.148 203 6455	177.85	.037 426	6.42	7
	1.076 618	8.264 453	.121 000 1490	.928 834	7.676 307	.130 270 9823	156.33	.042 168	6.33	8
	1.086 600	9.341 071	.107 054 1055	.920 302	8.596 609	.116 324 9388	139.59	.046 924	6.26	9
	1.096 673	10.427 671	.095 898 6956	.911 849	9.508 458	.105 169 5289	126.21	.051 695	6.20	10
	1.106 840	11.524 344	.086 772 8372	.903 473	10.411 930	.096 043 6705	115.26	.056 480	6.16	11
	1.117 102	12.631 184	.079 169 1422	.895 174	11.307 104	.088 439 9755	106.13	.061 280	6.13	12
1	1.117 102	12.631 184	.079 169 1422	.895 174	11.307 104	.088 439 9755	106.13	.061 280	6.13	12
2	1.247 916	26.741 500	.037 395 0604	.801 336	21.428 926	.046 665 8937	56.00	.119 981	6.00	24
3	1.394 049	42.504 156	.023 527 1110	.717 335	30.489 716	.032 797 9443	39.36	.180 726	6.02	36
4	1.557 294	60.112 645	.016 635 4350	.642 139	38.600 696	.025 906 2684	31.09	.243 501	6.09	48
5	1.739 656	79.783 116	.012 533 9803	.574 826	45.861 433	.021 804 8136	26.17	.308 289	6.17	60
6	1.943 372	101.757 031	.009 827 3308	.514 569	52.361 054	.019 098 1641	22.92	.375 068	6.25	72
7	2.170 944	126.304 126	.007 917 3977	.460 629	58.179 344	.017 188 2311	20.63	.443 811	6.34	84
8	2.425 166	153.725 725	.006 505 0921	.412 343	63.387 724	.015 775 9254	18.94	.514 489	6.43	96
9	2.709 156	184.358 438	.005 424 2161	.369 119	68.050 128	.014 695 0494	17.64	.587 065	6.52	108
10	3.026 403	218.578 290	.004 575 0198	.330 425	72.223 791	.013 845 8531	16.62	.661 502	6.62	120
11	3.380 800	256.805 342	.003 894 0000	.295 788	75.959 944	.013 164 8333	15.80	.737 758	6.71	132
12	3.776 697	299.508 842	.003 338 7996	.264 782	79.304 450	.012 609 6329	15.14	.815 787	6.80	144
13	4.218 954	347.212 992	.002 880 0766	.237 026	82.298 364	.012 150 9099	14.59	.895 542	6.89	156
14	4.713 000	400.503 373	.002 496 8579	.212 179	84.978 437	.011 767 6912	14.13	.976 972	6.98	168
15	5.264 900	460.034 143	.002 173 7517	.189 937	87.377 567	.011 444 5850	13.74	1.060 025	7.07	180
16	5.881 428	526.536 062	.001 899 2051	.170 027	89.525 206	.011 170 0385	13.41	1.144 647	7.15	192
17	6.570 153	600.825 462	.001 664 3769	.152 203	91.447 716	.010 935 2102	13.13	1.230 783	7.24	204
18	7.339 528	683.814 270	.001 462 3854	.136 249	93.168 697	.010 733 2187	12.88	1.318 375	7.32	216
19	8.198 999	776.521 200	.001 287 7948	.121 966	94.709 273	.010 558 6282	12.68	1.407 367	7.41	228
20	9.159 114	880.084 260	.001 136 2548	.109 181	96.088 357	.010 407 0882	12.49	1.497 701	7.49	240
21	10.231 661	995.774 720	.001 004 2432	.097 736	97.322 876	.010 275 0765	12.34	1.589 319	7.57	252
22	11.429 805	1125.012 719	.000 888 8788	.087 491	98.427 985	.010 159 7122	12.20	1.682 164	7.65	264
23	12.768 254	1269.384 693	.000 787 7833	.078 319	99.417 250	.010 058 6166	12.08	1.776 178	7.72	276
24	14.263 437	1430.662 858	.000 698 9767	.070 109	100.302 814	.009 969 8100	11.97	1.871 305	7.80	288
25	15.933 708	1610.826 954	.000 620 7991	.062 760	101.095 547	.009 891 6325	11.87	1.967 490	7.87	300
26	17.799 571	1812.088 553	.000 551 8494	.056 181	101.805 182	.009 822 6827	11.79	2.064 677	7.94	312
27	19.883 929	2036.918 209	.000 490 9377	.050 292	102.440 427	.009 761 7711	11.72	2.162 814	8.01	324
28	22.212 369	2288.075 777	.000 437 0485	.045 020	103.009 083	.009 707 8818	11.65	2.261 848	8.08	336
29	24.813 473	2568.644 299	.000 389 3104	.040 301	103.518 128	.009 660 1438	11.60	2.361 730	8.14	348
30	27.719 171	2882.067 844	.000 346 9731	.036 076	103.973 812	.009 617 8064	11.55	2.462 410	8.21	360
31	30.965 130	3232.193 788	.000 309 3874	.032 294	104.381 729	.009 580 2207	11.50	2.563 842	8.27	372
32	34.591 196	3623.320 040	.000 275 9900	.028 909	104.746 885	.009 546 8233	11.46	2.665 980	8.33	384
33	38.641 881	4060.247 803	.000 246 2904	.025 879	105.073 763	.009 517 1237	11.43	2.768 781	8.39	396
34	43.166 907	4548.340 507	.000 219 8604	.023 166	105.366 375	.009 490 6937	11.39	2.872 203	8.45	408
35	48.221 821	5093.589 648	.000 196 3252	.020 737	105.628 315	.009 467 1585	11.37	2.976 207	8.50	420
36	53.868 673	5702.688 337	.000 175 3559	.018 564	105.862 796	.009 446 1892	11.34	3.080 754	8.56	432
37	60.176 781	6383.113 458	.000 156 6634	.016 618	106.072 697	.009 427 4967	11.32	3.185 809	8.61	444
38	67.223 578	7143.217 450	.000 139 9929	.014 876	106.260 595	.009 410 8263	11.30	3.291 337	8.66	456
39	75.095 567	7992.330 837	.000 125 1199	.013 316	106.428 797	.009 395 9533	11.28	3.397 306	8.71	468
40	83.889 378	8940.876 761	.000 111 8459	.011 920	106.579 366	.009 382 6792	11.26	3.503 686	8.76	480
41	93.712 959	10000.498 931	.000 099 9950	.010 671	106.714 152	.009 370 8283	11.25	3.610 448	8.81	492
42	104.686 896	11184.204 555	.000 089 4118	.009 552	106.834 809	.009 360 2451	11.24	3.717 564	8.85	504
43	116.945 900	12506.524 003	.000 079 9583	.008 551	106.942 818	.009 350 7916	11.23	3.825 008	8.90	516
44	130.640 452	13983.689 176	.000 071 5119	.007 655	107.039 504	.009 342 3452	11.22	3.932 758	8.94	528
45	145.938 658	15633.832 757	.000 063 9638	.006 852	107.126 055	.009 334 7972	11.21	4.040 790	8.98	540
46	163.028 308	17477.210 793	.000 057 2174	.006 134	107.203 534	.009 328 0507	11.20	4.149 084	9.02	552
47	182.119 184	19536.451 349	.000 051 1864	.005 491	107.272 891	.009 322 0197	11.19	4.257 619	9.06	564
48	203.445 633	21836.832 272	.000 045 7942	.004 915	107.334 977	.009 316 6275	11.18	4.366 377	9.10	576
49	227.269 442	24406.591 485	.000 040 9725	.004 400	107.390 555	.009 311 8059	11.18	4.475 342	9.13	588
50	253.883 057	27277.273 618	.000 036 6606	.003 939	107.440 307	.009 307 4939	11.17	4.584 496	9.17	600

Effective Rate is 11.71 %

Annual Percentage Rate is 11.125%

	Amount Of 1	Amount Of 1 Per Period	Sinking Fund Payment	Present Worth Of 1	Present Worth of 1 Per Period	Periodic Payment To Amortize 1	Constant Annual Percent	Total Interest	Annual Add On Rate	
	What a single $ 1 deposit grows to in the future. The deposit is made at the beginning of the first period.	What a series of $ 1 deposits grow to in the future. A deposit is made at the end of each period.	The amount to be deposited at the end of each period that grows to $ 1 in the future.	What $ 1 to be paid in the future is worth today. Value today of a single $ 1 payment tomorrow.	What $ 1 to be paid at the end of each period is worth today. Value today of a series of $ 1 payments tomorrow.	The mortgage payment to amortize a loan of $ 1. An annuity certain, payable at the end of each period, worth $ 1 today.	The annual payment, including interest and principal, to amortize completely a loan of $ 100.	The total interest paid over the term on a loan of $1. The loan is amortized by regular periodic payments.	The average annual interest rate on a loan that is completely amortized by regular periodic payments.	
	$S = (1+i)^n$	$S\overline{n}| = \dfrac{(1+i)^n - 1}{i}$	$\dfrac{1}{S\overline{n}|} = \dfrac{i}{(1+i)^n - 1}$	$V^n = \dfrac{1}{(1+i)^n}$	$A\overline{n}| = \dfrac{1 - V^n}{i}$	$\dfrac{1}{A\overline{n}|} = \dfrac{i}{1 - V^n}$				

YEAR										PERIODS
	1.009 292	1.000 000	1.000 000 0000	.990 794	.990 794	1.009 291 6667	1211.15	.009 292	11.15	1
	1.018 670	2.009 292	.497 687 8253	.981 672	1.972 466	.506 979 4920	608.38	.013 959	8.38	2
	1.028 135	3.027 961	.330 255 2078	.972 635	2.945 101	.339 546 8745	407.46	.018 641	7.46	3
	1.037 688	4.056 096	.246 542 4795	.963 651	3.908 782	.255 834 1462	307.01	.023 337	7.00	4
	1.047 330	5.093 784	.196 317 7066	.954 809	4.863 591	.205 609 3733	246.74	.028 047	6.73	5
	1.057 061	6.141 114	.162 836 9113	.946 019	5.809 611	.172 128 5780	206.56	.032 771	6.55	6
	1.066 883	7.198 175	.138 924 1030	.937 310	6.746 920	.148 215 7697	177.86	.037 510	6.43	7
	1.076 796	8.265 058	.120 991 2864	.928 681	7.675 601	.130 282 9531	156.34	.042 264	6.34	8
	1.086 801	9.341 854	.107 045 1307	.920 131	8.595 733	.116 336 7973	139.61	.047 031	6.27	9
	1.096 900	10.428 656	.095 889 6374	.911 660	9.507 393	.105 181 3040	126.22	.051 813	6.22	10
	1.107 092	11.525 555	.086 763 7165	.903 268	10.410 661	.096 055 3832	115.27	.056 609	6.18	11
	1.117 378	12.632 647	.079 159 9748	.894 952	11.305 613	.088 451 6415	106.15	.061 420	6.14	12
1	1.117 378	12.632 647	.079 159 9748	.894 952	11.305 613	.088 451 6415	106.15	.061 420	6.14	12
2	1.248 534	26.748 093	.037 385 8432	.800 939	21.423 594	.046 677 5099	56.02	.120 260	6.01	24
3	1.395 085	42.520 386	.023 518 1307	.716 802	30.478 701	.032 809 7973	39.38	.181 153	6.04	36
4	1.558 838	60.144 005	.016 626 7609	.641 503	38.582 587	.025 918 4276	31.11	.244 085	6.10	48
5	1.741 812	79.836 256	.012 525 6375	.574 115	45.835 177	.021 817 3041	26.19	.309 038	6.18	60
6	1.946 263	101.839 950	.009 819 3292	.513 805	52.325 897	.019 110 9959	22.94	.375 992	6.27	72
7	2.174 712	126.426 402	.007 909 7403	.459 831	58.134 780	.017 201 4069	20.65	.444 918	6.36	84
8	2.429 976	153.898 770	.006 497 7777	.411 527	63.333 451	.015 789 4444	18.95	.515 787	6.45	96
9	2.715 203	184.595 799	.005 417 2414	.368 297	67.986 012	.014 708 9080	17.66	.588 562	6.54	108
10	3.033 909	218.895 995	.004 568 3796	.329 608	72.149 831	.013 860 0463	16.64	.663 206	6.63	120
11	3.390 024	257.222 291	.003 887 6879	.294 983	75.876 250	.013 179 3546	15.82	.739 675	6.72	132
12	3.787 939	300.047 264	.003 332 8083	.263 996	79.211 215	.012 624 4749	15.15	.817 924	6.82	144
13	4.232 561	347.898 961	.002 874 3978	.236 264	82.195 849	.012 166 0644	14.60	.897 906	6.91	156
14	4.729 372	401.367 412	.002 491 4828	.211 445	84.866 954	.011 783 1495	14.14	.979 569	7.00	168
15	5.284 498	461.111 900	.002 168 6710	.189 233	87.257 464	.011 460 3377	13.76	1.062 861	7.09	180
16	5.904 784	527.869 098	.001 894 4091	.169 354	89.396 856	.011 186 0757	13.43	1.147 727	7.17	192
17	6.597 877	602.462 144	.001 659 8553	.151 564	91.311 509	.010 951 5220	13.15	1.234 110	7.26	204
18	7.372 325	685.810 799	.001 458 1281	.135 642	93.025 032	.010 749 7948	12.90	1.321 956	7.34	216
19	8.237 677	778.942 781	.001 283 7913	.121 393	94.558 552	.010 575 4580	12.70	1.411 204	7.43	228
20	9.204 602	883.006 441	.001 132 4946	.108 641	95.930 980	.010 424 1612	12.51	1.501 799	7.51	240
21	10.285 022	999.284 920	.001 000 7156	.097 229	97.159 236	.010 292 3823	12.36	1.593 680	7.59	252
22	11.492 261	1129.211 975	.000 885 5733	.087 015	98.258 467	.010 177 2400	12.22	1.686 791	7.67	264
23	12.841 204	1274.389 652	.000 784 6894	.077 874	99.242 226	.010 076 3560	12.10	1.781 074	7.74	276
24	14.348 483	1436.608 045	.000 696 0841	.069 694	100.122 643	.009 987 7508	11.99	1.876 472	7.82	288
25	16.032 684	1617.867 363	.000 618 0976	.062 373	100.910 574	.009 909 7643	11.90	1.972 929	7.89	300
26	17.914 574	1820.402 600	.000 549 3290	.055 820	101.615 734	.009 840 9957	11.81	2.070 391	7.96	312
27	20.017 357	2046.711 088	.000 488 5887	.049 957	102.246 819	.009 780 2554	11.74	2.168 803	8.03	324
28	22.366 961	2299.583 290	.000 434 8614	.044 709	102.811 609	.009 726 5281	11.68	2.268 113	8.10	336
29	24.992 358	2582.137 213	.000 387 2761	.040 012	103.317 069	.009 678 9428	11.62	2.368 272	8.17	348
30	27.925 920	2897.856 847	.000 345 0826	.035 809	103.769 432	.009 636 7493	11.57	2.469 230	8.23	360
31	31.203 818	3250.635 129	.000 307 6322	.032 047	104.174 275	.009 599 2989	11.52	2.570 939	8.29	372
32	34.866 471	3644.821 940	.000 274 3618	.028 681	104.536 590	.009 566 0285	11.48	2.673 355	8.35	384
33	38.959 039	4085.277 747	.000 244 7814	.025 668	104.860 845	.009 536 4481	11.45	2.776 433	8.41	396
34	43.531 987	4577.433 526	.000 218 4630	.022 972	105.151 037	.009 510 1297	11.42	2.880 133	8.47	408
35	48.641 699	5127.357 734	.000 195 0322	.020 558	105.410 745	.009 486 6989	11.39	2.984 414	8.53	420
36	54.351 181	5741.831 135	.000 174 1605	.018 399	105.643 172	.009 465 8271	11.36	3.089 237	8.58	432
37	60.730 833	6428.430 406	.000 155 5590	.016 466	105.851 182	.009 447 2256	11.34	3.194 568	8.63	444
38	67.859 317	7195.621 562	.000 138 9734	.014 736	106.037 341	.009 430 6401	11.32	3.300 372	8.69	456
39	75.824 531	8052.864 343	.000 124 1794	.013 188	106.203 945	.009 415 8461	11.30	3.406 616	8.73	468
40	84.724 689	9010.728 862	.000 110 9788	.011 803	106.353 047	.009 402 6455	11.29	3.513 270	8.78	480
41	94.669 533	10081.025 932	.000 099 1963	.010 563	106.486 487	.009 390 8629	11.27	3.620 305	8.83	492
42	105.781 685	11276.952 697	.000 088 6764	.009 453	106.605 909	.009 380 3431	11.26	3.727 693	8.88	504
43	118.198 164	12613.255 364	.000 079 2817	.008 460	106.712 785	.009 370 9483	11.25	3.835 409	8.92	516
44	132.072 069	14106.411 025	.000 070 8898	.007 572	106.808 435	.009 362 5564	11.24	3.943 430	8.96	528
45	147.574 470	15774.830 822	.000 063 3921	.006 776	106.894 037	.009 355 0588	11.23	4.051 732	9.00	540
46	164.896 516	17639.086 970	.000 056 6923	.006 064	106.970 647	.009 348 3589	11.22	4.160 294	9.04	552
47	184.251 796	19722.166 416	.000 050 7044	.005 427	107.039 208	.009 342 3710	11.22	4.269 097	9.08	564
48	205.878 967	22049.774 275	.000 045 3520	.004 857	107.100 568	.009 337 0186	11.21	4.378 123	9.12	576
49	230.044 699	24650.550 540	.000 040 5670	.004 347	107.155 482	.009 332 2337	11.20	4.487 353	9.16	588
50	257.046 964	27556.623 961	.000 036 2889	.003 890	107.204 627	.009 327 9556	11.20	4.596 773	9.19	600

MONTHLY COMPOUND INTEREST AND ANNUITY

	Amount Of 1	Amount Of 1 Per Period	Sinking Fund Payment	Present Worth Of 1	Present Worth of 1 Per Period	Periodic Payment To Amortize 1	Constant Annual Percent	Total Interest	Annual Add On Rate
	What a single $1 deposit grows to in the future. The deposit is made at the beginning of the first period.	What a series of $1 deposits grow to in the future. A deposit is made at the end of each period.	The amount to be deposited at the end of each period that grows to $1 in the future.	What $1 to be paid in the future is worth today. Value today of a single $1 payment tomorrow.	What $1 to be paid at the end of each period is worth today. Value today of a series of $1 payments tomorrow.	The mortgage payment to amortize a loan of $1. An annuity certain, payable at the end of each period, worth $1 today.	The annual payment, including interest and principal, to amortize completely a loan of $100.	The total interest paid over the term on a loan of $1. The loan is amortized by regular periodic payments.	The average annual interest rate on a loan that is completely amortized by regular periodic payments.

$$S = (1+i)^n \qquad S\overline{n} = \frac{(1+i)^n - 1}{i} \qquad \frac{1}{S\overline{n}} = \frac{i}{(1+i)^n - 1} \qquad V^n = \frac{1}{(1+i)^n} \qquad A\overline{n} = \frac{1 - V^n}{i} \qquad \frac{1}{A\overline{n}} = \frac{i}{1 - V^n}$$

YEAR									**PERIODS**
	1.009 333	1.000 000	1.000 000 0000	.990 753	.990 753	1.009 333 3333	1211.20	.009 333	11.20 1
	1.018 754	2.009 333	.497 677 5050	.981 591	1.972 344	.507 010 8383	608.42	.014 022	8.41 2
	1.028 262	3.028 087	.330 241 4902	.972 515	2.944 859	.339 574 8235	407.49	.018 724	7.49 3
	1.037 859	4.056 349	.246 527 0953	.963 522	3.908 381	.255 860 4286	307.04	.023 442	7.03 4
	1.047 546	5.094 209	.196 301 3482	.954 612	4.862 993	.205 634 6815	246.77	.028 173	6.76 5
	1.057 323	6.141 754	.162 819 9248	.945 785	5.808 778	.172 153 2582	206.59	.032 920	6.58 6
	1.067 191	7.199 078	.138 906 6862	.937 039	6.745 817	.148 240 0195	177.89	.037 680	6.46 7
	1.077 152	8.266 269	.120 973 5629	.928 374	7.674 191	.130 306 8962	156.37	.042 455	6.37 8
	1.087 205	9.343 421	.107 027 1829	.919 790	8.593 980	.116 360 5162	139.64	.047 245	6.30 9
	1.097 353	10.430 626	.095 871 5230	.911 284	9.505 265	.105 204 8563	126.25	.052 049	6.25 10
	1.107 594	11.527 979	.086 745 4775	.902 858	10.408 122	.096 078 8108	115.30	.056 867	6.20 11
	1.117 932	12.635 573	.079 141 6426	.894 509	11.302 631	.088 474 9759	106.17	.061 700	6.17 12
1	1.117 932	12.635 573	.079 141 6426	.894 509	11.302 631	.088 474 9759	106.17	.061 700	6.17 12
2	1.249 772	26.761 285	.037 367 4141	.800 146	21.412 934	.046 700 7474	56.05	.120 818	6.04 24
3	1.397 160	42.552 870	.023 500 1777	.715 738	30.456 688	.032 833 5110	39.41	.182 006	6.07 36
4	1.561 930	60.206 788	.016 609 4228	.640 234	38.546 406	.025 942 7561	31.14	.245 252	6.13 48
5	1.746 132	79.942 669	.012 508 9644	.572 695	45.782 729	.021 842 2977	26.22	.310 538	6.21 60
6	1.952 056	102.006 042	.009 803 3409	.512 280	52.255 684	.019 136 6742	22.97	.377 841	6.30 72
7	2.182 266	126.671 393	.007 894 4423	.458 239	58.045 799	.017 227 7756	20.68	.447 133	6.39 84
8	2.439 625	154.245 579	.006 483 1680	.409 899	63.225 108	.015 816 5013	18.98	.518 384	6.48 96
9	2.727 335	185.071 643	.005 403 3129	.366 658	67.858 045	.014 736 6462	17.69	.591 558	6.57 108
10	3.048 975	219.533 088	.004 555 1220	.327 979	72.002 248	.013 888 4553	16.67	.666 615	6.67 120
11	3.408 547	258.058 640	.003 875 0882	.293 380	75.709 273	.013 208 4216	15.86	.743 512	6.76 132
12	3.810 524	301.127 589	.003 320 8515	.262 431	79.025 241	.012 654 1848	15.19	.822 203	6.85 144
13	4.259 907	349.275 745	.002 863 0674	.234 747	81.991 402	.012 196 4007	14.64	.902 639	6.94 156
14	4.762 286	403.102 110	.002 480 7610	.209 983	84.644 660	.011 814 0944	14.18	.984 768	7.03 168
15	5.323 912	463.276 327	.002 158 5390	.187 832	87.018 022	.011 491 8723	13.80	1.068 537	7.12 180
16	5.951 772	530.547 010	.001 884 8471	.168 017	89.141 016	.011 218 1804	13.47	1.153 891	7.21 192
17	6.653 677	605.751 061	.001 650 8432	.150 293	91.040 052	.010 984 1765	13.19	1.240 772	7.30 204
18	7.438 358	689.824 077	.001 449 6450	.134 438	92.738 757	.010 782 9783	12.94	1.329 123	7.38 216
19	8.315 579	783.811 992	.001 275 8162	.120 256	94.258 263	.010 609 1495	12.74	1.418 886	7.47 228
20	9.296 252	888.884 093	.001 125 0061	.107 570	95.617 474	.010 458 3394	12.56	1.510 001	7.55 240
21	10.392 577	1006.347 557	.000 993 6925	.096 223	96.833 301	.010 327 0258	12.40	1.602 411	7.63 252
22	11.618 195	1137.663 725	.000 878 9944	.086 072	97.920 869	.010 212 3277	12.26	1.696 055	7.71 264
23	12.988 352	1284.466 273	.000 778 5335	.076 992	98.893 708	.010 111 8668	12.14	1.790 875	7.79 276
24	14.520 094	1448.581 541	.000 690 3305	.068 870	99.763 920	.010 023 6638	12.03	1.886 815	7.86 288
25	16.232 478	1632.051 253	.000 612 7259	.061 605	100.542 334	.009 946 0592	11.94	1.983 818	7.94 300
26	18.146 807	1837.157 917	.000 544 3190	.055 106	101.238 631	.009 877 6524	11.86	2.081 828	8.01 312
27	20.286 897	2066.453 224	.000 483 9209	.049 293	101.861 475	.009 817 2543	11.79	2.180 790	8.08 324
28	22.679 371	2322.789 789	.000 430 5168	.044 093	102.418 614	.009 763 8501	11.72	2.280 654	8.15 336
29	25.353 995	2609.356 641	.000 383 2362	.039 442	102.916 980	.009 716 5696	11.66	2.381 366	8.21 348
30	28.344 043	2929.718 899	.000 341 3297	.035 281	103.362 773	.009 674 6630	11.61	2.482 879	8.28 360
31	31.686 713	3287.862 123	.000 304 1490	.031 559	103.761 539	.009 637 4823	11.57	2.585 143	8.34 372
32	35.423 591	3688.241 899	.000 271 1319	.028 230	104.118 238	.009 604 4652	11.53	2.688 115	8.40 384
33	39.601 167	4135.839 269	.000 241 7889	.025 252	104.437 309	.009 575 1222	11.50	2.791 748	8.46 396
34	44.271 412	4636.222 698	.000 215 6928	.022 588	104.722 721	.009 549 0262	11.46	2.896 003	8.52 408
35	49.492 429	5195.617 354	.000 192 4699	.020 205	104.978 024	.009 525 8032	11.44	3.000 837	8.57 420
36	55.329 170	5820.982 547	.000 171 7923	.018 074	105.206 395	.009 505 1256	11.41	3.106 214	8.63 432
37	61.854 251	6520.098 318	.000 153 3719	.016 167	105.410 675	.009 486 7053	11.39	3.212 097	8.68 444
38	69.148 847	7301.662 220	.000 136 9551	.014 462	105.593 405	.009 470 2884	11.37	3.318 452	8.73 456
39	77.303 710	8175.397 527	.000 122 3182	.012 936	105.756 858	.009 455 6515	11.35	3.425 245	8.78 468
40	86.420 293	9152.174 199	.000 109 2637	.011 571	105.903 069	.009 442 5970	11.34	3.532 447	8.83 480
41	96.612 012	10244.144 112	.000 097 6167	.010 351	106.033 856	.009 430 9501	11.32	3.640 027	8.88 492
42	108.005 661	11464.892 236	.000 087 2228	.009 259	106.150 846	.009 420 5561	11.31	3.747 960	8.92 504
43	120.742 986	12829.605 645	.000 077 9447	.008 282	106.255 494	.009 411 2781	11.30	3.856 219	8.97 516
44	134.982 450	14355.262 456	.000 069 6609	.007 408	106.349 103	.009 402 9942	11.29	3.964 781	9.01 528
45	150.901 202	16060.843 048	.000 062 2632	.006 627	106.432 837	.009 395 5966	11.28	4.073 622	9.05 540
46	168.697 284	17967.566 195	.000 055 6558	.005 928	106.507 738	.009 388 9892	11.27	4.182 722	9.09 552
47	188.592 095	20099.153 043	.000 049 7533	.005 302	106.574 738	.009 383 0867	11.26	4.292 061	9.13 564
48	210.833 141	22482.122 223	.000 044 4798	.004 743	106.634 669	.009 377 8131	11.26	4.401 620	9.17 576
49	235.697 118	25146.119 758	.000 039 7676	.004 243	106.688 279	.009 373 1009	11.25	4.511 383	9.21 588
50	263.493 354	28124.287 889	.000 035 5565	.003 795	106.736 233	.009 368 8898	11.25	4.621 334	9.24 600

Effective Rate is 11.79 %

Annual Percentage Rate is 11.20 %

	Amount Of 1	Amount Of 1 Per Period	Sinking Fund Payment	Present Worth Of 1	Present Worth of 1 Per Period	Periodic Payment To Amortize 1	Constant Annual Percent	Total Interest	Annual Add On Rate	
	What a single $ 1 deposit grows to in the future. The deposit is made at the beginning of the first period.	What a series of $ 1 deposits grow to in the future. A deposit is made at the end of each period.	The amount to be deposited at the end of each period that grows to $ 1 in the future.	What $ 1 to be paid in the future is worth today. Value today of a single $ 1 payment tomorrow.	What $ 1 to be paid at the end of each period is worth today. Value today of a series of $ 1 payments tomorrow.	The mortgage payment to amortize a loan of $ 1. An annuity certain, payable at the end of each period, worth $ 1 today.	The annual payment, including interest and principal, to amortize completely a loan of $ 100.	The total interest paid over the term on a loan of $1. The loan is amortized by regular periodic payments.	The average annual interest rate on a loan that is completely amortized by regular periodic payments.	
	$S = (1+i)^n$	$S\overline{n}| = \dfrac{(1+i)^n - 1}{i}$	$\dfrac{1}{S\overline{n}|} = \dfrac{i}{(1+i)^n - 1}$	$V^n = \dfrac{1}{(1+i)^n}$	$A\overline{n}| = \dfrac{1-V^n}{i}$	$\dfrac{1}{A\overline{n}|} = \dfrac{i}{1-V^n}$				

YEAR										PERIODS
	1.009 375	1.000 000	1.000 000 0000	.990 712	.990 712	1.009 375 0000	1211.25	.009 375	11.25	1
	1.018 838	2.009 375	.497 667 1851	.981 510	1.972 222	.507 042 1851	608.46	.014 084	8.45	2
	1.028 389	3.028 213	.330 227 7733	.972 394	2.944 617	.339 602 7733	407.53	.018 808	7.52	3
	1.038 031	4.056 602	.246 511 7122	.963 363	3.907 979	.255 886 7122	307.07	.023 547	7.06	4
	1.047 762	5.094 633	.196 284 9912	.954 415	4.862 394	.205 659 9912	246.80	.028 300	6.79	5
	1.057 585	6.142 395	.162 802 9400	.945 551	5.807 945	.172 177 9400	206.62	.033 068	6.61	6
	1.067 500	7.199 980	.138 889 2713	.936 768	6.744 713	.148 264 2713	177.92	.037 850	6.49	7
	1.077 508	8.267 480	.120 955 8416	.928 068	7.672 781	.130 330 8416	156.40	.042 647	6.40	8
	1.087 609	9.344 988	.107 009 2376	.919 448	8.592 229	.116 384 2376	139.67	.047 458	6.33	9
	1.097 806	10.432 597	.095 853 4114	.910 908	9.503 137	.105 228 4114	126.28	.052 284	6.27	10
	1.108 098	11.530 402	.086 727 2416	.902 448	10.405 585	.096 102 2416	115.33	.057 125	6.23	11
	1.118 486	12.638 500	.079 123 3137	.894 066	11.299 650	.088 498 3137	106.20	.061 980	6.20	12
1	1.118 486	12.638 500	.079 123 3137	.894 066	11.299 650	.088 498 3137	106.20	.061 980	6.20	12
2	1.251 011	26.774 484	.037 348 9917	.799 354	21.402 281	.046 723 9917	56.07	.121 376	6.07	24
3	1.399 238	42.585 384	.023 482 2349	.714 675	30.434 697	.032 857 2349	39.43	.182 860	6.10	36
4	1.565 028	60.269 654	.016 592 0980	.638 966	38.510 272	.025 967 0980	31.17	.246 421	6.16	48
5	1.750 462	80.049 260	.012 492 3079	.571 278	45.730 366	.021 867 3079	26.25	.312 038	6.24	60
6	1.957 867	102.172 472	.009 787 3721	.510 760	52.185 606	.019 162 3721	23.00	.379 691	6.33	72
7	2.189 847	126.916 973	.007 879 1668	.456 653	57.957 015	.017 254 1668	20.71	.449 350	6.42	84
8	2.449 313	154.593 349	.006 468 5836	.408 278	63.117 034	.015 843 5836	19.02	.520 984	6.51	96
9	2.739 522	185.548 987	.005 389 4123	.365 027	67.730 430	.014 764 4123	17.72	.594 557	6.61	108
10	3.064 117	220.172 433	.004 541 8947	.326 358	71.855 110	.013 916 8947	16.71	.670 027	6.70	120
11	3.427 171	258.898 270	.003 862 5210	.291 786	75.542 845	.013 237 5210	15.89	.747 353	6.79	132
12	3.833 243	302.212 574	.003 308 9292	.260 876	78.839 923	.012 683 9292	15.23	.826 486	6.89	144
13	4.287 428	350.659 014	.002 851 7733	.233 240	81.787 728	.012 226 7733	14.68	.907 377	6.98	156
14	4.795 428	404.845 676	.002 470 0770	.208 532	84.423 259	.011 845 0770	14.22	.989 973	7.07	168
15	5.363 619	465.452 695	.002 148 4460	.186 441	86.779 597	.011 523 4460	13.83	1.074 220	7.16	180
16	5.999 132	533.240 794	.001 875 3254	.166 691	88.886 318	.011 250 3254	13.51	1.160 062	7.25	192
17	6.709 945	609.060 830	.001 641 8721	.149 033	90.769 865	.011 016 8721	13.23	1.247 442	7.34	204
18	7.504 979	693.864 473	.001 441 2036	.133 245	92.453 881	.010 816 2036	12.98	1.336 300	7.42	216
19	8.394 214	788.716 155	.001 267 8832	.119 130	93.959 501	.010 642 8832	12.78	1.426 577	7.51	228
20	9.388 810	894.806 428	.001 117 5601	.106 510	95.305 625	.010 492 5601	12.60	1.518 214	7.59	240
21	10.501 252	1013.466 907	.000 986 7120	.095 227	96.509 148	.010 361 7120	12.44	1.611 151	7.67	252
22	11.745 503	1146.186 983	.000 872 4580	.085 139	97.585 177	.010 247 4580	12.30	1.705 329	7.75	264
23	13.137 180	1294.632 522	.000 772 4200	.076 120	98.547 217	.010 147 4200	12.18	1.800 688	7.83	276
24	14.693 751	1460.666 770	.000 684 6188	.068 056	99.407 345	.010 059 6188	12.08	1.897 170	7.90	288
25	16.434 754	1646.373 742	.000 607 3955	.060 847	100.176 355	.009 982 3955	11.98	1.994 719	7.98	300
26	18.382 041	1854.084 378	.000 539 3498	.054 401	100.863 902	.009 914 3498	11.90	2.093 277	8.05	312
27	20.560 054	2086.405 804	.000 479 2931	.048 638	101.478 613	.009 854 2931	11.83	2.192 791	8.12	324
28	22.996 132	2346.254 051	.000 426 2113	.043 486	102.028 205	.009 801 2113	11.77	2.293 207	8.19	336
29	25.720 850	2636.890 662	.000 379 2345	.038 879	102.519 577	.009 754 2345	11.71	2.394 474	8.26	348
30	28.768 409	2961.963 624	.000 337 6139	.034 760	102.958 896	.009 712 6139	11.66	2.496 541	8.32	360
31	32.177 061	3325.553 160	.000 300 7019	.031 078	103.351 676	.009 675 7019	11.62	2.599 361	8.39	372
32	35.989 590	3732.222 944	.000 267 9368	.027 786	103.702 847	.009 642 9368	11.58	2.702 888	8.45	384
33	40.253 850	4187.077 378	.000 238 8301	.024 842	104.016 817	.009 613 8301	11.54	2.807 077	8.51	396
34	45.023 366	4695.825 666	.000 212 9551	.022 211	104.297 526	.009 587 9551	11.51	2.911 886	8.56	408
35	50.358 001	5264.853 472	.000 189 9388	.019 858	104.548 499	.009 564 9388	11.48	3.017 274	8.62	420
36	56.324 716	5901.303 071	.000 169 4541	.017 754	104.772 886	.009 544 4541	11.46	3.123 204	8.68	432
37	62.998 403	6613.162 997	.000 151 2136	.015 873	104.973 502	.009 526 2136	11.44	3.229 639	8.73	444
38	70.462 828	7409.368 314	.000 134 9643	.014 192	105.152 866	.009 509 9643	11.42	3.336 544	8.78	456
39	78.811 682	8299.912 764	.000 120 4832	.012 688	105.313 229	.009 495 4832	11.40	3.443 886	8.83	468
40	88.149 758	9295.974 209	.000 107 5734	.011 344	105.456 605	.009 482 5734	11.38	3.551 635	8.88	480
41	98.594 265	10410.054 927	.000 096 0610	.010 143	105.584 792	.009 471 0610	11.37	3.659 762	8.93	492
42	110.276 299	11656.138 543	.000 085 7917	.009 068	105.699 399	.009 460 7917	11.36	3.768 239	8.97	504
43	123.342 489	13049.865 545	.000 076 6291	.008 108	105.801 866	.009 451 6291	11.35	3.877 041	9.02	516
44	137.956 840	14608.729 598	.000 068 4522	.007 249	105.893 478	.009 443 4522	11.34	3.986 143	9.06	528
45	154.302 785	16352.297 118	.000 061 1535	.006 481	105.975 385	.009 436 1535	11.33	4.095 523	9.10	540
46	172.585 496	18302.452 871	.000 054 6375	.005 794	106.048 616	.009 429 6375	11.32	4.205 160	9.14	552
47	193.034 450	20483.674 656	.000 048 8194	.005 180	106.114 088	.009 423 8194	11.31	4.315 034	9.18	564
48	215.906 318	22923.340 550	.000 043 6237	.004 632	106.172 625	.009 418 6237	11.31	4.425 127	9.22	576
49	241.488 180	25652.072 543	.000 038 9832	.004 141	106.224 961	.009 413 9832	11.30	4.535 422	9.26	588
50	270.101 133	28704.120 905	.000 034 8382	.003 702	106.271 753	.009 409 8382	11.30	4.645 903	9.29	600

Effective Rate is 11.85 %

Annual Percentage Rate is 11.25 %

MONTHLY COMPOUND INTEREST AND ANNUITY

11.30 % M

Amount Of 1	Amount Of 1 Per Period	Sinking Fund Payment	Present Worth Of 1	Present Worth of 1 Per Period	Periodic Payment To Amortize 1	Constant Annual Percent	Total Interest	Annual Add On Rate	
What a single $ 1 deposit grows to in the future. The deposit is made at the beginning of the first period.	What a series of $ 1 deposits grow to in the future. A deposit is made at the end of each period.	The amount to be deposited at the end of each period that grows to $ 1 in the future.	What $ 1 to be paid in the future is worth today. Value today of a single $ 1 payment tomorrow.	What $ 1 to be paid at the end of each period is worth today. Value today of a series of $ 1 payments tomorrow.	The mortgage payment to amortize a loan of $ 1. An annuity certain, payable at the end of each period, worth $ 1 today.	The annual payment, including interest and principal, to amortize completely a loan of $ 100.	The total interest paid over the term on a loan of $1. The loan is amortized by regular periodic payments.	The average annual interest rate on a loan that is completely amortized by regular periodic payments.	

$$S = (1+i)^n \qquad S\overline{n}| = \frac{(1+i)^n - 1}{i} \qquad \frac{1}{S\overline{n}|} = \frac{i}{(1+i)^n - 1} \qquad V^n = \frac{1}{(1+i)^n} \qquad A\overline{n}| = \frac{1-V^n}{i} \qquad \frac{1}{A\overline{n}|} = \frac{i}{1-V^n}$$

PERIODS

YEAR

	Amount Of 1	Amount Of 1 Per Period	Sinking Fund Payment	Present Worth Of 1	Present Worth of 1 Per Period	Periodic Payment To Amortize 1	Constant Annual Percent	Total Interest	Annual Add On Rate	PERIODS
	1.009 417	1.000 000	1.000 000 0000	.990 671	.990 671	1.009 416 6667	1211.30	.009 417	11.30	1
	1.018 922	2.009 417	.497 656 8656	.981 429	1.972 101	.507 073 5323	608.49	.014 147	8.49	2
	1.028 517	3.028 339	.330 214 0572	.972 274	2.944 374	.339 630 7239	407.56	.018 892	7.56	3
	1.038 202	4.056 856	.246 496 3302	.963 204	3.907 578	.255 912 9968	307.10	.023 652	7.10	4
	1.047 978	5.095 058	.196 268 6355	.954 218	4.861 796	.205 685 3021	246.83	.028 427	6.82	5
	1.057 847	6.143 036	.162 785 9568	.945 316	5.807 112	.172 202 6234	206.65	.033 216	6.64	6
	1.067 808	7.200 883	.138 871 8584	.936 498	6.743 610	.148 288 5251	177.95	.038 020	6.52	7
	1.077 864	8.268 691	.120 938 1226	.927 761	7.671 371	.130 354 7893	156.43	.042 838	6.43	8
	1.088 013	9.346 555	.106 991 2949	.919 106	8.590 478	.116 407 9616	139.69	.047 672	6.36	9
	1.098 259	10.434 568	.095 835 3027	.910 532	9.501 010	.105 251 9693	126.31	.052 520	6.30	10
	1.108 601	11.532 827	.086 709 0087	.902 038	10.403 048	.096 125 6754	115.36	.057 382	6.26	11
	1.119 040	12.641 428	.079 104 9883	.893 623	11.296 671	.088 521 6550	106.23	.062 260	6.23	12
1	1.119 040	12.641 428	.079 104 9883	.893 623	11.296 671	.088 521 6550	106.23	.062 260	6.23	12
2	1.252 251	26.787 693	.037 330 5762	.798 562	21.391 636	.046 747 2428	56.10	.121 934	6.10	24
3	1.401 319	42.617 930	.023 464 3023	.713 613	30.412 729	.032 880 9689	39.46	.183 715	6.12	36
4	1.568 132	60.332 601	.016 574 7867	.637 701	38.474 186	.025 991 4534	31.19	.247 590	6.19	48
5	1.754 803	80.156 029	.012 475 6679	.569 865	45.678 089	.021 892 3346	26.28	.313 540	6.27	60
6	1.963 695	102.339 239	.009 771 4230	.509 244	52.115 662	.019 188 0897	23.03	.381 542	6.36	72
7	2.197 453	127.163 142	.007 863 9139	.455 072	57.868 426	.017 280 5806	20.74	.451 569	6.45	84
8	2.459 038	154.942 084	.006 454 0245	.406 663	63.009 228	.015 870 6911	19.05	.523 586	6.54	96
9	2.751 762	186.027 835	.005 375 5396	.363 404	67.603 167	.014 792 2063	17.76	.597 558	6.64	108
10	3.079 332	220.814 037	.004 528 6976	.324 746	71.708 417	.013 945 3643	16.74	.673 444	6.73	120
11	3.445 896	259.741 193	.003 849 9862	.290 200	75.376 963	.013 266 6528	15.92	.751 198	6.83	132
12	3.856 096	303.302 241	.003 297 0412	.259 330	78.655 260	.012 713 7079	15.26	.830 774	6.92	144
13	4.315 126	352.048 802	.002 840 5153	.231 743	81.584 821	.012 257 1819	14.71	.912 120	7.02	156
14	4.828 799	406.598 158	.002 459 4307	.207 091	84.202 745	.011 876 0974	14.26	.995 184	7.11	168
15	5.403 620	467.641 076	.002 138 3921	.185 061	86.542 182	.011 555 0588	13.87	1.079 911	7.20	180
16	6.046 868	535.950 550	.001 865 8438	.165 375	88.632 756	.011 282 5104	13.54	1.166 242	7.29	192
17	6.766 687	612.391 592	.001 632 9421	.147 783	90.500 942	.011 049 6087	13.26	1.254 120	7.38	204
18	7.572 195	697.932 183	.001 432 8040	.132 062	92.170 396	.010 849 4706	13.02	1.343 684	7.46	216
19	8.473 590	793.655 536	.001 259 9625	.118 014	93.662 258	.010 676 6591	12.82	1.434 278	7.55	228
20	9.482 287	900.773 808	.001 110 1566	.105 460	94.995 420	.010 526 8233	12.64	1.526 438	7.63	240
21	10.611 059	1020.643 451	.000 979 7741	.094 241	96.186 765	.010 396 4407	12.48	1.619 903	7.71	252
22	11.874 201	1154.782 389	.000 865 9640	.084 216	97.251 378	.010 282 6307	12.34	1.714 615	7.79	264
23	13.287 707	1304.889 242	.000 766 3486	.075 258	98.202 740	.010 183 0152	12.22	1.810 512	7.87	276
24	14.869 477	1472.864 831	.000 678 9489	.067 252	99.052 900	.010 095 6156	12.12	1.907 537	7.95	288
25	16.639 541	1660.836 253	.000 602 1063	.060 098	99.812 622	.010 018 7730	12.03	2.005 632	8.02	300
26	18.620 314	1871.183 815	.000 534 4210	.053 705	100.491 527	.009 951 0877	11.95	2.104 739	8.10	312
27	20.836 879	2106.571 173	.000 474 7051	.047 992	101.098 212	.009 891 3717	11.87	2.204 804	8.17	324
28	23.317 303	2369.979 069	.000 421 9447	.042 887	101.640 360	.009 838 6113	11.81	2.305 773	8.23	336
29	26.092 997	2664.743 071	.000 375 2707	.038 324	102.124 836	.009 791 9374	11.76	2.407 594	8.30	348
30	29.199 111	2994.595 812	.000 333 9349	.034 248	102.557 775	.009 750 6015	11.71	2.510 217	8.37	360
31	32.674 976	3363.714 261	.000 297 2904	.030 604	102.944 659	.009 713 9571	11.66	2.613 592	8.43	372
32	36.564 609	3776.772 611	.000 264 7763	.027 349	103.290 388	.009 681 4430	11.62	2.717 674	8.49	384
33	40.917 264	4239.001 474	.000 235 9046	.024 440	103.599 339	.009 652 5713	11.59	2.822 418	8.55	396
34	45.788 060	4756.254 112	.000 210 2495	.021 840	103.875 424	.009 626 9162	11.56	2.927 782	8.61	408
35	51.238 675	5335.080 561	.000 187 4386	.019 517	104.122 141	.009 604 1053	11.53	3.033 724	8.67	420
36	57.338 133	5982.810 577	.000 167 1455	.017 440	104.342 612	.009 583 8122	11.51	3.140 207	8.72	432
37	64.163 671	6707.646 446	.000 149 0836	.015 585	104.539 631	.009 565 7503	11.48	3.247 193	8.78	444
38	71.801 721	7518.766 857	.000 133 0005	.013 927	104.715 691	.009 549 6672	11.46	3.354 648	8.83	456
39	80.349 006	8426.443 134	.000 118 6740	.012 446	104.873 023	.009 535 3407	11.45	3.462 539	8.88	468
40	89.913 761	9442.169 296	.000 105 9079	.011 122	105.013 618	.009 522 5745	11.43	3.570 836	8.93	480
41	100.617 105	10578.807 614	.000 094 5286	.009 939	105.139 256	.009 511 1953	11.42	3.679 508	8.97	492
42	112.594 576	11850.751 485	.000 084 3828	.008 881	105.251 530	.009 501 0495	11.41	3.788 529	9.02	504
43	125.997 847	13274.107 697	.000 075 3346	.007 937	105.351 861	.009 492 0013	11.40	3.897 873	9.06	516
44	140.996 645	14866.900 391	.000 067 2635	.007 092	105.441 519	.009 483 9302	11.39	4.007 515	9.11	528
45	157.780 902	16649.299 306	.000 060 0626	.006 338	105.521 639	.009 476 7293	11.38	4.117 434	9.15	540
46	176.563 158	18643.875 188	.000 053 6369	.005 664	105.593 236	.009 470 3036	11.37	4.227 608	9.19	552
47	197.581 256	20875.885 606	.000 047 9022	.005 061	105.657 217	.009 464 5688	11.36	4.338 017	9.23	564
48	221.101 351	23373.594 794	.000 042 7833	.004 523	105.714 392	.009 459 4500	11.36	4.448 643	9.27	576
49	247.421 281	26168.631 563	.000 038 2137	.004 042	105.765 484	.009 454 8804	11.35	4.559 470	9.31	588
50	276.874 337	29296.389 822	.000 034 1339	.003 612	105.811 142	.009 450 8006	11.35	4.670 480	9.34	600

	Amount Of 1	Amount Of 1 Per Period	Sinking Fund Payment	Present Worth Of 1	Present Worth of 1 Per Period	Periodic Payment To Amortize 1	Constant Annual Percent	Total Interest	Annual Add On Rate	
	What a single $ 1 deposit grows to in the future. The deposit is made at the beginning of the first period.	What a series of $ 1 deposits grow to in the future. A deposit is made at the end of each period.	The amount to be deposited at the end of each period that grows to $ 1 in the future.	What $ 1 to be paid in the future is worth today. Value today of a single $ 1 payment tomorrow.	What $ 1 to be paid at the end of each period is worth today. Value today of a series of $ 1 payments tomorrow.	The mortgage payment to amortize a loan of $ 1. An annuity certain, payable at the end of each period, worth $ 1 today.	The annual payment, including interest and principal, to amortize completely a loan of $ 100.	The total interest paid over the term on a loan of $1. The loan is amortized by regular periodic payments.	The average annual interest rate on a loan that is completely amortized by regular periodic payments.	
	$S = (1+i)^n$	$S\overline{n}| = \dfrac{(1+i)^n - 1}{i}$	$\dfrac{1}{S\overline{n}|} = \dfrac{i}{(1+i)^n - 1}$	$V^n = \dfrac{1}{(1+i)^n}$	$A\overline{n}| = \dfrac{1-V^n}{i}$	$\dfrac{1}{A\overline{n}|} = \dfrac{i}{1-V^n}$				

YEAR										PERIODS
	1.009 458	1.000 000	1.000 000 0000	.990 630	.990 630	1.009 458 3333	1211.35	.009 458	11.35	1
	1.019 006	2.009 458	.497 646 5465	.981 348	1.971 979	.507 104 8799	608.53	.014 210	8.53	2
	1.028 644	3.028 464	.330 200 3419	.972 153	2.944 132	.339 658 6752	407.60	.018 976	7.59	3
	1.038 373	4.057 109	.246 480 9492	.963 045	3.907 177	.255 939 2825	307.13	.023 757	7.13	4
	1.048 195	5.095 482	.196 252 2812	.954 021	4.861 198	.205 710 6145	246.86	.028 553	6.85	5
	1.058 109	6.143 677	.162 768 9752	.945 082	5.806 280	.172 227 3086	206.68	.033 364	6.67	6
	1.068 117	7.201 786	.138 854 4475	.936 227	6.742 507	.148 312 7808	177.98	.038 189	6.55	7
	1.078 219	8.269 903	.120 920 4058	.927 455	7.669 962	.130 378 7392	156.46	.043 030	6.45	8
	1.088 418	9.348 122	.106 973 3547	.918 765	8.588 727	.116 431 6880	139.72	.047 885	6.38	9
	1.098 712	10.436 540	.095 817 1968	.910 156	9.498 884	.105 275 5301	126.34	.052 755	6.33	10
	1.109 104	11.535 252	.086 690 7790	.901 628	10.400 512	.096 149 1124	115.38	.057 640	6.29	11
	1.119 595	12.644 356	.079 086 6663	.893 180	11.293 693	.088 544 9996	106.26	.062 540	6.25	12
1	1.119 595	12.644 356	.079 086 6663	.893 180	11.293 693	.088 544 9996	106.26	.062 540	6.25	12
2	1.253 492	26.800 909	.037 312 1674	.797 771	21.380 998	.046 770 5008	56.13	.122 492	6.12	24
3	1.403 403	42.650 508	.023 446 3798	.712 554	30.390 783	.032 904 7131	39.49	.184 570	6.15	36
4	1.571 242	60.395 632	.016 557 4888	.636 439	38.438 147	.026 015 8221	31.22	.248 759	6.22	48
5	1.759 154	80.262 976	.012 459 0446	.568 455	45.625 896	.021 917 3779	26.31	.315 043	6.30	60
6	1.969 539	102.506 346	.009 755 4936	.507 733	52.045 852	.019 213 8269	23.06	.383 396	6.39	72
7	2.205 085	127.409 902	.007 848 6836	.453 497	57.780 033	.017 307 0169	20.77	.453 789	6.48	84
8	2.468 801	155.291 787	.006 439 4906	.405 055	62.901 690	.015 897 8239	19.08	.526 191	6.58	96
9	2.764 057	186.508 193	.005 361 6948	.361 787	67.476 255	.014 820 0281	17.79	.600 563	6.67	108
10	3.094 623	221.457 910	.004 515 5307	.323 141	71.562 167	.013 973 8641	16.77	.676 864	6.77	120
11	3.464 723	260.587 423	.003 837 4837	.288 623	75.211 624	.013 295 8171	15.96	.755 048	6.86	132
12	3.879 085	304.396 612	.003 285 1877	.257 793	78.471 248	.012 743 5210	15.30	.835 067	6.96	144
13	4.343 002	353.445 141	.002 829 2934	.230 255	81.382 681	.012 287 6267	14.75	.916 870	7.05	156
14	4.862 401	408.359 606	.002 448 8220	.205 660	83.983 115	.011 907 1554	14.29	1.000 402	7.15	168
15	5.443 918	469.841 541	.002 128 3772	.183 691	86.305 773	.011 586 7105	13.91	1.085 608	7.24	180
16	6.094 981	538.676 379	.001 856 4022	.164 069	88.380 325	.011 314 7355	13.58	1.172 429	7.33	192
17	6.823 907	615.743 489	.001 624 0529	.146 544	90.233 275	.011 082 3862	13.30	1.260 807	7.42	204
18	7.640 009	702.027 403	.001 424 4458	.130 890	91.888 293	.010 882 7792	13.06	1.350 680	7.50	216
19	8.553 713	798.630 403	.001 252 1437	.116 908	93.366 523	.010 710 4770	12.86	1.441 989	7.59	228
20	9.576 690	906.786 593	.001 102 7953	.104 420	94.686 850	.010 561 1286	12.68	1.534 671	7.67	240
21	10.722 010	1027.877 674	.000 972 8784	.093 266	95.866 139	.010 431 2117	12.52	1.628 665	7.76	252
22	12.004 303	1163.450 586	.000 859 5122	.083 303	96.919 458	.010 317 8456	12.39	1.723 911	7.84	264
23	13.439 953	1315.237 278	.000 760 3191	.074 405	97.860 262	.010 218 6524	12.27	1.820 348	7.91	276
24	15.047 298	1485.176 830	.000 673 3205	.066 457	98.700 569	.010 131 6538	12.16	1.917 916	7.99	288
25	16.846 872	1675.440 223	.000 596 8581	.059 358	99.451 115	.010 055 1914	12.07	2.016 557	8.07	300
26	18.861 666	1888.458 079	.000 529 5325	.053 018	100.121 489	.009 987 8659	11.99	2.116 214	8.14	312
27	21.117 418	2126.951 708	.000 470 1564	.047 354	100.720 253	.009 928 4898	11.92	2.216 831	8.21	324
28	23.642 946	2393.967 872	.000 417 7165	.042 296	101.255 058	.009 876 0499	11.86	2.318 353	8.28	336
29	26.470 513	2692.917 710	.000 371 3444	.037 778	101.732 735	.009 829 6778	11.80	2.420 728	8.35	348
30	29.636 242	3027.620 317	.000 330 2924	.033 742	102.159 386	.009 788 6257	11.75	2.523 905	8.41	360
31	33.180 575	3402.351 527	.000 293 9144	.030 138	102.540 464	.009 752 2477	11.71	2.627 836	8.48	372
32	37.148 790	3821.898 543	.000 261 6501	.026 919	102.880 834	.009 719 9834	11.67	2.732 474	8.54	384
33	41.591 583	4291.621 091	.000 233 0122	.024 043	103.184 847	.009 691 3455	11.63	2.837 773	8.60	396
34	46.565 709	4817.519 890	.000 207 5757	.021 475	103.456 384	.009 665 9090	11.60	2.943 691	8.66	408
35	52.134 713	5406.313 314	.000 184 9689	.019 181	103.698 917	.009 643 3023	11.58	3.050 187	8.71	420
36	58.369 740	6065.523 214	.000 164 8662	.017 132	103.915 542	.009 623 1996	11.55	3.157 222	8.77	432
37	65.350 443	6803.571 019	.000 146 9816	.015 302	104.109 027	.009 605 3150	11.53	3.264 760	8.82	444
38	73.165 999	7629.885 310	.000 131 0636	.013 668	104.281 845	.009 589 3969	11.51	3.372 765	8.88	456
39	81.916 252	8555.022 276	.000 116 8904	.012 208	104.436 202	.009 575 2237	11.50	3.481 205	8.93	468
40	91.712 989	9590.800 572	.000 104 2666	.010 904	104.574 071	.009 562 5999	11.48	3.590 048	8.98	480
41	102.681 361	10750.452 294	.000 093 0193	.009 739	104.697 212	.009 551 3527	11.47	3.699 266	9.02	492
42	114.961 491	12048.792 028	.000 082 9959	.008 699	104.807 200	.009 541 3292	11.45	3.808 830	9.07	504
43	128.710 258	13502.406 103	.000 074 0609	.007 769	104.905 439	.009 532 3942	11.44	3.918 715	9.11	516
44	144.103 302	15129.864 483	.000 066 0944	.006 939	104.993 184	.009 524 4278	11.43	4.028 898	9.16	528
45	161.337 269	16951.957 996	.000 058 9902	.006 198	105.071 556	.009 517 3236	11.43	4.139 355	9.20	540
46	180.632 326	18991.963 941	.000 052 6538	.005 536	105.141 557	.009 510 9872	11.42	4.250 065	9.24	552
47	202.234 965	21275.943 455	.000 047 0014	.004 945	105.204 080	.009 505 3348	11.41	4.361 009	9.28	564
48	226.421 162	23833.074 444	.000 041 9585	.004 417	105.259 924	.009 500 2918	11.41	4.472 168	9.32	576
49	253.499 897	26696.024 334	.000 037 4588	.003 945	105.309 804	.009 495 7921	11.40	4.583 526	9.35	588
50	283.817 100	29901.367 393	.000 033 4433	.003 523	105.354 355	.009 491 7766	11.40	4.695 066	9.39	600

MONTHLY COMPOUND INTEREST AND ANNUITY

Amount Of 1	Amount Of 1 Per Period	Sinking Fund Payment	Present Worth Of 1	Present Worth of 1 Per Period	Periodic Payment To Amortize 1	Constant Annual Percent	Total Interest	Annual Add On Rate	PERIODS
What a single $ 1 deposit grows to in the future. The deposit is made at the beginning of the first period.	What a series of $ 1 deposits grow to in the future. A deposit is made at the end of each period.	The amount to be deposited at the end of each period that grows to $ 1 in the future.	What $ 1 to be paid in the future is worth today. Value today of a single $ 1 payment tomorrow.	What $ 1 to be paid at the end of each period is worth today. Value today of a series of $ 1 payments tomorrow.	The mortgage payment to amortize a loan of $ 1. An annuity certain, payable at the end of each period, worth $ 1 today.	The annual payment, including interest and principal, to amortize completely a loan of $ 100.	The total interest paid over the term on a loan of $1. The loan is amortized by regular periodic payments.	The average annual interest rate on a loan that is completely amortized by regular periodic payments.	
$S = (1+i)^n$	$S\overline{n}| = \dfrac{(1+i)^n - 1}{i}$	$\dfrac{1}{S\overline{n}|} = \dfrac{i}{(1+i)^n - 1}$	$V^n = \dfrac{1}{(1+i)^n}$	$A\overline{n}| = \dfrac{1 - V^n}{i}$	$\dfrac{1}{A\overline{n}|} = \dfrac{i}{1 - V^n}$				

YEAR

	Amount Of 1	Amount Of 1 Per Period	Sinking Fund Payment	Present Worth Of 1	Present Worth of 1 Per Period	Periodic Payment To Amortize 1	Constant Annual Percent	Total Interest	Annual Add On Rate	PERIODS
	1.009 479	1.000 000	1.000 000 0000	.990 610	.990 610	1.009 479 1667	1211.38	.009 479	11.38	1
	1.019 048	2.009 479	.497 641 3872	.981 308	1.971 918	.507 120 5538	608.55	.014 241	8.54	2
	1.028 708	3.028 527	.330 193 4845	.972 093	2.944 011	.339 672 6511	407.61	.019 018	7.61	3
	1.038 459	4.057 235	.246 473 2591	.962 965	3.906 976	.255 952 4258	307.15	.023 810	7.14	4
	1.048 303	5.095 694	.196 244 1045	.953 923	4.860 899	.205 723 2712	246.87	.028 616	6.87	5
	1.058 240	6.143 997	.162 760 4851	.944 965	5.805 864	.172 239 6518	206.69	.033 438	6.69	6
	1.068 271	7.202 237	.138 845 7427	.936 092	6.741 956	.148 324 9094	177.99	.038 274	6.56	7
	1.078 398	8.270 509	.120 911 5483	.927 302	7.669 258	.130 390 7149	156.47	.043 126	6.47	8
	1.088 620	9.348 906	.106 964 3856	.918 594	8.587 852	.116 443 5522	139.74	.047 992	6.40	9
	1.098 939	10.437 526	.095 808 1449	.909 969	9.497 821	.105 287 3115	126.35	.052 873	6.34	10
	1.109 356	11.536 465	.086 681 6653	.901 424	10.399 244	.096 160 8320	115.40	.057 769	6.30	11
	1.119 872	12.645 821	.079 077 5065	.892 959	11.292 204	.088 556 6732	106.27	.062 680	6.27	12
1	1.119 872	12.645 821	.079 077 5065	.892 959	11.292 204	.088 556 6732	106.27	.062 680	6.27	12
2	1.254 113	26.807 520	.037 302 9656	.797 376	21.375 682	.046 782 1323	56.14	.122 771	6.14	24
3	1.404 446	42.666 808	.023 437 4223	.712 025	30.379 819	.032 916 5890	39.50	.184 997	6.17	36
4	1.572 799	60.427 178	.016 548 8449	.635 809	38.420 146	.026 028 0116	31.24	.249 345	6.23	48
5	1.761 334	80.316 517	.012 450 7392	.567 752	45.599 831	.021 929 9058	26.32	.315 794	6.32	60
6	1.972 468	102.590 027	.009 747 5362	.506 979	52.010 998	.019 226 7029	23.08	.384 323	6.41	72
7	2.208 911	127.533 504	.007 841 0768	.452 712	57.735 909	.017 320 2435	20.79	.454 900	6.50	84
8	2.473 698	155.467 002	.006 432 2331	.404 253	62.848 022	.015 911 3998	19.10	.527 494	6.59	96
9	2.770 224	186.748 939	.005 354 7828	.360 982	67.412 930	.014 833 9494	17.81	.602 067	6.69	108
10	3.102 296	221.780 700	.004 508 9586	.322 342	71.489 208	.013 988 1253	16.79	.678 575	6.79	120
11	3.474 174	261.011 783	.003 831 2447	.287 838	75.129 158	.013 310 4113	15.98	.756 974	6.88	132
12	3.890 630	304.945 568	.003 279 2738	.257 028	78.379 486	.012 758 4404	15.32	.837 215	6.98	144
13	4.357 007	354.145 778	.002 823 6960	.229 515	81.281 896	.012 302 8626	14.77	.919 247	7.07	156
14	4.879 289	409.243 707	.002 443 5318	.204 948	83.873 630	.011 922 6984	14.31	1.003 013	7.16	168
15	5.464 179	470.946 326	.002 123 3842	.183 010	86.187 943	.011 602 5509	13.93	1.088 459	7.26	180
16	6.119 180	540.045 353	.001 851 6963	.163 421	88.254 531	.011 330 8630	13.60	1.175 526	7.35	192
17	6.852 697	617.427 407	.001 619 6236	.145 928	90.099 910	.011 098 7903	13.32	1.264 153	7.44	204
18	7.674 143	704.085 391	.001 420 2823	.130 308	91.747 758	.010 899 4489	13.08	1.354 281	7.52	216
19	8.594 056	801.131 228	.001 248 2350	.116 359	93.219 219	.010 727 4016	12.88	1.445 848	7.61	228
20	9.624 242	909.810 128	.001 099 1304	.103 904	94.533 174	.010 578 2971	12.70	1.538 591	7.69	240
21	10.777 917	1031.516 568	.000 969 4464	.092 782	95.706 482	.010 448 6130	12.54	1.633 050	7.78	252
22	12.069 886	1167.812 184	.000 856 3021	.082 851	96.754 199	.010 335 4687	12.41	1.728 564	7.86	264
23	13.516 726	1320.445 807	.000 757 3200	.073 982	97.689 767	.010 236 4867	12.29	1.825 270	7.94	276
24	15.137 001	1491.375 905	.000 670 5218	.066 063	98.525 192	.010 149 6884	12.18	1.923 110	8.01	288
25	16.951 501	1682.795 708	.000 594 2492	.058 992	99.271 192	.010 073 4159	12.09	2.022 025	8.09	300
26	18.983 509	1897.161 357	.000 527 1033	.052 677	99.937 340	.010 006 2700	12.01	2.121 956	8.16	312
27	21.259 097	2137.223 412	.000 467 8968	.047 039	100.532 183	.009 947 0635	11.94	2.222 849	8.23	324
28	23.807 464	2406.062 148	.000 415 6169	.042 004	101.063 353	.009 894 7835	11.88	2.324 647	8.30	336
29	26.661 309	2707.127 080	.000 369 3953	.037 508	101.537 667	.009 848 5620	11.82	2.427 300	8.37	348
30	29.857 249	3044.281 221	.000 328 4848	.033 493	101.961 209	.009 807 6514	11.77	2.530 755	8.44	360
31	33.436 293	3421.850 651	.000 292 2395	.029 908	102.339 416	.009 771 4062	11.73	2.634 963	8.50	372
32	37.444 363	3844.680 025	.000 260 0997	.026 706	102.677 139	.009 739 2663	11.69	2.739 878	8.56	384
33	41.932 888	4318.194 737	.000 231 5783	.023 848	102.978 712	.009 710 7449	11.66	2.845 455	8.62	396
34	46.959 460	4848.470 532	.000 206 2506	.021 295	103.248 004	.009 685 4173	11.63	2.951 650	8.68	408
35	52.588 577	5442.311 465	.000 183 7455	.019 016	103.488 471	.009 662 9121	11.60	3.058 423	8.74	420
36	58.892 467	6107.337 207	.000 163 7375	.016 980	103.703 198	.009 642 9041	11.58	3.165 735	8.79	432
37	65.952 016	6852.080 812	.000 145 9411	.015 163	103.894 941	.009 625 1077	11.56	3.273 548	8.85	444
38	73.857 806	7686.098 207	.000 130 1050	.013 540	104.066 159	.009 609 2717	11.54	3.381 828	8.90	456
39	82.711 277	8620.090 807	.000 116 0081	.012 090	104.219 051	.009 595 1747	11.52	3.490 542	8.95	468
40	92.626 031	9666.042 824	.000 103 4550	.010 796	104.355 576	.009 582 6216	11.50	3.599 658	9.00	480
41	103.729 284	10837.375 039	.000 092 2733	.009 640	104.477 488	.009 571 4399	11.49	3.709 148	9.05	492
42	116.163 505	12149.117 010	.000 082 3105	.008 609	104.586 350	.009 561 4772	11.48	3.818 984	9.09	504
43	130.088 239	13618.099 911	.000 073 4317	.007 687	104.683 560	.009 552 5983	11.47	3.929 141	9.14	516
44	145.682 156	15263.172 505	.000 065 5172	.006 864	104.770 364	.009 544 6838	11.46	4.039 593	9.18	528
45	163.145 345	17105.442 986	.000 058 4609	.006 130	104.847 877	.009 537 6276	11.45	4.150 319	9.22	540
46	182.701 879	19168.549 831	.000 052 1688	.005 473	104.917 092	.009 531 3355	11.44	4.261 297	9.26	552
47	204.602 690	21478.965 101	.000 046 5572	.004 888	104.978 999	.009 525 7238	11.44	4.372 508	9.30	564
48	229.128 792	24066.334 114	.000 041 5518	.004 364	105.034 090	.009 520 7185	11.43	4.483 934	9.34	576
49	256.594 883	26963.855 827	.000 037 0867	.003 897	105.083 373	.009 516 2534	11.42	4.595 557	9.38	588
50	287.353 386	30208.708 815	.000 033 1030	.003 480	105.127 381	.009 512 2697	11.42	4.707 362	9.41	600

Effective Rate is 11.99 %

Annual Percentage Rate is 11.375%

	Amount Of 1	Amount Of 1 Per Period	Sinking Fund Payment	Present Worth Of 1	Present Worth of 1 Per Period	Periodic Payment To Amortize 1	Constant Annual Percent	Total Interest	Annual Add On Rate	
	What a single $ 1 deposit grows to in the future. The deposit is made at the beginning of the first period.	What a series of $ 1 deposits grow to in the future. A deposit is made at the end of each period.	The amount to be deposited at the end of each period that grows to $ 1 in the future.	What $ 1 to be paid in the future is worth today. Value today of a single $ 1 payment tomorrow.	What $ 1 to be paid at the end of each period is worth today. Value today of a series of $ 1 payments tomorrow.	The mortgage payment to amortize a loan of $ 1. An annuity certain, payable at the end of each period, worth $ 1 today.	The annual payment, including interest and principal, to amortize completely a loan of $ 100.	The total interest paid over the term on a loan of $1. The loan is amortized by regular periodic payments.	The average annual interest rate on a loan that is completely amortized by regular periodic payments.	
	$S = (1+i)^n$	$S\overline{n}| = \frac{(1+i)^n - 1}{i}$	$\frac{1}{S\overline{n}|} = \frac{i}{(1+i)^n - 1}$	$V^n = \frac{1}{(1+i)^n}$	$A\overline{n}| = \frac{1-V^n}{i}$	$\frac{1}{A\overline{n}|} = \frac{i}{1-V^n}$				

YEAR										PERIODS
	1.009 500	1.000 000	1.000 000 0000	.990 589	.990 589	1.009 500 0000	1211.40	.009 500	11.40	1
	1.019 090	2.009 500	.497 636 2279	.981 267	1.971 857	.507 136 2279	608.57	.014 272	8.56	2
	1.028 772	3.028 590	.330 186 6273	.972 033	2.943 890	.339 686 6273	407.63	.019 060	7.62	3
	1.038 545	4.057 362	.246 465 5693	.962 886	3.906 775	.255 965 5693	307.16	.023 867	7.16	4
	1.048 411	5.095 907	.196 235 9282	.953 824	4.860 600	.205 735 9282	246.89	.028 680	6.88	5
	1.058 371	6.144 318	.162 751 9954	.944 848	5.805 448	.172 251 9954	206.71	.033 512	6.70	6
	1.068 426	7.202 689	.138 837 0385	.935 957	6.741 405	.148 337 0385	178.01	.038 359	6.58	7
	1.078 576	8.271 114	.120 902 6913	.927 149	7.668 553	.130 402 6913	156.49	.043 222	6.48	8
	1.088 822	9.349 690	.106 955 4171	.918 424	8.586 977	.116 455 4171	139.75	.048 099	6.41	9
	1.099 166	10.438 512	.095 799 0937	.909 781	9.496 758	.105 299 0937	126.36	.052 991	6.36	10
	1.109 608	11.537 678	.086 672 5524	.901 219	10.397 977	.096 172 5524	115.41	.057 898	6.32	11
	1.120 149	12.647 286	.079 068 3476	.892 738	11.290 715	.088 568 3476	106.29	.062 820	6.28	12
1	1.120 149	12.647 286	.079 068 3476	.892 738	11.290 715	.088 568 3476	106.29	.062 820	6.28	12
2	1.254 734	26.814 133	.037 293 7655	.796 982	21.370 368	.046 793 7655	56.16	.123 050	6.15	24
3	1.405 490	42.683 116	.023 428 4674	.711 496	30.368 860	.032 928 4674	39.52	.185 425	6.18	36
4	1.574 358	60.458 745	.016 540 2043	.635 180	38.402 156	.026 040 2043	31.25	.249 930	6.25	48
5	1.763 516	80.370 102	.012 442 4379	.567 049	45.573 788	.021 942 4379	26.34	.316 546	6.33	60
6	1.975 401	102.673 793	.009 739 5837	.506 226	51.976 177	.019 239 5837	23.09	.385 250	6.42	72
7	2.212 744	127.657 254	.007 833 4757	.451 928	57.691 834	.017 333 4757	20.81	.456 012	6.51	84
8	2.478 603	155.642 459	.006 424 9820	.403 453	62.794 419	.015 924 9820	19.11	.528 798	6.61	96
9	2.776 406	186.990 065	.005 347 8777	.360 178	67.349 693	.014 847 8777	17.82	.603 571	6.71	108
10	3.109 989	222.104 061	.004 502 3940	.321 545	71.416 359	.014 002 3940	16.81	.680 287	6.80	120
11	3.483 651	261.436 975	.003 825 0137	.287 055	75.046 827	.013 325 0137	16.00	.758 902	6.90	132
12	3.902 209	305.495 709	.003 273 3684	.256 265	78.287 885	.012 773 3684	15.33	.839 365	6.99	144
13	4.371 057	354.848 065	.002 818 1075	.228 778	81.181 301	.012 318 1075	14.79	.921 625	7.09	156
14	4.896 236	410.130 068	.002 438 2509	.204 239	83.764 365	.011 938 2509	14.33	1.005 626	7.18	168
15	5.484 515	472.054 160	.002 118 4010	.182 332	86.070 364	.011 618 4010	13.95	1.091 312	7.28	180
16	6.143 475	541.418 383	.001 847 0005	.162 774	88.129 017	.011 347 0005	13.62	1.178 624	7.37	192
17	6.881 608	619.116 663	.001 615 2045	.145 315	89.966 856	.011 115 2045	13.34	1.267 502	7.46	204
18	7.708 428	706.150 331	.001 416 1291	.129 728	91.607 565	.010 916 1291	13.10	1.357 884	7.54	216
19	8.634 590	803.641 026	.001 244 3367	.115 813	93.072 288	.010 744 3367	12.90	1.449 709	7.63	228
20	9.672 029	912.845 151	.001 095 4760	.103 391	94.379 903	.010 595 4760	12.72	1.542 914	7.71	240
21	10.834 116	1035.170 067	.000 966 0248	.092 301	95.547 260	.010 466 0248	12.56	1.637 438	7.80	252
22	12.135 826	1172.192 225	.000 853 1024	.082 401	96.589 405	.010 353 1024	12.43	1.733 219	7.88	264
23	13.593 936	1325.677 488	.000 754 3313	.073 562	97.519 767	.010 254 3313	12.31	1.830 195	7.96	276
24	15.227 237	1497.603 885	.000 667 7333	.065 672	98.350 337	.010 167 7333	12.21	1.928 307	8.03	288
25	17.056 777	1690.187 104	.000 591 6505	.058 628	99.091 819	.010 091 6505	12.11	2.027 495	8.11	300
26	19.106 136	1905.909 046	.000 524 6840	.052 339	99.753 768	.010 024 6840	12.03	2.127 701	8.18	312
27	21.401 723	2147.549 810	.000 465 6469	.046 725	100.344 715	.009 965 6469	11.96	2.228 870	8.26	324
28	23.973 123	2418.223 522	.000 413 5267	.041 713	100.872 276	.009 913 5267	11.90	2.330 945	8.32	336
29	26.853 475	2721.418 469	.000 367 4554	.037 239	101.343 250	.009 867 4554	11.85	2.433 874	8.39	348
30	30.079 899	3061.042 051	.000 326 6861	.033 245	101.763 706	.009 826 6861	11.80	2.537 607	8.46	360
31	33.693 976	3441.471 140	.000 290 5734	.029 679	102.139 064	.009 790 5734	11.75	2.642 093	8.52	372
32	37.742 281	3867.608 487	.000 258 5577	.026 495	102.474 160	.009 758 5577	11.72	2.747 286	8.59	384
33	42.276 986	4344.945 901	.000 230 1525	.023 654	102.773 313	.009 730 1525	11.68	2.853 140	8.65	396
34	47.356 533	4879.635 032	.000 204 9334	.021 116	103.040 378	.009 704 9334	11.65	2.959 613	8.70	408
35	53.046 383	5478.566 642	.000 182 5295	.018 851	103.278 797	.009 682 5295	11.62	3.066 662	8.76	420
36	59.419 864	6149.459 417	.000 162 6159	.016 829	103.491 643	.009 662 6159	11.60	3.174 250	8.82	432
37	66.559 115	6900.959 432	.000 144 9074	.015 024	103.681 659	.009 644 9074	11.58	3.282 339	8.87	444
38	74.556 140	7742.751 585	.000 129 1531	.013 413	103.851 294	.009 629 1531	11.56	3.390 894	8.92	456
39	83.514 002	8685.684 406	.000 115 1320	.011 974	104.002 733	.009 615 1320	11.54	3.499 882	8.97	468
40	93.548 144	9741.909 866	.000 102 6493	.010 690	104.137 928	.009 602 6493	11.53	3.609 272	9.02	480
41	104.787 880	10925.039 988	.000 091 5328	.009 543	104.258 622	.009 591 5328	11.51	3.719 034	9.07	492
42	117.378 062	12250.322 266	.000 081 6305	.008 519	104.366 371	.009 581 6305	11.50	3.829 142	9.12	504
43	131.480 944	13734.836 171	.000 072 8076	.007 606	104.462 562	.009 572 8076	11.49	3.939 569	9.16	516
44	147.278 276	15397.713 258	.000 064 9447	.006 790	104.548 435	.009 564 9447	11.48	4.050 291	9.21	528
45	164.973 645	17260.383 725	.000 057 9361	.006 062	104.625 097	.009 557 9361	11.47	4.161 286	9.25	540
46	184.795 100	19346.852 588	.000 051 6880	.005 411	104.693 537	.009 551 6880	11.47	4.272 532	9.29	552
47	206.998 086	21684.009 050	.000 046 1169	.004 831	104.754 636	.009 546 1169	11.46	4.384 010	9.33	564
48	231.868 744	24301.973 028	.000 041 1489	.004 313	104.809 181	.009 541 1489	11.45	4.495 702	9.37	576
49	259.727 592	27234.483 328	.000 036 7182	.003 850	104.857 875	.009 536 7182	11.45	4.607 590	9.40	588
50	290.933 658	30519.332 441	.000 032 7661	.003 437	104.901 346	.009 532 7661	11.44	4.719 660	9.44	600

MONTHLY COMPOUND INTEREST AND ANNUITY

	Amount Of 1	Amount Of 1 Per Period	Sinking Fund Payment	Present Worth Of 1	Present Worth of 1 Per Period	Periodic Payment To Amortize 1	Constant Annual Percent	Total Interest	Annual Add On Rate	

What a single $ 1 deposit grows to in the future. The deposit is made at the beginning of the first period.

What a series of $ 1 deposits grow to in the future. A deposit is made at the end of each period.

The amount to be deposited at the end of each period that grows to $ 1 in the future.

What $ 1 to be paid in the future is worth today. Value today of a single $ 1 payment tomorrow.

What $ 1 to be paid at the end of each period is worth today. Value today of a series of $ 1 payments tomorrow.

The mortgage payment to amortize a loan of $ 1. An annuity certain, payable at the end of each period, worth $ 1 today.

The annual payment, including interest and principal, to amortize completely a loan of $ 100.

The total interest paid over the term on a loan of $1. The loan is amortized by regular periodic payments.

The average annual interest rate on a loan that is completely amortized by regular periodic payments.

$S = (1+i)^n$

$S\overline{n}| = \dfrac{(1+i)^n - 1}{i}$

$\dfrac{1}{S\overline{n}|} = \dfrac{i}{(1+i)^n - 1}$

$V^n = \dfrac{1}{(1+i)^n}$

$A\overline{n}| = \dfrac{1 - V^n}{i}$

$\dfrac{1}{A\overline{n}|} = \dfrac{i}{1 - V^n}$

PERIODS

YEAR	Amount Of 1	Amount Of 1 Per Period	Sinking Fund Payment	Present Worth Of 1	Present Worth of 1 Per Period	Periodic Payment To Amortize 1	Constant Annual Percent	Total Interest	Annual Add On Rate	PERIODS
	1.009 542	1.000 000	1.000 000 0000	.990 549	.990 549	1.009 541 6667	1211.45	.009 542	11.45	1
	1.019 174	2.009 542	.497 625 9097	.981 186	1.971 735	.507 167 5764	608.61	.014 335	8.60	2
	1.028 899	3.028 716	.330 172 9134	.971 913	2.943 648	.339 714 5801	407.66	.019 144	7.66	3
	1.038 716	4.057 615	.246 450 1905	.962 727	3.906 374	.255 991 8571	307.20	.023 967	7.19	4
	1.048 627	5.096 331	.196 219 5766	.953 627	4.860 002	.205 761 2433	246.92	.028 806	6.91	5
	1.058 633	6.144 959	.162 735 0172	.944 614	5.804 616	.172 276 6838	206.74	.033 660	6.73	6
	1.068 734	7.203 592	.138 819 6314	.935 686	6.740 302	.148 361 2981	178.04	.038 529	6.60	7
	1.078 932	8.272 326	.120 884 9790	.926 843	7.667 145	.130 426 6457	156.52	.043 413	6.51	8
	1.089 227	9.351 258	.106 937 4819	.918 083	8.585 228	.116 479 1486	139.78	.048 312	6.44	9
	1.099 620	10.440 485	.095 780 9934	.909 405	9.494 633	.105 322 6601	126.39	.053 227	6.39	10
	1.110 112	11.540 104	.086 654 3290	.900 810	10.395 443	.096 195 9956	115.44	.058 156	6.34	11
	1.120 704	12.650 216	.079 050 0324	.892 296	11.287 739	.088 591 6991	106.32	.063 100	6.31	12
1	1.120 704	12.650 216	.079 050 0324	.892 296	11.287 739	.088 591 6991	106.32	.063 100	6.31	12
2	1.255 978	26.827 366	.037 275 3703	.796 192	21.359 746	.046 817 0370	56.19	.123 609	6.18	24
3	1.407 580	42.715 756	.023 410 5652	.710 439	30.346 958	.032 952 2318	39.55	.186 280	6.21	36
4	1.577 480	60.521 942	.016 522 9332	.633 922	38.366 213	.026 064 5999	31.28	.251 101	6.28	48
5	1.767 889	80.477 407	.012 425 8477	.565 647	45.521 764	.021 967 5143	26.37	.318 051	6.36	60
6	1.981 280	102.841 580	.009 723 6935	.504 724	51.906 634	.019 265 3601	23.12	.387 106	6.45	72
7	2.220 429	127.905 201	.007 818 2903	.450 363	57.603 829	.017 359 9570	20.84	.458 236	6.55	84
8	2.488 444	155.994 106	.006 410 4986	.401 858	62.687 415	.015 952 1653	19.15	.531 408	6.64	96
9	2.788 809	187.473 457	.005 334 0884	.358 576	67.223 478	.014 875 7551	17.86	.606 582	6.74	108
10	3.125 430	222.752 497	.004 489 2875	.319 956	71.270 990	.014 030 9542	16.84	.683 715	6.84	120
11	3.502 682	262.289 863	.003 812 5759	.285 495	74.882 570	.013 354 2425	16.03	.762 760	6.93	132
12	3.925 471	306.599 553	.003 261 5834	.254 747	78.105 168	.012 803 2500	15.37	.843 668	7.03	144
13	4.399 291	356.257 607	.002 806 9576	.227 309	80.980 681	.012 348 6243	14.82	.926 385	7.13	156
14	4.930 304	411.909 593	.002 427 7172	.202 827	83.546 489	.011 969 3839	14.37	1.010 856	7.22	168
15	5.525 412	474.279 005	.002 108 4636	.180 982	85.835 950	.011 650 1302	13.99	1.097 023	7.31	180
16	6.192 352	544.176 663	.001 837 6385	.161 490	87.878 828	.011 379 3052	13.66	1.184 827	7.41	192
17	6.939 795	622.511 259	.001 606 3966	.144 096	89.701 679	.011 148 0633	13.38	1.274 205	7.50	204
18	7.777 457	710.301 165	.001 407 8535	.128 577	91.328 203	.010 949 5202	13.14	1.365 096	7.58	216
19	8.716 228	808.687 677	.001 236 5713	.114 729	92.779 543	.010 778 2380	12.94	1.457 438	7.67	228
20	9.768 313	918.949 849	.001 088 1987	.102 372	94.074 569	.010 629 8653	12.76	1.551 168	7.76	240
21	10.947 389	1042.521 122	.000 959 2132	.091 346	95.230 115	.010 500 8798	12.61	1.646 222	7.84	252
22	12.268 784	1181.007 961	.000 846 7343	.081 508	96.261 205	.010 388 4010	12.47	1.742 538	7.92	264
23	13.749 677	1336.210 734	.000 748 3849	.072 729	97.181 242	.010 290 0516	12.35	1.840 054	8.00	276
24	15.409 320	1510.147 126	.000 662 1871	.064 896	98.002 188	.010 203 8538	12.25	1.938 710	8.08	288
25	17.269 289	1705.078 362	.000 586 4833	.057 906	98.734 715	.010 128 1500	12.16	2.038 445	8.15	300
26	19.353 764	1923.538 606	.000 519 8752	.051 670	99.388 346	.010 061 5419	12.08	2.139 201	8.23	312
27	21.689 844	2168.367 908	.000 461 1764	.046 105	99.971 578	.010 002 8430	12.01	2.240 921	8.30	324
28	24.307 898	2442.749 121	.000 409 3748	.041 139	100.491 994	.009 951 0415	11.95	2.343 550	8.37	336
29	27.241 962	2750.249 284	.000 363 6034	.036 708	100.956 359	.009 905 2701	11.89	2.447 034	8.44	348
30	30.530 180	3094.865 992	.000 323 1158	.032 754	101.370 710	.009 864 7824	11.84	2.551 322	8.50	360
31	34.215 299	3481.079 365	.000 287 2672	.029 227	101.740 434	.009 828 9339	11.80	2.656 363	8.57	372
32	38.345 227	3913.910 294	.000 255 4990	.026 079	102.070 337	.009 797 1656	11.76	2.762 112	8.63	384
33	42.973 655	4398.985 711	.000 227 3251	.023 270	102.364 709	.009 768 9918	11.73	2.868 521	8.69	396
34	48.160 754	4942.611 741	.000 202 3222	.020 764	102.627 375	.009 743 9889	11.70	2.975 547	8.75	408
35	53.973 956	5551.855 688	.000 180 1200	.018 527	102.861 752	.009 721 7866	11.67	3.083 150	8.81	420
36	60.488 837	6234.637 905	.000 160 3942	.016 532	103.070 885	.009 702 0609	11.65	3.191 290	8.86	432
37	67.790 090	6999.834 766	.000 142 8605	.014 751	103.257 493	.009 684 5272	11.63	3.299 530	8.92	444
38	75.972 635	7857.394 061	.000 127 2687	.013 163	103.424 003	.009 668 9353	11.61	3.409 035	8.97	456
39	85.142 847	8818.464 319	.000 113 3984	.011 745	103.572 580	.009 655 0651	11.59	3.518 570	9.02	468
40	95.419 942	9895.539 742	.000 101 0556	.010 480	103.705 154	.009 642 7223	11.58	3.628 507	9.07	480
41	106.937 524	11102.622 634	.000 090 0688	.009 351	103.823 449	.009 631 7355	11.56	3.738 814	9.12	492
42	119.845 327	12455.405 436	.000 080 2864	.008 344	103.929 004	.009 621 9531	11.55	3.849 464	9.17	504
43	134.311 155	13971.474 731	.000 071 5744	.007 445	104.023 190	.009 613 2411	11.54	3.960 432	9.21	516
44	150.523 068	15670.539 875	.000 063 8140	.006 643	104.107 231	.009 605 4807	11.53	4.071 694	9.25	528
45	168.691 826	17574.689 228	.000 056 9000	.005 928	104.182 222	.009 598 5667	11.52	4.183 226	9.30	540
46	189.053 629	19708.677 302	.000 050 7391	.005 290	104.249 135	.009 592 4057	11.52	4.295 008	9.34	552
47	211.873 186	22100.246 585	.000 045 2484	.004 720	104.308 841	.009 586 9150	11.51	4.407 020	9.38	564
48	237.447 158	24780.488 196	.000 040 3543	.004 211	104.362 117	.009 582 0210	11.50	4.519 244	9.42	576
49	266.108 015	27784.246 083	.000 035 9916	.003 758	104.409 655	.009 577 6583	11.50	4.631 663	9.45	588
50	298.228 355	31150.570 000	.000 032 1021	.003 353	104.452 073	.009 573 7688	11.49	4.744 261	9.49	600

Effective Rate is 12.07 %

Annual Percentage Rate is 11.45 %

MONTHLY COMPOUND INTEREST AND ANNUITY

	Amount Of 1	Amount Of 1 Per Period	Sinking Fund Payment	Present Worth Of 1	Present Worth of 1 Per Period	Periodic Payment To Amortize 1	Constant Annual Percent	Total Interest	Annual Add On Rate
	What a single $ 1 deposit grows to in the future. The deposit is made at the beginning of the first period.	What a series of $ 1 deposits grow to in the future. A deposit is made at the end of each period.	The amount to be deposited at the end of each period that grows to $ 1 in the future.	What $ 1 to be paid in the future is worth today. Value today of a single $ 1 payment tomorrow.	What $ 1 to be paid at the end of each period is worth today. Value today of a series of $ 1 payments tomorrow.	The mortgage payment to amortize a loan of $ 1. An annuity certain, payable at the end of each period, worth $ 1 today.	The annual payment, including interest and principal, to amortize completely a loan of $ 100.	The total interest paid over the term on a loan of $1. The loan is amortized by regular periodic payments.	The average annual interest rate on a loan that is completely amortized by regular periodic payments.

$$S = (1+i)^n \qquad S\overline{n}| = \frac{(1+i)^n - 1}{i} \qquad \frac{1}{S\overline{n}|} = \frac{i}{(1+i)^n - 1} \qquad V^n = \frac{1}{(1+i)^n} \qquad A\overline{n}| = \frac{1-V^n}{i} \qquad \frac{1}{A\overline{n}|} = \frac{i}{1-V^n}$$

YEAR									PERIODS
	1.009 583	1.000 000	1.000 000 0000	.990 508	.990 508	1.009 583 3333	1211.50	.009 583	11.50	1
	1.019 259	2.009 583	.497 615 5920	.981 105	1.971 613	.507 198 9253	608.64	.014 398	8.64	2
	1.029 026	3.028 842	.330 159 2004	.971 792	2.943 405	.339 742 5337	407.70	.019 228	7.69	3
	1.038 888	4.057 868	.246 434 8127	.962 568	3.905 973	.256 018 1460	307.23	.024 073	7.22	4
	1.048 844	5.096 756	.196 203 2264	.953 431	4.859 404	.205 786 5598	246.95	.028 933	6.94	5
	1.058 895	6.145 600	.162 718 0406	.944 380	5.803 784	.172 301 3740	206.77	.033 808	6.76	6
	1.069 043	7.204 495	.138 802 2263	.935 416	6.739 200	.148 385 5597	178.07	.038 699	6.63	7
	1.079 288	8.273 538	.120 867 2690	.926 537	7.665 737	.130 450 6023	156.55	.043 605	6.54	8
	1.089 631	9.352 827	.106 919 5494	.917 742	8.583 479	.116 502 8827	139.81	.048 526	6.47	9
	1.100 074	10.442 458	.095 762 8959	.909 030	9.492 509	.105 346 2293	126.42	.053 462	6.42	10
	1.110 616	11.542 531	.086 636 1086	.900 401	10.392 910	.096 219 4419	115.47	.058 414	6.37	11
	1.121 259	12.653 147	.079 031 7205	.891 854	11.284 764	.088 615 0539	106.34	.063 381	6.34	12
1	1.121 259	12.653 147	.079 031 7205	.891 854	11.284 764	.088 615 0539	106.34	.063 381	6.34	12
2	1.257 222	26.840 607	.037 256 9820	.795 404	21.349 130	.046 840 3153	56.21	.124 168	6.21	24
3	1.409 672	42.748 428	.023 392 6731	.709 385	30.325 079	.032 976 0064	39.58	.187 136	6.24	36
4	1.580 608	60.585 221	.016 505 6756	.632 668	38.330 318	.026 089 0089	31.31	.252 272	6.31	48
5	1.772 272	80.584 891	.012 409 2740	.564 248	45.469 825	.021 992 6074	26.40	.319 556	6.39	60
6	1.987 176	103.009 708	.009 707 8228	.503 227	51.837 225	.019 291 1562	23.15	.388 963	6.48	72
7	2.228 140	128.153 744	.007 803 1275	.448 805	57.516 018	.017 386 4608	20.87	.460 463	6.58	84
8	2.498 323	156.346 728	.006 396 0405	.400 269	62.580 675	.015 979 3738	19.18	.534 020	6.68	96
9	2.801 268	187.958 374	.005 320 3269	.356 981	67.097 611	.014 903 6603	17.89	.609 595	6.77	108
10	3.140 948	223.403 228	.004 476 2111	.318 375	71.126 060	.014 059 5444	16.88	.687 145	6.87	120
11	3.521 817	263.146 100	.003 800 1703	.283 944	74.718 850	.013 383 5037	16.07	.766 622	6.97	132
12	3.948 870	307.708 167	.003 249 8325	.253 237	77.923 095	.012 833 1658	15.40	.847 976	7.07	144
13	4.427 707	357.673 800	.002 795 8436	.225 851	80.780 815	.012 379 1769	14.86	.931 152	7.16	156
14	4.964 608	413.698 232	.002 417 2209	.201 426	83.329 485	.012 000 5542	14.41	1.016 093	7.26	168
15	5.566 613	476.516 149	.002 098 5648	.179 642	85.602 527	.011 681 8981	14.02	1.102 742	7.35	180
16	6.241 617	546.951 324	.001 828 3163	.160 215	87.629 750	.011 411 6496	13.70	1.191 037	7.44	192
17	6.998 471	625.927 421	.001 597 6293	.142 888	89.437 737	.011 180 9627	13.42	1.280 916	7.53	204
18	7.847 101	714.480 107	.001 399 6191	.127 436	91.050 199	.010 982 9524	13.18	1.372 318	7.62	216
19	8.798 635	813.770 632	.001 228 8475	.113 654	92.488 279	.010 812 1808	12.98	1.465 177	7.71	228
20	9.865 552	925.101 060	.001 080 9630	.101 363	93.770 838	.010 664 2963	12.80	1.559 431	7.80	240
21	11.061 842	1049.931 340	.000 952 4432	.090 401	94.914 693	.010 535 7766	12.65	1.655 016	7.88	252
22	12.403 194	1189.898 456	.000 840 4078	.080 624	95.934 846	.010 423 7412	12.51	1.751 868	7.96	264
23	13.907 196	1346.837 891	.000 742 4799	.071 905	96.844 673	.010 325 8132	12.40	1.849 924	8.04	276
24	15.593 574	1522.807 696	.000 656 6817	.064 129	97.656 106	.010 240 0151	12.29	1.949 124	8.12	288
25	17.484 440	1720.115 481	.000 581 3563	.057 194	98.379 787	.010 164 6896	12.20	2.049 407	8.20	300
26	19.604 591	1941.348 676	.000 515 1058	.051 008	99.025 204	.010 098 4392	12.12	2.150 713	8.27	312
27	21.981 831	2189.408 459	.000 456 7444	.045 492	99.600 823	.010 040 0777	12.05	2.252 985	8.34	324
28	24.647 333	2467.547 806	.000 405 2606	.040 572	100.114 191	.009 988 5940	11.99	2.356 168	8.41	336
29	27.636 052	2779.414 142	.000 359 7881	.036 185	100.572 040	.009 943 1214	11.94	2.460 206	8.48	348
30	30.987 181	3129.097 181	.000 319 5810	.032 271	100.980 375	.009 902 9143	11.89	2.565 049	8.55	360
31	34.744 666	3521.182 550	.000 283 9955	.028 781	101.344 550	.009 867 3288	11.85	2.670 646	8.61	372
32	38.957 781	3960.811 927	.000 252 4735	.025 669	101.669 341	.009 835 8068	11.81	2.776 950	8.68	384
33	43.681 775	4453.750 468	.000 224 5299	.022 893	101.959 008	.009 807 8632	11.77	2.883 514	8.74	396
34	48.978 598	5006.462 404	.000 199 7418	.020 417	102.217 348	.009 783 0752	11.74	2.991 495	8.80	408
35	54.917 710	5626.195 819	.000 177 7400	.018 209	102.447 750	.009 761 0733	11.72	3.099 651	8.86	420
36	61.576 995	6321.077 691	.000 158 2009	.016 240	102.653 235	.009 741 5342	11.69	3.208 343	8.91	432
37	69.043 780	7100.220 473	.000 140 8407	.014 484	102.836 498	.009 724 1740	11.67	3.317 533	8.97	444
38	77.415 982	7973.841 584	.000 125 4101	.012 917	102.999 941	.009 708 7434	11.66	3.427 187	9.02	456
39	86.803 392	8953.397 405	.000 111 6894	.011 520	103.145 709	.009 695 0228	11.64	3.537 271	9.07	468
40	97.329 113	10051.733 506	.000 099 4853	.010 274	103.275 713	.009 682 8187	11.62	3.647 753	9.12	480
41	109.131 176	11283.253 104	.000 088 6269	.009 163	103.391 657	.009 671 9603	11.61	3.758 604	9.17	492
42	122.364 349	12664.105 942	.000 078 9633	.008 172	103.495 063	.009 662 2967	11.60	3.869 798	9.21	504
43	137.202 167	14212.400 068	.000 070 3611	.007 289	103.587 285	.009 653 6944	11.59	3.981 306	9.26	516
44	153.839 210	15948.439 299	.000 062 7021	.006 500	103.669 535	.009 646 0354	11.58	4.093 107	9.30	528
45	172.493 649	17894.989 480	.000 055 8816	.005 797	103.742 889	.009 639 2149	11.57	4.205 176	9.34	540
46	193.410 113	20077.577 029	.000 049 8068	.005 170	103.808 310	.009 633 1401	11.56	4.317 493	9.39	552
47	216.862 894	22524.823 677	.000 044 3955	.004 611	103.866 657	.009 627 7288	11.56	4.430 039	9.43	564
48	243.159 542	25268.821 810	.000 039 5745	.004 113	103.918 693	.009 622 9078	11.55	4.542 795	9.46	576
49	272.644 905	28345.555 313	.000 035 2789	.003 668	103.965 102	.009 618 6122	11.55	4.655 744	9.50	588
50	305.705 643	31795.371 453	.000 031 4511	.003 271	104.006 492	.009 614 7845	11.54	4.768 871	9.54	600

Effective Rate is 12.13 %

Annual Percentage Rate is 11.50 %

MONTHLY COMPOUND INTEREST AND ANNUITY

Amount Of 1	Amount Of 1 Per Period	Sinking Fund Payment	Present Worth Of 1	Present Worth of 1 Per Period	Periodic Payment To Amortize 1	Constant Annual Percent	Total Interest	Annual Add On Rate
What a single $ 1 deposit grows to in the future. The deposit is made at the beginning of the first period.	What a series of $ 1 deposits grow to in the future. A deposit is made at the end of each period.	The amount to be deposited at the end of each period that grows to $ 1 in the future.	What $ 1 to be paid in the future is worth today. Value today of a single $ 1 payment tomorrow.	What $ 1 to be paid at the end of each period is worth today. Value today of a series of $ 1 payments tomorrow.	The mortgage payment to amortize a loan of $ 1. An annuity certain, payable at the end of each period, worth $ 1 today.	The annual payment, including interest and principal, to amortize completely a loan of $ 100.	The total interest paid over the term on a loan of $1. The loan is amortized by regular periodic payments.	The average annual interest rate on a loan that is completely amortized by regular periodic payments.

$$S = (1+i)^n \qquad S\overline{n}| = \frac{(1+i)^n - 1}{i} \qquad \frac{1}{S\overline{n}|} = \frac{i}{(1+i)^n - 1} \qquad V^n = \frac{1}{(1+i)^n} \qquad A\overline{n}| = \frac{1-V^n}{i} \qquad \frac{1}{A\overline{n}|} = \frac{i}{1-V^n}$$

YEAR									PERIODS
	1.009 625	1.000 000	1.000 000 0000	.990 467	.990 467	1.009 625 0000	1211.55	.009 625	11.55	1
	1.019 343	2.009 625	.497 605 2746	.981 024	1.971 491	.507 230 2746	608.68	.014 461	8.68	2
	1.029 154	3.028 968	.330 145 4880	.971 672	2.943 163	.339 770 4880	407.73	.019 311	7.72	3
	1.039 059	4.058 121	.246 419 4360	.962 409	3.905 572	.256 044 4360	307.26	.024 178	7.25	4
	1.049 060	5.097 181	.196 186 8776	.953 234	4.858 806	.205 811 8776	246.98	.029 059	6.97	5
	1.059 158	6.146 241	.162 701 0658	.944 147	5.802 953	.172 326 0658	206.80	.033 956	6.79	6
	1.069 352	7.205 399	.138 784 8232	.935 146	6.738 098	.148 409 8232	178.10	.038 869	6.66	7
	1.079 644	8.274 751	.120 849 5612	.926 231	7.664 329	.130 474 5612	156.57	.043 796	6.57	8
	1.090 036	9.354 395	.106 901 6193	.917 401	8.581 730	.116 526 6193	139.84	.048 740	6.50	9
	1.100 528	10.444 431	.095 744 8013	.908 655	9.490 385	.105 369 8013	126.45	.053 698	6.44	10
	1.111 120	11.544 959	.086 617 8913	.899 993	10.390 378	.096 242 8913	115.50	.058 672	6.40	11
	1.121 815	12.656 079	.079 013 4121	.891 413	11.281 791	.088 638 4121	106.37	.063 661	6.37	12
1	1.121 815	12.656 079	.079 013 4121	.891 413	11.281 791	.088 638 4121	106.37	.063 661	6.37	12
2	1.258 468	26.853 856	.037 238 6004	.794 617	21.338 523	.046 863 6004	56.24	.124 726	6.24	24
3	1.411 768	42.781 131	.023 374 7912	.708 331	30.303 222	.032 999 7912	39.60	.187 992	6.27	36
4	1.583 743	60.648 583	.016 488 4313	.631 416	38.294 470	.026 113 4313	31.34	.253 445	6.34	48
5	1.776 666	80.692 555	.012 392 7170	.562 852	45.417 970	.022 017 7170	26.43	.321 063	6.42	60
6	1.993 090	103.178 179	.009 691 9718	.501 733	51.767 948	.019 316 9718	23.19	.390 822	6.51	72
7	2.235 878	128.402 883	.007 787 9871	.447 252	57.428 401	.017 412 9871	20.90	.462 691	6.61	84
8	2.508 241	156.700 329	.006 381 6075	.398 686	62.474 200	.016 006 6075	19.21	.536 634	6.71	96
9	2.813 781	188.444 822	.005 306 5931	.355 394	66.972 090	.014 931 5931	17.92	.612 612	6.81	108
10	3.156 542	224.056 262	.004 463 1647	.316 802	70.981 567	.014 088 1647	16.91	.690 580	6.91	120
11	3.541 055	264.005 702	.003 787 7970	.282 402	74.555 665	.013 412 7970	16.10	.770 489	7.00	132
12	3.972 408	308.821 573	.003 238 1158	.251 737	77.741 662	.012 863 1158	15.44	.852 289	7.10	144
13	4.456 306	359.096 678	.002 784 7654	.224 401	80.581 701	.012 409 7654	14.90	.935 923	7.20	156
14	4.999 149	415.496 034	.002 406 7618	.200 034	83.113 347	.012 031 7618	14.44	1.021 336	7.30	168
15	5.608 120	478.765 664	.002 088 7045	.178 313	85.370 089	.011 713 7045	14.06	1.108 467	7.39	180
16	6.291 271	549.742 468	.001 819 0336	.158 950	87.381 778	.011 444 0336	13.74	1.197 254	7.48	192
17	7.057 641	629.365 295	.001 588 9024	.141 690	89.175 023	.011 213 9024	13.46	1.287 636	7.57	204
18	7.917 366	718.687 358	.001 391 4256	.126 305	90.773 544	.011 016 4256	13.22	1.379 548	7.66	216
19	8.881 818	818.890 167	.001 221 1650	.112 590	92.198 487	.010 846 1650	13.02	1.472 926	7.75	228
20	9.963 754	931.299 157	.001 073 7688	.100 364	93.468 699	.010 698 7688	12.84	1.567 705	7.84	240
21	11.177 487	1057.401 222	.000 945 7148	.089 466	94.600 982	.010 570 7148	12.69	1.663 820	7.92	252
22	12.539 070	1198.864 379	.000 834 1227	.079 751	95.610 313	.010 459 1227	12.56	1.761 208	8.01	264
23	14.066 513	1357.559 838	.000 736 6158	.071 091	96.510 044	.010 361 6158	12.44	1.859 806	8.09	276
24	15.780 022	1535.586 746	.000 651 2169	.063 371	97.312 076	.010 276 2169	12.34	1.959 550	8.16	288
25	17.702 262	1735.299 959	.000 576 2692	.056 490	98.027 018	.010 201 2692	12.25	2.060 381	8.24	300
26	19.858 659	1959.341 190	.000 510 3756	.050 356	98.664 325	.010 135 3756	12.17	2.162 237	8.32	312
27	22.277 737	2210.673 951	.000 452 3507	.044 888	99.232 430	.010 077 3507	12.10	2.265 062	8.39	324
28	24.991 494	2492.622 751	.000 401 1839	.040 014	99.738 845	.010 026 1839	12.04	2.368 798	8.46	336
29	28.035 827	2808.917 078	.000 356 0091	.035 669	100.190 270	.009 981 0091	11.98	2.473 391	8.53	348
30	31.451 004	3163.740 723	.000 316 0815	.031 795	100.592 677	.009 941 0815	11.93	2.578 789	8.60	360
31	35.282 201	3561.787 126	.000 280 7579	.028 343	100.951 387	.009 905 7579	11.89	2.684 942	8.66	372
32	39.580 094	4008.321 457	.000 249 4810	.025 265	101.271 145	.009 874 4810	11.85	2.791 801	8.72	384
33	44.401 534	4509.250 261	.000 221 7664	.022 522	101.556 182	.009 846 7664	11.82	2.899 319	8.79	396
34	49.810 296	5071.199 588	.000 197 1920	.020 076	101.810 268	.009 822 1920	11.79	3.007 454	8.85	408
35	55.877 925	5701.602 639	.000 175 3893	.017 896	102.036 763	.009 800 3893	11.77	3.116 163	8.90	420
36	62.684 682	6408.798 088	.000 156 0355	.015 953	102.238 664	.009 781 0355	11.74	3.225 407	8.96	432
37	70.320 601	7202.140 382	.000 138 8476	.014 221	102.418 641	.009 763 8476	11.72	3.335 148	9.01	444
38	78.886 688	8092.123 479	.000 123 5770	.012 676	102.579 074	.009 748 5770	11.70	3.445 351	9.07	456
39	88.496 252	9090.519 655	.000 110 0047	.011 300	102.722 087	.009 735 0047	11.69	3.555 982	9.12	468
40	99.276 402	10210.535 224	.000 097 9381	.010 073	102.849 570	.009 722 9381	11.67	3.667 010	9.17	480
41	111.369 733	11466.985 223	.000 087 2069	.008 979	102.963 210	.009 712 2069	11.66	3.778 406	9.22	492
42	124.936 210	12876.489 380	.000 077 6609	.008 004	103.064 511	.009 702 6609	11.65	3.890 141	9.26	504
43	140.155 285	14457.691 950	.000 069 1673	.007 135	103.154 811	.009 694 1673	11.64	4.002 190	9.31	516
44	157.228 268	16231.508 336	.000 061 6086	.006 360	103.235 306	.009 686 6086	11.63	4.114 529	9.35	528
45	176.380 992	18221.401 743	.000 054 8805	.005 670	103.307 060	.009 679 8805	11.62	4.227 135	9.39	540
46	197.866 800	20453.693 541	.000 048 8909	.005 054	103.371 023	.009 673 8909	11.61	4.339 988	9.43	552
47	221.969 898	22957.911 435	.000 043 5580	.004 505	103.428 040	.009 668 5580	11.61	4.453 067	9.47	564
48	249.009 108	25767.180 035	.000 038 8091	.004 016	103.478 866	.009 663 8091	11.60	4.566 354	9.51	576
49	279.342 093	28918.659 022	.000 034 5798	.003 580	103.524 172	.009 659 5798	11.60	4.679 833	9.55	588
50	313.370 084	32454.034 672	.000 030 8128	.003 191	103.564 559	.009 655 8128	11.59	4.793 488	9.59	600

Effective Rate is 12.18 %

Annual Percentage Rate is 11.55 %

	Amount Of 1	Amount Of 1 Per Period	Sinking Fund Payment	Present Worth Of 1	Present Worth of 1 Per Period	Periodic Payment To Amortize 1	Constant Annual Percent	Total Interest	Annual Add On Rate	
	What a single $ 1 deposit grows to in the future. The deposit is made at the beginning of the first period.	What a series of $ 1 deposits grow to in the future. A deposit is made at the end of each period.	The amount to be deposited at the end of each period that grows to $ 1 in the future.	What $ 1 to be paid in the future is worth today. Value today of a single $ 1 payment tomorrow.	What $ 1 to be paid at the end of each period is worth today. Value today of a series of $ 1 payments tomorrow.	The mortgage payment to amortize a loan of $ 1. An annuity certain, payable at the end of each period, worth $ 1 today.	The annual payment, including interest and principal, to amortize completely a loan of $ 100.	The total interest paid over the term on a loan of $1. The loan is amortized by regular periodic payments.	The average annual interest rate on a loan that is completely amortized by regular periodic payments.	
	$S = (1+i)^n$	$S\overline{n} = \dfrac{(1+i)^n - 1}{i}$	$\dfrac{1}{S\overline{n}} = \dfrac{i}{(1+i)^n - 1}$	$V^n = \dfrac{1}{(1+i)^n}$	$A\overline{n} = \dfrac{1-V^n}{i}$	$\dfrac{1}{A\overline{n}} = \dfrac{i}{1-V^n}$				

YEAR / **PERIODS**

YEAR	Amount Of 1	Amount Of 1 Per Period	Sinking Fund Payment	Present Worth Of 1	Present Worth of 1 Per Period	Periodic Payment To Amortize 1	Constant Annual Percent	Total Interest	Annual Add On Rate	PERIODS
	1.009 667	1.000 000	1.000 000 0000	.990 426	.990 426	1.009 666 6667	1211.60	.009 667	11.60	1
	1.019 427	2.009 667	.497 594 9577	.980 943	1.971 369	.507 261 6244	608.72	.014 523	8.71	2
	1.029 281	3.029 093	.330 131 7765	.971 552	2.942 921	.339 798 4432	407.76	.019 395	7.76	3
	1.039 231	4.058 375	.246 404 0604	.962 250	3.905 171	.256 070 7271	307.29	.024 283	7.28	4
	1.049 277	5.097 606	.196 170 5301	.953 037	4.858 208	.205 837 1968	247.01	.029 186	7.00	5
	1.059 420	6.146 882	.162 684 0925	.943 913	5.802 121	.172 350 7592	206.83	.034 105	6.82	6
	1.069 661	7.206 302	.138 767 4220	.934 876	6.736 997	.148 434 0887	178.13	.039 039	6.69	7
	1.080 001	8.275 963	.120 831 8556	.925 925	7.662 922	.130 498 5223	156.60	.043 988	6.60	8
	1.090 441	9.355 964	.106 883 6918	.917 060	8.579 982	.116 550 3585	139.87	.048 953	6.53	9
	1.100 982	10.446 405	.095 726 7095	.908 280	9.488 262	.105 393 3762	126.48	.053 934	6.47	10
	1.111 625	11.547 387	.086 599 6771	.899 584	10.387 846	.096 266 3438	115.52	.058 930	6.43	11
	1.122 370	12.659 012	.078 995 1070	.890 971	11.278 818	.088 661 7737	106.40	.063 941	6.39	12
1	1.122 370	12.659 012	.078 995 1070	.890 971	11.278 818	.088 661 7737	106.40	.063 941	6.39	12
2	1.259 715	26.867 113	.037 220 2257	.793 830	21.327 922	.046 886 8923	56.27	.125 285	6.26	24
3	1.413 867	42.813 865	.023 356 9194	.707 280	30.281 387	.033 023 5860	39.63	.188 849	6.29	36
4	1.586 883	60.712 029	.016 471 2004	.630 166	38.258 669	.026 137 8671	31.37	.254 618	6.37	48
5	1.781 071	80.800 399	.012 376 1765	.561 460	45.366 199	.022 042 8431	26.46	.322 571	6.45	60
6	1.999 021	103.346 992	.009 676 1403	.500 245	51.698 805	.019 342 8070	23.22	.392 682	6.54	72
7	2.243 642	128.652 622	.007 772 8692	.445 704	57.340 976	.017 439 5358	20.93	.464 921	6.64	84
8	2.518 197	157.054 913	.006 367 1997	.397 109	62.367 989	.016 033 8664	19.25	.539 251	6.74	96
9	2.826 350	188.932 805	.005 292 8871	.353 813	66.846 914	.014 959 5537	17.96	.615 632	6.84	108
10	3.172 212	224.711 609	.004 450 1484	.315 237	70.837 508	.014 116 8150	16.95	.694 018	6.94	120
11	3.560 397	264.868 681	.003 775 4558	.280 868	74.393 014	.013 442 1225	16.14	.774 360	7.04	132
12	3.996 085	309.939 792	.003 226 4331	.250 245	77.560 867	.012 893 0998	15.48	.856 606	7.14	144
13	4.485 087	360.526 275	.002 773 7229	.222 961	80.383 335	.012 440 3896	14.93	.940 701	7.24	156
14	5.033 929	417.303 049	.002 396 3400	.198 652	82.898 072	.012 063 0067	14.48	1.026 585	7.33	168
15	5.649 934	481.027 623	.002 078 8827	.176 993	85.138 632	.011 745 5494	14.10	1.114 199	7.43	180
16	6.341 319	552.550 200	.001 809 7903	.157 696	87.134 906	.011 476 4570	13.78	1.203 480	7.52	192
17	7.117 309	632.825 028	.001 580 2156	.140 503	88.913 529	.011 246 8823	13.50	1.294 364	7.61	204
18	7.988 257	722.923 122	.001 383 2729	.125 184	90.498 232	.011 049 9396	13.26	1.386 787	7.70	216
19	8.965 783	824.046 561	.001 213 5237	.111 535	91.910 157	.010 880 1903	13.06	1.480 683	7.79	228
20	10.062 930	937.544 520	.001 066 6160	.099 375	93.168 142	.010 733 2827	12.88	1.575 988	7.88	240
21	11.294 336	1064.931 275	.000 939 0277	.088 540	94.288 970	.010 605 6944	12.73	1.672 635	7.96	252
22	12.676 429	1207.906 405	.000 827 8787	.078 887	95.287 596	.010 494 5454	12.60	1.770 560	8.05	264
23	14.227 649	1368.377 465	.000 730 7925	.070 286	96.177 343	.010 397 4592	12.48	1.869 699	8.13	276
24	15.968 693	1548.485 441	.000 645 7923	.062 623	96.970 083	.010 312 4590	12.38	1.969 988	8.21	288
25	17.922 789	1750.633 311	.000 571 2219	.055 795	97.676 391	.010 237 8885	12.29	2.071 367	8.29	300
26	20.116 008	1977.518 106	.000 505 6844	.049 712	98.305 691	.010 172 3510	12.21	2.173 774	8.36	312
27	22.577 613	2232.166 895	.000 447 9952	.044 292	98.866 380	.010 114 6618	12.14	2.277 150	8.43	324
28	25.340 446	2517.977 171	.000 397 1442	.039 463	99.365 937	.010 063 8109	12.08	2.381 440	8.51	336
29	28.441 368	2838.762 178	.000 352 2662	.035 160	99.811 029	.010 018 9329	12.03	2.486 589	8.57	348
30	31.921 751	3198.801 790	.000 312 6171	.031 327	100.207 593	.009 979 2837	11.98	2.592 542	8.64	360
31	35.828 030	3602.899 612	.000 277 5542	.027 911	100.560 920	.009 944 2209	11.94	2.699 250	8.71	372
32	40.212 322	4056.447 065	.000 246 5212	.024 868	100.875 724	.009 913 1878	11.90	2.806 664	8.77	384
33	45.133 121	4565.495 323	.000 219 0469	.022 157	101.156 206	.009 885 7010	11.87	2.914 738	8.83	396
34	50.656 082	5136.836 045	.000 194 6724	.019 741	101.406 107	.009 861 3390	11.84	3.023 426	8.89	408
35	56.854 889	5778.091 987	.000 173 0675	.017 589	101.628 762	.009 839 7342	11.81	3.132 688	8.95	420
36	63.812 247	6497.818 706	.000 153 8978	.015 671	101.827 141	.009 820 5645	11.79	3.242 484	9.01	432
37	71.620 981	7305.618 706	.000 136 8809	.013 962	102.003 891	.009 803 5476	11.77	3.352 775	9.06	444
38	80.385 272	8212.269 555	.000 121 7690	.012 440	102.161 370	.009 788 4357	11.75	3.463 527	9.11	456
39	90.222 054	9229.867 675	.000 108 3439	.011 084	102.301 680	.009 775 0106	11.74	3.574 705	9.17	468
40	101.262 567	10371.989 733	.000 096 4135	.009 875	102.426 691	.009 763 0802	11.72	3.686 278	9.22	480
41	113.654 113	11653.873 780	.000 085 8084	.008 799	102.538 073	.009 752 4750	11.71	3.798 218	9.26	492
42	127.562 018	13092.622 551	.000 076 3789	.007 839	102.637 311	.009 743 0456	11.70	3.910 495	9.31	504
43	143.171 839	14707.431 656	.000 067 9928	.006 985	102.725 730	.009 734 6595	11.69	4.023 084	9.36	516
44	160.691 842	16519.845 674	.000 060 5333	.006 223	102.804 508	.009 727 1999	11.68	4.135 962	9.40	528
45	180.355 774	18554.045 609	.000 053 8966	.005 545	102.874 697	.009 720 5633	11.67	4.249 104	9.44	540
46	202.425 991	20837.171 502	.000 047 9912	.004 940	102.937 233	.009 714 6578	11.66	4.362 491	9.48	552
47	227.196 950	23399.684 534	.000 042 7356	.004 401	102.992 952	.009 709 4023	11.66	4.476 103	9.52	564
48	254.999 143	26275.773 434	.000 038 0579	.003 922	103.042 595	.009 704 7245	11.65	4.589 921	9.56	576
49	286.203 503	29503.810 624	.000 033 8939	.003 494	103.086 826	.009 700 5606	11.65	4.703 930	9.60	588
50	321.226 354	33126.864 171	.000 030 1870	.003 113	103.126 234	.009 696 8536	11.64	4.818 112	9.64	600

	Amount Of 1	Amount Of 1 Per Period	Sinking Fund Payment	Present Worth Of 1	Present Worth of 1 Per Period	Periodic Payment To Amortize 1	Constant Annual Percent	Total Interest	Annual Add On Rate	
	What a single $ 1 deposit grows to in the future. The deposit is made at the beginning of the first period.	What a series of $ 1 deposits grow to in the future. A deposit is made at the end of each period.	The amount to be deposited at the end of each period that grows to $ 1 in the future.	What $ 1 to be paid in the future is worth today. Value today of a single $ 1 payment tomorrow.	What $ 1 to be paid at the end of each period is worth today. Value today of a series of $ 1 payments tomorrow.	The mortgage payment to amortize a loan of $ 1. An annuity certain, payable at the end of each period, worth $ 1 today.	The annual payment, including interest and principal, to amortize completely a loan of $ 100.	The total interest paid over the term on a loan of $1. The loan is amortized by regular periodic payments.	The average annual interest rate on a loan that is completely amortized by regular periodic payments.	
	$S = (1+i)^n$	$S\overline{n}| = \dfrac{(1+i)^n - 1}{i}$	$\dfrac{1}{S\overline{n}|} = \dfrac{i}{(1+i)^n - 1}$	$V^n = \dfrac{1}{(1+i)^n}$	$A\overline{n}| = \dfrac{1-V^n}{i}$	$\dfrac{1}{A\overline{n}|} = \dfrac{i}{1-V^n}$			**PERIODS**	

YEAR										
	1.009 688	1.000 000	1.000 000 0000	.990 405	.990 405	1.009 687 5000	1211.63	.009 687	11.62	1
	1.019 469	2.009 688	.497 589 7994	.980 903	1.971 308	.507 277 2994	608.74	.014 555	8.73	2
	1.029 345	3.029 156	.330 124 9210	.971 492	2.942 800	.339 812 4210	407.78	.019 437	7.77	3
	1.039 317	4.058 501	.246 396 3730	.962 171	3.904 971	.256 083 8730	307.31	.024 335	7.30	4
	1.049 385	5.097 818	.196 162 3569	.952 939	4.857 910	.205 849 8569	247.02	.029 249	7.02	5
	1.059 551	6.147 203	.162 675 6066	.943 796	5.801 706	.172 363 1066	206.84	.034 179	6.84	6
	1.069 815	7.206 754	.138 758 7222	.934 741	6.736 446	.148 446 2222	178.14	.039 124	6.71	7
	1.080 179	8.276 570	.120 823 0037	.925 772	7.662 219	.130 510 5037	156.62	.044 084	6.61	8
	1.090 644	9.356 749	.106 874 7290	.916 890	8.579 108	.116 562 2290	139.88	.049 060	6.54	9
	1.101 209	10.447 392	.095 717 6646	.908 093	9.487 201	.105 405 1646	126.49	.054 052	6.49	10
	1.111 877	11.548 601	.086 590 5712	.899 380	10.386 581	.096 278 0712	115.54	.059 059	6.44	11
	1.122 648	12.660 479	.078 985 9558	.890 751	11.277 332	.088 673 4558	106.41	.064 081	6.41	12
1	1.122 648	12.660 479	.078 985 9558	.890 751	11.277 332	.088 673 4558	106.41	.064 081	6.41	12
2	1.260 339	26.873 744	.037 211 0408	.793 437	21.322 625	.046 898 5408	56.28	.125 565	6.28	24
3	1.414 918	42.830 244	.023 347 9873	.706 755	30.270 478	.033 035 4873	39.65	.189 278	6.31	36
4	1.588 455	60.743 783	.016 462 5900	.629 542	38.240 786	.026 150 0900	31.39	.255 204	6.38	48
5	1.783 277	80.854 389	.012 367 9124	.560 765	45.340 345	.022 055 4124	26.47	.323 325	6.47	60
6	2.001 993	103.431 528	.009 668 2319	.499 502	51.664 282	.019 355 7319	23.23	.393 613	6.56	72
7	2.247 534	128.777 716	.007 765 3186	.444 932	57.297 335	.017 452 8186	20.95	.466 037	6.66	84
8	2.523 191	157.232 574	.006 360 0053	.396 324	62.314 982	.016 047 5053	19.26	.540 561	6.76	96
9	2.832 656	189.177 374	.005 286 0444	.353 026	66.784 455	.014 973 5444	17.97	.617 143	6.86	108
10	3.180 076	225.040 152	.004 443 6515	.314 458	70.765 642	.014 131 1515	16.96	.695 738	6.96	120
11	3.570 108	265.301 442	.003 769 2973	.280 104	74.311 887	.013 456 7973	16.15	.776 297	7.06	132
12	4.007 976	310.500 714	.003 220 6045	.249 503	77.470 708	.012 908 1045	15.49	.858 767	7.16	144
13	4.499 547	361.243 604	.002 768 2151	.222 245	80.284 431	.012 455 7151	14.95	.943 092	7.25	156
14	5.051 410	418.210 028	.002 391 1430	.197 965	82.790 757	.012 078 6430	14.50	1.029 212	7.35	168
15	5.670 957	482.163 292	.002 073 9862	.176 337	85.023 269	.011 761 4862	14.12	1.117 068	7.45	180
16	6.366 491	553.960 320	.001 805 1834	.157 072	87.011 881	.011 492 6834	13.80	1.206 595	7.54	192
17	7.147 330	634.563 137	.001 575 8873	.139 912	88.783 238	.011 263 3873	13.52	1.297 731	7.63	204
18	8.023 939	725.051 761	.001 379 2119	.124 627	90.361 077	.011 066 7119	13.29	1.390 410	7.72	216
19	9.008 062	826.638 668	.001 209 7184	.111 012	91.766 537	.010 897 2184	13.08	1.484 566	7.81	228
20	10.112 886	940.685 045	.001 063 0551	.098 884	93.018 453	.010 750 5551	12.91	1.580 133	7.90	240
21	11.353 216	1068.719 026	.000 935 6996	.088 081	94.133 598	.010 623 1996	12.75	1.677 046	7.99	252
22	12.745 669	1212.456 168	.000 824 7721	.078 458	95.126 914	.010 512 2721	12.62	1.775 240	8.07	264
23	14.308 905	1373.822 439	.000 727 8961	.069 887	96.011 711	.010 415 3961	12.50	1.874 649	8.15	276
24	16.063 869	1554.980 022	.000 643 0951	.062 252	96.799 845	.010 330 5951	12.40	1.975 211	8.23	288
25	18.034 077	1758.356 291	.000 568 7130	.055 451	97.501 876	.010 256 2130	12.31	2.076 864	8.31	300
26	20.245 927	1986.676 331	.000 503 3533	.049 393	98.127 210	.010 190 8533	12.23	2.179 546	8.38	312
27	22.729 057	2242.999 455	.000 445 8316	.043 997	98.684 228	.010 133 3316	12.16	2.283 199	8.46	324
28	25.516 739	2530.760 197	.000 395 1382	.039 190	99.180 391	.010 082 6382	12.10	2.387 766	8.53	336
29	28.646 326	2853.814 330	.000 350 4082	.034 908	99.622 349	.010 037 9082	12.05	2.493 192	8.60	348
30	32.159 752	3216.490 530	.000 310 8979	.031 095	100.016 024	.009 998 3979	12.00	2.599 423	8.66	360
31	36.104 094	3623.648 381	.000 275 9650	.027 698	100.366 690	.009 963 4650	11.96	2.706 409	8.73	372
32	40.532 203	4080.743 486	.000 245 0534	.024 672	100.679 046	.009 932 5534	11.92	2.814 100	8.79	384
33	45.503 412	4593.900 567	.000 217 6799	.021 976	100.957 278	.009 905 1799	11.89	2.922 451	8.86	396
34	51.084 332	5169.995 536	.000 193 4238	.019 575	101.205 112	.009 880 9238	11.86	3.031 417	8.92	408
35	57.349 743	5816.747 624	.000 171 9174	.017 437	101.425 871	.009 859 4174	11.84	3.140 955	8.97	420
36	64.383 596	6542.822 811	.000 152 8392	.015 532	101.622 513	.009 840 3392	11.81	3.251 027	9.03	432
37	72.280 140	7357.949 948	.000 135 9074	.013 835	101.797 671	.009 823 4074	11.79	3.361 593	9.09	444
38	81.145 183	8273.051 113	.000 120 8744	.012 324	101.953 694	.009 808 3744	11.78	3.472 619	9.14	456
39	91.097 508	9300.387 959	.000 107 5224	.010 977	102.092 671	.009 795 0224	11.76	3.584 070	9.19	468
40	102.270 471	10453.726 011	.000 095 6597	.009 778	102.216 465	.009 783 1597	11.74	3.695 917	9.24	480
41	114.813 779	11748.519 113	.000 085 1171	.008 710	102.326 735	.009 772 6171	11.73	3.808 128	9.29	492
42	128.895 504	13202.116 501	.000 075 7454	.007 758	102.424 958	.009 763 2454	11.72	3.920 676	9.33	504
43	144.704 329	14833.995 262	.000 067 4127	.006 911	102.512 450	.009 754 9127	11.71	4.033 535	9.38	516
44	162.452 082	16666.021 319	.000 060 0023	.006 156	102.590 383	.009 747 5023	11.70	4.146 681	9.42	528
45	182.376 567	18722.742 415	.000 053 4110	.005 483	102.659 803	.009 740 9110	11.69	4.260 092	9.47	540
46	204.744 759	21031.717 035	.000 047 5472	.004 884	102.721 638	.009 735 0472	11.69	4.373 746	9.51	552
47	229.856 373	23623.883 666	.000 042 3300	.004 351	102.776 718	.009 729 8300	11.68	4.487 624	9.55	564
48	258.047 886	26533.975 350	.000 037 6875	.003 875	102.825 781	.009 725 1875	11.68	4.601 708	9.59	576
49	289.697 043	29800.985 083	.000 033 5559	.003 452	102.869 483	.009 721 0559	11.67	4.715 981	9.62	588
50	325.227 918	33468.688 287	.000 029 8787	.003 075	102.908 411	.009 717 3787	11.67	4.830 427	9.66	600

Effective Rate is 12.26 %   Annual Percentage Rate is 11.625%

Amount Of 1	Amount Of 1 Per Period	Sinking Fund Payment	Present Worth Of 1	Present Worth of 1 Per Period	Periodic Payment To Amortize 1	Constant Annual Percent	Total Interest	Annual Add On Rate
What a single $ 1 deposit grows to in the future. The deposit is made at the beginning of the first period.	What a series of $ 1 deposits grow to in the future. A deposit is made at the end of each period.	The amount to be deposited at the end of each period that grows to $ 1 in the future.	What $ 1 to be paid in the future is worth today. Value today of a single $ 1 payment tomorrow.	What $ 1 to be paid at the end of each period is worth today. Value today of a series of $ 1 payments tomorrow.	The mortgage payment to amortize a loan of $ 1. An annuity certain, payable at the end of each period, worth $ 1 today.	The annual payment, including interest and principal, to amortize completely a loan of $ 100.	The total interest paid over the term of $1. The loan is amortized by regular periodic payments.	The average annual interest rate on a loan that is completely amortized by regular periodic payments.

$$S = (1+i)^n \qquad S\overline{n}| = \frac{(1+i)^n - 1}{i} \qquad \frac{1}{S\overline{n}|} = \frac{i}{(1+i)^n - 1} \qquad V^n = \frac{1}{(1+i)^n} \qquad A\overline{n}| = \frac{1-V^n}{i} \qquad \frac{1}{A\overline{n}|} = \frac{i}{1-V^n}$$

YEAR / **PERIODS**

	Amount Of 1	Amount Of 1 Per Period	Sinking Fund Payment	Present Worth Of 1	Present Worth of 1 Per Period	Periodic Payment To Amortize 1	Constant Annual Percent	Total Interest	Annual Add On Rate	
	1.009 708	1.000 000	1.000 000 0000	.990 385	.990 385	1.009 708 3333	1211.65	.009 708	11.65	1
	1.019 511	2.009 708	.497 584 6412	.980 862	1.971 247	.507 292 9746	608.76	.014 586	8.75	2
	1.029 409	3.029 219	.330 118 0657	.971 431	2.942 679	.339 826 3990	407.80	.019 479	7.79	3
	1.039 403	4.058 628	.246 388 6858	.962 091	3.904 770	.256 097 0192	307.32	.024 388	7.32	4
	1.049 493	5.098 030	.196 154 1840	.952 841	4.857 611	.205 862 5173	247.04	.029 313	7.04	5
	1.059 682	6.147 524	.162 667 1210	.943 679	5.801 290	.172 375 4543	206.86	.034 253	6.85	6
	1.069 970	7.207 206	.138 750 0228	.934 606	6.735 896	.148 458 3561	178.16	.039 208	6.72	7
	1.080 358	8.277 176	.120 814 1523	.925 619	7.661 515	.130 522 4857	156.63	.044 180	6.63	8
	1.090 846	9.357 534	.106 865 7668	.916 720	8.578 235	.116 574 1001	139.89	.049 167	6.56	9
	1.101 436	10.448 380	.095 708 6205	.907 905	9.486 140	.105 416 9538	126.51	.054 170	6.50	10
	1.112 129	11.549 816	.086 581 4661	.899 176	10.385 316	.096 289 7994	115.55	.059 188	6.46	11
	1.122 926	12.661 945	.078 976 8053	.890 530	11.275 846	.088 685 1387	106.43	.064 222	6.42	12
1	1.122 926	12.661 945	.078 976 8053	.890 530	11.275 846	.088 685 1387	106.43	.064 222	6.42	12
2	1.260 964	26.880 378	.037 201 8577	.793 044	21.317 330	.046 910 1910	56.30	.125 845	6.29	24
3	1.415 969	42.846 631	.023 339 0577	.706 230	30.259 575	.033 047 3910	39.66	.189 706	6.32	36
4	1.590 029	60.775 558	.016 453 9830	.628 919	38.222 915	.026 162 3163	31.40	.255 791	6.39	48
5	1.785 486	80.908 424	.012 359 6525	.560 072	45.314 512	.022 067 9858	26.49	.324 079	6.48	60
6	2.004 969	103.516 149	.009 660 3284	.498 761	51.629 793	.019 368 6618	23.25	.394 544	6.58	72
7	2.251 433	128.902 961	.007 757 7737	.444 162	57.253 743	.017 466 1070	20.96	.467 153	6.67	84
8	2.528 193	157.410 481	.006 352 8171	.395 539	62.262 041	.016 061 1504	19.28	.541 870	6.77	96
9	2.838 975	189.422 329	.005 279 2087	.352 240	66.722 082	.014 987 5420	17.99	.618 655	6.87	108
10	3.187 960	225.369 277	.004 437 1620	.313 680	70.693 883	.014 145 4954	16.98	.697 459	6.97	120
11	3.579 844	265.735 053	.003 763 1467	.279 342	74.230 893	.013 471 4801	16.17	.778 235	7.07	132
12	4.019 902	311.062 848	.003 214 7844	.248 762	77.380 708	.012 923 1178	15.51	.860 929	7.17	144
13	4.514 054	361.962 626	.002 762 7162	.221 530	80.185 713	.012 471 0495	14.97	.945 484	7.27	156
14	5.068 950	419.119 329	.002 385 9553	.197 280	82.683 656	.012 094 2887	14.52	1.031 840	7.37	168
15	5.692 058	483.302 099	.002 069 0992	.175 683	84.908 149	.011 777 4326	14.14	1.119 938	7.47	180
16	6.391 762	555.374 625	.001 800 5864	.156 451	86.889 128	.011 508 9197	13.82	1.209 713	7.56	192
17	7.177 478	636.306 767	.001 571 5690	.139 325	88.653 250	.011 279 9023	13.54	1.301 100	7.65	204
18	8.059 780	727.187 604	.001 375 1610	.124 073	90.224 254	.011 083 4943	13.31	1.394 035	7.74	216
19	9.050 539	829.240 095	.001 205 9234	.110 491	91.623 280	.010 914 2567	13.10	1.488 451	7.83	228
20	10.163 089	943.837 529	.001 059 5044	.098 395	92.869 156	.010 767 8377	12.93	1.584 281	7.92	240
21	11.412 401	1072.522 011	.000 932 3818	.087 624	93.978 646	.010 640 7151	12.77	1.681 460	8.01	252
22	12.815 286	1217.025 213	.000 821 6757	.078 032	94.966 680	.010 530 0090	12.64	1.779 922	8.09	264
23	14.390 623	1379.291 670	.000 725 0098	.069 490	95.846 555	.010 433 3431	12.53	1.879 603	8.17	276
24	16.159 611	1561.504 957	.000 640 4078	.061 883	96.630 110	.010 348 7412	12.42	1.980 437	8.25	288
25	18.146 053	1766.117 065	.000 566 2139	.055 108	97.327 890	.010 274 5472	12.33	2.082 364	8.33	300
26	20.376 682	1995.881 401	.000 501 0318	.049 076	97.949 284	.010 209 3651	12.26	2.185 322	8.41	312
27	22.881 514	2253.889 835	.000 443 6774	.043 703	98.502 654	.010 152 0107	12.19	2.289 251	8.48	324
28	25.694 256	2543.614 315	.000 393 1414	.038 919	98.995 447	.010 101 4747	12.13	2.394 095	8.55	336
29	28.852 758	2868.953 578	.000 348 5591	.034 659	99.434 294	.010 056 8925	12.07	2.499 799	8.62	348
30	32.399 523	3234.285 621	.000 309 1873	.030 865	99.825 100	.010 017 5206	12.03	2.606 307	8.69	360
31	36.382 279	3644.526 612	.000 274 3841	.027 486	100.173 125	.009 982 7174	11.98	2.713 571	8.75	372
32	40.854 621	4105.197 046	.000 243 5937	.024 477	100.483 052	.009 951 9270	11.95	2.821 540	8.82	384
33	45.876 732	4622.496 032	.000 216 3333	.021 798	100.759 051	.009 924 6667	11.91	2.930 168	8.88	396
34	51.516 193	5203.384 713	.000 192 1826	.019 411	101.004 837	.009 900 5159	11.89	3.039 411	8.94	408
35	57.848 893	5855.679 941	.000 170 7744	.017 286	101.223 717	.009 879 1077	11.86	3.149 225	9.00	420
36	64.960 048	6588.159 465	.000 151 7875	.015 394	101.418 636	.009 860 1208	11.84	3.259 572	9.05	432
37	72.945 352	7410.680 050	.000 134 9404	.013 709	101.592 217	.009 843 2737	11.82	3.370 414	9.11	444
38	81.912 261	8334.310 119	.000 119 9859	.012 208	101.746 796	.009 828 3193	11.80	3.481 714	9.16	456
39	91.981 439	9371.478 695	.000 106 7067	.010 872	101.884 454	.009 815 0401	11.78	3.593 439	9.21	468
40	103.288 385	10536.142 657	.000 094 9114	.009 682	102.007 042	.009 803 2447	11.77	3.705 557	9.26	480
41	115.985 253	11843.974 551	.000 084 4311	.008 622	102.116 211	.009 792 7645	11.76	3.818 040	9.31	492
42	130.242 901	13312.573 495	.000 075 1170	.007 678	102.213 429	.009 783 4503	11.75	3.930 859	9.36	504
43	146.253 190	14961.702 001	.000 066 8373	.006 837	102.300 004	.009 775 1706	11.74	4.043 988	9.40	516
44	164.231 567	16813.551 916	.000 059 4758	.006 089	102.377 102	.009 767 8092	11.73	4.157 403	9.45	528
45	184.419 960	18893.043 051	.000 052 9295	.005 422	102.445 761	.009 761 2629	11.72	4.271 082	9.49	540
46	207.090 039	21228.158 517	.000 047 1072	.004 829	102.506 903	.009 755 4406	11.71	4.385 003	9.53	552
47	232.546 869	23850.321 290	.000 041 9282	.004 300	102.561 352	.009 750 2615	11.71	4.499 147	9.57	564
48	261.133 016	26794.817 059	.000 037 3207	.003 829	102.609 840	.009 745 6540	11.70	4.613 497	9.61	576
49	293.233 154	30101.269 055	.000 033 2212	.003 410	102.653 021	.009 741 5545	11.69	4.728 034	9.65	588
50	329.279 246	33814.171 248	.000 029 5734	.003 037	102.691 474	.009 737 9067	11.69	4.842 744	9.69	600

Effective Rate is 12.29 %

Annual Percentage Rate is 11.65 %

MONTHLY COMPOUND INTEREST AND ANNUITY

11.70 % M

	Amount Of 1	Amount Of 1 Per Period	Sinking Fund Payment	Present Worth Of 1	Present Worth of 1 Per Period	Periodic Payment To Amortize 1	Constant Annual Percent	Total Interest	Annual Add On Rate
	What a single $ 1 deposit grows to in the future. The deposit is made at the beginning of the first period.	What a series of $ 1 deposits grow to in the future. A deposit is made at the end of each period.	The amount to be deposited at the end of each period that grows to $ 1 in the future.	What $ 1 to be paid in the future is worth today. Value today of a single $ 1 payment tomorrow.	What $ 1 to be paid at the end of each period is worth today. Value today of a series of $ 1 payments tomorrow.	The mortgage payment to amortize a loan of $ 1. An annuity certain, payable at the end of each period, worth $ 1 today.	The annual payment, including interest and principal, to amortize completely a loan of $ 100.	The total interest paid over the term on a loan of $1. The loan is amortized by regular periodic payments.	The average annual interest rate on a loan that is completely amortized by regular periodic payments.

$$S = (1+i)^n \qquad S\overline{n}| = \frac{(1+i)^n - 1}{i} \qquad \frac{1}{S\overline{n}|} = \frac{i}{(1+i)^n - 1} \qquad V^n = \frac{1}{(1+i)^n} \qquad A\overline{n}| = \frac{1 - V^n}{i} \qquad \frac{1}{A\overline{n}|} = \frac{i}{1 - V^n}$$

YEAR									**PERIODS**
	1.009 750	1.000 000	1.000 000 0000	.990 344	.990 344	1.009 750 0000	1211.70	.009 750	11.70	1
	1.019 595	2.009 750	.497 574 3252	.980 782	1.971 126	.507 324 3252	608.79	.014 649	8.79	2
	1.029 536	3.029 345	.330 104 3557	.971 311	2.942 437	.339 854 3557	407.83	.019 563	7.83	3
	1.039 574	4.058 881	.246 373 3124	.961 932	3.904 369	.256 123 3124	307.35	.024 493	7.35	4
	1.049 710	5.098 455	.196 137 8393	.952 644	4.857 013	.205 887 8393	247.07	.029 439	7.07	5
	1.059 945	6.148 165	.162 650 1511	.943 446	5.800 459	.172 400 1511	206.89	.034 401	6.88	6
	1.070 279	7.208 110	.138 732 6255	.934 336	6.734 795	.148 482 6255	178.18	.039 378	6.75	7
	1.080 714	8.278 389	.120 796 4513	.925 314	7.660 109	.130 546 4513	156.66	.044 372	6.66	8
	1.091 251	9.359 103	.106 847 8444	.916 379	8.576 488	.116 597 8444	139.92	.049 381	6.58	9
	1.101 891	10.450 354	.095 690 5343	.907 531	9.484 019	.105 440 5343	126.53	.054 405	6.53	10
	1.112 634	11.552 245	.086 563 2581	.898 768	10.382 787	.096 313 2581	115.58	.059 446	6.49	11
	1.123 483	12.664 880	.078 958 5071	.890 089	11.272 876	.088 708 5071	106.46	.064 502	6.45	12
1	1.123 483	12.664 880	.078 958 5071	.890 089	11.272 876	.088 708 5071	106.46	.064 502	6.45	12
2	1.262 213	26.893 652	.037 183 4965	.792 259	21.306 744	.046 933 4965	56.33	.126 404	6.32	24
3	1.418 074	42.879 429	.023 321 2062	.705 182	30.237 784	.033 071 2062	39.69	.190 563	6.35	36
4	1.593 182	60.839 171	.016 436 7789	.627 675	38.187 209	.026 186 7789	31.43	.256 965	6.42	48
5	1.789 912	81.016 628	.012 343 1451	.558 687	45.262 908	.022 093 1451	26.52	.325 589	6.51	60
6	2.010 935	103.685 650	.009 644 5361	.497 281	51.560 914	.019 394 5361	23.28	.396 407	6.61	72
7	2.259 251	129.153 902	.007 742 7007	.442 625	57.166 702	.017 492 7007	21.00	.469 387	6.71	84
8	2.538 229	157.767 038	.006 338 4596	.393 976	62.156 355	.016 088 4596	19.31	.544 492	6.81	96
9	2.851 656	189.913 398	.005 265 5579	.350 673	66.597 592	.015 015 5579	18.02	.621 680	6.91	108
10	3.203 785	226.029 274	.004 424 2057	.312 131	70.550 691	.014 174 2057	17.01	.700 905	7.01	120
11	3.599 397	266.604 831	.003 750 8698	.277 824	74.069 302	.013 500 8698	16.21	.782 115	7.11	132
12	4.043 860	312.190 763	.003 203 1697	.247 288	77.201 181	.012 953 1697	15.55	.865 256	7.21	144
13	4.543 206	363.405 763	.002 751 7450	.220 109	79.988 833	.012 501 7450	15.01	.950 272	7.31	156
14	5.104 213	420.944 923	.002 375 6077	.195 917	82.470 093	.012 125 6077	14.56	1.037 102	7.41	168
15	5.734 494	485.589 167	.002 059 3540	.174 383	84.678 637	.011 809 3540	14.18	1.125 684	7.50	180
16	6.442 605	558.215 849	.001 791 4217	.155 217	86.644 438	.011 541 4217	13.85	1.215 953	7.60	192
17	7.238 154	639.810 661	.001 562 9624	.138 157	88.394 177	.011 312 9624	13.58	1.307 844	7.69	204
18	8.131 940	731.481 011	.001 367 0895	.122 972	89.951 601	.011 117 0895	13.35	1.401 291	7.78	216
19	9.136 093	834.471 051	.001 198 3639	.109 456	91.337 848	.010 948 3639	13.14	1.496 227	7.87	228
20	10.264 241	950.178 568	.001 052 4338	.097 426	92.571 732	.010 802 4338	12.97	1.592 584	7.96	240
21	11.531 696	1080.173 947	.000 925 7768	.086 718	93.669 999	.010 675 7768	12.82	1.690 296	8.05	252
22	12.955 660	1226.221 490	.000 815 5134	.077 186	94.647 554	.010 565 5134	12.68	1.789 296	8.13	264
23	14.555 458	1390.303 360	.000 719 2675	.068 703	95.517 666	.010 469 2675	12.57	1.889 518	8.22	276
24	16.352 803	1574.646 483	.000 635 0632	.061 152	96.292 144	.010 385 0632	12.47	1.990 898	8.30	288
25	18.372 090	1781.752 770	.000 561 2451	.054 430	96.981 498	.010 311 2451	12.38	2.093 374	8.37	300
26	20.640 722	2014.433 075	.000 496 4176	.048 448	97.595 085	.010 246 4176	12.30	2.196 882	8.45	312
27	23.189 492	2275.845 344	.000 439 3972	.043 123	98.141 233	.010 189 3972	12.23	2.301 365	8.52	324
28	26.052 990	2569.537 474	.000 389 1751	.038 383	98.627 353	.010 139 1751	12.17	2.406 763	8.60	336
29	29.270 081	2899.495 465	.000 344 8876	.034 165	99.060 043	.010 094 8876	12.12	2.513 021	8.67	348
30	32.884 426	3270.197 519	.000 305 7919	.030 410	99.445 176	.010 055 7919	12.07	2.620 085	8.73	360
31	36.945 079	3686.674 819	.000 271 2471	.027 067	99.787 979	.010 021 2471	12.03	2.727 904	8.80	372
32	41.507 153	4154.579 809	.000 240 6982	.024 092	100.093 104	.009 990 6982	11.99	2.836 428	8.86	384
33	46.632 563	4680.262 914	.000 213 6632	.021 444	100.364 693	.009 963 6632	11.96	2.945 611	8.93	396
34	52.390 873	5270.858 723	.000 189 7224	.019 087	100.606 431	.009 939 7224	11.93	3.055 407	8.99	408
35	58.860 233	5934.382 826	.000 168 5095	.016 989	100.821 600	.009 918 5095	11.91	3.165 774	9.05	420
36	66.128 446	6679.840 596	.000 149 7042	.015 122	101.013 119	.009 899 7042	11.88	3.276 672	9.10	432
37	74.294 157	7517.349 412	.000 133 0256	.013 460	101.183 589	.009 883 0256	11.86	3.388 063	9.16	444
38	83.468 191	8458.275 976	.000 118 2274	.011 981	101.335 322	.009 868 2274	11.85	3.499 912	9.21	456
39	93.775 058	9515.390 578	.000 105 0929	.010 664	101.470 378	.009 855 0929	11.83	3.612 183	9.26	468
40	105.354 644	10703.040 416	.000 093 4314	.009 492	101.590 590	.009 843 4314	11.82	3.724 847	9.31	480
41	118.364 107	12037.344 318	.000 083 0748	.008 449	101.697 589	.009 833 0748	11.80	3.837 873	9.36	492
42	132.980 012	13536.411 505	.000 073 8748	.007 520	101.792 828	.009 823 8748	11.79	3.951 233	9.41	504
43	149.400 727	15220.587 373	.000 065 7005	.006 693	101.877 599	.009 815 7005	11.78	4.064 901	9.45	516
44	167.849 114	17112.729 619	.000 058 4360	.005 958	101.953 053	.009 808 4360	11.78	4.178 850	9.50	528
45	188.575 555	19238.518 467	.000 051 9791	.005 303	102.020 214	.009 801 9791	11.77	4.293 069	9.54	540
46	211.861 351	21626.805 202	.000 046 2389	.004 720	102.079 993	.009 796 2389	11.76	4.407 524	9.58	552
47	238.022 536	24310.003 742	.000 041 1353	.004 201	102.133 202	.009 791 1353	11.75	4.522 200	9.62	564
48	267.414 173	27324.530 550	.000 036 5972	.003 740	102.180 562	.009 786 5972	11.75	4.637 080	9.66	576
49	300.435 164	30711.298 903	.000 032 5613	.003 329	102.222 717	.009 782 5613	11.74	4.752 146	9.70	588
50	337.533 673	34516.274 142	.000 028 9718	.002 963	102.260 239	.009 778 9718	11.74	4.867 383	9.73	600

Effective Rate is 12.35 %

Annual Percentage Rate is 11.70 %

Amount Of 1	Amount Of 1 Per Period	Sinking Fund Payment	Present Worth Of 1	Present Worth of 1 Per Period	Periodic Payment To Amortize 1	Constant Annual Percent	Total Interest	Annual Add On Rate
What a single $ 1 deposit grows to in the future. The deposit is made at the beginning of the first period.	What a series of $ 1 deposits grow to in the future. A deposit is made at the end of each period.	The amount to be deposited at the end of each period that grows to $ 1 in the future.	What $ 1 to be paid in the future is worth today. Value today of a single $ 1 payment tomorrow.	What $ 1 to be paid at the end of each period is worth today. Value today of a series of $ 1 payments tomorrow.	The mortgage payment to amortize a loan of $ 1. An annuity certain, payable at the end of each period, worth $ 1 today.	The annual payment, including interest and principal, to amortize completely a loan of $ 100.	The total interest paid over the term on a loan of $1. The loan is amortized by regular periodic payments.	The average annual interest rate on a loan that is completely amortized by regular periodic payments.
$S = (1+i)^n$	$S\overline{n}] = \dfrac{(1+i)^n - 1}{i}$	$\dfrac{1}{S\overline{n}]} = \dfrac{i}{(1+i)^n - 1}$	$V^n = \dfrac{1}{(1+i)^n}$	$A\overline{n}] = \dfrac{1 - V^n}{i}$	$\dfrac{1}{A\overline{n}]} = \dfrac{i}{1 - V^n}$			

YEAR								PERIODS
	1.009 792	1.000 000	1.000 000 0000	.990 303	.990 303	1.009 791 6667	1211.75	.009 792	11.75	1
	1.019 679	2.009 792	.497 564 0095	.980 701	1.971 004	.507 355 6762	608.83	.014 711	8.83	2
	1.029 664	3.029 471	.330 090 6464	.971 191	2.942 195	.339 882 3131	407.86	.019 647	7.86	3
	1.039 746	4.059 134	.246 357 9399	.961 774	3.903 969	.256 149 6066	307.38	.024 598	7.38	4
	1.049 927	5.098 880	.196 121 4959	.952 448	4.856 416	.205 913 1626	247.10	.029 566	7.10	5
	1.060 207	6.148 807	.162 633 1829	.943 212	5.799 628	.172 424 8496	206.91	.034 549	6.91	6
	1.070 588	7.209 014	.138 715 2302	.934 066	6.733 694	.148 506 8969	178.21	.039 548	6.78	7
	1.081 071	8.279 602	.120 778 7525	.925 009	7.658 703	.130 570 4191	156.69	.044 563	6.68	8
	1.091 657	9.360 673	.106 829 9244	.916 039	8.574 742	.116 621 5911	139.95	.049 594	6.61	9
	1.102 346	10.452 330	.095 672 4510	.907 156	9.481 898	.105 464 1177	126.56	.054 641	6.56	10
	1.113 140	11.554 675	.086 545 0533	.898 360	10.380 258	.096 336 7200	115.61	.059 704	6.51	11
	1.124 039	12.667 815	.078 940 2122	.889 649	11.269 907	.088 731 8789	106.48	.064 783	6.48	12
1	1.124 039	12.667 815	.078 940 2122	.889 649	11.269 907	.088 731 8789	106.48	.064 783	6.48	12
2	1.263 464	26.906 933	.037 165 1422	.791 475	21.296 166	.046 956 8088	56.35	.126 963	6.35	24
3	1.420 183	42.912 258	.023 303 3648	.704 135	30.216 016	.033 095 0315	39.72	.191 421	6.38	36
4	1.596 341	60.902 867	.016 419 5882	.626 433	38.151 550	.026 211 2548	31.46	.258 140	6.45	48
5	1.794 349	81.125 014	.012 326 6542	.557 305	45.211 389	.022 118 3209	26.55	.327 099	6.54	60
6	2.016 918	103.855 497	.009 628 7634	.495 806	51.492 166	.019 420 4300	23.31	.398 271	6.64	72
7	2.267 095	129.405 446	.007 727 6501	.441 093	57.079 852	.017 519 3167	21.03	.471 623	6.74	84
8	2.548 303	158.124 586	.006 324 1272	.392 418	62.050 930	.016 115 7939	19.34	.547 116	6.84	96
9	2.864 392	190.406 019	.005 251 9348	.349 114	66.473 444	.015 043 6015	18.06	.624 709	6.94	108
10	3.219 689	226.691 611	.004 411 2793	.310 589	70.407 928	.014 202 9459	17.05	.704 354	7.04	120
11	3.619 056	267.478 031	.003 738 6248	.276 315	73.908 238	.013 530 2915	16.24	.785 998	7.15	132
12	4.067 960	313.323 559	.003 191 5889	.245 823	77.022 284	.012 983 2556	15.58	.869 589	7.25	144
13	4.572 546	364.855 722	.002 740 8094	.218 697	79.792 692	.012 532 4761	15.04	.955 066	7.35	156
14	5.139 720	422.779 884	.002 365 2970	.194 563	82.257 381	.012 156 9637	14.59	1.042 370	7.45	168
15	5.777 245	487.888 901	.002 049 6470	.173 093	84.450 090	.011 841 3136	14.21	1.131 436	7.54	180
16	6.493 849	561.073 978	.001 782 2962	.153 992	86.400 830	.011 573 9628	13.89	1.222 201	7.64	192
17	7.299 340	643.336 860	.001 554 3956	.136 999	88.136 304	.011 346 0623	13.62	1.314 597	7.73	204
18	8.204 743	735.803 550	.001 359 0584	.121 881	89.680 267	.011 150 7251	13.39	1.408 557	7.83	216
19	9.222 451	839.739 717	.001 190 8452	.108 431	91.053 851	.010 982 5119	13.18	1.504 013	7.92	228
20	10.366 395	956.568 025	.001 045 4040	.096 466	92.275 859	.010 837 0706	13.01	1.600 897	8.00	240
21	11.652 233	1087.887 601	.000 919 2126	.085 820	93.363 017	.010 710 8793	12.86	1.699 142	8.09	252
22	13.097 564	1235.495 930	.000 809 3916	.076 350	94.330 205	.010 601 0582	12.73	1.798 679	8.18	264
23	14.722 173	1401.413 451	.000 713 5653	.067 925	95.190 663	.010 505 2320	12.61	1.899 044	8.26	276
24	16.548 297	1587.911 219	.000 629 7581	.060 429	95.956 169	.010 421 4248	12.51	2.001 370	8.34	288
25	18.600 932	1797.541 987	.000 556 3152	.053 761	96.637 200	.010 347 9819	12.42	2.104 395	8.42	300
26	20.908 173	2033.175 151	.000 491 8415	.047 828	97.243 079	.010 283 5082	12.35	2.208 455	8.49	312
27	23.501 603	2298.036 022	.000 435 1542	.042 550	97.782 098	.010 226 8209	12.28	2.313 490	8.57	324
28	26.416 719	2595.749 977	.000 385 2451	.037 855	98.261 636	.010 176 9118	12.22	2.419 442	8.64	336
29	29.693 422	2930.392 078	.000 341 2513	.033 677	98.688 256	.010 132 9179	12.16	2.526 255	8.71	348
30	33.376 565	3306.542 859	.000 302 4307	.029 961	99.067 798	.010 094 0973	12.12	2.633 875	8.78	360
31	37.516 562	3729.351 014	.000 268 1432	.026 655	99.405 458	.010 059 8098	12.08	2.742 249	8.85	372
32	42.170 080	4204.603 879	.000 237 8345	.023 713	99.705 856	.010 029 5012	12.04	2.851 328	8.91	384
33	47.400 815	4738.806 645	.000 211 0236	.021 097	99.973 105	.010 002 6903	12.01	2.961 065	8.97	396
34	53.280 366	5339.271 398	.000 187 2915	.018 769	100.210 862	.009 978 9581	11.98	3.071 415	9.03	408
35	59.889 210	6014.217 212	.000 166 2727	.016 697	100.422 383	.009 957 9393	11.95	3.182 335	9.09	420
36	67.317 809	6772.882 645	.000 147 6476	.014 855	100.610 562	.009 939 3143	11.93	3.293 784	9.15	432
37	75.667 844	7625.652 195	.000 131 1363	.013 216	100.777 976	.009 922 8030	11.91	3.405 725	9.20	444
38	85.053 610	8584.198 445	.000 116 4931	.011 757	100.926 915	.009 908 1598	11.89	3.518 121	9.26	456
39	95.603 576	9661.641 835	.000 103 5021	.010 460	101.059 419	.009 895 1687	11.88	3.630 939	9.31	468
40	107.462 150	10872.730 247	.000 091 9732	.009 306	101.177 300	.009 883 6399	11.87	3.744 147	9.36	480
41	120.791 650	12234.040 882	.000 081 7391	.008 279	101.282 173	.009 873 4058	11.85	3.857 716	9.41	492
42	135.774 528	13764.207 155	.000 072 6522	.007 365	101.375 474	.009 864 3189	11.84	3.971 617	9.46	504
43	152.615 868	15484.173 756	.000 064 5821	.006 552	101.458 478	.009 856 2487	11.83	4.085 824	9.50	516
44	171.546 191	17417.483 330	.000 057 4136	.005 829	101.532 323	.009 849 0802	11.82	4.200 314	9.55	528
45	192.824 613	19590.598 732	.000 051 0449	.005 186	101.598 019	.009 842 7116	11.82	4.315 064	9.59	540
46	216.742 389	22033.265 242	.000 045 3859	.004 614	101.656 466	.009 837 0526	11.81	4.430 053	9.63	552
47	243.626 903	24778.917 715	.000 040 3569	.004 105	101.708 463	.009 832 0236	11.80	4.545 261	9.67	564
48	273.846 145	27865.138 234	.000 035 8871	.003 652	101.754 721	.009 827 5538	11.80	4.660 671	9.71	576
49	307.813 753	31334.170 526	.000 031 9140	.003 249	101.795 876	.009 823 5807	11.79	4.776 265	9.75	588
50	345.994 670	35233.498 189	.000 028 3821	.002 890	101.832 488	.009 820 0487	11.79	4.892 029	9.78	600

Amount Of 1	Amount Of 1 Per Period	Sinking Fund Payment	Present Worth Of 1	Present Worth of 1 Per Period	Periodic Payment To Amortize 1	Constant Annual Percent	Total Interest	Annual Add On Rate
What a single $ 1 deposit grows to in the future. The deposit is made at the beginning of the first period.	What a series of $ 1 deposits grow to in the future. A deposit is made at the end of each period.	The amount to be deposited at the end of each period that grows to $ 1 in the future.	What $ 1 to be paid in the future is worth today. Value today of a single $ 1 payment tomorrow.	What $ 1 to be paid at the end of each period is worth today. Value today of a series of $ 1 payments tomorrow.	The mortgage payment to amortize a loan of $ 1. An annuity certain, payable at the end of each period, worth $ 1 today.	The annual interest payment, including interest and principal, to amortize completely a loan of $ 100.	The total interest paid over the term on a loan of $1. The loan is amortized by regular periodic payments.	The average annual interest rate on a loan that is completely amortized by regular periodic payments.
$S = (1+i)^n$	$S\overline{n} = \frac{(1+i)^n - 1}{i}$	$\frac{1}{S\overline{n}} = \frac{i}{(1+i)^n - 1}$	$V^n = \frac{1}{(1+i)^n}$	$A\overline{n} = \frac{1-V^n}{i}$	$\frac{1}{A\overline{n}} = \frac{i}{1-V^n}$			**PERIODS**

YEAR									
	1.009 833	1.000 000	1.000 000 0000	.990 262	.990 262	1.009 833 3333	1211.80	.009 833	11.80	1
	1.019 763	2.009 833	.497 553 6943	.980 620	1.970 882	.507 387 0277	608.87	.014 774	8.86	2
	1.029 791	3.029 597	.330 076 9379	.971 071	2.941 953	.339 910 2712	407.90	.019 731	7.89	3
	1.039 917	4.059 388	.246 342 5686	.961 615	3.903 568	.256 175 9019	307.42	.024 704	7.41	4
	1.050 143	5.099 305	.196 105 1539	.952 251	4.855 819	.205 938 4873	247.13	.029 692	7.13	5
	1.060 470	6.149 448	.162 616 2163	.942 978	5.798 797	.172 449 5497	206.94	.034 697	6.94	6
	1.070 898	7.209 918	.138 697 8368	.933 796	6.732 594	.148 531 1702	178.24	.039 718	6.81	7
	1.081 428	8.280 815	.120 761 0559	.924 703	7.657 297	.130 594 3892	156.72	.044 755	6.71	8
	1.092 062	9.362 243	.106 812 0071	.915 699	8.572 996	.116 645 3404	139.98	.049 808	6.64	9
	1.102 801	10.454 305	.095 654 3705	.906 782	9.479 778	.105 487 7038	126.59	.054 877	6.59	10
	1.113 645	11.557 106	.086 526 8516	.897 952	10.377 730	.096 360 1849	115.64	.059 962	6.54	11
	1.124 596	12.670 751	.078 921 9207	.889 208	11.266 939	.088 755 2540	106.51	.065 063	6.51	12
1	1.124 596	12.670 751	.078 921 9207	.889 208	11.266 939	.088 755 2540	106.51	.065 063	6.51	12
2	1.264 716	26.920 223	.037 146 7946	.790 692	21.285 596	.046 980 1279	56.38	.127 523	6.38	24
3	1.422 294	42.945 119	.023 285 5335	.703 090	30.194 270	.033 118 8669	39.75	.192 279	6.41	36
4	1.599 505	60.966 647	.016 402 4109	.625 193	38.115 938	.026 235 7442	31.49	.259 316	6.48	48
5	1.798 797	81.233 582	.012 310 1799	.555 927	45.159 952	.022 143 5132	26.58	.328 611	6.57	60
6	2.022 919	104.025 689	.009 613 0101	.494 335	51.423 549	.019 446 3435	23.34	.400 137	6.67	72
7	2.274 966	129.657 595	.007 712 6218	.439 567	56.993 192	.017 545 9552	21.06	.473 860	6.77	84
8	2.558 417	158.483 127	.006 309 8200	.390 867	61.945 766	.016 143 1533	19.38	.549 743	6.87	96
9	2.877 185	190.900 197	.005 238 3393	.347 562	66.349 637	.015 071 6726	18.09	.627 741	6.97	108
10	3.235 670	227.356 295	.004 398 3827	.309 055	70.265 595	.014 231 7161	17.08	.707 806	7.08	120
11	3.638 821	268.354 666	.003 726 4118	.274 814	73.747 699	.013 559 7451	16.28	.789 886	7.18	132
12	4.092 202	314.461 260	.003 180 0420	.244 367	76.844 015	.013 013 3753	15.62	.873 926	7.28	144
13	4.602 073	366.312 537	.002 729 9093	.217 293	79.597 285	.012 563 2426	15.08	.959 866	7.38	156
14	5.175 472	424.624 261	.002 355 0232	.193 219	82.045 516	.012 188 3566	14.63	1.047 644	7.48	168
15	5.820 314	490.201 376	.002 039 9780	.171 812	84.222 503	.011 873 3113	14.25	1.137 196	7.58	180
16	6.545 500	563.949 120	.001 773 2096	.152 777	86.158 299	.011 606 5429	13.93	1.228 456	7.68	192
17	7.361 041	646.885 516	.001 545 8686	.135 850	87.879 625	.011 379 2019	13.66	1.321 357	7.77	204
18	8.278 195	740.155 432	.001 351 0676	.120 799	89.410 243	.011 184 4009	13.43	1.415 831	7.87	216
19	9.309 623	845.046 379	.001 183 3670	.107 416	90.771 281	.011 016 7003	13.23	1.511 808	7.96	228
20	10.469 562	963.006 290	.001 038 4148	.095 515	91.981 527	.010 871 7481	13.05	1.609 220	8.05	240
21	11.774 024	1095.663 501	.000 912 6890	.084 933	93.057 689	.010 746 0223	12.90	1.707 998	8.13	252
22	13.241 017	1244.849 232	.000 803 3101	.075 523	94.014 621	.010 636 6435	12.77	1.808 074	8.22	264
23	14.890 792	1412.622 866	.000 707 9030	.067 156	94.865 532	.010 541 2364	12.65	1.909 381	8.30	276
24	16.746 120	1601.300 376	.000 624 4925	.059 715	95.622 170	.010 457 8258	12.55	2.011 854	8.38	288
25	18.832 615	1813.486 297	.000 551 4241	.053 099	96.294 979	.010 384 7574	12.47	2.115 427	8.46	300
26	21.179 078	2052.109 674	.000 487 3034	.047 216	96.893 247	.010 320 6367	12.39	2.220 039	8.54	312
27	23.817 901	2320.464 502	.000 430 9482	.041 985	97.425 231	.010 264 2815	12.32	2.325 627	8.61	324
28	26.785 509	2622.255 192	.000 381 3511	.037 334	97.898 276	.010 214 6845	12.26	2.432 134	8.69	336
29	30.122 869	2961.647 710	.000 337 6499	.033 197	98.318 912	.010 170 9832	12.21	2.539 502	8.76	348
30	33.876 050	3343.327 082	.000 299 1033	.029 519	98.692 944	.010 132 4366	12.16	2.647 677	8.83	360
31	38.096 860	3772.562 070	.000 265 0718	.026 249	99.025 537	.010 098 4052	12.12	2.756 607	8.89	372
32	42.843 566	4255.277 899	.000 235 0023	.023 341	99.321 282	.010 068 3356	12.09	2.866 241	8.96	384
33	48.181 691	4798.138 052	.000 208 4142	.020 755	99.584 260	.010 041 7475	12.06	2.976 532	9.02	396
34	54.184 923	5408.636 256	.000 184 8895	.018 455	99.818 103	.010 018 2228	12.03	3.087 435	9.08	408
35	60.936 133	6095.199 922	.000 164 0635	.016 411	100.026 038	.009 997 3969	12.00	3.198 907	9.14	420
36	68.528 514	6867.306 481	.000 145 6175	.014 592	100.210 936	.009 978 9508	11.98	3.310 907	9.20	432
37	77.066 873	7735.614 210	.000 129 2722	.012 976	100.375 348	.009 962 6056	11.96	3.423 397	9.25	444
38	86.669 075	8712.109 363	.000 114 7828	.011 538	100.521 545	.009 948 1161	11.94	3.536 341	9.31	456
39	97.467 671	9810.271 631	.000 101 9340	.010 260	100.651 545	.009 935 2673	11.93	3.649 705	9.36	468
40	109.611 725	11045.260 214	.000 090 5366	.009 123	100.767 141	.009 923 8699	11.91	3.763 458	9.41	480
41	123.268 877	12434.123 086	.000 080 4238	.008 112	100.869 931	.009 913 7572	11.90	3.877 569	9.46	492
42	138.627 651	13996.032 324	.000 071 4488	.007 214	100.961 332	.009 904 7822	11.89	3.992 010	9.50	504
43	155.900 063	15752.548 764	.000 063 4818	.006 414	101.042 607	.009 896 8151	11.88	4.106 757	9.55	516
44	175.324 543	17727.919 630	.000 056 4082	.005 704	101.114 877	.009 889 7415	11.87	4.221 784	9.59	528
45	197.169 230	19949.413 246	.000 050 1268	.005 072	101.179 140	.009 883 4601	11.87	4.337 068	9.64	540
46	221.735 672	22447.695 453	.000 044 5480	.004 510	101.236 284	.009 877 8813	11.86	4.452 590	9.68	552
47	249.362 987	25257.250 926	.000 039 5926	.004 010	101.287 096	.009 872 9259	11.85	4.568 330	9.72	564
48	280.432 547	28416.869 225	.000 035 1904	.003 566	101.332 279	.009 868 5237	11.85	4.684 270	9.76	576
49	315.373 242	31970.160 185	.000 031 2792	.003 171	101.372 456	.009 864 6125	11.84	4.800 392	9.80	588
50	354.667 397	35966.175 982	.000 027 8039	.002 820	101.408 182	.009 861 1372	11.84	4.916 682	9.83	600

MONTHLY COMPOUND INTEREST AND ANNUITY

Amount Of 1	Amount Of 1 Per Period	Sinking Fund Payment	Present Worth Of 1	Present Worth of 1 Per Period	Periodic Payment To Amortize 1	Constant Annual Percent	Total Interest	Annual Add On Rate
What a single $ 1 deposit grows to in the future. The deposit is made at the beginning of the first period.	What a series of $ 1 deposits grow to in the future. A deposit is made at the end of each period.	The amount to be deposited at the end of each period that grows to $ 1 in the future.	What $ 1 to be paid in the future is worth today. Value today of a single $ 1 payment tomorrow.	What $ 1 to be paid at the end of each period is worth today. Value today of a series of $ 1 payments tomorrow.	The mortgage payment to amortize a loan of $ 1. An annuity certain, payable at the end of each period, worth $ 1 today.	The annual payment, including interest and principal, to amortize completely a loan of $ 100.	The total interest paid over the term on a loan of $1. The loan is amortized by regular periodic payments.	The average annual interest rate on a loan that is completely amortized by regular periodic payments.

$$S = (1+i)^n \qquad S\overline{n}| = \frac{(1+i)^n - 1}{i} \qquad \frac{1}{S\overline{n}|} = \frac{i}{(1+i)^n - 1} \qquad V^n = \frac{1}{(1+i)^n} \qquad A\overline{n}| = \frac{1 - V^n}{i} \qquad \frac{1}{A\overline{n}|} = \frac{i}{1 - V^n}$$

YEAR									PERIODS
	1.009 875	1.000 000	1.000 000 0000	.990 222	.990 222	1.009 875 0000	1211.85	.009 875	11.85	1
	1.019 848	2.009 875	.497 543 3796	.980 539	1.970 760	.507 418 3796	608.91	.014 837	8.90	2
	1.029 919	3.029 723	.330 063 2302	.970 951	2.941 711	.339 938 2302	407.93	.019 815	7.93	3
	1.040 089	4.059 641	.246 327 1983	.961 456	3.903 167	.256 202 1983	307.45	.024 809	7.44	4
	1.050 360	5.099 730	.196 088 8133	.952 055	4.855 222	.205 963 8133	247.16	.029 819	7.16	5
	1.060 732	6.150 090	.162 599 2514	.942 745	5.797 967	.172 474 2514	206.97	.034 846	6.97	6
	1.071 207	7.210 822	.138 680 4454	.933 527	6.731 493	.148 555 4454	178.27	.039 888	6.84	7
	1.081 785	8.282 029	.120 743 3616	.924 398	7.655 891	.130 618 3616	156.75	.044 947	6.74	8
	1.092 468	9.363 814	.106 794 0922	.915 359	8.571 250	.116 669 0922	140.01	.050 022	6.67	9
	1.103 256	10.456 282	.095 636 2928	.906 408	9.477 658	.105 511 2928	126.62	.055 113	6.61	10
	1.114 150	11.559 537	.086 508 6529	.897 545	10.375 203	.096 383 6529	115.67	.060 220	6.57	11
	1.125 153	12.673 688	.078 903 6326	.888 768	11.263 972	.088 778 6326	106.54	.065 344	6.53	12
1	1.125 153	12.673 688	.078 903 6326	.888 768	11.263 972	.088 778 6326	106.54	.065 344	6.53	12
2	1.265 969	26.933 521	.037 128 4538	.789 909	21.275 032	.047 003 4538	56.41	.128 083	6.40	24
3	1.424 408	42.978 011	.023 267 7124	.702 046	30.172 546	.033 142 7124	39.78	.193 138	6.44	36
4	1.602 676	61.030 511	.016 385 2469	.623 956	38.080 373	.026 260 2469	31.52	.260 492	6.51	48
5	1.803 256	81.342 330	.012 293 7221	.554 553	45.108 599	.022 168 7221	26.61	.330 123	6.60	60
6	2.028 938	104.196 228	.009 597 2764	.492 869	51.355 064	.019 472 2764	23.37	.402 004	6.70	72
7	2.282 865	129.910 351	.007 697 6160	.438 046	56.906 723	.017 572 6160	21.09	.476 100	6.80	84
8	2.568 571	158.842 666	.006 295 5378	.389 321	61.840 862	.016 170 5378	19.41	.552 372	6.90	96
9	2.890 035	191.395 936	.005 224 7713	.346 017	66.226 168	.015 099 7713	18.12	.630 775	7.01	108
10	3.251 730	228.023 336	.004 385 5161	.307 529	70.123 690	.014 260 5161	17.12	.711 262	7.11	120
11	3.658 693	269.234 752	.003 714 2308	.273 322	73.587 683	.013 589 2308	16.31	.793 778	7.22	132
12	4.116 588	315.603 887	.003 168 5288	.242 920	76.666 370	.013 043 5288	15.66	.878 268	7.32	144
13	4.631 790	367.776 242	.002 719 0446	.215 899	79.402 609	.012 594 0446	15.12	.964 671	7.42	156
14	5.211 471	426.478 108	.002 344 7862	.191 884	81.834 492	.012 219 7862	14.67	1.052 924	7.52	168
15	5.863 701	492.526 668	.002 030 3469	.170 541	83.995 872	.011 905 3469	14.29	1.142 962	7.62	180
16	6.597 559	566.841 381	.001 764 1620	.151 571	85.916 839	.011 639 1620	13.97	1.234 719	7.72	192
17	7.423 261	650.456 779	.001 537 3812	.134 712	87.624 133	.011 412 3812	13.70	1.328 126	7.81	204
18	8.352 302	744.536 867	.001 343 1168	.119 727	89.141 521	.011 218 1168	13.47	1.423 113	7.91	216
19	9.397 614	850.391 328	.001 175 9292	.106 410	90.490 128	.011 050 9292	13.27	1.519 612	8.00	228
20	10.573 751	969.493 758	.001 031 4662	.094 574	91.688 727	.010 906 4662	13.09	1.617 552	8.09	240
21	11.897 084	1103.502 175	.000 906 2057	.084 054	92.754 004	.010 781 2057	12.94	1.716 864	8.18	252
22	13.386 036	1254.282 102	.000 797 2688	.074 705	93.700 788	.010 672 2688	12.81	1.817 479	8.26	264
23	15.061 334	1423.932 539	.000 702 2805	.066 395	94.542 260	.010 577 2805	12.70	1.919 329	8.34	276
24	16.946 300	1614.815 181	.000 619 2659	.059 010	95.290 133	.010 494 2659	12.60	2.022 349	8.43	288
25	19.067 175	1829.587 294	.000 546 5714	.052 446	95.954 820	.010 421 5714	12.51	2.126 471	8.51	300
26	21.453 482	2071.238 709	.000 482 8029	.046 612	96.545 572	.010 357 8029	12.43	2.231 634	8.58	312
27	24.138 443	2343.133 444	.000 426 7789	.041 428	97.070 613	.010 301 7789	12.37	2.337 776	8.66	324
28	27.159 433	2649.056 530	.000 377 4929	.036 820	97.537 254	.010 252 4929	12.31	2.444 838	8.73	336
29	30.558 509	2993.266 705	.000 334 0832	.032 724	97.951 989	.010 209 0832	12.26	2.552 761	8.80	348
30	34.382 988	3380.555 702	.000 295 8094	.029 084	98.320 592	.010 170 8094	12.21	2.661 491	8.87	360
31	38.686 110	3816.314 950	.000 262 0329	.025 849	98.648 195	.010 137 0329	12.17	2.770 976	8.94	372
32	43.527 780	4306.610 629	.000 232 2012	.022 974	98.939 359	.010 107 2012	12.13	2.881 165	9.00	384
33	48.975 398	4858.268 119	.000 205 8347	.020 418	99.198 135	.010 080 8347	12.10	2.992 011	9.07	396
34	55.104 799	5478.967 016	.000 182 5162	.018 147	99.428 128	.010 057 5162	12.07	3.103 467	9.13	408
35	62.001 312	6177.348 034	.000 161 8818	.016 129	99.632 538	.010 036 8818	12.05	3.215 490	9.19	420
36	69.760 941	6963.133 299	.000 143 6135	.014 335	99.814 211	.010 018 6135	12.03	3.328 041	9.24	432
37	78.491 709	7847.261 684	.000 127 4330	.012 740	99.975 676	.010 002 4330	12.01	3.441 080	9.30	444
38	88.315 156	8842.041 095	.000 113 0961	.011 323	100.119 181	.009 988 0961	11.99	3.554 572	9.35	456
39	99.368 033	9961.319 801	.000 100 3883	.010 064	100.246 724	.009 975 3883	11.98	3.668 482	9.41	468
40	111.804 207	11220.679 222	.000 089 1212	.008 944	100.360 080	.009 964 1212	11.96	3.782 778	9.46	480
41	125.796 802	12637.650 831	.000 079 1286	.007 949	100.460 828	.009 954 1286	11.95	3.897 431	9.51	492
42	141.540 607	14231.960 216	.000 070 2644	.007 065	100.550 369	.009 945 2644	11.94	4.012 413	9.55	504
43	159.254 792	16025.801 672	.000 062 3994	.006 279	100.629 950	.009 937 3994	11.93	4.127 698	9.60	516
44	179.185 953	18044.147 168	.000 055 4196	.005 581	100.700 679	.009 930 4196	11.92	4.243 262	9.64	528
45	201.611 553	20315.093 984	.000 049 2245	.004 960	100.763 541	.009 924 2245	11.91	4.359 081	9.69	540
46	226.843 777	22870.255 850	.000 043 7249	.004 408	100.819 411	.009 918 7249	11.91	4.475 136	9.73	552
47	255.233 880	25745.203 036	.000 038 8422	.003 918	100.869 066	.009 913 8422	11.90	4.591 407	9.77	564
48	287.177 081	28979.957 528	.000 034 5066	.003 482	100.913 198	.009 909 5066	11.90	4.707 876	9.81	576
49	323.118 058	32619.550 169	.000 030 6565	.003 095	100.952 421	.009 905 6565	11.89	4.824 526	9.85	588
50	363.557 144	36714.647 533	.000 027 2371	.002 751	100.987 281	.009 902 2371	11.89	4.941 342	9.88	600

Effective Rate is 12.52 %

Annual Percentage Rate is 11.85 %

MONTHLY COMPOUND INTEREST AND ANNUITY

Amount Of 1	Amount Of 1 Per Period	Sinking Fund Payment	Present Worth Of 1	Present Worth of 1 Per Period	Periodic Payment To Amortize 1	Constant Annual Percent	Total Interest	Annual Add On Rate
What a single $ 1 deposit grows to in the future. The deposit is made at the beginning of the first period.	What a series of $ 1 deposits grow to in the future. A deposit is made at the end of each period.	The amount to be deposited at the end of each period that grows to $ 1 in the future.	What $ 1 to be paid in the future is worth today. Value today of a single $ 1 payment tomorrow.	What $ 1 to be paid at the end of each period is worth today. Value today of a series of $ 1 payments tomorrow.	The mortgage payment to amortize a loan of $ 1. An annuity certain, payable at the end of each period, worth $ 1 today.	The annual payment, including interest and principal, to amortize completely a loan of $ 100.	The total interest paid over the term on a loan of $ 1. The loan is amortized by regular periodic payments.	The average annual interest rate on a loan that is completely amortized by regular periodic payments.

$$S = (1+i)^n \qquad S\overline{n}| = \frac{(1+i)^n - 1}{i} \qquad \frac{1}{S\overline{n}|} = \frac{i}{(1+i)^n - 1} \qquad V^n = \frac{1}{(1+i)^n} \qquad A\overline{n}| = \frac{1-V^n}{i} \qquad \frac{1}{A\overline{n}|} = \frac{i}{1-V^n}$$

PERIODS

YEAR

	Amount Of 1	Amount Of 1 Per Period	Sinking Fund Payment	Present Worth Of 1	Present Worth of 1 Per Period	Periodic Payment To Amortize 1	Constant Annual Percent	Total Interest	Annual Add On Rate	
	1.009 896	1.000 000	1.000 000 0000	.990 201	.990 201	1.009 895 8333	1211.88	.009 896	11.87	1
	1.019 890	2.009 896	.497 538 2223	.980 498	1.970 699	.507 434 0557	608.93	.014 868	8.92	2
	1.029 982	3.029 785	.330 056 3766	.970 891	2.941 590	.339 952 2099	407.95	.019 857	7.94	3
	1.040 175	4.059 768	.246 319 5136	.961 377	3.902 967	.256 215 3469	307.46	.024 861	7.46	4
	1.050 468	5.099 942	.196 080 6435	.951 956	4.854 923	.205 976 4768	247.18	.029 882	7.17	5
	1.060 863	6.150 411	.162 590 7696	.942 628	5.797 552	.172 486 6029	206.99	.034 920	6.98	6
	1.071 362	7.211 274	.138 671 7504	.933 392	6.730 943	.148 567 5838	178.29	.039 973	6.85	7
	1.081 964	8.282 636	.120 734 5152	.924 246	7.655 189	.130 630 3486	156.76	.045 043	6.76	8
	1.092 671	9.364 599	.106 785 1357	.915 189	8.570 378	.116 680 9691	140.02	.050 129	6.68	9
	1.103 483	10.457 270	.095 627 2550	.906 221	9.476 599	.105 523 0883	126.63	.055 231	6.63	10
	1.114 403	11.560 753	.086 499 5548	.897 341	10.373 940	.096 395 3881	115.68	.060 349	6.58	11
	1.125 431	12.675 156	.078 894 4898	.888 548	11.262 489	.088 790 3232	106.55	.065 484	6.55	12
1	1.125 431	12.675 156	.078 894 4898	.888 548	11.262 489	.088 790 3232	106.55	.065 484	6.55	12
2	1.266 595	26.940 173	.037 119 2860	.789 518	21.269 754	.047 015 1193	56.42	.128 363	6.42	24
3	1.425 466	42.994 469	.023 258 8057	.701 525	30.161 692	.033 154 6390	39.79	.193 567	6.45	36
4	1.604 264	61.062 475	.016 376 6700	.623 339	38.062 608	.026 272 5033	31.53	.261 080	6.53	48
5	1.805 489	81.396 773	.012 285 4993	.553 867	45.082 954	.022 181 3327	26.62	.330 880	6.62	60
6	2.031 954	104.281 627	.009 589 4169	.492 137	51.320 870	.019 485 2503	23.39	.402 938	6.72	72
7	2.286 824	130.036 957	.007 690 1215	.437 288	56.863 560	.017 585 9548	21.11	.477 220	6.82	84
8	2.573 663	159.022 810	.006 288 4061	.388 551	61.788 508	.016 184 2394	19.43	.553 687	6.92	96
9	2.896 481	191.644 393	.005 217 9977	.345 247	66.164 561	.015 113 8310	18.14	.632 294	7.03	108
10	3.259 790	228.357 743	.004 379 0939	.306 768	70.052 896	.014 274 9272	17.13	.712 991	7.13	120
11	3.668 670	269.676 093	.003 708 1522	.272 578	73.507 870	.013 603 9855	16.33	.795 726	7.23	132
12	4.128 835	316.177 055	.003 162 7849	.242 199	76.577 781	.013 058 6182	15.68	.880 441	7.34	144
13	4.646 720	368.510 690	.002 713 6255	.215 206	79.305 545	.012 609 4588	15.14	.967 076	7.44	156
14	5.229 564	427.408 598	.002 339 6815	.191 221	81.729 295	.012 235 5149	14.69	1.055 566	7.54	168
15	5.885 515	493.694 143	.002 025 5456	.169 909	83.882 914	.011 921 3789	14.31	1.145 848	7.64	180
16	6.623 742	568.293 965	.001 759 6527	.150 972	85.796 508	.011 655 4860	13.99	1.237 853	7.74	192
17	7.454 567	652.250 936	.001 533 1523	.134 146	87.496 829	.011 428 9856	13.72	1.331 513	7.83	204
18	8.389 602	746.738 733	.001 339 1565	.119 195	89.007 646	.011 234 9898	13.49	1.426 758	7.93	216
19	9.441 920	853.078 252	.001 172 2254	.105 911	90.350 081	.011 068 0587	13.29	1.523 517	8.02	228
20	10.626 232	972.756 067	.001 028 0070	.094 107	91.542 898	.010 923 8403	13.11	1.621 722	8.11	240
21	11.959 093	1107.445 219	.000 902 9792	.083 618	92.602 774	.010 798 8125	12.96	1.721 301	8.20	252
22	13.459 137	1259.028 597	.000 794 2631	.074 299	93.544 525	.010 690 0965	12.83	1.822 185	8.28	264
23	15.147 333	1429.625 266	.000 699 4840	.066 018	94.381 317	.010 595 3173	12.72	1.924 308	8.37	276
24	17.047 282	1621.620 086	.000 616 6673	.058 660	95.124 846	.010 512 5006	12.62	2.027 600	8.45	288
25	19.185 544	1837.697 054	.000 544 1593	.052 123	95.785 508	.010 439 9927	12.53	2.131 998	8.53	300
26	21.592 010	2080.876 822	.000 480 5666	.046 313	96.372 538	.010 376 4000	12.46	2.237 437	8.61	312
27	24.300 323	2354.558 929	.000 424 7080	.041 152	96.894 142	.010 320 5413	12.39	2.343 855	8.68	324
28	27.348 342	2662.569 321	.000 375 5771	.036 565	97.357 613	.010 271 4104	12.33	2.451 194	8.75	336
29	30.778 679	3009.213 837	.000 332 3127	.032 490	97.769 429	.010 228 1460	12.28	2.559 395	8.83	348
30	34.639 286	3399.338 403	.000 294 1749	.028 869	98.135 348	.010 190 0082	12.23	2.668 403	8.89	360
31	38.984 135	3838.396 775	.000 260 5254	.025 651	98.460 484	.010 156 3588	12.19	2.778 165	8.96	372
32	43.873 963	4332.526 781	.000 230 8122	.022 793	98.749 383	.010 126 6455	12.16	2.888 632	9.03	384
33	49.377 128	4888.636 125	.000 204 5560	.020 252	99.006 084	.010 100 3894	12.13	2.999 754	9.09	396
34	55.570 563	5514.498 950	.000 181 3401	.017 995	99.234 175	.010 077 1735	12.10	3.111 487	9.15	408
35	62.540 847	6218.864 523	.000 160 8011	.015 990	99.436 845	.010 056 6344	12.07	3.223 786	9.21	420
36	70.385 423	7011.579 540	.000 142 6212	.014 207	99.616 928	.010 038 4545	12.05	3.336 612	9.27	432
37	79.213 953	7903.725 781	.000 126 5226	.012 624	99.776 939	.010 022 3559	12.03	3.449 926	9.32	444
38	89.149 857	8907.775 027	.000 112 2615	.011 217	99.919 117	.010 008 0948	12.01	3.563 691	9.38	456
39	100.332 034	10037.763 411	.000 099 6238	.009 967	100.045 449	.009 995 4571	12.00	3.677 874	9.43	468
40	112.916 805	11309.487 633	.000 088 4213	.008 856	100.157 702	.009 984 2547	11.99	3.792 442	9.48	480
41	127.080 099	12740.725 796	.000 078 4885	.007 869	100.257 443	.009 974 3218	11.97	3.907 366	9.53	492
42	143.019 913	14351.485 931	.000 069 6792	.006 992	100.346 068	.009 965 5125	11.96	4.022 618	9.58	504
43	160.959 077	16164.285 698	.000 061 8648	.006 213	100.424 816	.009 957 6981	11.95	4.138 172	9.62	516
44	181.148 373	18204.467 181	.000 054 9316	.005 520	100.494 787	.009 950 7649	11.95	4.254 004	9.67	528
45	203.870 037	20500.551 148	.000 048 7792	.004 905	100.556 960	.009 944 6125	11.94	4.370 091	9.71	540
46	229.441 708	23084.635 763	.000 043 3189	.004 358	100.612 203	.009 939 1522	11.93	4.486 412	9.75	552
47	258.220 865	25992.845 304	.000 038 4721	.003 873	100.661 290	.009 934 3055	11.93	4.602 948	9.79	564
48	290.609 827	29265.835 161	.000 034 1695	.003 441	100.704 905	.009 930 0029	11.92	4.719 682	9.83	576
49	327.061 377	32949.360 179	.000 030 3496	.003 058	100.743 660	.009 926 1829	11.92	4.836 596	9.87	588
50	368.085 089	37094.914 292	.000 026 9579	.002 717	100.778 096	.009 922 7912	11.91	4.953 675	9.91	600

Effective Rate is 12.54 %

Annual Percentage Rate is 11.875%

	Amount Of 1	Amount Of 1 Per Period	Sinking Fund Payment	Present Worth Of 1	Present Worth of 1 Per Period	Periodic Payment To Amortize 1	Constant Annual Percent	Total Interest	Annual Add On Rate	
	What a single $ 1 deposit grows to in the future. The deposit is made at the beginning of the first period.	What a series of $ 1 deposits grow to in the future. A deposit is made at the end of each period.	The amount to be deposited at the end of each period that grows to $ 1 in the future.	What $ 1 to be paid in the future is worth today. Value today of a single $ 1 payment tomorrow.	What $ 1 to be paid at the end of each period is worth today. Value today of a series of $ 1 payments tomorrow.	The mortgage payment to amortize a loan of $ 1. An annuity certain, payable at the end of each period, worth $ 1 today.	The annual payment, including interest and principal, to amortize completely a loan of $ 100.	The total interest paid over the term on a loan of $1. The loan is amortized by regular periodic payments.	The average annual interest rate on a loan that is completely amortized by regular periodic payments.	
	$S = (1+i)^n$	$S\overline{n} = \dfrac{(1+i)^n - 1}{i}$	$\dfrac{1}{S\overline{n}} = \dfrac{i}{(1+i)^n - 1}$	$V^n = \dfrac{1}{(1+i)^n}$	$A\overline{n} = \dfrac{1-V^n}{i}$	$\dfrac{1}{A\overline{n}} = \dfrac{i}{1-V^n}$				

YEAR										PERIODS
	1.009 917	1.000 000	1.000 000 0000	.990 181	.990 181	1.009 916 6667	1211.90	.009 917	11.90	1
	1.019 932	2.009 917	.497 533 0652	.980 458	1.970 639	.507 449 7319	608.94	.014 899	8.94	2
	1.030 046	3.029 848	.330 049 5232	.970 830	2.941 469	.339 966 1898	407.96	.019 899	7.96	3
	1.040 261	4.059 894	.246 311 8291	.961 298	3.902 767	.256 228 4958	307.48	.024 914	7.47	4
	1.050 577	5.100 155	.196 072 4740	.951 858	4.854 625	.205 989 1407	247.19	.029 946	7.19	5
	1.060 995	6.150 731	.162 582 2882	.942 512	5.797 137	.172 498 9549	207.00	.034 994	7.00	6
	1.071 516	7.211 726	.138 663 0560	.933 257	6.730 394	.148 579 7226	178.30	.040 058	6.87	7
	1.082 142	8.283 243	.120 725 6695	.924 093	7.654 487	.130 642 3361	156.78	.045 139	6.77	8
	1.092 873	9.365 385	.106 776 1799	.915 019	8.569 506	.116 692 8466	140.04	.050 236	6.70	9
	1.103 711	10.458 258	.095 618 2179	.906 034	9.475 540	.105 534 8845	126.65	.055 349	6.64	10
	1.114 656	11.561 969	.086 490 4574	.897 138	10.372 677	.096 407 1241	115.69	.060 478	6.60	11
	1.125 710	12.676 625	.078 885 3479	.888 328	11.261 006	.088 802 0146	106.57	.065 624	6.56	12
1	1.125 710	12.676 625	.078 885 3479	.888 328	11.261 006	.088 802 0146	106.57	.065 624	6.56	12
2	1.267 223	26.946 828	.037 110 1198	.789 127	21.264 477	.047 026 7865	56.44	.128 643	6.43	24
3	1.426 525	43.010 935	.023 249 9014	.701 004	30.150 843	.033 166 5681	39.80	.193 996	6.47	36
4	1.605 853	61.094 459	.016 368 0964	.622 722	38.044 855	.026 284 7631	31.55	.261 669	6.54	48
5	1.807 725	81.451 261	.012 277 2808	.553 181	45.057 329	.022 193 9474	26.64	.331 637	6.63	60
6	2.034 974	104.367 114	.009 581 5623	.491 407	51.286 709	.019 498 2289	23.40	.403 872	6.73	72
7	2.290 790	130.163 715	.007 682 6326	.436 531	56.820 444	.017 599 2993	21.12	.478 341	6.83	84
8	2.578 765	159.203 204	.006 281 2806	.387 783	61.736 218	.016 197 9473	19.44	.555 003	6.94	96
9	2.902 941	191.893 243	.005 211 2309	.344 478	66.103 039	.015 127 8976	18.16	.633 813	7.04	108
10	3.267 870	228.692 743	.004 372 6792	.306 010	69.982 210	.014 289 3459	17.15	.714 722	7.15	120
11	3.678 673	270.118 302	.003 702 0816	.271 837	73.428 187	.013 618 7483	16.35	.797 675	7.25	132
12	4.141 119	316.751 464	.003 157 0493	.241 481	76.489 347	.013 073 7160	15.69	.882 615	7.36	144
13	4.661 698	369.246 874	.002 708 2152	.214 514	79.208 662	.012 624 8819	15.15	.969 482	7.46	156
14	5.247 720	428.341 475	.002 334 5860	.190 559	81.624 306	.012 251 2526	14.71	1.058 210	7.56	168
15	5.907 410	494.864 850	.002 020 7537	.169 279	83.770 192	.011 937 4204	14.33	1.148 736	7.66	180
16	6.650 029	569.750 871	.001 755 1531	.150 375	85.676 443	.011 671 8198	14.01	1.240 989	7.76	192
17	7.486 004	654.050 803	.001 528 9332	.133 583	87.369 820	.011 445 5999	13.74	1.334 902	7.85	204
18	8.427 068	748.948 068	.001 335 2061	.118 665	88.874 094	.011 251 8727	13.51	1.430 405	7.95	216
19	9.486 434	855.774 856	.001 168 5316	.105 414	90.210 384	.011 085 1983	13.31	1.527 425	8.04	228
20	10.678 972	976.030 826	.001 024 5578	.093 642	91.397 448	.010 941 2245	13.13	1.625 894	8.13	240
21	12.021 425	1111.404 157	.000 899 7627	.083 185	92.451 951	.010 816 4294	12.98	1.725 740	8.22	252
22	13.532 636	1263.795 253	.000 791 2674	.073 895	93.388 696	.010 707 9341	12.85	1.826 895	8.30	264
23	15.233 822	1435.343 412	.000 696 6974	.065 643	94.220 833	.010 613 3641	12.74	1.929 288	8.39	276
24	17.148 864	1628.456 868	.000 614 0783	.058 313	94.960 044	.010 530 7450	12.64	2.032 855	8.47	288
25	19.304 645	1845.846 592	.000 541 7568	.051 801	95.616 706	.010 458 4235	12.56	2.137 527	8.55	300
26	21.731 430	2090.564 348	.000 478 3397	.046 016	96.200 037	.010 395 0064	12.48	2.243 242	8.63	312
27	24.463 285	2366.045 542	.000 422 6461	.040 878	96.718 227	.010 339 3128	12.41	2.349 937	8.70	324
28	27.538 561	2676.157 439	.000 373 6701	.036 313	97.178 549	.010 290 3368	12.35	2.457 553	8.78	336
29	31.000 430	3025.253 463	.000 330 5508	.032 258	97.587 467	.010 247 2175	12.30	2.566 032	8.85	348
30	34.897 490	3418.234 302	.000 292 5487	.028 655	97.950 720	.010 209 2154	12.26	2.675 318	8.92	360
31	39.284 449	3860.616 710	.000 259 0260	.025 455	98.273 409	.010 175 6926	12.22	2.785 358	8.99	372
32	44.222 892	4358.610 952	.000 229 4309	.022 613	98.560 062	.010 146 0976	12.18	2.896 101	9.05	384
33	49.782 146	4919.207 984	.000 203 2848	.020 088	98.814 704	.010 119 9514	12.15	3.007 501	9.11	396
34	56.040 253	5550.277 596	.000 180 1712	.017 844	99.040 909	.010 096 8378	12.12	3.119 510	9.18	408
35	63.085 066	6260.678 884	.000 159 7271	.015 852	99.241 854	.010 076 3938	12.10	3.232 085	9.23	420
36	71.015 481	7060.384 625	.000 141 6353	.014 081	99.420 359	.010 058 3020	12.07	3.345 186	9.29	432
37	79.942 828	7960.621 270	.000 125 6183	.012 509	99.578 930	.010 042 2850	12.06	3.458 775	9.35	444
38	89.992 430	8974.026 543	.000 111 4327	.011 112	99.719 794	.010 028 0994	12.04	3.572 813	9.40	456
39	101.305 366	10114.826 860	.000 098 8648	.009 871	99.844 927	.010 015 5314	12.02	3.687 269	9.45	468
40	114.040 451	11399.037 034	.000 087 7267	.008 769	99.956 086	.010 004 3934	12.01	3.802 109	9.51	480
41	128.376 461	12844.685 100	.000 077 8532	.007 790	100.054 831	.009 994 5199	12.00	3.917 304	9.55	492
42	144.514 648	14472.065 393	.000 069 0986	.006 920	100.142 550	.009 985 7653	11.99	4.032 826	9.60	504
43	162.681 566	16304.023 447	.000 061 3346	.006 147	100.220 473	.009 978 0012	11.98	4.148 649	9.65	516
44	183.132 244	18366.276 707	.000 054 4476	.005 461	100.289 694	.009 971 1143	11.97	4.264 748	9.69	528
45	206.153 774	20687.775 552	.000 048 3377	.004 851	100.351 185	.009 965 0044	11.96	4.381 102	9.74	540
46	232.069 338	23301.109 709	.000 042 9164	.004 309	100.405 809	.009 959 5831	11.96	4.497 690	9.78	552
47	261.242 744	26242.965 759	.000 038 1054	.003 828	100.454 334	.009 954 7721	11.95	4.614 491	9.82	564
48	294.083 535	29554.642 144	.000 033 8356	.003 400	100.497 439	.009 950 5023	11.95	4.731 489	9.86	576
49	331.052 737	33282.628 930	.000 030 0457	.003 021	100.535 731	.009 946 7124	11.94	4.848 667	9.90	588
50	372.669 333	37479.260 442	.000 026 6814	.002 683	100.569 747	.009 943 3481	11.94	4.966 009	9.93	600

	Amount Of 1	Amount Of 1 Per Period	Sinking Fund Payment	Present Worth Of 1	Present Worth of 1 Per Period	Periodic Payment To Amortize 1	Constant Annual Percent	Total Interest	Annual Add On Rate	
	What a single $ 1 deposit grows to in the future. The deposit is made at the beginning of the first period.	What a series of $ 1 deposits grow to in the future. A deposit is made at the end of each period.	The amount to be deposited at the end of each period that grows to $ 1 in the future.	What $ 1 to be paid in the future is worth today. Value today of a single $ 1 payment tomorrow.	What $ 1 to be paid at the end of each period is worth today. Value today of a series of $ 1 payments tomorrow.	The mortgage payment to amortize a loan of $ 1. An annuity certain, payable at the end of each period, worth $ 1 today.	The annual payment, including interest and principal, to amortize completely a loan of $ 100.	The total interest paid over the term on a loan of $1. The loan is amortized by regular periodic payments.	The average annual interest rate on a loan that is completely amortized by regular periodic payments.	
	$S = (1+i)^n$	$S\overline{n} = \dfrac{(1+i)^n - 1}{i}$	$\dfrac{1}{S\overline{n}} = \dfrac{i}{(1+i)^n - 1}$	$V^n = \dfrac{1}{(1+i)^n}$	$A\overline{n} = \dfrac{1 - V^n}{i}$	$\dfrac{1}{A\overline{n}} = \dfrac{i}{1 - V^n}$				

YEAR										PERIODS
	1.009 958	1.000 000	1.000 000 0000	.990 140	.990 140	1.009 958 3333	1211.95	.009 958	11.95	1
	1.020 016	2.009 958	.497 522 7513	.980 377	1.970 517	.507 481 0846	608.98	.014 962	8.98	2
	1.030 173	3.029 974	.330 035 8169	.970 710	2.941 227	.339 994 1503	408.00	.019 982	7.99	3
	1.040 432	4.060 148	.246 296 4610	.961 139	3.902 366	.256 254 7943	307.51	.025 019	7.51	4
	1.050 793	5.100 580	.196 056 1361	.951 662	4.854 028	.206 014 4695	247.22	.030 072	7.22	5
	1.061 257	6.151 373	.162 565 3266	.942 278	5.796 306	.172 523 6600	207.03	.035 142	7.03	6
	1.071 826	7.212 631	.138 645 6685	.932 987	6.729 294	.148 604 0018	178.33	.040 228	6.90	7
	1.082 499	8.284 456	.120 707 9796	.923 788	7.653 082	.130 666 3130	156.80	.045 331	6.80	8
	1.093 279	9.366 956	.106 758 2701	.914 679	8.567 761	.116 716 6034	140.06	.050 449	6.73	9
	1.104 167	10.460 235	.095 600 1458	.905 661	9.473 422	.105 558 4791	126.68	.055 585	6.67	10
	1.115 162	11.564 402	.086 472 2650	.896 731	10.370 152	.096 430 5983	115.72	.060 737	6.63	11
	1.126 267	12.679 564	.078 867 0666	.887 889	11.258 041	.088 825 3999	106.60	.065 905	6.59	12
1	1.126 267	12.679 564	.078 867 0666	.887 889	11.258 041	.088 825 3999	106.60	.065 905	6.59	12
2	1.268 478	26.960 142	.037 091 7926	.788 346	21.253 928	.047 050 1260	56.47	.129 203	6.46	24
3	1.428 645	43.043 891	.023 232 1006	.699 964	30.129 163	.033 190 4339	39.83	.194 856	6.50	36
4	1.609 037	61.158 491	.016 350 9592	.621 490	38.009 384	.026 309 2926	31.58	.262 846	6.57	48
5	1.812 205	81.560 374	.012 260 8560	.551 814	45.006 143	.022 219 1893	26.67	.333 151	6.66	60
6	2.041 028	104.538 348	.009 565 8676	.489 949	51.218 485	.019 524 2010	23.43	.405 742	6.76	72
7	2.298 743	130.417 689	.007 667 6715	.435 020	56.734 354	.017 626 0049	21.16	.480 584	6.87	84
8	2.588 990	159.564 745	.006 267 0485	.386 250	61.631 831	.016 225 3818	19.48	.557 637	6.97	96
9	2.915 905	192.392 122	.005 197 7180	.342 947	65.980 246	.015 156 0514	18.19	.636 854	7.08	108
10	3.284 088	229.364 524	.004 359 8721	.304 499	69.841 154	.014 318 2055	17.19	.718 185	7.18	120
11	3.698 761	271.005 332	.003 689 9643	.270 361	73.269 211	.013 648 2976	16.38	.801 575	7.29	132
12	4.165 794	317.904 014	.003 145 6036	.240 050	76.312 944	.013 103 9369	15.73	.886 967	7.39	144
13	4.691 798	370.724 466	.002 697 4211	.213 138	79.015 440	.012 655 7544	15.19	.974 298	7.49	156
14	5.284 219	430.214 415	.002 324 4223	.189 243	81.414 955	.012 282 7557	14.74	1.063 503	7.60	168
15	5.951 443	497.216 002	.002 011 1983	.168 026	83.545 457	.011 969 5317	14.37	1.154 516	7.70	180
16	6.702 915	572.677 699	.001 746 1829	.149 189	85.437 107	.011 704 5162	14.05	1.247 267	7.80	192
17	7.549 275	657.667 742	.001 520 5246	.132 463	87.116 360	.011 478 8580	13.78	1.341 687	7.89	204
18	8.502 501	753.389 251	.001 327 3351	.117 612	88.607 955	.011 285 6684	13.55	1.437 704	7.99	216
19	9.576 089	861.197 258	.001 161 1742	.104 427	89.932 041	.011 119 5075	13.35	1.535 248	8.08	228
20	10.785 237	982.617 894	.001 017 6896	.092 719	91.107 681	.010 976 0229	13.18	1.634 246	8.17	240
21	12.147 059	1119.369 988	.000 893 3597	.082 324	92.151 520	.010 851 6930	13.03	1.734 627	8.26	252
22	13.680 836	1273.389 403	.000 785 3057	.073 095	93.078 332	.010 743 6391	12.90	1.836 321	8.35	264
23	15.408 279	1446.856 437	.000 691 1536	.064 900	93.901 238	.010 649 4869	12.78	1.939 258	8.43	276
24	17.353 841	1642.226 689	.000 608 9293	.057 624	94.631 886	.010 567 2627	12.69	2.043 372	8.51	288
25	19.545 064	1862.265 820	.000 536 9803	.051 164	95.280 621	.010 495 3136	12.60	2.148 594	8.59	300
26	22.012 967	2110.088 703	.000 473 9137	.045 428	95.856 626	.010 432 2471	12.52	2.254 861	8.67	312
27	24.792 485	2389.203 517	.000 418 5495	.040 335	96.368 053	.010 376 8829	12.46	2.362 110	8.75	324
28	27.922 966	2703.561 412	.000 369 8825	.035 813	96.822 144	.010 328 2158	12.40	2.470 281	8.82	336
29	31.448 724	3057.612 437	.000 327 0526	.031 798	97.225 326	.010 285 3859	12.35	2.579 314	8.89	348
30	35.419 670	3456.368 536	.000 289 3210	.028 233	97.583 307	.010 247 6543	12.30	2.689 156	8.96	360
31	39.892 017	3905.474 500	.000 256 0508	.025 068	97.901 154	.010 214 3842	12.26	2.799 751	9.03	372
32	44.929 075	4411.287 872	.000 226 6912	.022 257	98.183 367	.010 185 0245	12.23	2.911 049	9.10	384
33	50.602 149	4980.968 945	.000 200 7642	.019 762	98.433 941	.010 159 0975	12.20	3.023 003	9.16	396
34	56.991 547	5622.582 121	.000 177 8542	.017 546	98.656 422	.010 136 1876	12.17	3.135 565	9.22	408
35	64.187 717	6345.210 074	.000 157 5992	.015 579	98.853 961	.010 115 9325	12.14	3.248 692	9.28	420
36	72.292 528	7159.082 325	.000 139 6827	.013 833	99.029 353	.010 098 0160	12.12	3.362 343	9.34	432
37	81.420 712	8075.720 046	.000 123 8280	.012 282	99.185 082	.010 082 1613	12.10	3.476 480	9.40	444
38	91.701 487	9108.099 157	.000 109 7924	.010 905	99.323 352	.010 068 1257	12.09	3.591 065	9.45	456
39	103.280 389	10270.834 014	.000 097 3631	.009 682	99.446 121	.010 055 6964	12.07	3.706 066	9.50	468
40	116.321 327	11580.384 289	.000 086 3529	.008 597	99.555 125	.010 044 6863	12.06	3.821 449	9.55	480
41	131.008 909	13055.287 971	.000 076 5973	.007 633	99.651 909	.010 034 9306	12.05	3.937 186	9.60	492
42	147.551 054	14716.423 791	.000 067 9513	.006 777	99.737 843	.010 026 2846	12.04	4.053 247	9.65	504
43	166.181 930	16587.306 784	.000 060 2871	.006 018	99.814 142	.010 018 6204	12.03	4.169 608	9.70	516
44	187.165 277	18694.421 163	.000 053 4919	.005 343	99.881 887	.010 011 8252	12.02	4.286 244	9.74	528
45	210.798 136	21067.595 233	.000 047 4663	.004 744	99.942 038	.010 005 7996	12.01	4.403 132	9.78	540
46	237.415 052	23740.423 638	.000 042 1222	.004 212	99.995 444	.010 000 4556	12.01	4.520 251	9.83	552
47	267.392 815	26750.742 930	.000 037 3821	.003 740	100.042 864	.009 995 7155	12.00	4.637 584	9.87	564
48	301.155 790	30141.167 179	.000 033 1772	.003 321	100.084 967	.009 991 5105	11.99	4.755 110	9.91	576
49	339.181 925	33959.691 220	.000 029 4467	.002 948	100.122 349	.009 987 7800	11.99	4.872 815	9.94	588
50	382.009 519	38260.370 068	.000 026 1367	.002 618	100.155 541	.009 984 4700	11.99	4.990 682	9.98	600

MONTHLY COMPOUND INTEREST AND ANNUITY

	Amount Of 1	Amount Of 1 Per Period	Sinking Fund Payment	Present Worth Of 1	Present Worth of 1 Per Period	Periodic Payment To Amortize 1	Constant Annual Percent	Total Interest	Annual Add On Rate	
	What a single $ 1 deposit grows to in the future. The deposit is made at the beginning of the first period.	What a series of $ 1 deposits grow to in the future. A deposit is made at the end of each period.	The amount to be deposited at the end of each period that grows to $ 1 in the future.	What $ 1 to be paid in the future is worth today. Value today of a single $ 1 payment tomorrow.	What $ 1 to be paid at the end of each period is worth today. Value today of a series of $ 1 payments tomorrow.	The mortgage payment to amortize a loan of $ 1. An annuity certain, payable at the end of each period, worth $ 1 today.	The annual payment, including interest and principal, to amortize completely a loan of $ 100.	The total interest paid over the term on a loan of $1. The loan is amortized by regular periodic payments.	The average annual interest rate on a loan that is completely amortized by regular periodic payments.	
	$S = (1+i)^n$	$S\overline{n}| = \dfrac{(1+i)^n - 1}{i}$	$\dfrac{1}{S\overline{n}|} = \dfrac{i}{(1+i)^n - 1}$	$V^n = \dfrac{1}{(1+i)^n}$	$A\overline{n}| = \dfrac{1-V^n}{i}$	$\dfrac{1}{A\overline{n}|} = \dfrac{i}{1-V^n}$				

YEAR										PERIODS
	1.010 000	1.000 000	1.000 000 0000	.990 099	.990 099	1.010 000 0000	1212.00	.010 000	12.00	1
	1.020 100	2.010 000	.497 512 4378	.980 296	1.970 395	.507 512 4378	609.02	.015 025	9.01	2
	1.030 301	3.030 100	.330 022 1115	.970 590	2.940 985	.340 022 1115	408.03	.020 066	8.03	3
	1.040 604	4.060 401	.246 281 0939	.960 980	3.901 966	.256 281 0939	307.54	.025 124	7.54	4
	1.051 010	5.101 005	.196 039 7996	.951 466	4.853 431	.206 039 7996	247.25	.030 199	7.25	5
	1.061 520	6.152 015	.162 548 3667	.942 045	5.795 476	.172 548 3667	207.06	.035 290	7.06	6
	1.072 135	7.213 535	.138 628 2829	.932 718	6.728 195	.148 628 2829	178.36	.040 398	6.93	7
	1.082 857	8.285 671	.120 690 2920	.923 483	7.651 678	.130 690 2920	156.83	.045 522	6.83	8
	1.093 685	9.368 527	.106 740 3628	.914 340	8.566 018	.116 740 3628	140.09	.050 663	6.76	9
	1.104 622	10.462 213	.095 582 0766	.905 287	9.471 305	.105 582 0766	126.70	.055 821	6.70	10
	1.115 668	11.566 835	.086 454 0757	.896 324	10.367 628	.096 454 0757	115.75	.060 995	6.65	11
	1.126 825	12.682 503	.078 848 7887	.887 449	11.255 077	.088 848 7887	106.62	.066 185	6.62	12
1	1.126 825	12.682 503	.078 848 7887	.887 449	11.255 077	.088 848 7887	106.62	.066 185	6.62	12
2	1.269 735	26.973 465	.037 073 4722	.787 566	21.243 387	.047 073 4722	56.49	.129 763	6.49	24
3	1.430 769	43.076 878	.023 214 3098	.698 925	30.107 505	.033 214 3098	39.86	.195 715	6.52	36
4	1.612 226	61.222 608	.016 333 8354	.620 260	37.973 959	.026 333 8354	31.61	.264 024	6.60	48
5	1.816 697	81.669 670	.012 244 4477	.550 450	44.955 038	.022 244 4477	26.70	.334 667	6.69	60
6	2.047 099	104.709 931	.009 550 1925	.488 496	51.150 391	.019 550 1925	23.47	.407 614	6.79	72
7	2.306 723	130.672 274	.007 652 7328	.433 515	56.648 453	.017 652 7328	21.19	.482 830	6.90	84
8	2.599 273	159.927 293	.006 252 8414	.384 723	61.527 703	.016 252 8414	19.51	.560 273	7.00	96
9	2.928 926	192.892 579	.005 184 2326	.341 422	65.857 790	.015 184 2326	18.23	.639 897	7.11	108
10	3.300 387	230.038 689	.004 347 0948	.302 995	69.700 522	.014 347 0948	17.22	.721 651	7.22	120
11	3.718 959	271.895 856	.003 677 8788	.268 892	73.110 752	.013 677 8788	16.42	.805 480	7.32	132
12	4.190 616	319.061 559	.003 134 1914	.238 628	76.137 157	.013 134 1914	15.77	.891 324	7.43	144
13	4.722 091	372.209 054	.002 686 6622	.211 771	78.822 939	.012 686 6622	15.23	.979 119	7.53	156
14	5.320 970	432.096 982	.002 314 2953	.187 936	81.206 434	.012 314 2953	14.78	1.068 802	7.63	168
15	5.995 802	499.580 198	.002 001 6806	.166 783	83.321 664	.012 001 6806	14.41	1.160 303	7.74	180
16	6.756 220	575.621 974	.001 737 2513	.148 012	85.198 824	.011 737 2513	14.09	1.253 552	7.83	192
17	7.613 078	661.307 751	.001 512 1553	.131 353	86.864 707	.011 512 1553	13.82	1.348 480	7.93	204
18	8.578 606	757.860 630	.001 319 5038	.116 569	88.343 095	.011 319 5038	13.59	1.445 013	8.03	216
19	9.666 588	866.658 830	.001 153 8566	.103 449	89.655 089	.011 153 8566	13.39	1.543 079	8.12	228
20	10.892 554	989.255 365	.001 010 8613	.091 806	90.819 416	.011 010 8613	13.22	1.642 607	8.21	240
21	12.274 002	1127.400 210	.000 886 9965	.081 473	91.852 698	.010 886 9965	13.07	1.743 523	8.30	252
22	13.830 653	1283.065 279	.000 779 3836	.072 303	92.769 683	.010 779 3836	12.94	1.845 757	8.39	264
23	15.584 726	1458.472 574	.000 685 6488	.064 165	93.583 461	.010 685 6488	12.83	1.949 239	8.47	276
24	17.561 259	1656.125 905	.000 603 8188	.056 944	94.305 647	.010 603 8188	12.73	2.053 900	8.56	288
25	19.788 466	1878.846 626	.000 532 2414	.050 534	94.946 551	.010 532 2414	12.64	2.159 672	8.64	300
26	22.298 139	2129.813 909	.000 469 5246	.044 847	95.515 321	.010 469 5246	12.57	2.266 492	8.72	312
27	25.126 101	2412.610 125	.000 414 4889	.039 799	96.020 075	.010 414 4889	12.50	2.374 294	8.79	324
28	28.312 720	2731.271 980	.000 366 1298	.035 320	96.468 019	.010 366 1298	12.44	2.483 020	8.87	336
29	31.903 481	3090.348 134	.000 323 5881	.031 345	96.865 546	.010 323 5881	12.39	2.592 609	8.94	348
30	35.949 641	3494.964 133	.000 286 1260	.027 817	97.218 331	.010 286 1260	12.35	2.703 005	9.01	360
31	40.508 956	3950.895 567	.000 253 1072	.024 686	97.531 410	.010 253 1072	12.31	2.814 156	9.08	372
32	45.646 505	4464.650 520	.000 223 9817	.021 907	97.809 252	.010 223 9817	12.27	2.926 009	9.14	384
33	51.435 625	5043.562 459	.000 198 2726	.019 442	98.055 822	.010 198 2726	12.24	3.038 516	9.21	396
34	57.958 949	5695.894 923	.000 175 5650	.017 254	98.274 641	.010 175 5650	12.22	3.151 631	9.27	408
35	65.309 595	6430.959 471	.000 155 4978	.015 312	98.468 831	.010 155 4978	12.19	3.265 309	9.33	420
36	73.592 486	7259.248 603	.000 137 7553	.013 588	98.641 166	.010 137 7553	12.17	3.379 510	9.39	432
37	82.925 855	8192.585 529	.000 122 0616	.012 059	98.794 103	.010 122 0616	12.15	3.494 195	9.44	444
38	93.442 929	9244.292 939	.000 108 1748	.010 702	98.929 828	.010 108 1748	12.13	3.609 328	9.50	456
39	105.293 832	10429.383 172	.000 095 8829	.009 497	99.050 277	.010 095 8829	12.12	3.724 873	9.55	468
40	118.647 725	11764.772 510	.000 084 9995	.008 428	99.157 169	.010 084 9995	12.11	3.840 800	9.60	480
41	133.695 226	13269.522 641	.000 075 3607	.007 480	99.252 030	.010 075 3607	12.10	3.957 077	9.65	492
42	150.651 128	14965.112 753	.000 066 8221	.006 638	99.336 215	.010 066 8221	12.09	4.073 678	9.70	504
43	169.757 461	16875.746 132	.000 059 2566	.005 891	99.410 924	.010 059 2566	12.08	4.190 576	9.75	516
44	191.286 956	19028.695 647	.000 052 5522	.005 228	99.477 225	.010 052 5522	12.07	4.307 748	9.79	528
45	215.546 930	21454.693 049	.000 046 6098	.004 639	99.536 064	.010 046 6098	12.06	4.425 169	9.83	540
46	242.883 676	24188.367 644	.000 041 3422	.004 117	99.588 280	.010 041 3422	12.05	4.542 821	9.88	552
47	273.687 406	27268.740 602	.000 036 6720	.003 654	99.634 620	.010 036 6720	12.05	4.660 683	9.92	564
48	308.397 820	30739.781 954	.000 032 5311	.003 243	99.675 743	.010 032 5311	12.04	4.778 738	9.96	576
49	347.510 382	34651.038 229	.000 028 8592	.002 878	99.712 239	.010 028 8592	12.04	4.896 969	9.99	588
50	391.583 397	39058.339 700	.000 025 6027	.002 554	99.744 627	.010 025 6027	12.04	5.015 362	10.03	600

Effective Rate is 12.68 %   Annual Percentage Rate is 12.00 %

	Amount Of 1	Amount Of 1 Per Period	Sinking Fund Payment	Present Worth Of 1	Present Worth of 1 Per Period	Periodic Payment To Amortize 1	Constant Annual Percent	Total Interest	Annual Add On Rate	
	What a single $ 1 deposit grows to in the future. The deposit is made at the beginning of the first period.	What a series of $ 1 deposits grow to in the future. A deposit is made at the end of each period.	The amount to be deposited at the end of each period that grows to $ 1 in the future.	What $ 1 to be paid in the future is worth today. Value today of a single $ 1 payment tomorrow.	What $ 1 to be paid at the end of each period is worth today. Value today of a series of $ 1 payments tomorrow.	The mortgage payment to amortize a loan of $ 1. An annuity certain, payable at the end of each period, worth $ 1 today.	The annual payment, including interest and principal, to amortize completely a loan of $ 100.	The total interest paid over the term of a loan of $1. The loan is amortized by regular periodic payments.	The average annual interest rate on a loan that is completely amortized by regular periodic payments.	
	$S = (1+i)^n$	$S\overline{n} = \dfrac{(1+i)^n - 1}{i}$	$\dfrac{1}{S\overline{n}} = \dfrac{i}{(1+i)^n - 1}$	$V^n = \dfrac{1}{(1+i)^n}$	$A\overline{n} = \dfrac{1 - V^n}{i}$	$\dfrac{1}{A\overline{n}} = \dfrac{i}{1 - V^n}$				

YEAR										PERIODS
	1.010 042	1.000 000	1.000 000 0000	.990 058	.990 058	1.010 041 6667	1212.05	.010 042	12.05	1
	1.020 184	2.010 042	.497 502 1247	.980 215	1.970 273	.507 543 7914	609.06	.015 088	9.05	2
	1.030 429	3.030 226	.330 008 4068	.970 470	2.940 743	.340 050 0734	408.07	.020 150	8.06	3
	1.040 776	4.060 654	.246 265 7279	.960 822	3.901 565	.256 307 3946	307.57	.025 230	7.57	4
	1.051 227	5.101 430	.196 023 4645	.951 269	4.852 835	.206 065 1311	247.28	.030 326	7.28	5
	1.061 783	6.152 657	.162 531 4085	.941 812	5.794 647	.172 573 0751	207.09	.035 438	7.09	6
	1.072 445	7.214 440	.138 610 8993	.932 449	6.727 095	.148 652 5660	178.39	.040 568	6.95	7
	1.083 214	8.286 885	.120 672 6067	.923 178	7.650 274	.130 714 2734	156.86	.045 714	6.86	8
	1.094 091	9.370 099	.106 722 4581	.914 000	8.564 274	.116 764 1248	140.12	.050 877	6.78	9
	1.105 078	10.464 190	.095 564 0101	.904 914	9.469 188	.105 605 6768	126.73	.056 057	6.73	10
	1.116 175	11.569 268	.086 435 8895	.895 917	10.365 105	.096 477 5562	115.78	.061 253	6.68	11
	1.127 383	12.685 443	.078 830 5142	.887 010	11.252 115	.088 872 1808	106.65	.066 466	6.65	12
1	1.127 383	12.685 443	.078 830 5142	.887 010	11.252 115	.088 872 1808	106.65	.066 466	6.65	12
2	1.270 992	26.986 796	.037 055 1586	.786 787	21.232 854	.047 096 8253	56.52	.130 324	6.52	24
3	1.432 895	43.109 898	.023 196 5292	.697 888	30.085 869	.033 238 1959	39.89	.196 575	6.55	36
4	1.615 422	61.286 808	.016 316 7250	.619 033	37.938 582	.026 358 3917	31.64	.265 203	6.63	48
5	1.821 199	81.779 148	.012 228 0559	.549 089	44.904 017	.022 269 7226	26.73	.336 183	6.72	60
6	2.053 189	104.881 864	.009 534 5369	.487 047	51.082 428	.019 576 2035	23.50	.409 487	6.82	72
7	2.314 730	130.927 473	.007 637 8164	.432 016	56.562 740	.017 679 4831	21.22	.485 077	6.93	84
8	2.609 587	160.290 849	.006 238 6593	.383 202	61.423 831	.016 280 3260	19.54	.562 911	7.04	96
9	2.942 004	193.394 620	.005 170 7747	.339 904	65.735 668	.015 212 4413	18.26	.642 944	7.14	108
10	3.316 766	230.715 248	.004 334 3473	.301 499	69.560 311	.014 376 0139	17.26	.725 122	7.25	120
11	3.739 265	272.789 889	.003 665 8250	.267 432	72.952 807	.013 707 4917	16.45	.809 389	7.36	132
12	4.215 584	320.224 124	.003 122 8128	.237 215	75.961 986	.013 164 4795	15.80	.895 685	7.46	144
13	4.752 578	373.700 674	.002 675 9384	.210 412	78.631 157	.012 717 6051	15.27	.983 946	7.57	156
14	5.357 975	433.989 227	.002 304 2047	.186 638	80.998 738	.012 345 8713	14.82	1.074 106	7.67	168
15	6.040 490	501.957 515	.001 992 2005	.165 549	83.098 807	.012 033 8671	14.45	1.166 096	7.77	180
16	6.809 946	578.583 808	.001 728 3581	.146 844	84.961 589	.011 770 0247	14.13	1.259 845	7.87	192
17	7.677 417	664.970 987	.001 503 8250	.130 252	86.613 895	.011 545 4917	13.86	1.355 280	7.97	204
18	8.655 389	762.362 424	.001 311 7121	.115 535	88.079 507	.011 353 3787	13.63	1.452 330	8.07	216
19	9.757 939	872.159 872	.001 146 5788	.102 481	89.379 519	.011 188 2454	13.43	1.550 920	8.16	228
20	11.000 934	995.943 648	.001 004 0729	.090 901	90.532 644	.011 045 7395	13.26	1.650 977	8.25	240
21	12.402 266	1135.495 372	.000 880 6729	.080 630	91.555 476	.010 922 3396	13.11	1.752 430	8.34	252
22	13.982 104	1292.823 612	.000 773 5007	.071 520	92.462 739	.010 815 1674	12.98	1.855 204	8.43	264
23	15.763 186	1470.192 793	.000 680 1829	.063 439	93.267 490	.010 721 8496	12.87	1.959 230	8.52	276
24	17.771 148	1670.155 792	.000 598 7465	.056 271	93.981 313	.010 640 4132	12.77	2.064 439	8.60	288
25	20.034 890	1895.590 675	.000 527 5401	.049 913	94.614 480	.010 569 2067	12.69	2.170 762	8.68	300
26	22.586 994	2149.742 127	.000 465 1721	.044 273	95.176 106	.010 506 8387	12.61	2.278 134	8.76	312
27	25.464 193	2436.268 152	.000 410 4638	.039 271	95.674 274	.010 452 1305	12.55	2.386 490	8.84	324
28	28.707 898	2759.292 719	.000 362 4117	.034 834	96.116 154	.010 404 0784	12.49	2.495 770	8.91	336
29	32.364 796	3123.465 122	.000 320 1572	.030 898	96.508 106	.010 361 8239	12.44	2.605 915	8.99	348
30	36.487 520	3534.026 894	.000 282 9633	.027 407	96.855 771	.010 324 6300	12.39	2.716 867	9.06	360
31	41.135 409	3996.887 253	.000 250 1947	.024 310	97.164 154	.010 291 8614	12.36	2.828 572	9.12	372
32	46.375 361	4518.708 148	.000 221 3022	.021 563	97.437 692	.010 262 9689	12.32	2.940 980	9.19	384
33	52.282 793	5107.000 150	.000 195 8097	.019 127	97.680 323	.010 237 4763	12.29	3.054 041	9.25	396
34	58.942 732	5770.230 547	.000 173 3033	.016 966	97.895 540	.010 214 9700	12.26	3.167 708	9.32	408
35	66.451 033	6517.945 215	.000 153 4226	.015 049	98.086 439	.010 195 0893	12.24	3.281 937	9.38	420
36	74.915 765	7360.906 014	.000 135 8528	.013 348	98.255 768	.010 177 5195	12.22	3.396 688	9.44	432
37	84.458 759	8311.245 681	.000 120 3189	.011 840	98.405 965	.010 161 9856	12.20	3.511 922	9.49	444
38	95.217 368	9382.642 457	.000 106 5798	.010 502	98.539 191	.010 148 2464	12.18	3.627 600	9.55	456
39	107.346 441	10590.516 959	.000 094 4241	.009 316	98.657 364	.010 136 0908	12.17	3.743 690	9.60	468
40	121.020 552	11952.254 127	.000 083 6662	.008 263	98.762 185	.010 125 3329	12.16	3.860 160	9.65	480
41	136.436 512	13487.453 449	.000 074 1430	.007 329	98.855 162	.010 115 8096	12.14	3.976 978	9.70	492
42	153.816 203	15218.211 052	.000 065 7107	.006 501	98.937 633	.010 107 3774	12.13	4.094 118	9.75	504
43	173.409 771	17169.437 735	.000 058 2430	.005 767	99.010 786	.010 099 9097	12.12	4.211 553	9.79	516
44	195.499 226	19369.217 509	.000 051 6283	.005 115	99.075 674	.010 093 2950	12.12	4.329 260	9.84	528
45	220.402 502	21849.211 809	.000 045 7682	.004 537	99.133 230	.010 087 4349	12.11	4.447 215	9.88	540
46	248.478 032	24645.115 201	.000 040 5760	.004 025	99.184 282	.010 082 2427	12.10	4.565 398	9.92	552
47	280.129 907	27797.169 130	.000 035 9749	.003 570	99.229 566	.010 077 6416	12.10	4.683 790	9.97	564
48	315.813 692	31350.741 115	.000 031 8972	.003 166	99.269 734	.010 073 5638	12.09	4.802 373	10.00	576
49	356.042 985	35356.977 728	.000 028 2830	.002 809	99.305 363	.010 069 9496	12.09	4.921 130	10.04	588
50	401.396 805	39873.540 743	.000 025 0793	.002 491	99.336 966	.010 066 7460	12.09	5.040 048	10.08	600

MONTHLY COMPOUND INTEREST AND ANNUITY

12.10 % M

	Amount Of 1	Amount Of 1 Per Period	Sinking Fund Payment	Present Worth Of 1	Present Worth of 1 Per Period	Periodic Payment To Amortize 1	Constant Annual Percent	Total Interest	Annual Add On Rate	
	What a single $ 1 deposit grows to in the future. The deposit is made at the beginning of the first period.	What a series of $ 1 deposits grow to in the future. A deposit is made at the end of each period.	The amount to be deposited at the end of each period that grows to $ 1 in the future.	What $ 1 to be paid in the future is worth today. Value today of a single $ 1 payment tomorrow.	What $ 1 to be paid at the end of each period is worth today. Value today of a series of $ 1 payments tomorrow.	The mortgage payment to amortize a loan of $ 1. An annuity certain, payable at the end of each period, worth $ 1 today.	The annual payment, including interest and principal, to amortize completely a loan of $ 100.	The total interest paid over the term on a loan of $1. The loan is amortized by regular periodic payments.	The average annual interest rate on a loan that is completely amortized by regular periodic payments.	
	$S = (1+i)^n$	$S\overline{n}| = \dfrac{(1+i)^n - 1}{i}$	$\dfrac{1}{S\overline{n}|} = \dfrac{i}{(1+i)^n - 1}$	$V^n = \dfrac{1}{(1+i)^n}$	$A\overline{n}| = \dfrac{1-V^n}{i}$	$\dfrac{1}{A\overline{n}|} = \dfrac{i}{1-V^n}$				

YEAR										PERIODS
	1.010 083	1.000 000	1.000 000 0000	.990 017	.990 017	1.010 083 3333	1212.10	.010 083	12.10	1
	1.020 268	2.010 083	.497 491 8121	.980 134	1.970 152	.507 575 1454	609.10	.015 150	9.09	2
	1.030 556	3.030 352	.329 994 7028	.970 350	2.940 502	.340 078 0362	408.10	.020 234	8.09	3
	1.040 947	4.060 908	.246 250 3630	.960 663	3.901 165	.256 333 6963	307.61	.025 335	7.60	4
	1.051 444	5.101 855	.196 007 1307	.951 073	4.852 238	.206 090 4640	247.31	.030 452	7.31	5
	1.062 046	6.153 299	.162 514 4519	.941 579	5.793 817	.172 597 7852	207.12	.035 587	7.12	6
	1.072 755	7.215 345	.138 593 5177	.932 180	6.725 997	.148 676 8510	178.42	.040 738	6.98	7
	1.083 572	8.288 099	.120 654 9236	.922 874	7.648 871	.130 738 2569	156.89	.045 906	6.89	8
	1.094 498	9.371 671	.106 704 5559	.913 661	8.562 532	.116 787 8893	140.15	.051 091	6.81	9
	1.105 534	10.466 169	.095 545 9465	.904 540	9.467 072	.105 629 2798	126.76	.056 293	6.76	10
	1.116 681	11.571 703	.086 417 7064	.895 511	10.362 583	.096 501 0398	115.81	.061 511	6.71	11
	1.127 941	12.688 384	.078 812 2430	.886 571	11.249 154	.088 895 5764	106.68	.066 747	6.67	12
1	1.127 941	12.688 384	.078 812 2430	.886 571	11.249 154	.088 895 5764	106.68	.066 747	6.67	12
2	1.272 251	27.000 135	.037 036 8518	.786 008	21.222 327	.047 120 1851	56.55	.130 884	6.54	24
3	1.435 025	43.142 949	.023 178 7587	.696 852	30.064 255	.033 262 0920	39.92	.197 435	6.58	36
4	1.618 624	61.351 094	.016 299 6279	.617 809	37.903 251	.026 382 9613	31.66	.266 382	6.66	48
5	1.825 712	81.888 810	.012 211 6806	.547 731	44.853 078	.022 295 0140	26.76	.337 701	6.75	60
6	2.059 296	105.054 147	.009 518 9007	.485 603	51.014 593	.019 602 2341	23.53	.411 361	6.86	72
7	2.322 765	131.183 286	.007 622 9224	.430 521	56.477 214	.017 706 2557	21.25	.487 325	6.96	84
8	2.619 942	160.655 417	.006 224 5022	.381 688	61.320 216	.016 307 8355	19.57	.565 552	7.07	96
9	2.955 141	193.898 249	.005 157 3442	.338 393	65.613 881	.015 240 6775	18.29	.645 993	7.18	108
10	3.333 225	231.394 208	.004 321 6293	.300 010	69.420 520	.014 404 9627	17.29	.728 596	7.29	120
11	3.759 682	273.687 446	.003 653 8030	.265 980	72.795 376	.013 737 1363	16.49	.813 302	7.39	132
12	4.240 700	321.391 732	.003 111 4677	.235 810	75.787 425	.013 194 8011	15.84	.900 051	7.50	144
13	4.783 260	375.199 361	.002 665 2497	.209 062	78.440 090	.012 748 5831	15.30	.988 779	7.61	156
14	5.395 236	435.891 203	.002 294 1504	.185 349	80.791 865	.012 377 4838	14.86	1.079 417	7.71	168
15	6.085 509	504.348 033	.001 982 7578	.164 325	82.876 881	.012 066 0911	14.48	1.171 896	7.81	180
16	6.864 097	581.563 312	.001 719 5032	.145 686	84.725 396	.011 802 8366	14.17	1.266 145	7.91	192
17	7.742 298	668.657 607	.001 495 5337	.129 161	86.364 235	.011 578 8671	13.90	1.362 099	8.01	204
18	8.732 856	766.894 851	.001 303 9597	.114 510	87.817 183	.011 387 2931	13.67	1.459 655	8.11	216
19	9.850 149	877.700 686	.001 139 3406	.101 521	89.105 325	.011 222 6739	13.47	1.558 770	8.20	228
20	11.110 388	1002.683 153	.000 997 3240	.090 006	90.247 353	.011 080 6574	13.30	1.659 358	8.30	240
21	12.531 865	1143.656 028	.000 874 3888	.079 797	91.259 843	.010 957 7221	13.15	1.761 346	8.39	252
22	14.135 207	1302.665 142	.000 767 6570	.070 745	92.157 487	.010 850 9903	13.03	1.864 661	8.48	264
23	15.943 682	1482.018 074	.000 674 7556	.062 721	92.953 312	.010 758 0889	12.91	1.969 233	8.56	276
24	17.983 536	1684.317 636	.000 593 7122	.055 606	93.658 868	.010 677 0456	12.82	2.074 989	8.65	288
25	20.284 371	1912.499 648	.000 522 8759	.049 299	94.284 393	.010 606 2092	12.73	2.181 863	8.73	300
26	22.879 578	2169.875 541	.000 460 8559	.043 707	94.838 965	.010 544 1893	12.66	2.289 787	8.81	312
27	25.806 819	2460.180 416	.000 406 4743	.038 749	95.330 633	.010 489 8076	12.59	2.398 698	8.88	324
28	29.108 575	2787.627 247	.000 358 7280	.034 354	95.766 532	.010 442 0614	12.54	2.508 533	8.96	336
29	32.832 761	3156.968 020	.000 316 7596	.030 457	96.152 987	.010 400 0930	12.49	2.619 232	9.03	348
30	37.033 424	3573.562 696	.000 279 8328	.027 003	96.495 607	.010 363 1661	12.44	2.730 740	9.10	360
31	41.771 525	4043.456 997	.000 247 3131	.023 940	96.799 363	.010 330 6465	12.40	2.843 000	9.17	372
32	47.115 824	4573.470 141	.000 218 6524	.021 224	97.068 665	.010 301 9857	12.37	2.955 963	9.24	384
33	53.143 879	5171.293 805	.000 193 3752	.018 817	97.307 421	.010 276 7085	12.34	3.069 577	9.30	396
34	59.943 171	5845.603 750	.000 171 0687	.016 682	97.519 094	.010 254 4021	12.31	3.183 796	9.36	408
35	67.612 373	6606.185 721	.000 151 3733	.014 790	97.706 758	.010 234 7066	12.29	3.298 577	9.42	420
36	76.262 781	7464.077 466	.000 133 9750	.013 113	97.873 135	.010 217 3084	12.27	3.413 877	9.48	432
37	86.019 933	8431.728 914	.000 118 5996	.011 625	98.020 640	.010 201 9330	12.25	3.529 658	9.54	444
38	97.025 427	9523.182 855	.000 105 0069	.010 307	98.151 414	.010 188 3402	12.23	3.645 883	9.59	456
39	109.438 977	10754.278 727	.000 092 9862	.009 138	98.267 354	.010 176 3196	12.22	3.762 518	9.65	468
40	123.440 732	12142.882 490	.000 082 3528	.008 101	98.370 143	.010 165 6861	12.20	3.879 529	9.70	480
41	139.233 888	13709.145 890	.000 072 9440	.007 182	98.461 273	.010 156 2773	12.19	3.996 888	9.75	492
42	157.047 639	15475.798 918	.000 064 6170	.006 367	98.542 067	.010 147 9506	12.18	4.114 567	9.80	504
43	177.140 503	17468.479 662	.000 057 2460	.005 645	98.613 696	.010 140 5793	12.17	4.232 539	9.84	516
44	199.804 073	19716.106 382	.000 050 7200	.005 005	98.677 200	.010 134 0533	12.17	4.350 780	9.89	528
45	225.367 246	22251.297 172	.000 044 9412	.004 437	98.733 501	.010 128 2745	12.16	4.469 268	9.93	540
46	254.201 004	25110.843 327	.000 039 8234	.003 934	98.783 415	.010 123 1568	12.15	4.587 983	9.97	552
47	286.723 786	28336.243 262	.000 035 2905	.003 488	98.827 668	.010 118 6238	12.15	4.706 904	10.01	564
48	323.407 573	31974.304 752	.000 031 2751	.003 092	98.866 902	.010 114 6084	12.14	4.826 014	10.05	576
49	364.784 727	36077.824 211	.000 027 7179	.002 741	98.901 685	.010 111 0512	12.14	4.945 298	10.09	588
50	411.455 725	40706.352 895	.000 024 5662	.002 430	98.932 523	.010 107 8995	12.13	5.064 740	10.13	600

Effective Rate is 12.79 %   8 - 186   Annual Percentage Rate is 12.10 %

MONTHLY COMPOUND INTEREST AND ANNUITY

12.125% M

Amount Of 1	Amount Of 1 Per Period	Sinking Fund Payment	Present Worth Of 1	Present Worth of 1 Per Period	Periodic Payment To Amortize 1	Constant Annual Percent	Total Interest	Annual Add On Rate	
What a single $ 1 deposit grows to in the future. The deposit is made at the beginning of the first period.	What a series of $ 1 deposits grow to in the future. A deposit is made at the end of each period.	The amount to be deposited at the end of each period that grows to $ 1 in the future.	What $ 1 to be paid in the future is worth today. Value today of a single $ 1 payment tomorrow.	What $ 1 to be paid at the end of each period is worth today. Value today of a series of $ 1 payments tomorrow.	The mortgage payment to amortize a loan of $ 1. An annuity certain, payable at the end of each period, worth $ 1 today.	The annual payment, including interest and principal, to amortize completely a loan of $ 100.	The total interest paid over the term on a loan of $ 1. The loan is amortized by regular periodic payments.	The average annual interest rate on a loan that is completely amortized by regular periodic payments.	
$S = (1+i)^n$	$S\overline{n}| = \dfrac{(1+i)^n - 1}{i}$	$\dfrac{1}{S\overline{n}|} = \dfrac{i}{(1+i)^n - 1}$	$V^n = \dfrac{1}{(1+i)^n}$	$A\overline{n}| = \dfrac{1 - V^n}{i}$	$\dfrac{1}{A\overline{n}|} = \dfrac{i}{1 - V^n}$				

YEAR									PERIODS
	1.010 104	1.000 000	1.000 000 0000	.989 997	.989 997	1.010 104 1667	1212.13	.010 104	12.13	1
	1.020 310	2.010 104	.497 486 6560	.980 094	1.970 091	.507 590 8226	609.11	.015 182	9.11	2
	1.030 620	3.030 415	.329 987 8511	.970 290	2.940 381	.340 092 0178	408.12	.020 276	8.11	3
	1.041 033	4.061 034	.246 242 6809	.960 584	3.900 965	.256 346 8476	307.62	.025 387	7.62	4
	1.051 552	5.102 068	.195 998 9643	.950 975	4.851 940	.206 103 1310	247.33	.030 516	7.32	5
	1.062 177	6.153 620	.162 505 9742	.941 462	5.793 402	.172 610 1409	207.14	.035 661	7.13	6
	1.072 910	7.215 797	.138 584 8276	.932 045	6.725 447	.148 688 9943	178.43	.040 823	7.00	7
	1.083 750	8.288 707	.120 646 0829	.922 722	7.648 169	.130 750 2495	156.91	.046 002	6.90	8
	1.094 701	9.372 457	.106 695 6058	.913 492	8.561 661	.116 799 7725	140.16	.051 198	6.83	9
	1.105 762	10.467 158	.095 536 9158	.904 354	9.466 014	.105 641 0824	126.77	.056 411	6.77	10
	1.116 935	11.572 920	.086 408 6160	.895 307	10.361 322	.096 512 7827	115.82	.061 641	6.72	11
	1.128 220	12.689 855	.078 803 1087	.886 352	11.247 673	.088 907 2754	106.69	.066 887	6.69	12
1	1.128 220	12.689 855	.078 803 1087	.886 352	11.247 673	.088 907 2754	106.69	.066 887	6.69	12
2	1.272 881	27.006 808	.037 027 7009	.785 619	21.217 067	.047 131 8676	56.56	.131 165	6.56	24
3	1.436 091	43.159 486	.023 169 8772	.696 335	30.053 456	.033 274 0439	39.93	.197 866	6.60	36
4	1.620 227	61.383 268	.016 291 0844	.617 198	37.885 603	.026 395 2511	31.68	.266 972	6.67	48
5	1.827 973	81.943 710	.012 203 4992	.547 054	44.827 639	.022 307 6658	26.77	.338 650	6.77	60
6	2.062 356	105.140 421	.009 511 0900	.484 882	50.980 725	.019 615 2566	23.54	.412 298	6.87	72
7	2.326 793	131.311 423	.007 615 4837	.429 776	56.434 522	.017 719 6504	21.27	.488 451	6.98	84
8	2.625 135	160.838 082	.006 217 4330	.380 933	61.268 504	.016 321 5997	19.59	.566 874	7.09	96
9	2.961 731	194.150 661	.005 150 6392	.337 640	65.553 112	.015 254 8058	18.31	.647 519	7.19	108
10	3.341 485	231.734 592	.004 315 2815	.299 268	69.350 782	.014 419 4482	17.31	.730 334	7.30	120
11	3.769 932	274.137 551	.003 647 8038	.265 257	72.716 852	.013 751 9705	16.51	.815 260	7.41	132
12	4.253 314	321.977 434	.003 105 8077	.235 111	75.700 374	.013 209 9744	15.86	.902 236	7.52	144
13	4.798 675	375.951 366	.002 659 9185	.208 391	78.344 823	.012 764 0852	15.32	.991 197	7.62	156
14	5.413 963	436.845 858	.002 289 1370	.184 708	80.688 736	.012 393 3036	14.88	1.082 075	7.73	168
15	6.108 144	505.548 266	.001 978 0505	.163 716	82.766 266	.012 082 2172	14.50	1.174 799	7.83	180
16	6.891 333	583.059 725	.001 715 0902	.145 110	84.607 688	.011 819 2568	14.19	1.269 297	7.93	192
17	7.774 942	670.509 735	.001 491 4027	.128 618	86.239 836	.011 595 5693	13.92	1.365 496	8.03	204
18	8.771 848	769.172 621	.001 300 0983	.114 001	87.686 493	.011 404 2649	13.69	1.463 321	8.13	216
19	9.896 578	880.486 102	.001 135 7363	.101 045	88.968 740	.011 239 9029	13.49	1.562 698	8.22	228
20	11.165 522	1006.072 243	.000 993 9644	.089 561	90.105 261	.011 098 1311	13.32	1.663 551	8.32	240
21	12.597 169	1147.761 090	.000 871 2615	.079 383	91.112 619	.010 975 4281	13.18	1.765 808	8.41	252
22	14.212 384	1307.617 339	.000 764 7497	.070 361	92.005 492	.010 868 9164	13.05	1.869 394	8.50	264
23	16.034 701	1487.970 421	.000 672 0564	.062 365	92.796 892	.010 776 2230	12.94	1.974 238	8.58	276
24	18.090 677	1691.448 448	.000 591 2093	.055 277	93.498 350	.010 695 3759	12.84	2.080 268	8.67	288
25	20.410 271	1921.016 511	.000 520 5577	.048 995	94.120 088	.010 624 7244	12.75	2.187 417	8.75	300
26	23.027 284	2180.019 885	.000 458 7114	.043 427	94.671 168	.010 562 8781	12.68	2.295 618	8.83	312
27	25.979 852	2472.232 776	.000 404 4927	.038 491	95.159 617	.010 508 6593	12.62	2.404 806	8.91	324
28	29.310 999	2801.913 324	.000 356 8990	.034 117	95.592 556	.010 461 0656	12.56	2.514 918	8.98	336
29	33.069 267	3173.865 645	.000 315 0732	.030 240	95.976 291	.010 419 2399	12.51	2.625 895	9.05	348
30	37.309 422	3593.509 844	.000 278 2795	.026 803	96.316 416	.010 382 4461	12.46	2.737 681	9.13	360
31	42.093 252	4066.960 993	.000 245 8838	.023 757	96.617 886	.010 350 0505	12.43	2.850 219	9.19	372
32	47.490 466	4601.118 241	.000 217 3385	.021 057	96.885 094	.010 321 5051	12.39	2.963 458	9.26	384
33	53.579 712	5203.765 349	.000 192 1685	.018 664	97.121 935	.010 296 3352	12.36	3.077 349	9.33	396
34	60.449 725	5883.684 114	.000 169 9615	.016 543	97.331 859	.010 274 1282	12.33	3.191 844	9.39	408
35	68.200 613	6650.782 340	.000 150 3583	.014 663	97.517 926	.010 254 5249	12.31	3.306 900	9.45	420
36	76.945 324	7516.238 213	.000 133 0453	.012 996	97.682 846	.010 237 2119	12.29	3.422 476	9.51	432
37	86.811 284	8492.663 189	.000 117 7487	.011 519	97.829 024	.010 221 9154	12.27	3.538 530	9.56	444
38	97.942 263	9594.285 774	.000 104 2287	.010 210	97.958 588	.010 208 3954	12.26	3.655 028	9.62	456
39	110.500 459	10837.158 855	.000 092 2751	.009 050	98.073 428	.010 196 4418	12.24	3.771 935	9.67	468
40	124.668 873	12239.393 627	.000 081 7034	.008 021	98.175 217	.010 185 8701	12.23	3.889 218	9.72	480
41	140.653 967	13821.423 513	.000 072 3514	.007 110	98.265 437	.010 176 5181	12.22	4.006 847	9.77	492
42	158.688 676	15606.301 915	.000 064 0767	.006 302	98.345 404	.010 168 2433	12.21	4.124 795	9.82	504
43	179.035 802	17620.038 152	.000 056 7536	.005 585	98.416 283	.010 160 9202	12.20	4.243 035	9.87	516
44	201.991 846	19891.976 468	.000 050 2715	.004 951	98.479 106	.010 154 4382	12.19	4.361 543	9.91	528
45	227.891 322	22455.223 639	.000 044 5331	.004 388	98.534 790	.010 148 6997	12.18	4.480 298	9.96	540
46	257.111 640	25347.131 406	.000 039 4522	.003 889	98.584 146	.010 143 6189	12.18	4.599 278	10.00	552
47	290.078 599	28609.840 764	.000 034 9530	.003 447	98.627 892	.010 139 1197	12.17	4.718 463	10.04	564
48	327.272 595	32290.896 043	.000 030 9685	.003 056	98.666 667	.010 135 1351	12.17	4.837 838	10.08	576
49	369.235 621	36443.937 728	.000 027 4394	.002 708	98.701 034	.010 131 6061	12.16	4.957 384	10.12	588
50	416.579 162	41129.484 107	.000 024 3135	.002 401	98.731 496	.010 128 4801	12.16	5.077 088	10.15	600

MONTHLY COMPOUND INTEREST AND ANNUITY

12.15 % M

	Amount Of 1	Amount Of 1 Per Period	Sinking Fund Payment	Present Worth Of 1	Present Worth of 1 Per Period	Periodic Payment To Amortize 1	Constant Annual Percent	Total Interest	Annual Add On Rate	

Descriptions:
- Amount Of 1: What a single $1 deposit grows to in the future. The deposit is made at the beginning of the first period.
- Amount Of 1 Per Period: What a series of $1 deposits grow to in the future. A deposit is made at the end of each period.
- Sinking Fund Payment: The amount to be deposited at the end of each period that grows to $1 in the future.
- Present Worth Of 1: What $1 to be paid in the future is worth today. Value today of a single $1 payment tomorrow.
- Present Worth of 1 Per Period: What $1 to be paid at the end of each period is worth today. Value today of a series of $1 payments tomorrow.
- Periodic Payment To Amortize 1: The mortgage payment to amortize a loan of $1. An annuity certain, payable at the end of each period, worth $1 today.
- Constant Annual Percent: The annual payment, including interest and principal, to amortize completely a loan of $100.
- Total Interest: The total interest paid over the term on a loan of $1. The loan is amortized by regular periodic payments.
- Annual Add On Rate: The average annual interest rate on a loan that is completely amortized by regular periodic payments.

$$S = (1+i)^n \qquad S\overline{n}| = \frac{(1+i)^n - 1}{i} \qquad \frac{1}{S\overline{n}|} = \frac{i}{(1+i)^n - 1} \qquad V^n = \frac{1}{(1+i)^n} \qquad A\overline{n}| = \frac{1-V^n}{i} \qquad \frac{1}{A\overline{n}|} = \frac{i}{1-V^n}$$

YEAR	Amount Of 1	Amount Of 1 Per Period	Sinking Fund Payment	Present Worth Of 1	Present Worth of 1 Per Period	Periodic Payment To Amortize 1	Constant Annual Percent	Total Interest	Annual Add On Rate	PERIODS
	1.010 125	1.000 000	1.000 000 0000	.989 976	.989 976	1.010 125 0000	1212.15	.010 125	12.15	1
	1.020 353	2.010 125	.497 481 4999	.980 053	1.970 030	.507 606 4999	609.13	.015 213	9.13	2
	1.030 684	3.030 478	.329 980 9996	.970 230	2.940 260	.340 105 9996	408.13	.020 318	8.13	3
	1.041 119	4.061 161	.246 234 9991	.960 505	3.900 765	.256 359 9991	307.64	.025 440	7.63	4
	1.051 661	5.102 280	.195 990 7983	.950 877	4.851 642	.206 115 7983	247.34	.030 579	7.34	5
	1.062 309	6.153 941	.162 497 4970	.941 346	5.792 988	.172 622 4970	207.15	.035 735	7.15	6
	1.073 065	7.216 250	.138 576 1380	.931 910	6.724 898	.148 701 1380	178.45	.040 908	7.01	7
	1.083 929	8.289 314	.120 637 2427	.922 569	7.647 467	.130 762 2427	156.92	.046 098	6.91	8
	1.094 904	9.373 243	.106 686 6563	.913 322	8.560 789	.116 811 6563	140.18	.051 305	6.84	9
	1.105 990	10.468 148	.095 527 8857	.904 167	9.464 957	.105 652 8857	126.79	.056 529	6.78	10
	1.117 188	11.574 138	.086 399 5264	.895 104	10.360 061	.096 524 5264	115.83	.061 770	6.74	11
	1.128 500	12.691 326	.078 793 9753	.886 132	11.246 193	.088 918 9753	106.71	.067 028	6.70	12
1	1.128 500	12.691 326	.078 793 9753	.886 132	11.246 193	.088 918 9753	106.71	.067 028	6.70	12
2	1.273 512	27.013 482	.037 018 5518	.785 230	21.211 809	.047 143 5518	56.58	.131 445	6.57	24
3	1.437 157	43.176 032	.023 160 9983	.695 818	30.042 662	.033 285 9983	39.95	.198 296	6.61	36
4	1.621 832	61.415 463	.016 282 5442	.616 587	37.867 966	.026 407 5442	31.69	.267 562	6.69	48
5	1.830 236	81.998 656	.012 195 3218	.546 378	44.802 221	.022 320 3218	26.79	.339 219	6.78	60
6	2.065 421	105.226 782	.009 503 2841	.484 163	50.946 889	.019 628 2841	23.56	.413 236	6.89	72
7	2.330 827	131.439 715	.007 608 0506	.429 032	56.391 877	.017 733 0506	21.28	.489 576	6.99	84
8	2.630 338	161.021 001	.006 210 3701	.380 179	61.216 856	.016 335 3701	19.61	.568 196	7.10	96
9	2.968 335	194.403 472	.005 143 9410	.336 889	65.492 427	.015 268 9410	18.33	.649 046	7.21	108
10	3.349 765	232.075 580	.004 308 9411	.298 528	69.281 147	.014 433 9411	17.33	.732 073	7.32	120
11	3.780 209	274.588 542	.003 641 8126	.264 536	72.638 455	.013 766 8126	16.53	.817 219	7.43	132
12	4.265 965	322.564 405	.003 100 1561	.234 414	75.613 474	.013 225 1561	15.88	.904 422	7.54	144
13	4.814 140	376.705 151	.002 654 5960	.207 721	78.249 735	.012 779 5960	15.34	.993 617	7.64	156
14	5.432 755	437.802 965	.002 284 1325	.184 069	80.585 810	.012 409 1325	14.90	1.084 734	7.75	168
15	6.130 862	506.751 828	.001 973 3525	.163 109	82.655 882	.012 098 3525	14.52	1.177 703	7.85	180
16	6.918 676	584.560 598	.001 710 6866	.144 536	84.490 240	.011 835 6866	14.21	1.272 452	7.95	192
17	7.807 724	672.367 769	.001 487 2813	.128 078	86.115 723	.011 612 2813	13.94	1.368 905	8.05	204
18	8.811 014	771.458 132	.001 296 2466	.113 494	87.556 116	.011 421 2466	13.71	1.466 989	8.15	216
19	9.943 226	883.281 575	.001 132 1418	.100 571	88.832 496	.011 257 1418	13.51	1.566 628	8.25	228
20	11.220 927	1009.474 294	.000 990 6146	.089 119	89.963 536	.011 115 6146	13.34	1.667 748	8.34	240
21	12.662 813	1151.882 736	.000 868 1439	.078 971	90.965 788	.010 993 1439	13.20	1.770 272	8.43	252
22	14.289 980	1312.590 615	.000 761 8522	.069 979	91.853 916	.010 886 8522	13.07	1.874 129	8.52	264
23	16.126 238	1493.949 405	.000 669 3667	.062 011	92.640 914	.010 794 3667	12.96	1.979 245	8.61	276
24	18.198 454	1698.612 739	.000 588 7157	.054 950	93.338 299	.010 713 7157	12.86	2.085 550	8.69	288
25	20.536 949	1929.575 245	.000 518 2488	.048 693	93.956 274	.010 643 2488	12.78	2.192 975	8.77	300
26	23.175 941	2190.216 357	.000 456 5759	.043 148	94.503 882	.010 581 5759	12.70	2.301 452	8.85	312
27	26.154 041	2484.349 767	.000 402 5198	.038 235	94.989 135	.010 527 5198	12.64	2.410 916	8.93	324
28	29.514 827	2816.279 224	.000 355 0784	.033 881	95.419 133	.010 480 0784	12.58	2.521 306	9.00	336
29	33.307 473	3190.861 507	.000 313 3950	.030 023	95.800 169	.010 438 3950	12.53	2.632 561	9.08	348
30	37.587 472	3613.577 490	.000 276 7341	.026 605	96.137 816	.010 401 7341	12.49	2.744 624	9.15	360
31	42.417 450	4090.612 339	.000 244 4622	.023 575	96.437 017	.010 369 4622	12.45	2.857 440	9.22	372
32	47.868 078	4628.946 010	.000 216 0319	.020 891	96.702 148	.010 341 0319	12.41	2.970 956	9.28	384
33	54.019 111	5236.455 380	.000 190 9689	.018 512	96.937 090	.010 315 9689	12.38	3.085 124	9.35	396
34	60.960 549	5922.029 506	.000 168 8610	.016 404	97.145 279	.010 293 8610	12.36	3.199 895	9.41	408
35	68.793 959	6695.699 683	.000 149 3496	.014 536	97.329 762	.010 274 3496	12.33	3.315 227	9.47	420
36	77.633 961	7568.786 223	.000 132 1216	.012 881	97.493 238	.010 257 1216	12.31	3.431 077	9.53	432
37	87.609 899	8554.064 098	.000 116 9035	.011 414	97.638 100	.010 241 9035	12.30	3.547 405	9.59	444
38	98.867 742	9665.949 857	.000 103 4559	.010 115	97.766 467	.010 228 4559	12.28	3.664 176	9.64	456
39	111.572 215	10920.712 571	.000 091 5691	.008 963	97.880 217	.010 216 5691	12.26	3.781 354	9.70	468
40	125.909 208	12336.711 883	.000 081 0589	.007 942	97.981 014	.010 206 0589	12.25	3.898 908	9.75	480
41	142.088 500	13934.666 642	.000 071 7635	.007 038	98.070 334	.010 196 7635	12.24	4.016 808	9.80	492
42	160.346 825	15737.958 065	.000 063 5406	.006 236	98.149 483	.010 188 5406	12.23	4.135 024	9.85	504
43	180.951 340	17772.971 844	.000 056 2652	.005 526	98.219 620	.010 181 2652	12.22	4.253 533	9.89	516
44	204.203 528	20069.484 226	.000 049 8269	.004 897	98.281 770	.010 174 8269	12.21	4.372 309	9.94	528
45	230.443 614	22661.097 698	.000 044 1285	.004 339	98.336 844	.010 169 1285	12.21	4.491 329	9.98	540
46	260.055 543	25585.732 650	.000 039 0843	.003 845	98.385 646	.010 164 0843	12.20	4.610 575	10.02	552
47	293.472 595	28886.182 236	.000 034 6186	.003 407	98.428 892	.010 159 6186	12.20	4.730 025	10.06	564
48	331.183 727	32610.738 512	.000 030 6647	.003 019	98.467 213	.010 155 6647	12.19	4.849 663	10.10	576
49	373.740 728	36813.899 049	.000 027 1637	.002 676	98.501 170	.010 152 1637	12.19	4.969 472	10.14	588
50	421.766 289	41557.164 337	.000 024 0632	.002 371	98.531 261	.010 149 0632	12.18	5.089 438	10.18	600

Effective Rate is 12.85 %

8 - 188

Annual Percentage Rate is 12.15 %

MONTHLY COMPOUND INTEREST AND ANNUITY

	Amount Of 1	Amount Of 1 Per Period	Sinking Fund Payment	Present Worth Of 1	Present Worth of 1 Per Period	Periodic Payment To Amortize 1	Constant Annual Percent	Total Interest	Annual Add On Rate	
	What a single $ 1 deposit grows to in the future. The deposit is made at the beginning of the first period.	What a series of $ 1 deposits grow to in the future. A deposit is made at the end of each period.	The amount to be deposited at the end of each period that grows to $ 1 in the future.	What $ 1 to be paid in the future is worth today. Value today of a single $ 1 payment tomorrow.	What $ 1 to be paid at the end of each period is worth today. Value today of a series of $ 1 payments tomorrow.	The mortgage payment to amortize a loan of $ 1. An annuity certain, payable at the end of each period, worth $ 1 today.	The annual payment, including interest and principal, to amortize completely a loan of $ 100.	The total interest paid over the term on a loan of $1. The loan is amortized by regular periodic payments.	The average annual interest rate on a loan that is completely amortized by regular periodic payments.	
	$S = (1+i)^n$	$S\overline{n}| = \dfrac{(1+i)^n - 1}{i}$	$\dfrac{1}{S\overline{n}|} = \dfrac{i}{(1+i)^n - 1}$	$V^n = \dfrac{1}{(1+i)^n}$	$A\overline{n}| = \dfrac{1-V^n}{i}$	$\dfrac{1}{A\overline{n}|} = \dfrac{i}{1-V^n}$				

YEAR										PERIODS
	1.010 167	1.000 000	1.000 000 0000	.989 936	.989 936	1.010 166 6667	1212.20	.010 167	12.20	1
	1.020 437	2.010 167	.497 471 1881	.979 973	1.969 908	.507 637 8548	609.17	.015 276	9.17	2
	1.030 811	3.030 603	.329 967 2972	.970 110	2.940 018	.340 133 9639	408.17	.020 402	8.16	3
	1.041 291	4.061 414	.246 219 6363	.960 346	3.900 364	.256 386 3030	307.67	.025 545	7.66	4
	1.051 878	5.102 706	.195 974 4672	.950 681	4.851 045	.206 141 1339	247.37	.030 706	7.37	5
	1.062 572	6.154 583	.162 480 5437	.941 113	5.792 158	.172 647 2104	207.18	.035 883	7.18	6
	1.073 374	7.217 155	.138 558 7603	.931 641	6.723 800	.148 725 4269	178.48	.041 078	7.04	7
	1.084 287	8.290 529	.120 619 5641	.922 265	7.646 065	.130 786 2308	156.95	.046 290	6.94	8
	1.095 311	9.374 816	.106 668 7591	.912 983	8.559 048	.116 835 4258	140.21	.051 519	6.87	9
	1.106 446	10.470 127	.095 509 8278	.903 794	9.462 842	.105 676 4944	126.82	.056 765	6.81	10
	1.117 695	11.576 573	.086 381 3495	.894 698	10.357 541	.096 548 0162	115.86	.062 028	6.77	11
	1.129 058	12.694 268	.078 775 7109	.885 694	11.243 234	.088 942 3776	106.74	.067 309	6.73	12
1	1.129 058	12.694 268	.078 775 7109	.885 694	11.243 234	.088 942 3776	106.74	.067 309	6.73	12
2	1.274 773	27.026 838	.037 000 2585	.784 453	21.201 297	.047 166 9252	56.61	.132 006	6.60	24
3	1.439 293	43.209 147	.023 143 2481	.694 786	30.021 092	.033 309 9147	39.98	.199 157	6.64	36
4	1.625 046	61.479 918	.016 265 4739	.615 367	37.832 729	.026 432 1406	31.72	.268 743	6.72	48
5	1.834 772	82.108 685	.012 178 9795	.545 027	44.751 447	.022 345 6462	26.82	.340 739	6.81	60
6	2.071 564	105.399 769	.009 487 6869	.482 727	50.879 313	.019 654 3535	23.59	.415 113	6.92	72
7	2.338 917	131.696 762	.007 593 2011	.427 548	56.306 725	.017 759 8678	21.32	.491 829	7.03	84
8	2.640 774	161.387 602	.006 196 2628	.378 677	61.113 751	.016 362 9295	19.64	.570 841	7.14	96
9	2.981 588	194.910 295	.005 130 5653	.335 392	65.371 304	.015 297 2320	18.36	.652 101	7.25	108
10	3.366 387	232.759 373	.004 296 2824	.297 054	69.142 192	.014 462 9491	17.36	.735 554	7.36	120
11	3.800 847	275.493 191	.003 629 8538	.263 099	72.482 044	.013 796 5204	16.56	.821 141	7.46	132
12	4.291 379	323.742 168	.003 088 8778	.233 025	75.440 130	.013 255 5445	15.91	.908 798	7.57	144
13	4.845 217	378.218 080	.002 643 9773	.206 389	78.060 089	.012 810 6439	15.38	.998 460	7.68	156
14	5.470 533	439.724 566	.002 274 1509	.182 798	80.380 570	.012 440 8175	14.93	1.090 057	7.79	168
15	6.176 551	509.168 980	.001 963 9845	.161 903	82.435 805	.012 130 6512	14.56	1.183 517	7.89	180
16	6.973 687	587.575 779	.001 701 9081	.143 396	84.256 115	.011 868 5748	14.25	1.278 766	7.99	192
17	7.873 700	676.101 633	.001 479 0676	.127 005	85.868 351	.011 645 7342	13.98	1.375 730	8.09	204
18	8.889 867	776.052 491	.001 288 5726	.112 488	87.296 299	.011 455 2393	13.75	1.474 332	8.19	216
19	10.037 179	888.902 847	.001 124 9823	.099 630	88.561 024	.011 291 6490	13.55	1.574 496	8.29	228
20	11.332 561	1016.317 488	.000 983 9445	.088 241	89.681 183	.011 150 6112	13.39	1.676 147	8.38	240
21	12.795 123	1160.176 058	.000 861 9381	.078 155	90.673 301	.011 028 6048	13.24	1.779 208	8.47	252
22	14.446 441	1322.600 784	.000 756 0860	.069 221	91.552 013	.010 922 7527	13.11	1.883 607	8.56	264
23	16.310 876	1505.987 784	.000 664 0160	.061 309	92.330 283	.010 830 6827	13.00	1.989 268	8.65	276
24	18.415 931	1713.042 416	.000 583 7567	.054 301	93.019 592	.010 750 4234	12.91	2.096 122	8.73	288
25	20.792 662	1946.819 185	.000 513 6584	.048 094	93.630 109	.010 680 3251	12.82	2.204 098	8.82	300
26	23.476 129	2210.766 809	.000 452 3317	.042 596	94.170 840	.010 618 9984	12.75	2.313 128	8.90	312
27	26.505 921	2508.779 089	.000 398 6003	.037 727	94.649 762	.010 565 2669	12.68	2.423 146	8.97	324
28	29.926 732	2845.252 355	.000 351 4627	.033 415	95.073 940	.010 518 1293	12.63	2.534 091	9.05	336
29	33.789 028	3225.150 320	.000 310 0631	.029 595	95.449 632	.010 476 7297	12.58	2.645 902	9.12	348
30	38.149 786	3654.077 306	.000 273 6669	.026 212	95.782 380	.010 440 3336	12.53	2.758 520	9.20	360
31	43.073 336	4138.360 919	.000 241 6416	.023 216	96.077 093	.010 408 3082	12.49	2.871 891	9.26	372
32	48.632 312	4685.145 398	.000 213 4405	.020 562	96.338 119	.010 380 1072	12.46	2.985 961	9.33	384
33	54.908 720	5302.497 002	.000 188 5904	.018 212	96.569 307	.010 355 2571	12.43	3.100 682	9.40	396
34	61.995 151	5999.523 013	.000 166 6799	.016 130	96.774 069	.010 333 3466	12.41	3.216 005	9.46	408
35	69.996 145	6786.506 080	.000 147 3512	.014 287	96.955 426	.010 314 0179	12.38	3.331 888	9.52	420
36	79.029 735	7675.055 918	.000 130 2922	.012 653	97.116 053	.010 296 9589	12.36	3.448 286	9.58	432
37	89.229 186	8678.280 570	.000 115 2302	.011 207	97.258 318	.010 281 8969	12.34	3.565 162	9.64	444
38	100.744 961	9810.979 783	.000 101 9266	.009 926	97.384 322	.010 268 5933	12.33	3.682 479	9.69	456
39	113.746 944	11089.863 336	.000 090 1724	.008 791	97.495 923	.010 256 8391	12.31	3.800 201	9.74	468
40	128.426 942	12533.797 546	.000 079 7843	.007 787	97.594 768	.010 246 4509	12.30	3.918 296	9.80	480
41	145.001 516	14164.083 585	.000 070 6011	.006 896	97.682 313	.010 237 2678	12.29	4.036 736	9.85	492
42	163.715 179	16004.771 720	.000 062 4814	.006 108	97.759 852	.010 229 1480	12.28	4.155 491	9.89	504
43	184.843 997	18083.016 108	.000 055 3005	.005 410	97.828 528	.010 221 9672	12.27	4.274 535	9.94	516
44	208.699 666	20429.475 377	.000 048 9489	.004 792	97.889 353	.010 215 6155	12.26	4.393 845	9.99	528
45	235.634 110	23078.764 909	.000 043 3299	.004 244	97.943 226	.010 209 9965	12.26	4.513 398	10.03	540
46	266.044 669	26069.967 490	.000 038 3583	.003 759	97.990 941	.010 205 0250	12.25	4.633 174	10.07	552
47	300.379 967	29447.209 871	.000 033 9591	.003 329	98.033 202	.010 200 6257	12.25	4.753 153	10.11	564
48	339.146 523	33260.313 725	.000 030 0659	.002 949	98.070 632	.010 196 7325	12.24	4.873 318	10.15	576
49	382.916 228	37565.530 636	.000 026 6201	.002 612	98.103 783	.010 193 2868	12.24	4.993 653	10.19	588
50	432.334 781	42426.371 924	.000 023 5702	.002 313	98.133 145	.010 190 2369	12.23	5.114 142	10.23	600

Effective Rate is 12.91 %   Annual Percentage Rate is 12.20 %

MONTHLY COMPOUND INTEREST AND ANNUITY

Amount Of 1	Amount Of 1 Per Period	Sinking Fund Payment	Present Worth Of 1	Present Worth of 1 Per Period	Periodic Payment To Amortize 1	Constant Annual Percent	Total Interest	Annual Add On Rate
What a single $ 1 deposit grows to in the future. The deposit is made at the beginning of the first period.	What a series of $ 1 deposits grow to in the future. A deposit is made at the end of each period.	The amount to be deposited at the end of each period that grows to $ 1 in the future.	What $ 1 to be paid in the future is worth today. Value today of a single $ 1 payment tomorrow.	What $ 1 to be paid at the end of each period is worth today. Value today of a series of $ 1 payments tomorrow.	The mortgage payment to amortize a loan of $ 1. An annuity certain, payable at the end of each period, worth $ 1 today.	The annual payment, including interest and principal, to amortize completely a loan of $ 100.	The total interest paid over the term on a loan of $1. The loan is amortized by regular periodic payments.	The average annual interest rate on a loan that is completely amortized by regular periodic payments.
$S = (1+i)^n$	$S\overline{n}| = \dfrac{(1+i)^n - 1}{i}$	$\dfrac{1}{S\overline{n}|} = \dfrac{i}{(1+i)^n - 1}$	$V^n = \dfrac{1}{(1+i)^n}$	$A\overline{n}| = \dfrac{1 - V^n}{i}$	$\dfrac{1}{A\overline{n}|} = \dfrac{i}{1 - V^n}$			

YEAR / **PERIODS**

YEAR	Amount Of 1	Amount Of 1 Per Period	Sinking Fund Payment	Present Worth Of 1	Present Worth of 1 Per Period	Periodic Payment To Amortize 1	Constant Annual Percent	Total Interest	Annual Add On Rate	PERIODS
	1.010 208	1.000 000	1.000 000 0000	.989 895	.989 895	1.010 208 3333	1212.25	.010 208	12.25	1
	1.020 521	2.010 208	.497 460 8768	.979 892	1.969 787	.507 669 2101	609.21	.015 338	9.20	2
	1.030 939	3.030 729	.329 953 5955	.969 990	2.939 776	.340 161 9289	408.20	.020 486	8.19	3
	1.041 463	4.061 668	.246 204 2746	.960 188	3.899 964	.256 412 6079	307.70	.025 650	7.70	4
	1.052 094	5.103 131	.195 958 1375	.950 485	4.850 449	.206 166 4708	247.40	.030 832	7.40	5
	1.062 835	6.155 225	.162 463 5921	.940 880	5.791 329	.172 671 9254	207.21	.036 032	7.21	6
	1.073 684	7.218 060	.138 541 3845	.931 372	6.722 702	.148 749 7178	178.50	.041 248	7.07	7
	1.084 645	8.291 744	.120 601 8877	.921 961	7.644 663	.130 810 2211	156.98	.046 482	6.97	8
	1.095 717	9.376 389	.106 650 8645	.912 644	8.557 307	.116 859 1979	140.24	.051 733	6.90	9
	1.106 903	10.472 106	.095 491 7726	.903 422	9.460 728	.105 700 1059	126.85	.057 001	6.84	10
	1.118 202	11.579 009	.086 363 1758	.894 292	10.355 021	.096 571 5091	115.89	.062 287	6.79	11
	1.129 617	12.697 212	.078 757 4500	.885 256	11.240 276	.088 965 7833	106.76	.067 589	6.76	12
1	1.129 617	12.697 212	.078 757 4500	.885 256	11.240 276	.088 965 7833	106.76	.067 589	6.76	12
2	1.276 035	27.040 202	.036 981 9721	.783 677	21.190 793	.047 190 3054	56.63	.132 567	6.63	24
3	1.441 432	43.242 293	.023 125 5079	.693 755	29.999 543	.033 333 8413	40.01	.200 018	6.67	36
4	1.628 266	61.544 457	.016 248 4169	.614 150	37.797 537	.026 456 7503	31.75	.269 924	6.75	48
5	1.839 318	82.218 899	.012 162 6537	.543 680	44.700 755	.022 370 9870	26.85	.342 259	6.85	60
6	2.077 725	105.573 108	.009 472 1091	.481 296	50.811 866	.019 680 4425	23.62	.416 992	6.95	72
7	2.347 035	131.954 428	.007 578 3740	.426 070	56.221 761	.017 786 7073	21.35	.494 083	7.06	84
8	2.651 251	161.755 225	.006 182 1805	.377 180	61.010 900	.016 390 5138	19.67	.573 489	7.17	96
9	2.994 899	195.418 723	.005 117 2169	.333 901	65.250 512	.015 325 5503	18.40	.655 159	7.28	108
10	3.383 090	233.445 595	.004 283 6533	.295 588	69.003 652	.014 491 9867	17.40	.739 038	7.39	120
11	3.821 598	276.401 410	.003 617 9266	.261 671	72.326 139	.013 826 2599	16.60	.825 066	7.50	132
12	4.316 943	324.925 044	.003 077 6329	.231 645	75.267 390	.013 285 9662	15.95	.913 179	7.61	144
13	4.876 494	379.738 185	.002 633 3933	.205 065	77.871 148	.012 841 7267	15.42	1.003 309	7.72	156
14	5.508 572	441.656 060	.002 264 2053	.181 535	80.176 140	.012 472 5387	14.97	1.095 386	7.82	168
15	6.222 579	511.599 567	.001 954 6537	.160 705	82.216 646	.012 162 9871	14.60	1.189 338	7.93	180
16	7.029 133	590.608 968	.001 693 1677	.142 265	84.023 015	.011 901 5010	14.29	1.285 088	8.03	192
17	7.940 231	679.859 359	.001 470 8925	.125 941	85.622 114	.011 679 2258	14.02	1.382 562	8.13	204
18	8.969 423	780.678 151	.001 280 9376	.111 490	87.037 725	.011 489 2709	13.79	1.481 683	8.23	216
19	10.132 016	894.564 809	.001 117 8620	.098 697	88.290 902	.011 326 1953	13.60	1.582 373	8.33	228
20	11.445 301	1023.213 156	.000 977 3135	.087 372	89.400 284	.011 185 6468	13.43	1.684 555	8.42	240
21	12.928 811	1168.536 564	.000 855 7713	.077 347	90.382 370	.011 064 1046	13.28	1.788 154	8.52	252
22	14.604 609	1332.696 408	.000 750 3584	.068 472	91.251 768	.010 958 6918	13.16	1.893 095	8.60	264
23	16.497 620	1518.134 220	.000 658 7033	.060 615	92.021 407	.010 867 0366	13.05	1.999 302	8.69	276
24	18.635 998	1727.607 992	.000 578 8350	.053 660	92.702 734	.010 787 1683	12.95	2.106 704	8.78	288
25	21.051 547	1964.233 204	.000 509 1045	.047 502	93.305 883	.010 717 4379	12.87	2.215 231	8.86	300
26	23.780 193	2231.529 152	.000 448 1232	.042 052	93.839 823	.010 656 4565	12.79	2.324 814	8.94	312
27	26.862 519	2533.471 298	.000 394 7153	.037 227	94.312 497	.010 603 0487	12.73	2.435 388	9.02	324
28	30.344 369	2874.550 389	.000 347 8805	.032 955	94.730 934	.010 556 2138	12.67	2.546 888	9.10	336
29	34.277 526	3259.839 255	.000 306 7636	.029 174	95.101 358	.010 515 0969	12.62	2.659 254	9.17	348
30	38.720 488	3695.068 249	.000 270 6310	.025 826	95.429 278	.010 478 9643	12.58	2.772 427	9.24	360
31	43.739 336	4186.710 480	.000 238 8510	.022 863	95.719 571	.010 447 1843	12.54	2.886 353	9.31	372
32	49.408 714	4742.078 082	.000 210 8780	.020 239	95.976 554	.010 419 2113	12.51	3.000 977	9.38	384
33	55.812 941	5369.430 971	.000 186 2395	.017 917	96.204 050	.010 394 5728	12.48	3.116 251	9.44	396
34	63.047 268	6078.099 689	.000 164 5251	.015 861	96.405 442	.010 372 8584	12.45	3.232 126	9.51	408
35	71.219 289	6878.624 182	.000 145 3779	.014 041	96.583 725	.010 353 7112	12.43	3.348 559	9.57	420
36	80.450 545	7782.910 551	.000 128 4866	.012 430	96.741 551	.010 336 8200	12.41	3.465 506	9.63	432
37	90.878 333	8804.408 140	.000 113 5795	.011 004	96.881 268	.010 321 9128	12.39	3.582 929	9.68	444
38	102.657 743	9958.309 556	.000 100 4186	.009 741	97.004 953	.010 308 7520	12.38	3.700 791	9.74	456
39	115.963 970	11261.776 637	.000 088 7959	.008 623	97.114 446	.010 297 1293	12.36	3.819 056	9.79	468
40	130.994 914	12734.195 689	.000 078 5287	.007 634	97.211 375	.010 286 8620	12.35	3.937 694	9.84	480
41	147.974 130	14397.465 822	.000 069 4567	.006 758	97.297 182	.010 277 7900	12.34	4.056 673	9.89	492
42	167.154 147	16276.324 652	.000 061 4389	.005 983	97.373 143	.010 269 7723	12.33	4.175 965	9.94	504
43	188.820 228	18398.716 217	.000 054 3516	.005 296	97.440 388	.010 262 6850	12.32	4.295 545	9.99	516
44	213.294 609	20796.206 589	.000 048 0857	.004 688	97.499 917	.010 256 4190	12.31	4.415 389	10.03	528
45	240.941 295	23504.453 351	.000 042 5451	.004 150	97.552 615	.010 250 8785	12.31	4.535 474	10.08	540
46	272.171 471	26563.735 930	.000 037 6453	.003 674	97.599 267	.010 245 9786	12.30	4.655 780	10.12	552
47	307.449 621	30019.554 662	.000 033 3116	.003 253	97.640 565	.010 241 6450	12.29	4.776 288	10.16	564
48	347.300 431	33923.307 521	.000 029 4783	.002 879	97.677 125	.010 237 8116	12.29	4.896 979	10.20	576
49	392.316 599	38333.054 549	.000 026 0871	.002 549	97.709 489	.010 234 4205	12.29	5.017 839	10.24	588
50	443.167 643	43314.381 378	.000 023 0870	.002 256	97.738 140	.010 231 4204	12.28	5.138 852	10.28	600

MONTHLY COMPOUND INTEREST AND ANNUITY

	Amount Of 1	Amount Of 1 Per Period	Sinking Fund Payment	Present Worth Of 1	Present Worth of 1 Per Period	Periodic Payment To Amortize 1	Constant Annual Percent	Total Interest	Annual Add On Rate	
	What a single $ 1 deposit grows to in the future. The deposit is made at the beginning of the first period.	What a series of $ 1 deposits grow to in the future. A deposit is made at the end of each period.	The amount to be deposited at the end of each period that grows to $ 1 in the future.	What $ 1 to be paid in the future is worth today. Value today of a single $ 1 payment tomorrow.	What $ 1 to be paid at the end of each period is worth today. Value today of a series of $ 1 payments tomorrow.	The mortgage payment to amortize a loan of $ 1. An annuity certain, payable at the end of each period, worth $ 1 today.	The annual payment, including interest and principal, to amortize completely a loan of $ 100.	The total interest paid over the term on a loan of $1. The loan is amortized by regular periodic payments.	The average annual interest rate on a loan that is completely amortized by regular periodic payments.	
	$S = (1+i)^n$	$S\overline{n}| = \dfrac{(1+i)^n - 1}{i}$	$\dfrac{1}{S\overline{n}|} = \dfrac{i}{(1+i)^n - 1}$	$V^n = \dfrac{1}{(1+i)^n}$	$A\overline{n}| = \dfrac{1-V^n}{i}$	$\dfrac{1}{A\overline{n}|} = \dfrac{i}{1-V^n}$				

YEAR										PERIODS
	1.010 250	1.000 000	1.000 000 0000	.989 854	.989 854	1.010 250 0000	1212.30	.010 250	12.30	1
	1.020 605	2.010 250	.497 450 5659	.979 811	1.969 665	.507 700 5659	609.25	.015 401	9.24	2
	1.031 066	3.030 855	.329 939 8946	.969 870	2.939 535	.340 189 8946	408.23	.020 570	8.23	3
	1.041 635	4.061 921	.246 188 9139	.960 029	3.899 564	.256 438 9139	307.73	.025 756	7.73	4
	1.052 311	5.103 556	.195 941 8092	.950 289	4.849 853	.206 191 8092	247.44	.030 959	7.43	5
	1.063 098	6.155 867	.162 446 6422	.940 647	5.790 501	.172 696 6422	207.24	.036 180	7.24	6
	1.073 994	7.218 965	.138 524 0107	.931 104	6.721 604	.148 774 0107	178.53	.041 418	7.10	7
	1.085 003	8.292 960	.120 584 2136	.921 657	7.643 261	.130 834 2136	157.01	.046 674	7.00	8
	1.096 124	9.377 962	.106 632 9725	.912 305	8.555 566	.116 882 9725	140.26	.051 947	6.93	9
	1.107 359	10.474 086	.095 473 7203	.903 049	9.458 615	.105 723 7203	126.87	.057 237	6.87	10
	1.118 710	11.581 446	.086 345 0051	.893 887	10.352 502	.096 595 0051	115.92	.062 545	6.82	11
	1.130 177	12.700 156	.078 739 1924	.884 817	11.237 320	.088 989 1924	106.79	.067 870	6.79	12
1	1.130 177	12.700 156	.078 739 1924	.884 817	11.237 320	.088 989 1924	106.79	.067 870	6.79	12
2	1.277 299	27.053 574	.036 963 6924	.782 902	21.180 296	.047 213 6924	56.66	.133 129	6.66	24
3	1.443 574	43.275 472	.023 107 7779	.692 725	29.978 016	.033 357 7779	40.03	.200 880	6.70	36
4	1.631 493	61.609 082	.016 231 3733	.612 935	37.762 392	.026 481 3733	31.78	.271 106	6.78	48
5	1.843 875	82.329 298	.012 146 3444	.542 336	44.650 144	.022 396 3444	26.88	.343 781	6.88	60
6	2.083 905	105.746 801	.009 456 5508	.479 868	50.744 547	.019 706 5508	23.65	.418 872	6.98	72
7	2.355 180	132.212 715	.007 563 5690	.424 596	56.136 982	.017 813 5690	21.38	.496 340	7.09	84
8	2.661 770	162.123 872	.006 168 1231	.375 690	60.908 302	.016 418 1231	19.71	.576 140	7.20	96
9	3.008 270	195.928 761	.005 103 8959	.332 417	65.130 050	.015 353 8959	18.43	.658 221	7.31	108
10	3.399 876	234.134 256	.004 271 0538	.294 128	68.865 526	.014 521 0538	17.43	.742 526	7.43	120
11	3.842 460	277.313 212	.003 606 0309	.260 250	72.170 740	.013 856 0309	16.63	.828 996	7.54	132
12	4.342 659	326.113 058	.003 066 4212	.230 274	75.095 251	.013 316 4212	15.98	.917 565	7.65	144
13	4.907 971	381.265 501	.002 622 8442	.203 750	77.682 910	.012 872 8442	15.45	1.008 164	7.76	156
14	5.546 874	443.597 501	.002 254 2958	.180 282	79.972 516	.012 504 2958	15.01	1.100 722	7.86	168
15	6.268 948	514.043 670	.001 945 3600	.159 516	81.998 399	.012 195 3600	14.64	1.195 165	7.97	180
16	7.085 018	593.660 280	.001 684 4651	.141 143	83.790 936	.011 934 4651	14.33	1.291 417	8.07	192
17	8.007 321	683.641 110	.001 462 7558	.124 886	85.377 004	.011 712 7558	14.06	1.389 402	8.17	204
18	9.049 687	785.335 338	.001 273 3414	.110 501	86.780 385	.011 523 3414	13.83	1.489 042	8.27	216
19	10.227 745	900.267 774	.001 110 7806	.097 773	88.022 120	.011 360 7806	13.64	1.590 258	8.37	228
20	11.559 158	1030.161 724	.000 970 7214	.086 511	89.120 830	.011 220 7214	13.47	1.692 973	8.46	240
21	13.063 889	1176.964 825	.000 849 6431	.076 547	90.092 987	.011 099 6431	13.32	1.797 110	8.56	252
22	14.764 502	1342.878 255	.000 744 6691	.067 730	90.953 169	.010 994 6691	13.20	1.902 593	8.65	264
23	16.686 495	1530.389 730	.000 653 4283	.059 929	91.714 273	.010 903 4283	13.09	2.009 346	8.74	276
24	18.858 686	1742.310 810	.000 573 9504	.053 026	92.387 711	.010 823 9504	12.99	2.117 298	8.82	288
25	21.313 645	1981.819 056	.000 504 5869	.046 918	92.983 581	.010 754 5869	12.91	2.226 376	8.91	300
26	24.088 183	2252.505 669	.000 443 9500	.041 514	93.510 816	.010 693 9500	12.84	2.336 512	8.99	312
27	27.223 901	2558.429 344	.000 390 8648	.036 732	93.977 324	.010 640 8648	12.77	2.447 640	9.07	324
28	30.767 815	2904.177 121	.000 344 3316	.032 501	94.390 098	.010 594 3316	12.72	2.559 695	9.14	336
29	34.773 065	3294.933 167	.000 303 4963	.028 758	94.755 328	.010 553 4963	12.67	2.672 617	9.22	348
30	39.299 704	3736.556 505	.000 267 6261	.025 445	95.078 489	.010 517 6261	12.63	2.786 345	9.29	360
31	44.415 606	4235.668 865	.000 236 0902	.022 515	95.364 428	.010 486 0902	12.59	2.900 826	9.36	372
32	50.197 478	4799.753 974	.000 208 3440	.019 921	95.617 432	.010 458 3440	12.56	3.016 004	9.43	384
33	56.732 015	5437.269 761	.000 183 9158	.017 627	95.841 294	.010 433 9158	12.53	3.131 831	9.49	396
34	64.117 196	6157.775 183	.000 162 3963	.015 596	96.039 372	.010 412 3963	12.50	3.248 258	9.55	408
35	72.463 754	6972.073 547	.000 143 4294	.013 800	96.214 634	.010 393 4294	12.48	3.365 240	9.61	420
36	81.896 839	7892.374 501	.000 126 7046	.012 210	96.369 709	.010 376 7046	12.46	3.482 736	9.67	432
37	92.557 890	8932.477 100	.000 111 9510	.010 804	96.506 922	.010 361 9510	12.44	3.600 706	9.73	444
38	104.606 761	10107.976 714	.000 098 9318	.009 560	96.628 331	.010 348 9318	12.42	3.719 113	9.79	456
39	118.224 113	11436.498 865	.000 087 4393	.008 459	96.735 755	.010 337 4393	12.41	3.837 922	9.84	468
40	133.614 126	12937.963 508	.000 077 2919	.007 484	96.830 806	.010 327 2919	12.40	3.957 100	9.89	480
41	151.007 558	14634.883 705	.000 068 3299	.006 622	96.914 909	.010 318 3299	12.39	4.076 618	9.94	492
42	170.665 208	16552.703 197	.000 060 4131	.005 859	96.989 324	.010 310 4131	12.38	4.196 448	9.99	504
43	192.881 823	18720.177 902	.000 053 4183	.005 185	97.055 169	.010 303 4183	12.37	4.316 564	10.04	516
44	217.990 523	21169.807 084	.000 047 2371	.004 587	97.113 429	.010 297 2371	12.36	4.436 941	10.08	528
45	246.367 787	23938.320 653	.000 041 7740	.004 059	97.164 978	.010 291 7740	12.36	4.557 558	10.13	540
46	278.439 106	27067.229 893	.000 036 9450	.003 591	97.210 590	.010 286 9450	12.35	4.678 394	10.17	552
47	314.685 361	30603.449 886	.000 032 6761	.003 178	97.250 949	.010 282 6761	12.34	4.799 429	10.21	564
48	355.650 030	34600.002 958	.000 028 9017	.002 812	97.286 658	.010 278 9017	12.34	4.920 647	10.25	576
49	401.947 340	39116.813 703	.000 025 5645	.002 488	97.318 255	.010 275 5645	12.34	5.042 032	10.29	588
50	454.271 477	44221.607 493	.000 022 6134	.002 201	97.346 212	.010 272 6134	12.33	5.163 568	10.33	600

Effective Rate is 13.02 %

Annual Percentage Rate is 12.30 %

MONTHLY COMPOUND INTEREST AND ANNUITY

	Amount Of 1	Amount Of 1 Per Period	Sinking Fund Payment	Present Worth Of 1	Present Worth of 1 Per Period	Periodic Payment To Amortize 1	Constant Annual Percent	Total Interest	Annual Add On Rate	
	What a single $ 1 deposit grows to in the future. The deposit is made at the beginning of the first period.	What a series of $ 1 deposits grow to in the future. A deposit is made at the end of each period.	The amount to be deposited at the end of each period that grows to $ 1 in the future.	What $ 1 to be paid in the future is worth today. Value today of a single $ 1 payment tomorrow.	What $ 1 to be paid at the end of each period is worth today. Value today of a series of $ 1 payments tomorrow.	The mortgage payment to amortize a loan of $ 1. An annuity certain, payable at the end of each period, worth $ 1 today.	The annual payment, including interest and principal, to amortize completely a loan of $ 100.	The total interest paid over the term on a loan of $1. The loan is amortized by regular periodic payments.	The average annual interest rate on a loan that is completely amortized by regular periodic payments.	
	$S = (1+i)^n$	$S_{\overline{n}|} = \dfrac{(1+i)^n - 1}{i}$	$\dfrac{1}{S_{\overline{n}|}} = \dfrac{i}{(1+i)^n - 1}$	$V^n = \dfrac{1}{(1+i)^n}$	$A_{\overline{n}|} = \dfrac{1 - V^n}{i}$	$\dfrac{1}{A_{\overline{n}|}} = \dfrac{i}{1 - V^n}$				

YEAR										PERIODS
	1.010 292	1.000 000	1.000 000 0000	.989 813	.989 813	1.010 291 6667	1212.35	.010 292	12.35	1
	1.020 689	2.010 292	.497 440 2554	.979 730	1.969 543	.507 731 9220	609.28	.015 464	9.28	2
	1.031 194	3.030 981	.329 926 1945	.969 750	2.939 293	.340 217 8612	408.27	.020 654	8.26	3
	1.041 807	4.062 175	.246 173 5544	.959 871	3.899 164	.256 465 2210	307.76	.025 861	7.76	4
	1.052 528	5.103 981	.195 925 4822	.950 093	4.849 257	.206 217 1489	247.47	.031 086	7.46	5
	1.063 361	6.156 510	.162 429 6939	.940 415	5.789 672	.172 721 3605	207.27	.036 328	7.27	6
	1.074 305	7.219 871	.138 506 6388	.930 835	6.720 507	.148 798 3054	178.56	.041 588	7.13	7
	1.085 361	8.294 175	.120 566 5417	.921 353	7.641 859	.130 858 2084	157.03	.046 866	7.03	8
	1.096 531	9.379 536	.106 615 0829	.911 967	8.553 826	.116 906 7496	140.29	.052 161	6.95	9
	1.107 816	10.476 067	.095 455 6707	.902 677	9.456 503	.105 747 3374	126.90	.057 473	6.90	10
	1.119 217	11.583 883	.086 326 8375	.893 481	10.349 984	.096 618 5042	115.95	.062 804	6.85	11
	1.130 736	12.703 101	.078 720 9382	.884 380	11.234 364	.089 012 6049	106.82	.068 151	6.82	12
1	1.130 736	12.703 101	.078 720 9382	.884 380	11.234 364	.089 012 6049	106.82	.068 151	6.82	12
2	1.278 564	27.066 955	.036 945 4195	.782 127	21.169 807	.047 237 0862	56.69	.133 690	6.68	24
3	1.445 719	43.308 683	.023 090 0580	.691 698	29.956 511	.033 381 7246	40.06	.201 742	6.72	36
4	1.634 726	61.673 791	.016 214 3430	.611 723	37.727 293	.026 506 0097	31.81	.272 288	6.81	48
5	1.848 444	82.439 881	.012 130 0515	.540 996	44.599 615	.022 421 7181	26.91	.345 303	6.91	60
6	2.090 102	105.920 848	.009 441 0120	.478 446	50.677 357	.019 732 6787	23.68	.420 753	7.01	72
7	2.363 354	132.471 625	.007 548 7864	.423 128	56.052 388	.017 840 4531	21.41	.498 598	7.12	84
8	2.672 329	162.493 546	.006 154 0906	.374 205	60.805 957	.016 445 7572	19.74	.578 793	7.23	96
9	3.021 699	196.440 416	.005 090 6021	.330 940	65.009 916	.015 382 2688	18.46	.661 285	7.35	108
10	3.416 744	234.825 366	.004 258 4837	.292 676	68.727 812	.014 550 1504	17.47	.746 018	7.46	120
11	3.863 436	278.228 614	.003 594 1666	.258 837	72.015 844	.013 885 8333	16.67	.832 930	7.57	132
12	4.368 527	327.306 232	.003 055 2428	.228 910	74.923 712	.013 346 9094	16.02	.921 955	7.68	144
13	4.939 651	382.800 065	.002 612 3298	.202 443	77.495 372	.012 903 9964	15.49	1.013 023	7.79	156
14	5.585 441	445.548 945	.002 244 4223	.179 037	79.769 695	.012 536 0890	15.05	1.106 063	7.90	168
15	6.315 660	516.501 367	.001 936 1033	.158 337	81.781 061	.012 227 7700	14.68	1.200 999	8.01	180
16	7.141 345	596.729 830	.001 675 8003	.140 030	83.559 872	.011 967 4669	14.37	1.297 754	8.11	192
17	8.074 976	687.447 048	.001 454 6575	.123 839	85.133 016	.011 746 3242	14.10	1.396 250	8.21	204
18	9.130 667	790.024 279	.001 265 7839	.109 521	86.524 272	.011 557 4506	13.87	1.496 409	8.31	216
19	10.324 374	906.012 055	.001 103 7381	.096 858	87.754 672	.011 395 4047	13.68	1.598 152	8.41	228
20	11.674 142	1037.163 617	.000 964 1680	.085 659	88.842 811	.011 255 8347	13.51	1.701 400	8.51	240
21	13.200 374	1185.461 421	.000 843 5534	.075 755	89.805 140	.011 135 2201	13.37	1.806 075	8.60	252
22	14.926 139	1353.147 098	.000 739 0180	.066 997	90.656 204	.011 030 6846	13.24	1.912 101	8.69	264
23	16.877 524	1542.755 342	.000 648 1909	.059 250	91.408 868	.010 939 8576	13.13	2.019 401	8.78	276
24	19.084 025	1757.152 224	.000 569 1027	.052 400	92.074 509	.010 860 7693	13.04	2.127 902	8.87	288
25	21.578 996	1999.578 514	.000 500 1054	.046 341	92.663 188	.010 791 7721	12.96	2.237 532	8.95	300
26	24.400 149	2273.698 666	.000 439 8120	.040 983	93.183 803	.010 731 4787	12.88	2.348 221	9.03	312
27	27.590 129	2583.656 211	.000 387 0484	.036 245	93.644 225	.010 678 7151	12.82	2.459 904	9.11	324
28	31.197 154	2934.136 389	.000 340 8158	.032 054	94.051 413	.010 632 4825	12.76	2.572 514	9.19	336
29	35.275 747	3330.436 972	.000 300 2609	.028 348	94.411 522	.010 591 9276	12.72	2.685 991	9.26	348
30	39.887 560	3778.548 338	.000 264 6519	.025 070	94.729 995	.010 556 3186	12.67	2.800 275	9.33	360
31	45.102 303	4285.244 026	.000 233 3589	.022 172	95.011 645	.010 525 0256	12.64	2.915 310	9.40	372
32	50.998 801	4858.183 121	.000 205 8383	.019 608	95.260 732	.010 497 5049	12.60	3.031 042	9.47	384
33	57.666 185	5506.026 026	.000 181 6192	.017 341	95.481 018	.010 473 2859	12.57	3.147 421	9.54	396
34	65.205 235	6238.565 371	.000 160 2933	.015 336	95.675 836	.010 451 9599	12.55	3.264 400	9.60	408
35	73.729 912	7066.874 036	.000 141 5053	.013 563	95.848 128	.010 433 1719	12.52	3.381 932	9.66	420
36	83.369 071	8003.472 527	.000 124 9458	.011 995	96.000 500	.010 416 6124	12.50	3.499 977	9.72	432
37	94.268 417	9062.518 231	.000 110 3446	.010 608	96.135 254	.010 402 0113	12.49	3.618 493	9.78	444
38	106.592 700	10260.019 415	.000 097 4657	.009 382	96.254 429	.010 389 1324	12.47	3.737 444	9.84	456
39	120.528 211	11614.077 207	.000 086 1024	.008 297	96.359 824	.010 377 7691	12.46	3.856 796	9.89	468
40	136.285 597	13145.159 204	.000 076 0736	.007 338	96.453 033	.010 367 7403	12.45	3.976 515	9.94	480
41	154.103 041	14876.408 854	.000 067 2205	.006 489	96.535 466	.010 358 8872	12.44	4.096 572	9.99	492
42	174.249 868	16833.995 293	.000 059 4036	.005 739	96.608 367	.010 351 0703	12.43	4.216 939	10.04	504
43	197.030 612	19047.508 904	.000 052 5003	.005 075	96.672 840	.010 344 1670	12.42	4.337 590	10.09	516
44	222.789 622	21550.408 601	.000 046 4028	.004 489	96.729 859	.010 338 0695	12.41	4.458 501	10.13	528
45	251.916 263	24380.527 587	.000 041 0163	.003 970	96.780 284	.010 332 6830	12.40	4.579 649	10.18	540
46	284.850 807	27580.645 227	.000 036 2573	.003 511	96.824 880	.010 327 9240	12.40	4.701 014	10.22	552
47	322.091 084	31199.133 694	.000 032 0522	.003 105	96.864 319	.010 323 7188	12.39	4.822 577	10.26	564
48	364.200 009	35290.689 150	.000 028 3361	.002 746	96.899 199	.010 320 0028	12.39	4.944 322	10.30	576
49	411.814 090	39917.158 515	.000 025 0519	.002 428	96.930 046	.010 316 7186	12.39	5.066 231	10.34	588
50	465.653 048	45148.474 338	.000 022 1491	.002 148	96.957 326	.010 313 8158	12.38	5.188 289	10.38	600

	Amount Of 1	Amount Of 1 Per Period	Sinking Fund Payment	Present Worth Of 1	Present Worth of 1 Per Period	Periodic Payment To Amortize 1	Constant Annual Percent	Total Interest	Annual Add On Rate	
	What a single $ 1 deposit grows to in the future. The deposit is made at the beginning of the first period.	What a series of $ 1 deposits grow to in the future. A deposit is made at the end of each period.	The amount to be deposited at the end of each period that grows to $ 1 in the future.	What $ 1 to be paid in the future is worth today. Value today of a single $ 1 payment tomorrow.	What $ 1 to be paid at the end of each period is worth today. Value today of a series of $ 1 payments tomorrow.	The mortgage payment to amortize a loan of $ 1. An annuity certain, payable at the end of each period, worth $ 1 today.	The annual payment, including interest and principal, to amortize completely a loan of $ 100.	The total interest paid over the term on a loan of $1. The loan is amortized by regular periodic payments.	The average annual interest rate on a loan that is completely amortized by regular periodic payments.	
	$S = (1+i)^n$	$S\overline{n}| = \dfrac{(1+i)^n - 1}{i}$	$\dfrac{1}{S\overline{n}|} = \dfrac{i}{(1+i)^n - 1}$	$V^n = \dfrac{1}{(1+i)^n}$	$A\overline{n}| = \dfrac{1-V^n}{i}$	$\dfrac{1}{A\overline{n}|} = \dfrac{i}{1-V^n}$				

YEAR										PERIODS
	1.010 313	1.000 000	1.000 000 0000	.989 793	.989 793	1.010 312 5000	1212.38	.010 313	12.38	1
	1.020 731	2.010 312	.497 435 1003	.979 690	1.969 482	.507 747 6003	609.30	.015 495	9.30	2
	1.031 258	3.031 044	.329 919 3447	.969 690	2.939 172	.340 231 8447	408.28	.020 696	8.28	3
	1.041 892	4.062 301	.246 165 8750	.959 792	3.898 964	.256 478 3750	307.78	.025 913	7.77	4
	1.052 637	5.104 194	.195 917 3193	.949 995	4.848 959	.206 229 8193	247.48	.031 149	7.48	5
	1.063 492	6.156 831	.162 421 2204	.940 298	5.789 258	.172 733 7204	207.29	.036 402	7.28	6
	1.074 460	7.220 323	.138 497 9536	.930 700	6.719 958	.148 810 4536	178.58	.041 673	7.14	7
	1.085 540	8.294 783	.120 557 7066	.921 201	7.641 159	.130 870 2066	157.05	.046 962	7.04	8
	1.096 735	9.380 323	.106 606 1391	.911 798	8.552 956	.116 918 6391	140.31	.052 268	6.97	9
	1.108 045	10.477 057	.095 446 6470	.902 491	9.455 447	.105 759 1470	126.92	.057 591	6.91	10
	1.119 471	11.585 102	.086 317 7549	.893 279	10.348 726	.096 630 2549	115.96	.062 933	6.87	11
	1.131 016	12.704 573	.078 711 8124	.884 161	11.232 887	.089 024 3124	106.83	.068 292	6.83	12
1	1.131 016	12.704 573	.078 711 8124	.884 161	11.232 887	.089 024 3124	106.83	.068 292	6.83	12
2	1.279 197	27.073 648	.036 936 2856	.781 740	21.164 565	.047 248 7856	56.70	.133 971	6.70	24
3	1.446 792	43.325 300	.023 081 2018	.691 184	29.945 767	.033 393 7018	40.08	.202 173	6.74	36
4	1.636 345	61.706 178	.016 205 8329	.611 118	37.709 761	.026 518 3329	31.83	.272 880	6.82	48
5	1.850 732	82.495 242	.012 121 9112	.540 327	44.574 381	.022 434 4112	26.93	.346 065	6.92	60
6	2.093 208	106.008 005	.009 433 2499	.477 736	50.643 810	.019 745 7499	23.70	.421 694	7.03	72
7	2.367 451	132.601 314	.007 541 4034	.422 395	56.010 161	.017 853 9034	21.43	.499 728	7.14	84
8	2.677 625	162.678 770	.006 147 0836	.373 465	60.754 878	.016 459 5836	19.76	.580 120	7.25	96
9	3.028 436	196.696 851	.005 083 9655	.330 203	64.949 972	.015 396 4655	18.48	.662 818	7.36	108
10	3.425 210	235.171 842	.004 252 2098	.291 953	68.659 109	.014 564 7098	17.48	.747 765	7.48	120
11	3.873 967	278.687 669	.003 588 2463	.258 133	71.938 584	.013 900 7463	16.69	.834 899	7.59	132
12	4.381 518	327.904 762	.003 049 6660	.228 231	74.838 166	.013 362 1660	16.04	.924 152	7.70	144
13	4.955 566	383.570 077	.002 607 0855	.201 793	77.401 864	.012 919 5855	15.51	1.015 455	7.81	156
14	5.604 824	446.528 435	.002 239 4990	.178 418	79.668 585	.012 551 9990	15.07	1.108 736	7.92	168
15	6.339 146	517.735 339	.001 931 4888	.157 750	81.672 731	.012 243 9888	14.70	1.203 918	8.03	180
16	7.169 675	598.271 481	.001 671 4820	.139 476	83.444 718	.011 983 9820	14.39	1.300 925	8.13	192
17	8.109 016	689.359 138	.001 450 6227	.123 320	85.011 440	.011 763 1227	14.12	1.399 677	8.23	204
18	9.171 426	792.380 729	.001 262 0196	.109 034	86.396 674	.011 574 5196	13.89	1.500 096	8.33	216
19	10.373 029	908.899 787	.001 100 2313	.096 404	87.621 444	.011 412 7313	13.70	1.602 103	8.43	228
20	11.732 061	1040.684 697	.000 960 9058	.085 237	88.704 338	.011 273 4058	13.53	1.705 617	8.53	240
21	13.269 148	1189.735 526	.000 840 5229	.075 363	89.661 790	.011 153 0229	13.39	1.810 562	8.62	252
22	15.007 617	1358.314 386	.000 736 2066	.066 633	90.508 332	.011 048 7066	13.26	1.916 859	8.71	264
23	16.973 854	1548.979 760	.000 645 5862	.058 914	91.226 811	.010 958 0862	13.15	2.024 432	8.80	276
24	19.197 699	1764.625 331	.000 566 6925	.052 090	91.918 587	.010 879 1925	13.06	2.133 207	8.89	288
25	21.712 903	2008.523 904	.000 497 8781	.046 054	92.503 703	.010 810 3781	12.98	2.243 113	8.97	300
26	24.557 639	2284.377 072	.000 437 7561	.040 721	93.021 040	.010 750 2561	12.91	2.354 080	9.05	312
27	27.775 080	2596.371 394	.000 385 1529	.036 003	93.478 449	.010 697 6529	12.84	2.466 040	9.13	324
28	31.414 057	2949.241 937	.000 339 0702	.031 833	93.882 872	.010 651 5702	12.79	2.578 928	9.21	336
29	35.529 799	3348.344 137	.000 298 6551	.028 145	94.240 447	.010 611 1551	12.74	2.692 682	9.29	348
30	40.184 768	3799.735 076	.000 263 1762	.024 885	94.556 601	.010 575 6762	12.70	2.807 243	9.36	360
31	45.449 612	4310.265 411	.000 232 0043	.022 002	94.836 132	.010 544 5043	12.66	2.922 556	9.43	372
32	51.404 234	4887.683 344	.000 204 5959	.019 454	95.083 282	.010 517 0959	12.63	3.038 565	9.50	384
33	58.139 007	5540.752 215	.000 180 4809	.017 200	95.301 803	.010 492 9809	12.60	3.155 220	9.56	396
34	65.756 142	6279.383 501	.000 159 2513	.015 208	95.495 010	.010 471 7513	12.57	3.272 475	9.62	408
35	74.371 243	7114.787 240	.000 140 5523	.013 446	95.665 837	.010 453 0523	12.55	3.390 282	9.69	420
36	84.115 060	8059.642 162	.000 124 0750	.011 888	95.816 875	.010 436 5750	12.53	3.508 600	9.75	432
37	95.135 471	9128.288 115	.000 109 5496	.010 511	95.950 417	.010 422 0496	12.51	3.627 390	9.80	444
38	107.599 732	10336.943 694	.000 096 7404	.009 294	96.068 489	.010 409 2404	12.50	3.746 614	9.86	456
39	121.697 009	11703.952 387	.000 085 4412	.008 217	96.172 884	.010 397 9412	12.48	3.866 236	9.91	468
40	137.641 254	13250.060 973	.000 075 4714	.007 265	96.265 187	.010 387 9714	12.47	3.986 226	9.97	480
41	155.674 448	14998.734 388	.000 066 6723	.006 424	96.346 796	.010 379 1723	12.46	4.106 553	10.02	492
42	176.070 278	16976.511 847	.000 058 9049	.005 680	96.418 953	.010 371 4049	12.45	4.227 188	10.06	504
43	199.138 287	19213.409 627	.000 052 0470	.005 022	96.482 750	.010 364 5470	12.44	4.348 106	10.11	516
44	225.228 571	21743.376 612	.000 045 9910	.004 440	96.539 158	.010 358 4910	12.44	4.469 283	10.16	528
45	254.737 098	24604.809 533	.000 040 6425	.003 926	96.589 031	.010 353 1425	12.43	4.590 697	10.20	540
46	288.111 712	27841.135 702	.000 035 9181	.003 471	96.633 127	.010 348 4181	12.42	4.712 327	10.24	552
47	325.858 931	31501.472 100	.000 031 7445	.003 069	96.672 115	.010 344 2445	12.42	4.834 154	10.29	564
48	368.551 637	35641.370 814	.000 028 0573	.002 713	96.706 587	.010 340 5573	12.41	4.956 161	10.33	576
49	416.837 766	40323.662 141	.000 024 7993	.002 399	96.737 065	.010 337 2993	12.41	5.078 332	10.36	588
50	471.450 146	45619.408 142	.000 021 9205	.002 121	96.764 013	.010 334 4205	12.41	5.200 652	10.40	600

Effective Rate is 13.10 %   Annual Percentage Rate is 12.375%

	Amount Of 1	Amount Of 1 Per Period	Sinking Fund Payment	Present Worth Of 1	Present Worth of 1 Per Period	Periodic Payment To Amortize 1	Constant Annual Percent	Total Interest	Annual Add On Rate	
	What a single $ 1 deposit grows to in the future. The deposit is made at the beginning of the first period.	What a series of $ 1 deposits grow to in the future. A deposit is made at the end of each period.	The amount to be deposited at the end of each period that grows to $ 1 in the future.	What $ 1 to be paid in the future is worth today. Value today of a single $ 1 payment tomorrow.	What $ 1 to be paid at the end of each period is worth today. Value today of a series of $ 1 payments tomorrow.	The mortgage payment to amortize a loan of $ 1. An annuity certain, payable at the end of each period, worth $ 1 today.	The annual payment, including interest and principal, to amortize completely a loan of $ 100.	The total interest paid over the term on a loan of $1. The loan is amortized by regular periodic payments.	The average annual interest rate on a loan that is completely amortized by regular periodic payments.	
	$S = (1+i)^n$	$S\overline{n}\rceil = \dfrac{(1+i)^n - 1}{i}$	$\dfrac{1}{S\overline{n}\rceil} = \dfrac{i}{(1+i)^n - 1}$	$V^n = \dfrac{1}{(1+i)^n}$	$A\overline{n}\rceil = \dfrac{1-V^n}{i}$	$\dfrac{1}{A\overline{n}\rceil} = \dfrac{i}{1-V^n}$				

YEAR										PERIODS
	1.010 333	1.000 000	1.000 000 0000	.989 772	.989 772	1.010 333 3333	1212.40	.010 333	12.40	1
	1.020 773	2.010 333	.497 429 9453	.979 649	1.969 422	.507 763 2786	609.32	.015 527	9.32	2
	1.031 321	3.031 107	.329 912 4951	.969 630	2.939 051	.340 245 8284	408.30	.020 737	8.29	3
	1.041 978	4.062 428	.246 158 1958	.959 713	3.898 764	.256 491 5292	307.79	.025 966	7.79	4
	1.052 746	5.104 407	.195 909 1567	.949 897	4.848 661	.206 242 4900	247.50	.031 212	7.49	5
	1.063 624	6.157 152	.162 412 7473	.940 182	5.788 843	.172 746 0806	207.30	.036 476	7.30	6
	1.074 615	7.220 776	.138 489 2689	.930 566	6.719 409	.148 822 6022	178.59	.041 758	7.16	7
	1.085 719	8.295 391	.120 548 8720	.921 049	7.640 458	.130 882 2054	157.06	.047 058	7.06	8
	1.096 938	9.381 110	.106 597 1959	.911 628	8.552 086	.116 930 5293	140.32	.052 375	6.98	9
	1.108 273	10.478 048	.095 437 6241	.902 305	9.454 391	.105 770 9574	126.93	.057 710	6.93	10
	1.119 725	11.586 321	.086 308 6731	.893 076	10.347 467	.096 642 0064	115.98	.063 062	6.88	11
	1.131 296	12.706 046	.078 702 6874	.883 942	11.231 409	.089 036 0208	106.85	.068 432	6.84	12
1	1.131 296	12.706 046	.078 702 6874	.883 942	11.231 409	.089 036 0208	106.85	.068 432	6.84	12
2	1.279 830	27.080 344	.036 927 1534	.781 354	21.159 325	.047 260 4867	56.72	.134 252	6.71	24
3	1.447 867	43.341 926	.023 072 3482	.690 671	29.935 028	.033 405 6815	40.09	.202 605	6.75	36
4	1.637 965	61.738 585	.016 197 3261	.610 514	37.692 241	.026 530 6594	31.84	.273 472	6.84	48
5	1.853 023	82.550 650	.012 113 7750	.539 659	44.549 168	.022 447 1084	26.94	.346 827	6.94	60
6	2.096 318	106.095 251	.009 425 4926	.477 027	50.610 295	.019 758 8259	23.72	.422 635	7.04	72
7	2.371 555	132.731 159	.007 534 0260	.421 664	55.967 980	.017 867 3593	21.45	.500 858	7.16	84
8	2.682 931	162.864 251	.006 140 0829	.372 727	60.703 863	.016 473 4162	19.77	.581 448	7.27	96
9	3.035 188	196.953 692	.005 077 3356	.329 469	64.890 110	.015 410 6690	18.50	.664 352	7.38	108
10	3.433 696	235.518 933	.004 245 9431	.291 231	68.590 509	.014 579 2765	17.50	.749 015	7.50	120
11	3.884 526	279.147 630	.003 582 3338	.257 432	71.861 449	.013 915 6672	16.70	.836 868	7.61	132
12	4.394 547	328.504 591	.003 044 0975	.227 555	74.752 769	.013 377 4308	16.06	.926 350	7.72	144
13	4.971 533	384.341 915	.002 601 8500	.201 145	77.308 529	.012 935 1833	15.53	1.017 889	7.83	156
14	5.624 275	447.510 446	.002 234 5847	.177 801	79.567 674	.012 567 9180	15.09	1.111 410	7.94	168
15	6.362 718	518.972 740	.001 926 8835	.157 166	81.564 626	.012 260 2168	14.72	1.206 839	8.05	180
16	7.198 117	599.817 734	.001 667 1731	.138 925	83.329 816	.012 000 5064	14.41	1.304 097	8.15	192
17	8.143 199	691.277 337	.001 446 5974	.122 802	84.890 143	.011 779 9307	14.14	1.403 106	8.25	204
18	9.212 367	794.745 204	.001 258 2649	.108 550	86.269 381	.011 591 5982	13.91	1.503 785	8.35	216
19	10.421 912	911.797 968	.001 096 7342	.095 952	87.488 547	.011 430 0675	13.72	1.606 055	8.45	228
20	11.790 266	1044.219 270	.000 957 6533	.084 816	88.566 220	.011 290 9866	13.55	1.709 837	8.55	240
21	13.338 278	1194.026 934	.000 837 5020	.074 972	89.518 820	.011 170 8354	13.41	1.815 051	8.64	252
22	15.089 538	1363.503 718	.000 733 4047	.066 271	90.360 863	.011 066 7380	13.29	1.921 619	8.73	264
23	17.070 732	1555.232 093	.000 642 9908	.058 580	91.105 181	.010 976 3242	13.18	2.029 465	8.82	276
24	19.312 047	1772.133 602	.000 564 2915	.051 781	91.763 115	.010 897 6249	13.08	2.138 516	8.91	288
25	21.847 638	2017.513 370	.000 495 6597	.045 772	92.344 690	.010 828 9930	13.00	2.248 698	8.99	300
26	24.716 142	2295.110 475	.000 435 7089	.040 459	92.858 769	.010 769 0422	12.93	2.359 941	9.08	312
27	27.961 267	2609.154 917	.000 383 2659	.035 764	93.313 185	.010 716 5992	12.86	2.472 178	9.16	324
28	31.632 465	2964.432 079	.000 337 3327	.031 613	93.714 862	.010 670 6661	12.81	2.585 344	9.23	336
29	35.785 675	3366.355 646	.000 297 0571	.027 944	94.069 922	.010 630 3905	12.76	2.699 376	9.31	348
30	40.484 184	3821.050 094	.000 261 7082	.024 701	94.383 774	.010 595 0415	12.72	2.814 215	9.38	360
31	45.799 588	4335.444 018	.000 230 6569	.021 834	94.661 201	.010 563 9902	12.68	2.929 804	9.45	372
32	51.812 882	4917.375 712	.000 203 3605	.019 300	94.906 430	.010 536 6938	12.65	3.046 090	9.52	384
33	58.615 697	5575.712 600	.000 179 3493	.017 060	95.123 199	.010 512 6826	12.62	3.163 022	9.58	396
34	66.311 692	6320.486 366	.000 158 2157	.015 080	95.314 810	.010 491 5490	12.59	3.280 552	9.65	408
35	75.018 140	7163.045 808	.000 139 6054	.013 330	95.484 183	.010 472 9388	12.57	3.398 634	9.71	420
36	84.867 708	8116.229 777	.000 123 2099	.011 783	95.633 899	.010 456 5433	12.55	3.517 227	9.77	432
37	96.010 482	9194.562 811	.000 108 7599	.010 416	95.766 239	.010 442 0933	12.54	3.636 289	9.83	444
38	108.616 257	10414.476 457	.000 096 0202	.009 207	95.883 220	.010 429 3535	12.52	3.755 785	9.88	456
39	122.877 116	11794.559 656	.000 084 7849	.008 138	95.986 625	.010 418 1182	12.51	3.875 679	9.94	468
40	139.010 367	13355.842 002	.000 074 8736	.007 194	96.078 028	.010 408 2069	12.49	3.995 939	9.99	480
41	157.261 847	15122.114 182	.000 066 1283	.006 359	96.158 824	.010 399 4617	12.48	4.116 535	10.04	492
42	177.909 669	17120.290 505	.000 058 4102	.005 621	96.230 242	.010 391 7436	12.48	4.237 439	10.09	504
43	201.268 463	19380.819 012	.000 051 5974	.004 968	96.293 372	.010 384 9307	12.47	4.358 624	10.14	516
44	227.694 170	21938.145 447	.000 045 5827	.004 392	96.349 175	.010 378 9160	12.46	4.480 068	10.18	528
45	257.589 461	24831.238 135	.000 040 2719	.003 882	96.398 502	.010 373 6052	12.45	4.601 747	10.23	540
46	291.409 878	28104.181 780	.000 035 5819	.003 432	96.442 104	.010 368 9152	12.45	4.723 641	10.27	552
47	329.670 775	31806.849 222	.000 031 4398	.003 033	96.480 646	.010 364 7731	12.44	4.845 732	10.31	564
48	372.955 168	35995.661 396	.000 027 7811	.002 681	96.514 714	.010 361 1145	12.44	4.968 002	10.35	576
49	421.922 620	40734.447 070	.000 024 5492	.002 370	96.544 829	.010 357 8826	12.43	5.090 435	10.39	588
50	477.319 293	46095.415 462	.000 021 6941	.002 095	96.571 448	.010 355 0275	12.43	5.213 016	10.43	600

MONTHLY COMPOUND INTEREST AND ANNUITY

12.45 % M

	Amount Of 1	Amount Of 1 Per Period	Sinking Fund Payment	Present Worth Of 1	Present Worth of 1 Per Period	Periodic Payment To Amortize 1	Constant Annual Percent	Total Interest	Annual Add On Rate	
	What a single $ 1 deposit grows to in the future. The deposit is made at the beginning of the first period.	What a series of $ 1 deposits grow to in the future. A deposit is made at the end of each period.	The amount to be deposited at the end of each period that grows to $ 1 in the future.	What $ 1 to be paid in the future is worth today. Value today of a single $ 1 payment tomorrow.	What $ 1 to be paid at the end of each period is worth today. Value today of a series of $ 1 payments tomorrow.	The mortgage payment to amortize a loan of $ 1. An annuity certain, payable at the end of each period, worth $ 1 today.	The annual payment, including interest and principal, to amortize completely a loan of $ 100.	The total interest paid over the term on a loan of $1. The loan is amortized by regular periodic payments.	The average annual interest rate on a loan that is completely amortized by regular periodic payments.	
	$S = (1+i)^n$	$S\overline{n}| = \dfrac{(1+i)^n - 1}{i}$	$\dfrac{1}{S\overline{n}|} = \dfrac{i}{(1+i)^n - 1}$	$V^n = \dfrac{1}{(1+i)^n}$	$A\overline{n}| = \dfrac{1-V^n}{i}$	$\dfrac{1}{A\overline{n}|} = \dfrac{i}{1-V^n}$				

YEAR										PERIODS
	1.010 375	1.000 000	1.000 000 0000	.989 732	.989 732	1.010 375 0000	1212.45	.010 375	12.45	1
	1.020 858	2.010 375	.497 419 6356	.979 569	1.969 300	.507 794 6356	609.36	.015 589	9.35	2
	1.031 449	3.031 233	.329 898 7965	.969 510	2.938 810	.340 273 7965	408.33	.020 821	8.33	3
	1.042 150	4.062 682	.246 142 8384	.959 554	3.898 364	.256 517 8384	307.83	.026 071	7.82	4
	1.052 963	5.104 832	.195 892 8325	.949 701	4.848 066	.206 267 8325	247.53	.031 339	7.52	5
	1.063 887	6.157 795	.162 395 8023	.939 949	5.788 015	.172 770 8023	207.33	.036 625	7.32	6
	1.074 925	7.221 682	.138 471 9009	.930 298	6.718 313	.148 846 9009	178.62	.041 928	7.19	7
	1.086 077	8.296 607	.120 531 2046	.920 745	7.639 057	.130 906 2046	157.09	.047 250	7.09	8
	1.097 345	9.382 684	.106 579 3115	.911 290	8.550 347	.116 954 3115	140.35	.052 589	7.01	9
	1.108 730	10.480 029	.095 419 5802	.901 933	9.452 280	.105 794 5802	126.96	.057 946	6.95	10
	1.120 233	11.588 760	.086 290 5117	.892 671	10.344 951	.096 665 5117	116.00	.063 321	6.91	11
	1.131 856	12.708 993	.078 684 4400	.883 505	11.228 456	.089 059 4400	106.88	.068 713	6.87	12
1	1.131 856	12.708 993	.078 684 4400	.883 505	11.228 456	.089 059 4400	106.88	.068 713	6.87	12
2	1.281 098	27.093 741	.036 908 8941	.780 581	21.148 850	.047 283 8941	56.75	.134 813	6.74	24
3	1.450 018	43.375 200	.023 054 6485	.689 647	29.913 566	.033 429 6485	40.12	.203 467	6.78	36
4	1.641 211	61.803 465	.016 180 3225	.609 306	37.657 234	.026 555 3225	31.87	.274 655	6.87	48
5	1.857 614	82.661 604	.012 097 5151	.538 325	44.498 802	.022 472 5151	26.97	.348 351	6.97	60
6	2.102 551	106.270 009	.009 409 9926	.475 613	50.543 360	.019 784 9926	23.75	.424 519	7.08	72
7	2.379 785	132.991 319	.007 519 2878	.420 206	55.883 755	.017 894 2878	21.48	.503 120	7.19	84
8	2.693 573	163.235 990	.006 126 1000	.371 254	60.602 020	.016 501 1000	19.81	.584 106	7.30	96
9	3.048 737	197.468 595	.005 064 0964	.328 005	64.770 630	.015 439 0964	18.53	.667 422	7.42	108
10	3.450 730	236.214 968	.004 233 4320	.289 794	68.453 616	.014 608 4320	17.54	.753 012	7.53	120
11	3.905 729	280.070 276	.003 570 5324	.256 034	71.707 553	.013 945 5324	16.74	.840 810	7.64	132
12	4.420 722	329.708 160	.003 032 9853	.226 207	74.582 421	.013 407 9853	16.09	.930 750	7.76	144
13	5.003 620	385.891 087	.002 591 4048	.199 855	77.122 380	.012 966 4048	15.56	1.022 759	7.87	156
14	5.663 376	449.482 059	.002 224 7829	.176 573	79.366 447	.012 599 7829	15.12	1.116 764	7.98	168
15	6.410 125	521.457 869	.001 917 7005	.156 003	81.349 090	.012 292 7005	14.76	1.212 686	8.08	180
16	7.255 338	602.924 108	.001 658 5835	.137 830	83.100 765	.012 033 5835	14.45	1.310 448	8.19	192
17	8.211 996	695.132 143	.001 438 5754	.121 773	84.648 378	.011 813 5754	14.18	1.409 969	8.29	204
18	9.294 795	799.498 343	.001 250 7843	.107 587	86.015 702	.011 625 7843	13.96	1.511 169	8.40	216
19	10.520 368	917.625 832	.001 089 7688	.095 054	87.223 739	.011 464 7688	13.76	1.613 967	8.49	228
20	11.907 540	1051.329 116	.000 951 1769	.083 980	88.291 045	.011 326 1769	13.60	1.718 282	8.59	240
21	13.477 618	1202.661 953	.000 831 4888	.074 197	89.234 016	.011 206 4888	13.45	1.824 035	8.69	252
22	15.254 720	1373.948 903	.000 727 8291	.065 553	90.067 134	.011 102 8291	13.33	1.931 147	8.78	264
23	17.266 143	1567.821 032	.000 637 8279	.057 917	90.803 199	.011 012 8279	13.22	2.039 541	8.87	276
24	19.542 784	1787.256 325	.000 559 5168	.051 170	91.453 515	.010 934 5168	13.13	2.149 141	8.95	288
25	22.119 614	2035.625 436	.000 491 2495	.045 209	92.028 073	.010 866 2495	13.04	2.259 875	9.04	300
26	25.036 213	2316.743 455	.000 431 6404	.039 942	92.535 697	.010 806 6404	12.97	2.371 672	9.12	312
27	28.337 383	2634.928 515	.000 379 5169	.035 289	92.984 186	.010 754 5169	12.91	2.484 463	9.20	324
28	32.073 832	2995.068 123	.000 333 8822	.031 178	93.380 428	.010 708 8822	12.86	2.598 184	9.28	336
29	36.302 953	3402.694 227	.000 293 8848	.027 546	93.730 509	.010 668 8848	12.81	2.712 772	9.35	348
30	41.089 708	3864.068 199	.000 258 7946	.024 337	94.039 808	.010 633 7946	12.77	2.828 166	9.43	360
31	46.507 624	4386.277 006	.000 227 9838	.021 502	94.313 075	.010 602 9838	12.73	2.944 310	9.50	372
32	52.639 924	4977.342 074	.000 200 9104	.018 997	94.554 507	.010 575 9104	12.70	3.061 150	9.57	384
33	59.580 803	5646.342 501	.000 177 1058	.016 784	94.767 814	.010 552 1058	12.67	3.178 634	9.63	396
34	67.436 878	6403.554 517	.000 156 1633	.014 829	94.956 272	.010 531 1633	12.64	3.296 715	9.70	408
35	76.328 822	7260.609 331	.000 137 7295	.013 101	95.122 775	.010 512 7295	12.62	3.415 346	9.76	420
36	86.393 220	8230.671 795	.000 121 4968	.011 575	95.269 881	.010 496 4968	12.60	3.534 487	9.82	432
37	97.784 667	9328.642 624	.000 107 1967	.010 227	95.399 850	.010 482 1967	12.58	3.654 095	9.88	444
38	110.678 143	10571.387 278	.000 094 5950	.009 035	95.514 679	.010 469 5950	12.57	3.774 135	9.93	456
39	125.271 698	11977.995 026	.000 083 4864	.007 983	95.616 130	.010 458 4864	12.56	3.894 572	9.99	468
40	141.789 499	13570.072 167	.000 073 6916	.007 053	95.705 763	.010 448 6916	12.54	4.015 372	10.04	480
41	160.485 267	15372.073 918	.000 065 0530	.006 231	95.784 954	.010 440 0530	12.53	4.136 506	10.09	492
42	181.646 181	17411.680 057	.000 057 4327	.005 505	95.854 920	.010 432 4327	12.52	4.257 946	10.14	504
43	205.597 284	19720.220 099	.000 050 7094	.004 864	95.916 735	.010 425 7094	12.52	4.379 666	10.19	516
44	232.706 478	22333.154 542	.000 044 7765	.004 297	95.971 349	.010 419 7765	12.51	4.501 642	10.23	528
45	263.390 178	25290.619 553	.000 039 5404	.003 797	96.019 600	.010 414 5404	12.50	4.623 852	10.28	540
46	298.119 701	28638.043 487	.000 034 9186	.003 354	96.062 231	.010 409 9186	12.50	4.746 275	10.32	552
47	337.428 514	32426.844 691	.000 030 8386	.002 964	96.099 895	.010 405 8386	12.49	4.868 893	10.36	564
48	381.920 421	36715.221 319	.000 027 2367	.002 618	96.133 171	.010 402 2367	12.49	4.991 688	10.40	576
49	432.278 845	41569.045 289	.000 024 0564	.002 313	96.162 571	.010 399 0564	12.48	5.114 645	10.44	588
50	489.277 319	47062.874 115	.000 021 2482	.002 044	96.188 546	.010 396 2482	12.48	5.237 749	10.48	600

Effective Rate is 13.19 %   8 - 195   Annual Percentage Rate is 12.45 %

MONTHLY COMPOUND INTEREST AND ANNUITY

12.50 % M

	Amount Of 1	Amount Of 1 Per Period	Sinking Fund Payment	Present Worth Of 1	Present Worth of 1 Per Period	Periodic Payment To Amortize 1	Constant Annual Percent	Total Interest	Annual Add On Rate	
	What a single $ 1 deposit grows to in the future. The deposit is made at the beginning of the first period.	What a series of $ 1 deposits grow to in the future. A deposit is made at the end of each period.	The amount to be deposited at the end of each period that grows to $ 1 in the future.	What $ 1 to be paid in the future is worth today. Value today of a single $ 1 payment tomorrow.	What $ 1 to be paid at the end of each period is worth today. Value today of a series of $ 1 payments tomorrow.	The mortgage payment to amortize a loan of $ 1. An annuity certain, payable at the end of each period, worth $ 1 today.	The annual payment, including interest and principal, to amortize completely a loan of $ 100.	The total interest paid over the term on a loan of $1. The loan is amortized by regular periodic payments.	The average annual interest rate on a loan that is completely amortized by regular periodic payments.	
	$S = (1+i)^n$	$S\overline{n}| = \dfrac{(1+i)^n - 1}{i}$	$\dfrac{1}{S\overline{n}|} = \dfrac{i}{(1+i)^n - 1}$	$V^n = \dfrac{1}{(1+i)^n}$	$A\overline{n}| = \dfrac{1-V^n}{i}$	$\dfrac{1}{A\overline{n}|} = \dfrac{i}{1-V^n}$				

YEAR										PERIODS
	1.010 417	1.000 000	1.000 000 0000	.989 691	.989 691	1.010 416 6667	1212.50	.010 417	12.50	1
	1.020 942	2.010 417	.497 409 3264	.979 488	1.969 178	.507 825 9931	609.40	.015 652	9.39	2
	1.031 577	3.031 359	.329 885 0986	.969 390	2.938 568	.340 301 7653	408.37	.020 905	8.36	3
	1.042 322	4.062 935	.246 127 4820	.959 396	3.897 965	.256 544 1487	307.86	.026 177	7.85	4
	1.053 180	5.105 257	.195 876 5096	.949 506	4.847 470	.206 293 1763	247.56	.031 466	7.55	5
	1.064 150	6.158 437	.162 378 8590	.939 717	5.787 187	.172 795 5257	207.36	.036 773	7.35	6
	1.075 235	7.222 588	.138 454 5349	.930 029	6.717 216	.148 871 2015	178.65	.042 098	7.22	7
	1.086 436	8.297 823	.120 513 5395	.920 441	7.637 657	.130 930 2061	157.12	.047 442	7.12	8
	1.097 753	9.384 258	.106 561 4295	.910 952	8.548 609	.116 978 0962	140.38	.052 803	7.04	9
	1.109 188	10.482 011	.095 401 5391	.901 561	9.450 170	.105 818 2058	126.99	.058 182	6.98	10
	1.120 742	11.591 199	.086 272 3535	.892 266	10.342 436	.096 689 0201	116.03	.063 579	6.94	11
	1.132 416	12.711 940	.078 666 1960	.883 068	11.225 504	.089 082 8627	106.90	.068 994	6.90	12
1	1.132 416	12.711 940	.078 666 1960	.883 068	11.225 504	.089 082 8627	106.90	.068 994	6.90	12
2	1.282 366	27.107 146	.036 890 6416	.779 809	21.138 383	.047 307 3082	56.77	.135 375	6.77	24
3	1.452 172	43.408 507	.023 036 9589	.688 624	29.892 126	.033 453 6256	40.15	.204 331	6.81	36
4	1.644 463	61.868 431	.016 163 3322	.608 101	37.622 274	.026 579 9989	31.90	.275 840	6.90	48
5	1.862 216	82.772 744	.012 081 2716	.536 995	44.448 517	.022 497 9382	27.00	.349 876	7.00	60
6	2.108 803	106.445 124	.009 394 5120	.474 203	50.476 552	.019 811 1787	23.78	.426 405	7.11	72
7	2.388 043	133.252 107	.007 504 5718	.418 753	55.799 715	.017 921 2384	21.51	.505 384	7.22	84
8	2.704 258	163.608 765	.006 112 1420	.369 787	60.500 428	.016 528 8086	19.84	.586 766	7.33	96
9	3.062 345	197.985 131	.005 050 8844	.326 547	64.651 476	.015 467 5510	18.57	.670 496	7.45	108
10	3.467 849	236.913 480	.004 220 9502	.288 363	68.317 132	.014 637 6169	17.57	.756 514	7.57	120
11	3.927 048	280.996 567	.003 558 7623	.254 644	71.554 154	.013 975 4290	16.78	.844 757	7.68	132
12	4.447 052	330.916 961	.003 021 9061	.224 868	74.412 664	.013 438 5728	16.13	.935 154	7.79	144
13	5.035 913	387.447 618	.002 580 9941	.198 574	76.936 921	.012 997 6607	15.60	1.027 635	7.90	156
14	5.702 748	451.463 840	.002 215 0168	.175 354	79.166 011	.012 631 6835	15.16	1.122 123	8.02	168
15	6.457 884	523.956 837	.001 908 5542	.154 849	81.134 449	.012 325 2208	14.80	1.218 540	8.12	180
16	7.313 011	606.049 070	.001 650 0314	.136 743	82.872 712	.012 066 6981	14.49	1.316 806	8.23	192
17	8.281 371	699.011 633	.001 430 5914	.120 753	84.407 717	.011 847 2580	14.22	1.416 841	8.33	204
18	9.377 958	804.283 930	.001 243 3420	.106 633	85.763 229	.011 660 0087	14.00	1.518 562	8.44	216
19	10.619 750	923.495 968	.001 082 8418	.094 164	86.960 239	.011 499 5084	13.80	1.621 888	8.54	228
20	12.025 975	1058.493 594	.000 944 7388	.083 153	88.017 279	.011 361 4055	13.64	1.726 737	8.63	240
21	13.618 407	1211.367 071	.000 825 5136	.073 430	88.950 717	.011 242 1803	13.50	1.833 029	8.73	252
22	15.421 703	1384.483 450	.000 722 2910	.064 844	89.775 006	.011 138 9577	13.37	1.940 685	8.82	264
23	17.463 783	1580.523 215	.000 632 7019	.057 261	90.502 909	.011 049 3685	13.26	2.049 626	8.91	276
24	19.776 269	1802.521 791	.000 554 7783	.050 566	91.145 697	.010 971 4450	13.17	2.159 776	9.00	288
25	22.394 964	2053.916 541	.000 486 8747	.044 653	91.713 322	.010 903 5414	13.09	2.271 062	9.08	300
26	25.360 417	2338.599 989	.000 427 6063	.039 432	92.214 573	.010 844 2729	13.02	2.383 413	9.17	312
27	28.718 543	2660.980 094	.000 375 8014	.034 821	92.657 212	.010 792 4680	12.96	2.496 760	9.25	324
28	32.521 339	3026.048 499	.000 330 4640	.030 749	93.048 092	.010 747 1306	12.90	2.611 036	9.33	336
29	36.827 686	3439.457 817	.000 290 7435	.027 153	93.393 265	.010 707 4102	12.85	2.726 179	9.40	348
30	41.704 262	3907.609 164	.000 255 9110	.023 978	93.698 077	.010 672 5776	12.81	2.842 128	9.47	360
31	47.226 576	4437.751 261	.000 225 3394	.021 175	93.967 246	.010 642 0060	12.78	2.958 826	9.54	372
32	53.480 132	5038.092 678	.000 198 4878	.018 699	94.204 941	.010 615 1545	12.74	3.076 219	9.61	384
33	60.561 760	5717.928 933	.000 174 8885	.016 512	94.414 841	.010 591 5552	12.71	3.194 256	9.68	396
34	68.581 108	6487.786 416	.000 154 1358	.014 581	94.600 198	.010 570 8024	12.69	3.312 887	9.74	408
35	77.662 348	7359.585 384	.000 135 8772	.012 876	94.763 880	.010 552 5439	12.67	3.432 068	9.81	420
36	87.946 089	8346.824 524	.000 119 8060	.011 371	94.908 422	.010 536 4727	12.65	3.551 756	9.87	432
37	99.591 562	9464.789 968	.000 105 6547	.010 041	95.036 063	.010 522 3214	12.63	3.671 911	9.92	444
38	112.779 083	10730.791 976	.000 093 1898	.008 867	95.148 778	.010 509 8564	12.62	3.792 495	9.98	456
39	127.712 843	12164.432 965	.000 082 2069	.007 830	95.248 314	.010 498 8735	12.60	3.913 473	10.03	468
40	144.624 073	13787.911 025	.000 072 5273	.006 914	95.336 210	.010 489 1940	12.59	4.034 813	10.09	480
41	163.774 621	15626.363 632	.000 063 9944	.006 106	95.413 829	.010 480 6611	12.58	4.156 485	10.14	492
42	185.461 009	17708.256 865	.000 056 4708	.005 392	95.482 371	.010 473 1375	12.57	4.278 461	10.19	504
43	210.019 023	20065.826 168	.000 049 8360	.004 761	95.542 899	.010 466 5026	12.56	4.400 715	10.23	516
44	237.828 911	22735.575 478	.000 043 9839	.004 205	95.596 348	.010 460 6506	12.56	4.523 224	10.28	528
45	269.321 275	25758.842 436	.000 038 8216	.003 713	95.643 548	.010 455 4883	12.55	4.645 964	10.32	540
46	304.983 734	29182.438 452	.000 034 2672	.003 279	95.685 229	.010 450 9339	12.55	4.768 915	10.37	552
47	345.368 474	33059.373 517	.000 030 2486	.002 895	95.722 036	.010 446 9153	12.54	4.892 060	10.41	564
48	391.100 802	37449.676 995	.000 026 7025	.002 557	95.754 539	.010 443 3692	12.54	5.015 381	10.45	576
49	442.888 824	42421.327 103	.000 023 5730	.002 258	95.783 241	.010 440 2397	12.53	5.138 861	10.49	588
50	501.534 411	48051.303 462	.000 020 8111	.001 994	95.808 587	.010 437 4778	12.53	5.262 487	10.52	600

MONTHLY COMPOUND INTEREST AND ANNUITY

12.55 % M

	Amount Of 1	Amount Of 1 Per Period	Sinking Fund Payment	Present Worth Of 1	Present Worth of 1 Per Period	Periodic Payment To Amortize 1	Constant Annual Percent	Total Interest	Annual Add On Rate	
	What a single $ 1 deposit grows to in the future. The deposit is made at the beginning of the first period.	What a series of $ 1 deposits grow to in the future. A deposit is made at the end of each period.	The amount to be deposited at the end of each period that grows to $ 1 in the future.	What $ 1 to be paid in the future is worth today. Value today of a single $ 1 payment tomorrow.	What $ 1 to be paid at the end of each period is worth today. Value today of a series of $ 1 payments tomorrow.	The mortgage payment to amortize a loan of $ 1. An annuity certain, payable at the end of each period, worth $ 1 today.	The annual payment, including interest and principal, to amortize completely a loan of $ 100.	The total interest paid over the term on a loan of $1. The loan is amortized by regular periodic payments.	The average annual interest rate on a loan that is completely amortized by regular periodic payments.	
	$S = (1+i)^n$	$S\overline{n} = \dfrac{(1+i)^n - 1}{i}$	$\dfrac{1}{S\overline{n}} = \dfrac{i}{(1+i)^n - 1}$	$V^n = \dfrac{1}{(1+i)^n}$	$A\overline{n} = \dfrac{1-V^n}{i}$	$\dfrac{1}{A\overline{n}} = \dfrac{i}{1-V^n}$				

YEAR										PERIODS
	1.010 458	1.000 000	1.000 000 0000	.989 650	.989 650	1.010 458 3333	1212.55	.010 458	12.55	1
	1.021 026	2.010 458	.497 399 0176	.979 407	1.969 057	.507 857 3510	609.43	.015 715	9.43	2
	1.031 704	3.031 484	.329 871 4015	.969 270	2.938 327	.340 329 7348	408.40	.020 989	8.40	3
	1.042 494	4.063 189	.246 112 1267	.959 238	3.897 565	.256 570 4600	307.89	.026 282	7.88	4
	1.053 397	5.105 683	.195 860 1881	.949 310	4.846 875	.206 318 5215	247.59	.031 593	7.58	5
	1.064 414	6.159 080	.162 361 9174	.939 484	5.786 359	.172 820 2507	207.39	.036 922	7.38	6
	1.075 546	7.223 493	.138 437 1708	.929 761	6.716 120	.148 895 5042	178.68	.042 269	7.25	7
	1.086 794	8.299 039	.120 495 8765	.920 137	7.636 257	.130 954 2099	157.15	.047 634	7.15	8
	1.098 160	9.385 833	.106 543 5501	.910 614	8.546 871	.117 001 8834	140.41	.053 017	7.07	9
	1.109 645	10.483 993	.095 383 5009	.901 189	9.448 060	.105 841 8342	127.02	.058 418	7.01	10
	1.121 250	11.593 639	.086 254 1983	.891 862	10.339 922	.096 712 5316	116.06	.063 838	6.96	11
	1.132 977	12.714 889	.078 647 9554	.882 631	11.222 552	.089 106 2888	106.93	.069 275	6.93	12
1	1.132 977	12.714 889	.078 647 9554	.882 631	11.222 552	.089 106 2888	106.93	.069 275	6.93	12
2	1.283 636	27.120 559	.036 872 3958	.779 037	21.127 923	.047 330 7292	56.80	.135 937	6.80	24
3	1.454 329	43.441 846	.023 019 2794	.687 602	29.870 708	.033 477 6128	40.18	.205 194	6.84	36
4	1.647 721	61.933 482	.016 146 3553	.606 899	37.587 360	.026 604 6886	31.93	.277 025	6.93	48
5	1.866 829	82.884 071	.012 065 0445	.535 668	44.398 314	.022 523 3778	27.03	.351 403	7.03	60
6	2.115 074	106.620 597	.009 379 0509	.472 797	50.409 872	.019 837 3842	23.81	.428 292	7.14	72
7	2.396 329	133.513 524	.007 489 8780	.417 305	55.715 858	.017 948 2113	21.54	.507 650	7.25	84
8	2.714 984	163.982 580	.006 098 2087	.368 326	60.399 085	.016 556 5421	19.87	.589 428	7.37	96
9	3.076 014	198.503 305	.005 037 6995	.325 096	64.532 646	.015 496 0328	18.60	.673 572	7.48	108
10	3.485 051	237.614 477	.004 208 4978	.286 940	68.181 054	.014 666 8311	17.61	.760 020	7.60	120
11	3.948 482	281.926 518	.003 547 0236	.253 262	71.401 251	.014 005 3569	16.81	.848 707	7.72	132
12	4.473 537	332.131 021	.003 010 8600	.223 537	74.243 496	.013 469 1933	16.17	.939 564	7.83	144
13	5.068 412	389.011 545	.002 570 6178	.197 300	76.752 149	.013 028 9511	15.64	1.032 516	7.94	156
14	5.742 392	453.455 845	.002 205 2864	.174 143	78.966 364	.012 663 6197	15.20	1.127 488	8.05	168
15	6.505 996	526.469 725	.001 899 4445	.153 704	80.920 698	.012 357 7778	14.83	1.224 400	8.16	180
16	7.371 141	609.192 738	.001 641 5166	.135 664	82.645 653	.012 099 8499	14.52	1.323 171	8.27	192
17	8.351 330	702.915 972	.001 422 6452	.119 741	84.168 152	.011 880 9785	14.26	1.423 720	8.37	204
18	9.461 860	809.102 198	.001 235 9378	.105 687	85.511 956	.011 694 2711	14.04	1.525 963	8.48	216
19	10.720 066	929.408 701	.001 075 9529	.093 283	86.698 039	.011 534 2862	13.85	1.629 817	8.58	228
20	12.145 583	1065.713 147	.000 938 3388	.082 334	87.744 913	.011 396 6721	13.68	1.735 201	8.68	240
21	13.760 661	1220.142 887	.000 819 5761	.072 671	88.668 915	.011 277 9095	13.54	1.842 033	8.77	252
22	15.590 506	1395.108 161	.000 716 7903	.064 142	89.484 469	.011 175 1236	13.42	1.950 233	8.86	264
23	17.663 678	1593.339 712	.000 627 6126	.056 613	90.204 301	.011 085 9459	13.31	2.059 721	8.96	276
24	20.012 533	1817.931 409	.000 550 0758	.049 969	90.839 647	.011 008 4091	13.22	2.170 422	9.04	288
25	22.673 730	2072.388 535	.000 482 5350	.044 104	91.400 424	.010 940 8683	13.13	2.282 260	9.13	300
26	25.688 804	2360.682 489	.000 423 6063	.038 927	91.895 382	.010 881 9396	13.06	2.395 165	9.21	312
27	29.104 813	2687.312 778	.000 372 1189	.034 359	92.332 247	.010 830 4523	13.00	2.509 067	9.29	324
28	32.975 070	3057.377 233	.000 327 0777	.030 326	92.717 838	.010 785 4111	12.95	2.623 898	9.37	336
29	37.359 981	3476.651 581	.000 287 6331	.026 767	93.058 173	.010 745 9664	12.90	2.739 596	9.45	348
30	42.327 982	3951.679 583	.000 253 0570	.023 625	93.358 563	.010 711 3903	12.86	2.856 101	9.52	360
31	47.956 611	4489.875 167	.000 222 7233	.020 852	93.623 696	.010 681 0567	12.82	2.973 353	9.59	372
32	54.333 716	5099.638 140	.000 196 0923	.018 405	93.857 710	.010 654 4257	12.79	3.091 299	9.66	384
33	61.558 825	5790.485 286	.000 172 6971	.016 245	94.064 259	.010 631 0304	12.76	3.209 888	9.73	396
34	69.744 705	6573.198 898	.000 152 1329	.014 338	94.246 565	.010 610 4663	12.74	3.329 070	9.79	408
35	79.019 115	7459.995 062	.000 134 0483	.012 655	94.407 474	.010 592 3817	12.72	3.448 800	9.85	420
36	89.526 804	8464.714 314	.000 118 1375	.011 170	94.549 497	.010 576 4708	12.70	3.569 035	9.91	432
37	101.431 769	9603.037 662	.000 104 1337	.009 859	94.674 852	.010 562 4670	12.68	3.689 735	9.97	444
38	114.919 815	10892.731 314	.000 091 8043	.008 702	94.785 493	.010 550 1377	12.67	3.810 863	10.03	456
39	130.201 455	12353.923 971	.000 080 9459	.007 680	94.883 148	.010 539 2793	12.65	3.932 383	10.08	468
40	147.515 194	14009.420 979	.000 071 3805	.006 779	94.969 342	.010 529 7139	12.64	4.054 263	10.14	480
41	167.131 255	15885.060 258	.000 062 9522	.005 983	95.045 419	.010 521 2856	12.63	4.176 472	10.19	492
42	189.355 792	18010.115 566	.000 055 5244	.005 281	95.112 568	.010 513 8577	12.62	4.298 984	10.24	504
43	214.535 671	20417.753 387	.000 048 9770	.004 661	95.171 835	.010 507 3103	12.61	4.421 772	10.28	516
44	243.063 883	23145.550 564	.000 043 2048	.004 114	95.224 146	.010 501 5382	12.61	4.544 812	10.33	528
45	275.385 678	26236.080 784	.000 038 1154	.003 631	95.270 317	.010 496 4488	12.60	4.668 082	10.37	540
46	312.005 514	29737.579 033	.000 033 6275	.003 205	95.311 069	.010 491 9608	12.60	4.791 562	10.42	552
47	353.494 929	33704.694 419	.000 029 6695	.002 829	95.347 038	.010 488 0028	12.59	4.915 234	10.46	564
48	400.501 463	38199.343 100	.000 026 1785	.002 497	95.378 785	.010 484 5118	12.59	5.039 079	10.50	576
49	453.758 764	43291.674 630	.000 023 0991	.002 204	95.406 807	.010 481 4325	12.58	5.163 082	10.54	588
50	514.098 036	49061.166 811	.000 020 3827	.001 945	95.431 539	.010 478 7161	12.58	5.287 230	10.57	600

MONTHLY COMPOUND INTEREST AND ANNUITY

	Amount Of 1	Amount Of 1 Per Period	Sinking Fund Payment	Present Worth Of 1	Present Worth of 1 Per Period	Periodic Payment To Amortize 1	Constant Annual Percent	Total Interest	Annual Add On Rate
	What a single $1 deposit grows to in the future. The deposit is made at the beginning of the first period.	What a series of $1 deposits grow to in the future. A deposit is made at the end of each period.	The amount to be deposited at the end of each period that grows to $1 in the future.	What $1 to be paid in the future is worth today. Value today of a single $1 payment tomorrow.	What $1 to be paid at the end of each period is worth today. Value today of a series of $1 payments tomorrow.	The mortgage payment to amortize a loan of $1. An annuity certain, payable at the end of each period, worth $1 today.	The annual payment, including interest and principal, to amortize completely a loan of $100.	The total interest paid over the term on a loan of $1. The loan is amortized by regular periodic payments.	The average annual interest rate on a loan that is completely amortized by regular periodic payments.
	$S = (1+i)^n$	$S\overline{n}| = \dfrac{(1+i)^n - 1}{i}$	$\dfrac{1}{S\overline{n}|} = \dfrac{i}{(1+i)^n - 1}$	$V^n = \dfrac{1}{(1+i)^n}$	$A\overline{n}| = \dfrac{1 - V^n}{i}$	$\dfrac{1}{A\overline{n}|} = \dfrac{i}{1 - V^n}$			

YEAR									PERIODS
	1.010 500	1.000 000	1.000 000 0000	.989 609	.989 609	1.010 500 0000	1212.60	.010 500	12.60	1
	1.021 110	2.010 500	.497 388 7093	.979 326	1.968 935	.507 888 7093	609.47	.015 777	9.47	2
	1.031 832	3.031 610	.329 857 7052	.969 150	2.938 085	.340 357 7052	408.43	.021 073	8.43	3
	1.042 666	4.063 442	.246 096 7724	.959 080	3.897 165	.256 596 7724	307.92	.026 387	7.92	4
	1.053 614	5.106 108	.195 843 8680	.949 114	4.846 279	.206 343 8680	247.62	.031 719	7.61	5
	1.064 677	6.159 722	.162 344 9774	.939 252	5.785 531	.172 844 9774	207.42	.037 070	7.41	6
	1.075 856	7.224 400	.138 419 8087	.929 492	6.715 023	.148 919 8087	178.71	.042 439	7.28	7
	1.087 153	8.300 256	.120 478 2158	.919 834	7.634 857	.130 978 2158	157.18	.047 826	7.17	8
	1.098 568	9.387 408	.106 525 6732	.910 276	8.545 133	.117 025 6732	140.44	.053 231	7.10	9
	1.110 103	10.485 976	.095 365 4654	.900 818	9.445 951	.105 865 4654	127.04	.058 655	7.04	10
	1.121 759	11.596 079	.086 236 0463	.891 457	10.337 408	.096 736 0463	116.09	.064 097	6.99	11
	1.133 537	12.717 838	.078 629 7182	.882 194	11.219 602	.089 129 7182	106.96	.069 557	6.96	12
1	1.133 537	12.717 838	.078 629 7182	.882 194	11.219 602	.089 129 7182	106.96	.069 557	6.96	12
2	1.284 907	27.133 981	.036 854 1569	.778 267	21.117 470	.047 354 1569	56.83	.136 500	6.82	24
3	1.456 490	43.475 217	.023 001 6101	.686 582	29.849 312	.033 501 6101	40.21	.206 058	6.87	36
4	1.650 985	61.998 618	.016 129 3917	.605 699	37.552 491	.026 629 3917	31.96	.278 211	6.96	48
5	1.871 454	82.995 584	.012 048 8338	.534 344	44.348 191	.022 548 8338	27.06	.352 930	7.06	60
6	2.121 362	106.796 428	.009 363 6091	.471 395	50.343 319	.019 863 6091	23.84	.430 180	7.17	72
7	2.404 644	133.775 572	.007 475 2063	.415 862	55.632 185	.017 975 2063	21.58	.509 917	7.28	84
8	2.725 753	164.357 438	.006 084 3003	.366 871	60.297 992	.016 584 3003	19.91	.592 093	7.40	96
9	3.089 743	199.023 123	.005 024 5418	.323 652	64.414 139	.015 524 5418	18.63	.676 651	7.52	108
10	3.502 339	238.317 971	.004 196 0747	.285 523	68.045 381	.014 696 0747	17.64	.763 529	7.64	120
11	3.970 032	282.860 146	.003 535 3160	.251 887	71.248 841	.014 035 3160	16.85	.852 662	7.75	132
12	4.500 179	333.350 363	.002 999 8467	.222 213	74.074 915	.013 499 8467	16.20	.943 978	7.87	144
13	5.101 121	390.582 907	.002 560 2759	.196 035	76.568 061	.013 060 2759	15.68	1.037 403	7.98	156
14	5.782 310	455.458 130	.002 195 5915	.172 941	78.767 500	.012 695 5915	15.24	1.132 859	8.09	168
15	6.554 464	528.996 616	.001 890 3713	.152 568	80.707 832	.012 390 3713	14.87	1.230 267	8.20	180
16	7.429 730	612.355 231	.001 633 0390	.134 594	82.419 581	.012 133 0390	14.56	1.329 543	8.31	192
17	8.421 876	706.845 331	.001 414 7367	.118 738	83.929 677	.011 914 7367	14.30	1.430 606	8.42	204
18	9.546 511	813.953 384	.001 228 5716	.104 750	85.261 875	.011 728 5716	14.08	1.533 371	8.52	216
19	10.821 326	935.364 356	.001 069 1021	.092 410	86.437 132	.011 569 1021	13.89	1.637 755	8.62	228
20	12.266 376	1072.988 221	.000 931 9767	.081 524	87.473 936	.011 431 9767	13.72	1.743 674	8.72	240
21	13.904 395	1228.990 005	.000 813 6763	.071 920	88.388 599	.011 313 6763	13.58	1.851 046	8.81	252
22	15.761 150	1405.823 846	.000 711 3267	.063 447	89.195 510	.011 211 3267	13.46	1.959 790	8.91	264
23	17.865 852	1606.271 599	.000 622 5597	.055 973	89.907 362	.011 122 5597	13.35	2.069 826	9.00	276
24	20.251 609	1833.486 604	.000 545 4089	.049 379	90.535 353	.011 045 4089	13.26	2.181 078	9.09	288
25	22.955 955	2091.043 286	.000 478 2302	.043 562	91.089 364	.010 978 2302	13.18	2.293 469	9.17	300
26	26.021 431	2382.993 392	.000 419 6403	.038 430	91.578 108	.010 919 6403	13.11	2.406 928	9.26	312
27	29.496 262	2713.929 725	.000 368 4694	.033 903	92.009 276	.010 868 4694	13.05	2.521 384	9.34	324
28	33.435 113	3089.058 401	.000 323 7232	.029 909	92.389 650	.010 823 7232	12.99	2.636 771	9.42	336
29	37.899 948	3514.280 747	.000 284 5532	.026 385	92.725 213	.010 784 5532	12.95	2.753 025	9.49	348
30	42.961 004	3996.286 135	.000 250 2323	.023 277	93.021 245	.010 750 2323	12.91	2.870 084	9.57	360
31	48.697 901	4542.657 219	.000 220 1355	.020 535	93.282 403	.010 720 1355	12.87	2.987 890	9.64	372
32	55.200 887	5161.989 221	.000 193 7238	.018 116	93.512 795	.010 693 7238	12.84	3.106 390	9.71	384
33	62.572 264	5864.025 145	.000 170 5313	.015 982	93.716 046	.010 670 5313	12.81	3.225 530	9.77	396
34	70.927 995	6659.809 048	.000 150 1545	.014 099	93.895 352	.010 650 1545	12.79	3.345 263	9.84	408
35	80.399 528	7561.859 781	.000 132 2426	.012 438	94.053 535	.010 632 2426	12.76	3.465 542	9.90	420
36	91.135 863	8584.367 932	.000 116 4908	.010 973	94.193 083	.010 616 4908	12.74	3.586 324	9.96	432
37	103.305 900	9743.419 056	.000 102 6334	.009 680	94.316 192	.010 602 6334	12.73	3.707 569	10.02	444
38	117.101 091	11057.246 734	.000 090 4384	.008 540	94.424 797	.010 590 4384	12.71	3.829 240	10.08	456
39	132.738 454	12546.519 408	.000 079 7034	.007 534	94.520 608	.010 579 7034	12.70	3.951 301	10.13	468
40	150.463 988	14234.665 529	.000 070 2510	.006 646	94.605 133	.010 570 2510	12.69	4.073 720	10.18	480
41	170.556 542	16148.242 120	.000 061 9262	.005 863	94.679 699	.010 561 9262	12.68	4.196 468	10.24	492
42	193.332 202	18317.352 555	.000 054 5930	.005 172	94.745 482	.010 554 5930	12.67	4.319 515	10.28	504
43	219.149 261	20776.120 133	.000 048 1322	.004 563	94.803 514	.010 548 1322	12.66	4.442 836	10.33	516
44	248.413 861	23563.224 887	.000 042 4390	.004 026	94.854 710	.010 542 4390	12.66	4.566 408	10.38	528
45	281.586 377	26722.512 075	.000 037 4216	.003 551	94.899 875	.010 537 4216	12.65	4.690 208	10.42	540
46	319.188 660	30303.681 933	.000 032 9993	.003 133	94.939 720	.010 532 9993	12.64	4.814 216	10.47	552
47	361.812 251	34363.071 533	.000 029 1010	.002 764	94.974 870	.010 529 1010	12.64	4.938 413	10.51	564
48	410.127 681	38964.541 046	.000 025 6644	.002 438	95.005 880	.010 525 6644	12.64	5.062 783	10.55	576
49	464.895 023	44180.478 358	.000 022 6344	.002 151	95.033 236	.010 522 6344	12.63	5.187 309	10.59	588
50	526.975 847	50092.937 837	.000 019 9629	.001 898	95.057 370	.010 519 9629	12.63	5.311 978	10.62	600

Effective Rate is 13.35 %

Annual Percentage Rate is 12.60 %

MONTHLY COMPOUND INTEREST AND ANNUITY

12.625% M

Amount Of 1	Amount Of 1 Per Period	Sinking Fund Payment	Present Worth Of 1	Present Worth of 1 Per Period	Periodic Payment To Amortize 1	Constant Annual Percent	Total Interest	Annual Add On Rate	
What a single $ 1 deposit grows to in the future. The deposit is made at the beginning of the first period.	What a series of $ 1 deposits grow to in the future. A deposit is made at the end of each period.	The amount to be deposited at the end of each period that grows to $ 1 in the future.	What $ 1 to be paid in the future is worth today. Value today of a single $ 1 payment tomorrow.	What $ 1 to be paid at the end of each period is worth today. Value today of a series of $ 1 payments tomorrow.	The mortgage payment to amortize a loan of $ 1. An annuity certain, payable at the end of each period, worth $ 1 today.	The annual payment, including interest and principal, to amortize completely a loan of $ 100.	The total interest paid over the term on a loan of $1. The loan is amortized by regular periodic payments.	The average annual interest rate on a loan that is completely amortized by regular periodic payments.	

$$S = (1+i)^n \qquad S\overline{n}| = \frac{(1+i)^n - 1}{i} \qquad \frac{1}{S\overline{n}|} = \frac{i}{(1+i)^n - 1} \qquad V^n = \frac{1}{(1+i)^n} \qquad A\overline{n}| = \frac{1-V^n}{i} \qquad \frac{1}{A\overline{n}|} = \frac{i}{1-V^n}$$

PERIODS

YEAR	Amount Of 1	Amount Of 1 Per Period	Sinking Fund Payment	Present Worth Of 1	Present Worth of 1 Per Period	Periodic Payment To Amortize 1	Constant Annual Percent	Total Interest	Annual Add On Rate	PERIODS
	1.010 521	1.000 000	1.000 000 0000	.989 589	.989 589	1.010 520 8333	1212.63	.010 521	12.63	1
	1.021 152	2.010 521	.497 383 5553	.979 286	1.968 875	.507 904 3886	609.49	.015 809	9.49	2
	1.031 896	3.031 673	.329 850 8573	.969 090	2.937 965	.340 371 6906	408.45	.021 115	8.45	3
	1.042 752	4.063 569	.246 089 0957	.959 001	3.896 965	.256 609 9291	307.94	.026 440	7.93	4
	1.053 723	5.106 321	.195 835 7085	.949 016	4.845 982	.206 356 5418	247.63	.031 783	7.63	5
	1.064 809	6.160 044	.162 336 5081	.939 136	5.785 117	.172 857 3414	207.43	.037 144	7.43	6
	1.076 011	7.224 853	.138 411 1284	.929 358	6.714 475	.148 931 9617	178.72	.042 524	7.29	7
	1.087 332	8.300 864	.120 469 3863	.919 682	7.634 158	.130 990 2197	157.19	.047 922	7.19	8
	1.098 772	9.388 196	.106 516 7357	.910 107	8.544 265	.117 037 5691	140.45	.053 338	7.11	9
	1.110 332	10.486 968	.095 356 4488	.900 632	9.444 897	.105 877 2821	127.06	.058 773	7.05	10
	1.122 013	11.597 299	.086 226 9714	.891 255	10.336 152	.096 747 8047	116.10	.064 226	7.01	11
	1.133 818	12.719 313	.078 620 6009	.881 976	11.218 128	.089 141 4342	106.97	.069 697	6.97	12
1	1.133 818	12.719 313	.078 620 6009	.881 976	11.218 128	.089 141 4342	106.97	.069 697	6.97	12
2	1.285 543	27.140 695	.036 845 0399	.777 882	21.112 247	.047 365 8733	56.84	.136 781	6.84	24
3	1.457 571	43.491 915	.022 992 7792	.686 073	29.838 622	.033 513 6125	40.22	.206 490	6.88	36
4	1.652 620	62.031 219	.016 120 9149	.605 100	37.535 074	.026 641 7483	31.98	.278 804	6.97	48
5	1.873 770	83.051 411	.012 040 7347	.533 683	44.323 160	.022 561 5680	27.08	.353 694	7.07	60
6	2.124 514	106.884 478	.009 355 8955	.470 696	50.310 089	.019 876 7288	23.86	.431 124	7.19	72
7	2.408 811	133.906 832	.007 467 8788	.415 142	55.590 416	.017 988 7122	21.59	.511 052	7.30	84
8	2.731 153	164.545 259	.006 077 3553	.366 146	60.247 538	.016 598 1886	19.92	.593 426	7.42	96
9	3.096 630	199.283 650	.005 017 9731	.322 932	64.355 007	.015 538 8064	18.65	.678 191	7.54	108
10	3.511 014	238.670 656	.004 189 8741	.284 818	67.977 696	.014 710 7074	17.66	.765 285	7.65	120
11	3.980 850	283.328 343	.003 529 4739	.251 203	71.172 821	.014 050 3073	16.87	.854 641	7.77	132
12	4.513 559	333.962 023	.002 994 3524	.221 555	73.990 844	.013 515 1858	16.22	.946 187	7.88	144
13	5.117 553	391.371 388	.002 555 1178	.195 406	76.476 272	.013 075 9511	15.70	1.039 848	8.00	156
14	5.802 373	456.463 146	.002 190 7574	.172 343	78.668 361	.012 711 5907	15.26	1.135 547	8.11	168
15	6.578 833	530.265 338	.001 885 8483	.152 003	80.601 730	.012 406 6817	14.89	1.233 203	8.22	180
16	7.459 198	613.943 575	.001 628 8142	.134 063	82.306 915	.012 149 6475	14.58	1.332 732	8.33	192
17	8.457 371	708.819 446	.001 410 7965	.118 240	83.810 847	.011 931 6298	14.32	1.434 052	8.44	204
18	9.589 118	816.391 395	.001 224 9027	.104 285	85.137 279	.011 745 7360	14.10	1.537 079	8.54	216
19	10.872 312	938.358 382	.001 065 6909	.091 977	86.307 160	.011 586 5242	13.91	1.641 728	8.64	228
20	12.327 221	1076.646 719	.000 928 8098	.081 121	87.338 967	.011 449 6431	13.74	1.747 914	8.74	240
21	13.976 822	1233.440 492	.000 810 7404	.071 547	88.248 996	.011 331 5737	13.60	1.855 557	8.84	252
22	15.847 169	1411.216 059	.000 708 6407	.063 103	89.051 619	.011 229 4420	13.48	1.964 573	8.93	264
23	17.967 802	1612.781 155	.000 620 0469	.055 655	89.759 514	.011 140 8803	13.37	2.074 883	9.02	276
24	20.372 213	1841.319 242	.000 543 0889	.049 086	90.383 860	.011 063 9222	13.28	2.186 410	9.11	288
25	23.098 377	2100.439 786	.000 476 0908	.043 293	90.934 519	.010 996 9241	13.20	2.299 077	9.20	300
26	26.189 350	2394.235 263	.000 417 6699	.038 183	91.420 186	.010 938 5032	13.13	2.412 813	9.28	312
27	29.693 951	2727.345 794	.000 366 6568	.033 677	91.848 533	.010 887 4902	13.07	2.527 547	9.36	324
28	33.667 529	3105.032 434	.000 322 0578	.029 702	92.226 325	.010 842 8912	13.02	2.643 211	9.44	336
29	38.172 842	3533.260 257	.000 283 0247	.026 197	92.559 528	.010 803 8581	12.97	2.759 743	9.52	348
30	43.281 047	4018.792 571	.000 248 8310	.023 105	92.853 405	.010 769 6643	12.93	2.877 079	9.59	360
31	49.072 820	4569.297 736	.000 218 8520	.020 378	93.112 598	.010 739 6853	12.89	2.995 163	9.66	372
32	55.639 635	5193.470 274	.000 192 5495	.017 973	93.341 199	.010 713 3828	12.86	3.113 939	9.73	384
33	63.085 207	5901.168 187	.000 169 4580	.015 852	93.542 820	.010 690 2913	12.83	3.233 355	9.80	396
34	71.527 129	6703.568 655	.000 149 1743	.013 981	93.720 645	.010 670 0076	12.81	3.353 363	9.86	408
35	81.098 729	7613.344 564	.000 131 3483	.012 331	93.877 483	.010 652 1817	12.79	3.473 916	9.93	420
36	91.951 180	8644.864 654	.000 115 6756	.010 875	94.015 810	.010 636 5089	12.77	3.594 972	9.99	432
37	104.255 882	9814.420 460	.000 101 8909	.009 592	94.137 811	.010 622 7242	12.75	3.716 490	10.04	444
38	118.207 171	11140.483 613	.000 089 7627	.008 460	94.245 412	.010 610 5960	12.74	3.838 432	10.10	456
39	134.025 391	12643.997 579	.000 079 0889	.007 461	94.340 315	.010 599 9222	12.72	3.960 764	10.16	468
40	151.960 370	14348.708 427	.000 069 6927	.006 581	94.424 016	.010 590 5260	12.71	4.083 452	10.21	480
41	172.295 367	16281.539 876	.000 061 4193	.005 804	94.497 839	.010 582 2526	12.70	4.206 468	10.26	492
42	195.351 549	18473.018 516	.000 054 1330	.005 119	94.562 949	.010 574 9663	12.69	4.329 783	10.31	504
43	221.493 057	20957.755 937	.000 047 7150	.004 515	94.620 374	.010 568 5484	12.69	4.453 371	10.36	516
44	251.132 764	23774.995 373	.000 042 0610	.003 982	94.671 022	.010 562 8943	12.68	4.577 208	10.40	528
45	284.738 790	26969.231 503	.000 037 0793	.003 512	94.715 692	.010 557 9126	12.67	4.701 273	10.45	540
46	322.841 899	30590.913 183	.000 032 6894	.003 097	94.755 090	.010 553 5228	12.67	4.825 545	10.49	552
47	366.043 881	34694.240 222	.000 028 8207	.002 732	94.789 838	.010 549 6541	12.66	4.950 005	10.53	564
48	415.027 057	39353.066 780	.000 025 4110	.002 409	94.820 485	.010 546 2443	12.66	5.074 637	10.57	576
49	470.565 051	44631.925 657	.000 022 4055	.002 125	94.847 515	.010 543 2388	12.66	5.199 424	10.61	588
50	533.535 016	50617.189 647	.000 019 7561	.001 874	94.871 354	.010 540 5895	12.65	5.324 354	10.65	600

Effective Rate is 13.38 %

Annual Percentage Rate is 12.625%

Amount Of 1	Amount Of 1 Per Period	Sinking Fund Payment	Present Worth Of 1	Present Worth of 1 Per Period	Periodic Payment To Amortize 1	Constant Annual Percent	Total Interest	Annual Add On Rate
What a single $ 1 deposit grows to in the future. The deposit is made at the beginning of the first period.	What a series of $ 1 deposits grow to in the future. A deposit is made at the end of each period.	The amount to be deposited at the end of each period that grows to $ 1 in the future.	What $ 1 to be paid in the future is worth today. Value today of a single $ 1 payment tomorrow.	What $ 1 to be paid at the end of each period is worth today. Value today of a series of $ 1 payments tomorrow.	The mortgage payment to amortize a loan of $ 1. An annuity certain, payable at the end of each period, worth $ 1 today.	The annual payment, including interest and principal, to amortize completely a loan of $ 100.	The total interest paid over the term on a loan of $1. The loan is amortized by regular periodic payments.	The average annual interest rate on a loan that is completely amortized by regular periodic payments.

$$S = (1+i)^n \qquad S\overline{n}| = \frac{(1+i)^n - 1}{i} \qquad \frac{1}{S\overline{n}|} = \frac{i}{(1+i)^n - 1} \qquad V^n = \frac{1}{(1+i)^n} \qquad A\overline{n}| = \frac{1-V^n}{i} \qquad \frac{1}{A\overline{n}|} = \frac{i}{1-V^n}$$

YEAR   **PERIODS**

Year	Amount Of 1	Amount Of 1 Per Period	Sinking Fund Payment	Present Worth Of 1	Present Worth of 1 Per Period	Periodic Payment To Amortize 1	Constant Annual Percent	Total Interest	Annual Add On Rate	Periods
	1.010 542	1.000 000	1.000 000 0000	.989 568	.989 568	1.010 541 6667	1212.65	.010 542	12.65	1
	1.021 194	2.010 542	.497 378 4013	.979 245	1.968 814	.507 920 0680	609.51	.015 840	9.50	2
	1.031 960	3.031 736	.329 844 0096	.969 030	2.937 844	.340 385 6762	408.47	.021 157	8.46	3
	1.042 838	4.063 696	.246 081 4193	.958 922	3.896 766	.256 623 0859	307.95	.026 492	7.95	4
	1.053 831	5.106 534	.195 827 5493	.948 918	4.845 684	.206 369 2159	247.65	.031 846	7.64	5
	1.064 941	6.160 365	.162 328 0391	.939 020	5.784 704	.172 869 7058	207.45	.037 218	7.44	6
	1.076 167	7.225 306	.138 402 4485	.929 224	6.713 928	.148 944 1152	178.74	.042 609	7.30	7
	1.087 511	8.301 472	.120 460 5574	.919 531	7.633 458	.131 002 2241	157.21	.048 018	7.20	8
	1.098 976	9.388 984	.106 507 7989	.909 938	8.543 397	.117 049 4655	140.46	.053 445	7.13	9
	1.110 561	10.487 959	.095 347 4328	.900 446	9.443 843	.105 889 0995	127.07	.058 891	7.07	10
	1.122 268	11.598 520	.086 217 8973	.891 053	10.334 896	.096 759 5640	116.12	.064 355	7.02	11
	1.134 098	12.720 788	.078 611 4844	.881 758	11.216 653	.089 153 1510	106.99	.069 838	6.98	12
1	1.134 098	12.720 788	.078 611 4844	.881 758	11.216 653	.089 153 1510	106.99	.069 838	6.98	12
2	1.286 179	27.147 411	.036 835 9247	.777 497	21.107 025	.047 377 5913	56.86	.137 062	6.85	24
3	1.458 653	43.508 621	.022 983 9508	.685 564	29.827 937	.033 525 6175	40.24	.206 922	6.90	36
4	1.654 256	62.063 841	.016 112 4415	.604 501	37.517 669	.026 654 1081	31.99	.279 397	6.98	48
5	1.876 089	83.107 284	.012 032 6396	.533 024	44.298 150	.022 574 3063	27.09	.354 458	7.09	60
6	2.127 670	106.972 618	.009 348 1867	.469 998	50.276 892	.019 889 8534	23.87	.432 069	7.20	72
7	2.412 987	134.038 252	.007 460 5569	.414 424	55.548 694	.018 002 2235	21.61	.512 187	7.32	84
8	2.736 564	164.733 341	.006 070 4165	.365 487	60.197 146	.016 612 0832	19.94	.594 760	7.43	96
9	3.103 533	199.544 591	.005 011 4112	.322 213	64.295 955	.015 553 0779	18.67	.679 732	7.55	108
10	3.519 711	239.023 969	.004 183 6808	.284 114	67.910 112	.014 725 3475	17.68	.767 042	7.67	120
11	3.991 698	283.797 466	.003 523 6396	.250 520	71.096 923	.014 065 3063	16.88	.856 620	7.79	132
12	4.526 978	334.575 012	.002 988 8664	.220 898	73.906 918	.013 530 5330	16.24	.948 397	7.90	144
13	5.134 038	392.161 741	.002 549 9683	.194 778	76.384 654	.013 091 6349	15.71	1.042 295	8.02	156
14	5.822 504	457.470 753	.002 185 9321	.171 747	78.569 416	.012 727 5988	15.28	1.138 237	8.13	168
15	6.603 292	531.537 592	.001 881 3345	.151 440	80.495 847	.012 423 0011	14.91	1.236 140	8.24	180
16	7.488 782	615.536 669	.001 624 5986	.133 533	82.194 493	.012 166 2652	14.60	1.335 923	8.35	192
17	8.493 015	710.799 880	.001 406 8657	.117 744	83.692 287	.011 948 5324	14.34	1.437 501	8.46	204
18	9.631 914	818.837 725	.001 221 2432	.103 822	85.012 978	.011 762 9099	14.12	1.540 789	8.56	216
19	10.923 538	941.363 262	.001 062 2892	.091 545	86.177 508	.011 603 9558	13.93	1.645 702	8.66	228
20	12.388 366	1080.319 266	.000 925 6523	.080 721	87.204 342	.011 467 3190	13.77	1.752 157	8.76	240
21	14.049 624	1237.909 034	.000 807 8138	.071 176	88.109 760	.011 349 4805	13.62	1.860 069	8.86	252
22	15.933 655	1416.631 323	.000 705 9000	.062 760	88.908 120	.011 247 5666	13.50	1.969 358	8.95	264
23	18.070 331	1619.319 967	.000 617 5432	.055 339	89.612 080	.011 159 2098	13.40	2.079 942	9.04	276
24	20.493 532	1849.188 815	.000 540 7777	.048 796	90.232 802	.011 082 4443	13.30	2.191 744	9.13	288
25	23.241 680	2109.882 685	.000 473 9600	.043 026	90.780 128	.011 015 6267	13.22	2.304 688	9.22	300
26	26.358 350	2405.535 161	.000 415 7079	.037 939	91.262 738	.010 957 3746	13.15	2.418 701	9.30	312
27	29.892 960	2740.834 132	.000 364 8524	.033 453	91.688 282	.010 906 5191	13.09	2.533 712	9.38	324
28	33.901 555	3121.096 126	.000 320 4003	.029 497	92.063 509	.010 862 0669	13.04	2.649 654	9.46	336
29	38.447 696	3552.350 608	.000 281 5037	.026 009	92.394 369	.010 823 1704	12.99	2.766 463	9.54	348
30	43.603 467	4041.435 585	.000 247 4368	.022 934	92.686 107	.010 789 1035	12.95	2.884 077	9.61	360
31	49.450 618	4596.106 027	.000 217 5755	.020 222	92.943 349	.010 759 2422	12.92	3.002 438	9.69	372
32	56.081 862	5225.156 834	.000 191 3818	.017 831	93.170 175	.010 733 0485	12.88	3.121 491	9.75	384
33	63.602 344	5938.562 287	.000 168 3909	.015 723	93.370 180	.010 710 0576	12.86	3.241 183	9.82	396
34	72.131 311	6747.634 201	.000 148 2001	.013 864	93.546 535	.010 689 8668	12.83	3.361 466	9.89	408
35	81.803 997	7665.201 286	.000 130 4597	.012 224	93.702 039	.010 672 1264	12.81	3.482 293	9.95	420
36	92.773 774	8705.812 560	.000 114 8658	.010 779	93.839 155	.010 656 5325	12.79	3.603 622	10.01	432
37	105.214 580	9885.968 040	.000 101 1535	.009 504	93.960 058	.010 642 8201	12.78	3.725 412	10.07	444
38	119.323 676	11224.380 367	.000 089 0918	.008 381	94.066 666	.010 630 7584	12.76	3.847 626	10.13	456
39	135.324 779	12742.271 517	.000 078 4789	.007 390	94.160 668	.010 620 1456	12.75	3.970 228	10.18	468
40	153.471 602	14463.709 294	.000 069 1386	.006 516	94.243 554	.010 610 8052	12.74	4.093 187	10.23	480
41	174.051 884	16415.988 956	.000 060 9162	.005 745	94.316 641	.010 602 5829	12.73	4.216 471	10.28	492
42	197.391 946	18630.066 009	.000 053 6767	.005 066	94.381 085	.010 595 3433	12.72	4.340 053	10.33	504
43	223.861 871	21141.047 037	.000 047 3013	.004 467	94.437 909	.010 588 9680	12.71	4.463 907	10.38	516
44	253.881 368	23988.746 361	.000 041 6862	.003 939	94.488 014	.010 583 3529	12.71	4.588 010	10.43	528
45	287.926 429	27218.317 332	.000 036 7400	.003 473	94.532 195	.010 578 4066	12.70	4.712 340	10.47	540
46	326.536 874	30880.968 290	.000 032 3824	.003 062	94.571 152	.010 574 0491	12.69	4.836 875	10.51	552
47	370.324 915	35034.774 527	.000 028 5431	.002 700	94.605 502	.010 570 2097	12.69	4.961 598	10.56	564
48	419.984 858	39745.599 132	.000 025 1600	.002 381	94.635 791	.010 566 8267	12.69	5.086 492	10.60	576
49	476.304 114	45088.137 324	.000 022 1788	.002 099	94.662 498	.010 563 8454	12.68	5.211 541	10.64	588
50	540.175 688	51147.100 822	.000 019 5515	.001 851	94.686 047	.010 561 2181	12.68	5.336 731	10.67	600

Effective Rate is 13.41 %   8 - 200   Annual Percentage Rate is 12.65 %

MONTHLY COMPOUND INTEREST AND ANNUITY

Amount Of 1	Amount Of 1 Per Period	Sinking Fund Payment	Present Worth Of 1	Present Worth of 1 Per Period	Periodic Payment To Amortize 1	Constant Annual Percent	Total Interest	Annual Add On Rate
What a single $ 1 deposit grows to in the future. The deposit is made at the beginning of the first period.	What a series of $ 1 deposits grow to in the future. A deposit is made at the end of each period.	The amount to be deposited at the end of each period that grows to $ 1 in the future.	What $ 1 to be paid in the future is worth today. Value today of a single $ 1 payment tomorrow.	What $ 1 to be paid at the end of each period is worth today. Value today of a series of $ 1 payments tomorrow.	The mortgage payment to amortize a loan of $ 1. An annuity certain, payable at the end of each period, worth $ 1 today.	The annual payment, including interest and principal, to amortize completely a loan of $ 100.	The total interest paid over the term on a loan of $1. The loan is amortized completely by regular periodic payments.	The average annual interest rate on a loan that is completely amortized by regular periodic payments.

$$S = (1+i)^n \qquad S\overline{n}| = \frac{(1+i)^n - 1}{i} \qquad \frac{1}{S\overline{n}|} = \frac{i}{(1+i)^n - 1} \qquad V^n = \frac{1}{(1+i)^n} \qquad A\overline{n}| = \frac{1-V^n}{i} \qquad \frac{1}{A\overline{n}|} = \frac{i}{1-V^n}$$

PERIODS

YEAR	Amount Of 1	Amount Of 1 Per Period	Sinking Fund Payment	Present Worth Of 1	Present Worth of 1 Per Period	Periodic Payment To Amortize 1	Constant Annual Percent	Total Interest	Annual Add On Rate	
	1.010 583	1.000 000	1.000 000 0000	.989 528	.989 528	1.010 583 3333	1212.70	.010 583	12.70	1
	1.021 279	2.010 583	.497 368 0938	.979 165	1.968 692	.507 951 4272	609.55	.015 903	9.54	2
	1.032 087	3.031 862	.329 830 3147	.968 910	2.937 603	.340 413 6481	408.50	.021 241	8.50	3
	1.043 010	4.063 949	.246 066 0672	.958 763	3.896 366	.256 649 4005	307.98	.026 598	7.98	4
	1.054 049	5.106 959	.195 811 2319	.948 723	4.845 089	.206 394 5652	247.68	.031 973	7.67	5
	1.065 204	6.161 008	.162 311 1025	.938 787	5.783 876	.172 894 4358	207.48	.037 367	7.47	6
	1.076 477	7.226 212	.138 385 0903	.928 956	6.712 832	.148 968 4237	178.77	.042 779	7.33	7
	1.087 870	8.302 689	.120 442 9012	.919 227	7.632 059	.131 026 2345	157.24	.048 210	7.23	8
	1.099 383	9.390 560	.106 489 9270	.909 601	8.541 660	.117 073 2604	140.49	.053 659	7.15	9
	1.111 019	10.489 943	.095 329 4030	.900 075	9.441 735	.105 912 7364	127.10	.059 127	7.10	10
	1.122 777	11.600 962	.086 199 7515	.890 649	10.332 384	.096 783 0848	116.14	.064 614	7.05	11
	1.134 660	12.723 738	.078 593 2539	.881 322	11.213 706	.089 176 5872	107.02	.070 119	7.01	12
1	1.134 660	12.723 738	.078 593 2539	.881 322	11.213 706	.089 176 5872	107.02	.070 119	7.01	12
2	1.287 452	27.160 850	.036 817 6993	.776 728	21.096 587	.047 401 0326	56.89	.137 625	6.88	24
3	1.460 820	43.542 056	.022 966 3016	.684 547	29.806 584	.033 549 6350	40.26	.207 787	6.93	36
4	1.657 533	62.129 149	.016 095 5045	.603 306	37.482 892	.026 678 8379	32.02	.280 584	7.01	48
5	1.880 736	83.219 172	.012 016 4618	.531 707	44.248 189	.022 599 7952	27.12	.355 988	7.12	60
6	2.133 995	107.149 167	.009 332 7837	.468 605	50.210 591	.019 916 1170	23.90	.433 960	7.23	72
7	2.421 358	134.301 566	.007 445 9296	.412 991	55.465 385	.018 029 2629	21.64	.514 458	7.35	84
8	2.747 417	165.110 295	.006 056 5575	.363 978	60.096 548	.016 639 8909	19.97	.597 430	7.47	96
9	3.117 383	200.067 713	.004 998 3077	.320 782	64.178 092	.015 581 6411	18.70	.682 817	7.59	108
10	3.537 169	239.732 483	.004 171 3162	.282 712	67.775 246	.014 754 6496	17.71	.770 558	7.71	120
11	4.013 482	284.738 493	.003 511 9944	.249 160	70.945 495	.014 095 3278	16.92	.860 583	7.82	132
12	4.553 936	335.804 993	.002 977 9188	.219 590	73.739 504	.013 561 2521	16.28	.952 820	7.94	144
13	5.167 167	393.748 085	.002 539 6949	.193 530	76.201 924	.013 123 0282	15.75	1.047 192	8.06	156
14	5.862 976	459.493 769	.002 176 3081	.170 562	78.372 108	.012 759 6414	15.32	1.143 620	8.17	168
15	6.652 481	534.092 738	.001 872 3340	.150 320	80.284 739	.012 455 6673	14.95	1.242 020	8.28	180
16	7.548 302	618.737 172	.001 616 1951	.132 480	81.970 381	.012 199 5285	14.64	1.342 309	8.39	192
17	8.564 753	714.779 788	.001 399 0323	.116 758	83.455 975	.011 982 3656	14.38	1.444 403	8.50	204
18	9.718 079	823.755 461	.001 213 9525	.102 901	84.765 260	.011 797 2858	14.16	1.548 214	8.60	216
19	11.026 711	947.405 751	.001 055 5140	.090 689	85.919 161	.011 638 8473	13.97	1.653 657	8.70	228
20	12.511 563	1087.706 736	.000 919 3655	.079 926	86.936 120	.011 502 6988	13.81	1.760 648	8.80	240
21	14.196 365	1246.900 589	.000 801 9886	.070 441	87.832 387	.011 385 3219	13.67	1.869 101	8.90	252
22	16.108 041	1427.531 418	.000 700 5100	.062 081	88.622 287	.011 283 8433	13.55	1.978 935	9.00	264
23	18.277 143	1632.485 915	.000 612 5627	.054 713	89.318 443	.011 195 8960	13.44	2.090 067	9.09	276
24	20.738 335	1865.039 495	.000 536 1817	.048 220	89.931 980	.011 119 5150	13.35	2.202 420	9.18	288
25	23.530 950	2128.908 639	.000 469 7242	.042 497	90.472 703	.011 053 0576	13.27	2.315 917	9.26	300
26	26.699 617	2428.310 288	.000 411 8090	.037 454	90.949 255	.010 995 1423	13.20	2.430 484	9.35	312
27	30.294 976	2768.029 231	.000 361 2679	.033 009	91.369 250	.010 944 6012	13.14	2.546 051	9.43	324
28	34.374 484	3153.494 580	.000 317 1085	.029 091	91.739 400	.010 900 4419	13.09	2.662 548	9.51	336
29	39.003 337	3590.866 525	.000 278 4843	.025 639	92.065 622	.010 861 8176	13.04	2.779 913	9.59	348
30	44.255 510	4087.134 785	.000 244 6702	.022 596	92.353 129	.010 828 0035	13.00	2.898 081	9.66	360
31	50.214 937	4650.230 313	.000 215 0431	.019 914	92.606 514	.010 798 3764	12.96	3.016 996	9.73	372
32	56.976 859	5289.152 040	.000 189 0662	.017 551	92.829 828	.010 772 3996	12.93	3.136 601	9.80	384
33	64.649 338	6014.110 688	.000 166 2756	.015 468	93.026 640	.010 749 6090	12.90	3.256 845	9.87	396
34	73.354 990	6836.691 951	.000 146 2696	.013 632	93.200 094	.010 729 6029	12.88	3.377 678	9.93	408
35	83.232 941	7770.041 649	.000 128 6994	.012 014	93.352 963	.010 712 0328	12.86	3.499 054	10.00	420
36	94.441 052	8829.075 811	.000 113 2621	.010 589	93.487 690	.010 696 5955	12.84	3.620 929	10.06	432
37	107.158 443	10030.719 052	.000 099 6938	.009 332	93.606 427	.010 683 0271	12.82	3.743 264	10.12	444
38	121.588 353	11394.175 048	.000 087 7641	.008 224	93.711 074	.010 671 0975	12.81	3.866 020	10.17	456
39	137.961 387	12941.233 434	.000 077 2729	.007 248	93.803 300	.010 660 6057	12.80	3.989 163	10.23	468
40	156.539 207	14696.618 029	.000 068 0429	.006 388	93.884 582	.010 651 3762	12.79	4.112 661	10.28	480
41	177.618 709	16688.381 949	.000 059 9219	.005 630	93.956 217	.010 643 2553	12.78	4.236 482	10.33	492
42	201.536 767	18948.355 930	.000 052 7750	.004 962	94.019 351	.010 636 1084	12.77	4.360 599	10.38	504
43	228.675 620	21512.657 023	.000 046 4843	.004 373	94.074 992	.010 629 8176	12.76	4.484 986	10.43	516
44	259.468 980	24422.265 784	.000 040 9462	.003 854	94.124 029	.010 624 2796	12.75	4.609 620	10.48	528
45	294.408 959	27723.681 194	.000 036 0702	.003 397	94.167 247	.010 619 4036	12.75	4.734 478	10.52	540
46	334.053 941	31469.663 764	.000 031 7766	.002 994	94.205 336	.010 615 1100	12.74	4.859 541	10.56	552
47	379.037 500	35720.078 715	.000 027 9955	.002 638	94.238 904	.010 611 3288	12.74	4.984 789	10.61	564
48	430.078 524	40542.852 692	.000 024 6653	.002 325	94.268 489	.010 607 9986	12.73	5.110 207	10.65	576
49	487.992 711	46015.059 311	.000 021 7320	.002 049	94.294 563	.010 605 0653	12.73	5.235 778	10.69	588
50	553.705 597	52224.150 890	.000 019 1482	.001 806	94.317 542	.010 602 4816	12.73	5.361 489	10.72	600

Effective Rate is 13.47 %

Annual Percentage Rate is 12.70 %

MONTHLY COMPOUND INTEREST AND ANNUITY

12.75 % M

	Amount Of 1	Amount Of 1 Per Period	Sinking Fund Payment	Present Worth Of 1	Present Worth of 1 Per Period	Periodic Payment To Amortize 1	Constant Annual Percent	Total Interest	Annual Add On Rate	
	What a single $ 1 deposit grows to in the future. The deposit is made at the beginning of the first period.	What a series of $ 1 deposits grow to in the future. A deposit is made at the end of each period.	The amount to be deposited at the end of each period that grows to $ 1 in the future.	What $ 1 to be paid in the future is worth today. Value today of a single $ 1 payment tomorrow.	What $ 1 to be paid at the end of each period is worth today. Value today of a series of $ 1 payments tomorrow.	The mortgage payment to amortize a loan of $ 1. An annuity certain, payable at the end of each period, worth $ 1 today.	The annual payment, including interest and principal, to amortize completely a loan of $ 100.	The total interest paid over the term on a loan of $1. The loan is amortized by regular periodic payments.	The average annual interest rate on a loan that is completely amortized by regular periodic payments.	
	$S = (1+i)^n$	$S\overline{n}| = \dfrac{(1+i)^n - 1}{i}$	$\dfrac{1}{S\overline{n}|} = \dfrac{i}{(1+i)^n - 1}$	$V^n = \dfrac{1}{(1+i)^n}$	$A\overline{n}| = \dfrac{1 - V^n}{i}$	$\dfrac{1}{A\overline{n}|} = \dfrac{i}{1 - V^n}$				

YEAR										PERIODS
	1.010 625	1.000 000	1.000 000 0000	.989 487	.989 487	1.010 625 0000	1212.75	.010 625	12.75	1
	1.021 363	2.010 625	.497 357 7868	.979 084	1.968 571	.507 982 7868	609.58	.015 966	9.58	2
	1.032 215	3.031 988	.329 816 6207	.968 791	2.937 361	.340 441 6207	408.53	.021 325	8.53	3
	1.043 182	4.064 203	.246 050 7161	.958 605	3.895 967	.256 675 7161	308.02	.026 703	8.01	4
	1.054 266	5.107 385	.195 794 9159	.948 527	4.844 494	.206 419 9159	247.71	.032 100	7.70	5
	1.065 468	6.161 651	.162 294 1675	.938 555	5.783 049	.172 919 1675	207.51	.037 515	7.50	6
	1.076 788	7.227 118	.138 367 7341	.928 688	6.711 737	.148 992 7341	178.80	.042 949	7.36	7
	1.088 229	8.303 907	.120 425 2472	.918 924	7.630 661	.131 050 2472	157.27	.048 402	7.26	8
	1.099 791	9.392 136	.106 472 0578	.909 263	8.539 924	.117 097 0578	140.52	.053 874	7.18	9
	1.111 477	10.491 927	.095 311 3760	.899 704	9.439 628	.105 936 3760	127.13	.059 364	7.12	10
	1.123 286	11.603 404	.086 181 6087	.890 245	10.329 873	.096 806 6087	116.17	.064 873	7.08	11
	1.135 221	12.726 690	.078 575 0269	.880 886	11.210 759	.089 200 0269	107.05	.070 400	7.04	12
1	1.135 221	12.726 690	.078 575 0269	.880 886	11.210 759	.089 200 0269	107.05	.070 400	7.04	12
2	1.288 727	27.174 297	.036 799 4807	.775 960	21.086 156	.047 424 4807	56.91	.138 188	6.91	24
3	1.462 990	43.575 524	.022 948 6626	.683 532	29.785 252	.033 573 6626	40.29	.208 652	6.96	36
4	1.660 817	62.194 543	.016 078 5809	.602 113	37.448 161	.026 703 5809	32.05	.281 772	7.04	48
5	1.885 394	83.331 247	.012 000 3005	.530 393	44.198 308	.022 625 3005	27.16	.357 518	7.15	60
6	2.140 340	107.326 078	.009 317 4000	.467 216	50.144 416	.019 942 4000	23.94	.435 853	7.26	72
7	2.429 759	134.565 516	.007 431 3244	.411 564	55.382 257	.018 056 3244	21.67	.516 731	7.38	84
8	2.758 313	165.488 300	.006 042 7233	.362 540	59.996 197	.016 667 7233	20.01	.600 101	7.50	96
9	3.131 295	200.592 497	.004 985 2313	.319 357	64.060 550	.015 610 2313	18.74	.685 905	7.62	108
10	3.554 712	240.443 521	.004 158 9809	.281 317	67.640 780	.014 783 9809	17.75	.774 078	7.74	120
11	4.035 384	285.683 243	.003 500 3803	.247 808	70.794 554	.014 125 3803	16.96	.864 550	7.86	132
12	4.581 054	337.040 330	.002 967 0040	.218 290	73.572 668	.013 592 0040	16.32	.957 249	7.98	144
13	5.200 509	395.341 977	.002 529 4557	.192 289	76.019 869	.013 154 4557	15.79	1.052 095	8.09	156
14	5.903 727	461.527 236	.002 166 7194	.169 385	78.175 574	.012 791 7194	15.36	1.149 009	8.21	168
15	6.702 035	536.662 137	.001 863 3698	.149 208	80.074 503	.012 488 3698	14.99	1.247 907	8.32	180
16	7.608 292	621.956 861	.001 607 8286	.131 436	81.747 242	.012 232 8286	14.68	1.348 703	8.43	192
17	8.637 093	718.785 230	.001 391 2362	.115 780	83.220 735	.012 016 2362	14.42	1.451 312	8.54	204
18	9.805 010	828.706 835	.001 206 6994	.101 989	84.518 713	.011 831 6994	14.20	1.555 647	8.64	216
19	11.130 854	953.492 158	.001 048 7763	.089 840	85.662 083	.011 673 7763	14.01	1.661 621	8.75	228
20	12.635 980	1095.151 087	.000 913 1160	.079 139	86.669 262	.011 538 1160	13.85	1.769 148	8.85	240
21	14.344 631	1255.965 290	.000 796 2003	.069 712	87.556 471	.011 421 2003	13.71	1.878 142	8.94	252
22	16.284 328	1438.524 963	.000 695 1565	.061 409	88.338 001	.011 320 1565	13.59	1.988 521	9.04	264
23	18.486 312	1645.770 552	.000 607 6181	.054 094	89.026 440	.011 232 6181	13.48	2.100 203	9.13	276
24	20.986 051	1881.040 113	.000 531 6208	.047 651	89.632 875	.011 156 6208	13.39	2.213 107	9.22	288
25	23.823 808	2148.123 079	.000 465 5227	.041 975	90.167 076	.011 090 5227	13.31	2.327 157	9.31	300
26	27.045 289	2451.321 292	.000 407 9433	.036 975	90.637 645	.011 032 9433	13.24	2.442 278	9.39	312
27	30.702 382	2795.518 294	.000 357 7154	.032 571	91.052 163	.010 982 7154	13.18	2.558 400	9.48	324
28	34.853 991	3186.257 987	.000 313 8478	.028 691	91.417 306	.010 938 8478	13.13	2.675 453	9.56	336
29	39.566 985	3629.833 924	.000 275 4947	.025 274	91.738 956	.010 900 4947	13.09	2.793 372	9.63	348
30	44.917 276	4133.390 677	.000 241 9321	.022 263	92.022 292	.010 866 9321	13.05	2.912 096	9.71	360
31	50.991 039	4705.038 919	.000 212 5381	.019 611	92.271 879	.010 837 5381	13.01	3.031 564	9.78	372
32	57.886 102	5353.986 054	.000 186 7767	.017 275	92.491 736	.010 811 7767	12.98	3.151 722	9.85	384
33	65.713 523	6090.684 520	.000 164 1852	.015 218	92.685 405	.010 789 1852	12.95	3.272 517	9.92	396
34	74.599 377	6927.000 150	.000 144 3626	.013 405	92.856 006	.010 769 3626	12.93	3.393 900	9.98	408
35	84.686 785	7876.403 282	.000 126 9615	.011 808	93.006 285	.010 751 9615	12.91	3.515 824	10.05	420
36	96.138 223	8954.185 731	.000 111 6796	.010 402	93.138 664	.010 736 6796	12.89	3.638 246	10.11	432
37	109.138 133	10177.707 086	.000 098 2540	.009 163	93.255 275	.010 723 2540	12.87	3.761 125	10.17	444
38	123.895 915	11566.674 321	.000 086 4553	.008 071	93.357 996	.010 711 4553	12.86	3.884 424	10.22	456
39	140.649 254	13143.459 206	.000 076 0835	.007 110	93.448 481	.010 701 0835	12.85	4.008 107	10.28	468
40	159.667 998	14933.458 646	.000 066 9637	.006 263	93.528 189	.010 691 9637	12.84	4.132 143	10.33	480
41	181.258 477	16965.503 744	.000 058 9431	.005 517	93.598 402	.010 683 9431	12.83	4.256 500	10.38	492
42	205.768 444	19272.324 174	.000 051 8879	.004 860	93.660 251	.010 676 8879	12.82	4.381 151	10.43	504
43	233.592 676	21891.075 355	.000 045 6807	.004 281	93.714 734	.010 670 6807	12.81	4.506 071	10.48	516
44	265.179 330	24863.936 899	.000 040 2189	.003 771	93.762 726	.010 665 2189	12.80	4.631 236	10.53	528
45	301.037 165	28238.791 991	.000 035 4123	.003 322	93.805 002	.010 660 4123	12.80	4.756 623	10.57	540
46	341.743 735	32069.998 635	.000 031 1818	.002 926	93.842 243	.010 656 1818	12.79	4.882 212	10.61	552
47	387.954 693	36419.265 179	.000 027 4580	.002 578	93.875 047	.010 652 4580	12.79	5.007 986	10.66	564
48	440.414 345	41356.644 243	.000 024 1799	.002 271	93.903 945	.010 649 1799	12.78	5.133 928	10.70	576
49	499.967 649	46961.661 036	.000 021 2940	.002 000	93.929 400	.010 646 2940	12.78	5.260 021	10.73	588
50	567.573 814	53324.594 255	.000 018 7531	.001 762	93.951 823	.010 643 7531	12.78	5.386 252	10.77	600

Effective Rate is 13.52 %

Annual Percentage Rate is 12.75 %

MONTHLY COMPOUND INTEREST AND ANNUITY

12.80 % M

Amount Of 1	Amount Of 1 Per Period	Sinking Fund Payment	Present Worth Of 1	Present Worth of 1 Per Period	Periodic Payment To Amortize 1	Constant Annual Percent	Total Interest	Annual Add On Rate	PERIODS
What a single $ 1 deposit grows to in the future. The deposit is made at the beginning of the first period.	What a series of $ 1 deposits grow to in the future. A deposit is made at the end of each period.	The amount to be deposited at the end of each period that grows to $ 1 in the future.	What $ 1 to be paid in the future is worth today. Value today of a single $ 1 payment tomorrow.	What $ 1 to be paid at the end of each period is worth today. Value today of a series of $ 1 payments tomorrow.	The mortgage payment to amortize a loan of $ 1. An annuity certain, payable at the end of each period, worth $ 1 today.	The annual payment, including interest and principal, to amortize completely a loan of $ 100.	The total interest paid over the term on a loan of $1. The loan is amortized by regular periodic payments.	The average annual interest rate on a loan that is completely amortized by regular periodic payments.	
$S = (1+i)^n$	$S\overline{n}\|=\dfrac{(1+i)^n-1}{i}$	$\dfrac{1}{S\overline{n}\|}=\dfrac{i}{(1+i)^n-1}$	$V^n=\dfrac{1}{(1+i)^n}$	$A\overline{n}\|=\dfrac{1-V^n}{i}$	$\dfrac{1}{A\overline{n}\|}=\dfrac{i}{1-V^n}$				

YEAR

Amount Of 1	Amount Of 1 Per Period	Sinking Fund Payment	Present Worth Of 1	Present Worth of 1 Per Period	Periodic Payment To Amortize 1	Constant Annual Percent	Total Interest	Annual Add On Rate	PERIODS
1.010 667	1.000 000	1.000 000 0000	.989 446	.989 446	1.010 666 6667	1212.80	.010 667	12.80	1
1.021 447	2.010 667	.497 347 4801	.979 003	1.968 449	.508 014 1468	609.62	.016 028	9.62	2
1.032 343	3.032 114	.329 802 9274	.968 671	2.937 120	.340 469 5940	408.57	.021 409	8.56	3
1.043 456	4.064 456	.246 035 3661	.958 447	3.895 567	.256 702 0328	308.05	.026 808	8.04	4
1.054 483	5.107 811	.195 778 6012	.948 332	4.843 899	.206 445 2679	247.74	.032 226	7.73	5
1.065 731	6.162 294	.162 277 2341	.938 323	5.782 222	.172 943 9008	207.54	.037 663	7.53	6
1.077 099	7.228 025	.138 350 3798	.928 420	6.710 642	.149 017 0465	178.83	.043 119	7.39	7
1.088 588	8.305 124	.120 407 5955	.918 621	7.629 263	.131 074 2622	157.29	.048 594	7.29	8
1.100 200	9.393 712	.106 454 1910	.908 926	8.538 189	.117 120 8577	140.55	.054 088	7.21	9
1.111 935	10.493 911	.095 293 3519	.899 333	9.437 522	.105 960 0186	127.16	.059 600	7.15	10
1.123 796	11.605 847	.086 163 4691	.889 841	10.327 363	.096 830 1358	116.20	.065 131	7.11	11
1.135 783	12.729 642	.078 556 8032	.880 450	11.207 813	.089 223 4699	107.07	.070 682	7.07	12

	Amount Of 1	Amount Of 1 Per Period	Sinking Fund Payment	Present Worth Of 1	Present Worth of 1 Per Period	Periodic Payment To Amortize 1	Constant Annual Percent	Total Interest	Annual Add On Rate	PERIODS
1	1.135 783	12.729 642	.078 556 8032	.880 450	11.207 813	.089 223 4699	107.07	.070 682	7.07	12
2	1.290 003	27.187 752	.036 781 2688	.775 192	21.075 733	.047 447 9355	56.94	.138 750	6.94	24
3	1.465 163	43.609 024	.022 931 0336	.682 518	29.763 942	.033 597 7003	40.32	.209 517	6.98	36
4	1.664 107	62.260 024	.016 061 6706	.600 923	37.413 476	.026 728 3373	32.08	.282 960	7.07	48
5	1.890 064	83.443 510	.011 984 1555	.529 083	44.148 508	.022 650 8222	27.19	.359 049	7.18	60
6	2.146 702	107.503 350	.009 302 0357	.465 831	50.078 367	.019 968 7024	23.97	.437 747	7.30	72
7	2.438 188	134.830 103	.007 416 7413	.410 141	55.299 311	.018 083 4080	21.71	.519 006	7.41	84
8	2.769 252	165.867 361	.006 028 9137	.361 108	59.896 091	.016 695 5803	20.04	.602 776	7.53	96
9	3.145 269	201.118 947	.004 972 1820	.317 938	63.943 326	.015 638 8486	18.77	.688 996	7.66	108
10	3.572 342	241.157 093	.004 146 6746	.279 928	67.506 714	.014 813 3413	17.78	.777 601	7.78	120
11	4.057 405	286.631 732	.003 488 7972	.246 463	70.644 099	.014 155 4639	16.99	.868 521	7.90	132
12	4.608 331	338.281 048	.002 956 1219	.216 998	73.406 410	.013 622 7885	16.35	.961 692	8.01	144
13	5.234 064	396.943 456	.002 519 2505	.191 056	75.838 486	.013 185 9172	15.83	1.057 003	8.13	156
14	5.944 760	463.571 212	.002 157 1659	.168 215	77.979 808	.012 823 8325	15.39	1.154 404	8.25	168
15	6.751 956	539.245 875	.001 854 4416	.148 105	79.865 135	.012 521 1083	15.03	1.253 799	8.36	180
16	7.668 756	625.195 859	.001 599 4988	.130 399	81.525 070	.012 266 1654	14.72	1.355 104	8.47	192
17	8.710 041	722.816 377	.001 383 4772	.114 810	82.986 561	.012 050 1439	14.47	1.458 229	8.58	204
18	9.892 716	833.692 087	.001 199 4836	.101 084	84.273 330	.011 866 1503	14.24	1.563 088	8.68	216
19	11.235 977	959.622 818	.001 042 0761	.089 000	85.406 266	.011 708 7428	14.06	1.669 593	8.79	228
20	12.761 630	1102.652 782	.000 906 9038	.078 360	86.403 760	.011 573 5705	13.89	1.777 657	8.89	240
21	14.494 440	1265.103 762	.000 790 4490	.068 992	87.282 003	.011 457 1157	13.75	1.887 193	8.99	252
22	16.462 537	1449.612 799	.000 689 8394	.060 744	88.055 252	.011 356 5061	13.63	1.998 118	9.08	264
23	18.697 867	1659.174 999	.000 602 7092	.053 482	88.736 059	.011 269 3758	13.53	2.110 348	9.18	276
24	21.236 716	1897.192 152	.000 527 0947	.047 088	89.335 476	.011 193 7614	13.44	2.223 803	9.27	288
25	24.120 298	2167.527 953	.000 461 3551	.041 459	89.863 232	.011 128 0217	13.36	2.338 407	9.35	300
26	27.395 421	2474.570 720	.000 404 1105	.036 502	90.327 895	.011 070 7772	13.29	2.454 082	9.44	312
27	31.115 249	2823.304 628	.000 354 1949	.032 139	90.737 008	.011 020 8615	13.23	2.570 759	9.52	324
28	35.340 167	3219.390 621	.000 310 6178	.028 296	91.097 211	.010 977 2845	13.18	2.688 368	9.60	336
29	40.138 755	3669.258 298	.000 272 5346	.024 914	91.414 352	.010 939 2013	13.13	2.806 842	9.68	348
30	45.588 910	4180.210 292	.000 239 2224	.021 935	91.693 579	.010 905 8891	13.09	2.926 120	9.75	360
31	51.779 102	4760.540 803	.000 210 0602	.019 313	91.939 424	.010 876 7268	13.06	3.046 142	9.83	372
32	58.809 816	5419.670 246	.000 184 5131	.017 004	92.155 878	.010 851 1797	13.03	3.166 853	9.90	384
33	66.795 180	6168.298 163	.000 162 1193	.014 971	92.346 456	.010 828 7859	13.00	3.288 199	9.96	396
34	75.864 820	7018.576 913	.000 142 4790	.013 181	92.514 249	.010 809 1457	12.98	3.410 131	10.03	408
35	86.165 962	7984.308 935	.000 125 2457	.011 606	92.661 983	.010 791 9123	12.96	3.532 603	10.09	420
36	97.865 822	9081.170 805	.000 110 1180	.010 218	92.792 056	.010 776 7846	12.94	3.655 571	10.15	432
37	111.154 322	10326.967 705	.000 096 8338	.008 997	92.906 578	.010 763 5005	12.92	3.778 994	10.21	444
38	126.247 173	11741.922 460	.000 085 1649	.007 921	93.007 409	.010 751 8316	12.91	3.902 835	10.27	456
39	143.389 374	13349.003 805	.000 074 9120	.006 974	93.096 186	.010 741 5786	12.89	4.027 059	10.33	468
40	162.859 192	15174.299 236	.000 065 9009	.006 140	93.174 349	.010 732 5676	12.88	4.151 632	10.38	480
41	184.972 677	17247.438 483	.000 057 9796	.005 406	93.243 168	.010 724 6463	12.87	4.276 526	10.43	492
42	210.088 795	19602.074 487	.000 051 0150	.004 760	93.303 760	.010 717 6817	12.87	4.401 712	10.48	504
43	238.615 250	22276.429 680	.000 044 8905	.004 191	93.357 108	.010 711 5572	12.86	4.527 163	10.53	516
44	271.015 109	25313.916 445	.000 039 5040	.003 690	93.404 078	.010 706 1706	12.85	4.652 858	10.57	528
45	307.814 313	28763.841 820	.000 034 7659	.003 249	93.445 433	.010 701 4325	12.85	4.778 774	10.62	540
46	349.610 218	32682.207 898	.000 030 5977	.002 860	93.481 844	.010 697 2644	12.84	4.904 890	10.66	552
47	397.081 290	37132.620 891	.000 026 9305	.002 518	93.513 902	.010 693 5972	12.84	5.031 189	10.70	564
48	450.998 119	42187.323 646	.000 023 7038	.002 217	93.542 128	.010 690 3705	12.83	5.157 653	10.75	576
49	512.235 929	47928.368 350	.000 020 8645	.001 952	93.566 979	.010 687 5311	12.83	5.284 268	10.78	588
50	581.788 784	54448.948 469	.000 018 3658	.001 719	93.588 859	.010 685 0325	12.83	5.411 019	10.82	600

Effective Rate is 13.58 %

Annual Percentage Rate is 12.80 %

MONTHLY COMPOUND INTEREST AND ANNUITY

12.85 % M

	Amount Of 1	Amount Of 1 Per Period	Sinking Fund Payment	Present Worth Of 1	Present Worth of 1 Per Period	Periodic Payment To Amortize 1	Constant Annual Percent	Total Interest	Annual Add On Rate	
	What a single $ 1 deposit grows to in the future. The deposit is made at the beginning of the first period.	What a series of $ 1 deposits grow to in the future. A deposit is made at the end of each period.	The amount to be deposited at the end of each period that grows to $ 1 in the future.	What $ 1 to be paid in the future is worth today. Value today of a single $ 1 payment tomorrow.	What $ 1 to be paid at the end of each period is worth today. Value today of a series of $ 1 payments tomorrow.	The mortgage payment to amortize a loan of $ 1. An annuity certain, payable at the end of each period, worth $ 1 today.	The annual payment, including interest and principal, to amortize completely a loan of $ 100.	The total interest paid over the term on a loan of $1. The loan is amortized by regular periodic payments.	The average annual interest rate on a loan that is completely amortized by regular periodic payments.	
	$S = (1+i)^n$	$S\overline{n} = \dfrac{(1+i)^n - 1}{i}$	$\dfrac{1}{S\overline{n}} = \dfrac{i}{(1+i)^n - 1}$	$V^n = \dfrac{1}{(1+i)^n}$	$A\overline{n} = \dfrac{1 - V^n}{i}$	$\dfrac{1}{A\overline{n}} = \dfrac{i}{1-V^n}$				

YEAR / **PERIODS**

YEAR	Amount Of 1	Amount Of 1 Per Period	Sinking Fund Payment	Present Worth Of 1	Present Worth of 1 Per Period	Periodic Payment To Amortize 1	Constant Annual Percent	Total Interest	Annual Add On Rate	PERIODS
	1.010 708	1.000 000	1.000 000 0000	.989 405	.989 405	1.010 708 3333	1212.85	.010 708	12.85	1
	1.021 531	2.010 708	.497 337 1739	.978 922	1.968 328	.508 045 5072	609.66	.016 091	9.65	2
	1.032 470	3.032 240	.329 789 2348	.968 551	2.936 879	.340 497 5681	408.60	.021 493	8.60	3
	1.043 526	4.064 710	.246 020 0172	.958 289	3.895 168	.256 728 3506	308.08	.026 913	8.07	4
	1.054 701	5.108 236	.195 762 2879	.948 136	4.843 304	.206 470 6213	247.77	.032 353	7.76	5
	1.065 995	6.162 937	.162 260 3025	.938 091	5.781 395	.172 968 6358	207.57	.037 812	7.56	6
	1.077 410	7.228 932	.138 333 0274	.928 152	6.709 547	.149 041 3608	178.85	.043 290	7.42	7
	1.088 947	8.306 341	.120 389 9461	.918 318	7.627 865	.131 098 2794	157.32	.048 786	7.32	8
	1.100 608	9.395 289	.106 436 3268	.908 589	8.536 454	.117 144 6601	140.58	.054 302	7.24	9
	1.112 394	10.495 896	.095 275 3305	.898 962	9.435 416	.105 983 6639	127.19	.059 837	7.18	10
	1.124 305	11.608 290	.086 145 3326	.889 438	10.324 854	.096 853 6659	116.23	.065 390	7.13	11
	1.136 345	12.732 595	.078 538 5829	.880 015	11.204 869	.089 246 9162	107.10	.070 963	7.10	12
1	1.136 345	12.732 595	.078 538 5829	.880 015	11.204 869	.089 246 9162	107.10	.070 963	7.10	12
2	1.291 280	27.201 215	.036 763 0638	.774 426	21.065 316	.047 471 3971	56.97	.139 314	6.97	24
3	1.467 339	43.642 557	.022 913 4147	.681 506	29.742 653	.033 621 7481	40.35	.210 383	7.01	36
4	1.667 403	62.325 591	.016 044 7736	.599 735	37.378 836	.026 753 1070	32.11	.284 149	7.10	48
5	1.894 745	83.555 961	.011 968 0270	.527 775	44.098 788	.022 676 3603	27.22	.360 582	7.21	60
6	2.153 084	107.680 984	.009 286 6908	.464 450	50.012 443	.019 995 0241	24.00	.439 642	7.33	72
7	2.446 646	135.095 330	.007 402 1804	.408 723	55.216 545	.018 110 5137	21.74	.521 283	7.45	84
8	2.780 233	166.247 481	.006 015 1287	.359 682	59.796 231	.016 723 4621	20.07	.605 452	7.57	96
9	3.159 304	201.647 069	.004 959 1596	.316 525	63.826 421	.015 667 4929	18.81	.692 089	7.69	108
10	3.590 059	241.873 209	.004 134 3975	.278 547	67.373 047	.014 842 7309	17.82	.781 128	7.81	120
11	4.079 545	287.583 977	.003 477 2452	.245 125	70.494 129	.014 185 5785	17.03	.872 496	7.93	132
12	4.635 770	339.527 174	.002 945 2724	.215 714	73.240 726	.013 653 6057	16.39	.966 119	8.05	144
13	5.267 834	398.552 559	.002 509 0794	.189 831	75.657 772	.013 217 4127	15.87	1.061 916	8.17	156
14	5.986 076	465.625 754	.002 147 6475	.167 054	77.784 808	.012 855 9809	15.43	1.159 805	8.28	168
15	6.802 247	541.844 035	.001 845 5495	.147 010	79.656 630	.012 553 8829	15.07	1.259 699	8.40	180
16	7.729 698	628.454 288	.001 591 2056	.129 371	81.303 861	.012 299 5390	14.76	1.361 511	8.51	192
17	8.783 603	726.873 405	.001 375 7554	.113 849	82.753 447	.012 084 0887	14.51	1.465 154	8.62	204
18	9.981 202	838.711 465	.001 192 3052	.100 188	84.029 105	.011 900 6385	14.29	1.570 538	8.73	216
19	11.342 088	965.798 071	.001 035 4131	.088 167	85.151 702	.011 743 7465	14.10	1.677 574	8.83	228
20	12.888 523	1110.212 285	.000 900 7286	.077 588	86.139 604	.011 609 0620	13.94	1.786 175	8.93	240
21	14.645 807	1274.316 636	.000 784 7343	.068 279	87.008 972	.011 493 0677	13.80	1.896 253	9.03	252
22	16.642 688	1460.795 775	.000 684 5584	.060 086	87.774 028	.011 392 8917	13.68	2.007 723	9.13	264
23	18.911 833	1672.700 389	.000 597 8357	.052 877	88.447 289	.011 306 1690	13.57	2.120 503	9.22	276
24	21.490 365	1913.497 111	.000 522 6033	.046 532	89.039 768	.011 230 9367	13.48	2.234 510	9.31	288
25	24.420 466	2187.125 233	.000 457 2212	.040 949	89.561 159	.011 165 5545	13.40	2.349 666	9.40	300
26	27.750 071	2498.061 146	.000 400 3105	.036 036	90.019 990	.011 108 6438	13.34	2.465 897	9.48	312
27	31.533 651	2851.391 578	.000 350 7060	.031 712	90.423 768	.011 059 0393	13.28	2.583 129	9.57	324
28	35.833 103	3252.896 805	.000 307 4183	.027 907	90.779 098	.011 015 7516	13.22	2.701 293	9.65	336
29	40.718 763	3709.145 211	.000 269 6039	.024 559	91.091 794	.010 977 9372	13.18	2.820 322	9.73	348
30	46.270 558	4227.600 749	.000 236 5408	.021 612	91.366 971	.010 944 8741	13.14	2.940 155	9.80	360
31	52.579 312	4816.745 044	.000 207 6091	.019 019	91.609 131	.010 915 9424	13.10	3.060 731	9.87	372
32	59.748 231	5486.216 144	.000 182 2750	.016 737	91.822 235	.010 890 6083	13.07	3.181 994	9.94	384
33	67.894 596	6246.966 199	.000 160 0777	.014 729	92.009 770	.010 868 4110	13.05	3.303 891	10.01	396
34	77.151 677	7111.440 625	.000 140 6185	.012 961	92.174 803	.010 848 9518	13.02	3.426 372	10.08	408
35	87.670 912	8093.781 709	.000 123 5516	.011 406	92.320 035	.010 831 8850	13.00	3.549 392	10.14	420
36	99.624 392	9210.059 967	.000 108 5769	.010 038	92.447 841	.010 816 9103	12.99	3.672 905	10.20	432
37	113.207 668	10478.537 045	.000 095 4332	.008 833	92.560 312	.010 803 7665	12.97	3.796 872	10.26	444
38	128.642 953	11919.964 472	.000 083 8929	.007 773	92.659 288	.010 792 2262	12.96	3.921 255	10.32	456
39	146.182 760	13557.923 144	.000 073 7576	.006 841	92.746 389	.010 782 0909	12.94	4.046 019	10.37	468
40	166.114 031	15419.209 087	.000 064 8542	.006 020	92.823 039	.010 773 1875	12.93	4.171 130	10.43	480
41	188.762 828	17534.271 830	.000 057 0312	.005 298	92.890 492	.010 765 3645	12.92	4.296 559	10.48	492
42	214.499 672	19937.712 541	.000 050 1562	.004 662	92.949 851	.010 758 4895	12.92	4.422 279	10.53	504
43	243.745 603	22668.850 077	.000 044 1134	.004 103	93.002 088	.010 752 4467	12.91	4.548 263	10.58	516
44	276.979 067	25772.364 222	.000 038 8013	.003 610	93.048 058	.010 747 1346	12.90	4.674 487	10.62	528
45	314.743 743	29299.026 616	.000 034 1308	.003 177	93.088 512	.010 742 4642	12.90	4.800 931	10.67	540
46	357.657 440	33306.531 358	.000 030 0241	.002 796	93.124 112	.010 738 3575	12.89	4.927 573	10.71	552
47	406.422 199	37860.438 835	.000 026 4128	.002 460	93.155 440	.010 734 7461	12.89	5.054 397	10.75	564
48	461.835 783	43035.248 263	.000 023 2368	.002 165	93.183 010	.010 731 5701	12.88	5.181 384	10.79	576
49	524.804 726	48915.616 439	.000 020 4434	.001 905	93.207 271	.010 728 7767	12.88	5.308 521	10.83	588
50	596.359 161	55597.742 683	.000 017 9863	.001 677	93.228 622	.010 726 3197	12.88	5.435 792	10.87	600

Effective Rate is 13.63 %

8 - 204

Annual Percentage Rate is 12.85 %

MONTHLY COMPOUND INTEREST AND ANNUITY

12.875% M

	Amount Of 1	Amount Of 1 Per Period	Sinking Fund Payment	Present Worth Of 1	Present Worth of 1 Per Period	Periodic Payment To Amortize 1	Constant Annual Percent	Total Interest	Annual Add On Rate	

What a single $ 1 deposit grows to in the future. The deposit is made at the beginning of the first period.

What a series of $ 1 deposits grow to in the future. A deposit is made at the end of each period.

The amount to be deposited at the end of each period that grows to $ 1 in the future.

What $ 1 to be paid in the future is worth today. Value today of a single $ 1 payment tomorrow.

What $ 1 to be paid at the end of each period is worth today. Value today of a series of $ 1 payments tomorrow.

The mortgage payment to amortize a loan of $ 1. An annuity certain, payable at the end of each period, worth $ 1 today.

The annual payment, including interest and principal, to amortize completely a loan of $ 100.

The total interest paid over the term on a loan of $1. The loan is amortized by regular periodic payments.

The average annual interest rate on a loan that is completely amortized by regular periodic payments.

$$S = (1+i)^n \qquad S\overline{n}| = \frac{(1+i)^n - 1}{i} \qquad \frac{1}{S\overline{n}|} = \frac{i}{(1+i)^n - 1} \qquad V^n = \frac{1}{(1+i)^n} \qquad A\overline{n}| = \frac{1-V^n}{i} \qquad \frac{1}{A\overline{n}|} = \frac{i}{1-V^n}$$

PERIODS

YEAR										
	1.010 729	1.000 000	1.000 000 0000	.989 385	.989 385	1.010 729 1667	1212.88	.010 729	12.87	1
	1.021 573	2.010 729	.497 332 0209	.978 882	1.968 267	.508 061 1876	609.68	.016 122	9.67	2
	1.032 534	3.032 303	.329 782 3888	.968 491	2.936 758	.340 511 5555	408.62	.021 535	8.61	3
	1.043 612	4.064 837	.246 012 3432	.958 210	3.894 968	.256 741 5098	308.09	.026 966	8.09	4
	1.054 809	5.108 449	.195 754 1318	.948 039	4.843 007	.206 483 2985	247.78	.032 416	7.78	5
	1.066 127	6.163 258	.162 251 8373	.937 975	5.780 982	.172 981 0039	207.58	.037 886	7.58	6
	1.077 565	7.229 385	.138 324 3520	.928 018	6.709 000	.149 053 5187	178.87	.043 375	7.44	7
	1.089 127	8.306 950	.120 381 1222	.918 167	7.627 166	.131 110 2888	157.34	.048 882	7.33	8
	1.100 812	9.396 077	.106 427 3956	.908 420	8.535 587	.117 156 5622	140.59	.054 409	7.25	9
	1.112 623	10.496 889	.095 266 3209	.898 777	9.434 364	.105 994 4876	127.20	.059 955	7.19	10
	1.124 560	11.609 512	.086 136 2655	.889 236	10.323 600	.096 865 4321	116.24	.065 520	7.15	11
	1.136 626	12.734 072	.078 529 4740	.879 797	11.203 397	.089 258 6407	107.12	.071 104	7.11	12
1	1.136 626	12.734 072	.078 529 4740	.879 797	11.203 397	.089 258 6407	107.12	.071 104	7.11	12
2	1.291 919	27.207 950	.036 753 9638	.774 043	21.060 111	.047 483 1304	56.98	.139 595	6.98	24
3	1.468 428	43.659 335	.022 904 6091	.681 000	29.732 017	.033 633 7757	40.37	.210 816	7.03	36
4	1.669 054	62.358 407	.016 036 3301	.599 142	37.361 533	.026 765 4968	32.12	.284 744	7.12	48
5	1.897 090	83.612 258	.011 959 9689	.527 123	44.073 958	.022 689 1355	27.23	.361 348	7.23	60
6	2.156 282	107.769 937	.009 279 0255	.463 761	49.979 528	.020 008 1922	24.01	.440 590	7.34	72
7	2.450 886	135.228 183	.007 394 9082	.408 016	55.175 230	.018 124 0749	21.75	.522 422	7.46	84
8	2.785 740	166.437 939	.006 008 2455	.358 971	59.746 393	.016 737 4122	20.09	.606 792	7.58	96
9	3.166 345	201.911 759	.004 952 6586	.315 822	63.768 087	.015 681 8252	18.82	.693 637	7.71	108
10	3.598 950	242.232 224	.004 128 2699	.277 859	67.306 362	.014 857 4366	17.83	.782 892	7.83	120
11	4.090 660	288.061 512	.003 471 4808	.244 459	70.419 324	.014 200 6474	17.05	.874 485	7.95	132
12	4.649 550	340.152 272	.002 939 8598	.215 075	73.158 099	.013 669 0265	16.41	.968 340	8.07	144
13	5.284 800	399.359 983	.002 504 0065	.189 222	75.567 665	.013 233 1732	15.88	1.064 375	8.19	156
14	6.006 841	466.657 006	.002 142 9015	.166 477	77.687 594	.012 872 0682	15.45	1.162 507	8.30	168
15	6.827 531	543.148 551	.001 841 1169	.146 466	79.552 700	.012 570 2836	15.09	1.262 651	8.42	180
16	7.760 350	630.090 828	.001 587 0728	.128 860	81.193 615	.012 316 2394	14.78	1.364 718	8.53	192
17	8.820 615	728.911 680	.001 371 9083	.113 371	82.637 286	.012 101 0750	14.53	1.468 619	8.64	204
18	10.025 740	841.234 028	.001 188 7299	.099 743	83.907 424	.011 917 8965	14.31	1.574 266	8.75	216
19	11.395 517	968.902 527	.001 032 0956	.087 754	85.024 888	.011 761 2622	14.12	1.681 568	8.85	228
20	12.952 440	1114.013 861	.000 897 6549	.077 206	86.008 028	.011 626 8216	13.96	1.790 437	8.95	240
21	14.722 080	1278.951 173	.000 781 8907	.067 925	86.872 993	.011 511 0573	13.82	1.900 786	9.05	252
22	16.733 499	1466.423 208	.000 681 9314	.059 760	87.633 985	.011 411 0980	13.70	2.012 530	9.15	264
23	19.019 730	1679.508 794	.000 595 4122	.052 577	88.303 505	.011 324 5789	13.59	2.125 584	9.24	276
24	21.618 319	1921.707 408	.000 520 3706	.046 257	88.892 545	.011 249 5372	13.50	2.239 867	9.33	288
25	24.571 943	2196.996 646	.000 455 1668	.040 697	89.410 782	.011 184 3335	13.43	2.355 300	9.42	300
26	27.929 109	2509.897 547	.000 398 4226	.035 805	89.866 724	.011 127 5893	13.36	2.471 808	9.51	312
27	31.744 951	2865.548 841	.000 348 9733	.031 501	90.267 861	.011 078 1400	13.30	2.589 317	9.59	324
28	36.082 136	3269.791 344	.000 305 8299	.027 715	90.620 780	.011 034 9966	13.25	2.707 759	9.67	336
29	41.011 894	3729.263 876	.000 268 1494	.024 383	90.931 277	.010 997 3161	13.20	2.827 066	9.75	348
30	46.615 184	4251.512 295	.000 235 2104	.021 452	91.204 452	.010 964 3771	13.16	2.947 176	9.82	360
31	52.984 029	4845.113 419	.000 206 3935	.018 874	91.444 790	.010 935 5602	13.13	3.068 028	9.90	372
32	60.223 025	5519.815 879	.000 181 1655	.016 605	91.656 238	.010 910 3321	13.10	3.189 568	9.97	384
33	68.451 055	6286.700 228	.000 159 0660	.014 609	91.842 270	.010 888 2326	13.07	3.311 740	10.04	396
34	77.803 247	7158.360 906	.000 139 6968	.012 853	92.005 940	.010 868 8635	13.05	3.434 496	10.10	408
35	88.433 192	8149.113 081	.000 122 7127	.011 308	92.149 937	.010 851 8794	13.03	3.557 789	10.17	420
36	100.515 464	9275.227 747	.000 107 8141	.009 949	92.276 624	.010 836 9807	13.01	3.681 576	10.23	432
37	114.248 489	10555.198 937	.000 094 7400	.008 753	92.388 084	.010 823 9067	12.99	3.805 815	10.29	444
38	129.857 801	12010.047 451	.000 083 2636	.007 701	92.486 145	.010 812 4303	12.98	3.930 468	10.34	456
39	147.599 751	13663.666 075	.000 073 1868	.006 775	92.572 420	.010 802 3535	12.97	4.055 501	10.40	468
40	167.765 712	15543.211 971	.000 064 3368	.005 961	92.648 324	.010 793 5034	12.96	4.180 882	10.45	480
41	190.686 867	17679.552 674	.000 056 5625	.005 244	92.715 104	.010 785 7292	12.95	4.306 579	10.50	492
42	216.739 648	20107.773 028	.000 049 7320	.004 614	92.773 857	.010 778 8987	12.94	4.432 565	10.55	504
43	246.351 916	22867.751 378	.000 043 7297	.004 059	92.825 547	.010 772 8964	12.93	4.558 815	10.60	516
44	280.009 989	26004.814 485	.000 038 4544	.003 571	92.871 024	.010 767 6211	12.92	4.685 304	10.65	528
45	318.266 629	29570.481 927	.000 033 8175	.003 142	92.911 035	.010 762 9842	12.92	4.812 011	10.69	540
46	361.750 120	33623.312 191	.000 029 7413	.002 764	92.946 236	.010 758 9079	12.91	4.938 917	10.74	552
47	411.174 587	38229.864 379	.000 026 1576	.002 432	92.977 206	.010 755 3242	12.91	5.066 003	10.78	564
48	467.351 719	43465.791 292	.000 023 0066	.002 140	93.004 454	.010 752 1733	12.91	5.193 252	10.82	576
49	531.204 108	49417.081 872	.000 020 2359	.001 883	93.028 426	.010 749 4026	12.90	5.320 649	10.86	588
50	603.780 392	56181.473 384	.000 017 7995	.001 656	93.049 516	.010 746 9661	12.90	5.448 180	10.90	600

Effective Rate is 13.66 %

8 - 205

Annual Percentage Rate is 12.875%

MONTHLY COMPOUND INTEREST AND ANNUITY

12.90 % M

	Amount Of 1	Amount Of 1 Per Period	Sinking Fund Payment	Present Worth Of 1	Present Worth of 1 Per Period	Periodic Payment To Amortize 1	Constant Annual Percent	Total Interest	Annual Add On Rate	
	What a single $ 1 deposit grows to in the future. The deposit is made at the beginning of the first period.	What a series of $ 1 deposits grow to in the future. A deposit is made at the end of each period.	The amount to be deposited at the end of each period that grows to $ 1 in the future.	What $ 1 to be paid in the future is worth today. Value today of a single $ 1 payment tomorrow.	What $ 1 to be paid at the end of each period is worth today. Value today of a series of $ 1 payments tomorrow.	The mortgage payment to amortize a loan of $ 1. An annuity certain, payable at the end of each period, worth $ 1 today.	The annual payment, including interest and principal, to amortize completely a loan of $ 100.	The total interest paid over the term on a loan of $1. The loan is amortized completely by regular periodic payments.	The average annual interest rate on a loan that is completely amortized by regular periodic payments.	
	$S = (1+i)^n$	$S\overline{n}| = \frac{(1+i)^n - 1}{i}$	$\frac{1}{S\overline{n}|} = \frac{i}{(1+i)^n - 1}$	$V^n = \frac{1}{(1+i)^n}$	$A\overline{n}| = \frac{1 - V^n}{i}$	$\frac{1}{A\overline{n}|} = \frac{i}{1 - V^n}$				

YEAR / **PERIODS**

YEAR	Amount Of 1	Amount Of 1 Per Period	Sinking Fund Payment	Present Worth Of 1	Present Worth of 1 Per Period	Periodic Payment To Amortize 1	Constant Annual Percent	Total Interest	Annual Add On Rate	PERIODS
	1.010 750	1.000 000	1.000 000 0000	.989 364	.989 364	1.010 750 0000	1212.90	.010 750	12.90	1
	1.021 616	2.010 750	.497 326 8681	.978 842	1.968 206	.508 076 8681	609.70	.016 154	9.69	2
	1.032 598	3.032 366	.329 775 5430	.968 431	2.936 637	.340 525 5430	408.64	.021 577	8.63	3
	1.043 698	4.064 963	.246 004 6694	.958 131	3.894 769	.256 754 6694	308.11	.027 019	8.11	4
	1.054 918	5.108 662	.195 745 9760	.947 941	4.842 709	.206 495 9760	247.80	.032 480	7.80	5
	1.066 258	6.163 580	.162 243 3725	.937 859	5.780 568	.172 993 3725	207.60	.037 960	7.59	6
	1.077 721	7.229 838	.138 315 6770	.927 884	6.708 452	.149 065 6770	178.88	.043 460	7.45	7
	1.089 306	8.307 559	.120 372 2988	.918 015	7.626 468	.131 122 2988	157.35	.048 978	7.35	8
	1.101 016	9.396 865	.106 418 4650	.908 252	8.534 720	.117 168 4650	140.61	.054 516	7.27	9
	1.112 852	10.497 882	.095 257 3120	.898 592	9.433 312	.106 007 3120	127.21	.060 073	7.21	10
	1.124 815	11.610 734	.086 127 1991	.889 035	10.322 346	.096 877 1991	116.26	.065 649	7.16	11
	1.136 907	12.735 549	.078 520 3660	.879 579	11.201 926	.089 270 3660	107.13	.071 244	7.12	12
1	1.136 907	12.735 549	.078 520 3660	.879 579	11.201 926	.089 270 3660	107.13	.071 244	7.12	12
2	1.292 558	27.214 687	.036 744 8655	.773 660	21.054 908	.047 494 8655	57.00	.139 877	6.99	24
3	1.469 518	43.676 121	.022 895 8059	.680 495	29.721 386	.033 645 8059	40.38	.211 249	7.04	36
4	1.670 706	62.391 244	.016 027 8900	.598 549	37.344 242	.026 777 8900	32.14	.285 339	7.13	48
5	1.899 437	83.668 602	.011 951 9148	.526 472	44.049 148	.022 701 9148	27.25	.362 115	7.24	60
6	2.159 484	107.858 981	.009 271 3651	.463 074	49.946 644	.020 021 3651	24.03	.441 538	7.36	72
7	2.455 133	135.361 197	.007 387 6415	.407 310	55.133 960	.018 137 6415	21.77	.523 562	7.48	84
8	2.791 258	166.628 663	.006 001 3684	.358 261	59.696 615	.016 751 3684	20.11	.608 131	7.60	96
9	3.173 401	202.176 869	.004 946 1642	.315 119	63.709 833	.015 696 1642	18.84	.695 186	7.72	108
10	3.607 863	242.591 878	.004 122 1495	.277 172	67.239 776	.014 872 1495	17.85	.784 658	7.85	120
11	4.101 805	288.539 992	.003 465 7241	.243 795	70.344 640	.014 215 7241	17.06	.876 476	7.97	132
12	4.663 371	340.778 731	.002 934 4554	.214 437	73.075 615	.013 684 4554	16.43	.970 562	8.09	144
13	5.301 820	400.169 327	.002 498 9422	.188 614	75.477 724	.013 248 9422	15.90	1.066 835	8.21	156
14	6.027 677	467.690 921	.002 138 1642	.165 901	77.590 569	.012 888 1642	15.47	1.165 212	8.32	168
15	6.852 910	544.456 704	.001 836 6933	.145 923	79.448 984	.012 586 6933	15.11	1.265 605	8.44	180
16	7.791 122	631.732 273	.001 582 9490	.128 351	81.083 608	.012 332 9490	14.80	1.367 926	8.55	192
17	8.857 782	730.956 491	.001 368 0705	.112 895	82.521 388	.012 118 0705	14.55	1.472 086	8.66	204
18	10.070 476	843.765 215	.001 185 1638	.099 300	83.786 031	.011 935 1638	14.33	1.577 995	8.77	216
19	11.449 196	972.018 260	.001 028 7873	.087 342	84.898 384	.011 778 7873	14.14	1.685 563	8.87	228
20	13.016 673	1117.830 065	.000 894 5904	.076 825	85.876 786	.011 644 5904	13.98	1.794 702	8.97	240
21	14.798 749	1283.604 549	.000 779 0561	.067 573	86.737 369	.011 529 0561	13.84	1.905 322	9.07	252
22	16.824 804	1472.074 747	.000 679 3133	.059 436	87.494 320	.011 429 3133	13.72	2.017 339	9.17	264
23	19.128 240	1686.347 863	.000 592 9975	.052 279	88.160 118	.011 342 9975	13.62	2.130 667	9.26	276
24	21.747 032	1929.956 503	.000 518 1464	.045 983	88.745 741	.011 268 1464	13.53	2.245 226	9.36	288
25	24.724 357	2206.916 908	.000 453 1208	.040 446	89.260 842	.011 203 1208	13.45	2.360 936	9.44	300
26	28.109 298	2521.795 175	.000 396 5429	.035 575	89.713 915	.011 146 5429	13.38	2.477 721	9.53	312
27	31.957 662	2879.782 530	.000 347 2484	.031 291	90.112 428	.011 097 2484	13.32	2.595 508	9.61	324
28	36.332 895	3286.780 916	.000 304 2491	.027 523	90.462 952	.011 054 2491	13.27	2.714 228	9.69	336
29	41.307 128	3749.500 293	.000 266 7022	.024 209	90.771 265	.011 016 7022	13.23	2.833 812	9.77	348
30	46.962 370	4275.569 264	.000 233 8870	.021 294	91.042 452	.010 983 8870	13.19	2.954 199	9.85	360
31	53.391 854	4873.660 842	.000 205 1846	.018 729	91.280 982	.010 955 1846	13.15	3.075 329	9.92	372
32	60.701 581	5553.635 436	.000 180 0622	.016 474	91.490 787	.010 930 0622	13.12	3.197 144	9.99	384
33	69.012 062	6326.703 419	.000 158 0602	.014 490	91.675 328	.010 908 0602	13.09	3.319 592	10.06	396
34	78.460 307	7205.609 940	.000 138 7808	.012 745	91.837 647	.010 888 7808	13.07	3.442 623	10.13	408
35	89.202 084	8204.845 054	.000 121 8792	.011 211	91.980 419	.010 871 8792	13.05	3.566 189	10.19	420
36	101.414 488	9340.882 606	.000 107 0563	.009 861	92.105 998	.010 857 0563	13.03	3.690 248	10.25	432
37	115.298 857	10632.451 827	.000 094 0517	.008 673	92.216 455	.010 844 0517	13.02	3.814 759	10.31	444
38	131.084 096	12100.846 118	.000 082 6388	.007 629	92.313 610	.010 832 6388	13.00	3.939 683	10.37	456
39	149.030 447	13770.274 095	.000 072 6202	.006 710	92.399 066	.010 822 6202	12.99	4.064 986	10.42	468
40	169.433 781	15668.258 708	.000 063 8233	.005 902	92.474 232	.010 813 8233	12.98	4.190 635	10.48	480
41	192.630 478	17826.090 997	.000 056 0975	.005 191	92.540 345	.010 806 0975	12.97	4.316 600	10.53	492
42	219.002 969	20279.345 968	.000 049 3113	.004 566	92.598 498	.010 799 3113	12.96	4.442 853	10.58	504
43	248.986 043	23068.469 100	.000 043 3492	.004 016	92.649 647	.010 793 3492	12.96	4.569 368	10.63	516
44	283.074 014	26239.443 148	.000 038 1106	.003 533	92.694 638	.010 788 1106	12.95	4.696 122	10.67	528
45	321.828 872	29844.546 234	.000 033 5070	.003 107	92.734 210	.010 783 5070	12.95	4.823 094	10.72	540
46	365.889 548	33943.213 732	.000 029 4610	.002 733	92.769 017	.010 779 4610	12.94	4.950 262	10.76	552
47	415.962 445	38603.018 140	.000 025 9047	.002 404	92.799 633	.010 775 9047	12.94	5.077 610	10.80	564
48	472.933 419	43900.783 116	.000 022 7786	.002 114	92.826 562	.010 772 7786	12.93	5.205 120	10.84	576
49	537.681 388	49923.850 030	.000 020 0305	.001 860	92.850 248	.010 770 0305	12.93	5.332 778	10.88	588
50	611.293 817	56771.517 904	.000 017 6145	.001 636	92.871 081	.010 767 6145	12.93	5.460 569	10.92	600

Effective Rate is 13.69 %

Annual Percentage Rate is 12.90 %

MONTHLY COMPOUND INTEREST AND ANNUITY

12.95 % M

Amount Of 1	Amount Of 1 Per Period	Sinking Fund Payment	Present Worth Of 1	Present Worth of 1 Per Period	Periodic Payment To Amortize 1	Constant Annual Percent	Total Interest	Annual Add On Rate	
What a single $1 deposit grows to in the future. The deposit is made at the beginning of the first period.	What a series of $1 deposits grow to in the future. A deposit is made at the end of each period.	The amount to be deposited at the end of each period that grows to $1 in the future.	What $1 to be paid in the future is worth today. Value today of a single $1 payment tomorrow.	What $1 to be paid at the end of each period is worth today. Value today of a series of $1 payments tomorrow.	The mortgage payment to amortize a loan of $1. An annuity certain, payable at the end of each period, worth $1 today.	The annual payment, including interest and principal, to amortize completely a loan of $100.	The total interest paid over the term on a loan of $1. The loan is amortized by regular periodic payments.	The average annual interest rate on a loan that is completely amortized by regular periodic payments.	
$S = (1+i)^n$	$S\overline{n}| = \dfrac{(1+i)^n - 1}{i}$	$\dfrac{1}{S\overline{n}|} = \dfrac{i}{(1+i)^n - 1}$	$V^n = \dfrac{1}{(1+i)^n}$	$A\overline{n}| = \dfrac{1-V^n}{i}$	$\dfrac{1}{A\overline{n}|} = \dfrac{i}{1-V^n}$				**PERIODS**

YEAR

YEAR	Amount Of 1	Amount Of 1 Per Period	Sinking Fund Payment	Present Worth Of 1	Present Worth of 1 Per Period	Periodic Payment To Amortize 1	Constant Annual Percent	Total Interest	Annual Add On Rate	PERIODS
	1.010 792	1.000 000	1.000 000 0000	.989 324	.989 324	1.010 791 6667	1212.95	.010 792	12.95	1
	1.021 700	2.010 792	.497 316 5627	.978 761	1.968 085	.508 108 2294	609.73	.016 216	9.73	2
	1.032 726	3.032 491	.329 761 8520	.968 311	2.936 396	.340 553 5187	408.67	.021 661	8.66	3
	1.043 870	4.065 217	.245 989 3226	.957 973	3.894 369	.256 780 9893	308.14	.027 124	8.14	4
	1.055 136	5.109 088	.195 729 6655	.947 746	4.842 115	.206 521 3321	247.83	.032 607	7.83	5
	1.066 522	6.164 223	.162 226 4441	.937 627	5.779 742	.173 018 1108	207.63	.038 109	7.62	6
	1.078 032	7.230 745	.138 298 3286	.927 616	6.707 358	.149 089 9953	178.91	.043 630	7.48	7
	1.089 666	8.308 777	.120 354 6538	.917 713	7.625 071	.131 146 3205	157.38	.049 171	7.38	8
	1.101 425	9.398 443	.106 400 6059	.907 915	8.532 986	.117 192 2725	140.64	.054 730	7.30	9
	1.113 311	10.499 868	.095 239 2963	.898 222	9.431 207	.106 030 9630	127.24	.060 310	7.24	10
	1.125 326	11.613 179	.086 109 0688	.888 632	10.319 839	.096 900 7355	116.29	.065 908	7.19	11
	1.137 470	12.738 504	.078 502 1525	.879 144	11.198 983	.089 293 8192	107.16	.071 526	7.15	12
1	1.137 470	12.738 504	.078 502 1525	.879 144	11.198 983	.089 293 8192	107.16	.071 526	7.15	12
2	1.293 837	27.228 167	.036 726 6740	.772 895	21.044 506	.047 518 3406	57.03	.140 440	7.02	24
3	1.471 701	43.709 719	.022 878 2073	.679 486	29.700 141	.033 669 8739	40.41	.212 115	7.07	36
4	1.674 015	62.456 984	.016 011 0196	.597 366	37.309 693	.026 802 6863	32.17	.286 529	7.16	48
5	1.904 141	83.781 431	.011 935 8191	.525 171	43.999 588	.022 727 4857	27.28	.363 649	7.27	60
6	2.165 903	108.037 342	.009 256 0589	.461 701	49.880 970	.020 047 7255	24.06	.443 436	7.39	72
7	2.463 649	135.627 707	.007 373 1247	.405 902	55.051 554	.018 164 7914	21.80	.525 842	7.51	84
8	2.802 326	167.010 910	.005 987 6328	.356 846	59.597 244	.016 779 2995	20.14	.610 813	7.64	96
9	3.187 561	202.708 352	.004 933 1958	.313 719	63.593 561	.015 724 8625	18.87	.698 285	7.76	108
10	3.625 754	243.313 111	.004 109 9306	.275 805	67.106 900	.014 901 5973	17.89	.788 192	7.88	120
11	4.124 185	289.499 794	.003 454 2339	.242 472	70.195 632	.014 245 9006	17.10	.880 459	8.00	132
12	4.691 136	342.035 745	.002 923 6710	.213 168	72.911 074	.013 715 3377	16.46	.975 009	8.13	144
13	5.336 025	401.793 798	.002 488 8388	.187 405	75.298 339	.013 280 5055	15.94	1.071 759	8.24	156
14	6.069 566	469.766 771	.002 128 7159	.164 756	77.397 089	.012 920 3826	15.51	1.170 624	8.36	168
15	6.903 948	547.083 968	.001 827 8730	.144 845	79.242 193	.012 619 5396	15.15	1.271 517	8.48	180
16	7.853 031	635.029 937	.001 574 7289	.127 339	80.864 306	.012 366 3956	14.84	1.374 348	8.59	192
17	8.932 585	735.065 810	.001 360 4224	.111 950	82.290 378	.012 152 0891	14.59	1.479 026	8.70	204
18	10.160 545	848.853 585	.001 178 0595	.098 420	83.544 100	.011 969 7261	14.37	1.585 461	8.81	216
19	11.557 312	978.283 729	.001 022 1983	.086 525	84.646 303	.011 813 8650	14.18	1.693 561	8.91	228
20	13.146 092	1125.506 595	.000 888 4888	.076 068	85.615 299	.011 680 1555	14.02	1.803 237	9.02	240
21	14.953 281	1292.968 144	.000 773 4143	.066 875	86.467 186	.011 565 0809	13.88	1.914 400	9.12	252
22	17.008 904	1483.450 579	.000 674 1040	.058 793	87.216 117	.011 465 7707	13.76	2.026 963	9.21	264
23	19.347 113	1700.118 577	.000 588 1943	.051 687	87.874 536	.011 379 8609	13.66	2.140 842	9.31	276
24	22.006 755	1946.571 857	.000 513 7237	.045 441	88.453 381	.011 305 3903	13.57	2.255 952	9.40	288
25	25.032 016	2226.904 993	.000 449 0537	.039 949	88.962 270	.011 240 7204	13.49	2.372 216	9.49	300
26	28.473 160	2545.775 439	.000 392 8076	.035 121	89.409 656	.011 184 4743	13.43	2.489 556	9.58	312
27	32.387 356	2908.480 907	.000 343 8221	.030 876	89.802 973	.011 135 4888	13.37	2.607 898	9.66	324
28	36.839 636	3321.047 384	.000 301 1098	.027 145	90.148 756	.011 092 7765	13.32	2.727 173	9.74	336
29	41.903 970	3790.329 246	.000 263 8293	.023 864	90.452 749	.011 055 4960	13.27	2.847 313	9.82	348
30	47.664 496	4324.123 142	.000 231 2608	.020 980	90.720 002	.011 022 9274	13.23	2.968 254	9.89	360
31	54.216 919	4931.297 519	.000 202 7864	.018 444	90.954 957	.010 994 4531	13.20	3.089 937	9.97	372
32	61.670 102	5621.939 971	.000 177 8745	.016 215	91.161 515	.010 969 5412	13.17	3.212 304	10.04	384
33	70.147 872	6407.524 827	.000 156 0665	.014 256	91.343 110	.010 947 7332	13.14	3.335 302	10.11	396
34	79.791 078	7301.103 791	.000 136 9656	.012 533	91.502 759	.010 928 6323	13.12	3.458 882	10.17	408
35	90.759 933	8317.522 779	.000 120 2281	.011 018	91.643 112	.010 911 8948	13.10	3.582 996	10.24	420
36	103.236 673	9473.668 571	.000 105 5557	.009 686	91.766 504	.010 897 2224	13.08	3.707 600	10.30	432
37	117.428 587	10788.749 369	.000 092 6891	.008 516	91.874 982	.010 884 3558	13.07	3.832 654	10.36	444
38	133.571 459	12284.613 918	.000 081 4026	.007 487	91.970 351	.010 873 0693	13.05	3.958 120	10.42	456
39	151.933 486	13986.114 505	.000 071 4995	.006 582	92.054 194	.010 863 1662	13.04	4.083 962	10.47	468
40	172.819 735	15921.519 852	.000 062 8081	.005 786	92.127 903	.010 854 4747	13.03	4.210 148	10.53	480
41	196.577 211	18122.984 775	.000 055 1785	.005 087	92.192 705	.010 846 8452	13.02	4.336 648	10.58	492
42	223.600 619	20627.084 400	.000 048 4799	.004 472	92.249 675	.010 840 1466	13.01	4.463 434	10.63	504
43	254.338 927	23475.421 828	.000 042 5977	.003 932	92.299 760	.010 834 2644	13.01	4.590 480	10.68	516
44	289.302 821	26715.319 323	.000 037 4317	.003 457	92.343 791	.010 829 0984	13.00	4.717 764	10.72	528
45	329.073 191	30400.604 527	.000 032 8941	.003 039	92.382 502	.010 824 5607	12.99	4.845 263	10.77	540
46	374.310 780	34592.504 749	.000 028 9080	.002 672	92.416 533	.010 820 5747	12.99	4.972 957	10.81	552
47	425.767 168	39360.664 201	.000 025 4061	.002 349	92.446 452	.010 817 0727	12.99	5.100 829	10.85	564
48	484.297 249	44784.301 060	.000 022 3293	.002 065	92.472 755	.010 813 9959	12.98	5.228 862	10.89	576
49	550.873 442	50953.523 604	.000 019 6257	.001 815	92.495 880	.010 811 2924	12.98	5.357 040	10.93	588
50	626.601 844	57970.827 267	.000 017 2501	.001 596	92.516 209	.010 808 9167	12.98	5.485 350	10.97	600

Effective Rate is 13.75 %

Annual Percentage Rate is 12.95 %

MONTHLY COMPOUND INTEREST AND ANNUITY

	Amount Of 1	Amount Of 1 Per Period	Sinking Fund Payment	Present Worth Of 1	Present Worth of 1 Per Period	Periodic Payment To Amortize 1	Constant Annual Percent	Total Interest	Annual Add On Rate	
	What a single $ 1 deposit grows to in the future. The deposit is made at the beginning of the first period.	What a series of $ 1 deposits grow to in the future. A deposit is made at the end of each period.	The amount to be deposited at the end of each period that grows to $ 1 in the future.	What $ 1 to be paid in the future is worth today. Value today of a single $ 1 payment tomorrow.	What $ 1 to be paid at the end of each period is worth today. Value today of a series of $ 1 payments tomorrow.	The mortgage payment to amortize a loan of $ 1. An annuity certain, payable at the end of each period, worth $ 1 today.	The annual payment, including interest and principal, to amortize completely a loan of $ 100.	The total interest paid over the term on a loan of $1. The loan is amortized by regular periodic payments.	The average annual interest rate on a loan that is completely amortized by regular periodic payments.	
	$S = (1+i)^n$	$S\overline{n}| = \dfrac{(1+i)^n - 1}{i}$	$\dfrac{1}{S\overline{n}|} = \dfrac{i}{(1+i)^n - 1}$	$V^n = \dfrac{1}{(1+i)^n}$	$A\overline{n}| = \dfrac{1-V^n}{i}$	$\dfrac{1}{A\overline{n}|} = \dfrac{i}{1-V^n}$				

YEAR   **PERIODS**

YEAR	Amount Of 1	Amount Of 1 Per Period	Sinking Fund Payment	Present Worth Of 1	Present Worth of 1 Per Period	Periodic Payment To Amortize 1	Constant Annual Percent	Total Interest	Annual Add On Rate	PERIODS
	1.010 833	1.000 000	1.000 000 0000	.989 283	.989 283	1.010 833 3333	1213.00	.010 833	13.00	1
	1.021 784	2.010 833	.497 306 2578	.978 680	1.967 963	.508 139 5911	609.77	.016 279	9.77	2
	1.032 853	3.032 617	.329 748 1617	.968 192	2.936 155	.340 581 4950	408.70	.021 744	8.70	3
	1.044 043	4.065 471	.245 973 9769	.957 815	3.893 970	.256 807 3102	308.17	.027 229	8.17	4
	1.055 353	5.109 513	.195 713 3563	.947 550	4.841 520	.206 546 6896	247.86	.032 733	7.86	5
	1.066 786	6.164 866	.162 209 5174	.937 395	5.778 915	.173 042 8508	207.66	.038 257	7.65	6
	1.078 343	7.231 652	.138 280 9821	.927 349	6.706 264	.149 114 3154	178.94	.043 800	7.51	7
	1.090 025	8.309 995	.120 337 0111	.917 410	7.623 674	.131 170 3444	157.41	.049 363	7.40	8
	1.101 834	9.400 020	.106 382 7492	.907 578	8.531 253	.117 216 0825	140.66	.054 945	7.33	9
	1.113 770	10.501 854	.095 221 2834	.897 851	9.429 104	.106 054 6167	127.27	.060 546	7.27	10
	1.125 836	11.615 624	.086 090 9416	.888 229	10.317 333	.096 924 2749	116.31	.066 167	7.22	11
	1.138 032	12.741 460	.078 483 9424	.878 710	11.196 042	.089 317 2757	107.19	.071 807	7.18	12
1	1.138 032	12.741 460	.078 483 9424	.878 710	11.196 042	.089 317 2757	107.19	.071 807	7.18	12
2	1.295 118	27.241 655	.036 708 4893	.772 130	21.034 112	.047 541 8226	57.06	.141 004	7.05	24
3	1.473 886	43.743 348	.022 860 6187	.678 478	29.678 917	.033 693 9520	40.44	.212 982	7.10	36
4	1.677 330	62.522 811	.015 994 1626	.596 185	37.275 190	.026 827 4959	32.20	.287 720	7.19	48
5	1.908 857	83.894 449	.011 919 7397	.523 874	43.950 107	.022 753 0730	27.31	.365 184	7.30	60
6	2.172 341	108.216 068	.009 240 7719	.460 333	49.815 421	.020 074 1052	24.09	.445 336	7.42	72
7	2.472 194	135.894 861	.007 358 6300	.404 499	54.969 328	.018 191 9633	21.84	.528 125	7.54	84
8	2.813 437	167.394 225	.005 973 9217	.355 437	59.498 115	.016 807 2551	20.17	.613 496	7.67	96
9	3.201 783	203.241 525	.004 920 2544	.312 326	63.477 604	.015 753 5877	18.91	.701 387	7.79	108
10	3.643 733	244.036 917	.004 097 7407	.274 444	66.974 419	.014 931 0740	17.92	.791 729	7.92	120
11	4.146 687	290.463 399	.003 442 7746	.241 156	70.047 103	.014 276 1079	17.14	.884 446	8.04	132
12	4.719 064	343.298 242	.002 912 9191	.211 906	72.747 100	.013 746 2524	16.50	.979 460	8.16	144
13	5.370 448	403.426 010	.002 478 7693	.186 204	75.119 613	.013 312 1026	15.98	1.076 688	8.28	156
14	6.111 745	471.853 363	.002 119 3025	.163 619	77.204 363	.012 952 6358	15.55	1.176 043	8.40	168
15	6.955 364	549.725 914	.001 819 0883	.143 774	79.036 253	.012 652 4217	15.19	1.277 436	8.52	180
16	7.915 430	638.347 406	.001 566 5451	.126 336	80.645 952	.012 399 8784	14.88	1.380 777	8.63	192
17	9.008 017	739.201 542	.001 352 8110	.111 012	82.060 410	.012 186 1444	14.63	1.485 973	8.74	204
18	10.251 416	853.976 825	.001 170 9920	.097 548	83.303 307	.012 004 3253	14.41	1.592 934	8.85	216
19	11.666 444	984.594 826	.001 015 6462	.085 716	84.395 453	.011 848 9795	14.22	1.701 567	8.96	228
20	13.276 792	1133.242 353	.000 882 4238	.075 319	85.355 132	.011 715 7571	14.06	1.811 782	9.06	240
21	15.109 421	1302.408 067	.000 767 8085	.066 184	86.198 412	.011 601 1418	13.93	1.923 488	9.16	252
22	17.195 012	1494.924 144	.000 668 9303	.058 156	86.939 409	.011 502 2636	13.81	2.036 598	9.26	264
23	19.568 482	1714.013 694	.000 583 4259	.051 103	87.590 531	.011 416 7592	13.71	2.151 026	9.35	276
24	22.269 568	1963.344 717	.000 509 3349	.044 904	88.162 677	.011 342 6682	13.62	2.266 688	9.44	288
25	25.343 491	2247.091 520	.000 445 0197	.039 458	88.665 428	.011 278 3530	13.54	2.383 506	9.53	300
26	28.841 716	2570.004 599	.000 389 1044	.034 672	89.107 200	.011 222 4377	13.47	2.501 401	9.62	312
27	32.822 810	2937.490 172	.000 340 4267	.030 467	89.495 389	.011 173 7600	13.41	2.620 298	9.70	324
28	37.353 424	3355.700 690	.000 298 0004	.026 771	89.836 495	.011 131 3337	13.36	2.740 128	9.79	336
29	42.509 410	3831.637 843	.000 260 9850	.023 524	90.136 227	.011 094 3183	13.32	2.860 823	9.86	348
30	48.377 089	4373.269 783	.000 228 6619	.020 671	90.399 605	.011 061 9952	13.28	2.982 318	9.94	360
31	55.054 699	4989.664 524	.000 200 4143	.018 164	90.631 038	.011 033 7476	13.25	3.104 554	10.01	372
32	62.654 036	5691.141 761	.000 175 7117	.015 961	90.834 400	.011 009 0450	13.22	3.227 473	10.09	384
33	71.302 328	6489.445 641	.000 154 0964	.014 025	91.013 097	.010 987 4297	13.19	3.351 022	10.15	396
34	81.144 365	7397.941 387	.000 135 1727	.012 324	91.170 119	.010 968 5061	13.17	3.475 150	10.22	408
35	92.344 923	8431.839 055	.000 118 5981	.010 829	91.308 095	.010 951 9314	13.15	3.599 811	10.29	420
36	105.091 522	9608.448 184	.000 104 0751	.009 516	91.429 337	.010 937 4084	13.13	3.724 960	10.35	432
37	119.597 566	10947.467 591	.000 091 3453	.008 361	91.535 873	.010 924 6787	13.11	3.850 557	10.41	444
38	136.105 914	12471.315 170	.000 080 1840	.007 347	91.629 487	.010 913 5173	13.10	3.976 564	10.46	456
39	154.892 951	14205.503 212	.000 070 3953	.006 456	91.711 747	.010 903 7286	13.09	4.102 945	10.52	468
40	176.273 210	16179.065 533	.000 061 8083	.005 673	91.784 030	.010 895 1416	13.08	4.229 668	10.57	480
41	200.604 639	18425.043 558	.000 054 2740	.004 985	91.847 545	.010 887 6073	13.07	4.356 703	10.63	492
42	228.294 595	20981.039 504	.000 047 6621	.004 380	91.903 356	.010 880 9954	13.06	4.484 022	10.68	504
43	259.806 664	23889.845 914	.000 041 8588	.003 849	91.952 399	.010 875 1921	13.06	4.611 599	10.72	516
44	295.668 423	27200.162 091	.000 036 7645	.003 382	91.995 492	.010 870 0978	13.05	4.739 412	10.77	528
45	336.480 269	30967.409 424	.000 032 2920	.002 972	92.033 359	.010 865 6253	13.04	4.867 438	10.82	540
46	382.925 475	35254.659 256	.000 028 3650	.002 611	92.066 633	.010 861 6984	13.04	4.995 658	10.86	552
47	435.781 629	40133.688 821	.000 024 9167	.002 295	92.095 871	.010 858 2501	13.03	5.124 053	10.90	564
48	495.933 649	45686.182 945	.000 021 8885	.002 016	92.121 563	.010 855 2218	13.03	5.252 608	10.94	576
49	564.388 601	52005.101 613	.000 019 2289	.001 772	92.144 139	.010 852 5622	13.03	5.381 307	10.98	588
50	642.292 560	59196.236 305	.000 016 8930	.001 557	92.163 976	.010 850 2263	13.03	5.510 136	11.02	600

Effective Rate is 13.80 %

Annual Percentage Rate is 13.00 %

Amount Of 1	Amount Of 1 Per Period	Sinking Fund Payment	Present Worth Of 1	Present Worth of 1 Per Period	Periodic Payment To Amortize 1	Constant Annual Percent	Total Interest	Annual Add On Rate
What a single $ 1 deposit grows to in the future. The deposit is made at the beginning of the first period.	What a series of $ 1 deposits grow to in the future. A deposit is made at the end of each period.	The amount to be deposited at the end of each period that grows to $ 1 in the future.	What $ 1 to be paid in the future is worth today. Value today of a single $ 1 payment tomorrow.	What $ 1 to be paid at the end of each period is worth today. Value today of a series of $ 1 payments tomorrow.	The mortgage payment to amortize a loan of $ 1. An annuity certain, payable at the end of each period, worth $ 1 today.	The annual payment, including interest and principal, to amortize completely a loan of $ 100.	The total interest paid over the term on a loan of $1. The loan is amortized by regular periodic payments.	The average annual interest rate on a loan that is completely amortized by regular periodic payments.

$$S = (1 + i)^n \qquad S\overline{n}| = \frac{(1+i)^n - 1}{i} \qquad \frac{1}{S\overline{n}|} = \frac{i}{(1+i)^n - 1} \qquad V^n = \frac{1}{(1+i)^n} \qquad A\overline{n}| = \frac{1 - V^n}{i} \qquad \frac{1}{A\overline{n}|} = \frac{i}{1 - V^n}$$

YEAR									PERIODS
	1.010 875	1.000 000	1.000 000 0000	.989 242	.989 242	1.010 875 0000	1213.05	.010 875	13.05	1
	1.021 868	2.010 875	.497 295 9533	.978 600	1.967 842	.508 170 9533	609.81	.016 342	9.81	2
	1.032 981	3.032 743	.329 734 4722	.968 072	2.935 914	.340 609 4722	408.74	.021 828	8.73	3
	1.044 215	4.065 724	.245 958 6323	.957 657	3.893 571	.256 833 6323	308.21	.027 335	8.20	4
	1.055 571	5.109 939	.195 697 0485	.947 355	4.840 926	.206 572 0485	247.89	.032 860	7.89	5
	1.067 050	6.165 510	.162 192 5924	.937 163	5.778 089	.173 067 5924	207.69	.038 406	7.68	6
	1.078 654	7.232 560	.138 263 6376	.927 081	6.705 171	.149 138 6376	178.97	.043 970	7.54	7
	1.090 384	8.311 214	.120 319 3706	.917 108	7.622 278	.131 194 3706	157.44	.049 555	7.43	8
	1.102 242	9.401 598	.106 364 8951	.907 241	8.529 520	.117 239 8951	140.69	.055 159	7.35	9
	1.114 229	10.503 841	.095 203 2733	.897 481	9.427 001	.106 078 2733	127.30	.060 783	7.29	10
	1.126 347	11.618 070	.086 072 8175	.887 826	10.314 827	.096 947 8175	116.34	.066 426	7.25	11
	1.138 596	12.744 416	.078 465 7356	.878 275	11.193 102	.089 340 7356	107.21	.072 089	7.21	12
1	1.138 596	12.744 416	.078 465 7356	.878 275	11.193 102	.089 340 7356	107.21	.072 089	7.21	12
2	1.296 400	27.255 152	.036 690 3113	.771 367	21.023 724	.047 565 3113	57.08	.141 567	7.08	24
3	1.476 075	43.777 010	.022 843 0402	.677 472	29.657 714	.033 718 0402	40.47	.213 849	7.13	36
4	1.680 652	62.588 724	.015 977 3188	.595 007	37.240 732	.026 852 3188	32.23	.288 911	7.22	48
5	1.913 583	84.007 658	.011 903 6767	.522 580	43.900 706	.022 778 6767	27.34	.366 721	7.33	60
6	2.178 797	108.395 160	.009 225 5042	.458 969	49.749 996	.020 100 5042	24.13	.447 236	7.45	72
7	2.480 769	136.162 660	.007 344 1573	.403 101	54.887 281	.018 219 1573	21.87	.530 409	7.58	84
8	2.824 592	167.778 612	.005 960 2353	.354 033	59.399 229	.016 835 2353	20.21	.616 183	7.70	96
9	3.216 068	203.776 394	.004 907 3398	.310 939	63.361 961	.015 782 3398	18.94	.704 493	7.83	108
10	3.661 801	244.763 307	.004 085 5797	.273 090	66.842 330	.014 960 5797	17.96	.795 270	7.95	120
11	4.169 310	291.430 823	.003 431 3460	.239 848	69.899 050	.014 306 3460	17.17	.888 438	8.08	132
12	4.747 158	344.566 247	.002 902 1995	.210 652	72.583 691	.013 777 1995	16.54	.983 917	8.20	144
13	5.405 093	405.066 004	.002 468 7335	.185 011	74.941 545	.013 343 7335	16.02	1.081 622	8.32	156
14	6.154 214	473.590 757	.002 109 9238	.162 490	77.012 389	.012 984 9238	15.59	1.181 467	8.44	168
15	7.007 161	552.382 628	.001 810 3393	.142 711	78.831 159	.012 685 3393	15.23	1.283 361	8.56	180
16	7.978 322	641.684 806	.001 558 3975	.125 340	80.428 539	.012 433 3975	14.93	1.387 212	8.67	192
17	9.084 082	743.363 867	.001 345 2362	.110 083	81.831 479	.012 220 2362	14.67	1.492 928	8.78	204
18	10.343 095	859.135 190	.001 163 9612	.096 683	83.063 645	.012 038 9612	14.45	1.600 416	8.89	216
19	11.776 602	990.951 901	.001 009 1307	.084 914	84.145 826	.011 884 1307	14.27	1.709 582	9.00	228
20	13.408 786	1141.037 818	.000 876 3951	.074 578	85.096 279	.011 751 3951	14.11	1.820 335	9.10	240
21	15.267 184	1311.924 973	.000 762 2387	.065 500	85.931 038	.011 637 2387	13.97	1.932 584	9.20	252
22	17.383 148	1506.496 322	.000 663 7919	.057 527	86.664 186	.011 538 7919	13.85	2.046 241	9.30	264
23	19.792 374	1728.034 390	.000 578 6922	.050 525	87.308 091	.011 453 6922	13.75	2.161 219	9.40	276
24	22.535 509	1980.276 644	.000 504 9799	.044 374	87.873 617	.011 379 9799	13.66	2.277 434	9.49	288
25	25.658 829	2267.478 546	.000 441 0185	.038 973	88.370 304	.011 316 0185	13.58	2.394 806	9.58	300
26	29.215 028	2594.485 347	.000 385 4329	.034 229	88.806 533	.011 260 4329	13.52	2.513 255	9.67	312
27	33.264 100	2966.813 827	.000 337 0619	.030 062	89.189 661	.011 212 0619	13.46	2.632 708	9.75	324
28	37.874 356	3390.745 370	.000 294 9204	.026 403	89.526 153	.011 169 9204	13.41	2.753 093	9.83	336
29	43.123 572	3873.431 929	.000 258 1690	.023 189	89.821 685	.011 133 1690	13.36	2.874 343	9.91	348
30	49.100 306	4423.016 685	.000 226 0900	.020 366	90.081 244	.011 101 0900	13.33	2.996 392	9.99	360
31	55.905 389	5048.771 431	.000 198 0680	.017 887	90.309 208	.011 073 0680	13.29	3.119 181	10.06	372
32	63.653 626	5761.252 986	.000 173 5734	.015 710	90.509 423	.011 048 5734	13.26	3.242 652	10.13	384
33	72.475 734	6572.481 297	.000 152 1495	.013 798	90.685 267	.011 027 1495	13.24	3.366 751	10.20	396
34	82.520 547	7496.142 224	.000 133 4020	.012 118	90.839 706	.011 008 4020	13.22	3.491 428	10.27	408
35	93.957 525	8547.818 423	.000 116 9889	.010 643	90.975 346	.010 991 9889	13.20	3.616 635	10.33	420
36	106.979 618	9745.252 241	.000 102 6141	.009 348	91.094 476	.010 977 6141	13.18	3.742 329	10.40	432
37	121.806 515	11108.645 029	.000 090 0200	.008 210	91.199 104	.010 965 0200	13.16	3.868 469	10.46	444
38	138.688 353	12660.997 960	.000 078 9827	.007 210	91.290 997	.010 953 9827	13.15	3.995 016	10.51	456
39	157.909 938	14428.500 063	.000 069 3073	.006 333	91.371 704	.010 944 3073	13.14	4.121 936	10.57	468
40	179.795 549	16440.970 053	.000 060 8237	.005 562	91.442 586	.010 935 8237	13.13	4.249 195	10.62	480
41	204.714 408	18732.359 381	.000 053 3836	.004 885	91.504 841	.010 928 3836	13.12	4.376 765	10.68	492
42	233.086 910	21341.325 022	.000 046 8574	.004 290	91.559 518	.010 921 8574	13.11	4.504 616	10.73	504
43	265.391 713	24311.881 631	.000 041 1322	.003 768	91.607 539	.010 916 1322	13.10	4.632 724	10.77	516
44	302.173 817	27694.144 100	.000 036 1087	.003 309	91.649 715	.010 911 1087	13.10	4.761 065	10.82	528
45	344.053 757	31545.173 018	.000 031 7006	.002 907	91.686 757	.010 906 7006	13.09	4.889 618	10.87	540
46	391.738 068	35929.937 320	.000 027 8319	.002 553	91.719 290	.010 902 8319	13.09	5.018 363	10.91	552
47	446.031 212	40922.410 342	.000 024 4365	.002 242	91.747 862	.010 899 4365	13.08	5.147 282	10.95	564
48	507.849 144	46606.817 795	.000 021 4561	.001 969	91.772 957	.010 896 4561	13.08	5.276 359	10.99	576
49	578.234 763	53079.058 695	.000 018 8398	.001 729	91.794 998	.010 893 8398	13.08	5.405 578	11.03	588
50	658.375 515	60448.323 235	.000 016 5431	.001 519	91.814 355	.010 891 5431	13.07	5.534 926	11.07	600

MONTHLY COMPOUND INTEREST AND ANNUITY

	Amount Of 1	Amount Of 1 Per Period	Sinking Fund Payment	Present Worth Of 1	Present Worth of 1 Per Period	Periodic Payment To Amortize 1	Constant Annual Percent	Total Interest	Annual Add On Rate	
	What a single $1 deposit grows to in the future. The deposit is made at the beginning of the first period.	What a series of $1 deposits grow to in the future. A deposit is made at the end of each period.	The amount to be deposited at the end of each period that grows to $1 in the future.	What $1 to be paid in the future is worth today. Value today of a single $1 payment tomorrow.	What $1 to be paid at the end of each period is worth today. Value today of a series of $1 payments tomorrow.	The mortgage payment to amortize a loan of $1. An annuity certain, payable at the end of each period, worth $1 today.	The annual payment, including interest and principal, to amortize completely a loan of $100.	The total interest paid over the term on a loan of $1. The loan is amortized by regular periodic payments.	The average annual interest rate on a loan that is completely amortized by regular periodic payments.	
	$S = (1+i)^n$	$S\overline{n}] = \dfrac{(1+i)^n - 1}{i}$	$\dfrac{1}{S\overline{n}]} = \dfrac{i}{(1+i)^n - 1}$	$V^n = \dfrac{1}{(1+i)^n}$	$A\overline{n}] = \dfrac{1-V^n}{i}$	$\dfrac{1}{A\overline{n}]} = \dfrac{i}{1-V^n}$				

YEAR										PERIODS
	1.010 917	1.000 000	1.000 000 0000	.989 201	.989 201	1.010 916 6667	1213.10	.010 917	13.10	1
	1.021 953	2.010 917	.497 285 6492	.978 519	1.967 720	.508 202 3158	609.85	.016 405	9.84	2
	1.033 109	3.032 869	.329 720 7834	.967 952	2.935 673	.340 637 4501	408.77	.021 912	8.76	3
	1.044 387	4.065 978	.245 943 2887	.957 500	3.893 172	.256 859 9554	308.24	.027 440	8.23	4
	1.055 788	5.110 365	.195 680 7420	.947 160	4.840 332	.206 597 4087	247.92	.032 987	7.92	5
	1.067 314	6.166 153	.162 175 6691	.936 932	5.777 263	.173 092 3357	207.72	.038 554	7.71	6
	1.078 965	7.233 467	.138 246 2950	.926 814	6.704 077	.149 162 9616	179.00	.044 141	7.57	7
	1.090 744	8.312 432	.120 301 7323	.916 805	7.620 882	.131 218 3989	157.47	.049 747	7.46	8
	1.102 651	9.403 176	.106 347 0435	.906 905	8.527 787	.117 263 7102	140.72	.055 373	7.38	9
	1.114 689	10.505 828	.095 185 2661	.897 112	9.424 899	.106 101 9327	127.33	.061 019	7.32	10
	1.126 857	11.620 516	.086 054 6964	.887 424	10.312 323	.096 971 3631	116.37	.066 685	7.27	11
	1.139 159	12.747 374	.078 447 5323	.877 841	11.190 164	.089 364 1990	107.24	.072 370	7.24	12
1	1.139 159	12.747 374	.078 447 5323	.877 841	11.190 164	.089 364 1990	107.24	.072 370	7.24	12
2	1.297 683	27.268 657	.036 672 1401	.770 604	21.013 345	.047 588 8068	57.11	.142 131	7.11	24
3	1.478 267	43.810 705	.022 825 4717	.676 468	29.636 533	.033 742 1384	40.50	.214 717	7.16	36
4	1.683 981	62.654 724	.015 960 4883	.593 831	37.206 319	.026 877 1550	32.26	.290 103	7.25	48
5	1.918 322	84.121 056	.011 887 6301	.521 289	43.851 385	.022 804 2968	27.37	.368 258	7.37	60
6	2.185 273	108.574 617	.009 210 2558	.457 609	49.684 695	.020 126 9225	24.16	.449 138	7.49	72
7	2.489 373	136.431 107	.007 329 7067	.401 708	54.805 411	.018 246 3734	21.90	.532 695	7.61	84
8	2.835 791	168.164 074	.005 946 5733	.352 635	59.300 585	.016 863 2400	20.24	.618 871	7.74	96
9	3.230 417	204.312 963	.004 894 4520	.309 558	63.246 632	.015 811 1187	18.98	.707 601	7.86	108
10	3.679 957	245.492 289	.004 073 4477	.271 742	66.710 632	.014 990 1144	17.99	.798 814	7.99	120
11	4.192 056	292.402 082	.003 419 9483	.238 546	69.751 472	.014 336 6150	17.21	.892 433	8.11	132
12	4.775 418	345.839 786	.002 891 5123	.209 406	72.420 846	.013 808 1790	16.57	.988 378	8.24	144
13	5.439 959	406.713 819	.002 458 7313	.183 825	74.764 131	.013 375 3980	16.06	1.086 562	8.36	156
14	6.196 978	476.059 012	.002 100 5799	.161 369	76.821 161	.013 017 2466	15.63	1.186 897	8.48	168
15	7.059 342	555.054 199	.001 801 6259	.141 656	78.626 907	.012 718 2925	15.27	1.289 293	8.60	180
16	8.041 711	645.042 265	.001 550 2860	.124 352	80.212 064	.012 466 9527	14.97	1.393 655	8.71	192
17	9.160 787	747.552 964	.001 337 6979	.109 161	81.603 579	.012 254 3645	14.71	1.499 890	8.82	204
18	10.435 591	864.328 932	.001 156 9669	.095 826	82.825 107	.012 073 6336	14.49	1.607 905	8.93	216
19	11.887 795	997.355 307	.001 002 6517	.084 120	83.897 415	.011 919 3184	14.31	1.717 605	9.04	228
20	13.542 087	1148.893 476	.000 870 4027	.073 844	84.838 730	.011 787 0694	14.15	1.828 897	9.14	240
21	15.426 588	1321.519 520	.000 756 7047	.064 823	85.665 055	.011 673 3713	14.01	1.941 690	9.25	252
22	17.573 334	1518.168 001	.000 658 6886	.056 904	86.390 437	.011 575 3553	13.90	2.055 894	9.34	264
23	20.018 819	1742.181 855	.000 573 9929	.049 953	87.027 206	.011 490 6596	13.79	2.171 422	9.44	276
24	22.804 614	1997.369 214	.000 500 6586	.043 851	87.586 189	.011 417 3252	13.71	2.288 190	9.53	288
25	25.978 077	2288.068 146	.000 437 0499	.038 494	88.076 886	.011 353 7166	13.63	2.406 115	9.62	300
26	29.593 156	2619.220 402	.000 381 7930	.033 792	88.507 640	.011 298 4597	13.56	2.525 119	9.71	312
27	33.711 305	2996.455 417	.000 333 7276	.029 664	88.885 773	.011 250 3943	13.51	2.645 128	9.80	324
28	38.402 531	3426.186 015	.000 291 8697	.026 040	89.217 714	.011 208 5364	13.46	2.766 068	9.88	336
29	43.746 582	3915.717 420	.000 255 3810	.022 859	89.509 106	.011 172 0477	13.41	2.887 873	9.96	348
30	49.834 305	4473.371 441	.000 223 5450	.020 066	89.764 901	.011 140 2117	13.37	3.010 476	10.03	360
31	56.769 188	5108.627 942	.000 195 7473	.017 615	89.989 448	.011 112 4139	13.34	3.133 818	10.11	372
32	64.669 122	5832.285 994	.000 171 4594	.015 463	90.186 565	.011 088 1260	13.31	3.257 840	10.18	384
33	73.668 401	6656.647 452	.000 150 2258	.013 574	90.359 602	.011 066 8924	13.29	3.382 489	10.25	396
34	83.920 010	7595.726 084	.000 131 6530	.011 916	90.511 501	.011 048 3197	13.26	3.507 714	10.32	408
35	95.598 220	8665.485 799	.000 115 4003	.010 460	90.644 845	.011 032 0670	13.24	3.633 468	10.38	420
36	108.901 556	9884.112 022	.000 101 1725	.009 183	90.761 899	.011 017 8391	13.23	3.759 707	10.44	432
37	124.056 169	11272.320 841	.000 088 7129	.008 061	90.864 654	.011 005 3795	13.21	3.886 389	10.50	444
38	141.319 680	12853.711 174	.000 077 7985	.007 076	90.954 856	.010 994 4652	13.20	4.013 476	10.56	456
39	160.985 561	14655.165 932	.000 068 2353	.006 212	91.034 039	.010 984 9020	13.19	4.140 934	10.62	468
40	183.388 124	16707.309 023	.000 059 8540	.005 453	91.103 550	.010 976 5207	13.18	4.268 730	10.67	480
41	208.908 200	19045.025 942	.000 052 5071	.004 787	91.164 569	.010 969 1738	13.17	4.396 834	10.72	492
42	237.979 620	21708.056 808	.000 046 0658	.004 202	91.218 134	.010 962 7325	13.16	4.525 217	10.77	504
43	271.096 585	24741.671 928	.000 040 4176	.003 689	91.265 155	.010 957 0843	13.15	4.653 856	10.82	516
44	308.822 068	28197.441 374	.000 035 4642	.003 238	91.306 433	.010 952 1309	13.15	4.782 725	10.87	528
45	351.797 385	32134.111 646	.000 031 1196	.002 843	91.342 668	.010 947 7862	13.14	4.911 805	10.92	540
46	400.753 097	36618.604 341	.000 027 3085	.002 495	91.374 476	.010 943 9752	13.14	5.041 074	10.96	552
47	456.521 429	41727.153 783	.000 023 9652	.002 190	91.402 399	.010 940 6319	13.13	5.170 516	11.00	564
48	520.050 416	47546.602 979	.000 021 0320	.001 923	91.426 911	.010 937 6987	13.13	5.300 114	11.04	576
49	592.420 022	54175.879 907	.000 018 4584	.001 688	91.448 428	.010 935 1251	13.13	5.429 854	11.08	588
50	674.860 498	61727.679 242	.000 016 2002	.001 482	91.467 317	.010 932 8669	13.12	5.559 720	11.12	600

Effective Rate is 13.92 %

Annual Percentage Rate is 13.10 %

MONTHLY COMPOUND INTEREST AND ANNUITY

13.125% M

	Amount Of 1	Amount Of 1 Per Period	Sinking Fund Payment	Present Worth Of 1	Present Worth of 1 Per Period	Periodic Payment To Amortize 1	Constant Annual Percent	Total Interest	Annual Add On Rate	
	What a single $1 deposit grows to in the future. The deposit is made at the beginning of the first period.	What a series of $1 deposits grow to in the future. A deposit is made at the end of each period.	The amount to be deposited at the end of each period that grows to $1 in the future.	What $1 to be paid in the future is worth today. Value today of a single $1 payment tomorrow.	What $1 to be paid at the end of each period is worth today. Value today of a series of $1 payments tomorrow.	The mortgage payment to amortize a loan of $1. An annuity certain, payable at the end of each period, worth $1 today.	The annual payment, including interest and principal, to amortize completely a loan of $100.	The total interest paid over the term on a loan of $1. The loan is amortized by regular periodic payments.	The average annual interest rate on a loan that is completely amortized by regular periodic payments.	
	$S = (1+i)^n$	$S\overline{n}| = \dfrac{(1+i)^n - 1}{i}$	$\dfrac{1}{S\overline{n}|} = \dfrac{i}{(1+i)^n - 1}$	$V^n = \dfrac{1}{(1+i)^n}$	$A\overline{n}| = \dfrac{1-V^n}{i}$	$\dfrac{1}{A\overline{n}|} = \dfrac{i}{1-V^n}$				**PERIODS**

YEAR										PERIODS
	1.010 938	1.000 000	1.000 000 0000	.989 181	.989 181	1.010 937 5000	1213.13	.010 938	13.13	1
	1.021 995	2.010 938	.497 280 4973	.978 479	1.967 660	.508 217 9973	609.87	.016 436	9.86	2
	1.033 173	3.032 932	.329 713 9393	.967 892	2.935 552	.340 651 4393	408.79	.021 954	8.78	3
	1.044 473	4.066 105	.245 935 6173	.957 421	3.892 973	.256 873 1173	308.25	.027 492	8.25	4
	1.055 897	5.110 578	.195 672 5893	.947 062	4.840 035	.206 610 0893	247.94	.033 050	7.93	5
	1.067 446	6.166 475	.162 167 2080	.936 816	5.776 850	.173 104 7080	207.73	.038 628	7.73	6
	1.079 121	7.233 921	.138 237 6244	.926 680	6.703 531	.149 175 1244	179.02	.044 226	7.58	7
	1.090 924	8.313 042	.120 292 9140	.916 654	7.620 185	.131 230 4140	157.48	.049 843	7.48	8
	1.102 856	9.403 966	.106 338 1187	.906 737	8.526 922	.117 275 6187	140.74	.055 481	7.40	9
	1.114 918	10.506 821	.095 176 2635	.896 927	9.423 848	.106 113 7635	127.34	.061 138	7.34	10
	1.127 113	11.621 740	.086 045 6371	.887 223	10.311 071	.096 983 1371	116.38	.066 815	7.29	11
	1.139 441	12.748 853	.078 438 4319	.877 624	11.188 695	.089 375 9319	107.26	.072 511	7.25	12
1	1.139 441	12.748 853	.078 438 4319	.877 624	11.188 695	.089 375 9319	107.26	.072 511	7.25	12
2	1.298 325	27.275 412	.036 663 0571	.770 223	21.008 157	.047 600 5571	57.13	.142 413	7.12	24
3	1.479 364	43.827 564	.022 816 6913	.675 966	29.625 950	.033 754 1913	40.51	.215 151	7.17	36
4	1.685 647	62.687 757	.015 952 0781	.593 244	37.189 129	.026 889 5781	32.27	.290 700	7.27	48
5	1.920 695	84.177 827	.011 879 6130	.520 645	43.826 754	.022 817 1130	27.39	.369 027	7.38	60
6	2.188 518	108.664 484	.009 202 6389	.456 930	49.652 091	.020 140 1389	24.17	.450 090	7.50	72
7	2.493 686	136.565 574	.007 322 4896	.401 013	54.764 544	.018 259 9896	21.92	.533 839	7.63	84
8	2.841 407	168.357 209	.005 939 7516	.351 938	59.251 353	.016 877 2516	20.26	.620 216	7.75	96
9	3.237 614	204.581 887	.004 888 0183	.308 869	63.189 084	.015 825 5183	19.00	.709 156	7.88	108
10	3.689 069	245.857 756	.004 067 3925	.271 071	66.644 929	.015 004 8925	18.01	.800 587	8.01	120
11	4.203 475	292.889 155	.003 414 2609	.237 898	69.677 861	.014 351 7609	17.23	.894 432	8.13	132
12	4.789 610	346.478 639	.002 886 1808	.208 785	72.339 633	.013 823 6808	16.59	.990 610	8.26	144
13	5.457 476	407.540 672	.002 453 7428	.183 235	74.675 668	.013 391 2428	16.07	1.089 034	8.38	156
14	6.218 470	477.117 230	.002 095 9210	.160 811	76.725 827	.013 033 4210	15.65	1.189 615	8.50	168
15	7.085 577	556.395 584	.001 797 2824	.141 132	78.525 095	.012 734 7824	15.29	1.292 261	8.62	180
16	8.073 594	646.728 556	.001 546 2438	.123 861	80.104 175	.012 483 7438	14.99	1.396 879	8.73	192
17	9.199 380	749.657 610	.001 333 9423	.108 703	81.490 014	.012 271 4423	14.73	1.503 374	8.84	204
18	10.482 147	866.939 150	.001 153 4835	.095 400	82.706 258	.012 090 9835	14.51	1.611 652	8.95	216
19	11.943 784	1000.574 496	.000 999 4258	.083 726	83.773 663	.011 936 9258	14.33	1.721 619	9.06	228
20	13.609 232	1152.844 030	.000 867 4200	.073 480	84.710 443	.011 804 9200	14.17	1.833 181	9.17	240
21	15.506 911	1326.346 117	.000 753 9510	.064 487	85.532 583	.011 691 4510	14.03	1.946 246	9.27	252
22	17.669 203	1524.041 434	.000 656 1501	.056 596	86.254 112	.011 593 6501	13.92	2.060 724	9.37	264
23	20.133 007	1749.303 499	.000 571 6561	.049 670	86.887 344	.011 509 1561	13.82	2.176 527	9.46	276
24	22.940 365	2005.976 236	.000 498 5104	.043 591	87.443 082	.011 436 0104	13.73	2.293 571	9.56	288
25	26.139 183	2298.439 568	.000 435 0778	.038 257	87.930 812	.011 372 5778	13.65	2.411 773	9.65	300
26	29.784 045	2631.684 154	.000 379 9848	.033 575	88.358 855	.011 317 4848	13.59	2.531 055	9.73	312
27	33.937 150	3011.396 556	.000 332 0718	.029 466	88.734 516	.011 269 5718	13.53	2.651 341	9.82	324
28	38.669 366	3444.056 274	.000 290 3553	.025 860	89.064 204	.011 227 8553	13.48	2.772 559	9.90	336
29	44.061 444	3937.046 312	.000 253 9975	.022 696	89.353 547	.011 191 4975	13.43	2.894 641	9.98	348
30	50.205 397	4498.779 164	.000 222 2825	.019 918	89.607 481	.011 159 7825	13.40	3.017 522	10.06	360
31	57.206 067	5138.840 367	.000 194 5964	.017 481	89.830 339	.011 132 0964	13.36	3.141 140	10.13	372
32	65.182 913	5868.152 072	.000 170 4114	.015 341	90.025 925	.011 107 9114	13.33	3.265 438	10.20	384
33	74.272 056	6699.159 421	.000 149 2725	.013 464	90.197 576	.011 086 7725	13.31	3.390 362	10.27	396
34	84.628 594	7646.042 911	.000 130 7866	.011 816	90.348 221	.011 068 2866	13.29	3.515 861	10.34	408
35	96.429 254	8724.960 379	.000 114 6137	.010 370	90.480 430	.011 052 1137	13.27	3.641 888	10.41	420
36	109.875 405	9954.322 719	.000 100 4589	.009 101	90.596 460	.011 037 9589	13.25	3.768 398	10.47	432
37	125.196 494	11355.108 049	.000 088 0661	.007 987	90.698 291	.011 025 5661	13.24	3.895 351	10.53	444
38	142.653 965	12951.219 690	.000 077 2128	.007 010	90.787 660	.011 014 7128	13.22	4.022 709	10.59	456
39	162.545 716	14769.894 056	.000 067 7053	.006 152	90.866 092	.011 005 2053	13.21	4.150 436	10.64	468
40	185.211 184	16842.165 420	.000 059 3748	.005 399	90.934 926	.010 996 8748	13.20	4.278 500	10.70	480
41	211.037 138	19203.395 493	.000 052 0741	.004 739	90.995 337	.010 989 5741	13.19	4.406 870	10.75	492
42	240.464 278	21893.876 843	.000 045 6749	.004 159	91.048 355	.010 983 1749	13.18	4.535 520	10.80	504
43	273.994 755	24959.520 459	.000 040 0649	.003 650	91.094 884	.010 977 5649	13.18	4.664 423	10.85	516
44	312.200 741	28452.639 182	.000 035 1461	.003 203	91.135 720	.010 972 6461	13.17	4.793 557	10.89	528
45	355.734 192	32432.840 385	.000 030 8329	.002 811	91.171 558	.010 968 3329	13.17	4.922 900	10.94	540
46	405.337 972	36968.043 131	.000 027 0504	.002 467	91.203 010	.010 964 5504	13.16	5.052 432	10.98	552
47	461.858 531	42163.637 153	.000 023 7329	.002 165	91.230 613	.010 961 2329	13.16	5.182 135	11.03	564
48	526.260 350	48023.803 453	.000 020 8230	.001 900	91.254 839	.010 958 3230	13.15	5.311 994	11.07	576
49	599.642 396	54733.019 045	.000 018 2705	.001 668	91.276 100	.010 955 7705	13.15	5.441 993	11.11	588
50	683.256 876	62377.771 513	.000 016 0314	.001 464	91.294 759	.010 953 5314	13.15	5.572 119	11.14	600

Effective Rate is 13.94 %

Annual Percentage Rate is 13.125%

MONTHLY COMPOUND INTEREST AND ANNUITY

13.15 % M

	Amount Of 1	Amount Of 1 Per Period	Sinking Fund Payment	Present Worth Of 1	Present Worth of 1 Per Period	Periodic Payment To Amortize 1	Constant Annual Percent	Total Interest	Annual Add On Rate	
	What a single $ 1 deposit grows to in the future. The deposit is made at the beginning of the first period.	What a series of $ 1 deposits grow to in the future. A deposit is made at the end of each period.	The amount to be deposited at the end of each period that grows to $ 1 in the future.	What $ 1 to be paid in the future is worth today. Value today of a single $ 1 payment tomorrow.	What $ 1 to be paid at the end of each period is worth today. Value today of a series of $ 1 payments tomorrow.	The mortgage payment to amortize a loan of $ 1. An annuity certain, payable at the end of each period, worth $ 1 today.	The annual payment, including interest and principal, to amortize completely a loan of $ 100.	The total interest paid over the term on a loan of $1. The loan is amortized by regular periodic payments.	The average annual interest rate on a loan that is completely amortized by regular periodic payments.	
	$S = (1+i)^n$	$S\overline{n}| = \dfrac{(1+i)^n - 1}{i}$	$\dfrac{1}{S\overline{n}|} = \dfrac{i}{(1+i)^n - 1}$	$V^n = \dfrac{1}{(1+i)^n}$	$A\overline{n}| = \dfrac{1 - V^n}{i}$	$\dfrac{1}{A\overline{n}|} = \dfrac{i}{1 - V^n}$				

YEAR										PERIODS
	1.010 958	1.000 000	1.000 000 0000	.989 160	.989 160	1.010 958 3333	1213.15	.010 958	13.15	1
	1.022 037	2.010 958	.497 275 3455	.978 438	1.967 599	.508 233 6788	609.89	.016 467	9.88	2
	1.033 237	3.032 995	.329 707 0954	.967 833	2.935 431	.340 665 4288	408.80	.021 996	8.80	3
	1.044 559	4.066 232	.245 927 9462	.957 342	3.892 773	.256 886 2795	308.27	.027 545	8.26	4
	1.056 006	5.110 791	.195 664 4370	.946 965	4.839 738	.206 622 7703	247.95	.033 114	7.95	5
	1.067 578	6.166 797	.162 158 7474	.936 700	5.776 438	.173 117 0807	207.75	.038 702	7.74	6
	1.079 277	7.234 374	.138 228 9543	.926 546	6.702 984	.149 187 2876	179.03	.044 311	7.60	7
	1.091 104	8.313 651	.120 284 0962	.916 503	7.619 487	.131 242 4296	157.50	.049 939	7.49	8
	1.103 060	9.404 755	.106 329 1944	.906 569	8.526 056	.117 287 5278	140.75	.055 588	7.41	9
	1.115 148	10.507 815	.095 167 2616	.896 742	9.422 798	.106 125 5949	127.36	.061 256	7.35	10
	1.127 368	11.622 963	.086 036 5785	.887 022	10.309 819	.096 994 9119	116.40	.066 944	7.30	11
	1.139 722	12.750 332	.078 429 3323	.877 407	11.187 226	.089 387 6657	107.27	.072 652	7.27	12
1	1.139 722	12.750 332	.078 429 3323	.877 407	11.187 226	.089 387 6657	107.27	.072 652	7.27	12
2	1.298 967	27.282 170	.036 653 9757	.769 842	21.002 972	.047 612 3091	57.14	.142 695	7.13	24
3	1.480 462	43.844 432	.022 807 9134	.675 465	29.615 373	.033 766 2467	40.52	.215 585	7.19	36
4	1.687 316	62.720 812	.015 943 6712	.592 657	37.171 951	.026 902 0045	32.29	.291 296	7.28	48
5	1.923 071	84.234 645	.011 871 5999	.520 002	43.802 143	.022 829 9332	27.40	.369 796	7.40	60
6	2.191 767	108.754 442	.009 195 0267	.456 253	49.619 517	.020 153 3601	24.19	.451 042	7.52	72
7	2.498 006	136.700 204	.007 315 2781	.400 319	54.723 720	.018 273 6114	21.93	.534 983	7.64	84
8	2.847 034	168.550 614	.005 932 9360	.351 243	59.202 182	.016 891 2693	20.27	.621 562	7.77	96
9	3.244 828	204.851 239	.004 881 5912	.308 183	63.131 614	.015 839 9245	19.01	.710 712	7.90	108
10	3.698 203	246.223 874	.004 061 3446	.270 402	66.579 324	.015 019 6779	18.03	.802 361	8.02	120
11	4.214 925	293.377 193	.003 408 5813	.237 252	69.604 367	.014 366 9146	17.25	.896 433	8.15	132
12	4.803 844	347.118 885	.002 880 8574	.208 167	72.258 561	.013 839 1907	16.61	.992 843	8.27	144
13	5.475 049	408.369 496	.002 448 7627	.182 647	74.587 367	.013 407 0961	16.09	1.091 507	8.40	156
14	6.240 036	478.178 187	.002 091 2706	.160 255	76.630 678	.013 049 6040	15.66	1.192 333	8.52	168
15	7.111 909	557.740 715	.001 792 9478	.140 609	78.423 492	.012 751 2812	15.31	1.295 231	8.63	180
16	8.105 602	648.419 909	.001 542 2105	.123 371	79.996 520	.012 500 5438	15.01	1.400 104	8.75	192
17	9.238 135	751.769 017	.001 330 1958	.108 247	81.376 704	.012 288 5291	14.75	1.506 860	8.86	204
18	10.528 910	869.558 308	.001 150 0091	.094 977	82.587 687	.012 108 3425	14.54	1.615 402	8.97	216
19	12.000 034	1003.805 400	.000 996 2090	.083 333	83.650 212	.011 954 5424	14.35	1.725 636	9.08	228
20	13.676 708	1156.809 816	.000 864 4463	.073 117	84.582 478	.011 822 7797	14.19	1.837 467	9.19	240
21	15.587 650	1331.192 374	.000 751 2062	.064 153	85.400 454	.011 709 5396	14.06	1.950 804	9.29	252
22	17.765 593	1529.940 078	.000 653 6204	.056 289	86.118 153	.011 611 9537	13.94	2.065 556	9.39	264
23	20.247 844	1756.457 286	.000 569 3278	.049 388	86.747 866	.011 527 6612	13.84	2.181 634	9.49	276
24	23.076 922	2014.624 018	.000 496 3705	.043 333	87.300 380	.011 454 7039	13.75	2.298 955	9.58	288
25	26.301 284	2308.862 422	.000 433 1137	.038 021	87.785 160	.011 391 4471	13.67	2.417 434	9.67	300
26	29.976 162	2644.212 516	.000 378 1844	.033 360	88.210 509	.011 336 5178	13.61	2.536 994	9.76	312
27	34.164 503	3026.418 526	.000 330 4236	.029 270	88.583 713	.011 288 7569	13.55	2.657 557	9.84	324
28	38.938 049	3462.027 271	.000 288 8481	.025 682	88.911 165	.011 247 1814	13.50	2.779 053	9.93	336
29	44.378 566	3958.500 308	.000 252 6209	.022 533	89.198 452	.011 210 9543	13.46	2.901 412	10.00	348
30	50.579 245	4524.341 742	.000 221 0266	.019 771	89.450 559	.011 179 3600	13.42	3.024 570	10.08	360
31	57.646 298	5169.243 891	.000 193 4519	.017 347	89.671 741	.011 151 7852	13.39	3.148 464	10.16	372
32	65.700 776	5904.253 305	.000 169 3694	.015 221	89.865 808	.011 127 7028	13.36	3.273 038	10.23	384
33	74.880 645	6741.959 987	.000 148 3248	.013 355	90.036 083	.011 106 6582	13.33	3.398 237	10.30	396
34	85.343 147	7696.713 045	.000 129 9256	.011 717	90.185 484	.011 088 2589	13.31	3.524 010	10.36	408
35	97.267 495	8784.866 477	.000 113 8321	.010 281	90.316 569	.011 072 1655	13.29	3.650 309	10.43	420
36	110.857 942	10025.059 300	.000 099 7500	.009 021	90.431 584	.011 058 0834	13.27	3.777 092	10.49	432
37	126.347 277	11438.534 823	.000 087 4238	.007 915	90.532 499	.011 045 7571	13.26	3.904 316	10.55	444
38	144.000 820	13049.504 516	.000 076 6313	.006 944	90.621 043	.011 034 9646	13.25	4.031 944	10.61	456
39	164.120 958	14885.562 736	.000 067 1792	.006 093	90.698 732	.011 025 5125	13.24	4.159 940	10.67	468
40	187.052 330	16978.159 388	.000 058 8992	.005 346	90.766 896	.011 017 2325	13.23	4.288 272	10.72	480
41	213.187 728	19363.138 635	.000 051 6445	.004 691	90.826 704	.011 009 9779	13.22	4.416 909	10.77	492
42	242.974 825	22081.352 869	.000 045 2871	.004 116	90.879 180	.011 003 6204	13.21	4.545 825	10.82	504
43	276.923 847	25179.362 477	.000 039 7151	.003 611	90.925 223	.010 998 0484	13.20	4.674 993	10.87	516
44	315.616 307	28710.233 376	.000 034 8308	.003 168	90.965 621	.010 993 1641	13.20	4.804 391	10.92	528
45	359.714 970	32734.445 976	.000 030 5489	.002 780	91.001 067	.010 988 8822	13.19	4.933 996	10.96	540
46	409.975 204	37320.931 156	.000 026 7946	.002 439	91.032 167	.010 985 1279	13.19	5.063 791	11.01	552
47	467.257 917	42548.250 983	.000 023 5027	.002 140	91.059 454	.010 981 8361	13.18	5.193 756	11.05	564
48	532.544 307	48505.944 400	.000 020 6160	.001 878	91.083 397	.010 978 9494	13.18	5.323 875	11.09	576
49	606.952 668	55296.060 949	.000 018 0845	.001 648	91.104 404	.010 976 4178	13.18	5.454 134	11.13	588
50	691.757 542	63034.908 772	.000 015 8642	.001 446	91.122 836	.010 974 1976	13.17	5.584 519	11.17	600

Effective Rate is 13.97 %

Annual Percentage Rate is 13.15 %

MONTHLY COMPOUND INTEREST AND ANNUITY

	Amount Of 1	Amount Of 1 Per Period	Sinking Fund Payment	Present Worth Of 1	Present Worth of 1 Per Period	Periodic Payment To Amortize 1	Constant Annual Percent	Total Interest	Annual Add On Rate	
	What a single $1 deposit grows to in the future. The deposit is made at the beginning of the first period.	What a series of $1 deposits grow to in the future. A deposit is made at the end of each period.	The amount to be deposited at the end of each period that grows to $1 in the future.	What $1 to be paid in the future is worth today. Value today of a single $1 payment tomorrow.	What $1 to be paid at the end of each period is worth today. Value today of a series of $1 payments tomorrow.	The mortgage payment to amortize a loan of $1. An annuity certain, payable at the end of each period, worth $1 today.	The annual payment, including interest and principal, to amortize completely a loan of $100.	The total interest paid over the term on a loan of $1. The loan is amortized by regular periodic payments.	The average annual interest rate on a loan that is completely amortized by regular periodic payments.	
	$S = (1+i)^n$	$S\overline{n}| = \dfrac{(1+i)^n - 1}{i}$	$\dfrac{1}{S\overline{n}|} = \dfrac{i}{(1+i)^n - 1}$	$V^n = \dfrac{1}{(1+i)^n}$	$A\overline{n}| = \dfrac{1-V^n}{i}$	$\dfrac{1}{A\overline{n}|} = \dfrac{i}{1-V^n}$				PERIODS

YEAR										PERIODS
	1.011 000	1.000 000	1.000 000 0000	.989 120	.989 120	1.011 000 0000	1213.20	.011 000	13.20	1
	1.022 121	2.011 000	.497 265 0423	.978 358	1.967 477	.508 265 0423	609.92	.016 530	9.92	2
	1.033 364	3.033 121	.329 693 4082	.967 713	2.935 190	.340 693 4082	408.84	.022 080	8.83	3
	1.044 731	4.066 485	.245 912 6048	.957 184	3.892 374	.256 912 6048	308.30	.027 650	8.30	4
	1.056 223	5.111 217	.195 648 1332	.946 769	4.839 144	.206 648 1332	247.98	.033 241	7.98	5
	1.067 842	6.167 440	.162 141 8273	.936 468	5.775 612	.173 141 8273	207.78	.038 851	7.77	6
	1.079 588	7.235 282	.138 211 6156	.926 279	6.701 891	.149 211 6156	179.06	.044 481	7.63	7
	1.091 464	8.314 870	.120 266 4625	.916 201	7.618 092	.131 266 4625	157.52	.050 132	7.52	8
	1.103 470	9.406 334	.106 311 3479	.906 232	8.524 325	.117 311 3479	140.78	.055 802	7.44	9
	1.115 608	10.509 803	.095 149 2600	.896 372	9.420 697	.106 149 2600	127.38	.061 493	7.38	10
	1.127 880	11.625 411	.086 018 4637	.886 620	10.307 316	.097 018 4637	116.43	.067 203	7.33	11
	1.140 286	12.753 291	.078 411 1358	.876 973	11.184 289	.089 411 1358	107.30	.072 934	7.29	12
1	1.140 286	12.753 291	.078 411 1358	.876 973	11.184 289	.089 411 1358	107.30	.072 934	7.29	12
2	1.300 253	27.295 692	.036 635 8181	.769 081	20.992 607	.047 635 8181	57.17	.143 260	7.16	24
3	1.482 660	43.878 191	.022 790 3652	.674 463	29.594 235	.033 790 3652	40.55	.216 453	7.22	36
4	1.690 657	62.786 986	.015 926 8673	.591 486	37.137 629	.026 926 8673	32.32	.292 490	7.31	48
5	1.927 833	84.348 424	.011 855 5860	.518 717	43.752 980	.022 855 5860	27.43	.371 335	7.43	60
6	2.198 281	108.934 635	.009 179 8169	.454 901	49.554 464	.020 179 8169	24.22	.452 947	7.55	72
7	2.506 669	136.969 951	.007 300 8714	.398 936	54.642 207	.018 300 8714	21.97	.537 273	7.68	84
8	2.858 321	168.938 235	.005 919 3231	.349 856	59.104 019	.016 919 3231	20.31	.624 255	7.80	96
9	3.259 304	205.391 228	.004 868 7571	.306 814	63.016 908	.015 868 7571	19.05	.713 826	7.93	108
10	3.716 539	246.958 073	.004 049 2703	.269 068	66.448 404	.015 049 2703	18.06	.805 912	8.06	120
11	4.237 918	294.356 172	.003 397 2449	.235 965	69.457 734	.014 397 2449	17.28	.900 436	8.19	132
12	4.832 439	348.403 570	.002 870 2347	.206 935	72.096 834	.013 870 2347	16.65	.997 314	8.31	144
13	5.510 364	410.033 073	.002 438 8277	.181 476	74.411 253	.013 438 8277	16.13	1.096 457	8.43	156
14	6.283 392	480.308 343	.002 081 9959	.159 150	76.440 935	.013 081 9959	15.70	1.197 775	8.56	168
15	7.164 865	560.442 265	.001 784 3051	.139 570	78.220 912	.012 784 3051	15.35	1.301 175	8.67	180
16	8.169 997	651.817 869	.001 534 1709	.122 399	79.781 903	.012 534 1709	15.05	1.406 561	8.79	192
17	9.316 134	756.012 209	.001 322 7300	.107 341	81.150 849	.012 322 7300	14.79	1.513 837	8.90	204
18	10.623 059	874.823 577	.001 143 0876	.094 135	82.351 378	.012 143 0876	14.58	1.622 907	9.02	216
19	12.113 328	1010.302 540	.000 989 8025	.082 554	83.404 209	.011 989 8025	14.39	1.733 675	9.12	228
20	13.812 661	1164.787 331	.000 858 5258	.072 397	84.327 514	.011 858 5258	14.24	1.846 046	9.23	240
21	15.750 386	1340.944 206	.000 745 7432	.063 491	85.137 227	.011 745 7432	14.10	1.959 927	9.33	252
22	17.959 948	1541.813 459	.000 648 5869	.055 679	85.847 323	.011 648 5869	13.98	2.075 227	9.43	264
23	20.479 481	1770.861 895	.000 564 6968	.048 829	86.470 058	.011 564 6968	13.88	2.191 856	9.53	276
24	23.352 469	2032.042 666	.000 492 1157	.042 822	87.016 180	.011 492 1157	13.80	2.309 729	9.62	288
25	26.628 498	2329.863 493	.000 429 2097	.037 554	87.495 114	.011 429 2097	13.72	2.428 763	9.72	300
26	30.364 109	2669.464 471	.000 374 6070	.032 934	87.915 126	.011 374 6070	13.65	2.548 877	9.80	312
27	34.623 775	3056.706 779	.000 327 1495	.028 882	88.283 465	.011 327 1495	13.60	2.669 996	9.89	324
28	39.481 012	3498.273 838	.000 285 8553	.025 329	88.606 488	.011 285 8553	13.55	2.792 047	9.97	336
29	45.019 653	4001.786 659	.000 249 8884	.022 213	88.889 771	.011 249 8884	13.50	2.914 961	10.05	348
30	51.335 289	4575.935 379	.000 218 5346	.019 480	89.138 202	.011 218 5346	13.47	3.038 672	10.13	360
31	58.536 922	5230.629 240	.000 191 1816	.017 083	89.356 070	.011 191 1816	13.43	3.163 120	10.20	372
32	66.748 844	5977.167 612	.000 167 3033	.014 982	89.547 133	.011 167 3033	13.41	3.288 244	10.28	384
33	76.112 785	6828.435 012	.000 146 4464	.013 138	89.714 691	.011 146 4464	13.38	3.413 993	10.35	396
34	86.790 358	7799.123 479	.000 128 2195	.011 522	89.861 635	.011 128 2195	13.36	3.540 314	10.41	408
35	98.965 848	8905.986 138	.000 112 2840	.010 104	89.990 500	.011 112 2840	13.34	3.667 159	10.48	420
36	112.849 390	10168.126 350	.000 098 3465	.008 861	90.103 512	.011 098 3465	13.32	3.794 486	10.54	432
37	128.680 602	11607.327 412	.000 086 1525	.007 771	90.202 620	.011 086 1525	13.31	3.922 256	10.60	444
38	146.732 714	13248.428 517	.000 075 4807	.006 815	90.289 535	.011 075 4807	13.30	4.050 419	10.66	456
39	167.317 288	15119.753 454	.000 066 1386	.005 977	90.365 757	.011 066 1386	13.28	4.178 953	10.72	468
40	190.789 594	17253.599 449	.000 057 9589	.005 241	90.432 602	.011 057 9589	13.27	4.307 820	10.77	480
41	217.554 740	19686.794 582	.000 050 7955	.004 597	90.491 223	.011 050 7955	13.27	4.436 991	10.82	492
42	248.074 667	22461.333 406	.000 044 5210	.004 031	90.542 632	.011 044 5210	13.26	4.566 439	10.87	504
43	282.876 119	25625.101 728	.000 039 0242	.003 535	90.587 717	.011 039 0242	13.25	4.696 137	10.92	516
44	322.559 734	29232.703 075	.000 034 2083	.003 100	90.627 254	.011 034 2083	13.25	4.826 062	10.97	528
45	367.810 412	33346.401 093	.000 029 9882	.002 719	90.661 928	.011 029 9882	13.24	4.956 194	11.01	540
46	419.409 136	38037.194 160	.000 026 2901	.002 384	90.692 336	.011 026 2901	13.24	5.086 512	11.06	552
47	478.246 448	43386.040 745	.000 023 0489	.002 091	90.719 003	.011 023 0489	13.23	5.217 000	11.10	564
48	545.337 823	49485.256 673	.000 020 2080	.001 834	90.742 389	.011 020 2080	13.23	5.347 640	11.14	576
49	621.841 192	56440.108 405	.000 017 7179	.001 608	90.762 897	.011 017 7179	13.23	5.478 418	11.18	588
50	709.076 928	64370.629 834	.000 015 5350	.001 410	90.780 883	.011 015 5350	13.22	5.609 321	11.22	600

Effective Rate is 14.03 %

Annual Percentage Rate is 13.20 %

Amount Of 1	Amount Of 1 Per Period	Sinking Fund Payment	Present Worth Of 1	Present Worth of 1 Per Period	Periodic Payment To Amortize 1	Constant Annual Percent	Total Interest	Annual Add On Rate
What a single $ 1 deposit grows to in the future. The deposit is made at the beginning of the first period.	What a series of $ 1 deposits grow to in the future. A deposit is made at the end of each period.	The amount to be deposited at the end of each period that grows to $ 1 in the future.	What $ 1 to be paid in the future is worth today. Value today of a single $ 1 payment tomorrow.	What $ 1 to be paid at the end of each period is worth today. Value today of a series of $ 1 payments tomorrow.	The mortgage payment to amortize a loan of $ 1. An annuity certain, payable at the end of each period, worth $ 1 today.	The annual payment, including interest and principal, to amortize completely a loan of $ 100.	The total interest paid over the term on a loan of $1. The loan is amortized by regular periodic payments.	The average annual interest rate on a loan that is completely amortized by regular periodic payments.
$S = (1+i)^n$	$S\overline{n} = \dfrac{(1+i)^n - 1}{i}$	$\dfrac{1}{S\overline{n}} = \dfrac{i}{(1+i)^n - 1}$	$V^n = \dfrac{1}{(1+i)^n}$	$A\overline{n} = \dfrac{1 - V^n}{i}$	$\dfrac{1}{A\overline{n}} = \dfrac{i}{1 - V^n}$			

YEAR / **PERIODS**

YEAR	Amount Of 1	Amount Of 1 Per Period	Sinking Fund Payment	Present Worth Of 1	Present Worth of 1 Per Period	Periodic Payment To Amortize 1	Constant Annual Percent	Total Interest	Annual Add On Rate	PERIODS
	1.011 042	1.000 000	1.000 000 0000	.989 079	.989 079	1.011 041 6667	1213.25	.011 042	13.25	1
	1.022 205	2.011 042	.497 254 7395	.978 277	1.967 356	.508 296 4061	609.96	.016 593	9.96	2
	1.033 492	3.033 247	.329 679 7217	.967 593	2.934 949	.340 721 3884	408.87	.022 164	8.87	3
	1.044 904	4.066 739	.245 897 2644	.957 026	3.891 975	.256 938 9311	308.33	.027 756	8.33	4
	1.056 441	5.111 643	.195 631 8309	.946 574	4.838 550	.206 673 4976	248.01	.033 367	8.01	5
	1.068 106	6.168 084	.162 124 9089	.936 237	5.774 786	.173 166 5756	207.80	.038 999	7.80	6
	1.079 900	7.236 190	.138 194 2789	.926 012	6.700 798	.149 235 9455	179.09	.044 652	7.65	7
	1.091 823	8.316 089	.120 248 8309	.915 899	7.616 697	.131 290 4976	157.55	.050 324	7.55	8
	1.103 879	9.407 913	.106 293 5039	.905 894	8.522 594	.117 335 1706	140.81	.056 017	7.47	9
	1.116 068	10.511 792	.095 131 2611	.896 003	9.418 597	.106 172 9278	127.41	.061 729	7.41	10
	1.128 391	11.627 859	.086 000 3520	.886 218	10.304 814	.097 042 0186	116.46	.067 462	7.36	11
	1.140 850	12.756 250	.078 392 9426	.876 539	11.181 354	.089 434 6092	107.33	.073 215	7.32	12
1	1.140 850	12.756 250	.078 392 9426	.876 539	11.181 354	.089 434 6092	107.33	.073 215	7.32	12
2	1.301 539	27.309 222	.036 617 6672	.768 321	20.982 249	.047 659 3339	57.20	.143 824	7.19	24
3	1.484 861	43.911 983	.022 772 8270	.673 463	29.573 118	.033 814 4937	40.58	.217 322	7.24	36
4	1.694 005	62.853 248	.015 910 0767	.590 317	37.103 351	.026 951 7434	32.35	.293 684	7.34	48
5	1.932 606	84.462 395	.011 839 5885	.517 436	43.703 896	.022 881 2552	27.46	.372 875	7.46	60
6	2.204 814	109.115 196	.009 164 6263	.453 553	49.489 533	.020 206 2930	24.25	.454 853	7.58	72
7	2.515 362	137.240 351	.007 286 4868	.397 557	54.560 870	.018 328 1534	22.00	.539 565	7.71	84
8	2.869 652	169.326 941	.005 905 7348	.348 474	59.006 096	.016 947 4014	20.34	.626 951	7.84	96
9	3.273 843	205.932 935	.004 855 9498	.305 451	62.902 511	.015 897 6165	19.08	.716 943	7.97	108
10	3.734 964	247.694 894	.004 037 2249	.267 740	66.317 872	.015 078 8916	18.10	.809 467	8.09	120
11	4.261 035	295.339 035	.003 385 9391	.234 685	69.311 569	.014 427 6058	17.32	.904 444	8.22	132
12	4.861 203	349.693 867	.002 859 6441	.205 710	71.935 663	.013 901 3108	16.69	1.001 789	8.35	144
13	5.545 905	411.704 591	.002 428 9260	.180 313	74.235 783	.013 470 5927	16.17	1.101 412	8.47	156
14	6.327 047	482.449 541	.002 072 7556	.158 052	76.251 929	.013 114 4223	15.74	1.203 223	8.59	168
15	7.218 213	563.158 937	.001 775 6976	.138 538	78.019 160	.012 817 3643	15.39	1.307 126	8.71	180
16	8.234 901	655.236 272	.001 526 1670	.121 434	79.568 208	.012 567 8337	15.09	1.413 024	8.83	192
17	9.394 788	760.282 725	.001 315 3002	.106 442	80.926 008	.012 356 9668	14.83	1.520 821	8.95	204
18	10.718 047	880.124 998	.001 136 2022	.093 301	82.116 174	.012 177 8689	14.62	1.630 420	9.06	216
19	12.227 687	1016.847 086	.000 983 4320	.081 782	83.159 401	.012 025 0987	14.44	1.741 723	9.17	228
20	13.949 959	1172.826 517	.000 852 6410	.071 685	84.073 830	.011 894 3077	14.28	1.854 634	9.27	240
21	15.914 815	1350.775 692	.000 740 3154	.062 835	84.875 363	.011 781 9820	14.14	1.969 059	9.38	252
22	18.156 421	1553.789 056	.000 643 5880	.055 077	85.577 938	.011 685 2547	14.03	2.084 907	9.48	264
23	20.713 757	1785.396 905	.000 560 0995	.048 277	86.193 773	.011 601 7662	13.93	2.202 087	9.57	276
24	23.631 296	2049.626 781	.000 487 8937	.042 317	86.733 576	.011 529 5604	13.84	2.320 513	9.67	288
25	26.959 770	2351.073 504	.000 425 3376	.037 092	87.206 735	.011 467 0043	13.77	2.440 101	9.76	300
26	30.757 061	2694.979 079	.000 371 0604	.032 513	87.621 477	.011 412 7271	13.70	2.560 771	9.85	312
27	35.089 201	3087.323 844	.000 323 9051	.028 499	87.985 015	.011 365 5718	13.64	2.682 445	9.93	324
28	40.031 524	3534.930 473	.000 282 8910	.024 980	88.303 670	.011 324 5577	13.59	2.805 051	10.02	336
29	45.669 975	4045.582 614	.000 247 1832	.021 896	88.582 983	.011 288 8499	13.55	2.928 520	10.10	348
30	52.102 603	4628.160 244	.000 216 0686	.019 193	88.827 813	.011 257 7352	13.51	3.052 785	10.18	360
31	59.441 268	5292.794 087	.000 188 9361	.016 823	89.042 415	.011 230 6028	13.48	3.177 784	10.25	372
32	67.813 586	6051.041 783	.000 165 2608	.014 746	89.230 523	.011 206 9275	13.45	3.303 460	10.32	384
33	77.365 148	6916.088 866	.000 144 5904	.012 926	89.395 407	.011 186 2571	13.43	3.429 758	10.39	396
34	88.262 049	7902.978 060	.000 126 5346	.011 330	89.539 934	.011 168 2012	13.41	3.556 626	10.46	408
35	100.693 782	9028.870 858	.000 110 7558	.009 931	89.666 617	.011 152 4225	13.39	3.684 017	10.53	420
36	114.876 528	10313.345 953	.000 096 9617	.008 705	89.777 661	.011 138 6284	13.37	3.811 887	10.59	432
37	131.056 918	11778.739 704	.000 084 8987	.007 630	89.874 994	.011 126 5654	13.36	3.940 195	10.65	444
38	149.516 319	13450.534 553	.000 074 3465	.006 688	89.960 311	.011 116 0132	13.34	4.068 902	10.71	456
39	170.575 732	15357.802 147	.000 065 1135	.005 862	90.035 094	.011 106 7802	13.33	4.197 973	10.76	468
40	194.601 369	17533.708 886	.000 057 0330	.005 139	90.100 645	.011 098 6997	13.32	4.327 376	10.82	480
41	222.011 023	20016.092 664	.000 049 9598	.004 504	90.158 103	.011 091 6265	13.31	4.457 080	10.87	492
42	253.281 334	22848.120 853	.000 043 7673	.003 948	90.208 467	.011 085 4339	13.31	4.587 059	10.92	504
43	288.956 077	26079.040 959	.000 038 3450	.003 461	90.252 613	.011 080 0116	13.30	4.717 286	10.97	516
44	329.655 617	29765.037 017	.000 033 5965	.003 033	90.291 308	.011 075 2631	13.30	4.847 739	11.02	528
45	376.087 698	33970.206 592	.000 029 4376	.002 659	90.325 227	.011 071 1042	13.29	4.978 396	11.06	540
46	429.059 749	38767.675 413	.000 025 7947	.002 331	90.354 957	.011 067 4614	13.29	5.109 239	11.11	552
47	489.492 928	44240.868 984	.000 022 6035	.002 043	90.381 018	.011 064 2702	13.28	5.240 248	11.15	564
48	558.438 137	50484.963 315	.000 019 8079	.001 791	90.403 860	.011 061 4745	13.28	5.371 409	11.19	576
49	637.094 296	57608.539 981	.000 017 3585	.001 570	90.423 883	.011 059 0252	13.28	5.502 707	11.23	588
50	726.829 195	65735.474 303	.000 015 2125	.001 376	90.441 433	.011 056 8792	13.27	5.634 127	11.27	600

Effective Rate is 14.09 %

Annual Percentage Rate is 13.25 %

	Amount Of 1	Amount Of 1 Per Period	Sinking Fund Payment	Present Worth Of 1	Present Worth of 1 Per Period	Periodic Payment To Amortize 1	Constant Annual Percent	Total Interest	Annual Add On Rate
	What a single $ 1 deposit grows to in the future. The deposit is made at the beginning of the first period.	What a series of $ 1 deposits grow to in the future. A deposit is made at the end of each period.	The amount to be deposited at the end of each period that grows to $ 1 in the future.	What $ 1 to be paid in the future is worth today. Value today of a single $ 1 payment tomorrow.	What $ 1 to be paid at the end of each period is worth today. Value today of a series of $ 1 payments tomorrow.	The mortgage payment to amortize a loan of $ 1. An annuity certain, payable at the end of each period, worth $ 1 today.	The annual payment, including interest and principal, to amortize completely a loan of $ 100.	The total interest paid over the term on a loan of $1. The loan is amortized by regular periodic payments.	The average annual interest rate on a loan that is completely amortized by regular periodic payments.

Formulas:

$$S = (1+i)^n \qquad S\overline{n}| = \frac{(1+i)^n - 1}{i} \qquad \frac{1}{S\overline{n}|} = \frac{i}{(1+i)^n - 1} \qquad V^n = \frac{1}{(1+i)^n} \qquad A\overline{n}| = \frac{1-V^n}{i} \qquad \frac{1}{A\overline{n}|} = \frac{i}{1-V^n}$$

YEAR									PERIODS
	1.011 083	1.000 000	1.000 000 0000	.989 038	.989 038	1.011 083 3333	1213.30	.011 083	13.30	1
	1.022 290	2.011 083	.497 244 4371	.978 196	1.967 235	.508 327 7704	610.00	.016 656	9.99	2
	1.033 620	3.033 373	.329 666 0360	.967 474	2.934 708	.340 749 3693	408.90	.022 248	8.90	3
	1.045 076	4.066 993	.245 881 9251	.956 868	3.891 577	.256 965 2584	308.36	.027 861	8.36	4
	1.056 659	5.112 069	.195 615 5299	.946 379	4.837 956	.206 698 8632	248.04	.033 494	8.04	5
	1.068 370	6.168 727	.162 107 9922	.936 005	5.773 961	.173 191 3255	207.83	.039 148	7.83	6
	1.080 211	7.237 097	.138 176 9441	.925 745	6.699 706	.149 260 2774	179.12	.044 822	7.68	7
	1.092 184	8.317 309	.120 231 2016	.915 597	7.615 303	.131 314 5349	157.58	.050 516	7.58	8
	1.104 289	9.409 492	.106 275 6624	.905 560	8.520 864	.117 358 9957	140.84	.056 231	7.50	9
	1.116 528	10.513 781	.095 113 2651	.895 634	9.416 497	.106 196 5985	127.44	.061 966	7.44	10
	1.128 903	11.630 308	.085 982 2434	.885 816	10.302 313	.097 065 5767	116.48	.067 721	7.39	11
	1.141 415	12.759 211	.078 374 7528	.876 106	11.178 419	.089 458 0861	107.35	.073 497	7.35	12
1	1.141 415	12.759 211	.078 374 7528	.876 106	11.178 419	.089 458 0861	107.35	.073 497	7.35	12
2	1.302 827	27.322 760	.036 599 5232	.767 561	20.971 898	.047 682 8565	57.22	.144 389	7.22	24
3	1.487 066	43.945 808	.022 755 2989	.672 465	29.552 022	.033 838 6322	40.61	.218 191	7.27	36
4	1.697 359	62.919 597	.015 893 2994	.589 151	37.069 119	.026 976 6327	32.38	.294 878	7.37	48
5	1.937 390	84.576 557	.011 823 6073	.516 158	43.654 891	.022 906 9406	27.49	.374 416	7.49	60
6	2.211 365	109.296 127	.009 149 4550	.452 209	49.424 725	.020 232 7884	24.28	.456 761	7.61	72
7	2.524 085	137.511 405	.007 272 1241	.396 183	54.479 710	.018 355 4574	22.03	.541 858	7.74	84
8	2.881 027	169.716 734	.005 892 1709	.347 098	58.908 412	.016 975 5042	20.38	.629 648	7.87	96
9	3.288 446	206.476 367	.004 843 1693	.304 095	62.788 424	.015 926 5026	19.12	.720 062	8.00	108
10	3.753 481	248.434 348	.004 025 2083	.266 419	66.187 725	.015 108 5416	18.14	.813 025	8.13	120
11	4.284 278	296.325 800	.003 374 6640	.233 412	69.165 873	.014 457 9973	17.35	.908 456	8.26	132
12	4.890 137	350.989 801	.002 849 0856	.204 493	71.775 045	.013 932 4190	16.72	1.006 268	8.39	144
13	5.581 674	413.384 090	.002 419 0578	.179 158	74.060 956	.013 502 3911	16.21	1.106 373	8.51	156
14	6.371 004	484.601 842	.002 063 5497	.156 961	76.063 657	.013 146 8831	15.78	1.208 676	8.63	168
15	7.271 957	565.890 822	.001 767 1253	.137 515	77.818 234	.012 850 4587	15.43	1.313 083	8.75	180
16	8.300 317	658.675 250	.001 518 1988	.120 477	79.355 430	.012 601 5322	15.13	1.419 494	8.87	192
17	9.474 103	764.580 750	.001 307 9063	.105 551	80.702 176	.012 391 2397	14.87	1.527 813	8.99	204
18	10.813 880	885.462 832	.001 129 3529	.092 474	81.882 068	.012 212 6862	14.66	1.637 940	9.10	216
19	12.343 120	1023.439 405	.000 977 0974	.081 017	82.915 778	.012 060 4308	14.48	1.749 778	9.21	228
20	14.088 617	1180.927 877	.000 846 7918	.070 979	83.821 418	.011 930 1251	14.32	1.863 230	9.32	240
21	16.080 953	1360.687 516	.000 734 9226	.062 185	84.614 854	.011 818 2559	14.19	1.978 200	9.42	252
22	18.355 035	1565.867 791	.000 638 6235	.054 481	85.309 988	.011 721 9569	14.07	2.094 597	9.52	264
23	20.950 704	1800.063 549	.000 555 5359	.047 731	85.918 999	.011 638 8693	13.97	2.212 328	9.62	276
24	23.913 440	2067.378 004	.000 483 7045	.041 817	86.452 557	.011 567 0378	13.89	2.331 307	9.71	288
25	27.295 149	2372.494 623	.000 421 4973	.036 637	86.920 011	.011 504 8306	13.81	2.451 449	9.81	300
26	31.155 081	2720.759 182	.000 367 5445	.032 097	87.329 549	.011 450 8778	13.75	2.572 674	9.89	312
27	35.560 864	3118.273 431	.000 320 6903	.028 121	87.688 349	.011 404 0236	13.69	2.694 904	9.98	324
28	40.589 689	3572.001 992	.000 279 9551	.024 637	88.002 695	.011 363 2884	13.64	2.818 065	10.06	336
29	46.329 663	4089.894 392	.000 244 5051	.021 584	88.278 095	.011 327 8384	13.60	2.942 088	10.15	348
30	52.881 353	4681.024 331	.000 213 6285	.018 910	88.519 375	.011 296 9618	13.56	3.066 906	10.22	360
31	60.359 548	5355.748 666	.000 186 7153	.016 567	88.730 762	.011 270 0486	13.53	3.192 458	10.30	372
32	68.895 268	6125.888 866	.000 163 2416	.014 515	88.915 959	.011 246 5749	13.50	3.318 685	10.37	384
33	78.638 064	7004.938 123	.000 142 7564	.012 716	89.078 212	.011 226 0898	13.48	3.445 532	10.44	396
34	89.758 634	8008.297 769	.000 124 8705	.011 141	89.220 362	.011 208 2038	13.45	3.572 947	10.51	408
35	102.451 814	9153.547 106	.000 109 2473	.009 761	89.344 900	.011 192 5806	13.44	3.700 884	10.57	420
36	116.939 995	10460.751 405	.000 095 5954	.008 551	89.454 010	.011 178 9288	13.42	3.829 297	10.64	432
37	133.477 016	11952.813 460	.000 083 6623	.007 492	89.549 601	.011 166 9956	13.41	3.958 146	10.70	444
38	152.352 613	13655.874 856	.000 073 2286	.006 564	89.633 349	.011 156 5619	13.39	4.087 392	10.76	456
39	173.897 495	15599.773 976	.000 064 1035	.005 751	89.706 721	.011 147 4368	13.38	4.217 000	10.81	468
40	198.489 137	17818.568 788	.000 056 1212	.005 038	89.771 002	.011 139 4546	13.37	4.346 938	10.87	480
41	226.558 397	20351.133 554	.000 049 1373	.004 414	89.827 320	.011 132 4706	13.36	4.477 176	10.92	492
42	258.597 059	23241.839 921	.000 043 0259	.003 867	89.876 660	.011 126 3592	13.36	4.607 685	10.97	504
43	295.166 456	26541.334 337	.000 037 6771	.003 388	89.919 887	.011 121 0104	13.35	4.738 441	11.02	516
44	336.907 298	30307.425 395	.000 032 9952	.002 968	89.957 759	.011 116 3285	13.34	4.869 421	11.07	528
45	384.550 905	34606.096 665	.000 028 8966	.002 600	89.990 938	.011 112 2300	13.34	5.000 604	11.11	540
46	438.932 012	39512.662 760	.000 025 3083	.002 278	90.020 007	.011 108 6417	13.34	5.131 970	11.16	552
47	501.003 402	45113.088 876	.000 022 1665	.001 996	90.045 474	.011 105 4998	13.33	5.263 502	11.20	564
48	571.852 591	51505.496 940	.000 019 4154	.001 749	90.067 786	.011 102 7487	13.33	5.395 183	11.24	576
49	652.720 889	58801.884 754	.000 017 0063	.001 532	90.087 334	.011 100 3396	13.33	5.527 000	11.28	588
50	745.025 145	67130.088 241	.000 014 8964	.001 342	90.104 460	.011 098 2298	13.32	5.658 938	11.32	600

MONTHLY COMPOUND INTEREST AND ANNUITY

13.35 % M

	Amount Of 1	Amount Of 1 Per Period	Sinking Fund Payment	Present Worth Of 1	Present Worth of 1 Per Period	Periodic Payment To Amortize 1	Constant Annual Percent	Total Interest	Annual Add On Rate	
	What a single $ 1 deposit grows to in the future. The deposit is made at the beginning of the first period.	What a series of $ 1 deposits grow to in the future. A deposit is made at the end of each period.	The amount to be deposited at the end of each period that grows to $ 1 in the future.	What $ 1 to be paid in the future is worth today. Value today of a single $ 1 payment tomorrow.	What $ 1 to be paid at the end of each period is worth today. Value today of a series of $ 1 payments tomorrow.	The mortgage payment to amortize a loan of $ 1. An annuity certain, payable at the end of each period, worth $ 1 today.	The annual payment, including interest and principal, to amortize completely a loan of $ 100.	The total interest paid over the term on a loan of $1. The loan is amortized by regular periodic payments.	The average annual interest rate on a loan that is completely amortized by regular periodic payments.	
	$S = (1+i)^n$	$S\overline{n}| = \dfrac{(1+i)^n - 1}{i}$	$\dfrac{1}{S\overline{n}|} = \dfrac{i}{(1+i)^n - 1}$	$V^n = \dfrac{1}{(1+i)^n}$	$A\overline{n}| = \dfrac{1 - V^n}{i}$	$\dfrac{1}{A\overline{n}|} = \dfrac{i}{1 - V^n}$				

YEAR										PERIODS
	1.011 125	1.000 000	1.000 000 0000	.988 997	.988 997	1.011 125 0000	1213.35	.011 125	13.35	1
	1.022 374	2.011 125	.497 234 1351	.978 116	1.967 113	.508 359 1351	610.04	.016 718	10.03	2
	1.033 748	3.033 499	.329 652 3511	.967 354	2.934 467	.340 777 3511	408.94	.022 332	8.93	3
	1.045 248	4.067 246	.245 866 5869	.956 711	3.891 178	.256 991 5869	308.39	.027 966	8.39	4
	1.056 877	5.112 495	.195 599 2303	.946 184	4.837 362	.206 724 2303	248.07	.033 621	8.07	5
	1.068 634	6.169 371	.162 091 0771	.935 774	5.773 136	.173 216 0771	207.86	.039 296	7.86	6
	1.080 523	7.238 005	.138 159 6113	.925 478	6.698 614	.149 284 6113	179.15	.044 992	7.71	7
	1.092 544	8.318 528	.120 213 5745	.915 295	7.613 909	.131 338 5745	157.61	.050 709	7.61	8
	1.104 698	9.411 072	.106 257 8235	.905 225	8.519 134	.117 382 8235	140.86	.056 445	7.53	9
	1.116 988	10.515 770	.095 095 2719	.895 265	9.414 399	.106 220 2719	127.47	.062 203	7.46	10
	1.129 414	11.632 758	.085 964 1378	.885 415	10.299 813	.097 089 1378	116.51	.067 981	7.42	11
	1.141 979	12.762 172	.078 356 5664	.875 673	11.175 486	.089 481 5664	107.38	.073 779	7.38	12
1	1.141 979	12.762 172	.078 356 5664	.875 673	11.175 486	.089 481 5664	107.38	.073 779	7.38	12
2	1.304 116	27.336 307	.036 581 3858	.766 803	20.961 554	.047 706 3858	57.25	.144 953	7.25	24
3	1.489 274	43.979 666	.022 737 7809	.671 468	29.530 947	.033 862 7809	40.64	.219 060	7.30	36
4	1.700 720	62.986 034	.015 876 5354	.587 986	37.034 931	.027 001 5354	32.41	.296 074	7.40	48
5	1.942 186	84.690 911	.011 807 6425	.514 884	43.605 965	.022 932 6425	27.52	.375 959	7.52	60
6	2.217 936	109.477 428	.009 134 3030	.450 870	49.360 040	.020 259 3030	24.32	.458 670	7.64	72
7	2.532 837	137.783 115	.007 257 7834	.394 814	54.398 726	.018 382 7834	22.06	.544 154	7.77	84
8	2.892 447	170.107 619	.005 878 6315	.345 728	58.810 966	.017 003 6315	20.41	.632 349	7.90	96
9	3.303 115	207.021 529	.004 830 4155	.302 745	62.674 645	.015 955 4155	19.15	.723 185	8.04	108
10	3.772 088	249.176 446	.004 013 2204	.265 105	66.057 963	.015 138 2204	18.17	.816 586	8.17	120
11	4.307 646	297.316 482	.003 363 4193	.232 145	69.020 642	.014 488 4193	17.39	.912 471	8.30	132
12	4.919 242	352.291 401	.002 838 5592	.203 283	71.614 979	.013 963 5592	16.76	1.010 753	8.42	144
13	5.617 672	415.071 612	.002 409 2228	.178 010	73.886 769	.013 534 2228	16.25	1.111 339	8.55	156
14	6.415 264	486.765 306	.002 054 3781	.155 878	75.876 114	.013 179 3781	15.82	1.214 136	8.67	168
15	7.326 098	568.638 011	.001 758 5880	.136 498	77.618 129	.012 883 5880	15.47	1.319 046	8.79	180
16	8.366 251	662.134 934	.001 510 2662	.119 528	79.143 564	.012 635 2662	15.17	1.425 971	8.91	192
17	9.554 085	768.906 473	.001 300 5483	.104 667	80.479 346	.012 425 5483	14.92	1.534 812	9.03	204
18	10.910 565	890.837 346	.001 122 5394	.091 654	81.649 054	.012 247 5394	14.70	1.645 469	9.14	216
19	12.459 638	1030.079 862	.000 970 7985	.080 259	82.673 335	.012 095 7985	14.52	1.757 842	9.25	228
20	14.228 648	1189.091 915	.000 840 9779	.070 281	83.570 270	.011 965 9779	14.36	1.871 835	9.36	240
21	16.248 819	1370.680 366	.000 729 5647	.061 543	84.355 691	.011 854 5647	14.23	1.987 350	9.46	252
22	18.555 813	1578.050 591	.000 633 6932	.053 891	85.043 464	.011 758 6932	14.12	2.104 295	9.56	264
23	21.190 352	1814.863 075	.000 551 0058	.047 191	85.645 727	.011 676 0058	14.02	2.222 578	9.66	276
24	24.198 940	2085.297 995	.000 479 5478	.041 324	86.173 112	.011 604 5478	13.93	2.342 110	9.76	288
25	27.634 686	2394.129 039	.000 417 6884	.036 186	86.634 930	.011 542 6884	13.86	2.462 807	9.85	300
26	31.558 235	2746.807 657	.000 364 0590	.031 687	87.039 330	.011 489 0590	13.79	2.584 586	9.94	312
27	36.038 847	3149.559 292	.000 317 5047	.027 748	87.393 453	.011 442 5047	13.74	2.707 372	10.03	324
28	41.155 613	3609.493 268	.000 277 0472	.024 298	87.703 549	.011 402 0472	13.69	2.831 088	10.11	336
29	46.998 852	4134.728 287	.000 241 8539	.021 277	87.975 091	.011 366 8539	13.65	2.955 665	10.19	348
30	53.671 710	4734.535 736	.000 211 2140	.018 632	88.212 873	.011 336 2140	13.61	3.081 037	10.27	360
31	61.291 975	5419.503 347	.000 184 5188	.016 315	88.421 092	.011 309 5188	13.58	3.207 141	10.35	372
32	69.994 158	6201.722 088	.000 161 2455	.014 287	88.603 424	.011 286 2455	13.55	3.333 918	10.42	384
33	79.931 870	7094.999 595	.000 140 9443	.012 511	88.763 087	.011 265 9443	13.52	3.461 314	10.49	396
34	91.280 531	8115.103 897	.000 123 2270	.010 955	88.902 900	.011 248 2270	13.50	3.589 277	10.56	408
35	104.240 465	9280.041 759	.000 107 7581	.009 593	89.025 330	.011 232 7581	13.48	3.717 758	10.62	420
36	119.040 439	10610.376 527	.000 094 2474	.008 401	89.132 539	.011 219 2474	13.47	3.846 715	10.69	432
37	135.941 701	12129.591 118	.000 082 4430	.007 356	89.226 418	.011 207 4430	13.45	3.976 105	10.75	444
38	155.242 591	13864.502 529	.000 072 1266	.006 442	89.308 626	.011 197 1266	13.44	4.105 890	10.80	456
39	177.283 804	15845.735 218	.000 063 1085	.005 641	89.380 614	.011 188 1085	13.43	4.236 035	10.86	468
40	202.454 411	18108.261 673	.000 055 2234	.004 939	89.443 651	.011 180 2234	13.42	4.366 507	10.92	480
41	231.198 720	20692.019 748	.000 048 3278	.004 325	89.498 851	.011 173 3278	13.41	4.497 277	10.97	492
42	264.024 121	23642.617 642	.000 042 2965	.003 788	89.547 188	.011 167 2965	13.41	4.628 317	11.02	504
43	301.510 046	27012.138 966	.000 037 0204	.003 317	89.589 516	.011 162 0204	13.40	4.759 603	11.07	516
44	344.318 191	30860.062 121	.000 032 4043	.002 904	89.626 581	.011 157 4043	13.39	4.891 109	11.12	528
45	393.204 201	35254.310 198	.000 028 3653	.002 543	89.659 037	.011 153 3653	13.39	5.022 817	11.16	540
46	449.031 006	40272.449 956	.000 024 8309	.002 227	89.687 459	.011 149 8309	13.38	5.154 707	11.21	552
47	512.784 054	46003.061 015	.000 021 7377	.001 950	89.712 347	.011 146 7377	13.38	5.286 760	11.25	564
48	585.588 706	52547.299 457	.000 019 0305	.001 708	89.734 141	.011 144 0305	13.38	5.418 962	11.29	576
49	668.730 103	60020.683 420	.000 016 6609	.001 495	89.753 225	.011 141 6609	13.37	5.551 297	11.33	588
50	763.675 846	68555.132 211	.000 014 5868	.001 309	89.769 937	.011 139 5868	13.37	5.683 752	11.37	600

	Amount Of 1	Amount Of 1 Per Period	Sinking Fund Payment	Present Worth Of 1	Present Worth of 1 Per Period	Periodic Payment To Amortize 1	Constant Annual Percent	Total Interest	Annual Add On Rate	
	What a single $ 1 deposit grows to in the future. The deposit is made at the beginning of the first period.	What a series of $ 1 deposits grow to in the future. A deposit is made at the end of each period.	The amount to be deposited at the end of each period that grows to $ 1 in the future.	What $ 1 to be paid in the future is worth today. Value today of a single $ 1 payment tomorrow.	What $ 1 to be paid at the end of each period is worth today. Value today of a series of $ 1 payments tomorrow.	The mortgage payment to amortize a loan of $ 1. An annuity certain, payable at the end of each period, worth $ 1 today.	The annual payment, including interest and principal, to amortize completely a loan of $ 100.	The total interest paid over the term on a loan of $1. The loan is amortized by regular periodic payments.	The average annual interest rate on a loan that is completely amortized by regular periodic payments.	
	$S = (1+i)^n$	$S\overline{n} = \dfrac{(1+i)^n - 1}{i}$	$\dfrac{1}{S\overline{n}} = \dfrac{i}{(1+i)^n - 1}$	$V^n = \dfrac{1}{(1+i)^n}$	$A\overline{n} = \dfrac{1 - V^n}{i}$	$\dfrac{1}{A\overline{n}} = \dfrac{i}{1 - V^n}$				

YEAR	Amount Of 1	Amount Of 1 Per Period	Sinking Fund Payment	Present Worth Of 1	Present Worth of 1 Per Period	Periodic Payment To Amortize 1	Constant Annual Percent	Total Interest	Annual Add On Rate	PERIODS
	1.011 146	1.000 000	1.000 000 0000	.988 977	.988 977	1.011 145 8333	1213.38	.011 146	13.37	1
	1.022 416	2.011 146	.497 228 9843	.978 076	1.967 053	.508 374 8176	610.05	.016 750	10.05	2
	1.033 812	3.033 562	.329 645 5089	.967 294	2.934 347	.340 791 3422	408.95	.022 374	8.95	3
	1.045 334	4.067 373	.245 858 9182	.956 632	3.890 979	.257 004 7515	308.41	.028 019	8.41	4
	1.056 985	5.112 708	.195 591 0810	.946 087	4.837 066	.206 736 9143	248.09	.033 685	8.08	5
	1.068 766	6.169 693	.162 082 6202	.935 658	5.772 724	.173 228 4536	207.88	.039 371	7.87	6
	1.080 679	7.238 459	.138 150 9456	.925 344	6.698 068	.149 296 7789	179.16	.045 077	7.73	7
	1.092 724	8.319 138	.120 204 7618	.915 144	7.613 213	.131 350 5951	157.63	.050 805	7.62	8
	1.104 903	9.411 862	.106 248 9049	.905 057	8.518 269	.117 394 7383	140.88	.056 553	7.54	9
	1.117 218	10.516 765	.095 086 2764	.895 080	9.413 350	.106 232 1097	127.48	.062 321	7.48	10
	1.129 670	11.633 983	.085 955 0862	.885 214	10.298 564	.097 100 9196	116.53	.068 110	7.43	11
	1.142 262	12.763 653	.078 347 4744	.875 456	11.174 020	.089 493 3078	107.40	.073 920	7.39	12
1	1.142 262	12.763 653	.078 347 4744	.875 456	11.174 020	.089 493 3078	107.40	.073 920	7.39	12
2	1.304 761	27.343 084	.036 572 3197	.766 424	20.956 385	.047 718 1531	57.27	.145 236	7.26	24
3	1.490 379	43.996 607	.022 729 0257	.670 970	29.520 418	.033 874 8590	40.65	.219 495	7.32	36
4	1.702 402	63.019 285	.015 868 1584	.587 405	37.017 854	.027 013 9917	32.42	.296 672	7.42	48
5	1.944 589	84.748 160	.011 799 6662	.514 248	43.581 531	.022 945 4995	27.54	.376 730	7.53	60
6	2.221 229	109.568 218	.009 126 7342	.450 201	49.327 743	.020 272 5675	24.33	.459 625	7.66	72
7	2.537 225	137.919 216	.007 250 6212	.394 131	54.358 300	.018 396 4546	22.08	.545 302	7.79	84
8	2.898 174	170.303 471	.005 871 8709	.345 045	58.762 333	.017 017 7042	20.43	.633 700	7.92	96
9	3.310 473	207.294 761	.004 824 0486	.302 072	62.617 871	.015 969 8819	19.17	.724 747	8.05	108
10	3.781 426	249.548 489	.004 007 2373	.264 451	65.993 225	.015 153 0706	18.19	.818 368	8.18	120
11	4.319 377	297.813 297	.003 357 8084	.231 515	68.948 200	.014 503 6418	17.41	.914 481	8.31	132
12	4.933 859	352.944 333	.002 833 3080	.202 681	71.535 152	.013 979 1413	16.78	1.012 996	8.44	144
13	5.635 757	415.918 394	.002 404 3178	.177 438	73.799 915	.013 550 1511	16.27	1.113 824	8.57	156
14	6.437 509	487.851 244	.002 049 8052	.155 340	75.782 616	.013 195 6385	15.84	1.216 867	8.69	168
15	7.353 319	570.017 373	.001 754 3325	.135 993	77.518 383	.012 900 1658	15.49	1.322 030	8.81	180
16	8.399 413	663.872 582	.001 506 3131	.119 056	79.037 972	.012 652 1465	15.19	1.429 212	8.93	192
17	9.594 327	771.079 780	.001 296 8827	.104 228	80.368 305	.012 442 7160	14.94	1.538 314	9.05	204
18	10.959 231	893.538 440	.001 119 1460	.091 247	81.532 954	.012 264 9794	14.72	1.649 236	9.16	216
19	12.518 308	1033.418 258	.000 967 6624	.079 883	82.552 553	.012 113 4957	14.54	1.761 877	9.27	228
20	14.299 182	1193.197 597	.000 838 0842	.069 934	83.445 167	.011 983 9175	14.39	1.876 140	9.38	240
21	16.333 405	1375.707 393	.000 726 8988	.061 224	84.226 612	.011 872 7321	14.25	1.991 928	9.49	252
22	18.657 021	1584.181 315	.000 631 2409	.053 599	84.910 733	.011 777 0742	14.14	2.109 148	9.59	264
23	21.311 198	1822.313 062	.000 548 7531	.046 924	85.509 650	.011 694 5865	14.04	2.227 706	9.69	276
24	24.342 962	2094.321 800	.000 477 4815	.041 080	86.033 977	.011 623 3149	13.95	2.347 515	9.78	288
25	27.806 029	2405.026 924	.000 415 7958	.035 963	86.493 001	.011 561 6291	13.88	2.468 489	9.87	300
26	31.761 758	2759.933 441	.000 362 3276	.031 484	86.894 857	.011 508 1609	13.81	2.590 546	9.96	312
27	36.280 235	3165.329 510	.000 315 9229	.027 563	87.246 665	.011 461 7562	13.76	2.713 609	10.05	324
28	41.441 518	3628.397 853	.000 275 6037	.024 130	87.554 657	.011 421 4371	13.71	2.837 603	10.13	336
29	47.337 052	4157.343 017	.000 240 5382	.021 125	87.824 290	.011 386 3716	13.67	2.962 457	10.22	348
30	54.071 295	4761.536 741	.000 210 0162	.018 494	88.060 342	.011 355 8496	13.63	3.088 106	10.29	360
31	61.763 561	5451.684 003	.000 183 4296	.016 191	88.266 996	.011 329 2629	13.60	3.214 486	10.37	372
32	70.550 141	6240.012 686	.000 160 2561	.014 174	88.447 912	.011 306 0894	13.57	3.341 538	10.44	384
33	80.586 714	7140.490 230	.000 140 0464	.012 409	88.606 296	.011 285 8797	13.55	3.469 208	10.51	396
34	92.051 105	8169.071 108	.000 122 4129	.010 864	88.744 954	.011 268 2463	13.53	3.597 444	10.58	408
35	105.146 438	9343.979 498	.000 107 0208	.009 511	88.866 344	.011 252 8541	13.51	3.726 199	10.65	420
36	120.104 734	10686.032 180	.000 093 5801	.008 326	88.972 615	.011 239 4134	13.49	3.855 427	10.71	432
37	137.191 020	12219.007 359	.000 081 8397	.007 289	89.065 650	.011 227 6730	13.48	3.985 087	10.77	444
38	156.708 027	13970.065 968	.000 071 5816	.006 381	89.147 099	.011 217 4150	13.47	4.115 141	10.83	456
39	179.001 554	15970.232 892	.000 062 6165	.005 587	89.218 404	.011 208 4498	13.46	4.245 555	10.89	468
40	204.466 593	18254.946 667	.000 054 7797	.004 891	89.280 828	.011 200 6130	13.45	4.376 204	10.95	480
41	233.554 328	20864.687 371	.000 047 9279	.004 282	89.335 477	.011 193 7612	13.44	4.507 331	10.99	492
42	266.780 129	23845.693 839	.000 041 9363	.003 748	89.383 321	.011 187 7696	13.43	4.638 636	11.04	504
43	304.732 685	27250.782 914	.000 036 6962	.003 282	89.425 205	.011 182 5295	13.42	4.770 185	11.09	516
44	348.084 429	31140.285 247	.000 032 1127	.002 873	89.461 874	.011 177 9461	13.42	4.901 956	11.14	528
45	397.603 461	35583.114 220	.000 028 1032	.002 515	89.493 975	.011 173 9366	13.41	5.033 926	11.19	540
46	454.167 146	40657.986 939	.000 024 5954	.002 202	89.522 079	.011 170 4287	13.41	5.166 077	11.23	552
47	518.777 669	46454.818 929	.000 021 5263	.001 928	89.546 682	.011 167 3596	13.41	5.298 391	11.27	564
48	592.579 786	53076.317 236	.000 018 8408	.001 688	89.568 221	.011 164 6741	13.40	5.430 852	11.31	576
49	676.881 106	60639.800 172	.000 016 4908	.001 477	89.587 078	.011 162 3242	13.40	5.563 447	11.35	588
50	773.175 263	69279.275 931	.000 014 4343	.001 293	89.603 586	.011 160 2677	13.40	5.696 161	11.39	600

	Amount Of 1	Amount Of 1 Per Period	Sinking Fund Payment	Present Worth Of 1	Present Worth of 1 Per Period	Periodic Payment To Amortize 1	Constant Annual Percent	Total Interest	Annual Add On Rate	
	What a single $ 1 deposit grows to in the future. The deposit is made at the beginning of the first period.	What a series of $ 1 deposits grow to in the future. A deposit is made at the end of each period.	The amount to be deposited at the end of each period that grows to $ 1 in the future.	What $ 1 to be paid in the future is worth today. Value today of a single $ 1 payment tomorrow.	What $ 1 to be paid at the end of each period is worth today. Value today of a series of $ 1 payments tomorrow.	The mortgage payment to amortize a loan of $ 1. An annuity certain, payable at the end of each period, worth $ 1 today.	The annual payment, including interest and principal, to amortize completely a loan of $ 100.	The total interest paid over the term on a loan of $1. The loan is amortized by regular periodic payments.	The average annual interest rate on a loan that is completely amortized by regular periodic payments.	
	$S = (1+i)^n$	$S\overline{n}| = \dfrac{(1+i)^n - 1}{i}$	$\dfrac{1}{S\overline{n}|} = \dfrac{i}{(1+i)^n - 1}$	$V^n = \dfrac{1}{(1+i)^n}$	$A\overline{n}| = \dfrac{1-V^n}{i}$	$\dfrac{1}{A\overline{n}|} = \dfrac{i}{1-V^n}$				

YEAR										PERIODS
	1.011 167	1.000 000	1.000 000 0000	.988 957	.988 957	1.011 166 6667	1213.40	.011 167	13.40	1
	1.022 458	2.011 167	.497 223 8336	.978 035	1.966 992	.508 390 5003	610.07	.016 781	10.07	2
	1.033 875	3.033 625	.329 638 6669	.967 234	2.934 226	.340 805 3335	408.97	.022 416	8.97	3
	1.045 420	4.067 500	.245 851 2497	.956 553	3.890 779	.257 017 9164	308.43	.028 027	8.42	4
	1.057 094	5.112 921	.195 582 9320	.945 989	4.836 769	.206 749 5987	248.10	.033 748	8.10	5
	1.068 898	6.170 015	.162 074 1637	.935 543	5.772 311	.173 240 8304	207.89	.039 445	7.89	6
	1.080 835	7.238 913	.138 142 2804	.925 211	6.697 522	.149 308 9470	179.18	.045 163	7.74	7
	1.092 904	8.319 748	.120 195 9497	.914 994	7.612 516	.131 362 6163	157.64	.050 901	7.64	8
	1.105 108	9.412 652	.106 239 9870	.904 889	8.517 405	.117 406 6537	140.89	.056 660	7.55	9
	1.117 448	10.517 760	.095 077 2816	.894 896	9.412 301	.106 243 9482	127.50	.062 439	7.49	10
	1.129 926	11.635 208	.085 946 0354	.885 013	10.297 314	.097 112 7021	116.54	.068 240	7.44	11
	1.142 544	12.765 135	.078 338 3833	.875 240	11.172 554	.089 505 0500	107.41	.074 061	7.41	12
1	1.142 544	12.765 135	.078 338 3833	.875 240	11.172 554	.089 505 0500	107.41	.074 061	7.41	12
2	1.305 407	27.349 862	.036 563 2553	.766 045	20.951 218	.047 729 9220	57.28	.145 518	7.28	24
3	1.491 485	44.013 556	.022 720 2730	.670 473	29.509 894	.033 886 9396	40.67	.219 930	7.33	36
4	1.704 087	63.052 559	.015 859 7846	.586 825	37.000 788	.027 026 4513	32.44	.297 270	7.43	48
5	1.946 994	84.805 457	.011 791 6940	.513 612	43.557 117	.022 958 3607	27.56	.377 502	7.55	60
6	2.224 527	109.659 101	.009 119 1702	.449 534	49.295 477	.020 285 8368	24.35	.460 580	7.68	72
7	2.541 620	138.055 482	.007 243 4646	.393 450	54.317 918	.018 410 1313	22.10	.546 451	7.81	84
8	2.903 912	170.499 598	.005 865 1165	.344 363	58.713 758	.017 031 7831	20.44	.635 051	7.94	96
9	3.317 847	207.568 427	.004 817 6884	.301 400	62.561 173	.015 984 3550	19.19	.726 310	8.07	108
10	3.790 787	249.921 196	.004 001 2613	.263 797	65.928 583	.015 167 9279	18.21	.820 151	8.20	120
11	4.331 141	298.311 098	.003 352 2052	.230 886	68.875 875	.014 518 8718	17.43	.916 491	8.33	132
12	4.948 519	353.598 691	.002 828 0648	.202 081	71.455 462	.013 994 7314	16.80	1.015 241	8.46	144
13	5.653 900	416.767 197	.002 399 4211	.176 869	73.713 219	.013 566 0877	16.28	1.116 310	8.59	156
14	6.459 830	488.939 996	.002 045 2407	.154 803	75.689 298	.013 211 9074	15.86	1.219 600	8.71	168
15	7.380 640	571.400 594	.001 750 0857	.135 490	77.418 841	.012 916 7524	15.51	1.325 015	8.83	180
16	8.432 706	665.615 456	.001 502 3690	.118 586	78.932 606	.012 669 0356	15.21	1.432 455	8.95	192
17	9.634 738	773.260 082	.001 293 2259	.103 791	80.257 514	.012 459 8926	14.96	1.541 818	9.07	204
18	11.008 112	896.248 803	.001 115 7616	.090 842	81.417 125	.012 282 4283	14.74	1.653 005	9.18	216
19	12.577 252	1036.768 828	.000 964 5352	.079 509	82.432 063	.012 131 2018	14.56	1.765 914	9.29	228
20	14.370 064	1197.319 141	.000 835 1992	.069 589	83.320 378	.012 001 8659	14.41	1.880 448	9.40	240
21	16.418 430	1380.754 937	.000 724 2415	.060 907	84.097 866	.011 890 9081	14.27	1.996 509	9.51	252
22	18.758 779	1590.338 406	.000 628 7970	.053 308	84.778 355	.011 795 4637	14.16	2.114 002	9.61	264
23	21.432 730	1829.796 742	.000 546 5088	.046 658	85.373 945	.011 713 1755	14.06	2.232 836	9.71	276
24	24.487 837	2103.388 427	.000 475 4234	.040 837	85.895 230	.011 642 0900	13.98	2.352 922	9.80	288
25	27.978 432	2415.978 965	.000 413 9109	.035 742	86.351 479	.011 580 5776	13.90	2.474 173	9.90	300
26	31.966 589	2773.127 410	.000 360 6037	.031 283	86.750 806	.011 527 2704	13.84	2.596 508	9.99	312
27	36.523 235	3181.185 223	.000 314 3482	.027 380	87.100 314	.011 481 0149	13.78	2.719 849	10.07	324
28	41.729 403	3647.409 230	.000 274 1672	.023 964	87.406 216	.011 440 8339	13.73	2.844 120	10.16	336
29	47.677 679	4180.090 673	.000 239 2293	.020 974	87.673 954	.011 405 8959	13.69	2.969 252	10.24	348
30	54.473 846	4788.702 661	.000 208 8248	.018 357	87.908 290	.011 375 4915	13.66	3.095 177	10.32	360
31	62.238 766	5484.068 637	.000 182 3464	.016 067	88.113 389	.011 349 0130	13.62	3.221 833	10.39	372
32	71.110 529	6278.554 862	.000 159 2723	.014 063	88.292 900	.011 325 9390	13.60	3.349 161	10.47	384
33	81.246 909	7186.290 333	.000 139 1539	.012 308	88.450 015	.011 305 8205	13.57	3.477 105	10.54	396
34	92.828 168	8223.418 050	.000 121 6039	.010 773	88.587 529	.011 288 2706	13.55	3.605 614	10.60	408
35	106.060 267	9408.382 104	.000 106 2882	.009 429	88.707 886	.011 272 9549	13.53	3.734 641	10.67	420
36	121.178 522	10762.255 675	.000 092 9173	.008 252	88.813 228	.011 259 5840	13.52	3.864 140	10.73	432
37	138.451 793	12309.115 803	.000 081 2406	.007 223	88.905 427	.011 247 9073	13.50	3.994 071	10.79	444
38	158.187 266	14076.471 565	.000 071 0405	.006 322	88.986 123	.011 237 7072	13.49	4.124 394	10.85	456
39	180.735 912	16095.753 290	.000 062 1282	.005 533	89.056 752	.011 228 7949	13.48	4.255 076	10.91	468
40	206.498 732	18402.871 512	.000 054 3393	.004 843	89.118 569	.011 221 0060	13.47	4.386 083	10.97	480
41	235.933 888	21038.855 600	.000 047 5311	.004 238	89.172 674	.011 214 1978	13.46	4.517 385	11.02	492
42	269.564 848	24050.583 408	.000 041 5790	.003 710	89.220 028	.011 208 2457	13.45	4.648 956	11.07	504
43	307.989 700	27491.614 950	.000 036 3747	.003 247	89.261 475	.011 203 0414	13.45	4.780 769	11.12	516
44	351.891 785	31423.144 900	.000 031 8237	.002 842	89.297 751	.011 198 4903	13.44	4.912 803	11.17	528
45	402.051 848	35915.090 862	.000 027 8434	.002 487	89.329 501	.011 194 5101	13.44	5.045 035	11.21	540
46	459.361 927	41047.336 779	.000 024 3621	.002 177	89.357 290	.011 191 0288	13.43	5.177 448	11.26	552
47	524.841 215	46911.153 567	.000 021 3169	.001 905	89.381 612	.011 187 9836	13.43	5.310 023	11.30	564
48	599.654 182	53502.822 267	.000 018 6530	.001 668	89.402 899	.011 185 3196	13.43	5.442 744	11.34	576
49	685.131 289	61265.488 555	.000 016 3224	.001 460	89.421 531	.011 182 9891	13.42	5.575 598	11.38	588
50	782.792 645	70011.281 610	.000 014 2834	.001 277	89.437 838	.011 180 9501	13.42	5.708 570	11.42	600

	Amount Of 1	Amount Of 1 Per Period	Sinking Fund Payment	Present Worth Of 1	Present Worth of 1 Per Period	Periodic Payment To Amortize 1	Constant Annual Percent	Total Interest	Annual Add On Rate	
	What a single $ 1 deposit grows to in the future. The deposit is made at the beginning of the first period.	What a series of $ 1 deposits grow to in the future. A deposit is made at the end of each period.	The amount to be deposited at the end of each period that grows to $ 1 in the future.	What $ 1 to be paid in the future is worth today. Value today of a single $ 1 payment tomorrow.	What $ 1 to be paid at the end of each period is worth today. Value today of a series of $ 1 payments tomorrow.	The mortgage payment to amortize a loan of $ 1. An annuity certain, payable at the end of each period, worth $ 1 today.	The annual payment, including interest and principal, to amortize completely a loan of $ 100.	The total interest paid over the term on a loan of $1. The loan is amortized by regular periodic payments.	The average annual interest rate on a loan that is completely amortized by regular periodic payments.	
	$S = (1+i)^n$	$S\overline{n}| = \dfrac{(1+i)^n - 1}{i}$	$\dfrac{1}{S\overline{n}|} = \dfrac{i}{(1+i)^n - 1}$	$V^n = \dfrac{1}{(1+i)^n}$	$A\overline{n}| = \dfrac{1 - V^n}{i}$	$\dfrac{1}{A\overline{n}|} = \dfrac{i}{1 - V^n}$				

YEAR									PERIODS	
	1.011 208	1.000 000	1.000 000 0000	.988 916	.988 916	1.011 208 3333	1213.45	.011 208	13.45	1
	1.022 542	2.011 208	.497 213 5325	.977 955	1.966 871	.508 421 8658	610.11	.016 844	10.11	2
	1.034 003	3.033 751	.329 624 9834	.967 115	2.933 985	.340 833 3167	409.00	.022 500	9.00	3
	1.045 593	4.067 754	.245 835 9136	.956 395	3.890 381	.257 044 2469	308.46	.028 177	8.45	4
	1.057 312	5.113 347	.195 566 6351	.945 795	4.836 175	.206 774 9685	248.13	.033 875	8.13	5
	1.069 163	6.170 659	.162 057 2520	.935 311	5.771 487	.173 265 5853	207.92	.039 594	7.92	6
	1.081 146	7.239 822	.138 124 9514	.924 944	6.696 431	.149 333 2848	179.20	.045 333	7.77	7
	1.093 264	8.320 968	.120 178 3271	.914 692	7.611 123	.131 386 6604	157.67	.051 093	7.66	8
	1.105 518	9.414 232	.106 222 1531	.904 553	8.515 676	.117 430 4865	140.92	.056 874	7.58	9
	1.117 909	10.519 750	.095 059 2940	.894 527	9.410 204	.106 267 6273	127.53	.062 676	7.52	10
	1.130 439	11.637 659	.085 927 9361	.884 612	10.294 816	.097 136 2694	116.57	.068 499	7.47	11
	1.143 109	12.768 098	.078 320 2037	.874 807	11.169 623	.089 528 5370	107.44	.074 342	7.43	12
1	1.143 109	12.768 098	.078 320 2037	.874 807	11.169 623	.089 528 5370	107.44	.074 342	7.43	12
2	1.306 698	27.363 426	.036 545 1315	.765 288	20.940 889	.047 753 4649	57.31	.146 083	7.30	24
3	1.493 699	44.047 479	.022 702 7751	.669 479	29.488 862	.033 911 1084	40.70	.220 800	7.36	36
4	1.707 461	63.119 171	.015 843 0472	.585 665	36.966 690	.027 051 3805	32.47	.298 466	7.46	48
5	1.951 814	84.920 196	.011 775 7618	.512 344	43.508 347	.022 984 0952	27.59	.379 046	7.58	60
6	2.231 136	109.841 145	.009 104 0566	.448 202	49.231 036	.020 312 3899	24.38	.462 492	7.71	72
7	2.550 432	138.328 510	.007 229 1677	.392 090	54.237 285	.018 437 5011	22.13	.548 750	7.84	84
8	2.915 422	170.892 675	.005 851 6259	.343 004	58.616 787	.017 059 9592	20.48	.637 756	7.97	96
9	3.332 645	208.117 068	.004 804 9879	.300 062	62.448 007	.016 013 3213	19.22	.729 439	8.10	108
10	3.809 577	250.668 610	.003 989 3308	.262 496	65.799 586	.015 197 6641	18.24	.823 720	8.24	120
11	4.354 763	299.309 666	.003 341 0214	.229 634	68.731 570	.014 549 3547	17.46	.920 515	8.37	132
12	4.977 969	354.911 698	.002 817 6023	.200 885	71.296 492	.014 025 9356	16.84	1.019 735	8.50	144
13	5.690 361	418.470 887	.002 389 6525	.175 736	73.540 303	.013 597 9858	16.32	1.121 286	8.63	156
14	6.504 704	491.125 973	.002 036 1375	.153 735	75.503 205	.013 244 4708	15.90	1.225 071	8.75	168
15	7.435 586	574.178 664	.001 741 6182	.134 488	77.220 366	.012 949 9515	15.54	1.330 991	8.87	180
16	8.499 686	669.116 949	.001 494 5071	.117 651	78.722 551	.012 702 8404	15.25	1.438 945	8.99	192
17	9.716 068	777.641 767	.001 285 9392	.102 922	80.036 673	.012 494 2725	15.00	1.548 832	9.11	204
18	11.106 526	901.697 472	.001 109 0194	.090 037	81.186 276	.012 317 3527	14.79	1.660 548	9.23	216
19	12.695 971	1043.506 677	.000 958 3072	.078 765	82.191 957	.012 166 6406	14.60	1.773 994	9.34	228
20	14.512 880	1205.610 069	.000 829 4556	.068 904	83.071 734	.012 037 7889	14.45	1.889 069	9.45	240
21	16.589 805	1390.911 931	.000 718 9528	.060 278	83.841 369	.011 927 2861	14.32	2.005 676	9.55	252
22	18.963 956	1602.732 174	.000 623 9346	.052 732	84.514 652	.011 832 2679	14.20	2.123 719	9.65	264
23	21.677 871	1844.865 819	.000 542 0448	.046 130	85.103 644	.011 750 3782	14.11	2.243 104	9.75	276
24	24.780 172	2121.650 991	.000 471 3311	.040 355	85.618 899	.011 679 6644	14.02	2.363 743	9.85	288
25	28.326 439	2438.046 638	.000 410 1644	.035 303	86.069 647	.011 618 4978	13.95	2.485 549	9.94	300
26	32.380 210	2799.721 380	.000 357 1784	.030 883	86.463 965	.011 565 5117	13.88	2.608 440	10.03	312
27	37.014 113	3213.155 065	.000 311 2206	.027 017	86.808 917	.011 519 5539	13.83	2.732 335	10.12	324
28	42.311 169	3685.754 870	.000 271 3148	.023 634	87.110 684	.011 479 6482	13.78	2.857 162	10.20	336
29	48.366 282	4225.988 005	.000 236 6311	.020 676	87.374 671	.011 444 9644	13.74	2.982 848	10.29	348
30	55.287 937	4843.533 415	.000 206 4608	.018 087	87.605 609	.011 414 7942	13.70	3.109 326	10.36	360
31	63.200 144	5549.455 187	.000 180 1979	.015 823	87.807 636	.011 388 5312	13.67	3.236 534	10.44	372
32	72.244 659	6356.400 785	.000 157 3217	.013 842	87.984 370	.011 365 6551	13.64	3.364 412	10.51	384
33	82.583 526	7278.827 635	.000 137 3848	.012 109	88.138 978	.011 345 7181	13.62	3.492 904	10.58	396
34	94.401 980	8333.262 155	.000 120 0010	.010 593	88.274 231	.011 328 3344	13.60	3.621 960	10.65	408
35	107.911 762	9538.595 843	.000 104 8372	.009 267	88.392 550	.011 313 1706	13.58	3.751 532	10.72	420
36	123.354 916	10916.423 743	.000 091 6051	.008 107	88.496 057	.011 299 9384	13.56	3.881 573	10.78	432
37	141.008 126	12491.431 344	.000 080 0549	.007 092	88.586 606	.011 288 3882	13.55	4.012 044	10.84	444
38	161.187 671	14291.836 855	.000 069 9700	.006 204	88.665 819	.011 278 3033	13.54	4.142 906	10.90	456
39	184.255 093	16349.896 765	.000 061 1625	.005 427	88.735 114	.011 269 4958	13.53	4.274 124	10.96	468
40	210.623 672	18702.483 764	.000 053 4688	.004 748	88.795 735	.011 261 8022	13.52	4.405 665	11.01	480
41	240.765 835	21391.747 354	.000 046 7470	.004 153	88.848 766	.011 255 0803	13.51	4.537 500	11.07	492
42	275.221 615	24465.869 019	.000 040 8733	.003 633	88.895 158	.011 249 2066	13.50	4.669 600	11.12	504
43	314.608 331	27979.925 447	.000 035 7399	.003 179	88.935 742	.011 244 0732	13.50	4.801 942	11.17	516
44	359.631 644	31996.875 305	.000 031 2531	.002 781	88.971 246	.011 239 5864	13.49	4.934 502	11.21	528
45	411.098 203	36588.687 214	.000 027 3309	.002 433	89.002 304	.011 235 6642	13.49	5.067 259	11.26	540
46	469.930 094	41837.629 162	.000 023 9019	.002 128	89.029 474	.011 232 2353	13.48	5.200 194	11.30	552
47	537.181 363	47837.742 433	.000 020 9040	.001 862	89.053 243	.011 229 2373	13.48	5.333 290	11.35	564
48	614.056 901	54696.526 473	.000 018 2827	.001 629	89.074 036	.011 226 6160	13.48	5.466 531	11.39	576
49	701.934 027	62536.864 878	.000 015 9906	.001 425	89.092 226	.011 224 3239	13.47	5.599 902	11.43	588
50	802.387 169	71499.227 003	.000 013 9862	.001 246	89.108 138	.011 222 3195	13.47	5.733 392	11.47	600

Effective Rate is 14.31 %   Annual Percentage Rate is 13.45 %

MONTHLY COMPOUND INTEREST AND ANNUITY

13.50 % M

Amount Of 1	Amount Of 1 Per Period	Sinking Fund Payment	Present Worth Of 1	Present Worth of 1 Per Period	Periodic Payment To Amortize 1	Constant Annual Percent	Total Interest	Annual Add On Rate
What a single $ 1 deposit grows to in the future. The deposit is made at the beginning of the first period.	What a series of $ 1 deposits grow to in the future. A deposit is made at the end of each period.	The amount to be deposited at the end of each period that grows to $ 1 in the future.	What $ 1 to be paid in the future is worth today. Value today of a single $ 1 payment tomorrow.	What $ 1 to be paid at the end of each period is worth today. Value today of a series of $ 1 payments tomorrow.	The mortgage payment to amortize a loan of $ 1. An annuity certain, payable at the end of each period, worth $ 1 today.	The annual payment, including interest and principal, to amortize completely a loan of $ 100.	The total interest paid over the term on a loan of $1. The loan is amortized by regular periodic payments.	The average annual interest rate on a loan that is completely amortized by regular periodic payments.

$$S = (1+i)^n \qquad S\overline{n}| = \frac{(1+i)^n - 1}{i} \qquad \frac{1}{S\overline{n}|} = \frac{i}{(1+i)^n - 1} \qquad V^n = \frac{1}{(1+i)^n} \qquad A\overline{n}| = \frac{1-V^n}{i} \qquad \frac{1}{A\overline{n}|} = \frac{i}{1-V^n}$$

YEAR									PERIODS
	1.011 250	1.000 000	1.000 000 0000	.988 875	.988 875	1.011 250 0000	1213.50	.011 250	13.50	1
	1.022 627	2.011 250	.497 203 2318	.977 874	1.966 749	.508 453 2318	610.15	.016 906	10.14	2
	1.034 131	3.033 877	.329 611 3007	.966 995	2.933 745	.340 861 3007	409.04	.022 584	9.03	3
	1.045 765	4.068 008	.245 820 5786	.956 238	3.889 982	.257 070 5786	308.49	.028 282	8.48	4
	1.057 530	5.113 773	.195 550 3396	.945 600	4.835 582	.206 800 3396	248.17	.034 002	8.16	5
	1.069 427	6.171 303	.162 040 3419	.935 080	5.770 662	.173 290 3419	207.95	.039 742	7.95	6
	1.081 458	7.240 730	.138 107 6244	.924 677	6.695 339	.149 357 6244	179.23	.045 503	7.80	7
	1.093 625	8.322 188	.120 160 7067	.914 391	7.609 730	.131 410 7067	157.70	.051 286	7.69	8
	1.105 928	9.415 813	.106 204 3217	.904 218	8.513 948	.117 454 3217	140.95	.057 089	7.61	9
	1.118 370	10.521 741	.095 041 3092	.894 159	9.408 107	.106 291 3092	127.55	.062 913	7.55	10
	1.130 951	11.640 110	.085 909 8399	.884 211	10.292 318	.097 159 8399	116.60	.068 758	7.50	11
	1.143 674	12.771 061	.078 302 0274	.874 375	11.166 693	.089 552 0274	107.47	.074 624	7.46	12
1	1.143 674	12.771 061	.078 302 0274	.874 375	11.166 693	.089 552 0274	107.47	.074 624	7.46	12
2	1.307 991	27.376 998	.036 527 0145	.764 531	20.930 567	.047 777 0145	57.34	.146 648	7.33	24
3	1.495 916	44.081 434	.022 685 2873	.668 487	29.467 851	.033 935 2873	40.73	.221 670	7.39	36
4	1.710 841	63.185 871	.015 826 3230	.584 508	36.932 637	.027 076 3230	32.50	.299 664	7.49	48
5	1.956 645	85.035 127	.011 759 8460	.511 079	43.459 656	.023 009 8460	27.62	.380 591	7.61	60
6	2.237 765	110.023 563	.009 088 9622	.446 874	49.166 717	.020 338 9622	24.41	.464 405	7.74	72
7	2.559 275	138.602 198	.007 214 8928	.390 736	54.156 827	.018 464 8928	22.16	.551 051	7.87	84
8	2.926 977	171.286 853	.005 838 1597	.341 649	58.520 052	.017 088 1597	20.51	.640 463	8.01	96
9	3.347 509	208.667 457	.004 792 3141	.298 730	62.335 146	.016 042 3141	19.26	.732 570	8.14	108
10	3.828 460	251.418 698	.003 977 4289	.261 202	65.670 968	.015 227 4289	18.28	.827 291	8.27	120
11	4.378 512	300.312 201	.003 329 8680	.228 388	68.587 726	.014 579 8680	17.50	.924 543	8.40	132
12	5.007 593	356.230 450	.002 807 1716	.199 697	71.138 066	.014 057 1716	16.87	1.024 233	8.54	144
13	5.727 056	420.182 722	.002 379 9170	.174 610	73.368 018	.013 629 9170	16.36	1.126 267	8.66	156
14	6.549 887	493.323 301	.002 027 0683	.152 674	75.317 832	.013 277 0683	15.94	1.230 547	8.79	168
15	7.490 939	576.972 311	.001 733 1854	.133 495	77.022 700	.012 983 1854	15.58	1.336 973	8.91	180
16	8.567 195	672.639 547	.001 486 6804	.116 724	78.513 394	.012 736 6804	15.29	1.445 443	9.03	192
17	9.798 082	782.051 719	.001 278 6878	.102 061	79.816 818	.012 528 6878	15.04	1.555 852	9.15	204
18	11.205 816	907.183 624	.001 102 3127	.089 239	80.956 500	.012 352 3127	14.83	1.668 100	9.27	216
19	12.815 805	1050.293 785	.000 952 1146	.078 029	81.953 009	.012 202 1146	14.65	1.782 082	9.38	228
20	14.657 109	1213.965 218	.000 823 7468	.068 226	82.824 331	.012 073 7468	14.49	1.897 699	9.49	240
21	16.762 961	1401.152 054	.000 713 6984	.059 655	83.586 193	.011 963 6984	14.36	2.014 852	9.59	252
22	19.171 370	1615.232 853	.000 619 1058	.052 161	84.252 345	.011 869 1058	14.25	2.133 444	9.70	264
23	21.925 805	1860.071 591	.000 537 6137	.045 608	84.834 813	.011 787 6137	14.15	2.253 381	9.80	276
24	25.075 983	2140.087 398	.000 467 2706	.039 879	85.344 107	.011 717 2706	14.07	2.374 574	9.89	288
25	28.678 761	2460.334 319	.000 406 4488	.034 869	85.789 421	.011 656 4488	13.99	2.496 935	9.99	300
26	32.799 166	2826.592 538	.000 353 7829	.030 489	86.178 793	.011 603 7829	13.93	2.620 380	10.08	312
27	37.511 568	3245.472 702	.000 308 1215	.026 658	86.519 249	.011 558 1215	13.87	2.744 831	10.17	324
28	42.901 021	3724.535 238	.000 268 4899	.023 309	86.816 936	.011 518 4899	13.83	2.870 213	10.25	336
29	49.064 802	4272.426 817	.000 234 0590	.020 381	87.077 226	.011 484 0590	13.79	2.996 453	10.33	348
30	56.114 160	4899.036 412	.000 204 1218	.017 821	87.304 817	.011 454 1218	13.75	3.123 484	10.41	360
31	64.176 330	5615.673 790	.000 178 0730	.015 582	87.503 816	.011 428 0730	13.72	3.251 243	10.49	372
32	73.396 828	6435.273 643	.000 155 3935	.013 625	87.677 816	.011 405 3935	13.69	3.379 671	10.56	384
33	83.942 077	7372.629 046	.000 135 6368	.011 913	87.829 958	.011 385 6368	13.67	3.508 712	10.63	396
34	96.002 408	8444.658 462	.000 118 4181	.010 416	87.962 986	.011 368 4181	13.65	3.638 315	10.70	408
35	109.795 500	9670.711 105	.000 103 4050	.009 108	88.079 303	.011 353 4050	13.63	3.768 430	10.77	420
36	125.570 307	11072.916 176	.000 090 3104	.007 964	88.181 007	.011 340 3104	13.61	3.899 014	10.83	432
37	143.611 551	12676.582 277	.000 078 8856	.006 963	88.269 935	.011 328 8856	13.60	4.030 025	10.89	444
38	164.244 860	14510.654 207	.000 068 9149	.006 088	88.347 692	.011 318 9149	13.59	4.161 425	10.95	456
39	187.842 648	16608.235 397	.000 060 2111	.005 324	88.415 680	.011 310 2111	13.58	4.293 179	11.01	468
40	214.830 836	19007.185 391	.000 052 6117	.004 655	88.475 127	.011 302 6117	13.57	4.425 254	11.06	480
41	245.696 536	21750.803 183	.000 045 9753	.004 070	88.527 106	.011 295 9753	13.56	4.557 620	11.12	492
42	280.996 848	24888.608 727	.000 040 1790	.003 559	88.572 555	.011 290 1790	13.55	4.690 250	11.17	504
43	321.368 913	28477.236 729	.000 035 1158	.003 112	88.612 294	.011 285 1158	13.55	4.823 120	11.22	516
44	367.541 412	32581.458 851	.000 030 6923	.002 721	88.647 042	.011 280 6923	13.54	4.956 206	11.26	528
45	420.347 719	37275.352 791	.000 026 8274	.002 379	88.677 424	.011 276 8274	13.54	5.089 487	11.31	540
46	480.740 942	42643.639 319	.000 023 4502	.002 080	88.703 989	.011 273 4502	13.53	5.222 944	11.35	552
47	549.811 128	48783.211 410	.000 020 4989	.001 819	88.727 217	.011 270 4989	13.53	5.356 561	11.40	564
48	628.804 935	55804.883 089	.000 017 9196	.001 590	88.747 527	.011 267 9196	13.53	5.490 322	11.44	576
49	719.148 132	63835.389 519	.000 015 6653	.001 391	88.765 286	.011 265 6653	13.52	5.624 211	11.48	588
50	822.471 338	73019.674 469	.000 013 6949	.001 216	88.780 814	.011 263 6949	13.52	5.758 217	11.52	600

Effective Rate is 14.37 %

Annual Percentage Rate is 13.50 %

MONTHLY COMPOUND INTEREST AND ANNUITY

	Amount Of 1	Amount Of 1 Per Period	Sinking Fund Payment	Present Worth Of 1	Present Worth of 1 Per Period	Periodic Payment To Amortize 1	Constant Annual Percent	Total Interest	Annual Add On Rate	
	What a single $ 1 deposit grows to in the future. The deposit is made at the beginning of the first period.	What a series of $ 1 deposits grow to in the future. A deposit is made at the end of each period.	The amount to be deposited at the end of each period that grows to $ 1 in the future.	What $ 1 to be paid in the future is worth today. Value today of a single $ 1 payment tomorrow.	What $ 1 to be paid at the end of each period is worth today. Value today of a series of $ 1 payments tomorrow.	The mortgage payment to amortize a loan of $ 1. An annuity certain, payable at the end of each period, worth $ 1 today.	The annual payment, including interest and principal, to amortize completely a loan of $ 100.	The total interest paid over the term on a loan of $1. The loan is amortized by regular periodic payments.	The average annual interest rate on a loan that is completely amortized by regular periodic payments.	
	$S = (1+i)^n$	$S\overline{n} = \dfrac{(1+i)^n - 1}{i}$	$\dfrac{1}{S\overline{n}} = \dfrac{i}{(1+i)^n - 1}$	$V^n = \dfrac{1}{(1+i)^n}$	$A\overline{n} = \dfrac{1-V^n}{i}$	$\dfrac{1}{A\overline{n}} = \dfrac{i}{1-V^n}$				

YEAR										PERIODS
	1.011 292	1.000 000	1.000 000 0000	.988 834	.988 834	1.011 291 6667	1213.55	.011 292	13.55	1
	1.022 711	2.011 292	.497 192 9316	.977 793	1.966 628	.508 484 5982	610.19	.016 969	10.18	2
	1.034 259	3.034 003	.329 597 6188	.966 876	2.933 504	.340 889 2855	409.07	.022 668	9.07	3
	1.045 937	4.068 261	.245 805 2446	.956 080	3.889 584	.257 096 9113	308.52	.028 388	8.52	4
	1.057 748	5.114 199	.195 534 0455	.945 405	4.834 989	.206 825 7121	248.20	.034 129	8.19	5
	1.069 692	6.171 947	.162 023 4335	.934 849	5.769 838	.173 315 1001	207.98	.039 891	7.98	6
	1.081 770	7.241 638	.138 090 2994	.924 411	6.694 248	.149 381 9661	179.26	.045 674	7.83	7
	1.093 985	8.323 408	.120 143 0886	.914 089	7.608 338	.131 434 7553	157.73	.051 478	7.72	8
	1.106 338	9.417 394	.106 186 4929	.903 883	8.512 221	.117 478 1596	140.98	.057 303	7.64	9
	1.118 830	10.523 732	.095 023 3273	.893 790	9.406 011	.106 314 9940	127.58	.063 150	7.58	10
	1.131 464	11.642 562	.085 891 7468	.883 811	10.289 822	.097 183 4134	116.63	.069 018	7.53	11
	1.144 240	12.774 026	.078 283 8546	.873 942	11.163 764	.089 575 5212	107.50	.074 906	7.49	12
1	1.144 240	12.774 026	.078 283 8546	.873 942	11.163 764	.089 575 5212	107.50	.074 906	7.49	12
2	1.309 285	27.390 578	.036 508 9043	.763 775	20.920 252	.047 800 5710	57.37	.147 214	7.36	24
3	1.498 137	44.115 423	.022 667 8096	.667 496	29.446 862	.033 959 4763	40.76	.222 541	7.42	36
4	1.714 228	63.252 659	.015 809 6120	.583 353	36.898 628	.027 101 2787	32.53	.300 861	7.52	48
5	1.961 488	85.150 252	.011 743 9465	.509 817	43.411 043	.023 035 6132	27.65	.382 137	7.64	60
6	2.244 413	110.206 354	.009 073 8870	.445 551	49.102 520	.020 365 5537	24.44	.466 320	7.77	72
7	2.568 148	138.876 549	.007 200 6397	.389 386	54.076 543	.018 492 3064	22.20	.553 354	7.91	84
8	2.938 577	171.682 135	.005 824 7179	.340 301	58.423 553	.017 116 3845	20.54	.643 173	8.04	96
9	3.362 438	209.219 600	.004 779 6669	.297 403	62.222 590	.016 071 3336	19.29	.735 704	8.17	108
10	3.847 436	252.171 470	.003 965 5557	.259 913	65.542 730	.015 257 2223	18.31	.830 867	8.31	120
11	4.402 391	301.318 721	.003 318 7450	.227 149	68.444 341	.014 610 4117	17.54	.928 574	8.44	132
12	5.037 392	357.554 972	.002 796 7727	.198 515	70.980 182	.014 088 4394	16.91	1.028 735	8.57	144
13	5.763 985	421.902 744	.002 370 2145	.173 491	73.196 362	.013 661 8812	16.40	1.131 253	8.70	156
14	6.595 383	495.532 040	.002 018 0330	.151 621	75.133 176	.013 309 6996	15.98	1.236 030	8.83	168
15	7.546 701	579.781 630	.001 724 7873	.132 508	76.825 839	.013 016 4540	15.62	1.342 962	8.95	180
16	8.635 237	676.183 384	.001 478 8888	.115 805	78.305 130	.012 770 5554	15.33	1.451 947	9.07	192
17	9.880 784	786.490 131	.001 271 4718	.101 207	79.597 945	.012 563 1384	15.08	1.562 880	9.19	204
18	11.305 989	912.707 529	.001 095 6412	.088 449	80.727 791	.012 387 3079	14.87	1.675 659	9.31	216
19	12.936 766	1057.130 530	.000 945 9570	.077 299	81.715 211	.012 237 6236	14.69	1.790 178	9.42	228
20	14.802 765	1222.385 110	.000 818 0728	.067 555	82.578 160	.012 109 7395	14.54	1.906 337	9.53	240
21	16.937 917	1411.476 019	.000 708 4782	.059 039	83.332 327	.012 000 1449	14.41	2.024 037	9.64	252
22	19.381 043	1627.841 409	.000 614 3105	.051 597	83.991 426	.011 905 9771	14.29	2.143 178	9.74	264
23	22.176 565	1875.415 353	.000 533 2152	.045 093	84.567 441	.011 824 8819	14.19	2.263 667	9.84	276
24	25.375 314	2158.699 373	.000 463 2419	.039 408	85.070 845	.011 754 9086	14.11	2.385 414	9.94	288
25	29.035 450	2482.844 293	.000 402 7639	.034 441	85.510 790	.011 694 4305	14.04	2.508 329	10.03	300
26	33.223 525	2853.743 890	.000 350 4169	.030 099	85.895 278	.011 642 0835	13.98	2.632 330	10.12	312
27	38.015 687	3278.142 062	.000 305 0508	.026 305	86.231 298	.011 596 7175	13.92	2.757 336	10.21	324
28	43.499 072	3763.755 445	.000 265 6921	.022 989	86.524 960	.011 557 3587	13.87	2.883 273	10.30	336
29	49.773 380	4319.413 724	.000 231 5129	.020 091	86.781 603	.011 523 1796	13.83	3.010 066	10.38	348
30	56.952 695	4955.220 178	.000 201 8074	.017 558	87.005 895	.011 493 4740	13.80	3.137 651	10.46	360
31	65.167 554	5682.735 383	.000 175 9716	.015 345	87.201 914	.011 467 6383	13.77	3.265 961	10.54	372
32	74.567 325	6515.187 414	.000 153 4875	.013 411	87.373 222	.011 445 1542	13.74	3.394 939	10.61	384
33	85.322 919	7467.712 362	.000 133 9098	.011 720	87.522 936	.011 425 5765	13.72	3.524 528	10.68	396
34	97.629 900	8557.629 552	.000 116 8548	.010 243	87.653 777	.011 408 5215	13.70	3.654 677	10.75	408
35	111.712 042	9804.756 446	.000 101 9913	.008 952	87.768 125	.011 393 6580	13.68	3.785 336	10.82	420
36	127.825 391	11231.768 978	.000 089 0332	.007 823	87.868 059	.011 380 6998	13.66	3.916 462	10.88	432
37	146.262 932	12864.613 862	.000 077 7326	.006 837	87.955 395	.011 369 3993	13.65	4.048 013	10.94	444
38	167.359 903	14732.980 364	.000 067 8749	.005 975	88.031 721	.011 359 5416	13.64	4.179 951	11.00	456
39	191.499 903	16870.840 134	.000 059 2739	.005 222	88.098 426	.011 350 9405	13.63	4.312 240	11.06	468
40	219.121 858	19317.064 893	.000 051 7677	.004 564	88.156 723	.011 343 4344	13.62	4.444 848	11.11	480
41	250.728 004	22116.133 219	.000 045 2159	.003 988	88.207 671	.011 336 8825	13.61	4.577 746	11.17	492
42	286.893 023	25318.939 285	.000 039 4961	.003 486	88.252 196	.011 331 1628	13.60	4.710 906	11.22	504
43	328.274 485	28983.718 241	.000 034 5021	.003 046	88.291 109	.011 326 1688	13.60	4.844 303	11.27	516
44	375.624 811	33177.105 077	.000 030 1413	.002 662	88.325 116	.011 321 8079	13.59	4.977 915	11.31	528
45	429.804 951	37975.346 216	.000 026 3329	.002 327	88.354 837	.011 317 9995	13.59	5.111 720	11.36	540
46	491.800 036	43465.685 872	.000 023 0067	.002 033	88.380 811	.011 314 6733	13.58	5.245 700	11.40	552
47	562.737 295	49747.952 363	.000 020 1013	.001 777	88.403 510	.011 311 7680	13.58	5.379 837	11.45	564
48	643.906 548	56936.373 253	.000 017 5635	.001 553	88.423 349	.011 309 2301	13.58	5.514 117	11.49	576
49	736.783 657	65161.652 293	.000 015 3464	.001 357	88.440 686	.011 307 0131	13.57	5.648 524	11.53	588
50	843.057 365	74573.345 947	.000 013 4096	.001 186	88.455 838	.011 305 0763	13.57	5.783 046	11.57	600

Effective Rate is 14.42 %

Annual Percentage Rate is 13.55 %

MONTHLY COMPOUND INTEREST AND ANNUITY

	Amount Of 1	Amount Of 1 Per Period	Sinking Fund Payment	Present Worth Of 1	Present Worth of 1 Per Period	Periodic Payment To Amortize 1	Constant Annual Percent	Total Interest	Annual Add On Rate	
	What a single $ 1 deposit grows to in the future. The deposit is made at the beginning of the first period.	What a series of $ 1 deposits grow to in the future. A deposit is made at the end of each period.	The amount to be deposited at the end of each period that grows to $ 1 in the future.	What $ 1 to be paid in the future is worth today. Value today of a single $ 1 payment tomorrow.	What $ 1 to be paid at the end of each period is worth today. Value today of a series of $ 1 payments tomorrow.	The mortgage payment to amortize a loan of $ 1. An annuity certain, payable at the end of each period, worth $ 1 today.	The annual payment, including interest and principal, to amortize completely a loan of $ 100.	The total interest paid over the term on a loan of $1. The loan is amortized by regular periodic payments.	The average annual interest rate on a loan that is completely amortized by regular periodic payments.	
	$S = (1+i)^n$	$S\overline{n}\| = \dfrac{(1+i)^n - 1}{i}$	$\dfrac{1}{S\overline{n}\|} = \dfrac{i}{(1+i)^n - 1}$	$V^n = \dfrac{1}{(1+i)^n}$	$A\overline{n}\| = \dfrac{1 - V^n}{i}$	$\dfrac{1}{A\overline{n}\|} = \dfrac{i}{1 - V^n}$				

YEAR										PERIODS
	1.011 333	1.000 000	1.000 000 0000	.988 794	.988 794	1.011 333 3333	1213.60	.011 333	13.60	1
	1.022 795	2.011 333	.497 182 6318	.977 713	1.966 507	.508 515 9651	610.22	.017 032	10.22	2
	1.034 387	3.034 128	.329 583 9376	.966 756	2.933 263	.340 917 2710	409.11	.022 752	9.10	3
	1.046 110	4.068 515	.245 789 9117	.955 923	3.889 186	.257 123 2450	308.55	.028 493	8.55	4
	1.057 966	5.114 625	.195 517 7527	.945 210	4.834 396	.206 851 0860	248.23	.034 255	8.22	5
	1.069 956	6.172 591	.162 006 5267	.934 618	5.769 014	.173 339 8600	208.01	.040 039	8.01	6
	1.082 082	7.242 547	.138 072 9763	.924 144	6.693 158	.149 406 3096	179.29	.045 844	7.86	7
	1.094 346	8.324 629	.120 125 4727	.913 788	7.606 946	.131 458 8061	157.76	.051 670	7.75	8
	1.106 748	9.418 975	.106 168 6666	.903 548	8.510 493	.117 501 9999	141.01	.057 518	7.67	9
	1.119 292	10.525 723	.095 005 3482	.893 422	9.403 916	.106 338 6815	127.61	.063 387	7.61	10
	1.131 977	11.645 015	.085 873 6567	.883 410	10.287 326	.097 206 9901	116.65	.069 277	7.56	11
	1.144 806	12.776 992	.078 265 6851	.873 511	11.160 837	.089 599 0184	107.52	.075 188	7.52	12
1	1.144 806	12.776 992	.078 265 6851	.873 511	11.160 837	.089 599 0184	107.52	.075 188	7.52	12
2	1.310 581	27.404 167	.036 490 8008	.763 021	20.909 945	.047 824 1342	57.39	.147 779	7.39	24
3	1.500 360	44.149 444	.022 650 3420	.666 507	29.425 893	.033 983 6753	40.79	.223 412	7.45	36
4	1.717 621	63.319 536	.015 792 9143	.582 200	36.864 664	.027 126 2477	32.56	.302 060	7.55	48
5	1.966 343	85.265 570	.011 728 0633	.508 558	43.362 508	.023 061 3966	27.68	.383 684	7.67	60
6	2.251 081	110.389 519	.009 058 8310	.444 231	49.038 444	.020 392 1643	24.48	.468 236	7.80	72
7	2.577 051	139.151 565	.007 186 4086	.388 040	53.996 433	.018 519 7419	22.23	.555 658	7.94	84
8	2.950 223	172.078 525	.005 811 3004	.338 957	58.327 289	.017 144 6337	20.58	.645 885	8.07	96
9	3.377 433	209.773 503	.004 767 0463	.296 083	62.110 337	.016 100 3796	19.33	.738 841	8.21	108
10	3.866 505	252.926 937	.003 953 7110	.258 631	65.414 869	.015 287 0443	18.35	.834 445	8.34	120
11	4.426 398	302.329 242	.003 307 6523	.225 917	68.301 413	.014 640 9856	17.57	.932 610	8.48	132
12	5.067 367	358.885 293	.002 786 4056	.197 341	70.822 839	.014 119 7390	16.95	1.033 242	8.61	144
13	5.801 151	423.630 994	.002 360 5449	.172 380	73.025 331	.013 693 8783	16.44	1.136 245	8.74	156
14	6.641 192	497.752 255	.002 009 0316	.150 575	74.949 232	.013 342 3649	16.02	1.241 517	8.87	168
15	7.602 876	582.606 712	.001 716 4238	.131 529	76.629 779	.013 049 7571	15.66	1.348 956	8.99	180
16	8.703 817	679.748 596	.001 471 1321	.114 892	78.097 754	.012 804 4655	15.37	1.458 457	9.12	192
17	9.964 182	790.957 198	.001 264 2909	.100 359	79.380 047	.012 597 6242	15.12	1.569 915	9.23	204
18	11.407 054	918.269 462	.001 089 0050	.087 665	80.500 142	.012 422 3383	14.91	1.683 225	9.35	216
19	13.058 863	1064.017 294	.000 939 8343	.076 576	81.478 558	.012 273 1677	14.73	1.798 282	9.46	228
20	14.949 863	1230.870 273	.000 812 4333	.066 890	82.333 214	.012 145 7666	14.58	1.914 984	9.57	240
21	17.114 692	1421.884 548	.000 703 2920	.058 429	83.079 765	.012 036 6253	14.45	2.033 230	9.68	252
22	19.593 000	1640.558 818	.000 609 5484	.051 039	83.731 885	.011 942 8817	14.34	2.152 921	9.79	264
23	22.430 182	1890.898 413	.000 528 8491	.044 583	84.301 519	.011 862 1825	14.24	2.273 962	9.89	276
24	25.678 205	2177.488 660	.000 459 2446	.038 944	84.799 100	.011 792 5780	14.16	2.396 262	9.98	288
25	29.396 560	2505.578 867	.000 399 1094	.034 018	85.233 742	.011 732 4427	14.08	2.519 733	10.08	300
26	33.653 356	2881.178 473	.000 347 0802	.029 715	85.613 407	.011 680 4135	14.02	2.644 289	10.17	312
27	38.526 561	3311.167 120	.000 302 0083	.025 956	85.945 048	.011 635 3416	13.97	2.769 851	10.26	324
28	44.105 434	3803.420 662	.000 262 9212	.022 673	86.234 740	.011 596 2546	13.92	2.896 342	10.34	336
29	50.492 161	4366.955 424	.000 228 9925	.019 805	86.487 789	.011 562 3258	13.88	3.023 689	10.43	348
30	57.803 725	5012.093 347	.000 199 5174	.017 300	86.708 830	.011 532 8508	13.84	3.151 826	10.51	360
31	66.174 045	5750.651 050	.000 173 8934	.015 112	86.901 912	.011 507 2267	13.81	3.280 688	10.58	372
32	75.756 438	6596.156 269	.000 151 6034	.013 200	87.070 571	.011 484 9368	13.79	3.410 216	10.66	384
33	86.726 417	7564.095 637	.000 132 2035	.011 531	87.217 896	.011 465 5368	13.76	3.540 353	10.73	396
34	99.284 915	8672.198 341	.000 115 3110	.010 072	87.346 586	.011 448 6443	13.74	3.671 047	10.80	408
35	113.661 956	9940.760 859	.000 100 5959	.008 798	87.458 998	.011 433 9293	13.73	3.802 250	10.86	420
36	130.120 879	11393.018 720	.000 087 7730	.007 685	87.557 192	.011 421 1064	13.71	3.933 918	10.93	432
37	148.963 150	13055.572 095	.000 076 5956	.006 713	87.642 964	.011 409 9290	13.70	4.066 008	10.99	444
38	170.533 894	14958.873 015	.000 066 8500	.005 864	87.717 888	.011 400 1833	13.69	4.198 484	11.05	456
39	195.228 209	17137.783 147	.000 058 3506	.005 122	87.783 334	.011 391 6839	13.68	4.331 308	11.11	468
40	223.498 406	19632.212 332	.000 050 9367	.004 474	87.840 503	.011 384 2700	13.67	4.464 450	11.16	480
41	255.862 295	22487.849 592	.000 044 4685	.003 908	87.890 439	.011 377 8018	13.66	4.597 878	11.21	492
42	292.912 667	25756.999 988	.000 038 8244	.003 414	87.934 060	.011 372 1577	13.65	4.731 567	11.27	504
43	335.328 150	29499.542 666	.000 033 8988	.002 982	87.972 163	.011 367 2322	13.65	4.865 492	11.32	516
44	383.885 646	33784.027 622	.000 029 5998	.002 605	88.005 446	.011 362 9331	13.64	4.999 629	11.36	528
45	439.474 555	38688.931 298	.000 025 8472	.002 275	88.034 520	.011 359 1805	13.64	5.133 957	11.41	540
46	503.113 065	44304.093 988	.000 022 5713	.001 988	88.059 915	.011 355 9046	13.63	5.268 459	11.45	552
47	575.966 808	50732.365 392	.000 019 7113	.001 736	88.082 099	.011 353 0446	13.63	5.403 117	11.50	564
48	659.370 202	58091.488 452	.000 017 2142	.001 517	88.101 477	.011 350 5476	13.63	5.537 915	11.54	576
49	754.850 901	66516.255 985	.000 015 0339	.001 325	88.118 403	.011 348 3673	13.62	5.672 840	11.58	588
50	864.157 769	76160.979 602	.000 013 1301	.001 157	88.133 189	.011 346 4634	13.62	5.807 878	11.62	600

Effective Rate is 14.48 %

Annual Percentage Rate is 13.60 %

MONTHLY COMPOUND INTEREST AND ANNUITY

13.625% M

	Amount Of 1	Amount Of 1 Per Period	Sinking Fund Payment	Present Worth Of 1	Present Worth of 1 Per Period	Periodic Payment To Amortize 1	Constant Annual Percent	Total Interest	Annual Add On Rate	
	What a single $1 deposit grows to in the future. The deposit is made at the beginning of the first period.	What a series of $1 deposits grow to in the future. A deposit is made at the end of each period.	The amount to be deposited at the end of each period that grows to $1 in the future.	What $1 to be paid in the future is worth today. Value today of a single $1 payment tomorrow.	What $1 to be paid at the end of each period is worth today. Value today of a series of $1 payments tomorrow.	The mortgage payment to amortize a loan of $1. An annuity certain, payable at the end of each period, worth $1 today.	The annual payment, including interest and principal, to amortize completely a loan of $100.	The total interest paid over the term on a loan of $1. The loan is amortized by regular periodic payments.	The average annual interest rate on a loan that is completely amortized by regular periodic payments.	

$$S = (1+i)^n \qquad S\overline{n}| = \frac{(1+i)^n - 1}{i} \qquad \frac{1}{S\overline{n}|} = \frac{i}{(1+i)^n - 1} \qquad V^n = \frac{1}{(1+i)^n} \qquad A\overline{n}| = \frac{1-V^n}{i} \qquad \frac{1}{A\overline{n}|} = \frac{i}{1-V^n}$$

YEAR										PERIODS
	1.011 354	1.000 000	1.000 000 0000	.988 773	.988 773	1.011 354 1667	1213.63	.011 354	13.62	1
	1.022 837	2.011 354	.497 177 4820	.977 673	1.966 446	.508 531 6487	610.24	.017 063	10.24	2
	1.034 451	3.034 191	.329 577 0973	.966 697	2.933 143	.340 931 2640	409.12	.022 794	9.12	3
	1.046 196	4.068 642	.245 782 2457	.955 844	3.888 986	.257 136 4123	308.57	.028 546	8.56	4
	1.058 075	5.114 838	.195 509 6068	.945 113	4.834 099	.206 863 7735	248.24	.034 319	8.24	5
	1.070 088	6.172 913	.161 998 0739	.934 502	5.768 602	.173 352 2406	208.03	.040 113	8.02	6
	1.082 238	7.243 001	.138 064 3155	.924 011	6.692 612	.149 418 4822	179.31	.045 929	7.87	7
	1.094 526	8.325 239	.120 116 6656	.913 637	7.606 250	.131 470 8323	157.77	.051 767	7.76	8
	1.106 954	9.419 766	.106 159 7544	.903 380	8.509 630	.117 513 9210	141.02	.057 625	7.68	9
	1.119 522	10.526 719	.094 996 3597	.893 238	9.402 868	.106 350 5263	127.63	.063 505	7.62	10
	1.132 233	11.646 241	.085 864 6129	.883 210	10.286 079	.097 218 7796	116.67	.069 407	7.57	11
	1.145 089	12.778 475	.078 256 6016	.873 295	11.159 373	.089 610 7683	107.54	.075 329	7.53	12
1	1.145 089	12.778 475	.078 256 6016	.873 295	11.159 373	.089 610 7683	107.54	.075 329	7.53	12
2	1.311 229	27.410 965	.036 481 7516	.762 643	20.904 794	.047 835 9183	57.41	.148 062	7.40	24
3	1.501 473	44.166 467	.022 641 6119	.666 012	29.415 417	.033 995 7786	40.80	.223 848	7.46	36
4	1.719 321	63.353 007	.015 784 5705	.581 625	36.847 698	.027 138 7371	32.57	.302 659	7.57	48
5	1.968 775	85.323 302	.011 720 1278	.507 930	43.338 270	.023 074 2945	27.69	.384 458	7.69	60
6	2.254 422	110.481 243	.009 051 3102	.443 573	49.006 451	.020 405 4769	24.49	.469 194	7.82	72
7	2.581 514	139.289 323	.007 179 3012	.387 370	53.956 443	.018 533 4678	22.25	.556 811	7.95	84
8	2.956 063	172.277 136	.005 804 6008	.338 288	58.279 244	.017 158 7674	20.60	.647 242	8.09	96
9	3.384 955	210.051 117	.004 760 7459	.295 425	62.054 324	.016 114 9126	19.34	.740 411	8.23	108
10	3.876 075	253.305 683	.003 947 7993	.257 993	65.351 080	.015 301 9660	18.37	.836 236	8.36	120
11	4.438 451	302.836 009	.003 302 1172	.225 304	68.230 119	.014 656 2839	17.59	.934 629	8.50	132
12	5.082 421	359.552 636	.002 781 2340	.196 757	70.744 369	.014 135 4006	16.97	1.035 498	8.63	144
13	5.819 824	424.498 218	.002 355 7225	.171 827	72.940 050	.013 709 8892	16.46	1.138 743	8.76	156
14	6.664 215	498.866 686	.002 004 5436	.150 055	74.857 526	.013 358 7102	16.04	1.244 263	8.89	168
15	7.631 119	584.025 195	.001 712 2549	.131 042	76.532 048	.013 066 4216	15.68	1.351 956	9.01	180
16	8.738 310	681.539 260	.001 467 2669	.114 439	77.994 399	.012 821 4336	15.39	1.461 715	9.14	192
17	10.006 142	793.201 538	.001 260 7136	.099 939	79.271 462	.012 614 8803	15.14	1.573 436	9.26	204
18	11.457 923	921.064 776	.001 085 7000	.087 276	80.386 714	.012 439 8666	14.93	1.687 011	9.37	216
19	13.120 341	1067.479 554	.000 936 7861	.076 218	81.360 658	.012 290 9528	14.75	1.802 337	9.49	228
20	15.023 957	1235.137 496	.000 809 6265	.066 560	82.211 198	.012 163 7931	14.60	1.919 310	9.60	240
21	17.203 767	1427.120 750	.000 700 7116	.058 127	82.953 969	.012 054 8782	14.47	2.037 829	9.70	252
22	19.699 843	1646.958 648	.000 607 1798	.050 762	83.602 628	.011 961 3465	14.36	2.157 795	9.81	264
23	22.558 072	1898.692 592	.000 526 6782	.044 330	84.169 098	.011 880 8449	14.26	2.279 113	9.91	276
24	25.830 999	2186.950 346	.000 457 2578	.038 713	84.663 794	.011 811 4244	14.18	2.401 690	10.01	288
25	29.578 791	2517.031 108	.000 397 2935	.033 808	85.095 808	.011 751 4601	14.11	2.525 438	10.10	300
26	33.870 346	2895.002 935	.000 345 4228	.029 524	85.473 085	.011 699 5895	14.04	2.650 272	10.19	312
27	38.784 558	3327.814 291	.000 300 4975	.025 783	85.802 558	.011 654 6642	13.99	2.776 111	10.28	324
28	44.411 768	3823.421 784	.000 261 5458	.022 517	86.090 285	.011 615 7125	13.94	2.902 879	10.37	336
29	50.855 424	4390.936 438	.000 227 7419	.019 664	86.341 556	.011 581 9085	13.90	3.030 504	10.45	348
30	58.233 983	5040.791 186	.000 198 3816	.017 172	86.560 989	.011 552 5482	13.87	3.158 917	10.53	360
31	66.683 090	5784.932 665	.000 172 8629	.014 996	86.752 619	.011 527 0295	13.84	3.288 055	10.61	372
32	76.358 068	6637.040 836	.000 150 6696	.013 096	86.919 968	.011 504 8362	13.81	3.417 857	10.68	384
33	87.436 778	7612.780 471	.000 131 3581	.011 437	87.066 114	.011 485 5247	13.79	3.548 268	10.75	396
34	100.122 887	8730.089 125	.000 114 5464	.009 988	87.193 742	.011 468 7130	13.77	3.679 235	10.82	408
35	114.649 610	10009.506 899	.000 099 9050	.008 722	87.305 198	.011 454 0717	13.75	3.810 710	10.89	420
36	131.283 999	11474.554 029	.000 087 1494	.007 617	87.402 533	.011 441 3160	13.73	3.942 649	10.95	432
37	150.331 854	13152.163 281	.000 076 0331	.006 652	87.487 535	.011 430 1998	13.72	4.075 009	11.01	444
38	172.143 342	15073.175 066	.000 066 3430	.005 809	87.561 766	.011 420 5097	13.71	4.207 752	11.07	456
39	197.119 435	17272.904 398	.000 057 8941	.005 073	87.626 592	.011 412 0608	13.70	4.340 844	11.13	468
40	225.719 284	19791.790 107	.000 050 5260	.004 430	87.683 205	.011 404 6927	13.69	4.474 252	11.19	480
41	258.468 653	22676.138 250	.000 044 0992	.003 869	87.732 644	.011 398 2659	13.68	4.607 947	11.24	492
42	295.969 594	25978.973 382	.000 038 4927	.003 379	87.775 819	.011 392 6593	13.68	4.741 900	11.29	504
43	338.911 506	29761.013 333	.000 033 6010	.002 951	87.813 523	.011 387 7677	13.67	4.876 088	11.34	516
44	388.083 814	34091.785 417	.000 029 3326	.002 577	87.846 450	.011 383 4992	13.67	5.010 488	11.39	528
45	444.390 479	39050.904 593	.000 025 6076	.002 250	87.875 205	.011 379 7743	13.66	5.145 078	11.43	540
46	508.866 619	44729.537 069	.000 022 3566	.001 965	87.900 317	.011 376 5233	13.66	5.279 841	11.48	552
47	582.697 533	51232.076 261	.000 019 5190	.001 716	87.922 247	.011 373 6857	13.65	5.414 759	11.52	564
48	667.240 495	58678.061 912	.000 017 0421	.001 499	87.941 398	.011 371 2088	13.65	5.549 816	11.56	576
49	764.049 705	67204.377 662	.000 014 8800	.001 309	87.958 123	.011 369 0466	13.65	5.684 999	11.60	588
50	874.904 860	76967.767 449	.000 012 9925	.001 143	87.972 728	.011 367 1591	13.65	5.820 295	11.64	600

Effective Rate is 14.51 %　　　　8 - 223　　　　Annual Percentage Rate is 13.625%

MONTHLY COMPOUND INTEREST AND ANNUITY

13.65 % M

	Amount Of 1	Amount Of 1 Per Period	Sinking Fund Payment	Present Worth Of 1	Present Worth of 1 Per Period	Periodic Payment To Amortize 1	Constant Annual Percent	Total Interest	Annual Add On Rate	
	What a single $ 1 deposit grows to in the future. The deposit is made at the beginning of the first period.	What a series of $ 1 deposits grow to in the future. A deposit is made at the end of each period.	The amount to be deposited at the end of each period that grows to $ 1 in the future.	What $ 1 to be paid in the future is worth today. Value today of a single $ 1 payment tomorrow.	What $ 1 to be paid at the end of each period is worth today. Value today of a series of $ 1 payments tomorrow.	The mortgage payment to amortize a loan of $ 1. An annuity certain, payable at the end of each period, worth $ 1 today.	The annual payment, including interest and principal, to amortize completely a loan of $ 100.	The total interest paid over the term on a loan of $1. The loan is amortized by regular periodic payments.	The average annual interest rate on a loan that is completely amortized by regular periodic payments.	
	$S = (1+i)^n$	$S\overline{n} = \dfrac{(1+i)^n - 1}{i}$	$\dfrac{1}{S\overline{n}} = \dfrac{i}{(1+i)^n - 1}$	$V^n = \dfrac{1}{(1+i)^n}$	$A\overline{n} = \dfrac{1-V^n}{i}$	$\dfrac{1}{A\overline{n}} = \dfrac{i}{1-V^n}$				

YEAR										PERIODS
	1.011 375	1.000 000	1.000 000 0000	.988 753	.988 753	1.011 375 0000	1213.65	.011 375	13.65	1
	1.022 879	2.011 375	.497 172 3324	.977 632	1.966 385	.508 547 3324	610.26	.017 095	10.26	2
	1.034 515	3.034 254	.329 570 2572	.966 637	2.933 022	.340 945 2572	409.14	.022 836	9.13	3
	1.046 282	4.068 769	.245 774 5799	.955 765	3.888 787	.257 149 5799	308.58	.028 598	8.58	4
	1.058 184	5.115 051	.195 501 4612	.945 015	4.833 803	.206 876 4612	248.26	.034 382	8.25	5
	1.070 221	6.173 235	.161 989 6216	.934 387	5.768 190	.173 364 6216	208.04	.040 188	8.04	6
	1.082 394	7.243 456	.138 055 6552	.923 878	6.692 067	.149 430 6552	179.32	.046 015	7.89	7
	1.094 707	8.325 850	.120 107 8591	.913 487	7.605 554	.131 482 8591	157.78	.051 863	7.78	8
	1.107 159	9.420 556	.106 150 8428	.903 213	8.508 767	.117 525 8428	141.04	.057 733	7.70	9
	1.119 753	10.527 715	.094 987 3719	.893 054	9.401 821	.106 362 3719	127.64	.063 624	7.63	10
	1.132 490	11.647 468	.085 855 5698	.883 010	10.284 831	.097 230 5698	116.68	.069 536	7.59	11
	1.145 372	12.779 958	.078 247 5190	.873 079	11.157 910	.089 622 5190	107.55	.075 470	7.55	12
1	1.145 372	12.779 958	.078 247 5190	.873 079	11.157 910	.089 622 5190	107.55	.075 470	7.55	12
2	1.311 877	27.417 764	.036 472 7041	.762 267	20.899 644	.047 847 7041	57.42	.148 345	7.42	24
3	1.502 587	44.183 498	.022 632 8844	.665 519	29.404 946	.034 007 8844	40.81	.224 284	7.48	36
4	1.721 021	63.386 500	.015 776 2299	.581 050	36.830 744	.027 151 2299	32.59	.303 259	7.58	48
5	1.971 210	85.381 082	.011 712 1964	.507 303	43.314 051	.023 087 1964	27.71	.385 232	7.70	60
6	2.257 769	110.573 060	.009 043 7942	.442 915	48.974 488	.020 418 7942	24.51	.470 153	7.84	72
7	2.585 985	139.427 247	.007 172 1993	.386 700	53.916 496	.018 547 1993	22.26	.557 965	7.97	84
8	2.961 915	172.476 026	.005 797 9072	.337 619	58.231 258	.017 172 9072	20.61	.648 599	8.11	96
9	3.392 494	210.329 173	.004 754 4522	.294 768	61.998 386	.016 129 4522	19.36	.741 981	8.24	108
10	3.885 668	253.685 107	.003 941 8948	.257 356	65.287 385	.015 316 8948	18.39	.838 027	8.38	120
11	4.450 536	303.343 782	.003 296 5897	.224 692	68.158 940	.014 671 5897	17.61	.936 650	8.51	132
12	5.097 519	360.221 439	.002 776 0702	.196 174	70.666 033	.014 151 0702	16.99	1.037 754	8.65	144
13	5.838 555	425.367 516	.002 350 9082	.171 275	72.854 924	.013 725 9082	16.48	1.141 242	8.78	156
14	6.687 318	499.984 009	.002 000 0640	.149 537	74.765 998	.013 375 0640	16.06	1.247 011	8.91	168
15	7.659 467	585.447 653	.001 708 0946	.130 557	76.434 515	.013 083 0946	15.70	1.354 957	9.03	180
16	8.772 939	683.335 320	.001 463 4104	.113 987	77.891 263	.012 838 4104	15.41	1.464 975	9.16	192
17	10.048 279	795.453 115	.001 257 1451	.099 520	79.163 118	.012 632 1451	15.16	1.576 958	9.28	204
18	11.509 018	923.869 700	.001 082 4037	.086 888	80.273 548	.012 457 4037	14.95	1.690 799	9.39	216
19	13.182 107	1070.954 463	.000 933 7465	.075 860	81.243 041	.012 308 7465	14.78	1.806 394	9.51	228
20	15.098 417	1239.421 236	.000 806 8282	.066 232	82.089 485	.012 181 8282	14.62	1.923 639	9.62	240
21	17.293 304	1432.378 365	.000 698 1396	.057 826	82.828 497	.012 073 1396	14.49	2.042 431	9.73	252
22	19.807 266	1653.386 061	.000 604 8194	.050 487	83.473 712	.011 979 8194	14.38	2.162 672	9.83	264
23	22.686 689	1906.522 093	.000 524 5153	.044 079	84.037 036	.011 899 5153	14.28	2.284 266	9.93	276
24	25.984 699	2196.457 021	.000 455 2787	.038 484	84.528 863	.011 830 2787	14.20	2.407 120	10.03	288
25	29.762 147	2528.540 376	.000 395 4851	.033 600	84.958 266	.011 770 4851	14.13	2.531 146	10.12	300
26	34.088 730	2908.899 360	.000 343 7726	.029 335	85.333 169	.011 718 7726	14.07	2.656 257	10.22	312
27	39.044 278	3344.551 898	.000 298 9937	.025 612	85.660 488	.011 673 9937	14.01	2.782 374	10.31	324
28	44.720 223	3843.536 126	.000 260 1771	.022 361	85.946 264	.011 635 1771	13.97	2.909 419	10.39	336
29	51.221 293	4415.058 699	.000 226 4976	.019 523	86.195 769	.011 601 4976	13.93	3.037 321	10.47	348
30	58.667 436	5069.664 665	.000 197 2517	.017 045	86.413 606	.011 572 2517	13.89	3.166 011	10.55	360
31	67.196 039	5819.432 023	.000 171 8381	.014 882	86.603 795	.011 546 8381	13.86	3.295 424	10.63	372
32	76.964 463	6678.194 578	.000 149 7411	.012 993	86.769 845	.011 524 7411	13.83	3.425 501	10.70	384
33	88.152 943	7661.797 181	.000 130 5177	.011 344	86.914 820	.011 505 5177	13.81	3.556 185	10.78	396
34	100.967 914	8788.388 082	.000 113 7865	.009 904	87.041 395	.011 488 7865	13.79	3.687 425	10.85	408
35	115.645 824	10078.753 780	.000 099 2186	.008 647	87.151 904	.011 474 2186	13.77	3.819 172	10.91	420
36	132.457 491	11556.702 549	.000 086 5299	.007 550	87.248 388	.011 461 5299	13.76	3.951 381	10.98	432
37	151.713 105	13249.503 717	.000 075 4745	.006 591	87.332 625	.011 450 4745	13.75	4.084 011	11.04	444
38	173.767 945	15188.390 812	.000 065 8398	.005 755	87.406 171	.011 440 8398	13.73	4.217 023	11.10	456
39	199.028 943	17409.137 845	.000 057 4411	.005 024	87.470 383	.011 432 4411	13.72	4.350 382	11.15	468
40	227.962 183	19952.719 362	.000 050 1185	.004 387	87.526 445	.011 425 1185	13.72	4.484 057	11.21	480
41	261.101 506	22866.066 466	.000 043 7329	.003 830	87.575 391	.011 418 7329	13.71	4.618 017	11.26	492
42	299.058 360	26202.932 727	.000 038 1637	.003 344	87.618 125	.011 413 1637	13.70	4.752 234	11.31	504
43	342.533 078	30024.885 982	.000 033 3057	.002 919	87.655 435	.011 408 3057	13.69	4.886 686	11.36	516
44	392.327 804	34402.444 307	.000 029 0677	.002 549	87.688 010	.011 404 0677	13.69	5.021 348	11.41	528
45	449.361 290	39416.377 135	.000 025 3702	.002 225	87.716 450	.011 400 3702	13.69	5.156 200	11.46	540
46	514.685 849	45159.195 513	.000 022 1439	.001 943	87.741 281	.011 397 1439	13.68	5.291 223	11.50	552
47	589.506 771	51736.859 007	.000 019 3286	.001 696	87.762 960	.011 394 3286	13.68	5.426 401	11.55	564
48	675.204 562	59270.730 740	.000 016 8717	.001 481	87.781 887	.011 391 8717	13.68	5.561 718	11.59	576
49	773.360 414	67899.816 635	.000 014 7276	.001 293	87.798 412	.011 389 7276	13.67	5.697 160	11.63	588
50	885.785 381	77783.330 189	.000 012 8562	.001 129	87.812 840	.011 387 8562	13.67	5.832 714	11.67	600

Effective Rate is 14.54 %

Annual Percentage Rate is 13.65 %

Amount Of 1	Amount Of 1 Per Period	Sinking Fund Payment	Present Worth Of 1	Present Worth of 1 Per Period	Periodic Payment To Amortize 1	Constant Annual Percent	Total Interest	Annual Add On Rate
What a single $ 1 deposit grows to in the future. The deposit is made at the beginning of the first period.	What a series of $ 1 deposits grow to in the future. A deposit is made at the end of each period.	The amount to be deposited at the end of each period that grows to $ 1 in the future.	What $ 1 to be paid in the future is worth today. Value today of a single $ 1 payment tomorrow.	What $ 1 to be paid at the end of each period is worth today. Value today of a series of $ 1 payments tomorrow.	The mortgage payment to amortize a loan of $ 1. An annuity certain, payable at the end of each period, worth $ 1 today.	The annual payment, including interest and principal, to amortize completely a loan of $ 100.	The total interest paid over the term on a loan of $1. The loan is amortized by regular periodic payments.	The average annual interest rate on a loan that is completely amortized by regular periodic payments.
$S = (1+i)^n$	$S\overline{n}| = \dfrac{(1+i)^n - 1}{i}$	$\dfrac{1}{S\overline{n}|} = \dfrac{i}{(1+i)^n - 1}$	$V^n = \dfrac{1}{(1+i)^n}$	$A\overline{n}| = \dfrac{1-V^n}{i}$	$\dfrac{1}{A\overline{n}|} = \dfrac{i}{1-V^n}$			

YEAR									PERIODS
	1.011 417	1.000 000	1.000 000 0000	.988 712	.988 712	1.011 416 6667	1213.70	.011 417	13.70	1
	1.022 964	2.011 417	.497 162 0334	.977 552	1.966 264	.508 578 7001	610.30	.017 157	10.29	2
	1.034 643	3.034 380	.329 556 5776	.966 517	2.932 781	.340 973 2442	409.17	.022 920	9.17	3
	1.046 455	4.069 023	.245 759 2491	.955 608	3.888 389	.257 175 9158	308.62	.028 704	8.61	4
	1.058 402	5.115 478	.195 485 1712	.944 821	4.833 210	.206 901 8379	248.29	.034 509	8.28	5
	1.070 485	6.173 879	.161 972 7181	.934 156	5.767 366	.173 389 3848	208.07	.040 336	8.07	6
	1.082 706	7.244 364	.138 038 3360	.923 611	6.690 977	.149 455 0026	179.35	.046 185	7.92	7
	1.095 067	8.327 071	.120 090 2477	.913 186	7.604 163	.131 506 9144	157.81	.052 055	7.81	8
	1.107 569	9.422 138	.106 133 0215	.902 878	8.507 041	.117 549 6882	141.06	.057 947	7.73	9
	1.120 214	10.529 708	.094 969 3984	.892 686	9.399 727	.106 386 0650	127.67	.063 861	7.66	10
	1.133 003	11.649 922	.085 837 4860	.882 610	10.282 337	.097 254 1527	116.71	.069 796	7.61	11
	1.145 938	12.782 925	.078 229 3562	.872 647	11.154 985	.089 646 0229	107.58	.075 752	7.58	12
1	1.145 938	12.782 925	.078 229 3562	.872 647	11.154 985	.089 646 0229	107.58	.075 752	7.58	12
2	1.313 175	27.431 370	.036 454 6142	.761 513	20.889 351	.047 871 2808	57.45	.148 911	7.45	24
3	1.504 817	44.217 585	.022 615 4369	.664 532	29.384 020	.034 032 1036	40.84	.225 156	7.51	36
4	1.724 428	63.453 553	.015 759 5587	.579 902	36.796 869	.027 176 2254	32.62	.304 459	7.61	48
5	1.976 088	85.496 788	.011 696 3458	.506 050	43.265 671	.023 113 0125	27.74	.386 781	7.74	60
6	2.264 475	110.756 977	.009 028 7766	.441 603	48.910 654	.020 445 4432	24.54	.472 072	7.87	72
7	2.594 949	139.703 598	.007 158 0118	.385 364	53.836 733	.018 574 6785	22.29	.560 273	8.00	84
8	2.973 652	172.874 642	.005 784 5384	.336 287	58.135 462	.017 201 2051	20.65	.651 316	8.14	96
9	3.407 622	210.886 614	.004 741 8847	.293 460	61.886 736	.016 158 5513	19.40	.745 124	8.28	108
10	3.904 925	254.445 993	.003 930 1071	.256 087	65.160 275	.015 346 7737	18.42	.841 613	8.42	120
11	4.474 804	304.362 358	.003 285 5574	.223 473	68.016 920	.014 702 2241	17.65	.940 694	8.55	132
12	5.127 849	361.563 437	.002 765 7664	.195 014	70.509 763	.014 182 4330	17.02	1.042 270	8.69	144
13	5.876 199	427.112 350	.002 341 3043	.170 178	72.685 136	.013 757 9710	16.51	1.146 243	8.82	156
14	6.733 762	502.227 366	.001 991 1300	.148 505	74.583 470	.013 407 7967	16.09	1.252 510	8.95	168
15	7.716 477	588.304 546	.001 699 7999	.129 593	76.240 045	.013 116 4666	15.74	1.360 964	9.07	180
16	8.842 607	686.943 693	.001 455 7234	.113 089	77.685 651	.012 872 3901	15.45	1.471 499	9.20	192
17	10.133 083	799.978 078	.001 250 0343	.098 687	78.947 155	.012 666 7009	15.21	1.584 007	9.32	204
18	11.611 889	929.508 519	.001 075 8374	.086 119	80.048 003	.012 492 5040	15.00	1.698 381	9.44	216
19	13.306 509	1077.942 425	.000 927 6933	.075 151	81.008 655	.012 344 3600	14.82	1.814 514	9.55	228
20	15.248 440	1248.038 537	.000 801 2573	.065 580	81.846 965	.012 217 9240	14.67	1.932 302	9.66	240
21	17.473 773	1442.958 203	.000 693 0208	.057 229	82.578 515	.012 109 6874	14.54	2.051 641	9.77	252
22	20.023 867	1666.324 132	.000 600 1233	.049 940	83.216 899	.012 016 7900	14.43	2.172 433	9.87	264
23	22.946 118	1922.287 726	.000 520 2135	.043 580	83.773 983	.011 936 8802	14.33	2.294 579	9.98	276
24	26.294 838	2215.606 236	.000 451 3437	.038 030	84.260 122	.011 868 0104	14.25	2.417 987	10.07	288
25	30.132 264	2551.731 178	.000 391 8908	.033 187	84.684 349	.011 808 5575	14.18	2.542 567	10.17	300
26	34.529 719	2936.909 655	.000 340 4940	.028 961	85.054 549	.011 757 1606	14.11	2.668 234	10.26	312
27	39.568 930	3378.300 461	.000 296 0068	.025 272	85.377 604	.011 712 6735	14.06	2.794 906	10.35	324
28	45.343 556	3884.107 132	.000 257 4594	.022 054	85.659 517	.011 674 1261	14.01	2.922 506	10.44	336
29	51.960 922	4463.730 417	.000 224 0279	.019 245	85.905 527	.011 640 6945	13.97	3.050 962	10.52	348
30	59.544 016	5127.942 993	.000 195 0100	.016 794	86.120 207	.011 611 6766	13.94	3.180 204	10.60	360
31	68.233 774	5889.089 687	.000 169 8055	.014 655	86.307 548	.011 586 4722	13.91	3.310 168	10.68	372
32	78.191 701	6761.316 907	.000 147 9002	.012 789	86.471 029	.011 564 5668	13.88	3.440 794	10.75	384
33	89.602 873	7760.835 567	.000 128 8521	.011 160	86.613 691	.011 545 5188	13.86	3.572 025	10.82	396
34	102.679 372	8906.022 377	.000 112 2811	.009 739	86.738 185	.011 528 9477	13.84	3.703 811	10.89	408
35	117.664 235	10218.765 098	.000 097 8592	.008 499	86.846 824	.011 514 5258	13.82	3.836 101	10.96	420
36	134.835 964	11722.858 197	.000 085 3034	.007 416	86.941 628	.011 501 9701	13.81	3.968 851	11.02	432
37	154.513 709	13446.456 229	.000 074 3690	.006 472	87.024 358	.011 491 0357	13.79	4.102 020	11.09	444
38	177.063 191	15421.593 390	.000 064 8441	.005 648	87.096 552	.011 481 5108	13.78	4.235 569	11.15	456
39	202.903 509	17684.978 898	.000 056 5452	.004 928	87.159 552	.011 473 2118	13.77	4.369 463	11.20	468
40	232.514 921	20278.679 254	.000 049 3129	.004 301	87.214 529	.011 465 9795	13.76	4.503 670	11.26	480
41	266.447 776	23250.900 076	.000 043 0091	.003 753	87.262 504	.011 459 6758	13.76	4.638 160	11.31	492
42	305.332 737	26656.882 033	.000 037 5138	.003 275	87.304 369	.011 454 1804	13.75	4.772 907	11.36	504
43	349.892 506	30559.927 530	.000 032 7226	.002 858	87.340 903	.011 449 3893	13.74	4.907 885	11.41	516
44	400.955 257	35032.577 220	.000 028 5449	.002 494	87.372 784	.011 445 2115	13.74	5.043 072	11.46	528
45	459.470 023	40157.958 227	.000 024 9017	.002 176	87.400 605	.011 441 5683	13.73	5.178 447	11.51	540
46	526.524 341	46031.329 110	.000 021 7243	.001 899	87.424 883	.011 438 3910	13.73	5.313 992	11.55	552
47	603.364 458	52761.850 311	.000 018 9531	.001 657	87.446 070	.011 435 6198	13.73	5.449 690	11.60	564
48	691.418 498	60474.612 971	.000 016 5359	.001 446	87.464 557	.011 433 2025	13.72	5.585 525	11.64	576
49	792.323 004	69312.963 833	.000 014 4273	.001 262	87.480 691	.011 431 0940	13.72	5.721 483	11.68	588
50	907.953 351	79441.169 431	.000 012 5879	.001 101	87.494 770	.011 429 2546	13.72	5.857 553	11.72	600

Effective Rate is 14.59 %   Annual Percentage Rate is 13.70 %

Amount Of 1	Amount Of 1 Per Period	Sinking Fund Payment	Present Worth Of 1	Present Worth of 1 Per Period	Periodic Payment To Amortize 1	Constant Annual Percent	Total Interest	Annual Add On Rate
What a single $1 deposit grows to in the future. The deposit is made at the beginning of the first period.	What a series of $1 deposits grow to in the future. A deposit is made at the end of each period.	The amount to be deposited at the end of each period that grows to $1 in the future.	What $1 to be paid in the future is worth today. Value today of a single $1 payment tomorrow.	What $1 to be paid at the end of each period is worth today. Value today of a series of $1 payments tomorrow.	The mortgage payment to amortize a loan of $1. An annuity certain, payable at the end of each period, worth $1 today.	The annual payment, including interest and principal, to amortize completely a loan of $100.	The total interest paid over the term on a loan of $1. The loan is amortized by regular periodic payments.	The average annual interest rate on a loan that is completely amortized by regular periodic payments.
$S = (1+i)^n$	$S_{\overline{n}} = \dfrac{(1+i)^n - 1}{i}$	$\dfrac{1}{S_{\overline{n}}} = \dfrac{i}{(1+i)^n - 1}$	$V^n = \dfrac{1}{(1+i)^n}$	$A_{\overline{n}} = \dfrac{1-V^n}{i}$	$\dfrac{1}{A_{\overline{n}}} = \dfrac{i}{1-V^n}$			

YEAR ... **PERIODS**

Amount Of 1	Amount Of 1 Per Period	Sinking Fund Payment	Present Worth Of 1	Present Worth of 1 Per Period	Periodic Payment To Amortize 1	Constant Annual Percent	Total Interest	Annual Add On Rate	PERIODS
1.011 458	1.000 000	1.000 000 0000	.988 671	.988 671	1.011 458 3333	1213.75	.011 458	13.75	1
1.023 048	2.011 458	.497 151 7349	.977 471	1.966 143	.508 610 0682	610.34	.017 220	10.33	2
1.034 770	3.034 506	.329 542 8987	.966 398	2.932 541	.341 001 2320	409.21	.023 004	9.20	3
1.046 627	4.069 277	.245 743 9194	.955 450	3.887 991	.257 202 2527	308.65	.028 809	8.64	4
1.058 620	5.115 904	.195 468 8825	.944 626	4.832 617	.206 927 2158	248.32	.034 636	8.31	5
1.070 750	6.174 524	.161 955 8163	.933 925	5.766 542	.173 414 1497	208.10	.040 485	8.10	6
1.083 019	7.245 273	.138 021 0187	.923 345	6.689 887	.149 479 3521	179.38	.046 355	7.95	7
1.095 428	8.328 292	.120 072 6385	.912 885	7.602 772	.131 530 9719	157.84	.052 248	7.84	8
1.107 980	9.423 720	.106 115 2028	.902 543	8.505 315	.117 573 5361	141.09	.058 162	7.75	9
1.120 676	10.531 701	.094 951 4277	.892 319	9.397 634	.106 409 7610	127.70	.064 098	7.69	10
1.133 517	11.652 376	.085 819 4053	.882 210	10.279 844	.097 277 7386	116.74	.070 055	7.64	11
1.146 505	12.785 893	.078 211 1969	.872 216	11.152 060	.089 669 5302	107.61	.076 034	7.60	12

YEAR	Amount Of 1	Amount Of 1 Per Period	Sinking Fund Payment	Present Worth Of 1	Present Worth of 1 Per Period	Periodic Payment To Amortize 1	Constant Annual Percent	Total Interest	Annual Add On Rate	PERIODS
1	1.146 505	12.785 893	.078 211 1969	.872 216	11.152 060	.089 669 5302	107.61	.076 034	7.60	12
2	1.314 474	27.444 386	.036 436 5310	.760 761	20.879 065	.047 894 8643	57.48	.149 477	7.47	24
3	1.507 051	44.251 705	.022 597 9994	.663 548	29.363 115	.034 056 3328	40.87	.226 028	7.53	36
4	1.727 841	63.520 695	.015 742 9008	.578 757	36.763 038	.027 201 2341	32.65	.305 659	7.64	48
5	1.980 979	85.612 689	.011 680 5115	.504 801	43.217 369	.023 138 8449	27.77	.388 331	7.77	60
6	2.271 202	110.941 271	.009 013 7781	.440 295	48.846 940	.020 472 1114	24.57	.473 992	7.90	72
7	2.603 945	139.980 618	.007 143 8462	.384 033	53.757 142	.018 602 1795	22.33	.562 583	8.04	84
8	2.985 436	173.274 375	.005 771 1938	.334 960	58.039 898	.017 229 5271	20.68	.654 035	8.18	96
9	3.422 817	211.445 835	.004 729 3436	.292 157	61.775 387	.016 187 6769	19.43	.748 269	8.31	108
10	3.924 277	255.209 605	.003 918 3478	.254 824	65.033 539	.015 376 6812	18.46	.845 202	8.45	120
11	4.499 203	305.384 987	.003 274 5552	.222 262	67.875 352	.014 732 8885	17.68	.944 741	8.59	132
12	5.158 359	362.911 316	.002 755 4941	.193 860	70.354 027	.014 213 8275	17.06	1.046 791	8.72	144
13	5.914 084	428.865 540	.002 331 7332	.169 088	72.515 967	.013 790 0665	16.55	1.151 250	8.86	156
14	6.780 527	504.482 389	.001 982 2297	.147 481	74.401 645	.013 440 5631	16.13	1.258 015	8.99	168
15	7.773 909	591.177 487	.001 691 5394	.128 635	76.046 363	.013 149 8727	15.78	1.366 977	9.11	180
16	8.912 825	690.573 853	.001 448 0710	.112 198	77.480 913	.012 906 4044	15.49	1.478 030	9.24	192
17	10.218 599	804.532 285	.001 242 9582	.097 861	78.732 151	.012 701 2915	15.25	1.591 063	9.36	204
18	11.715 675	935.186 201	.001 069 3058	.085 356	79.823 500	.012 527 6391	15.04	1.705 970	9.48	216
19	13.432 081	1084.981 571	.000 921 6746	.074 449	80.775 392	.012 380 0080	14.86	1.822 642	9.59	228
20	15.399 948	1256.722 716	.000 795 7205	.064 935	81.605 648	.012 254 0538	14.71	1.940 973	9.70	240
21	17.656 118	1453.624 802	.000 687 9354	.056 638	82.329 810	.012 146 2688	14.58	2.060 860	9.81	252
22	20.242 827	1679.374 032	.000 595 4600	.049 400	82.961 436	.012 053 7933	14.47	2.182 201	9.92	264
23	23.208 503	1938.196 659	.000 515 9435	.043 088	83.512 350	.011 974 2768	14.37	2.304 900	10.02	276
24	26.608 666	2234.938 102	.000 447 4397	.037 582	83.992 866	.011 905 7730	14.29	2.428 863	10.12	288
25	30.506 969	2575.153 657	.000 388 3263	.032 779	84.411 980	.011 846 6597	14.22	2.553 998	10.22	300
26	34.976 393	2965.212 500	.000 337 2440	.028 591	84.777 538	.011 795 5773	14.16	2.680 220	10.31	312
27	40.100 611	3412.416 924	.000 293 0474	.024 937	85.096 383	.011 751 3808	14.11	2.807 447	10.40	324
28	45.975 552	3925.139 043	.000 254 7680	.021 751	85.374 485	.011 713 1014	14.06	2.935 602	10.48	336
29	52.711 201	4512.977 528	.000 221 5832	.018 971	85.617 050	.011 679 9165	14.02	3.064 611	10.57	348
30	60.433 657	5186.937 305	.000 192 7920	.016 547	85.828 619	.011 651 1253	13.99	3.194 405	10.65	360
31	69.287 491	5959.635 576	.000 167 7955	.014 433	86.013 153	.011 626 1288	13.96	3.324 920	10.73	372
32	79.438 457	6845.538 027	.000 146 0806	.012 588	86.174 107	.011 604 4139	13.93	3.456 095	10.80	384
33	91.076 590	7861.229 638	.000 127 2066	.010 980	86.314 493	.011 585 5399	13.91	3.587 874	10.87	396
34	104.419 768	9025.725 173	.000 110 7944	.009 577	86.436 940	.011 569 1278	13.89	3.720 204	10.94	408
35	119.717 788	10360.825 155	.000 096 5174	.008 353	86.543 740	.011 554 8507	13.87	3.853 037	11.01	420
36	137.257 046	11891.523 994	.000 084 0935	.007 286	86.636 893	.011 542 4268	13.86	3.986 328	11.07	432
37	157.365 893	13646.477 903	.000 073 2790	.006 355	86.718 143	.011 531 6123	13.84	4.120 036	11.14	444
38	180.420 787	15658.541 379	.000 063 8629	.005 543	86.789 010	.011 522 1962	13.83	4.254 121	11.20	456
39	206.853 338	17965.382 263	.000 055 6626	.004 834	86.850 821	.011 513 9959	13.82	4.388 550	11.25	468
40	237.158 392	20610.186 929	.000 048 5197	.004 217	86.904 734	.011 506 8530	13.81	4.523 289	11.31	480
41	271.903 288	23642.468 767	.000 042 2968	.003 678	86.951 758	.011 500 6301	13.81	4.658 310	11.36	492
42	311.738 486	27118.995 131	.000 036 8745	.003 208	86.992 772	.011 495 2079	13.80	4.793 585	11.41	504
43	357.409 740	31104.850 076	.000 032 1493	.002 798	87.028 546	.011 490 4827	13.79	4.929 089	11.46	516
44	409.772 063	35674.652 798	.000 028 0311	.002 440	87.059 749	.011 486 3644	13.79	5.064 800	11.51	528
45	469.805 730	40913.954 580	.000 024 4415	.002 129	87.086 964	.011 482 7749	13.78	5.200 698	11.56	540
46	538.634 630	46920.840 400	.000 021 3125	.001 857	87.110 701	.011 479 6458	13.78	5.336 764	11.60	552
47	617.547 309	53807.765 175	.000 018 5847	.001 619	87.131 406	.011 476 9180	13.78	5.472 982	11.64	564
48	708.021 093	61703.659 034	.000 016 2065	.001 412	87.149 464	.011 474 5398	13.77	5.609 335	11.69	576
49	811.749 741	70756.341 018	.000 014 1330	.001 232	87.165 215	.011 472 4663	13.77	5.745 810	11.73	588
50	930.675 157	81135.286 400	.000 012 3251	.001 074	87.178 954	.011 470 6584	13.77	5.882 395	11.76	600

Effective Rate is 14.65 %

Annual Percentage Rate is 13.75 %

MONTHLY COMPOUND INTEREST AND ANNUITY

13.80 % M

	Amount Of 1	Amount Of 1 Per Period	Sinking Fund Payment	Present Worth Of 1	Present Worth of 1 Per Period	Periodic Payment To Amortize 1	Constant Annual Percent	Total Interest	Annual Add On Rate	
	What a single $ 1 deposit grows to in the future. The deposit is made at the beginning of the first period.	What a series of $ 1 deposits grow to in the future. A deposit is made at the end of each period.	The amount to be deposited at the end of each period that grows to $ 1 in the future.	What $ 1 to be paid in the future is worth today. Value today of a single $ 1 payment tomorrow.	What $ 1 to be paid at the end of each period is worth today. Value today of a series of $ 1 payments tomorrow.	The mortgage payment to amortize a loan of $ 1. An annuity certain, payable at the end of each period, worth $ 1 today.	The annual payment, including interest and principal, to amortize completely a loan of $ 100.	The total interest paid over the term on a loan of $1. The loan is amortized by regular periodic payments.	The average annual interest rate on a loan that is completely amortized by regular periodic payments.	
	$S = (1+i)^n$	$S\overline{n}| = \dfrac{(1+i)^n - 1}{i}$	$\dfrac{1}{S\overline{n}|} = \dfrac{i}{(1+i)^n - 1}$	$V^n = \dfrac{1}{(1+i)^n}$	$A\overline{n}| = \dfrac{1-V^n}{i}$	$\dfrac{1}{A\overline{n}|} = \dfrac{i}{1-V^n}$				

YEAR										PERIODS
	1.011 500	1.000 000	1.000 000 0000	.988 631	.988 631	1.011 500 0000	1213.80	.011 500	13.80	1
	1.023 132	2.011 500	.497 141 4367	.977 391	1.966 021	.508 641 4367	610.37	.017 283	10.37	2
	1.034 898	3.034 632	.329 529 2206	.966 279	2.932 300	.341 029 2206	409.24	.023 088	9.24	3
	1.046 800	4.069 531	.245 728 5908	.955 293	3.887 593	.257 228 5908	308.68	.028 914	8.67	4
	1.058 838	5.116 330	.195 452 5952	.944 432	4.832 024	.206 952 5952	248.35	.034 763	8.34	5
	1.071 014	6.175 168	.161 938 9162	.933 694	5.765 719	.173 438 9162	208.13	.040 633	8.13	6
	1.083 331	7.246 182	.138 003 7034	.923 079	6.688 798	.149 503 7034	179.41	.046 526	7.98	7
	1.095 789	8.329 513	.120 055 0316	.912 584	7.601 382	.131 555 0316	157.87	.052 440	7.87	8
	1.108 391	9.425 303	.106 097 3866	.902 209	8.503 590	.117 597 3866	141.12	.058 376	7.78	9
	1.121 137	10.533 694	.094 933 4598	.891 951	9.395 542	.106 433 4598	127.73	.064 335	7.72	10
	1.134 031	11.654 831	.085 801 3276	.881 810	10.277 352	.097 301 3276	116.77	.070 315	7.67	11
	1.147 072	12.788 862	.078 193 0409	.871 785	11.149 137	.089 693 0409	107.64	.076 316	7.63	12
1	1.147 072	12.788 862	.078 193 0409	.871 785	11.149 137	.089 693 0409	107.64	.076 316	7.63	12
2	1.315 774	27.458 606	.036 418 4546	.760 009	20.868 787	.047 918 4546	57.51	.150 043	7.50	24
3	1.509 287	44.285 858	.022 580 5721	.662 564	29.342 230	.034 080 5721	40.90	.226 901	7.56	36
4	1.731 261	63.587 925	.015 726 2561	.577 614	36.729 251	.027 226 2561	32.68	.306 860	7.67	48
5	1.985 881	85.728 785	.011 664 6935	.503 555	43.169 144	.023 164 6935	27.80	.389 882	7.80	60
6	2.277 948	111.125 943	.008 998 7988	.438 992	48.783 346	.020 498 7988	24.60	.475 914	7.93	72
7	2.612 971	140.258 310	.007 129 7023	.382 706	53.677 723	.018 629 7023	22.36	.564 895	8.07	84
8	2.997 265	173.675 229	.005 757 8735	.333 637	57.944 567	.017 257 8735	20.71	.656 756	8.21	96
9	3.438 079	212.006 839	.004 716 8290	.290 860	61.664 337	.016 216 8290	19.47	.751 418	8.35	108
10	3.943 723	255.975 952	.003 906 6170	.253 567	64.907 176	.015 406 6170	18.49	.848 794	8.49	120
11	4.523 734	306.411 687	.003 263 5831	.221 056	67.734 235	.014 763 5831	17.72	.948 793	8.63	132
12	5.189 049	364.265 101	.002 745 2534	.192 714	70.198 822	.014 245 2534	17.10	1.051 316	8.76	144
13	5.952 212	430.627 128	.002 322 1946	.168 005	72.347 411	.013 822 1946	16.59	1.156 262	8.89	156
14	6.827 615	506.749 144	.001 973 3630	.146 464	74.220 520	.013 473 3630	16.17	1.263 525	9.03	168
15	7.831 766	594.066 571	.001 683 3130	.127 685	75.853 467	.013 183 3130	15.82	1.372 996	9.15	180
16	8.983 598	694.225 940	.001 440 4532	.111 314	77.277 046	.012 940 4532	15.53	1.484 567	9.28	192
17	10.304 833	809.115 937	.001 235 9168	.097 042	78.518 101	.012 735 9168	15.29	1.598 127	9.40	204
18	11.820 385	940.903 027	.001 062 8088	.084 600	79.600 034	.012 562 8088	15.08	1.713 567	9.52	216
19	13.558 831	1092.072 295	.000 915 6903	.073 753	80.543 246	.012 415 6903	14.90	1.830 777	9.64	228
20	15.552 955	1265.474 317	.000 790 2175	.064 296	81.365 525	.012 290 2175	14.75	1.949 652	9.75	240
21	17.840 357	1464.378 906	.000 682 8834	.056 053	82.082 375	.012 182 8834	14.62	2.070 087	9.86	252
22	20.464 173	1692.536 773	.000 590 8291	.048 866	82.707 314	.012 090 8291	14.51	2.191 979	9.96	264
23	23.473 878	1954.250 253	.000 511 7052	.042 601	83.252 126	.012 011 7052	14.42	2.315 231	10.07	276
24	26.926 226	2254.454 435	.000 443 5663	.037 139	83.727 086	.011 943 5663	14.34	2.439 747	10.17	288
25	30.886 318	2598.810 221	.000 384 7915	.032 377	84.141 148	.011 884 7915	14.27	2.565 437	10.26	300
26	35.428 827	2993.811 069	.000 334 0224	.028 226	84.502 122	.011 834 0224	14.21	2.692 215	10.35	312
27	40.639 413	3446.905 448	.000 290 1153	.024 607	84.816 813	.011 790 1153	14.15	2.819 997	10.44	324
28	46.616 329	3966.637 283	.000 252 1027	.021 452	85.091 156	.011 752 1027	14.11	2.948 707	10.53	336
29	53.472 281	4562.807 073	.000 219 1633	.018 701	85.330 324	.011 719 1633	14.07	3.078 269	10.61	348
30	61.336 552	5246.656 693	.000 190 5976	.016 303	85.538 827	.011 690 5976	14.03	3.208 615	10.70	360
31	70.357 436	6031.081 383	.000 165 8077	.014 213	85.720 597	.011 665 8077	14.00	3.339 680	10.77	372
32	80.705 038	6930.872 913	.000 144 2820	.012 391	85.879 061	.011 644 2820	13.98	3.471 404	10.85	384
33	92.574 483	7962.998 503	.000 125 5808	.010 802	86.017 208	.011 625 5808	13.96	3.603 730	10.92	396
34	106.189 589	9146.920 776	.000 109 3264	.009 417	86.137 642	.011 609 3264	13.94	3.736 605	10.99	408
35	121.807 095	10504.964 761	.000 095 1931	.008 210	86.242 635	.011 595 1931	13.92	3.869 981	11.06	420
36	139.721 497	12062.738 871	.000 082 8999	.007 157	86.334 166	.011 582 8999	13.90	4.003 813	11.12	432
37	160.270 605	13849.617 797	.000 072 2042	.006 239	86.413 961	.011 572 2042	13.89	4.138 059	11.18	444
38	183.841 909	15899.296 422	.000 062 8959	.005 439	86.483 526	.011 562 8959	13.88	4.272 681	11.24	456
39	210.879 890	18250.425 201	.000 054 7932	.004 742	86.544 171	.011 554 7932	13.87	4.407 643	11.30	468
40	241.894 398	20947.338 984	.000 047 7388	.004 134	86.597 040	.011 547 7388	13.86	4.542 915	11.36	480
41	277.470 270	24040.893 032	.000 041 5958	.003 604	86.643 131	.011 541 5958	13.85	4.678 465	11.41	492
42	318.278 353	27589.421 987	.000 036 2458	.003 142	86.683 313	.011 536 2458	13.85	4.814 268	11.46	504
43	365.088 159	31659.839 879	.000 031 5858	.002 739	86.718 342	.011 531 5858	13.84	4.950 298	11.51	516
44	418.782 372	36328.901 911	.000 027 5263	.002 388	86.748 880	.011 527 5263	13.84	5.086 534	11.56	528
45	480.373 496	41684.651 820	.000 023 9896	.002 082	86.775 503	.011 523 9896	13.83	5.222 954	11.61	540
46	551.022 944	47828.082 107	.000 020 9082	.001 815	86.798 712	.011 520 9082	13.83	5.359 541	11.65	552
47	632.062 942	54875.038 430	.000 018 2232	.001 582	86.818 946	.011 518 2232	13.83	5.496 278	11.69	564
48	725.021 647	62958.404 090	.000 015 8835	.001 379	86.836 585	.011 515 8835	13.82	5.633 149	11.74	576
49	831.651 967	72230.605 788	.000 013 8445	.001 202	86.851 963	.011 513 8445	13.82	5.770 141	11.78	588
50	953.964 611	82866.487 915	.000 012 0676	.001 048	86.865 369	.011 512 0676	13.82	5.907 241	11.81	600

Amount Of 1	Amount Of 1 Per Period	Sinking Fund Payment	Present Worth Of 1	Present Worth of 1 Per Period	Periodic Payment To Amortize 1	Constant Annual Percent	Total Interest	Annual Add On Rate
What a single $ 1 deposit grows to in the future. The deposit is made at the beginning of the first period.	What a series of $ 1 deposits grow to in the future. A deposit is made at the end of each period.	The amount to be deposited at the end of each period that grows to $ 1 in the future.	What $ 1 to be paid in the future is worth today. Value today of a single $ 1 payment tomorrow.	What $ 1 to be paid at the end of each period is worth today. Value today of a series of $ 1 payments tomorrow.	The mortgage payment to amortize a loan of $ 1. An annuity certain, payable at the end of each period, worth $ 1 today.	The annual payment, including interest and principal, to amortize completely a loan of $ 100.	The total interest paid over the term on a loan of $1. The loan is amortized by regular periodic payments.	The average annual interest rate on a loan that is completely amortized by regular periodic payments.

$$S = (1+i)^n \qquad S\overline{n}| = \frac{(1+i)^n - 1}{i} \qquad \frac{1}{S\overline{n}|} = \frac{i}{(1+i)^n - 1} \qquad V^n = \frac{1}{(1+i)^n} \qquad A\overline{n}| = \frac{1-V^n}{i} \qquad \frac{1}{A\overline{n}|} = \frac{i}{1-V^n}$$

YEAR	Amount Of 1	Amount Of 1 Per Period	Sinking Fund Payment	Present Worth Of 1	Present Worth of 1 Per Period	Periodic Payment To Amortize 1	Constant Annual Percent	Total Interest	Annual Add On Rate	PERIODS
	1.011 542	1.000 000	1.000 000 0000	.988 590	.988 590	1.011 541 6667	1213.85	.011 542	13.85	1
	1.023 217	2.011 542	.497 131 1391	.977 310	1.965 900	.508 672 8057	610.41	.017 346	10.41	2
	1.035 026	3.034 758	.329 515 5432	.966 159	2.932 059	.341 057 2098	409.27	.023 172	9.27	3
	1.046 972	4.069 784	.245 713 2632	.955 135	3.887 195	.257 254 9299	308.71	.029 020	8.71	4
	1.059 056	5.116 756	.195 436 3092	.944 237	4.831 432	.206 977 9759	248.38	.034 890	8.37	5
	1.071 279	6.175 812	.161 922 0177	.933 463	5.764 895	.173 463 6844	208.16	.040 782	8.16	6
	1.083 644	7.247 092	.137 986 3901	.922 813	6.687 708	.149 528 0568	179.44	.046 696	8.01	7
	1.096 151	8.330 735	.120 037 4269	.912 283	7.599 992	.131 579 0936	157.90	.052 633	7.89	8
	1.108 802	9.426 886	.106 079 5729	.901 874	8.501 866	.117 621 2395	141.15	.058 591	7.81	9
	1.121 599	10.535 688	.094 915 4947	.891 584	9.393 450	.106 457 1614	127.75	.064 572	7.75	10
	1.134 545	11.657 287	.085 783 2531	.881 411	10.274 861	.097 324 9198	116.79	.070 574	7.70	11
	1.147 639	12.791 832	.078 174 8884	.871 354	11.146 215	.089 716 5550	107.66	.076 599	7.66	12
1	1.147 639	12.791 832	.078 174 8884	.871 354	11.146 215	.089 716 5550	107.66	.076 599	7.66	12
2	1.317 075	27.472 237	.036 400 3850	.759 258	20.858 515	.047 942 0516	57.54	.150 609	7.53	24
3	1.511 527	44.320 044	.022 563 1547	.661 583	29.321 367	.034 104 8214	40.93	.227 774	7.59	36
4	1.734 688	63.655 244	.015 709 6247	.576 473	36.695 509	.027 251 2914	32.71	.308 062	7.70	48
5	1.990 795	85.845 076	.011 648 8918	.502 312	43.120 997	.023 190 5584	27.83	.391 434	7.83	60
6	2.284 714	111.310 994	.008 983 8386	.437 691	48.719 873	.020 525 5053	24.64	.477 836	7.96	72
7	2.622 027	140.536 675	.007 115 5803	.381 384	53.598 476	.018 657 2470	22.39	.567 209	8.10	84
8	3.009 141	174.077 208	.005 744 5774	.332 321	57.849 467	.017 286 2441	20.75	.659 479	8.24	96
9	3.453 408	212.569 634	.004 704 3408	.289 569	61.553 585	.016 246 0074	19.50	.754 569	8.38	108
10	3.963 266	256.745 046	.003 894 9145	.252 317	64.781 184	.015 436 5812	18.53	.852 390	8.52	120
11	4.548 399	307.442 474	.003 252 6410	.219 858	67.593 565	.014 794 3077	17.76	.952 849	8.66	132
12	5.219 920	365.624 821	.002 735 0441	.191 574	70.044 145	.014 276 7107	17.14	1.055 846	8.80	144
13	5.990 584	432.397 156	.002 312 6887	.166 929	72.179 468	.013 854 3553	16.63	1.161 279	8.93	156
14	6.875 028	509.027 695	.001 964 5296	.145 454	74.040 091	.013 506 1963	16.21	1.269 041	9.06	168
15	7.890 051	596.971 895	.001 675 1207	.126 742	75.661 352	.013 216 7874	15.87	1.379 022	9.19	180
16	9.054 930	697.900 093	.001 432 8698	.110 437	77.074 044	.012 974 5365	15.57	1.491 111	9.32	192
17	10.391 792	813.729 235	.001 228 9100	.096 230	78.304 999	.012 770 5767	15.33	1.605 198	9.44	204
18	11.926 026	946.659 282	.001 056 3463	.083 850	79.377 597	.012 598 0129	15.12	1.721 171	9.56	216
19	13.686 773	1099.214 995	.000 909 7401	.073 063	80.312 210	.012 451 4068	14.95	1.838 921	9.68	228
20	15.707 475	1274.293 890	.000 784 7483	.063 664	81.126 589	.012 326 4150	14.80	1.958 340	9.79	240
21	18.026 512	1475.221 268	.000 677 8644	.055 474	81.836 201	.012 219 5311	14.67	2.079 322	9.90	252
22	20.687 929	1705.813 374	.000 586 2306	.048 337	82.454 524	.012 127 8973	14.56	2.201 765	10.01	264
23	23.742 276	1970.449 881	.000 507 4983	.042 119	82.993 303	.012 049 1650	14.46	2.325 570	10.11	276
24	27.247 563	2274.157 071	.000 439 7234	.036 701	83.462 770	.011 981 3900	14.38	2.450 640	10.21	288
25	31.270 367	2622.703 304	.000 381 2860	.031 979	83.871 842	.011 922 9526	14.31	2.576 886	10.31	300
26	35.887 095	3022.708 574	.000 330 8291	.027 865	84.228 289	.011 872 4958	14.25	2.704 219	10.40	312
27	41.185 432	3481.770 243	.000 287 2102	.024 280	84.538 880	.011 828 8769	14.20	2.832 556	10.49	324
28	47.266 010	4008.607 344	.000 249 4632	.021 157	84.809 515	.011 791 1299	14.15	2.961 820	10.58	336
29	54.244 319	4613.226 177	.000 216 7680	.018 435	85.045 333	.011 758 4347	14.12	3.091 935	10.66	348
30	62.252 899	5307.110 364	.000 188 4265	.016 064	85.250 815	.011 730 0931	14.08	3.222 834	10.74	360
31	71.443 858	6103.438 956	.000 163 8421	.013 997	85.429 862	.011 705 5087	14.05	3.354 449	10.82	372
32	81.991 762	7017.336 749	.000 142 5042	.012 196	85.585 876	.011 684 1709	14.03	3.486 722	10.90	384
33	94.096 948	8066.161 548	.000 123 9747	.010 627	85.721 819	.011 665 6414	14.00	3.619 594	10.97	396
34	107.989 332	9269.833 851	.000 107 8768	.009 260	85.840 274	.011 649 5435	13.98	3.753 014	11.04	408
35	123.932 775	10651.215 195	.000 093 8860	.008 069	85.943 490	.011 635 5527	13.97	3.886 932	11.11	420
36	142.230 093	12236.542 375	.000 081 7224	.007 031	86.033 427	.011 623 3891	13.95	4.021 304	11.17	432
37	163.228 810	14055.925 763	.000 071 1444	.006 126	86.111 795	.011 612 8110	13.94	4.156 088	11.23	444
38	187.327 757	16143.921 196	.000 061 9428	.005 338	86.180 081	.011 603 6095	13.93	4.291 246	11.29	456
39	214.984 650	18540.186 302	.000 053 9369	.004 651	86.239 582	.011 595 6036	13.92	4.426 742	11.35	468
40	246.724 781	21290.233 724	.000 046 9699	.004 053	86.291 428	.011 588 6366	13.91	4.562 546	11.41	480
41	283.150 994	24446.295 550	.000 040 9060	.003 532	86.336 605	.011 582 5727	13.90	4.698 626	11.46	492
42	324.955 140	28068.315 362	.000 035 6274	.003 077	86.375 970	.011 577 2940	13.90	4.834 956	11.51	504
43	372.931 210	32225.086 757	.000 031 0317	.002 681	86.410 271	.011 572 6984	13.89	4.971 512	11.56	516
44	427.990 421	36995.559 954	.000 027 0303	.002 337	86.440 159	.011 568 6969	13.89	5.108 272	11.61	528
45	491.178 523	42470.341 308	.000 023 5458	.002 036	86.466 202	.011 565 2125	13.88	5.245 215	11.66	540
46	563.695 656	48753.414 208	.000 020 5114	.001 774	86.488 895	.011 562 1781	13.88	5.382 322	11.70	552
47	646.919 150	55964.114 056	.000 017 8686	.001 546	86.508 668	.011 559 5353	13.88	5.519 578	11.74	564
48	742.429 682	64239.394 817	.000 015 5668	.001 347	86.525 898	.011 557 2334	13.87	5.656 966	11.79	576
49	852.041 299	73736.430 213	.000 013 5618	.001 174	86.540 911	.011 555 2285	13.87	5.794 474	11.83	588
50	977.835 871	84635.598 942	.000 011 8154	.001 023	86.553 993	.011 553 4820	13.87	5.932 089	11.86	600

Effective Rate is 14.76 %
Annual Percentage Rate is 13.85 %

Amount Of 1	Amount Of 1 Per Period	Sinking Fund Payment	Present Worth Of 1	Present Worth of 1 Per Period	Periodic Payment To Amortize 1	Constant Annual Percent	Total Interest	Annual Add On Rate
What a single $ 1 deposit grows to in the future. The deposit is made at the beginning of the first period.	What a series of $ 1 deposits grow to in the future. A deposit is made at the end of each period.	The amount to be deposited at the end of each period that grows to $ 1 in the future.	What $ 1 to be paid in the future is worth today. Value today of a single $ 1 payment tomorrow.	What $ 1 to be paid at the end of each period is worth today. Value today of a series of $ 1 payments tomorrow.	The mortgage payment to amortize a loan of $ 1. An annuity certain, payable at the end of each period, worth $ 1 today.	The annual payment, including interest and principal, to amortize completely a loan of $ 100.	The total interest paid over the term on a loan of $1. The loan is amortized by regular periodic payments.	The average annual interest rate on a loan that is completely amortized by regular periodic payments.

$$S = (1+i)^n \qquad S\overline{n}| = \frac{(1+i)^n - 1}{i} \qquad \frac{1}{S\overline{n}|} = \frac{i}{(1+i)^n - 1} \qquad V^n = \frac{1}{(1+i)^n} \qquad A\overline{n}| = \frac{1-V^n}{i} \qquad \frac{1}{A\overline{n}|} = \frac{i}{1-V^n}$$

YEAR									PERIODS
	1.011 563	1.000 000	1.000 000 0000	.988 570	.988 570	1.011 562 5000	1213.88	.011 563	13.88	1
	1.023 259	2.011 562	.497 125 9904	.977 270	1.965 840	.508 688 4904	610.43	.017 377	10.43	2
	1.035 090	3.034 821	.329 508 7048	.966 099	2.931 939	.341 071 2048	409.29	.023 214	9.29	3
	1.047 058	4.069 911	.245 705 5998	.955 057	3.886 996	.257 268 0998	308.73	.029 072	8.72	4
	1.059 165	5.116 970	.195 428 1667	.944 140	4.831 136	.206 990 6667	248.39	.034 953	8.39	5
	1.071 412	6.176 135	.161 913 5691	.933 348	5.764 484	.173 476 0691	208.18	.040 856	8.17	6
	1.083 800	7.247 546	.137 977 7342	.922 680	6.687 164	.149 540 2342	179.45	.046 782	8.02	7
	1.096 331	8.331 346	.120 028 6254	.912 133	7.599 297	.131 591 1254	157.91	.052 729	7.91	8
	1.109 008	9.427 677	.106 070 6670	.901 707	8.501 004	.117 633 1670	141.16	.058 699	7.83	9
	1.121 830	10.536 685	.094 906 5132	.891 400	9.392 404	.106 469 0132	127.77	.064 690	7.76	10
	1.134 802	11.658 515	.085 774 2170	.881 211	10.273 615	.097 336 7170	116.81	.070 704	7.71	11
	1.147 923	12.793 317	.078 165 8133	.871 139	11.144 754	.089 728 3133	107.68	.076 740	7.67	12
1	1.147 923	12.793 317	.078 165 8133	.871 139	11.144 754	.089 728 3133	107.68	.076 740	7.67	12
2	1.317 727	27.479 056	.036 391 3527	.758 883	20.853 382	.047 953 8527	57.55	.150 892	7.54	24
3	1.512 648	44.337 149	.022 554 4498	.661 092	29.310 944	.034 116 9498	40.95	.228 210	7.61	36
4	1.736 403	63.688 937	.015 701 3140	.575 903	36.678 654	.027 263 8140	32.72	.308 663	7.72	48
5	1.993 257	85.903 295	.011 640 9970	.501 691	43.096 952	.023 203 4970	27.85	.392 210	7.84	60
6	2.288 105	111.403 661	.008 976 3657	.437 043	48.688 181	.020 538 8657	24.65	.478 798	7.98	72
7	2.626 568	140.676 111	.007 108 5275	.380 725	53.558 916	.018 671 0275	22.41	.568 366	8.12	84
8	3.015 097	174.278 621	.005 737 9385	.331 664	57.802 003	.017 300 4385	20.77	.660 842	8.26	96
9	3.461 098	212.851 706	.004 698 1066	.288 926	61.498 321	.016 260 6066	19.52	.756 146	8.40	108
10	3.973 073	257.130 626	.003 889 0739	.251 694	64.718 326	.015 451 5739	18.55	.854 189	8.54	120
11	4.560 781	307.959 405	.003 247 1812	.219 261	67.523 398	.014 809 6812	17.78	.954 878	8.68	132
12	5.235 424	366.306 916	.002 729 9512	.191 007	69.967 005	.014 292 4512	17.16	1.058 113	8.82	144
13	6.009 862	433.285 349	.002 307 9479	.166 393	72.095 725	.013 870 4479	16.65	1.163 790	8.95	156
14	6.898 857	510.171 415	.001 960 1255	.144 952	73.950 136	.013 522 6255	16.23	1.271 801	9.08	168
15	7.919 355	598.430 677	.001 671 0373	.126 273	75.565 586	.013 233 5373	15.89	1.382 037	9.21	180
16	9.090 807	699.745 489	.001 429 0910	.110 001	76.972 866	.012 991 5910	15.59	1.494 385	9.34	192
17	10.435 544	816.047 064	.001 225 4195	.095 826	78.198 803	.012 787 9195	15.35	1.608 736	9.46	204
18	11.979 198	949.552 285	.001 053 1279	.083 478	79.266 764	.012 615 6279	15.14	1.724 976	9.58	216
19	13.751 194	1102.805 961	.000 906 7778	.072 721	80.197 106	.012 469 2778	14.97	1.842 995	9.70	228
20	15.785 308	1278.729 339	.000 782 0263	.063 350	81.007 564	.012 344 5263	14.82	1.962 686	9.81	240
21	18.120 314	1480.675 783	.000 675 3673	.055 187	81.713 584	.012 237 8673	14.69	2.083 943	9.92	252
22	20.800 720	1712.494 694	.000 583 9434	.048 075	82.328 626	.012 146 4434	14.58	2.206 661	10.03	264
23	23.877 619	1978.604 890	.000 505 4066	.041 880	82.864 413	.012 067 9066	14.49	2.330 742	10.13	276
24	27.409 661	2284.078 830	.000 437 8133	.036 483	83.331 158	.012 000 3133	14.41	2.456 090	10.23	288
25	31.464 173	2634.739 308	.000 379 5442	.031 782	83.737 757	.011 942 0442	14.34	2.582 613	10.33	300
26	36.118 439	3037.270 439	.000 329 2430	.027 687	84.091 962	.011 891 7430	14.28	2.710 224	10.42	312
27	41.461 177	3499.345 072	.000 285 7678	.024 119	84.400 523	.011 848 2678	14.22	2.838 839	10.51	324
28	47.594 228	4029.771 042	.000 248 1531	.021 011	84.669 323	.011 810 6531	14.18	2.968 379	10.60	336
29	54.634 495	4638.659 066	.000 215 5795	.018 303	84.903 485	.011 778 0795	14.14	3.098 772	10.69	348
30	62.716 179	5337.615 466	.000 187 3496	.015 945	85.107 473	.011 749 8496	14.10	3.229 946	10.77	360
31	71.993 327	6139.963 400	.000 162 8674	.013 890	85.285 174	.011 725 3674	14.08	3.361 837	10.84	372
32	82.642 776	7060.996 825	.000 141 6231	.012 100	85.439 977	.011 704 1231	14.05	3.494 383	10.92	384
33	94.867 520	8118.272 023	.000 123 1789	.010 541	85.574 831	.011 685 6789	14.03	3.627 529	10.99	396
34	108.900 582	9331.942 248	.000 107 1588	.009 183	85.692 308	.011 669 6588	14.01	3.761 221	11.06	408
35	125.009 453	10725.141 878	.000 093 2389	.007 999	85.794 647	.011 655 7389	13.99	3.895 410	11.13	420
36	143.501 192	12324.427 392	.000 081 1397	.006 969	85.883 798	.011 643 6397	13.98	4.030 052	11.19	432
37	164.728 279	14160.283 574	.000 070 6201	.006 071	85.961 461	.011 633 1201	13.96	4.165 105	11.26	444
38	189.095 334	16267.704 604	.000 061 4715	.005 288	86.029 117	.011 623 9715	13.95	4.300 531	11.32	456
39	217.066 831	18686.861 091	.000 053 5135	.004 607	86.088 054	.011 616 0135	13.94	4.436 294	11.38	468
40	249.175 948	21463.865 795	.000 046 5899	.004 013	86.139 396	.011 609 0899	13.94	4.572 363	11.43	480
41	286.034 733	24651.652 599	.000 040 5652	.003 496	86.184 123	.011 603 0652	13.93	4.708 708	11.48	492
42	328.345 770	28310.985 508	.000 035 3220	.003 046	86.223 086	.011 597 8220	13.92	4.845 302	11.54	504
43	376.915 570	32511.616 908	.000 030 7582	.002 653	86.257 028	.011 593 2582	13.92	4.982 121	11.59	516
44	432.669 948	37333.617 145	.000 026 7855	.002 311	86.286 596	.011 589 2855	13.91	5.119 143	11.63	528
45	496.671 665	42868.900 790	.000 023 3269	.002 013	86.312 354	.011 585 8269	13.91	5.256 347	11.68	540
46	570.140 691	49222.978 667	.000 020 3157	.001 754	86.334 793	.011 582 8157	13.90	5.393 714	11.73	552
47	654.477 455	56516.969 050	.000 017 6938	.001 528	86.354 341	.011 580 1938	13.90	5.531 229	11.77	564
48	751.289 542	64889.906 356	.000 015 4107	.001 331	86.371 369	.011 577 9107	13.90	5.668 877	11.81	576
49	862.422 338	74501.391 353	.000 013 4226	.001 160	86.386 203	.011 575 9226	13.90	5.806 642	11.85	588
50	989.994 199	85534.633 388	.000 011 6912	.001 010	86.399 126	.011 574 1912	13.89	5.944 515	11.89	600

Effective Rate is 14.79 %

Annual Percentage Rate is 13.875%

MONTHLY COMPOUND INTEREST AND ANNUITY

13.90 % M

	Amount Of 1	Amount Of 1 Per Period	Sinking Fund Payment	Present Worth Of 1	Present Worth of 1 Per Period	Periodic Payment To Amortize 1	Constant Annual Percent	Total Interest	Annual Add On Rate
	What a single $ 1 deposit grows to in the future. The deposit is made at the beginning of the first period.	What a series of $ 1 deposits grow to in the future. A deposit is made at the end of each period.	The amount to be deposited at the end of each period that grows to $ 1 in the future.	What $ 1 to be paid in the future is worth today. Value today of a single $ 1 payment tomorrow.	What $ 1 to be paid at the end of each period is worth today. Value today of a series of $ 1 payments tomorrow.	The mortgage payment to amortize a loan of $ 1. An annuity certain, payable at the end of each period, worth $ 1 today.	The annual payment, including interest and principal, to amortize completely a loan of $ 100.	The total interest paid over the term on a loan of $1. The loan is amortized by regular periodic payments.	The average annual interest rate on a loan that is completely amortized by regular periodic payments.
	$S = (1+i)^n$	$S\overline{n} = \dfrac{(1+i)^n - 1}{i}$	$\dfrac{1}{S\overline{n}} = \dfrac{i}{(1+i)^n - 1}$	$V^n = \dfrac{1}{(1+i)^n}$	$A\overline{n} = \dfrac{1-V^n}{i}$	$\dfrac{1}{A\overline{n}} = \dfrac{i}{1-V^n}$			

YEAR									PERIODS
	1.011 583	1.000 000	1.000 000 0000	.988 549	.988 549	1.011 583 3333	1213.90	.011 583	13.90	1
	1.023 301	2.011 583	.497 120 8418	.977 230	1.965 779	.508 704 1751	610.45	.017 408	10.45	2
	1.035 154	3.034 884	.329 501 8666	.966 040	2.931 819	.341 085 1999	409.31	.023 256	9.30	3
	1.047 145	4.070 038	.245 697 9367	.954 978	3.886 797	.257 281 2700	308.74	.029 125	8.74	4
	1.059 274	5.117 183	.195 420 0246	.944 043	4.830 840	.207 003 3579	248.41	.035 017	8.40	5
	1.071 544	6.176 457	.161 905 1209	.933 233	5.764 072	.173 488 4542	208.19	.040 931	8.19	6
	1.083 956	7.248 001	.137 969 0787	.922 547	6.686 619	.149 552 4120	179.47	.046 867	8.03	7
	1.096 512	8.331 957	.120 019 8245	.911 983	7.598 602	.131 603 1578	157.93	.052 825	7.92	8
	1.109 213	9.428 469	.106 061 7617	.901 540	8.500 142	.117 645 0950	141.18	.058 806	7.84	9
	1.122 061	10.537 682	.094 897 5325	.891 217	9.391 359	.106 480 8658	127.78	.064 809	7.78	10
	1.135 059	11.659 743	.085 765 1817	.881 012	10.272 370	.097 348 5150	116.82	.070 834	7.73	11
	1.148 206	12.794 802	.078 156 7392	.870 924	11.143 294	.089 740 0725	107.69	.076 881	7.69	12
1	1.148 206	12.794 802	.078 156 7392	.870 924	11.143 294	.089 740 0725	107.69	.076 881	7.69	12
2	1.318 378	27.485 876	.036 382 3221	.758 508	20.848 251	.047 965 6554	57.56	.151 176	7.56	24
3	1.513 770	44.354 262	.022 545 7475	.660 602	29.300 525	.034 129 0808	40.96	.228 647	7.62	36
4	1.738 121	63.722 652	.015 693 0065	.575 334	36.661 810	.027 276 3398	32.74	.309 264	7.73	48
5	1.995 721	85.961 563	.011 633 1063	.501 072	43.072 927	.023 216 4396	27.86	.392 986	7.86	60
6	2.291 500	111.496 423	.008 968 8976	.436 395	48.656 518	.020 552 2309	24.67	.479 761	8.00	72
7	2.631 115	140.815 715	.007 101 4801	.380 067	53.519 400	.018 684 8134	22.43	.569 524	8.14	84
8	3.021 064	174.480 315	.005 731 3056	.331 009	57.754 598	.017 314 6389	20.78	.662 205	8.28	96
9	3.468 805	213.134 227	.004 691 8790	.288 284	61.443 131	.016 275 2123	19.54	.757 723	8.42	108
10	3.982 904	257.516 897	.003 883 2403	.251 073	64.655 561	.015 466 5737	18.56	.855 989	8.56	120
11	4.573 196	308.477 365	.003 241 7289	.218 665	67.453 342	.014 825 0623	17.80	.956 908	8.70	132
12	5.250 973	366.990 505	.002 724 8661	.190 441	69.889 996	.014 308 1995	17.17	1.060 381	8.84	144
13	6.029 201	434.175 669	.002 303 2152	.165 859	72.012 134	.013 886 5485	16.67	1.166 302	8.97	156
14	6.922 768	511.318 108	.001 955 7297	.144 451	73.860 355	.013 539 0630	16.25	1.274 563	9.10	168
15	7.948 767	599.893 554	.001 666 9624	.125 806	75.470 014	.013 250 2957	15.91	1.385 053	9.23	180
16	9.126 826	701.596 454	.001 425 3208	.109 567	76.871 903	.013 008 6541	15.62	1.497 662	9.36	192
17	10.479 480	818.372 380	.001 221 9376	.095 425	78.092 842	.012 805 2710	15.37	1.612 275	9.48	204
18	12.032 607	952.455 252	.001 049 9181	.083 108	79.156 186	.012 633 2514	15.16	1.728 782	9.60	216
19	13.815 917	1106.410 072	.000 903 8240	.072 380	80.082 277	.012 487 1574	14.99	1.847 072	9.72	228
20	15.863 525	1283.181 990	.000 779 3127	.063 038	80.888 832	.012 362 6460	14.84	1.967 035	9.84	240
21	18.214 601	1486.152 647	.000 672 8784	.054 901	81.591 280	.012 256 2117	14.71	2.088 565	9.95	252
22	20.914 123	1719.204 866	.000 581 6642	.047 815	82.203 058	.012 164 9976	14.60	2.211 559	10.05	264
23	24.013 731	1986.796 928	.000 503 3227	.041 643	82.735 870	.012 086 6560	14.51	2.335 917	10.16	276
24	27.572 721	2294.047 862	.000 435 9107	.036 268	83.199 908	.012 019 2440	14.43	2.461 542	10.26	288
25	31.659 176	2646.835 367	.000 377 8097	.031 586	83.604 050	.011 961 1430	14.36	2.588 343	10.35	300
26	36.351 271	3051.908 259	.000 327 6638	.027 509	83.956 027	.011 910 9972	14.30	2.716 231	10.45	312
27	41.738 764	3517.015 568	.000 284 3320	.023 959	84.262 572	.011 867 6653	14.25	2.845 124	10.54	324
28	47.924 718	4051.054 784	.000 246 8493	.020 866	84.529 549	.011 830 1826	14.20	2.974 941	10.62	336
29	55.027 471	4664.242 059	.000 214 3971	.018 173	84.762 065	.011 797 7304	14.16	3.105 610	10.71	348
30	63.182 897	5368.307 647	.000 186 2784	.015 827	84.964 570	.011 769 6118	14.13	3.237 060	10.79	360
31	72.547 010	6176.720 300	.000 161 8982	.013 784	85.140 935	.011 745 2315	14.10	3.369 226	10.87	372
32	83.298 945	7104.944 928	.000 140 7470	.012 005	85.294 536	.011 724 0804	14.07	3.502 047	10.94	384
33	95.644 387	8170.738 439	.000 122 3880	.010 455	85.428 311	.011 705 7213	14.05	3.635 466	11.02	396
34	109.819 503	9394.489 428	.000 106 4454	.009 106	85.544 819	.011 689 7787	14.03	3.769 430	11.09	408
35	126.095 462	10799.608 215	.000 092 5960	.007 930	85.646 288	.011 675 9293	14.02	3.903 890	11.15	420
36	144.783 623	12412.974 678	.000 080 5609	.006 907	85.734 660	.011 663 8942	14.00	4.038 802	11.22	432
37	166.241 491	14265.452 466	.000 070 0994	.006 015	85.811 625	.011 653 4328	13.99	4.174 124	11.28	444
38	190.879 553	16392.479 423	.000 061 0036	.005 239	85.878 656	.011 644 3369	13.98	4.309 818	11.34	456
39	219.169 135	18834.745 507	.000 053 0934	.004 563	85.937 034	.011 636 4267	13.97	4.445 848	11.40	468
40	251.651 416	21638.971 192	.000 046 2129	.003 974	85.987 878	.011 629 5463	13.96	4.582 182	11.46	480
41	288.947 781	24858.801 228	.000 040 2272	.003 461	86.032 158	.011 623 5605	13.95	4.718 792	11.51	492
42	331.771 707	28555.830 862	.000 035 0191	.003 014	86.070 723	.011 618 3525	13.95	4.855 650	11.56	504
43	380.942 416	32800.784 157	.000 030 4871	.002 625	86.104 311	.011 613 8204	13.94	4.992 731	11.61	516
44	437.400 542	37674.866 936	.000 026 5429	.002 286	86.133 563	.011 609 8762	13.94	5.130 015	11.66	528
45	502.226 126	43271.320 251	.000 023 1100	.001 991	86.159 039	.011 606 4433	13.93	5.267 479	11.71	540
46	576.659 281	49697.204 077	.000 020 1219	.001 734	86.181 227	.011 603 4552	13.93	5.405 107	11.75	552
47	662.123 909	57075.445 374	.000 017 5207	.001 510	86.200 550	.011 600 8540	13.93	5.542 882	11.79	564
48	760.254 947	65547.189 664	.000 015 2562	.001 315	86.217 380	.011 598 5895	13.92	5.680 788	11.83	576
49	872.929 638	75274.501 154	.000 013 2847	.001 146	86.232 037	.011 596 6180	13.92	5.818 811	11.88	588
50	1002.303 446	86443.463 006	.000 011 5683	.000 998	86.244 803	.011 594 9016	13.92	5.956 941	11.91	600

MONTHLY COMPOUND INTEREST AND ANNUITY

13.95 % M

	Amount Of 1	Amount Of 1 Per Period	Sinking Fund Payment	Present Worth Of 1	Present Worth of 1 Per Period	Periodic Payment To Amortize 1	Constant Annual Percent	Total Interest	Annual Add On Rate	
	What a single $ 1 deposit grows to in the future. The deposit is made at the beginning of the first period.	What a series of $ 1 deposits grow to in the future. A deposit is made at the end of each period.	The amount to be deposited at the end of each period that grows to $ 1 in the future.	What $ 1 to be paid in the future is worth today. Value today of a single $ 1 payment tomorrow.	What $ 1 to be paid at the end of each period is worth today. Value today of a series of $ 1 payments tomorrow.	The mortgage payment to amortize a loan of $ 1. An annuity certain, payable at the end of each period, worth $ 1 today.	The annual payment, including interest and principal, to amortize completely a loan of $ 100.	The total interest paid over the term on a loan of $1. The loan is amortized by regular periodic payments.	The average annual interest rate on a loan that is completely amortized by regular periodic payments.	

$$S = (1+i)^n \qquad S\overline{n}| = \frac{(1+i)^n - 1}{i} \qquad \frac{1}{S\overline{n}|} = \frac{i}{(1+i)^n - 1} \qquad V^n = \frac{1}{(1+i)^n} \qquad A\overline{n}| = \frac{1-V^n}{i} \qquad \frac{1}{A\overline{n}|} = \frac{i}{1-V^n}$$

YEAR									**PERIODS**	
	1.011 625	1.000 000	1.000 000 0000	.988 509	.988 509	1.011 625 0000	1213.95	.011 625	13.95	1
	1.023 385	2.011 625	.497 110 5450	.977 149	1.965 658	.508 735 5450	610.49	.017 471	10.48	2
	1.035 282	3.035 010	.329 488 1907	.965 920	2.931 578	.341 113 1907	409.34	.023 340	9.34	3
	1.047 317	4.070 292	.245 682 6113	.954 821	3.886 399	.257 307 6113	308.77	.029 230	8.77	4
	1.059 492	5.117 609	.195 403 7414	.943 848	4.830 247	.207 028 7414	248.44	.035 144	8.43	5
	1.071 809	6.177 101	.161 888 2257	.933 002	5.763 249	.173 513 2257	208.22	.041 079	8.22	6
	1.084 269	7.248 910	.137 951 7693	.922 281	6.685 530	.149 576 7693	179.50	.047 037	8.06	7
	1.096 873	8.333 179	.120 002 2243	.911 682	7.597 213	.131 627 2243	157.96	.053 018	7.95	8
	1.109 624	9.430 052	.106 043 9531	.901 206	8.498 418	.117 668 9531	141.21	.059 021	7.87	9
	1.122 524	10.539 676	.094 879 5730	.890 850	9.389 268	.106 504 5730	127.81	.065 046	7.81	10
	1.135 573	11.662 200	.085 747 1133	.880 613	10.269 881	.097 372 1133	116.85	.071 093	7.76	11
	1.148 774	12.797 773	.078 138 5934	.870 493	11.140 374	.089 763 5934	107.72	.077 163	7.72	12
1	1.148 774	12.797 773	.078 138 5934	.870 493	11.140 374	.089 763 5934	107.72	.077 163	7.72	12
2	1.319 682	27.499 524	.036 364 2660	.757 758	20.837 993	.047 989 2660	57.59	.151 742	7.59	24
3	1.516 016	44.388 514	.022 528 3502	.659 623	29.279 704	.034 153 3502	40.99	.229 521	7.65	36
4	1.741 560	63.790 150	.015 676 4016	.574 198	36.628 156	.027 301 4016	32.77	.310 467	7.76	48
5	2.000 660	86.078 246	.011 617 3371	.499 835	43.024 933	.023 242 3371	27.90	.394 540	7.89	60
6	2.298 306	111.682 234	.008 953 9756	.435 103	48.593 284	.020 578 9756	24.70	.481 686	8.03	72
7	2.640 234	141.095 432	.007 087 4016	.378 754	53.440 495	.018 712 4016	22.46	.571 842	8.17	84
8	3.033 033	174.884 554	.005 718 0579	.329 703	57.659 959	.017 343 0579	20.82	.664 934	8.31	96
9	3.484 270	213.700 621	.004 679 4436	.287 004	61.332 973	.016 304 4436	19.57	.760 880	8.45	108
10	4.002 639	258.291 515	.003 871 5945	.249 835	64.530 307	.015 496 5945	18.60	.859 591	8.60	120
11	4.598 128	309.516 380	.003 230 8468	.217 480	67.313 564	.014 855 8468	17.83	.960 972	8.74	132
12	5.282 210	368.362 178	.002 714 7195	.189 315	69.736 371	.014 339 7195	17.21	1.064 920	8.87	144
13	6.068 066	435.962 708	.002 293 7742	.164 797	71.845 407	.013 918 7742	16.71	1.171 329	9.01	156
14	6.970 838	513.620 447	.001 946 9630	.143 455	73.681 309	.013 571 9630	16.29	1.280 090	9.14	168
15	8.007 918	602.831 648	.001 658 8379	.124 876	75.279 449	.013 283 8379	15.95	1.391 091	9.27	180
16	9.199 289	705.315 165	.001 417 8059	.108 704	76.670 619	.013 042 8059	15.66	1.504 219	9.40	192
17	10.567 905	823.045 577	.001 214 9995	.094 626	77.881 623	.012 839 9995	15.41	1.619 360	9.53	204
18	12.140 136	958.291 227	.001 043 5241	.082 371	78.935 793	.012 668 5241	15.21	1.736 401	9.65	216
19	13.946 273	1113.657 928	.000 897 9418	.071 704	79.853 441	.012 522 9418	15.03	1.855 231	9.76	228
20	16.021 118	1292.139 173	.000 773 9104	.062 418	80.652 248	.012 398 9104	14.88	1.975 739	9.88	240
21	18.404 646	1497.173 807	.000 667 9251	.054 334	81.347 604	.012 292 9251	14.76	2.097 817	9.99	252
22	21.142 780	1732.712 287	.000 577 1299	.047 297	81.952 906	.012 202 1299	14.65	2.221 362	10.10	264
23	24.288 279	2003.292 796	.000 499 1782	.041 172	82.479 817	.012 124 1782	14.55	2.346 273	10.20	276
24	27.901 746	2314.128 680	.000 432 1281	.035 840	82.938 490	.012 057 1281	14.47	2.472 453	10.30	288
25	32.052 803	2671.208 897	.000 374 3623	.031 199	83.337 762	.011 999 3623	14.40	2.599 809	10.40	300
26	36.821 431	3081.413 408	.000 324 5264	.027 158	83.685 325	.011 949 5264	14.34	2.728 252	10.49	312
27	42.299 507	3552.645 731	.000 281 4804	.023 641	83.987 876	.011 906 4804	14.29	2.857 700	10.58	324
28	48.592 578	4093.985 225	.000 244 2608	.020 579	84.251 245	.011 869 2608	14.25	2.988 072	10.67	336
29	55.821 896	4715.862 023	.000 212 0503	.017 914	84.480 506	.011 837 0503	14.21	3.119 294	10.76	348
30	64.126 749	5430.257 990	.000 184 1533	.015 594	84.680 076	.011 809 1533	14.18	3.251 295	10.84	360
31	73.667 149	6250.937 585	.000 159 9760	.013 575	84.853 800	.011 784 9760	14.15	3.384 011	10.92	372
32	84.626 914	7193.713 060	.000 139 0103	.011 817	85.005 026	.011 764 0103	14.12	3.517 380	10.99	384
33	97.217 209	8276.749 120	.000 120 8204	.010 286	85.136 667	.011 745 8204	14.10	3.651 345	11.06	396
34	111.680 613	9520.912 910	.000 105 0319	.008 954	85.251 260	.011 730 0319	14.08	3.785 853	11.13	408
35	128.295 797	10950.176 067	.000 091 3227	.007 794	85.351 012	.011 716 3227	14.06	3.920 856	11.20	420
36	147.382 890	12592.076 583	.000 079 4150	.006 785	85.437 845	.011 704 4150	14.05	4.056 307	11.27	432
37	169.309 649	14478.249 393	.000 069 0691	.005 906	85.513 433	.011 694 0691	14.04	4.192 167	11.33	444
38	194.498 542	16645.035 893	.000 060 0780	.005 141	85.579 232	.011 685 0780	14.03	4.328 396	11.39	456
39	223.434 891	19134.184 134	.000 052 2625	.004 476	85.636 510	.011 677 2625	14.02	4.464 959	11.45	468
40	256.676 218	21993.653 199	.000 045 4677	.003 896	85.686 369	.011 670 4677	14.01	4.601 824	11.50	480
41	294.862 995	25278.537 241	.000 039 5593	.003 391	85.729 772	.011 664 5593	14.00	4.738 963	11.56	492
42	338.730 976	29052.126 997	.000 034 4209	.002 952	85.767 553	.011 659 4209	14.00	4.876 348	11.61	504
43	389.125 377	33387.129 224	.000 029 9517	.002 570	85.800 442	.011 654 9517	13.99	5.013 955	11.66	516
44	447.017 160	38367.067 568	.000 026 0640	.002 237	85.829 071	.011 651 0640	13.99	5.151 762	11.71	528
45	513.521 742	44087.891 827	.000 022 6820	.001 947	85.853 992	.011 647 6820	13.98	5.289 748	11.75	540
46	589.920 485	50659.826 646	.000 019 7395	.001 695	85.875 687	.011 644 7395	13.98	5.427 896	11.80	552
47	677.685 382	58209.495 245	.000 017 1793	.001 285	85.894 571	.011 642 1793	13.98	5.566 189	11.84	564
48	778.507 425	66882.359 101	.000 014 9516	.001 285	85.911 010	.011 639 9516	13.97	5.704 612	11.88	576
49	894.329 177	76845.520 594	.000 013 0131	.001 118	85.925 320	.011 638 0131	13.97	5.843 152	11.92	588
50	1027.382 208	88290.942 611	.000 011 3262	.000 973	85.937 777	.011 636 3262	13.97	5.981 796	11.96	600

MONTHLY COMPOUND INTEREST AND ANNUITY

	Amount Of 1	Amount Of 1 Per Period	Sinking Fund Payment	Present Worth Of 1	Present Worth of 1 Per Period	Periodic Payment To Amortize 1	Constant Annual Percent	Total Interest	Annual Add On Rate	
	What a single $ 1 deposit grows to in the future. The deposit is made at the beginning of the first period.	What a series of $ 1 deposits grow to in the future. A deposit is made at the end of each period.	The amount to be deposited at the end of each period that grows to $ 1 in the future.	What $ 1 to be paid in the future is worth today. Value today of a single $ 1 payment tomorrow.	What $ 1 to be paid at the end of each period is worth today. Value today of a series of $ 1 payments tomorrow.	The mortgage payment to amortize a loan of $ 1. An annuity certain, payable at the end of each period, worth $ 1 today.	The annual payment, including interest and principal, to amortize completely a loan of $ 100.	The total interest paid over the term on a loan of $1. The loan is amortized by regular periodic payments.	The average annual interest rate on a loan that is completely amortized by regular periodic payments.	

$$S = (1+i)^n \qquad S\overline{n}| = \frac{(1+i)^n - 1}{i} \qquad \frac{1}{S\overline{n}|} = \frac{i}{(1+i)^n - 1} \qquad V^n = \frac{1}{(1+i)^n} \qquad A\overline{n}| = \frac{1-V^n}{i} \qquad \frac{1}{A\overline{n}|} = \frac{i}{1-V^n}$$

YEAR										PERIODS
	1.011 667	1.000 000	1.000 000 0000	.988 468	.988 468	1.011 666 6667	1214.00	.011 667	14.00	1
	1.023 469	2.011 667	.497 100 2486	.977 069	1.965 537	.508 766 9152	610.53	.017 534	10.52	2
	1.035 410	3.035 136	.329 474 5156	.965 801	2.931 338	.341 141 1823	409.37	.023 424	9.37	3
	1.047 490	4.070 546	.245 667 2869	.954 663	3.886 001	.257 333 9536	308.81	.029 336	8.80	4
	1.059 710	5.118 036	.195 387 4595	.943 654	4.829 655	.207 054 1261	248.47	.035 271	8.46	5
	1.072 074	6.177 746	.161 871 3322	.932 772	5.762 427	.173 537 9989	208.25	.041 228	8.25	6
	1.084 581	7.249 820	.137 934 4618	.922 015	6.684 442	.149 601 1284	179.53	.047 208	8.09	7
	1.097 235	8.334 401	.119 984 6263	.911 382	7.595 824	.131 651 2929	157.99	.053 210	7.98	8
	1.110 036	9.431 636	.106 026 1469	.900 872	8.496 696	.117 692 8136	141.24	.059 235	7.90	9
	1.122 986	10.541 672	.094 861 6164	.890 483	9.387 178	.106 528 2831	127.84	.065 283	7.83	10
	1.136 088	11.664 658	.085 729 0481	.880 214	10.267 392	.097 395 7148	116.88	.071 353	7.78	11
	1.149 342	12.800 745	.078 120 4509	.870 063	11.137 455	.089 787 1176	107.75	.077 445	7.74	12
1	1.149 342	12.800 745	.078 120 4509	.870 063	11.137 455	.089 787 1176	107.75	.077 445	7.74	12
2	1.320 987	27.513 180	.036 346 2166	.757 010	20.827 743	.048 012 8833	57.62	.152 309	7.62	24
3	1.518 266	44.422 800	.022 510 9631	.658 646	29.258 904	.034 177 6298	41.02	.230 395	7.68	36
4	1.745 007	63.857 736	.015 659 8098	.573 064	36.594 546	.027 326 4765	32.80	.311 671	7.79	48
5	2.005 610	86.195 125	.011 601 5842	.498 601	42.977 016	.023 268 2508	27.93	.396 095	7.92	60
6	2.305 132	111.868 425	.008 939 0728	.433 815	48.530 168	.020 605 7395	24.73	.483 613	8.06	72
7	2.649 385	141.375 828	.007 073 3449	.377 446	53.361 760	.018 740 0116	22.49	.574 161	8.20	84
8	3.045 049	175.289 927	.005 704 8344	.328 402	57.565 549	.017 371 5010	20.85	.667 664	8.35	96
9	3.499 803	214.268 826	.004 667 0345	.285 730	61.223 111	.016 333 7012	19.61	.764 040	8.49	108
10	4.022 471	259.068 912	.003 859 9768	.248 603	64.405 420	.015 526 6435	18.64	.863 197	8.63	120
11	4.623 195	310.559 534	.003 219 9945	.216 301	67.174 230	.014 886 6612	17.87	.965 039	8.77	132
12	5.313 632	369.739 871	.002 704 6042	.188 195	69.583 269	.014 371 2708	17.25	1.069 463	8.91	144
13	6.107 180	437.758 319	.002 284 3655	.163 742	71.679 284	.013 951 0322	16.75	1.176 361	9.05	156
14	7.019 239	515.934 780	.001 938 2295	.142 466	73.502 950	.013 604 8961	16.33	1.285 623	9.18	168
15	8.067 507	605.786 272	.001 650 7472	.123 954	75.089 654	.013 317 4139	15.99	1.397 134	9.31	180
16	9.272 324	709.056 369	.001 410 3251	.107 848	76.470 187	.013 076 9918	15.70	1.510 782	9.44	192
17	10.657 072	827.749 031	.001 208 0956	.093 834	77.671 337	.012 874 7623	15.45	1.626 452	9.57	204
18	12.248 621	964.167 496	.001 037 1642	.081 642	78.716 413	.012 703 8309	15.25	1.744 027	9.69	216
19	14.077 855	1120.958 972	.000 892 0933	.071 034	79.625 696	.012 558 7600	15.08	1.863 397	9.81	228
20	16.180 270	1301.166 005	.000 768 5414	.061 804	80.416 829	.012 435 2081	14.93	1.984 450	9.92	240
21	18.596 664	1508.285 522	.000 663 0044	.053 773	81.105 164	.012 329 6711	14.80	2.107 077	10.03	252
22	21.373 928	1746.336 688	.000 572 6273	.046 798	81.704 060	.012 239 2939	14.69	2.231 174	10.14	264
23	24.565 954	2019.938 898	.000 495 0645	.040 707	82.225 136	.012 161 7311	14.60	2.356 638	10.25	276
24	28.234 683	2334.401 417	.000 428 3753	.035 417	82.678 506	.012 095 0420	14.52	2.483 372	10.35	288
25	32.451 308	2695.826 407	.000 370 9438	.030 815	83.072 966	.012 037 6104	14.45	2.611 283	10.45	300
26	37.297 652	3111.227 338	.000 321 4166	.026 811	83.416 171	.011 988 0832	14.39	2.740 282	10.54	312
27	42.867 759	3588.665 088	.000 278 6551	.023 328	83.714 781	.011 945 3218	14.34	2.870 284	10.63	324
28	49.269 718	4137.404 359	.000 241 6974	.020 296	83.974 591	.011 908 3641	14.30	3.001 210	10.72	336
29	56.627 757	4768.093 467	.000 209 7274	.017 659	84.200 641	.011 876 3941	14.26	3.132 985	10.80	348
30	65.084 661	5492.970 967	.000 182 0508	.015 365	84.397 320	.011 848 7175	14.22	3.265 538	10.89	360
31	74.804 537	6326.103 143	.000 158 0752	.013 368	84.568 442	.011 824 7419	14.19	3.398 804	10.96	372
32	85.975 998	7283.656 968	.000 137 2937	.011 631	84.717 330	.011 803 9603	14.17	3.532 721	11.04	384
33	98.815 828	8384.213 825	.000 119 2718	.010 120	84.846 871	.011 785 9384	14.15	3.667 232	11.11	396
34	113.573 184	9649.130 077	.000 103 6363	.008 805	84.959 580	.011 770 3030	14.13	3.802 284	11.18	408
35	130.534 434	11102.951 488	.000 090 0661	.007 661	85.057 645	.011 756 7328	14.11	3.937 828	11.25	420
36	150.028 711	12773.889 538	.000 078 2847	.006 665	85.142 966	.011 744 9514	14.10	4.073 819	11.32	432
37	172.434 303	14694.368 868	.000 068 0533	.005 799	85.217 202	.011 734 7199	14.09	4.210 216	11.38	444
38	198.185 992	16901.656 478	.000 059 1658	.005 046	85.281 792	.011 725 8325	14.08	4.346 980	11.44	456
39	227.783 490	19438.584 899	.000 051 4441	.004 390	85.337 989	.011 718 1107	14.07	4.484 076	11.50	468
40	261.801 139	22354.383 358	.000 044 7340	.003 820	85.386 883	.011 711 4006	14.06	4.621 472	11.55	480
41	300.899 053	25705.633 076	.000 038 9020	.003 323	85.429 425	.011 705 5686	14.05	4.759 140	11.61	492
42	345.835 928	29557.365 227	.000 033 8325	.002 892	85.466 439	.011 700 4992	14.05	4.897 052	11.66	504
43	397.483 767	33984.322 874	.000 029 4253	.002 516	85.498 643	.011 696 0920	14.04	5.035 183	11.71	516
44	456.844 799	39072.411 358	.000 025 5935	.002 189	85.526 663	.011 692 2602	14.04	5.173 513	11.76	528
45	525.070 929	44920.365 302	.000 022 2616	.001 905	85.551 042	.011 688 9283	14.03	5.312 021	11.80	540
46	603.486 086	51641.664 554	.000 019 3642	.001 657	85.572 254	.011 686 0309	14.03	5.450 689	11.85	552
47	693.611 923	59366.736 276	.000 016 8444	.001 442	85.590 709	.011 683 5111	14.03	5.589 500	11.89	564
48	797.197 335	68245.485 884	.000 014 6530	.001 254	85.606 766	.011 681 3197	14.02	5.728 440	11.93	576
49	916.252 403	78450.205 975	.000 012 7469	.001 091	85.620 737	.011 679 4136	14.02	5.867 495	11.97	588
50	1053.087 396	90178.919 673	.000 011 0891	.000 950	85.632 892	.011 677 7557	14.02	6.006 653	12.01	600

Effective Rate is 14.93 %

Annual Percentage Rate is 14.00 %

	Amount Of 1	Amount Of 1 Per Period	Sinking Fund Payment	Present Worth Of 1	Present Worth of 1 Per Period	Periodic Payment To Amortize 1	Constant Annual Percent	Total Interest	Annual Add On Rate	
	What a single $1 deposit grows to in the future. The deposit is made at the beginning of the first period.	What a series of $1 deposits grow to in the future. A deposit is made at the end of each period.	The amount to be deposited at the end of each period that grows to $1 in the future.	What $1 to be paid in the future is worth today. Value today of a single $1 payment tomorrow.	What $1 to be paid at the end of each period is worth today. Value today of a series of $1 payments tomorrow.	The mortgage payment to amortize a loan of $1. An annuity certain, payable at the end of each period, worth $1 today.	The annual payment, including interest and principal, to amortize completely a loan of $100.	The total interest paid over the term on a loan of $1. The loan is amortized by regular periodic payments.	The average annual interest rate on a loan that is completely amortized by regular periodic payments.	
	$S = (1+i)^n$	$Sn\rceil = \dfrac{(1+i)^n-1}{i}$	$\dfrac{1}{Sn\rceil} = \dfrac{i}{(1+i)^n-1}$	$V^n = \dfrac{1}{(1+i)^n}$	$An\rceil = \dfrac{1-V^n}{i}$	$\dfrac{1}{An\rceil} = \dfrac{i}{1-V^n}$				**PERIODS**

YEAR										
	1.011 708	1.000 000	1.000 000 0000	.988 427	.988 427	1.011 708 3333	1214.05	.011 708	14.05	1
	1.023 554	2.011 708	.497 089 9526	.976 988	1.965 415	.508 798 2859	610.56	.017 597	10.56	2
	1.035 538	3.035 262	.329 460 8413	.965 682	2.931 097	.341 169 1746	409.41	.023 508	9.40	3
	1.047 662	4.070 800	.245 651 9636	.954 506	3.885 603	.257 360 2969	308.84	.029 441	8.83	4
	1.059 929	5.118 462	.195 371 1790	.943 460	4.829 063	.207 079 5123	248.50	.035 398	8.50	5
	1.072 339	6.178 391	.161 854 4404	.932 541	5.761 604	.173 562 7737	208.28	.041 377	8.28	6
	1.084 894	7.250 730	.137 917 1562	.921 749	6.683 353	.149 625 4895	179.56	.047 378	8.12	7
	1.097 596	8.335 624	.119 967 0305	.911 082	7.594 435	.131 675 3639	158.02	.053 403	8.01	8
	1.110 447	9.433 220	.106 008 3434	.900 538	8.494 973	.117 716 6767	141.27	.059 450	7.93	9
	1.123 449	10.543 664	.094 843 6626	.890 116	9.385 089	.106 551 9959	127.87	.065 520	7.86	10
	1.136 602	11.667 116	.085 710 9860	.879 815	10.264 904	.097 419 3193	116.91	.071 613	7.81	11
	1.149 910	12.803 718	.078 102 3119	.869 633	11.134 538	.089 810 6452	107.78	.077 728	7.77	12
1	1.149 910	12.803 718	.078 102 3119	.869 633	11.134 538	.089 810 6452	107.78	.077 728	7.77	12
2	1.322 293	27.526 845	.036 328 1740	.756 262	20.817 500	.048 036 5073	57.65	.152 876	7.64	24
3	1.520 519	44.457 118	.022 493 5860	.657 670	29.238 125	.034 201 9193	41.05	.231 269	7.71	36
4	1.748 460	63.925 411	.015 643 2313	.571 932	36.560 980	.027 351 5647	32.83	.312 875	7.82	48
5	2.010 572	86.312 201	.011 585 8475	.497 371	42.929 176	.023 294 1808	27.96	.397 651	7.95	60
6	2.311 977	112.054 999	.008 924 1891	.432 530	48.467 171	.020 632 5224	24.76	.485 542	8.09	72
7	2.658 566	141.656 905	.007 059 3100	.376 143	53.283 195	.018 767 6433	22.53	.576 482	8.24	84
8	3.057 112	175.696 438	.005 691 6350	.327 106	57.471 369	.017 399 9684	20.88	.670 397	8.38	96
9	3.515 405	214.838 845	.004 654 6517	.284 462	61.113 544	.016 362 9851	19.64	.767 202	8.52	108
10	4.042 400	259.849 098	.003 848 3874	.247 378	64.280 899	.015 556 7208	18.67	.866 806	8.67	120
11	4.648 397	311.606 847	.003 209 1721	.215 128	67.035 337	.014 917 5054	17.91	.969 111	8.81	132
12	5.345 239	371.123 610	.002 694 5200	.187 082	69.430 687	.014 402 8534	17.29	1.074 011	8.95	144
13	6.146 545	439.562 544	.002 274 9891	.162 693	71.513 762	.013 983 3224	16.78	1.181 398	9.09	156
14	7.067 975	518.261 172	.001 929 5291	.141 483	73.325 274	.013 637 8624	16.37	1.291 161	9.22	168
15	8.127 536	608.757 527	.001 642 6902	.123 039	74.900 625	.013 351 0235	16.03	1.403 184	9.35	180
16	9.345 937	712.820 209	.001 402 8783	.106 998	76.270 602	.013 111 2116	15.74	1.517 353	9.48	192
17	10.746 988	832.482 949	.001 201 2258	.093 049	77.461 979	.012 909 5591	15.50	1.633 550	9.61	204
18	12.358 071	970.084 354	.001 030 8382	.080 919	78.498 040	.012 739 1715	15.29	1.751 661	9.73	216
19	14.210 672	1128.313 613	.000 886 2784	.070 370	79.399 033	.012 594 6117	15.12	1.871 571	9.85	228
20	16.340 997	1310.263 053	.000 763 2055	.061 196	80.182 567	.012 471 5389	14.97	1.993 169	9.97	240
21	18.790 679	1519.488 570	.000 658 1162	.053 218	80.863 954	.012 366 4495	14.84	2.116 345	10.08	252
22	21.607 593	1760.079 126	.000 568 1563	.046 280	81.456 510	.012 276 4896	14.74	2.240 993	10.19	264
23	24.846 792	2036.736 661	.000 490 9815	.040 247	81.971 817	.012 199 3148	14.64	2.367 011	10.29	276
24	28.571 579	2354.867 983	.000 424 6523	.035 000	82.419 945	.012 132 9856	14.56	2.494 300	10.39	288
25	32.854 751	2720.690 436	.000 367 5538	.030 437	82.809 651	.012 075 8871	14.50	2.622 766	10.49	300
26	37.780 013	3141.353 406	.000 318 3341	.026 469	83.148 553	.012 026 6675	14.44	2.752 320	10.59	312
27	43.443 622	3625.078 048	.000 275 8561	.023 018	83.443 274	.011 984 1895	14.39	2.882 877	10.68	324
28	49.956 264	4181.317 947	.000 239 1590	.020 018	83.699 572	.011 947 4924	14.34	3.014 357	10.77	336
29	57.445 218	4820.943 883	.000 207 4283	.017 408	83.922 458	.011 915 7616	14.30	3.146 685	10.85	348
30	66.056 842	5556.456 271	.000 179 9708	.015 138	84.116 287	.011 888 3042	14.27	3.279 789	10.93	360
31	75.959 437	6402.229 470	.000 156 1956	.013 165	84.284 847	.011 864 5289	14.24	3.413 605	11.01	372
32	87.346 531	7374.792 699	.000 135 5970	.011 449	84.431 432	.011 843 9304	14.22	3.548 069	11.09	384
33	100.440 667	8493.153 079	.000 117 7419	.009 956	84.558 907	.011 826 0752	14.20	3.683 126	11.16	396
34	115.497 748	9779.167 089	.000 102 2582	.008 658	84.669 764	.011 810 5915	14.18	3.818 721	11.23	408
35	132.812 039	11257.967 718	.000 088 8260	.007 529	84.766 169	.011 797 1593	14.16	3.954 807	11.30	420
36	152.721 918	12958.455 648	.000 077 1697	.006 548	84.850 006	.011 785 5030	14.15	4.091 337	11.36	432
37	175.616 492	14913.864 067	.000 067 0517	.005 694	84.922 913	.011 775 3850	14.14	4.228 271	11.43	444
38	201.943 195	17162.408 156	.000 058 2669	.004 952	84.986 316	.011 766 6002	14.12	4.365 570	11.49	456
39	232.216 541	19748.031 944	.000 050 6380	.004 306	85.041 453	.011 758 9713	14.12	4.503 199	11.55	468
40	267.028 169	22721.267 115	.000 044 0116	.003 745	85.089 402	.011 752 3450	14.11	4.641 126	11.60	480
41	307.058 416	26140.220 570	.000 038 2552	.003 257	85.131 100	.011 746 5886	14.10	4.779 322	11.66	492
42	353.089 605	30071.710 027	.000 033 2538	.002 832	85.167 362	.011 741 5872	14.09	4.917 760	11.71	504
43	406.021 339	34592.569 862	.000 028 9079	.002 463	85.198 896	.011 737 2413	14.09	5.056 416	11.76	516
44	466.888 080	39791.152 707	.000 025 1312	.002 142	85.226 320	.011 733 4645	14.09	5.195 269	11.81	528
45	536.879 366	45769.056 155	.000 021 8488	.001 863	85.250 168	.011 730 1822	14.08	5.334 298	11.85	540
46	617.363 060	52643.108 315	.000 018 9958	.001 620	85.270 907	.011 727 3292	14.08	5.473 486	11.90	552
47	709.912 081	60547.651 020	.000 016 5159	.001 409	85.288 943	.011 724 8493	14.07	5.612 815	11.94	564
48	816.335 144	69637.165 318	.000 014 3601	.001 225	85.304 627	.011 722 6935	14.07	5.752 271	11.98	576
49	938.712 110	80089.290 537	.000 012 4861	.001 065	85.318 267	.011 720 8194	14.07	5.891 842	12.02	588
50	1079.434 632	92108.295 957	.000 010 8568	.000 926	85.330 129	.011 719 1901	14.07	6.031 514	12.06	600

Effective Rate is 14.99 %

Annual Percentage Rate is 14.05 %

MONTHLY COMPOUND INTEREST AND ANNUITY

high

14.10 % M

Amount Of 1	Amount Of 1 Per Period	Sinking Fund Payment	Present Worth Of 1	Present Worth of 1 Per Period	Periodic Payment To Amortize 1	Constant Annual Percent	Total Interest	Annual Add On Rate	
What a single $ 1 deposit grows to in the future. The deposit is made at the beginning of the first period.	What a series of $ 1 deposits grow to in the future. A deposit is made at the end of each period.	The amount to be deposited at the end of each period that grows to $ 1 in the future.	What $ 1 to be paid in the future is worth today. Value today of a single $ 1 payment tomorrow.	What $ 1 to be paid at the end of each period is worth today. Value today of a series of $ 1 payments tomorrow.	The mortgage payment to amortize a loan of $ 1. An annuity certain, payable at the end of each period, worth $ 1 today.	The annual payment, including interest and principal, to amortize completely a loan of $ 100.	The total interest paid over the term on a loan of $1. The loan is amortized by regular periodic payments.	The average annual interest rate on a loan that is completely amortized by regular periodic payments.	
$S = (1+i)^n$	$S\overline{n}| = \frac{(1+i)^n - 1}{i}$	$\frac{1}{S\overline{n}|} = \frac{i}{(1+i)^n - 1}$	$V^n = \frac{1}{(1+i)^n}$	$A\overline{n}| = \frac{1-V^n}{i}$	$\frac{1}{A\overline{n}|} = \frac{i}{1-V^n}$				

YEAR									PERIODS
	1.011 750	1.000 000	1.000 000 0000	.988 386	.988 386	1.011 750 0000	1214.10	.011 750	14.10	1
	1.023 638	2.011 750	.497 079 6570	.976 908	1.965 294	.508 829 6570	610.60	.017 659	10.60	2
	1.035 666	3.035 388	.329 447 1677	.965 562	2.930 857	.341 197 1677	409.44	.023 592	9.44	3
	1.047 835	4.071 054	.245 636 6414	.954 349	3.885 206	.257 386 6414	308.87	.029 547	8.86	4
	1.060 147	5.118 889	.195 354 8998	.943 265	4.828 471	.207 104 8998	248.53	.035 524	8.53	5
	1.072 604	6.179 036	.161 837 5502	.932 311	5.760 782	.173 587 5502	208.31	.041 525	8.31	6
	1.085 207	7.251 639	.137 899 8526	.921 483	6.682 265	.149 649 8526	179.58	.047 549	8.15	7
	1.097 958	8.336 846	.119 949 4370	.910 782	7.593 047	.131 699 4370	158.04	.053 595	8.04	8
	1.110 859	9.434 804	.105 990 5423	.900 204	8.493 251	.117 740 5423	141.29	.059 665	7.96	9
	1.123 912	10.545 663	.094 825 7116	.889 750	9.383 001	.106 575 7116	127.90	.065 757	7.89	10
	1.137 118	11.669 575	.085 692 9269	.879 417	10.262 418	.097 442 9269	116.94	.071 872	7.84	11
	1.150 479	12.806 692	.078 084 1762	.869 203	11.131 621	.089 834 1762	107.81	.078 010	7.80	12
1	1.150 479	12.806 692	.078 084 1762	.869 203	11.131 621	.089 834 1762	107.81	.078 010	7.80	12
2	1.323 601	27.540 518	.036 310 1382	.755 515	20.807 264	.048 060 1382	57.68	.153 443	7.67	24
3	1.522 775	44.491 469	.022 476 2189	.656 696	29.217 367	.034 226 2189	41.08	.232 144	7.74	36
4	1.751 920	63.993 177	.015 626 6661	.570 802	36.527 457	.027 376 6661	32.86	.314 080	7.85	48
5	2.015 546	86.429 474	.011 570 1271	.496 143	42.881 413	.023 320 1271	27.99	.399 208	7.98	60
6	2.318 843	112.241 955	.008 909 3245	.431 250	48.404 293	.020 659 3245	24.80	.487 471	8.12	72
7	2.667 779	141.938 663	.007 045 2967	.374 844	53.204 800	.018 795 2967	22.56	.578 805	8.27	84
8	3.069 223	176.104 091	.005 678 4598	.325 815	57.377 417	.017 428 4598	20.92	.673 132	8.41	96
9	3.531 076	215.410 686	.004 642 2952	.283 200	61.004 270	.016 392 2952	19.68	.770 368	8.56	108
10	4.062 427	260.632 083	.003 836 8262	.246 158	64.156 743	.015 586 8262	18.71	.870 419	8.70	120
11	4.673 735	312.658 335	.003 198 3795	.213 962	66.896 883	.014 948 3795	17.94	.973 186	8.85	132
12	5.377 033	372.513 425	.002 684 4670	.185 976	69.278 623	.014 434 4670	17.33	1.078 563	8.99	144
13	6.186 161	441.375 428	.002 265 6449	.161 651	71.348 839	.014 015 6449	16.82	1.186 441	9.13	156
14	7.117 046	520.599 690	.001 920 8617	.140 508	73.148 279	.013 670 8617	16.41	1.296 705	9.26	168
15	8.188 010	611.745 511	.001 634 6667	.122 130	74.712 357	.013 384 6667	16.07	1.409 240	9.39	180
16	9.420 130	716.606 831	.001 395 4653	.106 156	76.071 860	.013 145 4653	15.78	1.523 929	9.52	192
17	10.837 659	837.247 538	.001 194 3899	.092 271	77.253 544	.012 944 3899	15.54	1.640 656	9.65	204
18	12.468 495	976.042 094	.001 024 5460	.080 202	78.280 669	.012 774 5460	15.33	1.759 302	9.77	216
19	14.344 737	1135.722 265	.000 880 4970	.069 712	79.173 448	.012 630 4970	15.16	1.879 753	9.89	228
20	16.503 313	1319.430 890	.000 757 9025	.060 594	79.949 456	.012 507 9025	15.01	2.001 897	10.01	240
21	18.986 709	1530.783 737	.000 653 2601	.052 668	80.623 964	.012 403 2601	14.89	2.125 622	10.12	252
22	21.843 803	1773.940 671	.000 563 7167	.045 780	81.210 249	.012 313 7167	14.78	2.250 821	10.23	264
23	25.130 828	2053.687 528	.000 486 9290	.039 792	81.719 850	.012 236 9290	14.69	2.377 392	10.34	276
24	28.912 481	2375.530 309	.000 420 9586	.034 587	82.162 797	.012 170 9586	14.61	2.505 236	10.44	288
25	33.263 192	2745.803 551	.000 364 1921	.030 063	82.547 808	.012 114 1921	14.54	2.634 258	10.54	300
26	38.268 591	3171.795 005	.000 315 2789	.026 131	82.882 460	.012 065 2789	14.48	2.764 367	10.63	312
27	44.027 197	3661.889 069	.000 273 0831	.022 713	83.173 342	.012 023 0831	14.43	2.895 479	10.72	324
28	50.652 349	4225.731 818	.000 236 6454	.019 742	83.426 177	.011 986 6454	14.39	3.027 513	10.81	336
29	58.274 445	4874.420 852	.000 205 1526	.017 160	83.645 942	.011 955 1526	14.35	3.160 393	10.90	348
30	67.043 504	5620.723 725	.000 177 9130	.014 916	83.836 963	.011 927 9130	14.32	3.294 049	10.98	360
31	77.132 118	6479.329 232	.000 154 3370	.012 965	84.002 998	.011 904 3370	14.29	3.428 413	11.06	372
32	88.738 854	7467.136 521	.000 133 9201	.011 269	84.147 317	.011 883 9201	14.27	3.563 425	11.14	384
33	102.092 155	8603.587 700	.000 116 2306	.009 795	84.272 760	.011 866 2306	14.24	3.699 027	11.21	396
34	117.454 843	9911.050 497	.000 100 8975	.008 514	84.381 795	.011 850 8975	14.23	3.835 166	11.28	408
35	135.129 287	11415.258 507	.000 087 6020	.007 400	84.476 568	.011 837 6020	14.21	3.971 793	11.35	420
36	155.463 358	13145.817 680	.000 076 0698	.006 432	84.558 946	.011 826 0698	14.20	4.108 862	11.41	432
37	178.857 271	15136.789 029	.000 066 0642	.005 591	84.630 549	.011 816 0642	14.18	4.246 333	11.48	444
38	205.771 469	17427.359 023	.000 057 3810	.004 860	84.692 786	.011 807 3810	14.17	4.384 166	11.54	456
39	236.735 678	20062.610 856	.000 049 8440	.004 224	84.746 883	.011 799 8440	14.16	4.522 327	11.60	468
40	272.359 338	23094.411 778	.000 043 3005	.003 672	84.793 905	.011 793 3005	14.16	4.660 784	11.65	480
41	313.343 599	26582.433 955	.000 037 6188	.003 191	84.834 776	.011 787 6188	14.15	4.799 508	11.71	492
42	360.495 115	30595.328 936	.000 032 6847	.002 774	84.870 301	.011 782 6847	14.14	4.938 473	11.76	504
43	414.741 927	35212.078 864	.000 028 3993	.002 411	84.901 180	.011 778 3993	14.14	5.077 654	11.81	516
44	477.151 724	40523.551 003	.000 024 6770	.002 096	84.928 020	.011 774 6770	14.13	5.217 029	11.86	528
45	548.952 863	46634.286 203	.000 021 4435	.001 822	84.951 349	.011 771 4435	14.13	5.356 579	11.90	540
46	631.558 539	53664.556 474	.000 018 6343	.001 583	84.971 627	.011 768 6343	14.13	5.496 286	11.95	552
47	726.594 603	61752.732 197	.000 016 1936	.001 376	84.989 252	.011 766 1936	14.12	5.636 133	11.99	564
48	835.931 565	71058.005 535	.000 014 0730	.001 196	85.004 573	.011 764 0730	14.12	5.776 106	12.03	576
49	961.721 403	81763.523 673	.000 012 2304	.001 040	85.017 889	.011 762 2304	14.12	5.916 191	12.07	588
50	1106.439 924	94079.993 532	.000 010 6293	.000 904	85.029 464	.011 760 6293	14.12	6.056 378	12.11	600

Effective Rate is 15.05 %

Annual Percentage Rate is 14.10 %

	Amount Of 1	Amount Of 1 Per Period	Sinking Fund Payment	Present Worth Of 1	Present Worth of 1 Per Period	Periodic Payment To Amortize 1	Constant Annual Percent	Total Interest	Annual Add On Rate	
	What a single $ 1 deposit grows to in the future. The deposit is made at the beginning of the first period.	What a series of $ 1 deposits grow to in the future. A deposit is made at the end of each period.	The amount to be deposited at the end of each period that grows to $ 1 in the future.	What $ 1 to be paid in the future is worth today. Value today of a single $ 1 payment tomorrow.	What $ 1 to be paid at the end of each period is worth today. Value today of a series of $ 1 payments tomorrow.	The mortgage payment to amortize a loan of $ 1. An annuity certain, payable at the end of each period, worth $ 1 today.	The annual payment, including interest and principal, to amortize completely a loan of $ 100.	The total interest paid over the term on a loan of $1. The loan is amortized by regular periodic payments.	The average annual interest rate on a loan that is completely amortized by regular periodic payments.	
	$S = (1+i)^n$	$Sn] = \dfrac{(1+i)^n - 1}{i}$	$\dfrac{1}{Sn]} = \dfrac{i}{(1+i)^n - 1}$	$V^n = \dfrac{1}{(1+i)^n}$	$An] = \dfrac{1-V^n}{i}$	$\dfrac{1}{An]} = \dfrac{i}{1-V^n}$				

YEAR									**PERIODS**	
	1.011 771	1.000 000	1.000 000 0000	.988 366	.988 366	1.011 770 8333	1214.13	.011 771	14.13	1
	1.023 680	2.011 771	.497 074 5094	.976 868	1.965 234	.508 845 3427	610.62	.017 691	10.61	2
	1.035 730	3.035 451	.329 440 3312	.965 503	2.930 736	.341 211 1645	409.46	.023 633	9.45	3
	1.047 921	4.071 181	.245 628 9806	.954 270	3.885 007	.257 399 8140	308.88	.029 599	8.88	4
	1.060 256	5.119 102	.195 346 7608	.943 168	4.828 175	.207 117 5941	248.55	.035 588	8.54	5
	1.072 736	6.179 358	.161 829 1057	.932 196	5.760 371	.173 599 9391	208.32	.041 600	8.32	6
	1.085 363	7.252 094	.137 891 2015	.921 351	6.681 721	.149 662 0349	179.60	.047 634	8.17	7
	1.098 139	8.337 458	.119 940 6411	.910 632	7.592 353	.131 711 4745	158.06	.053 692	8.05	8
	1.111 065	9.435 596	.105 981 6427	.900 037	8.492 390	.117 752 4760	141.31	.059 772	7.97	9
	1.124 143	10.546 661	.094 816 7371	.889 567	9.381 957	.106 587 5705	127.91	.065 876	7.91	10
	1.137 375	11.670 804	.085 683 8986	.879 217	10.261 174	.097 454 7319	116.95	.072 002	7.85	11
	1.150 763	12.808 179	.078 075 1097	.868 989	11.130 163	.089 845 9430	107.82	.078 151	7.82	12
1	1.150 763	12.808 179	.078 075 1097	.868 989	11.130 163	.089 845 9430	107.82	.078 151	7.82	12
2	1.324 255	27.547 357	.036 301 1228	.755 141	20.802 149	.048 071 9561	57.69	.153 727	7.69	24
3	1.523 904	44.508 657	.022 467 5392	.656 209	29.206 996	.034 238 3725	41.09	.232 581	7.75	36
4	1.753 652	64.027 093	.015 618 3884	.570 238	36.510 713	.027 389 2217	32.87	.314 683	7.87	48
5	2.018 038	86.488 185	.011 562 2729	.495 531	42.857 560	.023 333 1063	28.00	.399 986	8.00	60
6	2.322 283	112.335 577	.008 901 8993	.430 611	48.372 899	.020 672 7327	24.81	.488 437	8.14	72
7	2.672 398	142.079 799	.007 038 2982	.374 196	53.165 666	.018 809 1316	22.58	.579 967	8.29	84
8	3.075 296	176.308 347	.005 671 8812	.325 172	57.330 526	.017 442 7145	20.94	.674 501	8.43	96
9	3.538 937	215.697 291	.004 636 1268	.282 571	60.949 743	.016 406 9602	19.69	.771 952	8.58	108
10	4.072 477	261.024 629	.003 831 0561	.245 551	64.094 801	.015 601 8894	18.73	.872 227	8.72	120
11	4.686 456	313.185 650	.003 192 9943	.213 381	66.827 821	.014 963 8277	17.96	.975 225	8.87	132
12	5.393 000	373.210 619	.002 679 4522	.185 426	69.202 785	.014 450 2855	17.35	1.080 841	9.01	144
13	6.206 065	442.285 130	.002 260 9849	.161 133	71.266 602	.014 031 8182	16.84	1.188 964	9.15	156
14	7.141 709	521.773 517	.001 916 5404	.140 023	73.060 035	.013 687 3737	16.43	1.299 479	9.28	168
15	8.218 414	613.245 808	.001 630 6675	.121 678	74.618 508	.013 401 5008	16.09	1.412 270	9.42	180
16	9.457 447	718.508 730	.001 391 7715	.105 737	75.972 804	.013 162 6049	15.80	1.527 220	9.55	192
17	10.883 279	839.641 400	.001 190 9846	.091 884	77.149 672	.012 961 8180	15.56	1.644 211	9.67	204
18	12.524 074	979.036 388	.001 021 4125	.079 846	78.172 356	.012 792 2458	15.36	1.763 125	9.80	216
19	14.412 240	1139.446 975	.000 877 6187	.069 385	79.061 058	.012 648 4521	15.18	1.883 847	9.91	228
20	16.585 072	1324.041 534	.000 755 2633	.060 295	79.833 329	.012 526 0966	15.04	2.006 263	10.03	240
21	19.085 487	1536.466 112	.000 650 8442	.052 396	80.504 425	.012 421 6775	14.91	2.130 263	10.14	252
22	21.962 871	1780.916 445	.000 561 5087	.045 531	81.087 599	.012 332 3420	14.80	2.255 738	10.25	264
23	25.274 058	2062.220 829	.000 484 9141	.039 566	81.594 371	.012 255 7475	14.71	2.382 586	10.36	276
24	29.084 449	2385.935 490	.000 419 1228	.034 383	82.034 750	.012 189 9561	14.63	2.510 707	10.46	288
25	33.469 306	2758.454 326	.000 362 5219	.029 878	82.417 434	.012 133 3552	14.57	2.640 007	10.56	300
26	38.515 237	3187.135 199	.000 313 7614	.025 964	82.749 982	.012 084 5947	14.51	2.770 394	10.66	312
27	44.321 908	3680.445 261	.000 271 7063	.022 562	83.038 963	.012 042 5396	14.46	2.901 783	10.75	324
28	51.004 009	4248.128 200	.000 235 3978	.019 606	83.290 084	.012 006 2311	14.41	3.034 094	10.84	336
29	58.693 524	4901.396 691	.000 204 0235	.017 038	83.508 305	.011 974 8568	14.37	3.167 250	10.92	348
30	67.542 332	5653.153 861	.000 176 8924	.014 806	83.697 937	.011 947 7257	14.34	3.301 181	11.00	360
31	77.725 213	6518.248 156	.000 153 4155	.012 866	83.862 725	.011 924 2488	14.31	3.435 821	11.08	372
32	89.443 294	7513.766 612	.000 133 0890	.011 180	84.005 924	.011 903 9224	14.29	3.571 106	11.16	384
33	102.928 029	8659.372 361	.000 115 4818	.009 716	84.130 362	.011 886 3151	14.27	3.706 981	11.23	396
34	118.445 761	9977.693 004	.000 100 2236	.008 443	84.238 498	.011 871 0569	14.25	3.843 391	11.30	408
35	136.302 993	11494.767 548	.000 086 9961	.007 337	84.332 466	.011 857 8294	14.23	3.980 288	11.37	420
36	156.852 433	13240.560 716	.000 075 5255	.006 375	84.414 124	.011 846 3588	14.22	4.117 627	11.44	432
37	180.499 968	15249.554 799	.000 065 5757	.005 540	84.485 083	.011 836 4090	14.21	4.255 366	11.50	444
38	207.712 674	17561.430 744	.000 056 9430	.004 814	84.546 746	.011 827 7763	14.20	4.393 466	11.56	456
39	239.028 049	20221.851 911	.000 049 4515	.004 184	84.600 331	.011 820 2848	14.19	4.531 893	11.62	468
40	275.064 621	23283.366 003	.000 042 9491	.003 636	84.646 682	.011 813 7824	14.18	4.670 616	11.68	480
41	316.534 172	26806.442 970	.000 037 3045	.003 159	84.687 359	.011 808 1378	14.17	4.809 604	11.73	492
42	364.255 796	30860.669 391	.000 032 4037	.002 745	84.722 521	.011 803 2370	14.17	4.948 831	11.78	504
43	419.172 072	35526.122 920	.000 028 1483	.002 386	84.753 077	.011 798 9816	14.16	5.088 275	11.83	516
44	482.367 687	40894.953 955	.000 024 4529	.002 073	84.779 630	.011 795 2862	14.16	5.227 911	11.88	528
45	555.090 859	47073.205 758	.000 021 2435	.001 802	84.802 704	.011 792 0768	14.16	5.367 721	11.93	540
46	638.777 991	54182.908 988	.000 018 4560	.001 565	84.822 755	.011 789 2893	14.15	5.507 688	11.97	552
47	735.082 041	62364.492 002	.000 016 0348	.001 360	84.840 179	.011 786 8681	14.15	5.647 794	12.02	564
48	845.905 173	71779.554 553	.000 013 9315	.001 182	84.855 320	.011 784 7649	14.15	5.788 025	12.06	576
49	973.436 327	82614.059 645	.000 012 1045	.001 027	84.868 478	.011 782 9378	14.14	5.928 367	12.10	588
50	1120.194 453	95082.006 614	.000 010 5172	.000 893	84.879 912	.011 781 3506	14.14	6.068 810	12.14	600

MONTHLY COMPOUND INTEREST AND ANNUITY

	Amount Of 1	Amount Of 1 Per Period	Sinking Fund Payment	Present Worth Of 1	Present Worth of 1 Per Period	Periodic Payment To Amortize 1	Constant Annual Percent	Total Interest	Annual Add On Rate	
	What a single $ 1 deposit grows to in the future. The deposit is made at the beginning of the first period.	What a series of $ 1 deposits grow to in the future. A deposit is made at the end of each period.	The amount to be deposited at the end of each period that grows to $ 1 in the future.	What $ 1 to be paid in the future is worth today. Value today of a single $ 1 payment tomorrow.	What $ 1 to be paid at the end of each period is worth today. Value today of a series of $ 1 payments tomorrow.	The mortgage payment to amortize a loan of $ 1. An annuity certain, payable at the end of each period, worth $ 1 today.	The annual payment, including interest and principal, to amortize completely a loan of $ 100.	The total interest paid over the term on a loan of $1. The loan is amortized by regular periodic payments.	The average annual interest rate on a loan that is completely amortized by regular periodic payments.	
	$S = (1+i)^n$	$S\overline{n}| = \dfrac{(1+i)^n - 1}{i}$	$\dfrac{1}{S\overline{n}|} = \dfrac{i}{(1+i)^n - 1}$	$V^n = \dfrac{1}{(1+i)^n}$	$A\overline{n}| = \dfrac{1-V^n}{i}$	$\dfrac{1}{A\overline{n}|} = \dfrac{i}{1-V^n}$				

YEAR										PERIODS
	1.011 792	1.000 000	1.000 000 0000	.988 346	.988 346	1.011 791 6667	1214.15	.011 792	14.15	1
	1.023 722	2.011 792	.497 069 3619	.976 827	1.965 173	.508 861 0286	610.64	.017 722	10.63	2
	1.035 794	3.035 514	.329 433 4949	.965 443	2.930 616	.341 225 1615	409.48	.023 675	9.47	3
	1.048 008	4.071 308	.245 621 3202	.954 192	3.884 808	.257 412 9869	308.90	.029 652	8.90	4
	1.060 365	5.119 315	.195 338 6220	.943 071	4.827 879	.207 130 2887	248.56	.035 651	8.56	5
	1.072 869	6.179 681	.161 820 6617	.932 080	5.759 960	.173 612 3283	208.34	.041 674	8.33	6
	1.085 520	7.252 549	.137 882 5510	.921 218	6.681 177	.149 674 2176	179.61	.047 720	8.18	7
	1.098 320	8.338 069	.119 931 8458	.910 482	7.591 659	.131 723 5124	158.07	.053 788	8.07	8
	1.111 271	9.436 389	.105 972 7437	.899 871	8.491 530	.117 764 4104	141.32	.059 880	7.98	9
	1.124 374	10.547 659	.094 807 7634	.889 383	9.380 913	.106 599 4301	127.92	.065 994	7.92	10
	1.137 633	11.672 034	.085 674 8710	.879 018	10.259 932	.097 466 5376	116.96	.072 132	7.87	11
	1.151 047	12.809 667	.078 066 0440	.868 774	11.128 706	.089 857 7106	107.83	.078 293	7.83	12
1	1.151 047	12.809 667	.078 066 0440	.868 774	11.128 706	.089 857 7106	107.83	.078 293	7.83	12
2	1.324 910	27.554 199	.036 292 1091	.754 768	20.797 036	.048 083 7758	57.71	.154 011	7.70	24
3	1.525 034	44.525 854	.022 458 8619	.655 723	29.196 630	.034 250 5286	41.11	.233 019	7.77	36
4	1.755 386	64.061 031	.015 610 1140	.569 675	36.493 979	.027 401 7807	32.89	.315 285	7.88	48
5	2.020 533	86.546 945	.011 554 4229	.494 919	42.833 726	.023 346 0896	28.02	.400 765	8.02	60
6	2.325 729	112.429 296	.008 894 4789	.429 973	48.341 533	.020 686 1456	24.83	.489 402	8.16	72
7	2.677 024	142.221 106	.007 031 3052	.373 549	53.126 574	.018 822 9719	22.59	.581 130	8.30	84
8	3.081 381	176.512 889	.005 665 3087	.324 530	57.283 692	.017 456 9753	20.95	.675 870	8.45	96
9	3.546 816	215.984 355	.004 629 9650	.281 943	60.895 289	.016 421 6317	19.71	.773 536	8.59	108
10	4.082 552	261.417 879	.003 825 2931	.244 945	64.032 950	.015 616 9597	18.75	.874 035	8.74	120
11	4.699 211	313.714 016	.003 187 6166	.212 802	66.758 868	.014 979 2833	17.98	.977 265	8.88	132
12	5.409 014	373.909 343	.002 674 4451	.184 877	69.127 076	.014 466 1117	17.36	1.083 120	9.03	144
13	6.226 031	443.197 014	.002 256 3329	.160 616	71.184 512	.014 047 9996	16.86	1.191 488	9.17	156
14	7.166 457	522.950 401	.001 912 2272	.139 539	72.971 960	.013 703 8939	16.45	1.302 254	9.30	168
15	8.248 931	614.750 324	.001 626 6767	.121 228	74.524 848	.013 418 3433	16.11	1.415 302	9.44	180
16	9.494 910	720.416 380	.001 388 0862	.105 320	75.873 957	.013 179 7528	15.82	1.530 513	9.57	192
17	10.929 090	842.043 009	.001 187 5878	.091 499	77.046 028	.012 979 2545	15.58	1.647 768	9.69	204
18	12.579 900	982.041 015	.001 018 2874	.079 492	78.064 292	.012 809 9541	15.38	1.766 950	9.82	216
19	14.480 061	1143.185 344	.000 874 7488	.069 060	78.948 934	.012 666 4155	15.20	1.887 943	9.94	228
20	16.667 235	1328.670 003	.000 752 6323	.059 998	79.717 488	.012 544 2989	15.06	2.010 632	10.05	240
21	19.184 776	1542.171 815	.000 648 4362	.052 125	80.385 188	.012 440 1028	14.93	2.134 906	10.17	252
22	22.082 585	1787.922 400	.000 559 3084	.045 285	80.965 268	.012 350 9751	14.83	2.260 657	10.28	264
23	25.418 100	2070.792 953	.000 482 9068	.039 342	81.469 226	.012 274 5735	14.73	2.387 782	10.38	276
24	29.257 436	2396.390 343	.000 417 2943	.034 179	81.907 052	.012 208 9610	14.66	2.516 181	10.48	288
25	33.676 693	2771.168 347	.000 360 8586	.029 694	82.287 424	.012 152 5253	14.59	2.645 758	10.58	300
26	38.763 468	3202.555 564	.000 312 2506	.025 797	82.617 881	.012 103 9173	14.53	2.776 422	10.68	312
27	44.618 586	3699.102 664	.000 270 3358	.022 412	82.904 974	.012 062 0025	14.48	2.908 089	10.77	324
28	51.358 103	4270.651 871	.000 234 1563	.019 471	83.154 392	.012 025 8230	14.44	3.040 677	10.86	336
29	59.115 607	4928.532 055	.000 202 9002	.016 916	83.371 081	.011 994 5668	14.40	3.174 109	10.95	348
30	68.044 861	5685.783 276	.000 175 8773	.014 696	83.559 334	.011 967 5439	14.37	3.308 316	11.03	360
31	78.322 855	6557.415 265	.000 152 4991	.012 768	83.722 884	.011 944 1658	14.34	3.443 230	11.11	372
32	90.153 312	7560.704 929	.000 132 2628	.011 092	83.864 971	.011 923 9295	14.31	3.578 789	11.18	384
33	103.770 728	8715.538 806	.000 114 7376	.009 637	83.988 413	.011 906 4043	14.29	3.714 936	11.26	396
34	119.445 019	10044.807 246	.000 099 5539	.008 372	84.095 656	.011 891 2206	14.27	3.851 618	11.33	408
35	137.486 869	11574.858 120	.000 086 3941	.007 273	84.188 826	.011 878 0608	14.26	3.988 786	11.40	420
36	158.253 892	13336.019 076	.000 074 9849	.006 319	84.269 770	.011 866 6516	14.24	4.126 393	11.46	432
37	182.157 718	15363.198 674	.000 065 0906	.005 490	84.340 092	.011 856 7573	14.23	4.264 400	11.53	444
38	209.672 153	17696.578 316	.000 056 5081	.004 769	84.401 186	.011 848 1748	14.22	4.402 768	11.59	456
39	241.342 569	20382.408 697	.000 049 0619	.004 143	84.454 263	.011 840 7286	14.21	4.541 461	11.64	468
40	277.796 717	23473.926 558	.000 042 6005	.003 600	84.500 374	.011 834 2671	14.21	4.680 448	11.70	480
41	319.757 167	27032.409 904	.000 036 9926	.003 127	84.540 435	.011 828 6593	14.20	4.819 700	11.76	492
42	368.055 630	31128.392 620	.000 032 1250	.002 717	84.575 238	.011 823 7917	14.19	4.959 191	11.81	504
43	423.649 446	35843.062 546	.000 027 8994	.002 360	84.605 475	.011 819 5661	14.19	5.098 896	11.86	516
44	487.640 559	41269.870 724	.000 024 2308	.002 051	84.631 744	.011 815 8974	14.18	5.238 794	11.91	528
45	561.297 358	47516.383 731	.000 021 0454	.001 782	84.654 565	.011 812 7120	14.18	5.378 865	11.95	540
46	646.079 819	54706.415 782	.000 018 2794	.001 548	84.674 392	.011 809 9461	14.18	5.519 090	12.00	552
47	743.668 444	62982.482 899	.000 015 8771	.001 345	84.691 617	.011 807 5441	14.17	5.659 455	12.04	564
48	855.997 569	72508.627 769	.000 013 7915	.001 168	84.706 581	.011 805 4581	14.17	5.799 944	12.08	576
49	985.293 707	83473.671 284	.000 011 9798	.001 015	84.719 582	.011 803 6465	14.17	5.940 544	12.12	588
50	1134.119 680	96094.955 228	.000 010 4064	.000 882	84.730 877	.011 802 0730	14.17	6.081 244	12.16	600

Effective Rate is 15.10 %

Annual Percentage Rate is 14.15 %

	Amount Of 1	Amount Of 1 Per Period	Sinking Fund Payment	Present Worth Of 1	Present Worth of 1 Per Period	Periodic Payment To Amortize 1	Constant Annual Percent	Total Interest	Annual Add On Rate
	What a single $1 deposit grows to in the future. The deposit is made at the beginning of the first period.	What a series of $1 deposits grow to in the future. A deposit is made at the end of each period.	The amount to be deposited at the end of each period that grows to $1 in the future.	What $1 to be paid in the future is worth today. Value today of a single $1 payment tomorrow.	What $1 to be paid at the end of each period is worth today. Value today of a series of $1 payments tomorrow.	The mortgage payment to amortize a loan of $1. An annuity certain, payable at the end of each period, worth $1 today.	The annual payment, including interest and principal, to amortize completely a loan of $100.	The total interest paid over the term on a loan of $1. The loan is amortized by regular periodic payments.	The average annual interest rate on a loan that is completely amortized by regular periodic payments.

$$S = (1+i)^n \qquad S\overline{n}| = \frac{(1+i)^n - 1}{i} \qquad \frac{1}{S\overline{n}|} = \frac{i}{(1+i)^n - 1} \qquad V^n = \frac{1}{(1+i)^n} \qquad A\overline{n}| = \frac{1-V^n}{i} \qquad \frac{1}{A\overline{n}|} = \frac{i}{1-V^n}$$

PERIODS

YEAR	Amount Of 1	Amount Of 1 Per Period	Sinking Fund Payment	Present Worth Of 1	Present Worth of 1 Per Period	Periodic Payment To Amortize 1	Constant Annual Percent	Total Interest	Annual Add On Rate	PERIODS
	1.011 833	1.000 000	1.000 000 0000	.988 305	.988 305	1.011 833 3333	1214.20	.011 833	14.20	1
	1.023 807	2.011 833	.497 059 0672	.976 747	1.965 052	.508 892 4005	610.68	.017 785	10.67	2
	1.035 922	3.035 640	.329 419 8228	.965 324	2.930 376	.341 253 1561	409.51	.023 759	9.50	3
	1.048 180	4.071 562	.245 606 0001	.954 034	3.884 410	.257 439 3334	308.93	.029 757	8.93	4
	1.060 584	5.119 742	.195 322 3456	.942 877	4.827 287	.207 155 6790	248.59	.035 778	8.59	5
	1.073 134	6.180 326	.161 803 7748	.931 850	5.759 138	.173 637 1081	208.37	.041 823	8.36	6
	1.085 833	7.253 459	.137 865 2513	.920 952	6.680 090	.149 698 5846	179.64	.047 890	8.21	7
	1.098 682	8.339 292	.119 914 2568	.910 182	7.590 272	.131 747 5901	158.10	.053 981	8.10	8
	1.111 683	9.437 974	.105 954 9477	.899 537	8.489 809	.117 788 2811	141.35	.060 095	8.01	9
	1.124 838	10.549 656	.094 789 8180	.889 017	9.378 826	.106 623 1513	127.95	.066 232	7.95	10
	1.138 148	11.674 494	.085 656 8181	.878 620	10.257 446	.097 490 1515	116.99	.072 392	7.90	11
	1.151 616	12.812 642	.078 047 9151	.868 345	11.125 791	.089 881 2484	107.86	.078 575	7.86	12
1	1.151 616	12.812 642	.078 047 9151	.868 345	11.125 791	.089 881 2484	107.86	.078 575	7.86	12
2	1.326 220	27.567 889	.036 274 0868	.754 023	20.786 814	.048 107 4201	57.73	.154 578	7.73	24
3	1.527 297	44.560 271	.022 441 5150	.654 752	29.175 913	.034 274 8483	41.13	.233 895	7.80	36
4	1.758 860	64.128 975	.015 593 5752	.568 550	36.460 544	.027 426 9085	32.92	.316 492	7.91	48
5	2.025 531	86.664 613	.011 538 7349	.493 698	42.786 115	.023 372 0683	28.05	.402 324	8.05	60
6	2.332 635	112.617 020	.008 879 6525	.428 700	48.278 892	.020 712 9858	24.86	.491 335	8.19	72
7	2.686 300	142.504 234	.007 017 3353	.372 259	53.048 516	.018 850 6687	22.63	.583 456	8.34	84
8	3.093 587	176.922 836	.005 652 1816	.323 249	57.190 194	.017 485 5149	20.99	.678 609	8.48	96
9	3.562 625	216.559 858	.004 617 6610	.280 692	60.786 599	.016 450 9943	19.75	.776 707	8.63	108
10	4.102 777	262.206 496	.003 813 7880	.243 737	63.909 519	.015 647 1214	18.78	.877 655	8.78	120
11	4.724 825	314.773 908	.003 176 8834	.211 648	66.621 290	.015 010 2167	18.02	.981 349	8.92	132
12	5.441 185	375.311 394	.002 664 4541	.183 784	68.976 042	.014 497 7875	17.40	1.087 681	9.06	144
13	6.266 157	445.027 348	.002 247 0529	.159 587	71.020 779	.014 080 3863	16.90	1.196 540	9.20	156
14	7.216 208	525.313 374	.001 903 6256	.138 577	72.796 316	.013 736 9590	16.49	1.307 809	9.34	168
15	8.310 303	617.772 067	.001 618 7200	.120 333	74.338 094	.013 452 0533	16.15	1.421 370	9.48	180
16	9.570 280	724.249 002	.001 380 7406	.104 490	75.676 889	.013 214 0739	15.86	1.537 102	9.61	192
17	11.021 290	846.869 573	.001 180 8194	.090 733	76.839 424	.013 014 1527	15.62	1.654 887	9.73	204
18	12.692 297	988.081 416	.001 012 0624	.078 788	77.848 906	.012 845 3957	15.42	1.774 605	9.86	216
19	14.616 655	1150.703 271	.000 869 0338	.068 415	78.725 484	.012 702 3671	15.25	1.896 140	9.98	228
20	16.832 778	1337.981 245	.000 747 3946	.059 408	79.486 656	.012 580 7280	15.10	2.019 375	10.10	240
21	19.384 901	1553.653 605	.000 643 6441	.051 587	80.147 616	.012 476 9774	14.98	2.144 198	10.21	252
22	22.323 967	1802.025 403	.000 554 9311	.044 795	80.721 557	.012 388 2645	14.87	2.270 502	10.32	264
23	25.708 644	2088.054 406	.000 478 9147	.038 897	81.219 936	.012 312 2481	14.78	2.398 180	10.43	276
24	29.606 492	2417.450 057	.000 413 6590	.033 776	81.652 701	.012 246 9923	14.70	2.527 134	10.53	288
25	34.095 318	2796.787 446	.000 357 5531	.029 330	82.028 490	.012 190 8864	14.63	2.657 266	10.63	300
26	39.264 723	3233.638 553	.000 309 2492	.025 468	82.354 804	.012 142 5825	14.58	2.788 486	10.72	312
27	45.217 893	3736.723 393	.000 267 6141	.022 115	82.638 157	.012 100 9475	14.53	2.920 707	10.82	324
28	52.073 662	4316.084 078	.000 231 6915	.019 204	82.884 206	.012 065 0248	14.48	3.053 848	10.91	336
29	59.968 876	4983.285 265	.000 200 6708	.016 675	83.097 861	.012 034 0042	14.45	3.187 833	10.99	348
30	69.061 133	5751.645 004	.000 173 8633	.014 480	83.283 387	.012 007 1966	14.41	3.322 591	11.08	360
31	79.531 923	6636.500 576	.000 150 6818	.012 574	83.444 487	.011 984 0152	14.39	3.458 054	11.16	372
32	91.590 257	7655.514 645	.000 130 6248	.010 918	83.584 378	.011 963 9581	14.36	3.594 160	11.23	384
33	105.476 829	8829.027 820	.000 113 2628	.009 481	83.705 852	.011 946 5961	14.34	3.730 852	11.31	396
34	121.468 832	10180.464 680	.000 098 2273	.008 233	83.811 333	.011 931 5607	14.32	3.868 077	11.38	408
35	139.885 483	11736.801 347	.000 085 2021	.007 149	83.902 926	.011 918 5354	14.31	4.005 785	11.45	420
36	161.094 397	13529.103 966	.000 073 9147	.006 208	83.982 461	.011 907 2481	14.29	4.143 931	11.51	432
37	185.518 928	15593.148 814	.000 064 1307	.005 390	84.051 525	.011 897 4641	14.28	4.282 474	11.57	444
38	213.646 614	17970.136 431	.000 055 6479	.004 681	84.111 496	.011 888 9812	14.27	4.421 375	11.64	456
39	246.038 916	20707.514 031	.000 048 2916	.004 064	84.163 502	.011 881 6250	14.26	4.560 600	11.69	468
40	283.342 417	23859.922 597	.000 041 9113	.003 529	84.208 792	.011 875 2446	14.26	4.700 117	11.75	480
41	326.301 736	27490.287 575	.000 036 3765	.003 065	84.248 058	.011 869 7098	14.25	4.839 897	11.80	492
42	375.774 387	31671.074 929	.000 031 5746	.002 661	84.282 155	.011 864 9079	14.24	4.979 914	11.86	504
43	432.747 895	36485.737 644	.000 027 4080	.002 311	84.311 762	.011 860 7413	14.24	5.120 143	11.91	516
44	498.359 515	42030.381 535	.000 023 7923	.002 007	84.337 472	.011 857 1256	14.23	5.260 562	11.96	528
45	573.918 923	48415.683 620	.000 020 6545	.001 742	84.359 797	.011 853 9878	14.23	5.401 153	12.00	540
46	660.934 366	55769.101 355	.000 017 9311	.001 513	84.379 182	.011 851 2644	14.23	5.541 898	12.05	552
47	761.142 766	64237.416 819	.000 015 5673	.001 314	84.396 016	.011 848 9006	14.22	5.682 780	12.09	564
48	876.544 389	73989.666 640	.000 013 5154	.001 141	84.410 633	.011 846 8487	14.22	5.823 785	12.13	576
49	1009.442 774	85220.516 149	.000 011 7343	.000 991	84.423 326	.011 845 0676	14.22	5.964 900	12.17	588
50	1162.490 717	98154.145 108	.000 010 1881	.000 860	84.434 347	.011 843 5214	14.22	6.106 113	12.21	600

MONTHLY COMPOUND INTEREST AND ANNUITY

14.25 % M

Amount Of 1	Amount Of 1 Per Period	Sinking Fund Payment	Present Worth Of 1	Present Worth of 1 Per Period	Periodic Payment To Amortize 1	Constant Annual Percent	Total Interest	Annual Add On Rate
What a single $ 1 deposit grows to in the future. The deposit is made at the beginning of the first period.	What a series of $ 1 deposits grow to in the future. A deposit is made at the end of each period.	The amount to be deposited at the end of each period that grows to $ 1 in the future.	What $ 1 to be paid in the future is worth today. Value today of a single $ 1 payment tomorrow.	What $ 1 to be paid at the end of each period is worth today. Value today of a series of $ 1 payments tomorrow.	The mortgage payment to amortize a loan of $ 1. An annuity certain, payable at the end of each period, worth $ 1 today.	The annual payment, including interest and principal, to amortize completely a loan of $ 100.	The total interest paid over the term on a loan of $1. The loan is amortized by regular periodic payments.	The average annual interest rate on a loan that is completely amortized by regular periodic payments.
$S = (1+i)^n$	$S\overline{n} = \dfrac{(1+i)^n - 1}{i}$	$\dfrac{1}{S\overline{n}} = \dfrac{i}{(1+i)^n - 1}$	$V^n = \dfrac{1}{(1+i)^n}$	$A\overline{n} = \dfrac{1-V^n}{i}$	$\dfrac{1}{A\overline{n}} = \dfrac{i}{1-V^n}$			

YEAR / **PERIODS**

Amount Of 1	Amount Of 1 Per Period	Sinking Fund Payment	Present Worth Of 1	Present Worth of 1 Per Period	Periodic Payment To Amortize 1	Constant Annual Percent	Total Interest	Annual Add On Rate	PERIODS
1.011 875	1.000 000	1.000 000 0000	.988 264	.988 264	1.011 875 0000	1214.25	.011 875	14.25	1
1.023 891	2.011 875	.497 048 7729	.976 666	1.964 931	.508 923 7729	610.71	.017 848	10.71	2
1.036 050	3.035 766	.329 406 1515	.965 205	2.930 135	.341 281 1515	409.54	.023 843	9.54	3
1.048 353	4.071 816	.245 590 6811	.953 877	3.884 013	.257 465 6811	308.96	.029 863	8.96	4
1.060 802	5.120 169	.195 306 0706	.942 683	4.826 696	.207 181 0706	248.62	.035 905	8.62	5
1.073 399	6.180 971	.161 786 8896	.931 620	5.758 316	.173 661 8896	208.40	.041 971	8.39	6
1.086 146	7.254 370	.137 847 9535	.920 687	6.679 003	.149 722 9535	179.67	.048 061	8.24	7
1.099 044	8.340 515	.119 896 6700	.909 882	7.588 885	.131 771 6700	158.13	.054 173	8.13	8
1.112 095	9.439 559	.105 937 1542	.899 204	8.488 089	.117 812 1542	141.38	.060 309	8.04	9
1.125 301	10.551 654	.094 771 8754	.888 651	9.376 740	.106 646 8754	127.98	.066 469	7.98	10
1.138 664	11.676 954	.085 638 7684	.878 222	10.254 962	.097 513 7684	117.02	.072 651	7.93	11
1.152 185	12.815 618	.078 029 7895	.867 916	11.122 878	.089 904 7895	107.89	.078 857	7.89	12

YEAR	Amount Of 1	Amount Of 1 Per Period	Sinking Fund Payment	Present Worth Of 1	Present Worth of 1 Per Period	Periodic Payment To Amortize 1	Constant Annual Percent	Total Interest	Annual Add On Rate	PERIODS
1	1.152 185	12.815 618	.078 029 7895	.867 916	11.122 878	.089 904 7895	107.89	.078 857	7.89	12
2	1.327 531	27.581 587	.036 256 0712	.753 278	20.776 600	.048 131 0712	57.76	.155 146	7.76	24
3	1.529 562	44.594 723	.022 424 1781	.653 782	29.155 218	.034 299 1781	41.16	.234 770	7.83	36
4	1.762 339	64.197 010	.015 577 0496	.567 428	36.427 153	.027 452 0496	32.95	.317 698	7.94	48
5	2.030 542	86.782 480	.011 523 0632	.492 479	42.738 580	.023 398 0632	28.08	.403 884	8.08	60
6	2.339 561	112.805 130	.008 864 8450	.427 431	48.216 368	.020 739 8450	24.89	.493 269	8.22	72
7	2.695 608	142.788 050	.007 003 3872	.370 974	52.970 627	.018 878 3872	22.66	.585 785	8.37	84
8	3.105 840	177.333 935	.005 639 0786	.321 974	57.096 923	.017 514 0786	21.02	.681 352	8.52	96
9	3.578 504	217.137 201	.004 605 3831	.279 446	60.678 201	.016 480 3831	19.78	.779 881	8.67	108
10	4.123 101	262.997 946	.003 802 3111	.242 536	63.786 449	.015 677 3111	18.82	.881 277	8.81	120
11	4.750 577	315.838 029	.003 166 1798	.210 501	66.484 146	.015 041 1798	18.05	.985 436	8.96	132
12	5.473 545	376.719 606	.002 654 4942	.182 697	68.825 521	.014 529 4942	17.44	1.092 247	9.10	144
13	6.306 539	446.866 473	.002 237 8049	.158 566	70.857 636	.014 112 8049	16.94	1.201 598	9.24	156
14	7.266 303	527.688 675	.001 895 0568	.137 622	72.621 342	.013 770 0568	16.53	1.313 370	9.38	168
15	8.372 129	620.810 841	.001 610 7966	.119 444	74.152 090	.013 485 7966	16.19	1.427 443	9.52	180
16	9.646 245	728.104 847	.001 373 4286	.103 667	75.480 650	.013 248 4286	15.90	1.543 698	9.65	192
17	11.114 263	851.727 442	.001 174 0845	.089 974	76.633 729	.013 049 0845	15.66	1.662 013	9.78	204
18	12.805 693	994.163 599	.001 005 8707	.078 090	77.634 504	.012 880 8707	15.46	1.782 268	9.90	216
19	14.754 533	1158.276 469	.000 863 3517	.067 776	78.503 092	.012 738 3517	15.29	1.904 344	10.02	228
20	16.999 959	1347.364 934	.000 742 1894	.058 824	79.256 954	.012 617 1894	15.15	2.028 125	10.14	240
21	19.587 105	1565.229 914	.000 638 8838	.051 054	79.911 242	.012 513 8838	15.02	2.153 499	10.25	252
22	22.567 978	1816.250 779	.000 550 5848	.044 311	80.479 110	.012 425 5848	14.92	2.280 354	10.37	264
23	26.002 496	2105.473 371	.000 474 9526	.038 458	80.971 971	.012 349 9526	14.82	2.408 587	10.47	276
24	29.959 698	2438.711 438	.000 410 0526	.033 378	81.399 733	.012 285 0526	14.75	2.538 095	10.58	288
25	34.519 129	2822.663 497	.000 354 2753	.028 969	81.770 994	.012 229 2753	14.68	2.668 783	10.68	300
26	39.772 439	3265.047 479	.000 306 2743	.025 143	82.093 218	.012 181 2743	14.62	2.800 558	10.77	312
27	45.825 226	3774.755 874	.000 264 9178	.021 822	82.372 881	.012 139 9178	14.57	2.933 333	10.86	324
28	52.799 159	4362.034 480	.000 229 2508	.018 940	82.615 605	.012 104 2508	14.53	3.067 028	10.95	336
29	60.834 424	5038.688 355	.000 198 4643	.016 438	82.826 269	.012 073 4643	14.49	3.201 566	11.04	348
30	70.092 540	5818.319 116	.000 171 8709	.014 267	83.009 107	.012 046 8709	14.46	3.336 874	11.12	360
31	80.759 605	6716.598 349	.000 148 8849	.012 382	83.167 796	.012 023 8849	14.43	3.472 885	11.20	372
32	93.050 044	7751.582 627	.000 129 0059	.010 747	83.305 524	.012 004 0059	14.41	3.609 538	11.28	384
33	107.210 908	8944.076 471	.000 111 8058	.009 327	83.425 060	.011 986 8058	14.39	3.746 775	11.35	396
34	123.526 850	10318.050 549	.000 096 9175	.008 095	83.528 808	.011 971 9175	14.37	3.884 542	11.43	408
35	142.325 842	11901.123 513	.000 084 0257	.007 026	83.618 852	.011 959 0257	14.36	4.022 791	11.49	420
36	163.985 766	13725.117 177	.000 072 8591	.006 098	83.697 003	.011 947 8591	14.34	4.161 475	11.56	432
37	188.942 017	15826.696 169	.000 063 1844	.005 293	83.764 831	.011 938 1844	14.33	4.300 554	11.62	444
38	217.696 246	18248.104 943	.000 054 8002	.004 594	83.823 701	.011 929 8002	14.32	4.439 989	11.68	456
39	250.826 451	21038.016 943	.000 047 5330	.003 987	83.874 794	.011 922 5330	14.31	4.579 745	11.74	468
40	288.998 592	24252.513 005	.000 041 2328	.003 460	83.919 139	.011 916 2328	14.30	4.719 792	11.80	480
41	332.979 978	27956.208 652	.000 035 7702	.003 003	83.957 627	.011 910 7702	14.30	4.860 099	11.85	492
42	383.654 691	32223.552 953	.000 031 0332	.002 607	83.991 031	.011 906 0332	14.29	5.000 641	11.91	504
43	442.041 360	37140.325 042	.000 026 9249	.002 262	84.020 023	.011 901 9249	14.29	5.141 393	11.96	516
44	509.313 631	42805.358 390	.000 023 3616	.001 963	84.045 185	.011 898 3616	14.28	5.282 335	12.01	528
45	586.823 764	49332.527 485	.000 020 2706	.001 704	84.067 024	.011 895 2706	14.28	5.423 446	12.05	540
46	676.129 813	56853.036 861	.000 017 5892	.001 479	84.085 978	.011 892 5892	14.28	5.564 709	12.10	552
47	779.026 944	65518.058 472	.000 015 2630	.001 284	84.102 429	.011 890 2630	14.27	5.706 108	12.14	564
48	897.583 524	75501.770 448	.000 013 2447	.001 114	84.116 707	.011 888 2447	14.27	5.847 629	12.18	576
49	1034.182 692	87004.858 298	.000 011 4936	.000 967	84.129 099	.011 886 4936	14.27	5.989 258	12.22	588
50	1191.570 269	100258.549	.000 009 9742	.000 839	84.139 854	.011 884 9742	14.27	6.130 985	12.26	600

MONTHLY COMPOUND INTEREST AND ANNUITY

Amount Of 1	Amount Of 1 Per Period	Sinking Fund Payment	Present Worth Of 1	Present Worth of 1 Per Period	Periodic Payment To Amortize 1	Constant Annual Percent	Total Interest	Annual Add On Rate
What a single $ 1 deposit grows to in the future. The deposit is made at the beginning of the first period.	What a series of $ 1 deposits grow to in the future. A deposit is made at the end of each period.	The amount to be deposited at the end of each period that grows to $ 1 in the future.	What $ 1 to be paid in the future is worth today. Value today of a single $ 1 payment tomorrow.	What $ 1 to be paid at the end of each period is worth today. Value today of a series of $ 1 payments tomorrow.	The mortgage payment to amortize a loan of $ 1. An annuity certain, payable at the end of each period, worth $ 1 today.	The annual payment, including interest and principal, to amortize completely a loan of $ 100.	The total interest paid over the term on a loan of $1. The loan is amortized by regular periodic payments.	The average annual interest rate on a loan that is completely amortized by regular periodic payments.
$S = (1+i)^n$	$S\overline{n}| = \dfrac{(1+i)^n - 1}{i}$	$\dfrac{1}{S\overline{n}|} = \dfrac{i}{(1+i)^n - 1}$	$V^n = \dfrac{1}{(1+i)^n}$	$A\overline{n}| = \dfrac{1-V^n}{i}$	$\dfrac{1}{A\overline{n}|} = \dfrac{i}{1-V^n}$			

PERIODS

YEAR									
	1.011 917	1.000 000	1.000 000 0000	.988 224	.988 224	1.011 916 6667	1214.30	.011 917	14.30	1
	1.023 975	2.011 917	.497 038 4791	.976 586	1.964 810	.508 955 1457	610.75	.017 910	10.75	2
	1.036 178	3.035 892	.329 392 4809	.965 085	2.929 895	.341 309 1476	409.58	.023 927	9.57	3
	1.048 525	4.072 070	.245 575 3631	.953 720	3.883 615	.257 492 0298	309.00	.029 968	8.99	4
	1.061 020	5.120 595	.195 289 7969	.942 489	4.826 104	.207 206 4636	248.65	.036 032	8.65	5
	1.073 664	6.181 616	.161 770 0060	.931 390	5.757 494	.173 686 6727	208.43	.042 120	8.42	6
	1.086 459	7.255 280	.137 830 6577	.920 422	6.677 916	.149 747 3244	179.70	.048 231	8.27	7
	1.099 406	8.341 739	.119 879 0854	.909 582	7.587 498	.131 795 7521	158.16	.054 366	8.15	8
	1.112 507	9.441 144	.105 919 3633	.898 871	8.486 369	.117 836 0299	141.41	.060 524	8.07	9
	1.125 764	10.553 651	.094 753 9357	.888 285	9.374 654	.106 670 6023	128.01	.066 706	8.00	10
	1.139 180	11.679 416	.085 620 7217	.877 825	10.252 479	.097 537 3884	117.05	.072 911	7.95	11
	1.152 755	12.818 595	.078 011 6674	.867 487	11.119 966	.089 928 3341	107.92	.079 140	7.91	12
1	1.152 755	12.818 595	.078 011 6674	.867 487	11.119 966	.089 928 3341	107.92	.079 140	7.91	12
2	1.328 844	27.595 294	.036 238 0624	.752 534	20.766 392	.048 154 7291	57.79	.155 713	7.79	24
3	1.531 831	44.629 207	.022 406 8512	.652 813	29.134 543	.034 323 5179	41.19	.235 647	7.85	36
4	1.765 826	64.265 134	.015 560 5371	.566 307	36.393 805	.027 477 2038	32.98	.318 906	7.97	48
5	2.035 565	86.900 545	.011 507 4077	.491 264	42.691 121	.023 424 0744	28.11	.405 444	8.11	60
6	2.346 507	112.993 627	.008 850 0567	.426 165	48.153 962	.020 766 7233	24.93	.495 204	8.25	72
7	2.704 948	143.072 556	.006 989 4607	.369 693	52.892 905	.018 906 1273	22.69	.588 115	8.40	84
8	3.118 149	177.746 189	.005 625 9997	.320 704	57.003 877	.017 542 6663	21.06	.684 096	8.55	96
9	3.594 454	217.716 391	.004 593 1314	.278 206	60.570 093	.016 509 7981	19.82	.783 058	8.70	108
10	4.143 524	263.792 238	.003 790 8621	.241 340	63.663 738	.015 707 5288	18.85	.884 903	8.85	120
11	4.776 468	316.906 398	.003 155 5059	.209 360	66.347 436	.015 072 1725	18.09	.989 527	9.00	132
12	5.506 097	378.134 007	.002 644 5651	.181 617	68.675 509	.014 561 2318	17.48	1.096 817	9.14	144
13	6.347 180	448.714 436	.002 228 5889	.157 550	70.695 082	.014 145 2555	16.98	1.206 660	9.28	156
14	7.316 743	530.076 373	.001 886 5206	.136 673	72.447 036	.013 803 1873	16.57	1.318 935	9.42	168
15	8.434 412	623.866 746	.001 602 9064	.118 562	73.966 833	.013 519 5731	16.23	1.433 523	9.56	180
16	9.722 810	731.984 062	.001 366 1500	.102 851	75.285 237	.013 282 8166	15.94	1.550 301	9.69	192
17	11.208 017	856.616 830	.001 167 3831	.089 222	76.428 936	.013 084 0498	15.71	1.669 146	9.82	204
18	12.920 097	1000.287 868	.000 999 7122	.077 399	77.421 080	.012 916 3789	15.50	1.789 938	9.94	216
19	14.893 706	1165.905 365	.000 857 7025	.067 142	78.281 752	.012 774 3692	15.33	1.912 556	10.07	228
20	17.168 793	1356.821 751	.000 737 0165	.058 245	79.028 374	.012 653 6832	15.19	2.036 884	10.18	240
21	19.791 410	1576.901 556	.000 634 1550	.050 527	79.676 058	.012 550 8217	15.07	2.162 807	10.30	252
22	22.814 646	1830.599 635	.000 546 2691	.043 831	80.237 917	.012 462 9358	14.96	2.290 215	10.41	264
23	26.299 695	2123.051 347	.000 471 0202	.038 023	80.725 321	.012 387 6868	14.87	2.419 002	10.52	276
24	30.317 103	2460.176 498	.000 406 4749	.032 985	81.148 139	.012 323 1416	14.79	2.549 065	10.62	288
25	34.948 190	2848.799 179	.000 351 0251	.028 614	81.514 927	.012 267 6918	14.73	2.680 308	10.72	300
26	40.286 699	3296.785 888	.000 303 3257	.024 822	81.833 111	.012 219 9924	14.67	2.812 638	10.82	312
27	46.440 690	3813.204 776	.000 262 2466	.021 533	82.109 132	.012 178 9133	14.62	2.945 968	10.91	324
28	53.534 735	4408.509 194	.000 226 8341	.018 679	82.348 577	.012 143 5007	14.58	3.080 216	11.00	336
29	61.712 429	5094.749 295	.000 196 2805	.016 204	82.556 292	.012 112 9472	14.54	3.215 306	11.09	348
30	71.139 307	5885.815 954	.000 169 9000	.014 057	82.736 482	.012 086 5666	14.51	3.351 164	11.17	360
31	82.006 186	6797.721 944	.000 147 1081	.012 194	82.892 794	.012 063 7748	14.48	3.487 724	11.25	372
32	94.533 036	7848.926 068	.000 127 4060	.010 578	83.028 393	.012 044 0726	14.46	3.624 924	11.33	384
33	108.973 423	9060.706 803	.000 110 3667	.009 177	83.146 024	.012 027 0333	14.44	3.762 705	11.40	396
34	125.619 650	10457.593 016	.000 095 6243	.007 961	83.248 067	.012 012 2910	14.42	3.901 015	11.47	408
35	144.808 671	12067.860 484	.000 082 8647	.006 906	83.336 588	.011 999 5314	14.40	4.039 803	11.54	420
36	166.928 909	13924.104 243	.000 071 8179	.005 991	83.413 378	.011 988 4846	14.39	4.179 025	11.61	432
37	192.428 122	16063.898 385	.000 062 2514	.005 197	83.479 993	.011 978 9181	14.38	4.318 640	11.67	444
38	221.822 466	18530.556 627	.000 053 9649	.004 508	83.537 781	.011 970 6316	14.37	4.458 608	11.73	456
39	255.706 941	21374.009 072	.000 046 7858	.003 911	83.587 911	.011 963 4525	14.36	4.598 896	11.79	468
40	294.767 437	24651.812 892	.000 040 5650	.003 393	83.631 398	.011 957 2316	14.35	4.739 471	11.85	480
41	339.794 616	28430.317 400	.000 035 1737	.002 943	83.669 123	.011 951 8404	14.35	4.880 305	11.90	492
42	391.699 918	32786.007 093	.000 030 5008	.002 553	83.701 848	.011 947 1675	14.34	5.021 372	11.96	504
43	451.534 011	37807.049 854	.000 026 4501	.002 215	83.730 237	.011 943 1168	14.34	5.162 648	12.01	516
44	520.508 056	43595.081 641	.000 022 9384	.001 921	83.754 864	.011 939 6050	14.33	5.304 111	12.05	528
45	600.018 227	50267.263 809	.000 019 8937	.001 667	83.776 228	.011 936 5603	14.33	5.445 743	12.10	540
46	691.673 968	57958.654 687	.000 017 2537	.001 446	83.794 761	.011 933 9203	14.33	5.587 524	12.15	552
47	797.330 576	66824.943 427	.000 014 9645	.001 254	83.810 838	.011 931 6311	14.32	5.729 440	12.19	564
48	919.126 751	77045.601 468	.000 012 9793	.001 088	83.824 784	.011 929 6460	14.32	5.871 476	12.23	576
49	1059.527 892	88821.515 396	.000 011 2578	.000 944	83.836 883	.011 927 9244	14.32	6.013 620	12.27	588
50	1221.375 999	102409.175	.000 009 7648	.000 819	83.847 378	.011 926 4314	14.32	6.155 859	12.31	600

Amount Of 1	Amount Of 1 Per Period	Sinking Fund Payment	Present Worth Of 1	Present Worth of 1 Per Period	Periodic Payment To Amortize 1	Constant Annual Percent	Total Interest	Annual Add On Rate
What a single $ 1 deposit grows to in the future. The deposit is made at the beginning of the first period.	What a series of $ 1 deposits grow to in the future. A deposit is made at the end of each period.	The amount to be deposited at the end of each period that grows to $ 1 in the future.	What $ 1 to be paid in the future is worth today. Value today of a single $ 1 payment tomorrow.	What $ 1 to be paid at the end of each period is worth today. Value today of a series of $ 1 payments tomorrow.	The mortgage payment to amortize a loan of $ 1. An annuity certain, payable at the end of each period, worth $ 1 today.	The annual payment, including interest and principal, to amortize completely a loan of $ 100.	The total interest paid over the term on a loan of $ 1. The loan is amortized by regular periodic payments.	The average annual interest rate on a loan that is completely amortized by regular periodic payments.
$S = (1+i)^n$	$S\overline{n}| = \dfrac{(1+i)^n - 1}{i}$	$\dfrac{1}{S\overline{n}|} = \dfrac{i}{(1+i)^n - 1}$	$V^n = \dfrac{1}{(1+i)^n}$	$A\overline{n}| = \dfrac{1 - V^n}{i}$	$\dfrac{1}{A\overline{n}|} = \dfrac{i}{1 - V^n}$			

YEAR / **PERIODS**

YEAR	Amount Of 1	Amount Of 1 Per Period	Sinking Fund Payment	Present Worth Of 1	Present Worth of 1 Per Period	Periodic Payment To Amortize 1	Constant Annual Percent	Total Interest	Annual Add On Rate	PERIODS
	1.011 958	1.000 000	1.000 000 0000	.988 183	.988 183	1.011 958 3333	1214.35	.011 958	14.35	1
	1.024 060	2.011 958	.497 028 1856	.976 506	1.964 689	.508 986 5190	610.79	.017 973	10.78	2
	1.036 306	3.036 018	.329 378 8111	.964 966	2.929 655	.341 337 1445	409.61	.024 011	9.60	3
	1.048 698	4.072 324	.245 560 0462	.953 563	3.883 218	.257 518 3795	309.03	.030 074	9.02	4
	1.061 239	5.121 022	.195 273 5246	.942 295	4.825 513	.207 231 8579	248.68	.036 159	8.68	5
	1.073 930	6.182 261	.161 753 1241	.931 160	5.756 673	.173 711 4575	208.46	.042 269	8.45	6
	1.086 772	7.256 190	.137 813 3638	.920 156	6.676 829	.149 771 6972	179.73	.048 402	8.30	7
	1.099 768	8.342 962	.119 861 5031	.909 283	7.586 112	.131 819 8364	158.19	.054 559	8.18	8
	1.112 919	9.442 730	.105 901 5748	.898 538	8.484 649	.117 859 9082	141.44	.060 739	8.10	9
	1.126 228	10.555 650	.094 735 9987	.887 920	9.372 569	.106 694 3321	128.04	.066 943	8.03	10
	1.139 696	11.681 878	.085 602 6782	.877 427	10.249 996	.097 561 0115	117.08	.073 171	7.98	11
	1.153 325	12.821 573	.077 993 5487	.867 059	11.117 055	.089 951 8820	107.95	.079 423	7.94	12
1	1.153 325	12.821 573	.077 993 5487	.867 059	11.117 055	.089 951 8820	107.95	.079 423	7.94	12
2	1.330 158	27.609 010	.036 220 0603	.751 791	20.756 192	.048 178 3937	57.82	.156 281	7.81	24
3	1.534 104	44.663 725	.022 389 5344	.651 846	29.113 889	.034 347 8677	41.22	.236 523	7.88	36
4	1.769 320	64.333 348	.015 544 0379	.565 189	36.360 501	.027 502 3713	33.01	.320 114	8.00	48
5	2.040 600	87.018 809	.011 491 7684	.490 052	42.643 738	.023 450 1017	28.15	.407 006	8.14	60
6	2.353 474	113.182 511	.008 835 2873	.424 904	48.091 673	.020 793 6207	24.96	.497 141	8.29	72
7	2.714 320	143.357 752	.006 975 5558	.368 416	52.815 351	.018 933 8891	22.73	.590 447	8.43	84
8	3.130 492	178.159 602	.005 612 9447	.319 439	56.911 057	.017 571 2781	21.09	.686 843	8.59	96
9	3.610 473	218.297 434	.004 580 9059	.276 972	60.462 273	.016 539 2392	19.85	.786 238	8.74	108
10	4.164 048	264.589 384	.003 779 4411	.240 151	63.541 386	.015 737 7745	18.89	.888 533	8.89	120
11	4.802 499	317.979 031	.003 144 8615	.208 225	66.211 157	.015 103 1948	18.13	.993 622	9.03	132
12	5.538 841	379.554 628	.002 634 6669	.180 543	68.526 005	.014 593 0002	17.52	1.101 392	9.18	144
13	6.388 082	450.571 280	.002 219 4047	.156 542	70.533 113	.014 177 7380	17.02	1.211 727	9.32	156
14	7.367 532	532.476 536	.001 878 0170	.135 731	72.273 394	.013 836 3504	16.61	1.324 507	9.46	168
15	8.497 156	626.939 886	.001 595 0493	.117 686	73.782 319	.013 553 3826	16.27	1.439 609	9.60	180
16	9.799 980	735.886 797	.001 358 9047	.102 041	75.090 646	.013 317 2380	15.99	1.556 910	9.73	192
17	11.302 558	861.537 953	.001 160 7150	.088 476	76.225 041	.013 119 0483	15.75	1.676 286	9.86	204
18	13.035 519	1006.454 529	.000 993 5869	.076 713	77.208 629	.012 951 9202	15.55	1.797 615	9.99	216
19	15.034 185	1173.590 388	.000 852 0861	.066 515	78.061 457	.012 810 4194	15.38	1.920 776	10.11	228
20	17.339 296	1366.352 294	.000 731 8757	.057 672	78.800 909	.012 690 2090	15.23	2.045 650	10.23	240
21	19.997 838	1588.669 351	.000 629 4576	.050 005	79.442 057	.012 587 7909	15.11	2.172 123	10.34	252
22	23.063 999	1845.073 092	.000 541 9839	.043 358	79.997 969	.012 500 3173	15.01	2.300 084	10.45	264
23	26.600 279	2140.789 846	.000 467 1173	.037 594	80.479 978	.012 425 4506	14.92	2.429 424	10.56	276
24	30.678 757	2481.847 267	.000 402 9257	.032 596	80.897 908	.012 361 2590	14.84	2.560 043	10.67	288
25	35.382 566	2875.197 197	.000 347 8022	.028 263	81.260 278	.012 306 1356	14.77	2.691 841	10.77	300
26	40.807 586	3328.857 367	.000 300 4034	.024 505	81.574 474	.012 258 7367	14.72	2.824 726	10.86	312
27	47.064 395	3852.074 821	.000 259 6004	.021 247	81.846 900	.012 217 9337	14.67	2.958 611	10.96	324
28	54.280 526	4455.514 408	.000 224 4410	.018 423	82.083 110	.012 182 7743	14.62	3.093 412	11.05	336
29	62.603 069	5151.476 156	.000 194 1191	.015 974	82.287 917	.012 152 4524	14.59	3.229 053	11.13	348
30	72.201 663	5954.145 993	.000 167 9502	.013 850	82.465 497	.012 126 2835	14.56	3.365 462	11.22	360
31	83.271 957	6879.884 900	.000 145 3513	.012 009	82.619 469	.012 103 6846	14.53	3.502 571	11.30	372
32	96.039 600	7947.562 399	.000 125 8247	.010 412	82.752 972	.012 084 1581	14.51	3.640 317	11.38	384
33	110.764 838	9178.941 173	.000 108 9450	.009 028	82.868 727	.012 067 2784	14.49	3.778 642	11.45	396
34	127.747 818	10599.120 664	.000 094 3474	.007 828	82.969 094	.012 052 6808	14.47	3.917 494	11.52	408
35	147.334 707	12237.048 674	.000 081 7191	.006 787	83.056 117	.012 040 0524	14.45	4.056 822	11.59	420
36	169.924 749	14126.111 418	.000 070 7909	.005 885	83.131 571	.012 029 1242	14.44	4.196 582	11.66	432
37	195.978 401	16304.814 041	.000 061 3316	.005 103	83.196 995	.012 019 6649	14.43	4.336 731	11.72	444
38	226.026 720	18817.565 476	.000 053 1418	.004 424	83.253 721	.012 011 4752	14.42	4.477 233	11.78	456
39	260.682 188	21715.583 637	.000 046 0499	.003 836	83.302 905	.012 004 3832	14.41	4.618 051	11.84	468
40	300.651 192	25057.939 411	.000 039 9075	.003 326	83.345 551	.011 998 2408	14.40	4.759 156	11.90	480
41	346.748 430	28912.760 705	.000 034 5868	.002 884	83.382 528	.011 992 9201	14.40	4.900 517	11.95	492
42	399.913 511	33358.621 113	.000 029 9773	.002 501	83.414 589	.011 988 3106	14.39	5.042 109	12.01	504
43	461.230 109	38486.141 501	.000 025 9834	.002 168	83.442 388	.011 984 3167	14.39	5.183 907	12.06	516
44	531.948 052	44399.837 143	.000 022 5226	.001 880	83.466 491	.011 980 8559	14.38	5.325 892	12.12	528
45	613.508 800	51220.248 083	.000 019 5235	.001 630	83.487 389	.011 977 8569	14.38	5.468 043	12.15	540
46	707.574 820	59086.396 124	.000 016 9244	.001 413	83.505 510	.011 975 2577	14.38	5.610 342	12.20	552
47	816.063 480	68158.618 539	.000 014 6717	.001 225	83.521 221	.011 973 0050	14.37	5.752 775	12.24	564
48	941.186 125	78621.836 255	.000 012 7191	.001 062	83.534 844	.011 971 0524	14.37	5.895 326	12.28	576
49	1085.493 156	90689.323 136	.000 011 0267	.000 921	83.546 656	.011 969 3600	14.37	6.037 984	12.32	588
50	1251.926 011	104607.053	.000 009 5596	.000 799	83.556 897	.011 967 8929	14.37	6.180 736	12.36	600

Amount Of 1	Amount Of 1 Per Period	Sinking Fund Payment	Present Worth Of 1	Present Worth of 1 Per Period	Periodic Payment To Amortize 1	Constant Annual Percent	Total Interest	Annual Add On Rate	
What a single $ 1 deposit grows to in the future. The deposit is made at the beginning of the first period.	What a series of $ 1 deposits grow to in the future. A deposit is made at the end of each period.	The amount to be deposited at the end of each period that grows to $ 1 in the future.	What $ 1 to be paid in the future is worth today. Value today of a single $ 1 payment tomorrow.	What $ 1 to be paid at the end of each period is worth today. Value today of a series of $ 1 payments tomorrow.	The mortgage payment to amortize a loan of $ 1. An annuity certain, payable at the end of each period, worth $ 1 today.	The annual payment, including interest and principal, to amortize completely a loan of $ 100.	The total interest paid over the term on a loan of $1. The loan is amortized by regular periodic payments.	The average annual interest rate on a loan that is completely amortized by regular periodic payments.	
$S = (1+i)^n$	$S\overline{n}| = \dfrac{(1+i)^n - 1}{i}$	$\dfrac{1}{S\overline{n}|} = \dfrac{i}{(1+i)^n - 1}$	$V^n = \dfrac{1}{(1+i)^n}$	$A\overline{n}| = \dfrac{1-V^n}{i}$	$\dfrac{1}{A\overline{n}|} = \dfrac{i}{1-V^n}$				**PERIODS**

YEAR

Amount Of 1	Amount Of 1 Per Period	Sinking Fund Payment	Present Worth Of 1	Present Worth of 1 Per Period	Periodic Payment To Amortize 1	Constant Annual Percent	Total Interest	Annual Add On Rate	PERIODS
1.011 979	1.000 000	1.000 000 0000	.988 163	.988 163	1.011 979 1667	1214.38	.011 979	14.38	1
1.024 102	2.011 979	.497 023 0391	.976 465	1.964 628	.509 002 2058	610.81	.018 004	10.80	2
1.036 370	3.036 081	.329 371 9765	.964 907	2.929 535	.341 351 1432	409.63	.024 053	9.62	3
1.048 785	4.072 451	.245 552 3881	.953 485	3.883 019	.257 531 5548	309.04	.030 126	9.04	4
1.061 348	5.121 235	.195 265 3889	.942 198	4.825 217	.207 244 5556	248.70	.036 223	8.69	5
1.074 062	6.182 583	.161 744 6838	.931 045	5.756 262	.173 723 8505	208.47	.042 343	8.47	6
1.086 929	7.256 646	.137 804 7176	.920 024	6.676 286	.149 783 8843	179.75	.048 487	8.31	7
1.099 949	8.343 574	.119 852 7128	.909 133	7.585 419	.131 831 8794	158.20	.054 655	8.20	8
1.113 126	9.443 523	.105 892 6816	.898 371	8.483 790	.117 871 8482	141.45	.060 847	8.11	9
1.126 460	10.556 649	.094 727 0313	.887 737	9.371 527	.106 706 1980	128.05	.067 062	8.05	10
1.139 954	11.683 109	.085 593 6575	.877 228	10.248 755	.097 572 8242	117.09	.073 301	8.00	11
1.153 610	12.823 063	.077 984 4905	.866 844	11.115 600	.089 963 6572	107.96	.079 564	7.96	12

YEAR	Amount Of 1	Amount Of 1 Per Period	Sinking Fund Payment	Present Worth Of 1	Present Worth of 1 Per Period	Periodic Payment To Amortize 1	Constant Annual Percent	Total Interest	Annual Add On Rate	PERIODS
1	1.153 610	12.823 063	.077 984 4905	.866 844	11.115 600	.089 963 6572	107.96	.079 564	7.96	12
2	1.330 815	27.615 871	.036 211 0618	.751 419	20.751 095	.048 190 2285	57.83	.156 565	7.83	24
3	1.535 241	44.680 996	.022 380 8797	.651 363	29.103 570	.034 360 0464	41.24	.236 962	7.90	36
4	1.771 069	64.367 489	.015 535 7933	.564 631	36.343 865	.027 514 9600	33.02	.320 718	8.02	48
5	2.043 122	87.078 016	.011 483 9548	.489 447	42.620 075	.023 463 1215	28.16	.407 787	8.16	60
6	2.356 965	113.277 098	.008 827 9098	.424 274	48.060 572	.020 807 0765	24.97	.498 110	8.30	72
7	2.719 018	143.500 610	.006 968 6115	.367 780	52.776 637	.018 947 7781	22.74	.591 613	8.45	84
8	3.136 685	178.366 745	.005 606 4262	.318 808	56.864 730	.017 585 5929	21.11	.688 217	8.60	96
9	3.618 510	218.588 652	.004 574 8029	.276 357	60.408 472	.016 553 9696	19.87	.787 829	8.75	108
10	4.174 348	264.989 031	.003 773 7411	.239 558	63.480 344	.015 752 9078	18.91	.890 349	8.90	120
11	4.815 568	318.516 954	.003 139 5503	.207 660	66.143 179	.015 118 7170	18.15	.995 671	9.05	132
12	5.555 285	380.267 279	.002 629 7293	.180 009	68.451 442	.014 608 8960	17.54	1.103 681	9.20	144
13	6.408 630	451.503 047	.002 214 8245	.156 040	70.452 348	.014 193 9911	17.04	1.214 263	9.34	156
14	7.393 057	533.681 314	.001 873 7774	.135 262	72.186 821	.013 852 9441	16.63	1.327 295	9.48	168
15	8.528 702	628.482 952	.001 591 1331	.117 251	73.690 340	.013 570 2997	16.29	1.442 654	9.62	180
16	9.838 793	737.847 031	.001 355 2945	.101 638	74.993 657	.013 334 4611	16.01	1.560 217	9.75	192
17	11.350 126	864.010 484	.001 157 3934	.088 105	76.123 429	.013 136 5600	15.77	1.679 858	9.88	204
18	13.093 614	1009.553 854	.000 990 5366	.076 373	77.102 767	.012 969 7032	15.57	1.801 456	10.01	216
19	15.104 919	1177.454 084	.000 849 2900	.066 204	77.951 699	.012 828 4567	15.40	1.924 888	10.13	228
20	17.425 179	1371.145 401	.000 729 3173	.057 388	78.687 592	.012 708 4839	15.26	2.050 036	10.25	240
21	20.101 854	1594.589 565	.000 627 1206	.049 747	79.325 497	.012 606 2873	15.13	2.176 784	10.37	252
22	23.189 692	1852.356 898	.000 539 8528	.043 123	79.878 461	.012 519 0194	15.03	2.305 021	10.48	264
23	26.751 851	2149.719 769	.000 465 1769	.037 381	80.357 794	.012 444 3436	14.94	2.434 639	10.59	276
24	30.861 193	2492.760 433	.000 401 1617	.032 403	80.773 302	.012 380 3284	14.86	2.565 535	10.69	288
25	35.601 768	2888.495 437	.000 346 2010	.028 088	81.133 482	.012 325 3677	14.80	2.697 610	10.79	300
26	41.070 542	3345.019 138	.000 298 9520	.024 348	81.445 703	.012 278 1186	14.74	2.830 773	10.89	312
27	47.379 371	3871.669 264	.000 258 2865	.021 106	81.716 349	.012 237 4532	14.69	2.964 935	10.98	324
28	54.657 298	4479.217 907	.000 223 2533	.018 296	81.950 958	.012 202 4199	14.65	3.100 013	11.07	336
29	63.053 184	5180.091 855	.000 193 0468	.015 860	82.154 327	.012 172 2134	14.61	3.235 930	11.16	348
30	72.738 758	5988.626 774	.000 166 9832	.013 748	82.330 616	.012 146 1499	14.58	3.372 614	11.24	360
31	83.912 130	6921.360 420	.000 144 4803	.011 917	82.483 431	.012 123 6469	14.55	3.509 997	11.32	372
32	96.801 839	7997.370 912	.000 125 0411	.010 330	82.615 899	.012 104 2078	14.53	3.648 016	11.40	384
33	111.671 531	9238.666 949	.000 108 2407	.008 955	82.730 727	.012 087 4074	14.51	3.786 613	11.47	396
34	128.825 351	10670.637 978	.000 093 7151	.007 762	82.830 265	.012 072 8818	14.49	3.925 736	11.55	408
35	148.614 162	12322.573 508	.000 081 1519	.006 729	82.916 550	.012 060 3185	14.48	4.065 334	11.62	420
36	171.442 724	14228.262 201	.000 070 2827	.005 833	82.991 345	.012 049 4493	14.46	4.205 362	11.68	432
37	197.777 973	16426.682 978	.000 060 8766	.005 056	83.056 180	.012 040 0432	14.45	4.345 579	11.75	444
38	228.158 569	18962.802 298	.000 052 7348	.004 383	83.112 383	.012 031 9015	14.44	4.486 547	11.81	456
39	263.205 917	21888.493 902	.000 045 6861	.003 799	83.161 101	.012 024 8528	14.43	4.627 631	11.87	468
40	303.636 873	25263.599 832	.000 039 5826	.003 293	83.203 333	.012 018 7493	14.43	4.769 000	11.92	480
41	350.278 413	29157.154 447	.000 034 2969	.002 855	83.239 941	.012 013 4636	14.42	4.910 624	11.98	492
42	404.084 541	33648.796 441	.000 029 7187	.002 475	83.271 675	.012 008 8854	14.42	5.052 478	12.03	504
43	466.155 807	38830.397 781	.000 025 7530	.002 145	83.299 183	.012 004 9197	14.41	5.194 539	12.08	516
44	537.761 815	44807.942 848	.000 022 3175	.001 860	83.323 028	.012 001 4841	14.41	5.336 784	12.13	528
45	620.367 195	51703.696 242	.000 019 3410	.001 612	83.343 698	.011 998 5076	14.40	5.479 194	12.18	540
46	715.661 553	59658.703 581	.000 016 7620	.001 397	83.361 616	.011 995 9287	14.40	5.621 753	12.22	552
47	825.594 041	68835.676 442	.000 014 5274	.001 211	83.377 148	.011 993 6940	14.40	5.764 443	12.26	564
48	952.413 214	79422.320 465	.000 012 5909	.001 050	83.390 612	.011 991 7576	14.40	5.907 252	12.31	576
49	1098.713 030	91635.174 678	.000 010 9128	.000 910	83.402 283	.011 990 0795	14.39	6.050 167	12.35	588
50	1267.485 903	105724.041	.000 009 4586	.000 789	83.412 400	.011 988 6253	14.39	6.193 175	12.39	600

Effective Rate is 15.36 %

Annual Percentage Rate is 14.375%

MONTHLY COMPOUND INTEREST AND ANNUITY

14.40 % M

	Amount Of 1	Amount Of 1 Per Period	Sinking Fund Payment	Present Worth Of 1	Present Worth of 1 Per Period	Periodic Payment To Amortize 1	Constant Annual Percent	Total Interest	Annual Add On Rate	
	What a single $ 1 deposit grows to in the future. The deposit is made at the beginning of the first period.	What a series of $ 1 deposits grow to in the future. A deposit is made at the end of each period.	The amount to be deposited at the end of each period that grows to $ 1 in the future.	What $ 1 to be paid in the future is worth today. Value today of a single $ 1 payment tomorrow.	What $ 1 to be paid at the end of each period is worth today. Value today of a series of $ 1 payments tomorrow.	The mortgage payment to amortize a loan of $ 1. An annuity certain, payable at the end of each period, worth $ 1 today.	The annual payment, including interest and principal, to amortize completely a loan of $ 100.	The total interest paid over the term on a loan of $1. The loan is amortized by regular periodic payments.	The average annual interest rate on a loan that is completely amortized by regular periodic payments.	
	$S = (1+i)^n$	$S\overline{n} = \dfrac{(1+i)^n - 1}{i}$	$\dfrac{1}{S\overline{n}} = \dfrac{i}{(1+i)^n - 1}$	$V^n = \dfrac{1}{(1+i)^n}$	$A\overline{n} = \dfrac{1-V^n}{i}$	$\dfrac{1}{A\overline{n}} = \dfrac{i}{1-V^n}$				

YEAR										PERIODS
	1.012 000	1.000 000	1.000 000 0000	.988 142	.988 142	1.012 000 0000	1214.40	.012 000	14.40	1
	1.024 144	2.012 000	.497 017 8926	.976 425	1.964 567	.509 017 8926	610.83	.018 036	10.82	2
	1.036 434	3.036 144	.329 365 1421	.964 847	2.929 415	.341 365 1421	409.64	.024 095	9.64	3
	1.048 871	4.072 578	.245 544 7303	.953 406	3.882 821	.257 544 7303	309.06	.030 179	9.05	4
	1.061 457	5.121 449	.195 257 2536	.942 101	4.824 922	.207 257 2536	248.71	.036 286	8.71	5
	1.074 195	6.182 906	.161 736 2439	.930 930	5.755 851	.173 736 2439	208.49	.042 417	8.48	6
	1.087 085	7.257 101	.137 796 0719	.919 891	6.675 742	.149 796 0719	179.76	.048 573	8.33	7
	1.100 130	8.344 186	.119 843 9230	.908 983	7.584 726	.131 843 9230	158.22	.054 751	8.21	8
	1.113 332	9.444 316	.105 883 7889	.898 205	8.482 931	.117 883 7889	141.47	.060 954	8.13	9
	1.126 692	10.557 648	.094 718 0646	.887 554	9.370 485	.106 718 0646	128.07	.067 181	8.06	10
	1.140 212	11.684 340	.085 584 6377	.877 030	10.247 515	.097 584 6377	117.11	.073 431	8.01	11
	1.153 895	12.824 552	.077 975 4333	.866 630	11.114 145	.089 975 4333	107.98	.079 705	7.97	12
1	1.153 895	12.824 552	.077 975 4333	.866 630	11.114 145	.089 975 4333	107.98	.079 705	7.97	12
2	1.331 473	27.622 734	.036 202 0650	.751 048	20.745 999	.048 202 0650	57.85	.156 850	7.84	24
3	1.536 379	44.698 276	.022 372 2276	.650 881	29.093 256	.034 372 2276	41.25	.237 400	7.91	36
4	1.772 820	64.401 652	.015 527 5519	.564 073	36.327 241	.027 527 5519	33.04	.321 322	8.03	48
5	2.045 647	87.137 272	.011 476 1453	.488 843	42.596 431	.023 476 1453	28.18	.408 569	8.17	60
6	2.360 461	113.371 782	.008 820 5370	.423 646	48.029 501	.020 820 5370	24.99	.499 079	8.32	72
7	2.723 724	143.643 642	.006 961 6726	.367 144	52.737 964	.018 961 6726	22.76	.592 780	8.47	84
8	3.142 890	178.574 178	.005 599 9138	.318 178	56.818 460	.017 599 9138	21.12	.689 592	8.62	96
9	3.626 564	218.880 336	.004 568 7064	.275 743	60.354 742	.016 568 7064	19.89	.789 420	8.77	108
10	4.184 673	265.389 395	.003 768 0481	.238 967	63.419 391	.015 768 0481	18.93	.892 166	8.92	120
11	4.828 671	319.055 949	.003 134 2465	.207 096	66.075 308	.015 134 2465	18.17	.997 721	9.07	132
12	5.571 778	380.981 496	.002 624 7994	.179 476	68.377 006	.014 624 7994	17.55	1.105 971	9.22	144
13	6.429 245	452.437 052	.002 210 2522	.155 539	70.371 728	.014 210 2522	17.06	1.216 799	9.36	156
14	7.418 671	534.889 234	.001 869 5459	.134 795	72.100 414	.013 869 5459	16.65	1.330 084	9.50	168
15	8.560 364	630.030 364	.001 587 2251	.116 817	73.598 545	.013 587 2251	16.31	1.445 701	9.64	180
16	9.877 758	739.813 202	.001 351 6926	.101 238	74.896 871	.013 351 6926	16.03	1.563 525	9.77	192
17	11.397 892	866.491 029	.001 154 0800	.087 736	76.022 040	.013 154 0800	15.79	1.683 432	9.90	204
18	13.151 967	1012.663 892	.000 987 4945	.076 034	76.997 145	.012 987 4945	15.59	1.805 299	10.03	216
19	15.175 984	1181.331 973	.000 846 5021	.065 894	77.842 201	.012 846 5021	15.42	1.929 002	10.15	228
20	17.511 486	1375.957 165	.000 726 7668	.057 105	78.574 552	.012 726 7668	15.28	2.054 424	10.27	240
21	20.206 410	1600.534 128	.000 624 7914	.049 489	79.209 229	.012 624 7914	15.15	2.181 447	10.39	252
22	23.316 067	1859.672 279	.000 537 7292	.042 889	79.759 260	.012 537 7292	15.05	2.309 960	10.50	264
23	26.904 285	2158.690 397	.000 463 2438	.037 169	80.235 933	.012 463 2438	14.96	2.439 855	10.61	276
24	31.044 710	2503.725 796	.000 399 4048	.032 212	80.649 033	.012 399 4048	14.88	2.571 029	10.71	288
25	35.822 323	2901.860 289	.000 344 6065	.027 916	81.007 037	.012 344 6065	14.82	2.703 382	10.81	300
26	41.335 186	3361.265 539	.000 297 5070	.024 192	81.317 295	.012 297 5070	14.76	2.836 822	10.91	312
27	47.696 449	3891.370 788	.000 256 9789	.020 966	81.586 173	.012 256 9789	14.71	2.971 261	11.00	324
28	55.036 677	4503.056 385	.000 222 0714	.018 170	81.819 192	.012 222 0714	14.67	3.106 616	11.10	336
29	63.506 525	5208.877 108	.000 191 9800	.015 746	82.021 132	.012 191 9800	14.64	3.242 809	11.18	348
30	73.279 838	6023.319 845	.000 166 0214	.013 646	82.196 140	.012 166 0214	14.60	3.379 768	11.27	360
31	84.557 211	6963.100 940	.000 143 6142	.011 826	82.347 807	.012 143 6142	14.58	3.517 424	11.35	372
32	97.570 112	8047.509 295	.000 124 2620	.010 249	82.479 247	.012 124 2620	14.55	3.655 717	11.42	384
33	112.585 627	9298.802 265	.000 107 5407	.008 882	82.593 156	.012 107 5407	14.53	3.794 586	11.50	396
34	129.911 950	10742.662 497	.000 093 0868	.007 698	82.691 873	.012 093 0868	14.52	3.933 979	11.57	408
35	149.904 701	12408.725 057	.000 080 5885	.006 671	82.777 425	.012 080 5885	14.50	4.073 847	11.64	420
36	172.974 228	14331.185 688	.000 069 7779	.005 781	82.851 566	.012 069 7779	14.49	4.214 144	11.71	432
37	199.594 032	16549.502 676	.000 060 4248	.005 010	82.915 819	.012 060 4248	14.48	4.354 829	11.77	444
38	230.310 481	19109.206 723	.000 052 3308	.004 342	82.971 503	.012 052 3308	14.47	4.495 863	11.83	456
39	265.754 026	22062.835 462	.000 045 3251	.003 763	83.019 760	.012 045 3251	14.46	4.637 212	11.89	468
40	306.652 141	25471.011 785	.000 039 2603	.003 261	83.061 581	.012 039 2603	14.45	4.778 845	11.95	480
41	353.844 257	29403.688 124	.000 034 0093	.002 826	83.097 825	.012 034 0093	14.45	4.920 733	12.00	492
42	408.298 987	33941.582 209	.000 029 4624	.002 449	83.129 235	.012 029 4624	14.44	5.062 849	12.05	504
43	471.134 006	39177.833 799	.000 025 5246	.002 123	83.156 455	.012 025 5246	14.44	5.205 171	12.11	516
44	543.638 996	45219.916 360	.000 022 1141	.001 839	83.180 045	.012 022 1141	14.43	5.347 676	12.15	528
45	627.302 115	52191.842 946	.000 019 1601	.001 594	83.200 489	.012 019 1601	14.43	5.490 346	12.20	540
46	723.840 539	60236.711 553	.000 016 6012	.001 382	83.218 207	.012 016 6012	14.42	5.633 164	12.25	552
47	835.235 706	69519.642 192	.000 014 3844	.001 197	83.233 561	.012 014 3844	14.42	5.776 113	12.29	564
48	963.773 991	80231.165 952	.000 012 4640	.001 038	83.246 868	.012 012 4640	14.42	5.919 179	12.33	576
49	1112.093 628	92591.135 636	.000 010 8002	.000 899	83.258 400	.012 010 8002	14.42	6.062 350	12.37	588
50	1283.238 859	106853.238	.000 009 3586	.000 779	83.268 393	.012 009 3586	14.42	6.205 615	12.41	600

Effective Rate is 15.39 %

Annual Percentage Rate is 14.40 %

MONTHLY COMPOUND INTEREST AND ANNUITY

14.45 % M

Amount Of 1	Amount Of 1 Per Period	Sinking Fund Payment	Present Worth Of 1	Present Worth of 1 Per Period	Periodic Payment To Amortize 1	Constant Annual Percent	Total Interest	Annual Add On Rate
What a single $ 1 deposit grows to in the future. The deposit is made at the beginning of the first period.	What a series of $ 1 deposits grow to in the future. A deposit is made at the end of each period.	The amount to be deposited at the end of each period that grows to $ 1 in the future.	What $ 1 to be paid in the future is worth today. Value today of a single $ 1 payment tomorrow.	What $ 1 to be paid at the end of each period is worth today. Value today of a series of $ 1 payments tomorrow.	The mortgage payment to amortize a loan of $ 1. An annuity certain, payable at the end of each period, worth $ 1 today.	The annual payment, including interest and principal, to amortize completely a loan of $ 100.	The total interest paid over the term on a loan of $1. The loan is amortized by regular periodic payments.	The average annual interest rate on a loan that is completely amortized by regular periodic payments.
$S = (1+i)^n$	$S\overline{n} = \dfrac{(1+i)^n - 1}{i}$	$\dfrac{1}{S\overline{n}} = \dfrac{i}{(1+i)^n - 1}$	$V^n = \dfrac{1}{(1+i)^n}$	$A\overline{n} = \dfrac{1 - V^n}{i}$	$\dfrac{1}{A\overline{n}} = \dfrac{i}{1 - V^n}$			

PERIODS

YEAR	Amount Of 1	Amount Of 1 Per Period	Sinking Fund Payment	Present Worth Of 1	Present Worth of 1 Per Period	Periodic Payment To Amortize 1	Constant Annual Percent	Total Interest	Annual Add On Rate	PERIODS
	1.012 042	1.000 000	1.000 000 0000	.988 102	.988 102	1.012 041 6667	1214.45	.012 042	14.45	1
	1.024 228	2.012 042	.497 007 6001	.976 345	1.964 446	.509 049 2667	610.86	.018 099	10.86	2
	1.036 562	3.036 270	.329 351 4738	.964 728	2.929 174	.341 393 1405	409.68	.024 179	9.67	3
	1.049 044	4.072 832	.245 529 4156	.953 249	3.882 423	.257 571 0822	309.09	.030 284	9.09	4
	1.061 676	5.121 875	.195 240 9840	.941 907	4.824 330	.207 282 6507	248.74	.036 413	8.74	5
	1.074 460	6.183 551	.161 719 3653	.930 700	5.755 030	.173 761 0320	208.52	.042 566	8.51	6
	1.087 399	7.258 012	.137 778 7820	.919 626	6.674 656	.149 820 4486	179.79	.048 743	8.36	7
	1.100 493	8.345 410	.119 826 3452	.908 684	7.583 340	.131 868 0118	158.25	.054 944	8.24	8
	1.113 744	9.445 903	.105 866 0055	.897 872	8.481 212	.117 907 6722	141.49	.061 169	8.16	9
	1.127 156	10.559 647	.094 700 1332	.887 189	9.368 401	.106 741 7999	128.10	.067 418	8.09	10
	1.140 729	11.686 803	.085 566 6003	.876 633	10.245 034	.097 608 2670	117.13	.073 691	8.04	11
	1.154 465	12.827 532	.077 957 3213	.866 202	11.111 236	.089 998 9880	108.00	.079 988	8.00	12
1	1.154 465	12.827 532	.077 957 3213	.866 202	11.111 236	.089 998 9880	108.00	.079 988	8.00	12
2	1.332 789	27.636 466	.036 184 0765	.750 306	20.735 813	.048 225 7432	57.88	.157 418	7.87	24
3	1.538 658	44.732 860	.022 354 9308	.649 917	29.072 643	.034 396 5975	41.28	.238 278	7.94	36
4	1.776 327	64.470 047	.015 511 0791	.562 959	36.294 023	.027 552 7458	33.07	.322 532	8.06	48
5	2.050 707	87.255 935	.011 460 5384	.487 637	42.549 199	.023 502 2051	28.21	.410 132	8.20	60
6	2.367 469	113.561 443	.008 805 8057	.422 392	47.967 446	.020 847 4724	25.02	.501 018	8.35	72
7	2.733 160	143.930 226	.006 947 8109	.365 877	52.660 743	.018 989 4776	22.79	.595 116	8.50	84
8	3.155 337	178.989 920	.005 586 9068	.316 923	56.726 087	.017 628 5735	21.16	.692 343	8.65	96
9	3.642 726	219.465 105	.004 556 5330	.274 520	60.247 498	.016 598 1997	19.92	.792 606	8.81	108
10	4.205 399	266.192 283	.003 756 6829	.237 790	63.297 751	.015 798 3496	18.96	.895 802	8.96	120
11	4.854 985	320.137 168	.003 123 6610	.205 974	65.939 887	.015 165 3277	18.20	1.001 823	9.11	132
12	5.604 910	382.414 642	.002 614 9626	.178 415	68.228 511	.014 656 6293	17.59	1.110 555	9.25	144
13	6.470 671	454.311 797	.002 201 1315	.154 543	70.210 923	.014 242 7981	17.10	1.221 877	9.40	156
14	7.470 163	537.314 537	.001 861 1073	.133 866	71.928 092	.013 902 7740	16.69	1.335 666	9.54	168
15	8.624 040	633.138 283	.001 579 4338	.115 955	73.415 507	.013 621 1005	16.35	1.451 798	9.68	180
16	9.956 151	743.763 430	.001 344 5135	.100 440	74.703 910	.013 386 1802	16.07	1.570 147	9.81	192
17	11.494 027	871.476 275	.001 147 4782	.087 002	75.819 927	.013 189 1448	15.83	1.690 586	9.94	204
18	13.269 450	1018.916 267	.000 981 4349	.075 361	76.786 624	.013 023 1016	15.63	1.812 990	10.07	216
19	15.319 114	1189.130 557	.000 840 9506	.065 278	77.623 978	.012 882 6172	15.46	1.937 237	10.20	228
20	17.685 379	1385.636 972	.000 721 6897	.056 544	78.349 297	.012 763 3564	15.32	2.063 206	10.32	240
21	20.417 148	1612.496 724	.000 620 1563	.048 978	78.977 569	.012 661 8230	15.20	2.190 779	10.43	252
22	23.570 880	1874.398 335	.000 533 5045	.042 425	79.521 780	.012 575 1712	15.10	2.319 845	10.54	264
23	27.211 753	2176.754 542	.000 459 3995	.036 749	79.993 177	.012 501 0662	15.01	2.450 294	10.65	276
24	31.415 012	2525.814 158	.000 395 9119	.031 832	80.401 502	.012 437 5786	14.93	2.582 023	10.76	288
25	36.267 528	2928.791 218	.000 341 4378	.027 573	80.755 194	.012 383 1045	14.86	2.714 931	10.86	300
26	41.869 586	3394.014 073	.000 294 6364	.023 884	81.061 563	.012 336 3030	14.81	2.848 927	10.96	312
27	48.336 966	3931.097 511	.000 254 3819	.020 688	81.326 940	.012 296 0486	14.76	2.983 920	11.05	324
28	55.803 328	4551.141 467	.000 219 7251	.017 920	81.556 810	.012 261 3918	14.72	3.119 828	11.14	336
29	64.422 982	5266.960 425	.000 189 8628	.015 522	81.755 924	.012 231 5295	14.68	3.256 572	11.23	348
30	74.374 069	6093.348 257	.000 164 1134	.013 446	81.928 398	.012 205 7801	14.65	3.394 081	11.31	360
31	85.862 249	7047.383 971	.000 141 8966	.011 647	82.077 794	.012 183 5633	14.63	3.532 286	11.39	372
32	99.124 949	8148.784 676	.000 122 7177	.010 088	82.207 202	.012 164 3844	14.60	3.671 124	11.47	384
33	114.436 270	9420.313 086	.000 106 1536	.008 738	82.319 295	.012 147 8203	14.58	3.810 537	11.55	396
34	132.112 652	10888.247 953	.000 091 8421	.007 569	82.416 391	.012 133 5088	14.57	3.950 472	11.62	408
35	152.519 415	12582.927 174	.000 079 4728	.006 557	82.500 495	.012 121 1394	14.55	4.090 879	11.69	420
36	176.078 305	14539.374 781	.000 068 7787	.005 679	82.573 346	.012 110 4454	14.54	4.231 712	11.75	432
37	203.276 215	16798.024 793	.000 059 5308	.004 919	82.636 450	.012 101 1975	14.53	4.372 932	11.82	444
38	234.675 247	19405.556 862	.000 051 5316	.004 261	82.691 111	.012 093 1983	14.52	4.514 498	11.88	456
39	270.924 326	22415.861 004	.000 044 6113	.003 691	82.738 458	.012 086 2779	14.51	4.656 378	11.94	468
40	312.772 614	25891.151 353	.000 038 6232	.003 197	82.779 470	.012 080 2899	14.50	4.798 539	12.00	480
41	361.084 992	29903.251 936	.000 033 4412	.002 769	82.814 995	.012 075 1078	14.50	4.940 953	12.05	492
42	416.859 935	34535.081 072	.000 028 9561	.002 399	82.845 767	.012 070 6227	14.49	5.083 594	12.10	504
43	481.250 146	39882.365 044	.000 025 0737	.002 078	82.872 422	.012 066 7404	14.49	5.226 438	12.15	516
44	555.586 382	46055.616 482	.000 021 7129	.001 800	82.895 510	.012 063 3795	14.48	5.369 464	12.20	528
45	641.404 954	53182.418 335	.000 018 8032	.001 559	82.915 509	.012 060 4699	14.48	5.512 654	12.25	540
46	740.479 480	61410.060 634	.000 016 2840	.001 350	82.932 832	.012 057 9506	14.47	5.655 989	12.30	552
47	854.857 539	70908.584 544	.000 014 1027	.001 170	82.947 838	.012 055 7693	14.47	5.799 454	12.34	564
48	986.902 988	81874.296 613	.000 012 2138	.001 013	82.960 836	.012 053 8805	14.47	5.943 035	12.38	576
49	1139.344 820	94533.825 854	.000 010 5782	.000 878	82.972 094	.012 052 2449	14.47	6.086 720	12.42	588
50	1315.333 557	109148.807	.000 009 1618	.000 760	82.981 847	.012 050 8285	14.47	6.230 497	12.46	600

Effective Rate is 15.45 %

Annual Percentage Rate is 14.45 %

	Amount Of 1	Amount Of 1 Per Period	Sinking Fund Payment	Present Worth Of 1	Present Worth of 1 Per Period	Periodic Payment To Amortize 1	Constant Annual Percent	Total Interest	Annual Add On Rate	
	What a single $ 1 deposit grows to in the future. The deposit is made at the beginning of the first period.	What a series of $ 1 deposits grow to in the future. A deposit is made at the end of each period.	The amount to be deposited at the end of each period that grows to $ 1 in the future.	What $ 1 to be paid in the future is worth today. Value today of a single $ 1 payment tomorrow.	What $ 1 to be paid at the end of each period is worth today. Value today of a series of $ 1 payments tomorrow.	The mortgage payment to amortize a loan of $ 1. An annuity certain, payable at the end of each period, worth $ 1 today.	The annual payment, including interest and principal, to amortize completely a loan of $ 100.	The total interest paid over the term on a loan of $1. The loan is amortized by regular periodic payments.	The average annual interest rate on a loan that is completely amortized by regular periodic payments.	
	$S = (1+i)^n$	$S\overline{n}| = \frac{(1+i)^n - 1}{i}$	$\frac{1}{S\overline{n}|} = \frac{i}{(1+i)^n - 1}$	$V^n = \frac{1}{(1+i)^n}$	$A\overline{n}| = \frac{1-V^n}{i}$	$\frac{1}{A\overline{n}|} = \frac{i}{1-V^n}$				

YEAR										PERIODS
	1.012 083	1.000 000	1.000 000 0000	.988 061	.988 061	1.012 083 3333	1214.50	.012 083	14.50	1
	1.024 313	2.012 083	.496 997 3079	.976 264	1.964 325	.509 080 6413	610.90	.018 161	10.90	2
	1.036 690	3.036 396	.329 337 8063	.964 609	2.928 934	.341 421 1396	409.71	.024 263	9.71	3
	1.049 216	4.073 086	.245 514 1019	.953 092	3.882 026	.257 597 4352	309.12	.030 390	9.12	4
	1.061 894	5.122 302	.195 224 7158	.941 713	4.823 739	.207 308 0491	248.77	.036 540	8.77	5
	1.074 726	6.184 197	.161 702 4884	.930 470	5.754 209	.173 785 8217	208.55	.042 715	8.54	6
	1.087 712	7.258 922	.137 761 4940	.919 361	6.673 570	.149 844 8273	179.82	.048 914	8.39	7
	1.100 855	8.346 634	.119 808 7696	.908 385	7.581 955	.131 892 1029	158.28	.055 137	8.27	8
	1.114 157	9.447 490	.105 848 2246	.897 539	8.479 495	.117 931 5580	141.52	.061 384	8.18	9
	1.127 620	10.561 647	.094 682 2047	.886 824	9.366 318	.106 765 5381	128.12	.067 655	8.12	10
	1.141 245	11.689 267	.085 548 5660	.876 236	10.242 554	.097 631 8994	117.16	.073 951	8.07	11
	1.155 035	12.830 512	.077 939 2127	.865 774	11.108 328	.090 022 5460	108.03	.080 271	8.03	12
1	1.155 035	12.830 512	.077 939 2127	.865 774	11.108 328	.090 022 5460	108.03	.080 271	8.03	12
2	1.334 107	27.650 207	.036 166 0947	.749 565	20.725 634	.048 249 4280	57.90	.157 986	7.90	24
3	1.540 940	44.767 478	.022 337 6441	.648 954	29.052 051	.034 420 9774	41.31	.239 155	7.97	36
4	1.779 841	64.538 532	.015 494 6195	.561 848	36.260 850	.027 577 9529	33.10	.323 742	8.09	48
5	2.055 779	87.374 798	.011 444 9477	.486 434	42.502 042	.023 528 2811	28.24	.411 697	8.23	60
6	2.374 497	113.751 493	.008 791 0934	.421 142	47.905 507	.020 874 4268	25.05	.502 959	8.38	72
7	2.742 628	144.217 508	.006 933 9709	.364 614	52.583 688	.019 017 3042	22.83	.597 454	8.54	84
8	3.167 833	179.406 832	.005 573 9237	.315 673	56.633 938	.017 657 2571	21.19	.695 097	8.69	96
9	3.658 959	220.051 745	.004 544 3857	.273 302	60.140 540	.016 627 7190	19.96	.795 794	8.84	108
10	4.226 227	266.998 057	.003 745 3456	.236 618	63.176 466	.015 828 6789	19.00	.899 441	8.99	120
11	4.881 441	321.222 707	.003 113 1050	.204 858	65.804 893	.015 196 4383	18.24	1.005 930	9.14	132
12	5.638 237	383.854 095	.002 605 1565	.177 360	68.080 518	.014 688 4899	17.63	1.115 143	9.29	144
13	6.512 363	456.195 562	.002 192 0424	.153 554	70.050 696	.014 275 3757	17.14	1.226 959	9.44	156
14	7.522 010	539.752 513	.001 852 7010	.132 943	71.756 425	.013 936 0343	16.73	1.341 254	9.58	168
15	8.688 187	636.263 747	.001 571 6753	.115 099	73.233 202	.013 655 0086	16.39	1.457 902	9.72	180
16	10.035 163	747.737 633	.001 337 3675	.099 650	74.511 757	.013 420 7008	16.11	1.576 775	9.85	192
17	11.590 968	876.493 913	.001 140 9092	.086 274	75.618 698	.013 224 2426	15.87	1.697 745	9.99	204
18	13.387 978	1025.211 968	.000 975 4080	.074 694	76.577 058	.013 058 7414	15.68	1.820 688	10.11	216
19	15.463 588	1196.986 579	.000 835 4313	.064 668	77.406 782	.012 918 7646	15.51	1.945 478	10.24	228
20	17.860 991	1395.392 327	.000 716 6443	.055 988	78.125 136	.012 799 9777	15.36	2.071 995	10.36	240
21	20.630 076	1624.557 981	.000 615 5521	.048 473	78.747 069	.012 698 8854	15.24	2.200 119	10.48	252
22	23.828 467	1889.252 413	.000 529 3099	.041 967	79.285 522	.012 612 6432	15.14	2.329 738	10.59	264
23	27.522 721	2194.983 839	.000 455 5842	.036 334	79.751 701	.012 538 9176	15.05	2.460 741	10.70	276
24	31.789 716	2548.114 445	.000 392 4471	.031 457	80.155 306	.012 475 7804	14.98	2.593 025	10.80	288
25	36.718 246	2955.992 779	.000 338 2958	.027 234	80.504 738	.012 421 6292	14.91	2.726 489	10.91	300
26	42.410 872	3427.106 674	.000 291 7913	.023 579	80.807 267	.012 375 1247	14.86	2.861 039	11.00	312
27	48.986 057	3971.259 878	.000 251 8093	.020 414	81.069 189	.012 335 1426	14.81	2.996 586	11.10	324
28	56.580 627	4599.776 067	.000 217 4019	.017 674	81.295 954	.012 300 7352	14.77	3.133 047	11.19	336
29	65.352 625	5325.734 484	.000 187 7675	.015 302	81.492 281	.012 271 1009	14.73	3.270 343	11.28	348
30	75.484 592	6164.242 121	.000 162 2259	.013 248	81.662 256	.012 245 5593	14.70	3.408 401	11.36	360
31	87.187 373	7132.748 085	.000 140 1984	.011 470	81.809 416	.012 223 5318	14.67	3.547 154	11.44	372
32	100.704 498	8251.406 712	.000 121 1915	.009 930	81.936 824	.012 204 5248	14.65	3.686 538	11.52	384
33	116.317 255	9543.496 975	.000 104 7834	.008 597	82.047 130	.012 188 1167	14.63	3.826 494	11.60	396
34	134.350 542	11035.906 907	.000 090 6133	.007 443	82.142 630	.012 173 9466	14.61	3.966 970	11.67	408
35	155.179 625	12759.693 140	.000 078 3718	.006 444	82.225 312	.012 161 7051	14.60	4.107 916	11.74	420
36	179.237 953	14750.727 180	.000 067 7933	.005 579	82.296 896	.012 151 1266	14.59	4.249 287	11.80	432
37	207.026 173	17050.441 884	.000 058 6495	.004 830	82.358 871	.012 141 9828	14.58	4.391 040	11.87	444
38	239.122 549	19706.693 669	.000 050 7442	.004 182	82.412 528	.012 134 0775	14.57	4.533 139	11.93	456
39	276.194 997	22774.758 387	.000 043 9083	.003 621	82.458 982	.012 127 2416	14.56	4.675 549	11.99	468
40	319.014 986	26318.481 600	.000 037 9961	.003 135	82.499 201	.012 121 3294	14.55	4.818 238	12.05	480
41	368.473 587	30411.607 192	.000 032 8822	.002 714	82.534 022	.012 116 2155	14.54	4.961 178	12.10	492
42	425.600 019	35139.311 955	.000 028 4582	.002 350	82.564 169	.012 111 7915	14.54	5.104 343	12.15	504
43	491.583 069	40599.978 093	.000 024 6306	.002 034	82.590 269	.012 107 9639	14.53	5.247 709	12.20	516
44	567.795 823	46907.240 532	.000 021 3187	.001 761	82.612 866	.012 104 6520	14.53	5.391 256	12.25	528
45	655.824 249	54192.351 629	.000 018 4528	.001 525	82.632 430	.012 101 7861	14.53	5.534 965	12.30	540
46	757.500 193	62606.912 495	.000 015 9727	.001 320	82.649 368	.012 099 3060	14.52	5.678 817	12.35	552
47	874.939 502	72326.027 774	.000 013 8263	.001 143	82.664 033	.012 097 1596	14.52	5.822 798	12.39	564
48	1010.586 057	83551.949 519	.000 011 9686	.000 990	82.676 729	.012 095 3019	14.52	5.966 894	12.43	576
49	1167.262 623	96518.286 002	.000 010 3607	.000 857	82.687 721	.012 093 6941	14.52	6.111 092	12.47	588
50	1348.229 595	111494.863	.000 008 9690	.000 742	82.697 238	.012 092 3024	14.52	6.255 381	12.51	600

Effective Rate is 15.50 %

Annual Percentage Rate is 14.50 %

MONTHLY COMPOUND INTEREST AND ANNUITY

14.55 % M

	Amount Of 1	Amount Of 1 Per Period	Sinking Fund Payment	Present Worth Of 1	Present Worth of 1 Per Period	Periodic Payment To Amortize 1	Constant Annual Percent	Total Interest	Annual Add On Rate	
	What a single $1 deposit grows to in the future. The deposit is made at the beginning of the first period.	What a series of $1 deposits grow to in the future. A deposit is made at the end of each period.	The amount to be deposited at the end of each period that grows to $1 in the future.	What $1 to be paid in the future is worth today. Value today of a single $1 payment tomorrow.	What $1 to be paid at the end of each period is worth today. Value today of a series of $1 payments tomorrow.	The mortgage payment to amortize a loan of $1. An annuity certain, payable at the end of each period, worth $1 today.	The annual payment, including interest and principal, to amortize completely a loan of $100.	The total interest paid over the term on a loan of $1. The loan is amortized by regular periodic payments.	The average annual interest rate on a loan that is completely amortized by regular periodic payments.	
	$S = (1+i)^n$	$S\overline{n}| = \frac{(1+i)^n - 1}{i}$	$\frac{1}{S\overline{n}|} = \frac{i}{(1+i)^n - 1}$	$V^n = \frac{1}{(1+i)^n}$	$A\overline{n}| = \frac{1-V^n}{i}$	$\frac{1}{A\overline{n}|} = \frac{i}{1-V^n}$				

YEAR										PERIODS
	1.012 125	1.000 000	1.000 000 0000	.988 020	.988 020	1.012 125 0000	1214.55	.012 125	14.55	1
	1.024 397	2.012 125	.496 987 0162	.976 184	1.964 204	.509 112 0162	610.94	.018 224	10.93	2
	1.036 818	3.036 522	.329 324 1395	.964 490	2.928 694	.341 449 1395	409.74	.024 347	9.74	3
	1.049 389	4.073 340	.245 498 7892	.952 935	3.881 629	.257 623 7892	309.15	.030 495	9.15	4
	1.062 113	5.122 729	.195 208 4489	.941 519	4.823 148	.207 333 4489	248.81	.036 667	8.80	5
	1.074 991	6.184 842	.161 685 6131	.930 240	5.753 389	.173 810 6131	208.58	.042 864	8.57	6
	1.088 025	7.259 833	.137 744 2079	.919 096	6.672 485	.149 869 2079	179.85	.049 084	8.41	7
	1.101 218	8.347 859	.119 791 1962	.908 086	7.580 570	.131 916 1962	158.30	.055 330	8.30	8
	1.114 570	9.449 077	.105 830 4463	.897 207	8.477 777	.117 955 4463	141.55	.061 599	8.21	9
	1.128 084	10.563 647	.094 664 2790	.886 459	9.364 236	.106 789 2790	128.15	.067 893	8.15	10
	1.141 762	11.691 731	.085 530 5349	.875 839	10.240 075	.097 655 5349	117.19	.074 211	8.10	11
	1.155 606	12.833 493	.077 921 1074	.865 347	11.105 422	.090 046 1074	108.06	.080 553	8.06	12
1	1.155 606	12.833 493	.077 921 1074	.865 347	11.105 422	.090 046 1074	108.06	.080 553	8.06	12
2	1.335 425	27.663 956	.036 148 1197	.748 825	20.715 462	.048 273 1197	57.93	.158 555	7.93	24
3	1.543 226	44.802 130	.022 320 3674	.647 993	29.031 480	.034 445 3674	41.34	.240 033	8.00	36
4	1.783 361	64.607 108	.015 478 1731	.560 739	36.227 719	.027 603 1731	33.13	.324 952	8.12	48
5	2.060 863	87.493 862	.011 429 3732	.485 234	42.454 961	.023 554 3732	28.27	.413 262	8.27	60
6	2.381 546	113.941 934	.008 776 4001	.419 895	47.843 685	.020 901 4001	25.09	.504 901	8.42	72
7	2.752 129	144.505 487	.006 920 1524	.363 355	52.506 799	.019 045 1524	22.86	.599 793	8.57	84
8	3.180 377	179.824 916	.005 560 9646	.314 428	56.542 011	.017 685 9646	21.23	.697 853	8.72	96
9	3.675 263	220.640 264	.004 532 2643	.272 089	60.033 868	.016 657 2643	19.99	.798 985	8.88	108
10	4.247 157	267.806 730	.003 734 0361	.235 452	63.055 535	.015 859 0361	19.04	.903 084	9.03	120
11	4.908 040	322.312 585	.003 102 5782	.203 747	65.670 324	.015 227 5782	18.28	1.010 040	9.18	132
12	5.671 761	385.299 884	.002 595 3810	.176 312	67.933 024	.014 720 3810	17.67	1.119 735	9.33	144
13	6.554 322	458.088 391	.002 182 9848	.152 571	69.891 044	.014 307 9848	17.17	1.232 046	9.48	156
14	7.574 214	542.203 234	.001 844 3269	.132 027	71.585 411	.013 969 3269	16.77	1.346 847	9.62	168
15	8.752 808	639.406 861	.001 563 9494	.114 249	73.051 625	.013 688 9494	16.43	1.464 011	9.76	180
16	10.114 799	751.735 965	.001 330 2543	.098 865	74.320 409	.013 455 2543	16.15	1.583 409	9.90	192
17	11.688 723	881.544 163	.001 134 3731	.085 553	75.418 347	.013 259 3731	15.92	1.704 912	10.03	204
18	13.507 560	1031.551 310	.000 969 4137	.074 033	76.368 444	.013 094 4137	15.72	1.828 393	10.16	216
19	15.609 418	1204.900 484	.000 829 9441	.064 064	77.190 607	.012 954 9441	15.55	1.953 727	10.28	228
20	18.038 339	1405.223 848	.000 711 6304	.055 437	77.902 064	.012 836 6304	15.41	2.080 791	10.40	240
21	20.845 215	1636.718 750	.000 610 9785	.047 973	78.517 720	.012 735 9785	15.29	2.209 467	10.52	252
22	24.088 858	1904.235 672	.000 525 1451	.041 513	79.050 477	.012 650 1451	15.19	2.339 638	10.63	264
23	27.837 231	2213.379 861	.000 451 7977	.035 923	79.511 496	.012 576 7977	15.10	2.471 196	10.74	276
24	32.168 874	2570.628 773	.000 389 0099	.031 086	79.910 437	.012 514 0099	15.02	2.604 035	10.85	288
25	37.174 547	2983.467 796	.000 335 1804	.026 900	80.255 660	.012 460 1804	14.96	2.738 054	10.95	300
26	42.959 133	3460.547 091	.000 288 9716	.023 278	80.554 397	.012 413 9716	14.90	2.873 159	11.05	312
27	49.643 837	4011.862 837	.000 249 2608	.020 143	80.812 908	.012 374 2608	14.85	3.009 260	11.15	324
28	57.368 721	4648.966 679	.000 215 1016	.017 431	81.036 610	.012 340 1016	14.81	3.146 274	11.24	336
29	66.295 644	5385.207 767	.000 185 6939	.015 084	81.230 190	.012 310 6939	14.78	3.284 121	11.32	348
30	76.611 651	6236.012 464	.000 160 3589	.013 053	81.397 704	.012 285 3589	14.75	3.422 729	11.41	360
31	88.532 892	7219.207 566	.000 138 5194	.011 295	81.542 661	.012 263 5194	14.72	3.562 029	11.49	372
32	102.309 150	8355.393 827	.000 119 6832	.009 774	81.668 099	.012 244 6832	14.70	3.701 958	11.57	384
33	118.229 078	9668.377 607	.000 103 4300	.008 458	81.776 647	.012 228 4300	14.68	3.842 458	11.64	396
34	136.626 245	11185.669 678	.000 089 4001	.007 319	81.870 578	.012 214 4001	14.66	3.983 475	11.72	408
35	157.886 123	12939.061 658	.000 077 2854	.006 334	81.951 862	.012 202 2854	14.65	4.124 960	11.79	420
36	182.454 167	14965.292 134	.000 066 8213	.005 481	82.022 200	.012 191 8213	14.64	4.266 867	11.85	432
37	210.845 149	17306.816 441	.000 057 7807	.004 743	82.083 067	.012 182 7807	14.62	4.409 155	11.92	444
38	243.653 942	20012.696 225	.000 049 9683	.004 104	82.135 738	.012 174 9683	14.61	4.551 786	11.98	456
39	281.567 982	23139.627 422	.000 043 2159	.003 552	82.181 316	.012 168 2159	14.61	4.694 725	12.04	468
40	325.381 679	26753.128 203	.000 037 3788	.003 073	82.220 758	.012 162 3788	14.60	4.837 942	12.09	480
41	376.013 055	30928.911 763	.000 032 3322	.002 659	82.254 888	.012 157 3322	14.59	4.981 407	12.15	492
42	434.522 982	35754.472 738	.000 027 9685	.002 301	82.284 423	.012 152 9685	14.59	5.125 096	12.20	504
43	502.137 411	41330.920 459	.000 024 1950	.001 991	82.309 980	.012 149 1950	14.58	5.268 985	12.25	516
44	580.273 057	47775.097 487	.000 020 9314	.001 723	82.332 097	.012 145 9314	14.58	5.413 052	12.30	528
45	670.567 087	55222.027 801	.000 018 1087	.001 491	82.351 235	.012 143 1087	14.58	5.557 279	12.35	540
46	774.911 419	63827.745 933	.000 015 6672	.001 290	82.367 796	.012 140 6672	14.57	5.701 648	12.39	552
47	895.492 367	73772.566 342	.000 013 5552	.001 117	82.382 127	.012 138 5552	14.57	5.846 145	12.44	564
48	1034.836 446	85264.861 516	.000 011 7282	.000 966	82.394 529	.012 136 7282	14.57	5.990 755	12.48	576
49	1195.863 314	98545.427 975	.000 010 1476	.000 836	82.405 261	.012 135 1476	14.57	6.135 467	12.52	588
50	1381.946 946	113892.532	.000 008 7802	.000 724	82.414 547	.012 133 7802	14.57	6.280 268	12.56	600

Effective Rate is 15.56 %   8 - 245   Annual Percentage Rate is 14.55 %

Amount Of 1	Amount Of 1 Per Period	Sinking Fund Payment	Present Worth Of 1	Present Worth Of 1 Per Period	Periodic Payment To Amortize 1	Constant Annual Percent	Total Interest	Annual Add On Rate	
What a single $1 deposit grows to in the future. The deposit is made at the beginning of the first period.	What a series of $1 deposits grow to in the future. A deposit is made at the end of each period.	The amount to be deposited at the end of each period that grows to $1 in the future.	What $1 to be paid in the future is worth today. Value today of a single $1 payment tomorrow.	What $1 to be paid at the end of each period is worth today. Value today of a series of $1 payments tomorrow.	The mortgage payment to amortize a loan of $1. An annuity certain, payable at the end of each period, worth $1 today.	The annual interest payment, including interest and principal, to amortize completely a loan of $100.	The total interest paid over the term on a loan of $1. The loan is amortized by regular periodic payments.	The average annual interest rate on a loan that is completely amortized by regular periodic payments.	
$S = (1+i)^n$	$S\overline{n} = \dfrac{(1+i)^n - 1}{i}$	$\dfrac{1}{S\overline{n}} = \dfrac{i}{(1+i)^n - 1}$	$V^n = \dfrac{1}{(1+i)^n}$	$A\overline{n} = \dfrac{1-V^n}{i}$	$\dfrac{1}{A\overline{n}} = \dfrac{i}{1-V^n}$				

YEAR   **PERIODS**

	Amount Of 1	Amount Of 1 Per Period	Sinking Fund Payment	Present Worth Of 1	Present Worth Of 1 Per Period	Periodic Payment To Amortize 1	Constant Annual Percent	Total Interest	Annual Add On Rate	PERIODS
	1.012 167	1.000 000	1.000 000 0000	.987 980	.987 980	1.012 166 6667	1214.60	.012 167	14.60	1
	1.024 481	2.012 167	.496 976 7249	.976 104	1.964 083	.509 143 3916	610.98	.018 287	10.97	2
	1.036 946	3.036 648	.329 310 4735	.964 370	2.928 454	.341 477 1402	409.78	.024 431	9.77	3
	1.049 562	4.073 594	.245 483 4776	.952 778	3.881 232	.257 650 1443	309.19	.030 601	9.18	4
	1.062 332	5.123 156	.195 192 1834	.941 326	4.822 558	.207 358 8501	248.84	.036 794	8.83	5
	1.075 257	6.185 488	.161 668 7395	.930 010	5.752 568	.173 835 4062	208.61	.043 012	8.60	6
	1.088 339	7.260 744	.137 726 9238	.918 831	6.671 399	.149 893 5904	179.88	.049 255	8.44	7
	1.101 581	8.349 084	.119 773 6251	.907 787	7.579 186	.131 940 2917	158.33	.055 522	8.33	8
	1.114 983	9.450 664	.105 812 6705	.896 875	8.476 061	.117 979 3371	141.58	.061 814	8.24	9
	1.128 549	10.565 647	.094 646 3561	.886 094	9.362 154	.106 813 0228	128.18	.068 130	8.18	10
	1.142 279	11.694 196	.085 512 5068	.875 443	10.237 597	.097 679 1734	117.22	.074 471	8.12	11
	1.156 177	12.836 475	.077 903 0056	.864 919	11.102 516	.090 069 6722	108.09	.080 836	8.08	12
1	1.156 177	12.836 475	.077 903 0056	.864 919	11.102 516	.090 069 6722	108.09	.080 836	8.08	12
2	1.336 746	27.677 714	.036 130 1514	.748 086	20.705 298	.048 296 8180	57.96	.159 124	7.96	24
3	1.545 515	44.836 815	.022 303 1008	.647 034	29.010 930	.034 469 7674	41.37	.240 912	8.03	36
4	1.786 889	64.675 774	.015 461 7399	.559 632	36.194 632	.027 628 4065	33.16	.326 164	8.15	48
5	2.065 960	87.613 126	.011 413 8149	.484 037	42.407 955	.023 580 4816	28.30	.414 829	8.30	60
6	2.388 615	114.132 766	.008 761 7258	.418 653	47.781 979	.020 928 3925	25.12	.506 844	8.45	72
7	2.761 662	144.794 167	.006 906 3555	.362 101	52.430 076	.019 073 0222	22.89	.602 134	8.60	84
8	3.192 971	180.244 178	.005 548 0294	.313 188	56.450 305	.017 714 6961	21.26	.700 611	8.76	96
9	3.691 640	221.230 669	.004 520 1690	.270 882	59.927 480	.016 686 8356	20.03	.802 178	8.91	108
10	4.268 189	268.618 312	.003 722 7544	.234 291	62.934 955	.015 889 4211	19.07	.906 731	9.07	120
11	4.934 783	323.406 820	.003 092 0807	.202 643	65.536 179	.015 258 7474	18.32	1.014 155	9.22	132
12	5.705 483	386.752 039	.002 585 6360	.175 270	67.786 028	.014 752 3027	17.71	1.124 332	9.37	144
13	6.596 549	459.990 332	.002 173 9587	.151 594	69.731 966	.014 340 6254	17.21	1.237 138	9.52	156
14	7.626 779	544.666 770	.001 835 9850	.131 117	71.415 045	.014 002 6516	16.81	1.352 445	9.66	168
15	8.817 907	642.567 730	.001 556 2562	.113 406	72.870 773	.013 722 9228	16.47	1.470 126	9.80	180
16	10.195 063	755.758 580	.001 323 1739	.098 087	74.129 861	.013 489 8405	16.19	1.590 049	9.94	192
17	11.787 298	886.627 250	.001 127 8697	.084 837	75.218 870	.013 294 5364	15.96	1.712 085	10.07	204
18	13.628 204	1037.934 611	.000 963 4518	.073 377	76.160 775	.013 130 1185	15.76	1.836 106	10.20	216
19	15.756 618	1212.872 719	.000 824 4888	.063 465	76.975 447	.012 991 1555	15.59	1.961 983	10.33	228
20	18.217 441	1415.132 157	.000 706 6478	.054 892	77.680 073	.012 873 3144	15.45	2.089 595	10.45	240
21	21.062 589	1648.979 889	.000 606 4355	.047 478	78.289 517	.012 773 1022	15.33	2.218 822	10.57	252
22	24.352 083	1919.349 287	.000 521 0099	.041 064	78.816 637	.012 687 6766	15.23	2.349 547	10.68	264
23	28.155 321	2231.944 196	.000 448 0399	.035 517	79.272 554	.012 614 7065	15.14	2.481 659	10.79	276
24	32.552 538	2593.359 277	.000 385 6003	.030 720	79.666 885	.012 552 2669	15.07	2.615 053	10.90	288
25	37.636 499	3011.219 122	.000 332 0914	.026 570	80.007 949	.012 498 7581	15.00	2.749 627	11.00	300
26	43.514 459	3494.339 113	.000 286 1771	.022 981	80.302 942	.012 452 8438	14.95	2.885 287	11.10	312
27	50.310 422	4052.911 390	.000 246 7362	.019 877	80.558 088	.012 413 4029	14.90	3.021 943	11.19	324
28	58.167 758	4698.719 874	.000 212 8239	.017 192	80.778 768	.012 379 4906	14.86	3.159 509	11.28	336
29	67.252 231	5445.388 863	.000 183 6416	.014 869	80.969 639	.012 350 3083	14.83	3.297 907	11.37	348
30	77.755 491	6308.670 462	.000 158 5120	.012 861	81.134 726	.012 325 1787	14.80	3.437 064	11.46	360
31	89.899 119	7306.776 890	.000 136 8592	.011 124	81.277 514	.012 303 5259	14.77	3.576 912	11.54	372
32	103.939 304	8460.764 700	.000 118 1926	.009 621	81.401 014	.012 284 8593	14.75	3.717 386	11.62	384
33	120.172 244	9794.978 998	.000 102 0931	.008 321	81.507 831	.012 268 7598	14.73	3.858 429	11.69	396
34	138.940 399	11337.567 035	.000 088 2023	.007 197	81.600 219	.012 254 8690	14.71	3.999 987	11.76	408
35	160.639 710	13121.072 021	.000 076 2133	.006 225	81.680 128	.012 242 8800	14.70	4.142 010	11.83	420
36	185.727 956	15183.119 672	.000 065 8626	.005 384	81.749 242	.012 232 5293	14.68	4.284 453	11.90	432
37	214.734 412	17567.211 975	.000 056 9242	.004 657	81.809 021	.012 223 5909	14.67	4.427 274	11.97	444
38	248.271 013	20323.644 937	.000 049 2038	.004 028	81.860 724	.012 215 8704	14.66	4.570 437	12.03	456
39	287.045 264	23510.569 646	.000 042 5341	.003 484	81.905 443	.012 209 2007	14.66	4.713 906	12.09	468
40	331.875 165	27195.219 062	.000 036 7712	.003 013	81.944 122	.012 203 4378	14.65	4.857 650	12.14	480
41	383.706 471	31455.326 394	.000 031 7911	.002 606	81.977 576	.012 198 4578	14.64	5.001 641	12.20	492
42	443.632 641	36380.765 000	.000 027 4871	.002 254	82.006 511	.012 194 1537	14.64	5.145 853	12.25	504
43	512.917 907	42075.444 397	.000 023 7668	.001 950	82.031 537	.012 190 4335	14.63	5.290 264	12.30	516
44	593.023 946	48659.502 394	.000 020 5510	.001 686	82.053 183	.012 187 2176	14.63	5.434 851	12.35	528
45	685.640 715	56271.839 574	.000 017 7709	.001 458	82.071 905	.012 184 4375	14.63	5.579 596	12.40	540
46	792.722 104	65073.049 614	.000 015 3673	.001 261	82.088 098	.012 182 0340	14.62	5.724 483	12.44	552
47	916.527 155	75248.807 247	.000 013 2892	.001 091	82.102 103	.012 179 9559	14.62	5.869 495	12.49	564
48	1059.667 722	87013.785 351	.000 011 4924	.000 944	82.114 217	.012 178 1591	14.62	6.014 620	12.53	576
49	1225.163 569	100616.184	.000 009 9388	.000 816	82.124 694	.012 176 6054	14.62	6.159 844	12.57	588
50	1416.506 081	116342.966	.000 008 5953	.000 706	82.133 757	.012 175 2619	14.62	6.305 157	12.61	600

Effective Rate is 15.62 %   Annual Percentage Rate is 14.60 %

	Amount Of 1	Amount Of 1 Per Period	Sinking Fund Payment	Present Worth Of 1	Present Worth of 1 Per Period	Periodic Payment To Amortize 1	Constant Annual Percent	Total Interest	Annual Add On Rate	
	What a single $ 1 deposit grows to in the future. The deposit is made at the beginning of the first period.	What a series of $ 1 deposits grow to in the future. A deposit is made at the end of each period.	The amount to be deposited at the end of each period that grows to $ 1 in the future.	What $ 1 to be paid in the future is worth today. Value today of a single $ 1 payment tomorrow.	What $ 1 to be paid at the end of each period is worth today. Value today of a series of $ 1 payments tomorrow.	The mortgage payment to amortize a loan of $ 1. An annuity certain, payable at the end of each period, worth $ 1 today.	The annual payment, including interest and principal, to amortize completely a loan of $ 100.	The total interest paid over the term on a loan of $1. The loan is amortized by regular periodic payments.	The average annual interest rate on a loan that is completely amortized by regular periodic payments.	
	$S = (1+i)^n$	$S\overline{n}| = \dfrac{(1+i)^n - 1}{i}$	$\dfrac{1}{S\overline{n}|} = \dfrac{i}{(1+i)^n - 1}$	$V^n = \dfrac{1}{(1+i)^n}$	$A\overline{n}| = \dfrac{1 - V^n}{i}$	$\dfrac{1}{A\overline{n}|} = \dfrac{i}{1 - V^n}$				

YEAR										PERIODS
	1.012 188	1.000 000	1.000 000 0000	.987 959	.987 959	1.012 187 5000	1214.63	.012 187	14.62	1
	1.024 524	2.012 188	.496 971 5794	.976 063	1.964 023	.509 159 0794	611.00	.018 318	10.99	2
	1.037 010	3.036 711	.329 303 6408	.964 311	2.928 334	.341 491 1408	409.79	.024 473	9.79	3
	1.049 648	4.073 721	.245 475 8222	.952 700	3.881 034	.257 663 3222	309.20	.030 653	9.20	4
	1.062 441	5.123 369	.195 184 0512	.941 229	4.822 262	.207 371 5512	248.85	.036 858	8.85	5
	1.075 390	6.185 810	.161 660 3033	.929 896	5.752 158	.173 847 8033	208.62	.043 087	8.62	6
	1.088 496	7.261 200	.137 718 2824	.918 699	6.670 857	.149 905 7824	179.89	.049 340	8.46	7
	1.101 762	8.349 696	.119 764 8403	.907 637	7.578 494	.131 952 3403	158.35	.055 619	8.34	8
	1.115 190	9.451 458	.105 803 7835	.896 708	8.475 202	.117 991 2835	141.59	.061 922	8.26	9
	1.128 781	10.566 647	.094 637 3957	.885 911	9.361 114	.106 824 8957	128.19	.068 249	8.19	10
	1.142 538	11.695 429	.085 503 4939	.875 244	10.236 358	.097 690 9939	117.23	.074 601	8.14	11
	1.156 463	12.837 967	.077 893 9559	.864 706	11.101 064	.090 081 4559	108.10	.080 977	8.10	12
1	1.156 463	12.837 967	.077 893 9559	.864 706	11.101 064	.090 081 4559	108.10	.080 977	8.10	12
2	1.337 406	27.684 596	.036 121 1698	.747 716	20.700 218	.048 308 6698	57.98	.159 408	7.97	24
3	1.546 660	44.854 170	.022 294 4712	.646 554	29.000 662	.034 481 9712	41.38	.241 351	8.05	36
4	1.788 655	64.710 142	.015 453 5282	.559 079	36.178 104	.027 641 0282	33.17	.326 769	8.17	48
5	2.068 513	87.672 833	.011 406 0418	.483 439	42.384 480	.023 593 5418	28.32	.415 613	8.31	60
6	2.392 158	114.228 329	.008 754 3958	.418 033	47.751 169	.020 941 8958	25.14	.507 816	8.46	72
7	2.766 441	144.938 770	.006 899 4652	.361 475	52.391 776	.019 086 9652	22.91	.603 305	8.62	84
8	3.199 286	180.454 251	.005 541 5708	.312 570	56.404 535	.017 729 0708	21.28	.701 991	8.77	96
9	3.699 855	221.526 580	.004 514 1310	.270 281	59.874 392	.016 701 6310	20.05	.803 776	8.93	108
10	4.278 745	269.025 197	.003 717 1239	.233 713	62.874 797	.015 904 6239	19.09	.908 555	9.09	120
11	4.948 209	323.955 577	.003 086 8430	.202 093	65.469 264	.015 274 3430	18.33	1.016 213	9.24	132
12	5.722 419	387.480 513	.002 580 7749	.174 751	67.712 716	.014 768 2749	17.73	1.126 632	9.39	144
13	6.617 764	460.944 734	.002 169 4575	.151 108	69.652 641	.014 356 9575	17.23	1.239 685	9.54	156
14	7.653 197	545.903 366	.001 831 8260	.130 664	71.330 105	.014 019 3260	16.83	1.355 247	9.68	168
15	8.850 637	644.154 856	.001 552 4217	.112 986	72.780 618	.013 739 9217	16.49	1.473 186	9.82	180
16	10.235 432	757.779 042	.001 319 6459	.097 700	74.034 886	.013 507 1459	16.21	1.593 372	9.96	192
17	11.836 896	889.181 177	.001 124 6302	.084 482	75.119 458	.013 312 1302	15.98	1.715 675	10.09	204
18	13.688 928	1041.142 846	.000 960 4830	.073 052	76.057 293	.013 147 9830	15.78	1.839 964	10.22	216
19	15.830 735	1216.880 851	.000 821 7731	.063 168	76.868 245	.013 009 2731	15.62	1.966 114	10.35	228
20	18.307 655	1420.115 303	.000 704 1682	.054 622	77.569 480	.012 891 6682	15.48	2.094 000	10.47	240
21	21.172 121	1655.148 368	.000 604 1754	.047 232	78.175 842	.012 791 6754	15.36	2.223 502	10.59	252
22	24.484 768	1926.955 346	.000 518 9534	.040 842	78.700 167	.012 706 4534	15.25	2.354 504	10.70	264
23	28.315 722	2241.289 982	.000 446 1716	.035 316	79.153 553	.012 633 6716	15.17	2.486 893	10.81	276
24	32.746 076	2604.806 269	.000 383 9057	.030 538	79.545 599	.012 571 4057	15.09	2.620 565	10.92	288
25	37.869 616	3025.199 302	.000 330 5567	.026 406	79.884 604	.012 518 0567	15.03	2.755 417	11.02	300
26	43.794 800	3511.368 172	.000 284 7893	.022 834	80.177 743	.012 472 2893	14.97	2.891 354	11.12	312
27	50.647 053	4073.604 344	.000 245 4828	.019 744	80.431 222	.012 432 9828	14.92	3.028 286	11.22	324
28	58.571 428	4723.809 515	.000 211 6935	.017 073	80.650 407	.012 399 1935	14.88	3.166 129	11.31	336
29	67.735 673	5475.747 554	.000 182 6235	.014 763	80.839 937	.012 370 1235	14.85	3.304 803	11.40	348
30	78.333 781	6345.335 862	.000 157 5961	.012 766	81.003 825	.012 345 0961	14.82	3.444 235	11.48	360
31	90.590 097	7350.982 320	.000 136 0362	.011 039	81.145 540	.012 323 5362	14.79	3.584 355	11.56	372
32	104.764 070	8513.974 954	.000 117 4540	.009 545	81.268 081	.012 304 9540	14.77	3.725 102	11.64	384
33	121.155 741	9858.932 577	.000 101 4309	.008 254	81.374 044	.012 288 9309	14.75	3.866 411	11.72	396
34	140.112 097	11414.325 924	.000 087 6092	.007 137	81.465 670	.012 275 1092	14.74	4.008 245	11.79	408
35	162.034 417	13213.080 340	.000 075 6826	.006 172	81.544 900	.012 263 1826	14.72	4.150 537	11.86	420
36	187.386 762	15293.272 760	.000 065 3882	.005 337	81.613 411	.012 252 8882	14.71	4.293 248	11.93	432
37	216.705 804	17698.937 738	.000 056 5006	.004 615	81.672 652	.012 244 0006	14.70	4.436 336	11.99	444
38	250.612 183	20480.999 595	.000 048 8257	.003 990	81.723 879	.012 236 3257	14.69	4.579 765	12.05	456
39	289.823 646	23698.350 411	.000 042 1970	.003 450	81.768 174	.012 229 6970	14.68	4.723 498	12.11	468
40	335.170 241	27419.096 677	.000 036 4709	.002 984	81.806 477	.012 223 9709	14.67	4.867 506	12.17	480
41	387.611 887	31722.001 014	.000 031 5239	.002 580	81.839 598	.012 219 0239	14.67	5.011 760	12.22	492
42	448.258 696	36698.149 456	.000 027 2493	.002 231	81.868 238	.012 214 7493	14.66	5.156 234	12.28	504
43	518.394 470	42452.879 605	.000 023 5555	.001 929	81.893 002	.012 211 0555	14.66	5.300 905	12.33	516
44	599.503 878	49108.010 469	.000 020 3633	.001 668	81.914 417	.012 207 8633	14.65	5.445 752	12.38	528
45	693.303 883	56804.421 193	.000 017 6043	.001 442	81.932 934	.012 205 1043	14.65	5.590 756	12.42	540
46	801.780 093	65705.033 251	.000 015 2195	.001 247	81.948 946	.012 202 7195	14.65	5.735 901	12.47	552
47	927.228 785	75998.259 257	.000 013 1582	.001 078	81.962 791	.012 200 6582	14.65	5.881 171	12.51	564
48	1072.305 520	87901.991 374	.000 011 3763	.000 933	81.974 763	.012 198 8763	14.64	6.026 553	12.56	576
49	1240.081 355	101668.214	.000 009 8359	.000 806	81.985 116	.012 197 3359	14.64	6.172 034	12.60	588
50	1434.107 854	117588.337	.000 008 5042	.000 697	81.994 068	.012 196 0042	14.64	6.317 603	12.64	600

Effective Rate is 15.65 %

Annual Percentage Rate is 14.625%

MONTHLY COMPOUND INTEREST AND ANNUITY

14.65 % M

	Amount Of 1	Amount Of 1 Per Period	Sinking Fund Payment	Present Worth Of 1	Present Worth of 1 Per Period	Periodic Payment To Amortize 1	Constant Annual Percent	Total Interest	Annual Add On Rate	
	What a single $1 deposit grows to in the future. The deposit is made at the beginning of the first period.	What a series of $1 deposits grow to in the future. A deposit is made at the end of each period.	The amount to be deposited at the end of each period that grows to $1 in the future.	What $1 to be paid in the future is worth today. Value today of a single $1 payment tomorrow.	What $1 to be paid at the end of each period is worth today. Value today of a series of $1 payments tomorrow.	The mortgage payment to amortize a loan of $1. An annuity certain, payable at the end of each period, worth $1 today.	The annual payment, including interest and principal, to amortize completely a loan of $100.	The total interest paid over the term on a loan of $1. The loan is amortized by regular periodic payments.	The average annual interest rate on a loan that is completely amortized by regular periodic payments.	
	$S = (1+i)^n$	$S\overline{n} = \frac{(1+i)^n - 1}{i}$	$\frac{1}{S\overline{n}} = \frac{i}{(1+i)^n - 1}$	$V^n = \frac{1}{(1+i)^n}$	$A\overline{n} = \frac{1-V^n}{i}$	$\frac{1}{A\overline{n}} = \frac{i}{1-V^n}$				

YEAR										PERIODS
	1.012 208	1.000 000	1.000 000 0000	.987 939	.987 939	1.012 208 3333	1214.65	.012 208	14.65	1
	1.024 566	2.012 208	.496 966 4341	.976 023	1.963 962	.509 174 7674	611.01	.018 350	11.01	2
	1.037 074	3.036 774	.329 296 8083	.964 251	2.928 214	.341 505 1416	409.81	.024 515	9.81	3
	1.049 735	4.073 848	.245 468 1671	.952 621	3.880 835	.257 676 5005	309.22	.030 706	9.21	4
	1.062 550	5.123 583	.195 175 9193	.941 132	4.821 967	.207 384 2526	248.87	.036 921	8.86	5
	1.075 522	6.186 133	.161 651 8675	.929 781	5.751 748	.173 860 2009	208.64	.043 161	8.63	6
	1.088 653	7.261 656	.137 709 6416	.918 567	6.670 314	.149 917 9749	179.91	.049 426	8.47	7
	1.101 943	8.350 308	.119 756 0562	.907 488	7.577 802	.131 964 3895	158.36	.055 715	8.36	8
	1.115 396	9.452 252	.105 794 8971	.896 542	8.474 344	.118 003 2305	141.61	.062 029	8.27	9
	1.129 013	10.567 648	.094 628 4360	.885 729	9.360 073	.106 836 7693	128.21	.068 368	8.20	10
	1.142 797	11.696 661	.085 494 4818	.875 046	10.235 120	.097 702 8151	117.25	.074 731	8.15	11
	1.156 748	12.839 458	.077 884 9071	.864 492	11.099 612	.090 093 2404	108.12	.081 119	8.11	12
1	1.156 748	12.839 458	.077 884 9071	.864 492	11.099 612	.090 093 2404	108.12	.081 119	8.11	12
2	1.338 067	27.691 480	.036 112 1898	.747 347	20.695 140	.048 320 5232	57.99	.159 693	7.98	24
3	1.547 807	44.871 533	.022 285 8442	.646 076	28.990 400	.034 494 1775	41.40	.241 790	8.06	36
4	1.790 423	64.744 532	.015 445 3198	.558 527	36.161 588	.027 653 6531	33.19	.327 375	8.18	48
5	2.071 069	87.732 591	.011 398 2728	.482 843	42.361 024	.023 606 6061	28.33	.416 396	8.33	60
6	2.395 705	114.323 991	.008 747 0705	.417 414	47.720 388	.020 955 4038	25.15	.508 789	8.48	72
7	2.771 228	145.083 549	.006 892 5802	.360 851	52.353 517	.019 100 9135	22.93	.604 477	8.64	84
8	3.205 614	180.664 619	.005 535 1181	.311 953	56.358 821	.017 743 4514	21.30	.703 371	8.79	96
9	3.708 089	221.822 965	.004 508 0995	.269 681	59.821 375	.016 716 4329	20.06	.805 375	8.95	108
10	4.289 326	269.432 814	.003 711 5004	.233 137	62.814 726	.015 919 8337	19.11	.910 380	9.10	120
11	4.961 670	324.505 430	.003 081 6125	.201 545	65.402 455	.015 289 9459	18.35	1.018 273	9.26	132
12	5.739 404	388.210 590	.002 575 9215	.174 234	67.639 527	.014 784 2548	17.75	1.128 933	9.41	144
13	6.639 047	461.901 431	.002 164 9641	.150 624	69.573 458	.014 373 2974	17.25	1.242 234	9.56	156
14	7.679 706	547.143 192	.001 827 6751	.130 213	71.245 326	.014 036 0085	16.85	1.358 049	9.70	168
15	8.883 488	645.746 461	.001 548 5954	.112 568	72.690 643	.013 756 9287	16.51	1.476 247	9.84	180
16	10.275 960	759.805 634	.001 316 1261	.097 315	73.940 109	.013 524 4594	16.23	1.596 696	9.98	192
17	11.886 701	891.743 397	.001 121 3988	.084 128	75.020 262	.013 329 7322	16.00	1.719 265	10.11	204
18	13.749 922	1044.362 192	.000 957 5222	.072 728	75.954 046	.013 165 8555	15.80	1.843 825	10.24	216
19	15.905 200	1220.903 736	.000 819 0654	.062 873	76.761 295	.013 027 3987	15.64	1.970 247	10.37	228
20	18.398 314	1425.117 882	.000 701 6963	.054 353	77.459 156	.012 910 0297	15.50	2.098 407	10.49	240
21	21.282 220	1661.342 265	.000 601 9229	.046 988	78.062 451	.012 810 2563	15.38	2.228 185	10.61	252
22	24.618 174	1934.594 438	.000 516 9042	.040 620	78.583 995	.012 725 2375	15.28	2.359 463	10.72	264
23	28.477 033	2250.678 448	.000 444 3105	.035 116	79.034 865	.012 652 6438	15.19	2.492 130	10.84	276
24	32.940 762	2616.308 116	.000 382 2180	.030 358	79.424 640	.012 590 5513	15.11	2.626 079	10.94	288
25	38.104 173	3039.249 644	.000 329 0286	.026 244	79.761 596	.012 537 3619	15.05	2.761 209	11.04	300
26	44.076 940	3528.486 573	.000 283 4076	.022 688	80.052 893	.012 491 7410	15.00	2.897 423	11.14	312
27	50.985 929	4094.410 599	.000 244 2354	.019 613	80.304 716	.012 452 5687	14.95	3.034 632	11.24	324
28	58.977 891	4749.042 303	.000 210 5688	.016 956	80.522 416	.012 418 9021	14.91	3.172 751	11.33	336
29	68.222 581	5506.286 468	.000 181 6106	.014 658	80.710 615	.012 389 9439	14.87	3.311 700	11.42	348
30	78.916 360	6382.227 432	.000 156 6851	.012 672	80.873 312	.012 365 0184	14.84	3.451 407	11.50	360
31	91.286 372	7395.470 727	.000 135 2179	.010 955	81.013 963	.012 343 5512	14.82	3.591 801	11.59	372
32	105.595 363	8567.538 271	.000 116 7196	.009 470	81.135 554	.012 325 0530	14.80	3.732 820	11.67	384
33	122.147 266	9923.325 509	.000 100 7727	.008 187	81.240 668	.012 309 1060	14.78	3.874 406	11.74	396
34	141.293 652	11491.630 206	.000 087 0199	.007 077	81.331 539	.012 295 3532	14.76	4.016 504	11.81	408
35	163.441 204	13305.764 129	.000 075 1554	.006 118	81.410 096	.012 283 4887	14.75	4.159 065	11.88	420
36	189.060 348	15404.260 614	.000 064 9171	.005 289	81.478 008	.012 273 2504	14.73	4.302 044	11.95	432
37	218.695 252	17831.693 031	.000 056 0799	.004 573	81.536 718	.012 264 4133	14.72	4.445 399	12.01	444
38	252.975 380	20639.621 557	.000 048 4505	.003 953	81.587 471	.012 256 7838	14.71	4.589 093	12.08	456
39	292.628 862	23887.688 343	.000 041 8626	.003 417	81.631 348	.012 250 1959	14.71	4.733 092	12.14	468
40	338.497 963	27644.884 349	.000 036 1731	.002 954	81.669 278	.012 244 5064	14.70	4.877 363	12.19	480
41	391.556 972	31991.014 757	.000 031 2588	.002 554	81.702 069	.012 239 5921	14.69	5.021 879	12.25	492
42	452.932 894	37018.394 084	.000 027 0136	.002 208	81.730 416	.012 235 3469	14.69	5.166 615	12.30	504
43	523.929 394	42833.806 997	.000 023 3460	.001 909	81.754 923	.012 231 6794	14.68	5.311 547	12.35	516
44	606.054 480	49560.776 486	.000 020 1772	.001 650	81.776 108	.012 228 5106	14.68	5.456 654	12.40	528
45	701.052 540	57342.187 574	.000 017 4392	.001 426	81.794 422	.012 225 7725	14.68	5.601 917	12.45	540
46	810.941 393	66343.322 274	.000 015 0731	.001 233	81.810 255	.012 223 4064	14.67	5.747 320	12.49	552
47	938.055 146	76755.370 295	.000 013 0284	.001 066	81.823 942	.012 221 3617	14.67	5.892 848	12.54	564
48	1085.093 774	88799.490 018	.000 011 2613	.000 922	81.835 775	.012 219 5947	14.67	6.038 487	12.58	576
49	1255.180 470	102731.506	.000 009 7341	.000 797	81.846 004	.012 218 0674	14.67	6.184 224	12.62	588
50	1451.927 980	118847.343	.000 008 4142	.000 689	81.854 847	.012 216 7475	14.67	6.330 048	12.66	600

Effective Rate is 15.67 %

8 - 248

Annual Percentage Rate is 14.65 %

MONTHLY COMPOUND INTEREST AND ANNUITY

Amount Of 1	Amount Of 1 Per Period	Sinking Fund Payment	Present Worth Of 1	Present Worth of 1 Per Period	Periodic Payment To Amortize 1	Constant Annual Percent	Total Interest	Annual Add On Rate
What a single $1 deposit grows to in the future. The deposit is made at the beginning of the first period.	What a series of $1 deposits grow to in the future. A deposit is made at the end of each period.	The amount to be deposited at the end of each period that grows to $1 in the future.	What $1 to be paid in the future is worth today. Value today of a single $1 payment tomorrow.	What $1 to be paid at the end of each period is worth today. Value today of a series of $1 payments tomorrow.	The mortgage payment to amortize a loan of $1. An annuity certain, payable at the end of each period, worth $1 today.	The annual payment, including interest and principal, to amortize completely a loan of $100.	The total interest paid over the term on a loan of $1. The loan is amortized by regular periodic payments.	The average annual interest rate on a loan that is completely amortized by regular periodic payments.

$$S = (1+i)^n \qquad S\overline{n}| = \frac{(1+i)^n - 1}{i} \qquad \frac{1}{S\overline{n}|} = \frac{i}{(1+i)^n - 1} \qquad V^n = \frac{1}{(1+i)^n} \qquad A\overline{n}| = \frac{1 - V^n}{i} \qquad \frac{1}{A\overline{n}|} = \frac{i}{1 - V^n}$$

YEAR / **PERIODS**

YEAR	Amount Of 1	Amount Of 1 Per Period	Sinking Fund Payment	Present Worth Of 1	Present Worth of 1 Per Period	Periodic Payment To Amortize 1	Constant Annual Percent	Total Interest	Annual Add On Rate	PERIODS
	1.012 250	1.000 000	1.000 000 0000	.987 898	.987 898	1.012 250 0000	1214.70	.012 250	14.70	1
	1.024 650	2.012 250	.496 956 1436	.975 943	1.963 841	.509 206 1436	611.05	.018 412	11.05	2
	1.037 202	3.036 900	.329 283 1438	.964 132	2.927 974	.341 533 1438	409.84	.024 599	9.84	3
	1.049 908	4.074 102	.245 452 8577	.952 465	3.880 438	.257 702 8577	309.25	.030 811	9.24	4
	1.062 769	5.124 010	.195 159 6565	.940 938	4.821 376	.207 409 6565	248.90	.037 048	8.89	5
	1.075 788	6.186 779	.161 634 9972	.929 551	5.750 927	.173 884 9972	208.67	.043 310	8.66	6
	1.088 966	7.262 567	.137 692 3614	.918 302	6.669 229	.149 942 3614	179.94	.049 597	8.50	7
	1.102 306	8.351 533	.119 738 4895	.907 189	7.576 418	.131 988 4895	158.39	.055 908	8.39	8
	1.115 810	9.453 840	.105 777 1264	.896 210	8.472 629	.118 027 1264	141.64	.062 244	8.30	9
	1.129 478	10.569 649	.094 610 5187	.885 365	9.357 993	.106 860 5187	128.24	.068 605	8.23	10
	1.143 314	11.699 127	.085 476 4599	.874 650	10.232 643	.097 726 4599	117.28	.074 991	8.18	11
	1.157 320	12.842 442	.077 866 8120	.864 065	11.096 709	.090 116 8120	108.15	.081 402	8.14	12
1	1.157 320	12.842 442	.077 866 8120	.864 065	11.096 709	.090 116 8120	108.15	.081 402	8.14	12
2	1.339 389	27.705 255	.036 094 2351	.746 609	20.684 990	.048 344 2351	58.02	.160 262	8.01	24
3	1.550 102	44.906 285	.022 268 5976	.645 119	28.969 891	.034 518 5976	41.43	.242 670	8.09	36
4	1.793 964	64.813 380	.015 428 9129	.557 425	36.128 586	.027 678 9129	33.22	.328 588	8.21	48
5	2.076 190	87.852 257	.011 382 7468	.481 651	42.314 167	.023 632 7468	28.36	.417 965	8.36	60
6	2.402 816	114.515 608	.008 732 4341	.416 178	47.658 913	.020 982 4341	25.18	.510 735	8.51	72
7	2.780 827	145.373 636	.006 878 8264	.359 605	52.277 122	.019 128 8264	22.96	.606 821	8.67	84
8	3.218 306	181.086 245	.005 522 2306	.310 722	56.267 557	.017 772 2306	21.33	.706 134	8.83	96
9	3.724 610	222.417 159	.004 496 0560	.268 484	59.715 553	.016 746 0560	20.10	.808 574	8.98	108
10	4.310 566	270.250 248	.003 700 2741	.231 988	62.694 847	.015 950 2741	19.15	.914 033	9.14	120
11	4.988 703	325.608 435	.003 071 1735	.200 453	65.269 152	.015 321 1735	18.39	1.022 395	9.29	132
12	5.773 526	389.675 567	.002 566 2374	.173 204	67.493 519	.014 816 2374	17.78	1.133 538	9.45	144
13	6.681 816	463.821 735	.002 156 0007	.149 660	69.415 518	.014 406 0007	17.29	1.247 336	9.59	156
14	7.732 999	549.632 571	.001 819 3973	.129 316	71.076 250	.014 069 3973	16.89	1.363 659	9.74	168
15	8.949 554	648.943 161	.001 540 9670	.111 737	72.511 231	.013 790 9670	16.55	1.482 374	9.88	180
16	10.357 497	763.877 284	.001 309 1108	.096 548	73.751 149	.013 559 1108	16.28	1.603 349	10.02	192
17	11.986 937	896.892 832	.001 114 9604	.083 424	74.822 519	.013 364 9604	16.04	1.726 452	10.16	204
18	13.872 721	1050.834 375	.000 951 6248	.072 084	75.748 252	.013 201 6248	15.85	1.851 551	10.29	216
19	16.055 176	1228.993 988	.000 813 6736	.062 285	76.548 146	.013 063 6736	15.68	1.978 518	10.41	228
20	18.580 975	1435.181 656	.000 696 7759	.053 818	77.239 307	.012 946 7759	15.54	2.107 226	10.54	240
21	21.504 133	1673.806 749	.000 597 4405	.046 503	77.836 515	.012 847 4405	15.42	2.237 555	10.66	252
22	24.887 161	1949.972 322	.000 512 8278	.040 181	78.352 542	.012 762 8278	15.32	2.369 387	10.77	264
23	28.802 407	2269.584 237	.000 440 6093	.034 719	78.798 423	.012 690 6093	15.23	2.502 608	10.88	276
24	33.333 599	2639.477 471	.000 378 8629	.030 000	79.183 693	.012 628 8629	15.16	2.637 113	10.99	288
25	38.577 638	3067.562 276	.000 325 9918	.025 922	79.516 592	.012 575 9918	15.10	2.772 798	11.09	300
26	44.646 668	3562.993 344	.000 280 6629	.022 398	79.804 238	.012 530 6629	15.04	2.909 567	11.19	312
27	51.670 478	4136.365 585	.000 241 7581	.019 353	80.052 783	.012 491 7581	15.00	3.047 330	11.29	324
28	59.799 274	4799.940 696	.000 208 3359	.016 723	80.267 542	.012 458 3359	14.96	3.186 001	11.38	336
29	69.206 890	5567.909 385	.000 179 6006	.014 449	80.453 108	.012 429 6006	14.92	3.325 501	11.47	348
30	80.094 512	6456.694 841	.000 154 8780	.012 485	80.613 449	.012 404 8780	14.89	3.465 756	11.55	360
31	92.694 973	7485.303 946	.000 133 5951	.010 788	80.751 994	.012 383 5951	14.87	3.606 697	11.63	372
32	107.277 738	8675.733 744	.000 115 2640	.009 322	80.871 706	.012 365 2640	14.84	3.748 261	11.71	384
33	124.154 663	10053.441 854	.000 099 4684	.008 054	80.975 145	.012 349 4684	14.82	3.890 389	11.79	396
34	143.686 663	11647.890 882	.000 085 8525	.006 960	81.064 523	.012 335 8525	14.81	4.033 028	11.86	408
35	166.291 437	13493.178 491	.000 074 1115	.006 014	81.141 752	.012 324 1115	14.79	4.176 127	11.93	420
36	192.452 391	15628.766 583	.000 063 9846	.005 196	81.208 482	.012 313 9846	14.78	4.319 641	12.00	432
37	222.728 984	18100.325 206	.000 055 2476	.004 490	81.266 142	.012 305 2476	14.77	4.463 530	12.06	444
38	257.768 688	20960.709 214	.000 047 7083	.003 879	81.315 963	.012 297 7083	14.76	4.607 755	12.13	456
39	298.320 835	24271.088 582	.000 041 2013	.003 352	81.359 013	.012 291 2013	14.75	4.752 282	12.19	468
40	345.252 643	28102.256 540	.000 035 5843	.002 896	81.396 210	.012 285 5843	14.75	4.897 080	12.24	480
41	399.567 758	32536.143 503	.000 030 7351	.002 503	81.428 351	.012 280 7351	14.74	5.042 122	12.30	492
42	462.427 722	37667.569 173	.000 026 5480	.002 163	81.456 122	.012 276 5480	14.74	5.187 380	12.35	504
43	535.176 811	43606.270 277	.000 022 9325	.001 869	81.480 119	.012 272 9325	14.73	5.332 833	12.40	516
44	619.370 780	50479.247 315	.000 019 8101	.001 615	81.500 854	.012 269 8101	14.73	5.478 460	12.45	528
45	716.810 136	58433.480 495	.000 017 1135	.001 395	81.518 770	.012 267 1135	14.73	5.624 241	12.50	540
46	829.578 643	67639.072 937	.000 014 7844	.001 205	81.534 251	.012 264 7844	14.72	5.770 161	12.54	552
47	960.087 883	78292.888 371	.000 012 7726	.001 042	81.547 627	.012 262 7726	14.72	5.916 204	12.59	564
48	1111.128 824	90622.761 111	.000 011 0348	.000 900	81.559 185	.012 261 0348	14.72	6.062 356	12.63	576
49	1285.931 512	104892.368	.000 009 5336	.000 778	81.569 172	.012 259 5336	14.72	6.208 606	12.67	588
50	1488.234 144	121406.869	.000 008 2368	.000 672	81.577 801	.012 258 2368	14.71	6.354 942	12.71	600

Effective Rate is 15.73 % 8 - 249 Annual Percentage Rate is 14.70 %

MONTHLY COMPOUND INTEREST AND ANNUITY

	Amount Of 1	Amount Of 1 Per Period	Sinking Fund Payment	Present Worth Of 1	Present Worth of 1 Per Period	Periodic Payment To Amortize 1	Constant Annual Percent	Total Interest	Annual Add On Rate	
	What a single $ 1 deposit grows to in the future. The deposit is made at the beginning of the first period.	What a series of $ 1 deposits grow to in the future. A deposit is made at the end of each period.	The amount to be deposited at the end of each period that grows to $ 1 in the future.	What $ 1 to be paid in the future is worth today. Value today of a single $ 1 payment tomorrow.	What $ 1 to be paid at the end of each period is worth today. Value today of a series of $ 1 payments tomorrow.	The mortgage payment to amortize a loan of $ 1. An annuity certain, payable at the end of each period, worth $ 1 today.	The annual payment, including interest and principal, to amortize completely a loan of $ 100.	The total interest paid over the term on a loan of $1. The loan is amortized by regular periodic payments.	The average annual interest rate on a loan that is completely amortized by regular periodic payments.	
	$S = (1+i)^n$	$S\overline{n}| = \dfrac{(1+i)^n - 1}{i}$	$\dfrac{1}{S\overline{n}|} = \dfrac{i}{(1+i)^n - 1}$	$V^n = \dfrac{1}{(1+i)^n}$	$A\overline{n}| = \dfrac{1-V^n}{i}$	$\dfrac{1}{A\overline{n}|} = \dfrac{i}{1-V^n}$				

YEAR										PERIODS
	1.012 292	1.000 000	1.000 000 0000	.987 858	.987 858	1.012 291 6667	1214.75	.012 292	14.75	1
	1.024 734	2.012 292	.496 945 8536	.975 863	1.963 720	.509 237 5203	611.09	.018 475	11.09	2
	1.037 330	3.037 026	.329 269 4801	.964 013	2.927 733	.341 561 1467	409.88	.024 683	9.87	3
	1.050 081	4.074 356	.245 437 5493	.952 308	3.880 041	.257 729 2160	309.28	.030 917	9.28	4
	1.062 988	5.124 437	.195 143 3951	.940 745	4.820 786	.207 435 0617	248.93	.037 175	8.92	5
	1.076 054	6.187 425	.161 618 1286	.929 322	5.750 107	.173 909 7953	208.70	.043 459	8.69	6
	1.089 280	7.263 478	.137 675 0831	.918 037	6.668 145	.149 966 7497	179.97	.049 767	8.53	7
	1.102 669	8.352 759	.119 720 9251	.906 890	7.575 035	.132 012 5917	158.42	.056 101	8.42	8
	1.116 223	9.455 428	.105 759 3581	.895 878	8.470 913	.118 051 0248	141.67	.062 459	8.33	9
	1.129 943	10.571 651	.094 592 6042	.885 000	9.355 914	.106 884 2709	128.27	.068 843	8.26	10
	1.143 832	11.701 594	.085 458 4411	.874 254	10.230 168	.097 750 1077	117.31	.075 251	8.21	11
	1.157 892	12.845 426	.077 848 7203	.863 639	11.093 806	.090 140 3869	108.17	.081 685	8.17	12
1	1.157 892	12.845 426	.077 848 7203	.863 639	11.093 806	.090 140 3869	108.17	.081 685	8.17	12
2	1.340 713	27.719 039	.036 076 2870	.745 872	20.674 846	.048 367 9537	58.05	.160 831	8.04	24
3	1.552 401	44.941 071	.022 251 3610	.644 164	28.949 402	.034 543 0277	41.46	.243 549	8.12	36
4	1.797 512	64.882 320	.015 412 5192	.556 325	36.095 628	.027 704 1859	33.25	.329 801	8.25	48
5	2.081 324	87.972 126	.011 367 2370	.480 463	42.267 385	.023 658 9037	28.40	.419 534	8.39	60
6	2.409 948	114.707 620	.008 717 8166	.414 947	47.597 553	.021 009 4833	25.22	.512 683	8.54	72
7	2.790 459	145.664 428	.006 865 0941	.358 364	52.200 892	.019 156 7608	22.99	.609 168	8.70	84
8	3.231 049	181.509 058	.005 509 3669	.309 497	56.176 513	.017 801 0336	21.37	.708 899	8.86	96
9	3.741 205	223.013 257	.004 484 0384	.267 294	59.610 013	.016 775 7050	20.14	.811 776	9.02	108
10	4.331 910	271.070 626	.003 689 0755	.230 845	62.575 317	.015 980 7422	19.18	.917 689	9.18	120
11	5.015 882	326.715 854	.003 060 7636	.199 367	65.136 267	.015 352 4303	18.43	1.026 521	9.33	132
12	5.807 849	391.147 001	.002 556 5836	.172 181	67.348 003	.014 848 2502	17.82	1.138 148	9.48	144
13	6.724 860	465.751 291	.002 147 0687	.148 702	69.258 143	.014 438 7353	17.33	1.252 443	9.63	156
14	7.786 659	552.134 980	.001 811 1513	.128 425	70.907 814	.014 102 8180	16.93	1.369 273	9.78	168
15	9.016 108	652.157 936	.001 533 3709	.110 913	72.332 534	.013 825 0376	16.60	1.488 507	9.92	180
16	10.439 677	767.973 687	.001 302 1279	.095 788	73.562 977	.013 593 7946	16.32	1.610 009	10.06	192
17	12.088 015	902.075 783	.001 108 5543	.082 727	74.625 635	.013 400 2210	16.09	1.733 645	10.20	204
18	13.996 612	1057.351 487	.000 945 7593	.071 446	75.543 388	.013 237 4260	15.89	1.859 284	10.33	216
19	16.206 561	1237.143 935	.000 808 3134	.061 703	76.335 994	.013 099 9801	15.72	1.986 795	10.46	228
20	18.765 442	1445.324 119	.000 691 8863	.053 289	77.020 520	.012 983 5530	15.59	2.116 053	10.58	240
21	21.728 350	1686.374 225	.000 592 9882	.046 023	77.611 703	.012 884 6549	15.47	2.246 933	10.70	252
22	25.159 076	1965.484 142	.000 508 7805	.039 747	78.122 271	.012 800 4472	15.37	2.379 318	10.82	264
23	29.131 485	2288.663 198	.000 436 9363	.034 327	78.563 217	.012 728 6030	15.28	2.513 094	10.93	276
24	33.731 105	2662.869 543	.000 375 5347	.029 646	78.944 036	.012 667 2014	15.21	2.648 154	11.03	288
25	39.056 966	3096.159 965	.000 322 9807	.025 604	79.272 925	.012 614 6474	15.14	2.784 394	11.14	300
26	45.223 737	3597.863 346	.000 277 9427	.022 112	79.556 967	.012 569 6094	15.09	2.921 718	11.24	312
27	52.364 190	4178.781 527	.000 239 3042	.019 097	79.802 276	.012 530 9709	15.04	3.060 035	11.33	324
28	60.632 060	4851.421 866	.000 206 1251	.016 493	80.014 135	.012 497 7918	15.00	3.199 258	11.43	336
29	70.205 359	5630.266 531	.000 177 6115	.014 244	80.197 104	.012 469 2782	14.97	3.339 309	11.51	348
30	81.290 203	6532.084 302	.000 153 0905	.012 302	80.355 124	.012 444 7572	14.94	3.480 113	11.60	360
31	94.125 251	7576.291 614	.000 131 9907	.010 624	80.491 595	.012 423 6574	14.91	3.621 601	11.68	372
32	108.986 847	8785.370 591	.000 113 8256	.009 175	80.609 457	.012 405 4923	14.89	3.763 709	11.76	384
33	126.194 965	10185.353 101	.000 098 1802	.007 924	80.711 248	.012 389 8469	14.87	3.906 379	11.84	396
34	146.120 103	11806.381 228	.000 084 7000	.006 844	80.799 158	.012 376 3666	14.86	4.049 558	11.91	408
35	169.191 254	13683.356 239	.000 073 0815	.005 910	80.875 080	.012 364 7482	14.84	4.193 194	11.98	420
36	195.905 148	15856.690 022	.000 063 0649	.005 105	80.940 650	.012 354 7315	14.83	4.337 244	12.05	432
37	226.836 945	18373.175 168	.000 054 4272	.004 408	80.997 278	.012 346 0938	14.82	4.481 666	12.11	444
38	262.652 615	21286.992 427	.000 046 9770	.003 807	81.046 185	.012 338 6437	14.81	4.626 422	12.17	456
39	304.123 283	24660.877 243	.000 040 5501	.003 288	81.088 422	.012 332 2167	14.80	4.771 477	12.23	468
40	352.141 824	28567.470 462	.000 035 0048	.002 840	81.124 900	.012 326 6715	14.80	4.916 802	12.29	480
41	407.742 095	33090.882 320	.000 030 2198	.002 453	81.156 404	.012 321 8865	14.79	5.062 368	12.35	492
42	472.121 187	38328.503 359	.000 026 0902	.002 118	81.183 612	.012 317 7569	14.79	5.208 149	12.40	504
43	546.665 203	44393.101 279	.000 022 5260	.001 829	81.207 110	.012 314 1927	14.78	5.354 123	12.45	516
44	632.979 101	51415.248 866	.000 019 4495	.001 580	81.227 404	.012 311 1161	14.78	5.500 269	12.50	528
45	732.921 246	59546.135 262	.000 016 7937	.001 364	81.244 930	.012 308 4604	14.78	5.646 569	12.55	540
46	848.643 426	68960.821 120	.000 014 5010	.001 178	81.260 066	.012 306 1677	14.77	5.793 005	12.59	552
47	982.637 178	79862.007 720	.000 012 5216	.001 018	81.273 139	.012 304 1883	14.77	5.939 562	12.64	564
48	1137.787 431	92484.401 186	.000 010 8126	.000 879	81.284 429	.012 302 4793	14.77	6.086 228	12.68	576
49	1317.434 621	107099.766	.000 009 3371	.000 759	81.294 179	.012 301 0038	14.77	6.232 990	12.72	588
50	1525.446 611	124022.775	.000 008 0630	.000 656	81.302 600	.012 299 7297	14.76	6.379 838	12.76	600

Amount Of 1	Amount Of 1 Per Period	Sinking Fund Payment	Present Worth Of 1	Present Worth of 1 Per Period	Periodic Payment To Amortize 1	Constant Annual Percent	Total Interest	Annual Add On Rate	
What a single $ 1 deposit grows to in the future. The deposit is made at the beginning of the first period.	What a series of $ 1 deposits grow to in the future. A deposit is made at the end of each period.	The amount to be deposited at the end of each period that grows to $ 1 in the future.	What $ 1 to be paid in the future is worth today. Value today of a single $ 1 payment tomorrow.	What $ 1 to be paid at the end of each period is worth today. Value today of a series of $ 1 payments tomorrow.	The mortgage payment to amortize a loan of $ 1. An annuity certain, payable at the end of each period, worth $ 1 today.	The annual payment, including interest and principal, to amortize completely a loan of $ 100.	The total interest paid over the term on a loan of $1. The loan is amortized by regular periodic payments.	The average annual interest rate on a loan that is completely amortized by regular periodic payments.	
$S = (1+i)^n$	$S\overline{n}| = \dfrac{(1+i)^n - 1}{i}$	$\dfrac{1}{S\overline{n}|} = \dfrac{i}{(1+i)^n - 1}$	$V^n = \dfrac{1}{(1+i)^n}$	$A\overline{n}| = \dfrac{1-V^n}{i}$	$\dfrac{1}{A\overline{n}|} = \dfrac{i}{1-V^n}$				

YEAR									PERIODS
	1.012 333	1.000 000	1.000 000 0000	.987 817	.987 817	1.012 333 3333	1214.80	.012 333	14.80	1
	1.024 819	2.012 333	.496 935 5640	.975 782	1.963 599	.509 268 8974	611.13	.018 538	11.12	2
	1.037 458	3.037 152	.329 255 8171	.963 894	2.927 493	.341 589 1504	409.91	.024 767	9.91	3
	1.050 254	4.074 610	.245 422 2420	.952 151	3.879 644	.257 755 5753	309.31	.031 022	9.31	4
	1.063 207	5.124 864	.195 127 1350	.940 551	4.820 195	.207 460 4684	248.96	.037 302	8.95	5
	1.076 320	6.188 071	.161 601 2616	.929 092	5.749 288	.173 934 5949	208.73	.043 608	8.72	6
	1.089 594	7.264 390	.137 657 8067	.917 773	6.667 060	.149 991 1401	179.99	.049 938	8.56	7
	1.103 032	8.353 984	.119 703 3629	.906 592	7.573 652	.132 036 6962	158.45	.056 294	8.44	8
	1.116 637	9.457 017	.105 741 5924	.895 547	8.469 199	.118 074 9257	141.69	.062 674	8.36	9
	1.130 408	10.573 653	.094 574 6926	.884 636	9.353 835	.106 908 0259	128.29	.069 080	8.29	10
	1.144 350	11.704 062	.085 440 4254	.873 858	10.227 693	.097 773 7587	117.33	.075 511	8.24	11
	1.158 464	12.848 412	.077 830 6319	.863 212	11.090 905	.090 163 9653	108.20	.081 968	8.20	12
1	1.158 464	12.848 412	.077 830 6319	.863 212	11.090 905	.090 163 9653	108.20	.081 968	8.20	12
2	1.342 038	27.732 831	.036 058 3457	.745 135	20.664 710	.048 391 6791	58.08	.161 400	8.07	24
3	1.554 703	44.975 891	.022 234 1345	.643 210	28.928 934	.034 567 4678	41.49	.244 429	8.15	36
4	1.801 067	64.951 350	.015 396 1387	.555 227	36.062 713	.027 729 4721	33.28	.331 015	8.28	48
5	2.086 470	88.092 196	.011 351 7433	.479 278	42.220 678	.023 685 0767	28.43	.421 105	8.42	60
6	2.417 100	114.900 027	.008 703 2181	.413 719	47.536 308	.021 036 5515	25.25	.514 632	8.58	72
7	2.800 123	145.955 927	.006 851 3833	.357 127	52.124 825	.019 184 7166	23.03	.611 516	8.74	84
8	3.243 841	181.933 062	.005 496 5271	.308 277	56.085 689	.017 829 8604	21.40	.711 667	8.90	96
9	3.757 872	223.611 267	.004 472 0466	.266 108	59.504 754	.016 805 3799	20.17	.814 981	9.06	108
10	4.353 359	271.893 958	.003 677 9045	.229 708	62.456 133	.016 011 2378	19.22	.921 349	9.21	120
11	5.043 208	327.827 704	.003 050 3828	.198 286	65.003 799	.015 383 7162	18.47	1.030 651	9.37	132
12	5.842 374	392.624 921	.002 546 9601	.171 163	67.202 976	.014 880 2934	17.86	1.142 762	9.52	144
13	6.768 178	467.690 147	.002 138 1678	.147 750	69.101 332	.014 471 5011	17.37	1.257 554	9.67	156
14	7.840 689	554.650 491	.001 802 9372	.127 540	70.740 016	.014 136 2705	16.97	1.374 893	9.82	168
15	9.083 154	655.390 896	.001 525 8070	.110 094	72.154 548	.013 859 1403	16.64	1.494 645	9.96	180
16	10.522 505	772.095 003	.001 295 1774	.095 034	73.375 589	.013 628 5107	16.36	1.616 674	10.10	192
17	12.189 941	907.292 479	.001 102 1804	.082 035	74.429 606	.013 435 5137	16.13	1.740 845	10.24	204
18	14.121 604	1063.913 854	.000 939 9257	.070 813	75.339 447	.013 273 2591	15.93	1.867 024	10.37	216
19	16.359 366	1245.354 038	.000 802 9845	.061 127	76.124 833	.013 136 3178	15.77	1.995 080	10.50	228
20	18.951 733	1455.545 913	.000 687 0275	.052 766	76.802 787	.013 020 3608	15.63	2.124 887	10.62	240
21	21.954 895	1699.045 580	.000 588 5657	.045 548	77.388 006	.012 921 8991	15.51	2.256 319	10.74	252
22	25.433 950	1981.131 115	.000 504 7621	.039 318	77.893 174	.012 838 0955	15.41	2.389 257	10.86	264
23	29.464 309	2307.916 981	.000 433 2911	.033 939	78.329 241	.012 766 6245	15.32	2.523 588	10.97	276
24	34.133 334	2686.486 558	.000 372 2334	.029 297	78.705 659	.012 705 5667	15.25	2.659 203	11.08	288
25	39.542 230	3125.045 688	.000 319 9953	.025 289	79.030 588	.012 653 3287	15.19	2.795 999	11.18	300
26	45.808 240	3633.100 540	.000 275 2470	.021 830	79.311 070	.012 608 5803	15.14	2.933 877	11.28	312
27	53.067 185	4221.663 665	.000 236 8734	.018 844	79.553 186	.012 570 2068	15.09	3.072 747	11.38	324
28	61.476 410	4903.492 707	.000 203 9363	.016 266	79.762 184	.012 537 2696	15.05	3.212 523	11.47	336
29	71.218 192	5693.366 932	.000 175 6430	.014 041	79.942 593	.012 508 9763	15.02	3.353 124	11.56	348
30	82.503 694	6608.407 583	.000 151 3224	.012 121	80.098 324	.012 484 6557	14.99	3.494 476	11.65	360
31	95.577 538	7668.449 003	.000 130 4045	.010 463	80.232 753	.012 463 7378	14.96	3.636 510	11.73	372
32	110.723 112	8896.468 554	.000 112 4042	.009 032	80.348 794	.012 445 7375	14.94	3.779 163	11.81	384
33	128.268 711	10319.084 681	.000 096 9078	.007 796	80.448 962	.012 430 2412	14.92	3.922 375	11.89	396
34	148.594 651	11967.133 885	.000 083 5622	.006 730	80.535 428	.012 416 8955	14.91	4.066 093	11.96	408
35	172.141 516	13876.339 137	.000 072 0651	.005 809	80.610 067	.012 405 3985	14.89	4.210 267	12.03	420
36	199.419 705	16088.084 201	.000 062 1578	.005 015	80.674 496	.012 395 4911	14.88	4.354 852	12.10	432
37	231.020 498	18650.310 669	.000 053 6184	.004 329	80.730 112	.012 386 9517	14.87	4.499 807	12.16	444
38	267.628 871	21618.557 136	.000 046 2566	.003 737	80.778 120	.012 379 5899	14.86	4.645 093	12.22	456
39	310.038 344	25057.163 051	.000 039 9087	.003 225	80.819 562	.012 373 2421	14.85	4.790 677	12.28	468
40	359.168 181	29040.663 333	.000 034 4345	.002 784	80.855 334	.012 367 7678	14.85	4.936 529	12.34	480
41	416.083 316	33655.403 984	.000 029 7129	.002 403	80.886 214	.012 363 0462	14.84	5.082 619	12.40	492
42	482.017 436	39001.413 717	.000 025 6401	.002 075	80.912 869	.012 358 9734	14.84	5.228 923	12.45	504
43	558.399 723	45194.572 166	.000 022 1266	.001 791	80.935 879	.012 355 4599	14.83	5.375 417	12.50	516
44	646.885 834	52369.121 691	.000 019 0952	.001 546	80.955 740	.012 352 4286	14.83	5.522 082	12.55	528
45	749.393 785	60680.577 195	.000 016 4797	.001 334	80.972 886	.012 349 8131	14.82	5.668 899	12.60	540
46	868.145 530	70309.097 057	.000 014 2229	.001 152	80.987 685	.012 347 5562	14.82	5.815 851	12.64	552
47	1005.715 121	81463.388 224	.000 012 2755	.000 994	81.000 461	.012 345 6088	14.82	5.962 923	12.69	564
48	1165.084 505	94385.230 131	.000 010 5949	.000 858	81.011 489	.012 343 9282	14.82	6.110 103	12.73	576
49	1349.708 158	109354.715	.000 009 1446	.000 741	81.021 008	.012 342 4779	14.82	6.257 377	12.77	588
50	1563.587 966	126696.322	.000 007 8929	.000 640	81.029 225	.012 341 2262	14.81	6.404 736	12.81	600

MONTHLY COMPOUND INTEREST AND ANNUITY

Amount Of 1	Amount Of 1 Per Period	Sinking Fund Payment	Present Worth Of 1	Present Worth of 1 Per Period	Periodic Payment To Amortize 1	Constant Annual Percent	Total Interest	Annual Add On Rate
What a single $ 1 deposit grows to in the future. The deposit is made at the beginning of the first period.	What a series of $ 1 deposits grow to in the future. A deposit is made at the end of each period.	The amount to be deposited at the end of each period that grows to $ 1 in the future.	What $ 1 to be paid in the future is worth today. Value today of a single $ 1 payment tomorrow.	What $ 1 to be paid at the end of each period is worth today. Value today of a series of $ 1 payments tomorrow.	The mortgage payment to amortize a loan of $ 1. An annuity certain, payable at the end of each period, worth $ 1 today.	The annual payment, including interest and principal, to amortize completely a loan of $ 100.	The total interest paid over the term on a loan of $1. The loan is amortized by regular periodic payments.	The average annual interest rate on a loan that is completely amortized by regular periodic payments.
$S = (1+i)^n$	$S\overline{n}| = \dfrac{(1+i)^n - 1}{i}$	$\dfrac{1}{S\overline{n}|} = \dfrac{i}{(1+i)^n - 1}$	$V^n = \dfrac{1}{(1+i)^n}$	$A\overline{n}| = \dfrac{1-V^n}{i}$	$\dfrac{1}{A\overline{n}|} = \dfrac{i}{1-V^n}$			

YEAR									PERIODS
	1.012 375	1.000 000	1.000 000 0000	.987 776	.987 776	1.012 375 0000	1214.85	.012 375	14.85	1
	1.024 903	2.012 375	.496 925 2749	.975 702	1.963 478	.509 300 2749	611.17	.018 601	11.16	2
	1.037 586	3.037 278	.329 242 1549	.963 775	2.927 253	.341 617 1549	409.95	.024 851	9.94	3
	1.050 426	4.074 864	.245 406 9357	.951 994	3.879 248	.257 781 9357	309.34	.031 128	9.34	4
	1.063 425	5.125 291	.195 110 8763	.940 357	4.819 605	.207 485 8763	248.99	.037 429	8.98	5
	1.076 585	6.188 716	.161 584 3963	.928 863	5.748 468	.173 959 3963	208.76	.043 756	8.75	6
	1.089 908	7.265 302	.137 640 5324	.917 509	6.665 976	.150 015 5324	180.02	.050 109	8.59	7
	1.103 396	8.355 210	.119 685 8029	.906 293	7.572 270	.132 060 8029	158.48	.056 486	8.47	8
	1.117 050	9.458 606	.105 723 8292	.895 215	8.467 484	.118 098 8292	141.72	.062 889	8.39	9
	1.130 874	10.575 656	.094 556 7837	.884 272	9.351 756	.106 931 7837	128.32	.069 318	8.32	10
	1.144 868	11.706 530	.085 422 4127	.873 463	10.225 219	.097 797 4127	117.36	.075 772	8.27	11
	1.159 036	12.851 398	.077 812 5470	.862 786	11.088 005	.090 187 5470	108.23	.082 251	8.23	12
1	1.159 036	12.851 398	.077 812 5470	.862 786	11.088 005	.090 187 5470	108.23	.082 251	8.23	12
2	1.343 365	27.746 631	.036 040 4112	.744 400	20.654 580	.048 415 4112	58.10	.161 970	8.10	24
3	1.557 008	45.010 744	.022 216 9179	.642 257	28.908 487	.034 591 9179	41.52	.245 309	8.18	36
4	1.804 628	65.020 472	.015 379 7714	.554 131	36.029 841	.027 754 7714	33.31	.332 229	8.31	48
5	2.091 629	88.212 469	.011 336 2658	.478 096	42.174 045	.023 711 2658	28.46	.422 676	8.45	60
6	2.424 274	115.092 830	.008 688 6386	.412 495	47.475 178	.021 063 6386	25.28	.516 582	8.61	72
7	2.809 821	146.248 136	.006 837 6940	.355 895	52.048 921	.019 212 6940	23.06	.613 866	8.77	84
8	3.256 683	182.358 260	.005 483 7110	.307 061	55.995 083	.017 858 7110	21.44	.714 436	8.93	96
9	3.774 614	224.211 195	.004 460 0806	.264 928	59.399 775	.016 835 0806	20.21	.818 189	9.09	108
10	4.374 913	272.720 255	.003 666 7610	.228 576	62.337 296	.016 041 7610	19.26	.925 011	9.25	120
11	5.070 682	328.944 005	.003 040 0311	.197 212	64.871 747	.015 415 0311	18.50	1.034 784	9.41	132
12	5.877 103	394.109 358	.002 537 3668	.170 152	67.058 436	.014 912 3668	17.90	1.147 381	9.56	144
13	6.811 775	469.638 350	.002 129 2980	.146 805	68.945 081	.014 504 2980	17.41	1.262 670	9.71	156
14	7.895 092	557.179 176	.001 794 7548	.126 661	70.572 851	.014 169 7548	17.01	1.380 519	9.86	168
15	9.150 697	658.642 148	.001 518 2751	.109 281	71.977 269	.013 893 2751	16.68	1.500 790	10.01	180
16	10.605 987	776.241 391	.001 288 2591	.094 286	73.188 980	.013 663 2591	16.40	1.623 346	10.15	192
17	12.292 722	912.543 152	.001 095 8386	.081 349	74.234 428	.013 470 8386	16.17	1.748 051	10.28	204
18	14.247 707	1070.521 807	.000 934 1239	.070 187	75.136 426	.013 309 1239	15.98	1.874 771	10.42	216
19	16.513 606	1253.624 763	.000 797 6869	.060 556	75.914 657	.013 172 6869	15.81	2.003 373	10.54	228
20	19.139 865	1465.847 689	.000 682 1991	.052 247	76.586 103	.013 057 1991	15.67	2.133 728	10.67	240
21	22.183 794	1711.821 712	.000 584 1730	.045 078	77.165 418	.012 959 1730	15.56	2.265 712	10.79	252
22	25.711 817	1996.914 470	.000 500 7726	.038 893	77.665 243	.012 875 7726	15.46	2.399 204	10.91	264
23	29.800 922	2327.347 255	.000 429 6737	.033 556	78.096 484	.012 804 6737	15.37	2.534 090	11.02	276
24	34.540 343	2710.330 764	.000 368 9587	.028 952	78.468 553	.012 743 9587	15.30	2.670 260	11.13	288
25	40.033 503	3154.222 457	.000 317 0353	.024 979	78.789 569	.012 692 0353	15.24	2.807 611	11.23	300
26	46.400 273	3668.708 930	.000 272 5755	.021 552	79.066 538	.012 647 5755	15.18	2.946 044	11.33	312
27	53.779 589	4265.017 300	.000 234 4656	.018 594	79.305 502	.012 609 4656	15.14	3.085 467	11.43	324
28	62.332 482	4956.160 196	.000 201 7691	.016 043	79.511 677	.012 576 7691	15.10	3.225 794	11.52	336
29	72.245 594	5757.219 728	.000 173 6950	.013 842	79.689 562	.012 548 6950	15.06	3.366 946	11.61	348
30	83.735 248	6685.676 602	.000 149 5735	.011 942	79.843 038	.012 524 5735	15.03	3.508 846	11.70	360
31	97.052 171	7761.791 589	.000 128 8362	.010 304	79.975 456	.012 503 8362	15.01	3.651 427	11.78	372
32	112.486 965	9009.047 651	.000 110 9995	.008 890	80.089 704	.012 485 9995	14.99	3.794 624	11.86	384
33	130.376 447	10454.662 389	.000 095 6511	.007 670	80.188 275	.012 470 6511	14.97	3.938 378	11.93	396
34	151.111 002	12130.181 982	.000 082 4390	.006 618	80.273 321	.012 457 4390	14.95	4.082 635	12.01	408
35	175.143 099	14072.169 591	.000 071 0622	.005 710	80.346 698	.012 446 0622	14.94	4.227 346	12.08	420
36	202.997 165	16323.003 235	.000 061 2632	.004 926	80.410 006	.012 436 2632	14.93	4.372 466	12.15	432
37	235.281 032	18931.800 568	.000 052 8212	.004 250	80.464 627	.012 427 8212	14.92	4.517 953	12.21	444
38	272.699 198	21955.490 721	.000 045 5467	.003 667	80.511 754	.012 420 5467	14.91	4.663 769	12.27	456
39	316.068 201	25460.056 608	.000 039 2772	.003 164	80.552 414	.012 414 2772	14.90	4.809 882	12.33	468
40	366.334 438	29521.974 805	.000 033 8731	.002 730	80.587 495	.012 408 8731	14.90	4.956 259	12.39	480
41	424.594 820	34229.884 422	.000 029 2142	.002 355	80.617 763	.012 404 2142	14.89	5.102 873	12.45	492
42	492.120 702	39686.521 381	.000 025 1975	.002 032	80.643 877	.012 400 1975	14.89	5.249 700	12.50	504
43	570.385 634	46010.960 321	.000 021 7340	.001 753	80.666 408	.012 396 7340	14.88	5.396 715	12.55	516
44	661.097 511	53341.213 039	.000 018 7472	.001 513	80.685 848	.012 393 7472	14.88	5.543 899	12.60	528
45	766.235 847	61837.240 185	.000 016 1715	.001 305	80.702 620	.012 391 1715	14.87	5.691 233	12.65	540
46	888.094 969	71684.441 917	.000 013 9500	.001 126	80.717 090	.012 388 9500	14.87	5.838 700	12.69	552
47	1029.334 083	83097.703 702	.000 012 0340	.000 972	80.729 576	.012 387 0340	14.87	5.986 287	12.74	564
48	1193.035 309	96326.085 542	.000 010 3814	.000 838	80.740 348	.012 385 3814	14.87	6.133 980	12.78	576
49	1382.770 930	111658.257	.000 008 9559	.000 723	80.749 642	.012 383 9559	14.87	6.281 766	12.82	588
50	1602.681 355	129428.796	.000 007 7263	.000 624	80.757 660	.012 382 7263	14.86	6.429 636	12.86	600

Effective Rate is 15.90 %   Annual Percentage Rate is 14.85 %

Amount Of 1	Amount Of 1 Per Period	Sinking Fund Payment	Present Worth Of 1	Present Worth of 1 Per Period	Periodic Payment To Amortize 1	Constant Annual Percent	Total Interest	Annual Add On Rate
What a single $ 1 deposit grows to in the future. The deposit is made at the beginning of the first period.	What a series of $ 1 deposits grow to in the future. A deposit is made at the end of each period.	The amount to be deposited at the end of each period that grows to $ 1 in the future.	What $ 1 to be paid in the future is worth today. Value today of a single $ 1 payment tomorrow.	What $ 1 to be paid at the end of each period is worth today. Value today of a series of $ 1 payments tomorrow.	The mortgage payment to amortize a loan of $ 1. An annuity certain, payable at the end of each period, worth $ 1 today.	The annual payment, including interest and principal, to amortize completely a loan of $ 100.	The total interest paid over the term on a loan of $1. The loan is amortized by regular periodic payments.	The average annual interest rate on a loan that is completely amortized by regular periodic payments.

$$ S = (1+i)^n \qquad S\overline{n}| = \frac{(1+i)^n - 1}{i} \qquad \frac{1}{S\overline{n}|} = \frac{i}{(1+i)^n - 1} \qquad V^n = \frac{1}{(1+i)^n} \qquad A\overline{n}| = \frac{1-V^n}{i} \qquad \frac{1}{A\overline{n}|} = \frac{i}{1-V^n} $$

YEAR									PERIODS
	1.012 396	1.000 000	1.000 000 0000	.987 756	.987 756	1.012 395 8333	1214.88	.012 396	14.87	1
	1.024 945	2.012 396	.496 920 1304	.975 662	1.963 418	.509 315 9638	611.18	.018 632	11.18	2
	1.037 650	3.037 341	.329 235 3241	.963 716	2.927 133	.341 631 1574	409.96	.024 893	9.96	3
	1.050 513	4.074 992	.245 399 2830	.951 916	3.879 049	.257 795 1163	309.36	.031 180	9.35	4
	1.063 535	5.125 504	.195 102 7475	.940 261	4.819 310	.207 498 5808	249.00	.037 493	9.00	5
	1.076 718	6.189 039	.161 575 9642	.928 748	5.748 058	.173 971 7976	208.77	.043 831	8.77	6
	1.090 065	7.265 758	.137 631 8959	.917 376	6.665 434	.150 027 7292	180.04	.050 194	8.60	7
	1.103 577	8.355 823	.119 677 0238	.906 144	7.571 578	.132 072 8571	158.49	.056 583	8.49	8
	1.117 257	9.459 400	.105 714 9485	.895 049	8.466 628	.118 110 7818	141.74	.062 997	8.40	9
	1.131 106	10.576 657	.094 547 8303	.884 090	9.350 718	.106 943 6637	128.34	.069 437	8.33	10
	1.145 127	11.707 764	.085 413 4076	.873 265	10.223 983	.097 809 2409	117.38	.075 902	8.28	11
	1.159 322	12.852 891	.077 803 5058	.862 573	11.086 556	.090 199 3391	108.24	.082 392	8.24	12
1	1.159 322	12.852 891	.077 803 5058	.862 573	11.086 556	.090 199 3391	108.24	.082 392	8.24	12
2	1.344 028	27.753 535	.036 031 4465	.744 032	20.649 518	.048 427 2798	58.12	.162 255	8.11	24
3	1.558 162	45.028 183	.022 208 3134	.641 782	28.898 271	.034 604 1468	41.53	.245 749	8.19	36
4	1.806 412	65.055 068	.015 371 5926	.553 584	36.013 421	.027 767 4260	33.33	.332 836	8.32	48
5	2.094 213	88.272 682	.011 328 5331	.477 506	42.150 757	.023 724 3664	28.47	.423 462	8.47	60
6	2.427 868	115.189 380	.008 681 3559	.411 884	47.444 656	.021 077 1892	25.30	.517 558	8.63	72
7	2.814 682	146.394 508	.006 830 8574	.355 280	52.011 031	.019 226 6907	23.08	.615 042	8.79	84
8	3.263 124	182.571 308	.005 477 3119	.306 455	55.949 861	.017 873 1452	21.45	.715 822	8.95	96
9	3.783 012	224.511 880	.004 454 1073	.264 340	59.347 390	.016 849 9406	20.22	.819 794	9.11	108
10	4.385 730	273.134 520	.003 661 1996	.228 012	62.278 006	.016 057 0330	19.27	.926 844	9.27	120
11	5.084 475	329.503 831	.003 034 8661	.196 677	64.805 876	.015 430 6994	18.52	1.036 852	9.43	132
12	5.894 545	394.854 029	.002 532 5815	.169 648	66.986 349	.014 928 4148	17.92	1.149 692	9.58	144
13	6.833 677	470.615 972	.002 124 8748	.146 334	68.867 165	.014 520 7081	17.43	1.265 230	9.73	156
14	7.922 434	558.448 482	.001 790 6755	.126 224	70.489 506	.014 186 5088	17.03	1.383 333	9.88	168
15	9.184 655	660.274 668	.001 514 5212	.108 877	71.888 894	.013 910 3546	16.70	1.503 864	10.03	180
16	10.647 975	778.324 037	.001 284 8119	.093 915	73.095 967	.013 680 6453	16.42	1.626 684	10.17	192
17	12.344 435	915.181 302	.001 092 6797	.081 008	74.137 157	.013 488 5130	16.19	1.751 657	10.30	204
18	14.311 179	1073.842 982	.000 931 2348	.069 875	75.035 258	.013 327 0682	16.00	1.878 647	10.44	216
19	16.591 268	1257.783 005	.000 795 0497	.060 273	75.809 936	.013 190 8830	15.83	2.007 521	10.57	228
20	19.234 628	1471.028 775	.000 679 7964	.051 990	76.478 152	.013 075 6297	15.70	2.138 151	10.69	240
21	22.299 133	1718.249 351	.000 581 9877	.044 845	77.054 538	.012 977 8210	15.58	2.270 411	10.81	252
22	25.851 882	2004.857 678	.000 498 7885	.038 682	77.551 712	.012 894 6219	15.48	2.404 180	10.93	264
23	29.970 663	2337.129 101	.000 427 8754	.033 366	77.980 561	.012 823 7087	15.39	2.539 344	11.04	276
24	34.745 658	2722.338 772	.000 367 3312	.028 781	78.350 475	.012 763 1645	15.32	2.675 791	11.15	288
25	40.281 416	3168.920 932	.000 315 5648	.024 825	78.669 552	.012 711 3982	15.26	2.813 419	11.25	300
26	46.699 143	3686.653 589	.000 271 2487	.021 414	78.944 780	.012 667 0820	15.21	2.952 130	11.35	312
27	54.139 358	4286.872 602	.000 233 2703	.018 471	79.182 183	.012 629 1036	15.16	3.091 830	11.45	324
28	62.764 965	4982.719 888	.000 200 6936	.015 932	79.386 962	.012 596 5269	15.12	3.232 433	11.54	336
29	72.764 824	5789.431 162	.000 172 7285	.013 743	79.563 598	.012 568 5619	15.09	3.373 860	11.63	348
30	84.357 883	6724.669 530	.000 148 7062	.011 854	79.715 959	.012 544 5395	15.06	3.516 034	11.72	360
31	97.797 974	7808.912 225	.000 128 0588	.010 225	79.847 382	.012 523 8921	15.03	3.658 888	11.80	372
32	113.379 372	9065.898 957	.000 110 3035	.008 820	79.960 744	.012 506 1368	15.01	3.802 357	11.88	384
33	131.443 235	10523.151 704	.000 095 0286	.007 608	80.058 527	.012 490 8619	14.99	3.946 381	11.96	396
34	152.385 073	12212.577 307	.000 081 8828	.006 562	80.142 871	.012 477 7161	14.98	4.090 908	12.03	408
35	176.663 413	14171.166 080	.000 070 5658	.005 660	80.215 625	.012 466 3992	14.96	4.235 888	12.10	420
36	204.809 834	16441.801 717	.000 060 8206	.004 883	80.278 380	.012 456 6539	14.95	4.381 274	12.17	432
37	237.440 607	19074.200 242	.000 052 4268	.004 212	80.332 511	.012 448 2602	14.94	4.527 028	12.24	444
38	275.270 190	22125.998 549	.000 045 1957	.003 633	80.379 203	.012 441 0290	14.93	4.673 109	12.30	456
39	319.126 870	25664.016 376	.000 038 9651	.003 134	80.419 478	.012 434 7984	14.93	4.819 486	12.36	468
40	369.970 896	29765.719 333	.000 033 5957	.002 703	80.454 219	.012 429 4290	14.92	4.966 126	12.42	480
41	428.915 509	34520.915 032	.000 028 9679	.002 331	80.484 185	.012 424 8013	14.91	5.113 002	12.47	492
42	497.251 314	40033.719 437	.000 024 9789	.002 011	80.510 032	.012 420 8123	14.91	5.260 089	12.52	504
43	576.474 536	46424.836 508	.000 021 5402	.001 735	80.532 328	.012 417 3735	14.91	5.407 365	12.58	516
44	668.319 784	53834.201 038	.000 018 5756	.001 496	80.551 560	.012 414 4089	14.90	5.554 808	12.62	528
45	774.798 027	62424.042 552	.000 016 0195	.001 291	80.568 149	.012 411 8528	14.90	5.702 401	12.67	540
46	898.240 630	72382.437 356	.000 013 8155	.001 113	80.582 457	.012 409 6488	14.90	5.850 126	12.72	552
47	1041.350 391	83927.426 505	.000 011 9151	.000 960	80.594 800	.012 407 7484	14.89	5.997 970	12.76	564
48	1207.260 728	97311.789 857	.000 010 2762	.000 828	80.605 446	.012 406 1096	14.89	6.145 919	12.80	576
49	1399.604 282	112828.581	.000 008 8630	.000 714	80.614 630	.012 404 6963	14.89	6.293 961	12.84	588
50	1622.592 453	130817.542	.000 007 6442	.000 616	80.622 551	.012 403 4776	14.89	6.442 087	12.88	600

	Amount Of 1	Amount Of 1 Per Period	Sinking Fund Payment	Present Worth Of 1	Present Worth of 1 Per Period	Periodic Payment To Amortize 1	Constant Annual Percent	Total Interest	Annual Add On Rate	
	What a single $ 1 deposit grows to in the future. The deposit is made at the beginning of the first period.	What a series of $ 1 deposits grow to in the future. A deposit is made at the end of each period.	The amount to be deposited at the end of each period that grows to $ 1 in the future.	What $ 1 to be paid in the future is worth today. Value today of a single $ 1 payment tomorrow.	What $ 1 to be paid at the end of each period is worth today. Value today of a series of $ 1 payments tomorrow.	The mortgage payment to amortize a loan of $ 1. An annuity certain, payable at the end of each period, worth $ 1 today.	The annual payment, including interest and principal, to amortize completely a loan of $ 100.	The total interest paid over the term on a loan of $ 1. The loan is amortized by regular periodic payments.	The average annual interest rate on a loan that is completely amortized by regular periodic payments.	
	$S = (1+i)^n$	$S\overline{n}| = \dfrac{(1+i)^n - 1}{i}$	$\dfrac{1}{S\overline{n}|} = \dfrac{i}{(1+i)^n - 1}$	$V^n = \dfrac{1}{(1+i)^n}$	$A\overline{n}| = \dfrac{1-V^n}{i}$	$\dfrac{1}{A\overline{n}|} = \dfrac{i}{1-V^n}$				

YEAR									PERIODS	
	1.012 417	1.000 000	1.000 000 0000	.987 736	.987 736	1.012 416 6667	1214.90	.012 417	14.90	1
	1.024 988	2.012 417	.496 914 9861	.975 622	1.963 357	.509 331 6528	611.20	.018 663	11.20	2
	1.037 714	3.037 404	.329 228 4934	.963 656	2.927 014	.341 645 1601	409.98	.024 935	9.97	3
	1.050 599	4.075 119	.245 391 6305	.951 838	3.878 851	.257 808 2972	309.37	.031 233	9.37	4
	1.063 644	5.125 718	.195 094 6190	.940 164	4.819 015	.207 511 2857	249.02	.037 556	9.01	5
	1.076 851	6.189 362	.161 567 5326	.928 633	5.747 648	.173 984 1993	208.79	.043 905	8.78	6
	1.090 222	7.266 214	.137 623 2599	.917 244	6.664 893	.150 039 9266	180.05	.050 279	8.62	7
	1.103 759	8.356 436	.119 668 2452	.905 995	7.570 887	.132 084 9119	158.51	.056 679	8.50	8
	1.117 464	9.460 195	.105 706 0685	.894 883	8.465 771	.118 122 7351	141.75	.063 105	8.41	9
	1.131 339	10.577 659	.094 538 8777	.883 908	9.349 679	.106 955 5443	128.35	.069 555	8.35	10
	1.145 387	11.708 998	.085 404 4032	.873 068	10.222 747	.097 821 0699	117.39	.076 032	8.29	11
	1.159 609	12.854 385	.077 794 4654	.862 360	11.085 106	.090 211 1321	108.26	.082 534	8.25	12
1	1.159 609	12.854 385	.077 794 4654	.862 360	11.085 106	.090 211 1321	108.26	.082 534	8.25	12
2	1.344 692	27.760 440	.036 022 4834	.743 665	20.644 458	.048 439 1501	58.13	.162 540	8.13	24
3	1.559 317	45.045 631	.022 199 7114	.641 307	28.888 060	.034 616 3781	41.54	.246 190	8.21	36
4	1.808 197	65.089 686	.015 363 4172	.553 037	35.997 012	.027 780 0838	33.34	.333 444	8.34	48
5	2.096 801	88.332 945	.011 320 8044	.476 917	42.127 487	.023 737 4711	28.49	.424 248	8.48	60
6	2.431 468	115.286 029	.008 674 0779	.411 274	47.414 163	.021 090 7446	25.31	.518 534	8.64	72
7	2.819 551	146.541 057	.006 824 0261	.354 666	51.973 181	.019 240 6928	23.09	.616 218	8.80	84
8	3.269 576	182.784 657	.005 470 9187	.305 850	55.904 695	.017 887 5854	21.47	.717 208	8.97	96
9	3.791 429	224.813 047	.004 448 1404	.263 753	59.295 075	.016 864 8071	20.24	.821 399	9.13	108
10	4.396 573	273.549 530	.003 655 6451	.227 450	62.218 803	.016 072 3118	19.29	.928 677	9.29	120
11	5.098 304	330.064 776	.003 029 7083	.196 144	64.740 109	.015 446 3750	18.54	1.038 921	9.44	132
12	5.912 038	395.600 342	.002 527 8037	.169 146	66.914 382	.014 944 4703	17.94	1.152 004	9.60	144
13	6.855 650	471.595 949	.002 120 4593	.145 865	68.789 388	.014 537 1259	17.45	1.267 792	9.75	156
14	7.949 870	559.721 108	.001 786 6041	.125 788	70.406 318	.014 203 2707	17.05	1.386 149	9.90	168
15	9.218 738	661.911 803	.001 510 7753	.108 475	71.800 694	.013 927 4420	16.72	1.506 940	10.05	180
16	10.690 128	780.413 012	.001 281 3728	.093 544	73.003 148	.013 698 0395	16.44	1.630 024	10.19	192
17	12.396 365	917.828 035	.001 089 5287	.080 669	74.040 096	.013 506 1954	16.21	1.755 264	10.33	204
18	14.374 931	1077.175 678	.000 928 3537	.069 566	74.934 318	.013 345 0203	16.02	1.882 524	10.46	216
19	16.669 294	1261.956 578	.000 792 4203	.059 991	75.705 460	.013 209 0870	15.86	2.011 672	10.59	228
20	19.329 857	1476.230 102	.000 677 4012	.051 733	76.370 461	.013 094 0678	15.72	2.142 576	10.71	240
21	22.415 069	1724.703 525	.000 579 8098	.044 613	76.943 932	.012 996 4765	15.60	2.275 112	10.83	252
22	25.992 707	2012.835 446	.000 496 8116	.038 472	77.438 470	.012 913 4783	15.50	2.409 158	10.95	264
23	30.141 367	2346.955 703	.000 426 0839	.033 177	77.864 940	.012 842 7506	15.42	2.544 599	11.06	276
24	34.952 188	2734.404 431	.000 365 7103	.028 611	78.232 710	.012 782 3770	15.34	2.681 325	11.17	288
25	40.530 859	3183.693 312	.000 314 1006	.024 673	78.549 861	.012 730 7673	15.28	2.819 230	11.28	300
26	46.999 933	3704.692 569	.000 269 9279	.021 277	78.823 359	.012 686 5946	15.23	2.958 218	11.38	312
27	54.501 527	4308.847 794	.000 232 0806	.018 348	79.059 213	.012 648 7473	15.18	3.098 194	11.47	324
28	63.200 440	5009.431 396	.000 199 6235	.015 823	79.262 603	.012 616 2901	15.14	3.239 073	11.57	336
29	73.287 774	5821.834 174	.000 171 7672	.013 645	79.437 999	.012 588 4338	15.11	3.380 775	11.66	348
30	84.985 134	6763.903 433	.000 147 8436	.011 767	79.589 254	.012 564 5103	15.08	3.523 224	11.74	360
31	98.549 494	7856.335 058	.000 127 2858	.010 147	79.719 690	.012 543 9525	15.06	3.666 350	11.83	372
32	114.278 842	9123.128 180	.000 109 6115	.008 751	79.832 172	.012 526 2782	15.04	3.810 091	11.91	384
33	132.518 729	10592.112 393	.000 094 4099	.007 546	79.929 173	.012 511 0765	15.02	3.954 386	11.98	396
34	153.669 859	12295.559 139	.000 081 3302	.006 507	80.012 822	.012 497 9968	15.00	4.099 183	12.06	408
35	178.196 892	14270.890 656	.000 070 0727	.005 612	80.084 958	.012 486 7394	14.99	4.244 431	12.13	420
36	206.638 651	16561.502 095	.000 060 3810	.004 839	80.147 165	.012 477 0477	14.98	4.390 085	12.19	432
37	239.619 959	19217.714 847	.000 052 0353	.004 173	80.200 810	.012 468 7020	14.97	4.536 104	12.26	444
38	277.865 369	22297.882 031	.000 044 8473	.003 599	80.247 071	.012 461 5140	14.96	4.682 450	12.32	456
39	322.215 074	25869.670 424	.000 038 6553	.003 104	80.286 965	.012 455 3220	14.95	4.829 091	12.38	468
40	373.643 375	30011.547 007	.000 033 3205	.002 676	80.321 368	.012 449 9872	14.94	4.975 994	12.44	480
41	433.280 076	34814.502 763	.000 028 7237	.002 308	80.351 035	.012 445 3903	14.94	5.123 132	12.50	492
42	502.435 308	40384.051 622	.000 024 7623	.001 990	80.376 620	.012 441 4289	14.93	5.270 480	12.55	504
43	582.628 310	46842.548 447	.000 021 3481	.001 716	80.398 682	.012 438 0148	14.93	5.418 016	12.60	516
44	675.620 806	54331.876 987	.000 018 4054	.001 480	80.417 708	.012 435 0721	14.93	5.565 718	12.65	528
45	783.455 705	63016.566 863	.000 015 8688	.001 276	80.434 116	.012 432 5355	14.92	5.713 569	12.70	540
46	908.501 983	73087.408 038	.000 013 6822	.001 101	80.448 265	.012 430 3489	14.92	5.861 553	12.74	552
47	1053.506 724	84765.642 198	.000 011 7972	.000 949	80.460 466	.012 428 4639	14.92	6.009 654	12.79	564
48	1221.655 470	98307.823 107	.000 010 1721	.000 819	80.470 988	.012 426 8388	14.92	6.157 859	12.83	576
49	1416.642 205	114011.453	.000 008 7710	.000 706	80.480 062	.012 425 4377	14.92	6.306 157	12.87	588
50	1642.750 501	132221.517	.000 007 5631	.000 609	80.487 887	.012 424 2297	14.91	6.454 538	12.91	600

MONTHLY COMPOUND INTEREST AND ANNUITY

	Amount Of 1	Amount Of 1 Per Period	Sinking Fund Payment	Present Worth Of 1	Present Worth of 1 Per Period	Periodic Payment To Amortize 1	Constant Annual Percent	Total Interest	Annual Add On Rate	
	What a single $ 1 deposit grows to in the future. The deposit is made at the beginning of the first period.	What a series of $ 1 deposits grow to in the future. A deposit is made at the end of each period.	The amount to be deposited at the end of each period that grows to $ 1 in the future.	What $ 1 to be paid in the future is worth today. Value today of a single $ 1 payment tomorrow.	What $ 1 to be paid at the end of each period is worth today. Value today of a series of $ 1 payments tomorrow.	The mortgage payment to amortize a loan of $ 1. An annuity certain, payable at the end of each period, worth $ 1 today.	The annual payment, including interest and principal, to amortize completely a loan of $ 100.	The total interest paid over the term on a loan of $ 1. The loan is amortized by regular periodic payments.	The average annual interest rate on a loan that is completely amortized by regular periodic payments.	
	$S = (1+i)^n$	$S\overline{n}| = \dfrac{(1+i)^n - 1}{i}$	$\dfrac{1}{S\overline{n}|} = \dfrac{i}{(1+i)^n - 1}$	$V^n = \dfrac{1}{(1+i)^n}$	$A\overline{n}| = \dfrac{1-V^n}{i}$	$\dfrac{1}{A\overline{n}|} = \dfrac{i}{1-V^n}$				

YEAR										PERIODS
	1.012 458	1.000 000	1.000 000 0000	.987 695	.987 695	1.012 458 3333	1214.95	.012 458	14.95	1
	1.025 072	2.012 458	.496 904 6978	.975 541	1.963 236	.509 363 0312	611.24	.018 726	11.24	2
	1.037 843	3.037 530	.329 214 8327	.963 537	2.926 774	.341 673 1661	410.01	.025 019	10.01	3
	1.050 772	4.075 373	.245 376 3264	.951 681	3.878 455	.257 834 6597	309.41	.031 339	9.40	4
	1.063 863	5.126 145	.195 078 3630	.939 970	4.818 425	.207 536 6964	249.05	.037 683	9.04	5
	1.077 117	6.190 008	.161 550 6706	.928 404	5.746 829	.174 009 0039	208.82	.044 054	8.81	6
	1.090 536	7.267 126	.137 605 9894	.916 980	6.663 809	.150 064 3228	180.08	.050 450	8.65	7
	1.104 123	8.357 662	.119 650 6897	.905 697	7.569 506	.132 109 0230	158.54	.056 872	8.53	8
	1.117 878	9.461 784	.105 688 3103	.894 552	8.464 058	.118 146 6436	141.78	.063 320	8.44	9
	1.131 805	10.579 662	.094 520 9744	.883 544	9.347 602	.106 979 3077	128.38	.069 793	8.38	10
	1.145 905	11.711 467	.085 386 3968	.872 672	10.220 274	.097 844 7301	117.42	.076 292	8.32	11
	1.160 181	12.857 373	.077 776 3872	.861 934	11.082 209	.090 234 7205	108.29	.082 817	8.28	12
1	1.160 181	12.857 373	.077 776 3872	.861 934	11.082 209	.090 234 7205	108.29	.082 817	8.28	12
2	1.346 021	27.774 258	.036 004 5624	.742 930	20.634 343	.048 462 8957	58.16	.163 109	8.16	24
3	1.561 629	45.080 551	.022 182 5150	.640 357	28.867 653	.034 640 8483	41.57	.247 071	8.24	36
4	1.811 772	65.158 991	.015 347 0761	.551 946	35.964 225	.027 805 4095	33.37	.334 660	8.37	48
5	2.101 985	88.453 625	.011 305 3592	.475 741	42.081 002	.023 763 6925	28.52	.425 822	8.52	60
6	2.438 684	115.479 626	.008 659 5362	.410 057	47.353 262	.021 117 8695	25.35	.520 487	8.67	72
7	2.829 316	146.834 691	.006 810 3797	.353 442	51.897 602	.019 268 7130	23.13	.618 572	8.84	84
8	3.282 519	183.212 255	.005 458 1502	.304 644	55.814 524	.017 916 4835	21.50	.719 982	9.00	96
9	3.808 318	225.416 830	.004 436 2260	.262 583	59.190 653	.016 894 5593	20.28	.824 612	9.16	108
10	4.418 340	274.381 794	.003 644 5567	.226 329	62.100 654	.016 102 8900	19.33	.932 347	9.32	120
11	5.126 076	331.190 037	.003 019 4145	.195 081	64.608 883	.015 477 7478	18.58	1.043 063	9.48	132
12	5.947 178	397.097 905	.002 518 2707	.168 147	66.770 811	.014 976 6040	17.98	1.156 631	9.64	144
13	6.899 806	473.562 990	.002 111 6515	.144 932	68.634 251	.014 569 9848	17.49	1.272 918	9.79	156
14	8.005 026	562.276 362	.001 778 4849	.124 922	70.240 414	.014 236 8182	17.09	1.391 785	9.94	168
15	9.287 283	665.199 969	.001 503 3073	.107 674	71.624 820	.013 961 6407	16.76	1.513 095	10.09	180
16	10.774 933	784.610 028	.001 274 5185	.092 808	72.818 087	.013 732 8518	16.48	1.636 708	10.23	192
17	12.500 878	923.147 361	.001 083 2507	.079 994	73.846 605	.013 541 5840	16.25	1.762 483	10.37	204
18	14.503 286	1083.875 803	.000 922 6149	.068 950	74.733 119	.013 380 9483	16.06	1.890 285	10.50	216
19	16.826 443	1270.349 958	.000 787 1847	.059 430	75.497 236	.013 245 5180	15.90	2.019 978	10.63	228
20	19.521 727	1486.693 810	.000 672 6335	.051 225	76.155 855	.013 130 9668	15.76	2.151 432	10.76	240
21	22.648 745	1737.691 932	.000 575 4760	.044 153	76.723 541	.013 033 8093	15.65	2.284 520	10.88	252
22	26.276 654	2028.895 292	.000 492 8791	.038 057	77.212 848	.012 951 2124	15.55	2.419 120	11.00	264
23	30.485 686	2366.744 025	.000 422 5214	.032 802	77.634 600	.012 880 8547	15.46	2.555 116	11.11	276
24	35.368 927	2758.709 853	.000 362 4883	.028 273	77.998 121	.012 820 8216	15.39	2.692 397	11.22	288
25	41.034 372	3213.461 329	.000 311 1909	.024 370	78.311 453	.012 769 5243	15.33	2.830 857	11.32	300
26	47.607 317	3741.055 550	.000 267 3042	.021 005	78.581 524	.012 725 6376	15.28	2.970 399	11.42	312
27	55.233 125	4353.160 570	.000 229 7182	.018 105	78.814 308	.012 688 0515	15.23	3.110 929	11.52	324
28	64.080 447	5063.313 452	.000 197 4991	.015 605	79.014 952	.012 655 8325	15.19	3.252 360	11.62	336
29	74.344 945	5887.219 641	.000 169 8595	.013 451	79.187 895	.012 628 1928	15.16	3.394 611	11.71	348
30	86.253 625	6843.100 305	.000 146 1326	.011 594	79.336 959	.012 604 4659	15.13	3.537 608	11.79	360
31	100.069 854	7952.095 307	.000 125 7530	.009 993	79.465 443	.012 584 0864	15.11	3.681 280	11.88	372
32	116.099 187	9238.730 720	.000 108 2400	.008 613	79.576 188	.012 566 5733	15.08	3.825 564	11.95	384
33	134.696 121	10731.461 240	.000 093 1840	.007 424	79.671 643	.012 551 5173	15.07	3.970 401	12.03	396
34	156.271 939	12463.299 478	.000 080 2356	.006 399	79.753 918	.012 538 5689	15.05	4.115 736	12.11	408
35	181.303 803	14472.546 050	.000 069 0963	.005 516	79.824 834	.012 527 4297	15.04	4.261 520	12.18	420
36	210.345 306	16803.636 622	.000 059 5109	.004 754	79.885 960	.012 517 8443	15.03	4.407 709	12.24	432
37	244.038 719	19508.124 628	.000 051 2607	.004 098	79.938 645	.012 509 5940	15.02	4.554 260	12.31	444
38	283.129 192	22645.821 404	.000 044 1583	.003 532	79.984 057	.012 502 4916	15.01	4.701 136	12.37	456
39	328.481 232	26286.118 954	.000 038 0429	.003 044	80.023 199	.012 496 3762	15.00	4.848 304	12.43	468
40	381.097 827	30509.524 590	.000 032 7766	.002 624	80.056 937	.012 491 1100	14.99	4.995 733	12.49	480
41	442.142 624	35409.441 403	.000 028 2411	.002 262	80.086 016	.012 486 5744	14.99	5.143 395	12.54	492
42	512.965 664	41094.233 924	.000 024 3343	.001 949	80.111 081	.012 482 6676	14.98	5.291 264	12.60	504
43	595.133 241	47689.624 671	.000 020 9689	.001 680	80.132 685	.012 479 3023	14.98	5.439 320	12.65	516
44	690.462 537	55341.474 574	.000 018 0696	.001 448	80.151 307	.012 476 4030	14.98	5.587 541	12.70	528
45	801.061 818	64219.008 778	.000 015 5717	.001 248	80.167 357	.012 473 9050	14.97	5.735 909	12.75	540
46	929.377 049	74518.559 153	.000 013 4195	.001 076	80.181 191	.012 471 7528	14.97	5.884 408	12.79	552
47	1078.245 999	86467.906 290	.000 011 5650	.000 927	80.193 116	.012 469 8983	14.97	6.033 023	12.84	564
48	1250.960 991	100331.317	.000 009 9670	.000 799	80.203 394	.012 468 3003	14.97	6.181 741	12.88	576
49	1451.341 718	116415.389	.000 008 5899	.000 689	80.212 253	.012 466 9233	14.97	6.330 551	12.92	588
50	1683.819 718	135075.830	.000 007 4032	.000 594	80.219 889	.012 465 7366	14.96	6.479 442	12.96	600

Effective Rate is 16.02 %

Annual Percentage Rate is 14.95 %

MONTHLY COMPOUND INTEREST AND ANNUITY

15.00 % M

	Amount Of 1	Amount Of 1 Per Period	Sinking Fund Payment	Present Worth Of 1	Present Worth of 1 Per Period	Periodic Payment To Amortize 1	Constant Annual Percent	Total Interest	Annual Add On Rate
	What a single $ 1 deposit grows to in the future. The deposit is made at the beginning of the first period.	What a series of $ 1 deposits grow to in the future. A deposit is made at the end of each period.	The amount to be deposited at the end of each period that grows to $ 1 in the future.	What $ 1 to be paid in the future is worth today. Value today of a single $ 1 payment tomorrow.	What $ 1 to be paid at the end of each period is worth today. Value today of a series of $ 1 payments tomorrow.	The mortgage payment to amortize a loan of $ 1. An annuity certain, payable at the end of each period, worth $ 1 today.	The annual payment, including interest and principal, to amortize completely a loan of $ 100.	The total interest paid over the term on a loan of $1. The loan is amortized by regular periodic payments.	The average annual interest rate on a loan that is completely amortized by regular periodic payments.
	$S = (1+i)^n$	$S\overline{n} = \dfrac{(1+i)^n - 1}{i}$	$\dfrac{1}{S\overline{n}} = \dfrac{i}{(1+i)^n - 1}$	$V^n = \dfrac{1}{(1+i)^n}$	$A\overline{n} = \dfrac{1-V^n}{i}$	$\dfrac{1}{A\overline{n}} = \dfrac{i}{1-V^n}$			

YEAR									PERIODS
	1.012 500	1.000 000	1.000 000 0000	.987 654	.987 654	1.012 500 0000	1215.00	.012 500	15.00	1
	1.025 156	2.012 500	.496 894 4099	.975 461	1.963 115	.509 394 4099	611.28	.018 789	11.27	2
	1.037 971	3.037 656	.329 201 1728	.963 418	2.926 534	.341 701 1728	410.05	.025 104	10.04	3
	1.050 945	4.075 627	.245 361 0233	.951 524	3.878 058	.257 861 0233	309.44	.031 444	9.43	4
	1.064 082	5.126 572	.195 062 1084	.939 777	4.817 835	.207 562 1084	249.08	.037 811	9.07	5
	1.077 383	6.190 654	.161 533 8102	.928 175	5.746 010	.174 033 8102	208.85	.044 203	8.84	6
	1.090 850	7.268 038	.137 588 7209	.916 716	6.662 726	.150 088 7209	180.11	.050 621	8.68	7
	1.104 486	8.358 888	.119 633 1365	.905 398	7.568 124	.132 133 1365	158.56	.057 065	8.56	8
	1.118 292	9.463 374	.105 670 5546	.894 221	8.462 345	.118 170 5546	141.81	.063 535	8.47	9
	1.132 271	10.581 666	.094 503 0740	.883 181	9.345 526	.107 003 0740	128.41	.070 031	8.40	10
	1.146 424	11.713 937	.085 368 3935	.872 277	10.217 803	.097 868 3935	117.45	.076 552	8.35	11
	1.160 755	12.860 361	.077 758 3123	.861 509	11.079 312	.090 258 3123	108.31	.083 100	8.31	12
1	1.160 755	12.860 361	.077 758 3123	.861 509	11.079 312	.090 258 3123	108.31	.083 100	8.31	12
2	1.347 351	27.788 084	.035 986 6480	.742 197	20.624 235	.048 486 6480	58.19	.163 680	8.18	24
3	1.563 944	45.115 505	.022 165 3285	.639 409	28.847 267	.034 665 3285	41.60	.247 952	8.27	36
4	1.815 355	65.228 388	.015 330 7483	.550 856	35.931 481	.027 830 7483	33.40	.335 876	8.40	48
5	2.107 181	88.574 508	.011 289 9301	.474 568	42.034 592	.023 789 9301	28.55	.427 396	8.55	60
6	2.445 920	115.673 621	.008 645 0133	.408 844	47.292 474	.021 145 0133	25.38	.522 441	8.71	72
7	2.839 113	147.129 040	.006 796 7547	.352 223	51.822 185	.019 296 7547	23.16	.620 927	8.87	84
8	3.295 513	183.641 059	.005 445 4053	.303 443	55.724 570	.017 945 4053	21.54	.722 759	9.03	96
9	3.825 282	226.022 551	.004 424 3373	.261 419	59.086 509	.016 924 3373	20.31	.827 828	9.20	108
10	4.440 213	275.217 058	.003 633 4957	.225 214	61.982 847	.016 133 4957	19.37	.936 019	9.36	120
11	5.153 998	332.319 805	.003 009 1496	.194 024	64.478 068	.015 509 1496	18.62	1.047 208	9.52	132
12	5.982 526	398.602 077	.002 508 7677	.167 153	66.627 722	.015 008 7677	18.02	1.161 263	9.68	144
13	6.944 244	475.539 523	.002 102 8746	.144 004	68.479 668	.014 602 8746	17.53	1.278 048	9.83	156
14	8.060 563	564.845 011	.001 770 3972	.124 061	70.075 134	.014 270 3972	17.13	1.397 427	9.98	168
15	9.356 334	668.506 759	.001 495 8712	.106 879	71.449 643	.013 995 8712	16.80	1.519 257	10.13	180
16	10.860 408	788.832 603	.001 267 6961	.092 078	72.633 794	.013 767 6961	16.53	1.643 398	10.27	192
17	12.606 267	928.501 369	.001 077 0043	.079 326	73.653 950	.013 577 0043	16.30	1.769 709	10.41	204
18	14.632 781	1090.622 520	.000 916 9075	.068 340	74.532 823	.013 416 9075	16.11	1.898 052	10.54	216
19	16.985 067	1278.805 378	.000 781 9798	.058 875	75.289 980	.013 281 9798	15.94	2.028 291	10.68	228
20	19.715 494	1497.239 481	.000 667 8958	.050 722	75.942 278	.013 167 8958	15.81	2.160 295	10.80	240
21	22.884 848	1750.787 854	.000 571 1714	.043 697	76.504 237	.013 071 1714	15.69	2.293 935	10.92	252
22	26.563 691	2045.095 272	.000 488 9748	.037 645	76.988 370	.012 988 9748	15.59	2.429 089	11.04	264
23	30.833 924	2386.713 938	.000 418 9861	.032 432	77.405 455	.012 918 9861	15.51	2.565 640	11.15	276
24	35.790 617	2783.249 347	.000 359 2923	.027 940	77.764 777	.012 859 2923	15.44	2.703 476	11.26	288
25	41.544 120	3243.529 615	.000 308 3061	.024 071	78.074 336	.012 808 3061	15.37	2.842 492	11.37	300
26	48.222 525	3777.802 015	.000 264 7042	.020 737	78.341 024	.012 764 7042	15.32	2.982 588	11.47	312
27	55.974 514	4397.961 118	.000 227 3781	.017 865	78.570 778	.012 727 3781	15.28	3.123 671	11.57	324
28	64.972 670	5117.813 598	.000 195 3959	.015 391	78.768 713	.012 695 3959	15.24	3.265 653	11.66	336
29	75.417 320	5953.385 616	.000 167 9716	.013 260	78.939 236	.012 667 9716	15.21	3.408 454	11.75	348
30	87.540 995	6923.279 611	.000 144 4402	.011 423	79.086 142	.012 644 4402	15.18	3.551 998	11.84	360
31	101.613 606	8049.088 447	.000 124 2377	.009 841	79.212 704	.012 624 2377	15.15	3.696 216	11.92	372
32	117.948 452	9355.876 140	.000 106 8847	.008 478	79.321 738	.012 606 8847	15.13	3.841 044	12.00	384
33	136.909 198	10872.735 858	.000 091 9732	.007 304	79.415 671	.012 591 9732	15.12	3.986 421	12.08	396
34	158.917 970	12633.437 629	.000 079 1550	.006 293	79.496 596	.012 579 1550	15.10	4.132 295	12.15	408
35	184.464 752	14677.180 163	.000 068 1330	.005 421	79.566 313	.012 568 1330	15.09	4.278 616	12.22	420
36	214.118 294	17049.463 544	.000 058 6529	.004 670	79.626 375	.012 558 6529	15.08	4.425 338	12.29	432
37	248.538 777	19803.102 194	.000 050 4971	.004 024	79.678 119	.012 550 4971	15.07	4.572 421	12.36	444
38	288.492 509	22999.400 699	.000 043 4794	.003 466	79.722 696	.012 543 4794	15.06	4.719 827	12.42	456
39	334.868 983	26709.518 627	.000 037 4398	.002 986	79.761 101	.012 537 4398	15.05	4.867 522	12.48	468
40	388.700 685	31016.054 774	.000 032 2414	.002 573	79.794 186	.012 532 2414	15.04	5.015 476	12.54	480
41	451.186 076	36014.886 062	.000 027 7663	.002 216	79.822 690	.012 527 7663	15.04	5.163 661	12.59	492
42	523.716 276	41817.302 064	.000 023 9135	.001 909	79.847 246	.012 523 9135	15.03	5.312 052	12.65	504
43	607.906 033	48552.482 651	.000 020 5963	.001 645	79.868 401	.012 520 5963	15.03	5.460 028	12.70	516
44	705.629 674	56370.373 945	.000 017 7398	.001 417	79.886 626	.012 517 7398	15.03	5.609 367	12.75	528
45	819.062 832	65445.026 584	.000 015 2800	.001 221	79.902 327	.012 515 2800	15.02	5.758 251	12.80	540
46	950.730 883	75978.470 631	.000 013 1616	.001 052	79.915 854	.012 513 1616	15.02	5.907 265	12.84	552
47	1103.565 167	88205.213 396	.000 011 3372	.000 906	79.927 508	.012 511 3372	15.02	6.056 394	12.89	564
48	1280.968 254	102397.460	.000 009 7659	.000 781	79.937 547	.012 509 7659	15.02	6.205 625	12.93	576
49	1486.889 688	118871.175	.000 008 4125	.000 673	79.946 196	.012 508 4125	15.02	6.354 947	12.97	588
50	1725.913 922	137993.114	.000 007 2467	.000 579	79.953 648	.012 507 2467	15.01	6.504 348	13.01	600

Effective Rate is 16.08 %

Annual Percentage Rate is 15.00 %

	Amount Of 1	Amount Of 1 Per Period	Sinking Fund Payment	Present Worth Of 1	Present Worth of 1 Per Period	Periodic Payment To Amortize 1	Constant Annual Percent	Total Interest	Annual Add On Rate	
	What a single $ 1 deposit grows to in the future. The deposit is made at the beginning of the first period.	What a series of $ 1 deposits grow to in the future. A deposit is made at the end of each period.	The amount to be deposited at the end of each period that grows to $ 1 in the future.	What $ 1 to be paid in the future is worth today. Value today of a single $ 1 payment tomorrow.	What $ 1 to be paid at the end of each period is worth today. Value today of a series of $ 1 payments tomorrow.	The mortgage payment to amortize a loan of $ 1. An annuity certain, payable at the end of each period, worth $ 1 today.	The annual payment, including interest and principal, to amortize completely a loan of $ 100.	The total interest paid over the term on a loan of $1. The loan is amortized by regular periodic payments.	The average annual interest rate on a loan that is completely amortized by regular periodic payments.	
	$S = (1+i)^n$	$S\overline{n}| = \dfrac{(1+i)^n - 1}{i}$	$\dfrac{1}{S\overline{n}|} = \dfrac{i}{(1+i)^n - 1}$	$V^n = \dfrac{1}{(1+i)^n}$	$A\overline{n}| = \dfrac{1 - V^n}{i}$	$\dfrac{1}{A\overline{n}|} = \dfrac{i}{1 - V^n}$				

YEAR										PERIODS
	1.013 333	1.000 000	1.000 000 0000	.986 842	.986 842	1.013 333 3333	1216.00	.013 333	16.00	1
	1.026 844	2.013 333	.496 688 7417	.973 857	1.960 699	.510 022 0751	612.03	.020 044	12.03	2
	1.040 536	3.040 178	.328 928 1329	.961 043	2.921 743	.342 261 4662	410.72	.026 784	10.71	3
	1.054 410	4.080 713	.245 055 1857	.948 398	3.870 141	.258 388 5190	310.07	.033 554	10.07	4
	1.068 468	5.135 123	.194 737 3025	.935 919	4.806 060	.208 070 6358	249.69	.040 353	9.68	5
	1.082 715	6.203 591	.161 196 9505	.923 604	5.729 665	.174 530 2839	209.44	.047 182	9.44	6
	1.097 151	7.286 306	.137 243 7584	.911 452	6.641 116	.150 577 0917	180.70	.054 040	9.26	7
	1.111 779	8.383 457	.119 282 5404	.899 459	7.540 575	.132 615 8737	159.14	.060 927	9.14	8
	1.126 603	9.495 236	.105 315 9709	.887 624	8.428 199	.118 649 3042	142.38	.067 844	9.05	9
	1.141 625	10.621 839	.094 145 6545	.875 945	9.304 144	.107 478 9878	128.98	.074 790	8.97	10
	1.156 846	11.763 464	.085 008 9758	.864 419	10.168 563	.098 342 3091	118.02	.081 765	8.92	11
	1.172 271	12.920 310	.077 397 5245	.853 045	11.021 609	.090 730 8579	108.88	.088 770	8.88	12
1	1.172 271	12.920 310	.077 397 5245	.853 045	11.021 609	.090 730 8579	108.88	.088 770	8.88	12
2	1.374 219	28.066 412	.035 629 7772	.727 686	20.423 539	.048 963 1105	58.76	.175 115	8.76	24
3	1.610 957	45.821 745	.021 823 6997	.620 749	28.443 811	.035 157 0330	42.19	.265 653	8.86	36
4	1.888 477	66.635 803	.015 006 9475	.529 527	35.285 465	.028 340 2808	34.01	.360 333	9.01	48
5	2.213 807	91.035 516	.010 984 7238	.451 711	41.121 706	.024 318 0571	29.19	.459 083	9.18	60
6	2.595 181	119.638 587	.008 358 5073	.385 330	46.100 283	.021 691 8406	26.04	.561 813	9.36	72
7	3.042 255	153.169 132	.006 528 7306	.328 704	50.347 235	.019 862 0639	23.84	.668 413	9.55	84
8	3.566 347	192.476 010	.005 195 4527	.280 399	53.970 077	.018 528 7860	22.24	.778 763	9.73	96
9	4.180 724	238.554 316	.004 191 9174	.239 193	57.060 524	.017 525 2508	21.04	.892 727	9.92	108
10	4.900 941	292.570 569	.003 417 9788	.204 042	59.696 816	.016 751 3121	20.11	1.010 157	10.10	120
11	5.745 230	355.892 244	.002 809 8393	.174 057	61.945 692	.016 143 1726	19.38	1.130 899	10.28	132
12	6.734 965	430.122 395	.002 324 9196	.148 479	63.864 085	.015 658 2530	18.79	1.254 788	10.46	144
13	7.895 203	517.140 233	.001 933 7115	.126 659	65.500 561	.015 267 0448	18.33	1.381 659	10.63	156
14	9.255 316	619.148 703	.001 615 1209	.108 046	66.896 549	.014 948 4542	17.94	1.511 340	10.80	168
15	10.849 737	738.730 255	.001 353 6741	.092 168	68.087 390	.014 687 0074	17.63	1.643 661	10.96	180
16	12.718 830	878.912 215	.001 137 7701	.078 624	69.103 231	.014 471 1034	17.37	1.778 452	11.12	192
17	14.909 912	1043.243 434	.000 958 5490	.067 069	69.969 789	.014 291 8824	17.16	1.915 544	11.27	204
18	17.478 455	1235.884 123	.000 809 1373	.057 213	70.709 003	.014 142 4707	16.98	2.054 774	11.42	216
19	20.489 482	1461.711 177	.000 684 1297	.048 806	71.339 585	.014 017 4630	16.83	2.195 982	11.56	228
20	24.019 222	1726.441 638	.000 579 2261	.041 633	71.877 501	.013 912 5594	16.70	2.339 014	11.70	240
21	28.157 032	2036.777 427	.000 490 9717	.035 515	72.336 367	.013 824 3050	16.59	2.483 725	11.83	252
22	33.007 667	2400.575 011	.000 416 5669	.030 296	72.727 801	.013 749 9002	16.50	2.629 974	11.95	264
23	38.693 924	2827.044 294	.000 353 7263	.025 844	73.061 711	.013 687 0597	16.43	2.777 628	12.08	276
24	45.359 757	3326.981 781	.000 300 5727	.022 046	73.346 552	.013 633 9061	16.37	2.926 565	12.19	288
25	53.173 919	3913.043 898	.000 255 5555	.018 806	73.589 534	.013 588 8889	16.31	3.076 667	12.31	300
26	62.334 232	4600.067 404	.000 217 3881	.016 043	73.796 809	.013 550 7215	16.27	3.227 825	12.41	312
27	73.072 600	5405.444 997	.000 184 9986	.013 685	73.973 623	.013 518 3320	16.23	3.379 940	12.52	324
28	85.660 875	6349.565 632	.000 157 4911	.011 674	74.124 454	.013 490 8244	16.19	3.532 917	12.62	336
29	100.417 742	7456.330 682	.000 134 1142	.009 958	74.253 120	.013 467 4476	16.17	3.686 672	12.71	348
30	117.716 787	8753.759 030	.000 114 2366	.008 495	74.362 878	.013 447 5700	16.14	3.841 125	12.80	360
31	137.995 952	10274.696 396	.000 097 3265	.007 247	74.456 506	.013 430 6598	16.12	3.996 205	12.89	372
32	161.768 025	12057.646 856	.000 082 9349	.006 182	74.536 375	.013 416 2683	16.10	4.151 847	12.97	384
33	189.636 635	14147.747 615	.000 070 6826	.005 273	74.604 507	.013 404 0160	16.09	4.307 990	13.05	396
34	222.305 489	16597.911 700	.000 060 2485	.004 498	74.662 626	.013 393 5819	16.08	4.464 581	13.13	408
35	260.602 233	19470.167 508	.000 051 3606	.003 837	74.712 205	.013 384 6940	16.07	4.621 571	13.20	420
36	305.496 388	22837.229 116	.000 043 7881	.003 273	74.754 498	.013 377 1215	16.06	4.778 916	13.27	432
37	358.124 495	26784.337 116	.000 037 3353	.002 792	74.790 576	.013 370 6686	16.05	4.936 577	13.34	444
38	419.818 887	31411.416 562	.000 031 8356	.002 382	74.821 352	.013 365 1689	16.04	5.094 517	13.41	456
39	492.141 422	36835.606 677	.000 027 1476	.002 032	74.847 605	.013 360 4810	16.04	5.252 705	13.47	468
40	576.923 018	43194.226 353	.000 023 1512	.001 733	74.870 000	.013 356 4846	16.03	5.411 113	13.53	480
41	676.310 007	50648.250 517	.000 019 7440	.001 479	74.889 104	.013 353 0774	16.03	5.569 714	13.58	492
42	792.818 472	59386.385 374	.000 016 8389	.001 261	74.905 401	.013 350 1722	16.03	5.728 487	13.64	504
43	929.397 943	69629.845 698	.000 014 3617	.001 076	74.919 303	.013 347 6950	16.02	5.887 411	13.69	516
44	1089.506 068	81637.955 109	.000 012 2492	.000 918	74.931 161	.013 345 5825	16.02	6.046 468	13.74	528
45	1277.196 148	95714.711 114	.000 010 4477	.000 783	74.941 278	.013 343 7810	16.02	6.205 642	13.79	540
46	1497.219 748	112216.481	.000 008 9113	.000 668	74.949 907	.013 342 2447	16.02	6.364 919	13.84	552
47	1755.146 989	131561.024	.000 007 6010	.000 570	74.957 269	.013 340 9344	16.01	6.524 287	13.88	564
48	2057.507 562	154238.067	.000 006 4835	.000 486	74.963 548	.013 339 8168	16.01	6.683 734	13.92	576
49	2411.956 032	180821.702	.000 005 5303	.000 415	74.968 905	.013 338 8636	16.01	6.843 252	13.97	588
50	2827.465 624	211984.922	.000 004 7173	.000 354	74.973 474	.013 338 0506	16.01	7.002 830	14.01	600

MONTHLY COMPOUND INTEREST AND ANNUITY

17.00 % M

	Amount Of 1	Amount Of 1 Per Period	Sinking Fund Payment	Present Worth Of 1	Present Worth of 1 Per Period	Periodic Payment To Amortize 1	Constant Annual Percent	Total Interest	Annual Add On Rate	
	What a single $1 deposit grows to in the future. The deposit is made at the beginning of the first period.	What a series of $1 deposits grow to in the future. A deposit is made at the end of each period.	The amount to be deposited at the end of each period that grows to $1 in the future.	What $1 to be paid in the future is worth today. Value today of a single $1 payment tomorrow.	What $1 to be paid at the end of each period is worth today. Value today of a series of $1 payments tomorrow.	The mortgage payment to amortize a loan of $1. An annuity certain, payable at the end of each period, worth $1 today.	The annual payment, including interest and principal, to amortize completely a loan of $100.	The total interest paid over the term on a loan of $1. The loan is amortized by regular periodic payments.	The average annual interest rate on a loan that is completely amortized by regular periodic payments.	
	$S = (1+i)^n$	$S\overline{n}\rceil = \dfrac{(1+i)^n - 1}{i}$	$\dfrac{1}{S\overline{n}\rceil} = \dfrac{i}{(1+i)^n - 1}$	$V^n = \dfrac{1}{(1+i)^n}$	$A\overline{n}\rceil = \dfrac{1 - V^n}{i}$	$\dfrac{1}{A\overline{n}\rceil} = \dfrac{i}{1 - V^n}$				
YEAR										**PERIODS**
	1.014 167	1.000 000	1.000 000 0000	.986 031	.986 031	1.014 166 6667	1217.00	.014 167	17.00	1
	1.028 534	2.014 167	.496 483 2437	.972 258	1.958 289	.510 649 9104	612.78	.021 300	12.78	2
	1.043 105	3.042 701	.328 655 3955	.958 676	2.916 965	.342 822 0621	411.39	.028 466	11.39	3
	1.057 882	4.085 806	.244 749 7734	.945 285	3.862 250	.258 916 4401	310.70	.035 666	10.70	4
	1.072 869	5.143 688	.194 413 0410	.932 080	4.794 330	.208 579 7076	250.30	.042 899	10.30	5
	1.088 068	6.216 557	.160 860 7523	.919 060	5.713 391	.175 027 4189	210.04	.050 165	10.03	6
	1.103 482	7.304 625	.136 899 5733	.906 222	6.619 613	.151 066 2400	181.28	.057 464	9.85	7
	1.119 115	8.408 107	.118 932 8368	.893 563	7.513 176	.133 099 5035	159.72	.064 796	9.72	8
	1.134 969	9.527 222	.104 962 3943	.881 081	8.394 257	.119 129 0609	142.96	.072 162	9.62	9
	1.151 048	10.662 191	.093 789 3563	.868 774	9.263 031	.107 956 0230	129.55	.079 560	9.55	10
	1.167 354	11.813 238	.084 650 7933	.856 638	10.119 669	.098 817 4600	118.59	.086 992	9.49	11
	1.183 892	12.980 593	.077 038 0854	.844 672	10.964 341	.091 204 7521	109.45	.094 457	9.45	12
1	1.183 892	12.980 593	.077 038 0854	.844 672	10.964 341	.091 204 7521	109.45	.094 457	9.45	12
2	1.401 600	28.348 209	.035 275 5974	.713 471	20.225 611	.049 442 2641	59.34	.186 614	9.33	24
3	1.659 342	46.541 802	.021 486 0609	.602 648	28.048 345	.035 652 7275	42.79	.283 498	9.45	36
4	1.964 482	68.081 048	.014 688 3756	.509 040	34.655 988	.028 855 0423	34.63	.385 042	9.63	48
5	2.325 733	93.581 182	.010 685 9091	.429 972	40.237 278	.024 852 5758	29.83	.491 155	9.82	60
6	2.753 417	123.770 579	.008 079 4645	.363 185	44.951 636	.022 246 1311	26.70	.601 721	10.03	72
7	3.259 747	159.511 558	.006 269 1382	.306 772	48.933 722	.020 435 8049	24.53	.716 608	10.24	84
8	3.859 188	201.825 006	.004 954 7874	.259 122	52.297 278	.019 121 4541	22.95	.835 660	10.45	96
9	4.568 860	251.919 548	.003 969 5213	.218 873	55.138 379	.018 136 1879	21.77	.958 708	10.65	108
10	5.409 036	311.226 062	.003 213 0985	.184 876	57.538 177	.017 379 7652	20.86	1.085 572	10.86	120
11	6.403 713	381.438 553	.002 621 6542	.156 159	59.565 218	.016 788 3209	20.15	1.216 058	11.06	132
12	7.581 303	464.562 540	.002 152 5627	.131 903	61.277 403	.016 319 2294	19.59	1.349 969	11.25	144
13	8.975 441	562.972 341	.001 776 2862	.111 415	62.723 638	.015 942 9529	19.14	1.487 101	11.44	156
14	10.625 951	679.478 890	.001 471 7161	.094 109	63.945 231	.015 638 3827	18.77	1.627 248	11.62	168
15	12.579 975	817.410 030	.001 223 3762	.079 491	64.977 077	.015 390 0429	18.47	1.770 208	11.80	180
16	14.893 329	980.705 566	.001 019 6740	.067 144	65.848 648	.015 186 3407	18.23	1.915 777	11.97	192
17	17.632 089	1174.029 800	.000 851 7671	.056 715	66.584 839	.015 018 4338	18.03	2.063 760	12.14	204
18	20.874 484	1402.904 761	.000 712 8068	.047 905	67.206 679	.014 879 4734	17.86	2.213 966	12.30	216
19	24.713 129	1673.867 935	.000 597 4187	.040 464	67.731 930	.014 764 0854	17.72	2.366 211	12.45	228
20	29.257 669	1994.658 995	.000 501 3388	.034 179	68.175 595	.014 668 0055	17.61	2.520 321	12.60	240
21	34.637 912	2374.440 878	.000 421 1518	.028 870	68.550 346	.014 587 8184	17.51	2.676 130	12.74	252
22	41.007 538	2824.061 507	.000 354 0999	.024 386	68.866 887	.014 520 7666	17.43	2.833 482	12.88	264
23	48.548 485	3356.363 651	.000 297 9415	.020 598	69.134 261	.014 464 6082	17.36	2.992 232	13.01	276
24	57.476 150	3986.551 756	.000 250 8434	.017 399	69.360 104	.014 417 5100	17.31	3.152 243	13.13	288
25	68.045 538	4732.626 240	.000 211 2992	.014 696	69.550 868	.014 377 9658	17.26	3.313 390	13.25	300
26	80.558 550	5615.897 651	.000 178 0659	.012 413	69.712 000	.014 344 7326	17.22	3.475 557	13.37	312
27	95.372 601	6661.595 368	.000 150 1142	.010 485	69.848 104	.014 316 7809	17.19	3.638 637	13.48	324
28	112.910 833	7899.588 246	.000 126 5889	.008 857	69.963 067	.014 293 2555	17.16	3.802 534	13.58	336
29	133.674 202	9365.237 774	.000 106 7779	.007 481	70.060 174	.014 273 4445	17.13	3.967 159	13.68	348
30	158.255 782	11100.408 126	.000 090 0868	.006 319	70.142 196	.014 256 7534	17.11	4.132 431	13.77	360
31	187.357 711	13154.661 953	.000 076 0187	.005 337	70.211 479	.014 242 6853	17.10	4.298 279	13.87	372
32	221.811 244	15586.676 066	.000 064 1574	.004 508	70.270 000	.014 230 8240	17.08	4.464 636	13.95	384
33	262.600 497	18465.917 458	.000 054 1538	.003 808	70.319 431	.014 220 8205	17.07	4.631 445	14.03	396
34	310.890 557	21874.627 526	.000 045 7151	.003 217	70.361 184	.014 212 3817	17.06	4.798 652	14.11	408
35	368.060 758	25910.171 179	.000 038 5949	.002 717	70.396 451	.014 205 2615	17.05	4.966 210	14.19	420
36	435.744 087	30687.817 929	.000 032 5862	.002 295	70.426 241	.014 199 2529	17.04	5.134 077	14.26	432
37	515.873 821	36344.034 396	.000 027 5148	.001 938	70.451 403	.014 194 1815	17.04	5.302 217	14.33	444
38	610.738 749	43040.382 285	.000 023 2340	.001 637	70.472 657	.014 189 9007	17.03	5.470 595	14.40	456
39	723.048 553	50968.133 160	.000 019 6201	.001 383	70.490 609	.014 186 2868	17.03	5.639 182	14.46	468
40	856.011 201	60353.731 845	.000 016 5690	.001 168	70.505 773	.014 183 2357	17.02	5.807 953	14.52	480
41	1013.424 580	71465.264 492	.000 013 9928	.000 987	70.518 582	.014 180 6595	17.02	5.976 884	14.58	492
42	1199.784 978	84620.116 081	.000 011 8175	.000 833	70.529 401	.014 178 4842	17.02	6.145 956	14.63	504
43	1420.415 511	100194.036	.000 009 9806	.000 704	70.538 540	.014 176 6473	17.02	6.315 150	14.69	516
44	1681.618 174	118631.871	.000 008 4294	.000 595	70.546 259	.014 175 0961	17.02	6.484 451	14.74	528
45	1990.853 846	140460.272	.000 007 1195	.000 502	70.552 779	.014 173 7861	17.01	6.653 845	14.79	540
46	2356.955 401	166302.734	.000 006 0131	.000 424	70.558 286	.014 172 6798	17.01	6.823 319	14.83	552
47	2790.380 003	196997.412	.000 005 0788	.000 358	70.562 938	.014 171 7455	17.01	6.992 864	14.88	564
48	3303.507 804	233118.198	.000 004 2897	.000 303	70.566 868	.014 170 9563	17.01	7.162 471	14.92	576
49	3910.995 563	275999.687	.000 003 6232	.000 256	70.570 187	.014 170 2899	17.01	7.332 130	14.96	588
50	4630.195 297	326766.727	.000 003 0603	.000 216	70.572 990	.014 169 7270	17.01	7.501 836	15.00	600

	Amount Of 1	Amount Of 1 Per Period	Sinking Fund Payment	Present Worth Of 1	Present Worth of 1 Per Period	Periodic Payment To Amortize 1	Constant Annual Percent	Total Interest	Annual Add On Rate	
	What a single $1 deposit grows to in the future. The deposit is made at the beginning of the first period.	What a series of $1 deposits grow to in the future. A deposit is made at the end of each period.	The amount to be deposited at the end of each period that grows to $1 in the future.	What $1 to be paid in the future is worth today. Value today of a single $1 payment tomorrow.	What $1 to be paid at the end of each period is worth today. Value today of a series of $1 payments tomorrow.	The mortgage payment to amortize a loan of $1. An annuity certain, payable at the end of each period, worth $1 today.	The annual payment, including interest and principal, to amortize completely a loan of $100.	The total interest paid over the term on a loan of $1. The loan is amortized by regular periodic payments.	The average annual interest rate on a loan that is completely amortized by regular periodic payments.	
	$S = (1+i)^n$	$S\overline{n}| = \dfrac{(1+i)^n - 1}{i}$	$\dfrac{1}{S\overline{n}|} = \dfrac{i}{(1+i)^n - 1}$	$V^n = \dfrac{1}{(1+i)^n}$	$A\overline{n}| = \dfrac{1 - V^n}{i}$	$\dfrac{1}{A\overline{n}|} = \dfrac{i}{1 - V^n}$				

YEAR										PERIODS
	1.015 000	1.000 000	1.000 000 0000	.985 222	.985 222	1.015 000 0000	1218.00	.015 000	18.00	1
	1.030 225	2.015 000	.496 277 9156	.970 662	1.955 883	.511 277 9156	613.54	.022 556	13.53	2
	1.045 678	3.045 225	.328 382 9602	.956 317	2.912 200	.343 382 9602	412.06	.030 149	12.06	3
	1.061 364	4.090 903	.244 444 7860	.942 184	3.854 385	.259 444 7860	311.34	.037 779	11.33	4
	1.077 284	5.152 267	.194 089 3231	.928 260	4.782 645	.209 089 3231	250.91	.045 447	10.91	5
	1.093 443	6.229 551	.160 525 2146	.914 542	5.697 187	.175 525 2146	210.64	.053 151	10.63	6
	1.109 845	7.322 994	.136 556 1645	.901 027	6.598 214	.151 556 1645	181.87	.060 893	10.44	7
	1.126 493	8.432 839	.118 584 0246	.887 711	7.485 925	.133 584 0246	160.31	.068 672	10.30	8
	1.143 390	9.559 332	.104 609 8234	.874 592	8.360 517	.119 609 8234	143.54	.076 488	10.20	9
	1.160 541	10.702 722	.093 434 1779	.861 667	9.222 185	.108 434 1779	130.13	.084 342	10.12	10
	1.177 949	11.863 262	.084 293 8442	.848 933	10.071 118	.099 293 8442	119.16	.092 232	10.06	11
	1.195 618	13.041 211	.076 679 9929	.836 387	10.907 505	.091 679 9929	110.02	.100 160	10.02	12
1	1.195 618	13.041 211	.076 679 9929	.836 387	10.907 505	.091 679 9929	110.02	.100 160	10.02	12
2	1.429 503	28.633 521	.034 924 1020	.699 544	20.030 405	.049 924 1020	59.91	.198 178	9.91	24
3	1.709 140	47.275 969	.021 152 3955	.585 090	27.660 684	.036 152 3955	43.39	.301 486	10.05	36
4	2.043 478	69.565 219	.014 374 9996	.489 362	34.042 554	.029 374 9996	35.25	.410 000	10.25	48
5	2.443 220	96.214 652	.010 393 4274	.409 296	39.380 269	.025 393 4274	30.48	.523 606	10.47	60
6	2.921 158	128.077 197	.007 807 7911	.342 330	43.844 667	.022 807 7911	27.37	.642 161	10.70	72
7	3.492 590	166.172 636	.006 017 8380	.286 321	47.578 633	.021 017 8380	25.23	.765 498	10.94	84
8	4.175 804	211.720 235	.004 723 2141	.239 475	50.701 675	.019 723 2141	23.67	.893 429	11.17	96
9	4.992 667	266.177 771	.003 756 8877	.200 294	53.313 749	.018 756 8877	22.51	1.025 744	11.40	108
10	5.969 323	331.288 191	.003 018 5199	.167 523	55.498 454	.018 018 5199	21.63	1.162 222	11.62	120
11	7.137 031	409.135 393	.002 444 1787	.140 114	57.325 714	.017 444 1787	20.94	1.302 632	11.84	132
12	8.533 164	502.210 922	.001 991 1952	.117 190	58.854 011	.016 991 1952	20.39	1.446 732	12.06	144
13	10.202 406	613.493 716	.001 630 0085	.098 016	60.132 260	.016 630 0085	19.96	1.594 281	12.26	156
14	12.198 182	746.545 446	.001 339 5032	.081 979	61.201 371	.016 339 5032	19.61	1.745 037	12.46	168
15	14.584 368	905.624 513	.001 104 2104	.068 567	62.095 562	.016 104 2104	19.33	1.898 758	12.66	180
16	17.437 335	1095.822 335	.000 912 5567	.057 348	62.843 452	.015 912 5567	19.10	2.055 211	12.85	192
17	20.848 395	1323.226 308	.000 755 7286	.047 965	63.468 978	.015 755 7286	18.91	2.214 169	13.02	204
18	24.926 719	1595.114 630	.000 626 9142	.040 118	63.992 160	.015 626 9142	18.76	2.375 413	13.20	216
19	29.802 839	1920.189 249	.000 520 7820	.033 554	64.429 743	.015 520 7820	18.63	2.538 738	13.36	228
20	35.632 816	2308.854 370	.000 433 1152	.028 064	64.795 732	.015 433 1152	18.52	2.703 948	13.52	240
21	42.603 242	2773.549 452	.000 360 5488	.023 472	65.101 841	.015 360 5488	18.44	2.870 858	13.67	252
22	50.937 210	3329.147 335	.000 300 3772	.019 632	65.357 866	.015 300 3772	18.37	3.039 300	13.81	264
23	60.901 454	3993.430 261	.000 250 4113	.016 420	65.572 002	.015 250 4113	18.31	3.209 114	13.95	276
24	72.814 885	4787.658 998	.000 208 8703	.013 733	65.751 103	.015 208 8703	18.26	3.380 155	14.08	288
25	87.058 800	5737.253 308	.000 174 2994	.011 486	65.900 901	.015 174 2994	18.21	3.552 290	14.21	300
26	104.089 083	6872.605 521	.000 145 5052	.009 607	66.026 190	.015 145 5052	18.18	3.725 398	14.33	312
27	124.450 799	8230.053 258	.000 121 5059	.008 035	66.130 980	.015 121 5059	18.15	3.899 368	14.44	324
28	148.795 637	9853.042 439	.000 101 4915	.006 721	66.218 625	.015 101 4915	18.13	4.074 101	14.55	336
29	177.902 767	11793.517 795	.000 084 7923	.005 621	66.291 930	.015 084 7923	18.11	4.249 508	14.65	348
30	212.703 781	14113.585 393	.000 070 8537	.004 701	66.353 242	.015 070 8537	18.09	4.425 507	14.75	360
31	254.312 506	16887.500 372	.000 059 2154	.003 932	66.404 522	.015 059 2154	18.08	4.602 028	14.85	372
32	304.060 653	20204.043 526	.000 049 4950	.003 289	66.447 412	.015 049 4950	18.06	4.779 006	14.93	384
33	363.540 442	24169.362 788	.000 041 3747	.002 751	66.483 285	.015 041 3747	18.05	4.956 384	15.02	396
34	434.655 558	28910.370 554	.000 034 5897	.002 301	66.513 289	.015 034 5897	18.05	5.134 113	15.10	408
35	519.682 084	34578.805 589	.000 028 9194	.001 924	66.538 383	.015 028 9194	18.04	5.312 146	15.18	420
36	621.341 343	41356.089 521	.000 024 1802	.001 609	66.559 372	.015 024 1802	18.03	5.490 446	15.25	432
37	742.887 000	49459.133 344	.000 020 2187	.001 346	66.576 927	.015 020 2187	18.03	5.668 977	15.32	444
38	888.209 197	59147.279 782	.000 016 9069	.001 126	66.591 609	.015 016 9069	18.03	5.847 710	15.39	456
39	1061.959 056	70730.603 711	.000 014 1382	.000 942	66.603 890	.015 014 1382	18.02	6.026 617	15.45	468
40	1269.697 544	84579.836 287	.000 011 8231	.000 788	66.614 161	.015 011 8231	18.02	6.205 675	15.51	480
41	1518.073 456	101138.230	.000 009 8875	.000 659	66.622 751	.015 009 8875	18.02	6.384 865	15.57	492
42	1815.036 210	120935.747	.000 008 2689	.000 551	66.629 936	.015 008 2689	18.01	6.564 168	15.63	504
43	2170.090 274	144606.018	.000 006 9153	.000 461	66.635 946	.015 006 9153	18.01	6.743 568	15.68	516
44	2594.599 366	172906.624	.000 005 7835	.000 385	66.640 972	.015 005 7835	18.01	6.923 054	15.73	528
45	3102.150 149	206743.343	.000 004 8369	.000 322	66.645 176	.015 004 8369	18.01	7.102 612	15.78	540
46	3708.987 089	247199.139	.000 004 0453	.000 270	66.648 692	.015 004 0453	18.01	7.282 233	15.83	552
47	4434.532 362	295568.824	.000 003 3833	.000 226	66.651 633	.015 003 3833	18.01	7.461 908	15.88	564
48	5302.007 473	353400.498	.000 002 8297	.000 189	66.654 093	.015 002 8297	18.01	7.641 630	15.92	576
49	6339.176 480	422545.099	.000 002 3666	.000 158	66.656 150	.015 002 3666	18.01	7.821 392	15.96	588
50	7579.234 592	505215.639	.000 001 9794	.000 132	66.657 871	.015 001 9794	18.01	8.001 188	16.00	600

	Amount Of 1	Amount Of 1 Per Period	Sinking Fund Payment	Present Worth Of 1	Present Worth of 1 Per Period	Periodic Payment To Amortize 1	Constant Annual Percent	Total Interest	Annual Add On Rate	
	What a single $ 1 deposit grows to in the future. The deposit is made at the beginning of the first period.	What a series of $ 1 deposits grow to in the future. A deposit is made at the end of each period.	The amount to be deposited at the end of each period that grows to $ 1 in the future.	What $ 1 to be paid in the future is worth today. Value today of a single $ 1 payment tomorrow.	What $ 1 to be paid at the end of each period is worth today. Value today of a series of $ 1 payments tomorrow.	The mortgage payment to amortize a loan of $ 1. An annuity certain, payable at the end of each period, worth $ 1 today.	The annual payment, including interest and principal, to amortize completely a loan of $ 100.	The total interest paid over the term on a loan of $1. The loan is amortized by regular periodic payments.	The average annual interest rate on a loan that is completely amortized by regular periodic payments.	
	$S = (1+i)^n$	$S\overline{n}| = \dfrac{(1+i)^n - 1}{i}$	$\dfrac{1}{S\overline{n}|} = \dfrac{i}{(1+i)^n - 1}$	$V^n = \dfrac{1}{(1+i)^n}$	$A\overline{n}| = \dfrac{1-V^n}{i}$	$\dfrac{1}{A\overline{n}|} = \dfrac{i}{1-V^n}$				

YEAR										PERIODS
	1.015 833	1.000 000	1.000 000 0000	.984 413	.984 413	1.015 833 3333	1219.00	.015 833	19.00	1
	1.031 917	2.015 833	.496 072 7573	.969 070	1.953 483	.511 906 0907	614.29	.023 812	14.29	2
	1.048 256	3.047 751	.328 110 8267	.953 965	2.907 449	.343 944 1601	412.74	.031 832	12.73	3
	1.064 853	4.096 007	.244 140 2228	.939 096	3.846 545	.259 973 5562	311.97	.039 894	11.97	4
	1.081 714	5.160 860	.193 766 1482	.924 459	4.771 004	.209 599 4816	251.52	.047 997	11.52	5
	1.098 841	6.242 574	.160 190 3367	.910 050	5.681 054	.176 023 6700	211.23	.056 142	11.23	6
	1.116 239	7.341 415	.136 213 5311	.895 865	6.576 920	.152 046 8644	182.46	.064 328	11.03	7
	1.133 913	8.457 654	.118 236 1024	.881 902	7.458 822	.134 069 4358	160.89	.072 555	10.88	8
	1.151 866	9.591 566	.104 258 2568	.868 156	8.326 978	.120 091 5901	144.11	.080 824	10.78	9
	1.170 104	10.743 433	.093 080 1175	.854 625	9.181 602	.108 913 4508	130.70	.089 135	10.70	10
	1.188 631	11.913 537	.083 938 1265	.841 304	10.022 906	.099 771 4598	119.73	.097 486	10.63	11
	1.207 451	13.102 168	.076 323 2449	.828 191	10.851 097	.092 156 5782	110.59	.105 879	10.59	12
1	1.207 451	13.102 168	.076 323 2449	.828 191	10.851 097	.092 156 5782	110.59	.105 879	10.59	12
2	1.457 938	28.922 394	.034 575 2839	.685 900	19.837 878	.050 408 6172	60.50	.209 807	10.49	24
3	1.760 389	48.024 542	.020 822 6867	.568 056	27.280 649	.036 656 0200	43.99	.319 617	10.65	36
4	2.125 583	71.089 450	.014 066 7849	.470 459	33.444 684	.029 900 1182	35.89	.435 206	10.88	48
5	2.566 537	98.939 196	.010 107 2178	.389 630	38.549 682	.025 940 5511	31.13	.556 433	11.13	60
6	3.098 968	132.566 399	.007 543 3896	.322 688	42.777 596	.023 376 7230	28.06	.683 124	11.39	72
7	3.741 852	173.169 599	.005 774 6857	.267 247	46.279 115	.021 608 0190	25.93	.815 074	11.64	84
8	4.518 103	222.195 973	.004 500 5316	.221 332	49.179 042	.020 333 8649	24.41	.952 051	11.90	96
9	5.455 388	281.392 918	.003 553 7497	.183 305	51.580 735	.019 387 0830	23.27	1.093 805	12.15	108
10	6.587 114	352.870 328	.002 833 9022	.151 812	53.569 796	.018 667 2355	22.41	1.240 068	12.40	120
11	7.953 617	439.175 798	.002 276 9925	.125 729	55.217 118	.018 110 3258	21.74	1.390 563	12.64	132
12	9.603 603	543.385 424	.001 840 3144	.104 128	56.581 415	.017 673 6477	21.21	1.545 005	12.88	144
13	11.595 879	669.213 441	.001 494 2916	.086 238	57.711 314	.017 327 6249	20.80	1.703 109	13.10	156
14	14.001 456	821.144 606	.001 217 8123	.071 421	58.647 086	.017 051 1456	20.47	1.864 592	13.32	168
15	16.906 072	1004.594 042	.000 995 4270	.059 150	59.422 084	.016 828 7603	20.20	2.029 177	13.53	180
16	20.413 254	1226.100 247	.000 815 5940	.048 988	60.063 930	.016 648 9273	19.98	2.196 594	13.73	192
17	24.648 004	1493.558 135	.000 669 5421	.040 571	60.595 501	.016 502 8754	19.81	2.366 587	13.92	204
18	29.761 257	1816.500 430	.000 550 5091	.033 601	61.035 743	.016 383 8424	19.67	2.538 910	14.11	216
19	35.935 259	2206.437 425	.000 453 2193	.027 828	61.400 348	.016 286 5526	19.55	2.713 334	14.28	228
20	43.390 065	2677.267 240	.000 373 5152	.023 047	61.702 310	.016 206 8485	19.45	2.889 644	14.45	240
21	52.391 377	3245.771 169	.000 308 0932	.019 087	61.952 393	.016 141 4265	19.37	3.067 639	14.61	252
22	63.260 020	3932.211 806	.000 254 3098	.015 808	62.159 509	.016 087 6431	19.31	3.247 138	14.76	264
23	76.383 375	4761.055 238	.000 210 0375	.013 092	62.331 041	.016 043 3708	19.26	3.427 970	14.90	276
24	92.229 182	5761.843 068	.000 173 5556	.010 843	62.473 102	.016 006 8889	19.21	3.609 984	15.04	288
25	111.362 218	6970.245 332	.000 143 4670	.008 980	62.590 755	.015 976 8003	19.18	3.793 040	15.17	300
26	134.464 421	8429.331 851	.000 118 6334	.007 437	62.688 195	.015 951 9667	19.15	3.977 014	15.30	312
27	162.359 199	10191.107 326	.000 098 1248	.006 159	62.768 894	.015 931 4581	19.12	4.161 792	15.41	324
28	196.040 777	12318.364 881	.000 081 1796	.005 101	62.835 728	.015 914 5129	19.10	4.347 276	15.53	336
29	236.709 632	14886.924 139	.000 067 1730	.004 225	62.891 079	.015 900 5064	19.09	4.533 376	15.63	348
30	285.815 282	17988.333 579	.000 055 5916	.003 499	62.936 920	.015 888 9249	19.07	4.720 013	15.73	360
31	345.107 947	21733.133 503	.000 046 0127	.002 898	62.974 886	.015 879 3460	19.06	4.907 117	15.83	372
32	416.700 935	26254.795 909	.000 038 0883	.002 400	63.006 328	.015 871 4216	19.05	5.094 626	15.92	384
33	503.145 960	31714.481 694	.000 031 5313	.001 987	63.032 369	.015 864 8647	19.04	5.282 486	16.01	396
34	607.524 092	38306.784 745	.000 026 1050	.001 646	63.053 935	.015 859 4384	19.04	5.470 651	16.09	408
35	733.555 571	46266.667 644	.000 021 6138	.001 363	63.071 796	.015 854 9472	19.03	5.659 078	16.17	420
36	885.732 406	55877.836 195	.000 017 8962	.001 129	63.086 589	.015 851 2295	19.03	5.847 731	16.24	432
37	1069.478 478	67482.851 256	.000 014 8186	.000 935	63.098 840	.015 848 1519	19.02	6.036 579	16.32	444
38	1291.342 856	81495.338 274	.000 012 2706	.000 774	63.108 986	.015 845 6040	19.02	6.225 595	16.38	456
39	1559.233 220	98414.729 710	.000 010 1611	.000 641	63.117 389	.015 843 4944	19.02	6.414 755	16.45	468
40	1882.697 708	118844.066	.000 008 4144	.000 531	63.124 348	.015 841 7477	19.02	6.604 039	16.51	480
41	2273.265 227	143511.488	.000 006 9681	.000 440	63.130 112	.015 840 3014	19.01	6.793 428	16.57	492
42	2744.856 367	173296.192	.000 005 7705	.000 364	63.134 885	.015 839 1038	19.01	6.982 908	16.63	504
43	3314.279 561	209259.762	.000 004 7787	.000 302	63.138 838	.015 838 1121	19.01	7.172 466	16.68	516
44	4001.830 163	252684.010	.000 003 9575	.000 250	63.142 112	.015 837 2908	19.01	7.362 090	16.73	528
45	4832.013 825	305116.663	.000 003 2774	.000 207	63.144 824	.015 836 6108	19.01	7.551 770	16.78	540
46	5834.419 916	368426.521	.000 002 7142	.000 171	63.147 070	.015 836 0476	19.01	7.741 498	16.83	552
47	7044.776 151	444870.073	.000 002 2478	.000 142	63.148 930	.015 835 5812	19.01	7.931 268	16.88	564
48	8506.221 996	537171.916	.000 001 8616	.000 118	63.150 470	.015 835 1949	19.01	8.121 072	16.92	576
49	10270.846	648621.868	.000 001 5417	.000 097	63.151 745	.015 834 8751	19.01	8.310 907	16.96	588
50	12401.544	783192.224	.000 001 2768	.000 081	63.152 802	.015 834 6102	19.01	8.500 766	17.00	600

Effective Rate is 20.75 %

Annual Percentage Rate is 19.00 %

MONTHLY COMPOUND INTEREST AND ANNUITY

20.00 % M

	Amount Of 1	Amount Of 1 Per Period	Sinking Fund Payment	Present Worth Of 1	Present Worth of 1 Per Period	Periodic Payment To Amortize 1	Constant Annual Percent	Total Interest	Annual Add On Rate	
	What a single $ 1 deposit grows to in the future. The deposit is made at the beginning of the first period.	What a series of $ 1 deposits grow to in the future. A deposit is made at the end of each period.	The amount to be deposited at the end of each period that grows to $ 1 in the future.	What $ 1 to be paid in the future is worth today. Value today of a single $ 1 payment tomorrow.	What $ 1 to be paid at the end of each period is worth today. Value today of a series of $ 1 payments tomorrow.	The mortgage payment to amortize a loan of $ 1. An annuity certain, payable at the end of each period, worth $ 1 today.	The annual payment, including interest and principal, to amortize completely a loan of $ 100.	The total interest paid over the term on a loan of $1. The loan is amortized by regular periodic payments.	The average annual interest rate on a loan that is completely amortized by regular periodic payments.	
	$S = (1+i)^n$	$S\overline{n}| = \dfrac{(1+i)^n - 1}{i}$	$\dfrac{1}{S\overline{n}|} = \dfrac{i}{(1+i)^n - 1}$	$V^n = \dfrac{1}{(1+i)^n}$	$A\overline{n}| = \dfrac{1-V^n}{i}$	$\dfrac{1}{A\overline{n}|} = \dfrac{i}{1-V^n}$				

YEAR										PERIODS
	1.016 667	1.000 000	1.000 000 0000	.983 607	.983 607	1.016 666 6667	1220.00	.016 667	20.00	1
	1.033 611	2.016 667	.495 867 7686	.967 482	1.951 088	.512 534 4353	615.05	.025 069	15.04	2
	1.050 838	3.050 278	.327 838 9946	.951 622	2.902 710	.344 505 6613	413.41	.033 517	13.41	3
	1.068 352	4.101 116	.243 836 0835	.936 021	3.838 731	.260 502 7501	312.61	.042 011	12.60	4
	1.086 158	5.169 468	.193 443 5156	.920 677	4.759 408	.210 110 1823	252.14	.050 551	12.13	5
	1.104 260	6.255 625	.159 856 1176	.905 583	5.664 991	.176 522 7843	211.83	.059 137	11.83	6
	1.122 665	7.359 886	.135 871 6718	.890 738	6.555 729	.152 538 3385	183.05	.067 768	11.62	7
	1.141 376	8.482 551	.117 889 0691	.876 136	7.431 865	.134 555 7358	161.47	.076 446	11.47	8
	1.160 399	9.623 926	.103 907 6930	.861 773	8.293 637	.120 574 3597	144.69	.085 169	11.36	9
	1.179 739	10.784 325	.092 727 1734	.847 645	9.141 283	.109 393 8401	131.28	.093 938	11.27	10
	1.199 401	11.964 064	.083 583 6383	.833 749	9.975 032	.100 250 3049	120.31	.102 753	11.21	11
	1.219 391	13.163 465	.075 967 8392	.820 081	10.795 113	.092 634 5059	111.17	.111 614	11.16	12
1	1.219 391	13.163 465	.075 967 8392	.820 081	10.795 113	.092 634 5059	111.17	.111 614	11.16	12
2	1.486 915	29.214 877	.034 229 1360	.672 534	19.647 986	.050 895 8026	61.08	.221 499	11.07	24
3	1.813 130	48.787 826	.020 496 9167	.551 532	26.908 062	.037 163 5834	44.60	.337 889	11.26	36
4	2.210 915	72.654 905	.013 763 6957	.452 301	32.861 916	.030 430 3623	36.52	.460 657	11.52	48
5	2.695 970	101.758 208	.009 827 2170	.370 924	37.744 561	.026 493 8837	31.80	.589 633	11.79	60
6	3.287 442	137.246 517	.007 286 1594	.304 188	41.748 727	.023 952 8261	28.75	.724 603	12.08	72
7	4.008 677	180.520 645	.005 539 5326	.249 459	45.032 470	.022 206 1993	26.65	.865 321	12.36	84
8	4.888 145	233.288 730	.004 286 5337	.204 577	47.725 406	.020 953 2004	25.15	1.011 507	12.64	96
9	5.960 561	297.633 662	.003 359 8350	.167 769	49.933 833	.020 026 5017	24.04	1.162 862	12.92	108
10	7.268 255	376.095 300	.002 658 9006	.137 585	51.744 924	.019 325 5672	23.20	1.319 068	13.19	120
11	8.862 845	471.770 720	.002 119 6737	.112 831	53.230 165	.018 786 3404	22.55	1.479 797	13.45	132
12	10.807 275	588.436 476	.001 699 4188	.092 530	54.448 184	.018 366 0855	22.04	1.644 716	13.71	144
13	13.178 294	730.697 658	.001 368 5551	.075 882	55.447 059	.018 035 2218	21.65	1.813 495	13.95	156
14	16.069 495	904.169 675	.001 105 9871	.062 230	56.266 217	.017 772 6538	21.33	1.985 806	14.18	168
15	19.594 998	1115.699 905	.000 896 2984	.051 033	56.937 994	.017 562 9650	21.08	2.161 334	14.41	180
16	23.893 966	1373.637 983	.000 727 9938	.041 852	57.488 906	.017 394 6605	20.88	2.339 775	14.62	192
17	29.136 090	1688.165 376	.000 592 3590	.034 322	57.940 698	.017 259 0257	20.72	2.520 841	14.83	204
18	35.528 288	2071.697 274	.000 482 6960	.028 147	58.311 205	.017 149 3627	20.58	2.704 262	15.02	216
19	43.322 878	2539.372 652	.000 393 7981	.023 082	58.615 050	.017 060 4647	20.48	2.889 786	15.21	228
20	52.827 531	3109.651 838	.000 321 5794	.018 930	58.864 229	.016 988 2461	20.39	3.077 179	15.39	240
21	64.417 420	3805.045 193	.000 262 8090	.015 524	59.068 575	.016 929 4756	20.32	3.266 228	15.55	252
22	78.550 028	4653.001 652	.000 214 9150	.012 731	59.236 156	.016 881 5817	20.26	3.456 738	15.71	264
23	95.783 203	5686.992 197	.000 175 8399	.010 440	59.373 585	.016 842 5065	20.22	3.648 532	15.86	276
24	116.797 184	6947.831 050	.000 143 9298	.008 562	59.486 289	.016 810 5965	20.18	3.841 452	16.01	288
25	142.421 445	8485.286 707	.000 117 8511	.007 021	59.578 715	.016 784 5177	20.15	4.035 355	16.14	300
26	173.667 440	10360.046 428	.000 096 5247	.005 758	59.654 512	.016 763 1913	20.12	4.230 116	16.27	312
27	211.768 529	12646.111 719	.000 079 0757	.004 722	59.716 672	.016 745 7424	20.10	4.425 621	16.39	324
28	258.228 656	15433.719 354	.000 064 7932	.003 873	59.767 648	.016 731 4599	20.08	4.621 771	16.51	336
29	314.881 721	18832.903 252	.000 053 0986	.003 176	59.809 452	.016 719 7652	20.07	4.818 478	16.62	348
30	383.963 963	22977.837 794	.000 043 5202	.002 604	59.843 735	.016 710 1869	20.06	5.015 667	16.72	360
31	468.202 234	28032.134 021	.000 035 6733	.002 136	59.871 850	.016 702 3400	20.05	5.213 270	16.82	372
32	570.921 630	34195.297 782	.000 029 2408	.001 752	59.894 907	.016 695 9105	20.04	5.411 230	16.91	384
33	696.176 745	41710.604 726	.000 023 9747	.001 436	59.913 815	.016 690 6414	20.03	5.609 494	17.00	396
34	848.911 717	50874.703 014	.000 019 6561	.001 178	59.929 321	.016 686 3228	20.03	5.808 020	17.08	408
35	1035.155 379	62049.322 767	.000 016 1162	.000 966	59.942 038	.016 682 7829	20.02	6.006 769	17.16	420
36	1262.259 241	75675.554 472	.000 013 2143	.000 792	59.952 466	.016 679 8810	20.02	6.205 709	17.24	432
37	1539.187 666	92291.259 933	.000 010 8353	.000 650	59.961 018	.016 677 5019	20.02	6.404 811	17.31	444
38	1876.871 717	112552.303	.000 008 8848	.000 533	59.968 032	.016 675 5514	20.02	6.604 051	17.38	456
39	2288.640 640	137258.438	.000 007 2855	.000 437	59.973 784	.016 673 9522	20.01	6.803 410	17.44	468
40	2790.747 993	167384.880	.000 005 9743	.000 358	59.978 500	.016 672 6409	20.01	7.002 868	17.51	480
41	3403.013 222	204120.793	.000 004 8991	.000 294	59.982 369	.016 671 5657	20.01	7.202 410	17.57	492
42	4149.603 985	248916.239	.000 004 0174	.000 241	59.985 541	.016 670 6841	20.01	7.402 025	17.62	504
43	5059.990 105	303539.406	.000 003 2945	.000 198	59.988 142	.016 669 9611	20.01	7.601 700	17.68	516
44	6170.106 824	370146.409	.000 002 7016	.000 162	59.990 276	.016 669 3683	20.01	7.801 426	17.73	528
45	7523.773 254	451366.395	.000 002 2155	.000 133	59.992 025	.016 668 8822	20.01	8.001 196	17.78	540
46	9174.422 031	550405.322	.000 001 8168	.000 109	59.993 460	.016 668 4835	20.01	8.201 003	17.83	552
47	11187.208	671172.506	.000 001 4899	.000 089	59.994 637	.016 668 1566	20.01	8.400 840	17.87	564
48	13641.582	818434.934	.000 001 2218	.000 073	59.995 602	.016 667 8885	20.01	8.600 704	17.92	576
49	16634.424	998005.425	.000 001 0020	.000 060	59.996 393	.016 667 6687	20.01	8.800 589	17.96	588
50	20283.868	1216972.082	.000 000 8217	.000 049	59.997 042	.016 667 4884	20.01	9.000 493	18.00	600

Effective Rate is 21.94 %

Annual Percentage Rate is 20.00 %

QUARTERLY COMPOUND INTEREST AND ANNUITY

	Amount Of 1	Amount Of 1 Per Period	Sinking Fund Payment	Present Worth Of 1	Present Worth of 1 Per Period	Periodic Payment To Amortize 1	Constant Annual Percent	Total Interest	Annual Add On Rate	
	What a single $ 1 deposit grows to in the future. The deposit is made at the beginning of the first period.	What a series of $ 1 deposits grow to in the future. A deposit is made at the end of each period.	The amount to be deposited at the end of each period that grows to $ 1 in the future.	What $ 1 to be paid in the future is worth today. Value today of a single $ 1 payment tomorrow.	What $ 1 to be paid at the end of each period is worth today. Value today of a series of $ 1 payments tomorrow.	The mortgage payment to amortize a loan of $ 1. An annuity certain, payable at the end of each period, worth $ 1 today.	The annual payment, including interest and principal, to amortize completely a loan of $ 100.	The total interest paid over the term on a loan of $1. The loan is amortized by regular periodic payments.	The average annual interest rate on a loan that is completely amortized by regular periodic payments.	
	$S = (1+i)^n$	$S\overline{n}| = \dfrac{(1+i)^n - 1}{i}$	$\dfrac{1}{S\overline{n}|} = \dfrac{i}{(1+i)^n - 1}$	$V^n = \dfrac{1}{(1+i)^n}$	$A\overline{n}| = \dfrac{1 - V^n}{i}$	$\dfrac{1}{A\overline{n}|} = \dfrac{i}{1 - V^n}$				

YEAR										PERIODS
	1.000 000	1.000 000	1.000 000 0000	1.000 000	1.000 000	1.000 000 0000	400.00	0.000 000	0.00	1
	1.000 000	2.000 000	.500 000 0000	1.000 000	2.000 000	.500 000 0000	200.00	0.000 000	0.00	2
	1.000 000	3.000 000	.333 333 3333	1.000 000	3.000 000	.333 333 3333	133.34	0.000 000	0.00	3
	1.000 000	4.000 000	.250 000 0000	1.000 000	4.000 000	.250 000 0000	100.00	0.000 000	0.00	4
1	1.000 000	4.000 000	.250 000 0000	1.000 000	4.000 000	.250 000 0000	100.00	0.000 000	0.00	4
2	1.000 000	8.000 000	.125 000 0000	1.000 000	8.000 000	.125 000 0000	50.00	0.000 000	0.00	8
3	1.000 000	12.000 000	.083 333 3333	1.000 000	12.000 000	.083 333 3333	33.34	0.000 000	0.00	12
4	1.000 000	16.000 000	.062 500 0000	1.000 000	16.000 000	.062 500 0000	25.00	0.000 000	0.00	16
5	1.000 000	20.000 000	.050 000 0000	1.000 000	20.000 000	.050 000 0000	20.00	0.000 000	0.00	20
6	1.000 000	24.000 000	.041 666 6667	1.000 000	24.000 000	.041 666 6667	16.67	0.000 000	0.00	24
7	1.000 000	28.000 000	.035 714 2857	1.000 000	28.000 000	.035 714 2857	14.29	0.000 000	0.00	28
8	1.000 000	32.000 000	.031 250 0000	1.000 000	32.000 000	.031 250 0000	12.50	0.000 000	0.00	32
9	1.000 000	36.000 000	.027 777 7778	1.000 000	36.000 000	.027 777 7778	11.12	0.000 000	0.00	36
10	1.000 000	40.000 000	.025 000 0000	1.000 000	40.000 000	.025 000 0000	10.00	0.000 000	0.00	40
11	1.000 000	44.000 000	.022 727 2727	1.000 000	44.000 000	.022 727 2727	9.10	0.000 000	0.00	44
12	1.000 000	48.000 000	.020 833 3333	1.000 000	48.000 000	.020 833 3333	8.34	0.000 000	0.00	48
13	1.000 000	52.000 000	.019 230 7692	1.000 000	52.000 000	.019 230 7692	7.70	0.000 000	0.00	52
14	1.000 000	56.000 000	.017 857 1429	1.000 000	56.000 000	.017 857 1429	7.15	0.000 000	0.00	56
15	1.000 000	60.000 000	.016 666 6667	1.000 000	60.000 000	.016 666 6667	6.67	0.000 000	0.00	60
16	1.000 000	64.000 000	.015 625 0000	1.000 000	64.000 000	.015 625 0000	6.25	0.000 000	0.00	64
17	1.000 000	68.000 000	.014 705 8824	1.000 000	68.000 000	.014 705 8824	5.89	0.000 000	0.00	68
18	1.000 000	72.000 000	.013 888 8889	1.000 000	72.000 000	.013 888 8889	5.56	0.000 000	0.00	72
19	1.000 000	76.000 000	.013 157 8947	1.000 000	76.000 000	.013 157 8947	5.27	0.000 000	0.00	76
20	1.000 000	80.000 000	.012 500 0000	1.000 000	80.000 000	.012 500 0000	5.00	0.000 000	0.00	80
21	1.000 000	84.000 000	.011 904 7619	1.000 000	84.000 000	.011 904 7619	4.77	0.000 000	0.00	84
22	1.000 000	88.000 000	.011 363 6364	1.000 000	88.000 000	.011 363 6364	4.55	0.000 000	0.00	88
23	1.000 000	92.000 000	.010 869 5652	1.000 000	92.000 000	.010 869 5652	4.35	0.000 000	0.00	92
24	1.000 000	96.000 000	.010 416 6667	1.000 000	96.000 000	.010 416 6667	4.17	0.000 000	0.00	96
25	1.000 000	100.000 000	.010 000 0000	1.000 000	100.000 000	.010 000 0000	4.00	0.000 000	0.00	100
26	1.000 000	104.000 000	.009 615 3846	1.000 000	104.000 000	.009 615 3846	3.85	0.000 000	0.00	104
27	1.000 000	108.000 000	.009 259 2593	1.000 000	108.000 000	.009 259 2593	3.71	0.000 000	0.00	108
28	1.000 000	112.000 000	.008 928 5714	1.000 000	112.000 000	.008 928 5714	3.58	0.000 000	0.00	112
29	1.000 000	116.000 000	.008 620 6897	1.000 000	116.000 000	.008 620 6897	3.45	0.000 000	0.00	116
30	1.000 000	120.000 000	.008 333 3333	1.000 000	120.000 000	.008 333 3333	3.34	0.000 000	0.00	120
31	1.000 000	124.000 000	.008 064 5161	1.000 000	124.000 000	.008 064 5161	3.23	0.000 000	0.00	124
32	1.000 000	128.000 000	.007 812 5000	1.000 000	128.000 000	.007 812 5000	3.13	0.000 000	0.00	128
33	1.000 000	132.000 000	.007 575 7576	1.000 000	132.000 000	.007 575 7576	3.04	0.000 000	0.00	132
34	1.000 000	136.000 000	.007 352 9412	1.000 000	136.000 000	.007 352 9412	2.95	0.000 000	0.00	136
35	1.000 000	140.000 000	.007 142 8571	1.000 000	140.000 000	.007 142 8571	2.86	0.000 000	0.00	140
36	1.000 000	144.000 000	.006 944 4444	1.000 000	144.000 000	.006 944 4444	2.78	0.000 000	0.00	144
37	1.000 000	148.000 000	.006 756 7568	1.000 000	148.000 000	.006 756 7568	2.71	0.000 000	0.00	148
38	1.000 000	152.000 000	.006 578 9474	1.000 000	152.000 000	.006 578 9474	2.64	0.000 000	0.00	152
39	1.000 000	156.000 000	.006 410 2564	1.000 000	156.000 000	.006 410 2564	2.57	0.000 000	0.00	156
40	1.000 000	160.000 000	.006 250 0000	1.000 000	160.000 000	.006 250 0000	2.50	0.000 000	0.00	160
41	1.000 000	164.000 000	.006 097 5610	1.000 000	164.000 000	.006 097 5610	2.44	0.000 000	0.00	164
42	1.000 000	168.000 000	.005 952 3810	1.000 000	168.000 000	.005 952 3810	2.39	0.000 000	0.00	168
43	1.000 000	172.000 000	.005 813 9535	1.000 000	172.000 000	.005 813 9535	2.33	0.000 000	0.00	172
44	1.000 000	176.000 000	.005 681 8182	1.000 000	176.000 000	.005 681 8182	2.28	0.000 000	0.00	176
45	1.000 000	180.000 000	.005 555 5556	1.000 000	180.000 000	.005 555 5556	2.23	0.000 000	0.00	180
46	1.000 000	184.000 000	.005 434 7826	1.000 000	184.000 000	.005 434 7826	2.18	0.000 000	0.00	184
47	1.000 000	188.000 000	.005 319 1489	1.000 000	188.000 000	.005 319 1489	2.13	0.000 000	0.00	188
48	1.000 000	192.000 000	.005 208 3333	1.000 000	192.000 000	.005 208 3333	2.09	0.000 000	0.00	192
49	1.000 000	196.000 000	.005 102 0408	1.000 000	196.000 000	.005 102 0408	2.05	0.000 000	0.00	196
50	1.000 000	200.000 000	.005 000 0000	1.000 000	200.000 000	.005 000 0000	2.00	0.000 000	0.00	200

Effective Rate is 0.00 %

Annual Percentage Rate is 0.00 %

QUARTERLY COMPOUND INTEREST AND ANNUITY

1.00 % Q

	Amount Of 1	Amount Of 1 Per Period	Sinking Fund Payment	Present Worth Of 1	Present Worth of 1 Per Period	Periodic Payment To Amortize 1	Constant Annual Percent	Total Interest	Annual Add On Rate
	What a single $ 1 deposit grows to in the future. The deposit is made at the beginning of the first period.	What a series of $ 1 deposits grow to in the future. A deposit is made at the end of each period.	The amount to be deposited at the end of each period that grows to $ 1 in the future.	What $ 1 to be paid in the future is worth today. Value today of a single $ 1 payment tomorrow.	What $ 1 to be paid at the end of each period is worth today. Value today of a series of $ 1 payments tomorrow.	The mortgage payment to amortize a loan of $ 1. An annuity certain, payable at the end of each period, worth $ 1 today.	The annual payment, including interest and principal, to amortize completely a loan of $ 100.	The total interest paid over the term on a loan of $1. The loan is amortized by regular periodic payments.	The average annual interest rate on a loan that is completely amortized by regular periodic payments.
	$S = (1+i)^n$	$S\overline{n}| = \dfrac{(1+i)^n - 1}{i}$	$\dfrac{1}{S\overline{n}|} = \dfrac{i}{(1+i)^n - 1}$	$V^n = \dfrac{1}{(1+i)^n}$	$A\overline{n}| = \dfrac{1-V^n}{i}$	$\dfrac{1}{A\overline{n}|} = \dfrac{i}{1-V^n}$			

YEAR									PERIODS
	1.002 500	1.000 000	1.000 000 0000	.997 506	.997 506	1.002 500 0000	401.00	.002 500	1.00	1
	1.005 006	2.002 500	.499 375 7803	.995 019	1.992 525	.501 875 7803	200.76	.003 752	.75	2
	1.007 519	3.007 506	.332 501 3872	.992 537	2.985 062	.335 001 3872	134.01	.005 004	.67	3
	1.010 038	4.015 025	.249 064 4507	.990 062	3.975 124	.251 564 4507	100.63	.006 258	.63	4
1	1.010 038	4.015 025	.249 064 4507	.990 062	3.975 124	.251 564 4507	100.63	.006 258	.63	4
2	1.020 176	8.070 351	.123 910 3464	.980 223	7.910 745	.126 410 3464	50.57	.011 283	.56	8
3	1.030 416	12.166 383	.082 193 6988	.970 482	11.807 254	.084 693 6988	33.88	.016 324	.54	12
4	1.040 759	16.303 529	.061 336 4152	.960 837	15.665 040	.063 836 4152	25.54	.021 383	.53	16
5	1.051 206	20.482 201	.048 822 8772	.951 289	19.484 488	.051 322 8772	20.53	.026 458	.53	20
6	1.061 757	24.702 818	.040 481 2120	.941 835	23.265 980	.042 981 2120	17.20	.031 549	.53	24
7	1.072 414	28.965 799	.034 523 4739	.932 475	27.009 891	.037 023 4739	14.81	.036 657	.52	28
8	1.083 179	33.271 570	.030 055 6903	.923 209	30.716 596	.032 555 6903	13.03	.041 782	.52	32
9	1.094 051	37.620 560	.026 581 2096	.914 034	34.386 465	.029 081 2096	11.64	.046 924	.52	36
10	1.105 033	42.013 204	.023 802 0409	.904 950	38.019 863	.026 302 0409	10.53	.052 082	.52	40
11	1.116 125	46.449 939	.021 528 5535	.895 957	41.617 154	.024 028 5535	9.62	.057 256	.52	44
12	1.127 328	50.931 208	.019 634 3270	.887 053	45.178 695	.022 134 3270	8.86	.062 448	.52	48
13	1.138 644	55.457 459	.018 031 8396	.878 238	48.704 842	.020 531 8396	8.22	.067 656	.52	52
14	1.150 073	60.029 141	.016 658 5758	.869 510	52.195 947	.019 158 5758	7.67	.072 880	.52	56
15	1.161 617	64.646 713	.015 468 6907	.860 869	55.652 358	.017 968 6907	7.19	.078 121	.52	60
16	1.173 277	69.310 633	.014 427 8007	.852 314	59.074 420	.016 927 8007	6.78	.083 379	.52	64
17	1.185 053	74.021 368	.013 509 6125	.843 844	62.462 474	.016 009 6125	6.41	.088 654	.52	68
18	1.196 948	78.779 387	.012 693 6758	.835 458	65.816 858	.015 193 6758	6.08	.093 945	.52	72
19	1.208 963	83.585 165	.011 963 8455	.827 155	69.137 907	.014 463 8455	5.79	.099 252	.52	76
20	1.221 098	88.439 181	.011 307 2055	.818 935	72.425 952	.013 807 2055	5.53	.104 576	.52	80
21	1.233 355	93.341 920	.010 713 3001	.810 797	75.681 321	.013 213 3001	5.29	.109 917	.52	84
22	1.245 735	98.293 871	.010 173 5743	.802 739	78.904 339	.012 673 5743	5.07	.115 275	.52	88
23	1.258 239	103.295 526	.009 680 9614	.794 762	82.095 327	.012 180 9614	4.88	.120 648	.52	92
24	1.270 868	108.347 387	.009 229 5719	.786 863	85.254 603	.011 729 5719	4.70	.126 039	.53	96
25	1.283 625	113.449 955	.008 814 4592	.779 044	88.382 483	.011 314 4592	4.53	.131 446	.53	100
26	1.296 509	118.603 742	.008 431 4372	.771 302	91.479 279	.010 931 4372	4.38	.136 869	.53	104
27	1.309 523	123.809 259	.008 076 9404	.763 637	94.545 300	.010 576 9404	4.24	.142 310	.53	108
28	1.322 668	129.067 027	.007 747 9122	.756 048	97.580 851	.010 247 9122	4.10	.147 766	.53	112
29	1.335 944	134.377 571	.007 441 7181	.748 534	100.586 236	.009 941 7181	3.98	.153 239	.53	116
30	1.349 354	139.741 419	.007 156 0745	.741 096	103.561 753	.009 656 0745	3.87	.158 729	.53	120
31	1.362 898	145.159 107	.006 888 9925	.733 731	106.507 700	.009 388 9925	3.76	.164 235	.53	124
32	1.376 578	150.631 176	.006 638 7320	.726 439	109.424 371	.009 138 7320	3.66	.169 758	.53	128
33	1.390 395	156.158 171	.006 403 7635	.719 220	112.312 057	.008 903 7635	3.57	.175 297	.53	132
34	1.404 352	161.740 643	.006 182 7379	.712 072	115.171 046	.008 682 7379	3.48	.180 852	.53	136
35	1.418 448	167.379 150	.005 974 4598	.704 996	118.001 622	.008 474 4598	3.39	.186 424	.53	140
36	1.432 686	173.074 254	.005 777 8669	.697 990	120.804 069	.008 277 8669	3.32	.192 013	.53	144
37	1.447 066	178.826 522	.005 592 0117	.691 053	123.578 665	.008 092 0117	3.24	.197 618	.53	148
38	1.461 591	184.636 530	.005 416 0463	.684 186	126.325 668	.007 916 0463	3.17	.203 239	.53	152
39	1.476 262	190.504 855	.005 249 2100	.677 386	129.045 412	.007 749 2100	3.10	.208 877	.54	156
40	1.491 080	196.432 085	.005 090 8180	.670 655	131.738 107	.007 590 8180	3.04	.214 531	.54	160
41	1.506 047	202.418 809	.004 940 2524	.663 990	134.404 043	.007 440 2524	2.98	.220 201	.54	164
42	1.521 164	208.465 626	.004 796 9539	.657 391	137.043 486	.007 296 9539	2.92	.225 888	.54	168
43	1.536 433	214.573 137	.004 660 4156	.650 858	139.656 698	.007 160 4156	2.87	.231 591	.54	172
44	1.551 855	220.741 954	.004 530 1764	.644 390	142.243 940	.007 030 1764	2.82	.237 311	.54	176
45	1.567 432	226.972 690	.004 405 8164	.637 986	144.805 471	.006 905 8164	2.77	.243 047	.54	180
46	1.583 165	233.265 967	.004 286 9520	.631 646	147.341 546	.006 786 9520	2.72	.248 799	.54	184
47	1.599 056	239.622 414	.004 173 2323	.625 369	149.852 418	.006 673 2323	2.67	.254 568	.54	188
48	1.615 107	246.042 664	.004 064 3358	.619 154	152.338 338	.006 564 3358	2.63	.260 352	.54	192
49	1.631 318	252.527 358	.003 959 9670	.613 001	154.799 553	.006 459 9670	2.59	.266 154	.54	196
50	1.647 693	259.077 142	.003 859 8542	.606 909	157.236 308	.006 359 8542	2.55	.271 971	.54	200

QUARTERLY COMPOUND INTEREST AND ANNUITY

2.00 % Q

	Amount Of 1	Amount Of 1 Per Period	Sinking Fund Payment	Present Worth Of 1	Present Worth of 1 Per Period	Periodic Payment To Amortize 1	Constant Annual Percent	Total Interest	Annual Add On Rate	
	What a single $ 1 deposit grows to in the future. The deposit is made at the beginning of the first period.	What a series of $ 1 deposits grow to in the future. A deposit is made at the end of each period.	The amount to be deposited at the end of each period that grows to $ 1 in the future.	What $ 1 to be paid in the future is worth today. Value today of a single $ 1 payment tomorrow.	What $ 1 to be paid at the end of each period is worth today. Value today of a series of $ 1 payments tomorrow.	The mortgage payment to amortize a loan of $ 1. An annuity certain, payable at the end of each period, worth $ 1 today.	The annual payment, including interest and principal, to amortize completely a loan of $ 100.	The total interest paid over the term on a loan of $1. The loan is amortized by regular periodic payments.	The average annual interest rate on a loan that is completely amortized by regular periodic payments.	
	$S = (1+i)^n$	$S\overline{n} = \dfrac{(1+i)^n - 1}{i}$	$\dfrac{1}{S\overline{n}} = \dfrac{i}{(1+i)^n - 1}$	$V^n = \dfrac{1}{(1+i)^n}$	$A\overline{n} = \dfrac{1 - V^n}{i}$	$\dfrac{1}{A\overline{n}} = \dfrac{i}{1 - V^n}$				
YEAR										**PERIODS**
	1.005 000	1.000 000	1.000 000 0000	.995 025	.995 025	1.005 000 0000	402.00	.005 000	2.00	1
	1.010 025	2.005 000	.498 753 1172	.990 075	1.985 099	.503 753 1172	201.51	.007 506	1.50	2
	1.015 075	3.015 025	.331 672 2084	.985 149	2.970 248	.336 672 2084	134.67	.010 017	1.34	3
	1.020 151	4.030 100	.248 132 7930	.980 248	3.950 496	.253 132 7930	101.26	.012 531	1.25	4
1	1.020 151	4.030 100	.248 132 7930	.980 248	3.950 496	.253 132 7930	101.26	.012 531	1.25	4
2	1.040 707	8.141 409	.122 828 8649	.960 885	7.822 959	.127 828 8649	51.14	.022 631	1.13	8
3	1.061 678	12.335 562	.081 066 4297	.941 905	11.618 932	.086 066 4297	34.43	.032 797	1.09	12
4	1.083 071	16.614 230	.060 189 3669	.923 300	15.339 925	.065 189 3669	26.08	.043 030	1.08	16
5	1.104 896	20.979 115	.047 666 4520	.905 063	18.987 419	.052 666 4520	21.07	.053 329	1.07	20
6	1.127 160	25.431 955	.039 320 6103	.887 186	22.562 866	.044 320 6103	17.73	.063 695	1.06	24
7	1.149 873	29.974 522	.033 361 6663	.869 662	26.067 689	.038 361 6663	15.35	.074 127	1.06	28
8	1.173 043	34.608 624	.028 894 5324	.852 484	29.503 284	.033 894 5324	13.56	.084 625	1.06	32
9	1.196 681	39.336 105	.025 421 9375	.835 645	32.871 016	.030 421 9375	12.17	.095 190	1.06	36
10	1.220 794	44.158 847	.022 645 5186	.819 139	36.172 228	.027 645 5186	11.06	.105 821	1.06	40
11	1.245 394	49.078 770	.020 375 4086	.802 959	39.408 232	.025 375 4086	10.16	.116 518	1.06	44
12	1.270 489	54.097 832	.018 485 0290	.787 098	42.580 318	.023 485 0290	9.40	.127 281	1.06	48
13	1.296 090	59.218 031	.016 886 7486	.771 551	45.689 747	.021 886 7486	8.76	.138 111	1.06	52
14	1.322 207	64.441 404	.015 517 9735	.756 311	48.737 757	.020 517 9735	8.21	.149 007	1.06	56
15	1.348 850	69.770 031	.014 332 8015	.741 372	51.725 561	.019 332 8015	7.74	.159 968	1.07	60
16	1.376 030	75.206 032	.013 296 8058	.726 728	54.654 348	.018 296 8058	7.32	.170 996	1.07	64
17	1.403 758	80.751 571	.012 383 6600	.712 374	57.525 285	.017 383 6600	6.96	.182 089	1.07	68
18	1.432 044	86.408 856	.011 572 8879	.698 302	60.339 514	.016 572 8879	6.63	.193 248	1.07	72
19	1.460 901	92.180 138	.010 848 3240	.684 509	63.098 155	.015 848 3240	6.34	.204 473	1.08	76
20	1.490 339	98.067 714	.010 197 0359	.670 988	65.802 305	.015 197 0359	6.08	.215 763	1.08	80
21	1.520 370	104.073 927	.009 608 5545	.657 735	68.453 042	.014 608 5545	5.85	.227 119	1.08	84
22	1.551 006	110.201 169	.009 074 3139	.644 743	71.051 421	.014 074 3139	5.63	.238 540	1.08	88
23	1.582 259	116.451 878	.008 587 2381	.632 008	73.598 475	.013 587 2381	5.44	.250 026	1.09	92
24	1.614 143	122.828 542	.008 141 4302	.619 524	76.095 218	.013 141 4302	5.26	.261 577	1.09	96
25	1.646 668	129.333 698	.007 731 9369	.607 287	78.542 645	.012 731 9369	5.10	.273 194	1.09	100
26	1.679 850	135.969 937	.007 354 5669	.595 291	80.941 729	.012 354 5669	4.95	.284 875	1.10	104
27	1.713 699	142.739 900	.007 005 7496	.583 533	83.293 424	.012 005 7496	4.81	.296 621	1.10	108
28	1.748 231	149.646 280	.006 682 4247	.572 007	85.598 669	.011 682 4247	4.68	.308 432	1.10	112
29	1.783 459	156.691 828	.006 381 9538	.560 708	87.858 378	.011 381 9538	4.56	.320 307	1.10	116
30	1.819 397	163.879 347	.006 102 0502	.549 633	90.073 453	.011 102 0502	4.45	.332 246	1.11	120
31	1.856 058	171.211 698	.005 840 7224	.538 776	92.244 775	.010 840 7224	4.34	.344 250	1.11	124
32	1.893 459	178.691 799	.005 596 2277	.528 134	94.373 208	.010 596 2277	4.24	.356 317	1.11	128
33	1.931 613	186.322 629	.005 367 0346	.517 702	96.459 599	.010 367 0346	4.15	.368 449	1.12	132
34	1.970 536	194.107 223	.005 151 7918	.507 476	98.504 778	.010 151 7918	4.07	.380 644	1.12	136
35	2.010 243	202.048 681	.004 949 3023	.497 452	100.509 560	.009 949 3023	3.98	.392 902	1.12	140
36	2.050 751	210.150 163	.004 758 5021	.487 626	102.474 743	.009 758 5021	3.91	.405 224	1.13	144
37	2.092 074	218.414 894	.004 578 4423	.477 994	104.401 109	.009 578 4423	3.84	.417 609	1.13	148
38	2.134 231	226.846 164	.004 408 2738	.468 553	106.289 424	.009 408 2738	3.77	.430 058	1.13	152
39	2.177 237	235.447 328	.004 247 2344	.459 298	108.140 440	.009 247 2344	3.70	.442 569	1.13	156
40	2.221 109	244.221 809	.004 094 6384	.450 226	109.954 894	.009 094 6384	3.64	.455 142	1.14	160
41	2.265 866	253.173 101	.003 949 8667	.441 332	111.733 508	.008 949 8667	3.58	.467 778	1.14	164
42	2.311 524	262.304 766	.003 812 3592	.432 615	113.476 990	.008 812 3592	3.53	.480 476	1.14	168
43	2.358 102	271.620 439	.003 681 6081	.424 070	115.186 034	.008 681 6081	3.48	.493 237	1.15	172
44	2.405 619	281.123 826	.003 557 1514	.415 693	116.861 320	.008 557 1514	3.43	.506 059	1.15	176
45	2.454 094	290.818 712	.003 438 5683	.407 482	118.503 515	.008 438 5683	3.38	.518 942	1.15	180
46	2.503 545	300.708 955	.003 325 4746	.399 434	120.113 272	.008 325 4746	3.34	.531 887	1.16	184
47	2.553 992	310.798 491	.003 217 5188	.391 544	121.691 233	.008 217 5188	3.29	.544 894	1.16	188
48	2.605 457	321.091 337	.003 114 3786	.383 810	123.238 025	.008 114 3786	3.25	.557 961	1.16	192
49	2.657 958	331.591 588	.003 015 7580	.376 229	124.754 265	.008 015 7580	3.21	.571 089	1.17	196
50	2.711 517	342.303 425	.002 921 3847	.368 797	126.240 554	.007 921 3847	3.17	.584 277	1.17	200

Effective Rate is 2.02 %

Annual Percentage Rate is 2.00 %

QUARTERLY COMPOUND INTEREST AND ANNUITY

	Amount Of 1	Amount Of 1 Per Period	Sinking Fund Payment	Present Worth Of 1	Present Worth of 1 Per Period	Periodic Payment To Amortize 1	Constant Annual Percent	Total Interest	Annual Add On Rate	
	What a single $ 1 deposit grows to in the future. The deposit is made at the beginning of the first period.	What a series of $ 1 deposits grow to in the future. A deposit is made at the end of each period.	The amount to be deposited at the end of each period that grows to $ 1 in the future.	What $ 1 to be paid in the future is worth today. Value today of a single $ 1 payment tomorrow.	What $ 1 to be paid at the end of each period is worth today. Value today of a series of $ 1 payments tomorrow.	The mortgage payment to amortize a loan of $ 1. An annuity certain, payable at the end of each period, worth $ 1 today.	The annual payment, including interest and principal, to amortize completely a loan of $ 100.	The total interest paid over the term on a loan of $1. The loan is amortized by regular periodic payments.	The average annual interest rate on a loan that is completely amortized by regular periodic payments.	
	$S = (1+i)^n$	$S\overline{n}| = \dfrac{(1+i)^n - 1}{i}$	$\dfrac{1}{S\overline{n}|} = \dfrac{i}{(1+i)^n - 1}$	$V^n = \dfrac{1}{(1+i)^n}$	$A\overline{n}| = \dfrac{1-V^n}{i}$	$\dfrac{1}{A\overline{n}|} = \dfrac{i}{1-V^n}$				

YEAR										PERIODS
	1.005 625	1.000 000	1.000 000 0000	.994 406	.994 406	1.005 625 0000	402.25	.005 625	2.25	1
	1.011 282	2.005 625	.498 597 6940	.988 844	1.983 251	.504 222 6940	201.69	.008 445	1.69	2
	1.016 970	3.016 907	.331 465 3448	.983 313	2.966 564	.337 090 3448	134.84	.011 271	1.50	3
	1.022 691	4.033 877	.247 900 4849	.977 813	3.944 377	.253 525 4849	101.42	.014 102	1.41	4
1	1.022 691	4.033 877	.247 900 4849	.977 813	3.944 377	.253 525 4849	101.42	.014 102	1.41	4
2	1.045 896	8.159 284	.122 559 7678	.956 118	7.801 239	.128 184 7678	51.28	.025 478	1.27	8
3	1.069 628	12.378 300	.080 786 5388	.934 905	11.572 529	.086 411 5388	34.57	.036 938	1.23	12
4	1.093 898	16.693 047	.059 905 1806	.914 162	15.260 144	.065 530 1806	26.22	.048 483	1.21	16
5	1.118 720	21.105 698	.047 380 5691	.893 879	18.865 942	.053 005 5691	21.21	.060 111	1.20	20
6	1.144 104	25.618 475	.039 034 3295	.874 046	22.391 738	.044 659 3295	17.87	.071 824	1.20	24
7	1.170 064	30.233 649	.033 075 7292	.854 654	25.839 306	.038 700 7292	15.49	.083 620	1.19	28
8	1.196 614	34.953 544	.028 609 4019	.835 692	29.210 383	.034 234 4019	13.70	.095 501	1.19	32
9	1.223 766	39.780 537	.025 137 9214	.817 150	32.506 666	.030 762 9214	12.31	.107 465	1.19	36
10	1.251 533	44.717 056	.022 362 8319	.799 020	35.729 813	.027 987 8319	11.20	.119 513	1.20	40
11	1.279 931	49.765 587	.020 094 2067	.781 292	38.881 448	.025 719 2067	10.29	.131 645	1.20	44
12	1.308 974	54.928 673	.018 205 4280	.763 957	41.963 157	.023 830 4280	9.54	.143 861	1.20	48
13	1.338 675	60.208 912	.016 608 8369	.747 007	44.976 493	.022 233 8369	8.90	.156 160	1.20	52
14	1.369 050	65.608 962	.015 241 8201	.730 433	47.922 970	.020 866 8201	8.35	.168 542	1.20	56
15	1.400 115	71.131 543	.014 058 4607	.714 227	50.804 074	.019 683 4607	7.88	.181 008	1.21	60
16	1.431 884	76.779 434	.013 024 3211	.698 380	53.621 255	.018 649 3211	7.46	.193 557	1.21	64
17	1.464 375	82.555 479	.012 113 0664	.682 885	56.375 931	.017 738 0664	7.10	.206 189	1.21	68
18	1.497 602	88.462 585	.011 304 2140	.667 734	59.069 488	.016 929 2140	6.78	.218 903	1.22	72
19	1.531 583	94.503 728	.010 581 5932	.652 919	61.703 283	.016 206 5932	6.49	.231 701	1.22	76
20	1.566 336	100.681 946	.009 932 2673	.638 433	64.278 641	.015 557 2673	6.23	.244 581	1.22	80
21	1.601 877	107.000 353	.009 345 7636	.624 268	66.796 860	.014 970 7636	5.99	.257 544	1.23	84
22	1.638 224	113.462 127	.008 813 5136	.610 417	69.259 207	.014 438 5136	5.78	.270 589	1.23	88
23	1.675 397	120.070 522	.008 328 4388	.596 874	71.666 921	.013 953 4388	5.59	.283 716	1.23	92
24	1.713 412	126.828 866	.007 884 6404	.583 631	74.021 215	.013 509 6404	5.41	.296 925	1.24	96
25	1.752 291	133.740 560	.007 477 1632	.570 682	76.323 274	.013 102 1632	5.25	.310 216	1.24	100
26	1.792 051	140.809 085	.007 101 8145	.558 020	78.574 258	.012 726 8145	5.10	.323 589	1.24	104
27	1.832 714	148.037 998	.006 755 0224	.545 639	80.775 298	.012 380 0224	4.96	.337 042	1.25	108
28	1.874 299	155.430 940	.006 433 7255	.533 533	82.927 503	.012 058 7255	4.83	.350 577	1.25	112
29	1.916 828	162.991 631	.006 135 2843	.521 695	85.031 958	.011 760 2843	4.71	.364 193	1.26	116
30	1.960 322	170.723 878	.005 857 4114	.510 120	87.089 720	.011 482 4114	4.60	.377 889	1.26	120
31	2.004 803	178.631 575	.005 598 1144	.498 802	89.101 827	.011 223 1144	4.49	.391 666	1.26	124
32	2.050 293	186.718 702	.005 355 6499	.487 735	91.069 291	.010 980 6499	4.40	.405 523	1.27	128
33	2.096 815	194.989 330	.005 128 4858	.476 914	92.993 102	.010 753 4858	4.31	.419 460	1.27	132
34	2.144 393	203.447 623	.004 915 2700	.466 332	94.874 230	.010 540 2700	4.22	.433 477	1.27	136
35	2.193 050	212.097 839	.004 714 8052	.455 986	96.713 621	.010 339 8052	4.14	.447 573	1.28	140
36	2.242 812	220.944 334	.004 526 0269	.445 869	98.512 201	.010 151 0269	4.07	.461 748	1.28	144
37	2.293 703	229.991 561	.004 347 9856	.435 976	100.270 876	.009 972 9856	3.99	.476 002	1.29	148
38	2.345 748	239.244 074	.004 179 8318	.426 303	101.990 530	.009 804 8318	3.93	.490 334	1.29	152
39	2.398 974	248.706 532	.004 020 8031	.416 845	103.672 031	.009 645 8031	3.86	.504 745	1.29	156
40	2.453 408	258.383 698	.003 870 2132	.407 596	105.316 224	.009 495 2132	3.80	.519 234	1.30	160
41	2.509 078	268.280 445	.003 727 4427	.398 553	106.923 937	.009 352 4427	3.75	.533 801	1.30	164
42	2.566 010	278.401 755	.003 591 9314	.389 710	108.495 980	.009 216 9314	3.69	.548 444	1.31	168
43	2.624 234	288.752 722	.003 463 1708	.381 064	110.033 143	.009 088 1708	3.64	.563 165	1.31	172
44	2.683 779	299.338 559	.003 340 6989	.372 609	111.536 201	.008 965 6989	3.59	.577 963	1.31	176
45	2.744 676	310.164 594	.003 224 0946	.364 342	113.005 911	.008 849 0946	3.54	.592 837	1.32	180
46	2.806 954	321.236 278	.003 112 9734	.356 258	114.443 012	.008 737 9734	3.50	.607 787	1.32	184
47	2.870 645	332.559 185	.003 006 9836	.348 354	115.848 228	.008 631 9836	3.46	.622 813	1.33	188
48	2.935 782	344.139 015	.002 905 8025	.340 625	117.222 266	.008 530 8025	3.42	.637 914	1.33	192
49	3.002 396	355.981 597	.002 809 1340	.333 067	118.565 819	.008 434 1340	3.38	.653 090	1.33	196
50	3.070 523	368.092 895	.002 716 7055	.325 677	119.879 561	.008 341 7055	3.34	.668 341	1.34	200

Effective Rate is 2.27 %

Annual Percentage Rate is 2.25 %

QUARTERLY COMPOUND INTEREST AND ANNUITY

2.50 % Q

	Amount Of 1	Amount Of 1 Per Period	Sinking Fund Payment	Present Worth Of 1	Present Worth of 1 Per Period	Periodic Payment To Amortize 1	Constant Annual Percent	Total Interest	Annual Add On Rate	
	What a single $ 1 deposit grows to in the future. The deposit is made at the beginning of the first period.	What a series of $ 1 deposits grow to in the future. A deposit is made at the end of each period.	The amount to be deposited at the end of each period that grows to $ 1 in the future.	What $ 1 to be paid in the future is worth today. Value today of a single $ 1 payment tomorrow.	What $ 1 to be paid at the end of each period is worth today. Value today of a series of $ 1 payments tomorrow.	The mortgage payment to amortize a loan of $ 1. An annuity certain, payable at the end of each period, worth $ 1 today.	The annual payment, including interest and principal, to amortize completely a loan of $ 100.	The total interest paid over the term on a loan of $1. The loan is amortized by regular periodic payments.	The average annual interest rate on a loan that is completely amortized by regular periodic payments.	
	$S = (1+i)^n$	$Sn] = \dfrac{(1+i)^n - 1}{i}$	$\dfrac{1}{Sn]} = \dfrac{i}{(1+i)^n - 1}$	$V^n = \dfrac{1}{(1+i)^n}$	$An] = \dfrac{1 - V^n}{i}$	$\dfrac{1}{An]} = \dfrac{i}{1 - V^n}$				

YEAR										PERIODS
	1.006 250	1.000 000	1.000 000 0000	.993 789	.993 789	1.006 250 0000	402.50	.006 250	2.50	1
	1.012 539	2.006 250	.498 442 3676	.987 616	1.981 405	.504 692 3676	201.88	.009 385	1.88	2
	1.018 867	3.018 789	.331 258 6535	.981 482	2.962 887	.337 508 6535	135.01	.012 526	1.67	3
	1.025 235	4.037 656	.247 668 4189	.975 386	3.938 273	.253 918 4189	101.57	.015 674	1.57	4
1	1.025 235	4.037 656	.247 668 4189	.975 386	3.938 273	.253 918 4189	101.57	.015 674	1.57	4
2	1.051 108	8.177 205	.122 291 1789	.951 377	7.779 608	.128 541 1789	51.42	.028 329	1.42	8
3	1.077 633	12.421 216	.080 507 4169	.927 960	11.526 392	.086 757 4169	34.71	.041 089	1.37	12
4	1.104 827	16.772 326	.059 622 0223	.905 119	15.180 952	.065 872 0223	26.35	.053 952	1.35	16
5	1.132 708	21.233 238	.047 095 9725	.882 840	18.745 558	.053 345 9725	21.34	.066 919	1.34	20
6	1.161 292	25.806 723	.038 749 5927	.861 110	22.222 423	.044 999 5927	18.00	.079 990	1.33	24
7	1.190 598	30.495 621	.032 791 5931	.839 914	25.613 709	.039 041 5931	15.62	.093 165	1.33	28
8	1.220 643	35.302 845	.028 326 3286	.819 240	28.921 521	.034 576 3286	13.84	.106 443	1.33	32
9	1.251 446	40.231 382	.024 856 2182	.799 076	32.147 913	.031 106 2182	12.45	.119 824	1.33	36
10	1.283 027	45.284 291	.022 082 7128	.779 407	35.294 891	.028 332 7128	11.34	.133 309	1.33	40
11	1.315 404	50.464 713	.019 815 8266	.760 222	38.364 408	.026 065 8266	10.43	.146 896	1.34	44
12	1.348 599	55.775 864	.017 928 9019	.741 510	41.358 371	.024 178 9019	9.68	.160 587	1.34	48
13	1.382 632	61.221 044	.016 334 2526	.723 258	44.278 641	.022 584 2526	9.04	.174 381	1.34	52
14	1.417 523	66.803 636	.014 969 2452	.705 456	47.127 030	.021 219 2452	8.49	.188 278	1.34	56
15	1.453 294	72.527 105	.013 787 9486	.688 092	49.905 308	.020 037 9486	8.02	.202 277	1.35	60
16	1.489 969	78.395 009	.012 755 9141	.671 155	52.615 201	.019 005 9141	7.61	.216 379	1.35	64
17	1.527 569	84.410 991	.011 846 7985	.654 635	55.258 393	.018 096 7985	7.24	.230 582	1.36	68
18	1.566 117	90.578 789	.011 040 1123	.638 522	57.836 524	.017 290 1123	6.92	.244 888	1.36	72
19	1.605 639	96.902 233	.010 319 6796	.622 805	60.351 197	.016 569 6796	6.63	.259 296	1.36	76
20	1.646 158	103.385 252	.009 672 5595	.607 475	62.803 973	.015 922 5595	6.37	.273 805	1.37	80
21	1.687 699	110.031 871	.009 088 2759	.592 523	65.196 376	.015 338 2759	6.14	.288 415	1.37	84
22	1.730 289	116.846 221	.008 558 2571	.577 938	67.529 892	.014 808 2571	5.93	.303 127	1.38	88
23	1.773 953	123.832 533	.008 075 4223	.563 713	69.805 970	.014 325 4223	5.74	.317 939	1.38	92
24	1.818 720	130.995 147	.007 633 8706	.549 837	72.026 024	.013 883 8706	5.56	.332 852	1.39	96
25	1.864 616	138.338 513	.007 228 6450	.536 304	74.191 434	.013 478 6450	5.40	.347 865	1.39	100
26	1.911 670	145.867 190	.006 855 5513	.523 103	76.303 543	.013 105 5513	5.25	.362 977	1.40	104
27	1.959 912	153.585 857	.006 511 0162	.510 227	78.363 665	.012 761 0162	5.11	.378 190	1.40	108
28	2.009 371	161.499 307	.006 191 9770	.497 668	80.373 079	.012 441 9770	4.98	.393 501	1.41	112
29	2.060 078	169.612 455	.005 895 7934	.485 419	82.333 032	.012 145 7934	4.86	.408 912	1.41	116
30	2.112 065	177.930 342	.005 620 1769	.473 470	84.244 743	.011 870 1769	4.75	.424 421	1.41	120
31	2.165 363	186.458 133	.005 363 1342	.461 816	86.109 398	.011 613 1342	4.65	.440 029	1.42	124
32	2.220 007	195.201 127	.005 122 9212	.450 449	87.928 157	.011 372 9212	4.55	.455 734	1.42	128
33	2.276 030	204.164 753	.004 898 0051	.439 362	89.702 148	.011 148 0051	4.46	.471 537	1.43	132
34	2.333 466	213.354 579	.004 687 0332	.428 547	91.432 473	.010 937 0332	4.38	.487 437	1.43	136
35	2.392 352	222.776 313	.004 488 8076	.417 999	93.120 209	.010 738 8076	4.30	.503 433	1.44	140
36	2.452 724	232.435 809	.004 302 2631	.407 710	94.766 401	.010 552 2631	4.23	.519 526	1.44	144
37	2.514 619	242.339 065	.004 126 4499	.397 675	96.372 075	.010 376 4499	4.16	.535 715	1.45	148
38	2.578 076	252.492 233	.003 960 5179	.387 886	97.938 225	.010 210 5179	4.09	.551 999	1.45	152
39	2.643 135	262.901 620	.003 803 7042	.378 339	99.465 827	.010 053 7042	4.03	.568 378	1.46	156
40	2.709 836	273.573 692	.003 655 3222	.369 026	100.955 827	.009 905 3222	3.97	.584 852	1.46	160
41	2.778 219	284.515 077	.003 514 7522	.359 943	102.409 153	.009 764 7522	3.91	.601 419	1.47	164
42	2.848 329	295.732 572	.003 381 4334	.351 083	103.826 706	.009 631 4334	3.86	.618 081	1.47	168
43	2.920 207	307.233 145	.003 254 8572	.342 441	105.209 366	.009 504 8572	3.81	.634 835	1.48	172
44	2.993 900	319.023 938	.003 134 5610	.334 013	106.557 994	.009 384 5610	3.76	.651 683	1.48	176
45	3.069 452	331.112 276	.003 020 1236	.325 791	107.873 427	.009 270 1236	3.71	.668 622	1.49	180
46	3.146 910	343.505 668	.002 911 1601	.317 772	109.156 481	.009 161 1601	3.67	.685 653	1.49	184
47	3.226 324	356.211 811	.002 807 3185	.309 950	110.407 954	.009 057 3185	3.63	.702 776	1.50	188
48	3.307 741	369.238 599	.002 708 2759	.302 321	111.628 623	.008 958 2759	3.59	.719 989	1.50	192
49	3.391 213	382.594 122	.002 613 7359	.294 880	112.819 246	.008 863 7359	3.55	.737 292	1.50	196
50	3.476 792	396.286 676	.002 523 4257	.287 621	113.980 562	.008 773 4257	3.51	.754 685	1.51	200

Effective Rate is 2.52 %

Annual Percentage Rate is 2.50 %

QUARTERLY COMPOUND INTEREST AND ANNUITY

2.75 % Q

Amount Of 1	Amount Of 1 Per Period	Sinking Fund Payment	Present Worth Of 1	Present Worth of 1 Per Period	Periodic Payment To Amortize 1	Constant Annual Percent	Total Interest	Annual Add On Rate
What a single $1 deposit grows to in the future. The deposit is made at the beginning of the first period.	What a series of $1 deposits grow to in the future. A deposit is made at the end of each period.	The amount to be deposited at the end of each period that grows to $1 in the future.	What $1 to be paid in the future is worth today. Value today of a single $1 payment tomorrow.	What $1 to be paid at the end of each period is worth today. Value today of a series of $1 payments tomorrow.	The mortgage payment to amortize a loan of $1. An annuity certain, payable at the end of each period, worth $1 today.	The annual payment, including interest and principal, to amortize completely a loan of $100.	The total interest paid over the term on a loan of $1. The loan is amortized by regular periodic payments.	The average annual interest rate on a loan that is completely amortized by regular periodic payments.

$$S = (1+i)^n \qquad S\overline{n}| = \frac{(1+i)^n - 1}{i} \qquad \frac{1}{S\overline{n}|} = \frac{i}{(1+i)^n - 1} \qquad V^n = \frac{1}{(1+i)^n} \qquad A\overline{n}| = \frac{1-V^n}{i} \qquad \frac{1}{A\overline{n}|} = \frac{i}{1-V^n}$$

YEAR   **PERIODS**

	Amount Of 1	Amount Of 1 Per Period	Sinking Fund Payment	Present Worth Of 1	Present Worth of 1 Per Period	Periodic Payment To Amortize 1	Constant Annual Percent	Total Interest	Annual Add On Rate	Periods
	1.006 875	1.000 000	1.000 000 0000	.993 172	.993 172	1.006 875 0000	402.75	.006 875	2.75	1
	1.013 797	2.006 875	.498 287 1380	.986 391	1.979 562	.505 162 1380	202.07	.010 324	2.06	2
	1.020 767	3.020 672	.331 052 1341	.979 655	2.959 218	.337 927 1341	135.18	.013 781	1.84	3
	1.027 785	4.041 439	.247 436 5948	.972 966	3.932 184	.254 311 5948	101.73	.017 246	1.72	4
1	1.027 785	4.041 439	.247 436 5948	.972 966	3.932 184	.254 311 5948	101.73	.017 246	1.72	4
2	1.056 342	8.195 170	.122 023 0979	.946 663	7.758 066	.128 898 0979	51.56	.031 185	1.56	8
3	1.085 692	12.464 311	.080 229 0631	.921 071	11.480 521	.087 104 0631	34.85	.045 249	1.51	12
4	1.115 858	16.852 070	.059 339 8910	.896 171	15.102 343	.066 214 8910	26.49	.059 438	1.49	16
5	1.146 862	21.361 742	.046 812 6607	.871 945	18.626 254	.053 687 6607	21.48	.073 753	1.48	20
6	1.178 727	25.996 716	.038 466 3976	.848 373	22.054 900	.045 341 3976	18.14	.088 194	1.47	24
7	1.211 478	30.760 471	.032 509 2551	.825 438	25.390 857	.039 384 2551	15.76	.102 759	1.47	28
8	1.245 139	35.656 587	.028 045 3091	.803 213	28.636 631	.034 920 3091	13.97	.117 450	1.47	32
9	1.279 735	40.688 741	.024 576 8234	.781 412	31.794 659	.031 451 8234	12.59	.132 266	1.47	36
10	1.315 292	45.860 713	.021 805 1561	.760 287	34.867 314	.028 680 1561	11.48	.147 206	1.47	40
11	1.351 838	51.176 387	.019 540 2617	.739 734	37.856 903	.026 415 2617	10.57	.162 272	1.48	44
12	1.389 398	56.639 757	.017 655 4429	.719 736	40.765 672	.024 530 4429	9.82	.177 461	1.48	48
13	1.428 003	62.254 926	.016 062 9859	.700 279	43.595 807	.022 937 9859	9.18	.192 775	1.48	52
14	1.467 680	68.026 112	.014 700 2374	.681 348	46.349 432	.021 575 2374	8.64	.208 213	1.49	56
15	1.508 459	73.957 650	.013 521 2517	.662 928	49.028 616	.020 396 2517	8.16	.223 775	1.49	60
16	1.550 371	80.053 995	.012 491 5690	.645 007	51.635 372	.019 366 5690	7.75	.239 460	1.50	64
17	1.593 448	86.319 726	.011 584 8375	.627 570	54.171 658	.018 459 8375	7.39	.255 269	1.50	68
18	1.637 722	92.759 550	.010 780 5611	.610 604	56.639 378	.017 655 5611	7.07	.271 200	1.51	72
19	1.683 226	99.378 304	.010 062 5585	.594 097	59.040 386	.016 937 5585	6.78	.287 254	1.51	76
20	1.729 994	106.180 959	.009 417 8844	.578 037	61.376 487	.016 292 8844	6.52	.303 431	1.52	80
21	1.778 062	113.172 626	.008 836 0590	.562 410	63.649 433	.015 711 0590	6.29	.319 729	1.52	84
22	1.827 465	120.358 555	.008 308 5079	.547 206	65.860 933	.015 183 5079	6.08	.336 149	1.53	88
23	1.878 241	127.744 144	.007 828 1475	.532 413	68.012 648	.014 703 1475	5.89	.352 690	1.53	92
24	1.930 428	135.334 941	.007 389 0748	.518 020	70.106 194	.014 264 0748	5.71	.369 351	1.54	96
25	1.984 064	143.136 648	.006 986 3310	.504 016	72.143 144	.013 861 3310	5.55	.386 133	1.54	100
26	2.039 191	151.155 124	.006 615 7202	.490 390	74.125 027	.013 490 7202	5.40	.403 035	1.55	104
27	2.095 850	159.396 393	.006 273 6677	.477 133	76.053 333	.013 148 6677	5.26	.420 056	1.56	108
28	2.154 083	167.866 644	.005 957 1096	.464 235	77.929 509	.012 832 1096	5.14	.437 196	1.56	112
29	2.213 934	176.572 241	.005 663 4044	.451 685	79.754 965	.012 538 4044	5.02	.454 455	1.57	116
30	2.275 448	185.519 722	.005 390 2625	.439 474	81.531 072	.012 265 2625	4.91	.471 832	1.57	120
31	2.338 671	194.715 807	.005 135 6899	.427 593	83.259 164	.012 010 6899	4.81	.489 326	1.58	124
32	2.403 651	204.167 405	.004 897 9415	.416 034	84.940 539	.011 772 9415	4.71	.506 937	1.58	128
33	2.470 436	213.881 614	.004 675 4837	.404 787	86.576 461	.011 550 4837	4.63	.524 664	1.59	132
34	2.539 077	223.865 732	.004 466 9633	.393 844	88.168 157	.011 341 9633	4.54	.542 507	1.60	136
35	2.609 625	234.127 258	.004 271 1815	.383 197	89.716 824	.011 146 1815	4.46	.560 465	1.60	140
36	2.682 133	244.673 898	.004 087 0727	.372 838	91.223 625	.010 962 0727	4.39	.578 538	1.61	144
37	2.756 656	255.513 577	.003 913 6864	.362 758	92.689 691	.010 788 6864	4.32	.596 726	1.61	148
38	2.833 249	266.654 434	.003 750 1720	.352 952	94.116 123	.010 625 1720	4.26	.615 026	1.62	152
39	2.911 971	278.104 393	.003 595 7663	.343 410	95.503 994	.010 470 7663	4.19	.633 440	1.62	156
40	2.992 880	289.873 392	.003 449 7820	.334 126	96.854 346	.010 324 7820	4.13	.651 965	1.63	160
41	3.076 036	301.968 934	.003 311 5989	.325 094	98.168 192	.010 186 5989	4.08	.670 602	1.64	164
42	3.161 504	314.400 549	.003 180 6560	.316 305	99.446 520	.010 055 6560	4.03	.689 350	1.64	168
43	3.249 346	327.177 574	.003 056 4442	.307 754	100.690 290	.009 931 4442	3.98	.708 208	1.65	172
44	3.339 629	340.309 609	.002 938 5006	.299 434	101.900 437	.009 813 5006	3.93	.727 176	1.65	176
45	3.432 420	353.806 515	.002 826 4036	.291 340	103.077 868	.009 701 4036	3.89	.746 253	1.66	180
46	3.527 789	367.678 432	.002 719 7679	.283 464	104.223 469	.009 594 7679	3.84	.765 437	1.66	184
47	3.625 808	381.935 778	.002 618 2412	.275 801	105.338 101	.009 493 2412	3.80	.784 729	1.67	188
48	3.726 551	396.589 263	.002 521 5004	.268 345	106.422 599	.009 396 5004	3.76	.804 128	1.68	192
49	3.830 093	411.649 894	.002 429 2488	.261 090	107.477 780	.009 304 2488	3.73	.823 633	1.68	196
50	3.936 512	427.128 983	.002 341 2132	.254 032	108.504 435	.009 216 2132	3.69	.843 243	1.69	200

Effective Rate is 2.78 %   8 - 267   Annual Percentage Rate is 2.75 %

QUARTERLY COMPOUND INTEREST AND ANNUITY

	Amount Of 1	Amount Of 1 Per Period	Sinking Fund Payment	Present Worth Of 1	Present Worth of 1 Per Period	Periodic Payment To Amortize 1	Constant Annual Percent	Total Interest	Annual Add On Rate	
	What a single $ 1 deposit grows to in the future. The deposit is made at the beginning of the first period.	What a series of $ 1 deposits grow to in the future. A deposit is made at the end of each period.	The amount to be deposited at the end of each period that grows to $ 1 in the future.	What $ 1 to be paid in the future is worth today. Value today of a single $ 1 payment tomorrow.	What $ 1 to be paid at the end of each period is worth today. Value today of a series of $ 1 payments tomorrow.	The mortgage payment to amortize a loan of $ 1. An annuity certain, payable at the end of each period, worth $ 1 today.	The annual payment, including interest and principal, to amortize completely a loan of $ 100.	The total interest paid over the term on a loan of $1. The loan is amortized by regular periodic payments.	The average annual interest rate on a loan that is completely amortized by regular periodic payments.	
	$S = (1+i)^n$	$S\overline{n|} = \dfrac{(1+i)^n - 1}{i}$	$\dfrac{1}{S\overline{n|}} = \dfrac{i}{(1+i)^n - 1}$	$V^n = \dfrac{1}{(1+i)^n}$	$A\overline{n|} = \dfrac{1 - V^n}{i}$	$\dfrac{1}{A\overline{n|}} = \dfrac{i}{1 - V^n}$				

YEAR										PERIODS
	1.007 500	1.000 000	1.000 000 0000	.992 556	.992 556	1.007 500 0000	403.00	.007 500	3.00	1
	1.015 056	2.007 500	.498 132 0050	.985 167	1.977 723	.505 632 0050	202.26	.011 264	2.25	2
	1.022 669	3.022 556	.330 845 7866	.977 833	2.955 556	.338 345 7866	135.34	.015 037	2.00	3
	1.030 339	4.045 225	.247 205 0123	.970 554	3.926 110	.254 705 0123	101.89	.018 820	1.88	4
1	1.030 339	4.045 225	.247 205 0123	.970 554	3.926 110	.254 705 0123	101.89	.018 820	1.88	4
2	1.061 599	8.213 180	.121 755 5241	.941 975	7.736 613	.129 255 5241	51.71	.034 044	1.70	8
3	1.093 807	12.507 586	.079 951 4768	.914 238	11.434 913	.087 451 4768	34.99	.049 418	1.65	12
4	1.126 992	16.932 282	.059 058 7855	.887 318	15.024 313	.066 558 7855	26.63	.064 941	1.62	16
5	1.161 184	21.491 219	.046 530 6319	.861 190	18.508 020	.054 030 6319	21.62	.080 613	1.61	20
6	1.196 414	26.188 471	.038 184 7423	.835 831	21.889 146	.045 684 7423	18.28	.096 434	1.61	24
7	1.232 712	31.028 233	.032 228 7125	.811 220	25.170 713	.039 728 7125	15.90	.112 404	1.61	28
8	1.270 111	36.014 830	.027 766 3397	.787 333	28.355 650	.035 266 3397	14.11	.128 523	1.61	32
9	1.308 645	41.152 716	.024 299 7327	.764 149	31.446 805	.031 799 7327	12.72	.144 790	1.61	36
10	1.348 349	46.446 482	.021 530 1561	.741 648	34.446 938	.029 030 1561	11.62	.161 206	1.61	40
11	1.389 256	51.900 856	.019 267 5051	.719 810	37.358 730	.026 767 5051	10.71	.177 770	1.62	44
12	1.431 405	57.520 711	.017 385 0424	.698 614	40.184 782	.024 885 0424	9.96	.194 482	1.62	48
13	1.474 833	63.311 068	.015 795 0265	.678 043	42.927 618	.023 295 0265	9.32	.211 341	1.63	52
14	1.519 578	69.277 100	.014 434 7843	.658 077	45.589 689	.021 934 7843	8.78	.228 348	1.63	56
15	1.565 681	75.424 137	.013 258 3552	.638 700	48.173 374	.020 758 3552	8.31	.245 501	1.64	60
16	1.613 183	81.757 670	.012 231 2684	.619 893	50.680 979	.019 731 2684	7.90	.262 801	1.64	64
17	1.662 125	88.283 357	.011 327 1633	.601 639	53.114 746	.018 827 1633	7.54	.280 247	1.65	68
18	1.712 553	95.007 028	.010 525 5372	.583 924	55.476 849	.018 025 5372	7.22	.297 839	1.65	72
19	1.764 510	101.934 689	.009 810 2030	.566 730	57.769 397	.017 310 2030	6.93	.315 575	1.66	76
20	1.818 044	109.072 531	.009 168 2112	.550 042	59.994 440	.016 668 2112	6.67	.333 457	1.67	80
21	1.873 202	116.426 928	.008 589 0783	.533 845	62.153 965	.016 089 0783	6.44	.351 483	1.67	84
22	1.930 033	124.004 453	.008 064 2266	.518 126	64.249 900	.015 564 2266	6.23	.369 652	1.68	88
23	1.988 589	131.811 873	.007 586 5700	.502 869	66.284 119	.015 086 5700	6.04	.387 964	1.69	92
24	2.048 921	139.856 164	.007 150 2033	.488 062	68.258 439	.014 650 2033	5.87	.406 420	1.69	96
25	2.111 084	148.144 512	.006 750 1657	.473 690	70.174 623	.014 250 1657	5.71	.425 017	1.70	100
26	2.175 132	156.684 322	.006 382 2595	.459 742	72.034 383	.013 882 2595	5.56	.443 755	1.71	104
27	2.241 124	165.483 223	.006 042 9087	.446 205	73.839 382	.013 542 9087	5.42	.462 634	1.71	108
28	2.309 118	174.549 075	.005 729 0478	.433 066	75.591 230	.013 229 0478	5.30	.481 653	1.72	112
29	2.379 175	183.889 979	.005 438 0342	.420 314	77.291 494	.012 938 0342	5.18	.500 812	1.73	116
30	2.451 357	193.514 277	.005 167 5774	.407 937	78.941 693	.012 667 5774	5.07	.520 109	1.73	120
31	2.525 729	203.430 569	.004 915 6821	.395 925	80.543 300	.012 415 6821	4.97	.539 545	1.74	124
32	2.602 358	213.647 713	.004 680 6024	.384 267	82.097 746	.012 180 6024	4.88	.559 117	1.75	128
33	2.681 311	224.174 837	.004 460 8039	.372 952	83.606 420	.011 960 8039	4.79	.578 826	1.75	132
34	2.762 660	235.021 346	.004 254 9327	.361 970	85.070 670	.011 754 9327	4.71	.598 671	1.76	136
35	2.846 477	246.196 929	.004 061 7891	.351 311	86.491 804	.011 561 7891	4.63	.618 650	1.77	140
36	2.932 837	257.711 570	.003 880 3070	.340 967	87.871 092	.011 380 3070	4.56	.638 764	1.77	144
37	3.021 817	269.575 556	.003 709 5352	.330 927	89.209 765	.011 209 5352	4.49	.659 011	1.78	148
38	3.113 496	281.799 485	.003 548 6225	.321 182	90.509 020	.011 048 6225	4.42	.679 391	1.79	152
39	3.207 957	294.394 279	.003 396 8051	.311 725	91.770 018	.010 896 8051	4.36	.699 902	1.79	156
40	3.305 284	307.371 189	.003 253 3954	.302 546	92.993 884	.010 753 3954	4.31	.720 543	1.80	160
41	3.405 564	320.741 807	.003 117 7725	.293 637	94.181 712	.010 617 7725	4.25	.741 315	1.81	164
42	3.508 886	334.518 079	.002 989 3750	.284 991	95.334 564	.010 489 3750	4.20	.762 215	1.81	168
43	3.615 342	348.712 313	.002 867 6934	.276 599	96.453 470	.010 367 6934	4.15	.783 243	1.82	172
44	3.725 029	363.337 187	.002 752 2644	.268 454	97.539 428	.010 252 2644	4.11	.804 399	1.83	176
45	3.838 043	378.405 769	.002 642 6658	.260 549	98.593 409	.010 142 6658	4.06	.825 680	1.83	180
46	3.954 486	393.931 519	.002 538 5123	.252 877	99.616 355	.010 038 5123	4.02	.847 086	1.84	184
47	4.074 462	409.928 308	.002 439 4509	.245 431	100.609 179	.009 939 4509	3.98	.868 617	1.85	188
48	4.198 078	426.410 427	.002 345 1584	.238 204	101.572 769	.009 845 1584	3.94	.890 270	1.85	192
49	4.325 444	443.392 599	.002 255 3376	.231 190	102.507 985	.009 755 3376	3.91	.912 046	1.86	196
50	4.456 675	460.889 997	.002 169 7151	.224 383	103.415 663	.009 669 7151	3.87	.933 943	1.87	200

Effective Rate is 3.03 %

Annual Percentage Rate is 3.00 %

Amount Of 1	Amount Of 1 Per Period	Sinking Fund Payment	Present Worth Of 1	Present Worth of 1 Per Period	Periodic Payment To Amortize 1	Constant Annual Percent	Total Interest	Annual Add On Rate	
What a single $ 1 deposit grows to in the future. The deposit is made at the beginning of the first period.	What a series of $ 1 deposits grow to in the future. A deposit is made at the end of each period.	The amount to be deposited at the end of each period that grows to $ 1 in the future.	What $ 1 to be paid in the future is worth today. Value today of a single $ 1 payment tomorrow.	What $ 1 to be paid at the end of each period is worth today. Value today of a series of $ 1 payments tomorrow.	The mortgage payment to amortize a loan of $ 1. An annuity certain, payable at the end of each period, worth $ 1 today.	The annual payment, including interest and principal, to amortize completely a loan of $ 100.	The total interest paid over the term on a loan of $1. The loan is amortized by regular periodic payments.	The average annual interest rate on a loan that is completely amortized by regular periodic payments.	
$S = (1+i)^n$	$S\overline{n}| = \dfrac{(1+i)^n - 1}{i}$	$\dfrac{1}{S\overline{n}|} = \dfrac{i}{(1+i)^n - 1}$	$V^n = \dfrac{1}{(1+i)^n}$	$A\overline{n}| = \dfrac{1 - V^n}{i}$	$\dfrac{1}{A\overline{n}|} = \dfrac{i}{1 - V^n}$				

YEAR									PERIODS
	1.008 125	1.000 000	1.000 000 0000	.991 940	.991 940	1.008 125 0000	403.25	.008 125	3.25	1
	1.016 316	2.008 125	.497 976 9686	.983 946	1.975 886	.506 101 9686	202.45	.012 204	2.44	2
	1.024 574	3.024 441	.330 639 6107	.976 016	2.951 902	.338 764 6107	135.51	.016 294	2.17	3
	1.032 898	4.049 015	.246 973 6711	.968 150	3.920 052	.255 098 6711	102.04	.020 395	2.04	4

YEAR									PERIODS
1	1.032 898	4.049 015	.246 973 6711	.968 150	3.920 052	.255 098 6711	102.04	.020 395	2.04	4
2	1.066 879	8.231 235	.121 488 4571	.937 314	7.715 248	.129 613 4571	51.85	.036 908	1.85	8
3	1.101 977	12.551 042	.079 674 6570	.907 460	11.389 566	.087 799 6570	35.12	.053 596	1.79	12
4	1.138 230	17.012 964	.058 778 7045	.878 557	14.946 855	.066 903 7045	26.77	.070 459	1.76	16
5	1.175 676	21.621 676	.046 249 8847	.850 574	18.390 844	.054 374 8847	21.75	.087 498	1.75	20
6	1.214 354	26.382 005	.037 904 6244	.823 483	21.725 139	.046 029 6244	18.42	.104 711	1.75	24
7	1.254 304	31.298 942	.031 949 9623	.797 255	24.953 236	.040 074 9623	16.03	.122 099	1.74	28
8	1.295 568	36.377 636	.027 489 4166	.771 862	28.078 517	.035 614 4166	14.25	.139 661	1.75	32
9	1.338 190	41.623 411	.024 024 9410	.747 278	31.104 256	.032 149 9410	12.86	.157 398	1.75	36
10	1.382 214	47.041 763	.021 257 7067	.723 477	34.033 624	.029 382 7067	11.76	.175 308	1.75	40
11	1.427 687	52.638 369	.018 997 5491	.700 434	36.869 691	.027 122 5491	10.85	.193 392	1.76	44
12	1.474 655	58.419 093	.017 117 6912	.678 125	39.615 427	.025 242 6912	10.10	.211 649	1.76	48
13	1.523 169	64.389 994	.015 530 3634	.656 526	42.273 711	.023 655 3634	9.47	.230 079	1.77	52
14	1.573 278	70.557 326	.014 172 8727	.635 615	44.847 327	.022 297 8727	8.92	.248 681	1.78	56
15	1.625 036	76.927 553	.012 999 2437	.615 371	47.338 973	.021 124 2437	8.45	.267 455	1.78	60
16	1.678 497	83.507 349	.011 974 9940	.595 771	49.751 259	.020 099 9940	8.04	.286 400	1.79	64
17	1.733 717	90.303 608	.011 073 7546	.576 795	52.086 712	.019 198 7546	7.68	.305 515	1.80	68
18	1.790 753	97.323 453	.010 275 0156	.558 424	54.347 780	.018 400 0156	7.37	.324 801	1.80	72
19	1.849 666	104.574 238	.009 562 5846	.540 638	56.536 832	.017 687 5846	7.08	.344 256	1.81	76
20	1.910 516	112.063 562	.008 923 5072	.523 419	58.656 162	.017 048 5072	6.82	.363 881	1.82	80
21	1.973 369	119.799 271	.008 347 2962	.506 748	60.707 990	.016 472 2962	6.59	.383 673	1.83	84
22	2.038 289	127.789 471	.007 825 3709	.490 607	62.694 467	.015 950 3709	6.39	.403 633	1.83	88
23	2.105 346	136.042 534	.007 350 6422	.474 981	64.617 674	.015 475 6422	6.20	.423 759	1.84	92
24	2.174 608	144.567 109	.006 917 2027	.459 853	66.479 625	.015 042 2027	6.02	.444 051	1.85	96
25	2.246 149	153.372 128	.006 520 0895	.445 207	68.282 273	.014 645 0895	5.86	.464 509	1.86	100
26	2.320 043	162.466 816	.006 155 1031	.431 027	70.027 506	.014 280 1031	5.72	.485 131	1.87	104
27	2.396 368	171.860 704	.005 818 6658	.417 298	71.717 152	.013 943 6658	5.58	.505 916	1.87	108
28	2.475 205	181.563 634	.005 507 7109	.404 007	73.352 982	.013 632 7109	5.46	.526 864	1.88	112
29	2.556 634	191.585 773	.005 219 5943	.391 139	74.936 711	.013 344 5943	5.34	.547 973	1.89	116
30	2.640 743	201.937 623	.004 952 0242	.378 681	76.469 997	.013 077 0242	5.24	.569 243	1.90	120
31	2.727 619	212.630 031	.004 703 0045	.366 620	77.954 447	.012 828 0045	5.14	.590 673	1.91	124
32	2.817 353	223.674 200	.004 470 7883	.354 943	79.391 617	.012 595 7883	5.04	.612 261	1.91	128
33	2.910 039	235.081 703	.004 253 8402	.343 638	80.783 012	.012 378 8402	4.96	.634 007	1.92	132
34	3.005 774	246.864 492	.004 050 8053	.332 693	82.130 091	.012 175 8053	4.88	.655 910	1.93	136
35	3.104 659	259.034 915	.003 860 4834	.322 097	83.434 265	.011 985 4834	4.80	.677 968	1.94	140
36	3.206 797	271.605 724	.003 681 8075	.311 838	84.696 900	.011 806 8075	4.73	.700 180	1.94	144
37	3.312 294	284.590 090	.003 513 8258	.301 906	85.919 320	.011 638 8258	4.66	.722 546	1.95	148
38	3.421 263	298.001 618	.003 355 6865	.292 290	87.102 805	.011 480 6865	4.60	.745 064	1.96	152
39	3.533 817	311.854 363	.003 206 6250	.282 980	88.248 596	.011 331 6250	4.54	.767 734	1.97	156
40	3.650 073	326.162 838	.003 065 9532	.273 967	89.357 893	.011 190 9532	4.48	.790 553	1.98	160
41	3.770 154	340.942 037	.002 933 0499	.265 241	90.431 858	.011 058 0499	4.43	.813 520	1.98	164
42	3.894 185	356.207 446	.002 807 3529	.256 793	91.471 617	.010 932 3529	4.38	.836 635	1.99	168
43	4.022 297	371.975 060	.002 688 3523	.248 614	92.478 260	.010 813 3523	4.33	.859 897	2.00	172
44	4.154 624	388.261 401	.002 575 5844	.240 696	93.452 840	.010 700 5844	4.29	.883 303	2.01	176
45	4.291 304	405.083 533	.002 468 6266	.233 029	94.396 379	.010 593 6266	4.24	.906 853	2.02	180
46	4.432 480	422.459 085	.002 367 0931	.225 607	95.309 867	.010 492 0931	4.20	.930 545	2.02	184
47	4.578 301	440.406 261	.002 270 6308	.218 422	96.194 259	.010 395 6308	4.16	.954 379	2.03	188
48	4.728 919	458.943 868	.002 178 9157	.211 465	97.050 483	.010 303 9157	4.13	.978 352	2.04	192
49	4.884 492	478.091 330	.002 091 6506	.204 730	97.879 436	.010 216 6506	4.09	1.002 464	2.05	196
50	5.045 183	497.868 710	.002 008 5617	.198 209	98.681 987	.010 133 5617	4.06	1.026 712	2.05	200

QUARTERLY COMPOUND INTEREST AND ANNUITY

3.50 % Q

Amount Of 1	Amount Of 1 Per Period	Sinking Fund Payment	Present Worth Of 1	Present Worth of 1 Per Period	Periodic Payment To Amortize 1	Constant Annual Percent	Total Interest	Annual Add On Rate	
What a single $ 1 deposit grows to in the future. The deposit is made at the beginning of the first period.	What a series of $ 1 deposits grow to in the future. A deposit is made at the end of each period.	The amount to be deposited at the end of each period that grows to $ 1 in the future.	What $ 1 to be paid in the future is worth today. Value today of a single $ 1 payment tomorrow.	What $ 1 to be paid at the end of each period is worth today. Value today of a series of $ 1 payments tomorrow.	The mortgage payment to amortize a loan of $ 1. An annuity certain, payable at the end of each period, worth $ 1 today.	The annual payment, including interest and principal, to amortize completely a loan of $ 100.	The total interest paid over the term on a loan of $1. The loan is amortized by regular periodic payments.	The average annual interest rate on a loan that is completely amortized by regular periodic payments.	
$S = (1+i)^n$	$S\overline{n]} = \dfrac{(1+i)^n - 1}{i}$	$\dfrac{1}{S\overline{n]}} = \dfrac{i}{(1+i)^n - 1}$	$V^n = \dfrac{1}{(1+i)^n}$	$A\overline{n]} = \dfrac{1 - V^n}{i}$	$\dfrac{1}{A\overline{n]}} = \dfrac{i}{1 - V^n}$				

YEAR									PERIODS
	1.008 750	1.000 000	1.000 000 0000	.991 326	.991 326	1.008 750 0000	403.50	.008 750	3.50	1
	1.017 577	2.008 750	.497 822 0286	.982 727	1.974 053	.506 572 0286	202.63	.013 144	2.63	2
	1.026 480	3.026 327	.330 433 6063	.974 203	2.948 256	.339 183 6063	135.68	.017 551	2.34	3
	1.035 462	4.052 807	.246 742 5712	.965 752	3.914 008	.255 492 5712	102.20	.021 970	2.20	4

YEAR	Amount Of 1	Amount Of 1 Per Period	Sinking Fund Payment	Present Worth Of 1	Present Worth of 1 Per Period	Periodic Payment To Amortize 1	Constant Annual Percent	Total Interest	Annual Add On Rate	PERIODS
1	1.035 462	4.052 807	.246 742 5712	.965 752	3.914 008	.255 492 5712	102.20	.021 970	2.20	4
2	1.072 182	8.249 335	.121 221 8965	.932 678	7.693 971	.129 971 8965	51.99	.039 775	1.99	8
3	1.110 203	12.594 680	.079 398 6029	.900 736	11.344 479	.088 148 6029	35.26	.057 783	1.93	12
4	1.149 574	17.094 120	.058 499 6469	.869 888	14.869 967	.067 249 6469	26.90	.075 994	1.90	16
5	1.190 340	21.753 120	.045 970 4173	.840 096	18.274 714	.054 720 4173	21.89	.094 408	1.89	20
6	1.232 552	26.577 337	.037 626 0416	.811 325	21.562 858	.046 376 0416	18.56	.113 025	1.88	24
7	1.276 261	31.572 631	.031 673 0015	.783 539	24.738 391	.040 423 0015	16.17	.131 844	1.88	28
8	1.321 519	36.745 069	.027 214 5360	.756 705	27.805 169	.035 964 5360	14.39	.150 865	1.89	32
9	1.368 383	42.100 932	.023 752 4435	.730 789	30.766 918	.032 502 4435	13.01	.170 088	1.89	36
10	1.416 909	47.646 724	.020 987 8017	.705 762	33.627 233	.029 737 8017	11.90	.189 512	1.90	40
11	1.467 155	53.389 182	.018 730 3861	.681 591	36.389 591	.027 480 3861	11.00	.209 137	1.90	44
12	1.519 184	59.335 280	.016 853 3798	.658 248	39.057 344	.025 603 3798	10.25	.228 962	1.91	48
13	1.573 057	65.492 238	.015 268 9850	.635 705	41.633 733	.024 018 9850	9.61	.248 987	1.92	52
14	1.628 841	71.867 534	.013 914 4888	.613 933	44.121 886	.022 664 4888	9.07	.269 211	1.92	56
15	1.686 603	78.446 912	.012 743 9004	.592 908	46.524 827	.021 493 9004	8.60	.289 634	1.93	60
16	1.746 413	85.304 388	.011 722 7263	.572 602	48.845 473	.020 472 7263	8.19	.310 254	1.94	64
17	1.808 345	92.382 265	.010 824 5885	.552 992	51.086 642	.019 574 5885	7.83	.331 072	1.95	68
18	1.872 472	99.711 137	.010 028 9700	.534 053	53.251 057	.018 778 9700	7.52	.352 086	1.96	72
19	1.938 874	107.299 906	.009 319 6726	.515 763	55.341 346	.018 069 6726	7.23	.373 295	1.96	76
20	2.007 631	115.157 789	.008 683 7374	.498 100	57.360 047	.017 433 7374	6.98	.394 699	1.97	80
21	2.078 825	123.294 329	.008 110 6731	.481 041	59.309 613	.016 860 6731	6.75	.416 297	1.98	84
22	2.152 545	131.719 406	.007 591 8957	.464 566	61.192 411	.016 341 8957	6.54	.438 087	1.99	88
23	2.228 878	140.443 255	.007 120 3135	.448 656	63.010 728	.015 870 3135	6.35	.460 069	2.00	92
24	2.307 919	149.476 469	.006 690 0162	.433 291	64.766 771	.015 440 0162	6.18	.482 242	2.01	96
25	2.389 763	158.830 020	.006 296 0390	.418 452	66.462 675	.015 046 0390	6.02	.504 604	2.02	100
26	2.474 509	168.515 266	.005 934 1805	.404 121	68.100 498	.014 684 1805	5.88	.527 155	2.03	104
27	2.562 260	178.543 972	.005 600 8612	.390 280	69.682 229	.014 350 8612	5.75	.549 893	2.04	108
28	2.653 123	188.928 316	.005 293 0128	.376 914	71.209 790	.014 043 0128	5.62	.572 817	2.05	112
29	2.747 208	199.680 910	.005 007 9900	.364 006	72.685 036	.013 757 9900	5.51	.595 927	2.05	116
30	2.844 630	210.814 814	.004 743 4997	.351 540	74.109 758	.013 493 4997	5.40	.619 220	2.06	120
31	2.945 506	222.343 548	.004 497 5445	.339 500	75.485 687	.013 247 5445	5.30	.642 696	2.07	124
32	3.049 960	234.281 115	.004 268 3765	.327 873	76.814 494	.013 018 3765	5.21	.666 352	2.08	128
33	3.158 118	246.642 013	.004 054 4593	.316 644	78.097 792	.012 804 4593	5.13	.690 189	2.09	132
34	3.270 111	259.441 254	.003 854 4371	.305 800	79.337 141	.012 604 4371	5.05	.714 203	2.10	136
35	3.386 076	272.694 383	.003 667 1089	.295 327	80.534 044	.012 417 1089	4.97	.738 395	2.11	140
36	3.506 153	286.417 494	.003 491 4068	.285 213	81.689 957	.012 241 4068	4.90	.762 763	2.12	144
37	3.630 488	300.627 256	.003 326 3784	.275 445	82.806 283	.012 076 3784	4.84	.787 304	2.13	148
38	3.759 233	315.340 925	.003 171 1710	.266 012	83.884 377	.011 921 1710	4.77	.812 018	2.14	152
39	3.892 543	330.576 371	.003 025 0196	.256 901	84.925 549	.011 775 0196	4.72	.836 903	2.15	156
40	4.030 581	346.352 097	.002 887 2353	.248 103	85.931 063	.011 637 2353	4.66	.861 958	2.15	160
41	4.173 514	362.687 263	.002 757 1964	.239 606	86.902 141	.011 507 1964	4.61	.887 180	2.16	164
42	4.321 515	379.601 707	.002 634 3401	.231 400	87.839 962	.011 384 3401	4.56	.912 569	2.17	168
43	4.474 765	397.115 973	.002 518 1561	.223 475	88.745 665	.011 268 1561	4.51	.938 123	2.18	172
44	4.633 449	415.251 331	.002 408 1801	.215 822	89.620 349	.011 158 1801	4.47	.963 840	2.19	176
45	4.797 761	434.029 805	.002 303 9892	.208 431	90.465 078	.011 053 9892	4.43	.989 718	2.20	180
46	4.967 899	453.474 203	.002 205 1971	.201 292	91.280 877	.010 955 1971	4.39	1.015 756	2.21	184
47	5.144 071	473.608 140	.002 111 4502	.194 399	92.068 737	.010 861 4502	4.35	1.041 953	2.22	188
48	5.326 491	494.456 068	.002 022 4244	.187 741	92.829 614	.010 772 4244	4.31	1.068 305	2.23	192
49	5.515 379	516.043 305	.001 937 8219	.181 311	93.564 434	.010 687 8219	4.28	1.094 813	2.23	196
50	5.710 966	538.396 071	.001 857 3687	.175 102	94.274 087	.010 607 3687	4.25	1.121 474	2.24	200

Amount Of 1	Amount Of 1 Per Period	Sinking Fund Payment	Present Worth Of 1	Present Worth of 1 Per Period	Periodic Payment To Amortize 1	Constant Annual Percent	Total Interest	Annual Add On Rate
What a single $ 1 deposit grows to in the future. The deposit is made at the beginning of the first period.	What a series of $ 1 deposits grow to in the future. A deposit is made at the end of each period.	The amount to be deposited at the end of each period that grows to $ 1 in the future.	What $ 1 to be paid in the future is worth today. Value today of a single $ 1 payment tomorrow.	What $ 1 to be paid at the end of each period is worth today. Value today of a series of $ 1 payments tomorrow.	The mortgage payment to amortize a loan of $ 1. An annuity certain, payable at the end of each period, worth $ 1 today.	The annual payment, including interest and principal, to amortize completely a loan of $ 100.	The total interest paid over the term on a loan of $1. The loan is amortized by regular periodic payments.	The average annual interest rate on a loan that is completely amortized by regular periodic payments.
$S = (1+i)^n$	$S\overline{n} = \dfrac{(1+i)^n - 1}{i}$	$\dfrac{1}{S\overline{n}} = \dfrac{i}{(1+i)^n - 1}$	$V^n = \dfrac{1}{(1+i)^n}$	$A\overline{n} = \dfrac{1 - V^n}{i}$	$\dfrac{1}{A\overline{n}} = \dfrac{i}{1 - V^n}$			

YEAR								PERIODS
	1.009 375	1.000 000	1.000 000 0000	.990 712	.990 712	1.009 375 0000	403.75	.009 375	3.75	1
	1.018 838	2.009 375	.497 667 1851	.981 510	1.972 222	.507 042 1851	202.82	.014 084	2.82	2
	1.028 389	3.028 213	.330 227 7733	.972 394	2.944 617	.339 602 7733	135.85	.018 808	2.51	3
	1.038 031	4.056 602	.246 511 7122	.963 363	3.907 979	.255 886 7122	102.36	.023 547	2.35	4

YEAR									PERIODS
1	1.038 031	4.056 602	.246 511 7122	.963 363	3.907 979	.255 886 7122	102.36	.023 547	2.35	4
2	1.077 508	8.267 480	.120 955 8416	.928 068	7.672 781	.130 330 8416	52.14	.042 647	2.13	8
3	1.118 486	12.638 500	.079 123 3137	.894 066	11.299 650	.088 498 3137	35.40	.061 980	2.07	12
4	1.161 023	17.175 753	.058 221 6114	.861 310	14.793 641	.067 596 6114	27.04	.081 546	2.04	16
5	1.205 177	21.885 560	.045 692 2279	.829 754	18.159 621	.055 067 2279	22.03	.101 345	2.03	20
6	1.251 011	26.774 484	.037 348 9917	.799 354	21.402 281	.046 723 9917	18.69	.121 376	2.02	24
7	1.298 588	31.849 338	.031 397 8270	.770 067	24.526 138	.040 772 8270	16.31	.141 639	2.02	28
8	1.347 974	37.117 191	.026 941 6938	.741 854	27.535 546	.036 316 6938	14.53	.162 134	2.03	32
9	1.399 238	42.585 384	.023 482 2349	.714 675	30.434 697	.032 857 2349	13.15	.182 860	2.03	36
10	1.452 452	48.261 537	.020 720 4344	.688 491	33.227 631	.030 095 4344	12.04	.203 817	2.04	40
11	1.507 690	54.153 556	.018 466 0079	.663 267	35.918 240	.027 841 0079	11.14	.225 004	2.05	44
12	1.565 028	60.269 654	.016 592 0980	.638 966	38.510 272	.025 967 0980	10.39	.246 421	2.05	48
13	1.624 547	66.618 350	.015 010 8792	.615 556	41.007 338	.024 385 8792	9.76	.268 066	2.06	52
14	1.686 330	73.208 491	.013 659 6177	.593 004	43.412 919	.023 034 6177	9.22	.289 939	2.07	56
15	1.750 462	80.049 260	.012 492 3079	.571 278	45.730 366	.021 867 3079	8.75	.312 038	2.08	60
16	1.817 033	87.150 188	.011 474 4446	.550 348	47.962 908	.020 849 4446	8.34	.334 364	2.09	64
17	1.886 184	94.521 168	.010 579 6407	.530 184	50.113 656	.019 954 6407	7.99	.356 916	2.10	68
18	1.957 867	102.172 472	.009 787 3721	.510 760	52.185 606	.019 162 3721	7.67	.379 691	2.11	72
19	2.032 326	110.114 759	.009 081 4347	.492 047	54.181 645	.018 456 4347	7.39	.402 689	2.12	76
20	2.109 617	118.359 097	.008 448 8647	.474 020	56.104 555	.017 823 8647	7.13	.425 909	2.13	80
21	2.189 847	126.916 973	.007 879 1668	.456 653	57.957 015	.017 254 1668	6.91	.449 350	2.14	84
22	2.273 128	135.800 310	.007 363 7535	.439 922	59.741 605	.016 738 7535	6.70	.473 010	2.15	88
23	2.359 576	145.021 486	.006 895 5300	.423 805	61.460 813	.016 270 5300	6.51	.496 889	2.16	92
24	2.449 313	154.593 349	.006 468 5836	.408 278	63.117 034	.015 843 5836	6.34	.520 984	2.17	96
25	2.542 462	164.529 237	.006 077 9471	.393 320	64.712 575	.015 452 9471	6.19	.545 295	2.18	100
26	2.639 153	174.842 992	.005 719 4171	.378 909	66.249 660	.015 094 4171	6.04	.569 819	2.19	104
27	2.739 522	185.548 987	.005 389 4123	.365 027	67.730 430	.014 764 4123	5.91	.594 557	2.20	108
28	2.843 708	196.662 137	.005 084 8629	.351 654	69.156 949	.014 459 8629	5.79	.619 505	2.21	112
29	2.951 856	208.197 928	.004 803 1218	.338 770	70.531 204	.014 178 1218	5.68	.644 662	2.22	116
30	3.064 117	220.172 433	.004 541 8947	.326 358	71.855 110	.013 916 8947	5.57	.670 027	2.23	120
31	3.180 647	232.602 335	.004 299 1830	.314 401	73.130 512	.013 674 1830	5.47	.695 599	2.24	124
32	3.301 609	245.504 955	.004 073 2375	.302 883	74.359 186	.013 448 2375	5.38	.721 374	2.25	128
33	3.427 171	258.898 270	.003 862 5210	.291 786	75.542 845	.013 237 5210	5.30	.747 353	2.26	132
34	3.557 509	272.800 941	.003 665 6765	.281 096	76.683 138	.013 040 6765	5.22	.773 532	2.28	136
35	3.692 803	287.232 340	.003 481 5021	.270 797	77.781 654	.012 856 5021	5.15	.799 910	2.29	140
36	3.833 243	302.212 574	.003 308 9292	.260 876	78.839 923	.012 683 9292	5.08	.826 486	2.30	144
37	3.979 024	317.762 516	.003 147 0043	.251 318	79.859 420	.012 522 0043	5.01	.853 257	2.31	148
38	4.130 348	333.903 833	.002 994 8743	.242 110	80.841 565	.012 369 8743	4.95	.880 221	2.32	152
39	4.287 428	350.659 014	.002 851 7733	.233 240	81.787 728	.012 226 7733	4.90	.907 377	2.33	156
40	4.450 482	368.051 406	.002 717 0118	.224 695	82.699 225	.012 092 0118	4.84	.934 722	2.34	160
41	4.619 737	386.105 241	.002 589 9674	.216 463	83.577 327	.011 964 9674	4.79	.962 255	2.35	164
42	4.795 428	404.845 676	.002 470 0770	.208 532	84.423 259	.011 845 0770	4.74	.989 973	2.36	168
43	4.977 801	424.298 821	.002 356 8295	.200 892	85.238 197	.011 731 8295	4.70	1.017 875	2.37	172
44	5.167 110	444.491 783	.002 249 7604	.193 532	86.023 279	.011 624 7604	4.65	1.045 958	2.38	176
45	5.363 619	465.452 695	.002 148 4460	.186 441	86.779 597	.011 523 4460	4.61	1.074 220	2.39	180
46	5.567 601	487.210 765	.002 052 4998	.179 611	87.508 205	.011 427 4998	4.58	1.102 660	2.40	184
47	5.779 340	509.796 308	.001 961 5678	.173 030	88.210 120	.011 336 5678	4.54	1.131 275	2.41	188
48	5.999 132	533.240 794	.001 875 3254	.166 691	88.886 318	.011 250 3254	4.51	1.160 062	2.42	192
49	6.227 283	557.576 889	.001 793 4746	.160 584	89.537 742	.011 168 4746	4.47	1.189 021	2.43	196
50	6.464 111	582.838 502	.001 715 7411	.154 700	90.165 300	.011 090 7411	4.44	1.218 148	2.44	200

Amount Of 1	Amount Of 1 Per Period	Sinking Fund Payment	Present Worth Of 1	Present Worth of 1 Per Period	Periodic Payment To Amortize 1	Constant Annual Percent	Total Interest	Annual Add On Rate
What a single $1 deposit grows to in the future. The deposit is made at the beginning of the first period.	What a series of $1 deposits grow to in the future. A deposit is made at the end of each period.	The amount to be deposited at the end of each period that grows to $1 in the future.	What $1 to be paid in the future is worth today. Value today of a single $1 payment tomorrow.	What $1 to be paid at the end of each period is worth today. Value today of a series of $1 payments tomorrow.	The mortgage payment to amortize a loan of $1. An annuity certain, payable at the end of each period, worth $1 today.	The annual payment, including interest and principal, to amortize completely a loan of $100.	The total interest paid over the term on a loan of $1. The loan is amortized by regular periodic payments.	The average annual interest rate on a loan that is completely amortized by regular periodic payments.

$$S = (1+i)^n \quad S\overline{n}| = \frac{(1+i)^n - 1}{i} \quad \frac{1}{S\overline{n}|} = \frac{i}{(1+i)^n - 1} \quad V^n = \frac{1}{(1+i)^n} \quad A\overline{n}| = \frac{1-V^n}{i} \quad \frac{1}{A\overline{n}|} = \frac{i}{1-V^n}$$

YEAR / **PERIODS**

YEAR	Amount Of 1	Amount Of 1 Per Period	Sinking Fund Payment	Present Worth Of 1	Present Worth of 1 Per Period	Periodic Payment To Amortize 1	Constant Annual Percent	Total Interest	Annual Add On Rate	PERIODS
	1.010 000	1.000 000	1.000 000 0000	.990 099	.990 099	1.010 000 0000	404.00	.010 000	4.00	1
	1.020 100	2.010 000	.497 512 4378	.980 296	1.970 395	.507 512 4378	203.01	.015 025	3.00	2
	1.030 301	3.030 100	.330 022 1115	.970 590	2.940 985	.340 022 1115	136.01	.020 066	2.68	3
	1.040 604	4.060 401	.246 281 0939	.960 980	3.901 966	.256 281 0939	102.52	.025 124	2.51	4
1	1.040 604	4.060 401	.246 281 0939	.960 980	3.901 966	.256 281 0939	102.52	.025 124	2.51	4
2	1.082 857	8.285 671	.120 690 2920	.923 483	7.651 678	.130 690 2920	52.28	.045 522	2.28	8
3	1.126 825	12.682 503	.078 848 7887	.887 449	11.255 077	.088 848 7887	35.54	.066 185	2.21	12
4	1.172 579	17.257 864	.057 944 5968	.852 821	14.717 874	.067 944 5968	27.18	.087 114	2.18	16
5	1.220 190	22.019 004	.045 415 3149	.819 544	18.045 553	.055 415 3149	22.17	.108 306	2.17	20
6	1.269 735	26.973 465	.037 073 4722	.787 566	21.243 387	.047 073 4722	18.83	.129 763	2.16	24
7	1.321 291	32.129 097	.031 124 4356	.756 836	24.316 443	.041 124 4356	16.45	.151 484	2.16	28
8	1.374 941	37.494 068	.026 670 8857	.727 304	27.269 589	.036 670 8857	14.67	.173 468	2.17	32
9	1.430 769	43.076 878	.023 214 3098	.698 925	30.107 505	.033 214 3098	13.29	.195 715	2.17	36
10	1.488 864	48.886 373	.020 455 5980	.671 653	32.834 686	.030 455 5980	12.19	.218 224	2.18	40
11	1.549 318	54.931 757	.018 204 4058	.645 445	35.455 454	.028 204 4058	11.29	.240 994	2.19	44
12	1.612 226	61.222 608	.016 333 8354	.620 260	37.973 959	.026 333 8354	10.54	.264 024	2.20	48
13	1.677 689	67.768 892	.014 756 0329	.596 058	40.394 194	.024 756 0329	9.91	.287 314	2.21	52
14	1.745 810	74.580 982	.013 408 2440	.572 800	42.719 992	.023 408 2440	9.37	.310 862	2.22	56
15	1.816 697	81.669 670	.012 244 4477	.550 450	44.955 038	.022 244 4477	8.90	.334 667	2.23	60
16	1.890 462	89.046 187	.011 230 1271	.528 971	47.102 874	.021 230 1271	8.50	.358 728	2.24	64
17	1.967 222	96.722 220	.010 338 8859	.508 331	49.166 901	.020 338 8859	8.14	.383 044	2.25	68
18	2.047 099	104.709 931	.009 550 1925	.488 496	51.150 391	.019 550 1925	7.83	.407 614	2.26	72
19	2.130 220	113.021 975	.008 847 8369	.469 435	53.056 486	.018 847 8369	7.54	.432 436	2.28	76
20	2.216 715	121.671 522	.008 218 8501	.451 118	54.888 206	.018 218 8501	7.29	.457 508	2.29	80
21	2.306 723	130.672 274	.007 652 7328	.433 515	56.648 453	.017 652 7328	7.07	.482 830	2.30	84
22	2.400 385	140.038 494	.007 140 8937	.416 600	58.340 015	.017 140 8937	6.86	.508 399	2.31	88
23	2.497 850	149.785 019	.006 676 2351	.400 344	59.965 573	.016 676 2351	6.68	.534 214	2.32	92
24	2.599 273	159.927 293	.006 252 8414	.384 723	61.527 703	.016 252 8414	6.51	.560 273	2.33	96
25	2.704 814	170.481 383	.005 865 7431	.369 711	63.028 879	.015 865 7431	6.35	.586 574	2.35	100
26	2.814 640	181.464 012	.005 510 7346	.355 285	64.471 479	.015 510 7346	6.21	.613 116	2.36	104
27	2.928 926	192.892 579	.005 184 2326	.341 422	65.857 790	.015 184 2326	6.08	.639 897	2.37	108
28	3.047 852	204.785 192	.004 883 1656	.328 100	67.190 007	.014 883 1656	5.96	.666 915	2.38	112
29	3.171 607	217.160 693	.004 604 8849	.315 298	68.470 242	.014 604 8849	5.85	.694 167	2.39	116
30	3.300 387	230.038 689	.004 347 0948	.302 995	69.700 522	.014 347 0948	5.74	.721 651	2.41	120
31	3.434 396	243.439 584	.004 107 7954	.291 172	70.882 797	.014 107 7954	5.65	.749 367	2.42	124
32	3.573 846	257.384 608	.003 885 2362	.279 811	72.018 940	.013 885 2362	5.56	.777 310	2.43	128
33	3.718 959	271.895 856	.003 677 8788	.268 892	73.110 752	.013 677 8788	5.48	.805 480	2.44	132
34	3.869 963	286.996 319	.003 484 3652	.258 400	74.159 961	.013 484 3652	5.40	.833 874	2.45	136
35	4.027 099	302.709 922	.003 303 4926	.248 318	75.168 230	.013 303 4926	5.33	.862 489	2.46	140
36	4.190 616	319.061 559	.003 134 1914	.238 628	76.137 157	.013 134 1914	5.26	.891 324	2.48	144
37	4.360 771	336.077 139	.002 975 5074	.229 317	77.068 277	.012 975 5074	5.20	.920 375	2.49	148
38	4.537 836	353.783 620	.002 826 5865	.220 369	77.963 065	.012 826 5865	5.14	.949 641	2.50	152
39	4.722 091	372.209 054	.002 686 6622	.211 771	78.822 939	.012 686 6622	5.08	.979 119	2.51	156
40	4.913 826	391.382 635	.002 555 0444	.203 507	79.649 261	.012 555 0444	5.03	1.008 807	2.52	160
41	5.113 347	411.334 741	.002 431 1100	.195 567	80.443 339	.012 431 1100	4.98	1.038 702	2.53	164
42	5.320 970	432.096 982	.002 314 2953	.187 936	81.206 434	.012 314 2953	4.93	1.068 802	2.54	168
43	5.537 023	453.702 253	.002 204 0887	.180 602	81.939 752	.012 204 0887	4.89	1.099 103	2.56	172
44	5.761 848	476.184 785	.002 100 0251	.173 555	82.644 457	.012 100 0251	4.85	1.129 604	2.57	176
45	5.995 802	499.580 198	.002 001 6806	.166 783	83.321 664	.012 001 6806	4.81	1.160 303	2.58	180
46	6.239 256	523.925 558	.001 908 6681	.160 276	83.972 447	.011 908 6681	4.77	1.191 195	2.59	184
47	6.492 594	549.259 437	.001 820 6333	.154 022	84.597 837	.011 820 6333	4.73	1.222 279	2.60	188
48	6.756 220	575.621 771	.001 737 2513	.148 012	85.198 824	.011 737 2513	4.70	1.253 552	2.61	192
49	7.030 549	603.054 936	.001 658 2237	.142 236	85.776 360	.011 658 2237	4.67	1.285 012	2.62	196
50	7.316 018	631.601 785	.001 583 2761	.136 686	86.331 362	.011 583 2761	4.64	1.316 655	2.63	200

Effective Rate is 4.06 %   8 - 272   Annual Percentage Rate is 4.00 %

	Amount Of 1	Amount Of 1 Per Period	Sinking Fund Payment	Present Worth Of 1	Present Worth of 1 Per Period	Periodic Payment To Amortize 1	Constant Annual Percent	Total Interest	Annual Add On Rate	
	What a single $ 1 deposit grows to in the future. The deposit is made at the beginning of the first period.	What a series of $ 1 deposits grow to in the future. A deposit is made at the end of each period.	The amount to be deposited at the end of each period that grows to $ 1 in the future.	What $ 1 to be paid in the future is worth today. Value today of a single $ 1 payment tomorrow.	What $ 1 to be paid at the end of each period is worth today. Value today of a series of $ 1 payments tomorrow.	The mortgage payment to amortize a loan of $ 1. An annuity certain, payable at the end of each period, worth $ 1 today.	The annual payment, including interest and principal, to amortize completely a loan of $ 100.	The total interest paid over the term on a loan of $1. The loan is amortized by regular periodic payments.	The average annual interest rate on a loan that is completely amortized by regular periodic payments.	
	$S = (1+i)^n$	$S\overline{n} = \dfrac{(1+i)^n - 1}{i}$	$\dfrac{1}{S\overline{n}} = \dfrac{i}{(1+i)^n - 1}$	$V^n = \dfrac{1}{(1+i)^n}$	$A\overline{n} = \dfrac{1 - V^n}{i}$	$\dfrac{1}{A\overline{n}} = \dfrac{i}{1 - V^n}$				

YEAR										PERIODS
	1.010 625	1.000 000	1.000 000 0000	.989 487	.989 487	1.010 625 0000	404.25	.010 625	4.25	1
	1.021 363	2.010 625	.497 357 7868	.979 084	1.968 571	.507 982 7868	203.20	.015 966	3.19	2
	1.032 215	3.031 988	.329 816 6207	.968 791	2.937 361	.340 441 6207	136.18	.021 325	2.84	3
	1.043 182	4.064 203	.246 050 7161	.958 605	3.895 967	.256 675 7161	102.68	.026 703	2.67	4
1	1.043 182	4.064 203	.246 050 7161	.958 605	3.895 967	.256 675 7161	102.68	.026 703	2.67	4
2	1.088 229	8.303 907	.120 425 2472	.918 924	7.630 661	.131 050 2472	52.43	.048 402	2.42	8
3	1.135 221	12.726 690	.078 575 0269	.880 886	11.210 759	.089 200 0269	35.69	.070 400	2.35	12
4	1.184 242	17.340 459	.057 668 6019	.844 422	14.642 660	.068 293 6019	27.32	.092 698	2.32	16
5	1.235 381	22.153 460	.045 139 6764	.809 467	17.932 499	.055 764 6764	22.31	.115 294	2.31	20
6	1.288 727	27.174 297	.036 799 4807	.775 960	21.086 156	.047 424 4807	18.97	.138 188	2.30	24
7	1.344 377	32.411 944	.030 852 8239	.743 839	24.109 269	.041 477 8239	16.60	.161 379	2.31	28
8	1.402 430	37.875 764	.026 402 1075	.713 048	27.007 241	.037 027 1075	14.82	.184 867	2.31	32
9	1.462 990	43.575 524	.022 948 6626	.683 532	29.785 252	.033 573 6626	13.43	.208 652	2.32	36
10	1.526 165	49.521 412	.020 193 2853	.655 237	32.448 269	.030 818 2853	12.33	.232 731	2.33	40
11	1.592 068	55.724 056	.017 945 5710	.628 114	35.001 051	.028 570 5710	11.43	.257 105	2.34	44
12	1.660 817	62.194 543	.016 078 5809	.602 113	37.448 161	.026 703 5809	10.69	.281 772	2.35	48
13	1.732 535	68.944 441	.014 504 4327	.577 189	39.793 974	.025 129 4327	10.06	.306 731	2.36	52
14	1.807 349	75.985 813	.013 160 3514	.553 296	42.042 683	.023 785 3514	9.52	.331 980	2.37	56
15	1.885 394	83.331 247	.012 000 3005	.530 393	44.198 308	.022 625 3005	9.06	.357 518	2.38	60
16	1.966 810	90.993 872	.010 989 7510	.508 438	46.264 701	.021 614 7510	8.65	.383 344	2.40	64
17	2.051 741	98.987 386	.010 102 2972	.487 391	48.245 557	.020 727 2972	8.30	.409 456	2.41	68
18	2.140 340	107.326 078	.009 317 4000	.467 216	50.144 416	.019 942 4000	7.98	.435 853	2.42	72
19	2.232 764	116.024 852	.008 618 8432	.447 875	51.964 672	.019 243 8432	7.70	.462 532	2.43	76
20	2.329 180	125.099 258	.007 993 6526	.429 336	53.709 580	.018 618 6526	7.45	.489 492	2.45	80
21	2.429 759	134.565 516	.007 431 3244	.411 564	55.382 257	.018 056 3244	7.23	.516 731	2.46	84
22	2.534 681	144.440 547	.006 923 2637	.394 527	56.985 695	.017 548 2637	7.02	.544 247	2.47	88
23	2.644 134	154.742 004	.006 462 3694	.378 196	58.522 759	.017 087 3694	6.84	.572 038	2.49	92
24	2.758 313	165.488 300	.006 042 7233	.362 540	59.996 197	.016 667 7233	6.67	.600 101	2.50	96
25	2.877 423	176.698 644	.005 659 3530	.347 533	61.408 642	.016 284 3530	6.52	.628 435	2.51	100
26	3.001 676	188.393 075	.005 308 0507	.333 147	62.762 619	.015 933 0507	6.38	.657 037	2.53	104
27	3.131 295	200.592 497	.004 985 2313	.319 357	64.060 550	.015 610 2313	6.25	.685 905	2.54	108
28	3.266 511	213.318 716	.004 687 8212	.306 137	65.304 753	.015 312 8212	6.13	.715 036	2.55	112
29	3.407 566	226.594 480	.004 413 1702	.293 465	66.497 452	.015 038 1702	6.02	.744 428	2.57	116
30	3.554 712	240.443 521	.004 158 9809	.281 317	67.640 780	.014 783 9809	5.92	.774 078	2.58	120
31	3.708 213	254.890 593	.003 923 2519	.269 672	68.736 781	.014 548 2519	5.82	.803 983	2.59	124
32	3.868 341	269.961 520	.003 704 2316	.258 509	69.787 413	.014 329 2316	5.74	.834 142	2.61	128
33	4.035 384	285.683 243	.003 500 3803	.247 808	70.794 554	.014 125 3803	5.66	.864 550	2.62	132
34	4.209 641	302.083 864	.003 310 3390	.237 550	71.760 005	.013 935 3390	5.58	.895 206	2.63	136
35	4.391 422	319.192 699	.003 132 9037	.227 717	72.685 492	.013 757 9037	5.51	.926 107	2.65	140
36	4.581 054	337.040 330	.002 967 0040	.218 290	73.572 668	.013 592 0040	5.44	.957 249	2.66	144
37	4.778 873	355.658 660	.002 811 6847	.209 254	74.423 120	.013 436 6847	5.38	.988 629	2.67	148
38	4.985 235	375.080 970	.002 666 0910	.200 592	75.238 368	.013 291 0910	5.32	1.020 246	2.68	152
39	5.200 509	395.341 977	.002 529 4557	.192 289	76.019 869	.013 154 4557	5.27	1.052 095	2.70	156
40	5.425 078	416.477 898	.002 401 0878	.184 329	76.769 020	.013 026 0878	5.22	1.084 174	2.71	160
41	5.659 344	438.526 514	.002 280 3638	.176 699	77.487 161	.012 905 3638	5.17	1.116 480	2.72	164
42	5.903 727	461.527 236	.002 166 7194	.169 385	78.175 574	.012 791 7194	5.12	1.149 009	2.74	168
43	6.158 663	485.521 179	.002 059 6424	.162 373	78.835 490	.012 684 6424	5.08	1.181 758	2.75	172
44	6.424 607	510.551 232	.001 958 6673	.155 652	79.468 090	.012 583 6673	5.04	1.214 725	2.76	176
45	6.702 035	536.662 137	.001 863 3698	.149 208	80.074 503	.012 488 3698	5.00	1.247 907	2.77	180
46	6.991 444	563.900 567	.001 773 3623	.143 032	80.655 814	.012 398 3623	4.96	1.281 299	2.79	184
47	7.293 349	592.315 211	.001 688 2903	.137 111	81.213 062	.012 313 2903	4.93	1.314 899	2.80	188
48	7.608 292	621.956 861	.001 607 8286	.131 436	81.747 242	.012 232 8286	4.90	1.348 703	2.81	192
49	7.936 834	652.878 501	.001 531 6786	.125 995	82.259 311	.012 156 6786	4.87	1.382 709	2.82	196
50	8.279 564	685.135 404	.001 459 5655	.120 779	82.750 182	.012 084 5655	4.84	1.416 913	2.83	200

Effective Rate is 4.32 %

Annual Percentage Rate is 4.25 %

	Amount Of 1	Amount Of 1 Per Period	Sinking Fund Payment	Present Worth Of 1	Present Worth of 1 Per Period	Periodic Payment To Amortize 1	Constant Annual Percent	Total Interest	Annual Add On Rate	
	What a single $ 1 deposit grows to in the future. The deposit is made at the beginning of the first period.	What a series of $ 1 deposits grow to in the future. A deposit is made at the end of each period.	The amount to be deposited at the end of each period that grows to $ 1 in the future.	What $ 1 to be paid in the future is worth today. Value today of a single $ 1 payment tomorrow.	What $ 1 to be paid at the end of each period is worth today. Value today of a series of $ 1 payments tomorrow.	The mortgage payment to amortize a loan of $ 1. An annuity certain, payable at the end of each period, worth $ 1 today.	The annual payment, including interest and principal, to amortize completely a loan of $ 100.	The total interest paid over the term on a loan of $1. The loan is amortized by regular periodic payments.	The average annual interest rate on a loan that is completely amortized by regular periodic payments.	
	$S = (1+i)^n$	$S\overline{n}| = \dfrac{(1+i)^n - 1}{i}$	$\dfrac{1}{S\overline{n}|} = \dfrac{i}{(1+i)^n - 1}$	$V^n = \dfrac{1}{(1+i)^n}$	$A\overline{n}| = \dfrac{1-V^n}{i}$	$\dfrac{1}{A\overline{n}|} = \dfrac{i}{1-V^n}$				

YEAR										PERIODS
	1.011 250	1.000 000	1.000 000 0000	.988 875	.988 875	1.011 250 0000	404.50	.011 250	4.50	1
	1.022 627	2.011 250	.497 203 2318	.977 874	1.966 749	.508 453 2318	203.39	.016 906	3.38	2
	1.034 131	3.033 877	.329 611 3007	.966 995	2.933 745	.340 861 3007	136.35	.022 584	3.01	3
	1.045 765	4.068 008	.245 820 5786	.956 238	3.889 982	.257 070 5786	102.83	.028 282	2.83	4
1	1.045 765	4.068 008	.245 820 5786	.956 238	3.889 982	.257 070 5786	102.83	.028 282	2.83	4
2	1.093 625	8.322 188	.120 160 7067	.914 391	7.609 730	.131 410 7067	52.57	.051 286	2.56	8
3	1.143 674	12.771 061	.078 302 0274	.874 375	11.166 693	.089 552 0274	35.83	.074 624	2.49	12
4	1.196 015	17.423 538	.057 393 6253	.836 110	14.567 995	.068 643 6253	27.46	.098 298	2.46	16
5	1.250 751	22.288 935	.044 865 3106	.799 520	17.820 448	.056 115 3106	22.45	.122 306	2.45	20
6	1.307 991	27.376 998	.036 527 0145	.764 531	20.930 567	.047 777 0145	19.12	.146 648	2.44	24
7	1.367 852	32.697 916	.030 582 9886	.731 073	23.904 579	.041 832 9886	16.74	.171 324	2.45	28
8	1.430 451	38.262 347	.026 135 3545	.699 080	26.748 442	.037 385 3545	14.96	.196 331	2.45	32
9	1.495 916	44.081 434	.022 685 2873	.668 487	29.467 851	.033 935 2873	13.58	.221 670	2.46	36
10	1.564 377	50.166 832	.019 933 4889	.639 232	32.068 253	.031 183 4889	12.48	.247 340	2.47	40
11	1.635 971	56.530 730	.017 689 4940	.611 258	34.554 854	.028 939 4940	11.58	.273 338	2.48	44
12	1.710 841	63.185 871	.015 826 3230	.584 508	36.932 637	.027 076 3230	10.84	.299 664	2.50	48
13	1.789 138	70.145 585	.014 256 0646	.558 928	39.206 362	.025 506 0646	10.21	.326 315	2.51	52
14	1.871 018	77.423 812	.012 915 9231	.534 468	41.380 584	.024 165 9231	9.67	.353 292	2.52	56
15	1.956 645	85.035 127	.011 759 8460	.511 079	43.459 656	.023 009 8460	9.21	.380 591	2.54	60
16	2.046 191	92.994 775	.010 753 2924	.488 713	45.447 744	.022 003 2924	8.81	.408 211	2.55	64
17	2.139 835	101.318 696	.009 869 8467	.467 326	47.348 829	.021 119 8467	8.45	.436 150	2.57	68
18	2.237 765	110.023 563	.009 088 9622	.446 874	49.166 717	.020 338 9622	8.14	.464 405	2.58	72
19	2.340 177	119.126 808	.008 394 4161	.427 318	50.905 051	.019 644 4161	7.86	.492 976	2.59	76
20	2.447 275	128.646 665	.007 773 2291	.408 618	52.567 311	.019 023 2291	7.61	.521 858	2.61	80
21	2.559 275	138.602 198	.007 214 8928	.390 736	54.156 827	.018 464 8928	7.39	.551 051	2.62	84
22	2.676 400	149.013 347	.006 710 8083	.373 636	55.676 782	.017 960 8083	7.19	.580 551	2.64	88
23	2.798 886	159.900 964	.006 253 8710	.357 285	57.130 220	.017 503 8710	7.01	.610 356	2.65	92
24	2.926 977	171.286 853	.005 838 1597	.341 649	58.520 052	.017 088 1597	6.84	.640 463	2.67	96
25	3.060 930	183.193 818	.005 458 6995	.326 698	59.849 063	.016 708 6995	6.69	.670 870	2.68	100
26	3.201 014	195.645 707	.005 111 2801	.312 401	61.119 912	.016 361 2801	6.55	.701 573	2.70	104
27	3.347 509	208.667 457	.004 792 3141	.298 730	62.335 146	.016 042 3141	6.42	.732 570	2.71	108
28	3.500 708	222.285 149	.004 498 7261	.285 657	63.497 199	.015 748 7261	6.30	.763 857	2.73	112
29	3.660 918	236.526 055	.004 227 8640	.273 156	64.608 398	.015 477 8640	6.20	.795 432	2.74	116
30	3.828 460	251.418 698	.003 977 4289	.261 202	65.670 968	.015 227 4289	6.10	.827 291	2.76	120
31	4.003 670	266.992 905	.003 745 4179	.249 771	66.687 038	.014 995 4179	6.00	.859 432	2.77	124
32	4.186 898	283.279 866	.003 530 0779	.238 840	67.658 642	.014 780 0779	5.92	.891 850	2.79	128
33	4.378 512	300.312 201	.003 329 8680	.228 388	68.587 726	.014 579 8680	5.84	.924 543	2.80	132
34	4.578 895	318.124 022	.003 143 4281	.218 393	69.476 152	.014 393 4281	5.76	.957 506	2.82	136
35	4.788 449	336.751 003	.002 969 5531	.208 836	70.325 698	.014 219 5531	5.69	.990 737	2.83	140
36	5.007 593	356.230 450	.002 807 1716	.199 697	71.138 066	.014 057 1716	5.63	1.024 233	2.85	144
37	5.236 765	376.601 375	.002 655 3275	.190 958	71.914 883	.013 905 3275	5.57	1.057 988	2.86	148
38	5.476 426	397.904 577	.002 513 1654	.182 601	72.657 704	.013 763 1654	5.51	1.092 001	2.87	152
39	5.727 056	420.182 722	.002 379 9170	.174 610	73.368 018	.013 629 9170	5.46	1.126 267	2.89	156
40	5.989 155	443.480 428	.002 254 8909	.166 968	74.047 247	.013 504 8909	5.41	1.160 783	2.90	160
41	6.263 249	467.844 356	.002 137 4630	.159 662	74.696 752	.013 387 4630	5.36	1.195 544	2.92	164
42	6.549 887	493.323 301	.002 027 0683	.152 674	75.317 832	.013 277 0683	5.32	1.230 547	2.93	168
43	6.849 643	519.968 292	.001 923 1942	.145 993	75.911 733	.013 173 1942	5.27	1.265 789	2.94	172
44	7.163 118	547.832 693	.001 825 3748	.139 604	76.479 643	.013 075 3748	5.24	1.301 266	2.96	176
45	7.490 939	576.972 311	.001 733 1854	.133 495	77.022 700	.012 983 1854	5.20	1.336 973	2.97	180
46	7.833 762	607.445 507	.001 646 2382	.127 653	77.541 992	.012 896 2382	5.16	1.372 908	2.98	184
47	8.192 275	639.313 310	.001 564 1783	.122 066	78.038 558	.012 814 1783	5.13	1.409 066	3.00	188
48	8.567 195	672.639 547	.001 486 6804	.116 724	78.513 394	.012 736 6804	5.10	1.445 443	3.01	192
49	8.959 273	707.490 961	.001 413 4456	.111 616	78.967 449	.012 663 4456	5.07	1.482 035	3.02	196
50	9.369 295	743.937 354	.001 344 1992	.106 732	79.401 634	.012 594 1992	5.04	1.518 840	3.04	200

Effective Rate is 4.58 %

Annual Percentage Rate is 4.50 %

	Amount Of 1	Amount Of 1 Per Period	Sinking Fund Payment	Present Worth Of 1	Present Worth of 1 Per Period	Periodic Payment To Amortize 1	Constant Annual Percent	Total Interest	Annual Add On Rate	
	What a single $ 1 deposit grows to in the future. The deposit is made at the beginning of the first period.	What a series of $ 1 deposits grow to in the future. A deposit is made at the end of each period.	The amount to be deposited at the end of each period that grows to $ 1 in the future.	What $ 1 to be paid in the future is worth today. Value today of a single $ 1 payment tomorrow.	What $ 1 to be paid at the end of each period is worth today. Value today of a series of $ 1 payments tomorrow.	The mortgage payment to amortize a loan of $ 1. An annuity certain, payable at the end of each period, worth $ 1 today.	The annual payment, including interest and principal, to amortize completely a loan of $ 100.	The total interest paid over the term on a loan of $ 1. The loan is amortized by regular periodic payments.	The average annual interest rate on a loan that is completely amortized by regular periodic payments.	

$$S = (1+i)^n \qquad S\overline{n}| = \frac{(1+i)^n - 1}{i} \qquad \frac{1}{S\overline{n}|} = \frac{i}{(1+i)^n - 1} \qquad V^n = \frac{1}{(1+i)^n} \qquad A\overline{n}| = \frac{1-V^n}{i} \qquad \frac{1}{A\overline{n}|} = \frac{i}{1-V^n}$$

YEAR										PERIODS
	1.011 875	1.000 000	1.000 000 0000	.988 264	.988 264	1.011 875 0000	404.75	.011 875	4.75	1
	1.023 891	2.011 875	.497 048 7729	.976 666	1.964 931	.508 923 7729	203.57	.017 848	3.57	2
	1.036 050	3.035 766	.329 406 1515	.965 205	2.930 135	.341 281 1515	136.52	.023 843	3.18	3
	1.048 353	4.071 816	.245 590 6811	.953 877	3.884 013	.257 465 6811	102.99	.029 863	2.99	4
1	1.048 353	4.071 816	.245 590 6811	.953 877	3.884 013	.257 465 6811	102.99	.029 863	2.99	4
2	1.099 044	8.340 515	.119 896 6700	.909 882	7.588 885	.131 771 6700	52.71	.054 173	2.71	8
3	1.152 185	12.815 618	.078 029 7895	.867 916	11.122 878	.089 904 7895	35.97	.078 857	2.63	12
4	1.207 897	17.507 105	.057 119 6658	.827 885	14.493 874	.068 994 6658	27.60	.103 915	2.60	16
5	1.266 302	22.425 439	.044 592 2156	.789 701	17.709 391	.056 467 2156	22.59	.129 344	2.59	20
6	1.327 531	27.581 587	.036 256 0712	.753 278	20.776 600	.048 131 0712	19.26	.155 146	2.59	24
7	1.391 721	32.987 051	.030 314 9261	.718 535	23.702 341	.042 189 9261	16.88	.181 318	2.59	28
8	1.459 015	38.653 883	.025 870 6222	.685 394	26.493 139	.037 745 6222	15.10	.207 860	2.60	32
9	1.529 562	44.594 723	.022 424 1781	.653 782	29.155 218	.034 299 1781	13.72	.234 770	2.61	36
10	1.603 521	50.822 819	.019 676 2011	.623 628	31.694 514	.031 551 2011	12.63	.262 048	2.62	40
11	1.681 056	57.352 060	.017 436 1652	.594 864	34.116 692	.029 311 1652	11.73	.289 691	2.63	44
12	1.762 339	64.197 010	.015 577 0496	.567 428	36.427 153	.027 452 0496	10.99	.317 698	2.65	48
13	1.847 554	71.372 931	.014 010 9140	.541 256	38.631 049	.025 885 9140	10.36	.346 068	2.66	52
14	1.936 888	78.895 829	.012 674 9413	.516 292	40.733 295	.024 549 9413	9.82	.374 797	2.68	56
15	2.030 542	86.782 480	.011 523 0632	.492 479	42.738 580	.023 398 0632	9.36	.403 884	2.69	60
16	2.128 724	95.050 473	.010 520 7262	.469 765	44.651 376	.022 395 7262	8.96	.433 326	2.71	64
17	2.231 654	103.718 246	.009 641 5051	.448 098	46.475 949	.021 516 5051	8.61	.463 122	2.72	68
18	2.339 561	112.805 130	.008 864 8450	.427 431	48.216 368	.020 739 8450	8.30	.493 269	2.74	72
19	2.452 685	122.331 391	.008 174 5167	.407 716	49.876 514	.020 049 5167	8.02	.523 763	2.76	76
20	2.571 280	132.318 274	.007 557 5351	.388 911	51.460 090	.019 432 5351	7.78	.554 603	2.77	80
21	2.695 608	142.788 050	.007 003 3872	.370 974	52.970 627	.018 878 3872	7.56	.585 785	2.79	84
22	2.825 948	153.764 070	.006 503 4699	.353 864	54.411 494	.018 378 4699	7.36	.617 305	2.81	88
23	2.962 591	165.270 811	.006 050 6752	.337 542	55.785 904	.017 925 6752	7.18	.649 162	2.82	92
24	3.105 840	177.333 935	.005 639 0786	.321 974	57.096 923	.017 514 0786	7.01	.681 352	2.84	96
25	3.256 017	189.980 345	.005 263 7024	.307 124	58.347 474	.017 138 7024	6.86	.713 870	2.86	100
26	3.413 454	203.238 244	.004 920 3338	.292 958	59.540 347	.016 795 3338	6.72	.746 715	2.87	104
27	3.578 504	217.137 201	.004 605 3831	.279 446	60.678 201	.016 480 3831	6.60	.779 881	2.89	108
28	3.751 535	231.708 211	.004 315 7728	.266 558	61.763 574	.016 190 7728	6.48	.813 367	2.90	112
29	3.932 932	246.983 770	.004 048 8490	.254 263	62.798 887	.015 923 8490	6.37	.847 166	2.92	116
30	4.123 101	262.997 946	.003 802 3111	.242 536	63.786 449	.015 677 3111	6.28	.881 277	2.94	120
31	4.322 464	279.786 451	.003 574 1545	.231 350	64.728 461	.015 449 1545	6.18	.915 695	2.95	124
32	4.531 467	297.386 729	.003 362 6248	.220 679	65.627 026	.015 237 6248	6.10	.950 416	2.97	128
33	4.750 577	315.838 029	.003 166 1798	.210 501	66.484 146	.015 041 1798	6.02	.985 436	2.99	132
34	4.980 280	335.181 502	.002 983 4582	.200 792	67.301 734	.014 858 4582	5.95	1.020 750	3.00	136
35	5.221 091	355.460 286	.002 813 2538	.191 531	68.081 612	.014 688 2538	5.88	1.056 356	3.02	140
36	5.473 545	376.719 606	.002 654 4942	.182 697	68.825 521	.014 529 4942	5.82	1.092 247	3.03	144
37	5.738 207	399.006 874	.002 506 2225	.174 270	69.535 118	.014 381 2225	5.76	1.128 421	3.05	148
38	6.015 665	422.371 794	.002 367 5823	.166 233	70.211 987	.014 242 5823	5.70	1.164 873	3.07	152
39	6.306 539	446.866 473	.002 237 8049	.158 566	70.857 636	.014 112 8049	5.65	1.201 598	3.08	156
40	6.611 478	472.545 539	.002 116 1982	.151 252	71.473 507	.013 991 1982	5.60	1.238 592	3.10	160
41	6.931 162	499.466 261	.002 002 1372	.144 276	72.060 972	.013 877 1372	5.56	1.275 851	3.11	164
42	7.266 303	527.688 675	.001 895 0568	.137 622	72.621 342	.013 770 0568	5.51	1.313 370	3.13	168
43	7.617 649	557.275 722	.001 794 4439	.131 274	73.155 866	.013 669 4439	5.47	1.351 144	3.14	172
44	7.985 984	588.293 385	.001 699 8321	.125 219	73.665 736	.013 574 8321	5.43	1.389 170	3.16	176
45	8.372 129	620.810 841	.001 610 7966	.119 444	74.152 090	.013 485 7966	5.40	1.427 443	3.17	180
46	8.776 945	654.900 606	.001 526 9493	.113 935	74.616 011	.013 401 9493	5.37	1.465 959	3.19	184
47	9.201 335	690.638 708	.001 447 9351	.108 680	75.058 536	.013 322 9351	5.33	1.504 712	3.20	188
48	9.646 245	728.104 847	.001 373 4286	.103 667	75.480 650	.013 248 4286	5.30	1.543 698	3.22	192
49	10.112 668	767.382 579	.001 303 1310	.098 886	75.883 295	.013 178 1310	5.28	1.582 914	3.23	196
50	10.601 644	808.559 501	.001 236 7674	.094 325	76.267 369	.013 111 7674	5.25	1.622 353	3.24	200

Effective Rate is 4.84 %

Annual Percentage Rate is 4.75 %

QUARTERLY COMPOUND INTEREST AND ANNUITY

5.00 % Q

	Amount Of 1	Amount Of 1 Per Period	Sinking Fund Payment	Present Worth Of 1	Present Worth of 1 Per Period	Periodic Payment To Amortize 1	Constant Annual Percent	Total Interest	Annual Add On Rate
	What a single $ 1 deposit grows to in the future. The deposit is made at the beginning of the first period.	What a series of $ 1 deposits grow to in the future. A deposit is made at the end of each period.	The amount to be deposited at the end of each period that grows to $ 1 in the future.	What $ 1 to be paid in the future is worth today. Value today of a single $ 1 payment tomorrow.	What $ 1 to be paid at the end of each period is worth today. Value today of a series of $ 1 payments tomorrow.	The mortgage payment to amortize a loan of $ 1. An annuity certain, payable at the end of each period, worth $ 1 today.	The annual payment, including interest and principal, to amortize completely a loan of $ 100.	The total interest paid over the term on a loan of $1. The loan is amortized by regular periodic payments.	The average annual interest rate on a loan that is completely amortized by regular periodic payments.
	$S = (1+i)^n$	$S\overline{n} = \dfrac{(1+i)^n - 1}{i}$	$\dfrac{1}{S\overline{n}} = \dfrac{i}{(1+i)^n - 1}$	$V^n = \dfrac{1}{(1+i)^n}$	$A\overline{n} = \dfrac{1 - V^n}{i}$	$\dfrac{1}{A\overline{n}} = \dfrac{i}{1 - V^n}$			

YEAR   **PERIODS**

YEAR	Amount Of 1	Amount Of 1 Per Period	Sinking Fund Payment	Present Worth Of 1	Present Worth of 1 Per Period	Periodic Payment To Amortize 1	Constant Annual Percent	Total Interest	Annual Add On Rate	PERIODS
	1.012 500	1.000 000	1.000 000 0000	.987 654	.987 654	1.012 500 0000	405.00	.012 500	5.00	1
	1.025 156	2.012 500	.496 894 4099	.975 461	1.963 115	.509 394 4099	203.76	.018 789	3.76	2
	1.037 971	3.037 656	.329 201 1728	.963 418	2.926 534	.341 701 1728	136.69	.025 104	3.35	3
	1.050 945	4.075 627	.245 361 0233	.951 524	3.878 058	.257 861 0233	103.15	.031 444	3.14	4
1	1.050 945	4.075 627	.245 361 0233	.951 524	3.878 058	.257 861 0233	103.15	.031 444	3.14	4
2	1.104 486	8.358 888	.119 633 1365	.905 398	7.568 124	.132 133 1365	52.86	.057 065	2.85	8
3	1.160 755	12.860 361	.077 758 3123	.861 509	11.079 312	.090 258 3123	36.11	.083 100	2.77	12
4	1.219 890	17.591 164	.056 846 7221	.819 746	14.420 292	.069 346 7221	27.74	.109 548	2.74	16
5	1.282 037	22.562 979	.044 320 3896	.780 009	17.599 316	.056 820 3896	22.73	.136 408	2.73	20
6	1.347 351	27.788 084	.035 986 6480	.742 197	20.624 235	.048 486 6480	19.40	.163 680	2.73	24
7	1.415 992	33.279 384	.030 048 6329	.706 219	23.502 518	.042 548 6329	17.02	.191 362	2.73	28
8	1.488 131	39.050 441	.025 607 9056	.671 984	26.241 274	.038 107 9056	15.25	.219 453	2.74	32
9	1.563 944	45.115 505	.022 165 3285	.639 409	28.847 267	.034 665 3285	13.87	.247 592	2.76	36
10	1.643 619	51.489 557	.019 421 4139	.608 413	31.326 933	.031 921 4139	12.77	.276 857	2.77	40
11	1.727 354	58.188 337	.017 185 5745	.578 920	33.686 395	.029 685 5745	11.88	.306 165	2.78	44
12	1.815 355	65.228 388	.015 330 7483	.550 856	35.931 481	.027 830 7483	11.14	.335 876	2.80	48
13	1.907 839	72.627 097	.013 768 9655	.524 153	38.067 734	.026 268 9655	10.51	.365 986	2.82	52
14	2.005 034	80.402 736	.012 437 3877	.498 745	40.100 431	.024 937 3877	9.98	.396 494	2.83	56
15	2.107 181	88.574 508	.011 289 9301	.474 568	42.034 592	.023 789 9301	9.52	.427 396	2.85	60
16	2.214 532	97.162 593	.010 292 0267	.451 563	43.874 992	.022 792 0267	9.12	.458 690	2.87	64
17	2.327 353	106.188 201	.009 417 2421	.429 673	45.626 178	.021 917 2421	8.77	.490 372	2.88	68
18	2.445 920	115.673 621	.008 645 0133	.408 844	47.292 474	.021 145 0133	8.46	.522 441	2.90	72
19	2.570 529	125.642 280	.007 959 1042	.389 025	48.877 995	.020 459 1042	8.19	.554 892	2.92	76
20	2.701 485	136.118 795	.007 346 5240	.370 167	50.386 657	.019 846 5240	7.94	.587 722	2.94	80
21	2.839 113	147.129 040	.006 796 7547	.352 223	51.822 185	.019 296 7547	7.72	.620 927	2.96	84
22	2.983 753	158.700 206	.006 301 1891	.335 148	53.188 125	.018 801 1891	7.53	.654 505	2.98	88
23	3.135 761	170.860 868	.005 852 7152	.318 902	54.487 850	.018 352 7152	7.35	.688 450	2.99	92
24	3.295 513	183.641 059	.005 445 4053	.303 443	55.724 570	.017 945 4053	7.18	.722 759	3.01	96
25	3.463 404	197.072 342	.005 074 2788	.288 733	56.901 339	.017 574 2788	7.03	.757 428	3.03	100
26	3.639 849	211.187 886	.004 735 1201	.274 737	58.021 064	.017 235 1201	6.90	.792 452	3.05	104
27	3.825 282	226.022 551	.004 424 3373	.261 419	59.086 509	.016 924 3373	6.77	.827 828	3.07	108
28	4.020 162	241.612 973	.004 138 8506	.248 746	60.100 305	.016 638 8506	6.66	.863 551	3.08	112
29	4.224 971	257.997 654	.003 876 0042	.236 688	61.064 957	.016 376 0042	6.56	.899 616	3.10	116
30	4.440 213	275.217 058	.003 633 4957	.225 214	61.982 847	.016 133 4957	6.46	.936 019	3.12	120
31	4.666 421	293.313 711	.003 409 3190	.214 297	62.856 242	.015 909 3190	6.37	.972 756	3.14	124
32	4.904 154	312.332 304	.003 201 7181	.203 909	63.687 298	.015 701 7181	6.29	1.009 820	3.16	128
33	5.153 998	332.319 805	.003 009 1496	.194 024	64.478 068	.015 509 1496	6.21	1.047 208	3.17	132
34	5.416 570	353.325 577	.002 830 2508	.184 619	65.230 505	.015 330 2508	6.14	1.084 914	3.19	136
35	5.692 519	375.401 494	.002 663 8147	.175 669	65.946 467	.015 163 8147	6.07	1.122 934	3.21	140
36	5.982 526	398.602 077	.002 508 7677	.167 153	66.627 722	.015 008 7677	6.01	1.161 263	3.23	144
37	6.287 308	422.984 621	.002 364 1521	.159 051	67.275 953	.014 864 1521	5.95	1.199 895	3.24	148
38	6.607 617	448.609 342	.002 229 1110	.151 340	67.892 760	.014 729 1110	5.90	1.238 825	3.26	152
39	6.944 244	475.539 523	.002 102 8746	.144 004	68.479 668	.014 602 8746	5.85	1.278 048	3.28	156
40	7.298 021	503.841 671	.001 984 7505	.137 023	69.038 124	.014 484 7505	5.80	1.317 560	3.29	160
41	7.669 821	533.585 681	.001 874 1133	.130 381	69.569 509	.014 374 1133	5.75	1.357 355	3.31	164
42	8.060 563	564.845 011	.001 770 3972	.124 061	70.075 134	.014 270 3972	5.71	1.397 427	3.33	168
43	8.471 211	597.696 857	.001 673 0889	.118 047	70.556 250	.014 173 0889	5.67	1.437 771	3.34	172
44	8.902 779	632.222 352	.001 581 7220	.112 324	71.014 042	.014 081 7220	5.64	1.478 383	3.36	176
45	9.356 334	668.506 759	.001 495 8712	.106 879	71.449 643	.013 995 8712	5.60	1.519 257	3.38	180
46	9.832 996	706.639 688	.001 415 1484	.101 698	71.864 128	.013 915 1484	5.57	1.560 387	3.39	184
47	10.333 941	746.715 312	.001 339 1985	.096 768	72.258 520	.013 839 1985	5.54	1.601 769	3.41	188
48	10.860 408	788.832 603	.001 267 6961	.092 078	72.633 794	.013 767 6961	5.51	1.643 398	3.42	192
49	11.413 695	833.095 572	.001 200 3425	.087 614	72.990 876	.013 700 3425	5.49	1.685 267	3.44	196
50	11.995 169	879.613 534	.001 136 8629	.083 367	73.330 648	.013 636 8629	5.46	1.727 373	3.45	200

Effective Rate is 5.09 %

Annual Percentage Rate is 5.00 %

QUARTERLY COMPOUND INTEREST AND ANNUITY

Amount Of 1	Amount Of 1 Per Period	Sinking Fund Payment	Present Worth Of 1	Present Worth of 1 Per Period	Periodic Payment To Amortize 1	Constant Annual Percent	Total Interest	Annual Add On Rate	
What a single $ 1 deposit grows to in the future. The deposit is made at the beginning of the first period.	What a series of $ 1 deposits grow to in the future. A deposit is made at the end of each period.	The amount to be deposited at the end of each period that grows to $ 1 in the future.	What $ 1 to be paid in the future is worth today. Value today of a single $ 1 payment tomorrow.	What $ 1 to be paid at the end of each period is worth today. Value today of a series of $ 1 payments tomorrow.	The mortgage payment to amortize a loan of $ 1. An annuity certain, payable at the end of each period, worth $ 1 today.	The annual payment, including interest and principal, to amortize completely a loan of $ 100.	The total interest paid over the term on a loan of $1. The loan is amortized by regular periodic payments.	The average annual interest rate on a loan that is completely amortized by regular periodic payments.	

$$S = (1+i)^n \qquad S\overline{n}| = \frac{(1+i)^n - 1}{i} \qquad \frac{1}{S\overline{n}|} = \frac{i}{(1+i)^n - 1} \qquad V^n = \frac{1}{(1+i)^n} \qquad A\overline{n}| = \frac{1 - V^n}{i} \qquad \frac{1}{A\overline{n}|} = \frac{i}{1 - V^n}$$

YEAR   **PERIODS**

	Amount Of 1	Amount Of 1 Per Period	Sinking Fund Payment	Present Worth Of 1	Present Worth of 1 Per Period	Periodic Payment To Amortize 1	Constant Annual Percent	Total Interest	Annual Add On Rate	PERIODS
	1.012 812	1.000 000	1.000 000 0000	.987 350	.987 350	1.012 812 5000	405.13	.012 813	5.13	1
	1.025 789	2.012 812	.496 817 2644	.974 859	1.962 209	.509 629 7644	203.86	.019 260	3.85	2
	1.038 932	3.038 602	.329 098 7473	.962 527	2.924 736	.341 911 2473	136.77	.025 734	3.43	3
	1.052 243	4.077 534	.245 246 2843	.950 350	3.875 086	.258 058 7843	103.23	.032 235	3.22	4
1	1.052 243	4.077 534	.245 246 2843	.950 350	3.875 086	.258 058 7843	103.23	.032 235	3.22	4
2	1.107 216	8.368 092	.119 501 5583	.903 166	7.557 776	.132 314 0583	52.93	.058 512	2.93	8
3	1.165 061	12.882 803	.077 622 8587	.858 324	11.057 622	.090 435 3587	36.18	.085 224	2.84	12
4	1.225 928	17.633 378	.056 710 6307	.815 709	14.383 702	.069 523 1307	27.81	.112 370	2.81	16
5	1.289 974	22.632 140	.044 184 9519	.775 209	17.544 644	.056 997 4519	22.80	.139 949	2.80	20
6	1.357 367	27.892 053	.035 852 5057	.736 720	20.548 647	.048 665 0057	19.47	.167 960	2.80	24
7	1.428 280	33.426 763	.029 916 1485	.700 143	23.403 502	.042 728 6485	17.10	.196 402	2.81	28
8	1.502 899	39.250 624	.025 477 3018	.665 381	26.116 615	.038 289 8018	15.32	.225 274	2.82	32
9	1.581 415	45.378 744	.022 036 7491	.632 345	28.695 023	.034 849 2491	13.94	.254 573	2.83	36
10	1.664 034	51.827 018	.019 294 9554	.600 949	31.145 414	.032 107 4554	12.85	.284 298	2.84	40
11	1.750 968	58.612 171	.017 061 3028	.571 113	33.474 145	.029 873 8028	11.95	.314 447	2.86	44
12	1.842 445	65.751 804	.015 208 7082	.542 757	35.687 255	.028 021 2082	11.21	.345 018	2.88	48
13	1.938 701	73.264 436	.013 649 1872	.515 809	37.790 485	.026 461 6872	10.59	.376 008	2.89	52
14	2.039 985	81.169 553	.012 319 8905	.490 200	39.789 291	.025 132 3905	10.06	.407 414	2.91	56
15	2.146 561	89.487 660	.011 174 7251	.465 862	41.688 857	.023 987 2251	9.60	.439 234	2.93	60
16	2.258 704	98.240 334	.010 179 1185	.442 732	43.494 111	.022 991 6185	9.20	.471 464	2.95	64
17	2.376 707	107.450 276	.009 306 6303	.420 750	45.209 734	.022 119 1303	8.85	.504 101	2.97	68
18	2.500 874	117.141 378	.008 536 6932	.399 860	46.840 178	.021 349 1932	8.54	.537 142	2.98	72
19	2.631 528	127.338 776	.007 853 0675	.380 007	48.389 670	.020 665 5675	8.27	.570 583	3.00	76
20	2.769 008	138.068 920	.007 242 7596	.361 140	49.862 232	.020 055 2596	8.03	.604 421	3.02	80
21	2.913 670	149.359 644	.006 695 2490	.343 210	51.261 681	.019 507 7490	7.81	.638 651	3.04	84
22	3.065 890	161.240 234	.006 201 9260	.326 170	52.591 648	.019 014 4260	7.61	.673 269	3.06	88
23	3.226 063	173.741 506	.005 755 6771	.309 975	53.855 583	.018 568 1771	7.43	.708 272	3.08	92
24	3.394 604	186.895 886	.005 350 5726	.294 585	55.056 764	.018 163 0726	7.27	.743 655	3.10	96
25	3.571 949	200.737 497	.004 981 6303	.279 959	56.198 307	.017 794 1303	7.12	.779 413	3.12	100
26	3.758 560	215.302 240	.004 644 6335	.266 059	57.283 173	.017 457 1335	6.99	.815 542	3.14	104
27	3.954 920	230.627 895	.004 335 9889	.252 850	58.314 176	.017 148 4889	6.86	.852 037	3.16	108
28	4.161 538	246.754 215	.004 052 6157	.240 296	59.293 990	.016 865 1157	6.75	.888 893	3.17	112
29	4.378 951	263.723 028	.003 791 8570	.228 365	60.225 157	.016 604 3570	6.65	.926 105	3.19	116
30	4.607 723	281.578 349	.003 551 4094	.217 027	61.110 091	.016 363 9094	6.55	.963 669	3.21	120
31	4.848 446	300.366 494	.003 329 2661	.206 252	61.951 090	.016 141 7661	6.46	1.001 579	3.23	124
32	5.101 745	320.136 195	.003 123 6705	.196 011	62.750 332	.015 936 1705	6.38	1.039 830	3.25	128
33	5.368 278	340.938 732	.002 933 0783	.186 279	63.509 893	.015 745 5783	6.30	1.078 416	3.27	132
34	5.648 735	362.828 065	.002 756 1264	.177 031	64.231 742	.015 568 6264	6.23	1.117 333	3.29	136
35	5.943 844	385.860 971	.002 591 6070	.168 241	64.917 752	.015 404 1070	6.17	1.156 575	3.30	140
36	6.254 370	410.097 194	.002 438 4463	.159 888	65.569 702	.015 250 9463	6.11	1.196 136	3.32	144
37	6.581 120	435.599 600	.002 295 6862	.151 950	66.189 282	.015 108 1862	6.05	1.236 012	3.34	148
38	6.924 940	462.434 338	.002 162 4692	.144 406	66.778 101	.014 974 9692	5.99	1.276 195	3.36	152
39	7.286 722	490.671 015	.002 038 0254	.137 236	67.337 685	.014 850 5254	5.95	1.316 682	3.38	156
40	7.667 406	520.382 871	.001 921 6620	.130 422	67.869 486	.014 734 1620	5.90	1.357 466	3.39	160
41	8.067 977	551.646 976	.001 812 7535	.123 947	68.374 883	.014 625 2535	5.86	1.398 542	3.41	164
42	8.489 475	584.544 424	.001 710 7340	.117 793	68.855 188	.014 523 2340	5.81	1.439 903	3.43	168
43	8.932 994	619.160 546	.001 615 0900	.111 945	69.311 645	.014 427 5900	5.78	1.481 545	3.45	172
44	9.399 685	655.585 133	.001 525 3549	.106 387	69.745 440	.014 337 8549	5.74	1.523 462	3.46	176
45	9.890 756	693.912 663	.001 441 1035	.101 105	70.157 697	.014 253 6035	5.71	1.565 649	3.48	180
46	10.407 483	734.242 555	.001 361 9478	.096 085	70.549 486	.014 174 4478	5.67	1.608 098	3.50	184
47	10.951 205	776.679 417	.001 287 5325	.091 314	70.921 822	.014 100 0325	5.65	1.650 806	3.51	188
48	11.523 333	821.333 325	.001 217 5325	.086 780	71.275 672	.014 030 0325	5.62	1.693 766	3.53	192
49	12.125 351	868.320 105	.001 151 6490	.082 472	71.611 954	.013 964 1490	5.59	1.736 973	3.54	196
50	12.758 821	917.761 634	.001 089 6075	.078 377	71.931 540	.013 902 1075	5.57	1.780 422	3.56	200

Effective Rate is 5.22 %

Annual Percentage Rate is 5.125%

QUARTERLY COMPOUND INTEREST AND ANNUITY

5.25 % Q

Amount Of 1	Amount Of 1 Per Period	Sinking Fund Payment	Present Worth Of 1	Present Worth of 1 Per Period	Periodic Payment To Amortize 1	Constant Annual Percent	Total Interest	Annual Add On Rate	
What a single $ 1 deposit grows to in the future. The deposit is made at the beginning of the first period.	What a series of $ 1 deposits grow to in the future. A deposit is made at the end of each period.	The amount to be deposited at the end of each period that grows to $ 1 in the future.	What $ 1 to be paid in the future is worth today. Value today of a single $ 1 payment tomorrow.	What $ 1 to be paid at the end of each period is worth today. Value today of a series of $ 1 payments tomorrow.	The mortgage payment to amortize a loan of $ 1. An annuity certain, payable at the end of each period, worth $ 1 today.	The annual payment, including interest and principal, to amortize completely a loan of $ 100.	The total interest paid over the term on a loan of $1. The loan is amortized by regular periodic payments.	The average annual interest rate on a loan that is completely amortized by regular periodic payments.	
$S = (1+i)^n$	$S\overline{n} = \dfrac{(1+i)^n - 1}{i}$	$\dfrac{1}{S\overline{n}} = \dfrac{i}{(1+i)^n - 1}$	$V^n = \dfrac{1}{(1+i)^n}$	$A\overline{n} = \dfrac{1-V^n}{i}$	$\dfrac{1}{A\overline{n}} = \dfrac{i}{1-V^n}$				

YEAR / **PERIODS**

Amount Of 1	Amount Of 1 Per Period	Sinking Fund Payment	Present Worth Of 1	Present Worth of 1 Per Period	Periodic Payment To Amortize 1	Constant Annual Percent	Total Interest	Annual Add On Rate	PERIODS
1.013 125	1.000 000	1.000 000 0000	.987 045	.987 045	1.013 125 0000	405.25	.013 125	5.25	1
1.026 422	2.013 125	.496 740 1428	.974 258	1.961 303	.509 865 1428	203.95	.019 730	3.95	2
1.039 894	3.039 547	.328 996 3645	.961 636	2.922 939	.342 121 3645	136.85	.026 364	3.52	3
1.053 543	4.079 441	.245 131 6052	.949 178	3.872 118	.258 256 6052	103.31	.033 026	3.30	4

YEAR	Amount Of 1	Amount Of 1 Per Period	Sinking Fund Payment	Present Worth Of 1	Present Worth of 1 Per Period	Periodic Payment To Amortize 1	Constant Annual Percent	Total Interest	Annual Add On Rate	PERIODS
1	1.053 543	4.079 441	.245 131 6052	.949 178	3.872 118	.258 256 6052	103.31	.033 026	3.30	4
2	1.109 952	8.377 307	.119 370 1057	.900 940	7.547 449	.132 495 1057	53.00	.059 961	3.00	8
3	1.169 382	12.905 291	.077 487 5950	.855 153	11.035 993	.090 612 5950	36.25	.087 351	2.91	12
4	1.231 994	17.675 717	.056 574 7927	.811 692	14.347 245	.069 699 7927	27.88	.115 197	2.88	16
5	1.297 958	22.701 563	.044 049 8306	.770 441	17.490 214	.057 174 8306	22.87	.143 497	2.87	20
6	1.367 454	27.996 506	.035 718 7423	.731 286	20.473 452	.048 843 7423	19.54	.172 250	2.87	24
7	1.440 671	33.574 955	.029 784 1051	.694 121	23.305 077	.042 909 1051	17.17	.201 455	2.88	28
8	1.517 809	39.452 089	.025 347 2000	.658 845	25.992 795	.038 472 2000	15.39	.231 110	2.89	32
9	1.599 076	45.643 901	.021 908 7322	.625 361	28.543 919	.035 033 7322	14.02	.261 214	2.90	36
10	1.684 695	52.167 238	.019 169 1190	.593 579	30.965 390	.032 294 1190	12.92	.291 765	2.92	40
11	1.774 898	59.039 853	.016 937 7116	.563 413	33.263 799	.030 062 7116	12.03	.322 759	2.93	44
12	1.869 931	66.280 445	.015 087 4062	.534 779	35.445 399	.028 212 4062	11.29	.354 195	2.95	48
13	1.970 052	73.908 718	.013 530 2035	.507 601	37.516 127	.026 655 2035	10.67	.386 071	2.97	52
14	2.075 534	81.945 430	.012 203 2431	.481 804	39.481 617	.025 328 2431	10.14	.418 382	2.99	56
15	2.186 663	90.412 448	.011 060 4239	.457 318	41.347 218	.024 185 4239	9.68	.451 125	3.01	60
16	2.303 743	99.332 813	.010 067 1668	.434 076	43.118 006	.023 192 1668	9.28	.484 299	3.03	64
17	2.427 092	108.730 798	.009 197 0262	.412 016	44.798 801	.022 322 0262	8.93	.517 898	3.05	68
18	2.557 045	118.631 976	.008 429 4305	.391 076	46.394 174	.021 554 4305	8.63	.551 919	3.07	72
19	2.693 956	129.063 290	.007 748 1366	.371 201	47.908 468	.020 873 1366	8.35	.586 358	3.09	76
20	2.838 197	140.053 124	.007 140 1478	.352 336	49.345 804	.020 265 1478	8.11	.621 212	3.11	80
21	2.990 162	151.631 383	.006 594 9408	.334 430	50.710 091	.019 719 9408	7.89	.656 475	3.13	84
22	3.150 263	163.829 573	.006 103 9041	.317 434	52.005 044	.019 228 9041	7.70	.692 144	3.15	88
23	3.318 937	176.680 887	.005 659 9218	.301 301	53.234 185	.018 784 9218	7.52	.728 213	3.17	92
24	3.496 641	190.220 294	.005 257 0626	.285 989	54.400 859	.018 382 0626	7.36	.764 678	3.19	96
25	3.683 861	204.484 637	.004 890 3429	.271 454	55.508 241	.018 015 3429	7.21	.801 534	3.21	100
26	3.881 105	219.512 732	.004 555 5444	.257 659	56.559 344	.017 680 5444	7.08	.838 777	3.23	104
27	4.088 909	235.345 470	.004 249 0726	.244 564	57.557 029	.017 374 0726	6.95	.876 400	3.25	108
28	4.307 840	252.025 936	.003 967 8456	.232 135	58.504 009	.017 092 8456	6.84	.914 399	3.27	112
29	4.538 494	269.599 518	.003 709 2054	.220 337	59.402 863	.016 834 2054	6.74	.952 768	3.29	116
30	4.781 497	288.114 037	.003 470 8479	.209 140	60.256 035	.016 595 8479	6.64	.991 502	3.31	120
31	5.037 511	307.619 872	.003 250 7653	.198 511	61.065 848	.016 375 7653	6.56	1.030 595	3.32	124
32	5.307 233	328.170 102	.003 047 2002	.188 422	61.834 505	.016 172 2002	6.47	1.070 042	3.34	128
33	5.591 396	349.820 646	.002 858 6077	.178 846	62.564 098	.015 983 6077	6.40	1.109 836	3.36	132
34	5.890 774	372.630 417	.002 683 6242	.169 757	63.256 612	.015 808 6242	6.33	1.149 973	3.38	136
35	6.206 182	396.661 485	.002 521 0413	.161 130	63.913 931	.015 646 0413	6.26	1.190 446	3.40	140
36	6.538 478	421.979 241	.002 369 7848	.152 941	64.537 844	.015 494 7848	6.20	1.231 249	3.42	144
37	6.888 565	448.652 576	.002 228 8962	.145 168	65.130 048	.015 353 8962	6.15	1.272 377	3.44	148
38	7.257 397	476.754 073	.002 097 5175	.137 790	65.692 156	.015 222 5175	6.09	1.313 823	3.46	152
39	7.645 978	506.360 199	.001 974 8788	.130 788	66.225 697	.015 099 8788	6.04	1.355 581	3.48	156
40	8.055 364	537.551 516	.001 860 2868	.124 141	66.732 123	.014 985 2868	6.00	1.397 646	3.49	160
41	8.486 669	570.412 899	.001 753 1160	.117 832	67.212 811	.014 878 1160	5.96	1.440 011	3.51	164
42	8.941 068	605.033 769	.001 652 8003	.111 843	67.669 070	.014 777 8003	5.92	1.482 670	3.53	168
43	9.419 797	641.508 332	.001 558 8262	.106 159	68.102 141	.014 683 8262	5.88	1.525 618	3.55	172
44	9.924 158	679.935 841	.001 470 7270	.100 764	68.513 203	.014 595 7270	5.84	1.568 848	3.57	176
45	10.455 524	720.420 860	.001 388 0775	.095 643	68.903 373	.014 513 0775	5.81	1.612 354	3.58	180
46	11.015 340	763.073 556	.001 310 4897	.090 782	69.273 715	.014 435 4897	5.78	1.656 130	3.60	184
47	11.605 131	808.009 991	.001 237 6085	.086 169	69.625 236	.014 362 6085	5.75	1.700 170	3.62	188
48	12.226 501	855.352 443	.001 169 1087	.081 790	69.958 891	.014 294 1087	5.72	1.744 469	3.63	192
49	12.881 140	905.229 735	.001 104 6919	.077 633	70.275 590	.014 229 6919	5.70	1.789 020	3.65	196
50	13.570 831	957.777 591	.001 044 0837	.073 687	70.576 194	.014 169 0837	5.67	1.833 817	3.67	200

Effective Rate is 5.35 %

Annual Percentage Rate is 5.25 %

	Amount Of 1	Amount Of 1 Per Period	Sinking Fund Payment	Present Worth Of 1	Present Worth of 1 Per Period	Periodic Payment To Amortize 1	Constant Annual Percent	Total Interest	Annual Add On Rate	
	What a single $ 1 deposit grows to in the future. The deposit is made at the beginning of the first period.	What a series of $ 1 deposits grow to in the future. A deposit is made at the end of each period.	The amount to be deposited at the end of each period that grows to $ 1 in the future.	What $ 1 to be paid in the future is worth today. Value today of a single $ 1 payment tomorrow.	What $ 1 to be paid at the end of each period is worth today. Value today of a series of $ 1 payments tomorrow.	The mortgage payment to amortize a loan of $ 1. An annuity certain, payable at the end of each period, worth $ 1 today.	The annual payment, including interest and principal, to amortize completely a loan of $ 100.	The total interest paid over the term on a loan of $1. The loan is amortized by regular periodic payments.	The average annual interest rate on a loan that is completely amortized by regular periodic payments.	
	$S = (1+i)^n$	$S\overline{n}| = \dfrac{(1+i)^n - 1}{i}$	$\dfrac{1}{S\overline{n}|} = \dfrac{i}{(1+i)^n - 1}$	$V^n = \dfrac{1}{(1+i)^n}$	$A\overline{n}| = \dfrac{1-V^n}{i}$	$\dfrac{1}{A\overline{n}|} = \dfrac{i}{1-V^n}$				

YEAR | | | | | | | | | **PERIODS** |

	Amount Of 1	Amount Of 1 Per Period	Sinking Fund Payment	Present Worth Of 1	Present Worth of 1 Per Period	Periodic Payment To Amortize 1	Constant Annual Percent	Total Interest	Annual Add On Rate	PERIODS
	1.013 438	1.000 000	1.000 000 0000	.986 741	.986 741	1.013 437 5000	405.38	.013 437	5.37	1
	1.027 056	2.013 437	.496 663 0452	.973 657	1.960 398	.510 100 5452	204.05	.020 201	4.04	2
	1.040 857	3.040 493	.328 894 0241	.960 747	2.921 145	.342 331 5241	136.94	.026 995	3.60	3
	1.054 843	4.081 350	.245 016 9859	.948 008	3.869 153	.258 454 4859	103.39	.033 818	3.38	4
1	1.054 843	4.081 350	.245 016 9859	.948 008	3.869 153	.258 454 4859	103.39	.033 818	3.38	4
2	1.112 694	8.386 533	.119 238 7787	.898 720	7.537 142	.132 676 2787	53.08	.061 410	3.07	8
3	1.173 718	12.927 827	.077 352 5209	.851 994	11.014 426	.090 790 0209	36.32	.089 480	2.98	12
4	1.238 088	17.718 179	.056 439 2081	.807 697	14.310 920	.069 876 7081	27.96	.118 027	2.95	16
5	1.305 989	22.771 249	.043 915 0256	.765 703	17.436 024	.057 352 5256	22.95	.147 051	2.94	20
6	1.377 613	28.101 446	.035 585 3577	.725 893	20.398 648	.049 022 8577	19.61	.176 549	2.94	24
7	1.453 166	33.723 967	.029 652 5021	.688 153	23.207 240	.043 090 0021	17.24	.206 520	2.95	28
8	1.532 862	39.654 845	.025 217 5997	.652 374	25.869 808	.038 655 0997	15.47	.236 963	2.96	32
9	1.616 929	45.910 990	.021 781 2770	.618 456	28.393 945	.035 218 7770	14.09	.267 876	2.98	36
10	1.705 606	52.510 243	.019 043 9035	.586 302	30.786 847	.032 481 4035	13.00	.299 256	2.99	40
11	1.799 147	59.471 419	.016 814 7997	.555 819	33.055 338	.030 252 2997	12.11	.331 101	3.01	44
12	1.897 818	66.814 368	.014 966 8407	.526 921	35.205 887	.028 404 3407	11.37	.363 408	3.03	48
13	2.001 900	74.560 027	.013 412 0123	.499 525	37.244 624	.026 849 5123	10.74	.396 175	3.05	52
14	2.111 691	82.730 482	.012 087 4431	.473 554	39.177 365	.025 524 9431	10.21	.429 397	3.07	56
15	2.227 503	91.349 031	.010 947 0236	.448 933	41.009 618	.024 384 5236	9.76	.463 071	3.09	60
16	2.349 666	100.440 248	.009 956 1681	.425 592	42.746 610	.023 393 6681	9.36	.497 195	3.11	64
17	2.478 529	110.030 056	.009 088 4258	.403 465	44.393 292	.022 525 9258	9.02	.531 763	3.13	68
18	2.614 459	120.145 799	.008 323 2207	.382 488	45.954 360	.021 760 7207	8.71	.566 772	3.15	72
19	2.757 844	130.816 322	.007 644 3061	.362 602	47.434 266	.021 081 8061	8.44	.602 217	3.17	76
20	2.909 093	142.072 049	.007 038 6822	.343 750	48.837 229	.020 476 1822	8.20	.638 095	3.19	80
21	3.068 637	153.945 075	.006 495 8233	.325 878	50.167 249	.019 933 3233	7.98	.674 399	3.21	84
22	3.236 931	166.469 256	.006 007 1152	.308 935	51.428 120	.019 444 6152	7.78	.711 126	3.23	88
23	3.414 454	179.680 301	.005 565 4404	.292 873	52.623 435	.019 002 9404	7.61	.748 271	3.25	92
24	3.601 713	193.615 882	.005 164 8655	.277 646	53.756 604	.018 602 3655	7.45	.785 827	3.27	96
25	3.799 243	208.315 734	.004 800 4055	.263 210	54.830 858	.018 237 9055	7.30	.823 791	3.30	100
26	4.007 605	223.821 772	.004 467 8406	.249 526	55.849 259	.017 905 3406	7.17	.862 155	3.32	104
27	4.227 395	240.178 210	.004 163 5750	.236 552	56.814 711	.017 601 0750	7.05	.900 916	3.34	108
28	4.459 238	257.431 686	.003 884 5257	.224 254	57.729 969	.017 322 0257	6.93	.940 067	3.36	112
29	4.703 797	275.631 397	.003 628 0337	.212 594	58.597 640	.017 065 5337	6.83	.979 602	3.38	116
30	4.961 768	294.829 237	.003 391 7939	.201 541	59.420 200	.016 829 2939	6.74	1.019 515	3.40	120
31	5.233 887	315.079 946	.003 173 7977	.191 063	60.199 993	.016 611 2977	6.65	1.059 801	3.42	124
32	5.520 930	336.441 269	.002 972 2870	.181 129	60.939 243	.016 409 7870	6.57	1.100 453	3.44	128
33	5.823 715	358.974 113	.002 785 7162	.171 712	61.640 059	.016 223 2162	6.49	1.141 465	3.46	132
34	6.143 105	382.742 729	.002 612 7211	.162 784	62.304 438	.016 050 2211	6.43	1.182 830	3.48	136
35	6.480 013	407.814 890	.002 452 0929	.154 321	62.934 274	.015 889 5929	6.36	1.224 543	3.50	140
36	6.835 397	434.262 088	.002 302 7569	.146 297	63.531 365	.015 740 2569	6.30	1.266 597	3.52	144
37	7.210 271	462.159 732	.002 163 7541	.138 691	64.097 411	.015 601 2541	6.25	1.308 986	3.54	148
38	7.605 705	491.587 371	.002 034 2264	.131 480	64.634 028	.015 471 7264	6.19	1.351 702	3.56	152
39	8.022 826	522.628 914	.001 913 4035	.124 644	65.142 745	.015 350 9035	6.15	1.394 741	3.58	156
40	8.462 823	555.372 873	.001 800 5921	.118 164	65.625 014	.015 238 0921	6.10	1.438 095	3.60	160
41	8.926 951	589.912 613	.001 695 1663	.112 020	66.082 208	.015 132 6663	6.06	1.481 757	3.61	164
42	9.416 533	626.346 620	.001 596 5601	.106 196	66.515 632	.015 034 0601	6.02	1.525 722	3.63	168
43	9.932 965	664.778 783	.001 504 2598	.100 675	66.926 521	.014 941 7598	5.98	1.569 983	3.65	172
44	10.477 720	705.318 686	.001 417 7988	.095 441	67.316 047	.014 855 2988	5.95	1.614 533	3.67	176
45	11.052 351	748.081 925	.001 336 7520	.090 478	67.685 322	.014 774 2520	5.91	1.659 365	3.69	180
46	11.658 496	793.190 434	.001 260 7313	.085 774	68.035 397	.014 698 2313	5.88	1.704 475	3.71	184
47	12.297 885	840.772 835	.001 189 3819	.081 315	68.367 271	.014 626 8819	5.86	1.749 854	3.72	188
48	12.972 340	890.964 804	.001 122 3788	.077 087	68.681 890	.014 559 8788	5.83	1.795 497	3.74	192
49	13.683 783	943.909 458	.001 059 4236	.073 079	68.980 152	.014 496 9236	5.80	1.841 397	3.76	196
50	14.434 245	999.757 763	.001 000 2423	.069 280	69.262 907	.014 437 7423	5.78	1.887 548	3.78	200

QUARTERLY COMPOUND INTEREST AND ANNUITY

5.50 % Q

Amount Of 1	Amount Of 1 Per Period	Sinking Fund Payment	Present Worth Of 1	Present Worth of 1 Per Period	Periodic Payment To Amortize 1	Constant Annual Percent	Total Interest	Annual Add On Rate
What a single $ 1 deposit grows to in the future. The deposit is made at the beginning of the first period.	What a series of $ 1 deposits grow to in the future. A deposit is made at the end of each period.	The amount to be deposited at the end of each period that grows to $ 1 in the future.	What $ 1 to be paid in the future is worth today. Value today of a single $ 1 payment tomorrow.	What $ 1 to be paid at the end of each period is worth today. Value today of a series of $ 1 payments tomorrow.	The mortgage payment to amortize a loan of $ 1. An annuity certain, payable at the end of each period, worth $ 1 today.	The annual payment, including interest and principal, to amortize completely a loan of $ 100.	The total interest paid over the term on a loan of $1. The loan is amortized by regular periodic payments.	The average annual interest rate on a loan that is completely amortized by regular periodic payments.
$S = (1+i)^n$	$S\overline{n} = \dfrac{(1+i)^n - 1}{i}$	$\dfrac{1}{S\overline{n}} = \dfrac{i}{(1+i)^n - 1}$	$V^n = \dfrac{1}{(1+i)^n}$	$A\overline{n} = \dfrac{1-V^n}{i}$	$\dfrac{1}{A\overline{n}} = \dfrac{i}{1-V^n}$			

YEAR / **PERIODS**

Amount Of 1	Amount Of 1 Per Period	Sinking Fund Payment	Present Worth Of 1	Present Worth of 1 Per Period	Periodic Payment To Amortize 1	Constant Annual Percent	Total Interest	Annual Add On Rate	PERIODS
1.013 750	1.000 000	1.000 000 0000	.986 436	.986 436	1.013 750 0000	405.50	.013 750	5.50	1
1.027 689	2.013 750	.496 585 9714	.973 057	1.959 493	.510 335 9714	204.14	.020 672	4.13	2
1.041 820	3.041 439	.328 791 7264	.959 859	2.919 352	.342 541 7264	137.02	.027 625	3.68	3
1.056 145	4.083 259	.244 902 4264	.946 840	3.866 192	.258 652 4264	103.47	.034 610	3.46	4

YEAR	Amount Of 1	Amount Of 1 Per Period	Sinking Fund Payment	Present Worth Of 1	Present Worth of 1 Per Period	Periodic Payment To Amortize 1	Constant Annual Percent	Total Interest	Annual Add On Rate	PERIODS
1	1.056 145	4.083 259	.244 902 4264	.946 840	3.866 192	.258 652 4264	103.47	.034 610	3.46	4
2	1.115 442	8.395 771	.119 107 5771	.896 506	7.526 857	.132 857 5771	53.15	.062 861	3.14	8
3	1.178 068	12.950 409	.077 217 6365	.848 847	10.992 921	.090 967 6365	36.39	.091 612	3.05	12
4	1.244 211	17.760 766	.056 303 8765	.803 722	14.274 728	.070 053 8765	28.03	.120 862	3.02	16
5	1.314 067	22.841 200	.043 780 5367	.760 996	17.382 073	.057 530 5367	23.02	.150 611	3.01	20
6	1.387 845	28.206 874	.035 452 3513	.720 542	20.324 232	.049 202 3513	19.69	.180 856	3.01	24
7	1.465 765	33.873 802	.029 521 3391	.682 238	23.109 985	.043 271 3391	17.31	.211 597	3.02	28
8	1.548 060	39.858 899	.025 088 5002	.645 970	25.747 647	.038 838 5002	15.54	.242 832	3.04	32
9	1.634 975	46.180 028	.021 654 3826	.611 630	28.245 091	.035 404 3826	14.17	.274 558	3.05	36
10	1.726 771	52.856 056	.018 919 3079	.579 116	30.609 770	.032 669 3079	13.07	.306 772	3.07	40
11	1.823 720	59.906 908	.016 692 5657	.548 330	32.848 742	.030 442 5657	12.18	.339 473	3.09	44
12	1.926 112	67.353 629	.014 847 0100	.519 181	34.968 691	.028 597 0100	11.44	.372 656	3.11	48
13	2.034 254	75.218 444	.013 294 6116	.491 581	36.975 942	.027 044 6116	10.82	.406 320	3.13	52
14	2.148 466	83.524 828	.011 972 4879	.465 448	38.876 488	.025 722 4879	10.29	.440 459	3.15	56
15	2.269 092	92.297 573	.010 834 5211	.440 705	40.676 001	.024 584 5211	9.84	.475 071	3.17	60
16	2.396 489	101.562 861	.009 846 1188	.417 277	42.379 851	.023 596 1188	9.44	.510 152	3.19	64
17	2.531 040	111.348 348	.008 980 8248	.395 095	43.993 124	.022 730 8248	9.10	.545 696	3.21	68
18	2.673 145	121.683 238	.008 218 0587	.374 091	45.520 636	.021 968 0587	8.79	.581 700	3.23	72
19	2.823 228	132.598 379	.007 541 5703	.354 205	46.966 944	.021 291 5703	8.52	.618 159	3.25	76
20	2.981 737	144.126 349	.006 938 3566	.335 375	48.336 367	.020 688 3566	8.28	.655 069	3.28	80
21	3.149 146	156.301 554	.006 397 8890	.317 546	49.632 991	.020 147 8890	8.06	.692 423	3.30	84
22	3.325 955	169.160 334	.005 911 5514	.300 666	50.860 687	.019 661 5514	7.87	.730 217	3.32	88
23	3.512 690	182.741 067	.005 472 2237	.284 682	52.023 117	.019 222 2237	7.69	.768 445	3.34	92
24	3.709 909	197.084 288	.005 073 9712	.269 548	53.123 753	.018 823 9712	7.53	.807 101	3.36	96
25	3.918 201	212.232 807	.004 711 8069	.255 219	54.165 879	.018 461 8069	7.39	.846 181	3.38	100
26	4.138 188	228.231 836	.004 381 5097	.241 652	55.152 605	.018 131 5097	7.26	.885 677	3.41	104
27	4.370 526	245.129 128	.004 079 4825	.228 805	56.086 877	.017 829 4825	7.14	.925 584	3.43	108
28	4.615 908	262.975 115	.003 802 6412	.216 642	56.971 483	.017 552 6412	7.03	.965 896	3.45	112
29	4.875 067	281.823 062	.003 548 3257	.205 125	57.809 063	.017 298 3257	6.92	1.006 606	3.47	116
30	5.148 777	301.729 222	.003 314 2299	.194 221	58.602 117	.017 064 2299	6.83	1.047 708	3.49	120
31	5.437 854	322.753 011	.003 098 3444	.183 896	59.353 013	.016 848 3444	6.74	1.089 195	3.51	124
32	5.743 161	344.957 176	.002 898 9106	.174 120	60.063 990	.016 648 9106	6.66	1.131 061	3.53	128
33	6.065 610	368.407 990	.002 714 3820	.164 864	60.737 172	.016 464 3820	6.59	1.173 298	3.56	132
34	6.406 162	393.175 445	.002 543 3938	.156 100	61.374 568	.016 293 3938	6.52	1.215 902	3.58	136
35	6.765 835	419.333 464	.002 384 7369	.147 801	61.978 079	.016 134 7369	6.46	1.258 863	3.60	140
36	7.145 702	446.960 120	.002 237 3361	.139 944	62.549 508	.015 987 3361	6.40	1.302 176	3.62	144
37	7.546 896	476.137 870	.002 100 2320	.132 505	63.090 559	.015 850 2320	6.35	1.345 834	3.64	148
38	7.970 615	506.953 798	.001 972 5663	.125 461	63.602 848	.015 722 5663	6.29	1.389 830	3.66	152
39	8.418 123	539.499 881	.001 853 5685	.118 791	64.087 904	.015 603 5685	6.25	1.434 157	3.68	156
40	8.890 757	573.873 258	.001 742 5450	.112 476	64.547 174	.015 492 5450	6.20	1.478 807	3.70	160
41	9.389 927	610.176 522	.001 638 8700	.106 497	64.982 029	.015 388 8700	6.16	1.523 775	3.72	164
42	9.917 123	648.518 025	.001 541 9772	.100 836	65.393 767	.015 291 9772	6.12	1.569 052	3.74	168
43	10.473 918	689.012 205	.001 451 3531	.095 475	65.783 618	.015 201 3531	6.09	1.614 633	3.75	172
44	11.061 974	731.779 922	.001 366 5311	.090 400	66.152 743	.015 116 5311	6.05	1.660 509	3.77	176
45	11.683 046	776.948 825	.001 287 0861	.085 594	66.502 246	.015 037 0861	6.02	1.706 675	3.79	180
46	12.338 989	824.653 727	.001 212 6302	.081 044	66.833 170	.014 962 6302	5.99	1.753 124	3.81	184
47	13.031 759	875.037 012	.001 142 8088	.076 736	67.146 501	.014 892 8088	5.96	1.799 848	3.83	188
48	13.763 425	928.249 057	.001 077 2971	.072 656	67.443 176	.014 827 2971	5.94	1.846 841	3.85	192
49	14.536 169	984.448 682	.001 015 7970	.068 794	67.724 079	.014 765 7970	5.91	1.894 096	3.87	196
50	15.352 300	1043.803 625	.000 958 0346	.065 137	67.990 049	.014 708 0346	5.89	1.941 607	3.88	200

Effective Rate is 5.61 %

Annual Percentage Rate is 5.50 %

Amount Of 1	Amount Of 1 Per Period	Sinking Fund Payment	Present Worth Of 1	Present Worth of 1 Per Period	Periodic Payment To Amortize 1	Constant Annual Percent	Total Interest	Annual Add On Rate
What a single $ 1 deposit grows to in the future. The deposit is made at the beginning of the first period.	What a series of $ 1 deposits grow to in the future. A deposit is made at the end of each period.	The amount to be deposited at the end of each period that grows to $ 1 in the future.	What $ 1 to be paid in the future is worth today. Value today of a single $ 1 payment tomorrow.	What $ 1 to be paid at the end of each period is worth today. Value today of a series of $ 1 payments tomorrow.	The mortgage payment to amortize a loan of $ 1. An annuity certain, payable at the end of each period, worth $ 1 today.	The annual payment, including interest and principal, to amortize completely a loan of $ 100.	The total interest paid over the term on a loan of $1. The loan is amortized by regular periodic payments.	The average annual interest rate on a loan that is completely amortized by regular periodic payments.
$S = (1+i)^n$	$S\overline{n} = \dfrac{(1+i)^n - 1}{i}$	$\dfrac{1}{S\overline{n}} = \dfrac{i}{(1+i)^n - 1}$	$V^n = \dfrac{1}{(1+i)^n}$	$A\overline{n} = \dfrac{1-V^n}{i}$	$\dfrac{1}{A\overline{n}} = \dfrac{i}{1-V^n}$			

YEAR   **PERIODS**

	1.014 063	1.000 000	1.000 000 0000	.986 133	.986 133	1.014 062 5000	405.63	.014 062	5.62	1
	1.028 323	2.014 063	.496 508 9216	.972 457	1.958 590	.510 571 4216	204.23	.021 143	4.23	2
	1.042 784	3.042 385	.328 689 4711	.958 972	2.917 562	.342 751 9711	137.11	.028 256	3.77	3
	1.057 448	4.085 169	.244 787 9267	.945 673	3.863 235	.258 850 4267	103.55	.035 402	3.54	4

YEAR										PERIODS
1	1.057 448	4.085 169	.244 787 9267	.945 673	3.863 235	.258 850 4267	103.55	.035 402	3.54	4
2	1.118 196	8.405 021	.118 976 5010	.894 298	7.516 593	.133 039 0010	53.22	.064 312	3.22	8
3	1.182 433	12.973 039	.077 082 9416	.845 714	10.971 476	.091 145 4416	36.46	.093 745	3.12	12
4	1.250 361	17.803 479	.056 168 7979	.799 769	14.238 666	.070 231 2979	28.10	.123 701	3.09	16
5	1.322 192	22.911 416	.043 646 3635	.756 320	17.328 361	.057 708 8635	23.09	.154 177	3.08	20
6	1.398 149	28.312 793	.035 319 7230	.715 232	20.250 202	.049 382 2230	19.76	.185 173	3.09	24
7	1.478 469	34.024 466	.029 390 6155	.676 375	23.013 310	.043 453 1155	17.39	.216 687	3.10	28
8	1.563 404	40.064 262	.024 959 9008	.639 630	25.626 306	.039 022 4008	15.61	.248 717	3.11	32
9	1.653 218	46.451 030	.021 528 0481	.604 881	28.097 348	.035 590 5481	14.24	.281 260	3.13	36
10	1.748 191	53.204 703	.018 795 3311	.572 020	30.434 145	.032 857 8311	13.15	.314 313	3.14	40
11	1.848 621	60.346 359	.016 571 0082	.540 944	32.643 992	.030 633 5082	12.26	.347 874	3.16	44
12	1.954 820	67.898 286	.014 727 9123	.511 556	34.733 785	.028 790 4123	11.52	.381 940	3.18	48
13	2.067 120	75.884 054	.013 177 9991	.483 765	36.710 047	.027 240 4991	10.90	.416 506	3.20	52
14	2.185 871	84.328 586	.011 858 3750	.457 484	38.578 945	.025 920 8750	10.37	.451 569	3.23	56
15	2.311 444	93.258 237	.010 722 9134	.432 630	40.346 311	.024 785 4134	9.92	.487 125	3.25	60
16	2.444 231	102.700 876	.009 737 0153	.409 127	42.017 662	.023 799 5153	9.52	.523 169	3.27	64
17	2.584 646	112.685 973	.008 874 2190	.386 900	43.598 215	.022 936 7190	9.18	.559 697	3.29	68
18	2.733 128	123.244 690	.008 113 9399	.365 881	45.092 901	.022 176 4399	8.88	.596 704	3.32	72
19	2.890 140	134.409 981	.007 439 9237	.346 004	46.506 385	.021 502 4237	8.61	.634 184	3.34	76
20	3.056 172	146.216 692	.006 839 1644	.327 207	47.843 080	.020 901 6644	8.37	.672 133	3.36	80
21	3.231 742	158.701 671	.006 301 1309	.309 431	49.107 156	.020 363 6309	8.15	.710 545	3.38	84
22	3.417 398	171.903 884	.005 817 2042	.292 620	50.302 559	.019 879 7042	7.96	.749 414	3.41	88
23	3.613 720	185.864 533	.005 380 2626	.276 723	51.433 020	.019 442 7626	7.78	.788 734	3.43	92
24	3.821 320	200.627 189	.004 984 3693	.261 690	52.502 067	.019 046 8693	7.62	.828 499	3.45	96
25	4.040 846	216.237 926	.004 624 5357	.247 473	53.513 035	.018 687 0357	7.48	.868 704	3.47	100
26	4.272 983	232.745 463	.004 296 5392	.234 029	54.469 081	.018 359 0392	7.35	.909 340	3.50	104
27	4.518 456	250.201 320	.003 996 7815	.221 315	55.373 189	.018 059 2815	7.23	.950 402	3.52	108
28	4.778 031	268.659 976	.003 722 1771	.209 291	56.228 179	.017 784 6771	7.12	.991 884	3.54	112
29	5.052 518	288.179 039	.003 470 0650	.197 921	57.036 720	.017 532 5650	7.02	1.033 778	3.56	116
30	5.342 773	308.819 427	.003 238 1383	.187 169	57.801 336	.017 300 6383	6.93	1.076 077	3.59	120
31	5.649 703	330.645 557	.003 024 3866	.177 000	58.524 412	.017 086 8866	6.84	1.118 774	3.61	124
32	5.974 266	353.725 548	.002 827 0505	.167 385	59.208 207	.016 889 5505	6.76	1.161 862	3.63	128
33	6.317 473	378.131 431	.002 644 5831	.158 291	59.854 853	.016 707 0831	6.69	1.205 335	3.65	132
34	6.680 397	403.939 376	.002 475 6190	.149 692	60.466 369	.016 538 1190	6.62	1.249 184	3.67	136
35	7.064 171	431.229 927	.002 318 9485	.141 559	61.044 663	.016 381 4485	6.56	1.293 403	3.70	140
36	7.469 991	460.088 257	.002 173 4960	.133 869	61.591 540	.016 235 9960	6.50	1.337 983	3.72	144
37	7.899 125	490.604 432	.002 038 3020	.126 596	62.108 707	.016 100 8020	6.45	1.382 919	3.74	148
38	8.352 911	522.873 690	.001 912 5078	.119 719	62.597 779	.015 975 0078	6.40	1.428 201	3.76	152
39	8.832 767	556.996 743	.001 795 3426	.113 215	63.060 280	.015 857 8426	6.35	1.473 823	3.78	156
40	9.340 189	593.080 086	.001 686 1129	.107 064	63.497 656	.015 748 6129	6.30	1.519 778	3.80	160
41	9.876 761	631.236 333	.001 584 1927	.101 248	63.911 270	.015 646 6927	6.26	1.566 058	3.82	164
42	10.444 158	671.584 569	.001 489 0157	.095 747	64.302 414	.015 551 5157	6.23	1.612 655	3.84	168
43	11.044 151	714.250 717	.001 400 0686	.090 546	64.672 308	.015 462 5686	6.19	1.659 562	3.86	172
44	11.678 612	759.367 937	.001 316 8847	.085 627	65.022 107	.015 379 3847	6.16	1.706 772	3.88	176
45	12.349 521	807.077 037	.001 239 0391	.080 975	65.352 903	.015 301 5391	6.13	1.754 277	3.90	180
46	13.058 972	857.526 914	.001 166 1442	.076 576	65.665 728	.015 228 6442	6.10	1.802 071	3.92	184
47	13.809 180	910.875 020	.001 097 8455	.072 416	65.961 558	.015 160 3455	6.07	1.850 145	3.94	188
48	14.602 485	967.287 851	.001 033 8184	.068 481	66.241 316	.015 096 3184	6.04	1.898 493	3.96	192
49	15.441 364	1026.941 469	.000 973 7653	.064 761	66.505 876	.015 036 2653	6.02	1.947 108	3.97	196
50	16.328 435	1090.022 049	.000 917 4126	.061 243	66.756 064	.014 979 9126	6.00	1.995 983	3.99	200

	Amount Of 1	Amount Of 1 Per Period	Sinking Fund Payment	Present Worth Of 1	Present Worth of 1 Per Period	Periodic Payment To Amortize 1	Constant Annual Percent	Total Interest	Annual Add On Rate	
	What a single $ 1 deposit grows to in the future. The deposit is made at the beginning of the first period.	What a series of $ 1 deposits grow to in the future. A deposit is made at the end of each period.	The amount to be deposited at the end of each period that grows to $ 1 in the future.	What $ 1 to be paid in the future is worth today. Value today of a single $ 1 payment tomorrow.	What $ 1 to be paid at the end of each period is worth today. Value today of a series of $ 1 payments tomorrow.	The mortgage payment to amortize a loan of $ 1. An annuity certain, payable at the end of each period, worth $ 1 today.	The annual payment, including interest and principal, to amortize completely a loan of $ 100.	The total interest paid over the term on a loan of $1. The loan is amortized by regular periodic payments.	The average annual interest rate on a loan that is completely amortized by regular periodic payments.	
	$S = (1+i)^n$	$S\overline{n}| = \dfrac{(1+i)^n - 1}{i}$	$\dfrac{1}{S\overline{n}|} = \dfrac{i}{(1+i)^n - 1}$	$V^n = \dfrac{1}{(1+i)^n}$	$A\overline{n}| = \dfrac{1 - V^n}{i}$	$\dfrac{1}{A\overline{n}|} = \dfrac{i}{1 - V^n}$				

YEAR										PERIODS
	1.014 375	1.000 000	1.000 000 0000	.985 829	.985 829	1.014 375 0000	405.75	.014 375	5.75	1
	1.028 957	2.014 375	.496 431 8957	.971 858	1.957 687	.510 806 8957	204.33	.021 614	4.32	2
	1.043 748	3.043 332	.328 587 2583	.958 086	2.915 773	.342 962 2583	137.19	.028 887	3.85	3
	1.058 752	4.087 080	.244 673 4868	.944 508	3.860 281	.259 048 4868	103.62	.036 194	3.62	4
1	1.058 752	4.087 080	.244 673 4868	.944 508	3.860 281	.259 048 4868	103.62	.036 194	3.62	4
2	1.120 955	8.414 282	.118 845 5503	.892 096	7.506 349	.133 220 5503	53.29	.065 764	3.29	8
3	1.186 813	12.995 716	.076 948 4361	.842 592	10.950 092	.091 323 4361	36.53	.095 881	3.20	12
4	1.256 541	17.846 317	.056 033 9720	.795 836	14.202 735	.070 408 9720	28.17	.126 544	3.16	16
5	1.330 365	22.981 899	.043 512 5058	.751 674	17.274 885	.057 887 5058	23.16	.157 750	3.16	20
6	1.408 526	28.419 205	.035 187 4722	.709 962	20.176 556	.049 562 4722	19.83	.189 499	3.16	24
7	1.491 279	34.175 964	.029 260 3309	.670 565	22.917 209	.043 635 3309	17.46	.221 789	3.17	28
8	1.578 895	40.270 941	.024 831 8010	.633 354	25.505 779	.039 206 8010	15.69	.254 618	3.18	32
9	1.671 658	46.724 010	.021 402 2727	.598 209	27.950 705	.035 777 2727	14.32	.287 982	3.20	36
10	1.769 870	53.556 208	.018 671 9718	.565 013	30.259 959	.033 046 9718	13.22	.321 879	3.22	40
11	1.873 854	60.789 809	.016 450 1257	.533 660	32.441 068	.030 825 1257	12.34	.356 306	3.24	44
12	1.983 946	68.448 397	.014 609 5459	.504 046	34.501 144	.028 984 5459	11.60	.391 258	3.26	48
13	2.100 506	76.556 941	.013 062 1728	.476 076	36.446 904	.027 437 1728	10.98	.426 733	3.28	52
14	2.223 914	85.141 877	.011 745 1017	.449 658	38.284 690	.026 120 1017	10.45	.462 726	3.31	56
15	2.354 573	94.231 192	.010 612 1973	.424 705	40.020 495	.024 987 1973	10.00	.499 232	3.33	60
16	2.492 909	103.854 521	.009 628 8539	.401 138	41.659 977	.024 003 8539	9.61	.536 247	3.35	64
17	2.639 372	114.043 237	.008 768 6042	.378 878	43.208 482	.023 143 6042	9.26	.573 765	3.38	68
18	2.794 439	124.830 558	.008 010 8590	.357 854	44.671 058	.022 385 8590	8.96	.611 782	3.40	72
19	2.958 618	136.251 654	.007 339 3605	.337 996	46.052 473	.021 714 3605	8.69	.650 291	3.42	76
20	3.132 442	148.343 759	.006 741 0992	.319 240	47.357 231	.021 116 0992	8.45	.689 288	3.45	80
21	3.316 478	161.146 296	.006 205 5413	.301 525	48.589 587	.020 580 5413	8.24	.728 765	3.47	84
22	3.511 327	174.701 006	.005 724 0655	.284 793	49.753 557	.020 099 0655	8.04	.768 718	3.49	88
23	3.717 624	189.052 078	.005 289 5478	.268 989	50.852 937	.019 664 5478	7.87	.809 138	3.52	92
24	3.936 041	204.246 302	.004 896 0495	.254 062	51.891 310	.019 271 0495	7.71	.850 021	3.54	96
25	4.167 290	220.333 213	.004 538 5804	.239 964	52.872 062	.018 913 5804	7.57	.891 358	3.57	100
26	4.412 126	237.365 258	.004 212 9164	.226 648	53.798 391	.018 587 9164	7.44	.933 143	3.59	104
27	4.671 346	255.397 966	.003 915 4580	.214 071	54.673 317	.018 290 4580	7.32	.975 369	3.61	108
28	4.945 796	274.490 128	.003 643 1183	.202 192	55.499 691	.018 018 1183	7.21	1.018 029	3.64	112
29	5.236 370	294.703 988	.003 393 2354	.190 972	56.280 209	.017 768 2354	7.11	1.061 115	3.66	116
30	5.544 016	316.105 448	.003 163 5013	.180 375	57.017 415	.017 538 5013	7.02	1.104 620	3.68	120
31	5.869 737	338.764 282	.002 951 9051	.170 365	57.713 711	.017 326 9051	6.94	1.148 536	3.70	124
32	6.214 594	362.754 362	.002 756 6864	.160 912	58.371 370	.017 131 6864	6.86	1.192 856	3.73	128
33	6.579 712	388.153 901	.002 576 2977	.151 982	58.992 534	.016 951 2977	6.79	1.237 571	3.75	132
34	6.966 282	415.045 709	.002 409 3732	.143 549	59.579 228	.016 784 3732	6.72	1.282 675	3.77	136
35	7.375 563	443.517 458	.002 254 7027	.135 583	60.133 366	.016 629 7027	6.66	1.328 158	3.79	140
36	7.808 891	473.661 972	.002 111 2102	.128 059	60.656 754	.016 486 2102	6.60	1.374 014	3.82	144
37	8.267 677	505.577 530	.001 977 9360	.120 953	61.151 098	.016 352 9360	6.55	1.420 235	3.84	148
38	8.753 418	539.368 184	.001 854 0211	.114 241	61.618 011	.016 229 0211	6.50	1.466 811	3.86	152
39	9.267 696	575.144 098	.001 738 6947	.107 902	62.059 014	.016 113 6947	6.45	1.513 736	3.88	156
40	9.812 190	613.021 910	.001 631 2631	.101 914	62.475 544	.016 006 2631	6.41	1.561 002	3.90	160
41	10.388 673	653.125 111	.001 531 1002	.096 259	62.868 961	.015 906 1002	6.37	1.608 600	3.92	164
42	10.999 026	695.584 446	.001 437 6400	.090 917	63.240 547	.015 812 6400	6.33	1.656 524	3.94	168
43	11.645 239	740.538 341	.001 350 3690	.085 872	63.591 513	.015 725 3690	6.30	1.704 763	3.96	172
44	12.329 417	788.133 358	.001 268 8208	.081 107	63.923 003	.015 643 8208	6.26	1.753 312	3.98	176
45	13.053 792	838.524 666	.001 192 5708	.076 606	64.236 098	.015 567 5708	6.23	1.802 163	4.00	180
46	13.820 725	891.876 552	.001 121 2314	.072 355	64.531 819	.015 496 2314	6.20	1.851 307	4.02	184
47	14.632 717	948.362 956	.001 054 4486	.068 340	64.811 130	.015 429 4486	6.18	1.900 736	4.04	188
48	15.492 416	1008.168 036	.000 991 8981	.064 548	65.074 942	.015 366 8981	6.15	1.950 444	4.06	192
49	16.402 622	1071.486 771	.000 933 2826	.060 966	65.324 114	.015 308 2826	6.13	2.000 423	4.08	196
50	17.366 305	1138.525 593	.000 878 3290	.057 583	65.559 459	.015 253 3290	6.11	2.050 666	4.10	200

Effective Rate is 5.88 %

Annual Percentage Rate is 5.75 %

Amount Of 1	Amount Of 1 Per Period	Sinking Fund Payment	Present Worth Of 1	Present Worth of 1 Per Period	Periodic Payment To Amortize 1	Constant Annual Percent	Total Interest	Annual Add On Rate
What a single $ 1 deposit grows to in the future. The deposit is made at the beginning of the first period.	What a series of $ 1 deposits grow to in the future. A deposit is made at the end of each period.	The amount to be deposited at the end of each period that grows to $ 1 in the future.	What $ 1 to be paid in the future is worth today. Value today of a single $ 1 payment tomorrow.	What $ 1 to be paid at the end of each period is worth today. Value today of a series of $ 1 payments tomorrow.	The mortgage payment to amortize a loan of $ 1. An annuity certain, payable at the end of each period, worth $ 1 today.	The annual payment, including interest and principal, to amortize completely a loan of $ 100.	The total interest paid over the term on a loan of $1. The loan is amortized by regular periodic payments.	The average annual interest rate on a loan that is completely amortized by regular periodic payments.
$S = (1+i)^n$	$S\overline{n} = \dfrac{(1+i)^n - 1}{i}$	$\dfrac{1}{S\overline{n}} = \dfrac{i}{(1+i)^n - 1}$	$V^n = \dfrac{1}{(1+i)^n}$	$A\overline{n} = \dfrac{1-V^n}{i}$	$\dfrac{1}{A\overline{n}} = \dfrac{i}{1-V^n}$			

YEAR									PERIODS
	1.014 687	1.000 000	1.000 000 0000	.985 525	.985 525	1.014 687 5000	405.88	.014 688	5.88	1
	1.029 591	2.014 687	.496 354 8937	.971 260	1.956 785	.511 042 3937	204.42	.022 085	4.42	2
	1.044 713	3.044 278	.328 485 0880	.957 201	2.913 986	.343 172 5880	137.27	.029 518	3.94	3
	1.060 057	4.088 991	.244 559 1065	.943 345	3.857 331	.259 246 6065	103.70	.036 986	3.70	4

YEAR	Amount Of 1	Amount Of 1 Per Period	Sinking Fund Payment	Present Worth Of 1	Present Worth of 1 Per Period	Periodic Payment To Amortize 1	Constant Annual Percent	Total Interest	Annual Add On Rate	PERIODS
1	1.060 057	4.088 991	.244 559 1065	.943 345	3.857 331	.259 246 6065	103.70	.036 986	3.70	4
2	1.123 721	8.423 555	.118 714 7248	.889 901	7.496 127	.133 402 2248	53.37	.067 218	3.36	8
3	1.191 208	13.018 440	.076 814 1199	.839 484	10.928 768	.091 501 6199	36.61	.098 019	3.27	12
4	1.262 749	17.889 280	.055 899 3987	.791 923	14.166 935	.070 586 8987	28.24	.129 390	3.23	16
5	1.338 586	23.052 649	.043 378 9633	.747 057	17.221 645	.058 066 4633	23.23	.161 329	3.23	20
6	1.418 977	28.526 114	.035 055 5986	.704 733	20.103 291	.049 743 0986	19.90	.193 834	3.23	24
7	1.504 197	34.328 299	.029 130 4847	.664 807	22.821 679	.043 817 9847	17.53	.226 904	3.24	28
8	1.594 535	40.478 947	.024 704 1999	.627 142	25.386 059	.039 391 6999	15.76	.260 534	3.26	32
9	1.690 298	46.998 985	.021 277 0555	.591 612	27.805 154	.035 964 5555	14.39	.294 724	3.27	36
10	1.791 812	53.910 596	.018 549 2291	.558 094	30.087 197	.033 236 7291	13.30	.329 469	3.29	40
11	1.899 423	61.237 299	.016 329 9168	.526 476	32.239 951	.031 017 4168	12.41	.364 766	3.32	44
12	2.013 497	69.004 022	.014 491 9089	.496 648	34.270 742	.029 179 4089	11.68	.400 612	3.34	48
13	2.134 421	77.237 191	.012 947 1305	.468 511	36.186 480	.027 634 6305	11.06	.437 001	3.36	52
14	2.262 608	85.964 821	.011 632 6654	.441 968	37.993 682	.026 320 1654	10.53	.473 929	3.39	56
15	2.398 494	95.216 606	.010 502 3697	.416 928	39.698 498	.025 189 8697	10.08	.511 392	3.41	60
16	2.542 540	105.024 026	.009 521 6308	.393 307	41.306 729	.024 209 1308	9.69	.549 384	3.43	64
17	2.695 238	115.420 451	.008 663 9758	.371 025	42.823 846	.023 351 4758	9.35	.587 900	3.46	68
18	2.857 106	126.441 255	.007 908 8111	.350 005	44.255 011	.022 596 3111	9.04	.626 934	3.48	72
19	3.028 695	138.123 935	.007 239 8748	.330 175	45.605 094	.021 927 3748	8.78	.666 480	3.51	76
20	3.210 590	150.508 243	.006 644 1544	.311 469	46.878 689	.021 331 6544	8.54	.706 532	3.53	80
21	3.403 408	163.636 316	.006 111 1129	.293 823	48.080 129	.020 798 6129	8.32	.747 083	3.56	84
22	3.607 807	177.552 823	.005 632 1267	.277 177	49.213 502	.020 319 6267	8.13	.788 127	3.58	88
23	3.824 481	192.305 114	.005 200 0697	.261 473	50.282 665	.019 887 5697	7.96	.829 656	3.61	92
24	4.054 168	207.943 384	.004 809 0013	.246 660	51.291 254	.019 496 5013	7.80	.871 664	3.63	96
25	4.297 650	224.520 842	.004 453 9295	.232 685	52.242 702	.019 141 4295	7.66	.914 143	3.66	100
26	4.555 754	242.093 894	.004 130 6288	.219 503	53.140 246	.018 818 1288	7.53	.957 085	3.68	104
27	4.829 359	260.722 332	.003 835 4981	.207 067	53.986 941	.018 522 9981	7.41	1.000 484	3.71	108
28	5.119 396	280.469 539	.003 565 4496	.195 336	54.785 666	.018 252 9496	7.31	1.044 330	3.73	112
29	5.426 852	301.402 704	.003 317 8203	.184 269	55.539 140	.018 005 3203	7.21	1.088 617	3.75	116
30	5.752 773	323.593 055	.003 090 3012	.173 829	56.249 926	.017 777 8012	7.12	1.133 336	3.78	120
31	6.098 268	347.116 092	.002 880 8806	.163 981	56.920 443	.017 568 3806	7.03	1.178 479	3.80	124
32	6.464 512	372.051 854	.002 687 7974	.154 691	57.552 972	.017 375 2974	6.96	1.224 038	3.83	128
33	6.852 751	398.485 184	.002 509 5036	.145 927	58.149 665	.017 197 0036	6.88	1.270 004	3.85	132
34	7.264 307	426.506 022	.002 344 6328	.137 659	58.712 553	.017 032 1328	6.82	1.316 370	3.87	136
35	7.700 580	456.209 709	.002 191 9744	.129 860	59.243 551	.016 879 4744	6.76	1.363 126	3.89	140
36	8.163 054	487.697 312	.002 050 4521	.122 503	59.744 465	.016 737 9521	6.70	1.410 265	3.92	144
37	8.653 303	521.075 968	.001 919 1060	.115 563	60.217 001	.016 606 6060	6.65	1.457 778	3.94	148
38	9.172 995	556.459 248	.001 797 0768	.109 016	60.662 765	.016 484 5768	6.60	1.505 656	3.96	152
39	9.723 898	593.967 543	.001 683 5937	.102 839	61.083 274	.016 371 0937	6.55	1.553 891	3.98	156
40	10.307 887	633.728 477	.001 577 9629	.097 013	61.479 960	.016 265 4629	6.51	1.602 474	4.01	160
41	10.926 948	675.877 334	.001 479 5584	.091 517	61.854 171	.016 167 0584	6.47	1.651 398	4.03	164
42	11.583 189	720.557 529	.001 387 8142	.086 332	62.207 182	.016 075 3142	6.44	1.700 653	4.05	168
43	12.278 841	767.921 084	.001 302 2171	.081 441	62.540 193	.015 989 7171	6.40	1.750 231	4.07	172
44	13.016 272	818.129 154	.001 222 3009	.076 827	62.854 338	.015 909 8009	6.37	1.800 125	4.09	176
45	13.797 991	871.352 574	.001 147 6411	.072 474	63.150 685	.015 835 1411	6.34	1.850 325	4.11	180
46	14.626 658	927.772 435	.001 077 8505	.068 368	63.430 242	.015 765 3505	6.31	1.900 824	4.13	184
47	15.505 092	987.580 708	.001 012 5755	.064 495	63.693 961	.015 700 0755	6.29	1.951 614	4.15	188
48	16.436 282	1050.980 889	.000 951 4921	.060 841	63.942 740	.015 638 9921	6.26	2.002 686	4.17	192
49	17.423 397	1118.188 698	.000 894 3034	.057 394	64.177 424	.015 581 8034	6.24	2.054 033	4.19	196
50	18.469 794	1189.432 811	.000 840 7369	.054 142	64.398 812	.015 528 2369	6.22	2.105 647	4.21	200

QUARTERLY COMPOUND INTEREST AND ANNUITY

6.00 % Q

	Amount Of 1	Amount Of 1 Per Period	Sinking Fund Payment	Present Worth Of 1	Present Worth of 1 Per Period	Periodic Payment To Amortize 1	Constant Annual Percent	Total Interest	Annual Add On Rate	
	What a single $ 1 deposit grows to in the future. The deposit is made at the beginning of the first period.	What a series of $ 1 deposits grow to in the future. A deposit is made at the end of each period.	The amount to be deposited at the end of each period that grows to $ 1 in the future.	What $ 1 to be paid in the future is worth today. Value today of a single $ 1 payment tomorrow.	What $ 1 to be paid at the end of each period is worth today. Value today of a series of $ 1 payments tomorrow.	The mortgage payment to amortize a loan of $ 1. An annuity certain, payable at the end of each period, worth $ 1 today.	The annual payment, including interest and principal, to amortize completely a loan of $ 100.	The total interest paid over the term on a loan of $1. The loan is amortized by regular periodic payments.	The average annual interest rate on a loan that is completely amortized by regular periodic payments.	
	$S = (1+i)^n$	$S\overline{n}| = \dfrac{(1+i)^n - 1}{i}$	$\dfrac{1}{S\overline{n}|} = \dfrac{i}{(1+i)^n - 1}$	$V^n = \dfrac{1}{(1+i)^n}$	$A\overline{n}| = \dfrac{1-V^n}{i}$	$\dfrac{1}{A\overline{n}|} = \dfrac{i}{1-V^n}$				

YEAR										PERIODS
	1.015 000	1.000 000	1.000 000 0000	.985 222	.985 222	1.015 000 0000	406.00	.015 000	6.00	1
	1.030 225	2.015 000	.496 277 9156	.970 662	1.955 883	.511 277 9156	204.52	.022 556	4.51	2
	1.045 678	3.045 225	.328 382 9602	.956 317	2.912 200	.343 382 9602	137.36	.030 149	4.02	3
	1.061 364	4.090 903	.244 444 7860	.942 184	3.854 385	.259 444 7860	103.78	.037 779	3.78	4
1	1.061 364	4.090 903	.244 444 7860	.942 184	3.854 385	.259 444 7860	103.78	.037 779	3.78	4
2	1.126 493	8.432 839	.118 584 0246	.887 711	7.485 925	.133 584 0246	53.44	.068 672	3.43	8
3	1.195 618	13.041 211	.076 679 9929	.836 387	10.907 505	.091 679 9929	36.68	.100 160	3.34	12
4	1.268 986	17.932 370	.055 765 0778	.788 031	14.131 264	.070 765 0778	28.31	.132 241	3.31	16
5	1.346 855	23.123 667	.043 245 7359	.742 470	17.168 639	.058 245 7359	23.30	.164 915	3.30	20
6	1.429 503	28.633 521	.034 924 1020	.699 544	20.030 405	.049 924 1020	19.97	.198 178	3.30	24
7	1.517 222	34.481 479	.029 001 0765	.659 099	22.726 717	.044 001 0765	17.61	.232 030	3.31	28
8	1.610 324	40.688 288	.024 577 0970	.620 993	25.267 139	.039 577 0970	15.84	.266 467	3.33	32
9	1.709 140	47.275 969	.021 152 3955	.585 090	27.660 684	.036 152 3955	14.47	.301 486	3.35	36
10	1.814 018	54.267 894	.018 427 1017	.551 262	29.915 845	.033 427 1017	13.38	.337 084	3.37	40
11	1.925 333	61.688 868	.016 210 3801	.519 391	32.040 622	.031 210 3801	12.49	.373 257	3.39	44
12	2.043 478	69.565 219	.014 374 9996	.489 362	34.042 554	.029 374 9996	11.75	.410 000	3.42	48
13	2.168 873	77.924 892	.012 832 8700	.461 069	35.928 742	.027 832 8700	11.14	.447 309	3.44	52
14	2.301 963	86.797 543	.011 521 0635	.434 412	37.705 879	.026 521 0635	10.61	.485 180	3.47	56
15	2.443 220	96.214 652	.010 393 4274	.409 296	39.380 269	.025 393 4274	10.16	.523 606	3.49	60
16	2.593 144	106.209 628	.009 415 3423	.385 632	40.957 853	.024 415 3423	9.77	.562 582	3.52	64
17	2.752 269	116.817 931	.008 560 3297	.363 337	42.444 228	.023 560 3297	9.43	.602 102	3.54	68
18	2.921 158	128.077 197	.007 807 7911	.342 330	43.844 667	.022 807 7911	9.13	.642 161	3.57	72
19	3.100 411	140.027 372	.007 141 4609	.322 538	45.164 138	.022 141 4609	8.86	.682 751	3.59	76
20	3.290 663	152.710 852	.006 548 3231	.303 890	46.407 323	.021 548 3231	8.62	.723 866	3.62	80
21	3.492 590	166.172 636	.006 017 8380	.286 321	47.578 633	.021 017 8380	8.41	.765 498	3.65	84
22	3.706 907	180.460 482	.005 541 3794	.269 767	48.682 222	.020 541 3794	8.22	.807 641	3.67	88
23	3.934 376	195.625 082	.005 111 8190	.254 170	49.722 007	.020 111 8190	8.05	.850 287	3.70	92
24	4.175 804	211.720 235	.004 723 2141	.239 475	50.701 675	.019 723 2141	7.89	.893 429	3.72	96
25	4.432 046	228.803 043	.004 370 5712	.225 629	51.624 704	.019 370 5712	7.75	.937 057	3.75	100
26	4.704 012	246.934 114	.004 049 6632	.212 585	52.494 366	.019 049 6632	7.62	.981 165	3.77	104
27	4.992 667	266.177 771	.003 756 8877	.200 294	53.313 749	.018 756 8877	7.51	1.025 744	3.80	108
28	5.299 034	286.602 288	.003 489 1557	.188 714	54.085 758	.018 489 1557	7.40	1.070 785	3.82	112
29	5.624 202	308.280 125	.003 243 8030	.177 803	54.813 133	.018 243 8030	7.30	1.116 281	3.85	116
30	5.969 323	331.288 191	.003 018 5199	.167 523	55.498 454	.018 018 5199	7.21	1.162 222	3.87	120
31	6.335 622	355.708 115	.002 811 2938	.157 838	56.144 153	.017 811 2938	7.13	1.208 600	3.90	124
32	6.724 398	381.626 531	.002 620 3629	.148 712	56.752 520	.017 620 3629	7.05	1.255 406	3.92	128
33	7.137 031	409.135 393	.002 444 1787	.140 114	57.325 714	.017 444 1787	6.98	1.302 632	3.95	132
34	7.574 984	438.332 297	.002 281 3742	.132 013	57.865 769	.017 281 3742	6.92	1.350 267	3.97	136
35	8.039 812	469.320 826	.002 130 7386	.124 381	58.374 599	.017 130 7386	6.86	1.398 303	4.00	140
36	8.533 164	502.210 922	.001 991 1952	.117 190	58.854 011	.016 991 1952	6.80	1.446 732	4.02	144
37	9.056 789	537.119 271	.001 861 7839	.110 414	59.305 706	.016 861 7839	6.75	1.495 544	4.04	148
38	9.612 546	574.169 720	.001 741 6453	.104 031	59.731 286	.016 741 6453	6.70	1.544 730	4.07	152
39	10.202 406	613.493 716	.001 630 0085	.098 016	60.132 260	.016 630 0085	6.66	1.594 281	4.09	156
40	10.828 462	655.230 772	.001 526 1798	.092 349	60.510 052	.016 526 1798	6.62	1.644 189	4.11	160
41	11.492 934	699.528 962	.001 429 5334	.087 010	60.866 001	.016 429 5334	6.58	1.694 443	4.13	164
42	12.198 182	746.545 446	.001 339 5032	.081 979	61.201 371	.016 339 5032	6.54	1.745 037	4.15	168
43	12.946 705	796.447 029	.001 255 5763	.077 240	61.517 351	.016 255 5763	6.51	1.795 959	4.18	172
44	13.741 161	849.410 750	.001 177 2867	.072 774	61.815 063	.016 177 2867	6.48	1.847 202	4.20	176
45	14.584 368	905.624 513	.001 104 2104	.068 567	62.095 562	.016 104 2104	6.45	1.898 758	4.22	180
46	15.479 316	965.287 752	.001 035 9605	.064 602	62.359 844	.016 035 9605	6.42	1.950 617	4.24	184
47	16.429 182	1028.612 139	.000 972 1837	.060 867	62.608 846	.015 972 1837	6.39	2.002 771	4.26	188
48	17.437 335	1095.822 335	.000 912 5567	.057 348	62.843 452	.015 912 5567	6.37	2.055 211	4.28	192
49	18.507 352	1167.156 788	.000 856 7829	.054 033	63.064 495	.015 856 7829	6.35	2.107 929	4.30	196
50	19.643 029	1242.868 576	.000 804 5903	.050 909	63.272 757	.015 804 5903	6.33	2.160 918	4.32	200

Effective Rate is 6.14 %

Annual Percentage Rate is 6.00 %

	Amount Of 1	Amount Of 1 Per Period	Sinking Fund Payment	Present Worth Of 1	Present Worth of 1 Per Period	Periodic Payment To Amortize 1	Constant Annual Percent	Total Interest	Annual Add On Rate	
	What a single $ 1 deposit grows to in the future. The deposit is made at the beginning of the first period.	What a series of $ 1 deposits grow to in the future. A deposit is made at the end of each period.	The amount to be deposited at the end of each period that grows to $ 1 in the future.	What $ 1 to be paid in the future is worth today. Value today of a single $ 1 payment tomorrow.	What $ 1 to be paid at the end of each period is worth today. Value today of a series of $ 1 payments tomorrow.	The mortgage payment to amortize a loan of $ 1. An annuity certain, payable at the end of each period, worth $ 1 today.	The annual payment, including interest and principal, to amortize completely a loan of $ 100.	The total interest paid over the term on a loan of $1. The loan is amortized by regular periodic payments.	The average annual interest rate on a loan that is completely amortized by regular periodic payments.	
	$S = (1+i)^n$	$S\overline{n}] = \dfrac{(1+i)^n - 1}{i}$	$\dfrac{1}{S\overline{n}]} = \dfrac{i}{(1+i)^n - 1}$	$V^n = \dfrac{1}{(1+i)^n}$	$A\overline{n}] = \dfrac{1-V^n}{i}$	$\dfrac{1}{A\overline{n}]} = \dfrac{i}{1-V^n}$				

YEAR										PERIODS
	1.015 313	1.000 000	1.000 000 0000	.984 918	.984 918	1.015 312 5000	406.13	.015 312	6.12	1
	1.030 859	2.015 313	.496 200 9614	.970 064	1.954 983	.511 513 4614	204.61	.023 027	4.61	2
	1.046 645	3.046 172	.328 280 8748	.955 434	2.910 417	.343 593 3748	137.44	.030 780	4.10	3
	1.062 671	4.092 816	.244 330 5251	.941 025	3.851 442	.259 643 0251	103.86	.038 572	3.86	4
1	1.062 671	4.092 816	.244 330 5251	.941 025	3.851 442	.259 643 0251	103.86	.038 572	3.86	4
2	1.129 270	8.442 135	.118 453 4495	.885 528	7.475 744	.133 765 9495	53.51	.070 128	3.51	8
3	1.200 043	13.064 031	.076 546 0550	.833 303	10.886 302	.091 858 5550	36.75	.102 303	3.41	12
4	1.275 251	17.975 586	.055 631 0092	.784 159	14.095 722	.070 943 5092	28.38	.135 096	3.38	16
5	1.355 173	23.194 955	.043 112 8232	.737 913	17.115 866	.058 425 3232	23.38	.168 506	3.37	20
6	1.440 103	28.741 429	.034 792 9818	.694 395	19.957 896	.050 105 4818	20.05	.202 532	3.38	24
7	1.530 356	34.635 506	.028 872 1057	.653 443	22.632 317	.044 184 6057	17.68	.237 169	3.39	28
8	1.626 266	40.898 973	.024 450 4915	.614 906	25.149 013	.039 762 9915	15.91	.272 416	3.41	32
9	1.728 186	47.554 980	.021 028 2920	.578 642	27.517 287	.036 340 7920	14.54	.308 269	3.43	36
10	1.836 493	54.628 126	.018 305 5885	.544 516	29.745 891	.033 618 0885	13.45	.344 724	3.45	40
11	1.951 589	62.144 556	.016 091 5141	.512 403	31.843 063	.031 404 0141	12.57	.381 777	3.47	44
12	2.073 897	70.132 050	.014 258 8161	.482 184	33.816 554	.029 571 3161	11.83	.419 423	3.50	48
13	2.203 871	78.620 129	.012 719 3889	.453 747	35.673 657	.028 031 8889	11.22	.457 658	3.52	52
14	2.341 990	87.640 168	.011 410 2931	.426 987	37.421 238	.026 722 7931	10.69	.496 476	3.55	56
15	2.488 766	97.225 503	.010 285 3672	.401 806	39.065 755	.025 597 8672	10.24	.535 872	3.57	60
16	2.644 740	107.411 564	.009 309 9845	.378 109	40.613 286	.024 622 4845	9.85	.575 839	3.60	64
17	2.810 489	118.235 998	.008 457 6611	.355 810	42.069 551	.023 770 1611	9.51	.616 371	3.63	68
18	2.986 626	129.738 812	.007 707 7937	.334 826	43.439 932	.023 020 2937	9.21	.657 461	3.65	72
19	3.173 801	141.962 523	.007 044 1126	.315 080	44.729 495	.022 356 6126	8.95	.699 103	3.68	76
20	3.372 707	154.952 308	.006 453 5986	.296 498	45.943 006	.021 766 0986	8.71	.741 288	3.71	80
21	3.584 079	168.756 180	.005 925 7089	.279 012	47.084 950	.021 238 2089	8.50	.784 010	3.73	84
22	3.808 698	183.425 157	.005 451 8149	.262 557	48.159 547	.020 764 3149	8.31	.827 260	3.76	88
23	4.047 394	199.013 458	.005 024 7858	.247 073	49.170 770	.020 337 2858	8.14	.871 030	3.79	92
24	4.301 049	215.578 697	.004 638 6773	.232 501	50.122 356	.019 951 1773	7.99	.915 313	3.81	96
25	4.570 601	233.182 101	.004 288 4938	.218 790	51.017 821	.019 600 9938	7.85	.960 099	3.84	100
26	4.857 046	251.888 732	.003 970 0069	.205 886	51.860 477	.019 282 5069	7.72	1.005 381	3.87	104
27	5.161 443	271.767 730	.003 679 6127	.193 744	52.653 436	.018 992 1127	7.60	1.051 148	3.89	108
28	5.484 917	292.892 571	.003 414 2211	.182 318	53.399 631	.018 726 7211	7.50	1.097 393	3.92	112
29	5.828 664	315.341 331	.003 171 1669	.171 566	54.101 819	.018 483 6669	7.40	1.144 105	3.95	116
30	6.193 954	339.196 984	.002 948 1394	.161 448	54.762 595	.018 260 6394	7.31	1.191 277	3.97	120
31	6.582 137	364.547 700	.002 743 1252	.151 926	55.384 402	.018 055 6252	7.23	1.238 898	4.00	124
32	6.994 647	391.487 178	.002 554 3621	.142 966	55.969 537	.017 866 8621	7.15	1.286 958	4.02	128
33	7.433 011	420.114 986	.002 380 3007	.134 535	56.520 164	.017 692 8007	7.08	1.335 450	4.05	132
34	7.898 847	450.536 935	.002 219 5739	.126 601	57.038 318	.017 532 0739	7.02	1.384 362	4.07	136
35	8.393 877	482.865 465	.002 070 9702	.119 134	57.525 913	.017 383 4702	6.96	1.433 686	4.10	140
36	8.919 932	517.220 065	.001 933 4130	.112 108	57.984 753	.017 245 9130	6.90	1.483 411	4.12	144
37	9.478 956	553.727 711	.001 805 9418	.105 497	58.416 532	.017 118 4418	6.85	1.533 529	4.14	148
38	10.073 014	592.523 336	.001 687 6972	.099 275	58.822 847	.017 000 1972	6.81	1.584 030	4.17	152
39	10.704 302	633.750 332	.001 577 9084	.093 420	59.205 199	.016 890 4084	6.76	1.634 904	4.19	156
40	11.375 154	677.561 076	.001 475 8817	.087 911	59.565 003	.016 788 3817	6.72	1.686 141	4.22	160
41	12.088 049	724.117 494	.001 380 9914	.082 726	59.903 586	.016 693 4914	6.68	1.737 733	4.24	164
42	12.845 622	773.591 660	.001 292 6716	.077 848	60.222 202	.016 605 1716	6.65	1.789 669	4.26	168
43	13.650 674	826.166 435	.001 210 4099	.073 256	60.522 027	.016 522 9099	6.61	1.841 940	4.28	172
44	14.506 178	882.036 137	.001 133 7404	.068 936	60.804 170	.016 446 2404	6.58	1.894 538	4.31	176
45	15.415 299	941.407 262	.001 062 2395	.064 871	61.069 674	.016 374 7395	6.55	1.947 453	4.33	180
46	16.381 395	1004.499 251	.000 995 5209	.061 045	61.319 519	.016 308 0209	6.53	2.000 676	4.35	184
47	17.408 037	1071.545 293	.000 933 2317	.057 445	61.554 630	.016 245 7317	6.50	2.054 198	4.37	188
48	18.499 021	1142.793 195	.000 875 0490	.054 057	61.775 875	.016 187 5490	6.48	2.108 009	4.39	192
49	19.658 378	1218.506 293	.000 820 6769	.050 869	61.984 072	.016 133 1769	6.46	2.162 103	4.41	196
50	20.890 393	1298.964 424	.000 769 8440	.047 869	62.179 991	.016 082 3440	6.44	2.216 469	4.43	200

Effective Rate is 6.27 %

Annual Percentage Rate is 6.125%

QUARTERLY COMPOUND INTEREST AND ANNUITY

6.25 % Q

	Amount Of 1	Amount Of 1 Per Period	Sinking Fund Payment	Present Worth Of 1	Present Worth of 1 Per Period	Periodic Payment To Amortize 1	Constant Annual Percent	Total Interest	Annual Add On Rate	
	What a single $ 1 deposit grows to in the future. The deposit is made at the beginning of the first period.	What a series of $ 1 deposits grow to in the future. A deposit is made at the end of each period.	The amount to be deposited at the end of each period that grows to $ 1 in the future.	What $ 1 to be paid in the future is worth today. Value today of a single $ 1 payment tomorrow.	What $ 1 to be paid at the end of each period is worth today. Value today of a series of $ 1 payments tomorrow.	The mortgage payment to amortize a loan of $ 1. An annuity certain, payable at the end of each period, worth $ 1 today.	The annual payment, including interest and principal, to amortize completely a loan of $ 100.	The total interest paid over the term on a loan that is amortized by regular periodic payments.	The average annual interest rate on a loan that is completely amortized by regular periodic payments.	
	$S = (1+i)^n$	$S\overline{n} = \dfrac{(1+i)^n - 1}{i}$	$\dfrac{1}{S\overline{n}} = \dfrac{i}{(1+i)^n - 1}$	$V^n = \dfrac{1}{(1+i)^n}$	$A\overline{n} = \dfrac{1 - V^n}{i}$	$\dfrac{1}{A\overline{n}} = \dfrac{i}{1 - V^n}$				

YEAR										PERIODS
	1.015 625	1.000 000	1.000 000 0000	.984 615	.984 615	1.015 625 0000	406.25	.015 625	6.25	1
	1.031 494	2.015 625	.496 124 0310	.969 467	1.954 083	.511 749 0310	204.70	.023 498	4.70	2
	1.047 611	3.047 119	.328 178 8318	.954 553	2.908 635	.343 803 8318	137.53	.031 411	4.19	3
	1.063 980	4.094 730	.244 216 3239	.939 867	3.848 503	.259 841 3239	103.94	.039 365	3.94	4
1	1.063 980	4.094 730	.244 216 3239	.939 867	3.848 503	.259 841 3239	103.94	.039 365	3.94	4
2	1.132 054	8.451 442	.118 322 9996	.883 350	7.465 584	.133 947 9996	53.58	.071 584	3.58	8
3	1.204 483	13.086 897	.076 412 3060	.830 232	10.865 159	.092 037 3060	36.82	.104 448	3.48	12
4	1.281 546	18.018 929	.055 497 1926	.780 308	14.060 309	.071 122 1926	28.45	.137 955	3.45	16
5	1.363 539	23.266 514	.042 980 2249	.733 386	17.063 325	.058 605 2249	23.45	.172 104	3.44	20
6	1.450 779	28.849 840	.034 662 2378	.689 285	19.885 761	.050 287 2378	20.12	.206 894	3.45	24
7	1.543 600	34.790 387	.028 743 5719	.647 836	22.538 476	.044 368 5719	17.75	.242 320	3.46	28
8	1.642 360	41.111 012	.024 324 3827	.608 880	25.031 676	.039 949 3827	15.98	.278 380	3.48	32
9	1.747 438	47.836 032	.020 904 7439	.572 266	27.374 952	.036 529 7439	14.62	.315 071	3.50	36
10	1.859 239	54.991 319	.018 184 6882	.537 854	29.577 321	.033 809 6882	13.53	.352 388	3.52	40
11	1.978 194	62.604 403	.015 973 3173	.505 512	31.647 255	.031 598 3173	12.64	.390 326	3.55	44
12	2.104 759	70.704 574	.014 143 3566	.475 114	33.592 718	.029 768 3566	11.91	.428 881	3.57	48
13	2.239 422	79.322 994	.012 606 6850	.446 544	35.421 194	.028 231 6850	11.30	.468 048	3.60	52
14	2.382 700	88.492 823	.011 300 3515	.419 692	37.139 719	.026 925 3515	10.78	.507 820	3.63	56
15	2.535 146	98.249 338	.010 178 1856	.394 455	38.754 905	.025 803 1856	10.33	.548 191	3.65	60
16	2.697 345	108.630 077	.009 205 5536	.370 735	40.272 964	.024 830 5536	9.94	.589 155	3.68	64
17	2.869 922	119.674 977	.008 355 9657	.348 442	41.699 739	.023 980 9657	9.60	.630 706	3.71	68
18	3.053 540	131.426 532	.007 608 8137	.327 489	43.040 717	.023 233 8137	9.30	.672 835	3.74	72
19	3.248 906	143.929 953	.006 947 8241	.307 796	44.301 058	.022 572 8241	9.03	.715 535	3.77	76
20	3.456 771	157.233 345	.006 359 9741	.289 287	45.485 612	.021 984 9741	8.80	.758 798	3.79	80
21	3.677 936	171.387 891	.005 834 7179	.271 892	46.598 935	.021 459 7179	8.59	.802 616	3.82	84
22	3.913 251	186.448 046	.005 363 4244	.255 542	47.645 311	.020 988 4244	8.40	.846 981	3.85	88
23	4.163 621	202.471 753	.004 938 9606	.240 176	48.628 765	.020 563 9606	8.23	.891 884	3.88	92
24	4.430 010	219.520 659	.004 555 3799	.225 733	49.553 081	.020 180 3799	8.08	.937 316	3.91	96
25	4.713 443	237.660 356	.004 207 6853	.212 159	50.421 815	.019 832 6853	7.94	.983 269	3.93	100
26	5.015 010	256.960 635	.003 891 6467	.199 401	51.238 310	.019 516 6467	7.81	1.029 731	3.96	104
27	5.335 871	277.495 748	.003 603 6588	.187 411	52.005 707	.019 228 6588	7.70	1.076 695	3.99	108
28	5.677 261	299.344 702	.003 340 6304	.176 141	52.726 958	.018 965 6304	7.59	1.124 151	4.01	112
29	6.040 493	322.591 555	.003 099 8952	.165 549	53.404 838	.018 724 8952	7.49	1.172 088	4.04	116
30	6.426 965	347.325 745	.002 879 1416	.155 594	54.041 956	.018 504 1416	7.41	1.220 497	4.07	120
31	6.838 163	373.642 433	.002 676 3556	.146 238	54.640 761	.018 301 3556	7.33	1.269 368	4.09	124
32	7.275 670	401.642 867	.002 489 7741	.137 444	55.203 559	.018 114 7741	7.25	1.318 691	4.12	128
33	7.741 168	431.434 773	.002 317 8475	.129 179	55.732 514	.017 942 8475	7.18	1.368 456	4.15	132
34	8.236 450	463.132 770	.002 159 2080	.121 412	56.229 662	.017 784 2080	7.12	1.418 652	4.17	136
35	8.763 419	496.858 810	.002 012 6442	.114 111	56.696 914	.017 637 6442	7.06	1.469 270	4.20	140
36	9.324 104	532.742 648	.001 877 0789	.107 249	57.136 070	.017 502 0789	7.01	1.520 299	4.22	144
37	9.920 662	570.922 339	.001 751 5517	.100 800	57.548 817	.017 376 5517	6.96	1.571 730	4.25	148
38	10.555 387	611.544 773	.001 635 2032	.094 738	57.936 745	.017 260 2032	6.91	1.623 551	4.27	152
39	11.230 722	654.766 237	.001 527 2626	.089 041	58.301 346	.017 152 2626	6.87	1.675 753	4.30	156
40	11.949 266	700.753 018	.001 427 0363	.083 687	58.644 022	.017 052 0363	6.83	1.728 326	4.32	160
41	12.713 782	749.682 040	.001 333 8988	.078 655	58.966 093	.016 958 8988	6.79	1.781 259	4.34	164
42	13.527 212	801.741 549	.001 247 2847	.073 925	59.268 796	.016 872 2847	6.75	1.834 544	4.37	168
43	14.392 685	857.131 833	.001 166 6817	.069 480	59.553 297	.016 791 6817	6.72	1.888 169	4.39	172
44	15.313 531	916.065 997	.001 091 6244	.065 302	59.820 690	.016 716 6244	6.69	1.942 126	4.41	176
45	16.293 293	978.770 779	.001 021 6897	.061 375	60.072 003	.016 646 6897	6.66	1.996 404	4.44	180
46	17.335 741	1045.487 422	.000 956 4917	.057 684	60.308 205	.016 581 4917	6.64	2.050 994	4.46	184
47	18.444 884	1116.472 608	.000 895 6780	.054 216	60.530 203	.016 520 6780	6.61	2.105 887	4.48	188
48	19.624 991	1191.999 436	.000 838 9266	.050 955	60.738 852	.016 463 9266	6.59	2.161 074	4.50	192
49	20.880 601	1272.358 484	.000 785 9420	.047 891	60.934 954	.016 410 9420	6.57	2.216 545	4.52	196
50	22.216 546	1357.858 916	.000 736 4535	.045 011	61.119 264	.016 361 4535	6.55	2.272 291	4.54	200

Effective Rate is 6.40 %

Annual Percentage Rate is 6.25 %

QUARTERLY COMPOUND INTEREST AND ANNUITY

6.375% Q

	Amount Of 1	Amount Of 1 Per Period	Sinking Fund Payment	Present Worth Of 1	Present Worth of 1 Per Period	Periodic Payment To Amortize 1	Constant Annual Percent	Total Interest	Annual Add On Rate	
	What a single $ 1 deposit grows to in the future. The deposit is made at the beginning of the first period.	What a series of $ 1 deposits grow to in the future. A deposit is made at the end of each period.	The amount to be deposited at the end of each period that grows to $ 1 in the future.	What $ 1 to be paid in the future is worth today. Value today of a single $ 1 payment tomorrow.	What $ 1 to be paid at the end of each period is worth today. Value today of a series of $ 1 payments tomorrow.	The mortgage payment to amortize a loan of $ 1. An annuity certain, payable at the end of each period, worth $ 1 today.	The annual payment, including interest and principal, to amortize completely a loan of $ 100.	The total interest paid over the term on a loan of $1. The loan is amortized by regular periodic payments.	The average annual interest rate on a loan that is completely amortized by regular periodic payments.	
	$S = (1+i)^n$	$S\overline{n}| = \dfrac{(1+i)^n - 1}{i}$	$\dfrac{1}{S\overline{n}|} = \dfrac{i}{(1+i)^n - 1}$	$V^n = \dfrac{1}{(1+i)^n}$	$A\overline{n}| = \dfrac{1 - V^n}{i}$	$\dfrac{1}{A\overline{n}|} = \dfrac{i}{1 - V^n}$				

YEAR										PERIODS
	1.015 937	1.000 000	1.000 000 0000	.984 313	.984 313	1.015 937 5000	406.38	.015 938	6.38	1
	1.032 129	2.015 937	.496 047 1245	.968 871	1.953 184	.511 984 6245	204.80	.023 969	4.79	2
	1.048 579	3.048 067	.328 076 8312	.953 672	2.906 856	.344 014 3312	137.61	.032 043	4.27	3
	1.065 290	4.096 645	.244 102 1823	.938 711	3.845 567	.260 039 6823	104.02	.040 159	4.02	4
1	1.065 290	4.096 645	.244 102 1823	.938 711	3.845 567	.260 039 6823	104.02	.040 159	4.02	4
2	1.134 843	8.460 761	.118 192 6747	.881 179	7.455 444	.134 130 1747	53.66	.073 041	3.65	8
3	1.208 938	13.109 812	.076 278 7458	.827 173	10.844 076	.092 216 2458	36.89	.106 595	3.55	12
4	1.287 870	18.062 400	.055 363 6279	.776 476	14.025 024	.071 301 1279	28.53	.140 818	3.52	16
5	1.371 955	23.338 344	.042 847 9409	.728 887	17.011 015	.058 785 4409	23.52	.175 709	3.51	20
6	1.461 530	28.958 756	.034 531 8695	.684 214	19.813 998	.050 469 3695	20.19	.211 265	3.52	24
7	1.556 954	34.946 127	.028 615 4744	.642 280	22.445 191	.044 552 9744	17.83	.247 483	3.54	28
8	1.658 608	41.324 414	.024 198 7700	.602 915	24.915 120	.040 136 2700	16.06	.284 361	3.55	32
9	1.766 899	48.119 142	.020 781 7504	.565 963	27.233 671	.036 719 2504	14.69	.321 893	3.58	36
10	1.882 260	55.357 499	.018 064 3998	.531 276	29.410 121	.034 001 8998	13.61	.360 076	3.60	40
11	2.005 153	63.068 451	.015 855 7881	.498 715	31.453 180	.031 793 2881	12.72	.398 905	3.63	44
12	2.136 070	71.282 853	.014 028 6192	.468 149	33.371 021	.029 966 1192	11.99	.438 374	3.65	48
13	2.275 535	80.033 576	.012 494 7560	.439 457	35.171 321	.028 432 2560	11.38	.478 477	3.68	52
14	2.424 105	89.355 635	.011 191 2360	.412 523	36.861 282	.027 128 7360	10.86	.519 209	3.71	56
15	2.582 376	99.286 335	.010 071 8795	.387 240	38.447 668	.026 009 3795	10.41	.560 563	3.74	60
16	2.750 980	109.865 413	.009 102 0456	.363 507	39.936 827	.025 039 5456	10.02	.602 531	3.77	64
17	2.930 592	121.135 201	.008 255 2387	.341 228	41.334 717	.024 192 7387	9.68	.645 106	3.79	68
18	3.121 931	133.140 798	.007 510 8458	.320 315	42.646 932	.023 448 3458	9.38	.688 281	3.82	72
19	3.325 763	145.930 243	.006 852 5892	.300 683	43.878 723	.022 790 0892	9.12	.732 047	3.85	76
20	3.542 903	159.554 714	.006 267 4425	.282 254	45.035 019	.022 204 9425	8.89	.776 395	3.88	80
21	3.774 220	174.068 732	.005 744 8572	.264 955	46.120 447	.021 682 3572	8.68	.821 318	3.91	84
22	4.020 640	189.530 373	.005 276 1992	.248 717	47.139 350	.021 213 6992	8.49	.866 806	3.94	88
23	4.283 149	206.001 509	.004 854 3334	.233 473	48.095 807	.020 791 8334	8.32	.912 849	3.97	92
24	4.562 797	223.548 051	.004 473 3112	.219 164	48.993 643	.020 410 8112	8.17	.959 438	4.00	96
25	4.860 703	242.240 211	.004 128 1338	.205 732	49.836 452	.020 065 6338	8.03	1.006 563	4.03	100
26	5.178 060	262.152 787	.003 814 5694	.193 123	50.627 607	.019 752 0694	7.91	1.054 215	4.05	104
27	5.516 137	283.365 461	.003 529 0116	.181 286	51.370 272	.019 466 5116	7.79	1.102 383	4.08	108
28	5.876 287	305.963 117	.003 268 3678	.170 175	52.067 421	.019 205 8678	7.69	1.151 057	4.11	112
29	6.259 952	330.036 180	.003 029 9708	.159 746	52.721 842	.018 967 4708	7.59	1.200 227	4.14	116
30	6.668 666	355.680 980	.002 811 5082	.149 955	53.336 155	.018 749 0082	7.50	1.249 881	4.17	120
31	7.104 065	383.000 136	.002 610 9651	.140 764	53.912 817	.018 548 4651	7.42	1.300 010	4.19	124
32	7.567 891	412.102 967	.002 426 5780	.132 137	54.454 136	.018 364 0780	7.35	1.350 602	4.22	128
33	8.062 001	443.105 931	.002 256 7967	.124 039	54.962 278	.018 194 2967	7.28	1.401 647	4.25	132
34	8.588 371	476.133 086	.002 100 2531	.116 437	55.439 277	.018 037 7531	7.22	1.453 134	4.27	136
35	9.149 108	511.316 594	.001 955 7355	.109 300	55.887 042	.017 893 2355	7.16	1.505 053	4.30	140
36	9.746 456	548.797 243	.001 822 1666	.102 601	56.307 363	.017 759 6666	7.11	1.557 392	4.33	144
37	10.382 805	588.725 014	.001 698 5859	.096 313	56.701 924	.017 636 0859	7.06	1.610 141	4.35	148
38	11.060 701	631.259 681	.001 584 1341	.090 410	57.072 302	.017 521 6341	7.01	1.663 288	4.38	152
39	11.782 857	676.571 448	.001 478 0405	.084 869	57.419 981	.017 415 5405	6.97	1.716 824	4.40	156
40	12.552 164	724.841 632	.001 379 6117	.079 668	57.746 350	.017 317 1117	6.93	1.770 738	4.43	160
41	13.371 698	776.263 391	.001 288 2225	.074 785	58.052 717	.017 225 7225	6.90	1.825 018	4.45	164
42	14.244 740	831.042 491	.001 203 3079	.070 201	58.340 307	.017 140 8079	6.86	1.879 656	4.48	168
43	15.174 783	889.398 134	.001 124 3559	.065 899	58.610 271	.017 061 8559	6.83	1.934 639	4.50	172
44	16.165 549	951.563 832	.001 050 9016	.061 860	58.863 690	.016 988 4016	6.80	1.989 959	4.52	176
45	17.221 002	1017.788 347	.000 982 5225	.058 069	59.101 576	.016 920 0225	6.77	2.045 604	4.55	180
46	18.345 366	1088.336 679	.000 918 8333	.054 510	59.324 883	.016 856 3333	6.75	2.101 565	4.57	184
47	19.543 140	1163.491 132	.000 859 4823	.051 169	59.534 504	.016 796 9823	6.72	2.157 833	4.59	188
48	20.819 117	1243.552 439	.000 804 1478	.048 033	59.731 277	.016 741 6478	6.70	2.214 396	4.61	192
49	22.178 403	1328.840 972	.000 752 5355	.045 089	59.915 990	.016 690 0355	6.68	2.271 247	4.64	196
50	23.626 437	1419.698 017	.000 704 3751	.042 325	60.089 382	.016 641 8751	6.66	2.328 375	4.66	200

Effective Rate is 6.53 %

Annual Percentage Rate is 6.375%

QUARTERLY COMPOUND INTEREST AND ANNUITY

6.50 % Q

Amount Of 1	Amount Of 1 Per Period	Sinking Fund Payment	Present Worth Of 1	Present Worth of 1 Per Period	Periodic Payment To Amortize 1	Constant Annual Percent	Total Interest	Annual Add On Rate	
What a single $ 1 deposit grows to in the future. The deposit is made at the beginning of the first period.	What a series of $ 1 deposits grow to in the future. A deposit is made at the end of each period.	The amount to be deposited at the end of each period that grows to $ 1 in the future.	What $ 1 to be paid in the future is worth today. Value today of a single $ 1 payment tomorrow.	What $ 1 to be paid at the end of each period is worth today. Value today of a series of $ 1 payments tomorrow.	The mortgage payment to amortize a loan of $ 1. An annuity certain, payable at the end of each period, worth $ 1 today.	The annual payment, including interest and principal, to amortize completely a loan of $ 100.	The total interest paid over the term on a loan of $1. The loan is amortized by regular periodic payments.	The average annual interest rate on a loan that is completely amortized by regular periodic payments.	
$S = (1+i)^n$	$S\overline{n}| = \dfrac{(1+i)^n - 1}{i}$	$\dfrac{1}{S\overline{n}|} = \dfrac{i}{(1+i)^n - 1}$	$V^n = \dfrac{1}{(1+i)^n}$	$A\overline{n}| = \dfrac{1 - V^n}{i}$	$\dfrac{1}{A\overline{n}|} = \dfrac{i}{1 - V^n}$				

YEAR										PERIODS
	1.016 250	1.000 000	1.000 000 0000	.984 010	.984 010	1.016 250 0000	406.50	.016 250	6.50	1
	1.032 764	2.016 250	.495 970 2418	.968 275	1.952 285	.512 220 2418	204.89	.024 440	4.89	2
	1.049 546	3.049 014	.327 974 8730	.952 792	2.905 078	.344 224 8730	137.69	.032 675	4.36	3
	1.066 602	4.098 561	.243 988 1002	.937 557	3.842 635	.260 238 1002	104.10	.040 952	4.10	4
1	1.066 602	4.098 561	.243 988 1002	.937 557	3.842 635	.260 238 1002	104.10	.040 952	4.10	4
2	1.137 639	8.470 092	.118 062 4747	.879 013	7.445 325	.134 312 4747	53.73	.074 500	3.72	8
3	1.213 408	13.132 774	.076 145 3744	.824 125	10.823 053	.092 395 3744	36.96	.108 744	3.62	12
4	1.294 222	18.105 999	.055 230 3149	.772 665	13.989 866	.071 480 3149	28.60	.143 685	3.59	16
5	1.380 420	23.410 448	.042 715 9708	.724 417	16.958 934	.058 965 9708	23.59	.179 319	3.59	20
6	1.472 358	29.068 182	.034 401 8766	.679 183	19.742 605	.050 651 8766	20.27	.215 645	3.59	24
7	1.570 419	35.102 730	.028 487 8128	.636 773	22.352 456	.044 737 8128	17.90	.252 659	3.61	28
8	1.675 012	41.539 189	.024 073 6526	.597 011	24.799 341	.040 323 6526	16.13	.290 357	3.63	32
9	1.786 570	48.404 326	.020 659 3105	.559 732	27.093 435	.036 909 3105	14.77	.328 735	3.65	36
10	1.905 559	55.726 693	.017 944 7219	.524 780	29.244 279	.034 194 7219	13.68	.367 789	3.68	40
11	2.032 472	63.536 741	.015 738 9251	.492 012	31.260 819	.031 988 9251	12.80	.407 513	3.70	44
12	2.167 838	71.866 950	.013 914 6019	.461 289	33.151 440	.030 164 6019	12.07	.447 901	3.73	48
13	2.312 219	80.751 965	.012 383 5995	.432 485	34.924 006	.028 633 5995	11.46	.488 947	3.76	52
14	2.466 217	90.228 737	.011 082 9436	.405 479	36.585 887	.027 332 9436	10.94	.530 645	3.79	56
15	2.630 471	100.336 676	.009 966 4454	.380 160	38.143 997	.026 216 4454	10.49	.572 987	3.82	60
16	2.805 665	111.117 821	.008 999 4566	.356 422	39.604 813	.025 249 4566	10.10	.615 965	3.85	64
17	2.992 526	122.617 007	.008 155 4755	.334 166	40.974 412	.024 405 4755	9.77	.659 572	3.88	68
18	3.191 833	134.882 057	.007 413 8845	.313 300	42.258 489	.023 663 8845	9.47	.703 800	3.91	72
19	3.404 415	147.963 980	.006 758 4016	.293 736	43.462 385	.023 008 4016	9.21	.748 639	3.94	76
20	3.631 154	161.917 180	.006 175 9969	.275 395	44.591 106	.022 425 9969	8.98	.794 080	3.97	80
21	3.872 995	176.799 685	.005 656 1187	.258 198	45.649 346	.021 906 1187	8.77	.840 114	4.00	84
22	4.130 943	192.673 389	.005 190 1303	.242 076	46.641 508	.021 440 1303	8.58	.886 731	4.03	88
23	4.406 070	209.604 307	.004 770 8943	.226 960	47.571 715	.021 020 8943	8.41	.933 922	4.06	92
24	4.699 521	227.662 852	.004 392 4601	.212 788	48.443 838	.020 642 4601	8.26	.981 676	4.09	96
25	5.012 517	246.924 124	.004 049 8271	.199 501	49.261 503	.020 299 8271	8.12	1.029 983	4.12	100
26	5.346 359	267.468 229	.003 738 7618	.187 043	50.028 111	.019 988 7618	8.00	1.078 831	4.15	104
27	5.702 435	289.380 604	.003 455 6566	.175 364	50.746 850	.019 705 6566	7.89	1.128 211	4.18	108
28	6.082 226	312.752 378	.003 197 4177	.164 413	51.420 709	.019 447 4177	7.78	1.178 111	4.21	112
29	6.487 312	337.680 750	.002 961 3770	.154 147	52.052 490	.019 211 3770	7.69	1.228 520	4.24	116
30	6.919 378	364.269 392	.002 745 2210	.144 522	52.644 820	.018 995 2210	7.60	1.279 427	4.26	120
31	7.380 219	392.628 880	.002 546 9344	.135 497	53.200 164	.018 796 9344	7.52	1.330 820	4.29	124
32	7.871 754	422.877 155	.002 364 7529	.127 036	53.720 831	.018 614 7529	7.45	1.382 688	4.32	128
33	8.396 025	455.140 015	.002 197 1261	.119 104	54.208 986	.018 447 1261	7.38	1.435 021	4.35	132
34	8.955 214	489.551 633	.002 042 6855	.111 667	54.666 659	.018 292 6855	7.32	1.487 805	4.38	136
35	9.551 646	526.255 119	.001 900 2190	.104 694	55.095 754	.018 150 2190	7.27	1.541 031	4.40	140
36	10.187 801	565.403 117	.001 768 6496	.098 157	55.498 055	.018 018 6496	7.21	1.594 686	4.43	144
37	10.866 325	607.158 435	.001 647 0166	.092 027	55.875 235	.017 897 0166	7.16	1.648 758	4.46	148
38	11.590 039	651.694 724	.001 534 4608	.086 281	56.228 862	.017 784 4608	7.12	1.703 238	4.48	152
39	12.361 955	699.197 202	.001 430 2117	.080 893	56.560 409	.017 680 2117	7.08	1.758 113	4.51	156
40	13.185 281	749.863 421	.001 333 5762	.075 842	56.871 252	.017 583 5762	7.04	1.813 372	4.53	160
41	14.063 441	803.904 092	.001 243 9295	.071 106	57.162 686	.017 493 9295	7.00	1.869 004	4.56	164
42	15.000 089	861.543 958	.001 160 7069	.066 666	57.435 922	.017 410 7069	6.97	1.924 999	4.58	168
43	15.999 119	923.022 732	.001 083 3969	.062 503	57.692 096	.017 333 3969	6.94	1.981 344	4.61	172
44	17.064 686	988.596 092	.001 011 5355	.058 601	57.932 274	.017 261 5355	6.91	2.038 030	4.63	176
45	18.201 222	1058.536 743	.000 944 7003	.054 941	58.157 454	.017 194 7003	6.88	2.095 046	4.66	180
46	19.413 453	1133.135 553	.000 882 5069	.051 511	58.368 574	.017 132 5069	6.86	2.152 381	4.68	184
47	20.706 420	1212.702 765	.000 824 6044	.048 294	58.566 511	.017 074 6044	6.83	2.210 026	4.70	188
48	22.085 501	1297.569 280	.000 770 6718	.045 279	58.752 088	.017 020 6718	6.81	2.267 969	4.72	192
49	23.556 431	1388.088 042	.000 720 4154	.042 451	58.926 077	.016 970 4154	6.79	2.326 201	4.75	196
50	25.125 327	1484.635 500	.000 673 5660	.039 800	59.089 201	.016 923 5660	6.77	2.384 713	4.77	200

QUARTERLY COMPOUND INTEREST AND ANNUITY

	Amount Of 1	Amount Of 1 Per Period	Sinking Fund Payment	Present Worth Of 1	Present Worth of 1 Per Period	Periodic Payment To Amortize 1	Constant Annual Percent	Total Interest	Annual Add On Rate	
	What a single $ 1 deposit grows to in the future. The deposit is made at the beginning of the first period.	What a series of $ 1 deposits grow to in the future. A deposit is made at the end of each period.	The amount to be deposited at the end of each period that grows to $ 1 in the future.	What $ 1 to be paid in the future is worth today. Value today of a single $ 1 payment tomorrow.	What $ 1 to be paid at the end of each period is worth today. Value today of a series of $ 1 payments tomorrow.	The mortgage payment to amortize a loan of $ 1. An annuity certain, payable at the end of each period, worth $ 1 today.	The annual payment, including interest and principal, to amortize completely a loan of $ 100.	The total interest paid over the term on a loan of $1. The loan is amortized by regular periodic payments.	The average annual interest rate on a loan that is completely amortized by regular periodic payments.	
	$S = (1+i)^n$	$S\overline{n}| = \dfrac{(1+i)^n - 1}{i}$	$\dfrac{1}{S\overline{n}|} = \dfrac{i}{(1+i)^n - 1}$	$V^n = \dfrac{1}{(1+i)^n}$	$A\overline{n}| = \dfrac{1 - V^n}{i}$	$\dfrac{1}{A\overline{n}|} = \dfrac{i}{1 - V^n}$				

YEAR										PERIODS
	1.016 563	1.000 000	1.000 000 0000	.983 707	.983 707	1.016 562 5000	406.63	.016 562	6.62	1
	1.033 399	2.016 563	.495 893 3829	.967 680	1.951 387	.512 455 8829	204.99	.024 912	4.98	2
	1.050 515	3.049 962	.327 872 9572	.951 914	2.903 302	.344 435 4572	137.78	.033 306	4.44	3
	1.067 914	4.100 477	.243 874 0777	.936 405	3.839 706	.260 436 5777	104.18	.041 746	4.17	4
1	1.067 914	4.100 477	.243 874 0777	.936 405	3.839 706	.260 436 5777	104.18	.041 746	4.17	4
2	1.140 441	8.479 434	.117 932 3997	.876 854	7.435 226	.134 494 8997	53.80	.075 959	3.80	8
3	1.217 893	13.155 784	.076 012 1916	.821 090	10.802 088	.092 574 6916	37.03	.110 896	3.70	12
4	1.300 605	18.149 725	.055 097 2535	.768 873	13.954 835	.071 659 7535	28.67	.146 556	3.66	16
5	1.388 934	23.482 825	.042 584 3144	.719 976	16.907 081	.059 146 8144	23.66	.182 936	3.66	20
6	1.483 263	29.178 118	.034 272 2587	.674 189	19.671 580	.050 834 7587	20.34	.220 034	3.67	24
7	1.583 997	35.260 202	.028 360 5866	.631 314	22.260 269	.044 923 0866	17.97	.257 846	3.68	28
8	1.691 573	41.755 345	.023 949 0298	.591 166	24.684 331	.040 511 5298	16.21	.296 369	3.70	32
9	1.806 455	48.691 600	.020 537 4232	.553 571	26.954 234	.037 099 9232	14.84	.335 597	3.73	36
10	1.929 138	56.098 926	.017 825 6533	.518 366	29.079 782	.034 388 1533	13.76	.375 526	3.76	40
11	2.060 154	64.009 313	.015 622 7266	.485 401	31.070 156	.032 185 2266	12.88	.416 150	3.78	44
12	2.200 068	72.456 928	.013 801 3028	.454 531	32.933 951	.030 363 8028	12.15	.457 463	3.81	48
13	2.349 484	81.478 255	.012 273 2132	.425 625	34.679 218	.028 835 7132	11.54	.499 457	3.84	52
14	2.509 047	91.112 258	.010 975 4716	.398 558	36.313 495	.027 537 9716	11.02	.542 126	3.87	56
15	2.679 447	101.400 546	.009 861 8798	.373 211	37.843 840	.026 424 3798	10.57	.585 463	3.90	60
16	2.861 419	112.387 555	.008 897 7823	.349 477	39.276 862	.025 460 2823	10.19	.629 458	3.93	64
17	3.055 750	124.120 763	.008 056 6715	.327 252	40.618 751	.024 619 1715	9.85	.674 104	3.97	68
18	3.263 278	136.650 767	.007 317 9245	.306 440	41.875 302	.023 880 4245	9.56	.719 391	4.00	72
19	3.484 901	150.031 764	.006 665 2552	.286 952	43.051 943	.023 227 7552	9.30	.765 309	4.03	76
20	3.721 575	164.321 520	.006 085 6302	.268 703	44.153 755	.022 648 1302	9.06	.811 850	4.06	80
21	3.974 323	179.581 753	.005 568 4945	.251 615	45.185 498	.022 130 9945	8.86	.859 004	4.09	84
22	4.244 236	195.878 372	.005 105 2089	.235 614	46.151 626	.021 667 7089	8.67	.906 758	4.12	88
23	4.532 479	213.281 761	.004 688 6335	.220 630	47.056 314	.021 251 1335	8.51	.955 104	4.15	92
24	4.840 299	231.867 087	.004 312 8156	.206 599	47.903 467	.020 875 3156	8.36	1.004 030	4.18	96
25	5.169 023	251.714 619	.003 972 7530	.193 460	48.696 746	.020 535 2530	8.22	1.053 525	4.21	100
26	5.520 073	272.910 079	.003 664 2106	.181 157	49.439 576	.020 226 7106	8.10	1.103 578	4.24	104
27	5.894 964	295.545 012	.003 383 5794	.169 636	50.135 166	.019 946 0794	7.98	1.154 177	4.27	108
28	6.295 316	319.717 176	.003 127 7644	.158 848	50.786 520	.019 690 2644	7.88	1.205 310	4.30	112
29	6.722 857	345.530 972	.002 894 0966	.148 746	51.396 450	.019 456 5966	7.79	1.256 965	4.33	116
30	7.179 434	373.097 890	.002 680 2617	.139 287	51.967 592	.019 242 7617	7.70	1.309 131	4.36	120
31	7.667 019	402.536 992	.002 484 2437	.130 429	52.502 413	.019 046 7437	7.62	1.361 796	4.39	124
32	8.187 718	433.975 425	.002 304 2779	.122 134	53.003 221	.018 866 7779	7.55	1.414 948	4.42	128
33	8.743 780	467.548 973	.002 138 8134	.114 367	53.472 180	.018 701 3134	7.49	1.468 573	4.45	132
34	9.337 606	503.402 639	.001 986 4814	.107 094	53.911 316	.018 548 9814	7.42	1.522 661	4.48	136
35	9.971 762	541.691 277	.001 846 0700	.100 283	54.322 525	.018 408 5700	7.37	1.577 200	4.51	140
36	10.648 985	582.580 255	.001 716 5017	.093 906	54.707 583	.018 279 0017	7.32	1.632 176	4.53	144
37	11.372 202	626.246 173	.001 596 8161	.087 934	55.068 153	.018 159 3161	7.27	1.687 579	4.56	148
38	12.144 536	672.877 624	.001 486 1543	.082 342	55.405 793	.018 048 6543	7.22	1.743 395	4.59	152
39	12.969 321	722.676 011	.001 383 7459	.077 105	55.721 960	.017 946 2459	7.18	1.799 614	4.61	156
40	13.850 122	775.856 413	.001 288 8983	.072 202	56.018 021	.017 851 3983	7.15	1.856 224	4.64	160
41	14.790 741	832.648 516	.001 200 9869	.067 610	56.295 253	.017 763 4869	7.11	1.913 212	4.67	164
42	15.795 242	893.297 607	.001 119 4478	.063 310	56.554 855	.017 681 9478	7.08	1.970 567	4.69	168
43	16.867 962	958.065 629	.001 043 7698	.059 284	56.797 948	.017 606 2698	7.05	2.028 278	4.72	172
44	18.013 535	1027.232 316	.000 973 4896	.055 514	57.025 581	.017 535 9896	7.02	2.086 334	4.74	176
45	19.236 909	1101.096 399	.000 908 1857	.051 983	57.238 738	.017 470 6857	6.99	2.144 723	4.77	180
46	20.543 367	1179.976 899	.000 847 4742	.048 678	57.438 339	.017 409 9742	6.97	2.203 435	4.79	184
47	21.938 553	1264.214 501	.000 791 0050	.045 582	57.625 246	.017 353 5050	6.95	2.262 459	4.81	188
48	23.428 491	1354.173 027	.000 738 4581	.042 683	57.800 267	.017 300 9581	6.93	2.321 784	4.84	192
49	25.019 617	1450.241 010	.000 689 5406	.039 969	57.964 158	.017 252 0406	6.91	2.381 400	4.86	196
50	26.718 803	1552.833 368	.000 643 9841	.037 427	58.117 626	.017 206 4841	6.89	2.441 297	4.88	200

Effective Rate is 6.79 %

Annual Percentage Rate is 6.625%

Amount Of 1	Amount Of 1 Per Period	Sinking Fund Payment	Present Worth Of 1	Present Worth of 1 Per Period	Periodic Payment To Amortize 1	Constant Annual Percent	Total Interest	Annual Add On Rate
What a single $ 1 deposit grows to in the future. The deposit is made at the beginning of the first period.	What a series of $ 1 deposits grow to in the future. A deposit is made at the end of each period.	The amount to be deposited at the end of each period that grows to $ 1 in the future.	What $ 1 to be paid in the future is worth today. Value today of a single $ 1 payment tomorrow.	What $ 1 to be paid at the end of each period is worth today. Value today of a series of $ 1 payments tomorrow.	The mortgage payment to amortize a loan of $ 1. An annuity certain, payable at the end of each period, worth $ 1 today.	The annual payment, including interest and principal, to amortize completely a loan of $ 100.	The total interest paid over the term on a loan of $1. The loan is amortized by regular periodic payments.	The average annual interest rate on a loan that is completely amortized by regular periodic payments.
$S = (1+i)^n$	$S\overline{n} = \dfrac{(1+i)^n - 1}{i}$	$\dfrac{1}{S\overline{n}} = \dfrac{i}{(1+i)^n - 1}$	$V^n = \dfrac{1}{(1+i)^n}$	$A\overline{n} = \dfrac{1 - V^n}{i}$	$\dfrac{1}{A\overline{n}} = \dfrac{i}{1 - V^n}$			

YEAR									PERIODS
	1.016 875	1.000 000	1.000 000 0000	.983 405	.983 405	1.016 875 0000	406.75	.016 875	6.75	1
	1.034 035	2.016 875	.495 816 5479	.967 085	1.950 491	.512 691 5479	205.08	.025 383	5.08	2
	1.051 484	3.050 910	.327 771 0837	.951 037	2.901 527	.344 646 0837	137.86	.033 938	4.53	3
	1.069 228	4.102 394	.243 760 1148	.935 254	3.836 782	.260 635 1148	104.26	.042 540	4.25	4
1	1.069 228	4.102 394	.243 760 1148	.935 254	3.836 782	.260 635 1148	104.26	.042 540	4.25	4
2	1.143 248	8.488 788	.117 802 4495	.874 701	7.425 148	.134 677 4495	53.88	.077 420	3.87	8
3	1.222 393	13.178 843	.075 879 1973	.818 068	10.781 183	.092 754 1973	37.11	.113 050	3.77	12
4	1.307 017	18.193 580	.054 964 4434	.765 101	13.919 930	.071 839 4434	28.74	.149 431	3.74	16
5	1.397 499	23.555 477	.042 452 9714	.715 564	16.855 456	.059 327 9714	23.74	.186 559	3.73	20
6	1.494 245	29.288 567	.034 143 0154	.669 234	19.600 919	.051 018 0154	20.41	.224 432	3.74	24
7	1.597 688	35.418 547	.028 233 7952	.625 904	22.168 626	.045 108 7952	18.05	.263 046	3.76	28
8	1.708 293	41.972 892	.023 824 9009	.585 380	24.570 084	.040 699 9009	16.28	.302 397	3.78	32
9	1.826 554	48.980 981	.020 416 0875	.547 479	26.816 059	.037 291 0875	14.92	.342 479	3.81	36
10	1.953 003	56.474 225	.017 707 1928	.512 032	28.916 616	.034 582 1928	13.84	.383 288	3.83	40
11	2.088 205	64.486 211	.015 507 1911	.478 880	30.881 172	.032 382 1911	12.96	.424 816	3.86	44
12	2.232 767	73.052 850	.013 688 7199	.447 875	32.718 530	.030 563 7199	12.23	.467 059	3.89	48
13	2.387 337	82.212 539	.012 163 5947	.418 877	34.436 928	.029 038 5947	11.62	.510 007	3.92	52
14	2.552 607	92.006 334	.010 868 8170	.391 756	36.044 067	.027 743 8170	11.10	.553 654	3.95	56
15	2.729 318	102.478 133	.009 758 1794	.366 392	37.547 151	.026 633 1794	10.66	.597 991	3.99	60
16	2.918 263	113.674 872	.008 797 0189	.342 670	38.952 916	.025 672 0189	10.27	.643 009	4.02	64
17	3.120 289	125.646 738	.007 958 8218	.320 483	40.267 664	.024 833 8218	9.94	.688 700	4.05	68
18	3.336 300	138.447 391	.007 222 9602	.299 733	41.497 288	.024 097 9602	9.64	.735 053	4.08	72
19	3.567 265	152.134 207	.006 573 1437	.280 327	42.647 299	.023 448 1437	9.38	.782 059	4.12	76
20	3.814 219	166.768 532	.005 996 3351	.262 177	43.722 852	.022 871 3351	9.15	.829 707	4.15	80
21	4.078 269	182.415 960	.005 481 9765	.245 202	44.728 767	.022 356 9765	8.95	.877 986	4.18	84
22	4.360 599	199.146 628	.005 021 4257	.229 326	45.669 554	.021 896 4257	8.76	.926 885	4.21	88
23	4.662 474	217.035 524	.004 607 5407	.214 478	46.549 429	.021 482 5407	8.60	.976 394	4.25	92
24	4.985 248	236.162 830	.004 234 3666	.200 592	47.372 336	.021 109 3666	8.45	1.026 499	4.28	96
25	5.330 366	256.614 280	.003 896 8993	.187 604	48.141 963	.020 771 8993	8.31	1.077 190	4.31	100
26	5.699 376	278.481 541	.003 590 9023	.175 458	48.861 760	.020 465 9023	8.19	1.128 454	4.34	104
27	6.093 932	301.862 626	.003 312 7652	.164 098	49.534 953	.020 187 7652	8.08	1.180 279	4.37	108
28	6.515 802	326.862 334	.003 059 3920	.153 473	50.164 560	.019 934 3920	7.98	1.232 652	4.40	112
29	6.966 877	353.592 720	.002 828 1125	.143 536	50.753 402	.019 703 1125	7.89	1.285 561	4.43	116
30	7.449 179	382.173 594	.002 616 6120	.134 243	51.304 120	.019 491 6120	7.80	1.338 993	4.46	120
31	7.964 870	412.733 062	.002 422 8735	.125 551	51.819 181	.019 297 8735	7.72	1.392 936	4.49	124
32	8.516 262	445.408 098	.002 245 1321	.117 422	52.300 894	.019 120 1321	7.65	1.447 377	4.52	128
33	9.105 825	480.345 157	.002 081 8363	.109 820	52.751 418	.018 956 8363	7.59	1.502 302	4.55	132
34	9.736 202	517.700 836	.001 931 6175	.102 709	53.172 773	.018 806 6175	7.53	1.557 700	4.58	136
35	10.410 218	557.642 570	.001 793 2634	.096 059	53.566 847	.018 668 2634	7.47	1.613 557	4.61	140
36	11.130 896	600.349 386	.001 665 6967	.089 840	53.935 406	.018 540 6967	7.42	1.669 860	4.64	144
37	11.901 464	646.012 705	.001 547 9572	.084 023	54.280 102	.018 422 9572	7.37	1.726 598	4.67	148
38	12.725 378	694.837 199	.001 439 1860	.078 583	54.602 481	.018 314 1860	7.33	1.783 756	4.69	152
39	13.606 329	747.041 711	.001 338 6133	.073 495	54.903 988	.018 213 6133	7.29	1.841 324	4.72	156
40	14.548 266	802.860 231	.001 245 5468	.068 737	55.185 973	.018 120 5468	7.25	1.899 287	4.75	160
41	15.555 412	862.542 950	.001 159 3626	.064 286	55.449 700	.018 034 3626	7.22	1.957 635	4.77	164
42	16.632 281	926.357 378	.001 079 4970	.060 124	55.696 353	.017 954 4970	7.19	2.016 355	4.80	168
43	17.783 699	994.589 544	.001 005 4399	.056 231	55.927 036	.017 880 4399	7.16	2.075 436	4.83	172
44	19.014 827	1067.545 280	.000 936 7284	.052 591	56.142 783	.017 811 7284	7.13	2.134 864	4.85	176
45	20.331 183	1145.551 588	.000 872 9419	.049 186	56.344 561	.017 747 9419	7.10	2.194 630	4.88	180
46	21.738 668	1228.958 109	.000 813 6974	.046 001	56.533 275	.017 688 6974	7.08	2.254 720	4.90	184
47	23.243 590	1318.138 688	.000 758 6455	.043 023	56.709 771	.017 633 6455	7.06	2.315 125	4.93	188
48	24.852 695	1413.493 050	.000 707 4672	.040 237	56.874 839	.017 582 4672	7.04	2.375 834	4.95	192
49	26.573 195	1515.448 595	.000 659 8706	.037 632	57.029 220	.017 534 8706	7.02	2.436 835	4.97	196
50	28.412 801	1624.462 307	.000 615 5883	.035 195	57.173 606	.017 490 5883	7.00	2.498 118	5.00	200

Effective Rate is 6.92 %   Annual Percentage Rate is 6.75 %

	Amount Of 1	Amount Of 1 Per Period	Sinking Fund Payment	Present Worth Of 1	Present Worth of 1 Per Period	Periodic Payment To Amortize 1	Constant Annual Percent	Total Interest	Annual Add On Rate	
	What a single $ 1 deposit grows to in the future. The deposit is made at the beginning of the first period.	What a series of $ 1 deposits grow to in the future. A deposit is made at the end of each period.	The amount to be deposited at the end of each period that grows to $ 1 in the future.	What $ 1 to be paid in the future is worth today. Value today of a single $ 1 payment tomorrow.	What $ 1 to be paid at the end of each period is worth today. Value today of a series of $ 1 payments tomorrow.	The mortgage payment to amortize a loan of $ 1. An annuity certain, payable at the end of each period, worth $ 1 today.	The annual payment, including interest and principal, to amortize completely a loan of $ 100.	The total interest paid over the term on a loan of $1. The loan is amortized by regular periodic payments.	The average annual interest rate on a loan that is completely amortized by regular periodic payments.	
	$S = (1+i)^n$	$S\overline{n} = \dfrac{(1+i)^n - 1}{i}$	$\dfrac{1}{S\overline{n}} = \dfrac{i}{(1+i)^n - 1}$	$V^n = \dfrac{1}{(1+i)^n}$	$A\overline{n} = \dfrac{1 - V^n}{i}$	$\dfrac{1}{A\overline{n}} = \dfrac{i}{1 - V^n}$				

YEAR										PERIODS
	1.017 187	1.000 000	1.000 000 0000	.983 103	.983 103	1.017 187 5000	406.88	.017 188	6.88	1
	1.034 670	2.017 187	.495 739 7366	.966 491	1.949 594	.512 927 2366	205.18	.025 854	5.17	2
	1.052 454	3.051 858	.327 669 2524	.950 160	2.899 755	.344 856 7524	137.95	.034 570	4.61	3
	1.070 543	4.104 312	.243 646 2113	.934 106	3.833 860	.260 833 7113	104.34	.043 335	4.33	4
1	1.070 543	4.104 312	.243 646 2113	.934 106	3.833 860	.260 833 7113	104.34	.043 335	4.33	4
2	1.146 062	8.498 153	.117 672 6241	.872 553	7.415 090	.134 860 1241	53.95	.078 881	3.94	8
3	1.226 908	13.201 949	.075 746 3914	.815 057	10.760 337	.092 933 8914	37.18	.115 207	3.84	12
4	1.313 458	18.237 564	.054 831 8844	.761 349	13.885 151	.072 019 3844	28.81	.152 310	3.81	16
5	1.406 113	23.628 406	.042 321 9416	.711 180	16.804 056	.059 509 4416	23.81	.190 189	3.80	20
6	1.505 304	29.399 533	.034 014 1463	.664 317	19.530 622	.051 201 6463	20.49	.228 840	3.81	24
7	1.611 493	35.577 771	.028 107 4380	.620 543	22.077 522	.045 294 9380	18.12	.268 258	3.83	28
8	1.725 172	42.191 841	.023 701 2651	.579 652	24.456 596	.040 888 7651	16.36	.308 440	3.86	32
9	1.846 871	49.272 485	.020 295 3026	.541 456	26.678 902	.037 482 8026	15.00	.349 381	3.88	36
10	1.977 154	56.852 619	.017 589 3392	.505 777	28.754 770	.034 776 8392	13.92	.391 074	3.91	40
11	2.116 629	64.967 477	.015 392 3170	.472 449	30.693 850	.032 579 8170	13.04	.433 512	3.94	44
12	2.265 942	73.654 780	.013 576 8513	.441 318	32.505 155	.030 764 3513	12.31	.476 689	3.97	48
13	2.425 788	82.954 911	.012 054 7415	.412 237	34.197 105	.029 242 2415	11.70	.520 597	4.00	52
14	2.596 910	92.911 099	.010 762 9768	.385 073	35.777 565	.027 950 4768	11.19	.565 227	4.04	56
15	2.780 103	103.569 625	.009 655 3406	.359 699	37.253 881	.026 842 8406	10.74	.610 570	4.07	60
16	2.976 219	114.980 034	.008 697 1622	.335 997	38.632 917	.025 884 6622	10.36	.656 618	4.10	64
17	3.186 170	127.195 366	.007 861 9217	.313 856	39.921 081	.025 049 4217	10.02	.703 361	4.14	68
18	3.410 932	140.272 402	.007 128 9861	.293 175	41.124 363	.024 316 4861	9.73	.750 787	4.17	72
19	3.651 549	154.271 930	.006 482 0606	.273 856	42.248 355	.023 669 5606	9.47	.798 887	4.20	76
20	3.909 139	169.259 024	.005 908 1045	.255 811	43.298 282	.023 095 6045	9.24	.847 648	4.24	80
21	4.184 901	185.303 351	.005 396 5565	.238 954	44.279 025	.022 584 0565	9.04	.897 061	4.27	84
22	4.480 116	202.479 491	.004 938 7718	.223 208	45.195 142	.022 126 2718	8.86	.947 112	4.31	88
23	4.796 156	220.867 285	.004 527 6058	.208 500	46.050 892	.021 715 1058	8.69	.997 790	4.34	92
24	5.134 491	240.552 206	.004 157 1018	.194 761	46.850 253	.021 344 6018	8.54	1.049 082	4.37	96
25	5.496 693	261.625 758	.003 822 2536	.181 928	47.596 941	.021 009 7536	8.41	1.100 975	4.40	100
26	5.884 445	284.185 898	.003 518 8234	.169 940	48.294 426	.020 706 3234	8.29	1.153 458	4.44	104
27	6.299 551	308.337 495	.003 243 1995	.158 741	48.945 950	.020 430 6995	8.18	1.206 516	4.47	108
28	6.743 939	334.192 815	.002 992 2846	.148 281	49.554 543	.020 179 7846	8.08	1.260 136	4.50	112
29	7.219 676	361.872 042	.002 763 4077	.138 510	50.123 033	.019 950 9077	7.99	1.314 305	4.53	116
30	7.728 972	391.503 842	.002 554 2533	.129 383	50.654 062	.019 741 7533	7.90	1.369 010	4.56	120
31	8.274 196	423.225 954	.002 362 8041	.120 858	51.150 100	.019 550 3041	7.83	1.424 238	4.59	124
32	8.857 882	457.185 834	.002 187 2944	.112 894	51.613 451	.019 374 7944	7.75	1.479 979	4.62	128
33	9.482 742	493.541 341	.002 026 1727	.105 455	52.046 270	.019 213 6727	7.69	1.536 205	4.66	132
34	10.151 681	532.461 469	.001 878 0702	.098 506	52.450 569	.019 065 5702	7.63	1.592 918	4.69	136
35	10.867 810	574.127 134	.001 741 7745	.092 015	52.828 226	.018 929 2745	7.58	1.650 098	4.71	140
36	11.634 456	618.732 015	.001 616 2086	.085 952	53.180 999	.018 803 7086	7.53	1.707 734	4.74	144
37	12.455 184	666.483 451	.001 500 4123	.080 288	53.510 525	.018 687 9123	7.48	1.765 811	4.77	148
38	13.333 809	717.603 410	.001 393 5274	.074 997	53.818 337	.018 581 0274	7.44	1.824 316	4.80	152
39	14.274 414	772.329 516	.001 294 7841	.070 055	54.105 867	.018 482 2841	7.40	1.883 236	4.83	156
40	15.281 371	830.916 159	.001 203 4909	.065 439	54.374 449	.018 390 9909	7.36	1.942 559	4.86	160
41	16.359 363	893.635 671	.001 119 0243	.061 127	54.625 334	.018 306 5243	7.33	2.002 270	4.88	164
42	17.513 399	960.779 597	.001 040 8214	.057 099	54.859 687	.018 228 3214	7.30	2.062 358	4.91	168
43	18.748 845	1032.660 047	.000 968 3729	.053 337	55.078 597	.018 155 8729	7.27	2.122 810	4.94	172
44	20.071 442	1109.611 150	.000 901 2166	.049 822	55.283 082	.018 088 7166	7.24	2.183 614	4.96	176
45	21.487 338	1191.990 603	.000 838 9328	.046 539	55.474 093	.018 026 4328	7.22	2.244 758	4.99	180
46	23.003 117	1280.181 338	.000 781 1393	.043 472	55.652 517	.017 968 6393	7.19	2.306 230	5.01	184
47	24.625 822	1374.593 299	.000 727 4879	.040 608	55.819 184	.017 914 9879	7.17	2.368 018	5.04	188
48	26.362 998	1475.665 351	.000 677 6604	.037 932	55.974 868	.017 865 1604	7.15	2.430 111	5.06	192
49	28.222 719	1583.867 313	.000 631 3660	.035 432	56.120 294	.017 818 8660	7.13	2.492 498	5.09	196
50	30.213 631	1699.702 151	.000 588 3384	.033 098	56.256 137	.017 775 8384	7.12	2.555 168	5.11	200

	Amount Of 1	Amount Of 1 Per Period	Sinking Fund Payment	Present Worth Of 1	Present Worth of 1 Per Period	Periodic Payment To Amortize 1	Constant Annual Percent	Total Interest	Annual Add On Rate	
	What a single $ 1 deposit grows to in the future. The deposit is made at the beginning of the first period.	What a series of $ 1 deposits grow to in the future. A deposit is made at the end of each period.	The amount to be deposited at the end of each period that grows to $ 1 in the future.	What $ 1 to be paid in the future is worth today. Value today of a single $ 1 payment tomorrow.	What $ 1 to be paid at the end of each period is worth today. Value today of a series of $ 1 payments tomorrow.	The mortgage payment to amortize a loan of $ 1. An annuity certain, payable at the end of each period, worth $ 1 today.	The annual payment, including interest and principal, to amortize completely a loan of $ 100.	The total interest paid over the term on a loan of $1. The loan is amortized by regular periodic payments.	The average annual interest rate on a loan that is completely amortized by regular periodic payments.	
	$S = (1+i)^n$	$S\overline{n}| = \dfrac{(1+i)^n - 1}{i}$	$\dfrac{1}{S\overline{n}|} = \dfrac{i}{(1+i)^n - 1}$	$V^n = \dfrac{1}{(1+i)^n}$	$A\overline{n}| = \dfrac{1-V^n}{i}$	$\dfrac{1}{A\overline{n}|} = \dfrac{i}{1-V^n}$				

YEAR										PERIODS
	1.017 500	1.000 000	1.000 000 0000	.982 801	.982 801	1.017 500 0000	407.00	.017 500	7.00	1
	1.035 306	2.017 500	.495 662 9492	.965 898	1.948 699	.513 162 9492	205.27	.026 326	5.27	2
	1.053 424	3.052 806	.327 567 4635	.949 285	2.897 984	.345 067 4635	138.03	.035 202	4.69	3
	1.071 859	4.106 230	.243 532 3673	.932 959	3.830 943	.261 032 3673	104.42	.044 129	4.41	4
1	1.071 859	4.106 230	.243 532 3673	.932 959	3.830 943	.261 032 3673	104.42	.044 129	4.41	4
2	1.148 882	8.507 530	.117 542 9233	.870 412	7.405 053	.135 042 9233	54.02	.080 343	4.02	8
3	1.231 439	13.225 104	.075 613 7738	.812 058	10.739 550	.093 113 7738	37.25	.117 365	3.91	12
4	1.319 929	18.281 677	.054 699 5764	.757 616	13.850 497	.072 199 5764	28.88	.155 193	3.88	16
5	1.414 778	23.701 611	.042 191 2246	.706 825	16.752 881	.059 691 2246	23.88	.193 824	3.88	20
6	1.516 443	29.511 016	.033 885 6510	.659 438	19.460 686	.051 385 6510	20.56	.233 256	3.89	24
7	1.625 413	35.737 880	.027 981 5145	.615 228	21.986 955	.045 481 5145	18.20	.273 482	3.91	28
8	1.742 213	42.412 200	.023 578 1216	.573 982	24.343 859	.041 078 1216	16.44	.314 500	3.93	32
9	1.867 407	49.566 129	.020 175 0673	.535 502	26.542 753	.037 675 0673	15.08	.356 302	3.96	36
10	2.001 597	57.234 134	.017 472 0911	.499 601	28.594 230	.034 972 0911	13.99	.398 884	3.99	40
11	2.145 430	65.453 154	.015 278 1026	.466 107	30.508 172	.032 778 1026	13.12	.442 237	4.02	44
12	2.299 599	74.262 784	.013 465 6950	.434 858	32.293 801	.030 965 6950	12.39	.486 353	4.05	48
13	2.464 846	83.705 466	.011 946 6511	.405 705	33.959 719	.029 446 6511	11.78	.531 226	4.09	52
14	2.641 967	93.826 690	.010 657 9481	.378 506	35.513 951	.028 157 9481	11.27	.576 845	4.12	56
15	2.831 816	104.675 216	.009 553 3598	.353 130	36.963 986	.027 053 3598	10.83	.623 202	4.15	60
16	3.035 308	116.303 306	.008 598 2079	.329 456	38.316 807	.026 098 2079	10.44	.670 285	4.19	64
17	3.253 422	128.766 979	.007 765 9661	.307 369	39.578 934	.025 265 9661	10.11	.718 086	4.22	68
18	3.487 210	142.126 280	.007 035 9964	.286 762	40.756 445	.024 535 9964	9.82	.766 592	4.26	72
19	3.737 797	156.445 567	.006 391 9996	.267 537	41.855 015	.023 891 9996	9.56	.815 792	4.29	76
20	4.006 392	171.793 824	.005 820 9310	.249 601	42.879 935	.023 320 9310	9.33	.865 674	4.33	80
21	4.294 287	188.244 992	.005 312 2263	.232 868	43.836 142	.022 812 2263	9.13	.916 227	4.36	84
22	4.602 871	205.878 326	.004 857 2379	.217 256	44.728 244	.022 357 2379	8.95	.967 437	4.40	88
23	4.933 629	224.778 773	.004 448 8187	.202 691	45.560 539	.021 948 8187	8.78	1.019 291	4.43	92
24	5.288 154	245.037 388	.004 081 0099	.189 102	46.337 035	.021 581 0099	8.64	1.071 777	4.47	96
25	5.668 156	266.751 768	.003 748 8036	.176 424	47.061 473	.021 248 8036	8.50	1.124 880	4.50	100
26	6.075 464	290.026 522	.003 447 9605	.164 596	47.737 344	.020 947 9605	8.38	1.178 588	4.53	104
27	6.512 041	314.973 777	.003 174 8675	.153 562	48.367 904	.020 674 8675	8.27	1.232 886	4.57	108
28	6.979 990	341.713 718	.002 926 4263	.143 267	48.956 190	.020 426 4263	8.18	1.287 760	4.60	112
29	7.481 565	370.375 165	.002 699 9650	.133 662	49.505 036	.020 199 9650	8.08	1.343 196	4.63	116
30	8.019 183	401.096 196	.002 493 1675	.124 701	50.017 087	.019 993 1675	8.00	1.399 180	4.66	120
31	8.595 434	434.024 811	.002 304 0158	.116 341	50.494 809	.019 804 0158	7.93	1.455 698	4.70	124
32	9.213 094	469.319 643	.002 130 7440	.108 541	50.940 504	.019 630 7440	7.86	1.512 735	4.73	128
33	9.875 138	507.150 729	.001 971 8004	.101 264	51.356 319	.019 471 8004	7.79	1.570 278	4.76	132
34	10.584 756	547.700 319	.001 825 8160	.094 475	51.744 258	.019 325 8160	7.74	1.628 311	4.79	136
35	11.345 366	591.163 764	.001 691 5786	.088 142	52.106 188	.019 191 5786	7.68	1.686 821	4.82	140
36	12.160 633	637.750 450	.001 568 0114	.082 233	52.443 854	.019 068 0114	7.63	1.745 794	4.85	144
37	13.034 484	687.684 809	.001 454 1546	.076 720	52.758 882	.018 954 1546	7.59	1.805 215	4.88	148
38	13.971 130	741.207 404	.001 349 1500	.071 576	53.052 790	.018 849 1500	7.54	1.865 071	4.91	152
39	14.975 081	798.576 080	.001 252 2288	.066 778	53.326 994	.018 752 2288	7.51	1.925 348	4.94	156
40	16.051 176	860.067 214	.001 162 6998	.062 301	53.582 815	.018 662 6998	7.47	1.986 032	4.97	160
41	17.204 598	925.977 042	.001 079 9404	.058 124	53.821 486	.018 579 9404	7.44	2.047 110	4.99	164
42	18.440 904	996.623 085	.001 003 3884	.054 227	54.044 156	.018 503 3884	7.41	2.108 569	5.02	168
43	19.766 049	1072.345 685	.000 932 5351	.050 592	54.251 897	.018 432 5351	7.38	2.170 396	5.05	172
44	21.186 419	1153.509 637	.000 866 9195	.047 200	54.445 711	.018 366 9195	7.35	2.232 578	5.07	176
45	22.708 854	1240.505 953	.000 806 1227	.044 036	54.626 532	.018 306 1227	7.33	2.295 102	5.10	180
46	24.340 690	1333.753 739	.000 749 7636	.041 083	54.795 230	.018 249 7636	7.30	2.357 957	5.13	184
47	26.089 789	1433.702 221	.000 697 4949	.038 329	54.952 619	.018 197 4949	7.28	2.421 129	5.15	188
48	27.964 576	1540.832 905	.000 648 9996	.035 760	55.099 456	.018 148 9996	7.26	2.484 608	5.18	192
49	29.974 083	1655.661 895	.000 603 9881	.033 362	55.236 448	.018 103 9881	7.25	2.548 382	5.20	196
50	32.127 992	1778.742 385	.000 562 1950	.031 126	55.364 257	.018 062 1950	7.23	2.612 439	5.22	200

	Amount Of 1	Amount Of 1 Per Period	Sinking Fund Payment	Present Worth Of 1	Present Worth of 1 Per Period	Periodic Payment To Amortize 1	Constant Annual Percent	Total Interest	Annual Add On Rate	
	What a single $ 1 deposit grows to in the future. The deposit is made at the beginning of the first period.	What a series of $ 1 deposits grow to in the future. A deposit is made at the end of each period.	The amount to be deposited at the end of each period that grows to $ 1 in the future.	What $ 1 to be paid in the future is worth today. Value today of a single $ 1 payment tomorrow.	What $ 1 to be paid at the end of each period is worth today. Value today of a series of $ 1 payments tomorrow.	The mortgage payment to amortize a loan of $ 1. An annuity certain, payable at the end of each period, worth $ 1 today.	The annual payment, including interest and principal, to amortize completely a loan of $ 100.	The total interest paid over the term on a loan of $1. The loan is amortized by regular periodic payments.	The average annual interest rate on a loan that is completely amortized by regular periodic payments.	
	$S = (1+i)^n$	$S\overline{n} = \dfrac{(1+i)^n - 1}{i}$	$\dfrac{1}{S\overline{n}} = \dfrac{i}{(1+i)^n - 1}$	$V^n = \dfrac{1}{(1+i)^n}$	$A\overline{n} = \dfrac{1-V^n}{i}$	$\dfrac{1}{A\overline{n}} = \dfrac{i}{1-V^n}$				

YEAR										PERIODS
	1.017 813	1.000 000	1.000 000 0000	.982 499	.982 499	1.017 812 5000	407.13	.017 812	7.12	1
	1.035 942	2.017 813	.495 586 1855	.965 305	1.947 804	.513 398 6855	205.36	.026 797	5.36	2
	1.054 395	3.053 755	.327 465 7169	.948 411	2.896 215	.345 278 2169	138.12	.035 835	4.78	3
	1.073 176	4.108 150	.243 418 5827	.931 813	3.828 028	.261 231 0827	104.50	.044 924	4.49	4
1	1.073 176	4.108 150	.243 418 5827	.931 813	3.828 028	.261 231 0827	104.50	.044 924	4.49	4
2	1.151 708	8.516 919	.117 413 3473	.868 276	7.395 036	.135 225 8473	54.10	.081 807	4.09	8
3	1.235 985	13.248 307	.075 481 3443	.809 071	10.718 821	.093 293 8443	37.32	.119 526	3.98	12
4	1.326 430	18.325 920	.054 567 5193	.753 903	13.815 968	.072 380 0193	28.96	.158 080	3.95	16
5	1.423 494	23.775 095	.042 060 8202	.702 497	16.701 930	.059 873 3202	23.95	.197 466	3.95	20
6	1.527 660	29.623 021	.033 757 5291	.654 596	19.391 108	.051 570 0291	20.63	.237 681	3.96	24
7	1.639 449	35.898 878	.027 856 0241	.609 961	21.896 920	.045 668 5241	18.27	.278 719	3.98	28
8	1.759 418	42.633 979	.023 455 4698	.568 370	24.231 868	.041 267 9698	16.51	.320 575	4.01	32
9	1.888 166	49.861 930	.020 055 3808	.529 615	26.407 604	.037 867 8808	15.15	.363 244	4.04	36
10	2.026 335	57.618 798	.017 355 4472	.493 502	28.434 984	.035 167 9472	14.07	.406 718	4.07	40
11	2.174 615	65.943 285	.015 164 5464	.459 852	30.324 123	.032 977 0464	13.20	.450 990	4.10	44
12	2.333 745	74.876 928	.013 355 2488	.428 496	32.084 447	.031 167 7488	12.47	.496 052	4.13	48
13	2.504 520	84.464 303	.011 839 3211	.399 278	33.724 741	.029 651 8211	11.87	.541 895	4.17	52
14	2.687 792	94.753 248	.010 553 7279	.372 053	35.253 189	.028 366 2279	11.35	.588 509	4.20	56
15	2.884 475	105.795 101	.009 452 2335	.346 684	36.677 417	.027 264 7335	10.91	.635 884	4.24	60
16	3.095 551	117.644 957	.008 500 1518	.323 044	38.004 531	.026 312 6518	10.53	.684 010	4.28	64
17	3.322 072	130.361 944	.007 670 9504	.301 017	39.241 154	.025 483 4504	10.20	.732 875	4.31	68
18	3.565 169	144.009 514	.006 943 9857	.280 492	40.393 455	.024 756 4857	9.91	.782 467	4.35	72
19	3.826 056	158.655 764	.006 302 9541	.261 366	41.467 185	.024 115 4541	9.65	.832 775	4.38	76
20	4.106 033	174.373 774	.005 734 8073	.243 544	42.467 701	.023 547 3073	9.42	.883 785	4.42	80
21	4.406 498	191.241 972	.005 228 9777	.226 938	43.399 994	.023 041 4777	9.22	.935 484	4.45	84
22	4.728 949	209.344 524	.004 776 8147	.211 463	44.268 718	.022 589 3147	9.04	.987 860	4.49	88
23	5.074 997	228.771 757	.004 371 1690	.197 044	45.078 206	.022 183 6690	8.88	1.040 898	4.53	92
24	5.446 367	249.620 604	.004 006 0796	.183 609	45.832 498	.021 818 5796	8.73	1.094 584	4.56	96
25	5.844 913	271.995 096	.003 676 5369	.171 089	46.535 357	.021 489 0369	8.60	1.148 904	4.60	100
26	6.272 622	296.006 872	.003 378 2999	.159 423	47.190 290	.021 190 7999	8.48	1.203 843	4.63	104
27	6.731 630	321.775 745	.003 107 7544	.148 552	47.800 566	.020 920 2544	8.37	1.259 387	4.66	108
28	7.224 227	349.430 291	.002 861 8011	.138 423	48.369 229	.020 674 3011	8.27	1.315 522	4.70	112
29	7.752 870	379.108 498	.002 637 7673	.128 984	48.899 116	.020 450 2673	8.19	1.372 231	4.73	116
30	8.320 197	410.958 450	.002 433 3360	.120 189	49.392 873	.020 245 8360	8.10	1.429 500	4.77	120
31	8.929 040	445.139 067	.002 246 4890	.111 994	49.852 961	.020 058 9890	8.03	1.487 315	4.80	124
32	9.582 435	481.820 899	.002 075 4600	.104 358	50.281 678	.019 887 9600	7.96	1.545 659	4.83	128
33	10.283 643	521.186 976	.001 918 6972	.097 242	50.681 162	.019 731 1972	7.90	1.604 518	4.86	132
34	11.036 163	563.433 722	.001 774 8316	.090 611	51.053 406	.019 587 3316	7.84	1.663 877	4.89	136
35	11.843 750	608.771 934	.001 642 6513	.084 433	51.400 269	.019 455 1513	7.79	1.723 721	4.92	140
36	12.710 433	657.427 833	.001 521 0795	.078 676	51.723 479	.019 333 5795	7.74	1.784 035	4.96	144
37	13.640 537	709.644 197	.001 409 1569	.073 311	52.024 651	.019 221 6569	7.69	1.844 805	4.99	148
38	14.638 703	765.681 567	.001 306 0260	.068 312	52.305 288	.019 118 5260	7.65	1.906 016	5.02	152
39	15.709 911	825.819 552	.001 210 9183	.063 654	52.566 788	.019 023 4183	7.61	1.967 653	5.05	156
40	16.859 506	890.358 218	.001 123 1434	.059 314	52.810 458	.018 935 6434	7.58	2.029 703	5.07	160
41	18.093 224	959.619 594	.001 042 0796	.055 269	53.037 512	.018 854 5796	7.55	2.092 151	5.10	164
42	19.417 221	1033.949 268	.000 967 1654	.051 501	53.249 085	.018 779 6654	7.52	2.154 984	5.13	168
43	20.838 104	1113.718 122	.000 897 8933	.047 989	53.446 231	.018 710 3933	7.49	2.218 188	5.16	172
44	22.362 962	1199.324 175	.000 833 8029	.044 717	53.629 934	.018 646 3029	7.46	2.281 749	5.19	176
45	23.999 403	1291.194 572	.000 774 4766	.041 668	53.801 111	.018 586 9766	7.44	2.345 656	5.21	180
46	25.755 594	1389.787 715	.000 719 5343	.038 827	53.960 617	.018 532 0343	7.42	2.409 894	5.24	184
47	27.640 296	1495.595 552	.000 668 6300	.036 179	54.109 246	.018 481 1300	7.40	2.474 452	5.26	188
48	29.662 914	1609.146 028	.000 621 4476	.033 712	54.247 740	.018 433 9476	7.38	2.539 318	5.29	192
49	31.833 539	1731.005 720	.000 577 6988	.031 413	54.376 791	.018 390 1988	7.36	2.604 479	5.32	196
50	34.163 004	1861.782 668	.000 537 1196	.029 271	54.497 042	.018 349 6196	7.34	2.669 924	5.34	200

Effective Rate is 7.32 %

Annual Percentage Rate is 7.125%

QUARTERLY COMPOUND INTEREST AND ANNUITY

7.25 % Q

	Amount Of 1	Amount Of 1 Per Period	Sinking Fund Payment	Present Worth Of 1	Present Worth of 1 Per Period	Periodic Payment To Amortize 1	Constant Annual Percent	Total Interest	Annual Add On Rate	
	What a single $ 1 deposit grows to in the future. The deposit is made at the beginning of the first period.	What a series of $ 1 deposits grow to in the future. A deposit is made at the end of each period.	The amount to be deposited at the end of each period that grows to $ 1 in the future.	What $ 1 to be paid in the future is worth today. Value today of a single $ 1 payment tomorrow.	What $ 1 to be paid at the end of each period is worth today. Value today of a series of $ 1 payments tomorrow.	The mortgage payment to amortize a loan of $ 1. An annuity certain, payable at the end of each period, worth $ 1 today.	The annual payment, including interest and principal, to amortize completely a loan of $ 100.	The total interest paid over the term on a loan of $1. The loan is amortized by regular periodic payments.	The average annual interest rate on a loan that is completely amortized by regular periodic payments.	
	$S = (1+i)^n$	$S\overline{n}| = \dfrac{(1+i)^n - 1}{i}$	$\dfrac{1}{S\overline{n}|} = \dfrac{i}{(1+i)^n - 1}$	$V^n = \dfrac{1}{(1+i)^n}$	$A\overline{n}| = \dfrac{1-V^n}{i}$	$\dfrac{1}{A\overline{n}|} = \dfrac{i}{1-V^n}$				

YEAR										PERIODS
	1.018 125	1.000 000	1.000 000 0000	.982 198	.982 198	1.018 125 0000	407.25	.018 125	7.25	1
	1.036 579	2.018 125	.495 509 4456	.964 712	1.946 910	.513 634 4456	205.46	.027 269	5.45	2
	1.055 367	3.054 704	.327 364 0125	.947 538	2.894 448	.345 489 0125	138.20	.036 467	4.86	3
	1.074 495	4.110 070	.243 304 8576	.930 670	3.825 118	.261 429 8576	104.58	.045 719	4.57	4
1	1.074 495	4.110 070	.243 304 8576	.930 670	3.825 118	.261 429 8576	104.58	.045 719	4.57	4
2	1.154 540	8.526 320	.117 283 8958	.866 146	7.385 039	.135 408 8958	54.17	.083 271	4.16	8
3	1.240 547	13.271 558	.075 349 1029	.806 096	10.698 150	.093 474 1029	37.39	.121 689	4.06	12
4	1.332 962	18.370 293	.054 435 7127	.750 209	13.781 563	.072 560 7127	29.03	.160 971	4.02	16
5	1.432 261	23.848 858	.041 930 7281	.698 197	16.651 201	.060 055 7281	24.03	.201 115	4.02	20
6	1.538 957	29.735 550	.033 629 7802	.649 791	19.321 887	.051 754 7802	20.71	.242 115	4.04	24
7	1.653 601	36.060 770	.027 730 9663	.604 741	21.807 413	.045 855 9663	18.35	.283 967	4.06	28
8	1.776 787	42.857 188	.023 333 3089	.562 814	24.120 617	.041 458 3089	16.59	.326 666	4.08	32
9	1.909 148	50.159 905	.019 936 2420	.523 794	26.273 446	.038 061 2420	15.23	.370 205	4.11	36
10	2.051 370	58.006 638	.017 239 4063	.487 479	28.277 019	.035 364 4063	14.15	.414 576	4.15	40
11	2.204 187	66.437 914	.015 051 6467	.453 682	30.141 684	.033 176 6467	13.28	.459 772	4.18	44
12	2.368 388	75.497 277	.013 245 5108	.422 228	31.877 071	.031 370 5108	12.55	.505 785	4.21	48
13	2.544 821	85.231 518	.011 732 7489	.392 955	33.492 143	.029 857 7489	11.95	.552 603	4.25	52
14	2.734 398	95.690 912	.010 450 3132	.365 711	34.995 242	.028 575 3132	11.44	.600 218	4.29	56
15	2.938 097	106.929 478	.009 351 9581	.340 356	36.394 131	.027 476 9581	11.00	.648 617	4.32	60
16	3.156 970	119.005 262	.008 402 9898	.316 759	37.696 034	.026 527 9898	10.62	.697 791	4.36	64
17	3.392 149	131.980 694	.007 576 8694	.294 798	38.907 676	.025 701 8694	10.29	.747 727	4.40	68
18	3.644 847	145.922 601	.006 852 9480	.274 360	40.035 314	.024 977 9480	10.00	.798 412	4.44	72
19	3.916 370	160.903 178	.006 214 9177	.255 338	41.084 773	.024 339 9177	9.74	.849 834	4.47	76
20	4.208 120	176.999 733	.005 649 7260	.237 636	42.061 473	.023 774 7260	9.51	.901 978	4.51	80
21	4.521 604	194.295 401	.005 146 8022	.221 160	42.970 458	.023 271 8022	9.31	.954 831	4.55	84
22	4.858 441	212.879 511	.004 697 4929	.205 827	43.816 423	.022 822 4929	9.13	1.008 379	4.58	88
23	5.220 371	232.848 044	.004 294 6463	.191 557	44.603 737	.022 419 6463	8.97	1.062 607	4.62	92
24	5.609 262	254.304 134	.003 932 2994	.178 277	45.336 466	.022 057 2994	8.83	1.117 501	4.66	96
25	6.027 125	277.358 595	.003 605 4408	.165 917	46.018 395	.021 730 4408	8.70	1.173 044	4.69	100
26	6.476 115	302.130 499	.003 309 8280	.154 414	46.653 045	.021 434 8280	8.58	1.229 222	4.73	104
27	6.958 554	328.747 786	.003 041 8456	.143 708	47.243 695	.021 166 8456	8.47	1.286 019	4.76	108
28	7.476 931	357.347 929	.002 798 3932	.133 745	47.793 395	.020 923 3932	8.37	1.343 420	4.80	112
29	8.033 925	388.078 640	.002 576 7973	.124 472	48.304 985	.020 701 7973	8.29	1.401 408	4.83	116
30	8.632 413	421.098 635	.002 374 7405	.115 842	48.781 105	.020 499 7405	8.20	1.459 969	4.87	120
31	9.275 485	456.578 456	.002 190 2041	.107 811	49.224 216	.020 315 2041	8.13	1.519 085	4.90	124
32	9.966 462	494.701 347	.002 021 4216	.100 337	49.636 606	.020 146 4216	8.06	1.578 742	4.93	128
33	10.708 914	535.664 203	.001 866 8412	.093 380	50.020 405	.019 991 8412	8.00	1.638 923	4.97	132
34	11.506 674	579.678 588	.001 725 0939	.086 906	50.377 595	.019 850 0939	7.95	1.699 613	5.00	136
35	12.363 864	626.971 826	.001 594 9680	.080 881	50.710 021	.019 719 9680	7.89	1.760 796	5.03	140
36	13.284 911	677.788 174	.001 475 3872	.075 273	51.019 400	.019 600 3872	7.85	1.822 456	5.06	144
37	14.274 570	732.390 087	.001 365 3926	.070 055	51.307 330	.019 490 3926	7.80	1.884 578	5.09	148
38	15.337 955	791.059 570	.001 264 1273	.065 198	51.575 297	.019 389 1273	7.76	1.947 147	5.12	152
39	16.480 556	854.099 638	.001 170 8236	.060 678	51.824 686	.019 295 8236	7.72	2.010 148	5.15	156
40	17.708 275	921.835 877	.001 084 7918	.056 471	52.056 785	.019 209 7918	7.69	2.073 567	5.18	160
41	19.027 454	994.618 128	.001 005 4110	.052 556	52.272 792	.019 130 4110	7.66	2.137 387	5.21	164
42	20.444 904	1072.822 295	.000 932 1208	.048 912	52.473 824	.019 057 1208	7.63	2.201 596	5.24	168
43	21.967 948	1156.852 282	.000 864 4146	.045 521	52.660 918	.018 989 4146	7.60	2.266 179	5.27	172
44	23.604 450	1247.142 085	.000 801 8333	.042 365	52.835 040	.018 926 8333	7.58	2.331 123	5.30	176
45	25.362 864	1344.158 028	.000 743 9601	.039 428	52.997 091	.018 868 9601	7.55	2.396 413	5.33	180
46	27.252 271	1448.401 176	.000 690 4165	.036 694	53.147 907	.018 815 4165	7.53	2.462 037	5.35	184
47	29.282 430	1560.409 920	.000 640 8572	.034 150	53.288 266	.018 765 8572	7.51	2.527 981	5.38	188
48	31.463 825	1680.762 756	.000 594 9680	.031 783	53.418 895	.018 719 9680	7.49	2.594 234	5.40	192
49	33.807 723	1810.081 280	.000 552 4614	.029 579	53.540 467	.018 677 4614	7.48	2.660 782	5.43	196
50	36.326 230	1949.033 389	.000 513 0748	.027 528	53.653 610	.018 638 0748	7.46	2.727 615	5.46	200

Effective Rate is 7.45 %   Annual Percentage Rate is 7.25 %

Amount Of 1	Amount Of 1 Per Period	Sinking Fund Payment	Present Worth Of 1	Present Worth of 1 Per Period	Periodic Payment To Amortize 1	Constant Annual Percent	Total Interest	Annual Add On Rate
What a single $ 1 deposit grows to in the future. The deposit is made at the beginning of the first period.	What a series of $ 1 deposits grow to in the future. A deposit is made at the end of each period.	The amount to be deposited at the end of each period that grows to $ 1 in the future.	What $ 1 to be paid in the future is worth today. Value today of a single $ 1 payment tomorrow.	What $ 1 to be paid at the end of each period is worth today. Value today of a series of $ 1 payments tomorrow.	The mortgage payment to amortize a loan of $ 1. An annuity certain, payable at the end of each period, worth $ 1 today.	The annual payment, including interest and principal, to amortize completely a loan of $ 100.	The total interest paid over the term of a loan of $1. The loan is amortized by regular periodic payments.	The average annual interest rate on a loan that is completely amortized by regular periodic payments.
$S = (1+i)^n$	$S\overline{n} = \dfrac{(1+i)^n - 1}{i}$	$\dfrac{1}{S\overline{n}} = \dfrac{i}{(1+i)^n - 1}$	$V^n = \dfrac{1}{(1+i)^n}$	$A\overline{n} = \dfrac{1 - V^n}{i}$	$\dfrac{1}{A\overline{n}} = \dfrac{i}{1 - V^n}$			

YEAR								PERIODS
	1.018 438	1.000 000	1.000 000 0000	.981 896	.981 896	1.018 437 5000	407.38	.018 437	7.37	1
	1.037 215	2.018 438	.495 432 7295	.964 120	1.946 017	.513 870 2295	205.55	.027 740	5.55	2
	1.056 339	3.055 652	.327 262 3504	.946 666	2.892 683	.345 699 8504	138.28	.037 100	4.95	3
	1.075 815	4.111 991	.243 191 1918	.929 528	3.822 211	.261 628 6918	104.66	.046 515	4.65	4

YEAR	Amount Of 1	Amount Of 1 Per Period	Sinking Fund Payment	Present Worth Of 1	Present Worth of 1 Per Period	Periodic Payment To Amortize 1	Constant Annual Percent	Total Interest	Annual Add On Rate	PERIODS
1	1.075 815	4.111 991	.243 191 1918	.929 528	3.822 211	.261 628 6918	104.66	.046 515	4.65	4
2	1.157 378	8.535 732	.117 154 5688	.864 022	7.375 063	.135 592 0688	54.24	.084 737	4.24	8
3	1.245 124	13.294 858	.075 217 0493	.803 133	10.677 538	.093 654 5493	37.47	.123 855	4.13	12
4	1.339 523	18.414 797	.054 304 1566	.746 535	13.747 281	.072 741 6566	29.10	.163 867	4.10	16
5	1.441 079	23.922 902	.041 800 9480	.693 925	16.600 693	.060 238 4480	24.10	.204 769	4.10	20
6	1.550 334	29.848 604	.033 502 4039	.645 022	19.253 020	.051 939 9039	20.78	.246 558	4.11	24
7	1.667 872	36.223 562	.027 606 3406	.599 566	21.718 432	.046 043 8406	18.42	.289 228	4.13	28
8	1.794 321	43.081 837	.023 211 6380	.557 314	24.010 101	.041 649 1380	16.66	.332 772	4.16	32
9	1.930 358	50.460 070	.019 817 6498	.518 039	26.140 271	.038 255 1498	15.31	.377 185	4.19	36
10	2.076 707	58.397 683	.017 123 9670	.481 532	28.120 325	.035 561 4670	14.23	.422 459	4.22	40
11	2.234 153	66.937 085	.014 939 4017	.447 597	29.960 840	.033 376 9017	13.36	.468 584	4.26	44
12	2.403 534	76.123 900	.013 136 4788	.416 054	31.671 650	.031 573 9788	12.63	.515 551	4.30	48
13	2.585 758	86.007 212	.011 626 9320	.386 734	33.261 896	.030 064 4320	12.03	.563 350	4.33	52
14	2.781 797	96.639 825	.010 347 7008	.359 480	34.740 074	.028 785 2008	11.52	.611 971	4.37	56
15	2.992 698	108.078 549	.009 252 5299	.334 147	36.114 082	.027 690 0299	11.08	.661 402	4.41	60
16	3.219 589	120.384 497	.008 306 7174	.310 599	37.391 260	.026 744 2174	10.70	.711 630	4.45	64
17	3.463 682	133.623 419	.007 483 7181	.288 710	38.578 434	.025 921 2181	10.37	.762 643	4.49	68
18	3.726 280	147.866 047	.006 762 8777	.268 364	39.681 945	.025 200 3777	10.09	.814 427	4.52	72
19	4.008 788	163.188 478	.006 127 8836	.249 452	40.707 689	.024 565 3836	9.83	.866 969	4.56	76
20	4.312 713	179.672 577	.005 565 6796	.231 873	41.661 147	.024 003 1796	9.61	.920 254	4.60	80
21	4.639 681	197.406 415	.005 065 6915	.215 532	42.547 413	.023 503 1915	9.41	.974 268	4.64	84
22	4.991 437	216.484 740	.004 619 2632	.200 343	43.371 222	.023 056 7632	9.23	1.028 995	4.68	88
23	5.369 862	237.009 486	.004 219 2404	.186 225	44.136 976	.022 656 7404	9.07	1.084 420	4.71	92
24	5.776 978	259.090 312	.003 859 6580	.173 101	44.848 765	.022 297 1580	8.92	1.140 527	4.75	96
25	6.214 958	282.845 192	.003 535 5029	.160 902	45.510 393	.021 973 0029	8.79	1.197 300	4.79	100
26	6.686 144	308.401 045	.003 242 5312	.149 563	46.125 395	.021 680 0312	8.68	1.254 723	4.83	104
27	7.193 053	335.894 410	.002 977 1261	.139 023	46.697 056	.021 414 6261	8.57	1.312 780	4.86	108
28	7.738 393	365.472 180	.002 736 1864	.129 226	47.228 432	.021 173 6864	8.47	1.371 453	4.90	112
29	8.325 078	397.292 384	.002 517 0379	.120 119	47.722 360	.020 954 5379	8.39	1.430 726	4.93	116
30	8.956 243	431.525 032	.002 317 3627	.111 654	48.181 480	.020 754 8627	8.31	1.490 584	4.97	120
31	9.635 259	468.353 022	.002 135 1416	.103 785	48.608 245	.020 572 6416	8.23	1.551 008	5.00	124
32	10.365 754	507.973 120	.001 968 6081	.096 472	49.004 935	.020 406 1081	8.17	1.611 982	5.04	128
33	11.151 632	550.597 009	.001 816 2104	.089 673	49.373 669	.020 253 7104	8.11	1.673 490	5.07	132
34	11.997 092	596.452 421	.001 676 5797	.083 354	49.716 418	.020 114 0797	8.05	1.735 515	5.10	136
35	12.906 649	645.784 354	.001 548 5045	.077 479	50.035 013	.019 986 0045	8.00	1.798 041	5.14	140
36	13.885 164	698.856 379	.001 430 9092	.072 019	50.331 156	.019 868 4092	7.95	1.861 051	5.17	144
37	14.937 866	755.952 051	.001 322 8352	.066 944	50.606 429	.019 760 3352	7.91	1.924 530	5.20	148
38	16.070 378	817.376 422	.001 223 4265	.062 226	50.862 303	.019 660 9265	7.87	1.988 461	5.23	152
39	17.288 751	883.457 671	.001 131 9161	.057 841	51.100 145	.019 569 4161	7.83	2.052 829	5.26	156
40	18.599 495	954.548 859	.001 047 6153	.053 765	51.321 226	.019 485 1153	7.80	2.117 618	5.29	160
41	20.009 612	1031.029 814	.000 969 9041	.049 976	51.526 726	.019 407 4041	7.77	2.182 814	5.32	164
42	21.526 638	1113.309 160	.000 898 2231	.046 454	51.717 745	.019 335 7231	7.74	2.248 401	5.35	168
43	23.158 676	1201.826 501	.000 832 0669	.043 180	51.895 302	.019 269 5669	7.71	2.314 365	5.38	172
44	24.914 447	1297.054 770	.000 770 9775	.040 137	52.060 347	.019 208 4775	7.69	2.380 692	5.41	176
45	26.803 332	1399.502 754	.000 714 5395	.037 309	52.213 760	.019 152 0395	7.67	2.447 367	5.44	180
46	28.835 422	1509.717 815	.000 662 3754	.034 680	52.356 362	.019 099 8754	7.64	2.514 377	5.47	184
47	31.021 575	1628.288 812	.000 614 1417	.032 236	52.488 915	.019 051 6417	7.63	2.581 709	5.49	188
48	33.373 471	1755.849 250	.000 569 5250	.029 964	52.612 126	.019 007 0250	7.61	2.649 349	5.52	192
49	35.903 675	1893.080 662	.000 528 2395	.027 852	52.726 655	.018 965 7395	7.59	2.717 285	5.55	196
50	38.625 706	2040.716 250	.000 490 0240	.025 889	52.833 112	.018 927 5240	7.58	2.785 505	5.57	200

Effective Rate is 7.58 %

Annual Percentage Rate is 7.375%

	Amount Of 1	Amount Of 1 Per Period	Sinking Fund Payment	Present Worth Of 1	Present Worth of 1 Per Period	Periodic Payment To Amortize 1	Constant Annual Percent	Total Interest	Annual Add On Rate	
	What a single $ 1 deposit grows to in the future. The deposit is made at the beginning of the first period.	What a series of $ 1 deposits grow to in the future. A deposit is made at the end of each period.	The amount to be deposited at the end of each period that grows to $ 1 in the future.	What $ 1 to be paid in the future is worth today. Value today of a single $ 1 payment tomorrow.	What $ 1 to be paid at the end of each period is worth today. Value today of a series of $ 1 payments tomorrow.	The mortgage payment to amortize a loan of $ 1. An annuity certain, payable at the end of each period, worth $ 1 today.	The annual payment, including interest and principal, to amortize completely a loan of $ 100.	The total interest paid over the term on a loan of $1. The loan is amortized by regular periodic payments.	The average annual interest rate on a loan that is completely amortized by regular periodic payments.	
	$S = (1+i)^n$	$S\overline{n}| = \dfrac{(1+i)^n - 1}{i}$	$\dfrac{1}{S\overline{n}|} = \dfrac{i}{(1+i)^n - 1}$	$V^n = \dfrac{1}{(1+i)^n}$	$A\overline{n}| = \dfrac{1 - V^n}{i}$	$\dfrac{1}{A\overline{n}|} = \dfrac{i}{1 - V^n}$				

YEAR										PERIODS
	1.018 750	1.000 000	1.000 000 0000	.981 595	.981 595	1.018 750 0000	407.50	.018 750	7.50	1
	1.037 852	2.018 750	.495 356 0372	.963 529	1.945 124	.514 106 0372	205.65	.028 212	5.64	2
	1.057 311	3.056 602	.327 160 7305	.945 795	2.890 919	.345 910 7305	138.37	.037 732	5.03	3
	1.077 136	4.113 913	.243 077 5854	.928 388	3.819 307	.261 827 5854	104.74	.047 310	4.73	4
1	1.077 136	4.113 913	.243 077 5854	.928 388	3.819 307	.261 827 5854	104.74	.047 310	4.73	4
2	1.160 222	8.545 156	.117 025 3662	.861 904	7.365 106	.135 775 3662	54.32	.086 203	4.31	8
3	1.249 716	13.318 207	.075 085 1837	.800 182	10.656 983	.093 835 1837	37.54	.126 022	4.20	12
4	1.346 114	18.459 431	.054 172 8507	.742 879	13.713 123	.072 922 8507	29.17	.166 766	4.17	16
5	1.449 948	23.997 228	.041 671 4797	.689 680	16.550 406	.060 421 4797	24.17	.208 430	4.17	20
6	1.561 791	29.962 188	.033 375 3999	.640 291	19.184 505	.052 125 3999	20.86	.251 010	4.18	24
7	1.682 261	36.387 260	.027 482 1462	.594 438	21.629 971	.046 232 1462	18.50	.294 500	4.21	28
8	1.812 024	43.307 936	.023 090 4564	.551 869	23.900 313	.041 840 4564	16.74	.338 895	4.24	32
9	1.951 796	50.762 444	.019 699 6033	.512 349	26.008 071	.038 449 6033	15.38	.384 186	4.27	36
10	2.102 349	58.791 961	.017 009 1280	.475 658	27.964 888	.035 759 1280	14.31	.430 365	4.30	40
11	2.264 516	67.440 843	.014 827 8099	.441 596	29.781 573	.033 577 8099	13.44	.477 424	4.34	44
12	2.439 191	76.756 864	.013 028 1508	.409 972	31.468 162	.031 778 1508	12.72	.525 351	4.38	48
13	2.627 340	86.791 484	.011 521 8678	.380 613	33.033 971	.030 271 8678	12.11	.574 137	4.42	52
14	2.830 002	97.600 133	.010 245 8877	.353 357	34.487 649	.028 995 8877	11.60	.623 770	4.46	56
15	3.048 297	109.242 516	.009 153 9451	.328 052	35.837 226	.027 903 9451	11.17	.674 237	4.49	60
16	3.283 430	121.782 945	.008 211 3304	.304 560	37.090 158	.026 961 3304	10.79	.725 525	4.53	64
17	3.536 700	135.290 691	.007 391 4915	.282 749	38.253 364	.026 141 4915	10.46	.777 621	4.57	68
18	3.809 507	149.840 369	.006 673 7690	.262 501	39.333 271	.025 423 7690	10.17	.830 511	4.61	72
19	4.103 357	165.512 348	.006 041 8453	.243 703	40.335 844	.024 791 8453	9.92	.884 180	4.65	76
20	4.419 872	182.393 199	.005 482 6606	.226 251	41.266 620	.024 232 6606	9.70	.938 613	4.69	80
21	4.760 803	200.576 169	.004 985 6371	.210 049	42.130 742	.023 735 6371	9.50	.993 794	4.73	84
22	5.128 032	220.161 699	.004 542 1161	.195 007	42.932 982	.023 292 1161	9.32	1.049 706	4.77	88
23	5.523 587	241.257 975	.004 144 9407	.181 042	43.677 772	.022 894 9407	9.16	1.106 335	4.81	92
24	5.949 654	263.981 530	.003 788 1438	.168 077	44.369 226	.022 538 1438	9.02	1.163 662	4.85	96
25	6.408 585	288.457 887	.003 466 7105	.156 041	45.011 164	.022 216 7105	8.89	1.221 671	4.89	100
26	6.902 917	314.822 249	.003 176 3956	.144 866	45.607 131	.021 926 3956	8.78	1.280 345	4.92	104
27	7.435 380	343.220 248	.002 913 5810	.134 492	46.160 420	.021 663 5810	8.67	1.339 667	4.96	108
28	8.008 914	373.808 752	.002 675 1648	.124 861	46.674 087	.021 425 1648	8.58	1.399 618	5.00	112
29	8.626 689	406.756 727	.002 458 4719	.115 919	47.150 969	.021 208 4719	8.49	1.460 183	5.04	116
30	9.292 116	442.246 172	.002 261 1841	.107 618	47.593 700	.021 011 1841	8.41	1.521 342	5.07	120
31	10.008 871	480.473 126	.002 081 2819	.099 911	48.004 727	.020 831 2819	8.34	1.583 079	5.11	124
32	10.780 914	521.648 749	.001 916 9987	.092 757	48.386 319	.020 666 9987	8.27	1.645 376	5.14	128
33	11.612 509	566.000 490	.001 766 7829	.086 114	48.740 585	.020 516 7829	8.21	1.708 215	5.18	132
34	12.508 250	613.773 341	.001 629 2659	.079 947	49.069 481	.020 379 2659	8.16	1.771 580	5.21	136
35	13.473 085	665.231 192	.001 503 2368	.074 222	49.374 824	.020 253 2368	8.11	1.835 453	5.24	140
36	14.512 343	720.658 289	.001 387 6202	.068 907	49.658 301	.020 137 6202	8.06	1.899 817	5.28	144
37	15.631 765	780.360 802	.001 281 4585	.063 972	49.921 477	.020 031 4585	8.02	1.964 656	5.31	148
38	16.837 535	844.668 521	.001 183 8964	.059 391	50.165 807	.019 933 8964	7.98	2.029 952	5.34	152
39	18.136 313	913.936 672	.001 094 1677	.055 138	50.392 640	.019 844 1677	7.94	2.095 690	5.37	156
40	19.535 273	988.547 881	.001 011 5848	.051 189	50.603 229	.019 761 5848	7.91	2.161 854	5.40	160
41	21.042 143	1068.914 291	.000 935 5287	.047 524	50.798 737	.019 685 5287	7.88	2.228 427	5.44	164
42	22.665 247	1155.479 833	.000 865 4413	.044 120	50.980 245	.019 615 4413	7.85	2.295 394	5.47	168
43	24.413 550	1248.722 683	.000 800 8183	.040 961	51.148 754	.019 550 8183	7.83	2.362 741	5.49	172
44	26.296 711	1349.157 901	.000 741 2031	.038 028	51.305 196	.019 491 2031	7.80	2.430 452	5.52	176
45	28.325 130	1457.340 277	.000 686 1815	.035 304	51.450 435	.019 436 1815	7.78	2.498 513	5.55	180
46	30.510 014	1573.867 394	.000 635 3775	.032 776	51.585 273	.019 385 3775	7.76	2.566 909	5.58	184
47	32.863 430	1699.382 930	.000 588 4489	.030 429	51.710 455	.019 338 4489	7.74	2.635 628	5.61	188
48	35.398 379	1834.580 217	.000 545 0838	.028 250	51.826 673	.019 295 0838	7.72	2.704 656	5.63	192
49	38.128 864	1980.206 063	.000 504 9979	.026 227	51.934 568	.019 254 9979	7.71	2.773 980	5.66	196
50	41.069 967	2137.064 885	.000 467 9315	.024 349	52.034 736	.019 217 9315	7.69	2.843 586	5.69	200

Effective Rate is 7.71 %   8 - 296   Annual Percentage Rate is 7.50 %

QUARTERLY COMPOUND INTEREST AND ANNUITY

7.625% Q

	Amount Of 1	Amount Of 1 Per Period	Sinking Fund Payment	Present Worth Of 1	Present Worth of 1 Per Period	Periodic Payment To Amortize 1	Constant Annual Percent	Total Interest	Annual Add On Rate	
	What a single $ 1 deposit grows to in the future. The deposit is made at the beginning of the first period.	What a series of $ 1 deposits grow to in the future. A deposit is made at the end of each period.	The amount to be deposited at the end of each period that grows to $ 1 in the future.	What $ 1 to be paid in the future is worth today. Value today of a single $ 1 payment tomorrow.	What $ 1 to be paid at the end of each period is worth today. Value today of a series of $ 1 payments tomorrow.	The mortgage payment to amortize a loan of $ 1. An annuity certain, payable at the end of each period, worth $ 1 today.	The annual payment, including interest and principal, to amortize completely a loan of $ 100.	The total interest paid over the term on a loan of $1. The loan is amortized by regular periodic payments.	The average annual interest rate on a loan that is completely amortized by regular periodic payments.	

$$S = (1+i)^n \qquad S\overline{n}| = \frac{(1+i)^n - 1}{i} \qquad \frac{1}{S\overline{n}|} = \frac{i}{(1+i)^n - 1} \qquad V^n = \frac{1}{(1+i)^n} \qquad A\overline{n}| = \frac{1 - V^n}{i} \qquad \frac{1}{A\overline{n}|} = \frac{i}{1 - V^n}$$

YEAR										PERIODS
	1.019 063	1.000 000	1.000 000 0000	.981 294	.981 294	1.019 062 5000	407.63	.019 063	7.63	1
	1.038 488	2.019 063	.495 279 3685	.962 938	1.944 232	.514 341 8685	205.74	.028 684	5.74	2
	1.058 285	3.057 551	.327 059 1528	.944 925	2.889 158	.346 121 6528	138.45	.038 365	5.12	3
	1.078 458	4.115 835	.242 964 0383	.927 250	3.816 407	.262 026 5383	104.82	.048 106	4.81	4
1	1.078 458	4.115 835	.242 964 0383	.927 250	3.816 407	.262 026 5383	104.82	.048 106	4.81	4
2	1.163 072	8.554 592	.116 896 2880	.859 792	7.355 170	.135 958 7880	54.39	.087 670	4.38	8
3	1.254 324	13.341 604	.074 953 5056	.797 242	10.636 487	.094 016 0056	37.61	.128 192	4.27	12
4	1.352 736	18.504 197	.054 041 7949	.739 242	13.679 087	.073 104 2949	29.25	.169 669	4.24	16
5	1.458 869	24.071 836	.041 542 3228	.685 462	16.500 337	.060 604 8228	24.25	.212 096	4.24	20
6	1.573 330	30.076 303	.033 248 7676	.635 595	19.116 340	.052 311 2676	20.93	.255 470	4.26	24
7	1.696 770	36.551 868	.027 358 3828	.589 355	21.542 029	.046 420 8828	18.57	.299 785	4.28	28
8	1.829 895	43.535 494	.022 969 7634	.546 479	23.791 248	.042 032 2634	16.82	.345 032	4.31	32
9	1.973 465	51.067 042	.019 582 1014	.506 723	25.876 836	.038 644 6014	15.46	.391 206	4.35	36
10	2.128 300	59.189 502	.016 894 8880	.469 859	27.810 696	.035 957 3880	14.39	.438 296	4.38	40
11	2.295 282	67.949 234	.014 716 8694	.435 676	29.603 868	.033 779 3694	13.52	.486 292	4.42	44
12	2.475 366	77.396 238	.012 920 5247	.403 981	31.266 586	.031 983 0247	12.80	.535 185	4.46	48
13	2.669 578	87.584 436	.011 417 5537	.374 591	32.808 341	.030 480 0537	12.20	.584 963	4.50	52
14	2.879 028	98.571 981	.010 144 8707	.347 339	34.237 933	.029 207 3707	11.69	.635 613	4.54	56
15	3.104 912	110.421 588	.009 056 2001	.322 070	35.563 522	.028 118 7001	11.25	.687 122	4.58	60
16	3.348 517	123.200 893	.008 116 8243	.298 640	36.792 673	.027 179 3243	10.88	.739 477	4.62	64
17	3.611 235	136.982 838	.007 300 1846	.276 914	37.932 404	.026 362 6846	10.55	.792 663	4.66	68
18	3.894 566	151.846 088	.006 585 6158	.256 768	38.989 219	.025 648 1158	10.26	.846 664	4.70	72
19	4.200 126	167.875 482	.005 956 7960	.238 088	39.969 150	.025 019 2960	10.01	.901 466	4.74	76
20	4.529 660	185.162 510	.005 400 6613	.220 767	40.877 791	.024 463 1613	9.79	.957 053	4.79	80
21	4.885 049	203.805 847	.004 906 6306	.204 706	41.720 328	.023 969 1306	9.59	1.013 407	4.83	84
22	5.268 321	223.911 905	.004 466 0421	.189 814	42.501 571	.023 528 5421	9.42	1.070 512	4.87	88
23	5.681 663	245.595 446	.004 071 7367	.176 005	43.225 978	.023 134 2367	9.26	1.128 350	4.91	92
24	6.127 436	268.980 236	.003 717 7453	.163 200	43.897 684	.022 780 2453	9.12	1.186 904	4.95	96
25	6.608 183	294.199 754	.003 399 0511	.151 328	44.520 523	.022 461 5511	8.99	1.246 155	4.98	100
26	7.126 648	321.397 947	.003 111 4076	.140 318	45.098 050	.022 173 9076	8.87	1.306 086	5.02	104
27	7.685 792	350.730 059	.002 851 1956	.130 110	45.633 563	.021 913 6956	8.77	1.366 679	5.06	108
28	8.288 804	382.363 513	.002 615 3123	.120 645	46.130 116	.021 677 8123	8.68	1.427 915	5.10	112
29	8.939 128	416.478 868	.002 401 0822	.111 868	46.590 545	.021 463 5822	8.59	1.489 776	5.14	116
30	9.640 476	453.270 849	.002 206 1864	.103 729	47.017 478	.021 268 6864	8.51	1.552 242	5.17	120
31	10.396 849	492.949 460	.002 028 6055	.096 183	47.413 352	.021 091 1055	8.44	1.615 297	5.21	124
32	11.212 566	535.741 180	.001 866 5730	.089 186	47.780 425	.020 929 0730	8.38	1.678 921	5.25	128
33	12.092 283	581.890 258	.001 718 5371	.082 697	48.120 794	.020 781 0371	8.32	1.743 097	5.28	132
34	13.041 021	631.660 105	.001 583 1299	.076 681	48.436 401	.020 645 6299	8.26	1.807 806	5.32	136
35	14.064 195	685.334 801	.001 459 1408	.071 103	48.729 047	.020 521 6408	8.21	1.873 030	5.35	140
36	15.167 645	743.220 711	.001 345 4953	.065 930	49.000 403	.020 407 9953	8.17	1.938 751	5.39	144
37	16.357 670	805.648 241	.001 241 2365	.061 133	49.252 018	.020 303 7365	8.13	2.004 953	5.42	148
38	17.641 061	872.973 718	.001 145 5099	.056 686	49.485 328	.020 208 0099	8.09	2.071 617	5.45	152
39	19.025 146	945.581 424	.001 057 5504	.052 562	49.701 665	.020 120 0504	8.05	2.138 728	5.48	156
40	20.517 823	1023.885 794	.000 976 6714	.048 738	49.902 263	.020 039 1714	8.02	2.206 267	5.52	160
41	22.127 613	1108.333 777	.000 902 2553	.045 192	50.088 267	.019 964 7553	7.99	2.274 220	5.55	164
42	23.863 703	1199.407 389	.000 833 7451	.041 905	50.260 740	.019 896 2451	7.96	2.342 569	5.58	168
43	25.736 004	1297.626 465	.000 770 6378	.038 856	50.420 665	.019 833 1378	7.94	2.411 300	5.61	172
44	27.755 203	1403.551 624	.000 712 4782	.036 029	50.568 956	.019 774 9782	7.91	2.480 396	5.64	176
45	29.932 824	1517.787 472	.000 658 8538	.033 408	50.706 458	.019 721 3538	7.89	2.549 844	5.67	180
46	32.281 297	1640.986 048	.000 609 3897	.030 978	50.833 957	.019 671 8897	7.87	2.619 628	5.69	184
47	34.814 026	1773.850 553	.000 563 7453	.028 724	50.952 181	.019 626 2453	7.86	2.689 734	5.72	188
48	37.545 469	1917.139 356	.000 521 6105	.026 634	51.061 803	.019 584 1105	7.84	2.760 149	5.75	192
49	40.491 216	2071.670 328	.000 482 7023	.024 697	51.163 451	.019 545 2023	7.82	2.830 860	5.78	196
50	43.668 080	2238.325 508	.000 446 7625	.022 900	51.257 704	.019 509 2625	7.81	2.901 853	5.80	200

Effective Rate is 7.85 %

Annual Percentage Rate is 7.625%

QUARTERLY COMPOUND INTEREST AND ANNUITY

Amount Of 1	Amount Of 1 Per Period	Sinking Fund Payment	Present Worth Of 1	Present Worth of 1 Per Period	Periodic Payment To Amortize 1	Constant Annual Percent	Total Interest	Annual Add On Rate
What a single $ 1 deposit grows to in the future. The deposit is made at the beginning of the first period.	What a series of $ 1 deposits grow to in the future. A deposit is made at the end of each period.	The amount to be deposited at the end of each period that grows to $ 1 in the future.	What $ 1 to be paid in the future is worth today. Value today of a single $ 1 payment tomorrow.	What $ 1 to be paid at the end of each period is worth today. Value today of a series of $ 1 payments tomorrow.	The mortgage payment to amortize a loan of $ 1. An annuity certain, payable at the end of each period, worth $ 1 today.	The annual payment, including interest and principal, to amortize completely a loan of $ 100.	The total interest paid over the term on a loan of $1. The loan is amortized by regular periodic payments.	The average annual interest rate on a loan that is completely amortized by regular periodic payments.
$S = (1+i)^n$	$S\overline{n}| = \dfrac{(1+i)^n - 1}{i}$	$\dfrac{1}{S\overline{n}|} = \dfrac{i}{(1+i)^n - 1}$	$V^n = \dfrac{1}{(1+i)^n}$	$A\overline{n}| = \dfrac{1-V^n}{i}$	$\dfrac{1}{A\overline{n}|} = \dfrac{i}{1-V^n}$			

YEAR									PERIODS
	1.019 375	1.000 000	1.000 000 0000	.980 993	.980 993	1.019 375 0000	407.75	.019 375	7.75	1
	1.039 125	2.019 375	.495 202 7236	.962 348	1.943 341	.514 577 7236	205.84	.029 155	5.83	2
	1.059 258	3.058 500	.326 957 6172	.944 057	2.887 398	.346 332 6172	138.54	.038 998	5.20	3
	1.079 782	4.117 759	.242 850 5505	.926 113	3.813 511	.262 225 5505	104.90	.048 902	4.89	4

YEAR	Amount Of 1	Amount Of 1 Per Period	Sinking Fund Payment	Present Worth Of 1	Present Worth of 1 Per Period	Periodic Payment To Amortize 1	Constant Annual Percent	Total Interest	Annual Add On Rate	PERIODS
1	1.079 782	4.117 759	.242 850 5505	.926 113	3.813 511	.262 225 5505	104.90	.048 902	4.89	4
2	1.165 928	8.564 039	.116 767 3342	.857 686	7.345 254	.136 142 3342	54.46	.089 139	4.46	8
3	1.258 948	13.365 050	.074 822 0152	.794 314	10.616 048	.094 197 0152	37.68	.130 364	4.35	12
4	1.359 389	18.549 094	.053 910 9889	.735 625	13.645 173	.073 285 9889	29.32	.172 576	4.31	16
5	1.467 843	24.146 729	.041 413 4771	.681 272	16.450 486	.060 788 4771	24.32	.215 770	4.32	20
6	1.584 950	30.190 952	.033 122 5067	.630 935	19.048 524	.052 497 5067	21.00	.259 940	4.33	24
7	1.711 399	36.717 392	.027 235 0496	.584 317	21.454 601	.046 610 0496	18.65	.305 081	4.36	28
8	1.847 938	43.764 523	.022 849 5580	.541 144	23.682 900	.042 224 5580	16.89	.351 186	4.39	32
9	1.995 369	51.373 884	.019 465 1430	.501 160	25.746 558	.038 840 1430	15.54	.398 245	4.42	36
10	2.154 563	59.590 332	.016 781 2455	.464 131	27.657 739	.036 156 2455	14.47	.446 250	4.46	40
11	2.326 457	68.462 302	.014 606 5787	.429 838	29.427 709	.033 981 5787	13.60	.495 189	4.50	44
12	2.512 066	78.042 091	.012 813 5982	.398 079	31.066 901	.032 188 5982	12.88	.545 053	4.54	48
13	2.712 482	88.386 171	.011 313 9871	.368 666	32.584 979	.030 688 9871	12.28	.595 827	4.58	52
14	2.928 888	99.555 518	.010 044 6466	.341 426	33.990 891	.029 419 6466	11.77	.647 500	4.63	56
15	3.162 559	111.615 973	.008 959 2911	.316 200	35.292 925	.028 334 2911	11.34	.700 057	4.67	60
16	3.414 873	124.638 631	.008 023 1947	.292 837	36.498 755	.027 398 1947	10.96	.753 484	4.71	64
17	3.687 317	138.700 256	.007 209 7920	.271 200	37.615 491	.026 584 7920	10.64	.807 766	4.75	68
18	3.981 497	153.883 740	.006 498 4124	.251 162	38.649 714	.025 873 4124	10.35	.862 886	4.79	72
19	4.299 148	170.278 587	.005 872 7290	.232 604	39.607 523	.025 247 7290	10.10	.918 827	4.84	76
20	4.642 140	187.981 440	.005 319 6741	.215 418	40.494 562	.024 694 6741	9.88	.975 574	4.88	80
21	5.012 498	207.096 654	.004 828 6632	.199 501	41.316 060	.024 203 6632	9.69	1.033 108	4.92	84
22	5.412 403	227.736 911	.004 391 0317	.184 761	42.076 860	.023 766 0317	9.51	1.091 411	4.96	88
23	5.844 213	250.023 880	.003 999 6180	.171 109	42.781 448	.023 374 6180	9.35	1.150 465	5.00	92
24	6.310 473	274.088 938	.003 648 4508	.158 467	43.433 976	.023 023 4508	9.21	1.210 251	5.04	96
25	6.813 933	300.073 945	.003 332 5119	.146 758	44.038 290	.022 707 5119	9.09	1.270 751	5.08	100
26	7.357 559	328.132 076	.003 047 5533	.135 915	44.597 954	.022 422 5533	8.97	1.331 946	5.12	104
27	7.944 557	358.428 730	.002 789 9549	.125 872	45.116 266	.022 164 9549	8.87	1.393 815	5.16	108
28	8.578 386	391.142 498	.002 556 6130	.116 572	45.596 281	.021 931 6130	8.78	1.456 341	5.20	112
29	9.262 783	426.466 222	.002 344 8516	.107 959	46.040 830	.021 719 8516	8.69	1.519 503	5.24	116
30	10.001 783	464.608 129	.002 152 3515	.099 982	46.452 533	.021 527 3515	8.62	1.583 282	5.28	120
31	10.799 740	505.793 057	.001 977 0932	.092 595	46.833 816	.021 352 0932	8.55	1.647 660	5.32	124
32	11.661 361	550.263 784	.001 817 3102	.085 753	47.186 927	.021 192 3102	8.48	1.712 616	5.35	128
33	12.591 723	598.282 456	.001 671 4513	.079 417	47.513 948	.021 046 4513	8.42	1.778 132	5.39	132
34	13.596 310	650.132 133	.001 538 1489	.073 549	47.816 807	.020 913 1489	8.37	1.844 188	5.42	136
35	14.681 045	706.118 459	.001 416 1930	.068 115	48.097 288	.020 791 1930	8.32	1.910 767	5.46	140
36	15.852 322	766.571 462	.001 304 5098	.063 082	48.357 046	.020 679 5098	8.28	1.977 849	5.49	144
37	17.117 045	831.847 501	.001 202 1434	.058 421	48.597 610	.020 577 1434	8.24	2.045 417	5.53	148
38	18.482 670	902.331 366	.001 108 2403	.054 105	48.820 401	.020 483 2403	8.20	2.113 453	5.56	152
39	19.957 247	978.438 544	.001 022 0366	.050 107	49.026 730	.020 397 0366	8.16	2.181 938	5.59	156
40	21.549 467	1060.617 674	.000 942 8468	.046 405	49.217 814	.020 317 8468	8.13	2.250 855	5.63	160
41	23.268 718	1149.353 184	.000 870 0546	.042 976	49.394 779	.020 245 0546	8.10	2.320 189	5.66	164
42	25.125 133	1245.168 152	.000 803 1044	.039 801	49.558 669	.020 178 1044	8.08	2.389 922	5.69	168
43	27.129 656	1348.627 391	.000 741 4947	.036 860	49.710 450	.020 116 4947	8.05	2.460 037	5.72	172
44	29.294 102	1460.340 770	.000 684 7717	.034 137	49.851 016	.020 059 7717	8.03	2.530 520	5.75	176
45	31.631 232	1580.966 819	.000 632 5243	.031 614	49.981 196	.020 007 5243	8.01	2.601 354	5.78	180
46	34.154 822	1711.216 605	.000 584 3796	.029 278	50.101 758	.019 959 3796	7.99	2.672 526	5.81	184
47	36.879 747	1851.857 924	.000 539 9982	.027 115	50.213 411	.019 914 9982	7.97	2.744 020	5.84	188
48	39.822 072	2003.719 829	.000 499 0718	.025 112	50.316 815	.019 874 0718	7.95	2.815 822	5.87	192
49	42.999 139	2167.697 516	.000 461 3190	.023 256	50.412 579	.019 836 3190	7.94	2.887 919	5.89	196
50	46.429 679	2344.757 602	.000 426 4833	.021 538	50.501 267	.019 801 4833	7.93	2.960 297	5.92	200

QUARTERLY COMPOUND INTEREST AND ANNUITY

Amount Of 1	Amount Of 1 Per Period	Sinking Fund Payment	Present Worth Of 1	Present Worth of 1 Per Period	Periodic Payment To Amortize 1	Constant Annual Percent	Total Interest	Annual Add On Rate
What a single $ 1 deposit grows to in the future. The deposit is made at the beginning of the first period.	What a series of $ 1 deposits grow to in the future. A deposit is made at the end of each period.	The amount to be deposited at the end of each period that grows to $ 1 in the future.	What $ 1 to be paid in the future is worth today. Value today of a single $ 1 payment tomorrow.	What $ 1 to be paid at the end of each period is worth today. Value today of a series of $ 1 payments tomorrow.	The mortgage payment to amortize a loan of $ 1. An annuity certain, payable at the end of each period, worth $ 1 today.	The annual payment, including interest and principal, to amortize completely a loan of $ 100.	The total interest paid over the term on a loan of $1. The loan is amortized by regular periodic payments.	The average annual interest rate on a loan that is completely amortized by regular periodic payments.

$$S = (1+i)^n \qquad S\overline{n}| = \frac{(1+i)^n - 1}{i} \qquad \frac{1}{S\overline{n}|} = \frac{i}{(1+i)^n - 1} \qquad V^n = \frac{1}{(1+i)^n} \qquad A\overline{n}| = \frac{1-V^n}{i} \qquad \frac{1}{A\overline{n}|} = \frac{i}{1-V^n}$$

YEAR									PERIODS
	1.019 688	1.000 000	1.000 000 0000	.980 693	.980 693	1.019 687 5000	407.88	.019 687	7.87	1
	1.039 763	2.019 688	.495 126 1024	.961 758	1.942 451	.514 813 6024	205.93	.029 627	5.93	2
	1.060 233	3.059 450	.326 856 1238	.943 189	2.885 640	.346 543 6238	138.62	.039 631	5.28	3
	1.081 106	4.119 683	.242 737 1220	.924 978	3.810 618	.262 424 6220	104.97	.049 698	4.97	4
1	1.081 106	4.119 683	.242 737 1220	.924 978	3.810 618	.262 424 6220	104.97	.049 698	4.97	4
2	1.168 791	8.573 498	.116 638 5046	.855 585	7.335 358	.136 326 0046	54.54	.090 608	4.53	8
3	1.263 587	13.388 546	.074 690 7123	.791 398	10.595 666	.094 378 2123	37.76	.132 539	4.42	12
4	1.366 072	18.594 123	.053 780 4327	.732 026	13.611 381	.073 467 9327	29.39	.175 487	4.39	16
5	1.476 869	24.221 906	.041 284 9423	.677 108	16.400 852	.060 972 4423	24.39	.219 449	4.39	20
6	1.596 652	30.306 137	.032 996 6167	.626 311	18.981 053	.052 684 1167	21.08	.264 419	4.41	24
7	1.726 151	36.883 838	.027 112 1461	.579 324	21.367 683	.046 799 6461	18.72	.310 390	4.43	28
8	1.866 152	43.995 031	.022 729 8396	.535 862	23.575 264	.042 417 3396	16.97	.357 355	4.47	32
9	2.017 509	51.682 986	.019 348 7271	.495 661	25.617 230	.039 036 2271	15.62	.405 304	4.50	36
10	2.181 141	59.994 483	.016 668 1993	.458 476	27.506 004	.036 355 6993	14.55	.454 228	4.54	40
11	2.358 046	68.980 094	.014 496 9358	.424 080	29.253 079	.034 184 4358	13.68	.504 115	4.58	44
12	2.549 298	78.694 495	.012 707 3692	.392 265	30.869 086	.032 394 8692	12.96	.554 954	4.62	48
13	2.756 062	89.196 794	.011 211 1653	.362 837	32.363 857	.030 898 6653	12.36	.606 731	4.67	52
14	2.979 596	100.550 895	.009 945 2123	.335 616	33.746 489	.029 632 7123	11.86	.659 432	4.71	56
15	3.221 260	112.825 885	.008 863 2143	.310 438	35.025 393	.028 550 7143	11.43	.713 043	4.75	60
16	3.482 524	126.096 454	.007 930 4371	.287 148	36.208 352	.027 617 9371	11.05	.767 548	4.80	64
17	3.764 978	140.443 349	.007 120 3087	.265 606	37.302 564	.026 807 8087	10.73	.822 931	4.84	68
18	4.070 342	155.953 866	.006 412 1527	.245 680	38.314 686	.026 099 6527	10.44	.879 175	4.88	72
19	4.400 472	172.722 384	.005 789 6375	.227 248	39.250 877	.025 477 1375	10.20	.936 262	4.93	76
20	4.757 378	190.850 934	.005 239 6914	.210 200	40.116 834	.024 927 1914	9.98	.994 175	4.97	80
21	5.143 231	210.449 822	.004 751 7265	.194 430	40.917 825	.024 439 2265	9.78	1.052 895	5.01	84
22	5.560 379	231.638 303	.004 317 0753	.179 844	41.658 725	.024 004 5753	9.61	1.112 403	5.06	88
23	6.011 361	254.545 302	.003 928 5738	.166 352	42.344 041	.023 616 0738	9.45	1.172 679	5.10	92
24	6.498 920	279.310 202	.003 580 2487	.153 872	42.977 944	.023 267 7487	9.31	1.233 704	5.14	96
25	7.026 023	306.083 691	.003 267 0803	.142 328	43.564 290	.022 954 5803	9.19	1.295 458	5.18	100
26	7.595 877	335.028 678	.002 984 8191	.131 650	44.106 648	.022 672 3191	9.07	1.357 921	5.22	104
27	8.211 950	366.321 283	.002 729 8441	.121 774	44.608 317	.022 417 3441	8.97	1.421 073	5.26	108
28	8.877 991	400.151 915	.002 499 0509	.112 638	45.072 351	.022 186 5509	8.88	1.484 894	5.30	112
29	9.598 051	436.726 424	.002 289 7630	.104 188	45.501 571	.021 977 2630	8.80	1.549 363	5.34	116
30	10.376 514	476.267 353	.002 099 6610	.096 371	45.898 591	.021 787 1610	8.72	1.614 459	5.38	120
31	11.218 114	519.015 300	.001 926 7255	.089 142	46.265 826	.021 614 2255	8.65	1.680 164	5.42	124
32	12.127 973	565.230 372	.001 769 1901	.082 454	46.605 511	.021 456 6901	8.59	1.746 456	5.46	128
33	13.111 627	615.193 777	.001 625 5041	.076 268	46.919 711	.021 313 0041	8.53	1.813 317	5.49	132
34	14.175 063	669.209 526	.001 494 3003	.070 546	47.210 340	.021 181 8003	8.48	1.880 725	5.53	136
35	15.324 749	727.606 290	.001 374 3696	.065 254	47.479 166	.021 061 8696	8.43	1.948 662	5.57	140
36	16.567 682	790.739 398	.001 264 6391	.060 358	47.727 824	.020 952 1391	8.39	2.017 108	5.60	144
37	17.911 425	858.992 996	.001 164 1538	.055 830	47.957 827	.020 851 6538	8.35	2.086 045	5.64	148
38	19.364 153	932.782 388	.001 072 0614	.051 642	48.170 575	.020 759 5614	8.31	2.155 453	5.67	152
39	20.934 707	1012.556 561	.000 987 5992	.047 768	48.367 362	.020 675 0992	8.28	2.225 315	5.71	156
40	22.632 643	1098.800 919	.000 910 0830	.044 184	48.549 386	.020 597 5830	8.24	2.295 613	5.74	160
41	24.468 292	1192.040 235	.000 838 8979	.040 869	48.717 754	.020 526 3979	8.22	2.366 329	5.77	164
42	26.452 824	1292.841 842	.000 773 4898	.037 803	48.873 491	.020 460 9898	8.19	2.437 446	5.80	168
43	28.598 313	1401.819 091	.000 713 3588	.034 967	49.017 544	.020 400 8588	8.17	2.508 948	5.83	172
44	30.917 816	1519.635 077	.000 658 0527	.032 344	49.150 791	.020 345 5527	8.14	2.580 817	5.87	176
45	33.425 444	1647.006 677	.000 607 1621	.029 917	49.274 040	.020 294 6621	8.12	2.653 039	5.90	180
46	36.136 457	1784.708 911	.000 560 3155	.027 673	49.388 044	.020 247 8155	8.10	2.725 598	5.93	184
47	39.067 350	1933.579 658	.000 517 1755	.025 597	49.493 495	.020 204 6755	8.09	2.798 479	5.95	188
48	42.235 956	2094.524 755	.000 477 4353	.023 677	49.591 034	.020 164 9353	8.07	2.871 668	5.98	192
49	45.661 557	2268.523 506	.000 440 8154	.021 900	49.681 257	.020 128 3154	8.06	2.945 150	6.01	196
50	49.364 995	2456.634 645	.000 407 0609	.020 257	49.764 710	.020 094 5609	8.04	3.018 912	6.04	200

Effective Rate is 8.11 %

Annual Percentage Rate is 7.875%

QUARTERLY COMPOUND INTEREST AND ANNUITY

8.00 % Q

Amount Of 1	Amount Of 1 Per Period	Sinking Fund Payment	Present Worth Of 1	Present Worth of 1 Per Period	Periodic Payment To Amortize 1	Constant Annual Percent	Total Interest	Annual Add On Rate
What a single $ 1 deposit grows to in the future. The deposit is made at the beginning of the first period.	What a series of $ 1 deposits grow to in the future. A deposit is made at the end of each period.	The amount to be deposited at the end of each period that grows to $ 1 in the future.	What $ 1 to be paid in the future is worth today. Value today of a single $ 1 payment tomorrow.	What $ 1 to be paid at the end of each period is worth today. Value today of a series of $ 1 payments tomorrow.	The mortgage payment to amortize a loan of $ 1. An annuity certain, payable at the end of each period, worth $ 1 today.	The annual payment, including interest and principal, to amortize completely a loan of $ 100.	The total interest paid over the term on a loan of $1. The loan is amortized by regular periodic payments.	The average annual interest rate on a loan that is completely amortized by regular periodic payments.

$$S = (1+i)^n \qquad S\overline{n}| = \frac{(1+i)^n - 1}{i} \qquad \frac{1}{S\overline{n}|} = \frac{i}{(1+i)^n - 1} \qquad V^n = \frac{1}{(1+i)^n} \qquad A\overline{n}| = \frac{1-V^n}{i} \qquad \frac{1}{A\overline{n}|} = \frac{i}{1-V^n}$$

YEAR / **PERIODS**

	1.020 000	1.000 000	1.000 000 0000	.980 392	.980 392	1.020 000 0000	408.00	.020 000	8.00	1
	1.040 400	2.020 000	.495 049 5050	.961 169	1.941 561	.515 049 5050	206.02	.030 099	6.02	2
	1.061 208	3.060 400	.326 754 6726	.942 322	2.883 883	.346 754 6726	138.71	.040 264	5.37	3
	1.082 432	4.121 608	.242 623 7527	.923 845	3.807 729	.262 623 7527	105.05	.050 495	5.05	4

YEAR	Amount Of 1	Amount Of 1 Per Period	Sinking Fund Payment	Present Worth Of 1	Present Worth of 1 Per Period	Periodic Payment To Amortize 1	Constant Annual Percent	Total Interest	Annual Add On Rate	PERIODS
1	1.082 432	4.121 608	.242 623 7527	.923 845	3.807 729	.262 623 7527	105.05	.050 495	5.05	4
2	1.171 659	8.582 969	.116 509 7991	.853 490	7.325 481	.136 509 7991	54.61	.092 078	4.60	8
3	1.268 242	13.412 090	.074 559 5966	.788 493	10.575 341	.094 559 5966	37.83	.134 715	4.49	12
4	1.372 786	18.639 285	.053 650 1259	.728 446	13.577 709	.073 650 1259	29.47	.178 402	4.46	16
5	1.485 947	24.297 370	.041 156 7181	.672 971	16.351 433	.061 156 7181	24.47	.223 134	4.46	20
6	1.608 437	30.421 862	.032 871 0973	.621 721	18.913 926	.052 871 0973	21.15	.268 906	4.48	24
7	1.741 024	37.051 210	.026 989 6716	.574 375	21.281 272	.046 989 6716	18.80	.315 711	4.51	28
8	1.884 541	44.227 030	.022 610 6073	.530 633	23.468 335	.042 610 6073	17.05	.363 539	4.54	32
9	2.039 887	51.994 367	.019 232 8526	.490 223	25.488 842	.039 232 8526	15.70	.412 383	4.58	36
10	2.208 040	60.401 983	.016 555 7478	.452 890	27.355 479	.036 555 7478	14.63	.462 230	4.62	40
11	2.390 053	69.502 657	.014 387 9391	.418 401	29.079 963	.034 387 9391	13.76	.513 069	4.66	44
12	2.587 070	79.353 519	.012 601 8355	.386 538	30.673 120	.032 601 8355	13.05	.564 888	4.71	48
13	2.800 328	90.016 409	.011 109 0856	.357 101	32.144 950	.031 109 0856	12.45	.617 672	4.75	52
14	3.031 165	101.558 264	.009 846 5645	.329 906	33.504 694	.029 846 5645	11.94	.671 408	4.80	56
15	3.281 031	114.051 539	.008 767 9658	.304 782	34.760 887	.028 767 9658	11.51	.726 078	4.84	60
16	3.551 493	127.574 662	.007 838 5471	.281 572	35.921 415	.027 838 5471	11.14	.781 667	4.89	64
17	3.844 251	142.212 525	.007 031 7294	.260 129	36.993 564	.027 031 7294	10.82	.838 158	4.93	68
18	4.161 140	158.057 019	.006 326 8307	.240 319	37.984 063	.026 326 8307	10.54	.895 532	4.98	72
19	4.504 152	175.207 608	.005 707 5147	.222 017	38.899 132	.025 707 5147	10.29	.953 771	5.02	76
20	4.875 439	193.771 958	.005 160 7055	.205 110	39.744 514	.025 160 7055	10.07	1.012 856	5.06	80
21	5.277 332	213.866 607	.004 675 8118	.189 490	40.525 516	.024 675 8118	9.88	1.072 768	5.11	84
22	5.712 354	235.617 701	.004 244 1633	.175 059	41.247 041	.024 244 1633	9.70	1.133 486	5.15	88
23	6.183 236	259.161 785	.003 858 5936	.161 728	41.913 619	.023 858 5936	9.55	1.194 991	5.20	92
24	6.692 933	284.646 659	.003 513 1275	.149 411	42.529 434	.023 513 1275	9.41	1.257 260	5.24	96
25	7.244 646	312.232 306	.003 202 7435	.138 033	43.098 352	.023 202 7435	9.29	1.320 274	5.28	100
26	7.841 838	342.091 897	.002 923 1911	.127 521	43.623 944	.022 923 1911	9.17	1.384 012	5.32	104
27	8.488 258	374.412 879	.002 670 8483	.117 810	44.109 510	.022 670 8483	9.07	1.448 452	5.36	108
28	9.187 963	409.398 150	.002 442 6100	.108 838	44.558 097	.022 442 6100	8.98	1.513 572	5.41	112
29	9.945 347	447.267 331	.002 235 7993	.100 550	44.972 523	.022 235 7993	8.90	1.579 353	5.45	116
30	10.765 163	488.258 152	.002 048 0969	.092 892	45.355 389	.022 048 0969	8.82	1.645 772	5.49	120
31	11.652 559	532.627 934	.001 877 4832	.085 818	45.709 097	.021 877 4832	8.76	1.712 808	5.53	124
32	12.613 104	580.655 213	.001 722 1924	.079 283	46.035 869	.021 722 1924	8.69	1.780 441	5.56	128
33	13.652 830	632.641 484	.001 580 6741	.073 245	46.337 756	.021 580 6741	8.64	1.848 649	5.60	132
34	14.778 262	688.913 096	.001 451 5619	.067 667	46.616 652	.021 451 5619	8.59	1.917 412	5.64	136
35	15.996 466	749.823 299	.001 333 6475	.062 514	46.874 310	.021 333 6475	8.54	1.986 711	5.68	140
36	17.315 089	815.754 461	.001 225 8591	.057 753	47.112 345	.021 225 8591	8.50	2.056 524	5.71	144
37	18.742 409	887.120 471	.001 127 2426	.053 355	47.332 253	.021 127 2426	8.46	2.126 832	5.75	148
38	20.287 387	964.369 336	.001 036 9471	.049 292	47.535 414	.021 036 9471	8.42	2.197 616	5.78	152
39	21.959 720	1047.985 991	.000 954 2112	.045 538	47.723 104	.020 954 2112	8.39	2.268 857	5.82	156
40	23.769 907	1138.495 348	.000 878 3523	.042 070	47.896 500	.020 878 3523	8.36	2.340 536	5.85	160
41	25.729 312	1236.465 587	.000 808 7568	.038 866	48.056 691	.020 808 7568	8.33	2.412 636	5.88	164
42	27.850 234	1342.511 724	.000 744 8725	.035 906	48.204 683	.020 744 8725	8.30	2.485 139	5.92	168
43	30.145 989	1457.299 473	.000 686 2008	.033 172	48.341 405	.020 686 2008	8.28	2.558 027	5.95	172
44	32.630 988	1581.549 425	.000 632 2913	.030 646	48.467 714	.020 632 2913	8.26	2.631 283	5.98	176
45	35.320 831	1716.041 568	.000 582 7365	.028 312	48.584 405	.020 582 7365	8.24	2.704 893	6.01	180
46	38.232 404	1861.620 189	.000 537 1665	.026 156	48.692 209	.020 537 1665	8.22	2.778 839	6.04	184
47	41.383 983	2019.199 170	.000 495 2458	.024 164	48.791 803	.020 495 2458	8.20	2.853 106	6.07	188
48	44.795 355	2189.767 727	.000 456 6694	.022 324	48.883 813	.020 456 6694	8.19	2.927 681	6.10	192
49	48.487 932	2374.396 619	.000 421 1596	.020 624	48.968 816	.020 421 1596	8.17	3.002 547	6.13	196
50	52.484 897	2574.244 869	.000 388 4634	.019 053	49.047 345	.020 388 4634	8.16	3.077 693	6.16	200

Effective Rate is 8.24 %   8 - 300   Annual Percentage Rate is 8.00 %

QUARTERLY COMPOUND INTEREST AND ANNUITY

Amount Of 1	Amount Of 1 Per Period	Sinking Fund Payment	Present Worth Of 1	Present Worth of 1 Per Period	Periodic Payment To Amortize 1	Constant Annual Percent	Total Interest	Annual Add On Rate	
What a single $ 1 deposit grows to in the future. The deposit is made at the beginning of the first period.	What a series of $ 1 deposits grow to in the future. A deposit is made at the end of each period.	The amount to be deposited at the end of each period that grows to $ 1 in the future.	What $ 1 to be paid in the future is worth today. Value today of a single $ 1 payment tomorrow.	What $ 1 to be paid at the end of each period is worth today. Value today of a series of $ 1 payments tomorrow.	The mortgage payment to amortize a loan of $ 1. An annuity certain, payable at the end of each period, worth $ 1 today.	The annual payment, including interest and principal, to amortize completely a loan of $ 100.	The total interest paid over the term on a loan of $1. The loan is amortized by regular periodic payments.	The average annual interest rate on a loan that is completely amortized by regular periodic payments.	

$$S = (1+i)^n \qquad S\overline{n}| = \frac{(1+i)^n - 1}{i} \qquad \frac{1}{S\overline{n}|} = \frac{i}{(1+i)^n - 1} \qquad V^n = \frac{1}{(1+i)^n} \qquad A\overline{n}| = \frac{1-V^n}{i} \qquad \frac{1}{A\overline{n}|} = \frac{i}{1-V^n}$$

YEAR										PERIODS
	1.020 313	1.000 000	1.000 000 0000	.980 092	.980 092	1.020 312 5000	408.13	.020 313	8.13	1
	1.041 038	2.020 312	.494 972 9312	.960 580	1.940 672	.515 285 4312	206.12	.030 571	6.11	2
	1.062 184	3.061 350	.326 653 2635	.941 457	2.882 129	.346 965 7635	138.79	.040 897	5.45	3
	1.083 759	4.123 534	.242 510 4426	.922 714	3.804 843	.262 822 9426	105.13	.051 292	5.13	4
1	1.083 759	4.123 534	.242 510 4426	.922 714	3.804 843	.262 822 9426	105.13	.051 292	5.13	4
2	1.174 534	8.592 452	.116 381 2178	.851 401	7.315 625	.136 693 7178	54.68	.093 550	4.68	8
3	1.272 912	13.435 683	.074 428 6682	.785 600	10.555 074	.094 741 1682	37.90	.136 894	4.56	12
4	1.379 531	18.684 580	.053 520 0684	.724 884	13.544 158	.073 832 5684	29.54	.181 321	4.53	16
5	1.495 079	24.373 121	.041 028 8042	.668 861	16.302 229	.061 341 3042	24.54	.226 826	4.54	20
6	1.620 306	30.538 130	.032 745 9479	.617 167	18.847 140	.053 058 4479	21.23	.273 403	4.56	24
7	1.756 021	37.219 515	.026 867 6257	.569 469	21.195 365	.047 180 1257	18.88	.321 044	4.59	28
8	1.903 104	44.460 529	.022 491 8603	.525 457	23.362 106	.042 804 3603	17.13	.369 740	4.62	32
9	2.062 507	52.308 044	.019 117 5184	.484 847	25.361 388	.039 430 0184	15.78	.419 481	4.66	36
10	2.235 261	60.812 862	.016 443 8897	.447 375	27.206 154	.036 756 3897	14.71	.470 256	4.70	40
11	2.422 485	70.030 037	.014 279 5868	.412 799	28.908 346	.034 592 0868	13.84	.522 052	4.75	44
12	2.625 391	80.019 237	.012 496 9950	.380 896	30.478 982	.032 809 4950	13.13	.574 856	4.79	48
13	2.845 292	90.845 124	.011 007 7454	.351 458	31.928 230	.031 320 2454	12.53	.628 653	4.84	52
14	3.083 611	102.577 780	.009 748 7000	.324 295	33.265 472	.030 061 2000	12.03	.683 427	4.88	56
15	3.341 892	115.293 155	.008 673 5418	.299 232	34.499 364	.028 986 0418	11.60	.739 163	4.93	60
16	3.621 807	129.073 560	.007 747 5201	.276 105	35.637 893	.028 060 0201	11.23	.795 841	4.97	64
17	3.925 167	144.008 202	.006 944 0489	.254 766	36.688 430	.027 256 5489	10.91	.853 445	5.02	68
18	4.253 936	160.193 759	.006 242 4404	.235 076	37.657 776	.026 554 9404	10.63	.911 956	5.07	72
19	4.610 242	177.735 007	.005 626 3536	.216 908	38.552 205	.025 938 8536	10.38	.971 353	5.11	76
20	4.996 393	196.745 497	.005 082 7084	.200 144	39.377 507	.025 395 2084	10.16	1.031 617	5.16	80
21	5.414 887	217.348 292	.004 600 9103	.184 676	40.139 025	.024 913 4103	9.97	1.092 726	5.20	84
22	5.868 434	239.676 762	.004 172 2860	.170 403	40.841 688	.024 484 7860	9.80	1.154 661	5.25	88
23	6.359 970	263.875 449	.003 789 6667	.157 233	41.490 046	.024 102 1667	9.65	1.217 399	5.29	92
24	6.892 677	290.101 000	.003 447 0753	.145 082	42.088 294	.023 759 5753	9.51	1.280 919	5.34	96
25	7.470 002	318.523 185	.003 139 4889	.133 869	42.640 307	.023 451 9889	9.39	1.345 199	5.38	100
26	8.095 684	349.325 991	.002 862 6556	.123 523	43.149 656	.023 175 1556	9.28	1.410 216	5.42	104
27	8.773 773	382.708 818	.002 612 9526	.113 976	43.619 640	.022 925 4526	9.18	1.475 949	5.47	108
28	9.508 658	418.887 767	.002 387 2743	.105 167	44.053 301	.022 699 7743	9.08	1.542 375	5.51	112
29	10.305 096	458.097 038	.002 182 9436	.097 039	44.453 447	.022 495 4436	9.00	1.609 471	5.55	116
30	11.168 244	500.590 450	.001 997 6410	.089 540	44.822 666	.022 310 1410	8.93	1.677 217	5.59	120
31	12.103 688	546.643 079	.001 829 3472	.082 619	45.163 350	.022 141 8472	8.86	1.745 589	5.63	124
32	13.117 484	596.553 044	.001 676 2969	.076 234	45.477 704	.021 988 7969	8.80	1.814 566	5.67	128
33	14.216 195	650.643 431	.001 536 9401	.070 342	45.767 763	.021 849 4401	8.74	1.884 126	5.71	132
34	15.406 933	709.264 390	.001 409 9115	.064 906	46.035 405	.021 722 4115	8.69	1.954 248	5.75	136
35	16.697 407	772.795 398	.001 294 0036	.059 890	46.282 361	.021 606 5036	8.65	2.024 910	5.79	140
36	18.095 969	841.647 718	.001 188 1456	.055 261	46.510 231	.021 500 6456	8.61	2.096 093	5.82	144
37	19.611 675	916.267 058	.001 091 3849	.050 990	46.720 491	.021 403 8849	8.57	2.167 775	5.86	148
38	21.254 334	997.136 461	.001 002 8718	.047 049	46.914 500	.021 315 3718	8.53	2.239 937	5.89	152
39	23.034 582	1084.779 426	.000 921 8464	.043 413	47.093 515	.021 234 3464	8.50	2.312 558	5.93	156
40	24.963 942	1179.763 303	.000 847 6277	.040 058	47.258 694	.021 160 1277	8.47	2.385 620	5.96	160
41	27.054 904	1282.702 962	.000 779 6037	.036 962	47.411 108	.021 092 1037	8.44	2.459 105	6.00	164
42	29.321 003	1394.264 772	.000 717 2239	.034 105	47.551 742	.021 029 7239	8.42	2.532 994	6.03	168
43	31.776 909	1515.170 918	.000 659 9915	.031 469	47.681 507	.020 972 4915	8.39	2.607 269	6.06	172
44	34.438 520	1646.204 077	.000 607 4581	.029 037	47.801 243	.020 919 9581	8.37	2.681 913	6.10	176
45	37.323 066	1788.212 478	.000 559 2177	.026 793	47.911 725	.020 871 7177	8.35	2.756 909	6.13	180
46	40.449 219	1942.115 401	.000 514 9025	.024 722	48.013 669	.020 827 4025	8.34	2.832 242	6.16	184
47	43.837 217	2108.909 122	.000 474 1788	.022 812	48.107 733	.020 786 6788	8.32	2.907 896	6.19	188
48	47.508 990	2289.673 365	.000 436 7435	.021 049	48.194 528	.020 749 2435	8.30	2.983 855	6.22	192
49	51.488 309	2485.578 291	.000 402 3209	.019 422	48.274 615	.020 714 8209	8.29	3.060 105	6.25	196
50	55.800 933	2697.892 072	.000 370 6597	.017 921	48.348 512	.020 683 1597	8.28	3.136 632	6.27	200

Effective Rate is 8.38 %

Annual Percentage Rate is 8.125%

Amount Of 1	Amount Of 1 Per Period	Sinking Fund Payment	Present Worth Of 1	Present Worth of 1 Per Period	Periodic Payment To Amortize 1	Constant Annual Percent	Total Interest	Annual Add On Rate
What a single $ 1 deposit grows to in the future. The deposit is made at the beginning of the first period.	What a series of $ 1 deposits grow to in the future. A deposit is made at the end of each period.	The amount to be deposited at the end of each period that grows to $ 1 in the future.	What $ 1 to be paid in the future is worth today. Value today of a single $ 1 payment tomorrow.	What $ 1 to be paid at the end of each period is worth today. Value today of a series of $ 1 payments tomorrow.	The mortgage payment to amortize a loan of $ 1. An annuity certain, payable at the end of each period, worth $ 1 today.	The annual payment, including interest and principal, to amortize completely a loan of $ 100.	The total interest paid over the term on a loan of $1. The loan is amortized by regular periodic payments.	The average annual interest rate on a loan that is completely amortized by regular periodic payments.
$S = (1+i)^n$	$S\overline{n}| = \dfrac{(1+i)^n - 1}{i}$	$\dfrac{1}{S\overline{n}|} = \dfrac{i}{(1+i)^n - 1}$	$V^n = \dfrac{1}{(1+i)^n}$	$A\overline{n}| = \dfrac{1 - V^n}{i}$	$\dfrac{1}{A\overline{n}|} = \dfrac{i}{1 - V^n}$			

YEAR / **PERIODS**

	1.020 625	1.000 000	1.000 000 0000	.979 792	.979 792	1.020 625 0000	408.25	.020 625	8.25	1
	1.041 675	2.020 625	.494 896 3811	.959 992	1.939 784	.515 521 3811	206.21	.031 043	6.21	2
	1.063 160	3.062 300	.326 551 8964	.940 592	2.880 376	.347 176 8964	138.88	.041 531	5.54	3
	1.085 088	4.125 460	.242 397 1917	.921 585	3.801 961	.263 022 1917	105.21	.052 089	5.21	4

YEAR	Amount Of 1	Amount Of 1 Per Period	Sinking Fund Payment	Present Worth Of 1	Present Worth of 1 Per Period	Periodic Payment To Amortize 1	Constant Annual Percent	Total Interest	Annual Add On Rate	PERIODS
1	1.085 088	4.125 460	.242 397 1917	.921 585	3.801 961	.263 022 1917	105.21	.052 089	5.21	4
2	1.177 415	8.601 946	.116 252 7605	.849 318	7.305 789	.136 877 7605	54.76	.095 022	4.75	8
3	1.277 599	13.459 326	.074 297 9269	.782 718	10.534 863	.094 922 9269	37.97	.139 075	4.64	12
4	1.386 306	18.730 008	.053 390 2600	.721 341	13.510 727	.074 015 2600	29.61	.184 244	4.61	16
5	1.504 264	24.449 160	.040 901 2004	.664 777	16.253 238	.061 526 2004	24.62	.230 524	4.61	20
6	1.632 258	30.654 941	.032 621 1682	.612 648	18.780 694	.053 246 1682	21.30	.277 908	4.63	24
7	1.771 143	37.388 758	.026 746 0077	.564 607	21.109 958	.047 371 0077	18.95	.326 388	4.66	28
8	1.921 845	44.695 538	.022 373 5978	.520 333	23.256 572	.042 998 5978	17.20	.375 955	4.70	32
9	2.085 371	52.624 036	.019 002 7235	.479 531	25.234 859	.039 627 7235	15.86	.426 598	4.74	36
10	2.262 810	61.227 150	.016 332 6237	.441 928	27.058 017	.036 957 6237	14.79	.478 305	4.78	40
11	2.455 347	70.562 283	.014 171 8771	.407 274	28.738 211	.034 796 8771	13.92	.531 063	4.83	44
12	2.664 267	80.691 720	.012 392 8453	.375 338	30.286 652	.033 017 8453	13.21	.584 857	4.87	48
13	2.890 963	91.683 046	.010 907 1419	.345 906	31.713 672	.031 532 1419	12.62	.639 671	4.92	52
14	3.136 948	103.609 599	.009 651 6154	.318 781	33.028 791	.030 276 6154	12.12	.695 490	4.97	56
15	3.403 863	116.550 953	.008 579 9384	.293 784	34.240 784	.029 204 9384	11.69	.752 296	5.02	60
16	3.693 490	130.593 457	.007 657 3515	.270 747	35.357 739	.028 282 3515	11.32	.810 070	5.06	64
17	4.007 760	145.830 804	.006 857 2618	.249 516	36.387 107	.027 482 2618	11.00	.868 794	5.11	68
18	4.348 771	162.364 660	.006 158 9757	.229 950	37.335 757	.026 783 9757	10.72	.928 446	5.16	72
19	4.718 798	180.305 343	.005 546 1474	.211 918	38.210 018	.026 171 1474	10.47	.989 007	5.21	76
20	5.120 309	199.772 555	.005 005 6926	.195 301	39.015 723	.025 630 6926	10.26	1.050 455	5.25	80
21	5.555 984	220.896 187	.004 527 0134	.179 986	39.758 249	.025 152 0134	10.07	1.112 769	5.30	84
22	6.028 729	243.817 178	.004 101 4337	.165 872	40.442 549	.024 726 4337	9.90	1.175 926	5.35	88
23	6.541 700	268.688 461	.003 721 7825	.152 865	41.073 189	.024 346 7825	9.74	1.239 904	5.39	92
24	7.098 317	295.675 983	.003 382 0806	.140 878	41.654 378	.024 007 0806	9.61	1.304 680	5.44	96
25	7.702 296	324.959 809	.003 077 3036	.129 831	42.189 992	.023 702 3036	9.49	1.370 230	5.48	100
26	8.357 666	356.735 326	.002 803 1987	.119 651	42.683 606	.023 428 1987	9.38	1.436 533	5.53	104
27	9.068 800	391.214 546	.002 556 1422	.110 268	43.138 513	.023 181 1422	9.28	1.503 563	5.57	108
28	9.840 443	428.627 521	.002 333 0280	.101 621	43.557 748	.022 958 0280	9.19	1.571 299	5.61	112
29	10.677 742	469.223 876	.002 131 1788	.093 653	43.944 109	.022 756 1788	9.11	1.639 717	5.65	116
30	11.586 286	513.274 479	.001 948 2753	.086 309	44.300 173	.022 573 2753	9.03	1.708 793	5.70	120
31	12.572 136	561.073 243	.001 782 2985	.079 541	44.628 316	.022 407 2985	8.97	1.778 505	5.74	124
32	13.641 869	612.939 090	.001 631 4835	.073 304	44.930 728	.022 256 4835	8.91	1.848 830	5.78	128
33	14.802 623	669.218 079	.001 494 2812	.067 556	45.209 426	.022 119 2812	8.85	1.919 745	5.82	132
34	16.062 143	730.285 712	.001 369 3271	.062 258	45.466 269	.021 994 3271	8.80	1.991 228	5.86	136
35	17.428 832	796.549 445	.001 255 4148	.057 376	45.702 973	.021 880 4148	8.76	2.063 258	5.90	140
36	18.911 810	868.451 402	.001 151 4749	.052 877	45.921 115	.021 776 4749	8.72	2.135 812	5.93	144
37	20.520 971	946.471 324	.001 056 5560	.048 731	46.122 151	.021 681 5560	8.68	2.208 870	5.97	148
38	22.267 052	1031.129 776	.000 969 8100	.044 909	46.307 423	.021 594 8100	8.64	2.282 411	6.01	152
39	24.161 702	1122.991 615	.000 890 4786	.041 388	46.478 167	.021 515 4786	8.61	2.356 415	6.04	156
40	26.217 564	1222.669 758	.000 817 8823	.038 142	46.635 521	.021 442 8823	8.58	2.430 861	6.08	160
41	28.448 354	1330.829 278	.000 751 4112	.035 151	46.780 537	.021 376 4112	8.56	2.505 731	6.11	164
42	30.868 957	1448.191 833	.000 690 5163	.032 395	46.914 182	.021 315 5163	8.53	2.581 007	6.15	168
43	33.495 523	1575.540 489	.000 634 7028	.029 855	47.037 346	.021 259 7028	8.51	2.656 669	6.18	172
44	36.345 577	1713.724 939	.000 583 5242	.027 514	47.150 853	.021 208 5242	8.49	2.732 700	6.21	176
45	39.438 135	1863.667 175	.000 536 5765	.025 356	47.255 459	.021 161 5765	8.47	2.809 084	6.24	180
46	42.793 833	2026.367 638	.000 493 4939	.023 368	47.351 862	.021 118 4939	8.45	2.885 803	6.27	184
47	46.435 058	2202.911 897	.000 453 9446	.021 535	47.440 705	.021 078 9446	8.44	2.962 842	6.30	188
48	50.386 106	2394.477 886	.000 417 6276	.019 847	47.522 582	.021 042 6276	8.42	3.040 184	6.33	192
49	54.673 340	2602.343 770	.000 384 2690	.018 290	47.598 039	.021 009 2690	8.41	3.117 817	6.36	196
50	59.325 365	2827.896 467	.000 353 6197	.016 856	47.667 578	.020 978 6197	8.40	3.195 724	6.39	200

QUARTERLY COMPOUND INTEREST AND ANNUITY

8.375% Q

	Amount Of 1	Amount Of 1 Per Period	Sinking Fund Payment	Present Worth Of 1	Present Worth of 1 Per Period	Periodic Payment To Amortize 1	Constant Annual Percent	Total Interest	Annual Add On Rate	
	What a single $ 1 deposit grows to in the future. The deposit is made at the beginning of the first period.	What a series of $ 1 deposits grow to in the future. A deposit is made at the end of each period.	The amount to be deposited at the end of each period that grows to $ 1 in the future.	What $ 1 to be paid in the future is worth today. Value today of a single $ 1 payment tomorrow.	What $ 1 to be paid at the end of each period is worth today. Value today of a series of $ 1 payments tomorrow.	The mortgage payment to amortize a loan of $ 1. An annuity certain, payable at the end of each period, worth $ 1 today.	The annual payment, including interest and principal, to amortize completely a loan of $ 100.	The total interest paid over the term on a loan of $1. The loan is amortized by regular periodic payments.	The average annual interest rate on a loan that is completely amortized by regular periodic payments.	
	$S = (1+i)^n$	$S\overline{n} = \dfrac{(1+i)^n - 1}{i}$	$\dfrac{1}{S\overline{n}} = \dfrac{i}{(1+i)^n - 1}$	$V^n = \dfrac{1}{(1+i)^n}$	$A\overline{n} = \dfrac{1-V^n}{i}$	$\dfrac{1}{A\overline{n}} = \dfrac{i}{1-V^n}$				

YEAR										PERIODS
	1.020 938	1.000 000	1.000 000 0000	.979 492	.979 492	1.020 937 5000	408.38	.020 938	8.38	1
	1.042 313	2.020 938	.494 819 8546	.959 404	1.938 896	.515 757 3546	206.31	.031 515	6.30	2
	1.064 137	3.063 251	.326 450 5715	.939 729	2.878 625	.347 388 0715	138.96	.042 164	5.62	3
	1.086 417	4.127 388	.242 284 0000	.920 457	3.799 082	.263 221 5000	105.29	.052 886	5.29	4
1	1.086 417	4.127 388	.242 284 0000	.920 457	3.799 082	.263 221 5000	105.29	.052 886	5.29	4
2	1.180 302	8.611 453	.116 124 4272	.847 241	7.295 972	.137 061 9272	54.83	.096 495	4.82	8
3	1.282 301	13.483 018	.074 167 3726	.779 848	10.514 708	.095 104 8726	38.05	.141 258	4.71	12
4	1.393 113	18.775 570	.053 260 7005	.717 817	13.477 416	.074 198 2005	29.68	.187 171	4.68	16
5	1.513 502	24.525 489	.040 773 9062	.660 719	16.204 460	.061 711 4062	24.69	.234 228	4.68	20
6	1.644 295	30.772 301	.032 496 7578	.608 163	18.714 586	.053 434 2578	21.38	.282 422	4.71	24
7	1.786 390	37.558 944	.026 624 8169	.559 788	21.025 048	.047 562 3169	19.03	.331 745	4.74	28
8	1.940 765	44.932 069	.022 255 8189	.515 261	23.151 729	.043 193 3189	17.28	.382 186	4.78	32
9	2.108 481	52.942 360	.018 888 4667	.474 275	25.109 246	.039 825 9667	15.94	.433 735	4.82	36
10	2.290 690	61.644 877	.016 221 9482	.436 550	26.911 056	.037 159 4482	14.87	.486 378	4.86	40
11	2.488 645	71.099 441	.014 064 8082	.401 825	28.569 544	.035 002 3082	14.01	.540 102	4.91	44
12	2.703 706	81.371 042	.012 289 3842	.369 863	30.096 111	.033 226 8842	13.30	.594 890	4.96	48
13	2.937 353	92.530 286	.010 807 2724	.340 443	31.501 250	.031 744 7724	12.70	.650 728	5.01	52
14	3.191 191	104.653 880	.009 555 3075	.313 363	32.794 619	.030 492 8075	12.20	.707 597	5.05	56
15	3.466 964	117.825 160	.008 487 1516	.288 437	33.985 109	.029 424 6516	11.77	.765 479	5.10	60
16	3.766 570	132.134 666	.007 568 0367	.265 494	35.080 904	.028 505 5367	11.41	.824 354	5.15	64
17	4.092 066	147.680 759	.006 771 3628	.244 375	36.089 536	.027 708 8628	11.09	.884 203	5.20	68
18	4.445 691	164.570 302	.006 076 4305	.224 937	37.017 938	.027 013 9305	10.81	.945 003	5.25	72
19	4.829 875	182.919 391	.005 466 8890	.207 045	37.872 492	.026 404 3890	10.57	1.006 734	5.30	76
20	5.247 259	202.854 156	.004 929 6500	.190 576	38.659 071	.025 867 1500	10.35	1.069 372	5.35	80
21	5.700 712	224.511 628	.004 454 1123	.175 417	39.383 084	.025 391 6123	10.16	1.132 895	5.39	84
22	6.193 352	248.040 677	.004 031 5968	.161 463	40.049 506	.024 969 0968	9.99	1.197 281	5.44	88
23	6.728 564	273.603 041	.003 654 9301	.148 620	40.662 919	.024 592 4301	9.84	1.262 504	5.49	92
24	7.310 027	301.374 432	.003 318 1315	.136 798	41.227 539	.024 255 6315	9.71	1.328 541	5.54	96
25	7.941 739	331.545 748	.003 016 1750	.125 917	41.747 248	.023 953 6750	9.59	1.395 368	5.58	100
26	8.628 042	364.324 384	.002 744 8067	.115 901	42.225 617	.023 682 3067	9.48	1.462 960	5.63	104
27	9.373 653	399.935 658	.002 500 4022	.106 682	42.665 934	.023 437 9022	9.38	1.531 293	5.67	108
28	10.183 697	438.624 357	.002 279 8552	.098 196	43.071 228	.023 217 3552	9.29	1.600 344	5.72	112
29	11.063 744	480.656 425	.002 080 4882	.090 385	43.444 283	.023 017 9882	9.21	1.670 087	5.76	116
30	12.019 841	526.320 785	.001 899 9820	.083 196	43.787 665	.022 837 4820	9.14	1.740 498	5.80	120
31	13.058 562	575.931 331	.001 736 3181	.076 578	44.103 732	.022 673 8181	9.07	1.811 553	5.84	124
32	14.187 046	629.829 080	.001 587 7323	.070 487	44.394 659	.022 525 2323	9.02	1.883 230	5.89	128
33	15.413 051	688.384 520	.001 452 6765	.064 880	44.662 444	.022 390 1765	8.96	1.955 503	5.93	132
34	16.745 003	752.000 157	.001 329 7870	.059 719	44.908 929	.022 267 2870	8.91	2.028 351	5.97	136
35	18.192 059	821.113 278	.001 217 8588	.054 969	45.135 807	.022 155 3588	8.87	2.101 750	6.01	140
36	19.764 166	896.198 959	.001 115 8237	.050 597	45.344 639	.022 053 3237	8.83	2.175 679	6.04	144
37	21.472 129	977.773 333	.001 022 7319	.046 572	45.536 860	.021 960 2319	8.79	2.250 114	6.08	148
38	23.327 690	1066.397 135	.000 937 7370	.042 868	45.713 791	.021 875 2370	8.76	2.325 036	6.12	152
39	25.343 603	1162.679 556	.000 860 0822	.039 458	45.876 648	.021 797 5822	8.72	2.400 423	6.15	156
40	27.533 726	1267.282 432	.000 789 0901	.036 319	46.026 551	.021 726 5901	8.70	2.476 254	6.19	160
41	29.913 113	1380.924 793	.000 724 1524	.033 430	46.164 530	.021 661 6524	8.67	2.552 511	6.23	164
42	32.498 120	1504.387 807	.000 664 7222	.030 771	46.291 534	.021 602 2222	8.65	2.629 173	6.26	168
43	35.306 516	1638.520 146	.000 610 3068	.028 323	46.408 435	.021 547 8068	8.62	2.706 223	6.29	172
44	38.357 605	1784.243 824	.000 560 4615	.026 070	46.516 038	.021 497 9615	8.60	2.783 641	6.33	176
45	41.672 361	1942.560 532	.000 514 7845	.023 997	46.615 082	.021 452 2845	8.59	2.861 411	6.36	180
46	45.273 569	2114.558 522	.000 472 9120	.022 088	46.706 248	.021 410 4120	8.57	2.939 516	6.39	184
47	49.185 983	2301.420 094	.000 434 5143	.020 331	46.790 161	.021 372 0143	8.55	3.017 939	6.42	188
48	53.436 497	2504.429 716	.000 399 2925	.018 714	46.867 401	.021 336 7925	8.54	3.096 664	6.45	192
49	58.054 329	2724.982 857	.000 366 9748	.017 225	46.938 496	.021 304 4748	8.53	3.175 677	6.48	196
50	63.071 220	2964.595 578	.000 337 3141	.015 855	47.003 936	.021 274 8141	8.51	3.254 963	6.51	200

Effective Rate is 8.64 %

Annual Percentage Rate is 8.375%

Amount Of 1	Amount Of 1 Per Period	Sinking Fund Payment	Present Worth Of 1	Present Worth of 1 Per Period	Periodic Payment To Amortize 1	Constant Annual Percent	Total Interest	Annual Add On Rate	
What a single $ 1 deposit grows to in the future. The deposit is made at the beginning of the first period.	What a series of $ 1 deposits grow to in the future. A deposit is made at the end of each period.	The amount to be deposited at the end of each period that grows to $ 1 in the future.	What $ 1 to be paid in the future is worth today. Value today of a single $ 1 payment tomorrow.	What $ 1 to be paid at the end of each period is worth today. Value today of a series of $ 1 payments tomorrow.	The mortgage payment to amortize a loan of $ 1. An annuity certain, payable at the end of each period, worth $ 1 today.	The annual payment, including interest and principal, to amortize completely a loan of $ 100.	The total interest paid over the term on a loan that is amortized by regular periodic payments.	The average annual interest rate on a loan that is completely amortized by regular periodic payments.	
$S = (1+i)^n$	$S\overline{n} = \dfrac{(1+i)^n - 1}{i}$	$\dfrac{1}{S\overline{n}} = \dfrac{i}{(1+i)^n - 1}$	$V^n = \dfrac{1}{(1+i)^n}$	$A\overline{n} = \dfrac{1 - V^n}{i}$	$\dfrac{1}{A\overline{n}} = \dfrac{i}{1 - V^n}$				

YEAR									PERIODS
	1.021 250	1.000 000	1.000 000 0000	.979 192	.979 192	1.021 250 0000	408.50	.021 250	8.50	1
	1.042 952	2.021 250	.494 743 3519	.958 817	1.938 009	.515 993 3519	206.40	.031 987	6.40	2
	1.065 114	3.064 202	.326 349 2886	.938 866	2.876 876	.347 599 2886	139.04	.042 798	5.71	3
	1.087 748	4.129 316	.242 170 8674	.919 331	3.796 206	.263 420 8674	105.37	.053 683	5.37	4

YEAR	Amount Of 1	Amount Of 1 Per Period	Sinking Fund Payment	Present Worth Of 1	Present Worth of 1 Per Period	Periodic Payment To Amortize 1	Constant Annual Percent	Total Interest	Annual Add On Rate	PERIODS
1	1.087 748	4.129 316	.242 170 8674	.919 331	3.796 206	.263 420 8674	105.37	.053 683	5.37	4
2	1.183 196	8.620 971	.115 996 2178	.845 169	7.286 175	.137 246 2178	54.90	.097 970	4.90	8
3	1.287 019	13.506 759	.074 037 0051	.776 990	10.494 610	.095 287 0051	38.12	.143 444	4.78	12
4	1.399 952	18.821 266	.053 131 3898	.714 310	13.444 223	.074 381 3898	29.76	.190 102	4.75	16
5	1.522 795	24.602 109	.040 646 9215	.656 687	16.155 892	.061 896 9215	24.76	.237 938	4.76	20
6	1.656 417	30.890 210	.032 372 7162	.603 713	18.648 813	.053 622 7162	21.45	.286 945	4.78	24
7	1.801 764	37.730 079	.026 504 0528	.555 012	20.940 631	.047 754 0528	19.11	.337 113	4.82	28
8	1.959 865	45.170 132	.022 138 5228	.510 239	23.047 570	.043 388 5228	17.36	.388 433	4.86	32
9	2.131 839	53.263 035	.018 774 7469	.469 078	24.984 543	.040 024 7469	16.01	.440 891	4.90	36
10	2.318 904	62.066 074	.016 111 8618	.431 238	26.765 261	.037 361 8618	14.95	.494 474	4.94	40
11	2.522 383	71.641 561	.013 958 3782	.396 450	28.402 331	.035 208 3782	14.09	.549 169	4.99	44
12	2.743 717	82.057 278	.012 186 6095	.364 469	29.907 339	.033 436 6095	13.38	.604 957	5.04	48
13	2.984 473	93.386 952	.010 708 1340	.335 068	31.290 938	.031 958 1340	12.79	.661 823	5.09	52
14	3.246 354	105.710 783	.009 459 7729	.308 038	32.562 924	.030 709 7729	12.29	.719 747	5.14	56
15	3.531 215	119.116 005	.008 395 1775	.283 189	33.732 299	.029 645 1775	11.86	.778 711	5.19	60
16	3.841 072	133.697 507	.007 479 5710	.260 344	34.807 342	.028 729 5710	11.50	.838 693	5.24	64
17	4.178 118	149.558 507	.006 686 3465	.239 342	35.795 661	.027 936 3465	11.18	.899 672	5.29	68
18	4.544 740	166.811 276	.005 994 7986	.220 035	36.704 254	.027 244 7986	10.90	.961 625	5.34	72
19	4.943 531	185.577 942	.005 388 5715	.202 285	37.539 551	.026 638 5715	10.66	1.024 531	5.39	76
20	5.377 316	205.991 344	.004 854 5729	.185 966	38.307 464	.026 104 5729	10.45	1.088 366	5.44	80
21	5.849 165	228.195 980	.004 382 1981	.170 965	39.013 431	.025 632 1981	10.26	1.153 105	5.49	84
22	6.362 417	252.349 028	.003 962 7654	.157 173	39.662 448	.025 212 7654	10.09	1.218 723	5.54	88
23	6.920 706	278.621 457	.003 589 0990	.144 494	40.259 109	.024 839 0990	9.94	1.285 197	5.59	92
24	7.527 984	307.199 238	.003 255 2164	.132 838	40.807 638	.024 505 2164	9.81	1.352 501	5.64	96
25	8.188 549	338.284 660	.002 956 0903	.122 122	41.311 917	.024 206 0903	9.69	1.420 609	5.68	100
26	8.907 078	372.097 766	.002 687 4657	.112 270	41.775 517	.023 937 4657	9.58	1.489 496	5.73	104
27	9.688 655	408.877 902	.002 445 7179	.103 213	42.201 718	.023 695 7179	9.48	1.559 138	5.77	108
28	10.538 815	448.885 420	.002 227 7400	.094 887	42.593 538	.023 477 7400	9.40	1.629 507	5.82	112
29	11.463 575	492.403 517	.002 030 8547	.087 233	42.953 749	.023 280 8547	9.32	1.700 579	5.86	116
30	12.469 480	539.740 238	.001 852 7431	.080 196	43.284 903	.023 102 7431	9.25	1.772 329	5.91	120
31	13.563 652	591.230 659	.001 691 3873	.073 726	43.589 343	.022 941 3873	9.18	1.844 732	5.95	124
32	14.753 834	647.239 261	.001 545 0237	.067 779	43.869 224	.022 795 0237	9.12	1.917 763	5.99	128
33	16.048 453	708.162 502	.001 412 1053	.062 311	44.126 527	.022 662 1053	9.07	1.991 398	6.03	132
34	17.456 672	774.431 634	.001 291 2696	.057 285	44.363 074	.022 541 2696	9.02	2.065 613	6.08	136
35	18.988 460	846.515 747	.001 181 3129	.052 664	44.580 538	.022 431 3129	8.98	2.140 384	6.12	140
36	20.654 658	924.925 095	.001 081 1686	.048 415	44.780 460	.022 331 1686	8.94	2.215 688	6.15	144
37	22.467 062	1010.214 702	.000 989 8886	.044 510	44.964 254	.022 239 8886	8.90	2.291 504	6.19	148
38	24.438 501	1102.988 299	.000 906 6279	.040 919	45.133 222	.022 156 6279	8.87	2.367 807	6.23	152
39	26.582 930	1203.902 590	.000 830 6320	.037 618	45.288 559	.022 080 6320	8.84	2.444 579	6.27	156
40	28.915 528	1313.671 904	.000 761 2251	.034 583	45.431 365	.022 011 2251	8.81	2.521 796	6.30	160
41	31.452 807	1433.073 252	.000 697 8010	.031 794	45.562 651	.021 947 8010	8.78	2.599 439	6.34	164
42	34.212 726	1562.951 825	.000 639 8150	.029 229	45.683 346	.021 889 8150	8.76	2.677 489	6.37	168
43	37.214 823	1704.226 978	.000 586 7763	.026 871	45.794 305	.021 836 7763	8.74	2.755 926	6.41	172
44	40.480 348	1857.898 737	.000 538 2425	.024 703	45.896 313	.021 788 2425	8.72	2.834 731	6.44	176
45	44.032 416	2025.054 880	.000 493 8138	.022 711	45.990 092	.021 743 8138	8.70	2.913 886	6.48	180
46	47.896 171	2206.878 634	.000 453 1287	.020 878	46.076 306	.021 703 1287	8.69	2.993 376	6.51	184
47	52.098 962	2404.657 052	.000 415 8597	.019 194	46.155 565	.021 665 8597	8.67	3.073 182	6.54	188
48	56.670 540	2619.790 123	.000 381 7100	.017 646	46.228 430	.021 631 7100	8.66	3.153 288	6.57	192
49	61.643 264	2853.800 682	.000 350 4099	.016 222	46.295 418	.021 600 4099	8.65	3.233 680	6.60	196
50	67.052 335	3108.345 191	.000 321 7146	.014 914	46.357 001	.021 571 7146	8.63	3.314 343	6.63	200

Effective Rate is 8.77 %

Annual Percentage Rate is 8.50 %

QUARTERLY COMPOUND INTEREST AND ANNUITY

8.625% Q

Amount Of 1	Amount Of 1 Per Period	Sinking Fund Payment	Present Worth Of 1	Present Worth of 1 Per Period	Periodic Payment To Amortize 1	Constant Annual Percent	Total Interest	Annual Add On Rate
What a single $ 1 deposit grows to in the future. The deposit is made at the beginning of the first period.	What a series of $ 1 deposits grow to in the future. A deposit is made at the end of each period.	The amount to be deposited at the end of each period that grows to $ 1 in the future.	What $ 1 to be paid in the future is worth today. Value today of a single $ 1 payment tomorrow.	What $ 1 to be paid at the end of each period is worth today. Value today of a series of $ 1 payments tomorrow.	The mortgage payment to amortize a loan of $ 1. An annuity certain, payable at the end of each period, worth $ 1 today.	The annual payment, including interest and principal, to amortize completely a loan of $ 100.	The total interest paid over the term on a loan of $1. The loan is amortized by regular periodic payments.	The average annual interest rate on a loan that is completely amortized by regular periodic payments.
$S = (1+i)^n$	$S\overline{n}| = \dfrac{(1+i)^n - 1}{i}$	$\dfrac{1}{S\overline{n}|} = \dfrac{i}{(1+i)^n - 1}$	$V^n = \dfrac{1}{(1+i)^n}$	$A\overline{n}| = \dfrac{1-V^n}{i}$	$\dfrac{1}{A\overline{n}|} = \dfrac{i}{1-V^n}$			

YEAR / **PERIODS**

YEAR	Amount Of 1	Amount Of 1 Per Period	Sinking Fund Payment	Present Worth Of 1	Present Worth of 1 Per Period	Periodic Payment To Amortize 1	Constant Annual Percent	Total Interest	Annual Add On Rate	PERIODS
	1.021 563	1.000 000	1.000 000 0000	.978 893	.978 893	1.021 562 5000	408.63	.021 563	8.63	1
	1.043 590	2.021 562	.494 666 8728	.958 231	1.937 123	.516 229 3728	206.50	.032 459	6.49	2
	1.066 092	3.065 152	.326 248 0477	.938 005	2.875 128	.347 810 5477	139.13	.043 432	5.79	3
	1.089 080	4.131 245	.242 057 7939	.918 206	3.793 335	.263 620 2939	105.45	.054 481	5.45	4
1	1.089 080	4.131 245	.242 057 7939	.918 206	3.793 335	.263 620 2939	105.45	.054 481	5.45	4
2	1.186 095	8.630 501	.115 868 1323	.843 103	7.276 398	.137 430 6323	54.98	.099 445	4.97	8
3	1.291 752	13.530 550	.073 906 8244	.774 142	10.474 569	.095 469 3244	38.19	.145 632	4.85	12
4	1.406 822	18.867 096	.053 002 3275	.710 822	13.411 149	.074 564 8275	29.83	.193 037	4.83	16
5	1.532 141	24.679 021	.040 520 2459	.652 681	16.107 535	.062 082 7459	24.84	.241 655	4.83	20
6	1.668 624	31.008 672	.032 249 0429	.599 296	18.583 373	.053 811 5429	21.53	.291 477	4.86	24
7	1.817 266	37.902 168	.026 383 7148	.550 277	20.856 704	.047 946 2148	19.18	.342 494	4.89	28
8	1.979 147	45.409 737	.022 021 7087	.505 268	22.944 090	.043 584 2087	17.44	.394 695	4.93	32
9	2.155 450	53.586 080	.018 661 5630	.463 940	24.860 741	.040 224 0630	16.09	.448 066	4.98	36
10	2.347 457	62.490 771	.016 002 3631	.425 993	26.620 621	.037 564 8631	15.03	.502 595	5.03	40
11	2.556 569	72.188 691	.013 852 5853	.391 149	28.236 555	.035 415 0853	14.17	.558 264	5.08	44
12	2.784 308	82.750 502	.012 084 5188	.359 156	29.720 315	.033 647 0188	13.46	.615 057	5.13	48
13	3.032 334	94.253 159	.010 609 7240	.329 779	31.082 713	.032 172 2240	12.87	.672 956	5.18	52
14	3.302 454	106.780 472	.009 365 0083	.302 805	32.333 675	.030 927 5083	12.38	.731 940	5.23	56
15	3.596 636	120.423 717	.008 304 0121	.278 038	33.482 316	.029 866 5121	11.95	.791 991	5.28	60
16	3.917 025	135.282 303	.007 391 9499	.255 296	34.537 006	.028 954 4499	11.59	.853 085	5.33	64
17	4.265 953	151.464 490	.006 602 2075	.234 414	35.505 428	.028 164 7075	11.27	.915 200	5.38	68
18	4.645 964	169.088 187	.005 914 0737	.215 241	36.394 640	.027 476 5737	11.00	.978 313	5.44	72
19	5.059 826	188.281 801	.005 311 1878	.197 635	37.211 119	.026 873 6878	10.75	1.042 400	5.49	76
20	5.510 556	209.185 183	.004 780 4533	.181 470	37.960 816	.026 342 9533	10.54	1.107 436	5.54	80
21	6.001 436	231.950 636	.004 311 2622	.166 627	38.649 192	.025 873 7622	10.35	1.173 396	5.59	84
22	6.536 043	256.744 036	.003 894 9298	.152 998	39.281 263	.025 457 4298	10.19	1.240 254	5.64	88
23	7.118 274	283.746 031	.003 524 2784	.140 483	39.861 635	.025 086 7784	10.04	1.307 984	5.69	92
24	7.752 369	313.153 362	.003 193 3235	.128 993	40.394 536	.024 755 8235	9.91	1.376 559	5.74	96
25	8.442 950	345.180 298	.002 897 0367	.118 442	40.883 849	.024 459 5367	9.79	1.445 954	5.78	100
26	9.195 048	380.060 192	.002 631 1622	.108 754	41.333 139	.024 193 6622	9.68	1.516 141	5.83	104
27	10.014 142	418.047 185	.002 392 0745	.099 859	41.745 680	.023 954 5745	9.59	1.587 094	5.88	108
28	10.906 202	459.418 059	.002 176 6667	.091 691	42.124 478	.023 739 1667	9.50	1.658 787	5.92	112
29	11.877 726	504.474 249	.001 982 2617	.084 191	42.472 292	.023 544 7617	9.42	1.731 192	5.97	116
30	12.935 793	553.544 042	.001 806 5410	.077 305	42.791 658	.023 369 0410	9.35	1.804 285	6.01	120
31	14.088 113	606.984 972	.001 647 4872	.070 982	43.084 901	.023 209 9872	9.29	1.878 038	6.06	124
32	15.343 082	665.186 417	.001 503 3380	.065 176	43.354 129	.023 065 8380	9.23	1.952 427	6.10	128
33	16.709 843	728.572 445	.001 372 5471	.059 845	43.601 393	.022 935 0471	9.18	2.027 426	6.14	132
34	18.198 356	797.604 898	.001 253 7536	.054 950	43.828 405	.022 816 2536	9.13	2.103 010	6.19	136
35	19.819 465	872.786 760	.001 145 7552	.050 455	44.036 849	.022 708 2552	9.09	2.179 156	6.23	140
36	21.584 982	954.665 820	.001 047 4870	.046 329	44.228 243	.022 609 9870	9.05	2.255 838	6.27	144
37	23.507 771	1043.838 663	.000 958 0025	.042 539	44.403 983	.022 520 5025	9.01	2.333 034	6.31	148
38	25.601 843	1140.955 020	.000 876 4587	.039 060	44.565 348	.022 438 9587	8.98	2.410 722	6.34	152
39	27.882 454	1246.722 499	.000 802 1031	.035 865	44.713 514	.022 364 6031	8.95	2.488 878	6.38	156
40	30.366 222	1361.911 742	.000 734 2620	.032 931	44.849 562	.022 296 7620	8.92	2.567 482	6.42	160
41	33.071 244	1487.362 038	.000 672 3313	.030 238	44.974 481	.022 234 8313	8.90	2.646 512	6.45	164
42	36.017 229	1623.987 442	.000 615 7683	.027 764	45.089 183	.022 178 2683	8.88	2.725 949	6.49	168
43	39.225 643	1772.783 433	.000 564 0847	.025 494	45.194 503	.022 126 5847	8.86	2.805 773	6.53	172
44	42.719 862	1934.834 165	.000 516 8402	.023 408	45.291 209	.022 079 3402	8.84	2.885 964	6.56	176
45	46.525 345	2111.320 371	.000 473 6373	.021 494	45.380 004	.022 036 1373	8.82	2.966 505	6.59	180
46	50.669 822	2303.527 962	.000 434 1167	.019 736	45.461 537	.021 996 6167	8.80	3.047 377	6.62	184
47	55.183 488	2512.857 399	.000 397 9533	.018 121	45.536 401	.021 960 4533	8.79	3.128 565	6.66	188
48	60.099 231	2740.833 895	.000 364 8525	.016 639	45.605 141	.021 927 3525	8.78	3.210 052	6.69	192
49	65.452 868	2989.118 529	.000 334 5468	.015 278	45.668 259	.021 897 0468	8.76	3.291 821	6.72	196
50	71.283 408	3259.520 351	.000 306 7936	.014 029	45.726 214	.021 869 2936	8.75	3.373 859	6.75	200

Effective Rate is 8.91 %

Annual Percentage Rate is 8.625%

QUARTERLY COMPOUND INTEREST AND ANNUITY

Amount Of 1	Amount Of 1 Per Period	Sinking Fund Payment	Present Worth Of 1	Present Worth of 1 Per Period	Periodic Payment To Amortize 1	Constant Annual Percent	Total Interest	Annual Add On Rate
What a single $ 1 deposit grows to in the future. The deposit is made at the beginning of the first period.	What a series of $ 1 deposits grow to in the future. A deposit is made at the end of each period.	The amount to be deposited at the end of each period that grows to $ 1 in the future.	What $ 1 to be paid in the future is worth today. Value today of a single $ 1 payment tomorrow.	What $ 1 to be paid at the end of each period is worth today. Value today of a series of $ 1 payments tomorrow.	The mortgage payment to amortize a loan of $ 1. An annuity certain, payable at the end of each period, worth $ 1 today.	The annual payment, including interest and principal, to amortize completely a loan of $ 100.	The total interest paid over the term on a loan of $1. The loan is amortized by regular periodic payments.	The average annual interest rate on a loan that is completely amortized by regular periodic payments.
$S = (1+i)^n$	$S\overline{n} = \dfrac{(1+i)^n - 1}{i}$	$\dfrac{1}{S\overline{n}} = \dfrac{i}{(1+i)^n - 1}$	$V^n = \dfrac{1}{(1+i)^n}$	$A\overline{n} = \dfrac{1-V^n}{i}$	$\dfrac{1}{A\overline{n}} = \dfrac{i}{1-V^n}$			

YEAR									PERIODS
	1.021 875	1.000 000	1.000 000 0000	.978 593	.978 593	1.021 875 0000	408.75	.021 875	8.75	1
	1.044 229	2.021 875	.494 590 4173	.957 645	1.936 238	.516 465 4173	206.59	.032 931	6.59	2
	1.067 071	3.066 104	.326 146 8489	.937 145	2.873 383	.348 021 8489	139.21	.044 066	5.88	3
	1.090 413	4.133 175	.241 944 7794	.917 084	3.790 466	.263 819 7794	105.53	.055 279	5.53	4

YEAR									PERIODS
1	1.090 413	4.133 175	.241 944 7794	.917 084	3.790 466	.263 819 7794	105.53	.055 279	5.53	4
2	1.189 001	8.640 043	.115 740 1705	.841 042	7.266 641	.137 615 1705	55.05	.100 921	5.05	8
3	1.296 502	13.554 391	.073 776 8303	.771 306	10.454 583	.095 651 8303	38.27	.147 822	4.93	12
4	1.413 723	18.913 061	.052 873 5136	.707 352	13.378 192	.074 748 5136	29.90	.195 976	4.90	16
5	1.541 542	24.756 226	.040 393 8791	.648 701	16.059 387	.062 268 8791	24.91	.245 378	4.91	20
6	1.680 918	31.127 690	.032 125 7376	.594 913	18.518 266	.054 000 7376	21.61	.296 018	4.93	24
7	1.832 895	38.075 218	.026 263 8021	.545 585	20.773 263	.048 138 8021	19.26	.347 886	4.97	28
8	1.998 613	45.650 895	.021 905 3756	.500 347	22.841 284	.043 780 3756	17.52	.400 972	5.01	32
9	2.179 314	53.911 513	.018 548 9138	.458 860	24.737 832	.040 423 9138	16.17	.455 261	5.06	36
10	2.376 353	62.918 999	.015 893 4505	.420 813	26.477 125	.037 768 4505	15.11	.510 738	5.11	40
11	2.591 207	72.740 881	.013 747 4276	.385 921	28.072 202	.035 622 4276	14.25	.567 387	5.16	44
12	2.825 486	83.450 791	.011 983 1099	.353 921	29.535 021	.033 858 1099	13.55	.625 189	5.21	48
13	3.080 947	95.129 018	.010 512 0395	.324 575	30.876 549	.032 387 0395	12.96	.684 126	5.26	52
14	3.359 506	107.863 111	.009 271 0102	.297 663	32.106 841	.031 146 0102	12.46	.744 177	5.32	56
15	3.663 249	121.748 534	.008 213 6513	.272 982	33.235 122	.030 088 6513	12.04	.805 319	5.37	60
16	3.994 455	136.889 382	.007 305 1685	.250 347	34.269 850	.029 180 1685	11.68	.867 531	5.42	64
17	4.355 607	153.399 162	.006 518 9404	.229 589	35.218 782	.028 393 9404	11.36	.930 788	5.48	68
18	4.749 411	171.401 645	.005 834 2497	.210 552	36.089 032	.027 709 2497	11.09	.995 046	5.53	72
19	5.178 820	191.031 790	.005 234 7308	.193 094	36.887 124	.027 109 7308	10.85	1.060 340	5.58	76
20	5.647 054	212.436 758	.004 707 2833	.177 083	37.619 041	.026 582 2833	10.64	1.126 583	5.63	80
21	6.157 622	235.777 018	.004 241 2955	.162 400	38.290 270	.026 116 2955	10.45	1.193 769	5.68	84
22	6.714 353	261.227 546	.003 828 0802	.148 935	38.905 843	.025 703 0802	10.29	1.261 871	5.74	88
23	7.321 419	288.979 137	.003 460 4574	.136 586	39.470 375	.025 335 4574	10.14	1.330 862	5.79	92
24	7.983 371	319.239 838	.003 132 4411	.125 260	39.988 098	.025 007 4411	10.01	1.400 714	5.84	96
25	8.705 174	352.236 505	.002 839 0016	.114 874	40.462 893	.024 714 0016	9.89	1.471 400	5.89	100
26	9.492 236	388.216 507	.002 575 8822	.105 349	40.898 320	.024 450 8822	9.79	1.542 892	5.93	104
27	10.350 459	427.449 575	.002 339 4572	.096 614	41.297 643	.024 214 4572	9.69	1.615 161	5.98	108
28	11.286 278	470.229 831	.002 126 6197	.088 603	41.663 855	.024 001 6197	9.61	1.688 181	6.03	112
29	12.306 706	516.877 986	.001 934 6926	.081 257	41.999 702	.023 809 6926	9.53	1.761 924	6.08	116
30	13.419 395	567.743 749	.001 761 3580	.074 519	42.307 702	.023 636 3580	9.46	1.836 363	6.12	120
31	14.632 685	623.208 449	.001 604 5996	.068 340	42.590 164	.023 479 5996	9.40	1.911 470	6.17	124
32	15.955 673	683.687 889	.001 462 6557	.062 674	42.849 205	.023 337 6557	9.34	1.987 220	6.21	128
33	17.398 276	749.635 469	.001 333 9817	.057 477	43.086 768	.023 208 9817	9.29	2.063 586	6.25	132
34	18.971 310	821.545 579	.001 217 2179	.052 711	43.304 632	.023 092 2179	9.24	2.140 542	6.30	136
35	20.686 566	899.957 313	.001 111 1638	.048 341	43.504 432	.022 986 1638	9.20	2.218 063	6.34	140
36	22.556 905	985.458 501	.001 014 7561	.044 332	43.687 665	.022 889 7561	9.16	2.296 125	6.38	144
37	24.596 346	1078.690 125	.000 927 0503	.040 656	43.855 705	.022 802 0503	9.13	2.374 703	6.42	148
38	26.820 181	1180.351 118	.000 847 2055	.037 285	44.009 812	.022 722 2055	9.09	2.453 775	6.46	152
39	29.245 079	1291.203 606	.000 774 4712	.034 194	44.151 141	.022 649 4712	9.06	2.533 318	6.50	156
40	31.889 220	1412.078 621	.000 708 1759	.031 359	44.280 752	.022 583 1759	9.04	2.613 308	6.53	160
41	34.772 426	1543.882 332	.000 647 7178	.028 758	44.399 615	.022 522 7178	9.01	2.693 726	6.57	164
42	37.916 312	1687.602 838	.000 592 5565	.026 374	44.508 623	.022 467 5565	8.99	2.774 549	6.61	168
43	41.344 447	1844.317 573	.000 542 2060	.024 187	44.608 592	.022 417 2060	8.97	2.855 759	6.64	172
44	45.082 530	2015.201 388	.000 496 2283	.022 182	44.700 272	.022 371 2283	8.95	2.937 336	6.68	176
45	49.158 586	2201.535 355	.000 454 2285	.020 342	44.784 351	.022 329 2285	8.94	3.019 261	6.71	180
46	53.603 171	2404.716 370	.000 415 8495	.018 656	44.861 458	.022 290 8495	8.92	3.101 516	6.74	184
47	58.449 604	2626.267 629	.000 380 7685	.017 109	44.932 171	.022 255 7685	8.91	3.184 084	6.77	188
48	63.734 220	2867.850 045	.000 348 6933	.015 690	44.997 021	.022 223 6933	8.89	3.266 949	6.81	192
49	69.496 634	3131.274 699	.000 319 3588	.014 389	45.056 494	.022 194 3588	8.88	3.350 094	6.84	196
50	75.780 047	3418.516 417	.000 292 5246	.013 196	45.111 036	.022 167 5246	8.87	3.433 505	6.87	200

Effective Rate is 9.04 %

Annual Percentage Rate is 8.75 %

	Amount Of 1	Amount Of 1 Per Period	Sinking Fund Payment	Present Worth Of 1	Present Worth of 1 Per Period	Periodic Payment To Amortize 1	Constant Annual Percent	Total Interest	Annual Add On Rate	
	What a single $ 1 deposit grows to in the future. The deposit is made at the beginning of the first period.	What a series of $ 1 deposits grow to in the future. A deposit is made at the end of each period.	The amount to be deposited at the end of each period that grows to $ 1 in the future.	What $ 1 to be paid in the future is worth today. Value today of a single $ 1 payment tomorrow.	What $ 1 to be paid at the end of each period is worth today. Value today of a series of $ 1 payments tomorrow.	The mortgage payment to amortize a loan of $ 1. An annuity certain, payable at the end of each period, worth $ 1 today.	The annual payment, including interest and principal, to amortize completely a loan of $ 100.	The total interest paid over the term on a loan of $1. The loan is amortized by regular periodic payments.	The average annual interest rate on a loan that is completely amortized by regular periodic payments.	
	$S = (1+i)^n$	$S\overline{n} = \dfrac{(1+i)^n - 1}{i}$	$\dfrac{1}{S\overline{n}} = \dfrac{i}{(1+i)^n - 1}$	$V^n = \dfrac{1}{(1+i)^n}$	$A\overline{n} = \dfrac{1-V^n}{i}$	$\dfrac{1}{A\overline{n}} = \dfrac{i}{1-V^n}$				

YEAR										PERIODS
	1.022 188	1.000 000	1.000 000 0000	.978 294	.978 294	1.022 187 5000	408.88	.022 187	8.87	1
	1.044 867	2.022 188	.494 513 9855	.957 059	1.935 353	.516 701 4855	206.69	.033 403	6.68	2
	1.068 050	3.067 055	.326 045 6921	.936 286	2.871 639	.348 233 1921	139.30	.044 700	5.96	3
	1.091 748	4.135 105	.241 831 8240	.915 963	3.787 602	.264 019 3240	105.61	.056 077	5.61	4
1	1.091 748	4.135 105	.241 831 8240	.915 963	3.787 602	.264 019 3240	105.61	.056 077	5.61	4
2	1.191 913	8.649 596	.115 612 3325	.838 987	7.256 903	.137 799 8325	55.12	.102 399	5.12	8
3	1.301 268	13.578 281	.073 647 0228	.768 481	10.434 653	.095 834 5228	38.34	.150 014	5.00	12
4	1.420 656	18.959 162	.052 744 9478	.703 900	13.345 353	.074 932 4478	29.98	.198 919	4.97	16
5	1.550 998	24.833 725	.040 267 8208	.644 746	16.011 446	.062 455 3208	24.99	.249 106	4.98	20
6	1.693 299	31.247 266	.032 002 7997	.590 563	18.453 487	.054 190 2997	21.68	.300 567	5.01	24
7	1.848 655	38.249 234	.026 144 3143	.540 934	20.690 305	.048 331 8143	19.34	.353 291	5.05	28
8	2.018 265	45.893 616	.021 789 5228	.495 475	22.739 147	.043 977 0228	17.60	.407 265	5.09	32
9	2.203 436	54.239 353	.018 436 7982	.453 837	24.615 810	.040 624 2982	16.25	.462 475	5.14	36
10	2.405 596	63.350 790	.015 785 1227	.415 697	26.334 762	.037 972 6227	15.19	.518 905	5.19	40
11	2.626 303	73.298 181	.013 642 9033	.380 763	27.909 259	.035 830 4033	14.34	.576 538	5.24	44
12	2.867 261	84.158 222	.011 882 3803	.348 765	29.351 439	.034 069 8803	13.63	.635 354	5.29	48
13	3.130 325	96.014 645	.010 415 0778	.319 456	30.672 421	.032 602 5778	13.05	.695 334	5.35	52
14	3.417 525	108.958 868	.009 177 7752	.292 609	31.882 392	.031 365 2752	12.55	.756 455	5.40	56
15	3.731 075	123.090 692	.008 124 0911	.268 019	32.990 680	.030 311 5911	12.13	.818 695	5.46	60
16	4.073 392	138.519 078	.007 219 2222	.245 496	34.005 830	.029 406 7222	11.77	.882 030	5.51	64
17	4.447 116	155.362 982	.006 436 5397	.224 865	34.935 670	.028 624 0397	11.45	.946 435	5.57	68
18	4.855 129	173.752 275	.005 755 3203	.205 968	35.787 368	.027 942 8203	11.18	1.011 883	5.62	72
19	5.300 575	193.828 742	.005 159 1936	.188 659	36.567 492	.027 346 6936	10.94	1.078 349	5.68	76
20	5.786 890	215.747 177	.004 635 0548	.172 804	37.282 056	.026 822 5548	10.73	1.145 804	5.73	80
21	6.317 824	239.676 577	.004 172 2892	.158 282	37.936 570	.026 359 7892	10.55	1.214 222	5.78	84
22	6.897 470	265.801 444	.003 762 2068	.144 981	38.536 081	.025 949 7068	10.38	1.283 574	5.83	88
23	7.530 296	294.323 205	.003 397 6254	.132 797	39.085 210	.025 585 1254	10.24	1.353 832	5.89	92
24	8.221 183	325.461 771	.003 072 5575	.121 637	39.588 192	.025 260 0575	10.11	1.424 966	5.94	96
25	8.975 457	359.457 226	.002 781 9722	.111 415	40.048 904	.024 969 4722	9.99	1.496 947	5.99	100
26	9.798 934	396.571 685	.002 521 6122	.102 052	40.470 900	.024 709 1122	9.89	1.569 748	6.04	104
27	10.697 963	437.091 307	.002 287 8515	.093 476	40.857 432	.024 475 3515	9.80	1.643 338	6.09	108
28	11.679 476	481.328 510	.002 077 5831	.085 620	41.211 480	.024 265 0831	9.71	1.717 689	6.13	112
29	12.751 041	529.624 371	.001 888 1306	.078 425	41.535 776	.024 075 6306	9.64	1.792 773	6.18	116
30	13.920 919	582.351 265	.001 717 1767	.071 834	41.832 818	.023 904 6767	9.57	1.868 561	6.23	120
31	15.198 130	639.915 726	.001 562 7058	.065 798	42.104 898	.023 750 2058	9.51	1.945 026	6.27	124
32	16.592 523	702.761 591	.001 422 9577	.060 268	42.354 113	.023 610 4577	9.45	2.022 139	6.32	128
33	18.114 848	771.373 416	.001 296 3890	.055 203	42.582 385	.023 483 8890	9.40	2.099 873	6.36	132
34	19.776 842	846.280 214	.001 181 6417	.050 564	42.791 473	.023 369 1417	9.35	2.178 203	6.41	136
35	21.591 321	928.059 535	.001 077 5171	.046 315	42.982 990	.023 265 0171	9.31	2.257 102	6.45	140
36	23.572 274	1017.341 915	.000 982 9537	.042 423	43.158 413	.023 170 4537	9.27	2.336 545	6.49	144
37	25.734 974	1114.815 744	.000 897 0092	.038 858	43.319 093	.023 084 5092	9.24	2.416 507	6.53	148
38	28.096 098	1221.232 566	.000 818 8449	.035 592	43.466 270	.023 006 3449	9.21	2.496 964	6.57	152
39	30.673 848	1337.412 882	.000 747 7123	.032 601	43.601 079	.022 935 2123	9.18	2.577 893	6.61	156
40	33.488 102	1464.252 467	.000 682 9423	.029 861	43.724 559	.022 870 4423	9.15	2.659 271	6.65	160
41	36.560 556	1602.729 286	.000 623 9357	.027 352	43.837 662	.022 811 4357	9.13	2.741 075	6.69	164
42	39.914 901	1753.911 026	.000 570 1543	.025 053	43.941 260	.022 757 6543	9.11	2.823 286	6.72	168
43	43.576 999	1918.963 335	.000 521 1147	.022 948	44.036 152	.022 708 6147	9.09	2.905 882	6.76	172
44	47.575 086	2099.158 804	.000 476 3813	.021 019	44.123 069	.022 663 8813	9.07	2.988 843	6.79	176
45	51.939 988	2295.886 783	.000 435 5615	.019 253	44.202 682	.022 623 0615	9.05	3.072 151	6.83	180
46	56.705 360	2510.664 090	.000 398 3010	.017 635	44.275 605	.022 585 8010	9.04	3.155 787	6.86	184
47	61.907 943	2745.146 709	.000 364 2793	.016 153	44.342 399	.022 551 7793	9.03	3.239 735	6.89	188
48	67.587 850	3001.142 556	.000 333 2064	.014 796	44.403 580	.022 520 7064	9.01	3.323 976	6.92	192
49	73.788 876	3280.625 419	.000 304 8199	.013 552	44.459 620	.022 492 3199	9.00	3.408 495	6.96	196
50	80.558 832	3585.750 176	.000 278 8817	.012 413	44.510 950	.022 466 3817	8.99	3.493 276	6.99	200

Effective Rate is 9.17 %

Annual Percentage Rate is 8.875%

Amount Of 1	Amount Of 1 Per Period	Sinking Fund Payment	Present Worth Of 1	Present Worth of 1 Per Period	Periodic Payment To Amortize 1	Constant Annual Percent	Total Interest	Annual Add On Rate
What a single $ 1 deposit grows to in the future. The deposit is made at the beginning of the first period.	What a series of $ 1 deposits grow to in the future. A deposit is made at the end of each period.	The amount to be deposited at the end of each period that grows to $ 1 in the future.	What $ 1 to be paid in the future is worth today. Value today of a single $ 1 payment tomorrow.	What $ 1 to be paid at the end of each period is worth today. Value today of a series of $ 1 payments tomorrow.	The mortgage payment to amortize a loan of $ 1. An annuity certain, payable at the end of each period, worth $ 1 today.	The annual payment, including interest and principal, to amortize completely a loan of $ 100.	The total interest paid over the term on a loan of $1. The loan is amortized by regular periodic payments.	The average annual interest rate on a loan that is completely amortized by regular periodic payments.

$$S = (1+i)^n \qquad S\overline{n}| = \frac{(1+i)^n - 1}{i} \qquad \frac{1}{S\overline{n}|} = \frac{i}{(1+i)^n - 1} \qquad V^n = \frac{1}{(1+i)^n} \qquad A\overline{n}| = \frac{1-V^n}{i} \qquad \frac{1}{A\overline{n}|} = \frac{i}{1-V^n}$$

YEAR / **PERIODS**

YEAR	Amount Of 1	Amount Of 1 Per Period	Sinking Fund Payment	Present Worth Of 1	Present Worth of 1 Per Period	Periodic Payment To Amortize 1	Constant Annual Percent	Total Interest	Annual Add On Rate	PERIODS
	1.022 500	1.000 000	1.000 000 0000	.977 995	.977 995	1.022 500 0000	409.00	.022 500	9.00	1
	1.045 506	2.022 500	.494 437 5773	.956 474	1.934 470	.516 937 5773	206.78	.033 875	6.78	2
	1.069 030	3.068 006	.325 944 5772	.935 427	2.869 897	.348 444 5772	139.38	.045 334	6.04	3
	1.093 083	4.137 036	.241 718 9277	.914 843	3.784 740	.264 218 9277	105.69	.056 876	5.69	4
1	1.093 083	4.137 036	.241 718 9277	.914 843	3.784 740	.264 218 9277	105.69	.056 876	5.69	4
2	1.194 831	8.659 162	.115 484 6181	.836 938	7.247 185	.137 984 6181	55.20	.103 877	5.19	8
3	1.306 050	13.602 222	.073 517 4015	.765 667	10.414 779	.096 017 4015	38.41	.152 209	5.07	12
4	1.427 621	19.005 398	.052 616 6300	.700 466	13.312 631	.075 116 6300	30.05	.201 866	5.05	16
5	1.560 509	24.911 520	.040 142 0708	.640 816	15.963 712	.062 642 0708	25.06	.252 841	5.06	20
6	1.705 767	31.367 403	.031 880 2289	.586 247	18.389 036	.054 380 2289	21.76	.305 125	5.09	24
7	1.864 545	38.424 222	.026 025 2506	.536 324	20.607 828	.048 525 2506	19.42	.358 707	5.12	28
8	2.038 103	46.137 912	.021 674 1493	.490 652	22.637 674	.044 174 1493	17.67	.413 573	5.17	32
9	2.227 816	54.569 619	.018 325 2151	.448 870	24.494 666	.040 825 2151	16.34	.469 708	5.22	36
10	2.435 189	63.786 176	.015 677 3781	.410 646	26.193 522	.038 177 3781	15.28	.527 095	5.27	40
11	2.661 864	73.860 642	.013 539 0105	.375 677	27.747 710	.036 039 0105	14.42	.585 716	5.32	44
12	2.909 640	84.872 872	.011 782 3279	.343 685	29.169 548	.034 282 3279	13.72	.645 552	5.38	48
13	3.180 479	96.910 157	.010 318 8359	.314 418	30.470 307	.032 818 8359	13.13	.706 579	5.44	52
14	3.476 528	110.067 912	.009 085 3000	.287 643	31.660 298	.031 585 3000	12.64	.768 777	5.49	56
15	3.800 135	124.450 435	.008 035 3275	.263 149	32.748 953	.030 535 3275	12.22	.832 120	5.55	60
16	4.153 864	140.171 731	.007 134 1061	.240 740	33.744 902	.029 634 1061	11.86	.896 583	5.60	64
17	4.540 519	157.356 417	.006 354 9998	.220 239	34.656 039	.028 854 9998	11.55	.962 140	5.66	68
18	4.963 166	176.140 711	.005 677 2792	.201 484	35.489 587	.028 177 2792	11.28	1.028 764	5.72	72
19	5.425 154	196.673 509	.005 084 5689	.184 327	36.252 153	.027 584 5689	11.04	1.096 427	5.77	76
20	5.930 145	219.117 569	.004 563 7600	.168 630	36.949 781	.027 063 7600	10.83	1.165 101	5.83	80
21	6.482 143	243.650 796	.004 104 2345	.154 270	37.588 001	.026 604 2345	10.65	1.234 756	5.88	84
22	7.085 522	270.467 657	.003 697 2998	.141 133	38.171 873	.026 197 2998	10.48	1.305 362	5.93	88
23	7.745 066	299.780 720	.003 335 7716	.129 114	38.706 024	.025 835 7716	10.34	1.376 891	5.99	92
24	8.466 003	331.822 341	.003 013 6609	.118 119	39.194 689	.025 513 6609	10.21	1.449 311	6.04	96
25	9.254 046	366.846 502	.002 725 9358	.108 061	39.641 741	.025 225 9358	10.10	1.522 594	6.09	100
26	10.115 444	405.130 828	.002 468 3384	.098 859	40.050 723	.024 968 3384	9.99	1.596 707	6.14	104
27	11.057 023	446.978 787	.002 237 2426	.090 440	40.424 877	.024 737 2426	9.90	1.671 622	6.19	108
28	12.086 247	492.722 092	.002 029 5416	.082 739	40.767 170	.024 529 5416	9.82	1.747 309	6.24	112
29	13.211 275	542.722 336	.001 842 5594	.075 693	41.080 315	.024 342 5594	9.74	1.823 737	6.29	116
30	14.441 024	597.378 862	.001 673 9796	.069 247	41.366 793	.024 173 9796	9.67	1.900 878	6.34	120
31	15.785 243	657.121 905	.001 521 7877	.063 350	41.628 875	.024 021 7877	9.61	1.978 702	6.38	124
32	17.254 586	722.426 029	.001 384 2248	.057 956	41.868 640	.023 884 2248	9.56	2.057 181	6.43	128
33	18.860 700	793.808 878	.001 259 7491	.053 020	42.087 987	.023 759 7491	9.51	2.136 287	6.47	132
34	20.616 316	871.836 279	.001 147 0043	.048 505	42.288 655	.023 647 0043	9.46	2.215 993	6.52	136
35	22.535 351	957.126 730	.001 044 7937	.044 375	42.472 234	.023 544 7937	9.42	2.296 271	6.56	140
36	24.633 017	1050.356 299	.000 952 0579	.040 596	42.640 181	.023 452 0579	9.39	2.377 096	6.60	144
37	26.925 940	1152.263 986	.000 867 8567	.037 139	42.793 826	.023 367 8567	9.35	2.458 443	6.64	148
38	29.432 296	1263.657 578	.000 791 3536	.033 976	42.934 387	.023 291 3536	9.32	2.540 286	6.68	152
39	32.171 951	1385.420 056	.000 721 8027	.031 083	43.062 979	.023 221 8027	9.29	2.622 601	6.72	156
40	35.166 623	1518.516 589	.000 658 5374	.028 436	43.180 620	.023 158 5374	9.27	2.705 366	6.76	160
41	38.440 049	1664.002 189	.000 600 9607	.026 015	43.288 243	.023 100 9607	9.25	2.788 558	6.80	164
42	42.018 177	1823.030 071	.000 548 5373	.023 799	43.386 701	.023 048 5373	9.22	2.872 154	6.84	168
43	45.929 368	1996.860 797	.000 500 7860	.021 773	43.476 775	.023 000 7860	9.21	2.956 135	6.87	172
44	50.204 626	2186.872 264	.000 457 2741	.019 918	43.559 179	.022 957 2741	9.19	3.040 480	6.91	176
45	54.877 839	2394.570 628	.000 417 6114	.018 222	43.634 565	.022 917 6114	9.17	3.125 170	6.94	180
46	59.986 051	2621.602 246	.000 381 4461	.016 671	43.703 531	.022 881 4461	9.16	3.210 186	6.98	184
47	65.569 751	2869.766 720	.000 348 4604	.015 251	43.766 625	.022 848 4604	9.14	3.295 511	7.01	188
48	71.673 201	3141.031 167	.000 318 3668	.013 952	43.824 346	.022 818 3668	9.13	3.381 126	7.04	192
49	78.344 781	3437.545 808	.000 290 9052	.012 764	43.877 151	.022 790 9052	9.12	3.467 017	7.08	196
50	85.637 373	3761.661 017	.000 265 8400	.011 677	43.925 460	.022 765 8400	9.11	3.553 168	7.11	200

Effective Rate is 9.31 %

Annual Percentage Rate is 9.00 %

	Amount Of 1	Amount Of 1 Per Period	Sinking Fund Payment	Present Worth Of 1	Present Worth of 1 Per Period	Periodic Payment To Amortize 1	Constant Annual Percent	Total Interest	Annual Add On Rate	
	What a single $ 1 deposit grows to in the future. The deposit is made at the beginning of the first period.	What a series of $ 1 deposits grow to in the future. A deposit is made at the end of each period.	The amount to be deposited at the end of each period that grows to $ 1 in the future.	What $ 1 to be paid in the future is worth today. Value today of a single $ 1 payment tomorrow.	What $ 1 to be paid at the end of each period is worth today. Value today of a series of $ 1 payments tomorrow.	The mortgage payment to amortize a loan of $ 1. An annuity certain, payable at the end of each period, worth $ 1 today.	The annual payment, including interest and principal, to amortize completely a loan of $ 100.	The total interest paid over the term on a loan of $1. The loan is amortized by regular periodic payments.	The average annual interest rate on a loan that is completely amortized by regular periodic payments.	
	$S = (1+i)^n$	$S\overline{n}| = \dfrac{(1+i)^n - 1}{i}$	$\dfrac{1}{S\overline{n}|} = \dfrac{i}{(1+i)^n - 1}$	$V^n = \dfrac{1}{(1+i)^n}$	$A\overline{n}| = \dfrac{1-V^n}{i}$	$\dfrac{1}{A\overline{n}|} = \dfrac{i}{1-V^n}$				

YEAR										PERIODS
	1.022 812	1.000 000	1.000 000 0000	.977 696	.977 696	1.022 812 5000	409.13	.022 813	9.13	1
	1.046 145	2.022 812	.494 361 1926	.955 890	1.933 586	.517 173 6926	206.87	.034 347	6.87	2
	1.070 011	3.068 958	.325 843 5043	.934 570	2.868 157	.348 656 0043	139.47	.045 968	6.13	3
	1.094 420	4.138 969	.241 606 0903	.913 726	3.781 882	.264 418 5903	105.77	.057 674	5.77	4
1	1.094 420	4.138 969	.241 606 0903	.913 726	3.781 882	.264 418 5903	105.77	.057 674	5.77	4
2	1.197 756	8.668 739	.115 357 0272	.834 895	7.237 486	.138 169 5272	55.27	.105 356	5.27	8
3	1.310 848	13.626 212	.073 387 9666	.762 865	10.394 960	.096 200 4666	38.49	.154 406	5.15	12
4	1.434 619	19.051 771	.052 488 5599	.697 049	13.280 026	.075 301 0599	30.13	.204 817	5.12	16
5	1.570 076	24.989 611	.040 016 6286	.636 912	15.916 184	.062 829 1286	25.14	.256 583	5.13	20
6	1.718 322	31.488 105	.031 758 0247	.581 963	18.324 911	.054 570 5247	21.83	.309 693	5.16	24
7	1.880 567	38.600 187	.025 906 6104	.531 755	20.525 826	.048 719 1104	19.49	.364 135	5.20	28
8	2.058 130	46.383 793	.021 559 2544	.485 878	22.536 860	.044 371 7544	17.75	.419 896	5.25	32
9	2.252 459	54.902 330	.018 214 1633	.443 959	24.374 393	.041 026 6633	16.42	.476 960	5.30	36
10	2.465 137	64.225 188	.015 570 2151	.405 657	26.053 394	.038 382 7151	15.36	.535 309	5.35	40
11	2.697 896	74.428 313	.013 435 7472	.370 659	27.587 541	.036 248 2472	14.50	.594 923	5.41	44
12	2.952 632	85.594 819	.011 682 9501	.338 681	28.989 330	.034 495 4501	13.80	.655 782	5.46	48
13	3.231 420	97.815 670	.010 223 3109	.309 461	30.270 182	.033 035 8109	13.22	.717 862	5.52	52
14	3.536 531	111.190 415	.008 993 5810	.282 763	31.440 529	.031 806 0810	12.73	.781 141	5.58	56
15	3.870 451	125.828 007	.007 947 3563	.258 368	32.509 905	.030 759 8563	12.31	.845 591	5.64	60
16	4.235 900	141.847 683	.007 049 8155	.236 077	33.487 021	.029 862 3155	11.95	.911 188	5.69	64
17	4.635 855	159.379 941	.006 274 3153	.215 710	34.379 838	.029 086 8153	11.64	.977 903	5.75	68
18	5.073 573	178.567 599	.005 600 1201	.197 100	35.195 628	.028 412 6201	11.37	1.045 709	5.81	72
19	5.552 621	199.566 959	.005 010 8495	.180 095	35.941 036	.027 823 3495	11.13	1.114 575	5.87	76
20	6.076 901	222.549 084	.004 493 3908	.164 558	36.622 134	.027 305 8908	10.93	1.184 471	5.92	80
21	6.650 683	247.701 185	.004 037 1224	.150 360	37.244 472	.026 849 6224	10.74	1.255 368	5.98	84
22	7.278 642	275.228 154	.003 633 3492	.137 388	37.813 117	.026 445 8492	10.58	1.327 235	6.03	88
23	7.965 893	305.354 225	.003 274 8851	.125 535	38.332 704	.026 087 3851	10.44	1.400 039	6.09	92
24	8.718 035	338.324 807	.002 955 7395	.114 705	38.807 463	.025 768 2395	10.31	1.473 751	6.14	96
25	9.541 193	374.408 478	.002 670 8797	.104 809	39.241 263	.025 483 3797	10.20	1.548 338	6.19	100
26	10.442 075	413.899 177	.002 416 0473	.095 766	39.637 637	.025 228 5473	10.10	1.623 769	6.25	104
27	11.428 018	457.118 596	.002 187 6161	.087 504	39.999 814	.025 000 1161	10.01	1.700 013	6.30	108
28	12.507 054	504.418 803	.001 982 4796	.079 955	40.330 745	.024 794 9796	9.92	1.777 038	6.35	112
29	13.687 973	556.185 105	.001 797 9626	.073 057	40.633 125	.024 610 4626	9.85	1.854 814	6.40	116
30	14.980 394	612.839 193	.001 631 7494	.066 754	40.909 417	.024 444 2494	9.78	1.933 310	6.44	120
31	16.394 846	674.842 573	.001 481 8271	.060 995	41.161 873	.024 294 3271	9.72	2.012 497	6.49	124
32	17.942 851	742.700 325	.001 346 4381	.055 733	41.392 548	.024 158 9381	9.67	2.092 344	6.54	128
33	19.637 019	816.965 221	.001 224 0423	.050 924	41.603 322	.024 036 5423	9.62	2.172 824	6.58	132
34	21.491 151	898.242 224	.001 113 2855	.046 531	41.795 911	.023 925 7855	9.58	2.253 907	6.63	136
35	23.520 350	987.193 421	.001 012 9727	.042 516	41.971 885	.023 825 4727	9.54	2.335 566	6.67	140
36	25.741 146	1084.543 408	.000 922 0470	.038 848	42.132 677	.023 734 5470	9.50	2.417 775	6.72	144
37	28.171 631	1191.085 203	.000 839 5705	.035 497	42.279 597	.023 652 0705	9.47	2.500 506	6.76	148
38	30.831 603	1307.686 697	.000 764 7092	.032 434	42.413 841	.023 577 2092	9.44	2.583 736	6.80	152
39	33.742 729	1435.297 731	.000 696 7196	.029 636	42.536 504	.023 509 2196	9.41	2.667 438	6.84	156
40	36.928 725	1574.957 825	.000 634 9376	.027 079	42.648 583	.023 447 4376	9.38	2.751 590	6.88	160
41	40.415 544	1727.804 657	.000 578 7691	.024 743	42.750 994	.023 391 2691	9.36	2.836 168	6.92	164
42	44.231 588	1895.083 320	.000 527 6813	.022 608	42.844 569	.023 340 1813	9.34	2.921 150	6.96	168
43	48.407 944	2078.156 471	.000 481 1957	.020 658	42.930 071	.023 293 6957	9.32	3.006 516	6.99	172
44	52.978 633	2278.515 429	.000 438 8823	.018 876	43.008 196	.023 251 3823	9.31	3.092 243	7.03	176
45	57.980 887	2497.792 324	.000 400 3535	.017 247	43.079 581	.023 212 8535	9.29	3.178 314	7.06	180
46	63.455 455	2737.773 391	.000 365 2603	.015 759	43.144 807	.023 177 7603	9.28	3.264 708	7.10	184
47	69.446 933	3000.413 523	.000 333 2874	.014 399	43.204 406	.023 145 7874	9.26	3.351 408	7.13	188
48	76.004 128	3287.852 194	.000 304 1499	.013 157	43.258 863	.023 116 6499	9.25	3.438 397	7.16	192
49	83.180 455	3602.430 888	.000 277 5903	.012 022	43.308 622	.023 090 0903	9.24	3.525 658	7.20	196
50	91.034 371	3946.712 170	.000 253 3755	.010 985	43.354 088	.023 065 8755	9.23	3.613 175	7.23	200

Effective Rate is 9.44 %   8 - 309   Annual Percentage Rate is 9.125%

Amount Of 1	Amount Of 1 Per Period	Sinking Fund Payment	Present Worth Of 1	Present Worth of 1 Per Period	Periodic Payment To Amortize 1	Constant Annual Percent	Total Interest	Annual Add On Rate
What a single $ 1 deposit grows to in the future. The deposit is made at the beginning of the first period.	What a series of $ 1 deposits grow to in the future. A deposit is made at the end of each period.	The amount to be deposited at the end of each period that grows to $ 1 in the future.	What $ 1 to be paid in the future is worth today. Value today of a single $ 1 payment tomorrow.	What $ 1 to be paid at the end of each period is worth today. Value today of a series of $ 1 payments tomorrow.	The mortgage payment to amortize a loan of $ 1. An annuity certain, payable at the end of each period, worth $ 1 today.	The annual payment, including interest and principal, to amortize completely a loan of $ 100.	The total interest paid over the term on a loan of $1. The loan is amortized by regular periodic payments.	The average annual interest rate on a loan that is completely amortized by regular periodic payments.
$S = (1+i)^n$	$S\overline{n}| = \dfrac{(1+i)^n - 1}{i}$	$\dfrac{1}{S\overline{n}|} = \dfrac{i}{(1+i)^n - 1}$	$V^n = \dfrac{1}{(1+i)^n}$	$A\overline{n}| = \dfrac{1-V^n}{i}$	$\dfrac{1}{A\overline{n}|} = \dfrac{i}{1-V^n}$			

YEAR									PERIODS
	1.023 125	1.000 000	1.000 000 0000	.977 398	.977 398	1.023 125 0000	409.25	.023 125	9.25	1
	1.046 785	2.023 125	.494 284 8316	.955 306	1.932 704	.517 409 8316	206.97	.034 820	6.96	2
	1.070 992	3.069 910	.325 742 4733	.933 714	2.866 418	.348 867 4733	139.55	.046 602	6.21	3
	1.095 758	4.140 901	.241 493 3118	.912 610	3.779 028	.264 618 3118	105.85	.058 473	5.85	4
1	1.095 758	4.140 901	.241 493 3118	.912 610	3.779 028	.264 618 3118	105.85	.058 473	5.85	4
2	1.200 686	8.678 329	.115 229 5599	.832 857	7.227 807	.138 354 5599	55.35	.106 836	5.34	8
3	1.315 662	13.650 253	.073 258 7178	.760 074	10.375 196	.096 383 7178	38.56	.156 605	5.22	12
4	1.441 648	19.098 280	.052 360 7373	.693 651	13.247 536	.075 485 7373	30.20	.207 772	5.19	16
5	1.579 698	25.068 001	.039 891 4941	.633 033	15.868 861	.063 016 4941	25.21	.260 330	5.21	20
6	1.730 967	31.609 372	.031 636 1865	.577 712	18.261 109	.054 761 1865	21.91	.314 268	5.24	24
7	1.896 721	38.777 135	.025 788 3931	.527 226	20.444 298	.048 913 3931	19.57	.369 575	5.28	28
8	2.078 348	46.631 271	.021 444 8370	.481 151	22.436 699	.044 569 8370	17.83	.426 235	5.33	32
9	2.277 367	55.237 505	.018 103 6416	.439 104	24.254 983	.041 228 6416	16.50	.484 231	5.38	36
10	2.495 444	64.667 859	.015 463 6324	.400 730	25.914 367	.038 588 6324	15.44	.543 545	5.44	40
11	2.734 404	75.001 248	.013 333 1115	.365 710	27.428 738	.036 458 1115	14.59	.604 157	5.49	44
12	2.996 246	86.324 144	.011 584 2445	.333 751	28.810 768	.034 709 2445	13.89	.666 044	5.55	48
13	3.283 161	98.731 303	.010 128 5000	.304 584	30.072 023	.033 253 5000	13.31	.729 182	5.61	52
14	3.597 551	112.326 551	.008 902 6147	.277 967	31.223 056	.032 027 6147	12.82	.793 546	5.67	56
15	3.942 047	127.223 657	.007 860 1734	.253 675	32.273 500	.030 985 1734	12.40	.859 110	5.73	60
16	4.319 531	143.547 285	.006 966 3456	.231 507	33.232 146	.030 091 3456	12.04	.925 846	5.79	64
17	4.733 162	161.434 037	.006 194 4805	.211 275	34.107 016	.029 319 4805	11.73	.993 725	5.85	68
18	5.186 402	181.033 595	.005 523 8366	.192 812	34.905 431	.028 648 8366	11.46	1.062 716	5.90	72
19	5.683 043	202.509 974	.004 938 0284	.175 962	35.634 073	.028 063 0284	11.23	1.132 790	5.96	76
20	6.227 242	226.042 895	.004 423 9391	.160 585	36.299 038	.027 548 9391	11.02	1.203 915	6.02	80
21	6.823 552	251.829 291	.003 970 9440	.146 551	36.905 893	.027 095 9440	10.84	1.276 059	6.08	84
22	7.476 964	280.084 948	.003 570 3454	.133 744	37.459 714	.026 695 3454	10.68	1.349 190	6.13	88
23	8.192 946	311.046 321	.003 214 9552	.122 056	37.965 137	.026 339 9552	10.54	1.423 276	6.19	92
24	8.977 489	344.972 503	.002 898 7818	.111 390	38.426 390	.026 023 7818	10.41	1.498 283	6.24	96
25	9.837 159	382.147 401	.002 616 7913	.101 655	38.847 335	.025 741 7913	10.30	1.574 179	6.30	100
26	10.779 149	422.882 105	.002 364 7253	.092 772	39.231 494	.025 489 7253	10.20	1.650 931	6.35	104
27	11.811 342	467.517 498	.002 138 9574	.084 664	39.582 081	.025 263 9574	10.11	1.728 507	6.40	108
28	12.942 377	516.427 101	.001 936 3817	.077 266	39.902 030	.025 061 3817	10.03	1.806 875	6.45	112
29	14.181 717	570.020 207	.001 754 3238	.070 513	40.194 019	.024 879 3238	9.96	1.886 002	6.50	116
30	15.539 735	628.745 301	.001 590 4691	.064 351	40.460 490	.024 715 4691	9.89	1.965 856	6.55	120
31	17.027 794	693.093 812	.001 442 8061	.058 728	40.703 675	.024 567 8061	9.83	2.046 408	6.60	124
32	18.658 348	763.604 230	.001 309 5789	.053 595	40.925 608	.024 434 5789	9.78	2.127 626	6.65	128
33	20.445 040	840.866 609	.001 189 2493	.048 912	41.128 146	.024 314 2493	9.73	2.209 481	6.70	132
34	22.402 824	925.527 506	.001 080 4649	.044 637	41.312 985	.024 205 4649	9.69	2.291 943	6.74	136
35	24.548 081	1018.295 390	.000 982 0333	.040 736	41.481 670	.024 107 0333	9.65	2.374 985	6.79	140
36	26.898 765	1119.946 573	.000 892 8997	.037 176	41.635 614	.024 017 8997	9.61	2.458 578	6.83	144
37	29.474 546	1231.331 706	.000 812 1288	.033 928	41.776 105	.023 937 1288	9.58	2.542 695	6.87	148
38	32.296 979	1353.382 894	.000 738 8892	.030 963	41.904 318	.023 863 8892	9.55	2.627 311	6.91	152
39	35.389 685	1487.121 503	.000 672 4400	.028 257	42.021 327	.023 797 4400	9.52	2.712 401	6.95	156
40	38.778 542	1633.666 699	.000 612 1200	.025 787	42.128 110	.023 737 1200	9.50	2.797 939	6.99	160
41	42.491 911	1794.244 820	.000 557 3375	.023 534	42.225 561	.023 682 3375	9.48	2.883 903	7.03	164
42	46.560 867	1970.199 637	.000 507 5628	.021 477	42.314 497	.023 632 5628	9.46	2.970 271	7.07	168
43	51.019 458	2163.003 596	.000 462 3201	.019 600	42.395 660	.023 587 3201	9.44	3.057 019	7.11	172
44	55.904 997	2374.270 144	.000 421 1821	.017 887	42.469 730	.023 546 1821	9.42	3.144 128	7.15	176
45	61.258 367	2605.767 226	.000 383 7641	.016 324	42.537 328	.023 508 7641	9.41	3.231 578	7.18	180
46	67.124 367	2859.432 086	.000 349 7198	.014 898	42.599 018	.023 474 7198	9.39	3.319 348	7.22	184
47	73.552 085	3137.387 473	.000 318 7365	.013 596	42.655 316	.023 443 7365	9.38	3.407 422	7.25	188
48	80.595 311	3441.959 408	.000 290 5322	.012 408	42.706 695	.023 415 5322	9.37	3.495 782	7.28	192
49	88.312 985	3775.696 648	.000 264 8518	.011 323	42.753 584	.023 389 8518	9.36	3.584 411	7.32	196
50	96.769 690	4141.392 014	.000 241 4647	.010 334	42.796 376	.023 366 4647	9.35	3.673 293	7.35	200

Effective Rate is 9.58 %

Annual Percentage Rate is 9.25 %

QUARTERLY COMPOUND INTEREST AND ANNUITY

	Amount Of 1	Amount Of 1 Per Period	Sinking Fund Payment	Present Worth Of 1	Present Worth of 1 Per Period	Periodic Payment To Amortize 1	Constant Annual Percent	Total Interest	Annual Add On Rate	
	What a single $ 1 deposit grows to in the future. The deposit is made at the beginning of the first period.	What a series of $ 1 deposits grow to in the future. A deposit is made at the end of each period.	The amount to be deposited at the end of each period that grows to $ 1 in the future.	What $ 1 to be paid in the future is worth today. Value today of a single $ 1 payment tomorrow.	What $ 1 to be paid at the end of each period is worth today. Value today of a series of $ 1 payments tomorrow.	The mortgage payment to amortize a loan of $ 1. An annuity certain, payable at the end of each period, worth $ 1 today.	The annual payment, including interest and principal, to amortize completely a loan of $ 100.	The total interest paid over the term on a loan of $1. The loan is amortized by regular periodic payments.	The average annual interest rate on a loan that is completely amortized by regular periodic payments.	
	$S = (1+i)^n$	$S\overline{n}\| = \dfrac{(1+i)^n - 1}{i}$	$\dfrac{1}{S\overline{n}\|} = \dfrac{i}{(1+i)^n - 1}$	$V^n = \dfrac{1}{(1+i)^n}$	$A\overline{n}\| = \dfrac{1-V^n}{i}$	$\dfrac{1}{A\overline{n}\|} = \dfrac{i}{1-V^n}$				

YEAR										PERIODS
	1.023 438	1.000 000	1.000 000 0000	.977 099	.977 099	1.023 437 5000	409.38	.023 437	9.37	1
	1.047 424	2.023 438	.494 208 4942	.954 723	1.931 822	.517 645 9942	207.06	.035 292	7.06	2
	1.071 973	3.070 862	.325 641 4843	.932 859	2.864 681	.349 078 9843	139.64	.047 237	6.30	3
	1.097 098	4.142 835	.241 380 5923	.911 496	3.776 177	.264 818 0923	105.93	.059 272	5.93	4
1	1.097 098	4.142 835	.241 380 5923	.911 496	3.776 177	.264 818 0923	105.93	.059 272	5.93	4
2	1.203 623	8.687 930	.115 102 2160	.830 825	7.218 147	.138 539 7160	55.42	.108 318	5.42	8
3	1.320 492	13.674 343	.073 129 6550	.757 293	10.355 488	.096 567 1550	38.63	.158 806	5.29	12
4	1.448 709	19.144 926	.052 233 1620	.690 270	13.215 161	.075 670 6620	30.27	.210 731	5.27	16
5	1.589 376	25.146 689	.039 766 6668	.629 178	15.821 742	.063 204 1668	25.29	.264 083	5.28	20
6	1.743 700	31.731 210	.031 514 7140	.573 493	18.197 629	.054 952 2140	21.99	.318 853	5.31	24
7	1.913 010	38.955 072	.025 670 5980	.522 737	20.363 240	.049 108 0980	19.65	.375 027	5.36	28
8	2.098 758	46.880 355	.021 330 8964	.476 472	22.337 186	.044 768 3964	17.91	.432 589	5.41	32
9	2.302 543	55.575 165	.017 993 6488	.434 302	24.136 429	.041 431 1488	16.58	.491 521	5.46	36
10	2.526 115	65.114 221	.015 357 6283	.395 865	25.776 432	.038 795 1283	15.52	.551 805	5.52	40
11	2.771 394	75.579 497	.013 231 1016	.360 829	27.271 288	.036 668 6016	14.67	.613 418	5.58	44
12	3.040 490	87.060 927	.011 486 2089	.328 894	28.633 843	.034 923 7089	13.97	.676 338	5.64	48
13	3.335 715	99.657 178	.010 034 4001	.299 786	29.875 806	.033 471 9001	13.39	.740 539	5.70	52
14	3.659 605	113.476 496	.008 812 3976	.273 254	31.007 850	.032 249 8976	12.90	.805 994	5.76	56
15	4.014 945	128.637 638	.007 773 7746	.249 069	32.039 704	.031 211 2746	12.49	.872 676	5.82	60
16	4.404 787	145.270 891	.006 883 6915	.227 026	32.980 234	.030 321 1915	12.13	.940 556	5.88	64
17	4.832 481	163.519 196	.006 115 4900	.206 933	33.837 524	.029 552 9900	11.83	1.009 603	5.94	68
18	5.301 704	183.539 368	.005 448 4224	.188 619	34.618 940	.028 885 9224	11.56	1.079 786	6.00	72
19	5.816 487	205.503 454	.004 866 0983	.171 925	35.331 197	.028 303 5983	11.33	1.151 073	6.06	76
20	6.381 255	229.600 201	.004 355 3969	.156 709	35.980 416	.027 792 8969	11.12	1.223 432	6.12	80
21	7.000 860	256.036 688	.003 905 6903	.142 840	36.572 177	.027 343 1903	10.94	1.296 828	6.18	84
22	7.680 627	285.040 096	.003 508 2784	.130 198	37.111 565	.026 945 7784	10.78	1.371 228	6.23	88
23	8.426 398	316.859 668	.003 155 9712	.118 675	37.603 214	.026 593 4712	10.64	1.446 599	6.29	92
24	9.244 582	351.768 848	.002 842 7759	.108 171	38.051 351	.026 280 2759	10.52	1.522 906	6.35	96
25	10.142 210	390.067 629	.002 563 6580	.098 598	38.459 826	.026 001 1580	10.41	1.600 116	6.40	100
26	11.126 995	432.085 133	.002 314 3587	.089 872	38.832 148	.025 751 8587	10.31	1.678 193	6.45	104
27	12.207 401	478.182 440	.002 091 2520	.081 918	39.171 519	.025 528 7520	10.22	1.757 105	6.51	108
28	13.392 711	528.755 690	.001 891 2326	.074 667	39.480 854	.025 328 7326	10.14	1.836 818	6.56	112
29	14.693 113	584.239 486	.001 711 6269	.068 059	39.762 812	.025 149 1269	10.06	1.917 299	6.61	116
30	16.119 780	645.110 630	.001 550 1217	.062 036	40.019 815	.024 987 6217	10.00	1.998 515	6.66	120
31	17.684 974	711.892 223	.001 404 7070	.056 545	40.254 072	.024 842 2070	9.94	2.080 434	6.71	124
32	19.402 144	785.158 154	.001 273 6288	.051 541	40.467 597	.024 711 1288	9.89	2.163 024	6.76	128
33	21.286 048	865.538 039	.001 155 3507	.046 979	40.662 224	.024 592 8507	9.84	2.246 256	6.81	132
34	23.352 874	953.722 626	.001 048 5229	.042 821	40.839 625	.024 486 0229	9.80	2.330 099	6.85	136
35	25.620 384	1050.469 733	.000 951 9551	.039 031	41.001 326	.024 389 4551	9.76	2.414 524	6.90	140
36	28.108 065	1156.610 762	.000 864 5951	.035 577	41.148 716	.024 302 0951	9.73	2.499 502	6.94	144
37	30.837 293	1273.057 841	.000 785 5103	.032 428	41.283 061	.024 223 0103	9.69	2.585 006	6.99	148
38	33.831 523	1400.811 662	.000 713 8718	.029 558	41.405 515	.024 151 3718	9.67	2.671 009	7.03	152
39	37.116 486	1540.970 086	.000 648 9419	.026 942	41.517 133	.024 086 4419	9.64	2.757 485	7.07	156
40	40.720 412	1694.737 570	.000 590 0619	.024 558	41.618 871	.024 027 5619	9.62	2.844 410	7.11	160
41	44.674 270	1863.435 523	.000 536 6432	.022 384	41.711 605	.023 974 1432	9.59	2.931 759	7.15	164
42	49.012 039	2048.513 659	.000 488 1588	.020 403	41.796 132	.023 925 6588	9.58	3.019 511	7.19	168
43	53.770 995	2251.562 456	.000 444 1360	.018 597	41.873 178	.023 881 6360	9.56	3.107 641	7.23	172
44	58.992 035	2474.326 824	.000 404 1503	.016 951	41.943 405	.023 841 6503	9.54	3.196 130	7.26	176
45	64.720 026	2718.721 099	.000 367 8200	.015 451	42.007 417	.023 805 3200	9.53	3.284 958	7.30	180
46	71.004 191	2986.845 496	.000 334 8014	.014 084	42.065 763	.023 772 3014	9.51	3.374 103	7.34	184
47	77.898 535	3281.004 155	.000 304 7847	.012 837	42.118 946	.023 742 2847	9.50	3.463 550	7.37	188
48	85.462 303	3603.724 942	.000 277 4907	.011 701	42.167 421	.023 714 9907	9.49	3.553 278	7.40	192
49	93.760 496	3957.781 176	.000 252 6668	.010 665	42.211 607	.023 690 1668	9.48	3.643 273	7.44	196
50	102.864 425	4346.215 455	.000 230 0852	.009 722	42.251 881	.023 667 5852	9.47	3.733 517	7.47	200

Effective Rate is 9.71 %   8 - 311   Annual Percentage Rate is 9.375%

QUARTERLY COMPOUND INTEREST AND ANNUITY

9.50 % Q

Amount Of 1	Amount Of 1 Per Period	Sinking Fund Payment	Present Worth Of 1	Present Worth of 1 Per Period	Periodic Payment To Amortize 1	Constant Annual Percent	Total Interest	Annual Add On Rate	
What a single $ 1 deposit grows to in the future. The deposit is made at the beginning of the first period.	What a series of $ 1 deposits grow to in the future. A deposit is made at the end of each period.	The amount to be deposited at the end of each period that grows to $ 1 in the future.	What $ 1 to be paid in the future is worth today. Value today of a single $ 1 payment tomorrow.	What $ 1 to be paid at the end of each period is worth today. Value today of a series of $ 1 payments tomorrow.	The mortgage payment to amortize a loan of $ 1. An annuity certain, payable at the end of each period, worth $ 1 today.	The annual payment, including interest and principal, to amortize completely a loan of $ 100.	The total interest paid over the term on a loan of $1. The loan is amortized by regular periodic payments.	The average annual interest rate on a loan that is completely amortized by regular periodic payments.	
$S = (1+i)^n$	$S\overline{n}| = \dfrac{(1+i)^n - 1}{i}$	$\dfrac{1}{S\overline{n}|} = \dfrac{i}{(1+i)^n - 1}$	$V^n = \dfrac{1}{(1+i)^n}$	$A\overline{n}| = \dfrac{1-V^n}{i}$	$\dfrac{1}{A\overline{n}|} = \dfrac{i}{1-V^n}$				

YEAR / **PERIODS**

	Amount Of 1	Amount Of 1 Per Period	Sinking Fund Payment	Present Worth Of 1	Present Worth of 1 Per Period	Periodic Payment To Amortize 1	Constant Annual Percent	Total Interest	Annual Add On Rate	
	1.023 750	1.000 000	1.000 000 0000	.976 801	.976 801	1.023 750 0000	409.50	.023 750	9.50	1
	1.048 064	2.023 750	.494 132 1804	.954 140	1.930 941	.517 882 1804	207.16	.035 764	7.15	2
	1.072 956	3.071 814	.325 540 5372	.932 005	2.862 946	.349 290 5372	139.72	.047 872	6.38	3
	1.098 438	4.144 770	.241 267 9317	.910 383	3.773 330	.265 017 9317	106.01	.060 072	6.01	4
1	1.098 438	4.144 770	.241 267 9317	.910 383	3.773 330	.265 017 9317	106.01	.060 072	6.01	4
2	1.206 567	8.697 543	.114 974 9955	.828 798	7.208 506	.138 724 9955	55.49	.109 800	5.49	8
3	1.325 339	13.698 484	.073 000 7781	.754 524	10.335 834	.096 750 7781	38.71	.161 009	5.37	12
4	1.455 803	19.191 709	.052 105 8339	.686 906	13.182 902	.075 855 8339	30.35	.213 693	5.34	16
5	1.599 110	25.225 677	.039 642 1465	.625 348	15.774 825	.063 392 1465	25.36	.267 843	5.36	20
6	1.756 523	31.853 619	.031 393 6068	.569 306	18.134 469	.055 143 6068	22.06	.323 447	5.39	24
7	1.929 433	39.134 004	.025 553 2245	.518 287	20.282 649	.049 303 2245	19.73	.380 490	5.44	28
8	2.119 363	47.131 058	.021 217 4315	.471 840	22.238 317	.044 967 4315	17.99	.438 958	5.49	32
9	2.327 989	55.915 328	.017 884 1837	.429 555	24.018 725	.041 634 1837	16.66	.498 831	5.54	36
10	2.557 152	65.564 306	.015 252 2013	.391 060	25.639 578	.039 002 2013	15.61	.560 088	5.60	40
11	2.808 874	76.163 114	.013 129 7153	.356 015	27.115 177	.036 879 7153	14.76	.622 707	5.66	44
12	3.085 375	87.805 249	.011 388 8408	.324 110	28.458 537	.035 138 8408	14.06	.686 664	5.72	48
13	3.389 094	100.593 416	.009 941 0084	.295 064	29.681 510	.033 691 0084	13.48	.751 932	5.78	52
14	3.722 710	114.640 429	.008 722 9262	.268 622	30.794 884	.032 472 9262	12.99	.818 484	5.85	56
15	4.089 167	130.070 205	.007 688 1558	.244 549	31.808 482	.031 438 1558	12.58	.886 289	5.91	60
16	4.491 698	147.018 862	.006 801 8483	.222 633	32.731 244	.030 551 8483	12.23	.955 318	5.97	64
17	4.933 853	165.635 915	.006 037 3380	.202 681	33.571 311	.029 787 3380	11.92	1.025 539	6.03	68
18	5.419 533	186.085 599	.005 373 8710	.184 518	34.336 095	.029 123 8710	11.65	1.096 919	6.09	72
19	5.953 022	208.548 315	.004 795 0519	.167 982	35.032 341	.028 545 0519	11.42	1.169 424	6.15	76
20	6.539 028	233.222 222	.004 287 7561	.152 928	35.666 192	.028 037 7561	11.22	1.243 020	6.22	80
21	7.182 718	260.324 986	.003 841 3524	.139 223	36.243 240	.027 591 3524	11.04	1.317 674	6.27	84
22	7.889 773	290.095 699	.003 447 1383	.126 746	36.768 574	.027 197 1383	10.88	1.393 348	6.33	88
23	8.666 429	322.796 990	.003 097 9223	.115 388	37.246 830	.026 847 9223	10.74	1.470 009	6.39	92
24	9.519 537	358.717 340	.002 787 7102	.105 047	37.682 226	.026 537 7102	10.62	1.547 620	6.45	96
25	10.456 624	398.173 627	.002 511 4672	.095 633	38.078 604	.026 261 4672	10.51	1.626 147	6.50	100
26	11.485 956	441.513 923	.002 264 9342	.087 063	38.439 459	.026 014 9342	10.41	1.705 553	6.56	104
27	12.616 613	489.120 564	.002 044 4857	.079 261	38.767 976	.025 794 4857	10.32	1.785 804	6.61	108
28	13.858 571	541.413 520	.001 847 0170	.072 158	39.067 052	.025 597 0170	10.24	1.866 866	6.67	112
29	15.222 785	598.854 105	.001 669 8558	.065 691	39.339 326	.025 419 8558	10.17	1.948 703	6.72	116
30	16.721 290	661.949 042	.001 510 6903	.059 804	39.587 200	.025 260 6903	10.11	2.031 283	6.77	120
31	18.367 305	731.254 936	.001 367 5121	.054 445	39.812 860	.025 117 5121	10.05	2.114 572	6.82	124
32	20.175 351	807.383 183	.001 238 5693	.049 565	40.018 298	.024 988 5693	10.00	2.198 537	6.87	128
33	22.161 377	891.005 364	.001 122 3277	.045 124	40.205 324	.024 872 3277	9.95	2.283 147	6.92	132
34	24.342 905	982.859 168	.001 017 4398	.041 080	40.375 590	.024 767 4398	9.91	2.368 372	6.97	136
35	26.739 179	1083.754 903	.000 922 7179	.037 398	40.530 598	.024 672 7179	9.87	2.454 180	7.01	140
36	29.371 338	1194.582 640	.000 837 1124	.034 047	40.671 714	.024 587 1124	9.84	2.540 544	7.06	144
37	32.262 602	1316.320 069	.000 759 6937	.030 996	40.800 184	.024 509 6937	9.81	2.627 435	7.10	148
38	35.438 477	1450.041 121	.000 689 6356	.028 218	40.917 140	.024 439 6356	9.78	2.714 825	7.14	152
39	38.926 979	1596.925 443	.000 626 2033	.025 689	41.023 616	.024 376 2033	9.76	2.802 688	7.19	156
40	42.758 884	1758.268 805	.000 568 7413	.023 387	41.120 549	.024 318 7413	9.73	2.890 999	7.23	160
41	46.967 995	1935.494 530	.000 516 6638	.021 291	41.208 796	.024 266 6638	9.71	2.979 733	7.27	164
42	51.591 444	2130.166 051	.000 469 4470	.019 383	41.289 134	.024 219 4470	9.69	3.068 867	7.31	168
43	56.670 017	2344.000 701	.000 426 6210	.017 646	41.362 273	.024 176 6210	9.68	3.158 379	7.35	172
44	62.248 516	2578.884 866	.000 387 7645	.016 065	41.428 857	.024 137 7645	9.66	3.248 247	7.38	176
45	68.376 152	2836.890 623	.000 352 4986	.014 625	41.489 474	.024 102 4986	9.65	3.338 450	7.42	180
46	75.106 983	3120.294 024	.000 320 4826	.013 314	41.544 659	.024 070 4826	9.63	3.428 969	7.45	184
47	82.500 385	3431.595 168	.000 291 4097	.012 121	41.594 899	.024 041 4097	9.62	3.519 785	7.49	188
48	90.621 581	3773.540 260	.000 265 0031	.011 035	41.640 636	.024 015 0031	9.61	3.610 881	7.52	192
49	99.542 214	4149.145 839	.000 241 0135	.010 046	41.682 274	.023 991 0135	9.60	3.702 239	7.56	196
50	109.340 978	4561.725 385	.000 219 2153	.009 146	41.720 181	.023 969 2153	9.59	3.793 843	7.59	200

Effective Rate is 9.84 %

Annual Percentage Rate is 9.50 %

QUARTERLY COMPOUND INTEREST AND ANNUITY

9.625% Q

	Amount Of 1	Amount Of 1 Per Period	Sinking Fund Payment	Present Worth Of 1	Present Worth of 1 Per Period	Periodic Payment To Amortize 1	Constant Annual Percent	Total Interest	Annual Add On Rate	
	What a single $ 1 deposit grows to in the future. The deposit is made at the beginning of the first period.	What a series of $ 1 deposits grow to in the future. A deposit is made at the end of each period.	The amount to be deposited at the end of each period that grows to $ 1 in the future.	What $ 1 to be paid in the future is worth today. Value today of a single $ 1 payment tomorrow.	What $ 1 to be paid at the end of each period is worth today. Value today of a series of $ 1 payments tomorrow.	The mortgage payment to amortize a loan of $ 1. An annuity certain, payable at the end of each period, worth $ 1 today.	The annual payment, including interest and principal, to amortize completely a loan of $ 100.	The total interest paid over the term on a loan of $1. The loan is amortized by regular periodic payments.	The average annual interest rate on a loan that is completely amortized by regular periodic payments.	
	$S = (1+i)^n$	$S\overline{n} = \dfrac{(1+i)^n - 1}{i}$	$\dfrac{1}{S\overline{n}} = \dfrac{i}{(1+i)^n - 1}$	$V^n = \dfrac{1}{(1+i)^n}$	$A\overline{n} = \dfrac{1 - V^n}{i}$	$\dfrac{1}{A\overline{n}} = \dfrac{i}{1 - V^n}$				

YEAR										PERIODS
	1.024 063	1.000 000	1.000 000 0000	.976 503	.976 503	1.024 062 5000	409.63	.024 062	9.62	1
	1.048 704	2.024 063	.494 055 8901	.953 558	1.930 061	.518 118 3901	207.25	.036 237	7.25	2
	1.073 938	3.072 767	.325 439 6319	.931 152	2.861 213	.349 502 1319	139.81	.048 506	6.47	3
	1.099 780	4.146 705	.241 155 3300	.909 273	3.770 486	.265 217 8300	106.09	.060 871	6.09	4
1	1.099 780	4.146 705	.241 155 3300	.909 273	3.770 486	.265 217 8300	106.09	.060 871	6.09	4
2	1.209 516	8.707 168	.114 847 8983	.826 777	7.198 885	.138 910 3983	55.57	.111 283	5.56	8
3	1.330 202	13.722 675	.072 872 0870	.751 766	10.316 235	.096 934 5870	38.78	.163 215	5.44	12
4	1.462 930	19.238 630	.051 978 7527	.683 560	13.150 757	.076 041 2527	30.42	.216 660	5.42	16
5	1.608 901	25.304 967	.039 517 9329	.621 542	15.728 109	.063 580 4329	25.44	.271 609	5.43	20
6	1.769 437	31.976 604	.031 272 8642	.565 152	18.071 626	.055 335 3642	22.14	.328 049	5.47	24
7	1.945 992	39.313 937	.025 436 2718	.513 877	20.202 521	.049 498 7718	19.80	.385 966	5.51	28
8	2.140 163	47.383 391	.021 104 4416	.467 254	22.140 087	.045 166 9416	18.07	.445 342	5.57	32
9	2.353 708	56.258 014	.017 775 2452	.424 861	23.901 862	.041 837 7452	16.74	.506 159	5.62	36
10	2.588 562	66.018 149	.015 147 3499	.386 315	25.503 796	.039 209 8499	15.69	.568 394	5.68	40
11	2.846 849	76.752 151	.013 028 9509	.351 266	26.960 390	.037 091 4509	14.84	.632 024	5.75	44
12	3.130 907	88.557 192	.011 292 1377	.319 396	28.284 832	.035 354 6377	14.15	.697 023	5.81	48
13	3.443 310	101.540 141	.009 848 3219	.290 418	29.489 111	.033 910 8219	13.57	.763 363	5.87	52
14	3.786 883	115.818 530	.008 634 1969	.264 069	30.584 129	.032 696 6969	13.08	.831 015	5.94	56
15	4.164 739	131.521 618	.007 603 3128	.240 111	31.579 799	.031 665 8128	12.67	.899 949	6.00	60
16	4.580 297	148.791 562	.006 720 8112	.218 326	32.485 134	.030 783 3112	12.32	.970 132	6.06	64
17	5.037 319	167.784 702	.005 960 0189	.198 518	33.308 331	.030 022 5189	12.01	1.041 531	6.13	68
18	5.539 944	188.672 979	.005 300 1760	.180 507	34.056 841	.029 362 6760	11.75	1.114 113	6.19	72
19	6.092 720	211.645 491	.004 724 8821	.164 130	34.737 441	.028 787 3821	11.52	1.187 841	6.25	76
20	6.700 652	236.910 201	.004 221 0086	.149 239	35.356 292	.028 283 5086	11.32	1.262 681	6.31	80
21	7.369 243	264.695 827	.003 777 9213	.135 699	35.918 997	.027 840 4213	11.14	1.338 595	6.37	84
22	8.104 547	295.253 905	.003 386 9154	.123 388	36.430 648	.027 449 4154	10.98	1.415 549	6.43	88
23	8.913 220	328.861 070	.003 040 7977	.112 193	36.895 879	.027 103 2977	10.85	1.493 503	6.49	92
24	9.802 581	365.821 562	.002 733 5732	.102 014	37.318 901	.026 796 0732	10.72	1.572 423	6.55	96
25	10.780 684	406.469 974	.002 460 2063	.092 758	37.703 543	.026 522 7063	10.61	1.652 271	6.61	100
26	11.856 381	451.174 289	.002 216 4384	.084 343	38.053 288	.026 278 9384	10.52	1.733 010	6.67	104
27	13.039 412	500.339 204	.001 998 6441	.076 691	38.371 301	.026 061 1441	10.43	1.814 604	6.72	108
28	14.340 486	554.409 798	.001 803 7199	.069 733	38.660 462	.025 866 2199	10.35	1.897 017	6.78	112
29	15.771 381	613.875 562	.001 628 9946	.063 406	38.923 387	.025 691 4946	10.28	1.980 213	6.83	116
30	17.345 050	679.274 824	.001 472 1582	.057 653	39.162 459	.025 534 6582	10.22	2.064 159	6.88	120
31	19.075 741	751.199 631	.001 331 2041	.052 423	39.379 840	.025 393 7041	10.16	2.148 819	6.93	124
32	20.979 120	830.301 101	.001 204 3824	.047 666	39.577 499	.025 266 8824	10.11	2.234 161	6.98	128
33	23.072 419	917.295 322	.001 090 1615	.043 342	39.757 224	.025 152 6615	10.07	2.320 151	7.03	132
34	25.374 587	1012.969 835	.000 987 1962	.039 410	39.920 644	.025 049 6962	10.02	2.406 759	7.08	136
35	27.906 465	1118.190 759	.000 894 3018	.035 834	40.069 237	.024 956 8018	9.99	2.493 952	7.13	140
36	30.690 975	1233.910 636	.000 810 4315	.032 583	40.204 348	.024 872 9315	9.95	2.581 702	7.17	144
37	33.753 323	1361.177 053	.000 734 6583	.029 627	40.327 202	.024 797 1583	9.92	2.669 979	7.22	148
38	37.121 232	1501.142 124	.000 666 1594	.026 939	40.438 909	.024 728 6594	9.90	2.758 756	7.26	152
39	40.825 192	1655.072 922	.000 604 2030	.024 495	40.540 481	.024 666 7030	9.87	2.848 006	7.30	156
40	44.898 733	1824.362 948	.000 548 1365	.022 272	40.632 838	.024 610 6365	9.85	2.937 702	7.34	160
41	49.378 733	2010.544 748	.000 497 3776	.020 252	40.716 815	.024 559 8776	9.83	3.027 820	7.38	164
42	54.305 747	2215.303 784	.000 451 4054	.018 414	40.793 174	.024 513 9054	9.81	3.118 336	7.42	168
43	59.724 380	2440.493 696	.000 409 7532	.016 744	40.862 604	.024 472 2532	9.79	3.209 228	7.46	172
44	65.683 683	2688.153 076	.000 372 0026	.015 224	40.925 736	.024 434 5026	9.78	3.300 472	7.50	176
45	72.237 607	2960.523 931	.000 337 7780	.013 843	40.983 140	.024 400 2780	9.77	3.392 050	7.54	180
46	79.445 482	3260.071 973	.000 306 7417	.012 587	41.035 335	.024 369 2417	9.75	3.483 940	7.57	184
47	87.372 559	3589.508 946	.000 278 5896	.011 445	41.082 795	.024 341 0896	9.74	3.576 125	7.61	188
48	96.090 601	3951.817 169	.000 253 0481	.010 407	41.125 949	.024 315 5481	9.73	3.668 585	7.64	192
49	105.678 529	4350.276 538	.000 229 8704	.009 463	41.165 188	.024 292 3704	9.72	3.761 305	7.68	196
50	116.223 142	4788.494 218	.000 208 8339	.008 604	41.200 867	.024 271 3339	9.71	3.854 267	7.71	200

Effective Rate is 9.98 %

8 - 313

Annual Percentage Rate is 9.625%

	Amount Of 1	Amount Of 1 Per Period	Sinking Fund Payment	Present Worth Of 1	Present Worth of 1 Per Period	Periodic Payment To Amortize 1	Constant Annual Percent	Total Interest	Annual Add On Rate	
	What a single $ 1 deposit grows to in the future. The deposit is made at the beginning of the first period.	What a series of $ 1 deposits grow to in the future. A deposit is made at the end of each period.	The amount to be deposited at the end of each period that grows to $ 1 in the future.	What $ 1 to be paid in the future is worth today. Value today of a single $ 1 payment tomorrow.	What $ 1 to be paid at the end of each period is worth today. Value today of a series of $ 1 payments tomorrow.	The mortgage payment to amortize a loan of $ 1. An annuity certain, payable at the end of each period, worth $ 1 today.	The annual payment, including interest and principal, to amortize completely a loan of $ 100.	The total interest paid over the term on a loan of $1. The loan is amortized by regular periodic payments.	The average annual interest rate on a loan that is completely amortized by regular periodic payments.	
	$S = (1 + i)^n$	$S\overline{n}| = \dfrac{(1 + i)^n - 1}{i}$	$\dfrac{1}{S\overline{n}|} = \dfrac{i}{(1 + i)^n - 1}$	$V^n = \dfrac{1}{(1 + i)^n}$	$A\overline{n}| = \dfrac{1 - V^n}{i}$	$\dfrac{1}{A\overline{n}|} = \dfrac{i}{1 - V^n}$				

YEAR										PERIODS
	1.024 375	1.000 000	1.000 000 0000	.976 205	.976 205	1.024 375 0000	409.75	.024 375	9.75	1
	1.049 344	2.024 375	.493 979 6233	.952 976	1.929 181	.518 354 6233	207.35	.036 709	7.34	2
	1.074 922	3.073 719	.325 338 7685	.930 300	2.859 481	.349 713 7685	139.89	.049 141	6.55	3
	1.101 123	4.148 641	.241 042 7871	.908 164	3.767 645	.265 417 7871	106.17	.061 671	6.17	4
1	1.101 123	4.148 641	.241 042 7871	.908 164	3.767 645	.265 417 7871	106.17	.061 671	6.17	4
2	1.212 472	8.716 806	.114 720 9243	.824 761	7.189 283	.139 095 9243	55.64	.112 767	5.64	8
3	1.335 081	13.746 917	.072 743 5815	.749 018	10.296 691	.097 118 5815	38.85	.165 423	5.51	12
4	1.470 089	19.285 690	.051 851 9182	.680 231	13.118 725	.076 226 9182	30.50	.219 631	5.49	16
5	1.618 749	25.384 560	.039 394 0256	.617 761	15.681 594	.063 769 0256	25.51	.275 381	5.51	20
6	1.782 442	32.100 167	.031 152 4860	.561 028	18.009 099	.055 527 4860	22.22	.332 660	5.54	24
7	1.962 688	39.494 847	.025 319 7395	.509 505	20.122 854	.049 694 7395	19.88	.391 453	5.59	28
8	2.161 161	47.637 364	.020 991 9257	.462 714	22.042 490	.045 366 9257	18.15	.451 742	5.65	32
9	2.379 704	56.603 244	.017 666 8320	.420 220	23.785 833	.042 041 8320	16.82	.513 506	5.71	36
10	2.620 347	66.475 782	.015 043 0724	.381 629	25.369 074	.039 418 0724	15.77	.576 723	5.77	40
11	2.885 325	77.346 662	.012 928 8062	.346 581	26.806 916	.037 303 8062	14.93	.641 367	5.83	44
12	3.177 098	89.316 839	.011 196 0971	.314 753	28.112 712	.035 571 0971	14.23	.707 413	5.90	48
13	3.498 376	102.497 478	.009 756 3376	.285 847	29.298 588	.034 131 3376	13.66	.774 830	5.96	52
14	3.852 143	117.010 984	.008 546 2062	.259 596	30.375 558	.032 921 2062	13.17	.843 588	6.03	56
15	4.241 683	132.992 142	.007 519 2413	.235 755	31.353 622	.031 894 2413	12.76	.913 654	6.09	60
16	4.670 616	150.589 364	.006 640 5752	.214 105	32.241 865	.031 015 5752	12.41	.984 997	6.16	64
17	5.142 923	169.966 072	.005 883 5272	.194 442	33.048 535	.030 258 5272	12.11	1.057 580	6.22	68
18	5.662 991	191.302 213	.005 227 3311	.176 585	33.781 123	.029 602 3311	11.85	1.131 368	6.29	72
19	6.235 651	214.795 932	.004 655 5817	.160 368	34.446 433	.029 030 5817	11.62	1.206 324	6.35	76
20	6.866 219	240.665 409	.004 155 1464	.145 641	35.050 644	.028 530 1464	11.42	1.282 412	6.41	80
21	7.560 553	269.150 888	.003 715 3881	.132 265	35.599 366	.028 090 3881	11.24	1.359 593	6.47	84
22	8.325 100	300.516 909	.003 327 5998	.120 119	36.097 695	.027 702 5998	11.09	1.437 829	6.54	88
23	9.166 960	335.054 759	.002 984 5868	.109 087	36.550 260	.027 359 5868	10.95	1.517 082	6.60	92
24	10.093 951	373.085 184	.002 680 3530	.099 069	36.961 262	.027 055 3530	10.83	1.597 314	6.66	96
25	11.114 683	414.961 365	.002 409 8629	.089 971	37.334 520	.026 784 8629	10.72	1.678 486	6.71	100
26	12.238 635	461.072 196	.002 168 8577	.081 708	37.673 499	.026 543 8577	10.62	1.760 561	6.77	104
27	13.476 244	511.845 899	.001 953 7130	.074 205	37.981 348	.026 328 7130	10.54	1.843 501	6.83	108
28	14.839 004	567.753 997	.001 761 3262	.067 390	38.260 924	.026 136 3262	10.46	1.927 269	6.88	112
29	16.339 570	629.315 697	.001 589 0276	.061 201	38.514 826	.025 964 0276	10.39	2.011 827	6.94	116
30	17.991 879	697.102 708	.001 434 5088	.055 581	38.745 410	.025 809 5088	10.33	2.097 141	6.99	120
31	19.811 273	771.744 554	.001 295 7655	.050 476	38.954 818	.025 670 7655	10.27	2.183 175	7.04	124
32	21.814 651	853.934 416	.001 170 5001	.045 841	39.144 995	.025 546 0501	10.22	2.269 894	7.09	128
33	24.020 617	944.435 574	.001 058 8335	.041 631	39.317 707	.025 433 8335	10.18	2.357 266	7.14	132
34	26.449 657	1044.088 492	.000 957 7732	.037 808	39.474 557	.025 332 7732	10.14	2.445 257	7.19	136
35	29.124 329	1153.818 625	.000 866 6873	.034 336	39.617 003	.025 241 6873	10.10	2.533 836	7.24	140
36	32.069 472	1274.645 011	.000 784 5322	.031 182	39.746 367	.025 159 5322	10.07	2.622 973	7.29	144
37	35.312 437	1407.689 740	.000 710 3838	.028 319	39.863 851	.025 085 3838	10.04	2.712 637	7.33	148
38	38.883 341	1554.188 367	.000 643 4227	.025 718	39.970 545	.025 018 4227	10.01	2.802 800	7.38	152
39	42.815 346	1715.501 393	.000 582 9200	.023 356	40.067 442	.024 957 9200	9.99	2.893 436	7.42	156
40	47.144 968	1893.126 897	.000 528 2266	.021 211	40.155 439	.024 903 2266	9.97	2.984 516	7.46	160
41	51.912 415	2088.714 447	.000 478 7634	.019 263	40.235 355	.024 853 7634	9.95	3.076 017	7.50	164
42	57.161 960	2304.080 421	.000 434 0126	.017 494	40.307 932	.024 809 0126	9.93	3.167 914	7.54	168
43	62.942 356	2541.224 875	.000 393 5110	.015 888	40.373 844	.024 768 5110	9.91	3.260 184	7.58	172
44	69.307 284	2802.350 118	.000 356 8433	.014 428	40.433 703	.024 731 8433	9.90	3.352 804	7.62	176
45	76.315 853	3089.881 162	.000 323 6370	.013 103	40.488 064	.024 698 6370	9.88	3.445 755	7.66	180
46	84.033 151	3406.488 243	.000 293 5574	.011 900	40.537 433	.024 668 5574	9.87	3.539 015	7.69	184
47	92.530 846	3755.111 622	.000 266 3037	.010 807	40.582 268	.024 641 3037	9.86	3.632 565	7.73	188
48	101.887 854	4138.988 887	.000 241 6049	.009 815	40.622 986	.024 616 6049	9.85	3.726 388	7.76	192
49	112.191 072	4561.685 021	.000 219 2172	.008 913	40.659 965	.024 594 2172	9.85	3.820 467	7.80	196
50	123.536 184	5027.125 508	.000 198 9208	.008 095	40.693 547	.024 573 9208	9.83	3.914 784	7.83	200

Amount Of 1	Amount Of 1 Per Period	Sinking Fund Payment	Present Worth Of 1	Present Worth of 1 Per Period	Periodic Payment To Amortize 1	Constant Annual Percent	Total Interest	Annual Add On Rate
What a single $ 1 deposit grows to in the future. The deposit is made at the beginning of the first period.	What a series of $ 1 deposits grow to in the future. A deposit is made at the end of each period.	The amount to be deposited at the end of each period that grows to $ 1 in the future.	What $ 1 to be paid in the future is worth today. Value today of a single $ 1 payment tomorrow.	What $ 1 to be paid at the end of each period is worth today. Value today of a series of $ 1 payments tomorrow.	The mortgage payment to amortize a loan of $ 1. An annuity certain, payable at the end of each period, worth $ 1 today.	The annual payment, including interest and principal, to amortize completely a loan of $ 100.	The total interest paid over the term on a loan of $1. The loan is amortized by regular periodic payments.	The average annual interest rate on a loan that is completely amortized by regular periodic payments.
$S = (1+i)^n$	$S\overline{n}| = \dfrac{(1+i)^n - 1}{i}$	$\dfrac{1}{S\overline{n}|} = \dfrac{i}{(1+i)^n - 1}$	$V^n = \dfrac{1}{(1+i)^n}$	$A\overline{n}| = \dfrac{1 - V^n}{i}$	$\dfrac{1}{A\overline{n}|} = \dfrac{i}{1 - V^n}$			

YEAR   **PERIODS**

	Amount Of 1	Amount Of 1 Per Period	Sinking Fund Payment	Present Worth Of 1	Present Worth of 1 Per Period	Periodic Payment To Amortize 1	Constant Annual Percent	Total Interest	Annual Add On Rate	
	1.024 687	1.000 000	1.000 000 0000	.975 907	.975 907	1.024 687 5000	409.88	.024 687	9.87	1
	1.049 984	2.024 687	.493 903 3802	.952 395	1.928 302	.518 590 8802	207.44	.037 182	7.44	2
	1.075 906	3.074 672	.325 237 9470	.929 449	2.857 752	.349 925 4470	139.98	.049 776	6.64	3
	1.102 467	4.150 578	.240 930 3030	.907 056	3.764 808	.265 617 8030	106.25	.062 471	6.25	4
1	1.102 467	4.150 578	.240 930 3030	.907 056	3.764 808	.265 617 8030	106.25	.062 471	6.25	4
2	1.215 434	8.726 455	.114 594 0735	.822 751	7.179 701	.139 281 5735	55.72	.114 253	5.71	8
3	1.339 977	13.771 210	.072 615 2615	.746 282	10.277 201	.097 302 7615	38.93	.167 633	5.59	12
4	1.477 281	19.332 888	.051 725 3303	.676 919	13.086 807	.076 412 8303	30.57	.222 605	5.57	16
5	1.628 654	25.464 456	.039 270 4243	.614 004	15.635 279	.063 957 9243	25.59	.279 158	5.58	20
6	1.795 538	32.224 311	.031 032 4715	.556 936	17.946 886	.055 719 9715	22.29	.337 279	5.62	24
7	1.979 522	39.676 830	.025 203 6266	.505 173	20.043 644	.049 891 1266	19.96	.396 952	5.67	28
8	2.182 358	47.892 989	.020 879 8829	.458 220	21.945 522	.045 567 3829	18.23	.458 156	5.73	32
9	2.405 979	56.951 036	.017 558 9429	.415 631	23.670 632	.042 246 4429	16.90	.520 872	5.79	36
10	2.652 513	66.937 239	.014 939 3674	.377 001	25.235 404	.039 626 8674	15.86	.585 075	5.85	40
11	2.924 309	77.946 701	.012 829 2793	.341 961	26.654 740	.037 516 7793	15.01	.650 738	5.92	44
12	3.223 956	90.084 274	.011 100 7166	.310 178	27.942 158	.035 788 2166	14.32	.717 834	5.98	48
13	3.554 306	103.465 553	.009 665 0525	.281 349	29.109 918	.034 352 5525	13.75	.786 333	6.05	52
14	3.918 506	118.217 976	.008 458 9504	.255 199	30.169 143	.033 146 4504	13.26	.856 201	6.12	56
15	4.320 025	134.482 042	.007 435 9371	.231 480	31.129 919	.032 123 4371	12.85	.927 406	6.18	60
16	4.762 687	152.412 644	.006 561 1354	.209 966	32.001 397	.031 248 6354	12.50	.999 913	6.25	64
17	5.250 707	172.180 548	.005 807 8570	.190 451	32.791 877	.030 495 3570	12.20	1.073 684	6.32	68
18	5.788 734	193.974 018	.005 155 3296	.172 749	33.508 887	.029 842 8296	11.94	1.148 684	6.38	72
19	6.381 890	218.000 608	.004 587 1432	.156 693	34.159 255	.029 274 6432	11.71	1.224 873	6.45	76
20	7.035 826	244.489 140	.004 090 1612	.142 130	34.749 175	.028 777 6612	11.52	1.302 213	6.51	80
21	7.756 768	273.691 882	.003 653 7437	.128 920	35.284 267	.028 341 2437	11.34	1.380 664	6.57	84
22	8.551 584	305.886 954	.003 269 1816	.116 937	35.769 624	.027 956 6816	11.19	1.460 188	6.64	88
23	9.427 843	341.380 970	.002 929 2787	.106 069	36.209 871	.027 616 7787	11.05	1.540 744	6.70	92
24	10.393 889	380.511 966	.002 628 0382	.096 210	36.609 200	.027 315 5382	10.93	1.622 292	6.76	96
25	11.458 924	423.652 613	.002 360 4245	.087 268	36.971 413	.027 047 9245	10.82	1.704 792	6.82	100
26	12.633 090	471.213 770	.002 122 1791	.079 157	37.299 962	.026 809 6791	10.73	1.788 207	6.88	104
27	13.927 570	523.648 394	.001 909 6783	.071 800	37.597 973	.026 597 1783	10.64	1.872 495	6.94	108
28	15.354 691	581.455 858	.001 719 8210	.065 127	37.868 287	.026 407 3210	10.57	1.957 620	6.99	112
29	16.928 047	645.186 702	.001 549 9390	.059 074	38.113 476	.026 237 4390	10.50	2.043 543	7.05	116
30	18.662 620	715.447 879	.001 397 7259	.053 583	38.335 877	.026 085 2259	10.44	2.130 227	7.10	120
31	20.574 929	792.908 536	.001 261 1795	.048 603	38.537 606	.025 948 6795	10.38	2.217 636	7.15	124
32	22.683 189	878.306 384	.001 138 5549	.044 086	38.720 587	.025 826 0549	10.34	2.305 735	7.21	128
33	25.007 476	972.454 727	.001 028 3255	.039 988	38.886 560	.025 715 8255	10.29	2.394 489	7.26	132
34	27.569 927	1076.250 206	.000 929 1520	.036 271	39.037 108	.025 616 6520	10.25	2.483 865	7.31	136
35	30.394 945	1190.681 336	.000 839 8553	.032 900	39.173 662	.025 527 3553	10.22	2.573 830	7.35	140
36	33.509 436	1316.837 927	.000 759 3949	.029 842	39.297 525	.025 446 8949	10.18	2.664 353	7.40	144
37	36.943 061	1455.921 454	.000 686 8502	.027 069	39.409 876	.025 374 3502	10.15	2.755 404	7.45	148
38	40.728 520	1609.256 507	.000 621 4050	.024 553	39.511 785	.025 308 9050	10.13	2.846 954	7.49	152
39	44.901 865	1778.303 404	.000 562 3337	.022 271	39.604 221	.025 249 8337	10.10	2.938 974	7.54	156
40	49.502 842	1964.672 095	.000 508 9908	.020 201	39.688 066	.025 196 4908	10.08	3.031 439	7.58	160
41	54.575 270	2170.137 500	.000 460 8003	.018 323	39.764 119	.025 148 3003	10.06	3.124 321	7.62	164
42	60.167 455	2396.656 410	.000 417 2480	.016 620	39.833 103	.025 104 7480	10.05	3.217 598	7.66	168
43	66.332 657	2646.386 122	.000 377 8738	.015 076	39.895 675	.025 065 3738	10.03	3.311 244	7.70	172
44	73.129 592	2921.704 986	.000 342 2659	.013 674	39.952 431	.025 029 7659	10.02	3.405 239	7.74	176
45	80.622 990	3225.235 056	.000 310 0549	.012 403	40.003 913	.024 997 5549	10.00	3.499 560	7.78	180
46	88.884 218	3559.867 062	.000 280 9094	.011 251	40.050 609	.024 968 4094	9.99	3.594 187	7.81	184
47	97.991 952	3928.787 936	.000 254 5314	.010 205	40.092 965	.024 942 0314	9.98	3.689 100	7.85	188
48	108.032 932	4335.511 171	.000 230 6533	.009 256	40.131 385	.024 918 1533	9.97	3.784 285	7.88	192
49	119.102 785	4783.910 275	.000 209 0340	.008 396	40.166 234	.024 896 5340	9.96	3.879 721	7.92	196
50	131.306 937	5278.255 667	.000 189 4565	.007 616	40.197 843	.024 876 9565	9.96	3.975 391	7.95	200

Effective Rate is 10.25 %

Annual Percentage Rate is 9.875%

QUARTERLY COMPOUND INTEREST AND ANNUITY

10.00 % Q

	Amount Of 1	Amount Of 1 Per Period	Sinking Fund Payment	Present Worth Of 1	Present Worth of 1 Per Period	Periodic Payment To Amortize 1	Constant Annual Percent	Total Interest	Annual Add On Rate	
	What a single $1 deposit grows to in the future. The deposit is made at the beginning of the first period.	What a series of $1 deposits grow to in the future. A deposit is made at the end of each period.	The amount to be deposited at the end of each period that grows to $1 in the future.	What $1 to be paid in the future is worth today. Value today of a single $1 payment tomorrow.	What $1 to be paid at the end of each period is worth today. Value today of a series of $1 payments tomorrow.	The mortgage payment to amortize a loan of $1. An annuity certain, payable at the end of each period, worth $1 today.	The annual payment, including interest and principal, to amortize completely a loan of $100.	The total interest paid over the term of a loan of $1. The loan is amortized by regular periodic payments.	The average annual interest rate on a loan that is completely amortized by regular periodic payments.	
	$S = (1+i)^n$	$S\overline{n} = \dfrac{(1+i)^n - 1}{i}$	$\dfrac{1}{S\overline{n}} = \dfrac{i}{(1+i)^n - 1}$	$V^n = \dfrac{1}{(1+i)^n}$	$A\overline{n} = \dfrac{1-V^n}{i}$	$\dfrac{1}{A\overline{n}} = \dfrac{i}{1-V^n}$				

YEAR										PERIODS
	1.025 000	1.000 000	1.000 000 0000	.975 610	.975 610	1.025 000 0000	410.00	.025 000	10.00	1
	1.050 625	2.025 000	.493 827 1605	.951 814	1.927 424	.518 827 1605	207.54	.037 654	7.53	2
	1.076 891	3.075 625	.325 137 1672	.928 599	2.856 024	.350 137 1672	140.06	.050 412	6.72	3
	1.103 813	4.152 516	.240 817 8777	.905 951	3.761 974	.265 817 8777	106.33	.063 272	6.33	4
1	1.103 813	4.152 516	.240 817 8777	.905 951	3.761 974	.265 817 8777	106.33	.063 272	6.33	4
2	1.218 403	8.736 116	.114 467 3458	.820 747	7.170 137	.139 467 3458	55.79	.115 739	5.79	8
3	1.344 889	13.795 553	.072 487 1270	.743 556	10.257 765	.097 487 1270	39.00	.169 846	5.66	12
4	1.484 506	19.380 225	.051 598 9886	.673 625	13.055 003	.076 598 9886	30.64	.225 584	5.64	16
5	1.638 616	25.544 658	.039 147 1287	.610 271	15.589 162	.064 147 1287	25.66	.282 943	5.66	20
6	1.808 726	32.349 038	.030 912 8204	.552 875	17.884 986	.055 912 8204	22.37	.341 908	5.70	24
7	1.996 495	39.859 801	.025 087 9327	.500 878	19.964 889	.050 087 9327	20.04	.402 462	5.75	28
8	2.203 757	48.150 278	.020 768 3123	.453 771	21.849 178	.045 768 3123	18.31	.464 586	5.81	32
9	2.432 535	57.301 413	.017 451 5767	.411 094	23.556 251	.042 451 5767	16.99	.528 257	5.87	36
10	2.685 064	67.402 554	.014 836 2332	.372 431	25.102 775	.039 836 2332	15.94	.593 449	5.93	40
11	2.963 808	78.552 323	.012 730 3683	.337 404	26.503 849	.037 730 3683	15.10	.660 136	6.00	44
12	3.271 490	90.859 582	.011 005 9938	.305 671	27.773 154	.036 005 9938	14.41	.728 288	6.07	48
13	3.611 112	104.444 494	.009 574 4635	.276 923	28.923 081	.034 574 4635	13.83	.797 872	6.14	52
14	3.985 992	119.439 694	.008 372 4260	.250 879	29.964 858	.033 372 4260	13.35	.868 856	6.21	56
15	4.399 790	135.991 992	.007 353 3959	.227 284	30.908 656	.032 353 3959	12.95	.941 204	6.27	60
16	4.856 545	154.261 786	.006 482 4869	.205 908	31.763 691	.031 482 4869	12.60	1.014 879	6.34	64
17	5.360 717	174.428 663	.005 733 0027	.186 542	32.538 311	.030 733 0027	12.30	1.089 844	6.41	68
18	5.917 228	196.689 122	.005 084 1652	.168 998	33.240 078	.030 084 1652	12.04	1.166 060	6.48	72
19	6.531 513	221.260 504	.004 519 5594	.153 104	33.875 844	.029 519 5594	11.81	1.243 487	6.54	76
20	7.209 568	248.382 713	.004 026 0451	.138 705	34.451 817	.029 026 0451	11.62	1.322 084	6.61	80
21	7.958 014	278.320 556	.003 592 9793	.125 659	34.973 620	.028 592 9793	11.44	1.401 810	6.68	84
22	8.784 158	311.366 333	.003 211 6510	.113 841	35.446 348	.028 211 6510	11.29	1.482 625	6.74	88
23	9.696 067	347.842 687	.002 874 8628	.103 135	35.874 616	.027 874 8628	11.15	1.564 487	6.80	92
24	10.702 644	388.105 758	.002 576 6173	.093 435	36.262 606	.027 576 6173	11.04	1.647 355	6.86	96
25	11.813 716	432.548 654	.002 311 8787	.084 647	36.614 105	.027 311 8787	10.93	1.731 188	6.92	100
26	13.040 132	481.605 296	.002 076 3891	.076 686	36.932 546	.027 076 3891	10.84	1.815 944	6.98	104
27	14.393 866	535.754 649	.001 866 5260	.069 474	37.221 039	.026 866 5260	10.75	1.901 585	7.04	108
28	15.888 135	595.525 404	.001 679 1895	.062 940	37.482 398	.026 679 1895	10.68	1.988 069	7.10	112
29	17.537 528	661.501 133	.001 511 7132	.057 021	37.719 177	.026 511 7132	10.61	2.075 359	7.16	116
30	19.358 150	734.325 993	.001 361 7930	.051 658	37.933 687	.026 361 7930	10.55	2.163 415	7.21	120
31	21.367 775	814.711 013	.001 227 4291	.046 799	38.128 022	.026 227 4291	10.50	2.252 201	7.27	124
32	23.586 026	903.441 034	.001 106 8791	.042 398	38.304 081	.026 106 8791	10.45	2.341 681	7.32	128
33	26.034 559	1001.382 375	.000 998 6195	.038 410	38.463 581	.025 998 6195	10.40	2.431 818	7.37	132
34	28.737 282	1109.491 289	.000 901 3140	.034 798	38.608 080	.025 901 3140	10.37	2.522 579	7.42	136
35	31.720 583	1228.823 303	.000 813 7867	.031 525	38.738 989	.025 813 7867	10.33	2.613 930	7.47	140
36	35.013 588	1360.543 518	.000 735 0004	.028 560	38.857 586	.025 735 0004	10.30	2.705 840	7.52	144
37	38.648 450	1505.937 989	.000 664 0380	.025 874	38.965 030	.025 664 0380	10.27	2.798 278	7.56	148
38	42.660 657	1666.426 280	.000 600 0866	.023 441	39.062 368	.025 600 0866	10.25	2.891 213	7.61	152
39	47.089 383	1843.575 325	.000 542 4243	.021 236	39.150 552	.025 542 4243	10.22	2.984 618	7.65	156
40	51.977 868	2039.114 724	.000 490 4089	.019 239	39.230 442	.025 490 4089	10.20	3.078 465	7.70	160
41	57.373 841	2254.953 633	.000 443 4681	.017 430	39.302 818	.025 443 4681	10.18	3.172 729	7.74	164
42	63.329 985	2493.199 404	.000 401 0911	.015 790	39.368 388	.025 401 0911	10.17	3.267 383	7.78	168
43	69.904 454	2756.178 156	.000 362 8212	.014 305	39.427 790	.025 362 8212	10.15	3.362 405	7.82	172
44	77.161 437	3046.457 494	.000 328 2501	.012 960	39.481 606	.025 328 2501	10.14	3.457 772	7.86	176
45	85.171 789	3366.871 568	.000 297 0116	.011 741	39.530 361	.025 297 0116	10.12	3.553 462	7.90	180
46	94.013 719	3720.548 753	.000 268 7776	.010 637	39.574 530	.025 268 7776	10.11	3.649 455	7.93	184
47	103.773 555	4110.942 190	.000 243 2532	.009 636	39.614 545	.025 243 2532	10.10	3.745 732	7.97	188
48	114.546 587	4541.863 497	.000 220 1739	.008 730	39.650 797	.025 220 1739	10.09	3.842 273	8.00	192
49	126.438 000	5017.519 991	.000 199 3016	.007 909	39.683 639	.025 199 3016	10.08	3.939 063	8.04	196
50	139.563 894	5542.555 761	.000 180 4222	.007 165	39.713 393	.025 180 4222	10.08	4.036 084	8.07	200

Effective Rate is 10.38 %

Annual Percentage Rate is 10.00 %

QUARTERLY COMPOUND INTEREST AND ANNUITY

	Amount Of 1	Amount Of 1 Per Period	Sinking Fund Payment	Present Worth Of 1	Present Worth of 1 Per Period	Periodic Payment To Amortize 1	Constant Annual Percent	Total Interest	Annual Add On Rate	
	What a single $ 1 deposit grows to in the future. The deposit is made at the beginning of the first period.	What a series of $ 1 deposits grow to in the future. A deposit is made at the end of each period.	The amount to be deposited at the end of each period that grows to $ 1 in the future.	What $ 1 to be paid in the future is worth today. Value today of a single $ 1 payment tomorrow.	What $ 1 to be paid at the end of each period is worth today. Value today of a series of $ 1 payments tomorrow.	The mortgage payment to amortize a loan of $ 1. An annuity certain, payable at the end of each period, worth $ 1 today.	The annual payment, including interest and principal, to amortize completely a loan of $ 100.	The total interest paid over the term on a loan of $1. The loan is amortized by regular periodic payments.	The average annual interest rate on a loan that is completely amortized by regular periodic payments.	
	$S = (1+i)^n$	$S\overline{n}| = \dfrac{(1+i)^n - 1}{i}$	$\dfrac{1}{S\overline{n}|} = \dfrac{i}{(1+i)^n - 1}$	$V^n = \dfrac{1}{(1+i)^n}$	$A\overline{n}| = \dfrac{1-V^n}{i}$	$\dfrac{1}{A\overline{n}|} = \dfrac{i}{1-V^n}$				

YEAR										PERIODS
	1.025 313	1.000 000	1.000 000 0000	.975 312	.975 312	1.025 312 5000	410.13	.025 312	10.12	1
	1.051 266	2.025 313	.493 750 9644	.951 234	1.926 547	.519 063 4644	207.63	.038 127	7.63	2
	1.077 876	3.076 578	.325 036 4293	.927 751	2.854 297	.350 348 9293	140.14	.051 047	6.81	3
	1.105 160	4.154 454	.240 705 5112	.904 847	3.759 144	.266 018 0112	106.41	.064 072	6.41	4
1	1.105 160	4.154 454	.240 705 5112	.904 847	3.759 144	.266 018 0112	106.41	.064 072	6.41	4
2	1.221 378	8.745 789	.114 340 7412	.818 747	7.160 593	.139 653 2412	55.87	.117 226	5.86	8
3	1.349 817	13.819 947	.072 359 1777	.740 841	10.238 383	.097 671 6777	39.07	.172 060	5.74	12
4	1.491 764	19.427 701	.051 472 8931	.670 347	13.023 310	.076 785 3931	30.72	.228 566	5.71	16
5	1.648 637	25.625 165	.039 024 1386	.606 562	15.543 243	.064 336 6386	25.74	.286 733	5.73	20
6	1.822 007	32.474 352	.030 793 5321	.548 845	17.823 396	.056 106 0321	22.45	.346 545	5.78	24
7	2.013 609	40.043 797	.024 972 6570	.496 621	19.886 584	.050 285 1570	20.12	.407 984	5.83	28
8	2.225 359	48.409 241	.020 657 2129	.449 366	21.753 453	.045 969 7129	18.39	.471 031	5.89	32
9	2.459 377	57.654 393	.017 344 7322	.406 607	23.442 684	.042 657 2322	17.07	.535 660	5.95	36
10	2.718 004	67.871 761	.014 733 6682	.367 917	24.971 178	.040 046 1682	16.02	.601 847	6.02	40
11	3.003 828	79.163 583	.012 632 0709	.332 909	26.354 231	.037 944 5709	15.18	.669 561	6.09	44
12	3.319 710	91.642 850	.010 911 9260	.301 231	27.605 682	.036 224 4260	14.49	.738 772	6.16	48
13	3.668 809	105.434 431	.009 484 5677	.272 568	28.738 054	.034 797 0677	13.92	.809 448	6.23	52
14	4.054 620	120.676 330	.008 286 6292	.246 632	29.762 676	.033 599 1292	13.44	.881 551	6.30	56
15	4.481 002	137.521 061	.007 271 6135	.223 164	30.689 802	.032 584 1135	13.04	.955 047	6.37	60
16	4.952 222	156.137 178	.006 404 6245	.201 930	31.528 709	.031 717 1245	12.69	1.029 896	6.44	64
17	5.472 996	176.710 958	.005 658 9586	.182 715	32.287 792	.030 971 4586	12.39	1.106 059	6.51	68
18	6.048 534	199.448 269	.005 013 8314	.165 329	32.974 645	.030 326 3314	12.14	1.183 496	6.57	72
19	6.684 596	224.576 627	.004 452 8231	.149 598	33.596 141	.029 765 3231	11.91	1.262 165	6.64	76
20	7.387 545	252.347 474	.003 962 7898	.135 363	34.158 500	.029 275 2898	11.72	1.342 023	6.71	80
21	8.164 417	283.038 693	.003 533 0858	.122 483	34.667 349	.028 845 5858	11.54	1.423 029	6.78	84
22	9.022 984	316.957 388	.003 154 9982	.110 828	35.127 779	.028 467 4982	11.39	1.505 140	6.84	88
23	9.971 837	354.442 961	.002 821 3284	.100 282	35.544 398	.028 133 8284	11.26	1.588 312	6.91	92
24	11.020 472	395.870 502	.002 526 0786	.090 740	35.921 374	.027 838 5786	11.14	1.672 504	6.97	96
25	12.179 381	441.654 547	.002 264 2131	.082 106	36.262 480	.027 576 7131	11.04	1.757 671	7.03	100
26	13.460 160	492.253 225	.002 031 4748	.074 293	36.571 128	.027 343 9748	10.94	1.843 773	7.09	104
27	14.875 625	548.172 841	.001 824 2421	.067 224	36.850 407	.027 136 7421	10.86	1.930 768	7.15	108
28	16.439 940	609.972 943	.001 639 4170	.060 827	37.103 112	.026 951 9170	10.79	2.018 615	7.21	112
29	18.168 758	678.271 920	.001 474 3350	.055 040	37.331 771	.026 786 8350	10.72	2.107 273	7.27	116
30	20.079 378	753.753 191	.001 326 6942	.049 802	37.538 673	.026 639 1942	10.66	2.196 703	7.32	120
31	22.190 917	837.172 044	.001 194 4976	.045 063	37.725 887	.026 506 9976	10.61	2.286 868	7.38	124
32	24.524 506	929.363 192	.001 076 0056	.040 776	37.895 287	.026 388 5056	10.56	2.377 729	7.43	128
33	27.103 493	1031.249 126	.000 969 6978	.036 896	38.048 568	.026 282 1978	10.52	2.469 250	7.48	132
34	29.953 687	1143.849 346	.000 874 2410	.033 385	38.187 264	.026 186 7410	10.48	2.561 397	7.53	136
35	33.103 605	1268.290 562	.000 788 4629	.030 208	38.312 763	.026 100 9629	10.45	2.654 135	7.58	140
36	36.584 767	1405.817 969	.000 711 3296	.027 334	38.426 320	.026 023 8296	10.41	2.747 431	7.63	144
37	40.432 008	1557.807 706	.000 641 9278	.024 733	38.529 071	.025 954 4278	10.39	2.841 255	7.68	148
38	44.683 822	1725.780 626	.000 579 4479	.022 379	38.622 046	.025 891 9479	10.36	2.935 576	7.73	152
39	49.382 756	1911.417 514	.000 523 1719	.020 250	38.706 173	.025 835 6719	10.34	3.030 365	7.77	156
40	54.575 828	2116.575 907	.000 472 4612	.018 323	38.782 296	.025 784 9612	10.32	3.125 594	7.81	160
41	60.315 001	2343.308 679	.000 426 7470	.016 580	38.851 175	.025 739 2470	10.30	3.221 237	7.86	164
42	66.657 703	2593.884 582	.000 385 5222	.015 002	38.913 501	.025 698 0222	10.28	3.317 268	7.90	168
43	73.667 402	2870.810 952	.000 348 3336	.013 575	38.969 895	.025 660 8336	10.27	3.413 663	7.94	172
44	81.414 238	3176.858 794	.000 314 7763	.012 283	39.020 924	.025 627 2763	10.26	3.510 401	7.98	176
45	89.975 729	3515.090 511	.000 284 4877	.011 114	39.067 097	.025 596 9877	10.24	3.607 458	8.02	180
46	99.437 542	3888.890 546	.000 257 1427	.010 057	39.108 876	.025 569 6427	10.23	3.704 814	8.05	184
47	109.894 356	4301.999 251	.000 232 4501	.009 100	39.146 681	.025 544 9501	10.22	3.802 451	8.09	188
48	121.450 805	4758.550 309	.000 210 1480	.008 234	39.180 887	.025 522 6480	10.21	3.900 348	8.13	192
49	134.222 525	5263.112 104	.000 190 0017	.007 450	39.211 839	.025 502 5017	10.21	3.998 490	8.16	196
50	148.337 315	5820.733 425	.000 171 7997	.006 741	39.239 846	.025 484 2997	10.20	4.096 860	8.19	200

Effective Rate is 10.52 %

Annual Percentage Rate is 10.125%

QUARTERLY COMPOUND INTEREST AND ANNUITY

	Amount Of 1	Amount Of 1 Per Period	Sinking Fund Payment	Present Worth Of 1	Present Worth of 1 Per Period	Periodic Payment To Amortize 1	Constant Annual Percent	Total Interest	Annual Add On Rate	
	What a single $ 1 deposit grows to in the future. The deposit is made at the beginning of the first period.	What a series of $ 1 deposits grow to in the future. A deposit is made at the end of each period.	The amount to be deposited at the end of each period that grows to $ 1 in the future.	What $ 1 to be paid in the future is worth today. Value today of a single $ 1 payment tomorrow.	What $ 1 to be paid at the end of each period is worth today. Value today of a series of $ 1 payments tomorrow.	The mortgage payment to amortize a loan of $ 1. An annuity certain, payable at the end of each period, worth $ 1 today.	The annual payment, including interest and principal, to amortize completely a loan of $ 100.	The total interest paid over the term on a loan of $1. The loan is amortized by regular periodic payments.	The average annual interest rate on a loan that is completely amortized by regular periodic payments.	
	$S = (1+i)^n$	$S\overline{n}| = \dfrac{(1+i)^n - 1}{i}$	$\dfrac{1}{S\overline{n}|} = \dfrac{i}{(1+i)^n - 1}$	$V^n = \dfrac{1}{(1+i)^n}$	$A\overline{n}| = \dfrac{1-V^n}{i}$	$\dfrac{1}{A\overline{n}|} = \dfrac{i}{1-V^n}$				

YEAR										PERIODS
	1.025 625	1.000 000	1.000 000 0000	.975 015	.975 015	1.025 625 0000	410.25	.025 625	10.25	1
	1.051 907	2.025 625	.493 674 7917	.950 655	1.925 670	.519 299 7917	207.72	.038 600	7.72	2
	1.078 862	3.077 532	.324 935 7332	.926 903	2.852 573	.350 560 7332	140.23	.051 682	6.89	3
	1.106 508	4.156 393	.240 593 2034	.903 744	3.756 317	.266 218 2034	106.49	.064 873	6.49	4
1	1.106 508	4.156 393	.240 593 2034	.903 744	3.756 317	.266 218 2034	106.49	.064 873	6.49	4
2	1.224 359	8.755 474	.114 214 2595	.816 754	7.151 068	.139 839 2595	55.94	.118 714	5.94	8
3	1.354 763	13.844 392	.072 231 4136	.738 137	10.219 054	.097 856 4136	39.15	.174 277	5.81	12
4	1.499 055	19.475 318	.051 347 0434	.667 087	12.991 730	.076 972 0434	30.79	.231 553	5.79	16
5	1.658 716	25.705 980	.038 901 4534	.602 876	15.497 520	.064 526 4534	25.82	.290 529	5.81	20
6	1.835 382	32.600 256	.030 674 6061	.544 846	17.762 114	.056 299 6061	22.52	.351 191	5.85	24
7	2.030 864	40.228 823	.024 857 7989	.492 401	19.808 727	.050 482 7989	20.20	.413 518	5.91	28
8	2.247 166	48.669 891	.020 546 5838	.445 005	21.658 343	.046 171 5838	18.47	.477 491	5.97	32
9	2.486 506	58.009 997	.017 238 4080	.402 171	23.329 923	.042 863 4080	17.15	.543 083	6.03	36
10	2.751 338	68.344 895	.014 631 6707	.363 460	24.840 604	.040 256 6707	16.11	.610 267	6.10	40
11	3.044 376	79.780 538	.012 534 3853	.328 475	26.205 873	.038 159 3853	15.27	.679 013	6.17	44
12	3.368 625	92.434 163	.010 818 5109	.296 857	27.439 727	.036 443 5109	14.58	.749 289	6.24	48
13	3.727 410	106.435 496	.009 395 3619	.268 283	28.554 816	.035 020 3619	14.01	.821 059	6.32	52
14	4.124 407	121.928 076	.008 201 5565	.242 459	29.562 572	.033 826 5565	13.54	.894 287	6.39	56
15	4.563 688	139.070 734	.007 190 5855	.219 121	30.473 325	.032 815 5855	13.13	.968 935	6.46	60
16	5.049 755	158.039 215	.006 327 5435	.198 029	31.296 413	.031 952 5435	12.79	1.044 963	6.53	64
17	5.587 592	179.027 983	.005 585 7190	.178 968	32.040 274	.031 210 7190	12.49	1.122 329	6.60	68
18	6.182 713	202.252 213	.004 944 3217	.161 741	32.712 535	.030 569 3217	12.23	1.200 991	6.67	72
19	6.841 219	227.950 001	.004 386 9269	.146 173	33.320 086	.030 011 9269	12.01	1.280 906	6.74	76
20	7.569 860	256.384 797	.003 900 3873	.132 103	33.869 158	.029 525 3873	11.82	1.362 031	6.81	80
21	8.376 108	287.848 115	.003 474 0544	.119 387	34.365 378	.029 099 0544	11.64	1.444 321	6.88	84
22	9.268 227	322.662 514	.003 099 2134	.107 896	34.813 834	.028 724 2134	11.49	1.527 731	6.94	88
23	10.255 363	361.184 912	.002 768 6649	.097 510	35.219 124	.028 393 6649	11.36	1.612 217	7.01	92
24	11.347 637	403.810 236	.002 476 4107	.088 124	35.585 402	.028 101 4107	11.25	1.697 735	7.07	96
25	12.556 247	450.975 481	.002 217 4155	.079 642	35.916 424	.027 842 4155	11.14	1.784 242	7.14	100
26	13.893 582	503.164 181	.001 987 4229	.071 976	36.215 583	.027 612 4229	11.05	1.871 692	7.20	104
27	15.373 354	560.911 374	.001 782 8128	.065 048	36.485 947	.027 407 8128	10.97	1.960 044	7.26	108
28	17.010 733	624.809 081	.001 600 4889	.058 786	36.730 286	.027 225 4889	10.90	2.049 255	7.32	112
29	18.822 505	695.512 378	.001 437 7889	.053 128	36.951 107	.027 062 7889	10.83	2.139 284	7.38	116
30	20.827 244	773.746 112	.001 292 4136	.048 014	37.150 672	.026 917 4136	10.77	2.230 090	7.43	120
31	23.045 504	860.312 332	.001 162 3686	.043 392	37.331 028	.026 787 3686	10.72	2.321 634	7.49	124
32	25.500 024	956.098 511	.001 045 9173	.039 216	37.494 023	.026 670 9173	10.67	2.413 877	7.54	128
33	28.215 970	1062.086 643	.000 941 5428	.035 441	37.641 330	.026 566 5428	10.63	2.506 784	7.60	132
34	31.221 185	1179.363 315	.000 847 9151	.032 030	37.774 457	.026 472 9151	10.59	2.600 316	7.65	136
35	34.546 478	1309.130 842	.000 763 8656	.028 947	37.894 770	.026 388 8656	10.56	2.694 441	7.70	140
36	38.225 940	1452.719 594	.000 688 3641	.026 160	38.003 503	.026 313 3641	10.53	2.789 124	7.75	144
37	42.297 292	1611.601 637	.000 620 5007	.023 642	38.101 769	.026 245 5007	10.50	2.884 334	7.80	148
38	46.802 274	1787.405 821	.000 559 4700	.021 366	38.190 576	.026 184 4700	10.48	2.980 039	7.84	152
39	51.787 071	1981.934 484	.000 504 5575	.019 310	38.270 836	.026 129 5575	10.46	3.076 211	7.89	156
40	57.302 787	2197.181 920	.000 455 1284	.017 451	38.343 369	.026 080 1284	10.44	3.172 821	7.93	160
41	63.405 968	2435.354 849	.000 410 6178	.015 771	38.408 922	.026 035 6178	10.42	3.269 841	7.98	164
42	70.159 184	2698.894 995	.000 370 5220	.014 253	38.468 164	.025 995 5220	10.40	3.367 248	8.02	168
43	77.631 669	2990.504 164	.000 334 3918	.012 881	38.521 704	.025 959 3918	10.39	3.465 015	8.06	172
44	85.900 030	3313.171 921	.000 301 8256	.011 641	38.570 090	.025 926 8256	10.38	3.563 121	8.10	176
45	95.049 035	3670.206 240	.000 272 4643	.010 521	38.613 819	.025 897 4643	10.36	3.661 544	8.14	180
46	105.172 478	4065.267 420	.000 245 9863	.009 508	38.653 339	.025 870 9863	10.35	3.760 261	8.17	184
47	116.374 144	4502.405 611	.000 222 1035	.008 593	38.689 055	.025 847 1035	10.34	3.859 255	8.21	188
48	128.768 872	4986.102 333	.000 200 5575	.007 766	38.721 333	.025 825 5575	10.34	3.958 507	8.25	192
49	142.483 733	5521.516 422	.000 181 1162	.007 018	38.750 504	.025 806 1162	10.33	4.057 999	8.28	196
50	157.659 331	6113.434 869	.000 163 5715	.006 343	38.776 867	.025 788 5715	10.32	4.157 714	8.32	200

Effective Rate is 10.65 %

Annual Percentage Rate is 10.25 %

QUARTERLY COMPOUND INTEREST AND ANNUITY

10.375% Q

	Amount Of 1	Amount Of 1 Per Period	Sinking Fund Payment	Present Worth Of 1	Present Worth of 1 Per Period	Periodic Payment To Amortize 1	Constant Annual Percent	Total Interest	Annual Add On Rate	
	What a single $ 1 deposit grows to in the future. The deposit is made at the beginning of the first period.	What a series of $ 1 deposits grow to in the future. A deposit is made at the end of each period.	The amount to be deposited at the end of each period that grows to $ 1 in the future.	What $ 1 to be paid in the future is worth today. Value today of a single $ 1 payment tomorrow.	What $ 1 to be paid at the end of each period is worth today. Value today of a series of $ 1 payments tomorrow.	The mortgage payment to amortize a loan of $ 1. An annuity certain, payable at the end of each period, worth $ 1 today.	The annual payment, including interest and principal, to amortize completely a loan of $ 100.	The total interest paid over the term on a loan of $1. The loan is amortized by regular periodic payments.	The average annual interest rate on a loan that is completely amortized by regular periodic payments.	
	$S = (1+i)^n$	$S\overline{n}| = \dfrac{(1+i)^n - 1}{i}$	$\dfrac{1}{S\overline{n}|} = \dfrac{i}{(1+i)^n - 1}$	$V^n = \dfrac{1}{(1+i)^n}$	$A\overline{n}| = \dfrac{1-V^n}{i}$	$\dfrac{1}{A\overline{n}|} = \dfrac{i}{1-V^n}$				

YEAR										PERIODS
	1.025 937	1.000 000	1.000 000 0000	.974 718	.974 718	1.025 937 5000	410.38	.025 938	10.38	1
	1.052 548	2.025 938	.493 598 6426	.950 076	1.924 794	.519 536 1426	207.82	.039 072	7.81	2
	1.079 848	3.078 485	.324 835 0788	.926 056	2.850 850	.350 772 5788	140.31	.052 318	6.98	3
	1.107 857	4.158 333	.240 480 9543	.902 644	3.753 494	.266 418 4543	106.57	.065 674	6.57	4
1	1.107 857	4.158 333	.240 480 9543	.902 644	3.753 494	.266 418 4543	106.57	.065 674	6.57	4
2	1.227 347	8.765 171	.114 087 9007	.814 766	7.141 561	.140 025 4007	56.02	.120 203	6.01	8
3	1.359 724	13.868 888	.072 103 8345	.735 443	10.199 780	.098 041 3345	39.22	.176 496	5.88	12
4	1.506 380	19.523 075	.051 221 4395	.663 843	12.960 261	.077 158 9395	30.87	.234 543	5.86	16
5	1.668 853	25.787 104	.038 779 0730	.599 214	15.451 992	.064 716 5730	25.89	.294 331	5.89	20
6	1.848 850	32.726 752	.030 556 0421	.540 877	17.701 138	.056 493 5421	22.60	.355 845	5.93	24
7	2.048 261	40.414 887	.024 743 3576	.488 219	19.731 316	.050 680 8576	20.28	.419 064	5.99	28
8	2.269 180	48.932 240	.020 436 4240	.440 688	21.563 843	.046 373 9240	18.55	.483 966	6.05	32
9	2.513 926	58.368 247	.017 132 6030	.397 784	23.217 962	.043 070 1030	17.23	.550 524	6.12	36
10	2.785 070	68.821 991	.014 530 2393	.359 057	24.711 042	.040 467 7393	16.19	.618 710	6.19	40
11	3.085 459	80.403 242	.012 437 3094	.324 101	26.058 761	.038 374 8094	15.35	.688 492	6.26	44
12	3.418 247	93.233 610	.010 725 7458	.292 548	27.275 272	.036 663 2458	14.67	.759 836	6.33	48
13	3.786 928	107.447 820	.009 306 8431	.264 066	28.373 348	.035 244 3431	14.10	.832 706	6.41	52
14	4.195 374	123.195 129	.008 117 2041	.238 358	29.364 519	.034 054 7041	13.63	.907 063	6.48	56
15	4.647 873	140.640 892	.007 110 3076	.215 152	30.259 193	.033 047 8076	13.22	.982 868	6.55	60
16	5.149 178	159.968 298	.006 251 2386	.194 206	31.066 766	.032 188 7386	12.88	1.060 079	6.63	64
17	5.704 551	181.380 296	.005 513 2780	.175 299	31.795 716	.031 450 7780	12.59	1.138 653	6.70	68
18	6.319 826	205.101 723	.004 875 6294	.158 232	32.453 698	.030 813 1294	12.33	1.218 545	6.77	72
19	7.001 462	231.381 667	.004 321 8636	.142 827	33.047 622	.030 259 3636	12.11	1.299 712	6.84	76
20	7.756 617	260.496 081	.003 838 8294	.128 922	33.583 723	.029 776 3294	11.92	1.382 106	6.91	80
21	8.593 221	292.750 681	.003 415 8759	.116 371	34.067 632	.029 353 3759	11.75	1.465 684	6.98	84
22	9.520 058	328.484 159	.003 044 2868	.105 041	34.504 429	.028 981 7868	11.60	1.550 397	7.05	88
23	10.546 861	368.071 734	.002 716 8617	.094 815	34.898 701	.028 654 3617	11.47	1.636 201	7.11	92
24	11.684 411	411.929 097	.002 427 6022	.085 584	35.254 588	.028 365 1022	11.35	1.723 050	7.18	96
25	12.944 654	460.516 774	.002 171 4736	.077 252	35.575 828	.028 108 9736	11.25	1.810 897	7.24	100
26	14.340 822	514.344 961	.001 944 2205	.069 731	35.865 792	.027 881 7205	11.16	1.899 699	7.31	104
27	15.887 577	573.978 883	.001 742 2244	.062 942	36.127 527	.027 679 7244	11.08	1.989 410	7.37	108
28	17.601 160	640.044 728	.001 562 3908	.056 814	36.363 781	.027 499 8908	11.00	2.079 988	7.43	112
29	19.499 564	713.236 221	.001 402 0600	.051 283	36.577 033	.027 339 5600	10.94	2.171 389	7.49	116
30	21.602 725	794.321 912	.001 258 9354	.046 290	36.769 525	.027 196 4354	10.88	2.263 572	7.55	120
31	23.932 725	884.153 245	.001 131 0257	.041 784	36.943 275	.027 068 5257	10.83	2.356 497	7.60	124
32	26.514 031	983.673 495	.001 016 5975	.037 716	37.100 111	.026 954 0975	10.79	2.450 124	7.66	128
33	29.373 749	1093.927 679	.000 914 1372	.034 044	37.241 677	.026 851 6372	10.75	2.544 416	7.71	132
34	32.541 907	1216.073 523	.000 822 3187	.030 730	37.369 461	.026 759 8187	10.71	2.639 335	7.76	136
35	36.051 772	1351.393 624	.000 739 9769	.027 738	37.484 804	.026 677 4769	10.68	2.734 847	7.81	140
36	39.940 200	1501.308 915	.000 666 0854	.025 037	37.588 918	.026 603 5854	10.65	2.830 916	7.86	144
37	44.248 021	1667.393 585	.000 599 7384	.022 600	37.682 896	.026 537 2384	10.62	2.927 511	7.91	148
38	49.020 470	1851.391 612	.000 540 1342	.020 400	37.767 725	.026 477 6342	10.60	3.024 600	7.96	152
39	54.307 660	2055.235 072	.000 486 5623	.018 414	37.844 295	.026 424 0623	10.57	3.122 154	8.01	156
40	60.165 109	2281.064 431	.000 438 3918	.016 621	37.913 410	.026 375 8918	10.56	3.220 143	8.05	160
41	66.654 323	2531.251 016	.000 395 0616	.015 003	37.975 797	.026 332 5616	10.54	3.318 540	8.09	164
42	73.843 444	2808.421 919	.000 356 0719	.013 542	38.032 109	.026 293 5719	10.52	3.417 320	8.14	168
43	81.807 959	3115.487 581	.000 320 9770	.012 224	38.082 940	.026 258 4770	10.51	3.516 458	8.18	172
44	90.631 502	3455.672 355	.000 289 3793	.011 034	38.128 822	.026 226 8793	10.50	3.615 931	8.22	176
45	100.406 723	3832.548 362	.000 260 9230	.009 959	38.170 236	.026 198 4230	10.48	3.715 716	8.26	180
46	111.236 268	4250.072 999	.000 235 2901	.008 990	38.207 619	.026 172 7901	10.47	3.815 793	8.30	184
47	123.233 853	4712.630 496	.000 212 1957	.008 115	38.241 363	.026 149 6957	10.46	3.916 143	8.33	188
48	136.525 459	5225.077 953	.000 191 3847	.007 325	38.271 821	.026 128 8847	10.46	4.016 746	8.37	192
49	151.250 655	5792.796 340	.000 172 6282	.006 612	38.299 314	.026 110 1282	10.45	4.117 585	8.40	196
50	167.564 063	6421.747 000	.000 155 7209	.005 968	38.324 130	.026 093 2209	10.44	4.218 644	8.44	200

Effective Rate is 10.79 %

Annual Percentage Rate is 10.375%

QUARTERLY COMPOUND INTEREST AND ANNUITY

Amount Of 1	Amount Of 1 Per Period	Sinking Fund Payment	Present Worth Of 1	Present Worth of 1 Per Period	Periodic Payment To Amortize 1	Constant Annual Percent	Total Interest	Annual Add On Rate	
What a single $ 1 deposit grows to in the future. The deposit is made at the beginning of the first period.	What a series of $ 1 deposits grow to in the future. A deposit is made at the end of each period.	The amount to be deposited at the end of each period that grows to $ 1 in the future.	What $ 1 to be paid in the future is worth today. Value today of a single $ 1 payment tomorrow.	What $ 1 to be paid at the end of each period is worth today. Value today of a series of $ 1 payments tomorrow.	The mortgage payment to amortize a loan of $ 1. An annuity certain, payable at the end of each period, worth $ 1 today.	The annual payment, including interest and principal, to amortize completely a loan of $ 100.	The total interest paid over the term on a loan of $1. The loan is amortized by regular periodic payments.	The average annual interest rate on a loan that is completely amortized by regular periodic payments.	
$S = (1+i)^n$	$S\overline{n}| = \dfrac{(1+i)^n - 1}{i}$	$\dfrac{1}{S\overline{n}|} = \dfrac{i}{(1+i)^n - 1}$	$V^n = \dfrac{1}{(1+i)^n}$	$A\overline{n}| = \dfrac{1 - V^n}{i}$	$\dfrac{1}{A\overline{n}|} = \dfrac{i}{1 - V^n}$				

YEAR / **PERIODS**

YEAR	Amount Of 1	Amount Of 1 Per Period	Sinking Fund Payment	Present Worth Of 1	Present Worth of 1 Per Period	Periodic Payment To Amortize 1	Constant Annual Percent	Total Interest	Annual Add On Rate	PERIODS
	1.026 250	1.000 000	1.000 000 0000	.974 421	.974 421	1.026 250 0000	410.50	.026 250	10.50	1
	1.053 189	2.026 250	.493 522 5170	.949 497	1.923 919	.519 772 5170	207.91	.039 545	7.91	2
	1.080 835	3.079 439	.324 734 4661	.925 210	2.849 129	.350 984 4661	140.40	.052 953	7.06	3
	1.109 207	4.160 274	.240 368 7639	.901 545	3.750 674	.266 618 7639	106.65	.066 475	6.65	4
1	1.109 207	4.160 274	.240 368 7639	.901 545	3.750 674	.266 618 7639	106.65	.066 475	6.65	4
2	1.230 341	8.774 881	.113 961 6647	.812 783	7.132 074	.140 211 6647	56.09	.121 693	6.08	8
3	1.364 703	13.893 435	.071 976 4402	.732 760	10.180 558	.098 226 4402	39.30	.178 717	5.96	12
4	1.513 738	19.570 973	.051 096 0810	.660 616	12.928 903	.077 346 0810	30.94	.237 537	5.94	16
5	1.679 049	25.868 538	.038 656 9971	.595 575	15.406 659	.064 906 9971	25.97	.298 140	5.96	20
6	1.862 413	32.853 843	.030 437 8394	.536 938	17.640 468	.056 687 8394	22.68	.360 508	6.01	24
7	2.065 802	40.601 994	.024 629 3325	.484 073	19.654 346	.050 879 3325	20.36	.424 621	6.07	28
8	2.291 403	49.196 298	.020 326 7327	.436 414	21.469 947	.046 576 7327	18.64	.490 455	6.13	32
9	2.541 641	58.729 162	.017 027 3159	.393 447	23.106 793	.043 277 3159	17.32	.557 983	6.20	36
10	2.819 206	69.303 084	.014 429 3722	.354 710	24.582 484	.040 679 3722	16.28	.627 175	6.27	40
11	3.127 084	81.031 754	.012 340 8410	.319 787	25.912 884	.038 590 8410	15.44	.697 997	6.35	44
12	3.468 584	94.041 280	.010 633 6281	.288 302	27.112 300	.036 883 6281	14.76	.770 414	6.42	48
13	3.847 378	108.471 539	.009 219 0081	.259 917	28.193 627	.035 469 0081	14.19	.844 388	6.50	52
14	4.267 539	124.477 687	.008 033 5683	.234 327	29.168 492	.034 283 5683	13.72	.919 880	6.57	56
15	4.733 585	142.231 821	.007 030 7755	.211 256	30.047 377	.033 280 7755	13.32	.996 847	6.65	60
16	5.250 527	161.924 834	.006 175 7049	.190 457	30.839 730	.032 425 7049	12.98	1.075 245	6.72	64
17	5.823 922	183.768 467	.005 441 6300	.171 706	31.554 073	.031 691 6300	12.68	1.155 031	6.79	68
18	6.459 937	207.997 581	.004 807 7482	.154 800	32.198 084	.031 057 7482	12.43	1.236 158	6.87	72
19	7.165 408	234.872 689	.004 257 6257	.139 559	32.778 690	.030 507 6257	12.21	1.318 580	6.94	76
20	7.947 922	264.682 753	.003 778 1079	.125 819	33.302 132	.030 028 1079	12.02	1.402 249	7.01	80
21	8.815 893	297.748 290	.003 358 5415	.113 432	33.774 038	.029 608 5415	11.85	1.487 117	7.08	84
22	9.778 652	334.424 821	.002 990 2087	.102 264	34.199 482	.029 240 2087	11.70	1.573 138	7.15	88
23	10.846 551	375.106 694	.002 665 9082	.092 195	34.583 040	.028 915 9082	11.57	1.660 264	7.22	92
24	12.031 072	420.231 321	.002 379 6418	.083 118	34.928 834	.028 629 6418	11.46	1.748 446	7.29	96
25	13.344 952	470.283 882	.002 126 3752	.074 935	35.240 583	.028 376 3752	11.36	1.837 638	7.35	100
26	14.802 317	525.802 543	.001 901 8546	.067 557	35.521 638	.028 151 8546	11.27	1.927 793	7.41	104
27	16.418 836	587.384 241	.001 702 4631	.060 906	35.775 023	.027 952 4631	11.19	2.018 866	7.48	108
28	18.211 892	655.691 105	.001 525 1084	.054 909	36.003 460	.027 775 1084	11.12	2.110 812	7.54	112
29	20.200 761	731.457 570	.001 367 1333	.049 503	36.209 406	.027 617 1333	11.05	2.203 587	7.60	116
30	22.406 830	815.498 278	.001 226 2442	.044 629	36.395 076	.027 476 2442	11.00	2.297 149	7.66	120
31	24.853 817	908.716 837	.001 100 4528	.040 235	36.562 466	.027 350 4528	10.95	2.391 456	7.71	124
32	27.568 033	1012.115 534	.000 988 0295	.036 274	36.713 375	.027 238 0295	10.90	2.486 468	7.77	128
33	30.578 660	1126.806 113	.000 887 4641	.032 703	36.849 427	.027 137 4641	10.86	2.582 145	7.82	132
34	33.918 070	1254.021 730	.000 797 4343	.029 483	36.972 083	.027 047 4343	10.82	2.678 451	7.88	136
35	37.622 168	1395.130 208	.000 716 7790	.026 580	37.082 664	.026 966 7790	10.79	2.775 349	7.93	140
36	41.730 780	1551.648 748	.000 644 4758	.023 963	37.182 357	.026 894 4758	10.76	2.872 805	7.98	144
37	46.288 081	1725.260 239	.000 579 6227	.021 604	37.272 235	.026 829 6227	10.74	2.970 784	8.03	148
38	51.343 073	1917.831 356	.000 521 4223	.019 477	37.353 264	.026 771 4223	10.71	3.069 256	8.08	152
39	56.950 106	2131.432 625	.000 469 1680	.017 559	37.426 315	.026 719 1680	10.69	3.168 190	8.12	156
40	63.169 468	2368.360 691	.000 422 2330	.015 830	37.492 174	.026 672 2330	10.67	3.267 557	8.17	160
41	70.068 029	2631.163 009	.000 380 0601	.014 272	37.551 549	.026 630 0601	10.66	3.367 330	8.21	164
42	77.719 962	2922.665 232	.000 342 1535	.012 867	37.605 078	.026 592 1535	10.64	3.467 482	8.26	168
43	86.207 542	3246.001 596	.000 308 0713	.011 600	37.653 337	.026 558 0713	10.63	3.567 988	8.30	172
44	95.622 026	3604.648 621	.000 277 4196	.010 458	37.696 844	.026 527 4196	10.62	3.668 826	8.34	176
45	106.064 640	4002.462 483	.000 249 8462	.009 428	37.736 068	.026 499 8462	10.60	3.769 972	8.38	180
46	117.647 663	4443.720 483	.000 225 0367	.008 500	37.771 430	.026 475 0367	10.60	3.871 407	8.42	184
47	130.495 635	4933.167 035	.000 202 7095	.007 663	37.803 311	.026 452 7095	10.59	3.973 109	8.45	188
48	144.746 698	5476.064 676	.000 182 6129	.006 909	37.832 053	.026 432 6129	10.58	4.075 062	8.49	192
49	160.554 080	6078.250 648	.000 164 5210	.006 228	37.857 965	.026 414 5210	10.57	4.177 246	8.52	196
50	178.087 741	6746.199 665	.000 148 2316	.005 615	37.881 325	.026 398 2316	10.56	4.279 646	8.56	200

Effective Rate is 10.92 %

Annual Percentage Rate is 10.50 %

	Amount Of 1	Amount Of 1 Per Period	Sinking Fund Payment	Present Worth Of 1	Present Worth of 1 Per Period	Periodic Payment To Amortize 1	Constant Annual Percent	Total Interest	Annual Add On Rate	
	What a single $ 1 deposit grows to in the future. The deposit is made at the beginning of the first period.	What a series of $ 1 deposits grow to in the future. A deposit is made at the end of each period.	The amount to be deposited at the end of each period that grows to $ 1 in the future.	What $ 1 to be paid in the future is worth today. Value today of a single $ 1 payment tomorrow.	What $ 1 to be paid at the end of each period is worth today. Value today of a series of $ 1 payments tomorrow.	The mortgage payment to amortize a loan of $ 1. An annuity certain, payable at the end of each period, worth $ 1 today.	The annual payment, including interest and principal, to amortize completely a loan of $ 100.	The total interest paid over the term on a loan of $1. The loan is amortized by regular periodic payments.	The average annual interest rate on a loan that is completely amortized by regular periodic payments.	
	$S = (1+i)^n$	$S\overline{n}| = \dfrac{(1+i)^n - 1}{i}$	$\dfrac{1}{S\overline{n}|} = \dfrac{i}{(1+i)^n - 1}$	$V^n = \dfrac{1}{(1+i)^n}$	$A\overline{n}| = \dfrac{1 - V^n}{i}$	$\dfrac{1}{A\overline{n}|} = \dfrac{i}{1 - V^n}$				

YEAR										PERIODS
	1.026 563	1.000 000	1.000 000 0000	.974 125	.974 125	1.026 562 5000	410.63	.026 562	10.62	1
	1.053 831	2.026 563	.493 446 4148	.948 919	1.923 044	.520 008 9148	208.01	.040 018	8.00	2
	1.081 823	3.080 393	.324 633 8952	.924 366	2.847 410	.351 196 3952	140.48	.053 589	7.15	3
	1.110 559	4.162 216	.240 256 6321	.900 448	3.747 857	.266 819 1321	106.73	.067 277	6.73	4
1	1.110 559	4.162 216	.240 256 6321	.900 448	3.747 857	.266 819 1321	106.73	.067 277	6.73	4
2	1.233 341	8.784 602	.113 835 5515	.810 806	7.122 606	.140 398 0515	56.16	.123 184	6.16	8
3	1.369 698	13.918 033	.071 849 2308	.730 088	10.161 390	.098 411 7308	39.37	.180 941	6.03	12
4	1.521 130	19.619 011	.050 970 9678	.657 406	12.897 656	.077 533 4678	31.02	.240 535	6.01	16
5	1.689 304	25.950 283	.038 535 2252	.591 960	15.361 520	.065 097 7252	26.04	.301 955	6.04	20
6	1.876 072	32.981 533	.030 319 9977	.533 029	17.580 100	.056 882 4977	22.76	.365 180	6.09	24
7	2.083 488	40.790 150	.024 515 7228	.479 964	19.577 815	.051 078 2228	20.44	.430 190	6.15	28
8	2.313 836	49.462 078	.020 217 5088	.432 183	21.376 653	.046 780 0088	18.72	.496 960	6.21	32
9	2.569 652	59.092 765	.016 922 5453	.389 158	22.996 412	.043 485 0453	17.40	.565 462	6.28	36
10	2.853 749	69.788 210	.014 329 0679	.350 416	24.454 919	.040 891 5679	16.36	.635 663	6.36	40
11	3.169 257	81.666 131	.012 244 9782	.315 531	25.768 229	.038 807 4782	15.53	.707 529	6.43	44
12	3.519 646	94.857 262	.010 542 1554	.284 119	26.950 796	.037 104 6554	14.85	.781 023	6.51	48
13	3.908 774	109.506 789	.009 131 8539	.255 835	28.015 635	.035 694 3539	14.28	.856 106	6.59	52
14	4.340 924	125.775 951	.007 950 6455	.230 366	28.974 467	.034 513 1455	13.81	.932 736	6.66	56
15	4.820 851	143.843 813	.006 951 9848	.207 432	29.837 845	.033 514 4848	13.41	1.010 869	6.74	60
16	5.353 839	163.909 238	.006 100 9374	.186 782	30.615 271	.032 663 4374	13.07	1.090 460	6.82	64
17	5.945 753	186.193 072	.005 370 7691	.168 187	31.315 303	.031 933 2691	12.78	1.171 462	6.89	68
18	6.603 109	210.940 583	.004 740 6715	.151 444	31.945 645	.031 303 1715	12.53	1.253 828	6.97	72
19	7.333 141	238.424 150	.004 194 2060	.136 367	32.513 235	.030 756 7060	12.31	1.337 510	7.04	76
20	8.143 885	268.946 269	.003 718 2148	.122 792	33.024 319	.030 280 7148	12.12	1.422 457	7.11	80
21	9.044 264	302.842 878	.003 302 0423	.110 567	33.484 525	.029 864 5423	11.95	1.508 622	7.18	84
22	10.044 187	340.487 058	.002 936 9692	.099 560	33.898 915	.029 499 4692	11.80	1.595 953	7.25	88
23	11.154 661	382.293 136	.002 615 7938	.089 649	34.272 052	.029 178 2938	11.68	1.684 403	7.32	92
24	12.387 908	428.721 247	.002 332 5179	.080 724	34.608 042	.028 895 0179	11.56	1.773 922	7.39	96
25	13.757 501	480.282 396	.002 082 1084	.072 688	34.910 584	.028 644 6084	11.46	1.864 461	7.46	100
26	15.278 515	537.544 087	.001 860 3125	.065 451	35.183 007	.028 422 8125	11.37	1.955 973	7.52	104
27	16.967 690	601.136 566	.001 663 5155	.058 936	35.428 309	.028 226 0155	11.30	2.048 410	7.59	108
28	18.843 619	671.759 758	.001 488 6274	.053 068	35.649 191	.028 051 1274	11.23	2.141 726	7.65	112
29	20.926 948	750.190 968	.001 332 9939	.047 785	35.848 084	.027 895 4939	11.16	2.235 877	7.71	116
30	23.240 607	837.293 445	.001 194 3244	.043 028	36.027 176	.027 756 8244	11.11	2.330 819	7.77	120
31	25.810 062	934.025 872	.001 070 6342	.038 745	36.188 439	.027 633 1342	11.06	2.426 509	7.83	124
32	28.663 593	1041.452 926	.000 960 1970	.034 887	36.333 649	.027 522 6970	11.01	2.522 905	7.88	128
33	31.832 608	1160.756 993	.000 861 5068	.031 414	36.464 402	.027 424 0068	10.97	2.619 969	7.94	132
34	35.351 985	1293.251 182	.000 773 2450	.028 287	36.582 138	.027 335 7450	10.94	2.717 661	7.99	136
35	39.260 460	1440.393 778	.000 694 2546	.025 471	36.688 154	.027 256 7546	10.91	2.815 946	8.05	140
36	43.601 051	1603.804 291	.000 623 5175	.022 935	36.783 615	.027 186 0175	10.88	2.914 787	8.10	144
37	48.421 534	1785.281 286	.000 560 1358	.020 652	36.869 573	.027 122 6358	10.85	3.014 150	8.15	148
38	53.774 964	1986.822 170	.000 503 3163	.018 596	36.946 974	.027 065 8163	10.83	3.114 004	8.19	152
39	59.720 263	2210.645 186	.000 452 3566	.016 745	37.016 669	.027 014 8566	10.81	3.214 318	8.24	156
40	66.322 867	2459.213 820	.000 406 6340	.015 078	37.079 426	.026 969 1340	10.79	3.315 061	8.29	160
41	73.655 448	2735.263 919	.000 365 5954	.013 577	37.135 935	.026 928 0954	10.78	3.416 208	8.33	164
42	81.798 710	3041.833 803	.000 328 7491	.012 225	37.186 819	.026 891 2491	10.76	3.517 730	8.38	168
43	90.842 283	3382.297 704	.000 295 6570	.011 008	37.232 637	.026 858 1570	10.75	3.619 603	8.42	172
44	100.885 702	3760.402 908	.000 265 9290	.009 912	37.273 893	.026 828 4290	10.74	3.721 803	8.46	176
45	112.039 511	4180.310 993	.000 239 2167	.008 925	37.311 043	.026 801 7167	10.73	3.824 309	8.50	180
46	124.426 472	4646.643 638	.000 215 2091	.008 037	37.344 494	.026 777 7091	10.72	3.927 098	8.54	184
47	138.182 921	5164.533 490	.000 193 6283	.007 237	37.374 615	.026 756 1283	10.71	4.030 152	8.57	188
48	153.460 267	5739.680 655	.000 174 2207	.006 516	37.401 738	.026 736 7207	10.70	4.133 451	8.61	192
49	170.426 660	6378.415 436	.000 156 7788	.005 868	37.426 160	.026 719 2788	10.69	4.236 979	8.65	196
50	189.268 838	7087.768 008	.000 141 0881	.005 283	37.448 151	.026 703 5881	10.69	4.340 718	8.68	200

QUARTERLY COMPOUND INTEREST AND ANNUITY

10.75 % Q

	Amount Of 1	Amount Of 1 Per Period	Sinking Fund Payment	Present Worth Of 1	Present Worth of 1 Per Period	Periodic Payment To Amortize 1	Constant Annual Percent	Total Interest	Annual Add On Rate
	What a single $ 1 deposit grows to in the future. The deposit is made at the beginning of the first period.	What a series of $ 1 deposits grow to in the future. A deposit is made at the end of each period.	The amount to be deposited at the end of each period that grows to $ 1 in the future.	What $ 1 to be paid in the future is worth today. Value today of a single $ 1 payment tomorrow.	What $ 1 to be paid at the end of each period is worth today. Value today of a series of $ 1 payments tomorrow.	The mortgage payment to amortize a loan of $ 1. An annuity certain, payable at the end of each period, worth $ 1 today.	The annual interest payment, including interest and principal, to amortize completely a loan of $ 100.	The total interest paid over the term on a loan is amortized by regular periodic payments.	The average annual interest rate on a loan that is completely amortized by regular periodic payments.

$$S = (1+i)^n \qquad S\overline{n}| = \frac{(1+i)^n - 1}{i} \qquad \frac{1}{S\overline{n}|} = \frac{i}{(1+i)^n - 1} \qquad V^n = \frac{1}{(1+i)^n} \qquad A\overline{n}| = \frac{1 - V^n}{i} \qquad \frac{1}{A\overline{n}|} = \frac{i}{1 - V^n}$$

YEAR ... **PERIODS**

	1.026 875	1.000 000	1.000 000 0000	.973 828	.973 828	1.026 875 0000	410.75	.026 875	10.75 1
	1.054 472	2.026 875	.493 370 3361	.948 342	1.922 170	.520 245 3361	208.10	.040 491	8.10 2
	1.082 811	3.081 347	.324 533 3660	.923 522	2.845 692	.351 408 3660	140.57	.054 225	7.23 3
	1.111 912	4.164 158	.240 144 5590	.899 352	3.745 044	.267 019 5590	106.81	.068 078	6.81 4

YEAR	Amount Of 1	Amount Of 1 Per Period	Sinking Fund Payment	Present Worth Of 1	Present Worth of 1 Per Period	Periodic Payment To Amortize 1	Constant Annual Percent	Total Interest	Annual Add On Rate	PERIODS
1	1.111 912	4.164 158	.240 144 5590	.899 352	3.745 044	.267 019 5590	106.81	.068 078	6.81	4
2	1.236 348	8.794 335	.113 709 5610	.808 834	7.113 157	.140 584 5610	56.24	.124 676	6.23	8
3	1.374 710	13.942 683	.071 722 2060	.727 426	10.142 275	.098 597 2060	39.44	.183 166	6.11	12
4	1.528 556	19.667 192	.050 846 0996	.654 212	12.866 519	.077 721 0996	31.09	.243 538	6.09	16
5	1.699 619	26.032 340	.038 413 7570	.588 367	15.316 573	.065 288 7570	26.12	.305 775	6.12	20
6	1.889 827	33.109 824	.030 202 5164	.529 149	17.520 034	.057 077 5164	22.84	.369 860	6.16	24
7	2.101 320	40.979 361	.024 402 5279	.475 891	19.501 720	.051 277 5279	20.52	.435 771	6.23	28
8	2.336 483	49.729 592	.020 108 7514	.427 994	21.283 954	.046 983 7514	18.80	.503 480	6.29	32
9	2.597 963	59.459 076	.016 818 2902	.384 917	22.886 809	.043 693 2902	17.48	.572 958	6.37	36
10	2.888 705	70.277 405	.014 229 3245	.346 176	24.328 340	.041 104 3245	16.45	.644 173	6.44	40
11	3.211 985	82.306 431	.012 149 7189	.311 334	25.624 784	.039 024 7189	15.61	.717 088	6.52	44
12	3.571 444	95.681 647	.010 451 3251	.279 999	26.790 743	.037 326 3251	14.94	.791 664	6.60	48
13	3.971 131	110.553 707	.009 045 3774	.251 817	27.839 351	.035 920 3774	14.37	.867 860	6.68	52
14	4.415 547	127.090 125	.007 868 4319	.226 473	28.782 419	.034 743 4319	13.90	.945 632	6.75	56
15	4.909 699	145.477 163	.006 873 9311	.203 678	29.630 568	.033 748 9311	13.50	1.024 936	6.83	60
16	5.459 152	165.921 927	.006 026 9310	.183 179	30.393 353	.032 901 9310	13.17	1.105 724	6.91	64
17	6.070 095	188.654 700	.005 300 6896	.164 742	31.079 365	.032 175 6896	12.88	1.187 947	6.99	68
18	6.749 410	213.931 538	.004 674 3926	.148 161	31.696 331	.031 549 3926	12.62	1.271 556	7.06	72
19	7.504 748	242.037 151	.004 131 5971	.133 249	32.251 201	.031 006 5971	12.41	1.356 501	7.14	76
20	8.344 618	273.288 113	.003 659 1420	.119 838	32.750 224	.030 534 1420	12.22	1.442 731	7.21	80
21	9.278 479	308.036 425	.003 246 3693	.107 776	33.199 022	.030 121 3693	12.05	1.530 195	7.29	84
22	10.316 850	346.673 482	.002 884 5587	.096 929	33.602 649	.029 759 5587	11.91	1.618 841	7.36	88
23	11.471 427	389.634 479	.002 566 5080	.087 173	33.965 652	.029 441 5080	11.78	1.708 619	7.43	92
24	12.755 214	437.403 318	.002 286 2195	.078 399	34.292 119	.029 161 2195	11.67	1.799 477	7.50	96
25	14.182 673	490.518 051	.002 038 6610	.070 509	34.585 728	.028 913 6610	11.57	1.891 366	7.57	100
26	15.769 880	549.576 947	.001 819 5814	.063 412	34.849 785	.028 694 5814	11.48	1.984 236	7.63	104
27	17.534 716	615.245 228	.001 625 3682	.057 030	35.087 266	.028 500 3682	11.41	2.078 040	7.70	108
28	19.497 056	688.262 563	.001 452 9339	.051 290	35.300 845	.028 327 9339	11.34	2.172 729	7.76	112
29	21.679 006	769.451 395	.001 299 6272	.046 128	35.492 927	.028 174 6272	11.27	2.268 257	7.82	116
30	24.105 142	859.726 213	.001 163 1610	.041 485	35.665 677	.028 038 1610	11.22	2.364 579	7.88	120
31	26.802 791	960.103 844	.001 041 5540	.037 310	35.821 040	.027 916 5540	11.17	2.461 653	7.94	124
32	29.802 338	1071.714 912	.000 933 0840	.033 554	35.960 766	.027 808 0840	11.13	2.559 435	8.00	128
33	33.137 570	1195.816 571	.000 836 2487	.030 177	36.086 429	.027 711 2487	11.09	2.657 885	8.05	132
34	36.846 054	1333.806 666	.000 749 7338	.027 140	36.199 444	.027 624 7338	11.05	2.756 964	8.11	136
35	40.969 561	1487.239 474	.000 672 3867	.024 408	36.301 084	.027 547 3867	11.02	2.856 634	8.16	140
36	45.554 536	1657.843 219	.000 603 1933	.021 952	36.392 494	.027 478 1933	11.00	2.956 860	8.21	144
37	50.652 625	1847.539 528	.000 541 2604	.019 742	36.474 705	.027 416 2604	10.97	3.057 607	8.26	148
38	56.321 249	2058.465 084	.000 485 7989	.017 755	36.548 640	.027 360 7989	10.95	3.158 841	8.31	152
39	62.624 259	2292.995 691	.000 436 1107	.015 968	36.615 135	.027 311 1107	10.93	3.260 533	8.36	156
40	69.632 650	2553.773 031	.000 391 5775	.014 361	36.674 937	.027 266 5775	10.91	3.362 652	8.41	160
41	77.425 363	2843.734 421	.000 351 6503	.012 916	36.728 719	.027 226 6503	10.90	3.465 171	8.45	164
42	86.090 171	3166.145 901	.000 315 8414	.011 616	36.777 089	.027 190 8414	10.88	3.568 061	8.50	168
43	95.724 674	3524.639 016	.000 283 7170	.010 447	36.820 591	.027 158 7170	10.87	3.671 299	8.54	172
44	106.437 390	3923.251 727	.000 254 8906	.009 395	36.859 714	.027 129 8906	10.86	3.774 861	8.58	176
45	118.348 986	4366.473 887	.000 229 0177	.008 450	36.894 899	.027 104 0177	10.85	3.878 723	8.62	180
46	131.593 629	4859.297 819	.000 205 7910	.007 599	36.926 543	.027 080 7910	10.84	3.982 866	8.66	184
47	146.320 503	5407.274 543	.000 184 9361	.006 834	36.955 002	.027 059 9361	10.83	4.087 268	8.70	188
48	162.695 488	6016.576 307	.000 166 2075	.006 146	36.980 597	.027 041 2075	10.82	4.191 912	8.73	192
49	180.903 027	6694.066 103	.000 149 3860	.005 528	37.003 616	.027 024 3860	10.81	4.296 780	8.77	196
50	201.148 202	7447.374 974	.000 134 2755	.004 971	37.024 318	.027 009 2755	10.81	4.401 855	8.80	200

Effective Rate is 11.19 %

Annual Percentage Rate is 10.75 %

QUARTERLY COMPOUND INTEREST AND ANNUITY

	Amount Of 1	Amount Of 1 Per Period	Sinking Fund Payment	Present Worth Of 1	Present Worth of 1 Per Period	Periodic Payment To Amortize 1	Constant Annual Percent	Total Interest	Annual Add On Rate	
	What a single $ 1 deposit grows to in the future. The deposit is made at the beginning of the first period.	What a series of $ 1 deposits grow to in the future. A deposit is made at the end of each period.	The amount to be deposited at the end of each period that grows to $ 1 in the future.	What $ 1 to be paid in the future is worth today. Value today of a single $ 1 payment tomorrow.	What $ 1 to be paid at the end of each period is worth today. Value today of a series of $ 1 payments tomorrow.	The mortgage payment to amortize a loan of $ 1. An annuity certain, payable at the end of each period, worth $ 1 today.	The annual payment, including interest and principal, to amortize completely a loan of $ 100.	The total interest paid over the term on a loan of $1. The loan is amortized by regular periodic payments.	The average annual interest rate on a loan that is completely amortized by regular periodic payments.	
	$S = (1+i)^n$	$S\overline{n}| = \dfrac{(1+i)^n - 1}{i}$	$\dfrac{1}{S\overline{n}|} = \dfrac{i}{(1+i)^n - 1}$	$V^n = \dfrac{1}{(1+i)^n}$	$A\overline{n}| = \dfrac{1-V^n}{i}$	$\dfrac{1}{A\overline{n}|} = \dfrac{i}{1-V^n}$				

YEAR										PERIODS
	1.027 187	1.000 000	1.000 000 0000	.973 532	.973 532	1.027 187 5000	410.88	.027 188	10.88	1
	1.055 114	2.027 187	.493 294 2809	.947 765	1.921 297	.520 481 7809	208.20	.040 964	8.19	2
	1.083 800	3.082 302	.324 432 8785	.922 679	2.843 976	.351 620 3785	140.65	.054 861	7.31	3
	1.113 266	4.166 102	.240 032 5444	.898 258	3.742 234	.267 220 0444	106.89	.068 880	6.89	4
1	1.113 266	4.166 102	.240 032 5444	.898 258	3.742 234	.267 220 0444	106.89	.068 880	6.89	4
2	1.239 361	8.804 081	.113 583 6931	.806 867	7.103 726	.140 771 1931	56.31	.126 170	6.31	8
3	1.379 738	13.967 384	.071 595 3657	.724 775	10.123 213	.098 782 8657	39.52	.185 394	6.18	12
4	1.536 016	19.715 514	.050 721 4763	.651 035	12.835 491	.077 908 9763	31.17	.246 544	6.16	16
5	1.709 994	26.114 712	.038 292 5923	.584 797	15.271 817	.065 480 0923	26.20	.309 602	6.19	20
6	1.903 678	33.238 719	.030 085 3950	.525 299	17.460 266	.057 272 8950	22.91	.374 549	6.24	24
7	2.119 299	41.169 634	.024 289 7470	.471 854	19.426 058	.051 477 2470	20.60	.441 363	6.31	28
8	2.359 344	49.998 851	.020 000 4595	.423 847	21.191 847	.047 187 9595	18.88	.510 015	6.38	32
9	2.626 577	59.828 117	.016 714 5490	.380 724	22.777 980	.043 902 0490	17.57	.580 474	6.45	36
10	2.924 079	70.770 704	.014 130 1406	.341 988	24.202 737	.041 317 6406	16.53	.652 706	6.53	40
11	3.255 277	82.952 713	.012 055 0608	.307 194	25.482 537	.039 242 5608	15.70	.726 673	6.61	44
12	3.623 989	96.514 527	.010 361 1345	.275 939	26.632 127	.037 548 6345	15.02	.802 334	6.69	48
13	4.034 463	111.612 433	.008 959 5753	.247 864	27.664 755	.036 147 0753	14.46	.879 648	6.77	52
14	4.491 430	128.420 417	.007 786 9238	.222 646	28.592 322	.034 974 4238	13.99	.958 568	6.85	56
15	5.000 156	147.132 171	.006 796 6101	.199 994	29.425 517	.033 984 1101	13.60	1.039 047	6.93	60
16	5.566 503	167.963 329	.005 953 6805	.179 646	30.173 940	.033 141 1805	13.26	1.121 036	7.01	64
17	6.196 998	191.153 947	.005 231 3856	.161 368	30.846 218	.032 418 8856	12.97	1.204 484	7.09	68
18	6.898 906	216.971 271	.004 608 9051	.144 951	31.450 096	.031 796 4051	12.72	1.289 341	7.16	72
19	7.680 317	245.712 817	.004 069 7918	.130 203	31.992 535	.031 257 2918	12.51	1.375 554	7.24	76
20	8.550 235	277.709 800	.003 600 8812	.116 956	32.479 785	.030 788 3812	12.32	1.463 070	7.32	80
21	9.518 685	313.330 950	.003 191 5136	.105 057	32.917 461	.030 379 0136	12.16	1.551 837	7.39	84
22	10.596 828	352.986 761	.002 832 9674	.094 368	33.310 607	.030 020 4674	12.01	1.641 801	7.46	88
23	11.797 087	397.134 222	.002 518 0404	.084 767	33.663 754	.029 705 5404	11.89	1.732 910	7.53	92
24	13.133 294	446.282 086	.002 240 7352	.076 142	33.980 971	.029 428 2352	11.78	1.825 111	7.60	96
25	14.620 848	500.996 725	.001 996 0210	.068 395	34.265 913	.029 183 5210	11.68	1.918 352	7.67	100
26	16.276 892	561.908 668	.001 779 6486	.061 437	34.521 865	.028 967 1486	11.59	2.012 583	7.74	104
27	18.120 509	629.719 855	.001 588 0077	.055 186	34.751 776	.028 775 5077	11.52	2.107 755	7.81	108
28	20.172 944	705.211 737	.001 418 0138	.049 571	34.958 295	.028 605 5138	11.45	2.203 818	7.87	112
29	22.457 851	789.254 275	.001 267 0188	.044 528	35.143 803	.028 454 5188	11.39	2.300 724	7.93	116
30	25.001 559	882.815 965	.001 132 7389	.039 998	35.310 437	.028 320 2389	11.33	2.398 429	7.99	120
31	27.833 383	986.975 004	.001 013 1969	.035 928	35.460 117	.028 200 6969	11.29	2.496 886	8.05	124
32	30.985 956	1102.931 709	.000 906 6744	.032 273	35.594 568	.028 094 1744	11.24	2.596 054	8.11	128
33	34.495 608	1232.022 353	.000 811 6736	.028 989	35.715 340	.027 999 1736	11.20	2.695 891	8.17	132
34	38.402 783	1375.734 564	.000 726 8844	.026 040	35.823 824	.027 914 3844	11.17	2.796 356	8.22	136
35	42.752 509	1535.724 467	.000 651 1585	.023 390	35.921 271	.027 838 6585	11.14	2.897 412	8.28	140
36	47.594 910	1713.835 769	.000 583 4865	.021 011	36.008 804	.027 770 9865	11.11	2.999 022	8.33	144
37	52.985 790	1912.121 006	.000 522 9795	.018 873	36.087 430	.027 710 4795	11.09	3.101 151	8.38	148
38	58.987 273	2132.865 197	.000 468 8529	.016 953	36.158 058	.027 656 3529	11.07	3.203 766	8.43	152
39	65.668 519	2378.612 176	.000 420 4132	.015 228	36.221 499	.027 607 9132	11.05	3.306 834	8.48	156
40	73.106 522	2652.193 905	.000 377 0463	.013 679	36.278 486	.027 564 5463	11.03	3.410 327	8.53	160
41	81.386 997	2956.763 113	.000 338 2077	.012 287	36.329 617	.027 525 7077	11.02	3.514 216	8.57	164
42	90.605 368	3295.829 623	.000 303 4137	.011 037	36.375 655	.027 490 9137	11.00	3.618 474	8.62	168
43	100.867 866	3673.300 803	.000 272 2347	.009 914	36.416 958	.027 459 7347	10.99	3.723 074	8.66	172
44	112.292 754	4093.526 593	.000 244 2881	.008 905	36.454 058	.027 431 7881	10.98	3.827 995	8.70	176
45	125.011 693	4561.349 631	.000 219 2334	.007 999	36.487 384	.027 406 7334	10.97	3.933 212	8.74	180
46	139.171 254	5082.161 063	.000 196 7667	.007 185	36.517 319	.027 384 2667	10.96	4.038 705	8.78	184
47	154.934 610	5661.962 666	.000 176 6172	.006 454	36.544 208	.027 364 1172	10.95	4.144 454	8.82	188
48	172.483 417	6307.436 013	.000 158 5430	.005 798	36.568 362	.027 346 0430	10.94	4.250 440	8.86	192
49	192.019 904	7026.019 475	.000 142 3281	.005 208	36.590 058	.027 329 8281	10.94	4.356 646	8.90	196
50	213.769 210	7825.993 932	.000 127 7793	.004 678	36.609 547	.027 315 2793	10.93	4.463 056	8.93	200

Effective Rate is 11.33 %

8 - 323

Annual Percentage Rate is 10.875%

	Amount Of 1	Amount Of 1 Per Period	Sinking Fund Payment	Present Worth Of 1	Present Worth of 1 Per Period	Periodic Payment To Amortize 1	Constant Annual Percent	Total Interest	Annual Add On Rate	
	What a single $ 1 deposit grows to in the future. The deposit is made at the beginning of the first period.	What a series of $ 1 deposits grow to in the future. A deposit is made at the end of each period.	The amount to be deposited at the end of each period that grows to $ 1 in the future.	What $ 1 to be paid in the future is worth today. Value today of a single $ 1 payment tomorrow.	What $ 1 to be paid at the end of each period is worth today. Value today of a series of $ 1 payments tomorrow.	The mortgage payment to amortize a loan of $ 1. An annuity certain, payable at the end of each period, worth $ 1 today.	The annual payment, including interest and principal, to amortize completely a loan of $ 100.	The total interest paid over the term on a loan of $1. The loan is amortized by regular periodic payments.	The average annual interest rate on a loan that is completely amortized by regular periodic payments.	
	$S = (1+i)^n$	$S\overline{n} = \dfrac{(1+i)^n - 1}{i}$	$\dfrac{1}{S\overline{n}} = \dfrac{i}{(1+i)^n - 1}$	$V^n = \dfrac{1}{(1+i)^n}$	$A\overline{n} = \dfrac{1 - V^n}{i}$	$\dfrac{1}{A\overline{n}} = \dfrac{i}{1 - V^n}$				

YEAR										PERIODS
	1.027 500	1.000 000	1.000 000 0000	.973 236	.973 236	1.027 500 0000	411.00	.027 500	11.00	1
	1.055 756	2.027 500	.493 218 2491	.947 188	1.920 424	.520 718 2491	208.29	.041 436	8.29	2
	1.084 790	3.083 256	.324 332 4326	.921 838	2.842 262	.351 832 4326	140.74	.055 497	7.40	3
	1.114 621	4.168 046	.239 920 5884	.897 166	3.739 428	.267 420 5884	106.97	.069 682	6.97	4
1	1.114 621	4.168 046	.239 920 5884	.897 166	3.739 428	.267 420 5884	106.97	.069 682	6.97	4
2	1.242 381	8.813 838	.113 457 9478	.804 906	7.094 314	.140 957 9478	56.39	.127 664	6.38	8
3	1.384 784	13.992 137	.071 468 7098	.722 134	10.104 204	.098 968 7098	39.59	.187 625	6.25	12
4	1.543 509	19.763 979	.050 597 0977	.647 874	12.804 573	.078 097 0977	31.24	.249 554	6.24	16
5	1.720 428	26.197 398	.038 171 7306	.581 251	15.227 252	.065 671 7306	26.27	.313 435	6.27	20
6	1.917 626	33.368 222	.029 968 6330	.521 478	17.400 797	.057 468 6330	22.99	.379 247	6.32	24
7	2.137 427	41.360 975	.024 177 3795	.467 852	19.350 826	.051 677 3795	20.68	.446 967	6.39	28
8	2.382 421	50.269 868	.019 892 6322	.419 741	21.100 326	.047 392 6322	18.96	.516 564	6.46	32
9	2.655 498	60.199 910	.016 611 3206	.376 577	22.669 918	.044 111 3206	17.65	.588 008	6.53	36
10	2.959 874	71.268 145	.014 031 5144	.337 852	24.078 101	.041 531 5144	16.62	.661 261	6.61	40
11	3.299 138	83.605 035	.011 961 0021	.303 109	25.341 475	.039 461 0021	15.79	.736 284	6.69	44
12	3.677 290	97.355 996	.010 271 5811	.271 939	26.474 931	.037 771 5811	15.11	.813 036	6.78	48
13	4.098 785	112.683 108	.008 874 4446	.243 975	27.491 829	.036 374 4446	14.55	.891 471	6.86	52
14	4.568 593	129.767 034	.007 706 1174	.218 886	28.404 155	.035 206 1174	14.09	.971 543	6.94	56
15	5.092 251	148.809 140	.006 720 0173	.196 377	29.222 662	.034 220 0173	13.69	1.053 201	7.02	60
16	5.675 932	170.033 877	.005 881 1810	.176 183	29.956 999	.033 381 1810	13.36	1.136 396	7.10	64
17	6.326 514	193.691 420	.005 162 8513	.158 065	30.615 821	.032 662 8513	13.07	1.221 074	7.18	68
18	7.051 667	220.060 621	.004 544 2024	.141 810	31.206 893	.032 044 2024	12.82	1.307 183	7.26	72
19	7.859 938	249.452 292	.004 008 7826	.127 227	31.737 183	.031 508 7826	12.61	1.394 667	7.34	76
20	8.760 854	282.212 873	.003 543 4245	.114 144	32.212 941	.031 043 4245	12.42	1.483 474	7.42	80
21	9.765 034	318.728 514	.003 137 4664	.102 406	32.639 775	.030 637 4664	12.26	1.573 547	7.49	84
22	10.884 315	359.429 624	.002 782 1858	.091 875	33.022 715	.030 282 1858	12.12	1.664 832	7.57	88
23	12.131 889	404.795 946	.002 470 3805	.082 427	33.366 276	.029 970 3805	11.99	1.757 275	7.64	92
24	13.522 461	455.362 213	.002 196 0540	.073 951	33.674 508	.029 696 0540	11.88	1.850 821	7.71	96
25	15.072 422	511.724 449	.001 954 1767	.066 346	33.951 042	.029 454 1767	11.79	1.945 418	7.78	100
26	16.800 042	574.546 995	.001 740 5017	.059 524	34.199 140	.029 240 5017	11.70	2.041 012	7.85	104
27	18.725 684	644.570 341	.001 551 4211	.053 403	34.421 724	.029 051 4211	11.63	2.137 553	7.92	108
28	20.872 046	722.619 851	.001 383 8535	.047 911	34.621 419	.028 883 8535	11.56	2.234 992	7.98	112
29	23.264 426	809.615 495	.001 235 1542	.042 984	34.800 579	.028 735 1542	11.50	2.333 278	8.05	116
30	25.931 024	906.582 688	.001 103 0433	.038 564	34.961 315	.028 603 0433	11.45	2.432 365	8.11	120
31	28.903 271	1014.664 383	.000 985 5476	.034 598	35.105 521	.028 485 5476	11.40	2.532 208	8.17	124
32	32.216 200	1135.134 539	.000 880 9528	.031 040	35.234 899	.028 380 9528	11.36	2.632 762	8.23	128
33	35.908 861	1269.413 135	.000 787 7656	.027 848	35.350 972	.028 287 7656	11.32	2.733 985	8.28	132
34	40.024 780	1419.082 913	.000 704 6805	.024 985	35.455 108	.028 204 6805	11.29	2.835 837	8.34	136
35	44.612 471	1585.908 029	.000 630 5536	.022 415	35.548 536	.028 130 5536	11.26	2.938 278	8.40	140
36	49.726 008	1771.854 851	.000 564 3803	.020 110	35.632 356	.028 064 3803	11.23	3.041 271	8.45	144
37	55.425 666	1979.115 131	.000 505 2763	.018 042	35.707 557	.028 005 2763	11.21	3.144 781	8.50	148
38	61.778 626	2210.131 846	.000 452 4617	.016 187	35.775 024	.027 952 4617	11.19	3.248 774	8.55	152
39	68.859 770	2467.627 987	.000 405 2475	.014 522	35.835 554	.027 905 2475	11.17	3.353 219	8.60	156
40	76.752 563	2754.638 660	.000 363 0240	.013 029	35.889 859	.027 863 0240	11.15	3.458 084	8.65	160
41	85.550 039	3074.546 859	.000 325 2512	.011 689	35.938 579	.027 825 2512	11.14	3.563 341	8.69	164
42	95.355 892	3431.123 337	.000 291 4497	.010 487	35.982 290	.027 791 4497	11.12	3.668 964	8.74	168
43	106.285 704	3828.571 061	.000 261 1941	.009 409	36.021 505	.027 761 1941	11.11	3.774 925	8.78	172
44	118.468 305	4271.574 744	.000 234 1057	.008 441	36.056 688	.027 734 1057	11.10	3.881 203	8.82	176
45	132.047 292	4765.356 067	.000 209 8479	.007 573	36.088 253	.027 709 8479	11.09	3.987 773	8.86	180
46	147.182 719	5315.735 226	.000 188 1207	.006 794	36.116 572	.027 688 1207	11.08	4.094 614	8.90	184
47	164.052 987	5929.199 539	.000 168 6568	.006 096	36.141 978	.027 668 6568	11.07	4.201 707	8.94	188
48	182.856 947	6612.979 903	.000 151 2178	.005 469	36.164 773	.027 651 2178	11.07	4.309 034	8.98	192
49	203.816 241	7375.136 033	.000 135 5907	.004 906	36.185 223	.027 635 5907	11.06	4.416 576	9.01	196
50	227.177 915	8224.651 460	.000 121 5857	.004 402	36.203 570	.027 621 5857	11.05	4.524 317	9.05	200

QUARTERLY COMPOUND INTEREST AND ANNUITY

Amount Of 1	Amount Of 1 Per Period	Sinking Fund Payment	Present Worth Of 1	Present Worth of 1 Per Period	Periodic Payment To Amortize 1	Constant Annual Percent	Total Interest	Annual Add On Rate
What a single $ 1 deposit grows to in the future. The deposit is made at the beginning of the first period.	What a series of $ 1 deposits grow to in the future. A deposit is made at the end of each period.	The amount to be deposited at the end of each period that grows to $ 1 in the future.	What $ 1 to be paid in the future is worth today. Value today of a single $ 1 payment tomorrow.	What $ 1 to be paid at the end of each period is worth today. Value today of a series of $ 1 payments tomorrow.	The mortgage payment to amortize a loan of $ 1. An annuity certain, payable at the end of each period, worth $ 1 today.	The annual payment, including interest and principal, to amortize completely a loan of $ 100.	The total interest paid over the term on a loan of $1. The loan is amortized by regular periodic payments.	The average annual interest rate on a loan that is completely amortized by regular periodic payments.

$$S = (1+i)^n \qquad S\overline{n}| = \frac{(1+i)^n - 1}{i} \qquad \frac{1}{S\overline{n}|} = \frac{i}{(1+i)^n - 1} \qquad V^n = \frac{1}{(1+i)^n} \qquad A\overline{n}| = \frac{1-V^n}{i} \qquad \frac{1}{A\overline{n}|} = \frac{i}{1-V^n}$$

YEAR … **PERIODS**

Amount Of 1	Amount Of 1 Per Period	Sinking Fund Payment	Present Worth Of 1	Present Worth of 1 Per Period	Periodic Payment To Amortize 1	Constant Annual Percent	Total Interest	Annual Add On Rate	
1.027 813	1.000 000	1.000 000 0000	.972 940	.972 940	1.027 812 5000	411.13	.027 813	11.13	1
1.056 399	2.027 813	.493 142 2407	.946 612	1.919 553	.520 954 7407	208.39	.041 909	8.38	2
1.085 780	3.084 211	.324 232 0284	.920 997	2.840 550	.352 044 5284	140.82	.056 134	7.48	3
1.115 978	4.169 991	.239 808 6909	.896 075	3.736 625	.267 621 1909	107.05	.070 485	7.05	4

YEAR	Amount Of 1	Amount Of 1 Per Period	Sinking Fund Payment	Present Worth Of 1	Present Worth of 1 Per Period	Periodic Payment To Amortize 1	Constant Annual Percent	Total Interest	Annual Add On Rate	PERIODS
1	1.115 978	4.169 991	.239 808 6909	.896 075	3.736 625	.267 621 1909	107.05	.070 485	7.05	4
2	1.245 407	8.823 608	.113 332 3249	.802 951	7.084 921	.141 144 8249	56.46	.129 159	6.46	8
3	1.389 846	14.016 942	.071 342 2382	.719 504	10.085 247	.099 154 7382	39.67	.189 857	6.33	12
4	1.551 038	19.812 587	.050 472 9634	.644 730	12.773 764	.078 285 4634	31.32	.252 567	6.31	16
5	1.730 924	26.280 400	.038 051 1717	.577 726	15.182 877	.065 863 6717	26.35	.317 273	6.35	20
6	1.931 672	33.498 335	.029 852 2300	.517 686	17.341 623	.057 664 7300	23.07	.383 954	6.40	24
7	2.155 704	41.553 391	.024 065 4246	.463 886	19.276 022	.051 877 9246	20.76	.452 582	6.47	28
8	2.405 718	50.542 655	.019 785 2684	.415 676	21.009 388	.047 597 7684	19.04	.523 129	6.54	32
9	2.684 728	60.574 475	.016 508 6036	.372 477	22.562 615	.044 321 1036	17.73	.595 560	6.62	36
10	2.996 097	71.769 764	.013 933 4442	.333 768	23.954 423	.041 745 9442	16.70	.669 838	6.70	40
11	3.343 577	84.263 459	.011 867 5404	.299 081	25.201 587	.039 680 0404	15.88	.745 922	6.78	44
12	3.731 358	98.206 145	.010 182 6621	.267 999	26.319 140	.037 995 1621	15.20	.823 768	6.86	48
13	4.164 113	113.765 875	.008 789 9820	.240 147	27.320 552	.036 602 4820	14.65	.903 329	6.95	52
14	4.647 058	131.130 189	.007 626 0090	.215 190	28.217 891	.035 438 5090	14.18	.984 557	7.03	56
15	5.186 014	150.508 379	.006 644 1484	.192 826	29.021 975	.034 456 6484	13.79	1.067 399	7.12	60
16	5.787 477	172.134 010	.005 809 4272	.172 787	29.742 495	.033 621 9272	13.45	1.151 803	7.20	64
17	6.458 696	196.267 736	.005 095 0809	.154 830	30.388 135	.032 907 5809	13.17	1.237 716	7.28	68
18	7.207 762	223.200 440	.004 480 2779	.138 739	30.966 676	.032 292 7779	12.92	1.325 080	7.36	72
19	8.043 703	253.256 741	.003 948 5622	.124 321	31.485 093	.031 761 0622	12.71	1.413 841	7.44	76
20	8.976 595	286.798 908	.003 486 7636	.111 401	31.949 633	.031 299 2636	12.52	1.503 941	7.52	80
21	10.017 681	324.231 223	.003 084 2187	.099 824	32.365 897	.030 896 7187	12.36	1.595 324	7.60	84
22	11.179 510	366.004 859	.002 732 2042	.089 449	32.738 900	.030 544 7042	12.22	1.687 934	7.67	88
23	12.476 086	412.623 312	.002 423 5179	.080 153	33.073 138	.030 236 0179	12.10	1.781 714	7.75	92
24	13.923 036	464.648 473	.002 152 1646	.071 823	33.372 641	.029 964 6646	11.99	1.876 608	7.82	96
25	15.537 800	522.707 402	.001 913 1162	.064 359	33.641 018	.029 725 6162	11.90	1.972 562	7.89	100
26	17.339 840	587.499 881	.001 702 1280	.057 671	33.881 504	.029 514 6280	11.81	2.069 521	7.96	104
27	19.350 878	659.806 854	.001 515 5950	.051 677	34.096 998	.029 328 0950	11.74	2.167 434	8.03	108
28	21.595 152	740.499 835	.001 350 4392	.046 307	34.290 097	.029 162 9392	11.67	2.266 249	8.09	112
29	24.099 711	830.551 415	.001 204 0194	.041 494	34.463 127	.029 016 5194	11.61	2.365 916	8.16	116
30	26.894 744	931.046 986	.001 074 0597	.037 182	34.618 176	.028 886 5597	11.56	2.466 387	8.22	120
31	30.013 939	1043.197 818	.000 958 5910	.033 318	34.757 111	.028 771 0910	11.51	2.567 615	8.28	124
32	33.494 892	1168.355 665	.000 855 9038	.029 855	34.881 607	.028 668 4038	11.47	2.669 556	8.34	128
33	37.379 558	1308.029 051	.000 764 5090	.026 753	34.993 165	.028 577 0090	11.44	2.772 165	8.40	132
34	41.714 759	1463.901 458	.000 683 1061	.023 972	35.093 130	.028 495 6061	11.40	2.875 402	8.46	136
35	46.552 748	1637.851 615	.000 610 5559	.021 481	35.182 705	.028 423 0559	11.37	2.979 228	8.51	140
36	51.951 836	1831.976 139	.000 545 8586	.019 249	35.262 972	.028 358 3586	11.35	3.083 604	8.57	144
37	57.977 099	2048.614 811	.000 488 1347	.017 248	35.334 897	.028 300 6347	11.33	3.188 494	8.62	148
38	64.701 160	2290.378 774	.000 436 6090	.015 456	35.399 347	.028 249 1090	11.30	3.293 865	8.67	152
39	72.205 062	2560.182 005	.000 390 5972	.013 849	35.457 099	.028 203 0972	11.29	3.399 683	8.72	156
40	80.579 251	2861.276 439	.000 349 4944	.012 410	35.508 849	.028 161 9944	11.27	3.505 919	8.76	160
41	89.924 660	3197.291 163	.000 312 7648	.011 120	35.555 221	.028 125 2648	11.26	3.612 543	8.81	164
42	100.353 931	3572.276 156	.000 279 9336	.009 965	35.596 774	.028 092 4336	11.24	3.719 529	8.86	168
43	111.992 765	3990.751 109	.000 250 5794	.008 929	35.634 008	.028 063 0794	11.23	3.826 850	8.90	172
44	124.981 447	4457.759 894	.000 224 3279	.008 001	35.667 373	.028 036 8279	11.22	3.934 482	8.94	176
45	139.476 528	4978.931 360	.000 200 8463	.007 170	35.697 270	.028 013 3463	11.21	4.042 402	8.98	180
46	155.652 718	5560.547 180	.000 179 8384	.006 425	35.724 061	.027 992 3384	11.20	4.150 590	9.02	184
47	173.704 988	6209.617 561	.000 161 0405	.005 757	35.748 067	.027 973 5405	11.19	4.259 026	9.06	188
48	193.850 922	6933.965 740	.000 144 2176	.005 159	35.769 578	.027 956 7176	11.19	4.367 690	9.10	192
49	216.333 338	7742.322 273	.000 129 1602	.004 622	35.788 854	.027 941 6602	11.18	4.476 565	9.14	196
50	241.423 217	8644.430 272	.000 115 6814	.004 142	35.806 127	.027 928 1814	11.18	4.585 636	9.17	200

Effective Rate is 11.60 %

Annual Percentage Rate is 11.125%

Amount Of 1	Amount Of 1 Per Period	Sinking Fund Payment	Present Worth Of 1	Present Worth of 1 Per Period	Periodic Payment To Amortize 1	Constant Annual Percent	Total Interest	Annual Add On Rate
What a single $ 1 deposit grows to in the future. The deposit is made at the beginning of the first period.	What a series of $ 1 deposits grow to in the future. A deposit is made at the end of each period.	The amount to be deposited at the end of each period that grows to $ 1 in the future.	What $ 1 to be paid in the future is worth today. Value today of a single $ 1 payment tomorrow.	What $ 1 to be paid at the end of each period is worth today. Value today of a series of $ 1 payments tomorrow.	The mortgage payment to amortize a loan of $ 1. An annuity certain, payable at the end of each period, worth $ 1 today.	The annual payment, including interest and principal, to amortize completely a loan of $ 100.	The total interest paid over the term on a loan of $1. The loan is amortized by regular periodic payments.	The average annual interest rate on a loan that is completely amortized by regular periodic payments.

$$S = (1+i)^n \qquad S\overline{n}| = \frac{(1+i)^n - 1}{i} \qquad \frac{1}{S\overline{n}|} = \frac{i}{(1+i)^n - 1} \qquad V^n = \frac{1}{(1+i)^n} \qquad A\overline{n}| = \frac{1-V^n}{i} \qquad \frac{1}{A\overline{n}|} = \frac{i}{1-V^n}$$

YEAR									PERIODS
	1.028 125	1.000 000	1.000 000 0000	.972 644	.972 644	1.028 125 0000	411.25	.028 125	11.25	1
	1.057 041	2.028 125	.493 066 2558	.946 037	1.918 681	.521 191 2558	208.48	.042 383	8.48	2
	1.086 770	3.085 166	.324 131 6658	.920 158	2.838 839	.352 256 6658	140.91	.056 770	7.57	3
	1.117 336	4.171 936	.239 696 8520	.894 986	3.733 825	.267 821 8520	107.13	.071 287	7.13	4
1	1.117 336	4.171 936	.239 696 8520	.894 986	3.733 825	.267 821 8520	107.13	.071 287	7.13	4
2	1.248 439	8.833 390	.113 206 8245	.801 000	7.075 547	.141 331 8245	56.54	.130 655	6.53	8
3	1.394 926	14.041 798	.071 215 9507	.716 884	10.066 342	.099 340 9507	39.74	.192 091	6.40	12
4	1.558 600	19.861 339	.050 349 0734	.641 601	12.743 062	.078 474 0734	31.39	.255 585	6.39	16
5	1.741 480	26.363 719	.037 930 9152	.574 224	15.138 690	.066 055 9152	26.43	.321 118	6.42	20
6	1.945 817	33.629 061	.029 736 1854	.513 923	17.282 743	.057 861 1854	23.15	.388 668	6.48	24
7	2.174 131	41.746 887	.023 953 8817	.459 954	19.201 641	.052 078 8817	20.84	.458 209	6.55	28
8	2.429 234	50.817 224	.019 678 3672	.411 652	20.919 028	.047 803 3672	19.13	.529 708	6.62	32
9	2.714 270	60.951 836	.016 406 3968	.368 423	22.456 066	.044 531 3968	17.82	.603 130	6.70	36
10	3.032 751	72.275 599	.013 835 9283	.329 734	23.831 694	.041 960 9283	16.79	.678 437	6.78	40
11	3.388 601	84.928 044	.011 774 6737	.295 107	25.062 862	.039 899 6737	15.96	.755 586	6.87	44
12	3.786 205	99.065 072	.010 094 3751	.264 117	26.164 740	.038 219 3751	15.29	.834 530	6.95	48
13	4.230 462	114.860 879	.008 706 1845	.236 381	27.150 905	.036 831 1845	14.74	.915 222	7.04	52
14	4.726 847	132.510 098	.007 546 5947	.211 558	28.033 510	.035 671 5947	14.27	.997 609	7.13	56
15	5.281 474	152.230 200	.006 568 9988	.189 341	28.823 429	.034 693 9988	13.88	1.081 640	7.21	60
16	5.901 180	174.264 175	.005 738 4141	.169 458	29.530 395	.033 863 4141	13.55	1.167 259	7.30	64
17	6.593 599	198.883 522	.005 028 0686	.151 662	30.163 120	.033 153 0686	13.27	1.254 409	7.38	68
18	7.367 264	226.391 597	.004 417 1251	.135 736	30.729 401	.032 542 1251	13.02	1.343 033	7.46	72
19	8.231 707	257.127 352	.003 889 1234	.121 481	31.236 214	.032 014 1234	12.81	1.433 073	7.54	76
20	9.197 580	291.469 508	.003 430 8906	.108 724	31.689 804	.031 555 8906	12.63	1.524 471	7.62	80
21	10.276 784	329.841 226	.003 031 7617	.097 307	32.095 762	.031 156 7617	12.47	1.617 168	7.70	84
22	11.482 618	372.715 316	.002 683 0129	.087 088	32.459 088	.030 808 0129	12.33	1.711 105	7.78	88
23	12.829 939	420.620 069	.002 377 4424	.077 943	32.784 260	.030 502 4424	12.21	1.806 225	7.85	92
24	14.335 349	474.145 759	.002 109 0561	.069 758	33.075 284	.030 234 0561	12.10	1.902 469	7.93	96
25	16.017 398	533.951 924	.001 872 8278	.062 432	33.335 747	.029 997 8278	12.00	1.999 783	8.00	100
26	17.896 811	600.775 487	.001 664 5153	.055 876	33.568 858	.029 789 5153	11.92	2.098 110	8.07	104
27	19.996 746	675.439 841	.001 480 5168	.050 008	33.777 488	.029 605 5168	11.85	2.197 396	8.14	108
28	22.343 078	758.864 990	.001 317 7575	.044 757	33.964 210	.029 442 7575	11.78	2.297 589	8.21	112
29	24.964 719	852.078 888	.001 173 6003	.040 057	34.131 323	.029 298 6003	11.72	2.398 638	8.27	116
30	27.893 972	956.230 104	.001 045 7734	.035 850	34.280 887	.029 170 7734	11.67	2.500 493	8.33	120
31	31.166 931	1072.601 977	.000 932 3123	.032 085	34.414 745	.029 057 3123	11.63	2.603 107	8.40	124
32	34.823 925	1202.628 427	.000 831 5120	.028 716	34.534 546	.028 956 5120	11.59	2.706 434	8.46	128
33	38.910 014	1347.911 622	.000 741 8884	.025 700	34.641 766	.028 866 8884	11.55	2.810 429	8.52	132
34	43.475 548	1510.241 724	.000 662 1457	.023 001	34.737 727	.028 787 1457	11.52	2.915 052	8.57	136
35	48.576 783	1691.618 943	.000 591 1497	.020 586	34.823 610	.028 716 1497	11.49	3.020 261	8.63	140
36	54.276 574	1894.278 187	.000 527 9056	.018 424	34.900 474	.028 652 9056	11.47	3.126 018	8.68	144
37	60.645 154	2120.716 597	.000 471 5387	.016 489	34.969 267	.028 596 5387	11.44	3.232 288	8.74	148
38	67.760 996	2373.724 318	.000 421 2789	.014 758	35.030 835	.028 546 2789	11.42	3.339 034	8.79	152
39	75.711 781	2656.418 879	.000 376 4467	.013 208	35.085 938	.028 501 4467	11.41	3.446 226	8.84	156
40	84.505 476	2972.283 608	.000 336 4416	.011 821	35.135 255	.028 461 4416	11.39	3.553 831	8.88	160
41	94.521 547	3325.210 547	.000 300 7328	.010 580	35.179 392	.028 425 7328	11.38	3.661 820	8.93	164
42	105.612 299	3719.548 420	.000 268 8498	.009 469	35.218 894	.028 393 8498	11.36	3.770 169	8.98	168
43	118.004 393	4160.156 206	.000 240 3756	.008 474	35.254 249	.028 365 3756	11.35	3.878 845	9.02	172
44	131.850 522	4652.463 019	.000 214 9399	.007 584	35.285 890	.028 339 9399	11.34	3.987 829	9.06	176
45	147.321 297	5202.535 001	.000 192 2140	.006 788	35.314 209	.028 317 2140	11.33	4.097 099	9.10	180
46	164.607 346	5817.150 069	.000 171 9055	.006 075	35.339 553	.028 296 9055	11.32	4.206 631	9.14	184
47	183.921 665	6503.881 431	.000 153 7543	.005 437	35.362 237	.028 278 7543	11.32	4.316 406	9.18	188
48	205.502 244	7271.190 905	.000 137 5291	.004 866	35.382 538	.028 262 5291	11.31	4.426 406	9.22	192
49	229.614 996	8128.533 179	.000 123 0234	.004 355	35.400 707	.028 248 0234	11.30	4.536 613	9.26	196
50	256.557 034	9086.472 317	.000 110 0537	.003 898	35.416 968	.028 235 0537	11.30	4.647 011	9.29	200

QUARTERLY COMPOUND INTEREST AND ANNUITY

11.375% Q

	Amount Of 1	Amount Of 1 Per Period	Sinking Fund Payment	Present Worth Of 1	Present Worth of 1 Per Period	Periodic Payment To Amortize 1	Constant Annual Percent	Total Interest	Annual Add On Rate
	What a single $ 1 deposit grows to in the future. The deposit is made at the beginning of the first period.	What a series of $ 1 deposits grow to in the future. A deposit is made at the end of each period.	The amount to be deposited at the end of each period that grows to $ 1 in the future.	What $ 1 to be paid in the future is worth today. Value today of a single $ 1 payment tomorrow.	What $ 1 to be paid at the end of each period is worth today. Value today of a series of $ 1 payments tomorrow.	The mortgage payment to amortize a loan of $ 1. An annuity certain, payable at the end of each period, worth $ 1 today.	The annual payment, including interest and principal, to amortize completely a loan of $ 100.	The total interest paid over the term on a loan of $1. The loan is amortized by regular periodic payments.	The average annual interest rate on a loan that is completely amortized by regular periodic payments.
	$S = (1+i)^n$	$S\overline{n} = \dfrac{(1+i)^n - 1}{i}$	$\dfrac{1}{S\overline{n}} = \dfrac{i}{(1+i)^n - 1}$	$V^n = \dfrac{1}{(1+i)^n}$	$A\overline{n} = \dfrac{1-V^n}{i}$	$\dfrac{1}{A\overline{n}} = \dfrac{i}{1-V^n}$			

YEAR									**PERIODS**
	1.028 437	1.000 000	1.000 000 0000	.972 349	.972 349	1.028 437 5000	411.38	.028 438	11.38 1
	1.057 684	2.028 437	.492 990 2943	.945 462	1.917 811	.521 427 7943	208.58	.042 856	8.57 2
	1.087 762	3.086 121	.324 031 3448	.919 319	2.837 130	.352 468 8448	140.99	.057 407	7.65 3
	1.118 695	4.173 883	.239 585 0715	.893 899	3.731 029	.268 022 5715	107.21	.072 090	7.21 4

YEAR	Amount Of 1	Amount Of 1 Per Period	Sinking Fund Payment	Present Worth Of 1	Present Worth of 1 Per Period	Periodic Payment To Amortize 1	Constant Annual Percent	Total Interest	Annual Add On Rate	PERIODS
1	1.118 695	4.173 883	.239 585 0715	.893 899	3.731 029	.268 022 5715	107.21	.072 090	7.21	4
2	1.251 478	8.843 184	.113 081 4464	.799 055	7.066 192	.141 518 9464	56.61	.132 152	6.61	8
3	1.400 022	14.066 706	.071 089 8473	.714 275	10.047 490	.099 527 3473	39.82	.194 328	6.48	12
4	1.566 197	19.910 234	.050 225 4273	.638 489	12.712 469	.078 662 9273	31.47	.258 607	6.47	16
5	1.752 097	26.447 358	.037 810 9607	.570 745	15.094 690	.066 248 4607	26.50	.324 969	6.50	20
6	1.960 061	33.760 404	.029 620 4987	.510 188	17.224 156	.058 057 9987	23.23	.393 392	6.56	24
7	2.192 711	41.941 471	.023 842 7499	.456 057	19.127 682	.052 280 2499	20.92	.463 847	6.63	28
8	2.452 974	51.093 588	.019 571 9276	.407 668	20.829 242	.048 009 4276	19.21	.536 302	6.70	32
9	2.744 129	61.332 013	.016 304 6988	.364 414	22.350 265	.044 742 1988	17.90	.610 719	6.79	36
10	3.069 843	72.785 686	.013 738 9650	.325 750	23.709 905	.042 176 4650	16.88	.687 059	6.87	40
11	3.434 217	85.598 851	.011 682 3998	.291 187	24.925 287	.040 119 8998	16.05	.765 276	6.96	44
12	3.841 841	99.932 872	.010 006 7174	.260 292	26.011 714	.038 444 2174	15.38	.845 322	7.04	48
13	4.297 848	115.968 266	.008 623 0487	.232 675	26.982 871	.037 060 5487	14.83	.927 149	7.13	52
14	4.807 980	133.906 977	.007 467 8708	.207 988	27.850 987	.035 905 3708	14.37	1.010 701	7.22	56
15	5.378 662	153.974 921	.006 494 5641	.185 920	28.626 994	.034 932 0641	13.98	1.095 924	7.31	60
16	6.017 081	176.424 825	.005 668 1366	.166 194	29.320 667	.034 105 6366	13.65	1.182 761	7.39	64
17	6.731 277	201.539 415	.004 961 8086	.148 560	29.940 740	.033 399 3086	13.36	1.271 153	7.48	68
18	7.530 245	229.634 977	.004 354 7373	.132 798	30.495 022	.032 792 2373	13.12	1.361 041	7.56	72
19	8.424 045	261.065 335	.003 830 4588	.118 708	30.990 495	.032 267 9588	12.91	1.452 365	7.64	76
20	9.423 936	296.226 313	.003 375 7973	.106 113	31.433 397	.031 813 2973	12.73	1.545 064	7.73	80
21	10.542 508	335.560 716	.002 980 0866	.094 854	31.829 307	.031 417 5866	12.57	1.639 077	7.81	84
22	11.793 849	379.563 908	.002 634 6024	.084 790	32.183 210	.031 072 1024	12.43	1.734 345	7.88	88
23	13.193 717	428.790 050	.002 332 1437	.075 794	32.499 564	.030 769 6437	12.31	1.830 807	7.96	92
24	14.759 743	483.859 078	.002 066 7175	.067 752	32.782 352	.030 504 2175	12.21	1.928 405	8.04	96
25	16.511 647	545.464 513	.001 833 2998	.060 563	33.035 136	.030 270 7998	12.11	2.027 080	8.11	100
26	18.471 494	614.382 192	.001 627 6513	.054 137	33.261 100	.030 065 1513	12.03	2.126 776	8.18	104
27	20.663 964	691.480 041	.001 446 1733	.048 393	33.463 088	.029 883 6733	11.96	2.227 437	8.25	108
28	23.116 669	777.729 002	.001 285 7949	.043 259	33.643 646	.029 723 2949	11.89	2.329 009	8.32	112
29	25.860 497	874.215 266	.001 143 8830	.038 669	33.805 046	.029 581 3830	11.84	2.431 440	8.38	116
30	28.930 003	982.153 948	.001 018 1703	.034 566	33.949 321	.029 455 6703	11.79	2.534 680	8.45	120
31	32.363 844	1102.904 388	.000 906 6969	.030 899	34.078 288	.029 344 1969	11.74	2.638 680	8.51	124
32	36.205 263	1237.987 277	.000 807 7627	.027 620	34.193 572	.029 245 2627	11.70	2.743 394	8.57	128
33	40.502 639	1389.103 800	.000 719 8886	.024 690	34.296 624	.029 157 3886	11.67	2.848 775	8.63	132
34	45.310 092	1558.157 069	.000 641 7838	.022 070	34.388 742	.029 079 2838	11.64	2.954 783	8.69	136
35	50.688 163	1747.276 079	.000 572 3194	.019 728	34.471 087	.029 009 8194	11.61	3.061 375	8.75	140
36	56.704 584	1958.842 531	.000 510 5056	.017 635	34.544 694	.028 948 0056	11.58	3.168 513	8.80	144
37	63.435 123	2195.520 819	.000 455 4728	.015 764	34.610 492	.028 892 9728	11.56	3.276 160	8.85	148
38	70.964 542	2460.291 586	.000 406 4559	.014 092	34.669 308	.028 843 9559	11.54	3.384 281	8.91	152
39	79.387 663	2756.489 265	.000 362 7803	.012 596	34.721 884	.028 800 2803	11.53	3.492 844	8.96	156
40	88.810 566	3087.844 065	.000 323 8506	.011 260	34.768 882	.028 761 3506	11.51	3.601 816	9.00	160
41	99.351 917	3458.528 954	.000 289 1403	.010 065	34.810 893	.028 726 6403	11.50	3.711 169	9.05	164
42	111.144 472	3873.212 208	.000 258 1836	.008 997	34.848 447	.028 695 6836	11.48	3.820 875	9.10	168
43	124.336 742	4337.116 205	.000 230 5680	.008 043	34.882 016	.028 668 0680	11.47	3.930 908	9.14	172
44	139.094 866	4856.083 189	.000 205 9273	.007 189	34.912 023	.028 643 4273	11.46	4.041 243	9.18	176
45	155.604 702	5436.648 852	.000 183 9368	.006 427	34.938 847	.028 621 4368	11.45	4.151 859	9.23	180
46	174.074 169	6086.124 634	.000 164 3082	.005 745	34.962 825	.028 601 8082	11.45	4.262 733	9.27	184
47	194.735 866	6812.689 809	.000 146 7849	.005 135	34.984 258	.028 584 2849	11.44	4.373 846	9.31	188
48	217.849 999	7625.494 485	.000 131 1390	.004 590	35.003 418	.028 568 6390	11.43	4.485 179	9.34	192
49	243.707 660	8534.774 842	.000 117 1677	.004 103	35.020 544	.028 554 6677	11.43	4.596 715	9.38	196
50	272.634 489	9551.982 042	.000 104 6903	.003 668	35.035 854	.028 542 1903	11.42	4.708 438	9.42	200

Amount Of 1	Amount Of 1 Per Period	Sinking Fund Payment	Present Worth Of 1	Present Worth of 1 Per Period	Periodic Payment To Amortize 1	Constant Annual Percent	Total Interest	Annual Add On Rate
What a single $ 1 deposit grows to in the future. The deposit is made at the beginning of the first period.	What a series of $ 1 deposits grow to in the future. A deposit is made at the end of each period.	The amount to be deposited at the end of each period that grows to $ 1 in the future.	What $ 1 to be paid in the future is worth today. Value today of a single $ 1 payment tomorrow.	What $ 1 to be paid at the end of each period is worth today. Value today of a series of $ 1 payments tomorrow.	The mortgage payment to amortize a loan of $ 1. An annuity certain, payable at the end of each period, worth $ 1 today.	The annual payment, including interest and principal, to amortize completely a loan of $ 100.	The total interest paid over the term on a loan of $1. The loan is amortized by regular periodic payments.	The average annual interest rate on a loan that is completely amortized by regular periodic payments.
$S = (1+i)^n$	$S\overline{n} = \dfrac{(1+i)^n - 1}{i}$	$\dfrac{1}{S\overline{n}} = \dfrac{i}{(1+i)^n - 1}$	$V^n = \dfrac{1}{(1+i)^n}$	$A\overline{n} = \dfrac{1-V^n}{i}$	$\dfrac{1}{A\overline{n}} = \dfrac{i}{1-V^n}$			

YEAR / **PERIODS**

	Amount Of 1	Amount Of 1 Per Period	Sinking Fund Payment	Present Worth Of 1	Present Worth of 1 Per Period	Periodic Payment To Amortize 1	Constant Annual Percent	Total Interest	Annual Add On Rate	
	1.028 750	1.000 000	1.000 000 0000	.972 053	.972 053	1.028 750 0000	411.50	.028 750	11.50	1
	1.058 327	2.028 750	.492 914 3561	.944 888	1.916 941	.521 664 3561	208.67	.043 329	8.67	2
	1.088 753	3.087 077	.323 931 0654	.918 482	2.835 423	.352 681 0654	141.08	.058 043	7.74	3
	1.120 055	4.175 830	.239 473 3494	.892 813	3.728 236	.268 223 3494	107.29	.072 893	7.29	4
1	1.120 055	4.175 830	.239 473 3494	.892 813	3.728 236	.268 223 3494	107.29	.072 893	7.29	4
2	1.254 523	8.852 990	.112 956 1906	.797 115	7.056 855	.141 706 1906	56.69	.133 650	6.68	8
3	1.405 135	14.091 666	.070 963 9277	.711 675	10.028 689	.099 713 9277	39.89	.196 567	6.55	12
4	1.573 829	19.959 273	.050 102 0250	.635 393	12.681 982	.078 852 0250	31.55	.261 632	6.54	16
5	1.762 775	26.531 316	.037 691 3080	.567 287	15.050 878	.066 441 3080	26.58	.328 826	6.58	20
6	1.974 406	33.892 366	.029 505 1694	.506 482	17.165 859	.058 255 1694	23.31	.398 124	6.64	24
7	2.211 443	42.137 148	.023 732 0286	.452 193	19.054 142	.052 482 0286	21.00	.469 497	6.71	28
8	2.476 938	51.371 758	.019 465 9486	.403 724	20.740 025	.048 215 9486	19.29	.542 910	6.79	32
9	2.774 307	61.715 030	.016 203 5082	.360 450	22.245 205	.044 953 5082	17.99	.618 326	6.87	36
10	3.107 377	73.300 065	.013 642 5527	.321 815	23.589 049	.042 392 5527	16.96	.695 702	6.96	40
11	3.480 433	86.275 943	.011 590 7166	.287 321	24.788 851	.040 340 7166	16.14	.774 992	7.05	44
12	3.898 277	100.809 641	.009 919 6862	.256 524	25.860 050	.038 669 6862	15.47	.856 145	7.13	48
13	4.366 285	117.088 184	.008 540 5715	.229 028	26.816 430	.037 290 5715	14.92	.939 110	7.22	52
14	4.890 480	135.321 049	.007 389 8334	.204 479	27.670 299	.036 139 8334	14.46	1.023 831	7.31	56
15	5.477 607	155.742 862	.006 420 8400	.182 561	28.432 645	.035 170 8400	14.07	1.110 250	7.40	60
16	6.135 222	178.616 419	.005 598 5894	.162 993	29.113 277	.034 348 5894	13.74	1.198 310	7.49	64
17	6.871 787	204.236 064	.004 896 2949	.145 523	29.720 954	.033 646 2949	13.46	1.287 948	7.58	68
18	7.696 780	232.931 477	.004 293 1080	.129 924	30.263 497	.033 043 1080	13.22	1.379 104	7.66	72
19	8.620 818	265.071 922	.003 772 5610	.115 998	30.747 886	.032 522 5610	13.01	1.471 715	7.75	76
20	9.655 791	301.070 992	.003 321 4758	.103 565	31.180 355	.032 071 4758	12.83	1.565 718	7.83	80
21	10.815 018	341.391 934	.002 929 1846	.092 464	31.566 469	.031 679 1846	12.68	1.661 052	7.91	84
22	12.113 416	386.553 611	.002 586 9633	.082 553	31.911 197	.031 336 9633	12.54	1.757 653	7.99	88
23	13.567 694	437.137 178	.002 287 6114	.073 704	32.218 974	.031 037 6114	12.42	1.855 860	8.07	92
24	15.196 565	493.793 562	.002 025 1378	.065 804	32.493 762	.030 775 1378	12.32	1.954 413	8.14	96
25	17.020 990	557.251 834	.001 794 5208	.058 751	32.739 096	.030 544 5208	12.22	2.054 452	8.22	100
26	19.064 447	628.328 595	.001 591 5239	.052 454	32.958 134	.030 341 5239	12.14	2.155 518	8.29	104
27	21.353 231	707.938 486	.001 412 5521	.046 831	33.153 693	.030 162 5521	12.07	2.257 556	8.36	108
28	23.916 796	797.105 951	.001 254 5384	.041 812	33.328 291	.030 004 5384	12.01	2.360 508	8.43	112
29	26.788 130	896.978 426	.001 114 8540	.037 330	33.484 175	.029 864 8540	11.95	2.464 323	8.50	116
30	30.004 182	1008.841 102	.000 991 2364	.033 329	33.623 350	.029 741 2364	11.90	2.568 948	8.56	120
31	33.606 337	1134.133 464	.000 881 7304	.029 756	33.747 607	.029 631 7304	11.86	2.674 335	8.63	124
32	37.640 950	1274.467 815	.000 784 6412	.026 567	33.858 546	.029 534 6412	11.82	2.780 434	8.69	128
33	42.159 938	1431.650 023	.000 698 4947	.023 719	33.957 593	.029 448 4947	11.78	2.887 201	8.75	132
34	47.221 454	1607.702 758	.000 622 0055	.021 177	34.046 024	.029 372 0055	11.75	2.994 593	8.81	136
35	52.890 631	1804.891 524	.000 554 0499	.018 907	34.124 976	.029 304 0499	11.73	3.102 567	8.86	140
36	59.240 422	2025.753 809	.000 493 6434	.016 880	34.195 466	.029 243 6434	11.70	3.211 085	8.92	144
37	66.352 538	2273.131 742	.000 439 9217	.015 071	34.258 400	.029 189 9217	11.68	3.320 108	8.97	148
38	74.318 499	2550.208 660	.000 392 1248	.013 456	34.314 588	.029 142 1248	11.66	3.429 603	9.03	152
39	83.240 815	2860.550 078	.000 349 5831	.012 013	34.364 753	.029 099 5831	11.64	3.539 535	9.08	156
40	93.234 300	3208.149 571	.000 311 7062	.010 726	34.409 542	.029 061 7062	11.63	3.649 873	9.12	160
41	104.427 555	3597.480 160	.000 277 9723	.009 576	34.449 530	.029 027 9723	11.62	3.760 587	9.17	164
42	116.964 616	4033.551 876	.000 247 9205	.008 550	34.485 232	.028 997 9205	11.60	3.871 651	9.22	168
43	131.006 817	4521.976 232	.000 221 1423	.007 633	34.517 106	.028 971 1423	11.59	3.983 036	9.26	172
44	146.734 855	5069.038 429	.000 197 2761	.006 815	34.545 565	.028 947 2761	11.58	4.094 721	9.31	176
45	164.351 124	5681.778 240	.000 176 0012	.006 085	34.570 973	.028 926 0012	11.58	4.206 680	9.35	180
46	184.082 317	6368.080 598	.000 157 0332	.005 432	34.593 657	.028 907 0332	11.57	4.318 894	9.39	184
47	206.182 341	7136.777 064	.000 140 1193	.004 850	34.613 910	.028 890 1193	11.56	4.431 342	9.43	188
48	230.935 585	7997.759 470	.000 125 0350	.004 330	34.631 993	.028 875 0350	11.56	4.544 007	9.47	192
49	258.660 582	8962.107 216	.000 111 5809	.003 866	34.648 137	.028 861 5809	11.55	4.656 870	9.50	196
50	289.714 108	10042.229 839	.000 099 5795	.003 452	34.662 550	.028 849 5795	11.54	4.769 916	9.54	200

Effective Rate is 12.01 %

Annual Percentage Rate is 11.50 %

QUARTERLY COMPOUND INTEREST AND ANNUITY

	Amount Of 1	Amount Of 1 Per Period	Sinking Fund Payment	Present Worth Of 1	Present Worth of 1 Per Period	Periodic Payment To Amortize 1	Constant Annual Percent	Total Interest	Annual Add On Rate	
	What a single $ 1 deposit grows to in the future. The deposit is made at the beginning of the first period.	What a series of $ 1 deposits grow to in the future. A deposit is made at the end of each period.	The amount to be deposited at the end of each period that grows to $ 1 in the future.	What $ 1 to be paid in the future is worth today. Value today of a single $ 1 payment tomorrow.	What $ 1 to be paid at the end of each period is worth today. Value today of a series of $ 1 payments tomorrow.	The mortgage payment to amortize a loan of $ 1. An annuity certain, payable at the end of each period, worth $ 1 today.	The annual payment, including interest and principal, to amortize completely a loan of $ 100.	The total interest paid over the term on a loan of $1. The loan is amortized by regular periodic payments.	The average annual interest rate on a loan that is completely amortized by regular periodic payments.	
	$S = (1+i)^n$	$S\overline{n} = \dfrac{(1+i)^n - 1}{i}$	$\dfrac{1}{S\overline{n}} = \dfrac{i}{(1+i)^n - 1}$	$V^n = \dfrac{1}{(1+i)^n}$	$A\overline{n} = \dfrac{1-V^n}{i}$	$\dfrac{1}{A\overline{n}} = \dfrac{i}{1-V^n}$				

YEAR										PERIODS
	1.029 063	1.000 000	1.000 000 0000	.971 758	.971 758	1.029 062 5000	411.63	.029 063	11.63	1
	1.058 970	2.029 063	.492 838 4414	.944 314	1.916 072	.521 900 9414	208.77	.043 802	8.76	2
	1.089 746	3.088 032	.323 830 8276	.917 645	2.833 718	.352 893 3276	141.16	.058 680	7.82	3
	1.121 417	4.177 778	.239 361 6858	.891 729	3.725 447	.268 424 1858	107.37	.073 697	7.37	4
1	1.121 417	4.177 778	.239 361 6858	.891 729	3.725 447	.268 424 1858	107.37	.073 697	7.37	4
2	1.257 575	8.862 808	.112 831 0570	.795 181	7.047 536	.141 893 5570	56.76	.135 148	6.76	8
3	1.410 266	14.116 679	.070 838 1918	.709 086	10.009 941	.099 900 6918	39.97	.198 808	6.63	12
4	1.581 496	20.008 457	.049 978 8663	.632 313	12.651 603	.079 041 3663	31.62	.264 662	6.62	16
5	1.773 516	26.615 595	.037 571 9567	.563 852	15.007 251	.066 634 4567	26.66	.332 689	6.65	20
6	1.988 850	34.024 951	.029 390 1970	.502 803	17.107 850	.058 452 6970	23.39	.402 865	6.71	24
7	2.230 330	42.333 925	.023 621 7171	.448 364	18.981 017	.052 684 2171	21.08	.475 158	6.79	28
8	2.501 129	51.651 748	.019 360 4292	.399 819	20.651 374	.048 422 9292	19.37	.549 534	6.87	32
9	2.804 808	62.100 909	.016 102 8239	.356 531	22.140 880	.045 165 3239	18.07	.625 952	6.96	36
10	3.145 358	73.818 773	.013 546 6895	.317 929	23.469 116	.042 609 1895	17.05	.704 368	7.04	40
11	3.527 257	86.959 381	.011 499 6219	.283 506	24.653 543	.040 562 1219	16.23	.784 733	7.13	44
12	3.955 525	101.695 478	.009 833 2789	.252 811	25.709 731	.038 895 7789	15.56	.866 997	7.22	48
13	4.435 792	118.220 783	.008 458 7496	.225 439	26.651 564	.037 521 2496	15.01	.951 105	7.32	52
14	4.974 371	136.752 535	.007 312 4787	.201 030	27.491 425	.036 374 9787	14.55	1.036 999	7.41	56
15	5.578 342	157.534 351	.006 347 8219	.179 265	28.240 353	.035 410 3219	14.17	1.124 619	7.50	60
16	6.255 646	180.839 427	.005 529 7676	.159 856	28.908 195	.034 592 2676	13.84	1.213 905	7.59	64
17	7.015 186	206.974 127	.004 831 5218	.142 548	29.503 728	.033 894 0218	13.56	1.304 793	7.68	68
18	7.866 946	236.282 015	.004 232 2307	.127 114	30.034 783	.033 294 7307	13.32	1.397 221	7.76	72
19	8.822 124	269.148 369	.003 715 4228	.113 351	30.508 340	.032 777 9228	13.12	1.491 122	7.85	76
20	9.893 278	306.005 248	.003 267 9178	.101 079	30.930 624	.032 330 4178	12.94	1.586 433	7.93	80
21	11.094 486	347.337 165	.002 879 0469	.090 135	31.307 188	.031 941 5469	12.78	1.683 090	8.01	84
22	12.441 542	393.687 467	.002 540 0859	.080 376	31.642 980	.031 602 5859	12.65	1.781 028	8.10	88
23	13.952 153	445.665 468	.002 243 8355	.071 674	31.942 416	.031 306 3355	12.53	1.880 183	8.17	92
24	15.646 177	503.954 466	.001 984 3063	.063 913	32.209 432	.031 046 8063	12.42	1.980 493	8.25	96
25	17.545 883	569.320 719	.001 756 4792	.056 993	32.447 538	.030 818 9792	12.33	2.081 898	8.33	100
26	19.676 246	642.623 526	.001 556 1211	.050 823	32.659 864	.030 618 6211	12.25	2.184 337	8.40	104
27	22.065 271	724.826 516	.001 379 6405	.045 320	32.849 201	.030 442 1405	12.18	2.287 751	8.47	108
28	24.744 362	817.010 320	.001 223 9747	.040 413	33.018 039	.030 286 4747	12.12	2.392 085	8.54	112
29	27.748 741	920.386 774	.001 086 4997	.036 038	33.168 596	.030 148 9997	12.06	2.497 284	8.61	116
30	31.117 900	1036.314 854	.000 964 9577	.032 136	33.302 853	.030 027 4577	12.02	2.603 295	8.68	120
31	34.896 132	1166.318 536	.000 857 3987	.028 656	33.422 573	.029 919 8987	11.97	2.710 067	8.74	124
32	39.133 105	1312.106 832	.000 762 1331	.025 554	33.529 331	.029 824 6331	11.93	2.817 553	8.80	128
33	43.884 516	1475.596 259	.000 677 6921	.022 787	33.624 531	.029 740 1921	11.90	2.925 705	8.87	132
34	49.212 828	1658.936 029	.000 602 7960	.020 320	33.709 423	.029 665 2960	11.87	3.034 480	8.92	136
35	55.188 086	1864.536 303	.000 536 3264	.018 120	33.785 123	.029 598 8264	11.84	3.143 836	8.98	140
36	61.888 840	2095.099 880	.000 477 3042	.016 158	33.852 628	.029 539 8042	11.82	3.253 732	9.04	144
37	69.403 177	2353.657 719	.000 424 8706	.014 409	33.912 824	.029 487 3706	11.80	3.364 131	9.09	148
38	77.829 880	2643.608 791	.000 378 2708	.012 849	33.966 502	.029 440 7708	11.78	3.474 997	9.14	152
39	87.279 726	2968.764 758	.000 336 8404	.011 457	34.014 369	.029 399 3404	11.76	3.586 297	9.20	156
40	97.876 940	3333.400 082	.000 299 9940	.010 217	34.057 053	.029 362 4940	11.75	3.697 999	9.24	160
41	109.760 832	3742.308 214	.000 267 2148	.009 111	34.095 115	.029 329 7148	11.74	3.810 073	9.29	164
42	123.087 628	4200.864 613	.000 238 0462	.008 124	34.129 057	.029 300 5462	11.73	3.922 492	9.34	168
43	138.032 518	4715.097 404	.000 212 0847	.007 245	34.159 323	.029 274 5847	11.71	4.035 229	9.38	172
44	154.791 968	5291.766 631	.000 188 9728	.006 460	34.186 313	.029 251 4728	11.71	4.148 259	9.43	176
45	173.586 294	5938.453 118	.000 168 3940	.005 761	34.210 380	.029 230 8940	11.70	4.261 561	9.47	180
46	194.662 564	6663.658 127	.000 150 0677	.005 137	34.231 842	.029 212 5677	11.69	4.375 112	9.51	184
47	218.297 846	7476.915 118	.000 133 7450	.004 581	34.250 980	.029 196 2450	11.68	4.488 894	9.55	188
48	244.802 844	8388.915 069	.000 119 2049	.004 085	34.268 046	.029 181 7049	11.68	4.602 887	9.59	192
49	274.525 992	9411.647 021	.000 106 2513	.003 643	34.283 264	.029 168 7513	11.67	4.717 075	9.63	196
50	307.858 025	10558.555 686	.000 094 7099	.003 248	34.296 834	.029 157 2099	11.67	4.831 442	9.66	200

Effective Rate is 12.14 %

Annual Percentage Rate is 11.625%

QUARTERLY COMPOUND INTEREST AND ANNUITY

11.75 % Q

	Amount Of 1	Amount Of 1 Per Period	Sinking Fund Payment	Present Worth Of 1	Present Worth of 1 Per Period	Periodic Payment To Amortize 1	Constant Annual Percent	Total Interest	Annual Add On Rate	
	What a single $ 1 deposit grows to in the future. The deposit is made at the beginning of the first period.	What a series of $ 1 deposits grow to in the future. A deposit is made at the end of each period.	The amount to be deposited at the end of each period that grows to $ 1 in the future.	What $ 1 to be paid in the future is worth today. Value today of a single $ 1 payment tomorrow.	What $ 1 to be paid at the end of each period is worth today. Value today of a series of $ 1 payments tomorrow.	The mortgage payment to amortize a loan of $ 1. An annuity certain, payable at the end of each period, worth $ 1 today.	The annual payment, including interest and principal, to amortize completely a loan of $ 100.	The total interest paid over the term on a loan of $1. The loan is amortized by regular periodic payments.	The average annual interest rate on a loan that is completely amortized by regular periodic payments.	
	$S = (1+i)^n$	$S\overline{n} = \frac{(1+i)^n - 1}{i}$	$\frac{1}{S\overline{n}} = \frac{i}{(1+i)^n - 1}$	$V^n = \frac{1}{(1+i)^n}$	$A\overline{n} = \frac{1-V^n}{i}$	$\frac{1}{A\overline{n}} = \frac{i}{1-V^n}$				

YEAR

PERIODS

YEAR	Amount Of 1	Amount Of 1 Per Period	Sinking Fund Payment	Present Worth Of 1	Present Worth of 1 Per Period	Periodic Payment To Amortize 1	Constant Annual Percent	Total Interest	Annual Add On Rate	PERIODS
	1.029 375	1.000 000	1.000 000 0000	.971 463	.971 463	1.029 375 0000	411.75	.029 375	11.75	1
	1.059 613	2.029 375	.492 762 5500	.943 741	1.915 204	.522 137 5500	208.86	.044 275	8.86	2
	1.090 739	3.088 988	.323 730 6313	.916 810	2.832 014	.353 105 6313	141.25	.059 317	7.91	3
	1.122 779	4.179 727	.239 250 0806	.890 647	3.722 661	.268 625 0806	107.46	.074 500	7.45	4
1	1.122 779	4.179 727	.239 250 0806	.890 647	3.722 661	.268 625 0806	107.46	.074 500	7.45	4
2	1.260 634	8.872 639	.112 706 0456	.793 252	7.038 236	.142 081 0456	56.84	.136 648	6.83	8
3	1.415 414	14.141 743	.070 712 6396	.706 507	9.991 244	.100 087 6396	40.04	.201 052	6.70	12
4	1.589 197	20.057 786	.049 855 9509	.629 248	12.621 330	.079 230 9509	31.70	.267 695	6.69	16
5	1.784 318	26.700 198	.037 452 9064	.560 438	14.963 809	.066 827 9064	26.74	.336 558	6.73	20
6	2.003 396	34.158 161	.029 275 5809	.499 152	17.050 129	.058 650 5809	23.47	.407 614	6.79	24
7	2.249 372	42.531 809	.023 511 8145	.444 569	18.908 305	.052 886 8145	21.16	.480 831	6.87	28
8	2.525 549	51.933 569	.019 255 3683	.395 954	20.563 282	.048 630 3683	19.46	.556 172	6.95	32
9	2.835 634	62.489 672	.016 002 6443	.352 655	22.037 283	.045 377 6443	18.16	.633 595	7.04	36
10	3.183 792	74.341 849	.013 451 3739	.314 091	23.350 097	.042 826 3739	17.14	.713 055	7.13	40
11	3.574 696	87.649 229	.011 409 1135	.279 744	24.519 351	.040 784 1135	16.32	.794 501	7.22	44
12	4.013 595	102.590 482	.009 747 4929	.249 153	25.560 743	.039 122 4929	15.65	.877 880	7.32	48
13	4.506 383	119.366 215	.008 377 5799	.221 907	26.488 256	.037 752 5799	15.11	.963 134	7.41	52
14	5.059 674	138.201 664	.007 235 8029	.197 641	27.314 342	.036 610 8029	14.65	1.050 205	7.50	56
15	5.680 898	159.349 719	.006 275 5053	.176 029	28.050 093	.035 650 5053	14.27	1.139 030	7.59	60
16	6.378 396	183.094 321	.005 461 6658	.156 779	28.705 388	.034 836 6658	13.94	1.229 547	7.68	64
17	7.161 532	209.754 273	.004 767 4833	.139 635	29.289 024	.034 142 4833	13.66	1.321 689	7.77	68
18	8.040 821	239.687 520	.004 172 0987	.124 365	29.808 837	.033 547 0987	13.42	1.415 391	7.86	72
19	9.028 069	273.295 956	.003 659 0370	.110 766	30.271 807	.033 034 0370	13.22	1.510 587	7.95	76
20	10.136 530	311.030 817	.003 215 1155	.098 653	30.684 150	.032 590 1155	13.04	1.607 209	8.04	80
21	11.381 088	353.398 746	.002 829 6648	.087 865	31.051 402	.032 204 6648	12.89	1.705 192	8.12	84
22	12.778 452	400.968 586	.002 493 9610	.078 257	31.378 494	.031 868 9610	12.75	1.804 469	8.20	88
23	14.347 384	454.379 027	.002 200 8058	.069 699	31.669 817	.031 575 8058	12.64	1.904 974	8.28	92
24	16.108 948	514.347 173	.001 944 2121	.062 077	31.929 283	.031 319 2121	12.53	2.006 644	8.36	96
25	18.086 796	581.678 178	.001 719 1637	.055 289	32.160 376	.031 094 1637	12.44	2.109 416	8.44	100
26	20.307 484	657.276 047	.001 521 4308	.049 243	32.366 198	.030 896 4308	12.36	2.213 229	8.51	104
27	22.800 826	742.155 784	.001 347 4260	.043 858	32.549 513	.030 722 4260	12.29	2.318 022	8.59	108
28	25.600 300	837.457 011	.001 194 0911	.039 062	32.712 782	.030 569 0911	12.23	2.423 738	8.66	112
29	28.743 491	944.459 273	.001 058 8069	.034 790	32.858 196	.030 433 8069	12.18	2.530 322	8.73	116
30	32.272 602	1064.599 216	.000 939 3206	.030 986	32.987 709	.030 314 3206	12.13	2.637 718	8.79	120
31	36.235 015	1199.489 879	.000 833 6877	.027 598	33.103 060	.030 208 6877	12.09	2.745 877	8.86	124
32	40.683 931	1350.942 347	.000 740 2240	.024 580	33.205 796	.030 115 2240	12.05	2.854 749	8.92	128
33	45.679 083	1520.990 070	.000 657 4665	.021 892	33.297 298	.030 032 4665	12.02	2.964 286	8.98	132
34	51.287 537	1711.916 164	.000 584 1408	.019 498	33.378 794	.029 959 1408	11.99	3.074 443	9.04	136
35	57.584 594	1926.284 063	.000 519 1342	.017 366	33.451 379	.029 894 1342	11.96	3.185 179	9.10	140
36	64.654 801	2166.971 942	.000 461 4734	.015 467	33.516 025	.029 836 4734	11.94	3.296 452	9.16	144
37	72.593 083	2437.211 353	.000 410 3050	.013 775	33.573 603	.029 785 3050	11.92	3.408 225	9.21	148
38	81.506 024	2740.630 617	.000 364 8795	.012 269	33.624 884	.029 739 8795	11.90	3.520 462	9.26	152
39	91.513 292	3081.303 541	.000 324 5380	.010 927	33.670 557	.029 699 5380	11.88	3.633 128	9.32	156
40	102.749 246	3463.804 108	.000 288 6999	.009 732	33.711 236	.029 663 6999	11.87	3.746 192	9.37	160
41	115.364 744	3893.267 895	.000 256 8536	.008 668	33.747 467	.029 631 8536	11.86	3.859 624	9.41	164
42	129.529 168	4375.461 022	.000 228 5473	.007 720	33.779 736	.029 603 5473	11.85	3.973 396	9.46	168
43	145.432 691	4916.857 569	.000 203 3819	.006 876	33.808 475	.029 578 3819	11.84	4.087 482	9.51	172
44	163.288 841	5524.726 501	.000 181 0044	.006 124	33.834 073	.029 556 0044	11.83	4.201 857	9.55	176
45	183.337 360	6207.229 264	.000 161 1025	.005 454	33.856 871	.029 536 1025	11.82	4.316 498	9.59	180
46	205.847 425	6973.529 360	.000 143 3994	.004 858	33.877 176	.029 518 3994	11.81	4.431 385	9.63	184
47	231.121 264	7833.915 381	.000 127 6501	.004 327	33.895 260	.029 502 6501	11.81	4.546 498	9.67	188
48	259.498 213	8799.939 149	.000 113 6371	.003 853	33.911 367	.029 488 6371	11.80	4.661 818	9.71	192
49	291.359 268	9884.570 811	.000 101 1678	.003 432	33.925 713	.029 476 1678	11.80	4.777 329	9.75	196
50	327.132 206	11102.372 982	.000 090 0708	.003 057	33.938 490	.029 465 0708	11.79	4.893 014	9.79	200

Effective Rate is 12.28 %

8 - 330

Annual Percentage Rate is 11.75 %

Amount Of 1	Amount Of 1 Per Period	Sinking Fund Payment	Present Worth Of 1	Present Worth of 1 Per Period	Periodic Payment To Amortize 1	Constant Annual Percent	Total Interest	Annual Add On Rate
What a single $ 1 deposit grows to in the future. The deposit is made at the beginning of the first period.	What a series of $ 1 deposits grow to in the future. A deposit is made at the end of each period.	The amount to be deposited at the end of each period that grows to $ 1 in the future.	What $ 1 to be paid in the future is worth today. Value today of a single $ 1 payment tomorrow.	What $ 1 to be paid at the end of each period is worth today. Value today of a series of $ 1 payments tomorrow.	The mortgage payment to amortize a loan of $ 1. An annuity certain, payable at the end of each period, worth $ 1 today.	The annual payment, including interest and principal, to amortize completely a loan of $ 100.	The total interest paid over the term on a loan of $1. The loan is amortized by regular periodic payments.	The average annual interest rate on a loan that is completely amortized by regular periodic payments.

$$ S = (1+i)^n \qquad S\overline{n} = \frac{(1+i)^n - 1}{i} \qquad \frac{1}{S\overline{n}} = \frac{i}{(1+i)^n - 1} \qquad V^n = \frac{1}{(1+i)^n} \qquad A\overline{n} = \frac{1-V^n}{i} \qquad \frac{1}{A\overline{n}} = \frac{i}{1-V^n} $$

PERIODS

YEAR									
	1.029 688	1.000 000	1.000 000 0000	.971 168	.971 168	1.029 687 5000	411.88	.029 687	11.87	1
	1.060 256	2.029 688	.492 686 6821	.943 168	1.914 337	.522 374 1821	208.95	.044 748	8.95	2
	1.091 733	3.089 944	.323 630 4766	.915 975	2.830 312	.353 317 9766	141.33	.059 954	7.99	3
	1.124 144	4.181 677	.239 138 5337	.889 566	3.719 878	.268 826 0337	107.54	.075 304	7.53	4
1	1.124 144	4.181 677	.239 138 5337	.889 566	3.719 878	.268 826 0337	107.54	.075 304	7.53	4
2	1.263 699	8.882 481	.112 581 1562	.791 328	7.028 955	.142 268 6562	56.91	.138 149	6.91	8
3	1.420 579	14.166 860	.070 587 2708	.703 938	9.972 598	.100 274 7708	40.11	.203 297	6.78	12
4	1.596 934	20.107 261	.049 733 2786	.626 200	12.591 163	.079 420 7786	31.77	.270 732	6.77	16
5	1.795 183	26.785 123	.037 334 1568	.557 046	14.920 550	.067 021 6568	26.81	.340 433	6.81	20
6	2.018 044	34.292 000	.029 161 3208	.495 529	16.992 694	.058 848 8208	23.54	.412 372	6.87	24
7	2.268 571	42.730 806	.023 402 3202	.440 806	18.836 003	.053 089 8202	21.24	.486 515	6.95	28
8	2.550 199	52.217 235	.019 150 7650	.392 126	20.475 748	.048 838 2650	19.54	.562 824	7.04	32
9	2.866 790	62.881 343	.015 902 9682	.348 822	21.934 410	.045 590 4682	18.24	.641 257	7.13	36
10	3.222 683	74.869 331	.013 356 6039	.310 300	23.231 986	.043 044 1039	17.22	.721 764	7.22	40
11	3.622 759	88.345 550	.011 319 1892	.276 033	24.386 265	.041 006 6892	16.41	.804 294	7.31	44
12	4.072 501	103.494 755	.009 662 3254	.245 549	25.413 073	.039 349 8254	15.74	.888 792	7.41	48
13	4.578 075	120.524 635	.008 297 0590	.218 432	26.326 487	.037 984 5590	15.20	.975 197	7.50	52
14	5.146 413	139.668 664	.007 159 8022	.194 310	27.139 029	.036 847 3022	14.74	1.063 449	7.60	56
15	5.785 307	161.189 300	.006 203 8857	.172 852	27.861 839	.035 891 3857	14.36	1.153 483	7.69	60
16	6.503 516	185.381 585	.005 394 2791	.153 763	28.504 826	.035 081 7791	14.04	1.245 234	7.78	64
17	7.310 885	212.577 184	.004 704 1737	.136 782	29.076 805	.034 391 6737	13.76	1.338 634	7.87	68
18	8.218 484	243.148 941	.004 112 7056	.121 677	29.585 619	.033 800 2056	13.53	1.433 615	7.96	72
19	9.238 756	277.515 984	.003 603 3961	.108 240	30.038 242	.033 290 8961	13.32	1.530 108	8.05	76
20	10.385 687	316.149 472	.003 163 0608	.096 286	30.440 881	.032 850 5608	13.15	1.628 045	8.14	80
21	11.675 003	359.579 058	.002 781 0296	.085 653	30.799 054	.032 468 5296	12.99	1.727 356	8.23	84
22	13.124 379	408.400 145	.002 448 5790	.076 194	31.117 673	.032 136 0790	12.86	1.827 975	8.31	88
23	14.753 686	463.282 055	.002 158 5123	.067 780	31.401 106	.031 846 0123	12.74	1.929 833	8.39	92
24	16.585 261	524.977 197	.001 904 8446	.060 295	31.653 238	.031 592 3446	12.64	2.032 865	8.47	96
25	18.644 213	594.331 393	.001 682 5630	.053 636	31.877 526	.031 370 0630	12.55	2.137 006	8.55	100
26	20.958 772	672.295 462	.001 487 4412	.047 713	32.077 045	.031 174 9412	12.47	2.242 194	8.62	104
27	23.560 667	759.938 266	.001 315 8964	.042 444	32.254 531	.031 003 3964	12.41	2.348 367	8.70	108
28	26.485 571	858.461 355	.001 164 8748	.037 756	32.412 416	.030 852 3748	12.35	2.455 466	8.77	112
29	29.773 584	969.215 449	.001 031 7623	.033 587	32.552 865	.030 719 2623	12.29	2.563 434	8.84	116
30	33.469 781	1093.718 946	.000 914 3117	.029 878	32.677 804	.030 601 8117	12.25	2.672 217	8.91	120
31	37.624 838	1233.678 745	.000 810 5838	.026 578	32.788 945	.030 498 0838	12.20	2.781 762	8.97	124
32	42.295 718	1391.013 647	.000 718 9002	.023 643	32.887 813	.030 406 4002	12.17	2.892 019	9.04	128
33	47.546 457	1567.880 658	.000 637 8036	.021 032	32.975 762	.030 325 3036	12.14	3.002 940	9.10	132
34	53.449 042	1766.704 562	.000 566 0256	.018 709	33.053 999	.030 253 5256	12.11	3.114 479	9.16	136
35	60.084 394	1990.211 167	.000 502 4592	.016 643	33.123 596	.030 189 9592	12.08	3.226 594	9.22	140
36	67.543 482	2241.464 669	.000 446 1369	.014 805	33.185 506	.030 133 6369	12.06	3.339 244	9.28	144
37	75.928 568	2523.909 665	.000 396 2107	.013 170	33.240 580	.030 083 7107	12.04	3.452 389	9.33	148
38	85.354 608	2841.418 379	.000 351 9369	.011 716	33.289 572	.030 039 4369	12.02	3.565 994	9.38	152
39	95.950 830	3198.343 742	.000 312 6618	.010 422	33.333 154	.030 000 1618	12.01	3.680 025	9.44	156
40	107.862 504	3599.579 078	.000 277 8103	.009 271	33.371 922	.029 965 3103	11.99	3.794 450	9.49	160
41	121.252 935	4050.625 182	.000 246 8755	.008 247	33.406 409	.029 934 3755	11.98	3.909 238	9.53	164
42	136.305 702	4557.665 738	.000 219 4106	.007 336	33.437 088	.029 906 9106	11.97	4.024 361	9.58	168
43	153.227 172	5127.652 094	.000 195 0210	.006 526	33.464 379	.029 882 5210	11.96	4.139 791	9.63	172
44	172.249 332	5768.398 565	.000 173 3583	.005 806	33.488 656	.029 860 8583	11.95	4.255 511	9.67	176
45	193.632 971	6488.689 560	.000 154 1143	.005 164	33.510 251	.029 841 6143	11.94	4.371 491	9.71	180
46	217.671 251	7298.400 017	.000 137 0163	.004 594	33.529 462	.029 824 5163	11.93	4.487 711	9.76	184
47	244.693 726	8208.630 782	.000 121 8230	.004 087	33.546 552	.029 809 3230	11.93	4.604 153	9.80	188
48	275.070 868	9231.860 801	.000 108 3205	.003 635	33.561 754	.029 795 8205	11.92	4.720 798	9.83	192
49	309.219 134	10382.118 199	.000 096 3195	.003 234	33.575 277	.029 783 8195	11.92	4.837 629	9.87	196
50	347.606 687	11675.172 602	.000 085 6518	.002 877	33.587 307	.029 773 1518	11.91	4.954 630	9.91	200

Effective Rate is 12.41 %   Annual Percentage Rate is 11.875%

QUARTERLY COMPOUND INTEREST AND ANNUITY

	Amount Of 1	Amount Of 1 Per Period	Sinking Fund Payment	Present Worth Of 1	Present Worth of 1 Per Period	Periodic Payment To Amortize 1	Constant Annual Percent	Total Interest	Annual Add On Rate	
	What a single $ 1 deposit grows to in the future. The deposit is made at the beginning of the first period.	What a series of $ 1 deposits grow to in the future. A deposit is made at the end of each period.	The amount to be deposited at the end of each period that grows to $ 1 in the future.	What $ 1 to be paid in the future is worth today. Value today of a single $ 1 payment tomorrow.	What $ 1 to be paid at the end of each period is worth today. Value today of a series of $ 1 payments tomorrow.	The mortgage payment to amortize a loan of $ 1. An annuity certain, payable at the end of each period, worth $ 1 today.	The annual payment, including interest and principal, to amortize completely a loan of $ 100.	The total interest paid over the term on a loan of $1. The loan is amortized by regular periodic payments.	The average annual interest rate on a loan that is completely amortized by regular periodic payments.	
	$S = (1+i)^n$	$S\overline{n}| = \dfrac{(1+i)^n - 1}{i}$	$\dfrac{1}{S\overline{n}|} = \dfrac{i}{(1+i)^n - 1}$	$V^n = \dfrac{1}{(1+i)^n}$	$A\overline{n}| = \dfrac{1-V^n}{i}$	$\dfrac{1}{A\overline{n}|} = \dfrac{i}{1-V^n}$				

YEAR										PERIODS
	1.030 000	1.000 000	1.000 000 0000	.970 874	.970 874	1.030 000 0000	412.00	.030 000	12.00	1
	1.060 900	2.030 000	.492 610 8374	.942 596	1.913 470	.522 610 8374	209.05	.045 222	9.04	2
	1.092 727	3.090 900	.323 530 3633	.915 142	2.828 611	.353 530 3633	141.42	.060 591	8.08	3
	1.125 509	4.183 627	.239 027 0452	.888 487	3.717 098	.269 027 0452	107.62	.076 108	7.61	4
1	1.125 509	4.183 627	.239 027 0452	.888 487	3.717 098	.269 027 0452	107.62	.076 108	7.61	4
2	1.266 770	8.892 336	.112 456 3888	.789 409	7.019 692	.142 456 3888	56.99	.139 651	6.98	8
3	1.425 761	14.192 030	.070 462 0855	.701 380	9.954 004	.100 462 0855	40.19	.205 545	6.85	12
4	1.604 706	20.156 881	.049 610 8493	.623 167	12.561 102	.079 610 8493	31.85	.273 774	6.84	16
5	1.806 111	26.870 374	.037 215 7076	.553 676	14.877 475	.067 215 7076	26.89	.344 314	6.89	20
6	2.032 794	34.426 470	.029 047 4159	.491 934	16.935 542	.059 047 4159	23.62	.417 138	6.95	24
7	2.287 928	42.930 923	.023 293 2334	.437 077	18.764 108	.053 293 2334	21.32	.492 211	7.03	28
8	2.575 083	52.502 759	.019 046 6183	.388 337	20.388 766	.049 046 6183	19.62	.569 492	7.12	32
9	2.898 278	63.275 944	.015 803 7942	.345 032	21.832 252	.045 803 7942	18.33	.648 937	7.21	36
10	3.262 038	75.401 260	.013 262 3779	.306 557	23.114 772	.043 262 3779	17.31	.730 495	7.30	40
11	3.671 452	89.048 409	.011 229 8469	.272 372	24.254 274	.041 229 8469	16.50	.814 113	7.40	44
12	4.132 252	104.408 396	.009 577 7738	.241 999	25.266 707	.039 577 7738	15.84	.899 733	7.50	48
13	4.650 886	121.696 197	.008 217 1837	.215 013	26.166 240	.038 217 1837	15.29	.987 294	7.59	52
14	5.234 613	141.153 768	.007 084 4726	.191 036	26.965 464	.037 084 4726	14.84	1.076 730	7.69	56
15	5.891 603	163.053 437	.006 132 9587	.169 733	27.675 564	.036 132 9587	14.46	1.167 978	7.79	60
16	6.631 051	187.701 707	.005 327 6021	.150 806	28.306 478	.035 327 6021	14.14	1.260 967	7.88	64
17	7.463 307	215.443 551	.004 641 5871	.133 989	28.867 038	.034 641 5871	13.86	1.355 628	7.97	68
18	8.400 017	246.667 242	.004 054 0446	.119 047	29.365 088	.034 054 0446	13.63	1.451 891	8.07	72
19	9.454 293	281.809 781	.003 548 4929	.105 772	29.807 598	.033 548 4929	13.42	1.549 685	8.16	76
20	10.640 891	321.363 019	.003 111 7457	.093 977	30.200 763	.033 111 7457	13.25	1.648 940	8.24	80
21	11.976 416	365.880 536	.002 733 1325	.083 497	30.550 086	.032 733 1325	13.10	1.749 583	8.33	84
22	13.479 562	415.985 393	.002 403 9306	.074 186	30.860 454	.032 403 9306	12.97	1.851 546	8.42	88
23	15.171 366	472.378 852	.002 116 9449	.065 914	31.136 212	.032 116 9449	12.85	1.954 759	8.50	92
24	17.075 506	535.850 186	.001 866 1932	.058 563	31.381 219	.031 866 1932	12.75	2.059 155	8.58	96
25	19.218 632	607.287 733	.001 646 6659	.052 033	31.598 905	.031 646 6659	12.66	2.164 667	8.66	100
26	21.630 740	687.691 320	.001 454 1408	.046 231	31.792 317	.031 454 1408	12.59	2.271 231	8.74	104
27	24.345 588	778.186 267	.001 285 0394	.041 075	31.964 160	.031 285 0394	12.52	2.378 784	8.81	108
28	27.401 174	880.039 126	.001 136 3131	.036 495	32.116 840	.031 136 3131	12.46	2.487 267	8.88	112
29	30.840 262	994.675 416	.001 005 3531	.032 425	32.252 495	.031 005 3531	12.41	2.596 621	8.95	116
30	34.710 987	1123.699 571	.000 889 9176	.028 809	32.373 023	.030 889 9176	12.36	2.706 790	9.02	120
31	39.067 522	1268.917 394	.000 788 0734	.025 597	32.480 110	.030 788 0734	12.32	2.817 721	9.09	124
32	43.970 840	1432.361 333	.000 698 1479	.022 742	32.575 255	.030 698 1479	12.28	2.929 363	9.15	128
33	49.489 568	1616.318 927	.000 618 6898	.020 206	32.659 791	.030 618 6898	12.25	3.041 667	9.22	132
34	55.700 945	1823.364 819	.000 548 4366	.017 953	32.734 899	.030 548 4366	12.22	3.154 587	9.28	136
35	62.691 904	2056.396 794	.000 486 2875	.015 951	32.801 633	.030 486 2875	12.20	3.268 080	9.34	140
36	70.560 290	2318.676 336	.000 431 2805	.014 172	32.860 924	.030 431 2805	12.18	3.382 104	9.39	144
37	79.416 228	2613.874 271	.000 382 5739	.012 592	32.913 604	.030 382 5739	12.16	3.496 621	9.45	148
38	89.383 664	2946.122 147	.000 339 4292	.011 188	32.960 409	.030 339 4292	12.14	3.611 593	9.50	152
39	100.602 102	3320.070 059	.000 301 1985	.009 940	33.001 995	.030 301 1985	12.13	3.726 987	9.56	156
40	113.228 552	3740.951 728	.000 267 3117	.008 832	33.038 944	.030 267 3117	12.11	3.842 770	9.61	160
41	127.439 733	4214.657 754	.000 237 2672	.007 847	33.071 772	.030 237 2672	12.10	3.958 912	9.66	164
42	143.434 542	4747.818 061	.000 210 6231	.006 972	33.100 939	.030 210 6231	12.09	4.075 385	9.70	168
43	161.436 840	5347.894 683	.000 186 9895	.006 194	33.126 854	.030 186 9895	12.08	4.192 162	9.75	172
44	181.698 586	6023.286 207	.000 166 0223	.005 504	33.149 879	.030 166 0223	12.07	4.309 220	9.79	176
45	204.503 360	6783.445 318	.000 147 4177	.004 890	33.170 337	.030 147 4177	12.06	4.426 535	9.84	180
46	230.170 333	7639.011 095	.000 130 9070	.004 345	33.188 513	.030 130 9070	12.06	4.544 087	9.88	184
47	259.058 737	8601.957 914	.000 116 2526	.003 860	33.204 662	.030 116 2526	12.05	4.661 855	9.92	188
48	291.572 891	9685.763 043	.000 103 2443	.003 430	33.219 011	.030 103 2443	12.05	4.779 823	9.96	192
49	328.167 858	10905.595 263	.000 091 6960	.003 047	33.231 759	.030 091 6960	12.04	4.897 972	10.00	196
50	369.355 815	12278.527 174	.000 081 4430	.002 707	33.243 086	.030 081 4430	12.04	5.016 289	10.03	200

Effective Rate is 12.55 %

Annual Percentage Rate is 12.00 %

QUARTERLY COMPOUND INTEREST AND ANNUITY

12.125% Q

Amount Of 1	Amount Of 1 Per Period	Sinking Fund Payment	Present Worth Of 1	Present Worth of 1 Per Period	Periodic Payment To Amortize 1	Constant Annual Percent	Total Interest	Annual Add On Rate	
What a single $ 1 deposit grows to in the future. The deposit is made at the beginning of the first period.	What a series of $ 1 deposits grow to in the future. A deposit is made at the end of each period.	The amount to be deposited at the end of each period that grows to $ 1 in the future.	What $ 1 to be paid in the future is worth today. Value today of a single $ 1 payment tomorrow.	What $ 1 to be paid at the end of each period is worth today. Value today of a series of $ 1 payments tomorrow.	The mortgage payment to amortize a loan of $ 1. An annuity certain, payable at the end of each period, worth $ 1 today.	The annual payment, including interest and principal, to amortize completely a loan of $ 100.	The total interest paid over the term on a loan of $1. The loan is amortized by regular periodic payments.	The average annual interest rate on a loan that is completely amortized by regular periodic payments.	
$S = (1+i)^n$	$S\overline{n}| = \dfrac{(1+i)^n - 1}{i}$	$\dfrac{1}{S\overline{n}|} = \dfrac{i}{(1+i)^n - 1}$	$V^n = \dfrac{1}{(1+i)^n}$	$A\overline{n}| = \dfrac{1-V^n}{i}$	$\dfrac{1}{A\overline{n}|} = \dfrac{i}{1-V^n}$				**PERIODS**

YEAR

1.030 313	1.000 000	1.000 000 0000	.970 579	.970 579	1.030 312 5000	412.13	.030 312	12.12	1
1.061 544	2.030 312	.492 535 0162	.942 024	1.912 604	.522 847 5162	209.14	.045 695	9.14	2
1.093 722	3.091 856	.323 430 2916	.914 309	2.826 913	.353 742 7916	141.50	.061 228	8.16	3
1.126 875	4.185 578	.238 915 6150	.887 410	3.714 322	.269 228 1150	107.70	.076 912	7.69	4

YEAR	Amount Of 1	Amount Of 1 Per Period	Sinking Fund Payment	Present Worth Of 1	Present Worth of 1 Per Period	Periodic Payment To Amortize 1	Constant Annual Percent	Total Interest	Annual Add On Rate	PERIODS
1	1.126 875	4.185 578	.238 915 6150	.887 410	3.714 322	.269 228 1150	107.70	.076 912	7.69	4
2	1.269 848	8.902 203	.112 331 7434	.787 496	7.010 448	.142 644 2434	57.06	.141 154	7.06	8
3	1.430 960	14.217 251	.070 337 0833	.698 831	9.935 461	.100 649 5833	40.26	.207 795	6.93	12
4	1.612 514	20.206 648	.049 488 6626	.620 150	12.531 146	.079 801 1626	31.93	.276 819	6.92	16
5	1.817 102	26.955 952	.037 097 5584	.550 327	14.834 581	.067 410 0584	26.97	.348 201	6.96	20
6	2.047 648	34.561 576	.028 933 8659	.488 365	16.878 672	.059 246 3659	23.70	.421 913	7.03	24
7	2.307 444	43.132 166	.023 184 5534	.433 380	18.692 618	.053 497 0534	21.40	.497 917	7.11	28
8	2.600 201	52.790 152	.018 942 9270	.384 586	20.302 331	.049 255 4270	19.71	.576 174	7.20	32
9	2.930 103	63.673 499	.015 705 1209	.341 285	21.730 806	.046 017 6209	18.41	.656 634	7.30	36
10	3.301 861	75.937 674	.013 168 6941	.302 860	22.998 448	.043 481 1941	17.40	.739 248	7.39	40
11	3.720 785	89.757 871	.011 141 0843	.268 760	24.123 366	.041 453 5843	16.59	.823 958	7.49	44
12	4.192 861	105.331 509	.009 493 8353	.238 501	25.121 629	.039 806 3353	15.93	.910 704	7.59	48
13	4.724 832	122.881 058	.008 137 9507	.211 648	26.007 497	.038 450 4507	15.39	.999 423	7.69	52
14	5.324 297	142.657 213	.007 009 8103	.187 818	26.793 625	.037 322 3103	14.93	1.090 049	7.79	56
15	5.999 819	164.942 474	.006 062 7198	.166 672	27.491 243	.036 375 2198	14.56	1.182 513	7.88	60
16	6.761 048	190.055 184	.005 261 6297	.147 906	28.110 315	.035 574 1297	14.23	1.276 744	7.98	64
17	7.618 858	218.354 079	.004 579 7175	.131 253	28.659 686	.034 892 2175	13.96	1.372 671	8.07	68
18	8.585 503	250.243 405	.003 996 1093	.116 475	29.147 203	.034 308 6093	13.73	1.470 220	8.17	72
19	9.674 792	286.178 701	.003 494 3202	.103 361	29.579 830	.033 806 8202	13.53	1.569 318	8.26	76
20	10.902 284	326.673 299	.003 061 1623	.091 724	29.963 748	.033 373 6623	13.35	1.669 893	8.35	80
21	12.285 515	372.305 663	.002 685 9651	.081 397	30.304 440	.032 998 4651	13.20	1.771 871	8.44	84
22	13.844 244	423.727 649	.002 360 0065	.072 232	30.606 773	.032 672 5065	13.07	1.875 181	8.52	88
23	15.600 738	481.673 817	.002 076 0937	.064 100	30.875 067	.032 388 5937	12.96	1.979 751	8.61	92
24	17.580 086	546.971 925	.001 828 2474	.056 883	31.113 153	.032 140 7474	12.86	2.085 512	8.69	96
25	19.810 566	620.554 752	.001 611 4614	.050 478	31.324 433	.031 923 9614	12.77	2.192 396	8.77	100
26	22.324 038	703.473 426	.001 421 5178	.044 795	31.511 925	.031 734 0178	12.70	2.300 338	8.85	104
27	25.156 408	796.912 435	.001 254 8430	.039 751	31.678 308	.031 567 3430	12.63	2.409 273	8.92	108
28	28.348 136	902.206 550	.001 108 3936	.035 276	31.825 957	.031 420 8936	12.57	2.519 140	9.00	112
29	31.944 815	1020.859 891	.000 979 5664	.031 304	31.956 982	.031 292 0664	12.52	2.629 880	9.07	116
30	35.997 825	1154.567 416	.000 866 1253	.027 779	32.073 255	.031 178 6253	12.48	2.741 435	9.14	120
31	40.565 061	1305.239 128	.000 766 1431	.024 652	32.176 437	.031 078 6431	12.44	2.853 752	9.21	124
32	45.711 767	1475.027 365	.000 677 9535	.021 876	32.268 001	.030 990 4535	12.40	2.966 778	9.27	128
33	51.511 463	1666.357 542	.000 600 1113	.019 413	32.349 257	.030 912 6113	12.37	3.080 465	9.33	132
34	58.046 997	1881.962 801	.000 531 3601	.017 227	32.421 363	.030 843 8601	12.34	3.194 765	9.40	136
35	65.411 730	2124.923 051	.000 470 6053	.015 288	32.485 352	.030 783 1053	12.32	3.309 635	9.46	140
36	73.710 865	2398.708 964	.000 416 8909	.013 567	32.542 135	.030 729 3909	12.30	3.425 032	9.51	144
37	83.062 957	2707.231 559	.000 369 3810	.012 039	32.592 526	.030 681 8810	12.28	3.540 918	9.57	148
38	93.601 598	3054.898 063	.000 327 3432	.010 684	32.637 243	.030 639 8432	12.26	3.657 256	9.62	152
39	105.477 332	3446.674 874	.000 290 1347	.009 481	32.676 925	.030 602 6347	12.25	3.774 011	9.68	156
40	118.859 805	3888.158 500	.000 257 1912	.008 413	32.712 139	.030 569 6912	12.23	3.891 151	9.73	160
41	133.940 183	4385.655 512	.000 228 0161	.007 466	32.743 389	.030 540 5161	12.22	4.008 645	9.78	164
42	150.933 889	4946.272 627	.000 202 1724	.006 625	32.771 120	.030 514 6724	12.21	4.126 465	9.82	168
43	170.083 678	5578.018 228	.000 179 2751	.005 879	32.795 729	.030 491 7751	12.20	4.244 585	9.87	172
44	191.663 102	6289.916 769	.000 158 9846	.005 217	32.817 567	.030 471 4846	12.19	4.362 981	9.92	176
45	215.980 423	7092.137 679	.000 141 0012	.004 630	32.836 947	.030 453 5012	12.19	4.481 630	9.96	180
46	243.383 013	7996.140 640	.000 125 0603	.004 109	32.854 144	.030 437 5603	12.18	4.600 511	10.00	184
47	274.262 316	9014.839 284	.000 110 9282	.003 646	32.869 406	.030 423 4282	12.17	4.719 605	10.04	188
48	309.059 441	10162.785 666	.000 098 3982	.003 236	32.882 949	.030 410 8982	12.17	4.838 892	10.08	192
49	348.271 462	11456.378 136	.000 087 2876	.002 871	32.894 967	.030 399 7876	12.16	4.958 358	10.12	196
50	392.458 523	12914.095 592	.000 077 4348	.002 548	32.905 632	.030 389 9348	12.16	5.077 987	10.16	200

QUARTERLY COMPOUND INTEREST AND ANNUITY

Amount Of 1	Amount Of 1 Per Period	Sinking Fund Payment	Present Worth Of 1	Present Worth of 1 Per Period	Periodic Payment To Amortize 1	Constant Annual Percent	Total Interest	Annual Add On Rate
What a single $ 1 deposit grows to in the future. The deposit is made at the beginning of the first period.	What a series of $ 1 deposits grow to in the future. A deposit is made at the end of each period.	The amount to be deposited at the end of each period that grows to $ 1 in the future.	What $ 1 to be paid in the future is worth today. Value today of a single $ 1 payment tomorrow.	What $ 1 to be paid at the end of each period is worth today. Value today of a series of $ 1 payments tomorrow.	The mortgage payment to amortize a loan of $ 1. An annuity certain, payable at the end of each period, worth $ 1 today.	The annual payment, including interest and principal, to amortize completely a loan of $ 100.	The total interest paid over the term on a loan of $1. The loan is amortized by regular periodic payments.	The average annual interest rate on a loan that is completely amortized by regular periodic payments.
$S = (1+i)^n$	$S\overline{n}| = \dfrac{(1+i)^n - 1}{i}$	$\dfrac{1}{S\overline{n}|} = \dfrac{i}{(1+i)^n - 1}$	$V^n = \dfrac{1}{(1+i)^n}$	$A\overline{n}| = \dfrac{1-V^n}{i}$	$\dfrac{1}{A\overline{n}|} = \dfrac{i}{1-V^n}$			

YEAR / **PERIODS**

Amount Of 1	Amount Of 1 Per Period	Sinking Fund Payment	Present Worth Of 1	Present Worth of 1 Per Period	Periodic Payment To Amortize 1	Constant Annual Percent	Total Interest	Annual Add On Rate	
1.030 625	1.000 000	1.000 000 0000	.970 285	.970 285	1.030 625 0000	412.25	.030 625	12.25	1
1.062 188	2.030 625	.492 459 2182	.941 453	1.911 738	.523 084 2182	209.24	.046 168	9.23	2
1.094 717	3.092 813	.323 330 2613	.913 478	2.825 216	.353 955 2613	141.59	.061 866	8.25	3
1.128 243	4.187 530	.238 804 2430	.886 334	3.711 550	.269 429 2430	107.78	.077 717	7.77	4

YEAR	Amount Of 1	Amount Of 1 Per Period	Sinking Fund Payment	Present Worth Of 1	Present Worth of 1 Per Period	Periodic Payment To Amortize 1	Constant Annual Percent	Total Interest	Annual Add On Rate	PERIODS
1	1.128 243	4.187 530	.238 804 2430	.886 334	3.711 550	.269 429 2430	107.78	.077 717	7.77	4
2	1.272 933	8.912 082	.112 207 2198	.785 588	7.001 221	.142 832 2198	57.14	.142 658	7.13	8
3	1.436 177	14.242 526	.070 212 2643	.696 293	9.916 969	.100 837 2643	40.34	.210 047	7.00	12
4	1.620 357	20.256 562	.049 366 7183	.617 148	12.501 294	.079 991 7183	32.00	.279 867	7.00	16
5	1.828 157	27.041 857	.036 979 7088	.546 999	14.791 869	.067 604 7088	27.05	.352 094	7.04	20
6	2.062 605	34.697 319	.028 820 6702	.484 824	16.822 083	.059 445 6702	23.78	.426 696	7.11	24
7	2.327 120	43.334 542	.023 076 2794	.429 716	18.621 530	.053 701 2794	21.49	.503 636	7.19	28
8	2.625 558	53.079 429	.018 839 6903	.380 871	20.216 441	.049 464 6903	19.79	.582 870	7.29	32
9	2.962 267	64.074 031	.015 606 9470	.337 579	21.630 065	.046 231 9470	18.50	.664 350	7.38	36
10	3.342 158	76.478 614	.013 075 5508	.299 208	22.883 007	.043 700 5508	17.49	.748 022	7.48	40
11	3.770 766	90.474 000	.011 052 8992	.265 198	23.993 532	.041 677 8992	16.68	.833 828	7.58	44
12	4.254 341	106.264 198	.009 410 5072	.235 054	24.977 828	.040 035 5072	16.02	.921 704	7.68	48
13	4.799 931	124.079 380	.008 059 3568	.208 336	25.850 242	.038 684 3568	15.48	1.011 587	7.78	52
14	5.415 489	144.179 236	.006 935 8115	.184 656	26.623 493	.037 560 8115	15.03	1.103 405	7.88	56
15	6.109 988	166.856 761	.005 993 1644	.163 666	27.308 851	.036 618 1644	14.65	1.197 090	7.98	60
16	6.893 552	192.442 522	.005 196 3568	.145 063	27.916 307	.035 821 3568	14.33	1.292 567	8.08	64
17	7.777 603	221.309 481	.004 518 5592	.128 574	28.454 716	.035 143 5592	14.06	1.389 762	8.18	68
18	8.775 027	253.878 429	.003 938 8931	.113 960	28.931 926	.034 563 8931	13.83	1.488 600	8.27	72
19	9.900 364	290.624 119	.003 440 8706	.101 006	29.354 893	.034 065 8706	13.63	1.589 006	8.36	76
20	11.170 017	332.082 192	.003 011 3027	.089 525	29.729 784	.033 636 3027	13.46	1.690 904	8.45	80
21	12.602 495	378.856 977	.002 639 5185	.079 349	30.062 061	.033 264 5185	13.31	1.794 220	8.54	84
22	14.218 678	431.630 306	.002 316 7975	.070 330	30.356 571	.032 941 7975	13.18	1.898 878	8.63	88
23	16.042 126	491.171 451	.002 035 9489	.062 336	30.617 604	.032 660 9489	13.07	2.004 807	8.72	92
24	18.099 418	558.348 339	.001 790 9966	.055 250	30.848 967	.032 415 9966	12.97	2.111 936	8.80	96
25	20.420 544	634.140 199	.001 576 9384	.048 970	31.054 031	.032 201 9384	12.89	2.220 194	8.88	100
26	23.039 338	719.651 844	.001 389 5608	.043 404	31.235 787	.032 014 5608	12.81	2.329 514	8.96	104
27	25.993 974	816.129 768	.001 225 2953	.038 470	31.396 883	.031 850 2953	12.75	2.439 832	9.04	108
28	29.327 522	924.980 322	.001 081 1041	.034 098	31.539 668	.031 706 1041	12.69	2.551 084	9.11	112
29	33.088 575	1047.790 210	.000 954 3895	.030 222	31.666 223	.031 579 3895	12.64	2.663 209	9.18	116
30	37.331 957	1186.349 621	.000 842 9218	.026 787	31.778 393	.031 467 9218	12.59	2.776 151	9.25	120
31	42.119 524	1342.678 322	.000 744 7800	.023 742	31.877 814	.031 369 7800	12.55	2.889 853	9.32	124
32	47.521 063	1519.055 103	.000 658 3040	.021 043	31.965 503	.031 283 3040	12.52	3.004 263	9.39	128
33	53.615 312	1718.050 992	.000 582 0549	.018 651	32.044 036	.031 207 0549	12.49	3.119 331	9.45	132
34	60.491 106	1942.566 733	.000 514 7828	.016 531	32.113 262	.031 139 7828	12.46	3.235 010	9.51	136
35	68.248 674	2195.875 072	.000 455 3993	.014 652	32.174 619	.031 080 3993	12.44	3.351 256	9.58	140
36	77.001 097	2481.668 462	.000 402 9547	.012 987	32.229 002	.031 027 9547	12.42	3.468 025	9.63	144
37	86.875 957	2804.112 886	.000 356 6190	.011 511	32.277 203	.030 981 6190	12.40	3.585 280	9.69	148
38	98.017 200	3167.908 587	.000 315 6657	.010 202	32.319 925	.030 940 6657	12.38	3.702 981	9.74	152
39	110.587 232	3578.358 583	.000 279 4577	.009 043	32.357 792	.030 904 4577	12.37	3.821 095	9.80	156
40	124.769 283	4041.445 964	.000 247 4362	.008 015	32.391 354	.030 872 4362	12.35	3.939 590	9.85	160
41	140.770 084	4563.921 114	.000 219 1098	.007 104	32.421 101	.030 844 1098	12.34	4.058 434	9.90	164
42	158.822 878	5153.400 105	.000 194 0466	.006 296	32.447 467	.030 819 0466	12.33	4.177 600	9.95	168
43	179.190 819	5818.475 717	.000 171 8663	.005 581	32.470 836	.030 796 8663	12.32	4.297 061	9.99	172
44	202.170 808	6568.842 698	.000 152 2338	.004 946	32.491 549	.030 777 2338	12.32	4.416 793	10.04	176
45	228.097 822	7415.439 078	.000 134 8538	.004 384	32.509 907	.030 759 8538	12.31	4.536 774	10.08	180
46	257.349 797	8370.605 614	.000 119 4657	.003 886	32.526 179	.030 744 4657	12.30	4.656 982	10.12	184
47	290.353 137	9448.265 683	.000 105 8395	.003 444	32.540 601	.030 730 8395	12.30	4.777 398	10.16	188
48	327.588 927	10664.128 236	.000 093 7723	.003 053	32.553 384	.030 718 7723	12.29	4.898 004	10.20	192
49	369.599 952	12035.916 789	.000 083 0847	.002 706	32.564 714	.030 708 0847	12.29	5.018 785	10.24	196
50	416.998 601	13583.627 781	.000 073 6180	.002 398	32.574 756	.030 698 6180	12.28	5.139 724	10.28	200

Effective Rate is 12.82 %

Annual Percentage Rate is 12.25 %

QUARTERLY COMPOUND INTEREST AND ANNUITY

12.375% Q

Amount Of 1	Amount Of 1 Per Period	Sinking Fund Payment	Present Worth Of 1	Present Worth of 1 Per Period	Periodic Payment To Amortize 1	Constant Annual Percent	Total Interest	Annual Add On Rate	
What a single $ 1 deposit grows to in the future. The deposit is made at the beginning of the first period.	What a series of $ 1 deposits grow to in the future. A deposit is made at the end of each period.	The amount to be deposited at the end of each period that grows to $ 1 in the future.	What $ 1 to be paid in the future is worth today. Value today of a single $ 1 payment tomorrow.	What $ 1 to be paid at the end of each period is worth today. Value today of a series of $ 1 payments tomorrow.	The mortgage payment to amortize a loan of $ 1. An annuity certain, payable at the end of each period, worth $ 1 today.	The annual payment, including interest and principal, to amortize completely a loan of $ 100.	The total interest paid over the term on a loan of $1. The loan is amortized by regular periodic payments.	The average annual interest rate on a loan that is completely amortized by regular periodic payments.	

$$S = (1+i)^n \qquad S\overline{n}| = \frac{(1+i)^n - 1}{i} \qquad \frac{1}{S\overline{n}|} = \frac{i}{(1+i)^n - 1} \qquad V^n = \frac{1}{(1+i)^n} \qquad A\overline{n}| = \frac{1-V^n}{i} \qquad \frac{1}{A\overline{n}|} = \frac{i}{1-V^n}$$

PERIODS

YEAR	Amount Of 1	Amount Of 1 Per Period	Sinking Fund Payment	Present Worth Of 1	Present Worth of 1 Per Period	Periodic Payment To Amortize 1	Constant Annual Percent	Total Interest	Annual Add On Rate	PERIODS
	1.030 938	1.000 000	1.000 000 0000	.969 991	.969 991	1.030 937 5000	412.38	.030 937	12.37	1
	1.062 832	2.030 938	.492 383 4436	.940 882	1.910 873	.523 320 9436	209.33	.046 642	9.33	2
	1.095 713	3.093 770	.323 230 2724	.912 647	2.823 521	.354 167 7724	141.67	.062 503	8.33	3
	1.129 612	4.189 483	.238 692 9294	.885 260	3.708 780	.269 630 4294	107.86	.078 522	7.85	4
1	1.129 612	4.189 483	.238 692 9294	.885 260	3.708 780	.269 630 4294	107.86	.078 522	7.85	4
2	1.276 024	8.921 974	.112 082 8180	.783 685	6.992 014	.143 020 3180	57.21	.144 163	7.21	8
3	1.441 412	14.267 853	.070 087 6282	.693 764	9.898 527	.101 025 1282	40.42	.212 302	7.08	12
4	1.628 236	20.306 623	.049 245 0163	.614 162	12.471 547	.080 182 5163	32.08	.282 920	7.07	16
5	1.839 275	27.128 091	.036 862 1584	.543 692	14.749 337	.067 799 6584	27.12	.355 993	7.12	20
6	2.077 668	34.833 704	.028 707 8283	.481 309	16.765 772	.059 645 3283	23.86	.431 488	7.19	24
7	2.346 959	43.538 058	.022 968 4107	.426 083	18.550 841	.053 905 9107	21.57	.509 365	7.28	28
8	2.651 153	53.370 602	.018 736 9069	.377 194	20.131 091	.049 674 4069	19.87	.589 581	7.37	32
9	2.994 775	64.477 563	.015 509 2711	.333 915	21.530 022	.046 446 7711	18.58	.672 084	7.47	36
10	3.382 934	77.024 120	.012 982 9461	.295 601	22.768 439	.043 920 4461	17.57	.756 818	7.57	40
11	3.821 403	91.196 864	.010 965 2893	.261 684	23.864 760	.041 902 7893	16.77	.843 723	7.67	44
12	4.316 703	107.206 567	.009 327 7868	.231 658	24.835 288	.040 265 2868	16.11	.932 734	7.77	48
13	4.876 200	125.291 322	.007 981 3987	.205 078	25.694 458	.038 918 8987	15.57	1.023 783	7.88	52
14	5.508 215	145.720 081	.006 862 4722	.181 547	26.455 046	.037 799 9722	15.12	1.116 798	7.98	56
15	6.222 147	168.796 655	.005 924 2880	.160 716	27.128 364	.036 861 7880	14.75	1.211 707	8.08	60
16	7.028 612	194.864 233	.005 131 7781	.142 276	27.724 425	.036 069 2781	14.43	1.308 434	8.18	64
17	7.939 606	224.310 485	.004 458 1064	.125 951	28.252 094	.035 395 6064	14.16	1.406 901	8.28	68
18	8.968 675	257.573 329	.003 882 3895	.111 499	28.719 218	.034 819 8895	13.93	1.507 032	8.37	72
19	10.131 124	295.147 441	.003 388 1371	.098 706	29.132 744	.034 325 6371	13.74	1.608 748	8.47	76
20	11.444 241	337.591 614	.002 962 1589	.087 380	29.498 822	.033 899 6589	13.56	1.711 973	8.56	80
21	12.927 553	385.537 067	.002 593 7843	.077 354	29.822 896	.033 531 2843	13.42	1.816 628	8.65	84
22	14.603 121	439.696 832	.002 274 2943	.068 479	30.109 785	.033 211 7943	13.29	1.922 638	8.74	88
23	16.495 862	500.876 360	.001 996 5007	.060 621	30.363 757	.032 934 0007	13.18	2.029 928	8.83	92
24	18.633 926	569.985 497	.001 754 4306	.053 666	30.588 588	.032 691 9306	13.08	2.138 425	8.91	96
25	21.049 109	648.052 017	.001 543 0860	.047 508	30.787 622	.032 480 5860	13.00	2.248 059	8.99	100
26	23.777 329	736.236 905	.001 358 2585	.042 057	30.963 818	.032 295 7585	12.92	2.358 759	9.07	104
27	26.859 160	835.851 624	.001 196 3846	.037 231	31.119 798	.032 133 8846	12.86	2.470 460	9.15	108
28	30.340 433	948.377 621	.001 054 4323	.032 959	31.257 881	.031 991 9323	12.80	2.583 096	9.23	112
29	34.272 921	1075.488 351	.000 929 8102	.029 178	31.380 119	.031 867 3102	12.75	2.696 608	9.30	116
30	38.715 107	1219.074 175	.000 820 2946	.025 830	31.488 333	.031 757 7946	12.71	2.810 935	9.37	120
31	43.733 055	1381.270 463	.000 723 9712	.022 866	31.584 129	.031 661 4712	12.67	2.926 022	9.44	124
32	49.401 390	1564.489 359	.000 639 1862	.020 242	31.668 934	.031 576 6862	12.64	3.041 816	9.51	128
33	55.804 409	1771.455 647	.000 564 5075	.017 920	31.744 009	.031 502 0075	12.61	3.158 265	9.57	132
34	63.037 338	2005.247 278	.000 498 6916	.015 864	31.810 469	.031 436 1916	12.58	3.275 322	9.63	136
35	71.207 742	2269.341 140	.000 440 6565	.014 043	31.869 304	.031 378 1565	12.56	3.392 942	9.69	140
36	80.437 129	2567.664 772	.000 389 4589	.012 432	31.921 388	.031 326 9589	12.54	3.511 082	9.75	144
37	90.862 757	2904.654 766	.000 344 2750	.011 006	31.967 495	.031 281 7750	12.52	3.629 703	9.81	148
38	102.639 673	3285.322 752	.000 304 3841	.009 743	32.008 313	.031 241 8841	12.50	3.748 766	9.87	152
39	115.943 020	3715.329 929	.000 269 1551	.008 625	32.044 447	.031 206 6551	12.49	3.868 238	9.92	156
40	130.970 642	4201.071 254	.000 238 0345	.007 635	32.076 435	.031 175 5345	12.48	3.988 086	9.97	160
41	147.946 026	4749.770 548	.000 210 5365	.006 759	32.104 752	.031 148 0365	12.46	4.108 278	10.02	164
42	167.121 627	5369.587 929	.000 186 2340	.005 984	32.129 821	.031 123 7340	12.45	4.228 787	10.07	168
43	188.782 617	6069.741 164	.000 164 7517	.005 297	32.152 013	.031 102 2517	12.45	4.349 587	10.12	172
44	213.251 135	6860.642 753	.000 145 7589	.004 689	32.171 659	.031 083 2589	12.44	4.470 654	10.16	176
45	240.891 070	7754.054 786	.000 128 9648	.004 151	32.189 050	.031 066 4648	12.43	4.591 964	10.20	180
46	272.113 476	8763.263 859	.000 114 1127	.003 675	32.204 446	.031 051 6127	12.43	4.713 497	10.25	184
47	307.382 684	9903.288 673	.000 100 9767	.003 253	32.218 076	.031 038 4767	12.42	4.835 234	10.29	188
48	347.223 210	11191.053 241	.000 089 3571	.002 880	32.230 142	.031 026 8571	12.42	4.957 157	10.33	192
49	392.227 551	12645.739 019	.000 079 0780	.002 550	32.240 823	.031 016 5780	12.41	5.079 249	10.37	196
50	443.065 001	14288.969 726	.000 069 9841	.002 257	32.250 279	.031 007 4841	12.41	5.201 497	10.40	200

Effective Rate is 12.96 %

Annual Percentage Rate is 12.375%

QUARTERLY COMPOUND INTEREST AND ANNUITY

	Amount Of 1	Amount Of 1 Per Period	Sinking Fund Payment	Present Worth Of 1	Present Worth of 1 Per Period	Periodic Payment To Amortize 1	Constant Annual Percent	Total Interest	Annual Add On Rate	
	What a single $ 1 deposit grows to in the future. The deposit is made at the beginning of the first period.	What a series of $ 1 deposits grow to in the future. A deposit is made at the end of each period.	The amount to be deposited at the end of each period that grows to $ 1 in the future.	What $ 1 to be paid in the future is worth today. Value today of a single $ 1 payment tomorrow.	What $ 1 to be paid at the end of each period is worth today. Value today of a series of $ 1 payments tomorrow.	The mortgage payment to amortize a loan of $ 1. An annuity certain, payable at the end of each period, worth $ 1 today.	The annual payment, including interest and principal, to amortize completely a loan of $ 100.	The total interest paid over the term on a loan of $1. The loan is amortized by regular periodic payments.	The average annual interest rate on a loan that is completely amortized by regular periodic payments.	
	$S = (1+i)^n$	$S\overline{n} = \dfrac{(1+i)^n - 1}{i}$	$\dfrac{1}{S\overline{n}} = \dfrac{i}{(1+i)^n - 1}$	$V^n = \dfrac{1}{(1+i)^n}$	$A\overline{n} = \dfrac{1-V^n}{i}$	$\dfrac{1}{A\overline{n}} = \dfrac{i}{1-V^n}$				

YEAR										PERIODS
	1.031 250	1.000 000	1.000 000 0000	.969 697	.969 697	1.031 250 0000	412.50	.031 250	12.50	1
	1.063 477	2.031 250	.492 307 6923	.940 312	1.910 009	.523 557 6923	209.43	.047 115	9.42	2
	1.096 710	3.094 727	.323 130 3250	.911 818	2.821 827	.354 380 3250	141.76	.063 141	8.42	3
	1.130 982	4.191 437	.238 581 6739	.884 187	3.706 014	.269 831 6739	107.94	.079 327	7.93	4
1	1.130 982	4.191 437	.238 581 6739	.884 187	3.706 014	.269 831 6739	107.94	.079 327	7.93	4
2	1.279 121	8.931 878	.111 958 5380	.781 787	6.982 824	.143 208 5380	57.29	.145 668	7.28	8
3	1.446 664	14.293 234	.069 963 1750	.691 246	9.880 137	.101 213 1750	40.49	.214 558	7.15	12
4	1.636 151	20.356 832	.049 123 5563	.611 191	12.441 903	.080 373 5563	32.15	.285 977	7.15	16
5	1.850 458	27.214 656	.036 744 9071	.540 407	14.706 984	.067 994 9071	27.20	.359 898	7.20	20
6	2.092 835	34.970 734	.028 595 3396	.477 821	16.709 739	.059 845 3396	23.94	.436 288	7.27	24
7	2.366 960	43.742 721	.022 860 9465	.422 483	18.480 549	.054 110 9465	21.65	.515 107	7.36	28
8	2.676 990	53.663 684	.018 634 5760	.373 554	20.046 276	.049 884 5760	19.96	.596 306	7.45	32
9	3.027 629	64.884 119	.015 412 0918	.330 291	21.430 672	.046 662 0918	18.67	.679 835	7.55	36
10	3.424 195	77.574 233	.012 890 8783	.292 039	22.654 737	.044 140 8783	17.66	.765 635	7.66	40
11	3.872 704	91.926 529	.010 878 2525	.258 218	23.737 040	.042 128 2525	16.86	.853 643	7.76	44
12	4.379 960	108.158 723	.009 245 6713	.228 313	24.693 997	.040 495 6713	16.20	.943 792	7.86	48
13	4.953 658	126.517 049	.007 904 0731	.201 871	25.540 127	.039 154 0731	15.67	1.036 012	7.97	52
14	5.602 500	147.279 993	.006 789 7885	.178 492	26.288 264	.038 039 7885	15.22	1.130 228	8.07	56
15	6.336 329	170.762 516	.005 856 0861	.157 820	26.949 757	.037 106 0861	14.85	1.226 365	8.18	60
16	7.166 276	197.320 837	.005 067 8885	.139 542	27.534 640	.036 317 8885	14.53	1.324 345	8.28	64
17	8.104 932	227.357 830	.004 398 3530	.123 382	28.051 787	.035 648 3530	14.26	1.424 088	8.38	68
18	9.166 536	261.329 141	.003 826 5920	.109 092	28.509 041	.035 076 5920	14.04	1.525 515	8.48	72
19	10.367 190	299.750 096	.003 336 1124	.096 458	28.913 339	.034 586 1124	13.84	1.628 545	8.57	76
20	11.725 110	343.203 519	.002 913 7230	.085 287	29.270 815	.034 163 7230	13.67	1.733 098	8.67	80
21	13.260 893	392.348 576	.002 548 7540	.075 410	29.586 890	.033 798 7540	13.52	1.839 095	8.76	84
22	14.997 837	447.930 771	.002 232 4878	.066 676	29.866 359	.033 482 4878	13.40	1.946 459	8.85	88
23	16.962 289	510.793 254	.001 957 7392	.058 954	30.113 462	.033 207 7392	13.29	2.055 112	8.94	92
24	19.184 051	581.889 617	.001 718 5390	.052 127	30.331 948	.032 968 5390	13.19	2.164 980	9.02	96
25	21.696 823	662.298 352	.001 509 8935	.046 090	30.525 130	.032 759 8935	13.11	2.275 989	9.10	100
26	24.538 725	753.239 215	.001 327 5995	.040 752	30.695 939	.032 577 5995	13.04	2.388 070	9.18	104
27	27.752 867	856.091 731	.001 168 0991	.036 032	30.846 966	.032 418 0991	12.97	2.501 155	9.26	108
28	31.388 004	972.416 117	.001 028 3663	.031 859	30.980 502	.032 278 3663	12.92	2.615 177	9.34	112
29	35.499 280	1103.976 950	.000 905 8160	.028 170	31.098 573	.032 155 8160	12.87	2.730 075	9.41	116
30	40.149 060	1252.769 936	.000 798 2312	.024 907	31.202 970	.032 048 2312	12.82	2.845 788	9.49	120
31	45.407 881	1421.052 184	.000 703 7039	.022 023	31.295 277	.031 953 7039	12.79	2.962 259	9.56	124
32	51.355 514	1611.376 445	.000 620 5875	.019 472	31.376 893	.031 870 5875	12.75	3.079 435	9.62	128
33	58.082 182	1826.629 834	.000 547 4563	.017 217	31.449 057	.031 797 4563	12.72	3.197 264	9.69	132
34	65.689 926	2070.077 628	.000 483 0737	.015 223	31.512 863	.031 733 0737	12.70	3.315 698	9.75	136
35	74.294 150	2345.412 799	.000 426 3642	.013 460	31.569 280	.031 676 3642	12.68	3.434 691	9.81	140
36	84.025 376	2656.812 031	.000 376 3909	.011 901	31.619 163	.031 626 3909	12.66	3.554 200	9.87	144
37	95.031 221	3008.999 081	.000 332 3364	.010 523	31.663 269	.031 582 3364	12.64	3.674 186	9.93	148
38	107.478 639	3407.316 436	.000 293 4861	.009 304	31.702 266	.031 543 4861	12.62	3.794 610	9.99	152
39	121.556 449	3857.806 354	.000 259 2147	.008 227	31.736 748	.031 509 2147	12.61	3.915 437	10.04	156
40	137.478 204	4367.302 521	.000 228 9743	.007 274	31.767 236	.031 478 9743	12.60	4.036 636	10.09	160
41	155.485 429	4943.533 720	.000 202 2845	.006 431	31.794 193	.031 452 2845	12.59	4.158 175	10.14	164
42	175.851 283	5595.241 062	.000 178 7233	.005 687	31.818 028	.031 428 7233	12.58	4.280 026	10.19	168
43	198.884 706	6332.310 596	.000 157 9202	.005 028	31.839 103	.031 407 9202	12.57	4.402 162	10.24	172
44	224.935 102	7165.923 266	.000 139 5494	.004 446	31.857 737	.031 389 5494	12.56	4.524 561	10.28	176
45	254.397 641	8108.724 523	.000 123 3240	.003 931	31.874 213	.031 373 3240	12.55	4.647 198	10.33	180
46	287.719 255	9175.016 151	.000 108 9916	.003 476	31.888 780	.031 358 9916	12.55	4.770 054	10.37	184
47	325.405 413	10380.973 214	.000 096 3301	.003 073	31.901 661	.031 346 3301	12.54	4.893 110	10.41	188
48	368.027 795	11744.889 426	.000 085 1434	.002 717	31.913 050	.031 335 1434	12.54	5.016 348	10.45	192
49	416.232 958	13287.454 656	.000 075 2590	.002 403	31.923 120	.031 325 2590	12.54	5.139 751	10.45	196
50	470.752 149	15032.068 780	.000 066 5244	.002 124	31.932 024	.031 316 5244	12.53	5.263 305	10.53	200

Effective Rate is 13.10 %

Annual Percentage Rate is 12.50 %

QUARTERLY COMPOUND INTEREST AND ANNUITY

Amount Of 1	Amount Of 1 Per Period	Sinking Fund Payment	Present Worth Of 1	Present Worth of 1 Per Period	Periodic Payment To Amortize 1	Constant Annual Percent	Total Interest	Annual Add On Rate
What a single $ 1 deposit grows to in the future. The deposit is made at the beginning of the first period.	What a series of $ 1 deposits grow to in the future. A deposit is made at the end of each period.	The amount to be deposited at the end of each period that grows to $ 1 in the future.	What $ 1 to be paid in the future is worth today. Value today of a single $ 1 payment tomorrow.	What $ 1 to be paid at the end of each period is worth today. Value today of a series of $ 1 payments tomorrow.	The mortgage payment to amortize a loan of $ 1. An annuity certain, payable at the end of each period, worth $ 1 today.	The annual payment, including interest and principal, to amortize completely a loan of $ 100.	The total interest paid over the term on a loan of $1. The loan is amortized by regular periodic payments.	The average annual interest rate on a loan that is completely amortized by regular periodic payments.
$S = (1+i)^n$	$S\overline{n} = \dfrac{(1+i)^n - 1}{i}$	$\dfrac{1}{S\overline{n}} = \dfrac{i}{(1+i)^n - 1}$	$V^n = \dfrac{1}{(1+i)^n}$	$A\overline{n} = \dfrac{1-V^n}{i}$	$\dfrac{1}{A\overline{n}} = \dfrac{i}{1-V^n}$			

YEAR									PERIODS
	1.031 563	1.000 000	1.000 000 0000	.969 403	.969 403	1.031 562 5000	412.63	.031 563	12.63	1
	1.064 121	2.031 563	.492 231 9643	.939 743	1.909 146	.523 794 4643	209.52	.047 589	9.52	2
	1.097 708	3.095 684	.323 030 4190	.910 989	2.820 135	.354 592 9190	141.84	.063 779	8.50	3
	1.132 354	4.193 391	.238 470 4766	.883 116	3.703 251	.270 032 9766	108.02	.080 132	8.01	4
1	1.132 354	4.193 391	.238 470 4766	.883 116	3.703 251	.270 032 9766	108.02	.080 132	8.01	4
2	1.282 225	8.941 794	.111 834 3796	.779 894	6.973 652	.143 396 8796	57.36	.147 175	7.36	8
3	1.451 933	14.318 667	.069 838 9045	.688 737	9.861 796	.101 401 4045	40.57	.216 817	7.23	12
4	1.644 102	20.407 190	.049 002 3381	.608 235	12.412 363	.080 564 8381	32.23	.289 037	7.23	16
5	1.861 705	27.301 552	.036 627 9543	.537 142	14.664 809	.068 190 4543	27.28	.363 809	7.28	20
6	2.108 109	35.108 410	.028 483 2036	.474 359	16.653 981	.060 045 7036	24.02	.441 097	7.35	24
7	2.387 126	43.948 537	.022 753 8860	.418 914	18.410 651	.054 316 3860	21.73	.520 859	7.44	28
8	2.703 071	53.958 689	.018 532 6964	.369 950	19.961 994	.050 095 1964	20.04	.603 046	7.54	32
9	3.060 833	65.293 724	.015 315 4077	.326 708	21.332 010	.046 877 9077	18.76	.687 605	7.64	36
10	3.465 946	78.128 994	.012 799 3456	.288 521	22.541 894	.044 361 8456	17.75	.774 474	7.74	40
11	3.924 678	92.663 064	.010 791 7865	.254 798	23.610 361	.042 354 2865	16.95	.863 589	7.85	44
12	4.444 124	109.120 773	.009 164 1579	.225 016	24.553 942	.040 726 6579	16.30	.954 880	7.96	48
13	5.032 322	127.756 726	.007 827 3766	.198 715	25.387 234	.039 389 8766	15.76	1.048 274	8.06	52
14	5.698 369	148.859 219	.006 717 7566	.175 489	26.123 127	.038 280 2566	15.32	1.143 694	8.17	56
15	6.452 571	172.754 710	.005 788 5542	.154 977	26.773 006	.037 351 0542	14.95	1.241 063	8.27	60
16	7.306 593	199.812 863	.005 004 6828	.136 863	27.346 925	.036 567 1828	14.63	1.340 300	8.38	64
17	8.273 650	230.452 267	.004 339 2934	.120 866	27.853 762	.035 901 7934	14.37	1.441 322	8.48	68
18	9.368 700	265.146 917	.003 771 4940	.106 738	28.301 358	.035 333 9940	14.14	1.544 048	8.58	72
19	10.608 684	304.433 540	.003 284 7892	.094 262	28.696 637	.034 847 2892	13.94	1.648 394	8.68	76
20	12.012 784	348.919 900	.002 865 9873	.083 245	29.045 714	.034 428 4873	13.78	1.754 279	8.77	80
21	13.602 723	399.294 204	.002 504 4190	.073 515	29.353 990	.034 066 9190	13.63	1.861 621	8.86	84
22	15.403 097	456.335 745	.002 191 3690	.064 922	29.626 233	.033 753 8690	13.51	1.970 340	8.96	88
23	17.441 757	520.926 956	.001 919 6549	.057 334	29.866 656	.033 482 1549	13.40	2.080 358	9.05	92
24	19.750 242	594.067 067	.001 683 3116	.050 632	30.078 977	.033 245 8116	13.30	2.191 598	9.13	96
25	22.364 264	676.887 557	.001 477 3502	.044 714	30.266 481	.033 039 8502	13.22	2.303 985	9.22	100
26	25.324 261	770.669 663	.001 297 5728	.039 488	30.432 069	.032 860 0728	13.15	2.417 448	9.30	104
27	28.676 026	876.864 198	.001 140 4274	.034 872	30.578 302	.032 702 9274	13.09	2.531 916	9.38	108
28	32.471 410	997.113 994	.001 002 8944	.030 796	30.707 443	.032 565 3944	13.03	2.647 324	9.45	112
29	36.769 129	1133.279 321	.000 882 3950	.027 197	30.821 490	.032 444 8950	12.98	2.763 608	9.53	116
30	41.635 667	1287.466 662	.000 776 7191	.024 018	30.922 206	.032 339 2191	12.94	2.880 706	9.60	120
31	47.146 310	1462.061 299	.000 683 9659	.021 211	31.011 150	.032 246 4659	12.90	2.998 562	9.67	124
32	53.386 308	1659.764 220	.000 602 4952	.018 731	31.089 698	.032 164 9952	12.87	3.117 119	9.74	128
33	60.452 195	1883.633 896	.000 530 8887	.016 542	31.159 065	.032 093 3887	12.84	3.236 327	9.81	132
34	68.453 279	2137.133 598	.000 467 9165	.014 609	31.220 325	.032 030 4165	12.82	3.356 137	9.87	136
35	77.513 338	2424.184 977	.000 412 5098	.012 901	31.274 424	.031 975 0098	12.80	3.476 501	9.93	140
36	87.772 532	2749.228 729	.000 363 7384	.011 393	31.322 199	.031 926 2384	12.78	3.597 378	9.99	144
37	99.389 570	3117.293 291	.000 320 7911	.010 061	31.364 391	.031 883 2911	12.76	3.718 727	10.05	148
38	112.544 168	3534.072 638	.000 282 9597	.008 885	31.401 651	.031 845 4597	12.74	3.840 510	10.11	152
39	127.439 828	4006.014 362	.000 249 6247	.007 847	31.434 556	.031 812 1247	12.73	3.962 691	10.16	156
40	144.306 988	4540.419 417	.000 220 2440	.006 930	31.463 614	.031 782 7440	12.72	4.085 239	10.21	160
41	163.406 582	5145.555 071	.000 194 3425	.006 120	31.489 277	.031 756 8425	12.71	4.208 122	10.26	164
42	185.034 082	5830.782 795	.000 171 5036	.005 404	31.511 939	.031 734 0036	12.70	4.331 313	10.31	168
43	209.524 066	6606.703 088	.000 151 3614	.004 773	31.531 953	.031 713 8614	12.69	4.454 784	10.36	172
44	237.255 396	7485.319 465	.000 133 5948	.004 215	31.549 628	.031 696 0948	12.68	4.578 513	10.41	176
45	268.657 075	8480.224 155	.000 117 9214	.003 722	31.565 237	.031 680 4214	12.68	4.702 476	10.45	180
46	304.214 889	9606.808 370	.000 104 0928	.003 287	31.579 021	.031 666 5928	12.67	4.826 653	10.49	184
47	344.478 919	10882.500 412	.000 091 8906	.002 903	31.591 194	.031 654 3906	12.67	4.951 025	10.53	188
48	390.072 051	12327.035 283	.000 081 1225	.002 564	31.601 944	.031 643 6225	12.66	5.075 576	10.57	192
49	441.699 612	13962.759 993	.000 071 6191	.002 264	31.611 438	.031 634 1191	12.66	5.200 287	10.61	196
50	500.160 283	15814.979 264	.000 063 2312	.001 999	31.619 822	.031 625 7312	12.66	5.325 146	10.65	200

Effective Rate is 13.24 %

Annual Percentage Rate is 12.625%

QUARTERLY COMPOUND INTEREST AND ANNUITY

12.75 % Q

Amount Of 1	Amount Of 1 Per Period	Sinking Fund Payment	Present Worth Of 1	Present Worth of 1 Per Period	Periodic Payment To Amortize 1	Constant Annual Percent	Total Interest	Annual Add On Rate	
What a single $ 1 deposit grows to in the future. The deposit is made at the beginning of the first period.	What a series of $ 1 deposits grow to in the future. A deposit is made at the end of each period.	The amount to be deposited at the end of each period that grows to $ 1 in the future.	What $ 1 to be paid in the future is worth today. Value today of a single $ 1 payment tomorrow.	What $ 1 to be paid at the end of each period is worth today. Value today of a series of $ 1 payments tomorrow.	The mortgage payment to amortize a loan of $ 1. An annuity certain, payable at the end of each period, worth $ 1 today.	The annual payment, including interest and principal, to amortize completely a loan of $ 100.	The total interest paid over the term on a loan of $1. The loan is amortized by regular periodic payments.	The average annual interest rate on a loan that is completely amortized by regular periodic payments.	
$S = (1+i)^n$	$S\overline{n}| = \dfrac{(1+i)^n - 1}{i}$	$\dfrac{1}{S\overline{n}|} = \dfrac{i}{(1+i)^n - 1}$	$V^n = \dfrac{1}{(1+i)^n}$	$A\overline{n}| = \dfrac{1-V^n}{i}$	$\dfrac{1}{A\overline{n}|} = \dfrac{i}{1-V^n}$				

YEAR									PERIODS
	1.031 875	1.000 000	1.000 000 0000	.969 110	.969 110	1.031 875 0000	412.75	.031 875	12.75	1
	1.064 766	2.031 875	.492 156 2596	.939 173	1.908 283	.524 031 2596	209.62	.048 063	9.61	2
	1.098 705	3.096 641	.322 930 5544	.910 162	2.818 445	.354 805 5544	141.93	.064 417	8.59	3
	1.133 727	4.195 346	.238 359 3375	.882 047	3.700 492	.270 234 3375	108.10	.080 937	8.09	4

YEAR	Amount Of 1	Amount Of 1 Per Period	Sinking Fund Payment	Present Worth Of 1	Present Worth of 1 Per Period	Periodic Payment To Amortize 1	Constant Annual Percent	Total Interest	Annual Add On Rate	PERIODS
1	1.133 727	4.195 346	.238 359 3375	.882 047	3.700 492	.270 234 3375	108.10	.080 937	8.09	4
2	1.285 336	8.951 723	.111 710 3428	.778 007	6.964 499	.143 585 3428	57.44	.148 683	7.43	8
3	1.457 220	14.344 153	.069 714 8165	.686 238	9.843 506	.101 589 8165	40.64	.219 078	7.30	12
4	1.652 089	20.457 695	.048 881 3615	.605 294	12.382 925	.080 756 3615	32.31	.292 102	7.30	16
5	1.873 017	27.388 781	.036 511 2997	.533 898	14.622 812	.068 386 2997	27.36	.367 726	7.35	20
6	2.123 490	35.246 738	.028 371 4197	.470 923	16.598 497	.060 246 4197	24.10	.445 914	7.43	24
7	2.407 457	44.155 513	.022 647 2285	.415 376	18.341 143	.054 522 2285	21.81	.526 622	7.52	28
8	2.729 398	54.255 630	.018 431 2671	.366 381	19.878 239	.050 306 2671	20.13	.609 801	7.62	32
9	3.094 392	65.706 401	.015 219 2175	.323 165	21.234 029	.047 094 2175	18.84	.695 392	7.73	36
10	3.508 194	78.688 445	.012 708 3462	.285 047	22.429 900	.044 583 3462	17.84	.783 334	7.83	40
11	3.977 333	93.406 535	.010 705 8890	.251 425	23.484 714	.042 580 8890	17.04	.873 559	7.94	44
12	4.509 209	110.092 826	.009 083 2440	.221 768	24.415 109	.040 958 2440	16.39	.965 996	8.05	48
13	5.112 210	129.010 519	.007 751 3059	.195 610	25.235 761	.039 626 3059	15.86	1.060 568	8.16	52
14	5.795 849	150.458 013	.006 646 3725	.172 537	25.959 615	.038 521 3725	15.41	1.157 197	8.27	56
15	6.570 909	174.773 608	.005 721 6877	.152 186	26.598 088	.037 596 6877	15.04	1.255 801	8.37	60
16	7.449 614	202.340 847	.004 942 1559	.134 235	27.161 251	.036 817 1559	14.73	1.356 298	8.48	64
17	8.445 827	233.594 560	.004 280 9216	.118 402	27.657 987	.036 155 9216	14.47	1.458 603	8.58	68
18	9.575 259	269.027 729	.003 717 0890	.104 436	28.096 131	.035 592 0890	14.24	1.562 630	8.68	72
19	10.855 726	309.199 257	.003 234 1604	.092 117	28.482 595	.035 109 1604	14.05	1.668 296	8.78	76
20	12.307 426	354.742 790	.002 818 9438	.081 252	28.823 474	.034 693 9438	13.88	1.775 516	8.88	80
21	13.953 258	406.376 708	.002 460 7710	.071 668	29.124 146	.034 335 7710	13.74	1.884 205	8.97	84
22	15.819 180	464.915 457	.002 150 9287	.063 214	29.389 352	.034 025 9287	13.62	1.994 282	9.06	88
23	17.934 626	531.282 399	.001 882 2382	.055 758	29.623 277	.033 757 2382	13.51	2.105 666	9.16	92
24	20.332 964	606.524 370	.001 648 7384	.049 181	29.829 609	.033 523 7384	13.41	2.218 279	9.24	96
25	23.052 024	691.828 200	.001 445 4456	.043 380	30.011 603	.033 320 4456	13.33	2.332 045	9.33	100
26	26.134 694	788.539 426	.001 268 1674	.038 263	30.172 131	.033 143 1674	13.26	2.446 889	9.41	104
27	29.629 600	898.183 523	.001 113 3582	.033 750	30.313 724	.032 988 3582	13.20	2.562 743	9.49	108
28	33.591 867	1022.489 959	.000 978 0047	.029 769	30.438 616	.032 853 0047	13.15	2.679 537	9.57	112
29	38.083 996	1163.419 481	.000 859 5352	.026 258	30.548 777	.032 734 5352	13.10	2.797 206	9.65	116
30	43.176 842	1323.195 038	.000 755 7465	.023 161	30.645 943	.032 630 7465	13.06	2.915 690	9.72	120
31	48.950 737	1504.336 848	.000 664 7447	.020 429	30.731 649	.032 539 7447	13.02	3.034 928	9.79	124
32	55.496 756	1709.702 149	.000 584 8972	.018 019	30.807 245	.032 459 8972	12.99	3.154 867	9.86	128
33	62.918 152	1942.530 267	.000 514 7925	.015 894	30.873 924	.032 389 7925	12.96	3.275 453	9.93	132
34	71.331 987	2206.493 714	.000 453 2077	.014 019	30.932 739	.032 328 2077	12.94	3.396 636	9.99	136
35	80.870 976	2505.756 113	.000 399 0811	.012 365	30.984 616	.032 274 0811	12.91	3.518 371	10.05	140
36	91.685 582	2845.037 875	.000 351 4892	.010 907	31.030 374	.032 226 4892	12.90	3.640 614	10.11	144
37	103.946 390	3229.690 657	.000 309 6272	.009 620	31.070 734	.032 184 6272	12.88	3.763 325	10.17	148
38	117.846 794	3665.781 774	.000 272 7931	.008 486	31.106 334	.032 147 7931	12.86	3.886 465	10.23	152
39	133.606 053	4160.189 902	.000 240 3736	.007 485	31.137 735	.032 115 3736	12.85	4.009 998	10.28	156
40	151.472 745	4720.713 583	.000 211 8324	.006 602	31.165 432	.032 086 8324	12.84	4.133 893	10.33	160
41	171.728 691	5356.194 227	.000 186 6997	.005 823	31.189 862	.032 061 6997	12.83	4.258 119	10.39	164
42	194.693 397	6076.655 581	.000 164 5642	.005 136	31.211 411	.032 039 5642	12.82	4.382 647	10.43	168
43	220.729 096	6893.461 831	.000 145 0650	.004 530	31.230 418	.032 020 0650	12.81	4.507 451	10.48	172
44	250.246 462	7819.496 860	.000 127 8855	.003 996	31.247 182	.032 002 8855	12.81	4.632 508	10.53	176
45	283.711 088	8869.367 467	.000 112 7476	.003 525	31.261 970	.031 987 7476	12.80	4.757 795	10.57	180
46	321.650 826	10059.633 772	.000 099 4072	.003 109	31.275 013	.031 974 4072	12.79	4.883 291	10.62	184
47	364.664 120	11409.070 425	.000 087 6496	.002 742	31.286 518	.031 962 6496	12.79	5.008 978	10.66	188
48	413.429 437	12938.962 744	.000 077 2859	.002 419	31.296 665	.031 952 2859	12.79	5.134 839	10.70	192
49	468.715 979	14673.442 466	.000 068 1503	.002 133	31.305 616	.031 943 1503	12.78	5.260 857	10.74	196
50	531.395 805	16639.868 382	.000 060 0966	.001 882	31.313 511	.031 935 0966	12.78	5.387 019	10.77	200

Effective Rate is 13.37 %

Annual Percentage Rate is 12.75 %

QUARTERLY COMPOUND INTEREST AND ANNUITY

12.875% Q

	Amount Of 1	Amount Of 1 Per Period	Sinking Fund Payment	Present Worth Of 1	Present Worth of 1 Per Period	Periodic Payment To Amortize 1	Constant Annual Percent	Total Interest	Annual Add On Rate	
	What a single $ 1 deposit grows to in the future. The deposit is made at the beginning of the first period.	What a series of $ 1 deposits grow to in the future. A deposit is made at the end of each period.	The amount to be deposited at the end of each period that grows to $ 1 in the future.	What $ 1 to be paid in the future is worth today. Value today of a single $ 1 payment tomorrow.	What $ 1 to be paid at the end of each period is worth today. Value today of a series of $ 1 payments tomorrow.	The mortgage payment to amortize a loan of $ 1. An annuity certain, payable at the end of each period, worth $ 1 today.	The annual payment, including interest and principal, to amortize completely a loan of $ 100.	The total interest paid over the term on a loan of $1. The loan is amortized by regular periodic payments.	The average annual interest rate on a loan that is completely amortized by regular periodic payments.	

$$S = (1+i)^n \qquad S\overline{n}| = \frac{(1+i)^n - 1}{i} \qquad \frac{1}{S\overline{n}|} = \frac{i}{(1+i)^n - 1} \qquad V^n = \frac{1}{(1+i)^n} \qquad A\overline{n}| = \frac{1-V^n}{i} \qquad \frac{1}{A\overline{n}|} = \frac{i}{1-V^n}$$

YEAR / **PERIODS**

	Amount Of 1	Amount Of 1 Per Period	Sinking Fund Payment	Present Worth Of 1	Present Worth of 1 Per Period	Periodic Payment To Amortize 1	Constant Annual Percent	Total Interest	Annual Add On Rate	
	1.032 188	1.000 000	1.000 000 0000	.968 816	.968 816	1.032 187 5000	412.88	.032 188	12.88	1
	1.065 411	2.032 188	.492 080 5782	.938 605	1.907 421	.524 268 0782	209.71	.048 536	9.71	2
	1.099 704	3.097 599	.322 830 7312	.909 336	2.816 757	.355 018 2312	142.01	.065 055	8.67	3
	1.135 101	4.197 302	.238 248 2566	.880 979	3.697 736	.270 435 7566	108.18	.081 743	8.17	4
1	1.135 101	4.197 302	.238 248 2566	.880 979	3.697 736	.270 435 7566	108.18	.081 743	8.17	4
2	1.288 454	8.961 663	.111 586 4275	.776 124	6.955 364	.143 773 9275	57.51	.150 191	7.51	8
3	1.462 524	14.369 693	.069 590 9110	.683 749	9.825 266	.101 778 4110	40.72	.221 341	7.38	12
4	1.660 113	20.508 350	.048 760 6261	.602 369	12.353 590	.080 948 1261	32.38	.295 170	7.38	16
5	1.884 395	27.476 345	.036 394 9430	.530 674	14.580 991	.068 582 4430	27.44	.371 649	7.43	20
6	2.138 978	35.385 720	.028 259 9875	.467 513	16.543 285	.060 447 4875	24.18	.450 740	7.51	24
7	2.427 955	44.363 657	.022 540 9731	.411 869	18.272 024	.054 728 4731	21.90	.532 397	7.61	28
8	2.755 974	54.554 519	.018 330 2870	.362 848	19.795 008	.050 517 7870	20.21	.616 569	7.71	32
9	3.128 307	66.122 174	.015 123 5196	.319 662	21.136 725	.047 311 0196	18.93	.703 197	7.81	36
10	3.550 944	79.252 627	.012 617 8783	.281 615	22.318 749	.044 805 3783	17.93	.792 215	7.92	40
11	4.030 679	94.157 013	.010 620 5578	.248 097	23.360 088	.042 808 0578	17.13	.883 555	8.03	44
12	4.575 226	111.074 991	.009 002 9267	.218 568	24.277 486	.041 190 4267	16.48	.977 140	8.14	48
13	5.193 342	130.278 600	.007 675 8578	.192 554	25.085 694	.039 863 3578	15.95	1.072 895	8.25	52
14	5.894 966	152.076 629	.006 575 6323	.169 636	25.797 709	.038 763 1323	15.51	1.170 735	8.36	56
15	6.691 380	176.819 586	.005 655 4821	.149 446	26.424 979	.037 842 9821	15.14	1.270 579	8.47	60
16	7.595 390	204.905 334	.004 880 3024	.131 659	26.977 591	.037 067 8024	14.83	1.372 339	8.58	64
17	8.621 533	236.785 485	.004 223 2318	.115 989	27.464 430	.036 410 7318	14.57	1.475 930	8.68	68
18	9.786 308	272.972 666	.003 663 3705	.102 184	27.893 326	.035 850 8705	14.35	1.581 263	8.78	72
19	11.108 444	314.048 760	.003 184 2189	.090 022	28.271 173	.035 371 7189	14.15	1.688 251	8.89	76
20	12.609 203	360.674 262	.002 772 5849	.079 307	28.604 050	.034 960 0849	13.99	1.796 807	8.98	80
21	14.312 715	413.598 900	.002 417 8014	.069 868	28.897 306	.034 605 3014	13.85	1.906 845	9.08	84
22	16.246 372	473.673 693	.002 111 1580	.061 552	29.155 660	.034 298 6580	13.72	2.018 282	9.17	88
23	18.441 268	541.864 630	.001 845 4794	.054 226	29.383 263	.034 032 9794	13.62	2.131 034	9.27	92
24	20.932 695	619.268 209	.001 614 8092	.047 772	29.583 778	.033 802 3092	13.53	2.245 022	9.35	96
25	23.760 717	707.129 064	.001 414 1690	.042 086	29.760 426	.033 601 6690	13.45	2.360 167	9.44	100
26	26.970 806	806.859 980	.001 239 3724	.037 077	29.916 050	.033 426 8724	13.38	2.476 395	9.52	104
27	30.614 580	920.064 609	.001 086 8802	.032 664	30.053 152	.033 274 3802	13.31	2.593 633	9.61	108
28	34.750 630	1048.563 260	.000 953 6859	.028 776	30.173 935	.033 141 1859	13.26	2.711 813	9.69	112
29	39.445 463	1194.422 166	.000 837 2249	.025 351	30.280 343	.033 024 7249	13.21	2.830 868	9.76	116
30	44.774 572	1359.986 708	.000 735 3013	.022 334	30.374 086	.032 922 8013	13.17	2.950 736	9.84	120
31	50.823 647	1547.919 131	.000 646 0286	.019 676	30.456 672	.032 833 5286	13.14	3.071 358	9.91	124
32	57.689 956	1761.241 351	.000 567 7814	.017 334	30.529 428	.032 755 2814	13.11	3.192 676	9.98	128
33	65.483 908	2003.383 547	.000 499 1555	.015 271	30.593 525	.032 686 6555	13.08	3.314 639	10.04	132
34	74.330 828	2278.239 316	.000 438 9355	.013 453	30.649 992	.032 626 4355	13.06	3.437 195	10.11	136
35	84.372 973	2590.228 285	.000 386 0664	.011 852	30.699 739	.032 573 5664	13.03	3.560 299	10.17	140
36	95.771 818	2944.367 175	.000 339 6316	.010 441	30.743 566	.032 527 1316	13.02	3.683 907	10.23	144
37	108.710 656	3346.350 466	.000 298 8330	.009 199	30.782 175	.032 486 3330	13.00	3.807 977	10.29	148
38	123.397 538	3802.641 972	.000 262 9751	.008 104	30.816 190	.032 450 4751	12.99	3.932 472	10.35	152
39	140.068 629	4320.578 767	.000 231 4505	.007 139	30.846 156	.032 418 9505	12.97	4.057 356	10.40	156
40	158.991 995	4908.489 172	.000 203 7287	.006 290	30.872 555	.032 391 2287	12.96	4.182 597	10.46	160
41	180.471 921	5575.826 669	.000 179 3456	.005 541	30.895 813	.032 366 8456	12.95	4.308 163	10.51	164
42	204.853 799	6333.321 912	.000 157 8950	.004 882	30.916 302	.032 345 3950	12.94	4.434 026	10.56	168
43	232.529 685	7193.155 272	.000 139 0211	.004 301	30.934 353	.032 326 5211	12.94	4.560 162	10.61	172
44	263.944 603	8169.152 699	.000 122 4117	.003 789	30.950 255	.032 309 9117	12.93	4.686 544	10.65	176
45	299.603 696	9277.008 036	.000 107 7934	.003 338	30.964 264	.032 295 2934	12.92	4.813 153	10.70	180
46	340.080 357	10534.535 375	.000 094 9259	.002 940	30.976 606	.032 282 4259	12.92	4.939 966	10.74	184
47	386.025 443	11961.955 505	.000 083 5984	.002 591	30.987 480	.032 271 0984	12.91	5.066 966	10.78	188
48	438.177 740	13582.221 057	.000 073 6257	.002 282	30.997 059	.032 261 1257	12.91	5.194 136	10.82	192
49	497.375 848	15421.385 576	.000 064 8450	.002 011	31.005 497	.032 252 3450	12.91	5.321 460	10.86	196
50	564.571 660	17509.022 462	.000 057 1134	.001 771	31.012 932	.032 244 6134	12.90	5.448 923	10.90	200

Effective Rate is 13.51 %　　　　8 - 339　　　　Annual Percentage Rate is 12.875%

QUARTERLY COMPOUND INTEREST AND ANNUITY

13.00 % Q

Amount Of 1	Amount Of 1 Per Period	Sinking Fund Payment	Present Worth Of 1	Present Worth of 1 Per Period	Periodic Payment To Amortize 1	Constant Annual Percent	Total Interest	Annual Add On Rate
What a single $ 1 deposit grows to in the future. The deposit is made at the beginning of the first period.	What a series of $ 1 deposits grow to in the future. A deposit is made at the end of each period.	The amount to be deposited at the end of each period that grows to $ 1 in the future.	What $ 1 to be paid in the future is worth today. Value today of a single $ 1 payment tomorrow.	What $ 1 to be paid at the end of each period is worth today. Value today of a series of $ 1 payments tomorrow.	The mortgage payment to amortize a loan of $ 1. An annuity certain, payable at the end of each period, worth $ 1 today.	The annual payment, including interest and principal, to amortize completely a loan of $ 100.	The total interest paid over the term on a loan of $1. The loan is amortized by regular periodic payments.	The average annual interest rate on a loan that is completely amortized by regular periodic payments.
$S = (1+i)^n$	$S\overline{n} = \dfrac{(1+i)^n - 1}{i}$	$\dfrac{1}{S\overline{n}} = \dfrac{i}{(1+i)^n - 1}$	$V^n = \dfrac{1}{(1+i)^n}$	$A\overline{n} = \dfrac{1-V^n}{i}$	$\dfrac{1}{A\overline{n}} = \dfrac{i}{1-V^n}$			

YEAR ... **PERIODS**

	Amount Of 1	Amount Of 1 Per Period	Sinking Fund Payment	Present Worth Of 1	Present Worth of 1 Per Period	Periodic Payment To Amortize 1	Constant Annual Percent	Total Interest	Annual Add On Rate	PERIODS
	1.032 500	1.000 000	1.000 000 0000	.968 523	.968 523	1.032 500 0000	413.00	.032 500	13.00	1
	1.066 056	2.032 500	.492 004 9200	.938 037	1.906 560	.524 504 9200	209.81	.049 010	9.80	2
	1.100 703	3.098 556	.322 730 9493	.908 510	2.815 070	.355 230 9493	142.10	.065 693	8.76	3
	1.136 476	4.199 259	.238 137 2337	.879 913	3.694 983	.270 637 2337	108.26	.082 549	8.25	4
1	1.136 476	4.199 259	.238 137 2337	.879 913	3.694 983	.270 637 2337	108.26	.082 549	8.25	4
2	1.291 578	8.971 616	.111 462 6337	.774 247	6.946 247	.143 962 6337	57.59	.151 701	7.59	8
3	1.467 847	14.395 285	.069 467 1878	.681 270	9.807 076	.101 967 1878	40.79	.223 606	7.45	12
4	1.668 173	20.559 155	.048 640 1319	.599 458	12.324 358	.081 140 1319	32.46	.298 242	7.46	16
5	1.895 838	27.564 244	.036 278 8839	.527 471	14.539 346	.068 778 8839	27.52	.375 578	7.51	20
6	2.154 574	35.525 359	.028 148 9063	.464 129	16.488 343	.060 648 9063	24.26	.455 574	7.59	24
7	2.448 622	44.572 975	.022 435 1193	.408 393	18.203 292	.054 935 1193	21.98	.538 183	7.69	28
8	2.782 800	54.855 372	.018 229 7552	.359 350	19.712 297	.050 729 7552	20.30	.623 352	7.79	32
9	3.162 585	66.541 069	.015 028 3128	.316 197	21.040 090	.047 528 3128	19.02	.711 019	7.90	36
10	3.594 201	79.821 583	.012 527 9400	.278 226	22.208 433	.045 027 9400	18.02	.801 118	8.01	40
11	4.084 723	94.914 566	.010 535 7906	.244 815	23.236 473	.043 035 7906	17.22	.893 575	8.12	44
12	4.642 190	112.067 379	.008 923 2032	.215 416	24.141 059	.041 423 2032	16.57	.988 314	8.24	48
13	5.275 737	131.561 138	.007 601 0288	.189 547	24.937 016	.040 101 0288	16.05	1.085 253	8.35	52
14	5.995 748	153.715 326	.006 505 5322	.166 785	25.637 389	.039 005 5322	15.61	1.184 310	8.46	56
15	6.814 023	178.893 027	.005 589 9328	.146 756	26.253 656	.038 089 9328	15.24	1.285 396	8.57	60
16	7.743 974	207.506 879	.004 819 1174	.129 133	26.795 918	.037 319 1174	14.93	1.388 424	8.68	64
17	8.800 840	240.025 832	.004 166 2182	.113 626	27.273 061	.036 666 2182	14.67	1.493 303	8.78	68
18	10.001 942	276.982 839	.003 610 3320	.099 981	27.692 905	.036 110 3320	14.45	1.599 944	8.89	72
19	11.366 967	318.983 589	.003 134 9575	.087 974	28.062 332	.035 634 9575	14.26	1.708 257	8.99	76
20	12.918 284	366.716 429	.002 726 9026	.077 410	28.387 395	.035 226 9026	14.10	1.818 152	9.09	80
21	14.681 319	420.963 654	.002 375 5020	.068 114	28.673 422	.034 875 5020	13.96	1.929 542	9.19	84
22	16.684 965	482.614 318	.002 072 0479	.059 934	28.925 102	.034 572 0479	13.83	2.042 340	9.28	88
23	18.962 061	552.678 815	.001 809 3692	.052 737	29.146 557	.034 309 3692	13.73	2.156 462	9.38	92
24	21.549 926	632.305 428	.001 581 5142	.046 404	29.341 419	.034 081 5142	13.64	2.271 825	9.47	96
25	24.490 973	722.799 158	.001 383 5102	.040 831	29.512 881	.033 883 5102	13.56	2.388 351	9.55	100
26	27.833 401	825.643 103	.001 211 1771	.035 928	29.663 752	.033 711 1771	13.49	2.505 962	9.64	104
27	31.631 990	942.522 771	.001 060 9823	.031 614	29.796 506	.033 560 9823	13.43	2.624 586	9.72	108
28	35.948 995	1075.353 700	.000 929 9266	.027 817	29.913 317	.033 429 9266	13.38	2.744 152	9.80	112
29	40.855 168	1226.312 854	.000 815 4526	.024 477	30.016 101	.033 315 4526	13.33	2.864 593	9.88	116
30	46.430 915	1397.874 298	.000 715 3719	.021 537	30.106 542	.033 215 3719	13.29	2.985 845	9.95	120
31	52.767 617	1592.849 750	.000 627 8056	.018 951	30.186 123	.033 127 8056	13.26	3.107 848	10.03	124
32	59.969 126	1814.434 657	.000 551 1359	.016 675	30.256 146	.033 051 1359	13.23	3.230 545	10.10	128
33	68.153 469	2066.260 571	.000 483 9661	.014 673	30.317 761	.032 983 9661	13.20	3.353 884	10.16	132
34	77.454 776	2352.454 659	.000 425 0879	.012 911	30.371 977	.032 925 0879	13.18	3.477 812	10.23	136
35	88.025 489	2677.707 352	.000 373 4538	.011 360	30.419 682	.032 873 4538	13.15	3.602 284	10.29	140
36	100.038 849	3047.349 207	.000 328 1541	.009 996	30.461 658	.032 828 1541	13.14	3.727 254	10.35	144
37	113.691 744	3467.438 278	.000 288 3973	.008 796	30.498 593	.032 788 3973	13.12	3.852 683	10.41	148
38	129.207 930	3944.859 395	.000 253 4945	.007 739	30.531 093	.032 753 4945	13.11	3.978 531	10.47	152
39	146.841 703	4487.437 001	.000 222 8444	.006 810	30.559 691	.032 722 8444	13.09	4.104 764	10.53	156
40	166.882 060	5104.063 390	.000 195 9223	.005 992	30.584 854	.032 695 9223	13.08	4.231 348	10.58	160
41	189.657 444	5804.844 438	.000 172 2699	.005 273	30.606 995	.032 672 2699	13.07	4.358 252	10.63	164
42	215.541 120	6601.265 230	.000 151 4861	.004 639	30.626 477	.032 651 4861	13.07	4.485 450	10.68	168
43	244.957 294	7506.378 289	.000 133 2200	.004 082	30.643 620	.032 633 2200	13.06	4.612 914	10.73	172
44	278.388 068	8535.017 492	.000 117 1644	.003 592	30.658 704	.032 617 1644	13.05	4.740 621	10.77	176
45	316.381 339	9704.041 186	.000 103 0499	.003 161	30.671 977	.032 603 0499	13.05	4.868 549	10.82	180
46	359.559 775	11032.608 473	.000 090 6404	.002 781	30.683 656	.032 590 6404	13.04	4.996 678	10.86	184
47	408.631 029	12542.493 214	.000 079 7290	.002 447	30.693 932	.032 579 7290	13.04	5.124 989	10.90	188
48	464.399 328	14258.440 876	.000 070 1339	.002 153	30.702 975	.032 570 1339	13.03	5.253 466	10.94	192
49	527.778 658	16208.574 088	.000 061 6957	.001 895	30.710 931	.032 561 6957	13.03	5.382 092	10.98	196
50	599.807 740	18424.853 540	.000 054 2745	.001 667	30.717 932	.032 554 2745	13.03	5.510 855	11.02	200

Effective Rate is 13.65 %

Annual Percentage Rate is 13.00 %

	Amount Of 1	Amount Of 1 Per Period	Sinking Fund Payment	Present Worth Of 1	Present Worth of 1 Per Period	Periodic Payment To Amortize 1	Constant Annual Percent	Total Interest	Annual Add On Rate
	What a single $ 1 deposit grows to in the future. The deposit is made at the beginning of the first period.	What a series of $ 1 deposits grow to in the future. A deposit is made at the end of each period.	The amount to be deposited at the end of each period that grows to $ 1 in the future.	What $ 1 to be paid in the future is worth today. Value today of a single $ 1 payment tomorrow.	What $ 1 to be paid at the end of each period is worth today. Value today of a series of $ 1 payments tomorrow.	The mortgage payment to amortize a loan of $ 1. An annuity certain, payable at the end of each period, worth $ 1 today.	The annual payment, including interest and principal, to amortize completely a loan of $ 100.	The total interest paid over the term on a loan of $1. The loan is amortized by regular periodic payments.	The average annual interest rate on a loan that is completely amortized by regular periodic payments.
	$S = (1+i)^n$	$S\overline{n}] = \dfrac{(1+i)^n - 1}{i}$	$\dfrac{1}{S\overline{n}]} = \dfrac{i}{(1+i)^n - 1}$	$V^n = \dfrac{1}{(1+i)^n}$	$A\overline{n}] = \dfrac{1 - V^n}{i}$	$\dfrac{1}{A\overline{n}]} = \dfrac{i}{1 - V^n}$			

YEAR									PERIODS
	1.032 812	1.000 000	1.000 000 0000	.968 230	.968 230	1.032 812 5000	413.13	.032 813	13.13	1
	1.066 702	2.032 813	.491 929 2852	.937 469	1.905 699	.524 741 7852	209.90	.049 484	9.90	2
	1.101 703	3.099 514	.322 631 2087	.907 686	2.813 385	.355 443 7087	142.18	.066 331	8.84	3
	1.137 852	4.201 217	.238 026 2689	.878 849	3.692 234	.270 838 7689	108.34	.083 355	8.34	4

YEAR	Amount Of 1	Amount Of 1 Per Period	Sinking Fund Payment	Present Worth Of 1	Present Worth of 1 Per Period	Periodic Payment To Amortize 1	Constant Annual Percent	Total Interest	Annual Add On Rate	PERIODS
1	1.137 852	4.201 217	.238 026 2689	.878 849	3.692 234	.270 838 7689	108.34	.083 355	8.34	4
2	1.294 708	8.981 582	.111 338 9612	.772 375	6.937 148	.144 151 4612	57.67	.153 212	7.66	8
3	1.473 187	14.420 932	.069 343 6468	.678 801	9.788 936	.102 156 1468	40.87	.225 874	7.53	12
4	1.676 269	20.610 109	.048 519 8786	.596 563	12.295 226	.081 332 3786	32.54	.301 318	7.53	16
5	1.907 347	27.652 480	.036 163 1218	.524 288	14.497 876	.068 975 6218	27.60	.379 512	7.59	20
6	2.170 279	35.665 658	.028 038 1757	.460 770	16.433 671	.060 850 6757	24.35	.460 416	7.67	24
7	2.469 458	44.783 473	.022 329 6660	.404 947	18.134 942	.055 142 1660	22.06	.543 981	7.77	28
8	2.809 878	55.158 201	.018 129 6704	.355 887	19.630 102	.050 942 1704	20.38	.630 149	7.88	32
9	3.197 227	66.963 110	.014 933 5955	.312 771	20.944 121	.047 746 0955	19.10	.718 859	7.99	36
10	3.637 973	80.395 354	.012 438 5296	.274 878	22.098 945	.045 251 0296	18.11	.810 041	8.10	40
11	4.139 476	95.679 267	.010 451 5851	.241 576	23.113 860	.043 264 0851	17.31	.903 620	8.21	44
12	4.710 113	113.070 103	.008 844 0708	.212 309	24.005 817	.041 656 5708	16.67	.999 515	8.33	48
13	5.359 413	132.858 309	.007 526 8157	.186 588	24.789 712	.040 339 3157	16.14	1.097 644	8.44	52
14	6.098 221	155.374 367	.006 436 0681	.163 982	25.478 637	.039 248 5681	15.70	1.197 920	8.56	56
15	6.938 876	180.994 318	.005 525 0353	.144 116	26.084 097	.038 337 5353	15.34	1.300 252	8.67	60
16	7.895 417	210.146 042	.004 758 5955	.126 656	26.616 206	.037 571 0955	15.03	1.404 550	8.78	64
17	8.983 819	243.316 402	.004 109 8750	.111 311	27.083 848	.036 922 3750	14.77	1.510 722	8.89	68
18	10.222 261	281.059 376	.003 557 9671	.097 826	27.494 835	.036 370 4671	14.55	1.618 674	8.99	72
19	11.631 424	324.005 312	.003 086 3692	.085 974	27.856 031	.035 898 8692	14.36	1.728 314	9.10	76
20	13.234 844	372.871 449	.002 681 8894	.075 558	28.173 467	.035 494 3894	14.20	1.839 551	9.20	80
21	15.059 300	428.473 902	.002 333 8644	.066 404	28.452 445	.035 146 3644	14.06	1.952 295	9.30	84
22	17.135 261	491.741 288	.002 033 5897	.058 359	28.697 625	.034 846 0897	13.94	2.066 456	9.39	88
23	19.497 398	563.730 237	.001 773 8981	.051 289	28.913 100	.034 586 3981	13.84	2.181 949	9.49	92
24	22.185 162	645.643 038	.001 548 8435	.045 075	29.102 471	.034 361 3435	13.75	2.298 689	9.58	96
25	25.243 441	738.847 718	.001 353 4589	.039 614	29.268 899	.034 165 9589	13.67	2.416 596	9.67	100
26	28.723 310	844.900 890	.001 183 5708	.034 815	29.415 164	.033 996 0708	13.60	2.535 591	9.75	104
27	32.682 889	965.573 749	.001 035 6537	.030 597	29.543 709	.033 848 1537	13.54	2.655 601	9.84	108
28	37.188 304	1102.881 655	.000 906 7156	.026 890	29.656 680	.033 719 2156	13.49	2.776 552	9.92	112
29	42.314 803	1259.117 791	.000 794 2069	.023 632	29.755 965	.033 606 7069	13.45	2.898 378	9.99	116
30	48.148 001	1436.891 457	.000 695 9468	.020 769	29.843 222	.033 508 4468	13.41	3.021 014	10.07	120
31	54.785 320	1639.171 655	.000 610 0642	.018 253	29.919 907	.033 422 5642	13.37	3.144 398	10.14	124
32	62.337 610	1869.336 671	.000 534 9491	.016 042	29.987 301	.033 347 4491	13.34	3.268 473	10.21	128
33	70.931 001	2131.230 494	.000 469 2125	.014 098	30.046 531	.033 281 7125	13.32	3.393 186	10.28	132
34	80.709 012	2429.227 017	.000 411 6536	.012 390	30.098 585	.033 224 1536	13.29	3.518 485	10.35	136
35	91.834 945	2768.303 086	.000 361 2321	.010 889	30.144 332	.033 173 7321	13.27	3.644 322	10.41	140
36	104.494 615	3154.121 615	.000 317 0455	.009 570	30.184 537	.033 129 5455	13.26	3.770 655	10.47	144
37	118.899 452	3593.126 167	.000 278 3092	.008 410	30.219 871	.033 090 8092	13.24	3.897 440	10.53	148
38	135.290 031	4092.648 564	.000 244 3405	.007 392	30.250 925	.033 056 8405	13.23	4.024 640	10.59	152
39	153.940 091	4661.031 337	.000 214 5448	.006 496	30.278 216	.033 027 0448	13.22	4.152 219	10.65	156
40	175.161 107	5307.767 059	.000 188 4031	.005 709	30.302 201	.033 000 9031	13.21	4.280 145	10.70	160
41	199.307 491	6043.656 872	.000 165 4627	.005 017	30.323 280	.032 977 9627	13.20	4.408 386	10.75	164
42	226.782 513	6880.990 886	.000 145 3279	.004 410	30.341 805	.032 957 8279	13.19	4.536 915	10.80	168
43	258.045 034	7833.753 430	.000 127 6527	.003 875	30.358 086	.032 940 1527	13.18	4.665 706	10.85	172
44	293.617 170	8917.856 607	.000 112 1346	.003 406	30.372 395	.032 924 6346	13.17	4.794 736	10.90	176
45	334.093 011	10151.406 043	.000 098 5085	.002 993	30.384 970	.032 911 0085	13.17	4.923 982	10.94	180
46	380.148 545	11555.003 269	.000 086 5426	.002 631	30.396 021	.032 899 0426	13.16	5.053 424	10.99	184
47	432.552 946	13152.089 786	.000 076 0335	.002 312	30.405 734	.032 888 5335	13.16	5.183 044	11.03	188
48	492.181 422	14969.338 563	.000 066 8032	.002 032	30.414 270	.032 879 3032	13.16	5.312 826	11.07	192
49	560.029 827	17037.099 503	.000 058 6954	.001 786	30.421 772	.032 871 1954	13.15	5.442 754	11.11	196
50	637.231 301	19389.906 317	.000 051 5732	.001 569	30.428 365	.032 864 0732	13.15	5.572 815	11.15	200

Effective Rate is 13.79 %

Annual Percentage Rate is 13.125%

Amount Of 1	Amount Of 1 Per Period	Sinking Fund Payment	Present Worth Of 1	Present Worth of 1 Per Period	Periodic Payment To Amortize 1	Constant Annual Percent	Total Interest	Annual Add On Rate
What a single $ 1 deposit grows to in the future. The deposit is made at the beginning of the first period.	What a series of $ 1 deposits grow to in the future. A deposit is made at the end of each period.	The amount to be deposited at the end of each period that grows to $ 1 in the future.	What $ 1 to be paid in the future is worth today. Value today of a single $ 1 payment tomorrow.	What $ 1 to be paid at the end of each period is worth today. Value today of a series of $ 1 payments tomorrow.	The mortgage payment to amortize a loan of $ 1. An annuity certain, payable at the end of each period, worth $ 1 today.	The annual payment, including interest and principal, to amortize completely a loan of $ 100.	The total interest paid over the term on a loan of $1. The loan is amortized by regular periodic payments.	The average annual interest rate on a loan that is completely amortized by regular periodic payments.
$S = (1+i)^n$	$S\overline{n} = \dfrac{(1+i)^n - 1}{i}$	$\dfrac{1}{S\overline{n}} = \dfrac{i}{(1+i)^n - 1}$	$V^n = \dfrac{1}{(1+i)^n}$	$A\overline{n} = \dfrac{1-V^n}{i}$	$\dfrac{1}{A\overline{n}} = \dfrac{i}{1-V^n}$			

YEAR									PERIODS
	1.033 125	1.000 000	1.000 000 0000	.967 937	.967 937	1.033 125 0000	413.25	.033 125	13.25	1
	1.067 347	2.033 125	.491 853 6735	.936 902	1.904 839	.524 978 6735	210.00	.049 957	9.99	2
	1.102 703	3.100 472	.322 531 5095	.906 862	2.811 702	.355 656 5095	142.27	.066 970	8.93	3
	1.139 230	4.203 175	.237 915 3622	.877 786	3.689 487	.271 040 3622	108.42	.084 161	8.42	4
1	1.139 230	4.203 175	.237 915 3622	.877 786	3.689 487	.271 040 3622	108.42	.084 161	8.42	4
2	1.297 845	8.991 560	.111 215 4100	.770 508	6.928 067	.144 340 4100	57.74	.154 723	7.74	8
3	1.478 545	14.446 632	.069 220 2878	.676 341	9.770 846	.102 345 2878	40.94	.228 143	7.60	12
4	1.684 403	20.661 214	.048 399 8659	.593 682	12.266 196	.081 524 8659	32.61	.304 398	7.61	16
5	1.918 922	27.741 054	.036 047 6566	.521 126	14.456 579	.069 172 6566	27.67	.383 453	7.67	20
6	2.186 094	35.806 622	.027 927 7951	.457 437	16.379 266	.061 052 7951	24.43	.465 267	7.75	24
7	2.490 465	44.995 160	.022 224 6126	.401 531	18.066 974	.055 349 6126	22.14	.549 789	7.85	28
8	2.837 213	55.463 020	.018 030 0316	.352 459	19.548 419	.051 155 0316	20.47	.636 961	7.96	32
9	3.232 238	67.388 322	.014 839 3664	.309 383	20.848 811	.047 964 3664	19.19	.726 717	8.07	36
10	3.682 263	80.973 986	.012 349 6453	.271 572	21.990 276	.045 474 6453	18.19	.818 986	8.19	40
11	4.194 945	96.451 184	.010 367 9391	.238 382	22.992 238	.043 492 9391	17.40	.913 689	8.31	44
12	4.779 009	114.083 276	.008 765 5267	.209 248	23.871 746	.041 890 5267	16.76	1.010 745	8.42	48
13	5.444 391	134.170 287	.007 453 2150	.183 675	24.643 765	.040 578 2150	16.24	1.110 067	8.54	52
14	6.202 414	157.054 016	.006 367 2361	.161 228	25.321 433	.039 492 2361	15.80	1.211 565	8.65	56
15	7.065 978	183.123 851	.005 460 7851	.141 523	25.916 280	.038 585 7851	15.44	1.315 147	8.77	60
16	8.049 775	212.823 395	.004 698 7316	.124 227	26.438 428	.037 823 7316	15.13	1.420 719	8.88	64
17	9.170 547	246.658 011	.004 054 1963	.109 045	26.896 762	.037 179 1963	14.88	1.528 185	8.99	68
18	10.447 364	285.203 427	.003 506 2692	.095 718	27.299 081	.036 631 2692	14.66	1.637 451	9.10	72
19	11.901 952	329.115 528	.003 038 4467	.084 020	27.652 231	.036 163 4467	14.47	1.748 422	9.20	76
20	13.559 063	379.141 519	.002 637 5376	.073 751	27.962 222	.035 762 5376	14.31	1.861 003	9.31	80
21	15.446 894	436.132 639	.002 292 8804	.064 738	28.234 326	.035 417 8804	14.17	1.975 102	9.41	84
22	17.597 568	501.058 643	.001 995 7744	.056 826	28.473 176	.035 120 7744	14.05	2.090 628	9.50	88
23	20.047 680	575.024 306	.001 739 0569	.049 881	28.682 835	.034 864 0569	13.95	2.207 493	9.60	92
24	22.838 922	659.288 222	.001 516 7873	.043 785	28.866 871	.034 641 7873	13.86	2.325 612	9.69	96
25	26.018 790	755.284 219	.001 324 0049	.038 434	29.028 415	.034 449 0049	13.78	2.444 900	9.78	100
26	29.641 391	864.645 756	.001 156 5430	.033 737	29.170 216	.034 281 5430	13.72	2.565 280	9.87	104
27	33.768 367	989.233 720	.001 010 8835	.029 614	29.294 686	.034 135 8835	13.66	2.686 675	9.95	108
28	38.469 943	1131.168 090	.000 884 0419	.025 994	29.403 945	.034 009 0419	13.61	2.809 013	10.03	112
29	43.826 120	1292.864 008	.000 773 4766	.022 817	29.499 851	.033 898 4766	13.56	2.932 223	10.11	116
30	49.928 039	1477.072 879	.000 677 0147	.020 029	29.584 035	.033 802 0147	13.53	3.056 242	10.19	120
31	56.879 529	1686.929 185	.000 592 7931	.017 581	29.657 932	.033 717 7931	13.49	3.181 006	10.26	124
32	64.798 877	1926.003 824	.000 519 2098	.015 432	29.722 796	.033 644 2098	13.46	3.306 459	10.33	128
33	73.820 836	2198.364 869	.000 454 8835	.013 546	29.779 734	.033 579 8835	13.44	3.432 545	10.40	132
34	84.098 925	2508.646 793	.000 398 6213	.011 891	29.829 713	.033 523 6213	13.41	3.559 212	10.47	136
35	95.808 034	2862.129 326	.000 349 3902	.010 438	29.873 584	.033 474 3902	13.39	3.686 415	10.53	140
36	109.147 404	3264.827 299	.000 306 2949	.009 162	29.912 093	.033 431 2949	13.38	3.814 106	10.59	144
37	124.344 018	3723.592 984	.000 268 5578	.008 042	29.945 896	.033 393 5578	13.36	3.942 247	10.65	148
38	141.656 458	4246.232 702	.000 235 5029	.007 059	29.975 567	.033 360 5029	13.35	4.070 796	10.71	152
39	161.379 313	4841.639 643	.000 206 5416	.006 197	30.001 613	.033 331 5416	13.34	4.199 720	10.77	156
40	183.848 185	5519.945 204	.000 181 1612	.005 439	30.024 475	.033 306 1612	13.33	4.328 986	10.82	160
41	209.445 402	6292.691 374	.000 158 9145	.004 775	30.044 543	.033 283 9145	13.32	4.458 562	10.87	164
42	238.606 524	7173.027 136	.000 139 4112	.004 191	30.062 158	.033 264 4112	13.31	4.588 421	10.92	168
43	271.827 754	8175.932 210	.000 122 3102	.003 679	30.077 621	.033 247 3102	13.30	4.718 537	10.97	172
44	309.674 383	9318.471 943	.000 107 3137	.003 229	30.091 194	.033 232 3137	13.30	4.848 887	11.02	176
45	352.790 405	10620.087 695	.000 094 1612	.002 835	30.103 108	.033 219 1612	13.29	4.979 449	11.07	180
46	401.909 478	12102.927 650	.000 082 6246	.002 488	30.113 566	.033 207 6246	13.29	5.110 203	11.11	184
47	457.867 410	13792.223 886	.000 072 5046	.002 184	30.122 746	.033 197 5046	13.28	5.241 131	11.15	188
48	521.616 374	15716.720 723	.000 063 6265	.001 917	30.130 804	.033 188 6265	13.28	5.372 216	11.19	192
49	594.241 118	17909.165 839	.000 055 8373	.001 683	30.137 877	.033 180 8373	13.28	5.503 444	11.23	196
50	676.977 420	20406.865 495	.000 049 0031	.001 477	30.144 086	.033 174 0031	13.27	5.634 801	11.27	200

Effective Rate is 13.92 %

Annual Percentage Rate is 13.25 %

QUARTERLY COMPOUND INTEREST AND ANNUITY

13.375% Q

	Amount Of 1	Amount Of 1 Per Period	Sinking Fund Payment	Present Worth Of 1	Present Worth of 1 Per Period	Periodic Payment To Amortize 1	Constant Annual Percent	Total Interest	Annual Add On Rate	
	What a single $ 1 deposit grows to in the future. The deposit is made at the beginning of the first period.	What a series of $ 1 deposits grow to in the future. A deposit is made at the end of each period.	The amount to be deposited at the end of each period that grows to $ 1 in the future.	What $ 1 to be paid in the future is worth today. Value today of a single $ 1 payment tomorrow.	What $ 1 to be paid at the end of each period is worth today. Value today of a series of $ 1 payments tomorrow.	The mortgage payment to amortize a loan of $ 1. An annuity certain, payable at the end of each period, worth $ 1 today.	The annual payment, including interest and principal, to amortize completely a loan of $ 100.	The total interest paid over the term on a loan of $1. The loan is amortized by regular periodic payments.	The average annual interest rate on a loan that is completely amortized by regular periodic payments.	

$$S = (1+i)^n \qquad S\overline{n}| = \frac{(1+i)^n - 1}{i} \qquad \frac{1}{S\overline{n}|} = \frac{i}{(1+i)^n - 1} \qquad V^n = \frac{1}{(1+i)^n} \qquad A\overline{n}| = \frac{1 - V^n}{i} \qquad \frac{1}{A\overline{n}|} = \frac{i}{1 - V^n}$$

YEAR										PERIODS
	1.033 438	1.000 000	1.000 000 0000	.967 644	.967 644	1.033 437 5000	413.38	.033 437	13.37	1
	1.067 993	2.033 438	.491 778 0851	.936 336	1.903 980	.525 215 5851	210.09	.050 431	10.09	2
	1.103 704	3.101 431	.322 431 8516	.906 040	2.810 020	.355 869 3516	142.35	.067 608	9.01	3
	1.140 609	4.205 135	.237 804 5135	.876 724	3.686 744	.271 242 0135	108.50	.084 968	8.50	4
1	1.140 609	4.205 135	.237 804 5135	.876 724	3.686 744	.271 242 0135	108.50	.084 968	8.50	4
2	1.300 989	9.001 550	.111 091 9801	.768 646	6.919 004	.144 529 4801	57.82	.156 236	7.81	8
3	1.483 920	14.472 385	.069 097 1107	.673 891	9.752 804	.102 534 6107	41.02	.230 415	7.68	12
4	1.692 573	20.712 470	.048 280 0937	.590 816	12.237 267	.081 717 5937	32.69	.307 481	7.69	16
5	1.930 565	27.829 968	.035 932 4877	.517 983	14.415 456	.069 369 9877	27.75	.387 400	7.75	20
6	2.202 020	35.948 252	.027 817 7639	.454 129	16.325 128	.061 255 2639	24.51	.470 126	7.84	24
7	2.511 644	45.208 042	.022 119 9583	.398 146	17.999 384	.055 557 4583	22.23	.555 609	7.94	28
8	2.864 804	55.769 843	.017 930 8378	.349 064	19.467 245	.051 368 3378	20.55	.643 787	8.05	32
9	3.267 622	67.816 730	.014 745 6241	.306 033	20.754 154	.048 183 1241	19.28	.734 592	8.16	36
10	3.727 080	81.557 520	.012 261 2851	.268 307	21.882 420	.045 698 7851	18.28	.827 951	8.28	40
11	4.251 141	97.230 391	.010 284 8501	.235 231	22.871 598	.043 722 3501	17.49	.923 783	8.40	44
12	4.848 891	115.107 012	.008 687 5680	.206 233	23.738 834	.042 125 0680	16.86	1.022 003	8.52	48
13	5.530 689	135.497 251	.007 380 2236	.180 809	24.499 161	.040 817 7236	16.33	1.122 522	8.63	52
14	6.308 355	158.754 544	.006 299 0323	.158 520	25.165 759	.039 736 5323	15.90	1.225 246	8.75	56
15	7.195 368	185.282 026	.005 397 1776	.138 978	25.750 182	.038 834 6776	15.54	1.330 081	8.87	60
16	8.207 103	215.539 517	.004 639 5205	.121 846	26.262 559	.038 077 0205	15.24	1.436 929	8.98	64
17	9.361 097	250.051 488	.003 999 1764	.106 825	26.711 773	.037 436 6764	14.98	1.545 694	9.09	68
18	10.677 353	289.416 160	.003 455 2321	.093 656	27.105 610	.036 892 7321	14.76	1.656 277	9.20	72
19	12.178 687	334.315 866	.002 991 1832	.082 111	27.450 896	.036 428 6832	14.58	1.768 580	9.31	76
20	13.891 122	385.528 884	.002 593 8394	.071 988	27.753 617	.036 031 3394	14.42	1.882 507	9.41	80
21	15.844 341	443.942 923	.002 252 5418	.063 114	28.019 020	.035 690 0418	14.28	1.997 964	9.51	84
22	18.072 202	510.570 512	.001 958 5933	.055 334	28.251 705	.035 396 0933	14.16	2.114 856	9.61	88
23	20.613 319	586.566 553	.001 704 8364	.048 512	28.455 706	.035 142 3364	14.06	2.233 095	9.71	92
24	23.511 741	673.248 335	.001 485 3360	.042 532	28.634 559	.034 922 8360	13.97	2.352 592	9.80	96
25	26.817 708	772.118 373	.001 295 1382	.037 289	28.791 363	.034 732 6382	13.90	2.473 264	9.89	100
26	30.588 524	884.890 447	.001 130 0834	.032 692	28.928 837	.034 567 5834	13.83	2.595 029	9.98	104
27	34.889 552	1013.519 310	.000 986 6610	.028 662	29.049 364	.034 424 1610	13.77	2.717 809	10.07	108
28	39.795 344	1160.234 574	.000 861 8947	.025 129	29.155 033	.034 299 3947	13.72	2.841 532	10.15	112
29	45.390 935	1327.579 352	.000 753 2506	.022 031	29.247 676	.034 190 7506	13.68	2.966 127	10.23	116
30	51.773 317	1518.454 344	.000 658 5644	.019 315	29.328 898	.034 096 0644	13.64	3.091 528	10.31	120
31	59.053 121	1736.168 114	.000 575 9811	.016 934	29.400 107	.034 013 4811	13.61	3.217 672	10.38	124
32	67.356 533	1984.494 441	.000 503 9067	.014 846	29.462 538	.033 941 4067	13.58	3.344 500	10.45	128
33	76.827 480	2267.737 731	.000 440 9681	.013 016	29.517 273	.033 878 4681	13.56	3.471 958	10.52	132
34	87.630 130	2590.807 631	.000 385 9800	.011 412	29.565 261	.033 823 4800	13.53	3.599 993	10.59	136
35	99.951 732	2959.304 128	.000 337 9173	.010 005	29.607 332	.033 775 4173	13.52	3.728 558	10.65	140
36	114.005 864	3379.614 618	.000 295 8917	.008 771	29.644 217	.033 733 3917	13.50	3.857 608	10.72	144
37	130.036 136	3859.024 627	.000 259 1328	.007 690	29.676 556	.033 696 6328	13.48	3.987 102	10.78	148
38	148.320 412	4405.844 088	.000 226 9713	.006 742	29.704 907	.033 664 4713	13.47	4.117 000	10.83	152
39	169.175 625	5029.551 390	.000 198 8249	.005 911	29.729 764	.033 636 3249	13.46	4.247 267	10.89	156
40	192.963 272	5740.957 672	.000 174 1870	.005 182	29.751 556	.033 611 6870	13.45	4.377 870	10.94	160
41	220.095 682	6552.394 214	.000 152 6160	.004 543	29.770 662	.033 590 1160	13.44	4.508 779	11.00	164
42	251.043 157	7477.926 191	.000 133 7269	.003 983	29.787 413	.033 571 2269	13.43	4.639 966	11.05	168
43	286.342 132	8533.596 469	.000 117 1839	.003 492	29.802 099	.033 554 6839	13.43	4.771 406	11.10	172
44	326.604 467	9737.703 690	.000 102 6936	.003 062	29.814 974	.033 540 1936	13.42	4.903 074	11.14	176
45	372.528 057	11111.119 452	.000 089 9999	.002 684	29.826 262	.033 527 4999	13.42	5.034 950	11.19	180
46	424.908 925	12677.650 092	.000 078 8790	.002 353	29.836 159	.033 516 3790	13.41	5.167 014	11.23	184
47	484.655 025	14464.449 335	.000 069 1350	.002 063	29.844 835	.033 506 6350	13.41	5.299 247	11.27	188
48	552.801 975	16502.488 973	.000 060 5969	.001 809	29.852 442	.033 498 0969	13.40	5.431 635	11.32	192
49	630.531 013	18827.095 714	.000 053 1149	.001 586	29.859 111	.033 490 6149	13.40	5.564 161	11.36	196
50	719.189 468	21478.563 525	.000 046 5580	.001 390	29.864 958	.033 484 0580	13.40	5.696 812	11.39	200

QUARTERLY COMPOUND INTEREST AND ANNUITY

Amount Of 1	Amount Of 1 Per Period	Sinking Fund Payment	Present Worth Of 1	Present Worth of 1 Per Period	Periodic Payment To Amortize 1	Constant Annual Percent	Total Interest	Annual Add On Rate	
What a single $ 1 deposit grows to in the future. The deposit is made at the beginning of the first period.	What a series of $ 1 deposits grow to in the future. A deposit is made at the end of each period.	The amount to be deposited at the end of each period that grows to $ 1 in the future.	What $ 1 to be paid in the future is worth today. Value today of a single $ 1 payment tomorrow.	What $ 1 to be paid at the end of each period is worth today. Value today of a series of $ 1 payments tomorrow.	The mortgage payment to amortize a loan of $ 1. An annuity certain, payable at the end of each period, worth $ 1 today.	The annual payment, including interest and principal, to amortize completely a loan of $ 100.	The total interest paid over the term on a loan of $1. The loan is amortized by regular periodic payments.	The average annual interest rate on a loan that is completely amortized by regular periodic payments.	
$S = (1+i)^n$	$S\overline{n}| = \dfrac{(1+i)^n - 1}{i}$	$\dfrac{1}{S\overline{n}|} = \dfrac{i}{(1+i)^n - 1}$	$V^n = \dfrac{1}{(1+i)^n}$	$A\overline{n}| = \dfrac{1-V^n}{i}$	$\dfrac{1}{A\overline{n}|} = \dfrac{i}{1-V^n}$				

YEAR / **PERIODS**

	Amount Of 1	Amount Of 1 Per Period	Sinking Fund Payment	Present Worth Of 1	Present Worth of 1 Per Period	Periodic Payment To Amortize 1	Constant Annual Percent	Total Interest	Annual Add On Rate	PERIODS
	1.033 750	1.000 000	1.000 000 0000	.967 352	.967 352	1.033 750 0000	413.50	.033 750	13.50	1
	1.068 639	2.033 750	.491 702 5200	.935 770	1.903 122	.525 452 5200	210.19	.050 905	10.18	2
	1.104 706	3.102 389	.322 332 2349	.905 219	2.808 340	.356 082 2349	142.44	.068 247	9.10	3
	1.141 989	4.207 095	.237 693 7228	.875 665	3.684 005	.271 443 7228	108.58	.085 775	8.58	4
1	1.141 989	4.207 095	.237 693 7228	.875 665	3.684 005	.271 443 7228	108.58	.085 775	8.58	4
2	1.304 140	9.011 552	.110 968 6713	.766 789	6.909 958	.144 718 6713	57.89	.157 749	7.89	8
3	1.489 314	14.498 192	.068 974 1154	.671 450	9.734 812	.102 724 1154	41.09	.232 689	7.76	12
4	1.700 781	20.763 877	.048 160 5616	.587 965	12.208 438	.081 910 5616	32.77	.310 569	7.76	16
5	1.942 274	27.919 224	.035 817 6149	.514 860	14.374 505	.069 567 6149	27.83	.391 352	7.83	20
6	2.218 056	36.090 553	.027 708 0816	.450 845	16.271 253	.061 458 0816	24.59	.474 994	7.92	24
7	2.532 997	45.422 126	.022 015 7023	.394 789	17.932 169	.055 765 7023	22.31	.561 440	8.02	28
8	2.892 656	56.078 683	.017 832 0878	.345 703	19.386 575	.051 582 0878	20.64	.650 627	8.13	32
9	3.303 382	68.248 359	.014 652 3670	.302 720	20.660 147	.048 402 3670	19.37	.742 485	8.25	36
10	3.772 428	82.146 000	.012 173 4473	.265 081	21.775 369	.045 923 4473	18.37	.836 938	8.37	40
11	4.308 072	98.016 960	.010 202 3160	.232 122	22.751 930	.043 952 3160	17.59	.933 902	8.49	44
12	4.919 773	116.141 428	.008 610 1920	.203 261	23.607 070	.042 360 1920	16.95	1.033 289	8.61	48
13	5.618 329	136.839 380	.007 307 8378	.177 989	24.355 886	.041 057 8378	16.43	1.135 008	8.73	52
14	6.416 073	160.476 223	.006 231 4528	.155 859	25.011 597	.039 981 4528	16.00	1.238 961	8.85	56
15	7.327 087	187.469 247	.005 334 2082	.136 480	25.585 781	.039 084 2082	15.64	1.345 052	8.97	60
16	8.367 456	218.294 996	.004 580 9570	.119 511	26.088 574	.038 330 9570	15.34	1.453 181	9.08	64
17	9.555 547	253.497 677	.003 944 8093	.104 651	26.528 852	.037 694 8093	15.08	1.563 247	9.20	68
18	10.912 333	293.698 766	.003 404 8492	.091 639	26.914 387	.037 154 8492	14.87	1.675 149	9.31	72
19	12.461 770	339.607 986	.002 944 5715	.080 245	27.251 987	.036 694 5715	14.68	1.788 787	9.41	76
20	14.231 209	392.035 830	.002 550 7873	.070 268	27.547 612	.036 300 7873	14.53	1.904 063	9.52	80
21	16.251 891	451.907 875	.002 212 8404	.061 531	27.806 480	.035 962 8404	14.39	2.020 879	9.62	84
22	18.559 488	520.281 119	.001 922 0378	.053 881	28.033 162	.035 672 0378	14.27	2.139 139	9.72	88
23	21.194 739	598.362 641	.001 671 2273	.047 182	28.231 659	.035 421 2273	14.17	2.258 753	9.82	92
24	24.204 168	687.530 915	.001 454 4800	.041 315	28.405 476	.035 204 4800	14.09	2.379 630	9.92	96
25	27.640 905	789.360 144	.001 266 8489	.036 178	28.557 681	.035 016 8489	14.01	2.501 685	10.01	100
26	31.565 622	905.648 048	.001 104 1817	.031 680	28.690 962	.034 854 1817	13.95	2.624 835	10.10	104
27	36.047 607	1038.447 607	.000 962 9759	.027 741	28.807 671	.034 712 9759	13.89	2.749 001	10.18	108
28	41.165 986	1190.103 302	.000 840 2632	.024 292	28.909 870	.034 590 2632	13.84	2.874 109	10.26	112
29	47.011 122	1363.292 505	.000 733 5183	.021 272	28.999 361	.034 483 5183	13.80	3.000 088	10.35	116
30	53.686 205	1561.072 748	.000 640 5851	.018 627	29.077 726	.034 390 5851	13.76	3.126 870	10.42	120
31	61.309 080	1786.935 697	.000 559 6172	.016 311	29.146 347	.034 309 6172	13.73	3.254 393	10.50	124
32	70.014 322	2044.868 801	.000 489 0289	.014 283	29.206 436	.034 239 0289	13.70	3.382 596	10.57	128
33	79.955 617	2339.425 684	.000 427 4553	.012 507	29.259 054	.034 177 4553	13.68	3.511 424	10.64	132
34	91.308 471	2675.806 535	.000 373 7191	.010 952	29.305 129	.034 123 7191	13.65	3.640 826	10.71	136
35	104.273 310	3059.949 917	.000 326 8027	.009 590	29.345 476	.034 076 8027	13.64	3.770 752	10.77	140
36	119.079 019	3498.637 605	.000 285 8255	.008 398	29.380 806	.034 035 8255	13.62	3.901 159	10.84	144
37	135.986 983	3999.614 314	.000 250 0241	.007 354	29.411 744	.034 000 0241	13.61	4.032 004	10.90	148
38	155.295 699	4571.724 429	.000 218 7358	.006 439	29.438 835	.033 968 7358	13.59	4.163 248	10.96	152
39	177.346 050	5225.068 142	.000 191 3851	.005 639	29.462 557	.033 941 3851	13.58	4.294 856	11.01	156
40	202.527 317	5971.179 767	.000 167 4711	.004 938	29.483 330	.033 917 4711	13.57	4.426 795	11.07	160
41	231.284 059	6823.231 368	.000 146 5581	.004 324	29.501 520	.033 896 5581	13.56	4.559 036	11.12	164
42	264.123 954	7796.265 304	.000 128 2665	.003 786	29.517 449	.033 878 2665	13.56	4.691 549	11.17	168
43	301.626 768	8907.459 790	.000 112 2655	.003 315	29.531 397	.033 862 2655	13.55	4.824 310	11.22	172
44	344.454 586	10176.432 164	.000 098 2663	.002 903	29.543 611	.033 848 2663	13.54	4.957 295	11.27	176
45	393.363 501	11625.585 223	.000 086 0172	.002 542	29.554 306	.033 836 0172	13.54	5.090 483	11.31	180
46	449.216 967	13280.502 722	.000 075 2984	.002 226	29.563 671	.033 825 2984	13.54	5.223 855	11.36	184
47	513.001 035	15170.401 040	.000 065 9178	.001 949	29.571 872	.033 815 9178	13.53	5.357 393	11.40	188
48	585.841 768	17328.644 972	.000 057 7079	.001 707	29.579 053	.033 807 7079	13.53	5.491 080	11.44	192
49	669.025 116	19793.336 765	.000 050 5221	.001 495	29.585 342	.033 800 5221	13.53	5.624 902	11.48	196
50	764.019 621	22607.988 779	.000 044 2322	.001 309	29.590 848	.033 794 2322	13.52	5.758 846	11.52	200

Effective Rate is 14.20 %

Annual Percentage Rate is 13.50 %

Amount Of 1	Amount Of 1 Per Period	Sinking Fund Payment	Present Worth Of 1	Present Worth of 1 Per Period	Periodic Payment To Amortize 1	Constant Annual Percent	Total Interest	Annual Add On Rate
What a single $ 1 deposit grows to in the future. The deposit is made at the beginning of the first period.	What a series of $ 1 deposits grow to in the future. A deposit is made at the end of each period.	The amount to be deposited at the end of each period that grows to $ 1 in the future.	What $ 1 to be paid in the future is worth today. Value today of a single $ 1 payment tomorrow.	What $ 1 to be paid at the end of each period is worth today. Value today of a series of $ 1 payments tomorrow.	The mortgage payment to amortize a loan of $ 1. An annuity certain, payable at the end of each period, worth $ 1 today.	The annual payment, including interest and principal, to amortize completely a loan of $ 100.	The total interest paid over the term on a loan of $1. The loan is amortized by regular periodic payments.	The average annual interest rate on a loan that is completely amortized by regular periodic payments.

$$S = (1+i)^n \qquad S\overline{n}| = \frac{(1+i)^n - 1}{i} \qquad \frac{1}{S\overline{n}|} = \frac{i}{(1+i)^n - 1} \qquad V^n = \frac{1}{(1+i)^n} \qquad A\overline{n}| = \frac{1 - V^n}{i} \qquad \frac{1}{A\overline{n}|} = \frac{i}{1 - V^n}$$

YEAR									PERIODS
	1.034 063	1.000 000	1.000 000 0000	.967 060	.967 060	1.034 062 5000	413.63	.034 062	13.62	1
	1.069 285	2.034 063	.491 626 9780	.935 204	1.902 264	.525 689 4780	210.28	.051 379	10.28	2
	1.105 708	3.103 348	.322 232 6595	.904 398	2.806 662	.356 295 1595	142.52	.068 885	9.18	3
	1.143 371	4.209 056	.237 582 9901	.874 607	3.681 269	.271 645 4901	108.66	.086 582	8.66	4
1	1.143 371	4.209 056	.237 582 9901	.874 607	3.681 269	.271 645 4901	108.66	.086 582	8.66	4
2	1.307 297	9.021 567	.110 845 4837	.764 937	6.900 931	.144 907 9837	57.97	.159 264	7.96	8
3	1.494 726	14.524 054	.068 851 3017	.669 019	9.716 870	.102 913 8017	41.17	.234 966	7.83	12
4	1.709 026	20.815 437	.048 041 2695	.585 129	12.179 709	.082 103 7695	32.85	.313 660	7.84	16
5	1.954 050	28.008 821	.035 703 0378	.511 758	14.333 725	.069 765 5378	27.91	.395 311	7.91	20
6	2.234 205	36.233 528	.027 598 7477	.447 587	16.217 641	.061 661 2477	24.67	.479 870	8.00	24
7	2.554 525	45.637 419	.021 911 8438	.391 462	17.865 328	.055 974 3438	22.39	.567 282	8.10	28
8	2.920 769	56.389 555	.017 733 7807	.342 376	19.306 406	.051 796 2807	20.72	.657 481	8.22	32
9	3.339 523	68.683 235	.014 559 5938	.299 444	20.566 782	.048 622 0938	19.45	.750 395	8.34	36
10	3.818 313	82.739 471	.012 086 1299	.261 896	21.669 116	.046 148 6299	18.46	.845 945	8.46	40
11	4.365 748	98.810 964	.010 120 3344	.229 056	22.633 224	.044 182 8344	17.68	.944 045	8.58	44
12	4.991 670	117.186 642	.008 533 3958	.200 334	23.476 440	.042 595 8958	17.04	1.044 603	8.71	48
13	5.707 330	138.196 858	.007 236 0545	.175 213	24.213 923	.041 298 5545	16.52	1.147 525	8.83	52
14	6.525 596	162.219 329	.006 164 4935	.153 243	24.858 930	.040 226 9935	16.10	1.252 712	8.95	56
15	7.461 177	189.685 924	.005 271 8725	.134 027	25.423 057	.039 334 3725	15.74	1.360 046	9.07	60
16	8.530 893	221.090 431	.004 523 0361	.117 221	25.916 447	.038 585 5361	15.44	1.469 474	9.18	64
17	9.753 975	256.997 433	.003 891 0894	.102 522	26.347 969	.037 953 5894	15.19	1.580 844	9.30	68
18	11.152 412	298.052 456	.003 355 1141	.089 667	26.725 381	.037 417 6141	14.97	1.694 068	9.41	72
19	12.751 344	344.993 576	.002 898 6047	.078 423	27.055 468	.036 961 1047	14.79	1.809 044	9.52	76
20	14.579 516	398.664 690	.002 508 3736	.068 589	27.344 165	.036 570 8736	14.63	1.925 670	9.63	80
21	16.669 795	460.030 683	.002 173 7680	.059 989	27.596 661	.036 236 2680	14.50	2.043 847	9.73	84
22	19.059 760	530.194 776	.001 886 0993	.052 467	27.817 496	.035 948 5993	14.38	2.163 477	9.83	88
23	21.792 375	610.418 363	.001 638 2207	.045 888	28.010 639	.035 700 7207	14.29	2.284 466	9.93	92
24	24.916 769	702.143 682	.001 424 2099	.040 134	28.179 564	.035 486 7099	14.20	2.406 724	10.03	96
25	28.489 110	807.019 747	.001 239 1271	.035 101	28.327 306	.035 301 6271	14.13	2.530 163	10.12	100
26	32.573 621	926.931 993	.001 078 8278	.030 700	28.456 523	.035 141 3278	14.06	2.654 698	10.21	104
27	37.243 732	1064.036 173	.000 939 8177	.026 850	28.569 537	.035 002 3177	14.01	2.780 250	10.30	108
28	42.583 402	1220.797 110	.000 819 1369	.023 483	28.668 379	.034 881 6369	13.96	2.906 743	10.38	112
29	48.688 624	1400.033 013	.000 714 2689	.020 539	28.754 828	.034 776 7689	13.92	3.034 105	10.46	116
30	55.669 159	1604.966 137	.000 623 0661	.017 963	28.830 436	.034 685 5661	13.88	3.162 268	10.54	120
31	63.650 500	1839.280 719	.000 543 6908	.015 711	28.896 564	.034 606 1908	13.85	3.291 168	10.62	124
32	72.776 132	2107.189 207	.000 474 5658	.013 741	28.954 399	.034 537 0658	13.82	3.420 744	10.69	128
33	83.210 116	2413.507 989	.000 414 3347	.012 018	29.004 983	.034 476 8347	13.80	3.550 942	10.76	132
34	95.140 030	2763.743 988	.000 361 8280	.010 511	29.049 224	.034 424 3280	13.77	3.681 709	10.83	136
35	108.780 346	3164.193 657	.000 316 0363	.009 193	29.087 917	.034 378 5363	13.76	3.812 995	10.89	140
36	124.376 289	3622.056 176	.000 276 0863	.008 040	29.121 758	.034 338 5863	13.74	3.944 756	10.96	144
37	142.208 236	4145.562 882	.000 241 2218	.007 032	29.151 356	.034 303 7218	13.73	4.076 951	11.02	148
38	162.596 766	4744.125 244	.000 210 7870	.006 150	29.177 242	.034 273 2870	13.71	4.209 540	11.08	152
39	185.908 420	5428.504 062	.000 184 2128	.005 379	29.199 883	.034 246 7128	13.70	4.342 487	11.13	156
40	212.562 287	6211.002 925	.000 161 0046	.004 705	29.219 684	.034 223 5046	13.69	4.475 761	11.19	160
41	243.037 545	7105.689 397	.000 140 7323	.004 115	29.237 003	.034 203 2323	13.69	4.609 330	11.24	164
42	277.882 070	8128.647 922	.000 123 0217	.003 599	29.252 150	.034 185 5217	13.68	4.743 168	11.29	168
43	317.722 287	9298.268 987	.000 107 5469	.003 147	29.265 397	.034 170 0469	13.67	4.877 248	11.34	172
44	363.274 435	10635.579 739	.000 094 0240	.002 753	29.276 984	.034 156 5240	13.67	5.011 548	11.39	176
45	415.357 437	12164.622 011	.000 082 2056	.002 408	29.287 117	.034 144 7056	13.66	5.146 047	11.44	180
46	474.907 629	13912.884 532	.000 071 8758	.002 106	29.295 980	.034 134 3758	13.66	5.280 725	11.48	184
47	542.995 589	15911.797 118	.000 062 8465	.001 842	29.303 732	.034 125 3465	13.66	5.415 565	11.52	188
48	620.845 385	18197.295 710	.000 054 9532	.001 611	29.310 511	.034 117 4532	13.65	5.550 551	11.56	192
49	709.856 580	20810.468 416	.000 048 0527	.001 409	29.316 441	.034 110 5527	13.65	5.685 668	11.60	196
50	811.629 396	23798.294 186	.000 042 0198	.001 232	29.321 627	.034 104 5198	13.65	5.820 904	11.64	200

QUARTERLY COMPOUND INTEREST AND ANNUITY

13.75 % Q

	Amount Of 1	Amount Of 1 Per Period	Sinking Fund Payment	Present Worth Of 1	Present Worth of 1 Per Period	Periodic Payment To Amortize 1	Constant Annual Percent	Total Interest	Annual Add On Rate	
	What a single $ 1 deposit grows to in the future. The deposit is made at the beginning of the first period.	What a series of $ 1 deposits grow to in the future. A deposit is made at the end of each period.	The amount to be deposited at the end of each period that grows to $ 1 in the future.	What $ 1 to be paid in the future is worth today. Value today of a single $ 1 payment tomorrow.	What $ 1 to be paid at the end of each period is worth today. Value today of a series of $ 1 payments tomorrow.	The mortgage payment to amortize a loan of $ 1. An annuity certain, payable at the end of each period, worth $ 1 today.	The annual payment, including interest and principal, to amortize completely a loan of $ 100.	The total interest paid over the term on a loan of $1. The loan is amortized completely by regular periodic payments.	The average annual interest rate on a loan that is completely amortized by regular periodic payments.	
	$S = (1+i)^n$	$S\overline{n}| = \dfrac{(1+i)^n - 1}{i}$	$\dfrac{1}{S\overline{n}|} = \dfrac{i}{(1+i)^n - 1}$	$V^n = \dfrac{1}{(1+i)^n}$	$A\overline{n}| = \dfrac{1 - V^n}{i}$	$\dfrac{1}{A\overline{n}|} = \dfrac{i}{1 - V^n}$				

YEAR										PERIODS
	1.034 375	1.000 000	1.000 000 0000	.966 767	.966 767	1.034 375 0000	413.75	.034 375	13.75	1
	1.069 932	2.034 375	.491 551 4593	.934 639	1.901 407	.525 926 4593	210.38	.051 853	10.37	2
	1.106 711	3.104 307	.322 133 1253	.903 579	2.804 985	.356 508 1253	142.61	.069 524	9.27	3
	1.144 754	4.211 017	.237 472 3153	.873 550	3.678 535	.271 847 3153	108.74	.087 389	8.74	4
1	1.144 754	4.211 017	.237 472 3153	.873 550	3.678 535	.271 847 3153	108.74	.087 389	8.74	4
2	1.310 461	9.031 595	.110 722 4170	.763 090	6.891 921	.145 097 4170	58.04	.160 779	8.04	8
3	1.500 155	14.549 969	.068 728 6696	.666 598	9.698 976	.103 103 6696	41.25	.237 244	7.91	12
4	1.717 308	20.867 148	.047 922 2171	.582 307	12.151 079	.082 297 2171	32.92	.316 755	7.92	16
5	1.965 895	28.098 762	.035 588 7560	.508 674	14.293 115	.069 963 7560	27.99	.399 275	7.99	20
6	2.250 466	36.377 180	.027 489 7615	.444 353	16.164 291	.061 864 7615	24.75	.484 754	8.08	24
7	2.576 229	45.853 929	.021 808 3820	.388 164	17.798 857	.056 183 3820	22.48	.573 135	8.19	28
8	2.949 148	56.702 473	.017 635 9152	.339 081	19.226 733	.052 010 9152	20.81	.664 349	8.30	32
9	3.376 048	69.121 384	.014 467 3030	.296 204	20.474 055	.048 842 3030	19.54	.758 323	8.43	36
10	3.864 743	83.337 978	.011 999 3312	.258 749	21.563 653	.046 374 3312	18.55	.854 973	8.55	40
11	4.424 179	99.612 477	.010 038 9031	.226 031	22.515 472	.044 413 9031	17.77	.954 212	8.67	44
12	5.064 595	118.242 770	.008 457 1767	.197 449	23.346 934	.042 832 1767	17.14	1.055 944	8.80	48
13	5.797 714	139.569 868	.007 164 8703	.172 482	24.073 258	.041 539 8703	16.62	1.160 073	8.92	52
14	6.636 955	163.984 142	.006 098 1506	.150 672	24.707 738	.040 473 1506	16.19	1.266 496	9.05	56
15	7.597 679	191.932 473	.005 210 1658	.131 619	25.261 988	.039 585 1658	15.84	1.375 110	9.17	60
16	8.697 471	223.926 429	.004 465 7525	.114 976	25.746 154	.038 840 7525	15.54	1.485 808	9.29	64
17	9.956 462	260.551 629	.003 838 0109	.100 437	26.169 097	.038 213 0109	15.29	1.598 485	9.40	68
18	11.397 697	302.478 462	.003 306 0205	.087 737	26.538 559	.037 681 0205	15.08	1.713 033	9.52	72
19	13.047 556	350.474 361	.002 853 2758	.076 643	26.861 303	.037 228 2758	14.90	1.829 349	9.63	76
20	14.936 238	405.417 844	.002 466 5910	.066 951	27.143 236	.036 841 5910	14.74	1.947 327	9.74	80
21	17.098 314	468.314 600	.002 135 3167	.058 485	27.389 519	.036 510 3167	14.61	2.066 867	9.84	84
22	19.573 359	540.315 896	.001 850 7692	.051 090	27.604 659	.036 225 7692	14.50	2.187 868	9.94	88
23	22.406 675	622.739 647	.001 605 8075	.044 630	27.792 595	.035 980 8075	14.40	2.310 234	10.04	92
24	25.650 125	717.094 542	.001 394 5163	.038 986	27.956 766	.035 769 5163	14.31	2.433 874	10.14	96
25	29.363 076	825.107 658	.001 211 9631	.034 056	28.100 178	.035 586 9631	14.24	2.558 696	10.23	100
26	33.613 490	948.756 075	.001 054 0117	.029 750	28.225 456	.035 429 0117	14.18	2.684 617	10.33	104
27	38.479 168	1090.303 059	.000 917 1762	.025 988	28.334 892	.035 292 1762	14.12	2.811 555	10.41	108
28	44.049 170	1252.339 495	.000 798 5055	.022 702	28.430 490	.035 173 5055	14.07	2.939 433	10.50	112
29	50.425 451	1437.831 308	.000 695 4919	.019 831	28.514 000	.035 070 4919	14.03	3.068 177	10.58	116
30	57.724 723	1650.173 749	.000 605 9968	.017 324	28.586 950	.034 980 9968	14.00	3.197 720	10.66	120
31	66.080 591	1893.253 548	.000 528 1913	.015 133	28.650 675	.034 903 1913	13.97	3.327 996	10.74	124
32	75.646 002	2171.520 050	.000 460 5069	.013 219	28.706 343	.034 835 5069	13.94	3.458 945	10.81	128
33	86.596 042	2490.066 663	.000 401 5957	.011 548	28.754 971	.034 776 5957	13.92	3.590 511	10.88	132
34	99.131 140	2854.724 082	.000 350 2966	.010 088	28.797 450	.034 725 2966	13.90	3.722 640	10.95	136
35	113.480 741	3272.167 017	.000 305 6079	.008 812	28.834 558	.034 680 6079	13.88	3.855 285	11.02	140
36	129.907 500	3750.036 368	.000 266 6641	.007 698	28.866 974	.034 641 6641	13.86	3.988 400	11.08	144
37	148.712 093	4297.079 084	.000 232 7162	.006 724	28.895 290	.034 607 7162	13.85	4.121 942	11.14	148
38	170.238 722	4923.308 264	.000 203 1155	.005 874	28.920 026	.034 578 1155	13.84	4.255 874	11.20	152
39	194.881 409	5640.186 446	.000 177 2991	.005 131	28.941 634	.034 552 2991	13.83	4.390 159	11.26	156
40	223.091 217	6460.835 408	.000 154 7787	.004 482	28.960 510	.034 529 7787	13.82	4.524 765	11.31	160
41	255.384 500	7400.276 356	.000 135 1301	.003 916	28.976 999	.034 510 1301	13.81	4.659 661	11.37	164
42	292.352 355	8475.704 873	.000 117 9843	.003 421	28.991 403	.034 492 9843	13.80	4.794 821	11.42	168
43	334.671 445	9706.805 663	.000 103 0205	.002 988	29.003 985	.034 478 0205	13.80	4.930 220	11.47	172
44	383.116 380	11116.112 866	.000 089 9595	.002 610	29.014 977	.034 464 9595	13.79	5.065 833	11.51	176
45	438.573 899	12729.422 524	.000 078 5582	.002 280	29.024 578	.034 453 5582	13.79	5.201 640	11.56	180
46	502.059 101	14576.264 749	.000 068 6047	.001 992	29.032 966	.034 443 6047	13.78	5.337 623	11.60	184
47	574.734 021	16690.444 248	.000 059 9145	.001 740	29.040 293	.034 434 9145	13.78	5.473 764	11.65	188
48	657.928 906	19110.659 085	.000 052 3268	.001 520	29.046 693	.034 427 3268	13.78	5.610 047	11.69	192
49	753.166 560	21881.209 013	.000 045 7013	.001 328	29.052 284	.034 420 7013	13.77	5.746 457	11.73	196
50	862.190 218	25052.806 337	.000 039 9157	.001 160	29.057 168	.034 414 9157	13.77	5.882 983	11.77	200

Effective Rate is 14.48 %

Annual Percentage Rate is 13.75 %

Amount Of 1	Amount Of 1 Per Period	Sinking Fund Payment	Present Worth Of 1	Present Worth of 1 Per Period	Periodic Payment To Amortize 1	Constant Annual Percent	Total Interest	Annual Add On Rate	
What a single $ 1 deposit grows to in the future. The deposit is made at the beginning of the first period.	What a series of $ 1 deposits grow to in the future. A deposit is made at the end of each period.	The amount to be deposited at the end of each period that grows to $ 1 in the future.	What $ 1 to be paid in the future is worth today. Value today of a single $ 1 payment tomorrow.	What $ 1 to be paid at the end of each period is worth today. Value today of a series of $ 1 payments tomorrow.	The mortgage payment to amortize a loan of $ 1. An annuity certain, payable at the end of each period, worth $ 1 today.	The annual payment, including interest and principal, to amortize completely a loan of $ 100.	The total interest paid over the term on a loan of $1. The loan is amortized by regular periodic payments.	The average annual interest rate on a loan that is completely amortized by regular periodic payments.	
$S = (1+i)^n$	$S\overline{n}| = \dfrac{(1+i)^n - 1}{i}$	$\dfrac{1}{S\overline{n}|} = \dfrac{i}{(1+i)^n - 1}$	$V^n = \dfrac{1}{(1+i)^n}$	$A\overline{n}| = \dfrac{1-V^n}{i}$	$\dfrac{1}{A\overline{n}|} = \dfrac{i}{1-V^n}$				

YEAR									PERIODS
	1.034 687	1.000 000	1.000 000 0000	.966 475	.966 475	1.034 687 5000	413.88	.034 688	13.88	1
	1.070 578	2.034 688	.491 475 9638	.934 075	1.900 550	.526 163 4638	210.47	.052 327	10.47	2
	1.107 714	3.105 266	.322 033 6323	.902 760	2.803 310	.356 721 1323	142.69	.070 163	9.36	3
	1.146 138	4.212 980	.237 361 6985	.872 495	3.675 806	.272 049 1985	108.82	.088 197	8.82	4
1	1.146 138	4.212 980	.237 361 6985	.872 495	3.675 806	.272 049 1985	108.82	.088 197	8.82	4
2	1.313 632	9.041 635	.110 599 4714	.761 248	6.882 930	.145 286 9714	58.12	.162 296	8.11	8
3	1.505 603	14.575 938	.068 606 2188	.664 186	9.681 131	.103 293 7188	41.32	.239 525	7.98	12
4	1.725 628	20.919 012	.047 803 4043	.579 499	12.122 549	.082 490 9043	33.00	.319 854	8.00	16
5	1.977 808	28.189 049	.035 474 7691	.505 610	14.252 675	.070 162 2691	28.07	.403 245	8.06	20
6	2.266 840	36.521 512	.027 381 1226	.441 143	16.111 200	.062 068 6226	24.83	.489 647	8.16	24
7	2.598 111	46.071 663	.021 705 3161	.384 895	17.732 755	.056 392 8161	22.56	.578 999	8.27	28
8	2.977 793	57.017 451	.017 538 4902	.335 819	19.147 555	.052 225 9902	20.90	.671 232	8.39	32
9	3.412 961	69.562 831	.014 375 4931	.293 001	20.381 961	.049 062 9931	19.63	.766 268	8.51	36
10	3.911 723	83.941 565	.011 913 0493	.255 642	21.458 975	.046 600 5493	18.65	.864 022	8.64	40
11	4.483 373	100.421 574	.009 958 0195	.223 046	22.398 664	.044 645 5195	17.86	.964 403	8.77	44
12	5.138 563	119.309 935	.008 381 5317	.194 607	23.218 539	.043 069 0317	17.23	1.067 314	8.89	48
13	5.889 501	140.958 598	.007 094 2817	.169 794	23.933 876	.041 781 7817	16.72	1.172 653	9.02	52
14	6.750 180	165.770 947	.006 032 4201	.148 144	24.558 005	.040 719 9201	16.29	1.280 316	9.15	56
15	7.736 636	194.209 317	.005 149 0836	.129 255	25.102 554	.039 836 5836	15.94	1.390 195	9.27	60
16	8.867 250	226.803 605	.004 409 1010	.112 775	25.577 671	.039 096 6010	15.64	1.502 182	9.39	64
17	10.163 090	264.161 149	.003 785 5680	.098 395	25.992 208	.038 473 0680	15.39	1.616 169	9.51	68
18	11.648 301	306.978 040	.003 257 5620	.085 849	26.353 890	.037 945 0620	15.18	1.732 044	9.62	72
19	13.350 557	356.052 093	.002 808 5778	.074 903	26.669 456	.037 496 0778	15.00	1.849 702	9.74	76
20	15.301 577	412.297 718	.002 425 4318	.065 353	26.944 786	.037 112 9318	14.85	1.969 035	9.85	80
21	17.537 715	476.762 950	.002 097 4784	.057 020	27.185 010	.036 784 9784	14.72	2.089 938	9.95	84
22	20.100 637	550.648 986	.001 816 0389	.049 750	27.394 604	.036 503 5389	14.61	2.212 311	10.06	88
23	23.038 098	635.332 559	.001 573 9788	.043 406	27.577 474	.036 261 4788	14.51	2.336 056	10.16	92
24	26.404 834	732.391 597	.001 365 3898	.037 872	27.737 028	.036 052 8898	14.43	2.461 077	10.25	96
25	30.263 576	843.634 622	.001 185 3473	.033 043	27.876 237	.035 872 8473	14.35	2.587 285	10.35	100
26	34.686 226	971.134 451	.001 029 7235	.028 830	27.997 697	.035 717 2235	14.29	2.714 591	10.44	104
27	39.755 193	1117.266 816	.000 895 0414	.025 154	28.103 670	.035 582 5414	14.24	2.842 914	10.53	108
28	45.564 926	1284.754 633	.000 778 3587	.021 947	28.196 131	.035 465 8587	14.19	2.972 176	10.61	112
29	52.223 681	1476.718 739	.000 677 1770	.019 148	28.276 803	.035 364 6770	14.15	3.102 303	10.70	116
30	59.855 532	1696.736 044	.000 589 3669	.016 707	28.347 189	.035 276 8669	14.12	3.233 224	10.78	120
31	68.602 683	1948.906 179	.000 513 1083	.014 577	28.408 600	.035 200 6083	14.09	3.364 875	10.85	124
32	78.628 124	2237.927 886	.000 446 8419	.012 718	28.462 181	.035 134 3419	14.06	3.497 196	10.93	128
33	90.118 659	2569.186 568	.000 389 2283	.011 096	28.508 930	.035 076 7283	14.04	3.630 128	11.00	132
34	103.288 395	2948.854 643	.000 339 1147	.009 682	28.549 719	.035 026 6147	14.02	3.763 620	11.07	136
35	118.382 727	3384.006 549	.000 295 5077	.008 447	28.585 307	.034 983 0077	14.00	3.897 621	11.14	140
36	135.682 910	3882.750 566	.000 257 5494	.007 370	28.616 357	.034 945 0494	13.98	4.032 087	11.20	144
37	155.511 303	4454.379 903	.000 224 4981	.006 430	28.643 448	.034 911 9981	13.97	4.166 976	11.26	148
38	178.237 372	5109.545 854	.000 195 7121	.005 610	28.667 085	.034 883 2121	13.96	4.302 248	11.32	152
39	204.284 577	5860.456 270	.000 170 6352	.004 895	28.687 708	.034 858 1352	13.95	4.437 869	11.38	156
40	234.138 261	6721.103 031	.000 148 7851	.004 271	28.705 701	.034 836 2851	13.94	4.573 806	11.43	160
41	268.354 696	7707.522 756	.000 129 7434	.003 726	28.721 401	.034 817 2434	13.93	4.710 028	11.49	164
42	307.571 442	8838.095 622	.000 113 1465	.003 251	28.735 098	.034 800 6465	13.93	4.846 509	11.54	168
43	352.519 234	10133.887 840	.000 098 6788	.002 837	28.747 049	.034 786 1788	13.92	4.983 223	11.59	172
44	404.035 595	11619.044 194	.000 086 0656	.002 475	28.757 477	.034 773 5656	13.91	5.120 148	11.64	176
45	463.080 441	13321.237 926	.000 075 0681	.002 159	28.766 574	.034 762 5681	13.91	5.257 262	11.68	180
46	530.753 965	15272.186 388	.000 065 4785	.001 884	28.774 512	.034 752 9785	13.91	5.394 548	11.73	184
47	608.317 145	17508.242 031	.000 057 1160	.001 644	28.781 438	.034 744 6160	13.90	5.531 988	11.77	188
48	697.215 233	20071.069 772	.000 049 8230	.001 434	28.787 480	.034 737 3230	13.90	5.669 566	11.81	192
49	799.104 685	23008.423 343	.000 043 4623	.001 251	28.792 752	.034 730 9623	13.90	5.807 269	11.85	196
50	915.884 030	26375.035 100	.000 037 9146	.001 092	28.797 352	.034 725 4146	13.90	5.945 083	11.89	200

Effective Rate is 14.61 %

Annual Percentage Rate is 13.875%

Amount Of 1	Amount Of 1 Per Period	Sinking Fund Payment	Present Worth Of 1	Present Worth of 1 Per Period	Periodic Payment To Amortize 1	Constant Annual Percent	Total Interest	Annual Add On Rate	
What a single $ 1 deposit grows to in the future. The deposit is made at the beginning of the first period.	What a series of $ 1 deposits grow to in the future. A deposit is made at the end of each period.	The amount to be deposited at the end of each period that grows to $ 1 in the future.	What $ 1 to be paid in the future is worth today. Value today of a single $ 1 payment tomorrow.	What $ 1 to be paid at the end of each period is worth today. Value today of a series of $ 1 payments tomorrow.	The mortgage payment to amortize a loan of $ 1. An annuity certain, payable at the end of each period, worth $ 1 today.	The annual payment, including interest and principal, to amortize completely a loan of $ 100.	The total interest paid over the term on a loan of $1. The loan is amortized by regular periodic payments.	The average annual interest rate on a loan that is completely amortized by regular periodic payments.	
$S = (1+i)^n$	$S\overline{n}| = \dfrac{(1+i)^n - 1}{i}$	$\dfrac{1}{S\overline{n}|} = \dfrac{i}{(1+i)^n - 1}$	$V^n = \dfrac{1}{(1+i)^n}$	$A\overline{n}| = \dfrac{1-V^n}{i}$	$\dfrac{1}{A\overline{n}|} = \dfrac{i}{1-V^n}$				

YEAR									PERIODS
	1.035 000	1.000 000	1.000 000 0000	.966 184	.966 184	1.035 000 0000	414.00	.035 000	14.00	1
	1.071 225	2.035 000	.491 400 4914	.933 511	1.899 694	.526 400 4914	210.57	.052 801	10.56	2
	1.108 718	3.106 225	.321 934 1806	.901 943	2.801 637	.356 934 1806	142.78	.070 803	9.44	3
	1.147 523	4.214 943	.237 251 1395	.871 442	3.673 079	.272 251 1395	108.91	.089 005	8.90	4

YEAR	Amount Of 1	Amount Of 1 Per Period	Sinking Fund Payment	Present Worth Of 1	Present Worth of 1 Per Period	Periodic Payment To Amortize 1	Constant Annual Percent	Total Interest	Annual Add On Rate	PERIODS
1	1.147 523	4.214 943	.237 251 1395	.871 442	3.673 079	.272 251 1395	108.91	.089 005	8.90	4
2	1.316 809	9.051 687	.110 476 6465	.759 412	6.873 956	.145 476 6465	58.20	.163 813	8.19	8
3	1.511 069	14.601 962	.068 483 9493	.661 783	9.663 334	.103 483 9493	41.40	.241 807	8.06	12
4	1.733 986	20.971 030	.047 684 8306	.576 706	12.094 117	.082 684 8306	33.08	.322 957	8.07	16
5	1.989 789	28.279 682	.035 361 0768	.502 566	14.212 403	.070 361 0768	28.15	.407 222	8.14	20
6	2.283 328	36.666 528	.027 272 8303	.437 957	16.058 368	.062 272 8303	24.91	.494 548	8.24	24
7	2.620 172	46.290 627	.021 602 6452	.381 654	17.667 019	.056 602 6452	22.65	.584 874	8.36	28
8	3.006 708	57.334 502	.017 441 5048	.332 590	19.068 865	.052 441 5048	20.98	.678 128	8.48	32
9	3.450 266	70.007 603	.014 284 1628	.289 833	20.290 494	.049 284 1628	19.72	.774 230	8.60	36
10	3.959 260	84.550 278	.011 827 2823	.252 572	21.355 072	.046 827 2823	18.74	.873 091	8.73	40
11	4.543 342	101.238 331	.009 877 6816	.220 102	22.282 791	.044 877 6816	17.96	.974 618	8.86	44
12	5.213 589	120.388 257	.008 306 4580	.191 806	23.091 244	.043 306 4580	17.33	1.078 710	8.99	48
13	5.982 713	142.363 236	.007 024 2854	.167 148	23.795 765	.042 024 2854	16.81	1.185 263	9.12	52
14	6.865 301	167.580 031	.005 967 2981	.145 660	24.409 713	.040 967 2981	16.39	1.294 169	9.24	56
15	7.878 091	196.516 883	.005 088 6213	.126 934	24.944 734	.040 088 6213	16.04	1.405 317	9.37	60
16	9.040 291	229.722 586	.004 353 0765	.110 616	25.410 974	.039 353 0765	15.75	1.518 597	9.49	64
17	10.373 941	267.826 894	.003 733 7550	.096 395	25.817 275	.038 733 7550	15.50	1.633 895	9.61	68
18	11.904 336	311.552 464	.003 209 7323	.084 003	26.171 343	.038 209 7323	15.29	1.751 101	9.73	72
19	13.660 500	361.728 561	.002 764 5038	.073 204	26.479 892	.037 764 5038	15.11	1.870 102	9.84	76
20	15.675 738	419.306 787	.002 384 8887	.063 793	26.748 776	.037 384 8887	14.96	1.990 791	9.95	80
21	17.988 269	485.379 125	.002 060 2452	.055 592	26.983 092	.037 060 2452	14.83	2.113 061	10.06	84
22	20.641 953	561.198 653	.001 781 9002	.048 445	27.187 285	.036 781 9002	14.72	2.236 807	10.17	88
23	23.687 116	648.203 305	.001 542 7259	.042 217	27.365 227	.036 542 7259	14.62	2.361 931	10.27	92
24	27.181 510	748.043 145	.001 336 8213	.036 790	27.520 294	.036 336 8213	14.54	2.488 335	10.37	96
25	31.191 408	862.611 657	.001 159 2702	.032 060	27.655 425	.036 159 2702	14.47	2.615 927	10.46	100
26	35.792 858	994.081 659	.001 005 9536	.027 939	27.773 185	.036 005 9536	14.41	2.744 619	10.56	104
27	41.073 128	1144.946 512	.000 873 4032	.024 347	27.875 805	.035 873 4032	14.35	2.874 328	10.65	108
28	47.132 359	1318.067 399	.000 758 6865	.021 217	27.965 233	.035 758 6865	14.31	3.004 973	10.73	112
29	54.085 466	1516.727 600	.000 659 3142	.018 489	28.043 164	.035 659 3142	14.27	3.136 480	10.82	116
30	62.064 316	1744.694 750	.000 573 1662	.016 112	28.111 077	.035 573 1662	14.23	3.268 780	10.90	120
31	71.220 230	2006.292 297	.000 498 4319	.014 041	28.170 258	.035 498 4319	14.20	3.401 806	10.97	124
32	81.726 852	2306.481 500	.000 433 5608	.012 236	28.221 832	.035 433 5608	14.18	3.535 496	11.05	128
33	93.783 443	2650.955 515	.000 377 2225	.010 663	28.266 775	.035 377 2225	14.16	3.669 793	11.12	132
34	107.618 658	3046.247 370	.000 328 2727	.009 292	28.305 941	.035 328 2727	14.14	3.804 645	11.19	136
35	123.494 885	3499.853 865	.000 285 7262	.008 098	28.340 071	.035 285 7262	14.12	3.940 002	11.26	140
36	141.713 221	4020.377 752	.000 248 7328	.007 057	28.369 814	.035 248 7328	14.10	4.075 184	11.32	144
37	162.619 181	4617.690 884	.000 216 5585	.006 149	28.395 733	.035 216 5585	14.09	4.212 051	11.38	148
38	186.609 250	5303.121 442	.000 188 5682	.005 359	28.418 320	.035 188 5682	14.08	4.348 662	11.44	152
39	214.138 407	6089.668 773	.000 164 2125	.004 670	28.438 004	.035 164 2125	14.07	4.485 617	11.50	156
40	245.728 747	6992.249 926	.000 143 0155	.004 070	28.455 156	.035 143 0155	14.06	4.622 882	11.56	160
41	281.979 390	8027.982 559	.000 124 5643	.003 546	28.470 104	.035 124 5643	14.05	4.760 429	11.61	164
42	323.577 835	9216.509 578	.000 108 5009	.003 090	28.483 130	.035 108 5009	14.05	4.898 228	11.66	168
43	371.313 008	10580.371 669	.000 094 5146	.002 693	28.494 482	.035 094 5146	14.04	5.036 257	11.71	172
44	426.090 218	12145.434 789	.000 082 3355	.002 347	28.504 374	.035 082 3355	14.04	5.174 491	11.76	176
45	488.948 325	13941.380 715	.000 071 7289	.002 045	28.512 994	.035 071 7289	14.03	5.312 911	11.81	180
46	561.079 449	16002.269 974	.000 062 4911	.001 782	28.520 506	.035 062 4911	14.03	5.451 498	11.85	184
47	643.851 573	18367.187 800	.000 054 4449	.001 553	28.527 053	.035 054 4449	14.03	5.590 236	11.89	188
48	738.834 489	21080.985 401	.000 047 4361	.001 353	28.532 758	.035 047 4361	14.02	5.729 108	11.94	192
49	847.829 570	24195.130 566	.000 041 3306	.001 179	28.537 729	.035 041 3306	14.02	5.868 101	11.98	196
50	972.903 932	27768.683 771	.000 036 0118	.001 028	28.542 061	.035 036 0118	14.02	6.007 202	12.01	200

Effective Rate is 14.75 %   Annual Percentage Rate is 14.00 %

QUARTERLY COMPOUND INTEREST AND ANNUITY

14.125% Q

Amount Of 1	Amount Of 1 Per Period	Sinking Fund Payment	Present Worth Of 1	Present Worth of 1 Per Period	Periodic Payment To Amortize 1	Constant Annual Percent	Total Interest	Annual Add On Rate	
What a single $ 1 deposit grows to in the future. The deposit is made at the beginning of the first period.	What a series of $ 1 deposits grow to in the future. A deposit is made at the end of each period.	The amount to be deposited at the end of each period that grows to $ 1 in the future.	What $ 1 to be paid in the future is worth today. Value today of a single $ 1 payment tomorrow.	What $ 1 to be paid at the end of each period is worth today. Value today of a series of $ 1 payments tomorrow.	The mortgage payment to amortize a loan of $ 1. An annuity certain, payable at the end of each period, worth $ 1 today.	The annual payment, including interest and principal, to amortize completely a loan of $ 100.	The total interest paid over the term on a loan of $1. The loan is amortized by regular periodic payments.	The average annual interest rate on a loan that is completely amortized by regular periodic payments.	
$S = (1+i)^n$	$S\overline{n} = \dfrac{(1+i)^n - 1}{i}$	$\dfrac{1}{S\overline{n}} = \dfrac{i}{(1+i)^n - 1}$	$V^n = \dfrac{1}{(1+i)^n}$	$A\overline{n} = \dfrac{1-V^n}{i}$	$\dfrac{1}{A\overline{n}} = \dfrac{i}{1-V^n}$				

YEAR / **PERIODS**

	Amount Of 1	Amount Of 1 Per Period	Sinking Fund Payment	Present Worth Of 1	Present Worth of 1 Per Period	Periodic Payment To Amortize 1	Constant Annual Percent	Total Interest	Annual Add On Rate	PERIODS
	1.035 313	1.000 000	1.000 000 0000	.965 892	.965 892	1.035 312 5000	414.13	.035 312	14.12	1
	1.071 872	2.035 313	.491 325 0422	.932 947	1.898 839	.526 637 5422	210.66	.053 275	10.66	2
	1.109 722	3.107 184	.321 834 7700	.901 126	2.799 965	.357 147 2700	142.86	.071 442	9.53	3
	1.148 910	4.216 907	.237 140 6384	.870 391	3.670 356	.272 453 1384	108.99	.089 813	8.98	4
1	1.148 910	4.216 907	.237 140 6384	.870 391	3.670 356	.272 453 1384	108.99	.089 813	8.98	4
2	1.319 993	9.061 751	.110 353 9426	.757 580	6.864 999	.145 666 4426	58.27	.165 332	8.27	8
3	1.516 553	14.628 039	.068 361 8608	.659 390	9.645 586	.103 674 3608	41.47	.244 092	8.14	12
4	1.742 382	21.023 201	.047 566 4961	.573 927	12.065 783	.082 878 9961	33.16	.326 064	8.15	16
5	2.001 839	28.370 663	.035 247 6787	.499 541	14.172 300	.070 560 1787	28.23	.411 204	8.22	20
6	2.299 932	36.812 231	.027 164 8841	.434 795	16.005 792	.062 477 3841	25.00	.499 457	8.32	24
7	2.642 414	46.510 830	.021 500 3687	.378 442	17.601 646	.056 812 8687	22.73	.590 760	8.44	28
8	3.035 894	57.653 643	.017 344 9577	.329 392	18.990 662	.052 657 4577	21.07	.685 039	8.56	32
9	3.487 968	70.455 727	.014 193 3105	.286 700	20.199 649	.049 505 8105	19.81	.782 209	8.69	36
10	4.007 359	85.164 162	.011 742 0283	.249 541	21.251 940	.047 054 5283	18.83	.882 181	8.82	40
11	4.604 093	102.062 824	.009 797 8868	.217 198	22.167 844	.045 110 3868	18.05	.984 857	8.95	44
12	5.289 687	121.477 858	.008 231 9529	.189 047	22.965 038	.043 544 4529	17.42	1.090 134	9.08	48
13	6.077 372	143.783 975	.006 954 8780	.164 545	23.658 908	.042 267 3780	16.91	1.197 904	9.21	52
14	6.982 350	169.411 685	.005 902 7805	.143 218	24.262 846	.041 215 2805	16.49	1.308 056	9.34	56
15	8.022 089	198.855 606	.005 028 7745	.124 656	24.788 508	.040 341 2745	16.14	1.420 476	9.47	60
16	9.216 654	232.684 007	.004 297 6740	.108 499	25.246 039	.039 610 1740	15.85	1.535 051	9.59	64
17	10.589 102	271.549 779	.003 682 5661	.094 437	25.644 270	.038 995 0661	15.60	1.651 664	9.72	68
18	12.165 920	316.203 035	.003 162 5250	.082 197	25.990 886	.038 475 0250	15.40	1.770 202	9.83	72
19	13.977 541	367.505 586	.002 721 0471	.071 543	26.292 578	.038 033 5471	15.22	1.890 550	9.95	76
20	16.058 930	426.447 575	.002 344 9541	.062 271	26.555 167	.037 657 4541	15.07	2.012 596	10.06	80
21	18.450 258	494.166 588	.002 023 6091	.054 200	26.783 723	.037 336 1091	14.94	2.136 233	10.17	84
22	21.197 677	571.969 607	.001 748 3446	.047 175	26.982 655	.037 060 8446	14.83	2.261 354	10.28	88
23	24.354 213	661.358 237	.001 512 0398	.041 061	27.155 804	.036 824 5398	14.73	2.387 858	10.38	92
24	27.980 787	764.057 686	.001 308 8017	.035 739	27.306 512	.036 621 3017	14.65	2.515 645	10.48	96
25	32.147 393	882.050 060	.001 133 7225	.031 107	27.437 686	.036 446 2225	14.58	2.644 622	10.58	100
26	36.934 446	1017.612 624	.000 982 6922	.027 075	27.551 858	.036 295 1922	14.52	2.774 700	10.67	104
27	42.434 337	1173.361 744	.000 852 2521	.023 566	27.651 233	.036 164 7521	14.47	2.905 793	10.76	108
28	48.753 214	1352.303 391	.000 739 4790	.020 511	27.737 728	.036 051 9790	14.43	3.037 822	10.85	112
29	56.013 031	1557.891 155	.000 641 8934	.017 853	27.813 013	.035 954 3934	14.39	3.170 710	10.93	116
30	64.353 905	1794.092 895	.000 557 3847	.015 539	27.878 540	.035 869 8847	14.35	3.304 386	11.01	120
31	73.936 815	2065.467 324	.000 484 1519	.013 525	27.935 573	.035 796 6519	14.32	3.438 785	11.09	124
32	84.946 711	2377.251 991	.000 420 6538	.011 772	27.985 215	.035 733 1538	14.30	3.573 844	11.17	128
33	97.596 085	2735.464 364	.000 365 5686	.010 246	28.028 423	.035 678 0686	14.28	3.709 505	11.24	132
34	112.129 072	3147.017 972	.000 317 7611	.008 918	28.066 031	.035 630 2611	14.26	3.845 716	11.31	136
35	128.826 159	3619.855 833	.000 276 2541	.007 762	28.098 764	.035 588 7541	14.24	3.982 426	11.38	140
36	148.009 601	4163.103 755	.000 240 2054	.006 756	28.127 255	.035 552 7054	14.23	4.119 590	11.44	144
37	170.049 641	4787.246 468	.000 208 8883	.005 881	28.152 053	.035 521 3883	14.21	4.257 165	11.51	148
38	195.371 652	5504.329 977	.000 181 6752	.005 118	28.173 637	.035 494 1752	14.20	4.395 115	11.57	152
39	224.464 352	6328.194 050	.000 158 0230	.004 455	28.192 423	.035 470 5230	14.19	4.533 402	11.62	156
40	257.889 233	7274.739 332	.000 137 4620	.003 878	28.208 775	.035 449 9620	14.18	4.671 994	11.68	160
41	296.291 396	8362.234 223	.000 119 5853	.003 375	28.223 007	.035 432 0853	14.18	4.810 862	11.73	164
42	340.412 007	9611.667 462	.000 104 0402	.002 938	28.235 395	.035 416 5402	14.17	4.949 979	11.79	168
43	391.102 598	11047.153 213	.000 090 5211	.002 557	28.246 177	.035 403 0211	14.17	5.089 320	11.84	172
44	449.341 500	12696.396 465	.000 078 7625	.002 225	28.255 562	.035 391 2625	14.16	5.228 862	11.88	176
45	516.252 730	14591.227 749	.000 068 5343	.001 937	28.263 730	.035 381 0343	14.16	5.368 586	11.93	180
46	593.127 679	16768.217 460	.000 059 6366	.001 686	28.270 840	.035 372 1366	14.15	5.508 473	11.97	184
47	681.450 040	19269.381 677	.000 051 8958	.001 467	28.277 028	.035 364 3958	14.15	5.648 506	12.02	188
48	782.924 443	22142.093 071	.000 045 1610	.001 277	28.282 414	.035 357 6610	14.15	5.788 671	12.06	192
49	899.509 350	25444.512 576	.000 039 3012	.001 112	28.287 102	.035 351 8012	14.15	5.928 953	12.10	196
50	1033.454 861	29237.659 784	.000 034 2025	.000 968	28.291 182	.035 346 7025	14.14	6.069 340	12.14	200

QUARTERLY COMPOUND INTEREST AND ANNUITY

14.25 % Q

Amount Of 1	Amount Of 1 Per Period	Sinking Fund Payment	Present Worth Of 1	Present Worth of 1 Per Period	Periodic Payment To Amortize 1	Constant Annual Percent	Total Interest	Annual Add On Rate
What a single $ 1 deposit grows to in the future. The deposit is made at the beginning of the first period.	What a series of $ 1 deposits grow to in the future. A deposit is made at the end of each period.	The amount to be deposited at the end of each period that grows to $ 1 in the future.	What $ 1 to be paid in the future is worth today. Value today of a single $ 1 payment tomorrow.	What $ 1 to be paid at the end of each period is worth today. Value today of a series of $ 1 payments tomorrow.	The mortgage payment to amortize a loan of $ 1. An annuity certain, payable at the end of each period, worth $ 1 today.	The annual payment, including interest and principal, to amortize completely a loan of $ 100.	The total interest paid over the term on a loan of $1. The loan is amortized by regular periodic payments.	The average annual interest rate on a loan that is completely amortized by regular periodic payments.

$$S = (1 + i)^n \qquad S\overline{n}| = \frac{(1+i)^n - 1}{i} \qquad \frac{1}{S\overline{n}|} = \frac{i}{(1+i)^n - 1} \qquad V^n = \frac{1}{(1+i)^n} \qquad A\overline{n}| = \frac{1 - V^n}{i} \qquad \frac{1}{A\overline{n}|} = \frac{i}{1 - V^n}$$

YEAR	Amount Of 1	Amount Of 1 Per Period	Sinking Fund Payment	Present Worth Of 1	Present Worth of 1 Per Period	Periodic Payment To Amortize 1	Constant Annual Percent	Total Interest	Annual Add On Rate	PERIODS
	1.035 625	1.000 000	1.000 000 0000	.965 600	.965 600	1.035 625 0000	414.25	.035 625	14.25	1
	1.072 519	2.035 625	.491 249 6162	.932 384	1.897 985	.526 874 6162	210.75	.053 749	10.75	2
	1.110 728	3.108 144	.321 735 4005	.900 311	2.798 295	.357 360 4005	142.95	.072 081	9.61	3
	1.150 297	4.218 872	.237 030 1951	.869 340	3.667 636	.272 655 1951	109.07	.090 621	9.06	4
1	1.150 297	4.218 872	.237 030 1951	.869 340	3.667 636	.272 655 1951	109.07	.090 621	9.06	4
2	1.323 184	9.071 829	.110 231 3593	.755 753	6.856 060	.145 856 3593	58.35	.166 851	8.34	8
3	1.522 055	14.654 172	.068 239 9533	.657 007	9.627 887	.103 864 9533	41.55	.246 379	8.21	12
4	1.750 816	21.075 526	.047 448 4003	.571 162	12.037 547	.083 073 4003	33.23	.329 174	8.23	16
5	2.013 958	28.461 993	.035 134 5744	.496 535	14.132 363	.070 759 5744	28.31	.415 191	8.30	20
6	2.316 651	36.958 625	.027 057 2834	.431 658	15.953 471	.062 682 2834	25.08	.504 375	8.41	24
7	2.664 837	46.732 279	.021 398 4856	.375 257	17.536 634	.057 023 4856	22.81	.596 658	8.52	28
8	3.065 355	57.974 886	.017 248 8479	.326 226	18.912 942	.052 873 8479	21.15	.691 963	8.65	32
9	3.526 070	70.907 228	.014 102 9347	.283 602	20.109 422	.049 727 9347	19.90	.790 206	8.78	36
10	4.056 029	85.783 265	.011 657 2854	.246 547	21.149 570	.047 282 2854	18.92	.891 291	8.91	40
11	4.665 639	102.895 130	.009 718 6329	.214 333	22.053 813	.045 343 6329	18.14	.995 120	9.05	44
12	5.366 872	122.578 863	.008 158 0134	.186 328	22.839 908	.043 783 0134	17.52	1.101 585	9.18	48
13	6.173 498	145.221 008	.006 886 0561	.161 983	23.523 292	.042 511 0561	17.01	1.210 575	9.31	52
14	7.101 359	171.266 206	.005 838 8635	.140 818	24.117 386	.041 463 8635	16.59	1.321 976	9.44	56
15	8.168 674	201.225 927	.004 969 5385	.122 419	24.633 856	.040 594 5385	16.24	1.435 672	9.57	60
16	9.396 403	235.688 514	.004 242 8881	.106 424	25.082 844	.039 867 8881	15.95	1.551 545	9.70	64
17	10.808 657	275.330 734	.003 631 9955	.092 518	25.473 167	.039 256 9955	15.71	1.669 476	9.82	68
18	12.433 170	320.931 074	.003 115 9339	.080 430	25.812 491	.038 740 9339	15.50	1.789 347	9.94	72
19	14.301 841	373.385 022	.002 678 2006	.069 921	26.107 479	.038 303 2006	15.33	1.911 043	10.06	76
20	16.451 370	433.722 657	.002 305 6208	.060 785	26.363 924	.037 930 6208	15.18	2.034 450	10.17	80
21	18.923 966	503.128 876	.001 987 5623	.052 843	26.586 862	.037 612 5623	15.05	2.159 455	10.28	84
22	21.768 187	582.966 663	.001 715 3640	.045 939	26.780 671	.037 340 3640	14.94	2.285 952	10.39	88
23	25.039 887	674.803 855	.001 481 9121	.039 936	26.949 157	.037 106 9121	14.85	2.413 836	10.49	92
24	28.803 315	780.443 929	.001 281 3220	.034 718	27.095 629	.036 906 3220	14.77	2.543 007	10.60	96
25	33.132 376	901.961 421	.001 108 6949	.030 182	27.222 963	.036 733 6949	14.70	2.673 369	10.69	100
26	38.112 082	1041.742 665	.000 959 9300	.026 238	27.333 659	.036 584 9300	14.64	2.804 833	10.79	104
27	43.840 226	1202.532 654	.000 831 5782	.022 810	27.429 892	.036 456 5782	14.59	2.937 310	10.88	108
28	50.429 294	1387.488 946	.000 720 7265	.019 830	27.513 551	.036 345 7265	14.54	3.070 721	10.97	112
29	58.008 681	1600.243 670	.000 624 9048	.017 239	27.586 279	.036 249 9048	14.50	3.204 989	11.05	116
30	66.727 229	1844.974 855	.000 542 0128	.014 986	27.649 505	.036 167 0128	14.47	3.340 042	11.13	120
31	76.756 152	2126.488 479	.000 470 2588	.013 028	27.704 470	.036 095 2588	14.44	3.475 812	11.21	124
32	88.292 395	2450.312 843	.000 408 1112	.011 326	27.752 253	.036 033 1112	14.42	3.612 238	11.29	128
33	101.562 504	2822.807 136	.000 354 2573	.009 846	27.793 792	.035 979 2573	14.40	3.749 262	11.36	132
34	116.827 075	3251.286 319	.000 307 5706	.008 560	27.829 904	.035 932 5706	14.38	3.886 830	11.43	136
35	134.385 870	3744.164 769	.000 267 0823	.007 441	27.861 298	.035 892 0823	14.36	4.024 892	11.50	140
36	154.583 704	4311.121 522	.000 231 9582	.006 469	27.888 590	.035 856 9582	14.35	4.163 402	11.57	144
37	177.817 219	4963.290 349	.000 201 4792	.005 624	27.912 316	.035 826 4792	14.34	4.302 319	11.63	148
38	204.542 668	5713.478 394	.000 175 0247	.004 889	27.932 942	.035 800 0247	14.33	4.441 604	11.69	152
39	235.284 880	6576.417 682	.000 152 0585	.004 250	27.950 873	.035 777 0585	14.32	4.581 221	11.75	156
40	270.647 564	7569.054 422	.000 132 1169	.003 695	27.966 461	.035 757 1169	14.31	4.721 139	11.80	160
41	311.325 164	8710.881 789	.000 114 7989	.003 212	27.980 012	.035 739 7989	14.30	4.861 327	11.86	164
42	358.116 497	10024.322 736	.000 099 7574	.002 792	27.991 793	.035 724 7574	14.29	5.001 759	11.91	168
43	411.940 443	11535.170 319	.000 086 6914	.002 428	28.002 034	.035 711 6914	14.29	5.142 411	11.96	172
44	473.853 982	13273.094 226	.000 075 3404	.002 110	28.010 937	.035 700 3404	14.29	5.283 260	12.01	176
45	545.072 959	15272.223 416	.000 065 4784	.001 835	28.018 677	.035 690 4784	14.28	5.424 286	12.05	180
46	626.995 957	17571.816 339	.000 056 9093	.001 595	28.025 406	.035 681 9093	14.28	5.565 471	12.10	184
47	721.231 761	20217.031 886	.000 049 4632	.001 387	28.031 256	.035 674 4632	14.27	5.706 799	12.14	188
48	829.630 952	23259.816 205	.000 042 9926	.001 205	28.036 341	.035 667 9926	14.27	5.848 265	12.18	192
49	954.322 250	26759.922 814	.000 037 3693	.001 048	28.040 762	.035 662 3693	14.27	5.989 824	12.22	196
50	1097.754 314	30786.086 021	.000 032 4822	.000 911	28.044 605	.035 657 4822	14.27	6.131 496	12.26	200

Effective Rate is 15.03 %

Annual Percentage Rate is 14.25 %

	Amount Of 1	Amount Of 1 Per Period	Sinking Fund Payment	Present Worth Of 1	Present Worth of 1 Per Period	Periodic Payment To Amortize 1	Constant Annual Percent	Total Interest	Annual Add On Rate	
	What a single $ 1 deposit grows to in the future. The deposit is made at the beginning of the first period.	What a series of $ 1 deposits grow to in the future. A deposit is made at the end of each period.	The amount to be deposited at the end of each period that grows to $ 1 in the future.	What $ 1 to be paid in the future is worth today. Value today of a single $ 1 payment tomorrow.	What $ 1 to be paid at the end of each period is worth today. Value today of a series of $ 1 payments tomorrow.	The mortgage payment to amortize a loan of $ 1. An annuity certain, payable at the end of each period, worth $ 1 today.	The annual payment, including interest and principal, to amortize completely a loan of $ 100.	The total interest paid over the term on a loan of $1. The loan is amortized by regular periodic payments.	The average annual interest rate on a loan that is completely amortized by regular periodic payments.	

$$S = (1+i)^n \qquad S\overline{n}| = \frac{(1+i)^n - 1}{i} \qquad \frac{1}{S\overline{n}|} = \frac{i}{(1+i)^n - 1} \qquad V^n = \frac{1}{(1+i)^n} \qquad A\overline{n}| = \frac{1 - V^n}{i} \qquad \frac{1}{A\overline{n}|} = \frac{i}{1 - V^n}$$

YEAR										PERIODS
	1.035 937	1.000 000	1.000 000 0000	.965 309	.965 309	1.035 937 5000	414.38	.035 938	14.38	1
	1.073 167	2.035 938	.491 174 2134	.931 822	1.897 131	.527 111 7134	210.85	.054 223	10.84	2
	1.111 733	3.109 104	.321 636 0722	.899 496	2.796 627	.357 573 5722	143.03	.072 721	9.70	3
	1.151 686	4.220 837	.236 919 8096	.868 292	3.664 919	.272 857 3096	109.15	.091 429	9.14	4
1	1.151 686	4.220 837	.236 919 8096	.868 292	3.664 919	.272 857 3096	109.15	.091 429	9.14	4
2	1.326 381	9.081 918	.110 108 8967	.753 939	6.847 139	.146 046 3967	58.42	.168 371	8.42	8
3	1.527 575	14.680 359	.068 118 2267	.654 632	9.610 235	.104 055 7267	41.63	.248 669	8.29	12
4	1.759 288	21.128 006	.047 330 5430	.568 412	12.009 409	.083 268 0430	33.31	.332 289	8.31	16
5	2.026 148	28.553 674	.035 021 7635	.493 547	14.092 593	.070 959 2635	28.39	.419 185	8.38	20
6	2.333 487	37.105 713	.026 950 0277	.428 543	15.901 404	.062 887 5277	25.16	.509 301	8.49	24
7	2.687 445	46.954 981	.021 296 9952	.372 101	17.471 981	.057 234 4952	22.90	.602 566	8.61	28
8	3.095 093	58.298 248	.017 153 1743	.323 092	18.835 700	.053 090 6743	21.24	.698 902	8.74	32
9	3.564 577	71.362 133	.014 013 0340	.280 538	20.019 806	.049 950 5340	19.99	.798 219	8.87	36
10	4.105 274	86.407 632	.011 573 0518	.243 589	21.047 956	.047 510 5518	19.01	.900 422	9.00	40
11	4.727 988	103.735 327	.009 639 9176	.211 506	21.940 690	.045 577 4176	18.24	1.005 406	9.14	44
12	5.445 160	123.691 397	.008 084 6366	.183 649	22.715 844	.044 022 1366	17.61	1.113 063	9.28	48
13	6.271 116	146.674 530	.006 817 8163	.159 461	23.388 904	.042 755 3163	17.11	1.223 276	9.41	52
14	7.222 359	173.143 891	.005 775 5431	.138 459	23.973 317	.041 713 0431	16.69	1.335 930	9.54	56
15	8.317 892	203.628 293	.004 910 9089	.120 223	24.480 758	.040 848 4089	16.34	1.450 905	9.67	60
16	9.579 602	238.736 762	.004 188 7139	.104 388	24.921 364	.040 126 2139	16.06	1.568 078	9.80	64
17	11.032 697	279.170 706	.003 582 0377	.090 640	25.303 940	.039 519 5377	15.81	1.687 329	9.93	68
18	12.706 207	325.737 927	.003 069 9526	.078 702	25.636 127	.039 007 4526	15.61	1.808 537	10.05	72
19	14.633 565	379.368 761	.002 635 9577	.068 336	25.924 562	.038 573 4577	15.43	1.931 583	10.17	76
20	16.853 277	441.134 659	.002 266 8815	.059 336	26.175 008	.038 204 3815	15.29	2.056 351	10.28	80
21	19.409 689	512.269 600	.001 952 0971	.051 521	26.392 469	.037 889 5971	15.16	2.182 726	10.39	84
22	22.353 874	594.194 741	.001 682 9499	.044 735	26.581 288	.037 620 4499	15.05	2.310 600	10.50	88
23	25.744 651	688.546 807	.001 452 3341	.038 843	26.745 238	.037 389 8341	14.96	2.439 865	10.61	92
24	29.649 763	797.210 793	.001 254 3734	.033 727	26.887 594	.037 191 8734	14.88	2.570 420	10.71	96
25	34.147 227	922.357 622	.001 084 1782	.029 285	27.011 201	.037 021 6782	14.81	2.702 168	10.81	100
26	39.326 895	1066.487 516	.000 937 6575	.025 428	27.118 528	.036 875 1575	14.76	2.835 016	10.90	104
27	45.292 248	1232.479 947	.000 811 3722	.022 079	27.211 719	.036 748 8722	14.70	2.968 878	11.00	108
28	52.162 464	1423.651 163	.000 702 4193	.019 171	27.292 637	.036 639 9193	14.66	3.103 671	11.08	112
29	60.074 797	1643.820 442	.000 608 3389	.016 646	27.362 896	.036 545 8389	14.62	3.239 317	11.17	116
30	69.187 324	1897.386 394	.000 527 0408	.014 454	27.423 902	.036 464 5408	14.59	3.375 745	11.25	120
31	79.682 096	2189.414 839	.000 456 7430	.012 550	27.476 873	.036 394 2430	14.56	3.512 886	11.33	124
32	91.768 782	2525.740 011	.000 395 9236	.010 897	27.522 867	.036 333 4236	14.54	3.650 678	11.41	128
33	105.688 853	2913.081 119	.000 343 2791	.009 462	27.562 804	.036 280 7791	14.52	3.789 063	11.48	132
34	121.720 409	3359.176 585	.000 297 6920	.008 216	27.597 480	.036 235 1920	14.50	3.927 986	11.55	136
35	140.183 732	3872.938 641	.000 258 2019	.007 133	27.627 590	.036 195 7019	14.48	4.067 398	11.62	140
36	161.447 690	4464.631 385	.000 223 9827	.006 194	27.653 733	.036 161 4827	14.47	4.207 254	11.69	144
37	185.937 100	5146.075 840	.000 194 3228	.005 378	27.676 434	.036 131 8228	14.46	4.347 510	11.75	148
38	214.141 220	5930.886 113	.000 168 6089	.004 670	27.696 144	.036 106 1089	14.45	4.488 129	11.81	152
39	246.623 519	6834.741 388	.000 146 3113	.004 055	27.713 259	.036 083 8113	14.44	4.629 075	11.87	156
40	284.032 939	7875.699 167	.000 126 9729	.003 521	27.728 119	.036 064 4729	14.43	4.770 316	11.93	160
41	327.116 857	9074.556 026	.000 110 1982	.003 057	27.741 022	.036 047 6982	14.42	4.911 823	11.98	164
42	376.736 018	10455.263 100	.000 095 6456	.002 654	27.752 226	.036 033 1456	14.42	5.053 568	12.03	168
43	433.881 727	12045.404 585	.000 083 0192	.002 305	27.761 954	.036 020 5192	14.41	5.195 529	12.08	172
44	499.695 661	13876.748 819	.000 072 0630	.002 001	27.770 401	.036 009 5630	14.41	5.337 683	12.13	176
45	575.492 669	15985.882 967	.000 062 5552	.001 738	27.777 735	.036 000 0552	14.41	5.480 010	12.18	180
46	662.787 049	18414.943 965	.000 054 3037	.001 509	27.784 104	.035 991 8037	14.40	5.622 492	12.22	184
47	763.322 794	21212.460 347	.000 047 1421	.001 310	27.789 633	.035 984 6421	14.40	5.765 113	12.27	188
48	879.108 438	24434.321 765	.000 040 9260	.001 138	27.794 434	.035 978 4260	14.40	5.907 858	12.31	192
49	1012.457 184	28144.895 567	.000 035 5304	.000 988	27.798 603	.035 973 0304	14.39	6.050 714	12.35	196
50	1166.033 114	32418.312 746	.000 030 8468	.000 858	27.802 223	.035 968 3468	14.39	6.193 669	12.39	200

Effective Rate is 15.17 %   Annual Percentage Rate is 14.375%

Amount Of 1	Amount Of 1 Per Period	Sinking Fund Payment	Present Worth Of 1	Present Worth of 1 Per Period	Periodic Payment To Amortize 1	Constant Annual Percent	Total Interest	Annual Add On Rate
What a single $ 1 deposit grows to in the future. The deposit is made at the beginning of the first period.	What a series of $ 1 deposits grow to in the future. A deposit is made at the end of each period.	The amount to be deposited at the end of each period that grows to $ 1 in the future.	What $ 1 to be paid in the future is worth today. Value today of a single $ 1 payment tomorrow.	What $ 1 to be paid at the end of each period is worth today. Value today of a series of $ 1 payments tomorrow.	The mortgage payment to amortize a loan of $ 1. An annuity certain, payable at the end of each period, worth $ 1 today.	The annual payment, including interest and principal, to amortize completely a loan of $ 100.	The total interest paid over the term on a loan of $1. The loan is amortized by regular periodic payments.	The average annual interest rate on a loan that is completely amortized by regular periodic payments.
$S = (1+i)^n$	$S\overline{n} = \dfrac{(1+i)^n - 1}{i}$	$\dfrac{1}{S\overline{n}} = \dfrac{i}{(1+i)^n - 1}$	$V^n = \dfrac{1}{(1+i)^n}$	$A\overline{n} = \dfrac{1-V^n}{i}$	$\dfrac{1}{A\overline{n}} = \dfrac{i}{1-V^n}$			

YEAR									PERIODS
	1.036 250	1.000 000	1.000 000 0000	.965 018	.965 018	1.036 250 0000	414.50	.036 250	14.50	1
	1.073 814	2.036 250	.491 098 8336	.931 260	1.896 278	.527 348 8336	210.94	.054 698	10.94	2
	1.112 740	3.110 064	.321 536 7851	.898 683	2.794 961	.357 786 7851	143.12	.073 360	9.78	3
	1.153 077	4.222 804	.236 809 4819	.867 245	3.662 206	.273 059 4819	109.23	.092 238	9.22	4
1	1.153 077	4.222 804	.236 809 4819	.867 245	3.662 206	.273 059 4819	109.23	.092 238	9.22	4
2	1.329 586	9.092 020	.109 986 5548	.752 114	6.838 235	.146 236 5548	58.50	.169 892	8.49	8
3	1.533 114	14.706 600	.067 996 6807	.652 267	9.592 632	.104 246 6807	41.70	.250 960	8.37	12
4	1.767 798	21.180 641	.047 212 9241	.565 675	11.981 368	.083 462 9241	33.39	.335 407	8.39	16
5	2.038 407	28.645 706	.034 909 2457	.490 579	14.052 988	.071 159 2457	28.47	.423 185	8.46	20
6	2.350 439	37.253 499	.026 843 1163	.425 452	15.849 590	.063 093 1163	25.24	.514 235	8.57	24
7	2.710 237	47.178 943	.021 195 8966	.368 971	17.407 684	.057 445 8966	22.98	.608 485	8.69	28
8	3.125 111	58.623 741	.017 057 9356	.319 989	18.758 933	.053 307 9356	21.33	.705 854	8.82	32
9	3.603 492	71.820 470	.013 923 6070	.277 509	19.930 797	.050 173 6070	20.07	.806 250	8.96	36
10	4.155 103	87.037 311	.011 489 3256	.240 668	20.947 091	.047 739 3256	19.10	.909 573	9.10	40
11	4.791 152	104.583 494	.009 561 7383	.208 718	21.828 467	.045 811 7383	18.33	1.015 716	9.23	44
12	5.524 565	124.815 587	.008 011 8199	.181 010	22.592 835	.044 261 8199	17.71	1.124 567	9.37	48
13	6.370 247	148.144 742	.006 750 1552	.156 980	23.255 730	.043 000 1552	17.21	1.236 008	9.51	52
14	7.345 383	175.045 045	.005 712 8152	.136 140	23.830 622	.041 962 8152	16.79	1.349 918	9.64	56
15	8.469 789	206.063 157	.004 852 8811	.118 067	24.329 195	.041 102 8811	16.45	1.466 173	9.77	60
16	9.766 316	241.829 416	.004 135 1462	.102 393	24.761 579	.040 385 1462	16.16	1.584 649	9.90	64
17	11.261 311	283.070 655	.003 532 6869	.088 800	25.136 563	.039 782 6869	15.92	1.705 223	10.03	68
18	12.985 155	330.624 964	.003 024 5750	.077 011	25.461 765	.039 274 5750	15.71	1.827 769	10.15	72
19	14.972 879	385.458 727	.002 594 3115	.066 787	25.743 795	.038 844 3115	15.54	1.952 168	10.27	76
20	17.264 877	448.686 258	.002 228 7288	.057 921	25.988 384	.038 478 7288	15.40	2.078 298	10.39	80
21	19.907 726	521.592 447	.001 917 2057	.050 232	26.200 503	.038 167 2057	15.27	2.206 045	10.50	84
22	22.955 134	605.658 870	.001 651 0945	.043 563	26.384 462	.037 901 0945	15.17	2.335 296	10.61	88
23	26.469 029	702.593 899	.001 423 2973	.037 780	26.544 000	.037 673 2973	15.07	2.465 943	10.72	92
24	30.520 819	814.367 417	.001 227 9470	.032 765	26.682 358	.037 477 9470	15.00	2.597 883	10.82	96
25	35.192 843	943.250 850	.001 060 1634	.028 415	26.802 358	.037 310 1634	14.93	2.731 016	10.92	100
26	40.580 046	1091.863 325	.000 915 8655	.024 643	26.906 410	.037 165 8655	14.87	2.865 250	11.02	104
27	46.791 903	1263.224 899	.000 791 6247	.021 371	26.996 656	.037 041 6247	14.82	3.000 495	11.11	108
28	53.954 650	1460.817 927	.000 684 5480	.018 534	27.074 922	.036 934 5480	14.78	3.136 669	11.20	112
29	62.213 846	1688.657 832	.000 592 1863	.016 074	27.142 797	.036 842 1863	14.74	3.273 694	11.29	116
30	71.737 333	1951.374 705	.000 512 4592	.013 940	27.201 662	.036 762 4592	14.71	3.411 495	11.37	120
31	82.718 643	2254.307 393	.000 443 5952	.012 089	27.252 712	.036 693 5952	14.68	3.550 006	11.45	124
32	95.380 935	2603.612 000	.000 384 0818	.010 484	27.296 986	.036 634 0818	14.66	3.689 162	11.53	128
33	109.981 528	3006.386 983	.000 332 6252	.009 092	27.335 381	.036 582 6252	14.64	3.828 907	11.60	132
34	126.817 131	3470.817 407	.000 288 1166	.007 885	27.368 679	.036 538 1166	14.62	3.969 184	11.67	136
35	146.229 871	4006.341 281	.000 249 6043	.006 839	27.397 557	.036 499 6043	14.60	4.109 945	11.74	140
36	168.614 249	4623.841 350	.000 216 2704	.005 931	27.422 601	.036 466 2704	14.59	4.251 143	11.81	144
37	194.425 152	5335.866 256	.000 187 4110	.005 143	27.444 321	.036 437 4110	14.58	4.392 737	11.87	148
38	224.187 101	6156.885 542	.000 162 4198	.004 461	27.463 157	.036 412 4198	14.57	4.534 688	11.93	152
39	258.504 909	7103.583 702	.000 140 7740	.003 868	27.479 492	.036 390 7740	14.56	4.676 961	11.99	156
40	298.075 972	8195.199 237	.000 122 0227	.003 355	27.493 659	.036 372 0227	14.55	4.819 524	12.05	160
41	343.704 441	9453.915 611	.000 105 7763	.002 909	27.505 945	.036 355 7763	14.55	4.962 347	12.10	164
42	396.317 562	10905.312 059	.000 091 6984	.002 523	27.516 601	.036 341 6984	14.54	5.105 405	12.16	168
43	456.984 523	12578.883 401	.000 079 4983	.002 188	27.525 841	.036 329 4983	14.54	5.248 674	12.21	172
44	526.938 179	14508.639 421	.000 068 9245	.001 898	27.533 855	.036 318 9245	14.53	5.392 131	12.25	176
45	607.600 105	16733.796 010	.000 059 7593	.001 646	27.540 805	.036 309 7593	14.53	5.535 757	12.30	180
46	700.609 488	19299.572 095	.000 051 8146	.001 427	27.546 832	.036 301 8146	14.53	5.679 534	12.35	184
47	807.856 435	22258.108 565	.000 044 9274	.001 238	27.552 059	.036 294 9274	14.52	5.823 446	12.39	188
48	931.520 385	25669.527 859	.000 038 9567	.001 074	27.556 593	.036 288 9567	14.52	5.967 480	12.43	192
49	1074.114 396	29603.155 759	.000 033 7802	.000 931	27.560 524	.036 283 7802	14.52	6.111 621	12.47	196
50	1238.536 220	34138.930 204	.000 029 2921	.000 807	27.563 934	.036 279 2921	14.52	6.255 858	12.51	200

Effective Rate is 15.31 %

Annual Percentage Rate is 14.50 %

	Amount Of 1	Amount Of 1 Per Period	Sinking Fund Payment	Present Worth Of 1	Present Worth of 1 Per Period	Periodic Payment To Amortize 1	Constant Annual Percent	Total Interest	Annual Add On Rate	
	What a single $ 1 deposit grows to in the future. The deposit is made at the beginning of the first period.	What a series of $ 1 deposits grow to in the future. A deposit is made at the end of each period.	The amount to be deposited at the end of each period that grows to $ 1 in the future.	What $ 1 to be paid in the future is worth today. Value today of a single $ 1 payment tomorrow.	What $ 1 to be paid at the end of each period is worth today. Value today of a series of $ 1 payments tomorrow.	The mortgage payment to amortize a loan of $ 1. An annuity certain, payable at the end of each period, worth $ 1 today.	The annual payment, including interest and principal, to amortize completely a loan of $ 100.	The total interest paid over the term on a loan of $1. The loan is amortized by regular periodic payments.	The average annual interest rate on a loan that is completely amortized by regular periodic payments.	
	$S = (1+i)^n$	$S\overline{n} = \dfrac{(1+i)^n - 1}{i}$	$\dfrac{1}{S\overline{n}} = \dfrac{i}{(1+i)^n - 1}$	$V^n = \dfrac{1}{(1+i)^n}$	$A\overline{n} = \dfrac{1-V^n}{i}$	$\dfrac{1}{A\overline{n}} = \dfrac{i}{1-V^n}$				

YEAR										PERIODS
	1.036 563	1.000 000	1.000 000 0000	.964 727	.964 727	1.036 562 5000	414.63	.036 562	14.62	1
	1.074 462	2.036 563	.491 023 4771	.930 698	1.895 426	.527 585 9771	211.04	.055 172	11.03	2
	1.113 747	3.111 024	.321 437 5390	.897 870	2.793 296	.358 000 0390	143.21	.074 000	9.87	3
	1.154 468	4.224 771	.236 699 2119	.866 200	3.659 495	.273 261 7119	109.31	.093 047	9.30	4
1	1.154 468	4.224 771	.236 699 2119	.866 200	3.659 495	.273 261 7119	109.31	.093 047	9.30	4
2	1.332 797	9.102 135	.109 864 3333	.750 302	6.829 349	.146 426 8333	58.58	.171 415	8.57	8
3	1.538 672	14.732 897	.067 875 3153	.649 911	9.575 076	.104 437 8153	41.78	.253 254	8.44	12
4	1.776 347	21.233 432	.047 095 5433	.562 953	11.953 423	.083 658 0433	33.47	.338 529	8.46	16
5	2.050 737	28.738 093	.034 797 0205	.487 630	14.013 547	.071 359 5205	28.55	.427 190	8.54	20
6	2.367 510	37.401 985	.026 736 5488	.422 385	15.798 026	.063 299 0488	25.32	.519 177	8.65	24
7	2.733 215	47.404 173	.021 095 1891	.365 869	17.343 741	.057 657 6891	23.07	.614 415	8.78	28
8	3.155 410	58.951 382	.016 963 1309	.316 916	18.682 638	.053 525 6309	21.42	.712 820	8.91	32
9	3.642 820	72.282 266	.013 834 6520	.274 513	19.842 391	.050 397 1520	20.16	.814 297	9.05	36
10	4.205 520	87.672 349	.011 406 1048	.237 783	20.846 969	.047 968 6048	19.19	.918 744	9.19	40
11	4.855 139	105.439 709	.009 484 0929	.205 967	21.717 133	.046 046 5929	18.42	1.026 050	9.33	44
12	5.605 104	125.951 562	.007 939 5601	.178 409	22.470 870	.044 502 0601	17.81	1.136 099	9.47	48
13	6.470 914	149.631 843	.006 683 0694	.154 538	23.123 756	.043 245 5694	17.30	1.248 770	9.61	52
14	7.470 465	176.969 975	.005 650 6760	.133 860	23.689 286	.042 213 1760	16.89	1.363 938	9.74	56
15	8.624 414	208.530 979	.004 795 4506	.115 950	24.179 148	.041 357 9506	16.55	1.481 477	9.88	60
16	9.956 612	244.967 154	.004 082 1799	.100 436	24.603 466	.040 644 6799	16.26	1.601 260	10.01	64
17	11.494 591	287.031 559	.003 483 9375	.086 997	24.971 010	.040 046 4375	16.02	1.723 158	10.14	68
18	13.270 140	335.593 577	.002 979 7948	.075 357	25.289 377	.039 542 2948	15.82	1.847 045	10.26	72
19	15.319 955	391.656 883	.002 553 2553	.065 274	25.565 146	.039 115 7553	15.65	1.972 797	10.38	76
20	17.686 401	456.380 185	.002 191 1556	.056 541	25.804 017	.038 753 6556	15.51	2.100 292	10.50	80
21	20.418 387	531.101 180	.001 882 8804	.048 975	26.010 927	.038 445 3804	15.38	2.229 412	10.62	84
22	23.572 378	617.364 192	.001 619 7894	.042 423	26.190 153	.038 182 2894	15.28	2.360 041	10.73	88
23	27.213 561	716.952 095	.001 394 7933	.036 746	26.345 398	.037 957 2933	15.19	2.492 071	10.84	92
24	31.417 191	831.923 162	.001 202 0341	.031 830	26.479 871	.037 764 5341	15.11	2.625 395	10.94	96
25	36.270 147	964.653 603	.001 036 6415	.027 571	26.596 352	.037 599 1415	15.04	2.759 914	11.04	100
26	41.872 732	1117.886 675	.000 894 5451	.023 882	26.697 247	.037 457 0451	14.99	2.895 533	11.14	104
27	48.340 737	1294.789 383	.000 772 3264	.020 686	26.784 643	.037 334 8264	14.94	3.032 161	11.23	108
28	55.807 843	1499.017 932	.000 667 1034	.017 919	26.860 345	.037 229 6034	14.90	3.169 716	11.32	112
29	64.428 380	1734.793 298	.000 576 4376	.015 521	26.925 918	.037 138 9376	14.86	3.308 117	11.41	116
30	74.380 516	2006.988 458	.000 498 2590	.013 444	26.982 718	.037 060 7590	14.83	3.447 291	11.49	120
31	85.869 939	2321.229 114	.000 430 8062	.011 646	27.031 917	.036 993 3062	14.80	3.587 170	11.57	124
32	99.134 114	2684.009 956	.000 372 5769	.010 087	27.074 534	.036 935 0769	14.78	3.727 690	11.65	128
33	114.447 182	3102.828 900	.000 322 2865	.008 738	27.111 449	.036 884 7865	14.76	3.868 792	11.72	132
34	132.125 631	3586.342 051	.000 278 8356	.007 569	27.143 424	.036 841 3356	14.74	4.010 422	11.80	136
35	152.534 839	4144.542 605	.000 241 2811	.006 556	27.171 121	.036 803 7811	14.73	4.152 529	11.86	140
36	176.096 620	4788.967 391	.000 208 8133	.005 679	27.195 112	.036 771 3133	14.71	4.295 069	11.93	144
37	203.297 947	5532.935 310	.000 180 7359	.004 919	27.215 894	.036 743 2359	14.70	4.437 999	11.99	148
38	234.701 014	6391.822 611	.000 156 4499	.004 261	27.233 894	.036 718 9499	14.69	4.581 280	12.06	152
39	270.954 856	7383.380 683	.000 135 4393	.003 691	27.249 486	.036 697 9393	14.68	4.724 879	12.12	156
40	312.808 764	8528.102 941	.000 117 2594	.003 197	27.262 992	.036 679 7594	14.68	4.868 761	12.17	160
41	361.127 769	9849.648 379	.000 101 5265	.002 769	27.274 691	.036 664 0265	14.67	5.012 900	12.23	164
42	416.910 523	11375.330 556	.000 087 9095	.002 399	27.284 825	.036 650 4095	14.67	5.157 269	12.28	168
43	481.309 939	13136.682 105	.000 076 1227	.002 078	27.293 602	.036 638 6227	14.66	5.301 843	12.33	172
44	555.657 017	15170.106 448	.000 065 9191	.001 800	27.301 206	.036 628 4191	14.66	5.446 602	12.38	176
45	641.488 353	17517.630 179	.000 057 0853	.001 559	27.307 791	.036 619 5853	14.65	5.591 525	12.43	180
46	740.577 901	20227.771 663	.000 049 4370	.001 350	27.313 496	.036 611 9370	14.65	5.736 596	12.47	184
47	854.973 633	23356.543 810	.000 042 8146	.001 170	27.318 438	.036 605 3146	14.65	5.881 799	12.51	188
48	987.039 867	26968.611 743	.000 037 0801	.001 013	27.322 718	.036 599 5801	14.64	6.027 119	12.56	192
49	1139.506 133	31138.629 290	.000 032 1145	.000 878	27.326 425	.036 594 6145	14.64	6.172 544	12.60	196
50	1315.523 589	35952.781 919	.000 027 8143	.000 760	27.329 637	.036 590 3143	14.64	6.318 063	12.64	200

QUARTERLY COMPOUND INTEREST AND ANNUITY

Amount Of 1	Amount Of 1 Per Period	Sinking Fund Payment	Present Worth Of 1	Present Worth of 1 Per Period	Periodic Payment To Amortize 1	Constant Annual Percent	Total Interest	Annual Add On Rate
What a single $ 1 deposit grows to in the future. The deposit is made at the beginning of the first period.	What a series of $ 1 deposits grow to in the future. A deposit is made at the end of each period.	The amount to be deposited at the end of each period that grows to $ 1 in the future.	What $ 1 to be paid in the future is worth today. Value today of a single $ 1 payment tomorrow.	What $ 1 to be paid at the end of each period is worth today. Value today of a series of $ 1 payments tomorrow.	The mortgage payment to amortize a loan of $ 1. An annuity certain, payable at the end of each period, worth $ 1 today.	The annual payment, including interest and principal, to amortize completely a loan of $ 100.	The total interest paid over the term on a loan of $1. The loan is amortized by regular periodic payments.	The average annual interest rate on a loan that is completely amortized by regular periodic payments.
$S = (1+i)^n$	$S\overline{n}| = \dfrac{(1+i)^n - 1}{i}$	$\dfrac{1}{S\overline{n}|} = \dfrac{i}{(1+i)^n - 1}$	$V^n = \dfrac{1}{(1+i)^n}$	$A\overline{n}| = \dfrac{1-V^n}{i}$	$\dfrac{1}{A\overline{n}|} = \dfrac{i}{1-V^n}$			

YEAR   **PERIODS**

	Amount Of 1	Amount Of 1 Per Period	Sinking Fund Payment	Present Worth Of 1	Present Worth of 1 Per Period	Periodic Payment To Amortize 1	Constant Annual Percent	Total Interest	Annual Add On Rate	PERIODS
	1.036 875	1.000 000	1.000 000 0000	.964 436	.964 436	1.036 875 0000	414.75	.036 875	14.75	1
	1.075 110	2.036 875	.490 948 1436	.930 138	1.894 574	.527 823 1436	211.13	.055 646	11.13	2
	1.114 754	3.111 985	.321 338 3340	.897 059	2.791 633	.358 213 3340	143.29	.074 640	9.95	3
	1.155 861	4.226 739	.236 588 9996	.865 156	3.656 788	.273 463 9996	109.39	.093 856	9.39	4
1	1.155 861	4.226 739	.236 588 9996	.865 156	3.656 788	.273 463 9996	109.39	.093 856	9.39	4
2	1.336 015	9.112 262	.109 742 2323	.748 495	6.820 481	.146 617 2323	58.65	.172 938	8.65	8
3	1.544 247	14.759 248	.067 754 1303	.647 565	9.557 568	.104 629 1303	41.86	.255 550	8.52	12
4	1.784 935	21.286 378	.046 978 4003	.560 244	11.925 575	.083 853 4003	33.55	.341 654	8.54	16
5	2.063 137	28.830 834	.034 685 0877	.484 699	13.974 270	.071 560 0877	28.63	.431 202	8.62	20
6	2.384 700	37.551 176	.026 630 3245	.419 340	15.746 711	.063 505 3245	25.41	.524 128	8.74	24
7	2.756 381	47.630 679	.020 994 8717	.362 795	17.280 149	.057 869 8717	23.15	.620 356	8.86	28
8	3.185 994	59.281 184	.016 868 7589	.313 874	18.606 812	.053 743 7589	21.50	.719 800	9.00	32
9	3.682 566	72.747 548	.013 746 1677	.271 550	19.754 582	.050 621 1677	20.25	.822 362	9.14	36
10	4.256 534	88.312 794	.011 323 3877	.234 933	20.747 582	.048 198 3877	19.28	.927 936	9.28	40
11	4.919 962	106.304 054	.009 406 9790	.203 254	21.606 682	.046 281 9790	18.52	1.036 407	9.42	44
12	5.686 792	127.099 450	.007 867 8546	.175 846	22.349 937	.044 742 8546	17.90	1.147 657	9.56	48
13	6.573 141	151.136 038	.006 616 5556	.152 134	22.992 969	.043 491 5556	17.40	1.261 561	9.70	52
14	7.597 638	178.918 993	.005 589 1216	.131 620	23.549 292	.042 464 1216	16.99	1.377 991	9.84	56
15	8.781 813	211.032 226	.004 738 6128	.113 872	24.030 598	.041 613 6128	16.65	1.496 817	9.98	60
16	10.150 556	248.150 661	.004 029 8099	.098 517	24.447 003	.040 904 8099	16.37	1.617 908	10.11	64
17	11.732 631	291.054 412	.003 435 7837	.085 232	24.807 258	.040 310 7837	16.13	1.741 133	10.24	68
18	13.561 291	340.645 186	.002 935 6058	.073 739	25.118 934	.039 810 6058	15.93	1.866 364	10.37	72
19	15.674 968	397.965 227	.002 512 7824	.063 796	25.388 583	.039 387 7824	15.76	1.993 471	10.49	76
20	18.118 084	464.219 228	.002 154 1546	.055 193	25.621 872	.039 029 1546	15.62	2.122 332	10.61	80
21	20.941 987	540.799 644	.001 849 1136	.047 751	25.823 703	.038 724 1136	15.49	2.252 826	10.73	84
22	24.206 026	629.315 961	.001 589 0269	.041 312	25.998 318	.038 464 0269	15.39	2.384 834	10.84	88
23	27.978 802	731.628 520	.001 366 8139	.035 741	26.149 387	.038 241 8139	15.30	2.518 247	10.95	92
24	32.339 606	849.887 618	.001 176 6262	.030 922	26.280 086	.038 051 6262	15.23	2.652 960	11.05	96
25	37.380 089	986.578 698	.001 013 6039	.026 752	26.393 160	.037 888 6039	15.16	2.788 860	11.16	100
26	43.206 188	1144.574 588	.000 873 6871	.023 145	26.490 988	.037 748 6871	15.10	2.925 863	11.25	104
27	49.940 348	1327.195 876	.000 753 4683	.020 024	26.575 623	.037 628 4683	15.06	3.063 875	11.35	108
28	57.724 101	1538.280 703	.000 650 0764	.017 324	26.648 846	.037 525 0764	15.02	3.202 809	11.44	112
29	66.721 037	1782.265 423	.000 561 0837	.014 988	26.712 196	.037 436 0837	14.98	3.342 586	11.53	116
30	77.120 246	2064.277 848	.000 484 4309	.012 967	26.767 003	.037 359 4309	14.95	3.483 132	11.61	120
31	89.140 285	2390.245 014	.000 418 3672	.011 218	26.814 420	.037 293 3672	14.92	3.624 378	11.69	124
32	103.033 780	2767.017 750	.000 361 3999	.009 706	26.855 443	.037 236 3999	14.90	3.766 259	11.77	128
33	119.092 728	3202.514 666	.000 312 2546	.008 397	26.890 934	.037 187 2546	14.88	3.908 718	11.84	132
34	137.654 641	3705.888 569	.000 269 8408	.007 265	26.921 639	.037 144 8408	14.86	4.051 698	11.92	136
35	159.109 632	4287.718 837	.000 233 2242	.006 285	26.948 204	.037 108 2242	14.85	4.195 151	11.99	140
36	183.908 620	4960.233 757	.000 201 6034	.005 437	26.971 187	.037 076 6034	14.84	4.339 031	12.05	144
37	212.572 803	5737.567 530	.000 174 2899	.004 704	26.991 071	.037 049 2899	14.82	4.483 295	12.12	148
38	245.704 614	6636.057 329	.000 150 6919	.004 070	27.008 273	.037 025 6919	14.82	4.627 905	12.18	152
39	284.000 383	7674.586 653	.000 130 3002	.003 521	27.023 156	.037 005 3002	14.81	4.772 827	12.24	156
40	328.264 969	8874.982 205	.000 112 6763	.003 046	27.036 032	.036 987 6763	14.80	4.918 028	12.30	160
41	379.428 678	10262.472 618	.000 097 4424	.002 636	27.047 172	.036 972 4424	14.79	5.063 481	12.35	164
42	438.566 814	11866.218 686	.000 084 2728	.002 280	27.056 809	.036 959 2728	14.79	5.209 158	12.40	168
43	506.922 280	13719.926 232	.000 072 8867	.001 973	27.065 147	.036 947 8867	14.78	5.355 037	12.45	172
44	585.931 697	15862.554 505	.000 063 0415	.001 707	27.072 361	.036 938 0415	14.78	5.501 095	12.50	176
45	677.255 602	18339.134 981	.000 054 5282	.001 477	27.078 602	.036 929 5282	14.78	5.647 315	12.55	180
46	782.813 343	21201.717 787	.000 047 1660	.001 277	27.084 002	.036 922 1660	14.77	5.793 679	12.59	184
47	904.823 420	24510.465 635	.000 040 7989	.001 105	27.088 673	.036 915 7989	14.77	5.940 170	12.64	188
48	1045.050 111	28334.918 258	.000 035 2921	.000 956	27.092 714	.036 910 2921	14.77	6.086 776	12.68	192
49	1208.857 363	32755.453 923	.000 030 5293	.000 827	27.096 211	.036 905 5293	14.77	6.233 484	12.72	196
50	1397.271 091	37864.978 732	.000 026 4096	.000 716	27.099 236	.036 901 4096	14.77	6.380 282	12.76	200

Amount Of 1	Amount Of 1 Per Period	Sinking Fund Payment	Present Worth Of 1	Present Worth of 1 Per Period	Periodic Payment To Amortize 1	Constant Annual Percent	Total Interest	Annual Add On Rate	
What a single $ 1 deposit grows to in the future. The deposit is made at the beginning of the first period.	What a series of $ 1 deposits grow to in the future. A deposit is made at the end of each period.	The amount to be deposited at the end of each period that grows to $ 1 in the future.	What $ 1 to be paid in the future is worth today. Value today of a single $ 1 payment tomorrow.	What $ 1 to be paid at the end of each period is worth today. Value today of a series of $ 1 payments tomorrow.	The mortgage payment to amortize a loan of $ 1. An annuity certain, payable at the end of each period, worth $ 1 today.	The annual payment, including interest and principal, to amortize completely a loan of $ 100.	The total interest paid over the term on a loan of $ 1. The loan is amortized by regular periodic payments.	The average annual interest rate on a loan that is completely amortized by regular periodic payments.	
$S = (1+i)^n$	$S\overline{n}| = \dfrac{(1+i)^n - 1}{i}$	$\dfrac{1}{S\overline{n}|} = \dfrac{i}{(1+i)^n - 1}$	$V^n = \dfrac{1}{(1+i)^n}$	$A\overline{n}| = \dfrac{1-V^n}{i}$	$\dfrac{1}{A\overline{n}|} = \dfrac{i}{1-V^n}$				

YEAR									PERIODS
	1.037 187	1.000 000	1.000 000 0000	.964 146	.964 146	1.037 187 5000	414.88	.037 188	14.88	1
	1.075 758	2.037 188	.490 872 8333	.929 577	1.893 723	.528 060 3333	211.23	.056 121	11.22	2
	1.115 763	3.112 945	.321 239 1701	.896 248	2.789 971	.358 426 6701	143.38	.075 280	10.04	3
	1.157 255	4.228 708	.236 478 8451	.864 114	3.654 085	.273 666 3451	109.47	.094 665	9.47	4

YEAR	Amount Of 1	Amount Of 1 Per Period	Sinking Fund Payment	Present Worth Of 1	Present Worth of 1 Per Period	Periodic Payment To Amortize 1	Constant Annual Percent	Total Interest	Annual Add On Rate	PERIODS
1	1.157 255	4.228 708	.236 478 8451	.864 114	3.654 085	.273 666 3451	109.47	.094 665	9.47	4
2	1.339 239	9.122 402	.109 620 2517	.746 693	6.811 629	.146 807 7517	58.73	.174 462	8.72	8
3	1.549 842	14.785 654	.067 633 1256	.645 227	9.540 107	.104 820 6256	41.93	.257 848	8.59	12
4	1.793 562	21.339 481	.046 861 4950	.557 550	11.897 822	.084 048 9950	33.62	.344 784	8.62	16
5	2.075 609	28.923 931	.034 573 4467	.481 786	13.935 156	.071 760 9467	28.71	.435 219	8.70	20
6	2.402 009	37.701 075	.026 524 4429	.416 318	15.695 644	.063 711 9429	25.49	.529 087	8.82	24
7	2.779 737	47.858 468	.020 894 9437	.359 746	17.216 906	.058 082 4437	23.24	.626 308	8.95	28
8	3.216 865	59.613 164	.016 774 8185	.310 862	18.531 450	.053 962 3185	21.59	.726 794	9.08	32
9	3.722 733	73.216 345	.013 658 1525	.268 620	19.667 365	.050 845 6525	20.34	.830 443	9.23	36
10	4.308 151	88.958 695	.011 241 1721	.232 118	20.648 925	.048 428 6721	19.38	.937 147	9.37	40
11	4.985 630	107.176 610	.009 330 3940	.200 576	21.497 104	.046 517 8940	18.61	1.046 787	9.52	44
12	5.769 646	128.259 384	.007 796 7005	.173 321	22.230 027	.044 984 2005	18.00	1.159 242	9.66	48
13	6.676 952	152.657 532	.006 550 6103	.149 769	22.863 356	.043 738 1103	17.50	1.274 382	9.80	52
14	7.726 937	180.892 413	.005 528 1478	.129 417	23.410 625	.042 715 6478	17.09	1.392 076	9.94	56
15	8.942 037	213.567 372	.004 682 3632	.111 831	23.883 527	.041 869 8632	16.75	1.512 192	10.08	60
16	10.348 217	251.380 634	.003 978 0312	.096 635	24.292 168	.041 165 5312	16.47	1.634 594	10.22	64
17	11.975 527	295.140 225	.003 388 2200	.083 504	24.645 281	.040 575 7200	16.24	1.759 149	10.35	68
18	13.858 740	345.781 233	.002 892 0020	.072 157	24.950 410	.040 079 5020	16.04	1.885 724	10.48	72
19	16.038 097	404.385 797	.002 472 8861	.062 352	25.214 076	.039 660 3861	15.87	2.014 189	10.60	76
20	18.560 169	472.206 226	.002 117 7188	.053 879	25.441 914	.039 305 2188	15.73	2.144 418	10.72	80
21	21.478 850	550.691 763	.001 815 8979	.046 557	25.638 792	.039 003 3979	15.61	2.276 285	10.84	84
22	24.856 508	641.519 548	.001 558 7990	.040 231	25.808 917	.038 746 2990	15.50	2.409 674	10.95	88
23	28.765 320	746.630 465	.001 339 3507	.034 764	25.955 924	.038 526 8507	15.42	2.544 470	11.06	92
24	33.288 813	868.270 608	.001 151 7147	.030 040	26.082 955	.038 339 2147	15.34	2.680 565	11.17	96
25	38.523 648	1009.039 281	.000 991 0417	.025 958	26.192 724	.038 178 5417	15.28	2.817 854	11.27	100
26	44.581 688	1171.944 543	.000 853 2827	.022 431	26.287 577	.038 040 7827	15.22	2.956 241	11.37	104
27	51.592 385	1360.467 486	.000 735 0415	.019 383	26.369 541	.037 922 5415	15.17	3.095 634	11.47	108
28	59.705 549	1578.636 619	.000 633 4580	.016 749	26.440 367	.037 820 9580	15.13	3.235 947	11.56	112
29	69.094 550	1831.113 956	.000 546 1157	.014 473	26.501 568	.037 733 6157	15.10	3.377 099	11.65	116
30	79.960 019	2123.294 638	.000 470 9662	.012 506	26.554 454	.037 658 4662	15.07	3.519 016	11.73	120
31	92.534 139	2461.422 217	.000 406 2692	.010 807	26.600 153	.037 593 7692	15.04	3.661 627	11.81	124
32	107.085 602	2852.722 076	.000 350 5424	.009 338	26.639 642	.037 538 0424	15.02	3.804 869	11.89	128
33	123.925 357	3305.555 826	.000 302 5210	.008 069	26.673 765	.037 490 0210	15.00	3.948 683	11.97	132
34	143.413 249	3829.599 985	.000 261 1239	.006 973	26.703 251	.037 448 6239	14.98	4.093 013	12.04	136
35	165.965 712	4436.052 749	.000 225 4256	.006 025	26.728 730	.037 412 9256	14.97	4.237 810	12.11	140
36	192.064 663	5137.873 293	.000 194 6331	.005 207	26.750 747	.037 382 1331	14.96	4.383 027	12.18	144
37	222.267 807	5950.058 683	.000 168 0656	.004 499	26.769 773	.037 355 5656	14.95	4.528 624	12.24	148
38	257.220 549	6889.964 353	.000 145 1386	.003 888	26.786 213	.037 332 6386	14.94	4.674 561	12.30	152
39	297.669 788	7977.674 966	.000 125 3498	.003 359	26.800 419	.037 312 8498	14.93	4.820 805	12.36	156
40	344.479 874	9236.433 599	.000 108 2669	.002 903	26.812 694	.037 295 7669	14.92	4.967 323	12.42	160
41	398.651 085	10693.138 423	.000 093 5179	.002 508	26.823 302	.037 281 0179	14.92	5.114 087	12.47	164
42	461.340 994	12378.917 482	.000 080 7825	.002 168	26.832 468	.037 268 2825	14.91	5.261 071	12.53	168
43	533.889 209	14329.793 865	.000 069 7847	.001 873	26.840 389	.037 257 2847	14.91	5.408 253	12.58	172
44	617.846 000	16587.455 472	.000 060 2865	.001 619	26.847 233	.037 247 7865	14.90	5.555 610	12.63	176
45	715.005 423	19200.145 838	.000 052 0829	.001 399	26.853 147	.037 239 5829	14.90	5.703 125	12.67	180
46	827.443 659	22223.695 040	.000 044 9970	.001 209	26.858 258	.037 232 4970	14.90	5.850 779	12.72	184
47	957.563 379	25722.712 718	.000 038 8761	.001 044	26.862 674	.037 226 3761	14.90	5.998 559	12.76	188
48	1108.145 086	29771.968 705	.000 033 5886	.000 902	26.866 490	.037 221 0886	14.89	6.146 449	12.81	192
49	1282.406 532	34457.990 771	.000 029 0208	.000 780	26.869 787	.037 216 5208	14.89	6.294 438	12.85	196
50	1484.071 475	39880.913 618	.000 025 0747	.000 674	26.872 637	.037 212 5747	14.89	6.442 515	12.89	200

Effective Rate is 15.73 %   Annual Percentage Rate is 14.875%

	Amount Of 1	Amount Of 1 Per Period	Sinking Fund Payment	Present Worth Of 1	Present Worth of 1 Per Period	Periodic Payment To Amortize 1	Constant Annual Percent	Total Interest	Annual Add On Rate	
	What a single $ 1 deposit grows to in the future. The deposit is made at the beginning of the first period.	What a series of $ 1 deposits grow to in the future. A deposit is made at the end of each period.	The amount to be deposited at the end of each period that grows to $ 1 in the future.	What $ 1 to be paid in the future is worth today. Value today of a single $ 1 payment tomorrow.	What $ 1 to be paid at the end of each period is worth today. Value today of a series of $ 1 payments tomorrow.	The mortgage payment to amortize a loan of $ 1. An annuity certain, payable at the end of each period, worth $ 1 today.	The annual payment, including interest and principal, to amortize completely a loan of $ 100.	The total interest paid over the term on a loan of $1. The loan is amortized by regular periodic payments.	The average annual interest rate on a loan that is completely amortized by regular periodic payments.	
	$S = (1+i)^n$	$S\overline{n}| = \dfrac{(1+i)^n - 1}{i}$	$\dfrac{1}{S\overline{n}|} = \dfrac{i}{(1+i)^n - 1}$	$V^n = \dfrac{1}{(1+i)^n}$	$A\overline{n}| = \dfrac{1 - V^n}{i}$	$\dfrac{1}{A\overline{n}|} = \dfrac{i}{1 - V^n}$				

YEAR										PERIODS
	1.037 500	1.000 000	1.000 000 0000	.963 855	.963 855	1.037 500 0000	415.00	.037 500	15.00	1
	1.076 406	2.037 500	.490 797 5460	.929 017	1.892 873	.528 297 5460	211.32	.056 595	11.32	2
	1.116 771	3.113 906	.321 140 0472	.895 438	2.788 311	.358 640 0472	143.46	.075 920	10.12	3
	1.158 650	4.230 678	.236 368 7482	.863 073	3.651 384	.273 868 7482	109.55	.095 475	9.55	4
1	1.158 650	4.230 678	.236 368 7482	.863 073	3.651 384	.273 868 7482	109.55	.095 475	9.55	4
2	1.342 471	9.132 554	.109 498 3915	.744 895	6.802 796	.146 998 3915	58.80	.175 987	8.80	8
3	1.555 454	14.812 116	.067 512 3010	.642 899	9.522 694	.105 012 3010	42.01	.260 148	8.67	12
4	1.802 228	21.392 742	.046 744 8270	.554 869	11.870 165	.084 244 8270	33.70	.347 917	8.70	16
5	2.088 152	29.017 387	.034 462 0973	.478 892	13.896 204	.071 962 0973	28.79	.439 242	8.78	20
6	2.419 438	37.851 685	.026 418 9033	.413 319	15.644 824	.063 918 9033	25.57	.534 054	8.90	24
7	2.803 283	48.087 548	.020 795 4043	.356 725	17.154 011	.058 295 4043	23.32	.632 271	9.03	28
8	3.248 025	59.947 335	.016 681 3087	.307 879	18.456 549	.054 181 3087	21.68	.733 802	9.17	32
9	3.763 326	73.688 682	.013 570 6050	.265 722	19.580 735	.051 070 6050	20.43	.838 542	9.32	36
10	4.360 379	89.610 100	.011 159 4563	.229 338	20.550 990	.048 659 4563	19.47	.946 378	9.46	40
11	5.052 155	108.057 458	.009 254 3358	.197 935	21.388 391	.046 754 3358	18.71	1.057 191	9.61	44
12	5.853 681	129.431 496	.007 726 0947	.170 833	22.111 129	.045 226 0947	18.10	1.170 853	9.76	48
13	6.782 370	154.196 534	.006 485 2301	.147 441	22.734 904	.043 985 2301	17.60	1.287 232	9.90	52
14	7.858 396	182.890 556	.005 467 7509	.127 252	23.273 268	.042 967 7509	17.19	1.406 194	10.04	56
15	9.105 134	216.136 896	.004 626 6973	.109 828	23.737 916	.042 126 6973	16.86	1.527 602	10.18	60
16	10.549 667	254.657 782	.003 926 8386	.094 790	24.138 941	.041 426 8386	16.58	1.651 318	10.32	64
17	12.223 376	299.290 023	.003 341 2407	.081 810	24.485 054	.040 841 2407	16.34	1.777 204	10.45	68
18	14.162 620	351.003 187	.002 848 9770	.070 608	24.783 776	.040 348 9770	16.14	1.905 126	10.58	72
19	16.409 525	410.920 666	.002 433 5598	.060 940	25.041 594	.039 933 5598	15.98	2.034 951	10.71	76
20	19.012 903	480.344 078	.002 081 8410	.052 596	25.264 110	.039 581 8410	15.84	2.166 547	10.83	80
21	22.029 308	560.781 543	.001 783 2256	.045 394	25.456 158	.039 283 2256	15.72	2.299 791	10.95	84
22	25.524 267	653.980 445	.001 529 0977	.039 178	25.621 909	.039 029 0977	15.62	2.434 561	11.07	88
23	29.573 702	761.965 392	.001 312 3956	.033 814	25.764 965	.038 812 3956	15.53	2.570 740	11.18	92
24	34.265 582	887.082 195	.001 127 2913	.029 184	25.888 432	.038 627 2913	15.46	2.708 220	11.28	96
25	39.701 831	1032.048 832	.000 968 9464	.025 188	25.994 993	.038 468 9464	15.39	2.846 895	11.39	100
26	46.000 543	1200.014 485	.000 833 3233	.021 739	26.086 963	.038 333 3233	15.34	2.986 666	11.49	104
27	53.298 548	1394.627 959	.000 717 0371	.018 762	26.166 340	.038 217 0371	15.29	3.127 440	11.58	108
28	61.754 385	1620.116 941	.000 617 2394	.016 193	26.234 848	.038 117 2394	15.25	3.269 131	11.68	112
29	71.551 744	1881.379 844	.000 531 5248	.013 976	26.293 976	.038 031 5248	15.22	3.411 657	11.76	116
30	82.903 458	2184.092 215	.000 457 8561	.012 062	26.345 007	.037 957 8561	15.19	3.554 943	11.85	120
31	96.056 126	2534.830 029	.000 394 5038	.010 411	26.389 051	.037 894 5038	15.16	3.698 918	11.93	124
32	111.295 470	2941.212 542	.000 339 9958	.008 985	26.427 064	.037 839 9958	15.14	3.843 519	12.01	128
33	128.952 543	3412.067 811	.000 293 0774	.007 755	26.459 872	.037 793 0774	15.12	3.988 686	12.09	132
34	149.410 917	3957.624 463	.000 252 6768	.006 693	26.488 188	.037 752 6768	15.11	4.134 364	12.16	136
35	173.115 021	4589.733 904	.000 217 8776	.005 777	26.512 627	.037 717 8776	15.09	4.280 503	12.23	140
36	200.579 791	5322.127 771	.000 187 8948	.004 986	26.533 719	.037 687 8948	15.08	4.427 057	12.30	144
37	232.401 859	6170.716 228	.000 162 0557	.004 303	26.551 923	.037 662 0557	15.07	4.573 984	12.36	148
38	269.272 510	7153.933 596	.000 139 7832	.003 714	26.567 634	.037 639 7832	15.06	4.721 247	12.42	152
39	311.992 705	8293.138 808	.000 120 5816	.003 205	26.581 195	.037 620 5816	15.05	4.868 811	12.48	156
40	361.490 478	9613.079 400	.000 104 0249	.002 766	26.592 898	.037 604 0249	15.05	5.016 644	12.54	160
41	418.841 092	11142.429 115	.000 089 7470	.002 388	26.602 999	.037 589 7470	15.04	5.164 719	12.60	164
42	485.290 405	12914.410 796	.000 077 4329	.002 061	26.611 717	.037 577 4329	15.04	5.313 009	12.65	168
43	562.281 929	14967.518 106	.000 066 8113	.001 778	26.619 241	.037 566 8113	15.03	5.461 492	12.70	172
44	651.488 190	17346.351 744	.000 057 6490	.001 535	26.625 735	.037 557 6490	15.03	5.610 146	12.75	176
45	754.847 062	20102.588 325	.000 049 7448	.001 325	26.631 339	.037 549 7448	15.02	5.758 954	12.80	180
46	874.603 862	23296.102 984	.000 042 9256	.001 143	26.636 177	.037 542 9256	15.02	5.907 898	12.84	184
47	1013.360 128	26996.270 069	.000 037 0422	.000 987	26.640 352	.037 537 0422	15.02	6.056 964	12.89	188
48	1174.130 132	31283.470 197	.000 031 9658	.000 852	26.643 955	.037 531 9658	15.02	6.206 137	12.93	192
49	1360.406 365	36250.836 406	.000 027 5856	.000 735	26.647 065	.037 527 5856	15.02	6.355 407	12.97	196
50	1576.235 400	42006.277 325	.000 023 8060	.000 634	26.649 749	.037 523 8060	15.01	6.504 761	13.01	200

Effective Rate is 15.87 %

Annual Percentage Rate is 15.00 %

	Amount Of 1	Amount Of 1 Per Period	Sinking Fund Payment	Present Worth Of 1	Present Worth of 1 Per Period	Periodic Payment To Amortize 1	Constant Annual Percent	Total Interest	Annual Add On Rate	
	What a single $ 1 deposit grows to in the future. The deposit is made at the beginning of the first period.	What a series of $ 1 deposits grow to in the future. A deposit is made at the end of each period.	The amount to be deposited at the end of each period that grows to $ 1 in the future.	What $ 1 to be paid in the future is worth today. Value today of a single $ 1 payment tomorrow.	What $ 1 to be paid at the end of each period is worth today. Value today of a series of $ 1 payments tomorrow.	The mortgage payment to amortize a loan of $ 1. An annuity certain, payable at the end of each period, worth $ 1 today.	The annual payment, including interest and principal, to amortize completely a loan of $ 100.	The total interest paid over the term on a loan of $1. The loan is amortized by regular periodic payments.	The average annual interest rate on a loan that is completely amortized by regular periodic payments.	
	$S = (1+i)^n$	$S\overline{n}| = \dfrac{(1+i)^n - 1}{i}$	$\dfrac{1}{S\overline{n}|} = \dfrac{i}{(1+i)^n - 1}$	$V^n = \dfrac{1}{(1+i)^n}$	$A\overline{n}| = \dfrac{1-V^n}{i}$	$\dfrac{1}{A\overline{n}|} = \dfrac{i}{1-V^n}$				

YEAR										PERIODS
	1.040 000	1.000 000	1.000 000 0000	.961 538	.961 538	1.040 000 0000	416.00	.040 000	16.00	1
	1.081 600	2.040 000	.490 196 0784	.924 556	1.886 095	.530 196 0784	212.08	.060 392	12.08	2
	1.124 864	3.121 600	.320 348 5392	.888 996	2.775 091	.360 348 5392	144.14	.081 046	10.81	3
	1.169 859	4.246 464	.235 490 0454	.854 804	3.629 895	.275 490 0454	110.20	.101 960	10.20	4
1	1.169 859	4.246 464	.235 490 0454	.854 804	3.629 895	.275 490 0454	110.20	.101 960	10.20	4
2	1.368 569	9.214 226	.108 527 8320	.730 690	6.732 745	.148 527 8320	59.42	.188 223	9.41	8
3	1.601 032	15.025 805	.066 552 1727	.624 597	9.385 074	.106 552 1727	42.63	.278 626	9.29	12
4	1.872 981	21.824 531	.045 819 9992	.533 908	11.652 296	.085 819 9992	34.33	.373 120	9.33	16
5	2.191 123	29.778 079	.033 581 7503	.456 387	13.590 326	.073 581 7503	29.44	.471 635	9.43	20
6	2.563 304	39.082 604	.025 586 8313	.390 121	15.246 963	.065 586 8313	26.24	.574 084	9.57	24
7	2.998 703	49.967 583	.020 012 9752	.333 477	16.663 063	.060 012 9752	24.01	.680 363	9.72	28
8	3.508 059	62.701 469	.015 948 5897	.285 058	17.873 551	.055 948 5897	22.38	.790 355	9.88	32
9	4.103 933	77.598 314	.012 886 8780	.243 669	18.908 282	.052 886 8780	21.16	.903 928	10.04	36
10	4.801 021	95.025 516	.010 523 4893	.208 289	19.792 774	.050 523 4893	20.21	1.020 940	10.21	40
11	5.616 515	115.412 877	.008 664 5444	.178 046	20.548 841	.048 664 5444	19.47	1.141 240	10.37	44
12	6.570 528	139.263 206	.007 180 6476	.152 195	21.195 131	.047 180 6476	18.88	1.264 671	10.54	48
13	7.686 589	167.164 718	.005 982 1236	.130 097	21.747 582	.045 982 1236	18.40	1.391 070	10.70	52
14	8.992 222	199.805 540	.005 004 8662	.111 207	22.219 819	.045 004 8662	18.01	1.520 273	10.86	56
15	10.519 627	237.990 685	.004 201 8451	.095 060	22.623 490	.044 201 8451	17.69	1.652 111	11.01	60
16	12.306 476	282.661 904	.003 537 7955	.081 258	22.968 549	.043 537 7955	17.42	1.786 419	11.17	64
17	14.396 836	334.920 912	.002 985 7795	.069 460	23.263 507	.042 985 7795	17.20	1.923 033	11.31	68
18	16.842 262	396.056 560	.002 524 8919	.059 374	23.515 639	.042 524 8919	17.01	2.061 792	11.45	72
19	19.703 065	467.576 621	.002 138 6869	.050 754	23.731 162	.042 138 6869	16.86	2.202 540	11.59	76
20	23.049 799	551.244 977	.001 814 0755	.043 384	23.915 392	.041 814 0755	16.73	2.345 126	11.73	80
21	26.965 005	649.125 119	.001 540 5351	.037 085	24.072 872	.041 540 5351	16.62	2.489 405	11.85	84
22	31.545 242	763.631 041	.001 309 5329	.031 701	24.207 487	.041 309 5329	16.53	2.635 239	11.98	88
23	36.903 471	897.586 774	.001 114 0984	.027 098	24.322 557	.041 114 0984	16.45	2.782 497	12.10	92
24	43.171 841	1054.296 034	.000 948 5002	.023 163	24.420 919	.040 948 5002	16.38	2.931 056	12.21	96
25	50.504 948	1237.623 705	.000 808 0000	.019 800	24.504 999	.040 808 0000	16.33	3.080 800	12.32	100
26	59.083 646	1452.091 149	.000 688 6620	.016 925	24.576 871	.040 688 6620	16.28	3.231 621	12.43	104
27	69.119 509	1702.987 724	.000 587 2033	.014 468	24.638 308	.040 587 2033	16.24	3.383 418	12.53	108
28	80.860 049	1996.501 231	.000 500 8762	.012 367	24.690 824	.040 500 8762	16.21	3.536 098	12.63	112
29	94.594 821	2339.870 519	.000 427 3741	.010 571	24.735 715	.040 427 3741	16.18	3.689 575	12.72	116
30	110.662 561	2741.564 020	.000 364 7553	.009 036	24.774 088	.040 364 7553	16.15	3.843 771	12.81	120
31	129.459 544	3211.488 601	.000 311 3821	.007 724	24.806 889	.040 311 3821	16.13	3.998 611	12.90	124
32	151.449 356	3761.233 894	.000 265 8702	.006 603	24.834 928	.040 265 8702	16.11	4.154 031	12.98	128
33	177.174 325	4404.358 131	.000 227 0478	.005 644	24.858 896	.040 227 0478	16.10	4.309 970	13.06	132
34	207.268 901	5156.722 525	.000 193 9216	.004 825	24.879 384	.040 193 9216	16.08	4.466 373	13.14	136
35	242.475 298	6036.882 451	.000 165 6484	.004 124	24.896 897	.040 165 6484	16.07	4.623 191	13.21	140
36	283.661 803	7066.545 075	.000 141 5119	.003 525	24.911 867	.040 141 5119	16.06	4.780 378	13.28	144
37	331.844 188	8271.104 710	.000 120 9028	.003 013	24.924 663	.040 120 9028	16.05	4.937 894	13.35	148
38	388.210 764	9680.269 109	.000 103 3029	.002 576	24.935 602	.040 103 3029	16.05	5.095 702	13.41	152
39	454.151 686	11328.792 145	.000 088 2707	.002 202	24.944 952	.040 088 2707	16.04	5.253 770	13.47	156
40	531.293 237	13257.330 929	.000 075 4300	.001 882	24.952 945	.040 075 4300	16.04	5.412 069	13.53	160
41	621.537 941	15513.448 534	.000 064 4602	.001 609	24.959 777	.040 064 4602	16.03	5.570 571	13.59	164
42	727.111 481	18152.787 027	.000 055 0880	.001 375	24.965 617	.040 055 0880	16.03	5.729 255	13.64	168
43	850.617 590	21240.439 755	.000 047 0800	.001 176	24.970 610	.040 047 0800	16.02	5.888 098	13.69	172
44	995.102 269	24852.556 730	.000 040 2373	.001 005	24.974 877	.040 040 2373	16.02	6.047 082	13.74	176
45	1164.128 908	29078.222 692	.000 034 3900	.000 859	24.978 525	.040 034 3900	16.02	6.206 190	13.79	180
46	1361.866 168	34021.654 190	.000 029 3930	.000 734	24.981 643	.040 029 3930	16.02	6.365 408	13.84	184
47	1593.190 794	39804.769 843	.000 025 1226	.000 628	24.984 308	.040 025 1226	16.02	6.524 723	13.88	188
48	1863.807 888	46570.197 194	.000 021 4730	.000 537	24.986 587	.040 021 4730	16.01	6.684 123	13.93	192
49	2180.391 612	54484.790 292	.000 018 3537	.000 459	24.988 534	.040 018 3537	16.01	6.843 597	13.97	196
50	2550.749 791	63743.744 777	.000 015 6878	.000 392	24.990 199	.040 015 6878	16.01	7.003 138	14.01	200

QUARTERLY COMPOUND INTEREST AND ANNUITY

17.00 % Q

	Amount Of 1	Amount Of 1 Per Period	Sinking Fund Payment	Present Worth Of 1	Present Worth of 1 Per Period	Periodic Payment To Amortize 1	Constant Annual Percent	Total Interest	Annual Add On Rate	
	What a single $ 1 deposit grows to in the future. The deposit is made at the beginning of the first period.	What a series of $ 1 deposits grow to in the future. A deposit is made at the end of each period.	The amount to be deposited at the end of each period that grows to $ 1 in the future.	What $ 1 to be paid in the future is worth today. Value today of a single $ 1 payment tomorrow.	What $ 1 to be paid at the end of each period is worth today. Value today of a series of $ 1 payments tomorrow.	The mortgage payment to amortize a loan of $ 1. An annuity certain, payable at the end of each period, worth $ 1 today.	The annual payment, including interest and principal, to amortize completely a loan of $ 100.	The total interest paid over the term on a loan of $1. The loan is amortized by regular periodic payments.	The average annual interest rate on a loan that is completely amortized by regular periodic payments.	
	$S = (1+i)^n$	$S\overline{n} = \dfrac{(1+i)^n - 1}{i}$	$\dfrac{1}{S\overline{n}} = \dfrac{i}{(1+i)^n - 1}$	$V^n = \dfrac{1}{(1+i)^n}$	$A\overline{n} = \dfrac{1-V^n}{i}$	$\dfrac{1}{A\overline{n}} = \dfrac{i}{1-V^n}$				

YEAR — **PERIODS**

	1.042 500	1.000 000	1.000 000 0000	.959 233	.959 233	1.042 500 0000	417.00	.042 500	17.00	1
	1.086 806	2.042 500	.489 596 0832	.920 127	1.879 360	.532 096 0832	212.84	.064 192	12.84	2
	1.132 996	3.129 306	.319 559 6468	.882 616	2.761 976	.362 059 6468	144.83	.086 179	11.49	3
	1.181 148	4.262 302	.234 615 0167	.846 634	3.608 610	.277 115 0167	110.85	.108 460	10.85	4

YEAR	Amount Of 1	Amount Of 1 Per Period	Sinking Fund Payment	Present Worth Of 1	Present Worth of 1 Per Period	Periodic Payment To Amortize 1	Constant Annual Percent	Total Interest	Annual Add On Rate	PERIODS
1	1.181 148	4.262 302	.234 615 0167	.846 634	3.608 610	.277 115 0167	110.85	.108 460	10.85	4
2	1.395 110	9.296 710	.107 564 9316	.716 789	6.663 782	.150 064 9316	60.03	.200 519	10.03	8
3	1.647 831	15.243 091	.065 603 4928	.606 858	9.250 395	.108 103 4928	43.25	.297 242	9.91	12
4	1.946 332	22.266 645	.044 910 2226	.513 787	11.440 309	.087 410 2226	34.97	.398 564	9.96	16
5	2.298 906	30.562 501	.032 719 8348	.434 989	13.294 366	.075 219 8348	30.09	.504 397	10.09	20
6	2.715 348	40.361 134	.024 776 3108	.368 277	14.864 073	.067 276 3108	26.92	.614 631	10.24	24
7	3.207 228	51.934 767	.019 254 9240	.311 796	16.193 041	.061 754 9240	24.71	.729 138	10.42	28
8	3.788 210	65.604 939	.015 242 7548	.263 977	17.318 190	.057 742 7548	23.10	.847 768	10.60	32
9	4.474 436	81.751 433	.012 232 2015	.223 492	18.270 780	.054 732 2015	21.90	.970 359	10.78	36
10	5.284 970	100.822 829	.009 918 3886	.189 216	19.077 275	.052 418 3886	20.97	1.096 736	10.97	40
11	6.242 331	123.348 967	.008 107 0805	.160 197	19.760 081	.050 607 0805	20.25	1.226 712	11.15	44
12	7.373 116	149.955 666	.006 668 6377	.135 628	20.338 168	.049 168 6377	19.67	1.360 095	11.33	48
13	8.708 740	181.382 110	.005 513 2229	.114 827	20.827 596	.048 013 2229	19.21	1.496 688	11.51	52
14	10.286 309	218.501 387	.004 576 6300	.097 217	21.241 962	.047 076 6300	18.84	1.636 291	11.69	56
15	12.149 651	262.344 740	.003 811 7784	.082 307	21.592 779	.046 311 7784	18.53	1.778 707	11.86	60
16	14.350 534	314.130 221	.003 183 3932	.069 684	21.889 793	.045 683 3932	18.28	1.923 737	12.02	64
17	16.950 102	375.296 529	.002 664 5597	.058 997	22.141 254	.045 164 5597	18.07	2.071 190	12.18	68
18	20.020 577	447.542 980	.002 234 4223	.049 949	22.354 150	.044 734 4223	17.90	2.220 878	12.34	72
19	23.647 261	532.876 720	.001 876 6067	.042 288	22.534 395	.044 376 6067	17.76	2.372 622	12.49	76
20	27.930 910	633.668 480	.001 578 1123	.035 803	22.686 997	.044 078 1123	17.64	2.526 249	12.63	80
21	32.990 534	752.718 449	.001 328 5180	.030 312	22.816 195	.043 828 5180	17.54	2.681 596	12.77	84
22	38.966 698	893.334 060	.001 119 4021	.025 663	22.925 578	.043 619 4021	17.45	2.838 507	12.90	88
23	46.025 430	1059.421 884	.000 943 9110	.021 727	23.018 185	.043 443 9110	17.38	2.996 840	13.03	92
24	54.362 837	1255.596 156	.000 796 4344	.018 395	23.096 590	.043 296 4344	17.32	3.156 458	13.15	96
25	64.210 546	1487.306 971	.000 672 3562	.015 574	23.162 970	.043 172 3562	17.27	3.317 236	13.27	100
26	75.842 147	1760.991 695	.000 567 8618	.013 185	23.219 170	.043 067 8618	17.23	3.479 058	13.38	104
27	89.580 787	2084.253 813	.000 479 7880	.011 163	23.266 750	.042 979 7880	17.20	3.641 817	13.49	108
28	105.808 152	2466.074 159	.000 405 5028	.009 451	23.307 034	.042 905 5028	17.17	3.805 416	13.59	112
29	124.975 068	2917.060 432	.000 342 8109	.008 002	23.341 139	.042 842 8109	17.14	3.969 766	13.69	116
30	147.614 030	3449.741 886	.000 289 8768	.006 774	23.370 014	.042 789 8768	17.12	4.134 785	13.78	120
31	174.353 991	4078.917 427	.000 245 1631	.005 735	23.394 460	.042 745 1631	17.10	4.300 400	13.87	124
32	205.937 837	4822.066 750	.000 207 3800	.004 856	23.415 157	.042 707 3800	17.09	4.466 545	13.96	128
33	243.243 028	5699.835 955	.000 175 4436	.004 111	23.432 680	.042 675 4436	17.08	4.633 159	14.04	132
34	287.305 974	6736.611 143	.000 148 4426	.003 481	23.447 515	.042 648 4426	17.06	4.800 188	14.12	136
35	339.350 826	7961.195 902	.000 125 6093	.002 947	23.460 075	.042 625 6093	17.06	4.967 585	14.19	140
36	400.823 490	9407.611 526	.000 106 2969	.002 495	23.470 709	.042 606 2969	17.05	5.135 307	14.26	144
37	473.431 793	11116.042 195	.000 089 9601	.002 112	23.479 712	.042 589 9601	17.04	5.303 314	14.33	148
38	559.192 933	13133.951 363	.000 076 1385	.001 788	23.487 334	.042 576 1385	17.04	5.471 573	14.40	152
39	660.489 516	15517.400 388	.000 064 4438	.001 514	23.493 788	.042 564 4438	17.03	5.640 053	14.46	156
40	780.135 756	18332.606 021	.000 054 5476	.001 282	23.499 251	.042 554 5476	17.03	5.808 728	14.52	160
41	921.455 651	21657.780 030	.000 046 1728	.001 085	23.503 877	.042 546 1728	17.02	5.977 572	14.58	164
42	1088.375 338	25585.302 080	.000 039 0849	.000 919	23.507 793	.042 539 0849	17.02	6.146 566	14.63	168
43	1285.532 164	30224.286 206	.000 033 0860	.000 778	23.511 109	.042 533 0860	17.02	6.315 691	14.69	172
44	1518.403 519	35703.612 217	.000 028 0084	.000 659	23.513 916	.042 528 0084	17.02	6.484 929	14.74	176
45	1793.459 014	42175.506 218	.000 023 7104	.000 558	23.516 292	.042 523 7104	17.01	6.654 268	14.79	180
46	2118.340 214	49819.769 742	.000 020 0724	.000 472	23.518 304	.042 520 0724	17.01	6.823 693	14.83	184
47	2502.072 936	58848.774 974	.000 016 9927	.000 400	23.520 008	.042 516 9927	17.01	6.993 195	14.88	188
48	2955.318 007	69513.364 871	.000 014 3857	.000 338	23.521 450	.042 514 3857	17.01	7.162 762	14.92	192
49	3490.667 436	82109.822 030	.000 012 1788	.000 286	23.522 671	.042 512 1788	17.01	7.332 387	14.96	196
50	4122.994 250	96988.100 007	.000 010 3105	.000 243	23.523 705	.042 510 3105	17.01	7.502 062	15.00	200

Effective Rate is 18.11 %

Annual Percentage Rate is 17.00 %

QUARTERLY COMPOUND INTEREST AND ANNUITY

18.00 % Q

	Amount Of 1	Amount Of 1 Per Period	Sinking Fund Payment	Present Worth Of 1	Present Worth of 1 Per Period	Periodic Payment To Amortize 1	Constant Annual Percent	Total Interest	Annual Add On Rate	
	What a single $ 1 deposit grows to in the future. The deposit is made at the beginning of the first period.	What a series of $ 1 deposits grow to in the future. A deposit is made at the end of each period.	The amount to be deposited at the end of each period that grows to $ 1 in the future.	What $ 1 to be paid in the future is worth today. Value today of a single $ 1 payment tomorrow.	What $ 1 to be paid at the end of each period is worth today. Value today of a series of $ 1 payments tomorrow.	The mortgage payment to amortize a loan of $ 1. An annuity certain, payable at the end of each period, worth $ 1 today.	The annual payment, including interest and principal, to amortize completely a loan of $ 100.	The total interest paid over the term on a loan of $1. The loan is amortized by regular periodic payments.	The average annual interest rate on a loan that is completely amortized by regular periodic payments.	
	$S = (1+i)^n$	$S\overline{n} = \dfrac{(1+i)^n - 1}{i}$	$\dfrac{1}{S\overline{n}} = \dfrac{i}{(1+i)^n - 1}$	$V^n = \dfrac{1}{(1+i)^n}$	$A\overline{n} = \dfrac{1 - V^n}{i}$	$\dfrac{1}{A\overline{n}} = \dfrac{i}{1 - V^n}$				

YEAR										PERIODS
	1.045 000	1.000 000	1.000 000 0000	.956 938	.956 938	1.045 000 0000	418.00	.045 000	18.00	1
	1.092 025	2.045 000	.488 997 5550	.915 730	1.872 668	.533 997 5550	213.60	.067 995	13.60	2
	1.141 166	3.137 025	.318 773 3601	.876 297	2.748 964	.363 773 3601	145.51	.091 320	12.18	3
	1.192 519	4.278 191	.233 743 6479	.838 561	3.587 526	.278 743 6479	111.50	.114 975	11.50	4
1	1.192 519	4.278 191	.233 743 6479	.838 561	3.587 526	.278 743 6479	111.50	.114 975	11.50	4
2	1.422 101	9.380 014	.106 609 6533	.703 185	6.595 886	.151 609 6533	60.65	.212 877	10.64	8
3	1.695 881	15.464 032	.064 666 1886	.589 664	9.118 581	.109 666 1886	43.87	.315 994	10.53	12
4	2.022 370	22.719 337	.044 015 3694	.494 469	11.234 015	.089 015 3694	35.61	.424 246	10.61	16
5	2.411 714	31.371 423	.031 876 1443	.414 643	13.007 936	.076 876 1443	30.76	.537 523	10.75	20
6	2.876 014	41.689 196	.023 987 0299	.347 703	14.495 478	.068 987 0299	27.60	.655 689	10.93	24
7	3.429 700	53.993 343	.018 520 8051	.291 571	15.742 874	.063 520 8051	25.41	.778 583	11.12	28
8	4.089 981	68.666 245	.014 563 1962	.244 500	16.788 891	.059 563 1962	23.83	.906 022	11.33	32
9	4.877 378	86.163 966	.011 605 7796	.205 028	17.666 041	.056 605 7796	22.65	1.037 808	11.53	36
10	5.816 365	107.030 323	.009 343 1466	.171 929	18.401 584	.054 343 1466	21.74	1.173 726	11.74	40
11	6.936 123	131.913 842	.007 580 7056	.144 173	19.018 383	.052 580 7056	21.04	1.313 551	11.94	44
12	8.271 456	161.587 902	.006 188 5821	.120 898	19.535 607	.051 188 5821	20.48	1.457 052	12.14	48
13	9.863 865	196.974 769	.005 076 7923	.101 380	19.969 330	.050 076 7923	20.04	1.603 993	12.34	52
14	11.762 842	239.174 268	.004 181 0518	.085 013	20.333 034	.049 181 0518	19.68	1.754 139	12.53	56
15	14.027 408	289.497 954	.003 454 2558	.071 289	20.638 022	.048 454 2558	19.39	1.907 255	12.72	60
16	16.727 945	349.509 886	.002 861 1494	.059 780	20.893 773	.047 861 1494	19.15	2.063 114	12.89	64
17	19.948 385	421.075 231	.002 374 8725	.050 129	21.108 236	.047 374 8725	18.95	2.221 491	13.07	68
18	23.788 821	506.418 237	.001 974 6524	.042 037	21.288 077	.046 974 6524	18.79	2.382 175	13.23	72
19	28.368 611	608.191 358	.001 644 2194	.035 250	21.438 884	.046 644 2194	18.66	2.544 961	13.39	76
20	33.830 096	729.557 699	.001 370 6935	.029 559	21.565 345	.046 370 6935	18.55	2.709 655	13.55	80
21	40.343 019	874.289 317	.001 143 7861	.024 787	21.671 390	.046 143 7861	18.46	2.876 078	13.70	84
22	48.109 801	1046.884 464	.000 955 2152	.020 786	21.760 316	.045 955 2152	18.39	3.044 059	13.84	88
23	57.371 832	1252.707 387	.000 798 2710	.017 430	21.834 885	.045 798 2710	18.32	3.213 441	13.97	92
24	68.416 977	1498.155 051	.000 667 4877	.014 616	21.897 417	.045 667 4877	18.27	3.384 079	14.10	96
25	81.588 518	1790.855 956	.000 558 3922	.012 257	21.949 853	.045 558 3922	18.23	3.555 839	14.22	100
26	97.295 825	2139.907 230	.000 467 3100	.010 278	21.993 824	.045 467 3100	18.19	3.728 600	14.34	104
27	116.027 081	2556.157 367	.000 391 2122	.008 619	22.030 696	.045 391 2122	18.16	3.902 251	14.45	108
28	138.364 453	3052.543 397	.000 327 5957	.007 227	22.061 616	.045 327 5957	18.14	4.076 691	14.56	112
29	165.002 184	3644.492 971	.000 274 3866	.006 061	22.087 544	.045 274 3866	18.11	4.251 829	14.66	116
30	196.768 173	4350.403 849	.000 229 8637	.005 082	22.109 286	.045 229 8637	18.10	4.427 584	14.76	120
31	234.649 707	5192.215 701	.000 192 5960	.004 262	22.127 518	.045 192 5960	18.08	4.603 882	14.85	124
32	279.824 140	6196.091 993	.000 161 3921	.003 574	22.142 807	.045 161 3921	18.07	4.780 658	14.94	128
33	333.695 491	7393.233 144	.000 135 2588	.002 997	22.155 628	.045 135 2588	18.06	4.957 854	15.02	132
34	397.938 081	8820.846 235	.000 113 3678	.002 513	22.166 379	.045 113 3678	18.05	5.135 418	15.10	136
35	474.548 563	10523.301 399	.000 095 0272	.002 107	22.175 394	.045 095 0272	18.04	5.313 304	15.18	140
36	565.907 988	12553.510 849	.000 079 6590	.001 767	22.182 954	.045 079 6590	18.04	5.491 471	15.25	144
37	674.855 802	14974.573 382	.000 066 7799	.001 482	22.189 293	.045 066 7799	18.03	5.669 883	15.32	148
38	804.778 097	17861.735 486	.000 055 9856	.001 243	22.194 609	.045 055 9856	18.03	5.848 510	15.39	152
39	959.712 850	21304.729 997	.000 046 9379	.001 042	22.199 067	.045 046 9379	18.02	6.027 322	15.45	156
40	1144.475 425	25410.564 994	.000 039 3537	.000 874	22.202 805	.045 039 3537	18.02	6.206 297	15.52	160
41	1364.808 232	30306.849 599	.000 032 9958	.000 733	22.205 940	.045 032 9958	18.02	6.385 411	15.57	164
42	1627.559 203	36145.760 065	.000 027 6658	.000 614	22.208 569	.045 027 6658	18.02	6.564 648	15.63	168
43	1940.894 623	43108.769 402	.000 023 1971	.000 515	22.210 773	.045 023 1971	18.01	6.743 990	15.68	172
44	2314.552 940	51412.287 553	.000 019 4506	.000 432	22.212 621	.045 019 4506	18.01	6.923 423	15.74	176
45	2760.147 433	61314.387 399	.000 016 3094	.000 362	22.214 171	.045 016 3094	18.01	7.102 936	15.78	180
46	3291.527 154	73122.825 650	.000 013 6756	.000 304	22.215 471	.045 013 6756	18.01	7.282 516	15.83	184
47	3925.207 354	87204.607 909	.000 011 4673	.000 255	22.216 561	.045 011 4673	18.01	7.462 156	15.88	188
48	4680.882 783	103997.395	.000 009 6156	.000 214	22.217 475	.045 009 6156	18.01	7.641 846	15.92	192
49	5582.039 786	124023.106	.000 008 0630	.000 179	22.218 241	.045 008 0630	18.01	7.821 580	15.96	196
50	6656.686 275	147904.139	.000 006 7611	.000 150	22.218 884	.045 006 7611	18.01	8.001 352	16.00	200

Effective Rate is 19.25 %

Annual Percentage Rate is 18.00 %

QUARTERLY COMPOUND INTEREST AND ANNUITY

	Amount Of 1	Amount Of 1 Per Period	Sinking Fund Payment	Present Worth Of 1	Present Worth of 1 Per Period	Periodic Payment To Amortize 1	Constant Annual Percent	Total Interest	Annual Add On Rate	
	What a single $ 1 deposit grows to in the future. The deposit is made at the beginning of the first period.	What a series of $ 1 deposits grow to in the future. A deposit is made at the end of each period.	The amount to be deposited at the end of each period that grows to $ 1 in the future.	What $ 1 to be paid in the future is worth today. Value today of a single $ 1 payment tomorrow.	What $ 1 to be paid at the end of each period is worth today. Value today of a series of $ 1 payments tomorrow.	The mortgage payment to amortize a loan of $ 1. An annuity certain, payable at the end of each period, worth $ 1 today.	The annual payment, including interest and principal, to amortize completely a loan of $ 100.	The total interest paid over the term on a loan of $1. The loan is amortized by regular periodic payments.	The average annual interest rate on a loan that is completely amortized by regular periodic payments.	
	$S = (1+i)^n$	$S\overline{n}| = \dfrac{(1+i)^n - 1}{i}$	$\dfrac{1}{S\overline{n}|} = \dfrac{i}{(1+i)^n - 1}$	$V^n = \dfrac{1}{(1+i)^n}$	$A\overline{n}| = \dfrac{1 - V^n}{i}$	$\dfrac{1}{A\overline{n}|} = \dfrac{i}{1 - V^n}$				

YEAR										PERIODS
	1.047 500	1.000 000	1.000 000 0000	.954 654	.954 654	1.047 500 0000	419.00	.047 500	19.00	1
	1.097 256	2.047 500	.488 400 4884	.911 364	1.866 018	.535 900 4884	214.37	.071 801	14.36	2
	1.149 376	3.144 756	.317 989 6693	.870 037	2.736 055	.365 489 6693	146.20	.096 469	12.86	3
	1.203 971	4.294 132	.232 875 9246	.830 585	3.566 640	.280 375 9246	112.16	.121 504	12.15	4
1	1.203 971	4.294 132	.232 875 9246	.830 585	3.566 640	.280 375 9246	112.16	.121 504	12.15	4
2	1.449 547	9.464 144	.105 661 9598	.689 871	6.529 036	.153 161 9598	61.27	.225 296	11.26	8
3	1.745 213	15.688 690	.063 740 1861	.572 996	8.989 557	.111 240 1861	44.50	.334 882	11.16	12
4	2.101 186	23.182 864	.043 135 3090	.475 922	11.033 228	.090 635 3090	36.26	.450 165	11.25	16
5	2.529 768	32.205 635	.031 050 4673	.395 293	12.730 669	.078 550 4673	31.43	.571 009	11.42	20
6	3.045 768	43.068 791	.023 218 6689	.328 324	14.140 538	.070 718 6689	28.29	.697 248	11.62	24
7	3.667 017	56.147 720	.017 810 1623	.272 701	15.311 553	.065 310 1623	26.13	.828 685	11.84	28
8	4.414 983	71.894 374	.013 909 2942	.226 501	16.284 180	.061 409 2942	24.57	.965 097	12.06	32
9	5.315 512	90.852 894	.011 006 8041	.188 129	17.092 029	.058 506 8041	23.41	1.106 245	12.29	36
10	6.399 724	113.678 406	.008 796 7454	.156 257	17.763 016	.056 296 7454	22.52	1.251 870	12.52	40
11	7.705 084	141.159 669	.007 084 1765	.129 784	18.320 328	.054 584 1765	21.84	1.401 704	12.74	44
12	9.276 700	174.246 319	.005 739 0022	.107 797	18.783 222	.053 239 0022	21.30	1.555 472	12.96	48
13	11.168 881	214.081 695	.004 671 1140	.089 534	19.167 695	.052 171 1140	20.87	1.712 898	13.18	52
14	13.447 011	262.042 344	.003 816 1771	.074 366	19.487 032	.051 316 1771	20.53	1.873 706	13.38	56
15	16.189 815	319.785 589	.003 127 0953	.061 767	19.752 269	.050 627 0953	20.26	2.037 626	13.58	60
16	19.492 073	389.306 796	.002 568 6682	.051 303	19.972 570	.050 068 6682	20.03	2.204 395	13.78	64
17	23.467 896	473.008 333	.002 114 1277	.042 611	20.155 549	.049 614 1277	19.85	2.373 761	13.96	68
18	28.254 673	573.782 579	.001 742 8204	.035 392	20.307 529	.049 242 8204	19.70	2.545 483	14.14	72
19	34.017 814	695.111 877	.001 438 6173	.029 396	20.433 761	.048 938 6173	19.58	2.719 335	14.31	76
20	40.956 471	841.188 868	.001 188 7937	.024 416	20.538 607	.048 688 7937	19.48	2.895 103	14.48	80
21	49.310 415	1017.061 368	.000 983 2248	.020 280	20.625 691	.048 483 2248	19.40	3.072 591	14.63	84
22	59.368 323	1228.806 808	.000 813 7976	.016 844	20.698 021	.048 313 7976	19.33	3.251 614	14.78	88
23	71.477 756	1483.742 235	.000 673 9715	.013 990	20.758 098	.048 173 9715	19.27	3.432 005	14.92	92
24	86.057 165	1790.677 168	.000 558 4480	.011 620	20.807 996	.048 058 4480	19.23	3.613 611	15.06	96
25	103.610 356	2160.218 011	.000 462 9162	.009 652	20.849 441	.047 962 9162	19.19	3.796 292	15.19	100
26	124.743 892	2605.134 571	.000 383 8573	.008 016	20.883 865	.047 883 8573	19.16	3.979 921	15.31	104
27	150.188 063	3140.801 332	.000 318 3901	.006 658	20.912 456	.047 818 3901	19.13	4.164 386	15.42	108
28	180.822 114	3785.728 726	.000 264 1499	.005 530	20.936 204	.047 764 1499	19.11	4.349 585	15.53	112
29	217.704 632	4562.202 786	.000 219 1924	.004 593	20.955 929	.047 719 1924	19.09	4.535 426	15.64	116
30	262.110 124	5497.055 251	.000 181 9156	.003 815	20.972 312	.047 681 9156	19.08	4.721 830	15.74	120
31	315.573 062	6622.590 769	.000 150 9983	.003 169	20.985 919	.047 650 9983	19.07	4.908 724	15.83	124
32	379.940 902	7977.703 205	.000 125 3494	.002 632	20.997 221	.047 625 3494	19.06	5.096 045	15.93	128
33	457.437 934	9609.219 657	.000 104 0667	.002 186	21.006 609	.047 604 0667	19.05	5.283 737	16.01	132
34	550.742 134	11573.518 605	.000 086 4041	.001 816	21.014 406	.047 586 4041	19.04	5.471 751	16.09	136
35	663.077 711	13938.478 119	.000 071 7438	.001 508	21.020 882	.047 571 7438	19.03	5.660 044	16.17	140
36	798.326 519	16785.821 449	.000 059 5741	.001 253	21.026 261	.047 559 5741	19.03	5.848 579	16.25	144
37	961.162 199	20213.941 037	.000 049 4708	.001 040	21.030 728	.047 549 4708	19.02	6.037 322	16.32	148
38	1157.211 682	24341.298 560	.000 041 0824	.000 864	21.034 439	.047 541 0824	19.02	6.226 245	16.38	152
39	1393.249 627	29310.518 471	.000 034 1174	.000 718	21.037 521	.047 534 1174	19.02	6.415 322	16.45	156
40	1677.432 535	35293.316 520	.000 028 3340	.000 596	21.040 081	.047 528 3340	19.02	6.604 533	16.51	160
41	2019.580 593	42496.433 533	.000 023 5314	.000 495	21.042 207	.047 523 5314	19.01	6.793 859	16.57	164
42	2431.517 028	51168.779 530	.000 019 5432	.000 411	21.043 973	.047 519 5432	19.01	6.983 283	16.63	168
43	2927.476 664	61610.035 025	.000 016 2311	.000 342	21.045 440	.047 516 2311	19.01	7.172 792	16.68	172
44	3524.597 821	74181.006 750	.000 013 4805	.000 284	21.046 659	.047 513 4805	19.01	7.362 373	16.73	176
45	4243.514 543	89316.095 644	.000 011 1962	.000 236	21.047 670	.047 511 1962	19.01	7.552 015	16.78	180
46	5109.069 628	107538.308	.000 009 2990	.000 196	21.048 511	.047 509 2990	19.01	7.741 711	16.83	184
47	6151.173 091	129477.328	.000 007 7234	.000 163	21.049 209	.047 507 7234	19.01	7.931 452	16.88	188
48	7405.835 728	155891.278	.000 006 4147	.000 135	21.049 789	.047 506 4147	19.01	8.121 232	16.92	192
49	8916.413 508	187692.916	.000 005 3279	.000 112	21.050 270	.047 505 3279	19.01	8.311 044	16.96	196
50	10735.106	225981.174	.000 004 4251	.000 093	21.050 670	.047 504 4251	19.01	8.500 885	17.00	200

Effective Rate is 20.40 %

Annual Percentage Rate is 19.00 %

	Amount Of 1	Amount Of 1 Per Period	Sinking Fund Payment	Present Worth Of 1	Present Worth of 1 Per Period	Periodic Payment To Amortize 1	Constant Annual Percent	Total Interest	Annual Add On Rate	
	What a single $ 1 deposit grows to in the future. The deposit is made at the beginning of the first period.	What a series of $ 1 deposits grow to in the future. A deposit is made at the end of each period.	The amount to be deposited at the end of each period that grows to $ 1 in the future.	What $ 1 to be paid in the future is worth today. Value today of a single $ 1 payment tomorrow.	What $ 1 to be paid at the end of each period is worth today. Value today of a series of $ 1 payments tomorrow.	The mortgage payment to amortize a loan of $ 1. An annuity certain, payable at the end of each period, worth $ 1 today.	The annual payment, including interest and principal, to amortize completely a loan of $ 100.	The total interest paid over the term on a loan that is amortized by regular periodic payments.	The average annual interest rate on a loan that is completely amortized by regular periodic payments.	

$$S = (1+i)^n \qquad S\overline{n}| = \frac{(1+i)^n - 1}{i} \qquad \frac{1}{S\overline{n}|} = \frac{i}{(1+i)^n - 1} \qquad V^n = \frac{1}{(1+i)^n} \qquad A\overline{n}| = \frac{1-V^n}{i} \qquad \frac{1}{A\overline{n}|} = \frac{i}{1-V^n}$$

YEAR									**PERIODS**	
	1.050 000	1.000 000	1.000 000 0000	.952 381	.952 381	1.050 000 0000	420.00	.050 000	20.00	1
	1.102 500	2.050 000	.487 804 8780	.907 029	1.859 410	.537 804 8780	215.13	.075 610	15.12	2
	1.157 625	3.152 500	.317 208 5646	.863 838	2.723 248	.367 208 5646	146.89	.101 626	13.55	3
	1.215 506	4.310 125	.232 011 8326	.822 702	3.545 951	.282 011 8326	112.81	.128 047	12.80	4
1	1.215 506	4.310 125	.232 011 8326	.822 702	3.545 951	.282 011 8326	112.81	.128 047	12.80	4
2	1.477 455	9.549 109	.104 721 8136	.676 839	6.463 213	.154 721 8136	61.89	.237 775	11.89	8
3	1.795 856	15.917 127	.062 825 4100	.556 837	8.863 252	.112 825 4100	45.14	.353 905	11.80	12
4	2.182 875	23.657 492	.042 269 9080	.458 112	10.837 770	.092 269 9080	36.91	.476 319	11.91	16
5	2.653 298	33.065 954	.030 242 5872	.376 889	12.462 210	.080 242 5872	32.10	.604 852	12.10	20
6	3.225 100	44.501 999	.022 470 9008	.310 068	13.798 642	.072 470 9008	28.99	.739 302	12.32	24
7	3.920 129	58.402 583	.017 122 5304	.255 094	14.898 127	.067 122 5304	26.85	.879 431	12.56	28
8	4.764 941	75.298 829	.013 280 4189	.209 866	15.802 677	.063 280 4189	25.32	1.024 973	12.81	32
9	5.791 816	95.836 323	.010 434 4571	.172 657	16.546 852	.060 434 4571	24.18	1.175 640	13.06	36
10	7.039 989	120.799 774	.008 278 1612	.142 046	17.159 086	.058 278 1612	23.32	1.331 126	13.31	40
11	8.557 150	151.143 006	.006 616 2506	.116 861	17.662 773	.056 616 2506	22.65	1.491 115	13.56	44
12	10.401 270	188.025 393	.005 318 4306	.096 142	18.077 158	.055 318 4306	22.13	1.655 285	13.79	48
13	12.642 808	232.856 165	.004 294 4966	.079 096	18.418 073	.054 294 4966	21.72	1.823 314	14.03	52
14	15.367 412	287.348 249	.003 480 0978	.065 073	18.698 545	.053 480 0978	21.40	1.994 885	14.25	56
15	18.679 186	353.583 718	.002 828 1845	.053 536	18.929 290	.052 828 1845	21.14	2.169 691	14.46	60
16	22.704 667	434.093 344	.002 303 6520	.044 044	19.119 124	.052 303 6520	20.93	2.347 434	14.67	64
17	27.597 665	531.953 298	.001 879 8643	.036 235	19.275 301	.051 879 8643	20.76	2.527 831	14.87	68
18	33.545 134	650.902 683	.001 536 3280	.029 811	19.403 788	.051 536 3280	20.62	2.710 616	15.06	72
19	40.774 320	795.486 404	.001 257 0925	.024 525	19.509 495	.051 257 0925	20.51	2.895 539	15.24	76
20	49.561 441	971.228 821	.001 029 6235	.020 177	19.596 460	.051 029 6235	20.42	3.082 370	15.41	80
21	60.242 241	1184.844 828	.000 843 9924	.016 600	19.668 007	.050 843 9924	20.34	3.270 895	15.58	84
22	73.224 821	1444.496 418	.000 692 2828	.013 657	19.726 869	.050 692 2828	20.28	3.460 921	15.73	88
23	89.005 227	1760.104 549	.000 568 1481	.011 235	19.775 294	.050 568 1481	20.23	3.652 270	15.88	92
24	108.186 410	2143.728 205	.000 466 4770	.009 243	19.815 134	.050 466 4770	20.19	3.844 782	16.02	96
25	131.501 258	2610.025 157	.000 383 1381	.007 604	19.847 910	.050 383 1381	20.16	4.038 314	16.15	100
26	159.840 601	3176.812 016	.000 314 7810	.006 256	19.874 875	.050 314 7810	20.13	4.232 737	16.28	104
27	194.287 249	3865.744 985	.000 258 6824	.005 147	19.897 060	.050 258 6824	20.11	4.427 938	16.40	108
28	236.157 366	4703.147 316	.000 212 6236	.004 234	19.915 311	.050 212 6236	20.09	4.623 814	16.51	112
29	287.050 754	5721.015 082	.000 174 7942	.003 484	19.930 326	.050 174 7942	20.07	4.820 276	16.62	116
30	348.911 986	6958.239 713	.000 143 7145	.002 866	19.942 679	.050 143 7145	20.06	5.017 246	16.72	120
31	424.104 699	8462.093 986	.000 118 1741	.002 358	19.952 842	.050 118 1741	20.05	5.214 654	16.82	124
32	515.501 913	10290.038 253	.000 097 1814	.001 940	19.961 203	.050 097 1814	20.04	5.412 439	16.91	128
33	626.595 797	12511.915 934	.000 079 9238	.001 596	19.968 081	.050 079 9238	20.04	5.610 550	17.00	132
34	761.631 107	15212.622 142	.000 065 7349	.001 313	19.973 741	.050 065 7349	20.03	5.808 940	17.09	136
35	925.767 371	18495.347 417	.000 054 0677	.001 080	19.978 396	.050 054 0677	20.03	6.007 569	17.16	140
36	1125.276 025	22485.520 507	.000 044 4731	.000 889	19.982 227	.050 044 4731	20.02	6.206 404	17.24	144
37	1367.780 042	27335.600 835	.000 036 5823	.000 731	19.985 378	.050 036 5823	20.02	6.405 414	17.31	148
38	1662.545 189	33230.903 788	.000 030 0925	.000 601	19.987 970	.050 030 0925	20.02	6.604 574	17.38	152
39	2020.834 069	40396.681 372	.000 024 7545	.000 495	19.990 103	.050 024 7545	20.01	6.803 862	17.45	156
40	2456.336 441	49106.728 812	.000 020 3638	.000 407	19.991 858	.050 020 3638	20.01	7.003 258	17.51	160
41	2985.692 296	59693.845 914	.000 016 7521	.000 335	19.993 301	.050 016 7521	20.01	7.202 747	17.57	164
42	3629.127 646	72562.552 919	.000 013 7812	.000 276	19.994 489	.050 013 7812	20.01	7.402 315	17.62	168
43	4411.227 336	88204.546 715	.000 011 3373	.000 227	19.995 466	.050 011 3373	20.01	7.601 950	17.68	172
44	5361.874 397	107217.488	.000 009 3268	.000 187	19.996 270	.050 009 3268	20.01	7.801 642	17.73	176
45	6517.391 841	130327.837	.000 007 6730	.000 153	19.996 931	.050 007 6730	20.01	8.001 381	17.78	180
46	7921.930 516	158418.610	.000 006 3124	.000 126	19.997 475	.050 006 3124	20.01	8.201 161	17.83	184
47	9629.156 055	192563.121	.000 005 1931	.000 104	19.997 923	.050 005 1931	20.01	8.400 976	17.87	188
48	11704.299	234065.987	.000 004 2723	.000 085	19.998 291	.050 004 2723	20.01	8.600 820	17.92	192
49	14226.649	284512.981	.000 003 5148	.000 070	19.998 594	.050 003 5148	20.01	8.800 689	17.96	196
50	17292.581	345831.616	.000 002 8916	.000 058	19.998 843	.050 002 8916	20.01	9.000 578	18.00	200

Effective Rate is 21.55 %

Annual Percentage Rate is 20.00 %

SEMIANNUAL COMPOUND INTEREST AND ANNUITY

0.00 % S

	Amount Of 1	Amount Of 1 Per Period	Sinking Fund Payment	Present Worth Of 1	Present Worth of 1 Per Period	Periodic Payment To Amortize 1	Constant Annual Percent	Total Interest	Annual Add On Rate	
	What a single $ 1 deposit grows to in the future. The deposit is made at the beginning of the first period.	What a series of $ 1 deposits grow to in the future. A deposit is made at the end of each period.	The amount to be deposited at the end of each period that grows to $ 1 in the future.	What $ 1 to be paid in the future is worth today. Value today of a single $ 1 payment tomorrow.	What $ 1 to be paid at the end of each period is worth today. Value today of a series of $ 1 payments tomorrow.	The mortgage payment to amortize a loan of $ 1. An annuity certain, payable at the end of each period, worth $ 1 today.	The annual payment, including interest and principal, to amortize completely a loan of $ 100.	The total interest paid over the term on a loan of $1. The loan is amortized by regular periodic payments.	The average annual interest rate on a loan that is completely amortized by regular periodic payments.	

$$S = (1+i)^n \qquad S\overline{n}| = \frac{(1+i)^n - 1}{i} \qquad \frac{1}{S\overline{n}|} = \frac{i}{(1+i)^n - 1} \qquad V^n = \frac{1}{(1+i)^n} \qquad A\overline{n}| = \frac{1-V^n}{i} \qquad \frac{1}{A\overline{n}|} = \frac{i}{1-V^n}$$

YEAR   **PERIODS**

YEAR	Amount Of 1	Amount Of 1 Per Period	Sinking Fund Payment	Present Worth Of 1	Present Worth of 1 Per Period	Periodic Payment To Amortize 1	Constant Annual Percent	Total Interest	Annual Add On Rate	PERIODS
	1.000 000	1.000 000	1.000 000 0000	1.000 000	1.000 000	1.000 000 0000	200.00	0.000 000	0.00	1
	1.000 000	2.000 000	.500 000 0000	1.000 000	2.000 000	.500 000 0000	100.00	0.000 000	0.00	2
1	1.000 000	2.000 000	.500 000 0000	1.000 000	2.000 000	.500 000 0000	100.00	0.000 000	0.00	2
2	1.000 000	4.000 000	.250 000 0000	1.000 000	4.000 000	.250 000 0000	50.00	0.000 000	0.00	4
3	1.000 000	6.000 000	.166 666 6667	1.000 000	6.000 000	.166 666 6667	33.34	0.000 000	0.00	6
4	1.000 000	8.000 000	.125 000 0000	1.000 000	8.000 000	.125 000 0000	25.00	0.000 000	0.00	8
5	1.000 000	10.000 000	.100 000 0000	1.000 000	10.000 000	.100 000 0000	20.00	0.000 000	0.00	10
6	1.000 000	12.000 000	.083 333 3333	1.000 000	12.000 000	.083 333 3333	16.67	0.000 000	0.00	12
7	1.000 000	14.000 000	.071 428 5714	1.000 000	14.000 000	.071 428 5714	14.29	0.000 000	0.00	14
8	1.000 000	16.000 000	.062 500 0000	1.000 000	16.000 000	.062 500 0000	12.50	0.000 000	0.00	16
9	1.000 000	18.000 000	.055 555 5556	1.000 000	18.000 000	.055 555 5556	11.12	0.000 000	0.00	18
10	1.000 000	20.000 000	.050 000 0000	1.000 000	20.000 000	.050 000 0000	10.00	0.000 000	0.00	20
11	1.000 000	22.000 000	.045 454 5455	1.000 000	22.000 000	.045 454 5455	9.10	0.000 000	0.00	22
12	1.000 000	24.000 000	.041 666 6667	1.000 000	24.000 000	.041 666 6667	8.34	0.000 000	0.00	24
13	1.000 000	26.000 000	.038 461 5385	1.000 000	26.000 000	.038 461 5385	7.70	0.000 000	0.00	26
14	1.000 000	28.000 000	.035 714 2857	1.000 000	28.000 000	.035 714 2857	7.15	0.000 000	0.00	28
15	1.000 000	30.000 000	.033 333 3333	1.000 000	30.000 000	.033 333 3333	6.67	0.000 000	0.00	30
16	1.000 000	32.000 000	.031 250 0000	1.000 000	32.000 000	.031 250 0000	6.25	0.000 000	0.00	32
17	1.000 000	34.000 000	.029 411 7647	1.000 000	34.000 000	.029 411 7647	5.89	0.000 000	0.00	34
18	1.000 000	36.000 000	.027 777 7778	1.000 000	36.000 000	.027 777 7778	5.56	0.000 000	0.00	36
19	1.000 000	38.000 000	.026 315 7895	1.000 000	38.000 000	.026 315 7895	5.27	0.000 000	0.00	38
20	1.000 000	40.000 000	.025 000 0000	1.000 000	40.000 000	.025 000 0000	5.00	0.000 000	0.00	40
21	1.000 000	42.000 000	.023 809 5238	1.000 000	42.000 000	.023 809 5238	4.77	0.000 000	0.00	42
22	1.000 000	44.000 000	.022 727 2727	1.000 000	44.000 000	.022 727 2727	4.55	0.000 000	0.00	44
23	1.000 000	46.000 000	.021 739 1304	1.000 000	46.000 000	.021 739 1304	4.35	0.000 000	0.00	46
24	1.000 000	48.000 000	.020 833 3333	1.000 000	48.000 000	.020 833 3333	4.17	0.000 000	0.00	48
25	1.000 000	50.000 000	.020 000 0000	1.000 000	50.000 000	.020 000 0000	4.00	0.000 000	0.00	50
26	1.000 000	52.000 000	.019 230 7692	1.000 000	52.000 000	.019 230 7692	3.85	0.000 000	0.00	52
27	1.000 000	54.000 000	.018 518 5185	1.000 000	54.000 000	.018 518 5185	3.71	0.000 000	0.00	54
28	1.000 000	56.000 000	.017 857 1429	1.000 000	56.000 000	.017 857 1429	3.58	0.000 000	0.00	56
29	1.000 000	58.000 000	.017 241 3793	1.000 000	58.000 000	.017 241 3793	3.45	0.000 000	0.00	58
30	1.000 000	60.000 000	.016 666 6667	1.000 000	60.000 000	.016 666 6667	3.34	0.000 000	0.00	60
31	1.000 000	62.000 000	.016 129 0323	1.000 000	62.000 000	.016 129 0323	3.23	0.000 000	0.00	62
32	1.000 000	64.000 000	.015 625 0000	1.000 000	64.000 000	.015 625 0000	3.13	0.000 000	0.00	64
33	1.000 000	66.000 000	.015 151 5152	1.000 000	66.000 000	.015 151 5152	3.04	0.000 000	0.00	66
34	1.000 000	68.000 000	.014 705 8824	1.000 000	68.000 000	.014 705 8824	2.95	0.000 000	0.00	68
35	1.000 000	70.000 000	.014 285 7143	1.000 000	70.000 000	.014 285 7143	2.86	0.000 000	0.00	70
36	1.000 000	72.000 000	.013 888 8889	1.000 000	72.000 000	.013 888 8889	2.78	0.000 000	0.00	72
37	1.000 000	74.000 000	.013 513 5135	1.000 000	74.000 000	.013 513 5135	2.71	0.000 000	0.00	74
38	1.000 000	76.000 000	.013 157 8947	1.000 000	76.000 000	.013 157 8947	2.64	0.000 000	0.00	76
39	1.000 000	78.000 000	.012 820 5128	1.000 000	78.000 000	.012 820 5128	2.57	0.000 000	0.00	78
40	1.000 000	80.000 000	.012 500 0000	1.000 000	80.000 000	.012 500 0000	2.50	0.000 000	0.00	80
41	1.000 000	82.000 000	.012 195 1220	1.000 000	82.000 000	.012 195 1220	2.44	0.000 000	0.00	82
42	1.000 000	84.000 000	.011 904 7619	1.000 000	84.000 000	.011 904 7619	2.39	0.000 000	0.00	84
43	1.000 000	86.000 000	.011 627 9070	1.000 000	86.000 000	.011 627 9070	2.33	0.000 000	0.00	86
44	1.000 000	88.000 000	.011 363 6364	1.000 000	88.000 000	.011 363 6364	2.28	0.000 000	0.00	88
45	1.000 000	90.000 000	.011 111 1111	1.000 000	90.000 000	.011 111 1111	2.23	0.000 000	0.00	90
46	1.000 000	92.000 000	.010 869 5652	1.000 000	92.000 000	.010 869 5652	2.18	0.000 000	0.00	92
47	1.000 000	94.000 000	.010 638 2979	1.000 000	94.000 000	.010 638 2979	2.13	0.000 000	0.00	94
48	1.000 000	96.000 000	.010 416 6667	1.000 000	96.000 000	.010 416 6667	2.09	0.000 000	0.00	96
49	1.000 000	98.000 000	.010 204 0816	1.000 000	98.000 000	.010 204 0816	2.05	0.000 000	0.00	98
50	1.000 000	100.000 000	.010 000 0000	1.000 000	100.000 000	.010 000 0000	2.00	0.000 000	0.00	100

Effective Rate is 0.00 %

Annual Percentage Rate is 0.00 %

SEMIANNUAL COMPOUND INTEREST AND ANNUITY

Amount Of 1	Amount Of 1 Per Period	Sinking Fund Payment	Present Worth Of 1	Present Worth of 1 Per Period	Periodic Payment To Amortize 1	Constant Annual Percent	Total Interest	Annual Add On Rate
What a single $ 1 deposit grows to in the future. The deposit is made at the beginning of the first period.	What a series of $ 1 deposits grow to in the future. A deposit is made at the end of each period.	The amount to be deposited at the end of each period that grows to $ 1 in the future.	What $ 1 to be paid in the future is worth today. Value today of a single $ 1 payment tomorrow.	What $ 1 to be paid at the end of each period is worth today. Value today of a series of $ 1 payments tomorrow.	The mortgage payment to amortize a loan of $ 1. An annuity certain, payable at the end of each period, worth $ 1 today.	The annual payment, including interest and principal, to amortize completely a loan of $ 100.	The total interest paid over the term on a loan of $1. The loan is amortized by regular periodic payments.	The average annual interest rate on a loan that is completely amortized by regular periodic payments.
$S = (1+i)^n$	$S\overline{n}| = \dfrac{(1+i)^n - 1}{i}$	$\dfrac{1}{S\overline{n}|} = \dfrac{i}{(1+i)^n - 1}$	$V^n = \dfrac{1}{(1+i)^n}$	$A\overline{n}| = \dfrac{1 - V^n}{i}$	$\dfrac{1}{A\overline{n}|} = \dfrac{i}{1 - V^n}$			

PERIODS

YEAR

	1.005 000	1.000 000	1.000 000 0000	.995 025	.995 025	1.005 000 0000	201.00	.005 000	1.00	1
	1.010 025	2.005 000	.498 753 1172	.990 075	1.985 099	.503 753 1172	100.76	.007 506	.75	2

YEAR	Amount Of 1	Amount Of 1 Per Period	Sinking Fund Payment	Present Worth Of 1	Present Worth of 1 Per Period	Periodic Payment To Amortize 1	Constant Annual Percent	Total Interest	Annual Add On Rate	PERIODS
1	1.010 025	2.005 000	.498 753 1172	.990 075	1.985 099	.503 753 1172	100.76	.007 506	.75	2
2	1.020 151	4.030 100	.248 132 7930	.980 248	3.950 496	.253 132 7930	50.63	.012 531	.63	4
3	1.030 378	6.075 502	.164 595 4556	.970 518	5.896 384	.169 595 4556	33.92	.017 573	.59	6
4	1.040 707	8.141 409	.122 828 8649	.960 885	7.822 959	.127 828 8649	25.57	.022 631	.57	8
5	1.051 140	10.228 026	.097 770 5727	.951 348	9.730 412	.102 770 5727	20.56	.027 706	.55	10
6	1.061 678	12.335 562	.081 066 4297	.941 905	11.618 932	.086 066 4297	17.22	.032 797	.55	12
7	1.072 321	14.464 226	.069 136 0860	.932 556	13.488 708	.074 136 0860	14.83	.037 905	.54	14
8	1.083 071	16.614 230	.060 189 3669	.923 300	15.339 925	.065 189 3669	13.04	.043 030	.54	16
9	1.093 929	18.785 788	.053 231 7305	.914 136	17.172 768	.058 231 7305	11.65	.048 171	.54	18
10	1.104 896	20.979 115	.047 666 4520	.905 063	18.987 419	.052 666 4520	10.54	.053 329	.53	20
11	1.115 972	23.194 431	.043 113 7973	.896 080	20.784 059	.048 113 7973	9.63	.058 504	.53	22
12	1.127 160	25.431 955	.039 320 6103	.887 186	22.562 866	.044 320 6103	8.87	.063 695	.53	24
13	1.138 460	27.691 911	.036 111 6289	.878 380	24.324 018	.041 111 6289	8.23	.068 902	.53	26
14	1.149 873	29.974 522	.033 361 6663	.869 662	26.067 689	.038 361 6663	7.68	.074 127	.53	28
15	1.161 400	32.280 017	.030 978 9184	.861 030	27.794 054	.035 978 9184	7.20	.079 368	.53	30
16	1.173 043	34.608 624	.028 894 5324	.852 484	29.503 284	.033 894 5324	6.78	.084 625	.53	32
17	1.184 803	36.960 575	.027 055 8560	.844 022	31.195 548	.032 055 8560	6.42	.089 899	.53	34
18	1.196 681	39.336 105	.025 421 9375	.835 645	32.871 016	.030 421 9375	6.09	.095 190	.53	36
19	1.208 677	41.735 449	.023 960 4464	.827 351	34.529 854	.028 960 4464	5.80	.100 497	.53	38
20	1.220 794	44.158 847	.022 645 5186	.819 139	36.172 228	.027 645 5186	5.53	.105 821	.53	40
21	1.233 033	46.606 540	.021 456 2163	.811 009	37.798 300	.026 456 2163	5.30	.111 161	.53	42
22	1.245 394	49.078 770	.020 375 4086	.802 959	39.408 232	.025 375 4086	5.08	.116 518	.53	44
23	1.257 879	51.575 785	.019 388 9439	.794 989	41.002 185	.024 388 9439	4.88	.121 891	.53	46
24	1.270 489	54.097 832	.018 485 0290	.787 098	42.580 318	.023 485 0290	4.70	.127 281	.53	48
25	1.283 226	56.645 163	.017 653 7580	.779 286	44.142 786	.022 653 7580	4.54	.132 688	.53	50
26	1.296 090	59.218 031	.016 886 7486	.771 551	45.689 747	.021 886 7486	4.38	.138 111	.53	52
27	1.309 083	61.816 692	.016 176 8606	.763 893	47.221 353	.021 176 8606	4.24	.143 550	.53	54
28	1.322 207	64.441 404	.015 517 9735	.756 311	48.737 757	.020 517 9735	4.11	.149 007	.53	56
29	1.335 462	67.092 429	.014 904 8114	.748 804	50.239 109	.019 904 8114	3.99	.154 479	.53	58
30	1.348 850	69.770 031	.014 332 8015	.741 372	51.725 561	.019 332 8015	3.87	.159 968	.53	60
31	1.362 372	72.474 475	.013 797 9613	.734 014	53.197 258	.018 797 9613	3.76	.165 474	.53	62
32	1.376 030	75.206 032	.013 296 8058	.726 728	54.654 348	.018 296 8058	3.66	.170 996	.53	64
33	1.389 825	77.964 972	.012 826 2728	.719 515	56.096 976	.017 826 2728	3.57	.176 534	.54	66
34	1.403 758	80.751 571	.012 383 6600	.712 374	57.525 285	.017 383 6600	3.48	.182 089	.54	68
35	1.417 831	83.566 105	.011 966 5742	.705 303	58.939 418	.016 966 5742	3.40	.187 660	.54	70
36	1.432 044	86.408 856	.011 572 8879	.698 302	60.339 514	.016 572 8879	3.32	.193 248	.54	72
37	1.446 401	89.280 104	.011 200 7037	.691 371	61.725 714	.016 200 7037	3.25	.198 852	.54	74
38	1.460 901	92.180 138	.010 848 3240	.684 509	63.098 155	.015 848 3240	3.17	.204 473	.54	76
39	1.475 546	95.109 243	.010 514 2252	.677 715	64.456 973	.015 514 2252	3.11	.210 110	.54	78
40	1.490 339	98.067 714	.010 197 0359	.670 988	65.802 305	.015 197 0359	3.04	.215 763	.54	80
41	1.505 279	101.055 842	.009 895 5189	.664 329	67.134 284	.014 895 5189	2.98	.221 433	.54	82
42	1.520 370	104.073 927	.009 608 5545	.657 735	68.453 042	.014 608 5545	2.93	.227 119	.54	84
43	1.535 611	107.122 268	.009 335 1272	.651 206	69.758 711	.014 335 1272	2.87	.232 821	.54	86
44	1.551 006	110.201 169	.009 074 3139	.644 743	71.051 421	.014 074 3139	2.82	.238 540	.54	88
45	1.566 555	113.310 936	.008 825 2735	.638 344	72.331 300	.013 825 2735	2.77	.244 275	.54	90
46	1.582 259	116.451 878	.008 587 2381	.632 008	73.598 475	.013 587 2381	2.72	.250 026	.54	92
47	1.598 122	119.624 308	.008 359 5050	.625 735	74.853 073	.013 359 5050	2.68	.255 793	.54	94
48	1.614 143	122.828 542	.008 141 4302	.619 524	76.095 218	.013 141 4302	2.63	.261 577	.55	96
49	1.630 324	126.064 898	.007 932 4222	.613 375	77.325 035	.012 932 4222	2.59	.267 377	.55	98
50	1.646 668	129.333 698	.007 731 9369	.607 287	78.542 645	.012 731 9369	2.55	.273 194	.55	100

Effective Rate is 1.00 %

8 - 363

Annual Percentage Rate is 1.00 %

SEMIANNUAL COMPOUND INTEREST AND ANNUITY

2.00 % S

	Amount Of 1	Amount Of 1 Per Period	Sinking Fund Payment	Present Worth Of 1	Present Worth of 1 Per Period	Periodic Payment To Amortize 1	Constant Annual Percent	Total Interest	Annual Add On Rate	
	What a single $ 1 deposit grows to in the future. The deposit is made at the beginning of the first period.	What a series of $ 1 deposits grow to in the future. A deposit is made at the end of each period.	The amount to be deposited at the end of each period that grows to $ 1 in the future.	What $ 1 to be paid in the future is worth today. Value today of a single $ 1 payment tomorrow.	What $ 1 to be paid at the end of each period is worth today. Value today of a series of $ 1 payments tomorrow.	The mortgage payment to amortize a loan of $ 1. An annuity certain, payable at the end of each period, worth $ 1 today.	The annual payment, including interest and principal, to amortize completely a loan of $ 100.	The total interest paid over the term on a loan of $1. The loan is amortized by regular periodic payments.	The average annual interest rate on a loan that is completely amortized by regular periodic payments.	
	$S = (1+i)^n$	$S\overline{n} = \dfrac{(1+i)^n - 1}{i}$	$\dfrac{1}{S\overline{n}} = \dfrac{i}{(1+i)^n - 1}$	$V^n = \dfrac{1}{(1+i)^n}$	$A\overline{n} = \dfrac{1-V^n}{i}$	$\dfrac{1}{A\overline{n}} = \dfrac{i}{1-V^n}$				

YEAR										PERIODS
	1.010 000	1.000 000	1.000 000 0000	.990 099	.990 099	1.010 000 0000	202.00	.010 000	2.00	1
	1.020 100	2.010 000	.497 512 4378	.980 296	1.970 395	.507 512 4378	101.51	.015 025	1.50	2

YEAR										PERIODS
1	1.020 100	2.010 000	.497 512 4378	.980 296	1.970 395	.507 512 4378	101.51	.015 025	1.50	2
2	1.040 604	4.060 401	.246 281 0939	.960 980	3.901 966	.256 281 0939	51.26	.025 124	1.26	4
3	1.061 520	6.152 015	.162 548 3667	.942 045	5.795 476	.172 548 3667	34.51	.035 290	1.18	6
4	1.082 857	8.285 671	.120 690 2920	.923 483	7.651 678	.130 690 2920	26.14	.045 522	1.14	8
5	1.104 622	10.462 213	.095 582 0766	.905 287	9.471 305	.105 582 0766	21.12	.055 821	1.12	10
6	1.126 825	12.682 503	.078 848 7887	.887 449	11.255 077	.088 848 7887	17.77	.066 185	1.10	12
7	1.149 474	14.947 421	.066 901 1717	.869 963	13.003 703	.076 901 1717	15.39	.076 616	1.09	14
8	1.172 579	17.257 864	.057 944 5968	.852 821	14.717 874	.067 944 5968	13.59	.087 114	1.09	16
9	1.196 147	19.614 748	.050 982 0479	.836 017	16.398 269	.060 982 0479	12.20	.097 677	1.09	18
10	1.220 190	22.019 004	.045 415 3149	.819 544	18.045 553	.055 415 3149	11.09	.108 306	1.08	20
11	1.244 716	24.471 586	.040 863 7185	.803 396	19.660 379	.050 863 7185	10.18	.119 002	1.08	22
12	1.269 735	26.973 465	.037 073 4722	.787 566	21.243 387	.047 073 4722	9.42	.129 763	1.08	24
13	1.295 256	29.525 631	.033 868 8776	.772 048	22.795 204	.043 868 8776	8.78	.140 591	1.08	26
14	1.321 291	32.129 097	.031 124 4356	.756 836	24.316 443	.041 124 4356	8.23	.151 484	1.08	28
15	1.347 849	34.784 892	.028 748 1132	.741 923	25.807 708	.038 748 1132	7.75	.162 443	1.08	30
16	1.374 941	37.494 068	.026 670 8857	.727 304	27.269 589	.036 670 8857	7.34	.173 468	1.08	32
17	1.402 577	40.257 699	.024 839 9694	.712 973	28.702 666	.034 839 9694	6.97	.184 559	1.09	34
18	1.430 769	43.076 878	.023 214 3098	.698 925	30.107 505	.033 214 3098	6.65	.195 715	1.09	36
19	1.459 527	45.952 724	.021 761 4958	.685 153	31.484 663	.031 761 4958	6.36	.206 937	1.09	38
20	1.488 864	48.886 373	.020 455 5980	.671 653	32.834 686	.030 455 5980	6.10	.218 224	1.09	40
21	1.518 790	51.878 989	.019 275 6260	.658 419	34.158 108	.029 275 6260	5.86	.229 576	1.09	42
22	1.549 318	54.931 757	.018 204 4058	.645 445	35.455 454	.028 204 4058	5.65	.240 994	1.10	44
23	1.580 459	58.045 885	.017 227 7499	.632 728	36.727 236	.027 227 7499	5.45	.252 477	1.10	46
24	1.612 226	61.222 608	.016 333 8354	.620 260	37.973 959	.026 333 8354	5.27	.264 024	1.10	48
25	1.644 632	64.463 182	.015 512 7309	.608 039	39.196 118	.025 512 7309	5.11	.275 637	1.10	50
26	1.677 689	67.768 892	.014 756 0329	.596 058	40.394 194	.024 756 0329	4.96	.287 314	1.11	52
27	1.711 410	71.141 047	.014 056 5826	.584 313	41.568 664	.024 056 5826	4.82	.299 055	1.11	54
28	1.745 810	74.580 982	.013 408 2440	.572 800	42.719 992	.023 408 2440	4.69	.310 862	1.11	56
29	1.780 901	78.090 060	.012 805 7272	.561 514	43.848 635	.022 805 7272	4.57	.322 732	1.11	58
30	1.816 697	81.669 670	.012 244 4477	.550 450	44.955 038	.022 244 4477	4.45	.334 667	1.12	60
31	1.853 212	85.321 230	.011 720 4123	.539 604	46.039 642	.021 720 4123	4.35	.346 666	1.12	62
32	1.890 462	89.046 187	.011 230 1271	.528 971	47.102 874	.021 230 1271	4.25	.358 728	1.12	64
33	1.928 460	92.846 015	.010 770 5215	.518 548	48.145 156	.020 770 5215	4.16	.370 854	1.12	66
34	1.967 222	96.722 220	.010 338 8859	.508 331	49.166 901	.020 338 8859	4.07	.383 044	1.13	68
35	2.006 763	100.676 337	.009 932 8207	.498 315	50.168 514	.019 932 8207	3.99	.395 297	1.13	70
36	2.047 099	104.709 931	.009 550 1925	.488 496	51.150 391	.019 550 1925	3.92	.407 614	1.13	72
37	2.088 246	108.824 601	.009 189 0987	.478 871	52.112 922	.019 189 0987	3.84	.419 993	1.14	74
38	2.130 220	113.021 975	.008 847 8369	.469 435	53.056 486	.018 847 8369	3.77	.432 436	1.14	76
39	2.173 037	117.303 717	.008 524 8791	.460 185	53.981 449	.018 524 8791	3.71	.444 941	1.14	78
40	2.216 715	121.671 522	.008 218 8501	.451 118	54.888 206	.018 218 8501	3.65	.457 508	1.14	80
41	2.261 271	126.127 119	.007 928 5090	.442 229	55.777 087	.017 928 5090	3.59	.470 138	1.15	82
42	2.306 723	130.672 274	.007 652 7328	.433 515	56.648 453	.017 652 7328	3.54	.482 830	1.15	84
43	2.353 088	135.308 787	.007 390 5030	.424 974	57.502 650	.017 390 5030	3.48	.495 583	1.15	86
44	2.400 385	140.038 494	.007 140 8937	.416 600	58.340 015	.017 140 8937	3.43	.508 399	1.16	88
45	2.448 633	144.863 267	.006 903 0612	.408 391	59.160 881	.016 903 0612	3.39	.521 276	1.16	90
46	2.497 850	149.785 019	.006 676 2351	.400 344	59.965 573	.016 676 2351	3.34	.534 214	1.16	92
47	2.548 057	154.805 068	.006 459 7105	.392 456	60.754 410	.016 459 7105	3.30	.547 213	1.16	94
48	2.599 273	159.927 293	.006 252 8414	.384 722	61.527 703	.016 252 8414	3.26	.560 273	1.17	96
49	2.651 518	165.151 831	.006 055 0343	.377 142	62.285 759	.016 055 0343	3.22	.573 393	1.17	98
50	2.704 814	170.481 383	.005 865 7431	.369 711	63.028 879	.015 865 7431	3.18	.586 574	1.17	100

Effective Rate is 2.01 %

Annual Percentage Rate is 2.00 %

SEMIANNUAL COMPOUND INTEREST AND ANNUITY

2.25 % S

	Amount Of 1	Amount Of 1 Per Period	Sinking Fund Payment	Present Worth Of 1	Present Worth of 1 Per Period	Periodic Payment To Amortize 1	Constant Annual Percent	Total Interest	Annual Add On Rate	
	What a single $ 1 deposit grows to in the future. The deposit is made at the beginning of the first period.	What a series of $ 1 deposits grow to in the future. A deposit is made at the end of each period.	The amount to be deposited at the end of each period that grows to $ 1 in the future.	What $ 1 to be paid in the future is worth today. Value today of a single $ 1 payment tomorrow.	What $ 1 to be paid at the end of each period is worth today. Value today of a series of $ 1 payments tomorrow.	The mortgage payment to amortize a loan of $ 1. An annuity certain, payable at the end of each period, worth $ 1 today.	The annual payment, including interest and principal, to amortize completely a loan of $ 100.	The total interest paid over the term on a loan that is amortized by regular periodic payments.	The average annual interest rate on a loan that is completely amortized by regular periodic payments.	
	$S = (1+i)^n$	$S\overline{n}| = \dfrac{(1+i)^n - 1}{i}$	$\dfrac{1}{S\overline{n}|} = \dfrac{i}{(1+i)^n - 1}$	$V^n = \dfrac{1}{(1+i)^n}$	$A\overline{n}| = \dfrac{1-V^n}{i}$	$\dfrac{1}{A\overline{n}|} = \dfrac{i}{1-V^n}$				PERIODS
YEAR										
	1.011 250	1.000 000	1.000 000 0000	.988 875	.988 875	1.011 250 0000	202.25	.011 250	2.25	1
	1.022 627	2.011 250	.497 203 2318	.977 874	1.966 749	.508 453 2318	101.70	.016 906	1.69	2
1	1.022 627	2.011 250	.497 203 2318	.977 874	1.966 749	.508 453 2318	101.70	.016 906	1.69	2
2	1.045 765	4.068 008	.245 820 5786	.956 238	3.889 982	.257 070 5786	51.42	.028 282	1.41	4
3	1.069 427	6.171 303	.162 040 3419	.935 080	5.770 662	.173 290 3419	34.66	.039 742	1.32	6
4	1.093 625	8.322 188	.120 160 7067	.914 391	7.609 730	.131 410 7067	26.29	.051 286	1.28	8
5	1.118 370	10.521 741	.095 041 3092	.894 159	9.408 107	.106 291 3092	21.26	.062 913	1.26	10
6	1.143 674	12.771 061	.078 302 0274	.874 375	11.166 693	.089 552 0274	17.92	.074 624	1.24	12
7	1.169 552	15.071 277	.066 351 3799	.855 028	12.886 369	.077 601 3799	15.53	.086 419	1.23	14
8	1.196 015	17.423 538	.057 393 6253	.836 110	14.567 995	.068 643 6253	13.73	.098 298	1.23	16
9	1.223 077	19.829 023	.050 431 1292	.817 610	16.212 414	.061 681 1292	12.34	.110 260	1.23	18
10	1.250 751	22.288 935	.044 865 3106	.799 520	17.820 448	.056 115 3106	11.23	.122 306	1.22	20
11	1.279 051	24.804 507	.040 315 2537	.781 830	19.392 904	.051 565 2537	10.32	.134 436	1.22	22
12	1.307 991	27.376 998	.036 527 0145	.764 531	20.930 567	.047 777 0145	9.56	.146 648	1.22	24
13	1.337 587	30.007 695	.033 324 7852	.747 615	22.434 208	.044 574 7852	8.92	.158 944	1.22	26
14	1.367 852	32.697 916	.030 582 9886	.731 073	23.904 579	.041 832 9886	8.37	.171 324	1.22	28
15	1.398 801	35.449 008	.028 209 5343	.714 898	25.342 418	.039 459 5343	7.90	.183 786	1.23	30
16	1.430 451	38.262 347	.026 135 3545	.699 080	26.748 442	.037 385 3545	7.48	.196 331	1.23	32
17	1.462 818	41.139 342	.024 307 6322	.683 612	28.123 357	.035 557 6322	7.12	.208 960	1.23	34
18	1.495 916	44.081 434	.022 685 2873	.668 487	29.467 851	.033 935 2873	6.79	.221 670	1.23	36
19	1.529 764	47.090 095	.021 235 8881	.653 696	30.782 597	.032 485 8881	6.50	.234 464	1.23	38
20	1.564 377	50.166 832	.019 933 4889	.639 232	32.068 253	.031 183 4889	6.24	.247 340	1.24	40
21	1.599 773	53.313 185	.018 757 0859	.625 089	33.325 462	.030 007 0859	6.01	.260 298	1.24	42
22	1.635 971	56.530 730	.017 689 4940	.611 258	34.554 854	.028 939 4940	5.79	.273 338	1.24	44
23	1.672 987	59.821 076	.016 716 5165	.597 733	35.757 045	.027 966 5165	5.60	.286 460	1.25	46
24	1.710 841	63.185 871	.015 826 3230	.584 508	36.932 637	.027 076 3230	5.42	.299 664	1.25	48
25	1.749 552	66.626 800	.015 008 9754	.571 575	38.082 217	.026 258 9754	5.26	.312 949	1.25	50
26	1.789 138	70.145 585	.014 256 0646	.558 928	39.206 362	.025 506 0646	5.11	.326 315	1.26	52
27	1.829 620	73.743 989	.013 560 4273	.546 562	40.305 634	.024 810 4273	4.97	.339 763	1.26	54
28	1.871 018	77.423 812	.012 915 9231	.534 468	41.380 584	.024 165 9231	4.84	.353 292	1.26	56
29	1.913 353	81.186 897	.012 317 2586	.522 643	42.431 749	.023 567 2586	4.72	.366 901	1.27	58
30	1.956 645	85.035 127	.011 759 8460	.511 079	43.459 656	.023 009 8460	4.61	.380 591	1.27	60
31	2.000 917	88.970 430	.011 239 6895	.499 771	44.464 820	.022 489 6895	4.50	.394 361	1.27	62
32	2.046 191	92.994 775	.010 753 2924	.488 713	45.447 744	.022 003 2924	4.41	.408 211	1.28	64
33	2.092 489	97.110 177	.010 297 5819	.477 900	46.408 920	.021 547 5819	4.31	.422 140	1.28	66
34	2.139 835	101.318 696	.009 869 8467	.467 326	47.348 829	.021 119 8467	4.23	.436 150	1.28	68
35	2.188 252	105.622 440	.009 467 6851	.456 986	48.267 941	.020 717 6851	4.15	.450 238	1.29	70
36	2.237 765	110.023 563	.009 088 9622	.446 874	49.166 717	.020 338 9622	4.07	.464 405	1.29	72
37	2.288 398	114.524 268	.008 731 7738	.436 987	50.045 607	.019 981 7738	4.00	.478 651	1.29	74
38	2.340 177	119.126 808	.008 394 4161	.427 318	50.905 051	.019 644 4161	3.93	.492 976	1.30	76
39	2.393 127	123.833 488	.008 075 3600	.417 863	51.745 478	.019 325 3600	3.87	.507 378	1.30	78
40	2.447 275	128.646 665	.007 773 2291	.408 618	52.567 311	.019 023 2291	3.81	.521 858	1.30	80
41	2.502 648	133.568 746	.007 486 7814	.399 577	53.370 960	.018 736 7814	3.75	.536 416	1.31	82
42	2.559 275	138.602 198	.007 214 8928	.390 736	54.156 827	.018 464 8928	3.70	.551 051	1.31	84
43	2.617 182	143.749 539	.006 956 5440	.382 090	54.925 306	.018 206 5440	3.65	.565 763	1.32	86
44	2.676 400	149.013 347	.006 710 8083	.373 636	55.676 782	.017 960 8083	3.60	.580 551	1.32	88
45	2.736 958	154.396 257	.006 476 8409	.365 369	56.411 630	.017 726 8409	3.55	.595 416	1.32	90
46	2.798 886	159.900 964	.006 253 8710	.357 285	57.130 220	.017 503 8710	3.51	.610 356	1.33	92
47	2.862 215	165.530 223	.006 041 1929	.349 380	57.832 910	.017 291 1929	3.46	.625 372	1.33	94
48	2.926 977	171.286 853	.005 838 1597	.341 649	58.520 052	.017 088 1597	3.42	.640 463	1.33	96
49	2.993 205	177.173 735	.005 644 1774	.334 090	59.191 991	.016 894 1774	3.38	.655 629	1.34	98
50	3.060 930	183.193 818	.005 458 6995	.326 698	59.849 063	.016 708 6995	3.35	.670 870	1.34	100

Effective Rate is 2.26 %

Annual Percentage Rate is 2.25 %

SEMIANNUAL COMPOUND INTEREST AND ANNUITY

2.50 % S

	Amount Of 1	Amount Of 1 Per Period	Sinking Fund Payment	Present Worth Of 1	Present Worth of 1 Per Period	Periodic Payment To Amortize 1	Constant Annual Percent	Total Interest	Annual Add On Rate	
	What a single $ 1 deposit grows to in the future. The deposit is made at the beginning of the first period.	What a series of $ 1 deposits grow to in the future. A deposit is made at the end of each period.	The amount to be deposited at the end of each period that grows to $ 1 in the future.	What $ 1 to be paid in the future is worth today. Value today of a single $ 1 payment tomorrow.	What $ 1 to be paid at the end of each period is worth today. Value today of a series of $ 1 payments tomorrow.	The mortgage payment to amortize a loan of $ 1. An annuity certain, payable at the end of each period, worth $ 1 today.	The annual payment, including interest and principal, to amortize completely a loan of $ 100.	The total interest paid over the term on a loan of $1. The loan is amortized by regular periodic payments.	The average annual interest rate on a loan that is completely amortized by regular periodic payments.	
	$S = (1+i)^n$	$S\overline{n} = \dfrac{(1+i)^n - 1}{i}$	$\dfrac{1}{S\overline{n}} = \dfrac{i}{(1+i)^n - 1}$	$V^n = \dfrac{1}{(1+i)^n}$	$A\overline{n} = \dfrac{1-V^n}{i}$	$\dfrac{1}{A\overline{n}} = \dfrac{i}{1-V^n}$				

YEAR										PERIODS
	1.012 500	1.000 000	1.000 000 0000	.987 654	.987 654	1.012 500 0000	202.50	.012 500	2.50	1
	1.025 156	2.012 500	.496 894 4099	.975 461	1.963 115	.509 394 4099	101.88	.018 789	1.88	2

YEAR										PERIODS
1	1.025 156	2.012 500	.496 894 4099	.975 461	1.963 115	.509 394 4099	101.88	.018 789	1.88	2
2	1.050 945	4.075 627	.245 361 0233	.951 524	3.878 058	.257 861 0233	51.58	.031 444	1.57	4
3	1.077 383	6.190 654	.161 533 8102	.928 175	5.746 010	.174 033 8102	34.81	.044 203	1.47	6
4	1.104 486	8.358 888	.119 633 1365	.905 398	7.568 124	.132 133 1365	26.43	.057 065	1.43	8
5	1.132 271	10.581 666	.094 503 0740	.883 181	9.345 526	.107 003 0740	21.41	.070 031	1.40	10
6	1.160 755	12.860 361	.077 758 3123	.861 509	11.079 312	.090 258 3123	18.06	.083 100	1.39	12
7	1.189 955	15.196 380	.065 805 1462	.840 368	12.770 553	.078 305 1462	15.67	.096 272	1.38	14
8	1.219 890	17.591 164	.056 846 7221	.819 746	14.420 292	.069 346 7221	13.87	.109 548	1.37	16
9	1.250 577	20.046 192	.049 884 7873	.799 631	16.029 549	.062 384 7873	12.48	.122 926	1.37	18
10	1.282 037	22.562 979	.044 320 3896	.780 009	17.599 316	.056 820 3896	11.37	.136 408	1.36	20
11	1.314 288	25.143 078	.039 772 3772	.760 868	19.130 563	.052 272 3772	10.46	.149 992	1.36	22
12	1.347 351	27.788 084	.035 986 6480	.742 197	20.624 235	.048 486 6480	9.70	.163 680	1.36	24
13	1.381 245	30.499 628	.032 787 2851	.723 984	22.081 253	.045 287 2851	9.06	.177 469	1.37	26
14	1.415 992	33.279 384	.030 048 6329	.706 219	23.502 518	.042 548 6329	8.51	.191 362	1.37	28
15	1.451 613	36.129 069	.027 678 5434	.688 888	24.888 906	.040 178 5434	8.04	.205 356	1.37	30
16	1.488 131	39.050 441	.025 607 9056	.671 984	26.241 274	.038 107 9056	7.63	.219 453	1.37	32
17	1.525 566	42.045 303	.023 783 8693	.655 494	27.560 456	.036 283 8693	7.26	.233 652	1.37	34
18	1.563 944	45.115 505	.022 165 3285	.639 409	28.847 267	.034 665 3285	6.94	.247 952	1.38	36
19	1.603 287	48.262 942	.020 719 8308	.623 719	30.102 501	.033 219 8308	6.65	.262 354	1.38	38
20	1.643 619	51.489 557	.019 421 4139	.608 413	31.326 933	.031 921 4139	6.39	.276 857	1.38	40
21	1.684 967	54.797 341	.018 249 0606	.593 484	32.521 319	.030 749 0606	6.15	.291 461	1.39	42
22	1.727 354	58.188 337	.017 185 5745	.578 920	33.686 395	.029 685 5745	5.94	.306 165	1.39	44
23	1.770 808	61.664 637	.016 216 7499	.564 714	34.822 882	.028 716 7499	5.75	.320 971	1.40	46
24	1.815 355	65.228 388	.015 330 7483	.550 856	35.931 481	.027 830 7483	5.57	.335 876	1.40	48
25	1.861 022	68.881 790	.014 517 6251	.537 339	37.012 876	.027 017 6251	5.41	.350 881	1.40	50
26	1.907 839	72.627 097	.013 768 9655	.524 153	38.067 734	.026 268 9655	5.26	.365 986	1.41	52
27	1.955 833	76.466 623	.013 077 6012	.511 291	39.096 708	.025 577 6012	5.12	.381 190	1.41	54
28	2.005 034	80.402 736	.012 437 3877	.498 745	40.100 431	.024 937 3877	4.99	.396 494	1.42	56
29	2.055 473	84.437 868	.011 843 0276	.486 506	41.079 524	.024 343 0276	4.87	.411 896	1.42	58
30	2.107 181	88.574 508	.011 289 9301	.474 568	42.034 592	.023 789 9301	4.76	.427 396	1.42	60
31	2.160 190	92.815 210	.010 774 0962	.462 922	42.966 223	.023 274 0962	4.66	.442 994	1.43	62
32	2.214 532	97.162 593	.010 292 0267	.451 563	43.874 992	.022 792 0267	4.56	.458 690	1.43	64
33	2.270 242	101.619 339	.009 840 6465	.440 482	44.761 462	.022 340 6465	4.47	.474 483	1.44	66
34	2.327 353	106.188 201	.009 417 2421	.429 673	45.626 178	.021 917 2421	4.39	.490 372	1.44	68
35	2.385 900	110.871 998	.009 019 4100	.419 129	46.469 676	.021 519 4100	4.31	.506 359	1.45	70
36	2.445 920	115.673 621	.008 645 0133	.408 844	47.292 474	.021 145 0133	4.23	.522 441	1.45	72
37	2.507 450	120.596 036	.008 292 1465	.398 811	48.095 082	.020 792 1465	4.16	.538 619	1.46	74
38	2.570 529	125.642 280	.007 959 1042	.389 025	48.877 995	.020 459 1042	4.10	.554 892	1.46	76
39	2.635 193	130.815 469	.007 644 3559	.379 479	49.641 696	.020 144 3559	4.03	.571 260	1.46	78
40	2.701 485	136.118 795	.007 346 5240	.370 167	50.386 657	.019 846 5240	3.97	.587 722	1.47	80
41	2.769 444	141.555 534	.007 064 3653	.361 083	51.113 337	.019 564 3653	3.92	.604 278	1.47	82
42	2.839 113	147.129 040	.006 796 7547	.352 223	51.822 185	.019 296 7547	3.86	.620 927	1.48	84
43	2.910 534	152.842 755	.006 542 6719	.343 580	52.513 639	.019 042 6719	3.81	.637 670	1.48	86
44	2.983 753	158.700 206	.006 301 1891	.335 148	53.188 125	.018 801 1891	3.77	.654 505	1.49	88
45	3.058 813	164.705 008	.006 071 4608	.326 924	53.846 060	.018 571 4608	3.72	.671 431	1.49	90
46	3.135 761	170.860 868	.005 852 7152	.318 902	54.487 850	.018 352 7152	3.68	.688 450	1.50	92
47	3.214 645	177.141 568	.005 644 2459	.311 076	55.113 892	.018 144 2459	3.63	.705 559	1.50	94
48	3.295 513	183.641 059	.005 445 4053	.303 443	55.724 570	.017 945 4053	3.59	.722 759	1.51	96
49	3.378 416	190.273 280	.005 255 5987	.295 997	56.320 264	.017 755 5987	3.56	.740 049	1.51	98
50	3.463 404	197.072 342	.005 074 2788	.288 733	56.901 339	.017 574 2788	3.52	.757 428	1.51	100

Effective Rate is 2.52 %

Annual Percentage Rate is 2.50 %

	Amount Of 1	Amount Of 1 Per Period	Sinking Fund Payment	Present Worth Of 1	Present Worth of 1 Per Period	Periodic Payment To Amortize 1	Constant Annual Percent	Total Interest	Annual Add On Rate
	What a single $ 1 deposit grows to in the future. The deposit is made at the beginning of the first period.	What a series of $ 1 deposits grow to in the future. A deposit is made at the end of each period.	The amount to be deposited at the end of each period that grows to $ 1 in the future.	What $ 1 to be paid in the future is worth today. Value today of a single $ 1 payment tomorrow.	What $ 1 to be paid at the end of each period is worth today. Value today of a series of $ 1 payments tomorrow.	The mortgage payment to amortize a loan of $ 1. An annuity certain, payable at the end of each period, worth $ 1 today.	The annual payment, including interest and principal, to amortize completely a loan of $ 100.	The total interest paid over the term on a loan that is amortized by regular periodic payments.	The average annual interest rate on a loan that is completely amortized by regular periodic payments.

$$ S = (1+i)^n \qquad S\overline{n}| = \frac{(1+i)^n - 1}{i} \qquad \frac{1}{S\overline{n}|} = \frac{i}{(1+i)^n - 1} \qquad V^n = \frac{1}{(1+i)^n} \qquad A\overline{n}| = \frac{1 - V^n}{i} \qquad \frac{1}{A\overline{n}|} = \frac{i}{1 - V^n} $$

YEAR									PERIODS
	1.013 750	1.000 000	1.000 000 0000	.986 436	.986 436	1.013 750 0000	202.75	.013 750	2.75	1
	1.027 689	2.013 750	.496 585 9714	.973 057	1.959 493	.510 335 9714	102.07	.020 672	2.07	2

YEAR										PERIODS
1	1.027 689	2.013 750	.496 585 9714	.973 057	1.959 493	.510 335 9714	102.07	.020 672	2.07	2
2	1.056 145	4.083 259	.244 902 4264	.946 840	3.866 192	.258 652 4264	51.74	.034 610	1.73	4
3	1.085 388	6.210 070	.161 028 7688	.921 329	5.721 519	.174 778 7688	34.96	.048 673	1.62	6
4	1.115 442	8.395 771	.119 107 5771	.896 506	7.526 857	.132 857 5771	26.58	.062 861	1.57	8
5	1.146 327	10.641 993	.093 967 3653	.872 351	9.283 554	.107 717 3653	21.55	.077 174	1.54	10
6	1.178 068	12.950 409	.077 217 6365	.848 847	10.992 921	.090 967 6365	18.20	.091 612	1.53	12
7	1.210 688	15.322 744	.065 262 4620	.825 977	12.656 231	.079 012 4620	15.81	.106 174	1.52	14
8	1.244 211	17.760 766	.056 303 8765	.803 722	14.274 728	.070 053 8765	14.02	.120 862	1.51	16
9	1.278 662	20.266 295	.049 343 0092	.782 068	15.849 617	.063 093 0092	12.62	.135 674	1.51	18
10	1.314 067	22.841 200	.043 780 5367	.760 996	17.382 073	.057 530 5367	11.51	.150 611	1.51	20
11	1.350 452	25.487 402	.039 235 0706	.740 493	18.873 241	.052 985 0706	10.60	.165 672	1.51	22
12	1.387 845	28.206 874	.035 452 3513	.720 542	20.324 232	.049 202 3513	9.85	.180 856	1.51	24
13	1.426 273	31.001 646	.032 256 3521	.701 128	21.736 129	.046 006 3521	9.21	.196 165	1.51	26
14	1.465 765	33.873 802	.029 521 3391	.682 238	23.109 985	.043 271 3391	8.66	.211 598	1.51	28
15	1.506 350	36.825 486	.027 155 1066	.663 856	24.446 825	.040 905 1066	8.19	.227 153	1.51	30
16	1.548 060	39.858 899	.025 088 5002	.645 970	25.747 647	.038 838 5002	7.77	.242 832	1.52	32
17	1.590 924	42.976 305	.023 268 6362	.628 565	27.013 421	.037 018 6362	7.41	.258 634	1.52	34
18	1.634 975	46.180 028	.021 654 3826	.611 630	28.245 091	.035 404 3826	7.09	.274 558	1.53	36
19	1.680 246	49.472 460	.020 213 2661	.595 151	29.443 576	.033 963 2661	6.80	.290 604	1.53	38
20	1.726 771	52.856 056	.018 919 3079	.579 116	30.609 770	.032 669 3079	6.54	.306 772	1.53	40
21	1.774 583	56.333 341	.017 751 4770	.563 513	31.744 543	.031 501 4770	6.31	.323 062	1.54	42
22	1.823 720	59.906 908	.016 692 5657	.548 330	32.848 742	.030 442 5657	6.09	.339 473	1.54	44
23	1.874 217	63.579 424	.015 728 3589	.533 556	33.923 191	.029 478 3589	5.90	.356 005	1.55	46
24	1.926 112	67.353 629	.014 847 0100	.519 181	34.968 691	.028 597 0100	5.72	.372 656	1.55	48
25	1.979 445	71.232 338	.014 038 5678	.505 192	35.986 022	.027 788 5678	5.56	.389 428	1.56	50
26	2.034 254	75.218 444	.013 294 6116	.491 581	36.975 942	.027 044 6116	5.41	.406 320	1.56	52
27	2.090 580	79.314 923	.012 607 9679	.478 336	37.939 192	.026 357 9679	5.28	.423 330	1.57	54
28	2.148 466	83.524 828	.011 972 4879	.465 448	38.876 488	.025 722 4879	5.15	.440 459	1.57	56
29	2.207 955	87.851 303	.011 382 8705	.452 908	39.788 531	.025 132 8705	5.03	.457 706	1.58	58
30	2.269 092	92.297 573	.010 834 5211	.440 705	40.676 001	.024 584 5211	4.92	.475 071	1.58	60
31	2.331 921	96.866 956	.010 323 4378	.428 831	41.539 559	.024 073 4378	4.82	.492 553	1.59	62
32	2.396 489	101.562 861	.009 846 1188	.417 277	42.379 851	.023 596 1188	4.72	.510 152	1.59	64
33	2.462 846	106.388 792	.009 399 4864	.406 034	43.197 503	.023 149 4864	4.63	.527 866	1.60	66
34	2.531 040	111.348 348	.008 980 8248	.395 095	43.993 124	.022 730 8248	4.55	.545 696	1.61	68
35	2.601 122	116.445 229	.008 587 7284	.384 449	44.767 309	.022 337 7284	4.47	.563 641	1.61	70
36	2.673 145	121.683 238	.008 218 0587	.374 091	45.520 636	.021 968 0587	4.40	.581 700	1.62	72
37	2.747 161	127.066 283	.007 869 9083	.364 012	46.253 665	.021 619 9083	4.33	.599 873	1.62	74
38	2.823 228	132.598 379	.007 541 5703	.354 205	46.966 944	.021 291 5703	4.26	.618 159	1.63	76
39	2.901 400	138.283 654	.007 231 5127	.344 661	47.661 006	.020 981 5127	4.20	.636 558	1.63	78
40	2.981 737	144.126 349	.006 938 3566	.335 375	48.336 367	.020 688 3566	4.14	.655 069	1.64	80
41	3.064 299	150.130 822	.006 660 8574	.326 339	48.993 532	.020 410 8574	4.09	.673 690	1.64	82
42	3.149 146	156.301 554	.006 397 8890	.317 546	49.632 991	.020 147 8890	4.03	.692 423	1.65	84
43	3.236 343	162.643 147	.006 148 4300	.308 991	50.255 221	.019 898 4300	3.98	.711 265	1.65	86
44	3.325 955	169.160 334	.005 911 5514	.300 666	50.860 687	.019 661 5514	3.94	.730 217	1.66	88
45	3.418 047	175.857 975	.005 686 4069	.292 565	51.449 839	.019 436 4069	3.89	.749 277	1.67	90
46	3.512 690	182.741 067	.005 472 2237	.284 682	52.023 117	.019 222 2237	3.85	.768 445	1.67	92
47	3.609 953	189.814 746	.005 268 2946	.277 012	52.580 951	.019 018 2946	3.81	.787 720	1.68	94
48	3.709 909	197.084 288	.005 073 9712	.269 548	53.123 753	.018 823 9712	3.77	.807 101	1.68	96
49	3.812 633	204.555 118	.004 888 6579	.262 286	53.651 932	.018 638 6579	3.73	.826 588	1.69	98
50	3.918 201	212.232 807	.004 711 8069	.255 219	54.165 879	.018 461 8069	3.70	.846 181	1.69	100

Effective Rate is 2.77 %

Annual Percentage Rate is 2.75 %

SEMIANNUAL COMPOUND INTEREST AND ANNUITY

3.00 % S

Amount Of 1	Amount Of 1 Per Period	Sinking Fund Payment	Present Worth Of 1	Present Worth of 1 Per Period	Periodic Payment To Amortize 1	Constant Annual Percent	Total Interest	Annual Add On Rate
What a single $ 1 deposit grows to in the future. The deposit is made at the beginning of the first period.	What a series of $ 1 deposits grow to in the future. A deposit is made at the end of each period.	The amount to be deposited at the end of each period that grows to $ 1 in the future.	What $ 1 to be paid in the future is worth today. Value today of a single $ 1 payment tomorrow.	What $ 1 to be paid at the end of each period is worth today. Value today of a series of $ 1 payments tomorrow.	The mortgage payment to amortize a loan of $ 1. An annuity certain, payable at the end of each period, worth $ 1 today.	The annual payment, including interest and principal, to amortize a loan of $ 100.	The total interest paid over the term of a loan of $1. The loan is amortized by regular periodic payments.	The average annual interest rate on a loan that is completely amortized by regular periodic payments.
$S = (1+i)^n$	$S\overline{n}\rceil = \dfrac{(1+i)^n - 1}{i}$	$\dfrac{1}{S\overline{n}\rceil} = \dfrac{i}{(1+i)^n - 1}$	$V^n = \dfrac{1}{(1+i)^n}$	$A\overline{n}\rceil = \dfrac{1 - V^n}{i}$	$\dfrac{1}{A\overline{n}\rceil} = \dfrac{i}{1 - V^n}$			

YEAR   **PERIODS**

Amount Of 1	Amount Of 1 Per Period	Sinking Fund Payment	Present Worth Of 1	Present Worth of 1 Per Period	Periodic Payment To Amortize 1	Constant Annual Percent	Total Interest	Annual Add On Rate	PERIODS
1.015 000	1.000 000	1.000 000 0000	.985 222	.985 222	1.015 000 0000	203.00	.015 000	3.00	1
1.030 225	2.015 000	.496 277 9156	.970 662	1.955 883	.511 277 9156	102.26	.022 556	2.26	2

YEAR	Amount Of 1	Amount Of 1 Per Period	Sinking Fund Payment	Present Worth Of 1	Present Worth of 1 Per Period	Periodic Payment To Amortize 1	Constant Annual Percent	Total Interest	Annual Add On Rate	PERIODS
1	1.030 225	2.015 000	.496 277 9156	.970 662	1.955 883	.511 277 9156	102.26	.022 556	2.26	2
2	1.061 364	4.090 903	.244 444 7860	.942 184	3.854 385	.259 444 7860	51.89	.037 779	1.89	4
3	1.093 443	6.229 551	.160 525 2146	.914 542	5.697 187	.175 525 2146	35.11	.053 151	1.77	6
4	1.126 493	8.432 839	.118 584 0246	.887 711	7.485 925	.133 584 0246	26.72	.068 672	1.72	8
5	1.160 541	10.702 722	.093 434 1779	.861 667	9.222 185	.108 434 1779	21.69	.084 342	1.69	10
6	1.195 618	13.041 211	.076 679 9929	.836 387	10.907 505	.091 679 9929	18.34	.100 160	1.67	12
7	1.231 756	15.450 382	.064 723 3186	.811 849	12.543 382	.079 723 3186	15.95	.116 126	1.66	14
8	1.268 986	17.932 370	.055 765 0778	.788 031	14.131 264	.070 765 0778	14.16	.132 241	1.65	16
9	1.307 341	20.489 376	.048 805 7818	.764 912	15.672 561	.063 805 7818	12.77	.148 504	1.65	18
10	1.346 855	23.123 667	.043 245 7359	.742 470	17.168 639	.058 245 7359	11.65	.164 915	1.65	20
11	1.387 564	25.837 580	.038 703 3152	.720 688	18.620 824	.053 703 3152	10.75	.181 473	1.65	22
12	1.429 503	28.633 521	.034 924 1020	.699 544	20.030 405	.049 924 1020	9.99	.198 178	1.65	24
13	1.472 710	31.513 969	.031 731 9599	.679 021	21.398 632	.046 731 9599	9.35	.215 031	1.65	26
14	1.517 222	34.481 479	.029 001 0765	.659 099	22.726 717	.044 001 0765	8.81	.232 030	1.66	28
15	1.563 080	37.538 681	.026 639 1883	.639 762	24.015 838	.041 639 1883	8.33	.249 176	1.66	30
16	1.610 324	40.688 288	.024 577 0970	.620 993	25.267 139	.039 577 0970	7.92	.266 467	1.67	32
17	1.658 996	43.933 092	.022 761 8855	.602 774	26.481 728	.037 761 8855	7.56	.283 904	1.67	34
18	1.709 140	47.275 969	.021 152 3955	.585 090	27.660 684	.036 152 3955	7.24	.301 486	1.68	36
19	1.760 798	50.719 885	.019 716 1329	.567 924	28.805 052	.034 716 1329	6.95	.319 213	1.68	38
20	1.814 018	54.267 894	.018 427 1017	.551 262	29.915 845	.033 427 1017	6.69	.337 084	1.69	40
21	1.868 847	57.923 141	.017 264 2571	.535 089	30.994 050	.032 264 2571	6.46	.355 099	1.69	42
22	1.925 333	61.688 868	.016 210 3801	.519 391	32.040 622	.031 210 3801	6.25	.373 257	1.70	44
23	1.983 526	65.568 414	.015 251 2458	.504 153	33.056 490	.030 251 2458	6.06	.391 557	1.70	46
24	2.043 478	69.565 219	.014 374 9996	.489 362	34.042 554	.029 374 9996	5.88	.410 000	1.71	48
25	2.105 242	73.682 828	.013 571 6832	.475 005	34.999 688	.028 571 6832	5.72	.428 584	1.71	50
26	2.168 873	77.924 892	.012 832 8700	.461 069	35.928 742	.027 832 8700	5.57	.447 309	1.72	52
27	2.234 428	82.295 171	.012 151 3812	.447 542	36.830 539	.027 151 3812	5.44	.466 175	1.73	54
28	2.301 963	86.797 543	.011 521 0635	.434 412	37.705 879	.026 521 0635	5.31	.485 180	1.73	56
29	2.371 540	91.435 999	.010 936 6116	.421 667	38.555 538	.025 936 6116	5.19	.504 323	1.74	58
30	2.443 220	96.214 652	.010 393 4274	.409 296	39.380 269	.025 393 4274	5.08	.523 606	1.75	60
31	2.517 066	101.137 740	.009 887 5059	.397 288	40.180 804	.024 887 5059	4.98	.543 025	1.75	62
32	2.593 144	106.209 628	.009 415 3423	.385 632	40.957 853	.024 415 3423	4.89	.562 582	1.76	64
33	2.671 522	111.434 814	.008 973 8563	.374 318	41.712 105	.023 973 8563	4.80	.582 275	1.76	66
34	2.752 269	116.817 931	.008 560 3297	.363 337	42.444 228	.023 560 3297	4.72	.602 102	1.77	68
35	2.835 456	122.363 753	.008 172 3548	.352 677	43.154 872	.023 172 3548	4.64	.622 065	1.78	70
36	2.921 158	128.077 197	.007 807 7911	.342 330	43.844 667	.022 807 7911	4.57	.642 161	1.78	72
37	3.009 450	133.963 331	.007 464 7293	.332 287	44.514 224	.022 464 7293	4.50	.662 390	1.79	74
38	3.100 411	140.027 372	.007 141 4609	.322 538	45.164 138	.022 141 4609	4.43	.682 751	1.80	76
39	3.194 120	146.274 700	.006 836 4523	.313 075	45.794 985	.021 836 4523	4.37	.703 243	1.80	78
40	3.290 663	152.710 852	.006 548 3231	.303 890	46.407 323	.021 548 3231	4.31	.723 866	1.81	80
41	3.390 123	159.341 538	.006 275 8275	.294 975	47.001 697	.021 275 8275	4.26	.744 618	1.82	82
42	3.492 590	166.172 636	.006 017 8380	.286 321	47.578 633	.021 017 8380	4.21	.765 498	1.82	84
43	3.598 153	173.210 204	.005 773 3319	.277 920	48.138 643	.020 773 3319	4.16	.786 507	1.83	86
44	3.706 907	180.460 482	.005 541 3794	.269 767	48.682 222	.020 541 3794	4.11	.807 641	1.84	88
45	3.818 949	187.929 900	.005 321 1330	.261 852	49.209 855	.020 321 1330	4.07	.828 902	1.84	90
46	3.934 376	195.625 082	.005 111 8190	.254 170	49.722 007	.020 111 8190	4.03	.850 287	1.85	92
47	4.053 293	203.552 850	.004 912 7291	.246 713	50.219 134	.019 912 7291	3.99	.871 797	1.85	94
48	4.175 804	211.720 235	.004 723 2141	.239 475	50.701 675	.019 723 2141	3.95	.893 429	1.86	96
49	4.302 017	220.134 479	.004 542 6778	.232 449	51.170 060	.019 542 6778	3.91	.915 182	1.87	98
50	4.432 046	228.803 043	.004 370 5712	.225 629	51.624 704	.019 370 5712	3.88	.937 057	1.87	100

Effective Rate is 3.02 %

Annual Percentage Rate is 3.00 %

Amount Of 1	Amount Of 1 Per Period	Sinking Fund Payment	Present Worth Of 1	Present Worth of 1 Per Period	Periodic Payment To Amortize 1	Constant Annual Percent	Total Interest	Annual Add On Rate
What a single $ 1 deposit grows to in the future. The deposit is made at the beginning of the first period.	What a series of $ 1 deposits grow to in the future. A deposit is made at the end of each period.	The amount to be deposited at the end of each period that grows to $ 1 in the future.	What $ 1 to be paid in the future is worth today. Value today of a single $ 1 payment tomorrow.	What $ 1 to be paid at the end of each period is worth today. Value today of a series of $ 1 payments tomorrow.	The mortgage payment to amortize a loan of $ 1. An annuity certain, payable at the end of each period, worth $ 1 today.	The annual payment, including interest and principal, to amortize completely a loan of $ 100.	The total interest paid over the term on a loan of $1. The loan is amortized by regular periodic payments.	The average annual interest rate on a loan that is completely amortized by regular periodic payments.

$$S = (1+i)^n \qquad S\overline{n}| = \frac{(1+i)^n - 1}{i} \qquad \frac{1}{S\overline{n}|} = \frac{i}{(1+i)^n - 1} \qquad V^n = \frac{1}{(1+i)^n} \qquad A\overline{n}| = \frac{1-V^n}{i} \qquad \frac{1}{A\overline{n}|} = \frac{i}{1-V^n}$$

PERIODS

YEAR										
	1.016 250	1.000 000	1.000 000 0000	.984 010	.984 010	1.016 250 0000	203.25	.016 250	3.25	1
	1.032 764	2.016 250	.495 970 2418	.968 275	1.952 285	.512 220 2418	102.45	.024 440	2.44	2

YEAR	Amount Of 1	Amount Of 1 Per Period	Sinking Fund Payment	Present Worth Of 1	Present Worth of 1 Per Period	Periodic Payment To Amortize 1	Constant Annual Percent	Total Interest	Annual Add On Rate	PERIODS
1	1.032 764	2.016 250	.495 970 2418	.968 275	1.952 285	.512 220 2418	102.45	.024 440	2.44	2
2	1.066 602	4.098 561	.243 988 1002	.937 557	3.842 635	.260 238 1002	52.05	.040 952	2.05	4
3	1.101 548	6.249 096	.160 023 1449	.907 814	5.673 014	.176 273 1449	35.26	.057 639	1.92	6
4	1.137 639	8.470 092	.118 062 4747	.879 013	7.445 325	.134 312 4747	26.87	.074 500	1.86	8
5	1.174 913	10.763 856	.092 903 5060	.851 127	9.161 410	.109 153 5060	21.84	.091 535	1.83	10
6	1.213 408	13.132 774	.076 145 3744	.824 125	10.823 053	.092 395 3744	18.48	.108 745	1.81	12
7	1.253 164	15.579 307	.064 187 7070	.797 980	12.431 980	.080 437 7070	16.09	.126 128	1.80	14
8	1.294 222	18.105 999	.055 230 3149	.772 665	13.989 866	.071 480 3149	14.30	.143 685	1.80	16
9	1.336 626	20.715 475	.048 273 0915	.748 152	15.498 327	.064 523 0915	12.91	.161 416	1.79	18
10	1.380 420	23.410 448	.042 715 9708	.724 417	16.958 934	.058 965 9708	11.80	.179 319	1.79	20
11	1.425 648	26.193 719	.038 177 0912	.701 435	18.373 203	.054 427 0912	10.89	.197 396	1.79	22
12	1.472 358	29.068 182	.034 401 8766	.679 183	19.742 605	.050 651 8766	10.14	.215 645	1.80	24
13	1.520 598	32.036 823	.031 214 0810	.657 636	21.068 563	.047 464 0810	9.50	.234 066	1.80	26
14	1.570 419	35.102 730	.028 487 8128	.636 773	22.352 456	.044 737 8128	8.95	.252 659	1.80	28
15	1.621 873	38.269 088	.026 130 7508	.616 571	23.595 618	.042 380 7508	8.48	.271 423	1.81	30
16	1.675 012	41.539 189	.024 073 6526	.597 011	24.799 341	.040 323 6526	8.07	.290 357	1.81	32
17	1.729 892	44.916 431	.022 263 5675	.578 071	25.964 876	.038 513 5675	7.71	.309 461	1.82	34
18	1.786 570	48.404 326	.020 659 3105	.559 732	27.093 435	.036 909 3105	7.39	.328 735	1.83	36
19	1.845 106	52.006 498	.019 228 3663	.541 974	28.186 191	.035 478 3663	7.10	.348 178	1.83	38
20	1.905 559	55.726 693	.017 944 7219	.524 780	29.244 279	.034 194 7219	6.84	.367 789	1.84	40
21	1.967 993	59.568 775	.016 787 3184	.508 132	30.268 801	.033 037 3184	6.61	.387 567	1.85	42
22	2.032 472	63.536 741	.015 738 9251	.492 012	31.260 819	.031 988 9251	6.40	.407 513	1.85	44
23	2.099 064	67.634 712	.014 785 3072	.476 403	32.221 366	.031 035 3072	6.21	.427 624	1.86	46
24	2.167 838	71.866 950	.013 914 6019	.461 289	33.151 440	.030 164 6019	6.04	.447 901	1.87	48
25	2.238 865	76.237 853	.013 116 8436	.446 655	34.052 008	.029 366 8436	5.88	.468 342	1.87	50
26	2.312 219	80.751 965	.012 383 5995	.432 485	34.924 006	.028 633 5995	5.73	.488 947	1.88	52
27	2.387 977	85.413 978	.011 707 6856	.418 764	35.768 340	.027 957 6856	5.60	.509 715	1.89	54
28	2.466 217	90.228 737	.011 082 9436	.405 479	36.585 887	.027 332 9436	5.47	.530 645	1.90	56
29	2.547 020	95.201 247	.010 504 0641	.392 616	37.377 499	.026 754 0641	5.36	.551 736	1.90	58
30	2.630 471	100.336 676	.009 966 4454	.380 160	38.143 997	.026 216 4454	5.25	.572 987	1.91	60
31	2.716 656	105.640 363	.009 466 0788	.368 100	38.886 177	.025 716 0788	5.15	.594 397	1.92	62
32	2.805 665	111.117 821	.008 999 4566	.356 422	39.604 813	.025 249 4566	5.05	.615 965	1.92	64
33	2.897 590	116.774 742	.008 563 4957	.345 114	40.300 650	.024 813 4957	4.97	.637 691	1.93	66
34	2.992 526	122.617 007	.008 155 4755	.334 166	40.974 412	.024 405 4755	4.89	.659 572	1.94	68
35	3.090 574	128.650 688	.007 772 9860	.323 565	41.626 799	.024 022 9860	4.81	.681 609	1.95	70
36	3.191 833	134.882 057	.007 413 8845	.313 300	42.258 489	.023 663 8845	4.74	.703 800	1.96	72
37	3.296 411	141.317 592	.007 076 2599	.303 360	42.870 139	.023 326 2599	4.67	.726 143	1.96	74
38	3.404 415	147.963 980	.006 758 4016	.293 736	43.462 385	.023 008 4016	4.61	.748 639	1.97	76
39	3.515 957	154.828 131	.006 458 7746	.284 418	44.035 842	.022 708 7746	4.55	.771 284	1.98	78
40	3.631 154	161.917 180	.006 175 9969	.275 395	44.591 106	.022 425 9969	4.49	.794 080	1.99	80
41	3.750 126	169.238 494	.005 908 8212	.266 658	45.128 754	.022 158 8212	4.44	.817 023	1.99	82
42	3.872 995	176.799 685	.005 656 1187	.258 198	45.649 346	.021 906 1187	4.39	.840 114	2.00	84
43	3.999 890	184.608 611	.005 416 8654	.250 007	46.153 423	.021 666 8654	4.34	.863 350	2.01	86
44	4.130 943	192.673 389	.005 190 1303	.242 076	46.641 508	.021 440 1303	4.29	.886 731	2.02	88
45	4.266 289	201.002 402	.004 975 0649	.234 396	47.114 108	.021 225 0649	4.25	.910 256	2.02	90
46	4.406 070	209.604 307	.004 770 8943	.226 960	47.571 715	.021 020 8943	4.21	.933 922	2.03	92
47	4.550 431	218.488 046	.004 576 9094	.219 759	48.014 065	.020 826 9094	4.17	.957 729	2.04	94
48	4.699 521	227.662 852	.004 392 4601	.212 788	48.443 838	.020 642 4601	4.13	.981 676	2.05	96
49	4.853 497	237.138 261	.004 216 9492	.206 037	48.859 260	.020 466 9492	4.10	1.005 761	2.05	98
50	5.012 517	246.924 124	.004 049 8271	.199 501	49.261 503	.020 299 8271	4.06	1.029 983	2.06	100

Effective Rate is 3.28 %

Annual Percentage Rate is 3.25 %

	Amount Of 1	Amount Of 1 Per Period	Sinking Fund Payment	Present Worth Of 1	Present Worth of 1 Per Period	Periodic Payment To Amortize 1	Constant Annual Percent	Total Interest	Annual Add On Rate	
	What a single $ 1 deposit grows to in the future. The deposit is made at the beginning of the first period.	What a series of $ 1 deposits grow to in the future. A deposit is made at the end of each period.	The amount to be deposited at the end of each period that grows to $ 1 in the future.	What $ 1 to be paid in the future is worth today. Value today of a single $ 1 payment tomorrow.	What $ 1 to be paid at the end of each period is worth today. Value today of a series of $ 1 payments tomorrow.	The mortgage payment to amortize a loan of $ 1. An annuity certain, payable at the end of each period, worth $ 1 today.	The annual payment, including interest and principal, to amortize completely a loan of $ 100.	The total interest paid over the term on a loan of $1. The loan is amortized by regular periodic payments.	The average annual interest rate on a loan that is completely amortized by regular periodic payments.	
	$S = (1+i)^n$	$S\overline{n} = \dfrac{(1+i)^n - 1}{i}$	$\dfrac{1}{S\overline{n}} = \dfrac{i}{(1+i)^n - 1}$	$V^n = \dfrac{1}{(1+i)^n}$	$A\overline{n} = \dfrac{1-V^n}{i}$	$\dfrac{1}{A\overline{n}} = \dfrac{i}{1-V^n}$				

YEAR										PERIODS
	1.017 500	1.000 000	1.000 000 0000	.982 801	.982 801	1.017 500 0000	203.50	.017 500	3.50	1
	1.035 306	2.017 500	.495 662 9492	.965 898	1.948 699	.513 162 9492	102.64	.026 326	2.63	2

YEAR	Amount Of 1	Amount Of 1 Per Period	Sinking Fund Payment	Present Worth Of 1	Present Worth of 1 Per Period	Periodic Payment To Amortize 1	Constant Annual Percent	Total Interest	Annual Add On Rate	PERIODS
1	1.035 306	2.017 500	.495 662 9492	.965 898	1.948 699	.513 162 9492	102.64	.026 326	2.63	2
2	1.071 859	4.106 230	.243 532 3673	.932 959	3.830 943	.261 032 3673	52.21	.044 129	2.21	4
3	1.109 702	6.268 706	.159 522 5565	.901 143	5.648 998	.177 022 5565	35.41	.062 135	2.07	6
4	1.148 882	8.507 530	.117 542 9233	.870 412	7.405 053	.135 042 9233	27.01	.080 343	2.01	8
5	1.189 444	10.825 399	.092 375 3442	.840 729	9.101 223	.109 875 3442	21.98	.098 753	1.98	10
6	1.231 439	13.225 104	.075 613 7738	.812 058	10.739 550	.093 113 7738	18.63	.117 365	1.96	12
7	1.274 917	15.709 593	.063 655 6179	.784 365	12.322 006	.081 155 6179	16.24	.136 179	1.95	14
8	1.319 929	18.281 677	.054 699 5764	.757 616	13.850 497	.072 199 5764	14.44	.155 193	1.94	16
9	1.366 531	20.944 635	.047 744 9244	.731 780	15.326 863	.065 244 9244	13.05	.174 409	1.94	18
10	1.414 778	23.701 611	.042 191 2246	.706 825	16.752 881	.059 691 2246	11.94	.193 825	1.94	20
11	1.464 729	26.555 926	.037 656 3782	.682 720	18.130 269	.055 156 3782	11.04	.213 440	1.94	22
12	1.516 443	29.511 016	.033 885 6510	.659 438	19.460 686	.051 385 6510	10.28	.233 256	1.94	24
13	1.569 983	32.570 440	.030 702 6865	.636 950	20.745 732	.048 202 6865	9.65	.253 270	1.95	26
14	1.625 413	35.737 880	.027 981 5145	.615 228	21.986 955	.045 481 5145	9.10	.273 482	1.95	28
15	1.682 800	39.017 150	.025 629 7549	.594 248	23.185 849	.043 129 7549	8.63	.293 893	1.96	30
16	1.742 213	42.412 200	.023 578 1216	.573 982	24.343 859	.041 078 1216	8.22	.314 500	1.97	32
17	1.803 725	45.927 115	.021 773 6297	.554 408	25.462 378	.039 273 6297	7.86	.335 303	1.97	34
18	1.867 407	49.566 129	.020 175 0673	.535 502	26.542 753	.037 675 0673	7.54	.356 302	1.98	36
19	1.933 338	53.333 624	.018 749 8979	.517 240	27.586 285	.036 249 8979	7.25	.377 496	1.99	38
20	2.001 597	57.234 134	.017 472 0911	.499 601	28.594 230	.034 972 0911	7.00	.398 884	1.99	40
21	2.072 266	61.272 357	.016 320 5735	.482 563	29.567 801	.033 820 5735	6.77	.420 464	2.00	42
22	2.145 430	65.453 154	.015 278 1026	.466 107	30.508 172	.032 778 1026	6.56	.442 237	2.01	44
23	2.221 177	69.781 559	.014 330 4336	.450 212	31.416 474	.031 830 4336	6.37	.464 200	2.02	46
24	2.299 599	74.262 784	.013 465 6950	.434 858	32.293 801	.030 965 6950	6.20	.486 353	2.03	48
25	2.380 789	78.902 225	.012 673 9139	.420 029	33.141 209	.030 173 9139	6.04	.508 696	2.03	50
26	2.464 846	83.705 466	.011 946 6511	.405 705	33.959 719	.029 446 6511	5.89	.531 226	2.04	52
27	2.551 870	88.678 292	.011 276 7169	.391 869	34.750 316	.028 776 7169	5.76	.553 943	2.05	54
28	2.641 967	93.826 690	.010 657 9481	.378 506	35.513 951	.028 157 9481	5.64	.576 845	2.06	56
29	2.735 245	99.156 859	.010 085 0310	.365 598	36.251 545	.027 585 0310	5.52	.599 932	2.07	58
30	2.831 816	104.675 216	.009 553 3598	.353 130	36.963 986	.027 053 3598	5.42	.623 202	2.08	60
31	2.931 797	110.388 405	.009 058 9224	.341 088	37.652 130	.026 558 9224	5.32	.646 653	2.09	62
32	3.035 308	116.303 306	.008 598 2079	.329 456	38.316 807	.026 098 2079	5.22	.670 285	2.09	64
33	3.142 473	122.427 039	.008 168 1302	.318 221	38.958 817	.025 668 1302	5.14	.694 097	2.10	66
34	3.253 422	128.766 979	.007 765 9661	.307 369	39.578 934	.025 265 9661	5.06	.718 086	2.11	68
35	3.368 288	135.330 758	.007 389 3032	.296 887	40.177 903	.024 889 3032	4.98	.742 251	2.12	70
36	3.487 210	142.126 280	.007 035 9964	.286 762	40.756 445	.024 535 9964	4.91	.766 592	2.13	72
37	3.610 330	149.161 726	.006 704 1327	.276 983	41.315 259	.024 204 1327	4.85	.791 106	2.14	74
38	3.737 797	156.445 567	.006 391 9996	.267 537	41.855 015	.023 891 9996	4.78	.815 792	2.15	76
39	3.869 765	163.986 573	.006 098 0602	.258 414	42.376 364	.023 598 0602	4.72	.840 649	2.16	78
40	4.006 392	171.793 824	.005 820 9310	.249 601	42.879 935	.023 320 9310	4.67	.865 674	2.16	80
41	4.147 843	179.876 720	.005 559 3631	.241 089	43.366 332	.023 059 3631	4.62	.890 868	2.17	82
42	4.294 287	188.244 992	.005 312 2263	.232 868	43.836 142	.022 812 2263	4.57	.916 227	2.18	84
43	4.445 903	196.908 717	.005 078 4953	.224 926	44.289 931	.022 578 4953	4.52	.941 751	2.19	86
44	4.602 871	205.878 326	.004 857 2379	.217 256	44.728 244	.022 357 2379	4.48	.967 437	2.20	88
45	4.765 381	215.164 617	.004 647 6043	.209 847	45.151 610	.022 147 6043	4.43	.993 284	2.21	90
46	4.933 629	224.778 773	.004 448 8187	.202 691	45.560 539	.021 948 8187	4.39	1.019 291	2.22	92
47	5.107 816	234.732 369	.004 260 1709	.195 778	45.955 521	.021 760 1709	4.36	1.045 456	2.22	94
48	5.288 154	245.037 388	.004 081 0099	.189 102	46.337 035	.021 581 0099	4.32	1.071 777	2.23	96
49	5.474 859	255.706 239	.003 910 7376	.182 653	46.705 537	.021 410 7376	4.29	1.098 252	2.24	98
50	5.668 156	266.751 768	.003 748 8036	.176 424	47.061 473	.021 248 8036	4.25	1.124 880	2.25	100

Effective Rate is 3.53 %

Annual Percentage Rate is 3.50 %

Amount Of 1	Amount Of 1 Per Period	Sinking Fund Payment	Present Worth Of 1	Present Worth of 1 Per Period	Periodic Payment To Amortize 1	Constant Annual Percent	Total Interest	Annual Add On Rate	
What a single $ 1 deposit grows to in the future. The deposit is made at the beginning of the first period.	What a series of $ 1 deposits grow to in the future. A deposit is made at the end of each period.	The amount to be deposited at the end of each period that grows to $ 1 in the future.	What $ 1 to be paid in the future is worth today. Value today of a single $ 1 payment tomorrow.	What $ 1 to be paid at the end of each period is worth today. Value today of a series of $ 1 payments tomorrow.	The mortgage payment to amortize a loan of $ 1. An annuity certain, payable at the end of each period, worth $ 1 today.	The annual payment, including interest and principal, to amortize completely a loan of $ 100.	The total interest paid over the term on a loan of $1. The loan is amortized by regular periodic payments.	The average annual interest rate on a loan that is completely amortized by regular periodic payments.	
$S = (1+i)^n$	$S\overline{n}| = \dfrac{(1+i)^n - 1}{i}$	$\dfrac{1}{S\overline{n}|} = \dfrac{i}{(1+i)^n - 1}$	$V^n = \dfrac{1}{(1+i)^n}$	$A\overline{n}| = \dfrac{1-V^n}{i}$	$\dfrac{1}{A\overline{n}|} = \dfrac{i}{1-V^n}$				

YEAR									PERIODS
	1.018 750	1.000 000	1.000 000 0000	.981 595	.981 595	1.018 750 0000	203.75	.018 750	3.75	1
	1.037 852	2.018 750	.495 356 0372	.963 529	1.945 124	.514 106 0372	102.83	.028 212	2.82	2

YEAR	Amount Of 1	Amount Of 1 Per Period	Sinking Fund Payment	Present Worth Of 1	Present Worth of 1 Per Period	Periodic Payment To Amortize 1	Constant Annual Percent	Total Interest	Annual Add On Rate	PERIODS
1	1.037 852	2.018 750	.495 356 0372	.963 529	1.945 124	.514 106 0372	102.83	.028 212	2.82	2
2	1.077 136	4.113 913	.243 077 5854	.928 388	3.819 307	.261 827 5854	52.37	.047 310	2.37	4
3	1.117 907	6.288 381	.159 023 4467	.894 529	5.625 137	.177 773 4467	35.56	.066 641	2.22	6
4	1.160 222	8.545 156	.117 025 3662	.861 904	7.365 106	.135 775 3662	27.16	.086 203	2.16	8
5	1.204 138	10.887 353	.091 849 6867	.830 470	9.041 617	.110 599 6867	22.12	.105 997	2.12	10
6	1.249 716	13.318 207	.075 085 1837	.800 182	10.656 983	.093 835 1837	18.77	.126 022	2.10	12
7	1.297 020	15.841 072	.063 127 0421	.770 998	12.213 436	.081 877 0421	16.38	.146 279	2.09	14
8	1.346 114	18.459 431	.054 172 8507	.742 879	13.713 123	.072 922 8507	14.59	.166 766	2.08	16
9	1.397 067	21.176 899	.047 221 2662	.715 785	15.158 114	.065 971 2662	13.20	.187 483	2.08	18
10	1.449 948	23.997 228	.041 671 4797	.689 680	16.550 406	.060 421 4797	12.09	.208 430	2.08	20
11	1.504 831	26.924 311	.037 141 1552	.664 527	17.891 919	.055 891 1552	11.18	.229 605	2.09	22
12	1.561 791	29.962 188	.033 375 3999	.640 291	19.184 505	.052 125 3999	10.43	.251 010	2.09	24
13	1.620 907	33.115 053	.030 197 7468	.616 938	20.429 950	.048 947 7468	9.79	.272 641	2.10	26
14	1.682 261	36.387 260	.027 482 1462	.594 438	21.629 971	.046 232 1462	9.25	.294 500	2.10	28
15	1.745 937	39.783 325	.025 136 1597	.572 758	22.786 227	.043 886 1597	8.78	.316 585	2.11	30
16	1.812 024	43.307 936	.023 090 4564	.551 869	23.900 313	.041 840 4564	8.37	.338 895	2.12	32
17	1.880 612	46.965 959	.021 292 0172	.531 742	24.973 767	.040 042 0172	8.01	.361 429	2.13	34
18	1.951 796	50.762 444	.019 699 6033	.512 349	26.008 071	.038 449 6033	7.69	.384 186	2.13	36
19	2.025 674	54.702 631	.018 280 6562	.493 663	27.004 652	.037 030 6562	7.41	.407 165	2.14	38
20	2.102 349	58.791 961	.017 009 1280	.475 658	27.964 888	.035 759 1280	7.16	.430 365	2.15	40
21	2.181 926	63.036 079	.015 863 9309	.458 311	28.890 102	.034 613 9309	6.93	.453 785	2.16	42
22	2.264 516	67.440 843	.014 827 8099	.441 596	29.781 573	.033 577 8099	6.72	.477 424	2.17	44
23	2.350 231	72.012 334	.013 886 5100	.425 490	30.640 531	.032 636 5100	6.53	.501 279	2.18	46
24	2.439 191	76.756 864	.013 028 1508	.409 972	31.468 162	.031 778 1508	6.36	.525 351	2.19	48
25	2.531 518	81.680 981	.012 242 7521	.395 020	32.265 608	.030 992 7521	6.20	.549 638	2.20	50
26	2.627 340	86.791 484	.011 521 8678	.380 613	33.033 971	.030 271 8678	6.06	.574 137	2.21	52
27	2.726 789	92.095 427	.010 858 3024	.366 732	33.774 311	.029 608 3024	5.93	.598 848	2.22	54
28	2.830 002	97.600 133	.010 245 8877	.353 357	34.487 649	.028 995 8877	5.80	.623 770	2.23	56
29	2.937 123	103.313 200	.009 679 3052	.340 469	35.174 971	.028 429 3052	5.69	.648 900	2.24	58
30	3.048 297	109.242 516	.009 153 9451	.328 052	35.837 226	.027 903 9451	5.59	.674 237	2.25	60
31	3.163 680	115.396 266	.008 665 7916	.316 088	36.475 328	.027 415 7916	5.49	.699 779	2.26	62
32	3.283 430	121.782 945	.008 211 3304	.304 560	37.090 158	.026 961 3304	5.40	.725 525	2.27	64
33	3.407 713	128.411 370	.007 787 4724	.293 452	37.682 564	.026 537 4724	5.31	.751 473	2.28	66
34	3.536 700	135.290 691	.007 391 4915	.282 749	38.253 364	.026 141 4915	5.23	.777 621	2.29	68
35	3.670 570	142.430 405	.007 020 9728	.272 437	38.803 347	.025 770 9728	5.16	.803 968	2.30	70
36	3.809 507	149.840 369	.006 673 7690	.262 501	39.333 271	.025 423 7690	5.09	.830 511	2.31	72
37	3.953 703	157.530 811	.006 347 9645	.252 927	39.843 869	.025 097 9645	5.02	.857 249	2.32	74
38	4.103 357	165.512 348	.006 041 8453	.243 703	40.335 844	.024 791 8453	4.96	.884 180	2.33	76
39	4.258 675	173.795 999	.005 753 8724	.234 815	40.809 876	.024 503 8724	4.91	.911 302	2.34	78
40	4.419 872	182.393 199	.005 482 6606	.226 251	41.266 620	.024 232 6606	4.85	.938 613	2.35	80
41	4.587 172	191.315 817	.005 226 9594	.217 999	41.706 706	.023 976 9594	4.80	.966 111	2.36	82
42	4.760 803	200.576 169	.004 985 6371	.210 049	42.130 742	.023 735 6371	4.75	.993 794	2.37	84
43	4.941 007	210.187 041	.004 757 6673	.202 388	42.539 312	.023 507 6673	4.71	1.021 659	2.38	86
44	5.128 032	220.161 699	.004 542 1161	.195 007	42.932 982	.023 292 1161	4.66	1.049 706	2.39	88
45	5.322 136	230.513 913	.004 338 1329	.187 894	43.312 294	.023 088 1329	4.62	1.077 932	2.40	90
46	5.523 587	241.257 975	.004 144 9407	.181 042	43.677 772	.022 894 9407	4.58	1.106 335	2.41	92
47	5.732 663	252.408 716	.003 961 8283	.174 439	44.029 921	.022 711 8283	4.55	1.134 912	2.41	94
48	5.949 654	263.981 530	.003 788 1438	.168 077	44.369 226	.022 538 1438	4.51	1.163 662	2.42	96
49	6.174 857	275.992 394	.003 623 2883	.161 947	44.696 157	.022 373 2883	4.48	1.192 582	2.43	98
50	6.408 585	288.457 887	.003 466 7105	.156 041	45.011 164	.022 216 7105	4.45	1.221 671	2.44	100

SEMIANNUAL COMPOUND INTEREST AND ANNUITY

4.00 % S

	Amount Of 1	Amount Of 1 Per Period	Sinking Fund Payment	Present Worth Of 1	Present Worth of 1 Per Period	Periodic Payment To Amortize 1	Constant Annual Percent	Total Interest	Annual Add On Rate
	What a single $ 1 deposit grows to in the future. The deposit is made at the beginning of the first period.	What a series of $ 1 deposits grow to in the future. A deposit is made at the end of each period.	The amount to be deposited at the end of each period that grows to $ 1 in the future.	What $ 1 to be paid in the future is worth today. Value today of a single $ 1 payment tomorrow.	What $ 1 to be paid at the end of each period is worth today. Value today of a series of $ 1 payments tomorrow.	The mortgage payment to amortize a loan of $ 1. An annuity certain, payable at the end of each period, worth $ 1 today.	The annual payment, including interest and principal, to amortize completely a loan of $ 100.	The total interest paid over the term on a loan of $1. The loan is amortized by regular periodic payments.	The average annual interest rate on a loan that is completely amortized by regular periodic payments.
	$S = (1+i)^n$	$S\overline{n} = \dfrac{(1+i)^n - 1}{i}$	$\dfrac{1}{S\overline{n}} = \dfrac{i}{(1+i)^n - 1}$	$V^n = \dfrac{1}{(1+i)^n}$	$A\overline{n} = \dfrac{1-V^n}{i}$	$\dfrac{1}{A\overline{n}} = \dfrac{i}{1-V^n}$			

YEAR									PERIODS
	1.020 000	1.000 000	1.000 000 0000	.980 392	.980 392	1.020 000 0000	204.00	.020 000	4.00	1
	1.040 400	2.020 000	.495 049 5050	.961 169	1.941 561	.515 049 5050	103.01	.030 099	3.01	2

YEAR	Amount Of 1	Amount Of 1 Per Period	Sinking Fund Payment	Present Worth Of 1	Present Worth of 1 Per Period	Periodic Payment To Amortize 1	Constant Annual Percent	Total Interest	Annual Add On Rate	PERIODS
1	1.040 400	2.020 000	.495 049 5050	.961 169	1.941 561	.515 049 5050	103.01	.030 099	3.01	2
2	1.082 432	4.121 608	.242 623 7527	.923 845	3.807 729	.262 623 7527	52.53	.050 495	2.52	4
3	1.126 162	6.308 121	.158 525 8123	.887 971	5.601 431	.178 525 8123	35.71	.071 155	2.37	6
4	1.171 659	8.582 969	.116 509 7991	.853 490	7.325 481	.136 509 7991	27.31	.092 078	2.30	8
5	1.218 994	10.949 721	.091 326 5279	.820 348	8.982 585	.111 326 5279	22.27	.113 265	2.27	10
6	1.268 242	13.412 090	.074 559 5966	.788 493	10.575 341	.094 559 5966	18.92	.134 715	2.25	12
7	1.319 479	15.973 938	.062 601 9702	.757 875	12.106 249	.082 601 9702	16.53	.156 428	2.23	14
8	1.372 786	18.639 285	.053 650 1259	.728 446	13.577 709	.073 650 1259	14.74	.178 402	2.23	16
9	1.428 246	21.412 312	.046 702 1022	.700 159	14.992 031	.066 702 1022	13.35	.200 638	2.23	18
10	1.485 947	24.297 370	.041 156 7181	.672 971	16.351 433	.061 156 7181	12.24	.223 134	2.23	20
11	1.545 980	27.298 984	.036 631 4005	.646 839	17.658 048	.056 631 4005	11.33	.245 891	2.24	22
12	1.608 437	30.421 862	.032 871 0973	.621 721	18.913 926	.052 871 0973	10.58	.268 906	2.24	24
13	1.673 418	33.670 906	.029 699 2308	.597 579	20.121 036	.049 699 2308	9.94	.292 180	2.25	26
14	1.741 024	37.051 210	.026 989 6716	.574 375	21.281 272	.046 989 6716	9.40	.315 711	2.26	28
15	1.811 362	40.568 079	.024 649 9223	.552 071	22.396 456	.044 649 9223	8.93	.339 498	2.26	30
16	1.884 541	44.227 030	.022 610 6073	.530 633	23.468 335	.042 610 6073	8.53	.363 539	2.27	32
17	1.960 676	48.033 802	.020 818 6728	.510 028	24.498 592	.040 818 6728	8.17	.387 835	2.28	34
18	2.039 887	51.994 367	.019 232 8526	.490 223	25.488 842	.039 232 8526	7.85	.412 383	2.29	36
19	2.122 299	56.114 940	.017 820 5663	.471 187	26.440 641	.037 820 5663	7.57	.437 182	2.30	38
20	2.208 040	60.401 983	.016 555 7478	.452 890	27.355 479	.036 555 7478	7.32	.462 230	2.31	40
21	2.297 244	64.862 223	.015 417 2945	.435 304	28.234 794	.035 417 2945	7.09	.487 526	2.32	42
22	2.390 053	69.502 657	.014 387 9391	.418 401	29.079 963	.034 387 9391	6.88	.513 069	2.33	44
23	2.486 611	74.330 564	.013 453 4159	.402 154	29.892 314	.033 453 4159	6.70	.538 857	2.34	46
24	2.587 070	79.353 519	.012 601 8355	.386 538	30.673 120	.032 601 8355	6.53	.564 888	2.35	48
25	2.691 588	84.579 401	.011 823 2097	.371 528	31.423 606	.031 823 2097	6.37	.591 160	2.36	50
26	2.800 328	90.016 409	.011 109 0856	.357 101	32.144 950	.031 109 0856	6.23	.617 672	2.38	52
27	2.913 461	95.673 072	.010 452 2618	.343 234	32.838 283	.030 452 2618	6.10	.644 422	2.39	54
28	3.031 165	101.558 264	.009 846 5645	.329 906	33.504 694	.029 846 5645	5.97	.671 408	2.40	56
29	3.153 624	107.681 218	.009 286 6706	.317 095	34.145 226	.029 286 6706	5.86	.698 627	2.41	58
30	3.281 031	114.051 539	.008 767 9658	.304 782	34.760 887	.028 767 9658	5.76	.726 078	2.42	60
31	3.413 584	120.679 222	.008 286 4306	.292 947	35.352 640	.028 286 4306	5.66	.753 759	2.43	62
32	3.551 493	127.574 662	.007 838 5471	.281 572	35.921 415	.027 838 5471	5.57	.781 667	2.44	64
33	3.694 974	134.748 679	.007 421 2231	.270 638	36.468 103	.027 421 2231	5.49	.809 801	2.45	66
34	3.844 251	142.212 525	.007 031 7294	.260 129	36.993 564	.027 031 7294	5.41	.838 158	2.47	68
35	3.999 558	149.977 911	.006 667 6485	.250 028	37.498 619	.026 667 6485	5.34	.866 735	2.48	70
36	4.161 140	158.057 019	.006 326 8307	.240 319	37.984 063	.026 326 8307	5.27	.895 532	2.49	72
37	4.329 250	166.462 522	.006 007 3582	.230 987	38.450 657	.026 007 3582	5.21	.924 545	2.50	74
38	4.504 152	175.207 608	.005 707 5147	.222 017	38.899 132	.025 707 5147	5.15	.953 771	2.51	76
39	4.686 120	184.305 996	.005 425 7595	.213 396	39.330 192	.025 425 7595	5.09	.983 209	2.52	78
40	4.875 439	193.771 958	.005 160 7055	.205 110	39.744 514	.025 160 7055	5.04	1.012 856	2.53	80
41	5.072 407	203.620 345	.004 911 1006	.197 145	40.142 747	.024 911 1006	4.99	1.042 710	2.54	82
42	5.277 332	213.866 607	.004 675 8118	.189 490	40.525 516	.024 675 8118	4.94	1.072 768	2.55	84
43	5.490 536	224.526 818	.004 453 8110	.182 132	40.893 422	.024 453 8110	4.90	1.103 028	2.57	86
44	5.712 354	235.617 701	.004 244 1633	.175 059	41.247 041	.024 244 1633	4.85	1.133 486	2.58	88
45	5.943 133	247.156 656	.004 046 0169	.168 261	41.586 929	.024 046 0169	4.81	1.164 142	2.59	90
46	6.183 236	259.161 785	.003 858 5936	.161 728	41.913 619	.023 858 5936	4.78	1.194 991	2.60	92
47	6.433 048	271.651 925	.003 681 1814	.155 448	42.227 623	.023 681 1814	4.74	1.226 031	2.61	94
48	6.692 933	284.646 659	.003 513 1275	.149 411	42.529 434	.023 513 1275	4.71	1.257 260	2.62	96
49	6.963 328	298.166 384	.003 353 8321	.143 609	42.819 525	.023 353 8321	4.68	1.288 676	2.63	98
50	7.244 646	312.232 306	.003 202 7435	.138 033	43.098 352	.023 202 7435	4.65	1.320 274	2.64	100

Effective Rate is 4.04 %   8 - 372   Annual Percentage Rate is 4.00 %

Amount Of 1	Amount Of 1 Per Period	Sinking Fund Payment	Present Worth Of 1	Present Worth of 1 Per Period	Periodic Payment To Amortize 1	Constant Annual Percent	Total Interest	Annual Add On Rate
What a single $ 1 deposit grows to in the future. The deposit is made at the beginning of the first period.	What a series of $ 1 deposits grow to in the future. A deposit is made at the end of each period.	The amount to be deposited at the end of each period that grows to $ 1 in the future.	What $ 1 to be paid in the future is worth today. Value today of a single $ 1 payment tomorrow.	What $ 1 to be paid at the end of each period is worth today. Value today of a series of $ 1 payments tomorrow.	The mortgage payment to amortize a loan of $ 1. An annuity certain, payable at the end of each period, worth $ 1 today.	The annual payment, including interest and principal, to amortize completely a loan of $ 100.	The total interest paid over the term on a loan of $1. The loan is amortized by regular periodic payments.	The average annual interest rate on a loan that is completely amortized by regular periodic payments.

$$S = (1+i)^n \qquad S\overline{n}| = \frac{(1+i)^n - 1}{i} \qquad \frac{1}{S\overline{n}|} = \frac{i}{(1+i)^n - 1} \qquad V^n = \frac{1}{(1+i)^n} \qquad A\overline{n}| = \frac{1 - V^n}{i} \qquad \frac{1}{A\overline{n}|} = \frac{i}{1 - V^n}$$

YEAR									PERIODS
	1.021 250	1.000 000	1.000 000 0000	.979 192	.979 192	1.021 250 0000	204.25	.021 250	4.25 · 1
	1.042 952	2.021 250	.494 743 3519	.958 817	1.938 009	.515 993 3519	103.20	.031 987	3.20 · 2

YEAR	Amount Of 1	Amount Of 1 Per Period	Sinking Fund Payment	Present Worth Of 1	Present Worth of 1 Per Period	Periodic Payment To Amortize 1	Constant Annual Percent	Total Interest	Annual Add On Rate	PERIODS
1	1.042 952	2.021 250	.494 743 3519	.958 817	1.938 009	.515 993 3519	103.20	.031 987	3.20	2
2	1.087 748	4.129 316	.242 170 8674	.919 331	3.796 206	.263 420 8674	52.69	.053 683	2.68	4
3	1.134 468	6.327 926	.158 029 6506	.881 470	5.577 878	.179 279 6506	35.86	.075 678	2.52	6
4	1.183 196	8.620 971	.115 996 2178	.845 169	7.286 175	.137 246 2178	27.45	.097 970	2.45	8
5	1.234 016	11.012 505	.090 805 8619	.810 362	8.924 120	.112 055 8619	22.42	.120 559	2.41	10
6	1.287 019	13.506 759	.074 037 0051	.776 990	10.494 610	.095 287 0051	19.06	.143 444	2.39	12
7	1.342 298	16.108 146	.062 080 3924	.744 991	12.000 424	.083 330 3924	16.67	.166 626	2.38	14
8	1.399 952	18.821 266	.053 131 3898	.714 310	13.444 223	.074 381 3898	14.88	.190 102	2.38	16
9	1.460 082	21.650 918	.046 187 4172	.684 893	14.828 563	.067 437 4172	13.49	.213 874	2.38	18
10	1.522 795	24.602 109	.040 646 9215	.656 687	16.155 892	.061 896 9215	12.38	.237 938	2.38	20
11	1.588 201	27.680 058	.036 127 0917	.629 643	17.428 559	.057 377 0917	11.48	.262 296	2.38	22
12	1.656 417	30.890 210	.032 372 7162	.603 713	18.648 813	.053 622 7162	10.73	.286 945	2.39	24
13	1.727 563	34.238 243	.029 207 1064	.578 850	19.818 814	.050 457 1064	10.10	.311 885	2.40	26
14	1.801 764	37.730 079	.026 504 0528	.555 012	20.940 631	.047 754 0528	9.56	.337 113	2.41	28
15	1.879 153	41.371 895	.024 170 9984	.532 155	22.016 249	.045 420 9984	9.09	.362 630	2.42	30
16	1.959 865	45.170 132	.022 138 5228	.510 239	23.047 570	.043 388 5228	8.68	.388 433	2.43	32
17	2.044 045	49.131 510	.020 353 5369	.489 226	24.036 418	.041 603 5369	8.33	.414 520	2.44	34
18	2.131 839	53.263 035	.018 774 7469	.469 078	24.984 543	.040 024 7469	8.01	.440 891	2.45	36
19	2.223 405	57.572 016	.017 369 5500	.449 761	25.893 621	.038 619 5500	7.73	.467 543	2.46	38
20	2.318 904	62.066 074	.016 111 8618	.431 238	26.765 261	.037 361 8618	7.48	.494 474	2.47	40
21	2.418 505	66.753 158	.014 980 5646	.413 479	27.601 005	.036 230 5646	7.25	.521 684	2.48	42
22	2.522 383	71.641 561	.013 958 3782	.396 450	28.402 331	.035 208 3782	7.05	.549 169	2.50	44
23	2.630 723	76.739 928	.013 031 0261	.380 124	29.170 655	.034 281 0261	6.86	.576 927	2.51	46
24	2.743 717	82.057 278	.012 186 6095	.364 469	29.907 339	.033 436 6095	6.69	.604 957	2.52	48
25	2.861 564	87.603 016	.011 415 1321	.349 459	30.613 683	.032 665 1321	6.54	.633 257	2.53	50
26	2.984 473	93.386 952	.010 708 1340	.335 068	31.290 938	.031 958 1340	6.40	.661 823	2.55	52
27	3.112 661	99.419 318	.010 058 4074	.321 269	31.940 302	.031 308 4074	6.27	.690 654	2.56	54
28	3.246 354	105.710 783	.009 459 7729	.308 038	32.562 924	.030 709 7729	6.15	.719 747	2.57	56
29	3.385 790	112.272 476	.008 906 9025	.295 352	33.159 904	.030 156 9025	6.04	.749 100	2.58	58
30	3.531 215	119.116 005	.008 395 1775	.283 189	33.732 299	.029 645 1775	5.93	.778 711	2.60	60
31	3.682 886	126.253 473	.007 920 5742	.271 526	34.281 122	.029 170 5742	5.84	.808 576	2.61	62
32	3.841 072	133.697 507	.007 479 5710	.260 344	34.807 342	.028 729 5710	5.75	.838 693	2.62	64
33	4.006 052	141.461 274	.007 069 0725	.249 622	35.311 891	.028 319 0725	5.67	.869 059	2.63	66
34	4.178 118	149.558 507	.006 686 3465	.239 342	35.795 661	.027 936 3465	5.59	.899 672	2.65	68
35	4.357 575	158.003 528	.006 328 9726	.229 485	36.259 509	.027 578 9726	5.52	.930 528	2.66	70
36	4.544 740	166.811 276	.005 994 7986	.220 035	36.704 254	.027 244 7986	5.45	.961 626	2.67	72
37	4.739 943	175.997 331	.005 681 9043	.210 973	37.130 683	.026 931 9043	5.39	.992 961	2.68	74
38	4.943 531	185.577 942	.005 388 5715	.202 285	37.539 551	.026 638 5715	5.33	1.024 531	2.70	76
39	5.155 864	195.570 054	.005 113 2573	.193 954	37.931 580	.026 363 2573	5.28	1.056 334	2.71	78
40	5.377 316	205.991 344	.004 854 5729	.185 966	38.307 464	.026 104 5729	5.23	1.088 366	2.72	80
41	5.608 280	216.860 244	.004 611 2648	.178 308	38.667 869	.025 861 2648	5.18	1.120 624	2.73	82
42	5.849 165	228.195 980	.004 382 1981	.170 965	39.013 431	.025 632 1981	5.13	1.153 105	2.75	84
43	6.100 395	240.018 604	.004 166 3437	.163 924	39.344 762	.025 416 3437	5.09	1.185 806	2.76	86
44	6.362 417	252.349 028	.003 962 7654	.157 173	39.662 448	.025 212 7654	5.05	1.218 723	2.77	88
45	6.635 693	265.209 063	.003 770 6102	.150 700	39.967 051	.025 020 6102	5.01	1.251 855	2.78	90
46	6.920 706	278.621 457	.003 589 0990	.144 494	40.259 109	.024 839 0990	4.97	1.285 197	2.79	92
47	7.217 961	292.609 934	.003 417 5190	.138 543	40.539 140	.024 667 5190	4.94	1.318 747	2.81	94
48	7.527 984	307.199 238	.003 255 2164	.132 838	40.807 638	.024 505 2164	4.91	1.352 501	2.82	96
49	7.851 322	322.415 175	.003 101 5910	.127 367	41.065 079	.024 351 5910	4.88	1.386 456	2.83	98
50	8.188 549	338.284 660	.002 956 0903	.122 122	41.311 917	.024 206 0903	4.85	1.420 609	2.84	100

Effective Rate is 4.30 %

Annual Percentage Rate is 4.25 %

Amount Of 1	Amount Of 1 Per Period	Sinking Fund Payment	Present Worth Of 1	Present Worth of 1 Per Period	Periodic Payment To Amortize 1	Constant Annual Percent	Total Interest	Annual Add On Rate
What a single $ 1 deposit grows to in the future. The deposit is made at the beginning of the first period.	What a series of $ 1 deposits grow to in the future. A deposit is made at the end of each period.	The amount to be deposited at the end of each period that grows to $ 1 in the future.	What $ 1 to be paid in the future is worth today. Value today of a single $ 1 payment tomorrow.	What $ 1 to be paid at the end of each period is worth today. Value today of a series of $ 1 payments tomorrow.	The mortgage payment to amortize a loan of $ 1. An annuity certain, payable at the end of each period, worth $ 1 today.	The annual payment, including interest and principal, to amortize completely a loan of $ 100.	The total interest paid over the term on a loan of $1. The loan is amortized by regular periodic payments.	The average annual interest rate on a loan that is completely amortized by regular periodic payments.
$S = (1+i)^n$	$S\overline{n}| = \dfrac{(1+i)^n - 1}{i}$	$\dfrac{1}{S\overline{n}|} = \dfrac{i}{(1+i)^n - 1}$	$V^n = \dfrac{1}{(1+i)^n}$	$A\overline{n}| = \dfrac{1-V^n}{i}$	$\dfrac{1}{A\overline{n}|} = \dfrac{i}{1-V^n}$			

YEAR / **PERIODS**

	1.022 500	1.000 000	1.000 000 0000	.977 995	.977 995	1.022 500 0000	204.50	.022 500	4.50	1
	1.045 506	2.022 500	.494 437 5773	.956 474	1.934 470	.516 937 5773	103.39	.033 875	3.39	2

YEAR	Amount Of 1	Amount Of 1 Per Period	Sinking Fund Payment	Present Worth Of 1	Present Worth of 1 Per Period	Periodic Payment To Amortize 1	Constant Annual Percent	Total Interest	Annual Add On Rate	PERIODS
1	1.045 506	2.022 500	.494 437 5773	.956 474	1.934 470	.516 937 5773	103.39	.033 875	3.39	2
2	1.093 083	4.137 036	.241 718 9277	.914 843	3.784 740	.264 218 9277	52.85	.056 876	2.84	4
3	1.142 825	6.347 797	.157 534 9584	.875 024	5.554 477	.180 034 9584	36.01	.080 210	2.67	6
4	1.194 831	8.659 162	.115 484 6181	.836 938	7.247 185	.137 984 6181	27.60	.103 877	2.60	8
5	1.249 203	11.075 708	.090 287 6831	.800 510	8.866 216	.112 787 6831	22.56	.127 877	2.56	10
6	1.306 050	13.602 222	.073 517 4015	.765 667	10.414 779	.096 017 4015	19.21	.152 209	2.54	12
7	1.365 483	16.243 708	.061 562 2989	.732 341	11.895 939	.084 062 2989	16.82	.176 872	2.53	14
8	1.427 621	19.005 398	.052 616 6300	.700 466	13.312 631	.075 116 6300	15.03	.201 866	2.52	16
9	1.492 587	21.892 763	.045 677 1958	.669 978	14.667 661	.068 177 1958	13.64	.227 190	2.52	18
10	1.560 509	24.911 520	.040 142 0708	.640 816	15.963 712	.062 642 0708	12.53	.252 841	2.53	20
11	1.631 522	28.067 650	.035 628 2056	.612 925	17.203 352	.058 128 2056	11.63	.278 821	2.53	22
12	1.705 767	31.367 403	.031 880 2289	.586 247	18.389 036	.054 380 2289	10.88	.305 126	2.54	24
13	1.783 390	34.817 316	.028 721 3406	.560 730	19.523 113	.051 221 3406	10.25	.331 755	2.55	26
14	1.864 545	38.424 222	.026 025 2506	.536 324	20.607 828	.048 525 2506	9.71	.358 707	2.56	28
15	1.949 393	42.195 264	.023 699 3422	.512 980	21.645 330	.046 199 3422	9.24	.385 980	2.57	30
16	2.038 103	46.137 912	.021 674 1493	.490 652	22.637 674	.044 174 1493	8.84	.413 573	2.58	32
17	2.130 849	50.259 976	.019 896 5477	.469 296	23.586 826	.042 396 5477	8.48	.441 483	2.60	34
18	2.227 816	54.569 619	.018 325 2151	.448 870	24.494 666	.040 825 2151	8.17	.469 708	2.61	36
19	2.329 196	59.075 377	.016 927 5262	.429 333	25.362 991	.039 427 5262	7.89	.498 246	2.62	38
20	2.435 189	63.786 176	.015 677 3781	.410 646	26.193 522	.038 177 3781	7.64	.527 095	2.64	40
21	2.546 005	68.711 346	.014 553 6372	.392 772	26.987 904	.037 053 6372	7.42	.556 253	2.65	42
22	2.661 864	73.860 642	.013 539 0105	.375 677	27.747 710	.036 039 0105	7.21	.585 716	2.66	44
23	2.782 996	79.244 262	.012 619 2101	.359 325	28.474 444	.035 119 2101	7.03	.615 484	2.68	46
24	2.909 640	84.872 872	.011 782 3279	.343 685	29.169 548	.034 282 3279	6.86	.645 552	2.69	48
25	3.042 046	90.757 618	.011 018 3588	.328 726	29.834 396	.033 518 3588	6.71	.675 918	2.70	50
26	3.180 479	96.910 157	.010 318 8359	.314 418	30.470 307	.032 818 8359	6.57	.706 579	2.72	52
27	3.325 210	103.342 674	.009 676 5446	.300 733	31.078 539	.032 176 5446	6.44	.737 533	2.73	54
28	3.476 528	110.067 912	.009 085 3000	.287 643	31.660 298	.031 585 3000	6.32	.768 777	2.75	56
29	3.634 732	117.099 190	.008 539 7687	.275 123	32.216 735	.031 039 7687	6.21	.800 307	2.76	58
30	3.800 135	124.450 435	.008 035 3275	.263 149	32.748 953	.030 535 3275	6.11	.832 120	2.77	60
31	3.973 065	132.136 208	.007 567 9484	.251 695	33.258 006	.030 067 9484	6.02	.864 213	2.79	62
32	4.153 864	140.171 731	.007 134 1061	.240 740	33.744 902	.029 634 1061	5.93	.896 583	2.80	64
33	4.342 891	148.572 921	.006 730 7016	.230 261	34.210 605	.029 230 7016	5.85	.929 226	2.82	66
34	4.540 519	157.356 417	.006 354 9998	.220 239	34.656 039	.028 854 9998	5.78	.962 140	2.83	68
35	4.747 141	166.539 618	.006 004 5773	.210 653	35.082 085	.028 504 5773	5.71	.995 320	2.84	70
36	4.963 166	176.140 711	.005 677 2792	.201 484	35.489 587	.028 177 2792	5.64	1.028 764	2.86	72
37	5.189 021	186.178 714	.005 371 1833	.192 715	35.879 352	.027 871 1833	5.58	1.062 468	2.87	74
38	5.425 154	196.673 509	.005 084 5689	.184 327	36.252 153	.027 584 5689	5.52	1.096 427	2.89	76
39	5.672 032	207.645 883	.004 815 8913	.176 304	36.608 727	.027 315 8913	5.47	1.130 640	2.90	78
40	5.930 145	219.117 569	.004 563 7600	.168 630	36.949 781	.027 063 7600	5.42	1.165 101	2.91	80
41	6.200 004	231.111 288	.004 326 9198	.161 290	37.275 990	.026 826 9198	5.37	1.199 807	2.93	82
42	6.482 143	243.650 796	.004 104 2345	.154 270	37.588 001	.026 604 2345	5.33	1.234 756	2.94	84
43	6.777 121	256.760 930	.003 894 6735	.147 555	37.886 432	.026 394 6735	5.28	1.269 942	2.95	86
44	7.085 522	270.467 657	.003 697 2998	.141 133	38.171 873	.026 197 2998	5.24	1.305 362	2.97	88
45	7.407 958	284.798 126	.003 511 2591	.134 990	38.444 890	.026 011 2591	5.21	1.341 013	2.98	90
46	7.745 066	299.780 720	.003 335 7716	.129 114	38.706 024	.025 835 7716	5.17	1.376 891	2.99	92
47	8.097 515	315.445 117	.003 170 1236	.123 495	38.955 792	.025 670 1236	5.14	1.412 992	3.01	94
48	8.466 003	331.822 341	.003 013 6609	.118 119	39.194 689	.025 513 6609	5.11	1.449 311	3.02	96
49	8.851 259	348.944 831	.002 865 7825	.112 978	39.423 187	.025 365 7825	5.08	1.485 847	3.03	98
50	9.254 046	366.846 502	.002 725 9358	.108 061	39.641 741	.025 225 9358	5.05	1.522 594	3.05	100

Effective Rate is 4.55 %

Annual Percentage Rate is 4.50 %

SEMIANNUAL COMPOUND INTEREST AND ANNUITY

4.75 % S

	Amount Of 1	Amount Of 1 Per Period	Sinking Fund Payment	Present Worth Of 1	Present Worth of 1 Per Period	Periodic Payment To Amortize 1	Constant Annual Percent	Total Interest	Annual Add On Rate	
	What a single $ 1 deposit grows to in the future. The deposit is made at the beginning of the first period.	What a series of $ 1 deposits grow to in the future. A deposit is made at the end of each period.	The amount to be deposited at the end of each period that grows to $ 1 in the future.	What $ 1 to be paid in the future is worth today. Value today of a single $ 1 payment tomorrow.	What $ 1 to be paid at the end of each period is worth today. Value today of a series of $ 1 payments tomorrow.	The mortgage payment to amortize a loan of $ 1. An annuity, payable at the end of each period, worth $ 1 today.	The annual payment, including interest and principal, to amortize completely a loan of $ 100.	The total interest paid over the term on a loan of $1. The loan is amortized by regular periodic payments.	The average annual interest rate on a loan that is completely amortized by regular periodic payments.	
	$S = (1+i)^n$	$S\overline{n}\| = \dfrac{(1+i)^n - 1}{i}$	$\dfrac{1}{S\overline{n}\|} = \dfrac{i}{(1+i)^n - 1}$	$V^n = \dfrac{1}{(1+i)^n}$	$A\overline{n}\| = \dfrac{1-V^n}{i}$	$\dfrac{1}{A\overline{n}\|} = \dfrac{i}{1-V^n}$				

YEAR										PERIODS
	1.023 750	1.000 000	1.000 000 0000	.976 801	.976 801	1.023 750 0000	204.75	.023 750	4.75	1
	1.048 064	2.023 750	.494 132 1804	.954 140	1.930 941	.517 882 1804	103.58	.035 764	3.58	2

YEAR	Amount Of 1	Amount Of 1 Per Period	Sinking Fund Payment	Present Worth Of 1	Present Worth of 1 Per Period	Periodic Payment To Amortize 1	Constant Annual Percent	Total Interest	Annual Add On Rate	PERIODS
1	1.048 064	2.023 750	.494 132 1804	.954 140	1.930 941	.517 882 1804	103.58	.035 764	3.58	2
2	1.098 438	4.144 770	.241 267 9317	.910 383	3.773 330	.265 017 9317	53.01	.060 072	3.00	4
3	1.151 234	6.367 734	.157 041 7329	.868 633	5.531 226	.180 791 7329	36.16	.084 750	2.83	6
4	1.206 567	8.697 543	.114 974 9955	.828 798	7.208 506	.138 724 9955	27.75	.109 800	2.75	8
5	1.264 559	11.139 333	.089 771 9855	.790 789	8.808 866	.113 521 9855	22.71	.135 220	2.70	10
6	1.325 339	13.698 484	.073 000 7781	.754 524	10.335 834	.096 750 7781	19.36	.161 009	2.68	12
7	1.389 040	16.380 639	.061 047 6798	.719 922	11.792 775	.084 797 6798	16.96	.187 168	2.67	14
8	1.455 803	19.191 709	.052 105 8339	.686 906	13.182 902	.075 855 8339	15.18	.213 693	2.67	16
9	1.525 775	22.137 890	.045 171 4223	.655 405	14.509 277	.068 921 4223	13.79	.240 586	2.67	18
10	1.599 110	25.225 677	.039 642 1465	.625 348	15.774 825	.063 392 1465	12.68	.267 843	2.68	20
11	1.675 970	28.461 876	.035 134 7185	.596 670	16.982 335	.058 884 7185	11.78	.295 464	2.69	22
12	1.756 523	31.853 619	.031 393 6068	.569 306	18.134 469	.055 143 6068	11.03	.323 447	2.70	24
13	1.840 949	35.408 384	.028 241 8991	.543 198	19.233 766	.051 991 8991	10.40	.351 789	2.71	26
14	1.929 433	39.134 004	.025 553 2245	.518 287	20.282 649	.049 303 2245	9.87	.380 490	2.72	28
15	2.022 169	43.038 694	.023 234 9059	.494 519	21.283 431	.046 984 9059	9.40	.409 547	2.73	30
16	2.119 363	47.131 058	.021 217 4315	.471 840	22.238 317	.044 967 4315	9.00	.438 958	2.74	32
17	2.221 228	51.420 118	.019 447 6410	.450 201	23.149 412	.043 197 6410	8.64	.468 720	2.76	34
18	2.327 989	55.915 328	.017 884 1837	.429 555	24.018 725	.041 634 1837	8.33	.498 831	2.77	36
19	2.439 882	60.626 596	.016 494 4112	.409 856	24.848 171	.040 244 4112	8.05	.529 288	2.79	38
20	2.557 152	65.564 306	.015 252 2013	.391 060	25.639 578	.039 002 2013	7.81	.560 088	2.80	40
21	2.680 059	70.739 343	.014 136 4049	.373 126	26.394 692	.037 886 4049	7.58	.591 229	2.82	42
22	2.808 874	76.163 114	.013 129 7153	.356 015	27.115 177	.036 879 7153	7.38	.622 707	2.83	44
23	2.943 880	81.847 572	.012 217 8334	.339 688	27.802 620	.035 967 8334	7.20	.654 520	2.85	46
24	3.085 375	87.805 249	.011 388 8408	.324 110	28.458 537	.035 138 8408	7.03	.686 664	2.86	48
25	3.233 670	94.049 276	.010 632 7241	.309 246	29.084 374	.034 382 7241	6.88	.719 136	2.88	50
26	3.389 094	100.593 416	.009 941 0084	.295 064	29.681 510	.033 691 0084	6.74	.751 932	2.89	52
27	3.551 987	107.452 094	.009 306 4728	.281 533	30.251 261	.033 056 4728	6.62	.785 050	2.91	54
28	3.722 710	114.640 429	.008 722 9262	.268 622	30.794 884	.032 472 9262	6.50	.818 484	2.92	56
29	3.901 639	122.174 263	.008 185 0299	.256 303	31.313 576	.031 935 0299	6.39	.852 232	2.94	58
30	4.089 167	130.070 205	.007 688 1558	.244 549	31.808 482	.031 438 1558	6.29	.886 289	2.95	60
31	4.285 709	138.345 657	.007 228 2717	.233 334	32.280 690	.030 978 2717	6.20	.920 653	2.97	62
32	4.491 698	147.018 862	.006 801 8483	.222 633	32.731 244	.030 551 8483	6.12	.955 318	2.99	64
33	4.707 587	156.108 935	.006 405 7832	.212 423	33.161 135	.030 155 7832	6.04	.990 282	3.00	66
34	4.933 853	165.635 915	.006 037 3380	.202 681	33.571 311	.029 787 3380	5.96	1.025 539	3.02	68
35	5.170 994	175.620 800	.005 694 0864	.193 386	33.962 677	.029 444 0864	5.89	1.061 086	3.03	70
36	5.419 533	186.085 599	.005 373 8710	.184 518	34.336 095	.029 123 8710	5.83	1.096 919	3.05	72
37	5.680 018	197.053 379	.005 074 7671	.176 056	34.692 388	.028 824 7671	5.77	1.133 033	3.06	74
38	5.953 022	208.548 315	.004 795 0519	.167 982	35.032 341	.028 545 0519	5.71	1.169 424	3.08	76
39	6.239 149	220.595 744	.004 533 1790	.160 278	35.356 704	.028 283 1790	5.66	1.206 088	3.09	78
40	6.539 028	233.222 222	.004 287 7561	.152 928	35.666 192	.028 037 7561	5.61	1.243 020	3.11	80
41	6.853 320	246.455 579	.004 057 5263	.145 915	35.961 487	.027 807 5263	5.57	1.280 217	3.12	82
42	7.182 718	260.324 986	.003 841 3524	.139 223	36.243 240	.027 591 3524	5.52	1.317 674	3.14	84
43	7.527 949	274.861 012	.003 638 2024	.132 838	36.512 071	.027 388 2024	5.48	1.355 385	3.15	86
44	7.889 773	290.095 699	.003 447 1383	.126 746	36.768 574	.027 197 1383	5.44	1.393 348	3.17	88
45	8.268 987	306.062 627	.003 267 3052	.120 934	37.013 314	.027 017 3052	5.41	1.431 557	3.18	90
46	8.666 429	322.796 990	.003 097 9223	.115 388	37.246 830	.026 847 9223	5.37	1.470 009	3.20	92
47	9.082 972	340.335 674	.002 938 2756	.110 096	37.469 637	.026 688 2756	5.34	1.508 698	3.21	94
48	9.519 537	358.717 340	.002 787 7102	.105 047	37.682 226	.026 537 7102	5.31	1.547 620	3.22	96
49	9.977 084	377.982 502	.002 645 6251	.100 230	37.885 066	.026 395 6251	5.28	1.586 771	3.24	98
50	10.456 624	398.173 627	.002 511 4672	.095 633	38.078 604	.026 261 4672	5.26	1.626 147	3.25	100

Effective Rate is 4.81 %

Annual Percentage Rate is 4.75 %

SEMIANNUAL COMPOUND INTEREST AND ANNUITY

Amount Of 1	Amount Of 1 Per Period	Sinking Fund Payment	Present Worth Of 1	Present Worth of 1 Per Period	Periodic Payment To Amortize 1	Constant Annual Percent	Total Interest	Annual Add On Rate
What a single $ 1 deposit grows to in the future. The deposit is made at the beginning of the first period.	What a series of $ 1 deposits grow to in the future. A deposit is made at the end of each period.	The amount to be deposited at the end of each period that grows to $ 1 in the future.	What $ 1 to be paid in the future is worth today. Value today of a single $ 1 payment tomorrow.	What $ 1 to be paid at the end of each period is worth today. Value today of a series of $ 1 payments tomorrow.	The mortgage payment to amortize a loan of $ 1. An annuity certain, payable at the end of each period, worth $ 1 today.	The annual payment, including interest and principal, to amortize completely a loan of $ 100.	The total interest paid over the term of $1. The loan is amortized by regular periodic payments.	The average annual interest rate on a loan that is completely amortized by regular periodic payments.
$S = (1+i)^n$	$S\overline{n} = \dfrac{(1+i)^n - 1}{i}$	$\dfrac{1}{S\overline{n}} = \dfrac{i}{(1+i)^n - 1}$	$V^n = \dfrac{1}{(1+i)^n}$	$A\overline{n} = \dfrac{1-V^n}{i}$	$\dfrac{1}{A\overline{n}} = \dfrac{i}{1-V^n}$			

YEAR									PERIODS
	1.025 000	1.000 000	1.000 000 0000	.975 610	.975 610	1.025 000 0000	205.00	.025 000	5.00	1
	1.050 625	2.025 000	.493 827 1605	.951 814	1.927 424	.518 827 1605	103.77	.037 654	3.77	2

YEAR	Amount Of 1	Amount Of 1 Per Period	Sinking Fund Payment	Present Worth Of 1	Present Worth of 1 Per Period	Periodic Payment To Amortize 1	Constant Annual Percent	Total Interest	Annual Add On Rate	PERIODS
1	1.050 625	2.025 000	.493 827 1605	.951 814	1.927 424	.518 827 1605	103.77	.037 654	3.77	2
2	1.103 813	4.152 516	.240 817 8777	.905 951	3.761 974	.265 817 8777	53.17	.063 272	3.16	4
3	1.159 693	6.387 737	.156 549 9711	.862 297	5.508 125	.181 549 9711	36.31	.089 300	2.98	6
4	1.218 403	8.736 116	.114 467 3458	.820 747	7.170 137	.139 467 3458	27.90	.115 739	2.89	8
5	1.280 085	11.203 582	.089 258 7632	.781 198	8.752 064	.114 258 7632	22.86	.142 588	2.85	10
6	1.344 889	13.795 553	.072 487 1270	.743 556	10.257 765	.097 487 1270	19.50	.169 846	2.83	12
7	1.412 974	16.518 953	.060 536 5249	.707 727	11.690 912	.085 536 5249	17.11	.197 511	2.82	14
8	1.484 506	19.380 225	.051 598 9886	.673 625	13.055 003	.076 598 9886	15.32	.225 584	2.82	16
9	1.559 659	22.386 349	.044 670 0805	.641 166	14.353 364	.069 670 0805	13.94	.254 061	2.82	18
10	1.638 616	25.544 658	.039 147 1287	.610 271	15.589 162	.064 147 1287	12.83	.282 943	2.83	20
11	1.721 571	28.862 856	.034 646 6061	.580 865	16.765 413	.059 646 6061	11.93	.312 225	2.84	22
12	1.808 726	32.349 038	.030 912 8204	.552 875	17.884 986	.055 912 8204	11.19	.341 908	2.85	24
13	1.900 293	36.011 708	.027 768 7467	.526 235	18.950 611	.052 768 7467	10.56	.371 987	2.86	26
14	1.996 495	39.859 801	.025 087 9327	.500 878	19.964 889	.050 087 9327	10.02	.402 462	2.87	28
15	2.097 568	43.902 703	.022 777 6407	.476 743	20.930 293	.047 777 6407	9.56	.433 329	2.89	30
16	2.203 757	48.150 278	.020 768 3123	.453 771	21.849 178	.045 768 3123	9.16	.464 586	2.90	32
17	2.315 322	52.612 885	.019 006 7508	.431 905	22.723 786	.044 006 7508	8.81	.496 230	2.92	34
18	2.432 535	57.301 413	.017 451 5767	.411 094	23.556 251	.042 451 5767	8.50	.528 257	2.93	36
19	2.555 682	62.227 297	.016 070 1180	.391 285	24.348 603	.041 070 1180	8.22	.560 664	2.95	38
20	2.685 064	67.402 554	.014 836 2332	.372 431	25.102 775	.039 836 2332	7.97	.593 449	2.97	40
21	2.820 995	72.839 808	.013 728 7567	.354 485	25.820 607	.038 728 7567	7.75	.626 608	2.98	42
22	2.963 808	78.552 323	.012 730 3683	.337 404	26.503 849	.037 730 3683	7.55	.660 136	3.00	44
23	3.113 851	84.554 034	.011 826 7568	.321 146	27.154 170	.036 826 7568	7.37	.694 031	3.02	46
24	3.271 490	90.859 582	.011 005 9938	.305 671	27.773 154	.036 005 9938	7.21	.728 288	3.03	48
25	3.437 109	97.484 349	.010 258 0569	.290 942	28.362 312	.035 258 0569	7.06	.762 903	3.05	50
26	3.611 112	104.444 494	.009 574 4635	.276 923	28.923 081	.034 574 4635	6.92	.797 872	3.07	52
27	3.793 925	111.756 996	.008 947 9856	.263 579	29.456 829	.033 947 9856	6.79	.833 191	3.09	54
28	3.985 992	119.439 694	.008 372 4260	.250 879	29.964 858	.033 372 4260	6.68	.868 856	3.10	56
29	4.187 783	127.511 329	.007 842 4404	.238 790	30.448 407	.032 842 4404	6.57	.904 862	3.12	58
30	4.399 790	135.991 590	.007 353 3959	.227 284	30.908 656	.032 353 3959	6.48	.941 204	3.14	60
31	4.622 529	144.901 164	.006 901 2558	.216 332	31.346 728	.031 901 2558	6.39	.977 878	3.15	62
32	4.856 545	154.261 786	.006 482 4869	.205 908	31.763 691	.031 482 4869	6.30	1.014 879	3.17	64
33	5.102 407	164.096 289	.006 093 9830	.195 986	32.160 563	.031 093 9830	6.22	1.052 203	3.19	66
34	5.360 717	174.428 663	.005 733 0027	.186 542	32.538 311	.030 733 0027	6.15	1.089 844	3.21	68
35	5.632 103	185.284 114	.005 397 1168	.177 554	32.897 857	.030 397 1168	6.08	1.127 798	3.22	70
36	5.917 228	196.689 122	.005 084 1652	.168 998	33.240 078	.030 084 1652	6.02	1.166 060	3.24	72
37	6.216 788	208.671 509	.004 792 2211	.160 855	33.565 809	.029 792 2211	5.96	1.204 624	3.26	74
38	6.531 513	221.260 504	.004 519 5594	.153 104	33.877 844	.029 519 5594	5.91	1.243 487	3.27	76
39	6.862 170	234.486 818	.004 264 6321	.145 726	34.170 940	.029 264 6321	5.86	1.282 641	3.29	78
40	7.209 568	248.382 713	.004 026 0451	.138 705	34.451 817	.029 026 0451	5.81	1.322 084	3.31	80
41	7.574 552	262.982 087	.003 802 5404	.132 021	34.719 160	.028 802 5404	5.77	1.361 808	3.32	82
42	7.958 014	278.320 556	.003 592 9793	.125 659	34.973 620	.028 592 9793	5.72	1.401 810	3.34	84
43	8.360 888	294.435 534	.003 396 3292	.119 605	35.215 819	.028 396 3292	5.68	1.442 084	3.35	86
44	8.784 158	311.366 333	.003 211 6510	.113 841	35.446 348	.028 211 6510	5.65	1.482 625	3.37	88
45	9.228 856	329.154 253	.003 038 0893	.108 356	35.665 768	.028 038 0893	5.61	1.523 428	3.39	90
46	9.696 067	347.842 687	.002 874 8628	.103 135	35.874 616	.027 874 8628	5.58	1.564 487	3.40	92
47	10.186 931	367.477 223	.002 721 2571	.098 165	36.073 400	.027 721 2571	5.55	1.605 798	3.42	94
48	10.702 644	388.105 758	.002 576 6173	.093 435	36.262 606	.027 576 6173	5.52	1.647 355	3.43	96
49	11.244 465	409.778 612	.002 440 3421	.088 933	36.442 694	.027 440 3421	5.49	1.689 154	3.45	98
50	11.813 716	432.548 654	.002 311 8787	.084 647	36.614 105	.027 311 8787	5.47	1.731 188	3.46	100

Effective Rate is 5.06 %

Annual Percentage Rate is 5.00 %

	Amount Of 1	Amount Of 1 Per Period	Sinking Fund Payment	Present Worth Of 1	Present Worth of 1 Per Period	Periodic Payment To Amortize 1	Constant Annual Percent	Total Interest	Annual Add On Rate	
	What a single $ 1 deposit grows to in the future. The deposit is made at the beginning of the first period.	What a series of $ 1 deposits grow to in the future. A deposit is made at the end of each period.	The amount to be deposited at the end of each period that grows to $ 1 in the future.	What $ 1 to be paid in the future is worth today. Value today of a single $ 1 payment tomorrow.	What $ 1 to be paid at the end of each period is worth today. Value today of a series of $ 1 payments tomorrow.	The mortgage payment to amortize a loan of $ 1. An annuity certain, payable at the end of each period, worth $ 1 today.	The annual payment, including interest and principal, to amortize completely a loan of $ 100.	The total interest paid over the term on a loan of $1. The loan is amortized by regular periodic payments.	The average annual interest rate on a loan that is completely amortized by regular periodic payments.	
	$S = (1+i)^n$	$S\overline{n} = \dfrac{(1+i)^n - 1}{i}$	$\dfrac{1}{S\overline{n}} = \dfrac{i}{(1+i)^n - 1}$	$V^n = \dfrac{1}{(1+i)^n}$	$A\overline{n} = \dfrac{1-V^n}{i}$	$\dfrac{1}{A\overline{n}} = \dfrac{i}{1-V^n}$				

YEAR										PERIODS
	1.026 250	1.000 000	1.000 000 0000	.974 421	.974 421	1.026 250 0000	205.25	.026 250	5.25	1
	1.053 189	2.026 250	.493 522 5170	.949 497	1.923 919	.519 772 5170	103.96	.039 545	3.95	2
1	1.053 189	2.026 250	.493 522 5170	.949 497	1.923 919	.519 772 5170	103.96	.039 545	3.95	2
2	1.109 207	4.160 274	.240 368 7639	.901 545	3.750 674	.266 618 7639	53.33	.066 475	3.32	4
3	1.168 205	6.407 805	.156 059 6699	.856 014	5.485 173	.182 309 6699	36.47	.093 858	3.13	6
4	1.230 341	8.774 881	.113 961 6647	.812 783	7.132 074	.140 211 6647	28.05	.121 693	3.04	8
5	1.295 781	11.267 858	.088 748 0102	.771 735	8.695 803	.114 998 0102	23.00	.149 980	3.00	10
6	1.364 703	13.893 435	.071 976 4402	.732 760	10.180 558	.098 226 4402	19.65	.178 717	2.98	12
7	1.437 290	16.658 664	.060 028 8239	.695 754	11.590 330	.086 278 8239	17.26	.207 904	2.97	14
8	1.513 738	19.570 973	.051 096 0810	.660 616	12.928 903	.077 346 0810	15.47	.237 537	2.97	16
9	1.594 252	22.638 184	.044 173 1540	.627 253	14.199 875	.070 423 1540	14.09	.267 617	2.97	18
10	1.679 049	25.868 538	.038 656 9971	.595 575	15.406 659	.064 906 9971	12.99	.298 140	2.98	20
11	1.768 356	29.270 711	.034 163 8434	.565 497	16.552 498	.060 413 8434	12.09	.329 105	2.99	22
12	1.862 413	32.853 843	.030 437 8394	.536 938	17.640 468	.056 687 8394	11.34	.360 508	3.00	24
13	1.961 473	36.627 558	.027 301 8473	.509 821	18.673 492	.053 551 8473	10.72	.392 348	3.02	26
14	2.065 802	40.601 994	.024 629 3325	.484 073	19.654 346	.050 879 3325	10.18	.424 621	3.03	28
15	2.175 680	44.787 826	.022 327 4961	.459 626	20.585 664	.048 577 4961	9.72	.457 325	3.05	30
16	2.291 403	49.196 298	.020 326 7327	.436 414	21.469 947	.046 576 7327	9.32	.490 455	3.07	32
17	2.413 280	53.839 253	.018 573 8089	.414 374	22.309 572	.044 823 8089	8.97	.524 010	3.08	34
18	2.541 641	58.729 162	.017 027 3159	.393 447	23.106 793	.043 277 3159	8.66	.557 983	3.10	36
19	2.676 828	63.879 162	.015 654 5574	.373 576	23.863 753	.041 904 5574	8.39	.592 373	3.12	38
20	2.819 206	69.303 084	.014 429 3722	.354 710	24.582 484	.040 679 3722	8.14	.627 175	3.14	40
21	2.969 157	75.015 500	.013 330 5783	.336 796	25.264 916	.039 580 5783	7.92	.662 384	3.15	42
22	3.127 084	81.031 754	.012 340 8410	.319 787	25.912 884	.038 590 8410	7.72	.697 997	3.17	44
23	3.293 410	87.368 008	.011 445 8373	.303 637	26.528 128	.037 695 8373	7.54	.734 009	3.19	46
24	3.468 584	94.041 280	.010 633 6281	.288 302	27.112 300	.036 883 6281	7.38	.770 414	3.21	48
25	3.653 074	101.069 497	.009 894 1820	.273 742	27.666 970	.036 144 1820	7.23	.807 209	3.23	50
26	3.847 378	108.471 539	.009 219 0081	.259 917	28.193 627	.035 469 0081	7.10	.844 388	3.25	52
27	4.052 016	116.267 289	.008 600 8714	.246 791	28.693 687	.034 850 8714	6.98	.881 947	3.27	54
28	4.267 539	124.477 687	.008 033 5683	.234 327	29.168 492	.034 283 5683	6.86	.919 880	3.29	56
29	4.494 526	133.124 788	.007 511 7490	.222 493	29.619 319	.033 761 7490	6.76	.958 181	3.30	58
30	4.733 585	142.231 821	.007 030 7755	.211 256	30.047 377	.033 280 7755	6.66	.996 847	3.32	60
31	4.985 360	151.823 248	.006 586 6065	.200 587	30.453 817	.032 836 6065	6.57	1.035 870	3.34	62
32	5.250 527	161.924 834	.006 175 7049	.190 457	30.839 730	.032 425 7049	6.49	1.075 245	3.36	64
33	5.529 798	172.563 715	.005 794 9610	.180 838	31.206 154	.032 044 9610	6.41	1.114 967	3.38	66
34	5.823 922	183.768 467	.005 441 6300	.171 706	31.554 073	.031 691 6300	6.34	1.155 031	3.40	68
35	6.133 691	195.569 189	.005 113 2799	.163 034	31.884 420	.031 363 2799	6.28	1.195 430	3.42	70
36	6.459 937	207.997 581	.004 807 7482	.154 800	32.198 084	.031 057 7482	6.22	1.236 158	3.43	72
37	6.803 534	221.087 027	.004 523 1057	.146 982	32.495 908	.030 773 1057	6.16	1.277 210	3.45	74
38	7.165 408	234.872 689	.004 257 6257	.139 559	32.778 690	.030 507 6257	6.11	1.318 582	3.47	76
39	7.546 529	249.391 597	.004 009 7582	.132 511	33.047 191	.030 259 7582	6.06	1.360 261	3.49	78
40	7.947 922	264.682 753	.003 778 1079	.125 819	33.302 132	.030 028 1079	6.01	1.402 249	3.51	80
41	8.370 665	280.787 230	.003 561 4155	.119 465	33.544 197	.029 811 4155	5.97	1.444 536	3.52	82
42	8.815 893	297.748 290	.003 358 5415	.113 432	33.774 038	.029 608 5415	5.93	1.487 117	3.54	84
43	9.284 802	315.611 492	.003 168 4524	.107 703	33.992 271	.029 418 4524	5.89	1.529 987	3.56	86
44	9.778 652	334.424 821	.002 990 2087	.102 264	34.199 482	.029 240 2087	5.85	1.573 138	3.58	88
45	10.298 769	354.238 814	.002 822 9543	.097 099	34.396 229	.029 072 9543	5.82	1.616 566	3.59	90
46	10.846 551	375.106 694	.002 665 9082	.092 195	34.583 040	.028 915 9082	5.79	1.660 264	3.61	92
47	11.423 469	397.084 518	.002 518 3556	.087 539	34.760 416	.028 768 3556	5.76	1.704 225	3.63	94
48	12.031 072	420.231 321	.002 379 6418	.083 118	34.928 834	.028 629 6418	5.73	1.748 446	3.64	96
49	12.670 994	444.609 281	.002 249 1658	.078 920	35.088 746	.028 499 1658	5.70	1.792 918	3.66	98
50	13.344 952	470.283 882	.002 126 3752	.074 935	35.240 583	.028 376 3752	5.68	1.837 638	3.68	100

Effective Rate is 5.32 %

Annual Percentage Rate is 5.25 %

Amount Of 1	Amount Of 1 Per Period	Sinking Fund Payment	Present Worth Of 1	Present Worth of 1 Per Period	Periodic Payment To Amortize 1	Constant Annual Percent	Total Interest	Annual Add On Rate
What a single $ 1 deposit grows to in the future. The deposit is made at the beginning of the first period.	What a series of $ 1 deposits grow to in the future. A deposit is made at the end of each period.	The amount to be deposited at the end of each period that grows to $ 1 in the future.	What $ 1 to be paid in the future is worth today. Value today of a single $ 1 payment tomorrow.	What $ 1 to be paid at the end of each period is worth today. Value today of a series of $ 1 payments tomorrow.	The mortgage payment to amortize a loan of $ 1. An annuity certain, payable at the end of each period, worth $ 1 today.	The annual payment, including interest and principal, to amortize completely a loan of $ 100.	The total interest paid over the term on a loan of $1. The loan is amortized by regular periodic payments.	The average annual interest rate on a loan that is completely amortized by regular periodic payments.
$S = (1+i)^n$	$S\overline{n}| = \dfrac{(1+i)^n - 1}{i}$	$\dfrac{1}{S\overline{n}|} = \dfrac{i}{(1+i)^n - 1}$	$V^n = \dfrac{1}{(1+i)^n}$	$A\overline{n}| = \dfrac{1 - V^n}{i}$	$\dfrac{1}{A\overline{n}|} = \dfrac{i}{1 - V^n}$			

YEAR									PERIODS
	1.027 500	1.000 000	1.000 000 0000	.973 236	.973 236	1.027 500 0000	205.50	.027 500	5.50	1
	1.055 756	2.027 500	.493 218 2491	.947 188	1.920 424	.520 718 2491	104.15	.041 437	4.14	2

YEAR	Amount Of 1	Amount Of 1 Per Period	Sinking Fund Payment	Present Worth Of 1	Present Worth of 1 Per Period	Periodic Payment To Amortize 1	Constant Annual Percent	Total Interest	Annual Add On Rate	PERIODS
1	1.055 756	2.027 500	.493 218 2491	.947 188	1.920 424	.520 718 2491	104.15	.041 437	4.14	2
2	1.114 621	4.168 046	.239 920 5884	.897 166	3.739 428	.267 420 5884	53.49	.069 682	3.48	4
3	1.176 768	6.427 940	.155 570 8264	.849 785	5.462 367	.183 070 8264	36.62	.098 425	3.28	6
4	1.242 381	8.813 838	.113 457 9478	.804 906	7.094 314	.140 957 9478	28.20	.127 664	3.19	8
5	1.311 651	11.332 765	.088 239 7205	.762 398	8.640 076	.115 739 7205	23.15	.157 397	3.15	10
6	1.384 784	13.992 137	.071 468 7098	.722 134	10.104 204	.098 968 7098	19.80	.187 625	3.13	12
7	1.461 994	16.799 786	.059 524 5664	.683 997	11.491 008	.087 024 5664	17.41	.218 344	3.12	14
8	1.543 509	19.763 979	.050 597 0977	.647 874	12.804 573	.078 097 0977	15.62	.249 554	3.12	16
9	1.629 570	22.893 445	.043 680 6259	.613 659	14.048 767	.071 180 6259	14.24	.281 251	3.13	18
10	1.720 428	26.197 398	.038 171 7306	.581 251	15.227 252	.065 671 7306	13.14	.313 435	3.13	20
11	1.816 353	29.685 566	.033 686 4049	.550 554	16.343 500	.061 186 4049	12.24	.346 101	3.15	22
12	1.917 626	33.368 222	.029 968 6330	.521 478	17.400 797	.057 468 6330	11.50	.379 247	3.16	24
13	2.024 546	37.256 209	.026 841 1636	.493 938	18.402 256	.054 341 1636	10.87	.412 870	3.18	26
14	2.137 427	41.360 975	.024 177 3795	.467 852	19.350 826	.051 677 3795	10.34	.446 967	3.19	28
15	2.256 602	45.694 608	.021 884 4200	.443 144	20.249 301	.049 384 4200	9.88	.481 533	3.21	30
16	2.382 421	50.269 868	.019 892 6322	.419 741	21.100 326	.047 392 6322	9.48	.516 564	3.23	32
17	2.515 256	55.100 228	.018 148 7453	.397 574	21.906 407	.045 648 7453	9.13	.552 057	3.25	34
18	2.655 498	60.199 910	.016 611 3206	.376 577	22.669 918	.044 111 3206	8.83	.588 008	3.27	36
19	2.803 558	65.583 931	.015 247 6374	.356 690	23.393 106	.042 747 6374	8.55	.624 410	3.29	38
20	2.959 874	71.268 145	.014 031 5144	.337 852	24.078 101	.041 531 5144	8.31	.661 261	3.31	40
21	3.124 905	77.269 289	.012 941 7522	.320 010	24.726 921	.040 441 7522	8.09	.698 554	3.33	42
22	3.299 138	83.605 035	.011 961 0021	.303 109	25.341 475	.039 461 0021	7.90	.736 284	3.35	44
23	3.483 086	90.294 039	.011 074 9283	.287 102	25.923 574	.038 574 9283	7.72	.774 447	3.37	46
24	3.677 290	97.355 996	.010 271 5811	.271 939	26.474 931	.037 771 5811	7.56	.813 036	3.39	48
25	3.882 322	104.811 701	.009 540 9195	.257 578	26.997 170	.037 040 9195	7.41	.852 046	3.41	50
26	4.098 785	112.683 108	.008 874 4446	.243 975	27.491 829	.036 374 4446	7.28	.891 471	3.43	52
27	4.327 318	120.993 396	.008 264 9139	.231 090	27.960 364	.035 764 9139	7.16	.931 305	3.45	54
28	4.568 593	129.767 034	.007 706 1174	.218 886	28.404 155	.035 206 1174	7.05	.971 543	3.47	56
29	4.823 321	139.029 857	.007 192 6996	.207 326	28.824 508	.034 692 6996	6.94	1.012 177	3.49	58
30	5.092 251	148.809 140	.006 720 0173	.196 377	29.222 662	.034 220 0173	6.85	1.053 201	3.51	60
31	5.376 176	159.133 680	.006 284 0249	.186 006	29.599 789	.033 784 0249	6.76	1.094 610	3.53	62
32	5.675 932	170.033 877	.005 881 1810	.176 183	29.956 999	.033 381 1810	6.68	1.136 396	3.55	64
33	5.992 400	181.541 829	.005 508 3724	.166 878	30.295 344	.033 008 3724	6.61	1.178 553	3.57	66
34	6.326 514	193.691 420	.005 162 8513	.158 065	30.615 821	.032 662 8513	6.54	1.221 074	3.59	68
35	6.679 257	206.518 427	.004 842 1829	.149 717	30.919 372	.032 342 1829	6.47	1.263 953	3.61	70
36	7.051 667	220.060 621	.004 544 2024	.141 810	31.206 893	.032 044 2024	6.41	1.307 183	3.63	72
37	7.444 842	234.357 876	.004 266 9784	.134 321	31.479 229	.031 766 9784	6.36	1.350 756	3.65	74
38	7.859 938	249.452 292	.004 008 7826	.127 227	31.737 183	.031 508 7826	6.31	1.394 667	3.67	76
39	8.298 179	265.388 316	.003 768 0634	.120 508	31.981 514	.031 268 0634	6.26	1.438 909	3.69	78
40	8.760 854	282.212 873	.003 543 4245	.114 144	32.212 941	.031 043 4245	6.21	1.483 474	3.71	80
41	9.249 326	299.975 505	.003 333 6055	.108 116	32.432 146	.030 833 6055	6.17	1.528 356	3.73	82
42	9.765 034	318.728 514	.003 137 4664	.102 406	32.639 775	.030 637 4664	6.13	1.573 547	3.75	84
43	10.309 496	338.527 121	.002 953 9731	.096 998	32.836 438	.030 453 9731	6.10	1.619 042	3.77	86
44	10.884 315	359.429 624	.002 782 1858	.091 875	33.022 715	.030 282 1858	6.06	1.664 832	3.78	88
45	11.491 183	381.497 572	.002 621 2487	.087 023	33.199 155	.030 121 2487	6.03	1.710 912	3.80	90
46	12.131 889	404.795 946	.002 470 3805	.082 427	33.366 276	.029 970 3805	6.00	1.757 275	3.82	92
47	12.808 317	429.393 350	.002 328 8670	.078 074	33.524 572	.029 828 8670	5.97	1.803 914	3.84	94
48	13.522 461	455.362 213	.002 196 0540	.073 951	33.674 508	.029 696 0540	5.94	1.850 821	3.86	96
49	14.276 423	482.779 002	.002 071 3411	.070 046	33.816 525	.029 571 3411	5.92	1.897 991	3.87	98
50	15.072 422	511.724 449	.001 954 1767	.066 346	33.951 042	.029 454 1767	5.90	1.945 418	3.89	100

Effective Rate is 5.58 %

Annual Percentage Rate is 5.50 %

SEMIANNUAL COMPOUND INTEREST AND ANNUITY

5.75 % S

	Amount Of 1	Amount Of 1 Per Period	Sinking Fund Payment	Present Worth Of 1	Present Worth of 1 Per Period	Periodic Payment To Amortize 1	Constant Annual Percent	Total Interest	Annual Add On Rate	
	What a single $ 1 deposit grows to in the future. The deposit is made at the beginning of the first period.	What a series of $ 1 deposits grow to in the future. A deposit is made at the end of each period.	The amount to be deposited at the end of each period that grows to $ 1 in the future.	What $ 1 to be paid in the future is worth today. Value today of a single $ 1 payment tomorrow.	What $ 1 to be paid at the end of each period is worth today. Value today of a series of $ 1 payments tomorrow.	The mortgage payment to amortize a loan of $ 1. An annuity certain, payable at the end of each period, worth $ 1 today.	The annual payment, including interest and principal, to amortize completely a loan of $ 100.	The total interest paid over the term on a loan that is amortized by regular periodic payments.	The average annual interest rate on a loan that is completely amortized by regular periodic payments.	
	$S = (1+i)^n$	$S\overline{n}| = \dfrac{(1+i)^n - 1}{i}$	$\dfrac{1}{S\overline{n}|} = \dfrac{i}{(1+i)^n - 1}$	$V^n = \dfrac{1}{(1+i)^n}$	$A\overline{n}| = \dfrac{1 - V^n}{i}$	$\dfrac{1}{A\overline{n}|} = \dfrac{i}{1 - V^n}$				

YEAR										PERIODS
	1.028 750	1.000 000	1.000 000 0000	.972 053	.972 053	1.028 750 0000	205.75	.028 750	5.75	1
	1.058 327	2.028 750	.492 914 3561	.944 888	1.916 941	.521 664 3561	104.34	.043 329	4.33	2
1	1.058 327	2.028 750	.492 914 3561	.944 888	1.916 941	.521 664 3561	104.34	.043 329	4.33	2
2	1.120 055	4.175 830	.239 473 3494	.892 813	3.728 236	.268 223 3494	53.65	.072 893	3.64	4
3	1.185 384	6.448 142	.155 083 4376	.843 608	5.439 707	.183 833 4376	36.77	.103 001	3.43	6
4	1.254 523	8.852 990	.112 956 1906	.797 115	7.056 855	.141 706 1906	28.35	.133 650	3.34	8
5	1.327 695	11.398 104	.087 733 8880	.753 185	8.584 878	.116 483 8880	23.30	.164 839	3.30	10
6	1.405 135	14.091 666	.070 963 9277	.711 675	10.028 689	.099 713 9277	19.95	.196 567	3.28	12
7	1.487 092	16.942 335	.059 023 7416	.672 453	11.392 929	.087 773 7416	17.56	.228 832	3.27	14
8	1.573 829	19.959 273	.050 102 0250	.635 393	12.681 982	.078 852 0250	15.78	.261 632	3.27	16
9	1.665 625	23.152 179	.043 192 4790	.600 375	13.899 994	.071 942 4790	14.39	.294 965	3.28	18
10	1.762 775	26.531 316	.037 691 3080	.567 287	15.050 878	.066 441 3080	13.29	.328 826	3.29	20
11	1.865 592	30.107 546	.033 214 2642	.536 023	16.138 334	.061 964 2642	12.40	.363 214	3.30	22
12	1.974 406	33.892 366	.029 505 1694	.506 482	17.165 859	.058 255 1694	11.66	.398 124	3.32	24
13	2.089 566	37.897 941	.026 386 6576	.478 568	18.136 754	.055 136 6576	11.03	.433 553	3.34	26
14	2.211 443	42.137 148	.023 732 0286	.452 193	19.054 142	.052 482 0286	10.50	.469 497	3.35	28
15	2.340 429	46.623 613	.021 448 3593	.427 272	19.920 970	.050 198 3593	10.04	.505 951	3.37	30
16	2.476 938	51.371 758	.019 465 9486	.403 724	20.740 025	.048 215 9486	9.65	.542 910	3.39	32
17	2.621 409	56.396 846	.017 731 4880	.381 474	21.513 941	.046 481 4880	9.30	.580 371	3.41	34
18	2.774 307	61.715 030	.016 203 5082	.360 450	22.245 205	.044 953 5082	9.00	.618 326	3.44	36
19	2.936 123	67.343 406	.014 849 2639	.340 585	22.936 167	.043 599 2639	8.72	.656 772	3.46	38
20	3.107 377	73.300 065	.013 642 5527	.321 815	23.589 049	.042 392 5527	8.48	.695 702	3.48	40
21	3.288 619	79.604 156	.012 562 1582	.304 079	24.205 949	.041 312 1582	8.27	.735 111	3.50	42
22	3.480 433	86.275 943	.011 590 7166	.287 321	24.788 851	.040 340 7166	8.07	.774 992	3.52	44
23	3.683 435	93.336 872	.010 713 8795	.271 486	25.339 627	.039 463 8795	7.90	.815 338	3.55	46
24	3.898 277	100.809 641	.009 919 6862	.256 524	25.860 050	.038 669 6862	7.74	.856 145	3.57	48
25	4.125 650	108.718 271	.009 198 0860	.242 386	26.351 790	.037 948 0860	7.59	.897 404	3.59	50
26	4.366 285	117.088 184	.008 540 5715	.229 028	26.816 430	.037 290 5715	7.46	.939 110	3.61	52
27	4.620 956	125.946 285	.007 939 8928	.216 405	27.255 463	.036 689 8928	7.34	.981 254	3.63	54
28	4.890 480	135.321 049	.007 389 8334	.204 479	27.670 299	.036 139 8334	7.23	1.023 831	3.66	56
29	5.175 725	145.242 610	.006 885 0319	.193 210	28.062 273	.035 635 0319	7.13	1.066 832	3.68	58
30	5.477 607	155.742 862	.006 420 8400	.182 561	28.432 645	.035 170 8400	7.04	1.110 250	3.70	60
31	5.797 097	166.855 558	.005 993 2076	.172 500	28.782 604	.034 743 2076	6.95	1.154 079	3.72	62
32	6.135 222	178.616 419	.005 598 5894	.162 993	29.113 277	.034 348 5894	6.87	1.198 310	3.74	64
33	6.493 068	191.063 251	.005 233 8689	.154 010	29.425 726	.033 983 8689	6.80	1.242 935	3.77	66
34	6.871 787	204.236 064	.004 896 2949	.145 523	29.720 954	.033 646 2949	6.73	1.287 948	3.79	68
35	7.272 595	218.177 201	.004 583 4303	.137 503	29.999 913	.033 333 4303	6.67	1.333 340	3.81	70
36	7.696 780	232.931 477	.004 293 1080	.129 924	30.263 497	.033 043 1080	6.61	1.379 104	3.83	72
37	8.145 707	248.546 320	.004 023 3949	.122 764	30.512 555	.032 773 3949	6.56	1.425 231	3.85	74
38	8.620 818	265.071 922	.003 772 5610	.115 998	30.747 886	.032 522 5610	6.51	1.471 715	3.87	76
39	9.123 640	282.561 406	.003 539 0537	.109 605	30.970 248	.032 289 0537	6.46	1.518 546	3.89	78
40	9.655 791	301.070 992	.003 321 4758	.103 565	31.180 355	.032 071 4758	6.42	1.565 718	3.91	80
41	10.218 980	320.660 178	.003 118 5662	.097 857	31.378 883	.031 868 5662	6.38	1.613 222	3.93	82
42	10.815 018	341.391 934	.002 929 1846	.092 464	31.566 469	.031 679 1846	6.34	1.661 052	3.95	84
43	11.445 821	363.332 902	.002 752 2968	.087 368	31.743 717	.031 502 2968	6.31	1.709 198	3.97	86
44	12.113 416	386.553 611	.002 586 9633	.082 553	31.911 197	.031 336 9633	6.27	1.757 653	3.99	88
45	12.819 950	411.128 704	.002 432 3283	.078 003	32.069 446	.031 182 3283	6.24	1.806 410	4.01	90
46	13.567 694	437.137 178	.002 287 6114	.073 704	32.218 974	.031 037 6114	6.21	1.855 460	4.03	92
47	14.359 051	464.662 637	.002 152 0990	.069 642	32.360 261	.030 902 0990	6.19	1.904 797	4.05	94
48	15.196 565	493.793 562	.002 025 1378	.065 804	32.493 762	.030 775 1378	6.16	1.954 413	4.07	96
49	16.082 928	524.623 593	.001 906 1285	.062 178	32.619 905	.030 656 1285	6.14	2.004 301	4.09	98
50	17.020 990	557.251 834	.001 794 5208	.058 751	32.739 096	.030 544 5208	6.11	2.054 452	4.11	100

Effective Rate is 5.83 %

Annual Percentage Rate is 5.75 %

SEMIANNUAL COMPOUND INTEREST AND ANNUITY

	Amount Of 1	Amount Of 1 Per Period	Sinking Fund Payment	Present Worth Of 1	Present Worth of 1 Per Period	Periodic Payment To Amortize 1	Constant Annual Percent	Total Interest	Annual Add On Rate	
	What a single $ 1 deposit grows to in the future. The deposit is made at the beginning of the first period.	What a series of $ 1 deposits grow to in the future. A deposit is made at the end of each period.	The amount to be deposited at the end of each period that grows to $ 1 in the future.	What $ 1 to be paid in the future is worth today. Value today of a single $ 1 payment tomorrow.	What $ 1 to be paid at the end of each period is worth today. Value today of a series of $ 1 payments tomorrow.	The mortgage payment to amortize a loan of $ 1. An annuity certain, payable at the end of each period, worth $ 1 today.	The annual payment, including interest and principal, to amortize completely a loan of $ 100.	The total interest paid over the term on a loan of $1. The loan is amortized by regular periodic payments.	The average annual interest rate on a loan that is completely amortized by regular periodic payments.	
	$S = (1+i)^n$	$S\overline{n}| = \dfrac{(1+i)^n - 1}{i}$	$\dfrac{1}{S\overline{n}|} = \dfrac{i}{(1+i)^n - 1}$	$V^n = \dfrac{1}{(1+i)^n}$	$A\overline{n}| = \dfrac{1 - V^n}{i}$	$\dfrac{1}{A\overline{n}|} = \dfrac{i}{1 - V^n}$				

YEAR										PERIODS
	1.030 000	1.000 000	1.000 000 0000	.970 874	.970 874	1.030 000 0000	206.00	.030 000	6.00	1
	1.060 900	2.030 000	.492 610 8374	.942 596	1.913 470	.522 610 8374	104.53	.045 222	4.52	2

YEAR	Amount Of 1	Amount Of 1 Per Period	Sinking Fund Payment	Present Worth Of 1	Present Worth of 1 Per Period	Periodic Payment To Amortize 1	Constant Annual Percent	Total Interest	Annual Add On Rate	PERIODS
1	1.060 900	2.030 000	.492 610 8374	.942 596	1.913 470	.522 610 8374	104.53	.045 222	4.52	2
2	1.125 509	4.183 627	.239 027 0452	.888 487	3.717 098	.269 027 0452	53.81	.076 108	3.81	4
3	1.194 052	6.468 410	.154 597 5005	.837 484	5.417 191	.184 597 5005	36.92	.107 585	3.59	6
4	1.266 770	8.892 336	.112 456 3888	.789 409	7.019 692	.142 456 3888	28.50	.139 651	3.49	8
5	1.343 916	11.463 879	.087 230 5066	.744 094	8.530 203	.117 230 5066	23.45	.172 305	3.45	10
6	1.425 761	14.192 030	.070 462 0855	.701 380	9.954 004	.100 462 0855	20.10	.205 545	3.43	12
7	1.512 590	17.086 324	.058 526 3390	.661 118	11.296 073	.088 526 3390	17.71	.239 369	3.42	14
8	1.604 706	20.156 881	.049 610 8493	.623 167	12.561 102	.079 610 8493	15.93	.273 774	3.42	16
9	1.702 433	23.414 435	.042 708 6959	.587 395	13.753 513	.072 708 6959	14.55	.308 757	3.43	18
10	1.806 111	26.870 374	.037 215 7076	.553 676	14.877 475	.067 215 7076	13.45	.344 314	3.44	20
11	1.916 103	30.536 780	.032 747 3948	.521 893	15.936 917	.062 747 3948	12.55	.380 443	3.46	22
12	2.032 794	34.426 470	.029 047 4159	.491 934	16.935 542	.059 047 4159	11.81	.417 138	3.48	24
13	2.156 591	38.553 042	.025 938 2903	.463 695	17.876 842	.055 938 2903	11.19	.454 396	3.50	26
14	2.287 928	42.930 923	.023 293 2334	.437 077	18.764 108	.053 293 2334	10.66	.492 211	3.52	28
15	2.427 262	47.575 416	.021 019 2593	.411 987	19.600 441	.051 019 2593	10.21	.530 578	3.54	30
16	2.575 083	52.502 759	.019 046 6183	.388 337	20.388 766	.049 046 6183	9.81	.569 492	3.56	32
17	2.731 905	57.730 177	.017 321 9633	.366 045	21.131 837	.047 321 9633	9.47	.608 947	3.58	34
18	2.898 278	63.275 944	.015 803 7942	.345 032	21.832 252	.045 803 7942	9.17	.648 937	3.61	36
19	3.074 783	69.159 449	.014 459 3401	.325 226	22.492 462	.044 459 3401	8.90	.689 455	3.63	38
20	3.262 038	75.401 260	.013 262 3779	.306 557	23.114 772	.043 262 3779	8.66	.730 495	3.65	40
21	3.460 696	82.023 196	.012 191 6731	.288 959	23.701 359	.042 191 6731	8.44	.772 050	3.68	42
22	3.671 452	89.048 409	.011 229 8469	.272 372	24.254 274	.041 229 8469	8.25	.814 113	3.70	44
23	3.895 044	96.501 457	.010 362 5378	.256 737	24.775 449	.040 362 5378	8.08	.856 677	3.72	46
24	4.132 252	104.408 396	.009 577 7738	.241 999	25.266 707	.039 577 7738	7.92	.899 733	3.75	48
25	4.383 906	112.796 867	.008 865 4944	.228 107	25.729 764	.038 865 4944	7.78	.943 275	3.77	50
26	4.650 886	121.696 197	.008 217 1837	.215 013	26.166 240	.038 217 1837	7.65	.987 294	3.80	52
27	4.934 125	131.137 495	.007 625 5841	.202 670	26.577 660	.037 625 5841	7.53	1.031 782	3.82	54
28	5.234 613	141.153 768	.007 084 4726	.191 036	26.965 464	.037 084 4726	7.42	1.076 730	3.85	56
29	5.553 401	151.780 033	.006 588 4819	.180 070	27.331 005	.036 588 4819	7.32	1.122 132	3.87	58
30	5.891 603	163.053 437	.006 132 9587	.169 733	27.675 564	.036 132 9587	7.23	1.167 978	3.89	60
31	6.250 402	175.013 391	.005 713 8485	.159 990	28.000 343	.035 713 8485	7.15	1.214 259	3.92	62
32	6.631 051	187.701 707	.005 327 6021	.150 806	28.306 478	.035 327 6021	7.07	1.260 967	3.94	64
33	7.034 882	201.162 741	.004 971 0995	.142 149	28.595 040	.034 971 0995	7.00	1.308 093	3.96	66
34	7.463 307	215.443 551	.004 641 5871	.133 989	28.867 038	.034 641 5871	6.93	1.355 628	3.99	68
35	7.917 822	230.594 064	.004 336 6251	.126 297	29.123 421	.034 336 6251	6.87	1.403 564	4.01	70
36	8.400 017	246.667 242	.004 054 0446	.119 047	29.365 088	.034 054 0446	6.82	1.451 891	4.03	72
37	8.911 578	263.719 277	.003 791 9109	.112 214	29.592 881	.033 791 9109	6.76	1.500 601	4.06	74
38	9.454 293	281.809 781	.003 548 4929	.105 772	29.807 598	.033 548 4929	6.71	1.549 685	4.08	76
39	10.030 060	301.001 997	.003 322 2371	.099 700	30.009 990	.033 322 2371	6.67	1.599 135	4.10	78
40	10.640 891	321.363 019	.003 111 7457	.093 977	30.200 763	.033 111 7457	6.63	1.648 940	4.12	80
41	11.288 921	342.964 026	.002 915 7577	.088 582	30.380 586	.032 915 7577	6.59	1.699 092	4.14	82
42	11.976 416	365.880 536	.002 733 1325	.083 497	30.550 086	.032 733 1325	6.55	1.749 583	4.17	84
43	12.705 780	390.192 660	.002 562 8365	.078 704	30.709 855	.032 562 8365	6.52	1.800 404	4.19	86
44	13.479 562	415.985 393	.002 403 9306	.074 186	30.860 454	.032 403 9306	6.49	1.851 546	4.21	88
45	14.300 467	443.348 904	.002 255 5599	.069 928	31.002 407	.032 255 5599	6.46	1.903 000	4.23	90
46	15.171 366	472.378 852	.002 116 9449	.065 914	31.136 212	.032 116 9449	6.43	1.954 759	4.25	92
47	16.095 302	503.176 733	.001 987 3733	.062 130	31.262 336	.031 987 3733	6.40	2.006 813	4.27	94
48	17.075 506	535.850 186	.001 866 1932	.058 563	31.381 219	.031 866 1932	6.38	2.059 155	4.29	96
49	18.115 404	570.513 463	.001 752 8070	.055 202	31.493 279	.031 752 8070	6.36	2.111 775	4.31	98
50	19.218 632	607.287 733	.001 646 6659	.052 033	31.598 905	.031 646 6659	6.33	2.164 667	4.33	100

Effective Rate is 6.09 %

Annual Percentage Rate is 6.00 %

SEMIANNUAL COMPOUND INTEREST AND ANNUITY   6.25 % S

	Amount Of 1	Amount Of 1 Per Period	Sinking Fund Payment	Present Worth Of 1	Present Worth of 1 Per Period	Periodic Payment To Amortize 1	Constant Annual Percent	Total Interest	Annual Add On Rate	
	What a single $ 1 deposit grows to in the future. The deposit is made at the beginning of the first period.	What a series of $ 1 deposits grow to in the future. A deposit is made at the end of each period.	The amount to be deposited at the end of each period that grows to $ 1 in the future.	What $ 1 to be paid in the future is worth today. Value today of a single $ 1 payment tomorrow.	What $ 1 to be paid at the end of each period is worth today. Value today of a series of $ 1 payments tomorrow.	The mortgage payment to amortize a loan of $ 1. An annuity certain, payable at the end of each period, worth $ 1 today.	The annual payment, including interest and principal, to amortize completely a loan of $ 100.	The total interest paid over the term on a loan of $1. The loan is amortized by regular periodic payments.	The average annual interest rate on a loan that is completely amortized by regular periodic payments.	

$$S = (1+i)^n \qquad S\overline{n}| = \frac{(1+i)^n - 1}{i} \qquad \frac{1}{S\overline{n}|} = \frac{i}{(1+i)^n - 1} \qquad V^n = \frac{1}{(1+i)^n} \qquad A\overline{n}| = \frac{1 - V^n}{i} \qquad \frac{1}{A\overline{n}|} = \frac{i}{1 - V^n}$$

YEAR										PERIODS
	1.031 250	1.000 000	1.000 000 0000	.969 697	.969 697	1.031 250 0000	206.25	.031 250	6.25	1
	1.063 477	2.031 250	.492 307 6923	.940 312	1.910 009	.523 557 6923	104.72	.047 115	4.71	2

YEAR	Amount Of 1	Amount Of 1 Per Period	Sinking Fund Payment	Present Worth Of 1	Present Worth of 1 Per Period	Periodic Payment To Amortize 1	Constant Annual Percent	Total Interest	Annual Add On Rate	PERIODS
1	1.063 477	2.031 250	.492 307 6923	.940 312	1.910 009	.523 557 6923	104.72	.047 115	4.71	2
2	1.130 982	4.191 437	.238 581 6739	.884 187	3.706 014	.269 831 6739	53.97	.079 327	3.97	4
3	1.202 773	6.488 745	.154 113 0120	.831 412	5.394 820	.185 363 0120	37.08	.112 178	3.74	6
4	1.279 121	8.931 878	.111 958 5380	.781 787	6.982 824	.143 208 5380	28.65	.145 668	3.64	8
5	1.360 315	11.530 093	.086 729 5701	.735 124	8.476 044	.117 979 5701	23.60	.179 796	3.60	10
6	1.446 664	14.293 234	.069 963 1750	.691 246	9.880 137	.101 213 1750	20.25	.214 558	3.58	12
7	1.538 493	17.231 769	.058 032 3475	.649 987	11.200 422	.089 282 3475	17.86	.249 953	3.57	14
8	1.636 151	20.356 832	.049 123 5563	.611 191	12.441 903	.080 373 5563	16.08	.285 977	3.57	16
9	1.740 008	23.680 264	.042 229 2588	.574 710	13.609 283	.073 479 2588	14.70	.322 627	3.58	18
10	1.850 458	27.214 656	.036 744 9071	.540 407	14.706 984	.067 994 9071	13.60	.359 898	3.60	20
11	1.967 919	30.973 399	.032 285 7692	.508 151	15.739 166	.063 535 7692	12.71	.397 787	3.62	22
12	2.092 835	34.970 734	.028 595 3396	.477 821	16.709 739	.059 845 3396	11.97	.436 288	3.64	24
13	2.225 681	39.221 805	.025 496 0216	.449 301	17.622 381	.056 746 0216	11.35	.475 397	3.66	26
14	2.366 960	43.742 721	.022 860 9465	.422 483	18.480 549	.054 110 9465	10.83	.515 107	3.68	28
15	2.517 207	48.550 608	.020 597 0642	.397 266	19.287 495	.051 847 0642	10.37	.555 412	3.70	30
16	2.676 990	53.663 684	.018 634 5760	.373 554	20.046 276	.049 884 5760	9.98	.596 306	3.73	32
17	2.846 916	59.101 320	.016 920 0958	.351 257	20.759 768	.048 170 0958	9.64	.637 783	3.75	34
18	3.027 629	64.884 119	.015 412 0918	.330 291	21.430 672	.046 662 0918	9.34	.679 835	3.78	36
19	3.219 812	71.033 990	.014 077 7676	.310 577	22.061 532	.045 327 7676	9.07	.722 455	3.80	38
20	3.424 195	77.574 233	.012 890 8783	.292 039	22.654 737	.044 140 8783	8.83	.765 635	3.83	40
21	3.641 551	84.529 629	.011 830 1714	.274 608	23.212 535	.043 080 1714	8.62	.809 367	3.85	42
22	3.872 704	91.926 529	.010 878 2525	.258 218	23.737 040	.042 128 2525	8.43	.853 643	3.88	44
23	4.118 530	99.792 959	.010 020 7470	.242 805	24.230 237	.041 270 7470	8.26	.898 454	3.91	46
24	4.379 960	108.158 723	.009 245 6713	.228 313	24.693 997	.040 495 6713	8.10	.943 792	3.93	48
25	4.657 985	117.055 517	.008 542 9549	.214 685	25.130 077	.039 792 9549	7.96	.989 648	3.96	50
26	4.953 658	126.517 049	.007 904 0731	.201 871	25.540 127	.039 154 0731	7.84	1.036 012	3.98	52
27	5.268 099	136.579 167	.007 321 7609	.189 822	25.925 703	.038 571 7609	7.72	1.082 875	4.01	54
28	5.602 500	147.279 993	.006 789 7885	.178 492	26.288 264	.038 039 7885	7.61	1.130 228	4.04	56
29	5.958 127	158.660 070	.006 302 7830	.167 838	26.629 185	.037 552 7830	7.52	1.178 061	4.06	58
30	6.336 329	170.762 516	.005 856 0861	.157 820	26.949 757	.037 106 0861	7.43	1.226 365	4.09	60
31	6.738 537	183.633 184	.005 445 6389	.148 400	27.251 195	.036 695 6389	7.34	1.275 130	4.11	62
32	7.166 276	197.320 837	.005 067 8885	.139 542	27.534 640	.036 317 8885	7.27	1.324 345	4.14	64
33	7.621 167	211.877 335	.004 719 7120	.131 214	27.801 168	.035 969 7120	7.20	1.374 001	4.16	66
34	8.104 932	227.357 830	.004 398 3530	.123 382	28.051 787	.035 648 3530	7.13	1.424 088	4.19	68
35	8.619 405	243.820 974	.004 101 3699	.116 017	28.287 447	.035 351 3699	7.08	1.474 596	4.21	70
36	9.166 536	261.329 141	.003 826 5920	.109 092	28.509 041	.035 076 5920	7.02	1.525 515	4.24	72
37	9.748 396	279.948 667	.003 572 0835	.102 581	28.717 409	.034 822 0835	6.97	1.576 834	4.26	74
38	10.367 190	299.750 096	.003 336 1124	.096 458	28.913 339	.034 586 1124	6.92	1.628 545	4.29	76
39	11.025 264	320.808 451	.003 117 1249	.090 701	29.097 575	.034 367 1249	6.88	1.680 636	4.31	78
40	11.725 110	343.203 519	.002 913 7230	.085 287	29.270 815	.034 163 7230	6.84	1.733 098	4.33	80
41	12.469 380	367.020 149	.002 724 6461	.080 196	29.433 714	.033 974 6461	6.80	1.785 921	4.36	82
42	13.260 893	392.348 576	.002 548 7540	.075 410	29.586 890	.033 798 7540	6.76	1.839 095	4.38	84
43	14.102 649	419.284 765	.002 385 0139	.070 909	29.730 923	.033 635 0139	6.73	1.892 611	4.40	86
44	14.997 837	447.930 771	.002 232 4878	.066 676	29.866 359	.033 482 4878	6.70	1.946 459	4.42	88
45	15.949 848	478.395 126	.002 090 3223	.062 697	29.993 711	.033 340 3223	6.67	2.000 629	4.45	90
46	16.962 289	510.793 254	.001 957 7392	.058 954	30.113 462	.033 207 7392	6.65	2.055 112	4.47	92
47	18.038 997	545.247 904	.001 834 0281	.055 435	30.226 065	.033 084 0281	6.62	2.109 899	4.49	94
48	19.184 051	581.889 617	.001 718 5390	.052 127	30.331 948	.032 968 5390	6.60	2.164 980	4.51	96
49	20.401 788	620.857 219	.001 610 6763	.049 015	30.431 510	.032 860 6763	6.58	2.220 346	4.53	98
50	21.696 823	662.298 352	.001 509 8935	.046 090	30.525 130	.032 759 8935	6.56	2.275 989	4.55	100

SEMIANNUAL COMPOUND INTEREST AND ANNUITY

6.50 % S

Amount Of 1	Amount Of 1 Per Period	Sinking Fund Payment	Present Worth Of 1	Present Worth of 1 Per Period	Periodic Payment To Amortize 1	Constant Annual Percent	Total Interest	Annual Add On Rate
What a single $ 1 deposit grows to in the future. The deposit is made at the beginning of the first period.	What a series of $ 1 deposits grow to in the future. A deposit is made at the end of each period.	The amount to be deposited at the end of each period that grows to $ 1 in the future.	What $ 1 to be paid in the future is worth today. Value today of a single $ 1 payment tomorrow.	What $ 1 to be paid at the end of each period is worth today. Value today of a series of $ 1 payments tomorrow.	The mortgage payment to amortize a loan of $ 1. An annuity certain, payable at the end of each period, worth $ 1 today.	The annual payment, including interest and principal, to amortize completely a loan of $ 100.	The total interest paid over the term on a loan of $1. The loan is amortized by regular periodic payments.	The average annual interest rate on a loan that is completely amortized by regular periodic payments.
$S = (1+i)^n$	$S\overline{n}| = \dfrac{(1+i)^n - 1}{i}$	$\dfrac{1}{S\overline{n}|} = \dfrac{i}{(1+i)^n - 1}$	$V^n = \dfrac{1}{(1+i)^n}$	$A\overline{n}| = \dfrac{1-V^n}{i}$	$\dfrac{1}{A\overline{n}|} = \dfrac{i}{1-V^n}$			

YEAR									PERIODS
	1.032 500	1.000 000	1.000 000 0000	.968 523	.968 523	1.032 500 0000	206.50	.032 500	6.50	1
	1.066 056	2.032 500	.492 004 9200	.938 037	1.906 560	.524 504 9200	104.91	.049 010	4.90	2

YEAR	Amount Of 1	Amount Of 1 Per Period	Sinking Fund Payment	Present Worth Of 1	Present Worth of 1 Per Period	Periodic Payment To Amortize 1	Constant Annual Percent	Total Interest	Annual Add On Rate	PERIODS
1	1.066 056	2.032 500	.492 004 9200	.938 037	1.906 560	.524 504 9200	104.91	.049 010	4.90	2
2	1.136 476	4.199 259	.238 137 2337	.879 913	3.694 983	.270 637 2337	54.13	.082 549	4.13	4
3	1.211 547	6.509 147	.153 629 9692	.825 391	5.372 590	.186 129 9692	37.23	.116 780	3.89	6
4	1.291 578	8.971 616	.111 462 6337	.774 247	6.946 247	.143 962 6337	28.80	.151 701	3.79	8
5	1.376 894	11.596 748	.086 231 0724	.726 272	8.422 395	.118 731 0724	23.75	.187 311	3.75	10
6	1.467 847	14.395 285	.069 467 1878	.681 270	9.807 076	.101 967 1878	20.40	.223 606	3.73	12
7	1.564 807	17.378 684	.057 541 7561	.639 056	11.105 958	.090 041 7561	18.01	.260 585	3.72	14
8	1.668 173	20.559 155	.048 640 1319	.599 458	12.324 358	.081 140 1319	16.23	.298 242	3.73	16
9	1.778 366	23.949 715	.041 754 1496	.562 314	13.467 261	.074 254 1496	14.86	.336 575	3.74	18
10	1.895 838	27.564 244	.036 278 8839	.527 471	14.539 346	.068 778 8839	13.76	.375 578	3.76	20
11	2.021 070	31.417 534	.031 829 3596	.494 787	15.545 002	.064 329 3596	12.87	.415 246	3.78	22
12	2.154 574	35.525 359	.028 148 9063	.464 129	16.488 343	.060 648 9063	12.13	.455 574	3.80	24
13	2.296 897	39.904 531	.025 059 8109	.435 370	17.373 233	.057 559 8109	11.52	.496 555	3.82	26
14	2.448 622	44.572 975	.022 435 1193	.408 393	18.203 292	.054 935 1193	10.99	.538 183	3.84	28
15	2.610 368	49.549 798	.020 181 7169	.383 088	18.981 917	.052 681 7169	10.54	.580 452	3.87	30
16	2.782 800	54.855 372	.018 229 7552	.359 350	19.712 297	.050 729 7552	10.15	.623 352	3.90	32
17	2.966 621	60.511 412	.016 525 8084	.337 084	20.397 420	.049 025 8084	9.81	.666 877	3.92	34
18	3.162 585	66.541 069	.015 028 3128	.316 197	21.040 090	.047 528 3128	9.51	.711 019	3.95	36
19	3.371 493	72.969 023	.013 704 4456	.296 604	21.642 939	.046 204 4456	9.25	.755 769	3.98	38
20	3.594 201	79.821 583	.012 527 9400	.278 226	22.208 433	.045 027 9400	9.01	.801 118	4.01	40
21	3.831 621	87.126 797	.011 477 5251	.260 986	22.738 888	.043 977 5251	8.80	.847 056	4.03	42
22	4.084 723	94.914 566	.010 535 7906	.244 815	23.236 473	.043 035 7906	8.61	.893 575	4.06	44
23	4.354 545	103.216 767	.009 688 3484	.229 645	23.703 227	.042 188 3484	8.44	.940 664	4.09	46
24	4.642 190	112.067 379	.008 923 2032	.215 416	24.141 059	.041 423 2032	8.29	.988 314	4.12	48
25	4.948 835	121.502 630	.008 230 2745	.202 068	24.551 762	.040 730 2745	8.15	1.036 514	4.15	50
26	5.275 737	131.561 138	.007 601 0288	.189 547	24.937 016	.040 101 0288	8.03	1.085 254	4.17	52
27	5.624 232	142.284 074	.007 028 1935	.177 802	25.298 399	.039 528 1935	7.91	1.134 522	4.20	54
28	5.995 748	153.715 326	.006 505 5322	.166 785	25.637 389	.039 005 5322	7.81	1.184 310	4.23	56
29	6.391 805	165.901 684	.006 027 6664	.156 450	25.955 374	.038 527 6664	7.71	1.234 605	4.26	58
30	6.814 023	178.893 027	.005 589 9328	.146 756	26.253 656	.038 089 9328	7.62	1.285 396	4.28	60
31	7.264 132	192.742 530	.005 188 2685	.137 663	26.533 456	.037 688 2685	7.54	1.336 673	4.31	62
32	7.743 974	207.506 879	.004 819 1174	.129 133	26.795 918	.037 319 1174	7.47	1.388 424	4.34	64
33	8.255 511	223.246 505	.004 479 3534	.121 131	27.042 117	.036 979 3534	7.40	1.440 637	4.37	66
34	8.800 840	240.025 832	.004 166 2182	.113 626	27.273 061	.036 666 2182	7.34	1.493 303	4.39	68
35	9.382 190	257.913 538	.003 877 2684	.106 585	27.489 695	.036 377 2684	7.28	1.546 409	4.42	70
36	10.001 942	276.982 839	.003 610 3320	.099 981	27.692 905	.036 110 3320	7.23	1.599 944	4.44	72
37	10.662 633	297.311 787	.003 363 4724	.093 785	27.883 524	.035 863 4724	7.18	1.653 897	4.47	74
38	11.366 967	318.983 589	.003 134 9575	.087 974	28.062 332	.035 634 9575	7.13	1.708 257	4.50	76
39	12.117 826	342.086 948	.002 923 2334	.082 523	28.230 060	.035 423 2334	7.09	1.763 012	4.52	78
40	12.918 284	366.716 429	.002 726 9026	.077 410	28.387 395	.035 226 9026	7.05	1.818 152	4.55	80
41	13.771 617	392.972 841	.002 544 7051	.072 613	28.534 981	.035 044 7051	7.01	1.873 666	4.57	82
42	14.681 319	420.963 654	.002 375 5020	.068 114	28.673 422	.034 875 5020	6.98	1.929 542	4.59	84
43	15.651 112	450.803 434	.002 218 2617	.063 893	28.803 285	.034 718 2617	6.95	1.985 771	4.62	86
44	16.684 965	482.614 318	.002 072 0479	.059 934	28.925 102	.034 572 0479	6.92	2.042 340	4.64	88
45	17.787 112	516.526 510	.001 936 0091	.056 220	29.039 370	.034 436 0091	6.89	2.099 241	4.67	90
46	18.962 061	552.678 815	.001 809 3692	.052 737	29.146 557	.034 309 3692	6.87	2.156 462	4.69	92
47	20.214 624	591.219 205	.001 691 4200	.049 469	29.247 103	.034 191 4200	6.84	2.213 993	4.71	94
48	21.549 926	632.305 428	.001 581 5142	.046 404	29.341 419	.034 081 5142	6.82	2.271 825	4.73	96
49	22.973 434	676.105 654	.001 479 0588	.043 529	29.429 891	.033 979 0588	6.80	2.329 948	4.76	98
50	24.490 973	722.799 158	.001 383 5102	.040 831	29.512 881	.033 883 5102	6.78	2.388 351	4.78	100

Effective Rate is 6.61 %

Annual Percentage Rate is 6.50 %

Amount Of 1	Amount Of 1 Per Period	Sinking Fund Payment	Present Worth Of 1	Present Worth of 1 Per Period	Periodic Payment To Amortize 1	Constant Annual Percent	Total Interest	Annual Add On Rate
What a single $ 1 deposit grows to in the future. The deposit is made at the beginning of the first period.	What a series of $ 1 deposits grow to in the future. A deposit is made at the end of each period.	The amount to be deposited at the end of each period that grows to $ 1 in the future.	What $ 1 to be paid in the future is worth today. Value today of a single $ 1 payment tomorrow.	What $ 1 to be paid at the end of each period is worth today. Value today of a series of $ 1 payments tomorrow.	The mortgage payment to amortize a loan of $ 1. An annuity certain, payable at the end of each period, worth $ 1 today.	The annual payment, including interest and principal, to amortize completely a loan of $ 100.	The total interest paid over the term on a loan of $1. The loan is amortized by regular periodic payments.	The average annual interest rate on a loan that is completely amortized by regular periodic payments.
$S = (1+i)^n$	$S\overline{n}| = \dfrac{(1+i)^n - 1}{i}$	$\dfrac{1}{S\overline{n}|} = \dfrac{i}{(1+i)^n - 1}$	$V^n = \dfrac{1}{(1+i)^n}$	$A\overline{n}| = \dfrac{1-V^n}{i}$	$\dfrac{1}{A\overline{n}|} = \dfrac{i}{1-V^n}$			

YEAR									PERIODS
	1.033 750	1.000 000	1.000 000 0000	.967 352	.967 352	1.033 750 0000	206.75	.033 750	6.75	1
	1.068 639	2.033 750	.491 702 5200	.935 770	1.903 122	.525 452 5200	105.10	.050 905	5.09	2

YEAR	Amount Of 1	Amount Of 1 Per Period	Sinking Fund Payment	Present Worth Of 1	Present Worth of 1 Per Period	Periodic Payment To Amortize 1	Constant Annual Percent	Total Interest	Annual Add On Rate	PERIODS
1	1.068 639	2.033 750	.491 702 5200	.935 770	1.903 122	.525 452 5200	105.10	.050 905	5.09	2
2	1.141 989	4.207 095	.237 693 7228	.875 665	3.684 005	.271 443 7228	54.29	.085 775	4.29	4
3	1.220 375	6.529 616	.153 148 3691	.819 421	5.350 501	.186 898 3691	37.38	.121 390	4.05	6
4	1.304 140	9.011 552	.110 968 6713	.766 789	6.909 958	.144 718 6713	28.95	.157 749	3.94	8
5	1.393 655	11.663 847	.085 735 0071	.717 538	8.369 251	.119 485 0071	23.90	.194 850	3.90	10
6	1.489 314	14.498 192	.068 974 1154	.671 450	9.734 812	.102 724 1154	20.55	.232 689	3.88	12
7	1.591 539	17.527 085	.057 054 5536	.628 323	11.012 664	.090 804 5536	18.17	.271 264	3.88	14
8	1.700 781	20.763 877	.048 160 5616	.587 965	12.208 438	.081 910 5616	16.39	.310 569	3.88	16
9	1.817 521	24.222 841	.041 283 3498	.550 200	13.327 407	.075 033 3498	15.01	.350 600	3.90	18
10	1.942 274	27.919 224	.035 817 6149	.514 860	14.374 505	.069 567 6149	13.92	.391 352	3.91	20
11	2.075 590	31.869 323	.031 378 1376	.481 791	15.354 347	.065 128 1376	13.03	.432 819	3.93	22
12	2.218 056	36.090 553	.027 708 0816	.450 845	16.271 253	.061 458 0816	12.30	.474 994	3.96	24
13	2.370 301	40.601 525	.024 629 6167	.421 887	17.129 266	.058 379 6167	11.68	.517 870	3.98	26
14	2.532 997	45.422 126	.022 015 7023	.394 789	17.932 169	.055 765 7023	11.16	.561 440	4.01	28
15	2.706 859	50.573 608	.019 773 1592	.369 432	18.683 501	.053 523 1592	10.71	.605 695	4.04	30
16	2.892 656	56.078 683	.017 832 0878	.345 703	19.386 575	.051 582 0878	10.32	.650 627	4.07	32
17	3.091 205	61.961 621	.016 139 0225	.323 498	20.044 490	.049 889 0225	9.98	.696 227	4.10	34
18	3.303 382	68.248 359	.014 652 3670	.302 720	20.660 147	.048 402 3670	9.69	.742 485	4.13	36
19	3.530 123	74.966 612	.013 339 2716	.283 276	21.236 260	.047 089 2716	9.42	.789 392	4.15	38
20	3.772 428	82.146 000	.012 173 4473	.265 081	21.775 369	.045 923 4473	9.19	.836 938	4.18	40
21	4.031 363	89.818 175	.011 133 6041	.248 055	22.279 851	.044 883 6041	8.98	.885 111	4.21	42
22	4.308 072	98.016 960	.010 202 3160	.232 122	22.751 930	.043 952 3160	8.80	.933 902	4.25	44
23	4.603 774	106.778 502	.009 365 1810	.217 213	23.193 687	.043 115 1810	8.63	.983 298	4.28	46
24	4.919 773	116.141 428	.008 610 1920	.203 261	23.607 070	.042 360 1920	8.48	1.033 289	4.31	48
25	5.257 462	126.147 017	.007 927 2584	.190 206	23.993 901	.041 677 2584	8.34	1.083 863	4.34	50
26	5.618 329	136.839 380	.007 307 8378	.177 989	24.355 886	.041 057 8378	8.22	1.135 008	4.37	52
27	6.003 966	148.265 657	.006 744 6503	.166 557	24.694 620	.040 494 6503	8.10	1.186 711	4.40	54
28	6.416 073	160.476 223	.006 231 4528	.155 859	25.011 597	.039 981 4528	8.00	1.238 961	4.42	56
29	6.856 466	173.524 910	.005 762 8614	.145 848	25.308 215	.039 512 8614	7.91	1.291 746	4.45	58
30	7.327 087	187.469 247	.005 334 2082	.136 480	25.585 781	.039 084 2082	7.82	1.345 053	4.48	60
31	7.830 011	202.370 710	.004 941 4265	.127 714	25.845 519	.038 691 4265	7.74	1.398 868	4.51	62
32	8.367 456	218.294 996	.004 580 9570	.119 511	26.088 574	.038 330 9570	7.67	1.453 181	4.54	64
33	8.941 790	235.312 310	.004 249 6714	.111 834	26.316 017	.037 999 6714	7.60	1.507 978	4.57	66
34	9.555 547	253.497 677	.003 944 8093	.104 651	26.528 852	.037 694 8093	7.54	1.563 247	4.60	68
35	10.211 430	272.931 269	.003 663 9261	.097 929	26.728 016	.037 413 9261	7.49	1.618 975	4.63	70
36	10.912 333	293.698 766	.003 404 8492	.091 639	26.914 387	.037 154 8492	7.44	1.675 149	4.65	72
37	11.661 346	315.891 724	.003 165 6417	.085 753	27.088 788	.036 915 6417	7.39	1.731 757	4.68	74
38	12.461 770	339.607 986	.002 944 5715	.080 245	27.251 987	.036 694 5715	7.34	1.788 787	4.71	76
39	13.317 134	364.952 109	.002 740 0855	.075 091	27.404 704	.036 490 0855	7.30	1.846 227	4.73	78
40	14.231 209	392.035 830	.002 550 7873	.070 268	27.547 612	.036 300 7873	7.27	1.904 063	4.76	80
41	15.208 026	420.978 552	.002 375 4179	.065 755	27.681 341	.036 125 4179	7.23	1.962 284	4.79	82
42	16.251 891	451.907 875	.002 212 8404	.061 531	27.806 480	.035 962 8404	7.20	2.020 879	4.81	84
43	17.367 405	484.960 158	.002 062 0251	.057 579	27.923 581	.035 812 0251	7.17	2.079 834	4.84	86
44	18.559 488	520.281 119	.001 922 0378	.053 881	28.033 162	.035 672 0378	7.14	2.139 139	4.86	88
45	19.833 394	558.026 477	.001 792 0297	.050 420	28.135 703	.035 542 0297	7.11	2.198 783	4.89	90
46	21.194 739	598.362 641	.001 671 2273	.047 182	28.231 659	.035 421 2273	7.09	2.258 753	4.91	92
47	22.649 526	641.467 442	.001 558 9256	.044 151	28.321 451	.035 308 9256	7.07	2.319 039	4.93	94
48	24.204 168	687.530 915	.001 454 4800	.041 315	28.405 476	.035 204 4800	7.05	2.379 630	4.96	96
49	25.865 520	736.756 143	.001 357 3012	.038 662	28.484 103	.035 107 3012	7.03	2.440 516	4.98	98
50	27.640 905	789.360 144	.001 266 8489	.036 178	28.557 681	.035 016 8489	7.01	2.501 685	5.00	100

Effective Rate is 6.86 %   Annual Percentage Rate is 6.75 %

SEMIANNUAL COMPOUND INTEREST AND ANNUITY

7.00 % S

	Amount Of 1	Amount Of 1 Per Period	Sinking Fund Payment	Present Worth Of 1	Present Worth of 1 Per Period	Periodic Payment To Amortize 1	Constant Annual Percent	Total Interest	Annual Add On Rate	
	What a single $ 1 deposit grows to in the future. The deposit is made at the beginning of the first period.	What a series of $ 1 deposits grow to in the future. A deposit is made at the end of each period.	The amount to be deposited at the end of each period that grows to $ 1 in the future.	What $ 1 to be paid in the future is worth today. Value today of a single $ 1 payment tomorrow.	What $ 1 to be paid at the end of each period is worth today. Value today of a series of $ 1 payments tomorrow.	The mortgage payment to amortize a loan of $ 1. An annuity certain, payable at the end of each period, worth $ 1 today.	The annual payment, including interest and principal, to amortize completely a loan of $ 100.	The total interest paid over the term on a loan of $1. The loan is amortized by regular periodic payments.	The average annual interest rate on a loan that is completely amortized by regular periodic payments.	
	$S = (1+i)^n$	$S\overline{n} = \frac{(1+i)^n - 1}{i}$	$\frac{1}{S\overline{n}} = \frac{i}{(1+i)^n - 1}$	$V^n = \frac{1}{(1+i)^n}$	$A\overline{n} = \frac{1 - V^n}{i}$	$\frac{1}{A\overline{n}} = \frac{i}{1 - V^n}$				

YEAR										PERIODS
	1.035 000	1.000 000	1.000 000 0000	.966 184	.966 184	1.035 000 0000	207.00	.035 000	7.00	1
	1.071 225	2.035 000	.491 400 4914	.933 511	1.899 694	.526 400 4914	105.29	.052 801	5.28	2

YEAR										PERIODS
1	1.071 225	2.035 000	.491 400 4914	.933 511	1.899 694	.526 400 4914	105.29	.052 801	5.28	2
2	1.147 523	4.214 943	.237 251 1395	.871 442	3.673 079	.272 251 1395	54.46	.089 005	4.45	4
3	1.229 255	6.550 152	.152 668 2087	.813 501	5.328 553	.187 668 2087	37.54	.126 009	4.20	6
4	1.316 809	9.051 687	.110 476 6465	.759 412	6.873 956	.145 476 6465	29.10	.163 813	4.10	8
5	1.410 599	11.731 393	.085 241 3679	.708 919	8.316 605	.120 241 3679	24.05	.202 414	4.05	10
6	1.511 069	14.601 962	.068 483 9493	.661 783	9.663 334	.103 483 9493	20.70	.241 807	4.03	12
7	1.618 695	17.676 986	.056 570 7287	.617 782	10.920 520	.091 570 7287	18.32	.281 990	4.03	14
8	1.733 986	20.971 030	.047 684 8306	.576 706	12.094 117	.082 684 8306	16.54	.322 957	4.04	16
9	1.857 489	24.499 691	.040 816 8408	.538 361	13.189 682	.075 816 8408	15.17	.364 703	4.05	18
10	1.989 789	28.279 682	.035 361 0768	.502 566	14.212 403	.070 361 0768	14.08	.407 222	4.07	20
11	2.131 512	32.328 902	.030 932 0742	.469 151	15.167 125	.065 932 0742	13.19	.450 506	4.10	22
12	2.283 328	36.666 528	.027 272 8303	.437 957	16.058 368	.062 272 8303	12.46	.494 548	4.12	24
13	2.445 959	41.313 102	.024 205 3963	.408 838	16.890 352	.059 205 3963	11.85	.539 340	4.15	26
14	2.620 172	46.290 627	.021 602 6452	.381 654	17.667 019	.056 602 6452	11.33	.584 874	4.18	28
15	2.806 794	51.622 677	.019 371 3316	.356 278	18.392 045	.054 371 3316	10.88	.631 140	4.21	30
16	3.006 708	57.334 502	.017 441 5048	.332 590	19.068 865	.052 441 5048	10.49	.678 128	4.24	32
17	3.220 860	63.453 152	.015 759 6583	.310 476	19.700 684	.050 759 6583	10.16	.725 828	4.27	34
18	3.450 266	70.007 603	.014 284 1628	.289 833	20.290 494	.049 284 1628	9.86	.774 230	4.30	36
19	3.696 011	77.028 895	.012 982 1414	.270 562	20.841 087	.047 982 1414	9.60	.823 321	4.33	38
20	3.959 260	84.550 278	.011 827 2823	.252 572	21.355 072	.046 827 2823	9.37	.873 091	4.37	40
21	4.241 258	92.607 371	.010 798 2765	.235 779	21.834 883	.045 798 2765	9.16	.923 528	4.40	42
22	4.543 342	101.238 331	.009 877 6816	.220 102	22.282 791	.044 877 6816	8.98	.974 618	4.43	44
23	4.866 941	110.484 031	.009 051 0817	.205 468	22.700 918	.044 051 0817	8.82	1.026 350	4.46	46
24	5.213 589	120.388 257	.008 306 4580	.191 806	23.091 244	.043 306 4580	8.67	1.078 710	4.49	48
25	5.584 927	130.997 910	.007 633 7096	.179 053	23.455 618	.042 633 7096	8.53	1.131 685	4.53	50
26	5.982 713	142.363 236	.007 024 2854	.167 148	23.795 765	.042 024 2854	8.41	1.185 263	4.56	52
27	6.408 832	154.538 058	.006 470 8979	.156 035	24.113 295	.041 470 8979	8.30	1.239 428	4.59	54
28	6.865 301	167.580 031	.005 967 2981	.145 660	24.409 713	.040 967 2981	8.20	1.294 169	4.62	56
29	7.354 282	181.550 919	.005 508 0966	.135 975	24.686 423	.040 508 0966	8.11	1.349 470	4.65	58
30	7.878 091	196.516 883	.005 088 6213	.126 934	24.944 734	.040 088 6213	8.02	1.405 317	4.68	60
31	8.439 208	212.548 798	.004 704 8020	.118 495	25.185 870	.039 704 8020	7.95	1.461 698	4.72	62
32	9.040 291	229.722 586	.004 353 0765	.110 616	25.410 974	.039 353 0765	7.88	1.518 597	4.75	64
33	9.684 185	248.119 577	.004 030 3148	.103 261	25.621 110	.039 030 3148	7.81	1.576 001	4.78	66
34	10.373 941	267.826 894	.003 733 7550	.096 395	25.817 275	.038 733 7550	7.75	1.633 895	4.81	68
35	11.112 825	288.937 865	.003 460 9517	.089 986	26.000 397	.038 460 9517	7.70	1.692 267	4.84	70
36	11.904 336	311.552 464	.003 209 7323	.084 003	26.171 343	.038 209 7323	7.65	1.751 101	4.86	72
37	12.752 223	335.777 788	.002 978 1601	.078 418	26.330 923	.037 978 1601	7.60	1.810 384	4.89	74
38	13.660 500	361.728 561	.002 764 5038	.073 204	26.479 892	.037 764 5038	7.56	1.870 102	4.92	76
39	14.633 469	389.527 678	.002 567 2117	.068 336	26.618 957	.037 567 2117	7.52	1.930 243	4.95	78
40	15.675 738	419.306 787	.002 384 8887	.063 793	26.748 776	.037 384 8887	7.48	1.990 791	4.98	80
41	16.792 242	451.206 913	.002 216 2781	.059 551	26.869 963	.037 216 2781	7.45	2.051 735	5.00	82
42	17.988 269	485.379 125	.002 060 2452	.055 592	26.983 092	.037 060 2452	7.42	2.113 061	5.03	84
43	19.269 484	521.985 253	.001 915 7629	.051 896	27.088 699	.036 915 7629	7.39	2.174 756	5.06	86
44	20.641 953	561.198 653	.001 781 9002	.048 445	27.187 285	.036 781 9002	7.36	2.236 807	5.08	88
45	22.112 176	603.205 027	.001 657 8111	.045 224	27.279 316	.036 657 8111	7.34	2.299 203	5.11	90
46	23.687 116	648.203 305	.001 542 7259	.042 217	27.365 227	.036 542 7259	7.31	2.361 931	5.13	92
47	25.374 230	696.406 585	.001 435 9428	.039 410	27.445 427	.036 435 9428	7.29	2.424 979	5.16	94
48	27.181 510	748.043 145	.001 336 8213	.036 790	27.520 294	.036 336 8213	7.27	2.488 335	5.18	96
49	29.117 513	803.357 517	.001 244 7758	.034 344	27.590 183	.036 244 7758	7.25	2.551 988	5.21	98
50	31.191 408	862.611 657	.001 159 2702	.032 060	27.655 425	.036 159 2702	7.24	2.615 927	5.23	100

Effective Rate is 7.12 %

Annual Percentage Rate is 7.00 %

SEMIANNUAL COMPOUND INTEREST AND ANNUITY

	Amount Of 1	Amount Of 1 Per Period	Sinking Fund Payment	Present Worth Of 1	Present Worth of 1 Per Period	Periodic Payment To Amortize 1	Constant Annual Percent	Total Interest	Annual Add On Rate	
	What a single $ 1 deposit grows to in the future. The deposit is made at the beginning of the first period.	What a series of $ 1 deposits grow to in the future. A deposit is made at the end of each period.	The amount to be deposited at the end of each period that grows to $ 1 in the future.	What $ 1 to be paid in the future is worth today. Value today of a single $ 1 payment tomorrow.	What $ 1 to be paid at the end of each period is worth today. Value today of a series of $ 1 payments tomorrow.	The mortgage payment to amortize a loan of $ 1. An annuity certain, payable at the end of each period, worth $ 1 today.	The annual payment, including interest and principal, to amortize completely a loan of $ 100.	The total interest paid over the term on a loan of $1. The loan is amortized by regular periodic payments.	The average annual interest rate on a loan that is completely amortized by regular periodic payments.	

$$S = (1+i)^n \qquad S\overline{n}| = \frac{(1+i)^n - 1}{i} \qquad \frac{1}{S\overline{n}|} = \frac{i}{(1+i)^n - 1} \qquad V^n = \frac{1}{(1+i)^n} \qquad A\overline{n}| = \frac{1-V^n}{i} \qquad \frac{1}{A\overline{n}|} = \frac{i}{1-V^n}$$

YEAR									**PERIODS**	
	1.036 250	1.000 000	1.000 000 0000	.965 018	.965 018	1.036 250 0000	207.25	.036 250	7.25	1
	1.073 814	2.036 250	.491 098 8336	.931 260	1.896 278	.527 348 8336	105.47	.054 698	5.47	2
1	1.073 814	2.036 250	.491 098 8336	.931 260	1.896 278	.527 348 8336	105.47	.054 698	5.47	2
2	1.153 077	4.222 804	.236 809 4819	.867 245	3.662 206	.273 059 4819	54.62	.092 238	4.61	4
3	1.238 190	6.570 756	.152 189 4848	.807 631	5.306 743	.188 439 4848	37.69	.130 637	4.35	6
4	1.329 586	9.092 020	.109 986 5548	.752 114	6.838 235	.146 236 5548	29.25	.169 892	4.25	8
5	1.427 728	11.799 389	.084 750 1484	.700 414	8.264 453	.121 000 1484	24.21	.210 001	4.20	10
6	1.533 114	14.706 600	.067 996 6807	.652 267	9.592 632	.104 246 6807	20.85	.250 960	4.18	12
7	1.646 280	17.828 404	.056 090 2699	.607 430	10.829 511	.092 340 2699	18.47	.292 764	4.18	14
8	1.767 798	21.180 641	.047 212 9241	.565 675	11.981 368	.083 462 9241	16.70	.335 407	4.19	16
9	1.898 287	24.780 320	.040 354 6036	.526 791	13.054 046	.076 604 6036	15.33	.378 883	4.21	18
10	2.038 407	28.645 706	.034 909 2457	.490 579	14.052 988	.071 159 2457	14.24	.423 185	4.23	20
11	2.188 870	32.796 412	.030 491 1400	.456 857	14.983 262	.066 741 1400	13.35	.468 305	4.26	22
12	2.350 439	37.253 499	.026 843 1163	.425 452	15.849 590	.063 093 1163	12.62	.514 235	4.29	24
13	2.523 935	42.039 581	.023 787 1068	.396 207	16.656 366	.060 037 1068	12.01	.560 965	4.32	26
14	2.710 237	47.178 943	.021 195 8966	.368 971	17.407 684	.057 445 8966	11.49	.608 485	4.35	28
15	2.910 290	52.697 663	.018 976 1737	.343 608	18.107 356	.055 226 1737	11.05	.656 785	4.38	30
16	3.125 111	58.623 741	.017 057 9356	.319 989	18.758 933	.053 307 9356	10.67	.705 854	4.41	32
17	3.355 788	64.987 248	.015 387 6343	.297 993	19.365 721	.051 637 6343	10.33	.755 680	4.45	34
18	3.603 492	71.820 470	.013 923 6070	.277 509	19.930 797	.050 173 6070	10.04	.806 250	4.48	36
19	3.869 480	79.158 081	.012 632 9490	.258 433	20.457 031	.048 882 9490	9.78	.857 552	4.51	38
20	4.155 103	87.037 311	.011 489 3256	.240 668	20.947 091	.047 739 3256	9.55	.909 573	4.55	40
21	4.461 808	95.498 138	.010 471 4084	.224 124	21.403 464	.046 721 4084	9.35	.962 299	4.58	42
22	4.791 152	104.583 494	.009 561 7383	.208 718	21.828 467	.045 811 7383	9.17	1.015 716	4.62	44
23	5.144 806	114.339 476	.008 745 8858	.194 371	22.224 254	.044 995 8858	9.00	1.069 811	4.65	46
24	5.524 565	124.815 587	.008 011 8199	.181 010	22.592 835	.044 261 8199	8.86	1.124 567	4.69	48
25	5.932 356	136.064 983	.007 349 4295	.168 567	22.936 080	.043 599 4295	8.72	1.179 971	4.72	50
26	6.370 247	148.144 742	.006 750 1552	.156 980	23.255 730	.043 000 1552	8.61	1.236 008	4.75	52
27	6.840 461	161.116 157	.006 206 7022	.146 189	23.553 407	.042 456 7022	8.50	1.292 662	4.79	54
28	7.345 383	175.045 045	.005 712 8152	.136 140	23.830 622	.041 962 8152	8.40	1.349 918	4.82	56
29	7.887 575	190.002 081	.005 263 1002	.126 782	24.088 781	.041 513 1002	8.31	1.407 760	4.85	58
30	8.469 789	206.063 157	.004 852 8811	.118 067	24.329 195	.041 102 8811	8.23	1.466 173	4.89	60
31	9.094 979	223.309 766	.004 478 0845	.109 951	24.553 082	.040 728 0845	8.15	1.525 141	4.92	62
32	9.766 316	241.829 416	.004 135 1462	.102 393	24.761 579	.040 385 1462	8.08	1.584 649	4.95	64
33	10.487 208	261.716 078	.003 820 9345	.095 354	24.955 744	.040 070 9345	8.02	1.644 682	4.98	66
34	11.261 311	283.070 655	.003 532 6869	.088 800	25.136 563	.039 782 6869	7.96	1.705 223	5.02	68
35	12.092 554	306.001 500	.003 267 9578	.082 696	25.304 951	.039 517 9578	7.91	1.766 257	5.05	70
36	12.985 155	330.624 964	.003 024 5750	.077 011	25.461 765	.039 274 5750	7.86	1.827 769	5.08	72
37	13.943 642	357.065 986	.002 800 6028	.071 717	25.607 799	.039 050 6028	7.82	1.889 745	5.11	74
38	14.972 879	385.458 727	.002 594 3115	.066 787	25.743 795	.038 844 3115	7.77	1.952 168	5.14	76
39	16.078 088	415.947 251	.002 404 1510	.062 196	25.870 443	.038 654 1510	7.74	2.015 024	5.17	78
40	17.264 877	448.686 258	.002 228 7288	.057 921	25.988 384	.038 478 7288	7.70	2.078 298	5.20	80
41	18.539 268	483.841 863	.002 066 7910	.053 940	26.098 219	.038 316 7910	7.67	2.141 977	5.22	82
42	19.907 726	521.592 447	.001 917 2057	.050 232	26.200 503	.038 167 2057	7.64	2.206 045	5.25	84
43	21.377 196	562.129 554	.001 778 9493	.046 779	26.295 757	.038 028 9493	7.61	2.270 490	5.28	86
44	22.955 134	605.658 870	.001 651 0945	.043 563	26.384 462	.037 901 0945	7.59	2.335 296	5.31	88
45	24.649 546	652.401 262	.001 532 7990	.040 569	26.467 070	.037 782 7990	7.56	2.400 452	5.33	90
46	26.469 029	702.593 899	.001 423 2973	.037 780	26.544 000	.037 673 2973	7.54	2.465 943	5.36	92
47	28.422 815	756.491 459	.001 321 8920	.035 183	26.615 641	.037 571 8920	7.52	2.531 758	5.39	94
48	30.520 819	814.367 417	.001 227 9470	.032 765	26.682 358	.037 477 9470	7.50	2.597 883	5.41	96
49	32.773 685	876.515 435	.001 140 8812	.030 512	26.744 489	.037 390 8812	7.48	2.664 306	5.44	98
50	35.192 843	943.250 850	.001 060 1634	.028 415	26.802 348	.037 310 1634	7.47	2.731 016	5.46	100

Effective Rate is 7.38 %

Annual Percentage Rate is 7.25 %

SEMIANNUAL COMPOUND INTEREST AND ANNUITY

7.50 % S

Amount Of 1	Amount Of 1 Per Period	Sinking Fund Payment	Present Worth Of 1	Present Worth of 1 Per Period	Periodic Payment To Amortize 1	Constant Annual Percent	Total Interest	Annual Add On Rate
What a single $ 1 deposit grows to in the future. The deposit is made at the beginning of the first period.	What a series of $ 1 deposits grow to in the future. A deposit is made at the end of each period.	The amount to be deposited at the end of each period that grows to $ 1 in the future.	What $ 1 to be paid in the future is worth today. Value today of a single $ 1 payment tomorrow.	What $ 1 to be paid at the end of each period is worth today. Value today of a series of $ 1 payments tomorrow.	The mortgage payment to amortize a loan of $ 1. An annuity certain, payable at the end of each period, worth $ 1 today.	The annual payment, including interest and principal, to amortize completely a loan of $ 100.	The total interest paid over the term on a loan of $1. The loan is amortized by regular periodic payments.	The average annual interest rate on a loan that is completely amortized by regular periodic payments.
$S = (1+i)^n$	$S\overline{n} = \dfrac{(1+i)^n - 1}{i}$	$\dfrac{1}{S\overline{n}} = \dfrac{i}{(1+i)^n - 1}$	$V^n = \dfrac{1}{(1+i)^n}$	$A\overline{n} = \dfrac{1 - V^n}{i}$	$\dfrac{1}{A\overline{n}} = \dfrac{i}{1 - V^n}$			

YEAR									PERIODS
	1.037 500	1.000 000	1.000 000 0000	.963 855	.963 855	1.037 500 0000	207.50	.037 500	7.50	1
	1.076 406	2.037 500	.490 797 5460	.929 017	1.892 873	.528 297 5460	105.66	.056 595	5.66	2

YEAR	Amount Of 1	Amount Of 1 Per Period	Sinking Fund Payment	Present Worth Of 1	Present Worth of 1 Per Period	Periodic Payment To Amortize 1	Constant Annual Percent	Total Interest	Annual Add On Rate	PERIODS
1	1.076 406	2.037 500	.490 797 5460	.929 017	1.892 873	.528 297 5460	105.66	.056 595	5.66	2
2	1.158 650	4.230 678	.236 368 7482	.863 073	3.651 384	.273 868 7482	54.78	.095 475	4.77	4
3	1.247 179	6.591 428	.151 712 1945	.801 810	5.285 072	.189 212 1945	37.85	.135 273	4.51	6
4	1.342 471	9.132 554	.109 498 3915	.744 895	6.802 796	.146 998 3915	29.40	.175 987	4.40	8
5	1.445 044	11.867 838	.084 261 3423	.692 020	8.212 787	.121 761 3423	24.36	.217 613	4.35	10
6	1.555 454	14.812 116	.067 512 3010	.642 899	9.522 694	.105 012 3010	21.01	.260 148	4.34	12
7	1.674 301	17.981 354	.055 613 1655	.597 264	10.739 620	.093 113 1655	18.63	.303 584	4.34	14
8	1.802 228	21.392 742	.046 744 8270	.554 869	11.870 165	.084 244 8270	16.85	.347 917	4.35	16
9	1.939 929	25.064 781	.039 896 6188	.515 483	12.920 461	.077 396 6188	15.48	.393 139	4.37	18
10	2.088 152	29.017 387	.034 462 0973	.478 892	13.896 204	.071 962 0973	14.40	.439 242	4.39	20
11	2.247 700	33.271 996	.030 055 3051	.444 899	14.802 686	.067 555 3051	13.52	.486 217	4.42	22
12	2.419 438	37.851 685	.026 418 9033	.413 319	15.644 824	.063 918 9033	12.79	.534 054	4.45	24
13	2.604 298	42.781 290	.023 374 7042	.383 981	16.427 185	.060 874 7042	12.18	.582 742	4.48	26
14	2.803 283	48.087 548	.020 795 4043	.356 725	17.154 011	.058 295 4043	11.66	.632 271	4.52	28
15	3.017 471	53.799 237	.018 587 6242	.331 403	17.829 245	.056 087 6242	11.22	.682 629	4.55	30
16	3.248 025	59.947 335	.016 681 3087	.307 879	18.456 549	.054 181 3087	10.84	.733 802	4.59	32
17	3.496 194	66.565 186	.015 022 8679	.286 025	19.039 326	.052 522 8679	10.51	.785 778	4.62	34
18	3.763 326	73.688 682	.013 570 6050	.265 722	19.580 735	.051 070 6050	10.22	.838 542	4.66	36
19	4.050 867	81.356 458	.012 291 5872	.246 861	20.083 714	.049 791 5872	9.96	.892 080	4.70	38
20	4.360 379	89.610 100	.011 159 4563	.229 338	20.550 990	.048 659 4563	9.74	.946 378	4.73	40
21	4.693 539	98.494 372	.010 152 8644	.213 059	20.985 097	.047 652 8644	9.54	1.001 420	4.77	42
22	5.052 155	108.057 458	.009 254 3358	.197 935	21.388 391	.046 754 3358	9.36	1.057 191	4.81	44
23	5.438 171	118.351 223	.008 449 4269	.183 885	21.763 057	.045 949 4269	9.19	1.113 674	4.84	46
24	5.853 681	129.431 496	.007 726 0947	.170 833	22.111 129	.045 226 0947	9.05	1.170 853	4.88	48
25	6.300 939	141.358 371	.007 074 2185	.158 707	22.434 493	.044 574 2185	8.92	1.228 711	4.91	50
26	6.782 370	154.196 534	.006 485 2301	.147 441	22.734 904	.043 985 2301	8.80	1.287 232	4.95	52
27	7.300 585	168.015 613	.005 951 8278	.136 975	23.013 992	.043 451 8278	8.70	1.346 399	4.99	54
28	7.858 396	182.890 556	.005 467 7509	.127 252	23.273 268	.042 967 7509	8.60	1.406 194	5.02	56
29	8.458 826	198.902 037	.005 027 6006	.118 220	23.514 141	.042 527 6006	8.51	1.466 601	5.06	58
30	9.105 134	216.136 896	.004 626 6973	.109 828	23.737 916	.042 126 6973	8.43	1.527 602	5.09	60
31	9.800 823	234.688 606	.004 260 9653	.102 032	23.945 807	.041 760 9653	8.36	1.589 180	5.13	62
32	10.549 667	254.657 782	.003 926 8386	.094 790	24.138 941	.041 426 8386	8.29	1.651 318	5.16	64
33	11.355 727	276.152 728	.003 621 1846	.088 061	24.318 366	.041 121 1846	8.23	1.713 998	5.19	66
34	12.223 376	299.290 023	.003 341 2407	.081 810	24.485 054	.040 841 2407	8.17	1.777 204	5.23	68
35	13.157 318	324.195 151	.003 084 5619	.076 003	24.639 911	.040 584 5619	8.12	1.840 919	5.26	70
36	14.162 620	351.003 187	.002 848 9770	.070 608	24.783 776	.040 348 9770	8.07	1.905 126	5.29	72
37	15.244 732	379.859 524	.002 632 5521	.065 596	24.917 429	.040 132 5521	8.03	1.969 809	5.32	74
38	16.409 525	410.920 666	.002 433 5598	.060 940	25.041 594	.039 933 5598	7.99	2.034 951	5.36	76
39	17.663 315	444.355 073	.002 250 4525	.056 615	25.156 946	.039 750 4525	7.96	2.100 535	5.39	78
40	19.012 903	480.344 078	.002 081 8410	.052 596	25.264 110	.039 581 8410	7.92	2.166 547	5.42	80
41	20.465 608	519.082 868	.001 926 4747	.048 862	25.363 668	.039 426 4747	7.89	2.232 971	5.45	82
42	22.029 308	560.781 543	.001 783 2256	.045 394	25.456 158	.039 283 2256	7.86	2.299 791	5.48	84
43	23.712 485	605.666 258	.001 651 0743	.042 172	25.542 083	.039 151 0743	7.84	2.366 992	5.50	86
44	25.524 267	653.980 445	.001 529 0977	.039 178	25.621 909	.039 029 0977	7.81	2.434 561	5.53	88
45	27.474 480	705.986 139	.001 416 4584	.036 397	25.696 069	.038 916 4584	7.79	2.502 481	5.56	90
46	29.573 702	761.965 392	.001 312 3956	.033 814	25.764 965	.038 812 3956	7.77	2.570 740	5.59	92
47	31.833 318	822.221 810	.001 216 2168	.031 414	25.828 970	.038 716 2168	7.75	2.639 324	5.62	94
48	34.265 582	887.082 195	.001 127 2913	.029 184	25.888 432	.038 627 2913	7.73	2.708 220	5.64	96
49	36.883 687	956.898 319	.001 045 0431	.027 112	25.943 673	.038 545 0431	7.71	2.777 414	5.67	98
50	39.701 831	1032.048 832	.000 968 9464	.025 188	25.994 993	.038 468 9464	7.70	2.846 895	5.69	100

Effective Rate is 7.64 %

Annual Percentage Rate is 7.50 %

Amount Of 1	Amount Of 1 Per Period	Sinking Fund Payment	Present Worth Of 1	Present Worth of 1 Per Period	Periodic Payment To Amortize 1	Constant Annual Percent	Total Interest	Annual Add On Rate
What a single $ 1 deposit grows to in the future. The deposit is made at the beginning of the first period.	What a series of $ 1 deposits grow to in the future. A deposit is made at the end of each period.	The amount to be deposited at the end of each period that grows to $ 1 in the future.	What $ 1 to be paid in the future is worth today. Value today of a single $ 1 payment tomorrow.	What $ 1 to be paid at the end of each period is worth today. Value today of a series of $ 1 payments tomorrow.	The mortgage payment to amortize a loan of $ 1. An annuity certain, payable at the end of each period, worth $ 1 today.	The annual payment, including interest and principal, to amortize completely a loan of $ 100.	The total interest paid over the term on a loan of $1. The loan is amortized by regular periodic payments.	The average annual interest rate on a loan that is completely amortized by regular periodic payments.
$S = (1+i)^n$	$S\overline{n}| = \dfrac{(1+i)^n - 1}{i}$	$\dfrac{1}{S\overline{n}|} = \dfrac{i}{(1+i)^n - 1}$	$V^n = \dfrac{1}{(1+i)^n}$	$A\overline{n}| = \dfrac{1 - V^n}{i}$	$\dfrac{1}{A\overline{n}|} = \dfrac{i}{1 - V^n}$			

YEAR									PERIODS
	1.038 750	1.000 000	1.000 000 0000	.962 696	.962 696	1.038 750 0000	207.75	.038 750	7.75	1
	1.079 002	2.038 750	.490 496 6278	.926 783	1.889 478	.529 246 6278	105.85	.058 493	5.85	2

YEAR									PERIODS
1	1.079 002	2.038 750	.490 496 6278	.926 783	1.889 478	.529 246 6278	105.85	.058 493	5.85	2
2	1.164 244	4.238 564	.235 928 9366	.858 926	3.640 614	.274 678 9366	54.94	.098 716	4.94	4
3	1.256 221	6.612 168	.151 236 3348	.796 038	5.263 536	.189 986 3348	38.00	.139 918	4.66	6
4	1.355 465	9.173 289	.109 012 1521	.737 754	6.767 633	.147 762 1521	29.56	.182 097	4.55	8
5	1.462 549	11.936 743	.083 774 9431	.683 738	8.161 603	.122 524 9431	24.51	.225 249	4.51	10
6	1.578 092	14.918 515	.067 030 8013	.633 676	9.453 511	.105 780 8013	21.16	.269 370	4.49	12
7	1.702 764	18.135 851	.055 139 4039	.587 280	10.650 829	.093 889 4039	18.78	.314 452	4.49	14
8	1.837 285	21.607 361	.046 280 5238	.544 281	11.760 483	.085 030 5238	17.01	.360 488	4.51	16
9	1.982 434	25.353 127	.039 442 8670	.504 430	12.788 890	.078 192 8670	15.64	.407 472	4.53	18
10	2.139 049	29.394 813	.034 019 6072	.467 497	13.742 001	.072 769 6072	14.56	.455 392	4.55	20
11	2.308 037	33.755 799	.029 624 5391	.433 269	14.625 327	.068 374 5391	13.68	.504 240	4.58	22
12	2.490 376	38.461 310	.026 000 1542	.401 546	15.443 979	.064 750 1542	12.96	.554 004	4.62	24
13	2.687 119	43.538 564	.022 968 1439	.372 146	16.202 691	.061 718 1439	12.35	.604 672	4.65	26
14	2.899 406	49.016 928	.020 401 1151	.344 898	16.905 852	.059 151 1151	11.84	.656 231	4.69	28
15	3.128 464	54.928 092	.018 205 6204	.319 646	17.557 530	.056 955 6204	11.40	.708 669	4.72	30
16	3.375 617	61.306 248	.016 311 5513	.296 242	18.161 493	.055 061 5513	11.02	.761 970	4.76	32
17	3.642 296	68.188 287	.014 665 2753	.274 552	18.721 236	.053 415 2753	10.69	.816 119	4.80	34
18	3.930 043	75.614 018	.013 225 0610	.254 450	19.239 997	.051 975 0610	10.40	.871 102	4.84	36
19	4.240 523	83.626 394	.011 957 9472	.235 820	19.720 775	.050 707 9472	10.15	.926 902	4.88	38
20	4.575 531	92.271 759	.010 837 5521	.218 554	20.166 351	.049 587 5521	9.92	.983 502	4.92	40
21	4.937 005	101.600 123	.009 842 5078	.202 552	20.579 304	.048 592 5078	9.72	1.040 885	4.96	42
22	5.327 036	111.665 441	.008 955 3222	.187 722	20.962 022	.047 705 3222	9.55	1.099 034	5.00	44
23	5.747 880	122.525 935	.008 161 5374	.173 977	21.316 718	.046 911 5374	9.39	1.157 931	5.03	46
24	6.201 971	134.244 426	.007 449 0989	.161 239	21.645 444	.046 199 0989	9.24	1.217 557	5.07	48
25	6.691 937	146.888 695	.006 807 8758	.149 434	21.950 102	.045 557 8758	9.12	1.277 894	5.11	50
26	7.220 610	160.531 882	.006 229 2922	.138 492	22.232 453	.044 979 2922	9.00	1.338 923	5.15	52
27	7.791 050	175.252 901	.005 706 0396	.128 352	22.494 131	.044 456 0396	8.90	1.400 626	5.19	54
28	8.406 555	191.136 904	.005 231 8520	.118 955	22.736 651	.043 981 8520	8.80	1.462 984	5.23	56
29	9.070 686	208.275 768	.004 801 3267	.110 245	22.961 413	.043 551 3267	8.72	1.525 977	5.26	58
30	9.787 284	226.768 629	.004 409 7810	.102 173	23.169 719	.043 159 7810	8.64	1.589 587	5.30	60
31	10.560 495	246.722 455	.004 053 1374	.094 693	23.362 773	.042 803 1374	8.57	1.653 795	5.33	62
32	11.394 791	268.252 665	.003 727 8288	.087 759	23.541 693	.042 477 8288	8.50	1.718 581	5.37	64
33	12.294 997	291.483 794	.003 430 7225	.081 334	23.707 512	.042 180 7225	8.44	1.783 928	5.41	66
34	13.266 321	316.550 220	.003 159 0564	.075 379	23.861 191	.041 909 0564	8.39	1.849 816	5.44	68
35	14.314 381	343.596 932	.002 910 3869	.069 860	24.003 618	.041 660 3869	8.34	1.916 227	5.48	70
36	15.445 240	372.780 376	.002 682 5446	.064 745	24.135 616	.041 432 5446	8.29	1.983 143	5.51	72
37	16.665 438	404.269 358	.002 473 5983	.060 004	24.257 950	.041 223 5983	8.25	2.050 546	5.54	74
38	17.982 033	438.246 019	.002 281 8234	.055 611	24.371 327	.041 031 8234	8.21	2.118 419	5.57	76
39	19.402 642	474.906 889	.002 105 6759	.051 539	24.476 403	.040 855 6759	8.18	2.186 743	5.61	78
40	20.935 481	514.464 026	.001 943 7705	.047 766	24.573 786	.040 693 7705	8.14	2.255 502	5.64	80
41	22.589 417	557.146 238	.001 794 8609	.044 269	24.664 038	.040 544 8609	8.11	2.324 679	5.67	82
42	24.374 016	603.200 411	.001 657 8238	.041 027	24.747 683	.040 407 8238	8.09	2.394 257	5.70	84
43	26.299 601	652.892 936	.001 531 6447	.038 023	24.825 203	.040 281 6447	8.06	2.464 221	5.73	86
44	28.377 311	706.511 248	.001 415 4056	.035 239	24.897 047	.040 165 4056	8.04	2.534 556	5.76	88
45	30.619 163	764.365 491	.001 308 2747	.032 659	24.963 631	.040 058 2747	8.02	2.605 245	5.79	90
46	33.038 124	826.790 309	.001 209 4965	.030 268	25.025 340	.039 959 4965	8.00	2.676 274	5.82	92
47	35.648 188	894.146 785	.001 118 3846	.028 052	25.082 531	.039 868 3846	7.98	2.747 628	5.85	94
48	38.464 450	966.824 528	.001 034 3139	.025 998	25.135 535	.039 784 3139	7.96	2.819 294	5.87	96
49	41.503 202	1045.243 926	.000 956 7145	.024 095	25.184 657	.039 706 7145	7.95	2.891 258	5.90	98
50	44.782 020	1129.858 580	.000 885 0665	.022 330	25.230 183	.039 635 0665	7.93	2.963 507	5.93	100

SEMIANNUAL COMPOUND INTEREST AND ANNUITY

8.00 % S

	Amount Of 1	Amount Of 1 Per Period	Sinking Fund Payment	Present Worth Of 1	Present Worth of 1 Per Period	Periodic Payment To Amortize 1	Constant Annual Percent	Total Interest	Annual Add On Rate	
	What a single $ 1 deposit grows to in the future. The deposit is made at the beginning of the first period.	What a series of $ 1 deposits grow to in the future. A deposit is made at the end of each period.	The amount to be deposited at the end of each period that grows to $ 1 in the future.	What $ 1 to be paid in the future is worth today. Value today of a single $ 1 payment tomorrow.	What $ 1 to be paid at the end of each period is worth today. Value today of a series of $ 1 payments tomorrow.	The mortgage payment to amortize a loan of $ 1. An annuity certain, payable at the end of each period, worth $ 1 today.	The annual payment, including interest and principal, to amortize completely a loan of $ 100.	The total interest paid over the term on a loan of $1. The loan is amortized by regular periodic payments.	The average annual interest rate on a loan that is completely amortized by regular periodic payments.	
	$S = (1+i)^n$	$S\overline{n}| = \dfrac{(1+i)^n - 1}{i}$	$\dfrac{1}{S\overline{n}|} = \dfrac{i}{(1+i)^n - 1}$	$V^n = \dfrac{1}{(1+i)^n}$	$A\overline{n}| = \dfrac{1 - V^n}{i}$	$\dfrac{1}{A\overline{n}|} = \dfrac{i}{1 - V^n}$				

YEAR										PERIODS
	1.040 000	1.000 000	1.000 000 0000	.961 538	.961 538	1.040 000 0000	208.00	.040 000	8.00	1
	1.081 600	2.040 000	.490 196 0784	.924 556	1.886 095	.530 196 0784	106.04	.060 392	6.04	2

YEAR										PERIODS
1	1.081 600	2.040 000	.490 196 0784	.924 556	1.886 095	.530 196 0784	106.04	.060 392	6.04	2
2	1.169 859	4.246 464	.235 490 0454	.854 804	3.629 895	.275 490 0454	55.10	.101 960	5.10	4
3	1.265 319	6.632 975	.150 761 9025	.790 315	5.242 137	.190 761 9025	38.16	.144 571	4.82	6
4	1.368 569	9.214 226	.108 527 8320	.730 690	6.732 745	.148 527 8320	29.71	.188 223	4.71	8
5	1.480 244	12.006 107	.083 290 9443	.675 564	8.110 896	.123 290 9443	24.66	.232 909	4.66	10
6	1.601 032	15.025 805	.066 552 1727	.624 597	9.385 074	.106 552 1727	21.32	.278 626	4.64	12
7	1.731 676	18.291 911	.054 668 9731	.577 475	10.563 123	.094 668 9731	18.94	.325 366	4.65	14
8	1.872 981	21.824 531	.045 819 9992	.533 908	11.652 296	.085 819 9992	17.17	.373 120	4.66	16
9	2.025 817	25.645 413	.038 993 3281	.493 628	12.659 297	.078 993 3281	15.80	.421 880	4.69	18
10	2.191 123	29.778 079	.033 581 7503	.456 387	13.590 326	.073 581 7503	14.72	.471 635	4.72	20
11	2.369 919	34.247 970	.029 198 8111	.421 955	14.451 115	.069 198 8111	13.84	.522 374	4.75	22
12	2.563 304	39.082 604	.025 586 8313	.390 121	15.246 963	.065 586 8313	13.12	.574 084	4.78	24
13	2.772 470	44.311 745	.022 567 3805	.360 689	15.982 769	.062 567 3805	12.52	.626 752	4.82	26
14	2.998 703	49.967 583	.020 012 9752	.333 477	16.663 063	.060 012 9752	12.01	.680 363	4.86	28
15	3.243 398	56.084 938	.017 830 0991	.308 319	17.292 033	.057 830 0991	11.57	.734 903	4.90	30
16	3.508 059	62.701 469	.015 948 5897	.285 058	17.873 551	.055 948 5897	11.19	.790 355	4.94	32
17	3.794 316	69.857 909	.014 314 7715	.263 552	18.411 198	.054 314 7715	10.87	.846 702	4.98	34
18	4.103 933	77.598 314	.012 886 8780	.243 669	18.908 282	.052 886 8780	10.58	.903 928	5.02	36
19	4.438 813	85.970 336	.011 631 9191	.225 285	19.367 864	.051 631 9191	10.33	.962 013	5.06	38
20	4.801 021	95.025 516	.010 523 4893	.208 289	19.792 774	.050 523 4893	10.11	1.020 940	5.10	40
21	5.192 784	104.819 598	.009 540 2007	.192 575	20.185 627	.049 540 2007	9.91	1.080 688	5.15	42
22	5.616 515	115.412 877	.008 664 5444	.178 046	20.548 841	.048 664 5444	9.74	1.141 240	5.19	44
23	6.074 823	126.870 568	.007 882 0488	.164 614	20.884 654	.047 882 0488	9.58	1.202 574	5.23	46
24	6.570 528	139.263 206	.007 180 6476	.152 195	21.195 131	.047 180 6476	9.44	1.264 671	5.27	48
25	7.106 683	152.667 084	.006 550 2004	.140 713	21.482 185	.046 550 2004	9.32	1.327 510	5.31	50
26	7.686 589	167.164 718	.005 982 1236	.130 097	21.747 582	.045 982 1236	9.20	1.391 070	5.35	52
27	8.313 814	182.845 359	.005 469 1025	.120 282	21.992 957	.045 469 1025	9.10	1.455 332	5.39	54
28	8.992 222	199.805 540	.005 004 8662	.111 207	22.219 819	.045 004 8662	9.01	1.520 273	5.43	56
29	9.725 987	218.149 672	.004 584 0087	.102 817	22.429 567	.044 584 0087	8.92	1.585 873	5.47	58
30	10.519 627	237.990 685	.004 201 8451	.095 060	22.623 490	.044 201 8451	8.85	1.652 111	5.51	60
31	11.378 029	259.450 725	.003 854 2964	.087 889	22.802 783	.043 854 2964	8.78	1.718 966	5.55	62
32	12.306 476	282.661 904	.003 537 7955	.081 258	22.968 549	.043 537 7955	8.71	1.786 419	5.58	64
33	13.310 685	307.767 116	.003 249 2100	.075 128	23.121 810	.043 249 2100	8.65	1.854 648	5.62	66
34	14.396 836	334.920 912	.002 985 7795	.069 460	23.263 507	.042 985 7795	8.60	1.923 033	5.66	68
35	15.571 618	364.290 459	.002 745 0623	.064 219	23.394 515	.042 745 0623	8.55	1.992 154	5.69	70
36	16.842 262	396.056 560	.002 524 8919	.059 374	23.515 639	.042 524 8919	8.51	2.061 792	5.73	72
37	18.216 591	430.414 776	.002 323 3403	.054 895	23.627 625	.042 323 3403	8.47	2.131 927	5.76	74
38	19.703 065	467.576 621	.002 138 6869	.050 754	23.731 162	.042 138 6869	8.43	2.202 540	5.80	76
39	21.310 835	507.770 873	.001 969 3922	.046 924	23.826 888	.041 969 3922	8.40	2.273 613	5.83	78
40	23.049 799	551.244 977	.001 814 0755	.043 384	23.915 392	.041 814 0755	8.37	2.345 126	5.86	80
41	24.930 663	598.266 567	.001 671 4957	.040 111	23.997 219	.041 671 4957	8.34	2.417 063	5.90	82
42	26.965 005	649.125 119	.001 540 5351	.037 085	24.072 872	.041 540 5351	8.31	2.489 405	5.93	84
43	29.165 349	704.133 728	.001 420 1848	.034 287	24.142 818	.041 420 1848	8.29	2.562 136	5.96	86
44	31.545 242	763.631 041	.001 309 5329	.031 701	24.207 487	.041 309 5329	8.27	2.635 239	5.99	88
45	34.119 333	827.983 334	.001 207 7538	.029 309	24.267 278	.041 207 7538	8.25	2.708 698	6.02	90
46	36.903 471	897.586 774	.001 114 0984	.027 098	24.322 557	.041 114 0984	8.23	2.782 497	6.05	92
47	39.914 794	972.869 854	.001 027 8867	.025 053	24.373 666	.041 027 8867	8.21	2.856 621	6.08	94
48	43.171 841	1054.296 034	.000 948 5002	.023 163	24.420 919	.040 948 5002	8.19	2.931 056	6.11	96
49	46.694 664	1142.366 591	.000 875 3757	.021 416	24.464 607	.040 875 3757	8.18	3.005 787	6.13	98
50	50.504 948	1237.623 705	.000 808 0000	.019 800	24.504 999	.040 808 0000	8.17	3.080 800	6.16	100

Effective Rate is 8.16 %

Annual Percentage Rate is 8.00 %

SEMIANNUAL COMPOUND INTEREST AND ANNUITY

8.25 % S

	Amount Of 1	Amount Of 1 Per Period	Sinking Fund Payment	Present Worth Of 1	Present Worth of 1 Per Period	Periodic Payment To Amortize 1	Constant Annual Percent	Total Interest	Annual Add On Rate
	What a single $ 1 deposit grows to in the future. The deposit is made at the beginning of the first period.	What a series of $ 1 deposits grow to in the future. A deposit is made at the end of each period.	The amount to be deposited at the end of each period that grows to $ 1 in the future.	What $ 1 to be paid in the future is worth today. Value today of a single $ 1 payment tomorrow.	What $ 1 to be paid at the end of each period is worth today. Value today of a series of $ 1 payments tomorrow.	The mortgage payment to amortize a loan of $ 1. An annuity certain, payable at the end of each period, worth $ 1 today.	The annual payment, including interest and principal, to amortize completely a loan of $ 100.	The total interest paid over the term on a loan of $1. The loan is amortized by regular periodic payments.	The average annual interest rate on a loan that is completely amortized by regular periodic payments.
	$S = (1+i)^n$	$S\overline{n} = \dfrac{(1+i)^n - 1}{i}$	$\dfrac{1}{S\overline{n}} = \dfrac{i}{(1+i)^n - 1}$	$V^n = \dfrac{1}{(1+i)^n}$	$A\overline{n} = \dfrac{1 - V^n}{i}$	$\dfrac{1}{A\overline{n}} = \dfrac{i}{1 - V^n}$			

YEAR										PERIODS
	1.041 250	1.000 000	1.000 000 0000	.960 384	.960 384	1.041 250 0000	208.25	.041 250	8.25	1
	1.084 202	2.041 250	.489 895 8971	.922 338	1.882 722	.531 145 8971	106.23	.062 292	6.23	2

YEAR										PERIODS
1	1.084 202	2.041 250	.489 895 8971	.922 338	1.882 722	.531 145 8971	106.23	.062 292	6.23	2
2	1.175 493	4.254 376	.235 052 0727	.850 707	3.619 227	.276 302 0727	55.27	.105 208	5.26	4
3	1.274 471	6.653 852	.150 288 8947	.784 639	5.220 872	.191 538 8947	38.31	.149 233	4.97	6
4	1.381 784	9.255 366	.108 045 4268	.723 702	6.698 129	.149 295 4268	29.86	.194 363	4.86	8
5	1.498 132	12.075 933	.082 809 3394	.667 498	8.060 659	.124 059 3394	24.82	.240 593	4.81	10
6	1.624 277	15.133 995	.066 076 4062	.615 658	9.317 372	.107 326 4062	21.47	.287 917	4.80	12
7	1.761 044	18.449 551	.054 201 8611	.567 845	10.476 485	.095 451 8611	19.10	.336 326	4.80	14
8	1.909 327	22.044 282	.045 363 2375	.523 745	11.545 579	.086 613 2375	17.33	.385 812	4.82	16
9	2.070 095	25.941 695	.038 547 9823	.483 070	12.531 645	.079 797 9823	15.96	.436 364	4.85	18
10	2.244 400	30.167 276	.033 148 5014	.445 553	13.441 131	.074 398 5014	14.88	.487 970	4.88	20
11	2.433 382	34.748 658	.028 778 0897	.410 951	14.279 984	.070 028 0897	14.01	.540 618	4.91	22
12	2.638 277	39.715 799	.025 178 8965	.379 035	15.053 690	.066 428 8965	13.29	.594 294	4.95	24
13	2.860 424	45.101 182	.022 172 3680	.349 599	15.767 308	.063 422 3680	12.69	.648 982	4.99	26
14	3.101 276	50.940 022	.019 630 9300	.322 448	16.425 505	.060 880 9300	12.18	.704 666	5.03	28
15	3.362 408	57.270 501	.017 460 9962	.297 406	17.032 584	.058 710 9962	11.75	.761 330	5.08	30
16	3.645 528	64.134 017	.015 592 3494	.274 309	17.592 517	.056 842 3494	11.37	.818 955	5.12	32
17	3.952 487	71.575 451	.013 971 2706	.253 005	18.108 964	.055 221 2706	11.05	.877 523	5.16	34
18	4.285 293	79.643 466	.012 555 9578	.233 356	18.585 302	.053 805 9578	10.77	.937 014	5.21	36
19	4.646 121	88.390 820	.011 313 3920	.215 233	19.024 647	.052 563 3920	10.52	.997 409	5.25	38
20	5.037 332	97.874 716	.010 217 1434	.198 518	19.429 872	.051 467 1434	10.30	1.058 686	5.29	40
21	5.461 483	108.157 170	.009 245 8041	.183 100	19.803 626	.050 495 8041	10.10	1.120 824	5.34	42
22	5.921 349	119.305 422	.008 381 8487	.168 880	20.148 353	.049 631 8487	9.93	1.183 801	5.38	44
23	6.419 935	131.392 375	.007 610 7917	.155 765	20.466 308	.048 860 7917	9.78	1.247 596	5.42	46
24	6.960 504	144.497 068	.006 920 5556	.143 668	20.759 570	.048 170 5556	9.64	1.312 187	5.47	48
25	7.546 589	158.705 197	.006 300 9909	.132 510	21.030 056	.047 550 9909	9.52	1.377 550	5.51	50
26	8.182 024	174.109 673	.005 743 5063	.122 219	21.279 536	.046 993 5063	9.40	1.443 662	5.55	52
27	8.870 963	190.811 229	.005 240 7817	.112 727	21.509 640	.046 490 7817	9.30	1.510 502	5.59	54
28	9.617 912	208.919 083	.004 786 5422	.103 973	21.721 875	.046 036 5422	9.21	1.578 046	5.64	56
29	10.427 755	228.551 646	.004 375 3787	.095 898	21.917 626	.045 625 3787	9.13	1.646 272	5.68	58
30	11.305 789	249.837 302	.004 002 6049	.088 450	22.098 175	.045 252 6049	9.06	1.715 156	5.72	60
31	12.257 754	272.915 243	.003 664 1412	.081 581	22.264 703	.044 914 1412	8.99	1.784 677	5.76	62
32	13.289 876	297.936 383	.003 356 4212	.075 245	22.418 297	.044 606 4212	8.93	1.854 811	5.80	64
33	14.408 904	325.064 342	.003 076 3140	.069 402	22.559 963	.044 326 3140	8.87	1.925 537	5.84	66
34	15.622 156	354.476 518	.002 821 0613	.064 012	22.690 627	.044 071 0613	8.82	1.996 832	5.87	68
35	16.937 566	386.365 244	.002 588 2245	.059 040	22.811 143	.043 838 2245	8.77	2.068 676	5.91	70
36	18.363 736	420.939 052	.002 375 6408	.054 455	22.922 299	.043 625 6408	8.73	2.141 046	5.95	72
37	19.909 991	458.424 028	.002 181 3865	.050 226	23.024 823	.043 431 3865	8.69	2.213 923	5.98	74
38	21.586 444	499.065 297	.002 003 7458	.046 325	23.119 385	.043 253 7458	8.66	2.287 285	6.02	76
39	23.404 056	543.128 625	.001 841 1845	.042 728	23.206 603	.043 091 1845	8.62	2.361 112	6.05	78
40	25.374 714	590.902 154	.001 692 3276	.039 409	23.287 047	.042 942 3276	8.59	2.435 386	6.09	80
41	27.511 304	642.698 288	.001 555 9400	.036 349	23.361 244	.042 805 9400	8.57	2.510 087	6.12	82
42	29.827 799	698.855 738	.001 430 9105	.033 526	23.429 678	.042 680 9105	8.54	2.585 196	6.16	84
43	32.339 347	759.741 733	.001 316 2368	.030 922	23.492 798	.042 566 2368	8.52	2.660 696	6.19	86
44	35.062 370	825.754 424	.001 211 0138	.028 521	23.551 016	.042 461 0138	8.50	2.736 569	6.22	88
45	38.014 676	897.325 487	.001 114 4228	.026 306	23.604 712	.042 364 4228	8.48	2.812 798	6.25	90
46	41.215 571	974.922 945	.001 025 7221	.024 263	23.654 238	.042 275 7221	8.46	2.889 366	6.28	92
47	44.685 987	1059.054 231	.000 944 2387	.022 378	23.699 918	.042 194 2387	8.44	2.966 258	6.31	94
48	48.448 617	1150.269 502	.000 869 3615	.020 640	23.742 050	.042 119 3615	8.43	3.043 459	6.34	96
49	52.528 066	1249.165 241	.000 800 5346	.019 037	23.780 911	.042 050 5346	8.42	3.120 952	6.37	98
50	56.951 011	1356.388 156	.000 737 2521	.017 559	23.816 753	.041 987 2521	8.40	3.198 725	6.40	100

Effective Rate is 8.42 %

Annual Percentage Rate is 8.25 %

SEMIANNUAL COMPOUND INTEREST AND ANNUITY

8.50 % S

	Amount Of 1	Amount Of 1 Per Period	Sinking Fund Payment	Present Worth Of 1	Present Worth of 1 Per Period	Periodic Payment To Amortize 1	Constant Annual Percent	Total Interest	Annual Add On Rate	
	What a single $ 1 deposit grows to in the future. The deposit is made at the beginning of the first period.	What a series of $ 1 deposits grow to in the future. A deposit is made at the end of each period.	The amount to be deposited at the end of each period that grows to $ 1 in the future.	What $ 1 to be paid in the future is worth today. Value today of a single $ 1 payment tomorrow.	What $ 1 to be paid at the end of each period is worth today. Value today of a series of $ 1 payments tomorrow.	The mortgage payment to amortize a loan of $ 1. An annuity certain, payable at the end of each period, worth $ 1 today.	The annual payment, including interest and principal, to amortize completely a loan of $ 100.	The total interest paid over the term on a loan of $1. The loan is amortized by regular periodic payments.	The average annual interest rate on a loan that is completely amortized by regular periodic payments.	
	$S = (1+i)^n$	$S\overline{n|} = \dfrac{(1+i)^n - 1}{i}$	$\dfrac{1}{S\overline{n|}} = \dfrac{i}{(1+i)^n - 1}$	$V^n = \dfrac{1}{(1+i)^n}$	$A\overline{n|} = \dfrac{1 - V^n}{i}$	$\dfrac{1}{A\overline{n|}} = \dfrac{i}{1 - V^n}$				

YEAR										PERIODS
	1.042 500	1.000 000	1.000 000 0000	.959 233	.959 233	1.042 500 0000	208.50	.042 500	8.50	1
	1.086 806	2.042 500	.489 596 0832	.920 127	1.879 360	.532 096 0832	106.42	.064 192	6.42	2

YEAR										PERIODS
1	1.086 806	2.042 500	.489 596 0832	.920 127	1.879 360	.532 096 0832	106.42	.064 192	6.42	2
2	1.181 148	4.262 302	.234 615 0167	.846 634	3.608 610	.277 115 0167	55.43	.108 460	5.42	4
3	1.283 679	6.674 796	.149 817 3083	.779 011	5.199 740	.192 317 3083	38.47	.153 904	5.13	6
4	1.395 110	9.296 710	.107 564 9316	.716 789	6.663 782	.150 064 9316	30.02	.200 519	5.01	8
5	1.516 214	12.146 223	.082 330 1217	.659 537	8.010 887	.124 830 1217	24.97	.248 301	4.97	10
6	1.647 831	15.243 091	.065 603 4928	.606 858	9.250 395	.108 103 4928	21.63	.297 242	4.95	12
7	1.790 873	18.608 786	.053 738 0557	.558 387	10.390 900	.096 238 0557	19.25	.347 333	4.96	14
8	1.946 332	22.266 645	.044 910 2226	.513 787	11.440 309	.087 410 2226	17.49	.398 564	4.98	16
9	2.115 286	26.242 029	.038 106 8090	.472 749	12.405 900	.080 606 8090	16.13	.450 923	5.01	18
10	2.298 906	30.562 501	.032 719 8348	.434 989	13.294 366	.075 219 8348	15.05	.504 397	5.04	20
11	2.498 466	35.258 018	.028 362 3433	.400 246	14.111 868	.070 862 3433	14.18	.558 972	5.08	22
12	2.715 348	40.361 134	.024 776 3108	.368 277	14.864 073	.067 276 3108	13.46	.614 631	5.12	24
13	2.951 057	45.907 233	.021 783 0600	.338 862	15.556 198	.064 283 0600	12.86	.671 360	5.16	26
14	3.207 228	51.934 767	.019 254 9240	.311 796	16.193 041	.061 754 9240	12.36	.729 138	5.21	28
15	3.485 635	58.485 530	.017 098 2464	.286 892	16.779 017	.059 598 2464	11.92	.787 947	5.25	30
16	3.788 210	65.604 939	.015 242 7548	.263 977	17.318 190	.057 742 7548	11.55	.847 768	5.30	32
17	4.117 050	73.342 358	.013 634 6857	.242 892	17.814 298	.056 134 6857	11.23	.908 579	5.34	34
18	4.474 436	81.751 433	.012 232 2015	.223 492	18.270 780	.054 732 2015	10.95	.970 359	5.39	36
19	4.862 845	90.890 468	.011 002 2538	.205 641	18.690 801	.053 502 2538	10.71	1.033 086	5.44	38
20	5.284 970	100.822 829	.009 918 3886	.189 216	19.077 275	.052 418 3886	10.49	1.096 736	5.48	40
21	5.743 739	111.617 381	.008 959 1782	.174 103	19.432 879	.051 459 1782	10.30	1.161 285	5.53	42
22	6.242 331	123.348 967	.008 107 0805	.160 197	19.760 081	.050 607 0805	10.13	1.226 712	5.58	44
23	6.784 204	136.098 928	.007 347 5964	.147 401	20.061 148	.049 847 5964	9.97	1.292 989	5.62	46
24	7.373 116	149.955 666	.006 668 6377	.135 628	20.338 168	.049 168 6377	9.84	1.360 095	5.67	48
25	8.013 148	165.015 255	.006 060 0458	.124 795	20.593 061	.048 560 0458	9.72	1.428 002	5.71	50
26	8.708 740	181.382 110	.005 513 2229	.114 827	20.827 596	.048 013 2229	9.61	1.496 688	5.76	52
27	9.464 713	199.169 711	.005 020 8438	.105 656	21.043 397	.047 520 8438	9.51	1.566 126	5.80	54
28	10.286 309	218.501 387	.004 576 6300	.097 217	21.241 962	.047 076 6300	9.42	1.636 291	5.84	56
29	11.179 225	239.511 173	.004 175 1706	.089 452	21.424 667	.046 675 1706	9.34	1.707 160	5.89	58
30	12.149 651	262.344 740	.003 811 7784	.082 307	21.592 779	.046 311 7784	9.27	1.778 707	5.93	60
31	13.204 317	287.160 403	.003 482 3743	.075 733	21.747 463	.045 982 3743	9.20	1.850 907	5.97	62
32	14.350 534	314.130 221	.003 183 3932	.069 684	21.889 793	.045 683 3932	9.14	1.923 737	6.01	64
33	15.596 250	343.441 187	.002 911 7067	.064 118	22.020 754	.045 411 7067	9.09	1.997 173	6.05	66
34	16.950 102	375.296 529	.002 664 5597	.058 997	22.141 254	.045 164 5597	9.04	2.071 190	6.09	68
35	18.421 477	409.917 113	.002 439 5176	.054 284	22.252 130	.044 939 5176	8.99	2.145 766	6.13	70
36	20.020 577	447.542 980	.002 234 4223	.049 949	22.354 150	.044 734 4223	8.95	2.220 878	6.17	72
37	21.758 488	488.435 008	.002 047 3553	.045 959	22.448 022	.044 547 3553	8.91	2.296 504	6.21	74
38	23.647 261	532.876 720	.001 876 6067	.042 288	22.534 395	.044 376 6067	8.88	2.372 622	6.24	76
39	25.699 991	581.176 249	.001 720 6484	.038 911	22.613 870	.044 220 6484	8.85	2.449 211	6.28	78
40	27.930 910	633.668 480	.001 578 1123	.035 803	22.686 997	.044 078 1123	8.82	2.526 249	6.32	80
41	30.355 488	690.717 365	.001 447 7702	.032 943	22.754 283	.043 947 7702	8.79	2.603 717	6.35	82
42	32.990 534	752.718 449	.001 328 5180	.030 312	22.816 195	.043 828 5180	8.77	2.681 596	6.38	84
43	35.854 319	820.101 615	.001 219 3611	.027 891	22.873 161	.043 719 3611	8.75	2.759 865	6.42	86
44	38.966 698	893.334 060	.001 119 4021	.025 663	22.925 578	.043 619 4021	8.73	2.838 507	6.45	88
45	42.349 250	972.923 540	.001 027 8300	.023 613	22.973 808	.043 527 8300	8.71	2.917 505	6.48	90
46	46.025 430	1059.421 884	.000 943 9110	.021 727	23.018 185	.043 443 9110	8.69	2.996 840	6.51	92
47	50.020 725	1153.428 825	.000 866 9802	.019 992	23.059 019	.043 366 9802	8.68	3.076 496	6.55	94
48	54.362 837	1255.596 156	.000 796 4344	.018 395	23.096 590	.043 296 4344	8.66	3.156 458	6.58	96
49	59.081 871	1366.632 250	.000 731 7257	.016 926	23.131 161	.043 231 7257	8.65	3.236 709	6.61	98
50	64.210 546	1487.306 971	.000 672 3562	.015 574	23.162 970	.043 172 3562	8.64	3.317 236	6.63	100

Effective Rate is 8.68 %

Annual Percentage Rate is 8.50 %

SEMIANNUAL COMPOUND INTEREST AND ANNUITY

8.75 % S

	Amount Of 1	Amount Of 1 Per Period	Sinking Fund Payment	Present Worth Of 1	Present Worth of 1 Per Period	Periodic Payment To Amortize 1	Constant Annual Percent	Total Interest	Annual Add On Rate	
	What a single $ 1 deposit grows to in the future. The deposit is made at the beginning of the first period.	What a series of $ 1 deposits grow to in the future. A deposit is made at the end of each period.	The amount to be deposited at the end of each period that grows to $ 1 in the future.	What $ 1 to be paid in the future is worth today. Value today of a single $ 1 payment tomorrow.	What $ 1 to be paid at the end of each period is worth today. Value today of a series of $ 1 payments tomorrow.	The mortgage payment to amortize a loan of $ 1. An annuity certain, payable at the end of each period, worth $ 1 today.	The annual payment, including interest and principal, to amortize completely a loan of $ 100.	The total interest paid over the term of a loan of $ 1. The loan is amortized by regular periodic payments.	The average annual interest rate on a loan that is completely amortized by regular periodic payments.	
	$S = (1+i)^n$	$S\overline{n}| = \dfrac{(1+i)^n - 1}{i}$	$\dfrac{1}{S\overline{n}|} = \dfrac{i}{(1+i)^n - 1}$	$V^n = \dfrac{1}{(1+i)^n}$	$A\overline{n}| = \dfrac{1 - V^n}{i}$	$\dfrac{1}{A\overline{n}|} = \dfrac{i}{1 - V^n}$				

YEAR										PERIODS
	1.043 750	1.000 000	1.000 000 0000	.958 084	.958 084	1.043 750 0000	208.75	.043 750	8.75	1
	1.089 414	2.043 750	.489 296 6361	.917 925	1.876 008	.533 046 6361	106.61	.066 093	6.61	2
1	1.089 414	2.043 750	.489 296 6361	.917 925	1.876 008	.533 046 6361	106.61	.066 093	6.61	2
2	1.186 823	4.270 240	.234 178 8757	.842 586	3.598 043	.277 928 8757	55.59	.111 716	5.59	4
3	1.292 942	6.695 809	.149 347 1403	.773 430	5.178 741	.193 097 1403	38.62	.158 583	5.29	6
4	1.408 549	9.338 259	.107 086 3420	.709 951	6.629 702	.150 836 3420	30.17	.206 691	5.17	8
5	1.534 493	12.216 981	.081 853 2847	.651 681	7.961 575	.125 603 2847	25.13	.256 033	5.12	10
6	1.671 698	15.353 101	.065 133 4234	.598 194	9.184 134	.108 883 4234	21.78	.306 601	5.11	12
7	1.821 171	18.769 634	.053 277 5449	.549 097	10.306 352	.097 027 5449	19.41	.358 386	5.12	14
8	1.984 010	22.491 653	.044 460 9387	.504 030	11.336 463	.088 210 9387	17.65	.411 375	5.14	16
9	2.161 408	26.546 473	.037 669 7877	.462 661	12.282 027	.081 419 7877	16.29	.465 556	5.17	18
10	2.354 668	30.963 851	.032 295 7245	.424 688	13.149 983	.076 045 7245	15.21	.520 915	5.21	20
11	2.565 209	35.776 205	.027 951 5396	.389 832	13.946 702	.071 701 5396	14.35	.577 434	5.25	22
12	2.794 575	41.018 850	.024 379 0352	.357 836	14.678 030	.068 129 0352	13.63	.635 097	5.29	24
13	3.044 449	46.730 262	.021 399 4090	.328 467	15.349 333	.065 149 4090	13.03	.693 885	5.34	26
14	3.316 666	52.952 355	.018 884 9013	.301 508	15.965 540	.062 634 9013	12.53	.753 777	5.38	28
15	3.613 222	59.730 790	.016 741 7842	.276 761	16.531 171	.060 491 7842	12.10	.814 754	5.43	30
16	3.936 295	67.115 313	.014 899 7294	.254 046	17.050 377	.058 649 7294	11.73	.876 791	5.48	32
17	4.288 255	75.160 116	.013 304 9290	.233 195	17.526 970	.057 054 9290	11.42	.939 868	5.53	34
18	4.671 685	83.924 237	.011 915 5090	.214 056	17.964 445	.055 665 5090	11.14	1.003 958	5.58	36
19	5.089 400	93.471 994	.010 698 3917	.196 487	18.366 015	.054 448 3917	10.89	1.069 039	5.63	38
20	5.544 464	103.873 455	.009 627 0987	.180 360	18.734 626	.053 377 0987	10.68	1.135 084	5.68	40
21	6.040 217	115.204 952	.008 680 1824	.165 557	19.072 983	.052 430 1824	10.49	1.202 068	5.72	42
22	6.580 297	127.549 645	.007 840 0845	.151 969	19.383 570	.051 590 0845	10.32	1.269 964	5.77	44
23	7.168 668	140.998 127	.007 092 2928	.139 496	19.668 665	.050 842 2928	10.17	1.338 745	5.82	46
24	7.809 648	155.649 092	.006 424 7082	.128 047	19.930 360	.050 174 7082	10.04	1.408 386	5.87	48
25	8.507 940	171.610 060	.005 827 1642	.117 537	20.170 577	.049 577 1642	9.92	1.478 858	5.92	50
26	9.268 670	188.998 162	.005 291 0567	.107 890	20.391 078	.049 041 0567	9.81	1.550 135	5.96	52
27	10.097 419	207.941 006	.004 809 0563	.099 035	20.593 481	.048 559 0563	9.72	1.622 189	6.01	54
28	11.000 270	228.577 606	.004 374 8818	.090 907	20.779 272	.048 124 8818	9.63	1.694 993	6.05	56
29	11.983 849	251.059 408	.003 983 1210	.083 446	20.949 814	.047 733 1210	9.55	1.768 521	6.10	58
30	13.055 374	275.551 400	.003 629 0870	.076 597	21.106 359	.047 379 0870	9.48	1.842 745	6.14	60
31	14.222 708	302.233 320	.003 308 7020	.070 310	21.250 055	.047 058 7020	9.42	1.917 640	6.19	62
32	15.494 418	331.300 979	.003 018 4034	.064 539	21.381 957	.046 768 4034	9.36	1.993 178	6.23	64
33	16.879 837	362.967 696	.002 755 0661	.059 242	21.503 034	.046 505 0661	9.31	2.069 334	6.27	66
34	18.389 131	397.465 862	.002 515 9393	.054 380	21.614 173	.046 265 9393	9.26	2.146 084	6.31	68
35	20.033 378	435.048 649	.002 298 5935	.049 917	21.716 190	.046 048 5935	9.21	2.223 402	6.35	70
36	21.824 644	475.991 866	.002 100 8762	.045 820	21.809 834	.045 850 8762	9.18	2.301 263	6.39	72
37	23.776 074	520.595 983	.001 920 8754	.042 059	21.895 792	.045 670 8754	9.14	2.379 645	6.43	74
38	25.901 990	569.188 335	.001 756 8877	.038 607	21.974 695	.045 506 8877	9.11	2.458 523	6.47	76
39	28.217 992	622.125 526	.001 607 3927	.035 438	22.047 123	.045 357 3927	9.08	2.537 877	6.51	78
40	30.741 077	679.796 047	.001 471 0294	.032 530	22.113 605	.045 221 0294	9.05	2.617 682	6.54	80
41	33.489 762	742.623 123	.001 346 5781	.029 860	22.174 631	.045 096 5781	9.02	2.697 919	6.58	82
42	36.484 217	811.067 823	.001 232 9425	.027 409	22.230 649	.044 982 9425	9.00	2.778 567	6.62	84
43	39.746 419	885.632 442	.001 129 1366	.025 159	22.282 069	.044 879 1366	8.98	2.859 606	6.65	86
44	43.300 308	966.864 187	.001 034 2714	.023 095	22.329 268	.044 784 2714	8.96	2.941 016	6.68	88
45	47.171 965	1055.359 192	.000 947 5447	.021 199	22.372 594	.044 697 5447	8.94	3.022 779	6.72	90
46	51.389 802	1151.766 894	.000 868 2312	.019 459	22.412 363	.044 618 2312	8.93	3.104 877	6.75	92
47	55.984 773	1256.794 801	.000 795 6748	.017 862	22.448 869	.044 545 6748	8.91	3.187 293	6.78	94
48	60.990 599	1371.213 680	.000 729 2809	.016 396	22.482 378	.044 479 2809	8.90	3.270 011	6.81	96
49	66.444 016	1495.863 216	.000 668 5103	.015 050	22.513 137	.044 418 5103	8.89	3.353 014	6.84	98
50	72.385 045	1631.658 173	.000 612 8735	.013 815	22.541 371	.044 362 8735	8.88	3.436 287	6.87	100

Effective Rate is 8.94 %

Annual Percentage Rate is 8.75 %

SEMIANNUAL COMPOUND INTEREST AND ANNUITY

	Amount Of 1	Amount Of 1 Per Period	Sinking Fund Payment	Present Worth Of 1	Present Worth of 1 Per Period	Periodic Payment To Amortize 1	Constant Annual Percent	Total Interest	Annual Add On Rate	
	What a single $ 1 deposit grows to in the future. The deposit is made at the beginning of the first period.	What a series of $ 1 deposits grow to in the future. A deposit is made at the end of each period.	The amount to be deposited at the end of each period that grows to $ 1 in the future.	What $ 1 to be paid in the future is worth today. Value today of a single $ 1 payment tomorrow.	What $ 1 to be paid at the end of each period is worth today. Value today of a series of $ 1 payments tomorrow.	The mortgage payment to amortize a loan of $ 1. An annuity certain, payable at the end of each period, worth $ 1 today.	The annual payment, including interest and principal, to amortize completely a loan of $ 100.	The total interest paid over the term on a loan of $1. The loan is amortized by regular periodic payments.	The average annual interest rate on a loan that is completely amortized by regular periodic payments.	
	$S = (1+i)^n$	$S\overline{n}| = \dfrac{(1+i)^n - 1}{i}$	$\dfrac{1}{S\overline{n}|} = \dfrac{i}{(1+i)^n - 1}$	$V^n = \dfrac{1}{(1+i)^n}$	$A\overline{n}| = \dfrac{1-V^n}{i}$	$\dfrac{1}{A\overline{n}|} = \dfrac{i}{1-V^n}$				

YEAR										PERIODS
	1.045 000	1.000 000	1.000 000 0000	.956 938	.956 938	1.045 000 0000	209.00	.045 000	9.00	1
	1.092 025	2.045 000	.488 997 5550	.915 730	1.872 668	.533 997 5550	106.80	.067 995	6.80	2

YEAR										PERIODS
1	1.092 025	2.045 000	.488 997 5550	.915 730	1.872 668	.533 997 5550	106.80	.067 995	6.80	2
2	1.192 519	4.278 191	.233 743 6479	.838 561	3.587 526	.278 743 6479	55.75	.114 975	5.75	4
3	1.302 260	6.716 892	.148 878 3875	.767 896	5.157 872	.193 878 3875	38.78	.163 270	5.44	6
4	1.422 101	9.380 014	.106 609 6533	.703 185	6.595 886	.151 609 6533	30.33	.212 877	5.32	8
5	1.552 969	12.288 209	.081 378 8217	.643 928	7.912 718	.126 378 8217	25.28	.263 788	5.28	10
6	1.695 881	15.464 032	.064 666 1886	.589 664	9.118 581	.109 666 1886	21.94	.315 994	5.27	12
7	1.851 945	18.932 109	.052 820 3160	.539 973	10.222 825	.097 820 3160	19.57	.369 484	5.28	14
8	2.022 370	22.719 337	.044 015 3694	.494 469	11.234 015	.089 015 3694	17.81	.424 246	5.30	16
9	2.208 479	26.855 084	.037 236 8975	.452 800	12.159 992	.082 236 8975	16.45	.480 264	5.34	18
10	2.411 714	31.371 423	.031 876 1443	.414 643	13.007 936	.076 876 1443	15.38	.537 523	5.38	20
11	2.633 652	36.303 378	.027 545 6461	.379 701	13.784 425	.072 545 6461	14.51	.596 004	5.42	22
12	2.876 014	41.689 196	.023 987 0299	.347 703	14.495 478	.068 987 0299	13.80	.655 689	5.46	24
13	3.140 679	47.570 645	.021 021 3674	.318 402	15.146 611	.066 021 3674	13.21	.716 556	5.51	26
14	3.429 700	53.993 333	.018 520 8051	.291 571	15.742 874	.063 520 8051	12.71	.778 583	5.56	28
15	3.745 318	61.007 070	.016 391 5429	.267 000	16.288 889	.061 391 5429	12.28	.841 746	5.61	30
16	4.089 981	68.666 245	.014 563 1962	.244 500	16.788 891	.059 563 1962	11.92	.906 022	5.66	32
17	4.466 362	77.030 256	.012 981 9119	.223 896	17.246 758	.057 981 9119	11.60	.971 385	5.71	34
18	4.877 378	86.163 966	.011 605 7796	.205 028	17.666 041	.056 605 7796	11.33	1.037 808	5.77	36
19	5.326 219	96.138 205	.010 401 6920	.187 750	18.049 990	.055 401 6920	11.09	1.105 264	5.82	38
20	5.816 365	107.030 323	.009 343 1466	.171 929	18.401 584	.054 343 1466	10.87	1.173 726	5.87	40
21	6.351 615	118.924 789	.008 408 6759	.157 440	18.723 550	.053 408 6759	10.69	1.243 164	5.92	42
22	6.936 123	131.913 842	.007 580 7056	.144 173	19.018 383	.052 580 7056	10.52	1.313 551	5.97	44
23	7.574 420	146.098 214	.006 844 7107	.132 023	19.288 371	.051 844 7107	10.37	1.384 857	6.02	46
24	8.271 456	161.587 902	.006 188 5821	.120 898	19.535 607	.051 188 5821	10.24	1.457 052	6.07	48
25	9.032 636	178.503 028	.005 602 1459	.110 710	19.762 008	.050 602 1459	10.13	1.530 107	6.12	50
26	9.863 865	196.974 769	.005 076 7923	.101 380	19.969 330	.050 076 7923	10.02	1.603 993	6.17	52
27	10.771 587	217.146 373	.004 605 1886	.092 837	20.159 181	.049 605 1886	9.93	1.678 680	6.22	54
28	11.762 842	239.174 268	.004 181 0518	.085 013	20.333 034	.049 181 0518	9.84	1.754 139	6.26	56
29	12.845 318	263.229 280	.003 798 9695	.077 849	20.492 236	.048 798 9695	9.76	1.830 340	6.31	58
30	14.027 408	289.497 954	.003 454 2558	.071 289	20.638 022	.048 454 2558	9.70	1.907 255	6.36	60
31	15.318 280	318.184 003	.003 142 8356	.065 281	20.771 523	.048 142 8356	9.63	1.984 856	6.40	62
32	16.727 945	349.509 886	.002 861 1494	.059 780	20.893 773	.047 861 1494	9.58	2.063 114	6.45	64
33	18.267 334	383.718 533	.002 606 0769	.054 743	21.005 722	.047 606 0769	9.53	2.142 001	6.49	66
34	19.948 385	421.075 231	.002 374 8725	.050 129	21.108 236	.047 374 8725	9.48	2.221 491	6.53	68
35	21.784 136	461.869 680	.002 165 1129	.045 905	21.202 112	.047 165 1129	9.44	2.301 558	6.58	70
36	23.788 821	506.418 237	.001 974 6524	.042 037	21.288 077	.046 974 6524	9.40	2.382 175	6.62	72
37	25.977 987	555.066 375	.001 801 5863	.038 494	21.366 797	.046 801 5863	9.37	2.463 317	6.66	74
38	28.368 611	608.191 358	.001 644 2194	.035 250	21.438 884	.046 644 2194	9.33	2.544 961	6.70	76
39	30.979 233	666.205 168	.001 501 0391	.032 280	21.504 890	.046 501 0391	9.31	2.627 081	6.74	78
40	33.830 096	729.557 699	.001 370 6935	.029 559	21.565 345	.046 370 6935	9.28	2.709 655	6.77	80
41	36.943 311	798.740 246	.001 251 9715	.027 068	21.620 700	.046 251 9715	9.26	2.792 662	6.81	82
42	40.343 019	874.289 317	.001 143 7861	.024 787	21.671 390	.046 143 7861	9.23	2.876 078	6.85	84
43	44.055 586	956.790 791	.001 045 1606	.022 699	21.717 809	.046 045 1606	9.21	2.959 884	6.88	86
44	48.109 801	1046.884 464	.000 955 2152	.020 786	21.760 316	.045 955 2152	9.20	3.044 059	6.92	88
45	52.537 105	1145.269 007	.000 873 1573	.019 034	21.799 241	.045 873 1573	9.18	3.128 584	6.95	90
46	57.371 832	1252.707 387	.000 798 2710	.017 430	21.834 885	.045 798 2710	9.16	3.213 441	6.99	92
47	62.651 475	1370.032 784	.000 729 9095	.015 961	21.867 526	.045 729 9095	9.15	3.298 612	7.02	94
48	68.416 977	1498.155 051	.000 667 4877	.014 616	21.897 417	.045 667 4877	9.14	3.384 079	7.05	96
49	74.713 050	1638.067 770	.000 610 4754	.013 385	21.924 788	.045 610 4754	9.13	3.469 827	7.08	98
50	81.588 518	1790.855 956	.000 558 3922	.012 257	21.949 853	.045 558 3922	9.12	3.555 839	7.11	100

SEMIANNUAL COMPOUND INTEREST AND ANNUITY

Amount Of 1	Amount Of 1 Per Period	Sinking Fund Payment	Present Worth Of 1	Present Worth of 1 Per Period	Periodic Payment To Amortize 1	Constant Annual Percent	Total Interest	Annual Add On Rate
What a single $ 1 deposit grows to in the future. The deposit is made at the beginning of the first period.	What a series of $ 1 deposits grow to in the future. A deposit is made at the end of each period.	The amount to be deposited at the end of each period that grows to $ 1 in the future.	What $ 1 to be paid in the future is worth today. Value today of a single $ 1 payment tomorrow.	What $ 1 to be paid at the end of each period is worth today. Value today of a series of $ 1 payments tomorrow.	The mortgage payment to amortize a loan of $ 1. An annuity certain, payable at the end of each period, worth $ 1 today.	The annual payment, including interest and principal, to amortize completely a loan of $ 100.	The total interest paid over the term on a loan of $1. The loan is amortized by regular periodic payments.	The average annual interest rate on a loan that is completely amortized by regular periodic payments.

$$S = (1+i)^n \qquad S\overline{n}| = \frac{(1+i)^n - 1}{i} \qquad \frac{1}{S\overline{n}|} = \frac{i}{(1+i)^n - 1} \qquad V^n = \frac{1}{(1+i)^n} \qquad A\overline{n}| = \frac{1-V^n}{i} \qquad \frac{1}{A\overline{n}|} = \frac{i}{1-V^n}$$

PERIODS

YEAR

	Amount Of 1	Amount Of 1 Per Period	Sinking Fund Payment	Present Worth Of 1	Present Worth of 1 Per Period	Periodic Payment To Amortize 1	Constant Annual Percent	Total Interest	Annual Add On Rate	PERIODS
	1.046 250	1.000 000	1.000 000 0000	.955 795	.955 795	1.046 250 0000	209.25	.046 250	9.25	1
	1.094 639	2.046 250	.488 698 8393	.913 543	1.869 338	.534 948 8393	106.99	.069 898	6.99	2
1	1.094 639	2.046 250	.488 698 8393	.913 543	1.869 338	.534 948 8393	106.99	.069 898	6.99	2
2	1.198 235	4.286 155	.233 309 3315	.834 561	3.577 058	.279 559 3315	55.92	.118 237	5.91	4
3	1.311 634	6.738 043	.148 411 0470	.762 408	5.137 135	.194 661 0470	38.94	.167 966	5.60	6
4	1.435 766	9.421 975	.106 134 8608	.696 492	6.562 332	.152 384 8608	30.48	.219 079	5.48	8
5	1.571 646	12.359 912	.080 906 7260	.636 276	7.864 311	.127 156 7260	25.44	.271 567	5.43	10
6	1.720 385	15.575 892	.064 201 7793	.581 265	9.053 725	.110 451 7793	22.10	.325 421	5.42	12
7	1.883 201	19.096 230	.052 366 3567	.531 011	10.140 306	.098 616 3567	19.73	.380 629	5.44	14
8	2.061 425	22.949 729	.043 573 4984	.485 101	11.132 944	.089 823 4984	17.97	.437 176	5.46	16
9	2.256 516	27.167 920	.036 808 1173	.443 161	12.039 762	.083 058 1173	16.62	.495 046	5.50	18
10	2.470 071	31.785 317	.031 461 0675	.404 847	12.868 180	.077 711 0675	15.55	.554 221	5.54	20
11	2.703 836	36.839 699	.027 144 6297	.369 845	13.624 975	.073 394 6297	14.68	.614 682	5.59	22
12	2.959 725	42.372 424	.023 600 2547	.337 869	14.316 340	.069 850 2547	13.98	.676 406	5.64	24
13	3.239 830	48.428 761	.020 648 8869	.308 658	14.947 932	.066 898 8869	13.38	.739 371	5.69	26
14	3.546 445	55.058 263	.018 162 5781	.281 973	15.524 918	.064 412 5781	12.89	.803 552	5.74	28
15	3.882 077	62.315 175	.016 047 4554	.257 594	16.052 020	.062 297 4554	12.46	.868 924	5.79	30
16	4.249 473	70.258 875	.014 233 0773	.235 323	16.533 550	.060 483 0773	12.10	.935 458	5.85	32
17	4.651 639	78.954 359	.012 665 5451	.214 978	16.973 449	.058 915 5451	11.79	1.003 129	5.90	34
18	5.091 866	88.472 776	.011 302 9120	.196 392	17.375 315	.057 552 9120	11.52	1.071 905	5.96	36
19	5.573 755	98.892 006	.010 112 0408	.179 412	17.742 438	.056 362 0408	11.28	1.141 758	6.01	38
20	6.101 250	110.297 303	.009 066 4048	.163 901	18.077 820	.055 316 4048	11.07	1.212 656	6.06	40
21	6.678 667	122.781 987	.008 144 5172	.149 730	18.384 206	.054 394 5172	10.88	1.284 570	6.12	42
22	7.310 730	136.448 209	.007 328 7880	.136 785	18.664 103	.053 578 7880	10.72	1.357 467	6.17	44
23	8.002 610	151.407 789	.006 604 6800	.124 959	18.919 800	.052 854 6800	10.58	1.431 315	6.22	46
24	8.759 970	167.783 130	.005 960 0748	.114 156	19.153 391	.052 210 0748	10.45	1.506 084	6.28	48
25	9.589 005	185.708 219	.005 384 7913	.104 286	19.366 787	.051 634 7913	10.33	1.581 740	6.33	50
26	10.496 500	205.329 720	.004 870 2156	.095 270	19.561 733	.051 120 2156	10.23	1.658 251	6.38	52
27	11.489 878	226.808 183	.004 409 0120	.087 033	19.739 824	.050 659 0120	10.14	1.735 587	6.43	54
28	12.577 270	250.319 346	.003 994 8970	.079 509	19.902 519	.050 244 8970	10.05	1.813 714	6.48	56
29	13.767 571	276.055 585	.003 622 4589	.072 634	20.051 147	.049 872 4589	9.98	1.892 603	6.53	58
30	15.070 521	304.227 476	.003 287 0141	.066 355	20.186 925	.049 537 0141	9.91	1.972 221	6.57	60
31	16.496 781	335.065 529	.002 984 4908	.060 618	20.310 965	.049 234 4908	9.85	2.052 538	6.62	62
32	18.058 021	368.822 067	.002 711 3345	.055 377	20.424 280	.048 961 3345	9.80	2.133 525	6.67	64
33	19.767 015	405.773 292	.002 464 4303	.050 589	20.527 798	.048 714 4303	9.75	2.215 152	6.71	66
34	21.637 746	446.221 546	.002 241 0393	.046 216	20.622 367	.048 491 0393	9.70	2.297 391	6.76	68
35	23.685 523	490.497 784	.002 038 7452	.042 220	20.708 759	.048 288 7452	9.66	2.380 212	6.80	70
36	25.927 098	538.964 285	.001 855 4105	.038 570	20.787 682	.048 105 4105	9.63	2.463 066	6.84	72
37	28.380 814	592.017 609	.001 689 1389	.035 235	20.859 782	.047 939 1389	9.59	2.547 496	6.89	74
38	31.066 748	650.091 851	.001 538 2442	.032 189	20.925 649	.047 788 2442	9.56	2.631 907	6.93	76
39	34.006 876	713.662 184	.001 401 2232	.029 406	20.985 820	.047 651 2232	9.54	2.716 795	6.97	78
40	37.225 255	783.248 754	.001 276 7336	.026 863	21.040 790	.047 526 7336	9.51	2.802 139	7.01	80
41	40.748 218	859.420 932	.001 163 5742	.024 541	21.091 006	.047 413 5742	9.49	2.887 913	7.04	82
42	44.604 591	942.801 973	.001 060 6681	.022 419	21.136 882	.047 310 6681	9.47	2.974 096	7.08	84
43	48.825 928	1034.074 118	.000 967 0487	.020 481	21.178 791	.047 217 0487	9.45	3.060 666	7.12	86
44	53.446 768	1133.984 173	.000 881 8465	.018 710	21.217 077	.047 131 8465	9.43	3.147 603	7.15	88
45	58.504 920	1243.349 622	.000 804 2790	.017 093	21.252 052	.047 054 2790	9.42	3.234 885	7.19	90
46	64.041 771	1363.065 315	.000 733 6406	.015 615	21.284 004	.046 983 6406	9.40	3.322 495	7.22	92
47	70.102 624	1494.110 789	.000 669 2944	.014 265	21.313 193	.046 919 2944	9.39	3.410 414	7.26	94
48	76.737 071	1637.558 283	.000 610 6653	.013 032	21.339 859	.046 860 6653	9.38	3.498 624	7.29	96
49	83.999 395	1794.581 514	.000 557 2330	.011 905	21.364 220	.046 807 2330	9.37	3.587 109	7.32	98
50	91.949 019	1966.465 276	.000 508 5267	.010 876	21.386 474	.046 758 5267	9.36	3.675 853	7.35	100

Effective Rate is 9.46 %

Annual Percentage Rate is 9.25 %

Amount Of 1	Amount Of 1 Per Period	Sinking Fund Payment	Present Worth Of 1	Present Worth of 1 Per Period	Periodic Payment To Amortize 1	Constant Annual Percent	Total Interest	Annual Add On Rate
What a single $ 1 deposit grows to in the future. The deposit is made at the beginning of the first period.	What a series of $ 1 deposits grow to in the future. A deposit is made at the end of each period.	The amount to be deposited at the end of each period that grows to $ 1 in the future.	What $ 1 to be paid in the future is worth today. Value today of a single $ 1 payment tomorrow.	What $ 1 to be paid at the end of each period is worth today. Value today of a series of $ 1 payments tomorrow.	The mortgage payment to amortize a loan of $ 1. An annuity certain, payable at the end of each period, worth $ 1 today.	The annual payment, including interest and principal, to amortize completely a loan of $ 100.	The total interest paid over the term on a loan of $1. The loan is amortized by regular periodic payments.	The average annual interest rate on a loan that is completely amortized by regular periodic payments.

$$S = (1+i)^n \qquad S\overline{n}| = \frac{(1+i)^n - 1}{i} \qquad \frac{1}{S\overline{n}|} = \frac{i}{(1+i)^n - 1} \qquad V^n = \frac{1}{(1+i)^n} \qquad A\overline{n}| = \frac{1-V^n}{i} \qquad \frac{1}{A\overline{n}|} = \frac{i}{1-V^n}$$

YEAR

PERIODS

	Amount Of 1	Amount Of 1 Per Period	Sinking Fund Payment	Present Worth Of 1	Present Worth of 1 Per Period	Periodic Payment To Amortize 1	Constant Annual Percent	Total Interest	Annual Add On Rate	
	1.047 500	1.000 000	1.000 000 0000	.954 654	.954 654	1.047 500 0000	209.50	.047 500	9.50	1
	1.097 256	2.047 500	.488 400 4884	.911 364	1.866 018	.535 900 4884	107.19	.071 801	7.18	2
1	1.097 256	2.047 500	.488 400 4884	.911 364	1.866 018	.535 900 4884	107.19	.071 801	7.18	2
2	1.203 971	4.294 132	.232 875 9246	.830 585	3.566 640	.280 375 9246	56.08	.121 504	6.08	4
3	1.321 065	6.759 263	.147 945 1156	.756 965	5.116 526	.195 445 1156	39.09	.172 671	5.76	6
4	1.449 547	9.464 144	.105 661 9598	.689 871	6.529 036	.153 161 9598	30.64	.225 296	5.63	8
5	1.590 524	12.432 091	.080 436 9909	.628 723	7.816 348	.127 936 9909	25.59	.279 370	5.59	10
6	1.745 213	15.688 690	.063 740 1861	.572 996	8.989 557	.111 240 1861	22.25	.334 882	5.58	12
7	1.914 946	19.262 013	.051 916 6544	.522 208	10.058 778	.099 416 6544	19.89	.391 819	5.60	14
8	2.101 186	23.182 864	.043 135 3090	.475 922	11.033 228	.090 635 3090	18.13	.450 165	5.63	16
9	2.305 540	27.485 042	.036 383 4258	.433 738	11.921 306	.083 883 4258	16.78	.509 902	5.67	18
10	2.529 768	32.205 635	.031 050 4673	.395 293	12.730 669	.078 550 4673	15.72	.571 009	5.71	20
11	2.775 803	37.385 334	.026 748 4572	.360 256	13.468 293	.074 248 4572	14.85	.633 466	5.76	22
12	3.045 768	43.068 791	.023 218 6689	.328 324	14.140 538	.070 718 6689	14.15	.697 248	5.81	24
13	3.341 988	49.305 000	.020 281 9186	.299 223	14.753 197	.067 781 9186	13.56	.762 330	5.86	26
14	3.667 017	56.147 720	.017 810 1623	.272 701	15.311 553	.065 310 1623	13.07	.828 685	5.92	28
15	4.023 657	63.655 936	.015 709 4539	.248 530	15.820 418	.063 209 4539	12.65	.896 284	5.98	30
16	4.414 983	71.894 374	.013 909 2942	.226 501	16.284 180	.061 409 2942	12.29	.965 097	6.03	32
17	4.844 367	80.934 051	.012 355 7388	.206 425	16.706 836	.059 855 7388	11.98	1.035 095	6.09	34
18	5.315 512	90.852 894	.011 006 8041	.188 129	17.092 029	.058 506 8041	11.71	1.106 245	6.15	36
19	5.832 479	101.736 405	.009 829 3231	.171 454	17.443 081	.057 329 3231	11.47	1.178 514	6.20	38
20	6.399 724	113.678 406	.008 796 7454	.156 257	17.763 016	.056 296 7454	11.26	1.251 870	6.26	40
21	7.022 137	126.781 842	.007 887 5648	.142 407	18.054 594	.055 387 5648	11.08	1.326 278	6.32	42
22	7.705 084	141.159 669	.007 084 1765	.129 784	18.320 328	.054 584 1765	10.92	1.401 704	6.37	44
23	8.454 452	156.935 829	.006 372 0312	.118 281	18.562 508	.053 872 0312	10.78	1.478 113	6.43	46
24	9.276 700	174.246 319	.005 739 0022	.107 797	18.783 222	.053 239 0022	10.65	1.555 472	6.48	48
25	10.178 917	193.240 362	.005 174 9023	.098 242	18.984 373	.052 674 9023	10.54	1.633 745	6.54	50
26	11.168 881	214.081 695	.004 671 1140	.089 534	19.167 695	.052 171 1140	10.44	1.712 898	6.59	52
27	12.255 124	236.949 978	.004 220 3000	.081 599	19.334 768	.051 720 3000	10.35	1.792 896	6.64	54
28	13.447 011	262.042 344	.003 816 1771	.074 366	19.487 032	.051 316 1771	10.27	1.873 706	6.69	56
29	14.754 817	289.575 100	.003 453 3356	.067 774	19.625 801	.050 953 3356	10.20	1.955 293	6.74	58
30	16.189 815	319.785 589	.003 127 0953	.061 767	19.752 269	.050 627 0953	10.13	2.037 626	6.79	60
31	17.764 376	352.934 236	.002 833 3891	.056 292	19.867 528	.050 333 3891	10.07	2.120 670	6.84	62
32	19.492 073	389.306 796	.002 568 6682	.051 303	19.972 570	.050 068 6682	10.02	2.204 395	6.89	64
33	21.387 799	429.216 815	.002 329 8248	.046 756	20.068 303	.049 829 8248	9.97	2.288 768	6.94	66
34	23.467 896	473.008 333	.002 114 1277	.042 611	20.155 549	.049 614 1277	9.93	2.373 761	6.98	68
35	25.750 295	521.058 849	.001 919 1690	.038 835	20.235 063	.049 419 1690	9.89	2.459 342	7.03	70
36	28.254 673	573.782 579	.001 742 8204	.035 392	20.307 529	.049 242 8204	9.85	2.545 483	7.07	72
37	31.002 616	631.634 021	.001 583 1953	.032 255	20.373 572	.049 083 1953	9.82	2.632 156	7.11	74
38	34.017 814	695.111 877	.001 438 6173	.029 396	20.433 761	.048 938 6173	9.79	2.719 335	7.16	76
39	37.326 259	764.763 352	.001 307 5940	.026 791	20.488 615	.048 807 5940	9.77	2.806 992	7.20	78
40	40.956 471	841.188 868	.001 188 7937	.024 416	20.538 607	.048 688 7937	9.74	2.895 104	7.24	80
41	44.939 744	925.047 243	.001 081 0259	.022 252	20.584 168	.048 581 0259	9.72	2.983 644	7.28	82
42	49.310 415	1017.061 368	.000 983 2248	.020 280	20.625 691	.048 483 2248	9.70	3.072 591	7.32	84
43	54.106 161	1118.024 443	.000 894 4348	.018 482	20.663 533	.048 394 4348	9.68	3.161 921	7.35	86
44	59.368 323	1228.806 808	.000 813 7976	.016 844	20.698 021	.048 313 7976	9.67	3.251 614	7.39	88
45	65.142 264	1350.363 450	.000 740 5414	.015 351	20.729 452	.048 240 5414	9.65	3.341 649	7.43	90
46	71.477 756	1483.742 235	.000 673 9715	.013 990	20.758 098	.048 173 9715	9.64	3.432 005	7.46	92
47	78.429 415	1630.092 941	.000 613 4620	.012 750	20.784 204	.048 113 4620	9.63	3.522 665	7.50	94
48	86.057 165	1790.677 168	.000 558 4480	.011 620	20.807 996	.048 058 4480	9.62	3.613 611	7.53	96
49	94.426 763	1966.879 214	.000 508 4196	.010 590	20.829 680	.048 008 4196	9.61	3.704 825	7.56	98
50	103.610 356	2160.218 011	.000 462 9162	.009 652	20.849 441	.047 962 9162	9.60	3.796 292	7.59	100

Effective Rate is 9.73 %

Annual Percentage Rate is 9.50 %

SEMIANNUAL COMPOUND INTEREST AND ANNUITY

9.75 % S

	Amount Of 1	Amount Of 1 Per Period	Sinking Fund Payment	Present Worth Of 1	Present Worth of 1 Per Period	Periodic Payment To Amortize 1	Constant Annual Percent	Total Interest	Annual Add On Rate	
	What a single $ 1 deposit grows to in the future. The deposit is made at the beginning of the first period.	What a series of $ 1 deposits grow to in the future. A deposit is made at the end of each period.	The amount to be deposited at the end of each period that grows to $ 1 in the future.	What $ 1 to be paid in the future is worth today. Value today of a single $ 1 payment tomorrow.	What $ 1 to be paid at the end of each period is worth today. Value today of a series of $ 1 payments tomorrow.	The mortgage payment to amortize a loan of $ 1. An annuity certain, payable at the end of each period, worth $ 1 today.	The annual payment, including interest and principal, to amortize completely a loan of $ 100.	The total interest paid over the term on a loan of $1. The loan is amortized by regular periodic payments.	The average annual interest rate on a loan that is completely amortized by regular periodic payments.	

$$S = (1+i)^n \qquad S\overline{n}| = \frac{(1+i)^n - 1}{i} \qquad \frac{1}{S\overline{n}|} = \frac{i}{(1+i)^n - 1} \qquad V^n = \frac{1}{(1+i)^n} \qquad A\overline{n}| = \frac{1-V^n}{i} \qquad \frac{1}{A\overline{n}|} = \frac{i}{1-V^n}$$

PERIODS

YEAR

	Amount Of 1	Amount Of 1 Per Period	Sinking Fund Payment	Present Worth Of 1	Present Worth of 1 Per Period	Periodic Payment To Amortize 1	Constant Annual Percent	Total Interest	Annual Add On Rate	Periods
	1.048 750	1.000 000	1.000 000 0000	.953 516	.953 516	1.048 750 0000	209.75	.048 750	9.75	1
	1.099 877	2.048 750	.488 102 5015	.909 193	1.862 709	.536 852 5015	107.38	.073 705	7.37	2
1	1.099 877	2.048 750	.488 102 5015	.909 193	1.862 709	.536 852 5015	107.38	.073 705	7.37	2
2	1.209 728	4.302 122	.232 443 4256	.826 632	3.556 271	.281 193 4256	56.24	.124 774	6.24	4
3	1.330 552	6.780 553	.147 480 5904	.751 568	5.096 045	.196 230 5904	39.25	.177 384	5.91	6
4	1.463 443	9.506 522	.105 190 9457	.683 320	6.495 998	.153 940 9457	30.79	.231 528	5.79	8
5	1.609 607	12.504 750	.079 969 6094	.621 270	7.768 824	.128 719 6094	25.75	.287 196	5.74	10
6	1.770 369	15.802 432	.063 281 3995	.564 854	8.926 069	.112 031 3995	22.41	.344 377	5.74	12
7	1.947 187	19.429 474	.051 468 1962	.513 561	9.978 228	.100 218 1962	20.05	.403 055	5.76	14
8	2.141 665	23.418 773	.042 700 7845	.466 926	10.934 843	.091 450 7845	18.30	.463 213	5.79	16
9	2.355 567	27.806 510	.035 962 8014	.424 526	11.804 591	.084 712 8014	16.95	.524 830	5.83	18
10	2.590 833	32.632 479	.030 644 3163	.385 976	12.595 360	.079 394 3163	15.88	.587 886	5.88	20
11	2.849 597	37.940 449	.026 357 0948	.350 927	13.314 321	.075 107 0948	15.03	.652 356	5.93	22
12	3.134 205	43.778 560	.022 842 2314	.319 060	13.967 996	.071 592 2314	14.32	.718 214	5.99	24
13	3.447 238	50.199 762	.019 920 4131	.290 087	14.562 312	.068 670 4131	13.74	.785 431	6.04	26
14	3.791 537	57.262 292	.017 463 4994	.263 745	15.102 660	.066 213 4994	13.25	.853 978	6.10	28
15	4.170 222	65.030 203	.015 377 4701	.239 795	15.593 941	.064 127 4701	12.83	.923 824	6.16	30
16	4.586 730	73.573 946	.013 591 7680	.218 020	16.040 610	.062 341 7680	12.47	.994 937	6.22	32
17	5.044 837	82.971 009	.012 052 4026	.198 222	16.446 719	.060 802 4026	12.17	1.067 282	6.28	34
18	5.548 698	93.306 618	.010 717 3534	.180 222	16.815 949	.059 467 3534	11.90	1.140 825	6.34	36
19	6.102 882	104.674 512	.009 553 4240	.163 857	17.151 651	.058 303 4240	11.67	1.215 530	6.40	38
20	6.712 417	117.177 792	.008 534 0403	.148 978	17.456 869	.057 284 0403	11.46	1.291 362	6.46	40
21	7.382 831	130.929 858	.007 637 6773	.135 449	17.734 371	.056 387 6773	11.28	1.368 282	6.52	42
22	8.120 202	146.055 432	.006 846 7156	.123 150	17.986 674	.055 596 7156	11.12	1.446 255	6.57	44
23	8.931 220	162.691 696	.006 146 5952	.111 967	18.216 066	.054 896 5952	10.98	1.525 243	6.63	46
24	9.823 240	180.989 534	.005 525 1814	.101 799	18.424 628	.054 275 1814	10.86	1.605 209	6.69	48
25	10.804 351	201.114 896	.004 972 2821	.092 555	18.614 250	.053 722 2821	10.75	1.686 114	6.74	50
26	11.883 453	223.250 310	.004 479 2771	.084 151	18.786 654	.053 229 2771	10.65	1.767 922	6.80	52
27	13.070 331	247.596 534	.004 038 8287	.076 509	18.943 402	.052 788 8287	10.56	1.850 597	6.85	54
28	14.375 751	274.374 375	.003 644 6552	.069 562	19.085 916	.052 394 6552	10.48	1.934 101	6.91	56
29	15.811 551	303.826 694	.003 291 3500	.063 245	19.215 489	.052 041 3500	10.41	2.018 398	6.96	58
30	17.390 755	336.220 610	.002 974 2377	.057 502	19.333 296	.051 724 2377	10.35	2.103 454	7.01	60
31	19.127 684	371.849 919	.002 689 2570	.052 280	19.440 405	.051 439 2570	10.29	2.189 234	7.06	62
32	21.038 091	411.037 760	.002 432 8665	.047 533	19.537 788	.051 182 8665	10.24	2.275 703	7.11	64
33	23.139 303	454.139 549	.002 201 9663	.043 217	19.626 328	.050 951 9663	10.20	2.362 830	7.16	66
34	25.450 377	501.546 196	.001 993 8343	.039 292	19.706 828	.050 743 8343	10.15	2.450 581	7.21	68
35	27.992 273	553.687 656	.001 806 0724	.035 724	19.780 018	.050 556 0724	10.12	2.538 925	7.25	70
36	30.788 045	611.036 826	.001 636 5626	.032 480	19.846 561	.050 386 5626	10.08	2.627 833	7.30	72
37	33.863 049	674.113 833	.001 483 4290	.029 531	19.907 062	.050 233 4290	10.05	2.717 274	7.34	74
38	37.245 174	743.490 756	.001 345 0066	.026 849	19.962 069	.050 095 0066	10.02	2.807 221	7.39	76
39	40.965 094	819.796 807	.001 219 8145	.024 411	20.012 082	.049 969 8145	10.00	2.897 646	7.43	78
40	45.056 547	903.724 044	.001 106 5325	.022 194	20.057 552	.049 856 5325	9.98	2.988 523	7.47	80
41	49.556 640	996.033 645	.001 003 9821	.020 179	20.098 894	.049 753 9821	9.96	3.079 827	7.51	82
42	54.506 187	1097.562 811	.000 911 1096	.018 347	20.136 481	.049 661 1096	9.94	3.171 533	7.55	84
43	59.950 078	1209.232 362	.000 826 9709	.016 681	20.170 655	.049 576 9709	9.92	3.263 620	7.59	86
44	65.937 685	1332.055 084	.000 750 7197	.015 166	20.201 726	.049 500 7197	9.91	3.356 063	7.63	88
45	72.523 315	1467.144 916	.000 681 5959	.013 789	20.229 976	.049 431 5959	9.89	3.448 844	7.66	90
46	79.766 694	1615.727 057	.000 618 9164	.012 537	20.255 660	.049 368 9164	9.88	3.541 940	7.70	92
47	87.733 517	1779.149 072	.000 562 0664	.011 398	20.279 012	.049 312 0664	9.87	3.635 334	7.73	94
48	96.496 039	1958.893 115	.000 510 4924	.010 363	20.300 244	.049 260 4924	9.86	3.729 007	7.77	96
49	106.133 732	2156.589 376	.000 463 6951	.009 422	20.319 547	.049 213 6951	9.85	3.822 942	7.80	98
50	116.734 004	2374.030 860	.000 421 2245	.008 566	20.337 098	.049 171 2245	9.84	3.917 122	7.83	100

Effective Rate is 9.99 %

8 - 395

Annual Percentage Rate is 9.75 %

	Amount Of 1	Amount Of 1 Per Period	Sinking Fund Payment	Present Worth Of 1	Present Worth of 1 Per Period	Periodic Payment To Amortize 1	Constant Annual Percent	Total Interest	Annual Add On Rate	
	What a single $ 1 deposit grows to in the future. The deposit is made at the beginning of the first period.	What a series of $ 1 deposits grow to in the future. A deposit is made at the end of each period.	The amount to be deposited at the end of each period that grows to $ 1 in the future.	What $ 1 to be paid in the future is worth today. Value today of a single $ 1 payment tomorrow.	What $ 1 to be paid at the end of each period is worth today. Value today of a series of $ 1 payments tomorrow.	The mortgage payment to amortize a loan of $ 1. An annuity certain, payable at the end of each period, worth $ 1 today.	The annual payment, including interest and principal, to amortize completely a loan of $ 100.	The total interest paid over the term on a loan of $1. The loan is amortized by regular periodic payments.	The average annual interest rate on a loan that is completely amortized by regular periodic payments.	
	$S = (1+i)^n$	$S\overline{n}| = \dfrac{(1+i)^n - 1}{i}$	$\dfrac{1}{S\overline{n}|} = \dfrac{i}{(1+i)^n - 1}$	$V^n = \dfrac{1}{(1+i)^n}$	$A\overline{n}| = \dfrac{1-V^n}{i}$	$\dfrac{1}{A\overline{n}|} = \dfrac{i}{1-V^n}$				

YEAR   **PERIODS**

	Amount Of 1	Amount Of 1 Per Period	Sinking Fund Payment	Present Worth Of 1	Present Worth of 1 Per Period	Periodic Payment To Amortize 1	Constant Annual Percent	Total Interest	Annual Add On Rate	
	1.050 000	1.000 000	1.000 000 0000	.952 381	.952 381	1.050 000 0000	210.00	.050 000	10.00	1
	1.102 500	2.050 000	.487 804 8780	.907 029	1.859 410	.537 804 8780	107.57	.075 610	7.56	2
1	1.102 500	2.050 000	.487 804 8780	.907 029	1.859 410	.537 804 8780	107.57	.075 610	7.56	2
2	1.215 506	4.310 125	.232 011 8326	.822 702	3.545 951	.282 011 8326	56.41	.128 047	6.40	4
3	1.340 096	6.801 913	.147 017 4681	.746 215	5.075 692	.197 017 4681	39.41	.182 105	6.07	6
4	1.477 455	9.549 109	.104 721 8136	.676 839	6.463 213	.154 721 8136	30.95	.237 775	5.94	8
5	1.628 895	12.577 893	.079 504 5750	.613 913	7.721 735	.129 504 5750	25.91	.295 046	5.90	10
6	1.795 856	15.917 127	.062 825 4100	.556 837	8.863 252	.112 825 4100	22.57	.353 905	5.90	12
7	1.979 932	19.598 632	.051 023 9695	.505 068	9.898 641	.101 023 9695	20.21	.414 336	5.92	14
8	2.182 875	23.657 492	.042 269 9080	.458 112	10.837 770	.092 269 9080	18.46	.476 319	5.95	16
9	2.406 619	28.132 385	.035 546 2223	.415 521	11.689 587	.085 546 2223	17.11	.539 832	6.00	18
10	2.653 298	33.065 954	.030 242 5872	.376 889	12.462 210	.080 242 5872	16.05	.604 852	6.05	20
11	2.925 261	38.505 214	.025 970 5086	.341 850	13.163 003	.075 970 5086	15.20	.671 351	6.10	22
12	3.225 100	44.501 999	.022 470 9008	.310 068	13.798 642	.072 470 9008	14.50	.739 302	6.16	24
13	3.555 673	51.113 454	.019 564 3207	.281 241	14.375 185	.069 564 3207	13.92	.808 672	6.22	26
14	3.920 129	58.402 583	.017 122 5304	.255 094	14.898 127	.067 122 5304	13.43	.879 431	6.28	28
15	4.321 942	66.438 848	.015 051 4351	.231 377	15.372 451	.065 051 4351	13.02	.951 543	6.34	30
16	4.764 941	75.298 829	.013 280 4189	.209 866	15.802 677	.063 280 4189	12.66	1.024 973	6.41	32
17	5.253 348	85.066 959	.011 755 4454	.190 355	16.192 904	.061 755 4454	12.36	1.099 685	6.47	34
18	5.791 816	95.836 323	.010 434 4571	.172 657	16.546 852	.060 434 4571	12.09	1.175 640	6.53	36
19	6.385 477	107.709 546	.009 284 2282	.156 605	16.867 893	.059 284 2282	11.86	1.252 801	6.59	38
20	7.039 989	120.799 774	.008 278 1612	.142 046	17.159 086	.058 278 1612	11.66	1.331 126	6.66	40
21	7.761 588	135.231 751	.007 394 7131	.128 840	17.423 208	.057 394 7131	11.48	1.410 578	6.72	42
22	8.557 150	151.143 006	.006 616 2506	.116 861	17.662 773	.056 616 2506	11.33	1.491 115	6.78	44
23	9.434 258	168.685 164	.005 928 2036	.105 997	17.880 066	.055 928 2036	11.19	1.572 697	6.84	46
24	10.401 270	188.025 393	.005 318 4306	.096 142	18.077 158	.055 318 4306	11.07	1.655 285	6.90	48
25	11.467 400	209.347 996	.004 776 7355	.087 204	18.255 925	.054 776 7355	10.96	1.738 837	6.96	50
26	12.642 808	232.856 165	.004 294 4966	.079 096	18.418 073	.054 294 4966	10.86	1.823 314	7.01	52
27	13.938 696	258.773 922	.003 864 3770	.071 743	18.565 146	.053 864 3770	10.78	1.908 676	7.07	54
28	15.367 412	287.348 249	.003 480 0978	.065 073	18.698 545	.053 480 0978	10.70	1.994 885	7.12	56
29	16.942 572	318.851 445	.003 136 2568	.059 023	18.819 542	.053 136 2568	10.63	2.081 903	7.18	58
30	18.679 186	353.583 718	.002 828 1845	.053 536	18.929 290	.052 828 1845	10.57	2.169 691	7.23	60
31	20.593 802	391.876 049	.002 551 8273	.048 558	19.028 834	.052 551 8273	10.52	2.258 213	7.28	62
32	22.704 667	434.093 344	.002 303 6520	.044 044	19.119 124	.052 303 6520	10.47	2.347 434	7.34	64
33	25.031 896	480.637 912	.002 080 5683	.039 949	19.201 019	.052 080 5683	10.42	2.437 318	7.39	66
34	27.597 665	531.953 298	.001 879 8643	.036 235	19.275 301	.051 879 8643	10.38	2.527 831	7.43	68
35	30.426 426	588.528 511	.001 699 1530	.032 866	19.342 677	.051 699 1530	10.34	2.618 941	7.48	70
36	33.545 134	650.902 683	.001 536 3280	.029 811	19.403 788	.051 536 3280	10.31	2.710 616	7.53	72
37	36.983 510	719.670 208	.001 389 5254	.027 039	19.459 218	.051 389 5254	10.28	2.802 825	7.58	74
38	40.774 320	795.486 404	.001 257 0925	.024 525	19.509 495	.051 257 0925	10.26	2.895 539	7.62	76
39	44.953 688	879.073 761	.001 137 5610	.022 245	19.555 098	.051 137 5610	10.23	2.988 730	7.66	78
40	49.561 441	971.228 821	.001 029 6235	.020 177	19.596 460	.051 029 6235	10.21	3.082 370	7.71	80
41	54.641 489	1072.829 776	.000 932 1143	.018 301	19.633 978	.050 932 1143	10.19	3.176 433	7.75	82
42	60.242 241	1184.844 828	.000 843 9924	.016 600	19.668 007	.050 843 9924	10.17	3.270 895	7.79	84
43	66.417 071	1308.341 422	.000 764 3265	.015 056	19.698 873	.050 764 3265	10.16	3.365 732	7.83	86
44	73.224 821	1444.496 418	.000 692 2828	.013 657	19.726 869	.050 692 2828	10.14	3.460 921	7.87	88
45	80.730 365	1594.607 301	.000 627 1136	.012 387	19.752 262	.050 627 1136	10.13	3.556 440	7.90	90
46	89.005 227	1760.104 549	.000 568 1481	.011 235	19.775 294	.050 568 1481	10.12	3.652 270	7.94	92
47	98.128 263	1942.565 266	.000 514 7832	.010 191	19.796 185	.050 514 7832	10.11	3.748 390	7.98	94
48	108.186 410	2143.728 205	.000 466 4770	.009 243	19.815 134	.050 466 4770	10.10	3.844 782	8.01	96
49	119.275 517	2365.510 346	.000 422 7418	.008 384	19.832 321	.050 422 7418	10.09	3.941 429	8.04	98
50	131.501 258	2610.025 157	.000 383 1381	.007 604	19.847 910	.050 383 1381	10.08	4.038 314	8.08	100

Effective Rate is 10.25 %

Annual Percentage Rate is 10.00 %

Amount Of 1	Amount Of 1 Per Period	Sinking Fund Payment	Present Worth Of 1	Present Worth of 1 Per Period	Periodic Payment To Amortize 1	Constant Annual Percent	Total Interest	Annual Add On Rate
What a single $ 1 deposit grows to in the future. The deposit is made at the beginning of the first period.	What a series of $ 1 deposits grow to in the future. A deposit is made at the end of each period.	The amount to be deposited at the end of each period that grows to $ 1 in the future.	What $ 1 to be paid in the future is worth today. Value today of a single $ 1 payment tomorrow.	What $ 1 to be paid at the end of each period is worth today. Value today of a series of $ 1 payments tomorrow.	The mortgage payment to amortize a loan of $ 1. An annuity certain, payable at the end of each period, worth $ 1 today.	The annual payment, including interest and principal, to amortize completely a loan of $ 100.	The total interest paid over the term on a loan of $1. The loan is amortized by regular periodic payments.	The average annual interest rate on a loan that is completely amortized by regular periodic payments.
$S = (1+i)^n$	$S\overline{n}| = \dfrac{(1+i)^n - 1}{i}$	$\dfrac{1}{S\overline{n}|} = \dfrac{i}{(1+i)^n - 1}$	$V^n = \dfrac{1}{(1+i)^n}$	$A\overline{n}| = \dfrac{1-V^n}{i}$	$\dfrac{1}{A\overline{n}|} = \dfrac{i}{1-V^n}$			

YEAR									**PERIODS**
	1.051 250	1.000 000	1.000 000 0000	.951 249	.951 249	1.051 250 0000	210.25	.051 250	10.25	1
	1.105 127	2.051 250	.487 507 6173	.904 874	1.856 122	.538 757 6173	107.76	.077 515	7.75	2

YEAR	Amount Of 1	Amount Of 1 Per Period	Sinking Fund Payment	Present Worth Of 1	Present Worth of 1 Per Period	Periodic Payment To Amortize 1	Constant Annual Percent	Total Interest	Annual Add On Rate	PERIODS
1	1.105 127	2.051 250	.487 507 6173	.904 874	1.856 122	.538 757 6173	107.76	.077 515	7.75	2
2	1.221 305	4.318 141	.231 581 1439	.818 796	3.535 679	.282 831 1439	56.57	.131 325	6.57	4
3	1.349 696	6.823 342	.146 555 7458	.740 907	5.055 465	.197 805 7458	39.57	.186 834	6.23	6
4	1.491 585	9.591 907	.104 254 5590	.670 428	6.430 680	.155 504 5590	31.11	.244 036	6.10	8
5	1.648 390	12.651 521	.079 041 8806	.606 652	7.675 075	.130 291 8806	26.06	.302 919	6.06	10
6	1.821 680	16.032 782	.062 372 2081	.548 944	8.801 096	.113 622 2081	22.73	.363 467	6.06	12
7	2.013 187	19.769 503	.050 582 9611	.496 725	9.820 003	.101 832 9611	20.37	.425 661	6.08	14
8	2.224 826	23.899 053	.041 842 6624	.449 473	10.741 985	.093 092 6624	18.62	.489 483	6.12	16
9	2.458 715	28.462 728	.035 133 6666	.406 717	11.576 263	.086 383 6666	17.28	.554 906	6.17	18
10	2.717 191	33.506 167	.029 845 2521	.368 027	12.331 178	.081 095 2521	16.22	.621 905	6.22	20
11	3.002 840	39.079 805	.025 588 6640	.333 018	13.014 281	.076 838 6640	15.37	.690 451	6.28	22
12	3.318 518	45.239 381	.022 104 6351	.301 339	13.632 404	.073 354 6351	14.68	.760 511	6.34	24
13	3.667 383	52.046 491	.019 213 5911	.272 674	14.191 726	.070 463 5911	14.10	.832 053	6.40	26
14	4.052 922	59.569 210	.016 787 1960	.246 736	14.697 843	.068 037 1960	13.61	.905 041	6.46	28
15	4.478 992	67.882 766	.014 731 2795	.223 265	15.155 814	.065 981 2795	13.20	.979 438	6.53	30
16	4.949 853	77.070 298	.012 975 1672	.202 026	15.570 220	.064 225 1672	12.85	1.055 205	6.60	32
17	5.470 214	87.223 684	.011 464 7761	.182 808	15.945 206	.062 714 7761	12.55	1.132 302	6.66	34
18	6.045 279	98.444 460	.010 158 0120	.165 418	16.284 520	.061 408 0120	12.29	1.210 688	6.73	36
19	6.680 798	110.844 837	.009 021 6200	.149 683	16.591 557	.060 271 6200	12.06	1.290 322	6.79	38
20	7.383 127	124.548 824	.008 028 9799	.135 444	16.869 386	.059 278 9799	11.86	1.371 159	6.86	40
21	8.159 290	139.693 464	.007 158 5311	.122 560	17.120 787	.058 408 5311	11.69	1.453 158	6.92	42
22	9.017 048	156.430 207	.006 392 6272	.110 901	17.348 272	.057 642 6272	11.53	1.536 276	6.98	44
23	9.964 979	174.926 427	.005 716 6891	.100 351	17.554 118	.056 966 6891	11.40	1.620 468	7.05	46
24	11.012 563	195.367 091	.005 118 5693	.090 805	17.740 383	.056 368 5693	11.28	1.705 691	7.11	48
25	12.170 276	217.956 612	.004 588 0691	.082 167	17.908 929	.055 838 0691	11.17	1.791 903	7.17	50
26	13.449 696	242.920 891	.004 116 5665	.074 351	18.061 441	.055 366 5665	11.08	1.879 061	7.23	52
27	14.863 616	270.509 580	.003 696 7268	.067 278	18.199 446	.054 946 7268	10.99	1.967 123	7.29	54
28	16.426 177	300.998 572	.003 322 2749	.060 878	18.324 323	.054 572 2749	10.92	2.056 047	7.34	56
29	18.153 004	334.692 767	.002 987 8148	.055 087	18.437 321	.054 237 8148	10.85	2.145 793	7.40	58
30	20.061 367	371.929 117	.002 688 6844	.049 847	18.539 570	.053 938 6844	10.79	2.236 321	7.46	60
31	22.170 350	413.079 997	.002 420 8386	.045 105	18.632 092	.053 670 8386	10.74	2.327 592	7.51	62
32	24.501 042	458.556 927	.002 180 7543	.040 815	18.715 813	.053 430 7543	10.69	2.419 568	7.56	64
33	27.076 753	508.814 690	.001 965 3521	.036 932	18.791 570	.053 215 3521	10.65	2.512 213	7.61	66
34	29.923 239	564.355 880	.001 771 9316	.033 419	18.860 120	.053 021 9316	10.61	2.605 491	7.66	68
35	33.068 966	625.735 923	.001 598 1183	.030 240	18.922 150	.052 848 1183	10.57	2.699 368	7.71	70
36	36.545 393	693.568 640	.001 441 8184	.027 363	18.978 278	.052 691 8184	10.54	2.793 811	7.76	72
37	40.387 284	768.532 377	.001 301 1814	.024 760	19.029 068	.052 551 1814	10.52	2.888 787	7.81	74
38	44.633 061	851.376 794	.001 174 5681	.022 405	19.075 026	.052 424 5681	10.49	2.984 267	7.85	76
39	49.325 181	942.930 359	.001 060 5237	.020 274	19.116 612	.052 310 5237	10.47	3.080 221	7.90	78
40	54.510 568	1044.108 637	.000 957 7547	.018 345	19.154 243	.052 207 7547	10.45	3.176 620	7.94	80
41	60.241 076	1155.923 439	.000 865 1092	.016 600	19.188 293	.052 115 1092	10.43	3.273 439	7.98	82
42	66.574 013	1279.492 946	.000 781 5596	.015 021	19.219 105	.052 031 5596	10.41	3.370 651	8.03	84
43	73.572 711	1416.052 891	.000 706 1883	.013 592	19.246 985	.051 956 1883	10.40	3.468 232	8.07	86
44	81.307 157	1566.968 914	.000 638 1748	.012 299	19.272 214	.051 888 1748	10.38	3.566 159	8.11	88
45	89.854 699	1733.750 220	.000 576 7844	.011 129	19.295 042	.051 826 7844	10.37	3.664 411	8.14	90
46	99.300 814	1918.064 671	.000 521 3589	.010 070	19.315 699	.051 771 3589	10.36	3.762 965	8.18	92
47	109.739 968	2121.755 466	.000 471 3078	.009 112	19.334 391	.051 721 3078	10.35	3.861 803	8.22	94
48	121.276 553	2346.859 575	.000 426 1013	.008 246	19.351 305	.051 676 1013	10.34	3.960 906	8.25	96
49	134.025 940	2595.628 104	.000 385 2632	.007 461	19.366 610	.051 635 2632	10.33	4.060 256	8.29	98
50	148.115 627	2870.548 814	.000 348 3654	.006 751	19.380 459	.051 598 3654	10.32	4.159 837	8.32	100

Effective Rate is 10.51 %

Annual Percentage Rate is 10.25 %

Amount Of 1	Amount Of 1 Per Period	Sinking Fund Payment	Present Worth Of 1	Present Worth of 1 Per Period	Periodic Payment To Amortize 1	Constant Annual Percent	Total Interest	Annual Add On Rate	
What a single $ 1 deposit grows to in the future. The deposit is made at the beginning of the first period.	What a series of $ 1 deposits grow to in the future. A deposit is made at the end of each period.	The amount to be deposited at the end of each period that grows to $ 1 in the future.	What $ 1 to be paid in the future is worth today. Value today of a single $ 1 payment tomorrow.	What $ 1 to be paid at the end of each period is worth today. Value today of a series of $ 1 payments tomorrow.	The mortgage payment to amortize a loan of $ 1. An annuity certain, payable at the end of each period, worth $ 1 today.	The annual payment, including interest and principal, to amortize completely a loan of $ 100.	The total interest paid over the term on a loan is amortized by regular periodic payments.	The average annual interest rate on a loan that is completely amortized by regular periodic payments.	
$S = (1+i)^n$	$S\overline{n} = \dfrac{(1+i)^n - 1}{i}$	$\dfrac{1}{S\overline{n}} = \dfrac{i}{(1+i)^n - 1}$	$V^n = \dfrac{1}{(1+i)^n}$	$A\overline{n} = \dfrac{1 - V^n}{i}$	$\dfrac{1}{A\overline{n}} = \dfrac{i}{1 - V^n}$				

YEAR

PERIODS

	1.052 500	1.000 000	1.000 000 0000	.950 119	.950 119	1.052 500 0000	210.50	.052 500	10.50	1
	1.107 756	2.052 500	.487 210 7186	.902 726	1.852 844	.539 710 7186	107.95	.079 421	7.94	2

YEAR	Amount Of 1	Amount Of 1 Per Period	Sinking Fund Payment	Present Worth Of 1	Present Worth of 1 Per Period	Periodic Payment To Amortize 1	Constant Annual Percent	Total Interest	Annual Add On Rate	PERIODS
1	1.107 756	2.052 500	.487 210 7186	.902 726	1.852 844	.539 710 7186	107.95	.079 421	7.94	2
2	1.227 124	4.326 170	.231 151 3576	.814 914	3.525 455	.283 651 3576	56.74	.134 605	6.73	4
3	1.359 354	6.844 842	.146 095 4203	.735 643	5.035 363	.198 595 4203	39.72	.191 573	6.39	6
4	1.505 833	9.634 916	.103 789 1770	.664 084	6.398 396	.156 289 1770	31.26	.250 313	6.26	8
5	1.668 096	12.725 638	.078 581 5194	.599 486	7.628 840	.131 081 5194	26.22	.310 815	6.22	10
6	1.847 844	16.149 405	.061 921 7842	.541 171	8.739 595	.114 421 7842	22.89	.373 061	6.22	12
7	2.046 961	19.942 105	.050 145 1581	.488 529	9.742 301	.102 645 1581	20.53	.437 032	6.24	14
8	2.267 533	24.143 491	.041 419 0304	.441 008	10.647 469	.093 919 0304	18.79	.502 704	6.28	16
9	2.511 874	28.797 603	.034 725 1119	.398 109	11.464 588	.087 225 1119	17.45	.570 052	6.33	18
10	2.782 544	33.953 225	.029 452 2832	.359 383	12.202 223	.081 952 2832	16.40	.639 046	6.39	20
11	3.082 381	39.664 397	.025 211 5264	.324 425	12.868 104	.077 711 5264	15.55	.709 654	6.45	22
12	3.414 527	45.990 984	.021 743 3921	.292 866	13.469 212	.074 243 3921	14.85	.781 841	6.52	24
13	3.782 463	52.999 300	.018 868 1737	.264 378	14.011 848	.071 368 1737	14.28	.855 573	6.58	26
14	4.190 047	60.762 806	.016 457 4362	.238 661	14.501 699	.068 957 4362	13.80	.930 808	6.65	28
15	4.641 551	69.362 878	.014 416 9335	.215 445	14.943 901	.066 916 9335	13.39	1.007 508	6.72	30
16	5.141 707	78.889 662	.012 675 9322	.194 488	15.343 087	.065 175 9322	13.04	1.085 630	6.79	32
17	5.695 758	89.443 016	.011 180 3028	.175 569	15.703 443	.063 680 3028	12.74	1.165 130	6.85	34
18	6.309 512	101.133 560	.009 887 9146	.158 491	16.028 745	.062 387 9146	12.48	1.245 965	6.92	36
19	6.989 401	114.083 833	.008 765 4839	.143 074	16.322 404	.061 265 4839	12.26	1.328 088	6.99	38
20	7.742 553	128.429 579	.007 786 3683	.129 156	16.587 498	.060 286 3683	12.06	1.411 455	7.06	40
21	8.576 861	144.321 169	.006 928 9905	.116 593	16.826 804	.059 428 9905	11.89	1.496 018	7.12	42
22	9.501 072	161.925 176	.006 175 6919	.105 251	17.042 833	.058 675 6919	11.74	1.581 730	7.19	44
23	10.524 872	181.426 126	.005 511 8853	.095 013	17.237 847	.058 011 8853	11.61	1.668 547	7.25	46
24	11.658 992	203.028 425	.004 925 4187	.085 771	17.413 891	.057 425 4187	11.49	1.756 420	7.32	48
25	12.915 322	226.958 507	.004 406 0917	.077 427	17.572 811	.056 906 0917	11.39	1.845 305	7.38	50
26	14.307 028	253.467 205	.003 945 2836	.069 896	17.716 272	.056 445 2836	11.29	1.935 155	7.44	52
27	15.848 700	282.832 380	.003 535 6631	.063 097	17.845 778	.056 035 6631	11.21	2.025 926	7.50	54
28	17.556 496	315.361 837	.003 170 9607	.056 959	17.962 686	.055 670 9607	11.14	2.117 574	7.56	56
29	19.448 319	351.396 546	.002 845 7878	.051 418	18.068 222	.055 345 7878	11.07	2.210 056	7.62	58
30	21.543 997	391.314 220	.002 555 4911	.046 417	18.163 493	.055 055 4911	11.02	2.303 329	7.68	60
31	23.865 497	435.533 273	.002 296 0358	.041 901	18.249 495	.054 796 0358	10.96	2.397 354	7.73	62
32	26.437 153	484.517 205	.002 063 9102	.037 826	18.327 132	.054 563 9102	10.92	2.492 090	7.79	64
33	29.285 922	538.779 462	.001 856 0470	.034 146	18.397 217	.054 356 0470	10.88	2.587 499	7.84	66
34	32.441 663	598.888 816	.001 669 7590	.030 825	18.460 485	.054 169 7590	10.84	2.683 544	7.89	68
35	35.937 455	665.475 329	.001 502 6853	.027 826	18.517 598	.054 002 6853	10.81	2.780 188	7.94	70
36	39.809 940	739.236 955	.001 352 7462	.025 119	18.569 155	.053 852 7462	10.78	2.877 398	7.99	72
37	44.099 710	820.946 857	.001 218 1056	.022 676	18.615 697	.053 718 1056	10.75	2.975 140	8.04	74
38	48.851 729	911.461 512	.001 097 1390	.020 470	18.657 712	.053 597 1390	10.72	3.073 383	8.09	76
39	54.115 809	1011.729 687	.000 988 4063	.018 479	18.695 640	.053 488 4063	10.70	3.172 096	8.13	78
40	59.947 125	1122.802 384	.000 890 6287	.016 681	18.729 879	.053 390 6287	10.68	3.271 250	8.18	80
41	66.406 803	1245.843 858	.000 802 6688	.015 059	18.760 787	.053 302 6688	10.67	3.370 819	8.22	82
42	73.562 551	1382.143 820	.000 723 5137	.013 594	18.788 688	.053 223 5137	10.65	3.470 775	8.26	84
43	81.489 375	1533.130 955	.000 652 2600	.012 272	18.813 875	.053 152 2600	10.64	3.571 094	8.30	86
44	90.270 365	1700.387 898	.000 588 1011	.011 078	18.836 613	.053 088 1011	10.62	3.671 753	8.34	88
45	99.997 561	1885.667 821	.000 530 3161	.010 000	18.857 138	.053 030 3161	10.61	3.772 728	8.38	90
46	110.772 923	2090.912 814	.000 478 2600	.009 027	18.875 667	.052 978 2600	10.60	3.874 000	8.42	92
47	122.709 397	2318.274 238	.000 431 3554	.008 149	18.892 394	.052 931 3554	10.59	3.975 547	8.46	94
48	135.932 102	2570.135 276	.000 389 0846	.007 357	18.907 493	.052 889 0846	10.58	4.077 352	8.49	96
49	150.579 636	2849.135 916	.000 350 9836	.006 641	18.921 124	.052 850 9836	10.58	4.179 396	8.53	98
50	166.805 532	3158.200 618	.000 316 6360	.005 995	18.933 428	.052 816 6360	10.57	4.281 664	8.56	100

Effective Rate is 10.78 %

Annual Percentage Rate is 10.50 %

SEMIANNUAL COMPOUND INTEREST AND ANNUITY

	Amount Of 1	Amount Of 1 Per Period	Sinking Fund Payment	Present Worth Of 1	Present Worth of 1 Per Period	Periodic Payment To Amortize 1	Constant Annual Percent	Total Interest	Annual Add On Rate
	What a single $ 1 deposit grows to in the future. The deposit is made at the beginning of the first period.	What a series of $ 1 deposits grow to in the future. A deposit is made at the end of each period.	The amount to be deposited at the end of each period that grows to $ 1 in the future.	What $ 1 to be paid in the future is worth today. Value today of a single $ 1 payment tomorrow.	What $ 1 to be paid at the end of each period is worth today. Value today of a series of $ 1 payments tomorrow.	The mortgage payment to amortize a loan of $ 1. An annuity certain, payable at the end of each period, worth $ 1 today.	The annual payment, including interest and principal, to amortize completely a loan of $ 100.	The total interest paid over the term on a loan of $1. The loan is amortized by regular periodic payments.	The average annual interest rate on a loan that is completely amortized by regular periodic payments.
	$S = (1+i)^n$	$S\overline{n} = \dfrac{(1+i)^n - 1}{i}$	$\dfrac{1}{S\overline{n}} = \dfrac{i}{(1+i)^n - 1}$	$V^n = \dfrac{1}{(1+i)^n}$	$A\overline{n} = \dfrac{1-V^n}{i}$	$\dfrac{1}{A\overline{n}} = \dfrac{i}{1-V^n}$			

YEAR / **PERIODS**

YEAR	Amount Of 1	Amount Of 1 Per Period	Sinking Fund Payment	Present Worth Of 1	Present Worth of 1 Per Period	Periodic Payment To Amortize 1	Constant Annual Percent	Total Interest	Annual Add On Rate	PERIODS
	1.053 750	1.000 000	1.000 000 0000	.948 992	.948 992	1.053 750 0000	210.75	.053 750	10.75	1
	1.110 389	2.053 750	.486 914 1814	.900 585	1.849 577	.540 664 1814	108.14	.081 328	8.13	2

YEAR	Amount Of 1	Amount Of 1 Per Period	Sinking Fund Payment	Present Worth Of 1	Present Worth of 1 Per Period	Periodic Payment To Amortize 1	Constant Annual Percent	Total Interest	Annual Add On Rate	PERIODS
1	1.110 389	2.053 750	.486 914 1814	.900 585	1.849 577	.540 664 1814	108.14	.081 328	8.13	2
2	1.232 964	4.334 212	.230 722 4720	.811 054	3.515 279	.284 472 4720	56.90	.137 890	6.89	4
3	1.369 070	6.866 411	.145 636 4886	.730 423	5.015 385	.199 386 4886	39.88	.196 319	6.54	6
4	1.520 200	9.678 138	.103 325 6628	.657 808	6.366 359	.157 075 6628	31.42	.256 605	6.42	8
5	1.688 013	12.800 248	.078 123 4844	.592 412	7.583 026	.131 873 4844	26.38	.318 735	6.37	10
6	1.874 352	16.267 006	.061 474 1284	.533 518	8.678 738	.115 224 1284	23.05	.382 690	6.38	12
7	2.081 259	20.116 455	.049 710 5473	.480 478	9.665 520	.103 460 5473	20.70	.448 448	6.41	14
8	2.311 008	24.390 842	.040 998 9948	.432 712	10.554 202	.094 748 9948	18.95	.515 984	6.45	16
9	2.566 118	29.137 074	.034 320 5360	.389 694	11.354 535	.088 070 5360	17.62	.585 270	6.50	18
10	2.849 389	34.407 238	.029 063 6520	.350 952	12.075 304	.082 813 6520	16.57	.656 273	6.56	20
11	3.163 930	40.259 171	.024 839 0608	.316 063	12.724 417	.078 589 0608	15.72	.728 959	6.63	22
12	3.513 194	46.757 093	.021 387 1293	.284 641	13.308 999	.075 137 1293	15.03	.803 291	6.69	24
13	3.901 012	53.972 315	.018 528 0176	.256 344	13.835 465	.072 278 0176	14.46	.879 228	6.76	26
14	4.331 641	61.984 018	.016 133 1909	.230 859	14.309 593	.069 883 1909	13.98	.956 729	6.83	28
15	4.809 807	70.880 126	.014 108 3271	.207 909	14.736 585	.067 858 3271	13.58	1.035 750	6.91	30
16	5.340 757	80.758 267	.012 382 6333	.187 239	15.121 128	.066 132 6333	13.23	1.116 244	6.98	32
17	5.930 318	91.726 846	.010 901 9338	.168 625	15.467 441	.064 651 9338	12.94	1.198 166	7.05	34
18	6.584 960	103.906 236	.009 624 0614	.151 861	15.779 326	.063 374 0614	12.68	1.281 466	7.12	36
19	7.311 868	117.430 098	.008 515 7044	.136 764	16.060 205	.062 265 7044	12.46	1.366 097	7.19	38
20	8.119 018	132.446 847	.007 550 1986	.123 168	16.313 161	.061 300 1986	12.27	1.452 000	7.26	40
21	9.015 269	149.121 280	.006 705 9510	.110 923	16.540 969	.060 455 9510	12.10	1.539 150	7.33	42
22	10.010 456	167.636 388	.005 965 2920	.099 896	16.746 129	.059 715 2920	11.95	1.627 473	7.40	44
23	11.115 501	188.195 362	.005 313 6272	.089 964	16.930 894	.059 063 6272	11.82	1.716 927	7.46	46
24	12.342 530	211.023 822	.004 738 8015	.081 021	17.097 290	.058 488 8015	11.70	1.807 462	7.53	48
25	13.705 011	236.372 294	.004 230 6143	.072 966	17.247 144	.057 980 6143	11.60	1.899 031	7.60	50
26	15.217 894	264.518 960	.003 780 4474	.065 712	17.382 100	.057 530 4474	11.51	1.991 583	7.66	52
27	16.897 783	295.772 710	.003 380 9745	.059 179	17.503 640	.057 130 9745	11.43	2.085 073	7.72	54
28	18.763 114	330.476 532	.003 025 9335	.053 296	17.613 097	.056 775 9335	11.36	2.179 452	7.78	56
29	20.834 356	369.011 276	.002 709 9443	.047 998	17.711 672	.056 459 9443	11.30	2.274 677	7.84	58
30	23.134 241	411.799 835	.002 428 3643	.043 226	17.800 447	.056 178 3643	11.24	2.370 702	7.90	60
31	25.688 008	459.311 783	.002 177 1704	.038 929	17.880 397	.055 927 1704	11.19	2.467 485	7.96	62
32	28.523 683	512.068 530	.001 952 8636	.035 059	17.952 398	.055 702 8636	11.15	2.564 983	8.02	64
33	31.672 386	570.649 045	.001 752 3906	.031 573	18.017 242	.055 502 3906	11.11	2.663 158	8.07	66
34	35.168 671	635.696 208	.001 573 0784	.028 434	18.075 639	.055 323 0784	11.07	2.761 969	8.12	68
35	39.050 908	707.923 866	.001 412 5813	.025 608	18.128 231	.055 162 5813	11.04	2.861 381	8.18	70
36	43.361 701	788.124 668	.001 268 8348	.023 062	18.175 594	.055 018 8348	11.01	2.961 356	8.23	72
37	48.148 358	877.178 761	.001 140 0185	.020 769	18.218 249	.054 890 0185	10.98	3.061 861	8.28	74
38	53.463 411	976.063 452	.001 024 5236	.018 704	18.256 663	.054 774 5236	10.96	3.162 864	8.32	76
39	59.365 186	1085.863 932	.000 920 9257	.016 845	18.291 258	.054 670 9257	10.94	3.264 332	8.37	78
40	65.918 454	1207.785 183	.000 827 9618	.015 170	18.322 414	.054 577 9618	10.92	3.366 237	8.42	80
41	73.195 130	1343.165 208	.000 744 5101	.013 662	18.350 472	.054 494 5101	10.90	3.468 550	8.46	82
42	81.275 072	1493.489 706	.000 669 5727	.012 304	18.375 741	.054 419 5727	10.89	3.571 244	8.50	84
43	90.246 951	1660.408 384	.000 602 2615	.011 081	18.398 498	.054 352 2615	10.88	3.674 294	8.54	86
44	100.209 227	1845.753 059	.000 541 7843	.009 979	18.418 993	.054 291 7843	10.86	3.777 677	8.59	88
45	111.271 230	2051.557 759	.000 487 4345	.008 987	18.437 450	.054 237 4345	10.85	3.881 369	8.63	90
46	123.554 356	2280.081 046	.000 438 5809	.008 094	18.454 072	.054 188 5809	10.84	3.985 349	8.66	92
47	137.193 406	2533.830 805	.000 394 6593	.007 289	18.469 042	.054 144 6593	10.83	4.089 598	8.70	94
48	152.338 057	2815.591 763	.000 355 1651	.006 564	18.482 524	.054 105 1651	10.83	4.194 096	8.74	96
49	169.154 513	3128.456 048	.000 319 6465	.005 912	18.494 665	.054 069 6465	10.82	4.298 825	8.77	98
50	187.827 321	3475.857 128	.000 287 6988	.005 324	18.505 599	.054 037 6988	10.81	4.403 770	8.81	100

Effective Rate is 11.04 %

Annual Percentage Rate is 10.75 %

	Amount Of 1	Amount Of 1 Per Period	Sinking Fund Payment	Present Worth Of 1	Present Worth of 1 Per Period	Periodic Payment To Amortize 1	Constant Annual Percent	Total Interest	Annual Add On Rate
	What a single $ 1 deposit grows to in the future. The deposit is made at the beginning of the first period.	What a series of $ 1 deposits grow to in the future. A deposit is made at the end of each period.	The amount to be deposited at the end of each period that grows to $ 1 in the future.	What $ 1 to be paid in the future is worth today. Value today of a single $ 1 payment tomorrow.	What $ 1 to be paid at the end of each period is worth today. Value today of a series of $ 1 payments tomorrow.	The mortgage payment to amortize a loan of $ 1. An annuity certain, payable at the end of each period, worth $ 1 today.	The annual payment, including interest and principal, to amortize completely a loan of $ 100.	The total interest paid over the term on a loan of $1. The loan is amortized by regular periodic payments.	The average annual interest rate on a loan that is completely amortized by regular periodic payments.

$$S = (1+i)^n \qquad S\overline{n}| = \frac{(1+i)^n - 1}{i} \qquad \frac{1}{S\overline{n}|} = \frac{i}{(1+i)^n - 1} \qquad V^n = \frac{1}{(1+i)^n} \qquad A\overline{n}| = \frac{1-V^n}{i} \qquad \frac{1}{A\overline{n}|} = \frac{i}{1-V^n}$$

YEAR / **PERIODS**

	1.055 000	1.000 000	1.000 000 0000	.947 867	.947 867	1.055 000 0000	211.00	.055 000	11.00 / 1
	1.113 025	2.055 000	.486 618 0049	.898 452	1.846 320	.541 618 0049	108.33	.083 236	8.32 / 2

YEAR	Amount Of 1	Amount Of 1 Per Period	Sinking Fund Payment	Present Worth Of 1	Present Worth of 1 Per Period	Periodic Payment To Amortize 1	Constant Annual Percent	Total Interest	Annual Add On Rate	PERIODS
1	1.113 025	2.055 000	.486 618 0049	.898 452	1.846 320	.541 618 0049	108.33	.083 236	8.32	2
2	1.238 825	4.342 266	.230 294 4853	.807 217	3.505 150	.285 294 4853	57.06	.141 178	7.06	4
3	1.378 843	6.888 051	.145 178 9476	.725 246	4.995 530	.200 178 9476	40.04	.201 074	6.70	6
4	1.534 687	9.721 573	.102 864 0118	.651 599	6.334 566	.157 864 0118	31.58	.262 912	6.57	8
5	1.708 144	12.875 354	.077 667 7687	.585 431	7.537 626	.132 667 7687	26.54	.326 678	6.53	10
6	1.901 207	16.385 591	.061 029 2312	.525 982	8.618 518	.116 029 2312	23.21	.392 351	6.54	12
7	2.116 091	20.292 572	.049 279 1154	.472 569	9.589 648	.104 279 1154	20.86	.459 908	6.57	14
8	2.355 263	24.641 140	.040 582 5380	.424 581	10.462 162	.095 582 5380	19.12	.529 321	6.62	16
9	2.621 466	29.481 205	.033 919 9163	.381 466	11.246 074	.088 919 9163	17.79	.600 559	6.67	18
10	2.917 757	34.868 318	.028 679 3300	.342 729	11.950 382	.083 679 3300	16.74	.673 587	6.74	20
11	3.247 537	40.864 310	.024 471 2319	.307 926	12.583 170	.079 471 2319	15.90	.748 367	6.80	22
12	3.614 590	47.537 998	.021 035 8037	.276 657	13.151 699	.076 035 8037	15.21	.824 859	6.87	24
13	4.023 129	54.965 981	.018 193 0713	.248 563	13.662 495	.073 193 0713	14.64	.903 020	6.95	26
14	4.477 843	63.233 510	.015 814 3996	.223 322	14.121 422	.070 814 3996	14.17	.982 803	7.02	28
15	4.983 951	72.435 478	.013 805 3897	.200 644	14.533 745	.068 805 3897	13.77	1.064 162	7.09	30
16	5.547 262	82.677 498	.012 095 1895	.180 269	14.904 198	.067 095 1895	13.42	1.147 046	7.17	32
17	6.174 242	94.077 122	.010 629 5769	.161 963	15.237 033	.065 629 5769	13.13	1.231 406	7.24	34
18	6.872 085	106.765 189	.009 366 3488	.145 516	15.536 068	.064 366 3488	12.88	1.317 189	7.32	36
19	7.648 803	120.887 324	.008 272 1659	.130 739	15.804 738	.063 272 1659	12.66	1.404 342	7.39	38
20	8.513 309	136.605 614	.007 320 3434	.117 463	16.046 125	.062 320 3434	12.47	1.492 814	7.46	40
21	9.475 525	154.100 464	.006 489 2731	.105 535	16.262 999	.061 489 2731	12.30	1.582 549	7.54	42
22	10.546 497	173.572 669	.005 761 2757	.094 818	16.457 851	.060 761 2757	12.16	1.673 496	7.61	44
23	11.738 515	195.245 719	.005 121 7512	.085 190	16.632 915	.060 121 7512	12.03	1.765 601	7.68	46
24	13.065 260	219.368 367	.004 558 5424	.076 539	16.790 203	.059 558 5424	11.92	1.858 810	7.75	48
25	14.541 961	246.217 476	.004 061 4501	.068 767	16.931 518	.059 061 4501	11.82	1.953 073	7.81	50
26	16.185 566	276.101 207	.003 621 8603	.061 783	17.058 483	.058 621 8603	11.73	2.048 337	7.88	52
27	18.014 940	309.362 546	.003 232 4534	.055 509	17.172 555	.058 232 4534	11.65	2.144 552	7.94	54
28	20.051 079	346.383 247	.002 886 9756	.049 873	17.275 043	.057 886 9756	11.58	2.241 671	8.01	56
29	22.317 352	387.588 214	.002 580 0578	.044 808	17.367 124	.057 580 0578	11.52	2.339 643	8.07	58
30	24.839 770	433.450 372	.002 307 0692	.040 258	17.449 854	.057 307 0692	11.47	2.438 424	8.13	60
31	27.647 285	484.496 100	.002 064 0001	.036 170	17.524 183	.057 064 0001	11.42	2.537 968	8.19	62
32	30.772 120	541.311 272	.001 847 3659	.032 497	17.590 965	.056 847 3659	11.37	2.638 231	8.24	64
33	34.250 139	604.547 978	.001 654 1284	.029 197	17.650 964	.056 654 1284	11.34	2.739 172	8.30	66
34	38.121 261	674.932 013	.001 481 6307	.026 232	17.704 871	.056 481 6307	11.30	2.840 751	8.36	68
35	42.429 916	753.271 204	.001 327 5431	.023 568	17.753 304	.056 327 5431	11.27	2.942 928	8.41	70
36	47.225 558	840.464 682	.001 189 8180	.021 175	17.796 819	.056 189 8180	11.24	3.045 667	8.46	72
37	52.563 226	937.513 203	.001 066 6516	.019 025	17.835 914	.056 066 6516	11.22	3.148 932	8.51	74
38	58.504 185	1045.530 633	.000 956 4521	.017 093	17.871 040	.055 956 4521	11.20	3.252 690	8.56	76
39	65.116 620	1165.756 732	.000 857 8119	.015 357	17.902 599	.055 857 8119	11.18	3.356 909	8.61	78
40	72.476 426	1299.571 387	.000 769 4845	.013 798	17.930 953	.055 769 4845	11.16	3.461 559	8.65	80
41	80.668 074	1448.510 443	.000 690 3644	.012 396	17.956 428	.055 690 3644	11.14	3.566 610	8.70	82
42	89.785 583	1614.283 336	.000 619 4699	.011 138	17.979 316	.055 619 4699	11.13	3.672 035	8.74	84
43	99.933 599	1798.792 710	.000 555 9284	.010 007	17.999 879	.055 555 9284	11.12	3.777 810	8.79	86
44	111.228 594	2004.156 256	.000 498 9631	.008 990	18.018 355	.055 498 9631	11.10	3.883 909	8.83	88
45	123.800 206	2232.731 017	.000 447 8820	.008 078	18.034 954	.055 447 8820	11.09	3.990 309	8.87	90
46	137.792 724	2487.140 440	.000 402 0682	.007 257	18.049 868	.055 402 0682	11.09	4.096 990	8.91	92
47	153.366 747	2770.304 488	.000 360 9712	.006 520	18.063 267	.055 360 9712	11.08	4.203 931	8.94	94
48	170.701 023	3085.473 153	.000 324 0994	.005 858	18.075 306	.055 324 0994	11.07	4.311 114	8.98	96
49	189.994 507	3436.263 756	.000 291 0137	.005 263	18.086 122	.055 291 0137	11.06	4.418 519	9.02	98
50	211.468 636	3826.702 467	.000 261 3216	.004 729	18.095 839	.055 261 3216	11.06	4.526 132	9.05	100

Effective Rate is 11.30 %

Annual Percentage Rate is 11.00 %

SEMIANNUAL COMPOUND INTEREST AND ANNUITY

Amount Of 1	Amount Of 1 Per Period	Sinking Fund Payment	Present Worth Of 1	Present Worth of 1 Per Period	Periodic Payment To Amortize 1	Constant Annual Percent	Total Interest	Annual Add On Rate	
What a single $ 1 deposit grows to in the future. The deposit is made at the beginning of the first period.	What a series of $ 1 deposits grow to in the future. A deposit is made at the end of each period.	The amount to be deposited at the end of each period that grows to $ 1 in the future.	What $ 1 to be paid in the future is worth today. Value today of a single $ 1 payment tomorrow.	What $ 1 to be paid at the end of each period is worth today. Value today of a series of $ 1 payments tomorrow.	The mortgage payment to amortize a loan of $ 1. An annuity certain, payable at the end of each period, worth $ 1 today.	The annual payment, including interest and principal, to amortize completely a loan of $ 100.	The total interest paid over the term on a loan of $1. The loan is amortized by regular periodic payments.	The average annual interest rate on a loan that is completely amortized by regular periodic payments.	
$S = (1+i)^n$	$S\overline{n}| = \dfrac{(1+i)^n - 1}{i}$	$\dfrac{1}{S\overline{n}|} = \dfrac{i}{(1+i)^n - 1}$	$V^n = \dfrac{1}{(1+i)^n}$	$A\overline{n}| = \dfrac{1 - V^n}{i}$	$\dfrac{1}{A\overline{n}|} = \dfrac{i}{1 - V^n}$				PERIODS

YEAR

	1.056 250	1.000 000	1.000 000 0000	.946 746	.946 746	1.056 250 0000	211.25	.056 250	11.25	1
	1.115 664	2.056 250	.486 322 1884	.896 327	1.843 073	.542 572 1884	108.52	.085 144	8.51	2

YEAR	Amount Of 1	Amount Of 1 Per Period	Sinking Fund Payment	Present Worth Of 1	Present Worth of 1 Per Period	Periodic Payment To Amortize 1	Constant Annual Percent	Total Interest	Annual Add On Rate	PERIODS
1	1.115 664	2.056 250	.486 322 1884	.896 327	1.843 073	.542 572 1884	108.52	.085 144	8.51	2
2	1.244 706	4.350 334	.229 867 3958	.803 402	3.495 069	.286 117 3958	57.23	.144 470	7.22	4
3	1.388 674	6.909 762	.144 722 7942	.720 111	4.975 798	.200 972 7942	40.20	.205 837	6.86	6
4	1.549 294	9.765 223	.102 404 2191	.645 455	6.303 015	.158 654 2191	31.74	.269 234	6.73	8
5	1.728 491	12.950 958	.077 214 3653	.578 539	7.492 637	.133 464 3653	26.70	.334 644	6.69	10
6	1.928 416	16.505 168	.060 587 0826	.518 560	8.558 926	.116 837 0826	23.37	.402 045	6.70	12
7	2.151 464	20.470 473	.048 850 8492	.464 800	9.514 671	.105 100 8492	21.03	.471 412	6.73	14
8	2.400 311	24.894 421	.040 169 6423	.416 613	10.371 331	.096 419 6423	19.29	.542 714	6.78	16
9	2.677 941	29.830 061	.033 523 2299	.373 421	11.139 178	.089 773 2299	17.96	.615 918	6.84	18
10	2.987 682	35.336 577	.028 299 2886	.334 708	11.827 421	.084 549 2886	16.91	.690 986	6.91	20
11	3.333 250	41.479 999	.024 108 0042	.300 008	12.444 311	.080 358 0042	16.08	.767 876	6.98	22
12	3.718 787	48.333 995	.020 689 3721	.268 905	12.997 247	.076 939 3721	15.39	.846 545	7.05	24
13	4.148 917	55.980 751	.017 863 2831	.241 027	13.492 858	.074 113 2831	14.83	.926 945	7.13	26
14	4.628 798	64.511 962	.015 501 0012	.216 039	13.937 088	.071 751 0012	14.36	1.009 028	7.21	28
15	5.164 183	74.029 927	.013 508 0505	.193 641	14.335 263	.069 758 0505	13.96	1.092 742	7.29	30
16	5.761 494	84.648 780	.011 813 5194	.173 566	14.692 158	.068 063 5194	13.62	1.178 033	7.36	32
17	6.427 892	96.495 851	.010 363 1398	.155 572	15.012 053	.066 613 1398	13.33	1.264 847	7.44	34
18	7.171 368	109.713 203	.009 114 6732	.139 443	15.298 784	.065 364 6732	13.08	1.353 128	7.52	36
19	8.000 837	124.459 328	.008 034 7533	.124 987	15.555 788	.064 284 7533	12.86	1.442 821	7.59	38
20	8.926 247	140.911 050	.007 096 6755	.112 029	15.786 148	.063 346 6755	12.67	1.533 867	7.67	40
21	9.958 692	159.265 644	.006 278 8180	.100 415	15.992 626	.062 528 8180	12.51	1.626 210	7.74	42
22	11.110 555	179.743 206	.005 563 4926	.090 005	16.177 698	.061 813 4926	12.37	1.719 794	7.82	44
23	12.395 647	202.589 285	.004 936 0952	.080 673	16.343 583	.061 186 0952	12.24	1.814 560	7.89	46
24	13.829 378	228.077 835	.004 384 4681	.072 310	16.492 270	.060 634 4681	12.13	1.910 454	7.96	48
25	15.428 940	256.514 494	.003 898 4152	.064 813	16.625 542	.060 148 4152	12.03	2.007 421	8.03	50
26	17.213 514	288.240 252	.003 469 3281	.058 094	16.744 998	.059 719 3281	11.95	2.105 405	8.10	52
27	19.204 499	323.635 541	.003 089 8955	.052 071	16.852 069	.059 339 8955	11.87	2.204 354	8.16	54
28	21.425 770	363.124 792	.002 753 8742	.046 673	16.948 040	.059 003 8742	11.81	2.304 217	8.23	56
29	23.903 961	407.181 531	.002 455 9071	.041 834	17.034 061	.058 705 9071	11.75	2.404 943	8.29	58
30	26.668 790	456.334 051	.002 191 3771	.037 497	17.111 164	.058 441 3771	11.69	2.506 483	8.36	60
31	29.753 411	511.171 751	.001 956 2896	.033 610	17.180 274	.058 206 2896	11.65	2.608 790	8.42	62
32	33.194 811	572.352 202	.001 747 1759	.030 125	17.242 219	.057 997 1759	11.60	2.711 819	8.47	64
33	37.034 258	640.609 033	.001 561 0145	.027 002	17.297 742	.057 811 0145	11.57	2.815 527	8.53	66
34	41.317 791	716.760 727	.001 395 1657	.024 203	17.347 508	.057 645 1657	11.53	2.919 871	8.59	68
35	46.096 774	801.720 434	.001 247 3176	.021 693	17.392 116	.057 497 3176	11.50	3.024 812	8.64	70
36	51.428 515	896.506 926	.001 115 4404	.019 444	17.432 098	.057 365 4404	11.48	3.130 312	8.70	72
37	57.376 946	1002.256 810	.000 997 7483	.017 429	17.467 936	.057 247 7483	11.45	3.236 333	8.75	74
38	64.013 396	1120.238 154	.000 892 6673	.015 622	17.500 058	.057 142 6673	11.43	3.342 843	8.80	76
39	71.417 446	1251.865 700	.000 798 8077	.014 002	17.528 850	.057 048 8077	11.41	3.449 807	8.85	78
40	79.677 878	1398.717 822	.000 714 9405	.012 551	17.554 657	.056 964 9405	11.40	3.557 195	8.89	80
41	88.893 745	1562.555 458	.000 639 9773	.011 249	17.577 789	.056 889 9773	11.38	3.664 978	8.94	82
42	99.175 556	1745.343 220	.000 572 9532	.010 083	17.598 522	.056 822 9532	11.37	3.773 128	8.98	84
43	110.646 604	1949.272 957	.000 513 0118	.009 038	17.617 106	.056 763 0118	11.36	3.881 619	9.03	86
44	123.444 440	2176.790 036	.000 459 3920	.008 101	17.633 763	.056 709 3920	11.35	3.990 427	9.07	88
45	137.722 525	2430.622 665	.000 411 4172	.007 261	17.648 694	.056 661 4172	11.34	4.099 528	9.11	90
46	153.652 072	2713.814 607	.000 368 4850	.006 508	17.662 076	.056 618 4850	11.33	4.208 901	9.15	92
47	171.424 094	3029.761 679	.000 330 0590	.005 833	17.674 071	.056 580 0590	11.32	4.318 526	9.19	94
48	191.251 702	3382.252 474	.000 295 6610	.005 229	17.684 823	.056 545 6610	11.31	4.428 383	9.23	96
49	213.372 650	3775.513 785	.000 264 8646	.004 687	17.694 460	.056 514 8646	11.31	4.538 457	9.26	98
50	238.052 198	4214.261 298	.000 237 2895	.004 201	17.703 098	.056 487 2895	11.30	4.648 729	9.30	100

Effective Rate is 11.57 %

Annual Percentage Rate is 11.25 %

SEMIANNUAL COMPOUND INTEREST AND ANNUITY

11.50 % S

	Amount Of 1	Amount Of 1 Per Period	Sinking Fund Payment	Present Worth Of 1	Present Worth of 1 Per Period	Periodic Payment To Amortize 1	Constant Annual Percent	Total Interest	Annual Add On Rate	
	What a single $ 1 deposit grows to in the future. The deposit is made at the beginning of the first period.	What a series of $ 1 deposits grow to in the future. A deposit is made at the end of each period.	The amount to be deposited at the end of each period that grows to $ 1 in the future.	What $ 1 to be paid in the future is worth today. Value today of a single $ 1 payment tomorrow.	What $ 1 to be paid at the end of each period is worth today. Value today of a series of $ 1 payments tomorrow.	The mortgage payment to amortize a loan of $ 1. An annuity certain, payable at the end of each period, worth $ 1 today.	The annual payment, including interest and principal, to amortize completely a loan of $ 100.	The total interest paid over the term on a loan of $1. The loan is amortized by regular periodic payments.	The average annual interest rate on a loan that is completely amortized by regular periodic payments.	
	$S = (1+i)^n$	$S\overline{n}| = \dfrac{(1+i)^n - 1}{i}$	$\dfrac{1}{S\overline{n}|} = \dfrac{i}{(1+i)^n - 1}$	$V^n = \dfrac{1}{(1+i)^n}$	$A\overline{n}| = \dfrac{1 - V^n}{i}$	$\dfrac{1}{A\overline{n}|} = \dfrac{i}{1 - V^n}$				

YEAR										PERIODS
	1.057 500	1.000 000	1.000 000 0000	.945 626	.945 626	1.057 500 0000	211.50	.057 500	11.50	1
	1.118 306	2.057 500	.486 026 7315	.894 209	1.839 836	.543 526 7315	108.71	.087 053	8.71	2
1	1.118 306	2.057 500	.486 026 7315	.894 209	1.839 836	.543 526 7315	108.71	.087 053	8.71	2
2	1.250 609	4.358 415	.229 441 2017	.799 611	3.485 035	.286 941 2017	57.39	.147 765	7.39	4
3	1.398 564	6.931 543	.144 268 0253	.715 019	4.956 187	.201 768 0253	40.36	.210 608	7.02	6
4	1.564 023	9.809 088	.101 946 2799	.639 377	6.271 705	.159 446 2799	31.89	.275 570	6.89	8
5	1.749 056	13.027 064	.076 763 2671	.571 737	7.448 054	.134 263 2671	26.86	.342 633	6.85	10
6	1.955 980	16.625 747	.060 147 6727	.511 253	8.499 956	.117 647 6727	23.53	.411 772	6.86	12
7	2.187 385	20.650 177	.048 425 7351	.457 167	9.440 576	.105 925 7351	21.19	.482 960	6.90	14
8	2.446 167	25.150 722	.039 760 2900	.408 803	10.281 688	.097 260 2900	19.46	.556 165	6.95	16
9	2.735 563	30.183 710	.033 130 4539	.365 555	11.033 819	.090 630 4539	18.13	.631 348	7.02	18
10	3.059 198	35.812 131	.027 923 4988	.326 883	11.706 381	.085 423 4988	17.09	.708 470	7.08	20
11	3.421 120	42.106 430	.023 749 3418	.292 302	12.307 792	.081 249 3418	16.25	.787 486	7.16	22
12	3.825 860	49.145 384	.020 347 7910	.261 379	12.845 580	.077 847 7910	15.57	.868 347	7.24	24
13	4.278 483	57.017 090	.017 538 6012	.233 728	13.326 474	.075 038 6012	15.01	.951 004	7.32	26
14	4.784 654	65.820 068	.015 192 9348	.209 002	13.756 495	.072 692 9348	14.54	1.035 402	7.40	28
15	5.350 708	75.664 493	.013 216 2386	.186 891	14.141 024	.070 716 2386	14.15	1.121 487	7.48	30
16	5.983 731	86.673 576	.011 537 5417	.167 120	14.484 873	.069 037 5417	13.81	1.209 201	7.56	32
17	6.691 643	98.985 102	.010 102 5304	.149 440	14.792 346	.067 602 5304	13.53	1.298 486	7.64	34
18	7.483 307	112.753 158	.008 868 9312	.133 631	15.067 291	.066 368 9312	13.28	1.389 282	7.72	36
19	8.368 629	128.150 061	.007 803 3517	.119 494	15.313 150	.065 303 3517	13.07	1.481 527	7.80	38
20	9.358 690	145.368 514	.006 879 0687	.106 853	15.532 999	.064 379 0687	12.88	1.575 163	7.88	40
21	10.465 881	164.624 018	.006 074 4478	.095 549	15.729 590	.063 574 4478	12.72	1.670 127	7.95	42
22	11.704 060	186.157 568	.005 371 7934	.085 440	15.905 384	.062 871 7934	12.58	1.766 359	8.03	44
23	13.088 724	210.238 672	.004 756 4988	.076 402	16.062 580	.062 256 4988	12.46	1.863 799	8.10	46
24	14.637 201	237.168 721	.004 216 4076	.068 319	16.203 147	.061 716 4076	12.35	1.962 388	8.18	48
25	16.368 874	267.284 763	.003 741 3281	.061 092	16.328 842	.061 241 3281	12.25	2.062 066	8.25	50
26	18.305 414	300.963 721	.003 322 6596	.054 629	16.441 241	.060 822 6596	12.17	2.162 778	8.32	52
27	20.471 059	338.627 110	.002 953 1008	.048 849	16.541 749	.060 453 1008	12.10	2.264 467	8.39	54
28	22.892 913	380.746 314	.002 626 4207	.043 682	16.631 624	.060 126 4207	12.03	2.367 080	8.45	56
29	25.601 288	427.848 482	.002 337 2760	.039 061	16.711 991	.059 837 2760	11.97	2.470 562	8.52	58
30	28.630 080	480.523 132	.002 081 0653	.034 928	16.783 856	.059 581 0653	11.92	2.574 864	8.58	60
31	32.017 197	539.429 522	.001 853 8103	.031 233	16.848 118	.059 353 8103	11.88	2.679 936	8.65	62
32	35.805 032	605.304 906	.001 652 0600	.027 929	16.905 582	.059 152 0600	11.84	2.785 732	8.71	64
33	40.040 991	678.973 759	.001 472 8110	.024 974	16.956 967	.058 972 8110	11.80	2.892 206	8.76	66
34	44.778 091	761.358 098	.001 313 4424	.022 332	17.002 916	.058 813 4424	11.77	2.999 314	8.82	68
35	50.075 619	853.489 020	.001 171 6612	.019 970	17.044 004	.058 671 6612	11.74	3.107 016	8.88	70
36	55.999 877	956.519 605	.001 045 4569	.017 857	17.080 745	.058 545 4569	11.71	3.215 273	8.93	72
37	62.625 013	1071.739 353	.000 933 0627	.015 968	17.113 599	.058 433 0627	11.69	3.324 047	8.98	74
38	70.033 943	1200.590 316	.000 832 9236	.014 279	17.142 978	.058 332 9236	11.67	3.433 302	9.04	76
39	78.319 396	1344.685 155	.000 743 6685	.012 768	17.169 248	.058 243 6685	11.65	3.543 006	9.08	78
40	87.585 070	1505.827 313	.000 664 0868	.011 417	17.192 740	.058 164 0868	11.64	3.653 127	9.13	80
41	97.946 932	1686.033 595	.000 593 1080	.010 210	17.213 746	.058 093 1080	11.62	3.763 635	9.18	82
42	109.534 666	1887.559 407	.000 529 7847	.009 130	17.232 530	.058 029 7847	11.61	3.874 502	9.23	84
43	122.493 301	2112.926 982	.000 473 2771	.008 164	17.249 327	.057 973 2771	11.60	3.985 702	9.27	86
44	136.985 025	2364.956 950	.000 422 8407	.007 300	17.264 347	.057 922 8407	11.59	4.097 210	9.31	88
45	153.191 209	2646.803 638	.000 377 8142	.006 528	17.277 778	.057 877 8142	11.58	4.209 003	9.35	90
46	171.314 687	2961.994 551	.000 337 6103	.005 837	17.289 788	.057 837 6103	11.57	4.321 060	9.39	92
47	191.582 285	3314.474 519	.000 301 7070	.005 220	17.300 527	.057 801 7070	11.57	4.433 360	9.43	94
48	214.247 661	3708.655 070	.000 269 6395	.004 667	17.310 131	.057 769 6395	11.56	4.545 885	9.47	96
49	239.594 505	4149.469 644	.000 240 9947	.004 174	17.318 718	.057 740 9947	11.55	4.658 617	9.51	98
50	267.940 032	4642.435 337	.000 215 4042	.003 732	17.326 397	.057 715 4042	11.55	4.771 540	9.54	100

Effective Rate is 11.83 %

Annual Percentage Rate is 11.50 %

SEMIANNUAL COMPOUND INTEREST AND ANNUITY

11.75 % S

	Amount Of 1	Amount Of 1 Per Period	Sinking Fund Payment	Present Worth Of 1	Present Worth of 1 Per Period	Periodic Payment To Amortize 1	Constant Annual Percent	Total Interest	Annual Add On Rate	
	What a single $ 1 deposit grows to in the future. The deposit is made at the beginning of the first period.	What a series of $ 1 deposits grow to in the future. A deposit is made at the end of each period.	The amount to be deposited at the end of each period that grows to $ 1 in the future.	What $ 1 to be paid in the future is worth today. Value today of a single $ 1 payment tomorrow.	What $ 1 to be paid at the end of each period is worth today. Value today of a series of $ 1 payments tomorrow.	The mortgage payment to amortize a loan of $ 1. An annuity certain, payable at the end of each period, worth $ 1 today.	The annual payment, including interest and principal, to amortize completely a loan of $ 100.	The total interest paid over the term on a loan of $1. The loan is amortized by regular periodic payments.	The average annual interest rate on a loan that is completely amortized by regular periodic payments.	
	$S = (1+i)^n$	$S\overline{n} = \dfrac{(1+i)^n - 1}{i}$	$\dfrac{1}{S\overline{n}} = \dfrac{i}{(1+i)^n - 1}$	$V^n = \dfrac{1}{(1+i)^n}$	$A\overline{n} = \dfrac{1-V^n}{i}$	$\dfrac{1}{A\overline{n}} = \dfrac{i}{1-V^n}$				

YEAR										PERIODS
	1.058 750	1.000 000	1.000 000 0000	.944 510	.944 510	1.058 750 0000	211.75	.058 750	11.75	1
	1.120 952	2.058 750	.485 731 6333	.892 099	1.836 609	.544 481 6333	108.90	.088 963	8.90	2

YEAR										PERIODS
1	1.120 952	2.058 750	.485 731 6333	.892 099	1.836 609	.544 481 6333	108.90	.088 963	8.90	2
2	1.256 532	4.366 509	.229 015 9011	.795 841	3.475 047	.287 765 9011	57.56	.151 064	7.55	4
3	1.408 512	6.953 395	.143 814 6377	.709 969	4.936 696	.202 564 6377	40.52	.215 388	7.18	6
4	1.578 874	9.853 169	.101 490 1893	.633 363	6.240 632	.160 240 1893	32.05	.281 922	7.05	8
5	1.769 841	13.103 675	.076 314 4671	.565 023	7.403 872	.135 064 4671	27.02	.350 645	7.01	10
6	1.983 906	16.747 335	.059 710 9916	.504 056	8.441 597	.118 460 9916	23.70	.421 532	7.03	12
7	2.223 862	20.831 702	.048 003 7596	.449 668	9.367 352	.106 753 7596	21.36	.494 553	7.07	14
8	2.492 842	25.410 079	.039 354 4631	.401 149	10.193 216	.098 104 4631	19.63	.569 671	7.12	16
9	2.794 355	30.542 217	.032 741 5652	.357 864	10.929 969	.091 491 5652	18.30	.646 848	7.19	18
10	3.132 337	36.295 096	.027 551 9314	.319 250	11.587 226	.086 301 9314	17.27	.726 039	7.26	20
11	3.511 198	42.743 795	.023 395 2087	.284 803	12.173 565	.082 145 2087	16.43	.807 195	7.34	22
12	3.935 883	49.972 474	.020 011 0166	.254 073	12.696 637	.078 761 0166	15.76	.890 264	7.42	24
13	4.411 934	58.075 472	.017 218 9732	.226 658	13.163 269	.075 968 9732	15.20	.975 193	7.50	26
14	4.945 564	67.158 541	.014 890 1387	.202 201	13.579 551	.073 640 1387	14.73	1.061 924	7.59	28
15	5.543 738	77.340 222	.012 929 8827	.180 384	13.950 916	.071 679 8827	14.34	1.150 396	7.67	30
16	6.214 262	88.753 393	.011 267 1749	.160 920	14.282 210	.070 017 1749	14.01	1.240 550	7.75	32
17	6.965 886	101.547 004	.009 847 6563	.143 557	14.577 758	.068 597 6563	13.72	1.332 320	7.84	34
18	7.808 421	115.888 023	.008 629 0194	.128 067	14.841 415	.067 379 0194	13.48	1.425 645	7.92	36
19	8.752 862	131.963 610	.007 577 8466	.114 248	15.076 024	.066 327 8466	13.27	1.520 458	8.00	38
20	9.811 534	149.983 565	.006 667 3972	.101 921	15.286 453	.065 417 3972	13.09	1.616 696	8.08	40
21	10.998 255	170.183 062	.005 876 0254	.090 924	15.473 642	.064 626 0254	12.93	1.714 293	8.16	42
22	12.328 511	192.825 719	.005 186 0302	.081 113	15.640 633	.063 936 0302	12.79	1.813 185	8.24	44
23	13.819 664	218.207 041	.004 582 8035	.072 361	15.789 606	.063 332 8035	12.67	1.913 309	8.32	46
24	15.491 174	246.658 274	.004 054 1920	.064 553	15.922 504	.062 804 1920	12.57	2.014 601	8.39	48
25	17.364 855	278.550 727	.003 590 0104	.057 588	16.041 062	.062 340 0104	12.47	2.117 001	8.47	50
26	19.465 162	314.300 623	.003 181 6673	.051 374	16.146 828	.061 931 6673	12.39	2.220 447	8.54	52
27	21.819 503	354.374 524	.002 821 8733	.045 831	16.241 182	.061 571 8733	12.32	2.324 881	8.61	54
28	24.458 606	399.295 427	.002 504 4114	.040 885	16.325 355	.061 254 4114	12.26	2.430 247	8.68	56
29	27.416 913	449.649 583	.002 223 9540	.036 474	16.400 445	.060 973 9540	12.20	2.536 489	8.75	58
30	30.733 031	506.094 152	.001 975 9169	.032 538	16.467 434	.060 725 9169	12.15	2.643 555	8.81	60
31	34.450 240	569.365 781	.001 756 3402	.029 027	16.527 194	.060 506 3402	12.11	2.751 393	8.88	62
32	38.617 050	640.290 212	.001 561 7918	.025 895	16.580 506	.060 311 7918	12.07	2.859 955	8.94	64
33	43.287 842	719.793 063	.001 389 2882	.023 101	16.628 065	.060 139 2882	12.03	2.969 193	9.00	66
34	48.523 575	808.911 909	.001 236 2286	.020 609	16.670 493	.059 986 2286	12.00	3.079 064	9.06	68
35	54.392 577	908.809 818	.001 100 3402	.018 385	16.708 343	.059 850 3402	11.98	3.189 524	9.11	70
36	60.971 444	1020.790 536	.000 979 6329	.016 401	16.742 109	.059 729 6329	11.95	3.300 534	9.17	72
37	68.346 035	1146.315 496	.000 872 3602	.014 631	16.772 231	.059 622 3602	11.93	3.412 055	9.22	74
38	76.612 595	1287.022 896	.000 776 9870	.013 053	16.799 103	.059 526 9870	11.91	3.524 051	9.27	76
39	85.879 008	1444.749 076	.000 692 1617	.011 644	16.823 076	.059 442 1617	11.89	3.636 489	9.32	78
40	96.266 208	1621.552 485	.000 616 6930	.010 388	16.844 462	.059 366 6930	11.88	3.749 335	9.37	80
41	107.909 757	1819.740 541	.000 549 5289	.009 267	16.863 540	.059 299 5289	11.86	3.862 561	9.42	82
42	120.961 611	2041.899 753	.000 489 7400	.008 267	16.880 560	.059 239 7400	11.85	3.976 138	9.47	84
43	135.592 106	2290.929 469	.000 436 5041	.007 375	16.895 744	.059 186 5041	11.84	4.090 039	9.51	86
44	151.992 183	2570.079 718	.000 389 0930	.006 579	16.909 289	.059 139 0930	11.83	4.204 240	9.56	88
45	170.375 875	2882.993 625	.000 346 8617	.005 869	16.921 372	.059 096 8617	11.82	4.318 718	9.60	90
46	190.983 104	3233.754 959	.000 309 2380	.005 236	16.932 152	.059 059 2380	11.82	4.433 450	9.64	92
47	214.082 809	3626.941 424	.000 275 7144	.004 671	16.941 769	.059 025 7144	11.81	4.548 417	9.68	94
48	239.976 459	4067.684 406	.000 245 8401	.004 167	16.950 348	.058 995 8401	11.80	4.663 601	9.72	96
49	269.001 987	4561.735 941	.000 219 2148	.003 717	16.958 001	.058 969 2148	11.80	4.778 983	9.75	98
50	301.538 197	5115.543 781	.000 195 4826	.003 316	16.964 828	.058 945 4826	11.79	4.894 548	9.79	100

Effective Rate is 12.10 %

Annual Percentage Rate is 11.75 %

SEMIANNUAL COMPOUND INTEREST AND ANNUITY

12.00 % S

Amount Of 1	Amount Of 1 Per Period	Sinking Fund Payment	Present Worth Of 1	Present Worth of 1 Per Period	Periodic Payment To Amortize 1	Constant Annual Percent	Total Interest	Annual Add On Rate
What a single $ 1 deposit grows to in the future. The deposit is made at the beginning of the first period.	What a series of $ 1 deposits grow to in the future. A deposit is made at the end of each period.	The amount to be deposited at the end of each period that grows to $ 1 in the future.	What $ 1 to be paid in the future is worth today. Value today of a single $ 1 payment tomorrow.	What $ 1 to be paid at the end of each period is worth today. Value today of a series of $ 1 payments tomorrow.	The mortgage payment to amortize a loan of $ 1. An annuity certain, payable at the end of each period, worth $ 1 today.	The annual payment, including interest and principal, to amortize completely a loan of $ 100.	The total interest paid over the term on a loan of $1. The loan is amortized by regular periodic payments.	The average annual interest rate on a loan that is completely amortized by regular periodic payments.
$S = (1+i)^n$	$S\overline{n}| = \dfrac{(1+i)^n - 1}{i}$	$\dfrac{1}{S\overline{n}|} = \dfrac{i}{(1+i)^n - 1}$	$V^n = \dfrac{1}{(1+i)^n}$	$A\overline{n}| = \dfrac{1-V^n}{i}$	$\dfrac{1}{A\overline{n}|} = \dfrac{i}{1-V^n}$			

YEAR / **PERIODS**

	Amount Of 1	Amount Of 1 Per Period	Sinking Fund Payment	Present Worth Of 1	Present Worth of 1 Per Period	Periodic Payment To Amortize 1	Constant Annual Percent	Total Interest	Annual Add On Rate	PERIODS
	1.060 000	1.000 000	1.000 000 0000	.943 396	.943 396	1.060 000 0000	212.00	.060 000	12.00	1
	1.123 600	2.060 000	.485 436 8932	.889 996	1.833 393	.545 436 8932	109.09	.090 874	9.09	2
1	1.123 600	2.060 000	.485 436 8932	.889 996	1.833 393	.545 436 8932	109.09	.090 874	9.09	2
2	1.262 477	4.374 616	.228 591 4924	.792 094	3.465 106	.288 591 4924	57.72	.154 366	7.72	4
3	1.418 519	6.975 319	.143 362 6285	.704 961	4.917 324	.203 362 6285	40.68	.220 176	7.34	6
4	1.593 848	9.897 468	.101 035 9426	.627 412	6.209 794	.161 035 9426	32.21	.288 288	7.21	8
5	1.790 848	13.180 795	.075 867 9582	.558 395	7.360 087	.135 867 9582	27.18	.358 680	7.17	10
6	2.012 196	16.869 941	.059 277 0294	.496 969	8.383 844	.119 277 0294	23.86	.431 324	7.19	12
7	2.260 904	21.015 066	.047 584 9090	.442 301	9.294 984	.107 584 9090	21.52	.506 189	7.23	14
8	2.540 352	25.672 528	.038 952 1436	.393 646	10.105 895	.098 952 1436	19.80	.583 234	7.29	16
9	2.854 339	30.905 653	.032 356 5406	.350 344	10.827 603	.092 356 5406	18.48	.662 418	7.36	18
10	3.207 135	36.785 591	.027 184 5570	.311 805	11.469 921	.087 184 5570	17.44	.743 691	7.44	20
11	3.603 537	43.392 290	.023 045 5685	.277 505	12.041 582	.083 045 5685	16.61	.827 003	7.52	22
12	4.048 935	50.815 577	.019 679 0050	.246 979	12.550 358	.079 679 0050	15.94	.912 296	7.60	24
13	4.549 383	59.156 383	.016 904 3467	.219 810	13.003 166	.076 904 3467	15.39	.999 513	7.69	26
14	5.111 687	68.528 112	.014 592 5515	.195 630	13.406 164	.074 592 5515	14.92	1.088 591	7.78	28
15	5.743 491	79.058 186	.012 648 9115	.174 110	13.764 831	.072 648 9115	14.53	1.179 467	7.86	30
16	6.453 387	90.889 778	.011 002 3374	.154 957	14.084 043	.071 002 3374	14.21	1.272 075	7.95	32
17	7.251 025	104.183 755	.009 598 4254	.137 912	14.368 141	.069 598 4254	13.92	1.366 346	8.04	34
18	8.147 252	119.120 867	.008 394 8348	.122 741	14.620 987	.068 394 8348	13.68	1.462 214	8.12	36
19	9.154 252	135.904 206	.007 358 1240	.109 239	14.846 019	.067 358 1240	13.48	1.559 609	8.21	38
20	10.285 718	154.761 966	.006 461 5359	.097 222	15.046 297	.066 461 5359	13.30	1.658 461	8.29	40
21	11.557 033	175.950 545	.005 683 4152	.086 527	15.224 543	.065 683 4152	13.14	1.758 703	8.37	42
22	12.985 482	199.758 032	.005 006 0565	.077 009	15.383 182	.065 006 0565	13.01	1.860 266	8.46	44
23	14.590 487	226.508 125	.004 414 8527	.068 538	15.524 370	.064 414 8527	12.89	1.963 083	8.54	46
24	16.393 872	256.564 529	.003 897 6549	.060 998	15.650 027	.063 897 6549	12.78	2.067 087	8.61	48
25	18.420 154	290.335 905	.003 444 2864	.054 288	15.761 861	.063 444 2864	12.69	2.172 214	8.69	50
26	20.696 885	328.281 422	.003 046 1669	.048 316	15.861 393	.063 046 1669	12.61	2.278 401	8.76	52
27	23.255 020	370.917 006	.002 696 0209	.043 001	15.949 976	.062 696 0209	12.54	2.385 585	8.84	54
28	26.129 341	418.822 348	.002 387 6472	.038 271	16.028 814	.062 387 6472	12.48	2.493 708	8.91	56
29	29.358 927	472.648 790	.002 115 7359	.034 061	16.098 980	.062 115 7359	12.43	2.602 713	8.97	58
30	32.987 691	533.128 181	.001 875 7215	.030 314	16.161 428	.061 875 7215	12.38	2.712 543	9.04	60
31	37.064 969	601.082 824	.001 663 6642	.026 980	16.217 006	.061 663 6642	12.34	2.823 147	9.11	62
32	41.646 200	677.436 661	.001 476 1528	.024 012	16.266 470	.061 476 1528	12.30	2.934 474	9.17	64
33	46.793 670	763.227 832	.001 310 2248	.021 370	16.310 493	.061 310 2248	12.27	3.046 475	9.23	66
34	52.577 368	859.622 792	.001 163 3009	.019 020	16.349 673	.061 163 3009	12.24	3.159 104	9.29	68
35	59.075 930	967.932 170	.001 033 1302	.016 927	16.384 544	.061 033 1302	12.21	3.272 319	9.35	70
36	66.377 715	1089.628 586	.000 917 7439	.015 065	16.415 578	.060 917 7439	12.19	3.386 078	9.41	72
37	74.582 001	1226.366 679	.000 815 4168	.013 408	16.443 199	.060 815 4168	12.17	3.500 341	9.46	74
38	83.800 336	1380.005 601	.000 724 6347	.011 933	16.467 781	.060 724 6347	12.15	3.615 072	9.51	76
39	94.158 058	1552.634 293	.000 644 0667	.010 620	16.489 659	.060 644 0667	12.13	3.730 237	9.56	78
40	105.795 993	1746.599 891	.000 572 5410	.009 452	16.509 131	.060 572 5410	12.12	3.845 803	9.61	80
41	118.872 378	1964.539 638	.000 509 0251	.008 412	16.526 460	.060 509 0251	12.11	3.961 740	9.66	82
42	133.565 004	2209.416 737	.000 452 6081	.007 487	16.541 883	.060 452 6081	12.10	4.078 019	9.71	84
43	150.073 639	2484.560 646	.000 402 4856	.006 663	16.555 610	.060 402 4856	12.09	4.194 614	9.76	86
44	168.622 741	2793.712 342	.000 357 9467	.005 930	16.567 827	.060 357 9467	12.08	4.311 499	9.80	88
45	189.464 511	3141.075 187	.000 318 3623	.005 278	16.578 699	.060 318 3623	12.07	4.428 653	9.84	90
46	212.882 325	3531.372 080	.000 283 1761	.004 697	16.588 376	.060 283 1761	12.06	4.546 052	9.88	92
47	239.194 580	3969.909 669	.000 251 8949	.004 181	16.596 988	.060 251 8949	12.06	4.663 678	9.92	94
48	268.759 030	4462.650 505	.000 224 0821	.003 721	16.604 653	.060 224 0821	12.05	4.781 512	9.96	96
49	301.977 646	5016.294 107	.000 199 3504	.003 312	16.611 475	.060 199 3504	12.04	4.899 536	10.00	98
50	339.302 084	5638.368 059	.000 177 3563	.002 947	16.617 546	.060 177 3563	12.04	5.017 736	10.04	100

SEMIANNUAL COMPOUND INTEREST AND ANNUITY

	Amount Of 1	Amount Of 1 Per Period	Sinking Fund Payment	Present Worth Of 1	Present Worth of 1 Per Period	Periodic Payment To Amortize 1	Constant Annual Percent	Total Interest	Annual Add On Rate	
	What a single $ 1 deposit grows to in the future. The deposit is made at the beginning of the first period.	What a series of $ 1 deposits grow to in the future. A deposit is made at the end of each period.	The amount to be deposited at the end of each period that grows to $ 1 in the future.	What $ 1 to be paid in the future is worth today. Value today of a single $ 1 payment tomorrow.	What $ 1 to be paid at the end of each period is worth today. Value today of a series of $ 1 payments tomorrow.	The mortgage payment to amortize a loan of $ 1. An annuity certain, payable at the end of each period, worth $ 1 today.	The annual payment, including interest and principal, to amortize completely a loan of $ 100.	The total interest paid over the term on a loan of $1. The loan is amortized by regular periodic payments.	The average annual interest rate on a loan that is completely amortized by regular periodic payments.	
	$S = (1+i)^n$	$S\overline{n}| = \dfrac{(1+i)^n - 1}{i}$	$\dfrac{1}{S\overline{n}|} = \dfrac{i}{(1+i)^n - 1}$	$V^n = \dfrac{1}{(1+i)^n}$	$A\overline{n}| = \dfrac{1-V^n}{i}$	$\dfrac{1}{A\overline{n}|} = \dfrac{i}{1-V^n}$				PERIODS

YEAR										
	1.061 250	1.000 000	1.000 000 0000	.942 285	.942 285	1.061 250 0000	212.25	.061 250	12.25	1
	1.126 252	2.061 250	.485 142 5106	.887 901	1.830 186	.546 392 5106	109.28	.092 785	9.28	2
1	1.126 252	2.061 250	.485 142 5106	.887 901	1.830 186	.546 392 5106	109.28	.092 785	9.28	2
2	1.268 443	4.382 736	.228 167 9737	.788 368	3.455 210	.289 417 9737	57.89	.157 672	7.88	4
3	1.428 585	6.997 313	.142 911 9944	.699 993	4.898 071	.204 161 9944	40.84	.224 972	7.50	6
4	1.608 947	9.941 985	.100 583 5349	.621 525	6.179 189	.161 833 5349	32.37	.294 668	7.37	8
5	1.812 079	13.258 426	.075 423 7332	.551 852	7.316 695	.136 673 7332	27.34	.366 737	7.33	10
6	2.040 856	16.993 573	.058 845 7758	.489 990	8.326 688	.120 095 7758	24.02	.441 149	7.35	12
7	2.298 518	21.200 288	.047 169 1697	.435 063	9.223 461	.108 419 1697	21.69	.517 868	7.40	14
8	2.588 709	25.938 108	.038 553 3133	.386 293	10.019 707	.099 803 3133	19.97	.596 853	7.46	16
9	2.915 538	31.274 085	.031 975 3564	.342 990	10.726 695	.093 225 3564	18.65	.678 056	7.53	18
10	3.283 629	37.283 737	.026 821 3460	.304 541	11.354 431	.088 071 3460	17.62	.761 427	7.61	20
11	3.698 192	44.052 117	.022 700 3848	.270 402	11.911 798	.083 950 3848	16.80	.846 908	7.70	22
12	4.165 095	51.675 015	.019 351 7118	.240 091	12.406 684	.080 601 7118	16.13	.934 441	7.79	24
13	4.690 944	60.260 317	.016 594 6689	.213 177	12.846 095	.077 844 6689	15.57	1.023 961	7.88	26
14	5.283 183	69.929 526	.014 300 1113	.189 280	13.236 248	.075 550 1113	15.12	1.115 403	7.97	28
15	5.950 194	80.819 488	.012 373 2534	.168 062	13.582 665	.073 623 2534	14.73	1.208 698	8.06	30
16	6.701 415	93.084 324	.010 742 9474	.149 222	13.890 249	.071 992 9474	14.40	1.303 774	8.15	32
17	7.547 479	106.897 616	.009 354 7456	.132 495	14.163 354	.070 604 7456	14.13	1.400 561	8.24	34
18	8.500 360	122.454 857	.008 166 2747	.117 642	14.405 844	.069 416 2747	13.89	1.498 986	8.33	36
19	9.573 544	139.976 224	.007 144 0704	.104 455	14.621 151	.068 394 0704	13.68	1.598 975	8.42	38
20	10.782 219	159.709 690	.006 261 3608	.092 745	14.812 322	.067 511 3608	13.51	1.700 454	8.50	40
21	12.143 490	181.934 538	.005 496 4825	.082 349	14.982 063	.066 746 4825	13.35	1.803 352	8.59	42
22	13.676 625	206.965 308	.004 831 7276	.073 117	15.132 776	.066 081 7276	13.22	1.907 596	8.67	44
23	15.403 320	235.156 252	.004 252 4917	.064 921	15.266 595	.065 502 4917	13.11	2.013 115	8.75	46
24	17.348 014	266.906 346	.003 746 6325	.057 643	15.385 412	.064 996 6325	13.00	2.119 838	8.83	48
25	19.538 228	302.664 939	.003 303 9836	.051 182	15.490 911	.064 553 9836	12.92	2.227 699	8.91	50
26	22.004 959	342.938 111	.002 915 9780	.045 444	15.584 583	.064 165 9780	12.84	2.336 631	8.99	52
27	24.783 120	388.295 833	.002 575 3560	.040 350	15.667 754	.063 825 3560	12.77	2.446 569	9.06	54
28	27.912 027	439.380 038	.002 275 9341	.035 827	15.741 602	.063 525 9341	12.71	2.557 452	9.13	56
29	31.435 964	496.913 705	.002 012 4219	.031 811	15.807 172	.063 262 4219	12.66	2.669 220	9.20	58
30	35.404 804	561.711 087	.001 780 2746	.028 245	15.865 392	.063 030 2746	12.61	2.781 816	9.27	60
31	39.874 716	634.689 239	.001 575 5742	.025 079	15.917 085	.062 825 5742	12.57	2.895 186	9.34	62
32	44.908 961	716.880 997	.001 394 9317	.022 267	15.962 983	.062 644 9317	12.53	3.009 276	9.40	64
33	50.578 788	809.449 593	.001 235 4074	.019 771	16.003 737	.062 485 4074	12.50	3.124 037	9.47	66
34	56.964 439	913.705 119	.001 094 4450	.017 555	16.039 921	.062 344 4450	12.47	3.239 422	9.53	68
35	64.156 288	1031.123 068	.000 969 8163	.015 587	16.072 050	.062 219 8163	12.45	3.355 387	9.59	70
36	72.256 119	1163.365 216	.000 859 5753	.013 840	16.100 577	.062 109 5753	12.43	3.471 889	9.64	72
37	81.378 567	1312.303 143	.000 762 0191	.012 288	16.125 906	.062 012 0191	12.41	3.588 889	9.70	74
38	91.652 739	1480.044 715	.000 675 6553	.010 911	16.148 396	.061 925 6553	12.39	3.706 350	9.75	76
39	103.224 040	1668.963 923	.000 599 1741	.009 688	16.168 365	.061 849 1741	12.37	3.824 236	9.81	78
40	116.256 237	1881.734 476	.000 531 4246	.008 602	16.186 095	.061 781 4246	12.36	3.942 514	9.86	80
41	130.933 768	2121.367 643	.000 471 3940	.007 637	16.201 838	.061 721 3940	12.35	4.061 154	9.91	82
42	147.464 361	2391.254 873	.000 418 1905	.006 781	16.215 816	.061 668 1905	12.34	4.180 128	9.95	84
43	166.081 967	2695.215 787	.000 371 0278	.006 021	16.228 227	.061 621 0278	12.33	4.299 408	10.00	86
44	187.050 075	3037.552 241	.000 329 2124	.005 346	16.239 246	.061 579 2124	12.32	4.418 971	10.04	88
45	210.665 439	3423.109 208	.000 292 1321	.004 747	16.249 031	.061 542 1321	12.31	4.538 792	10.09	90
46	237.262 280	3857.343 344	.000 259 2458	.004 215	16.257 718	.061 509 2458	12.31	4.658 851	10.13	92
47	267.217 013	4346.400 219	.000 230 0755	.003 742	16.265 432	.061 480 0755	12.30	4.779 127	10.17	94
48	300.953 579	4897.201 287	.000 204 1983	.003 323	16.272 281	.061 454 1983	12.30	4.899 603	10.21	96
49	338.949 438	5517.541 852	.000 181 2401	.002 950	16.278 363	.061 431 2401	12.29	5.020 262	10.25	98
50	381.742 335	6216.201 382	.000 160 8699	.002 620	16.283 762	.061 410 8699	12.29	5.141 087	10.28	100

Effective Rate is 12.63 %

Annual Percentage Rate is 12.25 %

SEMIANNUAL COMPOUND INTEREST AND ANNUITY

12.50 % S

	Amount Of 1	Amount Of 1 Per Period	Sinking Fund Payment	Present Worth Of 1	Present Worth of 1 Per Period	Periodic Payment To Amortize 1	Constant Annual Percent	Total Interest	Annual Add On Rate	

	What a single $1 deposit grows to in the future. The deposit is made at the beginning of the first period.	What a series of $1 deposits grow to in the future. A deposit is made at the end of each period.	The amount to be deposited at the end of each period that grows to $1 in the future.	What $1 to be paid in the future is worth today. Value today of a single $1 payment tomorrow.	What $1 to be paid at the end of each period is worth today. Value today of a series of $1 payments tomorrow.	The mortgage payment to amortize a loan of $1. An annuity certain, payable at the end of each period, worth $1 today.	The annual payment, including interest and principal, to amortize completely a loan of $100.	The total interest paid over the term on a loan of $1. The loan is amortized by regular periodic payments.	The average annual interest rate on a loan that is completely amortized by regular periodic payments.	

$S = (1+i)^n$ $S\overline{n}| = \dfrac{(1+i)^n - 1}{i}$ $\dfrac{1}{S\overline{n}|} = \dfrac{i}{(1+i)^n - 1}$ $V^n = \dfrac{1}{(1+i)^n}$ $A\overline{n}| = \dfrac{1-V^n}{i}$ $\dfrac{1}{A\overline{n}|} = \dfrac{i}{1-V^n}$

YEAR   **PERIODS**

YEAR	Amount Of 1	Amount Of 1 Per Period	Sinking Fund Payment	Present Worth Of 1	Present Worth of 1 Per Period	Periodic Payment To Amortize 1	Constant Annual Percent	Total Interest	Annual Add On Rate	PERIODS
	1.062 500	1.000 000	1.000 000 0000	.941 176	.941 176	1.062 500 0000	212.50	.062 500	12.50	1
	1.128 906	2.062 500	.484 848 4848	.885 813	1.826 990	.547 348 4848	109.47	.094 697	9.47	2
1	1.128 906	2.062 500	.484 848 4848	.885 813	1.826 990	.547 348 4848	109.47	.094 697	9.47	2
2	1.274 429	4.390 869	.227 745 3433	.784 665	3.445 361	.290 245 3433	58.05	.160 981	8.05	4
3	1.438 711	7.019 380	.142 462 7324	.695 067	4.878 936	.204 962 7324	41.00	.229 776	7.66	6
4	1.624 170	9.986 722	.100 132 9614	.615 699	6.148 815	.162 632 9614	32.53	.301 064	7.53	8
5	1.833 536	13.336 572	.074 981 7850	.545 394	7.273 691	.137 481 7850	27.50	.374 818	7.50	10
6	2.069 890	17.118 240	.058 417 2209	.483 117	8.270 121	.120 917 2209	24.19	.451 007	7.52	12
7	2.336 712	21.387 388	.046 756 5278	.427 952	9.152 771	.109 256 5278	21.86	.529 591	7.57	14
8	2.637 928	26.206 856	.038 157 9538	.379 085	9.934 635	.100 657 9538	20.14	.610 527	7.63	16
9	2.977 974	31.647 583	.031 597 9892	.335 799	10.627 220	.094 097 9892	18.82	.693 764	7.71	18
10	3.361 853	37.789 655	.026 462 2687	.297 455	11.240 721	.088 962 2687	17.80	.779 245	7.79	20
11	3.795 217	44.723 477	.022 359 6209	.263 490	11.784 168	.084 859 6209	16.98	.866 912	7.88	22
12	4.284 445	52.551 113	.019 029 0926	.233 402	12.265 560	.081 529 0926	16.31	.956 698	7.97	24
13	4.836 736	61.387 780	.016 289 8870	.206 751	12.691 984	.078 789 8870	15.76	1.048 537	8.07	26
14	5.460 222	71.363 549	.014 012 7561	.183 143	13.069 716	.076 512 7561	15.31	1.142 357	8.16	28
15	6.164 079	82.625 256	.012 102 8369	.162 230	13.404 316	.074 602 8369	14.93	1.238 085	8.25	30
16	6.958 667	95.338 668	.010 488 9235	.143 706	13.700 709	.072 988 9235	14.60	1.335 646	8.35	32
17	7.855 682	109.690 918	.009 116 5250	.127 296	13.963 258	.071 616 5250	14.33	1.434 962	8.44	34
18	8.868 329	125.893 263	.007 943 2368	.112 761	14.195 827	.070 443 2368	14.09	1.535 957	8.53	36
19	10.011 512	144.184 192	.006 935 5731	.099 885	14.401 840	.069 435 5731	13.89	1.638 552	8.62	38
20	11.302 058	164.832 935	.006 066 7487	.088 479	14.584 329	.068 566 7487	13.72	1.742 670	8.71	40
21	12.758 964	188.143 431	.005 315 0939	.078 376	14.745 980	.067 815 0939	13.57	1.848 234	8.80	42
22	14.403 675	214.458 795	.004 662 9004	.069 427	14.889 172	.067 162 9004	13.44	1.955 168	8.89	44
23	16.260 398	244.166 374	.004 095 5681	.061 499	15.016 014	.066 595 5681	13.32	2.063 396	8.97	46
24	18.356 465	277.703 445	.003 600 9636	.054 477	15.128 372	.066 100 9636	13.23	2.172 846	9.05	48
25	20.722 728	315.563 655	.003 168 9327	.048 256	15.227 901	.065 668 9327	13.14	2.283 447	9.13	50
26	23.394 018	358.304 283	.002 790 9239	.042 746	15.316 064	.065 290 9239	13.06	2.395 128	9.21	52
27	26.409 653	406.554 444	.002 459 6952	.037 865	15.394 161	.064 959 6952	13.00	2.507 824	9.29	54
28	29.814 022	461.024 353	.002 169 0828	.033 541	15.463 340	.064 669 0828	12.94	2.621 469	9.36	56
29	33.657 236	522.515 773	.001 913 8178	.029 711	15.524 619	.064 413 8178	12.89	2.736 001	9.43	58
30	37.995 864	591.933 822	.001 689 3780	.026 319	15.578 902	.064 189 3780	12.84	2.851 363	9.50	60
31	42.893 768	670.300 292	.001 491 8687	.023 313	15.626 985	.063 991 8687	12.80	2.967 496	9.57	62
32	48.423 043	758.768 689	.001 317 9247	.020 651	15.669 579	.063 817 9247	12.77	3.084 347	9.64	64
33	54.665 076	858.641 215	.001 164 6308	.018 293	15.707 309	.063 664 6308	12.74	3.201 866	9.70	66
34	61.711 746	971.387 934	.001 029 4548	.016 204	15.740 730	.063 529 4548	12.71	3.320 003	9.76	68
35	69.666 776	1098.668 410	.000 910 1927	.014 354	15.770 335	.063 410 1927	12.69	3.438 714	9.82	70
36	78.647 258	1242.356 135	.000 804 9222	.012 715	15.796 560	.063 304 9222	12.67	3.557 954	9.88	72
37	88.785 382	1404.566 105	.000 711 9636	.011 263	15.819 790	.063 211 9636	12.65	3.677 685	9.94	74
38	100.230 372	1587.685 954	.000 629 8475	.009 977	15.840 368	.063 129 8475	12.63	3.797 868	9.99	76
39	113.150 694	1794.411 097	.000 557 2859	.008 838	15.858 596	.063 057 2859	12.62	3.918 468	10.05	78
40	127.736 525	2027.784 403	.000 493 1491	.007 829	15.874 742	.062 993 1491	12.60	4.039 452	10.10	80
41	144.202 562	2291.240 986	.000 436 4447	.006 935	15.889 045	.062 936 4447	12.59	4.160 788	10.15	82
42	162.791 173	2588.658 769	.000 386 3004	.006 143	15.901 715	.062 886 3004	12.58	4.282 449	10.20	84
43	183.775 973	2924.415 563	.000 341 9487	.005 441	15.912 937	.062 841 9487	12.57	4.404 408	10.24	86
44	207.465 844	3303.453 507	.000 302 7135	.004 820	15.922 879	.062 802 7135	12.57	4.526 639	10.29	88
45	234.209 488	3731.351 811	.000 267 9994	.004 270	15.931 685	.062 767 9994	12.56	4.649 120	10.33	90
46	264.400 555	4214.408 880	.000 237 2812	.003 782	15.939 486	.062 737 2812	12.55	4.771 830	10.37	92
47	298.483 439	4759.735 025	.000 210 0957	.003 350	15.946 396	.062 710 0957	12.55	4.894 749	10.41	94
48	336.959 820	5375.357 118	.000 186 0342	.002 968	15.952 517	.062 686 0342	12.54	5.017 859	10.45	96
49	380.396 047	6070.336 746	.000 164 7355	.002 629	15.957 939	.062 664 7355	12.54	5.141 144	10.49	98
50	429.431 475	6854.903 593	.000 145 8810	.002 329	15.962 741	.062 645 8810	12.53	5.264 588	10.53	100

Effective Rate is 12.89 %   8 - 406   Annual Percentage Rate is 12.50 %

	Amount Of 1	Amount Of 1 Per Period	Sinking Fund Payment	Present Worth Of 1	Present Worth of 1 Per Period	Periodic Payment To Amortize 1	Constant Annual Percent	Total Interest	Annual Add On Rate	
	What a single $ 1 deposit grows to in the future. The deposit is made at the beginning of the first period.	What a series of $ 1 deposits grow to in the future. A deposit is made at the end of each period.	The amount to be deposited at the end of each period that grows to $ 1 in the future.	What $ 1 to be paid in the future is worth today. Value today of a single $ 1 payment tomorrow.	What $ 1 to be paid at the end of each period is worth today. Value today of a series of $ 1 payments tomorrow.	The mortgage payment to amortize a loan of $ 1. An annuity certain, payable at the end of each period, worth $ 1 today.	The annual payment, including interest and principal, to amortize completely a loan of $ 100.	The total interest paid over the term on a loan of $1. The loan is amortized by regular periodic payments.	The average annual interest rate on a loan that is completely amortized by regular periodic payments.	
	$S = (1+i)^n$	$S\overline{n} = \dfrac{(1+i)^n - 1}{i}$	$\dfrac{1}{S\overline{n}} = \dfrac{i}{(1+i)^n - 1}$	$V^n = \dfrac{1}{(1+i)^n}$	$A\overline{n} = \dfrac{1-V^n}{i}$	$\dfrac{1}{A\overline{n}} = \dfrac{i}{1-V^n}$				

YEAR										PERIODS
	1.066 250	1.000 000	1.000 000 0000	.937 866	.937 866	1.066 250 0000	213.25	.066 250	13.25	1
	1.136 889	2.066 250	.483 968 5420	.879 593	1.817 460	.550 218 5420	110.05	.100 437	10.04	2
1	1.136 889	2.066 250	.483 968 5420	.879 593	1.817 460	.550 218 5420	110.05	.100 437	10.04	2
2	1.292 517	4.415 347	.226 482 7644	.773 684	3.416 085	.292 732 7644	58.55	.170 931	8.55	4
3	1.469 448	7.086 010	.141 123 1478	.680 528	4.822 225	.207 373 1478	41.48	.244 239	8.14	6
4	1.670 600	10.122 257	.098 792 1965	.598 588	6.059 057	.165 042 1965	33.01	.320 338	8.01	8
5	1.899 286	13.574 133	.073 669 5288	.526 514	7.146 965	.139 919 5288	27.99	.399 195	7.98	10
6	2.159 278	17.498 534	.057 147 6458	.463 118	8.103 882	.123 397 6458	24.68	.480 772	8.01	12
7	2.454 859	21.960 141	.045 537 0473	.407 355	8.945 580	.111 787 0473	22.36	.565 019	8.07	14
8	2.790 903	27.032 495	.036 992 5163	.358 307	9.685 932	.103 242 5163	20.65	.651 880	8.15	16
9	3.172 947	32.799 198	.030 488 5508	.315 164	10.337 141	.096 738 5508	19.35	.741 294	8.24	18
10	3.607 289	39.355 299	.025 409 5389	.277 217	10.909 939	.091 659 5389	18.34	.833 191	8.33	20
11	4.101 087	46.808 859	.021 363 4774	.243 838	11.413 769	.087 613 4774	17.53	.927 497	8.43	22
12	4.662 481	55.282 730	.018 088 8318	.214 478	11.856 934	.084 338 8318	16.87	1.024 132	8.53	24
13	5.300 723	64.916 581	.015 404 3850	.188 653	12.246 740	.081 654 3850	16.34	1.123 014	8.64	26
14	6.026 335	75.869 201	.013 180 5791	.165 938	12.589 610	.079 430 5791	15.89	1.224 056	8.74	28
15	6.851 274	88.321 114	.011 322 3209	.145 958	12.891 196	.077 572 3209	15.52	1.327 170	8.85	30
16	7.789 138	102.477 559	.009 758 2340	.128 384	13.156 469	.076 008 2340	15.21	1.432 263	8.95	32
17	8.855 386	118.571 866	.008 433 7038	.112 926	13.389 802	.074 683 7038	14.94	1.539 246	9.05	34
18	10.067 592	136.869 307	.007 306 2399	.099 329	13.595 040	.073 556 2399	14.72	1.648 025	9.16	36
19	11.445 735	157.671 469	.006 342 3016	.087 369	13.775 565	.072 592 3016	14.52	1.758 507	9.26	38
20	13.012 531	181.321 218	.005 515 0744	.076 849	13.934 355	.071 765 0744	14.36	1.870 603	9.35	40
21	14.793 804	208.208 360	.004 802 8811	.067 596	14.074 025	.071 052 8811	14.22	1.984 221	9.45	42
22	16.818 914	238.776 057	.004 188 0246	.059 457	14.196 877	.070 438 0246	14.09	2.099 273	9.54	44
23	19.121 239	273.528 137	.003 655 9310	.052 298	14.304 938	.069 905 9310	13.99	2.215 673	9.63	46
24	21.738 728	313.037 398	.003 194 5065	.046 001	14.399 987	.069 444 5065	13.89	2.333 336	9.72	48
25	24.714 522	357.955 043	.002 793 6469	.040 462	14.483 592	.069 043 6469	13.81	2.452 182	9.81	50
26	28.097 669	409.021 424	.002 444 8597	.035 590	14.557 130	.068 694 8597	13.74	2.572 133	9.89	52
27	31.943 933	467.078 233	.002 140 9690	.031 305	14.621 814	.068 390 9690	13.68	2.693 112	9.97	54
28	36.316 708	533.082 385	.001 875 8827	.027 536	14.678 709	.068 125 8827	13.63	2.815 049	10.05	56
29	41.288 068	608.121 782	.001 644 4075	.024 220	14.728 754	.067 894 4075	13.58	2.937 876	10.13	58
30	46.939 953	693.433 253	.001 442 0999	.021 304	14.772 773	.067 692 0999	13.54	3.061 526	10.21	60
31	53.365 519	790.422 931	.001 265 1455	.018 739	14.811 491	.067 515 1455	13.51	3.185 939	10.28	62
32	60.670 675	900.689 435	.001 110 2606	.016 482	14.845 548	.067 360 2606	13.48	3.311 057	10.35	64
33	68.975 827	1026.050 217	.000 974 6112	.014 498	14.875 504	.067 224 6112	13.45	3.436 824	10.41	66
34	78.417 863	1168.571 520	.000 855 7457	.012 752	14.901 854	.067 105 7457	13.43	3.563 191	10.48	68
35	89.152 411	1330.602 429	.000 751 5393	.011 217	14.925 030	.067 001 5393	13.41	3.690 108	10.54	70
36	101.356 401	1514.813 599	.000 660 1472	.009 866	14.945 416	.066 910 1472	13.39	3.817 531	10.60	72
37	115.230 984	1724.241 262	.000 579 9652	.008 678	14.963 348	.066 829 9652	13.37	3.945 417	10.66	74
38	131.004 845	1962.337 282	.000 509 5964	.007 633	14.979 120	.066 759 5964	13.36	4.073 729	10.72	76
39	148.937 975	2233.026 043	.000 447 8228	.006 714	14.992 993	.066 697 8228	13.34	4.202 430	10.78	78
40	169.325 955	2540.769 134	.000 393 5816	.005 906	15.005 196	.066 643 5816	13.33	4.331 487	10.83	80
41	192.504 826	2890.638 889	.000 345 9443	.005 195	15.015 929	.066 595 9443	13.32	4.460 867	10.88	82
42	218.856 632	3288.401 986	.000 304 0991	.004 569	15.025 371	.066 554 0991	13.32	4.590 544	10.93	84
43	248.815 711	3740.614 501	.000 267 3358	.004 019	15.033 675	.066 517 3358	13.31	4.720 491	10.98	86
44	282.875 860	4254.729 964	.000 235 0325	.003 535	15.040 979	.066 485 0325	13.30	4.850 683	11.02	88
45	321.598 471	4839.222 210	.000 206 6448	.003 109	15.047 404	.066 456 6448	13.30	4.981 098	11.07	90
46	365.621 785	5503.725 051	.000 181 6951	.002 735	15.053 056	.066 431 6951	13.29	5.111 716	11.11	92
47	415.671 408	6259.191 064	.000 159 7651	.002 406	15.058 026	.066 409 7651	13.29	5.242 518	11.15	94
48	472.572 277	7118.072 110	.000 140 4875	.002 116	15.062 399	.066 390 4875	13.28	5.373 487	11.19	96
49	537.262 253	8094.524 578	.000 123 5403	.001 861	15.066 245	.066 373 5403	13.28	5.504 607	11.23	98
50	610.807 579	9204.642 709	.000 108 6408	.001 637	15.069 628	.066 358 6408	13.28	5.635 864	11.27	100

Effective Rate is 13.69 %

Annual Percentage Rate is 13.25 %

Amount Of 1	Amount Of 1 Per Period	Sinking Fund Payment	Present Worth Of 1	Present Worth of 1 Per Period	Periodic Payment To Amortize 1	Constant Annual Percent	Total Interest	Annual Add On Rate
What a single $ 1 deposit grows to in the future. The deposit is made at the beginning of the first period.	What a series of $ 1 deposits grow to in the future. A deposit is made at the end of each period.	The amount to be deposited at the end of each period that grows to $ 1 in the future.	What $ 1 to be paid in the future is worth today. Value today of a single $ 1 payment tomorrow.	What $ 1 to be paid at the end of each period is worth today. Value today of a series of $ 1 payments tomorrow.	The mortgage payment to amortize a loan of $ 1. An annuity certain, payable at the end of each period, worth $ 1 today.	The annual payment, including interest and principal, to amortize completely a loan of $ 100.	The total interest paid over the term on a loan of $1. The loan is amortized by regular periodic payments.	The average annual interest rate on a loan that is completely amortized by regular periodic payments.
$S = (1 + i)^n$	$S\overline{n}| = \dfrac{(1+i)^n - 1}{i}$	$\dfrac{1}{S\overline{n}|} = \dfrac{i}{(1+i)^n - 1}$	$V^n = \dfrac{1}{(1+i)^n}$	$A\overline{n}| = \dfrac{1 - V^n}{i}$	$\dfrac{1}{A\overline{n}|} = \dfrac{i}{1 - V^n}$			

YEAR / **PERIODS**

	Amount Of 1	Amount Of 1 Per Period	Sinking Fund Payment	Present Worth Of 1	Present Worth of 1 Per Period	Periodic Payment To Amortize 1	Constant Annual Percent	Total Interest	Annual Add On Rate	
	1.067 500	1.000 000	1.000 000 0000	.936 768	.936 768	1.067 500 0000	213.50	.067 500	13.50	1
	1.139 556	2.067 500	.483 675 9371	.877 535	1.814 303	.551 175 9371	110.24	.102 352	10.24	2
1	1.139 556	2.067 500	.483 675 9371	.877 535	1.814 303	.551 175 9371	110.24	.102 352	10.24	2
2	1.298 588	4.423 533	.226 063 6696	.770 067	3.406 416	.293 563 6696	58.72	.174 255	8.71	4
3	1.479 815	7.108 364	.140 679 3430	.675 760	4.803 551	.208 179 3430	41.64	.249 076	8.30	6
4	1.686 332	10.167 881	.098 348 9106	.593 003	6.029 584	.165 848 9106	33.17	.326 791	8.17	8
5	1.921 670	13.654 372	.073 236 6154	.520 381	7.105 471	.140 736 6154	28.15	.407 366	8.15	10
6	2.189 851	17.627 425	.056 729 7830	.456 652	8.049 600	.124 229 7830	24.85	.490 757	8.18	12
7	2.495 459	22.154 942	.045 136 6553	.400 728	8.878 105	.112 636 6553	22.53	.576 913	8.24	14
8	2.843 715	27.314 303	.036 610 8553	.351 653	9.605 146	.104 110 8553	20.83	.665 774	8.32	16
9	3.240 574	33.193 685	.030 126 2124	.308 587	10.243 151	.097 626 2124	19.53	.757 272	8.41	18
10	3.692 816	39.893 571	.025 066 6956	.270 796	10.803 021	.092 566 6956	18.52	.851 334	8.51	20
11	4.208 172	47.528 468	.021 040 0217	.237 633	11.294 327	.088 540 0217	17.71	.947 880	8.62	22
12	4.795 448	56.228 863	.017 784 4606	.208 531	11.725 465	.085 284 4606	17.06	1.046 827	8.72	24
13	5.464 683	66.143 452	.015 118 6545	.182 993	12.103 804	.082 618 6545	16.53	1.148 085	8.83	26
14	6.227 314	77.441 684	.012 912 9423	.160 583	12.435 809	.080 412 9423	16.09	1.251 562	8.94	28
15	7.096 374	90.316 655	.011 072 1549	.140 917	12.727 155	.078 572 1549	15.72	1.357 165	9.05	30
16	8.086 718	104.988 409	.009 524 8610	.123 660	12.982 821	.077 024 8610	15.41	1.464 796	9.16	32
17	9.215 270	121.707 698	.008 216 4072	.108 516	13.207 177	.075 716 4072	15.15	1.574 358	9.26	34
18	10.501 318	140.760 268	.007 104 2775	.095 226	13.404 057	.074 604 2775	14.93	1.685 754	9.37	36
19	11.966 843	162.471 743	.006 154 9164	.083 564	13.576 826	.073 654 9164	14.74	1.798 887	9.47	38
20	13.636 890	187.213 190	.005 341 5040	.073 331	13.728 437	.072 841 5040	14.57	1.913 660	9.57	40
21	15.540 004	215.407 461	.004 642 3647	.064 350	13.861 481	.072 142 3647	14.43	2.029 979	9.67	42
22	17.708 708	247.536 418	.004 039 8096	.056 469	13.978 231	.071 539 8096	14.31	2.147 752	9.76	44
23	20.180 069	284.149 173	.003 519 2782	.049 554	14.080 684	.071 019 2782	14.21	2.266 887	9.86	46
24	22.996 324	325.871 466	.003 068 6946	.043 485	14.170 589	.070 568 6946	14.12	2.387 297	9.95	48
25	26.205 605	373.416 365	.002 677 9758	.038 160	14.249 485	.070 177 9758	14.04	2.508 899	10.04	50
26	29.862 761	427.596 453	.002 338 6536	.033 487	14.318 718	.069 838 6536	13.97	2.631 610	10.12	52
27	34.030 295	489.337 710	.002 043 5785	.029 386	14.379 473	.069 543 5785	13.91	2.755 353	10.21	54
28	38.779 436	559.695 346	.001 786 6863	.025 787	14.432 787	.069 286 6863	13.86	2.880 054	10.29	56
29	44.191 349	639.871 830	.001 562 8130	.022 629	14.479 572	.069 062 8130	13.82	3.005 643	10.36	58
30	50.358 527	731.237 443	.001 367 5449	.019 858	14.520 628	.068 867 5449	13.78	3.132 053	10.44	60
31	57.386 375	835.353 698	.001 197 0977	.017 426	14.556 656	.068 697 0977	13.74	3.259 220	10.51	62
32	65.395 002	954.000 028	.001 048 2180	.015 292	14.588 271	.068 548 2180	13.71	3.387 086	10.58	64
33	74.521 283	1089.204 194	.000 918 1015	.013 419	14.616 015	.068 418 1015	13.69	3.515 595	10.65	66
34	84.921 194	1243.276 947	.000 804 3260	.011 776	14.640 361	.068 304 3260	13.67	3.644 694	10.72	68
35	96.772 477	1418.851 516	.000 704 7954	.010 334	14.661 726	.068 204 7954	13.65	3.774 336	10.78	70
36	110.277 681	1618.928 612	.000 617 6925	.009 068	14.680 474	.068 117 6925	13.63	3.904 474	10.85	72
37	125.667 621	1846.927 719	.000 541 4397	.007 957	14.696 926	.068 041 4397	13.61	4.035 067	10.91	74
38	143.205 323	2106.745 525	.000 474 6658	.006 983	14.711 363	.067 974 6658	13.60	4.166 075	10.96	76
39	163.190 521	2402.822 530	.000 416 1772	.006 128	14.724 032	.067 916 1772	13.59	4.297 462	11.02	78
40	185.964 778	2740.218 932	.000 364 9343	.005 377	14.735 150	.067 864 9343	13.58	4.429 195	11.07	80
41	211.917 325	3124.701 110	.000 320 0306	.004 719	14.744 906	.067 820 0306	13.57	4.561 243	11.13	82
42	241.491 712	3562.840 179	.000 280 6750	.004 141	14.753 468	.067 780 6750	13.56	4.693 577	11.18	84
43	275.193 390	4062.124 294	.000 246 1766	.003 634	14.760 981	.067 746 1766	13.55	4.826 171	11.22	86
44	313.598 347	4631.086 628	.000 215 9320	.003 189	14.767 573	.067 715 9320	13.55	4.959 002	11.27	88
45	357.362 957	5279.451 211	.000 189 4136	.002 798	14.773 359	.067 689 4136	13.54	5.092 047	11.32	90
46	407.235 191	6018.299 124	.000 166 1599	.002 456	14.778 436	.067 666 1599	13.54	5.225 287	11.36	92
47	464.067 407	6860.257 881	.000 145 7671	.002 155	14.782 891	.067 645 7671	13.53	5.358 702	11.40	94
48	528.830 914	7819.717 245	.000 127 8819	.001 891	14.786 801	.067 627 8819	13.53	5.492 277	11.44	96
49	602.632 573	8913.075 160	.000 112 1947	.001 659	14.790 231	.067 612 1947	13.53	5.625 995	11.48	98
50	686.733 715	10159.018 005	.000 098 4347	.001 456	14.793 242	.067 598 4347	13.52	5.759 843	11.52	100

SEMIANNUAL COMPOUND INTEREST AND ANNUITY

13.75 % S

Amount Of 1	Amount Of 1 Per Period	Sinking Fund Payment	Present Worth Of 1	Present Worth of 1 Per Period	Periodic Payment To Amortize 1	Constant Annual Percent	Total Interest	Annual Add On Rate	
What a single $ 1 deposit grows to in the future. The deposit is made at the beginning of the first period.	What a series of $ 1 deposits grow to in the future. A deposit is made at the end of each period.	The amount to be deposited at the end of each period that grows to $ 1 in the future.	What $ 1 to be paid in the future is worth today. Value today of a single $ 1 payment tomorrow.	What $ 1 to be paid at the end of each period is worth today. Value today of a series of $ 1 payments tomorrow.	The mortgage payment to amortize a loan of $ 1. An annuity certain, payable at the end of each period, worth $ 1 today.	The annual interest payment, including interest and principal, to amortize completely a loan of $ 100.	The total interest paid over the term on a loan of $1. The loan is amortized by regular periodic payments.	The average annual interest rate on a loan that is completely amortized by regular periodic payments.	

$$S = (1+i)^n \qquad S\overline{n}| = \frac{(1+i)^n - 1}{i} \qquad \frac{1}{S\overline{n}|} = \frac{i}{(1+i)^n - 1} \qquad V^n = \frac{1}{(1+i)^n} \qquad A\overline{n}| = \frac{1-V^n}{i} \qquad \frac{1}{A\overline{n}|} = \frac{i}{1-V^n}$$

YEAR										PERIODS
	1.068 750	1.000 000	1.000 000 0000	.935 673	.935 673	1.068 750 0000	213.75	.068 750	13.75	1
	1.142 227	2.068 750	.483 383 6858	.875 483	1.811 156	.552 133 6858	110.43	.104 267	10.43	2
1	1.142 227	2.068 750	.483 383 6858	.875 483	1.811 156	.552 133 6858	110.43	.104 267	10.43	2
2	1.304 682	4.431 731	.225 645 4542	.766 471	3.396 792	.294 395 4542	58.88	.177 582	8.88	4
3	1.490 242	7.130 791	.140 236 8947	.671 032	4.784 989	.208 986 8947	41.80	.253 921	8.46	6
4	1.702 194	10.213 729	.097 907 4342	.587 477	6.000 332	.166 657 4342	33.34	.333 259	8.33	8
5	1.944 291	13.735 143	.072 805 9425	.514 326	7.064 345	.141 555 9425	28.32	.415 559	8.31	10
6	2.220 821	17.757 395	.056 314 5674	.450 284	7.995 870	.125 064 5674	25.02	.500 775	8.35	12
7	2.536 681	22.351 718	.044 739 2905	.394 216	8.811 404	.113 489 2905	22.70	.588 850	8.41	14
8	2.897 464	27.599 476	.036 232 5721	.345 129	9.525 391	.104 982 5721	21.00	.679 721	8.50	16
9	3.309 560	33.593 604	.029 767 5708	.302 155	10.150 474	.098 517 5708	19.71	.773 316	8.59	18
10	3.780 268	40.440 257	.024 727 8347	.264 532	10.697 723	.093 477 8347	18.70	.869 557	8.70	20
11	4.317 922	48.260 686	.020 720 7995	.231 593	11.176 831	.089 470 7995	17.90	.968 358	8.80	22
12	4.932 045	57.193 388	.017 484 5387	.202 756	11.596 282	.086 234 5387	17.25	1.069 629	8.91	24
13	5.633 513	67.396 557	.014 837 5533	.177 509	11.963 504	.083 587 5533	16.72	1.173 276	9.03	26
14	6.434 748	79.050 887	.012 650 0794	.155 406	12.285 000	.081 400 0794	16.29	1.279 202	9.14	28
15	7.349 941	92.362 773	.010 826 8729	.136 056	12.566 465	.079 576 8729	15.92	1.387 306	9.25	30
16	8.395 297	107.567 963	.009 296 4483	.119 114	12.812 883	.078 046 4483	15.61	1.497 486	9.36	32
17	9.589 332	124.935 734	.008 004 1151	.104 283	13.028 617	.076 754 1151	15.36	1.609 640	9.47	34
18	10.953 189	144.773 664	.006 907 3336	.091 298	13.217 489	.075 657 3336	15.14	1.723 664	9.58	36
19	12.511 024	167.433 075	.005 972 5356	.079 930	13.382 844	.074 722 5356	14.95	1.839 456	9.68	38
20	14.290 424	193.315 256	.005 172 8975	.069 977	13.527 608	.073 922 8975	14.79	1.956 916	9.78	40
21	16.322 902	222.878 570	.004 486 7481	.061 264	13.654 347	.073 236 7481	14.65	2.075 943	9.89	42
22	18.644 452	256.646 573	.003 896 4089	.053 635	13.765 305	.072 646 4089	14.53	2.196 442	9.98	44
23	21.296 188	295.217 283	.003 387 3356	.046 957	13.862 447	.072 137 3356	14.43	2.318 317	10.08	46
24	24.325 072	339.273 772	.002 947 4722	.041 110	13.947 493	.071 697 4722	14.34	2.441 479	10.17	48
25	27.784 743	389.596 264	.002 566 7597	.035 991	14.021 949	.071 316 7597	14.27	2.565 838	10.26	50
26	31.736 472	447.075 952	.002 236 7564	.031 509	14.087 135	.070 986 7564	14.20	2.691 311	10.35	52
27	36.250 241	512.730 778	.001 950 3413	.027 586	14.144 203	.070 700 3413	14.15	2.817 818	10.44	54
28	41.405 988	587.723 464	.001 701 4805	.024 151	14.194 166	.070 451 4805	14.10	2.945 283	10.52	56
29	47.295 019	673.382 102	.001 485 0410	.021 144	14.237 907	.070 235 0410	14.05	3.073 632	10.60	58
30	54.021 628	771.223 673	.001 296 6407	.018 511	14.276 202	.070 046 6407	14.01	3.202 798	10.68	60
31	61.704 938	882.980 915	.001 132 5273	.016 206	14.309 729	.069 882 5273	13.98	3.332 717	10.75	62
32	70.481 019	1010.633 005	.000 989 4789	.014 188	14.339 080	.069 739 4789	13.95	3.463 327	10.82	64
33	80.505 292	1156.440 614	.000 864 7223	.012 422	14.364 778	.069 614 7223	13.93	3.594 572	10.89	66
34	91.955 283	1322.985 937	.000 755 8659	.010 875	14.387 275	.069 505 8659	13.91	3.726 399	10.96	68
35	105.033 767	1513.218 429	.000 660 8431	.009 521	14.406 971	.069 410 8431	13.89	3.858 759	11.03	70
36	119.972 359	1730.507 034	.000 577 8653	.008 335	14.424 214	.069 327 8653	13.87	3.991 606	11.09	72
37	137.035 615	1978.699 851	.000 505 3824	.007 297	14.439 311	.069 255 3824	13.86	4.124 898	11.15	74
38	156.525 719	2262.192 279	.000 442 0491	.006 389	14.452 528	.069 192 0491	13.84	4.258 596	11.21	76
39	178.787 834	2586.004 861	.000 386 6969	.005 593	14.464 099	.069 136 6969	13.83	4.392 662	11.26	78
40	204.216 213	2955.872 193	.000 338 3096	.004 897	14.474 229	.069 088 3096	13.82	4.527 065	11.32	80
41	233.261 183	3378.344 484	.000 296 0030	.004 287	14.483 098	.069 046 0030	13.81	4.661 772	11.37	82
42	266.437 120	3860.903 557	.000 259 0067	.003 753	14.490 862	.069 009 0067	13.81	4.796 757	11.42	84
43	304.331 555	4412.095 348	.000 226 6497	.003 286	14.497 660	.068 976 6497	13.80	4.931 992	11.47	86
44	347.615 586	5041.681 253	.000 198 3465	.002 877	14.503 611	.068 948 3465	13.79	5.067 455	11.52	88
45	397.055 756	5760.810 997	.000 173 5867	.002 519	14.508 821	.068 923 5867	13.79	5.203 123	11.56	90
46	453.527 631	6582.220 092	.000 151 9244	.002 205	14.513 383	.068 901 9244	13.79	5.338 977	11.61	92
47	518.031 307	7520.455 379	.000 132 9707	.001 930	14.517 376	.068 882 9707	13.78	5.474 999	11.65	94
48	591.709 119	8592.132 646	.000 116 3855	.001 690	14.520 872	.068 866 3855	13.78	5.611 173	11.69	96
49	675.865 873	9816.230 887	.000 101 8721	.001 480	14.523 933	.068 851 8721	13.78	5.747 483	11.73	98
50	771.991 953	11214.428 413	.000 089 1708	.001 295	14.526 613	.068 839 1708	13.77	5.883 917	11.77	100

Effective Rate is 14.22 %

8 - 411

Annual Percentage Rate is 13.75 %

SEMIANNUAL COMPOUND INTEREST AND ANNUITY

14.00 % S

	Amount Of 1	Amount Of 1 Per Period	Sinking Fund Payment	Present Worth Of 1	Present Worth of 1 Per Period	Periodic Payment To Amortize 1	Constant Annual Percent	Total Interest	Annual Add On Rate
	What a single $ 1 deposit grows to in the future. The deposit is made at the beginning of the first period.	What a series of $ 1 deposits grow to in the future. A deposit is made at the end of each period.	The amount to be deposited at the end of each period that grows to $ 1 in the future.	What $ 1 to be paid in the future is worth today. Value today of a single $ 1 payment tomorrow.	What $ 1 to be paid at the end of each period is worth today. Value today of a series of $ 1 payments tomorrow.	The mortgage payment to amortize a loan of $ 1. An annuity certain, payable at the end of each period, worth $ 1 today.	The annual payment, including interest and principal, to amortize completely a loan of $ 100.	The total interest paid over the term on a loan of $1. The loan is amortized by regular periodic payments.	The average annual interest rate on a loan that is completely amortized by regular periodic payments.
	$S = (1+i)^n$	$S\overline{n}| = \dfrac{(1+i)^n - 1}{i}$	$\dfrac{1}{S\overline{n}|} = \dfrac{i}{(1+i)^n - 1}$	$V^n = \dfrac{1}{(1+i)^n}$	$A\overline{n}| = \dfrac{1 - V^n}{i}$	$\dfrac{1}{A\overline{n}|} = \dfrac{i}{1 - V^n}$			

YEAR — **PERIODS**

	1.070 000	1.000 000	1.000 000 0000	.934 579	.934 579	1.070 000 0000	214.00	.070 000	14.00	1
	1.144 900	2.070 000	.483 091 7874	.873 439	1.808 018	.553 091 7874	110.62	.106 184	10.62	2

YEAR	Amount Of 1	Amount Of 1 Per Period	Sinking Fund Payment	Present Worth Of 1	Present Worth of 1 Per Period	Periodic Payment To Amortize 1	Constant Annual Percent	Total Interest	Annual Add On Rate	PERIODS
1	1.144 900	2.070 000	.483 091 7874	.873 439	1.808 018	.553 091 7874	110.62	.106 184	10.62	2
2	1.310 796	4.439 943	.225 228 1167	.762 895	3.387 211	.295 228 1167	59.05	.180 912	9.05	4
3	1.500 730	7.153 291	.139 795 7998	.666 342	4.766 540	.209 795 7998	41.96	.258 775	8.63	6
4	1.718 186	10.259 803	.097 467 7625	.582 009	5.971 299	.167 467 7625	33.50	.339 742	8.49	8
5	1.967 151	13.816 448	.072 377 5027	.508 349	7.023 582	.142 377 5027	28.48	.423 775	8.48	10
6	2.252 192	17.888 451	.055 901 9887	.444 012	7.942 686	.125 901 9887	25.19	.510 824	8.51	12
7	2.578 534	22.550 488	.044 344 9386	.387 817	8.745 468	.114 344 9386	22.87	.600 829	8.58	14
8	2.952 164	27.888 054	.035 857 6477	.338 735	9.446 649	.105 857 6477	21.18	.693 722	8.67	16
9	3.379 932	33.999 033	.029 412 6017	.295 864	10.059 087	.099 412 6017	19.89	.789 427	8.77	18
10	3.869 684	40.995 492	.024 392 9257	.258 419	10.594 014	.094 392 9257	18.88	.887 859	8.88	20
11	4.430 402	49.005 739	.020 405 7732	.225 713	11.061 240	.090 405 7732	18.09	.988 927	8.99	22
12	5.072 367	58.176 671	.017 189 0207	.197 147	11.469 334	.087 189 0207	17.44	1.092 537	9.10	24
13	5.807 353	68.676 470	.014 561 0279	.172 195	11.825 779	.084 561 0279	16.92	1.198 587	9.22	26
14	6.648 838	80.697 691	.012 391 9283	.150 402	12.137 111	.082 391 9283	16.48	1.306 974	9.34	28
15	7.612 255	94.460 786	.010 586 4035	.131 367	12.409 041	.080 586 4035	16.12	1.417 592	9.45	30
16	8.715 271	110.218 154	.009 072 9155	.114 741	12.646 555	.079 072 9155	15.82	1.530 333	9.56	32
17	9.978 114	128.258 765	.007 796 7381	.100 219	12.854 009	.077 796 7381	15.56	1.645 089	9.68	34
18	11.423 942	148.913 460	.006 715 3097	.087 535	13.035 208	.076 715 3097	15.35	1.761 751	9.79	36
19	13.079 271	172.561 020	.005 795 0515	.076 457	13.193 473	.075 795 0515	15.16	1.880 212	9.90	38
20	14.974 458	199.635 112	.005 009 1389	.066 780	13.331 709	.075 009 1389	15.01	2.000 366	10.00	40
21	17.144 257	230.632 240	.004 335 9072	.058 329	13.452 449	.074 335 9072	14.87	2.122 108	10.11	42
22	19.628 460	266.120 851	.003 757 6913	.050 946	13.557 908	.073 757 6913	14.76	2.245 338	10.21	44
23	22.472 623	306.751 763	.003 259 9650	.044 499	13.650 020	.073 259 9650	14.66	2.369 958	10.30	46
24	25.728 907	353.270 093	.002 830 6953	.038 867	13.730 474	.072 830 6953	14.57	2.495 873	10.40	48
25	29.457 025	406.528 929	.002 459 8495	.033 948	13.800 746	.072 459 8495	14.50	2.622 992	10.49	50
26	33.725 348	467.504 971	.002 139 0147	.029 651	13.862 124	.072 139 0147	14.43	2.751 229	10.58	52
27	38.612 151	537.316 442	.001 861 1007	.025 899	13.915 735	.071 861 1007	14.38	2.880 499	10.67	54
28	44.207 052	617.243 594	.001 620 1059	.022 621	13.962 560	.071 620 1059	14.33	3.010 726	10.75	56
29	50.612 653	708.752 191	.001 410 9304	.019 758	14.003 458	.071 410 9304	14.29	3.141 834	10.83	58
30	57.946 427	813.520 383	.001 229 2255	.017 257	14.039 181	.071 229 2255	14.25	3.273 754	10.91	60
31	66.342 864	933.469 487	.001 071 2723	.015 073	14.070 383	.071 071 2723	14.22	3.406 419	10.99	62
32	75.955 945	1070.799 216	.000 933 8819	.013 166	14.097 635	.070 933 8819	14.19	3.539 768	11.06	64
33	86.961 962	1228.028 022	.000 814 3137	.011 499	14.121 439	.070 814 3137	14.17	3.673 745	11.13	66
34	99.562 750	1408.039 282	.000 710 2075	.010 044	14.142 230	.070 710 2075	14.15	3.808 294	11.20	68
35	113.989 392	1614.134 174	.000 619 5272	.008 773	14.160 389	.070 619 5272	14.13	3.943 367	11.27	70
36	130.506 455	1850.092 216	.000 540 5136	.007 662	14.176 251	.070 540 5136	14.11	4.078 917	11.33	72
37	149.416 840	2120.240 578	.000 471 6446	.006 693	14.190 104	.070 471 6446	14.10	4.214 902	11.39	74
38	171.067 341	2429.533 438	.000 411 6017	.005 846	14.202 205	.070 411 6017	14.09	4.351 282	11.45	76
39	195.854 998	2783.642 833	.000 359 2415	.005 106	14.212 774	.070 359 2415	14.08	4.488 021	11.51	78
40	224.234 388	3189.062 680	.000 313 5718	.004 460	14.222 005	.070 313 5718	14.07	4.625 086	11.56	80
41	256.725 950	3653.227 862	.000 273 7305	.003 895	14.230 069	.070 273 7305	14.06	4.762 446	11.62	82
42	293.925 541	4184.650 579	.000 238 9686	.003 402	14.237 111	.070 238 9686	14.05	4.900 073	11.67	84
43	336.515 351	4793.076 448	.000 208 6343	.002 972	14.243 262	.070 208 6343	14.05	5.037 943	11.72	86
44	385.276 426	5489.663 225	.000 182 1605	.002 596	14.248 635	.070 182 1605	14.04	5.176 030	11.76	88
45	441.102 980	6287.185 427	.000 159 0537	.002 267	14.253 328	.070 159 0537	14.04	5.314 315	11.81	90
46	505.018 802	7200.268 595	.000 138 8837	.001 980	14.257 427	.070 138 8837	14.03	5.452 777	11.85	92
47	578.196 026	8245.657 515	.000 121 2760	.001 730	14.261 007	.070 121 2760	14.03	5.591 400	11.90	94
48	661.976 630	9442.523 288	.000 105 9039	.001 511	14.264 134	.070 105 9039	14.03	5.730 167	11.94	96
49	757.897 044	10812.814 913	.000 092 4829	.001 319	14.266 865	.070 092 4829	14.02	5.869 063	11.98	98
50	867.716 326	12381.661 794	.000 080 7646	.001 152	14.269 251	.070 080 7646	14.02	6.008 076	12.02	100

Effective Rate is 14.49 %

Annual Percentage Rate is 14.00 %

Amount Of 1	Amount Of 1 Per Period	Sinking Fund Payment	Present Worth Of 1	Present Worth of 1 Per Period	Periodic Payment To Amortize 1	Constant Annual Percent	Total Interest	Annual Add On Rate
What a single $ 1 deposit grows to in the future. The deposit is made at the beginning of the first period.	What a series of $ 1 deposits grow to in the future. A deposit is made at the end of each period.	The amount to be deposited at the end of each period that grows to $ 1 in the future.	What $ 1 to be paid in the future is worth today. Value today of a single $ 1 payment tomorrow.	What $ 1 to be paid at the end of each period is worth today. Value today of a series of $ 1 payments tomorrow.	The mortgage payment to amortize a loan of $ 1. An annuity certain, payable at the end of each period, worth $ 1 today.	The annual payment, including interest and principal, to amortize completely a loan of $ 100.	The total interest paid over the term on a loan of $1. The loan is amortized by regular periodic payments.	The average annual interest rate on a loan that is completely amortized by regular periodic payments.
$S = (1+i)^n$	$S\overline{n} = \dfrac{(1+i)^n - 1}{i}$	$\dfrac{1}{S\overline{n}} = \dfrac{i}{(1+i)^n - 1}$	$V^n = \dfrac{1}{(1+i)^n}$	$A\overline{n} = \dfrac{1 - V^n}{i}$	$\dfrac{1}{A\overline{n}} = \dfrac{i}{1 - V^n}$			

YEAR									PERIODS
	1.071 250	1.000 000	1.000 000 0000	.933 489	.933 489	1.071 250 0000	214.25	.071 250	14.25	1
	1.147 577	2.071 250	.482 800 2414	.871 402	1.804 890	.554 050 2414	110.82	.108 100	10.81	2

YEAR	Amount Of 1	Amount Of 1 Per Period	Sinking Fund Payment	Present Worth Of 1	Present Worth of 1 Per Period	Periodic Payment To Amortize 1	Constant Annual Percent	Total Interest	Annual Add On Rate	PERIODS
1	1.147 577	2.071 250	.482 800 2414	.871 402	1.804 890	.554 050 2414	110.82	.108 100	10.81	2
2	1.316 932	4.448 168	.224 811 6551	.759 341	3.377 675	.296 061 6551	59.22	.184 247	9.21	4
3	1.511 280	7.175 863	.139 356 0551	.661 691	4.748 202	.210 606 0551	42.13	.263 636	8.79	6
4	1.734 310	10.306 103	.097 029 8905	.576 598	5.942 481	.168 279 8905	33.66	.346 239	8.66	8
5	1.990 253	13.898 292	.071 951 2887	.502 449	6.983 177	.143 201 2887	28.65	.432 013	8.64	10
6	2.283 968	18.020 604	.055 492 0362	.437 835	7.890 042	.126 742 0362	25.35	.520 904	8.68	12
7	2.621 028	22.751 273	.043 953 5853	.381 530	8.680 285	.115 203 5853	23.05	.612 850	8.76	14
8	3.007 831	28.180 077	.035 486 0632	.332 466	9.368 905	.106 736 0632	21.35	.707 777	8.85	16
9	3.451 716	34.410 046	.029 061 2804	.289 711	9.968 969	.100 311 2804	20.07	.805 603	8.95	18
10	3.961 108	41.559 412	.024 061 9379	.252 455	10.491 865	.095 311 9379	19.07	.906 239	9.06	20
11	4.545 675	49.763 858	.020 094 9052	.219 989	10.947 518	.091 344 9052	18.27	1.009 588	9.18	22
12	5.216 510	59.179 087	.016 897 8613	.191 699	11.344 575	.088 147 8613	17.63	1.115 549	9.30	24
13	5.986 345	69.983 783	.014 289 0247	.167 047	11.690 571	.085 539 0247	17.11	1.224 015	9.42	26
14	6.869 789	82.382 999	.012 138 4268	.145 565	11.992 072	.083 388 4268	16.68	1.334 876	9.53	28
15	7.883 608	96.612 049	.010 350 6758	.126 845	12.254 800	.081 600 6758	16.33	1.448 020	9.65	30
16	9.047 044	112.940 973	.008 854 1826	.110 533	12.483 743	.080 104 1826	16.03	1.563 334	9.77	32
17	10.382 176	131.679 663	.007 594 1871	.096 319	12.683 243	.078 844 1871	15.77	1.680 702	9.89	34
18	11.914 342	153.183 746	.006 528 1078	.083 932	12.857 088	.077 778 1078	15.56	1.800 012	10.00	36
19	13.672 619	177.861 326	.005 622 3577	.073 139	13.008 577	.076 872 3577	15.38	1.921 150	10.11	38
20	15.690 378	206.180 739	.004 850 1136	.063 733	13.140 585	.076 100 1136	15.23	2.044 005	10.22	40
21	18.005 910	238.679 434	.004 189 7200	.055 537	13.255 617	.075 439 7200	15.09	2.168 468	10.33	42
22	20.663 160	275.974 174	.003 623 5275	.048 395	13.355 855	.074 873 5275	14.98	2.294 435	10.43	44
23	23.712 558	318.772 744	.003 137 0311	.042 172	13.443 204	.074 387 0311	14.88	2.421 803	10.53	46
24	27.211 976	367.887 380	.002 718 2232	.036 749	13.519 319	.073 968 2232	14.80	2.550 475	10.63	48
25	31.227 826	424.250 185	.002 357 0997	.032 023	13.585 646	.073 607 0997	14.73	2.680 355	10.72	50
26	35.836 321	488.930 819	.002 045 2791	.027 905	13.643 444	.073 295 2791	14.66	2.811 355	10.81	52
27	41.124 922	563.156 799	.001 775 7044	.024 316	13.693 808	.073 025 7044	14.61	2.943 388	10.90	54
28	47.193 997	648.336 793	.001 542 4082	.021 189	13.737 696	.072 792 4082	14.56	3.076 375	10.99	56
29	54.158 724	746.087 359	.001 340 3256	.018 464	13.775 940	.072 590 3256	14.52	3.210 239	11.07	58
30	62.151 283	858.263 616	.001 165 1432	.016 090	13.809 266	.072 415 1432	14.49	3.344 909	11.15	60
31	71.323 355	986.994 460	.001 013 1769	.014 021	13.838 307	.072 263 1769	14.46	3.480 317	11.23	62
32	81.849 011	1134.722 960	.000 881 2724	.012 218	13.863 612	.072 131 2724	14.43	3.616 401	11.30	64
33	93.928 007	1304.252 724	.000 766 7226	.010 646	13.885 664	.072 016 7226	14.41	3.753 104	11.37	66
34	107.789 579	1498.801 108	.000 667 1999	.009 277	13.904 880	.071 917 1999	14.39	3.890 370	11.44	68
35	123.696 794	1722.060 273	.000 580 6998	.008 084	13.921 624	.071 830 6998	14.37	4.028 149	11.51	70
36	141.951 542	1978.267 258	.000 505 4929	.007 045	13.936 215	.071 755 4929	14.36	4.166 395	11.57	72
37	162.900 263	2272.284 390	.000 440 0858	.006 139	13.948 930	.071 690 0858	14.34	4.305 066	11.64	74
38	186.940 524	2609.691 559	.000 383 1870	.005 349	13.960 010	.071 633 1870	14.33	4.444 122	11.70	76
39	214.528 563	2996.892 119	.000 333 6790	.004 661	13.969 665	.071 583 6790	14.32	4.583 527	11.75	78
40	246.187 951	3441.234 406	.000 290 5934	.004 062	13.978 078	.071 540 5934	14.31	4.723 247	11.81	80
41	282.519 523	3951.151 200	.000 253 0908	.003 540	13.985 409	.071 503 0908	14.31	4.863 253	11.86	82
42	324.212 783	4536.319 762	.000 220 4430	.003 084	13.991 798	.071 470 4430	14.30	5.003 517	11.91	84
43	372.058 991	5207.845 489	.000 192 0180	.002 688	13.997 365	.071 442 0180	14.29	5.144 014	11.96	86
44	426.966 178	5978.472 675	.000 167 2668	.002 342	14.002 216	.071 417 2668	14.29	5.284 719	12.01	88
45	489.976 379	6862.826 371	.000 145 7126	.002 041	14.006 443	.071 395 7126	14.28	5.425 614	12.06	90
46	562.285 409	7877.689 946	.000 126 9408	.001 778	14.010 127	.071 376 9408	14.28	5.566 679	12.10	92
47	645.265 556	9042.323 599	.000 110 5910	.001 550	14.013 337	.071 360 5910	14.28	5.707 896	12.14	94
48	740.491 629	10378.829 882	.000 096 3500	.001 350	14.016 134	.071 346 3500	14.27	5.849 250	12.19	96
49	849.770 838	11912.573 169	.000 083 9449	.001 177	14.018 571	.071 333 9449	14.27	5.990 727	12.23	98
50	975.177 098	13672.661 018	.000 073 1387	.001 025	14.020 695	.071 323 1387	14.27	6.132 314	12.26	100

Effective Rate is 14.76 %

Annual Percentage Rate is 14.25 %

Amount Of 1	Amount Of 1 Per Period	Sinking Fund Payment	Present Worth Of 1	Present Worth of 1 Per Period	Periodic Payment To Amortize 1	Constant Annual Percent	Total Interest	Annual Add On Rate
What a single $ 1 deposit grows to in the future. The deposit is made at the beginning of the first period.	What a series of $ 1 deposits grow to in the future. A deposit is made at the end of each period.	The amount to be deposited at the end of each period that grows to $ 1 in the future.	What $ 1 to be paid in the future is worth today. Value today of a single $ 1 payment tomorrow.	What $ 1 to be paid at the end of each period is worth today. Value today of a series of $ 1 payments tomorrow.	The mortgage payment to amortize a loan of $ 1. An annuity certain, payable at the end of each period, worth $ 1 today.	The annual payment, including interest and principal, to amortize completely a loan of $ 100.	The total interest paid over the term on a loan of $1. The loan is amortized by regular periodic payments.	The average annual interest rate on a loan that is completely amortized by regular periodic payments.
$S = (1+i)^n$	$S\overline{n}| = \dfrac{(1+i)^n - 1}{i}$	$\dfrac{1}{S\overline{n}|} = \dfrac{i}{(1+i)^n - 1}$	$V^n = \dfrac{1}{(1+i)^n}$	$A\overline{n}| = \dfrac{1-V^n}{i}$	$\dfrac{1}{A\overline{n}|} = \dfrac{i}{1-V^n}$			

YEAR									PERIODS
	1.072 500	1.000 000	1.000 000 0000	.932 401	.932 401	1.072 500 0000	214.50	.072 500	14.50	1
	1.150 256	2.072 500	.482 509 0470	.869 371	1.801 772	.555 009 0470	111.01	.110 018	11.00	2

YEAR									PERIODS
1	1.150 256	2.072 500	.482 509 0470	.869 371	1.801 772	.555 009 0470	111.01	.110 018	11.00	2
2	1.323 089	4.456 406	.224 396 0677	.755 807	3.368 182	.296 896 0677	59.38	.187 584	9.38	4
3	1.521 892	7.198 509	.138 917 6575	.657 077	4.729 974	.211 417 6575	42.29	.268 506	8.95	6
4	1.750 566	10.352 630	.096 593 8133	.571 244	5.913 877	.169 093 8133	33.82	.352 751	8.82	8
5	2.013 599	13.980 677	.071 527 2931	.496 623	6.943 128	.144 027 2931	28.81	.440 273	8.81	10
6	2.316 155	18.153 861	.055 084 6995	.431 750	7.837 930	.127 584 6995	25.52	.531 016	8.85	12
7	2.664 172	22.954 093	.043 565 2161	.375 351	8.615 846	.116 065 2161	23.22	.624 913	8.93	14
8	3.064 480	28.475 588	.035 117 7994	.326 320	9.292 143	.107 617 7994	21.53	.721 885	9.02	16
9	3.524 937	34.826 724	.028 713 5825	.283 693	9.880 097	.101 213 5825	20.25	.821 844	9.13	18
10	4.054 581	42.132 156	.023 734 8402	.246 635	10.391 247	.096 234 8402	19.25	.924 697	9.25	20
11	4.663 808	50.535 276	.019 788 1574	.214 417	10.835 626	.092 288 1574	18.46	1.030 339	9.37	22
12	5.364 574	60.201 017	.016 611 0150	.186 408	11.221 957	.089 111 0150	17.83	1.138 664	9.49	24
13	6.170 634	71.319 096	.014 021 4900	.162 058	11.557 822	.086 521 4900	17.31	1.249 559	9.61	26
14	7.097 811	84.107 736	.011 889 5127	.140 889	11.849 814	.084 389 5127	16.88	1.362 906	9.74	28
15	8.164 301	98.817 949	.010 119 6190	.122 484	12.103 663	.082 619 6190	16.53	1.478 589	9.86	30
16	9.391 039	115.738 464	.008 640 1700	.106 484	12.324 352	.081 140 1700	16.23	1.596 485	9.98	32
17	10.802 101	135.201 392	.007 396 3736	.092 575	12.516 213	.079 896 3736	15.98	1.716 477	10.10	34
18	12.425 184	157.588 746	.006 345 6308	.080 482	12.683 011	.078 845 6308	15.77	1.838 443	10.21	36
19	14.292 146	183.339 940	.005 454 3489	.069 969	12.828 021	.077 954 3489	15.60	1.962 265	10.33	38
20	16.439 630	212.960 411	.004 695 7084	.060 829	12.954 088	.077 195 7084	15.44	2.087 828	10.44	40
21	18.909 787	247.031 544	.004 048 0660	.052 883	13.063 687	.076 548 0660	15.31	2.215 019	10.55	42
22	21.751 101	286.222 078	.003 493 7906	.045 975	13.158 970	.075 993 7906	15.20	2.343 727	10.65	44
23	25.019 339	331.301 234	.003 018 4011	.039 969	13.241 806	.075 518 4011	15.11	2.473 846	10.76	46
24	28.778 652	383.153 815	.002 609 9179	.034 748	13.313 821	.075 109 9179	15.03	2.605 276	10.86	48
25	33.102 824	442.797 570	.002 258 3683	.030 209	13.376 429	.074 758 3683	14.96	2.737 918	10.95	50
26	38.076 730	511.403 173	.001 955 4044	.026 263	13.430 858	.074 455 4044	14.90	2.871 681	11.05	52
27	43.797 997	590.317 195	.001 694 0045	.022 832	13.478 178	.074 194 0045	14.84	3.006 476	11.14	54
28	50.378 919	681.088 544	.001 468 2379	.019 850	13.519 316	.073 968 2379	14.80	3.142 221	11.22	56
29	57.948 667	785.498 854	.001 273 0763	.017 257	13.555 081	.073 773 0763	14.76	3.278 838	11.31	58
30	66.655 816	905.597 466	.001 104 2434	.015 002	13.586 173	.073 604 2434	14.73	3.416 255	11.39	60
31	76.671 269	1043.741 646	.000 958 0915	.013 043	13.613 204	.073 458 0915	14.70	3.554 402	11.47	62
32	88.191 607	1202.642 851	.000 831 5021	.011 339	13.636 704	.073 331 5021	14.67	3.693 216	11.54	64
33	101.442 947	1385.419 956	.000 721 8028	.009 858	13.657 134	.073 221 8028	14.65	3.832 639	11.61	66
34	116.685 384	1595.660 463	.000 626 6997	.008 570	13.674 896	.073 126 6997	14.63	3.972 616	11.68	68
35	134.218 092	1837.490 921	.000 544 2204	.007 451	13.690 337	.073 044 2204	14.61	4.113 095	11.75	70
36	154.385 199	2115.657 916	.000 472 6662	.006 477	13.703 761	.072 972 6662	14.60	4.254 032	11.82	72
37	177.582 540	2435.621 241	.000 410 5729	.005 631	13.715 432	.072 910 5729	14.59	4.395 382	11.88	74
38	204.265 426	2803.661 055	.000 356 6765	.004 896	13.725 578	.072 856 6765	14.58	4.537 107	11.94	76
39	234.957 583	3227.001 151	.000 309 8852	.004 256	13.734 399	.072 809 8852	14.57	4.679 171	12.00	78
40	270.261 429	3713.950 743	.000 269 2551	.003 700	13.742 067	.072 769 2551	14.56	4.821 540	12.05	80
41	310.869 898	4274.067 554	.000 233 9692	.003 217	13.748 734	.072 733 9692	14.55	4.964 185	12.11	82
42	357.580 043	4918.345 417	.000 203 3204	.002 797	13.754 530	.072 703 3204	14.55	5.107 079	12.16	84
43	411.308 679	5659.430 056	.000 176 6962	.002 431	13.759 569	.072 676 6962	14.54	5.250 196	12.21	86
44	473.110 379	6511.867 293	.000 153 5658	.002 114	13.763 949	.072 653 5658	14.54	5.393 514	12.26	88
45	544.198 170	7492.388 553	.000 133 4688	.001 838	13.767 758	.072 633 4688	14.53	5.537 012	12.30	90
46	625.967 346	8620.239 261	.000 116 0061	.001 598	13.771 069	.072 616 0061	14.53	5.680 673	12.35	92
47	720.022 852	9917.556 586	.000 100 8313	.001 389	13.773 947	.072 600 8313	14.53	5.824 478	12.39	94
48	828.210 786	11409.803 948	.000 087 6439	.001 207	13.776 449	.072 587 6439	14.52	5.968 414	12.43	96
49	952.654 633	13126.270 802	.000 076 1831	.001 050	13.778 625	.072 576 1831	14.52	6.112 466	12.47	98
50	1095.796 946	15100.647 530	.000 066 2223	.000 913	13.780 516	.072 566 2223	14.52	6.256 622	12.51	100

Effective Rate is 15.03 %

Annual Percentage Rate is 14.50 %

SEMIANNUAL COMPOUND INTEREST AND ANNUITY

Amount Of 1	Amount Of 1 Per Period	Sinking Fund Payment	Present Worth Of 1	Present Worth of 1 Per Period	Periodic Payment To Amortize 1	Constant Annual Percent	Total Interest	Annual Add On Rate	
What a single $1 deposit grows to in the future. The deposit is made at the beginning of the first period.	What a series of $1 deposits grow to in the future. A deposit is made at the end of each period.	The amount to be deposited at the end of each period that grows to $1 in the future.	What $1 to be paid in the future is worth today. Value today of a single $1 payment tomorrow.	What $1 to be paid at the end of each period is worth today. Value today of a series of $1 payments tomorrow.	The mortgage payment to amortize a loan of $1. An annuity certain, payable at the end of each period, worth $1 today.	The annual payment, including interest and principal, to amortize completely a loan of $100.	The total interest paid over the term on a loan of $1. The loan is amortized by regular periodic payments.	The average annual interest rate on a loan that is completely amortized by regular periodic payments.	
$S = (1+i)^n$	$S\overline{n} = \dfrac{(1+i)^n - 1}{i}$	$\dfrac{1}{S\overline{n}} = \dfrac{i}{(1+i)^n - 1}$	$V^n = \dfrac{1}{(1+i)^n}$	$A\overline{n} = \dfrac{1-V^n}{i}$	$\dfrac{1}{A\overline{n}} = \dfrac{i}{1-V^n}$				

YEAR / **PERIODS**

	Amount Of 1	Amount Of 1 Per Period	Sinking Fund Payment	Present Worth Of 1	Present Worth of 1 Per Period	Periodic Payment To Amortize 1	Constant Annual Percent	Total Interest	Annual Add On Rate	PERIODS
	1.073 750	1.000 000	1.000 000 0000	.931 315	.931 315	1.073 750 0000	214.75	.073 750	14.75	1
	1.152 939	2.073 750	.482 218 2037	.867 349	1.798 664	.555 968 2037	111.20	.111 936	11.19	2
1	1.152 939	2.073 750	.482 218 2037	.867 349	1.798 664	.555 968 2037	111.20	.111 936	11.19	2
2	1.329 268	4.464 657	.223 981 3528	.752 293	3.358 733	.297 731 3528	59.55	.190 925	9.55	4
3	1.532 566	7.221 228	.138 480 6039	.652 501	4.711 856	.212 230 6039	42.45	.273 384	9.11	6
4	1.766 955	10.399 386	.096 159 5259	.565 945	5.885 485	.169 909 5259	33.99	.359 276	8.98	8
5	2.037 191	14.063 608	.071 105 5085	.490 872	6.903 431	.144 855 5085	28.98	.448 555	8.97	10
6	2.348 757	18.288 233	.054 679 9681	.425 757	7.786 345	.128 429 9681	25.69	.541 160	9.02	12
7	2.707 974	23.158 968	.043 179 8165	.369 280	8.552 139	.116 929 8165	23.39	.637 017	9.10	14
8	3.122 129	28.774 629	.034 752 8371	.320 294	9.216 349	.108 502 8371	21.71	.736 045	9.20	16
9	3.599 624	35.249 144	.028 369 4833	.277 807	9.792 451	.102 119 4833	20.43	.838 151	9.31	18
10	4.150 148	42.713 865	.023 411 6018	.240 955	10.292 132	.097 161 6018	19.44	.943 232	9.43	20
11	4.784 867	51.320 233	.019 485 4920	.208 992	10.725 529	.093 235 4920	18.65	1.051 181	9.56	22
12	5.516 660	61.242 852	.016 328 4362	.181 269	11.101 436	.090 078 4362	18.02	1.161 882	9.68	24
13	6.360 373	72.683 026	.013 758 3704	.157 223	11.427 478	.087 508 3704	17.51	1.275 218	9.81	26
14	7.333 123	85.872 850	.011 645 1241	.136 368	11.710 270	.085 395 1241	17.08	1.391 063	9.94	28
15	8.454 644	101.079 913	.009 893 1624	.118 278	11.955 550	.083 643 1624	16.73	1.509 295	10.06	30
16	9.747 689	118.612 730	.008 430 7982	.102 588	12.168 293	.082 180 7982	16.44	1.629 786	10.19	32
17	11.238 491	138.827 000	.007 203 2097	.088 980	12.352 815	.080 953 2097	16.20	1.752 409	10.31	34
18	12.957 296	162.132 822	.006 167 7826	.077 177	12.512 860	.079 917 7826	15.99	1.877 040	10.43	36
19	14.938 972	189.003 013	.005 290 9209	.066 939	12.651 674	.079 040 9209	15.81	2.003 555	10.55	38
20	17.223 725	219.982 707	.004 545 8119	.058 059	12.772 075	.078 295 8119	15.66	2.131 832	10.66	40
21	19.857 905	255.700 406	.003 910 8268	.050 358	12.876 505	.077 660 8268	15.54	2.261 755	10.77	42
22	22.894 954	296.880 736	.003 368 3560	.043 678	12.967 081	.077 118 3560	15.43	2.393 208	10.88	44
23	26.396 487	344.359 148	.002 903 9449	.037 884	13.045 643	.076 653 9449	15.34	2.526 081	10.98	46
24	30.433 541	399.098 863	.002 505 6448	.032 858	13.113 783	.076 255 6448	15.26	2.660 271	11.08	48
25	35.088 018	462.210 419	.002 163 5168	.028 500	13.172 885	.075 913 5168	15.19	2.795 676	11.18	50
26	40.454 347	534.974 197	.001 869 2490	.024 719	13.224 146	.075 619 2490	15.13	2.932 201	11.28	52
27	46.641 397	618.866 399	.001 615 8576	.021 440	13.268 608	.075 365 8576	15.08	3.069 756	11.37	54
28	53.774 688	715.588 996	.001 397 4502	.018 596	13.307 171	.075 147 4502	15.03	3.208 257	11.46	56
29	61.998 939	827.104 256	.001 209 0374	.016 129	13.340 620	.074 959 0374	15.00	3.347 624	11.54	58
30	71.480 998	955.674 556	.001 046 3813	.013 990	13.369 631	.074 796 3813	14.96	3.487 783	11.63	60
31	82.413 235	1103.908 276	.000 905 8724	.012 134	13.394 794	.074 655 8724	14.94	3.628 664	11.71	62
32	95.017 438	1274.812 723	.000 784 4289	.010 524	13.416 619	.074 534 4289	14.91	3.770 203	11.78	64
33	109.549 316	1471.855 136	.000 679 4147	.009 128	13.435 548	.074 429 4147	14.89	3.912 341	11.86	66
34	126.303 686	1699.033 031	.000 588 5701	.007 917	13.451 967	.074 338 5701	14.87	4.055 023	11.93	68
35	145.620 453	1960.955 300	.000 509 9555	.006 867	13.466 208	.074 259 9555	14.86	4.198 197	11.99	70
36	167.891 509	2262.935 715	.000 441 9038	.005 956	13.478 560	.074 191 9038	14.84	4.341 817	12.06	72
37	193.568 679	2611.100 731	.000 382 9802	.005 166	13.489 273	.074 132 9802	14.83	4.485 841	12.12	74
38	223.172 891	3012.513 779	.000 331 9487	.004 481	13.498 565	.074 081 9487	14.82	4.630 228	12.18	76
39	257.304 744	3475.318 562	.000 287 7434	.003 886	13.506 625	.074 037 7434	14.81	4.774 944	12.24	78
40	296.656 690	4008.904 275	.000 249 4447	.003 371	13.513 615	.073 999 4447	14.80	4.919 956	12.30	80
41	342.027 086	4624.096 087	.000 216 2585	.002 924	13.519 678	.073 966 2585	14.80	5.065 233	12.35	82
42	394.336 388	5333.374 757	.000 187 4985	.002 536	13.524 937	.073 937 4985	14.79	5.210 750	12.41	84
43	454.645 826	6151.129 843	.000 162 5718	.002 200	13.529 498	.073 912 5718	14.79	5.356 481	12.46	86
44	524.178 932	7093.951 624	.000 140 9652	.001 908	13.533 454	.073 890 9652	14.78	5.502 405	12.51	88
45	604.346 367	8180.967 685	.000 122 2349	.001 655	13.536 886	.073 872 2349	14.78	5.648 501	12.55	90
46	696.774 534	9434.230 963	.000 105 9970	.001 435	13.539 862	.073 855 9970	14.78	5.794 752	12.60	92
47	803.338 577	10879.167 152	.000 091 9188	.001 245	13.542 443	.073 841 9188	14.77	5.941 140	12.64	94
48	926.200 426	12545.090 527	.000 079 7125	.001 080	13.544 682	.073 829 7125	14.77	6.087 652	12.68	96
49	1067.852 651	14465.798 661	.000 069 1286	.000 936	13.546 624	.073 819 1286	14.77	6.234 275	12.72	98
50	1231.169 035	16680.258 096	.000 059 9511	.000 812	13.548 309	.073 809 9511	14.77	6.380 995	12.76	100

Effective Rate is 15.29 %

Annual Percentage Rate is 14.75 %

SEMIANNUAL COMPOUND INTEREST AND ANNUITY

	Amount Of 1	Amount Of 1 Per Period	Sinking Fund Payment	Present Worth Of 1	Present Worth of 1 Per Period	Periodic Payment To Amortize 1	Constant Annual Percent	Total Interest	Annual Add On Rate	
	What a single $ 1 deposit grows to in the future. The deposit is made at the beginning of the first period.	What a series of $ 1 deposits grow to in the future. A deposit is made at the end of each period.	The amount to be deposited at the end of each period that grows to $ 1 in the future.	What $ 1 to be paid in the future is worth today. Value today of a single $ 1 payment tomorrow.	What $ 1 to be paid at the end of each period is worth today. Value today of a series of $ 1 payments tomorrow.	The mortgage payment to amortize a loan of $ 1. An annuity certain, payable at the end of each period, worth $ 1 today.	The annual payment, including interest and principal, to amortize a loan of $ 100.	The total interest paid over the term on a loan of $1. The loan is amortized by regular periodic payments.	The average annual interest rate on a loan that is completely amortized by regular periodic payments.	

| | $S = (1+i)^n$ | $S\overline{n} = \dfrac{(1+i)^n - 1}{i}$ | $\dfrac{1}{S\overline{n}} = \dfrac{i}{(1+i)^n - 1}$ | $V^n = \dfrac{1}{(1+i)^n}$ | $A\overline{n} = \dfrac{1 - V^n}{i}$ | $\dfrac{1}{A\overline{n}} = \dfrac{i}{1 - V^n}$ | | | | |

YEAR										PERIODS
	1.075 000	1.000 000	1.000 000 0000	.930 233	.930 233	1.075 000 0000	215.00	.075 000	15.00	1
	1.155 625	2.075 000	.481 927 7108	.865 333	1.795 565	.556 927 7108	111.39	.113 855	11.39	2
1	1.155 625	2.075 000	.481 927 7108	.865 333	1.795 565	.556 927 7108	111.39	.113 855	11.39	2
2	1.335 469	4.472 922	.223 567 5087	.748 801	3.349 326	.298 567 5087	59.72	.194 270	9.71	4
3	1.543 302	7.244 020	.138 044 8912	.647 962	4.693 846	.213 044 8912	42.61	.278 269	9.28	6
4	1.783 478	10.446 371	.095 727 0232	.560 702	5.857 304	.170 727 0232	34.15	.365 816	9.15	8
5	2.061 032	14.147 087	.070 685 9274	.485 194	6.864 081	.145 685 9274	29.14	.456 859	9.14	10
6	2.381 780	18.423 728	.054 277 8313	.419 854	7.735 278	.129 277 8313	25.86	.551 334	9.19	12
7	2.752 444	23.365 921	.042 797 3721	.363 313	8.489 154	.117 797 3721	23.56	.649 163	9.27	14
8	3.180 793	29.077 242	.034 391 1571	.314 387	9.141 507	.109 391 1571	21.88	.750 259	9.38	16
9	3.675 804	35.677 388	.028 028 9578	.272 049	9.706 009	.103 028 9578	20.61	.854 521	9.49	18
10	4.247 851	43.304 681	.023 092 1916	.235 413	10.194 491	.098 092 1916	19.62	.961 844	9.62	20
11	4.908 923	52.118 972	.019 186 8710	.203 711	10.617 191	.094 186 8710	18.84	1.072 111	9.75	22
12	5.672 874	62.304 987	.016 050 0795	.176 277	10.982 967	.091 050 0795	18.22	1.185 202	9.88	24
13	6.555 715	74.076 201	.013 499 6124	.152 539	11.299 485	.088 499 6124	17.70	1.300 990	10.01	26
14	7.575 948	87.679 310	.011 405 1993	.131 997	11.573 378	.086 405 1993	17.29	1.419 346	10.14	28
15	8.754 955	103.399 403	.009 671 2358	.114 221	11.810 386	.084 671 2358	16.94	1.540 137	10.27	30
16	10.117 445	121.565 935	.008 225 9887	.098 839	12.015 478	.083 225 9887	16.65	1.663 232	10.40	32
17	11.691 972	142.559 633	.007 014 6084	.085 529	12.192 950	.082 014 6084	16.41	1.788 497	10.52	34
18	13.511 536	166.820 476	.005 994 4680	.074 011	12.346 522	.080 994 4680	16.20	1.915 801	10.64	36
19	15.614 268	194.856 913	.005 131 9709	.064 044	12.479 414	.080 131 9709	16.03	2.045 015	10.76	38
20	18.044 239	227.256 520	.004 400 3138	.055 419	12.594 409	.079 400 3138	15.89	2.176 013	10.88	40
21	20.852 374	264.698 315	.003 777 8858	.047 956	12.693 918	.078 777 8858	15.76	2.308 671	10.99	42
22	24.097 524	307.966 991	.003 247 1012	.041 498	12.780 026	.078 247 1012	15.65	2.442 872	11.10	44
23	27.847 702	357.969 354	.002 793 5352	.035 910	12.854 539	.077 793 5352	15.56	2.578 503	11.21	46
24	32.181 500	415.753 334	.002 405 2724	.031 074	12.919 017	.077 405 2724	15.49	2.715 453	11.31	48
25	37.189 746	482.529 947	.002 072 4102	.026 889	12.974 812	.077 072 4102	15.42	2.853 621	11.41	50
26	42.977 400	559.698 670	.001 786 6757	.023 268	13.023 093	.076 786 6757	15.36	2.992 907	11.51	52
27	49.665 758	648.876 776	.001 541 1247	.020 135	13.064 872	.076 541 1247	15.31	3.133 221	11.60	54
28	57.394 992	751.933 224	.001 329 9053	.017 423	13.101 025	.076 329 9053	15.27	3.274 475	11.69	56
29	66.327 087	871.027 832	.001 148 0689	.015 077	13.132 309	.076 148 0689	15.23	3.416 588	11.78	58
30	76.649 240	1008.656 538	.000 991 4178	.013 046	13.159 381	.075 991 4178	15.20	3.559 485	11.87	60
31	88.577 778	1167.703 712	.000 856 3816	.011 290	13.182 806	.075 856 3816	15.18	3.703 096	11.95	62
32	102.362 695	1351.502 602	.000 739 9172	.009 769	13.203 078	.075 739 9172	15.15	3.847 355	12.02	64
33	118.292 890	1563.905 195	.000 639 4249	.008 454	13.220 619	.075 639 4249	15.13	3.992 202	12.10	66
34	136.702 221	1809.362 940	.000 552 6807	.007 315	13.235 798	.075 552 6807	15.12	4.137 582	12.17	68
35	157.976 504	2093.020 048	.000 477 7785	.006 330	13.248 933	.075 477 7785	15.10	4.283 445	12.24	70
36	182.561 597	2420.821 293	.000 413 0829	.005 478	13.260 299	.075 413 0829	15.09	4.429 742	12.30	72
37	210.972 746	2799.636 607	.000 357 1892	.004 740	13.270 134	.075 357 1892	15.08	4.576 432	12.37	74
38	243.805 379	3237.405 054	.000 308 8894	.004 102	13.278 645	.075 308 8894	15.07	4.723 476	12.43	76
39	281.747 591	3743.301 215	.000 267 1439	.003 549	13.286 010	.075 267 1439	15.06	4.870 837	12.49	78
40	325.594 560	4327.927 467	.000 231 0575	.003 071	13.292 383	.075 231 0575	15.05	5.018 485	12.55	80
41	376.265 213	5003.536 179	.000 199 8587	.002 658	13.297 897	.075 199 8587	15.04	5.166 388	12.60	82
42	434.821 487	5784.286 496	.000 172 8822	.002 300	13.302 669	.075 172 8822	15.04	5.314 522	12.65	84
43	502.490 581	6686.541 082	.000 149 5542	.001 990	13.306 799	.075 149 5542	15.03	5.462 862	12.70	86
44	580.690 678	7729.209 038	.000 129 3793	.001 722	13.310 372	.075 129 3793	15.03	5.611 385	12.75	88
45	671.060 665	8934.142 195	.000 111 9302	.001 490	13.313 464	.075 111 9302	15.03	5.760 074	12.80	90
46	775.494 481	10326.593 074	.000 096 8374	.001 289	13.316 140	.075 096 8374	15.02	5.908 909	12.85	92
47	896.180 809	11935.744 121	.000 083 7820	.001 116	13.318 455	.075 083 7820	15.02	6.057 876	12.89	94
48	1035.648 948	13795.319 300	.000 072 4884	.000 966	13.320 459	.075 072 4884	15.02	6.206 959	12.93	96
49	1196.821 815	15944.290 866	.000 062 7184	.000 836	13.322 193	.075 062 7184	15.02	6.356 146	12.97	98
50	1383.077 210	18427.696 132	.000 054 2661	.000 723	13.323 693	.075 054 2661	15.02	6.505 427	13.01	100

Effective Rate is 15.56 %

Annual Percentage Rate is 15.00 %

Amount Of 1	Amount Of 1 Per Period	Sinking Fund Payment	Present Worth Of 1	Present Worth of 1 Per Period	Periodic Payment To Amortize 1	Constant Annual Percent	Total Interest	Annual Add On Rate
What a single $ 1 deposit grows to in the future. The deposit is made at the beginning of the first period.	What a series of $ 1 deposits grow to in the future. A deposit is made at the end of each period.	The amount to be deposited at the end of each period that grows to $ 1 in the future.	What $ 1 to be paid in the future is worth today. Value today of a single $ 1 payment tomorrow.	What $ 1 to be paid at the end of each period is worth today. Value today of a series of $ 1 payments tomorrow.	The mortgage payment to amortize a loan of $ 1. An annuity certain, payable at the end of each period, worth $ 1 today.	The annual payment, including interest and principal, to amortize completely a loan of $ 100.	The total interest paid over the term on a loan of $1. The loan is amortized by regular periodic payments.	The average annual interest rate on a loan that is completely amortized by regular periodic payments.

$$S = (1+i)^n \qquad S\overline{n}| = \frac{(1+i)^n - 1}{i} \qquad \frac{1}{S\overline{n}|} = \frac{i}{(1+i)^n - 1} \qquad V^n = \frac{1}{(1+i)^n} \qquad A\overline{n}| = \frac{1-V^n}{i} \qquad \frac{1}{A\overline{n}|} = \frac{i}{1-V^n}$$

YEAR									PERIODS
	1.080 000	1.000 000	1.000 000 0000	.925 926	.925 926	1.080 000 0000	216.00	.080 000	16.00	1
	1.166 400	2.080 000	.480 769 2308	.857 339	1.783 265	.560 769 2308	112.16	.121 538	12.15	2

YEAR	Amount Of 1	Amount Of 1 Per Period	Sinking Fund Payment	Present Worth Of 1	Present Worth of 1 Per Period	Periodic Payment To Amortize 1	Constant Annual Percent	Total Interest	Annual Add On Rate	PERIODS
1	1.166 400	2.080 000	.480 769 2308	.857 339	1.783 265	.560 769 2308	112.16	.121 538	12.15	2
2	1.360 489	4.506 112	.221 920 8045	.735 030	3.312 127	.301 920 8045	60.39	.207 683	10.38	4
3	1.586 874	7.335 929	.136 315 3862	.630 170	4.622 880	.216 315 3862	43.27	.297 892	9.93	6
4	1.850 930	10.636 628	.094 014 7606	.540 269	5.746 639	.174 014 7606	34.81	.392 118	9.80	8
5	2.158 925	14.486 562	.069 029 4887	.463 193	6.710 081	.149 029 4887	29.81	.490 295	9.81	10
6	2.518 170	18.977 126	.052 695 0169	.397 114	7.536 078	.132 695 0169	26.54	.592 340	9.87	12
7	2.937 194	24.214 920	.041 296 8528	.340 461	8.244 237	.121 296 8528	24.26	.698 156	9.97	14
8	3.425 943	30.324 283	.032 976 8720	.291 890	8.851 369	.112 976 8720	22.60	.807 630	10.10	16
9	3.996 019	37.450 244	.026 702 0959	.250 249	9.371 887	.106 702 0959	21.35	.920 638	10.23	18
10	4.660 957	45.761 964	.021 852 2088	.214 548	9.818 147	.101 852 2088	20.38	1.037 044	10.37	20
11	5.436 540	55.456 755	.018 032 0684	.183 941	10.200 744	.098 032 0684	19.61	1.156 706	10.52	22
12	6.341 181	66.764 759	.014 977 9616	.157 699	10.528 758	.094 977 9616	19.00	1.279 471	10.66	24
13	7.396 353	79.954 415	.012 507 1267	.135 202	10.809 978	.092 507 1267	18.51	1.405 185	10.81	26
14	8.627 106	95.338 830	.010 488 9057	.115 914	11.051 078	.090 488 9057	18.10	1.533 689	10.96	28
15	10.062 657	113.283 211	.008 827 4334	.099 377	11.257 783	.088 827 4334	17.77	1.664 823	11.10	30
16	11.737 083	134.213 537	.007 450 8132	.085 200	11.434 999	.087 450 8132	17.50	1.798 426	11.24	32
17	13.690 134	158.626 670	.006 304 1101	.073 045	11.586 934	.086 304 1101	17.27	1.934 340	11.38	34
18	15.968 172	187.102 148	.005 344 6741	.062 625	11.717 193	.085 344 6741	17.07	2.072 408	11.51	36
19	18.625 276	220.315 945	.004 538 9361	.053 690	11.828 869	.084 538 9361	16.91	2.212 480	11.64	38
20	21.724 521	259.056 519	.003 860 1615	.046 031	11.924 613	.083 860 1615	16.78	2.354 406	11.77	40
21	25.339 482	304.243 523	.003 286 8407	.039 464	12.006 699	.083 286 8407	16.66	2.498 047	11.90	42
22	29.555 972	356.949 646	.002 801 5156	.033 834	12.077 074	.082 801 5156	16.57	2.643 267	12.01	44
23	34.474 085	418.426 067	.002 389 9085	.029 007	12.137 409	.082 389 9085	16.48	2.789 936	12.13	46
24	40.210 573	490.132 164	.002 040 2660	.024 869	12.189 136	.082 040 2660	16.41	2.937 933	12.24	48
25	46.901 613	573.770 156	.001 742 8582	.021 321	12.233 485	.081 742 8582	16.35	3.087 143	12.35	50
26	54.706 041	671.325 510	.001 489 5903	.018 280	12.271 506	.081 489 5903	16.30	3.237 459	12.45	52
27	63.809 126	785.114 075	.001 273 7003	.015 672	12.304 103	.081 273 7003	16.26	3.388 780	12.55	54
28	74.426 965	917.837 058	.001 089 5180	.013 436	12.332 050	.081 089 5180	16.22	3.541 013	12.65	56
29	86.811 612	1072.645 144	.000 932 2748	.011 519	12.356 010	.080 932 2748	16.19	3.694 072	12.74	58
30	101.257 064	1253.213 296	.000 797 9488	.009 876	12.376 552	.080 797 9488	16.16	3.847 877	12.83	60
31	118.106 239	1463.827 988	.000 683 1404	.008 467	12.394 163	.080 683 1404	16.14	4.002 355	12.91	62
32	137.759 117	1709.488 966	.000 584 9701	.007 259	12.409 262	.080 584 9701	16.12	4.157 438	12.99	64
33	160.682 234	1996.027 929	.000 500 9950	.006 223	12.422 207	.080 500 9950	16.11	4.313 066	13.07	66
34	187.419 758	2330.246 977	.000 429 1391	.005 336	12.433 305	.080 429 1391	16.09	4.469 181	13.14	68
35	218.606 406	2720.080 074	.000 367 6362	.004 574	12.442 820	.080 367 6362	16.08	4.625 735	13.22	70
36	254.982 512	3174.781 398	.000 314 9823	.003 922	12.450 977	.080 314 9823	16.07	4.782 679	13.29	72
37	297.411 602	3705.145 023	.000 269 8950	.003 362	12.457 971	.080 269 8950	16.06	4.939 972	13.35	74
38	346.900 892	4323.761 154	.000 231 2801	.002 883	12.463 967	.080 231 2801	16.05	5.097 577	13.41	76
39	404.625 201	5045.315 011	.000 198 2037	.002 471	12.469 107	.080 198 2037	16.04	5.255 460	13.48	78
40	471.954 834	5886.935 428	.000 169 8677	.002 119	12.473 514	.080 169 8677	16.04	5.413 589	13.53	80
41	550.488 119	6868.601 484	.000 145 5900	.001 817	12.477 293	.080 145 5900	16.03	5.571 938	13.59	82
42	642.089 342	8013.616 770	.000 124 7876	.001 557	12.480 532	.080 124 7876	16.03	5.730 482	13.64	84
43	748.933 008	9349.162 601	.000 106 9615	.001 335	12.483 310	.080 106 9615	16.03	5.889 199	13.70	86
44	873.555 461	10906.943 258	.000 091 6847	.001 145	12.485 691	.080 091 6847	16.02	6.048 068	13.75	88
45	1018.915 089	12723.938 616	.000 078 5920	.000 981	12.487 732	.080 078 5920	16.02	6.207 073	13.79	90
46	1188.462 560	14843.282 002	.000 067 3705	.000 841	12.489 482	.080 067 3705	16.02	6.366 198	13.84	92
47	1386.222 730	17315.284 127	.000 057 7524	.000 721	12.490 983	.080 057 7524	16.02	6.525 429	13.88	94
48	1616.890 192	20198.627 405	.000 049 5083	.000 618	12.492 269	.080 049 5083	16.01	6.684 753	13.93	96
49	1885.940 720	23561.759 006	.000 042 4417	.000 530	12.493 372	.080 042 4417	16.01	6.844 159	13.97	98
50	2199.761 256	27484.515 704	.000 036 3841	.000 455	12.494 318	.080 036 3841	16.01	7.003 638	14.01	100

SEMIANNUAL COMPOUND INTEREST AND ANNUITY

17.00 % S

	Amount Of 1	Amount Of 1 Per Period	Sinking Fund Payment	Present Worth Of 1	Present Worth of 1 Per Period	Periodic Payment To Amortize 1	Constant Annual Percent	Total Interest	Annual Add On Rate	
	What a single $ 1 deposit grows to in the future. The deposit is made at the beginning of the first period.	What a series of $ 1 deposits grow to in the future. A deposit is made at the end of each period.	The amount to be deposited at the end of each period that grows to $ 1 in the future.	What $ 1 to be paid in the future is worth today. Value today of a single $ 1 payment tomorrow.	What $ 1 to be paid at the end of each period is worth today. Value today of a series of $ 1 payments tomorrow.	The mortgage payment to amortize a loan of $ 1. An annuity certain, payable at the end of each period, worth $ 1 today.	The annual payment, including interest and principal, to amortize completely a loan of $ 100.	The total interest paid over the term on a loan of $1. The loan is amortized by regular periodic payments.	The average annual interest rate on a loan that is completely amortized by regular periodic payments.	

$$S = (1+i)^n \qquad S\overline{n}| = \frac{(1+i)^n - 1}{i} \qquad \frac{1}{S\overline{n}|} = \frac{i}{(1+i)^n - 1} \qquad V^n = \frac{1}{(1+i)^n} \qquad A\overline{n}| = \frac{1-V^n}{i} \qquad \frac{1}{A\overline{n}|} = \frac{i}{1-V^n}$$

YEAR										PERIODS
	1.085 000	1.000 000	1.000 000 0000	.921 659	.921 659	1.085 000 0000	217.00	.085 000	17.00	1
	1.177 225	2.085 000	.479 616 3070	.849 455	1.771 114	.564 616 3070	112.93	.129 233	12.92	2
1	1.177 225	2.085 000	.479 616 3070	.849 455	1.771 114	.564 616 3070	112.93	.129 233	12.92	2
2	1.385 859	4.539 514	.220 287 8926	.721 574	3.275 597	.305 287 8926	61.06	.221 152	11.06	4
3	1.631 468	7.429 030	.134 607 0840	.612 945	4.553 587	.219 607 0840	43.93	.317 643	10.59	6
4	1.920 604	10.830 639	.092 330 6533	.520 669	5.639 183	.177 330 6533	35.47	.418 645	10.47	8
5	2.260 983	14.835 099	.067 407 7051	.442 285	6.561 348	.152 407 7051	30.49	.524 077	10.48	10
6	2.661 686	19.549 250	.051 152 8581	.375 702	7.344 686	.136 152 8581	27.24	.633 834	10.56	12
7	3.133 404	25.098 866	.039 842 4382	.319 142	8.010 097	.124 842 4382	24.97	.747 794	10.68	14
8	3.688 721	31.632 012	.031 613 5439	.271 097	8.575 333	.116 613 5439	23.33	.865 817	10.82	16
9	4.342 455	39.322 995	.025 430 4127	.230 285	9.055 476	.110 430 4127	22.09	.987 747	10.98	18
10	5.112 046	48.377 013	.020 670 9744	.195 616	9.463 337	.105 670 9744	21.14	1.113 419	11.13	20
11	6.018 028	59.035 629	.016 938 9233	.166 167	9.809 796	.101 938 9233	20.39	1.242 656	11.30	22
12	7.084 574	71.583 219	.013 969 7546	.141 152	10.104 097	.098 969 7546	19.80	1.375 274	11.46	24
13	8.340 137	86.354 555	.011 580 1651	.119 902	10.354 093	.096 580 1651	19.32	1.511 084	11.62	26
14	9.818 218	103.743 741	.009 639 1357	.101 851	10.566 453	.094 639 1357	18.93	1.649 896	11.79	28
15	11.558 252	124.214 725	.008 050 5753	.086 518	10.746 844	.093 050 5753	18.62	1.791 517	11.94	30
16	13.606 663	148.313 680	.006 742 4664	.073 493	10.900 078	.091 742 4664	18.35	1.935 759	12.10	32
17	16.018 104	176.683 572	.005 659 8358	.062 429	11.030 243	.090 659 8358	18.14	2.082 434	12.25	34
18	18.856 912	210.081 318	.004 760 0615	.053 031	11.140 812	.089 760 0615	17.96	2.231 362	12.40	36
19	22.198 828	249.397 979	.004 009 6556	.045 047	11.234 736	.089 009 6556	17.81	2.382 367	12.54	38
20	26.133 016	295.682 536	.003 382 0056	.038 266	11.314 520	.088 382 0056	17.68	2.535 280	12.68	40
21	30.764 439	350.169 874	.002 855 7568	.032 505	11.382 293	.087 855 7568	17.58	2.689 942	12.81	42
22	36.216 667	414.313 730	.002 413 6299	.027 612	11.439 864	.087 413 6299	17.49	2.846 200	12.94	44
23	42.635 166	489.825 480	.002 041 5434	.023 455	11.488 767	.087 041 5434	17.41	3.003 911	13.06	46
24	50.191 183	578.719 801	.001 727 9519	.019 924	11.530 308	.086 727 9519	17.35	3.162 942	13.18	48
25	59.086 316	683.368 418	.001 463 3395	.016 924	11.565 595	.086 463 3395	17.30	3.323 167	13.29	50
26	69.557 888	806.563 386	.001 239 8282	.014 377	11.595 570	.086 239 8282	17.25	3.484 471	13.40	52
27	81.885 284	951.591 582	.001 050 8710	.012 212	11.621 033	.086 050 8710	17.22	3.646 747	13.51	54
28	96.397 404	1122.322 400	.000 891 0096	.010 374	11.642 662	.085 891 0096	17.18	3.809 897	13.61	56
29	113.481 434	1323.310 987	.000 755 6803	.008 812	11.661 035	.085 755 6803	17.16	3.973 829	13.70	58
30	133.593 181	1559.919 777	.000 641 0586	.007 485	11.676 642	.085 641 0586	17.13	4.138 464	13.79	60
31	157.269 233	1838.461 559	.000 543 9330	.006 359	11.689 900	.085 543 9330	17.11	4.303 724	13.88	62
32	185.141 272	2166.367 909	.000 461 6021	.005 401	11.701 161	.085 461 6021	17.10	4.469 543	13.97	64
33	217.952 934	2552.387 462	.000 391 7900	.004 588	11.710 728	.085 391 7900	17.08	4.635 858	14.05	66
34	256.579 643	3006.819 330	.000 332 5773	.003 897	11.718 854	.085 332 5773	17.07	4.802 615	14.13	68
35	302.051 970	3541.787 885	.000 282 3433	.003 311	11.725 757	.085 282 3433	17.06	4.969 764	14.20	70
36	355.583 131	4171.566 243	.000 239 7181	.002 812	11.731 620	.085 239 7181	17.05	5.137 260	14.27	72
37	418.601 351	4912.957 071	.000 203 5434	.002 389	11.736 601	.085 203 5434	17.05	5.305 062	14.34	74
38	492.787 975	5785.740 887	.000 172 8387	.002 029	11.740 832	.085 172 8387	17.04	5.473 136	14.40	76
39	580.122 324	6813.203 816	.000 146 7738	.001 724	11.744 426	.085 146 7738	17.03	5.641 448	14.47	78
40	682.934 503	8022.758 863	.000 124 6454	.001 464	11.747 479	.085 124 6454	17.03	5.809 972	14.53	80
41	803.967 571	9446.677 302	.000 105 8573	.001 244	11.750 073	.085 105 8573	17.03	5.978 680	14.58	82
42	946.450 723	11122.949 687	.000 089 9042	.001 057	11.752 276	.085 089 9042	17.02	6.147 552	14.64	84
43	1114.185 453	13096.299 445	.000 076 3574	.000 898	11.754 147	.085 076 3574	17.02	6.316 567	14.69	86
44	1311.646 970	15419.376 114	.000 064 8535	.000 762	11.755 736	.085 064 8535	17.02	6.485 707	14.74	88
45	1544.163 604	18154.160 046	.000 055 0838	.000 648	11.757 087	.085 055 0838	17.02	6.654 958	14.79	90
46	1817.757 365	21373.616 060	.000 046 7867	.000 550	11.758 234	.085 046 7867	17.01	6.824 304	14.84	92
47	2139.909 414	25163.640 167	.000 039 7399	.000 467	11.759 208	.085 039 7399	17.01	6.993 736	14.88	94
48	2519.154 860	29625.351 295	.000 033 7549	.000 397	11.760 036	.085 033 7549	17.01	7.163 240	14.92	96
49	2965.612 080	34877.789 178	.000 028 6715	.000 337	11.760 739	.085 028 6715	17.01	7.332 810	14.97	98
50	3491.192 681	41061.090 366	.000 024 3540	.000 286	11.761 336	.085 024 3540	17.01	7.502 435	15.00	100

Effective Rate is 17.72 %

Annual Percentage Rate is 17.00 %

SEMIANNUAL COMPOUND INTEREST AND ANNUITY

Amount Of 1	Amount Of 1 Per Period	Sinking Fund Payment	Present Worth Of 1	Present Worth of 1 Per Period	Periodic Payment To Amortize 1	Constant Annual Percent	Total Interest	Annual Add On Rate
What a single $ 1 deposit grows to in the future. The deposit is made at the beginning of the first period.	What a series of $ 1 deposits grow to in the future. A deposit is made at the end of each period.	The amount to be deposited at the end of each period that grows to $ 1 in the future.	What $ 1 to be paid in the future is worth today. Value today of a single $ 1 payment tomorrow.	What $ 1 to be paid at the end of each period is worth today. Value today of a series of $ 1 payments tomorrow.	The mortgage payment to amortize a loan of $ 1. An annuity certain, payable at the end of each period, worth $ 1 today.	The annual payment, including interest and principal, to amortize completely a loan of $ 100.	The total interest paid over the term on a loan of $1. The loan is amortized by regular periodic payments.	The average annual interest rate on a loan that is completely amortized by regular periodic payments.
$S = (1+i)^n$	$S\overline{n} = \dfrac{(1+i)^n - 1}{i}$	$\dfrac{1}{S\overline{n}} = \dfrac{i}{(1+i)^n - 1}$	$V^n = \dfrac{1}{(1+i)^n}$	$A\overline{n} = \dfrac{1-V^n}{i}$	$\dfrac{1}{A\overline{n}} = \dfrac{i}{1-V^n}$			

YEAR									PERIODS
	1.090 000	1.000 000	1.000 000 0000	.917 431	.917 431	1.090 000 0000	218.00	.090 000	18.00	1
	1.188 100	2.090 000	.478 468 8995	.841 680	1.759 111	.568 468 8995	113.70	.136 938	13.69	2

YEAR	Amount Of 1	Amount Of 1 Per Period	Sinking Fund Payment	Present Worth Of 1	Present Worth of 1 Per Period	Periodic Payment To Amortize 1	Constant Annual Percent	Total Interest	Annual Add On Rate	PERIODS
1	1.188 100	2.090 000	.478 468 8995	.841 680	1.759 111	.568 468 8995	113.70	.136 938	13.69	2
2	1.411 582	4.573 129	.218 668 6621	.708 425	3.239 720	.308 668 6621	61.74	.234 675	11.73	4
3	1.677 100	7.523 335	.132 919 7833	.596 267	4.485 919	.222 919 7833	44.59	.337 519	11.25	6
4	1.992 563	11.028 474	.090 674 3778	.501 866	5.534 819	.180 674 3778	36.14	.445 395	11.13	8
5	2.367 364	15.192 930	.065 820 0899	.422 411	6.417 658	.155 820 0899	31.17	.558 201	11.16	10
6	2.812 665	20.140 720	.049 650 6585	.355 535	7.160 725	.139 650 6585	27.94	.675 808	11.26	12
7	3.341 727	26.019 189	.038 433 1730	.299 246	7.786 150	.128 433 1730	25.69	.798 064	11.40	14
8	3.970 306	33.003 399	.030 299 9097	.251 870	8.312 558	.120 299 9097	24.06	.924 799	11.56	16
9	4.717 120	41.301 338	.024 212 2907	.211 994	8.755 625	.114 212 2907	22.85	1.055 821	11.73	18
10	5.604 411	51.160 120	.019 546 4750	.178 431	9.128 546	.109 546 4750	21.91	1.190 930	11.91	20
11	6.658 600	62.873 338	.015 904 9930	.150 182	9.442 425	.105 904 9930	21.19	1.329 910	12.09	22
12	7.911 083	76.789 813	.013 022 5607	.126 405	9.706 612	.103 022 5607	20.61	1.472 541	12.27	24
13	9.399 158	93.323 977	.010 715 3599	.106 393	9.928 972	.100 715 3599	20.15	1.618 599	12.45	26
14	11.167 140	112.968 217	.008 852 0473	.089 548	10.116 128	.098 852 0473	19.78	1.767 857	12.63	28
15	13.267 678	136.307 539	.007 336 3514	.075 371	10.273 654	.097 336 3514	19.47	1.920 091	12.80	30
16	15.763 329	164.036 987	.006 096 1861	.063 438	10.406 240	.096 096 1861	19.22	2.075 078	12.97	32
17	18.728 411	196.982 344	.005 076 5971	.053 395	10.517 835	.095 076 5971	19.02	2.232 604	13.13	34
18	22.251 225	236.124 723	.004 235 0500	.044 941	10.611 763	.094 235 0500	18.85	2.392 462	13.29	36
19	26.436 680	282.629 783	.003 538 1975	.037 826	10.690 820	.093 538 1975	18.71	2.554 452	13.44	38
20	31.409 420	337.882 445	.002 959 6092	.031 838	10.757 360	.092 959 6092	18.60	2.718 384	13.59	40
21	37.317 532	403.528 133	.002 478 1420	.026 797	10.813 366	.092 478 1420	18.50	2.884 082	13.73	42
22	44.336 960	481.521 775	.002 076 7493	.022 555	10.860 505	.092 076 7493	18.42	3.051 377	13.87	44
23	52.676 742	574.186 021	.001 741 5959	.018 984	10.900 181	.091 741 5959	18.35	3.220 113	14.00	46
24	62.585 237	684.280 411	.001 461 3892	.015 978	10.933 575	.091 461 3892	18.30	3.390 147	14.13	48
25	74.357 520	815.083 556	.001 226 8681	.013 449	10.961 683	.091 226 8681	18.25	3.561 343	14.25	50
26	88.344 170	970.490 773	.001 030 4065	.011 319	10.985 340	.091 030 4065	18.21	3.733 581	14.36	52
27	104.961 708	1155.130 088	.000 865 7034	.009 527	11.005 252	.090 865 7034	18.18	3.906 748	14.47	54
28	124.705 005	1374.500 057	.000 727 5373	.008 019	11.022 012	.090 727 5373	18.15	4.080 742	14.57	56
29	148.162 017	1635.133 518	.000 611 5709	.006 749	11.036 118	.090 611 5709	18.13	4.255 471	14.67	58
30	176.031 292	1944.792 133	.000 514 1938	.005 681	11.047 991	.090 514 1938	18.11	4.430 852	14.77	60
31	209.142 778	2312.697 533	.000 432 3955	.004 781	11.057 984	.090 432 3955	18.09	4.606 809	14.86	62
32	248.482 535	2749.805 939	.000 363 6620	.004 024	11.066 395	.090 363 6620	18.08	4.783 274	14.95	64
33	295.222 099	3269.134 436	.000 305 8914	.003 387	11.073 475	.090 305 8914	18.07	4.960 189	15.03	66
34	350.753 376	3886.148 624	.000 257 3242	.002 851	11.079 433	.090 257 3242	18.06	5.137 498	15.11	68
35	416.730 086	4619.223 180	.000 216 4866	.002 400	11.084 449	.090 216 4866	18.05	5.315 154	15.19	70
36	495.117 015	5490.189 060	.000 182 1431	.002 020	11.088 670	.090 182 1431	18.04	5.493 114	15.26	72
37	588.248 526	6524.983 622	.000 153 2571	.001 700	11.092 223	.090 153 2571	18.04	5.671 341	15.33	74
38	698.898 074	7754.423 041	.000 128 9587	.001 431	11.095 213	.090 128 9587	18.03	5.849 801	15.39	76
39	830.360 801	9215.120 015	.000 108 5173	.001 204	11.097 730	.090 108 5173	18.03	6.028 464	15.46	78
40	986.551 668	10950.574 090	.000 091 3194	.001 014	11.099 849	.090 091 3194	18.02	6.207 306	15.52	80
41	1172.122 037	13012.467 077	.000 076 8494	.000 853	11.101 632	.090 076 8494	18.02	6.386 302	15.58	82
42	1392.598 192	15462.202 134	.000 064 6738	.000 718	11.103 132	.090 064 6738	18.02	6.565 433	15.63	84
43	1654.545 912	18372.732 355	.000 054 4285	.000 604	11.104 396	.090 054 4285	18.02	6.744 681	15.69	86
44	1965.765 998	21830.733 311	.000 045 8070	.000 509	11.105 459	.090 045 8070	18.01	6.924 031	15.74	88
45	2335.526 582	25939.184 247	.000 038 5517	.000 428	11.106 354	.090 038 5517	18.01	7.103 470	15.79	90
46	2774.839 132	30820.434 804	.000 032 4460	.000 360	11.107 107	.090 032 4460	18.01	7.282 985	15.83	92
47	3296.786 373	36619.848 591	.000 027 3076	.000 303	11.107 741	.090 027 3076	18.01	7.462 567	15.88	94
48	3916.911 890	43510.132 110	.000 022 9832	.000 255	11.108 274	.090 022 9832	18.01	7.642 206	15.92	96
49	4653.683 016	51696.477 960	.000 019 3437	.000 215	11.108 724	.090 019 3437	18.01	7.821 896	15.96	98
50	5529.040 792	61422.675 465	.000 016 2806	.000 181	11.109 102	.090 016 2806	18.01	8.001 628	16.00	100

Amount Of 1	Amount Of 1 Per Period	Sinking Fund Payment	Present Worth Of 1	Present Worth of 1 Per Period	Periodic Payment To Amortize 1	Constant Annual Percent	Total Interest	Annual Add On Rate
What a single $ 1 deposit grows to in the future. The deposit is made at the beginning of the first period.	What a series of $ 1 deposits grow to in the future. A deposit is made at the end of each period.	The amount to be deposited at the end of each period that grows to $ 1 in the future.	What $ 1 to be paid in the future is worth today. Value today of a single $ 1 payment tomorrow.	What $ 1 to be paid at the end of each period is worth today. Value today of a series of $ 1 payments tomorrow.	The mortgage payment to amortize a loan of $ 1. An annuity certain, payable at the end of each period, worth $ 1 today.	The annual payment, including interest and principal, to amortize completely a loan of $ 100.	The total interest paid over the term on a loan of $1. The loan is amortized by regular periodic payments.	The average annual interest rate on a loan that is completely amortized by regular periodic payments.

$$S = (1+i)^n \qquad S\overline{n}| = \frac{(1+i)^n - 1}{i} \qquad \frac{1}{S\overline{n}|} = \frac{i}{(1+i)^n - 1} \qquad V^n = \frac{1}{(1+i)^n} \qquad A\overline{n}| = \frac{1 - V^n}{i} \qquad \frac{1}{A\overline{n}|} = \frac{i}{1 - V^n}$$

YEAR									PERIODS
	1.095 000	1.000 000	1.000 000 0000	.913 242	.913 242	1.095 000 0000	219.00	.095 000	19.00	1
	1.199 025	2.095 000	.477 326 9690	.834 011	1.747 253	.572 326 9690	114.47	.144 654	14.47	2

YEAR	Amount Of 1	Amount Of 1 Per Period	Sinking Fund Payment	Present Worth Of 1	Present Worth of 1 Per Period	Periodic Payment To Amortize 1	Constant Annual Percent	Total Interest	Annual Add On Rate	PERIODS
1	1.199 025	2.095 000	.477 326 9690	.834 011	1.747 253	.572 326 9690	114.47	.144 654	14.47	2
2	1.437 661	4.606 957	.217 063 0025	.695 574	3.204 481	.312 063 0025	62.42	.248 252	12.41	4
3	1.723 791	7.618 857	.131 253 2826	.580 117	4.419 825	.226 253 2826	45.26	.357 520	11.92	6
4	2.066 869	11.230 200	.089 045 6084	.483 824	5.433 436	.184 045 6084	36.81	.472 365	11.81	8
5	2.478 228	15.560 291	.064 266 1517	.403 514	6.278 798	.159 266 1517	31.86	.592 662	11.85	10
6	2.971 457	20.752 178	.048 187 7142	.336 535	6.983 839	.143 187 7142	28.64	.718 253	11.97	12
7	3.562 851	26.977 380	.037 068 0923	.280 674	7.571 852	.132 068 0923	26.42	.848 953	12.13	14
8	4.271 948	34.441 553	.029 034 6957	.234 085	8.062 260	.124 034 6957	24.81	.984 555	12.31	16
9	5.122 172	43.391 283	.023 046 1037	.195 230	8.471 266	.118 046 1037	23.61	1.124 830	12.50	18
10	6.141 612	54.122 233	.018 476 6953	.162 824	8.812 382	.113 476 6953	22.70	1.269 534	12.70	20
11	7.363 946	66.988 910	.014 927 8440	.135 797	9.096 876	.109 927 8440	21.99	1.418 413	12.89	22
12	8.829 556	82.416 378	.012 133 5107	.113 256	9.334 148	.107 133 5107	21.43	1.571 204	13.09	24
13	10.586 858	100.914 297	.009 909 3986	.094 457	9.532 034	.104 909 3986	20.99	1.727 644	13.29	26
14	12.693 908	123.093 766	.008 123 8883	.078 778	9.697 074	.103 123 8883	20.63	1.887 469	13.48	28
15	15.220 313	149.687 502	.006 680 5845	.065 702	9.834 719	.101 680 5845	20.34	2.050 418	13.67	30
16	18.249 535	181.574 057	.005 507 3947	.054 796	9.949 517	.100 507 3947	20.11	2.216 237	13.85	32
17	21.881 649	219.806 834	.004 549 4491	.045 700	10.045 259	.099 549 4491	19.91	2.384 681	14.03	34
18	26.236 644	265.648 889	.003 764 3673	.038 115	10.125 109	.098 764 3673	19.76	2.555 517	14.20	36
19	31.458 393	320.614 659	.003 119 0090	.031 788	10.191 705	.098 119 0090	19.63	2.728 522	14.36	38
20	37.719 399	386.519 992	.002 587 1883	.026 512	10.247 247	.097 587 1883	19.52	2.903 488	14.52	40
21	45.226 503	465.542 133	.002 148 0333	.022 111	10.293 569	.097 148 0333	19.43	3.080 217	14.67	42
22	54.227 707	560.291 656	.001 784 7847	.018 441	10.332 203	.096 784 7847	19.36	3.258 531	14.81	44
23	65.020 377	673.898 703	.001 483 9025	.015 380	10.364 423	.096 483 9025	19.30	3.438 260	14.95	46
24	77.961 057	810.116 393	.001 234 3905	.012 827	10.391 296	.096 234 3905	19.25	3.619 251	15.08	48
25	93.477 257	973.444 808	.001 027 2796	.010 698	10.413 707	.096 027 2796	19.21	3.801 364	15.21	50
26	112.081 568	1169.279 661	.000 855 2274	.008 922	10.432 399	.095 855 2274	19.18	3.984 472	15.32	52
27	134.388 602	1404.090 545	.000 712 2048	.007 441	10.447 988	.095 712 2048	19.15	4.168 459	15.44	54
28	161.135 293	1685.634 666	.000 593 2484	.006 206	10.460 990	.095 593 2484	19.12	4.353 222	15.55	56
29	193.205 245	2023.213 106	.000 494 2633	.005 176	10.471 833	.095 494 2633	19.10	4.538 667	15.65	58
30	231.657 919	2427.978 094	.000 411 8653	.004 317	10.480 877	.095 411 8653	19.09	4.724 712	15.75	60
31	277.763 636	2913.301 434	.000 343 2532	.003 600	10.488 419	.095 343 2532	19.07	4.911 282	15.84	62
32	333.045 544	3495.216 252	.000 286 1053	.003 003	10.494 710	.095 286 1053	19.06	5.098 311	15.93	64
33	399.329 933	4192.946 666	.000 238 4958	.002 504	10.499 956	.095 238 4958	19.05	5.285 741	16.02	66
34	478.806 573	5029.542 877	.000 198 8252	.002 089	10.504 331	.095 198 8252	19.04	5.473 520	16.10	68
35	574.101 052	6032.642 648	.000 165 7648	.001 742	10.507 980	.095 165 7648	19.04	5.661 604	16.18	70
36	688.361 513	7235.384 351	.000 138 2097	.001 453	10.511 024	.095 138 2097	19.03	5.849 951	16.25	72
37	825.362 664	8677.501 721	.000 115 2405	.001 212	10.513 562	.095 115 2405	19.03	6.038 528	16.32	74
38	989.630 468	10406.636 501	.000 096 0925	.001 010	10.515 679	.095 096 0925	19.02	6.227 303	16.39	76
39	1186.591 671	12479.912 331	.000 080 1288	.000 843	10.517 445	.095 080 1288	19.02	6.416 250	16.45	78
40	1422.753 079	14965.821 882	.000 066 8189	.000 703	10.518 917	.095 066 8189	19.02	6.605 346	16.51	80
41	1705.916 510	17946.489 583	.000 055 7212	.000 586	10.520 145	.095 055 7212	19.02	6.794 569	16.57	82
42	2045.436 544	21520.384 672	.000 046 4676	.000 489	10.521 170	.095 046 4676	19.01	6.983 903	16.63	84
43	2452.529 552	25805.574 231	.000 038 7513	.000 408	10.522 024	.095 038 7513	19.01	7.173 333	16.68	86
44	2940.644 246	30943.623 642	.000 032 3168	.000 340	10.522 736	.095 032 3168	19.01	7.362 844	16.73	88
45	3525.905 967	37104.273 338	.000 026 9511	.000 284	10.523 330	.095 026 9511	19.01	7.552 426	16.78	90
46	4227.649 402	44491.046 339	.000 022 4764	.000 237	10.523 826	.095 022 4764	19.01	7.742 068	16.83	92
47	5069.057 324	53347.971 836	.000 018 7449	.000 197	10.524 239	.095 018 7449	19.01	7.931 762	16.88	94
48	6077.926 458	63967.646 931	.000 015 6329	.000 165	10.524 584	.095 015 6329	19.01	8.121 501	16.92	96
49	7287.585 772	76700.902 861	.000 013 0377	.000 137	10.524 871	.095 013 0377	19.01	8.311 278	16.96	98
50	8737.997 530	91968.395 053	.000 010 8733	.000 114	10.525 111	.095 010 8733	19.01	8.501 087	17.00	100

SEMIANNUAL COMPOUND INTEREST AND ANNUITY

Amount Of 1	Amount Of 1 Per Period	Sinking Fund Payment	Present Worth Of 1	Present Worth of 1 Per Period	Periodic Payment To Amortize 1	Constant Annual Percent	Total Interest	Annual Add On Rate
What a single $ 1 deposit grows to in the future. The deposit is made at the beginning of the first period.	What a series of $ 1 deposits grow to in the future. A deposit is made at the end of each period.	The amount to be deposited at the end of each period that grows to $ 1 in the future.	What $ 1 to be paid in the future is worth today. Value today of a single $ 1 payment tomorrow.	What $ 1 to be paid at the end of each period is worth today. Value today of a series of $ 1 payments tomorrow.	The mortgage payment to amortize a loan of $ 1. An annuity certain, payable at the end of each period, worth $ 1 today.	The annual payment, including interest and principal, to amortize completely a loan of $ 100.	The total interest paid over the term on a loan of $1. The loan is amortized by regular periodic payments.	The average annual interest rate on a loan that is completely amortized by regular periodic payments.
$S = (1+i)^n$	$S_{\overline{n}|} = \dfrac{(1+i)^n - 1}{i}$	$\dfrac{1}{S_{\overline{n}|}} = \dfrac{i}{(1+i)^n - 1}$	$V^n = \dfrac{1}{(1+i)^n}$	$A_{\overline{n}|} = \dfrac{1-V^n}{i}$	$\dfrac{1}{A_{\overline{n}|}} = \dfrac{i}{1-V^n}$			

YEAR									PERIODS
	1.100 000	1.000 000	1.000 000 0000	.909 091	.909 091	1.100 000 0000	220.00	.100 000	20.00	1
	1.210 000	2.100 000	.476 190 4762	.826 446	1.735 537	.576 190 4762	115.24	.152 381	15.24	2

YEAR	Amount Of 1	Amount Of 1 Per Period	Sinking Fund Payment	Present Worth Of 1	Present Worth of 1 Per Period	Periodic Payment To Amortize 1	Constant Annual Percent	Total Interest	Annual Add On Rate	PERIODS
1	1.210 000	2.100 000	.476 190 4762	.826 446	1.735 537	.576 190 4762	115.24	.152 381	15.24	2
2	1.464 100	4.641 000	.215 470 8037	.683 013	3.169 865	.315 470 8037	63.10	.261 883	13.09	4
3	1.771 561	7.715 610	.129 607 3804	.564 474	4.355 261	.229 607 3804	45.93	.377 644	12.59	6
4	2.143 589	11.435 888	.087 444 0176	.466 507	5.334 926	.187 444 0176	37.49	.499 552	12.49	8
5	2.593 742	15.937 425	.062 745 3949	.385 543	6.144 567	.162 745 3949	32.55	.627 454	12.55	10
6	3.138 428	21.384 284	.046 763 3151	.318 631	6.813 692	.146 763 3151	29.36	.761 160	12.69	12
7	3.797 498	27.974 983	.035 746 2232	.263 331	7.366 687	.135 746 2232	27.15	.900 447	12.86	14
8	4.594 973	35.949 730	.027 816 6207	.217 629	7.823 709	.127 816 6207	25.57	1.045 066	13.06	16
9	5.559 917	45.599 173	.021 930 2222	.179 859	8.201 412	.121 930 2222	24.39	1.194 744	13.28	18
10	6.727 500	57.274 999	.017 459 6248	.148 644	8.513 564	.117 459 6248	23.50	1.349 193	13.49	20
11	8.140 275	71.402 749	.014 005 0630	.122 846	8.771 540	.114 005 0630	22.81	1.508 111	13.71	22
12	9.849 733	88.497 327	.011 299 7764	.101 526	8.984 744	.111 299 7764	22.26	1.671 195	13.93	24
13	11.918 177	109.181 765	.009 159 0386	.083 905	9.160 945	.109 159 0386	21.84	1.838 135	14.14	26
14	14.420 994	134.209 936	.007 451 0132	.069 343	9.306 567	.107 451 0132	21.50	2.008 628	14.35	28
15	17.449 402	164.494 023	.006 079 2483	.057 309	9.426 914	.106 079 2483	21.22	2.182 377	14.55	30
16	21.113 777	201.137 767	.004 971 7167	.047 362	9.526 376	.104 971 7167	21.00	2.359 095	14.74	32
17	25.547 670	245.476 699	.004 073 7064	.039 143	9.608 575	.104 073 7064	20.82	2.538 506	14.93	34
18	30.912 681	299.126 805	.003 343 0638	.032 349	9.676 508	.103 343 0638	20.67	2.720 350	15.11	36
19	37.404 343	364.043 434	.002 746 9250	.026 735	9.732 651	.102 746 9250	20.55	2.904 383	15.29	38
20	45.259 256	442.592 556	.002 259 4144	.022 095	9.779 051	.102 259 4144	20.46	3.090 377	15.45	40
21	54.763 699	537.636 992	.001 859 9911	.018 260	9.817 397	.101 859 9911	20.38	3.278 120	15.61	42
22	66.264 076	652.640 761	.001 532 2365	.015 091	9.849 089	.101 532 2365	20.31	3.467 418	15.76	44
23	80.179 532	791.795 321	.001 262 9527	.012 472	9.875 280	.101 262 9527	20.26	3.658 096	15.90	46
24	97.017 234	960.172 338	.001 041 4797	.010 307	9.896 926	.101 041 4797	20.21	3.849 991	16.04	48
25	117.390 853	1163.908 529	.000 859 1740	.008 519	9.914 814	.100 859 1740	20.18	4.042 959	16.17	50
26	142.042 932	1410.429 320	.000 709 0040	.007 040	9.929 599	.100 709 0040	20.15	4.236 868	16.30	52
27	171.871 948	1708.719 477	.000 585 2336	.005 818	9.941 817	.100 585 2336	20.12	4.431 603	16.41	54
28	207.965 057	2069.650 567	.000 483 1734	.004 809	9.951 915	.100 483 1734	20.10	4.627 058	16.53	56
29	251.637 719	2506.377 186	.000 398 9822	.003 974	9.960 260	.100 398 9822	20.08	4.823 141	16.63	58
30	304.481 640	3034.816 395	.000 329 5092	.003 284	9.967 157	.100 329 5092	20.07	5.019 771	16.73	60
31	368.422 784	3674.227 838	.000 272 1660	.002 714	9.972 857	.100 272 1660	20.06	5.216 874	16.83	62
32	445.791 568	4447.915 685	.000 224 8244	.002 243	9.977 568	.100 224 8244	20.05	5.414 389	16.92	64
33	539.407 798	5384.077 978	.000 185 7328	.001 854	9.981 461	.100 185 7328	20.04	5.612 258	17.01	66
34	652.683 435	6516.834 354	.000 153 4487	.001 532	9.984 679	.100 153 4487	20.04	5.810 435	17.09	68
35	789.746 957	7887.469 568	.000 126 7834	.001 266	9.987 338	.100 126 7834	20.03	6.008 875	17.17	70
36	955.593 818	9545.938 177	.000 104 7566	.001 046	9.989 535	.100 104 7566	20.03	6.207 542	17.24	72
37	1156.268 519	11552.685 195	.000 086 5600	.000 865	9.991 351	.100 086 5600	20.02	6.406 405	17.31	74
38	1399.084 909	13980.849 085	.000 071 5264	.000 715	9.992 852	.100 071 5264	20.02	6.605 436	17.38	76
39	1692.892 739	16918.927 393	.000 059 1054	.000 591	9.994 093	.100 059 1054	20.02	6.804 610	17.45	78
40	2048.400 215	20474.002 146	.000 048 8424	.000 488	9.995 118	.100 048 8424	20.01	7.003 907	17.51	80
41	2478.564 260	24775.642 596	.000 040 3622	.000 403	9.995 965	.100 040 3622	20.01	7.203 310	17.57	82
42	2999.062 754	29980.627 542	.000 033 3549	.000 333	9.996 666	.100 033 3549	20.01	7.402 802	17.63	84
43	3628.865 933	36278.659 326	.000 027 5644	.000 276	9.997 244	.100 027 5644	20.01	7.602 371	17.68	86
44	4390.927 778	43899.277 784	.000 022 7794	.000 228	9.997 723	.100 022 7794	20.01	7.802 005	17.73	88
45	5313.022 612	53120.226 118	.000 018 8252	.000 188	9.998 118	.100 018 8252	20.01	8.001 694	17.78	90
46	6428.757 360	64277.573 603	.000 015 5575	.000 156	9.998 444	.100 015 5575	20.01	8.201 431	17.83	92
47	7778.796 406	77777.964 060	.000 012 8571	.000 129	9.998 714	.100 012 8571	20.01	8.401 209	17.88	94
48	9412.343 651	94113.436 513	.000 010 6255	.000 106	9.998 938	.100 010 6255	20.01	8.601 020	17.92	96
49	11388.936	113879.358	.000 008 7812	.000 088	9.999 122	.100 008 7812	20.01	8.800 861	17.96	98
50	13780.612	137796.123	.000 007 2571	.000 073	9.999 274	.100 007 2571	20.01	9.000 726	18.00	100

ANNUAL COMPOUND INTEREST AND ANNUITY

0.00 % A

	Amount Of 1	Amount Of 1 Per Period	Sinking Fund Payment	Present Worth Of 1	Present Worth of 1 Per Period	Periodic Payment To Amortize 1	Constant Annual Percent	Total Interest	Annual Add On Rate	
	What a single $ 1 deposit grows to in the future. The deposit is made at the beginning of the first period.	What a series of $ 1 deposits grow to in the future. A deposit is made at the end of each period.	The amount to be deposited at the end of each period that grows to $ 1 in the future.	What $ 1 to be paid in the future is worth today. Value today of a single $ 1 payment tomorrow.	What $ 1 to be paid at the end of each period is worth today. Value today of a series of $ 1 payments tomorrow.	The mortgage payment to amortize a loan of $ 1. An annuity certain, payable at the end of each period, worth $ 1 today.	The annual payment, including interest and principal, to amortize completely a loan of $ 100.	The total interest paid over the term on a loan of $1. The loan is amortized by regular periodic payments.	The average annual interest rate on a loan that is completely amortized by regular periodic payments.	
	$S = (1+i)^n$	$S\overline{n} = \dfrac{(1+i)^n - 1}{i}$	$\dfrac{1}{S\overline{n}} = \dfrac{i}{(1+i)^n - 1}$	$V^n = \dfrac{1}{(1+i)^n}$	$A\overline{n} = \dfrac{1 - V^n}{i}$	$\dfrac{1}{A\overline{n}} = \dfrac{i}{1 - V^n}$				

YEAR										PERIODS
	1.000 000	1.000 000	1.000 000 0000	1.000 000	1.000 000	1.000 000 0000	100.00	0.000 000	0.00	1

YEAR	Amount Of 1	Amount Of 1 Per Period	Sinking Fund Payment	Present Worth Of 1	Present Worth of 1 Per Period	Periodic Payment To Amortize 1	Constant Annual Percent	Total Interest	Annual Add On Rate	PERIODS
1	1.000 000	1.000 000	1.000 000 0000	1.000 000	1.000 000	1.000 000 0000	100.00	0.000 000	0.00	1
2	1.000 000	2.000 000	.500 000 0000	1.000 000	2.000 000	.500 000 0000	50.00	0.000 000	0.00	2
3	1.000 000	3.000 000	.333 333 3333	1.000 000	3.000 000	.333 333 3333	33.34	0.000 000	0.00	3
4	1.000 000	4.000 000	.250 000 0000	1.000 000	4.000 000	.250 000 0000	25.00	0.000 000	0.00	4
5	1.000 000	5.000 000	.200 000 0000	1.000 000	5.000 000	.200 000 0000	20.00	0.000 000	0.00	5
6	1.000 000	6.000 000	.166 666 6667	1.000 000	6.000 000	.166 666 6667	16.67	0.000 000	0.00	6
7	1.000 000	7.000 000	.142 857 1429	1.000 000	7.000 000	.142 857 1429	14.29	0.000 000	0.00	7
8	1.000 000	8.000 000	.125 000 0000	1.000 000	8.000 000	.125 000 0000	12.50	0.000 000	0.00	8
9	1.000 000	9.000 000	.111 111 1111	1.000 000	9.000 000	.111 111 1111	11.12	0.000 000	0.00	9
10	1.000 000	10.000 000	.100 000 0000	1.000 000	10.000 000	.100 000 0000	10.00	0.000 000	0.00	10
11	1.000 000	11.000 000	.090 909 0909	1.000 000	11.000 000	.090 909 0909	9.10	0.000 000	0.00	11
12	1.000 000	12.000 000	.083 333 3333	1.000 000	12.000 000	.083 333 3333	8.34	0.000 000	0.00	12
13	1.000 000	13.000 000	.076 923 0769	1.000 000	13.000 000	.076 923 0769	7.70	0.000 000	0.00	13
14	1.000 000	14.000 000	.071 428 5714	1.000 000	14.000 000	.071 428 5714	7.15	0.000 000	0.00	14
15	1.000 000	15.000 000	.066 666 6667	1.000 000	15.000 000	.066 666 6667	6.67	0.000 000	0.00	15
16	1.000 000	16.000 000	.062 500 0000	1.000 000	16.000 000	.062 500 0000	6.25	0.000 000	0.00	16
17	1.000 000	17.000 000	.058 823 5294	1.000 000	17.000 000	.058 823 5294	5.89	0.000 000	0.00	17
18	1.000 000	18.000 000	.055 555 5556	1.000 000	18.000 000	.055 555 5556	5.56	0.000 000	0.00	18
19	1.000 000	19.000 000	.052 631 5789	1.000 000	19.000 000	.052 631 5789	5.27	0.000 000	0.00	19
20	1.000 000	20.000 000	.050 000 0000	1.000 000	20.000 000	.050 000 0000	5.00	0.000 000	0.00	20
21	1.000 000	21.000 000	.047 619 0476	1.000 000	21.000 000	.047 619 0476	4.77	0.000 000	0.00	21
22	1.000 000	22.000 000	.045 454 5455	1.000 000	22.000 000	.045 454 5455	4.55	0.000 000	0.00	22
23	1.000 000	23.000 000	.043 478 2609	1.000 000	23.000 000	.043 478 2609	4.35	0.000 000	0.00	23
24	1.000 000	24.000 000	.041 666 6667	1.000 000	24.000 000	.041 666 6667	4.17	0.000 000	0.00	24
25	1.000 000	25.000 000	.040 000 0000	1.000 000	25.000 000	.040 000 0000	4.00	0.000 000	0.00	25
26	1.000 000	26.000 000	.038 461 5385	1.000 000	26.000 000	.038 461 5385	3.85	0.000 000	0.00	26
27	1.000 000	27.000 000	.037 037 0370	1.000 000	27.000 000	.037 037 0370	3.71	0.000 000	0.00	27
28	1.000 000	28.000 000	.035 714 2857	1.000 000	28.000 000	.035 714 2857	3.58	0.000 000	0.00	28
29	1.000 000	29.000 000	.034 482 7586	1.000 000	29.000 000	.034 482 7586	3.45	0.000 000	0.00	29
30	1.000 000	30.000 000	.033 333 3333	1.000 000	30.000 000	.033 333 3333	3.34	0.000 000	0.00	30
31	1.000 000	31.000 000	.032 258 0645	1.000 000	31.000 000	.032 258 0645	3.23	0.000 000	0.00	31
32	1.000 000	32.000 000	.031 250 0000	1.000 000	32.000 000	.031 250 0000	3.13	0.000 000	0.00	32
33	1.000 000	33.000 000	.030 303 0303	1.000 000	33.000 000	.030 303 0303	3.04	0.000 000	0.00	33
34	1.000 000	34.000 000	.029 411 7647	1.000 000	34.000 000	.029 411 7647	2.95	0.000 000	0.00	34
35	1.000 000	35.000 000	.028 571 4286	1.000 000	35.000 000	.028 571 4286	2.86	0.000 000	0.00	35
36	1.000 000	36.000 000	.027 777 7778	1.000 000	36.000 000	.027 777 7778	2.78	0.000 000	0.00	36
37	1.000 000	37.000 000	.027 027 0270	1.000 000	37.000 000	.027 027 0270	2.71	0.000 000	0.00	37
38	1.000 000	38.000 000	.026 315 7895	1.000 000	38.000 000	.026 315 7895	2.64	0.000 000	0.00	38
39	1.000 000	39.000 000	.025 641 0256	1.000 000	39.000 000	.025 641 0256	2.57	0.000 000	0.00	39
40	1.000 000	40.000 000	.025 000 0000	1.000 000	40.000 000	.025 000 0000	2.50	0.000 000	0.00	40
41	1.000 000	41.000 000	.024 390 2439	1.000 000	41.000 000	.024 390 2439	2.44	0.000 000	0.00	41
42	1.000 000	42.000 000	.023 809 5238	1.000 000	42.000 000	.023 809 5238	2.39	0.000 000	0.00	42
43	1.000 000	43.000 000	.023 255 8140	1.000 000	43.000 000	.023 255 8140	2.33	0.000 000	0.00	43
44	1.000 000	44.000 000	.022 727 2727	1.000 000	44.000 000	.022 727 2727	2.28	0.000 000	0.00	44
45	1.000 000	45.000 000	.022 222 2222	1.000 000	45.000 000	.022 222 2222	2.23	0.000 000	0.00	45
46	1.000 000	46.000 000	.021 739 1304	1.000 000	46.000 000	.021 739 1304	2.18	0.000 000	0.00	46
47	1.000 000	47.000 000	.021 276 5957	1.000 000	47.000 000	.021 276 5957	2.13	0.000 000	0.00	47
48	1.000 000	48.000 000	.020 833 3333	1.000 000	48.000 000	.020 833 3333	2.09	0.000 000	0.00	48
49	1.000 000	49.000 000	.020 408 1633	1.000 000	49.000 000	.020 408 1633	2.05	0.000 000	0.00	49
50	1.000 000	50.000 000	.020 000 0000	1.000 000	50.000 000	.020 000 0000	2.00	0.000 000	0.00	50

Effective Rate is 0.00 %

Annual Percentage Rate is 0.00 %

Amount Of 1	Amount Of 1 Per Period	Sinking Fund Payment	Present Worth Of 1	Present Worth of 1 Per Period	Periodic Payment To Amortize 1	Constant Annual Percent	Total Interest	Annual Add On Rate
What a single $ 1 deposit grows to in the future. The deposit is made at the beginning of the first period.	What a series of $ 1 deposits grow to in the future. A deposit is made at the end of each period.	The amount to be deposited at the end of each period that grows to $ 1 in the future.	What $ 1 to be paid in the future is worth today. Value today of a single $ 1 payment tomorrow.	What $ 1 to be paid at the end of each period is worth today. Value today of a series of $ 1 payments tomorrow.	The mortgage payment to amortize a loan of $ 1. An annuity certain, payable at the end of each period, worth $ 1 today.	The annual payment, including interest and principal, to amortize completely a loan of $ 100.	The total interest paid over the term on a loan of $1. The loan is amortized by regular periodic payments.	The average annual interest rate on a loan that is completely amortized by regular periodic payments.

$$S = (1+i)^n \qquad S\overline{n}| = \frac{(1+i)^n - 1}{i} \qquad \frac{1}{S\overline{n}|} = \frac{i}{(1+i)^n - 1} \qquad V^n = \frac{1}{(1+i)^n} \qquad A\overline{n}| = \frac{1-V^n}{i} \qquad \frac{1}{A\overline{n}|} = \frac{i}{1-V^n}$$

YEAR   **PERIODS**

| | 1.010 000 | 1.000 000 | 1.000 000 0000 | .990 099 | .990 099 | 1.010 000 0000 | 101.00 | .010 000 | 1.00 | 1 |

YEAR	Amount Of 1	Amount Of 1 Per Period	Sinking Fund Payment	Present Worth Of 1	Present Worth of 1 Per Period	Periodic Payment To Amortize 1	Constant Annual Percent	Total Interest	Annual Add On Rate	PERIODS
1	1.010 000	1.000 000	1.000 000 0000	.990 099	.990 099	1.010 000 0000	101.00	.010 000	1.00	1
2	1.020 100	2.010 000	.497 512 4378	.980 296	1.970 395	.507 512 4378	50.76	.015 025	.75	2
3	1.030 301	3.030 100	.330 022 1115	.970 590	2.940 985	.340 022 1115	34.01	.020 066	.67	3
4	1.040 604	4.060 401	.246 281 0939	.960 980	3.901 966	.256 281 0939	25.63	.025 124	.63	4
5	1.051 010	5.101 005	.196 039 7996	.951 466	4.853 431	.206 039 7996	20.61	.030 199	.60	5
6	1.061 520	6.152 015	.162 548 3667	.942 045	5.795 476	.172 548 3667	17.26	.035 290	.59	6
7	1.072 135	7.213 535	.138 628 2829	.932 718	6.728 195	.148 628 2829	14.87	.040 398	.58	7
8	1.082 857	8.285 671	.120 690 2920	.923 483	7.651 678	.130 690 2920	13.07	.045 522	.57	8
9	1.093 685	9.368 527	.106 740 3628	.914 340	8.566 018	.116 740 3628	11.68	.050 663	.56	9
10	1.104 622	10.462 213	.095 582 0766	.905 287	9.471 305	.105 582 0766	10.56	.055 821	.56	10
11	1.115 668	11.566 835	.086 454 0757	.896 324	10.367 628	.096 454 0757	9.65	.060 995	.55	11
12	1.126 825	12.682 503	.078 848 7887	.887 449	11.255 077	.088 848 7887	8.89	.066 185	.55	12
13	1.138 093	13.809 328	.072 414 8197	.878 663	12.133 740	.082 414 8197	8.25	.071 393	.55	13
14	1.149 474	14.947 421	.066 901 1717	.869 963	13.003 703	.076 901 1717	7.70	.076 616	.55	14
15	1.160 969	16.096 896	.062 123 7802	.861 349	13.865 053	.072 123 7802	7.22	.081 857	.55	15
16	1.172 579	17.257 864	.057 944 5968	.852 821	14.717 874	.067 944 5968	6.80	.087 114	.54	16
17	1.184 304	18.430 443	.054 258 0551	.844 377	15.562 251	.064 258 0551	6.43	.092 387	.54	17
18	1.196 147	19.614 748	.050 982 0479	.836 017	16.398 269	.060 982 0479	6.10	.097 677	.54	18
19	1.208 109	20.810 895	.048 051 7536	.827 740	17.226 008	.058 051 7536	5.81	.102 983	.54	19
20	1.220 190	22.019 004	.045 415 3149	.819 544	18.045 553	.055 415 3149	5.55	.108 306	.54	20
21	1.232 392	23.239 194	.043 030 7522	.811 430	18.856 983	.053 030 7522	5.31	.113 646	.54	21
22	1.244 716	24.471 586	.040 863 7185	.803 396	19.660 379	.050 863 7185	5.09	.119 002	.54	22
23	1.257 163	25.716 302	.038 885 8401	.795 442	20.455 821	.048 885 8401	4.89	.124 374	.54	23
24	1.269 735	26.973 465	.037 073 4722	.787 566	21.243 387	.047 073 4722	4.71	.129 763	.54	24
25	1.282 432	28.243 200	.035 406 7534	.779 768	22.023 156	.045 406 7534	4.55	.135 169	.54	25
26	1.295 256	29.525 631	.033 868 8776	.772 048	22.795 204	.043 868 8776	4.39	.140 591	.54	26
27	1.308 209	30.820 888	.032 445 5287	.764 404	23.559 608	.042 445 5287	4.25	.146 029	.54	27
28	1.321 291	32.129 097	.031 124 4356	.756 836	24.316 443	.041 124 4356	4.12	.151 484	.54	28
29	1.334 504	33.450 388	.029 895 0198	.749 342	25.065 785	.039 895 0198	3.99	.156 956	.54	29
30	1.347 849	34.784 892	.028 748 1132	.741 923	25.807 708	.038 748 1132	3.88	.162 443	.54	30
31	1.361 327	36.132 740	.027 675 7309	.734 577	26.542 285	.037 675 7309	3.77	.167 948	.54	31
32	1.374 941	37.494 068	.026 670 8857	.727 304	27.269 589	.036 670 8857	3.67	.173 468	.54	32
33	1.388 690	38.869 009	.025 727 4378	.720 103	27.989 693	.035 727 4378	3.58	.179 005	.54	33
34	1.402 577	40.257 699	.024 839 9694	.712 973	28.702 666	.034 839 9694	3.49	.184 559	.54	34
35	1.416 603	41.660 276	.024 003 6818	.705 914	29.408 580	.034 003 6818	3.41	.190 129	.54	35
36	1.430 769	43.076 878	.023 214 3098	.698 925	30.107 505	.033 214 3098	3.33	.195 715	.54	36
37	1.445 076	44.507 647	.022 468 0491	.692 005	30.799 510	.032 468 0491	3.25	.201 318	.54	37
38	1.459 527	45.952 724	.021 761 4958	.685 153	31.484 663	.031 761 4958	3.18	.206 937	.54	38
39	1.474 123	47.412 251	.021 091 5951	.678 370	32.163 033	.031 091 5951	3.11	.212 572	.55	39
40	1.488 864	48.886 373	.020 455 5980	.671 653	32.834 686	.030 455 5980	3.05	.218 224	.55	40
41	1.503 752	50.375 237	.019 851 0232	.665 003	33.499 689	.029 851 0232	2.99	.223 892	.55	41
42	1.518 790	51.878 989	.019 275 6260	.658 419	34.158 108	.029 275 6260	2.93	.229 576	.55	42
43	1.533 978	53.397 779	.018 727 3705	.651 900	34.810 008	.028 727 3705	2.88	.235 277	.55	43
44	1.549 318	54.931 757	.018 204 4058	.645 445	35.455 454	.028 204 4058	2.83	.240 994	.55	44
45	1.564 811	56.481 075	.017 705 0455	.639 055	36.094 508	.027 705 0455	2.78	.246 727	.55	45
46	1.580 459	58.045 885	.017 227 7499	.632 728	36.727 236	.027 227 7499	2.73	.252 477	.55	46
47	1.596 263	59.626 344	.016 771 1103	.626 463	37.353 699	.026 771 1103	2.68	.258 242	.55	47
48	1.612 226	61.222 608	.016 333 8354	.620 260	37.973 959	.026 333 8354	2.64	.264 024	.55	48
49	1.628 348	62.834 834	.015 914 7393	.614 119	38.588 079	.025 914 7393	2.60	.269 822	.55	49
50	1.644 632	64.463 182	.015 512 7309	.608 039	39.196 118	.025 512 7309	2.56	.275 637	.55	50

Amount Of 1	Amount Of 1 Per Period	Sinking Fund Payment	Present Worth Of 1	Present Worth of 1 Per Period	Periodic Payment To Amortize 1	Constant Annual Percent	Total Interest	Annual Add On Rate
What a single $ 1 deposit grows to in the future. The deposit is made at the beginning of the first period.	What a series of $ 1 deposits grow to in the future. A deposit is made at the end of each period.	The amount to be deposited at the end of each period that grows to $ 1 in the future.	What $ 1 to be paid in the future is worth today. Value today of a single $ 1 payment tomorrow.	What $ 1 to be paid at the end of each period is worth today. Value today of a series of $ 1 payments tomorrow.	The mortgage payment to amortize a loan of $ 1. An annuity certain, payable at the end of each period, worth $ 1 today.	The annual payment, including interest and principal, to amortize completely a loan of $ 100.	The total interest paid over the term of a loan of $1. The loan is amortized by regular periodic payments.	The average annual interest rate on a loan that is completely amortized by regular periodic payments.
$S = (1+i)^n$	$S\overline{n} = \dfrac{(1+i)^n - 1}{i}$	$\dfrac{1}{S\overline{n}} = \dfrac{i}{(1+i)^n - 1}$	$V^n = \dfrac{1}{(1+i)^n}$	$A\overline{n} = \dfrac{1-V^n}{i}$	$\dfrac{1}{A\overline{n}} = \dfrac{i}{1-V^n}$			

YEAR									PERIODS
	1.020 000	1.000 000	1.000 000 0000	.980 392	.980 392	1.020 000 0000	102.00	.020 000	2.00	1

YEAR	Amount Of 1	Amount Of 1 Per Period	Sinking Fund Payment	Present Worth Of 1	Present Worth of 1 Per Period	Periodic Payment To Amortize 1	Constant Annual Percent	Total Interest	Annual Add On Rate	PERIODS
1	1.020 000	1.000 000	1.000 000 0000	.980 392	.980 392	1.020 000 0000	102.00	.020 000	2.00	1
2	1.040 400	2.020 000	.495 049 5050	.961 169	1.941 561	.515 049 5050	51.51	.030 099	1.51	2
3	1.061 208	3.060 400	.326 754 6726	.942 322	2.883 883	.346 754 6726	34.68	.040 264	1.34	3
4	1.082 432	4.121 608	.242 623 7527	.923 845	3.807 729	.262 623 7527	26.27	.050 495	1.26	4
5	1.104 081	5.204 040	.192 158 3941	.905 731	4.713 460	.212 158 3941	21.22	.060 792	1.22	5
6	1.126 162	6.308 121	.158 525 8123	.887 971	5.601 431	.178 525 8123	17.86	.071 155	1.19	6
7	1.148 686	7.434 283	.134 511 9561	.870 560	6.471 991	.154 511 9561	15.46	.081 584	1.17	7
8	1.171 659	8.582 969	.116 509 7991	.853 490	7.325 481	.136 509 7991	13.66	.092 078	1.15	8
9	1.195 093	9.754 628	.102 515 4374	.836 755	8.162 237	.122 515 4374	12.26	.102 639	1.14	9
10	1.218 994	10.949 721	.091 326 5279	.820 348	8.982 585	.111 326 5279	11.14	.113 265	1.13	10
11	1.243 374	12.168 715	.082 177 9428	.804 263	9.786 848	.102 177 9428	10.22	.123 957	1.13	11
12	1.268 242	13.412 090	.074 559 5966	.788 493	10.575 341	.094 559 5966	9.46	.134 715	1.12	12
13	1.293 607	14.680 332	.068 118 3527	.773 033	11.348 374	.088 118 3527	8.82	.145 539	1.12	13
14	1.319 479	15.973 938	.062 601 9702	.757 875	12.106 249	.082 601 9702	8.27	.156 428	1.12	14
15	1.345 868	17.293 417	.057 825 4723	.743 015	12.849 264	.077 825 4723	7.79	.167 382	1.12	15
16	1.372 786	18.639 285	.053 650 1259	.728 446	13.577 709	.073 650 1259	7.37	.178 402	1.12	16
17	1.400 241	20.012 071	.049 969 8408	.714 163	14.291 872	.069 969 8408	7.00	.189 487	1.11	17
18	1.428 246	21.412 312	.046 702 1022	.700 159	14.992 031	.066 702 1022	6.68	.200 638	1.11	18
19	1.456 811	22.840 559	.043 781 7663	.686 431	15.678 462	.063 781 7663	6.38	.211 854	1.12	19
20	1.485 947	24.297 370	.041 156 7181	.672 971	16.351 433	.061 156 7181	6.12	.223 134	1.12	20
21	1.515 666	25.783 317	.038 784 7689	.659 776	17.011 209	.058 784 7689	5.88	.234 480	1.12	21
22	1.545 980	27.298 984	.036 631 4005	.646 839	17.658 048	.056 631 4005	5.67	.245 891	1.12	22
23	1.576 899	28.844 963	.034 668 0976	.634 156	18.292 204	.054 668 0976	5.47	.257 366	1.12	23
24	1.608 437	30.421 862	.032 871 0973	.621 721	18.913 926	.052 871 0973	5.29	.268 906	1.12	24
25	1.640 606	32.030 300	.031 220 4384	.609 531	19.523 456	.051 220 4384	5.13	.280 511	1.12	25
26	1.673 418	33.670 906	.029 699 2308	.597 579	20.121 036	.049 699 2308	4.97	.292 180	1.12	26
27	1.706 886	35.344 324	.028 293 0862	.585 862	20.706 898	.048 293 0862	4.83	.303 913	1.13	27
28	1.741 024	37.051 210	.026 989 6716	.574 375	21.281 272	.046 989 6716	4.70	.315 711	1.13	28
29	1.775 845	38.792 235	.025 778 3552	.563 112	21.844 385	.045 778 3552	4.58	.327 572	1.13	29
30	1.811 362	40.568 079	.024 649 9223	.552 071	22.396 456	.044 649 9223	4.47	.339 498	1.13	30
31	1.847 589	42.379 441	.023 596 3472	.541 246	22.937 702	.043 596 3472	4.36	.351 487	1.13	31
32	1.884 541	44.227 030	.022 610 6073	.530 633	23.468 335	.042 610 6073	4.27	.363 539	1.14	32
33	1.922 231	46.111 570	.021 686 5311	.520 229	23.988 564	.041 686 5311	4.17	.375 656	1.14	33
34	1.960 676	48.033 802	.020 818 6728	.510 028	24.498 592	.040 818 6728	4.09	.387 835	1.14	34
35	1.999 890	49.994 478	.020 002 2092	.500 028	24.998 619	.040 002 2092	4.01	.400 077	1.14	35
36	2.039 887	51.994 367	.019 232 8526	.490 223	25.488 842	.039 232 8526	3.93	.412 383	1.15	36
37	2.080 685	54.034 255	.018 506 7789	.480 611	25.969 453	.038 506 7789	3.86	.424 751	1.15	37
38	2.122 299	56.114 940	.017 820 5663	.471 187	26.440 641	.037 820 5663	3.79	.437 182	1.15	38
39	2.164 745	58.237 238	.017 171 1439	.461 948	26.902 589	.037 171 1439	3.72	.449 675	1.15	39
40	2.208 040	60.401 983	.016 555 7478	.452 890	27.355 479	.036 555 7478	3.66	.462 230	1.16	40
41	2.252 200	62.610 023	.015 971 8836	.444 010	27.799 489	.035 971 8836	3.60	.474 847	1.16	41
42	2.297 244	64.862 223	.015 417 2945	.435 304	28.234 794	.035 417 2945	3.55	.487 526	1.16	42
43	2.343 189	67.159 468	.014 889 9334	.426 769	28.661 562	.034 889 9334	3.49	.500 267	1.16	43
44	2.390 053	69.502 657	.014 387 9391	.418 401	29.079 963	.034 387 9391	3.44	.513 069	1.17	44
45	2.437 854	71.892 710	.013 909 6161	.410 197	29.490 160	.033 909 6161	3.40	.525 933	1.17	45
46	2.486 611	74.330 564	.013 453 4159	.402 154	29.892 314	.033 453 4159	3.35	.538 857	1.17	46
47	2.536 344	76.817 176	.013 017 9220	.394 268	30.286 582	.033 017 9220	3.31	.551 842	1.17	47
48	2.587 070	79.353 519	.012 601 8355	.386 538	30.673 120	.032 601 8355	3.27	.564 888	1.18	48
49	2.638 812	81.940 590	.012 203 9639	.378 958	31.052 078	.032 203 9639	3.23	.577 994	1.18	49
50	2.691 588	84.579 401	.011 823 2097	.371 528	31.423 606	.031 823 2097	3.19	.591 160	1.18	50

Amount Of 1	Amount Of 1 Per Period	Sinking Fund Payment	Present Worth Of 1	Present Worth of 1 Per Period	Periodic Payment To Amortize 1	Constant Annual Percent	Total Interest	Annual Add On Rate	
What a single $ 1 deposit grows to in the future. The deposit is made at the beginning of the first period.	What a series of $ 1 deposits grow to in the future. A deposit is made at the end of each period.	The amount to be deposited at the end of each period that grows to $ 1 in the future.	What $ 1 to be paid in the future is worth today. Value today of a single $ 1 payment tomorrow.	What $ 1 to be paid at the end of each period is worth today. Value today of a series of $ 1 payments tomorrow.	The mortgage payment to amortize a loan of $ 1. An annuity certain, payable at the end of each period, worth $ 1 today.	The annual payment, including interest and principal, to amortize completely a loan of $ 100.	The total interest paid over the term on a loan of $1. The loan is amortized by regular periodic payments.	The average annual interest rate on a loan that is completely amortized by regular periodic payments.	

$$S = (1+i)^n \qquad S\overline{n|} = \frac{(1+i)^n - 1}{i} \qquad \frac{1}{S\overline{n|}} = \frac{i}{(1+i)^n - 1} \qquad V^n = \frac{1}{(1+i)^n} \qquad A\overline{n|} = \frac{1-V^n}{i} \qquad \frac{1}{A\overline{n|}} = \frac{i}{1-V^n}$$

YEAR									**PERIODS**	
	1.022 500	1.000 000	1.000 000 0000	.977 995	.977 995	1.022 500 0000	102.25	.022 500	2.25	1
1	1.022 500	1.000 000	1.000 000 0000	.977 995	.977 995	1.022 500 0000	102.25	.022 500	2.25	1
2	1.045 506	2.022 500	.494 437 5773	.956 474	1.934 470	.516 937 5773	51.70	.033 875	1.69	2
3	1.069 030	3.068 006	.325 944 5772	.935 427	2.869 897	.348 444 5772	34.85	.045 334	1.51	3
4	1.093 083	4.137 036	.241 718 9277	.914 843	3.784 740	.264 218 9277	26.43	.056 876	1.42	4
5	1.117 678	5.230 120	.191 200 2125	.894 712	4.679 453	.213 700 2125	21.38	.068 501	1.37	5
6	1.142 825	6.347 797	.157 534 9584	.875 024	5.554 477	.180 034 9584	18.01	.080 210	1.34	6
7	1.168 539	7.490 623	.133 500 2470	.855 769	6.410 246	.156 000 2470	15.61	.092 002	1.31	7
8	1.194 831	8.659 162	.115 484 6181	.836 938	7.247 185	.137 984 6181	13.80	.103 877	1.30	8
9	1.221 715	9.853 993	.101 481 7039	.818 522	8.065 706	.123 981 7039	12.40	.115 835	1.29	9
10	1.249 203	11.075 708	.090 287 6831	.800 510	8.866 216	.112 787 6831	11.28	.127 877	1.28	10
11	1.277 311	12.324 911	.081 136 4868	.782 895	9.649 111	.103 636 4868	10.37	.140 001	1.27	11
12	1.306 050	13.602 222	.073 517 4015	.765 667	10.414 779	.096 017 4015	9.61	.152 209	1.27	12
13	1.335 436	14.908 272	.067 076 8561	.748 819	11.163 598	.089 576 8561	8.96	.164 499	1.27	13
14	1.365 483	16.243 708	.061 562 2989	.732 341	11.895 939	.084 062 2989	8.41	.176 872	1.26	14
15	1.396 207	17.609 191	.056 788 5250	.716 226	12.612 166	.079 288 5250	7.93	.189 328	1.26	15
16	1.427 621	19.005 398	.052 616 6300	.700 466	13.312 631	.075 116 6300	7.52	.201 866	1.26	16
17	1.459 743	20.433 020	.048 940 3926	.685 052	13.997 683	.071 440 3926	7.15	.214 487	1.26	17
18	1.492 587	21.892 763	.045 677 1958	.669 978	14.667 661	.068 177 1958	6.82	.227 190	1.26	18
19	1.526 170	23.385 350	.042 761 8152	.655 235	15.322 896	.065 261 8152	6.53	.239 974	1.26	19
20	1.560 509	24.911 520	.040 142 0708	.640 816	15.963 712	.062 642 0708	6.27	.252 841	1.26	20
21	1.595 621	26.472 029	.037 775 7214	.626 715	16.590 428	.060 275 7214	6.03	.265 790	1.27	21
22	1.631 522	28.067 650	.035 628 2056	.612 925	17.203 352	.058 128 2056	5.82	.278 821	1.27	22
23	1.668 231	29.699 172	.033 670 9724	.599 437	17.802 790	.056 170 9724	5.62	.291 932	1.27	23
24	1.705 767	31.367 403	.031 880 2289	.586 247	18.389 036	.054 380 2289	5.44	.305 126	1.27	24
25	1.744 146	33.073 170	.030 235 9889	.573 346	18.962 383	.052 735 9889	5.28	.318 400	1.27	25
26	1.783 390	34.817 316	.028 721 3406	.560 730	19.523 113	.051 221 3406	5.13	.331 755	1.28	26
27	1.823 516	36.600 706	.027 321 8774	.548 391	20.071 504	.049 821 8774	4.99	.345 191	1.28	27
28	1.864 545	38.424 222	.026 025 2506	.536 324	20.607 828	.048 525 2506	4.86	.358 707	1.28	28
29	1.906 497	40.288 767	.024 820 8143	.524 522	21.132 350	.047 320 8143	4.74	.372 304	1.28	29
30	1.949 393	42.195 264	.023 699 3422	.512 980	21.645 330	.046 199 3422	4.62	.385 980	1.29	30
31	1.993 255	44.144 657	.022 652 7978	.501 692	22.147 022	.045 152 7978	4.52	.399 737	1.29	31
32	2.038 103	46.137 912	.021 674 1493	.490 652	22.637 674	.044 174 1493	4.42	.413 573	1.29	32
33	2.083 960	48.176 015	.020 757 2169	.479 856	23.117 530	.043 257 2169	4.33	.427 488	1.30	33
34	2.130 849	50.259 976	.019 896 5477	.469 296	23.586 826	.042 396 5477	4.24	.441 483	1.30	34
35	2.178 794	52.390 825	.019 087 3115	.458 970	24.045 796	.041 587 3115	4.16	.455 556	1.30	35
36	2.227 816	54.569 619	.018 325 2151	.448 870	24.494 666	.040 825 2151	4.09	.469 708	1.30	36
37	2.277 942	56.797 435	.017 606 4289	.438 993	24.933 658	.040 106 4289	4.02	.483 938	1.31	37
38	2.329 196	59.075 377	.016 927 5262	.429 333	25.362 991	.039 427 5262	3.95	.498 246	1.31	38
39	2.381 603	61.404 573	.016 285 4319	.419 885	25.782 876	.038 785 4319	3.88	.512 632	1.31	39
40	2.435 189	63.786 176	.015 677 3781	.410 646	26.193 522	.038 177 3781	3.82	.527 095	1.32	40
41	2.489 981	66.221 365	.015 100 8666	.401 610	26.595 132	.037 600 8666	3.77	.541 636	1.32	41
42	2.546 005	68.711 346	.014 553 6372	.392 772	26.987 904	.037 053 6372	3.71	.556 253	1.32	42
43	2.603 290	71.257 351	.014 033 6398	.384 129	27.372 033	.036 533 6398	3.66	.570 947	1.33	43
44	2.661 864	73.860 642	.013 539 0105	.375 677	27.747 710	.036 039 0105	3.61	.585 716	1.33	44
45	2.721 756	76.522 506	.013 068 0508	.367 410	28.115 120	.035 568 0508	3.56	.600 562	1.33	45
46	2.782 996	79.244 262	.012 619 2101	.359 325	28.474 444	.035 119 2101	3.52	.615 484	1.34	46
47	2.845 613	82.027 258	.012 191 0694	.351 418	28.825 863	.034 691 0694	3.47	.630 480	1.34	47
48	2.909 640	84.872 872	.011 782 3279	.343 685	29.169 548	.034 282 3279	3.43	.645 552	1.34	48
49	2.975 107	87.782 511	.011 391 7908	.336 122	29.505 670	.033 891 7908	3.39	.660 698	1.35	49
50	3.042 046	90.757 618	.011 018 3588	.328 726	29.834 396	.033 518 3588	3.36	.675 918	1.35	50

Effective Rate is 2.25 %   Annual Percentage Rate is 2.25 %

Amount Of 1	Amount Of 1 Per Period	Sinking Fund Payment	Present Worth Of 1	Present Worth of 1 Per Period	Periodic Payment To Amortize 1	Constant Annual Percent	Total Interest	Annual Add On Rate
What a single $ 1 deposit grows to in the future. The deposit is made at the beginning of the first period.	What a series of $ 1 deposits grow to in the future. A deposit is made at the end of each period.	The amount to be deposited at the end of each period that grows to $ 1 in the future.	What $ 1 to be paid in the future is worth today. Value today of a single $ 1 payment tomorrow.	What $ 1 to be paid at the end of each period is worth today. Value today of a series of $ 1 payments tomorrow.	The mortgage payment to amortize a loan of $ 1. An annuity certain, payable at the end of each period, worth $ 1 today.	The annual payment, including interest and principal, to amortize completely a loan of $ 100.	The total interest paid over the term of $1. The loan is amortized by regular periodic payments.	The average annual interest rate on a loan that is completely amortized by regular periodic payments.

$$S = (1+i)^n \qquad S\overline{n}| = \frac{(1+i)^n - 1}{i} \qquad \frac{1}{S\overline{n}|} = \frac{i}{(1+i)^n - 1} \qquad V^n = \frac{1}{(1+i)^n} \qquad A\overline{n}| = \frac{1-V^n}{i} \qquad \frac{1}{A\overline{n}|} = \frac{i}{1-V^n}$$

YEAR ... **PERIODS**

	1.025 000	1.000 000	1.000 000 0000	.975 610	.975 610	1.025 000 0000	102.50	.025 000	2.50	1

YEAR	Amount Of 1	Amount Of 1 Per Period	Sinking Fund Payment	Present Worth Of 1	Present Worth of 1 Per Period	Periodic Payment To Amortize 1	Constant Annual Percent	Total Interest	Annual Add On Rate	PERIODS
1	1.025 000	1.000 000	1.000 000 0000	.975 610	.975 610	1.025 000 0000	102.50	.025 000	2.50	1
2	1.050 625	2.025 000	.493 827 1605	.951 814	1.927 424	.518 827 1605	51.89	.037 654	1.88	2
3	1.076 891	3.075 625	.325 137 1672	.928 599	2.856 024	.350 137 1672	35.02	.050 412	1.68	3
4	1.103 813	4.152 516	.240 817 8777	.905 951	3.761 974	.265 817 8777	26.59	.063 272	1.58	4
5	1.131 408	5.256 329	.190 246 8609	.883 854	4.645 828	.215 246 8609	21.53	.076 234	1.52	5
6	1.159 693	6.387 737	.156 549 9711	.862 297	5.508 125	.181 549 9711	18.16	.089 300	1.49	6
7	1.188 686	7.547 430	.132 495 4296	.841 265	6.349 391	.157 495 4296	15.75	.102 468	1.46	7
8	1.218 403	8.736 116	.114 467 3458	.820 747	7.170 137	.139 467 3458	13.95	.115 739	1.45	8
9	1.248 863	9.954 519	.100 456 8900	.800 728	7.970 866	.125 456 8900	12.55	.129 112	1.43	9
10	1.280 085	11.203 382	.089 258 7632	.781 198	8.752 064	.114 258 7632	11.43	.142 588	1.43	10
11	1.312 087	12.483 466	.080 105 9558	.762 145	9.514 209	.105 105 9558	10.52	.156 166	1.42	11
12	1.344 889	13.795 553	.072 487 1270	.743 556	10.257 765	.097 487 1270	9.75	.169 846	1.42	12
13	1.378 511	15.140 442	.066 048 2708	.725 420	10.983 185	.091 048 2708	9.11	.183 628	1.41	13
14	1.412 974	16.518 953	.060 536 5249	.707 727	11.690 912	.085 536 5249	8.56	.197 511	1.41	14
15	1.448 298	17.931 927	.055 766 4561	.690 466	12.381 378	.080 766 4561	8.08	.211 497	1.41	15
16	1.484 506	19.380 225	.051 598 9886	.673 625	13.055 003	.076 598 9886	7.66	.225 584	1.41	16
17	1.521 618	20.864 730	.047 927 7699	.657 195	13.712 198	.072 927 7699	7.30	.239 772	1.41	17
18	1.559 659	22.386 349	.044 670 0805	.641 166	14.353 364	.069 670 0805	6.97	.254 061	1.41	18
19	1.598 650	23.946 007	.041 760 6151	.625 528	14.978 891	.066 760 6151	6.68	.268 452	1.41	19
20	1.638 616	25.544 658	.039 147 1287	.610 271	15.589 162	.064 147 1287	6.42	.282 943	1.41	20
21	1.679 582	27.183 274	.036 787 3273	.595 386	16.184 549	.061 787 3273	6.18	.297 534	1.42	21
22	1.721 571	28.862 856	.034 646 6061	.580 865	16.765 413	.059 646 6061	5.97	.312 225	1.42	22
23	1.764 611	30.584 427	.032 696 3781	.566 697	17.332 110	.057 696 3781	5.77	.327 017	1.42	23
24	1.808 726	32.349 038	.030 912 8204	.552 875	17.884 986	.055 912 8204	5.60	.341 908	1.42	24
25	1.853 944	34.157 764	.029 275 9210	.539 391	18.424 376	.054 275 9210	5.43	.356 898	1.43	25
26	1.900 293	36.011 708	.027 768 7467	.526 235	18.950 611	.052 768 7467	5.28	.371 987	1.43	26
27	1.947 800	37.912 001	.026 376 8722	.513 400	19.464 011	.051 376 8722	5.14	.387 176	1.43	27
28	1.996 495	39.859 801	.025 087 9327	.500 878	19.964 889	.050 087 9327	5.01	.402 462	1.44	28
29	2.046 407	41.856 296	.023 891 2685	.488 661	20.453 550	.048 891 2685	4.89	.417 847	1.44	29
30	2.097 568	43.902 703	.022 777 6407	.476 743	20.930 293	.047 777 6407	4.78	.433 329	1.44	30
31	2.150 007	46.000 271	.021 739 0025	.465 115	21.395 407	.046 739 0025	4.68	.448 909	1.45	31
32	2.203 757	48.150 278	.020 768 3123	.453 771	21.849 178	.045 768 3123	4.58	.464 586	1.45	32
33	2.258 851	50.354 034	.019 859 3819	.442 703	22.291 881	.044 859 3819	4.49	.480 360	1.46	33
34	2.315 322	52.612 885	.019 006 7508	.431 905	22.723 786	.044 006 7508	4.41	.496 230	1.46	34
35	2.373 205	54.928 207	.018 205 5823	.421 371	23.145 157	.043 205 5823	4.33	.512 195	1.46	35
36	2.432 535	57.301 413	.017 451 5767	.411 094	23.556 251	.042 451 5767	4.25	.528 257	1.47	36
37	2.493 349	59.733 948	.016 740 8992	.401 067	23.957 318	.041 740 8992	4.18	.544 413	1.47	37
38	2.555 682	62.227 297	.016 070 1180	.391 285	24.348 603	.041 070 1180	4.11	.560 664	1.48	38
39	2.619 574	64.782 979	.015 436 1534	.381 741	24.730 344	.040 436 1534	4.05	.577 010	1.48	39
40	2.685 064	67.402 554	.014 836 2332	.372 431	25.102 775	.039 836 2332	3.99	.593 449	1.48	40
41	2.752 190	70.087 617	.014 267 8555	.363 347	25.466 122	.039 267 8555	3.93	.609 982	1.49	41
42	2.820 995	72.839 808	.013 728 7567	.354 485	25.820 607	.038 728 7567	3.88	.626 608	1.49	42
43	2.891 520	75.660 803	.013 216 8833	.345 839	26.166 446	.038 216 8833	3.83	.643 326	1.50	43
44	2.963 808	78.552 323	.012 730 3683	.337 404	26.503 849	.037 730 3683	3.78	.660 136	1.50	44
45	3.037 903	81.516 131	.012 267 5106	.329 174	26.833 024	.037 267 5106	3.73	.677 038	1.50	45
46	3.113 851	84.554 034	.011 826 7568	.321 146	27.154 170	.036 826 7568	3.69	.694 031	1.51	46
47	3.191 697	87.667 885	.011 406 6855	.313 313	27.467 483	.036 406 6855	3.65	.711 114	1.51	47
48	3.271 490	90.859 582	.011 005 9938	.305 671	27.773 154	.036 005 9938	3.61	.728 288	1.52	48
49	3.353 277	94.131 072	.010 623 4847	.298 216	28.071 369	.035 623 4847	3.57	.745 551	1.52	49
50	3.437 109	97.484 349	.010 258 0569	.290 942	28.362 312	.035 258 0569	3.53	.762 903	1.53	50

Amount Of 1	Amount Of 1 Per Period	Sinking Fund Payment	Present Worth Of 1	Present Worth of 1 Per Period	Periodic Payment To Amortize 1	Constant Annual Percent	Total Interest	Annual Add On Rate
What a single $ 1 deposit grows to in the future. The deposit is made at the beginning of the first period.	What a series of $ 1 deposits grow to in the future. A deposit is made at the end of each period.	The amount to be deposited at the end of each period that grows to $ 1 in the future.	What $ 1 to be paid in the future is worth today. Value today of a single $ 1 payment tomorrow.	What $ 1 to be paid at the end of each period is worth today. Value today of a series of $ 1 payments tomorrow.	The mortgage payment to amortize a loan of $ 1. An annuity certain, payable at the end of each period, worth $ 1 today.	The annual payment, including interest and principal, to amortize completely a loan of $ 100.	The total interest paid over the term on a loan of $1. The loan is amortized completely by regular periodic payments.	The average annual interest rate on a loan that is completely amortized by regular periodic payments.
$S = (1+i)^n$	$S\overline{n} = \dfrac{(1+i)^n - 1}{i}$	$\dfrac{1}{S\overline{n}} = \dfrac{i}{(1+i)^n - 1}$	$V^n = \dfrac{1}{(1+i)^n}$	$A\overline{n} = \dfrac{1-V^n}{i}$	$\dfrac{1}{A\overline{n}} = \dfrac{i}{1-V^n}$			

YEAR / **PERIODS**

| | 1.027 500 | 1.000 000 | 1.000 000 0000 | .973 236 | .973 236 | 1.027 500 0000 | 102.75 | .027 500 | 2.75 | 1 |

YEAR	Amount Of 1	Amount Of 1 Per Period	Sinking Fund Payment	Present Worth Of 1	Present Worth of 1 Per Period	Periodic Payment To Amortize 1	Constant Annual Percent	Total Interest	Annual Add On Rate	PERIODS
1	1.027 500	1.000 000	1.000 000 0000	.973 236	.973 236	1.027 500 0000	102.75	.027 500	2.75	1
2	1.055 756	2.027 500	.493 218 2491	.947 188	1.920 424	.520 718 2491	52.08	.041 437	2.07	2
3	1.084 790	3.083 256	.324 332 4326	.921 838	2.842 262	.351 832 4326	35.19	.055 497	1.85	3
4	1.114 621	4.168 046	.239 920 5884	.897 166	3.739 428	.267 420 5884	26.75	.069 682	1.74	4
5	1.145 273	5.282 667	.189 298 3202	.873 154	4.612 582	.216 798 3202	21.68	.083 992	1.68	5
6	1.176 768	6.427 940	.155 570 8264	.849 785	5.462 367	.183 070 8264	18.31	.098 425	1.64	6
7	1.209 129	7.604 709	.131 497 4750	.827 041	6.289 408	.158 997 4750	15.90	.112 982	1.61	7
8	1.242 381	8.813 838	.113 457 9478	.804 906	7.094 314	.140 957 9478	14.10	.127 664	1.60	8
9	1.276 546	10.056 219	.099 440 9548	.783 364	7.877 678	.126 940 9548	12.70	.142 469	1.58	9
10	1.311 651	11.332 765	.088 239 7205	.762 398	8.640 076	.115 739 7205	11.58	.157 397	1.57	10
11	1.347 721	12.644 416	.079 086 2948	.741 993	9.382 069	.106 586 2948	10.66	.172 449	1.57	11
12	1.384 784	13.992 137	.071 468 7098	.722 134	10.104 204	.098 968 7098	9.90	.187 625	1.56	12
13	1.422 865	15.376 921	.065 032 5248	.702 807	10.807 011	.092 532 5248	9.26	.202 923	1.56	13
14	1.461 994	16.799 786	.059 524 5664	.683 997	11.491 008	.087 024 5664	8.71	.218 344	1.56	14
15	1.502 199	18.261 781	.054 759 1731	.665 691	12.156 699	.082 259 1731	8.23	.233 888	1.56	15
16	1.543 509	19.763 979	.050 597 0977	.647 874	12.804 573	.078 097 0977	7.81	.249 554	1.56	16
17	1.585 956	21.307 489	.046 931 8559	.630 535	13.435 108	.074 431 8559	7.45	.265 342	1.56	17
18	1.629 570	22.893 445	.043 680 6259	.613 659	14.048 767	.071 180 6259	7.12	.281 251	1.56	18
19	1.674 383	24.523 015	.040 778 0208	.597 235	14.646 002	.068 278 0208	6.83	.297 282	1.56	19
20	1.720 428	26.197 398	.038 171 7306	.581 251	15.227 252	.065 671 7306	6.57	.313 435	1.57	20
21	1.767 740	27.917 826	.035 819 4081	.565 694	15.792 946	.063 319 4081	6.34	.329 708	1.57	21
22	1.816 353	29.685 566	.033 686 4049	.550 554	16.343 500	.061 186 4049	6.12	.346 101	1.57	22
23	1.866 303	31.501 919	.031 744 0977	.535 819	16.879 319	.059 244 0977	5.93	.362 614	1.58	23
24	1.917 626	33.368 222	.029 968 6330	.521 478	17.400 797	.057 468 6330	5.75	.379 247	1.58	24
25	1.970 361	35.285 848	.028 339 9735	.507 521	17.908 318	.055 839 9735	5.59	.395 999	1.58	25
26	2.024 546	37.256 209	.026 841 1636	.493 938	18.402 256	.054 341 1636	5.44	.412 870	1.59	26
27	2.080 221	39.280 755	.025 457 7594	.480 718	18.882 974	.052 957 7594	5.30	.429 860	1.59	27
28	2.137 427	41.360 975	.024 177 3795	.467 852	19.350 826	.051 677 3795	5.17	.446 967	1.60	28
29	2.196 206	43.498 402	.022 989 3501	.455 331	19.806 157	.050 489 3501	5.05	.464 191	1.60	29
30	2.256 602	45.694 608	.021 884 4200	.443 144	20.249 301	.049 384 4200	4.94	.481 533	1.61	30
31	2.318 658	47.951 210	.020 854 5311	.431 284	20.680 585	.048 354 5311	4.84	.498 990	1.61	31
32	2.382 421	50.269 868	.019 892 6322	.419 741	21.100 326	.047 392 6322	4.74	.516 564	1.61	32
33	2.447 938	52.652 290	.018 992 5264	.408 507	21.508 833	.046 492 5264	4.65	.534 253	1.62	33
34	2.515 256	55.100 228	.018 148 7453	.397 574	21.906 407	.045 648 7453	4.57	.552 057	1.62	34
35	2.584 426	57.615 484	.017 356 4454	.386 933	22.293 340	.044 856 4454	4.49	.569 976	1.63	35
36	2.655 498	60.199 910	.016 611 3206	.376 577	22.669 918	.044 111 3206	4.42	.588 008	1.63	36
37	2.728 524	62.855 407	.015 909 5302	.366 499	23.036 416	.043 409 5302	4.35	.606 153	1.64	37
38	2.803 558	65.583 931	.015 247 6374	.356 690	23.393 106	.042 747 6374	4.28	.624 410	1.64	38
39	2.880 656	68.387 489	.014 622 5576	.347 143	23.740 249	.042 122 5576	4.22	.642 780	1.65	39
40	2.959 874	71.268 145	.014 031 5144	.337 852	24.078 101	.041 531 5144	4.16	.661 261	1.65	40
41	3.041 271	74.228 019	.013 472 0017	.328 810	24.406 911	.040 972 0017	4.10	.679 852	1.66	41
42	3.124 905	77.269 289	.012 941 7522	.320 010	24.726 921	.040 441 7522	4.05	.698 554	1.66	42
43	3.210 840	80.394 195	.012 438 7090	.311 445	25.038 366	.039 938 7090	4.00	.717 364	1.67	43
44	3.299 138	83.605 035	.011 961 0021	.303 109	25.341 475	.039 461 0021	3.95	.736 284	1.67	44
45	3.389 865	86.904 174	.011 506 9272	.294 997	25.636 472	.039 006 9272	3.91	.755 312	1.68	45
46	3.483 086	90.294 039	.011 074 9283	.287 102	25.923 574	.038 574 9283	3.86	.774 447	1.68	46
47	3.578 871	93.777 125	.010 663 5814	.279 418	26.202 992	.038 163 5814	3.82	.793 688	1.69	47
48	3.677 290	97.355 996	.010 271 5811	.271 939	26.474 931	.037 771 5811	3.78	.813 036	1.69	48
49	3.778 415	101.033 285	.009 897 7282	.264 661	26.739 592	.037 397 7282	3.74	.832 489	1.70	49
50	3.882 322	104.811 701	.009 540 9195	.257 578	26.997 170	.037 040 9195	3.71	.852 046	1.70	50

ANNUAL COMPOUND INTEREST AND ANNUITY

3.00 % A

Amount Of 1	Amount Of 1 Per Period	Sinking Fund Payment	Present Worth Of 1	Present Worth of 1 Per Period	Periodic Payment To Amortize 1	Constant Annual Percent	Total Interest	Annual Add On Rate
What a single $ 1 deposit grows to in the future. The deposit is made at the beginning of the first period.	What a series of $ 1 deposits grow to in the future. A deposit is made at the end of each period.	The amount to be deposited at the end of each period that grows to $ 1 in the future.	What $ 1 to be paid in the future is worth today. Value today of a single $ 1 payment tomorrow.	What $ 1 to be paid at the end of each period is worth today. Value today of a series of $ 1 payments tomorrow.	The mortgage payment to amortize a loan of $ 1. An annuity certain, payable at the end of each period, worth $ 1 today.	The annual payment, including interest and principal, to amortize completely a loan of $ 100.	The total interest paid over the term of $1. The loan is amortized by regular periodic payments.	The average annual interest rate on a loan that is completely amortized by regular periodic payments.

$$S = (1+i)^n \qquad S\overline{n}| = \frac{(1+i)^n - 1}{i} \qquad \frac{1}{S\overline{n}|} = \frac{i}{(1+i)^n - 1} \qquad V^n = \frac{1}{(1+i)^n} \qquad A\overline{n}| = \frac{1-V^n}{i} \qquad \frac{1}{A\overline{n}|} = \frac{i}{1-V^n}$$

YEAR									PERIODS
	1.030 000	1.000 000	1.000 000 0000	.970 874	.970 874	1.030 000 0000	103.00	.030 000	3.00	1

YEAR	Amount Of 1	Amount Of 1 Per Period	Sinking Fund Payment	Present Worth Of 1	Present Worth of 1 Per Period	Periodic Payment To Amortize 1	Constant Annual Percent	Total Interest	Annual Add On Rate	PERIODS
1	1.030 000	1.000 000	1.000 000 0000	.970 874	.970 874	1.030 000 0000	103.00	.030 000	3.00	1
2	1.060 900	2.030 000	.492 610 8374	.942 596	1.913 470	.522 610 8374	52.27	.045 222	2.26	2
3	1.092 727	3.090 900	.323 530 3633	.915 142	2.828 611	.353 530 3633	35.36	.060 591	2.02	3
4	1.125 509	4.183 627	.239 027 0452	.888 487	3.717 098	.269 027 0452	26.91	.076 108	1.90	4
5	1.159 274	5.309 136	.188 354 5714	.862 609	4.579 707	.218 354 5714	21.84	.091 773	1.84	5
6	1.194 052	6.468 410	.154 597 5005	.837 484	5.417 191	.184 597 5005	18.46	.107 585	1.79	6
7	1.229 874	7.662 462	.130 506 3538	.813 092	6.230 283	.160 506 3538	16.06	.123 544	1.77	7
8	1.266 770	8.892 336	.112 456 3888	.789 409	7.019 692	.142 456 3888	14.25	.139 651	1.75	8
9	1.304 773	10.159 106	.098 433 8570	.766 417	7.786 109	.128 433 8570	12.85	.155 905	1.73	9
10	1.343 916	11.463 879	.087 230 5066	.744 094	8.530 203	.117 230 5066	11.73	.172 305	1.72	10
11	1.384 234	12.807 796	.078 077 4478	.722 421	9.252 624	.108 077 4478	10.81	.188 852	1.72	11
12	1.425 761	14.192 030	.070 462 0855	.701 380	9.954 004	.100 462 0855	10.05	.205 545	1.71	12
13	1.468 534	15.617 790	.064 029 5440	.680 951	10.634 955	.094 029 5440	9.41	.222 384	1.71	13
14	1.512 590	17.086 324	.058 526 3390	.661 118	11.296 073	.088 526 3390	8.86	.239 369	1.71	14
15	1.557 967	18.598 914	.053 766 5805	.641 862	11.937 935	.083 766 5805	8.38	.256 499	1.71	15
16	1.604 706	20.156 881	.049 610 8493	.623 167	12.561 102	.079 610 8493	7.97	.273 774	1.71	16
17	1.652 848	21.761 588	.045 952 5294	.605 016	13.166 118	.075 952 5294	7.60	.291 193	1.71	17
18	1.702 433	23.414 435	.042 708 6959	.587 395	13.753 513	.072 708 6959	7.28	.308 757	1.72	18
19	1.753 506	25.116 868	.039 813 8806	.570 286	14.323 799	.069 813 8806	6.99	.326 464	1.72	19
20	1.806 111	26.870 374	.037 215 7076	.553 676	14.877 475	.067 215 7076	6.73	.344 314	1.72	20
21	1.860 295	28.676 486	.034 871 7765	.537 549	15.415 024	.064 871 7765	6.49	.362 307	1.73	21
22	1.916 103	30.536 780	.032 747 3948	.521 893	15.936 917	.062 747 3948	6.28	.380 443	1.73	22
23	1.973 587	32.452 884	.030 813 9027	.506 692	16.443 608	.060 813 9027	6.09	.398 720	1.73	23
24	2.032 794	34.426 470	.029 047 4159	.491 934	16.935 542	.059 047 4159	5.91	.417 138	1.74	24
25	2.093 778	36.459 264	.027 427 8710	.477 606	17.413 148	.057 427 8710	5.75	.435 697	1.74	25
26	2.156 591	38.553 042	.025 938 2903	.463 695	17.876 842	.055 938 2903	5.60	.454 396	1.75	26
27	2.221 289	40.709 634	.024 564 2103	.450 189	18.327 031	.054 564 2103	5.46	.473 234	1.75	27
28	2.287 928	42.930 923	.023 293 2334	.437 077	18.764 108	.053 293 2334	5.33	.492 211	1.76	28
29	2.356 566	45.218 850	.022 114 6711	.424 346	19.188 455	.052 114 6711	5.22	.511 325	1.76	29
30	2.427 262	47.575 416	.021 019 2593	.411 987	19.600 441	.051 019 2593	5.11	.530 578	1.77	30
31	2.500 080	50.002 678	.019 998 9288	.399 987	20.000 428	.049 998 9288	5.00	.549 967	1.77	31
32	2.575 083	52.502 759	.019 046 6183	.388 337	20.388 766	.049 046 6183	4.91	.569 492	1.78	32
33	2.652 335	55.077 841	.018 156 1219	.377 026	20.765 792	.048 156 1219	4.82	.589 152	1.79	33
34	2.731 905	57.730 177	.017 321 9633	.366 045	21.131 837	.047 321 9633	4.74	.608 947	1.79	34
35	2.813 862	60.462 082	.016 539 2916	.355 383	21.487 220	.046 539 2916	4.66	.628 875	1.80	35
36	2.898 278	63.275 944	.015 803 7942	.345 032	21.832 252	.045 803 7942	4.59	.648 937	1.80	36
37	2.985 227	66.174 223	.015 111 6244	.334 983	22.167 235	.045 111 6244	4.52	.669 130	1.81	37
38	3.074 783	69.159 449	.014 459 3401	.325 226	22.492 462	.044 459 3401	4.45	.689 455	1.81	38
39	3.167 027	72.234 233	.013 843 8516	.315 754	22.808 215	.043 843 8516	4.39	.709 910	1.82	39
40	3.262 038	75.401 260	.013 262 3779	.306 557	23.114 772	.043 262 3779	4.33	.730 495	1.83	40
41	3.359 899	78.663 298	.012 712 4089	.297 628	23.412 400	.042 712 4089	4.28	.751 209	1.83	41
42	3.460 696	82.023 196	.012 191 6731	.288 959	23.701 359	.042 191 6731	4.22	.772 050	1.84	42
43	3.564 517	85.483 892	.011 698 1103	.280 543	23.981 902	.041 698 1103	4.17	.793 019	1.84	43
44	3.671 452	89.048 409	.011 229 8469	.272 372	24.254 274	.041 229 8469	4.13	.814 113	1.85	44
45	3.781 596	92.719 861	.010 785 1757	.264 439	24.518 713	.040 785 1757	4.08	.835 333	1.86	45
46	3.895 044	96.501 457	.010 362 5378	.256 737	24.775 449	.040 362 5378	4.04	.856 677	1.86	46
47	4.011 895	100.396 501	.009 960 5065	.249 259	25.024 708	.039 960 5065	4.00	.878 144	1.87	47
48	4.132 252	104.408 396	.009 577 7738	.241 999	25.266 707	.039 577 7738	3.96	.899 733	1.87	48
49	4.256 219	108.540 648	.009 213 1383	.234 950	25.501 657	.039 213 1383	3.93	.921 444	1.88	49
50	4.383 906	112.796 867	.008 865 4944	.228 107	25.729 764	.038 865 4944	3.89	.943 275	1.89	50

Effective Rate is 3.00 %

Annual Percentage Rate is 3.00 %

ANNUAL COMPOUND INTEREST AND ANNUITY

3.25 % A

	Amount Of 1	Amount Of 1 Per Period	Sinking Fund Payment	Present Worth Of 1	Present Worth of 1 Per Period	Periodic Payment To Amortize 1	Constant Annual Percent	Total Interest	Annual Add On Rate	
	What a single $ 1 deposit grows to in the future. The deposit is made at the beginning of the first period.	What a series of $ 1 deposits grow to in the future. A deposit is made at the end of each period.	The amount to be deposited at the end of each period that grows to $ 1 in the future.	What $ 1 to be paid in the future is worth today. Value today of a single $ 1 payment tomorrow.	What $ 1 to be paid at the end of each period is worth today. Value today of a series of $ 1 payments tomorrow.	The mortgage payment to amortize a loan of $ 1. An annuity certain, payable at the end of each period, worth $ 1 today.	The annual payment, including interest and principal, to amortize completely a loan of $ 100.	The total interest paid over the term of $1. The loan is amortized by regular periodic payments.	The average annual interest rate on a loan that is completely amortized by regular periodic payments.	
	$S = (1+i)^n$	$S\overline{n}| = \dfrac{(1+i)^n - 1}{i}$	$\dfrac{1}{S\overline{n}|} = \dfrac{i}{(1+i)^n - 1}$	$V^n = \dfrac{1}{(1+i)^n}$	$A\overline{n}| = \dfrac{1-V^n}{i}$	$\dfrac{1}{A\overline{n}|} = \dfrac{i}{1-V^n}$				

YEAR										PERIODS
	1.032 500	1.000 000	1.000 000 0000	.968 523	.968 523	1.032 500 0000	103.25	.032 500	3.25	1

YEAR										PERIODS
1	1.032 500	1.000 000	1.000 000 0000	.968 523	.968 523	1.032 500 0000	103.25	.032 500	3.25	1
2	1.066 056	2.032 500	.492 004 9200	.938 037	1.906 560	.524 504 9200	52.46	.049 010	2.45	2
3	1.100 703	3.098 556	.322 730 9493	.908 510	2.815 070	.355 230 9493	35.53	.065 693	2.19	3
4	1.136 476	4.199 259	.238 137 2337	.879 913	3.694 983	.270 637 2337	27.07	.082 549	2.06	4
5	1.173 411	5.335 735	.187 415 5954	.852 216	4.547 199	.219 915 5954	22.00	.099 578	1.99	5
6	1.211 547	6.509 147	.153 629 9692	.825 391	5.372 590	.186 129 9692	18.62	.116 780	1.95	6
7	1.250 923	7.720 694	.129 522 0366	.799 410	6.172 000	.162 022 0366	16.21	.134 154	1.92	7
8	1.291 578	8.971 616	.111 462 6337	.774 247	6.946 247	.143 962 6337	14.40	.151 701	1.90	8
9	1.333 554	10.263 194	.097 435 5546	.749 876	7.696 123	.129 935 5546	13.00	.169 420	1.88	9
10	1.376 894	11.596 748	.086 231 0724	.726 272	8.422 395	.118 731 0724	11.88	.187 311	1.87	10
11	1.421 643	12.973 642	.077 079 3576	.703 411	9.125 806	.109 579 3576	10.96	.205 373	1.87	11
12	1.467 847	14.395 285	.069 467 1878	.681 270	9.807 076	.101 967 1878	10.20	.223 606	1.86	12
13	1.515 552	15.863 132	.063 039 2525	.659 826	10.466 902	.095 539 2525	9.56	.242 010	1.86	13
14	1.564 807	17.378 684	.057 541 7561	.639 056	11.105 958	.090 041 7561	9.01	.260 585	1.86	14
15	1.615 663	18.943 491	.052 788 5797	.618 941	11.724 899	.085 288 5797	8.53	.279 329	1.86	15
16	1.668 173	20.559 155	.048 640 1319	.599 458	12.324 358	.081 140 1319	8.12	.298 242	1.86	16
17	1.722 388	22.227 327	.044 989 6646	.580 589	12.904 947	.077 489 6646	7.75	.317 324	1.87	17
18	1.778 366	23.949 715	.041 754 1496	.562 314	13.467 261	.074 254 1496	7.43	.336 575	1.87	18
19	1.836 163	25.728 081	.038 868 0366	.544 614	14.011 875	.071 368 0366	7.14	.355 993	1.87	19
20	1.895 838	27.564 244	.036 278 8839	.527 471	14.539 346	.068 778 8839	6.88	.375 578	1.88	20
21	1.957 453	29.460 082	.033 944 2371	.510 868	15.050 214	.066 444 2371	6.65	.395 329	1.88	21
22	2.021 070	31.417 534	.031 829 3596	.494 787	15.545 002	.064 329 3596	6.44	.415 246	1.89	22
23	2.086 755	33.438 604	.029 905 5544	.479 213	16.024 215	.062 405 5544	6.25	.435 328	1.89	23
24	2.154 574	35.525 359	.028 148 9063	.464 129	16.488 343	.060 648 9063	6.07	.455 574	1.90	24
25	2.224 598	37.679 933	.026 539 3253	.449 519	16.937 863	.059 039 3253	5.91	.475 983	1.90	25
26	2.296 897	39.904 531	.025 059 8109	.435 370	17.373 233	.057 559 8109	5.76	.496 555	1.91	26
27	2.371 546	42.201 428	.023 695 8805	.421 666	17.794 899	.056 195 8805	5.62	.517 289	1.92	27
28	2.448 622	44.572 975	.022 435 1193	.408 393	18.203 292	.054 935 1193	5.50	.538 183	1.92	28
29	2.528 202	47.021 596	.021 266 8238	.395 538	18.598 830	.053 766 8238	5.38	.559 238	1.93	29
30	2.610 368	49.549 798	.020 181 7169	.383 088	18.981 917	.052 681 7169	5.27	.580 452	1.93	30
31	2.695 205	52.160 167	.019 171 7179	.371 029	19.352 947	.051 671 7179	5.17	.601 823	1.94	31
32	2.782 800	54.855 372	.018 229 7552	.359 350	19.712 297	.050 729 7552	5.08	.623 352	1.95	32
33	2.873 641	57.638 172	.017 349 6135	.348 029	20.060 336	.049 849 6135	4.99	.645 037	1.95	33
34	2.966 621	60.511 412	.016 525 8084	.337 084	20.397 420	.049 025 8084	4.91	.666 877	1.96	34
35	3.063 036	63.478 033	.015 753 4812	.326 473	20.723 893	.048 253 4812	4.83	.688 872	1.97	35
36	3.162 585	66.541 069	.015 028 3128	.316 197	21.040 090	.047 528 3128	4.76	.711 019	1.98	36
37	3.265 369	69.703 654	.014 346 4502	.306 244	21.346 335	.046 846 4502	4.69	.733 319	1.98	37
38	3.371 493	72.969 023	.013 704 4456	.296 604	21.642 939	.046 204 4456	4.63	.755 769	1.99	38
39	3.481 067	76.340 516	.013 099 2041	.287 268	21.930 207	.045 599 2041	4.56	.778 369	2.00	39
40	3.594 201	79.821 583	.012 527 9400	.278 226	22.208 433	.045 027 9400	4.51	.801 118	2.00	40
41	3.711 013	83.415 784	.011 988 1388	.269 468	22.477 901	.044 488 1388	4.45	.824 014	2.01	41
42	3.831 621	87.126 797	.011 477 5251	.260 986	22.738 888	.043 977 5251	4.40	.847 056	2.02	42
43	3.956 149	90.958 418	.010 994 0347	.252 771	22.991 659	.043 494 0347	4.35	.870 244	2.02	43
44	4.084 723	94.914 566	.010 535 7906	.244 815	23.236 473	.043 035 7906	4.31	.893 575	2.03	44
45	4.217 477	98.999 290	.010 101 0826	.237 109	23.473 582	.042 601 0826	4.27	.917 049	2.04	45
46	4.354 545	103.216 767	.009 688 3484	.229 645	23.703 227	.042 188 3484	4.22	.940 664	2.05	46
47	4.496 068	107.571 312	.009 296 1588	.222 417	23.925 644	.041 796 1588	4.18	.964 419	2.05	47
48	4.642 190	112.067 379	.008 923 2032	.215 416	24.141 059	.041 423 2032	4.15	.988 314	2.06	48
49	4.793 061	116.709 569	.008 568 2777	.208 635	24.349 694	.041 068 2777	4.11	1.012 346	2.07	49
50	4.948 835	121.502 630	.008 230 2745	.202 068	24.551 762	.040 730 2745	4.08	1.036 514	2.07	50

ANNUAL COMPOUND INTEREST AND ANNUITY

3.50 % A

	Amount Of 1	Amount Of 1 Per Period	Sinking Fund Payment	Present Worth Of 1	Present Worth of 1 Per Period	Periodic Payment To Amortize 1	Constant Annual Percent	Total Interest	Annual Add On Rate	
	What a single $ 1 deposit grows to in the future. The deposit is made at the beginning of the first period.	What a series of $ 1 deposits grow to in the future. A deposit is made at the end of each period.	The amount to be deposited at the end of each period that grows to $ 1 in the future.	What $ 1 to be paid in the future is worth today. Value today of a single $ 1 payment tomorrow.	What $ 1 to be paid at the end of each period is worth today. Value today of a series of $ 1 payments tomorrow.	The mortgage payment to amortize a loan of $ 1. An annuity certain, payable at the end of each period, worth $ 1 today.	The annual payment, including interest and principal, to amortize completely a loan of $ 100.	The total interest paid over the term on a loan of $1. The loan is amortized by regular periodic payments.	The average annual interest rate on a loan that is completely amortized by regular periodic payments.	
	$S = (1+i)^n$	$S\overline{n}| = \dfrac{(1+i)^n - 1}{i}$	$\dfrac{1}{S\overline{n}|} = \dfrac{i}{(1+i)^n - 1}$	$V^n = \dfrac{1}{(1+i)^n}$	$A\overline{n}| = \dfrac{1-V^n}{i}$	$\dfrac{1}{A\overline{n}|} = \dfrac{i}{1-V^n}$				

YEAR										PERIODS
	1.035 000	1.000 000	1.000 000 0000	.966 184	.966 184	1.035 000 0000	103.50	.035 000	3.50	1

YEAR	Amount Of 1	Amount Of 1 Per Period	Sinking Fund Payment	Present Worth Of 1	Present Worth of 1 Per Period	Periodic Payment To Amortize 1	Constant Annual Percent	Total Interest	Annual Add On Rate	PERIODS
1	1.035 000	1.000 000	1.000 000 0000	.966 184	.966 184	1.035 000 0000	103.50	.035 000	3.50	1
2	1.071 225	2.035 000	.491 400 4914	.933 511	1.899 694	.526 400 4914	52.65	.052 801	2.64	2
3	1.108 718	3.106 225	.321 934 1806	.901 943	2.801 637	.356 934 1806	35.70	.070 803	2.36	3
4	1.147 523	4.214 943	.237 251 1395	.871 442	3.673 079	.272 251 1395	27.23	.089 005	2.23	4
5	1.187 686	5.362 466	.186 481 3732	.841 973	4.515 052	.221 481 3732	22.15	.107 407	2.15	5
6	1.229 255	6.550 152	.152 668 2087	.813 501	5.328 553	.187 668 2087	18.77	.126 009	2.10	6
7	1.272 279	7.779 408	.128 544 4938	.785 991	6.114 544	.163 544 4938	16.36	.144 811	2.07	7
8	1.316 809	9.051 687	.110 476 6465	.759 412	6.873 956	.145 476 6465	14.55	.163 813	2.05	8
9	1.362 897	10.368 496	.096 446 0051	.733 731	7.607 687	.131 446 0051	13.15	.183 014	2.03	9
10	1.410 599	11.731 393	.085 241 3679	.708 919	8.316 605	.120 241 3679	12.03	.202 414	2.02	10
11	1.459 970	13.141 992	.076 091 9658	.684 946	9.001 551	.111 091 9658	11.11	.222 012	2.02	11
12	1.511 069	14.601 962	.068 483 9493	.661 783	9.663 334	.103 483 9493	10.35	.241 807	2.02	12
13	1.563 956	16.113 030	.062 061 5726	.639 404	10.302 738	.097 061 5726	9.71	.261 800	2.01	13
14	1.618 695	17.676 986	.056 570 7287	.617 782	10.920 520	.091 570 7287	9.16	.281 990	2.01	14
15	1.675 349	19.295 681	.051 825 0694	.596 891	11.517 411	.086 825 0694	8.69	.302 376	2.02	15
16	1.733 986	20.971 030	.047 684 8306	.576 706	12.094 117	.082 684 8306	8.27	.322 957	2.02	16
17	1.794 676	22.705 016	.044 043 1317	.557 204	12.651 321	.079 043 1317	7.91	.343 733	2.02	17
18	1.857 489	24.499 691	.040 816 8408	.538 361	13.189 682	.075 816 8408	7.59	.364 703	2.03	18
19	1.922 501	26.357 180	.037 940 3252	.520 156	13.709 837	.072 940 3252	7.30	.385 866	2.03	19
20	1.989 789	28.279 682	.035 361 0768	.502 566	14.212 403	.070 361 0768	7.04	.407 222	2.04	20
21	2.059 431	30.269 471	.033 036 5870	.485 571	14.697 974	.068 036 5870	6.81	.428 768	2.04	21
22	2.131 512	32.328 902	.030 932 0742	.469 151	15.167 125	.065 932 0742	6.60	.450 506	2.05	22
23	2.206 114	34.460 414	.029 018 8042	.453 286	15.620 410	.064 018 8042	6.41	.472 433	2.05	23
24	2.283 328	36.666 528	.027 272 8303	.437 957	16.058 368	.062 272 8303	6.23	.494 548	2.06	24
25	2.363 245	38.949 857	.025 674 0354	.423 147	16.481 515	.060 674 0354	6.07	.516 851	2.07	25
26	2.445 959	41.313 102	.024 205 3963	.408 838	16.890 352	.059 205 3963	5.93	.539 340	2.07	26
27	2.531 567	43.759 060	.022 852 4103	.395 012	17.285 365	.057 852 4103	5.79	.562 015	2.08	27
28	2.620 172	46.290 627	.021 602 6452	.381 654	17.667 019	.056 602 6452	5.67	.584 874	2.09	28
29	2.711 878	48.910 799	.020 445 3825	.368 748	18.035 767	.055 445 3825	5.55	.607 916	2.10	29
30	2.806 794	51.622 677	.019 371 3316	.356 278	18.392 045	.054 371 3316	5.44	.631 140	2.10	30
31	2.905 031	54.429 471	.018 372 3998	.344 230	18.736 276	.053 372 3998	5.34	.654 544	2.11	31
32	3.006 708	57.334 502	.017 441 5048	.332 590	19.068 865	.052 441 5048	5.25	.678 128	2.12	32
33	3.111 942	60.341 210	.016 572 4221	.321 343	19.390 208	.051 572 4221	5.16	.701 890	2.13	33
34	3.220 860	63.453 152	.015 759 6583	.310 476	19.700 684	.050 759 6583	5.08	.725 828	2.13	34
35	3.333 590	66.674 013	.014 998 3473	.299 977	20.000 661	.049 998 3473	5.00	.749 942	2.14	35
36	3.450 266	70.007 603	.014 284 1628	.289 833	20.290 494	.049 284 1628	4.93	.774 230	2.15	36
37	3.571 025	73.457 869	.013 613 2454	.280 032	20.570 525	.048 613 2454	4.87	.798 690	2.16	37
38	3.696 011	77.028 895	.012 982 1414	.270 562	20.841 087	.047 982 1414	4.80	.823 321	2.17	38
39	3.825 372	80.724 906	.012 387 7506	.261 413	21.102 500	.047 387 7506	4.74	.848 122	2.17	39
40	3.959 260	84.550 278	.011 827 2823	.252 572	21.355 072	.046 827 2823	4.69	.873 091	2.18	40
41	4.097 834	88.509 537	.011 298 2174	.244 031	21.599 104	.046 298 2174	4.63	.898 227	2.19	41
42	4.241 258	92.607 371	.010 798 2765	.235 779	21.834 883	.045 798 2765	4.58	.923 528	2.20	42
43	4.389 702	96.848 629	.010 325 3914	.227 806	22.062 689	.045 325 3914	4.54	.948 992	2.21	43
44	4.543 342	101.238 331	.009 877 6816	.220 102	22.282 791	.044 877 6816	4.49	.974 618	2.22	44
45	4.702 359	105.781 673	.009 453 4334	.212 659	22.495 450	.044 453 4334	4.45	1.000 405	2.22	45
46	4.866 941	110.484 031	.009 051 0817	.205 468	22.700 918	.044 051 0817	4.41	1.026 350	2.23	46
47	5.037 284	115.350 973	.008 669 1944	.198 520	22.899 438	.043 669 1944	4.37	1.052 452	2.24	47
48	5.213 589	120.388 257	.008 306 4580	.191 806	23.091 244	.043 306 4580	4.34	1.078 710	2.25	48
49	5.396 065	125.601 846	.007 961 6665	.185 320	23.276 564	.042 961 6665	4.30	1.105 122	2.26	49
50	5.584 927	130.997 910	.007 633 7096	.179 053	23.455 618	.042 633 7096	4.27	1.131 685	2.26	50

Effective Rate is 3.50 %

Annual Percentage Rate is 3.50 %

ANNUAL COMPOUND INTEREST AND ANNUITY

	Amount Of 1	Amount Of 1 Per Period	Sinking Fund Payment	Present Worth Of 1	Present Worth of 1 Per Period	Periodic Payment To Amortize 1	Constant Annual Percent	Total Interest	Annual Add On Rate
	What a single $ 1 deposit grows to in the future. The deposit is made at the beginning of the first period.	What a series of $ 1 deposits grow to in the future. A deposit is made at the end of each period.	The amount to be deposited at the end of each period that grows to $ 1 in the future.	What $ 1 to be paid in the future is worth today. Value today of a single $ 1 payment tomorrow.	What $ 1 to be paid at the end of each period is worth today. Value today of a series of $ 1 payments tomorrow.	The mortgage payment to amortize a loan of $ 1. An annuity certain, payable at the end of each period, worth $ 1 today.	The annual payment, including interest and principal, to amortize completely a loan of $ 100.	The total interest paid over the term on a loan of $1. The loan is amortized by regular periodic payments.	The average annual interest rate on a loan that is completely amortized by regular periodic payments.
	$S = (1+i)^n$	$S\overline{n} = \dfrac{(1+i)^n - 1}{i}$	$\dfrac{1}{S\overline{n}} = \dfrac{i}{(1+i)^n - 1}$	$V^n = \dfrac{1}{(1+i)^n}$	$A\overline{n} = \dfrac{1-V^n}{i}$	$\dfrac{1}{A\overline{n}} = \dfrac{i}{1-V^n}$			

YEAR									PERIODS
	1.037 500	1.000 000	1.000 000 0000	.963 855	.963 855	1.037 500 0000	103.75	.037 500	3.75	1

YEAR										PERIODS
1	1.037 500	1.000 000	1.000 000 0000	.963 855	.963 855	1.037 500 0000	103.75	.037 500	3.75	1
2	1.076 406	2.037 500	.490 797 5460	.929 017	1.892 873	.528 297 5460	52.83	.056 595	2.83	2
3	1.116 771	3.113 906	.321 140 0472	.895 438	2.788 311	.358 640 0472	35.87	.075 920	2.53	3
4	1.158 650	4.230 678	.236 368 7482	.863 073	3.651 384	.273 868 7482	27.39	.095 475	2.39	4
5	1.202 100	5.389 328	.185 551 8856	.831 878	4.483 262	.223 051 8856	22.31	.115 259	2.31	5
6	1.247 179	6.591 428	.151 712 1945	.801 810	5.285 072	.189 212 1945	18.93	.135 273	2.25	6
7	1.293 948	7.838 607	.127 573 6956	.772 829	6.057 900	.165 073 6956	16.51	.155 516	2.22	7
8	1.342 471	9.132 554	.109 498 3915	.744 895	6.802 796	.146 998 3915	14.70	.175 987	2.20	8
9	1.392 813	10.475 025	.095 465 1657	.717 971	7.520 767	.132 965 1657	13.30	.196 687	2.19	9
10	1.445 044	11.867 838	.084 261 3423	.692 020	8.212 787	.121 761 3423	12.18	.217 613	2.18	10
11	1.499 233	13.312 882	.075 115 2131	.667 008	8.879 795	.112 615 2131	11.27	.238 767	2.17	11
12	1.555 454	14.812 116	.067 512 3010	.642 899	9.522 694	.105 012 3010	10.51	.260 148	2.17	12
13	1.613 784	16.367 570	.061 096 4248	.619 662	10.142 356	.098 596 4248	9.86	.281 754	2.17	13
14	1.674 301	17.981 354	.055 613 1655	.597 264	10.739 620	.093 113 1655	9.32	.303 584	2.17	14
15	1.737 087	19.655 654	.050 875 9452	.575 676	11.315 296	.088 375 9452	8.84	.325 639	2.17	15
16	1.802 228	21.392 742	.046 744 8270	.554 869	11.870 165	.084 244 8270	8.43	.347 917	2.17	16
17	1.869 811	23.194 969	.043 112 7968	.534 813	12.404 978	.080 612 7968	8.07	.370 418	2.18	17
18	1.939 929	25.064 781	.039 896 6188	.515 483	12.920 461	.077 396 6188	7.74	.393 139	2.18	18
19	2.012 677	27.004 710	.037 030 5773	.496 851	13.417 312	.074 530 5773	7.46	.416 081	2.19	19
20	2.088 152	29.017 387	.034 462 0973	.478 892	13.896 204	.071 962 0973	7.20	.439 242	2.20	20
21	2.166 458	31.105 539	.032 148 6155	.461 583	14.357 787	.069 648 6155	6.97	.462 621	2.20	21
22	2.247 700	33.271 996	.030 055 3051	.444 899	14.802 686	.067 555 3051	6.76	.486 217	2.21	22
23	2.331 989	35.519 696	.028 153 3940	.428 819	15.231 505	.065 653 3940	6.57	.510 028	2.22	23
24	2.419 438	37.851 685	.026 418 9033	.413 319	15.644 824	.063 918 9033	6.40	.534 054	2.23	24
25	2.510 167	40.271 123	.024 831 6890	.398 380	16.043 204	.062 331 6890	6.24	.558 292	2.23	25
26	2.604 298	42.781 290	.023 374 7042	.383 981	16.427 185	.060 874 7042	6.09	.582 742	2.24	26
27	2.701 960	45.385 588	.022 033 4259	.370 102	16.797 286	.059 533 4259	5.96	.607 403	2.25	27
28	2.803 283	48.087 548	.020 795 4043	.356 725	17.154 011	.058 295 4043	5.83	.632 271	2.26	28
29	2.908 406	50.890 831	.019 649 9051	.343 831	17.497 842	.057 149 9051	5.72	.657 347	2.27	29
30	3.017 471	53.799 237	.018 587 6242	.331 403	17.829 245	.056 087 6242	5.61	.682 629	2.28	30
31	3.130 627	56.816 709	.017 600 4564	.319 425	18.148 670	.055 100 4564	5.52	.708 114	2.28	31
32	3.248 025	59.947 335	.016 681 3087	.307 879	18.456 549	.054 181 3087	5.42	.733 802	2.29	32
33	3.369 826	63.195 360	.015 823 9465	.296 751	18.753 301	.053 323 9465	5.34	.759 690	2.30	33
34	3.496 194	66.565 186	.015 022 8679	.286 025	19.039 326	.052 522 8679	5.26	.785 778	2.31	34
35	3.627 302	70.061 381	.014 273 1986	.275 687	19.315 013	.051 773 1986	5.18	.812 062	2.32	35
36	3.763 326	73.688 682	.013 570 6050	.265 722	19.580 735	.051 070 6050	5.11	.838 542	2.33	36
37	3.904 450	77.452 008	.012 911 2211	.256 118	19.836 853	.050 411 2211	5.05	.865 215	2.34	37
38	4.050 867	81.356 458	.012 291 5872	.246 861	20.083 714	.049 791 5872	4.98	.892 080	2.35	38
39	4.202 775	85.407 326	.011 708 5975	.237 938	20.321 652	.049 208 5975	4.93	.919 135	2.36	39
40	4.360 379	89.610 100	.011 159 4563	.229 338	20.550 990	.048 659 4563	4.87	.946 378	2.37	40
41	4.523 893	93.970 479	.010 641 6399	.221 049	20.772 039	.048 141 6399	4.82	.973 807	2.38	41
42	4.693 539	98.494 372	.010 152 8644	.213 059	20.985 097	.047 652 8644	4.77	1.001 420	2.38	42
43	4.869 547	103.187 911	.009 691 0577	.205 358	21.190 455	.047 191 0577	4.72	1.029 215	2.39	43
44	5.052 155	108.057 458	.009 254 3358	.197 935	21.388 391	.046 754 3358	4.68	1.057 191	2.40	44
45	5.241 610	113.109 612	.008 840 9816	.190 781	21.579 172	.046 340 9816	4.64	1.085 344	2.41	45
46	5.438 171	118.351 223	.008 449 4269	.183 885	21.763 057	.045 949 4269	4.60	1.113 674	2.42	46
47	5.642 102	123.789 394	.008 078 2365	.177 239	21.940 296	.045 578 2365	4.56	1.142 177	2.43	47
48	5.853 681	129.431 496	.007 726 0947	.170 833	22.111 129	.045 226 0947	4.53	1.170 853	2.44	48
49	6.073 194	135.285 177	.007 391 7928	.164 658	22.275 787	.044 891 7928	4.49	1.199 698	2.45	49
50	6.300 939	141.358 371	.007 074 2185	.158 707	22.434 493	.044 574 2185	4.46	1.228 711	2.46	50

Effective Rate is 3.75 %

Annual Percentage Rate is 3.75 %

	Amount Of 1	Amount Of 1 Per Period	Sinking Fund Payment	Present Worth Of 1	Present Worth of 1 Per Period	Periodic Payment To Amortize 1	Constant Annual Percent	Total Interest	Annual Add On Rate	
	What a single $ 1 deposit grows to in the future. The deposit is made at the beginning of the first period.	What a series of $ 1 deposits grow to in the future. A deposit is made at the end of each period.	The amount to be deposited at the end of each period that grows to $ 1 in the future.	What $ 1 to be paid in the future is worth today. Value today of a single $ 1 payment tomorrow.	What $ 1 to be paid at the end of each period is worth today. Value today of a series of $ 1 payments tomorrow.	The mortgage payment to amortize a loan of $ 1. An annuity certain, payable at the end of each period, worth $ 1 today.	The annual payment, including interest and principal, to amortize completely a loan of $ 100.	The total interest paid over the term on a loan of $1. The loan is amortized by regular periodic payments.	The average annual interest rate on a loan that is completely amortized by regular periodic payments.	
	$S = (1+i)^n$	$S\overline{n|} = \dfrac{(1+i)^n - 1}{i}$	$\dfrac{1}{S\overline{n|}} = \dfrac{i}{(1+i)^n - 1}$	$V^n = \dfrac{1}{(1+i)^n}$	$A\overline{n|} = \dfrac{1-V^n}{i}$	$\dfrac{1}{A\overline{n|}} = \dfrac{i}{1-V^n}$				

YEAR										PERIODS
	1.040 000	1.000 000	1.000 000 0000	.961 538	.961 538	1.040 000 0000	104.00	.040 000	4.00	1
1	1.040 000	1.000 000	1.000 000 0000	.961 538	.961 538	1.040 000 0000	104.00	.040 000	4.00	1
2	1.081 600	2.040 000	.490 196 0784	.924 556	1.886 095	.530 196 0784	53.02	.060 392	3.02	2
3	1.124 864	3.121 600	.320 348 5392	.888 996	2.775 091	.360 348 5392	36.04	.081 046	2.70	3
4	1.169 859	4.246 464	.235 490 0454	.854 804	3.629 895	.275 490 0454	27.55	.101 960	2.55	4
5	1.216 653	5.416 323	.184 627 1135	.821 927	4.451 822	.224 627 1135	22.47	.123 136	2.46	5
6	1.265 319	6.632 975	.150 761 9025	.790 315	5.242 137	.190 761 9025	19.08	.144 571	2.41	6
7	1.315 932	7.898 294	.126 609 6120	.759 918	6.002 055	.166 609 6120	16.67	.166 267	2.38	7
8	1.368 569	9.214 226	.108 527 8320	.730 690	6.732 745	.148 527 8320	14.86	.188 223	2.35	8
9	1.423 312	10.582 795	.094 492 9927	.702 587	7.435 332	.134 492 9927	13.45	.210 437	2.34	9
10	1.480 244	12.006 107	.083 290 9443	.675 564	8.110 896	.123 290 9443	12.33	.232 909	2.33	10
11	1.539 454	13.486 351	.074 149 0393	.649 581	8.760 477	.114 149 0393	11.42	.255 639	2.32	11
12	1.601 032	15.025 805	.066 552 1727	.624 597	9.385 074	.106 552 1727	10.66	.278 626	2.32	12
13	1.665 074	16.626 838	.060 143 7278	.600 574	9.985 648	.100 143 7278	10.02	.301 868	2.32	13
14	1.731 676	18.291 911	.054 668 9731	.577 475	10.563 123	.094 668 9731	9.47	.325 366	2.32	14
15	1.800 944	20.023 588	.049 941 1004	.555 265	11.118 387	.089 941 1004	9.00	.349 117	2.33	15
16	1.872 981	21.824 531	.045 819 9992	.533 908	11.652 296	.085 819 9992	8.59	.373 120	2.33	16
17	1.947 900	23.697 512	.042 198 5221	.513 373	12.165 669	.082 198 5221	8.22	.397 375	2.34	17
18	2.025 817	25.645 413	.038 993 3281	.493 628	12.659 297	.078 993 3281	7.90	.421 880	2.34	18
19	2.106 849	27.671 229	.036 138 6184	.474 642	13.133 939	.076 138 6184	7.62	.446 634	2.35	19
20	2.191 123	29.778 079	.033 581 7503	.456 387	13.590 326	.073 581 7503	7.36	.471 635	2.36	20
21	2.278 768	31.969 202	.031 280 1054	.438 834	14.029 160	.071 280 1054	7.13	.496 882	2.37	21
22	2.369 919	34.247 970	.029 198 8111	.421 955	14.451 115	.069 198 8111	6.92	.522 374	2.37	22
23	2.464 716	36.617 889	.027 309 0568	.405 726	14.856 842	.067 309 0568	6.74	.548 108	2.38	23
24	2.563 304	39.082 604	.025 586 8313	.390 121	15.246 963	.065 586 8313	6.56	.574 084	2.39	24
25	2.665 836	41.645 908	.024 011 9628	.375 117	15.622 080	.064 011 9628	6.41	.600 299	2.40	25
26	2.772 470	44.311 745	.022 567 3805	.360 689	15.982 769	.062 567 3805	6.26	.626 752	2.41	26
27	2.883 369	47.084 214	.021 238 5406	.346 817	16.329 586	.061 238 5406	6.13	.653 441	2.42	27
28	2.998 703	49.967 583	.020 012 9752	.333 477	16.663 063	.060 012 9752	6.01	.680 363	2.43	28
29	3.118 651	52.966 286	.018 879 9342	.320 651	16.983 715	.058 879 9342	5.89	.707 518	2.44	29
30	3.243 398	56.084 938	.017 830 0991	.308 319	17.292 033	.057 830 0991	5.79	.734 903	2.45	30
31	3.373 133	59.328 335	.016 855 3524	.296 460	17.588 494	.056 855 3524	5.69	.762 516	2.46	31
32	3.508 059	62.701 469	.015 948 5897	.285 058	17.873 551	.055 948 5897	5.60	.790 355	2.47	32
33	3.648 381	66.209 527	.015 103 5665	.274 094	18.147 646	.055 103 5665	5.52	.818 418	2.48	33
34	3.794 316	69.857 909	.014 314 7715	.263 552	18.411 198	.054 314 7715	5.44	.846 702	2.49	34
35	3.946 089	73.652 225	.013 577 3224	.253 415	18.664 613	.053 577 3224	5.36	.875 206	2.50	35
36	4.103 933	77.598 314	.012 886 8780	.243 669	18.908 282	.052 886 8780	5.29	.903 928	2.51	36
37	4.268 090	81.702 246	.012 239 5655	.234 297	19.142 579	.052 239 5655	5.23	.932 864	2.52	37
38	4.438 813	85.970 336	.011 631 9191	.225 285	19.367 864	.051 631 9191	5.17	.962 013	2.53	38
39	4.616 366	90.409 150	.011 060 8274	.216 621	19.584 485	.051 060 8274	5.11	.991 372	2.54	39
40	4.801 021	95.025 516	.010 523 4893	.208 289	19.792 774	.050 523 4893	5.06	1.020 940	2.55	40
41	4.993 061	99.826 536	.010 017 3765	.200 278	19.993 052	.050 017 3765	5.01	1.050 712	2.56	41
42	5.192 784	104.819 598	.009 540 2007	.192 575	20.185 627	.049 540 2007	4.96	1.080 688	2.57	42
43	5.400 495	110.012 382	.009 089 8859	.185 168	20.370 795	.049 089 8859	4.91	1.110 865	2.58	43
44	5.616 515	115.412 877	.008 664 5444	.178 046	20.548 841	.048 664 5444	4.87	1.141 240	2.59	44
45	5.841 176	121.029 392	.008 262 4558	.171 198	20.720 040	.048 262 4558	4.83	1.171 811	2.60	45
46	6.074 823	126.870 568	.007 882 0488	.164 614	20.884 654	.047 882 0488	4.79	1.202 574	2.61	46
47	6.317 816	132.945 390	.007 521 8855	.158 283	21.042 936	.047 521 8855	4.76	1.233 529	2.62	47
48	6.570 528	139.263 206	.007 180 6476	.152 195	21.195 131	.047 180 6476	4.72	1.264 671	2.63	48
49	6.833 349	145.833 734	.006 857 1240	.146 341	21.341 472	.046 857 1240	4.69	1.295 999	2.64	49
50	7.106 683	152.667 084	.006 550 2004	.140 713	21.482 185	.046 550 2004	4.66	1.327 510	2.66	50

Effective Rate is 4.00 %   Annual Percentage Rate is 4.00 %

Amount Of 1	Amount Of 1 Per Period	Sinking Fund Payment	Present Worth Of 1	Present Worth of 1 Per Period	Periodic Payment To Amortize 1	Constant Annual Percent	Total Interest	Annual Add On Rate	
What a single $ 1 deposit grows to in the future. The deposit is made at the beginning of the first period.	What a series of $ 1 deposits grow to in the future. A deposit is made at the end of each period.	The amount to be deposited at the end of each period that grows to $ 1 in the future.	What $ 1 to be paid in the future is worth today. Value today of a single $ 1 payment tomorrow.	What $ 1 to be paid at the end of each period is worth today. Value today of a series of $ 1 payments tomorrow.	The mortgage payment to amortize a loan of $ 1. An annuity certain, payable at the end of each period, worth $ 1 today.	The annual payment, including interest and principal, to amortize completely a loan of $ 100.	The total interest paid over the term on a loan of $1. The loan is amortized by regular periodic payments.	The average annual interest rate on a loan that is completely amortized by regular periodic payments.	
$S = (1+i)^n$	$S\overline{n}| = \dfrac{(1+i)^n - 1}{i}$	$\dfrac{1}{S\overline{n}|} = \dfrac{i}{(1+i)^n - 1}$	$V^n = \dfrac{1}{(1+i)^n}$	$A\overline{n}| = \dfrac{1-V^n}{i}$	$\dfrac{1}{A\overline{n}|} = \dfrac{i}{1-V^n}$				PERIODS

YEAR										
	1.042 500	1.000 000	1.000 000 0000	.959 233	.959 233	1.042 500 0000	104.25	.042 500	4.25	1

YEAR	Amount Of 1	Amount Of 1 Per Period	Sinking Fund Payment	Present Worth Of 1	Present Worth of 1 Per Period	Periodic Payment To Amortize 1	Constant Annual Percent	Total Interest	Annual Add On Rate	PERIODS
1	1.042 500	1.000 000	1.000 000 0000	.959 233	.959 233	1.042 500 0000	104.25	.042 500	4.25	1
2	1.086 806	2.042 500	.489 596 0832	.920 127	1.879 360	.532 096 0832	53.21	.064 192	3.21	2
3	1.132 996	3.129 306	.319 559 6468	.882 616	2.761 976	.362 059 6468	36.21	.086 179	2.87	3
4	1.181 148	4.262 302	.234 615 0167	.846 634	3.608 610	.277 115 0167	27.72	.108 460	2.71	4
5	1.231 347	5.443 450	.183 707 0379	.812 119	4.420 729	.226 207 0379	22.63	.131 035	2.62	5
6	1.283 679	6.674 796	.149 817 3083	.779 011	5.199 740	.192 317 3083	19.24	.153 904	2.57	6
7	1.338 235	7.958 475	.125 652 2129	.747 253	5.946 993	.168 152 2129	16.82	.177 066	2.53	7
8	1.395 110	9.296 710	.107 564 9316	.716 789	6.663 782	.150 064 9316	15.01	.200 519	2.51	8
9	1.454 402	10.691 820	.093 529 4423	.687 568	7.351 350	.136 029 4423	13.61	.224 265	2.49	9
10	1.516 214	12.146 223	.082 330 1217	.659 537	8.010 887	.124 830 1217	12.49	.248 301	2.48	10
11	1.580 654	13.662 437	.073 193 3829	.632 650	8.643 537	.115 693 3829	11.57	.272 627	2.48	11
12	1.647 831	15.243 091	.065 603 4928	.606 858	9.250 395	.108 103 4928	10.82	.297 242	2.48	12
13	1.717 864	16.890 922	.059 203 3987	.582 118	9.832 513	.101 703 3987	10.18	.322 144	2.48	13
14	1.790 873	18.608 786	.053 738 0557	.558 387	10.390 900	.096 238 0557	9.63	.347 333	2.48	14
15	1.866 986	20.399 660	.049 020 4253	.535 623	10.926 523	.091 520 4253	9.16	.372 806	2.49	15
16	1.946 332	22.266 645	.044 910 2226	.513 787	11.440 309	.087 410 2226	8.75	.398 564	2.49	16
17	2.029 052	24.212 978	.041 300 1659	.492 841	11.933 151	.083 800 1659	8.39	.424 603	2.50	17
18	2.115 286	26.242 029	.038 106 8090	.472 749	12.405 900	.080 606 8090	8.07	.450 923	2.51	18
19	2.205 186	28.357 316	.035 264 2688	.453 477	12.859 376	.077 764 2688	7.78	.477 521	2.51	19
20	2.298 906	30.562 501	.032 719 8348	.434 989	13.294 366	.075 219 8348	7.53	.504 397	2.52	20
21	2.396 610	32.861 408	.030 430 8326	.417 256	13.711 622	.072 930 8326	7.30	.531 547	2.53	21
22	2.498 466	35.258 018	.028 362 3433	.400 246	14.111 868	.070 862 3433	7.09	.558 972	2.54	22
23	2.604 651	37.756 483	.026 485 5175	.383 929	14.495 796	.068 985 5175	6.90	.586 667	2.55	23
24	2.715 348	40.361 134	.024 776 3108	.368 277	14.864 073	.067 276 3108	6.73	.614 631	2.56	24
25	2.830 750	43.076 482	.023 214 5234	.353 263	15.217 336	.065 714 5234	6.58	.642 863	2.57	25
26	2.951 057	45.907 233	.021 783 0600	.338 862	15.556 198	.064 283 0600	6.43	.671 360	2.58	26
27	3.076 477	48.858 290	.020 467 3557	.325 047	15.881 245	.062 967 3557	6.30	.700 119	2.59	27
28	3.207 228	51.934 767	.019 254 9240	.311 796	16.193 041	.061 754 9240	6.18	.729 138	2.60	28
29	3.343 535	55.141 995	.018 134 9986	.299 085	16.492 125	.060 634 9986	6.07	.758 415	2.62	29
30	3.485 635	58.485 530	.017 098 2464	.286 892	16.779 017	.059 598 2464	5.96	.787 947	2.63	30
31	3.633 775	61.971 165	.016 136 5371	.275 196	17.054 213	.058 636 5371	5.87	.817 733	2.64	31
32	3.788 210	65.604 939	.015 242 7548	.263 977	17.318 190	.057 742 7548	5.78	.847 768	2.65	32
33	3.949 209	69.393 149	.014 410 6445	.253 215	17.571 405	.056 910 6445	5.70	.878 051	2.66	33
34	4.117 050	73.342 358	.013 634 6857	.242 892	17.814 298	.056 134 6857	5.62	.908 579	2.67	34
35	4.292 025	77.459 408	.012 909 9876	.232 990	18.047 288	.055 409 9876	5.55	.939 350	2.68	35
36	4.474 436	81.751 433	.012 232 2015	.223 492	18.270 780	.054 732 2015	5.48	.970 359	2.70	36
37	4.664 599	86.225 869	.011 597 4476	.214 381	18.485 160	.054 097 4476	5.41	1.001 606	2.71	37
38	4.862 845	90.890 468	.011 002 2538	.205 641	18.690 801	.053 502 2538	5.36	1.033 086	2.72	38
39	5.069 516	95.753 313	.010 443 5028	.197 257	18.888 059	.052 943 5028	5.30	1.064 797	2.73	39
40	5.284 970	100.822 829	.009 918 3886	.189 216	19.077 275	.052 418 3886	5.25	1.096 736	2.74	40
41	5.509 581	106.107 799	.009 424 3779	.181 502	19.258 777	.051 924 3779	5.20	1.128 900	2.75	41
42	5.743 739	111.617 381	.008 959 1782	.174 103	19.432 879	.051 459 1782	5.15	1.161 285	2.77	42
43	5.987 848	117.361 119	.008 520 7095	.167 005	19.599 884	.051 020 7095	5.11	1.193 891	2.78	43
44	6.242 331	123.348 967	.008 107 0805	.160 197	19.760 081	.050 607 0805	5.07	1.226 712	2.79	44
45	6.507 630	129.591 298	.007 716 5675	.153 666	19.913 747	.050 216 5675	5.03	1.259 746	2.80	45
46	6.784 204	136.098 928	.007 347 5964	.147 401	20.061 148	.049 847 5964	4.99	1.292 989	2.81	46
47	7.072 533	142.883 133	.006 998 7267	.141 392	20.202 540	.049 498 7267	4.95	1.326 440	2.82	47
48	7.373 116	149.955 666	.006 668 6377	.135 628	20.338 168	.049 168 6377	4.92	1.360 095	2.83	48
49	7.686 473	157.328 782	.006 356 1161	.130 099	20.468 266	.048 856 1161	4.89	1.393 950	2.84	49
50	8.013 148	165.015 255	.006 060 0458	.124 795	20.593 061	.048 560 0458	4.86	1.428 002	2.86	50

	Amount Of 1	Amount Of 1 Per Period	Sinking Fund Payment	Present Worth Of 1	Present Worth of 1 Per Period	Periodic Payment To Amortize 1	Constant Annual Percent	Total Interest	Annual Add On Rate	
	What a single $ 1 deposit grows to in the future. The deposit is made at the beginning of the first period.	What a series of $ 1 deposits grow to in the future. A deposit is made at the end of each period.	The amount to be deposited at the end of each period that grows to $ 1 in the future.	What $ 1 to be paid in the future is worth today. Value today of a single $ 1 payment tomorrow.	What $ 1 to be paid at the end of each period is worth today. Value today of a series of $ 1 payments tomorrow.	The mortgage payment to amortize a loan of $ 1. An annuity certain, payable at the end of each period, worth $ 1 today.	The annual payment, including interest and principal, to amortize completely a loan of $ 100.	The total interest paid over the term on a loan that is amortized by regular periodic payments.	The average annual interest rate on a loan that is completely amortized by regular periodic payments.	
	$S = (1+i)^n$	$S\overline{n}| = \dfrac{(1+i)^n - 1}{i}$	$\dfrac{1}{S\overline{n}|} = \dfrac{i}{(1+i)^n - 1}$	$V^n = \dfrac{1}{(1+i)^n}$	$A\overline{n}| = \dfrac{1 - V^n}{i}$	$\dfrac{1}{A\overline{n}|} = \dfrac{i}{1 - V^n}$				

YEAR										PERIODS
	1.045 000	1.000 000	1.000 000 0000	.956 938	.956 938	1.045 000 0000	104.50	.045 000	4.50	1
1	1.045 000	1.000 000	1.000 000 0000	.956 938	.956 938	1.045 000 0000	104.50	.045 000	4.50	1
2	1.092 025	2.045 000	.488 997 5550	.915 730	1.872 668	.533 997 5550	53.40	.067 995	3.40	2
3	1.141 166	3.137 025	.318 773 3601	.876 297	2.748 964	.363 773 3601	36.38	.091 320	3.04	3
4	1.192 519	4.278 191	.233 743 6479	.838 561	3.587 526	.278 743 6479	27.88	.114 975	2.87	4
5	1.246 182	5.470 710	.182 791 6395	.802 451	4.389 977	.227 791 6395	22.78	.138 958	2.78	5
6	1.302 260	6.716 892	.148 878 3875	.767 896	5.157 872	.193 878 3875	19.39	.163 270	2.72	6
7	1.360 862	8.019 152	.124 701 4680	.734 828	5.892 701	.169 701 4680	16.98	.187 910	2.68	7
8	1.422 101	9.380 014	.106 609 6533	.703 185	6.595 886	.151 609 6533	15.17	.212 877	2.66	8
9	1.486 095	10.802 114	.092 574 4700	.672 904	7.268 790	.137 574 4700	13.76	.238 170	2.65	9
10	1.552 969	12.288 209	.081 378 8217	.643 928	7.912 718	.126 378 8217	12.64	.263 788	2.64	10
11	1.622 853	13.841 179	.072 248 1817	.616 199	8.528 917	.117 248 1817	11.73	.289 730	2.63	11
12	1.695 881	15.464 032	.064 666 1886	.589 664	9.118 581	.109 666 1886	10.97	.315 994	2.63	12
13	1.772 196	17.159 913	.058 275 3528	.564 272	9.682 852	.103 275 3528	10.33	.342 580	2.64	13
14	1.851 945	18.932 109	.052 820 3160	.539 973	10.222 825	.097 820 3160	9.79	.369 484	2.64	14
15	1.935 282	20.784 054	.048 113 8081	.516 720	10.739 546	.093 113 8081	9.32	.396 707	2.64	15
16	2.022 370	22.719 337	.044 015 3694	.494 469	11.234 015	.089 015 3694	8.91	.424 246	2.65	16
17	2.113 377	24.741 707	.040 417 5833	.473 176	11.707 191	.085 417 5833	8.55	.452 099	2.66	17
18	2.208 479	26.855 084	.037 236 8975	.452 800	12.159 992	.082 236 8975	8.23	.480 264	2.67	18
19	2.307 860	29.063 562	.034 407 3443	.433 302	12.593 294	.079 407 3443	7.95	.508 740	2.68	19
20	2.411 714	31.371 443	.031 876 1443	.414 643	13.007 936	.076 876 1443	7.69	.537 523	2.69	20
21	2.520 241	33.783 137	.029 600 5669	.396 787	13.404 724	.074 600 5669	7.47	.566 612	2.70	21
22	2.633 652	36.303 378	.027 545 6461	.379 701	13.784 425	.072 545 6461	7.26	.596 004	2.71	22
23	2.752 166	38.937 030	.025 682 4930	.363 350	14.147 775	.070 682 4930	7.07	.625 697	2.72	23
24	2.876 014	41.689 196	.023 987 0299	.347 703	14.495 478	.068 987 0299	6.90	.655 689	2.73	24
25	3.005 434	44.565 210	.022 439 0280	.332 731	14.828 209	.067 439 0280	6.75	.685 976	2.74	25
26	3.140 679	47.570 645	.021 021 3674	.318 402	15.146 611	.066 021 3674	6.61	.716 556	2.76	26
27	3.282 010	50.711 324	.019 719 4616	.304 691	15.451 303	.064 719 4616	6.48	.747 425	2.77	27
28	3.429 700	53.993 333	.018 520 8051	.291 571	15.742 874	.063 520 8051	6.36	.778 583	2.78	28
29	3.584 036	57.423 033	.017 414 6147	.279 015	16.021 889	.062 414 6147	6.25	.810 024	2.79	29
30	3.745 318	61.007 070	.016 391 5429	.267 000	16.288 889	.061 391 5429	6.14	.841 746	2.81	30
31	3.913 857	64.752 388	.015 443 4459	.255 502	16.544 391	.060 443 4459	6.05	.873 747	2.82	31
32	4.089 981	68.666 245	.014 563 1962	.244 500	16.788 891	.059 563 1962	5.96	.906 022	2.83	32
33	4.274 030	72.756 226	.013 744 5281	.233 971	17.022 862	.058 744 5281	5.88	.938 569	2.84	33
34	4.466 362	77.030 256	.012 981 9119	.223 896	17.246 758	.057 981 9119	5.80	.971 385	2.86	34
35	4.667 348	81.496 618	.012 270 4478	.214 254	17.461 012	.057 270 4478	5.73	1.004 466	2.87	35
36	4.877 378	86.163 966	.011 605 7796	.205 028	17.666 041	.056 605 7796	5.67	1.037 808	2.88	36
37	5.096 860	91.041 344	.010 984 0206	.196 199	17.862 240	.055 984 0206	5.60	1.071 409	2.90	37
38	5.326 219	96.138 205	.010 401 6920	.187 750	18.049 990	.055 401 6920	5.55	1.105 264	2.91	38
39	5.565 899	101.464 424	.009 855 6712	.179 665	18.229 656	.054 855 6712	5.49	1.139 371	2.92	39
40	5.816 365	107.030 323	.009 343 1466	.171 929	18.401 584	.054 343 1466	5.44	1.173 726	2.93	40
41	6.078 101	112.846 688	.008 861 5804	.164 525	18.566 109	.053 861 5804	5.39	1.208 325	2.95	41
42	6.351 615	118.924 789	.008 408 6759	.157 440	18.723 550	.053 408 6759	5.35	1.243 164	2.96	42
43	6.637 438	125.276 404	.007 982 3492	.150 661	18.874 210	.052 982 3492	5.30	1.278 241	2.97	43
44	6.936 123	131.913 842	.007 580 7056	.144 173	19.018 383	.052 580 7056	5.26	1.313 551	2.99	44
45	7.248 248	138.849 965	.007 202 0184	.137 964	19.156 347	.052 202 0184	5.23	1.349 091	3.00	45
46	7.574 420	146.098 214	.006 844 7107	.132 023	19.288 371	.051 844 7107	5.19	1.384 857	3.01	46
47	7.915 268	153.672 633	.006 507 3395	.126 338	19.414 709	.051 507 3395	5.16	1.420 845	3.02	47
48	8.271 456	161.587 902	.006 188 5821	.120 898	19.535 607	.051 188 5821	5.12	1.457 052	3.04	48
49	8.643 671	169.859 357	.005 887 2235	.115 692	19.651 298	.050 887 2235	5.09	1.493 474	3.05	49
50	9.032 636	178.503 028	.005 602 1459	.110 710	19.762 008	.050 602 1459	5.07	1.530 107	3.06	50

ANNUAL COMPOUND INTEREST AND ANNUITY

4.75 % A

	Amount Of 1	Amount Of 1 Per Period	Sinking Fund Payment	Present Worth Of 1	Present Worth of 1 Per Period	Periodic Payment To Amortize 1	Constant Annual Percent	Total Interest	Annual Add On Rate	
	What a single $ 1 deposit grows to in the future. The deposit is made at the beginning of the first period.	What a series of $ 1 deposits grow to in the future. A deposit is made at the end of each period.	The amount to be deposited at the end of each period that grows to $ 1 in the future.	What $ 1 to be paid in the future is worth today. Value today of a single $ 1 payment tomorrow.	What $ 1 to be paid at the end of each period is worth today. Value today of a series of $ 1 payments tomorrow.	The mortgage payment to amortize a loan of $ 1. An annuity certain, payable at the end of each period, worth $ 1 today.	The annual payment, including interest and principal, to amortize completely a loan of $ 100.	The total interest paid over the term on a loan of $1. The loan is amortized by regular periodic payments.	The average annual interest rate on a loan that is completely amortized by regular periodic payments.	
	$S = (1+i)^n$	$S\overline{n}| = \frac{(1+i)^n - 1}{i}$	$\frac{1}{S\overline{n}|} = \frac{i}{(1+i)^n - 1}$	$V^n = \frac{1}{(1+i)^n}$	$A\overline{n}| = \frac{1-V^n}{i}$	$\frac{1}{A\overline{n}|} = \frac{i}{1-V^n}$				

YEAR | | | | | | | | | **PERIODS** |

	1.047 500	1.000 000	1.000 000 0000	.954 654	.954 654	1.047 500 0000	104.75	.047 500	4.75	1

YEAR										PERIODS
1	1.047 500	1.000 000	1.000 000 0000	.954 654	.954 654	1.047 500 0000	104.75	.047 500	4.75	1
2	1.097 256	2.047 500	.488 400 4884	.911 364	1.866 018	.535 900 4884	53.60	.071 801	3.59	2
3	1.149 376	3.144 756	.317 989 6693	.870 037	2.736 055	.365 489 6693	36.55	.096 469	3.22	3
4	1.203 971	4.294 132	.232 875 9246	.830 585	3.566 640	.280 375 9246	28.04	.121 504	3.04	4
5	1.261 160	5.498 103	.181 880 8993	.792 921	4.359 561	.229 380 8993	22.94	.146 905	2.94	5
6	1.321 065	6.759 263	.147 945 1156	.756 965	5.116 526	.195 445 1156	19.55	.172 671	2.88	6
7	1.383 816	8.080 328	.123 757 3467	.722 640	5.839 166	.171 257 3467	17.13	.198 801	2.84	7
8	1.449 547	9.464 144	.105 661 9598	.689 871	6.529 036	.153 161 9598	15.32	.225 296	2.82	8
9	1.518 400	10.913 691	.091 628 0310	.658 588	7.187 624	.139 128 0310	13.92	.252 152	2.80	9
10	1.590 524	12.432 091	.080 436 9909	.628 723	7.816 348	.127 936 9909	12.80	.279 370	2.79	10
11	1.666 074	14.022 615	.071 313 3726	.600 213	8.416 561	.118 813 3726	11.89	.306 947	2.79	11
12	1.745 213	15.688 690	.063 740 1861	.572 996	8.989 557	.111 240 1861	11.13	.334 882	2.79	12
13	1.828 110	17.433 902	.057 359 5042	.547 013	9.536 570	.104 859 5042	10.49	.363 174	2.79	13
14	1.914 946	19.262 013	.051 915 6544	.522 208	10.058 778	.099 415 6544	9.95	.391 819	2.80	14
15	2.005 906	21.176 958	.047 221 1344	.498 528	10.557 306	.094 721 1344	9.48	.420 817	2.81	15
16	2.101 186	23.182 864	.043 135 3090	.475 922	11.033 228	.090 635 3090	9.07	.450 165	2.81	16
17	2.200 992	25.284 050	.039 550 6258	.454 341	11.487 568	.087 050 6258	8.71	.479 861	2.82	17
18	2.305 540	27.485 042	.036 383 4258	.433 738	11.921 306	.083 883 4258	8.39	.509 902	2.83	18
19	2.415 053	29.790 582	.033 567 6559	.414 070	12.335 376	.081 067 6559	8.11	.540 285	2.84	19
20	2.529 768	32.205 635	.031 050 4673	.395 293	12.730 669	.078 550 4673	7.86	.571 009	2.86	20
21	2.649 932	34.735 402	.028 789 0722	.377 368	13.108 037	.076 289 0722	7.63	.602 071	2.87	21
22	2.775 803	37.385 334	.026 748 4572	.360 256	13.468 293	.074 248 4572	7.43	.633 466	2.88	22
23	2.907 654	40.161 137	.024 899 6934	.343 920	13.812 213	.072 399 6934	7.24	.665 193	2.89	23
24	3.045 768	43.068 791	.023 218 6689	.328 324	14.140 538	.070 718 6689	7.08	.697 248	2.91	24
25	3.190 442	46.114 559	.021 685 1257	.313 436	14.453 974	.069 185 1257	6.92	.729 628	2.92	25
26	3.341 988	49.305 000	.020 281 9186	.299 223	14.753 197	.067 781 9186	6.78	.762 330	2.93	26
27	3.500 732	52.646 988	.018 994 4391	.285 655	15.038 852	.066 494 4391	6.65	.795 350	2.95	27
28	3.667 017	56.147 720	.017 810 1623	.272 701	15.311 553	.065 310 1623	6.54	.828 685	2.96	28
29	3.841 200	59.814 736	.016 718 2882	.260 335	15.571 888	.064 218 2882	6.43	.862 330	2.97	29
30	4.023 657	63.655 936	.015 709 4539	.248 530	15.820 418	.063 209 4539	6.33	.896 284	2.99	30
31	4.214 781	67.679 593	.014 775 5025	.237 260	16.057 679	.062 275 5025	6.23	.930 541	3.00	31
32	4.414 983	71.894 374	.013 909 2942	.226 501	16.284 180	.061 409 2942	6.15	.965 097	3.02	32
33	4.624 694	76.309 357	.013 104 5529	.216 231	16.500 410	.060 604 5529	6.07	.999 950	3.03	33
34	4.844 367	80.934 051	.012 355 7388	.206 425	16.706 836	.059 855 7388	5.99	1.035 095	3.04	34
35	5.074 475	85.778 419	.011 657 9440	.197 065	16.903 901	.059 157 9440	5.92	1.070 528	3.06	35
36	5.315 512	90.852 894	.011 006 8041	.188 129	17.092 029	.058 506 8041	5.86	1.106 245	3.07	36
37	5.567 999	96.168 406	.010 398 4255	.179 598	17.271 627	.057 898 4255	5.79	1.142 242	3.09	37
38	5.832 479	101.736 405	.009 829 3231	.171 454	17.443 081	.057 329 3231	5.74	1.178 514	3.10	38
39	6.109 522	107.568 884	.009 296 3686	.163 679	17.606 759	.056 796 3686	5.68	1.215 058	3.12	39
40	6.399 724	113.678 406	.008 796 7454	.156 257	17.763 016	.056 296 7454	5.63	1.251 870	3.13	40
41	6.703 711	120.078 131	.008 327 9111	.149 171	17.912 187	.055 827 9111	5.59	1.288 944	3.14	41
42	7.022 137	126.781 842	.007 887 5648	.142 407	18.054 594	.055 387 5648	5.54	1.326 278	3.16	42
43	7.355 689	133.803 980	.007 473 6193	.135 949	18.190 543	.054 973 6193	5.50	1.363 866	3.17	43
44	7.705 084	141.159 669	.007 084 1765	.129 784	18.320 328	.054 584 1765	5.46	1.401 704	3.19	44
45	8.071 076	148.864 753	.006 717 5069	.123 899	18.444 227	.054 217 5069	5.43	1.439 788	3.20	45
46	8.454 452	156.935 829	.006 372 0312	.118 281	18.562 508	.053 872 0312	5.39	1.478 113	3.21	46
47	8.856 038	165.390 280	.006 046 3045	.112 917	18.675 425	.053 546 3045	5.36	1.516 676	3.23	47
48	9.276 700	174.246 319	.005 739 0022	.107 797	18.783 222	.053 239 0022	5.33	1.555 472	3.24	48
49	9.717 343	183.523 019	.005 448 9078	.102 909	18.886 131	.052 948 9078	5.30	1.594 496	3.25	49
50	10.178 917	193.240 362	.005 174 9023	.098 242	18.984 373	.052 674 9023	5.27	1.633 745	3.27	50

Effective Rate is 4.75 %

Annual Percentage Rate is 4.75 %

ANNUAL COMPOUND INTEREST AND ANNUITY

5.00 % A

Amount Of 1	Amount Of 1 Per Period	Sinking Fund Payment	Present Worth Of 1	Present Worth of 1 Per Period	Periodic Payment To Amortize 1	Constant Annual Percent	Total Interest	Annual Add On Rate	
What a single $ 1 deposit grows to in the future. The deposit is made at the beginning of the first period.	What a series of $ 1 deposits grow to in the future. A deposit is made at the end of each period.	The amount to be deposited at the end of each period that grows to $ 1 in the future.	What $ 1 to be paid in the future is worth today. Value today of a single $ 1 payment tomorrow.	What $ 1 to be paid at the end of each period is worth today. Value today of a series of $ 1 payments tomorrow.	The mortgage payment to amortize a loan of $ 1. An annuity certain, payable at the end of each period, worth $ 1 today.	The annual payment, including interest and principal, to amortize completely a loan of $ 100.	The total interest paid over the term on a loan that is amortized by regular periodic payments.	The average annual interest rate on a loan that is completely amortized by regular periodic payments.	
$S = (1+i)^n$	$S\overline{n} = \dfrac{(1+i)^n - 1}{i}$	$\dfrac{1}{S\overline{n}} = \dfrac{i}{(1+i)^n - 1}$	$V^n = \dfrac{1}{(1+i)^n}$	$A\overline{n} = \dfrac{1 - V^n}{i}$	$\dfrac{1}{A\overline{n}} = \dfrac{i}{1 - V^n}$				

YEAR									PERIODS
	1.050 000	1.000 000	1.000 000 0000	.952 381	.952 381	1.050 000 0000	105.00	.050 000	5.00 1

YEAR	Amount Of 1	Amount Of 1 Per Period	Sinking Fund Payment	Present Worth Of 1	Present Worth of 1 Per Period	Periodic Payment To Amortize 1	Constant Annual Percent	Total Interest	Annual Add On Rate	PERIODS
1	1.050 000	1.000 000	1.000 000 0000	.952 381	.952 381	1.050 000 0000	105.00	.050 000	5.00	1
2	1.102 500	2.050 000	.487 804 8780	.907 029	1.859 410	.537 804 8780	53.79	.075 610	3.78	2
3	1.157 625	3.152 500	.317 208 5646	.863 838	2.723 248	.367 208 5646	36.73	.101 626	3.39	3
4	1.215 506	4.310 125	.232 011 8326	.822 702	3.545 951	.282 011 8326	28.21	.128 047	3.20	4
5	1.276 282	5.525 631	.180 974 7981	.783 526	4.329 477	.230 974 7981	23.10	.154 874	3.10	5
6	1.340 096	6.801 913	.147 017 4681	.746 215	5.075 692	.197 017 4681	19.71	.182 105	3.04	6
7	1.407 100	8.142 008	.122 819 8184	.710 681	5.786 373	.172 819 8184	17.29	.209 739	3.00	7
8	1.477 455	9.549 109	.104 721 8136	.676 839	6.463 213	.154 721 8136	15.48	.237 775	2.97	8
9	1.551 328	11.026 564	.090 690 0800	.644 609	7.107 822	.140 690 0800	14.07	.266 211	2.96	9
10	1.628 895	12.577 893	.079 504 5750	.613 913	7.721 735	.129 504 5750	12.96	.295 046	2.95	10
11	1.710 339	14.206 787	.070 388 8915	.584 679	8.306 414	.120 388 8915	12.04	.324 278	2.95	11
12	1.795 856	15.917 127	.062 825 4100	.556 837	8.863 252	.112 825 4100	11.29	.353 905	2.95	12
13	1.885 649	17.712 983	.056 455 7652	.530 321	9.393 573	.106 455 7652	10.65	.383 925	2.95	13
14	1.979 932	19.598 632	.051 023 9695	.505 068	9.898 641	.101 023 9695	10.11	.414 336	2.96	14
15	2.078 928	21.578 564	.046 342 2876	.481 017	10.379 658	.096 342 2876	9.64	.445 134	2.97	15
16	2.182 875	23.657 492	.042 269 9080	.458 112	10.837 770	.092 269 9080	9.23	.476 319	2.98	16
17	2.292 018	25.840 366	.038 699 1417	.436 297	11.274 066	.088 699 1417	8.87	.507 885	2.99	17
18	2.406 619	28.132 385	.035 546 2223	.415 521	11.689 587	.085 546 2223	8.56	.539 832	3.00	18
19	2.526 950	30.539 004	.032 745 0104	.395 734	12.085 321	.082 745 0104	8.28	.572 155	3.01	19
20	2.653 298	33.065 954	.030 242 5872	.376 889	12.462 210	.080 242 5872	8.03	.604 852	3.02	20
21	2.785 963	35.719 252	.027 996 1071	.358 942	12.821 153	.077 996 1071	7.80	.637 918	3.04	21
22	2.925 261	38.505 214	.025 970 5086	.341 850	13.163 003	.075 970 5086	7.60	.671 351	3.05	22
23	3.071 524	41.430 475	.024 136 8219	.325 571	13.488 574	.074 136 8219	7.42	.705 147	3.07	23
24	3.225 100	44.501 999	.022 470 9008	.310 068	13.798 642	.072 470 9008	7.25	.739 302	3.08	24
25	3.386 355	47.727 099	.020 952 4573	.295 303	14.093 945	.070 952 4573	7.10	.773 811	3.10	25
26	3.555 673	51.113 454	.019 564 3207	.281 241	14.375 185	.069 564 3207	6.96	.808 672	3.11	26
27	3.733 456	54.669 126	.018 291 8599	.267 848	14.643 034	.068 291 8599	6.83	.843 880	3.13	27
28	3.920 129	58.402 583	.017 122 5304	.255 094	14.898 127	.067 122 5304	6.72	.879 431	3.14	28
29	4.116 136	62.322 712	.016 045 5149	.242 946	15.141 074	.066 045 5149	6.61	.915 320	3.16	29
30	4.321 942	66.438 848	.015 051 4351	.231 377	15.372 451	.065 051 4351	6.51	.951 543	3.17	30
31	4.538 039	70.760 790	.014 132 1204	.220 359	15.592 811	.064 132 1204	6.42	.988 096	3.19	31
32	4.764 941	75.298 829	.013 280 4189	.209 866	15.802 677	.063 280 4189	6.33	1.024 973	3.20	32
33	5.003 189	80.063 771	.012 490 0437	.199 873	16.002 549	.062 490 0437	6.25	1.062 171	3.22	33
34	5.253 348	85.066 959	.011 755 4454	.190 355	16.192 904	.061 755 4454	6.18	1.099 685	3.23	34
35	5.516 015	90.320 307	.011 071 7072	.181 290	16.374 194	.061 071 7072	6.11	1.137 510	3.25	35
36	5.791 816	95.836 323	.010 434 4571	.172 657	16.546 852	.060 434 4571	6.05	1.175 640	3.27	36
37	6.081 407	101.628 139	.009 839 7945	.164 436	16.711 287	.059 839 7945	5.99	1.214 072	3.28	37
38	6.385 477	107.709 546	.009 284 2282	.156 605	16.867 893	.059 284 2282	5.93	1.252 801	3.30	38
39	6.704 751	114.095 023	.008 764 6242	.149 148	17.017 041	.058 764 6242	5.88	1.291 820	3.31	39
40	7.039 989	120.799 774	.008 278 1612	.142 046	17.159 086	.058 278 1612	5.83	1.331 126	3.33	40
41	7.391 988	127.839 763	.007 822 2924	.135 282	17.294 368	.057 822 2924	5.79	1.370 714	3.34	41
42	7.761 588	135.231 751	.007 394 7131	.128 840	17.423 208	.057 394 7131	5.74	1.410 578	3.36	42
43	8.149 667	142.993 339	.006 993 3328	.122 704	17.545 912	.056 993 3328	5.70	1.450 713	3.37	43
44	8.557 150	151.143 006	.006 616 2506	.116 861	17.662 773	.056 616 2506	5.67	1.491 115	3.39	44
45	8.985 008	159.700 156	.006 261 7347	.111 297	17.774 070	.056 261 7347	5.63	1.531 778	3.40	45
46	9.434 258	168.685 164	.005 928 2036	.105 997	17.880 066	.055 928 2036	5.60	1.572 697	3.42	46
47	9.905 971	178.119 422	.005 614 2109	.100 949	17.981 016	.055 614 2109	5.57	1.613 868	3.43	47
48	10.401 270	188.025 393	.005 318 4306	.096 142	18.077 158	.055 318 4306	5.54	1.655 285	3.45	48
49	10.921 333	198.426 663	.005 039 6453	.091 564	18.168 722	.055 039 6453	5.51	1.696 943	3.46	49
50	11.467 400	209.347 996	.004 776 7355	.087 204	18.255 925	.054 776 7355	5.48	1.738 837	3.48	50

Effective Rate is 5.00 %

Annual Percentage Rate is 5.00 %

ANNUAL COMPOUND INTEREST AND ANNUITY

5.25 % A

	Amount Of 1	Amount Of 1 Per Period	Sinking Fund Payment	Present Worth Of 1	Present Worth of 1 Per Period	Periodic Payment To Amortize 1	Constant Annual Percent	Total Interest	Annual Add On Rate	
	What a single $ 1 deposit grows to in the future. The deposit is made at the beginning of the first period.	What a series of $ 1 deposits grow to in the future. A deposit is made at the end of each period.	The amount to be deposited at the end of each period that grows to $ 1 in the future.	What $ 1 to be paid in the future is worth today. Value today of a single $ 1 payment tomorrow.	What $ 1 to be paid at the end of each period is worth today. Value today of a series of $ 1 payments tomorrow.	The mortgage payment to amortize a loan of $ 1. An annuity certain, payable at the end of each period, worth $ 1 today.	The annual payment, including interest and principal, to amortize completely a loan of $ 100.	The total interest paid over the term on a loan of $1. The loan is amortized by regular periodic payments.	The average annual interest rate on a loan that is completely amortized by regular periodic payments.	
	$S = (1+i)^n$	$S\overline{n} = \dfrac{(1+i)^n - 1}{i}$	$\dfrac{1}{S\overline{n}} = \dfrac{i}{(1+i)^n - 1}$	$V^n = \dfrac{1}{(1+i)^n}$	$A\overline{n} = \dfrac{1 - V^n}{i}$	$\dfrac{1}{A\overline{n}} = \dfrac{i}{1 - V^n}$				

YEAR										PERIODS
	1.052 500	1.000 000	1.000 000 0000	.950 119	.950 119	1.052 500 0000	105.25	.052 500	5.25	1

YEAR	Amount Of 1	Amount Of 1 Per Period	Sinking Fund Payment	Present Worth Of 1	Present Worth of 1 Per Period	Periodic Payment To Amortize 1	Constant Annual Percent	Total Interest	Annual Add On Rate	PERIODS
1	1.052 500	1.000 000	1.000 000 0000	.950 119	.950 119	1.052 500 0000	105.25	.052 500	5.25	1
2	1.107 756	2.052 500	.487 210 7186	.902 726	1.852 844	.539 710 7186	53.98	.079 421	3.97	2
3	1.165 913	3.160 256	.316 430 0363	.857 697	2.710 541	.368 930 0363	36.90	.106 790	3.56	3
4	1.227 124	4.326 170	.231 151 3576	.814 914	3.525 455	.283 651 3576	28.37	.134 605	3.37	4
5	1.291 548	5.553 294	.180 073 3168	.774 265	4.299 719	.232 573 3168	23.26	.162 867	3.26	5
6	1.359 354	6.844 842	.146 095 4203	.735 643	5.035 363	.198 595 4203	19.86	.191 573	3.19	6
7	1.430 720	8.204 196	.121 888 8524	.698 949	5.734 311	.174 388 8524	17.44	.220 722	3.15	7
8	1.505 833	9.634 916	.103 789 1770	.664 084	6.398 396	.156 289 1770	15.63	.250 313	3.13	8
9	1.584 889	11.140 749	.089 760 5712	.630 959	7.029 355	.142 260 5712	14.23	.280 345	3.12	9
10	1.668 096	12.725 638	.078 581 5194	.599 486	7.628 840	.131 081 5194	13.11	.310 815	3.11	10
11	1.755 671	14.393 734	.069 474 6736	.569 583	8.198 423	.121 974 6736	12.20	.341 721	3.11	11
12	1.847 844	16.149 405	.061 921 7842	.541 171	8.739 595	.114 421 7842	11.45	.373 061	3.11	12
13	1.944 856	17.997 249	.055 564 0468	.514 177	9.253 772	.108 064 0468	10.81	.404 833	3.11	13
14	2.046 961	19.942 105	.050 145 1581	.488 529	9.742 301	.102 645 1581	10.27	.437 032	3.12	14
15	2.154 426	21.989 065	.045 477 1489	.464 161	10.206 462	.097 977 1489	9.80	.469 657	3.13	15
16	2.267 533	24.143 491	.041 419 0304	.441 008	10.647 469	.093 919 0304	9.40	.502 704	3.14	16
17	2.386 579	26.411 025	.037 862 9764	.419 010	11.066 479	.090 362 9764	9.04	.536 171	3.15	17
18	2.511 874	28.797 603	.034 725 1119	.398 109	11.464 588	.087 225 1119	8.73	.570 052	3.17	18
19	2.643 748	31.309 478	.031 939 2107	.378 251	11.842 839	.084 439 2107	8.45	.604 345	3.18	19
20	2.782 544	33.953 225	.029 452 2832	.359 383	12.202 223	.081 952 2832	8.20	.639 046	3.20	20
21	2.928 628	36.735 769	.027 221 4252	.341 457	12.543 679	.079 721 4252	7.98	.674 150	3.21	21
22	3.082 381	39.664 397	.025 211 5264	.324 425	12.868 104	.077 711 5264	7.78	.709 654	3.23	22
23	3.244 206	42.746 778	.023 393 5759	.308 242	13.176 346	.075 893 5759	7.59	.745 552	3.24	23
24	3.414 527	45.990 984	.021 743 3921	.292 866	13.469 212	.074 243 3921	7.43	.781 841	3.26	24
25	3.593 789	49.405 511	.020 240 6571	.278 258	13.747 470	.072 740 6571	7.28	.818 516	3.27	25
26	3.782 463	52.999 300	.018 868 1737	.264 378	14.011 848	.071 368 1737	7.14	.855 573	3.29	26
27	3.981 043	56.781 763	.017 611 2882	.251 190	14.263 038	.070 111 2882	7.02	.893 005	3.31	27
28	4.190 047	60.762 806	.016 457 4362	.238 661	14.501 699	.068 957 4362	6.90	.930 808	3.32	28
29	4.410 025	64.952 853	.015 395 7825	.226 756	14.728 455	.067 895 7825	6.79	.968 978	3.34	29
30	4.641 551	69.362 878	.014 416 9335	.215 445	14.943 901	.066 916 9335	6.70	1.007 508	3.36	30
31	4.885 233	74.004 429	.013 512 7048	.204 699	15.148 599	.066 012 7048	6.61	1.046 394	3.38	31
32	5.141 707	78.889 662	.012 675 9322	.194 488	15.343 087	.065 175 9322	6.52	1.085 630	3.39	32
33	5.411 647	84.031 369	.011 900 3179	.184 787	15.527 874	.064 400 3179	6.45	1.125 210	3.41	33
34	5.695 758	89.443 016	.011 180 3028	.175 569	15.703 443	.063 680 3028	6.37	1.165 130	3.43	34
35	5.994 786	95.138 774	.010 510 9616	.166 812	15.870 255	.063 010 9616	6.31	1.205 384	3.44	35
36	6.309 512	101.133 560	.009 887 9146	.158 491	16.028 745	.062 387 9146	6.24	1.245 965	3.46	36
37	6.640 761	107.443 071	.009 307 2544	.150 585	16.179 331	.061 807 2544	6.19	1.286 868	3.48	37
38	6.989 401	114.083 833	.008 765 4839	.143 074	16.322 404	.061 265 4839	6.13	1.328 088	3.50	38
39	7.356 345	121.073 234	.008 259 4639	.135 937	16.458 341	.060 759 4639	6.08	1.369 619	3.51	39
40	7.742 553	128.429 579	.007 786 3683	.129 156	16.587 498	.060 286 3683	6.03	1.411 455	3.53	40
41	8.149 037	136.172 132	.007 343 6465	.122 714	16.710 212	.059 843 6465	5.99	1.453 590	3.55	41
42	8.576 861	144.321 169	.006 928 9905	.116 593	16.826 804	.059 428 9905	5.95	1.496 018	3.56	42
43	9.027 147	152.898 030	.006 540 3066	.110 777	16.937 581	.059 040 3066	5.91	1.538 733	3.58	43
44	9.501 072	161.925 176	.006 175 6919	.105 251	17.042 833	.058 675 6919	5.87	1.581 730	3.59	44
45	9.999 878	171.426 248	.005 833 4124	.100 001	17.142 834	.058 333 4124	5.84	1.625 004	3.61	45
46	10.524 872	181.426 126	.005 511 8853	.095 013	17.237 847	.058 011 8853	5.81	1.668 547	3.63	46
47	11.077 427	191.950 998	.005 209 6629	.090 274	17.328 121	.057 709 6629	5.78	1.712 354	3.64	47
48	11.658 992	203.028 425	.004 925 4187	.085 771	17.413 891	.057 425 4187	5.75	1.756 420	3.66	48
49	12.271 089	214.687 418	.004 657 9348	.081 492	17.495 384	.057 157 9348	5.72	1.800 739	3.68	49
50	12.915 322	226.958 507	.004 406 0917	.077 427	17.572 811	.056 906 0917	5.70	1.845 305	3.69	50

Effective Rate is 5.25 % 8 - 437 Annual Percentage Rate is 5.25 %

	Amount Of 1	Amount Of 1 Per Period	Sinking Fund Payment	Present Worth Of 1	Present Worth of 1 Per Period	Periodic Payment To Amortize 1	Constant Annual Percent	Total Interest	Annual Add On Rate	
	What a single $ 1 deposit grows to in the future. The deposit is made at the beginning of the first period.	What a series of $ 1 deposits grow to in the future. A deposit is made at the end of each period.	The amount to be deposited at the end of each period that grows to $ 1 in the future.	What $ 1 to be paid in the future is worth today. Value today of a single $ 1 payment tomorrow.	What $ 1 to be paid at the end of each period is worth today. Value today of a series of $ 1 payments tomorrow.	The mortgage payment to amortize a loan of $ 1. An annuity certain, payable at the end of each period, worth $ 1 today.	The annual payment, including interest and principal, to amortize a loan of $ 100.	The total interest paid over the term on a loan is amortized by regular periodic payments.	The average annual interest rate on a loan that is completely amortized by regular periodic payments.	
	$S = (1+i)^n$	$S\overline{n}| = \dfrac{(1+i)^n - 1}{i}$	$\dfrac{1}{S\overline{n}|} = \dfrac{i}{(1+i)^n - 1}$	$V^n = \dfrac{1}{(1+i)^n}$	$A\overline{n}| = \dfrac{1-V^n}{i}$	$\dfrac{1}{A\overline{n}|} = \dfrac{i}{1-V^n}$				

YEAR / **PERIODS**

	Amount Of 1	Amount Of 1 Per Period	Sinking Fund Payment	Present Worth Of 1	Present Worth of 1 Per Period	Periodic Payment To Amortize 1	Constant Annual Percent	Total Interest	Annual Add On Rate	
	1.055 000	1.000 000	1.000 000 0000	.947 867	.947 867	1.055 000 0000	105.50	.055 000	5.50	1

	Amount Of 1	Amount Of 1 Per Period	Sinking Fund Payment	Present Worth Of 1	Present Worth of 1 Per Period	Periodic Payment To Amortize 1	Constant Annual Percent	Total Interest	Annual Add On Rate	
1	1.055 000	1.000 000	1.000 000 0000	.947 867	.947 867	1.055 000 0000	105.50	.055 000	5.50	1
2	1.113 025	2.055 000	.486 618 0049	.898 452	1.846 320	.541 618 0049	54.17	.083 236	4.16	2
3	1.174 241	3.168 025	.315 654 0747	.851 614	2.697 933	.370 654 0747	37.07	.111 962	3.73	3
4	1.238 825	4.342 266	.230 294 4853	.807 217	3.505 150	.285 294 4853	28.53	.141 178	3.53	4
5	1.306 960	5.581 091	.179 176 4362	.765 134	4.270 284	.234 176 4362	23.42	.170 882	3.42	5
6	1.378 843	6.888 051	.145 178 9476	.725 246	4.995 530	.200 178 9476	20.02	.201 074	3.35	6
7	1.454 679	8.266 894	.120 964 4178	.687 437	5.682 967	.175 964 4178	17.60	.231 751	3.31	7
8	1.534 687	9.721 573	.102 864 0118	.651 599	6.334 566	.157 864 0118	15.79	.262 912	3.29	8
9	1.619 094	11.256 260	.088 839 4585	.617 629	6.952 195	.143 839 4585	14.39	.294 555	3.27	9
10	1.708 144	12.875 354	.077 667 7687	.585 431	7.537 626	.132 667 7687	13.27	.326 678	3.27	10
11	1.802 092	14.583 498	.068 570 6532	.554 911	8.092 536	.123 570 6532	12.36	.359 277	3.27	11
12	1.901 207	16.385 591	.061 029 2312	.525 982	8.618 518	.116 029 2312	11.61	.392 351	3.27	12
13	2.005 774	18.286 798	.054 684 2587	.498 561	9.117 079	.109 684 2587	10.97	.425 895	3.28	13
14	2.116 091	20.292 572	.049 279 1154	.472 569	9.589 648	.104 279 1154	10.43	.459 908	3.29	14
15	2.232 476	22.408 663	.044 625 5976	.447 933	10.037 581	.099 625 5976	9.97	.494 384	3.30	15
16	2.355 263	24.641 140	.040 582 5380	.424 581	10.462 162	.095 582 5380	9.56	.529 321	3.31	16
17	2.484 802	26.996 403	.037 041 9723	.402 447	10.864 609	.092 041 9723	9.21	.564 714	3.32	17
18	2.621 466	29.481 205	.033 919 9163	.381 466	11.246 074	.088 919 9163	8.90	.600 559	3.34	18
19	2.765 647	32.102 671	.031 150 0559	.361 579	11.607 654	.086 150 0559	8.62	.636 851	3.35	19
20	2.917 757	34.868 318	.028 679 3300	.342 729	11.950 382	.083 679 3300	8.37	.673 587	3.37	20
21	3.078 234	37.786 076	.026 464 7754	.324 862	12.275 244	.081 464 7754	8.15	.710 760	3.38	21
22	3.247 537	40.864 310	.024 471 2319	.307 926	12.583 170	.079 471 2319	7.95	.748 367	3.40	22
23	3.426 152	44.111 847	.022 669 6472	.291 873	12.875 042	.077 669 6472	7.77	.786 402	3.42	23
24	3.614 590	47.537 998	.021 035 8037	.276 657	13.151 699	.076 035 8037	7.61	.824 859	3.44	24
25	3.813 392	51.152 588	.019 549 3529	.262 234	13.413 933	.074 549 3529	7.46	.863 734	3.46	25
26	4.023 129	54.965 981	.018 193 0713	.248 563	13.662 495	.073 193 0713	7.32	.903 020	3.47	26
27	4.244 401	58.989 109	.016 952 2817	.235 605	13.898 100	.071 952 2817	7.20	.942 712	3.49	27
28	4.477 843	63.233 510	.015 814 3996	.223 322	14.121 422	.070 814 3996	7.09	.982 803	3.51	28
29	4.724 124	67.711 354	.014 768 5720	.211 679	14.333 101	.069 768 5720	6.98	1.023 289	3.53	29
30	4.983 951	72.435 478	.013 805 3897	.200 644	14.533 745	.068 805 3897	6.89	1.064 162	3.55	30
31	5.258 069	77.419 429	.012 916 6543	.190 184	14.723 929	.067 916 6543	6.80	1.105 416	3.57	31
32	5.547 262	82.677 498	.012 095 1895	.180 269	14.904 198	.067 095 1895	6.71	1.147 046	3.58	32
33	5.852 362	88.224 760	.011 334 6865	.170 871	15.075 069	.066 334 6865	6.64	1.189 045	3.60	33
34	6.174 242	94.077 122	.010 629 5769	.161 963	15.237 033	.065 629 5769	6.57	1.231 406	3.62	34
35	6.513 825	100.251 364	.009 974 9266	.153 520	15.390 552	.064 974 9266	6.50	1.274 122	3.64	35
36	6.872 085	106.765 189	.009 366 3488	.145 516	15.536 068	.064 366 3488	6.44	1.317 189	3.66	36
37	7.250 050	113.637 274	.008 799 9295	.137 930	15.673 999	.063 799 9295	6.38	1.360 597	3.68	37
38	7.648 803	120.887 324	.008 272 1659	.130 739	15.804 738	.063 272 1659	6.33	1.404 342	3.70	38
39	8.069 487	128.536 127	.007 779 9139	.123 924	15.928 662	.062 779 9139	6.28	1.448 417	3.71	39
40	8.513 309	136.605 614	.007 320 3434	.117 463	16.046 125	.062 320 3434	6.24	1.492 814	3.73	40
41	8.981 541	145.118 923	.006 890 9001	.111 339	16.157 464	.061 890 9001	6.19	1.537 527	3.75	41
42	9.475 525	154.100 464	.006 489 2731	.105 535	16.262 999	.061 489 2731	6.15	1.582 549	3.77	42
43	9.996 679	163.575 989	.006 113 3667	.100 033	16.363 032	.061 113 3667	6.12	1.627 875	3.79	43
44	10.546 497	173.572 669	.005 761 2757	.094 818	16.457 851	.060 761 2757	6.08	1.673 496	3.80	44
45	11.126 554	184.119 165	.005 431 2651	.089 875	16.547 726	.060 431 2651	6.05	1.719 407	3.82	45
46	11.738 515	195.245 719	.005 121 7512	.085 190	16.632 915	.060 121 7512	6.02	1.765 601	3.84	46
47	12.384 133	206.984 234	.004 831 2858	.080 748	16.713 664	.059 831 2858	5.99	1.812 070	3.86	47
48	13.065 260	219.368 367	.004 558 5424	.076 539	16.790 203	.059 558 5424	5.96	1.858 810	3.87	48
49	13.783 849	232.433 627	.004 302 3035	.072 549	16.862 751	.059 302 3035	5.94	1.905 813	3.89	49
50	14.541 961	246.217 476	.004 061 4501	.068 767	16.931 518	.059 061 4501	5.91	1.953 073	3.91	50

Effective Rate is 5.50 %

Annual Percentage Rate is 5.50 %

	Amount Of 1	Amount Of 1 Per Period	Sinking Fund Payment	Present Worth Of 1	Present Worth of 1 Per Period	Periodic Payment To Amortize 1	Constant Annual Percent	Total Interest	Annual Add On Rate	
	What a single $ 1 deposit grows to in the future. The deposit is made at the beginning of the first period.	What a series of $ 1 deposits grow to in the future. A deposit is made at the end of each period.	The amount to be deposited at the end of each period that grows to $ 1 in the future.	What $ 1 to be paid in the future is worth today. Value today of a single $ 1 payment tomorrow.	What $ 1 to be paid at the end of each period is worth today. Value today of a series of $ 1 payments tomorrow.	The mortgage payment to amortize a loan of $ 1. An annuity certain, payable at the end of each period, worth $ 1 today.	The annual payment, including interest and principal, to amortize completely a loan of $ 100.	The total interest paid over the term on a loan of $1. The loan is amortized by regular periodic payments.	The average annual interest rate on a loan that is completely amortized by regular periodic payments.	
	$S = (1+i)^n$	$S\overline{n} = \dfrac{(1+i)^n - 1}{i}$	$\dfrac{1}{S\overline{n}} = \dfrac{i}{(1+i)^n - 1}$	$V^n = \dfrac{1}{(1+i)^n}$	$A\overline{n} = \dfrac{1-V^n}{i}$	$\dfrac{1}{A\overline{n}} = \dfrac{i}{1-V^n}$				

YEAR										PERIODS
	1.057 500	1.000 000	1.000 000 0000	.945 626	.945 626	1.057 500 0000	105.75	.057 500	5.75	1

YEAR	Amount Of 1	Amount Of 1 Per Period	Sinking Fund Payment	Present Worth Of 1	Present Worth of 1 Per Period	Periodic Payment To Amortize 1	Constant Annual Percent	Total Interest	Annual Add On Rate	PERIODS
1	1.057 500	1.000 000	1.000 000 0000	.945 626	.945 626	1.057 500 0000	105.75	.057 500	5.75	1
2	1.118 306	2.057 500	.486 026 7315	.894 209	1.839 836	.543 526 7315	54.36	.087 053	4.35	2
3	1.182 609	3.175 806	.314 880 6701	.845 588	2.685 424	.372 380 6701	37.24	.117 142	3.90	3
4	1.250 609	4.358 415	.229 441 2017	.799 611	3.485 035	.286 941 2017	28.70	.147 765	3.69	4
5	1.322 519	5.609 024	.178 284 1371	.756 133	4.241 167	.235 784 1371	23.58	.178 921	3.58	5
6	1.398 564	6.931 543	.144 268 0253	.715 019	4.956 187	.201 768 0253	20.18	.210 608	3.51	6
7	1.478 981	8.330 107	.120 046 4834	.676 141	5.632 328	.177 546 4834	17.76	.242 825	3.47	7
8	1.564 023	9.809 088	.101 946 2799	.639 377	6.271 705	.159 446 2799	15.95	.275 570	3.44	8
9	1.653 954	11.373 110	.087 926 6954	.604 612	6.876 317	.145 426 6954	14.55	.308 840	3.43	9
10	1.749 056	13.027 064	.076 763 2671	.571 737	7.448 054	.134 263 2671	13.43	.342 633	3.43	10
11	1.849 627	14.776 120	.067 676 7637	.540 650	7.988 703	.125 176 7637	12.52	.376 944	3.43	11
12	1.955 980	16.625 747	.060 147 6727	.511 253	8.499 956	.117 647 6727	11.77	.411 772	3.43	12
13	2.068 449	18.581 728	.053 816 3092	.483 454	8.983 410	.111 316 3092	11.14	.447 112	3.44	13
14	2.187 385	20.650 177	.048 425 7351	.457 167	9.440 576	.105 925 7351	10.60	.482 960	3.45	14
15	2.313 160	22.837 562	.043 787 5108	.432 309	9.872 886	.101 287 5108	10.13	.519 313	3.46	15
16	2.446 167	25.150 722	.039 760 2900	.408 803	10.281 688	.097 260 2900	9.73	.556 165	3.48	16
17	2.586 821	27.596 888	.036 235 9691	.386 575	10.668 263	.093 735 9691	9.38	.593 511	3.49	17
18	2.735 563	30.183 710	.033 130 4539	.365 555	11.033 819	.090 630 4539	9.07	.631 348	3.51	18
19	2.892 858	32.919 273	.030 377 3417	.345 679	11.379 498	.087 877 3417	8.79	.669 670	3.52	19
20	3.059 198	35.812 131	.027 923 4988	.326 883	11.706 381	.085 423 4988	8.55	.708 470	3.54	20
21	3.235 101	38.871 329	.025 725 9022	.309 109	12.015 490	.083 225 9022	8.33	.747 744	3.56	21
22	3.421 120	42.106 430	.023 749 3418	.292 302	12.307 792	.081 249 3418	8.13	.787 486	3.58	22
23	3.617 834	45.527 550	.021 964 7226	.276 408	12.584 200	.079 464 7226	7.95	.827 689	3.60	23
24	3.825 860	49.145 384	.020 347 7910	.261 379	12.845 580	.077 847 7910	7.79	.868 347	3.62	24
25	4.045 846	52.971 243	.018 878 1674	.247 167	13.092 747	.076 378 1674	7.64	.909 454	3.64	25
26	4.278 483	57.017 090	.017 538 6012	.233 728	13.326 474	.075 038 6012	7.51	.951 004	3.66	26
27	4.524 495	61.295 573	.016 314 3920	.221 019	13.547 494	.073 814 3920	7.39	.992 989	3.68	27
28	4.784 654	65.820 068	.015 192 9348	.209 002	13.756 495	.072 692 9348	7.27	1.035 402	3.70	28
29	5.059 772	70.604 722	.014 163 3587	.197 637	13.954 132	.071 663 3587	7.17	1.078 237	3.72	29
30	5.350 708	75.664 493	.013 216 2386	.186 891	14.141 024	.070 716 2386	7.08	1.121 487	3.74	30
31	5.658 374	81.015 202	.012 343 3625	.176 729	14.317 753	.069 843 3625	6.99	1.165 144	3.76	31
32	5.983 731	86.673 576	.011 537 5417	.167 120	14.484 873	.069 037 5417	6.91	1.209 201	3.78	32
33	6.327 795	92.657 307	.010 792 4570	.158 033	14.642 906	.068 292 4570	6.83	1.253 651	3.80	33
34	6.691 643	98.985 102	.010 102 5304	.149 440	14.792 346	.067 602 5304	6.77	1.298 486	3.82	34
35	7.076 413	105.676 745	.009 462 8198	.141 315	14.933 660	.066 962 8198	6.70	1.343 699	3.84	35
36	7.483 307	112.753 158	.008 868 9312	.133 631	15.067 291	.066 368 9312	6.64	1.389 282	3.86	36
37	7.913 597	120.236 464	.008 316 9445	.126 365	15.193 656	.065 816 9445	6.59	1.435 227	3.88	37
38	8.368 629	128.150 061	.007 803 3517	.119 494	15.313 150	.065 303 3517	6.54	1.481 527	3.90	38
39	8.849 825	136.518 690	.007 325 0044	.112 997	15.426 146	.064 825 0044	6.49	1.528 175	3.92	39
40	9.358 690	145.368 514	.006 879 0687	.106 853	15.532 999	.064 379 0687	6.44	1.575 163	3.94	40
41	9.896 814	154.727 204	.006 462 9876	.101 043	15.634 041	.063 962 9876	6.40	1.622 483	3.96	41
42	10.465 881	164.624 018	.006 074 4478	.095 549	15.729 590	.063 574 4478	6.36	1.670 127	3.98	42
43	11.067 669	175.089 899	.005 711 3517	.090 353	15.819 943	.063 211 3517	6.33	1.718 088	4.00	43
44	11.704 060	186.157 568	.005 371 7934	.085 440	15.905 384	.062 871 7934	6.29	1.766 359	4.01	44
45	12.377 044	197.861 628	.005 054 0370	.080 795	15.986 178	.062 554 0370	6.26	1.814 932	4.03	45
46	13.088 724	210.238 672	.004 756 4988	.076 402	16.062 580	.062 256 4988	6.23	1.863 799	4.05	46
47	13.841 325	223.327 396	.004 477 7310	.072 247	16.134 828	.061 977 7310	6.20	1.912 953	4.07	47
48	14.637 201	237.168 721	.004 216 4076	.068 319	16.203 147	.061 716 4076	6.18	1.962 388	4.09	48
49	15.478 841	251.805 922	.003 971 3125	.064 604	16.267 751	.061 471 3125	6.15	2.012 094	4.11	49
50	16.368 874	267.284 763	.003 741 3281	.061 092	16.328 842	.061 241 3281	6.13	2.062 066	4.12	50

Amount Of 1	Amount Of 1 Per Period	Sinking Fund Payment	Present Worth Of 1	Present Worth of 1 Per Period	Periodic Payment To Amortize 1	Constant Annual Percent	Total Interest	Annual Add On Rate
What a single $ 1 deposit grows to in the future. The deposit is made at the beginning of the first period.	What a series of $ 1 deposits grow to in the future. A deposit is made at the end of each period.	The amount to be deposited at the end of each period that grows to $ 1 in the future.	What $ 1 to be paid in the future is worth today. Value today of a single $ 1 payment tomorrow.	What $ 1 to be paid at the end of each period is worth today. Value today of a series of $ 1 payments tomorrow.	The mortgage payment to amortize a loan of $ 1. An annuity certain, payable at the end of each period, worth $ 1 today.	The annual payment, including interest and principal, to amortize completely a loan of $ 100.	The total interest paid over the term on a loan of $1. The loan is amortized by regular periodic payments.	The average annual interest rate on a loan that is completely amortized by regular periodic payments.
$S = (1+i)^n$	$S\overline{n}| = \dfrac{(1+i)^n - 1}{i}$	$\dfrac{1}{S\overline{n}|} = \dfrac{i}{(1+i)^n - 1}$	$V^n = \dfrac{1}{(1+i)^n}$	$A\overline{n}| = \dfrac{1 - V^n}{i}$	$\dfrac{1}{A\overline{n}|} = \dfrac{i}{1 - V^n}$			

YEAR									PERIODS
	1.060 000	1.000 000	1.000 000 0000	.943 396	.943 396	1.060 000 0000	106.00	.060 000	6.00	1

YEAR	Amount Of 1	Amount Of 1 Per Period	Sinking Fund Payment	Present Worth Of 1	Present Worth of 1 Per Period	Periodic Payment To Amortize 1	Constant Annual Percent	Total Interest	Annual Add On Rate	PERIODS
1	1.060 000	1.000 000	1.000 000 0000	.943 396	.943 396	1.060 000 0000	106.00	.060 000	6.00	1
2	1.123 600	2.060 000	.485 436 8932	.889 996	1.833 393	.545 436 8932	54.55	.090 874	4.54	2
3	1.191 016	3.183 600	.314 109 8128	.839 619	2.673 012	.374 109 8128	37.42	.122 329	4.08	3
4	1.262 477	4.374 616	.228 591 4924	.792 094	3.465 106	.288 591 4924	28.86	.154 366	3.86	4
5	1.338 226	5.637 093	.177 396 4004	.747 258	4.212 364	.237 396 4004	23.74	.186 982	3.74	5
6	1.418 519	6.975 319	.143 362 6285	.704 961	4.917 324	.203 362 6285	20.34	.220 176	3.67	6
7	1.503 630	8.393 838	.119 135 0181	.665 057	5.582 381	.179 135 0181	17.92	.253 945	3.63	7
8	1.593 848	9.897 468	.101 035 9426	.627 412	6.209 794	.161 035 9426	16.11	.288 288	3.60	8
9	1.689 479	11.491 316	.087 022 2350	.591 898	6.801 692	.147 022 2350	14.71	.323 200	3.59	9
10	1.790 848	13.180 795	.075 867 9582	.558 395	7.360 087	.135 867 9582	13.59	.358 680	3.59	10
11	1.898 299	14.971 643	.066 792 9381	.526 788	7.886 875	.126 792 9381	12.68	.394 722	3.59	11
12	2.012 196	16.869 941	.059 277 0294	.496 969	8.383 844	.119 277 0294	11.93	.431 324	3.59	12
13	2.132 928	18.882 138	.052 960 1053	.468 839	8.852 683	.112 960 1053	11.30	.468 481	3.60	13
14	2.260 904	21.015 066	.047 584 9090	.442 301	9.294 984	.107 584 9090	10.76	.506 189	3.62	14
15	2.396 558	23.275 970	.042 962 7640	.417 265	9.712 249	.102 962 7640	10.30	.544 441	3.63	15
16	2.540 352	25.672 528	.038 952 1436	.393 646	10.105 895	.098 952 1436	9.90	.583 234	3.65	16
17	2.692 773	28.212 880	.035 444 8042	.371 364	10.477 260	.095 444 8042	9.55	.622 562	3.66	17
18	2.854 339	30.905 653	.032 356 5406	.350 344	10.827 603	.092 356 5406	9.24	.662 418	3.68	18
19	3.025 600	33.759 992	.029 620 8604	.330 513	11.158 116	.089 620 8604	8.97	.702 796	3.70	19
20	3.207 135	36.785 591	.027 184 5570	.311 805	11.469 921	.087 184 5570	8.72	.743 691	3.72	20
21	3.399 564	39.992 727	.025 004 5467	.294 155	11.764 077	.085 004 5467	8.51	.785 095	3.74	21
22	3.603 537	43.392 290	.023 045 5685	.277 505	12.041 582	.083 045 5685	8.31	.827 003	3.76	22
23	3.819 750	46.995 828	.021 278 4847	.261 797	12.303 379	.081 278 4847	8.13	.869 405	3.78	23
24	4.048 935	50.815 577	.019 679 0050	.246 979	12.550 358	.079 679 0050	7.97	.912 296	3.80	24
25	4.291 871	54.864 512	.018 226 7182	.232 999	12.783 356	.078 226 7182	7.83	.955 668	3.82	25
26	4.549 383	59.156 383	.016 904 3467	.219 810	13.003 166	.076 904 3467	7.70	.999 513	3.84	26
27	4.822 346	63.705 766	.015 697 1663	.207 368	13.210 534	.075 697 1663	7.57	1.043 824	3.87	27
28	5.111 687	68.528 112	.014 592 5515	.195 630	13.406 164	.074 592 5515	7.46	1.088 591	3.89	28
29	5.418 388	73.639 798	.013 579 6135	.184 557	13.590 721	.073 579 6135	7.36	1.133 809	3.91	29
30	5.743 491	79.058 186	.012 648 9115	.174 110	13.764 831	.072 648 9115	7.27	1.179 467	3.93	30
31	6.088 101	84.801 677	.011 792 2196	.164 255	13.929 086	.071 792 2196	7.18	1.225 559	3.95	31
32	6.453 387	90.889 778	.011 002 3374	.154 957	14.084 043	.071 002 3374	7.11	1.272 075	3.98	32
33	6.840 590	97.343 165	.010 272 9350	.146 186	14.230 230	.070 272 9350	7.03	1.319 007	4.00	33
34	7.251 025	104.183 755	.009 598 4254	.137 912	14.368 141	.069 598 4254	6.96	1.366 346	4.02	34
35	7.686 087	111.434 780	.008 973 8590	.130 105	14.498 246	.068 973 8590	6.90	1.414 085	4.04	35
36	8.147 252	119.120 867	.008 394 8348	.122 741	14.620 987	.068 394 8348	6.84	1.462 214	4.06	36
37	8.636 087	127.268 119	.007 857 4274	.115 793	14.736 780	.067 857 4274	6.79	1.510 725	4.08	37
38	9.154 252	135.904 206	.007 358 1240	.109 239	14.846 019	.067 358 1240	6.74	1.559 609	4.10	38
39	9.703 507	145.058 458	.006 893 7724	.103 056	14.949 075	.066 893 7724	6.69	1.608 857	4.13	39
40	10.285 718	154.761 966	.006 461 5359	.097 222	15.046 297	.066 461 5359	6.65	1.658 461	4.15	40
41	10.902 861	165.047 684	.006 058 8551	.091 719	15.138 016	.066 058 8551	6.61	1.708 413	4.17	41
42	11.557 033	175.950 545	.005 683 4152	.086 527	15.224 543	.065 683 4152	6.57	1.758 703	4.19	42
43	12.250 455	187.507 577	.005 333 1178	.081 630	15.306 173	.065 333 1178	6.54	1.809 324	4.21	43
44	12.985 482	199.758 032	.005 006 0565	.077 009	15.383 182	.065 006 0565	6.51	1.860 266	4.23	44
45	13.764 611	212.743 514	.004 700 4958	.072 650	15.455 832	.064 700 4958	6.48	1.911 522	4.25	45
46	14.590 487	226.508 125	.004 414 8527	.068 538	15.524 370	.064 414 8527	6.45	1.963 083	4.27	46
47	15.465 917	241.098 612	.004 147 6805	.064 658	15.589 028	.064 147 6805	6.42	2.014 941	4.29	47
48	16.393 872	256.564 529	.003 897 6549	.060 998	15.650 027	.063 897 6549	6.39	2.067 087	4.31	48
49	17.377 504	272.958 401	.003 663 5619	.057 546	15.707 572	.063 663 5619	6.37	2.119 515	4.33	49
50	18.420 154	290.335 905	.003 444 2864	.054 288	15.761 861	.063 444 2864	6.35	2.172 214	4.34	50

Effective Rate is 6.00 %

Annual Percentage Rate is 6.00 %

Amount Of 1	Amount Of 1 Per Period	Sinking Fund Payment	Present Worth Of 1	Present Worth of 1 Per Period	Periodic Payment To Amortize 1	Constant Annual Percent	Total Interest	Annual Add On Rate	
What a single $ 1 deposit grows to in the future. The deposit is made at the beginning of the first period.	What a series of $ 1 deposits grow to in the future. A deposit is made at the end of each period.	The amount to be deposited at the end of each period that grows to $ 1 in the future.	What $ 1 to be paid in the future is worth today. Value today of a single $ 1 payment tomorrow.	What $ 1 to be paid at the end of each period is worth today. Value today of a series of $ 1 payments tomorrow.	The mortgage payment to amortize a loan of $ 1. An annuity certain, payable at the end of each period, worth $ 1 today.	The annual payment, including interest and principal, to amortize completely a loan of $ 100.	The total interest paid over the term on a loan of $1. The loan is amortized by regular periodic payments.	The average annual interest rate on a loan that is completely amortized by regular periodic payments.	
$S = (1+i)^n$	$S\overline{n}\| = \dfrac{(1+i)^n - 1}{i}$	$\dfrac{1}{S\overline{n}\|} = \dfrac{i}{(1+i)^n - 1}$	$V^n = \dfrac{1}{(1+i)^n}$	$A\overline{n}\| = \dfrac{1-V^n}{i}$	$\dfrac{1}{A\overline{n}\|} = \dfrac{i}{1-V^n}$				

YEAR								**PERIODS**	
	1.062 500	1.000 000	1.000 000 0000	.941 176	.941 176	1.062 500 0000	106.25	.062 500	6.25 1

YEAR	Amount Of 1	Amount Of 1 Per Period	Sinking Fund Payment	Present Worth Of 1	Present Worth of 1 Per Period	Periodic Payment To Amortize 1	Constant Annual Percent	Total Interest	Annual Add On Rate	PERIODS
1	1.062 500	1.000 000	1.000 000 0000	.941 176	.941 176	1.062 500 0000	106.25	.062 500	6.25	1
2	1.128 906	2.062 500	.484 848 4848	.885 813	1.826 990	.547 348 4848	54.74	.094 697	4.73	2
3	1.199 463	3.191 406	.313 341 4933	.833 706	2.660 696	.375 841 4933	37.59	.127 524	4.25	3
4	1.274 429	4.390 869	.227 745 3433	.784 665	3.445 361	.290 245 3433	29.03	.160 981	4.02	4
5	1.354 081	5.665 298	.176 513 2070	.738 508	4.183 869	.239 013 2070	23.91	.195 066	3.90	5
6	1.438 711	7.019 380	.142 462 7324	.695 067	4.878 936	.204 962 7324	20.50	.229 776	3.83	6
7	1.528 631	8.458 091	.118 229 9905	.654 180	5.533 116	.180 729 9905	18.08	.265 110	3.79	7
8	1.624 170	9.986 722	.100 132 9614	.615 699	6.148 815	.162 632 9614	16.27	.301 064	3.76	8
9	1.725 681	11.610 892	.086 126 0300	.579 481	6.728 297	.148 626 0300	14.87	.337 634	3.75	9
10	1.833 536	13.336 572	.074 981 7850	.545 394	7.273 691	.137 481 7850	13.75	.374 818	3.75	10
11	1.948 132	15.170 108	.065 919 1083	.513 312	7.787 003	.128 419 1083	12.85	.412 610	3.75	11
12	2.069 890	17.118 240	.058 417 2209	.483 117	8.270 121	.120 917 2209	12.10	.451 007	3.76	12
13	2.199 258	19.188 130	.052 115 5531	.454 699	8.724 819	.114 615 5531	11.47	.490 002	3.77	13
14	2.336 712	21.387 388	.046 756 5278	.427 952	9.152 771	.109 256 5278	10.93	.529 591	3.78	14
15	2.482 756	23.724 100	.042 151 2307	.402 778	9.555 549	.104 651 2307	10.47	.569 768	3.80	15
16	2.637 928	26.206 856	.038 157 9538	.379 085	9.934 635	.100 657 9538	10.07	.610 527	3.82	16
17	2.802 799	28.844 784	.034 668 3124	.356 786	10.291 421	.097 168 3124	9.72	.651 861	3.83	17
18	2.977 974	31.647 583	.031 597 9892	.335 799	10.627 220	.094 097 9892	9.41	.693 764	3.85	18
19	3.164 097	34.625 557	.028 880 4015	.316 046	10.943 266	.091 380 4015	9.14	.736 228	3.87	19
20	3.361 853	37.789 655	.026 462 2687	.297 455	11.240 721	.088 962 2687	8.90	.779 245	3.90	20
21	3.571 969	41.151 508	.024 300 4459	.279 958	11.520 678	.086 800 4459	8.69	.822 809	3.92	21
22	3.795 217	44.723 477	.022 359 6209	.263 490	11.784 168	.084 859 6209	8.49	.866 912	3.94	22
23	4.032 418	48.518 695	.020 610 6121	.247 990	12.032 158	.083 110 6121	8.32	.911 544	3.96	23
24	4.284 445	52.551 113	.019 029 0926	.233 402	12.265 560	.081 529 0926	8.16	.956 698	3.99	24
25	4.552 222	56.835 558	.017 594 6193	.219 673	12.485 233	.080 094 6193	8.01	1.002 365	4.01	25
26	4.836 736	61.387 780	.016 289 8870	.206 751	12.691 984	.078 789 8870	7.88	1.048 537	4.03	26
27	5.139 032	66.224 516	.015 100 1480	.194 589	12.886 573	.077 600 1480	7.77	1.095 204	4.06	27
28	5.460 222	71.363 549	.014 012 7561	.183 143	13.069 716	.076 512 7561	7.66	1.142 357	4.08	28
29	5.801 486	76.823 771	.013 016 8045	.172 370	13.242 086	.075 516 8045	7.56	1.189 987	4.10	29
30	6.164 079	82.625 256	.012 102 8369	.162 230	13.404 316	.074 602 8369	7.47	1.238 085	4.13	30
31	6.549 333	88.789 335	.011 262 6140	.152 687	13.557 003	.073 762 6140	7.38	1.286 641	4.15	31
32	6.958 667	95.338 668	.010 488 9235	.143 706	13.700 709	.072 988 9235	7.30	1.335 646	4.17	32
33	7.393 583	102.297 335	.009 775 4257	.135 252	13.835 961	.072 275 4257	7.23	1.385 089	4.20	33
34	7.855 682	109.690 918	.009 116 5250	.127 296	13.963 258	.071 616 5250	7.17	1.434 962	4.22	34
35	8.346 663	117.546 601	.008 507 2643	.119 808	14.083 066	.071 007 2643	7.11	1.485 254	4.24	35
36	8.868 329	125.893 263	.007 943 2368	.112 761	14.195 827	.070 443 2368	7.05	1.535 957	4.27	36
37	9.422 600	134.761 592	.007 420 5119	.106 128	14.301 955	.069 920 5119	7.00	1.587 059	4.29	37
38	10.011 512	144.184 192	.006 935 5731	.099 885	14.401 840	.069 435 5731	6.95	1.638 552	4.31	38
39	10.637 231	154.195 704	.006 485 2650	.094 009	14.495 849	.068 985 2650	6.90	1.690 425	4.33	39
40	11.302 058	164.832 935	.006 066 7487	.088 479	14.584 329	.068 566 7487	6.86	1.742 670	4.36	40
41	12.008 437	176.134 994	.005 677 4635	.083 275	14.667 603	.068 177 4635	6.82	1.795 276	4.38	41
42	12.758 964	188.143 431	.005 315 0939	.078 376	14.745 980	.067 815 0939	6.79	1.848 234	4.40	42
43	13.556 400	200.902 395	.004 977 5415	.073 766	14.819 746	.067 477 5415	6.75	1.901 534	4.42	43
44	14.403 675	214.458 795	.004 662 9004	.069 427	14.889 172	.067 162 9004	6.72	1.955 168	4.44	44
45	15.303 904	228.862 470	.004 369 4364	.065 343	14.954 515	.066 869 4364	6.69	2.009 125	4.46	45
46	16.260 398	244.166 374	.004 095 5681	.061 499	15.016 014	.066 595 5681	6.66	2.063 396	4.49	46
47	17.276 673	260.426 772	.003 839 8510	.057 882	15.073 896	.066 339 8510	6.64	2.117 973	4.51	47
48	18.356 465	277.703 445	.003 600 9636	.054 477	15.128 372	.066 100 9636	6.62	2.172 846	4.53	48
49	19.503 744	296.059 911	.003 377 6947	.051 272	15.179 645	.065 877 6947	6.59	2.228 007	4.55	49
50	20.722 728	315.563 655	.003 168 9327	.048 256	15.227 901	.065 668 9327	6.57	2.283 447	4.57	50

Effective Rate is 6.25 %

Annual Percentage Rate is 6.25 %

ANNUAL COMPOUND INTEREST AND ANNUITY

6.50 % A

Amount Of 1	Amount Of 1 Per Period	Sinking Fund Payment	Present Worth Of 1	Present Worth of 1 Per Period	Periodic Payment To Amortize 1	Constant Annual Percent	Total Interest	Annual Add On Rate
What a single $ 1 deposit grows to in the future. The deposit is made at the beginning of the first period.	What a series of $ 1 deposits grow to in the future. A deposit is made at the end of each period.	The amount to be deposited at the end of each period that grows to $ 1 in the future.	What $ 1 to be paid in the future is worth today. Value today of a single $ 1 payment tomorrow.	What $ 1 to be paid at the end of each period is worth today. Value today of a series of $ 1 payments tomorrow.	The mortgage payment to amortize a loan of $ 1. An annuity certain, payable at the end of each period, worth $ 1 today.	The annual payment, including interest and principal, to amortize completely a loan of $ 100.	The total interest paid over the term on a loan of $1. The loan is amortized by regular periodic payments.	The average annual interest rate on a loan that is completely amortized by regular periodic payments.
$S = (1+i)^n$	$S\overline{n} = \dfrac{(1+i)^n - 1}{i}$	$\dfrac{1}{S\overline{n}} = \dfrac{i}{(1+i)^n - 1}$	$V^n = \dfrac{1}{(1+i)^n}$	$A\overline{n} = \dfrac{1 - V^n}{i}$	$\dfrac{1}{A\overline{n}} = \dfrac{i}{1 - V^n}$			

YEAR									PERIODS
	1.065 000	1.000 000	1.000 000 0000	.938 967	.938 967	1.065 000 0000	106.50	.065 000	6.50	1

YEAR	Amount Of 1	Amount Of 1 Per Period	Sinking Fund Payment	Present Worth Of 1	Present Worth of 1 Per Period	Periodic Payment To Amortize 1	Constant Annual Percent	Total Interest	Annual Add On Rate	PERIODS
1	1.065 000	1.000 000	1.000 000 0000	.938 967	.938 967	1.065 000 0000	106.50	.065 000	6.50	1
2	1.134 225	2.065 000	.484 261 5012	.881 659	1.820 626	.549 261 5012	54.93	.098 523	4.93	2
3	1.207 950	3.199 225	.312 575 7019	.827 849	2.648 476	.377 575 7019	37.76	.132 727	4.42	3
4	1.286 466	4.407 175	.226 902 7404	.777 323	3.425 799	.291 902 7404	29.20	.167 611	4.19	4
5	1.370 087	5.693 641	.175 634 5376	.729 881	4.155 679	.240 634 5376	24.07	.203 173	4.06	5
6	1.459 142	7.063 728	.141 568 3122	.685 334	4.841 014	.206 568 3122	20.66	.239 410	3.99	6
7	1.553 987	8.522 870	.117 331 3693	.643 506	5.484 520	.182 331 3693	18.24	.276 320	3.95	7
8	1.654 996	10.076 856	.099 237 2971	.604 231	6.088 751	.164 237 2971	16.43	.313 898	3.92	8
9	1.762 570	11.731 852	.085 238 0329	.567 353	6.656 104	.150 238 0329	15.03	.352 142	3.91	9
10	1.877 137	13.494 423	.074 104 6901	.532 726	7.188 830	.139 104 6901	13.92	.391 047	3.91	10
11	1.999 151	15.371 560	.065 055 2058	.500 212	7.689 042	.130 055 2058	13.01	.430 607	3.91	11
12	2.129 096	17.370 711	.057 568 1661	.469 683	8.158 725	.122 568 1661	12.26	.470 818	3.92	12
13	2.267 487	19.499 808	.051 282 5571	.441 017	8.599 742	.116 282 5571	11.63	.511 673	3.94	13
14	2.414 874	21.767 295	.045 940 4806	.414 100	9.013 842	.110 940 4806	11.10	.553 167	3.95	14
15	2.571 841	24.182 169	.041 352 7830	.388 827	9.402 669	.106 352 7830	10.64	.595 292	3.97	15
16	2.739 011	26.754 010	.037 377 5740	.365 095	9.767 764	.102 377 5740	10.24	.638 041	3.99	16
17	2.917 046	29.493 021	.033 906 3265	.342 813	10.110 577	.098 906 3265	9.90	.681 408	4.01	17
18	3.106 654	32.410 067	.030 854 6103	.321 890	10.432 466	.095 854 6103	9.59	.725 383	4.03	18
19	3.308 587	35.516 722	.028 155 7517	.302 244	10.734 710	.093 155 7517	9.32	.769 959	4.05	19
20	3.523 645	38.825 309	.025 756 3954	.283 797	11.018 507	.090 756 3954	9.08	.815 128	4.08	20
21	3.752 682	42.348 954	.023 613 3343	.266 476	11.284 983	.088 613 3343	8.87	.860 880	4.10	21
22	3.996 606	46.101 636	.021 691 2043	.250 212	11.535 196	.086 691 2043	8.67	.907 207	4.12	22
23	4.256 386	50.098 242	.019 960 7802	.234 941	11.770 137	.084 960 7802	8.50	.954 098	4.15	23
24	4.533 051	54.354 628	.018 397 6975	.220 602	11.990 739	.083 397 6975	8.34	1.001 545	4.17	24
25	4.827 699	58.887 679	.016 981 4811	.207 138	12.197 877	.081 981 4811	8.20	1.049 537	4.20	25
26	5.141 500	63.715 378	.015 694 7983	.194 496	12.392 373	.080 694 7983	8.07	1.098 065	4.22	26
27	5.475 697	68.856 877	.014 522 8776	.182 625	12.574 998	.079 522 8776	7.96	1.147 118	4.25	27
28	5.831 617	74.332 574	.013 453 0522	.171 479	12.746 477	.078 453 0522	7.85	1.196 685	4.27	28
29	6.210 672	80.164 192	.012 474 3976	.161 013	12.907 490	.077 474 3976	7.75	1.246 758	4.30	29
30	6.614 366	86.374 864	.011 577 4422	.151 186	13.058 676	.076 577 4422	7.66	1.297 323	4.32	30
31	7.044 300	92.989 230	.010 753 9335	.141 959	13.200 635	.075 753 9335	7.58	1.348 372	4.35	31
32	7.502 179	100.033 530	.009 996 6481	.133 295	13.333 929	.074 996 6481	7.50	1.399 893	4.37	32
33	7.989 821	107.535 710	.009 299 2365	.125 159	13.459 088	.074 299 2365	7.43	1.451 875	4.40	33
34	8.509 159	115.525 531	.008 656 0953	.117 520	13.576 609	.073 656 0953	7.37	1.504 307	4.42	34
35	9.062 255	124.034 690	.008 062 2606	.110 348	13.686 957	.073 062 2606	7.31	1.557 179	4.45	35
36	9.651 301	133.096 945	.007 513 3205	.103 613	13.790 570	.072 513 3205	7.26	1.610 480	4.47	36
37	10.278 636	142.748 247	.007 005 3400	.097 289	13.887 859	.072 005 3400	7.21	1.664 198	4.50	37
38	10.946 747	153.026 883	.006 534 7995	.091 351	13.979 210	.071 534 7995	7.16	1.718 322	4.52	38
39	11.658 286	163.973 630	.006 098 5416	.085 776	14.064 986	.071 098 5416	7.11	1.772 843	4.55	39
40	12.416 075	175.631 916	.005 693 7260	.080 541	14.145 527	.070 693 7260	7.07	1.827 749	4.57	40
41	13.223 119	188.047 990	.005 317 7915	.075 625	14.221 152	.070 317 7915	7.04	1.883 029	4.59	41
42	14.082 622	201.271 110	.004 968 4229	.071 010	14.292 161	.069 968 4229	7.00	1.938 674	4.62	42
43	14.997 993	215.353 732	.004 643 5230	.066 676	14.358 837	.069 643 5230	6.97	1.994 671	4.64	43
44	15.972 862	230.351 725	.004 341 1874	.062 606	14.421 443	.069 341 1874	6.94	2.051 012	4.66	44
45	17.011 098	246.324 587	.004 059 6841	.058 785	14.480 228	.069 059 6841	6.91	2.107 686	4.68	45
46	18.116 820	263.335 685	.003 797 4344	.055 197	14.535 426	.068 797 4344	6.88	2.164 682	4.71	46
47	19.294 413	281.452 504	.003 552 9973	.051 828	14.587 254	.068 552 9973	6.86	2.221 991	4.73	47
48	20.548 550	300.746 917	.003 325 0549	.048 665	14.635 919	.068 325 0549	6.84	2.279 603	4.75	48
49	21.884 205	321.295 467	.003 112 4000	.045 695	14.681 615	.068 112 4000	6.82	2.337 508	4.77	49
50	23.306 679	343.179 672	.002 913 9255	.042 906	14.724 521	.067 913 9255	6.80	2.395 696	4.79	50

Effective Rate is 6.50 %

Annual Percentage Rate is 6.50 %

Amount Of 1	Amount Of 1 Per Period	Sinking Fund Payment	Present Worth Of 1	Present Worth of 1 Per Period	Periodic Payment To Amortize 1	Constant Annual Percent	Total Interest	Annual Add On Rate	
What a single $ 1 deposit grows to in the future. The deposit is made at the beginning of the first period.	What a series of $ 1 deposits grow to in the future. A deposit is made at the end of each period.	The amount to be deposited at the end of each period that grows to $ 1 in the future.	What $ 1 to be paid in the future is worth today. Value today of a single $ 1 payment tomorrow.	What $ 1 to be paid at the end of each period is worth today. Value today of a series of $ 1 payments tomorrow.	The mortgage payment to amortize a loan of $ 1. An annuity certain, payable at the end of each period, worth $ 1 today.	The annual payment, including interest and principal, to amortize completely a loan of $ 100.	The total interest paid over the term on a loan of $1. The loan is amortized by regular periodic payments.	The average annual interest rate on a loan that is completely amortized by regular periodic payments.	
$S = (1+i)^n$	$S\overline{n}| = \dfrac{(1+i)^n - 1}{i}$	$\dfrac{1}{S\overline{n}|} = \dfrac{i}{(1+i)^n - 1}$	$V^n = \dfrac{1}{(1+i)^n}$	$A\overline{n}| = \dfrac{1 - V^n}{i}$	$\dfrac{1}{A\overline{n}|} = \dfrac{i}{1 - V^n}$				

YEAR — **PERIODS**

	Amount Of 1	Amount Of 1 Per Period	Sinking Fund Payment	Present Worth Of 1	Present Worth of 1 Per Period	Periodic Payment To Amortize 1	Constant Annual Percent	Total Interest	Annual Add On Rate	
	1.067 500	1.000 000	1.000 000 0000	.936 768	.936 768	1.067 500 0000	106.75	.067 500	6.75	1
1	1.067 500	1.000 000	1.000 000 0000	.936 768	.936 768	1.067 500 0000	106.75	.067 500	6.75	1
2	1.139 556	2.067 500	.483 675 9371	.877 535	1.814 303	.551 175 9371	55.12	.102 352	5.12	2
3	1.216 476	3.207 056	.311 812 4292	.822 046	2.636 349	.379 312 4292	37.94	.137 937	4.60	3
4	1.298 588	4.423 533	.226 063 6696	.770 067	3.406 416	.293 563 6696	29.36	.174 255	4.36	4
5	1.386 243	5.722 121	.174 760 3731	.721 374	4.127 790	.242 260 3731	24.23	.211 302	4.23	5
6	1.479 815	7.108 364	.140 679 3430	.675 760	4.803 551	.208 179 3430	20.82	.249 076	4.15	6
7	1.579 702	8.588 179	.116 439 1229	.633 031	5.436 581	.183 939 1229	18.40	.287 574	4.11	7
8	1.686 332	10.167 881	.098 348 9106	.593 003	6.029 584	.165 848 9106	16.59	.326 791	4.08	8
9	1.800 159	11.854 213	.084 358 1957	.555 506	6.585 091	.151 858 1957	15.19	.366 724	4.07	9
10	1.921 670	13.654 372	.073 236 6154	.520 381	7.105 471	.140 736 6154	14.08	.407 366	4.07	10
11	2.051 383	15.576 042	.064 201 1613	.487 476	7.592 947	.131 701 1613	13.18	.448 713	4.08	11
12	2.189 851	17.627 425	.056 729 7830	.456 652	8.049 600	.124 229 7830	12.43	.490 757	4.09	12
13	2.337 666	19.817 276	.050 461 0213	.427 777	8.477 377	.117 961 0213	11.80	.533 493	4.10	13
14	2.495 459	22.154 942	.045 136 6553	.400 728	8.878 105	.112 636 6553	11.27	.576 913	4.12	14
15	2.663 902	24.650 401	.040 567 2913	.375 389	9.253 494	.108 067 2913	10.81	.621 009	4.14	15
16	2.843 715	27.314 303	.036 610 8553	.351 653	9.605 146	.104 110 8553	10.42	.665 774	4.16	16
17	3.035 666	30.158 019	.033 158 6771	.329 417	9.934 563	.100 658 6771	10.07	.711 198	4.18	17
18	3.240 574	33.193 685	.030 126 2124	.308 587	10.243 151	.097 626 2124	9.77	.757 272	4.21	18
19	3.459 312	36.434 259	.027 446 6955	.289 075	10.532 225	.094 946 6955	9.50	.803 987	4.23	19
20	3.692 816	39.893 571	.025 066 6956	.270 796	10.803 021	.092 566 6956	9.26	.851 334	4.26	20
21	3.942 081	43.586 387	.022 942 9431	.253 673	11.056 695	.090 442 9431	9.05	.899 302	4.28	21
22	4.208 172	47.528 468	.021 040 0217	.237 633	11.294 327	.088 540 0217	8.86	.947 880	4.31	22
23	4.492 223	51.736 640	.019 328 6615	.222 607	11.516 934	.086 828 6615	8.69	.997 059	4.34	23
24	4.795 448	56.228 863	.017 784 4606	.208 531	11.725 465	.085 284 4606	8.53	1.046 827	4.36	24
25	5.119 141	61.024 311	.016 386 9117	.195 345	11.920 811	.083 886 9117	8.39	1.097 173	4.39	25
26	5.464 683	66.143 452	.015 118 6545	.182 993	12.103 804	.082 618 6545	8.27	1.148 085	4.42	26
27	5.833 549	71.608 135	.013 964 8937	.171 422	12.275 226	.081 464 8937	8.15	1.199 552	4.44	27
28	6.227 314	77.441 684	.012 912 9423	.160 583	12.435 809	.080 412 9423	8.05	1.251 562	4.47	28
29	6.647 657	83.668 998	.011 951 8582	.150 429	12.586 238	.079 451 8582	7.95	1.304 104	4.50	29
30	7.096 374	90.316 655	.011 072 1549	.140 917	12.727 155	.078 572 1549	7.86	1.357 165	4.52	30
31	7.575 380	97.413 030	.010 265 5672	.132 007	12.859 162	.077 765 5672	7.78	1.410 733	4.55	31
32	8.086 718	104.988 409	.009 524 8610	.123 660	12.982 821	.077 024 8610	7.71	1.464 796	4.58	32
33	8.632 571	113.075 127	.008 843 6779	.115 840	13.098 662	.076 343 6779	7.64	1.519 341	4.60	33
34	9.215 270	121.707 698	.008 216 4072	.108 516	13.207 177	.075 716 4072	7.58	1.574 358	4.63	34
35	9.837 300	130.922 967	.007 638 0792	.101 654	13.308 831	.075 138 0792	7.52	1.629 833	4.66	35
36	10.501 318	140.760 268	.007 104 2775	.095 226	13.404 057	.074 604 2775	7.47	1.685 754	4.68	36
37	11.210 157	151.261 586	.006 611 0638	.089 205	13.493 262	.074 111 0638	7.42	1.742 109	4.71	37
38	11.966 843	162.471 743	.006 154 9164	.083 564	13.576 826	.073 654 9164	7.37	1.798 887	4.73	38
39	12.774 605	174.438 586	.005 732 6766	.078 280	13.655 107	.073 232 6766	7.33	1.856 074	4.76	39
40	13.636 890	187.213 190	.005 341 5040	.073 331	13.728 437	.072 841 5040	7.29	1.913 660	4.78	40
41	14.557 380	200.850 080	.004 978 8379	.068 694	13.797 131	.072 478 8379	7.25	1.971 632	4.81	41
42	15.540 004	215.407 461	.004 642 3647	.064 350	13.861 481	.072 142 3647	7.22	2.029 979	4.83	42
43	16.588 954	230.947 464	.004 329 9891	.060 281	13.921 762	.071 829 9891	7.19	2.088 690	4.86	43
44	17.708 708	247.536 418	.004 039 8096	.056 469	13.978 231	.071 539 8096	7.16	2.147 752	4.88	44
45	18.904 046	265.245 127	.003 770 0975	.052 899	14.031 130	.071 270 0975	7.13	2.207 154	4.90	45
46	20.180 069	284.149 173	.003 519 2782	.049 554	14.080 684	.071 019 2782	7.11	2.266 887	4.93	46
47	21.542 224	304.329 242	.003 285 9149	.046 420	14.127 104	.070 785 9149	7.08	2.326 938	4.95	47
48	22.996 324	325.871 466	.003 068 6946	.043 485	14.170 589	.070 568 6946	7.06	2.387 297	4.97	48
49	24.548 576	348.867 789	.002 866 4154	.040 736	14.211 325	.070 366 4154	7.04	2.447 954	5.00	49
50	26.205 605	373.416 365	.002 677 9758	.038 160	14.249 485	.070 177 9758	7.02	2.508 899	5.02	50

ANNUAL COMPOUND INTEREST AND ANNUITY

7.00 % A

Amount Of 1	Amount Of 1 Per Period	Sinking Fund Payment	Present Worth Of 1	Present Worth of 1 Per Period	Periodic Payment To Amortize 1	Constant Annual Percent	Total Interest	Annual Add On Rate
What a single $ 1 deposit grows to in the future. The deposit is made at the beginning of the first period.	What a series of $ 1 deposits grow to in the future. A deposit is made at the end of each period.	The amount to be deposited at the end of each period that grows to $ 1 in the future.	What $ 1 to be paid in the future is worth today. Value today of a single $ 1 payment tomorrow.	What $ 1 to be paid at the end of each period is worth today. Value today of a series of $ 1 payments tomorrow.	The mortgage payment to amortize a loan of $ 1. An annuity certain, payable at the end of each period, worth $ 1 today.	The annual payment, including interest and principal, to amortize completely a loan of $ 100.	The total interest paid over the term on a loan of $1. The loan is amortized by regular periodic payments.	The average annual interest rate on a loan that is completely amortized by regular periodic payments.

$$S = (1+i)^n \qquad S\overline{n}| = \frac{(1+i)^n - 1}{i} \qquad \frac{1}{S\overline{n}|} = \frac{i}{(1+i)^n - 1} \qquad V^n = \frac{1}{(1+i)^n} \qquad A\overline{n}| = \frac{1 - V^n}{i} \qquad \frac{1}{A\overline{n}|} = \frac{i}{1 - V^n}$$

YEAR									PERIODS
	1.070 000	1.000 000	1.000 000 0000	.934 579	.934 579	1.070 000 0000	107.00	.070 000	7.00	1

YEAR	Amount Of 1	Amount Of 1 Per Period	Sinking Fund Payment	Present Worth Of 1	Present Worth of 1 Per Period	Periodic Payment To Amortize 1	Constant Annual Percent	Total Interest	Annual Add On Rate	PERIODS
1	1.070 000	1.000 000	1.000 000 0000	.934 579	.934 579	1.070 000 0000	107.00	.070 000	7.00	1
2	1.144 900	2.070 000	.483 091 7874	.873 439	1.808 018	.553 091 7874	55.31	.106 184	5.31	2
3	1.225 043	3.214 900	.311 051 6657	.816 298	2.624 316	.381 051 6657	38.11	.143 155	4.77	3
4	1.310 796	4.439 943	.225 228 1167	.762 895	3.387 211	.295 228 1167	29.53	.180 912	4.52	4
5	1.402 552	5.750 739	.173 890 6944	.712 986	4.100 197	.243 890 6944	24.39	.219 453	4.39	5
6	1.500 730	7.153 291	.139 795 7998	.666 342	4.766 540	.209 795 7998	20.98	.258 775	4.31	6
7	1.605 781	8.654 021	.115 553 2196	.622 750	5.389 289	.185 553 2196	18.56	.298 873	4.27	7
8	1.718 186	10.259 803	.097 467 7625	.582 009	5.971 299	.167 467 7625	16.75	.339 742	4.25	8
9	1.838 459	11.977 989	.083 486 4701	.543 934	6.515 232	.153 486 4701	15.35	.381 378	4.24	9
10	1.967 151	13.816 448	.072 377 5027	.508 349	7.023 582	.142 377 5027	14.24	.423 775	4.24	10
11	2.104 852	15.783 599	.063 356 9048	.475 093	7.498 674	.133 356 9048	13.34	.466 926	4.24	11
12	2.252 192	17.888 451	.055 901 9887	.444 012	7.942 686	.125 901 9887	12.60	.510 824	4.26	12
13	2.409 845	20.140 643	.049 650 8481	.414 964	8.357 651	.119 650 8481	11.97	.555 461	4.27	13
14	2.578 534	22.550 488	.044 344 9386	.387 817	8.745 468	.114 344 9386	11.44	.600 829	4.29	14
15	2.759 032	25.129 022	.039 794 6247	.362 446	9.107 914	.109 794 6247	10.98	.646 919	4.31	15
16	2.952 164	27.888 054	.035 857 6477	.338 735	9.446 649	.105 857 6477	10.59	.693 722	4.34	16
17	3.158 815	30.840 217	.032 425 1931	.316 574	9.763 223	.102 425 1931	10.25	.741 228	4.36	17
18	3.379 932	33.999 033	.029 412 6017	.295 864	10.059 087	.099 412 6017	9.95	.789 427	4.39	18
19	3.616 528	37.378 965	.026 753 0148	.276 508	10.335 595	.096 753 0148	9.68	.838 307	4.41	19
20	3.869 684	40.995 492	.024 392 9257	.258 419	10.594 014	.094 392 9257	9.44	.887 859	4.44	20
21	4.140 562	44.865 177	.022 289 0017	.241 513	10.835 527	.092 289 0017	9.23	.938 069	4.47	21
22	4.430 402	49.005 739	.020 405 7732	.225 713	11.061 240	.090 405 7732	9.05	.988 927	4.50	22
23	4.740 530	53.436 141	.018 713 9263	.210 947	11.272 187	.088 713 9263	8.88	1.040 420	4.52	23
24	5.072 367	58.176 671	.017 189 0207	.197 147	11.469 334	.087 189 0207	8.72	1.092 537	4.55	24
25	5.427 433	63.249 038	.015 810 5172	.184 249	11.653 583	.085 810 5172	8.59	1.145 263	4.58	25
26	5.807 353	68.676 470	.014 561 0279	.172 195	11.825 779	.084 561 0279	8.46	1.198 587	4.61	26
27	6.213 868	74.483 823	.013 425 7340	.160 930	11.986 709	.083 425 7340	8.35	1.252 495	4.64	27
28	6.648 838	80.697 691	.012 391 9283	.150 402	12.137 111	.082 391 9283	8.24	1.306 974	4.67	28
29	7.114 257	87.346 529	.011 448 6518	.140 563	12.277 674	.081 448 6518	8.15	1.362 011	4.70	29
30	7.612 255	94.460 786	.010 586 4035	.131 367	12.409 041	.080 586 4035	8.06	1.417 592	4.73	30
31	8.145 113	102.073 041	.009 796 9061	.122 773	12.531 814	.079 796 9061	7.98	1.473 704	4.75	31
32	8.715 271	110.218 154	.009 072 9155	.114 741	12.646 555	.079 072 9155	7.91	1.530 333	4.78	32
33	9.325 340	118.933 425	.008 408 0653	.107 235	12.753 790	.078 408 0653	7.85	1.587 466	4.81	33
34	9.978 114	128.258 765	.007 796 7381	.100 219	12.854 009	.077 796 7381	7.78	1.645 089	4.84	34
35	10.676 581	138.236 878	.007 233 9596	.093 663	12.947 672	.077 233 9596	7.73	1.703 189	4.87	35
36	11.423 942	148.913 460	.006 715 3097	.087 535	13.035 208	.076 715 3097	7.68	1.761 751	4.89	36
37	12.223 618	160.337 402	.006 236 8480	.081 809	13.117 017	.076 236 8480	7.63	1.820 763	4.92	37
38	13.079 271	172.561 020	.005 795 0515	.076 457	13.193 473	.075 795 0515	7.58	1.880 212	4.95	38
39	13.994 820	185.640 292	.005 386 7616	.071 455	13.264 928	.075 386 7616	7.54	1.940 084	4.97	39
40	14.974 458	199.635 112	.005 009 1389	.066 780	13.331 709	.075 009 1389	7.51	2.000 366	5.00	40
41	16.022 670	214.609 570	.004 659 6245	.062 412	13.394 120	.074 659 6245	7.47	2.061 045	5.03	41
42	17.144 257	230.632 240	.004 335 9072	.058 329	13.452 449	.074 335 9072	7.44	2.122 108	5.05	42
43	18.344 355	247.776 496	.004 035 8953	.054 513	13.506 962	.074 035 8953	7.41	2.183 544	5.08	43
44	19.628 460	266.120 851	.003 757 6913	.050 946	13.557 908	.073 757 6913	7.38	2.245 338	5.10	44
45	21.002 452	285.749 311	.003 499 5710	.047 613	13.605 522	.073 499 5710	7.35	2.307 481	5.13	45
46	22.472 623	306.751 763	.003 259 9650	.044 499	13.650 020	.073 259 9650	7.33	2.369 958	5.15	46
47	24.045 707	329.224 386	.003 037 4421	.041 587	13.691 608	.073 037 4421	7.31	2.432 760	5.18	47
48	25.728 907	353.270 093	.002 830 6953	.038 867	13.730 474	.072 830 6953	7.29	2.495 873	5.20	48
49	27.529 930	378.999 000	.002 638 5294	.036 324	13.766 799	.072 638 5294	7.27	2.559 288	5.22	49
50	29.457 025	406.528 929	.002 459 8495	.033 948	13.800 746	.072 459 8495	7.25	2.622 992	5.25	50

Effective Rate is 7.00 %

Annual Percentage Rate is 7.00 %

ANNUAL COMPOUND INTEREST AND ANNUITY

	Amount Of 1	Amount Of 1 Per Period	Sinking Fund Payment	Present Worth Of 1	Present Worth of 1 Per Period	Periodic Payment To Amortize 1	Constant Annual Percent	Total Interest	Annual Add On Rate	
	What a single $ 1 deposit grows to in the future. The deposit is made at the beginning of the first period.	What a series of $ 1 deposits grow to in the future. A deposit is made at the end of each period.	The amount to be deposited at the end of each period that grows to $ 1 in the future.	What $ 1 to be paid in the future is worth today. Value today of a single $ 1 payment tomorrow.	What $ 1 to be paid at the end of each period is worth today. Value today of a series of $ 1 payments tomorrow.	The mortgage payment to amortize a loan of $ 1. An annuity certain, payable at the end of each period, worth $ 1 today.	The annual payment, including interest and principal, to amortize completely a loan of $ 100.	The total interest paid over the term on a loan of $1. The loan is amortized by regular periodic payments.	The average annual interest rate on a loan that is completely amortized by regular periodic payments.	
	$S = (1 + i)^n$	$S\overline{n} = \dfrac{(1+i)^n - 1}{i}$	$\dfrac{1}{S\overline{n}} = \dfrac{i}{(1+i)^n - 1}$	$V^n = \dfrac{1}{(1+i)^n}$	$A\overline{n} = \dfrac{1 - V^n}{i}$	$\dfrac{1}{A\overline{n}} = \dfrac{i}{1 - V^n}$				

YEAR										PERIODS
	1.072 500	1.000 000	1.000 000 0000	.932 401	.932 401	1.072 500 0000	107.25	.072 500	7.25	1

YEAR	Amount Of 1	Amount Of 1 Per Period	Sinking Fund Payment	Present Worth Of 1	Present Worth of 1 Per Period	Periodic Payment To Amortize 1	Constant Annual Percent	Total Interest	Annual Add On Rate	PERIODS
1	1.072 500	1.000 000	1.000 000 0000	.932 401	.932 401	1.072 500 0000	107.25	.072 500	7.25	1
2	1.150 256	2.072 500	.482 509 0470	.869 371	1.801 772	.555 009 0470	55.51	.110 018	5.50	2
3	1.233 650	3.222 756	.310 293 4018	.810 603	2.612 375	.382 793 4018	38.28	.148 380	4.95	3
4	1.323 089	4.456 406	.224 396 0677	.755 807	3.368 182	.296 896 0677	29.69	.187 584	4.69	4
5	1.419 013	5.779 496	.173 025 4824	.704 715	4.072 897	.245 525 4824	24.56	.227 627	4.55	5
6	1.521 892	7.198 509	.138 917 6575	.657 077	4.729 974	.211 417 6575	21.15	.268 506	4.48	6
7	1.632 229	8.720 401	.114 673 6277	.612 659	5.342 633	.187 173 6277	18.72	.310 215	4.43	7
8	1.750 566	10.352 630	.096 593 8133	.571 244	5.913 877	.169 093 8133	16.91	.352 751	4.41	8
9	1.877 482	12.103 196	.082 622 8077	.532 628	6.446 505	.155 122 8077	15.52	.396 105	4.40	9
10	2.013 599	13.980 677	.071 527 2931	.496 623	6.943 128	.144 027 2931	14.41	.440 273	4.40	10
11	2.159 585	15.994 276	.062 522 3660	.463 052	7.406 180	.135 022 3660	13.51	.485 246	4.41	11
12	2.316 155	18.153 861	.055 084 6995	.431 750	7.837 930	.127 584 6995	12.76	.531 016	4.43	12
13	2.484 076	20.470 016	.048 851 9395	.402 564	8.240 495	.121 351 9395	12.14	.577 575	4.44	13
14	2.664 172	22.954 093	.043 565 2161	.375 351	8.615 846	.116 065 2161	11.61	.624 913	4.46	14
15	2.857 324	25.618 264	.039 034 6509	.349 978	8.965 824	.111 534 6509	11.16	.673 020	4.49	15
16	3.064 480	28.475 588	.035 117 7994	.326 320	9.292 143	.107 617 7994	10.77	.721 885	4.51	16
17	3.286 655	31.540 069	.031 705 7015	.304 261	9.596 404	.104 205 7015	10.43	.771 497	4.54	17
18	3.524 937	34.826 724	.028 713 5825	.283 693	9.880 097	.101 213 5825	10.13	.821 844	4.57	18
19	3.780 495	38.351 661	.026 074 4900	.264 516	10.144 612	.098 574 4900	9.86	.872 915	4.59	19
20	4.054 581	42.132 156	.023 734 8402	.246 635	10.391 247	.096 234 8402	9.63	.924 697	4.62	20
21	4.348 538	46.186 738	.021 651 2369	.229 962	10.621 209	.094 151 2369	9.42	.977 176	4.65	21
22	4.663 808	50.535 276	.019 788 1574	.214 417	10.835 626	.092 288 1574	9.23	1.030 339	4.68	22
23	5.001 934	55.199 084	.018 116 2427	.199 923	11.035 549	.090 616 2427	9.07	1.084 174	4.71	23
24	5.364 574	60.201 017	.016 611 0150	.186 408	11.221 957	.089 111 0150	8.92	1.138 664	4.74	24
25	5.753 505	65.565 591	.015 251 9025	.173 807	11.395 764	.087 751 9025	8.78	1.193 798	4.78	25
26	6.170 634	71.319 096	.014 021 4900	.162 058	11.557 822	.086 521 4900	8.66	1.249 559	4.81	26
27	6.618 005	77.489 731	.012 904 9358	.151 103	11.708 925	.085 404 9358	8.55	1.305 933	4.84	27
28	7.097 811	84.107 736	.011 889 5127	.140 889	11.849 814	.084 389 5127	8.44	1.362 906	4.87	28
29	7.612 402	91.205 547	.010 964 2454	.131 365	11.981 178	.083 464 2454	8.35	1.420 463	4.90	29
30	8.164 301	98.817 949	.010 119 6190	.122 484	12.103 663	.082 619 6190	8.27	1.478 589	4.93	30
31	8.756 213	106.982 251	.009 347 3449	.114 205	12.217 867	.081 847 3449	8.19	1.537 268	4.96	31
32	9.391 039	115.738 464	.008 640 1700	.106 484	12.324 352	.081 140 1700	8.12	1.596 485	4.99	32
33	10.071 889	125.129 503	.007 991 7204	.099 286	12.423 638	.080 491 7204	8.05	1.656 227	5.02	33
34	10.802 101	135.201 392	.007 396 3736	.092 575	12.516 213	.079 896 3736	7.99	1.716 477	5.05	34
35	11.585 253	146.003 492	.006 849 1512	.086 317	12.602 529	.079 349 1512	7.94	1.777 220	5.08	35
36	12.425 184	157.588 746	.006 345 6308	.080 482	12.683 011	.078 845 6308	7.89	1.838 443	5.11	36
37	13.326 010	170.013 930	.005 881 8710	.075 041	12.758 052	.078 381 8710	7.84	1.900 129	5.14	37
38	14.292 146	183.339 940	.005 454 3489	.069 969	12.828 021	.077 954 3489	7.80	1.962 265	5.16	38
39	15.328 326	197.632 085	.005 059 9071	.065 239	12.893 259	.077 559 9071	7.76	2.024 836	5.19	39
40	16.439 630	212.960 411	.004 695 7084	.060 829	12.954 088	.077 195 7084	7.72	2.087 828	5.22	40
41	17.631 503	229.400 041	.004 359 1971	.056 717	13.010 805	.076 859 1971	7.69	2.151 227	5.25	41
42	18.909 787	247.031 544	.004 048 0660	.052 883	13.063 687	.076 548 0660	7.66	2.215 019	5.27	42
43	20.280 747	265.941 331	.003 760 2278	.049 308	13.112 995	.076 260 2278	7.63	2.279 190	5.30	43
44	21.751 101	286.222 078	.003 493 7906	.045 975	13.158 970	.075 993 7906	7.60	2.343 727	5.33	44
45	23.328 055	307.973 178	.003 247 0360	.042 867	13.201 837	.075 747 0360	7.58	2.408 617	5.35	45
46	25.019 339	331.301 234	.003 018 4011	.039 969	13.241 806	.075 518 4011	7.56	2.473 846	5.38	46
47	26.833 242	356.320 573	.002 806 4616	.037 267	13.279 073	.075 306 4616	7.54	2.539 404	5.40	47
48	28.778 652	383.153 815	.002 609 9179	.034 748	13.313 821	.075 109 9179	7.52	2.605 276	5.43	48
49	30.865 104	411.932 466	.002 427 5824	.032 399	13.346 220	.074 927 5824	7.50	2.671 452	5.45	49
50	33.102 824	442.797 570	.002 258 3683	.030 209	13.376 429	.074 758 3683	7.48	2.737 918	5.48	50

Effective Rate is 7.25 %

Annual Percentage Rate is 7.25 %

ANNUAL COMPOUND INTEREST AND ANNUITY

7.50 % A

	Amount Of 1	Amount Of 1 Per Period	Sinking Fund Payment	Present Worth Of 1	Present Worth of 1 Per Period	Periodic Payment To Amortize 1	Constant Annual Percent	Total Interest	Annual Add On Rate	
	What a single $ 1 deposit grows to in the future. The deposit is made at the beginning of the first period.	What a series of $ 1 deposits grow to in the future. A deposit is made at the end of each period.	The amount to be deposited at the end of each period that grows to $ 1 in the future.	What $ 1 to be paid in the future is worth today. Value today of a single $ 1 payment tomorrow.	What $ 1 to be paid at the end of each period is worth today. Value today of a series of $ 1 payments tomorrow.	The mortgage payment to amortize a loan of $ 1. An annuity certain, payable at the end of each period, worth $ 1 today.	The annual payment, including interest and principal, to amortize a loan of $ 100.	The total interest paid over the term on a loan of $1. The loan is amortized by regular periodic payments.	The average annual interest rate on a loan that is completely amortized by regular periodic payments.	
	$S = (1+i)^n$	$S\overline{n} = \dfrac{(1+i)^n - 1}{i}$	$\dfrac{1}{S\overline{n}} = \dfrac{i}{(1+i)^n - 1}$	$V^n = \dfrac{1}{(1+i)^n}$	$A\overline{n} = \dfrac{1-V^n}{i}$	$\dfrac{1}{A\overline{n}} = \dfrac{i}{1-V^n}$				

YEAR										PERIODS
	1.075 000	1.000 000	1.000 000 0000	.930 233	.930 233	1.075 000 0000	107.50	.075 000	7.50	1

YEAR	Amount Of 1	Amount Of 1 Per Period	Sinking Fund Payment	Present Worth Of 1	Present Worth of 1 Per Period	Periodic Payment To Amortize 1	Constant Annual Percent	Total Interest	Annual Add On Rate	PERIODS
1	1.075 000	1.000 000	1.000 000 0000	.930 233	.930 233	1.075 000 0000	107.50	.075 000	7.50	1
2	1.155 625	2.075 000	.481 927 7108	.865 333	1.795 565	.556 927 7108	55.70	.113 855	5.69	2
3	1.242 297	3.230 625	.309 537 6282	.804 961	2.600 526	.384 537 6282	38.46	.153 613	5.12	3
4	1.335 469	4.472 922	.223 567 5087	.748 801	3.349 326	.298 567 5087	29.86	.194 270	4.86	4
5	1.435 629	5.808 391	.172 164 7178	.696 559	4.045 885	.247 164 7178	24.72	.235 824	4.72	5
6	1.543 302	7.244 020	.138 044 8912	.647 962	4.693 846	.213 044 8912	21.31	.278 269	4.64	6
7	1.659 049	8.787 322	.113 800 3154	.602 755	5.296 601	.188 800 3154	18.89	.321 602	4.59	7
8	1.783 478	10.446 371	.095 727 0232	.560 702	5.857 304	.170 727 0232	17.08	.365 816	4.57	8
9	1.917 239	12.229 849	.081 767 1595	.521 583	6.378 887	.156 767 1595	15.68	.410 904	4.57	9
10	2.061 032	14.147 087	.070 685 9274	.485 194	6.864 081	.145 685 9274	14.57	.456 859	4.57	10
11	2.215 609	16.208 119	.061 697 4737	.451 343	7.315 424	.136 697 4737	13.67	.503 672	4.58	11
12	2.381 780	18.423 728	.054 277 8313	.419 854	7.735 278	.129 277 8313	12.93	.551 334	4.59	12
13	2.560 413	20.805 508	.048 064 1963	.390 562	8.125 840	.123 064 1963	12.31	.599 835	4.61	13
14	2.752 444	23.365 921	.042 797 3721	.363 313	8.489 154	.117 797 3721	11.78	.649 163	4.64	14
15	2.958 877	26.118 365	.038 287 2363	.337 966	8.827 120	.113 287 2363	11.33	.699 309	4.66	15
16	3.180 793	29.077 242	.034 391 1571	.314 387	9.141 507	.109 391 1571	10.94	.750 259	4.69	16
17	3.419 353	32.258 035	.031 000 0282	.292 453	9.433 960	.106 000 0282	10.61	.802 000	4.72	17
18	3.675 804	35.677 388	.028 028 9578	.272 049	9.706 009	.103 028 9578	10.31	.854 521	4.75	18
19	3.951 489	39.353 192	.025 410 8994	.253 069	9.959 078	.100 410 8994	10.05	.907 807	4.78	19
20	4.247 851	43.304 681	.023 092 1916	.235 413	10.194 491	.098 092 1916	9.81	.961 844	4.81	20
21	4.566 440	47.552 532	.021 029 3742	.218 989	10.413 480	.096 029 3742	9.61	1.016 617	4.84	21
22	4.908 923	52.118 972	.019 186 8710	.203 711	10.617 191	.094 186 8710	9.42	1.072 111	4.87	22
23	5.277 092	57.027 895	.017 535 2780	.189 498	10.806 689	.092 535 2780	9.26	1.128 311	4.91	23
24	5.672 874	62.304 987	.016 050 0795	.176 277	10.982 967	.091 050 0795	9.11	1.185 202	4.94	24
25	6.098 340	67.977 862	.014 710 6716	.163 979	11.146 946	.089 710 6716	8.98	1.242 767	4.97	25
26	6.555 715	74.076 201	.013 499 6124	.152 539	11.299 485	.088 499 6124	8.85	1.300 990	5.00	26
27	7.047 394	80.631 916	.012 402 0369	.141 896	11.441 381	.087 402 0369	8.75	1.359 855	5.04	27
28	7.575 948	87.679 310	.011 405 1993	.131 997	11.573 378	.086 405 1993	8.65	1.419 346	5.07	28
29	8.144 144	95.255 258	.010 498 1081	.122 788	11.696 165	.085 498 1081	8.55	1.479 445	5.10	29
30	8.754 955	103.399 403	.009 671 2358	.114 221	11.810 386	.084 671 2358	8.47	1.540 137	5.13	30
31	9.411 577	112.154 358	.008 916 2831	.106 252	11.916 638	.083 916 2831	8.40	1.601 405	5.17	31
32	10.117 445	121.565 935	.008 225 9887	.098 839	12.015 478	.083 225 9887	8.33	1.663 232	5.20	32
33	10.876 253	131.683 380	.007 593 9728	.091 943	12.107 421	.082 593 9728	8.26	1.725 601	5.23	33
34	11.691 972	142.559 633	.007 014 6084	.085 529	12.192 950	.082 014 6084	8.21	1.788 497	5.26	34
35	12.568 870	154.251 606	.006 482 9147	.079 562	12.272 511	.081 482 9147	8.15	1.851 902	5.29	35
36	13.511 536	166.820 476	.005 994 4680	.074 011	12.346 522	.080 994 4680	8.10	1.915 801	5.32	36
37	14.524 901	180.332 012	.005 545 3271	.068 847	12.415 370	.080 545 3271	8.06	1.980 177	5.35	37
38	15.614 268	194.856 913	.005 131 9709	.064 044	12.479 414	.080 131 9709	8.02	2.045 015	5.38	38
39	16.785 339	210.471 181	.004 751 2443	.059 576	12.538 989	.079 751 2443	7.98	2.110 299	5.41	39
40	18.044 239	227.256 520	.004 400 3138	.055 419	12.594 409	.079 400 3138	7.95	2.176 013	5.44	40
41	19.397 557	245.300 759	.004 076 6282	.051 553	12.645 962	.079 076 6282	7.91	2.242 142	5.47	41
42	20.852 374	264.698 315	.003 777 8858	.047 956	12.693 918	.078 777 8858	7.88	2.308 671	5.50	42
43	22.416 302	285.550 689	.003 502 0052	.044 610	12.738 528	.078 502 0052	7.86	2.375 586	5.52	43
44	24.097 524	307.966 991	.003 247 1012	.041 498	12.780 026	.078 247 1012	7.83	2.442 872	5.55	44
45	25.904 839	332.064 515	.003 011 4630	.038 603	12.818 629	.078 011 4630	7.81	2.510 516	5.58	45
46	27.847 702	357.969 354	.002 793 5352	.035 910	12.854 539	.077 793 5352	7.78	2.578 503	5.61	46
47	29.936 279	385.817 055	.002 591 9020	.033 404	12.887 943	.077 591 9020	7.76	2.646 819	5.63	47
48	32.181 500	415.753 334	.002 405 2724	.031 074	12.919 017	.077 405 2724	7.75	2.715 453	5.66	48
49	34.595 113	447.934 835	.002 232 4676	.028 906	12.947 922	.077 232 4676	7.73	2.784 391	5.68	49
50	37.189 746	482.529 947	.002 072 4102	.026 889	12.974 812	.077 072 4102	7.71	2.853 621	5.71	50

Effective Rate is 7.50 %

Annual Percentage Rate is 7.50 %

Amount Of 1	Amount Of 1 Per Period	Sinking Fund Payment	Present Worth Of 1	Present Worth of 1 Per Period	Periodic Payment To Amortize 1	Constant Annual Percent	Total Interest	Annual Add On Rate
What a single $ 1 deposit grows to in the future. The deposit is made at the beginning of the first period.	What a series of $ 1 deposits grow to in the future. A deposit is made at the end of each period.	The amount to be deposited at the end of each period that grows to $ 1 in the future.	What $ 1 to be paid in the future is worth today. Value today of a single $ 1 payment tomorrow.	What $ 1 to be paid at the end of each period is worth today. Value today of a series of $ 1 payments tomorrow.	The mortgage payment to amortize a loan of $ 1. An annuity certain, payable at the end of each period, worth $ 1 today.	The annual payment, including interest and principal, to amortize completely a loan of $ 100.	The total interest paid over the term on a loan of $1. The loan is amortized by regular periodic payments.	The average annual interest rate on a loan that is completely amortized by regular periodic payments.
$S = (1+i)^n$	$S\overline{n}| = \dfrac{(1+i)^n - 1}{i}$	$\dfrac{1}{S\overline{n}|} = \dfrac{i}{(1+i)^n - 1}$	$V^n = \dfrac{1}{(1+i)^n}$	$A\overline{n}| = \dfrac{1 - V^n}{i}$	$\dfrac{1}{A\overline{n}|} = \dfrac{i}{1 - V^n}$			

YEAR								PERIODS
	1.077 500	1.000 000	1.000 000 0000	.928 074	.928 074	1.077 500 0000	107.75	.077 500	7.75	1

YEAR	Amount Of 1	Amount Of 1 Per Period	Sinking Fund Payment	Present Worth Of 1	Present Worth of 1 Per Period	Periodic Payment To Amortize 1	Constant Annual Percent	Total Interest	Annual Add On Rate	PERIODS
1	1.077 500	1.000 000	1.000 000 0000	.928 074	.928 074	1.077 500 0000	107.75	.077 500	7.75	1
2	1.161 006	2.077 500	.481 347 7738	.861 322	1.789 396	.558 847 7738	55.89	.117 696	5.88	2
3	1.250 984	3.238 506	.308 784 3354	.799 371	2.588 767	.386 284 3354	38.63	.158 853	5.30	3
4	1.347 936	4.489 490	.222 742 4256	.741 875	3.330 642	.300 242 4256	30.03	.200 970	5.02	4
5	1.452 401	5.837 426	.171 308 3816	.688 515	4.019 157	.248 808 3816	24.89	.244 042	4.88	5
6	1.564 962	7.289 827	.137 177 4758	.638 993	4.658 151	.214 677 4758	21.47	.288 065	4.80	6
7	1.686 246	8.854 788	.112 933 2506	.593 033	5.251 184	.190 433 2506	19.05	.333 033	4.76	7
8	1.816 930	10.541 034	.094 867 3523	.550 379	5.801 563	.172 367 3523	17.24	.378 939	4.74	8
9	1.957 742	12.357 964	.080 919 4764	.510 792	6.312 355	.158 419 4764	15.85	.425 775	4.73	9
10	2.109 467	14.315 707	.069 853 3459	.474 053	6.786 409	.147 353 3459	14.74	.473 533	4.74	10
11	2.272 951	16.425 174	.060 882 1565	.439 957	7.226 365	.138 382 1565	13.84	.522 204	4.75	11
12	2.449 105	18.698 125	.053 481 2990	.408 312	7.634 678	.130 981 2990	13.10	.571 776	4.76	12
13	2.638 910	21.147 229	.047 287 5184	.378 944	8.013 622	.124 787 5184	12.48	.622 238	4.79	13
14	2.843 426	23.786 140	.042 041 2901	.351 688	8.365 310	.119 541 2901	11.96	.673 578	4.81	14
15	3.063 791	26.629 566	.037 552 2462	.326 393	8.691 703	.115 052 2462	11.51	.725 784	4.84	15
16	3.301 235	29.693 357	.033 677 5665	.302 917	8.994 620	.111 177 5665	11.12	.778 841	4.87	16
17	3.557 081	32.994 592	.030 307 9971	.281 129	9.275 750	.107 807 9971	10.79	.832 736	4.90	17
18	3.832 755	36.551 673	.027 358 5289	.260 909	9.536 659	.104 858 5289	10.49	.887 454	4.93	18
19	4.129 793	40.384 428	.024 762 0199	.242 143	9.778 802	.102 262 0199	10.23	.942 978	4.96	19
20	4.449 852	44.514 221	.022 464 7312	.224 727	10.003 528	.099 964 7312	10.00	.999 295	5.00	20
21	4.794 716	48.964 073	.020 423 1377	.208 563	10.212 091	.097 923 1377	9.80	1.056 386	5.03	21
22	5.166 306	53.758 788	.018 601 6097	.193 562	10.405 653	.096 101 6097	9.62	1.114 235	5.06	22
23	5.566 695	58.925 095	.016 970 6983	.179 640	10.585 293	.094 470 6983	9.45	1.172 826	5.10	23
24	5.998 114	64.491 789	.015 505 8498	.166 719	10.752 012	.093 005 8498	9.31	1.232 140	5.13	24
25	6.462 967	70.489 903	.014 186 4289	.154 728	10.906 740	.091 686 4289	9.17	1.292 161	5.17	25
26	6.963 847	76.952 870	.012 994 9668	.143 599	11.050 338	.090 494 9668	9.05	1.352 869	5.20	26
27	7.503 546	83.916 718	.011 916 5766	.133 270	11.183 609	.089 416 5766	8.95	1.414 248	5.24	27
28	8.085 070	91.420 264	.010 938 4939	.123 685	11.307 293	.088 438 4939	8.85	1.476 278	5.27	28
29	8.711 663	99.505 334	.010 049 7125	.114 789	11.422 082	.087 549 7125	8.76	1.538 942	5.31	29
30	9.386 817	108.216 997	.009 240 6925	.106 532	11.528 614	.086 740 6925	8.68	1.602 221	5.34	30
31	10.114 296	117.603 815	.008 503 1255	.098 870	11.627 484	.086 003 1255	8.61	1.666 097	5.37	31
32	10.898 154	127.718 110	.007 829 7432	.091 759	11.719 243	.085 329 7432	8.54	1.730 552	5.41	32
33	11.742 760	138.616 264	.007 214 1607	.085 159	11.804 402	.084 714 1607	8.48	1.795 567	5.44	33
34	12.652 824	150.359 024	.006 650 7481	.079 034	11.883 436	.084 150 7481	8.42	1.861 125	5.47	34
35	13.633 418	163.011 849	.006 134 5234	.073 349	11.956 785	.083 634 5234	8.37	1.927 208	5.51	35
36	14.690 008	176.645 267	.005 661 0631	.068 073	12.024 858	.083 161 0631	8.32	1.993 798	5.54	36
37	15.828 484	191.335 275	.005 226 4278	.063 177	12.088 036	.082 726 4278	8.28	2.060 878	5.57	37
38	17.055 191	207.163 759	.004 827 0991	.058 633	12.146 669	.082 327 0991	8.24	2.128 430	5.60	38
39	18.376 969	224.218 950	.004 459 9263	.054 416	12.201 085	.081 959 9263	8.20	2.196 437	5.63	39
40	19.801 184	242.595 919	.004 122 0809	.050 502	12.251 587	.081 622 0809	8.17	2.264 883	5.66	40
41	21.335 775	262.397 103	.003 811 0177	.046 870	12.298 456	.081 311 0177	8.14	2.333 752	5.69	41
42	22.989 298	283.732 878	.003 524 4417	.043 499	12.341 955	.081 024 4417	8.11	2.403 027	5.72	42
43	24.770 969	306.722 176	.003 260 2794	.040 370	12.382 325	.080 760 2794	8.08	2.472 692	5.75	43
44	26.690 719	331.493 145	.003 016 6536	.037 466	12.419 791	.080 516 6536	8.06	2.542 733	5.78	44
45	28.759 249	358.183 864	.002 791 8622	.034 771	12.454 562	.080 291 8622	8.03	2.613 134	5.81	45
46	30.988 091	386.943 113	.002 584 3592	.032 270	12.486 833	.080 084 3592	8.01	2.683 881	5.83	46
47	33.389 668	417.931 204	.002 392 7383	.029 949	12.516 782	.079 892 7383	7.99	2.754 959	5.86	47
48	35.977 368	451.320 873	.002 215 7185	.027 795	12.544 577	.079 715 7185	7.98	2.826 354	5.89	48
49	38.765 614	487.298 240	.002 052 1314	.025 796	12.570 373	.079 552 1314	7.96	2.898 054	5.91	49
50	41.769 949	526.063 854	.001 900 9099	.023 941	12.594 314	.079 400 9099	7.95	2.970 046	5.94	50

Effective Rate is 7.75 %

Annual Percentage Rate is 7.75 %

ANNUAL COMPOUND INTEREST AND ANNUITY

8.00 % A

	Amount Of 1	Amount Of 1 Per Period	Sinking Fund Payment	Present Worth Of 1	Present Worth of 1 Per Period	Periodic Payment To Amortize 1	Constant Annual Percent	Total Interest	Annual Add On Rate
	What a single $ 1 deposit grows to in the future. The deposit is made at the beginning of the first period.	What a series of $ 1 deposits grow to in the future. A deposit is made at the end of each period.	The amount to be deposited at the end of each period that grows to $ 1 in the future.	What $ 1 to be paid in the future is worth today. Value today of a single $ 1 payment tomorrow.	What $ 1 to be paid at the end of each period is worth today. Value today of a series of $ 1 payments tomorrow.	The mortgage payment to amortize a loan of $ 1. An annuity certain, payable at the end of each period, worth $ 1 today.	The annual payment, including interest and principal, to amortize completely a loan of $ 100.	The total interest paid over the term on a loan of $1. The loan is amortized by regular periodic payments.	The average annual interest rate on a loan that is completely amortized by regular periodic payments.

$$S = (1+i)^n \qquad S\overline{n}| = \frac{(1+i)^n - 1}{i} \qquad \frac{1}{S\overline{n}|} = \frac{i}{(1+i)^n - 1} \qquad V^n = \frac{1}{(1+i)^n} \qquad A\overline{n}| = \frac{1 - V^n}{i} \qquad \frac{1}{A\overline{n}|} = \frac{i}{1 - V^n}$$

YEAR										PERIODS
	1.080 000	1.000 000	1.000 000 0000	.925 926	.925 926	1.080 000 0000	108.00	.080 000	8.00	1

YEAR	Amount Of 1	Amount Of 1 Per Period	Sinking Fund Payment	Present Worth Of 1	Present Worth of 1 Per Period	Periodic Payment To Amortize 1	Constant Annual Percent	Total Interest	Annual Add On Rate	PERIODS
1	1.080 000	1.000 000	1.000 000 0000	.925 926	.925 926	1.080 000 0000	108.00	.080 000	8.00	1
2	1.166 400	2.080 000	.480 769 2308	.857 339	1.783 265	.560 769 2308	56.08	.121 538	6.08	2
3	1.259 712	3.246 400	.308 033 5140	.793 832	2.577 097	.388 033 5140	38.81	.164 101	5.47	3
4	1.360 489	4.506 112	.221 920 8045	.735 030	3.312 127	.301 920 8045	30.20	.207 683	5.19	4
5	1.469 328	5.866 601	.170 456 4546	.680 583	3.992 710	.250 456 4546	25.05	.252 282	5.05	5
6	1.586 874	7.335 929	.136 315 3862	.630 170	4.622 880	.216 315 3862	21.64	.297 892	4.96	6
7	1.713 824	8.922 803	.112 072 4014	.583 490	5.206 370	.192 072 4014	19.21	.344 507	4.92	7
8	1.850 930	10.636 628	.094 014 7606	.540 269	5.746 639	.174 014 7606	17.41	.392 118	4.90	8
9	1.999 005	12.487 558	.080 079 7092	.500 249	6.246 888	.160 079 7092	16.01	.440 717	4.90	9
10	2.158 925	14.486 562	.069 029 4887	.463 193	6.710 081	.149 029 4887	14.91	.490 295	4.90	10
11	2.331 639	16.645 487	.060 076 3421	.428 883	7.138 964	.140 076 3421	14.01	.540 840	4.92	11
12	2.518 170	18.977 126	.052 695 0169	.397 114	7.536 078	.132 695 0169	13.27	.592 340	4.94	12
13	2.719 624	21.495 297	.046 521 8052	.367 698	7.903 776	.126 521 8052	12.66	.644 783	4.96	13
14	2.937 194	24.214 920	.041 296 8528	.340 461	8.244 237	.121 296 8528	12.13	.698 156	4.99	14
15	3.172 169	27.152 114	.036 829 5449	.315 242	8.559 479	.116 829 5449	11.69	.752 443	5.02	15
16	3.425 943	30.324 283	.032 976 8720	.291 890	8.851 369	.112 976 8720	11.30	.807 630	5.05	16
17	3.700 018	33.750 226	.029 629 4315	.270 269	9.121 638	.109 629 4315	10.97	.863 700	5.08	17
18	3.996 019	37.450 244	.026 702 0959	.250 249	9.371 887	.106 702 0959	10.68	.920 638	5.11	18
19	4.315 701	41.446 263	.024 127 6275	.231 712	9.603 599	.104 127 6275	10.42	.978 425	5.15	19
20	4.660 957	45.761 964	.021 852 2088	.214 548	9.818 147	.101 852 2088	10.19	1.037 044	5.19	20
21	5.033 834	50.422 921	.019 832 2503	.198 656	10.016 803	.099 832 2503	9.99	1.096 477	5.22	21
22	5.436 540	55.456 755	.018 032 0684	.183 941	10.200 744	.098 032 0684	9.81	1.156 706	5.26	22
23	5.871 464	60.893 296	.016 422 1692	.170 315	10.371 059	.096 422 1692	9.65	1.217 710	5.29	23
24	6.341 181	66.764 759	.014 977 9616	.157 699	10.528 758	.094 977 9616	9.50	1.279 471	5.33	24
25	6.848 475	73.105 940	.013 678 7791	.146 018	10.674 776	.093 678 7791	9.37	1.341 969	5.37	25
26	7.396 353	79.954 415	.012 507 1267	.135 202	10.809 978	.092 507 1267	9.26	1.405 185	5.40	26
27	7.988 061	87.350 768	.011 448 0962	.125 187	10.935 165	.091 448 0962	9.15	1.469 099	5.44	27
28	8.627 106	95.338 830	.010 488 9057	.115 914	11.051 078	.090 488 9057	9.05	1.533 689	5.48	28
29	9.317 275	103.965 936	.009 618 5350	.107 328	11.158 406	.089 618 5350	8.97	1.598 938	5.51	29
30	10.062 657	113.283 211	.008 827 4334	.099 377	11.257 783	.088 827 4334	8.89	1.664 823	5.55	30
31	10.867 669	123.345 868	.008 107 2841	.092 016	11.349 799	.088 107 2841	8.82	1.731 326	5.59	31
32	11.737 083	134.213 537	.007 450 8132	.085 200	11.434 999	.087 450 8132	8.75	1.798 426	5.62	32
33	12.676 050	145.950 620	.006 851 6324	.078 889	11.513 888	.086 851 6324	8.69	1.866 104	5.65	33
34	13.690 134	158.626 670	.006 304 1101	.073 045	11.586 934	.086 304 1101	8.64	1.934 340	5.69	34
35	14.785 344	172.316 804	.005 803 2646	.067 635	11.654 568	.085 803 2646	8.59	2.003 114	5.72	35
36	15.968 172	187.102 148	.005 344 6741	.062 625	11.717 193	.085 344 6741	8.54	2.072 408	5.76	36
37	17.245 626	203.070 320	.004 924 4025	.057 986	11.775 179	.084 924 4025	8.50	2.142 203	5.79	37
38	18.625 276	220.315 945	.004 538 9361	.053 690	11.828 869	.084 538 9361	8.46	2.212 480	5.82	38
39	20.115 298	238.941 221	.004 185 1297	.049 713	11.878 582	.084 185 1297	8.42	2.283 220	5.85	39
40	21.724 521	259.056 519	.003 860 1615	.046 031	11.924 613	.083 860 1615	8.39	2.354 406	5.89	40
41	23.462 483	280.781 040	.003 561 4940	.042 621	11.967 235	.083 561 4940	8.36	2.426 021	5.92	41
42	25.339 482	304.243 523	.003 286 8407	.039 464	12.006 699	.083 286 8407	8.33	2.498 047	5.95	42
43	27.366 640	329.583 005	.003 034 1370	.036 541	12.043 240	.083 034 1370	8.31	2.570 468	5.98	43
44	29.555 972	356.949 646	.002 801 5156	.033 834	12.077 074	.082 801 5156	8.29	2.643 267	6.01	44
45	31.920 449	386.505 617	.002 587 2845	.031 328	12.108 402	.082 587 2845	8.26	2.716 428	6.04	45
46	34.474 085	418.426 067	.002 389 9085	.029 007	12.137 409	.082 389 9085	8.24	2.789 936	6.07	46
47	37.232 012	452.900 152	.002 207 9922	.026 859	12.164 267	.082 207 9922	8.23	2.863 776	6.09	47
48	40.210 573	490.132 164	.002 040 2660	.024 869	12.189 136	.082 040 2660	8.21	2.937 933	6.12	48
49	43.427 419	530.342 737	.001 885 5731	.023 027	12.212 163	.081 885 5731	8.19	3.012 393	6.15	49
50	46.901 613	573.770 156	.001 742 8582	.021 321	12.233 485	.081 742 8582	8.18	3.087 143	6.17	50

Effective Rate is 8.00 %

Annual Percentage Rate is 8.00 %

ANNUAL COMPOUND INTEREST AND ANNUITY

Amount Of 1	Amount Of 1 Per Period	Sinking Fund Payment	Present Worth Of 1	Present Worth of 1 Per Period	Periodic Payment To Amortize 1	Constant Annual Percent	Total Interest	Annual Add On Rate
What a single $ 1 deposit grows to in the future. The deposit is made at the beginning of the first period.	What a series of $ 1 deposits grow to in the future. A deposit is made at the end of each period.	The amount to be deposited at the end of each period that grows to $ 1 in the future.	What $ 1 to be paid in the future is worth today. Value today of a single $ 1 payment tomorrow.	What $ 1 to be paid at the end of each period is worth today. Value today of a series of $ 1 payments tomorrow.	The mortgage payment to amortize a loan of $ 1. An annuity certain, payable at the end of each period, worth $ 1 today.	The annual payment, including interest and principal, to amortize completely a loan of $ 100.	The total interest paid over the term on a loan of $1. The loan is amortized by regular periodic payments.	The average annual interest rate on a loan that is completely amortized by regular periodic payments.
$S = (1+i)^n$	$S\overline{n} = \dfrac{(1+i)^n - 1}{i}$	$\dfrac{1}{S\overline{n}} = \dfrac{i}{(1+i)^n - 1}$	$V^n = \dfrac{1}{(1+i)^n}$	$A\overline{n} = \dfrac{1-V^n}{i}$	$\dfrac{1}{A\overline{n}} = \dfrac{i}{1-V^n}$			

YEAR									PERIODS
	1.082 500	1.000 000	1.000 000 0000	.923 788	.923 788	1.082 500 0000	108.25	.082 500	8.25	1

YEAR	Amount Of 1	Amount Of 1 Per Period	Sinking Fund Payment	Present Worth Of 1	Present Worth of 1 Per Period	Periodic Payment To Amortize 1	Constant Annual Percent	Total Interest	Annual Add On Rate	PERIODS
1	1.082 500	1.000 000	1.000 000 0000	.923 788	.923 788	1.082 500 0000	108.25	.082 500	8.25	1
2	1.171 806	2.082 500	.480 192 0768	.853 383	1.777 171	.562 692 0768	56.27	.125 384	6.27	2
3	1.268 480	3.254 306	.307 285 1549	.788 345	2.565 516	.389 785 1549	38.98	.169 355	5.65	3
4	1.373 130	4.522 787	.221 102 6314	.728 263	3.293 779	.303 602 6314	30.37	.214 411	5.36	4
5	1.486 413	5.895 916	.169 608 9177	.672 760	3.966 540	.252 108 9177	25.22	.260 545	5.21	5
6	1.609 042	7.382 330	.135 458 5973	.621 488	4.588 027	.217 958 5973	21.80	.307 752	5.13	6
7	1.741 788	8.991 372	.111 217 7357	.574 123	5.162 150	.193 717 7357	19.38	.356 024	5.09	7
8	1.885 486	10.733 160	.093 169 2077	.530 367	5.692 517	.175 669 2077	17.57	.405 354	5.07	8
9	2.041 038	12.618 646	.079 247 8081	.489 947	6.182 464	.161 747 8081	16.18	.455 730	5.06	9
10	2.209 424	14.659 684	.068 214 2953	.452 607	6.635 071	.150 714 2953	15.08	.507 143	5.07	10
11	2.391 701	16.869 108	.059 279 9582	.418 112	7.053 183	.141 779 9582	14.18	.559 580	5.09	11
12	2.589 017	19.260 809	.051 918 8989	.386 247	7.439 430	.134 418 8989	13.45	.613 027	5.11	12
13	2.802 611	21.849 826	.045 766 9552	.356 810	7.796 240	.128 266 9552	12.83	.667 470	5.13	13
14	3.033 826	24.652 436	.040 563 9419	.329 617	8.125 857	.123 063 9419	12.31	.722 895	5.16	14
15	3.284 117	27.686 262	.036 118 9958	.304 496	8.430 353	.118 618 9958	11.87	.779 285	5.20	15
16	3.555 056	30.970 379	.032 288 9169	.281 289	8.711 642	.114 788 9169	11.48	.836 623	5.23	16
17	3.848 348	34.525 435	.028 964 1532	.259 852	8.971 494	.111 464 1532	11.15	.894 891	5.26	17
18	4.165 837	38.373 784	.026 059 4578	.240 048	9.211 542	.108 559 4578	10.86	.954 070	5.30	18
19	4.509 519	42.539 621	.023 507 4967	.221 753	9.433 295	.106 007 4967	10.61	1.014 142	5.34	19
20	4.881 554	47.049 140	.021 254 3737	.204 853	9.638 148	.103 754 3737	10.38	1.075 087	5.38	20
21	5.284 282	51.930 694	.019 256 4344	.189 240	9.827 388	.101 756 4344	10.18	1.136 885	5.41	21
22	5.720 236	57.214 976	.017 477 9414	.174 818	10.002 206	.099 977 9414	10.00	1.199 515	5.45	22
23	6.192 155	62.935 212	.015 889 3563	.161 495	10.163 701	.098 389 3563	9.84	1.262 955	5.49	23
24	6.703 008	69.127 366	.014 466 0509	.149 187	10.312 888	.096 966 0509	9.70	1.327 185	5.53	24
25	7.256 006	75.830 374	.013 187 3278	.137 817	10.450 705	.095 687 3278	9.57	1.392 183	5.57	25
26	7.854 626	83.086 380	.012 035 6670	.127 314	10.578 018	.094 535 6670	9.46	1.457 927	5.61	26
27	8.502 633	90.941 006	.010 996 1396	.117 611	10.695 629	.093 496 1396	9.35	1.524 396	5.65	27
28	9.204 100	99.443 639	.010 055 9473	.108 647	10.804 276	.092 555 9473	9.26	1.591 567	5.68	28
29	9.963 439	108.647 740	.009 204 0571	.100 367	10.904 643	.091 704 0571	9.18	1.659 418	5.72	29
30	10.785 422	118.611 178	.008 430 9086	.092 718	10.997 361	.090 930 9086	9.10	1.727 927	5.76	30
31	11.675 220	129.396 600	.007 728 1783	.085 651	11.083 012	.090 228 1783	9.03	1.797 074	5.80	31
32	12.638 425	141.071 820	.007 088 5879	.079 124	11.162 136	.089 588 5879	8.96	1.866 835	5.83	32
33	13.681 095	153.710 245	.006 505 7472	.073 094	11.235 230	.089 005 7472	8.91	1.937 190	5.87	33
34	14.809 786	167.391 340	.005 974 0247	.067 523	11.302 752	.088 474 0247	8.85	2.008 117	5.91	34
35	16.031 593	182.201 126	.005 488 4403	.062 377	11.365 129	.087 988 4403	8.80	2.079 595	5.94	35
36	17.354 199	198.232 719	.005 044 5759	.057 623	11.422 752	.087 544 5759	8.76	2.151 605	5.98	36
37	18.785 921	215.586 918	.004 638 5004	.053 231	11.475 984	.087 138 5004	8.72	2.224 125	6.01	37
38	20.335 759	234.372 839	.004 266 7060	.049 174	11.525 158	.086 766 7060	8.68	2.297 135	6.05	38
39	22.013 459	254.708 598	.003 926 0551	.045 427	11.570 585	.086 426 0551	8.65	2.370 616	6.08	39
40	23.829 570	276.722 058	.003 613 7343	.041 965	11.612 549	.086 113 7343	8.62	2.444 549	6.11	40
41	25.795 509	300.551 627	.003 327 2154	.038 766	11.651 316	.085 827 2154	8.59	2.518 916	6.14	41
42	27.923 639	326.347 137	.003 064 2218	.035 812	11.687 128	.085 564 2218	8.56	2.593 697	6.18	42
43	30.227 339	354.270 775	.002 822 6997	.033 083	11.720 210	.085 322 6997	8.54	2.668 876	6.21	43
44	32.721 094	384.498 114	.002 600 7930	.030 561	11.750 772	.085 100 7930	8.52	2.744 435	6.24	44
45	35.420 585	417.219 209	.002 396 8216	.028 232	11.779 004	.084 896 8216	8.49	2.820 357	6.27	45
46	38.342 783	452.639 793	.002 209 2622	.026 081	11.805 085	.084 709 2622	8.48	2.896 626	6.30	46
47	41.506 063	490.982 576	.002 036 7322	.024 093	11.829 177	.084 536 7322	8.46	2.973 226	6.33	47
48	44.930 313	532.488 639	.001 877 9743	.022 257	11.851 434	.084 377 9743	8.44	3.050 143	6.35	48
49	48.637 064	577.418 952	.001 731 8448	.020 560	11.871 995	.084 231 8448	8.43	3.127 360	6.38	49
50	52.649 621	626.056 015	.001 597 3012	.018 993	11.890 988	.084 097 3012	8.41	3.204 865	6.41	50

Effective Rate is 8.25 %

Annual Percentage Rate is 8.25 %

ANNUAL COMPOUND INTEREST AND ANNUITY

8.50 % A

	Amount Of 1	Amount Of 1 Per Period	Sinking Fund Payment	Present Worth Of 1	Present Worth of 1 Per Period	Periodic Payment To Amortize 1	Constant Annual Percent	Total Interest	Annual Add On Rate	
	What a single $ 1 deposit grows to in the future. The deposit is made at the beginning of the first period.	What a series of $ 1 deposits grow to in the future. A deposit is made at the end of each period.	The amount to be deposited at the end of each period that grows to $ 1 in the future.	What $ 1 to be paid in the future is worth today. Value today of a single $ 1 payment tomorrow.	What $ 1 to be paid at the end of each period is worth today. Value today of a series of $ 1 payments tomorrow.	The mortgage payment to amortize a loan of $ 1. An annuity certain, payable at the end of each period, worth $ 1 today.	The annual payment, including interest and principal, to amortize completely a loan of $ 100.	The total interest paid over the term on a loan of $1. The loan is amortized by regular periodic payments.	The average annual interest rate on a loan that is completely amortized by regular periodic payments.	
	$S = (1+i)^n$	$S\overline{n}| = \dfrac{(1+i)^n - 1}{i}$	$\dfrac{1}{S\overline{n}|} = \dfrac{i}{(1+i)^n - 1}$	$V^n = \dfrac{1}{(1+i)^n}$	$A\overline{n}| = \dfrac{1 - V^n}{i}$	$\dfrac{1}{A\overline{n}|} = \dfrac{i}{1 - V^n}$				

YEAR / **PERIODS**

	Amount Of 1	Amount Of 1 Per Period	Sinking Fund Payment	Present Worth Of 1	Present Worth of 1 Per Period	Periodic Payment To Amortize 1	Constant Annual Percent	Total Interest	Annual Add On Rate	
	1.085 000	1.000 000	1.000 000 0000	.921 659	.921 659	1.085 000 0000	108.50	.085 000	8.50	1

YEAR	Amount Of 1	Amount Of 1 Per Period	Sinking Fund Payment	Present Worth Of 1	Present Worth of 1 Per Period	Periodic Payment To Amortize 1	Constant Annual Percent	Total Interest	Annual Add On Rate	PERIODS
1	1.085 000	1.000 000	1.000 000 0000	.921 659	.921 659	1.085 000 0000	108.50	.085 000	8.50	1
2	1.177 225	2.085 000	.479 616 3070	.849 455	1.771 114	.564 616 3070	56.47	.129 233	6.46	2
3	1.277 289	3.262 225	.306 539 2485	.782 908	2.554 022	.391 539 2485	39.16	.174 618	5.82	3
4	1.385 859	4.539 514	.220 287 8926	.721 574	3.275 597	.305 287 8926	30.53	.221 152	5.53	4
5	1.503 657	5.925 373	.168 765 7519	.665 045	3.940 642	.253 765 7519	25.38	.268 829	5.38	5
6	1.631 468	7.429 030	.134 607 0840	.612 945	4.553 587	.219 607 0840	21.97	.317 643	5.29	6
7	1.770 142	9.060 497	.110 369 2212	.564 926	5.118 514	.195 369 2212	19.54	.367 585	5.25	7
8	1.920 604	10.830 639	.092 330 6533	.520 669	5.639 183	.177 330 6533	17.74	.418 645	5.23	8
9	2.083 856	12.751 244	.078 423 7233	.479 880	6.119 063	.163 423 7233	16.35	.470 814	5.23	9
10	2.260 983	14.835 099	.067 407 7051	.442 285	6.561 348	.152 407 7051	15.25	.524 077	5.24	10
11	2.453 167	17.096 083	.058 492 9316	.407 636	6.968 984	.143 492 9316	14.35	.578 422	5.26	11
12	2.661 686	19.549 250	.051 152 8581	.375 702	7.344 686	.136 152 8581	13.62	.633 834	5.28	12
13	2.887 930	22.210 936	.045 022 8662	.346 269	7.690 955	.130 022 8662	13.01	.690 297	5.31	13
14	3.133 404	25.098 866	.039 842 4382	.319 142	8.010 097	.124 842 4382	12.49	.747 794	5.34	14
15	3.399 743	28.232 269	.035 420 4614	.294 140	8.304 237	.120 420 4614	12.05	.806 307	5.38	15
16	3.688 721	31.632 012	.031 613 5439	.271 097	8.575 333	.116 613 5439	11.67	.865 817	5.41	16
17	4.002 262	35.320 733	.028 311 9832	.249 859	8.825 192	.113 311 9832	11.34	.926 304	5.45	17
18	4.342 455	39.322 995	.025 430 4127	.230 285	9.055 476	.110 430 4127	11.05	.987 747	5.49	18
19	4.711 563	43.665 450	.022 901 4015	.212 244	9.267 720	.107 901 4015	10.80	1.050 127	5.53	19
20	5.112 046	48.377 013	.020 670 9744	.195 616	9.463 337	.105 670 9744	10.57	1.113 419	5.57	20
21	5.546 570	53.489 059	.018 695 4120	.180 292	9.643 628	.103 695 4120	10.37	1.177 604	5.61	21
22	6.018 028	59.035 629	.016 938 9233	.166 167	9.809 796	.101 938 9233	10.20	1.242 656	5.65	22
23	6.529 561	65.053 658	.015 371 9258	.153 150	9.962 945	.100 371 9258	10.04	1.308 554	5.69	23
24	7.084 574	71.583 219	.013 969 7546	.141 152	10.104 097	.098 969 7546	9.90	1.375 274	5.73	24
25	7.686 762	78.667 792	.012 711 6825	.130 094	10.234 191	.097 711 6825	9.78	1.442 792	5.77	25
26	8.340 137	86.354 555	.011 580 1651	.119 902	10.354 093	.096 580 1651	9.66	1.511 084	5.81	26
27	9.049 049	94.694 692	.010 560 2540	.110 509	10.464 602	.095 560 2540	9.56	1.580 127	5.85	27
28	9.818 218	103.743 741	.009 639 1357	.101 851	10.566 453	.094 639 1357	9.47	1.649 896	5.89	28
29	10.652 766	113.561 959	.008 805 7657	.093 872	10.660 326	.093 805 7657	9.39	1.720 367	5.93	29
30	11.558 252	124.214 725	.008 050 5753	.086 518	10.746 844	.093 050 5753	9.31	1.791 517	5.97	30
31	12.540 703	135.772 977	.007 365 2359	.079 740	10.826 584	.092 365 2359	9.24	1.863 322	6.01	31
32	13.606 663	148.313 680	.006 742 4664	.073 493	10.900 078	.091 742 4664	9.18	1.935 759	6.05	32
33	14.763 229	161.920 343	.006 175 8763	.067 736	10.967 813	.091 175 8763	9.12	2.008 804	6.09	33
34	16.018 104	176.683 572	.005 659 8358	.062 429	11.030 243	.090 659 8358	9.07	2.082 434	6.12	34
35	17.379 642	192.701 675	.005 189 3685	.057 539	11.087 781	.090 189 3685	9.02	2.156 628	6.16	35
36	18.856 912	210.081 318	.004 760 0615	.053 031	11.140 812	.089 760 0615	8.98	2.231 362	6.20	36
37	20.459 750	228.938 230	.004 367 9904	.048 876	11.189 689	.089 367 9904	8.94	2.306 616	6.23	37
38	22.198 828	249.397 979	.004 009 6556	.045 047	11.234 736	.089 009 6556	8.91	2.382 367	6.27	38
39	24.085 729	271.596 808	.003 681 9284	.041 518	11.276 255	.088 681 9284	8.87	2.458 595	6.30	39
40	26.133 016	295.682 536	.003 382 0056	.038 266	11.314 520	.088 382 0056	8.84	2.535 280	6.34	40
41	28.354 322	321.815 552	.003 107 3700	.035 268	11.349 788	.088 107 3700	8.82	2.612 402	6.37	41
42	30.764 439	350.169 874	.002 855 7568	.032 505	11.382 293	.087 855 7568	8.79	2.689 942	6.40	42
43	33.379 417	380.934 313	.002 625 1245	.029 959	11.412 252	.087 625 1245	8.77	2.767 880	6.44	43
44	36.216 667	414.313 730	.002 413 6299	.027 612	11.439 864	.087 413 6299	8.75	2.846 200	6.47	44
45	39.295 084	450.530 397	.002 219 6061	.025 448	11.465 312	.087 219 6061	8.73	2.924 882	6.50	45
46	42.635 166	489.825 480	.002 041 5434	.023 455	11.488 767	.087 041 5434	8.71	3.003 911	6.53	46
47	46.259 155	532.460 646	.001 878 0731	.021 617	11.510 384	.086 878 0731	8.69	3.083 269	6.56	47
48	50.191 183	578.719 801	.001 727 9519	.019 924	11.530 308	.086 727 9519	8.68	3.162 942	6.59	48
49	54.457 434	628.910 984	.001 590 0501	.018 363	11.548 671	.086 590 0501	8.66	3.242 912	6.62	49
50	59.086 316	683.368 418	.001 463 3395	.016 924	11.565 595	.086 463 3395	8.65	3.323 167	6.65	50

Effective Rate is 8.50 %

8 - 450

Annual Percentage Rate is 8.50 %

ANNUAL COMPOUND INTEREST AND ANNUITY

	Amount Of 1	Amount Of 1 Per Period	Sinking Fund Payment	Present Worth Of 1	Present Worth of 1 Per Period	Periodic Payment To Amortize 1	Constant Annual Percent	Total Interest	Annual Add On Rate	
	What a single $ 1 deposit grows to in the future. The deposit is made at the beginning of the first period.	What a series of $ 1 deposits grow to in the future. A deposit is made at the end of each period.	The amount to be deposited at the end of each period that grows to $ 1 in the future.	What $ 1 to be paid in the future is worth today. Value today of a single $ 1 payment tomorrow.	What $ 1 to be paid at the end of each period is worth today. Value today of a series of $ 1 payments tomorrow.	The mortgage payment to amortize a loan of $ 1. An annuity certain, payable at the end of each period, worth $ 1 today.	The annual payment, including interest and principal, to amortize a loan of $ 100.	The total interest paid over the term on a loan of $1. The loan is amortized by regular periodic payments.	The average annual interest rate on a loan that is completely amortized by regular periodic payments.	
	$S = (1+i)^n$	$S\overline{n} = \dfrac{(1+i)^n - 1}{i}$	$\dfrac{1}{S\overline{n}} = \dfrac{i}{(1+i)^n - 1}$	$V^n = \dfrac{1}{(1+i)^n}$	$A\overline{n} = \dfrac{1-V^n}{i}$	$\dfrac{1}{A\overline{n}} = \dfrac{i}{1-V^n}$				

YEAR									PERIODS	
	1.087 500	1.000 000	1.000 000 0000	.919 540	.919 540	1.087 500 0000	108.75	.087 500	8.75	1

YEAR	Amount Of 1	Amount Of 1 Per Period	Sinking Fund Payment	Present Worth Of 1	Present Worth of 1 Per Period	Periodic Payment To Amortize 1	Constant Annual Percent	Total Interest	Annual Add On Rate	PERIODS
1	1.087 500	1.000 000	1.000 000 0000	.919 540	.919 540	1.087 500 0000	108.75	.087 500	8.75	1
2	1.182 656	2.087 500	.479 041 9162	.845 554	1.765 094	.566 541 9162	56.66	.133 084	6.65	2
3	1.286 139	3.270 156	.305 795 7858	.777 521	2.542 616	.393 295 7858	39.33	.179 887	6.00	3
4	1.398 676	4.556 295	.219 476 5741	.714 962	3.257 578	.306 976 5741	30.70	.227 906	5.70	4
5	1.521 060	5.954 971	.167 926 9380	.657 436	3.915 014	.255 426 9380	25.55	.277 135	5.54	5
6	1.654 153	7.476 031	.133 760 8210	.604 539	4.519 553	.221 260 8210	22.13	.327 565	5.46	6
7	1.798 891	9.130 183	.109 526 8257	.555 898	5.075 451	.197 026 8257	19.71	.379 188	5.42	7
8	1.956 294	10.929 074	.091 499 0569	.511 171	5.586 622	.178 999 0569	17.90	.431 992	5.40	8
9	2.127 470	12.885 368	.077 607 4047	.470 042	6.056 664	.165 107 4047	16.52	.485 967	5.40	9
10	2.313 623	15.012 838	.066 609 6571	.432 222	6.488 886	.154 109 6571	15.42	.541 097	5.41	10
11	2.516 065	17.326 461	.057 715 1891	.397 446	6.886 332	.145 215 1891	14.53	.597 367	5.43	11
12	2.736 221	19.842 527	.050 396 8072	.365 468	7.251 800	.137 896 8072	13.79	.654 762	5.46	12
13	2.975 640	22.578 748	.044 289 4355	.336 062	7.587 862	.131 789 4355	13.18	.713 263	5.49	13
14	3.236 009	25.554 388	.039 132 2220	.309 023	7.896 884	.126 632 2220	12.67	.772 851	5.52	14
15	3.519 160	28.790 397	.034 733 8033	.284 159	8.181 043	.122 233 8033	12.23	.833 507	5.56	15
16	3.827 086	32.309 557	.030 950 5944	.261 295	8.442 338	.118 450 5944	11.85	.895 210	5.60	16
17	4.161 956	36.136 643	.027 672 7417	.240 272	8.682 610	.115 172 7417	11.52	.957 937	5.64	17
18	4.526 127	40.298 600	.024 814 7580	.220 939	8.903 549	.112 314 7580	11.24	1.021 666	5.68	18
19	4.922 164	44.824 727	.022 309 1151	.203 163	9.106 712	.109 809 1151	10.99	1.086 373	5.72	19
20	5.352 853	49.746 891	.020 101 7588	.186 816	9.293 528	.107 601 7588	10.77	1.152 035	5.76	20
21	5.821 228	55.099 744	.018 148 9047	.171 785	9.465 313	.105 648 9047	10.57	1.218 627	5.80	21
22	6.330 585	60.920 971	.016 414 7087	.157 963	9.623 277	.103 914 7087	10.40	1.286 124	5.85	22
23	6.884 511	67.251 556	.014 869 5444	.145 254	9.768 530	.102 369 5444	10.24	1.354 500	5.89	23
24	7.486 906	74.136 067	.013 488 7111	.133 567	9.902 097	.100 988 7111	10.10	1.423 729	5.93	24
25	8.142 010	81.622 973	.012 251 4527	.122 820	10.024 917	.099 751 4527	9.98	1.493 786	5.98	25
26	8.854 436	89.764 984	.011 140 2014	.112 938	10.137 854	.098 640 2014	9.87	1.564 645	6.02	26
27	9.629 199	98.619 420	.010 139 9907	.103 851	10.241 705	.097 639 9907	9.77	1.636 280	6.06	27
28	10.471 754	108.248 619	.009 237 9932	.095 495	10.337 200	.096 737 9932	9.68	1.708 664	6.10	28
29	11.388 033	118.720 373	.008 423 1541	.087 811	10.425 012	.095 923 1541	9.60	1.781 771	6.14	29
30	12.384 485	130.108 406	.007 685 8985	.080 746	10.505 758	.095 185 8985	9.52	1.855 577	6.19	30
31	13.468 128	142.492 891	.007 017 8940	.074 249	10.580 007	.094 517 8940	9.46	1.930 055	6.23	31
32	14.646 589	155.961 019	.006 411 8586	.068 275	10.648 282	.093 911 8586	9.40	2.005 179	6.27	32
33	15.928 166	170.607 608	.005 861 4033	.062 782	10.711 064	.093 361 4033	9.34	2.080 926	6.31	33
34	17.321 880	186.535 774	.005 360 9020	.057 730	10.768 795	.092 860 9020	9.29	2.157 271	6.35	34
35	18.837 545	203.857 654	.004 905 3836	.053 085	10.821 880	.092 405 3836	9.25	2.234 188	6.38	35
36	20.485 830	222.695 199	.004 490 4426	.048 814	10.870 695	.091 990 4426	9.20	2.311 656	6.42	36
37	22.278 340	243.181 029	.004 112 1629	.044 887	10.915 581	.091 612 1629	9.17	2.389 650	6.46	37
38	24.227 695	265.459 369	.003 767 0548	.041 275	10.956 856	.091 267 0548	9.13	2.468 148	6.50	38
39	26.347 618	289.687 064	.003 452 0009	.037 954	10.994 810	.090 952 0009	9.10	2.547 128	6.53	39
40	28.653 035	316.034 682	.003 164 2097	.034 900	11.029 711	.090 664 2097	9.07	2.626 568	6.57	40
41	31.160 175	344.687 716	.002 901 1768	.032 092	11.061 803	.090 401 1768	9.05	2.706 448	6.60	41
42	33.886 691	375.847 892	.002 660 6508	.029 510	11.091 313	.090 160 6508	9.02	2.786 747	6.64	42
43	36.851 776	409.734 582	.002 440 6043	.027 136	11.118 449	.089 940 6043	9.00	2.867 446	6.67	43
44	40.076 306	446.586 358	.002 239 2086	.024 952	11.143 401	.089 739 2086	8.98	2.948 525	6.70	44
45	43.582 983	486.662 664	.002 054 8114	.022 945	11.166 346	.089 554 8114	8.96	3.029 967	6.73	45
46	47.396 494	530.245 648	.001 885 9184	.021 099	11.187 444	.089 385 9184	8.94	3.111 752	6.76	46
47	51.543 687	577.642 142	.001 731 1756	.019 401	11.206 846	.089 231 1756	8.93	3.193 865	6.80	47
48	56.053 760	629.185 829	.001 589 3556	.017 840	11.224 686	.089 089 3556	8.91	3.276 289	6.83	48
49	60.958 464	685.239 589	.001 459 3436	.016 405	11.241 090	.088 959 3436	8.90	3.359 008	6.86	49
50	66.292 330	746.198 053	.001 340 1268	.015 085	11.256 175	.088 840 1268	8.89	3.442 006	6.88	50

Effective Rate is 8.75 %

Annual Percentage Rate is 8.75 %

ANNUAL COMPOUND INTEREST AND ANNUITY

	Amount Of 1	Amount Of 1 Per Period	Sinking Fund Payment	Present Worth Of 1	Present Worth of 1 Per Period	Periodic Payment To Amortize 1	Constant Annual Percent	Total Interest	Annual Add On Rate	
	What a single $ 1 deposit grows to in the future. The deposit is made at the beginning of the first period.	What a series of $ 1 deposits grow to in the future. A deposit is made at the end of each period.	The amount to be deposited at the end of each period that grows to $ 1 in the future.	What $ 1 to be paid in the future is worth today. Value today of a single $ 1 payment tomorrow.	What $ 1 to be paid at the end of each period is worth today. Value today of a series of $ 1 payments tomorrow.	The mortgage payment to amortize a loan of $ 1. An annuity certain, payable at the end of each period, worth $ 1 today.	The annual payment, including interest and principal, to amortize completely a loan of $ 100.	The total interest paid over the term on a loan of $1. The loan is amortized completely by regular periodic payments.	The average annual interest rate on a loan that is completely amortized by regular periodic payments.	
	$S = (1+i)^n$	$S\overline{n} = \dfrac{(1+i)^n - 1}{i}$	$\dfrac{1}{S\overline{n}} = \dfrac{i}{(1+i)^n - 1}$	$V^n = \dfrac{1}{(1+i)^n}$	$A\overline{n} = \dfrac{1-V^n}{i}$	$\dfrac{1}{A\overline{n}} = \dfrac{i}{1-V^n}$				

YEAR										PERIODS
	1.090 000	1.000 000	1.000 000 0000	.917 431	.917 431	1.090 000 0000	109.00	.090 000	9.00	1

YEAR	Amount Of 1	Amount Of 1 Per Period	Sinking Fund Payment	Present Worth Of 1	Present Worth of 1 Per Period	Periodic Payment To Amortize 1	Constant Annual Percent	Total Interest	Annual Add On Rate	PERIODS
1	1.090 000	1.000 000	1.000 000 0000	.917 431	.917 431	1.090 000 0000	109.00	.090 000	9.00	1
2	1.188 100	2.090 000	.478 468 8995	.841 680	1.759 111	.568 468 8995	56.85	.136 938	6.85	2
3	1.295 029	3.278 100	.305 054 7573	.772 183	2.531 295	.395 054 7573	39.51	.185 164	6.17	3
4	1.411 582	4.573 129	.218 668 6621	.708 425	3.239 720	.308 668 6621	30.87	.234 675	5.87	4
5	1.538 624	5.984 711	.167 092 4570	.649 931	3.889 651	.257 092 4570	25.71	.285 462	5.71	5
6	1.677 100	7.523 335	.132 919 7833	.596 267	4.485 919	.222 919 7833	22.30	.337 519	5.63	6
7	1.828 039	9.200 435	.108 690 5168	.547 034	5.032 953	.198 690 5168	19.87	.390 834	5.58	7
8	1.992 563	11.028 474	.090 674 3778	.501 866	5.534 819	.180 674 3778	18.07	.445 395	5.57	8
9	2.171 893	13.021 036	.076 798 8021	.460 428	5.995 247	.166 798 8021	16.68	.501 189	5.57	9
10	2.367 364	15.192 930	.065 820 0899	.422 411	6.417 658	.155 820 0899	15.59	.558 201	5.58	10
11	2.580 426	17.560 293	.056 946 6567	.387 533	6.805 191	.146 946 6567	14.70	.616 413	5.60	11
12	2.812 665	20.140 720	.049 650 6585	.355 535	7.160 725	.139 650 6585	13.97	.675 808	5.63	12
13	3.065 805	22.953 385	.043 566 5597	.326 179	7.486 904	.133 566 5597	13.36	.736 365	5.66	13
14	3.341 727	26.019 189	.038 433 1730	.299 246	7.786 150	.128 433 1730	12.85	.798 064	5.70	14
15	3.642 482	29.360 916	.034 058 8827	.274 538	8.060 688	.124 058 8827	12.41	.860 883	5.74	15
16	3.970 306	33.003 399	.030 299 9097	.251 870	8.312 558	.120 299 9097	12.03	.924 799	5.78	16
17	4.327 633	36.973 705	.027 046 2485	.231 073	8.543 631	.117 046 2485	11.71	.989 786	5.82	17
18	4.717 120	41.301 338	.024 212 2907	.211 994	8.755 625	.114 212 2907	11.43	1.055 821	5.87	18
19	5.141 661	46.018 458	.021 730 4107	.194 490	8.950 115	.111 730 4107	11.18	1.122 878	5.91	19
20	5.604 411	51.160 120	.019 546 4750	.178 431	9.128 546	.109 546 4750	10.96	1.190 930	5.95	20
21	6.108 808	56.764 530	.017 616 6348	.163 698	9.292 244	.107 616 6348	10.77	1.259 949	6.00	21
22	6.658 600	62.873 338	.015 904 9930	.150 182	9.442 425	.105 904 9930	10.60	1.329 910	6.05	22
23	7.257 874	69.531 939	.014 381 8800	.137 781	9.580 207	.104 381 8800	10.44	1.400 783	6.09	23
24	7.911 083	76.789 813	.013 022 5607	.126 405	9.706 612	.103 022 5607	10.31	1.472 541	6.14	24
25	8.623 081	84.700 896	.011 806 2505	.115 968	9.822 580	.101 806 2505	10.19	1.545 156	6.18	25
26	9.399 158	93.323 977	.010 715 3599	.106 393	9.928 972	.100 715 3599	10.08	1.618 599	6.23	26
27	10.245 082	102.723 135	.009 734 9054	.097 608	10.026 580	.099 734 9054	9.98	1.692 842	6.27	27
28	11.167 140	112.968 217	.008 852 0473	.089 548	10.116 128	.098 852 0473	9.89	1.767 857	6.31	28
29	12.172 182	124.135 356	.008 055 7226	.082 155	10.198 283	.098 055 7226	9.81	1.843 616	6.36	29
30	13.267 678	136.307 539	.007 336 3514	.075 371	10.273 654	.097 336 3514	9.74	1.920 091	6.40	30
31	14.461 770	149.575 217	.006 685 5995	.069 148	10.342 802	.096 685 5995	9.67	1.997 254	6.44	31
32	15.763 329	164.036 987	.006 096 1861	.063 438	10.406 240	.096 096 1861	9.61	2.075 078	6.48	32
33	17.182 028	179.800 315	.005 561 7255	.058 200	10.464 441	.095 561 7255	9.56	2.153 537	6.53	33
34	18.728 411	196.982 344	.005 076 5971	.053 395	10.517 835	.095 076 5971	9.51	2.232 604	6.57	34
35	20.413 968	215.710 755	.004 635 8375	.048 986	10.566 821	.094 635 8375	9.47	2.312 254	6.61	35
36	22.251 225	236.124 723	.004 235 0500	.044 941	10.611 763	.094 235 0500	9.43	2.392 462	6.65	36
37	24.253 835	258.375 948	.003 870 3293	.041 231	10.652 993	.093 870 3293	9.39	2.473 202	6.68	37
38	26.436 680	282.629 783	.003 538 1975	.037 826	10.690 820	.093 538 1975	9.36	2.554 452	6.72	38
39	28.815 982	309.066 463	.003 235 5500	.034 703	10.725 523	.093 235 5500	9.33	2.636 186	6.76	39
40	31.409 420	337.882 445	.002 959 6092	.031 838	10.757 360	.092 959 6092	9.30	2.718 384	6.80	40
41	34.236 268	369.291 865	.002 707 8853	.029 209	10.786 569	.092 707 8853	9.28	2.801 023	6.83	41
42	37.317 532	403.528 133	.002 478 1420	.026 797	10.813 366	.092 478 1420	9.25	2.884 082	6.87	42
43	40.676 110	440.845 665	.002 268 3675	.024 584	10.837 950	.092 268 3675	9.23	2.967 540	6.90	43
44	44.336 960	481.521 775	.002 076 7493	.022 555	10.860 505	.092 076 7493	9.21	3.051 377	6.94	44
45	48.327 286	525.858 734	.001 901 6514	.020 692	10.881 197	.091 901 6514	9.20	3.135 574	6.97	45
46	52.676 742	574.186 021	.001 741 5959	.018 984	10.900 181	.091 741 5959	9.18	3.220 113	7.00	46
47	57.417 649	626.862 762	.001 595 2455	.017 416	10.917 597	.091 595 2455	9.16	3.304 977	7.03	47
48	62.585 237	684.280 411	.001 461 3892	.015 978	10.933 575	.091 461 3892	9.15	3.390 147	7.06	48
49	68.217 908	746.865 648	.001 338 9289	.014 659	10.948 234	.091 338 9289	9.14	3.475 608	7.09	49
50	74.357 520	815.083 556	.001 226 8681	.013 449	10.961 683	.091 226 8681	9.13	3.561 343	7.12	50

Effective Rate is 9.00 %

Annual Percentage Rate is 9.00 %

ANNUAL COMPOUND INTEREST AND ANNUITY

	Amount Of 1	Amount Of 1 Per Period	Sinking Fund Payment	Present Worth Of 1	Present Worth of 1 Per Period	Periodic Payment To Amortize 1	Constant Annual Percent	Total Interest	Annual Add On Rate
	What a single $ 1 deposit grows to in the future. The deposit is made at the beginning of the first period.	What a series of $ 1 deposits grow to in the future. A deposit is made at the end of each period.	The amount to be deposited at the end of each period that grows to $ 1 in the future.	What $ 1 to be paid in the future is worth today. Value today of a single $ 1 payment tomorrow.	What $ 1 to be paid at the end of each period is worth today. Value today of a series of $ 1 payments tomorrow.	The mortgage payment to amortize a loan of $ 1. An annuity certain, payable at the end of each period, worth $ 1 today.	The annual payment, including interest and principal, to amortize completely a loan of $ 100.	The total interest paid over the term on a loan of $1. The loan is amortized by regular periodic payments.	The average annual interest rate on a loan that is completely amortized by regular periodic payments.

$$ S = (1+i)^n \qquad S\overline{n}| = \frac{(1+i)^n - 1}{i} \qquad \frac{1}{S\overline{n}|} = \frac{i}{(1+i)^n - 1} \qquad V^n = \frac{1}{(1+i)^n} \qquad A\overline{n}| = \frac{1 - V^n}{i} \qquad \frac{1}{A\overline{n}|} = \frac{i}{1 - V^n} $$

YEAR										PERIODS
	1.092 500	1.000 000	1.000 000 0000	.915 332	.915 332	1.092 500 0000	109.25	.092 500	9.25	1

YEAR	Amount Of 1	Amount Of 1 Per Period	Sinking Fund Payment	Present Worth Of 1	Present Worth of 1 Per Period	Periodic Payment To Amortize 1	Constant Annual Percent	Total Interest	Annual Add On Rate	PERIODS
1	1.092 500	1.000 000	1.000 000 0000	.915 332	.915 332	1.092 500 0000	109.25	.092 500	9.25	1
2	1.193 556	2.092 500	.477 897 2521	.837 832	1.753 164	.570 397 2521	57.04	.140 795	7.04	2
3	1.303 960	3.286 056	.304 316 1541	.766 895	2.520 059	.396 816 1541	39.69	.190 448	6.35	3
4	1.424 577	4.590 016	.217 864 1428	.701 963	3.222 022	.310 364 1428	31.04	.241 457	6.04	4
5	1.556 350	6.014 593	.166 262 2898	.642 529	3.864 551	.258 762 2898	25.88	.293 811	5.88	5
6	1.700 312	7.570 943	.132 083 9456	.588 127	4.452 678	.224 583 9456	22.46	.347 504	5.79	6
7	1.857 591	9.271 255	.107 860 2623	.538 332	4.991 010	.200 360 2623	20.04	.402 522	5.75	7
8	2.029 418	11.128 846	.089 856 5753	.492 752	5.483 762	.182 356 5753	18.24	.458 853	5.74	8
9	2.217 139	13.158 264	.075 997 8649	.451 032	5.934 793	.168 497 8649	16.85	.516 481	5.74	9
10	2.422 225	15.375 404	.065 038 9420	.412 844	6.347 637	.157 538 9420	15.76	.575 389	5.75	10
11	2.646 281	17.797 629	.056 187 2605	.377 889	6.725 526	.148 687 2605	14.87	.635 560	5.78	11
12	2.891 062	20.443 909	.048 914 3237	.345 894	7.071 419	.141 414 3237	14.15	.696 972	5.81	12
13	3.158 485	23.334 971	.042 854 1351	.316 608	7.388 027	.135 354 1351	13.54	.759 604	5.84	13
14	3.450 645	26.493 456	.037 745 1703	.289 801	7.677 828	.130 245 1703	13.03	.823 432	5.88	14
15	3.769 829	29.944 100	.033 395 5599	.265 264	7.943 092	.125 895 5599	12.59	.888 433	5.92	15
16	4.118 539	33.713 930	.029 661 3301	.242 805	8.185 896	.122 161 3301	12.22	.954 581	5.97	16
17	4.499 503	37.832 468	.026 432 3225	.222 247	8.408 143	.118 932 3225	11.90	1.021 849	6.01	17
18	4.915 707	42.331 972	.023 622 8071	.203 430	8.611 573	.116 122 8071	11.62	1.090 211	6.06	18
19	5.370 410	47.247 679	.021 165 0609	.186 206	8.797 778	.113 665 0609	11.37	1.159 636	6.10	19
20	5.867 173	52.618 089	.019 004 8710	.170 440	8.968 218	.111 504 8710	11.16	1.230 097	6.15	20
21	6.409 887	58.485 262	.017 098 3246	.156 009	9.124 227	.109 598 3246	10.96	1.301 565	6.20	21
22	7.002 801	64.895 149	.015 409 4722	.142 800	9.267 027	.107 909 4722	10.80	1.374 008	6.25	22
23	7.650 560	71.897 951	.013 908 6023	.130 709	9.397 736	.106 408 6023	10.65	1.447 398	6.29	23
24	8.358 237	79.548 511	.012 570 9455	.119 642	9.517 379	.105 070 9455	10.51	1.521 703	6.34	24
25	9.131 374	87.906 748	.011 375 6909	.109 513	9.626 891	.103 875 6909	10.39	1.596 892	6.39	25
26	9.976 026	97.038 122	.010 305 2282	.100 240	9.727 132	.102 805 2282	10.29	1.672 936	6.43	26
27	10.898 809	107.014 149	.009 344 5587	.091 753	9.818 885	.101 844 5587	10.19	1.749 803	6.48	27
28	11.906 949	117.912 958	.008 480 8321	.083 985	9.902 869	.100 980 8321	10.10	1.827 463	6.53	28
29	13.008 341	129.819 906	.007 702 9789	.076 874	9.979 743	.100 202 9789	10.03	1.905 886	6.57	29
30	14.211 613	142.828 247	.007 001 4162	.070 365	10.050 108	.099 501 4162	9.96	1.985 042	6.62	30
31	15.526 187	157.039 860	.006 367 8100	.064 407	10.114 516	.098 867 8100	9.89	2.064 902	6.66	31
32	16.962 359	172.566 047	.005 794 8827	.058 954	10.173 470	.098 294 8827	9.83	2.145 436	6.70	32
33	18.531 378	189.528 407	.005 276 2539	.053 963	10.227 432	.097 776 2539	9.78	2.226 616	6.75	33
34	20.245 530	208.059 784	.004 806 3109	.049 394	10.276 826	.097 306 3109	9.74	2.308 415	6.79	34
35	22.118 242	228.305 315	.004 380 0995	.045 212	10.322 037	.096 880 0995	9.69	2.390 803	6.83	35
36	24.164 179	250.423 556	.003 993 2346	.041 384	10.363 421	.096 493 2346	9.65	2.473 756	6.87	36
37	26.399 365	274.587 735	.003 641 8233	.037 880	10.401 301	.096 141 8233	9.62	2.557 247	6.91	37
38	28.841 307	300.987 101	.003 322 4015	.034 672	10.435 973	.095 822 4015	9.59	2.641 251	6.95	38
39	31.509 128	329.828 407	.003 031 8795	.031 737	10.467 710	.095 531 8795	9.56	2.725 743	6.99	39
40	34.423 722	361.337 535	.002 767 4955	.029 050	10.496 760	.095 267 4955	9.53	2.810 700	7.03	40
41	37.607 916	395.761 257	.002 526 7759	.026 590	10.523 350	.095 026 7759	9.51	2.896 098	7.06	41
42	41.086 649	433.369 173	.002 307 5015	.024 339	10.547 689	.094 807 5015	9.49	2.981 915	7.10	42
43	44.887 164	474.455 822	.002 107 6778	.022 278	10.569 967	.094 607 6778	9.47	3.068 130	7.14	43
44	49.039 226	519.342 985	.001 925 5098	.020 392	10.590 358	.094 425 5098	9.45	3.154 722	7.17	44
45	53.575 355	568.382 212	.001 759 3795	.018 665	10.609 024	.094 259 3795	9.43	3.241 672	7.20	45
46	58.531 075	621.957 566	.001 607 8267	.017 085	10.626 109	.094 107 8267	9.42	3.328 960	7.24	46
47	63.945 199	680.488 641	.001 469 5322	.015 638	10.641 747	.093 969 5322	9.40	3.416 568	7.27	47
48	69.860 130	744.433 840	.001 343 3027	.014 314	10.656 061	.093 843 3027	9.39	3.504 479	7.30	48
49	76.322 192	814.293 970	.001 228 0577	.013 102	10.669 164	.093 728 0577	9.38	3.592 675	7.33	49
50	83.381 995	890.616 163	.001 122 8182	.011 993	10.681 157	.093 622 8182	9.37	3.681 141	7.36	50

Effective Rate is 9.25 %

Annual Percentage Rate is 9.25 %

ANNUAL COMPOUND INTEREST AND ANNUITY

	Amount Of 1	Amount Of 1 Per Period	Sinking Fund Payment	Present Worth Of 1	Present Worth of 1 Per Period	Periodic Payment To Amortize 1	Constant Annual Percent	Total Interest	Annual Add On Rate	
	What a single $1 deposit grows to in the future. The deposit is made at the beginning of the first period.	What a series of $1 deposits grow to in the future. A deposit is made at the end of each period.	The amount to be deposited at the end of each period that grows to $1 in the future.	What $1 to be paid in the future is worth today. Value today of a single $1 payment tomorrow.	What $1 to be paid at the end of each period is worth today. Value today of a series of $1 payments tomorrow.	The mortgage payment to amortize a loan of $1. An annuity certain, payable at the end of each period, worth $1 today.	The annual payment, including interest and principal, to amortize completely a loan of $100.	The total interest paid over the term on a loan of $1. The loan is amortized by regular periodic payments.	The average annual interest rate on a loan that is completely amortized by regular periodic payments.	
	$S = (1+i)^n$	$S\overline{n}| = \dfrac{(1+i)^n - 1}{i}$	$\dfrac{1}{S\overline{n}|} = \dfrac{i}{(1+i)^n - 1}$	$V^n = \dfrac{1}{(1+i)^n}$	$A\overline{n}| = \dfrac{1 - V^n}{i}$	$\dfrac{1}{A\overline{n}|} = \dfrac{i}{1 - V^n}$				

YEAR

										PERIODS
	1.095 000	1.000 000	1.000 000 0000	.913 242	.913 242	1.095 000 0000	109.50	.095 000	9.50	1

YEAR	Amount Of 1	Amount Of 1 Per Period	Sinking Fund Payment	Present Worth Of 1	Present Worth of 1 Per Period	Periodic Payment To Amortize 1	Constant Annual Percent	Total Interest	Annual Add On Rate	PERIODS
1	1.095 000	1.000 000	1.000 000 0000	.913 242	.913 242	1.095 000 0000	109.50	.095 000	9.50	1
2	1.199 025	2.095 000	.477 326 9690	.834 011	1.747 253	.572 326 9690	57.24	.144 654	7.23	2
3	1.312 932	3.294 025	.303 579 9668	.761 654	2.508 907	.398 579 9668	39.86	.195 740	6.52	3
4	1.437 661	4.606 957	.217 063 0025	.695 574	3.204 481	.312 063 0025	31.21	.248 252	6.21	4
5	1.574 239	6.044 618	.165 436 4173	.635 228	3.839 709	.260 436 4173	26.05	.302 182	6.04	5
6	1.723 791	7.618 857	.131 253 2826	.580 117	4.419 825	.226 253 2826	22.63	.357 520	5.96	6
7	1.887 552	9.342 648	.107 036 0296	.529 787	4.949 612	.202 036 0296	20.21	.414 252	5.92	7
8	2.066 869	11.230 200	.089 045 6084	.483 824	5.433 436	.184 045 6084	18.41	.472 365	5.90	8
9	2.263 222	13.297 069	.075 204 5426	.441 848	5.875 284	.170 204 5426	17.03	.531 841	5.91	9
10	2.478 228	15.560 291	.064 266 1517	.403 514	6.278 798	.159 266 1517	15.93	.592 662	5.93	10
11	2.713 659	18.038 518	.055 436 9258	.368 506	6.647 304	.150 436 9258	15.05	.654 806	5.95	11
12	2.971 457	20.752 178	.048 187 7142	.336 535	6.983 839	.143 187 7142	14.32	.718 253	5.99	12
13	3.253 745	23.723 634	.042 152 0575	.307 338	7.291 178	.137 152 0575	13.72	.782 977	6.02	13
14	3.562 851	26.977 380	.037 068 0923	.280 674	7.571 852	.132 068 0923	13.21	.848 953	6.06	14
15	3.901 322	30.540 231	.032 743 6950	.256 323	7.828 175	.127 743 6950	12.78	.916 155	6.11	15
16	4.271 948	34.441 553	.029 034 6957	.234 085	8.062 260	.124 034 6957	12.41	.984 555	6.15	16
17	4.677 783	38.713 500	.025 830 7825	.213 777	8.276 037	.120 830 7825	12.09	1.054 123	6.20	17
18	5.122 172	43.391 283	.023 046 1037	.195 230	8.471 266	.118 046 1037	11.81	1.124 830	6.25	18
19	5.608 778	48.513 454	.020 612 8384	.178 292	8.649 558	.115 612 8384	11.57	1.196 644	6.30	19
20	6.141 612	54.122 233	.018 476 6953	.162 824	8.812 382	.113 476 6953	11.35	1.269 534	6.35	20
21	6.725 065	60.263 845	.016 593 6973	.148 697	8.961 080	.111 593 6973	11.16	1.343 468	6.40	21
22	7.363 946	66.988 910	.014 927 8440	.135 797	9.096 876	.109 927 8440	11.00	1.418 413	6.45	22
23	8.063 521	74.352 856	.013 449 3824	.124 015	9.220 892	.108 449 3824	10.85	1.494 336	6.50	23
24	8.829 556	82.416 378	.012 133 5107	.113 256	9.334 148	.107 133 5107	10.72	1.571 204	6.55	24
25	9.668 364	91.245 934	.010 959 3925	.103 430	9.437 578	.105 959 3925	10.60	1.648 985	6.60	25
26	10.586 858	100.914 297	.009 909 3986	.094 457	9.532 034	.104 909 3986	10.50	1.727 644	6.64	26
27	11.592 610	111.501 156	.008 968 5169	.086 262	9.618 296	.103 968 5169	10.40	1.807 150	6.69	27
28	12.693 908	123.093 766	.008 123 8883	.078 778	9.697 074	.103 123 8883	10.32	1.887 469	6.74	28
29	13.899 829	135.787 673	.007 364 4387	.071 943	9.769 018	.102 364 4387	10.24	1.968 569	6.79	29
30	15.220 313	149.687 502	.006 680 5845	.065 702	9.834 719	.101 680 5845	10.17	2.050 418	6.83	30
31	16.666 242	164.907 815	.006 063 9940	.060 002	9.894 721	.101 063 9940	10.11	2.132 984	6.88	31
32	18.249 535	181.574 057	.005 507 3947	.054 796	9.949 517	.100 507 3947	10.06	2.216 237	6.93	32
33	19.983 241	199.823 593	.005 004 4141	.050 042	9.999 559	.100 004 4141	10.01	2.300 146	6.97	33
34	21.881 649	219.806 834	.004 549 4491	.045 700	10.045 259	.099 549 4491	9.96	2.384 681	7.01	34
35	23.960 406	241.688 483	.004 137 5575	.041 736	10.086 995	.099 137 5575	9.92	2.469 815	7.06	35
36	26.236 644	265.648 889	.003 764 3673	.038 115	10.125 109	.098 764 3673	9.88	2.555 517	7.10	36
37	28.729 126	291.885 534	.003 426 0006	.034 808	10.159 917	.098 426 0006	9.85	2.641 762	7.14	37
38	31.458 393	320.614 659	.003 119 0090	.031 788	10.191 705	.098 119 0090	9.82	2.728 522	7.18	38
39	34.446 940	352.073 052	.002 840 3196	.029 030	10.220 735	.097 840 3196	9.79	2.815 772	7.22	39
40	37.719 399	386.519 992	.002 587 1883	.026 512	10.247 247	.097 587 1883	9.76	2.903 488	7.26	40
41	41.302 742	424.239 391	.002 357 1597	.024 211	10.271 458	.097 357 1597	9.74	2.991 644	7.30	41
42	45.226 503	465.542 133	.002 148 0333	.022 111	10.293 569	.097 148 0333	9.72	3.080 217	7.33	42
43	49.523 020	510.768 636	.001 957 8336	.020 193	10.313 762	.096 957 8336	9.70	3.169 187	7.37	43
44	54.227 707	560.291 656	.001 784 7847	.018 441	10.332 203	.096 784 7847	9.68	3.258 531	7.41	44
45	59.379 340	614.519 364	.001 627 2880	.016 841	10.349 043	.096 627 2880	9.67	3.348 228	7.44	45
46	65.020 377	673.898 703	.001 483 9025	.015 380	10.364 423	.096 483 9025	9.65	3.438 260	7.47	46
47	71.197 313	738.919 080	.001 353 3282	.014 045	10.378 469	.096 353 3282	9.64	3.528 606	7.51	47
48	77.961 057	810.116 393	.001 234 3905	.012 827	10.391 296	.096 234 3905	9.63	3.619 251	7.54	48
49	85.367 358	888.077 450	.001 126 0279	.011 714	10.403 010	.096 126 0279	9.62	3.710 175	7.57	49
50	93.477 257	973.444 808	.001 027 2796	.010 698	10.413 707	.096 027 2796	9.61	3.801 364	7.60	50

Effective Rate is 9.50 %

Annual Percentage Rate is 9.50 %

ANNUAL COMPOUND INTEREST AND ANNUITY

	Amount Of 1	Amount Of 1 Per Period	Sinking Fund Payment	Present Worth Of 1	Present Worth of 1 Per Period	Periodic Payment To Amortize 1	Constant Annual Percent	Total Interest	Annual Add On Rate	
	What a single $ 1 deposit grows to in the future. The deposit is made at the beginning of the first period.	What a series of $ 1 deposits grow to in the future. A deposit is made at the end of each period.	The amount to be deposited at the end of each period that grows to $ 1 in the future.	What $ 1 to be paid in the future is worth today. Value today of a single $ 1 payment tomorrow.	What $ 1 to be paid at the end of each period is worth today. Value today of a series of $ 1 payments tomorrow.	The mortgage payment to amortize a loan of $ 1. An annuity certain, payable at the end of each period, worth $ 1 today.	The annual payment, including interest and principal, to amortize completely a loan of $ 100.	The total interest paid over the term on a loan of $1. The loan is amortized by regular periodic payments.	The average annual interest rate on a loan that is completely amortized by regular periodic payments.	

$$S = (1+i)^n \qquad S\overline{n} = \frac{(1+i)^n - 1}{i} \qquad \frac{1}{S\overline{n}} = \frac{i}{(1+i)^n - 1} \qquad V^n = \frac{1}{(1+i)^n} \qquad A\overline{n} = \frac{1-V^n}{i} \qquad \frac{1}{A\overline{n}} = \frac{i}{1-V^n}$$

YEAR   **PERIODS**

| | 1.097 500 | 1.000 000 | 1.000 000 0000 | .911 162 | .911 162 | 1.097 500 0000 | 109.75 | .097 500 | 9.75 | 1 |

1	1.097 500	1.000 000	1.000 000 0000	.911 162	.911 162	1.097 500 0000	109.75	.097 500	9.75	1
2	1.204 506	2.097 500	.476 758 0453	.830 216	1.741 377	.574 258 0453	57.43	.148 516	7.43	2
3	1.321 946	3.302 006	.302 846 1863	.756 461	2.497 838	.400 346 1863	40.04	.201 039	6.70	3
4	1.450 835	4.623 952	.216 265 2273	.689 258	3.187 096	.313 765 2273	31.38	.255 061	6.38	4
5	1.592 292	6.074 787	.164 614 8207	.628 026	3.815 122	.262 114 8207	26.22	.310 574	6.21	5
6	1.747 540	7.667 079	.130 427 7693	.572 233	4.387 355	.227 927 7693	22.80	.367 567	6.13	6
7	1.917 925	9.414 619	.106 217 7862	.521 397	4.908 752	.203 717 7862	20.38	.426 025	6.09	7
8	2.104 923	11.332 544	.088 241 4362	.475 077	5.383 828	.185 741 4362	18.58	.485 931	6.07	8
9	2.310 153	13.437 468	.074 418 7843	.432 872	5.816 700	.171 918 7843	17.20	.547 269	6.08	9
10	2.535 393	15.747 621	.063 501 6567	.394 416	6.211 116	.161 001 6567	16.11	.610 017	6.10	10
11	2.782 594	18.283 014	.054 695 5780	.359 377	6.570 493	.152 195 5780	15.22	.674 151	6.13	11
12	3.053 897	21.065 607	.047 470 7411	.327 450	6.897 944	.144 970 7411	14.50	.739 649	6.16	12
13	3.351 652	24.119 504	.041 460 2220	.298 360	7.196 304	.138 960 2220	13.90	.806 483	6.20	13
14	3.678 438	27.471 156	.036 401 8174	.271 855	7.468 159	.133 901 8174	13.40	.874 625	6.25	14
15	4.037 085	31.149 594	.032 103 1476	.247 703	7.715 862	.129 603 1476	12.97	.944 047	6.29	15
16	4.430 701	35.186 679	.028 419 8461	.225 698	7.941 560	.125 919 8461	12.60	1.014 718	6.34	16
17	4.862 695	39.617 380	.025 241 4470	.205 647	8.147 207	.122 741 4470	12.28	1.086 605	6.39	17
18	5.336 807	44.480 075	.022 481 9766	.187 378	8.334 585	.119 981 9766	12.00	1.159 676	6.44	18
19	5.857 146	49.816 882	.020 073 5164	.170 732	8.505 317	.117 573 5164	11.76	1.233 897	6.49	19
20	6.428 218	55.674 028	.017 961 6966	.155 564	8.660 881	.115 461 6966	11.55	1.309 234	6.55	20
21	7.054 969	62.102 246	.016 102 4773	.141 744	8.802 625	.113 602 4773	11.37	1.385 652	6.60	21
22	7.742 828	69.157 215	.014 459 8073	.129 152	8.931 777	.111 959 8073	11.20	1.463 116	6.65	22
23	8.497 754	76.900 043	.013 003 8939	.117 678	9.049 455	.110 503 8939	11.06	1.541 590	6.70	23
24	9.326 285	85.397 797	.011 709 9039	.107 224	9.156 679	.109 209 9039	10.93	1.621 038	6.75	24
25	10.235 598	94.724 083	.010 556 9774	.097 698	9.254 377	.108 056 9774	10.81	1.701 424	6.81	25
26	11.233 569	104.959 681	.009 527 4680	.089 019	9.343 396	.107 027 4680	10.71	1.782 714	6.86	26
27	12.328 842	116.193 249	.008 606 3520	.081 111	9.424 506	.106 106 3520	10.62	1.864 872	6.91	27
28	13.530 904	128.522 091	.007 780 7635	.073 905	9.498 411	.105 280 7635	10.53	1.947 861	6.96	28
29	14.850 167	142.052 995	.007 039 6263	.067 339	9.565 751	.104 539 6263	10.46	2.031 649	7.01	29
30	16.298 058	156.903 162	.006 373 3578	.061 357	9.627 108	.103 873 3578	10.39	2.116 201	7.05	30
31	17.887 119	173.201 221	.005 773 6314	.055 906	9.683 014	.103 273 6314	10.33	2.201 483	7.10	31
32	19.631 113	191.088 340	.005 233 1817	.050 940	9.733 953	.102 733 1817	10.28	2.287 462	7.15	32
33	21.545 147	210.719 453	.004 745 6463	.046 414	9.780 368	.102 245 6463	10.23	2.374 106	7.19	33
34	23.645 798	232.264 599	.004 305 4344	.042 291	9.822 658	.101 805 4344	10.19	2.461 385	7.24	34
35	25.951 264	255.910 398	.003 907 6177	.038 534	9.861 192	.101 407 6177	10.15	2.549 267	7.28	35
36	28.481 512	281.861 661	.003 547 8397	.035 110	9.896 303	.101 047 8397	10.11	2.637 722	7.33	36
37	31.258 459	310.343 173	.003 222 2394	.031 991	9.928 294	.100 722 2394	10.08	2.726 723	7.37	37
38	34.306 159	341.601 633	.002 927 3865	.029 149	9.957 443	.100 427 3865	10.05	2.816 241	7.41	38
39	37.651 010	375.907 792	.002 660 2268	.026 560	9.984 003	.100 160 2268	10.02	2.906 249	7.45	39
40	41.321 983	413.558 802	.002 418 0358	.024 200	10.008 203	.099 918 0358	10.00	2.996 721	7.49	40
41	45.350 877	454.880 785	.002 198 3782	.022 050	10.030 253	.099 698 3782	9.97	3.087 634	7.53	41
42	49.772 587	500.231 662	.001 999 0738	.020 091	10.050 345	.099 499 0738	9.95	3.178 961	7.57	42
43	54.625 414	550.004 249	.001 818 1678	.018 306	10.068 651	.099 318 1678	9.94	3.270 681	7.61	43
44	59.951 392	604.629 663	.001 653 9050	.016 680	10.085 331	.099 153 9050	9.92	3.362 772	7.64	44
45	65.796 653	664.581 055	.001 504 7074	.015 198	10.100 530	.099 004 7074	9.91	3.455 212	7.68	45
46	72.211 827	730.377 708	.001 369 1546	.013 848	10.114 378	.098 869 1546	9.89	3.547 981	7.71	46
47	79.252 480	802.589 534	.001 245 9669	.012 618	10.126 996	.098 745 9669	9.88	3.641 060	7.75	47
48	86.979 596	881.842 014	.001 133 9900	.011 497	10.138 493	.098 633 9900	9.87	3.734 432	7.78	48
49	95.460 107	968.821 610	.001 032 1818	.010 476	10.148 968	.098 532 1818	9.86	3.828 077	7.81	49
50	104.767 467	1064.281 717	.000 939 6008	.009 545	10.158 513	.098 439 6008	9.85	3.921 980	7.84	50

Effective Rate is 9.75 %   **8 - 455**   Annual Percentage Rate is 9.75 %

ANNUAL COMPOUND INTEREST AND ANNUITY

10.00 % A

	Amount Of 1	Amount Of 1 Per Period	Sinking Fund Payment	Present Worth Of 1	Present Worth of 1 Per Period	Periodic Payment To Amortize 1	Constant Annual Percent	Total Interest	Annual Add On Rate	
	What a single $ 1 deposit grows to in the future. The deposit is made at the beginning of the first period.	What a series of $ 1 deposits grow to in the future. A deposit is made at the end of each period.	The amount to be deposited at the end of each period that grows to $ 1 in the future.	What $ 1 to be paid in the future is worth today. Value today of a single $ 1 payment tomorrow.	What $ 1 to be paid at the end of each period is worth today. Value today of a series of $ 1 payments tomorrow.	The mortgage payment to amortize a loan of $ 1. An annuity certain, payable at the end of each period, worth $ 1 today.	The annual payment, including interest and principal, to amortize completely a loan of $ 100.	The total interest paid over the term on a loan of $1. The loan is amortized by regular periodic payments.	The average annual interest rate on a loan that is completely amortized by regular periodic payments.	
	$S = (1+i)^n$	$S\overline{n}| = \dfrac{(1+i)^n - 1}{i}$	$\dfrac{1}{S\overline{n}|} = \dfrac{i}{(1+i)^n - 1}$	$V^n = \dfrac{1}{(1+i)^n}$	$A\overline{n}| = \dfrac{1 - V^n}{i}$	$\dfrac{1}{A\overline{n}|} = \dfrac{i}{1 - V^n}$				

YEAR | | | | | | | | | **PERIODS**

| | 1.100 000 | 1.000 000 | 1.000 000 0000 | .909 091 | .909 091 | 1.100 000 0000 | 110.00 | .100 000 | 10.00 | 1 |

YEAR	Amount Of 1	Amount Of 1 Per Period	Sinking Fund Payment	Present Worth Of 1	Present Worth of 1 Per Period	Periodic Payment To Amortize 1	Constant Annual Percent	Total Interest	Annual Add On Rate	PERIODS
1	1.100 000	1.000 000	1.000 000 0000	.909 091	.909 091	1.100 000 0000	110.00	.100 000	10.00	1
2	1.210 000	2.100 000	.476 190 4762	.826 446	1.735 537	.576 190 4762	57.62	.152 381	7.62	2
3	1.331 000	3.310 000	.302 114 8036	.751 315	2.486 852	.402 114 8036	40.22	.206 344	6.88	3
4	1.464 100	4.641 000	.215 470 8037	.683 013	3.169 865	.315 470 8037	31.55	.261 883	6.55	4
5	1.610 510	6.105 100	.163 797 4808	.620 921	3.790 787	.263 797 4808	26.38	.318 987	6.38	5
6	1.771 561	7.715 610	.129 607 3804	.564 474	4.355 261	.229 607 3804	22.97	.377 644	6.29	6
7	1.948 717	9.487 171	.105 405 4997	.513 158	4.868 419	.205 405 4997	20.55	.437 839	6.25	7
8	2.143 589	11.435 888	.087 444 0176	.466 507	5.334 926	.187 444 0176	18.75	.499 552	6.24	8
9	2.357 948	13.579 477	.073 640 5391	.424 098	5.759 024	.173 640 5391	17.37	.562 765	6.25	9
10	2.593 742	15.937 425	.062 745 3949	.385 543	6.144 567	.162 745 3949	16.28	.627 454	6.27	10
11	2.853 117	18.531 167	.053 963 1420	.350 494	6.495 061	.153 963 1420	15.40	.693 595	6.31	11
12	3.138 428	21.384 284	.046 763 3151	.318 631	6.813 692	.146 763 3151	14.68	.761 160	6.34	12
13	3.452 271	24.522 712	.040 778 5238	.289 664	7.103 356	.140 778 5238	14.08	.830 121	6.39	13
14	3.797 498	27.974 983	.035 746 2232	.263 331	7.366 687	.135 746 2232	13.58	.900 447	6.43	14
15	4.177 248	31.772 482	.031 473 7769	.239 392	7.606 080	.131 473 7769	13.15	.972 107	6.48	15
16	4.594 973	35.949 730	.027 816 6207	.217 629	7.823 709	.127 816 6207	12.79	1.045 066	6.53	16
17	5.054 470	40.544 703	.024 664 1344	.197 845	8.021 553	.124 664 1344	12.47	1.119 290	6.58	17
18	5.559 917	45.599 173	.021 930 2222	.179 859	8.201 412	.121 930 2222	12.20	1.194 744	6.64	18
19	6.115 909	51.159 090	.019 546 8682	.163 508	8.364 920	.119 546 8682	11.96	1.271 391	6.69	19
20	6.727 500	57.274 999	.017 459 6248	.148 644	8.513 564	.117 459 6248	11.75	1.349 193	6.75	20
21	7.400 250	64.002 499	.015 624 3898	.135 131	8.648 694	.115 624 3898	11.57	1.428 112	6.80	21
22	8.140 275	71.402 749	.014 005 0630	.122 846	8.771 540	.114 005 0630	11.41	1.508 111	6.86	22
23	8.954 302	79.543 024	.012 571 8127	.111 678	8.883 218	.112 571 8127	11.26	1.589 152	6.91	23
24	9.849 733	88.497 327	.011 299 7764	.101 526	8.984 744	.111 299 7764	11.13	1.671 195	6.96	24
25	10.834 706	98.347 059	.010 168 0722	.092 296	9.077 040	.110 168 0722	11.02	1.754 202	7.02	25
26	11.918 177	109.181 765	.009 159 0386	.083 905	9.160 945	.109 159 0386	10.92	1.838 135	7.07	26
27	13.109 994	121.099 942	.008 257 6423	.076 278	9.237 223	.108 257 6423	10.83	1.922 956	7.12	27
28	14.420 994	134.209 936	.007 451 0132	.069 343	9.306 567	.107 451 0132	10.75	2.008 628	7.17	28
29	15.863 093	148.630 930	.006 728 0747	.063 039	9.369 606	.106 728 0747	10.68	2.095 114	7.22	29
30	17.449 402	164.494 023	.006 079 2483	.057 309	9.426 914	.106 079 2483	10.61	2.182 377	7.27	30
31	19.194 342	181.943 425	.005 496 2140	.052 099	9.479 013	.105 496 2140	10.55	2.270 383	7.32	31
32	21.113 777	201.137 767	.004 971 7167	.047 362	9.526 376	.104 971 7167	10.50	2.359 095	7.37	32
33	23.225 154	222.251 544	.004 499 4063	.043 057	9.569 432	.104 499 4063	10.45	2.448 480	7.42	33
34	25.547 670	245.476 699	.004 073 7064	.039 143	9.608 575	.104 073 7064	10.41	2.538 506	7.47	34
35	28.102 437	271.024 368	.003 689 7051	.035 584	9.644 159	.103 689 7051	10.37	2.629 140	7.51	35
36	30.912 681	299.126 805	.003 343 0638	.032 349	9.676 508	.103 343 0638	10.34	2.720 350	7.56	36
37	34.003 949	330.039 486	.003 029 9405	.029 408	9.705 917	.103 029 9405	10.31	2.812 108	7.60	37
38	37.404 343	364.043 434	.002 746 9250	.026 735	9.732 651	.102 746 9250	10.28	2.904 383	7.64	38
39	41.144 778	401.447 778	.002 490 9840	.024 304	9.756 956	.102 490 9840	10.25	2.997 148	7.69	39
40	45.259 256	442.592 556	.002 259 4144	.022 095	9.779 051	.102 259 4144	10.23	3.090 377	7.73	40
41	49.785 181	487.851 811	.002 049 8028	.020 086	9.799 137	.102 049 8028	10.21	3.184 042	7.77	41
42	54.763 699	537.636 992	.001 859 9911	.018 260	9.817 397	.101 859 9911	10.19	3.278 120	7.81	42
43	60.240 069	592.400 692	.001 688 0466	.016 600	9.833 998	.101 688 0466	10.17	3.372 586	7.84	43
44	66.264 076	652.640 761	.001 532 2365	.015 091	9.849 089	.101 532 2365	10.16	3.467 418	7.88	44
45	72.890 484	718.904 837	.001 391 0047	.013 719	9.862 808	.101 391 0047	10.14	3.562 595	7.92	45
46	80.179 532	791.795 321	.001 262 9527	.012 472	9.875 280	.101 262 9527	10.13	3.658 096	7.95	46
47	88.197 485	871.974 853	.001 146 8221	.011 338	9.886 618	.101 146 8221	10.12	3.753 901	7.99	47
48	97.017 234	960.172 338	.001 041 4797	.010 307	9.896 926	.101 041 4797	10.11	3.849 991	8.02	48
49	106.718 957	1057.189 572	.000 945 9041	.009 370	9.906 296	.100 945 9041	10.10	3.946 349	8.05	49
50	117.390 853	1163.908 529	.000 859 1740	.008 519	9.914 814	.100 859 1740	10.09	4.042 959	8.09	50

Effective Rate is 10.00 %

8 - 456

Annual Percentage Rate is 10.00 %

ANNUAL COMPOUND INTEREST AND ANNUITY

Amount Of 1	Amount Of 1 Per Period	Sinking Fund Payment	Present Worth Of 1	Present Worth of 1 Per Period	Periodic Payment To Amortize 1	Constant Annual Percent	Total Interest	Annual Add On Rate
What a single $ 1 deposit grows to in the future. The deposit is made at the beginning of the first period.	What a series of $ 1 deposits grow to in the future. A deposit is made at the end of each period.	The amount to be deposited at the end of each period that grows to $ 1 in the future.	What $ 1 to be paid in the future is worth today. Value today of a single $ 1 payment tomorrow.	What $ 1 to be paid at the end of each period is worth today. Value today of a series of $ 1 payments tomorrow.	The mortgage payment to amortize a loan of $ 1. An annuity certain, payable at the end of each period, worth $ 1 today.	The annual payment, including interest and principal, to amortize completely a loan of $ 100.	The total interest paid over the term on a loan of $1. The loan is amortized by regular periodic payments.	The average annual interest rate on a loan that is completely amortized by regular periodic payments.
$S = (1+i)^n$	$S\overline{n} = \dfrac{(1+i)^n - 1}{i}$	$\dfrac{1}{S\overline{n}} = \dfrac{i}{(1+i)^n - 1}$	$V^n = \dfrac{1}{(1+i)^n}$	$A\overline{n} = \dfrac{1-V^n}{i}$	$\dfrac{1}{A\overline{n}} = \dfrac{i}{1-V^n}$			

YEAR   **PERIODS**

	Amount Of 1	Amount Of 1 Per Period	Sinking Fund Payment	Present Worth Of 1	Present Worth of 1 Per Period	Periodic Payment To Amortize 1	Constant Annual Percent	Total Interest	Annual Add On Rate	PERIODS
	1.102 500	1.000 000	1.000 000 0000	.907 029	.907 029	1.102 500 0000	110.25	.102 500	10.25	1
1	1.102 500	1.000 000	1.000 000 0000	.907 029	.907 029	1.102 500 0000	110.25	.102 500	10.25	1
2	1.215 506	2.102 500	.475 624 2568	.822 702	1.729 732	.578 124 2568	57.82	.156 249	7.81	2
3	1.340 096	3.318 006	.301 385 8096	.746 215	2.475 947	.403 885 8096	40.39	.211 657	7.06	3
4	1.477 455	4.658 102	.214 679 7179	.676 839	3.152 787	.317 179 7179	31.72	.268 719	6.72	4
5	1.628 895	6.135 557	.162 984 3787	.613 913	3.766 700	.265 484 3787	26.55	.327 422	6.55	5
6	1.795 856	7.764 452	.128 792 0905	.556 837	4.323 537	.231 292 0905	23.13	.387 753	6.46	6
7	1.979 932	9.560 308	.104 599 1374	.505 068	4.828 605	.207 099 1374	20.71	.449 694	6.42	7
8	2.182 875	11.540 240	.086 653 3114	.458 112	5.286 717	.189 153 3114	18.92	.513 227	6.42	8
9	2.406 619	13.723 114	.072 869 7558	.415 521	5.702 238	.175 369 7558	17.54	.578 328	6.43	9
10	2.653 298	16.129 734	.061 997 3037	.376 889	6.079 127	.164 497 3037	16.45	.644 973	6.45	10
11	2.925 261	18.783 031	.053 239 5425	.341 850	6.420 977	.155 739 5425	15.58	.713 135	6.48	11
12	3.225 100	21.708 292	.046 065 3465	.310 068	6.731 045	.148 565 3465	14.86	.782 784	6.52	12
13	3.555 673	24.933 392	.040 106 8574	.281 241	7.012 286	.142 606 8574	14.27	.853 889	6.57	13
14	3.920 129	28.489 065	.035 101 1874	.255 094	7.267 379	.137 601 1874	13.77	.926 417	6.62	14
15	4.321 942	32.409 194	.030 855 4419	.231 377	7.498 757	.133 355 4419	13.34	1.000 332	6.67	15
16	4.764 941	36.731 136	.027 224 8588	.209 866	7.708 623	.129 724 8588	12.98	1.075 598	6.72	16
17	5.253 348	41.496 078	.024 098 6632	.190 355	7.898 978	.126 598 6632	12.66	1.152 177	6.78	17
18	5.791 816	46.749 426	.021 390 6371	.172 657	8.071 635	.123 890 6371	12.39	1.230 031	6.83	18
19	6.385 477	52.541 242	.019 032 6678	.156 605	8.228 240	.121 532 6678	12.16	1.309 121	6.89	19
20	7.039 989	58.926 719	.016 970 2304	.142 046	8.370 286	.119 470 2304	11.95	1.389 405	6.95	20
21	7.761 588	65.966 708	.015 159 1618	.128 840	8.499 126	.117 659 1618	11.77	1.470 842	7.00	21
22	8.557 150	73.728 295	.013 563 3137	.116 861	8.615 987	.116 063 3137	11.61	1.553 393	7.06	22
23	9.434 258	82.285 446	.012 152 8174	.105 997	8.721 984	.114 652 8174	11.47	1.637 015	7.12	23
24	10.401 270	91.719 704	.010 902 7827	.096 142	8.818 126	.113 402 7827	11.35	1.721 667	7.17	24
25	11.467 400	102.120 974	.009 792 3077	.087 204	8.905 329	.112 292 3077	11.23	1.807 308	7.23	25
26	12.642 808	113.588 373	.008 803 7179	.079 096	8.984 426	.111 303 7179	11.14	1.893 897	7.28	26
27	13.938 696	126.231 182	.007 921 9729	.071 743	9.056 169	.110 421 9729	11.05	1.981 393	7.34	27
28	15.367 412	140.169 878	.007 134 2004	.065 073	9.121 241	.109 634 2004	10.97	2.069 758	7.39	28
29	16.942 572	155.537 290	.006 429 3264	.059 023	9.180 264	.108 929 3264	10.90	2.158 950	7.44	29
30	18.679 186	172.479 862	.005 797 7783	.053 536	9.233 800	.108 297 7783	10.83	2.248 933	7.50	30
31	20.593 802	191.159 048	.005 231 2460	.048 558	9.282 358	.107 731 2460	10.78	2.339 669	7.55	31
32	22.704 667	211.752 851	.004 722 4866	.044 044	9.326 402	.107 222 4866	10.73	2.431 120	7.60	32
33	25.031 896	234.457 518	.004 265 1650	.039 949	9.366 351	.106 765 1650	10.68	2.523 250	7.65	33
34	27.597 665	259.489 414	.003 853 7218	.036 235	9.402 586	.106 353 7218	10.64	2.616 027	7.69	34
35	30.426 426	287.087 078	.003 483 2637	.032 866	9.435 452	.105 983 2637	10.60	2.709 414	7.74	35
36	33.545 134	317.513 504	.003 149 4723	.029 811	9.465 263	.105 649 4723	10.57	2.803 381	7.79	36
37	36.983 510	351.058 638	.002 848 5270	.027 039	9.492 302	.105 348 5270	10.54	2.897 896	7.83	37
38	40.774 320	388.042 148	.002 577 0396	.024 525	9.516 827	.105 077 0396	10.51	2.992 928	7.88	38
39	44.953 688	428.816 469	.002 332 0000	.022 245	9.539 072	.104 832 0000	10.49	3.088 448	7.92	39
40	49.561 441	473.770 157	.002 110 7281	.020 177	9.559 249	.104 610 7281	10.47	3.184 429	7.96	40
41	54.641 489	523.331 598	.001 910 8344	.018 301	9.577 550	.104 410 8344	10.45	3.280 844	8.00	41
42	60.242 241	577.973 087	.001 730 1844	.016 600	9.594 150	.104 230 1844	10.43	3.377 668	8.04	42
43	66.417 071	638.215 328	.001 566 8693	.015 056	9.609 206	.104 066 8693	10.41	3.474 875	8.08	43
44	73.224 821	704.632 399	.001 419 1797	.013 657	9.622 863	.103 919 1797	10.40	3.572 444	8.12	44
45	80.730 365	777.857 220	.001 285 5830	.012 387	9.635 250	.103 785 5830	10.38	3.670 351	8.16	45
46	89.005 227	858.587 585	.001 164 7035	.011 235	9.646 485	.103 664 7035	10.37	3.768 576	8.19	46
47	98.128 263	947.592 813	.001 055 3056	.010 191	9.656 676	.103 555 3056	10.36	3.867 099	8.23	47
48	108.186 410	1045.721 076	.000 956 2779	.009 243	9.665 919	.103 456 2779	10.35	3.965 901	8.26	48
49	119.275 517	1153.907 486	.000 866 6206	.008 384	9.674 303	.103 366 6206	10.34	4.064 964	8.30	49
50	131.501 258	1273.183 003	.000 785 4330	.007 604	9.681 907	.103 285 4330	10.33	4.164 272	8.33	50

ANNUAL COMPOUND INTEREST AND ANNUITY

10.50 % A

Amount Of 1	Amount Of 1 Per Period	Sinking Fund Payment	Present Worth Of 1	Present Worth of 1 Per Period	Periodic Payment To Amortize 1	Constant Annual Percent	Total Interest	Annual Add On Rate
What a single $ 1 deposit grows to in the future. The deposit is made at the beginning of the first period.	What a series of $ 1 deposits grow to in the future. A deposit is made at the end of each period.	The amount to be deposited at the end of each period that grows to $ 1 in the future.	What $ 1 to be paid in the future is worth today. Value today of a single $ 1 payment tomorrow.	What $ 1 to be paid at the end of each period is worth today. Value today of a series of $ 1 payments tomorrow.	The mortgage payment to amortize a loan of $ 1. An annuity certain, payable at the end of each period, worth $ 1 today.	The annual payment, including interest and principal, to amortize completely a loan of $ 100.	The total interest paid over the term on a loan of $1. The loan is amortized by regular periodic payments.	The average annual interest rate on a loan that is completely amortized by regular periodic payments.

$$S = (1+i)^n \qquad S\overline{n}| = \frac{(1+i)^n - 1}{i} \qquad \frac{1}{S\overline{n}|} = \frac{i}{(1+i)^n - 1} \qquad V^n = \frac{1}{(1+i)^n} \qquad A\overline{n}| = \frac{1-V^n}{i} \qquad \frac{1}{A\overline{n}|} = \frac{i}{1-V^n}$$

YEAR   **PERIODS**

| | 1.105 000 | 1.000 000 | 1.000 000 0000 | .904 977 | .904 977 | 1.105 000 0000 | 110.50 | .105 000 | 10.50 | 1 |

YEAR	Amount Of 1	Amount Of 1 Per Period	Sinking Fund Payment	Present Worth Of 1	Present Worth of 1 Per Period	Periodic Payment To Amortize 1	Constant Annual Percent	Total Interest	Annual Add On Rate	PERIODS
1	1.105 000	1.000 000	1.000 000 0000	.904 977	.904 977	1.105 000 0000	110.50	.105 000	10.50	1
2	1.221 025	2.105 000	.475 059 3824	.818 984	1.723 961	.580 059 3824	58.01	.160 119	8.01	2
3	1.349 233	3.326 025	.300 659 1953	.741 162	2.465 123	.405 659 1953	40.57	.216 978	7.23	3
4	1.490 902	4.675 258	.213 891 9564	.670 735	3.135 858	.318 891 9564	31.89	.275 568	6.89	4
5	1.647 447	6.166 160	.162 175 4954	.607 000	3.742 858	.267 175 4954	26.72	.335 877	6.72	5
6	1.820 429	7.813 606	.127 981 8746	.549 321	4.292 179	.232 981 8746	23.30	.397 891	6.63	6
7	2.011 574	9.634 035	.103 798 6667	.497 123	4.789 303	.208 798 6667	20.88	.461 591	6.59	7
8	2.222 789	11.645 609	.085 869 2763	.449 885	5.239 188	.190 869 2763	19.09	.526 954	6.59	8
9	2.456 182	13.868 398	.072 106 3831	.407 136	5.646 324	.177 106 3831	17.72	.593 957	6.60	9
10	2.714 081	16.324 579	.061 257 3206	.368 449	6.014 773	.166 257 3206	16.63	.662 573	6.63	10
11	2.999 059	19.038 660	.052 524 7041	.333 438	6.348 211	.157 524 7041	15.76	.732 772	6.66	11
12	3.313 961	22.037 720	.045 376 7456	.301 754	6.649 964	.150 376 7456	15.04	.804 521	6.70	12
13	3.661 926	25.351 680	.039 445 1173	.273 080	6.923 045	.144 445 1173	14.45	.877 787	6.75	13
14	4.046 429	29.013 607	.034 466 5871	.247 132	7.170 176	.139 466 5871	13.95	.952 532	6.80	14
15	4.471 304	33.060 035	.030 248 0015	.223 648	7.393 825	.135 248 0015	13.53	1.028 720	6.86	15
16	4.940 791	37.531 339	.026 644 3997	.202 397	7.596 221	.131 644 3997	13.17	1.106 310	6.91	16
17	5.459 574	42.472 130	.023 544 8518	.183 164	7.779 386	.128 544 8518	12.86	1.185 262	6.97	17
18	6.032 829	47.931 703	.020 863 0182	.165 760	7.945 146	.125 863 0182	12.59	1.265 534	7.03	18
19	6.666 276	53.964 532	.018 530 6897	.150 009	8.095 154	.123 530 6897	12.36	1.347 083	7.09	19
20	7.366 235	60.630 808	.016 493 2653	.135 755	8.230 909	.121 493 2653	12.15	1.429 865	7.15	20
21	8.139 690	67.997 043	.014 706 5219	.122 855	8.353 764	.119 706 5219	11.98	1.513 837	7.21	21
22	8.994 357	76.136 732	.013 134 2647	.111 181	8.464 945	.118 134 2647	11.82	1.598 954	7.27	22
23	9.938 764	85.131 089	.011 746 5900	.100 616	8.565 561	.116 746 5900	11.68	1.685 172	7.33	23
24	10.982 335	95.069 854	.010 518 5815	.091 055	8.656 616	.115 518 5815	11.56	1.772 446	7.39	24
25	12.135 480	106.052 188	.009 429 3198	.082 403	8.739 019	.114 429 3198	11.45	1.860 733	7.44	25
26	13.409 705	118.187 668	.008 461 1196	.074 573	8.813 592	.113 461 1196	11.35	1.949 989	7.50	26
27	14.817 724	131.597 373	.007 598 9359	.067 487	8.881 079	.112 598 9359	11.26	2.040 171	7.56	27
28	16.373 585	146.415 097	.006 829 8968	.061 074	8.942 153	.111 829 8968	11.19	2.131 237	7.61	28
29	18.092 812	162.788 683	.006 142 9332	.055 271	8.997 423	.111 142 9332	11.12	2.223 145	7.67	29
30	19.992 557	180.881 494	.005 528 4815	.050 019	9.047 442	.110 528 4815	11.06	2.315 854	7.72	30
31	22.091 775	200.874 051	.004 978 2438	.045 266	9.092 707	.109 978 2438	11.00	2.409 326	7.77	31
32	24.411 412	222.965 827	.004 484 9922	.040 964	9.133 672	.109 484 9922	10.95	2.503 520	7.82	32
33	26.974 610	247.377 238	.004 042 4091	.037 072	9.170 744	.109 042 4091	10.91	2.598 400	7.87	33
34	29.806 944	274.351 848	.003 644 9545	.033 549	9.204 293	.108 644 9545	10.87	2.693 928	7.92	34
35	32.936 673	304.158 792	.003 287 7563	.030 361	9.234 654	.108 287 7563	10.83	2.790 071	7.97	35
36	36.395 024	337.095 466	.002 966 5187	.027 476	9.262 131	.107 966 5187	10.80	2.886 795	8.02	36
37	40.216 501	373.490 489	.002 677 4443	.024 865	9.286 996	.107 677 4443	10.77	2.984 065	8.07	37
38	44.439 234	413.706 991	.002 417 1697	.022 503	9.309 499	.107 417 1697	10.75	3.081 852	8.11	38
39	49.105 354	458.146 225	.002 182 7092	.020 364	9.329 863	.107 182 7092	10.72	3.180 126	8.15	39
40	54.261 416	507.251 579	.001 971 4084	.018 429	9.348 292	.106 971 4084	10.70	3.278 856	8.20	40
41	59.958 864	561.512 994	.001 780 9027	.016 678	9.364 970	.106 780 9027	10.68	3.378 017	8.24	41
42	66.254 545	621.471 859	.001 609 0833	.015 093	9.380 064	.106 609 0833	10.67	3.477 582	8.28	42
43	73.211 272	687.726 404	.001 454 0666	.013 659	9.393 723	.106 454 0666	10.65	3.577 525	8.32	43
44	80.898 456	760.937 676	.001 314 1681	.012 361	9.406 084	.106 314 1681	10.64	3.677 823	8.36	44
45	89.392 794	841.836 132	.001 187 8796	.011 187	9.417 271	.106 187 8796	10.62	3.778 455	8.40	45
46	98.779 037	931.228 926	.001 073 8498	.010 124	9.427 394	.106 073 8498	10.61	3.879 397	8.43	46
47	109.150 836	1030.007 963	.000 970 8663	.009 162	9.436 556	.105 970 8663	10.60	3.980 631	8.47	47
48	120.611 674	1139.158 800	.000 877 8407	.008 291	9.444 847	.105 877 8407	10.59	4.082 136	8.50	48
49	133.275 900	1259.770 473	.000 793 7954	.007 503	9.452 350	.105 793 7954	10.58	4.183 896	8.54	49
50	147.269 869	1393.046 373	.000 717 8512	.006 790	9.459 140	.105 717 8512	10.58	4.285 893	8.57	50

Effective Rate is 10.50 %

Annual Percentage Rate is 10.50 %

Amount Of 1	Amount Of 1 Per Period	Sinking Fund Payment	Present Worth Of 1	Present Worth of 1 Per Period	Periodic Payment To Amortize 1	Constant Annual Percent	Total Interest	Annual Add On Rate
What a single $ 1 deposit grows to in the future. The deposit is made at the beginning of the first period.	What a series of $ 1 deposits grow to in the future. A deposit is made at the end of each period.	The amount to be deposited at the end of each period that grows to $ 1 in the future.	What $ 1 to be paid in the future is worth today. Value today of a single $ 1 payment tomorrow.	What $ 1 to be paid at the end of each period is worth today. Value today of a series of $ 1 payments tomorrow.	The mortgage payment to amortize a loan of $ 1. An annuity certain, payable at the end of each period, worth $ 1 today.	The annual payment, including interest and principal, to amortize completely a loan of $ 100.	The total interest paid over the term on a loan of $1. The loan is amortized by regular periodic payments.	The average annual interest rate on a loan that is completely amortized by regular periodic payments.

$$S = (1+i)^n \qquad S\overline{n}| = \frac{(1+i)^n - 1}{i} \qquad \frac{1}{S\overline{n}|} = \frac{i}{(1+i)^n - 1} \qquad V^n = \frac{1}{(1+i)^n} \qquad A\overline{n}| = \frac{1-V^n}{i} \qquad \frac{1}{A\overline{n}|} = \frac{i}{1-V^n}$$

YEAR | | | | | | | | | **PERIODS**

YEAR									PERIODS
	1.107 500	1.000 000	1.000 000 0000	.902 935	.902 935	1.107 500 0000	110.75	.107 500	10.75	1

YEAR	Amount Of 1	Amount Of 1 Per Period	Sinking Fund Payment	Present Worth Of 1	Present Worth of 1 Per Period	Periodic Payment To Amortize 1	Constant Annual Percent	Total Interest	Annual Add On Rate	PERIODS
1	1.107 500	1.000 000	1.000 000 0000	.902 935	.902 935	1.107 500 0000	110.75	.107 500	10.75	1
2	1.226 556	2.107 500	.474 495 8482	.815 291	1.718 225	.581 995 8482	58.20	.163 992	8.20	2
3	1.358 411	3.334 056	.299 934 9516	.736 154	2.454 380	.407 434 9516	40.75	.222 305	7.41	3
4	1.504 440	4.692 467	.213 107 5054	.664 699	3.119 079	.320 607 5054	32.07	.282 430	7.06	4
5	1.666 168	6.196 908	.161 370 8120	.600 180	3.719 258	.268 870 8120	26.89	.344 354	6.89	5
6	1.845 281	7.863 075	.127 176 7074	.541 923	4.261 181	.234 676 7074	23.47	.408 060	6.80	6
7	2.043 648	9.708 356	.103 004 0549	.489 321	4.750 502	.210 504 0549	21.06	.473 528	6.76	7
8	2.263 340	11.752 004	.085 091 8710	.441 825	5.192 327	.192 591 8710	19.26	.540 735	6.76	8
9	2.506 650	14.015 344	.071 350 3698	.398 939	5.591 266	.178 850 3698	17.89	.609 653	6.77	9
10	2.776 114	16.521 994	.060 525 3827	.360 216	5.951 482	.168 025 3827	16.81	.680 254	6.80	10
11	3.074 547	19.298 108	.051 818 5509	.325 251	6.276 733	.159 318 5509	15.94	.752 504	6.84	11
12	3.405 060	22.372 655	.044 697 4223	.293 681	6.570 414	.152 197 4223	15.22	.826 369	6.89	12
13	3.771 104	25.777 715	.038 793 1976	.265 174	6.835 588	.146 293 1976	14.63	.901 812	6.94	13
14	4.176 498	29.548 820	.033 842 2994	.239 435	7.075 023	.141 342 2994	14.14	.978 792	6.99	14
15	4.625 472	33.725 318	.029 651 3145	.216 194	7.291 217	.137 151 3145	13.72	1.057 270	7.05	15
16	5.122 710	38.350 789	.026 075 0826	.195 209	7.486 426	.133 575 0826	13.36	1.137 201	7.11	16
17	5.673 401	43.473 499	.023 002 5192	.176 261	7.662 687	.130 502 5192	13.06	1.218 543	7.17	17
18	6.283 292	49.146 900	.020 347 1632	.159 152	7.821 840	.127 847 1632	12.79	1.301 249	7.23	18
19	6.958 746	55.430 192	.018 040 7096	.143 704	7.965 544	.125 540 7096	12.56	1.385 273	7.29	19
20	7.706 811	62.388 938	.016 028 4825	.129 755	8.095 299	.123 528 4825	12.36	1.470 570	7.35	20
21	8.535 293	70.095 749	.014 266 2005	.117 161	8.212 460	.121 766 2005	12.18	1.557 090	7.41	21
22	9.452 837	78.631 042	.012 717 6237	.105 788	8.318 248	.120 217 6237	12.03	1.644 788	7.48	22
23	10.469 017	88.083 879	.011 352 8153	.095 520	8.413 768	.118 852 8153	11.89	1.733 615	7.54	23
24	11.594 436	98.552 895	.010 146 8353	.086 248	8.500 016	.117 646 8353	11.77	1.823 524	7.60	24
25	12.840 838	110.147 332	.009 078 7492	.077 877	8.577 893	.116 578 7492	11.66	1.914 469	7.66	25
26	14.221 228	122.988 170	.008 130 8633	.070 317	8.648 210	.115 630 8633	11.57	2.006 402	7.72	26
27	15.750 010	137.209 398	.007 288 1305	.063 492	8.711 702	.114 788 1305	11.48	2.099 280	7.78	27
28	17.443 136	152.959 408	.006 537 6822	.057 329	8.769 031	.114 037 6822	11.41	2.193 055	7.83	28
29	19.318 274	170.402 545	.005 868 4570	.051 764	8.820 796	.113 368 4570	11.34	2.287 685	7.89	29
30	21.394 988	189.720 818	.005 270 9028	.046 740	8.867 536	.112 770 9028	11.28	2.383 127	7.94	30
31	23.694 949	211.115 806	.004 736 7368	.042 203	8.909 739	.112 236 7368	11.23	2.479 339	8.00	31
32	26.242 156	234.810 756	.004 258 7487	.038 107	8.947 845	.111 758 7487	11.18	2.576 280	8.05	32
33	29.063 188	261.052 912	.003 830 6410	.034 408	8.982 253	.111 330 6410	11.14	2.673 911	8.10	33
34	32.187 481	290.116 100	.003 446 8959	.031 068	9.013 321	.110 946 8959	11.10	2.772 194	8.15	34
35	35.647 635	322.303 581	.003 102 6649	.028 052	9.041 373	.110 602 6649	11.07	2.871 093	8.20	35
36	39.479 756	357.951 215	.002 793 6768	.025 329	9.066 703	.110 293 6768	11.03	2.970 572	8.25	36
37	43.723 829	397.430 971	.002 516 1602	.022 871	9.089 574	.110 016 1602	11.01	3.070 598	8.30	37
38	48.424 141	441.154 801	.002 266 7780	.020 651	9.110 225	.109 766 7780	10.98	3.171 138	8.35	38
39	53.629 736	489.578 942	.002 042 5715	.018 646	9.128 871	.109 542 5715	10.96	3.272 160	8.39	39
40	59.394 933	543.208 678	.001 840 9132	.016 836	9.145 707	.109 340 9132	10.94	3.373 637	8.43	40
41	65.779 888	602.603 611	.001 659 4657	.015 202	9.160 910	.109 159 4657	10.92	3.475 538	8.48	41
42	72.851 226	668.383 499	.001 496 1470	.013 727	9.174 636	.108 996 1470	10.90	3.577 838	8.52	42
43	80.682 733	741.234 725	.001 349 1003	.012 394	9.187 030	.108 849 1003	10.89	3.680 511	8.56	43
44	89.356 127	821.917 458	.001 216 6672	.011 191	9.198 222	.108 716 6672	10.88	3.783 533	8.60	44
45	98.961 910	911.273 585	.001 097 3653	.010 105	9.208 327	.108 597 3653	10.86	3.886 881	8.64	45
46	109.600 316	1010.235 495	.000 989 8682	.009 124	9.217 451	.108 489 8682	10.85	3.990 534	8.68	46
47	121.382 350	1119.835 811	.000 892 9881	.008 238	9.225 689	.108 392 9881	10.84	4.094 470	8.71	47
48	134.430 952	1241.218 160	.000 805 6601	.007 439	9.233 128	.108 305 6601	10.84	4.198 672	8.75	48
49	148.882 280	1375.649 113	.000 726 9296	.006 717	9.239 845	.108 226 9296	10.83	4.303 120	8.78	49
50	164.887 125	1524.531 392	.000 655 9393	.006 065	9.245 909	.108 155 9393	10.82	4.407 797	8.82	50

Effective Rate is 10.75 %

Annual Percentage Rate is 10.75 %

	Amount Of 1	Amount Of 1 Per Period	Sinking Fund Payment	Present Worth Of 1	Present Worth of 1 Per Period	Periodic Payment To Amortize 1	Constant Annual Percent	Total Interest	Annual Add On Rate	
	What a single $ 1 deposit grows to in the future. The deposit is made at the beginning of the first period.	What a series of $ 1 deposits grow to in the future. A deposit is made at the end of each period.	The amount to be deposited at the end of each period that grows to $ 1 in the future.	What $ 1 to be paid in the future is worth today. Value today of a single $ 1 payment tomorrow.	What $ 1 to be paid at the end of each period is worth today. Value today of a series of $ 1 payments tomorrow.	The mortgage payment to amortize a loan of $ 1. An annuity certain, payable at the end of each period, worth $ 1 today.	The annual payment, including interest and principal, to amortize completely a loan of $ 100.	The total interest paid over the term on a loan of $1. The loan is amortized by regular periodic payments.	The average annual interest rate on a loan that is completely amortized by regular periodic payments.	
	$S = (1+i)^n$	$S\overline{n}| = \dfrac{(1+i)^n - 1}{i}$	$\dfrac{1}{S\overline{n}|} = \dfrac{i}{(1+i)^n - 1}$	$V^n = \dfrac{1}{(1+i)^n}$	$A\overline{n}| = \dfrac{1-V^n}{i}$	$\dfrac{1}{A\overline{n}|} = \dfrac{i}{1-V^n}$				

YEAR										PERIODS
	1.110 000	1.000 000	1.000 000 0000	.900 901	.900 901	1.110 000 0000	111.00	.110 000	11.00	1

YEAR										PERIODS
1	1.110 000	1.000 000	1.000 000 0000	.900 901	.900 901	1.110 000 0000	111.00	.110 000	11.00	1
2	1.232 100	2.110 000	.473 933 6493	.811 622	1.712 523	.583 933 6493	58.40	.167 867	8.39	2
3	1.367 631	3.342 100	.299 213 0696	.731 191	2.443 715	.409 213 0696	40.93	.227 639	7.59	3
4	1.518 070	4.709 731	.212 326 3515	.658 731	3.102 446	.322 326 3515	32.24	.289 305	7.23	4
5	1.685 058	6.227 801	.160 570 3095	.593 451	3.695 897	.270 570 3095	27.06	.352 852	7.06	5
6	1.870 415	7.912 860	.126 376 5636	.534 641	4.230 538	.236 376 5636	23.64	.418 259	6.97	6
7	2.076 160	9.783 274	.102 215 2695	.481 658	4.712 196	.212 215 2695	21.23	.485 507	6.94	7
8	2.304 538	11.859 434	.084 321 0542	.433 926	5.146 123	.194 321 0542	19.44	.554 568	6.93	8
9	2.558 037	14.163 972	.070 601 6644	.390 925	5.537 048	.180 601 6644	18.07	.625 415	6.95	9
10	2.839 421	16.722 009	.059 801 4271	.352 184	5.889 232	.169 801 4271	16.99	.698 014	6.98	10
11	3.151 757	19.561 430	.051 121 0071	.317 283	6.206 515	.161 121 0071	16.12	.772 331	7.02	11
12	3.498 451	22.713 187	.044 027 2864	.285 841	6.492 356	.154 027 2864	15.41	.848 327	7.07	12
13	3.883 280	26.211 638	.038 150 9925	.257 514	6.749 870	.148 150 9925	14.82	.925 963	7.12	13
14	4.310 441	30.094 918	.033 228 2015	.231 995	6.981 865	.143 228 2015	14.33	1.005 195	7.18	14
15	4.784 589	34.405 359	.029 065 2395	.209 004	7.190 870	.139 065 2395	13.91	1.085 979	7.24	15
16	5.310 894	39.189 948	.025 516 7470	.188 292	7.379 162	.135 516 7470	13.56	1.168 268	7.30	16
17	5.895 093	44.500 843	.022 471 4845	.169 633	7.548 794	.132 471 4845	13.25	1.252 015	7.36	17
18	6.543 553	50.395 936	.019 842 8701	.152 822	7.701 617	.129 842 8701	12.99	1.337 172	7.43	18
19	7.263 344	56.939 488	.017 562 5041	.137 678	7.839 294	.127 562 5041	12.76	1.423 688	7.49	19
20	8.062 312	64.202 832	.015 575 6369	.124 034	7.963 328	.125 575 6369	12.56	1.511 513	7.56	20
21	8.949 166	72.265 144	.013 837 9300	.111 742	8.075 070	.123 837 9300	12.39	1.600 597	7.62	21
22	9.933 574	81.214 309	.012 313 1011	.100 669	8.175 739	.122 313 1011	12.24	1.690 888	7.69	22
23	11.026 267	91.147 884	.010 971 1818	.090 693	8.266 432	.120 971 1818	12.10	1.782 337	7.75	23
24	12.239 157	102.174 151	.009 787 2113	.081 705	8.348 137	.119 787 2113	11.98	1.874 893	7.81	24
25	13.585 464	114.413 307	.008 740 2421	.073 608	8.421 745	.118 740 2421	11.88	1.968 506	7.87	25
26	15.079 865	127.998 771	.007 812 5750	.066 314	8.488 058	.117 812 5750	11.79	2.063 127	7.94	26
27	16.738 650	143.078 636	.006 989 1636	.059 742	8.547 800	.116 989 1636	11.70	2.158 707	8.00	27
28	18.579 901	159.817 286	.006 257 1454	.053 822	8.601 622	.116 257 1454	11.63	2.255 200	8.05	28
29	20.623 691	178.397 187	.005 605 4695	.048 488	8.650 110	.115 605 4695	11.57	2.352 559	8.11	29
30	22.892 297	199.020 878	.005 024 5985	.043 683	8.693 793	.115 024 5985	11.51	2.450 738	8.17	30
31	25.410 449	221.913 174	.004 506 2669	.039 354	8.733 146	.114 506 2669	11.46	2.549 694	8.22	31
32	28.205 599	247.323 624	.004 043 2854	.035 454	8.768 600	.114 043 2854	11.41	2.649 385	8.28	32
33	31.308 214	275.529 222	.003 629 3791	.031 940	8.800 541	.113 629 3791	11.37	2.749 770	8.33	33
34	34.752 118	306.837 437	.003 259 0547	.028 775	8.829 316	.113 259 0547	11.33	2.850 808	8.38	34
35	38.574 851	341.589 555	.002 927 4900	.025 924	8.855 240	.112 927 4900	11.30	2.952 462	8.44	35
36	42.818 085	380.164 406	.002 630 4409	.023 355	8.878 594	.112 630 4409	11.27	3.054 696	8.49	36
37	47.528 074	422.982 490	.002 364 1641	.021 040	8.899 635	.112 364 1641	11.24	3.157 474	8.53	37
38	52.756 162	470.510 564	.002 125 3508	.018 955	8.918 590	.112 125 3508	11.22	3.260 763	8.58	38
39	58.559 340	523.266 726	.001 911 0713	.017 077	8.935 666	.111 911 0713	11.20	3.364 532	8.63	39
40	65.000 867	581.826 066	.001 718 7267	.015 384	8.951 051	.111 718 7267	11.18	3.468 749	8.67	40
41	72.150 963	646.826 934	.001 546 0086	.013 860	8.964 911	.111 546 0086	11.16	3.573 386	8.72	41
42	80.087 569	718.977 896	.001 390 8633	.012 486	8.977 397	.111 390 8633	11.14	3.678 416	8.76	42
43	88.897 201	799.065 465	.001 251 4619	.011 249	8.988 646	.111 251 4619	11.13	3.783 813	8.80	43
44	98.675 893	887.962 666	.001 126 1735	.010 134	8.998 780	.111 126 1735	11.12	3.889 552	8.84	44
45	109.530 242	986.638 559	.001 013 5424	.009 130	9.007 910	.111 013 5424	11.11	3.995 609	8.88	45
46	121.578 568	1096.168 801	.000 912 2683	.008 225	9.016 135	.110 912 2683	11.10	4.101 964	8.92	46
47	134.952 211	1217.747 369	.000 821 1884	.007 410	9.023 545	.110 821 1884	11.09	4.208 596	8.95	47
48	149.796 954	1352.699 580	.000 739 2624	.006 676	9.030 221	.110 739 2624	11.08	4.315 485	8.99	48
49	166.274 619	1502.496 533	.000 665 5589	.006 014	9.036 235	.110 665 5589	11.07	4.422 612	9.03	49
50	184.564 827	1668.771 152	.000 599 2433	.005 418	9.041 653	.110 599 2433	11.06	4.529 962	9.06	50

ANNUAL COMPOUND INTEREST AND ANNUITY

Amount Of 1	Amount Of 1 Per Period	Sinking Fund Payment	Present Worth Of 1	Present Worth of 1 Per Period	Periodic Payment To Amortize 1	Constant Annual Percent	Total Interest	Annual Add On Rate
What a single $ 1 deposit grows to in the future. The deposit is made at the beginning of the first period.	What a series of $ 1 deposits grow to in the future. A deposit is made at the end of each period.	The amount to be deposited at the end of each period that grows to $ 1 in the future.	What $ 1 to be paid in the future is worth today. Value today of a single $ 1 payment tomorrow.	What $ 1 to be paid at the end of each period is worth today. Value today of a series of $ 1 payments tomorrow.	The mortgage payment to amortize a loan of $ 1. An annuity certain, payable at the end of each period, worth $ 1 today.	The annual payment, including interest and principal, to amortize completely a loan of $ 100.	The total interest paid over the term on a loan of $1. The loan is amortized by regular periodic payments.	The average annual interest rate on a loan that is completely amortized by regular periodic payments.

$$S = (1+i)^n \qquad S\overline{n}| = \frac{(1+i)^n - 1}{i} \qquad \frac{1}{S\overline{n}|} = \frac{i}{(1+i)^n - 1} \qquad V^n = \frac{1}{(1+i)^n} \qquad A\overline{n}| = \frac{1-V^n}{i} \qquad \frac{1}{A\overline{n}|} = \frac{i}{1-V^n}$$

YEAR   **PERIODS**

	Amount Of 1	Amount Of 1 Per Period	Sinking Fund Payment	Present Worth Of 1	Present Worth of 1 Per Period	Periodic Payment To Amortize 1	Constant Annual Percent	Total Interest	Annual Add On Rate	
	1.112 500	1.000 000	1.000 000 0000	.898 876	.898 876	1.112 500 0000	111.25	.112 500	11.25	1
1	1.112 500	1.000 000	1.000 000 0000	.898 876	.898 876	1.112 500 0000	111.25	.112 500	11.25	1
2	1.237 656	2.112 500	.473 372 7811	.807 979	1.706 855	.585 872 7811	58.59	.171 746	8.59	2
3	1.376 893	3.350 156	.298 493 5404	.726 273	2.433 128	.410 993 5404	41.10	.232 981	7.77	3
4	1.531 793	4.727 049	.211 548 4812	.652 830	3.085 958	.324 048 4812	32.41	.296 194	7.40	4
5	1.704 120	6.258 842	.159 773 9691	.586 813	3.672 771	.272 273 9691	27.23	.361 370	7.23	5
6	1.895 833	7.962 962	.125 581 4180	.527 473	4.200 244	.238 081 4180	23.81	.428 489	7.14	6
7	2.109 114	9.858 795	.101 432 2775	.474 133	4.674 376	.213 932 2775	21.40	.497 526	7.11	7
8	2.346 390	11.967 909	.083 556 7844	.426 187	5.100 563	.196 056 7844	19.61	.568 454	7.11	8
9	2.610 359	14.314 299	.069 860 2152	.383 089	5.483 652	.182 360 2152	18.24	.641 242	7.13	9
10	2.904 024	16.924 657	.059 085 3907	.344 350	5.828 002	.171 585 3907	17.16	.715 854	7.16	10
11	3.230 727	19.828 681	.050 431 9968	.309 528	6.137 530	.162 931 9968	16.30	.792 252	7.20	11
12	3.594 183	23.059 408	.043 366 2475	.278 227	6.415 757	.155 866 2475	15.59	.870 395	7.25	12
13	3.998 529	26.653 592	.037 518 3959	.250 092	6.665 849	.150 018 3959	15.01	.950 239	7.31	13
14	4.448 364	30.652 121	.032 624 1702	.224 802	6.890 651	.145 124 1702	14.52	1.031 738	7.37	14
15	4.948 804	35.100 484	.028 489 6355	.202 069	7.092 720	.140 989 6355	14.10	1.114 845	7.43	15
16	5.505 545	40.049 289	.024 969 2325	.181 635	7.274 355	.137 469 2325	13.75	1.199 508	7.50	16
17	6.124 919	45.554 834	.021 951 5674	.163 267	7.437 622	.134 451 5674	13.45	1.285 677	7.56	17
18	6.813 972	51.679 752	.019 349 9379	.146 757	7.584 380	.131 849 9379	13.19	1.373 299	7.63	18
19	7.580 544	58.493 725	.017 095 8510	.131 917	7.716 296	.129 595 8510	12.96	1.462 321	7.70	19
20	8.433 355	66.074 269	.015 134 4846	.118 577	7.834 873	.127 634 4846	12.77	1.552 690	7.76	20
21	9.382 108	74.507 624	.013 421 4453	.106 586	7.941 459	.125 921 4453	12.60	1.644 350	7.83	21
22	10.437 595	83.889 731	.011 920 4101	.095 808	8.037 267	.124 420 4101	12.45	1.737 249	7.90	22
23	11.611 824	94.327 326	.010 601 3818	.086 119	8.123 386	.123 101 3818	12.32	1.831 332	7.96	23
24	12.918 154	105.939 150	.009 439 3810	.077 410	8.200 796	.121 939 3810	12.20	1.926 545	8.03	24
25	14.371 447	118.857 305	.008 413 4501	.069 582	8.270 379	.120 913 4501	12.10	2.022 836	8.09	25
26	15.988 235	133.228 752	.007 505 8873	.062 546	8.332 925	.120 005 8873	12.01	2.120 153	8.15	26
27	17.786 911	149.216 986	.006 701 6499	.056 221	8.389 146	.119 201 6499	11.93	2.218 445	8.22	27
28	19.787 938	167.003 897	.005 987 8842	.050 536	8.439 681	.118 487 8842	11.85	2.317 661	8.28	28
29	22.014 081	186.791 836	.005 353 5530	.045 425	8.485 107	.117 853 5530	11.79	2.417 753	8.34	29
30	24.490 666	208.805 917	.004 789 1363	.040 832	8.525 939	.117 289 1363	11.73	2.518 674	8.40	30
31	27.245 866	233.296 583	.004 286 3894	.036 703	8.562 642	.116 786 3894	11.68	2.620 378	8.45	31
32	30.311 025	260.542 448	.003 838 1462	.032 991	8.595 633	.116 338 1462	11.64	2.722 821	8.51	32
33	33.721 016	290.853 474	.003 438 1573	.029 655	8.625 288	.115 938 1573	11.60	2.825 959	8.56	33
34	37.514 630	324.574 489	.003 080 9569	.026 656	8.651 944	.115 580 9569	11.56	2.929 753	8.62	34
35	41.735 026	362.089 120	.002 761 7510	.023 961	8.675 905	.115 261 7510	11.53	3.034 161	8.67	35
36	46.430 216	403.824 145	.002 476 3254	.021 538	8.697 443	.114 976 3254	11.50	3.139 148	8.72	36
37	51.653 616	450.254 362	.002 220 9668	.019 360	8.716 802	.114 720 9668	11.48	3.244 676	8.77	37
38	57.464 647	501.907 978	.001 992 3971	.017 402	8.734 204	.114 492 3971	11.45	3.350 711	8.82	38
39	63.929 420	559.372 625	.001 787 7171	.015 642	8.749 847	.114 287 7171	11.43	3.457 221	8.86	39
40	71.121 480	623.302 045	.001 604 3586	.014 060	8.763 907	.114 104 3586	11.42	3.564 174	8.91	40
41	79.122 647	694.423 525	.001 440 0434	.012 639	8.776 546	.113 940 0434	11.40	3.671 542	8.96	41
42	88.023 944	773.546 172	.001 292 7477	.011 361	8.787 906	.113 792 7477	11.38	3.779 295	9.00	42
43	97.926 638	861.570 116	.001 160 6716	.010 212	8.798 118	.113 660 6716	11.37	3.887 409	9.04	43
44	108.943 385	959.496 755	.001 042 2130	.009 179	8.807 297	.113 542 2130	11.36	3.995 857	9.08	44
45	121.199 516	1068.440 139	.000 935 9439	.008 251	8.815 548	.113 435 9439	11.35	4.104 617	9.12	45
46	134.834 461	1189.639 655	.000 840 5907	.007 417	8.822 964	.113 340 5907	11.34	4.213 667	9.16	46
47	150.003 338	1324.474 116	.000 755 0166	.006 667	8.829 631	.113 255 0166	11.33	4.322 986	9.20	47
48	166.878 714	1474.477 454	.000 678 2064	.005 992	8.835 623	.113 178 2064	11.32	4.432 554	9.23	48
49	185.652 569	1641.356 168	.000 609 2523	.005 386	8.841 010	.113 109 2523	11.32	4.542 353	9.27	49
50	206.538 483	1827.008 737	.000 547 3428	.004 842	8.845 851	.113 047 3428	11.31	4.652 367	9.30	50

Effective Rate is 11.25 %   **8 - 461**   Annual Percentage Rate is 11.25 %

ANNUAL COMPOUND INTEREST AND ANNUITY

11.50 % A

	Amount Of 1	Amount Of 1 Per Period	Sinking Fund Payment	Present Worth Of 1	Present Worth of 1 Per Period	Periodic Payment To Amortize 1	Constant Annual Percent	Total Interest	Annual Add On Rate	
	What a single $ 1 deposit grows to in the future. The deposit is made at the beginning of the first period.	What a series of $ 1 deposits grow to in the future. A deposit is made at the end of each period.	The amount to be deposited at the end of each period that grows to $ 1 in the future.	What $ 1 to be paid in the future is worth today. Value today of a single $ 1 payment tomorrow.	What $ 1 to be paid at the end of each period is worth today. Value today of a series of $ 1 payments tomorrow.	The mortgage payment to amortize a loan of $ 1. An annuity certain, payable at the end of each period, worth $ 1 today.	The annual payment, including interest and principal, to amortize completely a loan of $ 100.	The total interest paid over the term on a loan of $1. The loan is amortized by regular periodic payments.	The average annual interest rate on a loan that is completely amortized by regular periodic payments.	
	$S = (1+i)^n$	$S\overline{n}| = \dfrac{(1+i)^n - 1}{i}$	$\dfrac{1}{S\overline{n}|} = \dfrac{i}{(1+i)^n - 1}$	$V^n = \dfrac{1}{(1+i)^n}$	$A\overline{n}| = \dfrac{1-V^n}{i}$	$\dfrac{1}{A\overline{n}|} = \dfrac{i}{1-V^n}$				

YEAR   **PERIODS**

	Amount Of 1	Amount Of 1 Per Period	Sinking Fund Payment	Present Worth Of 1	Present Worth of 1 Per Period	Periodic Payment To Amortize 1	Constant Annual Percent	Total Interest	Annual Add On Rate	
	1.115 000	1.000 000	1.000 000 0000	.896 861	.896 861	1.115 000 0000	111.50	.115 000	11.50	1

Year										Periods
1	1.115 000	1.000 000	1.000 000 0000	.896 861	.896 861	1.115 000 0000	111.50	.115 000	11.50	1
2	1.243 225	2.115 000	.472 813 2388	.804 360	1.701 221	.587 813 2388	58.79	.175 626	8.78	2
3	1.386 196	3.358 225	.297 776 3551	.721 399	2.422 619	.412 776 3551	41.28	.238 329	7.94	3
4	1.545 608	4.744 421	.210 773 8808	.646 994	3.069 614	.325 773 8808	32.58	.303 096	7.58	4
5	1.723 353	6.290 029	.158 981 7720	.580 264	3.649 878	.273 981 7720	27.40	.369 909	7.40	5
6	1.921 539	8.013 383	.124 791 2454	.520 416	4.170 294	.239 791 2454	23.98	.438 747	7.31	6
7	2.142 516	9.934 922	.100 655 0465	.466 741	4.637 035	.215 655 0465	21.57	.509 585	7.28	7
8	2.388 905	12.077 438	.082 799 0200	.418 602	5.055 637	.197 799 0200	19.78	.582 392	7.28	8
9	2.663 629	14.466 343	.069 125 9707	.375 428	5.431 064	.184 125 9707	18.42	.657 134	7.30	9
10	2.969 947	17.129 972	.058 377 2102	.336 706	5.767 771	.173 377 2102	17.34	.733 772	7.34	10
11	3.311 491	20.099 919	.049 751 4437	.301 979	6.069 750	.164 751 4437	16.48	.812 266	7.38	11
12	3.692 312	23.411 410	.042 714 2151	.270 833	6.340 583	.157 714 2151	15.78	.892 571	7.44	12
13	4.116 928	27.103 722	.036 895 3016	.242 900	6.583 482	.151 895 3016	15.19	.974 639	7.50	13
14	4.590 375	31.220 650	.032 030 0825	.217 847	6.801 329	.147 030 0825	14.71	1.058 421	7.56	14
15	5.118 268	35.811 025	.027 924 3614	.195 379	6.996 708	.142 924 3614	14.30	1.143 865	7.63	15
16	5.706 869	40.929 293	.024 432 3792	.175 227	7.171 935	.139 432 3792	13.95	1.230 918	7.69	16
17	6.363 159	46.636 161	.021 442 5881	.157 155	7.329 090	.136 442 5881	13.65	1.319 524	7.76	17
18	7.094 922	52.999 320	.018 868 1666	.140 946	7.470 036	.133 868 1666	13.39	1.409 627	7.83	18
19	7.910 838	60.094 242	.016 640 5294	.126 409	7.596 445	.131 640 5294	13.17	1.501 170	7.90	19
20	8.820 584	68.005 080	.014 704 7839	.113 371	7.709 816	.129 704 7839	12.98	1.594 096	7.97	20
21	9.834 951	76.825 664	.013 016 4837	.101 678	7.811 494	.128 016 4837	12.81	1.688 346	8.04	21
22	10.965 971	86.660 615	.011 539 2673	.091 191	7.902 685	.126 539 2673	12.66	1.783 864	8.11	22
23	12.227 057	97.626 586	.010 243 1115	.081 786	7.984 471	.125 243 1115	12.53	1.880 592	8.18	23
24	13.633 169	109.853 643	.009 103 0208	.073 351	8.057 822	.124 103 0208	12.42	1.978 473	8.24	24
25	15.200 983	123.486 812	.008 098 0307	.065 785	8.123 607	.123 098 0307	12.31	2.077 451	8.31	25
26	16.949 096	138.687 796	.007 210 4398	.059 000	8.182 607	.122 210 4398	12.23	2.177 471	8.37	26
27	18.898 243	155.636 892	.006 425 2118	.052 915	8.235 522	.121 425 2118	12.15	2.278 481	8.44	27
28	21.071 540	174.535 135	.005 729 5054	.047 457	8.282 979	.120 729 5054	12.08	2.380 426	8.50	28
29	23.494 768	195.606 675	.005 112 3000	.042 563	8.325 542	.120 112 3000	12.02	2.483 257	8.56	29
30	26.196 666	219.101 443	.004 564 0959	.038 173	8.363 715	.119 564 0959	11.96	2.586 923	8.62	30
31	29.209 282	245.298 109	.004 076 6723	.034 236	8.397 951	.119 076 6723	11.91	2.691 377	8.68	31
32	32.568 350	274.507 391	.003 642 8892	.030 705	8.428 655	.118 642 8892	11.87	2.796 572	8.74	32
33	36.313 710	307.075 741	.003 256 5256	.027 538	8.456 193	.118 256 5256	11.83	2.902 465	8.80	33
34	40.489 787	343.389 451	.002 912 1454	.024 698	8.480 891	.117 912 1454	11.80	3.009 013	8.85	34
35	45.146 112	383.879 238	.002 604 9859	.022 150	8.503 041	.117 604 9859	11.77	3.116 175	8.90	35
36	50.337 915	429.025 351	.002 330 8646	.019 866	8.522 907	.117 330 8646	11.74	3.223 911	8.96	36
37	56.126 776	479.363 266	.002 086 1006	.017 817	8.540 723	.117 086 1006	11.71	3.332 186	9.01	37
38	62.581 355	535.490 042	.001 867 4484	.015 979	8.556 703	.116 867 4484	11.69	3.440 963	9.06	38
39	69.778 211	598.071 396	.001 672 0412	.014 331	8.571 034	.116 672 0412	11.67	3.550 210	9.10	39
40	77.802 705	667.849 607	.001 497 3431	.012 853	8.583 887	.116 497 3431	11.65	3.659 894	9.15	40
41	86.750 016	745.652 312	.001 341 1076	.011 527	8.595 414	.116 341 1076	11.64	3.769 985	9.20	41
42	96.726 268	832.402 327	.001 201 3421	.010 338	8.605 753	.116 201 3421	11.63	3.880 456	9.24	42
43	107.849 788	929.128 595	.001 076 2773	.009 272	8.615 025	.116 076 2773	11.61	3.991 280	9.28	43
44	120.252 514	1036.978 384	.000 964 3403	.008 316	8.623 341	.115 964 3403	11.60	4.102 431	9.32	44
45	134.081 553	1157.230 898	.000 864 1318	.007 458	8.630 799	.115 864 1318	11.59	4.213 886	9.36	45
46	149.500 932	1291.312 451	.000 774 4059	.006 689	8.637 488	.115 774 4059	11.58	4.325 623	9.40	46
47	166.693 539	1440.813 383	.000 694 0524	.005 999	8.643 487	.115 694 0524	11.57	4.437 620	9.44	47
48	185.863 296	1607.506 922	.000 622 0813	.005 380	8.648 867	.115 622 0813	11.57	4.549 860	9.48	48
49	207.237 575	1793.370 218	.000 557 6093	.004 825	8.653 692	.115 557 6093	11.56	4.662 323	9.52	49
50	231.069 896	2000.607 793	.000 499 8481	.004 328	8.658 020	.115 499 8481	11.55	4.774 992	9.55	50

Effective Rate is 11.50 %

Annual Percentage Rate is 11.50 %

ANNUAL COMPOUND INTEREST AND ANNUITY

	Amount Of 1	Amount Of 1 Per Period	Sinking Fund Payment	Present Worth Of 1	Present Worth of 1 Per Period	Periodic Payment To Amortize 1	Constant Annual Percent	Total Interest	Annual Add On Rate	
	What a single $ 1 deposit grows to in the future. The deposit is made at the beginning of the first period.	What a series of $ 1 deposits grow to in the future. A deposit is made at the end of each period.	The amount to be deposited at the end of each period that grows to $ 1 in the future.	What $ 1 to be paid in the future is worth today. Value today of a single $ 1 payment tomorrow.	What $ 1 to be paid at the end of each period is worth today. Value today of a series of $ 1 payments tomorrow.	The mortgage payment to amortize a loan of $ 1. An annuity certain, payable at the end of each period, worth $ 1 today.	The annual payment, including interest and principal, to amortize completely a loan of $ 100.	The total interest paid over the term on a loan of $1. The loan is amortized by regular periodic payments.	The average annual interest rate on a loan that is completely amortized by regular periodic payments.	
	$S = (1+i)^n$	$S\overline{n}| = \dfrac{(1+i)^n - 1}{i}$	$\dfrac{1}{S\overline{n}|} = \dfrac{i}{(1+i)^n - 1}$	$V^n = \dfrac{1}{(1+i)^n}$	$A\overline{n}| = \dfrac{1-V^n}{i}$	$\dfrac{1}{A\overline{n}|} = \dfrac{i}{1-V^n}$				

YEAR										PERIODS
	1.117 500	1.000 000	1.000 000 0000	.894 855	.894 855	1.117 500 0000	111.75	.117 500	11.75	1

YEAR	Amount Of 1	Amount Of 1 Per Period	Sinking Fund Payment	Present Worth Of 1	Present Worth of 1 Per Period	Periodic Payment To Amortize 1	Constant Annual Percent	Total Interest	Annual Add On Rate	PERIODS
1	1.117 500	1.000 000	1.000 000 0000	.894 855	.894 855	1.117 500 0000	111.75	.117 500	11.75	1
2	1.248 806	2.117 500	.472 255 0177	.800 765	1.695 619	.589 755 0177	58.98	.179 510	8.98	2
3	1.395 541	3.366 306	.297 061 5047	.716 568	2.412 187	.414 561 5047	41.46	.243 685	8.12	3
4	1.559 517	4.761 847	.210 002 5370	.641 224	3.053 411	.327 502 5370	32.76	.310 010	7.75	4
5	1.742 760	6.321 364	.158 193 6992	.573 802	3.627 214	.275 693 6992	27.57	.378 469	7.57	5
6	1.947 535	8.064 125	.124 006 0206	.513 470	4.140 684	.241 506 0206	24.16	.449 036	7.48	6
7	2.176 370	10.011 659	.099 883 5435	.459 481	4.600 164	.217 383 5435	21.74	.521 685	7.45	7
8	2.432 093	12.188 029	.082 047 7195	.411 168	5.011 333	.199 547 7195	19.96	.596 382	7.45	8
9	2.717 864	14.620 123	.068 398 8792	.367 936	5.379 269	.185 898 8792	18.59	.673 090	7.48	9
10	3.037 213	17.337 987	.057 676 8225	.329 249	5.708 518	.175 176 8225	17.52	.751 768	7.52	10
11	3.394 086	20.375 200	.049 079 2716	.294 630	6.003 148	.166 579 2716	16.66	.832 372	7.57	11
12	3.792 891	23.769 287	.042 071 0987	.263 651	6.266 799	.159 571 0987	15.96	.914 853	7.62	12
13	4.238 556	27.562 178	.036 281 6034	.235 929	6.502 728	.153 781 6034	15.38	.999 161	7.69	13
14	4.736 586	31.800 734	.031 445 8154	.211 123	6.713 851	.148 945 8154	14.90	1.085 241	7.75	14
15	5.293 135	36.537 320	.027 369 2763	.188 924	6.902 775	.144 869 2763	14.49	1.173 039	7.82	15
16	5.915 078	41.830 455	.023 906 0274	.169 059	7.071 834	.141 406 0274	14.15	1.262 496	7.89	16
17	6.610 100	47.745 533	.020 944 3676	.151 284	7.223 118	.138 444 3676	13.85	1.353 554	7.96	17
18	7.386 787	54.355 634	.018 397 3571	.135 377	7.358 495	.135 897 3571	13.59	1.446 152	8.03	18
19	8.254 734	61.742 420	.016 196 3200	.121 143	7.479 637	.133 696 3200	13.37	1.540 230	8.11	19
20	9.224 666	69.997 155	.014 286 2950	.108 405	7.588 042	.131 786 2950	13.18	1.635 726	8.18	20
21	10.308 564	79.221 821	.012 622 7849	.097 007	7.685 049	.130 122 7849	13.02	1.732 578	8.25	21
22	11.519 820	89.530 384	.011 169 3924	.086 807	7.771 856	.128 669 3924	12.87	1.830 727	8.32	22
23	12.873 399	101.050 205	.009 896 0710	.077 680	7.849 536	.127 396 0710	12.74	1.930 110	8.39	23
24	14.386 023	113.923 604	.008 777 8122	.069 512	7.919 048	.126 277 8122	12.63	2.030 668	8.46	24
25	16.076 381	128.309 627	.007 793 6475	.062 203	7.981 251	.125 293 6475	12.53	2.132 341	8.53	25
26	17.965 356	144.386 008	.006 925 8788	.055 663	8.036 913	.124 425 8788	12.45	2.235 073	8.60	26
27	20.076 285	162.351 364	.006 159 4801	.049 810	8.086 723	.123 659 4801	12.37	2.338 806	8.66	27
28	22.435 249	182.427 650	.005 481 6252	.044 573	8.131 296	.122 981 6252	12.30	2.443 486	8.73	28
29	25.071 391	204.862 898	.004 881 3133	.039 886	8.171 182	.122 381 3133	12.24	2.549 058	8.79	29
30	28.017 279	229.934 289	.004 349 0686	.035 692	8.206 874	.121 849 0686	12.19	2.655 472	8.85	30
31	31.309 309	257.951 568	.003 876 6967	.031 939	8.238 814	.121 376 6967	12.14	2.762 678	8.91	31
32	34.988 153	289.260 877	.003 457 0869	.028 581	8.267 395	.120 957 0869	12.10	2.870 627	8.97	32
33	39.099 261	324.249 030	.003 084 0493	.025 576	8.292 971	.120 584 0493	12.06	2.979 274	9.03	33
34	43.693 424	363.348 291	.002 752 1803	.022 887	8.315 858	.120 252 1803	12.03	3.088 574	9.08	34
35	48.827 402	407.041 715	.002 456 7507	.020 480	8.336 338	.119 956 7507	12.00	3.198 486	9.14	35
36	54.564 621	455.869 117	.002 193 6121	.018 327	8.354 665	.119 693 6121	11.97	3.308 970	9.19	36
37	60.975 964	510.433 738	.001 959 1181	.016 400	8.371 065	.119 459 1181	11.95	3.419 987	9.24	37
38	68.140 640	571.409 702	.001 750 0578	.014 676	8.385 740	.119 250 0578	11.93	3.531 502	9.29	38
39	76.147 165	639.550 343	.001 563 5986	.013 132	8.398 873	.119 063 5986	11.91	3.643 480	9.34	39
40	85.094 457	715.697 508	.001 397 2383	.011 752	8.410 624	.118 897 2383	11.89	3.755 890	9.39	40
41	95.093 056	800.791 965	.001 248 7638	.010 516	8.421 140	.118 748 7638	11.88	3.868 699	9.44	41
42	106.266 490	895.885 021	.001 116 2147	.009 410	8.430 551	.118 616 2147	11.87	3.981 881	9.48	42
43	118.752 803	1002.151 511	.000 997 8531	.008 421	8.438 971	.118 497 8531	11.85	4.095 408	9.52	43
44	132.706 257	1120.904 313	.000 892 1368	.007 535	8.446 507	.118 392 1368	11.84	4.209 254	9.57	44
45	148.299 242	1253.610 570	.000 797 6959	.006 743	8.453 250	.118 297 6959	11.83	4.323 396	9.61	45
46	165.724 403	1401.909 812	.000 713 3126	.006 034	8.459 284	.118 213 3126	11.83	4.437 812	9.65	46
47	185.197 020	1567.634 215	.000 637 9039	.005 400	8.464 684	.118 137 9039	11.82	4.552 461	9.69	47
48	206.957 670	1752.831 235	.000 570 5056	.004 832	8.469 516	.118 070 5056	11.81	4.667 384	9.72	48
49	231.275 196	1959.788 905	.000 510 2590	.004 324	8.473 840	.118 010 2590	11.81	4.782 503	9.76	49
50	258.450 032	2191.064 102	.000 456 3992	.003 869	8.477 709	.117 956 3992	11.80	4.897 820	9.80	50

Effective Rate is 11.75 %

Annual Percentage Rate is 11.75 %

ANNUAL COMPOUND INTEREST AND ANNUITY

12.00 % A

	Amount Of 1	Amount Of 1 Per Period	Sinking Fund Payment	Present Worth Of 1	Present Worth of 1 Per Period	Periodic Payment To Amortize 1	Constant Annual Percent	Total Interest	Annual Add On Rate	
	What a single $ 1 deposit grows to in the future. The deposit is made at the beginning of the first period.	What a series of $ 1 deposits grow to in the future. A deposit is made at the end of each period.	The amount to be deposited at the end of each period that grows to $ 1 in the future.	What $ 1 to be paid in the future is worth today. Value today of a single $ 1 payment tomorrow.	What $ 1 to be paid at the end of each period is worth today. Value today of a series of $ 1 payments tomorrow.	The mortgage payment to amortize a loan of $ 1. An annuity certain, payable at the end of each period, worth $ 1 today.	The annual payment, including interest and principal, to amortize completely a loan of $ 100.	The total interest paid over the term on a loan of $1. The loan is amortized by regular periodic payments.	The average annual interest rate on a loan that is completely amortized by regular periodic payments.	
	$S = (1+i)^n$	$S\overline{n} = \dfrac{(1+i)^n - 1}{i}$	$\dfrac{1}{S\overline{n}} = \dfrac{i}{(1+i)^n - 1}$	$V^n = \dfrac{1}{(1+i)^n}$	$A\overline{n} = \dfrac{1-V^n}{i}$	$\dfrac{1}{A\overline{n}} = \dfrac{i}{1-V^n}$				

YEAR										PERIODS
	1.120 000	1.000 000	1.000 000 0000	.892 857	.892 857	1.120 000 0000	112.00	.120 000	12.00	1

YEAR	Amount Of 1	Amount Of 1 Per Period	Sinking Fund Payment	Present Worth Of 1	Present Worth of 1 Per Period	Periodic Payment To Amortize 1	Constant Annual Percent	Total Interest	Annual Add On Rate	PERIODS
1	1.120 000	1.000 000	1.000 000 0000	.892 857	.892 857	1.120 000 0000	112.00	.120 000	12.00	1
2	1.254 400	2.120 000	.471 698 1132	.797 194	1.690 051	.591 698 1132	59.17	.183 396	9.17	2
3	1.404 928	3.374 400	.296 348 9806	.711 780	2.401 831	.416 348 9806	41.64	.249 047	8.30	3
4	1.573 519	4.779 328	.209 234 4363	.635 518	3.037 349	.329 234 4363	32.93	.316 938	7.92	4
5	1.762 342	6.352 847	.157 409 7319	.567 427	3.604 776	.277 409 7319	27.75	.387 049	7.74	5
6	1.973 823	8.115 189	.123 225 7184	.506 631	4.111 407	.243 225 7184	24.33	.459 354	7.66	6
7	2.210 681	10.089 012	.099 117 7359	.452 349	4.563 757	.219 117 7359	21.92	.533 824	7.63	7
8	2.475 963	12.299 693	.081 302 8414	.403 883	4.967 640	.201 302 8414	20.14	.610 423	7.63	8
9	2.773 079	14.775 656	.067 678 8888	.360 610	5.328 250	.187 678 8888	18.77	.689 110	7.66	9
10	3.105 848	17.548 735	.056 984 1642	.321 973	5.650 223	.176 984 1642	17.70	.769 842	7.70	10
11	3.478 550	20.654 583	.048 415 4043	.287 476	5.937 699	.168 415 4043	16.85	.852 569	7.75	11
12	3.895 976	24.133 133	.041 436 8076	.256 675	6.194 374	.161 436 8076	16.15	.937 242	7.81	12
13	4.363 493	28.029 109	.035 677 1951	.229 174	6.423 548	.155 677 1951	15.57	1.023 804	7.88	13
14	4.887 112	32.392 602	.030 871 2461	.204 620	6.628 168	.150 871 2461	15.09	1.112 197	7.94	14
15	5.473 566	37.279 715	.026 824 2396	.182 696	6.810 864	.146 824 2396	14.69	1.202 364	8.02	15
16	6.130 394	42.753 280	.023 390 0180	.163 122	6.973 986	.143 390 0180	14.34	1.294 240	8.09	16
17	6.866 041	48.883 674	.020 456 7275	.145 644	7.119 630	.140 456 7275	14.05	1.387 764	8.16	17
18	7.689 966	55.749 715	.017 937 3114	.130 040	7.249 670	.137 937 3114	13.80	1.482 872	8.24	18
19	8.612 762	63.439 681	.015 763 0049	.116 107	7.365 777	.135 763 0049	13.58	1.579 497	8.31	19
20	9.646 293	72.052 442	.013 878 7800	.103 667	7.469 444	.133 878 7800	13.39	1.677 576	8.39	20
21	10.803 848	81.698 736	.012 240 0915	.092 560	7.562 003	.132 240 0915	13.23	1.777 042	8.46	21
22	12.100 310	92.502 584	.010 810 5088	.082 643	7.644 646	.130 810 5088	13.09	1.877 831	8.54	22
23	13.552 347	104.602 894	.009 559 9650	.073 788	7.718 434	.129 559 9650	12.96	1.979 879	8.61	23
24	15.178 629	118.155 241	.008 463 4417	.065 882	7.784 316	.128 463 4417	12.85	2.083 123	8.68	24
25	17.000 064	133.333 870	.007 499 9698	.058 823	7.843 139	.127 499 9698	12.75	2.187 499	8.75	25
26	19.040 072	150.333 934	.006 651 8581	.052 521	7.895 660	.126 651 8581	12.67	2.292 948	8.82	26
27	21.324 881	169.374 007	.005 904 0937	.046 894	7.942 554	.125 904 0937	12.60	2.399 411	8.89	27
28	23.883 866	190.698 887	.005 243 8691	.041 869	7.984 423	.125 243 8691	12.53	2.506 828	8.95	28
29	26.749 930	214.582 754	.004 660 2068	.037 383	8.021 806	.124 660 2068	12.47	2.615 146	9.02	29
30	29.959 922	241.332 684	.004 143 6576	.033 378	8.055 184	.124 143 6576	12.42	2.724 310	9.08	30
31	33.555 113	271.292 606	.003 686 0570	.029 802	8.084 986	.123 686 0570	12.37	2.834 268	9.14	31
32	37.581 726	304.847 719	.003 280 3263	.026 609	8.111 594	.123 280 3263	12.33	2.944 970	9.20	32
33	42.091 533	342.429 446	.002 920 3096	.023 758	8.135 352	.122 920 3096	12.30	3.056 370	9.26	33
34	47.142 517	384.520 979	.002 600 6383	.021 212	8.156 564	.122 600 6383	12.27	3.168 422	9.32	34
35	52.799 620	431.663 496	.002 316 6193	.018 940	8.175 504	.122 316 6193	12.24	3.281 082	9.37	35
36	59.135 574	484.463 116	.002 064 1406	.016 910	8.192 414	.122 064 1406	12.21	3.394 309	9.43	36
37	66.231 843	543.598 690	.001 839 5924	.015 098	8.207 513	.121 839 5924	12.19	3.508 065	9.48	37
38	74.179 664	609.830 533	.001 639 7998	.013 481	8.220 993	.121 639 7998	12.17	3.622 312	9.53	38
39	83.081 224	684.010 197	.001 461 9665	.012 036	8.233 030	.121 461 9665	12.15	3.737 017	9.58	39
40	93.050 970	767.091 420	.001 303 6256	.010 747	8.243 777	.121 303 6256	12.14	3.852 145	9.63	40
41	104.217 087	860.142 391	.001 162 5982	.009 595	8.253 372	.121 162 5982	12.12	3.967 667	9.68	41
42	116.723 137	964.359 478	.001 036 9577	.008 567	8.261 939	.121 036 9577	12.11	4.083 552	9.72	42
43	130.729 914	1081.082 615	.000 924 9987	.007 649	8.269 589	.120 924 9987	12.10	4.199 775	9.77	43
44	146.417 503	1211.812 529	.000 825 2102	.006 830	8.276 418	.120 825 2102	12.09	4.316 309	9.81	44
45	163.987 604	1358.230 032	.000 736 2523	.006 098	8.282 516	.120 736 2523	12.08	4.433 131	9.85	45
46	183.666 116	1522.217 636	.000 656 9363	.005 445	8.287 961	.120 656 9363	12.07	4.550 219	9.89	46
47	205.706 050	1705.883 752	.000 586 2064	.004 861	8.292 822	.120 586 2064	12.06	4.667 552	9.93	47
48	230.390 770	1911.589 803	.000 523 1248	.004 340	8.297 163	.120 523 1248	12.06	4.785 110	9.97	48
49	258.037 669	2141.980 579	.000 466 8576	.003 875	8.301 038	.120 466 8576	12.05	4.902 876	10.01	49
50	289.002 190	2400.018 249	.000 416 6635	.003 460	8.304 498	.120 416 6635	12.05	5.020 833	10.04	50

Effective Rate is 12.00 %

Annual Percentage Rate is 12.00 %

	Amount Of 1	Amount Of 1 Per Period	Sinking Fund Payment	Present Worth Of 1	Present Worth of 1 Per Period	Periodic Payment To Amortize 1	Constant Annual Percent	Total Interest	Annual Add On Rate	
	What a single $ 1 deposit grows to in the future. The deposit is made at the beginning of the first period.	What a series of $ 1 deposits grow to in the future. A deposit is made at the end of each period.	The amount to be deposited at the end of each period that grows to $ 1 in the future.	What $ 1 to be paid in the future is worth today. Value today of a single $ 1 payment tomorrow.	What $ 1 to be paid at the end of each period is worth today. Value today of a series of $ 1 payments tomorrow.	The mortgage payment to amortize a loan of $ 1. An annuity certain, payable at the end of each period, worth $ 1 today.	The annual payment, including interest and principal, to amortize completely a loan of $ 100.	The total interest paid over the term of $1. The loan is amortized by regular periodic payments.	The average annual interest rate on a loan that is completely amortized by regular periodic payments.	
	$S = (1+i)^n$	$S\overline{n} = \dfrac{(1+i)^n - 1}{i}$	$\dfrac{1}{S\overline{n}} = \dfrac{i}{(1+i)^n - 1}$	$V^n = \dfrac{1}{(1+i)^n}$	$A\overline{n} = \dfrac{1 - V^n}{i}$	$\dfrac{1}{A\overline{n}} = \dfrac{i}{1 - V^n}$				

YEAR / **PERIODS**

	Amount Of 1	Amount Of 1 Per Period	Sinking Fund Payment	Present Worth Of 1	Present Worth of 1 Per Period	Periodic Payment To Amortize 1	Constant Annual Percent	Total Interest	Annual Add On Rate	
	1.122 500	1.000 000	1.000 000 0000	.890 869	.890 869	1.122 500 0000	112.25	.122 500	12.25	1

YEAR	Amount Of 1	Amount Of 1 Per Period	Sinking Fund Payment	Present Worth Of 1	Present Worth of 1 Per Period	Periodic Payment To Amortize 1	Constant Annual Percent	Total Interest	Annual Add On Rate	PERIODS
1	1.122 500	1.000 000	1.000 000 0000	.890 869	.890 869	1.122 500 0000	112.25	.122 500	12.25	1
2	1.260 006	2.122 500	.471 142 5206	.793 642	1.684 515	.593 642 5206	59.37	.187 285	9.36	2
3	1.414 357	3.382 506	.295 638 7738	.707 035	2.391 551	.418 138 7738	41.82	.254 416	8.48	3
4	1.587 616	4.796 863	.208 469 5653	.629 875	3.021 426	.330 969 5653	33.10	.323 878	8.10	4
5	1.782 099	6.384 479	.156 629 8515	.561 136	3.582 562	.279 129 8515	27.92	.395 649	7.91	5
6	2.000 406	8.166 578	.122 450 3136	.499 899	4.082 461	.244 950 3136	24.50	.469 702	7.83	6
7	2.245 455	10.166 983	.098 357 5909	.445 344	4.527 805	.220 857 5909	22.09	.546 003	7.80	7
8	2.520 524	12.412 439	.080 564 3440	.396 743	4.924 547	.203 064 3440	20.31	.624 515	7.81	8
9	2.829 288	14.932 963	.066 965 9477	.353 446	5.277 993	.189 465 9477	18.95	.705 194	7.84	9
10	3.175 876	17.762 251	.056 299 1718	.314 874	5.592 867	.178 799 1718	17.88	.787 992	7.88	10
11	3.564 920	20.938 126	.047 759 7653	.280 511	5.873 378	.170 259 7653	17.03	.872 857	7.94	11
12	4.001 623	24.503 047	.040 811 2512	.249 899	6.123 277	.163 311 2512	16.34	.959 735	8.00	12
13	4.491 822	28.504 670	.035 081 9707	.222 627	6.345 904	.157 581 9707	15.76	1.048 566	8.07	13
14	5.042 070	32.996 492	.030 306 2518	.198 331	6.544 235	.152 806 2518	15.29	1.139 288	8.14	14
15	5.659 724	38.038 562	.026 289 1113	.176 687	6.720 922	.148 789 1113	14.88	1.231 837	8.21	15
16	6.353 040	43.698 286	.022 884 1926	.157 405	6.878 327	.145 384 1926	14.54	1.326 147	8.29	16
17	7.131 287	50.051 326	.019 979 4905	.140 227	7.018 554	.142 479 4905	14.25	1.422 151	8.37	17
18	8.004 870	57.182 614	.017 487 8330	.124 924	7.143 478	.139 987 8330	14.00	1.519 781	8.44	18
19	8.985 467	65.187 484	.015 340 3681	.111 291	7.254 769	.137 840 3681	13.79	1.618 967	8.52	19
20	10.086 186	74.172 951	.013 482 0037	.099 145	7.353 914	.135 982 0037	13.60	1.719 640	8.60	20
21	11.321 744	84.259 137	.011 868 1490	.088 326	7.442 240	.134 368 1490	13.44	1.821 731	8.68	21
22	12.708 658	95.580 882	.010 462 3433	.078 687	7.520 926	.132 962 3433	13.30	1.925 172	8.75	22
23	14.265 469	108.289 540	.009 234 5023	.070 099	7.591 026	.131 734 5023	13.18	2.029 894	8.83	23
24	16.012 989	122.555 008	.008 159 6013	.062 449	7.653 475	.130 659 6013	13.07	2.135 830	8.90	24
25	17.974 580	138.567 997	.007 216 6736	.055 634	7.709 109	.129 716 6736	12.98	2.242 917	8.97	25
26	20.176 466	156.542 576	.006 388 0385	.049 563	7.758 672	.128 888 0385	12.89	2.351 089	9.04	26
27	22.648 083	176.719 042	.005 658 6998	.044 154	7.802 826	.128 158 6998	12.82	2.460 285	9.11	27
28	25.422 473	199.367 125	.005 015 8721	.039 335	7.842 161	.127 515 8721	12.76	2.570 444	9.18	28
29	28.536 726	224.789 597	.004 448 6044	.035 043	7.877 204	.126 948 6044	12.70	2.681 510	9.25	29
30	32.032 475	253.326 323	.003 947 4777	.031 218	7.908 422	.126 447 4777	12.65	2.793 424	9.31	30
31	35.956 453	285.358 798	.003 504 3602	.027 811	7.936 233	.126 004 3602	12.61	2.906 135	9.37	31
32	40.361 118	321.315 250	.003 112 2083	.024 776	7.961 010	.125 612 2083	12.57	3.019 591	9.44	32
33	45.305 355	361.676 369	.002 764 9028	.022 072	7.983 082	.125 264 9028	12.53	3.133 742	9.50	33
34	50.855 261	406.981 724	.002 457 1128	.019 664	8.002 746	.124 957 1128	12.50	3.248 542	9.55	34
35	57.085 031	457.836 985	.002 184 1835	.017 518	8.020 263	.124 684 1835	12.47	3.363 946	9.61	35
36	64.077 947	514.922 016	.001 942 0416	.015 606	8.035 869	.124 442 0416	12.45	3.479 914	9.67	36
37	71.927 495	578.999 963	.001 727 1158	.013 903	8.049 772	.124 227 1158	12.43	3.596 403	9.72	37
38	80.738 614	650.927 458	.001 536 2695	.012 386	8.062 158	.124 036 2695	12.41	3.713 378	9.77	38
39	90.629 094	731.666 072	.001 366 7437	.011 034	8.073 192	.123 866 7437	12.39	3.830 803	9.82	39
40	101.731 158	822.295 165	.001 216 1083	.009 830	8.083 022	.123 716 1083	12.38	3.948 644	9.87	40
41	114.193 225	924.026 323	.001 082 2203	.008 757	8.091 779	.123 582 2203	12.36	4.066 871	9.92	41
42	128.181 895	1038.219 548	.000 963 1874	.007 801	8.099 580	.123 463 1874	12.35	4.185 454	9.97	42
43	143.884 177	1166.401 442	.000 857 3378	.006 950	8.106 530	.123 357 3378	12.34	4.304 366	10.01	43
44	161.509 988	1310.285 619	.000 763 1924	.006 192	8.112 722	.123 263 1924	12.33	4.423 580	10.05	44
45	181.294 962	1471.795 607	.000 679 4422	.005 516	8.118 238	.123 179 4422	12.32	4.543 075	10.10	45
46	203.503 595	1653.090 569	.000 604 9275	.004 914	8.123 152	.123 104 9275	12.32	4.662 827	10.14	46
47	228.432 785	1856.594 164	.000 538 6207	.004 378	8.127 529	.123 038 6207	12.31	4.782 815	10.18	47
48	256.415 801	2085.026 949	.000 479 6101	.003 900	8.131 429	.122 979 6101	12.30	4.903 021	10.21	48
49	287.826 737	2341.442 750	.000 427 0871	.003 474	8.134 904	.122 927 0871	12.30	5.023 427	10.25	49
50	323.085 512	2629.269 487	.000 380 3338	.003 095	8.137 999	.122 880 3338	12.29	5.144 017	10.29	50

Effective Rate is 12.25 %   **8 - 465**   Annual Percentage Rate is 12.25 %

ANNUAL COMPOUND INTEREST AND ANNUITY

12.50 % A

	Amount Of 1	Amount Of 1 Per Period	Sinking Fund Payment	Present Worth Of 1	Present Worth of 1 Per Period	Periodic Payment To Amortize 1	Constant Annual Percent	Total Interest	Annual Add On Rate	
	What a single $ 1 deposit grows to in the future. The deposit is made at the beginning of the first period.	What a series of $ 1 deposits grow to in the future. A deposit is made at the end of each period.	The amount to be deposited at the end of each period that grows to $ 1 in the future.	What $ 1 to be paid in the future is worth today. Value today of a single $ 1 payment tomorrow.	What $ 1 to be paid at the end of each period is worth today. Value today of a series of $ 1 payments tomorrow.	The mortgage payment to amortize a loan of $ 1. An annuity certain, payable at the end of each period, worth $ 1 today.	The annual payment, including interest and principal, to amortize completely a loan of $ 100.	The total interest paid over the term on a loan of $1. The loan is amortized by regular periodic payments.	The average annual interest rate on a loan that is completely amortized by regular periodic payments.	
	$S = (1+i)^n$	$S\overline{n}| = \dfrac{(1+i)^n - 1}{i}$	$\dfrac{1}{S\overline{n}|} = \dfrac{i}{(1+i)^n - 1}$	$V^n = \dfrac{1}{(1+i)^n}$	$A\overline{n}| = \dfrac{1-V^n}{i}$	$\dfrac{1}{A\overline{n}|} = \dfrac{i}{1-V^n}$				

YEAR										**PERIODS**
	1.125 000	1.000 000	1.000 000 0000	.888 889	.888 889	1.125 000 0000	112.50	.125 000	12.50	1

YEAR	Amount Of 1	Amount Of 1 Per Period	Sinking Fund Payment	Present Worth Of 1	Present Worth of 1 Per Period	Periodic Payment To Amortize 1	Constant Annual Percent	Total Interest	Annual Add On Rate	PERIODS
1	1.125 000	1.000 000	1.000 000 0000	.888 889	.888 889	1.125 000 0000	112.50	.125 000	12.50	1
2	1.265 625	2.125 000	.470 588 2353	.790 123	1.679 012	.595 588 2353	59.56	.191 176	9.56	2
3	1.423 828	3.390 625	.294 930 8756	.702 332	2.381 344	.419 930 8756	42.00	.259 793	8.66	3
4	1.601 807	4.814 453	.207 707 9108	.624 295	3.005 639	.332 707 9108	33.28	.330 832	8.27	4
5	1.802 032	6.416 260	.155 854 0390	.554 929	3.560 568	.280 854 0390	28.09	.404 270	8.09	5
6	2.027 287	8.218 292	.121 679 7811	.493 270	4.053 839	.246 679 7811	24.67	.480 079	8.00	6
7	2.280 697	10.245 579	.097 603 0757	.438 462	4.492 301	.222 603 0757	22.27	.558 222	7.97	7
8	2.565 785	12.526 276	.079 832 1856	.389 744	4.882 045	.204 832 1856	20.49	.638 657	7.98	8
9	2.886 508	15.092 061	.066 260 0042	.346 439	5.228 485	.191 260 0042	19.13	.721 340	8.01	9
10	3.247 321	17.978 568	.055 621 7819	.307 946	5.536 431	.180 621 7819	18.07	.806 218	8.06	10
11	3.653 236	21.225 889	.047 112 2783	.273 730	5.810 161	.172 112 2783	17.22	.893 235	8.12	11
12	4.109 891	24.879 125	.040 194 3390	.243 315	6.053 476	.165 194 3390	16.52	.982 332	8.19	12
13	4.623 627	28.989 016	.034 495 8241	.216 280	6.269 757	.159 495 8241	15.95	1.073 446	8.26	13
14	5.201 580	33.612 643	.029 750 7101	.192 249	6.462 006	.154 750 7101	15.48	1.166 510	8.33	14
15	5.851 778	38.814 223	.025 763 7513	.170 888	6.632 894	.150 763 7513	15.08	1.261 456	8.41	15
16	6.583 250	44.666 001	.022 388 3932	.151 901	6.784 795	.147 388 3932	14.74	1.358 214	8.49	16
17	7.406 156	51.249 252	.019 512 4801	.135 023	6.919 818	.144 512 4801	14.46	1.456 712	8.57	17
18	8.331 926	58.655 408	.017 048 7264	.120 020	7.039 838	.142 048 7264	14.21	1.556 877	8.65	18
19	9.373 417	66.987 334	.014 928 1952	.106 685	7.146 523	.139 928 1952	14.00	1.658 636	8.73	19
20	10.545 094	76.360 751	.013 095 7330	.094 831	7.241 353	.138 095 7330	13.81	1.761 915	8.81	20
21	11.863 231	86.905 845	.011 506 7060	.084 294	7.325 647	.136 506 7060	13.66	1.866 641	8.89	21
22	13.346 134	98.769 075	.010 124 6265	.074 928	7.400 575	.135 124 6265	13.52	1.972 742	8.97	22
23	15.014 401	112.115 210	.008 919 3964	.066 603	7.467 178	.133 919 3964	13.40	2.080 146	9.04	23
24	16.891 201	127.129 611	.007 865 9881	.059 202	7.526 381	.132 865 9881	13.29	2.188 784	9.12	24
25	19.002 602	144.020 812	.006 943 4409	.052 624	7.579 005	.131 943 4409	13.20	2.298 586	9.19	25
26	21.377 927	163.023 414	.006 134 0882	.046 777	7.625 782	.131 134 0882	13.12	2.409 486	9.27	26
27	24.050 168	184.401 340	.005 422 9541	.041 580	7.667 362	.130 422 9541	13.05	2.521 420	9.34	27
28	27.056 438	208.451 508	.004 797 2788	.036 960	7.704 322	.129 797 2788	12.98	2.634 324	9.41	28
29	30.438 493	235.507 946	.004 246 1412	.032 853	7.737 175	.129 246 1412	12.93	2.748 138	9.48	29
30	34.243 305	265.946 440	.003 760 1556	.029 203	7.766 378	.128 760 1556	12.88	2.862 805	9.54	30
31	38.523 718	300.189 745	.003 331 2264	.025 958	7.792 336	.128 331 2264	12.84	2.978 268	9.61	31
32	43.339 183	338.713 463	.002 952 3480	.023 074	7.815 410	.127 952 3480	12.80	3.094 475	9.67	32
33	48.756 581	382.052 645	.002 617 4403	.020 510	7.835 920	.127 617 4403	12.77	3.211 376	9.73	33
34	54.851 153	430.809 226	.002 321 2131	.018 231	7.854 151	.127 321 2131	12.74	3.328 921	9.79	34
35	61.707 547	485.660 379	.002 059 0521	.016 205	7.870 356	.127 059 0521	12.71	3.447 067	9.85	35
36	69.420 991	547.367 927	.001 826 9247	.014 405	7.884 761	.126 826 9247	12.69	3.565 769	9.91	36
37	78.098 615	616.788 918	.001 621 3002	.012 804	7.897 565	.126 621 3002	12.67	3.684 988	9.96	37
38	87.860 942	694.887 532	.001 439 0818	.011 382	7.908 947	.126 439 0818	12.65	3.804 685	10.01	38
39	98.843 559	782.748 474	.001 277 5496	.010 117	7.919 064	.126 277 5496	12.63	3.924 824	10.06	39
40	111.199 004	881.592 033	.001 134 3115	.008 993	7.928 057	.126 134 3115	12.62	4.045 372	10.11	40
41	125.098 880	992.791 037	.001 007 2613	.007 994	7.936 051	.126 007 2613	12.61	4.166 298	10.16	41
42	140.736 240	1117.889 917	.000 894 5425	.007 105	7.943 156	.125 894 5425	12.59	4.287 571	10.21	42
43	158.328 270	1258.626 157	.000 794 5171	.006 316	7.949 472	.125 794 5171	12.58	4.409 164	10.25	43
44	178.119 303	1416.954 426	.000 705 7390	.005 614	7.955 086	.125 705 7390	12.58	4.531 053	10.30	44
45	200.384 216	1595.073 729	.000 626 9303	.004 990	7.960 077	.125 626 9303	12.57	4.653 212	10.34	45
46	225.432 243	1795.457 946	.000 556 9610	.004 436	7.964 513	.125 556 9610	12.56	4.775 620	10.38	46
47	253.611 274	2020.890 189	.000 494 8314	.003 943	7.968 456	.125 494 8314	12.55	4.898 257	10.42	47
48	285.312 683	2274.501 462	.000 439 6568	.003 505	7.971 961	.125 439 6568	12.55	5.021 104	10.46	48
49	320.976 768	2559.814 145	.000 390 6534	.003 115	7.975 076	.125 390 6534	12.54	5.144 142	10.50	49
50	361.098 864	2880.790 913	.000 347 1269	.002 769	7.977 845	.125 347 1269	12.54	5.267 356	10.53	50

Effective Rate is 12.50 %

Annual Percentage Rate is 12.50 %

ANNUAL COMPOUND INTEREST AND ANNUITY

	Amount Of 1	Amount Of 1 Per Period	Sinking Fund Payment	Present Worth Of 1	Present Worth of 1 Per Period	Periodic Payment To Amortize 1	Constant Annual Percent	Total Interest	Annual Add On Rate	
	What a single $ 1 deposit grows to in the future. The deposit is made at the beginning of the first period.	What a series of $ 1 deposits grow to in the future. A deposit is made at the end of each period.	The amount to be deposited at the end of each period that grows to $ 1 in the future.	What $ 1 to be paid in the future is worth today. Value today of a single $ 1 payment tomorrow.	What $ 1 to be paid at the end of each period is worth today. Value today of a series of $ 1 payments tomorrow.	The mortgage payment to amortize a loan of $ 1. An annuity certain, payable at the end of each period, worth $ 1 today.	The annual payment, including interest and principal, to amortize completely a loan of $ 100.	The total interest paid over the term on a loan of $1. The loan is amortized by regular periodic payments.	The average annual interest rate on a loan that is completely amortized by regular periodic payments.	
	$S = (1+i)^n$	$S\overline{n} = \dfrac{(1+i)^n - 1}{i}$	$\dfrac{1}{S\overline{n}} = \dfrac{i}{(1+i)^n - 1}$	$V^n = \dfrac{1}{(1+i)^n}$	$A\overline{n} = \dfrac{1 - V^n}{i}$	$\dfrac{1}{A\overline{n}} = \dfrac{i}{1 - V^n}$				

YEAR										PERIODS
	1.127 500	1.000 000	1.000 000 0000	.886 918	.886 918	1.127 500 0000	112.75	.127 500	12.75	1

YEAR	Amount Of 1	Amount Of 1 Per Period	Sinking Fund Payment	Present Worth Of 1	Present Worth of 1 Per Period	Periodic Payment To Amortize 1	Constant Annual Percent	Total Interest	Annual Add On Rate	PERIODS
1	1.127 500	1.000 000	1.000 000 0000	.886 918	.886 918	1.127 500 0000	112.75	.127 500	12.75	1
2	1.271 256	2.127 500	.470 035 2526	.786 623	1.673 541	.597 535 2526	59.76	.195 071	9.75	2
3	1.433 341	3.398 756	.294 225 2773	.697 670	2.371 212	.421 725 2773	42.18	.265 176	8.84	3
4	1.616 092	4.832 098	.206 949 4592	.618 776	2.989 988	.334 449 4592	33.45	.337 798	8.45	4
5	1.822 144	6.448 190	.155 082 2759	.548 804	3.538 792	.282 582 2759	28.26	.412 911	8.26	5
6	2.054 468	8.270 334	.120 914 0956	.486 744	4.025 536	.248 414 0956	24.85	.490 485	8.17	6
7	2.316 412	10.324 802	.096 854 1576	.431 702	4.457 239	.224 354 1576	22.44	.570 479	8.15	7
8	2.611 755	12.641 214	.079 106 3248	.382 884	4.840 123	.206 606 3248	20.67	.652 851	8.16	8
9	2.944 754	15.252 969	.065 561 0062	.339 587	5.179 710	.193 061 0062	19.31	.737 549	8.20	9
10	3.320 210	18.197 723	.054 951 9311	.301 186	5.480 896	.182 451 9311	18.25	.824 519	8.25	10
11	3.743 536	21.517 932	.046 472 8668	.267 127	5.748 023	.173 972 8668	17.40	.913 702	8.31	11
12	4.220 837	25.261 469	.039 585 9803	.236 920	5.984 943	.167 085 9803	16.71	1.005 032	8.38	12
13	4.758 994	29.482 306	.033 918 6495	.210 128	6.195 071	.161 418 6495	16.15	1.098 442	8.45	13
14	5.365 766	34.241 300	.029 204 4988	.186 367	6.381 438	.156 704 4988	15.68	1.193 863	8.53	14
15	6.049 901	39.607 066	.025 248 0204	.165 292	6.546 730	.152 748 0204	15.28	1.291 220	8.61	15
16	6.821 263	45.656 966	.021 902 4626	.146 600	6.693 330	.149 402 4626	14.95	1.390 439	8.69	16
17	7.690 974	52.478 230	.019 055 5208	.130 023	6.823 353	.146 555 5208	14.66	1.491 444	8.77	17
18	8.671 574	60.169 204	.016 619 7977	.115 319	6.938 672	.144 119 7977	14.42	1.594 156	8.86	18
19	9.777 199	68.840 777	.014 526 2741	.102 279	7.040 951	.142 026 2741	14.21	1.698 499	8.94	19
20	11.023 792	78.617 977	.012 719 7372	.090 713	7.131 664	.140 219 7372	14.03	1.804 395	9.02	20
21	12.429 326	89.641 769	.011 155 5139	.080 455	7.212 119	.138 655 5139	13.87	1.911 766	9.10	21
22	14.014 065	102.071 094	.009 797 0930	.071 357	7.283 475	.137 297 0930	13.73	2.020 536	9.18	22
23	15.800 858	116.085 159	.008 614 3656	.063 288	7.346 763	.136 114 3656	13.62	2.130 630	9.26	23
24	17.815 467	131.886 016	.007 582 3050	.056 131	7.402 894	.135 082 3050	13.51	2.241 975	9.34	24
25	20.086 939	149.701 483	.006 679 9605	.049 784	7.452 678	.134 179 9605	13.42	2.354 499	9.42	25
26	22.648 024	169.788 423	.005 889 6831	.044 154	7.496 832	.133 389 6831	13.34	2.468 132	9.49	26
27	25.535 647	192.436 446	.005 196 5208	.039 161	7.535 993	.132 696 5208	13.27	2.582 806	9.57	27
28	28.791 442	217.972 093	.004 587 7432	.034 733	7.570 725	.132 087 7432	13.21	2.698 457	9.64	28
29	32.462 351	246.763 535	.004 052 4626	.030 805	7.601 530	.131 552 4626	13.16	2.815 021	9.71	29
30	36.601 300	279.225 886	.003 581 3298	.027 321	7.628 852	.131 081 3298	13.11	2.932 440	9.77	30
31	41.267 966	315.827 187	.003 166 2885	.024 232	7.653 083	.130 666 2885	13.07	3.050 655	9.84	31
32	46.529 632	357.095 153	.002 800 3741	.021 492	7.674 575	.130 300 3741	13.04	3.169 612	9.91	32
33	52.462 160	403.624 785	.002 477 5485	.019 061	7.693 636	.129 977 5485	13.00	3.289 259	9.97	33
34	59.151 085	456.086 945	.002 192 5644	.016 906	7.710 542	.129 692 5644	12.97	3.409 547	10.03	34
35	66.692 849	515.238 030	.001 940 8505	.014 994	7.725 536	.129 440 8505	12.95	3.530 430	10.09	35
36	75.196 187	581.930 879	.001 718 4171	.013 299	7.738 835	.129 218 4171	12.93	3.651 863	10.14	36
37	84.783 701	657.127 066	.001 521 7757	.011 795	7.750 630	.129 021 7757	12.91	3.773 806	10.20	37
38	95.593 623	741.910 767	.001 347 8710	.010 461	7.761 091	.128 847 8710	12.89	3.896 219	10.25	38
39	107.781 810	837.504 390	.001 194 0236	.009 278	7.770 369	.128 694 0236	12.87	4.019 067	10.31	39
40	121.523 990	945.286 200	.001 057 8807	.008 229	7.778 597	.128 557 8807	12.86	4.142 315	10.36	40
41	137.018 299	1066.810 190	.000 937 3739	.007 298	7.785 896	.128 437 3739	12.85	4.265 932	10.40	41
42	154.488 132	1203.828 490	.000 830 6831	.006 473	7.792 369	.128 330 6831	12.84	4.389 889	10.45	42
43	174.185 369	1358.316 622	.000 736 2054	.005 741	7.798 110	.128 236 2054	12.83	4.514 157	10.50	43
44	196.394 004	1532.501 991	.000 652 5277	.005 092	7.803 202	.128 152 5277	12.82	4.638 711	10.54	44
45	221.434 239	1728.895 995	.000 578 4038	.004 516	7.807 718	.128 078 4038	12.81	4.763 528	10.59	45
46	249.667 105	1950.330 235	.000 512 7337	.004 005	7.811 723	.128 012 7337	12.81	4.888 586	10.63	46
47	281.499 661	2199.997 339	.000 454 5460	.003 552	7.815 275	.127 954 5460	12.80	5.013 864	10.67	47
48	317.390 868	2481.497 000	.000 402 9826	.003 151	7.818 426	.127 902 9826	12.80	5.139 343	10.71	48
49	357.858 203	2798.887 868	.000 357 2848	.002 794	7.821 220	.127 857 2848	12.79	5.265 007	10.75	49
50	403.485 124	3156.746 071	.000 316 7819	.002 478	7.823 699	.127 816 7819	12.79	5.390 839	10.78	50

Effective Rate is 12.75 %

Annual Percentage Rate is 12.75 %

ANNUAL COMPOUND INTEREST AND ANNUITY

	Amount Of 1	Amount Of 1 Per Period	Sinking Fund Payment	Present Worth Of 1	Present Worth of 1 Per Period	Periodic Payment To Amortize 1	Constant Annual Percent	Total Interest	Annual Add On Rate	
	What a single $ 1 deposit grows to in the future. The deposit is made at the beginning of the first period.	What a series of $ 1 deposits grow to in the future. A deposit is made at the end of each period.	The amount to be deposited at the end of each period that grows to $ 1 in the future.	What $ 1 to be paid in the future is worth today. Value today of a single $ 1 payment tomorrow.	What $ 1 to be paid at the end of each period is worth today. Value today of a series of $ 1 payments tomorrow.	The mortgage payment to amortize a loan of $ 1. An annuity certain, payable at the end of each period, worth $ 1 today.	The annual payment, including interest and principal, to amortize completely a loan of $ 100.	The total interest paid over the term on a loan of $1. The loan is amortized by regular periodic payments.	The average annual interest rate on a loan that is completely amortized by regular periodic payments.	
	$S = (1+i)^n$	$S\overline{n}| = \dfrac{(1+i)^n - 1}{i}$	$\dfrac{1}{S\overline{n}|} = \dfrac{i}{(1+i)^n - 1}$	$V^n = \dfrac{1}{(1+i)^n}$	$A\overline{n}| = \dfrac{1 - V^n}{i}$	$\dfrac{1}{A\overline{n}|} = \dfrac{i}{1 - V^n}$				

YEAR										PERIODS
	1.130 000	1.000 000	1.000 000 0000	.884 956	.884 956	1.130 000 0000	113.00	.130 000	13.00	1

YEAR	Amount Of 1	Amount Of 1 Per Period	Sinking Fund Payment	Present Worth Of 1	Present Worth of 1 Per Period	Periodic Payment To Amortize 1	Constant Annual Percent	Total Interest	Annual Add On Rate	PERIODS
1	1.130 000	1.000 000	1.000 000 0000	.884 956	.884 956	1.130 000 0000	113.00	.130 000	13.00	1
2	1.276 900	2.130 000	.469 483 5681	.783 147	1.668 102	.599 483 5681	59.95	.198 967	9.95	2
3	1.442 897	3.406 900	.293 521 9701	.693 050	2.361 153	.423 521 9701	42.36	.270 566	9.02	3
4	1.630 474	4.849 797	.206 194 1974	.613 319	2.974 471	.336 194 1974	33.62	.344 777	8.62	4
5	1.842 435	6.480 271	.154 314 5434	.542 760	3.517 231	.284 314 5434	28.44	.421 573	8.43	5
6	2.081 952	8.322 706	.120 153 2321	.480 319	3.997 550	.250 153 2321	25.02	.500 919	8.35	6
7	2.352 605	10.404 658	.096 110 8038	.425 061	4.422 610	.226 110 8038	22.62	.582 776	8.33	7
8	2.658 444	12.757 263	.078 386 7196	.376 160	4.798 770	.208 386 7196	20.84	.667 094	8.34	8
9	3.004 042	15.415 707	.064 868 9020	.332 885	5.131 655	.194 868 9020	19.49	.753 820	8.38	9
10	3.394 567	18.419 749	.054 289 5558	.294 588	5.426 243	.184 289 5558	18.43	.842 896	8.43	10
11	3.835 861	21.814 317	.045 841 4545	.260 698	5.686 941	.175 841 4545	17.59	.934 256	8.49	11
12	4.334 523	25.650 178	.038 986 0847	.230 706	5.917 647	.168 986 0847	16.90	1.027 833	8.57	12
13	4.898 011	29.984 701	.033 350 3411	.204 165	6.121 812	.163 350 3411	16.34	1.123 554	8.64	13
14	5.534 753	34.882 712	.028 667 4959	.180 677	6.302 488	.158 667 4959	15.87	1.221 345	8.72	14
15	6.254 270	40.417 464	.024 741 7797	.159 891	6.462 379	.154 741 7797	15.48	1.321 127	8.81	15
16	7.067 326	46.671 735	.021 426 2445	.141 496	6.603 875	.151 426 2445	15.15	1.422 820	8.89	16
17	7.986 078	53.739 060	.018 608 4385	.125 218	6.729 093	.148 608 4385	14.87	1.526 343	8.98	17
18	9.024 268	61.725 138	.016 200 8548	.110 812	6.839 905	.146 200 8548	14.63	1.631 615	9.06	18
19	10.197 423	70.749 406	.014 134 3943	.098 064	6.937 969	.144 134 3943	14.42	1.738 554	9.15	19
20	11.523 088	80.946 829	.012 353 7884	.086 782	7.024 752	.142 353 7884	14.24	1.847 076	9.24	20
21	13.021 089	92.469 917	.010 814 3279	.076 798	7.101 550	.140 814 3279	14.09	1.957 101	9.32	21
22	14.713 831	105.491 006	.009 479 4811	.067 963	7.169 513	.139 479 4811	13.95	2.068 549	9.40	22
23	16.626 629	120.204 837	.008 319 1328	.060 144	7.229 658	.138 319 1328	13.84	2.181 340	9.48	23
24	18.788 091	136.831 465	.007 308 2605	.053 225	7.282 883	.137 308 2605	13.74	2.295 398	9.56	24
25	21.230 542	155.619 556	.006 425 9276	.047 102	7.329 985	.136 425 9276	13.65	2.410 648	9.64	25
26	23.990 513	176.850 098	.005 654 5063	.041 683	7.371 668	.135 654 5063	13.57	2.527 017	9.72	26
27	27.109 279	200.840 611	.004 979 0727	.036 888	7.408 556	.134 979 0727	13.50	2.644 435	9.79	27
28	30.633 486	227.949 890	.004 386 9291	.032 644	7.441 200	.134 386 9291	13.44	2.762 834	9.87	28
29	34.615 839	258.583 376	.003 867 2246	.028 889	7.470 088	.133 867 2246	13.39	2.882 150	9.94	29
30	39.115 898	293.199 215	.003 410 6503	.025 565	7.495 653	.133 410 6503	13.35	3.002 320	10.01	30
31	44.200 965	332.315 113	.003 009 1921	.022 624	7.518 277	.133 009 1921	13.31	3.123 285	10.08	31
32	49.947 090	376.516 078	.002 655 9291	.020 021	7.538 299	.132 655 9291	13.27	3.244 990	10.14	32
33	56.440 212	426.463 168	.002 344 8684	.017 718	7.556 016	.132 344 8684	13.24	3.367 381	10.20	33
34	63.777 439	482.903 380	.002 070 8076	.015 680	7.571 696	.132 070 8076	13.21	3.490 407	10.27	34
35	72.068 506	546.680 819	.001 829 2209	.013 876	7.585 572	.131 829 2209	13.19	3.614 023	10.33	35
36	81.437 412	618.749 325	.001 616 1634	.012 279	7.597 851	.131 616 1634	13.17	3.738 182	10.38	36
37	92.024 276	700.186 738	.001 428 1904	.010 867	7.608 718	.131 428 1904	13.15	3.862 843	10.44	37
38	103.987 432	792.211 014	.001 262 2899	.009 617	7.618 334	.131 262 2899	13.13	3.987 967	10.49	38
39	117.505 798	896.198 445	.001 115 8243	.008 510	7.626 844	.131 115 8243	13.12	4.113 517	10.55	39
40	132.781 552	1013.704 243	.000 986 4810	.007 531	7.634 376	.130 986 4810	13.10	4.239 459	10.60	40
41	150.043 153	1146.485 795	.000 872 2306	.006 665	7.641 040	.130 872 2306	13.09	4.365 761	10.65	41
42	169.548 763	1296.528 948	.000 771 2901	.005 898	7.646 938	.130 771 2901	13.08	4.492 394	10.70	42
43	191.590 103	1466.077 712	.000 682 0921	.005 219	7.652 158	.130 682 0921	13.07	4.619 330	10.74	43
44	216.496 816	1657.667 814	.000 603 2572	.004 619	7.656 777	.130 603 2572	13.07	4.746 543	10.79	44
45	244.641 402	1874.164 630	.000 533 5711	.004 088	7.660 864	.130 533 5711	13.06	4.874 011	10.83	45
46	276.444 784	2118.806 032	.000 471 9639	.003 617	7.664 482	.130 471 9639	13.05	5.001 710	10.87	46
47	312.382 606	2395.250 816	.000 417 4928	.003 201	7.667 683	.130 417 4928	13.05	5.129 622	10.91	47
48	352.992 345	2707.633 422	.000 369 3262	.002 833	7.670 516	.130 369 3262	13.04	5.257 728	10.95	48
49	398.881 350	3060.625 767	.000 326 7306	.002 507	7.673 023	.130 326 7306	13.04	5.386 010	10.99	49
50	450.735 925	3459.507 117	.000 289 0585	.002 219	7.675 242	.130 289 0585	13.03	5.514 453	11.03	50

Effective Rate is 13.00 %

Annual Percentage Rate is 13.00 %

ANNUAL COMPOUND INTEREST AND ANNUITY

13.25 % A

	Amount Of 1	Amount Of 1 Per Period	Sinking Fund Payment	Present Worth Of 1	Present Worth of 1 Per Period	Periodic Payment To Amortize 1	Constant Annual Percent	Total Interest	Annual Add On Rate	
	What a single $ 1 deposit grows to in the future. The deposit is made at the beginning of the first period.	What a series of $ 1 deposits grow to in the future. A deposit is made at the end of each period.	The amount to be deposited at the end of each period that grows to $ 1 in the future.	What $ 1 to be paid in the future is worth today. Value today of a single $ 1 payment tomorrow.	What $ 1 to be paid at the end of each period is worth today. Value today of a series of $ 1 payments tomorrow.	The mortgage payment to amortize a loan of $ 1. An annuity certain, payable at the end of each period, worth $ 1 today.	The annual payment, including interest and principal, to amortize completely a loan of $ 100.	The total interest paid over the term on a loan of $1. The loan is amortized by regular periodic payments.	The average annual interest rate on a loan that is completely amortized by regular periodic payments.	
	$S = (1+i)^n$	$S\overline{n}| = \dfrac{(1+i)^n - 1}{i}$	$\dfrac{1}{S\overline{n}|} = \dfrac{i}{(1+i)^n - 1}$	$V^n = \dfrac{1}{(1+i)^n}$	$A\overline{n}| = \dfrac{1-V^n}{i}$	$\dfrac{1}{A\overline{n}|} = \dfrac{i}{1-V^n}$				

YEAR										PERIODS
	1.132 500	1.000 000	1.000 000 0000	.883 002	.883 002	1.132 500 0000	113.25	.132 500	13.25	1

YEAR										PERIODS
1	1.132 500	1.000 000	1.000 000 0000	.883 002	.883 002	1.132 500 0000	113.25	.132 500	13.25	1
2	1.282 556	2.132 500	.468 933 1770	.779 693	1.662 695	.601 433 1770	60.15	.202 866	10.14	2
3	1.452 495	3.415 056	.292 820 9455	.688 471	2.351 166	.425 320 9455	42.54	.275 963	9.20	3
4	1.644 951	4.867 551	.205 442 1121	.607 921	2.959 087	.337 942 1121	33.80	.351 768	8.79	4
5	1.862 906	6.512 502	.153 550 8228	.536 796	3.495 882	.286 050 8228	28.61	.430 254	8.61	5
6	2.109 742	8.375 408	.119 397 1654	.473 992	3.969 874	.251 897 1654	25.19	.511 383	8.52	6
7	2.389 282	10.485 150	.095 372 9816	.418 536	4.388 410	.227 872 9816	22.79	.595 111	8.50	7
8	2.705 862	12.874 432	.077 673 3286	.369 568	4.757 978	.210 173 3286	21.02	.681 387	8.52	8
9	3.064 389	15.580 294	.064 183 6395	.326 329	5.084 307	.196 683 6395	19.67	.770 153	8.56	9
10	3.470 421	18.644 683	.053 634 5926	.288 150	5.372 456	.186 134 5926	18.62	.861 346	8.61	10
11	3.930 251	22.115 104	.045 217 9651	.254 437	5.626 893	.177 717 9651	17.78	.954 898	8.68	11
12	4.451 010	26.045 355	.038 394 5617	.224 668	5.851 561	.170 894 5617	17.09	1.050 735	8.76	12
13	5.040 768	30.496 365	.032 790 7934	.198 382	6.049 944	.165 290 7934	16.53	1.148 780	8.84	13
14	5.708 670	35.537 133	.028 139 5799	.175 172	6.225 116	.160 639 5799	16.07	1.248 954	8.92	14
15	6.465 069	41.245 803	.024 244 8909	.154 677	6.379 793	.156 744 8909	15.68	1.351 173	9.01	15
16	7.321 691	47.710 872	.020 959 5833	.136 580	6.516 374	.153 459 5833	15.35	1.455 353	9.10	16
17	8.291 815	55.032 563	.018 171 0600	.120 601	6.636 975	.150 671 0600	15.07	1.561 408	9.18	17
18	9.390 480	63.324 377	.015 791 7068	.106 491	6.743 465	.148 291 7068	14.83	1.669 251	9.27	18
19	10.634 719	72.714 857	.013 752 3477	.094 032	6.837 497	.146 252 3477	14.63	1.778 795	9.36	19
20	12.043 819	83.349 576	.011 997 6615	.083 030	6.920 527	.144 497 6615	14.45	1.889 953	9.45	20
21	13.639 625	95.393 395	.010 482 9061	.073 316	6.993 843	.142 982 9061	14.30	2.002 641	9.54	21
22	15.446 875	109.033 020	.009 171 5336	.064 738	7.058 581	.141 671 5336	14.17	2.116 774	9.62	22
23	17.493 586	124.479 895	.008 033 4258	.057 164	7.115 745	.140 533 4258	14.06	2.232 269	9.71	23
24	19.811 486	141.973 481	.007 043 5689	.050 476	7.166 221	.139 543 5689	13.96	2.349 046	9.79	24
25	22.436 508	161.784 967	.006 181 0440	.044 570	7.210 791	.138 681 0440	13.87	2.467 026	9.87	25
26	25.409 345	184.221 475	.005 428 2488	.039 356	7.250 146	.137 928 2488	13.80	2.586 134	9.95	26
27	28.776 084	209.630 821	.004 770 2909	.034 751	7.284 898	.137 270 2909	13.73	2.706 298	10.02	27
28	32.588 915	238.406 904	.004 194 5094	.030 685	7.315 583	.136 694 5094	13.67	2.827 446	10.10	28
29	36.906 946	270.995 819	.003 690 0938	.027 095	7.342 678	.136 190 0938	13.62	2.949 513	10.17	29
30	41.797 116	307.902 765	.003 247 7786	.023 925	7.366 603	.135 747 7786	13.58	3.072 433	10.24	30
31	47.335 234	349.699 882	.002 859 5949	.021 126	7.387 729	.135 359 5949	13.54	3.196 147	10.31	31
32	53.607 153	397.035 116	.002 518 6689	.018 654	7.406 383	.135 018 6689	13.51	3.320 597	10.38	32
33	60.710 101	450.642 269	.002 219 0550	.016 472	7.422 855	.134 719 0550	13.48	3.445 729	10.44	33
34	68.754 189	511.352 369	.001 955 5986	.014 545	7.437 399	.134 455 5986	13.45	3.571 490	10.50	34
35	77.864 119	580.106 558	.001 723 8212	.012 843	7.450 242	.134 223 8212	13.43	3.697 834	10.57	35
36	88.181 115	657.970 677	.001 519 8246	.011 340	7.461 583	.134 019 8246	13.41	3.824 714	10.62	36
37	99.865 112	746.151 792	.001 340 2099	.010 014	7.471 596	.133 840 2099	13.39	3.952 088	10.68	37
38	113.097 240	846.016 904	.001 182 0095	.008 842	7.480 438	.133 682 0095	13.37	4.079 916	10.74	38
39	128.082 624	959.114 144	.001 042 6288	.007 807	7.488 246	.133 542 6288	13.36	4.208 163	10.79	39
40	145.053 572	1087.196 768	.000 919 7967	.006 894	7.495 140	.133 419 7967	13.35	4.336 792	10.84	40
41	164.273 170	1232.250 340	.000 811 5234	.006 087	7.501 227	.133 311 5234	13.34	4.465 772	10.89	41
42	186.039 365	1396.523 510	.000 716 0638	.005 375	7.506 602	.133 216 0638	13.33	4.595 075	10.94	42
43	210.689 581	1582.562 875	.000 631 8864	.004 746	7.511 349	.133 131 8864	13.32	4.724 671	10.99	43
44	238.605 950	1793.252 456	.000 557 6460	.004 191	7.515 540	.133 057 6460	13.31	4.854 536	11.03	44
45	270.221 239	2031.858 407	.000 492 1603	.003 701	7.519 240	.132 992 1603	13.30	4.984 647	11.08	45
46	306.025 553	2302.079 646	.000 434 3898	.003 268	7.522 508	.132 934 3898	13.30	5.114 982	11.12	46
47	346.573 939	2608.105 199	.000 383 4201	.002 885	7.525 393	.132 883 4201	13.29	5.245 521	11.16	47
48	392.494 986	2954.679 138	.000 338 4462	.002 548	7.527 941	.132 838 4462	13.29	5.376 245	11.20	48
49	444.500 571	3347.174 124	.000 298 7595	.002 250	7.530 191	.132 798 7595	13.28	5.507 139	11.24	49
50	503.396 897	3791.674 695	.000 263 7357	.001 987	7.532 177	.132 763 7357	13.28	5.638 187	11.28	50

Effective Rate is 13.25 %

8 - 469

Annual Percentage Rate is 13.25 %

	Amount Of 1	Amount Of 1 Per Period	Sinking Fund Payment	Present Worth Of 1	Present Worth of 1 Per Period	Periodic Payment To Amortize 1	Constant Annual Percent	Total Interest	Annual Add On Rate
	What a single $ 1 deposit grows to in the future. The deposit is made at the beginning of the first period.	What a series of $ 1 deposits grow to in the future. A deposit is made at the end of each period.	The amount to be deposited at the end of each period that grows to $ 1 in the future.	What $ 1 to be paid in the future is worth today. Value today of a single $ 1 payment tomorrow.	What $ 1 to be paid at the end of each period is worth today. Value today of a series of $ 1 payments tomorrow.	The mortgage payment to amortize a loan of $ 1. An annuity certain, payable at the end of each period, worth $ 1 today.	The annual payment, including interest and principal, to amortize completely a loan of $ 100.	The total interest paid over the term on a loan of $1. The loan is amortized by regular periodic payments.	The average annual interest rate on a loan that is completely amortized by regular periodic payments.
	$S = (1+i)^n$	$S\overline{n}| = \dfrac{(1+i)^n - 1}{i}$	$\dfrac{1}{S\overline{n}|} = \dfrac{i}{(1+i)^n - 1}$	$V^n = \dfrac{1}{(1+i)^n}$	$A\overline{n}| = \dfrac{1 - V^n}{i}$	$\dfrac{1}{A\overline{n}|} = \dfrac{i}{1 - V^n}$			

YEAR | | | | | | | | | **PERIODS**

	Amount Of 1	Amount Of 1 Per Period	Sinking Fund Payment	Present Worth Of 1	Present Worth of 1 Per Period	Periodic Payment To Amortize 1	Constant Annual Percent	Total Interest	Annual Add On Rate	
	1.135 000	1.000 000	1.000 000 0000	.881 057	.881 057	1.135 000 0000	113.50	.135 000	13.50	1
1	1.135 000	1.000 000	1.000 000 0000	.881 057	.881 057	1.135 000 0000	113.50	.135 000	13.50	1
2	1.288 225	2.135 000	.468 384 0749	.776 262	1.657 319	.603 384 0749	60.34	.206 768	10.34	2
3	1.462 135	3.423 225	.292 122 1947	.683 931	2.341 250	.427 122 1947	42.72	.281 367	9.38	3
4	1.659 524	4.885 360	.204 693 1901	.602 583	2.943 833	.339 693 1901	33.97	.358 773	8.97	4
5	1.883 559	6.544 884	.152 791 0955	.530 910	3.474 743	.287 791 0955	28.78	.438 955	8.78	5
6	2.137 840	8.428 443	.118 645 8704	.467 762	3.942 505	.253 645 8704	25.37	.521 875	8.70	6
7	2.426 448	10.566 283	.094 640 6583	.412 125	4.354 630	.229 640 6583	22.97	.607 485	8.68	7
8	2.754 019	12.992 731	.076 966 1101	.363 106	4.717 735	.211 966 1101	21.20	.695 729	8.70	8
9	3.125 811	15.746 750	.063 505 1669	.319 917	5.037 652	.198 505 1669	19.86	.786 547	8.74	9
10	3.547 796	18.872 561	.052 986 9780	.281 865	5.319 517	.187 986 9780	18.80	.879 870	8.80	10
11	4.026 748	22.420 357	.044 602 3222	.248 339	5.567 857	.179 602 3222	17.97	.975 626	8.87	11
12	4.570 359	26.447 106	.037 811 3211	.218 801	5.786 658	.172 811 3211	17.29	1.073 736	8.95	12
13	5.187 358	31.017 465	.032 239 9012	.192 776	5.979 434	.167 239 9012	16.73	1.174 119	9.03	13
14	5.887 651	36.204 823	.027 620 6298	.169 847	6.149 281	.162 620 6298	16.27	1.276 689	9.12	14
15	6.682 484	42.092 474	.023 757 2163	.149 645	6.298 926	.158 757 2163	15.88	1.381 358	9.21	15
16	7.584 619	48.774 957	.020 502 3244	.131 846	6.430 772	.155 502 3244	15.56	1.488 037	9.30	16
17	8.608 543	56.359 577	.017 743 2135	.116 164	6.546 936	.152 743 2135	15.28	1.596 635	9.39	17
18	9.770 696	64.968 120	.015 392 1647	.102 347	6.649 283	.150 392 1647	15.04	1.707 059	9.48	18
19	11.089 740	74.738 816	.013 379 9284	.090 173	6.739 456	.148 379 9284	14.84	1.819 219	9.57	19
20	12.586 855	85.828 556	.011 651 1339	.079 448	6.818 904	.146 651 1339	14.67	1.933 023	9.67	20
21	14.286 080	98.415 411	.010 161 0103	.069 998	6.888 902	.145 161 0103	14.52	2.048 381	9.75	21
22	16.214 701	112.701 491	.008 872 9970	.061 672	6.950 575	.143 872 9970	14.39	2.165 206	9.84	22
23	18.403 686	128.916 193	.007 756 9775	.054 337	7.004 912	.142 756 9775	14.28	2.283 410	9.93	23
24	20.888 184	147.319 879	.006 787 9502	.047 874	7.052 786	.141 787 9502	14.18	2.402 911	10.01	24
25	23.708 088	168.208 062	.005 945 0182	.042 180	7.094 965	.140 945 0182	14.10	2.523 625	10.09	25
26	26.908 680	191.916 151	.005 210 6089	.037 163	7.132 128	.140 210 6089	14.03	2.645 476	10.18	26
27	30.541 352	218.824 831	.004 569 8653	.032 742	7.164 870	.139 569 8653	13.96	2.768 386	10.25	27
28	34.664 435	249.366 183	.004 010 1668	.028 848	7.193 718	.139 010 1668	13.91	2.892 285	10.33	28
29	39.344 133	284.030 618	.003 520 7472	.025 417	7.219 135	.138 520 7472	13.86	3.017 102	10.40	29
30	44.655 591	323.374 752	.003 092 3874	.022 394	7.241 529	.138 092 3874	13.81	3.142 772	10.48	30
31	50.684 096	368.030 343	.002 717 1673	.019 730	7.261 259	.137 717 1673	13.78	3.269 232	10.55	31
32	57.526 449	418.714 439	.002 388 2625	.017 383	7.278 642	.137 388 2625	13.74	3.396 424	10.61	32
33	65.292 520	476.240 889	.002 099 7777	.015 316	7.293 958	.137 099 7777	13.71	3.524 293	10.68	33
34	74.107 010	541.533 409	.001 846 6081	.013 494	7.307 452	.136 846 6081	13.69	3.652 785	10.74	34
35	84.111 457	615.640 419	.001 624 3248	.011 889	7.319 341	.136 624 3248	13.67	3.781 851	10.81	35
36	95.466 503	699.751 875	.001 429 0780	.010 475	7.329 816	.136 429 0780	13.65	3.911 447	10.87	36
37	108.354 481	795.218 378	.001 257 5162	.009 229	7.339 045	.136 257 5162	13.63	4.041 528	10.92	37
38	122.982 336	903.572 859	.001 106 7176	.008 131	7.347 176	.136 106 7176	13.62	4.172 055	10.98	38
39	139.584 951	1026.555 195	.000 974 1317	.007 164	7.354 340	.135 974 1317	13.60	4.302 991	11.03	39
40	158.428 920	1166.140 147	.000 857 5299	.006 312	7.360 652	.135 857 5299	13.59	4.434 301	11.09	40
41	179.816 824	1324.569 067	.000 754 9625	.005 561	7.366 213	.135 754 9625	13.58	4.565 953	11.14	41
42	204.092 095	1504.385 891	.000 664 7231	.004 900	7.371 113	.135 664 7231	13.57	4.697 918	11.19	42
43	231.644 528	1708.477 986	.000 585 3163	.004 317	7.375 430	.135 585 3163	13.56	4.830 169	11.23	43
44	262.916 539	1940.122 514	.000 515 4314	.003 803	7.379 233	.135 515 4314	13.56	4.962 679	11.28	44
45	298.410 272	2203.039 053	.000 453 9184	.003 351	7.382 585	.135 453 9184	13.55	5.095 426	11.32	45
46	338.695 659	2501.449 326	.000 399 7682	.002 953	7.385 537	.135 399 7682	13.54	5.228 389	11.37	46
47	384.419 573	2840.144 984	.000 352 0947	.002 601	7.388 138	.135 352 0947	13.54	5.361 548	11.41	47
48	436.316 215	3224.564 557	.000 310 1194	.002 292	7.390 430	.135 310 1194	13.54	5.494 886	11.45	48
49	495.218 904	3660.880 773	.000 273 1583	.002 019	7.392 450	.135 273 1583	13.53	5.628 385	11.49	49
50	562.073 456	4156.099 677	.000 240 6102	.001 779	7.394 229	.135 240 6102	13.53	5.762 031	11.52	50

Effective Rate is 13.50 %

Annual Percentage Rate is 13.50 %

ANNUAL COMPOUND INTEREST AND ANNUITY

13.75 % A

	Amount Of 1	Amount Of 1 Per Period	Sinking Fund Payment	Present Worth Of 1	Present Worth of 1 Per Period	Periodic Payment To Amortize 1	Constant Annual Percent	Total Interest	Annual Add On Rate	
	What a single $ 1 deposit grows to in the future. The deposit is made at the beginning of the first period.	What a series of $ 1 deposits grow to in the future. A deposit is made at the end of each period.	The amount to be deposited at the end of each period that grows to $ 1 in the future.	What $ 1 to be paid in the future is worth today. Value today of a single $ 1 payment tomorrow.	What $ 1 to be paid at the end of each period is worth today. Value today of a series of $ 1 payments tomorrow.	The mortgage payment to amortize a loan of $ 1. An annuity certain, payable at the end of each period, worth $ 1 today.	The annual payment, including interest and principal, to amortize completely a loan of $ 100.	The total interest paid over the term on a loan of $1. The loan is amortized by regular periodic payments.	The average annual interest rate on a loan that is completely amortized by regular periodic payments.	
	$S = (1+i)^n$	$S\overline{n}| = \dfrac{(1+i)^n - 1}{i}$	$\dfrac{1}{S\overline{n}|} = \dfrac{i}{(1+i)^n - 1}$	$V^n = \dfrac{1}{(1+i)^n}$	$A\overline{n}| = \dfrac{1-V^n}{i}$	$\dfrac{1}{A\overline{n}|} = \dfrac{i}{1-V^n}$				

YEAR										PERIODS
	1.137 500	1.000 000	1.000 000 0000	.879 121	.879 121	1.137 500 0000	113.75	.137 500	13.75	1

YEAR	Amount Of 1	Amount Of 1 Per Period	Sinking Fund Payment	Present Worth Of 1	Present Worth of 1 Per Period	Periodic Payment To Amortize 1	Constant Annual Percent	Total Interest	Annual Add On Rate	PERIODS
1	1.137 500	1.000 000	1.000 000 0000	.879 121	.879 121	1.137 500 0000	113.75	.137 500	13.75	1
2	1.293 906	2.137 500	.467 836 2573	.772 854	1.651 974	.605 336 2573	60.54	.210 673	10.53	2
3	1.471 818	3.431 406	.291 425 7092	.679 432	2.331 406	.428 925 7092	42.90	.286 777	9.56	3
4	1.674 193	4.903 225	.203 947 4182	.597 303	2.928 709	.341 447 4182	34.15	.365 790	9.14	4
5	1.904 395	6.577 418	.152 035 3429	.525 101	3.453 810	.289 535 3429	28.96	.447 677	8.95	5
6	2.166 249	8.481 813	.117 899 3222	.461 627	3.915 437	.255 399 3222	25.54	.532 396	8.87	6
7	2.464 109	10.648 062	.093 913 8011	.405 826	4.321 263	.231 413 8011	23.15	.619 897	8.86	7
8	2.802 923	13.112 171	.076 265 0224	.356 770	4.678 034	.213 765 0224	21.38	.710 120	8.88	8
9	3.188 325	15.915 094	.062 833 4323	.313 644	4.991 678	.200 333 4323	20.04	.803 001	8.92	9
10	3.626 720	19.103 420	.052 346 6485	.275 731	5.267 409	.189 846 6485	18.99	.898 466	8.98	10
11	4.125 394	22.730 140	.043 994 4497	.242 401	5.509 810	.181 494 4497	18.15	.996 439	9.06	11
12	4.692 636	26.855 534	.037 236 2729	.213 100	5.722 910	.174 736 2729	17.48	1.096 835	9.14	12
13	5.337 873	31.548 170	.031 697 5595	.187 341	5.910 251	.169 197 5595	16.92	1.199 568	9.23	13
14	6.071 831	36.886 044	.027 110 5248	.164 695	6.074 946	.164 610 5248	16.47	1.304 547	9.32	14
15	6.906 708	42.957 875	.023 278 6191	.144 787	6.219 732	.160 778 6191	16.08	1.411 679	9.41	15
16	7.856 380	49.864 582	.020 054 3142	.127 285	6.347 018	.157 554 3142	15.76	1.520 869	9.51	16
17	8.936 632	57.720 962	.017 324 7285	.111 899	6.458 917	.154 824 7285	15.49	1.632 020	9.60	17
18	10.165 419	66.657 595	.015 002 0415	.098 373	6.557 289	.152 502 0415	15.26	1.745 037	9.69	18
19	11.563 164	76.823 014	.013 016 9327	.086 482	6.643 771	.150 516 9327	15.06	1.859 822	9.79	19
20	13.153 100	88.386 178	.011 313 9862	.076 028	6.719 798	.148 813 9862	14.89	1.976 280	9.88	20
21	14.961 651	101.539 278	.009 848 4057	.066 838	6.786 636	.147 348 4057	14.74	2.094 317	9.97	21
22	17.018 878	116.500 929	.008 583 6226	.058 758	6.845 394	.146 083 6226	14.61	2.213 840	10.06	22
23	19.358 973	133.519 806	.007 489 5255	.051 656	6.897 050	.144 989 5255	14.50	2.334 759	10.15	23
24	22.020 832	152.878 780	.006 541 1302	.045 412	6.942 461	.144 041 1302	14.41	2.456 987	10.24	24
25	25.048 697	174.899 612	.005 717 5656	.039 922	6.982 384	.143 217 5656	14.33	2.580 439	10.32	25
26	28.492 892	199.948 309	.005 001 2926	.035 096	7.017 480	.142 501 2926	14.26	2.705 034	10.40	26
27	32.410 665	228.441 201	.004 377 4941	.030 854	7.048 334	.141 877 4941	14.19	2.830 692	10.48	27
28	36.867 132	260.851 866	.003 833 5934	.027 124	7.075 459	.141 333 5934	14.14	2.957 341	10.56	28
29	41.936 362	297.718 998	.003 358 8720	.023 846	7.099 304	.140 858 8720	14.09	3.084 907	10.64	29
30	47.702 612	339.655 360	.002 944 1608	.020 963	7.120 268	.140 444 1608	14.05	3.213 325	10.71	30
31	54.261 721	387.357 972	.002 581 5914	.018 429	7.138 697	.140 081 5914	14.01	3.342 529	10.78	31
32	61.722 708	441.619 693	.002 264 3918	.016 201	7.154 898	.139 764 3918	13.98	3.472 461	10.85	32
33	70.209 580	503.342 401	.001 986 7192	.014 243	7.169 141	.139 486 7192	13.95	3.603 062	10.92	33
34	79.863 397	573.551 981	.001 743 5211	.012 521	7.181 663	.139 243 5211	13.93	3.734 280	10.98	34
35	90.844 615	653.415 378	.001 530 4201	.011 008	7.192 670	.139 030 4201	13.91	3.866 065	11.05	35
36	103.335 749	744.259 993	.001 343 6165	.009 677	7.202 348	.138 843 6165	13.89	3.998 370	11.11	36
37	117.544 415	847.595 742	.001 179 8077	.008 507	7.210 855	.138 679 8077	13.87	4.131 153	11.17	37
38	133.706 772	965.140 157	.001 036 1189	.007 479	7.218 334	.138 536 1189	13.86	4.264 373	11.22	38
39	152.091 453	1098.846 928	.000 910 0449	.006 575	7.224 909	.138 410 0449	13.85	4.397 992	11.28	39
40	173.004 027	1250.938 381	.000 799 3999	.005 780	7.230 689	.138 299 3999	13.83	4.531 975	11.33	40
41	196.792 081	1423.942 408	.000 702 2756	.005 082	7.235 771	.138 202 2756	13.83	4.666 293	11.38	41
42	223.850 992	1620.734 489	.000 617 0042	.004 467	7.240 238	.138 117 0042	13.82	4.800 914	11.43	42
43	254.630 504	1844.585 481	.000 542 1272	.003 927	7.244 165	.138 042 1272	13.81	4.935 811	11.48	43
44	289.642 198	2099.215 985	.000 476 3683	.003 453	7.247 618	.137 976 3683	13.80	5.070 960	11.53	44
45	329.468 000	2388.858 183	.000 418 6100	.003 035	7.250 653	.137 918 6100	13.80	5.206 337	11.57	45
46	374.769 850	2718.326 183	.000 367 8734	.002 668	7.253 321	.137 867 8734	13.79	5.341 922	11.61	46
47	426.300 705	3093.096 034	.000 323 3007	.002 346	7.255 667	.137 823 3007	13.79	5.477 695	11.65	47
48	484.917 051	3519.396 738	.000 284 1396	.002 062	7.257 729	.137 784 1396	13.78	5.613 639	11.70	48
49	551.593 146	4004.313 790	.000 249 7307	.001 813	7.259 542	.137 749 7307	13.78	5.749 737	11.73	49
50	627.437 204	4555.906 936	.000 219 4953	.001 594	7.261 136	.137 719 4953	13.78	5.885 975	11.77	50

Effective Rate is 13.75 %

Annual Percentage Rate is 13.75 %

Amount Of 1	Amount Of 1 Per Period	Sinking Fund Payment	Present Worth Of 1	Present Worth of 1 Per Period	Periodic Payment To Amortize 1	Constant Annual Percent	Total Interest	Annual Add On Rate
What a single $ 1 deposit grows to in the future. The deposit is made at the beginning of the first period.	What a series of $ 1 deposits grow to in the future. A deposit is made at the end of each period.	The amount to be deposited at the end of each period that grows to $ 1 in the future.	What $ 1 to be paid in the future is worth today. Value today of a single $ 1 payment tomorrow.	What $ 1 to be paid at the end of each period is worth today. Value today of a series of $ 1 payments tomorrow.	The mortgage payment to amortize a loan of $ 1. An annuity certain, payable at the end of each period, worth $ 1 today.	The annual payment, including interest and principal, to amortize completely a loan of $ 100.	The total interest paid over the term on a loan of $1. The loan is amortized by regular periodic payments.	The average annual interest rate on a loan that is completely amortized by regular periodic payments.

$$S = (1+i)^n \qquad S\overline{n}| = \frac{(1+i)^n - 1}{i} \qquad \frac{1}{S\overline{n}|} = \frac{i}{(1+i)^n - 1} \qquad V^n = \frac{1}{(1+i)^n} \qquad A\overline{n}| = \frac{1-V^n}{i} \qquad \frac{1}{A\overline{n}|} = \frac{i}{1-V^n}$$

YEAR ... **PERIODS**

	Amount Of 1	Amount Of 1 Per Period	Sinking Fund Payment	Present Worth Of 1	Present Worth of 1 Per Period	Periodic Payment To Amortize 1	Constant Annual Percent	Total Interest	Annual Add On Rate	
	1.140 000	1.000 000	1.000 000 0000	.877 193	.877 193	1.140 000 0000	114.00	.140 000	14.00	1
1	1.140 000	1.000 000	1.000 000 0000	.877 193	.877 193	1.140 000 0000	114.00	.140 000	14.00	1
2	1.299 600	2.140 000	.467 289 7196	.769 468	1.646 661	.607 289 7196	60.73	.214 579	10.73	2
3	1.481 544	3.439 600	.290 731 4804	.674 972	2.321 632	.430 731 4804	43.08	.292 194	9.74	3
4	1.688 960	4.921 144	.203 204 7833	.592 080	2.913 712	.343 204 7833	34.33	.372 819	9.32	4
5	1.925 415	6.610 104	.151 283 5465	.519 369	3.433 081	.291 283 5465	29.13	.456 418	9.13	5
6	2.194 973	8.535 519	.117 157 4957	.455 587	3.888 668	.257 157 4957	25.72	.542 945	9.05	6
7	2.502 269	10.730 491	.093 192 3773	.399 637	4.288 305	.233 192 3773	23.32	.632 347	9.03	7
8	2.852 586	13.232 760	.075 570 0238	.350 559	4.638 864	.215 570 0238	21.56	.724 560	9.06	8
9	3.251 949	16.085 347	.062 168 3838	.307 508	4.946 372	.202 168 3838	20.22	.819 515	9.11	9
10	3.707 221	19.337 295	.051 713 5408	.269 744	5.216 116	.191 713 5408	19.18	.917 135	9.17	10
11	4.226 232	23.044 516	.043 394 2714	.236 617	5.452 733	.183 394 2714	18.34	1.017 337	9.25	11
12	4.817 905	27.270 749	.036 669 3269	.207 559	5.660 292	.176 669 3269	17.67	1.120 032	9.33	12
13	5.492 411	32.088 654	.031 163 6635	.182 069	5.842 362	.171 163 6635	17.12	1.225 128	9.42	13
14	6.261 349	37.581 065	.026 609 1448	.159 710	6.002 072	.166 609 1448	16.67	1.332 528	9.52	14
15	7.137 938	43.842 414	.022 808 9630	.140 096	6.142 168	.162 808 9630	16.29	1.442 134	9.61	15
16	8.137 249	50.980 352	.019 615 4000	.122 892	6.265 060	.159 615 4000	15.97	1.553 846	9.71	16
17	9.276 464	59.117 601	.016 915 4359	.107 800	6.372 859	.156 915 4359	15.70	1.667 562	9.81	17
18	10.575 169	68.394 066	.014 621 1516	.094 561	6.467 420	.154 621 1516	15.47	1.783 181	9.91	18
19	12.055 693	78.969 235	.012 663 1593	.082 948	6.550 369	.152 663 1593	15.27	1.900 600	10.00	19
20	13.743 490	91.024 928	.010 986 0016	.072 762	6.623 131	.150 986 0016	15.10	2.019 720	10.10	20
21	15.667 578	104.768 418	.009 544 8612	.063 826	6.686 957	.149 544 8612	14.96	2.140 442	10.19	21
22	17.861 039	120.435 996	.008 303 1654	.055 988	6.742 944	.148 303 1654	14.84	2.262 670	10.28	22
23	20.361 585	138.297 035	.007 230 8130	.049 112	6.792 056	.147 230 8130	14.73	2.386 309	10.38	23
24	23.212 207	158.658 620	.006 302 8406	.043 081	6.835 137	.146 302 8406	14.64	2.511 268	10.46	24
25	26.461 916	181.870 827	.005 498 4079	.037 790	6.872 927	.145 498 4079	14.55	2.637 460	10.55	25
26	30.166 584	208.332 743	.004 800 0136	.033 149	6.906 077	.144 800 0136	14.49	2.764 800	10.63	26
27	34.389 906	238.499 327	.004 192 8839	.029 078	6.935 155	.144 192 8839	14.42	2.893 208	10.72	27
28	39.204 493	272.889 233	.003 664 4905	.025 507	6.960 662	.143 664 4905	14.37	3.022 606	10.80	28
29	44.693 122	312.093 725	.003 204 1657	.022 375	6.983 037	.143 204 1657	14.33	3.152 921	10.87	29
30	50.950 159	356.786 847	.002 802 7939	.019 627	7.002 664	.142 802 7939	14.29	3.284 084	10.95	30
31	58.083 181	407.737 006	.002 452 5613	.017 217	7.019 881	.142 452 5613	14.25	3.416 029	11.02	31
32	66.214 826	465.820 186	.002 146 7511	.015 102	7.034 983	.142 146 7511	14.22	3.548 696	11.09	32
33	75.484 902	532.035 012	.001 879 5755	.013 248	7.048 231	.141 879 5755	14.19	3.682 026	11.16	33
34	86.052 788	607.519 914	.001 646 0366	.011 621	7.059 852	.141 646 0366	14.17	3.815 965	11.22	34
35	98.100 178	693.572 702	.001 441 8099	.010 194	7.070 045	.141 441 8099	14.15	3.950 463	11.29	35
36	111.834 203	791.672 881	.001 263 1480	.008 942	7.078 987	.141 263 1480	14.13	4.085 473	11.35	36
37	127.490 992	903.507 084	.001 106 7982	.007 844	7.086 831	.141 106 7982	14.12	4.220 952	11.41	37
38	145.339 731	1030.998 076	.000 969 9339	.006 880	7.093 711	.140 969 9339	14.10	4.356 857	11.47	38
39	165.687 293	1176.337 806	.000 850 0959	.006 035	7.099 747	.140 850 0959	14.09	4.493 154	11.52	39
40	188.883 514	1342.025 099	.000 745 1425	.005 294	7.105 041	.140 745 1425	14.08	4.629 806	11.57	40
41	215.327 206	1530.908 613	.000 653 2069	.004 644	7.109 685	.140 653 2069	14.07	4.766 781	11.63	41
42	245.473 015	1746.235 819	.000 572 6603	.004 074	7.113 759	.140 572 6603	14.06	4.904 052	11.68	42
43	279.839 237	1991.708 833	.000 502 0814	.003 573	7.117 332	.140 502 0814	14.06	5.041 590	11.72	43
44	319.016 730	2271.548 070	.000 440 2284	.003 135	7.120 467	.140 440 2284	14.05	5.179 370	11.77	44
45	363.679 072	2590.564 800	.000 386 0162	.002 750	7.123 217	.140 386 0162	14.04	5.317 371	11.82	45
46	414.594 142	2954.243 872	.000 338 4961	.002 412	7.125 629	.140 338 4961	14.04	5.455 571	11.86	46
47	472.637 322	3368.838 014	.000 296 8383	.002 116	7.127 744	.140 296 8383	14.03	5.593 951	11.90	47
48	538.806 547	3841.475 336	.000 260 3167	.001 856	7.129 600	.140 260 3167	14.03	5.732 495	11.94	48
49	614.239 464	4380.281 883	.000 228 2958	.001 628	7.131 228	.140 228 2958	14.03	5.871 187	11.98	49
50	700.232 988	4994.521 346	.000 200 2194	.001 428	7.132 656	.140 200 2194	14.03	6.010 011	12.02	50

Effective Rate is 14.00 %

Annual Percentage Rate is 14.00 %

Amount Of 1	Amount Of 1 Per Period	Sinking Fund Payment	Present Worth Of 1	Present Worth of 1 Per Period	Periodic Payment To Amortize 1	Constant Annual Percent	Total Interest	Annual Add On Rate
What a single $ 1 deposit grows to in the future. The deposit is made at the beginning of the first period.	What a series of $ 1 deposits grow to in the future. A deposit is made at the end of each period.	The amount to be deposited at the end of each period that grows to $ 1 in the future.	What $ 1 to be paid in the future is worth today. Value today of a single $ 1 payment tomorrow.	What $ 1 to be paid at the end of each period is worth today. Value today of a series of $ 1 payments tomorrow.	The mortgage payment to amortize a loan of $ 1. An annuity certain, payable at the end of each period, worth $ 1 today.	The annual payment, including interest and principal, to amortize completely a loan of $ 100.	The total interest paid over the term on a loan of $1. The loan is amortized by regular periodic payments.	The average annual interest rate on a loan that is completely amortized by regular periodic payments.

$$S = (1+i)^n \qquad S\overline{n}| = \frac{(1+i)^n - 1}{i} \qquad \frac{1}{S\overline{n}|} = \frac{i}{(1+i)^n - 1} \qquad V^n = \frac{1}{(1+i)^n} \qquad A\overline{n}| = \frac{1-V^n}{i} \qquad \frac{1}{A\overline{n}|} = \frac{i}{1-V^n}$$

YEAR									PERIODS
	1.142 500	1.000 000	1.000 000 0000	.875 274	.875 274	1.142 500 0000	114.25	.142 500	14.25	1

YEAR	Amount Of 1	Amount Of 1 Per Period	Sinking Fund Payment	Present Worth Of 1	Present Worth of 1 Per Period	Periodic Payment To Amortize 1	Constant Annual Percent	Total Interest	Annual Add On Rate	PERIODS
1	1.142 500	1.000 000	1.000 000 0000	.875 274	.875 274	1.142 500 0000	114.25	.142 500	14.25	1
2	1.305 306	2.142 500	.466 744 4574	.766 104	1.641 377	.609 244 4574	60.93	.218 489	10.92	2
3	1.491 312	3.447 806	.290 039 4998	.670 550	2.311 928	.432 539 4998	43.26	.297 619	9.92	3
4	1.703 824	4.939 119	.202 465 2722	.586 915	2.898 843	.344 965 2722	34.50	.379 861	9.50	4
5	1.946 619	6.642 943	.150 535 6877	.513 711	3.412 554	.293 035 6877	29.31	.465 178	9.30	5
6	2.224 013	8.589 562	.116 420 3658	.449 638	3.862 191	.258 920 3658	25.90	.553 522	9.23	6
7	2.540 934	10.813 575	.092 476 3543	.393 556	4.255 747	.234 976 3543	23.50	.644 834	9.21	7
8	2.903 018	13.354 510	.074 881 0728	.344 469	4.600 217	.217 381 0728	21.74	.739 049	9.24	8
9	3.316 698	16.257 527	.061 509 9696	.301 505	4.901 721	.204 009 9696	20.41	.836 090	9.29	9
10	3.789 327	19.574 225	.051 087 5916	.263 899	5.165 620	.193 587 5916	19.36	.935 876	9.36	10
11	4.329 306	23.363 552	.042 801 7114	.230 984	5.396 604	.185 301 7114	18.54	1.038 319	9.44	11
12	4.946 232	27.692 858	.036 110 3936	.202 174	5.598 778	.178 610 3936	17.87	1.143 325	9.53	12
13	5.651 070	32.639 090	.030 638 1089	.176 958	5.775 736	.173 138 1089	17.32	1.250 795	9.62	13
14	6.456 348	38.290 161	.026 116 3700	.154 886	5.930 622	.168 616 3700	16.87	1.360 629	9.72	14
15	7.376 377	44.746 508	.022 348 1124	.135 568	6.066 190	.164 848 1124	16.49	1.472 722	9.82	15
16	8.427 511	52.122 886	.019 185 4304	.118 659	6.184 849	.161 685 4304	16.17	1.586 967	9.92	16
17	9.628 432	60.550 397	.016 515 1683	.103 859	6.288 708	.159 015 1683	15.91	1.703 258	10.02	17
18	11.000 483	70.178 829	.014 249 3116	.090 905	6.379 613	.156 749 3116	15.68	1.821 488	10.12	18
19	12.568 052	81.179 312	.012 318 4094	.079 567	6.459 180	.154 818 4094	15.49	1.941 550	10.22	19
20	14.358 999	93.747 364	.010 666 9666	.069 643	6.528 823	.153 166 9666	15.32	2.063 339	10.32	20
21	16.405 157	108.106 363	.009 250 1493	.060 956	6.589 779	.151 750 1493	15.18	2.186 753	10.41	21
22	18.742 892	124.511 520	.008 031 3854	.053 354	6.643 133	.150 531 3854	15.06	2.311 690	10.51	22
23	21.413 754	143.254 411	.006 980 5878	.046 699	6.689 832	.149 480 5878	14.95	2.438 054	10.60	23
24	24.465 213	164.668 165	.006 072 8192	.040 874	6.730 706	.148 572 8192	14.86	2.565 748	10.69	24
25	27.951 506	189.133 378	.005 287 2740	.035 776	6.766 482	.147 787 2740	14.78	2.694 682	10.78	25
26	31.934 596	217.084 885	.004 606 4930	.031 314	6.797 796	.147 106 4930	14.72	2.824 769	10.86	26
27	36.485 276	249.019 481	.004 015 7501	.027 408	6.825 205	.146 515 7501	14.66	2.955 925	10.95	27
28	41.684 428	285.504 757	.003 502 5686	.023 990	6.849 195	.146 002 5686	14.61	3.088 072	11.03	28
29	47.624 459	327.189 185	.003 056 3357	.020 998	6.870 192	.145 556 3357	14.56	3.221 134	11.11	29
30	54.410 944	374.813 643	.002 667 9925	.018 379	6.888 571	.145 167 9925	14.52	3.355 040	11.18	30
31	62.164 504	429.224 588	.002 329 7827	.016 086	6.904 657	.144 829 7827	14.49	3.489 723	11.26	31
32	71.022 946	491.389 091	.002 035 0472	.014 080	6.918 737	.144 535 0472	14.46	3.625 122	11.33	32
33	81.143 715	562.412 037	.001 778 0558	.012 324	6.931 061	.144 278 0558	14.43	3.761 176	11.40	33
34	92.706 695	643.555 752	.001 553 8669	.010 787	6.941 848	.144 053 8669	14.41	3.897 831	11.46	34
35	105.917 399	736.262 447	.001 358 2113	.009 441	6.951 289	.143 858 2113	14.39	4.035 037	11.53	35
36	121.010 628	842.179 845	.001 187 3948	.008 264	6.959 553	.143 687 3948	14.37	4.172 746	11.59	36
37	138.254 642	963.190 473	.001 038 2162	.007 233	6.966 786	.143 538 2162	14.36	4.310 914	11.65	37
38	157.955 929	1101.445 116	.000 907 8982	.006 331	6.973 117	.143 407 8982	14.35	4.449 500	11.71	38
39	180.464 649	1259.401 045	.000 794 0282	.005 541	6.978 658	.143 294 0282	14.33	4.588 467	11.77	39
40	206.180 861	1439.865 694	.000 694 5092	.004 850	6.983 508	.143 194 5092	14.32	4.727 780	11.82	40
41	235.561 634	1646.046 555	.000 607 5162	.004 245	6.987 753	.143 107 5162	14.32	4.867 408	11.87	41
42	269.129 167	1881.608 189	.000 531 4603	.003 716	6.991 469	.143 031 4603	14.31	5.007 321	11.92	42
43	307.480 073	2150.737 356	.000 464 9568	.003 252	6.994 721	.142 964 9568	14.30	5.147 493	11.97	43
44	351.295 984	2458.217 430	.000 406 7988	.002 847	6.997 568	.142 906 7988	14.30	5.287 899	12.02	44
45	401.355 661	2809.513 413	.000 355 9335	.002 492	7.000 059	.142 855 9335	14.29	5.428 517	12.06	45
46	458.548 843	3210.869 075	.000 311 4422	.002 181	7.002 240	.142 811 4422	14.29	5.569 326	12.11	46
47	523.892 053	3669.417 918	.000 272 5228	.001 909	7.004 149	.142 772 5228	14.28	5.710 309	12.15	47
48	598.546 671	4193.309 971	.000 238 4751	.001 671	7.005 820	.142 738 4751	14.28	5.851 447	12.19	48
49	683.839 572	4791.856 642	.000 208 6874	.001 462	7.007 282	.142 708 6874	14.28	5.992 726	12.23	49
50	781.286 710	5475.696 214	.000 182 6252	.001 280	7.008 562	.142 682 6252	14.27	6.134 131	12.27	50

Effective Rate is 14.25 %

Annual Percentage Rate is 14.25 %

	Amount Of 1	Amount Of 1 Per Period	Sinking Fund Payment	Present Worth Of 1	Present Worth of 1 Per Period	Periodic Payment To Amortize 1	Constant Annual Percent	Total Interest	Annual Add On Rate	
	What a single $ 1 deposit grows to in the future. The deposit is made at the beginning of the first period.	What a series of $ 1 deposits grow to in the future. A deposit is made at the end of each period.	The amount to be deposited at the end of each period that grows to $ 1 in the future.	What $ 1 to be paid in the future is worth today. Value today of a single $ 1 payment tomorrow.	What $ 1 to be paid at the end of each period is worth today. Value today of a series of $ 1 payments tomorrow.	The mortgage payment to amortize a loan of $ 1. An annuity certain, payable at the end of each period, worth $ 1 today.	The annual payment, including interest and principal, to amortize completely a loan of $ 100.	The total interest paid over the term on a loan of $1. The loan is amortized by regular periodic payments.	The average annual interest rate on a loan that is completely amortized by regular periodic payments.	
	$S = (1+i)^n$	$S\overline{n}| = \dfrac{(1+i)^n - 1}{i}$	$\dfrac{1}{S\overline{n}|} = \dfrac{i}{(1+i)^n - 1}$	$V^n = \dfrac{1}{(1+i)^n}$	$A\overline{n}| = \dfrac{1-V^n}{i}$	$\dfrac{1}{A\overline{n}|} = \dfrac{i}{1-V^n}$				

YEAR										PERIODS
	1.145 000	1.000 000	1.000 000 0000	.873 362	.873 362	1.145 000 0000	114.50	.145 000	14.50	1
1	1.145 000	1.000 000	1.000 000 0000	.873 362	.873 362	1.145 000 0000	114.50	.145 000	14.50	1
2	1.311 025	2.145 000	.466 200 4662	.762 762	1.636 124	.611 200 4662	61.13	.222 401	11.12	2
3	1.501 124	3.456 025	.289 349 7588	.666 168	2.302 292	.434 349 7588	43.44	.303 049	10.10	3
4	1.718 787	4.957 149	.201 728 8719	.581 806	2.884 098	.346 728 8719	34.68	.386 915	9.67	4
5	1.968 011	6.675 935	.149 791 7481	.508 127	3.392 225	.294 791 7481	29.48	.473 959	9.48	5
6	2.253 372	8.643 946	.115 687 9076	.443 779	3.836 005	.260 687 9076	26.07	.564 127	9.40	6
7	2.580 111	10.897 318	.091 765 6994	.387 580	4.223 585	.236 765 6994	23.68	.657 360	9.39	7
8	2.954 227	13.477 429	.074 198 1278	.338 498	4.562 083	.219 198 1278	21.92	.753 585	9.42	8
9	3.382 590	16.431 656	.060 858 1379	.295 631	4.857 714	.205 858 1379	20.59	.852 723	9.47	9
10	3.873 066	19.814 246	.050 468 7376	.258 193	5.115 908	.195 468 7376	19.55	.954 687	9.55	10
11	4.434 660	23.687 312	.042 216 6937	.225 496	5.341 404	.187 216 6937	18.73	1.059 384	9.63	11
12	5.077 686	28.121 972	.035 559 3835	.196 940	5.538 344	.180 559 3835	18.06	1.166 713	9.72	12
13	5.813 950	33.199 658	.030 120 7919	.172 000	5.710 344	.175 120 7919	17.52	1.276 570	9.82	13
14	6.656 973	39.013 609	.025 632 0815	.150 218	5.860 563	.170 632 0815	17.07	1.388 849	9.92	14
15	7.622 234	45.670 582	.021 895 9329	.131 195	5.991 758	.166 895 9329	16.69	1.503 439	10.02	15
16	8.727 458	53.292 816	.018 764 2550	.114 581	6.106 339	.163 764 2550	16.38	1.620 228	10.13	16
17	9.992 940	62.020 275	.016 123 7596	.100 071	6.206 409	.161 123 7596	16.12	1.739 104	10.23	17
18	11.441 916	72.013 215	.013 886 3402	.087 398	6.293 807	.158 886 3402	15.89	1.859 954	10.33	18
19	13.100 994	83.455 131	.011 982 4868	.076 330	6.370 137	.156 982 4868	15.70	1.982 660	10.44	19
20	15.000 638	96.556 125	.010 356 6708	.066 664	6.436 801	.155 356 6708	15.54	2.107 133	10.54	20
21	17.175 731	111.556 763	.008 964 0464	.058 222	6.495 023	.153 964 0464	15.40	2.233 245	10.63	21
22	19.666 212	128.732 494	.007 768 0465	.050 849	6.545 871	.152 768 0465	15.28	2.360 897	10.73	22
23	22.517 812	148.398 705	.006 738 6033	.044 409	6.590 281	.151 738 6033	15.18	2.489 988	10.83	23
24	25.782 895	170.916 517	.005 850 8096	.038 785	6.629 066	.150 850 8096	15.09	2.620 419	10.92	24
25	29.521 415	196.699 412	.005 083 8993	.033 874	6.662 940	.150 083 8993	15.01	2.752 097	11.01	25
26	33.802 020	226.220 827	.004 420 4595	.029 584	6.692 524	.149 420 4595	14.95	2.884 932	11.10	26
27	38.703 313	260.022 847	.003 845 8159	.025 838	6.718 362	.148 845 8159	14.89	3.018 837	11.18	27
28	44.315 293	298.726 160	.003 347 5475	.022 566	6.740 927	.148 347 5475	14.84	3.153 731	11.26	28
29	50.741 011	343.041 453	.002 915 0996	.019 708	6.760 635	.147 915 0996	14.80	3.289 538	11.34	29
30	58.098 457	393.782 464	.002 539 4732	.017 212	6.777 847	.147 539 4732	14.76	3.426 184	11.42	30
31	66.522 734	451.880 921	.002 212 9724	.015 032	6.792 880	.147 212 9724	14.73	3.563 602	11.50	31
32	76.168 530	518.403 655	.001 928 9987	.013 129	6.806 008	.146 928 9987	14.70	3.701 728	11.57	32
33	87.212 967	594.572 185	.001 681 8816	.011 466	6.817 475	.146 681 8816	14.67	3.840 502	11.64	33
34	99.858 847	681.785 151	.001 466 7377	.010 014	6.827 489	.146 466 7377	14.65	3.979 869	11.71	34
35	114.338 380	781.643 998	.001 279 3548	.008 746	6.836 235	.146 279 3548	14.63	4.119 777	11.77	35
36	130.917 445	895.982 378	.001 116 0934	.007 638	6.843 873	.146 116 0934	14.62	4.260 179	11.83	36
37	149.900 474	1026.899 823	.000 973 8048	.006 671	6.850 544	.145 973 8048	14.60	4.401 031	11.89	37
38	171.636 043	1176.800 297	.000 849 7619	.005 826	6.856 370	.145 849 7619	14.59	4.542 291	11.95	38
39	196.523 269	1348.436 340	.000 741 5997	.005 088	6.861 459	.145 741 5997	14.58	4.683 922	12.01	39
40	225.019 143	1544.959 609	.000 647 2661	.004 444	6.865 903	.145 647 2661	14.57	4.825 891	12.06	40
41	257.646 919	1769.978 753	.000 564 9785	.003 881	6.869 784	.145 564 9785	14.56	4.968 164	12.12	41
42	295.005 722	2027.625 672	.000 493 1877	.003 390	6.873 174	.145 493 1877	14.55	5.110 714	12.17	42
43	337.781 552	2322.631 394	.000 430 5461	.002 960	6.876 135	.145 430 5461	14.55	5.253 513	12.22	43
44	386.759 877	2660.412 947	.000 375 8815	.002 586	6.878 720	.145 375 8815	14.54	5.396 539	12.26	44
45	442.840 059	3047.172 824	.000 328 1731	.002 258	6.880 978	.145 328 1731	14.54	5.539 768	12.31	45
46	507.051 868	3490.012 883	.000 286 5319	.001 972	6.882 950	.145 286 5319	14.53	5.683 180	12.35	46
47	580.574 389	3997.064 751	.000 250 1836	.001 722	6.884 673	.145 250 1836	14.53	5.826 759	12.40	47
48	664.757 675	4577.639 140	.000 218 4532	.001 504	6.886 177	.145 218 4532	14.53	5.970 486	12.44	48
49	761.147 538	5242.396 816	.000 190 7524	.001 314	6.887 491	.145 190 7524	14.52	6.114 347	12.48	49
50	871.513 931	6003.544 354	.000 166 5683	.001 147	6.888 638	.145 166 5683	14.52	6.258 328	12.52	50

Effective Rate is 14.50 %

Annual Percentage Rate is 14.50 %

ANNUAL COMPOUND INTEREST AND ANNUITY

14.75 % A

Amount Of 1	Amount Of 1 Per Period	Sinking Fund Payment	Present Worth Of 1	Present Worth of 1 Per Period	Periodic Payment To Amortize 1	Constant Annual Percent	Total Interest	Annual Add On Rate
What a single $ 1 deposit grows to in the future. The deposit is made at the beginning of the first period.	What a series of $ 1 deposits grow to in the future. A deposit is made at the end of each period.	The amount to be deposited at the end of each period that grows to $ 1 in the future.	What $ 1 to be paid in the future is worth today. Value today of a single $ 1 payment tomorrow.	What $ 1 to be paid at the end of each period is worth today. Value today of a series of $ 1 payments tomorrow.	The mortgage payment to amortize a loan of $ 1. An annuity certain, payable at the end of each period, worth $ 1 today.	The annual payment, including interest and principal, to amortize completely a loan of $ 100.	The total interest paid over the term on a loan of $1. The loan is amortized by regular periodic payments.	The average annual interest rate on a loan that is completely amortized by regular periodic payments.

$$S = (1+i)^n \qquad S\overline{n}| = \frac{(1+i)^n - 1}{i} \qquad \frac{1}{S\overline{n}|} = \frac{i}{(1+i)^n - 1} \qquad V^n = \frac{1}{(1+i)^n} \qquad A\overline{n}| = \frac{1-V^n}{i} \qquad \frac{1}{A\overline{n}|} = \frac{i}{1-V^n}$$

YEAR   **PERIODS**

	1.147 500	1.000 000	1.000 000 0000	.871 460	.871 460	1.147 500 0000	114.75	.147 500	14.75 1

Year	Amount Of 1	Amount Of 1 Per Period	Sinking Fund Payment	Present Worth Of 1	Present Worth of 1 Per Period	Periodic Payment To Amortize 1	Constant Annual Percent	Total Interest	Annual Add On Rate	Periods
1	1.147 500	1.000 000	1.000 000 0000	.871 460	.871 460	1.147 500 0000	114.75	.147 500	14.75	1
2	1.316 756	2.147 500	.465 657 7416	.759 442	1.630 902	.613 157 7416	61.32	.226 315	11.32	2
3	1.510 978	3.464 256	.288 662 2489	.661 823	2.292 725	.436 162 2489	43.62	.308 487	10.28	3
4	1.733 847	4.975 234	.200 995 5694	.576 752	2.869 477	.348 495 5694	34.85	.393 982	9.85	4
5	1.989 589	6.709 081	.149 051 7091	.502 616	3.372 093	.296 551 7091	29.66	.482 759	9.66	5
6	2.283 054	8.698 671	.114 960 0961	.438 010	3.810 103	.262 460 0961	26.25	.574 761	9.58	6
7	2.619 804	10.981 724	.091 060 3800	.381 708	4.191 811	.238 560 3800	23.86	.669 923	9.57	7
8	3.006 225	13.601 529	.073 521 1472	.332 643	4.524 454	.221 021 1472	22.11	.768 169	9.60	8
9	3.449 644	16.607 754	.060 212 8369	.289 885	4.814 339	.207 712 8369	20.78	.869 416	9.66	9
10	3.958 466	20.057 398	.049 856 9156	.252 623	5.066 962	.197 356 9156	19.74	.973 569	9.74	10
11	4.542 340	24.015 864	.041 639 1428	.220 151	5.287 113	.189 139 1428	18.92	1.080 531	9.82	11
12	5.212 335	28.558 204	.035 016 2073	.191 853	5.478 965	.182 516 2073	18.26	1.190 194	9.92	12
13	5.981 155	33.770 539	.029 611 6088	.167 192	5.646 157	.177 111 6088	17.72	1.302 451	10.02	13
14	6.863 375	39.751 694	.025 156 1607	.145 701	5.791 858	.172 656 1607	17.27	1.417 186	10.12	14
15	7.875 723	46.615 069	.021 452 2906	.126 972	5.918 831	.168 952 2906	16.90	1.534 284	10.23	15
16	9.037 392	54.490 791	.018 351 7247	.110 651	6.029 482	.165 851 7247	16.59	1.653 628	10.34	16
17	10.370 407	63.528 183	.015 741 0452	.096 428	6.125 910	.163 241 0452	16.33	1.775 098	10.44	17
18	11.900 042	73.898 590	.013 532 0579	.084 033	6.209 944	.161 032 0579	16.11	1.898 577	10.55	18
19	13.655 298	85.798 632	.011 655 1975	.073 232	6.283 175	.159 155 1975	15.92	2.023 949	10.65	19
20	15.669 455	99.453 930	.010 054 9068	.063 818	6.346 994	.157 554 9068	15.76	2.151 098	10.76	20
21	17.980 699	115.123 385	.008 686 3325	.055 615	6.402 609	.156 186 3325	15.62	2.279 913	10.86	21
22	20.632 852	133.104 084	.007 512 9175	.048 466	6.451 075	.155 012 9175	15.51	2.410 284	10.96	22
23	23.676 198	153.736 937	.006 504 6177	.042 237	6.493 312	.154 004 6177	15.41	2.542 106	11.05	23
24	27.168 437	177.413 135	.005 636 5612	.036 807	6.530 119	.153 136 5612	15.32	2.675 277	11.15	24
25	31.175 782	204.581 573	.004 888 0258	.032 076	6.562 195	.152 388 0258	15.24	2.809 701	11.24	25
26	35.774 210	235.757 354	.004 241 6492	.027 953	6.590 148	.151 741 6492	15.18	2.945 283	11.33	26
27	41.050 906	271.531 564	.003 682 8131	.024 360	6.614 508	.151 182 8131	15.12	3.081 936	11.41	27
28	47.105 914	312.582 470	.003 199 1557	.021 229	6.635 737	.150 699 1557	15.07	3.219 576	11.50	28
29	54.054 037	359.688 384	.002 780 1843	.018 500	6.654 237	.150 280 1843	15.03	3.358 125	11.58	29
30	62.027 007	413.742 421	.002 416 9627	.016 122	6.670 359	.149 916 9627	15.00	3.497 509	11.66	30
31	71.175 991	475.769 428	.002 101 8585	.014 050	6.684 409	.149 601 8585	14.97	3.637 658	11.73	31
32	81.674 449	546.945 419	.001 828 3360	.012 244	6.696 653	.149 328 3360	14.94	3.778 507	11.81	32
33	93.721 431	628.619 868	.001 590 7865	.010 670	6.707 323	.149 090 7865	14.91	3.919 996	11.88	33
34	107.545 342	722.341 299	.001 384 3871	.009 298	6.716 621	.148 884 3871	14.89	4.062 069	11.95	34
35	123.408 279	829.886 640	.001 204 9839	.008 103	6.724 724	.148 704 9839	14.88	4.204 674	12.01	35
36	141.611 001	953.294 920	.001 048 9933	.007 062	6.731 786	.148 548 9933	14.86	4.347 764	12.08	36
37	162.498 623	1094.905 920	.000 913 3205	.006 154	6.737 940	.148 413 3205	14.85	4.491 293	12.14	37
38	186.467 170	1257.404 543	.000 795 2890	.005 363	6.743 303	.148 295 2890	14.83	4.635 221	12.20	38
39	213.971 078	1443.871 714	.000 692 5823	.004 674	6.747 976	.148 192 5823	14.82	4.779 511	12.26	39
40	245.531 812	1657.842 791	.000 603 1935	.004 073	6.752 049	.148 103 1935	14.82	4.924 128	12.31	40
41	281.747 754	1903.374 603	.000 525 3827	.003 549	6.755 598	.148 025 3827	14.81	5.069 041	12.36	41
42	323.305 548	2185.122 357	.000 457 6403	.003 093	6.758 691	.147 957 6403	14.80	5.214 221	12.41	42
43	370.993 116	2508.427 905	.000 398 6561	.002 695	6.761 387	.147 898 6561	14.79	5.359 642	12.46	43
44	425.714 601	2879.421 020	.000 347 2920	.002 349	6.763 736	.147 847 2920	14.79	5.505 281	12.51	44
45	488.507 504	3305.135 621	.000 302 5594	.002 047	6.765 783	.147 802 5594	14.79	5.651 115	12.56	45
46	560.562 361	3793.643 125	.000 263 5989	.001 784	6.767 567	.147 763 5989	14.78	5.797 126	12.60	46
47	643.245 309	4354.205 486	.000 229 6630	.001 555	6.769 121	.147 729 6630	14.78	5.943 294	12.65	47
48	738.123 992	4997.450 795	.000 200 1020	.001 355	6.770 476	.147 700 1020	14.78	6.089 605	12.69	48
49	846.997 281	5735.574 787	.000 174 3504	.001 181	6.771 657	.147 674 3504	14.77	6.236 043	12.73	49
50	971.929 380	6582.572 069	.000 151 9163	.001 029	6.772 686	.147 651 9163	14.77	6.382 596	12.77	50

Effective Rate is 14.75 %

8 - 475

Annual Percentage Rate is 14.75 %

ANNUAL COMPOUND INTEREST AND ANNUITY

15.00 % A

Amount Of 1	Amount Of 1 Per Period	Sinking Fund Payment	Present Worth Of 1	Present Worth of 1 Per Period	Periodic Payment To Amortize 1	Constant Annual Percent	Total Interest	Annual Add On Rate
What a single $ 1 deposit grows to in the future. The deposit is made at the beginning of the first period.	What a series of $ 1 deposits grow to in the future. A deposit is made at the end of each period.	The amount to be deposited at the end of each period that grows to $ 1 in the future.	What $ 1 to be paid in the future is worth today. Value today of a single $ 1 payment tomorrow.	What $ 1 to be paid at the end of each period is worth today. Value today of a series of $ 1 payments tomorrow.	The mortgage payment to amortize a loan of $ 1. An annuity certain, payable at the end of each period, worth $ 1 today.	The annual payment, including interest and principal, to amortize completely a loan of $ 100.	The total interest paid over the term on a loan of $1. The loan is amortized by regular periodic payments.	The average annual interest rate on a loan that is completely amortized by regular periodic payments.
$S = (1+i)^n$	$S\overline{n}| = \dfrac{(1+i)^n - 1}{i}$	$\dfrac{1}{S\overline{n}|} = \dfrac{i}{(1+i)^n - 1}$	$V^n = \dfrac{1}{(1+i)^n}$	$A\overline{n}| = \dfrac{1 - V^n}{i}$	$\dfrac{1}{A\overline{n}|} = \dfrac{i}{1 - V^n}$			

YEAR / **PERIODS**

	Amount Of 1	Amount Of 1 Per Period	Sinking Fund Payment	Present Worth Of 1	Present Worth of 1 Per Period	Periodic Payment To Amortize 1	Constant Annual Percent	Total Interest	Annual Add On Rate	
	1.150 000	1.000 000	1.000 000 0000	.869 565	.869 565	1.150 000 0000	115.00	.150 000	15.00	1
1	1.150 000	1.000 000	1.000 000 0000	.869 565	.869 565	1.150 000 0000	115.00	.150 000	15.00	1
2	1.322 500	2.150 000	.465 116 2791	.756 144	1.625 709	.615 116 2791	61.52	.230 233	11.51	2
3	1.520 875	3.472 500	.287 976 9618	.657 516	2.283 225	.437 976 9618	43.80	.313 931	10.46	3
4	1.749 006	4.993 375	.200 265 3516	.571 753	2.854 978	.350 265 3516	35.03	.401 061	10.03	4
5	2.011 357	6.742 381	.148 315 5525	.497 177	3.352 155	.298 315 5525	29.84	.491 578	9.83	5
6	2.313 061	8.753 738	.114 236 9066	.432 328	3.784 483	.264 236 9066	26.43	.585 421	9.76	6
7	2.660 020	11.066 799	.090 360 3636	.375 937	4.160 420	.240 360 3636	24.04	.682 523	9.75	7
8	3.059 023	13.726 819	.072 850 0896	.326 902	4.487 322	.222 850 0896	22.29	.782 801	9.79	8
9	3.517 876	16.785 842	.059 574 0150	.284 262	4.771 584	.209 574 0150	20.96	.886 166	9.85	9
10	4.045 558	20.303 718	.049 252 0625	.247 185	5.018 769	.199 252 0625	19.93	.992 521	9.93	10
11	4.652 391	24.349 276	.041 068 9830	.214 943	5.233 712	.191 068 9830	19.11	1.101 759	10.02	11
12	5.350 250	29.001 667	.034 480 7761	.186 907	5.420 619	.184 480 7761	18.45	1.213 769	10.11	12
13	6.152 788	34.351 917	.029 110 4565	.162 528	5.583 147	.179 110 4565	17.92	1.328 436	10.22	13
14	7.075 706	40.504 705	.024 688 4898	.141 329	5.724 476	.174 688 4898	17.47	1.445 639	10.33	14
15	8.137 062	47.580 411	.021 017 0526	.122 894	5.847 370	.171 017 0526	17.11	1.565 256	10.44	15
16	9.357 621	55.717 472	.017 947 6914	.106 865	5.954 235	.167 947 6914	16.80	1.687 163	10.54	16
17	10.761 264	65.075 093	.015 366 8623	.092 926	6.047 161	.165 366 8623	16.54	1.811 237	10.65	17
18	12.375 454	75.836 357	.013 186 2874	.080 805	6.127 966	.163 186 2874	16.32	1.937 353	10.76	18
19	14.231 772	88.211 811	.011 336 3504	.070 265	6.198 231	.161 336 3504	16.14	2.065 391	10.87	19
20	16.366 537	102.443 583	.009 761 4704	.061 100	6.259 331	.159 761 4704	15.98	2.195 229	10.98	20
21	18.821 518	118.810 120	.008 416 7914	.053 131	6.312 462	.158 416 7914	15.85	2.326 753	11.08	21
22	21.644 746	137.631 638	.007 265 7713	.046 201	6.358 663	.157 265 7713	15.73	2.459 847	11.18	22
23	24.891 458	159.276 384	.006 278 3947	.040 174	6.398 837	.156 278 3947	15.63	2.594 403	11.28	23
24	28.625 176	184.167 841	.005 429 8296	.034 934	6.433 771	.155 429 8296	15.55	2.730 316	11.38	24
25	32.918 953	212.793 017	.004 699 4023	.030 378	6.464 149	.154 699 4023	15.47	2.867 485	11.47	25
26	37.856 796	245.711 970	.004 069 8058	.026 415	6.490 564	.154 069 8058	15.41	3.005 815	11.56	26
27	43.535 315	283.568 766	.003 526 4815	.022 970	6.513 534	.153 526 4815	15.36	3.145 215	11.65	27
28	50.065 612	327.104 080	.003 057 1309	.019 974	6.533 508	.153 057 1309	15.31	3.285 600	11.73	28
29	57.575 454	377.169 693	.002 651 3265	.017 369	6.550 877	.152 651 3265	15.27	3.426 888	11.82	29
30	66.211 772	434.745 146	.002 300 1982	.015 103	6.565 980	.152 300 1982	15.24	3.569 006	11.90	30
31	76.143 538	500.956 918	.001 996 1796	.013 133	6.579 113	.151 996 1796	15.20	3.711 882	11.97	31
32	87.565 068	577.100 456	.001 732 8006	.011 420	6.590 533	.151 732 8006	15.18	3.855 450	12.05	32
33	100.699 829	664.665 524	.001 504 5161	.009 931	6.600 463	.151 504 5161	15.16	3.999 649	12.12	33
34	115.804 803	765.365 353	.001 306 5655	.008 635	6.609 099	.151 306 5655	15.14	4.144 423	12.19	34
35	133.175 523	881.170 156	.001 134 8546	.007 509	6.616 607	.151 134 8546	15.12	4.289 720	12.26	35
36	153.151 852	1014.345 680	.000 985 8572	.006 529	6.623 137	.150 985 8572	15.10	4.435 491	12.32	36
37	176.124 630	1167.497 532	.000 856 5329	.005 678	6.628 815	.150 856 5329	15.09	4.581 692	12.38	37
38	202.543 324	1343.622 161	.000 744 2569	.004 937	6.633 752	.150 744 2569	15.08	4.728 282	12.44	38
39	232.924 823	1546.165 485	.000 646 7613	.004 293	6.638 045	.150 646 7613	15.07	4.875 224	12.50	39
40	267.863 546	1779.090 308	.000 562 0850	.003 733	6.641 778	.150 562 0850	15.06	5.022 483	12.56	40
41	308.043 078	2046.953 854	.000 488 5308	.003 246	6.645 025	.150 488 5308	15.05	5.170 030	12.61	41
42	354.249 540	2354.996 933	.000 424 6290	.002 823	6.647 848	.150 424 6290	15.05	5.317 834	12.66	42
43	407.386 971	2709.246 473	.000 369 1063	.002 455	6.650 302	.150 369 1063	15.04	5.465 872	12.71	43
44	468.495 017	3116.633 443	.000 320 8590	.002 134	6.652 437	.150 320 8590	15.04	5.614 118	12.76	44
45	538.769 269	3585.128 460	.000 278 9300	.001 856	6.654 293	.150 278 9300	15.03	5.762 552	12.81	45
46	619.584 659	4123.897 729	.000 242 4890	.001 614	6.655 907	.150 242 4890	15.03	5.911 155	12.85	46
47	712.522 358	4743.482 388	.000 210 8156	.001 403	6.657 310	.150 210 8156	15.03	6.059 908	12.89	47
48	819.400 712	5456.004 746	.000 183 2843	.001 220	6.658 531	.150 183 2843	15.02	6.208 798	12.94	48
49	942.310 819	6275.405 458	.000 159 3523	.001 061	6.659 592	.150 159 3523	15.02	6.357 808	12.98	49
50	1083.657 442	7217.716 277	.000 138 5480	.000 923	6.660 515	.150 138 5480	15.02	6.506 927	13.01	50

Effective Rate is 15.00 %

Annual Percentage Rate is 15.00 %

ANNUAL COMPOUND INTEREST AND ANNUITY

Amount Of 1	Amount Of 1 Per Period	Sinking Fund Payment	Present Worth Of 1	Present Worth of 1 Per Period	Periodic Payment To Amortize 1	Constant Annual Percent	Total Interest	Annual Add On Rate
What a single $ 1 deposit grows to in the future. The deposit is made at the beginning of the first period.	What a series of $ 1 deposits grow to in the future. A deposit is made at the end of each period.	The amount to be deposited at the end of each period that grows to $ 1 in the future.	What $ 1 to be paid in the future is worth today. Value today of a single $ 1 payment tomorrow.	What $ 1 to be paid at the end of each period is worth today. Value today of a series of $ 1 payments tomorrow.	The mortgage payment to amortize a loan of $ 1. An annuity certain, payable at the end of each period, worth $ 1 today.	The annual payment, including interest and principal, to amortize completely a loan of $ 100.	The total interest paid over the term on a loan of $1. The loan is amortized by regular periodic payments.	The average annual interest rate on a loan that is completely amortized by regular periodic payments.
$S = (1+i)^n$	$S\overline{n} = \dfrac{(1+i)^n - 1}{i}$	$\dfrac{1}{S\overline{n}} = \dfrac{i}{(1+i)^n - 1}$	$V^n = \dfrac{1}{(1+i)^n}$	$A\overline{n} = \dfrac{1-V^n}{i}$	$\dfrac{1}{A\overline{n}} = \dfrac{i}{1-V^n}$			

YEAR   **PERIODS**

	Amount Of 1	Amount Of 1 Per Period	Sinking Fund Payment	Present Worth Of 1	Present Worth of 1 Per Period	Periodic Payment To Amortize 1	Constant Annual Percent	Total Interest	Annual Add On Rate	
	1.160 000	1.000 000	1.000 000 0000	.862 069	.862 069	1.160 000 0000	116.00	.160 000	16.00	1
1	1.160 000	1.000 000	1.000 000 0000	.862 069	.862 069	1.160 000 0000	116.00	.160 000	16.00	1
2	1.345 600	2.160 000	.462 962 9630	.743 163	1.605 232	.622 962 9630	62.30	.245 926	12.30	2
3	1.560 896	3.505 600	.285 257 8731	.640 658	2.245 890	.445 257 8731	44.53	.335 774	11.19	3
4	1.810 639	5.066 496	.197 375 0695	.552 291	2.798 181	.357 375 0695	35.74	.429 500	10.74	4
5	2.100 342	6.877 135	.145 409 3816	.476 113	3.274 294	.305 409 3816	30.55	.527 047	10.54	5
6	2.436 396	8.977 477	.111 389 8702	.410 442	3.684 736	.271 389 8702	27.14	.628 339	10.47	6
7	2.826 220	11.413 873	.087 612 6771	.353 830	4.038 565	.247 612 6771	24.77	.733 289	10.48	7
8	3.278 415	14.240 093	.070 224 2601	.305 025	4.343 591	.230 224 2601	23.03	.841 794	10.52	8
9	3.802 961	17.518 508	.057 082 4868	.262 953	4.606 544	.217 082 4868	21.71	.953 742	10.60	9
10	4.411 435	21.321 469	.046 901 0831	.226 684	4.833 227	.206 901 0831	20.70	1.069 011	10.69	10
11	5.117 265	25.732 904	.038 860 7515	.195 417	5.028 644	.198 860 7515	19.89	1.187 468	10.80	11
12	5.936 027	30.850 169	.032 414 7333	.168 463	5.197 107	.192 414 7333	19.25	1.308 977	10.91	12
13	6.885 791	36.786 196	.027 184 1100	.145 227	5.342 334	.187 184 1100	18.72	1.433 393	11.03	13
14	7.987 518	43.671 987	.022 897 9733	.125 195	5.467 529	.182 897 9733	18.29	1.560 572	11.15	14
15	9.265 521	51.659 505	.019 357 5218	.107 927	5.575 456	.179 357 5218	17.94	1.690 363	11.27	15
16	10.748 004	60.925 026	.016 413 6162	.093 041	5.668 497	.176 413 6162	17.65	1.822 618	11.39	16
17	12.467 685	71.673 030	.013 952 2494	.080 207	5.748 704	.173 952 2494	17.40	1.957 188	11.51	17
18	14.462 514	84.140 715	.011 884 8526	.069 144	5.817 848	.171 884 8526	17.19	2.093 927	11.63	18
19	16.776 517	98.603 230	.010 141 6556	.059 607	5.877 455	.170 141 6556	17.02	2.232 691	11.75	19
20	19.460 759	115.379 747	.008 667 0324	.051 385	5.928 841	.168 667 0324	16.87	2.373 341	11.87	20
21	22.574 481	134.840 506	.007 416 1691	.044 298	5.973 139	.167 416 1691	16.75	2.515 740	11.98	21
22	26.186 398	157.414 987	.006 352 6353	.038 188	6.011 326	.166 352 6353	16.64	2.659 758	12.09	22
23	30.376 222	183.601 385	.005 446 5820	.032 920	6.044 247	.165 446 5820	16.55	2.805 271	12.20	23
24	35.236 417	213.977 607	.004 673 3862	.028 380	6.072 627	.164 673 3862	16.47	2.952 161	12.30	24
25	40.874 244	249.214 024	.004 012 6153	.024 465	6.097 092	.164 012 6153	16.41	3.100 315	12.40	25
26	47.414 123	290.088 267	.003 447 2266	.021 091	6.118 183	.163 447 2266	16.35	3.249 628	12.50	26
27	55.000 382	337.502 390	.002 962 9420	.018 182	6.136 364	.162 962 9420	16.30	3.399 999	12.59	27
28	63.800 444	392.502 773	.002 547 7527	.015 674	6.152 038	.162 547 7527	16.26	3.551 337	12.68	28
29	74.008 515	456.303 216	.002 191 5252	.013 512	6.165 550	.162 191 5252	16.22	3.703 554	12.77	29
30	85.849 877	530.311 731	.001 885 6833	.011 648	6.177 198	.161 885 6833	16.19	3.856 571	12.86	30
31	99.585 857	616.161 608	.001 622 9508	.010 042	6.187 240	.161 622 9508	16.17	4.010 311	12.94	31
32	115.519 594	715.747 465	.001 397 1408	.008 657	6.195 897	.161 397 1408	16.14	4.164 709	13.01	32
33	134.002 729	831.267 059	.001 202 9828	.007 463	6.203 359	.161 202 9828	16.13	4.319 698	13.09	33
34	155.443 166	965.269 789	.001 035 9798	.006 433	6.209 792	.161 035 9798	16.11	4.475 223	13.16	34
35	180.314 073	1120.712 955	.000 892 2891	.005 546	6.215 338	.160 892 2891	16.09	4.631 230	13.23	35
36	209.164 324	1301.027 028	.000 768 6235	.004 781	6.220 119	.160 768 6235	16.08	4.787 670	13.30	36
37	242.630 616	1510.191 352	.000 662 1677	.004 121	6.224 241	.160 662 1677	16.07	4.944 500	13.36	37
38	281.451 515	1752.821 968	.000 570 5086	.003 553	6.227 794	.160 570 5086	16.06	5.101 679	13.43	38
39	326.483 757	2034.273 483	.000 491 5760	.003 063	6.230 857	.160 491 5760	16.05	5.259 171	13.49	39
40	378.721 158	2360.757 241	.000 423 5929	.002 640	6.233 497	.160 423 5929	16.05	5.416 944	13.54	40
41	439.316 544	2739.478 399	.000 365 0330	.002 276	6.235 773	.160 365 0330	16.04	5.574 966	13.60	41
42	509.607 191	3178.794 943	.000 314 5846	.001 962	6.237 736	.160 314 5846	16.04	5.733 213	13.65	42
43	591.144 341	3688.402 134	.000 271 1201	.001 692	6.239 427	.160 271 1201	16.03	5.891 658	13.70	43
44	685.727 436	4279.546 475	.000 233 6696	.001 458	6.240 886	.160 233 6696	16.03	6.050 281	13.75	44
45	795.443 826	4965.273 911	.000 201 3988	.001 257	6.242 143	.160 201 3988	16.03	6.209 063	13.80	45
46	922.714 838	5760.717 737	.000 173 5895	.001 084	6.243 227	.160 173 5895	16.02	6.367 985	13.84	46
47	1070.349 212	6683.432 575	.000 149 6237	.000 934	6.244 161	.160 149 6237	16.02	6.527 032	13.89	47
48	1241.605 086	7753.781 787	.000 128 9693	.000 805	6.244 966	.160 128 9693	16.02	6.686 191	13.93	48
49	1440.261 900	8995.386 873	.000 111 1681	.000 694	6.245 661	.160 111 1681	16.02	6.845 447	13.97	49
50	1670.703 804	10435.648 773	.000 095 8254	.000 599	6.246 259	.160 095 8254	16.01	7.004 791	14.01	50

ANNUAL COMPOUND INTEREST AND ANNUITY

17.00 % A

	Amount Of 1	Amount Of 1 Per Period	Sinking Fund Payment	Present Worth Of 1	Present Worth of 1 Per Period	Periodic Payment To Amortize 1	Constant Annual Percent	Total Interest	Annual Add On Rate	
	What a single $ 1 deposit grows to in the future. The deposit is made at the beginning of the first period.	What a series of $ 1 deposits grow to in the future. A deposit is made at the end of each period.	The amount to be deposited at the end of each period that grows to $ 1 in the future.	What $ 1 to be paid in the future is worth today. Value today of a single $ 1 payment tomorrow.	What $ 1 to be paid at the end of each period is worth today. Value today of a series of $ 1 payments tomorrow.	The mortgage payment to amortize a loan of $ 1. An annuity certain, payable at the end of each period, worth $ 1 today.	The annual payment, including interest and principal, to amortize completely a loan of $ 100.	The total interest paid over the term on a loan of $1. The loan is amortized by regular periodic payments.	The average annual interest rate on a loan that is completely amortized by regular periodic payments.	
	$S = (1+i)^n$	$S\overline{n}| = \dfrac{(1+i)^n - 1}{i}$	$\dfrac{1}{S\overline{n}|} = \dfrac{i}{(1+i)^n - 1}$	$V^n = \dfrac{1}{(1+i)^n}$	$A\overline{n}| = \dfrac{1-V^n}{i}$	$\dfrac{1}{A\overline{n}|} = \dfrac{i}{1-V^n}$				

YEAR										PERIODS
	1.170 000	1.000 000	1.000 000 0000	.854 701	.854 701	1.170 000 0000	117.00	.170 000	17.00	1

YEAR	Amount Of 1	Amount Of 1 Per Period	Sinking Fund Payment	Present Worth Of 1	Present Worth of 1 Per Period	Periodic Payment To Amortize 1	Constant Annual Percent	Total Interest	Annual Add On Rate	PERIODS
1	1.170 000	1.000 000	1.000 000 0000	.854 701	.854 701	1.170 000 0000	117.00	.170 000	17.00	1
2	1.368 900	2.170 000	.460 829 4931	.730 514	1.585 214	.630 829 4931	63.09	.261 659	13.08	2
3	1.601 613	3.538 900	.282 573 6811	.624 371	2.209 585	.452 573 6811	45.26	.357 721	11.92	3
4	1.873 887	5.140 513	.194 533 1137	.533 650	2.743 235	.364 533 1137	36.46	.458 132	11.45	4
5	2.192 448	7.014 400	.142 563 8643	.456 111	3.199 346	.312 563 8643	31.26	.562 819	11.26	5
6	2.565 164	9.206 848	.108 614 8021	.389 839	3.589 185	.278 614 8021	27.87	.671 689	11.19	6
7	3.001 242	11.772 012	.084 947 2428	.333 195	3.922 380	.254 947 2428	25.50	.784 631	11.21	7
8	3.511 453	14.773 255	.067 689 8916	.284 782	4.207 163	.237 689 8916	23.77	.901 519	11.27	8
9	4.108 400	18.284 708	.054 690 5102	.243 404	4.450 566	.224 690 5102	22.47	1.022 215	11.36	9
10	4.806 828	22.393 108	.044 656 5967	.208 037	4.658 604	.214 656 5967	21.47	1.146 566	11.47	10
11	5.623 989	27.199 937	.036 764 7916	.177 810	4.836 413	.206 764 7916	20.68	1.274 413	11.59	11
12	6.580 067	32.823 926	.030 465 5819	.151 974	4.988 387	.200 465 5819	20.05	1.405 587	11.71	12
13	7.698 679	39.403 993	.025 378 1386	.129 892	5.118 280	.195 378 1386	19.54	1.539 916	11.85	13
14	9.007 454	47.102 672	.021 230 2181	.111 019	5.229 299	.191 230 2181	19.13	1.677 223	11.98	14
15	10.538 721	56.110 126	.017 822 0950	.094 888	5.324 187	.187 822 0950	18.79	1.817 331	12.12	15
16	12.330 304	66.648 848	.015 004 0103	.081 101	5.405 288	.185 004 0103	18.51	1.960 064	12.25	16
17	14.426 456	78.979 152	.012 661 5693	.069 317	5.474 605	.182 661 5693	18.27	2.105 247	12.38	17
18	16.878 953	93.405 608	.010 705 9953	.059 245	5.533 851	.180 705 9953	18.08	2.252 708	12.52	18
19	19.748 375	110.284 561	.009 067 4523	.050 637	5.584 488	.179 067 4523	17.91	2.402 282	12.64	19
20	23.105 599	130.032 936	.007 690 3593	.043 280	5.627 767	.177 690 3593	17.77	2.553 807	12.77	20
21	27.033 551	153.138 535	.006 530 0350	.036 991	5.664 758	.176 530 0350	17.66	2.707 131	12.89	21
22	31.629 255	180.172 086	.005 550 2493	.031 616	5.696 375	.175 550 2493	17.56	2.862 105	13.01	22
23	37.006 228	211.801 341	.004 721 4054	.027 022	5.723 397	.174 721 4054	17.48	3.018 592	13.12	23
24	43.297 287	248.807 569	.004 019 1703	.023 096	5.746 493	.174 019 1703	17.41	3.176 460	13.24	24
25	50.657 826	292.104 856	.003 423 4282	.019 740	5.766 234	.173 423 4282	17.35	3.335 586	13.34	25
26	59.269 656	342.762 681	.002 917 4705	.016 872	5.783 106	.172 917 4705	17.30	3.495 854	13.45	26
27	69.345 497	402.032 337	.002 487 3621	.014 421	5.797 526	.172 487 3621	17.25	3.657 159	13.55	27
28	81.134 232	471.377 835	.002 121 4404	.012 325	5.809 851	.172 121 4404	17.22	3.819 400	13.64	28
29	94.927 051	552.512 066	.001 809 9152	.010 534	5.820 386	.171 809 9152	17.19	3.982 488	13.73	29
30	111.064 650	647.439 118	.001 544 5468	.009 004	5.829 390	.171 544 5468	17.16	4.146 336	13.82	30
31	129.945 641	758.503 768	.001 318 3850	.007 696	5.837 085	.171 318 3850	17.14	4.310 870	13.91	31
32	152.036 399	888.449 408	.001 125 5565	.006 577	5.843 663	.171 125 5565	17.12	4.476 018	13.99	32
33	177.882 587	1040.485 808	.000 961 0895	.005 622	5.849 284	.170 961 0895	17.10	4.641 716	14.07	33
34	208.122 627	1218.368 395	.000 820 7698	.004 805	5.854 089	.170 820 7698	17.09	4.807 906	14.14	34
35	243.503 474	1426.491 022	.000 701 0209	.004 107	5.858 196	.170 701 0209	17.08	4.974 536	14.21	35
36	284.899 064	1669.994 496	.000 598 8044	.003 510	5.861 706	.170 598 8044	17.06	5.141 557	14.28	36
37	333.331 905	1954.893 560	.000 511 5368	.003 000	5.864 706	.170 511 5368	17.06	5.308 927	14.35	37
38	389.998 329	2288.225 465	.000 437 0199	.002 564	5.867 270	.170 437 0199	17.05	5.476 607	14.41	38
39	456.298 045	2678.223 794	.000 373 3818	.002 192	5.869 461	.170 373 3818	17.04	5.644 562	14.47	39
40	533.868 713	3134.521 839	.000 319 0279	.001 873	5.871 335	.170 319 0279	17.04	5.812 761	14.53	40
41	624.626 394	3668.390 552	.000 272 5991	.001 601	5.872 936	.170 272 5991	17.03	5.981 177	14.59	41
42	730.812 881	4293.016 946	.000 232 9364	.001 368	5.874 304	.170 232 9364	17.03	6.149 783	14.64	42
43	855.051 071	5023.829 827	.000 199 0513	.001 170	5.875 473	.170 199 0513	17.02	6.318 559	14.69	43
44	1000.409 753	5878.880 897	.000 170 1004	.001 000	5.876 473	.170 170 1004	17.02	6.487 484	14.74	44
45	1170.479 411	6879.290 650	.000 145 3638	.000 854	5.877 327	.170 145 3638	17.02	6.656 541	14.79	45
46	1369.460 910	8049.770 061	.000 124 2272	.000 730	5.878 058	.170 124 2272	17.02	6.825 714	14.84	46
47	1602.269 265	9419.230 971	.000 106 1658	.000 624	5.878 682	.170 106 1658	17.02	6.994 990	14.88	47
48	1874.655 040	11021.500 236	.000 090 7317	.000 533	5.879 215	.170 090 7317	17.01	7.164 355	14.93	48
49	2193.346 397	12896.155 276	.000 077 5425	.000 456	5.879 671	.170 077 5425	17.01	7.333 800	14.97	49
50	2566.215 284	15089.501 673	.000 066 2712	.000 390	5.880 061	.170 066 2712	17.01	7.503 314	15.01	50

	Amount Of 1	Amount Of 1 Per Period	Sinking Fund Payment	Present Worth Of 1	Present Worth of 1 Per Period	Periodic Payment To Amortize 1	Constant Annual Percent	Total Interest	Annual Add On Rate	
	What a single $ 1 deposit grows to in the future. The deposit is made at the beginning of the first period.	What a series of $ 1 deposits grow to in the future. A deposit is made at the end of each period.	The amount to be deposited at the end of each period that grows to $ 1 in the future.	What $ 1 to be paid in the future is worth today. Value today of a single $ 1 payment tomorrow.	What $ 1 to be paid at the end of each period is worth today. Value today of a series of $ 1 payments tomorrow.	The mortgage payment to amortize a loan of $ 1. An annuity certain, payable at the end of each period, worth $ 1 today.	The annual payment, including interest and principal, to amortize completely a loan of $ 100.	The total interest paid over the term on a loan of $1. The loan is amortized by regular periodic payments.	The average annual interest rate on a loan that is completely amortized by regular periodic payments.	
	$S = (1+i)^n$	$S\overline{n}| = \dfrac{(1+i)^n - 1}{i}$	$\dfrac{1}{S\overline{n}|} = \dfrac{i}{(1+i)^n - 1}$	$V^n = \dfrac{1}{(1+i)^n}$	$A\overline{n}| = \dfrac{1-V^n}{i}$	$\dfrac{1}{A\overline{n}|} = \dfrac{i}{1-V^n}$				

YEAR										PERIODS
	1.180 000	1.000 000	1.000 000 0000	.847 458	.847 458	1.180 000 0000	118.00	.180 000	18.00	1

1	1.180 000	1.000 000	1.000 000 0000	.847 458	.847 458	1.180 000 0000	118.00	.180 000	18.00	1
2	1.392 400	2.180 000	.458 715 5963	.718 184	1.565 642	.638 715 5963	63.88	.277 431	13.87	2
3	1.643 032	3.572 400	.279 923 8607	.608 631	2.174 273	.459 923 8607	46.00	.379 772	12.66	3
4	1.938 778	5.215 432	.191 738 6709	.515 789	2.690 062	.371 738 6709	37.18	.486 955	12.17	4
5	2.287 758	7.154 210	.139 777 8418	.437 109	3.127 171	.319 777 8418	31.98	.598 889	11.98	5
6	2.699 554	9.441 968	.105 910 1292	.370 432	3.497 603	.285 910 1292	28.60	.715 461	11.92	6
7	3.185 474	12.141 522	.082 361 9994	.313 925	3.811 528	.262 361 9994	26.24	.836 534	11.95	7
8	3.758 859	15.326 996	.065 244 3589	.266 038	4.077 566	.245 244 3589	24.53	.961 955	12.02	8
9	4.435 454	19.085 855	.052 394 8239	.225 456	4.303 022	.232 394 8239	23.24	1.091 553	12.13	9
10	5.233 836	23.521 309	.042 514 6413	.191 064	4.494 086	.222 514 6413	22.26	1.225 146	12.25	10
11	6.175 926	28.755 144	.034 776 3862	.161 919	4.656 005	.214 776 3862	21.48	1.362 540	12.39	11
12	7.287 593	34.931 070	.028 627 8089	.137 220	4.793 225	.208 627 8089	20.87	1.503 534	12.53	12
13	8.599 359	42.218 663	.023 686 2073	.116 288	4.909 513	.203 686 2073	20.37	1.647 921	12.68	13
14	10.147 244	50.818 022	.019 678 0583	.098 549	5.008 062	.199 678 0583	19.97	1.795 493	12.83	14
15	11.973 748	60.965 266	.016 402 7825	.083 516	5.091 578	.196 402 7825	19.65	1.946 042	12.97	15
16	14.129 023	72.939 014	.013 710 0839	.070 776	5.162 354	.193 710 0839	19.38	2.099 361	13.12	16
17	16.672 247	87.068 036	.011 485 2711	.059 980	5.222 334	.191 485 2711	19.15	2.255 250	13.27	17
18	19.673 251	103.740 283	.009 639 4570	.050 830	5.273 164	.189 639 4570	18.97	2.413 510	13.41	18
19	23.214 436	123.413 534	.008 102 8390	.043 077	5.316 241	.188 102 8390	18.82	2.573 954	13.55	19
20	27.393 035	146.627 970	.006 819 9812	.036 506	5.352 746	.186 819 9812	18.69	2.736 400	13.68	20
21	32.323 781	174.021 005	.005 746 4327	.030 937	5.383 683	.185 746 4327	18.58	2.900 675	13.81	21
22	38.142 061	206.344 785	.004 846 2577	.026 218	5.409 901	.184 846 2577	18.49	3.066 618	13.94	22
23	45.007 632	244.486 847	.004 090 1996	.022 218	5.432 120	.184 090 1996	18.41	3.234 075	14.06	23
24	53.109 006	289.494 479	.003 454 2973	.018 829	5.450 949	.183 454 2973	18.35	3.402 903	14.18	24
25	62.668 627	342.603 486	.002 918 8261	.015 957	5.466 906	.182 918 8261	18.30	3.572 971	14.29	25
26	73.948 980	405.272 113	.002 467 4779	.013 523	5.480 429	.182 467 4779	18.25	3.744 154	14.40	26
27	87.259 797	479.221 093	.002 086 7195	.011 460	5.491 889	.182 086 7195	18.21	3.916 341	14.51	27
28	102.966 560	566.480 890	.001 765 2846	.009 712	5.501 601	.181 765 2846	18.18	4.089 428	14.61	28
29	121.500 541	669.447 450	.001 493 7692	.008 230	5.509 831	.181 493 7692	18.15	4.263 319	14.70	29
30	143.370 638	790.947 991	.001 264 3056	.006 975	5.516 806	.181 264 3056	18.13	4.437 929	14.79	30
31	169.177 353	934.318 630	.001 070 2987	.005 911	5.522 717	.181 070 2987	18.11	4.613 179	14.88	31
32	199.629 277	1103.495 983	.000 906 2108	.005 009	5.527 726	.180 906 2108	18.10	4.788 999	14.97	32
33	235.562 547	1303.125 260	.000 767 3859	.004 245	5.531 971	.180 767 3859	18.08	4.965 324	15.05	33
34	277.963 805	1538.687 807	.000 649 9044	.003 598	5.535 569	.180 649 9044	18.07	5.142 097	15.12	34
35	327.997 290	1816.651 612	.000 550 4633	.003 049	5.538 618	.180 550 4633	18.06	5.319 266	15.20	35
36	387.036 802	2144.648 902	.000 466 2768	.002 584	5.541 201	.180 466 2768	18.05	5.496 786	15.27	36
37	456.703 427	2531.685 705	.000 394 9937	.002 190	5.543 391	.180 394 9937	18.04	5.674 615	15.34	37
38	538.910 044	2988.389 132	.000 334 6284	.001 856	5.545 247	.180 334 6284	18.04	5.852 716	15.40	38
39	635.913 852	3527.299 175	.000 283 5030	.001 573	5.546 819	.180 283 5030	18.03	6.031 057	15.46	39
40	750.378 345	4163.213 027	.000 240 1991	.001 333	5.548 152	.180 240 1991	18.03	6.209 608	15.52	40
41	885.446 447	4913.591 372	.000 203 5171	.001 129	5.549 281	.180 203 5171	18.03	6.388 344	15.58	41
42	1044.826 807	5799.037 819	.000 172 4424	.000 957	5.550 238	.180 172 4424	18.02	6.567 243	15.64	42
43	1232.895 633	6843.864 626	.000 146 1163	.000 811	5.551 049	.180 146 1163	18.02	6.746 283	15.69	43
44	1454.816 847	8076.760 259	.000 123 8120	.000 687	5.551 737	.180 123 8120	18.02	6.925 448	15.74	44
45	1716.683 879	9531.577 105	.000 104 9144	.000 583	5.552 319	.180 104 9144	18.02	7.104 721	15.79	45
46	2025.686 977	11248.260 984	.000 088 9026	.000 494	5.552 813	.180 088 9026	18.01	7.284 090	15.84	46
47	2390.310 633	13273.947 961	.000 075 3355	.000 418	5.553 231	.180 075 3355	18.01	7.463 541	15.88	47
48	2820.566 547	15664.258 594	.000 063 8396	.000 355	5.553 586	.180 063 8396	18.01	7.643 064	15.92	48
49	3328.268 525	18484.825 141	.000 054 0984	.000 300	5.553 886	.180 054 0984	18.01	7.822 651	15.96	49
50	3927.356 860	21813.093 666	.000 045 8440	.000 255	5.554 141	.180 045 8440	18.01	8.002 292	16.00	50

Effective Rate is 18.00 %   Annual Percentage Rate is 18.00 %

ANNUAL COMPOUND INTEREST AND ANNUITY

	Amount Of 1	Amount Of 1 Per Period	Sinking Fund Payment	Present Worth Of 1	Present Worth of 1 Per Period	Periodic Payment To Amortize 1	Constant Annual Percent	Total Interest	Annual Add On Rate	
	What a single $ 1 deposit grows to in the future. The deposit is made at the beginning of the first period.	What a series of $ 1 deposits grow to in the future. A deposit is made at the end of each period.	The amount to be deposited at the end of each period that grows to $ 1 in the future.	What $ 1 to be paid in the future is worth today. Value today of a single $ 1 payment tomorrow.	What $ 1 to be paid at the end of each period is worth today. Value today of a series of $ 1 payments tomorrow.	The mortgage payment to amortize a loan of $ 1. An annuity certain, payable at the end of each period, worth $ 1 today.	The annual payment, including interest and principal, to amortize completely a loan of $ 100.	The total interest paid over the term on a loan of $1. The loan is amortized by regular periodic payments.	The average annual interest rate on a loan that is completely amortized by regular periodic payments.	
	$S = (1+i)^n$	$S\overline{n} = \dfrac{(1+i)^n - 1}{i}$	$\dfrac{1}{S\overline{n}} = \dfrac{i}{(1+i)^n - 1}$	$V^n = \dfrac{1}{(1+i)^n}$	$A\overline{n} = \dfrac{1-V^n}{i}$	$\dfrac{1}{A\overline{n}} = \dfrac{i}{1-V^n}$				

YEAR										PERIODS
	1.190 000	1.000 000	1.000 000 0000	.840 336	.840 336	1.190 000 0000	119.00	.190 000	19.00	1

	Amount Of 1	Amount Of 1 Per Period	Sinking Fund Payment	Present Worth Of 1	Present Worth of 1 Per Period	Periodic Payment To Amortize 1	Constant Annual Percent	Total Interest	Annual Add On Rate	
1	1.190 000	1.000 000	1.000 000 0000	.840 336	.840 336	1.190 000 0000	119.00	.190 000	19.00	1
2	1.416 100	2.190 000	.456 621 0046	.706 165	1.546 501	.646 621 0046	64.67	.293 242	14.66	2
3	1.685 159	3.606 100	.277 307 8950	.593 416	2.139 917	.467 307 8950	46.74	.401 924	13.40	3
4	2.005 339	5.291 259	.188 990 9377	.498 669	2.638 586	.378 990 9377	37.90	.515 964	12.90	4
5	2.386 354	7.296 598	.137 050 1666	.419 049	3.057 635	.327 050 1666	32.71	.635 251	12.71	5
6	2.839 761	9.682 952	.103 274 2921	.352 142	3.409 777	.293 274 2921	29.33	.759 646	12.66	6
7	3.379 315	12.522 713	.079 854 9022	.295 918	3.705 695	.269 854 9022	26.99	.888 984	12.70	7
8	4.021 385	15.902 028	.062 885 0604	.248 671	3.954 366	.252 885 0604	25.29	1.023 080	12.79	8
9	4.785 449	19.923 413	.050 192 2023	.208 967	4.163 332	.240 192 2023	24.02	1.161 730	12.91	9
10	5.694 684	24.708 862	.040 471 3094	.175 602	4.338 935	.230 471 3094	23.05	1.304 713	13.05	10
11	6.776 674	30.403 546	.032 890 9005	.147 565	4.486 500	.222 890 9005	22.29	1.451 800	13.20	11
12	8.064 242	37.180 220	.026 896 0219	.124 004	4.610 504	.216 896 0219	21.69	1.602 752	13.36	12
13	9.596 448	45.244 461	.022 102 1529	.104 205	4.714 709	.212 102 1529	21.22	1.757 328	13.52	13
14	11.419 773	54.840 909	.018 234 5628	.087 567	4.802 277	.208 234 5628	20.83	1.915 284	13.68	14
15	13.589 530	66.260 682	.015 091 9063	.073 586	4.875 863	.205 091 9063	20.51	2.076 379	13.84	15
16	16.171 540	79.850 211	.012 523 4484	.061 837	4.937 700	.202 523 4484	20.26	2.240 375	14.00	16
17	19.244 133	96.021 751	.010 414 3070	.051 964	4.989 664	.200 414 3070	20.05	2.407 043	14.16	17
18	22.900 518	115.265 884	.008 675 5939	.043 667	5.033 331	.198 675 5939	19.87	2.576 161	14.31	18
19	27.251 616	138.166 402	.007 237 6496	.036 695	5.070 026	.197 237 6496	19.73	2.747 515	14.46	19
20	32.429 423	165.418 018	.006 045 2907	.030 836	5.100 862	.196 045 2907	19.61	2.920 906	14.60	20
21	38.591 014	197.847 442	.005 054 3994	.025 913	5.126 775	.195 054 3994	19.51	3.096 142	14.74	21
22	45.923 307	236.438 456	.004 229 4304	.021 775	5.148 550	.194 229 4304	19.43	3.273 047	14.88	22
23	54.648 735	282.361 762	.003 541 5560	.018 299	5.166 849	.193 541 5560	19.36	3.451 456	15.01	23
24	65.031 994	337.010 497	.002 967 2666	.015 377	5.182 226	.192 967 2666	19.30	3.631 214	15.13	24
25	77.388 073	402.042 491	.002 487 2993	.012 922	5.195 148	.192 487 2993	19.25	3.812 182	15.25	25
26	92.091 807	479.430 565	.002 085 8078	.010 859	5.206 007	.192 085 8078	19.21	3.994 231	15.36	26
27	109.589 251	571.522 372	.001 749 7128	.009 125	5.215 132	.191 749 7128	19.18	4.177 242	15.47	27
28	130.411 208	681.111 623	.001 468 1881	.007 668	5.222 800	.191 468 1881	19.15	4.361 109	15.58	28
29	155.189 338	811.522 831	.001 232 2512	.006 444	5.229 243	.191 232 2512	19.13	4.545 735	15.68	29
30	184.675 312	966.712 169	.001 034 4341	.005 415	5.234 658	.191 034 4341	19.11	4.731 033	15.77	30
31	219.763 621	1151.387 481	.000 868 5173	.004 550	5.239 209	.190 868 5173	19.09	4.916 924	15.86	31
32	261.518 710	1371.151 103	.000 729 3142	.003 824	5.243 033	.190 729 3142	19.08	5.103 338	15.95	32
33	311.207 264	1632.669 812	.000 612 4937	.003 213	5.246 246	.190 612 4937	19.07	5.290 212	16.03	33
34	370.336 645	1943.877 077	.000 514 4358	.002 700	5.248 946	.190 514 4358	19.06	5.477 491	16.11	34
35	440.700 607	2314.213 721	.000 432 1122	.002 269	5.251 215	.190 432 1122	19.05	5.665 124	16.19	35
36	524.433 722	2754.914 328	.000 362 9877	.001 907	5.253 122	.190 362 9877	19.04	5.853 068	16.26	36
37	624.076 130	3279.348 051	.000 304 9387	.001 602	5.254 724	.190 304 9387	19.04	6.041 283	16.33	37
38	742.650 594	3903.424 180	.000 256 1853	.001 347	5.256 071	.190 256 1853	19.03	6.229 735	16.39	38
39	883.754 207	4646.074 775	.000 215 2355	.001 132	5.257 202	.190 215 2355	19.03	6.418 394	16.46	39
40	1051.667 507	5529.828 982	.000 180 8374	.000 951	5.258 153	.190 180 8374	19.02	6.607 234	16.52	40
41	1251.484 333	6581.496 488	.000 151 9411	.000 799	5.258 952	.190 151 9411	19.02	6.796 230	16.58	41
42	1489.266 356	7832.980 821	.000 127 6653	.000 671	5.259 624	.190 127 6653	19.02	6.985 362	16.63	42
43	1772.226 964	9322.247 177	.000 107 2703	.000 564	5.260 188	.190 107 2703	19.02	7.174 613	16.69	43
44	2108.950 087	11094.474 141	.000 090 1350	.000 474	5.260 662	.190 090 1350	19.01	7.363 966	16.74	44
45	2509.650 603	13203.424 228	.000 075 7379	.000 398	5.261 061	.190 075 7379	19.01	7.553 408	16.79	45
46	2986.484 218	15713.074 831	.000 063 6413	.000 335	5.261 396	.190 063 6413	19.01	7.742 928	16.83	46
47	3553.916 219	18699.559 049	.000 053 4772	.000 281	5.261 677	.190 053 4772	19.01	7.932 513	16.88	47
48	4229.160 301	22253.475 268	.000 044 9368	.000 236	5.261 913	.190 044 9368	19.01	8.122 157	16.92	48
49	5032.700 758	26482.635 569	.000 037 7606	.000 199	5.262 112	.190 037 7606	19.01	8.311 850	16.96	49
50	5988.913 902	31515.336 327	.000 031 7306	.000 167	5.262 279	.190 031 7306	19.01	8.501 587	17.00	50

Effective Rate is 19.00 %

Annual Percentage Rate is 19.00 %

ANNUAL COMPOUND INTEREST AND ANNUITY

20.00 % A

	Amount Of 1	Amount Of 1 Per Period	Sinking Fund Payment	Present Worth Of 1	Present Worth of 1 Per Period	Periodic Payment To Amortize 1	Constant Annual Percent	Total Interest	Annual Add On Rate	
	What a single $ 1 deposit grows to in the future. The deposit is made at the beginning of the first period.	What a series of $ 1 deposits grow to in the future. A deposit is made at the end of each period.	The amount to be deposited at the end of each period that grows to $ 1 in the future.	What $ 1 to be paid in the future is worth today. Value today of a single $ 1 payment tomorrow.	What $ 1 to be paid at the end of each period is worth today. Value today of a series of $ 1 payments tomorrow.	The mortgage payment to amortize a loan of $ 1. An annuity certain, payable at the end of each period, worth $ 1 today.	The annual payment, including interest and principal, to amortize completely a loan of $ 100.	The total interest paid over the term on a loan of $1. The loan is amortized by regular periodic payments.	The average annual interest rate on a loan that is completely amortized by regular periodic payments.	

$$S = (1+i)^n \qquad S\overline{n}| = \frac{(1+i)^n - 1}{i} \qquad \frac{1}{S\overline{n}|} = \frac{i}{(1+i)^n - 1} \qquad V^n = \frac{1}{(1+i)^n} \qquad A\overline{n}| = \frac{1-V^n}{i} \qquad \frac{1}{A\overline{n}|} = \frac{i}{1-V^n}$$

YEAR   **PERIODS**

1.200 000	1.000 000	1.000 000 0000	.833 333	.833 333	1.200 000 0000	120.00	.200 000	20.00	1

YEAR	Amount Of 1	Amount Of 1 Per Period	Sinking Fund Payment	Present Worth Of 1	Present Worth of 1 Per Period	Periodic Payment To Amortize 1	Constant Annual Percent	Total Interest	Annual Add On Rate	PERIODS
1	1.200 000	1.000 000	1.000 000 0000	.833 333	.833 333	1.200 000 0000	120.00	.200 000	20.00	1
2	1.440 000	2.200 000	.454 545 4545	.694 444	1.527 778	.654 545 4545	65.46	.309 091	15.45	2
3	1.728 000	3.640 000	.274 725 2747	.578 704	2.106 481	.474 725 2747	47.48	.424 176	14.14	3
4	2.073 600	5.368 000	.186 289 1207	.482 253	2.588 735	.386 289 1207	38.63	.545 156	13.63	4
5	2.488 320	7.441 600	.134 379 7033	.401 878	2.990 612	.334 379 7033	33.44	.671 899	13.44	5
6	2.985 984	9.929 920	.100 705 7459	.334 898	3.325 510	.300 705 7459	30.08	.804 234	13.40	6
7	3.583 181	12.915 904	.077 423 9263	.279 082	3.604 592	.277 423 9263	27.75	.941 967	13.46	7
8	4.299 817	16.499 085	.060 609 4224	.232 568	3.837 160	.260 609 4224	26.07	1.084 875	13.56	8
9	5.159 780	20.798 902	.048 079 4617	.193 807	4.030 967	.248 079 4617	24.81	1.232 715	13.70	9
10	6.191 736	25.958 682	.038 522 7569	.161 506	4.192 472	.238 522 7569	23.86	1.385 228	13.85	10
11	7.430 084	32.150 419	.031 103 7942	.134 588	4.327 060	.231 103 7942	23.12	1.542 142	14.02	11
12	8.916 100	39.580 502	.025 264 9649	.112 157	4.439 217	.225 264 9649	22.53	1.703 180	14.19	12
13	10.699 321	48.496 603	.020 620 0011	.093 464	4.532 681	.220 620 0011	22.07	1.868 060	14.37	13
14	12.839 185	59.195 923	.016 893 0552	.077 887	4.610 567	.216 893 0552	21.69	2.036 503	14.55	14
15	15.407 022	72.035 108	.013 882 1198	.064 905	4.675 473	.213 882 1198	21.39	2.208 232	14.72	15
16	18.488 426	87.442 129	.011 436 1350	.054 088	4.729 561	.211 436 1350	21.15	2.382 978	14.89	16
17	22.186 111	105.930 555	.009 440 1469	.045 073	4.774 634	.209 440 1469	20.95	2.560 483	15.06	17
18	26.623 333	128.116 666	.007 805 3857	.037 561	4.812 195	.207 805 3857	20.79	2.740 497	15.23	18
19	31.948 000	154.740 000	.006 462 4532	.031 301	4.843 496	.206 462 4532	20.65	2.922 787	15.38	19
20	38.337 600	186.688 000	.005 356 5307	.026 084	4.869 580	.205 356 5307	20.54	3.107 131	15.54	20
21	46.005 120	225.025 600	.004 443 9388	.021 737	4.891 316	.204 443 9388	20.45	3.293 323	15.68	21
22	55.206 144	271.030 719	.003 689 6187	.018 114	4.909 430	.203 689 6187	20.37	3.481 172	15.82	22
23	66.247 373	326.236 863	.003 065 2575	.015 095	4.924 525	.203 065 2575	20.31	3.670 501	15.96	23
24	79.496 847	392.484 236	.002 547 8730	.012 579	4.937 104	.202 547 8730	20.26	3.861 149	16.09	24
25	95.396 217	471.981 083	.002 118 7290	.010 483	4.947 587	.202 118 7290	20.22	4.052 968	16.21	25
26	114.475 460	567.377 300	.001 762 4956	.008 735	4.956 323	.201 762 4956	20.18	4.245 825	16.33	26
27	137.370 552	681.852 760	.001 466 5923	.007 280	4.963 602	.201 466 5923	20.15	4.439 598	16.44	27
28	164.844 662	819.223 312	.001 220 6684	.006 066	4.969 668	.201 220 6684	20.13	4.634 179	16.55	28
29	197.813 595	984.067 974	.001 016 1900	.005 055	4.974 724	.201 016 1900	20.11	4.829 470	16.65	29
30	237.376 314	1181.881 569	.000 846 1085	.004 213	4.978 936	.200 846 1085	20.09	5.025 383	16.75	30
31	284.851 577	1419.257 883	.000 704 5936	.003 511	4.982 447	.200 704 5936	20.08	5.221 842	16.84	31
32	341.821 892	1704.109 459	.000 586 8168	.002 926	4.985 372	.200 586 8168	20.06	5.418 778	16.93	32
33	410.186 270	2045.931 351	.000 488 7750	.002 438	4.987 810	.200 488 7750	20.05	5.616 130	17.02	33
34	492.223 524	2456.117 621	.000 407 1466	.002 032	4.989 842	.200 407 1466	20.05	5.813 843	17.10	34
35	590.668 229	2948.341 146	.000 339 1738	.001 693	4.991 535	.200 339 1738	20.04	6.011 871	17.18	35
36	708.801 875	3539.009 375	.000 282 5649	.001 411	4.992 946	.200 282 5649	20.03	6.210 172	17.25	36
37	850.562 250	4247.811 250	.000 235 4154	.001 176	4.994 122	.200 235 4154	20.03	6.408 710	17.32	37
38	1020.674 700	5098.373 500	.000 196 1410	.000 980	4.995 101	.200 196 1410	20.02	6.607 453	17.39	38
39	1224.809 640	6119.048 200	.000 163 4241	.000 816	4.995 918	.200 163 4241	20.02	6.806 374	17.45	39
40	1469.771 568	7343.857 840	.000 136 1682	.000 680	4.996 598	.200 136 1682	20.02	7.005 447	17.51	40
41	1763.725 882	8813.629 408	.000 113 4606	.000 567	4.997 165	.200 113 4606	20.02	7.204 652	17.57	41
42	2116.471 058	10577.355 289	.000 094 5416	.000 472	4.997 638	.200 094 5416	20.01	7.403 971	17.63	42
43	2539.765 269	12693.826 347	.000 078 7785	.000 394	4.998 031	.200 078 7785	20.01	7.603 387	17.68	43
44	3047.718 323	15233.591 617	.000 065 6444	.000 328	4.998 359	.200 065 6444	20.01	7.802 888	17.73	44
45	3657.261 988	18281.309 940	.000 054 7007	.000 273	4.998 633	.200 054 7007	20.01	8.002 462	17.78	45
46	4388.714 386	21938.571 928	.000 045 5818	.000 228	4.998 861	.200 045 5818	20.01	8.202 097	17.83	46
47	5266.457 263	26327.286 314	.000 037 9834	.000 190	4.999 051	.200 037 9834	20.01	8.401 785	17.88	47
48	6319.748 715	31593.743 576	.000 031 6518	.000 158	4.999 209	.200 031 6518	20.01	8.601 519	17.92	48
49	7583.698 458	37913.492 292	.000 026 3758	.000 132	4.999 341	.200 026 3758	20.01	8.801 292	17.96	49
50	9100.438 150	45497.190 750	.000 021 9794	.000 110	4.999 451	.200 021 9794	20.01	9.001 099	18.00	50

Effective Rate is 20.00 %

8 - 481

Annual Percentage Rate is 20.00 %

TABLE **9**

Days of the Year

This table shows the days of the year, numbered sequentially, for 2 years. The number of days between 2 dates can be found by subtraction. If February 29 falls between the 2 dates, add 1 day.

Example: There are 156 days between June 28 and December 1.

$$December\ 1\ =\ 335$$
$$June\ 28\ \ \ =\ \underline{179}$$
$$156$$

THIS YEAR

DAYS IN EACH MONTH

| | 31 | 28 | 31 | 30 | 31 | 30 | 31 | 31 | 30 | 31 | 30 | 31 |
DAY	JAN	FEB	MAR	APR	MAY	JUN	JUL	AUG	SEP	OCT	NOV	DEC
1	1	32	60	91	121	152	182	213	244	274	305	335
2	2	33	61	92	122	153	183	214	245	275	306	336
3	3	34	62	93	123	154	184	215	246	276	307	337
4	4	35	63	94	124	155	185	216	247	277	308	338
5	5	36	64	95	125	156	186	217	248	278	309	339
6	6	37	65	96	126	157	187	218	249	279	310	340
7	7	38	66	97	127	158	188	219	250	280	311	341
8	8	39	67	98	128	159	189	220	251	281	312	342
9	9	40	68	99	129	160	190	221	252	282	313	343
10	10	41	69	100	130	161	191	222	253	283	314	344
11	11	42	70	101	131	162	192	223	254	284	315	345
12	12	43	71	102	132	163	193	224	255	285	316	346
13	13	44	72	103	133	164	194	225	256	286	317	347
14	14	45	73	104	134	165	195	226	257	287	318	348
15	15	46	74	105	135	166	196	227	258	288	319	349
16	16	47	75	106	136	167	197	228	259	289	320	350
17	17	48	76	107	137	168	198	229	260	290	321	351
18	18	49	77	108	138	169	199	230	261	291	322	352
19	19	50	78	109	139	170	200	231	262	292	323	353
20	20	51	79	110	140	171	201	232	263	293	324	354
21	21	52	80	111	141	172	202	233	264	294	325	355
22	22	53	81	112	142	173	203	234	265	295	326	356
23	23	54	82	113	143	174	204	235	266	296	327	357
24	24	55	83	114	144	175	205	236	267	297	328	358
25	25	56	84	115	145	176	206	237	268	298	329	359
26	26	57	85	116	146	177	207	238	269	299	330	360
27	27	58	86	117	147	178	208	239	270	300	331	361
28	28	59	87	118	148	179	209	240	271	301	332	362
29	29	0	88	119	149	180	210	241	272	302	333	363
30	30	0	89	120	150	181	211	242	273	303	334	364
31	31	0	90	0	151	0	212	243	0	304	0	365

NEXT YEAR

DAYS IN EACH MONTH

| | 31 | 28 | 31 | 30 | 31 | 30 | 31 | 31 | 30 | 31 | 30 | 31 |
	JAN	FEB	MAR	APR	MAY	JUN	JUL	AUG	SEP	OCT	NOV	DEC
1	366	397	425	456	486	517	547	578	609	639	670	700
2	367	398	426	457	487	518	548	579	610	640	671	701
3	368	399	427	458	488	519	549	580	611	641	672	702
4	369	400	428	459	489	520	550	581	612	642	673	703
5	370	401	429	460	490	521	551	582	613	643	674	704
6	371	402	430	461	491	522	552	583	614	644	675	705
7	372	403	431	462	492	523	553	584	615	645	676	706
8	373	404	432	463	493	524	554	585	616	646	677	707
9	374	405	433	464	494	525	555	586	617	647	678	708
10	375	406	434	465	495	526	556	587	618	648	679	709
11	376	407	435	466	496	527	557	588	619	649	680	710
12	377	408	436	467	497	528	558	589	620	650	681	711
13	378	409	437	468	498	529	559	590	621	651	682	712
14	379	410	438	469	499	530	560	591	622	652	683	713
15	380	411	439	470	500	531	561	592	623	653	684	714
16	381	412	440	471	501	532	562	593	624	654	685	715
17	382	413	441	472	502	533	563	594	625	655	686	716
18	383	414	442	473	503	534	564	595	626	656	687	717
19	384	415	443	474	504	535	565	596	627	657	688	718
20	385	416	444	475	505	536	566	597	628	658	689	719
21	386	417	445	476	506	537	567	598	629	659	690	720
22	387	418	446	477	507	538	568	599	630	660	691	721
23	388	419	447	478	508	539	569	600	631	661	692	722
24	389	420	448	479	509	540	570	601	632	662	693	723
25	390	421	449	480	510	541	571	602	633	663	694	724
26	391	422	450	481	511	542	572	603	634	664	695	725
27	392	423	451	482	512	543	573	604	635	665	696	726
28	393	424	452	483	513	544	574	605	636	666	697	727
29	394	0	453	484	514	545	575	606	637	667	698	728
30	395	0	454	485	515	546	576	607	638	668	699	729
31	396	0	455	0	516	0	577	608	0	669	0	730

ADD 1 DAY FOR LEAP YEAR IF FEBRUARY 29 FALLS BETWEEN THE TWO DATES.

TABLE **10**

Days Between Dates

This table shows the number of days between today and the first day of a month within the next year. If February 29 falls between the 2 dates, add 1 day.

Example: There are 156 days between June 28 and December 1. This number can be read directly from the **MAY & JUN** table on page 10-4.

There are 160 days between June 28 and December 5. This is computed by reading the number 156 directly from the table and adding 4, the number of midnights between December 1 and December 5.

Days Between Dates. When the year is evenly divisible by the number of periods, such as 12, 4, or 2, then interest is computed for the period, and the actual number of days in the period is not considered. The rub comes when there is a partial period for which interest is due and the number of days must be computed for interest.

The number of days between dates can be computed by months and days or by exact days.

Months and Days. For this method, a year is 12 30-day months. Days between dates are computed by subtracting 1 date from another. For example, in calculating the 94 days between August 27 and December 1, the arithmetic looks like this:

	Month	*Day*
August 27	8	27
December 1	12	1
Difference	3	4

Based on a 30-day month, the 3 months and 4 days add up to 94 days.

Exact Days. For this method, the days between dates are the exact number of days shown on the calendar. There is no simple way to calculate exact days. Therefore, Tables 9 and 10 number the days of a year so that the days between dates can be found by subtraction. In calculating the actual 96 days between December 1 and August 27, the arithmetic looks like this:

	Day
December 1	335
August 27	− 239
	96

A Day. What is a day? A day is the shortest practical period of time for computing interest; for this purpose, a day includes 1 midnight. For example, money borrowed on Friday and repaid on Monday is at interest for 3 days; however, money borrowed at 12:01 A.M. today and repaid at 11:59 P.M. tomorrow is at interest for 1 day. When counting the days between dates, count the first day but not the last, count the last day but not the first, or count the number of midnights.

A Year. The basis year for calculating interest may be 360 days, 365 days, or, in the case of leap year, 366 days. The basis year is the denominator in the formula for computing interest for 1 day. The formula is:

$$\text{Interest for 1 day} = \frac{\text{Interest rate}}{\text{Basis year}}$$

Depending on which basis year is used in the calculation, interest for 1 day at 8% may be:

$$.08/360 = .00022222,$$
$$.08/365 = .00021918, \text{ or}$$
$$.08/366 = .00021858.$$

The most commonly used basis year, however, is 360 days.

Time Factor. The time factor is the fraction of a year during which money earns interest. In the computation of daily interest, the time factor is expressed as a fraction in which the number of days between dates is the numerator and the basis year is the denominator. The time factor for 1 year may be any one of the following: 360/360, 365/360, 366/360, 365/365, 366/365, or 366/366. The formula is:

$$\text{Time factor} = \frac{\text{Days between dates}}{\text{Basis year}}$$

Days in a Period. The days in a period are the actual number of days in a month, a quarter, or a half year, as shown in the following tables.

Month	*Days*	*Month*	*Days*
Jan	31	July	31
Feb	28*	Aug	31
Mar	31	Sept	30
Apr	30	Oct	31
May	31	Nov	30
June	30	Dec	31

*Add 1 day for leap year. A leap year is a year evenly divisible by 4 (e.g., 1984).

DAYS BETWEEN DATES

Quarter	Days
Jan, Feb, Mar	90*
Feb, Mar, Apr	89*
Mar, Apr, May	92
Apr, May, June	91
May, June, July	92
June, July, Aug	92
July, Aug, Sept	92
Aug, Sept, Oct	92
Sept, Oct, Nov	91
Oct, Nov, Dec	92
Nov, Dec, Jan	92
Dec, Jan, Feb	90*

Semiannual Period	Days
Jan, Feb, Mar, Apr, May, June	181*
Feb, Mar, Apr, May, June, July	181*
Mar, Apr, May, June, July, Aug	184
Apr, May, June, July, Aug, Sept	183
May, June, July, Aug, Sept, Oct	184
June, July, Aug, Sept, Oct, Nov	183
July, Aug, Sept, Oct, Nov, Dec	184
Aug, Sept, Oct, Nov, Dec, Jan	184
Sept, Oct, Nov, Dec, Jan, Feb	181*
Oct, Nov, Dec, Jan, Feb, Mar	182*
Nov, Dec, Jan, Feb, Mar, Apr	181*
Dec, Jan, Feb, Mar, Apr, May	182*

*Add 1 day for leap year. A leap year is a year evenly divisible by 4 (e.g., 1984).

DAYS BETWEEN DATES

DAYS BETWEEN DATES

Description: This table shows the number of days FROM TODAY to the first day in a month within the next year.

Example: The number of days from JAN 1 this year to APR 15 next year is 469. The number is the sum of 455 + 14.

FROM TODAY	THIS YEAR — TO THE FIRST DAY IN THE MONTH OF												NEXT YEAR — TO THE FIRST DAY IN THE MONTH OF											
JAN	JAN	FEB	MAR	APR	MAY	JUN	JUL	AUG	SEP	OCT	NOV	DEC	JAN	FEB	MAR	APR	MAY	JUN	JUL	AUG	SEP	OCT	NOV	DEC
1	0	31	59	90	120	151	181	212	243	273	304	334	365	396	424	455	485	516	546	577	608	638	669	699
2	0	30	58	89	119	150	180	211	242	272	303	333	364	395	423	454	484	515	545	576	607	637	668	698
3	0	29	57	88	118	149	179	210	241	271	302	332	363	394	422	453	483	514	544	575	606	636	667	697
4	0	28	56	87	117	148	178	209	240	270	301	331	362	393	421	452	482	513	543	574	605	635	666	696
5	0	27	55	86	116	147	177	208	239	269	300	330	361	392	420	451	481	512	542	573	604	634	665	695
6	0	26	54	85	115	146	176	207	238	268	299	329	360	391	419	450	480	511	541	572	603	633	664	694
7	0	25	53	84	114	145	175	206	237	267	298	328	359	390	418	449	479	510	540	571	602	632	663	693
8	0	24	52	83	113	144	174	205	236	266	297	327	358	389	417	448	478	509	539	570	601	631	662	692
9	0	23	51	82	112	143	173	204	235	265	296	326	357	388	416	447	477	508	538	569	600	630	661	691
10	0	22	50	81	111	142	172	203	234	264	295	325	356	387	415	446	476	507	537	568	599	629	660	690
11	0	21	49	80	110	141	171	202	233	263	294	324	355	386	414	445	475	506	536	567	598	628	659	689
12	0	20	48	79	109	140	170	201	232	262	293	323	354	385	413	444	474	505	535	566	597	627	658	688
13	0	19	47	78	108	139	169	200	231	261	292	322	353	384	412	443	473	504	534	565	596	626	657	687
14	0	18	46	77	107	138	168	199	230	260	291	321	352	383	411	442	472	503	533	564	595	625	656	686
15	0	17	45	76	106	137	167	198	229	259	290	320	351	382	410	441	471	502	532	563	594	624	655	685
16	0	16	44	75	105	136	166	197	228	258	289	319	350	381	409	440	470	501	531	562	593	623	654	684
17	0	15	43	74	104	135	165	196	227	257	288	318	349	380	408	439	469	500	530	561	592	622	653	683
18	0	14	42	73	103	134	164	195	226	256	287	317	348	379	407	438	468	499	529	560	591	621	652	682
19	0	13	41	72	102	133	163	194	225	255	286	316	347	378	406	437	467	498	528	559	590	620	651	681
20	0	12	40	71	101	132	162	193	224	254	285	315	346	377	405	436	466	497	527	558	589	619	650	680
21	0	11	39	70	100	131	161	192	223	253	284	314	345	376	404	435	465	496	526	557	588	618	649	679
22	0	10	38	69	99	130	160	191	222	252	283	313	344	375	403	434	464	495	525	556	587	617	648	678
23	0	9	37	68	98	129	159	190	221	251	282	312	343	374	402	433	463	494	524	555	586	616	647	677
24	0	8	36	67	97	128	158	189	220	250	281	311	342	373	401	432	462	493	523	554	585	615	646	676
25	0	7	35	66	96	127	157	188	219	249	280	310	341	372	400	431	461	492	522	553	584	614	645	675
26	0	6	34	65	95	126	156	187	218	248	279	309	340	371	399	430	460	491	521	552	583	613	644	674
27	0	5	33	64	94	125	155	186	217	247	278	308	339	370	398	429	459	490	520	551	582	612	643	673
28	0	4	32	63	93	124	154	185	216	246	277	307	338	369	397	428	458	489	519	550	581	611	642	672
29	0	3	31	62	92	123	153	184	215	245	276	306	337	368	396	427	457	488	518	549	580	610	641	671
30	0	2	30	61	91	122	152	183	214	244	275	305	336	367	395	426	456	487	517	548	579	609	640	670
31	0	1	29	60	90	121	151	182	213	243	274	304	335	366	394	425	455	486	516	547	578	608	639	669

FROM TODAY	THIS YEAR — TO THE FIRST DAY IN THE MONTH OF												NEXT YEAR — TO THE FIRST DAY IN THE MONTH OF											
FEB	JAN	FEB	MAR	APR	MAY	JUN	JUL	AUG	SEP	OCT	NOV	DEC	JAN	FEB	MAR	APR	MAY	JUN	JUL	AUG	SEP	OCT	NOV	DEC
1	0	0	28	59	89	120	150	181	212	242	273	303	334	365	393	424	454	485	515	546	577	607	638	668
2	0	0	27	58	88	119	149	180	211	241	272	302	333	364	392	423	453	484	514	545	576	606	637	667
3	0	0	26	57	87	118	148	179	210	240	271	301	332	363	391	422	452	483	513	544	575	605	636	666
4	0	0	25	56	86	117	147	178	209	239	270	300	331	362	390	421	451	482	512	543	574	604	635	665
5	0	0	24	55	85	116	146	177	208	238	269	299	330	361	389	420	450	481	511	542	573	603	634	664
6	0	0	23	54	84	115	145	176	207	237	268	298	329	360	388	419	449	480	510	541	572	602	633	663
7	0	0	22	53	83	114	144	175	206	236	267	297	328	359	387	418	448	479	509	540	571	601	632	662
8	0	0	21	52	82	113	143	174	205	235	266	296	327	358	386	417	447	478	508	539	570	600	631	661
9	0	0	20	51	81	112	142	173	204	234	265	295	326	357	385	416	446	477	507	538	569	599	630	660
10	0	0	19	50	80	111	141	172	203	233	264	294	325	356	384	415	445	476	506	537	568	598	629	659
11	0	0	18	49	79	110	140	171	202	232	263	293	324	355	383	414	444	475	505	536	567	597	628	658
12	0	0	17	48	78	109	139	170	201	231	262	292	323	354	382	413	443	474	504	535	566	596	627	657
13	0	0	16	47	77	108	138	169	200	230	261	291	322	353	381	412	442	473	503	534	565	595	626	656
14	0	0	15	46	76	107	137	168	199	229	260	290	321	352	380	411	441	472	502	533	564	594	625	655
15	0	0	14	45	75	106	136	167	198	228	259	289	320	351	379	410	440	471	501	532	563	593	624	654
16	0	0	13	44	74	105	135	166	197	227	258	288	319	350	378	409	439	470	500	531	562	592	623	653
17	0	0	12	43	73	104	134	165	196	226	257	287	318	349	377	408	438	469	499	530	561	591	622	652
18	0	0	11	42	72	103	133	164	195	225	256	286	317	348	376	407	437	468	498	529	560	590	621	651
19	0	0	10	41	71	102	132	163	194	224	255	285	316	347	375	406	436	467	497	528	559	589	620	650
20	0	0	9	40	70	101	131	162	193	223	254	284	315	346	374	405	435	466	496	527	558	588	619	649
21	0	0	8	39	69	100	130	161	192	222	253	283	314	345	373	404	434	465	495	526	557	587	618	648
22	0	0	7	38	68	99	129	160	191	221	252	282	313	344	372	403	433	464	494	525	556	586	617	647
23	0	0	6	37	67	98	128	159	190	220	251	281	312	343	371	402	432	463	493	524	555	585	616	646
24	0	0	5	36	66	97	127	158	189	219	250	280	311	342	370	401	431	462	492	523	554	584	615	645
25	0	0	4	35	65	96	126	157	188	218	249	279	310	341	369	400	430	461	491	522	553	583	614	644
26	0	0	3	34	64	95	125	156	187	217	248	278	309	340	368	399	429	460	490	521	552	582	613	643
27	0	0	2	33	63	94	124	155	186	216	247	277	308	339	367	398	428	459	489	520	551	581	612	642
28	0	0	1	32	62	93	123	154	185	215	246	276	307	338	366	397	427	458	488	519	550	580	611	641

ADD 1 DAY FOR LEAP YEAR IF FEBRUARY 29 FALLS BETWEEN THE TWO DATES.

Description: This table shows the number of days FROM TODAY to the first day in a month within the next year.

Example: The number of days from MAR 1 this year to APR 15 next year is 410. The number is the sum of 396 + 14.

FROM TODAY — MAR

MAR	THIS YEAR JAN	FEB	MAR	APR	MAY	JUN	JUL	AUG	SEP	OCT	NOV	DEC	NEXT YEAR JAN	FEB	MAR	APR	MAY	JUN	JUL	AUG	SEP	OCT	NOV	DEC
1	0	0	0	31	61	92	122	153	184	214	245	275	306	337	365	396	426	457	487	518	549	579	610	640
2	0	0	0	30	60	91	121	152	183	213	244	274	305	336	364	395	425	456	486	517	548	578	609	639
3	0	0	0	29	59	90	120	151	182	212	243	273	304	335	363	394	424	455	485	516	547	577	608	638
4	0	0	0	28	58	89	119	150	181	211	242	272	303	334	362	393	423	454	484	515	546	576	607	637
5	0	0	0	27	57	88	118	149	180	210	241	271	302	333	361	392	422	453	483	514	545	575	606	636
6	0	0	0	26	56	87	117	148	179	209	240	270	301	332	360	391	421	452	482	513	544	574	605	635
7	0	0	0	25	55	86	116	147	178	208	239	269	300	331	359	390	420	451	481	512	543	573	604	634
8	0	0	0	24	54	85	115	146	177	207	238	268	299	330	358	389	419	450	480	511	542	572	603	633
9	0	0	0	23	53	84	114	145	176	206	237	267	298	329	357	388	418	449	479	510	541	571	602	632
10	0	0	0	22	52	83	113	144	175	205	236	266	297	328	356	387	417	448	478	509	540	570	601	631
11	0	0	0	21	51	82	112	143	174	204	235	265	296	327	355	386	416	447	477	508	539	569	600	630
12	0	0	0	20	50	81	111	142	173	203	234	264	295	326	354	385	415	446	476	507	538	568	599	629
13	0	0	0	19	49	80	110	141	172	202	233	263	294	325	353	384	414	445	475	506	537	567	598	628
14	0	0	0	18	48	79	109	140	171	201	232	262	293	324	352	383	413	444	474	505	536	566	597	627
15	0	0	0	17	47	78	108	139	170	200	231	261	292	323	351	382	412	443	473	504	535	565	596	626
16	0	0	0	16	46	77	107	138	169	199	230	260	291	322	350	381	411	442	472	503	534	564	595	625
17	0	0	0	15	45	76	106	137	168	198	229	259	290	321	349	380	410	441	471	502	533	563	594	624
18	0	0	0	14	44	75	105	136	167	197	228	258	289	320	348	379	409	440	470	501	532	562	593	623
19	0	0	0	13	43	74	104	135	166	196	227	257	288	319	347	378	408	439	469	500	531	561	592	622
20	0	0	0	12	42	73	103	134	165	195	226	256	287	318	346	377	407	438	468	499	530	560	591	621
21	0	0	0	11	41	72	102	133	164	194	225	255	286	317	345	376	406	437	467	498	529	559	590	620
22	0	0	0	10	40	71	101	132	163	193	224	254	285	316	344	375	405	436	466	497	528	558	589	619
23	0	0	0	9	39	70	100	131	162	192	223	253	284	315	343	374	404	435	465	496	527	557	588	618
24	0	0	0	8	38	69	99	130	161	191	222	252	283	314	342	373	403	434	464	495	526	556	587	617
25	0	0	0	7	37	68	98	129	160	190	221	251	282	313	341	372	402	433	463	494	525	555	586	616
26	0	0	0	6	36	67	97	128	159	189	220	250	281	312	340	371	401	432	462	493	524	554	585	615
27	0	0	0	5	35	66	96	127	158	188	219	249	280	311	339	370	400	431	461	492	523	553	584	614
28	0	0	0	4	34	65	95	126	157	187	218	248	279	310	338	369	399	430	460	491	522	552	583	613
29	0	0	0	3	33	64	94	125	156	186	217	247	278	309	337	368	398	429	459	490	521	551	582	612
30	0	0	0	2	32	63	93	124	155	185	216	246	277	308	336	367	397	428	458	489	520	550	581	611
31	0	0	0	1	31	62	92	123	154	184	215	245	276	307	335	366	396	427	457	488	519	549	580	610

FROM TODAY — APR

APR	THIS YEAR JAN	FEB	MAR	APR	MAY	JUN	JUL	AUG	SEP	OCT	NOV	DEC	NEXT YEAR JAN	FEB	MAR	APR	MAY	JUN	JUL	AUG	SEP	OCT	NOV	DEC
1	0	0	0	0	30	61	91	122	153	183	214	244	275	306	334	365	395	426	456	487	518	548	579	609
2	0	0	0	0	29	60	90	121	152	182	213	243	274	305	333	364	394	425	455	486	517	547	578	608
3	0	0	0	0	28	59	89	120	151	181	212	242	273	304	332	363	393	424	454	485	516	546	577	607
4	0	0	0	0	27	58	88	119	150	180	211	241	272	303	331	362	392	423	453	484	515	545	576	606
5	0	0	0	0	26	57	87	118	149	179	210	240	271	302	330	361	391	422	452	483	514	544	575	605
6	0	0	0	0	25	56	86	117	148	178	209	239	270	301	329	360	390	421	451	482	513	543	574	604
7	0	0	0	0	24	55	85	116	147	177	208	238	269	300	328	359	389	420	450	481	512	542	573	603
8	0	0	0	0	23	54	84	115	146	176	207	237	268	299	327	358	388	419	449	480	511	541	572	602
9	0	0	0	0	22	53	83	114	145	175	206	236	267	298	326	357	387	418	448	479	510	540	571	601
10	0	0	0	0	21	52	82	113	144	174	205	235	266	297	325	356	386	417	447	478	509	539	570	600
11	0	0	0	0	20	51	81	112	143	173	204	234	265	296	324	355	385	416	446	477	508	538	569	599
12	0	0	0	0	19	50	80	111	142	172	203	233	264	295	323	354	384	415	445	476	507	537	568	598
13	0	0	0	0	18	49	79	110	141	171	202	232	263	294	322	353	383	414	444	475	506	536	567	597
14	0	0	0	0	17	48	78	109	140	170	201	231	262	293	321	352	382	413	443	474	505	535	566	596
15	0	0	0	0	16	47	77	108	139	169	200	230	261	292	320	351	381	412	442	473	504	534	565	595
16	0	0	0	0	15	46	76	107	138	168	199	229	260	291	319	350	380	411	441	472	503	533	564	594
17	0	0	0	0	14	45	75	106	137	167	198	228	259	290	318	349	379	410	440	471	502	532	563	593
18	0	0	0	0	13	44	74	105	136	166	197	227	258	289	317	348	378	409	439	470	501	531	562	592
19	0	0	0	0	12	43	73	104	135	165	196	226	257	288	316	347	377	408	438	469	500	530	561	591
20	0	0	0	0	11	42	72	103	134	164	195	225	256	287	315	346	376	407	437	468	499	529	560	590
21	0	0	0	0	10	41	71	102	133	163	194	224	255	286	314	345	375	406	436	467	498	528	559	589
22	0	0	0	0	9	40	70	101	132	162	193	223	254	285	313	344	374	405	435	466	497	527	558	588
23	0	0	0	0	8	39	69	100	131	161	192	222	253	284	312	343	373	404	434	465	496	526	557	587
24	0	0	0	0	7	38	68	99	130	160	191	221	252	283	311	342	372	403	433	464	495	525	556	586
25	0	0	0	0	6	37	67	98	129	159	190	220	251	282	310	341	371	402	432	463	494	524	555	585
26	0	0	0	0	5	36	66	97	128	158	189	219	250	281	309	340	370	401	431	462	493	523	554	584
27	0	0	0	0	4	35	65	96	127	157	188	218	249	280	308	339	369	400	430	461	492	522	553	583
28	0	0	0	0	3	34	64	95	126	156	187	217	248	279	307	338	368	399	429	460	491	521	552	582
29	0	0	0	0	2	33	63	94	125	155	186	216	247	278	306	337	367	398	428	459	490	520	551	581
30	0	0	0	0	1	32	62	93	124	154	185	215	246	277	305	336	366	397	427	458	489	519	550	580

ADD 1 DAY FOR LEAP YEAR IF FEBRUARY 29 FALLS BETWEEN THE TWO DATES.

Description: This table shows the number of days FROM TODAY to the first day in a month within the next year.

Example: The number of days from MAY 1 this year to APR 15 next year is 349. The number is the sum of 335 + 14.

FROM TODAY MAY	THIS YEAR — TO THE FIRST DAY IN THE MONTH OF												NEXT YEAR — TO THE FIRST DAY IN THE MONTH OF											
	JAN	FEB	MAR	APR	MAY	JUN	JUL	AUG	SEP	OCT	NOV	DEC	JAN	FEB	MAR	APR	MAY	JUN	JUL	AUG	SEP	OCT	NOV	DEC
1	0	0	0	0	0	31	61	92	123	153	184	214	245	276	304	335	365	396	426	457	488	518	549	579
2	0	0	0	0	0	30	60	91	122	152	183	213	244	275	303	334	364	395	425	456	487	517	548	578
3	0	0	0	0	0	29	59	90	121	151	182	212	243	274	302	333	363	394	424	455	486	516	547	577
4	0	0	0	0	0	28	58	89	120	150	181	211	242	273	301	332	362	393	423	454	485	515	546	576
5	0	0	0	0	0	27	57	88	119	149	180	210	241	272	300	331	361	392	422	453	484	514	545	575
6	0	0	0	0	0	26	56	87	118	148	179	209	240	271	299	330	360	391	421	452	483	513	544	574
7	0	0	0	0	0	25	55	86	117	147	178	208	239	270	298	329	359	390	420	451	482	512	543	573
8	0	0	0	0	0	24	54	85	116	146	177	207	238	269	297	328	358	389	419	450	481	511	542	572
9	0	0	0	0	0	23	53	84	115	145	176	206	237	268	296	327	357	388	418	449	480	510	541	571
10	0	0	0	0	0	22	52	83	114	144	175	205	236	267	295	326	356	387	417	448	479	509	540	570
11	0	0	0	0	0	21	51	82	113	143	174	204	235	266	294	325	355	386	416	447	478	508	539	569
12	0	0	0	0	0	20	50	81	112	142	173	203	234	265	293	324	354	385	415	446	477	507	538	568
13	0	0	0	0	0	19	49	80	111	141	172	202	233	264	292	323	353	384	414	445	476	506	537	567
14	0	0	0	0	0	18	48	79	110	140	171	201	232	263	291	322	352	383	413	444	475	505	536	566
15	0	0	0	0	0	17	47	78	109	139	170	200	231	262	290	321	351	382	412	443	474	504	535	565
16	0	0	0	0	0	16	46	77	108	138	169	199	230	261	289	320	350	381	411	442	473	503	534	564
17	0	0	0	0	0	15	45	76	107	137	168	198	229	260	288	319	349	380	410	441	472	502	533	563
18	0	0	0	0	0	14	44	75	106	136	167	197	228	259	287	318	348	379	409	440	471	501	532	562
19	0	0	0	0	0	13	43	74	105	135	166	196	227	258	286	317	347	378	408	439	470	500	531	561
20	0	0	0	0	0	12	42	73	104	134	165	195	226	257	285	316	346	377	407	438	469	499	530	560
21	0	0	0	0	0	11	41	72	103	133	164	194	225	256	284	315	345	376	406	437	468	498	529	559
22	0	0	0	0	0	10	40	71	102	132	163	193	224	255	283	314	344	375	405	436	467	497	528	558
23	0	0	0	0	0	9	39	70	101	131	162	192	223	254	282	313	343	374	404	435	466	496	527	557
24	0	0	0	0	0	8	38	69	100	130	161	191	222	253	281	312	342	373	403	434	465	495	526	556
25	0	0	0	0	0	7	37	68	99	129	160	190	221	252	280	311	341	372	402	433	464	494	525	555
26	0	0	0	0	0	6	36	67	98	128	159	189	220	251	279	310	340	371	401	432	463	493	524	554
27	0	0	0	0	0	5	35	66	97	127	158	188	219	250	278	309	339	370	400	431	462	492	523	553
28	0	0	0	0	0	4	34	65	96	126	157	187	218	249	277	308	338	369	399	430	461	491	522	552
29	0	0	0	0	0	3	33	64	95	125	156	186	217	248	276	307	337	368	398	429	460	490	521	551
30	0	0	0	0	0	2	32	63	94	124	155	185	216	247	275	306	336	367	397	428	459	489	520	550
31	0	0	0	0	0	1	31	62	93	123	154	184	215	246	274	305	335	366	396	427	458	488	519	549

FROM TODAY JUN	THIS YEAR — TO THE FIRST DAY IN THE MONTH OF												NEXT YEAR — TO THE FIRST DAY IN THE MONTH OF											
	JAN	FEB	MAR	APR	MAY	JUN	JUL	AUG	SEP	OCT	NOV	DEC	JAN	FEB	MAR	APR	MAY	JUN	JUL	AUG	SEP	OCT	NOV	DEC
1	0	0	0	0	0	0	30	61	92	122	153	183	214	245	273	304	334	365	395	426	457	487	518	548
2	0	0	0	0	0	0	29	60	91	121	152	182	213	244	272	303	333	364	394	425	456	486	517	547
3	0	0	0	0	0	0	28	59	90	120	151	181	212	243	271	302	332	363	393	424	455	485	516	546
4	0	0	0	0	0	0	27	58	89	119	150	180	211	242	270	301	331	362	392	423	454	484	515	545
5	0	0	0	0	0	0	26	57	88	118	149	179	210	241	269	300	330	361	391	422	453	483	514	544
6	0	0	0	0	0	0	25	56	87	117	148	178	209	240	268	299	329	360	390	421	452	482	513	543
7	0	0	0	0	0	0	24	55	86	116	147	177	208	239	267	298	328	359	389	420	451	481	512	542
8	0	0	0	0	0	0	23	54	85	115	146	176	207	238	266	297	327	358	388	419	450	480	511	541
9	0	0	0	0	0	0	22	53	84	114	145	175	206	237	265	296	326	357	387	418	449	479	510	540
10	0	0	0	0	0	0	21	52	83	113	144	174	205	236	264	295	325	356	386	417	448	478	509	539
11	0	0	0	0	0	0	20	51	82	112	143	173	204	235	263	294	324	355	385	416	447	477	508	538
12	0	0	0	0	0	0	19	50	81	111	142	172	203	234	262	293	323	354	384	415	446	476	507	537
13	0	0	0	0	0	0	18	49	80	110	141	171	202	233	261	292	322	353	383	414	445	475	506	536
14	0	0	0	0	0	0	17	48	79	109	140	170	201	232	260	291	321	352	382	413	444	474	505	535
15	0	0	0	0	0	0	16	47	78	108	139	169	200	231	259	290	320	351	381	412	443	473	504	534
16	0	0	0	0	0	0	15	46	77	107	138	168	199	230	258	289	319	350	380	411	442	472	503	533
17	0	0	0	0	0	0	14	45	76	106	137	167	198	229	257	288	318	349	379	410	441	471	502	532
18	0	0	0	0	0	0	13	44	75	105	136	166	197	228	256	287	317	348	378	409	440	470	501	531
19	0	0	0	0	0	0	12	43	74	104	135	165	196	227	255	286	316	347	377	408	439	469	500	530
20	0	0	0	0	0	0	11	42	73	103	134	164	195	226	254	285	315	346	376	407	438	468	499	529
21	0	0	0	0	0	0	10	41	72	102	133	163	194	225	253	284	314	345	375	406	437	467	498	528
22	0	0	0	0	0	0	9	40	71	101	132	162	193	224	252	283	313	344	374	405	436	466	497	527
23	0	0	0	0	0	0	8	39	70	100	131	161	192	223	251	282	312	343	373	404	435	465	496	526
24	0	0	0	0	0	0	7	38	69	99	130	160	191	222	250	281	311	342	372	403	434	464	495	525
25	0	0	0	0	0	0	6	37	68	98	129	159	190	221	249	280	310	341	371	402	433	463	494	524
26	0	0	0	0	0	0	5	36	67	97	128	158	189	220	248	279	309	340	370	401	432	462	493	523
27	0	0	0	0	0	0	4	35	66	96	127	157	188	219	247	278	308	339	369	400	431	461	492	522
28	0	0	0	0	0	0	3	34	65	95	126	156	187	218	246	277	307	338	368	399	430	460	491	521
29	0	0	0	0	0	0	2	33	64	94	125	155	186	217	245	276	306	337	367	398	429	459	490	520
30	0	0	0	0	0	0	1	32	63	93	124	154	185	216	244	275	305	336	366	397	428	458	489	519

ADD 1 DAY FOR LEAP YEAR IF FEBRUARY 29 FALLS BETWEEN THE TWO DATES.

DAYS BETWEEN DATES

Description: This table shows the number of days FROM TODAY to the first day in a month within the next year.

Example: The number of days from JUL 1 this year to APR 15 next year is 288. The number is the sum of 274 + 14.

FROM TODAY: JUL

THIS YEAR / NEXT YEAR — TO THE FIRST DAY IN THE MONTH OF

JUL	JAN	FEB	MAR	APR	MAY	JUN	JUL	AUG	SEP	OCT	NOV	DEC	JAN	FEB	MAR	APR	MAY	JUN	JUL	AUG	SEP	OCT	NOV	DEC
1	0	0	0	0	0	0	0	31	62	92	123	153	184	215	243	274	304	335	365	396	427	457	488	518
2	0	0	0	0	0	0	0	30	61	91	122	152	183	214	242	273	303	334	364	395	426	456	487	517
3	0	0	0	0	0	0	0	29	60	90	121	151	182	213	241	272	302	333	363	394	425	455	486	516
4	0	0	0	0	0	0	0	28	59	89	120	150	181	212	240	271	301	332	362	393	424	454	485	515
5	0	0	0	0	0	0	0	27	58	88	119	149	180	211	239	270	300	331	361	392	423	453	484	514
6	0	0	0	0	0	0	0	26	57	87	118	148	179	210	238	269	299	330	360	391	422	452	483	513
7	0	0	0	0	0	0	0	25	56	86	117	147	178	209	237	268	298	329	359	390	421	451	482	512
8	0	0	0	0	0	0	0	24	55	85	116	146	177	208	236	267	297	328	358	389	420	450	481	511
9	0	0	0	0	0	0	0	23	54	84	115	145	176	207	235	266	296	327	357	388	419	449	480	510
10	0	0	0	0	0	0	0	22	53	83	114	144	175	206	234	265	295	326	356	387	418	448	479	509
11	0	0	0	0	0	0	0	21	52	82	113	143	174	205	233	264	294	325	355	386	417	447	478	508
12	0	0	0	0	0	0	0	20	51	81	112	142	173	204	232	263	293	324	354	385	416	446	477	507
13	0	0	0	0	0	0	0	19	50	80	111	141	172	203	231	262	292	323	353	384	415	445	476	506
14	0	0	0	0	0	0	0	18	49	79	110	140	171	202	230	261	291	322	352	383	414	444	475	505
15	0	0	0	0	0	0	0	17	48	78	109	139	170	201	229	260	290	321	351	382	413	443	474	504
16	0	0	0	0	0	0	0	16	47	77	108	138	169	200	228	259	289	320	350	381	412	442	473	503
17	0	0	0	0	0	0	0	15	46	76	107	137	168	199	227	258	288	319	349	380	411	441	472	502
18	0	0	0	0	0	0	0	14	45	75	106	136	167	198	226	257	287	318	348	379	410	440	471	501
19	0	0	0	0	0	0	0	13	44	74	105	135	166	197	225	256	286	317	347	378	409	439	470	500
20	0	0	0	0	0	0	0	12	43	73	104	134	165	196	224	255	285	316	346	377	408	438	469	499
21	0	0	0	0	0	0	0	11	42	72	103	133	164	195	223	254	284	315	345	376	407	437	468	498
22	0	0	0	0	0	0	0	10	41	71	102	132	163	194	222	253	283	314	344	375	406	436	467	497
23	0	0	0	0	0	0	0	9	40	70	101	131	162	193	221	252	282	313	343	374	405	435	466	496
24	0	0	0	0	0	0	0	8	39	69	100	130	161	192	220	251	281	312	342	373	404	434	465	495
25	0	0	0	0	0	0	0	7	38	68	99	129	160	191	219	250	280	311	341	372	403	433	464	494
26	0	0	0	0	0	0	0	6	37	67	98	128	159	190	218	249	279	310	340	371	402	432	463	493
27	0	0	0	0	0	0	0	5	36	66	97	127	158	189	217	248	278	309	339	370	401	431	462	492
28	0	0	0	0	0	0	0	4	35	65	96	126	157	188	216	247	277	308	338	369	400	430	461	491
29	0	0	0	0	0	0	0	3	34	64	95	125	156	187	215	246	276	307	337	368	399	429	460	490
30	0	0	0	0	0	0	0	2	33	63	94	124	155	186	214	245	275	306	336	367	398	428	459	489
31	0	0	0	0	0	0	0	1	32	62	93	123	154	185	213	244	274	305	335	366	397	427	458	488

FROM TODAY: AUG

THIS YEAR / NEXT YEAR — TO THE FIRST DAY IN THE MONTH OF

AUG	JAN	FEB	MAR	APR	MAY	JUN	JUL	AUG	SEP	OCT	NOV	DEC	JAN	FEB	MAR	APR	MAY	JUN	JUL	AUG	SEP	OCT	NOV	DEC
1	0	0	0	0	0	0	0	0	31	61	92	122	153	184	212	243	273	304	334	365	396	426	457	487
2	0	0	0	0	0	0	0	0	30	60	91	121	152	183	211	242	272	303	333	364	395	425	456	486
3	0	0	0	0	0	0	0	0	29	59	90	120	151	182	210	241	271	302	332	363	394	424	455	485
4	0	0	0	0	0	0	0	0	28	58	89	119	150	181	209	240	270	301	331	362	393	423	454	484
5	0	0	0	0	0	0	0	0	27	57	88	118	149	180	208	239	269	300	330	361	392	422	453	483
6	0	0	0	0	0	0	0	0	26	56	87	117	148	179	207	238	268	299	329	360	391	421	452	482
7	0	0	0	0	0	0	0	0	25	55	86	116	147	178	206	237	267	298	328	359	390	420	451	481
8	0	0	0	0	0	0	0	0	24	54	85	115	146	177	205	236	266	297	327	358	389	419	450	480
9	0	0	0	0	0	0	0	0	23	53	84	114	145	176	204	235	265	296	326	357	388	418	449	479
10	0	0	0	0	0	0	0	0	22	52	83	113	144	175	203	234	264	295	325	356	387	417	448	478
11	0	0	0	0	0	0	0	0	21	51	82	112	143	174	202	233	263	294	324	355	386	416	447	477
12	0	0	0	0	0	0	0	0	20	50	81	111	142	173	201	232	262	293	323	354	385	415	446	476
13	0	0	0	0	0	0	0	0	19	49	80	110	141	172	200	231	261	292	322	353	384	414	445	475
14	0	0	0	0	0	0	0	0	18	48	79	109	140	171	199	230	260	291	321	352	383	413	444	474
15	0	0	0	0	0	0	0	0	17	47	78	108	139	170	198	229	259	290	320	351	382	412	443	473
16	0	0	0	0	0	0	0	0	16	46	77	107	138	169	197	228	258	289	319	350	381	411	442	472
17	0	0	0	0	0	0	0	0	15	45	76	106	137	168	196	227	257	288	318	349	380	410	441	471
18	0	0	0	0	0	0	0	0	14	44	75	105	136	167	195	226	256	287	317	348	379	409	440	470
19	0	0	0	0	0	0	0	0	13	43	74	104	135	166	194	225	255	286	316	347	378	408	439	469
20	0	0	0	0	0	0	0	0	12	42	73	103	134	165	193	224	254	285	315	346	377	407	438	468
21	0	0	0	0	0	0	0	0	11	41	72	102	133	164	192	223	253	284	314	345	376	406	437	467
22	0	0	0	0	0	0	0	0	10	40	71	101	132	163	191	222	252	283	313	344	375	405	436	466
23	0	0	0	0	0	0	0	0	9	39	70	100	131	162	190	221	251	282	312	343	374	404	435	465
24	0	0	0	0	0	0	0	0	8	38	69	99	130	161	189	220	250	281	311	342	373	403	434	464
25	0	0	0	0	0	0	0	0	7	37	68	98	129	160	188	219	249	280	310	341	372	402	433	463
26	0	0	0	0	0	0	0	0	6	36	67	97	128	159	187	218	248	279	309	340	371	401	432	462
27	0	0	0	0	0	0	0	0	5	35	66	96	127	158	186	217	247	278	308	339	370	400	431	461
28	0	0	0	0	0	0	0	0	4	34	65	95	126	157	185	216	246	277	307	338	369	399	430	460
29	0	0	0	0	0	0	0	0	3	33	64	94	125	156	184	215	245	276	306	337	368	398	429	459
30	0	0	0	0	0	0	0	0	2	32	63	93	124	155	183	214	244	275	305	336	367	397	428	458
31	0	0	0	0	0	0	0	0	1	31	62	92	123	154	182	213	243	274	304	335	366	396	427	457

ADD 1 DAY FOR LEAP YEAR IF FEBRUARY 29 FALLS BETWEEN THE TWO DATES.

DAYS BETWEEN DATES

Description: This table shows the number of days FROM TODAY to the first day in a month within the next year.

Example: The number of days from SEP 1 this year to APR 15 next year is 226. The number is the sum of 212 + 14.

FROM TODAY SEP

TO THE FIRST DAY IN THE MONTH OF

SEP	JAN	FEB	MAR	APR	MAY	JUN	JUL	AUG	SEP	OCT	NOV	DEC	JAN	FEB	MAR	APR	MAY	JUN	JUL	AUG	SEP	OCT	NOV	DEC
	THIS YEAR												NEXT YEAR											
1	0	0	0	0	0	0	0	0	0	30	61	91	122	153	181	212	242	273	303	334	365	395	426	456
2	0	0	0	0	0	0	0	0	0	29	60	90	121	152	180	211	241	272	302	333	364	394	425	455
3	0	0	0	0	0	0	0	0	0	28	59	89	120	151	179	210	240	271	301	332	363	393	424	454
4	0	0	0	0	0	0	0	0	0	27	58	88	119	150	178	209	239	270	300	331	362	392	423	453
5	0	0	0	0	0	0	0	0	0	26	57	87	118	149	177	208	238	269	299	330	361	391	422	452
6	0	0	0	0	0	0	0	0	0	25	56	86	117	148	176	207	237	268	298	329	360	390	421	451
7	0	0	0	0	0	0	0	0	0	24	55	85	116	147	175	206	236	267	297	328	359	389	420	450
8	0	0	0	0	0	0	0	0	0	23	54	84	115	146	174	205	235	266	296	327	358	388	419	449
9	0	0	0	0	0	0	0	0	0	22	53	83	114	145	173	204	234	265	295	326	357	387	418	448
10	0	0	0	0	0	0	0	0	0	21	52	82	113	144	172	203	233	264	294	325	356	386	417	447
11	0	0	0	0	0	0	0	0	0	20	51	81	112	143	171	202	232	263	293	324	355	385	416	446
12	0	0	0	0	0	0	0	0	0	19	50	80	111	142	170	201	231	262	292	323	354	384	415	445
13	0	0	0	0	0	0	0	0	0	18	49	79	110	141	169	200	230	261	291	322	353	383	414	444
14	0	0	0	0	0	0	0	0	0	17	48	78	109	140	168	199	229	260	290	321	352	382	413	443
15	0	0	0	0	0	0	0	0	0	16	47	77	108	139	167	198	228	259	289	320	351	381	412	442
16	0	0	0	0	0	0	0	0	0	15	46	76	107	138	166	197	227	258	288	319	350	380	411	441
17	0	0	0	0	0	0	0	0	0	14	45	75	106	137	165	196	226	257	287	318	349	379	410	440
18	0	0	0	0	0	0	0	0	0	13	44	74	105	136	164	195	225	256	286	317	348	378	409	439
19	0	0	0	0	0	0	0	0	0	12	43	73	104	135	163	194	224	255	285	316	347	377	408	438
20	0	0	0	0	0	0	0	0	0	11	42	72	103	134	162	193	223	254	284	315	346	376	407	437
21	0	0	0	0	0	0	0	0	0	10	41	71	102	133	161	192	222	253	283	314	345	375	406	436
22	0	0	0	0	0	0	0	0	0	9	40	70	101	132	160	191	221	252	282	313	344	374	405	435
23	0	0	0	0	0	0	0	0	0	8	39	69	100	131	159	190	220	251	281	312	343	373	404	434
24	0	0	0	0	0	0	0	0	0	7	38	68	99	130	158	189	219	250	280	311	342	372	403	433
25	0	0	0	0	0	0	0	0	0	6	37	67	98	129	157	188	218	249	279	310	341	371	402	432
26	0	0	0	0	0	0	0	0	0	5	36	66	97	128	156	187	217	248	278	309	340	370	401	431
27	0	0	0	0	0	0	0	0	0	4	35	65	96	127	155	186	216	247	277	308	339	369	400	430
28	0	0	0	0	0	0	0	0	0	3	34	64	95	126	154	185	215	246	276	307	338	368	399	429
29	0	0	0	0	0	0	0	0	0	2	33	63	94	125	153	184	214	245	275	306	337	367	398	428
30	0	0	0	0	0	0	0	0	0	1	32	62	93	124	152	183	213	244	274	305	336	366	397	427

FROM TODAY OCT

TO THE FIRST DAY IN THE MONTH OF

OCT	JAN	FEB	MAR	APR	MAY	JUN	JUL	AUG	SEP	OCT	NOV	DEC	JAN	FEB	MAR	APR	MAY	JUN	JUL	AUG	SEP	OCT	NOV	DEC
	THIS YEAR												NEXT YEAR											
1	0	0	0	0	0	0	0	0	0	0	31	61	92	123	151	182	212	243	273	304	335	365	396	426
2	0	0	0	0	0	0	0	0	0	0	30	60	91	122	150	181	211	242	272	303	334	364	395	425
3	0	0	0	0	0	0	0	0	0	0	29	59	90	121	149	180	210	241	271	302	333	363	394	424
4	0	0	0	0	0	0	0	0	0	0	28	58	89	120	148	179	209	240	270	301	332	362	393	423
5	0	0	0	0	0	0	0	0	0	0	27	57	88	119	147	178	208	239	269	300	331	361	392	422
6	0	0	0	0	0	0	0	0	0	0	26	56	87	118	146	177	207	238	268	299	330	360	391	421
7	0	0	0	0	0	0	0	0	0	0	25	55	86	117	145	176	206	237	267	298	329	359	390	420
8	0	0	0	0	0	0	0	0	0	0	24	54	85	116	144	175	205	236	266	297	328	358	389	419
9	0	0	0	0	0	0	0	0	0	0	23	53	84	115	143	174	204	235	265	296	327	357	388	418
10	0	0	0	0	0	0	0	0	0	0	22	52	83	114	142	173	203	234	264	295	326	356	387	417
11	0	0	0	0	0	0	0	0	0	0	21	51	82	113	141	172	202	233	263	294	325	355	386	416
12	0	0	0	0	0	0	0	0	0	0	20	50	81	112	140	171	201	232	262	293	324	354	385	415
13	0	0	0	0	0	0	0	0	0	0	19	49	80	111	139	170	200	231	261	292	323	353	384	414
14	0	0	0	0	0	0	0	0	0	0	18	48	79	110	138	169	199	230	260	291	322	352	383	413
15	0	0	0	0	0	0	0	0	0	0	17	47	78	109	137	168	198	229	259	290	321	351	382	412
16	0	0	0	0	0	0	0	0	0	0	16	46	77	108	136	167	197	228	258	289	320	350	381	411
17	0	0	0	0	0	0	0	0	0	0	15	45	76	107	135	166	196	227	257	288	319	349	380	410
18	0	0	0	0	0	0	0	0	0	0	14	44	75	106	134	165	195	226	256	287	318	348	379	409
19	0	0	0	0	0	0	0	0	0	0	13	43	74	105	133	164	194	225	255	286	317	347	378	408
20	0	0	0	0	0	0	0	0	0	0	12	42	73	104	132	163	193	224	254	285	316	346	377	407
21	0	0	0	0	0	0	0	0	0	0	11	41	72	103	131	162	192	223	253	284	315	345	376	406
22	0	0	0	0	0	0	0	0	0	0	10	40	71	102	130	161	191	222	252	283	314	344	375	405
23	0	0	0	0	0	0	0	0	0	0	9	39	70	101	129	160	190	221	251	282	313	343	374	404
24	0	0	0	0	0	0	0	0	0	0	8	38	69	100	128	159	189	220	250	281	312	342	373	403
25	0	0	0	0	0	0	0	0	0	0	7	37	68	99	127	158	188	219	249	280	311	341	372	402
26	0	0	0	0	0	0	0	0	0	0	6	36	67	98	126	157	187	218	248	279	310	340	371	401
27	0	0	0	0	0	0	0	0	0	0	5	35	66	97	125	156	186	217	247	278	309	339	370	400
28	0	0	0	0	0	0	0	0	0	0	4	34	65	96	124	155	185	216	246	277	308	338	369	399
29	0	0	0	0	0	0	0	0	0	0	3	33	64	95	123	154	184	215	245	276	307	337	368	398
30	0	0	0	0	0	0	0	0	0	0	2	32	63	94	122	153	183	214	244	275	306	336	367	397
31	0	0	0	0	0	0	0	0	0	0	1	31	62	93	121	152	182	213	243	274	305	335	366	396

ADD 1 DAY FOR LEAP YEAR IF FEBRUARY 29 FALLS BETWEEN THE TWO DATES.

Description: This table shows the number of days FROM TODAY to the first day in a month within the next year.

Example: The number of days from NOV 1 this year to APR 15 next year is 165. The number is the sum of 151 + 14.

FROM TODAY — THIS YEAR / NEXT YEAR — TO THE FIRST DAY IN THE MONTH OF

NOV	JAN	FEB	MAR	APR	MAY	JUN	JUL	AUG	SEP	OCT	NOV	DEC	JAN	FEB	MAR	APR	MAY	JUN	JUL	AUG	SEP	OCT	NOV	DEC
1	0	0	0	0	0	0	0	0	0	0	0	30	61	92	120	151	181	212	242	273	304	334	365	395
2	0	0	0	0	0	0	0	0	0	0	0	29	60	91	119	150	180	211	241	272	303	333	364	394
3	0	0	0	0	0	0	0	0	0	0	0	28	59	90	118	149	179	210	240	271	302	332	363	393
4	0	0	0	0	0	0	0	0	0	0	0	27	58	89	117	148	178	209	239	270	301	331	362	392
5	0	0	0	0	0	0	0	0	0	0	0	26	57	88	116	147	177	208	238	269	300	330	361	391
6	0	0	0	0	0	0	0	0	0	0	0	25	56	87	115	146	176	207	237	268	299	329	360	390
7	0	0	0	0	0	0	0	0	0	0	0	24	55	86	114	145	175	206	236	267	298	328	359	389
8	0	0	0	0	0	0	0	0	0	0	0	23	54	85	113	144	174	205	235	266	297	327	358	388
9	0	0	0	0	0	0	0	0	0	0	0	22	53	84	112	143	173	204	234	265	296	326	357	387
10	0	0	0	0	0	0	0	0	0	0	0	21	52	83	111	142	172	203	233	264	295	325	356	386
11	0	0	0	0	0	0	0	0	0	0	0	20	51	82	110	141	171	202	232	263	294	324	355	385
12	0	0	0	0	0	0	0	0	0	0	0	19	50	81	109	140	170	201	231	262	293	323	354	384
13	0	0	0	0	0	0	0	0	0	0	0	18	49	80	108	139	169	200	230	261	292	322	353	383
14	0	0	0	0	0	0	0	0	0	0	0	17	48	79	107	138	168	199	229	260	291	321	352	382
15	0	0	0	0	0	0	0	0	0	0	0	16	47	78	106	137	167	198	228	259	290	320	351	381
16	0	0	0	0	0	0	0	0	0	0	0	15	46	77	105	136	166	197	227	258	289	319	350	380
17	0	0	0	0	0	0	0	0	0	0	0	14	45	76	104	135	165	196	226	257	288	318	349	379
18	0	0	0	0	0	0	0	0	0	0	0	13	44	75	103	134	164	195	225	256	287	317	348	378
19	0	0	0	0	0	0	0	0	0	0	0	12	43	74	102	133	163	194	224	255	286	316	347	377
20	0	0	0	0	0	0	0	0	0	0	0	11	42	73	101	132	162	193	223	254	285	315	346	376
21	0	0	0	0	0	0	0	0	0	0	0	10	41	72	100	131	161	192	222	253	284	314	345	375
22	0	0	0	0	0	0	0	0	0	0	0	9	40	71	99	130	160	191	221	252	283	313	344	374
23	0	0	0	0	0	0	0	0	0	0	0	8	39	70	98	129	159	190	220	251	282	312	343	373
24	0	0	0	0	0	0	0	0	0	0	0	7	38	69	97	128	158	189	219	250	281	311	342	372
25	0	0	0	0	0	0	0	0	0	0	0	6	37	68	96	127	157	188	218	249	280	310	341	371
26	0	0	0	0	0	0	0	0	0	0	0	5	36	67	95	126	156	187	217	248	279	309	340	370
27	0	0	0	0	0	0	0	0	0	0	0	4	35	66	94	125	155	186	216	247	278	308	339	369
28	0	0	0	0	0	0	0	0	0	0	0	3	34	65	93	124	154	185	215	246	277	307	338	368
29	0	0	0	0	0	0	0	0	0	0	0	2	33	64	92	123	153	184	214	245	276	306	337	367
30	0	0	0	0	0	0	0	0	0	0	0	1	32	63	91	122	152	183	213	244	275	305	336	366

FROM TODAY — THIS YEAR / NEXT YEAR — TO THE FIRST DAY IN THE MONTH OF

DEC	JAN	FEB	MAR	APR	MAY	JUN	JUL	AUG	SEP	OCT	NOV	DEC	JAN	FEB	MAR	APR	MAY	JUN	JUL	AUG	SEP	OCT	NOV	DEC
1	0	0	0	0	0	0	0	0	0	0	0	0	31	62	90	121	151	182	212	243	274	304	335	365
2	0	0	0	0	0	0	0	0	0	0	0	0	30	61	89	120	150	181	211	242	273	303	334	364
3	0	0	0	0	0	0	0	0	0	0	0	0	29	60	88	119	149	180	210	241	272	302	333	363
4	0	0	0	0	0	0	0	0	0	0	0	0	28	59	87	118	148	179	209	240	271	301	332	362
5	0	0	0	0	0	0	0	0	0	0	0	0	27	58	86	117	147	178	208	239	270	300	331	361
6	0	0	0	0	0	0	0	0	0	0	0	0	26	57	85	116	146	177	207	238	269	299	330	360
7	0	0	0	0	0	0	0	0	0	0	0	0	25	56	84	115	145	176	206	237	268	298	329	359
8	0	0	0	0	0	0	0	0	0	0	0	0	24	55	83	114	144	175	205	236	267	297	328	358
9	0	0	0	0	0	0	0	0	0	0	0	0	23	54	82	113	143	174	204	235	266	296	327	357
10	0	0	0	0	0	0	0	0	0	0	0	0	22	53	81	112	142	173	203	234	265	295	326	356
11	0	0	0	0	0	0	0	0	0	0	0	0	21	52	80	111	141	172	202	233	264	294	325	355
12	0	0	0	0	0	0	0	0	0	0	0	0	20	51	79	110	140	171	201	232	263	293	324	354
13	0	0	0	0	0	0	0	0	0	0	0	0	19	50	78	109	139	170	200	231	262	292	323	353
14	0	0	0	0	0	0	0	0	0	0	0	0	18	49	77	108	138	169	199	230	261	291	322	352
15	0	0	0	0	0	0	0	0	0	0	0	0	17	48	76	107	137	168	198	229	260	290	321	351
16	0	0	0	0	0	0	0	0	0	0	0	0	16	47	75	106	136	167	197	228	259	289	320	350
17	0	0	0	0	0	0	0	0	0	0	0	0	15	46	74	105	135	166	196	227	258	288	319	349
18	0	0	0	0	0	0	0	0	0	0	0	0	14	45	73	104	134	165	195	226	257	287	318	348
19	0	0	0	0	0	0	0	0	0	0	0	0	13	44	72	103	133	164	194	225	256	286	317	347
20	0	0	0	0	0	0	0	0	0	0	0	0	12	43	71	102	132	163	193	224	255	285	316	346
21	0	0	0	0	0	0	0	0	0	0	0	0	11	42	70	101	131	162	192	223	254	284	315	345
22	0	0	0	0	0	0	0	0	0	0	0	0	10	41	69	100	130	161	191	222	253	283	314	344
23	0	0	0	0	0	0	0	0	0	0	0	0	9	40	68	99	129	160	190	221	252	282	313	343
24	0	0	0	0	0	0	0	0	0	0	0	0	8	39	67	98	128	159	189	220	251	281	312	342
25	0	0	0	0	0	0	0	0	0	0	0	0	7	38	66	97	127	158	188	219	250	280	311	341
26	0	0	0	0	0	0	0	0	0	0	0	0	6	37	65	96	126	157	187	218	249	279	310	340
27	0	0	0	0	0	0	0	0	0	0	0	0	5	36	64	95	125	156	186	217	248	278	309	339
28	0	0	0	0	0	0	0	0	0	0	0	0	4	35	63	94	124	155	185	216	247	277	308	338
29	0	0	0	0	0	0	0	0	0	0	0	0	3	34	62	93	123	154	184	215	246	276	307	337
30	0	0	0	0	0	0	0	0	0	0	0	0	2	33	61	92	122	153	183	214	245	275	306	336
31	0	0	0	0	0	0	0	0	0	0	0	0	1	32	60	91	121	152	182	213	244	274	305	335

ADD 1 DAY FOR LEAP YEAR IF FEBRUARY 29 FALLS BETWEEN THE TWO DATES.

TABLE 11

Simple Interest on $100

Interest Rates: 4 to 15% by .25%; 16, 17, 18%.

Terms: 1 to 366 days.

Basis Years: 360 and 365 day years.

This table shows the simple interest on $100 from 1 to 366 days. In the 360 day table, interest is computed on the basis of a 360 day year. This means that the interest rate is divided by 360 to get the 1 day interest factor. At 8%, the 1 day factor is .08/360 = .000 222 2222. In the 365 day table, interest is computed on the basis of a 365 day year. At 8%, the 1 day factor is .08/365 = .000 219 1781.

Example: To find the interest factor at 8% for 30 days in a 360 day year, scan the day index on page 11-4 that corresponds to 8%. The value to the right of 30 in the index reads .666667. This is the value for $100. To get the factor for $1, move the decimal point 2 places to the left: .00666667.

To calculate the interest on $11,000 at 8% for 30 days, multiply the amount by the factor, as follows:

$$\$11,000 \times .00666667 = 73.333$$

The interest is $73.33. Calculate interest on $10,000:

$$\$10,000 \times .00666667 = 66.666$$

The interest is $66.67. Interest calculations of .005 or more are rounded to the next higher cent.

For Days Not Shown.   The interest factor for a number of days not shown in the index can be calculated by adding daily factors for the required number of days, and then multiplying the amount by the new factor.

Example: To calculate the interest on $11,000 at 8% for 65 days, add the factors for 10 days and 55 days:

$$1.222222 + .222222 = 1.444444$$

The sum 1.444444 is the factor per $100 for 65 days. Now, multiply the amount by the new factor for $1:

$$11,000 \times .01444444 = 158.888$$

The interest is $158.89.

Time Factor.   The time factor is the fraction of a year during which money earns interest. In the computation of daily interest, the time factor is expressed as a fraction in which the number of days between dates is the numerator and the basis year is the denominator. The time factor for 1 year may be any one of the following: 360/360, 365/360, 366/360, 365/365, 366/365, or 366/366.

Interest Factor.   The interest factor is the interest ratio multiplied by the time factor. At a 6% interest rate, the daily interest factor is .06 × (1/360) = .000166667, and the monthly interest factor is .06 × (30/360) = .005.

Interest.   Interest is money paid for the use of money; it is the difference between what is loaned and what is repaid. If $100 is loaned and later $104 is repaid, then the $4 difference is interest. Interest, expressed as a percent, which means "by the hundred," is by convention understood to be per year. If the $100 is loaned for 1 year, then the interest rate is 4%. An interest rate of 4% means an annual rate of 4%. If interest is expressed for a period of less than 1 year, then it is qualified. A 1.50% per month rate, for example, is qualified, and equals an annual rate of 18%. "Interest" is defined by the following general interest equation:

$$\text{Interest} = \text{Principal} \times \text{Rate} \times \text{Time}$$

For the equation to work, the rate must be converted to a ratio, or a value per 1. To change a percent to a ratio, move the decimal point 2 places to the left and drop the percent sign: 4% = .04. Time is the time factor described previously.

Simple Interest.   Simple interest is interest that is earned and immediately paid out. Interest on a savings account that is computed and paid out monthly, the interest portion on a mortgage loan payment, coupon interest clipped from a bond, and the discount received at maturity from a Treasury bill are examples of simple interest.

Compound Interest.   When simple interest is not paid out but left in the account, it is said to be converted to principal. When interest is computed again at the end of the period, it includes interest on the original principal and on the interest that was converted to principal. This is interest on interest, or compound interest.

Variations of Simple Interest. There are 4 variations of simple interest. They are different in the calculation of the number of days in the interest period and the number of days in a year.

Ordinary Interest. Ordinary interest counts months and days in the interest period and is computed on a 360 day year. It is used for corporate and municipal bonds, mortgages, installment loans, and U.S. agency bonds and notes.

Exact Day Interest. Exact day interest counts each day in the interest period and is computed on a 365 or 366 day year. It is used for U.S. Treasury bonds and notes and in some municipalities, such as Boston.

Bank Interest. Bank interest also counts each day in the interest period but is computed on a 360 day year. It is used for commercial paper, certificates of deposit, repurchase agreements, corporate loans, and personal loans.

Discount. Discount interest is computed from bank interest. Once bank interest is calculated, the interest from the face of the note is subtracted. The difference is the price. The discount interest is the difference between the price and the face amount at maturity. It is used for U.S. Treasury bills, banker's acceptances, commercial paper, and municipal tax and revenue anticipation notes.

Loan agreements usually describe how interest is to be computed. The rule is: Follow the maker of the note.

SIMPLE INTEREST ON $100

Description: This table shows the simple interest on $100. Interest is computed on the basis of a 360 day year.

Example: The interest on $100 at 4% for 40 days is $ .44. On $10,000 the interest is $ 44.44.

Interest on $100

DAY	4.00 %	4.25 %	4.50 %	4.75 %	5.00 %	5.25 %	5.50 %	5.75 %
1	.011111	.011806	.012500	.013194	.013889	.014583	.015278	.015972
2	.022222	.023611	.025000	.026389	.027778	.029167	.030556	.031944
3	.033333	.035417	.037500	.039583	.041667	.043750	.045833	.047917
4	.044444	.047222	.050000	.052778	.055556	.058333	.061111	.063889
5	.055556	.059028	.062500	.065972	.069444	.072917	.076389	.079861
6	.066667	.070833	.075000	.079167	.083333	.087500	.091667	.095833
7	.077778	.082639	.087500	.092361	.097222	.102083	.106944	.111806
8	.088889	.094444	.100000	.105556	.111111	.116667	.122222	.127778
9	.100000	.106250	.112500	.118750	.125000	.131250	.137500	.143750
10	.111111	.118056	.125000	.131944	.138889	.145833	.152778	.159722
11	.122222	.129861	.137500	.145139	.152778	.160417	.168056	.175694
12	.133333	.141667	.150000	.158333	.166667	.175000	.183333	.191667
13	.144444	.153472	.162500	.171528	.180556	.189583	.198611	.207639
14	.155556	.165278	.175000	.184722	.194444	.204167	.213889	.223611
15	.166667	.177083	.187500	.197917	.208333	.218750	.229167	.239583
16	.177778	.188889	.200000	.211111	.222222	.233333	.244444	.255556
17	.188889	.200694	.212500	.224306	.236111	.247917	.259722	.271528
18	.200000	.212500	.225000	.237500	.250000	.262500	.275000	.287500
19	.211111	.224306	.237500	.250694	.263889	.277083	.290278	.303472
20	.222222	.236111	.250000	.263889	.277778	.291667	.305556	.319444
21	.233333	.247917	.262500	.277083	.291667	.306250	.320833	.335417
22	.244444	.259722	.275000	.290278	.305556	.320833	.336111	.351389
23	.255556	.271528	.287500	.303472	.319444	.335417	.351389	.367361
24	.266667	.283333	.300000	.316667	.333333	.350000	.366667	.383333
25	.277778	.295139	.312500	.329861	.347222	.364583	.381944	.399306
26	.288889	.306944	.325000	.343056	.361111	.379167	.397222	.415278
27	.300000	.318750	.337500	.356250	.375000	.393750	.412500	.431250
28	.311111	.330556	.350000	.369444	.388889	.408333	.427778	.447222
29	.322222	.342361	.362500	.382639	.402778	.422917	.443056	.463194
30	.333333	.354167	.375000	.395833	.416667	.437500	.458333	.479167
31	.344444	.365972	.387500	.409028	.430556	.452083	.473611	.495139
32	.355556	.377778	.400000	.422222	.444444	.466667	.488889	.511111
33	.366667	.389583	.412500	.435417	.458333	.481250	.504167	.527083
34	.377778	.401389	.425000	.448611	.472222	.495833	.519444	.543056
35	.388889	.413194	.437500	.461806	.486111	.510417	.534722	.559028
36	.400000	.425000	.450000	.475000	.500000	.525000	.550000	.575000
37	.411111	.436806	.462500	.488194	.513889	.539583	.565278	.590972
38	.422222	.448611	.475000	.501389	.527778	.554167	.580556	.606944
39	.433333	.460417	.487500	.514583	.541667	.568750	.595833	.622917
40	.444444	.472222	.500000	.527778	.555556	.583333	.611111	.638889
41	.455556	.484028	.512500	.540972	.569444	.597917	.626389	.654861
42	.466667	.495833	.525000	.554167	.583333	.612500	.641667	.670833
43	.477778	.507639	.537500	.567361	.597222	.627083	.656944	.686806
44	.488889	.519444	.550000	.580556	.611111	.641667	.672222	.702778
45	.500000	.531250	.562500	.593750	.625000	.656250	.687500	.718750
46	.511111	.543056	.575000	.606944	.638889	.670833	.702778	.734722
47	.522222	.554861	.587500	.620139	.652778	.685417	.718056	.750694
48	.533333	.566667	.600000	.633333	.666667	.700000	.733333	.766667
49	.544444	.578472	.612500	.646528	.680556	.714583	.748611	.782639
50	.555556	.590278	.625000	.659722	.694444	.729167	.763889	.798611
51	.566667	.602083	.637500	.672917	.708333	.743750	.779167	.814583
52	.577778	.613889	.650000	.686111	.722222	.758333	.794444	.830556
53	.588889	.625694	.662500	.699306	.736111	.772917	.809722	.846528
54	.600000	.637500	.675000	.712500	.750000	.787500	.825000	.862500
55	.611111	.649306	.687500	.725694	.763889	.802083	.840278	.878472
89	.988889	1.050694	1.112500	1.174306	1.236111	1.297917	1.359722	1.421528
90	1.000000	1.062500	1.125000	1.187500	1.250000	1.312500	1.375000	1.437500
91	1.011111	1.074306	1.137500	1.200694	1.263889	1.327083	1.390278	1.453472
92	1.022222	1.086111	1.150000	1.213889	1.277778	1.341667	1.405556	1.469444
120	1.333333	1.416667	1.500000	1.583333	1.666667	1.750000	1.833333	1.916667
180	2.000000	2.125000	2.250000	2.375000	2.500000	2.625000	2.750000	2.875000
181	2.011111	2.136806	2.262500	2.388194	2.513889	2.639583	2.765278	2.890972
182	2.022222	2.148611	2.275000	2.401389	2.527778	2.654167	2.780556	2.906944
183	2.033333	2.160417	2.287500	2.414583	2.541667	2.668750	2.795833	2.922917
184	2.044444	2.172222	2.300000	2.427778	2.555556	2.683333	2.811111	2.938889
270	3.000000	3.187500	3.375000	3.562500	3.750000	3.937500	4.125000	4.312500
300	3.333333	3.541667	3.750000	3.958333	4.166667	4.375000	4.583333	4.791667
360	4.000000	4.250000	4.500000	4.750000	5.000000	5.250000	5.500000	5.750000
365	4.055556	4.309028	4.562500	4.815972	5.069444	5.322917	5.576389	5.829861
366	4.066667	4.320833	4.575000	4.829167	5.083333	5.337500	5.591667	5.845833

Description: This table shows the simple interest on $100. Interest is computed on the basis of a 360 day year.

Example: The interest on $100 at 6% for 40 days is $ .67. On $10,000 the interest is $ 66.67.

Interest on $100

DAY	6.00 %	6.25 %	6.50 %	6.75 %	7.00 %	7.25 %	7.50 %	7.75 %
1	.016667	.017361	.018056	.018750	.019444	.020139	.020833	.021528
2	.033333	.034722	.036111	.037500	.038889	.040278	.041667	.043056
3	.050000	.052083	.054167	.056250	.058333	.060417	.062500	.064583
4	.066667	.069444	.072222	.075000	.077778	.080556	.083333	.086111
5	.083333	.086806	.090278	.093750	.097222	.100694	.104167	.107639
6	.100000	.104167	.108333	.112500	.116667	.120833	.125000	.129167
7	.116667	.121528	.126389	.131250	.136111	.140972	.145833	.150694
8	.133333	.138889	.144444	.150000	.155556	.161111	.166667	.172222
9	.150000	.156250	.162500	.168750	.175000	.181250	.187500	.193750
10	.166667	.173611	.180556	.187500	.194444	.201389	.208333	.215278
11	.183333	.190972	.198611	.206250	.213889	.221528	.229167	.236806
12	.200000	.208333	.216667	.225000	.233333	.241667	.250000	.258333
13	.216667	.225694	.234722	.243750	.252778	.261806	.270833	.279861
14	.233333	.243056	.252778	.262500	.272222	.281944	.291667	.301389
15	.250000	.260417	.270833	.281250	.291667	.302083	.312500	.322917
16	.266667	.277778	.288889	.300000	.311111	.322222	.333333	.344444
17	.283333	.295139	.306944	.318750	.330556	.342361	.354167	.365972
18	.300000	.312500	.325000	.337500	.350000	.362500	.375000	.387500
19	.316667	.329861	.343056	.356250	.369444	.382639	.395833	.409028
20	.333333	.347222	.361111	.375000	.388889	.402778	.416667	.430556
21	.350000	.364583	.379167	.393750	.408333	.422917	.437500	.452083
22	.366667	.381944	.397222	.412500	.427778	.443056	.458333	.473611
23	.383333	.399306	.415278	.431250	.447222	.463194	.479167	.495139
24	.400000	.416667	.433333	.450000	.466667	.483333	.500000	.516667
25	.416667	.434028	.451389	.468750	.486111	.503472	.520833	.538194
26	.433333	.451389	.469444	.487500	.505556	.523611	.541667	.559722
27	.450000	.468750	.487500	.506250	.525000	.543750	.562500	.581250
28	.466667	.486111	.505556	.525000	.544444	.563889	.583333	.602778
29	.483333	.503472	.523611	.543750	.563889	.584028	.604167	.624306
30	.500000	.520833	.541667	.562500	.583333	.604167	.625000	.645833
31	.516667	.538194	.559722	.581250	.602778	.624306	.645833	.667361
32	.533333	.555556	.577778	.600000	.622222	.644444	.666667	.688889
33	.550000	.572917	.595833	.618750	.641667	.664583	.687500	.710417
34	.566667	.590278	.613889	.637500	.661111	.684722	.708333	.731944
35	.583333	.607639	.631944	.656250	.680556	.704861	.729167	.753472
36	.600000	.625000	.650000	.675000	.700000	.725000	.750000	.775000
37	.616667	.642361	.668056	.693750	.719444	.745139	.770833	.796528
38	.633333	.659722	.686111	.712500	.738889	.765278	.791667	.818056
39	.650000	.677083	.704167	.731250	.758333	.785417	.812500	.839583
40	.666667	.694444	.722222	.750000	.777778	.805556	.833333	.861111
41	.683333	.711806	.740278	.768750	.797222	.825694	.854167	.882639
42	.700000	.729167	.758333	.787500	.816667	.845833	.875000	.904167
43	.716667	.746528	.776389	.806250	.836111	.865972	.895833	.925694
44	.733333	.763889	.794444	.825000	.855556	.886111	.916667	.947222
45	.750000	.781250	.812500	.843750	.875000	.906250	.937500	.968750
46	.766667	.798611	.830556	.862500	.894444	.926389	.958333	.990278
47	.783333	.815972	.848611	.881250	.913889	.946528	.979167	1.011806
48	.800000	.833333	.866667	.900000	.933333	.966667	1.000000	1.033333
49	.816667	.850694	.884722	.918750	.952778	.986806	1.020833	1.054861
50	.833333	.868056	.902778	.937500	.972222	1.006944	1.041667	1.076389
51	.850000	.885417	.920833	.956250	.991667	1.027083	1.062500	1.097917
52	.866667	.902778	.938889	.975000	1.011111	1.047222	1.083333	1.119444
53	.883333	.920139	.956944	.993750	1.030556	1.067361	1.104167	1.140972
54	.900000	.937500	.975000	1.012500	1.050000	1.087500	1.125000	1.162500
55	.916667	.954861	.993056	1.031250	1.069444	1.107639	1.145833	1.184028
89	1.483333	1.545139	1.606944	1.668750	1.730556	1.792361	1.854167	1.915972
90	1.500000	1.562500	1.625000	1.687500	1.750000	1.812500	1.875000	1.937500
91	1.516667	1.579861	1.643056	1.706250	1.769444	1.832639	1.895833	1.959028
92	1.533333	1.597222	1.661111	1.725000	1.788889	1.852778	1.916667	1.980556
120	2.000000	2.083333	2.166667	2.250000	2.333333	2.416667	2.500000	2.583333
180	3.000000	3.125000	3.250000	3.375000	3.500000	3.625000	3.750000	3.875000
181	3.016667	3.142361	3.268056	3.393750	3.519444	3.645139	3.770833	3.896528
182	3.033333	3.159722	3.286111	3.412500	3.538889	3.665278	3.791667	3.918056
183	3.050000	3.177083	3.304167	3.431250	3.558333	3.685417	3.812500	3.939583
184	3.066667	3.194444	3.322222	3.450000	3.577778	3.705556	3.833333	3.961111
270	4.500000	4.687500	4.875000	5.062500	5.250000	5.437500	5.625000	5.812500
300	5.000000	5.208333	5.416667	5.625000	5.833333	6.041667	6.250000	6.458333
360	6.000000	6.250000	6.500000	6.750000	7.000000	7.250000	7.500000	7.750000
365	6.083333	6.336806	6.590278	6.843750	7.097222	7.350694	7.604167	7.857639
366	6.100000	6.354167	6.608333	6.862500	7.116667	7.370833	7.625000	7.879167

Description: This table shows the simple interest on $100. Interest is computed on the basis of a 360 day year.

Example: The interest on $100 at 8% for 40 days is $ .89. On $10,000 the interest is $ 88.89.

Interest on $100

DAY	8.00 %	DAY	8.25 %	DAY	8.50 %	DAY	8.75 %	DAY	9.00 %	DAY	9.25 %	DAY	9.50 %	DAY	9.75 %
1	.022222	1	.022917	1	.023611	1	.024306	1	.025000	1	.025694	1	.026389	1	.027083
2	.044444	2	.045833	2	.047222	2	.048611	2	.050000	2	.051389	2	.052778	2	.054167
3	.066667	3	.068750	3	.070833	3	.072917	3	.075000	3	.077083	3	.079167	3	.081250
4	.088889	4	.091667	4	.094444	4	.097222	4	.100000	4	.102778	4	.105556	4	.108333
5	.111111	5	.114583	5	.118056	5	.121528	5	.125000	5	.128472	5	.131944	5	.135417
6	.133333	6	.137500	6	.141667	6	.145833	6	.150000	6	.154167	6	.158333	6	.162500
7	.155556	7	.160417	7	.165278	7	.170139	7	.175000	7	.179861	7	.184722	7	.189583
8	.177778	8	.183333	8	.188889	8	.194444	8	.200000	8	.205556	8	.211111	8	.216667
9	.200000	9	.206250	9	.212500	9	.218750	9	.225000	9	.231250	9	.237500	9	.243750
10	.222222	10	.229167	10	.236111	10	.243056	10	.250000	10	.256944	10	.263889	10	.270833
11	.244444	11	.252083	11	.259722	11	.267361	11	.275000	11	.282639	11	.290278	11	.297917
12	.266667	12	.275000	12	.283333	12	.291667	12	.300000	12	.308333	12	.316667	12	.325000
13	.288889	13	.297917	13	.306944	13	.315972	13	.325000	13	.334028	13	.343056	13	.352083
14	.311111	14	.320833	14	.330556	14	.340278	14	.350000	14	.359722	14	.369444	14	.379167
15	.333333	15	.343750	15	.354167	15	.364583	15	.375000	15	.385417	15	.395833	15	.406250
16	.355556	16	.366667	16	.377778	16	.388889	16	.400000	16	.411111	16	.422222	16	.433333
17	.377778	17	.389583	17	.401389	17	.413194	17	.425000	17	.436806	17	.448611	17	.460417
18	.400000	18	.412500	18	.425000	18	.437500	18	.450000	18	.462500	18	.475000	18	.487500
19	.422222	19	.435417	19	.448611	19	.461806	19	.475000	19	.488194	19	.501389	19	.514583
20	.444444	20	.458333	20	.472222	20	.486111	20	.500000	20	.513889	20	.527778	20	.541667
21	.466667	21	.481250	21	.495833	21	.510417	21	.525000	21	.539583	21	.554167	21	.568750
22	.488889	22	.504167	22	.519444	22	.534722	22	.550000	22	.565278	22	.580556	22	.595833
23	.511111	23	.527083	23	.543056	23	.559028	23	.575000	23	.590972	23	.606944	23	.622917
24	.533333	24	.550000	24	.566667	24	.583333	24	.600000	24	.616667	24	.633333	24	.650000
25	.555556	25	.572917	25	.590278	25	.607639	25	.625000	25	.642361	25	.659722	25	.677083
26	.577778	26	.595833	26	.613889	26	.631944	26	.650000	26	.668056	26	.686111	26	.704167
27	.600000	27	.618750	27	.637500	27	.656250	27	.675000	27	.693750	27	.712500	27	.731250
28	.622222	28	.641667	28	.661111	28	.680556	28	.700000	28	.719444	28	.738889	28	.758333
29	.644444	29	.664583	29	.684722	29	.704861	29	.725000	29	.745139	29	.765278	29	.785417
30	.666667	30	.687500	30	.708333	30	.729167	30	.750000	30	.770833	30	.791667	30	.812500
31	.688889	31	.710417	31	.731944	31	.753472	31	.775000	31	.796528	31	.818056	31	.839583
32	.711111	32	.733333	32	.755556	32	.777778	32	.800000	32	.822222	32	.844444	32	.866667
33	.733333	33	.756250	33	.779167	33	.802083	33	.825000	33	.847917	33	.870833	33	.893750
34	.755556	34	.779167	34	.802778	34	.826389	34	.850000	34	.873611	34	.897222	34	.920833
35	.777778	35	.802083	35	.826389	35	.850694	35	.875000	35	.899306	35	.923611	35	.947917
36	.800000	36	.825000	36	.850000	36	.875000	36	.900000	36	.925000	36	.950000	36	.975000
37	.822222	37	.847917	37	.873611	37	.899306	37	.925000	37	.950694	37	.976389	37	1.002083
38	.844444	38	.870833	38	.897222	38	.923611	38	.950000	38	.976389	38	1.002778	38	1.029167
39	.866667	39	.893750	39	.920833	39	.947917	39	.975000	39	1.002083	39	1.029167	39	1.056250
40	.888889	40	.916667	40	.944444	40	.972222	40	1.000000	40	1.027778	40	1.055556	40	1.083333
41	.911111	41	.939583	41	.968056	41	.996528	41	1.025000	41	1.053472	41	1.081944	41	1.110417
42	.933333	42	.962500	42	.991667	42	1.020833	42	1.050000	42	1.079167	42	1.108333	42	1.137500
43	.955556	43	.985417	43	1.015278	43	1.045139	43	1.075000	43	1.104861	43	1.134722	43	1.164583
44	.977778	44	1.008333	44	1.038889	44	1.069444	44	1.100000	44	1.130556	44	1.161111	44	1.191667
45	1.000000	45	1.031250	45	1.062500	45	1.093750	45	1.125000	45	1.156250	45	1.187500	45	1.218750
46	1.022222	46	1.054167	46	1.086111	46	1.118056	46	1.150000	46	1.181944	46	1.213889	46	1.245833
47	1.044444	47	1.077083	47	1.109722	47	1.142361	47	1.175000	47	1.207639	47	1.240278	47	1.272917
48	1.066667	48	1.100000	48	1.133333	48	1.166667	48	1.200000	48	1.233333	48	1.266667	48	1.300000
49	1.088889	49	1.122917	49	1.156944	49	1.190972	49	1.225000	49	1.259028	49	1.293056	49	1.327083
50	1.111111	50	1.145833	50	1.180556	50	1.215278	50	1.250000	50	1.284722	50	1.319444	50	1.354167
51	1.133333	51	1.168750	51	1.204167	51	1.239583	51	1.275000	51	1.310417	51	1.345833	51	1.381250
52	1.155556	52	1.191667	52	1.227778	52	1.263889	52	1.300000	52	1.336111	52	1.372222	52	1.408333
53	1.177778	53	1.214583	53	1.251389	53	1.288194	53	1.325000	53	1.361806	53	1.398611	53	1.435417
54	1.200000	54	1.237500	54	1.275000	54	1.312500	54	1.350000	54	1.387500	54	1.425000	54	1.462500
55	1.222222	55	1.260417	55	1.298611	55	1.336806	55	1.375000	55	1.413194	55	1.451389	55	1.489583
89	1.977778	89	2.039583	89	2.101389	89	2.163194	89	2.225000	89	2.286806	89	2.348611	89	2.410417
90	2.000000	90	2.062500	90	2.125000	90	2.187500	90	2.250000	90	2.312500	90	2.375000	90	2.437500
91	2.022222	91	2.085417	91	2.148611	91	2.211806	91	2.275000	91	2.338194	91	2.401389	91	2.464583
92	2.044444	92	2.108333	92	2.172222	92	2.236111	92	2.300000	92	2.363889	92	2.427778	92	2.491667
120	2.666667	120	2.750000	120	2.833333	120	2.916667	120	3.000000	120	3.083333	120	3.166667	120	3.250000
180	4.000000	180	4.125000	180	4.250000	180	4.375000	180	4.500000	180	4.625000	180	4.750000	180	4.875000
181	4.022222	181	4.147917	181	4.273611	181	4.399306	181	4.525000	181	4.650694	181	4.776389	181	4.902083
182	4.044444	182	4.170833	182	4.297222	182	4.423611	182	4.550000	182	4.676389	182	4.802778	182	4.929167
183	4.066667	183	4.193750	183	4.320833	183	4.447917	183	4.575000	183	4.702083	183	4.829167	183	4.956250
184	4.088889	184	4.216667	184	4.344444	184	4.472222	184	4.600000	184	4.727778	184	4.855556	184	4.983333
270	6.000000	270	6.187500	270	6.375000	270	6.562500	270	6.750000	270	6.937500	270	7.125000	270	7.312500
300	6.666667	300	6.875000	300	7.083333	300	7.291667	300	7.500000	300	7.708333	300	7.916667	300	8.125000
360	8.000000	360	8.250000	360	8.500000	360	8.750000	360	9.000000	360	9.250000	360	9.500000	360	9.750000
365	8.111111	365	8.364583	365	8.618056	365	8.871528	365	9.125000	365	9.378472	365	9.631944	365	9.885417
366	8.133333	366	8.387500	366	8.641667	366	8.895833	366	9.150000	366	9.404167	366	9.658333	366	9.912500

Description: This table shows the simple interest on $100. Interest is computed on the basis of a 360 day year.

Example: The interest on $100 at 10% for 40 days is $ 1.11. On $10,000 the interest is $111.11.

Interest on $100

DAY	10.00 %	10.25 %	10.50 %	10.75 %	11.00 %	11.25 %	11.50 %	11.75 %
1	.027778	.028472	.029167	.029861	.030556	.031250	.031944	.032639
2	.055556	.056944	.058333	.059722	.061111	.062500	.063889	.065278
3	.083333	.085417	.087500	.089583	.091667	.093750	.095833	.097917
4	.111111	.113889	.116667	.119444	.122222	.125000	.127778	.130556
5	.138889	.142361	.145833	.149306	.152778	.156250	.159722	.163194
6	.166667	.170833	.175000	.179167	.183333	.187500	.191667	.195833
7	.194444	.199306	.204167	.209028	.213889	.218750	.223611	.228472
8	.222222	.227778	.233333	.238889	.244444	.250000	.255556	.261111
9	.250000	.256250	.262500	.268750	.275000	.281250	.287500	.293750
10	.277778	.284722	.291667	.298611	.305556	.312500	.319444	.326389
11	.305556	.313194	.320833	.328472	.336111	.343750	.351389	.359028
12	.333333	.341667	.350000	.358333	.366667	.375000	.383333	.391667
13	.361111	.370139	.379167	.388194	.397222	.406250	.415278	.424306
14	.388889	.398611	.408333	.418056	.427778	.437500	.447222	.456944
15	.416667	.427083	.437500	.447917	.458333	.468750	.479167	.489583
16	.444444	.455556	.466667	.477778	.488889	.500000	.511111	.522222
17	.472222	.484028	.495833	.507639	.519444	.531250	.543056	.554861
18	.500000	.512500	.525000	.537500	.550000	.562500	.575000	.587500
19	.527778	.540972	.554167	.567361	.580556	.593750	.606944	.620139
20	.555556	.569444	.583333	.597222	.611111	.625000	.638889	.652778
21	.583333	.597917	.612500	.627083	.641667	.656250	.670833	.685417
22	.611111	.626389	.641667	.656944	.672222	.687500	.702778	.718056
23	.638889	.654861	.670833	.686806	.702778	.718750	.734722	.750694
24	.666667	.683333	.700000	.716667	.733333	.750000	.766667	.783333
25	.694444	.711806	.729167	.746528	.763889	.781250	.798611	.815972
26	.722222	.740278	.758333	.776389	.794444	.812500	.830556	.848611
27	.750000	.768750	.787500	.806250	.825000	.843750	.862500	.881250
28	.777778	.797222	.816667	.836111	.855556	.875000	.894444	.913889
29	.805556	.825694	.845833	.865972	.886111	.906250	.926389	.946528
30	.833333	.854167	.875000	.895833	.916667	.937500	.958333	.979167
31	.861111	.882639	.904167	.925694	.947222	.968750	.990278	1.011806
32	.888889	.911111	.933333	.955556	.977778	1.000000	1.022222	1.044444
33	.916667	.939583	.962500	.985417	1.008333	1.031250	1.054167	1.077083
34	.944444	.968056	.991667	1.015278	1.038889	1.062500	1.086111	1.109722
35	.972222	.996528	1.020833	1.045139	1.069444	1.093750	1.118056	1.142361
36	1.000000	1.025000	1.050000	1.075000	1.100000	1.125000	1.150000	1.175000
37	1.027778	1.053472	1.079167	1.104861	1.130556	1.156250	1.181944	1.207639
38	1.055556	1.081944	1.108333	1.134722	1.161111	1.187500	1.213889	1.240278
39	1.083333	1.110417	1.137500	1.164583	1.191667	1.218750	1.245833	1.272917
40	1.111111	1.138889	1.166667	1.194444	1.222222	1.250000	1.277778	1.305556
41	1.138889	1.167361	1.195833	1.224306	1.252778	1.281250	1.309722	1.338194
42	1.166667	1.195833	1.225000	1.254167	1.283333	1.312500	1.341667	1.370833
43	1.194444	1.224306	1.254167	1.284028	1.313889	1.343750	1.373611	1.403472
44	1.222222	1.252778	1.283333	1.313889	1.344444	1.375000	1.405556	1.436111
45	1.250000	1.281250	1.312500	1.343750	1.375000	1.406250	1.437500	1.468750
46	1.277778	1.309722	1.341667	1.373611	1.405556	1.437500	1.469444	1.501389
47	1.305556	1.338194	1.370833	1.403472	1.436111	1.468750	1.501389	1.534028
48	1.333333	1.366667	1.400000	1.433333	1.466667	1.500000	1.533333	1.566667
49	1.361111	1.395139	1.429167	1.463194	1.497222	1.531250	1.565278	1.599306
50	1.388889	1.423611	1.458333	1.493056	1.527778	1.562500	1.597222	1.631944
51	1.416667	1.452083	1.487500	1.522917	1.558333	1.593750	1.629167	1.664583
52	1.444444	1.480556	1.516667	1.552778	1.588889	1.625000	1.661111	1.697222
53	1.472222	1.509028	1.545833	1.582639	1.619444	1.656250	1.693056	1.729861
54	1.500000	1.537500	1.575000	1.612500	1.650000	1.687500	1.725000	1.762500
55	1.527778	1.565972	1.604167	1.642361	1.680556	1.718750	1.756944	1.795139
89	2.472222	2.534028	2.595833	2.657639	2.719444	2.781250	2.843056	2.904861
90	2.500000	2.562500	2.625000	2.687500	2.750000	2.812500	2.875000	2.937500
91	2.527778	2.590972	2.654167	2.717361	2.780556	2.843750	2.906944	2.970139
92	2.555556	2.619444	2.683333	2.747222	2.811111	2.875000	2.938889	3.002778
120	3.333333	3.416667	3.500000	3.583333	3.666667	3.750000	3.833333	3.916667
180	5.000000	5.125000	5.250000	5.375000	5.500000	5.625000	5.750000	5.875000
181	5.027778	5.153472	5.279167	5.404861	5.530556	5.656250	5.781944	5.907639
182	5.055556	5.181944	5.308333	5.434722	5.561111	5.687500	5.813889	5.940278
183	5.083333	5.210417	5.337500	5.464583	5.591667	5.718750	5.845833	5.972917
184	5.111111	5.238889	5.366667	5.494444	5.622222	5.750000	5.877778	6.005556
270	7.500000	7.687500	7.875000	8.062500	8.250000	8.437500	8.625000	8.812500
300	8.333333	8.541667	8.750000	8.958333	9.166667	9.375000	9.583333	9.791667
360	10.000000	10.250000	10.500000	10.750000	11.000000	11.250000	11.500000	11.750000
365	10.138889	10.392361	10.645833	10.899306	11.152778	11.406250	11.659722	11.913194
366	10.166667	10.420833	10.675000	10.929167	11.183333	11.437500	11.691667	11.945833

SIMPLE INTEREST, 360 DAY YEAR

12.00 %

Description: This table shows the simple interest on $100. Interest is computed on the basis of a 360 day year.

Example: The interest on $100 at 12% for 40 days is $ 1.33. On $10,000 the interest is $133.33.

Interest on $100

DAY	12.00 %	12.25 %	12.50 %	12.75 %	13.00 %	13.25 %	13.50 %	13.75 %
1	.033333	.034028	.034722	.035417	.036111	.036806	.037500	.038194
2	.066667	.068056	.069444	.070833	.072222	.073611	.075000	.076389
3	.100000	.102083	.104167	.106250	.108333	.110417	.112500	.114583
4	.133333	.136111	.138889	.141667	.144444	.147222	.150000	.152778
5	.166667	.170139	.173611	.177083	.180556	.184028	.187500	.190972
6	.200000	.204167	.208333	.212500	.216667	.220833	.225000	.229167
7	.233333	.238194	.243056	.247917	.252778	.257639	.262500	.267361
8	.266667	.272222	.277778	.283333	.288889	.294444	.300000	.305556
9	.300000	.306250	.312500	.318750	.325000	.331250	.337500	.343750
10	.333333	.340278	.347222	.354167	.361111	.368056	.375000	.381944
11	.366667	.374306	.381944	.389583	.397222	.404861	.412500	.420139
12	.400000	.408333	.416667	.425000	.433333	.441667	.450000	.458333
13	.433333	.442361	.451389	.460417	.469444	.478472	.487500	.496528
14	.466667	.476389	.486111	.495833	.505556	.515278	.525000	.534722
15	.500000	.510417	.520833	.531250	.541667	.552083	.562500	.572917
16	.533333	.544444	.555556	.566667	.577778	.588889	.600000	.611111
17	.566667	.578472	.590278	.602083	.613889	.625694	.637500	.649306
18	.600000	.612500	.625000	.637500	.650000	.662500	.675000	.687500
19	.633333	.646528	.659722	.672917	.686111	.699306	.712500	.725694
20	.666667	.680556	.694444	.708333	.722222	.736111	.750000	.763889
21	.700000	.714583	.729167	.743750	.758333	.772917	.787500	.802083
22	.733333	.748611	.763889	.779167	.794444	.809722	.825000	.840278
23	.766667	.782639	.798611	.814583	.830556	.846528	.862500	.878472
24	.800000	.816667	.833333	.850000	.866667	.883333	.900000	.916667
25	.833333	.850694	.868056	.885417	.902778	.920139	.937500	.954861
26	.866667	.884722	.902778	.920833	.938889	.956944	.975000	.993056
27	.900000	.918750	.937500	.956250	.975000	.993750	1.012500	1.031250
28	.933333	.952778	.972222	.991667	1.011111	1.030556	1.050000	1.069444
29	.966667	.986806	1.006944	1.027083	1.047222	1.067361	1.087500	1.107639
30	1.000000	1.020833	1.041667	1.062500	1.083333	1.104167	1.125000	1.145833
31	1.033333	1.054861	1.076389	1.097917	1.119444	1.140972	1.162500	1.184028
32	1.066667	1.088889	1.111111	1.133333	1.155556	1.177778	1.200000	1.222222
33	1.100000	1.122917	1.145833	1.168750	1.191667	1.214583	1.237500	1.260417
34	1.133333	1.156944	1.180556	1.204167	1.227778	1.251389	1.275000	1.298611
35	1.166667	1.190972	1.215278	1.239583	1.263889	1.288194	1.312500	1.336806
36	1.200000	1.225000	1.250000	1.275000	1.300000	1.325000	1.350000	1.375000
37	1.233333	1.259028	1.284722	1.310417	1.336111	1.361806	1.387500	1.413194
38	1.266667	1.293056	1.319444	1.345833	1.372222	1.398611	1.425000	1.451389
39	1.300000	1.327083	1.354167	1.381250	1.408333	1.435417	1.462500	1.489583
40	1.333333	1.361111	1.388889	1.416667	1.444444	1.472222	1.500000	1.527778
41	1.366667	1.395139	1.423611	1.452083	1.480556	1.509028	1.537500	1.565972
42	1.400000	1.429167	1.458333	1.487500	1.516667	1.545833	1.575000	1.604167
43	1.433333	1.463194	1.493056	1.522917	1.552778	1.582639	1.612500	1.642361
44	1.466667	1.497222	1.527778	1.558333	1.588889	1.619444	1.650000	1.680556
45	1.500000	1.531250	1.562500	1.593750	1.625000	1.656250	1.687500	1.718750
46	1.533333	1.565278	1.597222	1.629167	1.661111	1.693056	1.725000	1.756944
47	1.566667	1.599306	1.631944	1.664583	1.697222	1.729861	1.762500	1.795139
48	1.600000	1.633333	1.666667	1.700000	1.733333	1.766667	1.800000	1.833333
49	1.633333	1.667361	1.701389	1.735417	1.769444	1.803472	1.837500	1.871528
50	1.666667	1.701389	1.736111	1.770833	1.805556	1.840278	1.875000	1.909722
51	1.700000	1.735417	1.770833	1.806250	1.841667	1.877083	1.912500	1.947917
52	1.733333	1.769444	1.805556	1.841667	1.877778	1.913889	1.950000	1.986111
53	1.766667	1.803472	1.840278	1.877083	1.913889	1.950694	1.987500	2.024306
54	1.800000	1.837500	1.875000	1.912500	1.950000	1.987500	2.025000	2.062500
55	1.833333	1.871528	1.909722	1.947917	1.986111	2.024306	2.062500	2.100694
89	2.966667	3.028472	3.090278	3.152083	3.213889	3.275694	3.337500	3.399306
90	3.000000	3.062500	3.125000	3.187500	3.250000	3.312500	3.375000	3.437500
91	3.033333	3.096528	3.159722	3.222917	3.286111	3.349306	3.412500	3.475694
92	3.066667	3.130556	3.194444	3.258333	3.322222	3.386111	3.450000	3.513889
120	4.000000	4.083333	4.166667	4.250000	4.333333	4.416667	4.500000	4.583333
180	6.000000	6.125000	6.250000	6.375000	6.500000	6.625000	6.750000	6.875000
181	6.033333	6.159028	6.284722	6.410417	6.536111	6.661806	6.787500	6.913194
182	6.066667	6.193056	6.319444	6.445833	6.572222	6.698611	6.825000	6.951389
183	6.100000	6.227083	6.354167	6.481250	6.608333	6.735417	6.862500	6.989583
184	6.133333	6.261111	6.388889	6.516667	6.644444	6.772222	6.900000	7.027778
270	9.000000	9.187500	9.375000	9.562500	9.750000	9.937500	10.125000	10.312500
300	10.000000	10.208333	10.416667	10.625000	10.833333	11.041667	11.250000	11.458333
360	12.000000	12.250000	12.500000	12.750000	13.000000	13.250000	13.500000	13.750000
365	12.166667	12.420139	12.673611	12.927083	13.180556	13.434028	13.687500	13.940972
366	12.200000	12.454167	12.708333	12.962500	13.216667	13.470833	13.725000	13.979167

SIMPLE INTEREST, 360 DAY YEAR

Description: This table shows the simple interest on $100. Interest is computed on the basis of a 360 day year.

Example: The interest on $100 at 14% for 40 days is $ 1.56. On $10,000 the interest is $155.56.

Interest on $100

DAY	14.00 %	14.25 %	14.50 %	14.75 %	15.00 %	16.00 %	17.00 %	18.00 %
1	.038889	.039583	.040278	.040972	.041667	.044444	.047222	.050000
2	.077778	.079167	.080556	.081944	.083333	.088889	.094444	.100000
3	.116667	.118750	.120833	.122917	.125000	.133333	.141667	.150000
4	.155556	.158333	.161111	.163889	.166667	.177778	.188889	.200000
5	.194444	.197917	.201389	.204861	.208333	.222222	.236111	.250000
6	.233333	.237500	.241667	.245833	.250000	.266667	.283333	.300000
7	.272222	.277083	.281944	.286806	.291667	.311111	.330556	.350000
8	.311111	.316667	.322222	.327778	.333333	.355556	.377778	.400000
9	.350000	.356250	.362500	.368750	.375000	.400000	.425000	.450000
10	.388889	.395833	.402778	.409722	.416667	.444444	.472222	.500000
11	.427778	.435417	.443056	.450694	.458333	.488889	.519444	.550000
12	.466667	.475000	.483333	.491667	.500000	.533333	.566667	.600000
13	.505556	.514583	.523611	.532639	.541667	.577778	.613889	.650000
14	.544444	.554167	.563889	.573611	.583333	.622222	.661111	.700000
15	.583333	.593750	.604167	.614583	.625000	.666667	.708333	.750000
16	.622222	.633333	.644444	.655556	.666667	.711111	.755556	.800000
17	.661111	.672917	.684722	.696528	.708333	.755556	.802778	.850000
18	.700000	.712500	.725000	.737500	.750000	.800000	.850000	.900000
19	.738889	.752083	.765278	.778472	.791667	.844444	.897222	.950000
20	.777778	.791667	.805556	.819444	.833333	.888889	.944444	1.000000
21	.816667	.831250	.845833	.860417	.875000	.933333	.991667	1.050000
22	.855556	.870833	.886111	.901389	.916667	.977778	1.038889	1.100000
23	.894444	.910417	.926389	.942361	.958333	1.022222	1.086111	1.150000
24	.933333	.950000	.966667	.983333	1.000000	1.066667	1.133333	1.200000
25	.972222	.989583	1.006944	1.024306	1.041667	1.111111	1.180556	1.250000
26	1.011111	1.029167	1.047222	1.065278	1.083333	1.155556	1.227778	1.300000
27	1.050000	1.068750	1.087500	1.106250	1.125000	1.200000	1.275000	1.350000
28	1.088889	1.108333	1.127778	1.147222	1.166667	1.244444	1.322222	1.400000
29	1.127778	1.147917	1.168056	1.188194	1.208333	1.288889	1.369444	1.450000
30	1.166667	1.187500	1.208333	1.229167	1.250000	1.333333	1.416667	1.500000
31	1.205556	1.227083	1.248611	1.270139	1.291667	1.377778	1.463889	1.550000
32	1.244444	1.266667	1.288889	1.311111	1.333333	1.422222	1.511111	1.600000
33	1.283333	1.306250	1.329167	1.352083	1.375000	1.466667	1.558333	1.650000
34	1.322222	1.345833	1.369444	1.393056	1.416667	1.511111	1.605556	1.700000
35	1.361111	1.385417	1.409722	1.434028	1.458333	1.555556	1.652778	1.750000
36	1.400000	1.425000	1.450000	1.475000	1.500000	1.600000	1.700000	1.800000
37	1.438889	1.464583	1.490278	1.515972	1.541667	1.644444	1.747222	1.850000
38	1.477778	1.504167	1.530556	1.556944	1.583333	1.688889	1.794444	1.900000
39	1.516667	1.543750	1.570833	1.597917	1.625000	1.733333	1.841667	1.950000
40	1.555556	1.583333	1.611111	1.638889	1.666667	1.777778	1.888889	2.000000
41	1.594444	1.622917	1.651389	1.679861	1.708333	1.822222	1.936111	2.050000
42	1.633333	1.662500	1.691667	1.720833	1.750000	1.866667	1.983333	2.100000
43	1.672222	1.702083	1.731944	1.761806	1.791667	1.911111	2.030556	2.150000
44	1.711111	1.741667	1.772222	1.802778	1.833333	1.955556	2.077778	2.200000
45	1.750000	1.781250	1.812500	1.843750	1.875000	2.000000	2.125000	2.250000
46	1.788889	1.820833	1.852778	1.884722	1.916667	2.044444	2.172222	2.300000
47	1.827778	1.860417	1.893056	1.925694	1.958333	2.088889	2.219444	2.350000
48	1.866667	1.900000	1.933333	1.966667	2.000000	2.133333	2.266667	2.400000
49	1.905556	1.939583	1.973611	2.007639	2.041667	2.177778	2.313889	2.450000
50	1.944444	1.979167	2.013889	2.048611	2.083333	2.222222	2.361111	2.500000
51	1.983333	2.018750	2.054167	2.089583	2.125000	2.266667	2.408333	2.550000
52	2.022222	2.058333	2.094444	2.130556	2.166667	2.311111	2.455556	2.600000
53	2.061111	2.097917	2.134722	2.171528	2.208333	2.355556	2.502778	2.650000
54	2.100000	2.137500	2.175000	2.212500	2.250000	2.400000	2.550000	2.700000
55	2.138889	2.177083	2.215278	2.253472	2.291667	2.444444	2.597222	2.750000
89	3.461111	3.522917	3.584722	3.646528	3.708333	3.955556	4.202778	4.450000
90	3.500000	3.562500	3.625000	3.687500	3.750000	4.000000	4.250000	4.500000
91	3.538889	3.602083	3.665278	3.728472	3.791667	4.044444	4.297222	4.550000
92	3.577778	3.641667	3.705556	3.769444	3.833333	4.088889	4.344444	4.600000
120	4.666667	4.750000	4.833333	4.916667	5.000000	5.333333	5.666667	6.000000
180	7.000000	7.125000	7.250000	7.375000	7.500000	8.000000	8.500000	9.000000
181	7.038889	7.164583	7.290278	7.415972	7.541667	8.044444	8.547222	9.050000
182	7.077778	7.204167	7.330556	7.456944	7.583333	8.088889	8.594444	9.100000
183	7.116667	7.243750	7.370833	7.497917	7.625000	8.133333	8.641667	9.150000
184	7.155556	7.283333	7.411111	7.538889	7.666667	8.177778	8.688889	9.200000
270	10.500000	10.687500	10.875000	11.062500	11.250000	12.000000	12.750000	13.500000
300	11.666667	11.875000	12.083333	12.291667	12.500000	13.333333	14.166667	15.000000
360	14.000000	14.250000	14.500000	14.750000	15.000000	16.000000	17.000000	18.000000
365	14.194444	14.447917	14.701389	14.954861	15.208333	16.222222	17.236111	18.250000
366	14.233333	14.487500	14.741667	14.995833	15.250000	16.266667	17.283333	18.300000

Description: This table shows the simple interest on $100. Interest is computed on the basis of a 365 day year.

Example: The interest on $100 at 4% for 40 days is $ .44. On $10,000 the interest is $ 43.84.

Interest on $100

DAY	4.00 %		4.25 %		4.50 %		4.75 %		5.00 %		5.25 %		5.50 %		5.75 %
1	.010959	1	.011644	1	.012329	1	.013014	1	.013699	1	.014384	1	.015068	1	.015753
2	.021918	2	.023288	2	.024658	2	.026027	2	.027397	2	.028767	2	.030137	2	.031507
3	.032877	3	.034932	3	.036986	3	.039041	3	.041096	3	.043151	3	.045205	3	.047260
4	.043836	4	.046575	4	.049315	4	.052055	4	.054795	4	.057534	4	.060274	4	.063014
5	.054795	5	.058219	5	.061644	5	.065068	5	.068493	5	.071918	5	.075342	5	.078767
6	.065753	6	.069863	6	.073973	6	.078082	6	.082192	6	.086301	6	.090411	6	.094521
7	.076712	7	.081507	7	.086301	7	.091096	7	.095890	7	.100685	7	.105479	7	.110274
8	.087671	8	.093151	8	.098630	8	.104110	8	.109589	8	.115068	8	.120548	8	.126027
9	.098630	9	.104795	9	.110959	9	.117123	9	.123288	9	.129452	9	.135616	9	.141781
10	.109589	10	.116438	10	.123288	10	.130137	10	.136986	10	.143836	10	.150685	10	.157534
11	.120548	11	.128082	11	.135616	11	.143151	11	.150685	11	.158219	11	.165753	11	.173288
12	.131507	12	.139726	12	.147945	12	.156164	12	.164384	12	.172603	12	.180822	12	.189041
13	.142466	13	.151370	13	.160274	13	.169178	13	.178082	13	.186986	13	.195890	13	.204795
14	.153425	14	.163014	14	.172603	14	.182192	14	.191781	14	.201370	14	.210959	14	.220548
15	.164384	15	.174658	15	.184932	15	.195205	15	.205479	15	.215753	15	.226027	15	.236301
16	.175342	16	.186301	16	.197260	16	.208219	16	.219178	16	.230137	16	.241096	16	.252055
17	.186301	17	.197945	17	.209589	17	.221233	17	.232877	17	.244521	17	.256164	17	.267808
18	.197260	18	.209589	18	.221918	18	.234247	18	.246575	18	.258904	18	.271233	18	.283562
19	.208219	19	.221233	19	.234247	19	.247260	19	.260274	19	.273288	19	.286301	19	.299315
20	.219178	20	.232877	20	.246575	20	.260274	20	.273973	20	.287671	20	.301370	20	.315068
21	.230137	21	.244521	21	.258904	21	.273288	21	.287671	21	.302055	21	.316438	21	.330822
22	.241096	22	.256164	22	.271233	22	.286301	22	.301370	22	.316438	22	.331507	22	.346575
23	.252055	23	.267808	23	.283562	23	.299315	23	.315068	23	.330822	23	.346575	23	.362329
24	.263014	24	.279452	24	.295890	24	.312329	24	.328767	24	.345205	24	.361644	24	.378082
25	.273973	25	.291096	25	.308219	25	.325342	25	.342466	25	.359589	25	.376712	25	.393836
26	.284932	26	.302740	26	.320548	26	.338356	26	.356164	26	.373973	26	.391781	26	.409589
27	.295890	27	.314384	27	.332877	27	.351370	27	.369863	27	.388356	27	.406849	27	.425342
28	.306849	28	.326027	28	.345205	28	.364384	28	.383562	28	.402740	28	.421918	28	.441096
29	.317808	29	.337671	29	.357534	29	.377397	29	.397260	29	.417123	29	.436986	29	.456849
30	.328767	30	.349315	30	.369863	30	.390411	30	.410959	30	.431507	30	.452055	30	.472603
31	.339726	31	.360959	31	.382192	31	.403425	31	.424658	31	.445890	31	.467123	31	.488356
32	.350685	32	.372603	32	.394521	32	.416438	32	.438356	32	.460274	32	.482192	32	.504110
33	.361644	33	.384247	33	.406849	33	.429452	33	.452055	33	.474658	33	.497260	33	.519863
34	.372603	34	.395890	34	.419178	34	.442466	34	.465753	34	.489041	34	.512329	34	.535616
35	.383562	35	.407534	35	.431507	35	.455479	35	.479452	35	.503425	35	.527397	35	.551370
36	.394521	36	.419178	36	.443836	36	.468493	36	.493151	36	.517808	36	.542466	36	.567123
37	.405479	37	.430822	37	.456164	37	.481507	37	.506849	37	.532192	37	.557534	37	.582877
38	.416438	38	.442466	38	.468493	38	.494521	38	.520548	38	.546575	38	.572603	38	.598630
39	.427397	39	.454110	39	.480822	39	.507534	39	.534247	39	.560959	39	.587671	39	.614384
40	.438356	40	.465753	40	.493151	40	.520548	40	.547945	40	.575342	40	.602740	40	.630137
41	.449315	41	.477397	41	.505479	41	.533562	41	.561644	41	.589726	41	.617808	41	.645890
42	.460274	42	.489041	42	.517808	42	.546575	42	.575342	42	.604110	42	.632877	42	.661644
43	.471233	43	.500685	43	.530137	43	.559589	43	.589041	43	.618493	43	.647945	43	.677397
44	.482192	44	.512329	44	.542466	44	.572603	44	.602740	44	.632877	44	.663014	44	.693151
45	.493151	45	.523973	45	.554795	45	.585616	45	.616438	45	.647260	45	.678082	45	.708904
46	.504110	46	.535616	46	.567123	46	.598630	46	.630137	46	.661644	46	.693151	46	.724658
47	.515068	47	.547260	47	.579452	47	.611644	47	.643836	47	.676027	47	.708219	47	.740411
48	.526027	48	.558904	48	.591781	48	.624658	48	.657534	48	.690411	48	.723288	48	.756164
49	.536986	49	.570548	49	.604110	49	.637671	49	.671233	49	.704795	49	.738356	49	.771918
50	.547945	50	.582192	50	.616438	50	.650685	50	.684932	50	.719178	50	.753425	50	.787671
51	.558904	51	.593836	51	.628767	51	.663699	51	.698630	51	.733562	51	.768493	51	.803425
52	.569863	52	.605479	52	.641096	52	.676712	52	.712329	52	.747945	52	.783562	52	.819178
53	.580822	53	.617123	53	.653425	53	.689726	53	.726027	53	.762329	53	.798630	53	.834932
54	.591781	54	.628767	54	.665753	54	.702740	54	.739726	54	.776712	54	.813699	54	.850685
55	.602740	55	.640411	55	.678082	55	.715753	55	.753425	55	.791096	55	.828767	55	.866438
89	.975342	89	1.036301	89	1.097260	89	1.158219	89	1.219178	89	1.280137	89	1.341096	89	1.402055
90	.986301	90	1.047945	90	1.109589	90	1.171233	90	1.232877	90	1.294521	90	1.356164	90	1.417808
91	.997260	91	1.059589	91	1.121918	91	1.184247	91	1.246575	91	1.308904	91	1.371233	91	1.433562
92	1.008219	92	1.071233	92	1.134247	92	1.197260	92	1.260274	92	1.323288	92	1.386301	92	1.449315
120	1.315068	120	1.397260	120	1.479452	120	1.561644	120	1.643836	120	1.726027	120	1.808219	120	1.890411
180	1.972603	180	2.095890	180	2.219178	180	2.342466	180	2.465753	180	2.589041	180	2.712329	180	2.835616
181	1.983562	181	2.107534	181	2.231507	181	2.355479	181	2.479452	181	2.603425	181	2.727397	181	2.851370
182	1.994521	182	2.119178	182	2.243836	182	2.368493	182	2.493151	182	2.617808	182	2.742466	182	2.867123
183	2.005479	183	2.130822	183	2.256164	183	2.381507	183	2.506849	183	2.632192	183	2.757534	183	2.882877
184	2.016438	184	2.142466	184	2.268493	184	2.394521	184	2.520548	184	2.646575	184	2.772603	184	2.898630
270	2.958904	270	3.143836	270	3.328767	270	3.513699	270	3.698630	270	3.883562	270	4.068493	270	4.253425
300	3.287671	300	3.493151	300	3.698630	300	3.904110	300	4.109589	300	4.315068	300	4.520548	300	4.726027
360	3.945205	360	4.191781	360	4.438356	360	4.684932	360	4.931507	360	5.178082	360	5.424658	360	5.671233
365	4.000000	365	4.250000	365	4.500000	365	4.750000	365	5.000000	365	5.250000	365	5.500000	365	5.750000
366	4.010959	366	4.261644	366	4.512329	366	4.763014	366	5.013699	366	5.264384	366	5.515068	366	5.765753

Description: This table shows the simple interest on $100. Interest is computed on the basis of a 365 day year.

Example: The interest on $100 at 6% for 40 days is $ .66. On $10,000 the interest is $ 65.75.

Interest on $100

DAY	6.00 %		6.25 %		6.50 %		6.75 %		7.00 %		7.25 %		7.50 %		7.75 %
1	.016438	1	.017123	1	.017808	1	.018493	1	.019178	1	.019863	1	.020548	1	.021233
2	.032877	2	.034247	2	.035616	2	.036986	2	.038356	2	.039726	2	.041096	2	.042466
3	.049315	3	.051370	3	.053425	3	.055479	3	.057534	3	.059589	3	.061644	3	.063699
4	.065753	4	.068493	4	.071233	4	.073973	4	.076712	4	.079452	4	.082192	4	.084932
5	.082192	5	.085616	5	.089041	5	.092466	5	.095890	5	.099315	5	.102740	5	.106164
6	.098630	6	.102740	6	.106849	6	.110959	6	.115068	6	.119178	6	.123288	6	.127397
7	.115068	7	.119863	7	.124658	7	.129452	7	.134247	7	.139041	7	.143836	7	.148630
8	.131507	8	.136986	8	.142466	8	.147945	8	.153425	8	.158904	8	.164384	8	.169863
9	.147945	9	.154110	9	.160274	9	.166438	9	.172603	9	.178767	9	.184932	9	.191096
10	.164384	10	.171233	10	.178082	10	.184932	10	.191781	10	.198630	10	.205479	10	.212329
11	.180822	11	.188356	11	.195890	11	.203425	11	.210959	11	.218493	11	.226027	11	.233562
12	.197260	12	.205479	12	.213699	12	.221918	12	.230137	12	.238356	12	.246575	12	.254795
13	.213699	13	.222603	13	.231507	13	.240411	13	.249315	13	.258219	13	.267123	13	.276027
14	.230137	14	.239726	14	.249315	14	.258904	14	.268493	14	.278082	14	.287671	14	.297260
15	.246575	15	.256849	15	.267123	15	.277397	15	.287671	15	.297945	15	.308219	15	.318493
16	.263014	16	.273973	16	.284932	16	.295890	16	.306849	16	.317808	16	.328767	16	.339726
17	.279452	17	.291096	17	.302740	17	.314384	17	.326027	17	.337671	17	.349315	17	.360959
18	.295890	18	.308219	18	.320548	18	.332877	18	.345205	18	.357534	18	.369863	18	.382192
19	.312329	19	.325342	19	.338356	19	.351370	19	.364384	19	.377397	19	.390411	19	.403425
20	.328767	20	.342466	20	.356164	20	.369863	20	.383562	20	.397260	20	.410959	20	.424658
21	.345205	21	.359589	21	.373973	21	.388356	21	.402740	21	.417123	21	.431507	21	.445890
22	.361644	22	.376712	22	.391781	22	.406849	22	.421918	22	.436986	22	.452055	22	.467123
23	.378082	23	.393836	23	.409589	23	.425342	23	.441096	23	.456849	23	.472603	23	.488356
24	.394521	24	.410959	24	.427397	24	.443836	24	.460274	24	.476712	24	.493151	24	.509589
25	.410959	25	.428082	25	.445205	25	.462329	25	.479452	25	.496575	25	.513699	25	.530822
26	.427397	26	.445205	26	.463014	26	.480822	26	.498630	26	.516438	26	.534247	26	.552055
27	.443836	27	.462329	27	.480822	27	.499315	27	.517808	27	.536301	27	.554795	27	.573288
28	.460274	28	.479452	28	.498630	28	.517808	28	.536986	28	.556164	28	.575342	28	.594521
29	.476712	29	.496575	29	.516438	29	.536301	29	.556164	29	.576027	29	.595890	29	.615753
30	.493151	30	.513699	30	.534247	30	.554795	30	.575342	30	.595890	30	.616438	30	.636986
31	.509589	31	.530822	31	.552055	31	.573288	31	.594521	31	.615753	31	.636986	31	.658219
32	.526027	32	.547945	32	.569863	32	.591781	32	.613699	32	.635616	32	.657534	32	.679452
33	.542466	33	.565068	33	.587671	33	.610274	33	.632877	33	.655479	33	.678082	33	.700685
34	.558904	34	.582192	34	.605479	34	.628767	34	.652055	34	.675342	34	.698630	34	.721918
35	.575342	35	.599315	35	.623288	35	.647260	35	.671233	35	.695205	35	.719178	35	.743151
36	.591781	36	.616438	36	.641096	36	.665753	36	.690411	36	.715068	36	.739726	36	.764384
37	.608219	37	.633562	37	.658904	37	.684247	37	.709589	37	.734932	37	.760274	37	.785616
38	.624658	38	.650685	38	.676712	38	.702740	38	.728767	38	.754795	38	.780822	38	.806849
39	.641096	39	.667808	39	.694521	39	.721233	39	.747945	39	.774658	39	.801370	39	.828082
40	.657534	40	.684932	40	.712329	40	.739726	40	.767123	40	.794521	40	.821918	40	.849315
41	.673973	41	.702055	41	.730137	41	.758219	41	.786301	41	.814384	41	.842466	41	.870548
42	.690411	42	.719178	42	.747945	42	.776712	42	.805479	42	.834247	42	.863014	42	.891781
43	.706849	43	.736301	43	.765753	43	.795205	43	.824658	43	.854110	43	.883562	43	.913014
44	.723288	44	.753425	44	.783562	44	.813699	44	.843836	44	.873973	44	.904110	44	.934247
45	.739726	45	.770548	45	.801370	45	.832192	45	.863014	45	.893836	45	.924658	45	.955479
46	.756164	46	.787671	46	.819178	46	.850685	46	.882192	46	.913699	46	.945205	46	.976712
47	.772603	47	.804795	47	.836986	47	.869178	47	.901370	47	.933562	47	.965753	47	.997945
48	.789041	48	.821918	48	.854795	48	.887671	48	.920548	48	.953425	48	.986301	48	1.019178
49	.805479	49	.839041	49	.872603	49	.906164	49	.939726	49	.973288	49	1.006849	49	1.040411
50	.821918	50	.856164	50	.890411	50	.924658	50	.958904	50	.993151	50	1.027397	50	1.061644
51	.838356	51	.873288	51	.908219	51	.943151	51	.978082	51	1.013014	51	1.047945	51	1.082877
52	.854795	52	.890411	52	.926027	52	.961644	52	.997260	52	1.032877	52	1.068493	52	1.104110
53	.871233	53	.907534	53	.943836	53	.980137	53	1.016438	53	1.052740	53	1.089041	53	1.125342
54	.887671	54	.924658	54	.961644	54	.998630	54	1.035616	54	1.072603	54	1.109589	54	1.146575
55	.904110	55	.941781	55	.979452	55	1.017123	55	1.054795	55	1.092466	55	1.130137	55	1.167808
89	1.463014	89	1.523973	89	1.584932	89	1.645890	89	1.706849	89	1.767808	89	1.828767	89	1.889726
90	1.479452	90	1.541096	90	1.602740	90	1.664384	90	1.726027	90	1.787671	90	1.849315	90	1.910959
91	1.495890	91	1.558219	91	1.620548	91	1.682877	91	1.745205	91	1.807534	91	1.869863	91	1.932192
92	1.512329	92	1.575342	92	1.638356	92	1.701370	92	1.764384	92	1.827397	92	1.890411	92	1.953425
120	1.972603	120	2.054795	120	2.136986	120	2.219178	120	2.301370	120	2.383562	120	2.465753	120	2.547945
180	2.958904	180	3.082192	180	3.205479	180	3.328767	180	3.452055	180	3.575342	180	3.698630	180	3.821918
181	2.975342	181	3.099315	181	3.223288	181	3.347260	181	3.471233	181	3.595205	181	3.719178	181	3.843151
182	2.991781	182	3.116438	182	3.241096	182	3.365753	182	3.490411	182	3.615068	182	3.739726	182	3.864384
183	3.008219	183	3.133562	183	3.258904	183	3.384247	183	3.509589	183	3.634932	183	3.760274	183	3.885616
184	3.024658	184	3.150685	184	3.276712	184	3.402740	184	3.528767	184	3.654795	184	3.780822	184	3.906849
270	4.438356	270	4.623288	270	4.808219	270	4.993151	270	5.178082	270	5.363014	270	5.547945	270	5.732877
300	4.931507	300	5.136986	300	5.342466	300	5.547945	300	5.753425	300	5.958904	300	6.164384	300	6.369863
360	5.917808	360	6.164384	360	6.410959	360	6.657534	360	6.904110	360	7.150685	360	7.397260	360	7.643836
365	6.000000	365	6.250000	365	6.500000	365	6.750000	365	7.000000	365	7.250000	365	7.500000	365	7.750000
366	6.016438	366	6.267123	366	6.517808	366	6.768493	366	7.019178	366	7.269863	366	7.520548	366	7.771233

Description: This table shows the simple interest on $100. Interest is computed on the basis of a 365 day year.

Example: The interest on $100 at 8% for 40 days is $ .88. On $10,000 the interest is $ 87.67.

Interest on $100

DAY	8.00 %	8.25 %	8.50 %	8.75 %	9.00 %	9.25 %	9.50 %	9.75 %
1	.021918	.022603	.023288	.023973	.024658	.025342	.026027	.026712
2	.043836	.045205	.046575	.047945	.049315	.050685	.052055	.053425
3	.065753	.067808	.069863	.071918	.073973	.076027	.078082	.080137
4	.087671	.090411	.093151	.095890	.098630	.101370	.104110	.106849
5	.109589	.113014	.116438	.119863	.123288	.126712	.130137	.133562
6	.131507	.135616	.139726	.143836	.147945	.152055	.156164	.160274
7	.153425	.158219	.163014	.167808	.172603	.177397	.182192	.186986
8	.175342	.180822	.186301	.191781	.197260	.202740	.208219	.213699
9	.197260	.203425	.209589	.215753	.221918	.228082	.234247	.240411
10	.219178	.226027	.232877	.239726	.246575	.253425	.260274	.267123
11	.241096	.248630	.256164	.263699	.271233	.278767	.286301	.293836
12	.263014	.271233	.279452	.287671	.295890	.304110	.312329	.320548
13	.284932	.293836	.302740	.311644	.320548	.329452	.338356	.347260
14	.306849	.316438	.326027	.335616	.345205	.354795	.364384	.373973
15	.328767	.339041	.349315	.359589	.369863	.380137	.390411	.400685
16	.350685	.361644	.372603	.383562	.394521	.405479	.416438	.427397
17	.372603	.384247	.395890	.407534	.419178	.430822	.442466	.454110
18	.394521	.406849	.419178	.431507	.443836	.456164	.468493	.480822
19	.416438	.429452	.442466	.455479	.468493	.481507	.494521	.507534
20	.438356	.452055	.465753	.479452	.493151	.506849	.520548	.534247
21	.460274	.474658	.489041	.503425	.517808	.532192	.546575	.560959
22	.482192	.497260	.512329	.527397	.542466	.557534	.572603	.587671
23	.504110	.519863	.535616	.551370	.567123	.582877	.598630	.614384
24	.526027	.542466	.558904	.575342	.591781	.608219	.624658	.641096
25	.547945	.565068	.582192	.599315	.616438	.633562	.650685	.667808
26	.569863	.587671	.605479	.623288	.641096	.658904	.676712	.694521
27	.591781	.610274	.628767	.647260	.665753	.684247	.702740	.721233
28	.613699	.632877	.652055	.671233	.690411	.709589	.728767	.747945
29	.635616	.655479	.675342	.695205	.715068	.734932	.754795	.774658
30	.657534	.678082	.698630	.719178	.739726	.760274	.780822	.801370
31	.679452	.700685	.721918	.743151	.764384	.785616	.806849	.828082
32	.701370	.723288	.745205	.767123	.789041	.810959	.832877	.854795
33	.723288	.745890	.768493	.791096	.813699	.836301	.858904	.881507
34	.745205	.768493	.791781	.815068	.838356	.861644	.884932	.908219
35	.767123	.791096	.815068	.839041	.863014	.886986	.910959	.934932
36	.789041	.813699	.838356	.863014	.887671	.912329	.936986	.961644
37	.810959	.836301	.861644	.886986	.912329	.937671	.963014	.988356
38	.832877	.858904	.884932	.910959	.936986	.963014	.989041	1.015068
39	.854795	.881507	.908219	.934932	.961644	.988356	1.015068	1.041781
40	.876712	.904110	.931507	.958904	.986301	1.013699	1.041096	1.068493
41	.898630	.926712	.954795	.982877	1.010959	1.039041	1.067123	1.095205
42	.920548	.949315	.978082	1.006849	1.035616	1.064384	1.093151	1.121918
43	.942466	.971918	1.001370	1.030822	1.060274	1.089726	1.119178	1.148630
44	.964384	.994521	1.024658	1.054795	1.084932	1.115068	1.145205	1.175342
45	.986301	1.017123	1.047945	1.078767	1.109589	1.140411	1.171233	1.202055
46	1.008219	1.039726	1.071233	1.102740	1.134247	1.165753	1.197260	1.228767
47	1.030137	1.062329	1.094521	1.126712	1.158904	1.191096	1.223288	1.255479
48	1.052055	1.084932	1.117808	1.150685	1.183562	1.216438	1.249315	1.282192
49	1.073973	1.107534	1.141096	1.174658	1.208219	1.241781	1.275342	1.308904
50	1.095890	1.130137	1.164384	1.198630	1.232877	1.267123	1.301370	1.335616
51	1.117808	1.152740	1.187671	1.222603	1.257534	1.292466	1.327397	1.362329
52	1.139726	1.175342	1.210959	1.246575	1.282192	1.317808	1.353425	1.389041
53	1.161644	1.197945	1.234247	1.270548	1.306849	1.343151	1.379452	1.415753
54	1.183562	1.220548	1.257534	1.294521	1.331507	1.368493	1.405479	1.442466
55	1.205479	1.243151	1.280822	1.318493	1.356164	1.393836	1.431507	1.469178
89	1.950685	2.011644	2.072603	2.133562	2.194521	2.255479	2.316438	2.377397
90	1.972603	2.034247	2.095890	2.157534	2.219178	2.280822	2.342466	2.404110
91	1.994521	2.056849	2.119178	2.181507	2.243836	2.306164	2.368493	2.430822
92	2.016438	2.079452	2.142466	2.205479	2.268493	2.331507	2.394521	2.457534
120	2.630137	2.712329	2.794521	2.876712	2.958904	3.041096	3.123288	3.205479
180	3.945205	4.068493	4.191781	4.315068	4.438356	4.561644	4.684932	4.808219
181	3.967123	4.091096	4.215068	4.339041	4.463014	4.586986	4.710959	4.834932
182	3.989041	4.113699	4.238356	4.363014	4.487671	4.612329	4.736986	4.861644
183	4.010959	4.136301	4.261644	4.386986	4.512329	4.637671	4.763014	4.888356
184	4.032877	4.158904	4.284932	4.410959	4.536986	4.663014	4.789041	4.915068
270	5.917808	6.102740	6.287671	6.472603	6.657534	6.842466	7.027397	7.212329
300	6.575342	6.780822	6.986301	7.191781	7.397260	7.602740	7.808219	8.013699
360	7.890411	8.136986	8.383562	8.630137	8.876712	9.123288	9.369863	9.616438
365	8.000000	8.250000	8.500000	8.750000	9.000000	9.250000	9.500000	9.750000
366	8.021918	8.272603	8.523288	8.773973	9.024658	9.275342	9.526027	9.776712

Description: This table shows the simple interest on $100. Interest is computed on the basis of a 365 day year.

Example: The interest on $100 at 10% for 40 days is $ 1.10. On $10,000 the interest is $109.59.

Interest on $100

DAY	10.00 %	10.25 %	10.50 %	10.75 %	11.00 %	11.25 %	11.50 %	11.75 %
1	.027397	.028082	.028767	.029452	.030137	.030822	.031507	.032192
2	.054795	.056164	.057534	.058904	.060274	.061644	.063014	.064384
3	.082192	.084247	.086301	.088356	.090411	.092466	.094521	.096575
4	.109589	.112329	.115068	.117808	.120548	.123288	.126027	.128767
5	.136986	.140411	.143836	.147260	.150685	.154110	.157534	.160959
6	.164384	.168493	.172603	.176712	.180822	.184932	.189041	.193151
7	.191781	.196575	.201370	.206164	.210959	.215753	.220548	.225342
8	.219178	.224658	.230137	.235616	.241096	.246575	.252055	.257534
9	.246575	.252740	.258904	.265068	.271233	.277397	.283562	.289726
10	.273973	.280822	.287671	.294521	.301370	.308219	.315068	.321918
11	.301370	.308904	.316438	.323973	.331507	.339041	.346575	.354110
12	.328767	.336986	.345205	.353425	.361644	.369863	.378082	.386301
13	.356164	.365068	.373973	.382877	.391781	.400685	.409589	.418493
14	.383562	.393151	.402740	.412329	.421918	.431507	.441096	.450685
15	.410959	.421233	.431507	.441781	.452055	.462329	.472603	.482877
16	.438356	.449315	.460274	.471233	.482192	.493151	.504110	.515068
17	.465753	.477397	.489041	.500685	.512329	.523973	.535616	.547260
18	.493151	.505479	.517808	.530137	.542466	.554795	.567123	.579452
19	.520548	.533562	.546575	.559589	.572603	.585616	.598630	.611644
20	.547945	.561644	.575342	.589041	.602740	.616438	.630137	.643836
21	.575342	.589726	.604110	.618493	.632877	.647260	.661644	.676027
22	.602740	.617808	.632877	.647945	.663014	.678082	.693151	.708219
23	.630137	.645890	.661644	.677397	.693151	.708904	.724658	.740411
24	.657534	.673973	.690411	.706849	.723288	.739726	.756164	.772603
25	.684932	.702055	.719178	.736301	.753425	.770548	.787671	.804795
26	.712329	.730137	.747945	.765753	.783562	.801370	.819178	.836986
27	.739726	.758219	.776712	.795205	.813699	.832192	.850685	.869178
28	.767123	.786301	.805479	.824658	.843836	.863014	.882192	.901370
29	.794521	.814384	.834247	.854110	.873973	.893836	.913699	.933562
30	.821918	.842466	.863014	.883562	.904110	.924658	.945205	.965753
31	.849315	.870548	.891781	.913014	.934247	.955479	.976712	.997945
32	.876712	.898630	.920548	.942466	.964384	.986301	1.008219	1.030137
33	.904110	.926712	.949315	.971918	.994521	1.017123	1.039726	1.062329
34	.931507	.954795	.978082	1.001370	1.024658	1.047945	1.071233	1.094521
35	.958904	.982877	1.006849	1.030822	1.054795	1.078767	1.102740	1.126712
36	.986301	1.010959	1.035616	1.060274	1.084932	1.109589	1.134247	1.158904
37	1.013699	1.039041	1.064384	1.089726	1.115068	1.140411	1.165753	1.191096
38	1.041096	1.067123	1.093151	1.119178	1.145205	1.171233	1.197260	1.223288
39	1.068493	1.095205	1.121918	1.148630	1.175342	1.202055	1.228767	1.255479
40	1.095890	1.123288	1.150685	1.178082	1.205479	1.232877	1.260274	1.287671
41	1.123288	1.151370	1.179452	1.207534	1.235616	1.263699	1.291781	1.319863
42	1.150685	1.179452	1.208219	1.236986	1.265753	1.294521	1.323288	1.352055
43	1.178082	1.207534	1.236986	1.266438	1.295890	1.325342	1.354795	1.384247
44	1.205479	1.235616	1.265753	1.295890	1.326027	1.356164	1.386301	1.416438
45	1.232877	1.263699	1.294521	1.325342	1.356164	1.386986	1.417808	1.448630
46	1.260274	1.291781	1.323288	1.354795	1.386301	1.417808	1.449315	1.480822
47	1.287671	1.319863	1.352055	1.384247	1.416438	1.448630	1.480822	1.513014
48	1.315068	1.347945	1.380822	1.413699	1.446575	1.479452	1.512329	1.545205
49	1.342466	1.376027	1.409589	1.443151	1.476712	1.510274	1.543836	1.577397
50	1.369863	1.404110	1.438356	1.472603	1.506849	1.541096	1.575342	1.609589
51	1.397260	1.432192	1.467123	1.502055	1.536986	1.571918	1.606849	1.641781
52	1.424658	1.460274	1.495890	1.531507	1.567123	1.602740	1.638356	1.673973
53	1.452055	1.488356	1.524658	1.560959	1.597260	1.633562	1.669863	1.706164
54	1.479452	1.516438	1.553425	1.590411	1.627397	1.664384	1.701370	1.738356
55	1.506849	1.544521	1.582192	1.619863	1.657534	1.695205	1.732877	1.770548
89	2.438356	2.499315	2.560274	2.621233	2.682192	2.743151	2.804110	2.865068
90	2.465753	2.527397	2.589041	2.650685	2.712329	2.773973	2.835616	2.897260
91	2.493151	2.555479	2.617808	2.680137	2.742466	2.804795	2.867123	2.929452
92	2.520548	2.583562	2.646575	2.709589	2.772603	2.835616	2.898630	2.961644
120	3.287671	3.369863	3.452055	3.534247	3.616438	3.698630	3.780822	3.863014
180	4.931507	5.054795	5.178082	5.301370	5.424658	5.547945	5.671233	5.794521
181	4.958904	5.082877	5.206849	5.330822	5.454795	5.578767	5.702740	5.826712
182	4.986301	5.110959	5.235616	5.360274	5.484932	5.609589	5.734247	5.858904
183	5.013699	5.139041	5.264384	5.389726	5.515068	5.640411	5.765753	5.891096
184	5.041096	5.167123	5.293151	5.419178	5.545205	5.671233	5.797260	5.923288
270	7.397260	7.582192	7.767123	7.952055	8.136986	8.321918	8.506849	8.691781
300	8.219178	8.424658	8.630137	8.835616	9.041096	9.246575	9.452055	9.657534
360	9.863014	10.109589	10.356164	10.602740	10.849315	11.095890	11.342466	11.589041
365	10.000000	10.250000	10.500000	10.750000	11.000000	11.250000	11.500000	11.750000
366	10.027397	10.278082	10.528767	10.779452	11.030137	11.280822	11.531507	11.782192

SIMPLE INTEREST, 365 DAY YEAR

12.00 %

Description: This table shows the simple interest on $100. Interest is computed on the basis of a 365 day year.

Example: The interest on $100 at 12% for 40 days is $ 1.32. On $10,000 the interest is $131.51.

Interest on $100

DAY	12.00 %	12.25 %	12.50 %	12.75 %	13.00 %	13.25 %	13.50 %	13.75 %
1	.032877	.033562	.034247	.034932	.035616	.036301	.036986	.037671
2	.065753	.067123	.068493	.069863	.071233	.072603	.073973	.075342
3	.098630	.100685	.102740	.104795	.106849	.108904	.110959	.113014
4	.131507	.134247	.136986	.139726	.142466	.145205	.147945	.150685
5	.164384	.167808	.171233	.174658	.178082	.181507	.184932	.188356
6	.197260	.201370	.205479	.209589	.213699	.217808	.221918	.226027
7	.230137	.234932	.239726	.244521	.249315	.254110	.258904	.263699
8	.263014	.268493	.273973	.279452	.284932	.290411	.295890	.301370
9	.295890	.302055	.308219	.314384	.320548	.326712	.332877	.339041
10	.328767	.335616	.342466	.349315	.356164	.363014	.369863	.376712
11	.361644	.369178	.376712	.384247	.391781	.399315	.406849	.414384
12	.394521	.402740	.410959	.419178	.427397	.435616	.443836	.452055
13	.427397	.436301	.445205	.454110	.463014	.471918	.480822	.489726
14	.460274	.469863	.479452	.489041	.498630	.508219	.517808	.527397
15	.493151	.503425	.513699	.523973	.534247	.544521	.554795	.565068
16	.526027	.536986	.547945	.558904	.569863	.580822	.591781	.602740
17	.558904	.570548	.582192	.593836	.605479	.617123	.628767	.640411
18	.591781	.604110	.616438	.628767	.641096	.653425	.665753	.678082
19	.624658	.637671	.650685	.663699	.676712	.689726	.702740	.715753
20	.657534	.671233	.684932	.698630	.712329	.726027	.739726	.753425
21	.690411	.704795	.719178	.733562	.747945	.762329	.776712	.791096
22	.723288	.738356	.753425	.768493	.783562	.798630	.813699	.828767
23	.756164	.771918	.787671	.803425	.819178	.834932	.850685	.866438
24	.789041	.805479	.821918	.838356	.854795	.871233	.887671	.904110
25	.821918	.839041	.856164	.873288	.890411	.907534	.924658	.941781
26	.854795	.872603	.890411	.908219	.926027	.943836	.961644	.979452
27	.887671	.906164	.924658	.943151	.961644	.980137	.998630	1.017123
28	.920548	.939726	.958904	.978082	.997260	1.016438	1.035616	1.054795
29	.953425	.973288	.993151	1.013014	1.032877	1.052740	1.072603	1.092466
30	.986301	1.006849	1.027397	1.047945	1.068493	1.089041	1.109589	1.130137
31	1.019178	1.040411	1.061644	1.082877	1.104110	1.125342	1.146575	1.167808
32	1.052055	1.073973	1.095890	1.117808	1.139726	1.161644	1.183562	1.205479
33	1.084932	1.107534	1.130137	1.152740	1.175342	1.197945	1.220548	1.243151
34	1.117808	1.141096	1.164384	1.187671	1.210959	1.234247	1.257534	1.280822
35	1.150685	1.174658	1.198630	1.222603	1.246575	1.270548	1.294521	1.318493
36	1.183562	1.208219	1.232877	1.257534	1.282192	1.306849	1.331507	1.356164
37	1.216438	1.241781	1.267123	1.292466	1.317808	1.343151	1.368493	1.393836
38	1.249315	1.275342	1.301370	1.327397	1.353425	1.379452	1.405479	1.431507
39	1.282192	1.308904	1.335616	1.362329	1.389041	1.415753	1.442466	1.469178
40	1.315068	1.342466	1.369863	1.397260	1.424658	1.452055	1.479452	1.506849
41	1.347945	1.376027	1.404110	1.432192	1.460274	1.488356	1.516438	1.544521
42	1.380822	1.409589	1.438356	1.467123	1.495890	1.524658	1.553425	1.582192
43	1.413699	1.443151	1.472603	1.502055	1.531507	1.560959	1.590411	1.619863
44	1.446575	1.476712	1.506849	1.536986	1.567123	1.597260	1.627397	1.657534
45	1.479452	1.510274	1.541096	1.571918	1.602740	1.633562	1.664384	1.695205
46	1.512329	1.543836	1.575342	1.606849	1.638356	1.669863	1.701370	1.732877
47	1.545205	1.577397	1.609589	1.641781	1.673973	1.706164	1.738356	1.770548
48	1.578082	1.610959	1.643836	1.676712	1.709589	1.742466	1.775342	1.808219
49	1.610959	1.644521	1.678082	1.711644	1.745205	1.778767	1.812329	1.845890
50	1.643836	1.678082	1.712329	1.746575	1.780822	1.815068	1.849315	1.883562
51	1.676712	1.711644	1.746575	1.781507	1.816438	1.851370	1.886301	1.921233
52	1.709589	1.745205	1.780822	1.816438	1.852055	1.887671	1.923288	1.958904
53	1.742466	1.778767	1.815068	1.851370	1.887671	1.923973	1.960274	1.996575
54	1.775342	1.812329	1.849315	1.886301	1.923288	1.960274	1.997260	2.034247
55	1.808219	1.845890	1.883562	1.921233	1.958904	1.996575	2.034247	2.071918
89	2.926027	2.986986	3.047945	3.108904	3.169863	3.230822	3.291781	3.352740
90	2.958904	3.020548	3.082192	3.143836	3.205479	3.267123	3.328767	3.390411
91	2.991781	3.054110	3.116438	3.178767	3.241096	3.303425	3.365753	3.428082
92	3.024658	3.087671	3.150685	3.213699	3.276712	3.339726	3.402740	3.465753
120	3.945205	4.027397	4.109589	4.191781	4.273973	4.356164	4.438356	4.520548
180	5.917808	6.041096	6.164384	6.287671	6.410959	6.534247	6.657534	6.780822
181	5.950685	6.074658	6.198630	6.322603	6.446575	6.570548	6.694521	6.818493
182	5.983562	6.108219	6.232877	6.357534	6.482192	6.606849	6.731507	6.856164
183	6.016438	6.141781	6.267123	6.392466	6.517808	6.643151	6.768493	6.893836
184	6.049315	6.175342	6.301370	6.427397	6.553425	6.679452	6.805479	6.931507
270	8.876712	9.061644	9.246575	9.431507	9.616438	9.801370	9.986301	10.171233
300	9.863014	10.068493	10.273973	10.479452	10.684932	10.890411	11.095890	11.301370
360	11.835616	12.082192	12.328767	12.575342	12.821918	13.068493	13.315068	13.561644
365	12.000000	12.250000	12.500000	12.750000	13.000000	13.250000	13.500000	13.750000
366	12.032877	12.283562	12.534247	12.784932	13.035616	13.286301	13.536986	13.787671

SIMPLE INTEREST, 365 DAY YEAR

14.00 %

Description: This table shows the simple interest on $100. Interest is computed on the basis of a 365 day year.

Example: The interest on $100 at 14% for 40 days is $ 1.53. On $10,000 the interest is $153.42.

Interest on $100

DAY	14.00 %		14.25 %		14.50 %		14.75 %		15.00 %		16.00 %		17.00 %		18.00 %
1	.038356	1	.039041	1	.039726	1	.040411	1	.041096	1	.043836	1	.046575	1	.049315
2	.076712	2	.078082	2	.079452	2	.080822	2	.082192	2	.087671	2	.093151	2	.098630
3	.115068	3	.117123	3	.119178	3	.121233	3	.123288	3	.131507	3	.139726	3	.147945
4	.153425	4	.156164	4	.158904	4	.161644	4	.164384	4	.175342	4	.186301	4	.197260
5	.191781	5	.195205	5	.198630	5	.202055	5	.205479	5	.219178	5	.232877	5	.246575
6	.230137	6	.234247	6	.238356	6	.242466	6	.246575	6	.263014	6	.279452	6	.295890
7	.268493	7	.273288	7	.278082	7	.282877	7	.287671	7	.306849	7	.326027	7	.345205
8	.306849	8	.312329	8	.317808	8	.323288	8	.328767	8	.350685	8	.372603	8	.394521
9	.345205	9	.351370	9	.357534	9	.363699	9	.369863	9	.394521	9	.419178	9	.443836
10	.383562	10	.390411	10	.397260	10	.404110	10	.410959	10	.438356	10	.465753	10	.493151
11	.421918	11	.429452	11	.436986	11	.444521	11	.452055	11	.482192	11	.512329	11	.542466
12	.460274	12	.468493	12	.476712	12	.484932	12	.493151	12	.526027	12	.558904	12	.591781
13	.498630	13	.507534	13	.516438	13	.525342	13	.534247	13	.569863	13	.605479	13	.641096
14	.536986	14	.546575	14	.556164	14	.565753	14	.575342	14	.613699	14	.652055	14	.690411
15	.575342	15	.585616	15	.595890	15	.606164	15	.616438	15	.657534	15	.698630	15	.739726
16	.613699	16	.624658	16	.635616	16	.646575	16	.657534	16	.701370	16	.745205	16	.789041
17	.652055	17	.663699	17	.675342	17	.686986	17	.698630	17	.745205	17	.791781	17	.838356
18	.690411	18	.702740	18	.715068	18	.727397	18	.739726	18	.789041	18	.838356	18	.887671
19	.728767	19	.741781	19	.754795	19	.767808	19	.780822	19	.832877	19	.884932	19	.936986
20	.767123	20	.780822	20	.794521	20	.808219	20	.821918	20	.876712	20	.931507	20	.986301
21	.805479	21	.819863	21	.834247	21	.848630	21	.863014	21	.920548	21	.978082	21	1.035616
22	.843836	22	.858904	22	.873973	22	.889041	22	.904110	22	.964384	22	1.024658	22	1.084932
23	.882192	23	.897945	23	.913699	23	.929452	23	.945205	23	1.008219	23	1.071233	23	1.134247
24	.920548	24	.936986	24	.953425	24	.969863	24	.986301	24	1.052055	24	1.117808	24	1.183562
25	.958904	25	.976027	25	.993151	25	1.010274	25	1.027397	25	1.095890	25	1.164384	25	1.232877
26	.997260	26	1.015068	26	1.032877	26	1.050685	26	1.068493	26	1.139726	26	1.210959	26	1.282192
27	1.035616	27	1.054110	27	1.072603	27	1.091096	27	1.109589	27	1.183562	27	1.257534	27	1.331507
28	1.073973	28	1.093151	28	1.112329	28	1.131507	28	1.150685	28	1.227397	28	1.304110	28	1.380822
29	1.112329	29	1.132192	29	1.152055	29	1.171918	29	1.191781	29	1.271233	29	1.350685	29	1.430137
30	1.150685	30	1.171233	30	1.191781	30	1.212329	30	1.232877	30	1.315068	30	1.397260	30	1.479452
31	1.189041	31	1.210274	31	1.231507	31	1.252740	31	1.273973	31	1.358904	31	1.443836	31	1.528767
32	1.227397	32	1.249315	32	1.271233	32	1.293151	32	1.315068	32	1.402740	32	1.490411	32	1.578082
33	1.265753	33	1.288356	33	1.310959	33	1.333562	33	1.356164	33	1.446575	33	1.536986	33	1.627397
34	1.304110	34	1.327397	34	1.350685	34	1.373973	34	1.397260	34	1.490411	34	1.583562	34	1.676712
35	1.342466	35	1.366438	35	1.390411	35	1.414384	35	1.438356	35	1.534247	35	1.630137	35	1.726027
36	1.380822	36	1.405479	36	1.430137	36	1.454795	36	1.479452	36	1.578082	36	1.676712	36	1.775342
37	1.419178	37	1.444521	37	1.469863	37	1.495205	37	1.520548	37	1.621918	37	1.723288	37	1.824658
38	1.457534	38	1.483562	38	1.509589	38	1.535616	38	1.561644	38	1.665753	38	1.769863	38	1.873973
39	1.495890	39	1.522603	39	1.549315	39	1.576027	39	1.602740	39	1.709589	39	1.816438	39	1.923288
40	1.534247	40	1.561644	40	1.589041	40	1.616438	40	1.643836	40	1.753425	40	1.863014	40	1.972603
41	1.572603	41	1.600685	41	1.628767	41	1.656849	41	1.684932	41	1.797260	41	1.909589	41	2.021918
42	1.610959	42	1.639726	42	1.668493	42	1.697260	42	1.726027	42	1.841096	42	1.956164	42	2.071233
43	1.649315	43	1.678767	43	1.708219	43	1.737671	43	1.767123	43	1.884932	43	2.002740	43	2.120548
44	1.687671	44	1.717808	44	1.747945	44	1.778082	44	1.808219	44	1.928767	44	2.049315	44	2.169863
45	1.726027	45	1.756849	45	1.787671	45	1.818493	45	1.849315	45	1.972603	45	2.095890	45	2.219178
46	1.764384	46	1.795890	46	1.827397	46	1.858904	46	1.890411	46	2.016438	46	2.142466	46	2.268493
47	1.802740	47	1.834932	47	1.867123	47	1.899315	47	1.931507	47	2.060274	47	2.189041	47	2.317808
48	1.841096	48	1.873973	48	1.906849	48	1.939726	48	1.972603	48	2.104110	48	2.235616	48	2.367123
49	1.879452	49	1.913014	49	1.946575	49	1.980137	49	2.013699	49	2.147945	49	2.282192	49	2.416438
50	1.917808	50	1.952055	50	1.986301	50	2.020548	50	2.054795	50	2.191781	50	2.328767	50	2.465753
51	1.956164	51	1.991096	51	2.026027	51	2.060959	51	2.095890	51	2.235616	51	2.375342	51	2.515068
52	1.994521	52	2.030137	52	2.065753	52	2.101370	52	2.136986	52	2.279452	52	2.421918	52	2.564384
53	2.032877	53	2.069178	53	2.105479	53	2.141781	53	2.178082	53	2.323288	53	2.468493	53	2.613699
54	2.071233	54	2.108219	54	2.145205	54	2.182192	54	2.219178	54	2.367123	54	2.515068	54	2.663014
55	2.109589	55	2.147260	55	2.184932	55	2.222603	55	2.260274	55	2.410959	55	2.561644	55	2.712329
89	3.413699	89	3.474658	89	3.535616	89	3.596575	89	3.657534	89	3.901370	89	4.145205	89	4.389041
90	3.452055	90	3.513699	90	3.575342	90	3.636986	90	3.698630	90	3.945205	90	4.191781	90	4.438356
91	3.490411	91	3.552740	91	3.615068	91	3.677397	91	3.739726	91	3.989041	91	4.238356	91	4.487671
92	3.528767	92	3.591781	92	3.654795	92	3.717808	92	3.780822	92	4.032877	92	4.284932	2	4.536986
120	4.602740	120	4.684932	120	4.767123	120	4.849315	120	4.931507	120	5.260274	120	5.589041	120	5.917808
180	6.904110	180	7.027397	180	7.150685	180	7.273973	180	7.397260	180	7.890411	180	8.383562	180	8.876712
181	6.942466	181	7.066438	181	7.190411	181	7.314384	181	7.438356	181	7.934247	181	8.430137	181	8.926027
182	6.980822	182	7.105479	182	7.230137	182	7.354795	182	7.479452	182	7.978082	182	8.476712	182	8.975342
183	7.019178	183	7.144521	183	7.269863	183	7.395205	183	7.520548	183	8.021918	183	8.523288	183	9.024658
184	7.057534	184	7.183562	184	7.309589	184	7.435616	184	7.561644	184	8.065753	184	8.569863	184	9.073973
270	10.356164	270	10.541096	270	10.726027	270	10.910959	270	11.095890	270	11.835616	270	12.575342	270	13.315068
300	11.506849	300	11.712329	300	11.917808	300	12.123288	300	12.328767	300	13.150685	300	13.972603	300	14.794521
360	13.808219	360	14.054795	360	14.301370	360	14.547945	360	14.794521	360	15.780822	360	16.767123	360	17.753425
365	14.000000	365	14.250000	365	14.500000	365	14.750000	365	15.000000	365	16.000000	365	17.000000	365	18.000000
366	14.038356	366	14.289041	366	14.539726	366	14.790411	366	15.041096	366	16.043836	366	17.046575	366	18.049315

TABLE **12**

Daily Compound Interest on $100

Interest Rates:	4 to 15% by .25%; 16, 17, 18%.
Terms:	1 to 366 days.
Basis Years:	360 and 365 day years.

This table shows the daily compound interest on $100 from 1 to 366 days. In the first table, interest is computed on the basis of a 360 day year. This means that the interest rate is divided by 360 to get the 1 day interest factor. At 8%, the 1 day factor is .08/360 = .000 222 2222. In the second table, interest is computed on the basis of a 365 day year. At 8%, the 1 day factor is .08/365 = .000 219 1781.

Example: To find the compound interest factor at 8% for 30 days in a 360 day year, scan the day index on page 12-4 that corresponds to 8%. The value to the right of 30 in the index reads .668819. This is the value for $100. To get the factor for $1, move the decimal point 2 places to the left: .00668819.

To calculate the compound interest on $11,000 at 8% for 30 days, multiply the amount by the factor, as follows:

$$11,000 \times .006668819 = 73.570$$

The interest is $73.57. Calculate interest on $12,000:

$$12,000 \times .006668819 = 80.258$$

The interest is $80.26. Interest amounts of .005 or more are rounded to the next higher cent.

For Days Not Shown. The interest factor for a number of days not shown in the index can be calculated by multiplying daily factors for the required number of days, and then multiplying the amount by the new factor.

Example: To calculate the interest on $11,000 at 8% for 65 days, follow these steps to multiply the factors for 10 days and 55 days:

1. Get the factor for $1 for each term:
   10 days = .00222445
   55 days = .01229584

2. Add 1 to each factor:
   10 days = 1.00222445
   55 days = 1.01229584

3. Multiply the 2 factors:
   65 days = 1.00222445 × 1.01229584
   = 1.01454764

4. Subtract 1 from the product:
   65 days = .01454764

The factor per $1 for 65 days is .01454764. Multiply the amount by this factor, as follows:

$$11,000 \times .01454764 = 160.024$$

The interest is $160.02.

Compound Interest. Interest on a balance for a single period is always simple interest. Interest is compounded when the interest for a period is added to the balance to make a new balance and interest is then computed on the new balance. Compounding takes place when the interest is converted to the new balance; this gives the impression that compound interest is interest computed on interest.

Example: Find the interest on $100 at 4% computed annually for 2 years.

Year 1   100 × .04 = 4.00
          New balance = 104.00

Year 2   104 × .04 = 4.16
          New balance = 108.16

The interest computed each year is actually simple interest. The $.16 portion of year 2 interest is the simple interest on year 1 interest. If the $.16 is left on deposit, it is immediately converted to principal. Interest computed by this process is compound interest.

There is an apocryphal story told about Albert Einstein who, when asked what he thought was the greatest invention to come from the mind of man, paused for a moment of reflection and replied, "Compound interest." It is truly remarkable that $100, deposited in a savings institution and left, will have produced on the saver's return an amount greater than $100.

DAILY COMPOUND INTEREST, 360 DAY YEAR

4.00 %

Description: This table shows the compound interest on $100. Interest is compounded daily on the basis of a 360 day year.

Example: The interest on $100 at 4% for 40 days is $ .45. On $10,000 the daily compound interest is $ 44.54.

Interest on $100

DAY	4.00 %		4.25 %		4.50 %		4.75 %		5.00 %		5.25 %		5.50 %		5.75 %
1	.011111	1	.011806	1	.012500	1	.013194	1	.013889	1	.014583	1	.015278	1	.015972
2	.022223	2	.023613	2	.025002	2	.026391	2	.027780	2	.029169	2	.030558	2	.031947
3	.033337	3	.035421	3	.037505	3	.039589	3	.041672	3	.043756	3	.045840	3	.047924
4	.044452	4	.047231	4	.050009	4	.052788	4	.055567	4	.058346	4	.061125	4	.063904
5	.055568	5	.059042	5	.062516	5	.065990	5	.069464	5	.072938	5	.076412	5	.079887
6	.066685	6	.070854	6	.075023	6	.079193	6	.083362	6	.087532	6	.091702	6	.095872
7	.077804	7	.082668	7	.087533	7	.092398	7	.097263	7	.102128	7	.106993	7	.111859
8	.088923	8	.094483	8	.100044	8	.105604	8	.111165	8	.116726	8	.122288	8	.127849
9	.100044	9	.106300	9	.112556	9	.118813	9	.125069	9	.131327	9	.137584	9	.143842
10	.111167	10	.118118	10	.125070	10	.132023	10	.138976	10	.145929	10	.152883	10	.159837
11	.122290	11	.129938	11	.137586	11	.145235	11	.152884	11	.160534	11	.168184	11	.175835
12	.133415	12	.141759	12	.150103	12	.158448	12	.166794	12	.175140	12	.183487	12	.191835
13	.144541	13	.153581	13	.162622	13	.171664	13	.180706	13	.189749	13	.198793	13	.207838
14	.155668	14	.165405	14	.175142	14	.184881	14	.194620	14	.204360	14	.214101	14	.223843
15	.166796	15	.177230	15	.187664	15	.198100	15	.208536	15	.218973	15	.229412	15	.239851
16	.177926	16	.189056	16	.200188	16	.211320	16	.222454	16	.233589	16	.244725	16	.255862
17	.189057	17	.200884	17	.212713	17	.224542	17	.236374	17	.248206	17	.260040	17	.271875
18	.200189	18	.212713	18	.225239	18	.237767	18	.250295	18	.262826	18	.275357	18	.287891
19	.211322	19	.224544	19	.237767	19	.250992	19	.264219	19	.277447	19	.290677	19	.303909
20	.222457	20	.236376	20	.250297	20	.264220	20	.278145	20	.292071	20	.305999	20	.319930
21	.233593	21	.248210	21	.262828	21	.277449	21	.292072	21	.306697	21	.321324	21	.335953
22	.244730	22	.260044	22	.275361	22	.290680	22	.306002	22	.321325	22	.336651	22	.351979
23	.255868	23	.271881	23	.287896	23	.303913	23	.319933	23	.335955	23	.351980	23	.368007
24	.267008	24	.283718	24	.300432	24	.317148	24	.333866	24	.350588	24	.367312	24	.384038
25	.278148	25	.295557	25	.312969	25	.330384	25	.347802	25	.365222	25	.382645	25	.400072
26	.289290	26	.307398	26	.325508	26	.343622	26	.361739	26	.379859	26	.397982	26	.416108
27	.300434	27	.319240	27	.338049	27	.356862	27	.375678	27	.394497	27	.413320	27	.432147
28	.311578	28	.331083	28	.350591	28	.370103	28	.389619	28	.409138	28	.428661	28	.448188
29	.322724	29	.342928	29	.363135	29	.383347	29	.403562	29	.423781	29	.444005	29	.464232
30	.333871	30	.354774	30	.375680	30	.396592	30	.417507	30	.438426	30	.459350	30	.480278
31	.345019	31	.366621	31	.388227	31	.409838	31	.431454	31	.453074	31	.474698	31	.496327
32	.356169	32	.378470	32	.400776	32	.423087	32	.445403	32	.467723	32	.490048	32	.512378
33	.367319	33	.390320	33	.413326	33	.436337	33	.459353	33	.482375	33	.505401	33	.528433
34	.378471	34	.402172	34	.425878	34	.449589	34	.473306	34	.497028	34	.520756	34	.544489
35	.389624	35	.414025	35	.438431	35	.462843	35	.487261	35	.511684	35	.536113	35	.560548
36	.400779	36	.425879	36	.450986	36	.476098	36	.501217	36	.526342	36	.551473	36	.576610
37	.411934	37	.437735	37	.463542	37	.489356	37	.515176	37	.541002	37	.566835	37	.592674
38	.423091	38	.449592	38	.476100	38	.502615	38	.529136	38	.555664	38	.582199	38	.608741
39	.434249	39	.461451	39	.488660	39	.515875	39	.543099	39	.570329	39	.597566	39	.624811
40	.445409	40	.473311	40	.501221	40	.529138	40	.557063	40	.584995	40	.612935	40	.640883
41	.456569	41	.485172	41	.513783	41	.542402	41	.571029	41	.599664	41	.628307	41	.656957
42	.467731	42	.497035	42	.526348	42	.555668	42	.584997	42	.614335	42	.643680	42	.673035
43	.478894	43	.508899	43	.538913	43	.568936	43	.598967	43	.629008	43	.659057	43	.689114
44	.490059	44	.520765	44	.551481	44	.582206	44	.612940	44	.643683	44	.674435	44	.705197
45	.501224	45	.532632	45	.564050	45	.595477	45	.626914	45	.658360	45	.689816	45	.721281
46	.512391	46	.544501	46	.576620	46	.608750	46	.640889	46	.673039	46	.705199	46	.737369
47	.523559	47	.556370	47	.589192	47	.622025	47	.654867	47	.687721	47	.720585	47	.753459
48	.534728	48	.568242	48	.601766	48	.635301	48	.668847	48	.702404	48	.735972	48	.769551
49	.545899	49	.580114	49	.614341	49	.648579	49	.682829	49	.717090	49	.751363	49	.785647
50	.557071	50	.591988	50	.626918	50	.661859	50	.696813	50	.731778	50	.766755	50	.801744
51	.568244	51	.603864	51	.639496	51	.675141	51	.710798	51	.746468	51	.782150	51	.817845
52	.579418	52	.615741	52	.652076	52	.688425	52	.724786	52	.761160	52	.797547	52	.833947
53	.590593	53	.627619	53	.664658	53	.701710	53	.738776	53	.775855	53	.812947	53	.850053
54	.601770	54	.639498	54	.677241	54	.714997	54	.752767	54	.790551	54	.828349	54	.866161
55	.612948	55	.651380	55	.689825	55	.728286	55	.766761	55	.805250	55	.843753	55	.882271
89	.993739	89	1.056171	89	1.118641	89	1.181149	89	1.243696	89	1.306280	89	1.368903	89	1.431564
90	1.004961	90	1.068101	90	1.131281	90	1.194500	90	1.257757	90	1.321054	90	1.384390	90	1.447765
91	1.016183	91	1.080033	91	1.143922	91	1.207852	91	1.271821	91	1.335830	91	1.399879	91	1.463969
92	1.027407	92	1.091966	92	1.156565	92	1.221205	92	1.285886	92	1.350608	92	1.415371	92	1.480175
120	1.342187	120	1.426664	120	1.511211	120	1.595828	120	1.680515	120	1.765272	120	1.850099	120	1.934997
180	2.020021	180	2.147611	180	2.275360	180	2.403267	180	2.531334	180	2.659560	180	2.787946	180	2.916491
181	2.031356	181	2.159670	181	2.288144	181	2.416779	181	2.545575	181	2.674531	181	2.803649	181	2.932929
182	2.042693	182	2.171730	182	2.300930	182	2.430292	182	2.559817	182	2.689505	182	2.819355	182	2.949370
183	2.054031	183	2.183792	183	2.313718	183	2.443807	183	2.574061	183	2.704480	183	2.835064	183	2.965813
184	2.065370	184	2.195856	184	2.326507	184	2.457324	184	2.588308	184	2.719458	184	2.850775	184	2.982259
270	3.045282	270	3.238651	270	3.432381	270	3.626474	270	3.820929	270	4.015748	270	4.210932	270	4.406480
300	3.389320	300	3.604914	300	3.820956	300	4.037448	300	4.254389	300	4.471781	300	4.689625	300	4.907921
360	4.080846	360	4.341344	360	4.602492	360	4.864292	360	5.126745	360	5.389853	360	5.653618	360	5.918041
365	4.138682	365	4.402949	365	4.667885	365	4.933491	365	5.199770	365	5.466722	365	5.734350	365	6.002655
366	4.150253	366	4.415274	366	4.680968	366	4.947336	366	5.214381	366	5.482103	366	5.750504	366	6.019586

DAILY COMPOUND INTEREST, 360 DAY YEAR

6.00 %

Description: This table shows the compound interest on $100. Interest is compounded daily on the basis of a 360 day year.

Example: The interest on $100 at 6% for 40 days is $ .67. On $10,000 the daily compound interest is $ 66.88.

Interest on $100

DAY	6.00 %		6.25 %		6.50 %		6.75 %		7.00 %		7.25 %		7.50 %		7.75 %
1	.016667	1	.017361	1	.018056	1	.018750	1	.019444	1	.020139	1	.020833	1	.021528
2	.033336	2	.034725	2	.036114	2	.037504	2	.038893	2	.040282	2	.041671	2	.043060
3	.050008	3	.052092	3	.054176	3	.056261	3	.058345	3	.060429	3	.062513	3	.064597
4	.066683	4	.069463	4	.072242	4	.075021	4	.077800	4	.080580	4	.083359	4	.086139
5	.083361	5	.086836	5	.090310	5	.093785	5	.097260	5	.100735	5	.104210	5	.107685
6	.100042	6	.104212	6	.108382	6	.112553	6	.116723	6	.120894	6	.125065	6	.129236
7	.116725	7	.121591	7	.126457	7	.131324	7	.136191	7	.141057	7	.145925	7	.150792
8	.133411	8	.138973	8	.144536	8	.150098	8	.155661	8	.161225	8	.166788	8	.172352
9	.150100	9	.156359	9	.162617	9	.168877	9	.175136	9	.181396	9	.187656	9	.193917
10	.166792	10	.173747	10	.180702	10	.187658	10	.194615	10	.201571	10	.208529	10	.215486
11	.183486	11	.191138	11	.198791	11	.206443	11	.214097	11	.221751	11	.229406	11	.237061
12	.200183	12	.208532	12	.216882	12	.225232	12	.233583	12	.241935	12	.250287	12	.258639
13	.216883	13	.225930	13	.234977	13	.244024	13	.253073	13	.262122	13	.271172	13	.280223
14	.233586	14	.243330	14	.253075	14	.262820	14	.272567	14	.282314	14	.292062	14	.301811
15	.250292	15	.260733	15	.271176	15	.281619	15	.292064	15	.302510	15	.312956	15	.323404
16	.267000	16	.278140	16	.289280	16	.300422	16	.311565	16	.322709	16	.333855	16	.345001
17	.283711	17	.295549	17	.307388	17	.319229	17	.331070	17	.342913	17	.354758	17	.366603
18	.300425	18	.312962	18	.325499	18	.338038	18	.350579	18	.363121	18	.375665	18	.388210
19	.317142	19	.330377	19	.343614	19	.356852	19	.370092	19	.383333	19	.396576	19	.409821
20	.333862	20	.347795	20	.361731	20	.375669	20	.389608	20	.403549	20	.417492	20	.431437
21	.350584	21	.365217	21	.379852	21	.394489	21	.409128	21	.423769	21	.438413	21	.453058
22	.367309	22	.382642	22	.397976	22	.413313	22	.428652	22	.443994	22	.459337	22	.474683
23	.384037	23	.400069	23	.416104	23	.432141	23	.448180	23	.464222	23	.480266	23	.496313
24	.400768	24	.417500	24	.434234	24	.450972	24	.467712	24	.484454	24	.501200	24	.517948
25	.417501	25	.434933	25	.452368	25	.469806	25	.487247	25	.504691	25	.522137	25	.539587
26	.434237	26	.452370	26	.470505	26	.488644	26	.506786	26	.524931	26	.543080	26	.561231
27	.450976	27	.469809	27	.488646	27	.507486	27	.526329	27	.545176	27	.564026	27	.582880
28	.467718	28	.487252	28	.506790	28	.526331	28	.545876	28	.565425	28	.584977	28	.604533
29	.484463	29	.504698	29	.524937	29	.545180	29	.565427	29	.585677	29	.605932	29	.626191
30	.501210	30	.522147	30	.543087	30	.564032	30	.584981	30	.605934	30	.626892	30	.647853
31	.517960	31	.539598	31	.561241	31	.582888	31	.604539	31	.626195	31	.647856	31	.669521
32	.534713	32	.557053	32	.579398	32	.601747	32	.624101	32	.646460	32	.668824	32	.691193
33	.551469	33	.574511	33	.597558	33	.620610	33	.643667	33	.666729	33	.689797	33	.712869
34	.568228	34	.591972	34	.615721	34	.639476	34	.663237	34	.687002	34	.710774	34	.734550
35	.584989	35	.609436	35	.633888	35	.658346	35	.682810	35	.707280	35	.731755	35	.756236
36	.601753	36	.626903	36	.652058	36	.677220	36	.702387	36	.727561	36	.752741	36	.777927
37	.618520	37	.644373	37	.670231	37	.696097	37	.721968	37	.747846	37	.773731	37	.799622
38	.635290	38	.661846	38	.688408	38	.714977	38	.741553	38	.768136	38	.794726	38	.821322
39	.652063	39	.679322	39	.706588	39	.733861	39	.761142	39	.788429	39	.815724	39	.843027
40	.668838	40	.696801	40	.724771	40	.752749	40	.780734	40	.808727	40	.836728	40	.864736
41	.685616	41	.714283	41	.742957	41	.771640	41	.800330	41	.829029	41	.857735	41	.886450
42	.702397	42	.731768	42	.761147	42	.790535	42	.819930	42	.849335	42	.878747	42	.908168
43	.719181	43	.749256	43	.779340	43	.809433	43	.839534	43	.869645	43	.899764	43	.929892
44	.735967	44	.766747	44	.797536	44	.828335	44	.859142	44	.889959	44	.920785	44	.951620
45	.752757	45	.784241	45	.815736	45	.847240	45	.878754	45	.910277	45	.941810	45	.973352
46	.769549	46	.801739	46	.833939	46	.866149	46	.898369	46	.930599	46	.962839	46	.995090
47	.786344	47	.819239	47	.852145	47	.885061	47	.917988	47	.950925	47	.983873	47	1.016832
48	.803141	48	.836742	48	.870354	48	.903977	48	.937611	48	.971256	48	1.004912	48	1.038578
49	.819942	49	.854249	49	.888567	49	.922897	49	.957238	49	.991590	49	1.025954	49	1.060330
50	.836745	50	.871758	50	.906783	50	.941820	50	.976868	50	1.011929	50	1.047001	50	1.082086
51	.853551	51	.889271	51	.925002	51	.960746	51	.996503	51	1.032271	51	1.068053	51	1.103846
52	.870360	52	.906786	52	.943225	52	.979676	52	1.016141	52	1.052618	52	1.089109	52	1.125612
53	.887172	53	.924305	53	.961451	53	.998610	53	1.035783	53	1.072969	53	1.110169	53	1.147382
54	.903987	54	.941826	54	.979680	54	1.017547	54	1.055429	54	1.093324	54	1.131233	54	1.169157
55	.920804	55	.959351	55	.997912	55	1.036488	55	1.075078	55	1.113683	55	1.152302	55	1.190936
89	1.494264	89	1.557002	89	1.619778	89	1.682592	89	1.745445	89	1.808337	89	1.871266	89	1.934235
90	1.511180	90	1.574633	90	1.638126	90	1.701658	90	1.765229	90	1.828840	90	1.892490	90	1.956179
91	1.528098	91	1.592268	91	1.656477	91	1.720727	91	1.785017	91	1.849347	91	1.913717	91	1.978128
92	1.545019	92	1.609905	92	1.674832	92	1.739800	92	1.804808	92	1.869858	92	1.934949	92	2.000081
120	2.019964	120	2.105002	120	2.190109	120	2.275288	120	2.360536	120	2.445855	120	2.531245	120	2.616705
180	3.045196	180	3.174061	180	3.303086	180	3.432272	180	3.561619	180	3.691126	180	3.820794	180	3.950624
181	3.062370	181	3.191973	181	3.321738	181	3.451666	181	3.581756	181	3.712008	181	3.842424	181	3.973002
182	3.079547	182	3.209888	182	3.340394	182	3.471063	182	3.601896	182	3.732895	182	3.864057	182	3.995385
183	3.096727	183	3.227807	183	3.359052	183	3.490464	183	3.622041	183	3.753785	183	3.885696	183	4.017773
184	3.113910	184	3.245728	184	3.377714	184	3.509868	184	3.642190	184	3.774680	184	3.907339	184	4.040166
270	4.602394	270	4.798674	270	4.995321	270	5.192335	270	5.389718	270	5.587470	270	5.785592	270	5.984084
300	5.126672	300	5.345877	300	5.565537	300	5.785654	300	6.006228	300	6.227261	300	6.448753	300	6.670705
360	6.183124	360	6.448868	360	6.715276	360	6.982349	360	7.250088	360	7.518496	360	7.787573	360	8.057322
365	6.271639	365	6.541304	365	6.811651	365	7.082683	365	7.354400	365	7.626805	365	7.899899	365	8.173684
366	6.289351	366	6.559801	366	6.830937	366	7.102761	366	7.375274	366	7.648479	366	7.922378	366	8.196971

Description: This table shows the compound interest on $100. Interest is compounded daily on the basis of a 360 day year.

Example: The interest on $100 at 8% for 40 days is $ .89. On $10,000 the daily compound interest is $ 89.28.

Interest on $100

DAY	8.00 %		8.25 %		8.50 %		8.75 %		9.00 %		9.25 %		9.50 %		9.75 %
1	.022222	1	.022917	1	.023611	1	.024306	1	.025000	1	.025694	1	.026389	1	.027083
2	.044449	2	.045839	2	.047228	2	.048617	2	.050006	2	.051395	2	.052785	2	.054174
3	.066681	3	.068766	3	.070850	3	.072934	3	.075019	3	.077103	3	.079188	3	.081272
4	.088919	4	.091698	4	.094478	4	.097258	4	.100038	4	.102817	4	.105597	4	.108377
5	.111161	5	.114636	5	.118111	5	.121587	5	.125063	5	.128538	5	.132014	5	.135490
6	.133407	6	.137579	6	.141750	6	.145922	6	.150094	6	.154266	6	.158438	6	.162610
7	.155659	7	.160527	7	.165395	7	.170263	7	.175131	7	.180000	7	.184869	7	.189737
8	.177916	8	.183480	8	.189045	8	.194610	8	.200175	8	.205741	8	.211306	8	.216872
9	.200178	9	.206439	9	.212701	9	.218963	9	.225225	9	.231488	9	.237751	9	.244014
10	.222445	10	.229403	10	.236362	10	.243322	10	.250281	10	.257242	10	.264202	10	.271164
11	.244716	11	.252372	11	.260029	11	.267686	11	.275344	11	.283002	11	.290661	11	.298320
12	.266993	12	.275347	12	.283702	12	.292057	12	.300413	12	.308769	12	.317127	12	.325485
13	.289274	13	.298327	13	.307380	13	.316433	13	.325488	13	.334543	13	.343599	13	.352656
14	.311561	14	.321312	14	.331063	14	.340816	14	.350569	14	.360324	14	.370079	14	.379835
15	.333852	15	.344302	15	.354753	15	.365204	15	.375657	15	.386111	15	.396565	15	.407021
16	.356149	16	.367298	16	.378447	16	.389599	16	.400751	16	.411904	16	.423059	16	.434215
17	.378450	17	.390298	17	.402148	17	.413999	17	.425851	17	.437705	17	.449559	17	.461416
18	.400756	18	.413304	18	.425854	18	.438405	18	.450958	18	.463511	18	.476067	18	.488624
19	.423068	19	.436316	19	.449566	19	.462817	19	.476070	19	.489325	19	.502581	19	.515840
20	.445384	20	.459333	20	.473283	20	.487235	20	.501189	20	.515145	20	.529103	20	.543063
21	.467705	21	.482354	21	.497006	21	.511659	21	.526315	21	.540972	21	.555631	21	.570293
22	.490031	22	.505382	22	.520734	22	.536089	22	.551446	22	.566805	22	.582167	22	.597531
23	.512362	23	.528414	23	.544468	23	.560525	23	.576584	23	.592646	23	.608710	23	.624776
24	.534699	24	.551452	24	.568208	24	.584967	24	.601728	24	.618492	24	.635259	24	.652029
25	.557040	25	.574495	25	.591953	25	.609414	25	.626879	25	.644346	25	.661816	25	.679288
26	.579386	26	.597543	26	.615704	26	.633868	26	.652035	26	.670206	26	.688379	26	.706556
27	.601737	27	.620597	27	.639461	27	.658328	27	.677198	27	.696072	27	.714950	27	.733830
28	.624092	28	.643656	28	.663223	28	.682793	28	.702368	28	.721946	28	.741527	28	.761113
29	.646453	29	.666720	29	.686990	29	.707265	29	.727543	29	.747826	29	.768112	29	.788402
30	.668819	30	.689789	30	.710764	30	.731742	30	.752725	30	.773712	30	.794703	30	.815699
31	.691190	31	.712864	31	.734543	31	.756226	31	.777913	31	.799605	31	.821302	31	.843003
32	.713566	32	.735944	32	.758327	32	.780715	32	.803108	32	.825505	32	.847908	32	.870315
33	.735947	33	.759029	33	.782117	33	.805210	33	.828309	33	.851412	33	.874520	33	.897634
34	.758333	34	.782120	34	.805913	34	.829712	34	.853516	34	.877325	34	.901140	34	.924960
35	.780723	35	.805216	35	.829715	35	.854219	35	.878729	35	.903245	35	.927767	35	.952294
36	.803119	36	.828317	36	.853522	36	.878732	36	.903949	36	.929171	36	.954400	36	.979635
37	.825520	37	.851424	37	.877334	37	.903251	37	.929175	37	.955105	37	.981041	37	1.006984
38	.847925	38	.874535	38	.901152	38	.927776	38	.954407	38	.981044	38	1.007689	38	1.034340
39	.870336	39	.897653	39	.924976	39	.952307	39	.979646	39	1.006991	39	1.034344	39	1.061703
40	.892752	40	.920775	40	.948806	40	.976844	40	1.004890	40	1.032944	40	1.061005	40	1.089074
41	.915172	41	.943903	41	.972641	41	1.001387	41	1.030142	41	1.058904	41	1.087674	41	1.116453
42	.937598	42	.967036	42	.996482	42	1.025936	42	1.055399	42	1.084871	42	1.114350	42	1.143838
43	.960028	43	.990174	43	1.020328	43	1.050491	43	1.080663	43	1.110844	43	1.141033	43	1.171231
44	.982464	44	1.013317	44	1.044180	44	1.075052	44	1.105933	44	1.136824	44	1.167723	44	1.198632
45	1.004904	45	1.036466	45	1.068038	45	1.099619	45	1.131210	45	1.162810	45	1.194420	45	1.226040
46	1.027350	46	1.059621	46	1.091901	46	1.124192	46	1.156493	46	1.188803	46	1.221124	46	1.253455
47	1.049801	47	1.082780	47	1.115770	47	1.148771	47	1.181782	47	1.214803	47	1.247835	47	1.280878
48	1.072256	48	1.105945	48	1.139645	48	1.173355	48	1.207077	48	1.240810	48	1.274554	48	1.308308
49	1.094717	49	1.129115	49	1.163525	49	1.197946	49	1.232379	49	1.266823	49	1.301279	49	1.335746
50	1.117182	50	1.152290	50	1.187411	50	1.222543	50	1.257687	50	1.292843	50	1.328011	50	1.363191
51	1.139653	51	1.175471	51	1.211302	51	1.247146	51	1.283001	51	1.318870	51	1.354750	51	1.390644
52	1.162128	52	1.198657	52	1.235199	52	1.271754	52	1.308322	52	1.344903	52	1.381497	52	1.418104
53	1.184608	53	1.221849	53	1.259102	53	1.296369	53	1.333649	53	1.370943	53	1.408250	53	1.445571
54	1.207094	54	1.245045	54	1.283010	54	1.320990	54	1.358983	54	1.396990	54	1.435011	54	1.473046
55	1.229584	55	1.268247	55	1.306924	55	1.345616	55	1.384322	55	1.423043	55	1.461778	55	1.500528
89	1.997241	89	2.060286	89	2.123370	89	2.186493	89	2.249653	89	2.312853	89	2.376091	89	2.439368
90	2.019907	90	2.083675	90	2.147483	90	2.211330	90	2.275216	90	2.339142	90	2.403107	90	2.467112
91	2.042578	91	2.107069	91	2.171601	91	2.236173	91	2.300785	91	2.365437	91	2.430130	91	2.494863
92	2.065255	92	2.130469	92	2.195725	92	2.261022	92	2.326360	92	2.391739	92	2.457160	92	2.522622
120	2.702236	120	2.787838	120	2.873510	120	2.959253	120	3.045067	120	3.130952	120	3.216908	120	3.302935
180	4.080615	180	4.210768	180	4.341082	180	4.471559	180	4.602198	180	4.732999	180	4.863963	180	4.995090
181	4.103744	181	4.234649	181	4.365718	181	4.496951	181	4.628348	181	4.759910	181	4.891635	181	5.023526
182	4.126878	182	4.258536	182	4.390360	182	4.522350	182	4.654505	182	4.786827	182	4.919315	182	5.051970
183	4.150017	183	4.282429	183	4.415008	183	4.547755	183	4.680669	183	4.813751	183	4.947002	183	5.080421
184	4.173162	184	4.306327	184	4.439661	184	4.573165	184	4.706839	184	4.840683	184	4.974697	184	5.108881
270	6.182947	270	6.382182	270	6.581789	270	6.781769	270	6.982123	270	7.182852	270	7.383956	270	7.585436
300	6.893119	300	7.115995	300	7.339334	300	7.563137	300	7.787405	300	8.012139	300	8.237340	300	8.463009
360	8.327744	360	8.598841	360	8.870614	360	9.143066	360	9.416198	360	9.690011	360	9.964507	360	10.239689
365	8.448162	365	8.723334	365	8.999203	365	9.275770	365	9.553036	365	9.831004	365	10.109676	365	10.389053
366	8.472261	366	8.748250	366	9.024939	366	9.302330	366	9.580425	366	9.859225	366	10.138733	366	10.418950

DAILY COMPOUND INTEREST, 360 DAY YEAR 10.00 %

Description: This table shows the compound interest on $100. Interest is compounded daily on the basis of a 360 day year.

Example: The interest on $100 at 10% for 40 days is $ 1.12. On $10,000 the daily compound interest is $111.72.

Interest on $100

DAY	10.00 %		10.25 %		10.50 %		10.75 %		11.00 %		11.25 %		11.50 %		11.75 %
1	.027778	1	.028472	1	.029167	1	.029861	1	.030556	1	.031250	1	.031944	1	.032639
2	.055563	2	.056953	2	.058342	2	.059731	2	.061120	2	.062510	2	.063899	2	.065288
3	.083356	3	.085441	3	.087526	3	.089610	3	.091695	3	.093779	3	.095864	3	.097949
4	.111157	4	.113938	4	.116718	4	.119498	4	.122278	4	.125059	4	.127839	4	.130619
5	.138966	5	.142442	5	.145918	5	.149395	5	.152871	5	.156348	5	.159824	5	.163301
6	.166782	6	.170955	6	.175128	6	.179300	6	.183473	6	.187647	6	.191820	6	.195993
7	.194607	7	.199476	7	.204345	7	.209215	7	.214085	7	.218955	7	.223826	7	.228696
8	.222438	8	.228005	8	.233572	8	.239139	8	.244706	8	.250274	8	.255841	8	.261410
9	.250278	9	.256542	9	.262806	9	.269071	9	.275336	9	.281602	9	.287868	9	.294134
10	.278125	10	.285087	10	.292050	10	.299013	10	.305976	10	.312940	10	.319904	10	.326869
11	.305980	11	.313641	11	.321302	11	.328963	11	.336625	11	.344288	11	.351951	11	.359614
12	.333843	12	.342202	12	.350562	12	.358922	12	.367283	12	.375645	12	.384008	12	.392371
13	.361714	13	.370772	13	.379831	13	.388891	13	.397951	13	.407013	13	.416075	13	.425137
14	.389592	14	.399350	14	.409108	14	.418868	14	.428628	14	.438390	14	.448152	14	.457915
15	.417478	15	.427936	15	.438394	15	.448854	15	.459315	15	.469777	15	.480240	15	.490703
16	.445372	16	.456530	16	.467689	16	.478849	16	.490011	16	.501174	16	.512337	16	.523503
17	.473273	17	.485132	17	.496992	17	.508853	17	.520716	17	.532580	17	.544446	17	.556312
18	.501182	18	.513742	18	.526304	18	.538866	18	.551431	18	.563997	18	.576564	18	.589133
19	.529099	19	.542361	19	.555624	19	.568888	19	.582155	19	.595423	19	.608693	19	.621964
20	.557024	20	.570987	20	.584952	20	.598919	20	.612888	20	.626859	20	.640831	20	.654806
21	.584957	21	.599622	21	.614290	21	.628959	21	.643631	21	.658305	21	.672981	21	.687658
22	.612897	22	.628265	22	.643636	22	.659008	22	.674383	22	.689761	22	.705140	22	.720522
23	.640845	23	.656916	23	.672990	23	.689066	23	.705145	23	.721226	23	.737310	23	.753396
24	.668801	24	.685575	24	.702353	24	.719133	24	.735916	24	.752701	24	.769490	24	.786281
25	.696764	25	.714243	25	.731724	25	.749209	25	.766696	25	.784187	25	.801680	25	.819176
26	.724736	26	.742918	26	.761105	26	.779294	26	.797486	26	.815682	26	.833881	26	.852082
27	.752715	27	.771602	27	.790493	27	.809388	27	.828285	27	.847187	27	.866091	27	.884999
28	.780701	28	.800294	28	.819890	28	.839490	28	.859094	28	.878701	28	.898312	28	.917927
29	.808696	29	.828994	29	.849296	29	.869602	29	.889912	29	.910226	29	.930544	29	.950866
30	.836699	30	.857702	30	.878711	30	.899723	30	.920740	30	.941760	30	.962786	30	.983815
31	.864709	31	.886419	31	.908134	31	.929853	31	.951577	31	.973305	31	.995038	31	1.016775
32	.892727	32	.915143	32	.937565	32	.959992	32	.982423	32	1.004859	32	1.027300	32	1.049746
33	.920752	33	.943876	33	.967005	33	.990139	33	1.013279	33	1.036423	33	1.059572	33	1.082727
34	.948786	34	.972617	34	.996454	34	1.020296	34	1.044144	34	1.067997	34	1.091855	34	1.115719
35	.976827	35	1.001366	35	1.025911	35	1.050462	35	1.075018	35	1.099581	35	1.124149	35	1.148722
36	1.004876	36	1.030124	36	1.055377	36	1.080637	36	1.105902	36	1.131174	36	1.156452	36	1.181736
37	1.032933	37	1.058889	37	1.084852	37	1.110820	37	1.136796	37	1.162778	37	1.188766	37	1.214761
38	1.060998	38	1.087663	38	1.114335	38	1.141013	38	1.167699	38	1.194391	38	1.221090	38	1.247796
39	1.089071	39	1.116445	39	1.143826	39	1.171215	39	1.198611	39	1.226014	39	1.253425	39	1.280842
40	1.117151	40	1.145235	40	1.173327	40	1.201426	40	1.229533	40	1.257647	40	1.285770	40	1.313899
41	1.145239	41	1.174033	41	1.202836	41	1.231646	41	1.260464	41	1.289290	41	1.318125	41	1.346967
42	1.173335	42	1.202840	42	1.232353	42	1.261875	42	1.291405	42	1.320943	42	1.350490	42	1.380046
43	1.201439	43	1.231654	43	1.261879	43	1.292113	43	1.322355	43	1.352606	43	1.382866	43	1.413135
44	1.229550	44	1.260477	44	1.291414	44	1.322360	44	1.353315	44	1.384279	44	1.415252	44	1.446235
45	1.257669	45	1.289308	45	1.320957	45	1.352616	45	1.384284	45	1.415961	45	1.447649	45	1.479346
46	1.285797	46	1.318148	46	1.350509	46	1.382881	46	1.415262	46	1.447654	46	1.480056	46	1.512468
47	1.313931	47	1.346995	47	1.380070	47	1.413155	47	1.446250	47	1.479356	47	1.512473	47	1.545600
48	1.342074	48	1.375851	48	1.409639	48	1.443438	48	1.477248	48	1.511069	48	1.544901	48	1.578744
49	1.370225	49	1.404715	49	1.439217	49	1.473730	49	1.508255	49	1.542791	49	1.577339	49	1.611898
50	1.398383	50	1.433587	50	1.468803	50	1.504031	50	1.539271	50	1.574523	50	1.609787	50	1.645063
51	1.426549	51	1.462468	51	1.498398	51	1.534341	51	1.570297	51	1.606265	51	1.642246	51	1.678239
52	1.454723	52	1.491356	52	1.528002	52	1.564661	52	1.601332	52	1.638017	52	1.674715	52	1.711425
53	1.482905	53	1.520253	53	1.557614	53	1.594989	53	1.632377	53	1.669779	53	1.707194	53	1.744623
54	1.511095	54	1.549158	54	1.587235	54	1.625326	54	1.663431	54	1.701551	54	1.739684	54	1.777831
55	1.539293	55	1.578071	55	1.616865	55	1.655673	55	1.694495	55	1.733332	55	1.772184	55	1.811050
89	2.502683	89	2.566037	89	2.629430	89	2.692862	89	2.756332	89	2.819841	89	2.883389	89	2.946976
90	2.531156	90	2.595240	90	2.659364	90	2.723527	90	2.787730	90	2.851972	90	2.916255	90	2.980577
91	2.559637	91	2.624451	91	2.689306	91	2.754201	91	2.819137	91	2.884114	91	2.949131	91	3.014188
92	2.588126	92	2.653671	92	2.719257	92	2.784885	92	2.850554	92	2.916265	92	2.982017	92	3.047811
120	3.389033	120	3.475202	120	3.561442	120	3.647754	120	3.734137	120	3.820592	120	3.907117	120	3.993715
180	5.126380	180	5.257833	180	5.389449	180	5.521230	180	5.653174	180	5.785282	180	5.917555	180	6.049991
181	5.155581	181	5.287802	181	5.420188	181	5.552740	181	5.685457	181	5.818340	181	5.951389	181	6.084605
182	5.184791	182	5.317780	182	5.450936	182	5.584259	182	5.717750	182	5.851408	182	5.985235	182	6.119230
183	5.214009	183	5.347766	183	5.481692	183	5.615787	183	5.750052	183	5.884487	183	6.019091	183	6.153866
184	5.243235	184	5.377761	184	5.512458	184	5.647325	184	5.782365	184	5.917576	184	6.052958	184	6.188513
270	7.787293	270	7.989526	270	8.192138	270	8.395129	270	8.598499	270	8.802249	270	9.006380	270	9.210893
300	8.689147	300	8.915755	300	9.142834	300	9.370385	300	9.598408	300	9.826906	300	10.055878	300	10.285326
360	10.515557	360	10.792114	360	11.069361	360	11.347299	360	11.625931	360	11.905259	360	12.185284	360	12.466007
365	10.669136	365	10.949929	365	11.231431	365	11.513646	365	11.796575	365	12.080220	365	12.364583	365	12.649665
366	10.699878	366	10.981518	366	11.263874	366	11.546945	366	11.830735	366	12.115245	366	12.400477	366	12.686433

Description: This table shows the compound interest on $100. Interest is compounded daily on the basis of a 360 day year.

Example: The interest on $100 at 12% for 40 days is $ 1.34. On $10,000 the daily compound interest is $134.20.

Interest on $100

DAY	12.00 %		12.25 %		12.50 %		12.75 %		13.00 %		13.25 %		13.50 %		13.75 %
1	.033333	1	.034028	1	.034722	1	.035417	1	.036111	1	.036806	1	.037500	1	.038194
2	.066678	2	.068067	2	.069457	2	.070846	2	.072235	2	.073625	2	.075014	2	.076403
3	.100033	3	.102118	3	.104203	3	.106288	3	.108372	3	.110457	3	.112542	3	.114627
4	.133400	4	.136181	4	.138961	4	.141742	4	.144523	4	.147304	4	.150084	4	.152865
5	.166778	5	.170255	5	.173732	5	.177209	5	.180686	5	.184163	5	.187641	5	.191118
6	.200167	6	.204340	6	.208514	6	.212688	6	.216862	6	.221037	6	.225211	6	.229386
7	.233567	7	.238438	7	.243309	7	.248180	7	.253052	7	.257924	7	.262795	7	.267668
8	.266978	8	.272547	8	.278116	8	.283685	8	.289254	8	.294824	8	.300394	8	.305964
9	.300400	9	.306667	9	.312934	9	.319202	9	.325470	9	.331738	9	.338007	9	.344276
10	.333834	10	.340799	10	.347765	10	.354732	10	.361698	10	.368666	10	.375633	10	.382602
11	.367278	11	.374943	11	.382608	11	.390274	11	.397940	11	.405607	11	.413274	11	.420942
12	.400734	12	.409098	12	.417463	12	.425829	12	.434195	12	.442562	12	.450929	12	.459297
13	.434201	13	.443265	13	.452330	13	.461396	13	.470463	13	.479530	13	.488598	13	.497667
14	.467679	14	.477461	14	.487210	14	.496976	14	.506744	14	.516512	14	.526282	14	.536052
15	.501168	15	.511634	15	.522101	15	.532569	15	.543038	15	.553508	15	.563979	15	.574451
16	.534669	16	.545836	16	.557005	16	.568174	16	.579345	16	.590517	16	.601690	16	.612865
17	.568180	17	.580050	17	.591920	17	.603792	17	.615666	17	.627540	17	.639416	17	.651293
18	.601703	18	.614275	18	.626848	18	.639423	18	.651999	18	.664577	18	.677156	18	.689737
19	.635237	19	.648512	19	.661788	19	.675066	19	.688346	19	.701627	19	.714910	19	.728194
20	.668782	20	.682760	20	.696740	20	.710722	20	.724705	20	.738691	20	.752678	20	.766667
21	.702338	21	.717020	21	.731704	21	.746390	21	.761078	21	.775768	21	.790460	21	.805154
22	.735906	22	.751292	22	.766680	22	.782071	22	.797464	22	.812859	22	.828257	22	.843656
23	.769484	23	.785575	23	.801669	23	.817765	23	.833863	23	.849964	23	.866067	23	.882173
24	.803074	24	.819870	24	.836669	24	.853471	24	.870275	24	.887082	24	.903892	24	.920704
25	.836675	25	.854177	25	.871682	25	.889190	25	.906701	25	.924214	25	.941731	25	.959250
26	.870287	26	.888496	26	.906707	26	.924922	26	.943139	26	.961360	26	.979584	26	.997811
27	.903911	27	.922826	27	.941744	27	.960666	27	.979591	27	.998519	27	1.017451	27	1.036387
28	.937545	28	.957168	28	.976793	28	.996423	28	1.016056	28	1.035692	28	1.055333	28	1.074977
29	.971191	29	.991521	29	1.011855	29	1.032192	29	1.052534	29	1.072879	29	1.093229	29	1.113582
30	1.004848	30	1.025886	30	1.046928	30	1.067974	30	1.089025	30	1.110080	30	1.131139	30	1.152202
31	1.038517	31	1.060263	31	1.082014	31	1.103769	31	1.125529	31	1.147294	31	1.169063	31	1.190836
32	1.072196	32	1.094652	32	1.117112	32	1.139577	32	1.162047	32	1.184522	32	1.207001	32	1.229486
33	1.105887	33	1.129052	33	1.152222	33	1.175397	33	1.198578	33	1.221763	33	1.244954	33	1.268150
34	1.139589	34	1.163464	34	1.187344	34	1.211230	34	1.235122	34	1.259018	34	1.282921	34	1.306829
35	1.173302	35	1.197888	35	1.222479	35	1.247076	35	1.271679	35	1.296287	35	1.320902	35	1.345522
36	1.207027	36	1.232323	36	1.257625	36	1.282934	36	1.308249	36	1.333570	36	1.358897	36	1.384230
37	1.240762	37	1.266770	37	1.292784	37	1.318805	37	1.344833	37	1.370866	37	1.396907	37	1.422954
38	1.274509	38	1.301229	38	1.327955	38	1.354689	38	1.381429	38	1.408176	38	1.434931	38	1.461692
39	1.308267	39	1.335699	39	1.363139	39	1.390585	39	1.418039	39	1.445500	39	1.472969	39	1.500444
40	1.342037	40	1.370182	40	1.398334	40	1.426495	40	1.454662	40	1.482838	40	1.511021	40	1.539212
41	1.375817	41	1.404676	41	1.433542	41	1.462416	41	1.491299	41	1.520189	41	1.549088	41	1.577994
42	1.409609	42	1.439181	42	1.468762	42	1.498351	42	1.527948	42	1.557554	42	1.587169	42	1.616791
43	1.443413	43	1.473699	43	1.503994	43	1.534298	43	1.564611	43	1.594933	43	1.625264	43	1.655603
44	1.477227	44	1.508228	44	1.539239	44	1.570258	44	1.601287	44	1.632326	44	1.663373	44	1.694430
45	1.511053	45	1.542769	45	1.574495	45	1.606231	45	1.637977	45	1.669732	45	1.701497	45	1.733272
46	1.544890	46	1.577322	46	1.609764	46	1.642217	46	1.674679	46	1.707152	46	1.739635	46	1.772128
47	1.578738	47	1.611886	47	1.645045	47	1.678215	47	1.711395	47	1.744586	47	1.777787	47	1.810999
48	1.612598	48	1.646463	48	1.680339	48	1.714226	48	1.748124	48	1.782034	48	1.815954	48	1.849886
49	1.646468	49	1.681051	49	1.715645	49	1.750250	49	1.784867	49	1.819495	49	1.854135	49	1.888787
50	1.680351	50	1.715651	50	1.750962	50	1.786286	50	1.821622	50	1.856970	50	1.892330	50	1.927702
51	1.714244	51	1.750262	51	1.786293	51	1.822336	51	1.858391	51	1.894459	51	1.930540	51	1.966633
52	1.748149	52	1.784886	52	1.821635	52	1.858398	52	1.895174	52	1.931962	52	1.968764	52	2.005579
53	1.782065	53	1.819521	53	1.856990	53	1.894473	53	1.931969	53	1.969479	53	2.007002	53	2.044539
54	1.815992	54	1.854168	54	1.892357	54	1.930560	54	1.968778	54	2.007009	54	2.045255	54	2.083515
55	1.849931	55	1.888826	55	1.927736	55	1.966661	55	2.005600	55	2.044554	55	2.083522	55	2.122505
89	3.010601	89	3.074266	89	3.137969	89	3.201712	89	3.265493	89	3.329313	89	3.393172	89	3.457071
90	3.044938	90	3.109340	90	3.173781	90	3.238262	90	3.302783	90	3.367344	90	3.431945	90	3.496586
91	3.079287	91	3.144426	91	3.209605	91	3.274826	91	3.340087	91	3.405389	91	3.470732	91	3.536116
92	3.113646	92	3.179523	92	3.245442	92	3.311402	92	3.377404	92	3.443448	92	3.509533	92	3.575661
120	4.080384	120	4.167124	120	4.253937	120	4.340821	120	4.427776	120	4.514804	120	4.601904	120	4.689075
180	6.182593	180	6.315360	180	6.448291	180	6.581388	180	6.714650	180	6.848078	180	6.981672	180	7.115432
181	6.217987	181	6.351536	181	6.485252	181	6.619136	181	6.753186	181	6.887404	181	7.021790	181	7.156344
182	6.253393	182	6.387725	182	6.522226	182	6.656896	182	6.791736	182	6.926745	182	7.061924	182	7.197272
183	6.288811	183	6.423927	183	6.559213	183	6.694671	183	6.830300	183	6.966100	183	7.102072	183	7.238216
184	6.324241	184	6.460140	184	6.596213	184	6.732459	184	6.868877	184	7.005469	184	7.142235	184	7.279175
270	9.415787	270	9.621065	270	9.826727	270	10.032773	270	10.239204	270	10.446021	270	10.653224	270	10.860815
300	10.515250	300	10.745653	300	10.976534	300	11.207895	300	11.439736	300	11.672060	300	11.904866	300	12.138156
360	12.747431	360	13.029557	360	13.312387	360	13.595923	360	13.880166	360	14.165118	360	14.450782	360	14.737158
365	12.935468	365	13.221995	365	13.509246	365	13.797225	365	14.085931	365	14.375369	365	14.665538	365	14.956442
366	12.973114	366	13.260522	366	13.548659	366	13.837528	366	14.127129	366	14.417465	366	14.708538	366	15.000349

Description: This table shows the compound interest on $100. Interest is compounded daily on the basis of a 360 day year.

Example: The interest on $100 at 14% for 40 days is $ 1.57. On $10,000 the daily compound interest is $156.74.

Interest on $100

DAY	14.00 %		14.25 %		14.50 %		14.75 %		15.00 %		16.00 %		17.00 %		18.00 %
1	.038889	1	.039583	1	.040278	1	.040972	1	.041667	1	.044444	1	.047222	1	.050000
2	.077793	2	.079182	2	.080572	2	.081961	2	.083351	2	.088909	2	.094467	2	.100025
3	.116712	3	.118797	3	.120882	3	.122967	3	.125052	3	.133393	3	.141734	3	.150075
4	.155646	4	.158427	4	.161208	4	.163990	4	.166771	4	.177896	4	.189023	4	.200150
5	.194596	5	.198073	5	.201551	5	.205029	5	.208507	5	.222420	5	.236334	5	.250250
6	.233560	6	.237735	6	.241910	6	.246085	6	.250261	6	.266963	6	.283668	6	.300375
7	.272540	7	.277413	7	.282285	7	.287158	7	.292032	7	.311526	7	.331024	7	.350525
8	.311535	8	.317106	8	.322677	8	.328248	8	.333820	8	.356109	8	.378403	8	.400701
9	.350545	9	.356815	9	.363085	9	.369355	9	.375626	9	.400712	9	.425804	9	.450901
10	.389570	10	.396539	10	.403509	10	.410478	10	.417449	10	.445334	10	.473227	10	.501127
11	.428611	11	.436279	11	.443949	11	.451619	11	.459289	11	.489977	11	.520673	11	.551377
12	.467666	12	.476035	12	.484405	12	.492776	12	.501147	12	.534639	12	.568141	12	.601653
13	.506737	13	.515807	13	.524878	13	.533950	13	.543023	13	.579321	13	.615631	13	.651954
14	.545823	14	.555595	14	.565368	14	.575141	14	.584916	14	.624023	14	.663144	14	.702280
15	.584924	15	.595398	15	.605873	15	.616349	15	.626826	15	.668745	15	.710680	15	.752631
16	.624040	16	.635217	16	.646395	16	.657574	16	.668754	16	.713486	16	.758237	16	.803007
17	.663172	17	.675052	17	.686933	17	.698816	17	.710699	17	.758248	17	.805818	17	.853409
18	.702319	18	.714902	18	.727487	18	.740074	18	.752662	18	.803029	18	.853420	18	.903835
19	.741481	19	.754769	19	.768058	19	.781350	19	.794642	19	.847831	19	.901046	19	.954287
20	.780658	20	.794651	20	.808645	20	.822642	20	.836640	20	.892652	20	.948693	20	1.004764
21	.819850	21	.834549	21	.849249	21	.863951	21	.878655	21	.937493	21	.996364	21	1.055267
22	.859058	22	.874462	22	.889869	22	.905277	22	.920688	22	.982354	22	1.044056	22	1.105794
23	.898281	23	.914392	23	.930505	23	.946620	23	.962739	23	1.027235	23	1.091772	23	1.156347
24	.937519	24	.954337	24	.971157	24	.987981	24	1.004806	24	1.072136	24	1.139509	24	1.206925
25	.976773	25	.994298	25	1.011826	25	1.029358	25	1.046892	25	1.117057	25	1.187270	25	1.257529
26	1.016042	26	1.034275	26	1.052512	26	1.070752	26	1.088995	26	1.161998	26	1.235053	26	1.308158
27	1.055326	27	1.074268	27	1.093213	27	1.112162	27	1.131115	27	1.206959	27	1.282858	27	1.358812
28	1.094625	28	1.114276	28	1.133932	28	1.153590	28	1.173253	28	1.251940	28	1.330686	28	1.409491
29	1.133939	29	1.154301	29	1.174666	29	1.195035	29	1.215408	29	1.296941	29	1.378537	29	1.460196
30	1.173269	30	1.194341	30	1.215417	30	1.236497	30	1.257582	30	1.341962	30	1.426410	30	1.510926
31	1.212614	31	1.234397	31	1.256184	31	1.277976	31	1.299772	31	1.387003	31	1.474306	31	1.561681
32	1.251975	32	1.274469	32	1.296968	32	1.319472	32	1.341980	32	1.432063	32	1.522224	32	1.612462
33	1.291351	33	1.314557	33	1.337768	33	1.360985	33	1.384206	33	1.477144	33	1.570165	33	1.663268
34	1.330742	34	1.354661	34	1.378585	34	1.402514	34	1.426450	34	1.522245	34	1.618129	34	1.714100
35	1.370148	35	1.394780	35	1.419418	35	1.444061	35	1.468711	35	1.567366	35	1.666115	35	1.764957
36	1.409570	36	1.434916	36	1.460267	36	1.485625	36	1.510989	36	1.612507	36	1.714124	36	1.815840
37	1.449007	37	1.475067	37	1.501133	37	1.527206	37	1.553286	37	1.657668	37	1.762156	37	1.866748
38	1.488459	38	1.515234	38	1.542016	38	1.568804	38	1.595599	38	1.702850	38	1.810210	38	1.917681
39	1.527927	39	1.555417	39	1.582915	39	1.610419	39	1.637931	39	1.748051	39	1.858287	39	1.968640
40	1.567410	40	1.595616	40	1.623830	40	1.652051	40	1.680280	40	1.793272	40	1.906387	40	2.019624
41	1.606909	41	1.635831	41	1.664762	41	1.693700	41	1.722647	41	1.838514	41	1.954509	41	2.070634
42	1.646422	42	1.676062	42	1.705710	42	1.735366	42	1.765031	42	1.883775	42	2.002655	42	2.121669
43	1.685952	43	1.716309	43	1.746675	43	1.777050	43	1.807433	43	1.929057	43	2.050822	43	2.172730
44	1.725496	44	1.756571	44	1.787656	44	1.818750	44	1.849853	44	1.974359	44	2.099013	44	2.223816
45	1.765056	45	1.796850	45	1.828654	45	1.860467	45	1.892291	45	2.019681	45	2.147227	45	2.274928
46	1.804631	46	1.837145	46	1.869668	46	1.902202	46	1.934746	46	2.065023	46	2.195463	46	2.326066
47	1.844222	47	1.877455	47	1.910699	47	1.943953	47	1.977219	47	2.110385	47	2.243722	47	2.377229
48	1.883828	48	1.917782	48	1.951746	48	1.985722	48	2.019709	48	2.155767	48	2.292003	48	2.428417
49	1.923450	49	1.958124	49	1.992810	49	2.027508	49	2.062217	49	2.201170	49	2.340308	49	2.479632
50	1.963086	50	1.998483	50	2.033891	50	2.069311	50	2.104743	50	2.246593	50	2.388635	50	2.530871
51	2.002739	51	2.038857	51	2.074988	51	2.111131	51	2.147287	51	2.292036	51	2.436986	51	2.582137
52	2.042407	52	2.079247	52	2.116101	52	2.152968	52	2.189848	52	2.337499	52	2.485359	52	2.633428
53	2.082090	53	2.119654	53	2.157231	53	2.194823	53	2.232427	53	2.382982	53	2.533754	53	2.684745
54	2.121788	54	2.160076	54	2.198378	54	2.236694	54	2.275024	54	2.428486	54	2.582173	54	2.736087
55	2.161502	55	2.200514	55	2.239541	55	2.278583	55	2.317639	55	2.474009	55	2.630615	55	2.787455
89	3.521008	89	3.584984	89	3.649000	89	3.713055	89	3.777148	89	4.033915	89	4.291310	89	4.549335
90	3.561266	90	3.625987	90	3.690748	90	3.755548	90	3.820389	90	4.080153	90	4.340559	90	4.601610
91	3.601540	91	3.667006	91	3.732512	91	3.798059	91	3.863647	91	4.126410	91	4.389831	91	4.653910
92	3.641830	92	3.708040	92	3.774293	92	3.840587	92	3.906924	92	4.172689	92	4.439126	92	4.706237
120	4.776319	120	4.863635	120	4.951022	120	5.038483	120	5.126015	120	5.476868	120	5.828883	120	6.182062
180	7.249359	180	7.383452	180	7.517711	180	7.652138	180	7.786731	180	8.326782	180	8.869522	180	9.414967
181	7.291067	181	7.425958	181	7.561017	181	7.696245	181	7.831643	181	8.374227	181	8.920933	181	9.469675
182	7.332791	182	7.468480	182	7.604340	182	7.740371	182	7.876572	182	8.423093	182	8.972368	182	9.524410
183	7.374532	183	7.511020	183	7.647681	183	7.784514	183	7.921521	183	8.471281	183	9.023827	183	9.579172
184	7.416288	184	7.553576	184	7.691039	184	7.828676	184	7.966488	184	8.519491	184	9.075311	184	9.633961
270	11.068794	270	11.277161	270	11.485918	270	11.695066	270	11.904604	270	12.746679	270	13.595068	270	14.449817
300	12.371930	300	12.606190	300	12.840937	300	13.076172	300	13.311895	300	14.259697	300	15.215399	300	16.179069
360	15.024249	360	15.312057	360	15.600582	360	15.889828	360	16.179795	360	17.346916	360	18.525729	360	19.716351
365	15.248082	365	15.540459	365	15.833577	365	16.127435	365	16.422038	365	17.607919	365	18.805846	365	20.015941
366	15.292900	366	15.586194	366	15.880232	366	16.175015	366	16.470547	366	17.660189	366	18.861949	366	20.075949

DAILY COMPOUND INTEREST, 365 DAY YEAR

4.00 %

Description: This table shows the compound interest on $100. Interest is compounded daily on the basis of a 365 day year.

Example: The interest on $100 at 4% for 40 days is $ .44. On $10,000 the daily compound interest is $ 43.93.

Interest on $100

DAY	4.00 %		4.25 %		4.50 %		4.75 %		5.00 %		5.25 %		5.50 %		5.75 %
1	.010959	1	.011644	1	.012329	1	.013014	1	.013699	1	.014384	1	.015068	1	.015753
2	.021919	2	.023289	2	.024659	2	.026029	2	.027399	2	.028769	2	.030139	2	.031509
3	.032880	3	.034936	3	.036991	3	.039046	3	.041102	3	.043157	3	.045212	3	.047268
4	.043843	4	.046583	4	.049324	4	.052065	4	.054806	4	.057547	4	.060288	4	.063029
5	.054807	5	.058233	5	.061659	5	.065085	5	.068512	5	.071938	5	.075365	5	.078792
6	.065771	6	.069883	6	.073995	6	.078108	6	.082220	6	.086332	6	.090445	6	.094558
7	.076738	7	.081535	7	.086333	7	.091131	7	.095930	7	.100728	7	.105527	7	.110326
8	.087705	8	.093189	8	.098673	8	.104157	8	.109642	8	.115126	8	.120612	8	.126097
9	.098673	9	.104843	9	.111014	9	.117184	9	.123355	9	.129527	9	.135698	9	.141870
10	.109643	10	.116499	10	.123356	10	.130213	10	.137071	10	.143929	10	.150787	10	.157646
11	.120614	11	.128157	11	.135700	11	.143244	11	.150788	11	.158333	11	.165878	11	.173424
12	.131586	12	.139816	12	.148046	12	.156276	12	.164507	12	.172739	12	.180972	12	.189205
13	.142559	13	.151476	13	.160393	13	.169310	13	.178229	13	.187148	13	.196068	13	.204988
14	.153534	14	.163137	14	.172741	14	.182346	14	.191952	14	.201558	14	.211166	14	.220774
15	.164510	15	.174800	15	.185091	15	.195383	15	.205677	15	.215971	15	.226266	15	.236562
16	.175487	16	.186464	16	.197443	16	.208423	16	.219403	16	.230385	16	.241369	16	.252353
17	.186465	17	.198130	17	.209796	17	.221463	17	.233132	17	.244802	17	.256473	17	.268146
18	.197444	18	.209797	18	.222151	18	.234506	18	.246863	18	.259221	18	.271581	18	.283942
19	.208425	19	.221465	19	.234507	19	.247550	19	.260595	19	.273642	19	.286690	19	.299740
20	.219406	20	.233134	20	.246864	20	.260596	20	.274329	20	.288065	20	.301802	20	.315540
21	.230389	21	.244805	21	.259224	21	.273644	21	.288066	21	.302490	21	.316916	21	.331344
22	.241374	22	.256474	22	.271584	22	.286693	22	.301804	22	.316917	22	.332032	22	.347149
23	.252359	23	.268152	23	.283947	23	.299744	23	.315544	23	.331346	23	.347150	23	.362957
24	.263345	24	.279827	24	.296310	24	.312797	24	.329286	24	.345777	24	.362271	24	.378768
25	.274333	25	.291503	25	.308676	25	.325851	25	.343029	25	.360210	25	.377394	25	.394581
26	.285322	26	.303181	26	.321042	26	.338907	26	.356775	26	.374646	26	.392520	26	.410397
27	.296312	27	.314860	27	.333411	27	.351965	27	.370522	27	.389083	27	.407647	27	.426215
28	.307304	28	.326540	28	.345781	28	.365024	28	.384272	28	.403523	28	.422777	28	.442035
29	.318296	29	.338222	29	.358152	29	.378086	29	.398023	29	.417964	29	.437909	29	.457858
30	.329290	30	.349905	30	.370525	30	.391149	30	.411776	30	.432408	30	.453044	30	.473684
31	.340285	31	.361590	31	.382899	31	.404213	31	.425531	31	.446854	31	.468181	31	.489512
32	.351281	32	.373276	32	.395275	32	.417279	32	.439288	32	.461302	32	.483320	32	.505342
33	.362279	33	.384963	33	.407653	33	.430347	33	.453047	33	.475752	33	.498461	33	.521175
34	.373277	34	.396652	34	.420032	34	.443417	34	.466808	34	.490204	34	.513605	34	.537011
35	.384277	35	.408342	35	.432412	35	.456489	35	.480570	35	.504658	35	.528751	35	.552849
36	.395278	36	.420033	36	.444795	36	.469562	36	.494335	36	.519114	36	.543899	36	.568690
37	.406280	37	.431726	37	.457178	37	.482636	37	.508101	37	.533572	37	.559049	37	.584533
38	.417284	38	.443420	38	.469563	38	.495713	38	.521869	38	.548032	38	.574202	38	.600378
39	.428288	39	.455116	39	.481950	39	.508791	39	.535639	39	.562495	39	.589357	39	.616226
40	.439294	40	.466813	40	.494338	40	.521871	40	.549411	40	.576959	40	.604514	40	.632077
41	.450301	41	.478511	41	.506728	41	.534953	41	.563185	41	.591426	41	.619674	41	.647930
42	.461310	42	.490210	42	.519119	42	.548036	42	.576961	42	.605894	42	.634836	42	.663785
43	.472319	43	.501911	43	.531512	43	.561121	43	.590739	43	.620365	43	.650000	43	.679643
44	.483330	44	.513613	44	.543906	44	.574208	44	.604518	44	.634838	44	.665166	44	.695504
45	.494342	45	.525317	45	.556302	45	.587296	45	.618300	45	.649313	45	.680335	45	.711367
46	.505355	46	.537022	46	.568699	46	.600386	46	.632083	46	.663790	46	.695506	46	.727232
47	.516369	47	.548728	47	.581098	47	.613478	47	.645868	47	.678269	47	.710679	47	.743100
48	.527384	48	.560436	48	.593499	48	.626572	48	.659655	48	.692750	48	.725855	48	.758971
49	.538401	49	.572145	49	.605901	49	.639667	49	.673444	49	.707233	49	.741033	49	.774844
50	.549419	50	.583856	50	.618304	50	.652764	50	.687235	50	.721718	50	.756213	50	.790719
51	.560438	51	.595568	51	.630709	51	.665863	51	.701028	51	.736206	51	.771395	51	.806597
52	.571458	52	.607281	52	.643116	52	.678963	52	.714823	52	.750695	52	.786580	52	.822477
53	.582480	53	.618995	53	.655524	53	.692065	53	.728619	53	.765187	53	.801767	53	.838360
54	.593503	54	.630711	54	.667933	54	.705169	54	.742418	54	.779680	54	.816956	54	.854246
55	.604527	55	.642428	55	.680344	55	.718274	55	.756218	55	.794176	55	.832148	55	.870134
89	.980060	89	1.041629	89	1.103234	89	1.164876	89	1.226556	89	1.288273	89	1.350027	89	1.411818
90	.991127	90	1.053394	90	1.115699	90	1.178042	90	1.240422	90	1.302841	90	1.365298	90	1.427794
91	1.002194	91	1.065160	91	1.128165	91	1.191209	91	1.254291	91	1.317412	91	1.380573	91	1.443772
92	1.013263	92	1.076928	92	1.140633	92	1.204377	92	1.268161	92	1.331985	92	1.395849	92	1.459753
120	1.323681	120	1.406985	120	1.490358	120	1.573798	120	1.657306	120	1.740883	120	1.824528	120	1.908241
180	1.992077	180	2.117884	180	2.243845	180	2.369961	180	2.496231	180	2.622657	180	2.749237	180	2.875973
181	2.003254	181	2.129774	181	2.256451	181	2.383283	181	2.510272	181	2.637418	181	2.764720	181	2.892179
182	2.014433	182	2.141666	182	2.269058	182	2.396607	182	2.524315	182	2.652181	182	2.780205	182	2.908389
183	2.025612	183	2.153559	183	2.281666	183	2.409933	183	2.538359	183	2.666946	183	2.795693	183	2.924600
184	2.036793	184	2.165454	184	2.294276	184	2.423260	184	2.552405	184	2.681713	184	2.811182	184	2.940814
270	3.002948	270	3.193587	270	3.384578	270	3.575922	270	3.767618	270	3.959667	270	4.152071	270	4.344829
300	3.342126	300	3.554667	300	3.767644	300	3.981057	300	4.194908	300	4.409197	300	4.623926	300	4.839094
360	4.023837	360	4.280622	360	4.538039	360	4.796089	360	5.054775	360	5.314097	360	5.574058	360	5.834658
365	4.080849	365	4.341347	365	4.602496	365	4.864296	365	5.126750	365	5.389858	365	5.653624	365	5.918047
366	4.092255	366	4.353497	366	4.615392	366	4.877943	366	5.141151	366	5.405017	366	5.669544	366	5.934733

Description: This table shows the compound interest on $100. Interest is compounded daily on the basis of a 365 day year.

Example: The interest on $100 at 6% for 40 days is $ .66. On $10,000 the daily compound interest is $ 65.96.

Interest on $100

DAY	6.00 %		6.25 %		6.50 %		6.75 %		7.00 %		7.25 %		7.50 %		7.75 %
1	.016438	1	.017123	1	.017808	1	.018493	1	.019178	1	.019863	1	.020548	1	.021233
2	.032879	2	.034250	2	.035620	2	.036990	2	.038360	2	.039730	2	.041100	2	.042470
3	.049323	3	.051379	3	.053434	3	.055490	3	.057545	3	.059601	3	.061657	3	.063712
4	.065770	4	.068511	4	.071252	4	.073993	4	.076734	4	.079476	4	.082217	4	.084959
5	.082219	5	.085646	5	.089073	5	.092500	5	.095927	5	.099355	5	.102782	5	.106209
6	.098671	6	.102784	6	.106897	6	.111010	6	.115124	6	.119237	6	.123351	6	.127465
7	.115125	7	.119925	7	.124724	7	.129524	7	.134324	7	.139124	7	.143924	7	.148725
8	.131583	8	.137068	8	.142555	8	.148041	8	.153528	8	.159015	8	.164502	8	.169989
9	.148043	9	.154215	9	.160388	9	.166562	9	.172735	9	.178909	9	.185084	9	.191258
10	.164505	10	.171365	10	.178225	10	.185085	10	.191946	10	.198808	10	.205670	10	.212532
11	.180971	11	.188518	11	.196065	11	.203613	11	.211161	11	.218710	11	.226260	11	.233810
12	.197439	12	.205673	12	.213908	12	.222144	12	.230380	12	.238617	12	.246854	12	.255092
13	.213910	13	.222832	13	.231754	13	.240678	13	.249602	13	.258527	13	.267453	13	.276379
14	.230383	14	.239993	14	.249604	14	.259216	14	.268828	14	.278442	14	.288056	14	.297671
15	.246859	15	.257157	15	.267457	15	.277757	15	.288058	15	.298360	15	.308663	15	.318967
16	.263338	16	.274325	16	.285312	16	.296301	16	.307291	16	.318282	16	.329274	16	.340268
17	.279820	17	.291495	17	.303171	17	.314849	17	.326528	17	.338208	17	.349890	17	.361573
18	.296304	18	.308668	18	.321034	18	.333400	18	.345769	18	.358139	18	.370510	18	.382882
19	.312791	19	.325844	19	.338899	19	.351955	19	.365013	19	.378073	19	.391134	19	.404197
20	.329281	20	.343023	20	.356768	20	.370514	20	.384261	20	.398011	20	.411762	20	.425515
21	.345774	21	.360205	21	.374639	21	.389075	21	.403513	21	.417953	21	.432395	21	.446838
22	.362269	22	.377390	22	.392514	22	.407640	22	.422769	22	.437899	22	.453031	22	.468166
23	.378767	23	.394578	23	.410392	23	.426209	23	.442028	23	.457849	23	.473672	23	.489498
24	.395267	24	.411769	24	.428274	24	.444781	24	.461291	24	.477803	24	.494318	24	.510835
25	.411771	25	.428963	25	.446158	25	.463356	25	.480557	25	.497761	25	.514967	25	.532177
26	.428277	26	.446160	26	.464046	26	.481935	26	.499827	26	.517723	26	.535621	26	.553523
27	.444785	27	.463359	27	.481937	27	.500517	27	.519101	27	.537688	27	.556279	27	.574873
28	.461297	28	.480562	28	.499831	28	.519103	28	.538379	28	.557658	28	.576941	28	.596228
29	.477811	29	.497768	29	.517728	29	.537692	29	.557660	29	.577632	29	.597608	29	.617587
30	.494328	30	.514976	30	.535628	30	.556285	30	.576945	30	.597610	30	.618279	30	.638951
31	.510848	31	.532188	31	.553532	31	.574881	31	.596234	31	.617592	31	.638954	31	.660320
32	.527370	32	.549402	32	.571439	32	.593480	32	.615526	32	.637577	32	.659633	32	.681693
33	.543895	33	.566619	33	.589349	33	.612083	33	.634823	33	.657567	33	.680316	33	.703071
34	.560423	34	.583840	34	.607262	34	.630690	34	.654122	34	.677561	34	.701004	34	.724453
35	.576953	35	.601063	35	.625178	35	.649299	35	.673426	35	.697558	35	.721696	35	.745839
36	.593486	36	.618289	36	.643098	36	.667913	36	.692733	36	.717560	36	.742392	36	.767231
37	.610022	37	.635518	37	.661021	37	.686529	37	.712044	37	.737565	37	.763093	37	.788626
38	.626561	38	.652750	38	.678947	38	.705149	38	.731359	38	.757575	38	.783797	38	.810027
39	.643102	39	.669985	39	.696876	39	.723773	39	.750677	39	.777588	39	.804506	39	.831432
40	.659646	40	.687223	40	.714808	40	.742400	40	.769999	40	.797606	40	.825220	40	.852841
41	.676193	41	.704464	41	.732744	41	.761030	41	.789325	41	.817627	41	.845937	41	.874255
42	.692743	42	.721708	42	.750682	42	.779664	42	.808654	42	.837653	42	.866659	42	.895674
43	.709295	43	.738955	43	.768624	43	.798302	43	.827987	43	.857682	43	.887385	43	.917097
44	.725850	44	.756205	44	.786569	44	.816942	44	.847324	44	.877715	44	.908115	44	.938524
45	.742408	45	.773458	45	.804518	45	.835587	45	.866665	45	.897753	45	.928850	45	.959956
46	.758968	46	.790714	46	.822469	46	.854234	46	.886009	46	.917794	46	.949589	46	.981393
47	.775531	47	.807972	47	.840424	47	.872885	47	.905357	47	.937839	47	.970332	47	1.002834
48	.792097	48	.825234	48	.858382	48	.891540	48	.924709	48	.957889	48	.991079	48	1.024280
49	.808665	49	.842498	49	.876343	49	.910198	49	.944064	49	.977942	49	1.011831	49	1.045730
50	.825237	50	.859766	50	.894307	50	.928859	50	.963424	50	.997999	50	1.032586	50	1.067185
51	.841811	51	.877037	51	.912274	51	.947524	51	.982786	51	1.018060	51	1.053347	51	1.088645
52	.858387	52	.894310	52	.930245	52	.966193	52	1.002153	52	1.038126	52	1.074111	52	1.110109
53	.874967	53	.911586	53	.948219	53	.984865	53	1.021523	53	1.058195	53	1.094880	53	1.131577
54	.891549	54	.928866	54	.966196	54	1.003540	54	1.040897	54	1.078268	54	1.115653	54	1.153051
55	.908134	55	.946148	55	.984176	55	1.022219	55	1.060275	55	1.098345	55	1.136430	55	1.174528
89	1.473646	89	1.535512	89	1.597415	89	1.659355	89	1.721333	89	1.783348	89	1.845400	89	1.907490
90	1.490327	90	1.552898	90	1.615507	90	1.678155	90	1.740841	90	1.803565	90	1.866327	90	1.929128
91	1.507010	91	1.570287	91	1.633603	91	1.696959	91	1.760353	91	1.823786	91	1.887259	91	1.950770
92	1.523696	92	1.587679	92	1.651703	92	1.715766	92	1.779869	92	1.844012	92	1.908194	92	1.972417
120	1.992022	120	2.075871	120	2.159789	120	2.243775	120	2.327830	120	2.411953	120	2.496145	120	2.580405
180	3.002864	180	3.129911	180	3.257114	180	3.384472	180	3.511987	180	3.639658	180	3.767486	180	3.895471
181	3.019796	181	3.147570	181	3.275502	181	3.403591	181	3.531839	181	3.660244	181	3.788808	181	3.917531
182	3.036731	182	3.165232	182	3.293893	182	3.422714	182	3.551694	182	3.680834	182	3.810135	182	3.939596
183	3.053668	183	3.182898	183	3.312288	183	3.441840	183	3.571553	183	3.701429	183	3.831466	183	3.961665
184	3.070609	184	3.200566	184	3.330686	184	3.460970	184	3.591416	184	3.722027	184	3.852801	184	3.983739
270	4.537943	270	4.731413	270	4.925240	270	5.119424	270	5.313966	270	5.508867	270	5.704127	270	5.899747
300	5.054704	300	5.270755	300	5.487249	300	5.704187	300	5.921570	300	6.139398	300	6.357673	300	6.576395
360	6.095900	360	6.357785	360	6.620315	360	6.883491	360	7.147315	360	7.411788	360	7.676912	360	7.942689
365	6.183131	365	6.448876	365	6.715285	365	6.982358	365	7.250098	365	7.518507	365	7.787585	365	8.057334
366	6.200586	366	6.467104	366	6.734289	366	7.002143	366	7.270667	366	7.539863	366	7.809733	366	8.080278

Description: This table shows the compound interest on $100. Interest is compounded daily on the basis of a 365 day year.

Example: The interest on $100 at 8% for 40 days is $ .88. On $10,000 the daily compound interest is $ 88.05.

Interest on $100

DAY	8.00 %		8.25 %		8.50 %		8.75 %		9.00 %		9.25 %		9.50 %		9.75 %
1	.021918	1	.022603	1	.023288	1	.023973	1	.024658	1	.025342	1	.026027	1	.026712
2	.043840	2	.045211	2	.046581	2	.047951	2	.049321	2	.050691	2	.052062	2	.053432
3	.065768	3	.067824	3	.069879	3	.071935	3	.073991	3	.076047	3	.078103	3	.080158
4	.087700	4	.090442	4	.093183	4	.095925	4	.098667	4	.101408	4	.104150	4	.106892
5	.109637	5	.113065	5	.116493	5	.119920	5	.123348	5	.126777	5	.130205	5	.133633
6	.131579	6	.135693	6	.139807	6	.143922	6	.148036	6	.152151	6	.156266	6	.160381
7	.153526	7	.158327	7	.163128	7	.167929	7	.172730	7	.177532	7	.182334	7	.187136
8	.175477	8	.180965	8	.186453	8	.191942	8	.197431	8	.202920	8	.208409	8	.213899
9	.197433	9	.203609	9	.209784	9	.215960	9	.222137	9	.228314	9	.234491	9	.240668
10	.219394	10	.226257	10	.233121	10	.239985	10	.246849	10	.253714	10	.260579	10	.267445
11	.241360	11	.248911	11	.256463	11	.264015	11	.271568	11	.279121	11	.286674	11	.294228
12	.263331	12	.271570	12	.279810	12	.288051	12	.296292	12	.304534	12	.312776	12	.321019
13	.285307	13	.294234	13	.303163	13	.312092	13	.321023	13	.329953	13	.338885	13	.347817
14	.307287	14	.316904	14	.326521	14	.336140	14	.345759	14	.355380	14	.365001	14	.374623
15	.329272	15	.339578	15	.349885	15	.360193	15	.370502	15	.380812	15	.391123	15	.401435
16	.351262	16	.362258	16	.373254	16	.384252	16	.395251	16	.406251	16	.417252	16	.428255
17	.373257	17	.384942	17	.396629	17	.408317	17	.420006	17	.431696	17	.443388	17	.455081
18	.395256	18	.407632	18	.420009	18	.432387	18	.444767	18	.457148	18	.469531	18	.481915
19	.417261	19	.430327	19	.443394	19	.456464	19	.469534	19	.482607	19	.495681	19	.508756
20	.439270	20	.453027	20	.466785	20	.480546	20	.494308	20	.508071	20	.521837	20	.535604
21	.461284	21	.475732	21	.490182	21	.504633	21	.519087	21	.533543	21	.548000	21	.562460
22	.483303	22	.498442	22	.513583	22	.528727	22	.543873	22	.559020	22	.574170	22	.589322
23	.505327	23	.521158	23	.536991	23	.552826	23	.568664	23	.584504	23	.600347	23	.616192
24	.527355	24	.543878	24	.560403	24	.576931	24	.593462	24	.609995	24	.626531	24	.643069
25	.549389	25	.566604	25	.583822	25	.601042	25	.618266	25	.635492	25	.652721	25	.669953
26	.571427	26	.589335	26	.607245	26	.625159	26	.643076	26	.660996	26	.678919	26	.696845
27	.593470	27	.612071	27	.630674	27	.649281	27	.667892	27	.686506	27	.705123	27	.723743
28	.615518	28	.634812	28	.654109	28	.673410	28	.692714	28	.712022	28	.731334	28	.750649
29	.637571	29	.657558	29	.677549	29	.697544	29	.717542	29	.737545	29	.757551	29	.777562
30	.659628	30	.680309	30	.700994	30	.721684	30	.742377	30	.763074	30	.783776	30	.804482
31	.681691	31	.703066	31	.724445	31	.745829	31	.767217	31	.788610	31	.810007	31	.831409
32	.703758	32	.725827	32	.747902	32	.769981	32	.792064	32	.814153	32	.836246	32	.858343
33	.725830	33	.748594	33	.771363	33	.794138	33	.816917	33	.839701	33	.862491	33	.885285
34	.747907	34	.771366	34	.794831	34	.818301	34	.841776	34	.865257	34	.888742	34	.912234
35	.769989	35	.794143	35	.818304	35	.842470	35	.866641	35	.890818	35	.915001	35	.939190
36	.792075	36	.816925	36	.841782	36	.866644	36	.891512	36	.916387	36	.941267	36	.966153
37	.814166	37	.839713	37	.865265	37	.890824	37	.916390	37	.941961	37	.967539	37	.993123
38	.836263	38	.862505	38	.888755	38	.915011	38	.941273	38	.967542	38	.993818	38	1.020101
39	.858364	39	.885303	39	.912249	39	.939203	39	.966163	39	.993130	39	1.020104	39	1.047086
40	.880470	40	.908106	40	.935749	40	.963400	40	.991059	40	1.018724	40	1.046397	40	1.074078
41	.902581	41	.930914	41	.959255	41	.987604	41	1.015960	41	1.044325	41	1.072697	41	1.101077
42	.924696	42	.953727	42	.982766	42	1.011813	42	1.040869	42	1.069932	42	1.099004	42	1.128083
43	.946817	43	.976545	43	1.006283	43	1.036028	43	1.065783	43	1.095546	43	1.125317	43	1.155097
44	.968942	44	.999369	44	1.029805	44	1.060249	44	1.090703	44	1.121166	44	1.151637	44	1.182118
45	.991072	45	1.022197	45	1.053332	45	1.084476	45	1.115630	45	1.146792	45	1.177964	45	1.209146
46	1.013207	46	1.045031	46	1.076865	46	1.108709	46	1.140562	46	1.172425	46	1.204298	46	1.236181
47	1.035347	47	1.067870	47	1.100404	47	1.132947	47	1.165501	47	1.198065	47	1.230639	47	1.263224
48	1.057492	48	1.090714	48	1.123947	48	1.157191	48	1.190446	48	1.223711	48	1.256987	48	1.290274
49	1.079641	49	1.113564	49	1.147497	49	1.181441	49	1.215397	49	1.249364	49	1.283342	49	1.317331
50	1.101796	50	1.136418	50	1.171052	50	1.205697	50	1.240354	50	1.275023	50	1.309703	50	1.344395
51	1.123955	51	1.159278	51	1.194612	51	1.229959	51	1.265317	51	1.300688	51	1.336071	51	1.371466
52	1.146119	52	1.182142	52	1.218178	52	1.254226	52	1.290287	52	1.326360	52	1.362446	52	1.398545
53	1.168288	53	1.205012	53	1.241749	53	1.278499	53	1.315263	53	1.352039	53	1.388828	53	1.425631
54	1.190462	54	1.227887	54	1.265326	54	1.302779	54	1.340245	54	1.377724	54	1.415217	54	1.452724
55	1.212641	55	1.250768	55	1.288909	55	1.327063	55	1.365233	55	1.403416	55	1.441613	55	1.479824
89	1.969617	89	2.031782	89	2.093984	89	2.156224	89	2.218501	89	2.280815	89	2.343168	89	2.405558
90	1.991967	90	2.054844	90	2.117759	90	2.180713	90	2.243705	90	2.306736	90	2.369805	90	2.432912
91	2.014321	91	2.077911	91	2.141540	91	2.205208	91	2.268916	91	2.332663	91	2.396449	91	2.460275
92	2.036680	92	2.100983	92	2.165327	92	2.229710	92	2.294133	92	2.358597	92	2.423100	92	2.487644
120	2.664734	120	2.749132	120	2.833599	120	2.918135	120	3.002739	120	3.087412	120	3.172155	120	3.256966
180	4.023613	180	4.151911	180	4.280368	180	4.408981	180	4.537753	180	4.666682	180	4.795770	180	4.925016
181	4.046412	181	4.175453	181	4.304652	181	4.434011	181	4.563529	181	4.693207	181	4.823045	181	4.953043
182	4.069217	182	4.198999	182	4.328942	182	4.459046	182	4.589312	182	4.719739	182	4.850328	182	4.981079
183	4.092027	183	4.222551	183	4.353238	183	4.484088	183	4.615101	183	4.746278	183	4.877618	183	5.009122
184	4.114841	184	4.246108	184	4.377539	184	4.509136	184	4.640897	184	4.772823	184	4.904915	184	5.037172
270	6.095728	270	6.292071	270	6.488775	270	6.685842	270	6.883272	270	7.081066	270	7.279225	270	7.477749
300	6.795566	300	7.015185	300	7.235255	300	7.455776	300	7.676749	300	7.898174	300	8.120054	300	8.342388
360	8.209120	360	8.476207	360	8.743951	360	9.012354	360	9.281418	360	9.551144	360	9.821533	360	10.092589
365	8.327757	365	8.598855	365	8.870629	365	9.143082	365	9.416214	365	9.690029	365	9.964526	365	10.239709
366	8.351500	366	8.623401	366	8.895983	366	9.169246	366	9.443194	366	9.717827	366	9.993147	366	10.269156

DAILY COMPOUND INTEREST, 365 DAY YEAR

10.00 %

Description: This table shows the compound interest on $100. Interest is compounded daily on the basis of a 365 day year.

Example: The interest on $100 at 10% for 40 days is $ 1.10. On $10,000 the daily compound interest is $110.18.

Interest on $100

DAY	10.00 %		10.25 %		10.50 %		10.75 %		11.00 %		11.25 %		11.50 %		11.75 %
1	.027397	1	.028082	1	.028767	1	.029452	1	.030137	1	.030822	1	.031507	1	.032192
2	.054802	2	.056172	2	.057543	2	.058913	2	.060283	2	.061653	2	.063024	2	.064394
3	.082214	3	.084270	3	.086326	3	.088382	3	.090438	3	.092494	3	.094550	3	.096606
4	.109634	4	.112376	4	.115118	4	.117860	4	.120602	4	.123345	4	.126087	4	.128829
5	.137061	5	.140490	5	.143918	5	.147347	5	.150776	5	.154205	5	.157634	5	.161063
6	.164496	6	.168611	6	.172727	6	.176842	6	.180958	6	.185074	6	.189190	6	.193306
7	.191939	7	.196741	7	.201544	7	.206347	7	.211150	7	.215953	7	.220757	7	.225560
8	.219388	8	.224878	8	.230369	8	.235859	8	.241350	8	.246842	8	.252333	8	.257825
9	.246846	9	.253024	9	.259202	9	.265381	9	.271560	9	.277740	9	.283919	9	.290099
10	.274311	10	.281177	10	.288044	10	.294911	10	.301779	10	.308647	10	.315516	10	.322385
11	.301783	11	.309338	11	.316894	11	.324450	11	.332007	11	.339564	11	.347122	11	.354680
12	.329263	12	.337507	12	.345752	12	.353998	12	.362244	12	.370491	12	.378738	12	.386986
13	.356750	13	.365684	13	.374619	13	.383554	13	.392490	13	.401427	13	.410364	13	.419302
14	.384245	14	.393869	14	.403494	14	.413119	14	.422745	14	.432372	14	.442000	14	.451629
15	.411748	15	.422062	15	.432377	15	.442693	15	.453010	15	.463328	15	.473646	15	.483966
16	.439258	16	.450263	16	.461268	16	.472275	16	.483283	16	.494292	16	.505303	16	.516314
17	.466776	17	.478471	17	.490168	17	.501866	17	.513566	17	.525267	17	.536969	17	.548672
18	.494301	18	.506688	18	.519076	18	.531466	18	.543858	18	.556250	18	.568645	18	.581040
19	.521833	19	.534912	19	.547993	19	.561075	19	.574158	19	.587244	19	.600331	19	.613419
20	.549374	20	.563145	20	.576918	20	.590692	20	.604469	20	.618247	20	.632027	20	.645808
21	.576921	21	.591385	21	.605851	21	.620318	21	.634788	21	.649259	21	.663733	21	.678208
22	.604477	22	.619633	22	.634792	22	.649953	22	.665116	22	.680281	22	.695449	22	.710618
23	.632024	23	.647890	23	.663742	23	.679596	23	.695453	23	.711313	23	.727175	23	.743039
24	.659610	24	.676154	24	.692700	24	.709249	24	.725800	24	.742354	24	.758911	24	.775470
25	.687188	25	.704426	25	.721666	25	.738910	25	.756156	25	.773405	25	.790656	25	.807911
26	.714774	26	.732706	26	.750641	26	.768579	26	.786521	26	.804465	26	.822412	26	.840363
27	.742367	27	.760994	27	.779624	27	.798258	27	.816895	27	.835535	27	.854178	27	.872825
28	.769967	28	.789290	28	.808615	28	.827945	28	.847278	28	.866614	28	.885954	28	.905298
29	.797576	29	.817593	29	.837615	29	.857641	29	.877670	29	.897703	29	.917740	29	.937781
30	.825191	30	.845905	30	.866623	30	.887345	30	.908072	30	.928802	30	.949536	30	.970275
31	.852815	31	.874225	31	.895640	31	.917059	31	.938482	31	.959910	31	.981342	31	1.002779
32	.880446	32	.902553	32	.924664	32	.946781	32	.968902	32	.991028	32	1.013158	32	1.035294
33	.908084	33	.930888	33	.953698	33	.976512	33	.999331	33	1.022155	33	1.044984	33	1.067819
34	.935730	34	.959232	34	.982739	34	1.006251	34	1.029769	34	1.053292	34	1.076821	34	1.100354
35	.963384	35	.987583	35	1.011789	35	1.036000	35	1.060216	35	1.084439	35	1.108667	35	1.132900
36	.991045	36	1.015943	36	1.040847	36	1.065757	36	1.090673	36	1.115595	36	1.140523	36	1.165457
37	1.018714	37	1.044310	37	1.069914	37	1.095523	37	1.121139	37	1.146761	37	1.172389	37	1.198024
38	1.046390	38	1.072686	38	1.098988	38	1.125298	38	1.151614	38	1.177936	38	1.204265	38	1.230601
39	1.074074	39	1.101069	39	1.128072	39	1.155081	39	1.182098	39	1.209121	39	1.236152	39	1.263189
40	1.101766	40	1.129461	40	1.157163	40	1.184873	40	1.212591	40	1.240316	40	1.268048	40	1.295788
41	1.129465	41	1.157860	41	1.186263	41	1.214674	41	1.243093	41	1.271520	41	1.299954	41	1.328396
42	1.157171	42	1.186267	42	1.215372	42	1.244484	42	1.273605	42	1.302734	42	1.331871	42	1.361016
43	1.184886	43	1.214683	43	1.244489	43	1.274303	43	1.304126	43	1.333957	43	1.363797	43	1.393646
44	1.212608	44	1.243106	44	1.273614	44	1.304130	44	1.334656	44	1.365190	44	1.395734	44	1.426286
45	1.240337	45	1.271537	45	1.302747	45	1.333966	45	1.365195	45	1.396433	45	1.427680	45	1.458937
46	1.268074	46	1.299977	46	1.331889	46	1.363811	46	1.395743	46	1.427685	46	1.459637	46	1.491599
47	1.295819	47	1.328424	47	1.361039	47	1.393665	47	1.426301	47	1.458947	47	1.491604	47	1.524271
48	1.323571	48	1.356879	48	1.390198	48	1.423528	48	1.456868	48	1.490219	48	1.523581	48	1.556953
49	1.351331	49	1.385342	49	1.419365	49	1.453399	49	1.487444	49	1.521500	49	1.555567	49	1.589646
50	1.379098	50	1.413814	50	1.448540	50	1.483279	50	1.518029	50	1.552791	50	1.587564	50	1.622349
51	1.406874	51	1.442293	51	1.477724	51	1.513168	51	1.548624	51	1.584091	51	1.619571	51	1.655064
52	1.434656	52	1.470780	52	1.506916	52	1.543066	52	1.579227	52	1.615402	52	1.651589	52	1.687788
53	1.462447	53	1.499275	53	1.536117	53	1.572972	53	1.609840	53	1.646721	53	1.683616	53	1.720523
54	1.490244	54	1.527778	54	1.565326	54	1.602887	54	1.640462	54	1.678051	54	1.715653	54	1.753269
55	1.518050	55	1.556290	55	1.594544	55	1.632812	55	1.671094	55	1.709390	55	1.747700	55	1.786025
89	2.467985	89	2.530450	89	2.592953	89	2.655493	89	2.718071	89	2.780687	89	2.843341	89	2.906032
90	2.496058	90	2.559243	90	2.622466	90	2.685727	90	2.749027	90	2.812366	90	2.875743	90	2.939159
91	2.524140	91	2.588044	91	2.651987	91	2.715970	91	2.779993	91	2.844055	91	2.908156	91	2.972297
92	2.552228	92	2.616853	92	2.681517	92	2.746222	92	2.810968	92	2.875753	92	2.940579	92	3.005446
120	3.341847	120	3.426797	120	3.511816	120	3.596904	120	3.682062	120	3.767289	120	3.852586	120	3.937952
180	5.054420	180	5.183983	180	5.313705	180	5.443586	180	5.573626	180	5.703826	180	5.834186	180	5.964705
181	5.083202	181	5.213521	181	5.344001	181	5.474641	181	5.605443	181	5.736406	181	5.867531	181	5.998817
182	5.111992	182	5.243067	182	5.374305	182	5.505706	182	5.637269	182	5.768996	182	5.900886	182	6.032940
183	5.140790	183	5.272622	183	5.404618	183	5.536779	183	5.669105	183	5.801596	183	5.934252	183	6.067074
184	5.169595	184	5.302185	184	5.434940	184	5.567862	184	5.700951	184	5.834206	184	5.967629	184	6.101219
270	7.676640	270	7.875896	270	8.075521	270	8.275513	270	8.475874	270	8.676605	270	8.877705	270	9.079176
300	8.565178	300	8.788424	300	9.012128	300	9.236291	300	9.460913	300	9.685995	300	9.911539	300	10.137544
360	10.364311	360	10.636703	360	10.909764	360	11.183498	360	11.457906	360	11.732989	360	12.008748	360	12.285187
365	10.515578	365	10.792136	365	11.069384	365	11.347324	365	11.625957	365	11.905286	365	12.185312	365	12.466036
366	10.545856	366	10.823249	366	11.101335	366	11.380118	366	11.659598	366	11.939777	366	12.220658	366	12.502241

DAILY COMPOUND INTEREST, 365 DAY YEAR

12.00 %

Description: This table shows the compound interest on $100. Interest is compounded daily on the basis of a 365 day year.

Example: The interest on $100 at 12% for 40 days is $ 1.32. On $10,000 the daily compound interest is $132.35.

Interest on $100

DAY	12.00 %		12.25 %		12.50 %		12.75 %		13.00 %		13.25 %		13.50 %		13.75 %
1	.032877	1	.033562	1	.034247	1	.034932	1	.035616	1	.036301	1	.036986	1	.037671
2	.065764	2	.067135	2	.068505	2	.069875	2	.071246	2	.072616	2	.073986	2	.075357
3	.098663	3	.100719	3	.102775	3	.104831	3	.106887	3	.108944	3	.111000	3	.113056
4	.131572	4	.134314	4	.137057	4	.139799	4	.142542	4	.145285	4	.148027	4	.150770
5	.164492	5	.167921	5	.171350	5	.174780	5	.178209	5	.181639	5	.185068	5	.188498
6	.197422	6	.201539	6	.205655	6	.209772	6	.213889	6	.218006	6	.222123	6	.226240
7	.230364	7	.235168	7	.239972	7	.244777	7	.249582	7	.254386	7	.259192	7	.263997
8	.263317	8	.268809	8	.274301	8	.279794	8	.285287	8	.290780	8	.296274	8	.301768
9	.296280	9	.302461	9	.308642	9	.314823	9	.321005	9	.327187	9	.333370	9	.339552
10	.329254	10	.336124	10	.342994	10	.349865	10	.356736	10	.363607	10	.370479	10	.377352
11	.362239	11	.369798	11	.377358	11	.384918	11	.392479	11	.400041	11	.407603	11	.415165
12	.395235	12	.403484	12	.411734	12	.419984	12	.428235	12	.436487	12	.444740	12	.452993
13	.428241	13	.437181	13	.446121	13	.455063	13	.464004	13	.472947	13	.481890	13	.490834
14	.461259	14	.470889	14	.480521	14	.490153	14	.499786	14	.509420	14	.519055	14	.528691
15	.494287	15	.504609	15	.514932	15	.525256	15	.535581	15	.545906	15	.556233	15	.566561
16	.527326	16	.538340	16	.549355	16	.560371	16	.571388	16	.582406	16	.593425	16	.604446
17	.560377	17	.572082	17	.583790	17	.595498	17	.607208	17	.618919	17	.630631	17	.642345
18	.593437	18	.605836	18	.618236	18	.630638	18	.643040	18	.655445	18	.667851	18	.680258
19	.626509	19	.639601	19	.652694	19	.665789	19	.678886	19	.691984	19	.705084	19	.718185
20	.659592	20	.673377	20	.687164	20	.700953	20	.714744	20	.728537	20	.742331	20	.756127
21	.692686	21	.707165	21	.721646	21	.736130	21	.750615	21	.765102	21	.779592	21	.794083
22	.725790	22	.740964	22	.756140	22	.771318	22	.786499	22	.801682	22	.816866	22	.832054
23	.758905	23	.774774	23	.790646	23	.806519	23	.822395	23	.838274	23	.854155	23	.870038
24	.792032	24	.808596	24	.825163	24	.841733	24	.858305	24	.874880	24	.891457	24	.908037
25	.825169	25	.842429	25	.859692	25	.876958	25	.894227	25	.911499	25	.928773	25	.946051
26	.858317	26	.876273	26	.894233	26	.912196	26	.930162	26	.948131	26	.966103	26	.984078
27	.891476	27	.910129	27	.928786	27	.947446	27	.966110	27	.984776	27	1.003447	27	1.022120
28	.924645	28	.943996	28	.963351	28	.982709	28	1.002070	28	1.021435	28	1.040804	28	1.060176
29	.957826	29	.977875	29	.997927	29	1.017983	29	1.038043	29	1.058107	29	1.078175	29	1.098247
30	.991018	30	1.011764	30	1.032515	30	1.053270	30	1.074030	30	1.094793	30	1.115560	30	1.136332
31	1.024220	31	1.045666	31	1.067116	31	1.088570	31	1.110029	31	1.131492	31	1.152959	31	1.174431
32	1.057434	32	1.079578	32	1.101728	32	1.123882	32	1.146040	32	1.168204	32	1.190372	32	1.212545
33	1.090658	33	1.113502	33	1.136351	33	1.159206	33	1.182065	33	1.204929	33	1.227799	33	1.250673
34	1.123893	34	1.147438	34	1.170987	34	1.194542	34	1.218102	34	1.241668	34	1.265239	34	1.288815
35	1.157139	35	1.181384	35	1.205635	35	1.229891	35	1.254153	35	1.278420	35	1.302693	35	1.326972
36	1.190397	36	1.215342	36	1.240294	36	1.265252	36	1.290216	36	1.315186	36	1.340161	36	1.365143
37	1.223665	37	1.249312	37	1.274966	37	1.300626	37	1.326292	37	1.351964	37	1.377643	37	1.403329
38	1.256944	38	1.283293	38	1.309649	38	1.336011	38	1.362381	38	1.388757	38	1.415139	38	1.441529
39	1.290234	39	1.317285	39	1.344344	39	1.371410	39	1.398482	39	1.425562	39	1.452649	39	1.479743
40	1.323535	40	1.351289	40	1.379051	40	1.406820	40	1.434597	40	1.462381	40	1.490173	40	1.517971
41	1.356846	41	1.385304	41	1.413770	41	1.442243	41	1.470724	41	1.499213	41	1.527710	41	1.556215
42	1.390169	42	1.419331	42	1.448500	42	1.477678	42	1.506865	42	1.536059	42	1.565261	42	1.594472
43	1.423503	43	1.453369	43	1.483243	43	1.513126	43	1.543018	43	1.572918	43	1.602827	43	1.632744
44	1.456848	44	1.487418	44	1.517998	44	1.548586	44	1.579184	44	1.609790	44	1.640406	44	1.671030
45	1.490203	45	1.521479	45	1.552764	45	1.584059	45	1.615363	45	1.646676	45	1.677999	45	1.709331
46	1.523570	46	1.555551	46	1.587542	46	1.619543	46	1.651554	46	1.683575	46	1.715606	46	1.747646
47	1.556948	47	1.589635	47	1.622333	47	1.655041	47	1.687759	47	1.720488	47	1.753226	47	1.785976
48	1.590336	48	1.623730	48	1.657135	48	1.690550	48	1.723977	48	1.757413	48	1.790861	48	1.824320
49	1.623736	49	1.657837	49	1.691949	49	1.726072	49	1.760207	49	1.794353	49	1.828510	49	1.862678
50	1.657146	50	1.691955	50	1.726775	50	1.761607	50	1.796450	50	1.831306	50	1.866173	50	1.901051
51	1.690568	51	1.726084	51	1.761613	51	1.797154	51	1.832707	51	1.868272	51	1.903849	51	1.939439
52	1.724000	52	1.760225	52	1.796463	52	1.832713	52	1.868976	52	1.905251	52	1.941539	52	1.977840
53	1.757444	53	1.794378	53	1.831325	53	1.868285	53	1.905258	53	1.942244	53	1.979244	53	2.016257
54	1.790898	54	1.828541	54	1.866198	54	1.903869	54	1.941553	54	1.979251	54	2.016962	54	2.054687
55	1.824364	55	1.862717	55	1.901084	55	1.939465	55	1.977861	55	2.016271	55	2.054695	55	2.093133
89	2.968761	89	3.031528	89	3.094333	89	3.157175	89	3.220056	89	3.282974	89	3.345930	89	3.408925
90	3.002614	90	3.066107	90	3.129639	90	3.193210	90	3.256819	90	3.320467	90	3.384154	90	3.447880
91	3.036478	91	3.100698	91	3.164957	91	3.229257	91	3.293595	91	3.357974	91	3.422392	91	3.486850
92	3.070353	92	3.135300	92	3.200288	92	3.265316	92	3.330385	92	3.395494	92	3.460644	92	3.525835
120	4.023388	120	4.108893	120	4.194468	120	4.280113	120	4.365828	120	4.451612	120	4.537467	120	4.623391
180	6.095384	180	6.226224	180	6.357224	180	6.488385	180	6.619707	180	6.751189	180	6.882833	180	7.014639
181	6.130265	181	6.261875	181	6.393648	181	6.525583	181	6.657681	181	6.789942	181	6.922365	181	7.054953
182	6.165157	182	6.297539	182	6.430084	182	6.562794	182	6.695669	182	6.828708	182	6.961912	182	7.095281
183	6.200061	183	6.333214	183	6.466533	183	6.600018	183	6.733670	183	6.867488	183	7.001473	183	7.135626
184	6.234976	184	6.368901	184	6.502994	184	6.637255	184	6.771684	184	6.906282	184	7.041049	184	7.175985
270	9.281019	270	9.483234	270	9.685821	270	9.888782	270	10.092118	270	10.295828	270	10.499913	270	10.704375
300	10.364013	300	10.590946	300	10.818344	300	11.046209	300	11.274540	300	11.503339	300	11.732607	300	11.962344
360	12.562306	360	12.840107	360	13.118592	360	13.397762	360	13.677619	360	13.958165	360	14.239401	360	14.521329
365	12.747462	365	13.029589	365	13.312420	365	13.595958	365	13.880203	365	14.165157	365	14.450822	365	14.737200
366	12.784529	366	13.067524	366	13.351226	366	13.635639	366	13.920763	366	14.206600	366	14.493153	366	14.780423

DAILY COMPOUND INTEREST, 365 DAY YEAR

14.00 %

Description: This table shows the compound interest on $100. Interest is compounded daily on the basis of a 365 day year.

Example: The interest on $100 at 14% for 40 days is $ 1.55. On $10,000 the daily compound interest is $154.58.

Interest on $100

DAY	14.00 %	DAY	14.25 %	DAY	14.50 %	DAY	14.75 %	DAY	15.00 %	DAY	16.00 %	DAY	17.00 %	DAY	18.00 %
1	.038356	1	.039041	1	.039726	1	.040411	1	.041096	1	.043836	1	.046575	1	.049315
2	.076727	2	.078097	2	.079468	2	.080838	2	.082209	2	.087690	2	.093172	2	.098654
3	.115113	3	.117169	3	.119225	3	.121282	3	.123338	3	.131565	3	.139791	3	.148018
4	.153513	4	.156256	4	.158999	4	.161742	4	.164485	4	.175458	4	.186432	4	.197406
5	.191928	5	.195358	5	.198788	5	.202218	5	.205648	5	.219370	5	.233094	5	.246819
6	.230358	6	.234475	6	.238593	6	.242711	6	.246829	6	.263302	6	.279778	6	.296255
7	.268802	7	.273608	7	.278414	7	.283220	7	.288026	7	.307253	7	.326483	7	.345717
8	.307262	8	.312756	8	.318250	8	.323745	8	.329240	8	.351223	8	.373211	8	.395202
9	.345736	9	.351919	9	.358103	9	.364287	9	.370472	9	.395213	9	.419960	9	.444712
10	.384224	10	.391098	10	.397971	10	.404845	10	.411720	10	.439222	10	.466731	10	.494247
11	.422728	11	.430291	11	.437855	11	.445420	11	.452985	11	.483250	11	.513524	11	.543805
12	.461246	12	.469500	12	.477755	12	.486011	12	.494267	12	.527297	12	.560338	12	.593389
13	.499779	13	.508725	13	.517671	13	.526618	13	.535566	13	.571364	13	.607174	13	.642996
14	.538327	14	.547965	14	.557603	14	.567242	14	.576882	14	.615450	14	.654033	14	.692628
15	.576890	15	.587220	15	.597550	15	.607882	15	.618215	15	.659556	15	.700912	15	.742285
16	.615467	16	.626490	16	.637514	16	.648539	16	.659565	16	.703680	16	.747814	16	.791966
17	.654059	17	.665776	17	.677493	17	.689212	17	.700932	17	.747825	17	.794738	17	.841672
18	.692666	18	.705077	18	.717488	18	.729901	18	.742316	18	.791988	18	.841683	18	.891402
19	.731288	19	.744393	19	.757499	19	.770607	19	.783717	19	.836171	19	.888651	19	.941157
20	.769925	20	.783725	20	.797526	20	.811330	20	.825135	20	.880373	20	.935640	20	.990936
21	.808576	21	.823072	21	.837569	21	.852068	21	.866570	21	.924594	21	.982651	21	1.040740
22	.847243	22	.862434	22	.877628	22	.892824	22	.908022	22	.968835	22	1.029684	22	1.090568
23	.885924	23	.901812	23	.917702	23	.933595	23	.949491	23	1.013096	23	1.076739	23	1.140421
24	.924620	24	.941205	24	.957793	24	.974384	24	.990977	24	1.057375	24	1.123816	24	1.190298
25	.963331	25	.980614	25	.997900	25	1.015188	25	1.032480	25	1.101675	25	1.170915	25	1.240200
26	1.002056	26	1.020038	26	1.038022	26	1.056010	26	1.074000	26	1.145993	26	1.218035	26	1.290127
27	1.040797	27	1.059477	27	1.078160	27	1.096847	27	1.115537	27	1.190331	27	1.265178	27	1.340078
28	1.079552	28	1.098932	28	1.118315	28	1.137701	28	1.157092	28	1.234688	28	1.312343	28	1.390054
29	1.118322	29	1.138402	29	1.158485	29	1.178572	29	1.198663	29	1.279065	29	1.359529	29	1.440055
30	1.157108	30	1.177887	30	1.198671	30	1.219459	30	1.240252	30	1.323462	30	1.406738	30	1.490080
31	1.195908	31	1.217388	31	1.238874	31	1.260363	31	1.281857	31	1.367877	31	1.453968	31	1.540130
32	1.234722	32	1.256905	32	1.279092	32	1.301283	32	1.323480	32	1.412313	32	1.501221	32	1.590204
33	1.273552	33	1.296437	33	1.319326	33	1.342220	33	1.365120	33	1.456767	33	1.548495	33	1.640304
34	1.312397	34	1.335984	34	1.359576	34	1.383174	34	1.406777	34	1.501241	34	1.595792	34	1.690428
35	1.351256	35	1.375546	35	1.399842	35	1.424144	35	1.448451	35	1.545735	35	1.643110	35	1.740576
36	1.390131	36	1.415125	36	1.440124	36	1.465130	36	1.490142	36	1.590248	36	1.690451	36	1.790750
37	1.429020	37	1.454718	37	1.480422	37	1.506133	37	1.531850	37	1.634781	37	1.737814	37	1.840948
38	1.467925	38	1.494327	38	1.520737	38	1.547153	38	1.573575	38	1.679333	38	1.785199	38	1.891171
39	1.506844	39	1.533952	39	1.561067	39	1.588189	39	1.615318	39	1.723905	39	1.832605	39	1.941419
40	1.545778	40	1.573592	40	1.601413	40	1.629242	40	1.657078	40	1.768496	40	1.880034	40	1.991691
41	1.584727	41	1.613247	41	1.641775	41	1.670311	41	1.698855	41	1.813107	41	1.927485	41	2.041988
42	1.623691	42	1.652918	42	1.682153	42	1.711397	42	1.740649	42	1.857738	42	1.974958	42	2.092311
43	1.662670	43	1.692604	43	1.722548	43	1.752499	43	1.782460	43	1.902388	43	2.022453	43	2.142657
44	1.701664	44	1.732306	44	1.762958	44	1.793619	44	1.824288	44	1.947057	44	2.069971	44	2.193029
45	1.740673	45	1.772024	45	1.803384	45	1.834754	45	1.866134	45	1.991746	45	2.117510	45	2.243426
46	1.779696	46	1.811757	46	1.843827	46	1.875907	46	1.907997	46	2.036455	46	2.165072	46	2.293847
47	1.818735	47	1.851505	47	1.884285	47	1.917076	47	1.949877	47	2.081183	47	2.212655	47	2.344293
48	1.857789	48	1.891269	48	1.924760	48	1.958261	48	1.991774	48	2.125931	48	2.260261	48	2.394765
49	1.896858	49	1.931049	49	1.965251	49	1.999464	49	2.033688	49	2.170699	49	2.307889	49	2.445261
50	1.935941	50	1.970844	50	2.005757	50	2.040683	50	2.075620	50	2.215486	50	2.355540	50	2.495782
51	1.975040	51	2.010654	51	2.046280	51	2.081918	51	2.117569	51	2.260293	51	2.403212	51	2.546327
52	2.014154	52	2.050480	52	2.086819	52	2.123171	52	2.159535	52	2.305119	52	2.450907	52	2.596898
53	2.053283	53	2.090322	53	2.127374	53	2.164440	53	2.201518	53	2.349965	53	2.498624	53	2.647494
54	2.092426	54	2.130179	54	2.167945	54	2.205725	54	2.243519	54	2.394831	54	2.546363	54	2.698115
55	2.131585	55	2.170052	55	2.208532	55	2.247028	55	2.285537	55	2.439716	55	2.594124	55	2.748760
89	3.471957	89	3.535027	89	3.598135	89	3.661281	89	3.724466	89	3.977584	89	4.231313	89	4.485654
90	3.511645	90	3.575448	90	3.639291	90	3.703172	90	3.767092	90	4.023163	90	4.279859	90	4.537181
91	3.551348	91	3.615885	91	3.680462	91	3.745079	91	3.809736	91	4.068762	91	4.328428	91	4.588734
92	3.591066	92	3.656338	92	3.721651	92	3.787004	92	3.852398	92	4.114381	92	4.377019	92	4.640312
120	4.709386	120	4.795450	120	4.881585	120	4.967790	120	5.054065	120	5.399870	120	5.746803	120	6.094869
180	7.146606	180	7.278735	180	7.411026	180	7.543479	180	7.676094	180	8.208185	180	8.742890	180	9.280222
181	7.187703	181	7.320617	181	7.453696	181	7.586938	181	7.720345	181	8.255618	181	8.793537	181	9.334114
182	7.228816	182	7.362517	182	7.496383	182	7.630415	182	7.764613	182	8.303073	182	8.844208	182	9.388032
183	7.269945	183	7.404432	183	7.539087	183	7.673909	183	7.808900	183	8.350548	183	8.894903	183	9.441977
184	7.311090	184	7.446364	184	7.581808	184	7.717421	184	7.853205	184	8.398044	184	8.945621	184	9.495948
270	10.909214	270	11.114430	270	11.320025	270	11.525999	270	11.732352	270	12.561576	270	13.396932	270	14.238464
300	12.192553	300	12.423233	300	12.654386	300	12.886013	300	13.118114	300	14.051286	300	14.992129	300	15.940708
360	14.803951	360	15.087269	360	15.371284	360	15.655998	360	15.941413	360	17.090112	360	18.250160	360	19.421670
365	15.024292	365	15.312101	365	15.600628	365	15.889875	365	16.179844	365	17.346973	365	18.525794	365	19.716424
366	15.068411	366	15.357120	366	15.646552	366	15.936708	366	16.227589	366	17.398413	366	18.580998	366	19.775463

TABLE **13**

Compensating Balances, Effective Rate

Interest Rates:	4 to 20% by 1%.
Term:	1 year.
Balances:	5, 10, 15, 20%.

This table shows the effective interest rate on the funds in use from a loan where a compensating balance is required. The compensating balance can be a function of the line of credit, the loan outstanding, or both.

The table assumes that the line of credit is the only source of funds for both the loan and the compensating balance.

Example: A bank requires that 20% of the loan be kept on deposit as a compensating balance. At an 8% interest rate, with half of the loan outstanding, the effective rate on funds in use is 10%.

If the bank requires 10% of the loan plus 10% of the line of credit as a compensating balance and the rate and loan balances are the same, the effective rate is 10.67%.

If the bank requires 20% of the line of credit as a compensating balance, all else being the same, the effective rate is 11.20%.

Source of Compensating Balance. If the compensating balance is a function of the line of credit, when the line is arranged, a deposit is made into a demand deposit account. If no other funds are available, then the compensating balance is drawn from the line of credit.

If the compensating balance is a function of the loan, when a withdrawal occurs, an amount is deposited into a demand deposit account. If no other funds are available, the amount is drawn from the line of credit.

Allocation of Loan Between Funds in Use and Compensating Balance
Line of Credit = 100

Compensating Balance, % Line	Compensating Balance, % Loan	% of Funds in Use	Compensating Balance for Line	Compensating Balance for Loan	Demand Deposit Balance	Loan Balance
0	20	0	0	0	0	0
—	—	50	0	12.5	12.5	62.5
—	—	80	0	20.0	20.0	100.0
10	10	0	10	1.1	11.0	11.1
—	—	50	10	6.6	16.6	66.6
—	—	80	10	11.1	21.1	101.1
20	0	0	20	0	20	20
—	—	50	20	0	20	70
—	—	80	20	0	20	100

Description: This table shows the effective rate on funds in use when a compensating balance is required.

Example: The effective rate is 8.42 % for an 8 % loan rate when the compensating balance is 5 % of the loan.

Compensating Balance: 0.00 % of LINE plus 5.00 % of LOAN

% LINE IN USE	4 %	5 %	6 %	7 %	8 %	9 %	10 %	11 %	12 %	13 %	14 %	15 %	16 %	17 %	18 %	19 %	20 %
25	4.21	5.26	6.32	7.37	8.42	9.47	10.53	11.58	12.63	13.68	14.74	15.79	16.84	17.89	18.95	20.00	21.05
30	4.21	5.26	6.32	7.37	8.42	9.47	10.53	11.58	12.63	13.68	14.74	15.79	16.84	17.89	18.95	20.00	21.05
35	4.21	5.26	6.32	7.37	8.42	9.47	10.53	11.58	12.63	13.68	14.74	15.79	16.84	17.89	18.95	20.00	21.05
40	4.21	5.26	6.32	7.37	8.42	9.47	10.53	11.58	12.63	13.68	14.74	15.79	16.84	17.89	18.95	20.00	21.05
45	4.21	5.26	6.32	7.37	8.42	9.47	10.53	11.58	12.63	13.68	14.74	15.79	16.84	17.89	18.95	20.00	21.05
50	4.21	5.26	6.32	7.37	8.42	9.47	10.53	11.58	12.63	13.68	14.74	15.79	16.84	17.89	18.95	20.00	21.05
55	4.21	5.26	6.32	7.37	8.42	9.47	10.53	11.58	12.63	13.68	14.74	15.79	16.84	17.89	18.95	20.00	21.05
60	4.21	5.26	6.32	7.37	8.42	9.47	10.53	11.58	12.63	13.68	14.74	15.79	16.84	17.89	18.95	20.00	21.05
65	4.21	5.26	6.32	7.37	8.42	9.47	10.53	11.58	12.63	13.68	14.74	15.79	16.84	17.89	18.95	20.00	21.05
70	4.21	5.26	6.32	7.37	8.42	9.47	10.53	11.58	12.63	13.68	14.74	15.79	16.84	17.89	18.95	20.00	21.05
75	4.21	5.26	6.32	7.37	8.42	9.47	10.53	11.58	12.63	13.68	14.74	15.79	16.84	17.89	18.95	20.00	21.05
80	4.21	5.26	6.32	7.37	8.42	9.47	10.53	11.58	12.63	13.68	14.74	15.79	16.84	17.89	18.95	20.00	21.05

Compensating Balance: 1.25 % of LINE plus 3.75 % of LOAN

% LINE IN USE	4 %	5 %	6 %	7 %	8 %	9 %	10 %	11 %	12 %	13 %	14 %	15 %	16 %	17 %	18 %	19 %	20 %
25	4.36	5.45	6.55	7.64	8.73	9.82	10.91	12.00	13.09	14.18	15.27	16.36	17.45	18.55	19.64	20.73	21.82
30	4.33	5.41	6.49	7.58	8.66	9.74	10.82	11.90	12.99	14.07	15.15	16.23	17.32	18.40	19.48	20.56	21.65
35	4.30	5.38	6.46	7.53	8.61	9.68	10.76	11.84	12.91	13.99	15.06	16.14	17.22	18.29	19.37	20.45	21.52
40	4.29	5.36	6.43	7.50	8.57	9.64	10.71	11.79	12.86	13.93	15.00	16.07	17.14	18.21	19.29	20.36	21.43
45	4.27	5.34	6.41	7.47	8.54	9.61	10.68	11.75	12.81	13.88	14.95	16.02	17.09	18.15	19.22	20.29	21.36
50	4.26	5.32	6.39	7.45	8.52	9.58	10.65	11.71	12.78	13.84	14.91	15.97	17.04	18.10	19.17	20.23	21.30
55	4.25	5.31	6.38	7.44	8.50	9.56	10.63	11.69	12.75	13.81	14.88	15.94	17.00	18.06	19.13	20.19	21.25
60	4.24	5.30	6.36	7.42	8.48	9.55	10.61	11.67	12.73	13.79	14.85	15.91	16.97	18.03	19.09	20.15	21.21
65	4.24	5.29	6.35	7.41	8.47	9.53	10.59	11.65	12.71	13.77	14.83	15.88	16.94	18.00	19.06	20.12	21.18
70	4.23	5.29	6.35	7.40	8.46	9.52	10.58	11.63	12.69	13.75	14.81	15.86	16.92	17.98	19.04	20.09	21.15
75	4.23	5.28	6.34	7.39	8.45	9.51	10.56	11.62	12.68	13.73	14.79	15.84	16.90	17.96	19.01	20.07	21.13
80	4.22	5.28	6.33	7.39	8.44	9.50	10.55	11.61	12.66	13.72	14.77	15.83	16.88	17.94	18.99	20.05	21.10

Compensating Balance: 2.50 % of LINE plus 2.50 % of LOAN

% LINE IN USE	4 %	5 %	6 %	7 %	8 %	9 %	10 %	11 %	12 %	13 %	14 %	15 %	16 %	17 %	18 %	19 %	20 %
25	4.51	5.64	6.77	7.90	9.03	10.15	11.28	12.41	13.54	14.67	15.79	16.92	18.05	19.18	20.31	21.44	22.56
30	4.44	5.56	6.67	7.78	8.89	10.00	11.11	12.22	13.33	14.44	15.56	16.67	17.78	18.89	20.00	21.11	22.22
35	4.40	5.49	6.59	7.69	8.79	9.89	10.99	12.09	13.19	14.29	15.38	16.48	17.58	18.68	19.78	20.88	21.98
40	4.36	5.45	6.54	7.63	8.72	9.81	10.90	11.99	13.08	14.17	15.26	16.35	17.44	18.53	19.62	20.71	21.79
45	4.33	5.41	6.50	7.58	8.66	9.74	10.83	11.91	12.99	14.07	15.16	16.24	17.32	18.40	19.49	20.57	21.65
50	4.31	5.38	6.46	7.54	8.62	9.69	10.77	11.85	12.92	14.00	15.08	16.15	17.23	18.31	19.38	20.46	21.54
55	4.29	5.36	6.43	7.51	8.58	9.65	10.72	11.79	12.87	13.94	15.01	16.08	17.16	18.23	19.30	20.37	21.45
60	4.27	5.34	6.41	7.48	8.55	9.62	10.68	11.75	12.82	13.89	14.96	16.03	17.09	18.16	19.23	20.30	21.37
65	4.26	5.33	6.39	7.46	8.52	9.59	10.65	11.72	12.78	13.85	14.91	15.98	17.04	18.11	19.17	20.24	21.30
70	4.25	5.31	6.37	7.44	8.50	9.56	10.62	11.68	12.75	13.81	14.87	15.93	17.00	18.06	19.12	20.18	21.25
75	4.24	5.30	6.36	7.42	8.48	9.54	10.60	11.66	12.72	13.78	14.84	15.90	16.96	18.02	19.08	20.14	21.20
80	4.23	5.29	6.35	7.40	8.46	9.52	10.58	11.63	12.69	13.75	14.81	15.87	16.92	17.98	19.04	20.10	21.15

Compensating Balance: 3.75 % of LINE plus 1.25 % of LOAN

% LINE IN USE	4 %	5 %	6 %	7 %	8 %	9 %	10 %	11 %	12 %	13 %	14 %	15 %	16 %	17 %	18 %	19 %	20 %
25	4.66	5.82	6.99	8.15	9.32	10.48	11.65	12.81	13.97	15.14	16.30	17.47	18.63	19.80	20.96	22.13	23.29
30	4.56	5.70	6.84	7.97	9.11	10.25	11.39	12.53	13.67	14.81	15.95	17.09	18.23	19.37	20.51	21.65	22.78
35	4.48	5.61	6.73	7.85	8.97	10.09	11.21	12.33	13.45	14.58	15.70	16.82	17.94	19.06	20.18	21.30	22.42
40	4.43	5.54	6.65	7.75	8.86	9.97	11.08	12.18	13.29	14.40	15.51	16.61	17.72	18.83	19.94	21.04	22.15
45	4.39	5.49	6.58	7.68	8.78	9.87	10.97	12.07	13.16	14.26	15.36	16.46	17.55	18.65	19.75	20.84	21.94
50	4.35	5.44	6.53	7.62	8.71	9.80	10.89	11.97	13.06	14.15	15.24	16.33	17.42	18.51	19.59	20.68	21.77
55	4.33	5.41	6.49	7.57	8.65	9.74	10.82	11.90	12.98	14.06	15.14	16.23	17.31	18.39	19.47	20.55	21.63
60	4.30	5.38	6.46	7.53	8.61	9.68	10.76	11.84	12.91	13.99	15.06	16.14	17.22	18.29	19.37	20.44	21.52
65	4.28	5.36	6.43	7.50	8.57	9.64	10.71	11.78	12.85	13.92	15.00	16.07	17.14	18.21	19.28	20.35	21.42
70	4.27	5.33	6.40	7.47	8.54	9.60	10.67	11.74	12.80	13.87	14.94	16.00	17.07	18.14	19.20	20.27	21.34
75	4.25	5.32	6.38	7.44	8.51	9.57	10.63	11.70	12.76	13.82	14.89	15.95	17.01	18.08	19.14	20.20	21.27
80	4.24	5.30	6.36	7.42	8.48	9.54	10.60	11.66	12.72	13.78	14.84	15.90	16.96	18.02	19.08	20.14	21.20

Compensating Balance: 5.00 % of LINE plus 0.00 % of LOAN

% LINE IN USE	4 %	5 %	6 %	7 %	8 %	9 %	10 %	11 %	12 %	13 %	14 %	15 %	16 %	17 %	18 %	19 %	20 %
25	4.80	6.00	7.20	8.40	9.60	10.80	12.00	13.20	14.40	15.60	16.80	18.00	19.20	20.40	21.60	22.80	24.00
30	4.67	5.83	7.00	8.17	9.33	10.50	11.67	12.83	14.00	15.17	16.33	17.50	18.67	19.83	21.00	22.17	23.33
35	4.57	5.71	6.86	8.00	9.14	10.29	11.43	12.57	13.71	14.86	16.00	17.14	18.29	19.43	20.57	21.71	22.86
40	4.50	5.63	6.75	7.88	9.00	10.13	11.25	12.37	13.50	14.63	15.75	16.88	18.00	19.13	20.25	21.38	22.50
45	4.44	5.56	6.67	7.78	8.89	10.00	11.11	12.22	13.33	14.44	15.56	16.67	17.78	18.89	20.00	21.11	22.22
50	4.40	5.50	6.60	7.70	8.80	9.90	11.00	12.10	13.20	14.30	15.40	16.50	17.60	18.70	19.80	20.90	22.00
55	4.36	5.45	6.55	7.64	8.73	9.82	10.91	12.00	13.09	14.18	15.27	16.36	17.45	18.55	19.64	20.73	21.82
60	4.33	5.42	6.50	7.58	8.67	9.75	10.83	11.92	13.00	14.08	15.17	16.25	17.33	18.42	19.50	20.58	21.67
65	4.31	5.38	6.46	7.54	8.62	9.69	10.77	11.85	12.92	14.00	15.08	16.15	17.23	18.31	19.38	20.46	21.54
70	4.29	5.36	6.43	7.50	8.57	9.64	10.71	11.79	12.86	13.93	15.00	16.07	17.14	18.21	19.29	20.36	21.43
75	4.27	5.33	6.40	7.47	8.53	9.60	10.67	11.73	12.80	13.87	14.93	16.00	17.07	18.13	19.20	20.27	21.33
80	4.25	5.31	6.38	7.44	8.50	9.56	10.62	11.69	12.75	13.81	14.87	15.94	17.00	18.06	19.12	20.19	21.25

Description: This table shows the effective rate on funds in use when a compensating balance is required.

Example: The effective rate is 8.89 % for an 8 % loan rate when the compensating balance is 10 % of the loan.

Compensating Balance: 0.00 % of LINE plus 10.00 % of LOAN

% LINE IN USE	4 %	5 %	6 %	7 %	8 %	9 %	10 %	11 %	12 %	13 %	14 %	15 %	16 %	17 %	18 %	19 %	20 %
25	4.44	5.56	6.67	7.78	8.89	10.00	11.11	12.22	13.33	14.44	15.56	16.67	17.78	18.89	20.00	21.11	22.22
30	4.44	5.56	6.67	7.78	8.89	10.00	11.11	12.22	13.33	14.44	15.56	16.67	17.78	18.89	20.00	21.11	22.22
35	4.44	5.56	6.67	7.78	8.89	10.00	11.11	12.22	13.33	14.44	15.56	16.67	17.78	18.89	20.00	21.11	22.22
40	4.44	5.56	6.67	7.78	8.89	10.00	11.11	12.22	13.33	14.44	15.56	16.67	17.78	18.89	20.00	21.11	22.22
45	4.44	5.56	6.67	7.78	8.89	10.00	11.11	12.22	13.33	14.44	15.56	16.67	17.78	18.89	20.00	21.11	22.22
50	4.44	5.56	6.67	7.78	8.89	10.00	11.11	12.22	13.33	14.44	15.56	16.67	17.78	18.89	20.00	21.11	22.22
55	4.44	5.56	6.67	7.78	8.89	10.00	11.11	12.22	13.33	14.44	15.56	16.67	17.78	18.89	20.00	21.11	22.22
60	4.44	5.56	6.67	7.78	8.89	10.00	11.11	12.22	13.33	14.44	15.56	16.67	17.78	18.89	20.00	21.11	22.22
65	4.44	5.56	6.67	7.78	8.89	10.00	11.11	12.22	13.33	14.44	15.56	16.67	17.78	18.89	20.00	21.11	22.22
70	4.44	5.56	6.67	7.78	8.89	10.00	11.11	12.22	13.33	14.44	15.56	16.67	17.78	18.89	20.00	21.11	22.22
75	4.44	5.56	6.67	7.78	8.89	10.00	11.11	12.22	13.33	14.44	15.56	16.67	17.78	18.89	20.00	21.11	22.22
80	4.44	5.56	6.67	7.78	8.89	10.00	11.11	12.22	13.33	14.44	15.56	16.67	17.78	18.89	20.00	21.11	22.22

Compensating Balance: 2.50 % of LINE plus 7.50 % of LOAN

% LINE IN USE	4 %	5 %	6 %	7 %	8 %	9 %	10 %	11 %	12 %	13 %	14 %	15 %	16 %	17 %	18 %	19 %	20 %
25	4.76	5.95	7.14	8.32	9.51	10.70	11.89	13.08	14.27	15.46	16.65	17.84	19.03	20.22	21.41	22.59	23.78
30	4.68	5.86	7.03	8.20	9.37	10.54	11.71	12.88	14.05	15.23	16.40	17.57	18.74	19.91	21.08	22.25	23.42
35	4.63	5.79	6.95	8.11	9.27	10.42	11.58	12.74	13.90	15.06	16.22	17.37	18.53	19.69	20.85	22.01	23.17
40	4.59	5.74	6.89	8.04	9.19	10.34	11.49	12.64	13.78	14.93	16.08	17.23	18.38	19.53	20.68	21.82	22.97
45	4.56	5.71	6.85	7.99	9.13	10.27	11.41	12.55	13.69	14.83	15.98	17.12	18.26	19.40	20.54	21.68	22.82
50	4.54	5.68	6.81	7.95	9.08	10.22	11.35	12.49	13.62	14.76	15.89	17.03	18.16	19.30	20.43	21.57	22.70
55	4.52	5.65	6.78	7.91	9.04	10.17	11.30	12.43	13.56	14.69	15.82	16.95	18.08	19.21	20.34	21.47	22.60
60	4.50	5.63	6.76	7.88	9.01	10.14	11.26	12.39	13.51	14.64	15.77	16.89	18.02	19.14	20.27	21.40	22.52
65	4.49	5.61	6.74	7.86	8.98	10.10	11.23	12.35	13.47	14.59	15.72	16.84	17.96	19.09	20.21	21.33	22.45
70	4.48	5.60	6.72	7.84	8.96	10.08	11.20	12.32	13.44	14.56	15.68	16.80	17.92	19.03	20.15	21.27	22.39
75	4.47	5.59	6.70	7.82	8.94	10.05	11.17	12.29	13.41	14.52	15.64	16.76	17.87	18.99	20.11	21.23	22.34
80	4.46	5.57	6.69	7.80	8.92	10.03	11.15	12.26	13.38	14.49	15.61	16.72	17.84	18.95	20.07	21.18	22.30

Compensating Balance: 5.00 % of LINE plus 5.00 % of LOAN

% LINE IN USE	4 %	5 %	6 %	7 %	8 %	9 %	10 %	11 %	12 %	13 %	14 %	15 %	16 %	17 %	18 %	19 %	20 %
25	5.05	6.32	7.58	8.84	10.11	11.37	12.63	13.89	15.16	16.42	17.68	18.95	20.21	21.47	22.74	24.00	25.26
30	4.91	6.14	7.37	8.60	9.82	11.05	12.28	13.51	14.74	15.96	17.19	18.42	19.65	20.88	22.11	23.33	24.56
35	4.81	6.02	7.22	8.42	9.62	10.83	12.03	13.23	14.44	15.64	16.84	18.05	19.25	20.45	21.65	22.86	24.06
40	4.74	5.92	7.11	8.29	9.47	10.66	11.84	13.03	14.21	15.39	16.58	17.76	18.95	20.13	21.32	22.50	23.68
45	4.68	5.85	7.02	8.19	9.36	10.53	11.70	12.87	14.04	15.20	16.37	17.54	18.71	19.88	21.05	22.22	23.39
50	4.63	5.79	6.95	8.11	9.26	10.42	11.58	12.74	13.89	15.05	16.21	17.37	18.53	19.68	20.84	22.00	23.16
55	4.59	5.74	6.89	8.04	9.19	10.33	11.48	12.63	13.78	14.93	16.08	17.22	18.37	19.52	20.67	21.82	22.97
60	4.56	5.70	6.84	7.98	9.12	10.26	11.40	12.54	13.68	14.82	15.96	17.11	18.25	19.39	20.53	21.67	22.81
65	4.53	5.67	6.80	7.94	9.07	10.20	11.34	12.47	13.60	14.74	15.87	17.00	18.14	19.27	20.40	21.54	22.67
70	4.51	5.64	6.77	7.89	9.02	10.15	11.28	12.41	13.53	14.66	15.79	16.92	18.05	19.17	20.30	21.43	22.56
75	4.49	5.61	6.74	7.86	8.98	10.11	11.23	12.35	13.47	14.60	15.72	16.84	17.96	19.09	20.21	21.33	22.46
80	4.47	5.59	6.71	7.83	8.95	10.07	11.18	12.30	13.42	14.54	15.66	16.78	17.89	19.01	20.13	21.25	22.37

Compensating Balance: 7.50 % of LINE plus 2.50 % of LOAN

% LINE IN USE	4 %	5 %	6 %	7 %	8 %	9 %	10 %	11 %	12 %	13 %	14 %	15 %	16 %	17 %	18 %	19 %	20 %
25	5.33	6.67	8.00	9.33	10.67	12.00	13.33	14.67	16.00	17.33	18.67	20.00	21.33	22.67	24.00	25.33	26.67
30	5.13	6.41	7.69	8.97	10.26	11.54	12.82	14.10	15.38	16.67	17.95	19.23	20.51	21.79	23.08	24.36	25.64
35	4.98	6.23	7.47	8.72	9.96	11.21	12.45	13.70	14.95	16.19	17.44	18.68	19.93	21.17	22.42	23.66	24.91
40	4.87	6.09	7.31	8.53	9.74	10.96	12.18	13.40	14.62	15.83	17.05	18.27	19.49	20.71	21.92	23.14	24.36
45	4.79	5.98	7.18	8.38	9.57	10.77	11.97	13.16	14.36	15.56	16.75	17.95	19.15	20.34	21.54	22.74	23.93
50	4.72	5.90	7.08	8.26	9.44	10.62	11.79	12.97	14.15	15.33	16.51	17.69	18.87	20.05	21.23	22.41	23.59
55	4.66	5.83	6.99	8.16	9.32	10.49	11.66	12.82	13.99	15.15	16.32	17.48	18.65	19.81	20.98	22.14	23.31
60	4.62	5.77	6.92	8.08	9.23	10.38	11.54	12.69	13.85	15.00	16.15	17.31	18.46	19.62	20.77	21.92	23.08
65	4.58	5.72	6.86	8.01	9.15	10.30	11.44	12.58	13.73	14.87	16.02	17.16	18.30	19.45	20.59	21.74	22.88
70	4.54	5.68	6.81	7.95	9.08	10.22	11.36	12.49	13.63	14.76	15.90	17.03	18.17	19.30	20.44	21.58	22.71
75	4.51	5.64	6.77	7.90	9.03	10.15	11.28	12.41	13.54	14.67	15.79	16.92	18.05	19.18	20.31	21.44	22.56
80	4.49	5.61	6.73	7.85	8.97	10.10	11.22	12.34	13.46	14.58	15.71	16.83	17.95	19.07	20.19	21.31	22.44

Compensating Balance: 10.00 % of LINE plus 0.00 % of LOAN

% LINE IN USE	4 %	5 %	6 %	7 %	8 %	9 %	10 %	11 %	12 %	13 %	14 %	15 %	16 %	17 %	18 %	19 %	20 %
25	5.60	7.00	8.40	9.80	11.20	12.60	14.00	15.40	16.80	18.20	19.60	21.00	22.40	23.80	25.20	26.60	28.00
30	5.33	6.67	8.00	9.33	10.67	12.00	13.33	14.67	16.00	17.33	18.67	20.00	21.33	22.67	24.00	25.33	26.67
35	5.14	6.43	7.71	9.00	10.29	11.57	12.86	14.14	15.43	16.71	18.00	19.29	20.57	21.86	23.14	24.43	25.71
40	5.00	6.25	7.50	8.75	10.00	11.25	12.50	13.75	15.00	16.25	17.50	18.75	20.00	21.25	22.50	23.75	25.00
45	4.89	6.11	7.33	8.56	9.78	11.00	12.22	13.44	14.67	15.89	17.11	18.33	19.56	20.78	22.00	23.22	24.44
50	4.80	6.00	7.20	8.40	9.60	10.80	12.00	13.20	14.40	15.60	16.80	18.00	19.20	20.40	21.60	22.80	24.00
55	4.73	5.91	7.09	8.27	9.45	10.64	11.82	13.00	14.18	15.36	16.55	17.73	18.91	20.09	21.27	22.45	23.64
60	4.67	5.83	7.00	8.17	9.33	10.50	11.67	12.83	14.00	15.17	16.33	17.50	18.67	19.83	21.00	22.17	23.33
65	4.62	5.77	6.92	8.08	9.23	10.38	11.54	12.69	13.85	15.00	16.15	17.31	18.46	19.62	20.77	21.92	23.08
70	4.57	5.71	6.86	8.00	9.14	10.29	11.43	12.57	13.71	14.86	16.00	17.14	18.29	19.43	20.57	21.71	22.86
75	4.53	5.67	6.80	7.93	9.07	10.20	11.33	12.47	13.60	14.73	15.87	17.00	18.13	19.27	20.40	21.53	22.67
80	4.50	5.63	6.75	7.88	9.00	10.13	11.25	12.37	13.50	14.63	15.75	16.88	18.00	19.13	20.25	21.38	22.50

Description: This table shows the effective rate on funds in use when a compensating balance is required.

Example: The effective rate is 9.41 % for an 8 % loan rate when the compensating balance is 15 % of the loan.

% LINE IN USE	4 %	5 %	6 %	7 %	8 %	9 %	10 %	11 %	12 %	13 %	14 %	15 %	16 %	17 %	18 %	19 %	20 %
				NOMINAL INTEREST RATE					Compensating Balance: 0.00 % of LINE plus 15.00 % of LOAN							
25	4.71	5.88	7.06	8.24	9.41	10.59	11.76	12.94	14.12	15.29	16.47	17.65	18.82	20.00	21.18	22.35	23.53
30	4.71	5.88	7.06	8.24	9.41	10.59	11.76	12.94	14.12	15.29	16.47	17.65	18.82	20.00	21.18	22.35	23.53
35	4.71	5.88	7.06	8.24	9.41	10.59	11.76	12.94	14.12	15.29	16.47	17.65	18.82	20.00	21.18	22.35	23.53
40	4.71	5.88	7.06	8.24	9.41	10.59	11.76	12.94	14.12	15.29	16.47	17.65	18.82	20.00	21.18	22.35	23.53
45	4.71	5.88	7.06	8.24	9.41	10.59	11.76	12.94	14.12	15.29	16.47	17.65	18.82	20.00	21.18	22.35	23.53
50	4.71	5.88	7.06	8.24	9.41	10.59	11.76	12.94	14.12	15.29	16.47	17.65	18.82	20.00	21.18	22.35	23.53
55	4.71	5.88	7.06	8.24	9.41	10.59	11.76	12.94	14.12	15.29	16.47	17.65	18.82	20.00	21.18	22.35	23.53
60	4.71	5.88	7.06	8.24	9.41	10.59	11.76	12.94	14.12	15.29	16.47	17.65	18.82	20.00	21.18	22.35	23.53
65	4.71	5.88	7.06	8.24	9.41	10.59	11.76	12.94	14.12	15.29	16.47	17.65	18.82	20.00	21.18	22.35	23.53
70	4.71	5.88	7.06	8.24	9.41	10.59	11.76	12.94	14.12	15.29	16.47	17.65	18.82	20.00	21.18	22.35	23.53
75	4.71	5.88	7.06	8.24	9.41	10.59	11.76	12.94	14.12	15.29	16.47	17.65	18.82	20.00	21.18	22.35	23.53
80	4.71	5.88	7.06	8.24	9.41	10.59	11.76	12.94	14.12	15.29	16.47	17.65	18.82	20.00	21.18	22.35	23.53

% LINE IN USE	4 %	5 %	6 %	7 %	8 %	9 %	10 %	11 %	12 %	13 %	14 %	15 %	16 %	17 %	18 %	19 %	20 %
				NOMINAL INTEREST RATE					Compensating Balance: 3.75 % of LINE plus 11.25 % of LOAN							
25	5.18	6.48	7.77	9.07	10.37	11.66	12.96	14.25	15.55	16.85	18.14	19.44	20.73	22.03	23.32	24.62	25.92
30	5.07	6.34	7.61	8.87	10.14	11.41	12.68	13.94	15.21	16.48	17.75	19.01	20.28	21.55	22.82	24.08	25.35
35	4.99	6.24	7.48	8.73	9.98	11.23	12.47	13.72	14.97	16.22	17.46	18.71	19.96	21.21	22.45	23.70	24.95
40	4.93	6.16	7.39	8.63	9.86	11.09	12.32	13.56	14.79	16.02	17.25	18.49	19.72	20.95	22.18	23.42	24.65
45	4.88	6.10	7.32	8.54	9.77	10.99	12.21	13.43	14.65	15.87	17.09	18.31	19.53	20.75	21.97	23.19	24.41
50	4.85	6.06	7.27	8.48	9.69	10.90	12.11	13.32	14.54	15.75	16.96	18.17	19.38	20.59	21.80	23.01	24.23
55	4.81	6.02	7.22	8.43	9.63	10.83	12.04	13.24	14.44	15.65	16.85	18.05	19.26	20.46	21.66	22.87	24.07
60	4.79	5.99	7.18	8.38	9.58	10.77	11.97	13.17	14.37	15.56	16.76	17.96	19.15	20.35	21.55	22.75	23.94
65	4.77	5.96	7.15	8.34	9.53	10.73	11.92	13.11	14.30	15.49	16.68	17.88	19.07	20.26	21.45	22.64	23.84
70	4.75	5.94	7.12	8.31	9.50	10.68	11.87	13.06	14.25	15.43	16.62	17.81	18.99	20.18	21.37	22.56	23.74
75	4.73	5.92	7.10	8.28	9.46	10.65	11.83	13.01	14.20	15.38	16.56	17.75	18.93	20.11	21.30	22.48	23.66
80	4.72	5.90	7.08	8.26	9.44	10.62	11.80	12.98	14.15	15.33	16.51	17.69	18.87	20.05	21.23	22.41	23.59

% LINE IN USE	4 %	5 %	6 %	7 %	8 %	9 %	10 %	11 %	12 %	13 %	14 %	15 %	16 %	17 %	18 %	19 %	20 %
				NOMINAL INTEREST RATE					Compensating Balance: 7.50 % of LINE plus 7.50 % of LOAN							
25	5.62	7.03	8.43	9.84	11.24	12.65	14.05	15.46	16.86	18.27	19.68	21.08	22.49	23.89	25.30	26.70	28.11
30	5.41	6.76	8.11	9.46	10.81	12.16	13.51	14.86	16.22	17.57	18.92	20.27	21.62	22.97	24.32	25.68	27.03
35	5.25	6.56	7.88	9.19	10.50	11.81	13.13	14.44	15.75	17.07	18.38	19.69	21.00	22.32	23.63	24.94	26.25
40	5.14	6.42	7.70	8.99	10.27	11.55	12.84	14.12	15.41	16.69	17.97	19.26	20.54	21.82	23.11	24.39	25.68
45	5.05	6.31	7.57	8.83	10.09	11.35	12.61	13.87	15.14	16.40	17.66	18.92	20.18	21.44	22.70	23.96	25.23
50	4.97	6.22	7.46	8.70	9.95	11.19	12.43	13.68	14.92	16.16	17.41	18.65	19.89	21.14	22.38	23.62	24.86
55	4.91	6.14	7.37	8.60	9.83	11.06	12.29	13.51	14.74	15.97	17.20	18.43	19.66	20.88	22.11	23.34	24.57
60	4.86	6.08	7.30	8.51	9.73	10.95	12.16	13.38	14.59	15.81	17.03	18.24	19.46	20.68	21.89	23.11	24.32
65	4.82	6.03	7.23	8.44	9.65	10.85	12.06	13.26	14.47	15.68	16.88	18.09	19.29	20.50	21.70	22.91	24.12
70	4.79	5.98	7.18	8.38	9.58	10.77	11.97	13.17	14.36	15.56	16.76	17.95	19.15	20.35	21.54	22.74	23.94
75	4.76	5.95	7.14	8.32	9.51	10.70	11.89	13.08	14.27	15.46	16.65	17.84	19.03	20.22	21.41	22.59	23.78
80	4.73	5.91	7.09	8.28	9.46	10.64	11.82	13.01	14.19	15.37	16.55	17.74	18.92	20.10	21.28	22.47	23.65

% LINE IN USE	4 %	5 %	6 %	7 %	8 %	9 %	10 %	11 %	12 %	13 %	14 %	15 %	16 %	17 %	18 %	19 %	20 %
				NOMINAL INTEREST RATE					Compensating Balance: 11.25 % of LINE plus 3.75 % of LOAN							
25	6.03	7.53	9.04	10.55	12.05	13.56	15.06	16.57	18.08	19.58	21.09	22.60	24.10	25.61	27.12	28.62	30.13
30	5.71	7.14	8.57	10.00	11.43	12.86	14.29	15.71	17.14	18.57	20.00	21.43	22.86	24.29	25.71	27.14	28.57
35	5.49	6.86	8.24	9.61	10.98	12.36	13.73	15.10	16.47	17.85	19.22	20.59	21.97	23.34	24.71	26.09	27.46
40	5.32	6.66	7.99	9.32	10.65	11.98	13.31	14.64	15.97	17.31	18.64	19.97	21.30	22.63	23.96	25.29	26.62
45	5.19	6.49	7.79	9.09	10.39	11.69	12.99	14.29	15.58	16.88	18.18	19.48	20.78	22.08	23.38	24.68	25.97
50	5.09	6.36	7.64	8.91	10.18	11.45	12.73	14.00	15.27	16.55	17.82	19.09	20.36	21.64	22.91	24.18	25.45
55	5.01	6.26	7.51	8.76	10.01	11.26	12.51	13.77	15.02	16.27	17.52	18.77	20.02	21.28	22.53	23.78	25.03
60	4.94	6.17	7.40	8.64	9.87	11.10	12.34	13.57	14.81	16.04	17.27	18.51	19.74	20.97	22.21	23.44	24.68
65	4.88	6.09	7.31	8.53	9.75	10.97	12.19	13.41	14.63	15.84	17.06	18.28	19.50	20.72	21.94	23.16	24.38
70	4.82	6.03	7.24	8.44	9.65	10.85	12.06	13.27	14.47	15.68	16.88	18.09	19.29	20.50	21.71	22.91	24.12
75	4.78	5.97	7.17	8.36	9.56	10.75	11.95	13.14	14.34	15.53	16.73	17.92	19.12	20.31	21.51	22.70	23.90
80	4.74	5.93	7.11	8.30	9.48	10.67	11.85	13.04	14.22	15.41	16.59	17.78	18.96	20.15	21.33	22.52	23.70

% LINE IN USE	4 %	5 %	6 %	7 %	8 %	9 %	10 %	11 %	12 %	13 %	14 %	15 %	16 %	17 %	18 %	19 %	20 %
				NOMINAL INTEREST RATE					Compensating Balance: 15.00 % of LINE plus 0.00 % of LOAN							
25	6.40	8.00	9.60	11.20	12.80	14.40	16.00	17.60	19.20	20.80	22.40	24.00	25.60	27.20	28.80	30.40	32.00
30	6.00	7.50	9.00	10.50	12.00	13.50	15.00	16.50	18.00	19.50	21.00	22.50	24.00	25.50	27.00	28.50	30.00
35	5.71	7.14	8.57	10.00	11.43	12.86	14.29	15.71	17.14	18.57	20.00	21.43	22.86	24.29	25.71	27.14	28.57
40	5.50	6.88	8.25	9.63	11.00	12.37	13.75	15.12	16.50	17.88	19.25	20.63	22.00	23.38	24.75	26.12	27.50
45	5.33	6.67	8.00	9.33	10.67	12.00	13.33	14.67	16.00	17.33	18.67	20.00	21.33	22.67	24.00	25.33	26.67
50	5.20	6.50	7.80	9.10	10.40	11.70	13.00	14.30	15.60	16.90	18.20	19.50	20.80	22.10	23.40	24.70	26.00
55	5.09	6.36	7.64	8.91	10.18	11.45	12.73	14.00	15.27	16.55	17.82	19.09	20.36	21.64	22.91	24.18	25.45
60	5.00	6.25	7.50	8.75	10.00	11.25	12.50	13.75	15.00	16.25	17.50	18.75	20.00	21.25	22.50	23.75	25.00
65	4.92	6.15	7.38	8.62	9.85	11.08	12.31	13.54	14.77	16.00	17.23	18.46	19.69	20.92	22.15	23.38	24.62
70	4.86	6.07	7.29	8.50	9.71	10.93	12.14	13.36	14.57	15.79	17.00	18.21	19.43	20.64	21.86	23.07	24.29
75	4.80	6.00	7.20	8.40	9.60	10.80	12.00	13.20	14.40	15.60	16.80	18.00	19.20	20.40	21.60	22.80	24.00
80	4.75	5.94	7.13	8.31	9.50	10.69	11.88	13.06	14.25	15.44	16.63	17.81	19.00	20.19	21.37	22.56	23.75

Description: This table shows the effective rate on funds in use when a compensating balance is required.

Example: The effective rate is 10.00 % for an 8 % loan rate when the compensating balance is 20 % of the loan.

Compensating Balance: 0.00 % of LINE plus 20.00 % of LOAN

% LINE IN USE	4 %	5 %	6 %	7 %	8 %	9 %	10 %	11 %	12 %	13 %	14 %	15 %	16 %	17 %	18 %	19 %	20 %
25	5.00	6.25	7.50	8.75	10.00	11.25	12.50	13.75	15.00	16.25	17.50	18.75	20.00	21.25	22.50	23.75	25.00
30	5.00	6.25	7.50	8.75	10.00	11.25	12.50	13.75	15.00	16.25	17.50	18.75	20.00	21.25	22.50	23.75	25.00
35	5.00	6.25	7.50	8.75	10.00	11.25	12.50	13.75	15.00	16.25	17.50	18.75	20.00	21.25	22.50	23.75	25.00
40	5.00	6.25	7.50	8.75	10.00	11.25	12.50	13.75	15.00	16.25	17.50	18.75	20.00	21.25	22.50	23.75	25.00
45	5.00	6.25	7.50	8.75	10.00	11.25	12.50	13.75	15.00	16.25	17.50	18.75	20.00	21.25	22.50	23.75	25.00
50	5.00	6.25	7.50	8.75	10.00	11.25	12.50	13.75	15.00	16.25	17.50	18.75	20.00	21.25	22.50	23.75	25.00
55	5.00	6.25	7.50	8.75	10.00	11.25	12.50	13.75	15.00	16.25	17.50	18.75	20.00	21.25	22.50	23.75	25.00
60	5.00	6.25	7.50	8.75	10.00	11.25	12.50	13.75	15.00	16.25	17.50	18.75	20.00	21.25	22.50	23.75	25.00
65	5.00	6.25	7.50	8.75	10.00	11.25	12.50	13.75	15.00	16.25	17.50	18.75	20.00	21.25	22.50	23.75	25.00
70	5.00	6.25	7.50	8.75	10.00	11.25	12.50	13.75	15.00	16.25	17.50	18.75	20.00	21.25	22.50	23.75	25.00
75	5.00	6.25	7.50	8.75	10.00	11.25	12.50	13.75	15.00	16.25	17.50	18.75	20.00	21.25	22.50	23.75	25.00
80	5.00	6.25	7.50	8.75	10.00	11.25	12.50	13.75	15.00	16.25	17.50	18.75	20.00	21.25	22.50	23.75	25.00

Compensating Balance: 5.00 % of LINE plus 15.00 % of LOAN

% LINE IN USE	4 %	5 %	6 %	7 %	8 %	9 %	10 %	11 %	12 %	13 %	14 %	15 %	16 %	17 %	18 %	19 %	20 %
25	5.65	7.06	8.47	9.88	11.29	12.71	14.12	15.53	16.94	18.35	19.76	21.18	22.59	24.00	25.41	26.82	28.24
30	5.49	6.86	8.24	9.61	10.98	12.35	13.73	15.10	16.47	17.84	19.22	20.59	21.96	23.33	24.71	26.08	27.45
35	5.38	6.72	8.07	9.41	10.76	12.10	13.45	14.79	16.13	17.48	18.82	20.17	21.51	22.86	24.20	25.55	26.89
40	5.29	6.62	7.94	9.26	10.59	11.91	13.24	14.56	15.88	17.21	18.53	19.85	21.18	22.50	23.82	25.15	26.47
45	5.23	6.54	7.84	9.15	10.46	11.76	13.07	14.38	15.69	16.99	18.30	19.61	20.92	22.22	23.53	24.84	26.14
50	5.18	6.47	7.76	9.06	10.35	11.65	12.94	14.24	15.53	16.82	18.12	19.41	20.71	22.00	23.29	24.59	25.88
55	5.13	6.42	7.70	8.98	10.27	11.55	12.83	14.12	15.40	16.68	17.97	19.25	20.53	21.82	23.10	24.39	25.67
60	5.10	6.37	7.65	8.92	10.20	11.47	12.75	14.02	15.29	16.57	17.84	19.12	20.39	21.67	22.94	24.22	25.49
65	5.07	6.33	7.60	8.87	10.14	11.40	12.67	13.94	15.20	16.47	17.74	19.00	20.27	21.54	22.81	24.07	25.34
70	5.04	6.30	7.56	8.82	10.08	11.34	12.61	13.87	15.13	16.39	17.65	18.91	20.17	21.43	22.69	23.95	25.21
75	5.02	6.27	7.53	8.78	10.04	11.29	12.55	13.80	15.06	16.31	17.57	18.82	20.08	21.33	22.59	23.84	25.10
80	5.00	6.25	7.50	8.75	10.00	11.25	12.50	13.75	15.00	16.25	17.50	18.75	20.00	21.25	22.50	23.75	25.00

Compensating Balance: 10.00 % of LINE plus 10.00 % of LOAN

% LINE IN USE	4 %	5 %	6 %	7 %	8 %	9 %	10 %	11 %	12 %	13 %	14 %	15 %	16 %	17 %	18 %	19 %	20 %
25	6.22	7.78	9.33	10.89	12.44	14.00	15.56	17.11	18.67	20.22	21.78	23.33	24.89	26.44	28.00	29.56	31.11
30	5.93	7.41	8.89	10.37	11.85	13.33	14.81	16.30	17.78	19.26	20.74	22.22	23.70	25.19	26.67	28.15	29.63
35	5.71	7.14	8.57	10.00	11.43	12.86	14.29	15.71	17.14	18.57	20.00	21.43	22.86	24.29	25.71	27.14	28.57
40	5.56	6.94	8.33	9.72	11.11	12.50	13.89	15.28	16.67	18.06	19.44	20.83	22.22	23.61	25.00	26.39	27.78
45	5.43	6.79	8.15	9.51	10.86	12.22	13.58	14.94	16.30	17.65	19.01	20.37	21.73	23.09	24.44	25.80	27.16
50	5.33	6.67	8.00	9.33	10.67	12.00	13.33	14.67	16.00	17.33	18.67	20.00	21.33	22.67	24.00	25.33	26.67
55	5.25	6.57	7.88	9.19	10.51	11.82	13.13	14.44	15.76	17.07	18.38	19.70	21.01	22.32	23.64	24.95	26.26
60	5.19	6.48	7.78	9.07	10.37	11.67	12.96	14.26	15.56	16.85	18.15	19.44	20.74	22.04	23.33	24.63	25.93
65	5.13	6.41	7.69	8.97	10.26	11.54	12.82	14.10	15.38	16.67	17.95	19.23	20.51	21.79	23.08	24.36	25.64
70	5.08	6.35	7.62	8.89	10.16	11.43	12.70	13.97	15.24	16.51	17.78	19.05	20.32	21.59	22.86	24.13	25.40
75	5.04	6.30	7.56	8.81	10.07	11.33	12.59	13.85	15.11	16.37	17.63	18.89	20.15	21.41	22.67	23.93	25.19
80	5.00	6.25	7.50	8.75	10.00	11.25	12.50	13.75	15.00	16.25	17.50	18.75	20.00	21.25	22.50	23.75	25.00

Compensating Balance: 15.00 % of LINE plus 5.00 % of LOAN

% LINE IN USE	4 %	5 %	6 %	7 %	8 %	9 %	10 %	11 %	12 %	13 %	14 %	15 %	16 %	17 %	18 %	19 %	20 %
25	6.74	8.42	10.11	11.79	13.47	15.16	16.84	18.53	20.21	21.89	23.58	25.26	26.95	28.63	30.32	32.00	33.68
30	6.32	7.89	9.47	11.05	12.63	14.21	15.79	17.37	18.95	20.53	22.11	23.68	25.26	26.84	28.42	30.00	31.58
35	6.02	7.52	9.02	10.53	12.03	13.53	15.04	16.54	18.05	19.55	21.05	22.56	24.06	25.56	27.07	28.57	30.08
40	5.79	7.24	8.68	10.13	11.58	13.03	14.47	15.92	17.37	18.82	20.26	21.71	23.16	24.61	26.05	27.50	28.95
45	5.61	7.02	8.42	9.82	11.23	12.63	14.04	15.44	16.84	18.25	19.65	21.05	22.46	23.86	25.26	26.67	28.07
50	5.47	6.84	8.21	9.58	10.95	12.32	13.68	15.05	16.42	17.79	19.16	20.53	21.89	23.26	24.63	26.00	27.37
55	5.36	6.70	8.04	9.38	10.72	12.06	13.40	14.74	16.08	17.42	18.76	20.10	21.44	22.78	24.11	25.45	26.79
60	5.26	6.58	7.89	9.21	10.53	11.84	13.16	14.47	15.79	17.11	18.42	19.74	21.05	22.37	23.68	25.00	26.32
65	5.18	6.48	7.77	9.07	10.36	11.66	12.96	14.25	15.55	16.84	18.14	19.43	20.73	22.02	23.32	24.62	25.91
70	5.11	6.39	7.67	8.95	10.23	11.50	12.78	14.06	15.34	16.62	17.89	19.17	20.45	21.73	23.01	24.29	25.56
75	5.05	6.32	7.58	8.84	10.11	11.37	12.63	13.89	15.16	16.42	17.68	18.95	20.21	21.47	22.74	24.00	25.26
80	5.00	6.25	7.50	8.75	10.00	11.25	12.50	13.75	15.00	16.25	17.50	18.75	20.00	21.25	22.50	23.75	25.00

Compensating Balance: 20.00 % of LINE plus 0.00 % of LOAN

% LINE IN USE	4 %	5 %	6 %	7 %	8 %	9 %	10 %	11 %	12 %	13 %	14 %	15 %	16 %	17 %	18 %	19 %	20 %
25	7.20	9.00	10.80	12.60	14.40	16.20	18.00	19.80	21.60	23.40	25.20	27.00	28.80	30.60	32.40	34.20	36.00
30	6.67	8.33	10.00	11.67	13.33	15.00	16.67	18.33	20.00	21.67	23.33	25.00	26.67	28.33	30.00	31.67	33.33
35	6.29	7.86	9.43	11.00	12.57	14.14	15.71	17.29	18.86	20.43	22.00	23.57	25.14	26.71	28.29	29.86	31.43
40	6.00	7.50	9.00	10.50	12.00	13.50	15.00	16.50	18.00	19.50	21.00	22.50	24.00	25.50	27.00	28.50	30.00
45	5.78	7.22	8.67	10.11	11.56	13.00	14.44	15.89	17.33	18.78	20.22	21.67	23.11	24.56	26.00	27.44	28.89
50	5.60	7.00	8.40	9.80	11.20	12.60	14.00	15.40	16.80	18.20	19.60	21.00	22.40	23.80	25.20	26.60	28.00
55	5.45	6.82	8.18	9.55	10.91	12.27	13.64	15.00	16.36	17.73	19.09	20.45	21.82	23.18	24.55	25.91	27.27
60	5.33	6.67	8.00	9.33	10.67	12.00	13.33	14.67	16.00	17.33	18.67	20.00	21.33	22.67	24.00	25.33	26.67
65	5.23	6.54	7.85	9.15	10.46	11.77	13.08	14.38	15.69	17.00	18.31	19.62	20.92	22.23	23.54	24.85	26.15
70	5.14	6.43	7.71	9.00	10.29	11.57	12.86	14.14	15.43	16.71	18.00	19.29	20.57	21.86	23.14	24.43	25.71
75	5.07	6.33	7.60	8.87	10.13	11.40	12.67	13.93	15.20	16.47	17.73	19.00	20.27	21.53	22.80	24.07	25.33
80	5.00	6.25	7.50	8.75	10.00	11.25	12.50	13.75	15.00	16.25	17.50	18.75	20.00	21.25	22.50	23.75	25.00

TABLE **14**

Construction Loan, Average Interest

Interest Rates: 4 to 20% by 1%.

Terms: 6, 12, 18, 24, 36 months.

Points: 1, 2, 3, 4, 5.

This table shows the average interest rate on a construction loan when points are added to interest. The average rate for the original term is shown on the 0 line. The average rate for a loan that is repaid beyond the original term is shown on the corresponding month line.

Example: A borrower must pay 1 point up front for a construction loan to finance a project that is estimated to take 1 year to complete. Interest is charged at the rate of 8% on the outstanding balance; however, adding on the 1 point produces an average interest rate of 9.85%.

If, however, construction of the project takes 18 months, bringing completion of the building to 6 months beyond the original estimated term, what is the new average interest rate? Turn to page 14-2, to the 12 month table. Scan the months delay index to the 6 month line and find the corresponding rate under the 8% column. The average interest rate is 8.96%.

Points. Points are an additional finance charge paid to the lender at closing for granting the loan. A point is 1%: A point on $100,000 is $1,000. Points are added to the interest in computing the average rate.

Construction Loan. For the purpose of computing average rates, monthly draws are made in equal amounts over the original term. The following is the schedule for a $100,000 construction loan for a term of 1 year. The interest is 12% plus 1 point up front.

Month	Monthly Draw	Loan Balance	Interest
0	(1 point)		1,000.00
1	8,333	8,333	83.33
2	8,333	16,667	166.67
3	8,333	25,000	250.00
4	8,333	33,333	333.33
5	8,333	41,667	416.67
6	8,333	50,000	500.00

Month	Monthly Draw	Loan Balance	Interest
7	8,333	58,333	583.33
8	8,333	66,667	666.67
9	8,333	75,000	750.00
10	8,333	83,333	833.33
11	8,333	91,667	916.67
12	8,333	100,000	1,000.00
Total	100,000	650,000	7,500.00

To compute the average monthly rate, the interest is divided by the sum of the loan balances: $7,500 \div 650,000 = .011538$. Multiplying this factor by 12 produces an annual rate of 13.85%.

Extension Beyond Estimated Term. If there is an extension beyond the estimated term, the average rate declines. When the term of a construction loan is extended, the tables assume that the monthly interest is paid from a source other than the loan and that the loan balance remains the same. If the loan in the preceding example is extended 3 months, its previous schedule is continued in the following manner:

Month	Monthly Draw	Loan Balance	Interest + Point
(Previous balance)		650,000	7,500.00
13	0	100,000	1,000.00
14	0	100,000	1,000.00
15	0	100,000	1,000.00
Total		950,000	10,500.00*

*Including point.

The average rate is calculated as:

$$(10,500 \div 950,000) \times 12 \times 100 = 13.26\%$$

The actual rate on a construction loan can be determined only after it is paid off and all the cash flows have been related to the interest charges. Table 14, based on a simple model, is a first approximation of reality.

Description: This table shows the average rate when points are paid and when repayment is delayed.

Example: The average rate is 10.18 % when 1 point is paid for an 8 % 6 month loan and repayment is delayed two months.

Original Term: 6 MONTHS

MONTHS DELAY	4 %	5 %	6 %	7 %	8 %	9 %	10 %	11 %	12 %	13 %	14 %	15 %	16 %	17 %	18 %	19 %	20 %
0	7.43	8.43	9.43	10.43	11.43	12.43	13.43	14.43	15.43	16.43	17.43	18.43	19.43	20.43	21.43	22.43	23.43
1	6.67	7.67	8.67	9.67	10.67	11.67	12.67	13.67	14.67	15.67	16.67	17.67	18.67	19.67	20.67	21.67	22.67
2	6.18	7.18	8.18	9.18	10.18	11.18	12.18	13.18	14.18	15.18	16.18	17.18	18.18	19.18	20.18	21.18	22.18
3	5.85	6.85	7.85	8.85	9.85	10.85	11.85	12.85	13.85	14.85	15.85	16.85	17.85	18.85	19.85	20.85	21.85
4	5.60	6.60	7.60	8.60	9.60	10.60	11.60	12.60	13.60	14.60	15.60	16.60	17.60	18.60	19.60	20.60	21.60
5	5.41	6.41	7.41	8.41	9.41	10.41	11.41	12.41	13.41	14.41	15.41	16.41	17.41	18.41	19.41	20.41	21.41
6	5.26	6.26	7.26	8.26	9.26	10.26	11.26	12.26	13.26	14.26	15.26	16.26	17.26	18.26	19.26	20.26	21.26

Original Term: 12 MONTHS

MONTHS DELAY	4 %	5 %	6 %	7 %	8 %	9 %	10 %	11 %	12 %	13 %	14 %	15 %	16 %	17 %	18 %	19 %	20 %
0	5.85	6.85	7.85	8.85	9.85	10.85	11.85	12.85	13.85	14.85	15.85	16.85	17.85	18.85	19.85	20.85	21.85
1	5.60	6.60	7.60	8.60	9.60	10.60	11.60	12.60	13.60	14.60	15.60	16.60	17.60	18.60	19.60	20.60	21.60
2	5.41	6.41	7.41	8.41	9.41	10.41	11.41	12.41	13.41	14.41	15.41	16.41	17.41	18.41	19.41	20.41	21.41
3	5.26	6.26	7.26	8.26	9.26	10.26	11.26	12.26	13.26	14.26	15.26	16.26	17.26	18.26	19.26	20.26	21.26
4	5.14	6.14	7.14	8.14	9.14	10.14	11.14	12.14	13.14	14.14	15.14	16.14	17.14	18.14	19.14	20.14	21.14
5	5.04	6.04	7.04	8.04	9.04	10.04	11.04	12.04	13.04	14.04	15.04	16.04	17.04	18.04	19.04	20.04	21.04
6	4.96	5.96	6.96	7.96	8.96	9.96	10.96	11.96	12.96	13.96	14.96	15.96	16.96	17.96	18.96	19.96	20.96
7	4.89	5.89	6.89	7.89	8.89	9.89	10.89	11.89	12.89	13.89	14.89	15.89	16.89	17.89	18.89	19.89	20.89
8	4.83	5.83	6.83	7.83	8.83	9.83	10.83	11.83	12.83	13.83	14.83	15.83	16.83	17.83	18.83	19.83	20.83
9	4.77	5.77	6.77	7.77	8.77	9.77	10.77	11.77	12.77	13.77	14.77	15.77	16.77	17.77	18.77	19.77	20.77
10	4.73	5.73	6.73	7.73	8.73	9.73	10.73	11.73	12.73	13.73	14.73	15.73	16.73	17.73	18.73	19.73	20.73
11	4.69	5.69	6.69	7.69	8.69	9.69	10.69	11.69	12.69	13.69	14.69	15.69	16.69	17.69	18.69	19.69	20.69
12	4.65	5.65	6.65	7.65	8.65	9.65	10.65	11.65	12.65	13.65	14.65	15.65	16.65	17.65	18.65	19.65	20.65

Original Term: 18 MONTHS

MONTHS DELAY	4 %	5 %	6 %	7 %	8 %	9 %	10 %	11 %	12 %	13 %	14 %	15 %	16 %	17 %	18 %	19 %	20 %
0	5.26	6.26	7.26	8.26	9.26	10.26	11.26	12.26	13.26	14.26	15.26	16.26	17.26	18.26	19.26	20.26	21.26
1	5.14	6.14	7.14	8.14	9.14	10.14	11.14	12.14	13.14	14.14	15.14	16.14	17.14	18.14	19.14	20.14	21.14
2	5.04	6.04	7.04	8.04	9.04	10.04	11.04	12.04	13.04	14.04	15.04	16.04	17.04	18.04	19.04	20.04	21.04
3	4.96	5.96	6.96	7.96	8.96	9.96	10.96	11.96	12.96	13.96	14.96	15.96	16.96	17.96	18.96	19.96	20.96
4	4.89	5.89	6.89	7.89	8.89	9.89	10.89	11.89	12.89	13.89	14.89	15.89	16.89	17.89	18.89	19.89	20.89
5	4.83	5.83	6.83	7.83	8.83	9.83	10.83	11.83	12.83	13.83	14.83	15.83	16.83	17.83	18.83	19.83	20.83
6	4.77	5.77	6.77	7.77	8.77	9.77	10.77	11.77	12.77	13.77	14.77	15.77	16.77	17.77	18.77	19.77	20.77
7	4.73	5.73	6.73	7.73	8.73	9.73	10.73	11.73	12.73	13.73	14.73	15.73	16.73	17.73	18.73	19.73	20.73
8	4.69	5.69	6.69	7.69	8.69	9.69	10.69	11.69	12.69	13.69	14.69	15.69	16.69	17.69	18.69	19.69	20.69
9	4.65	5.65	6.65	7.65	8.65	9.65	10.65	11.65	12.65	13.65	14.65	15.65	16.65	17.65	18.65	19.65	20.65
10	4.62	5.62	6.62	7.62	8.62	9.62	10.62	11.62	12.62	13.62	14.62	15.62	16.62	17.62	18.62	19.62	20.62
11	4.59	5.59	6.59	7.59	8.59	9.59	10.59	11.59	12.59	13.59	14.59	15.59	16.59	17.59	18.59	19.59	20.59
12	4.56	5.56	6.56	7.56	8.56	9.56	10.56	11.56	12.56	13.56	14.56	15.56	16.56	17.56	18.56	19.56	20.56

Original Term: 24 MONTHS

MONTHS DELAY	4 %	5 %	6 %	7 %	8 %	9 %	10 %	11 %	12 %	13 %	14 %	15 %	16 %	17 %	18 %	19 %	20 %
0	4.96	5.96	6.96	7.96	8.96	9.96	10.96	11.96	12.96	13.96	14.96	15.96	16.96	17.96	18.96	19.96	20.96
1	4.89	5.89	6.89	7.89	8.89	9.89	10.89	11.89	12.89	13.89	14.89	15.89	16.89	17.89	18.89	19.89	20.89
2	4.83	5.83	6.83	7.83	8.83	9.83	10.83	11.83	12.83	13.83	14.83	15.83	16.83	17.83	18.83	19.83	20.83
3	4.77	5.77	6.77	7.77	8.77	9.77	10.77	11.77	12.77	13.77	14.77	15.77	16.77	17.77	18.77	19.77	20.77
4	4.73	5.73	6.73	7.73	8.73	9.73	10.73	11.73	12.73	13.73	14.73	15.73	16.73	17.73	18.73	19.73	20.73
5	4.69	5.69	6.69	7.69	8.69	9.69	10.69	11.69	12.69	13.69	14.69	15.69	16.69	17.69	18.69	19.69	20.69
6	4.65	5.65	6.65	7.65	8.65	9.65	10.65	11.65	12.65	13.65	14.65	15.65	16.65	17.65	18.65	19.65	20.65
7	4.62	5.62	6.62	7.62	8.62	9.62	10.62	11.62	12.62	13.62	14.62	15.62	16.62	17.62	18.62	19.62	20.62
8	4.59	5.59	6.59	7.59	8.59	9.59	10.59	11.59	12.59	13.59	14.59	15.59	16.59	17.59	18.59	19.59	20.59
9	4.56	5.56	6.56	7.56	8.56	9.56	10.56	11.56	12.56	13.56	14.56	15.56	16.56	17.56	18.56	19.56	20.56
10	4.53	5.53	6.53	7.53	8.53	9.53	10.53	11.53	12.53	13.53	14.53	15.53	16.53	17.53	18.53	19.53	20.53
11	4.51	5.51	6.51	7.51	8.51	9.51	10.51	11.51	12.51	13.51	14.51	15.51	16.51	17.51	18.51	19.51	20.51
12	4.49	5.49	6.49	7.49	8.49	9.49	10.49	11.49	12.49	13.49	14.49	15.49	16.49	17.49	18.49	19.49	20.49

Original Term: 36 MONTHS

MONTHS DELAY	4 %	5 %	6 %	7 %	8 %	9 %	10 %	11 %	12 %	13 %	14 %	15 %	16 %	17 %	18 %	19 %	20 %
0	4.65	5.65	6.65	7.65	8.65	9.65	10.65	11.65	12.65	13.65	14.65	15.65	16.65	17.65	18.65	19.65	20.65
1	4.62	5.62	6.62	7.62	8.62	9.62	10.62	11.62	12.62	13.62	14.62	15.62	16.62	17.62	18.62	19.62	20.62
2	4.59	5.59	6.59	7.59	8.59	9.59	10.59	11.59	12.59	13.59	14.59	15.59	16.59	17.59	18.59	19.59	20.59
3	4.56	5.56	6.56	7.56	8.56	9.56	10.56	11.56	12.56	13.56	14.56	15.56	16.56	17.56	18.56	19.56	20.56
4	4.53	5.53	6.53	7.53	8.53	9.53	10.53	11.53	12.53	13.53	14.53	15.53	16.53	17.53	18.53	19.53	20.53
5	4.51	5.51	6.51	7.51	8.51	9.51	10.51	11.51	12.51	13.51	14.51	15.51	16.51	17.51	18.51	19.51	20.51
6	4.49	5.49	6.49	7.49	8.49	9.49	10.49	11.49	12.49	13.49	14.49	15.49	16.49	17.49	18.49	19.49	20.49
7	4.47	5.47	6.47	7.47	8.47	9.47	10.47	11.47	12.47	13.47	14.47	15.47	16.47	17.47	18.47	19.47	20.47
8	4.45	5.45	6.45	7.45	8.45	9.45	10.45	11.45	12.45	13.45	14.45	15.45	16.45	17.45	18.45	19.45	20.45
9	4.44	5.44	6.44	7.44	8.44	9.44	10.44	11.44	12.44	13.44	14.44	15.44	16.44	17.44	18.44	19.44	20.44
10	4.42	5.42	6.42	7.42	8.42	9.42	10.42	11.42	12.42	13.42	14.42	15.42	16.42	17.42	18.42	19.42	20.42
11	4.41	5.41	6.41	7.41	8.41	9.41	10.41	11.41	12.41	13.41	14.41	15.41	16.41	17.41	18.41	19.41	20.41
12	4.39	5.39	6.39	7.39	8.39	9.39	10.39	11.39	12.39	13.39	14.39	15.39	16.39	17.39	18.39	19.39	20.39

Description: This table shows the average rate when points are paid and when repayment is delayed.

Example: The average rate is 12.36 % when 2 points are paid for an 8 % 6 month loan and repayment is delayed two months.

Original Term: 6 MONTHS

MONTHS DELAY	4 %	5 %	6 %	7 %	8 %	9 %	10 %	11 %	12 %	13 %	14 %	15 %	16 %	17 %	18 %	19 %	20 %
0	10.86	11.86	12.86	13.86	14.86	15.86	16.86	17.86	18.86	19.86	20.86	21.86	22.86	23.86	24.86	25.86	26.86
1	9.33	10.33	11.33	12.33	13.33	14.33	15.33	16.33	17.33	18.33	19.33	20.33	21.33	22.33	23.33	24.33	25.33
2	8.36	9.36	10.36	11.36	12.36	13.36	14.36	15.36	16.36	17.36	18.36	19.36	20.36	21.36	22.36	23.36	24.36
3	7.69	8.69	9.69	10.69	11.69	12.69	13.69	14.69	15.69	16.69	17.69	18.69	19.69	20.69	21.69	22.69	23.69
4	7.20	8.20	9.20	10.20	11.20	12.20	13.20	14.20	15.20	16.20	17.20	18.20	19.20	20.20	21.20	22.20	23.20
5	6.82	7.82	8.82	9.82	10.82	11.82	12.82	13.82	14.82	15.82	16.82	17.82	18.82	19.82	20.82	21.82	22.82
6	6.53	7.53	8.53	9.53	10.53	11.53	12.53	13.53	14.53	15.53	16.53	17.53	18.53	19.53	20.53	21.53	22.53

Original Term: 12 MONTHS

MONTHS DELAY	4 %	5 %	6 %	7 %	8 %	9 %	10 %	11 %	12 %	13 %	14 %	15 %	16 %	17 %	18 %	19 %	20 %
0	7.69	8.69	9.69	10.69	11.69	12.69	13.69	14.69	15.69	16.69	17.69	18.69	19.69	20.69	21.69	22.69	23.69
1	7.20	8.20	9.20	10.20	11.20	12.20	13.20	14.20	15.20	16.20	17.20	18.20	19.20	20.20	21.20	22.20	23.20
2	6.82	7.82	8.82	9.82	10.82	11.82	12.82	13.82	14.82	15.82	16.82	17.82	18.82	19.82	20.82	21.82	22.82
3	6.53	7.53	8.53	9.53	10.53	11.53	12.53	13.53	14.53	15.53	16.53	17.53	18.53	19.53	20.53	21.53	22.53
4	6.29	7.29	8.29	9.29	10.29	11.29	12.29	13.29	14.29	15.29	16.29	17.29	18.29	19.29	20.29	21.29	22.29
5	6.09	7.09	8.09	9.09	10.09	11.09	12.09	13.09	14.09	15.09	16.09	17.09	18.09	19.09	20.09	21.09	22.09
6	5.92	6.92	7.92	8.92	9.92	10.92	11.92	12.92	13.92	14.92	15.92	16.92	17.92	18.92	19.92	20.92	21.92
7	5.78	6.78	7.78	8.78	9.78	10.78	11.78	12.78	13.78	14.78	15.78	16.78	17.78	18.78	19.78	20.78	21.78
8	5.66	6.66	7.66	8.66	9.66	10.66	11.66	12.66	13.66	14.66	15.66	16.66	17.66	18.66	19.66	20.66	21.66
9	5.55	6.55	7.55	8.55	9.55	10.55	11.55	12.55	13.55	14.55	15.55	16.55	17.55	18.55	19.55	20.55	21.55
10	5.45	6.45	7.45	8.45	9.45	10.45	11.45	12.45	13.45	14.45	15.45	16.45	17.45	18.45	19.45	20.45	21.45
11	5.37	6.37	7.37	8.37	9.37	10.37	11.37	12.37	13.37	14.37	15.37	16.37	17.37	18.37	19.37	20.37	21.37
12	5.30	6.30	7.30	8.30	9.30	10.30	11.30	12.30	13.30	14.30	15.30	16.30	17.30	18.30	19.30	20.30	21.30

Original Term: 18 MONTHS

MONTHS DELAY	4 %	5 %	6 %	7 %	8 %	9 %	10 %	11 %	12 %	13 %	14 %	15 %	16 %	17 %	18 %	19 %	20 %
0	6.53	7.53	8.53	9.53	10.53	11.53	12.53	13.53	14.53	15.53	16.53	17.53	18.53	19.53	20.53	21.53	22.53
1	6.29	7.29	8.29	9.29	10.29	11.29	12.29	13.29	14.29	15.29	16.29	17.29	18.29	19.29	20.29	21.29	22.29
2	6.09	7.09	8.09	9.09	10.09	11.09	12.09	13.09	14.09	15.09	16.09	17.09	18.09	19.09	20.09	21.09	22.09
3	5.92	6.92	7.92	8.92	9.92	10.92	11.92	12.92	13.92	14.92	15.92	16.92	17.92	18.92	19.92	20.92	21.92
4	5.78	6.78	7.78	8.78	9.78	10.78	11.78	12.78	13.78	14.78	15.78	16.78	17.78	18.78	19.78	20.78	21.78
5	5.66	6.66	7.66	8.66	9.66	10.66	11.66	12.66	13.66	14.66	15.66	16.66	17.66	18.66	19.66	20.66	21.66
6	5.55	6.55	7.55	8.55	9.55	10.55	11.55	12.55	13.55	14.55	15.55	16.55	17.55	18.55	19.55	20.55	21.55
7	5.45	6.45	7.45	8.45	9.45	10.45	11.45	12.45	13.45	14.45	15.45	16.45	17.45	18.45	19.45	20.45	21.45
8	5.37	6.37	7.37	8.37	9.37	10.37	11.37	12.37	13.37	14.37	15.37	16.37	17.37	18.37	19.37	20.37	21.37
9	5.30	6.30	7.30	8.30	9.30	10.30	11.30	12.30	13.30	14.30	15.30	16.30	17.30	18.30	19.30	20.30	21.30
10	5.23	6.23	7.23	8.23	9.23	10.23	11.23	12.23	13.23	14.23	15.23	16.23	17.23	18.23	19.23	20.23	21.23
11	5.17	6.17	7.17	8.17	9.17	10.17	11.17	12.17	13.17	14.17	15.17	16.17	17.17	18.17	19.17	20.17	21.17
12	5.12	6.12	7.12	8.12	9.12	10.12	11.12	12.12	13.12	14.12	15.12	16.12	17.12	18.12	19.12	20.12	21.12

Original Term: 24 MONTHS

MONTHS DELAY	4 %	5 %	6 %	7 %	8 %	9 %	10 %	11 %	12 %	13 %	14 %	15 %	16 %	17 %	18 %	19 %	20 %
0	5.92	6.92	7.92	8.92	9.92	10.92	11.92	12.92	13.92	14.92	15.92	16.92	17.92	18.92	19.92	20.92	21.92
1	5.78	6.78	7.78	8.78	9.78	10.78	11.78	12.78	13.78	14.78	15.78	16.78	17.78	18.78	19.78	20.78	21.78
2	5.66	6.66	7.66	8.66	9.66	10.66	11.66	12.66	13.66	14.66	15.66	16.66	17.66	18.66	19.66	20.66	21.66
3	5.55	6.55	7.55	8.55	9.55	10.55	11.55	12.55	13.55	14.55	15.55	16.55	17.55	18.55	19.55	20.55	21.55
4	5.45	6.45	7.45	8.45	9.45	10.45	11.45	12.45	13.45	14.45	15.45	16.45	17.45	18.45	19.45	20.45	21.45
5	5.37	6.37	7.37	8.37	9.37	10.37	11.37	12.37	13.37	14.37	15.37	16.37	17.37	18.37	19.37	20.37	21.37
6	5.30	6.30	7.30	8.30	9.30	10.30	11.30	12.30	13.30	14.30	15.30	16.30	17.30	18.30	19.30	20.30	21.30
7	5.23	6.23	7.23	8.23	9.23	10.23	11.23	12.23	13.23	14.23	15.23	16.23	17.23	18.23	19.23	20.23	21.23
8	5.17	6.17	7.17	8.17	9.17	10.17	11.17	12.17	13.17	14.17	15.17	16.17	17.17	18.17	19.17	20.17	21.17
9	5.12	6.12	7.12	8.12	9.12	10.12	11.12	12.12	13.12	14.12	15.12	16.12	17.12	18.12	19.12	20.12	21.12
10	5.07	6.07	7.07	8.07	9.07	10.07	11.07	12.07	13.07	14.07	15.07	16.07	17.07	18.07	19.07	20.07	21.07
11	5.02	6.02	7.02	8.02	9.02	10.02	11.02	12.02	13.02	14.02	15.02	16.02	17.02	18.02	19.02	20.02	21.02
12	4.98	5.98	6.98	7.98	8.98	9.98	10.98	11.98	12.98	13.98	14.98	15.98	16.98	17.98	18.98	19.98	20.98

Original Term: 36 MONTHS

MONTHS DELAY	4 %	5 %	6 %	7 %	8 %	9 %	10 %	11 %	12 %	13 %	14 %	15 %	16 %	17 %	18 %	19 %	20 %
0	5.30	6.30	7.30	8.30	9.30	10.30	11.30	12.30	13.30	14.30	15.30	16.30	17.30	18.30	19.30	20.30	21.30
1	5.23	6.23	7.23	8.23	9.23	10.23	11.23	12.23	13.23	14.23	15.23	16.23	17.23	18.23	19.23	20.23	21.23
2	5.17	6.17	7.17	8.17	9.17	10.17	11.17	12.17	13.17	14.17	15.17	16.17	17.17	18.17	19.17	20.17	21.17
3	5.12	6.12	7.12	8.12	9.12	10.12	11.12	12.12	13.12	14.12	15.12	16.12	17.12	18.12	19.12	20.12	21.12
4	5.07	6.07	7.07	8.07	9.07	10.07	11.07	12.07	13.07	14.07	15.07	16.07	17.07	18.07	19.07	20.07	21.07
5	5.02	6.02	7.02	8.02	9.02	10.02	11.02	12.02	13.02	14.02	15.02	16.02	17.02	18.02	19.02	20.02	21.02
6	4.98	5.98	6.98	7.98	8.98	9.98	10.98	11.98	12.98	13.98	14.98	15.98	16.98	17.98	18.98	19.98	20.98
7	4.94	5.94	6.94	7.94	8.94	9.94	10.94	11.94	12.94	13.94	14.94	15.94	16.94	17.94	18.94	19.94	20.94
8	4.91	5.91	6.91	7.91	8.91	9.91	10.91	11.91	12.91	13.91	14.91	15.91	16.91	17.91	18.91	19.91	20.87
9	4.87	5.87	6.87	7.87	8.87	9.87	10.87	11.87	12.87	13.87	14.87	15.87	16.87	17.87	18.87	19.87	20.87
10	4.84	5.84	6.84	7.84	8.84	9.84	10.84	11.84	12.84	13.84	14.84	15.84	16.84	17.84	18.84	19.84	20.84
11	4.81	5.81	6.81	7.81	8.81	9.81	10.81	11.81	12.81	13.81	14.81	15.81	16.81	17.81	18.81	19.81	20.81
12	4.79	5.79	6.79	7.79	8.79	9.79	10.79	11.79	12.79	13.79	14.79	15.79	16.79	17.79	18.79	19.79	20.79

Description: This table shows the average rate when points are paid and when repayment is delayed.

Example: The average rate is 14.55 % when 3 points are paid for an 8 % 6 month loan and repayment is delayed two months.

Original Term: 6 MONTHS

MONTHS DELAY	4 %	5 %	6 %	7 %	8 %	9 %	10 %	11 %	12 %	13 %	14 %	15 %	16 %	17 %	18 %	19 %	20 %
0	14.29	15.29	16.29	17.29	18.29	19.29	20.29	21.29	22.29	23.29	24.29	25.29	26.29	27.29	28.29	29.29	30.29
1	12.00	13.00	14.00	15.00	16.00	17.00	18.00	19.00	20.00	21.00	22.00	23.00	24.00	25.00	26.00	27.00	28.00
2	10.55	11.55	12.55	13.55	14.55	15.55	16.55	17.55	18.55	19.55	20.55	21.55	22.55	23.55	24.55	25.55	26.55
3	9.54	10.54	11.54	12.54	13.54	14.54	15.54	16.54	17.54	18.54	19.54	20.54	21.54	22.54	23.54	24.54	25.54
4	8.80	9.80	10.80	11.80	12.80	13.80	14.80	15.80	16.80	17.80	18.80	19.80	20.80	21.80	22.80	23.80	24.80
5	8.24	9.24	10.24	11.24	12.24	13.24	14.24	15.24	16.24	17.24	18.24	19.24	20.24	21.24	22.24	23.24	24.24
6	7.79	8.79	9.79	10.79	11.79	12.79	13.79	14.79	15.79	16.79	17.79	18.79	19.79	20.79	21.79	22.79	23.79

Original Term: 12 MONTHS

MONTHS DELAY	4 %	5 %	6 %	7 %	8 %	9 %	10 %	11 %	12 %	13 %	14 %	15 %	16 %	17 %	18 %	19 %	20 %
0	9.54	10.54	11.54	12.54	13.54	14.54	15.54	16.54	17.54	18.54	19.54	20.54	21.54	22.54	23.54	24.54	25.54
1	8.80	9.80	10.80	11.80	12.80	13.80	14.80	15.80	16.80	17.80	18.80	19.80	20.80	21.80	22.80	23.80	24.80
2	8.24	9.24	10.24	11.24	12.24	13.24	14.24	15.24	16.24	17.24	18.24	19.24	20.24	21.24	22.24	23.24	24.24
3	7.79	8.79	9.79	10.79	11.79	12.79	13.79	14.79	15.79	16.79	17.79	18.79	19.79	20.79	21.79	22.79	23.79
4	7.43	8.43	9.43	10.43	11.43	12.43	13.43	14.43	15.43	16.43	17.43	18.43	19.43	20.43	21.43	22.43	23.43
5	7.13	8.13	9.13	10.13	11.13	12.13	13.13	14.13	15.13	16.13	17.13	18.13	19.13	20.13	21.13	22.13	23.13
6	6.88	7.88	8.88	9.88	10.88	11.88	12.88	13.88	14.88	15.88	16.88	17.88	18.88	19.88	20.88	21.88	22.88
7	6.67	7.67	8.67	9.67	10.67	11.67	12.67	13.67	14.67	15.67	16.67	17.67	18.67	19.67	20.67	21.67	22.67
8	6.48	7.48	8.48	9.48	10.48	11.48	12.48	13.48	14.48	15.48	16.48	17.48	18.48	19.48	20.48	21.48	22.48
9	6.32	7.32	8.32	9.32	10.32	11.32	12.32	13.32	14.32	15.32	16.32	17.32	18.32	19.32	20.32	21.32	22.32
10	6.18	7.18	8.18	9.18	10.18	11.18	12.18	13.18	14.18	15.18	16.18	17.18	18.18	19.18	20.18	21.18	22.18
11	6.06	7.06	8.06	9.06	10.06	11.06	12.06	13.06	14.06	15.06	16.06	17.06	18.06	19.06	20.06	21.06	22.06
12	5.95	6.95	7.95	8.95	9.95	10.95	11.95	12.95	13.95	14.95	15.95	16.95	17.95	18.95	19.95	20.95	21.95

Original Term: 18 MONTHS

MONTHS DELAY	4 %	5 %	6 %	7 %	8 %	9 %	10 %	11 %	12 %	13 %	14 %	15 %	16 %	17 %	18 %	19 %	20 %
0	7.79	8.79	9.79	10.79	11.79	12.79	13.79	14.79	15.79	16.79	17.79	18.79	19.79	20.79	21.79	22.79	23.79
1	7.43	8.43	9.43	10.43	11.43	12.43	13.43	14.43	15.43	16.43	17.43	18.43	19.43	20.43	21.43	22.43	23.43
2	7.13	8.13	9.13	10.13	11.13	12.13	13.13	14.13	15.13	16.13	17.13	18.13	19.13	20.13	21.13	22.13	23.13
3	6.88	7.88	8.88	9.88	10.88	11.88	12.88	13.88	14.88	15.88	16.88	17.88	18.88	19.88	20.88	21.88	22.88
4	6.67	7.67	8.67	9.67	10.67	11.67	12.67	13.67	14.67	15.67	16.67	17.67	18.67	19.67	20.67	21.67	22.67
5	6.48	7.48	8.48	9.48	10.48	11.48	12.48	13.48	14.48	15.48	16.48	17.48	18.48	19.48	20.48	21.48	22.48
6	6.32	7.32	8.32	9.32	10.32	11.32	12.32	13.32	14.32	15.32	16.32	17.32	18.32	19.32	20.32	21.32	22.32
7	6.18	7.18	8.18	9.18	10.18	11.18	12.18	13.18	14.18	15.18	16.18	17.18	18.18	19.18	20.18	21.18	22.18
8	6.06	7.06	8.06	9.06	10.06	11.06	12.06	13.06	14.06	15.06	16.06	17.06	18.06	19.06	20.06	21.06	22.06
9	5.95	6.95	7.95	8.95	9.95	10.95	11.95	12.95	13.95	14.95	15.95	16.95	17.95	18.95	19.95	20.95	21.95
10	5.85	6.85	7.85	8.85	9.85	10.85	11.85	12.85	13.85	14.85	15.85	16.85	17.85	18.85	19.85	20.85	21.85
11	5.76	6.76	7.76	8.76	9.76	10.76	11.76	12.76	13.76	14.76	15.76	16.76	17.76	18.76	19.76	20.76	21.76
12	5.67	6.67	7.67	8.67	9.67	10.67	11.67	12.67	13.67	14.67	15.67	16.67	17.67	18.67	19.67	20.67	21.67

Original Term: 24 MONTHS

MONTHS DELAY	4 %	5 %	6 %	7 %	8 %	9 %	10 %	11 %	12 %	13 %	14 %	15 %	16 %	17 %	18 %	19 %	20 %
0	6.88	7.88	8.88	9.88	10.88	11.88	12.88	13.88	14.88	15.88	16.88	17.88	18.88	19.88	20.88	21.88	22.88
1	6.67	7.67	8.67	9.67	10.67	11.67	12.67	13.67	14.67	15.67	16.67	17.67	18.67	19.67	20.67	21.67	22.67
2	6.48	7.48	8.48	9.48	10.48	11.48	12.48	13.48	14.48	15.48	16.48	17.48	18.48	19.48	20.48	21.48	22.48
3	6.32	7.32	8.32	9.32	10.32	11.32	12.32	13.32	14.32	15.32	16.32	17.32	18.32	19.32	20.32	21.32	22.32
4	6.18	7.18	8.18	9.18	10.18	11.18	12.18	13.18	14.18	15.18	16.18	17.18	18.18	19.18	20.18	21.18	22.18
5	6.06	7.06	8.06	9.06	10.06	11.06	12.06	13.06	14.06	15.06	16.06	17.06	18.06	19.06	20.06	21.06	22.06
6	5.95	6.95	7.95	8.95	9.95	10.95	11.95	12.95	13.95	14.95	15.95	16.95	17.95	18.95	19.95	20.95	21.95
7	5.85	6.85	7.85	8.85	9.85	10.85	11.85	12.85	13.85	14.85	15.85	16.85	17.85	18.85	19.85	20.85	21.85
8	5.76	6.76	7.76	8.76	9.76	10.76	11.76	12.76	13.76	14.76	15.76	16.76	17.76	18.76	19.76	20.76	21.76
9	5.67	6.67	7.67	8.67	9.67	10.67	11.67	12.67	13.67	14.67	15.67	16.67	17.67	18.67	19.67	20.67	21.67
10	5.60	6.60	7.60	8.60	9.60	10.60	11.60	12.60	13.60	14.60	15.60	16.60	17.60	18.60	19.60	20.60	21.60
11	5.53	6.53	7.53	8.53	9.53	10.53	11.53	12.53	13.53	14.53	15.53	16.53	17.53	18.53	19.53	20.53	21.53
12	5.47	6.47	7.47	8.47	9.47	10.47	11.47	12.47	13.47	14.47	15.47	16.47	17.47	18.47	19.47	20.47	21.47

Original Term: 36 MONTHS

MONTHS DELAY	4 %	5 %	6 %	7 %	8 %	9 %	10 %	11 %	12 %	13 %	14 %	15 %	16 %	17 %	18 %	19 %	20 %
0	5.95	6.95	7.95	8.95	9.95	10.95	11.95	12.95	13.95	14.95	15.95	16.95	17.95	18.95	19.95	20.95	21.95
1	5.85	6.85	7.85	8.85	9.85	10.85	11.85	12.85	13.85	14.85	15.85	16.85	17.85	18.85	19.85	20.85	21.85
2	5.76	6.76	7.76	8.76	9.76	10.76	11.76	12.76	13.76	14.76	15.76	16.76	17.76	18.76	19.76	20.76	21.76
3	5.67	6.67	7.67	8.67	9.67	10.67	11.67	12.67	13.67	14.67	15.67	16.67	17.67	18.67	19.67	20.67	21.67
4	5.60	6.60	7.60	8.60	9.60	10.60	11.60	12.60	13.60	14.60	15.60	16.60	17.60	18.60	19.60	20.60	21.60
5	5.53	6.53	7.53	8.53	9.53	10.53	11.53	12.53	13.53	14.53	15.53	16.53	17.53	18.53	19.53	20.53	21.53
6	5.47	6.47	7.47	8.47	9.47	10.47	11.47	12.47	13.47	14.47	15.47	16.47	17.47	18.47	19.47	20.47	21.47
7	5.41	6.41	7.41	8.41	9.41	10.41	11.41	12.41	13.41	14.41	15.41	16.41	17.41	18.41	19.41	20.41	21.41
8	5.36	6.36	7.36	8.36	9.36	10.36	11.36	12.36	13.36	14.36	15.36	16.36	17.36	18.36	19.36	20.36	21.36
9	5.31	6.31	7.31	8.31	9.31	10.31	11.31	12.31	13.31	14.31	15.31	16.31	17.31	18.31	19.31	20.31	21.31
10	5.26	6.26	7.26	8.26	9.26	10.26	11.26	12.26	13.26	14.26	15.26	16.26	17.26	18.26	19.26	20.26	21.26
11	5.22	6.22	7.22	8.22	9.22	10.22	11.22	12.22	13.22	14.22	15.22	16.22	17.22	18.22	19.22	20.22	21.22
12	5.18	6.18	7.18	8.18	9.18	10.18	11.18	12.18	13.18	14.18	15.18	16.18	17.18	18.18	19.18	20.18	21.18

Description: This table shows the average rate when points are paid and when repayment is delayed.

Example: The average rate is 16.73 % when 4 points are paid for an 8 % 6 month loan and repayment is delayed two months.

Original Term: 6 MONTHS

MONTHS DELAY	4 %	5 %	6 %	7 %	8 %	9 %	10 %	11 %	12 %	13 %	14 %	15 %	16 %	17 %	18 %	19 %	20 %
0	17.71	18.71	19.71	20.71	21.71	22.71	23.71	24.71	25.71	26.71	27.71	28.71	29.71	30.71	31.71	32.71	33.71
1	14.67	15.67	16.67	17.67	18.67	19.67	20.67	21.67	22.67	23.67	24.67	25.67	26.67	27.67	28.67	29.67	30.67
2	12.73	13.73	14.73	15.73	16.73	17.73	18.73	19.73	20.73	21.73	22.73	23.73	24.73	25.73	26.73	27.73	28.73
3	11.38	12.38	13.38	14.38	15.38	16.38	17.38	18.38	19.38	20.38	21.38	22.38	23.38	24.38	25.38	26.38	27.38
4	10.40	11.40	12.40	13.40	14.40	15.40	16.40	17.40	18.40	19.40	20.40	21.40	22.40	23.40	24.40	25.40	26.40
5	9.65	10.65	11.65	12.65	13.65	14.65	15.65	16.65	17.65	18.65	19.65	20.65	21.65	22.65	23.65	24.65	25.65
6	9.05	10.05	11.05	12.05	13.05	14.05	15.05	16.05	17.05	18.05	19.05	20.05	21.05	22.05	23.05	24.05	25.05

Original Term: 12 MONTHS

MONTHS DELAY	4 %	5 %	6 %	7 %	8 %	9 %	10 %	11 %	12 %	13 %	14 %	15 %	16 %	17 %	18 %	19 %	20 %
0	11.38	12.38	13.38	14.38	15.38	16.38	17.38	18.38	19.38	20.38	21.38	22.38	23.38	24.38	25.38	26.38	27.38
1	10.40	11.40	12.40	13.40	14.40	15.40	16.40	17.40	18.40	19.40	20.40	21.40	22.40	23.40	24.40	25.40	26.40
2	9.65	10.65	11.65	12.65	13.65	14.65	15.65	16.65	17.65	18.65	19.65	20.65	21.65	22.65	23.65	24.65	25.65
3	9.05	10.05	11.05	12.05	13.05	14.05	15.05	16.05	17.05	18.05	19.05	20.05	21.05	22.05	23.05	24.05	25.05
4	8.57	9.57	10.57	11.57	12.57	13.57	14.57	15.57	16.57	17.57	18.57	19.57	20.57	21.57	22.57	23.57	24.57
5	8.17	9.17	10.17	11.17	12.17	13.17	14.17	15.17	16.17	17.17	18.17	19.17	20.17	21.17	22.17	23.17	24.17
6	7.84	8.84	9.84	10.84	11.84	12.84	13.84	14.84	15.84	16.84	17.84	18.84	19.84	20.84	21.84	22.84	23.84
7	7.56	8.56	9.56	10.56	11.56	12.56	13.56	14.56	15.56	16.56	17.56	18.56	19.56	20.56	21.56	22.56	23.56
8	7.31	8.31	9.31	10.31	11.31	12.31	13.31	14.31	15.31	16.31	17.31	18.31	19.31	20.31	21.31	22.31	23.31
9	7.10	8.10	9.10	10.10	11.10	12.10	13.10	14.10	15.10	16.10	17.10	18.10	19.10	20.10	21.10	22.10	23.10
10	6.91	7.91	8.91	9.91	10.91	11.91	12.91	13.91	14.91	15.91	16.91	17.91	18.91	19.91	20.91	21.91	22.91
11	6.74	7.74	8.74	9.74	10.74	11.74	12.74	13.74	14.74	15.74	16.74	17.74	18.74	19.74	20.74	21.74	22.74
12	6.59	7.59	8.59	9.59	10.59	11.59	12.59	13.59	14.59	15.59	16.59	17.59	18.59	19.59	20.59	21.59	22.59

Original Term: 18 MONTHS

MONTHS DELAY	4 %	5 %	6 %	7 %	8 %	9 %	10 %	11 %	12 %	13 %	14 %	15 %	16 %	17 %	18 %	19 %	20 %
0	9.05	10.05	11.05	12.05	13.05	14.05	15.05	16.05	17.05	18.05	19.05	20.05	21.05	22.05	23.05	24.05	25.05
1	8.57	9.57	10.57	11.57	12.57	13.57	14.57	15.57	16.57	17.57	18.57	19.57	20.57	21.57	22.57	23.57	24.57
2	8.17	9.17	10.17	11.17	12.17	13.17	14.17	15.17	16.17	17.17	18.17	19.17	20.17	21.17	22.17	23.17	24.17
3	7.84	8.84	9.84	10.84	11.84	12.84	13.84	14.84	15.84	16.84	17.84	18.84	19.84	20.84	21.84	22.84	23.84
4	7.56	8.56	9.56	10.56	11.56	12.56	13.56	14.56	15.56	16.56	17.56	18.56	19.56	20.56	21.56	22.56	23.56
5	7.31	8.31	9.31	10.31	11.31	12.31	13.31	14.31	15.31	16.31	17.31	18.31	19.31	20.31	21.31	22.31	23.31
6	7.10	8.10	9.10	10.10	11.10	12.10	13.10	14.10	15.10	16.10	17.10	18.10	19.10	20.10	21.10	22.10	23.10
7	6.91	7.91	8.91	9.91	10.91	11.91	12.91	13.91	14.91	15.91	16.91	17.91	18.91	19.91	20.91	21.91	22.91
8	6.74	7.74	8.74	9.74	10.74	11.74	12.74	13.74	14.74	15.74	16.74	17.74	18.74	19.74	20.74	21.74	22.74
9	6.59	7.59	8.59	9.59	10.59	11.59	12.59	13.59	14.59	15.59	16.59	17.59	18.59	19.59	20.59	21.59	22.59
10	6.46	7.46	8.46	9.46	10.46	11.46	12.46	13.46	14.46	15.46	16.46	17.46	18.46	19.46	20.46	21.46	22.46
11	6.34	7.34	8.34	9.34	10.34	11.34	12.34	13.34	14.34	15.34	16.34	17.34	18.34	19.34	20.34	21.34	22.34
12	6.23	7.23	8.23	9.23	10.23	11.23	12.23	13.23	14.23	15.23	16.23	17.23	18.23	19.23	20.23	21.23	22.23

Original Term: 24 MONTHS

MONTHS DELAY	4 %	5 %	6 %	7 %	8 %	9 %	10 %	11 %	12 %	13 %	14 %	15 %	16 %	17 %	18 %	19 %	20 %
0	7.84	8.84	9.84	10.84	11.84	12.84	13.84	14.84	15.84	16.84	17.84	18.84	19.84	20.84	21.84	22.84	23.84
1	7.56	8.56	9.56	10.56	11.56	12.56	13.56	14.56	15.56	16.56	17.56	18.56	19.56	20.56	21.56	22.56	23.56
2	7.31	8.31	9.31	10.31	11.31	12.31	13.31	14.31	15.31	16.31	17.31	18.31	19.31	20.31	21.31	22.31	23.31
3	7.10	8.10	9.10	10.10	11.10	12.10	13.10	14.10	15.10	16.10	17.10	18.10	19.10	20.10	21.10	22.10	23.10
4	6.91	7.91	8.91	9.91	10.91	11.91	12.91	13.91	14.91	15.91	16.91	17.91	18.91	19.91	20.91	21.91	22.91
5	6.74	7.74	8.74	9.74	10.74	11.74	12.74	13.74	14.74	15.74	16.74	17.74	18.74	19.74	20.74	21.74	22.74
6	6.59	7.59	8.59	9.59	10.59	11.59	12.59	13.59	14.59	15.59	16.59	17.59	18.59	19.59	20.59	21.59	22.59
7	6.46	7.46	8.46	9.46	10.46	11.46	12.46	13.46	14.46	15.46	16.46	17.46	18.46	19.46	20.46	21.46	22.46
8	6.34	7.34	8.34	9.34	10.34	11.34	12.34	13.34	14.34	15.34	16.34	17.34	18.34	19.34	20.34	21.34	22.34
9	6.23	7.23	8.23	9.23	10.23	11.23	12.23	13.23	14.23	15.23	16.23	17.23	18.23	19.23	20.23	21.23	22.23
10	6.13	7.13	8.13	9.13	10.13	11.13	12.13	13.13	14.13	15.13	16.13	17.13	18.13	19.13	20.13	21.13	22.13
11	6.04	7.04	8.04	9.04	10.04	11.04	12.04	13.04	14.04	15.04	16.04	17.04	18.04	19.04	20.04	21.04	22.04
12	5.96	6.96	7.96	8.96	9.96	10.96	11.96	12.96	13.96	14.96	15.96	16.96	17.96	18.96	19.96	20.96	21.96

Original Term: 36 MONTHS

MONTHS DELAY	4 %	5 %	6 %	7 %	8 %	9 %	10 %	11 %	12 %	13 %	14 %	15 %	16 %	17 %	18 %	19 %	20 %
0	6.59	7.59	8.59	9.59	10.59	11.59	12.59	13.59	14.59	15.59	16.59	17.59	18.59	19.59	20.59	21.59	22.59
1	6.46	7.46	8.46	9.46	10.46	11.46	12.46	13.46	14.46	15.46	16.46	17.46	18.46	19.46	20.46	21.46	22.46
2	6.34	7.34	8.34	9.34	10.34	11.34	12.34	13.34	14.34	15.34	16.34	17.34	18.34	19.34	20.34	21.34	22.34
3	6.23	7.23	8.23	9.23	10.23	11.23	12.23	13.23	14.23	15.23	16.23	17.23	18.23	19.23	20.23	21.23	22.23
4	6.13	7.13	8.13	9.13	10.13	11.13	12.13	13.13	14.13	15.13	16.13	17.13	18.13	19.13	20.13	21.13	22.13
5	6.04	7.04	8.04	9.04	10.04	11.04	12.04	13.04	14.04	15.04	16.04	17.04	18.04	19.04	20.04	21.04	22.04
6	5.96	6.96	7.96	8.96	9.96	10.96	11.96	12.96	13.96	14.96	15.96	16.96	17.96	18.96	19.96	20.96	21.96
7	5.88	6.88	7.88	8.88	9.88	10.88	11.88	12.88	13.88	14.88	15.88	16.88	17.88	18.88	19.88	20.88	21.88
8	5.81	6.81	7.81	8.81	9.81	10.81	11.81	12.81	13.81	14.81	15.81	16.81	17.81	18.81	19.81	20.81	21.81
9	5.75	6.75	7.75	8.75	9.75	10.75	11.75	12.75	13.75	14.75	15.75	16.75	17.75	18.75	19.75	20.75	21.75
10	5.68	6.68	7.68	8.68	9.68	10.68	11.68	12.68	13.68	14.68	15.68	16.68	17.68	18.68	19.68	20.68	21.68
11	5.63	6.63	7.63	8.63	9.63	10.63	11.63	12.63	13.63	14.63	15.63	16.63	17.63	18.63	19.63	20.63	21.63
12	5.57	6.57	7.57	8.57	9.57	10.57	11.57	12.57	13.57	14.57	15.57	16.57	17.57	18.57	19.57	20.57	21.57

Description: This table shows the average rate when points are paid and when repayment is delayed.

Example: The average rate is 18.91 % when 5 points are paid for an 8 % 6 month loan and repayment is delayed two months.

Original Term: 6 MONTHS

MONTHS DELAY	4 %	5 %	6 %	7 %	8 %	9 %	10 %	11 %	12 %	13 %	14 %	15 %	16 %	17 %	18 %	19 %	20 %
0	21.14	22.14	23.14	24.14	25.14	26.14	27.14	28.14	29.14	30.14	31.14	32.14	33.14	34.14	35.14	36.14	37.14
1	17.33	18.33	19.33	20.33	21.33	22.33	23.33	24.33	25.33	26.33	27.33	28.33	29.33	30.33	31.33	32.33	33.33
2	14.91	15.91	16.91	17.91	18.91	19.91	20.91	21.91	22.91	23.91	24.91	25.91	26.91	27.91	28.91	29.91	30.91
3	13.23	14.23	15.23	16.23	17.23	18.23	19.23	20.23	21.23	22.23	23.23	24.23	25.23	26.23	27.23	28.23	29.23
4	12.00	13.00	14.00	15.00	16.00	17.00	18.00	19.00	20.00	21.00	22.00	23.00	24.00	25.00	26.00	27.00	28.00
5	11.06	12.06	13.06	14.06	15.06	16.06	17.06	18.06	19.06	20.06	21.06	22.06	23.06	24.06	25.06	26.06	27.06
6	10.32	11.32	12.32	13.32	14.32	15.32	16.32	17.32	18.32	19.32	20.32	21.32	22.32	23.32	24.32	25.32	26.32

Original Term: 12 MONTHS

MONTHS DELAY	4 %	5 %	6 %	7 %	8 %	9 %	10 %	11 %	12 %	13 %	14 %	15 %	16 %	17 %	18 %	19 %	20 %
0	13.23	14.23	15.23	16.23	17.23	18.23	19.23	20.23	21.23	22.23	23.23	24.23	25.23	26.23	27.23	28.23	29.23
1	12.00	13.00	14.00	15.00	16.00	17.00	18.00	19.00	20.00	21.00	22.00	23.00	24.00	25.00	26.00	27.00	28.00
2	11.06	12.06	13.06	14.06	15.06	16.06	17.06	18.06	19.06	20.06	21.06	22.06	23.06	24.06	25.06	26.06	27.06
3	10.32	11.32	12.32	13.32	14.32	15.32	16.32	17.32	18.32	19.32	20.32	21.32	22.32	23.32	24.32	25.32	26.32
4	9.71	10.71	11.71	12.71	13.71	14.71	15.71	16.71	17.71	18.71	19.71	20.71	21.71	22.71	23.71	24.71	25.71
5	9.22	10.22	11.22	12.22	13.22	14.22	15.22	16.22	17.22	18.22	19.22	20.22	21.22	22.22	23.22	24.22	25.22
6	8.80	9.80	10.80	11.80	12.80	13.80	14.80	15.80	16.80	17.80	18.80	19.80	20.80	21.80	22.80	23.80	24.80
7	8.44	9.44	10.44	11.44	12.44	13.44	14.44	15.44	16.44	17.44	18.44	19.44	20.44	21.44	22.44	23.44	24.44
8	8.14	9.14	10.14	11.14	12.14	13.14	14.14	15.14	16.14	17.14	18.14	19.14	20.14	21.14	22.14	23.14	24.14
9	7.87	8.87	9.87	10.87	11.87	12.87	13.87	14.87	15.87	16.87	17.87	18.87	19.87	20.87	21.87	22.87	23.87
10	7.64	8.64	9.64	10.64	11.64	12.64	13.64	14.64	15.64	16.64	17.64	18.64	19.64	20.64	21.64	22.64	23.64
11	7.43	8.43	9.43	10.43	11.43	12.43	13.43	14.43	15.43	16.43	17.43	18.43	19.43	20.43	21.43	22.43	23.43
12	7.24	8.24	9.24	10.24	11.24	12.24	13.24	14.24	15.24	16.24	17.24	18.24	19.24	20.24	21.24	22.24	23.24

Original Term: 18 MONTHS

MONTHS DELAY	4 %	5 %	6 %	7 %	8 %	9 %	10 %	11 %	12 %	13 %	14 %	15 %	16 %	17 %	18 %	19 %	20 %
0	10.32	11.32	12.32	13.32	14.32	15.32	16.32	17.32	18.32	19.32	20.32	21.32	22.32	23.32	24.32	25.32	26.32
1	9.71	10.71	11.71	12.71	13.71	14.71	15.71	16.71	17.71	18.71	19.71	20.71	21.71	22.71	23.71	24.71	25.71
2	9.22	10.22	11.22	12.22	13.22	14.22	15.22	16.22	17.22	18.22	19.22	20.22	21.22	22.22	23.22	24.22	25.22
3	8.80	9.80	10.80	11.80	12.80	13.80	14.80	15.80	16.80	17.80	18.80	19.80	20.80	21.80	22.80	23.80	24.80
4	8.44	9.44	10.44	11.44	12.44	13.44	14.44	15.44	16.44	17.44	18.44	19.44	20.44	21.44	22.44	23.44	24.44
5	8.14	9.14	10.14	11.14	12.14	13.14	14.14	15.14	16.14	17.14	18.14	19.14	20.14	21.14	22.14	23.14	24.14
6	7.87	8.87	9.87	10.87	11.87	12.87	13.87	14.87	15.87	16.87	17.87	18.87	19.87	20.87	21.87	22.87	23.87
7	7.64	8.64	9.64	10.64	11.64	12.64	13.64	14.64	15.64	16.64	17.64	18.64	19.64	20.64	21.64	22.64	23.64
8	7.43	8.43	9.43	10.43	11.43	12.43	13.43	14.43	15.43	16.43	17.43	18.43	19.43	20.43	21.43	22.43	23.43
9	7.24	8.24	9.24	10.24	11.24	12.24	13.24	14.24	15.24	16.24	17.24	18.24	19.24	20.24	21.24	22.24	23.24
10	7.08	8.08	9.08	10.08	11.08	12.08	13.08	14.08	15.08	16.08	17.08	18.08	19.08	20.08	21.08	22.08	23.08
11	6.93	7.93	8.93	9.93	10.93	11.93	12.93	13.93	14.93	15.93	16.93	17.93	18.93	19.93	20.93	21.93	22.93
12	6.79	7.79	8.79	9.79	10.79	11.79	12.79	13.79	14.79	15.79	16.79	17.79	18.79	19.79	20.79	21.79	22.79

Original Term: 24 MONTHS

MONTHS DELAY	4 %	5 %	6 %	7 %	8 %	9 %	10 %	11 %	12 %	13 %	14 %	15 %	16 %	17 %	18 %	19 %	20 %
0	8.80	9.80	10.80	11.80	12.80	13.80	14.80	15.80	16.80	17.80	18.80	19.80	20.80	21.80	22.80	23.80	24.80
1	8.44	9.44	10.44	11.44	12.44	13.44	14.44	15.44	16.44	17.44	18.44	19.44	20.44	21.44	22.44	23.44	24.44
2	8.14	9.14	10.14	11.14	12.14	13.14	14.14	15.14	16.14	17.14	18.14	19.14	20.14	21.14	22.14	23.14	24.14
3	7.87	8.87	9.87	10.87	11.87	12.87	13.87	14.87	15.87	16.87	17.87	18.87	19.87	20.87	21.87	22.87	23.87
4	7.64	8.64	9.64	10.64	11.64	12.64	13.64	14.64	15.64	16.64	17.64	18.64	19.64	20.64	21.64	22.64	23.64
5	7.43	8.43	9.43	10.43	11.43	12.43	13.43	14.43	15.43	16.43	17.43	18.43	19.43	20.43	21.43	22.43	23.43
6	7.24	8.24	9.24	10.24	11.24	12.24	13.24	14.24	15.24	16.24	17.24	18.24	19.24	20.24	21.24	22.24	23.24
7	7.08	8.08	9.08	10.08	11.08	12.08	13.08	14.08	15.08	16.08	17.08	18.08	19.08	20.08	21.08	22.08	23.08
8	6.93	7.93	8.93	9.93	10.93	11.93	12.93	13.93	14.93	15.93	16.93	17.93	18.93	19.93	20.93	21.93	22.93
9	6.79	7.79	8.79	9.79	10.79	11.79	12.79	13.79	14.79	15.79	16.79	17.79	18.79	19.79	20.79	21.79	22.79
10	6.67	7.67	8.67	9.67	10.67	11.67	12.67	13.67	14.67	15.67	16.67	17.67	18.67	19.67	20.67	21.67	22.67
11	6.55	7.55	8.55	9.55	10.55	11.55	12.55	13.55	14.55	15.55	16.55	17.55	18.55	19.55	20.55	21.55	22.55
12	6.45	7.45	8.45	9.45	10.45	11.45	12.45	13.45	14.45	15.45	16.45	17.45	18.45	19.45	20.45	21.45	22.45

Original Term: 36 MONTHS

MONTHS DELAY	4 %	5 %	6 %	7 %	8 %	9 %	10 %	11 %	12 %	13 %	14 %	15 %	16 %	17 %	18 %	19 %	20 %
0	7.24	8.24	9.24	10.24	11.24	12.24	13.24	14.24	15.24	16.24	17.24	18.24	19.24	20.24	21.24	22.24	23.24
1	7.08	8.08	9.08	10.08	11.08	12.08	13.08	14.08	15.08	16.08	17.08	18.08	19.08	20.08	21.08	22.08	23.08
2	6.93	7.93	8.93	9.93	10.93	11.93	12.93	13.93	14.93	15.93	16.93	17.93	18.93	19.93	20.93	21.93	22.93
3	6.79	7.79	8.79	9.79	10.79	11.79	12.79	13.79	14.79	15.79	16.79	17.79	18.79	19.79	20.79	21.79	22.79
4	6.67	7.67	8.67	9.67	10.67	11.67	12.67	13.67	14.67	15.67	16.67	17.67	18.67	19.67	20.67	21.67	22.67
5	6.55	7.55	8.55	9.55	10.55	11.55	12.55	13.55	14.55	15.55	16.55	17.55	18.55	19.55	20.55	21.55	22.55
6	6.45	7.45	8.45	9.45	10.45	11.45	12.45	13.45	14.45	15.45	16.45	17.45	18.45	19.45	20.45	21.45	22.45
7	6.35	7.35	8.35	9.35	10.35	11.35	12.35	13.35	14.35	15.35	16.35	17.35	18.35	19.35	20.35	21.35	22.35
8	6.26	7.26	8.26	9.26	10.26	11.26	12.26	13.26	14.26	15.26	16.26	17.26	18.26	19.26	20.26	21.26	22.26
9	6.18	7.18	8.18	9.18	10.18	11.18	12.18	13.18	14.18	15.18	16.18	17.18	18.18	19.18	20.18	21.18	22.18
10	6.11	7.11	8.11	9.11	10.11	11.11	12.11	13.11	14.11	15.11	16.11	17.11	18.11	19.11	20.11	21.11	22.11
11	6.03	7.03	8.03	9.03	10.03	11.03	12.03	13.03	14.03	15.03	16.03	17.03	18.03	19.03	20.03	21.03	22.03
12	5.97	6.97	7.97	8.97	9.97	10.97	11.97	12.97	13.97	14.97	15.97	16.97	17.97	18.97	19.97	20.97	21.97

Description: This table shows the average rate when points are paid and when repayment is delayed.

Example: The average rate is 21.09 % when 6 points are paid for an 8 % 6 month loan and repayment is delayed two months.

Original Term: 6 MONTHS

MONTHS DELAY	NOMINAL INTEREST RATE 4 %	5 %	6 %	7 %	8 %	9 %	10 %	11 %	12 %	13 %	14 %	15 %	16 %	17 %	18 %	19 %	20 %
0	24.57	25.57	26.57	27.57	28.57	29.57	30.57	31.57	32.57	33.57	34.57	35.57	36.57	37.57	38.57	39.57	40.57
1	20.00	21.00	22.00	23.00	24.00	25.00	26.00	27.00	28.00	29.00	30.00	31.00	32.00	33.00	34.00	35.00	36.00
2	17.09	18.09	19.09	20.09	21.09	22.09	23.09	24.09	25.09	26.09	27.09	28.09	29.09	30.09	31.09	32.09	33.09
3	15.08	16.08	17.08	18.08	19.08	20.08	21.08	22.08	23.08	24.08	25.08	26.08	27.08	28.08	29.08	30.08	31.08
4	13.60	14.60	15.60	16.60	17.60	18.60	19.60	20.60	21.60	22.60	23.60	24.60	25.60	26.60	27.60	28.60	29.60
5	12.47	13.47	14.47	15.47	16.47	17.47	18.47	19.47	20.47	21.47	22.47	23.47	24.47	25.47	26.47	27.47	28.47
6	11.58	12.58	13.58	14.58	15.58	16.58	17.58	18.58	19.58	20.58	21.58	22.58	23.58	24.58	25.58	26.58	27.58

Original Term: 12 MONTHS

MONTHS DELAY	NOMINAL INTEREST RATE 4 %	5 %	6 %	7 %	8 %	9 %	10 %	11 %	12 %	13 %	14 %	15 %	16 %	17 %	18 %	19 %	20 %
0	15.08	16.08	17.08	18.08	19.08	20.08	21.08	22.08	23.08	24.08	25.08	26.08	27.08	28.08	29.08	30.08	31.08
1	13.60	14.60	15.60	16.60	17.60	18.60	19.60	20.60	21.60	22.60	23.60	24.60	25.60	26.60	27.60	28.60	29.60
2	12.47	13.47	14.47	15.47	16.47	17.47	18.47	19.47	20.47	21.47	22.47	23.47	24.47	25.47	26.47	27.47	28.47
3	11.58	12.58	13.58	14.58	15.58	16.58	17.58	18.58	19.58	20.58	21.58	22.58	23.58	24.58	25.58	26.58	27.58
4	10.86	11.86	12.86	13.86	14.86	15.86	16.86	17.86	18.86	19.86	20.86	21.86	22.86	23.86	24.86	25.86	26.86
5	10.26	11.26	12.26	13.26	14.26	15.26	16.26	17.26	18.26	19.26	20.26	21.26	22.26	23.26	24.26	25.26	26.26
6	9.76	10.76	11.76	12.76	13.76	14.76	15.76	16.76	17.76	18.76	19.76	20.76	21.76	22.76	23.76	24.76	25.76
7	9.33	10.33	11.33	12.33	13.33	14.33	15.33	16.33	17.33	18.33	19.33	20.33	21.33	22.33	23.33	24.33	25.33
8	8.97	9.97	10.97	11.97	12.97	13.97	14.97	15.97	16.97	17.97	18.97	19.97	20.97	21.97	22.97	23.97	24.97
9	8.65	9.65	10.65	11.65	12.65	13.65	14.65	15.65	16.65	17.65	18.65	19.65	20.65	21.65	22.65	23.65	24.65
10	8.36	9.36	10.36	11.36	12.36	13.36	14.36	15.36	16.36	17.36	18.36	19.36	20.36	21.36	22.36	23.36	24.36
11	8.11	9.11	10.11	11.11	12.11	13.11	14.11	15.11	16.11	17.11	18.11	19.11	20.11	21.11	22.11	23.11	24.11
12	7.89	8.89	9.89	10.89	11.89	12.89	13.89	14.89	15.89	16.89	17.89	18.89	19.89	20.89	21.89	22.89	23.89

Original Term: 18 MONTHS

MONTHS DELAY	NOMINAL INTEREST RATE 4 %	5 %	6 %	7 %	8 %	9 %	10 %	11 %	12 %	13 %	14 %	15 %	16 %	17 %	18 %	19 %	20 %
0	11.58	12.58	13.58	14.58	15.58	16.58	17.58	18.58	19.58	20.58	21.58	22.58	23.58	24.58	25.58	26.58	27.58
1	10.86	11.86	12.86	13.86	14.86	15.86	16.86	17.86	18.86	19.86	20.86	21.86	22.86	23.86	24.86	25.86	26.86
2	10.26	11.26	12.26	13.26	14.26	15.26	16.26	17.26	18.26	19.26	20.26	21.26	22.26	23.26	24.26	25.26	26.26
3	9.76	10.76	11.76	12.76	13.76	14.76	15.76	16.76	17.76	18.76	19.76	20.76	21.76	22.76	23.76	24.76	25.76
4	9.33	10.33	11.33	12.33	13.33	14.33	15.33	16.33	17.33	18.33	19.33	20.33	21.33	22.33	23.33	24.33	25.33
5	8.97	9.97	10.97	11.97	12.97	13.97	14.97	15.97	16.97	17.97	18.97	19.97	20.97	21.97	22.97	23.97	24.97
6	8.65	9.65	10.65	11.65	12.65	13.65	14.65	15.65	16.65	17.65	18.65	19.65	20.65	21.65	22.65	23.65	24.65
7	8.36	9.36	10.36	11.36	12.36	13.36	14.36	15.36	16.36	17.36	18.36	19.36	20.36	21.36	22.36	23.36	24.36
8	8.11	9.11	10.11	11.11	12.11	13.11	14.11	15.11	16.11	17.11	18.11	19.11	20.11	21.11	22.11	23.11	24.11
9	7.89	8.89	9.89	10.89	11.89	12.89	13.89	14.89	15.89	16.89	17.89	18.89	19.89	20.89	21.89	22.89	23.89
10	7.69	8.69	9.69	10.69	11.69	12.69	13.69	14.69	15.69	16.69	17.69	18.69	19.69	20.69	21.69	22.69	23.69
11	7.51	8.51	9.51	10.51	11.51	12.51	13.51	14.51	15.51	16.51	17.51	18.51	19.51	20.51	21.51	22.51	23.51
12	7.35	8.35	9.35	10.35	11.35	12.35	13.35	14.35	15.35	16.35	17.35	18.35	19.35	20.35	21.35	22.35	23.35

Original Term: 24 MONTHS

MONTHS DELAY	NOMINAL INTEREST RATE 4 %	5 %	6 %	7 %	8 %	9 %	10 %	11 %	12 %	13 %	14 %	15 %	16 %	17 %	18 %	19 %	20 %
0	9.76	10.76	11.76	12.76	13.76	14.76	15.76	16.76	17.76	18.76	19.76	20.76	21.76	22.76	23.76	24.76	25.76
1	9.33	10.33	11.33	12.33	13.33	14.33	15.33	16.33	17.33	18.33	19.33	20.33	21.33	22.33	23.33	24.33	25.33
2	8.97	9.97	10.97	11.97	12.97	13.97	14.97	15.97	16.97	17.97	18.97	19.97	20.97	21.97	22.97	23.97	24.97
3	8.65	9.65	10.65	11.65	12.65	13.65	14.65	15.65	16.65	17.65	18.65	19.65	20.65	21.65	22.65	23.65	24.65
4	8.36	9.36	10.36	11.36	12.36	13.36	14.36	15.36	16.36	17.36	18.36	19.36	20.36	21.36	22.36	23.36	24.36
5	8.11	9.11	10.11	11.11	12.11	13.11	14.11	15.11	16.11	17.11	18.11	19.11	20.11	21.11	22.11	23.11	24.11
6	7.89	8.89	9.89	10.89	11.89	12.89	13.89	14.89	15.89	16.89	17.89	18.89	19.89	20.89	21.89	22.89	23.89
7	7.69	8.69	9.69	10.69	11.69	12.69	13.69	14.69	15.69	16.69	17.69	18.69	19.69	20.69	21.69	22.69	23.69
8	7.51	8.51	9.51	10.51	11.51	12.51	13.51	14.51	15.51	16.51	17.51	18.51	19.51	20.51	21.51	22.51	23.51
9	7.35	8.35	9.35	10.35	11.35	12.35	13.35	14.35	15.35	16.35	17.35	18.35	19.35	20.35	21.35	22.35	23.35
10	7.20	8.20	9.20	10.20	11.20	12.20	13.20	14.20	15.20	16.20	17.20	18.20	19.20	20.20	21.20	22.20	23.20
11	7.06	8.06	9.06	10.06	11.06	12.06	13.06	14.06	15.06	16.06	17.06	18.06	19.06	20.06	21.06	22.06	23.06
12	6.94	7.94	8.94	9.94	10.94	11.94	12.94	13.94	14.94	15.94	16.94	17.94	18.94	19.94	20.94	21.94	22.94

Original Term: 36 MONTHS

MONTHS DELAY	NOMINAL INTEREST RATE 4 %	5 %	6 %	7 %	8 %	9 %	10 %	11 %	12 %	13 %	14 %	15 %	16 %	17 %	18 %	19 %	20 %
0	7.89	8.89	9.89	10.89	11.89	12.89	13.89	14.89	15.89	16.89	17.89	18.89	19.89	20.89	21.89	22.89	23.89
1	7.69	8.69	9.69	10.69	11.69	12.69	13.69	14.69	15.69	16.69	17.69	18.69	19.69	20.69	21.69	22.69	23.69
2	7.51	8.51	9.51	10.51	11.51	12.51	13.51	14.51	15.51	16.51	17.51	18.51	19.51	20.51	21.51	22.51	23.51
3	7.35	8.35	9.35	10.35	11.35	12.35	13.35	14.35	15.35	16.35	17.35	18.35	19.35	20.35	21.35	22.35	23.35
4	7.20	8.20	9.20	10.20	11.20	12.20	13.20	14.20	15.20	16.20	17.20	18.20	19.20	20.20	21.20	22.20	23.20
5	7.06	8.06	9.06	10.06	11.06	12.06	13.06	14.06	15.06	16.06	17.06	18.06	19.06	20.06	21.06	22.06	23.06
6	6.94	7.94	8.94	9.94	10.94	11.94	12.94	13.94	14.94	15.94	16.94	17.94	18.94	19.94	20.94	21.94	22.94
7	6.82	7.82	8.82	9.82	10.82	11.82	12.82	13.82	14.82	15.82	16.82	17.82	18.82	19.82	20.82	21.82	22.82
8	6.72	7.72	8.72	9.72	10.72	11.72	12.72	13.72	14.72	15.72	16.72	17.72	18.72	19.72	20.72	21.72	22.72
9	6.62	7.62	8.62	9.62	10.62	11.62	12.62	13.62	14.62	15.62	16.62	17.62	18.62	19.62	20.62	21.62	22.62
10	6.53	7.53	8.53	9.53	10.53	11.53	12.53	13.53	14.53	15.53	16.53	17.53	18.53	19.53	20.53	21.53	22.53
11	6.44	7.44	8.44	9.44	10.44	11.44	12.44	13.44	14.44	15.44	16.44	17.44	18.44	19.44	20.44	21.44	22.44
12	6.36	7.36	8.36	9.36	10.36	11.36	12.36	13.36	14.36	15.36	16.36	17.36	18.36	19.36	20.36	21.36	22.36

TABLE **15**

Growth of 1

Interest Rates:	0, 1, 2, 3%; 4 to 4.875% by .25%, .125%; 5 to 9.50% by .25%, .125%, .10%; 9.75 to 11% by .25%; 12 to 16% by 1%.
Terms:	1 to 10 years, each year; 15, 20, 25, 30 years.
Compound Periods:	Continuous, daily, monthly, quarterly, semiannual, annual.

This table shows what a single $1 deposit made today will grow to in the future. Tables are shown for 6 compounding periods: continuous, daily, monthly, quarterly, semiannual, and annual.

Example: The balance in 5 years of a $1 deposit in a savings account that pays 5% interest compounded monthly is $1.28. To find the balance in 5 years of a $1,000 deposit, turn to the monthly compounding table on page 15-8. At 5%, the balance in 5 years is $1,283.40.

What amount must be deposited today to have $10,000 in 5 years in a savings account that pays 5% interest compounded monthly? The 5 year factor is 1.2834. To find the present balance, divide the future balance by the 5 year factor: 10,000 ÷ 1.2834 = 7,791.80. The amount to be deposited today is $7,791.80.

Example: An amount of $1,200 was deposited in a savings account 6 years ago; today, the balance is $1,700. Interest is compounded monthly. What is the rate at which the deposit earns interest? The answer is computed in the following 2 steps:

1. Find the Growth of 1 by dividing the balance today by the original balance:

$$1,700 \div 1,200 = 1.4166$$

2. Enter the monthly compounding table and scan the 6 year lines until the balance of 1.4166 is found. Because 1.4166 falls between 2 given values, the interest rate is computed by interpolation. As shown on page 15-8, the interest rate is about 5.82%.

Example: An investment of $1,000 made 6 years ago now has a value of $1,500. What is the rate of growth for this investment? First, find the Growth of 1 using the given formula: 1,500 ÷ 1,000 = 1.5000. Second, enter the monthly table and scan the 6 year lines until the balance is found. As shown on page 15-8, the Growth of 1 lies between 6.75% and 6.80%.

Example: A state university system offers a guaranteed tuition plan: A $3,000 payment into a trust fund today guarantees the payment of 4 years of tuition tomorrow. The payment must be made before the person is age 3. Today, the tuition is $1,500 per year. A look at the growth of these 2 amounts shows the assumptions that balance the equation.

Assume a 6% interest rate on the trust fund and a 3% inflation rate on the tuition. If the payment is made at age 3 and the person is ready for college at age 18, then the term for the Growth of 1 is 15 years. At 6% for 15 years compounded monthly, the Growth of 1 is 2.4541, and at 3%, it is 1.5674.

Payment to trust fund:
    3,000 × 2.4541 = 7,362
Tuition, 4 years:
    1,500 × 1.5674 = 2,351 × 4 = 9,404

To make the cash flows balance, either the interest rate must be increased to 7.7%, or the rate of inflation must be decreased to 1.3%.

$1 Million. If $1 million is the goal, an easy way to get there is to put a few dollars away at interest today, and then come back in 30 years and collect. The following table shows the deposits required today for interest rates of 4 to 16% to grow to $1 million in 30 years, with interest compounded monthly.

Interest Rate	Deposit Today	Interest Rate	Deposit Today
4%	$301,795	10%	$50,409
5	223,828	11	37,441
6	166,041	13	20,670
7	123,205	14	15,364
8	91,443	15	11,423
9	67,885	16	8,494

Rule of 72, the Number of Years for Money to Double. To calculate the number of years required for money to double, divide 72 by the interest rate.

Example: At an interest rate of 6%, money doubles in 12 years: $72 \div 6 = 12$.

To calculate the interest rate required for money to double, divide 72 by the number of years.

Example: To find the interest rate that must be paid to double money in 8 years, do the division: $72 \div 8 = 9$. The interest rate must be 9%.

Period. A "period" is the time interval between interest calculations. A "regular period" is usually 1 month, 1 quarter, 6 months, or 1 year. It is a discrete period of time.

Simple Interest. "Simple interest" is interest on an amount for a period. A rate of 4% on $100 for 1 year is $100 $\times .04 = \$4$. The interest on $100 at 4% for 1 month is $100 $\times (.04 \div 12) = \$.33$. Both the $4 and the $.33 are simple interest.

Compound Interest. Interest on a balance for a single period is always simple interest. Interest is "compounded" when the interest for a period is added to the principal balance to make a new balance, and interest is then computed on the new balance. Compounding takes place when the interest is converted to the new balance. This gives the impression that compound interest is interest computed on interest.

Continuous Compounding. "Continuous compounding" is interest computed for an infinitely small period of time for an infinitely large number of periods. The formula for continuous compounding for an Amount of 1 is:

$$\text{Amount of } 1 = e^{(\frac{Rate}{100} \times Time)}$$

$$= e^{R}$$

$$= 1 + \frac{R^1}{1!} + \frac{R^2}{2!} + \frac{R^3}{3!} + \cdots + \frac{R^N}{N!}$$

where R is the annual rate and N! is N factorial:

$$N! = 1 \times 2 \times 3 \times \cdots \times N$$

N can literally go on forever, depending on the degree of accuracy required; usually, however, N = 5 is adequate. By definition, the symbol e is the number $2.71828 \cdots$.

Example: The nominal annual rate is 6% and the time interval is 1 year; time = 1.

$$e^{.06} = 1 + .06 + \frac{(.06)^2}{1 \times 2} + \frac{(.06)^3}{1 \times 2 \times 3}$$

$$+ \frac{(.06)^4}{1 \times 2 \times 3 \times 4} + \frac{(.06)^5}{1 \times 2 \times 3 \times 4 \times 5}$$

$$= 1.06183654648$$

The Amount of 1, continuous compounding, is:

$$1.06183654648$$

When compounding is continuous there is only a rate and a term, 6% for 1 year, R = .06. At 6% for 2 years, R = .12. There are no intermediate periods—no days, months, or quarters—just a continuous interval of time.

Daily Compounding. Interest is computed each day. The rate per day is 1/360 or 1/365 of the nominal annual rate. A year is 365 days, which equals 365 periods.

Monthly Compounding. Interest is computed each month. The rate per month is 1/12 of the nominal annual rate; there are 12 periods per year.

Quarterly Compounding. Interest is computed each quarter. The rate per quarter is 1/4 of the nominal annual rate; there are 4 periods per year.

Semiannual Compounding. Interest is computed each 6 months. The rate per 6 months is 1/2 of the nominal annual rate; there are 2 periods per year.

Annual Compounding. Interest is computed once a year at the nominal annual rate; there is 1 period per year.

Bank Interest and Adjusted Annual Rate. The 1 day factor for bank interest is the interest rate divided by 360, 365, or 366. The adjusted annual rate may be different from the nominal rate, depending on the number of days in the basis year. For a nominal rate of 6%, the adjusted annual rate for the 3 years is shown in the following table:

		Adjusted Annual Rate
360 day year	$(365/360) \times 6 =$	6.0833
	$(366/360) \times 6 =$	6.1000
365 day year	$(365/365) \times 6 =$	6.0000
	$(366/365) \times 6 =$	6.0164
366 day year	$(366/366) \times 6 =$	6.0000

Example: At a nominal rate of 6%, compute the Amount of 1 for a 365 day year. Use 360 days in the basis year and continuous compounding.

$$\text{Amount of } 1 = e^{.060833} = 1.062721$$

Nominal Rate. The nominal rate is the named rate (e.g., a 5% passbook savings rate, a 6% mortgage loan, 8% coupon). The nominal rate is given per year, without regard for compounding frequency.

Effective Rate. The effective rate takes into account the effect of compounding interest. The effective rate and the Amount of 1 are computed by the same formula:

$$S = (1 + \frac{R}{m})^n$$

where:

R = nominal annual rate divided by 100
m = number of periods in the basis year
n = number of compounding periods in a year

The effective rate is the decimal portion of the result, minus 1, times 100.

Example: Compute the effective rate of a 6% nominal rate, for 365 days, on a 360 day basis year, compounded daily:

$$S = (1 + \frac{.06}{360})^{365} = 1.062716$$

The effective rate is 6.27%.

More Frequent Compounding Increases the Effective Rate. When interest is computed and compounded more frequently, the effective rate becomes higher. The following table shows the effective rate as the periods per year increase.

Compound Period	Periods Per Year	Effective Rate, %
Annual	1	6.00
Semiannual	2	6.09
Quarterly	4	6.136355
Monthly	12	6.167781
Weekly	52	6.179981
Daily	365	6.183131
Hourly	8,760	6.183632
Per minute	525,600	6.183654
Per second	31,536,000	6.183654
Continuous	Infinite	6.183654

The last 3 effective rates are identical carried out to 6 decimal places, but if carried out further, they differ. For example:

Per minute	6.183654255
Continuous	6.183654648

Beyond daily compounding, the difference among effective rates is very small. As the professor said when he stamped his foot on the platform, "Even that shakes the orbit of Mars—but not very much."

Description: This table shows what a single $ 1 deposit will grow to in the future.

Example: At 5 % one dollar will grow to $ 1.29 by the end of the fifth year.

YEAR	0.00 %	1.00 %	2.00 %	3.00 %	4.00 %	4.125%	4.25 %	4.375%	4.50 %	4.625%	4.75 %	4.875%
1	1.0000	1.0102	1.0205	1.0309	1.0414	1.0427	1.0440	1.0454	1.0467	1.0480	1.0493	1.0507
2	1.0000	1.0205	1.0414	1.0627	1.0845	1.0872	1.0900	1.0928	1.0955	1.0983	1.1011	1.1039
3	1.0000	1.0309	1.0627	1.0955	1.1294	1.1337	1.1380	1.1423	1.1467	1.1511	1.1554	1.1598
4	1.0000	1.0414	1.0845	1.1294	1.1761	1.1821	1.1881	1.1941	1.2002	1.2063	1.2124	1.2186
5	1.0000	1.0520	1.1067	1.1643	1.2248	1.2326	1.2404	1.2483	1.2562	1.2642	1.2723	1.2804
6	1.0000	1.0627	1.1294	1.2002	1.2755	1.2852	1.2950	1.3049	1.3149	1.3249	1.3350	1.3452
7	1.0000	1.0736	1.1525	1.2373	1.3283	1.3401	1.3521	1.3641	1.3763	1.3885	1.4009	1.4134
8	1.0000	1.0845	1.1761	1.2755	1.3833	1.3974	1.4116	1.4260	1.4405	1.4552	1.4700	1.4850
9	1.0000	1.0955	1.2002	1.3149	1.4405	1.4570	1.4738	1.4907	1.5078	1.5251	1.5426	1.5602
10	1.0000	1.1067	1.2248	1.3555	1.5001	1.5193	1.5386	1.5583	1.5781	1.5983	1.6187	1.6393
15	1.0000	1.1643	1.3555	1.5781	1.8374	1.8726	1.9086	1.9452	1.9825	2.0206	2.0594	2.0989
20	1.0000	1.2248	1.5001	1.8374	2.2504	2.3082	2.3674	2.4282	2.4905	2.5545	2.6201	2.6873
25	1.0000	1.2885	1.6602	2.1392	2.7563	2.8450	2.9366	3.0311	3.1287	3.2294	3.3334	3.4407
30	1.0000	1.3555	1.8374	2.4905	3.3759	3.5067	3.6426	3.7838	3.9304	4.0828	4.2410	4.4053

YEAR	5.00 %	5.10 %	5.125%	5.20 %	5.25 %	5.30 %	5.375%	5.40 %	5.50 %	5.60 %	5.625%	5.70 %
1	1.0520	1.0531	1.0533	1.0541	1.0547	1.0552	1.0560	1.0563	1.0573	1.0584	1.0587	1.0595
2	1.1067	1.1090	1.1095	1.1112	1.1123	1.1135	1.1152	1.1157	1.1180	1.1203	1.1208	1.1225
3	1.1643	1.1678	1.1687	1.1714	1.1731	1.1749	1.1776	1.1785	1.1821	1.1857	1.1866	1.1893
4	1.2248	1.2298	1.2310	1.2348	1.2373	1.2398	1.2436	1.2448	1.2499	1.2550	1.2562	1.2601
5	1.2885	1.2950	1.2967	1.3016	1.3049	1.3082	1.3132	1.3149	1.3216	1.3283	1.3300	1.3350
6	1.3555	1.3638	1.3658	1.3721	1.3763	1.3805	1.3868	1.3889	1.3974	1.4059	1.4080	1.4145
7	1.4260	1.4361	1.4387	1.4464	1.4515	1.4567	1.4644	1.4670	1.4775	1.4880	1.4907	1.4986
8	1.5001	1.5124	1.5154	1.5247	1.5309	1.5371	1.5465	1.5496	1.5622	1.5749	1.5781	1.5878
9	1.5781	1.5926	1.5962	1.6072	1.6146	1.6219	1.6331	1.6368	1.6518	1.6670	1.6708	1.6822
10	1.6602	1.6771	1.6814	1.6942	1.7028	1.7115	1.7245	1.7289	1.7465	1.7643	1.7688	1.7823
15	2.1392	2.1719	2.1802	2.2052	2.2221	2.2390	2.2647	2.2733	2.3082	2.3435	2.3525	2.3795
20	2.7563	2.8128	2.8271	2.8704	2.8996	2.9292	2.9741	2.9892	3.0504	3.1129	3.1287	3.1767
25	3.5515	3.6426	3.6658	3.7361	3.7838	3.8321	3.9056	3.9304	4.0313	4.1348	4.1611	4.2410
30	4.5760	4.7174	4.7534	4.8631	4.9376	5.0132	5.1289	5.1681	5.3277	5.4922	5.5341	5.6618

YEAR	5.75 %	5.80 %	5.875%	5.90 %	6.00 %	6.10 %	6.125%	6.20 %	6.25 %	6.30 %	6.375%	6.40 %
1	1.0600	1.0606	1.0614	1.0616	1.0627	1.0638	1.0641	1.0649	1.0654	1.0660	1.0668	1.0670
2	1.1237	1.1248	1.1265	1.1271	1.1294	1.1317	1.1322	1.1340	1.1351	1.1363	1.1380	1.1386
3	1.1911	1.1929	1.1957	1.1966	1.2002	1.2039	1.2048	1.2075	1.2094	1.2112	1.2140	1.2149
4	1.2626	1.2652	1.2690	1.2703	1.2755	1.2807	1.2820	1.2859	1.2885	1.2911	1.2950	1.2964
5	1.3384	1.3418	1.3469	1.3486	1.3555	1.3624	1.3641	1.3693	1.3728	1.3763	1.3815	1.3833
6	1.4188	1.4231	1.4296	1.4318	1.4405	1.4493	1.4515	1.4581	1.4626	1.4670	1.4738	1.4760
7	1.5039	1.5093	1.5173	1.5200	1.5309	1.5418	1.5445	1.5528	1.5583	1.5638	1.5722	1.5749
8	1.5942	1.6007	1.6105	1.6137	1.6269	1.6401	1.6435	1.6535	1.6602	1.6670	1.6771	1.6805
9	1.6899	1.6977	1.7093	1.7132	1.7289	1.7448	1.7488	1.7608	1.7688	1.7769	1.7891	1.7932
10	1.7914	1.8005	1.8142	1.8188	1.8374	1.8561	1.8608	1.8750	1.8845	1.8941	1.9086	1.9134
15	2.3976	2.4159	2.4436	2.4530	2.4905	2.5287	2.5383	2.5675	2.5871	2.6068	2.6367	2.6468
20	3.2090	3.2417	3.2914	3.3081	3.3759	3.4451	3.4626	3.5156	3.5515	3.5877	3.6426	3.6612
25	4.2951	4.3498	4.4333	4.4615	4.5760	4.6935	4.7233	4.8140	4.8754	4.9376	5.0323	5.0643
30	5.7486	5.8367	5.9714	6.0170	6.2028	6.3944	6.4432	6.5918	6.6929	6.7954	6.9522	7.0053

YEAR	6.50 %	6.60 %	6.625%	6.70 %	6.75 %	6.80 %	6.875%	6.90 %	7.00 %	7.10 %	7.125%	7.20 %
1	1.0681	1.0692	1.0695	1.0703	1.0708	1.0714	1.0722	1.0725	1.0736	1.0746	1.0749	1.0757
2	1.1409	1.1432	1.1438	1.1455	1.1467	1.1478	1.1496	1.1502	1.1525	1.1549	1.1554	1.1572
3	1.2186	1.2223	1.2232	1.2260	1.2279	1.2298	1.2326	1.2335	1.2373	1.2411	1.2420	1.2448
4	1.3016	1.3069	1.3082	1.3122	1.3149	1.3176	1.3216	1.3229	1.3283	1.3337	1.3350	1.3391
5	1.3903	1.3974	1.3991	1.4045	1.4080	1.4116	1.4170	1.4188	1.4260	1.4332	1.4350	1.4405
6	1.4850	1.4941	1.4963	1.5032	1.5078	1.5124	1.5193	1.5216	1.5309	1.5402	1.5426	1.5496
7	1.5862	1.5975	1.6003	1.6088	1.6146	1.6203	1.6289	1.6318	1.6435	1.6552	1.6581	1.6670
8	1.6942	1.7080	1.7115	1.7219	1.7289	1.7360	1.7465	1.7501	1.7643	1.7787	1.7823	1.7932
9	1.8096	1.8262	1.8304	1.8430	1.8514	1.8599	1.8726	1.8769	1.8941	1.9115	1.9158	1.9290
10	1.9329	1.9526	1.9576	1.9725	1.9825	1.9926	2.0078	2.0129	2.0334	2.0541	2.0594	2.0751
15	2.6873	2.7285	2.7389	2.7703	2.7915	2.8128	2.8450	2.8559	2.8996	2.9441	2.9553	2.9892
20	3.7361	3.8127	3.8321	3.8908	3.9304	3.9705	4.0313	4.0518	4.1348	4.2195	4.2410	4.3060
25	5.1943	5.3277	5.3616	5.4645	5.5341	5.6047	5.7123	5.7486	5.8962	6.0475	6.0860	6.2028
30	7.2216	7.4447	7.5015	7.6746	7.7922	7.9116	8.0942	8.1560	8.4079	8.6675	8.7337	8.9352

Description: This table shows what a single $ 1 deposit will grow to in the future.

Example: At 8 % one dollar will grow to $ 1.50 by the end of the fifth year.

YEAR	7.25 %	7.30 %	7.375%	7.40 %	7.50 %	7.60 %	7.625%	7.70 %	7.75 %	7.80 %	7.875%	7.90 %
1	1.0763	1.0768	1.0776	1.0779	1.0790	1.0801	1.0804	1.0812	1.0817	1.0823	1.0831	1.0834
2	1.1584	1.1595	1.1613	1.1619	1.1643	1.1666	1.1672	1.1690	1.1702	1.1714	1.1731	1.1737
3	1.2467	1.2486	1.2515	1.2524	1.2562	1.2601	1.2610	1.2639	1.2658	1.2678	1.2707	1.2716
4	1.3418	1.3445	1.3486	1.3500	1.3555	1.3610	1.3624	1.3665	1.3693	1.3721	1.3763	1.3777
5	1.4442	1.4478	1.4534	1.4552	1.4626	1.4700	1.4719	1.4775	1.4812	1.4850	1.4907	1.4926
6	1.5543	1.5591	1.5662	1.5686	1.5781	1.5878	1.5902	1.5975	1.6023	1.6072	1.6146	1.6170
7	1.6729	1.6788	1.6878	1.6908	1.7028	1.7150	1.7180	1.7272	1.7333	1.7395	1.7488	1.7519
8	1.8005	1.8078	1.8188	1.8225	1.8374	1.8523	1.8561	1.8674	1.8750	1.8826	1.8941	1.8980
9	1.9378	1.9467	1.9600	1.9645	1.9825	2.0007	2.0053	2.0190	2.0283	2.0376	2.0515	2.0562
10	2.0856	2.0962	2.1122	2.1176	2.1392	2.1610	2.1665	2.1830	2.1941	2.2052	2.2221	2.2277
15	3.0120	3.0350	3.0698	3.0815	3.1287	3.1767	3.1888	3.2254	3.2500	3.2748	3.3123	3.3250
20	4.3498	4.3942	4.4615	4.4842	4.5760	4.6698	4.6935	4.7654	4.8140	4.8631	4.9376	4.9627
25	6.2819	6.3620	6.4841	6.5253	6.6929	6.8647	6.9083	7.0409	7.1307	7.2216	7.3602	7.4070
30	9.0721	9.2112	9.4237	9.4956	9.7889	10.0912	10.1683	10.4029	10.5623	10.7242	10.9716	11.0554

YEAR	8.00 %	8.10 %	8.125%	8.20 %	8.25 %	8.30 %	8.375%	8.40 %	8.50 %	8.60 %	8.625%	8.70 %
1	1.0845	1.0856	1.0859	1.0867	1.0872	1.0878	1.0886	1.0889	1.0900	1.0911	1.0914	1.0922
2	1.1761	1.1785	1.1791	1.1809	1.1821	1.1833	1.1851	1.1857	1.1881	1.1905	1.1911	1.1929
3	1.2755	1.2794	1.2804	1.2833	1.2852	1.2872	1.2901	1.2911	1.2950	1.2990	1.3000	1.3029
4	1.3833	1.3889	1.3903	1.3945	1.3974	1.4002	1.4045	1.4059	1.4116	1.4173	1.4188	1.4231
5	1.5001	1.5078	1.5097	1.5154	1.5193	1.5231	1.5289	1.5309	1.5386	1.5465	1.5484	1.5543
6	1.6269	1.6368	1.6393	1.6468	1.6518	1.6568	1.6644	1.6670	1.6771	1.6874	1.6899	1.6977
7	1.7643	1.7769	1.7801	1.7896	1.7959	1.8023	1.8119	1.8151	1.8281	1.8411	1.8444	1.8542
8	1.9134	1.9290	1.9329	1.9447	1.9526	1.9605	1.9725	1.9765	1.9926	2.0088	2.0129	2.0252
9	2.0751	2.0941	2.0989	2.1133	2.1230	2.1327	2.1473	2.1522	2.1719	2.1919	2.1969	2.2120
10	2.2504	2.2733	2.2791	2.2965	2.3082	2.3199	2.3376	2.3435	2.3674	2.3916	2.3976	2.4159
15	3.3759	3.4277	3.4407	3.4802	3.5067	3.5335	3.5740	3.5877	3.6426	3.6985	3.7125	3.7551
20	5.0643	5.1681	5.1943	5.2739	5.3277	5.3820	5.4645	5.4922	5.6047	5.7195	5.7486	5.8367
25	7.5972	7.7922	7.8417	7.9922	8.0942	8.1974	8.3547	8.4079	8.6237	8.8451	8.9013	9.0721
30	11.3968	11.7488	11.8385	12.1116	12.2972	12.4857	12.7738	12.8713	13.2688	13.6786	13.7830	14.1011

YEAR	8.75 %	8.80 %	8.875%	8.90 %	9.00 %	9.10 %	9.125%	9.20 %	9.25 %	9.30 %	9.375%	9.40 %
1	1.0928	1.0933	1.0942	1.0944	1.0955	1.0967	1.0969	1.0978	1.0983	1.0989	1.0997	1.1000
2	1.1941	1.1954	1.1972	1.1978	1.2002	1.2027	1.2033	1.2051	1.2063	1.2075	1.2094	1.2100
3	1.3049	1.3069	1.3099	1.3109	1.3149	1.3189	1.3199	1.3229	1.3249	1.3269	1.3300	1.3310
4	1.4260	1.4289	1.4332	1.4347	1.4405	1.4464	1.4478	1.4522	1.4552	1.4581	1.4626	1.4641
5	1.5583	1.5622	1.5682	1.5702	1.5781	1.5862	1.5882	1.5942	1.5983	1.6023	1.6084	1.6105
6	1.7028	1.7080	1.7158	1.7184	1.7289	1.7395	1.7421	1.7501	1.7554	1.7608	1.7688	1.7715
7	1.8608	1.8674	1.8774	1.8807	1.8941	1.9076	1.9110	1.9212	1.9280	1.9349	1.9452	1.9487
8	2.0334	2.0417	2.0541	2.0583	2.0751	2.0920	2.0962	2.1090	2.1176	2.1262	2.1392	2.1435
9	2.2221	2.2322	2.2476	2.2527	2.2733	2.2942	2.2994	2.3152	2.3258	2.3364	2.3525	2.3578
10	2.4282	2.4405	2.4592	2.4654	2.4905	2.5159	2.5223	2.5416	2.5545	2.5675	2.5871	2.5936
15	3.7838	3.8127	3.8564	3.8711	3.9304	3.9907	4.0059	4.0518	4.0828	4.1139	4.1611	4.1770
20	5.8962	5.9563	6.0475	6.0783	6.2028	6.3299	6.3620	6.4595	6.5253	6.5918	6.6929	6.7269
25	9.1878	9.3050	9.4836	9.5439	9.7889	10.0402	10.1040	10.2979	10.4293	10.5623	10.7650	10.8335
30	14.3172	14.5366	14.8720	14.9855	15.4483	15.9254	16.0470	16.4173	16.6688	16.9243	17.3148	17.4470

YEAR	9.50 %	9.75 %	10.00 %	10.25 %	10.50 %	10.75 %	11.00 %	12.00 %	13.00 %	14.00 %	15.00 %	16.00 %
1	1.1011	1.1039	1.1067	1.1095	1.1123	1.1152	1.1180	1.1294	1.1409	1.1525	1.1643	1.1761
2	1.2124	1.2186	1.2248	1.2310	1.2373	1.2436	1.2499	1.2755	1.3016	1.3283	1.3555	1.3833
3	1.3350	1.3452	1.3555	1.3658	1.3763	1.3868	1.3974	1.4405	1.4850	1.5309	1.5781	1.6269
4	1.4700	1.4850	1.5001	1.5154	1.5309	1.5465	1.5622	1.6269	1.6942	1.7643	1.8374	1.9134
5	1.6187	1.6393	1.6602	1.6814	1.7028	1.7245	1.7465	1.8374	1.9329	2.0334	2.1392	2.2504
6	1.7823	1.8096	1.8374	1.8655	1.8941	1.9231	1.9526	2.0751	2.2052	2.3435	2.4905	2.6468
7	1.9625	1.9977	2.0334	2.0698	2.1069	2.1446	2.1830	2.3435	2.5159	2.7010	2.8996	3.1129
8	2.1610	2.2052	2.2504	2.2965	2.3435	2.3916	2.4405	2.6468	2.8704	3.1129	3.3759	3.6612
9	2.3795	2.4344	2.4905	2.5480	2.6068	2.6670	2.7285	2.9892	3.2748	3.5877	3.9304	4.3060
10	2.6201	2.6873	2.7563	2.8271	2.8996	2.9741	3.0504	3.3759	3.7361	4.1348	4.5760	5.0643
15	4.2410	4.4053	4.5760	4.7534	4.9376	5.1289	5.3277	6.2028	7.2216	8.4079	9.7889	11.3968
20	6.8647	7.2216	7.5972	7.9922	8.4079	8.8451	9.3050	11.3968	13.9588	17.0968	20.9401	25.6475
25	11.1116	11.8385	12.6129	13.4381	14.3172	15.2538	16.2517	20.9401	26.9812	34.7650	44.7944	57.7172
30	17.9858	19.4068	20.9401	22.5945	24.3797	26.3059	28.3842	38.4747	52.1522	70.6921	95.8227	129.8872

GROWTH OF 1

DAILY COMPOUNDING, 360 DAY YEAR

Description: This table shows what a single $ 1 deposit will grow to in the future.

Example: At 5 % one dollar will grow to $ 1.29 by the end of the fifth year.

YEAR	0.00 %	1.00 %	2.00 %	3.00 %	4.00 %	4.125%	4.25 %	4.375%	4.50 %	4.625%	4.75 %	4.875%
1	1.0000	1.0102	1.0205	1.0309	1.0414	1.0427	1.0440	1.0454	1.0467	1.0480	1.0493	1.0507
2	1.0000	1.0205	1.0414	1.0627	1.0845	1.0872	1.0900	1.0928	1.0955	1.0983	1.1011	1.1039
3	1.0000	1.0309	1.0627	1.0955	1.1294	1.1337	1.1380	1.1423	1.1467	1.1510	1.1554	1.1598
4	1.0000	1.0414	1.0845	1.1294	1.1761	1.1821	1.1881	1.1941	1.2002	1.2063	1.2124	1.2186
5	1.0000	1.0520	1.1067	1.1642	1.2248	1.2326	1.2404	1.2483	1.2562	1.2642	1.2722	1.2803
6	1.0000	1.0627	1.1294	1.2002	1.2755	1.2852	1.2950	1.3049	1.3149	1.3249	1.3350	1.3452
7	1.0000	1.0736	1.1525	1.2373	1.3283	1.3401	1.3520	1.3641	1.3762	1.3885	1.4009	1.4134
8	1.0000	1.0845	1.1761	1.2755	1.3832	1.3973	1.4116	1.4260	1.4405	1.4552	1.4700	1.4850
9	1.0000	1.0955	1.2002	1.3149	1.4405	1.4570	1.4737	1.4906	1.5077	1.5250	1.5425	1.5602
10	1.0000	1.1067	1.2248	1.3555	1.5001	1.5192	1.5386	1.5582	1.5781	1.5982	1.6186	1.6392
15	1.0000	1.1643	1.3555	1.5781	1.8373	1.8726	1.9085	1.9451	1.9824	2.0205	2.0593	2.0988
20	1.0000	1.2248	1.5001	1.8373	2.2503	2.3081	2.3673	2.4281	2.4904	2.5543	2.6199	2.6871
25	1.0000	1.2885	1.6602	2.1391	2.7561	2.8449	2.9364	3.0309	3.1285	3.2292	3.3331	3.4404
30	1.0000	1.3555	1.8373	2.4904	3.3757	3.5065	3.6424	3.7835	3.9301	4.0824	4.2406	4.4049

YEAR	5.00 %	5.10 %	5.125%	5.20 %	5.25 %	5.30 %	5.375%	5.40 %	5.50 %	5.60 %	5.625%	5.70 %
1	1.0520	1.0531	1.0533	1.0541	1.0547	1.0552	1.0560	1.0563	1.0573	1.0584	1.0587	1.0595
2	1.1067	1.1089	1.1095	1.1112	1.1123	1.1135	1.1151	1.1157	1.1180	1.1202	1.1208	1.1225
3	1.1642	1.1678	1.1687	1.1713	1.1731	1.1749	1.1776	1.1785	1.1821	1.1857	1.1866	1.1893
4	1.2248	1.2298	1.2310	1.2348	1.2373	1.2398	1.2435	1.2448	1.2499	1.2549	1.2562	1.2600
5	1.2885	1.2950	1.2967	1.3016	1.3049	1.3082	1.3132	1.3149	1.3215	1.3283	1.3299	1.3350
6	1.3555	1.3637	1.3658	1.3721	1.3762	1.3804	1.3867	1.3888	1.3973	1.4058	1.4080	1.4144
7	1.4259	1.4361	1.4387	1.4463	1.4515	1.4566	1.4644	1.4670	1.4774	1.4880	1.4906	1.4986
8	1.5001	1.5123	1.5154	1.5246	1.5308	1.5370	1.5464	1.5496	1.5622	1.5749	1.5781	1.5877
9	1.5781	1.5926	1.5962	1.6072	1.6145	1.6219	1.6330	1.6368	1.6518	1.6669	1.6707	1.6822
10	1.6602	1.6771	1.6813	1.6942	1.7028	1.7114	1.7245	1.7289	1.7465	1.7643	1.7687	1.7822
15	2.1391	2.1718	2.1801	2.2051	2.2219	2.2389	2.2646	2.2732	2.3080	2.3434	2.3523	2.3793
20	2.7561	2.8126	2.8268	2.8702	2.8994	2.9289	2.9738	2.9889	3.0502	3.1126	3.1284	3.1764
25	3.5512	3.6423	3.6655	3.7358	3.7834	3.8317	3.9052	3.9300	4.0309	4.1344	4.1606	4.2405
30	4.5756	4.7168	4.7528	4.8625	4.9370	5.0126	5.1283	5.1674	5.3270	5.4915	5.5334	5.6611

YEAR	5.75 %	5.80 %	5.875%	5.90 %	6.00 %	6.10 %	6.125%	6.20 %	6.25 %	6.30 %	6.375%	6.40 %
1	1.0600	1.0606	1.0614	1.0616	1.0627	1.0638	1.0641	1.0649	1.0654	1.0660	1.0668	1.0670
2	1.1237	1.1248	1.1265	1.1271	1.1294	1.1317	1.1322	1.1340	1.1351	1.1363	1.1380	1.1386
3	1.1911	1.1929	1.1956	1.1966	1.2002	1.2039	1.2048	1.2075	1.2094	1.2112	1.2140	1.2149
4	1.2626	1.2652	1.2690	1.2703	1.2755	1.2807	1.2819	1.2859	1.2885	1.2911	1.2950	1.2963
5	1.3384	1.3418	1.3469	1.3486	1.3555	1.3623	1.3641	1.3693	1.3727	1.3762	1.3815	1.3832
6	1.4187	1.4231	1.4296	1.4317	1.4405	1.4493	1.4515	1.4581	1.4625	1.4670	1.4737	1.4759
7	1.5039	1.5092	1.5173	1.5200	1.5308	1.5417	1.5445	1.5527	1.5582	1.5637	1.5721	1.5749
8	1.5942	1.6006	1.6104	1.6137	1.6268	1.6401	1.6434	1.6534	1.6601	1.6669	1.6771	1.6805
9	1.6899	1.6976	1.7092	1.7131	1.7288	1.7447	1.7487	1.7607	1.7687	1.7768	1.7890	1.7931
10	1.7913	1.8004	1.8141	1.8187	1.8373	1.8560	1.8607	1.8749	1.8844	1.8940	1.9085	1.9133
15	2.3975	2.4158	2.4435	2.4528	2.4904	2.5285	2.5381	2.5673	2.5868	2.6066	2.6365	2.6465
20	3.2087	3.2414	3.2911	3.3078	3.3756	3.4447	3.4622	3.5153	3.5511	3.5873	3.6422	3.6607
25	4.2946	4.3493	4.4328	4.4610	4.5755	4.6929	4.7227	4.8133	4.8747	4.9369	5.0316	5.0636
30	5.7478	5.8359	5.9705	6.0161	6.2019	6.3934	6.4422	6.5908	6.6918	6.7943	6.9510	7.0041

YEAR	6.50 %	6.60 %	6.625%	6.70 %	6.75 %	6.80 %	6.875%	6.90 %	7.00 %	7.10 %	7.125%	7.20 %
1	1.0681	1.0692	1.0695	1.0703	1.0708	1.0714	1.0722	1.0725	1.0735	1.0746	1.0749	1.0757
2	1.1409	1.1432	1.1438	1.1455	1.1467	1.1478	1.1496	1.1502	1.1525	1.1548	1.1554	1.1572
3	1.2186	1.2223	1.2232	1.2260	1.2279	1.2298	1.2326	1.2335	1.2373	1.2410	1.2420	1.2448
4	1.3016	1.3069	1.3082	1.3122	1.3149	1.3175	1.3215	1.3229	1.3282	1.3336	1.3350	1.3391
5	1.3903	1.3973	1.3991	1.4044	1.4080	1.4116	1.4169	1.4187	1.4259	1.4332	1.4350	1.4405
6	1.4849	1.4940	1.4963	1.5031	1.5077	1.5123	1.5192	1.5215	1.5308	1.5401	1.5425	1.5495
7	1.5861	1.5974	1.6002	1.6088	1.6145	1.6202	1.6289	1.6318	1.6434	1.6551	1.6580	1.6669
8	1.6941	1.7079	1.7114	1.7218	1.7288	1.7359	1.7465	1.7500	1.7642	1.7786	1.7822	1.7931
9	1.8095	1.8261	1.8303	1.8429	1.8513	1.8597	1.8725	1.8768	1.8940	1.9114	1.9157	1.9289
10	1.9328	1.9525	1.9574	1.9724	1.9824	1.9925	2.0077	2.0128	2.0333	2.0540	2.0592	2.0749
15	2.6871	2.7282	2.7386	2.7700	2.7912	2.8125	2.8447	2.8556	2.8993	2.9438	2.9550	2.9889
20	3.7357	3.8122	3.8316	3.8903	3.9299	3.9700	4.0308	4.0513	4.1343	4.2189	4.2404	4.3053
25	5.1936	5.3269	5.3607	5.4636	5.5333	5.6038	5.7113	5.7476	5.8952	6.0465	6.0849	6.2017
30	7.2204	7.4433	7.5001	7.6731	7.7907	7.9101	8.0926	8.1543	8.4061	8.6657	8.7318	8.9333

GROWTH OF 1

Description: This table shows what a single $ 1 deposit will grow to in the future.

Example: At 8 % one dollar will grow to $ 1.50 by the end of the fifth year.

YEAR	7.25 %	7.30 %	7.375%	7.40 %	7.50 %	7.60 %	7.625%	7.70 %	7.75 %	7.80 %	7.875%	7.90 %
1	1.0763	1.0768	1.0776	1.0779	1.0790	1.0801	1.0804	1.0812	1.0817	1.0823	1.0831	1.0834
2	1.1584	1.1595	1.1613	1.1619	1.1642	1.1666	1.1672	1.1690	1.1702	1.1713	1.1731	1.1737
3	1.2467	1.2486	1.2514	1.2524	1.2562	1.2600	1.2610	1.2639	1.2658	1.2677	1.2706	1.2716
4	1.3418	1.3445	1.3486	1.3500	1.3555	1.3610	1.3623	1.3665	1.3693	1.3720	1.3762	1.3776
5	1.4441	1.4478	1.4533	1.4551	1.4625	1.4700	1.4718	1.4774	1.4812	1.4849	1.4906	1.4925
6	1.5543	1.5590	1.5661	1.5685	1.5781	1.5877	1.5901	1.5974	1.6022	1.6071	1.6145	1.6169
7	1.6728	1.6787	1.6877	1.6907	1.7027	1.7149	1.7179	1.7271	1.7332	1.7394	1.7487	1.7518
8	1.8004	1.8077	1.8187	1.8224	1.8373	1.8522	1.8560	1.8673	1.8749	1.8825	1.8940	1.8978
9	1.9377	1.9465	1.9599	1.9644	1.9824	2.0006	2.0051	2.0189	2.0281	2.0374	2.0514	2.0561
10	2.0855	2.0961	2.1121	2.1174	2.1390	2.1608	2.1663	2.1828	2.1939	2.2050	2.2219	2.2275
15	3.0117	3.0346	3.0695	3.0811	3.1284	3.1763	3.1884	3.2249	3.2496	3.2744	3.3119	3.3245
20	4.3492	4.3935	4.4608	4.4835	4.5753	4.6690	4.6927	4.7646	4.8132	4.8622	4.9367	4.9618
25	6.2807	6.3608	6.4829	6.5241	6.6915	6.8633	6.9069	7.0394	7.1292	7.2201	7.3586	7.4054
30	9.0701	9.2091	9.4215	9.4934	9.7866	10.0888	10.1658	10.4003	10.5596	10.7214	10.9688	11.0525

YEAR	8.00 %	8.10 %	8.125%	8.20 %	8.25 %	8.30 %	8.375%	8.40 %	8.50 %	8.60 %	8.625%	8.70 %
1	1.0845	1.0856	1.0859	1.0867	1.0872	1.0878	1.0886	1.0889	1.0900	1.0911	1.0914	1.0922
2	1.1761	1.1785	1.1791	1.1809	1.1821	1.1833	1.1851	1.1857	1.1881	1.1905	1.1911	1.1929
3	1.2755	1.2793	1.2803	1.2832	1.2852	1.2871	1.2901	1.2911	1.2950	1.2989	1.2999	1.3029
4	1.3832	1.3888	1.3902	1.3945	1.3973	1.4001	1.4044	1.4058	1.4115	1.4173	1.4187	1.4230
5	1.5001	1.5077	1.5096	1.5154	1.5192	1.5231	1.5289	1.5308	1.5386	1.5464	1.5483	1.5542
6	1.6268	1.6367	1.6392	1.6467	1.6517	1.6568	1.6643	1.6669	1.6770	1.6873	1.6898	1.6976
7	1.7642	1.7768	1.7799	1.7894	1.7958	1.8022	1.8118	1.8150	1.8279	1.8410	1.8442	1.8541
8	1.9133	1.9289	1.9328	1.9446	1.9525	1.9604	1.9724	1.9764	1.9924	2.0087	2.0127	2.0250
9	2.0749	2.0939	2.0987	2.1131	2.1228	2.1325	2.1471	2.1520	2.1718	2.1917	2.1967	2.2117
10	2.2502	2.2731	2.2789	2.2963	2.3080	2.3197	2.3374	2.3433	2.3672	2.3913	2.3974	2.4157
15	3.3755	3.4272	3.4402	3.4797	3.5062	3.5330	3.5735	3.5871	3.6421	3.6979	3.7120	3.7545
20	5.0634	5.1671	5.1934	5.2729	5.3267	5.3809	5.4634	5.4911	5.6036	5.7184	5.7474	5.8355
25	7.5955	7.7904	7.8399	7.9904	8.0922	8.1954	8.3527	8.4058	8.6215	8.8428	8.8990	9.0697
30	11.3937	11.7455	11.8352	12.1082	12.2937	12.4821	12.7700	12.8675	13.2648	13.6743	13.7787	14.0966

YEAR	8.75 %	8.80 %	8.875%	8.90 %	9.00 %	9.10 %	9.125%	9.20 %	9.25 %	9.30 %	9.375%	9.40 %
1	1.0928	1.0933	1.0941	1.0944	1.0955	1.0966	1.0969	1.0978	1.0983	1.0989	1.0997	1.1000
2	1.1941	1.1953	1.1971	1.1978	1.2002	1.2026	1.2032	1.2051	1.2063	1.2075	1.2093	1.2100
3	1.3049	1.3069	1.3099	1.3108	1.3148	1.3188	1.3198	1.3229	1.3249	1.3269	1.3299	1.3309
4	1.4259	1.4288	1.4332	1.4346	1.4404	1.4463	1.4478	1.4522	1.4551	1.4581	1.4625	1.4640
5	1.5582	1.5621	1.5681	1.5701	1.5781	1.5861	1.5881	1.5941	1.5982	1.6022	1.6083	1.6104
6	1.7027	1.7079	1.7157	1.7183	1.7288	1.7394	1.7420	1.7500	1.7553	1.7606	1.7687	1.7714
7	1.8607	1.8673	1.8772	1.8806	1.8940	1.9074	1.9108	1.9210	1.9279	1.9347	1.9450	1.9485
8	2.0333	2.0415	2.0540	2.0581	2.0749	2.0918	2.0960	2.1088	2.1174	2.1260	2.1390	2.1433
9	2.2219	2.2320	2.2473	2.2525	2.2731	2.2939	2.2992	2.3150	2.3255	2.3362	2.3522	2.3576
10	2.4279	2.4403	2.4589	2.4651	2.4903	2.5156	2.5220	2.5413	2.5542	2.5671	2.5867	2.5933
15	3.7832	3.8121	3.8558	3.8705	3.9298	3.9900	4.0052	4.0511	4.0820	4.1132	4.1603	4.1762
20	5.8949	5.9550	6.0462	6.0769	6.2014	6.3284	6.3605	6.4580	6.5238	6.5902	6.6912	6.7252
25	9.1854	9.3025	9.4810	9.5412	9.7861	10.0373	10.1011	10.2949	10.4261	10.5591	10.7617	10.8301
30	14.3125	14.5318	14.8670	14.9805	15.4430	15.9199	16.0413	16.4114	16.6628	16.9181	17.3084	17.4405

YEAR	9.50 %	9.75 %	10.00 %	10.25 %	10.50 %	10.75 %	11.00 %	12.00 %	13.00 %	14.00 %	15.00 %	16.00 %
1	1.1011	1.1039	1.1067	1.1095	1.1123	1.1151	1.1180	1.1294	1.1409	1.1525	1.1642	1.1761
2	1.2124	1.2186	1.2248	1.2310	1.2372	1.2435	1.2498	1.2754	1.3016	1.3282	1.3554	1.3832
3	1.3350	1.3452	1.3554	1.3658	1.3762	1.3867	1.3973	1.4404	1.4849	1.5307	1.5780	1.6267
4	1.4699	1.4849	1.5001	1.5153	1.5308	1.5464	1.5621	1.6268	1.6941	1.7641	1.8371	1.9131
5	1.6186	1.6392	1.6601	1.6813	1.7027	1.7244	1.7464	1.8372	1.9327	2.0331	2.1388	2.2500
6	1.7822	1.8095	1.8372	1.8654	1.8939	1.9230	1.9524	2.0748	2.2049	2.3432	2.4901	2.6462
7	1.9624	1.9975	2.0332	2.0696	2.1067	2.1444	2.1827	2.3432	2.5155	2.7004	2.8990	3.1121
8	2.1607	2.2050	2.2502	2.2962	2.3433	2.3912	2.4402	2.6463	2.8698	3.1122	3.3751	3.6601
9	2.3792	2.4341	2.4902	2.5477	2.6064	2.6666	2.7281	2.9886	3.2741	3.5868	3.9293	4.3046
10	2.6197	2.6870	2.7559	2.8266	2.8992	2.9736	3.0499	3.3752	3.7353	4.1337	4.5746	5.0625
15	4.2402	4.4044	4.5751	4.7523	4.9364	5.1277	5.3263	6.2009	7.2191	8.4044	9.7843	11.3906
20	6.8629	7.2197	7.5950	7.9899	8.4052	8.8422	9.3019	11.3922	13.9522	17.0873	20.9269	25.6290
25	11.1080	11.8345	12.6085	13.4331	14.3116	15.2476	16.2447	20.9295	26.9651	34.7410	44.7590	57.6652
30	17.9790	19.3990	20.9313	22.5845	24.3683	26.2930	28.3697	38.4513	52.1150	70.6336	95.7317	129.7469

Description: This table shows what a single $ 1 deposit will grow to in the future.

Example: At 5 % one dollar will grow to $ 1.28 by the end of the fifth year.

YEAR	0.00 %	1.00 %	2.00 %	3.00 %	4.00 %	4.125%	4.25 %	4.375%	4.50 %	4.625%	4.75 %	4.875%
1	1.0000	1.0101	1.0202	1.0305	1.0408	1.0421	1.0434	1.0447	1.0460	1.0473	1.0486	1.0500
2	1.0000	1.0202	1.0408	1.0618	1.0833	1.0860	1.0887	1.0914	1.0942	1.0969	1.0997	1.1024
3	1.0000	1.0305	1.0618	1.0942	1.1275	1.1317	1.1360	1.1402	1.1445	1.1488	1.1531	1.1575
4	1.0000	1.0408	1.0833	1.1275	1.1735	1.1794	1.1853	1.1912	1.1972	1.2032	1.2092	1.2153
5	1.0000	1.0513	1.1052	1.1618	1.2214	1.2290	1.2368	1.2445	1.2523	1.2602	1.2681	1.2760
6	1.0000	1.0618	1.1275	1.1972	1.2712	1.2808	1.2904	1.3002	1.3099	1.3198	1.3297	1.3397
7	1.0000	1.0725	1.1503	1.2337	1.3231	1.3347	1.3465	1.3583	1.3702	1.3823	1.3944	1.4067
8	1.0000	1.0833	1.1735	1.2712	1.3771	1.3909	1.4049	1.4190	1.4333	1.4477	1.4622	1.4769
9	1.0000	1.0942	1.1972	1.3099	1.4333	1.4495	1.4659	1.4825	1.4993	1.5162	1.5334	1.5507
10	1.0000	1.1052	1.2214	1.3498	1.4918	1.5106	1.5296	1.5488	1.5683	1.5880	1.6080	1.6282
15	1.0000	1.1618	1.3498	1.5683	1.8221	1.8565	1.8917	1.9275	1.9640	2.0011	2.0390	2.0776
20	1.0000	1.2214	1.4918	1.8221	2.2254	2.2818	2.3395	2.3987	2.4595	2.5217	2.5855	2.6510
25	1.0000	1.2840	1.6487	2.1169	2.7181	2.8044	2.8934	2.9853	3.0800	3.1778	3.2786	3.3827
30	1.0000	1.3499	1.8221	2.4595	3.3199	3.4467	3.5784	3.7152	3.8571	4.0045	4.1575	4.3163

YEAR	5.00 %	5.10 %	5.125%	5.20 %	5.25 %	5.30 %	5.375%	5.40 %	5.50 %	5.60 %	5.625%	5.70 %
1	1.0513	1.0523	1.0526	1.0534	1.0539	1.0544	1.0552	1.0555	1.0565	1.0576	1.0579	1.0587
2	1.1052	1.1074	1.1079	1.1096	1.1107	1.1118	1.1135	1.1140	1.1163	1.1185	1.1191	1.1207
3	1.1618	1.1653	1.1662	1.1688	1.1706	1.1723	1.1750	1.1758	1.1794	1.1829	1.1838	1.1865
4	1.2214	1.2263	1.2275	1.2312	1.2337	1.2361	1.2398	1.2411	1.2461	1.2510	1.2523	1.2561
5	1.2840	1.2904	1.2921	1.2969	1.3002	1.3034	1.3083	1.3099	1.3165	1.3231	1.3248	1.3297
6	1.3498	1.3580	1.3600	1.3661	1.3702	1.3743	1.3805	1.3826	1.3909	1.3993	1.4014	1.4077
7	1.4190	1.4290	1.4315	1.4390	1.4441	1.4491	1.4568	1.4593	1.4696	1.4799	1.4825	1.4903
8	1.4918	1.5038	1.5068	1.5158	1.5219	1.5280	1.5372	1.5403	1.5527	1.5651	1.5683	1.5777
9	1.5683	1.5824	1.5860	1.5967	1.6039	1.6112	1.6221	1.6257	1.6404	1.6553	1.6590	1.6702
10	1.6487	1.6652	1.6694	1.6820	1.6904	1.6989	1.7117	1.7159	1.7332	1.7506	1.7550	1.7682
15	2.1169	2.1489	2.1570	2.1814	2.1978	2.2143	2.2394	2.2478	2.2817	2.3162	2.3249	2.3512
20	2.7181	2.7730	2.7869	2.8290	2.8574	2.8861	2.9298	2.9444	3.0039	3.0646	3.0799	3.1265
25	3.4900	3.5784	3.6008	3.6690	3.7151	3.7618	3.8330	3.8570	3.9547	4.0548	4.0802	4.1574
30	4.4812	4.6177	4.6524	4.7583	4.8302	4.9032	5.0147	5.0525	5.2063	5.3649	5.4052	5.5282

YEAR	5.75 %	5.80 %	5.875%	5.90 %	6.00 %	6.10 %	6.125%	6.20 %	6.25 %	6.30 %	6.375%	6.40 %
1	1.0592	1.0597	1.0605	1.0608	1.0618	1.0629	1.0632	1.0640	1.0645	1.0650	1.0658	1.0661
2	1.1219	1.1230	1.1247	1.1252	1.1275	1.1297	1.1303	1.1320	1.1331	1.1343	1.1360	1.1365
3	1.1883	1.1900	1.1927	1.1936	1.1972	1.2008	1.2017	1.2044	1.2062	1.2080	1.2107	1.2117
4	1.2586	1.2611	1.2649	1.2662	1.2712	1.2763	1.2776	1.2814	1.2840	1.2866	1.2904	1.2917
5	1.3331	1.3364	1.3414	1.3431	1.3498	1.3566	1.3583	1.3634	1.3668	1.3702	1.3754	1.3771
6	1.4120	1.4162	1.4226	1.4247	1.4333	1.4419	1.4441	1.4506	1.4549	1.4593	1.4659	1.4681
7	1.4955	1.5008	1.5087	1.5113	1.5219	1.5326	1.5353	1.5434	1.5488	1.5542	1.5624	1.5651
8	1.5840	1.5904	1.5999	1.6031	1.6160	1.6290	1.6322	1.6421	1.6487	1.6553	1.6652	1.6686
9	1.6778	1.6853	1.6967	1.7006	1.7159	1.7314	1.7353	1.7471	1.7550	1.7629	1.7748	1.7788
10	1.7771	1.7860	1.7994	1.8039	1.8220	1.8403	1.8449	1.8588	1.8681	1.8775	1.8916	1.8964
15	2.3689	2.3867	2.4137	2.4228	2.4594	2.4966	2.5060	2.5343	2.5534	2.5726	2.6017	2.6115
20	3.1579	3.1896	3.2378	3.2541	3.3198	3.3868	3.4038	3.4552	3.4900	3.5250	3.5783	3.5962
25	4.2097	4.2626	4.3433	4.3705	4.4811	4.5946	4.6234	4.7109	4.7701	4.8301	4.9215	4.9523
30	5.6118	5.6966	5.8262	5.8700	6.0488	6.2329	6.2798	6.4227	6.5198	6.6183	6.7689	6.8198

YEAR	6.50 %	6.60 %	6.625%	6.70 %	6.75 %	6.80 %	6.875%	6.90 %	7.00 %	7.10 %	7.125%	7.20 %
1	1.0672	1.0682	1.0685	1.0693	1.0698	1.0704	1.0712	1.0714	1.0725	1.0736	1.0738	1.0746
2	1.1388	1.1411	1.1417	1.1434	1.1445	1.1457	1.1474	1.1480	1.1503	1.1526	1.1531	1.1549
3	1.2153	1.2189	1.2199	1.2226	1.2244	1.2263	1.2290	1.2300	1.2337	1.2374	1.2383	1.2411
4	1.2969	1.3021	1.3034	1.3073	1.3099	1.3126	1.3165	1.3178	1.3231	1.3284	1.3297	1.3337
5	1.3840	1.3909	1.3927	1.3979	1.4014	1.4049	1.4102	1.4119	1.4190	1.4261	1.4279	1.4333
6	1.4769	1.4858	1.4880	1.4948	1.4992	1.5038	1.5105	1.5128	1.5219	1.5311	1.5334	1.5403
7	1.5761	1.5872	1.5900	1.5983	1.6039	1.6096	1.6180	1.6209	1.6322	1.6437	1.6466	1.6552
8	1.6819	1.6955	1.6989	1.7091	1.7159	1.7228	1.7332	1.7366	1.7506	1.7646	1.7682	1.7788
9	1.7949	1.8111	1.8152	1.8275	1.8357	1.8440	1.8565	1.8607	1.8775	1.8945	1.8987	1.9116
10	1.9154	1.9347	1.9395	1.9541	1.9639	1.9738	1.9886	1.9936	2.0136	2.0339	2.0389	2.0543
15	2.6509	2.6910	2.7011	2.7317	2.7522	2.7729	2.8043	2.8148	2.8574	2.9005	2.9114	2.9444
20	3.6689	3.7430	3.7617	3.8186	3.8569	3.8957	3.9546	3.9744	4.0547	4.1365	4.1573	4.2201
25	5.0777	5.2062	5.2388	5.3380	5.4051	5.4731	5.5766	5.6116	5.7536	5.8993	5.9362	6.0486
30	7.0275	7.2414	7.2960	7.4619	7.5747	7.6891	7.8641	7.9233	8.1645	8.4131	8.4764	8.6693

GROWTH OF 1

Description: This table shows what a single $ 1 deposit will grow to in the future.

Example: At 8 % one dollar will grow to $ 1.49 by the end of the fifth year.

YEAR	7.25 %	7.30 %	7.375%	7.40 %	7.50 %	7.60 %	7.625%	7.70 %	7.75 %	7.80 %	7.875%	7.90 %
1	1.0752	1.0757	1.0765	1.0768	1.0779	1.0790	1.0792	1.0800	1.0806	1.0811	1.0819	1.0822
2	1.1560	1.1572	1.1589	1.1595	1.1618	1.1641	1.1647	1.1665	1.1676	1.1688	1.1706	1.1711
3	1.2429	1.2448	1.2476	1.2485	1.2523	1.2561	1.2570	1.2598	1.2617	1.2636	1.2665	1.2674
4	1.3364	1.3391	1.3431	1.3444	1.3498	1.3552	1.3566	1.3607	1.3634	1.3661	1.3702	1.3716
5	1.4369	1.4405	1.4459	1.4477	1.4549	1.4622	1.4641	1.4696	1.4732	1.4769	1.4825	1.4843
6	1.5449	1.5495	1.5565	1.5589	1.5682	1.5777	1.5800	1.5872	1.5919	1.5967	1.6039	1.6063
7	1.6610	1.6669	1.6756	1.6786	1.6904	1.7022	1.7052	1.7142	1.7202	1.7262	1.7353	1.7384
8	1.7859	1.7931	1.8039	1.8075	1.8220	1.8366	1.8403	1.8514	1.8588	1.8663	1.8775	1.8812
9	1.9202	1.9289	1.9419	1.9463	1.9639	1.9816	1.9861	1.9996	2.0086	2.0176	2.0313	2.0359
10	2.0646	2.0749	2.0905	2.0958	2.1168	2.1381	2.1435	2.1596	2.1704	2.1813	2.1977	2.2032
15	2.9665	2.9889	3.0227	3.0340	3.0799	3.1264	3.1381	3.1736	3.1975	3.2216	3.2580	3.2703
20	4.2625	4.3053	4.3704	4.3923	4.4810	4.5715	4.5944	4.6638	4.7107	4.7580	4.8299	4.8541
25	6.1246	6.2017	6.3190	6.3586	6.5196	6.6846	6.7265	6.8538	6.9399	7.0272	7.1602	7.2051
30	8.8003	8.9333	9.1365	9.2053	9.4855	9.7744	9.8479	10.0720	10.2242	10.3786	10.6148	10.6946

YEAR	8.00 %	8.10 %	8.125%	8.20 %	8.25 %	8.30 %	8.375%	8.40 %	8.50 %	8.60 %	8.625%	8.70 %
1	1.0833	1.0844	1.0846	1.0854	1.0860	1.0865	1.0873	1.0876	1.0887	1.0898	1.0901	1.0909
2	1.1735	1.1758	1.1764	1.1782	1.1794	1.1806	1.1823	1.1829	1.1853	1.1877	1.1882	1.1900
3	1.2712	1.2750	1.2760	1.2789	1.2808	1.2827	1.2856	1.2866	1.2904	1.2943	1.2953	1.2982
4	1.3771	1.3826	1.3840	1.3881	1.3909	1.3937	1.3979	1.3993	1.4049	1.4105	1.4119	1.4162
5	1.4918	1.4992	1.5011	1.5067	1.5105	1.5143	1.5200	1.5219	1.5295	1.5372	1.5391	1.5449
6	1.6160	1.6257	1.6282	1.6355	1.6404	1.6453	1.6528	1.6552	1.6652	1.6752	1.6777	1.6853
7	1.7506	1.7629	1.7659	1.7752	1.7815	1.7877	1.7971	1.8003	1.8129	1.8256	1.8288	1.8385
8	1.8963	1.9116	1.9154	1.9269	1.9346	1.9424	1.9541	1.9580	1.9737	1.9896	1.9936	2.0055
9	2.0543	2.0728	2.0775	2.0916	2.1010	2.1105	2.1248	2.1296	2.1488	2.1682	2.1731	2.1878
10	2.2253	2.2477	2.2533	2.2703	2.2817	2.2931	2.3104	2.3161	2.3394	2.3629	2.3688	2.3867
15	3.3197	3.3698	3.3825	3.4208	3.4465	3.4724	3.5117	3.5249	3.5782	3.6322	3.6459	3.6871
20	4.9522	5.0522	5.0775	5.1542	5.2060	5.2583	5.3378	5.3645	5.4729	5.5834	5.6114	5.6962
25	7.3874	7.5744	7.6219	7.7661	7.8638	7.9627	8.1133	8.1642	8.3708	8.5827	8.6365	8.7999
30	11.0203	11.3558	11.4413	11.7016	11.8784	12.0579	12.3322	12.4250	12.8033	13.1931	13.2924	13.5948

YEAR	8.75 %	8.80 %	8.875%	8.90 %	9.00 %	9.10 %	9.125%	9.20 %	9.25 %	9.30 %	9.375%	9.40 %
1	1.0914	1.0920	1.0928	1.0931	1.0942	1.0953	1.0955	1.0964	1.0969	1.0974	1.0983	1.0985
2	1.1912	1.1924	1.1942	1.1948	1.1972	1.1996	1.2002	1.2020	1.2032	1.2044	1.2062	1.2068
3	1.3001	1.3021	1.3050	1.3060	1.3099	1.3139	1.3148	1.3178	1.3198	1.3218	1.3247	1.3257
4	1.4190	1.4218	1.4261	1.4275	1.4333	1.4390	1.4404	1.4448	1.4477	1.4506	1.4549	1.4564
5	1.5487	1.5526	1.5585	1.5604	1.5682	1.5761	1.5781	1.5840	1.5879	1.5919	1.5979	1.5999
6	1.6904	1.6954	1.7031	1.7056	1.7159	1.7262	1.7288	1.7366	1.7418	1.7471	1.7549	1.7576
7	1.8449	1.8514	1.8611	1.8644	1.8775	1.8906	1.8940	1.9039	1.9106	1.9173	1.9274	1.9308
8	2.0136	2.0217	2.0338	2.0379	2.0543	2.0707	2.0749	2.0874	2.0957	2.1041	2.1168	2.1210
9	2.1977	2.2076	2.2225	2.2276	2.2477	2.2680	2.2731	2.2885	2.2988	2.3092	2.3248	2.3301
10	2.3986	2.4106	2.4288	2.4349	2.4593	2.4840	2.4903	2.5090	2.5216	2.5342	2.5533	2.5597
15	3.7149	3.7428	3.7852	3.7994	3.8568	3.9151	3.9298	3.9742	4.0041	4.0343	4.0799	4.0952
20	5.7534	5.8112	5.8990	5.9286	6.0483	6.1705	6.2014	6.2951	6.3583	6.4222	6.5192	6.5519
25	8.9106	9.0226	9.1933	9.2510	9.4851	9.7252	9.7861	9.9713	10.0967	10.2237	10.4171	10.4824
30	13.8002	14.0087	14.3274	14.4353	14.8748	15.3277	15.4430	15.7943	16.0330	16.2752	16.6455	16.7708

YEAR	9.50 %	9.75 %	10.00 %	10.25 %	10.50 %	10.75 %	11.00 %	12.00 %	13.00 %	14.00 %	15.00 %	16.00 %
1	1.0996	1.1024	1.1052	1.1079	1.1107	1.1135	1.1163	1.1275	1.1388	1.1502	1.1618	1.1735
2	1.2092	1.2153	1.2214	1.2275	1.2336	1.2398	1.2460	1.2712	1.2969	1.3231	1.3498	1.3770
3	1.3297	1.3397	1.3498	1.3600	1.3702	1.3805	1.3909	1.4332	1.4769	1.5218	1.5682	1.6159
4	1.4622	1.4769	1.4917	1.5067	1.5219	1.5372	1.5526	1.6159	1.6819	1.7505	1.8219	1.8962
5	1.6079	1.6281	1.6486	1.6693	1.6903	1.7116	1.7331	1.8219	1.9153	2.0135	2.1167	2.2252
6	1.7681	1.7949	1.8220	1.8495	1.8774	1.9058	1.9346	2.0542	2.1812	2.3160	2.4591	2.6111
7	1.9443	1.9786	2.0136	2.0491	2.0853	2.1221	2.1595	2.3160	2.4839	2.6640	2.8570	3.0641
8	2.1381	2.1812	2.2253	2.2702	2.3161	2.3629	2.4106	2.6113	2.8287	3.0642	3.3193	3.5956
9	2.3511	2.4046	2.4593	2.5152	2.5725	2.6310	2.6908	2.9442	3.2213	3.5246	3.8564	4.2194
10	2.5854	2.6508	2.7179	2.7867	2.8572	2.9295	3.0037	3.3195	3.6684	4.0541	4.4803	4.9513
15	4.1571	4.3159	4.4808	4.6519	4.8296	5.0141	5.2057	6.0479	7.0262	8.1629	9.4834	11.0174
20	6.6842	7.0269	7.3870	7.7657	8.1637	8.5821	9.0220	11.0188	13.4575	16.4358	20.0732	24.5153
25	10.7477	11.4407	12.1783	12.9635	13.7994	14.6891	15.6362	20.0756	25.7754	33.0932	42.4883	54.5503
30	17.2814	18.6269	20.0773	21.6405	23.3255	25.1416	27.0992	36.5766	49.3682	66.6327	89.9340	121.3827

Description: This table shows what a single $ 1 deposit will grow to in the future.

Example: At 5 % one dollar will grow to $ 1.28 by the end of the fifth year.

YEAR	0.00 %	1.00 %	2.00 %	3.00 %	4.00 %	4.125%	4.25 %	4.375%	4.50 %	4.625%	4.75 %	4.875%
1	1.0000	1.0100	1.0202	1.0304	1.0407	1.0420	1.0433	1.0446	1.0459	1.0472	1.0485	1.0499
2	1.0000	1.0202	1.0408	1.0618	1.0831	1.0858	1.0886	1.0913	1.0940	1.0967	1.0995	1.1022
3	1.0000	1.0304	1.0618	1.0941	1.1273	1.1315	1.1357	1.1400	1.1442	1.1485	1.1528	1.1571
4	1.0000	1.0408	1.0832	1.1273	1.1732	1.1791	1.1849	1.1909	1.1968	1.2028	1.2088	1.2148
5	1.0000	1.0512	1.1051	1.1616	1.2210	1.2286	1.2363	1.2440	1.2518	1.2596	1.2675	1.2754
6	1.0000	1.0618	1.1274	1.1969	1.2707	1.2803	1.2899	1.2996	1.3093	1.3191	1.3290	1.3390
7	1.0000	1.0725	1.1501	1.2334	1.3225	1.3341	1.3458	1.3576	1.3695	1.3814	1.3935	1.4057
8	1.0000	1.0833	1.1734	1.2709	1.3764	1.3902	1.4041	1.4182	1.4324	1.4467	1.4612	1.4758
9	1.0000	1.0941	1.1970	1.3095	1.4325	1.4486	1.4650	1.4815	1.4982	1.5151	1.5321	1.5494
10	1.0000	1.1051	1.2212	1.3494	1.4908	1.5095	1.5284	1.5476	1.5670	1.5866	1.6065	1.6266
15	1.0000	1.1618	1.3495	1.5674	1.8203	1.8546	1.8896	1.9253	1.9616	1.9985	2.0362	2.0746
20	1.0000	1.2213	1.4913	1.8208	2.2226	2.2787	2.3361	2.3951	2.4555	2.5174	2.5809	2.6459
25	1.0000	1.2839	1.6480	2.1150	2.7138	2.7996	2.8882	2.9795	3.0737	3.1709	3.2712	3.3746
30	1.0000	1.3497	1.8212	2.4568	3.3135	3.4397	3.5706	3.7066	3.8477	3.9942	4.1462	4.3040

YEAR	5.00 %	5.10 %	5.125%	5.20 %	5.25 %	5.30 %	5.375%	5.40 %	5.50 %	5.60 %	5.625%	5.70 %
1	1.0512	1.0522	1.0525	1.0533	1.0538	1.0543	1.0551	1.0554	1.0564	1.0575	1.0577	1.0585
2	1.1049	1.1071	1.1077	1.1094	1.1105	1.1116	1.1132	1.1138	1.1160	1.1182	1.1188	1.1204
3	1.1615	1.1649	1.1658	1.1684	1.1702	1.1719	1.1746	1.1754	1.1789	1.1825	1.1834	1.1860
4	1.2209	1.2258	1.2270	1.2307	1.2331	1.2356	1.2393	1.2405	1.2455	1.2504	1.2517	1.2554
5	1.2834	1.2898	1.2914	1.2962	1.2994	1.3027	1.3075	1.3092	1.3157	1.3223	1.3239	1.3289
6	1.3490	1.3571	1.3591	1.3652	1.3693	1.3734	1.3796	1.3816	1.3899	1.3982	1.4003	1.4066
7	1.4180	1.4280	1.4304	1.4379	1.4430	1.4480	1.4556	1.4581	1.4683	1.4786	1.4812	1.4889
8	1.4906	1.5025	1.5055	1.5145	1.5206	1.5266	1.5358	1.5388	1.5511	1.5635	1.5667	1.5760
9	1.5668	1.5810	1.5845	1.5952	1.6023	1.6095	1.6204	1.6240	1.6386	1.6534	1.6571	1.6683
10	1.6470	1.6635	1.6676	1.6801	1.6885	1.6970	1.7097	1.7139	1.7311	1.7484	1.7527	1.7659
15	2.1137	2.1455	2.1535	2.1778	2.1941	2.2106	2.2355	2.2438	2.2776	2.3118	2.3205	2.3466
20	2.7126	2.7672	2.7810	2.8229	2.8511	2.8796	2.9230	2.9376	2.9966	3.0569	3.0721	3.1183
25	3.4813	3.5690	3.5913	3.6590	3.7048	3.7512	3.8219	3.8458	3.9427	4.0420	4.0672	4.1439
30	4.4677	4.6032	4.6377	4.7428	4.8142	4.8866	4.9973	5.0348	5.1874	5.3446	5.3847	5.5066

YEAR	5.75 %	5.80 %	5.875%	5.90 %	6.00 %	6.10 %	6.125%	6.20 %	6.25 %	6.30 %	6.375%	6.40 %
1	1.0590	1.0596	1.0604	1.0606	1.0617	1.0627	1.0630	1.0638	1.0643	1.0649	1.0656	1.0659
2	1.1216	1.1227	1.1244	1.1249	1.1272	1.1294	1.1300	1.1317	1.1328	1.1339	1.1356	1.1362
3	1.1878	1.1896	1.1922	1.1931	1.1967	1.2003	1.2012	1.2038	1.2056	1.2074	1.2101	1.2111
4	1.2579	1.2604	1.2642	1.2654	1.2705	1.2756	1.2768	1.2806	1.2832	1.2857	1.2896	1.2909
5	1.3322	1.3355	1.3405	1.3422	1.3489	1.3556	1.3573	1.3623	1.3657	1.3691	1.3742	1.3760
6	1.4108	1.4150	1.4214	1.4235	1.4320	1.4406	1.4428	1.4492	1.4536	1.4579	1.4645	1.4666
7	1.4941	1.4993	1.5072	1.5098	1.5204	1.5310	1.5337	1.5417	1.5471	1.5525	1.5606	1.5633
8	1.5823	1.5886	1.5982	1.6013	1.6141	1.6270	1.6303	1.6400	1.6466	1.6531	1.6630	1.6664
9	1.6758	1.6833	1.6946	1.6984	1.7137	1.7291	1.7330	1.7447	1.7525	1.7604	1.7722	1.7762
10	1.7747	1.7835	1.7969	1.8014	1.8194	1.8376	1.8422	1.8560	1.8652	1.8745	1.8886	1.8933
15	2.3642	2.3819	2.4087	2.4177	2.4541	2.4910	2.5003	2.5284	2.5474	2.5665	2.5953	2.6050
20	3.1495	3.1810	3.2289	3.2450	3.3102	3.3767	3.3936	3.4446	3.4790	3.5138	3.5666	3.5844
25	4.1957	4.2482	4.3283	4.3553	4.4650	4.5774	4.6060	4.6927	4.7514	4.8109	4.9015	4.9320
30	5.5894	5.6735	5.8020	5.8454	6.0226	6.2051	6.2515	6.3931	6.4892	6.5867	6.7358	6.7862

YEAR	6.50 %	6.60 %	6.625%	6.70 %	6.75 %	6.80 %	6.875%	6.90 %	7.00 %	7.10 %	7.125%	7.20 %
1	1.0670	1.0680	1.0683	1.0691	1.0696	1.0702	1.0710	1.0712	1.0723	1.0734	1.0736	1.0744
2	1.1384	1.1407	1.1413	1.1430	1.1441	1.1452	1.1470	1.1475	1.1498	1.1521	1.1527	1.1544
3	1.2147	1.2183	1.2192	1.2219	1.2238	1.2256	1.2283	1.2293	1.2329	1.2366	1.2375	1.2403
4	1.2960	1.3012	1.3025	1.3064	1.3090	1.3116	1.3155	1.3168	1.3221	1.3273	1.3286	1.3326
5	1.3828	1.3897	1.3914	1.3966	1.4001	1.4036	1.4088	1.4106	1.4176	1.4247	1.4265	1.4318
6	1.4754	1.4843	1.4865	1.4931	1.4976	1.5021	1.5088	1.5111	1.5201	1.5292	1.5315	1.5383
7	1.5742	1.5852	1.5880	1.5963	1.6019	1.6075	1.6159	1.6187	1.6300	1.6414	1.6442	1.6528
8	1.6797	1.6931	1.6965	1.7066	1.7134	1.7202	1.7305	1.7340	1.7478	1.7618	1.7653	1.7758
9	1.7922	1.8083	1.8123	1.8245	1.8327	1.8409	1.8533	1.8575	1.8742	1.8910	1.8953	1.9080
10	1.9122	1.9313	1.9361	1.9506	1.9603	1.9701	1.9848	1.9898	2.0097	2.0297	2.0348	2.0500
15	2.6442	2.6839	2.6940	2.7243	2.7447	2.7652	2.7963	2.8068	2.8489	2.8917	2.9025	2.9352
20	3.6564	3.7299	3.7485	3.8048	3.8429	3.8813	3.9396	3.9592	4.0387	4.1198	4.1404	4.2026
25	5.0562	5.1835	5.2158	5.3140	5.3804	5.4477	5.5503	5.5849	5.7254	5.8695	5.9061	6.0172
30	6.9918	7.2036	7.2575	7.4217	7.5332	7.6465	7.8195	7.8780	8.1165	8.3622	8.4248	8.6154

Description: This table shows what a single $ 1 deposit will grow to in the future.

Example: At 8 % one dollar will grow to $ 1.49 by the end of the fifth year.

YEAR	7.25 %	7.30 %	7.375%	7.40 %	7.50 %	7.60 %	7.625%	7.70 %	7.75 %	7.80 %	7.875%	7.90 %
1	1.0750	1.0755	1.0763	1.0766	1.0776	1.0787	1.0790	1.0798	1.0803	1.0808	1.0817	1.0819
2	1.1555	1.1567	1.1584	1.1590	1.1613	1.1636	1.1642	1.1659	1.1671	1.1682	1.1700	1.1706
3	1.2422	1.2440	1.2468	1.2477	1.2514	1.2552	1.2561	1.2589	1.2608	1.2627	1.2655	1.2665
4	1.3353	1.3379	1.3419	1.3432	1.3486	1.3540	1.3553	1.3594	1.3621	1.3648	1.3688	1.3702
5	1.4354	1.4389	1.4443	1.4461	1.4533	1.4605	1.4623	1.4678	1.4715	1.4751	1.4806	1.4825
6	1.5429	1.5476	1.5545	1.5568	1.5661	1.5755	1.5778	1.5849	1.5896	1.5944	1.6015	1.6039
7	1.6586	1.6644	1.6731	1.6760	1.6877	1.6995	1.7024	1.7113	1.7173	1.7233	1.7323	1.7353
8	1.7829	1.7900	1.8007	1.8043	1.8187	1.8332	1.8369	1.8479	1.8552	1.8626	1.8738	1.8775
9	1.9166	1.9252	1.9381	1.9425	1.9599	1.9775	1.9819	1.9953	2.0042	2.0132	2.0268	2.0313
10	2.0602	2.0705	2.0860	2.0912	2.1121	2.1332	2.1385	2.1545	2.1652	2.1760	2.1922	2.1977
15	2.9572	2.9793	3.0128	3.0240	3.0695	3.1155	3.1272	3.1623	3.1860	3.2098	3.2459	3.2580
20	4.2446	4.2870	4.3513	4.3730	4.4608	4.5504	4.5730	4.6417	4.6880	4.7349	4.8059	4.8299
25	6.0924	6.1686	6.2846	6.3238	6.4829	6.6460	6.6874	6.8131	6.8983	6.9845	7.1158	7.1601
30	8.7448	8.8761	9.0769	9.1448	9.4215	9.7066	9.7793	10.0004	10.1505	10.3029	10.5358	10.6146

YEAR	8.00 %	8.10 %	8.125%	8.20 %	8.25 %	8.30 %	8.375%	8.40 %	8.50 %	8.60 %	8.625%	8.70 %
1	1.0830	1.0841	1.0843	1.0852	1.0857	1.0862	1.0870	1.0873	1.0884	1.0895	1.0897	1.0906
2	1.1729	1.1752	1.1758	1.1776	1.1787	1.1799	1.1817	1.1822	1.1846	1.1869	1.1875	1.1893
3	1.2702	1.2740	1.2750	1.2778	1.2797	1.2816	1.2845	1.2855	1.2893	1.2931	1.2941	1.2970
4	1.3757	1.3811	1.3825	1.3866	1.3894	1.3922	1.3963	1.3977	1.4033	1.4088	1.4102	1.4145
5	1.4898	1.4973	1.4991	1.5047	1.5085	1.5122	1.5179	1.5197	1.5273	1.5349	1.5368	1.5425
6	1.6135	1.6231	1.6256	1.6328	1.6377	1.6426	1.6500	1.6524	1.6623	1.6722	1.6747	1.6822
7	1.7474	1.7596	1.7627	1.7719	1.7781	1.7843	1.7936	1.7967	1.8092	1.8219	1.8250	1.8346
8	1.8925	1.9076	1.9113	1.9228	1.9304	1.9381	1.9497	1.9536	1.9692	1.9849	1.9888	2.0007
9	2.0495	2.0679	2.0726	2.0865	2.0959	2.1052	2.1194	2.1241	2.1432	2.1624	2.1673	2.1819
10	2.2196	2.2418	2.2474	2.2642	2.2754	2.2868	2.3039	2.3096	2.3326	2.3559	2.3618	2.3794
15	3.3069	3.3566	3.3691	3.4069	3.4324	3.4581	3.4969	3.5100	3.5627	3.6161	3.6296	3.6704
20	4.9268	5.0257	5.0507	5.1265	5.1777	5.2293	5.3078	5.3342	5.4412	5.5504	5.5780	5.6617
25	7.3402	7.5247	7.5716	7.7139	7.8103	7.9079	8.0565	8.1066	8.3104	8.5193	8.5723	8.7334
30	10.9357	11.2665	11.3508	11.6073	11.7815	11.9583	12.2285	12.3200	12.6925	13.0763	13.1740	13.4716

YEAR	8.75 %	8.80 %	8.875%	8.90 %	9.00 %	9.10 %	9.125%	9.20 %	9.25 %	9.30 %	9.375%	9.40 %
1	1.0911	1.0916	1.0925	1.0927	1.0938	1.0949	1.0952	1.0960	1.0965	1.0971	1.0979	1.0982
2	1.1905	1.1917	1.1934	1.1940	1.1964	1.1988	1.1994	1.2012	1.2024	1.2036	1.2054	1.2059
3	1.2989	1.3009	1.3038	1.3048	1.3086	1.3125	1.3135	1.3165	1.3184	1.3204	1.3233	1.3243
4	1.4173	1.4201	1.4243	1.4257	1.4314	1.4371	1.4385	1.4428	1.4457	1.4486	1.4529	1.4543
5	1.5464	1.5502	1.5560	1.5579	1.5657	1.5735	1.5754	1.5813	1.5852	1.5892	1.5951	1.5971
6	1.6872	1.6923	1.6999	1.7024	1.7126	1.7228	1.7253	1.7331	1.7382	1.7434	1.7512	1.7538
7	1.8409	1.8474	1.8570	1.8602	1.8732	1.8863	1.8895	1.8994	1.9060	1.9127	1.9226	1.9260
8	2.0086	2.0166	2.0287	2.0327	2.0489	2.0653	2.0694	2.0817	2.0900	2.0983	2.1108	2.1150
9	2.1916	2.2014	2.2162	2.2212	2.2411	2.2612	2.2663	2.2815	2.2917	2.3020	2.3175	2.3226
10	2.3913	2.4032	2.4211	2.4271	2.4514	2.4758	2.4820	2.5005	2.5129	2.5254	2.5443	2.5506
15	3.6978	3.7254	3.7673	3.7813	3.8380	3.8956	3.9101	3.9540	3.9836	4.0133	4.0584	4.0735
20	5.7182	5.7752	5.8619	5.8910	6.0092	6.1296	6.1601	6.2525	6.3149	6.3778	6.4735	6.5057
25	8.8424	8.9529	9.1211	9.1778	9.4084	9.6448	9.7048	9.8871	10.0105	10.1354	10.3258	10.3900
30	13.6737	13.8789	14.1923	14.2984	14.7306	15.1758	15.2892	15.6344	15.8689	16.1068	16.4705	16.5935

YEAR	9.50 %	9.75 %	10.00 %	10.25 %	10.50 %	10.75 %	11.00 %	12.00 %	13.00 %	14.00 %	15.00 %	16.00 %
1	1.0992	1.1020	1.1047	1.1075	1.1102	1.1130	1.1157	1.1268	1.1380	1.1493	1.1608	1.1723
2	1.2083	1.2144	1.2204	1.2265	1.2326	1.2387	1.2448	1.2697	1.2951	1.3210	1.3474	1.3742
3	1.3283	1.3382	1.3482	1.3582	1.3684	1.3786	1.3889	1.4308	1.4739	1.5183	1.5639	1.6110
4	1.4601	1.4747	1.4894	1.5042	1.5192	1.5343	1.5496	1.6122	1.6773	1.7450	1.8154	1.8885
5	1.6050	1.6250	1.6453	1.6658	1.6866	1.7076	1.7289	1.8167	1.9089	2.0056	2.1072	2.2138
6	1.7643	1.7908	1.8176	1.8448	1.8725	1.9005	1.9290	2.0471	2.1723	2.3051	2.4459	2.5952
7	1.9394	1.9734	2.0079	2.0431	2.0788	2.1152	2.1522	2.3067	2.4722	2.6494	2.8391	3.0423
8	2.1319	2.1746	2.2182	2.2626	2.3079	2.3541	2.4013	2.5993	2.8134	3.0450	3.2955	3.5663
9	2.3435	2.3964	2.4504	2.5057	2.5623	2.6200	2.6791	2.9289	3.2018	3.4998	3.8253	4.1807
10	2.5761	2.6407	2.7070	2.7750	2.8446	2.9160	2.9891	3.3004	3.6437	4.0225	4.4402	4.9009
15	4.1346	4.2913	4.4539	4.6227	4.7978	4.9795	5.1680	5.9958	6.9554	8.0675	9.3563	10.8497
20	6.6361	6.9735	7.3281	7.7006	8.0919	8.5031	8.9350	10.8926	13.2768	16.1803	19.7155	24.0192
25	10.6509	11.3322	12.0569	12.8278	13.6479	14.5201	15.4479	19.7885	25.3435	32.4513	41.5441	53.1739
30	17.0949	18.4153	19.8374	21.3690	23.0185	24.7950	26.7081	35.9496	48.3771	65.0847	87.5410	117.7168

Description: This table shows what a single $ 1 deposit will grow to in the future.

Example: At 5 % one dollar will grow to $ 1.28 by the end of the fifth year.

YEAR	0.00 %	1.00 %	2.00 %	3.00 %	4.00 %	4.125%	4.25 %	4.375%	4.50 %	4.625%	4.75 %	4.875%
1	1.0000	1.0100	1.0202	1.0303	1.0406	1.0419	1.0432	1.0445	1.0458	1.0471	1.0484	1.0496
2	1.0000	1.0202	1.0407	1.0616	1.0829	1.0855	1.0882	1.0909	1.0936	1.0963	1.0990	1.1018
3	1.0000	1.0304	1.0617	1.0938	1.1268	1.1310	1.1352	1.1394	1.1437	1.1479	1.1522	1.1565
4	1.0000	1.0408	1.0831	1.1270	1.1726	1.1784	1.1842	1.1901	1.1960	1.2019	1.2079	1.2139
5	1.0000	1.0512	1.1049	1.1612	1.2202	1.2278	1.2354	1.2430	1.2508	1.2585	1.2663	1.2741
6	1.0000	1.0618	1.1272	1.1964	1.2697	1.2792	1.2887	1.2983	1.3080	1.3177	1.3275	1.3374
7	1.0000	1.0724	1.1499	1.2327	1.3213	1.3328	1.3444	1.3561	1.3679	1.3797	1.3917	1.4038
8	1.0000	1.0832	1.1730	1.2701	1.3749	1.3886	1.4024	1.4164	1.4305	1.4447	1.4590	1.4735
9	1.0000	1.0941	1.1967	1.3086	1.4308	1.4468	1.4630	1.4794	1.4959	1.5126	1.5296	1.5467
10	1.0000	1.1050	1.2208	1.3483	1.4889	1.5074	1.5262	1.5452	1.5644	1.5838	1.6035	1.6234
15	1.0000	1.1616	1.3489	1.5657	1.8167	1.8507	1.8854	1.9207	1.9566	1.9933	2.0305	2.0685
20	1.0000	1.2211	1.4903	1.8180	2.2167	2.2723	2.3292	2.3875	2.4473	2.5085	2.5713	2.6356
25	1.0000	1.2836	1.6467	2.1111	2.7048	2.7898	2.8774	2.9678	3.0609	3.1570	3.2560	3.3581
30	1.0000	1.3494	1.8194	2.4514	3.3004	3.4252	3.5547	3.6891	3.8285	3.9731	4.1231	4.2787

YEAR	5.00 %	5.10 %	5.125%	5.20 %	5.25 %	5.30 %	5.375%	5.40 %	5.50 %	5.60 %	5.625%	5.70 %
1	1.0509	1.0520	1.0522	1.0530	1.0535	1.0541	1.0548	1.0551	1.0561	1.0572	1.0574	1.0582
2	1.1045	1.1067	1.1072	1.1089	1.1100	1.1110	1.1127	1.1132	1.1154	1.1176	1.1182	1.1199
3	1.1608	1.1642	1.1651	1.1677	1.1694	1.1711	1.1737	1.1746	1.1781	1.1816	1.1824	1.1851
4	1.2199	1.2247	1.2259	1.2296	1.2320	1.2344	1.2381	1.2393	1.2442	1.2491	1.2504	1.2541
5	1.2820	1.2884	1.2900	1.2948	1.2980	1.3012	1.3060	1.3076	1.3141	1.3206	1.3222	1.3271
6	1.3474	1.3554	1.3574	1.3634	1.3675	1.3715	1.3776	1.3797	1.3878	1.3961	1.3981	1.4044
7	1.4160	1.4258	1.4283	1.4357	1.4407	1.4457	1.4532	1.4557	1.4658	1.4759	1.4785	1.4861
8	1.4881	1.4999	1.5029	1.5118	1.5178	1.5238	1.5329	1.5359	1.5481	1.5603	1.5634	1.5727
9	1.5639	1.5779	1.5814	1.5920	1.5991	1.6062	1.6169	1.6205	1.6350	1.6496	1.6532	1.6643
10	1.6436	1.6599	1.6640	1.6764	1.6847	1.6930	1.7056	1.7098	1.7268	1.7439	1.7482	1.7612
15	2.1072	2.1386	2.1466	2.1705	2.1867	2.2029	2.2275	2.2358	2.2691	2.3029	2.3114	2.3372
20	2.7015	2.7554	2.7690	2.8103	2.8382	2.8663	2.9091	2.9235	2.9817	3.0411	3.0562	3.1017
25	3.4634	3.5500	3.5719	3.6387	3.6839	3.7296	3.7992	3.8227	3.9182	4.0160	4.0408	4.1162
30	4.4402	4.5737	4.6077	4.7112	4.7815	4.8528	4.9618	4.9986	5.1488	5.3034	5.3428	5.4626

YEAR	5.75 %	5.80 %	5.875%	5.90 %	6.00 %	6.10 %	6.125%	6.20 %	6.25 %	6.30 %	6.375%	6.40 %
1	1.0588	1.0593	1.0601	1.0603	1.0614	1.0624	1.0627	1.0635	1.0640	1.0645	1.0653	1.0656
2	1.1210	1.1221	1.1237	1.1243	1.1265	1.1287	1.1293	1.1309	1.1321	1.1332	1.1348	1.1354
3	1.1868	1.1886	1.1912	1.1921	1.1956	1.1992	1.2000	1.2027	1.2045	1.2063	1.2089	1.2098
4	1.2565	1.2590	1.2627	1.2640	1.2690	1.2740	1.2753	1.2790	1.2815	1.2841	1.2879	1.2891
5	1.3304	1.3336	1.3386	1.3402	1.3469	1.3535	1.3552	1.3602	1.3635	1.3669	1.3720	1.3736
6	1.4085	1.4127	1.4190	1.4211	1.4295	1.4380	1.4401	1.4465	1.4508	1.4551	1.4615	1.4637
7	1.4913	1.4964	1.5042	1.5068	1.5172	1.5277	1.5304	1.5383	1.5436	1.5489	1.5570	1.5596
8	1.5789	1.5851	1.5945	1.5977	1.6103	1.6231	1.6263	1.6359	1.6424	1.6488	1.6586	1.6619
9	1.6717	1.6791	1.6903	1.6940	1.7091	1.7244	1.7282	1.7397	1.7474	1.7552	1.7669	1.7708
10	1.7699	1.7786	1.7918	1.7962	1.8140	1.8320	1.8365	1.8501	1.8592	1.8684	1.8823	1.8869
15	2.3546	2.3720	2.3985	2.4074	2.4432	2.4796	2.4888	2.5165	2.5351	2.5539	2.5824	2.5919
20	3.1324	3.1635	3.2106	3.2264	3.2907	3.3561	3.3727	3.4229	3.4568	3.4910	3.5429	3.5604
25	4.1673	4.2190	4.2976	4.3242	4.4320	4.5426	4.5706	4.6558	4.7134	4.7718	4.8607	4.8907
30	5.5440	5.6266	5.7528	5.7955	5.9693	6.1484	6.1940	6.3327	6.4270	6.5226	6.6687	6.7181

YEAR	6.50 %	6.60 %	6.625%	6.70 %	6.75 %	6.80 %	6.875%	6.90 %	7.00 %	7.10 %	7.125%	7.20 %
1	1.0666	1.0677	1.0679	1.0687	1.0692	1.0698	1.0705	1.0708	1.0719	1.0729	1.0732	1.0740
2	1.1376	1.1399	1.1404	1.1421	1.1432	1.1444	1.1461	1.1466	1.1489	1.1511	1.1517	1.1534
3	1.2134	1.2170	1.2179	1.2206	1.2224	1.2242	1.2269	1.2278	1.2314	1.2351	1.2360	1.2387
4	1.2942	1.2993	1.3006	1.3044	1.3070	1.3096	1.3135	1.3147	1.3199	1.3251	1.3264	1.3303
5	1.3804	1.3872	1.3889	1.3941	1.3975	1.4009	1.4061	1.4078	1.4148	1.4217	1.4235	1.4287
6	1.4724	1.4811	1.4833	1.4898	1.4942	1.4987	1.5053	1.5075	1.5164	1.5254	1.5277	1.5344
7	1.5704	1.5813	1.5840	1.5922	1.5977	1.6032	1.6115	1.6143	1.6254	1.6366	1.6394	1.6479
8	1.6750	1.6882	1.6916	1.7016	1.7083	1.7150	1.7252	1.7286	1.7422	1.7560	1.7594	1.7698
9	1.7866	1.8025	1.8065	1.8185	1.8266	1.8347	1.8469	1.8510	1.8674	1.8840	1.8882	1.9007
10	1.9056	1.9244	1.9291	1.9434	1.9530	1.9626	1.9772	1.9820	2.0016	2.0214	2.0263	2.0413
15	2.6305	2.6696	2.6794	2.7093	2.7293	2.7495	2.7801	2.7904	2.8318	2.8739	2.8845	2.9165
20	3.6312	3.7033	3.7216	3.7769	3.8142	3.8519	3.9091	3.9284	4.0064	4.0859	4.1060	4.1670
25	5.0125	5.1373	5.1690	5.2652	5.3304	5.3963	5.4967	5.5306	5.6682	5.8091	5.8449	5.9536
30	6.9194	7.1267	7.1794	7.3401	7.4492	7.5599	7.7290	7.7862	8.0192	8.2591	8.3202	8.5062

Description: This table shows what a single $ 1 deposit will grow to in the future.

Example: At 8 % one dollar will grow to $ 1.49 by the end of the fifth year.

YEAR	7.25 %	7.30 %	7.375%	7.40 %	7.50 %	7.60 %	7.625%	7.70 %	7.75 %	7.80 %	7.875%	7.90 %
1	1.0745	1.0750	1.0758	1.0761	1.0771	1.0782	1.0785	1.0793	1.0798	1.0803	1.0811	1.0814
2	1.1545	1.1557	1.1574	1.1579	1.1602	1.1625	1.1631	1.1648	1.1659	1.1671	1.1688	1.1694
3	1.2405	1.2424	1.2451	1.2460	1.2497	1.2534	1.2543	1.2571	1.2589	1.2608	1.2636	1.2645
4	1.3330	1.3356	1.3395	1.3408	1.3461	1.3514	1.3527	1.3567	1.3594	1.3621	1.3661	1.3674
5	1.4323	1.4358	1.4411	1.4428	1.4499	1.4571	1.4589	1.4642	1.4678	1.4714	1.4769	1.4787
6	1.5390	1.5435	1.5503	1.5526	1.5618	1.5710	1.5733	1.5803	1.5849	1.5896	1.5967	1.5990
7	1.6536	1.6593	1.6679	1.6707	1.6823	1.6939	1.6968	1.7055	1.7114	1.7173	1.7262	1.7291
8	1.7768	1.7838	1.7943	1.7978	1.8120	1.8263	1.8299	1.8407	1.8479	1.8552	1.8662	1.8698
9	1.9091	1.9176	1.9304	1.9346	1.9518	1.9691	1.9735	1.9866	1.9954	2.0042	2.0175	2.0220
10	2.0514	2.0615	2.0767	2.0818	2.1023	2.1231	2.1283	2.1440	2.1546	2.1652	2.1811	2.1865
15	2.9381	2.9598	2.9927	3.0037	3.0483	3.0935	3.1049	3.1394	3.1626	3.1859	3.2213	3.2331
20	4.2081	4.2497	4.3127	4.3339	4.4199	4.5075	4.5297	4.5968	4.6421	4.6879	4.7574	4.7808
25	6.0271	6.1016	6.2150	6.2532	6.4086	6.5678	6.6082	6.7309	6.8139	6.8980	7.0260	7.0692
30	8.6324	8.7605	8.9562	9.0224	9.2921	9.5698	9.6405	9.8557	10.0018	10.1500	10.3765	10.4531

YEAR	8.00 %	8.10 %	8.125%	8.20 %	8.25 %	8.30 %	8.375%	8.40 %	8.50 %	8.60 %	8.625%	8.70 %
1	1.0824	1.0835	1.0838	1.0846	1.0851	1.0856	1.0864	1.0867	1.0877	1.0888	1.0891	1.0899
2	1.1717	1.1740	1.1745	1.1763	1.1774	1.1786	1.1803	1.1809	1.1832	1.1855	1.1861	1.1878
3	1.2682	1.2720	1.2729	1.2757	1.2776	1.2795	1.2823	1.2832	1.2870	1.2908	1.2918	1.2946
4	1.3728	1.3782	1.3795	1.3836	1.3863	1.3890	1.3931	1.3945	1.4000	1.4054	1.4068	1.4110
5	1.4859	1.4932	1.4951	1.5006	1.5043	1.5080	1.5135	1.5154	1.5228	1.5303	1.5321	1.5378
6	1.6084	1.6179	1.6203	1.6275	1.6323	1.6371	1.6443	1.6467	1.6564	1.6662	1.6686	1.6760
7	1.7410	1.7530	1.7560	1.7651	1.7711	1.7772	1.7864	1.7895	1.8018	1.8142	1.8173	1.8266
8	1.8845	1.8994	1.9031	1.9143	1.9218	1.9294	1.9408	1.9446	1.9599	1.9753	1.9791	1.9908
9	2.0399	2.0580	2.0625	2.0762	2.0854	2.0946	2.1085	2.1131	2.1318	2.1507	2.1554	2.1697
10	2.2080	2.2298	2.2353	2.2518	2.2628	2.2739	2.2907	2.2963	2.3189	2.3417	2.3475	2.3648
15	3.2810	3.3296	3.3419	3.3789	3.4039	3.4290	3.4670	3.4797	3.5312	3.5835	3.5966	3.6365
20	4.8754	4.9720	4.9964	5.0704	5.1203	5.1707	5.2473	5.2730	5.3773	5.4836	5.5106	5.5921
25	7.2446	7.4244	7.4700	7.6085	7.7023	7.7972	7.9417	7.9905	8.1885	8.3915	8.4430	8.5993
30	10.7652	11.0864	11.1682	11.4172	11.5863	11.7578	12.0198	12.1085	12.4695	12.8412	12.9358	13.2238

YEAR	8.75 %	8.80 %	8.875%	8.90 %	9.00 %	9.10 %	9.125%	9.20 %	9.25 %	9.30 %	9.375%	9.40 %
1	1.0904	1.0909	1.0917	1.0920	1.0931	1.0942	1.0944	1.0952	1.0958	1.0963	1.0971	1.0974
2	1.1890	1.1902	1.1919	1.1925	1.1948	1.1972	1.1978	1.1995	1.2007	1.2019	1.2036	1.2042
3	1.2965	1.2984	1.3013	1.3022	1.3060	1.3099	1.3108	1.3137	1.3157	1.3176	1.3205	1.3215
4	1.4137	1.4165	1.4207	1.4220	1.4276	1.4332	1.4346	1.4388	1.4416	1.4445	1.4487	1.4501
5	1.5415	1.5453	1.5510	1.5529	1.5605	1.5682	1.5701	1.5758	1.5797	1.5836	1.5894	1.5913
6	1.6809	1.6859	1.6933	1.6958	1.7058	1.7158	1.7183	1.7259	1.7310	1.7360	1.7437	1.7463
7	1.8329	1.8392	1.8487	1.8518	1.8645	1.8774	1.8806	1.8902	1.8967	1.9032	1.9130	1.9163
8	1.9986	2.0065	2.0183	2.0222	2.0381	2.0541	2.0581	2.0702	2.0783	2.0865	2.0988	2.1029
9	2.1793	2.1889	2.2034	2.2083	2.2278	2.2475	2.2525	2.2674	2.2774	2.2874	2.3025	2.3076
10	2.3764	2.3880	2.4056	2.4115	2.4352	2.4591	2.4651	2.4833	2.4954	2.5077	2.5261	2.5323
15	3.6632	3.6902	3.7311	3.7448	3.8001	3.8563	3.8705	3.9133	3.9420	3.9710	4.0149	4.0297
20	5.6471	5.7026	5.7869	5.8153	5.9301	6.0473	6.0769	6.1667	6.2272	6.2884	6.3813	6.4125
25	8.7052	8.8123	8.9755	9.0305	9.2540	9.4831	9.5412	9.7177	9.8372	9.9581	10.1422	10.2043
30	13.4194	13.6178	13.9209	14.0234	14.4410	14.8709	14.9804	15.3136	15.5397	15.7692	16.1198	16.2383

YEAR	9.50 %	9.75 %	10.00 %	10.25 %	10.50 %	10.75 %	11.00 %	12.00 %	13.00 %	14.00 %	15.00 %	16.00 %
1	1.0984	1.1011	1.1038	1.1065	1.1092	1.1119	1.1146	1.1255	1.1365	1.1475	1.1587	1.1699
2	1.2066	1.2125	1.2184	1.2244	1.2303	1.2363	1.2424	1.2668	1.2916	1.3168	1.3425	1.3686
3	1.3253	1.3351	1.3449	1.3548	1.3647	1.3747	1.3848	1.4258	1.4678	1.5111	1.5555	1.6010
4	1.4558	1.4701	1.4845	1.4991	1.5137	1.5286	1.5435	1.6047	1.6682	1.7340	1.8022	1.8730
5	1.5991	1.6187	1.6386	1.6587	1.6790	1.6996	1.7204	1.8061	1.8958	1.9898	2.0882	2.1911
6	1.7565	1.7824	1.8087	1.8354	1.8624	1.8898	1.9176	2.0328	2.1546	2.2833	2.4194	2.5633
7	1.9294	1.9627	1.9965	2.0309	2.0658	2.1013	2.1374	2.2879	2.4486	2.6202	2.8033	2.9987
8	2.1194	2.1612	2.2038	2.2472	2.2914	2.3365	2.3824	2.5751	2.7828	3.0067	3.2480	3.5081
9	2.3280	2.3797	2.4325	2.4865	2.5416	2.5980	2.6555	2.8983	3.1626	3.4503	3.7633	4.1039
10	2.5572	2.6203	2.6851	2.7513	2.8192	2.8887	2.9599	3.2620	3.5942	3.9593	4.3604	4.8010
15	4.0892	4.2417	4.3998	4.5637	4.7336	4.9097	5.0923	5.8916	6.8140	7.8781	9.1051	10.5196
20	6.5390	6.8662	7.2096	7.5699	7.9479	8.3446	8.7609	10.6409	12.9183	15.6757	19.0129	23.0498
25	10.4566	11.1147	11.8137	12.5562	13.3450	14.1827	15.0724	19.2186	24.4910	31.1914	39.7018	50.5049
30	16.7213	17.9919	19.3581	20.8272	22.4068	24.1051	25.9310	34.7110	46.4309	62.0643	82.9035	110.6626

GROWTH OF 1

Description: This table shows what a single $ 1 deposit will grow to in the future.

Example: At 5 % one dollar will grow to $ 1.28 by the end of the fifth year.

YEAR	0.00 %	1.00 %	2.00 %	3.00 %	4.00 %	4.125%	4.25 %	4.375%	4.50 %	4.625%	4.75 %	4.875%
1	1.0000	1.0100	1.0201	1.0302	1.0404	1.0417	1.0430	1.0442	1.0455	1.0468	1.0481	1.0493
2	1.0000	1.0202	1.0406	1.0614	1.0824	1.0851	1.0877	1.0904	1.0931	1.0958	1.0984	1.1011
3	1.0000	1.0304	1.0615	1.0934	1.1262	1.1303	1.1345	1.1386	1.1428	1.1470	1.1512	1.1555
4	1.0000	1.0407	1.0829	1.1265	1.1717	1.1774	1.1832	1.1890	1.1948	1.2007	1.2066	1.2125
5	1.0000	1.0511	1.1046	1.1605	1.2190	1.2265	1.2340	1.2416	1.2492	1.2569	1.2646	1.2723
6	1.0000	1.0617	1.1268	1.1956	1.2682	1.2776	1.2870	1.2965	1.3060	1.3157	1.3253	1.3351
7	1.0000	1.0723	1.1495	1.2318	1.3195	1.3308	1.3423	1.3538	1.3655	1.3772	1.3890	1.4010
8	1.0000	1.0831	1.1726	1.2690	1.3728	1.3863	1.4000	1.4137	1.4276	1.4416	1.4558	1.4701
9	1.0000	1.0939	1.1961	1.3073	1.4282	1.4441	1.4601	1.4763	1.4926	1.5091	1.5258	1.5426
10	1.0000	1.1049	1.2202	1.3469	1.4859	1.5043	1.5228	1.5415	1.5605	1.5797	1.5991	1.6187
15	1.0000	1.1614	1.3478	1.5631	1.8114	1.8450	1.8792	1.9140	1.9494	1.9855	2.0222	2.0595
20	1.0000	1.2208	1.4889	1.8140	2.2080	2.2628	2.3189	2.3764	2.4352	2.4954	2.5572	2.6203
25	1.0000	1.2832	1.6446	2.1052	2.6916	2.7753	2.8616	2.9505	3.0420	3.1364	3.2337	3.3339
30	1.0000	1.3489	1.8167	2.4432	3.2810	3.4039	3.5312	3.6632	3.8001	3.9420	4.0892	4.2417

YEAR	5.00 %	5.10 %	5.125%	5.20 %	5.25 %	5.30 %	5.375%	5.40 %	5.50 %	5.60 %	5.625%	5.70 %
1	1.0506	1.0517	1.0519	1.0527	1.0532	1.0537	1.0545	1.0547	1.0558	1.0568	1.0570	1.0578
2	1.1038	1.1060	1.1065	1.1081	1.1092	1.1103	1.1119	1.1125	1.1146	1.1168	1.1173	1.1190
3	1.1597	1.1631	1.1639	1.1665	1.1682	1.1699	1.1725	1.1733	1.1768	1.1802	1.1811	1.1837
4	1.2184	1.2232	1.2244	1.2279	1.2303	1.2327	1.2363	1.2376	1.2424	1.2472	1.2484	1.2521
5	1.2801	1.2863	1.2879	1.2926	1.2958	1.2989	1.3037	1.3053	1.3117	1.3180	1.3197	1.3245
6	1.3449	1.3528	1.3548	1.3607	1.3647	1.3687	1.3747	1.3767	1.3848	1.3929	1.3949	1.4010
7	1.4130	1.4227	1.4251	1.4324	1.4373	1.4422	1.4496	1.4521	1.4620	1.4720	1.4745	1.4820
8	1.4845	1.4961	1.4991	1.5078	1.5137	1.5196	1.5286	1.5315	1.5435	1.5556	1.5586	1.5677
9	1.5597	1.5734	1.5769	1.5873	1.5943	1.6013	1.6118	1.6154	1.6296	1.6439	1.6475	1.6584
10	1.6386	1.6547	1.6587	1.6709	1.6790	1.6872	1.6996	1.7038	1.7204	1.7372	1.7415	1.7542
15	2.0976	2.1285	2.1363	2.1598	2.1757	2.1916	2.2158	2.2239	2.2566	2.2898	2.2981	2.3234
20	2.6851	2.7380	2.7513	2.7919	2.8192	2.8468	2.8887	2.9028	2.9599	3.0180	3.0328	3.0773
25	3.4371	3.5220	3.5435	3.6088	3.6531	3.6978	3.7660	3.7890	3.8823	3.9779	4.0022	4.0758
30	4.3998	4.5304	4.5637	4.6649	4.7336	4.8033	4.9097	4.9457	5.0923	5.2431	5.2815	5.3983

YEAR	5.75 %	5.80 %	5.875%	5.90 %	6.00 %	6.10 %	6.125%	6.20 %	6.25 %	6.30 %	6.375%	6.40 %
1	1.0583	1.0588	1.0596	1.0599	1.0609	1.0619	1.0622	1.0630	1.0635	1.0640	1.0648	1.0650
2	1.1201	1.1211	1.1228	1.1233	1.1255	1.1277	1.1282	1.1299	1.1310	1.1321	1.1337	1.1343
3	1.1854	1.1871	1.1897	1.1906	1.1941	1.1975	1.1984	1.2010	1.2028	1.2045	1.2072	1.2080
4	1.2545	1.2570	1.2606	1.2619	1.2668	1.2717	1.2729	1.2766	1.2791	1.2816	1.2853	1.2866
5	1.3277	1.3309	1.3358	1.3374	1.3439	1.3505	1.3521	1.3570	1.3603	1.3636	1.3686	1.3702
6	1.4051	1.4092	1.4154	1.4175	1.4258	1.4341	1.4362	1.4425	1.4467	1.4509	1.4572	1.4593
7	1.4871	1.4922	1.4998	1.5023	1.5126	1.5229	1.5255	1.5333	1.5385	1.5437	1.5516	1.5542
8	1.5738	1.5800	1.5892	1.5923	1.6047	1.6172	1.6204	1.6298	1.6362	1.6425	1.6521	1.6553
9	1.6656	1.6729	1.6839	1.6876	1.7024	1.7174	1.7211	1.7324	1.7400	1.7476	1.7591	1.7629
10	1.7628	1.7714	1.7843	1.7887	1.8061	1.8237	1.8282	1.8415	1.8505	1.8595	1.8730	1.8776
15	2.3404	2.3576	2.3835	2.3922	2.4273	2.4629	2.4718	2.4990	2.5172	2.5356	2.5634	2.5727
20	3.1074	3.1377	3.1838	3.1993	3.2620	3.3260	3.3422	3.3911	3.4242	3.4576	3.5082	3.5252
25	4.1257	4.1761	4.2529	4.2788	4.3839	4.4916	4.5189	4.6019	4.6580	4.7148	4.8013	4.8304
30	5.4776	5.5581	5.6809	5.7224	5.8916	6.0657	6.1100	6.2448	6.3363	6.4292	6.5709	6.6188

YEAR	6.50 %	6.60 %	6.625%	6.70 %	6.75 %	6.80 %	6.875%	6.90 %	7.00 %	7.10 %	7.125%	7.20 %
1	1.0661	1.0671	1.0673	1.0681	1.0686	1.0692	1.0699	1.0702	1.0712	1.0723	1.0725	1.0733
2	1.1365	1.1387	1.1392	1.1409	1.1420	1.1431	1.1448	1.1453	1.1475	1.1497	1.1503	1.1520
3	1.2115	1.2151	1.2160	1.2186	1.2204	1.2221	1.2248	1.2257	1.2293	1.2328	1.2337	1.2364
4	1.2916	1.2966	1.2978	1.3016	1.3041	1.3067	1.3105	1.3117	1.3168	1.3219	1.3232	1.3270
5	1.3769	1.3836	1.3853	1.3903	1.3937	1.3970	1.4021	1.4038	1.4106	1.4174	1.4191	1.4243
6	1.4678	1.4764	1.4785	1.4850	1.4893	1.4936	1.5002	1.5023	1.5111	1.5199	1.5221	1.5287
7	1.5648	1.5754	1.5781	1.5862	1.5915	1.5969	1.6051	1.6078	1.6187	1.6297	1.6324	1.6407
8	1.6682	1.6811	1.6844	1.6942	1.7008	1.7074	1.7173	1.7206	1.7340	1.7474	1.7508	1.7610
9	1.7784	1.7939	1.7978	1.8096	1.8175	1.8254	1.8374	1.8414	1.8575	1.8737	1.8778	1.8901
10	1.8958	1.9143	1.9189	1.9329	1.9423	1.9517	1.9659	1.9707	1.9898	2.0091	2.0140	2.0286
15	2.6104	2.6486	2.6582	2.6873	2.7069	2.7266	2.7564	2.7664	2.8068	2.8478	2.8581	2.8893
20	3.5942	3.6645	3.6823	3.7361	3.7724	3.8091	3.8647	3.8835	3.9593	4.0365	4.0560	4.1152
25	4.9488	5.0701	5.1009	5.1943	5.2575	5.3214	5.4188	5.4516	5.5849	5.7214	5.7561	5.8612
30	6.8140	7.0149	7.0660	7.2215	7.3271	7.4342	7.5977	7.6530	7.8781	8.1097	8.1687	8.3481

Description: This table shows what a single $ 1 deposit will grow to in the future.

Example: At 8 % one dollar will grow to $ 1.48 by the end of the fifth year.

YEAR	7.25 %	7.30 %	7.375%	7.40 %	7.50 %	7.60 %	7.625%	7.70 %	7.75 %	7.80 %	7.875%	7.90 %
1	1.0738	1.0743	1.0751	1.0754	1.0764	1.0774	1.0777	1.0785	1.0790	1.0795	1.0803	1.0806
2	1.1531	1.1542	1.1559	1.1564	1.1587	1.1609	1.1614	1.1631	1.1642	1.1654	1.1670	1.1676
3	1.2382	1.2400	1.2427	1.2436	1.2472	1.2508	1.2517	1.2544	1.2562	1.2580	1.2608	1.2617
4	1.3296	1.3322	1.3360	1.3373	1.3425	1.3477	1.3490	1.3529	1.3555	1.3581	1.3620	1.3633
5	1.4277	1.4312	1.4364	1.4381	1.4450	1.4520	1.4538	1.4590	1.4625	1.4661	1.4714	1.4731
6	1.5331	1.5376	1.5442	1.5465	1.5555	1.5645	1.5667	1.5735	1.5781	1.5827	1.5895	1.5918
7	1.6463	1.6518	1.6602	1.6630	1.6743	1.6856	1.6885	1.6970	1.7028	1.7085	1.7172	1.7201
8	1.7678	1.7746	1.7849	1.7884	1.8022	1.8162	1.8197	1.8302	1.8373	1.8444	1.8551	1.8586
9	1.8983	1.9065	1.9190	1.9232	1.9399	1.9568	1.9611	1.9739	1.9824	1.9910	2.0040	2.0084
10	2.0384	2.0483	2.0631	2.0681	2.0882	2.1084	2.1135	2.1288	2.1390	2.1494	2.1649	2.1702
15	2.9103	2.9314	2.9634	2.9741	3.0175	3.0614	3.0725	3.1060	3.1285	3.1511	3.1854	3.1969
20	4.1551	4.1954	4.2565	4.2771	4.3604	4.4452	4.4667	4.5317	4.5755	4.6198	4.6870	4.7096
25	5.9324	6.0043	6.1139	6.1509	6.3009	6.4546	6.4936	6.6119	6.6919	6.7729	6.8963	6.9378
30	8.4698	8.5933	8.7818	8.8456	9.1051	9.3722	9.4402	9.6470	9.7873	9.9296	10.1470	10.2204

YEAR	8.00 %	8.10 %	8.125%	8.20 %	8.25 %	8.30 %	8.375%	8.40 %	8.50 %	8.60 %	8.625%	8.70 %
1	1.0816	1.0826	1.0829	1.0837	1.0842	1.0847	1.0855	1.0858	1.0868	1.0878	1.0881	1.0889
2	1.1699	1.1721	1.1727	1.1744	1.1755	1.1766	1.1783	1.1789	1.1811	1.1834	1.1840	1.1857
3	1.2653	1.2690	1.2699	1.2726	1.2745	1.2763	1.2791	1.2800	1.2837	1.2874	1.2883	1.2911
4	1.3686	1.3738	1.3752	1.3791	1.3818	1.3844	1.3884	1.3898	1.3951	1.4005	1.4018	1.4059
5	1.4802	1.4874	1.4892	1.4945	1.4981	1.5017	1.5071	1.5090	1.5162	1.5235	1.5253	1.5308
6	1.6010	1.6103	1.6126	1.6196	1.6243	1.6290	1.6360	1.6384	1.6478	1.6573	1.6597	1.6669
7	1.7317	1.7434	1.7463	1.7551	1.7610	1.7670	1.7759	1.7789	1.7909	1.8029	1.8060	1.8151
8	1.8730	1.8874	1.8911	1.9020	1.9093	1.9167	1.9277	1.9315	1.9463	1.9613	1.9651	1.9764
9	2.0258	2.0434	2.0478	2.0612	2.0701	2.0791	2.0926	2.0971	2.1153	2.1336	2.1382	2.1521
10	2.1911	2.2123	2.2176	2.2336	2.2444	2.2552	2.2715	2.2770	2.2989	2.3211	2.3266	2.3434
15	3.2434	3.2905	3.3024	3.3383	3.3624	3.3867	3.4235	3.4358	3.4856	3.5361	3.5489	3.5873
20	4.8010	4.8942	4.9178	4.9892	5.0373	5.0859	5.1597	5.1845	5.2850	5.3873	5.4132	5.4916
25	7.1067	7.2795	7.3234	7.4565	7.5466	7.6377	7.7764	7.8232	8.0131	8.2076	8.2569	8.4066
30	10.5196	10.8274	10.9057	11.1441	11.3058	11.4698	11.7203	11.8049	12.1497	12.5043	12.5945	12.8691

YEAR	8.75 %	8.80 %	8.875%	8.90 %	9.00 %	9.10 %	9.125%	9.20 %	9.25 %	9.30 %	9.375%	9.40 %
1	1.0894	1.0899	1.0907	1.0910	1.0920	1.0931	1.0933	1.0941	1.0946	1.0952	1.0959	1.0962
2	1.1868	1.1880	1.1897	1.1902	1.1925	1.1948	1.1954	1.1971	1.1982	1.1994	1.2011	1.2017
3	1.2929	1.2948	1.2976	1.2985	1.3023	1.3060	1.3069	1.3098	1.3116	1.3135	1.3163	1.3173
4	1.4085	1.4113	1.4153	1.4167	1.4221	1.4276	1.4289	1.4330	1.4358	1.4385	1.4426	1.4440
5	1.5345	1.5382	1.5437	1.5456	1.5530	1.5604	1.5623	1.5679	1.5716	1.5754	1.5811	1.5829
6	1.6717	1.6765	1.6837	1.6862	1.6959	1.7056	1.7081	1.7155	1.7204	1.7253	1.7328	1.7352
7	1.8212	1.8273	1.8365	1.8396	1.8519	1.8644	1.8675	1.8769	1.8832	1.8895	1.8990	1.9022
8	1.9840	1.9916	2.0031	2.0069	2.0224	2.0379	2.0418	2.0536	2.0614	2.0693	2.0812	2.0852
9	2.1614	2.1707	2.1848	2.1895	2.2085	2.2276	2.2324	2.2468	2.2565	2.2662	2.2809	2.2858
10	2.3547	2.3660	2.3830	2.3887	2.4117	2.4349	2.4407	2.4583	2.4701	2.4819	2.4997	2.5057
15	3.6132	3.6393	3.6787	3.6919	3.7453	3.7995	3.8131	3.8543	3.8821	3.9100	3.9523	3.9664
20	5.5445	5.5978	5.6788	5.7061	5.8164	5.9287	5.9571	6.0432	6.1013	6.1598	6.2487	6.2787
25	8.5079	8.6104	8.7664	8.8191	9.0326	9.2513	9.3067	9.4751	9.5890	9.7042	9.8796	9.9388
30	13.0554	13.2443	13.5328	13.6303	14.0274	14.4358	14.5398	14.8560	15.0705	15.2881	15.6203	15.7326

YEAR	9.50 %	9.75 %	10.00 %	10.25 %	10.50 %	10.75 %	11.00 %	12.00 %	13.00 %	14.00 %	15.00 %	16.00 %
1	1.0973	1.0999	1.1025	1.1051	1.1078	1.1104	1.1130	1.1236	1.1342	1.1449	1.1556	1.1664
2	1.2040	1.2097	1.2155	1.2213	1.2271	1.2330	1.2388	1.2625	1.2865	1.3108	1.3355	1.3605
3	1.3211	1.3306	1.3401	1.3497	1.3594	1.3691	1.3788	1.4185	1.4591	1.5007	1.5433	1.5869
4	1.4495	1.4634	1.4775	1.4916	1.5058	1.5202	1.5347	1.5938	1.6550	1.7182	1.7835	1.8509
5	1.5905	1.6096	1.6289	1.6484	1.6681	1.6880	1.7081	1.7908	1.8771	1.9672	2.0610	2.1589
6	1.7452	1.7704	1.7959	1.8217	1.8478	1.8744	1.9012	2.0122	2.1291	2.2522	2.3818	2.5182
7	1.9149	1.9472	1.9799	2.0132	2.0470	2.0813	2.1161	2.2609	2.4149	2.5785	2.7524	2.9372
8	2.1012	2.1417	2.1829	2.2248	2.2675	2.3110	2.3553	2.5404	2.7390	2.9522	3.1808	3.4259
9	2.3055	2.3556	2.4066	2.4587	2.5119	2.5661	2.6215	2.8543	3.1067	3.3799	3.6758	3.9960
10	2.5298	2.5908	2.6533	2.7172	2.7825	2.8494	2.9178	3.2071	3.5236	3.8697	4.2479	4.6610
15	4.0237	4.1702	4.3219	4.4790	4.6416	4.8098	4.9840	5.7435	6.6144	7.6123	8.7550	10.0627
20	6.3997	6.7124	7.0400	7.3831	7.7426	8.1190	8.5133	10.2857	12.4161	14.9745	18.0442	21.7245
25	10.1789	10.8044	11.4674	12.1703	12.9153	13.7050	14.5420	18.4202	23.3067	29.4570	37.1897	46.9016
30	16.1898	17.3908	18.6792	20.0614	21.5440	23.1342	24.8398	32.9877	43.7498	57.9464	76.6492	101.2571

Description: This table shows what a single $ 1 deposit will grow to in the future.

Example: At 5 % one dollar will grow to $ 1.28 by the end of the fifth year.

YEAR	0.00 %	1.00 %	2.00 %	3.00 %	4.00 %	4.125%	4.25 %	4.375%	4.50 %	4.625%	4.75 %	4.875%
1	1.0000	1.0100	1.0200	1.0300	1.0400	1.0413	1.0425	1.0437	1.0450	1.0462	1.0475	1.0488
2	1.0000	1.0201	1.0404	1.0609	1.0816	1.0842	1.0868	1.0894	1.0920	1.0946	1.0973	1.0999
3	1.0000	1.0303	1.0612	1.0927	1.1249	1.1289	1.1330	1.1371	1.1412	1.1453	1.1494	1.1535
4	1.0000	1.0406	1.0824	1.1255	1.1699	1.1755	1.1811	1.1868	1.1925	1.1982	1.2040	1.2097
5	1.0000	1.0510	1.1041	1.1593	1.2167	1.2240	1.2313	1.2387	1.2462	1.2537	1.2612	1.2687
6	1.0000	1.0615	1.1262	1.1941	1.2653	1.2745	1.2837	1.2929	1.3023	1.3116	1.3211	1.3306
7	1.0000	1.0721	1.1487	1.2299	1.3159	1.3270	1.3382	1.3495	1.3609	1.3723	1.3838	1.3954
8	1.0000	1.0829	1.1717	1.2668	1.3686	1.3818	1.3951	1.4085	1.4221	1.4358	1.4495	1.4634
9	1.0000	1.0937	1.1951	1.3048	1.4233	1.4388	1.4544	1.4702	1.4861	1.5022	1.5184	1.5348
10	1.0000	1.1046	1.2190	1.3439	1.4802	1.4981	1.5162	1.5345	1.5530	1.5716	1.5905	1.6096
15	1.0000	1.1610	1.3459	1.5580	1.8009	1.8337	1.8670	1.9008	1.9353	1.9703	2.0059	2.0421
20	1.0000	1.2202	1.4859	1.8061	2.1911	2.2444	2.2989	2.3547	2.4117	2.4701	2.5298	2.5908
25	1.0000	1.2824	1.6406	2.0938	2.6658	2.7471	2.8308	2.9168	3.0054	3.0966	3.1904	3.2870
30	1.0000	1.3478	1.8114	2.4273	3.2434	3.3624	3.4856	3.6132	3.7453	3.8821	4.0237	4.1702

YEAR	5.00 %	5.10 %	5.125%	5.20 %	5.25 %	5.30 %	5.375%	5.40 %	5.50 %	5.60 %	5.625%	5.70 %
1	1.0500	1.0510	1.0513	1.0520	1.0525	1.0530	1.0537	1.0540	1.0550	1.0560	1.0562	1.0570
2	1.1025	1.1046	1.1051	1.1067	1.1078	1.1088	1.1104	1.1109	1.1130	1.1151	1.1157	1.1172
3	1.1576	1.1609	1.1618	1.1643	1.1659	1.1676	1.1701	1.1709	1.1742	1.1776	1.1784	1.1809
4	1.2155	1.2201	1.2213	1.2248	1.2271	1.2295	1.2330	1.2341	1.2388	1.2435	1.2447	1.2482
5	1.2763	1.2824	1.2839	1.2885	1.2915	1.2946	1.2992	1.3008	1.3070	1.3132	1.3147	1.3194
6	1.3401	1.3478	1.3497	1.3555	1.3594	1.3632	1.3691	1.3710	1.3788	1.3867	1.3887	1.3946
7	1.4071	1.4165	1.4189	1.4260	1.4307	1.4355	1.4427	1.4451	1.4547	1.4644	1.4668	1.4741
8	1.4775	1.4887	1.4916	1.5001	1.5058	1.5116	1.5202	1.5231	1.5347	1.5464	1.5493	1.5581
9	1.5513	1.5647	1.5680	1.5781	1.5849	1.5917	1.6019	1.6053	1.6191	1.6330	1.6364	1.6469
10	1.6289	1.6445	1.6484	1.6602	1.6681	1.6760	1.6880	1.6920	1.7081	1.7244	1.7285	1.7408
15	2.0789	2.1088	2.1164	2.1391	2.1544	2.1698	2.1931	2.2009	2.2325	2.2644	2.2725	2.2968
20	2.6533	2.7043	2.7172	2.7562	2.7825	2.8091	2.8494	2.8629	2.9178	2.9736	2.9877	3.0304
25	3.3864	3.4679	3.4886	3.5514	3.5938	3.6367	3.7020	3.7240	3.8134	3.9048	3.9280	3.9983
30	4.3219	4.4471	4.4790	4.5759	4.6416	4.7082	4.8098	4.8442	4.9840	5.1276	5.1642	5.2753

YEAR	5.75 %	5.80 %	5.875%	5.90 %	6.00 %	6.10 %	6.125%	6.20 %	6.25 %	6.30 %	6.375%	6.40 %
1	1.0575	1.0580	1.0588	1.0590	1.0600	1.0610	1.0613	1.0620	1.0625	1.0630	1.0637	1.0640
2	1.1183	1.1194	1.1210	1.1215	1.1236	1.1257	1.1263	1.1278	1.1289	1.1300	1.1316	1.1321
3	1.1826	1.1843	1.1868	1.1876	1.1910	1.1944	1.1952	1.1978	1.1995	1.2012	1.2037	1.2046
4	1.2506	1.2530	1.2565	1.2577	1.2625	1.2672	1.2684	1.2720	1.2744	1.2768	1.2804	1.2816
5	1.3225	1.3256	1.3304	1.3319	1.3382	1.3445	1.3461	1.3509	1.3541	1.3573	1.3621	1.3637
6	1.3986	1.4025	1.4085	1.4105	1.4185	1.4266	1.4286	1.4347	1.4387	1.4428	1.4489	1.4509
7	1.4790	1.4839	1.4913	1.4937	1.5036	1.5136	1.5161	1.5236	1.5286	1.5337	1.5413	1.5438
8	1.5640	1.5699	1.5789	1.5819	1.5938	1.6059	1.6089	1.6181	1.6242	1.6303	1.6395	1.6426
9	1.6540	1.6610	1.6716	1.6752	1.6895	1.7039	1.7075	1.7184	1.7257	1.7330	1.7440	1.7477
10	1.7491	1.7573	1.7698	1.7740	1.7908	1.8078	1.8121	1.8249	1.8335	1.8422	1.8552	1.8596
15	2.3132	2.3296	2.3545	2.3629	2.3966	2.4307	2.4393	2.4653	2.4828	2.5003	2.5269	2.5359
20	3.0592	3.0883	3.1323	3.1472	3.2071	3.2682	3.2836	3.3304	3.3619	3.3936	3.4418	3.4581
25	4.0458	4.0939	4.1671	4.1918	4.2919	4.3942	4.4202	4.4990	4.5522	4.6061	4.6880	4.7156
30	5.3507	5.4271	5.5437	5.5831	5.7435	5.9083	5.9502	6.0776	6.1641	6.2517	6.3854	6.4306

YEAR	6.50 %	6.60 %	6.625%	6.70 %	6.75 %	6.80 %	6.875%	6.90 %	7.00 %	7.10 %	7.125%	7.20 %
1	1.0650	1.0660	1.0662	1.0670	1.0675	1.0680	1.0688	1.0690	1.0700	1.0710	1.0713	1.0720
2	1.1342	1.1364	1.1369	1.1385	1.1396	1.1406	1.1422	1.1428	1.1449	1.1470	1.1476	1.1492
3	1.2079	1.2114	1.2122	1.2148	1.2165	1.2182	1.2208	1.2216	1.2250	1.2285	1.2293	1.2319
4	1.2865	1.2913	1.2925	1.2962	1.2986	1.3010	1.3047	1.3059	1.3108	1.3157	1.3169	1.3206
5	1.3701	1.3765	1.3781	1.3830	1.3862	1.3895	1.3944	1.3960	1.4026	1.4091	1.4108	1.4157
6	1.4591	1.4674	1.4694	1.4757	1.4798	1.4840	1.4902	1.4923	1.5007	1.5092	1.5113	1.5176
7	1.5540	1.5642	1.5668	1.5745	1.5797	1.5849	1.5927	1.5953	1.6058	1.6163	1.6190	1.6269
8	1.6550	1.6675	1.6706	1.6800	1.6863	1.6927	1.7022	1.7054	1.7182	1.7311	1.7343	1.7440
9	1.7626	1.7775	1.7813	1.7926	1.8002	1.8078	1.8192	1.8231	1.8385	1.8540	1.8579	1.8696
10	1.8771	1.8948	1.8993	1.9127	1.9217	1.9307	1.9443	1.9488	1.9672	1.9856	1.9903	2.0042
15	2.5718	2.6083	2.6175	2.6452	2.6639	2.6827	2.7111	2.7206	2.7590	2.7980	2.8078	2.8374
20	3.5236	3.5904	3.6073	3.6584	3.6928	3.7276	3.7803	3.7980	3.8697	3.9427	3.9611	4.0169
25	4.8277	4.9423	4.9714	5.0595	5.1191	5.1794	5.2711	5.3020	5.4274	5.5557	5.5882	5.6868
30	6.6144	6.8032	6.8513	6.9973	7.0964	7.1968	7.3499	7.4017	7.6123	7.8286	7.8836	8.0509

GROWTH OF 1

Description: This table shows what a single $ 1 deposit will grow to in the future.

Example: At 8 % one dollar will grow to $ 1.47 by the end of the fifth year.

YEAR	7.25 %	7.30 %	7.375%	7.40 %	7.50 %	7.60 %	7.625%	7.70 %	7.75 %	7.80 %	7.875%	7.90 %
1	1.0725	1.0730	1.0737	1.0740	1.0750	1.0760	1.0762	1.0770	1.0775	1.0780	1.0788	1.0790
2	1.1503	1.1513	1.1529	1.1535	1.1556	1.1578	1.1583	1.1599	1.1610	1.1621	1.1637	1.1642
3	1.2336	1.2354	1.2380	1.2388	1.2423	1.2458	1.2466	1.2492	1.2510	1.2527	1.2553	1.2562
4	1.3231	1.3256	1.3293	1.3305	1.3355	1.3404	1.3417	1.3454	1.3479	1.3504	1.3542	1.3555
5	1.4190	1.4223	1.4273	1.4290	1.4356	1.4423	1.4440	1.4490	1.4524	1.4558	1.4608	1.4625
6	1.5219	1.5262	1.5326	1.5347	1.5433	1.5519	1.5541	1.5606	1.5650	1.5693	1.5759	1.5781
7	1.6322	1.6376	1.6456	1.6483	1.6590	1.6699	1.6726	1.6808	1.6862	1.6917	1.7000	1.7027
8	1.7506	1.7571	1.7670	1.7702	1.7835	1.7968	1.8001	1.8102	1.8169	1.8237	1.8339	1.8373
9	1.8775	1.8854	1.8973	1.9012	1.9172	1.9333	1.9374	1.9496	1.9577	1.9659	1.9783	1.9824
10	2.0136	2.0230	2.0372	2.0419	2.0610	2.0803	2.0851	2.0997	2.1095	2.1193	2.1341	2.1390
15	2.8573	2.8774	2.9077	2.9179	2.9589	3.0004	3.0109	3.0425	3.0638	3.0852	3.1175	3.1284
20	4.0546	4.0926	4.1501	4.1695	4.2479	4.3276	4.3477	4.4087	4.4499	4.4913	4.5542	4.5754
25	5.7535	5.8209	5.9235	5.9581	6.0983	6.2418	6.2781	6.3884	6.4630	6.5384	6.6530	6.6917
30	8.1643	8.2793	8.4546	8.5139	8.7550	9.0026	9.0656	9.2570	9.3868	9.5184	9.7191	9.7869

YEAR	8.00 %	8.10 %	8.125%	8.20 %	8.25 %	8.30 %	8.375%	8.40 %	8.50 %	8.60 %	8.625%	8.70 %
1	1.0800	1.0810	1.0813	1.0820	1.0825	1.0830	1.0837	1.0840	1.0850	1.0860	1.0862	1.0870
2	1.1664	1.1686	1.1691	1.1707	1.1718	1.1729	1.1745	1.1751	1.1772	1.1794	1.1799	1.1816
3	1.2597	1.2632	1.2641	1.2667	1.2685	1.2702	1.2729	1.2738	1.2773	1.2808	1.2817	1.2844
4	1.3605	1.3655	1.3668	1.3706	1.3731	1.3757	1.3795	1.3808	1.3859	1.3910	1.3923	1.3961
5	1.4693	1.4761	1.4779	1.4830	1.4864	1.4898	1.4950	1.4967	1.5037	1.5106	1.5123	1.5176
6	1.5869	1.5957	1.5979	1.6046	1.6090	1.6135	1.6202	1.6225	1.6315	1.6405	1.6428	1.6496
7	1.7138	1.7250	1.7278	1.7362	1.7418	1.7474	1.7559	1.7588	1.7701	1.7816	1.7845	1.7931
8	1.8509	1.8647	1.8681	1.8785	1.8855	1.8925	1.9030	1.9065	1.9206	1.9348	1.9384	1.9491
9	1.9990	2.0157	2.0199	2.0326	2.0410	2.0495	2.0623	2.0666	2.0839	2.1012	2.1056	2.1187
10	2.1589	2.1790	2.1840	2.1992	2.2094	2.2197	2.2351	2.2402	2.2610	2.2819	2.2872	2.3030
15	3.1722	3.2165	3.2277	3.2614	3.2841	3.3069	3.3415	3.3530	3.3997	3.4470	3.4590	3.4950
20	4.6610	4.7480	4.7700	4.8367	4.8816	4.9268	4.9955	5.0186	5.1120	5.2071	5.2311	5.3038
25	6.8485	7.0088	7.0494	7.1727	7.2560	7.3403	7.4684	7.5116	7.6868	7.8658	7.9112	8.0489
30	10.0627	10.3460	10.4180	10.6370	10.7854	10.9359	11.1654	11.2429	11.5583	11.8821	11.9645	12.2148

YEAR	8.75 %	8.80 %	8.875%	8.90 %	9.00 %	9.10 %	9.125%	9.20 %	9.25 %	9.30 %	9.375%	9.40 %
1	1.0875	1.0880	1.0888	1.0890	1.0900	1.0910	1.0913	1.0920	1.0925	1.0930	1.0938	1.0940
2	1.1827	1.1837	1.1854	1.1859	1.1881	1.1903	1.1908	1.1925	1.1936	1.1946	1.1963	1.1968
3	1.2861	1.2879	1.2906	1.2915	1.2950	1.2986	1.2995	1.3022	1.3040	1.3058	1.3084	1.3093
4	1.3987	1.4012	1.4051	1.4064	1.4116	1.4168	1.4181	1.4220	1.4246	1.4272	1.4311	1.4324
5	1.5211	1.5246	1.5298	1.5316	1.5386	1.5457	1.5475	1.5528	1.5563	1.5599	1.5653	1.5671
6	1.6542	1.6587	1.6656	1.6679	1.6771	1.6864	1.6887	1.6956	1.7003	1.7050	1.7120	1.7144
7	1.7989	1.8047	1.8134	1.8163	1.8280	1.8398	1.8428	1.8516	1.8576	1.8636	1.8725	1.8755
8	1.9563	1.9635	1.9744	1.9780	1.9926	2.0072	2.0109	2.0220	2.0294	2.0369	2.0481	2.0518
9	2.1275	2.1363	2.1496	2.1540	2.1719	2.1899	2.1944	2.2080	2.2171	2.2263	2.2401	2.2447
10	2.3136	2.3243	2.3404	2.3457	2.3674	2.3892	2.3947	2.4112	2.4222	2.4333	2.4501	2.4557
15	3.5192	3.5435	3.5803	3.5927	3.6425	3.6929	3.7056	3.7440	3.7698	3.7958	3.8350	3.8482
20	5.3529	5.4023	5.4773	5.5025	5.6044	5.7081	5.7344	5.8137	5.8672	5.9211	6.0029	6.0304
25	8.1420	8.2361	8.3792	8.4275	8.6231	8.8231	8.8737	9.0275	9.1314	9.2364	9.3962	9.4500
30	12.3845	12.5564	12.8187	12.9073	13.2677	13.6377	13.7318	14.0178	14.2116	14.4080	14.7076	14.8088

YEAR	9.50 %	9.75 %	10.00 %	10.25 %	10.50 %	10.75 %	11.00 %	12.00 %	13.00 %	14.00 %	15.00 %	16.00 %
1	1.0950	1.0975	1.1000	1.1025	1.1050	1.1075	1.1100	1.1200	1.1300	1.1400	1.1500	1.1600
2	1.1990	1.2045	1.2100	1.2155	1.2210	1.2266	1.2321	1.2544	1.2769	1.2996	1.3225	1.3456
3	1.3129	1.3219	1.3310	1.3401	1.3492	1.3584	1.3676	1.4049	1.4429	1.4815	1.5209	1.5609
4	1.4377	1.4508	1.4641	1.4775	1.4909	1.5044	1.5181	1.5735	1.6305	1.6890	1.7490	1.8106
5	1.5742	1.5923	1.6105	1.6289	1.6474	1.6662	1.6851	1.7623	1.8424	1.9254	2.0114	2.1003
6	1.7238	1.7475	1.7716	1.7959	1.8204	1.8453	1.8704	1.9738	2.0820	2.1950	2.3131	2.4364
7	1.8876	1.9179	1.9487	1.9799	2.0116	2.0436	2.0762	2.2107	2.3526	2.5023	2.6600	2.8262
8	2.0669	2.1049	2.1436	2.1829	2.2228	2.2633	2.3045	2.4760	2.6584	2.8526	3.0590	3.2784
9	2.2632	2.3102	2.3579	2.4066	2.4562	2.5066	2.5580	2.7731	3.0040	3.2519	3.5179	3.8030
10	2.4782	2.5354	2.5937	2.6533	2.7141	2.7761	2.8394	3.1058	3.3946	3.7072	4.0456	4.4114
15	3.9013	4.0371	4.1772	4.3219	4.4713	4.6255	4.7846	5.4736	6.2543	7.1379	8.1371	9.2655
20	6.1416	6.4282	6.7275	7.0400	7.3662	7.7068	8.0623	9.6463	11.5231	13.7435	16.3665	19.4608
25	9.6684	10.2356	10.8347	11.4674	12.1355	12.8408	13.5855	17.0001	21.2305	26.4619	32.9190	40.8742
30	15.2203	16.2981	17.4494	18.6792	19.9926	21.3950	22.8923	29.9599	39.1159	50.9502	66.2118	85.8499

TABLE **16**

Savings Growth

Interest Rates:	0, 1, 2, 3%; 4 to 4.875% by .25%, .125%; 5 to 9.50% by .25%, .125%, .10%; 9.75 to 11% by .25%; 12 to 16% by 1%.
Terms:	1 to 10 years, each year; 15, 20, 25, 30 years.
Compound Periods:	Daily 360 and 365 day year, monthly, quarterly, semiannual, annual.
Deposit Periods:	Weekly, monthly, quarterly, semiannual, annual.

This table shows what a series of $1 deposits will grow to in the future. Deposits are made at the beginning of the period. Tables are shown for 6 compounding periods—daily 360 day year, daily 365 day year, monthly, quarterly, semiannual, and annual—and for 5 deposit periods—weekly, monthly, quarterly, semiannual, and annual.

Example: The balance in 5 years of $1 deposited each week in a savings account that pays 5% interest compounded monthly is $295.34. If the deposits were $10 per week, then the balance in 5 years would be $2,953.34, shown in the monthly compounding table for weekly deposits on page 16-22. A comparison with the 0% column shows that, of the $2,953, only $353 is interest.

What amount must be deposited weekly to have $10,000 in 5 years in a savings account that pays 5% interest compounded monthly? The 5 year factor is 295.3424. To find the weekly deposit of $33.98, divide the future balance by the 5 year factor:

$$10,000 \div 295.3424 = 33.975$$

Example: For the past 6 years, $10 per week has been deposited regularly in a savings account. Interest was compounded monthly. Today, the balance is $3,700. What is the average rate at which the deposit earned interest? The answer is computed in 2 steps:

1. Find the Savings Growth by dividing the balance today by the weekly deposit:
$$3,700 \div 10 = 370$$

2. Enter the monthly table for weekly deposits and scan the 6 year lines for a balance of 370. The balance lies between 2 given values in the monthly compounding table on page 16-22. By interpolation, the interest rate is 5.54%.

Example: For the past 6 years, $10 per week has been invested in a stock purchase plan. The market value of the stock today is $3,900. What is the growth rate of the investment? Find the Savings Growth as follows:

$$3,900 \div 10 = 390$$

Enter the table and scan the 6 year lines to find the amount. The growth rate is 7.20%.

$1 Million. If $1 million is the goal, an easy way to get there is to put a few dollars at interest every month and then come back 1 month after the 360th deposit and collect. The following table shows the monthly deposits required at interest rates of 4 to 16% to grow to $1 million tomorrow, with interest compounded monthly.

Interest Rate	Monthly Deposit	Interest Rate	Monthly Deposit
4%	$1,436	10%	$438
5	1,196	11	353
6	990	13	283
7	814	14	226
8	666	15	179
9	530	16	142

Period. A period is the time interval between interest calculations. A regular period is usually 1 month, 1 quarter, 6 months, or 1 year. It is a discrete period of time.

Simple Interest. Simple interest is interest on an amount for a period. A rate of 4% on $100 for 1 year is $100 × .04 = $4.00. The interest on $100 at 4% for 1 month is $100 × (.04 ÷ 12) = $.33. Both the $4 and the $.33 are simple interest.

SAVINGS GROWTH

Compound Interest. Interest on a balance for a single period is always simple interest. Interest is compounded when the interest for a period is added to the principal balance to make a new balance and interest is then computed on the new balance. Compounding takes place when the interest is converted to the new balance. This gives the impression that compound interest is interest computed on interest.

Daily Compounding. Interest is computed each day. The rate per day is 1/360 or 1/365 of the nominal annual rate. A year is 365 days, which equals 365 periods.

Monthly Compounding. Interest is computed each month. The rate per month is 1/12 of the nominal annual rate; there are 12 periods per year.

Quarterly Compounding. Interest is computed each quarter. The rate per quarter is 1/4 of the nominal annual rate; there are 4 periods per year.

Semiannual Compounding. Interest is computed each 6 months. The rate per 6 months is 1/2 of the nominal annual rate; there are 2 periods per year.

Annual Compounding. Interest is computed once a year at the nominal annual rate; there is 1 period per year.

The Calendar. The Savings Growth tables are computed using a 365 day year that begins on January 1. For daily compounding, the exact days in each month, quarter, and semiannual period are used. For monthly compounding and weekly deposits, each quarter contains first a 4 week month, then a 5 week month, then a 4 week month.

SAVINGS GROWTH

Description: This table shows what a series of $ 1 deposits grow to in the future. The deposit is made at the beginning of a period.

Example: At 5 % a regular one dollar deposit will grow to $ 296.08 by the end of the fifth year.

YEAR	0.00 %	1.00 %	2.00 %	3.00 %	4.00 %	4.125%	4.25 %	4.375%	4.50 %	4.625%	4.75 %	4.875%
1	52.0000	52.2703	52.5425	52.8165	53.0924	53.1270	53.1616	53.1963	53.2310	53.2657	53.3005	53.3353
2	104.0000	105.0733	106.1612	107.2641	108.3820	108.5229	108.6639	108.8052	108.9468	109.0886	109.2306	109.3729
3	156.0000	158.4143	160.8783	163.3931	165.9600	166.2845	166.6100	166.9362	167.2633	167.5912	167.9200	168.2496
4	208.0000	212.2989	216.7162	221.2556	225.9209	226.5131	227.1073	227.7036	228.3019	228.9023	229.5048	230.1093
5	260.0000	266.7326	273.6979	280.9050	288.3634	289.3138	290.2684	291.2270	292.1898	293.1568	294.1279	295.1032
6	312.0000	321.7210	331.8469	342.3966	353.3902	354.7966	356.2103	357.6314	359.0599	360.4958	361.9392	363.3901
7	364.0000	377.2697	391.1869	405.7872	421.1082	423.0760	425.0557	427.0475	429.0514	431.0675	433.0959	435.1367
8	416.0000	433.3845	451.7425	471.1355	491.6289	494.2714	496.9323	499.6118	502.3100	505.0271	507.7632	510.5184
9	468.0000	490.0712	513.5386	538.5019	565.0682	568.5074	571.9736	575.4672	578.9883	582.5372	586.1141	589.7193
10	520.0000	547.3355	576.6005	607.9487	641.5469	645.9138	650.3189	654.7628	659.2458	663.7682	668.3305	672.9330
15	780.0000	842.5299	911.8239	988.7092	1074.1214	1085.4487	1096.9278	1108.5610	1120.3505	1132.2986	1144.4078	1156.6803
20	1040.0000	1153.0746	1282.8169	1432.0097	1603.9327	1627.2069	1650.9041	1675.0328	1699.6015	1724.6190	1750.0945	1776.0369
25	1300.0000	1479.7678	1693.3963	1948.1221	2252.8385	2294.9626	2338.0596	2382.1539	2427.2707	2473.4359	2520.6761	2569.0185
30	1560.0000	1823.3493	2147.7861	2549.0060	3047.6094	3118.0192	3190.4113	3264.8462	3341.3866	3420.0971	3501.0444	3584.2974

YEAR	5.00 %	5.10 %	5.125%	5.20 %	5.25 %	5.30 %	5.375%	5.40 %	5.50 %	5.60 %	5.625%	5.70 %
1	53.3701	53.3980	53.4050	53.4259	53.4399	53.4538	53.4748	53.4818	53.5097	53.5377	53.5447	53.5657
2	109.5154	109.6296	109.6581	109.7439	109.8011	109.8584	109.9444	109.9731	110.0879	110.2029	110.2316	110.3180
3	168.5800	168.8450	168.9114	169.1106	169.2435	169.3766	169.5765	169.6433	169.9104	170.1782	170.2452	170.4464
4	230.7159	231.2027	231.3247	231.6909	231.9355	232.1804	232.5484	232.6712	233.1634	233.6570	233.7806	234.1519
5	296.0828	296.8695	297.0666	297.5689	298.0546	298.4510	299.0469	299.2459	300.0435	300.8439	301.0445	301.6471
6	364.8485	366.0207	366.3146	367.1979	367.7883	368.3799	369.2697	369.5669	370.7588	371.9557	372.2557	373.1576
7	437.1899	438.8415	439.2557	440.5012	441.3341	442.1690	443.4252	443.8450	445.5291	447.2216	447.6459	448.9223
8	513.2929	515.5265	516.0869	517.7727	518.9005	520.0314	521.7338	522.3029	524.5871	526.8841	527.4604	529.1941
9	593.3531	596.2808	597.0156	599.2271	600.7072	602.1920	604.4280	605.1758	608.1784	611.2002	611.9587	614.2412
10	677.5762	681.3203	682.2604	685.0908	686.9860	688.8880	691.7535	692.7121	696.5633	700.4417	701.4156	704.3477
15	1169.1186	1179.1904	1181.7253	1189.3711	1194.5027	1199.6621	1207.4535	1210.0646	1220.5801	1231.2099	1233.8853	1241.9553
20	1802.4558	1823.9403	1829.3606	1845.7409	1856.7612	1867.8625	1884.6675	1890.3103	1913.0897	1936.2059	1942.0382	1959.6643
25	2618.4910	2658.9021	2669.1225	2700.0699	2720.9423	2742.0098	2773.9809	2784.7375	2828.2692	2872.6211	2883.8391	2917.8099
30	3669.9270	3740.1912	3758.0068	3812.0621	3848.6123	3885.5792	3941.8218	3960.7832	4037.7160	4116.4201	4136.3781	4196.9396

YEAR	5.75 %	5.80 %	5.875%	5.90 %	6.00 %	6.10 %	6.125%	6.20 %	6.25 %	6.30 %	6.375%	6.40 %
1	53.5797	53.5937	53.6147	53.6217	53.6498	53.6779	53.6849	53.7060	53.7200	53.7341	53.7552	53.7622
2	110.3756	110.4333	110.5198	110.5487	110.6643	110.7801	110.8090	110.8960	110.9540	111.0121	111.0992	111.1283
3	170.5808	170.7153	170.9172	170.9846	171.2546	171.5251	171.5928	171.7961	171.9319	172.0678	172.2718	172.3399
4	234.3999	234.6482	235.0213	235.1458	235.6449	236.1453	236.2706	236.4471	236.8985	237.1502	237.5286	237.6548
5	302.0498	302.4531	303.0594	303.2619	304.0734	304.8878	305.0919	305.7051	306.1148	306.5251	307.1421	307.3481
6	373.7605	374.3646	375.2731	375.5766	376.7936	378.0158	378.3221	379.2431	379.8587	380.4755	381.4032	381.7131
7	449.7757	450.6313	451.9186	452.3487	454.0746	455.8089	456.2438	457.5518	458.4264	459.3032	460.6224	461.0632
8	530.3539	531.5170	533.2678	533.8531	536.2023	538.5648	539.1575	540.9405	542.1335	543.3298	545.1305	545.7325
9	615.7689	617.3015	619.6096	620.3813	623.4808	626.6000	627.3829	629.7390	631.3161	632.8982	635.2807	636.0775
10	706.3111	708.2815	711.2501	712.2432	716.2330	720.2513	721.2603	724.2982	726.3324	728.3739	731.4497	732.4787
15	1247.3718	1252.8177	1261.0421	1263.7985	1274.8991	1286.1210	1288.9456	1297.4656	1303.1843	1308.9343	1317.6183	1320.5287
20	1971.5236	1983.4706	2001.5569	2007.6302	2032.1490	2057.0326	2063.3112	2082.2871	2095.0552	2107.9183	2127.3927	2133.9325
25	2940.7236	2963.8529	2998.9561	3010.7674	3058.5713	3107.2827	3119.6046	3156.9204	3182.0925	3207.5032	3246.0723	3259.0506
30	4237.8942	4279.3195	4342.3530	4363.6059	4449.8463	4538.0893	4560.4687	4628.3847	4674.3180	4720.7837	4791.4950	4815.3388

YEAR	6.50 %	6.60 %	6.625%	6.70 %	6.75 %	6.80 %	6.875%	6.90 %	7.00 %	7.10 %	7.125%	7.20 %
1	53.7904	53.8185	53.8256	53.8467	53.8608	53.8749	53.8961	53.9031	53.9314	53.9597	53.9667	53.9879
2	111.2447	111.3613	111.3904	111.4780	111.5364	111.5949	111.6826	111.7119	111.8291	111.9465	111.9758	112.0640
3	172.6127	172.8860	172.9544	173.1598	173.2970	173.4343	173.6405	173.7093	173.9849	174.2610	174.3301	174.5377
4	238.1608	238.6682	238.7952	239.1770	239.4319	239.6872	240.0707	240.1988	240.7118	241.2262	241.3551	241.7421
5	308.1738	309.0025	309.2101	309.8340	310.2509	310.6685	311.2962	311.5058	312.3461	313.1893	313.4005	314.0354
6	382.9559	384.2039	384.5168	385.4572	386.0858	386.7157	387.6631	387.9795	389.2487	390.5231	390.8426	391.8030
7	462.8319	464.6093	465.0550	466.3955	467.2918	468.1904	469.5425	469.9942	471.8070	473.6286	474.0854	475.4593
8	548.1487	550.5787	551.1883	553.0224	554.2494	555.4800	557.3322	557.9514	560.4369	562.9365	563.5636	565.4503
9	639.2771	642.4972	643.3054	645.7379	647.3660	648.9993	651.4591	652.2817	655.5851	658.9097	659.7442	662.2556
10	736.6128	740.7764	741.8219	744.9698	747.0777	749.1931	752.3805	753.4467	757.7308	762.0456	763.1291	766.3913
15	1332.2503	1344.1006	1347.0834	1356.0811	1362.1207	1368.1934	1377.3651	1380.4391	1392.8198	1405.3370	1408.4879	1417.9926
20	2160.3359	2187.1346	2193.8969	2214.3353	2228.0883	2241.9443	2262.9231	2269.9684	2298.4143	2327.2889	2334.5753	2356.5991
25	3311.5824	3365.1189	3378.6624	3419.6808	3447.3527	3475.2890	3517.6950	3531.9654	3589.7318	3648.6109	3663.5071	3708.6255
30	4912.1039	5011.1343	5036.2524	5112.4866	5164.0516	5216.2190	5295.6161	5322.3912	5431.0646	5542.3018	5570.5192	5656.1675

SAVINGS GROWTH

Description: This table shows what a series of $ 1 deposits grow to in the future. The deposit is made at the beginning of a period.

Example: At 8 % a regular one dollar deposit will grow to $ 320.91 by the end of the fifth year.

YEAR	7.25 %	7.30 %	7.375%	7.40 %	7.50 %	7.60 %	7.625%	7.70 %	7.75 %	7.80 %	7.875%	7.90 %
1	54.0021	54.0162	54.0375	54.0446	54.0729	54.1013	54.1084	54.1297	54.1438	54.1581	54.1794	54.1865
2	112.1228	112.1817	112.2700	112.2995	112.4175	112.5357	112.5653	112.6540	112.7132	112.7725	112.8615	112.8912
3	174.6763	174.8150	175.0233	175.0929	175.3713	175.6503	175.7202	175.9299	176.0699	176.2101	176.4206	176.4908
4	242.0006	242.2594	242.6484	242.7782	243.2984	243.8200	243.9506	244.3431	244.6052	244.8676	245.2620	245.3936
5	314.4596	314.8845	315.5233	315.7366	316.5916	317.4496	317.6646	318.3106	318.7423	319.1747	319.8247	320.0417
6	392.4449	393.0882	394.0557	394.3788	395.6749	396.9765	397.3027	398.2835	398.9391	399.5961	400.5841	400.9142
7	476.3780	477.2990	478.6847	479.1478	481.0058	482.8729	483.3411	484.7493	485.6910	486.6350	488.0554	488.5300
8	566.7125	567.9783	569.8838	570.5207	573.0776	575.6491	576.2942	578.2351	579.5337	580.8359	582.7962	583.4515
9	663.9367	665.6231	668.1629	669.0122	672.4231	675.8560	676.7176	679.3109	681.0468	682.7882	685.4109	686.2879
10	768.5759	770.7683	774.0716	775.1767	779.6167	784.0888	785.2118	788.5930	790.8572	793.1296	796.5536	797.6990
15	1424.3727	1430.7881	1440.4775	1443.7251	1456.8055	1470.0309	1473.3602	1483.4032	1490.1449	1496.9240	1507.1631	1510.5951
20	2371.4198	2386.3520	2408.9617	2416.5550	2447.2153	2478.3405	2486.1953	2509.9380	2525.9164	2542.0158	2566.3939	2574.5815
25	3739.0660	3769.7993	3816.4547	3832.1562	3895.7207	3960.5180	3976.9129	4026.9735	4060.0813	4093.9135	4145.2775	4162.5647
30	5714.1065	5772.7277	5861.9570	5892.0504	6014.2053	6139.2639	6170.9907	6267.2995	6332.4571	6398.3874	6498.7529	6532.6050

YEAR	8.00 %	8.10 %	8.125%	8.20 %	8.25 %	8.30 %	8.375%	8.40 %	8.50 %	8.60 %	8.625%	8.70 %
1	54.2149	54.2434	54.2505	54.2719	54.2861	54.3003	54.3217	54.3289	54.3574	54.3860	54.3931	54.4145
2	113.0100	113.1290	113.1587	113.2481	113.3078	113.3674	113.4570	113.4869	113.6065	113.7263	113.7563	113.8463
3	176.7722	177.0541	177.1247	177.3366	177.4781	177.6197	177.8324	177.9034	178.1876	178.4725	178.5438	178.7579
4	245.9211	246.4500	246.5825	246.9804	247.2462	247.5123	247.9122	248.0456	248.5805	249.1168	249.2511	249.6547
5	320.9118	321.7849	322.0037	322.6611	323.1004	323.5404	324.2018	324.4227	325.3082	326.1967	326.4193	327.0884
6	402.2379	403.5671	403.9003	404.9020	405.5716	406.2426	407.2517	407.5888	408.9407	410.2983	410.6387	411.6617
7	490.4345	492.3484	492.8283	494.2718	495.2370	496.2047	497.6607	498.1473	500.0995	502.0614	502.5534	504.0331
8	586.0821	588.7276	589.3914	591.3883	592.7243	594.0642	596.0811	596.7553	599.4619	602.1839	602.8669	604.9216
9	689.8102	693.3552	694.2450	696.9231	698.7157	700.5142	703.2227	704.1284	707.7661	711.4273	712.3463	715.1123
10	802.3014	806.9369	808.1010	811.6060	813.9532	816.3088	819.8582	821.0456	825.8168	830.6225	831.8293	835.4630
15	1524.4185	1538.3958	1541.9144	1552.5291	1559.6547	1566.8201	1577.6431	1581.2708	1595.8832	1610.6591	1614.3789	1625.6006
20	2607.6433	2641.2092	2649.6805	2675.2876	2692.5216	2709.8869	2736.1833	2745.0156	2780.6825	2816.8963	2826.0363	2853.6662
25	4232.5543	4303.9102	4321.9660	4376.6610	4413.5685	4450.8357	4507.4190	4526.4640	4603.5764	4682.2038	4702.1011	4762.3780
30	6670.0314	6810.7482	6846.4512	6954.8388	7028.1760	7102.3889	7215.3747	7253.4866	7408.2220	7566.6879	7606.8984	7728.9794

YEAR	8.75 %	8.80 %	8.875%	8.90 %	9.00 %	9.10 %	9.125%	9.20 %	9.25 %	9.30 %	9.375%	9.40 %
1	54.4288	54.4431	54.4646	54.4717	54.5004	54.5290	54.5362	54.5577	54.5721	54.5864	54.6079	54.6151
2	113.9064	113.9664	114.0566	114.0867	114.2072	114.3278	114.3580	114.4486	114.5091	114.5696	114.6604	114.6907
3	178.9009	179.0440	179.2589	179.3306	179.6178	179.9057	179.9777	180.1941	180.3385	180.4831	180.7003	180.7728
4	249.9241	250.1940	250.5995	250.7348	251.2772	251.8210	251.9572	252.3664	252.6397	252.9133	253.3245	253.4618
5	327.5354	327.9831	328.6563	328.8811	329.7822	330.6864	330.9130	331.5938	332.0488	332.5045	333.1895	333.4183
6	412.3456	413.0309	414.0616	414.4059	415.7868	417.1734	417.5210	418.5660	419.2645	419.9645	421.0173	421.3690
7	505.0227	506.0147	507.5073	508.0061	510.0074	512.0187	512.5231	514.0400	515.0545	516.0715	517.6017	518.1131
8	606.2962	607.6749	609.7502	610.4440	613.2290	616.0299	616.7327	618.8470	620.2616	621.6802	623.8159	624.5298
9	716.9637	718.8212	721.6186	722.5541	726.3113	730.0930	731.0422	733.8992	735.8116	737.7302	740.6198	741.5862
10	837.8965	840.3387	844.0187	845.2498	850.1965	855.1792	856.4305	860.1982	862.7213	865.2536	869.0694	870.3460
15	1633.1341	1640.7097	1652.1528	1655.9884	1671.4389	1687.0631	1690.9965	1702.8631	1710.8298	1718.8413	1730.9430	1734.9996
20	2872.2625	2891.0012	2919.3790	2928.9108	2967.4044	3006.4916	3016.3573	3046.1822	3066.2570	3086.4863	3117.1231	3127.4141
25	4803.0553	4844.1314	4906.5027	4927.4971	5012.5090	5099.2015	5121.1414	5187.6100	5232.4690	5277.7706	5346.5630	5369.7202
30	7811.5901	7895.1940	8022.4898	8065.4320	8239.7962	8418.3922	8463.7151	8601.3283	8694.4585	8788.7157	8932.2459	8980.6685

YEAR	9.50 %	9.75 %	10.00 %	10.25 %	10.50 %	10.75 %	11.00 %	12.00 %	13.00 %	14.00 %	15.00 %	16.00 %
1	54.6439	54.7158	54.7878	54.8600	54.9323	55.0047	55.0772	55.3686	55.6620	55.9574	56.2549	56.5544
2	114.8120	115.1160	115.4210	115.7271	116.0342	116.3424	116.6517	117.8994	119.1646	120.4473	121.7480	123.0669
3	181.0630	181.7912	182.5232	183.2591	183.9988	184.7423	185.4898	188.5189	191.6120	194.7707	197.9964	201.2909
4	254.0117	255.3934	256.7847	258.1858	259.5967	261.0176	262.4484	268.2733	274.2644	280.4269	286.7664	293.2884
5	334.3353	336.6421	338.9692	341.3169	343.6854	346.0749	348.4856	358.3443	368.5591	379.1441	390.1142	401.4849
6	422.7794	426.3318	429.9221	433.5509	437.2185	440.9254	444.6722	460.0664	476.1361	492.9138	510.4338	528.7324
7	520.1649	525.3394	530.5789	535.8844	541.2567	546.6967	552.2055	574.9468	598.8663	624.0311	650.5124	678.3856
8	627.3957	634.6329	641.9749	649.4233	656.9798	664.6461	672.4240	704.6875	738.8842	775.1413	813.5947	854.3897
9	745.4672	755.2811	765.2559	775.3947	785.7003	796.1758	806.8242	851.2107	898.6250	949.2929	1003.4584	1061.3843
10	875.4754	888.4634	901.6899	915.1598	928.8780	942.8494	957.0791	1016.6874	1080.8667	1149.9994	1224.5016	1304.8264
15	1751.3403	1793.0049	1835.8590	1879.9394	1925.2841	1971.9321	2019.9238	2226.1825	2457.5310	2717.2605	3009.1133	3337.3464
20	3168.9757	3275.7227	3386.6672	3501.9858	3621.8628	3746.4908	3876.0706	4448.2430	5118.1856	5903.7309	6826.0919	7910.5196
25	5463.4964	5706.1831	5961.1541	6229.0690	6510.6240	6806.5544	7117.6362	8530.5689	10260.39	12382.29	14989.95	18200.17
30	9177.3039	9690.1762	10235.04	10814.01	11429.31	12083.35	12778.69	16030.54	20198.62	25554.14	32451.06	41351.89

Description: This table shows what a series of $ 1 deposits grow to in the future. The deposit is made at the beginning of a period.

Example: At 5 % a regular one dollar deposit will grow to $ 68.44 by the end of the fifth year.

YEAR	0.00 %	1.00 %	2.00 %	3.00 %	4.00 %	4.125%	4.25 %	4.375%	4.50 %	4.625%	4.75 %	4.875%
1	12.0000	12.0664	12.1333	12.2006	12.2684	12.2769	12.2855	12.2940	12.3025	12.3111	12.3196	12.3282
2	24.0000	24.2558	24.5151	24.7780	25.0446	25.0782	25.1118	25.1455	25.1793	25.2131	25.2470	25.2809
3	36.0000	36.5693	37.1505	37.7438	38.3495	38.4262	38.5030	38.5800	38.6572	38.7346	38.8122	38.8900
4	48.0000	49.0084	50.0448	51.1101	52.2051	52.3442	52.4837	52.6237	52.7641	52.9051	53.0466	53.1885
5	60.0000	61.5742	63.2032	64.8891	66.6342	66.8566	67.0800	67.3043	67.5296	67.7559	67.9832	68.2115
6	72.0000	74.2681	76.6311	79.0937	81.6604	81.9888	82.3189	82.6508	82.9843	83.3197	83.6568	83.9956
7	84.0000	87.0913	90.3341	93.7369	97.3085	97.7672	98.2288	98.6932	99.1605	99.6306	100.1036	100.5794
8	96.0000	100.0452	104.3178	108.8323	113.6042	114.2196	114.8392	115.4633	116.0917	116.7245	117.3618	118.0035
9	108.0000	113.1311	118.5879	124.3940	130.5743	131.3745	132.1810	132.9939	133.8132	134.6390	135.4714	136.3104
10	120.0000	126.3503	133.1504	140.4362	148.2468	149.2621	150.2863	151.3196	152.3620	153.4136	154.4745	155.5448
15	180.0000	194.4948	210.5612	228.3919	248.2049	250.8328	253.4960	256.1951	258.9305	261.7028	264.5125	267.3603
20	240.0000	266.1828	296.2321	330.7944	370.6321	376.0259	381.5179	387.1101	392.8044	398.6030	404.5078	410.5211
25	300.0000	341.5987	391.0444	450.0164	520.5794	530.3354	540.3170	550.5300	560.9801	571.6735	582.6161	593.8145
30	360.0000	420.9363	495.9735	588.8206	704.2327	720.5328	737.2924	754.5255	772.2466	790.4707	809.2134	828.4906

YEAR	5.00 %	5.10 %	5.125%	5.20 %	5.25 %	5.30 %	5.375%	5.40 %	5.50 %	5.60 %	5.625%	5.70 %
1	12.3367	12.3436	12.3453	12.3504	12.3539	12.3573	12.3625	12.3642	12.3711	12.3779	12.3797	12.3848
2	25.3149	25.3422	25.3490	25.3694	25.3831	25.3968	25.4173	25.4241	25.4515	25.4789	25.4858	25.5064
3	38.9680	39.0305	39.0462	39.0932	39.1246	39.1560	39.2032	39.2190	39.2820	39.3452	39.3611	39.4086
4	53.3309	53.4452	53.4739	53.5599	53.6173	53.6748	53.7612	53.7901	53.9057	54.0216	54.0506	54.1378
5	68.4408	68.6249	68.6710	68.8097	68.9023	68.9951	69.1346	69.1811	69.3679	69.5552	69.6022	69.7432
6	84.3362	84.6100	84.6786	84.8850	85.0229	85.1610	85.3689	85.4383	85.7167	85.9963	86.0664	86.2770
7	101.0583	101.4434	101.5400	101.8305	102.0247	102.2194	102.5124	102.6103	103.0031	103.3978	103.4968	103.7944
8	118.6498	119.1701	119.3006	119.6933	119.9560	120.2194	120.6160	120.7486	121.2807	121.8158	121.9500	122.3539
9	137.1560	137.8374	138.0084	138.5230	138.8675	139.2131	139.7335	139.9075	140.6064	141.3097	141.4862	142.0175
10	156.6245	157.4952	157.7139	158.3721	158.8129	159.2552	159.9217	160.1446	161.0403	161.9424	162.1689	162.8509
15	270.2466	272.5838	273.1720	274.9463	276.1372	277.3345	279.1427	279.7487	282.1891	284.6561	285.2771	287.1501
20	416.6451	421.6254	422.8819	426.6790	429.2338	431.8073	435.7031	437.0113	442.2922	447.6515	449.0036	453.0902
25	605.2750	614.6366	617.0044	624.1739	629.0094	633.8902	641.2972	643.7894	653.8750	664.1510	666.7501	674.6211
30	848.3187	864.5894	868.7149	881.2326	889.6967	898.2574	911.2822	915.6734	933.4902	951.7177	956.3400	970.3662

YEAR	5.75 %	5.80 %	5.875%	5.90 %	6.00 %	6.10 %	6.125%	6.20 %	6.25 %	6.30 %	6.375%	6.40 %
1	12.3883	12.3917	12.3969	12.3986	12.4055	12.4124	12.4141	12.4193	12.4228	12.4262	12.4314	12.4332
2	25.5202	25.5339	25.5546	25.5615	25.5890	25.6167	25.6236	25.6443	25.6582	25.6720	25.6928	25.6998
3	39.4403	39.4721	39.5197	39.5357	39.5994	39.6633	39.6793	39.7273	39.7593	39.7914	39.8396	39.8557
4	54.1960	54.2544	54.3420	54.3712	54.4884	54.6060	54.6354	54.7238	54.7829	54.8420	54.9309	54.9605
5	69.8375	69.9319	70.0739	70.1213	70.3113	70.5019	70.5497	70.6932	70.7892	70.8852	71.0297	71.0779
6	86.4179	86.5590	86.7712	86.8421	87.1264	87.4119	87.4835	87.6987	87.8425	87.9866	88.2033	88.2757
7	103.9935	104.1931	104.4933	104.5936	104.9962	105.4007	105.5022	105.8073	106.0113	106.2158	106.5236	106.6264
8	122.6241	122.8951	123.3030	123.4394	123.9867	124.5371	124.6752	125.0906	125.3686	125.6473	126.0669	126.2072
9	142.3731	142.7298	143.2671	143.4467	144.1682	144.8943	145.0765	145.6250	145.9921	146.3604	146.9151	147.1005
10	163.3075	163.7658	164.4563	164.6873	165.6154	166.5501	166.7848	167.4915	167.9647	168.4396	169.1551	169.3945
15	288.4072	289.6712	291.5801	292.2198	294.7964	297.4012	298.0568	300.0345	301.3619	302.6967	304.7125	305.3881
20	455.8397	458.6096	462.8030	464.2112	469.8962	475.6659	477.1217	481.5217	484.4824	487.4651	491.9810	493.4975
25	679.9303	685.2895	693.4232	696.1600	707.2370	718.5245	721.3798	730.0270	735.8602	741.7488	750.6869	753.6945
30	979.8515	989.4461	1004.0455	1008.9680	1028.9431	1049.3826	1054.5664	1070.2981	1080.9380	1091.7014	1108.0814	1113.6048

YEAR	6.50 %	6.60 %	6.625%	6.70 %	6.75 %	6.80 %	6.875%	6.90 %	7.00 %	7.10 %	7.125%	7.20 %
1	12.4401	12.4470	12.4487	12.4539	12.4574	12.4609	12.4661	12.4678	12.4748	12.4817	12.4835	12.4887
2	25.7275	25.7553	25.7623	25.7832	25.7971	25.8111	25.8320	25.8390	25.8670	25.8950	25.9020	25.9231
3	39.9201	39.9846	40.0008	40.0493	40.0817	40.1141	40.1628	40.1790	40.2441	40.3093	40.3257	40.3747
4	55.0794	55.1986	55.2284	55.3181	55.3780	55.4379	55.5280	55.5581	55.6786	55.7995	55.8297	55.9207
5	71.2713	71.4653	71.5139	71.6600	71.7576	71.8554	72.0024	72.0515	72.2482	72.4457	72.4951	72.6438
6	88.5661	88.8577	88.9308	89.1505	89.2974	89.4446	89.6659	89.7399	90.0364	90.3342	90.4089	90.6333
7	107.0390	107.4536	107.5576	107.8703	108.0794	108.2891	108.6045	108.7099	109.1328	109.5578	109.6644	109.9850
8	126.7702	127.3364	127.4785	127.9058	128.1918	128.4785	128.9102	129.0545	129.6337	130.2162	130.3623	130.8020
9	147.8454	148.5951	148.7832	149.3495	149.7286	150.1089	150.6816	150.8731	151.6422	152.4163	152.6106	153.1954
10	170.3562	171.3248	171.5681	172.3004	172.7908	173.2830	174.0245	174.2726	175.2694	176.2733	176.5254	177.2844
15	308.1091	310.8601	311.5525	313.6414	315.0435	316.4533	318.5826	319.2963	322.1707	325.0768	325.8084	328.0152
20	499.6202	505.8348	507.4030	512.1428	515.3322	518.5456	523.4109	525.0449	531.6421	538.3390	540.0290	545.1371
25	765.8686	778.2759	781.4148	790.9212	797.3346	803.8094	813.6379	816.9454	830.3345	843.9818	847.4346	857.8927
30	1136.0207	1158.9621	1164.7810	1182.4420	1194.3881	1206.4739	1224.8685	1231.0718	1256.2499	1282.0227	1288.5606	1308.4052

SAVINGS GROWTH

Description: This table shows what a series of $ 1 deposits grow to in the future. The deposit is made at the beginning of a period.

Example: At 8 % a regular one dollar deposit will grow to $ 74.25 by the end of the fifth year.

YEAR	7.25 %	7.30 %	7.375%	7.40 %	7.50 %	7.60 %	7.625%	7.70 %	7.75 %	7.80 %	7.875%	7.90 %
1	12.4922	12.4957	12.5009	12.5026	12.5096	12.5166	12.5183	12.5236	12.5270	12.5305	12.5358	12.5375
2	25.9371	25.9511	25.9722	25.9793	26.0074	26.0356	26.0427	26.0639	26.0780	26.0922	26.1134	26.1205
3	40.4074	40.4402	40.4894	40.5058	40.5716	40.6375	40.6540	40.7035	40.7366	40.7697	40.8194	40.8360
4	55.9814	56.0422	56.1336	56.1641	56.2863	56.4088	56.4395	56.5317	56.5933	56.6550	56.7477	56.7786
5	72.7432	72.8427	72.9922	73.0422	73.2424	73.4434	73.4937	73.6450	73.7461	73.8474	73.9996	74.0505
6	90.7833	90.9336	91.1597	91.2352	91.5381	91.8423	91.9185	92.1477	92.3010	92.4545	92.6854	92.7626
7	110.1993	110.4142	110.7376	110.8456	111.2791	111.7148	111.8241	112.1527	112.3724	112.5927	112.9241	113.0349
8	131.0962	131.3912	131.8353	131.9837	132.5797	133.1790	133.3293	133.7817	134.0844	134.3879	134.8449	134.9976
9	153.5868	153.9795	154.5709	154.7686	155.5629	156.3623	156.5630	157.1669	157.5711	157.9766	158.5874	158.7916
10	177.7927	178.3029	179.0715	179.3286	180.3618	181.4024	181.6638	182.4506	182.9775	183.5063	184.3031	184.5697
15	329.4966	330.9861	333.2359	333.9900	337.0272	340.0982	340.8713	343.2034	344.7689	346.3431	348.7209	349.5179
20	548.5746	552.0380	557.2823	559.0436	566.1553	573.3751	575.1972	580.7047	584.4113	588.1459	593.8011	595.7005
25	864.9488	872.0727	882.8877	886.5274	901.2624	916.2835	920.0842	931.5968	939.3649	947.2083	959.1164	963.1242
30	1321.8299	1335.4129	1356.0883	1363.0614	1391.3669	1420.3461	1427.6982	1450.0161	1465.1155	1480.3942	1503.6533	1511.4984

YEAR	8.00 %	8.10 %	8.125%	8.20 %	8.25 %	8.30 %	8.375%	8.40 %	8.50 %	8.60 %	8.625%	8.70 %
1	12.5445	12.5515	12.5533	12.5585	12.5621	12.5656	12.5708	12.5726	12.5796	12.5866	12.5884	12.5937
2	26.1489	26.1773	26.1844	26.2057	26.2199	26.2342	26.2556	26.2627	26.2913	26.3199	26.3270	26.3485
3	40.9025	40.9691	40.9858	41.0358	41.0692	41.1027	41.1529	41.1697	41.2369	41.3042	41.3210	41.3716
4	56.9025	57.0268	57.0579	57.1514	57.2139	57.2764	57.3704	57.4018	57.5275	57.6535	57.6851	57.7799
5	74.2543	74.4588	74.5100	74.6640	74.7669	74.8700	75.0249	75.0767	75.2841	75.4922	75.5444	75.7011
6	93.0719	93.3826	93.4605	93.6946	93.8511	94.0080	94.2438	94.3226	94.6386	94.9560	95.0355	95.2747
7	113.4793	113.9260	114.0380	114.3748	114.6001	114.8260	115.1658	115.2793	115.7350	116.1929	116.3077	116.6531
8	135.6108	136.2275	136.3822	136.8477	137.1591	137.4715	137.9416	138.0988	138.7298	139.3644	139.5236	140.0026
9	159.6119	160.4375	160.6448	161.2685	161.6860	162.1049	162.7357	162.9467	163.7940	164.6467	164.8608	165.5051
10	185.6407	186.7196	186.9905	187.8062	188.3525	188.9007	189.7269	190.0032	191.1137	192.2323	192.5132	193.3590
15	352.7280	355.9741	356.7912	359.2564	360.9113	362.5754	365.0890	365.9316	369.3254	372.7574	373.6214	376.2278
20	603.3703	611.1574	613.1227	619.0635	623.0618	627.0907	633.1917	635.2409	643.5163	651.9187	654.0395	660.4504
25	979.3509	995.8948	1000.0811	1012.7625	1021.3200	1029.9609	1043.0808	1047.4969	1065.3774	1083.6098	1088.2237	1102.2013
30	1543.3473	1575.9596	1584.2342	1609.3548	1626.3521	1643.5527	1669.7403	1678.5739	1714.4393	1751.1705	1760.4911	1788.7894

YEAR	8.75 %	8.80 %	8.875%	8.90 %	9.00 %	9.10 %	9.125%	9.20 %	9.25 %	9.30 %	9.375%	9.40 %
1	12.5972	12.6007	12.6060	12.6077	12.6148	12.6218	12.6236	12.6289	12.6324	12.6360	12.6413	12.6430
2	26.3628	26.3772	26.3987	26.4059	26.4347	26.4635	26.4707	26.4923	26.5068	26.5212	26.5429	26.5501
3	41.4054	41.4392	41.4900	41.5069	41.5748	41.6428	41.6598	41.7109	41.7451	41.7792	41.8306	41.8477
4	57.8432	57.9066	58.0019	58.0338	58.1612	58.2890	58.3211	58.4172	58.4815	58.5458	58.6424	58.6747
5	75.8058	75.9107	76.0684	76.1211	76.3322	76.5440	76.5971	76.7566	76.8632	76.9700	77.1305	77.1841
6	95.4346	95.5948	95.8357	95.9162	96.2390	96.5632	96.6445	96.8888	97.0521	97.2157	97.4619	97.5441
7	116.8840	117.1156	117.4640	117.5804	118.0475	118.5170	118.6348	118.9889	119.2257	119.4631	119.8203	119.9397
8	140.3231	140.6445	141.1284	141.2901	141.9395	142.5925	142.7564	143.2494	143.5792	143.9100	144.4080	144.5744
9	165.9363	166.3690	167.0206	167.2385	168.1138	168.9947	169.2158	169.8814	170.3269	170.7739	171.4471	171.6722
10	193.9254	194.4939	195.3505	195.6370	196.7885	197.9484	198.2397	199.1168	199.7042	200.2937	201.1820	201.4792
15	377.9777	379.7373	382.3953	383.2863	386.8753	390.5047	391.4184	394.1751	396.0258	397.8869	400.6983	401.6407
20	664.7654	669.1135	675.6984	677.9102	686.8426	695.9130	698.2024	705.1237	709.7824	714.4770	721.5870	723.9753
25	1111.6342	1121.1596	1135.6237	1140.4924	1160.2074	1180.3128	1185.4011	1200.8167	1211.2208	1221.7276	1237.6830	1243.0540
30	1807.9389	1827.3189	1856.8275	1866.7822	1907.2031	1948.6063	1959.1135	1991.0169	2012.6080	2034.4607	2067.7375	2078.9642

YEAR	9.50 %	9.75 %	10.00 %	10.25 %	10.50 %	10.75 %	11.00 %	12.00 %	13.00 %	14.00 %	15.00 %	16.00 %
1	12.6501	12.6678	12.6855	12.7033	12.7211	12.7389	12.7568	12.8286	12.9008	12.9736	13.0469	13.1208
2	26.5791	26.6517	26.7245	26.7976	26.8710	26.9446	27.0185	27.3166	27.6189	27.9255	28.2365	28.5519
3	41.9163	42.0883	42.2613	42.4353	42.6101	42.7858	42.9625	43.6787	44.4101	45.1572	45.9204	46.7000
4	58.8040	59.1287	59.4558	59.7852	60.1169	60.4510	60.7874	62.1573	63.5665	65.0165	66.5084	68.0437
5	77.3990	77.9395	78.4848	79.0350	79.5900	80.1501	80.7151	83.0262	85.4213	87.9039	90.4774	93.1456
6	97.8738	98.7044	99.5440	100.3925	101.2502	102.1172	102.9935	106.5946	110.3546	114.2812	118.3826	122.6674
7	120.4187	121.6267	122.8500	124.0888	125.3432	126.6135	127.9000	133.2116	138.7999	144.6805	150.8704	157.3873
8	145.2427	146.9304	148.6426	150.3797	152.1421	153.9303	155.7446	163.2718	171.2520	179.7152	188.6933	198.2207
9	172.5764	174.8629	177.1870	179.5495	181.9510	184.3922	186.8740	197.2203	208.2753	220.0919	232.7276	246.2441
10	202.6734	205.6973	208.7769	211.9133	215.1078	218.3615	221.6755	235.5602	250.5136	266.6254	283.9931	302.7233
15	405.4370	415.1169	425.0739	435.3166	445.8537	456.6943	467.8481	515.7928	569.5845	629.9921	697.8901	774.2735
20	733.6210	758.3962	784.1474	810.9157	838.7442	867.6775	897.7626	1030.6306	1186.2472	1368.7697	1583.1447	1835.2623
25	1264.8047	1321.0970	1380.2429	1442.3959	1507.7180	1576.3803	1648.5633	1976.4804	2378.0603	2870.8124	3476.5526	4222.4886
30	2124.5548	2243.4721	2369.8173	2504.0789	2646.7785	2798.4732	2959.7580	3714.1771	4681.4564	5924.6841	7526.2276	9593.7517

SAVINGS GROWTH

Description: This table shows what a series of $ 1 deposits grow to in the future. The deposit is made at the beginning of a period.

Example: At 5 % a regular one dollar deposit will grow to $ 22.91 by the end of the fifth year.

YEAR	0.00 %	1.00 %	2.00 %	3.00 %	4.00 %	4.125%	4.25 %	4.375%	4.50 %	4.625%	4.75 %	4.875%
1	4.0000	4.0255	4.0513	4.0772	4.1033	4.1066	4.1099	4.1132	4.1165	4.1198	4.1231	4.1264
2	8.0000	8.0921	8.1855	8.2803	8.3765	8.3886	8.4008	8.4129	8.4251	8.4373	8.4495	8.4618
3	12.0000	12.2001	12.4045	12.6133	12.8265	12.8535	12.8805	12.9077	12.9349	12.9621	12.9895	13.0169
4	16.0000	16.3500	16.7099	17.0800	17.4607	17.5091	17.5576	17.6063	17.6551	17.7042	17.7534	17.8028
5	20.0000	20.5421	21.1034	21.6847	22.2867	22.3634	22.4405	22.5180	22.5957	22.6738	22.7523	22.8311
6	24.0000	24.7770	25.5870	26.4316	27.3124	27.4251	27.5385	27.6524	27.7670	27.8821	27.9979	28.1142
7	28.0000	29.0550	30.1624	31.3251	32.5461	32.7030	32.8609	33.0197	33.1796	33.3404	33.5022	33.6650
8	32.0000	33.3766	34.8315	36.3697	37.9964	38.2063	38.4176	38.6305	38.8448	39.0607	39.2781	39.4970
9	36.0000	37.7423	39.5963	41.5701	43.6723	43.9446	44.2191	44.4957	44.7745	45.0556	45.3389	45.6245
10	40.0000	42.1525	44.4587	46.9311	49.5831	49.9280	50.2759	50.6269	50.9810	51.3383	51.6988	52.0625
15	60.0000	64.8865	70.3060	76.3242	83.0154	83.9033	84.8031	85.7150	86.6394	87.5762	88.5258	89.4884
20	80.0000	88.8028	98.9114	110.5451	123.9629	125.7802	127.6307	129.5152	131.4342	133.3885	135.3788	137.4058
25	100.0000	113.9627	130.5690	150.3868	174.1148	177.3965	180.7545	184.1905	187.7066	191.3048	194.9873	198.7561
30	120.0000	140.4310	165.6047	196.7726	235.5401	241.0173	246.6494	252.4411	258.3974	264.5232	270.8238	277.3047

YEAR	5.00 %	5.10 %	5.125%	5.20 %	5.25 %	5.30 %	5.375%	5.40 %	5.50 %	5.60 %	5.625%	5.70 %
1	4.1297	4.1323	4.1330	4.1350	4.1363	4.1376	4.1396	4.1403	4.1429	4.1456	4.1462	4.1482
2	8.4741	8.4839	8.4864	8.4938	8.4987	8.5036	8.5110	8.5135	8.5234	8.5333	8.5358	8.5432
3	13.0444	13.0664	13.0719	13.0885	13.0996	13.1106	13.1273	13.1328	13.1551	13.1773	13.1829	13.1997
4	17.8523	17.8921	17.9021	17.9320	17.9520	17.9720	18.0021	18.0121	18.0523	18.0927	18.1028	18.1331
5	22.9103	22.9739	22.9898	23.0377	23.0696	23.1017	23.1499	23.1659	23.2304	23.2951	23.3114	23.3601
6	28.2312	28.3253	28.3488	28.4197	28.4671	28.5145	28.5859	28.6098	28.7054	28.8015	28.8256	28.8980
7	33.8289	33.9607	33.9937	34.0931	34.1596	34.2262	34.3265	34.3600	34.4944	34.6295	34.6634	34.7653
8	39.7175	39.8951	39.9396	40.0736	40.1633	40.2532	40.3885	40.4338	40.6154	40.7980	40.8438	40.9817
9	45.9124	46.1444	46.2026	46.3779	46.4952	46.6128	46.7901	46.8493	47.0873	47.3268	47.3870	47.5679
10	52.4294	52.7254	52.7997	53.0234	53.1732	53.3236	53.5501	53.6259	53.9304	54.2370	54.3141	54.5459
15	90.4640	91.2541	91.4529	92.0528	92.4554	92.8602	93.4715	93.6764	94.5016	95.3358	95.5458	96.1792
20	139.4703	141.1494	141.5730	142.8533	143.7147	144.5824	145.8961	146.3372	148.1181	149.9255	150.3815	151.7598
25	202.6134	205.7646	206.5616	208.9750	210.6029	212.2460	214.7397	215.5788	218.9745	222.4346	223.3098	225.9603
30	283.9714	289.4424	290.8296	295.0390	297.8854	300.7643	305.1448	306.6216	312.6141	318.7452	320.3000	325.0183

YEAR	5.75 %	5.80 %	5.875%	5.90 %	6.00 %	6.10 %	6.125%	6.20 %	6.25 %	6.30 %	6.375%	6.40 %
1	4.1495	4.1509	4.1529	4.1535	4.1562	4.1589	4.1595	4.1615	4.1629	4.1642	4.1662	4.1669
2	8.5482	8.5532	8.5606	8.5631	8.5731	8.5830	8.5855	8.5930	8.5980	8.6030	8.6106	8.6131
3	13.2109	13.2220	13.2389	13.2445	13.2669	13.2895	13.2951	13.3120	13.3233	13.3346	13.3516	13.3573
4	18.1534	18.1737	18.2042	18.2144	18.2552	18.2961	18.3064	18.3372	18.3577	18.3783	18.4092	18.4196
5	23.3926	23.4253	23.4743	23.4907	23.5563	23.6222	23.6387	23.6883	23.7214	23.7546	23.8045	23.8212
6	28.9464	28.9949	29.0678	29.0922	29.1899	29.2880	29.3126	29.3865	29.4360	29.4855	29.5600	29.5849
7	34.8335	34.9018	35.0046	35.0389	35.1767	35.3153	35.3500	35.4545	35.5243	35.5944	35.6998	35.7350
8	41.0739	41.1665	41.3057	41.3522	41.5391	41.7270	41.7742	41.9160	42.0110	42.1061	42.2494	42.2973
9	47.6890	47.8105	47.9935	48.0547	48.3005	48.5478	48.6099	48.7968	48.9219	49.0474	49.2364	49.2996
10	54.7012	54.8570	55.0918	55.1703	55.4859	55.8038	55.8836	56.1239	56.2849	56.4464	56.6898	56.7712
15	96.6043	97.0318	97.6774	97.8938	98.7653	99.6464	99.8681	100.5372	100.9862	101.4378	102.1198	102.3483
20	152.6872	153.6215	155.0360	155.5110	157.4287	159.3752	159.8664	161.3509	162.3498	163.3562	164.8800	165.3917
25	227.7482	229.5530	232.2922	233.2140	236.9448	240.7467	241.7085	244.6214	246.5864	248.5701	251.5813	252.5946
30	328.2092	331.4370	336.3487	338.0048	344.7256	351.6031	353.3474	358.6412	362.2218	365.8440	371.3567	373.2156

YEAR	6.50 %	6.60 %	6.625%	6.70 %	6.75 %	6.80 %	6.875%	6.90 %	7.00 %	7.10 %	7.125%	7.20 %
1	4.1695	4.1722	4.1729	4.1749	4.1762	4.1776	4.1796	4.1803	4.1829	4.1856	4.1863	4.1883
2	8.6231	8.6332	8.6357	8.6432	8.6483	8.6533	8.6609	8.6634	8.6735	8.6836	8.6862	8.6938
3	13.3800	13.4028	13.4085	13.4256	13.4370	13.4485	13.4656	13.4714	13.4943	13.5173	13.5231	13.5404
4	18.4610	18.5025	18.5129	18.5441	18.5650	18.5858	18.6172	18.6277	18.6697	18.7118	18.7223	18.7540
5	23.8880	23.9551	23.9719	24.0223	24.0561	24.0899	24.1407	24.1577	24.2257	24.2939	24.3110	24.3624
6	29.6847	29.7850	29.8101	29.8856	29.9361	29.9867	30.0629	30.0883	30.1903	30.2927	30.3183	30.3955
7	35.8763	36.0183	36.0539	36.1610	36.2326	36.3045	36.4125	36.4486	36.5935	36.7391	36.7756	36.8855
8	42.4896	42.6830	42.7315	42.8775	42.9751	43.0731	43.2205	43.2698	43.4677	43.6667	43.7166	43.8668
9	49.5534	49.8088	49.8730	50.0660	50.1951	50.3248	50.5200	50.5852	50.8474	51.1113	51.1775	51.3769
10	57.0983	57.4278	57.5106	57.7597	57.9265	58.0940	58.3463	58.4307	58.7698	59.1115	59.1972	59.4556
15	103.2690	104.1998	104.4341	105.1410	105.6154	106.0926	106.8132	107.0547	108.0276	109.0112	109.2588	110.0059
20	167.4578	169.5550	170.0843	171.6839	172.7604	173.8450	175.4872	176.0388	178.2658	180.5265	181.0971	182.8216
25	256.6963	260.8769	261.9346	265.1379	267.2992	269.4811	272.7934	273.9082	278.4208	283.0207	284.1846	287.7099
30	380.7603	388.4823	390.4410	396.3862	400.4077	404.4764	410.6693	412.7578	421.2351	429.9133	432.1148	438.7974

Description: This table shows what a series of $ 1 deposits grow to in the future. The deposit is made at the beginning of a period.

Example: At 8 % a regular one dollar deposit will grow to $ 24.92 by the end of the fifth year.

YEAR	7.25 %	7.30 %	7.375%	7.40 %	7.50 %	7.60 %	7.625%	7.70 %	7.75 %	7.80 %	7.875%	7.90 %
1	4.1897	4.1910	4.1930	4.1937	4.1964	4.1991	4.1997	4.2018	4.2031	4.2045	4.2065	4.2072
2	8.6988	8.7039	8.7115	8.7141	8.7243	8.7345	8.7370	8.7447	8.7498	8.7549	8.7626	8.7652
3	13.5519	13.5635	13.5809	13.5867	13.6099	13.6331	13.6389	13.6564	13.6681	13.6798	13.6973	13.7032
4	18.7752	18.7964	18.8282	18.8388	18.8814	18.9241	18.9348	18.9669	18.9884	19.0099	19.0422	19.0530
5	24.3968	24.4312	24.4829	24.5002	24.5694	24.6389	24.6563	24.7086	24.7436	24.7786	24.8313	24.8488
6	30.4471	30.4988	30.5766	30.6025	30.7067	30.8114	30.8376	30.9164	30.9692	31.0220	31.1014	31.1280
7	36.9589	37.0325	37.1433	37.1804	37.3289	37.4782	37.5157	37.6283	37.7036	37.7791	37.8927	37.9307
8	43.9673	44.0681	44.2199	44.2706	44.4742	44.6791	44.7304	44.8851	44.9885	45.0922	45.2484	45.3006
9	51.5103	51.6442	51.8458	51.9132	52.1840	52.4566	52.5250	52.7310	52.8688	53.0071	53.2154	53.2851
10	59.6285	59.8021	60.0637	60.1513	60.5029	60.8571	60.9461	61.2139	61.3933	61.5733	61.8446	61.9353
15	110.5073	111.0116	111.7732	112.0285	113.0568	114.0966	114.3583	115.1480	115.6781	116.2112	117.0164	117.2864
20	183.9822	185.1516	186.9223	187.5170	189.9185	192.3566	192.9720	194.8320	196.0838	197.3452	199.2553	199.8969
25	290.0885	292.4901	296.1361	297.3632	302.3312	307.3960	308.6775	312.5596	315.1792	317.8242	321.8402	323.1919
30	443.3183	447.8927	454.8559	457.2045	466.7382	476.4995	478.9761	486.4942	491.5810	496.7283	504.5645	507.2077

YEAR	8.00 %	8.10 %	8.125%	8.20 %	8.25 %	8.30 %	8.375%	8.40 %	8.50 %	8.60 %	8.625%	8.70 %
1	4.2099	4.2126	4.2133	4.2153	4.2166	4.2180	4.2200	4.2207	4.2234	4.2261	4.2268	4.2289
2	8.7754	8.7857	8.7883	8.7960	8.8011	8.8063	8.8140	8.8166	8.8269	8.8373	8.8399	8.8476
3	13.7266	13.7502	13.7560	13.7737	13.7855	13.7973	13.8151	13.8210	13.8447	13.8685	13.8744	13.8923
4	19.0962	19.1395	19.1503	19.1829	19.2047	19.2265	19.2593	19.2702	19.3140	19.3580	19.3690	19.4021
5	24.9193	24.9901	25.0078	25.0611	25.0966	25.1323	25.1859	25.2038	25.2756	25.3476	25.3656	25.4199
6	31.2344	31.3413	31.3681	31.4487	31.5025	31.5565	31.6377	31.6648	31.7736	31.8828	31.9102	31.9925
7	38.0830	38.2361	38.2745	38.3900	38.4673	38.5447	38.6612	38.7001	38.8564	39.0134	39.0528	39.1712
8	45.5102	45.7210	45.7739	45.9331	46.0395	46.1463	46.3071	46.3608	46.5766	46.7936	46.8480	47.0118
9	53.5649	53.8465	53.9172	54.1299	54.2724	54.4153	54.6305	54.7024	54.9915	55.2825	55.3555	55.5753
10	62.3000	62.6673	62.7596	63.0373	63.2234	63.4101	63.6914	63.7855	64.1637	64.5447	64.6404	64.9285
15	118.3736	119.4730	119.7498	120.5848	121.1453	121.7090	122.5606	122.8460	123.9958	125.1586	125.4513	126.3345
20	202.4877	205.1183	205.7822	207.7893	209.1401	210.5013	212.5628	213.2552	216.0515	218.8909	219.6076	221.7743
25	328.6647	334.2449	335.6570	339.9347	342.8215	345.7365	350.1627	351.6526	357.6854	363.8373	365.3942	370.1109
30	517.9387	528.9278	531.7162	540.1815	545.9097	551.7066	560.5326	563.5100	575.5987	587.9802	591.1222	600.6619

YEAR	8.75 %	8.80 %	8.875%	8.90 %	9.00 %	9.10 %	9.125%	9.20 %	9.25 %	9.30 %	9.375%	9.40 %
1	4.2302	4.2316	4.2336	4.2343	4.2370	4.2397	4.2404	4.2425	4.2438	4.2452	4.2473	4.2479
2	8.8528	8.8580	8.8658	8.8684	8.8788	8.8892	8.8918	8.8997	8.9049	8.9101	8.9180	8.9206
3	13.9042	13.9161	13.9341	13.9401	13.9640	13.9880	13.9941	14.0121	14.0242	14.0362	14.0544	14.0604
4	19.4241	19.4463	19.4795	19.4906	19.5350	19.5796	19.5908	19.6243	19.6467	19.6692	19.7029	19.7141
5	25.4561	25.4924	25.5470	25.5652	25.6382	25.7116	25.7299	25.7852	25.8220	25.8590	25.9146	25.9331
6	32.0476	32.1027	32.1857	32.2134	32.3245	32.4361	32.4641	32.5482	32.6045	32.6608	32.7456	32.7739
7	39.2504	39.3298	39.4493	39.4893	39.6495	39.8105	39.8509	39.9724	40.0536	40.1351	40.2576	40.2986
8	47.1214	47.2313	47.3968	47.4521	47.6742	47.8976	47.9537	48.1223	48.2352	48.3483	48.5187	48.5756
9	55.7225	55.8702	56.0925	56.1669	56.4656	56.7663	56.8417	57.0689	57.2210	57.3736	57.6034	57.6802
10	65.1214	65.3151	65.6069	65.7045	66.0968	66.4920	66.5912	66.8901	67.0902	67.2911	67.5938	67.6951
15	126.9274	127.5237	128.4244	128.7263	129.9426	131.1727	131.4824	132.4168	133.0441	133.6750	134.6280	134.9475
20	223.2326	224.7022	226.9279	227.6755	230.6948	233.7611	234.5350	236.8749	238.4500	240.0372	242.4412	243.2488
25	373.2941	376.5086	381.3901	383.0332	389.6873	396.4737	398.1912	403.3950	406.9072	410.4543	415.8409	417.6543
30	607.1178	613.6515	623.6005	626.9569	640.5862	654.5478	658.0910	668.8500	676.1317	683.5018	694.7255	698.5122

YEAR	9.50 %	9.75 %	10.00 %	10.25 %	10.50 %	10.75 %	11.00 %	12.00 %	13.00 %	14.00 %	15.00 %	16.00 %
1	4.2507	4.2575	4.2644	4.2712	4.2781	4.2850	4.2919	4.3197	4.3477	4.3759	4.4043	4.4330
2	8.9311	8.9574	8.9837	9.0102	9.0368	9.0634	9.0902	9.1982	9.3078	9.4191	9.5319	9.6465
3	14.0846	14.1455	14.2066	14.2680	14.3298	14.3920	14.4545	14.7078	14.9666	15.2312	15.5016	15.7780
4	19.7592	19.8725	19.9867	20.1016	20.2174	20.3341	20.4515	20.9300	21.4225	21.9296	22.4516	22.9892
5	26.0075	26.1946	26.3835	26.5740	26.7663	26.9603	27.1560	27.9571	28.7878	29.6493	30.5430	31.4701
6	32.8874	33.1735	33.4627	33.7551	34.0506	34.3494	34.6515	35.8932	37.1905	38.5462	39.9631	41.4443
7	40.4629	40.8775	41.2973	41.7225	42.1531	42.5893	43.0311	44.8559	46.7769	48.7997	50.9302	53.1747
8	48.8043	49.3818	49.9677	50.5623	51.1657	51.7779	52.3992	54.9779	57.7135	60.6166	63.6983	66.9707
9	57.9889	58.7696	59.5632	60.3701	61.1904	62.0245	62.8725	66.4093	70.1907	74.2354	78.5632	83.1958
10	68.1021	69.1327	70.1825	71.2518	72.3411	73.4508	74.5812	79.3193	84.4254	89.9307	95.8692	102.2778
15	136.2344	139.5164	142.8930	146.3669	149.9414	153.6194	157.4043	173.6810	191.9553	212.4917	235.5908	261.5953
20	246.5104	254.8890	263.5992	272.6550	282.0711	291.8628	302.0462	347.0404	399.7765	461.6759	534.4313	620.0600
25	424.9981	444.0068	463.9828	484.9782	507.0482	530.2510	554.6480	665.5329	801.4287	968.3037	1173.6000	1426.6060
30	713.8903	754.0074	796.6384	841.9489	890.1162	941.3294	995.7906	1250.6611	1577.6948	1998.3519	2540.6722	3241.3358

SAVINGS GROWTH

Description: This table shows what a series of $ 1 deposits grow to in the future. The deposit is made at the beginning of a period.

Example: At 5 % a regular one dollar deposit will grow to $ 11.53 by the end of the fifth year.

YEAR	0.00 %	1.00 %	2.00 %	3.00 %	4.00 %	4.125%	4.25 %	4.375%	4.50 %	4.625%	4.75 %	4.875%
1	2.0000	2.0153	2.0308	2.0463	2.0620	2.0640	2.0660	2.0680	2.0699	2.0719	2.0739	2.0759
2	4.0000	4.0512	4.1031	4.1559	4.2094	4.2162	4.2229	4.2297	4.2365	4.2433	4.2501	4.2570
3	6.0000	6.1078	6.2179	6.3305	6.4457	6.4602	6.4749	6.4895	6.5042	6.5189	6.5337	6.5485
4	8.0000	8.1853	8.3761	8.5724	8.7745	8.8002	8.8259	8.8518	8.8778	8.9038	8.9300	8.9562
5	10.0000	10.2840	10.5784	10.8834	11.1997	11.2400	11.2805	11.3212	11.3621	11.4032	11.4444	11.4859
6	12.0000	12.4042	12.8258	13.2659	13.7252	13.7841	13.8432	13.9026	13.9624	14.0225	14.0830	14.1437
7	14.0000	14.5459	15.1193	15.7219	16.3553	16.4367	16.5187	16.6011	16.6841	16.7676	16.8516	16.9362
8	16.0000	16.7094	17.4598	18.2538	19.0943	19.2027	19.3120	19.4220	19.5329	19.6445	19.7569	19.8702
9	18.0000	18.8950	19.8482	20.8638	21.9465	22.0868	22.2283	22.3708	22.5146	22.6595	22.8055	22.9528
10	20.0000	21.1029	22.2855	23.5545	24.9169	25.0941	25.2730	25.4534	25.6355	25.8192	26.0046	26.1916
15	30.0000	32.4843	35.2419	38.3068	41.7175	42.1703	42.6292	43.0945	43.5660	44.0440	44.5286	45.0198
20	40.0000	44.4575	49.5807	55.4821	62.2947	63.2179	64.1581	65.1156	66.0908	67.0840	68.0957	69.1261
25	50.0000	57.0534	65.4495	75.4785	87.4974	89.1606	90.8626	92.6044	94.3870	96.2114	98.0788	99.9902
30	60.0000	70.3042	83.0116	98.7593	118.3653	121.1368	123.9870	126.9184	129.9334	133.0346	136.2247	139.5065

YEAR	5.00 %	5.10 %	5.125%	5.20 %	5.25 %	5.30 %	5.375%	5.40 %	5.50 %	5.60 %	5.625%	5.70 %
1	2.0779	2.0795	2.0799	2.0811	2.0819	2.0827	2.0839	2.0843	2.0859	2.0874	2.0878	2.0890
2	4.2638	4.2693	4.2707	4.2748	4.2775	4.2803	4.2844	4.2858	4.2913	4.2968	4.2982	4.3024
3	6.5634	6.5753	6.5783	6.5873	6.5932	6.5992	6.6082	6.6112	6.6232	6.6353	6.6383	6.6474
4	8.9826	9.0037	9.0090	9.0249	9.0355	9.0462	9.0622	9.0675	9.0889	9.1103	9.1157	9.1319
5	11.5275	11.5610	11.5693	11.5945	11.6113	11.6282	11.6535	11.6620	11.6959	11.7300	11.7385	11.7642
6	14.2048	14.2539	14.2662	14.3032	14.3280	14.3528	14.3900	14.4025	14.4525	14.5027	14.5152	14.5531
7	17.0213	17.0898	17.1069	17.1586	17.1931	17.2277	17.2798	17.2972	17.3671	17.4373	17.4549	17.5079
8	19.9842	20.0761	20.0991	20.1685	20.2149	20.2614	20.3314	20.3548	20.4488	20.5434	20.5671	20.6384
9	23.1013	23.2209	23.2509	23.3413	23.4018	23.4625	23.5539	23.5845	23.7073	23.8309	23.8619	23.9553
10	26.3803	26.5326	26.5708	26.6859	26.7630	26.8403	26.9569	26.9959	27.1526	27.3104	27.3500	27.4694
15	45.5178	45.9211	46.0226	46.3288	46.5344	46.7410	47.0532	47.1578	47.5792	48.0052	48.1124	48.4359
20	70.1757	71.0295	71.2449	71.8960	72.3340	72.7753	73.4435	73.6679	74.5737	75.4932	75.7252	76.4264
25	101.9468	103.5453	103.9496	105.1741	106.0000	106.8337	108.0991	108.5249	110.2482	112.0043	112.4485	113.7939
30	142.8828	145.6538	146.3565	148.4888	149.9307	151.3893	153.6086	154.3569	157.3934	160.5003	161.2883	163.6796

YEAR	5.75 %	5.80 %	5.875%	5.90 %	6.00 %	6.10 %	6.125%	6.20 %	6.25 %	6.30 %	6.375%	6.40 %
1	2.0898	2.0906	2.0919	2.0923	2.0939	2.0955	2.0959	2.0971	2.0979	2.0987	2.0999	2.1003
2	4.3051	4.3079	4.3121	4.3135	4.3190	4.3246	4.3260	4.3302	4.3330	4.3358	4.3400	4.3414
3	6.6534	6.6595	6.6686	6.6716	6.6838	6.6959	6.6990	6.7082	6.7143	6.7204	6.7296	6.7327
4	9.1426	9.1534	9.1697	9.1751	9.1968	9.2186	9.2240	9.2404	9.2513	9.2623	9.2788	9.2843
5	11.7813	11.7985	11.8243	11.8329	11.8674	11.9021	11.9108	11.9369	11.9544	11.9719	11.9981	12.0069
6	14.5783	14.6037	14.6418	14.6545	14.7056	14.7569	14.7697	14.8084	14.8342	14.8601	14.8991	14.9121
7	17.5433	17.5788	17.6322	17.6501	17.7217	17.7937	17.8118	17.8661	17.9024	17.9389	17.9937	18.0120
8	20.6862	20.7341	20.8062	20.8303	20.9270	21.0243	21.0487	21.1222	21.1714	21.2207	21.2949	21.3197
9	24.0178	24.0805	24.1749	24.2065	24.3333	24.4610	24.4931	24.5895	24.6541	24.7189	24.8165	24.8491
10	27.5493	27.6295	27.7504	27.7908	27.9533	28.1170	28.1581	28.2818	28.3647	28.4479	28.5732	28.6151
15	48.6531	48.8715	49.2013	49.3118	49.7570	50.2072	50.3205	50.6624	50.8919	51.1226	51.4712	51.5880
20	76.8983	77.3737	78.0934	78.3352	79.3111	80.3018	80.5518	81.3074	81.8159	82.3283	83.1040	83.3646
25	114.7014	115.6176	117.0083	117.4763	119.3706	121.3012	121.7896	123.2689	124.2669	125.2744	126.8039	127.3186
30	165.2969	166.9330	169.4228	170.2623	173.6695	177.1565	178.0410	180.7254	182.5411	184.3781	187.1740	188.1168

YEAR	6.50 %	6.60 %	6.625%	6.70 %	6.75 %	6.80 %	6.875%	6.90 %	7.00 %	7.10 %	7.125%	7.20 %
1	2.1019	2.1035	2.1039	2.1051	2.1059	2.1067	2.1079	2.1083	2.1100	2.1116	2.1120	2.1132
2	4.3470	4.3526	4.3540	4.3582	4.3610	4.3638	4.3681	4.3695	4.3751	4.3808	4.3822	4.3864
3	6.7450	6.7573	6.7604	6.7696	6.7758	6.7820	6.7913	6.7944	6.8068	6.8193	6.8224	6.8318
4	9.3063	9.3284	9.3339	9.3505	9.3616	9.3728	9.3895	9.3951	9.4174	9.4398	9.4454	9.4623
5	12.0421	12.0774	12.0863	12.1129	12.1306	12.1484	12.1752	12.1841	12.2200	12.2559	12.2649	12.2920
6	14.9643	15.0167	15.0298	15.0693	15.0957	15.1222	15.1620	15.1753	15.2286	15.2822	15.2956	15.3360
7	18.0855	18.1593	18.1779	18.2336	18.2708	18.3082	18.3644	18.3832	18.4586	18.5343	18.5533	18.6105
8	21.4193	21.5195	21.5446	21.6202	21.6708	21.7216	21.7980	21.8235	21.9261	22.0292	22.0551	22.1329
9	24.9802	25.1121	25.1452	25.2449	25.3116	25.3786	25.4794	25.5131	25.6486	25.7849	25.8191	25.9221
10	28.7836	28.9534	28.9960	29.1243	29.2103	29.2966	29.4266	29.4701	29.6448	29.8209	29.8651	29.9982
15	52.0586	52.5344	52.6542	53.0155	53.2581	53.5020	53.8705	53.9940	54.4915	54.9946	55.1212	55.5033
20	84.4166	85.4845	85.7540	86.5687	87.1169	87.6693	88.5058	88.7867	89.9212	91.0730	91.3637	92.2424
25	129.4023	131.5262	132.0636	133.6912	134.7894	135.8982	137.5815	138.1481	140.4416	142.7798	143.3715	145.1636
30	191.9437	195.8610	196.8547	199.8709	201.9113	203.9758	207.1183	208.1781	212.4804	216.8850	218.0024	221.3946

Description: This table shows what a series of $ 1 deposits grow to in the future. The deposit is made at the beginning of a period.

Example: At 8 % a regular one dollar deposit will grow to $ 12.59 by the end of the fifth year.

YEAR	7.25 %	7.30 %	7.375%	7.40 %	7.50 %	7.60 %	7.625%	7.70 %	7.75 %	7.80 %	7.875%	7.90 %
1	2.1140	2.1148	2.1160	2.1164	2.1181	2.1197	2.1201	2.1213	2.1221	2.1230	2.1242	2.1246
2	4.3893	4.3921	4.3964	4.3978	4.4035	4.4092	4.4106	4.4149	4.4177	4.4206	4.4249	4.4263
3	6.8380	6.8443	6.8537	6.8568	6.8694	6.8820	6.8852	6.8946	6.9010	6.9073	6.9168	6.9200
4	9.4736	9.4849	9.5018	9.5075	9.5302	9.5529	9.5586	9.5757	9.5872	9.5986	9.6158	9.6216
5	12.3101	12.3283	12.3555	12.3646	12.4011	12.4377	12.4469	12.4745	12.4929	12.5114	12.5392	12.5484
6	15.3630	15.3901	15.4307	15.4443	15.4989	15.5536	15.5673	15.6086	15.6362	15.6638	15.7054	15.7193
7	18.6487	18.6870	18.7447	18.7640	18.8413	18.9190	18.9385	18.9972	19.0364	19.0757	19.1349	19.1546
8	22.1850	22.2373	22.3160	22.3423	22.4478	22.5540	22.5807	22.6609	22.7145	22.7683	22.8493	22.8764
9	25.9911	26.0602	26.1644	26.1993	26.3393	26.4802	26.5155	26.6220	26.6933	26.7648	26.8725	26.9085
10	30.0874	30.1769	30.3117	30.3568	30.5381	30.7207	30.7666	30.9047	30.9972	31.0901	31.2300	31.2768
15	55.7598	56.0177	56.4074	56.5380	57.0641	57.5961	57.7300	58.1341	58.4054	58.6782	59.0904	59.2285
20	92.8338	93.4296	94.3320	94.6351	95.8591	97.1018	97.4155	98.3637	99.0019	99.6450	100.6189	100.9460
25	146.3729	147.5939	149.4478	150.0717	152.5980	155.1738	155.8256	157.8002	159.1327	160.4782	162.5212	163.2088
30	223.6896	226.0119	229.5471	230.7396	235.5805	240.5375	241.7952	245.6136	248.1972	250.8117	254.7923	256.1351

YEAR	8.00 %	8.10 %	8.125%	8.20 %	8.25 %	8.30 %	8.375%	8.40 %	8.50 %	8.60 %	8.625%	8.70 %
1	2.1262	2.1278	2.1283	2.1295	2.1303	2.1311	2.1323	2.1328	2.1344	2.1360	2.1364	2.1377
2	4.4321	4.4378	4.4392	4.4435	4.4464	4.4493	4.4536	4.4551	4.4609	4.4666	4.4681	4.4724
3	6.9327	6.9454	6.9486	6.9582	6.9646	6.9710	6.9806	6.9838	6.9967	7.0096	7.0128	7.0225
4	9.6446	9.6677	9.6735	9.6908	9.7024	9.7141	9.7315	9.7374	9.7607	9.7842	9.7900	9.8077
5	12.5856	12.6229	12.6322	12.6603	12.6791	12.6979	12.7262	12.7356	12.7735	12.8115	12.8210	12.8496
6	15.7751	15.8310	15.8451	15.8873	15.9155	15.9437	15.9862	16.0004	16.0574	16.1146	16.1290	16.1721
7	19.2340	19.3137	19.3337	19.3939	19.4341	19.4744	19.5351	19.5554	19.6368	19.7186	19.7392	19.8009
8	22.9851	23.0945	23.1219	23.2045	23.2597	23.3151	23.3985	23.4264	23.5384	23.6510	23.6792	23.7643
9	27.0531	27.1988	27.2353	27.3454	27.4190	27.4929	27.6043	27.6415	27.7910	27.9416	27.9794	28.0931
10	31.4648	31.6543	31.7019	31.8452	31.9412	32.0375	32.1827	32.2312	32.4264	32.6230	32.6724	32.8211
15	59.7850	60.3478	60.4895	60.9170	61.2040	61.4927	61.9287	62.0749	62.6637	63.2592	63.4091	63.8615
20	102.2672	103.6087	103.9473	104.9710	105.6600	106.3544	107.4059	107.7592	109.1858	110.6346	111.0003	112.1059
25	165.9933	168.8327	169.5513	171.7282	173.1974	174.6810	176.9339	177.6923	180.7633	183.8952	184.6879	187.0895
30	261.5869	267.1703	268.5872	272.8889	275.7999	278.7460	283.2318	284.7451	290.8900	297.1844	298.7818	303.6320

YEAR	8.75 %	8.80 %	8.875%	8.90 %	9.00 %	9.10 %	9.125%	9.20 %	9.25 %	9.30 %	9.375%	9.40 %
1	2.1385	2.1393	2.1405	2.1410	2.1426	2.1442	2.1447	2.1459	2.1467	2.1475	2.1488	2.1492
2	4.4753	4.4782	4.4826	4.4841	4.4899	4.4957	4.4972	4.5016	4.5045	4.5074	4.5118	4.5133
3	7.0290	7.0354	7.0452	7.0484	7.0614	7.0744	7.0777	7.0875	7.0940	7.1006	7.1104	7.1137
4	9.8194	9.8312	9.8489	9.8549	9.8786	9.9024	9.9083	9.9262	9.9382	9.9501	9.9681	9.9741
5	12.8687	12.8879	12.9167	12.9263	12.9649	13.0036	13.0133	13.0424	13.0619	13.0814	13.1107	13.1205
6	16.2009	16.2298	16.2733	16.2878	16.3460	16.4045	16.4192	16.4633	16.4927	16.5223	16.5667	16.5815
7	19.8422	19.8835	19.9458	19.9666	20.0502	20.1341	20.1552	20.2185	20.2608	20.3033	20.3672	20.3886
8	23.8212	23.8782	23.9641	23.9929	24.1082	24.2241	24.2532	24.3408	24.3994	24.4582	24.5467	24.5762
9	28.1692	28.2457	28.3607	28.3992	28.5538	28.7094	28.7485	28.8661	28.9448	29.0238	29.1428	29.1826
10	32.9207	33.0206	33.1712	33.2216	33.4242	33.6282	33.6795	33.8338	33.9371	34.0409	34.1972	34.2495
15	64.1653	64.4707	64.9322	65.0869	65.7101	66.3404	66.4991	66.9779	67.2994	67.6228	68.1112	68.2750
20	112.8502	113.6002	114.7361	115.1177	116.6589	118.2243	118.6194	119.8140	120.6182	121.4287	122.6563	123.0687
25	188.7103	190.3473	192.8332	193.6700	197.0591	200.5159	201.3908	204.0418	205.8312	207.6384	210.3830	211.3071
30	306.9146	310.2370	315.2963	317.0032	323.9349	331.0364	332.8388	338.3120	342.0165	345.7662	351.4768	353.4036

YEAR	9.50 %	9.75 %	10.00 %	10.25 %	10.50 %	10.75 %	11.00 %	12.00 %	13.00 %	14.00 %	15.00 %	16.00 %
1	2.1508	2.1550	2.1591	2.1633	2.1674	2.1716	2.1758	2.1926	2.2095	2.2266	2.2439	2.2613
2	4.5191	4.5338	4.5486	4.5634	4.5783	4.5933	4.6082	4.6688	4.7303	4.7928	4.8563	4.9207
3	7.1268	7.1598	7.1930	7.2264	7.2600	7.2937	7.3277	7.4653	7.6062	7.7503	7.8976	8.0484
4	9.9982	10.0587	10.1196	10.1810	10.2428	10.3051	10.3679	10.6236	10.8871	11.1587	11.4385	11.7269
5	13.1598	13.2586	13.3584	13.4590	13.5606	13.6632	13.7667	14.1904	14.6302	15.0868	15.5608	16.0530
6	16.6411	16.7911	16.9427	17.0961	17.2511	17.4079	17.5665	18.2186	18.9006	19.6139	20.3601	21.1409
7	20.4743	20.6905	20.9095	21.1314	21.3561	21.5838	21.8145	22.7679	23.7725	24.8313	25.9475	27.1246
8	24.6950	24.9950	25.2995	25.6085	25.9222	26.2405	26.5637	27.9056	29.3306	30.8442	32.4525	34.1619
9	29.3424	29.7467	30.1578	30.5759	31.0010	31.4334	31.8731	33.7079	35.6716	37.7740	40.0258	42.4384
10	34.4597	34.9921	35.5345	36.0872	36.6503	37.2241	37.8088	40.2608	42.9059	45.7605	48.8427	52.1722
15	68.9347	70.6175	72.3491	74.1311	75.9651	77.8528	79.7958	88.1568	97.5536	108.1245	120.0269	133.4406
20	124.7345	129.0143	133.4646	138.0927	142.9063	147.9132	153.1216	176.1504	203.1704	234.9197	272.2779	316.2945
25	215.0494	224.7379	234.9221	245.6290	256.8869	268.7259	281.1776	337.8105	407.2942	492.7127	597.9165	727.7160
30	361.2291	381.6474	403.3511	426.4255	450.9615	477.0563	504.8138	634.8093	801.8004	1016.8437	1294.4016	1653.4151

Description: This table shows what a series of $ 1 deposits grow to in the future. The deposit is made at the beginning of a period.

Example: At 5 % a regular one dollar deposit will grow to $ 5.84 by the end of the fifth year.

YEAR	0.00 %	1.00 %	2.00 %	3.00 %	4.00 %	4.125%	4.25 %	4.375%	4.50 %	4.625%	4.75 %	4.875%
1	1.0000	1.0102	1.0205	1.0309	1.0414	1.0427	1.0440	1.0454	1.0467	1.0480	1.0493	1.0507
2	2.0000	2.0307	2.0619	2.0936	2.1259	2.1299	2.1340	2.1381	2.1422	2.1463	2.1504	2.1546
3	3.0000	3.0616	3.1246	3.1891	3.2552	3.2636	3.2720	3.2804	3.2889	3.2974	3.3059	3.3144
4	4.0000	4.1029	4.2091	4.3185	4.4314	4.4457	4.4601	4.4746	4.4891	4.5037	4.5183	4.5330
5	5.0000	5.1549	5.3158	5.4828	5.6561	5.6783	5.7005	5.7229	5.7453	5.7679	5.7905	5.8133
6	6.0000	6.2177	6.4452	6.6830	6.9316	6.9635	6.9955	7.0278	7.0602	7.0928	7.1255	7.1585
7	7.0000	7.2912	7.5977	7.9202	8.2599	8.3036	8.3476	8.3919	8.4364	8.4813	8.5264	8.5719
8	8.0000	8.3757	8.7738	9.1957	9.6431	9.7009	9.7591	9.8178	9.8769	9.9364	9.9964	10.0568
9	9.0000	9.4713	9.9740	10.5106	11.0836	11.1579	11.2329	11.3084	11.3846	11.4614	11.5389	11.6170
10	10.0000	10.5780	11.1988	11.8661	12.5837	12.6772	12.7715	12.8667	12.9627	13.0597	13.1575	13.2563
15	15.0000	16.2830	17.7095	19.2978	21.0685	21.3038	21.5423	21.7842	22.0294	22.2780	22.5301	22.7857
20	20.0000	22.2846	24.9150	27.9503	31.4605	31.9367	32.4217	32.9158	33.4192	33.9320	34.4544	34.9866
25	25.0000	28.5984	32.8893	38.0238	44.1886	45.0426	45.9166	46.8114	47.7273	48.6650	49.6249	50.6077
30	30.0000	35.2405	41.7145	49.7520	59.7777	61.1964	62.6558	64.1571	65.7015	67.2906	68.9256	70.6080

YEAR	5.00 %	5.10 %	5.125%	5.20 %	5.25 %	5.30 %	5.375%	5.40 %	5.50 %	5.60 %	5.625%	5.70 %
1	1.0520	1.0531	1.0533	1.0541	1.0547	1.0552	1.0560	1.0563	1.0573	1.0584	1.0587	1.0595
2	2.1587	2.1620	2.1628	2.1653	2.1670	2.1687	2.1712	2.1720	2.1753	2.1787	2.1795	2.1820
3	3.3229	3.3298	3.3315	3.3367	3.3401	3.3436	3.3487	3.3505	3.3574	3.3643	3.3661	3.3713
4	4.5477	4.5596	4.5625	4.5714	4.5774	4.5833	4.5923	4.5953	4.6073	4.6193	4.6223	4.6313
5	5.8362	5.8546	5.8592	5.8730	5.8823	5.8916	5.9055	5.9101	5.9288	5.9475	5.9522	5.9664
6	7.1917	7.2183	7.2250	7.2451	7.2585	7.2720	7.2922	7.2990	7.3261	7.3534	7.3602	7.3808
7	8.6176	8.6544	8.6636	8.6914	8.7100	8.7286	8.7566	8.7660	8.8036	8.8414	8.8508	8.8793
8	10.1177	10.1667	10.1790	10.2160	10.2408	10.2656	10.3030	10.3156	10.3658	10.4163	10.4289	10.4671
9	11.6958	11.7593	11.7752	11.8232	11.8553	11.8875	11.9361	11.9523	12.0175	12.0831	12.0996	12.1492
10	13.3559	13.4364	13.4565	13.5173	13.5581	13.5990	13.6605	13.6812	13.7640	13.8474	13.8684	13.9315
15	23.0449	23.2549	23.3077	23.4672	23.5742	23.6819	23.8444	23.8989	24.1185	24.3405	24.3963	24.5649
20	35.5289	35.9700	36.0813	36.4178	36.6443	36.8724	37.2179	37.3339	37.8023	38.2779	38.3979	38.7607
25	51.6140	52.4363	52.6444	53.2744	53.6994	54.1285	54.7798	54.9989	55.8861	56.7904	57.0192	57.7121
30	72.3392	73.7605	74.1209	75.2148	75.9546	76.7030	77.8420	78.2260	79.7846	81.3797	81.7843	83.0123

YEAR	5.75 %	5.80 %	5.875%	5.90 %	6.00 %	6.10 %	6.125%	6.20 %	6.25 %	6.30 %	6.375%	6.40 %
1	1.0600	1.0606	1.0614	1.0616	1.0627	1.0638	1.0641	1.0649	1.0654	1.0660	1.0668	1.0670
2	2.1837	2.1854	2.1879	2.1887	2.1921	2.1955	2.1963	2.1988	2.2005	2.2022	2.2047	2.2056
3	3.3748	3.3783	3.3835	3.3853	3.3923	3.3993	3.4011	3.4063	3.4099	3.4134	3.4187	3.4205
4	4.6374	4.6434	4.6525	4.6556	4.6677	4.6800	4.6830	4.6922	4.6983	4.7045	4.7137	4.7168
5	5.9758	5.9852	5.9994	6.0042	6.0232	6.0423	6.0471	6.0615	6.0711	6.0807	6.0952	6.1000
6	7.3945	7.4083	7.4290	7.4359	7.4637	7.4916	7.4986	7.5196	7.5336	7.5477	7.5689	7.5760
7	8.8984	8.9175	8.9463	8.9559	8.9945	9.0333	9.0430	9.0723	9.0918	9.1115	9.1410	9.1509
8	10.4926	10.5182	10.5567	10.5696	10.6213	10.6733	10.6864	10.7257	10.7520	10.7783	10.8180	10.8313
9	12.1824	12.2158	12.2659	12.2827	12.3502	12.4180	12.4351	12.4864	12.5207	12.5552	12.6071	12.6244
10	13.9737	14.0162	14.0801	14.1015	14.1874	14.2740	14.2958	14.3613	14.4051	14.4492	14.5155	14.5377
15	24.6781	24.7920	24.9639	25.0215	25.2537	25.4885	25.5476	25.7259	25.8457	25.9661	26.1480	26.2089
20	39.0048	39.2508	39.6233	39.7484	40.2536	40.7665	40.8960	41.2873	41.5506	41.8160	42.2178	42.3528
25	58.1796	58.6516	59.3681	59.6092	60.5854	61.5805	61.8323	62.5949	63.1095	63.6291	64.4179	64.6833
30	83.8430	84.6833	85.9623	86.3936	88.1443	89.9364	90.3910	91.7709	92.7044	93.6489	95.0866	95.5714

YEAR	6.50 %	6.60 %	6.625%	6.70 %	6.75 %	6.80 %	6.875%	6.90 %	7.00 %	7.10 %	7.125%	7.20 %
1	1.0681	1.0692	1.0695	1.0703	1.0708	1.0714	1.0722	1.0725	1.0735	1.0746	1.0749	1.0757
2	2.2090	2.2124	2.2132	2.2158	2.2175	2.2192	2.2218	2.2226	2.2260	2.2295	2.2303	2.2329
3	3.4276	3.4347	3.4365	3.4418	3.4454	3.4490	3.4543	3.4561	3.4633	3.4705	3.4723	3.4777
4	4.7292	4.7416	4.7447	4.7540	4.7602	4.7665	4.7759	4.7790	4.7915	4.8041	4.8073	4.8168
5	6.1194	6.1389	6.1438	6.1584	6.1682	6.1780	6.1928	6.1977	6.2175	6.2373	6.2423	6.2572
6	7.6044	7.6329	7.6400	7.6615	7.6759	7.6903	7.7120	7.7192	7.7483	7.7775	7.7848	7.8068
7	9.1905	9.2303	9.2403	9.2703	9.2904	9.3105	9.3409	9.3510	9.3917	9.4325	9.4428	9.4736
8	10.8846	10.9382	10.9517	10.9922	11.0192	11.0464	11.0873	11.1010	11.1559	11.2112	11.2250	11.2667
9	12.6941	12.7643	12.7820	12.8350	12.8705	12.9062	12.9598	12.9778	13.0499	13.1225	13.1407	13.1956
10	14.6269	14.7168	14.7394	14.8074	14.8529	14.8986	14.9675	14.9906	15.0832	15.1765	15.1999	15.2705
15	26.4545	26.7029	26.7655	26.9541	27.0808	27.2082	27.4007	27.4652	27.7251	27.9880	28.0542	28.2538
20	42.8978	43.4513	43.5910	44.0132	44.2975	44.5838	45.0176	45.1633	45.7516	46.3491	46.4999	46.9558
25	65.7582	66.8540	67.1313	67.9713	68.5381	69.1104	69.9794	70.2719	71.4563	72.6639	72.9695	73.8953
30	97.5398	99.5550	100.0663	101.6183	102.6684	103.7310	105.3486	105.8942	108.1093	110.3776	110.9532	112.7005

Description: This table shows what a series of $ 1 deposits grow to in the future. The deposit is made at the beginning of a period.

Example: At 8 % a regular one dollar deposit will grow to $ 6.42 by the end of the fifth year.

YEAR	7.25 %	7.30 %	7.375%	7.40 %	7.50 %	7.60 %	7.625%	7.70 %	7.75 %	7.80 %	7.875%	7.90 %
1	1.0763	1.0768	1.0776	1.0779	1.0790	1.0801	1.0804	1.0812	1.0817	1.0823	1.0831	1.0834
2	2.2346	2.2363	2.2389	2.2398	2.2432	2.2467	2.2476	2.2502	2.2519	2.2536	2.2562	2.2571
3	3.4813	3.4849	3.4904	3.4922	3.4995	3.5067	3.5086	3.5140	3.5177	3.5214	3.5269	3.5287
4	4.8231	4.8294	4.8390	4.8422	4.8549	4.8677	4.8709	4.8805	4.8870	4.8934	4.9031	4.9063
5	6.2672	6.2772	6.2923	6.2973	6.3174	6.3377	6.3427	6.3580	6.3681	6.3783	6.3937	6.3988
6	7.8215	7.8362	7.8584	7.8658	7.8955	7.9254	7.9328	7.9553	7.9704	7.9855	8.0081	8.0157
7	9.4943	9.5150	9.5461	9.5565	9.5982	9.6402	9.6507	9.6824	9.7036	9.7248	9.7568	9.7675
8	11.2946	11.3226	11.3648	11.3789	11.4355	11.4924	11.5067	11.5497	11.5785	11.6073	11.6508	11.6653
9	13.2323	13.2692	13.3247	13.3433	13.4179	13.4930	13.5118	13.5686	13.6066	13.6447	13.7022	13.7214
10	15.3178	15.3653	15.4368	15.4607	15.5569	15.6538	15.6781	15.7514	15.8005	15.8498	15.9240	15.9489
15	28.3879	28.5228	28.7265	28.7947	29.0699	29.3481	29.4182	29.6296	29.7715	29.9143	30.1299	30.2022
20	47.2627	47.5719	48.0403	48.1976	48.8330	49.4783	49.6412	50.1336	50.4651	50.7992	51.3052	51.4752
25	74.5200	75.1509	76.1090	76.4314	77.7372	79.0689	79.4059	80.4270	81.1161	81.8121	82.8689	83.2247
30	113.8828	115.0793	116.9010	117.5155	120.0106	122.5660	123.2145	125.1834	126.5158	127.8643	129.9176	130.6103

YEAR	8.00 %	8.10 %	8.125%	8.20 %	8.25 %	8.30 %	8.375%	8.40 %	8.50 %	8.60 %	8.625%	8.70 %
1	1.0845	1.0856	1.0859	1.0867	1.0872	1.0878	1.0886	1.0889	1.0900	1.0911	1.0914	1.0922
2	2.2606	2.2641	2.2649	2.2676	2.2693	2.2711	2.2737	2.2746	2.2781	2.2816	2.2825	2.2851
3	3.5360	3.5434	3.5453	3.5508	3.5545	3.5582	3.5638	3.5656	3.5731	3.5805	3.5824	3.5880
4	4.9193	4.9322	4.9355	4.9453	4.9518	4.9583	4.9682	4.9715	4.9846	4.9978	5.0011	5.0110
5	6.4193	6.4399	6.4451	6.4606	6.4710	6.4814	6.4970	6.5023	6.5232	6.5442	6.5495	6.5653
6	8.0461	8.0767	8.0843	8.1073	8.1227	8.1381	8.1614	8.1691	8.2002	8.2315	8.2393	8.2628
7	9.8103	9.8534	9.8643	9.8968	9.9185	9.9403	9.9732	9.9841	10.0282	10.0724	10.0835	10.1169
8	11.7236	11.7823	11.7970	11.8413	11.8710	11.9007	11.9455	11.9605	12.0206	12.0811	12.0963	12.1419
9	13.7985	13.8762	13.8957	13.9545	13.9938	14.0332	14.0926	14.1125	14.1924	14.2727	14.2929	14.3537
10	16.0487	16.1494	16.1746	16.2507	16.3017	16.3529	16.4300	16.4558	16.5595	16.6640	16.6903	16.7693
15	30.4935	30.7882	30.8624	31.0862	31.2365	31.3877	31.6161	31.6927	32.0012	32.3132	32.3918	32.6289
20	52.1617	52.8590	53.0350	53.5671	53.9254	54.2864	54.8333	55.0170	55.7591	56.5129	56.7032	57.2785
25	84.6654	86.1349	86.5068	87.6337	88.3943	89.1624	90.3290	90.7218	92.3124	93.9349	94.3456	95.5901
30	133.4232	136.3046	137.0359	139.2564	140.7592	142.2803	144.5967	145.3782	148.5520	151.8038	152.6291	155.1354

YEAR	8.75 %	8.80 %	8.875%	8.90 %	9.00 %	9.10 %	9.125%	9.20 %	9.25 %	9.30 %	9.375%	9.40 %
1	1.0928	1.0933	1.0941	1.0944	1.0955	1.0966	1.0969	1.0978	1.0983	1.0989	1.0997	1.1000
2	2.2869	2.2886	2.2913	2.2922	2.2957	2.2993	2.3002	2.3028	2.3046	2.3064	2.3090	2.3099
3	3.5918	3.5955	3.6011	3.6030	3.6106	3.6181	3.6200	3.6257	3.6295	3.6333	3.6390	3.6409
4	5.0177	5.0243	5.0343	5.0376	5.0510	5.0644	5.0678	5.0779	5.0846	5.0913	5.1015	5.1049
5	6.5759	6.5865	6.6024	6.6077	6.6291	6.6505	6.6559	6.6720	6.6828	6.6936	6.7098	6.7152
6	8.2786	8.2944	8.3181	8.3260	8.3579	8.3898	8.3979	8.4220	8.4381	8.4542	8.4785	8.4866
7	10.1392	10.1616	10.1954	10.2066	10.2518	10.2973	10.3087	10.3430	10.3659	10.3889	10.4235	10.4351
8	12.1725	12.2032	12.2493	12.2648	12.3267	12.3891	12.4047	12.4518	12.4833	12.5149	12.5625	12.5784
9	14.3943	14.4352	14.4966	14.5172	14.5998	14.6830	14.7039	14.7668	14.8088	14.8511	14.9147	14.9360
10	16.8223	16.8754	16.9556	16.9824	17.0901	17.1986	17.2259	17.3080	17.3630	17.4182	17.5014	17.5293
15	32.7881	32.9483	33.1902	33.2713	33.5982	33.9288	34.0120	34.2632	34.4319	34.6016	34.8580	34.9439
20	57.6659	58.0563	58.6476	58.8463	59.6488	60.4640	60.6698	61.2921	61.7111	62.1334	62.7731	62.9880
25	96.4301	97.2785	98.5671	99.0009	100.7581	102.5508	103.0046	104.3797	105.3080	106.2456	107.6699	108.1494
30	156.8319	158.5491	161.1644	162.0468	165.6309	169.3035	170.2358	173.0670	174.9835	176.9237	179.8789	180.8761

YEAR	9.50 %	9.75 %	10.00 %	10.25 %	10.50 %	10.75 %	11.00 %	12.00 %	13.00 %	14.00 %	15.00 %	16.00 %
1	1.1011	1.1039	1.1067	1.1095	1.1123	1.1151	1.1180	1.1294	1.1409	1.1525	1.1642	1.1761
2	2.3135	2.3225	2.3315	2.3405	2.3496	2.3587	2.3678	2.4048	2.4424	2.4807	2.5196	2.5592
3	3.6485	3.6676	3.6869	3.7063	3.7258	3.7454	3.7651	3.8452	3.9273	4.0114	4.0976	4.1859
4	5.1184	5.1526	5.1869	5.2216	5.2565	5.2917	5.3272	5.4720	5.6214	5.7756	5.9348	6.0991
5	6.7370	6.7918	6.8470	6.9029	6.9592	7.0161	7.0736	7.3092	7.5541	7.8087	8.0736	8.3491
6	8.5192	8.6012	8.6843	8.7682	8.8532	8.9391	9.0260	9.3840	9.7590	10.1519	10.5637	10.9953
7	10.4815	10.5987	10.7175	10.8379	10.9598	11.0834	11.2088	11.7272	12.2745	12.8523	13.4626	14.1074
8	12.6423	12.8037	12.9676	13.1341	13.3031	13.4747	13.6490	14.3735	15.1443	15.9646	16.8377	17.7675
9	15.0215	15.2378	15.4579	15.6817	15.9095	16.1413	16.3770	17.3622	18.4184	19.5513	20.7670	22.0720
10	17.6412	17.9247	18.2138	18.5084	18.8087	19.1148	19.4269	20.7374	22.1536	23.6850	25.3416	27.1346
15	35.2903	36.1739	37.0836	38.0203	38.9848	39.9779	41.0007	45.4075	50.3700	55.9638	62.2749	69.4019
20	63.8562	66.0877	68.4093	70.8249	73.3385	75.9544	78.6771	90.7309	104.9033	121.5913	141.2690	164.5034
25	110.0918	115.1222	120.4129	125.9780	131.8325	137.9926	144.4749	173.9982	210.2988	255.0215	310.2238	378.4820
30	184.9266	195.4993	206.7437	218.7047	231.4302	244.9717	259.3838	326.9752	413.9948	526.3046	671.5890	859.9343

Description: This table shows what a series of $ 1 deposits grow to in the future. The deposit is made at the beginning of a period.

Example: At 5 % a regular one dollar deposit will grow to $ 295.55 by the end of the fifth year.

YEAR	0.00 %	1.00 %	2.00 %	3.00 %	4.00 %	4.125%	4.25 %	4.375%	4.50 %	4.625%	4.75 %	4.875%
1	52.0000	52.2666	52.5350	52.8052	53.0772	53.1113	53.1455	53.1797	53.2139	53.2481	53.2824	53.3167
2	104.0000	105.0585	106.1312	107.2184	108.3204	108.4592	108.5982	108.7374	108.8769	109.0167	109.1566	109.2968
3	156.0000	158.3809	160.8101	163.2888	165.8180	166.1377	166.4583	166.7797	167.1019	167.4249	167.7487	168.0734
4	208.0000	212.2392	216.5936	221.0666	225.6619	226.2451	226.8303	227.4175	228.0066	228.5978	229.1909	229.7861
5	260.0000	266.6388	273.5039	280.6040	287.9480	288.8837	289.8233	290.7669	291.7145	292.6661	293.6219	294.5816
6	312.0000	321.5851	331.5639	341.9545	352.7759	354.1599	355.5510	356.9492	358.3545	359.7671	361.1869	362.6140
7	364.0000	377.0837	390.7967	405.1733	420.2494	422.1850	424.1322	426.0910	428.0617	430.0441	432.0385	434.0449
8	416.0000	433.1400	451.2261	470.3173	490.4763	493.0746	495.6907	498.3248	500.9771	503.6476	506.3365	509.0440
9	468.0000	489.7596	512.8762	537.4451	563.5691	566.9493	570.3558	573.7888	577.2484	580.7349	584.2486	587.7897
10	520.0000	546.9483	575.7717	606.6173	639.6447	643.9350	648.2624	652.6273	657.0301	661.4711	665.9506	670.4691
15	780.0000	841.6294	909.8283	985.3883	1069.2033	1080.3095	1091.5624	1102.9641	1114.5168	1126.2227	1138.0841	1150.1033
20	1040.0000	1151.4189	1279.0169	1425.4548	1593.8616	1616.6338	1639.8139	1663.4099	1687.4298	1711.8823	1736.7756	1762.1186
25	1300.0000	1477.0914	1687.0323	1936.7360	2234.6736	2275.8012	2317.8644	2360.8867	2404.8919	2449.9045	2495.9495	2543.0529
30	1560.0000	1819.4612	2137.9579	2530.7563	3017.3546	3085.9482	3156.4440	3228.8994	3303.3735	3379.9274	3458.6241	3539.5286

YEAR	5.00 %	5.10 %	5.125%	5.20 %	5.25 %	5.30 %	5.375%	5.40 %	5.50 %	5.60 %	5.625%	5.70 %
1	53.3510	53.3785	53.3854	53.4060	53.4198	53.4336	53.4542	53.4611	53.4887	53.5162	53.5231	53.5438
2	109.4373	109.5498	109.5779	109.6624	109.7188	109.7753	109.8600	109.8882	110.0014	110.1146	110.1430	110.2281
3	168.3989	168.6598	168.7252	168.9214	169.0523	169.1834	169.3803	169.4460	169.7091	169.9727	170.0387	170.2369
4	230.3833	230.8625	230.9825	231.3430	231.5838	231.8249	232.1871	232.3080	232.7925	233.2782	233.3999	233.7653
5	295.5455	296.3196	296.5135	297.0963	297.4856	297.8756	298.4619	298.6576	299.4423	300.2297	300.4270	301.0198
6	364.0484	365.2013	365.4902	366.3589	366.9395	367.5212	368.3961	368.6884	369.8603	371.0371	371.3320	372.2187
7	436.0633	437.6868	438.0939	439.3182	440.1368	440.9573	442.1919	442.6044	444.2595	445.9225	446.3395	447.5936
8	511.7702	513.9647	514.5153	516.1714	517.2793	518.3903	520.0625	520.6214	522.8649	525.1208	525.6868	527.3893
9	591.3584	594.2335	594.9550	597.1264	598.5797	600.0375	602.2327	602.9668	605.9144	608.8804	609.6249	611.8651
10	675.0270	678.7018	679.6245	682.4022	684.2621	686.1285	688.9402	689.8807	693.6592	697.4640	698.4194	701.2955
15	1162.2824	1172.1426	1174.6240	1182.1078	1187.1303	1192.1795	1199.8038	1202.3588	1212.6470	1223.0453	1225.6622	1233.5551
20	1787.9201	1808.8976	1814.1893	1830.1791	1840.9354	1851.7694	1868.1678	1873.6734	1895.8962	1918.4426	1924.1304	1941.3180
25	2591.2411	2630.5909	2640.5413	2670.6667	2690.9813	2711.4828	2742.5897	2753.0542	2795.3961	2838.5238	2849.4304	2882.4533
30	3622.7080	3690.9357	3708.2313	3760.7001	3796.1701	3832.0383	3886.5979	3904.9888	3979.5908	4055.8845	4075.2271	4133.9114

YEAR	5.75 %	5.80 %	5.875%	5.90 %	6.00 %	6.10 %	6.125%	6.20 %	6.25 %	6.30 %	6.375%	6.40 %
1	53.5576	53.5715	53.5922	53.5991	53.6267	53.6544	53.6613	53.6821	53.6960	53.7098	53.7306	53.7375
2	110.2848	110.3417	110.4270	110.4554	110.5693	110.6833	110.7119	110.7975	110.8547	110.9119	110.9978	111.0264
3	170.3692	170.5016	170.7005	170.7669	171.0327	171.2990	171.3657	171.5659	171.6995	171.8333	172.0342	172.1013
4	234.0094	234.2537	234.6209	234.7435	235.2346	235.7270	235.8503	236.2208	236.4682	236.7159	237.0881	237.2124
5	301.4158	301.8125	302.4089	302.6080	303.4062	304.2071	304.4078	305.0108	305.4137	305.8172	306.4239	306.6264
6	372.8114	373.4052	374.2983	374.5966	375.7929	376.9942	377.2953	378.2004	378.8054	379.4116	380.3233	380.6278
7	448.4322	449.2727	450.5374	450.9600	452.6554	454.3591	454.7863	456.0710	456.9300	457.7912	459.0868	459.5197
8	528.5282	529.6703	531.3894	531.9640	534.2705	536.5897	537.1716	538.9219	540.0928	541.2670	543.0345	543.6252
9	613.3644	614.8685	617.1333	617.8907	620.9319	623.9921	624.7602	627.0717	628.6187	630.1706	632.5076	633.2890
10	703.2213	705.1538	708.0652	709.0391	712.9516	716.8916	717.8809	720.8593	722.8535	724.8548	727.8698	728.8784
15	1238.8522	1244.1777	1252.2194	1254.9144	1265.7665	1276.7354	1279.4961	1287.8225	1293.4109	1299.0292	1307.5136	1310.3569
20	1952.8806	1964.5275	1982.1570	1988.0764	2011.9701	2036.2142	2042.3306	2060.8142	2073.2494	2085.7758	2104.7377	2111.1047
25	2904.7236	2927.2005	2961.3076	2972.7821	3019.2148	3066.5158	3078.4788	3114.7027	3139.1339	3163.7932	3201.2152	3213.8058
30	4173.5879	4213.7136	4274.7566	4295.3348	4378.8194	4464.2132	4485.8654	4551.5628	4595.9861	4640.9166	4709.2766	4732.3236

YEAR	6.50 %	6.60 %	6.625%	6.70 %	6.75 %	6.80 %	6.875%	6.90 %	7.00 %	7.10 %	7.125%	7.20 %
1	53.7653	53.7931	53.8000	53.8208	53.8347	53.8486	53.8695	53.8765	53.9043	53.9322	53.9391	53.9600
2	111.1411	111.2559	111.2846	111.3709	111.4284	111.4860	111.5724	111.6013	111.7167	111.8323	111.8612	111.9481
3	172.3698	172.6389	172.7062	172.9085	173.0435	173.1786	173.3816	173.4493	173.7206	173.9924	174.0605	174.2648
4	237.7102	238.2094	238.3344	238.7099	238.9607	239.2119	239.5892	239.7152	240.2198	240.7259	240.8526	241.2333
5	307.4384	308.2532	308.4573	309.0707	309.4806	309.8911	310.5082	310.7143	311.5403	312.3692	312.5768	313.2009
6	381.8491	383.0754	383.3827	384.3067	384.9243	385.5432	386.4739	386.7848	388.0316	389.2835	389.5973	390.5406
7	461.2566	463.0020	463.4396	464.7558	465.6359	466.5181	467.8455	468.2890	470.0686	471.8567	472.3051	473.6536
8	545.9966	548.3812	548.9794	550.7790	551.9830	553.1903	555.0076	555.6150	558.0533	560.5052	561.1203	562.9708
9	636.4271	639.5850	640.3775	642.7627	644.3592	645.9606	648.3722	649.1786	652.4170	655.6759	656.4938	658.9554
10	732.9303	737.0107	738.0353	741.1199	743.1854	745.2581	748.3808	749.4254	753.6222	757.8486	758.9099	762.1049
15	1321.8071	1333.3810	1336.2941	1345.0803	1350.9775	1356.9065	1365.8602	1368.8609	1380.9452	1393.1609	1396.2355	1405.5095
20	2136.8069	2162.8884	2169.4687	2189.3551	2202.7348	2216.2132	2236.6175	2243.4691	2271.1291	2299.1996	2306.2822	2327.6874
25	3264.7591	3316.6722	3329.8027	3369.5645	3396.3841	3423.4559	3464.5423	3478.3667	3534.3177	3591.3300	3605.7514	3649.4252
30	4825.8344	4921.5009	4945.7605	5019.3762	5069.1592	5119.5149	5196.1379	5221.9729	5326.8076	5434.0777	5461.2828	5543.8437

Description: This table shows what a series of $ 1 deposits grow to in the future. The deposit is made at the beginning of a period.

Example: At 8 % a regular one dollar deposit will grow to $ 319.96 by the end of the fifth year.

YEAR	7.25 %	7.30 %	7.375%	7.40 %	7.50 %	7.60 %	7.625%	7.70 %	7.75 %	7.80 %	7.875%	7.90 %
1	53.9740	53.9879	54.0089	54.0159	54.0438	54.0717	54.0787	54.0997	54.1137	54.1277	54.1487	54.1557
2	112.0060	112.0640	112.1510	112.1801	112.2963	112.4127	112.4418	112.5292	112.5875	112.6459	112.7335	112.7628
3	174.4012	174.5377	174.7428	174.8112	175.0852	175.3598	175.4286	175.6350	175.7728	175.9107	176.1179	176.1870
4	241.4875	241.7421	242.1247	242.2523	242.7639	243.2770	243.4054	243.7914	244.0491	244.3072	244.6950	244.8245
5	313.6178	314.0354	314.6632	314.8729	315.7132	316.5564	316.7677	317.4025	317.8267	318.2516	318.8903	319.1035
6	391.1711	391.8030	392.7532	393.0706	394.3434	395.6216	395.9419	396.9050	397.5487	398.1938	399.1639	399.4880
7	474.5554	475.4593	476.8193	477.2737	479.0970	480.9292	481.3887	482.7704	483.6943	484.6205	486.0140	486.4797
8	564.2088	565.4503	567.3190	567.9436	570.4509	572.9723	573.6048	575.5078	576.7809	578.0575	579.9792	580.6216
9	660.6029	662.2556	664.7445	665.5768	668.9190	672.2825	673.1267	675.6673	677.3677	679.0736	681.6425	682.5016
10	764.2444	766.3913	769.6261	770.7081	775.0555	779.4336	780.5330	783.8429	786.0592	788.2834	791.6345	792.7555
15	1411.7341	1417.9926	1427.4442	1430.6118	1443.3688	1456.2651	1459.5112	1469.3025	1475.8746	1482.4825	1492.4623	1495.8070
20	2342.0898	2356.5991	2378.5651	2385.9415	2415.7215	2445.9462	2453.5727	2476.6228	2492.1328	2507.7586	2531.4162	2539.3609
25	3678.8859	3708.6255	3753.7644	3768.9534	3830.4318	3893.0844	3908.9338	3956.9351	3989.3174	4022.0085	4071.6310	4088.3297
30	5599.6819	5656.1675	5742.1269	5771.1125	5888.7439	6009.1285	6039.6629	6132.3349	6195.0182	6258.4334	6354.9485	6387.4961

YEAR	8.00 %	8.10 %	8.125%	8.20 %	8.25 %	8.30 %	8.375%	8.40 %	8.50 %	8.60 %	8.625%	8.70 %
1	54.1837	54.2118	54.2188	54.2399	54.2539	54.2679	54.2890	54.2961	54.3242	54.3523	54.3594	54.3805
2	112.8798	112.9970	113.0263	113.1143	113.1730	113.2318	113.3200	113.3494	113.4672	113.5852	113.6147	113.7034
3	176.4639	176.7413	176.8108	177.0193	177.1585	177.2979	177.5071	177.5770	177.8567	178.1370	178.2071	178.4178
4	245.3431	245.8632	245.9934	246.3847	246.6460	246.9077	247.3008	247.4320	247.9579	248.4851	248.6172	249.0139
5	319.9584	320.8163	321.0312	321.6771	322.1086	322.5409	323.1907	323.4077	324.2775	325.1503	325.3689	326.0261
6	400.7876	402.0925	402.4196	403.4029	404.0602	404.7188	405.7093	406.0402	407.3671	408.6995	409.0335	410.0375
7	488.3459	490.2253	490.6961	492.1119	493.0587	494.0077	495.4357	495.9128	497.8273	499.7511	500.2336	501.6844
8	583.2001	585.7931	586.4436	588.4007	589.7100	591.0229	592.9993	593.6600	596.3119	598.9788	599.6478	601.6607
9	685.9513	689.4231	690.2944	692.9169	694.6722	696.4330	699.0848	699.9716	703.5327	707.1165	708.0161	710.7233
10	797.2594	801.7954	802.9344	806.3636	808.6599	810.9644	814.4365	815.5980	820.2646	824.9646	826.1448	829.6981
15	1509.2776	1522.8961	1526.3240	1536.6642	1543.6049	1550.5837	1561.1238	1564.6565	1578.8843	1593.2691	1596.8900	1607.8126
20	2571.4374	2603.9956	2612.2114	2637.0434	2653.7534	2670.5888	2696.0791	2704.6397	2739.2043	2774.2910	2783.1453	2809.9084
25	4155.9241	4224.8180	4242.2477	4295.0381	4330.6540	4366.6116	4421.1966	4439.5664	4513.9308	4589.7340	4608.9131	4667.0057
30	6519.5969	6654.8119	6689.1114	6793.2189	6863.6443	6934.8978	7043.3534	7079.9305	7228.4012	7380.3961	7418.9558	7536.0037

YEAR	8.75 %	8.80 %	8.875%	8.90 %	9.00 %	9.10 %	9.125%	9.20 %	9.25 %	9.30 %	9.375%	9.40 %
1	54.3946	54.4087	54.4298	54.4369	54.4651	54.4933	54.5004	54.5216	54.5357	54.5499	54.5711	54.5781
2	113.7625	113.8216	113.9105	113.9401	114.0587	114.1775	114.2072	114.2964	114.3559	114.4155	114.5049	114.5348
3	178.5584	178.6992	178.9107	178.9812	179.2638	179.5470	179.6178	179.8307	179.9728	180.1150	180.3286	180.3999
4	249.2788	249.5440	249.9426	250.0757	250.6087	251.1433	251.2772	251.6793	251.9479	252.2168	252.6210	252.7558
5	326.4651	326.9049	327.5660	327.7868	328.6717	329.5597	329.7822	330.4508	330.8974	331.3449	332.0176	332.2422
6	410.7086	411.3811	412.3925	412.7303	414.0852	415.4457	415.7868	416.8120	417.4972	418.1839	419.2166	419.5616
7	502.6546	503.6272	505.0905	505.5795	507.5414	509.5130	510.0074	511.4942	512.4885	513.4853	514.9849	515.4861
8	603.0073	604.3577	606.3905	607.0701	609.7977	612.5408	613.2290	615.2994	616.6845	618.0736	620.1646	620.8635
9	712.5353	714.3531	717.0907	718.0062	721.6826	725.3826	726.3113	729.1063	730.9771	732.8539	735.6804	736.6256
10	832.0776	834.4655	838.0634	839.2670	844.1029	848.9734	850.1965	853.8789	856.3447	858.8195	862.5482	863.7956
15	1615.1445	1622.5168	1633.6516	1637.3837	1652.4151	1667.6131	1671.4389	1682.9796	1690.7267	1698.5167	1710.2827	1714.2264
20	2827.9187	2846.0649	2873.5414	2882.7694	2920.0307	2957.8580	2967.4044	2996.2605	3015.6803	3035.2475	3064.8771	3074.8286
25	4706.2016	4745.7760	4805.8559	4826.0761	4907.9374	4991.3924	5012.5090	5076.4739	5119.6352	5163.2158	5229.3824	5251.6523
30	7615.1905	7695.3148	7817.2846	7858.4227	8025.4228	8196.4134	8239.7962	8371.4950	8460.6021	8550.7709	8688.0439	8734.3470

YEAR	9.50 %	9.75 %	10.00 %	10.25 %	10.50 %	10.75 %	11.00 %	12.00 %	13.00 %	14.00 %	15.00 %	16.00 %
1	54.6065	54.6773	54.7483	54.8194	54.8907	54.9620	55.0335	55.3206	55.6096	55.9006	56.1936	56.4886
2	114.6542	114.9535	115.2537	115.5550	115.8574	116.1607	116.4651	117.6931	118.9380	120.1999	121.4793	122.7763
3	180.6854	181.4017	182.1217	182.8453	183.5727	184.3039	185.0388	188.0166	191.0564	194.1598	197.3281	200.5629
4	253.2963	254.6540	256.0211	257.3977	258.7838	260.1795	261.5848	267.3045	273.1851	279.2315	285.4491	291.8430
5	333.1426	335.4072	337.6916	339.9958	342.3202	344.6649	347.0300	356.6996	366.7133	377.0847	387.8279	398.9576
6	420.9451	424.4292	427.9501	431.5081	435.1036	438.7371	442.4091	457.4903	473.2235	489.6397	506.7715	524.6533
7	517.4967	522.5669	527.6998	532.8964	538.1575	543.4840	548.8768	571.1293	594.5175	619.1052	644.9599	672.1533
8	623.6693	630.7536	637.9388	645.2268	652.6189	660.1170	667.7225	699.2544	732.6474	768.0220	805.5071	845.2402
9	740.4214	750.0182	759.7701	769.6799	779.7505	789.9846	800.3851	843.7122	889.9499	939.3125	992.0305	1048.3524
10	868.8074	881.4952	894.4127	907.5643	920.9547	934.5887	948.4710	1006.5846	1069.0864	1136.3382	1208.7331	1286.6984
15	1730.1108	1770.6000	1812.2278	1855.0288	1899.0387	1944.2945	1990.8341	2190.6355	2414.3550	2665.0817	2946.3217	3262.0556
20	3115.0134	3218.1822	3325.3454	3436.6686	3552.3246	3672.4935	3797.3634	4347.9042	4990.9738	5743.1800	6624.2300	7657.5234
25	5341.8188	5575.0408	5819.8838	6076.9626	6346.9254	6630.4561	6928.2762	8278.3165	9926.0211	11940.88	14409.16	17438.10
30	8922.3321	9412.3236	9932.4007	10484.51	11070.73	11693.27	12354.49	15439.29	19378.21	24419.83	30887.33	39201.37

SAVINGS GROWTH

DAILY COMPOUNDING, 365 DAY YEAR
Monthly Deposit

Description: This table shows what a series of $ 1 deposits grow to in the future. The deposit is made at the beginning of a period.

Example: At 5 % a regular one dollar deposit will grow to $ 68.32 by the end of the fifth year.

YEAR	0.00 %	1.00 %	2.00 %	3.00 %	4.00 %	4.125%	4.25 %	4.375 %	4.50 %	4.625%	4.75 %	4.875%
1	12.0000	12.0655	12.1314	12.1978	12.2647	12.2731	12.2815	12.2899	12.2983	12.3067	12.3152	12.3236
2	24.0000	24.2522	24.5079	24.7671	25.0299	25.0630	25.0962	25.1294	25.1626	25.1960	25.2294	25.2628
3	36.0000	36.5615	37.1344	37.7192	38.3160	38.3915	38.4672	38.5430	38.6191	38.6953	38.7717	38.8484
4	48.0000	48.9944	50.0160	51.0657	52.1443	52.2813	52.4186	52.5565	52.6948	52.8336	52.9729	53.1126
5	60.0000	61.5523	63.1578	64.8187	66.5370	66.7559	66.9758	67.1966	67.4184	67.6411	67.8648	68.0894
6	72.0000	74.2364	76.5651	78.9904	81.5170	81.8401	82.1649	82.4914	82.8196	83.1495	83.4811	83.8144
7	84.0000	87.0479	90.2432	93.5938	97.1082	97.5595	98.0135	98.4702	98.9297	99.3919	99.8570	100.3248
8	96.0000	99.9882	104.1976	108.6418	113.3358	113.9408	114.5501	115.1635	115.7812	116.4032	117.0295	117.6601
9	108.0000	113.0586	118.4339	124.1482	130.2255	131.0120	131.8046	132.6034	133.4084	134.2197	135.0373	135.8613
10	120.0000	126.2603	132.9578	140.1267	147.8045	148.8020	149.8082	150.8231	151.8468	152.8794	153.9211	154.9718
15	180.0000	194.2860	210.0985	227.6217	247.0639	249.6405	252.2512	254.8965	257.5769	260.2930	263.0452	265.8341
20	240.0000	265.7994	295.3519	329.2757	368.2982	373.5756	378.9477	384.4163	389.9834	395.6508	401.4207	407.2949
25	300.0000	340.9793	389.5712	447.3801	516.3725	525.8975	535.6396	545.6041	555.7966	566.2228	576.8884	587.7996
30	360.0000	420.0137	493.6994	584.5970	697.2288	713.1082	729.4285	746.2030	763.4455	781.1700	799.3913	818.1243

YEAR	5.00 %	5.10 %	5.125%	5.20 %	5.25 %	5.30 %	5.375%	5.40 %	5.50 %	5.60 %	5.625%	5.70 %
1	12.3320	12.3388	12.3405	12.3456	12.3489	12.3523	12.3574	12.3591	12.3659	12.3727	12.3744	12.3794
2	25.2963	25.3231	25.3299	25.3500	25.3635	25.3769	25.3971	25.4039	25.4309	25.4579	25.4647	25.4850
3	38.9252	38.9868	39.0022	39.0485	39.0795	39.1104	39.1569	39.1724	39.2345	39.2967	39.3123	39.3591
4	53.2528	53.3654	53.3935	53.4782	53.5347	53.5913	53.6764	53.7048	53.8185	53.9326	53.9612	54.0470
5	68.3150	68.4962	68.5416	68.6780	68.7691	68.8604	68.9976	69.0434	69.2271	69.4114	69.4576	69.5964
6	84.1494	84.4186	84.4861	84.6890	84.8246	84.9605	85.1648	85.2331	85.5068	85.7817	85.8506	86.0577
7	100.7955	101.1741	101.2691	101.5546	101.7455	101.9368	102.2247	102.3210	102.7069	103.0948	103.1921	103.4845
8	118.2951	118.8063	118.9345	119.3203	119.5783	119.8371	120.2267	120.3569	120.8795	121.4050	121.5369	121.9335
9	136.6918	137.3609	137.5288	138.0342	138.3724	138.7117	139.2226	139.3934	140.0794	140.7698	140.9430	141.4644
10	156.0317	156.8863	157.1009	157.7469	158.1794	158.6134	159.2674	159.4861	160.3649	161.2498	161.4720	162.1409
15	268.6602	270.9483	271.5241	273.2608	274.4263	275.5981	277.3674	277.9604	280.3480	282.7613	283.3686	285.2004
20	413.2757	418.1383	419.3650	423.0716	425.5650	428.0766	431.8780	433.1544	438.3062	443.5332	444.8519	448.8367
25	598.9624	608.0780	610.3831	617.3621	622.0683	626.8179	634.0246	636.4490	646.2588	656.2509	658.7778	666.4290
30	837.3847	853.1836	857.1886	869.3386	877.5524	885.8586	898.4933	902.7523	920.0290	937.6979	942.1775	955.7687

YEAR	5.75 %	5.80 %	5.875%	5.90 %	6.00 %	6.10 %	6.125%	6.20 %	6.25 %	6.30 %	6.375%	6.40 %
1	12.3828	12.3862	12.3913	12.3930	12.3998	12.4066	12.4083	12.4135	12.4169	12.4203	12.4254	12.4271
2	25.4985	25.5121	25.5324	25.5392	25.5664	25.5936	25.6004	25.6208	25.6345	25.6481	25.6686	25.6754
3	39.3904	39.4216	39.4686	39.4842	39.5470	39.6099	39.6256	39.6729	39.7045	39.7360	39.7835	39.7993
4	54.1043	54.1617	54.2480	54.2767	54.3921	54.5077	54.5367	54.6237	54.6818	54.7400	54.8274	54.8566
5	69.6891	69.7820	69.9216	69.9682	70.1550	70.3426	70.3895	70.5307	70.6250	70.7195	70.8615	70.9090
6	86.1962	86.3349	86.5435	86.6132	86.8927	87.1733	87.2436	87.4551	87.5964	87.7380	87.9510	88.0222
7	103.6801	103.8762	104.1712	104.2697	104.6652	105.0626	105.1622	105.4619	105.6622	105.8631	106.1653	106.2663
8	122.1988	122.4649	122.8654	122.9992	123.5366	124.0769	124.2125	124.6203	124.8931	125.1667	125.5785	125.7162
9	141.8134	142.1635	142.6907	142.8670	143.5749	144.2872	144.4660	145.0041	145.3642	145.7255	146.2695	146.4514
10	162.5889	163.0383	163.7155	163.9420	164.8521	165.7686	165.9987	166.6915	167.1554	167.6209	168.3223	168.5569
15	286.4299	287.6659	289.5323	290.1578	292.6766	295.2226	295.8634	297.7961	299.0933	300.3974	302.3669	303.0269
20	451.5174	454.2177	458.3051	459.6775	465.2174	470.8387	472.2569	476.5427	479.4261	482.3307	486.7276	488.2040
25	671.5890	676.7969	684.6997	687.3584	698.1174	709.0779	711.8500	720.2439	725.9053	731.6197	740.2917	743.2094
30	964.9578	974.2512	988.3892	993.1554	1012.4918	1032.2708	1037.2861	1052.5035	1062.7934	1073.2009	1089.0359	1094.3746

YEAR	6.50 %	6.60 %	6.625%	6.70 %	6.75 %	6.80 %	6.875%	6.90 %	7.00 %	7.10 %	7.125%	7.20 %
1	12.4339	12.4407	12.4425	12.4476	12.4510	12.4544	12.4595	12.4613	12.4681	12.4750	12.4767	12.4818
2	25.7028	25.7302	25.7371	25.7576	25.7714	25.7851	25.8057	25.8126	25.8402	25.8678	25.8747	25.8954
3	39.8627	39.9263	39.9422	39.9899	40.0218	40.0537	40.1017	40.1177	40.1817	40.2459	40.2620	40.3102
4	54.9735	55.0908	55.1202	55.2084	55.2673	55.3263	55.4149	55.4445	55.5630	55.6819	55.7117	55.8011
5	71.0991	71.2898	71.3376	71.4813	71.5772	71.6734	71.8179	71.8661	72.0595	72.2536	72.3022	72.4484
6	88.3075	88.5940	88.6658	88.8817	89.0260	89.1706	89.3881	89.4607	89.7520	90.0446	90.1179	90.3383
7	106.6715	107.0787	107.1808	107.4878	107.6931	107.8989	108.2086	108.3121	108.7272	109.1444	109.2491	109.5637
8	126.2687	126.8243	126.9637	127.3831	127.6636	127.9450	128.3684	128.5100	129.0782	129.6496	129.7929	130.2242
9	147.1819	147.9171	148.1016	148.6569	149.0286	149.4014	149.9629	150.1506	150.9046	151.6634	151.8538	152.4269
10	169.4995	170.4488	170.6871	171.4048	171.8853	172.3675	173.0940	173.3370	174.3134	175.2968	175.5437	176.2871
15	305.6848	308.3716	309.0478	311.0875	312.4565	313.8330	315.9116	316.6083	319.4138	322.2499	322.9637	325.1169
20	494.1640	500.2121	501.7381	506.3497	509.4525	512.5783	517.3102	518.8992	525.3140	531.8243	533.4669	538.4314
25	755.0174	767.0482	770.0912	779.3062	785.5219	791.7962	801.3186	804.5227	817.4906	830.7049	834.0476	844.1706
30	1116.0361	1138.1976	1143.8176	1160.8714	1172.4044	1184.0702	1201.8216	1207.8070	1232.0950	1256.9480	1263.2512	1282.3799

SAVINGS GROWTH

Description: This table shows what a series of $ 1 deposits grow to in the future. The deposit is made at the beginning of a period.

Example: At 8 % a regular one dollar deposit will grow to $ 74.03 by the end of the fifth year.

YEAR	7.25 %	7.30 %	7.375%	7.40 %	7.50 %	7.60 %	7.625%	7.70 %	7.75 %	7.80 %	7.875%	7.90 %
1	12.4853	12.4887	12.4938	12.4956	12.5024	12.5093	12.5110	12.5162	12.5196	12.5231	12.5282	12.5300
2	25.9092	25.9231	25.9438	25.9508	25.9785	26.0063	26.0132	26.0341	26.0480	26.0619	26.0829	26.0898
3	40.3425	40.3747	40.4231	40.4393	40.5040	40.5689	40.5851	40.6339	40.6664	40.6990	40.7479	40.7643
4	55.8609	55.9207	56.0105	56.0405	56.1607	56.2813	56.3114	56.4021	56.4627	56.5233	56.6144	56.6449
5	72.5460	72.6438	72.7908	72.8399	73.0367	73.2342	73.2837	73.4324	73.5317	73.6312	73.7808	73.8307
6	90.4856	90.6333	90.8553	90.9295	91.2269	91.5256	91.6005	91.8256	91.9760	92.1268	92.3535	92.4292
7	109.7741	109.9850	110.3023	110.4083	110.8338	111.2613	111.3685	111.6909	111.9065	112.1226	112.4478	112.5564
8	130.5127	130.8020	131.2375	131.3831	131.9675	132.5551	132.7025	133.1461	133.4428	133.7403	134.1883	134.3380
9	152.8106	153.1954	153.7749	153.9687	154.7470	155.5302	155.7267	156.3184	156.7143	157.1116	157.7098	157.9099
10	176.7849	177.2844	178.0371	178.2889	179.3004	180.3192	180.5750	181.3452	181.8610	182.3786	183.1584	183.4193
15	326.5621	328.0152	330.2097	330.9452	333.9073	336.9018	337.6555	339.9291	341.4552	342.9896	345.3070	346.0838
20	541.7718	545.1371	550.2319	551.9428	558.8502	565.8610	567.6300	572.9767	576.5745	580.1992	585.6871	587.5300
25	850.9993	857.8927	868.3558	871.8767	886.1277	900.6512	904.3254	915.4530	922.9599	930.5385	942.0425	945.9138
30	1295.3175	1308.4052	1328.3224	1335.0386	1362.2952	1390.1905	1397.2660	1418.7405	1433.2661	1447.9615	1470.3276	1477.8702

YEAR	8.00 %	8.10 %	8.125%	8.20 %	8.25 %	8.30 %	8.375%	8.40 %	8.50 %	8.60 %	8.625%	8.70 %
1	12.5369	12.5438	12.5455	12.5507	12.5541	12.5576	12.5628	12.5645	12.5714	12.5783	12.5801	12.5853
2	26.1178	26.1457	26.1527	26.1737	26.1878	26.2018	26.2229	26.2299	26.2580	26.2862	26.2932	26.3144
3	40.8297	40.8952	40.9116	40.9609	40.9937	41.0267	41.0761	41.0926	41.1587	41.2249	41.2415	41.2912
4	56.7667	56.8889	56.9195	57.0115	57.0729	57.1344	57.2267	57.2576	57.3811	57.5050	57.5361	57.6293
5	74.0310	74.2319	74.2822	74.4335	74.5346	74.6359	74.7881	74.8389	75.0426	75.2471	75.2983	75.4522
6	92.7330	93.0380	93.1144	93.3442	93.4979	93.6518	93.8833	93.9607	94.2708	94.5823	94.6603	94.8950
7	112.9924	113.4305	113.5404	113.8708	114.0917	114.3132	114.6465	114.7578	115.2046	115.6537	115.7662	116.1049
8	134.9390	135.5434	135.6951	136.1512	136.4564	136.7625	137.2232	137.3772	137.9954	138.6172	138.7731	139.2424
9	158.7133	159.5218	159.7247	160.3355	160.7443	161.1544	161.7720	161.9785	162.8079	163.6427	163.8522	164.4828
10	184.4674	185.5230	185.7881	186.5861	187.1206	187.6569	188.4650	188.7353	189.8214	190.9154	191.1901	192.0171
15	349.2119	352.3745	353.1706	355.5719	357.1838	358.8046	361.2524	362.0729	365.3773	368.7183	369.5593	372.0962
20	594.9711	602.5241	604.4301	610.1909	614.0676	617.9734	623.8872	625.8733	633.8926	642.0333	644.0877	650.2973
25	961.5847	977.5573	981.5983	993.8377	1002.0954	1010.4325	1023.0887	1027.3480	1044.5908	1062.1677	1066.6149	1080.0855
30	1508.4839	1539.8201	1547.7692	1571.8970	1588.2189	1604.7331	1629.8698	1638.3474	1672.7596	1707.9896	1716.9273	1744.0580

YEAR	8.75 %	8.80 %	8.875%	8.90 %	9.00 %	9.10 %	9.125%	9.20 %	9.25 %	9.30 %	9.375%	9.40 %
1	12.5887	12.5922	12.5974	12.5992	12.6061	12.6131	12.6148	12.6200	12.6235	12.6270	12.6322	12.6339
2	26.3285	26.3426	26.3638	26.3709	26.3992	26.4276	26.4347	26.4560	26.4702	26.4844	26.5058	26.5129
3	41.3245	41.3577	41.4077	41.4244	41.4911	41.5580	41.5748	41.6251	41.6586	41.6923	41.7427	41.7596
4	57.6916	57.7539	57.8476	57.8788	58.0041	58.1298	58.1612	58.2557	58.3189	58.3821	58.4771	58.5088
5	75.5551	75.6581	75.8130	75.8647	76.0720	76.2801	76.3322	76.4888	76.5935	76.6983	76.8559	76.9085
6	95.0519	95.2091	95.4455	95.5245	95.8412	96.1593	96.2390	96.4787	96.6389	96.7994	97.0409	97.1215
7	116.3313	116.6583	116.8999	117.0140	117.4719	117.9321	118.0475	118.3946	118.6267	118.8594	119.2095	119.3264
8	139.5563	139.8712	140.3451	140.5035	141.1394	141.7790	141.9395	142.4222	142.7452	143.0690	143.5566	143.7196
9	164.9048	165.3282	165.9659	166.1792	167.0355	167.8974	168.1138	168.7649	169.2007	169.6379	170.2964	170.5165
10	192.5710	193.1268	193.9643	194.2444	195.3701	196.5038	196.7885	197.6457	198.2198	198.7959	199.6639	199.9543
15	373.7992	375.5116	378.0979	378.9648	382.4563	385.9866	386.8753	389.5561	391.3558	393.1654	395.8987	396.8148
20	654.4762	658.6867	665.0622	667.2034	675.8496	684.6273	686.8426	693.5388	698.0453	702.5861	709.4621	711.7716
25	1089.1746	1098.3515	1112.2836	1116.9726	1135.9564	1155.3102	1160.2074	1175.0419	1185.0518	1195.1591	1210.5049	1215.6700
30	1762.4132	1780.9859	1809.2589	1818.7950	1857.5074	1897.1460	1907.2031	1937.7342	1958.3918	1979.2959	2011.1208	2021.8557

YEAR	9.50 %	9.75 %	10.00 %	10.25 %	10.50 %	10.75 %	11.00 %	12.00 %	13.00 %	14.00 %	15.00 %	16.00 %
1	12.6409	12.6583	12.6758	12.6933	12.7109	12.7284	12.7460	12.8167	12.8879	12.9596	13.0318	13.1046
2	26.5414	26.6129	26.6846	26.7565	26.8287	26.9012	26.9739	27.2673	27.5647	27.8664	28.1722	28.4824
3	41.8270	41.9963	42.1664	42.3375	42.5094	42.6822	42.8559	43.5599	44.2787	45.0127	45.7623	46.5277
4	58.6358	58.9549	59.2763	59.5999	59.9258	60.2539	60.5844	61.9294	63.3126	64.7352	66.1984	67.7034
5	77.1195	77.6501	78.1854	78.7254	79.2701	79.8196	80.3739	82.6406	84.9885	87.4209	89.9410	92.5525
6	97.4450	98.2596	99.0828	99.9148	100.7556	101.6054	102.4642	105.9919	109.6730	113.5149	117.5252	121.7121
7	119.7958	120.9794	122.1778	123.3911	124.6195	125.8633	127.1227	132.3199	137.7838	143.5293	149.5724	155.9300
8	144.3738	146.0257	147.7013	149.4010	151.1250	152.8739	154.6479	162.0041	169.7964	178.0532	186.8048	196.0837
9	171.4009	173.6367	175.9088	178.2178	180.5645	182.9494	185.3732	195.4722	206.2524	217.7641	230.0614	243.2029
10	201.1210	204.0749	207.0824	210.1447	213.2627	216.4377	219.6707	233.2067	247.7686	263.4412	280.3168	298.4958
15	400.5050	409.9115	419.5832	429.5282	439.7547	450.2715	461.0873	507.5290	559.5444	617.8551	683.2803	756.7506
20	721.0974	745.0412	769.9138	795.7537	822.6012	850.4982	879.4886	1007.3275	1156.6946	1331.4613	1536.2227	1776.4368
25	1236.5826	1290.6774	1347.4717	1407.1085	1469.7386	1535.5211	1604.6238	1917.9301	2300.4279	2768.2947	3341.6235	4045.3923
30	2065.4390	2179.0466	2299.6385	2427.6672	2563.6151	2707.9971	2861.3626	3576.9924	4491.0421	5661.3337	7163.0681	9094.1606

Description: This table shows what a series of $ 1 deposits grow to in the future. The deposit is made at the beginning of a period.

Example: At 5 % a regular one dollar deposit will grow to $ 22.87 by the end of the fifth year.

YEAR	0.00 %	1.00 %	2.00 %	3.00 %	4.00 %	4.125%	4.25 %	4.375%	4.50 %	4.625%	4.75 %	4.875%
1	4.0000	4.0252	4.0506	4.0761	4.1019	4.1051	4.1084	4.1116	4.1149	4.1181	4.1214	4.1246
2	8.0000	8.0908	8.1830	8.2764	8.3712	8.3831	8.3951	8.4071	8.4191	8.4311	8.4432	8.4553
3	12.0000	12.1973	12.3988	12.6046	12.8147	12.8413	12.8679	12.8947	12.9214	12.9483	12.9752	13.0022
4	16.0000	16.3451	16.6999	17.0646	17.4396	17.4872	17.5350	17.5829	17.6310	17.6793	17.7277	17.7764
5	20.0000	20.5346	21.0878	21.6604	22.2532	22.3287	22.4046	22.4808	22.5573	22.6342	22.7114	22.7890
6	24.0000	24.7661	25.5644	26.3962	27.2632	27.3741	27.4856	27.5977	27.7104	27.8237	27.9375	28.0520
7	28.0000	29.0402	30.1313	31.2762	32.4776	32.6320	32.7872	32.9435	33.1006	33.2587	33.4178	33.5779
8	32.0000	33.3573	34.7906	36.3048	37.9049	38.1112	38.3190	38.5282	38.7389	38.9511	39.1647	39.3799
9	36.0000	37.7177	39.5440	41.4865	43.5537	43.8213	44.0910	44.3628	44.6367	44.9129	45.1912	45.4717
10	40.0000	42.1220	44.3933	46.8260	49.4329	49.7717	50.1135	50.4582	50.8060	51.1568	51.5108	51.8678
15	60.0000	64.8161	70.1499	76.0642	82.6300	83.5004	84.3825	85.2763	86.1820	87.0998	88.0299	88.9725
20	80.0000	88.6738	98.6152	110.0338	123.1766	124.9546	126.7647	128.6074	130.4835	132.3935	134.3382	136.3183
25	100.0000	113.7548	130.0741	149.5006	172.6997	175.9037	179.1809	182.5332	185.9625	189.4707	193.0598	196.7317
30	120.0000	140.1216	164.8416	195.3543	233.1867	238.5224	244.0067	249.6441	255.4392	261.3968	267.5219	273.8196

YEAR	5.00 %	5.10 %	5.125%	5.20 %	5.25 %	5.30 %	5.375%	5.40 %	5.50 %	5.60 %	5.625%	5.70 %
1	4.1279	4.1305	4.1311	4.1331	4.1344	4.1357	4.1376	4.1383	4.1409	4.1435	4.1442	4.1461
2	8.4673	8.4770	8.4795	8.4867	8.4916	8.4965	8.5038	8.5062	8.5159	8.5257	8.5281	8.5355
3	13.0293	13.0510	13.0564	13.0728	13.0837	13.0946	13.1109	13.1164	13.1383	13.1602	13.1657	13.1822
4	17.8251	17.8643	17.8741	17.9036	17.9232	17.9429	17.9725	17.9824	18.0220	18.0617	18.0717	18.1015
5	22.8669	22.9294	22.9451	22.9922	23.0237	23.0552	23.1026	23.1184	23.1818	23.2455	23.2614	23.3094
6	28.1670	28.2595	28.2827	28.3524	28.3990	28.4457	28.5159	28.5393	28.6333	28.7278	28.7515	28.8226
7	33.7390	33.8685	33.9010	33.9987	34.0640	34.1295	34.2280	34.2610	34.3931	34.5258	34.5591	34.6592
8	39.5965	39.7709	39.8147	39.9463	40.0344	40.1227	40.2556	40.3001	40.4784	40.6578	40.7028	40.8382
9	45.7544	45.9822	46.0394	46.2114	46.3266	46.4421	46.6161	46.6742	46.9079	47.1430	47.2020	47.3795
10	52.2280	52.5184	52.5913	52.8109	52.9579	53.1054	53.3277	53.4020	53.7008	54.0016	54.0771	54.3046
15	89.9278	90.7012	90.8958	91.4829	91.8770	92.2731	92.8713	93.0718	93.8791	94.6951	94.9004	95.5199
20	138.3344	139.9737	140.3873	141.6370	142.4777	143.3245	144.6063	145.0367	146.7739	148.5366	148.9813	150.3252
25	200.4887	203.5569	204.3328	206.6820	208.2662	209.8651	212.2913	213.1075	216.4102	219.7745	220.6254	223.2017
30	280.2951	285.6071	286.9538	291.0393	293.8014	296.5946	300.8437	302.2760	308.0865	314.0294	315.5362	320.1079

YEAR	5.75 %	5.80 %	5.875%	5.90 %	6.00 %	6.10 %	6.125%	6.20 %	6.25 %	6.30 %	6.375%	6.40 %
1	4.1475	4.1488	4.1507	4.1514	4.1540	4.1566	4.1573	4.1593	4.1606	4.1619	4.1639	4.1645
2	8.5404	8.5453	8.5526	8.5551	8.5649	8.5747	8.5772	8.5845	8.5895	8.5944	8.6018	8.6043
3	13.1932	13.2043	13.2208	13.2263	13.2485	13.2706	13.2762	13.2929	13.3040	13.3151	13.3319	13.3374
4	18.1215	18.1415	18.1715	18.1815	18.2216	18.2619	18.2720	18.3023	18.3225	18.3428	18.3732	18.3834
5	23.3414	23.3735	23.4217	23.4378	23.5023	23.5671	23.5833	23.6321	23.6647	23.6973	23.7464	23.7628
6	28.8702	28.9179	28.9895	29.0135	29.1095	29.2060	29.2301	29.3028	29.3514	29.4001	29.4733	29.4977
7	34.7262	34.7933	34.8943	34.9280	35.0634	35.1995	35.2336	35.3362	35.4048	35.4736	35.5771	35.6117
8	40.9288	41.0196	41.1563	41.2020	41.3854	41.5699	41.6162	41.7554	41.8486	41.9420	42.0826	42.1296
9	47.4984	47.6176	47.7972	47.8572	48.0984	48.3410	48.4020	48.5853	48.7079	48.8310	49.0164	49.0784
10	54.4568	54.6097	54.8399	54.9169	55.2264	55.5380	55.6163	55.8519	56.0096	56.1680	56.4065	56.4863
15	95.9356	96.3536	96.9848	97.1964	98.0483	98.9095	99.1262	99.7800	100.2188	100.6599	101.3262	101.5495
20	151.2294	152.1401	153.5188	153.9817	155.8504	157.7467	158.2252	159.6710	160.6438	161.6238	163.1074	163.6055
25	224.9392	226.6930	229.3543	230.2497	233.8732	237.5648	238.4985	241.3259	243.2329	245.1579	248.0792	249.0622
30	323.1990	326.3252	331.0814	332.6849	339.1904	345.8453	347.5328	352.6532	356.1158	359.6181	364.9470	366.7436

YEAR	6.50 %	6.60 %	6.625%	6.70 %	6.75 %	6.80 %	6.875%	6.90 %	7.00 %	7.10 %	7.125%	7.20 %
1	4.1672	4.1698	4.1705	4.1724	4.1738	4.1751	4.1771	4.1777	4.1804	4.1830	4.1837	4.1857
2	8.6142	8.6241	8.6265	8.6340	8.6389	8.6439	8.6514	8.6539	8.6638	8.6738	8.6763	8.6838
3	13.3598	13.3822	13.3878	13.4047	13.4159	13.4272	13.4441	13.4497	13.4723	13.4950	13.5006	13.5176
4	18.4241	18.4649	18.4752	18.5059	18.5264	18.5470	18.5778	18.5881	18.6294	18.6708	18.6812	18.7124
5	23.8285	23.8944	23.9109	23.9606	23.9937	24.0270	24.0769	24.0936	24.1604	24.2275	24.2443	24.2949
6	29.5958	29.6943	29.7190	29.7932	29.8428	29.8925	29.9673	29.9923	30.0925	30.1931	30.2183	30.2941
7	35.7504	35.8899	35.9248	36.0300	36.1003	36.1708	36.2769	36.3123	36.4546	36.5975	36.6333	36.7411
8	42.3183	42.5081	42.5557	42.6989	42.7947	42.8908	43.0355	43.0838	43.2779	43.4731	43.5221	43.6694
9	49.3273	49.5778	49.6407	49.8299	49.9566	50.0836	50.2750	50.3390	50.5960	50.8546	50.9195	51.1149
10	56.8069	57.1298	57.2109	57.4550	57.6185	57.7825	58.0297	58.1124	58.4446	58.7792	58.8632	59.1162
15	102.4487	103.3578	103.5866	104.2768	104.7400	105.2058	105.9092	106.1450	107.0945	108.0544	108.2960	109.0248
20	165.6166	167.6575	168.1725	169.7288	170.7760	171.8309	173.4280	173.9644	176.1296	178.3272	178.8818	180.5577
25	253.0403	257.0938	258.1191	261.2241	263.3185	265.4328	268.6417	269.7215	274.0919	278.5456	279.6723	283.0844
30	374.0339	381.4930	383.3846	389.1250	393.0072	396.9343	402.9102	404.9252	413.1023	421.4702	423.5925	430.0336

Description: This table shows what a series of $ 1 deposits grow to in the future. The deposit is made at the beginning of a period.

Example: At 8 % a regular one dollar deposit will grow to $ 24.84 by the end of the fifth year.

YEAR	7.25 %	7.30 %	7.375%	7.40 %	7.50 %	7.60 %	7.625%	7.70 %	7.75 %	7.80 %	7.875%	7.90 %
1	4.1870	4.1883	4.1903	4.1910	4.1936	4.1963	4.1969	4.1989	4.2003	4.2016	4.2036	4.2042
2	8.6888	8.6938	8.7013	8.7038	8.7138	8.7239	8.7264	8.7339	8.7389	8.7440	8.7515	8.7541
3	13.5290	13.5404	13.5575	13.5632	13.5860	13.6089	13.6146	13.6318	13.6433	13.6548	13.6721	13.6779
4	18.7332	18.7540	18.7853	18.7958	18.8377	18.8797	18.8902	18.9218	18.9429	18.9640	18.9958	19.0064
5	24.3286	24.3624	24.4133	24.4302	24.4983	24.5665	24.5837	24.6351	24.6694	24.7038	24.7556	24.7728
6	30.3447	30.3955	30.4719	30.4974	30.5997	30.7024	30.7282	30.8056	30.8574	30.9092	30.9872	31.0133
7	36.8132	36.8855	36.9942	37.0305	37.1763	37.3228	37.3595	37.4700	37.5439	37.6180	37.7294	37.7667
8	43.7680	43.8668	44.0156	44.0654	44.2650	44.4658	44.5162	44.6678	44.7692	44.8709	45.0240	45.0752
9	51.2457	51.3769	51.5744	51.6405	51.9058	52.1729	52.2399	52.4416	52.5767	52.7121	52.9161	52.9844
10	59.2856	59.4556	59.7117	59.7974	60.1417	60.4884	60.5755	60.8376	61.0132	61.1894	61.4549	61.5437
15	109.5140	110.0059	110.7487	110.9977	112.0005	113.0143	113.2695	114.0393	114.5560	115.0756	115.8604	116.1234
20	181.6855	182.8216	184.5418	185.1194	187.4517	189.8191	190.4165	192.2221	193.4371	194.6612	196.5147	197.1372
25	285.3862	287.7099	291.2371	292.4240	297.2284	302.1251	303.3639	307.1159	309.6472	312.2028	316.0821	317.3877
30	434.3902	438.7974	445.5048	447.7667	456.9464	466.3420	468.7252	475.9587	480.8517	485.8021	493.3369	495.8779

YEAR	8.00 %	8.10 %	8.125%	8.20 %	8.25 %	8.30 %	8.375%	8.40 %	8.50 %	8.60 %	8.625%	8.70 %
1	4.2069	4.2096	4.2102	4.2122	4.2136	4.2149	4.2169	4.2176	4.2203	4.2229	4.2236	4.2256
2	8.7642	8.7743	8.7768	8.7844	8.7895	8.7946	8.8022	8.8047	8.8149	8.8251	8.8276	8.8353
3	13.7009	13.7241	13.7299	13.7473	13.7589	13.7705	13.7879	13.7938	13.8171	13.8405	13.8463	13.8639
4	19.0488	19.0914	19.1021	19.1341	19.1555	19.1770	19.2092	19.2199	19.2630	19.3062	19.3170	19.3495
5	24.8421	24.9116	24.9290	24.9813	25.0163	25.0513	25.1040	25.1215	25.1920	25.2628	25.2805	25.3337
6	31.1178	31.2227	31.2490	31.3281	31.3810	31.4340	31.5136	31.5402	31.6470	31.7542	31.7810	31.8618
7	37.9161	38.0663	38.1040	38.2172	38.2930	38.3689	38.4832	38.5213	38.6745	38.8285	38.8671	38.9832
8	45.2806	45.4872	45.5390	45.6950	45.7993	45.9039	46.0615	46.1141	46.3255	46.5380	46.5914	46.7518
9	53.2584	53.5341	53.6033	53.8117	53.9511	54.0910	54.3017	54.3721	54.6551	54.9399	55.0114	55.2265
10	61.9005	62.2599	62.3502	62.6219	62.8039	62.9865	63.2617	63.3537	63.7236	64.0962	64.1897	64.4714
15	117.1827	118.2538	118.5234	119.3368	119.8827	120.4317	121.2609	121.5388	122.6582	123.7901	124.0750	124.9345
20	199.6505	202.2019	202.8457	204.7918	206.1014	207.4210	209.4190	210.0900	212.7996	215.5504	216.2446	218.3430
25	322.6726	328.0597	329.4227	333.5510	336.3365	339.1487	343.4182	344.8550	350.6722	356.6024	358.1029	362.6481
30	506.1920	516.7502	519.4287	527.5588	533.0589	538.6240	547.0952	549.9523	561.5503	573.4247	576.4374	585.5827

YEAR	8.75 %	8.80 %	8.875%	8.90 %	9.00 %	9.10 %	9.125%	9.20 %	9.25 %	9.30 %	9.375%	9.40 %
1	4.2270	4.2283	4.2303	4.2310	4.2337	4.2363	4.2370	4.2390	4.2404	4.2417	4.2437	4.2444
2	8.8404	8.8455	8.8532	8.8557	8.8660	8.8762	8.8788	8.8865	8.8917	8.8968	8.9045	8.9071
3	13.8756	13.8874	13.9050	13.9109	13.9345	13.9581	13.9640	13.9818	13.9936	14.0055	14.0233	14.0293
4	19.3712	19.3930	19.4256	19.4366	19.4802	19.5241	19.5350	19.5680	19.5900	19.6121	19.6452	19.6563
5	25.3693	25.4050	25.4586	25.4765	25.5482	25.6202	25.6382	25.6925	25.7287	25.7650	25.8195	25.8377
6	31.9158	31.9699	32.0513	32.0785	32.1875	32.2970	32.3245	32.4070	32.4622	32.5175	32.6006	32.6284
7	39.0609	39.1387	39.2559	39.2950	39.4521	39.6099	39.6495	39.7685	39.8482	39.9280	40.0481	40.0882
8	46.8592	46.9669	47.1289	47.1831	47.4006	47.6194	47.6742	47.8394	47.9498	48.0606	48.2274	48.2832
9	55.3705	55.5150	55.7326	55.8054	56.0976	56.3918	56.4656	56.6878	56.8366	56.9858	57.2106	57.2857
10	64.6601	64.8494	65.1347	65.2301	65.6136	65.9998	66.0968	66.3889	66.5844	66.7807	67.0765	67.1754
15	125.5115	126.0918	126.9681	127.2619	128.4450	129.6414	129.9426	130.8512	131.4612	132.0745	133.0010	133.3116
20	219.7552	221.1782	223.3329	224.0566	226.9790	229.9460	230.6948	232.9584	234.4819	236.0170	238.3417	239.1225
25	365.7150	368.8117	373.5132	375.0956	381.5023	388.0344	389.6873	394.6945	398.0733	401.4852	406.6656	408.4092
30	591.7702	598.0312	607.5628	610.7778	623.8298	637.1951	640.5862	650.8815	657.8477	664.8972	675.6301	679.2506

YEAR	9.50 %	9.75 %	10.00 %	10.25 %	10.50 %	10.75 %	11.00 %	12.00 %	13.00 %	14.00 %	15.00 %	16.00 %
1	4.2471	4.2539	4.2606	4.2674	4.2742	4.2810	4.2878	4.3151	4.3427	4.3705	4.3985	4.4267
2	8.9174	8.9433	8.9693	8.9953	9.0215	9.0477	9.0740	9.1803	9.2882	9.3976	9.5086	9.6213
3	14.0531	14.1129	14.1730	14.2335	14.2943	14.3553	14.4168	14.6657	14.9201	15.1800	15.4456	15.7169
4	19.7006	19.8119	19.9240	20.0370	20.1507	20.2653	20.3806	20.8504	21.3338	21.8312	22.3431	22.8700
5	25.9108	26.0945	26.2798	26.4668	26.6554	26.8458	27.0378	27.8234	28.6376	29.4817	30.3567	31.2640
6	32.7398	33.0203	33.3039	33.5905	33.8802	34.1730	34.4690	35.6853	36.9553	38.2816	39.6668	41.1140
7	40.2492	40.6553	41.0666	41.4830	41.9047	42.3317	42.7641	44.5494	46.4275	48.4036	50.4833	52.6727
8	48.5070	49.0722	49.6456	50.2273	50.8175	51.4162	52.0237	54.5435	57.2144	60.0463	63.0499	66.2365
9	57.5876	58.3509	59.1267	59.9153	60.7168	61.5315	62.3597	65.8115	69.4986	73.4384	77.6498	82.1532
10	67.5730	68.5797	69.6049	70.6488	71.7119	72.7947	73.8974	78.5160	83.4878	88.8425	94.6119	100.8310
15	134.5624	137.7515	141.0309	144.4036	147.8724	151.4402	155.1100	170.8747	188.5435	208.3644	230.6191	255.6281
20	242.2757	250.3724	258.7846	267.5254	276.6087	286.0488	295.8605	339.1468	389.7586	449.0197	518.5022	600.0749
25	415.4694	433.7344	452.9142	473.0576	494.2158	516.4430	539.7964	645.7282	775.1498	933.5749	1127.8567	1366.5212
30	693.9502	732.2723	772.9579	816.1605	862.0438	910.7829	962.5641	1204.3010	1513.2970	1909.2183	2417.6614	3071.9798

Description: This table shows what a series of $ 1 deposits grow to in the future. The deposit is made at the beginning of a period.

Example: At 5 % a regular one dollar deposit will grow to $ 11.50 by the end of the fifth year.

YEAR	0.00 %	1.00 %	2.00 %	3.00 %	4.00 %	4.125%	4.25 %	4.375%	4.50 %	4.625%	4.75 %	4.875%
1	2.0000	2.0151	2.0303	2.0457	2.0612	2.0631	2.0651	2.0670	2.0690	2.0709	2.0729	2.0748
2	4.0000	4.0505	4.1017	4.1537	4.2065	4.2131	4.2198	4.2265	4.2332	4.2399	4.2466	4.2533
3	6.0000	6.1063	6.2149	6.3259	6.4393	6.4537	6.4681	6.4825	6.4970	6.5115	6.5260	6.5406
4	8.0000	8.1827	8.3708	8.5642	8.7633	8.7885	8.8139	8.8394	8.8649	8.8906	8.9163	8.9422
5	10.0000	10.2801	10.5702	10.8707	11.1820	11.2218	11.2616	11.3017	11.3419	11.3823	11.4229	11.4637
6	12.0000	12.3985	12.8140	13.2474	13.6995	13.7574	13.8156	13.8741	13.9329	13.9920	14.0515	14.1112
7	14.0000	14.5382	15.1032	15.6966	16.3198	16.3999	16.4805	16.5615	16.6431	16.7252	16.8078	16.8910
8	16.0000	16.6994	17.4387	18.2203	19.0469	19.1536	19.2610	19.3692	19.4781	19.5878	19.6983	19.8096
9	18.0000	18.8824	19.8213	20.8208	21.8854	22.0233	22.1623	22.3023	22.4435	22.5859	22.7294	22.8740
10	20.0000	21.0872	22.2520	23.5006	24.8397	25.0138	25.1895	25.3667	25.5455	25.7259	25.9079	26.0915
15	30.0000	32.4485	35.1624	38.1743	41.5210	41.9649	42.4147	42.8706	43.3327	43.8009	44.2755	44.7565
20	40.0000	44.3922	49.4305	55.2226	61.8953	62.7985	63.7181	64.6543	65.6077	66.5783	67.5668	68.5733
25	50.0000	56.9483	65.1992	75.0298	86.7803	88.4040	90.0650	91.7643	93.5027	95.2814	97.1013	98.9635
30	60.0000	70.1481	82.6262	98.0424	117.1746	119.8744	122.6496	125.5027	128.4359	131.4518	134.5528	137.7416

YEAR	5.00 %	5.10 %	5.125%	5.20 %	5.25 %	5.30 %	5.375%	5.40 %	5.50 %	5.60 %	5.625%	5.70 %
1	2.0768	2.0784	2.0788	2.0799	2.0807	2.0815	2.0827	2.0831	2.0846	2.0862	2.0866	2.0878
2	4.2601	4.2655	4.2668	4.2709	4.2736	4.2763	4.2804	4.2817	4.2872	4.2926	4.2940	4.2981
3	6.5552	6.5670	6.5699	6.5787	6.5846	6.5905	6.5994	6.6023	6.6142	6.6260	6.6290	6.6379
4	8.9681	8.9889	8.9941	9.0098	9.0203	9.0307	9.0465	9.0517	9.0728	9.0939	9.0992	9.1151
5	11.5047	11.5376	11.5458	11.5706	11.5871	11.6037	11.6287	11.6370	11.6704	11.7039	11.7122	11.7375
6	14.1713	14.2196	14.2317	14.2681	14.2924	14.3168	14.3534	14.3657	14.4148	14.4641	14.4765	14.5137
7	16.9746	17.0419	17.0588	17.1095	17.1434	17.1775	17.2287	17.2458	17.3144	17.3834	17.4007	17.4527
8	19.9216	20.0119	20.0345	20.1026	20.1482	20.1939	20.2627	20.2856	20.3780	20.4708	20.4941	20.5641
9	23.0198	23.1372	23.1667	23.2555	23.3148	23.3744	23.4642	23.4942	23.6147	23.7360	23.7664	23.8581
10	26.2767	26.4261	26.4636	26.5766	26.6522	26.7281	26.8425	26.8807	27.0344	27.1892	27.2281	27.3452
15	45.2441	45.6388	45.7382	46.0379	46.2391	46.4413	46.7467	46.8491	47.2613	47.6780	47.7829	48.0992
20	69.5982	70.4317	70.6420	71.2774	71.7049	72.1356	72.7875	73.0064	73.8900	74.7866	75.0129	75.6965
25	100.8690	102.4254	102.8190	104.0107	104.8145	105.6257	106.8567	107.2708	108.9468	110.6542	111.0860	112.3936
30	141.0209	143.7112	144.3933	146.4627	147.8619	149.2769	151.4295	152.1551	155.0992	158.1105	158.8741	161.1909

YEAR	5.75 %	5.80 %	5.875%	5.90 %	6.00 %	6.10 %	6.125%	6.20 %	6.25 %	6.30 %	6.375%	6.40 %
1	2.0886	2.0894	2.0906	2.0910	2.0925	2.0941	2.0945	2.0957	2.0965	2.0973	2.0985	2.0989
2	4.3008	4.3035	4.3076	4.3090	4.3145	4.3199	4.3213	4.3254	4.3282	4.3309	4.3351	4.3365
3	6.6439	6.6499	6.6588	6.6618	6.6738	6.6858	6.6888	6.6978	6.7038	6.7098	6.7189	6.7219
4	9.1257	9.1363	9.1523	9.1576	9.1790	9.2004	9.2057	9.2219	9.2326	9.2434	9.2596	9.2650
5	11.7543	11.7712	11.7966	11.8051	11.8390	11.8731	11.8817	11.9074	11.9245	11.9417	11.9675	11.9762
6	14.5385	14.5634	14.6009	14.6134	14.6636	14.7140	14.7266	14.7646	14.7900	14.8154	14.8537	14.8665
7	17.4875	17.5224	17.5749	17.5924	17.6628	17.7335	17.7513	17.8046	17.8403	17.8761	17.9299	17.9478
8	20.6110	20.6580	20.7288	20.7525	20.8475	20.9430	20.9669	21.0390	21.0873	21.1357	21.2085	21.2328
9	23.9194	23.9809	24.0736	24.1046	24.2290	24.3543	24.3857	24.4803	24.5437	24.6072	24.7029	24.7349
10	27.4235	27.5022	27.6207	27.6604	27.8197	27.9801	28.0204	28.1417	28.2230	28.3045	28.4273	28.4684
15	48.3115	48.5250	48.8475	48.9555	49.3907	49.8307	49.9414	50.2755	50.4997	50.7251	51.0656	51.1797
20	76.1565	76.6199	77.3214	77.5570	78.5079	79.4730	79.7165	80.4524	80.9475	81.4464	82.2016	82.4552
25	113.2756	114.1658	115.5168	115.9714	117.8110	119.6854	120.1595	121.5953	122.5637	123.5413	125.0251	125.5243
30	162.7575	164.3420	166.7528	167.5655	170.8633	174.2372	175.0928	177.6890	179.4448	181.2208	183.9232	184.8344

YEAR	6.50 %	6.60 %	6.625%	6.70 %	6.75 %	6.80 %	6.875%	6.90 %	7.00 %	7.10 %	7.125%	7.20 %
1	2.1005	2.1020	2.1024	2.1036	2.1044	2.1052	2.1064	2.1068	2.1084	2.1100	2.1104	2.1116
2	4.3420	4.3475	4.3489	4.3530	4.3558	4.3586	4.3627	4.3641	4.3697	4.3753	4.3767	4.3808
3	6.7340	6.7461	6.7492	6.7583	6.7644	6.7705	6.7796	6.7827	6.7949	6.8072	6.8102	6.8195
4	9.2867	9.3084	9.3138	9.3302	9.3411	9.3521	9.3685	9.3740	9.3960	9.4180	9.4235	9.4401
5	12.0108	12.0455	12.0542	12.0803	12.0978	12.1153	12.1416	12.1504	12.1856	12.2209	12.2298	12.2564
6	14.9178	14.9693	14.9822	15.0210	15.0469	15.0729	15.1120	15.1251	15.1775	15.2301	15.2433	15.2829
7	18.0200	18.0925	18.1107	18.1654	18.2020	18.2387	18.2938	18.3123	18.3863	18.4606	18.4793	18.5354
8	21.3306	21.4289	21.4535	21.5277	21.5774	21.6271	21.7021	21.7271	21.8277	21.9289	21.9543	22.0306
9	24.8634	24.9928	25.0253	25.1230	25.1884	25.2540	25.3529	25.3859	25.5187	25.6523	25.6858	25.7868
10	28.6335	28.7999	28.8416	28.9674	29.0516	29.1361	29.2634	29.3060	29.4772	29.6496	29.6929	29.8233
15	51.6393	52.1040	52.2209	52.5737	52.8105	53.0487	53.4083	53.5289	54.0143	54.5052	54.6288	55.0015
20	83.4791	84.5183	84.7805	85.5730	86.1063	86.6435	87.4570	87.7301	88.8330	89.9525	90.2350	91.0889
25	127.5450	129.6042	130.1251	131.7026	132.7668	133.8410	135.4717	136.0204	138.2414	140.5051	141.0777	142.8122
30	188.5319	192.3154	193.2749	196.1870	198.1566	200.1490	203.1811	204.2035	208.3530	212.5997	213.6768	216.9460

Description: This table shows what a series of $ 1 deposits grow to in the future. The deposit is made at the beginning of a period.

Example: At 8 % a regular one dollar deposit will grow to $ 12.54 by the end of the fifth year.

YEAR	7.25 %	7.30 %	7.375%	7.40 %	7.50 %	7.60 %	7.625%	7.70 %	7.75 %	7.80 %	7.875%	7.90 %
1	2.1124	2.1132	2.1144	2.1148	2.1164	2.1180	2.1184	2.1196	2.1204	2.1212	2.1224	2.1228
2	4.3836	4.3864	4.3906	4.3920	4.3976	4.4032	4.4046	4.4089	4.4117	4.4145	4.4187	4.4201
3	6.8256	6.8318	6.8410	6.8441	6.8565	6.8689	6.8720	6.8813	6.8875	6.8938	6.9031	6.9063
4	9.4512	9.4623	9.4790	9.4845	9.5069	9.5292	9.5348	9.5517	9.5629	9.5742	9.5911	9.5967
5	12.2742	12.2920	12.3188	12.3278	12.3636	12.3996	12.4086	12.4357	12.4538	12.4720	12.4992	12.5084
6	15.3094	15.3360	15.3760	15.3893	15.4428	15.4966	15.5101	15.5506	15.5777	15.6048	15.6457	15.6593
7	18.5729	18.6105	18.6671	18.6860	18.7619	18.8381	18.8573	18.9148	18.9532	18.9918	19.0498	19.0692
8	22.0817	22.1329	22.2101	22.2359	22.3394	22.4435	22.4696	22.5482	22.6008	22.6535	22.7329	22.7595
9	25.8543	25.9221	26.0242	26.0584	26.1955	26.3335	26.3681	26.4724	26.5422	26.6122	26.7177	26.7530
10	29.9106	29.9982	30.1302	30.1744	30.3519	30.5306	30.5755	30.7107	30.8012	30.8921	31.0290	31.0748
15	55.2517	55.5033	55.8833	56.0106	56.5236	57.0423	57.1729	57.5668	57.8312	58.0971	58.4987	58.6333
20	91.6635	92.2424	93.1189	93.4133	94.6018	95.8084	96.1129	97.0332	97.6526	98.2767	99.2216	99.5390
25	143.9823	145.1636	146.9568	147.5603	150.0032	152.4932	153.1232	155.0314	156.3188	157.6187	159.5920	160.2561
30	219.1574	221.3946	224.7996	225.9479	230.6086	235.3793	236.5895	240.2628	242.7478	245.2620	249.0891	250.3798

YEAR	8.00 %	8.10 %	8.125%	8.20 %	8.25 %	8.30 %	8.375%	8.40 %	8.50 %	8.60 %	8.625%	8.70 %
1	2.1244	2.1260	2.1264	2.1276	2.1284	2.1293	2.1305	2.1309	2.1325	2.1341	2.1345	2.1357
2	4.4258	4.4314	4.4328	4.4371	4.4399	4.4428	4.4470	4.4484	4.4541	4.4598	4.4613	4.4655
3	6.9188	6.9313	6.9344	6.9439	6.9502	6.9565	6.9659	6.9691	6.9817	6.9944	6.9976	7.0071
4	9.6194	9.6421	9.6477	9.6648	9.6762	9.6877	9.7048	9.7106	9.7335	9.7566	9.7623	9.7797
5	12.5449	12.5815	12.5907	12.6183	12.6367	12.6552	12.6830	12.6922	12.7294	12.7667	12.7761	12.8042
6	15.7140	15.7689	15.7827	15.8241	15.8518	15.8795	15.9213	15.9352	15.9911	16.0472	16.0613	16.1036
7	19.1471	19.2253	19.2449	19.3039	19.3433	19.3829	19.4424	19.4623	19.5421	19.6223	19.6424	19.7029
8	22.8660	22.9732	23.0000	23.0809	23.1351	23.1894	23.2711	23.2984	23.4081	23.5184	23.5461	23.6293
9	26.8946	27.0372	27.0730	27.1808	27.2529	27.3252	27.4342	27.4706	27.6170	27.7643	27.8013	27.9126
10	31.2588	31.4442	31.4907	31.6309	31.7248	31.8190	31.9609	32.0084	32.1993	32.3915	32.4398	32.5852
15	59.1755	59.7237	59.8617	60.2781	60.5576	60.8387	61.2632	61.4055	61.9787	62.5583	62.7043	63.1445
20	100.8204	102.1214	102.4497	103.4422	104.1101	104.7831	105.8023	106.1445	107.5268	108.9301	109.2843	110.3550
25	162.9447	165.6855	166.3790	168.4797	169.8971	171.3282	173.5011	174.2324	177.1932	180.2119	180.9758	183.2898
30	255.6191	260.9830	262.3439	266.4747	269.2695	272.0974	276.4024	277.8544	283.7490	289.7849	291.3163	295.9655

YEAR	8.75 %	8.80 %	8.875%	8.90 %	9.00 %	9.10 %	9.125%	9.20 %	9.25 %	9.30 %	9.375%	9.40 %
1	2.1365	2.1373	2.1385	2.1390	2.1406	2.1422	2.1426	2.1438	2.1446	2.1454	2.1467	2.1471
2	4.4684	4.4712	4.4755	4.4770	4.4827	4.4884	4.4899	4.4942	4.4971	4.5000	4.5043	4.5057
3	7.0135	7.0198	7.0294	7.0326	7.0454	7.0582	7.0614	7.0710	7.0775	7.0839	7.0936	7.0968
4	9.7912	9.8028	9.8202	9.8261	9.8494	9.8727	9.8786	9.8962	9.9079	9.9197	9.9373	9.9432
5	12.8230	12.8418	12.8701	12.8795	12.9174	12.9554	12.9649	12.9935	13.0126	13.0318	13.0606	13.0702
6	16.1319	16.1603	16.2029	16.2171	16.2743	16.3316	16.3460	16.3893	16.4182	16.4471	16.4907	16.5053
7	19.7434	19.7839	19.8450	19.8654	19.9472	20.0295	20.0502	20.1122	20.1537	20.1953	20.2579	20.2789
8	23.6851	23.7409	23.8251	23.8532	23.9661	24.0797	24.1082	24.1939	24.2513	24.3088	24.3954	24.4243
9	27.9871	28.0619	28.1745	28.2121	28.3634	28.5156	28.5538	28.6688	28.7458	28.8231	28.9394	28.9783
10	32.6825	32.7802	32.9275	32.9767	33.1747	33.3741	33.4242	33.5750	33.6759	33.7773	33.9300	33.9811
15	63.4400	63.7372	64.1861	64.3366	64.9427	65.5557	65.7101	66.1756	66.4882	66.8025	67.2773	67.4365
20	111.0756	111.8017	112.9014	113.2707	114.7622	116.2767	116.6589	117.8145	118.5923	119.3760	120.5630	120.9617
25	184.8512	186.4280	188.8219	189.6277	192.8904	196.2172	197.0591	199.6096	201.3307	203.0688	205.7080	206.5964
30	299.1112	302.2945	307.1409	308.7756	315.4129	322.2101	323.9349	329.1715	332.7150	336.3011	341.7613	343.6032

YEAR	9.50 %	9.75 %	10.00 %	10.25 %	10.50 %	10.75 %	11.00 %	12.00 %	13.00 %	14.00 %	15.00 %	16.00 %
1	2.1487	2.1528	2.1569	2.1609	2.1650	2.1692	2.1733	2.1898	2.2065	2.2234	2.2403	2.2575
2	4.5115	4.5260	4.5405	4.5551	4.5697	4.5844	4.5992	4.6588	4.7193	4.7808	4.8431	4.9065
3	7.1097	7.1422	7.1748	7.2076	7.2406	7.2738	7.3072	7.4425	7.5809	7.7224	7.8671	8.0151
4	9.9669	10.0263	10.0861	10.1464	10.2072	10.2683	10.3300	10.5811	10.8396	11.1060	11.3803	11.6629
5	13.1087	13.2057	13.3036	13.4024	13.5021	13.6027	13.7042	14.1197	14.5507	14.9979	15.4619	15.9435
6	16.5637	16.7107	16.8594	17.0097	17.1617	17.3154	17.4707	18.1094	18.7769	19.4746	20.2040	20.9667
7	20.3628	20.5746	20.7891	21.0064	21.2265	21.4494	21.6751	22.6077	23.5897	24.6239	25.7133	26.8612
8	24.5406	24.8342	25.1321	25.4344	25.7411	26.0524	26.3683	27.6795	29.0705	30.5468	32.1140	33.7783
9	29.1346	29.5299	29.9317	30.3402	30.7556	31.1778	31.6072	33.3977	35.3121	37.3596	39.5503	41.8952
10	34.1865	34.7064	35.2361	35.7755	36.3251	36.8848	37.4551	39.8449	42.4200	45.1959	48.1898	51.4202
15	68.0776	69.7125	71.3941	73.1239	74.9035	76.7343	78.6179	86.7147	95.7985	105.9992	117.4641	130.3613
20	122.5718	126.7070	131.0045	135.4710	140.1138	144.9400	149.9577	172.1086	198.0355	228.4253	264.0952	306.0171
25	210.1937	219.5018	229.2787	239.5496	250.3407	261.6801	273.5972	327.6911	393.8518	474.9283	574.4653	696.8776
30	351.0824	370.5842	391.2945	413.2920	436.6608	461.4909	487.8781	611.1529	768.9027	971.2578	1231.4176	1566.6014

Description: This table shows what a series of $ 1 deposits grow to in the future. The deposit is made at the beginning of a period.

Example: At 5 % a regular one dollar deposit will grow to $ 5.82 by the end of the fifth year.

YEAR	0.00 %	1.00 %	2.00 %	3.00 %	4.00 %	4.125%	4.25 %	4.375%	4.50 %	4.625%	4.75 %	4.875%
1	1.0000	1.0101	1.0202	1.0305	1.0408	1.0421	1.0434	1.0447	1.0460	1.0473	1.0486	1.0500
2	2.0000	2.0303	2.0610	2.0923	2.1241	2.1281	2.1321	2.1362	2.1402	2.1442	2.1483	2.1524
3	3.0000	3.0607	3.1228	3.1865	3.2516	3.2598	3.2681	3.2764	3.2847	3.2931	3.3014	3.3098
4	4.0000	4.1015	4.2061	4.3139	4.4251	4.4392	4.4534	4.4676	4.4819	4.4963	4.5107	4.5251
5	5.0000	5.1528	5.3113	5.4758	5.6465	5.6683	5.6901	5.7121	5.7342	5.7564	5.7787	5.8011
6	6.0000	6.2146	6.4388	6.6730	6.9177	6.9491	6.9806	7.0123	7.0442	7.0762	7.1085	7.1409
7	7.0000	7.2871	7.5891	7.9067	8.2408	8.2838	8.3271	8.3706	8.4144	8.4585	8.5029	8.5476
8	8.0000	8.3704	8.7626	9.1779	9.6179	9.6747	9.7320	9.7896	9.8477	9.9062	9.9651	10.0245
9	9.0000	9.4646	9.9598	10.4878	11.0512	11.1243	11.1979	11.2721	11.3470	11.4224	11.4985	11.5752
10	10.0000	10.5698	11.1812	11.8377	12.5430	12.6348	12.7274	12.8209	12.9152	13.0104	13.1065	13.2034
15	15.0000	16.2645	17.6684	19.2291	20.9664	21.1970	21.4308	21.6678	21.9080	22.1516	22.3985	22.6487
20	20.0000	22.2511	24.8378	27.8167	31.2546	31.7204	32.1947	32.6778	33.1698	33.6709	34.1812	34.7010
25	25.0000	28.5447	32.7613	37.7939	43.8205	44.6541	45.5070	46.3798	47.2729	48.1870	49.1224	50.0798
30	30.0000	35.1610	41.5180	49.3858	59.1683	60.5501	61.9710	63.4320	64.9344	66.4795	68.0687	69.7032

YEAR	5.00 %	5.10 %	5.125%	5.20 %	5.25 %	5.30 %	5.375%	5.40 %	5.50 %	5.60 %	5.625%	5.70 %
1	1.0513	1.0523	1.0526	1.0534	1.0539	1.0544	1.0552	1.0555	1.0565	1.0576	1.0579	1.0587
2	2.1564	2.1597	2.1605	2.1630	2.1646	2.1662	2.1687	2.1695	2.1728	2.1761	2.1769	2.1794
3	3.3183	3.3250	3.3267	3.3318	3.3352	3.3386	3.3437	3.3454	3.3522	3.3590	3.3607	3.3659
4	4.5396	4.5513	4.5542	4.5630	4.5688	4.5747	4.5835	4.5864	4.5982	4.6101	4.6130	4.6219
5	5.8236	5.8417	5.8463	5.8599	5.8690	5.8781	5.8918	5.8964	5.9147	5.9332	5.9378	5.9517
6	7.1735	7.1997	7.2062	7.2260	7.2392	7.2524	7.2723	7.2790	7.3057	7.3325	7.3392	7.3594
7	8.5925	8.6287	8.6378	8.6650	8.6833	8.7016	8.7291	8.7383	8.7752	8.8124	8.8217	8.8497
8	10.0843	10.1324	10.1445	10.1809	10.2052	10.2296	10.2663	10.2786	10.3279	10.3775	10.3899	10.4274
9	11.6526	11.7149	11.7305	11.7776	11.8091	11.8408	11.8884	11.9043	11.9683	12.0328	12.0489	12.0976
10	13.3012	13.3801	13.3999	13.4596	13.4995	13.5396	13.6001	13.6203	13.7015	13.7834	13.8039	13.8658
15	22.9025	23.1079	23.1597	23.3157	23.4204	23.5258	23.6848	23.7381	23.9528	24.1699	24.2246	24.3894
20	35.2305	35.6611	35.7698	36.0982	36.3191	36.5417	36.8787	36.9919	37.4487	37.9125	38.0295	38.3831
25	51.0597	51.8602	52.0627	52.6758	53.0893	53.5068	54.1403	54.3534	55.2161	56.0952	56.3175	56.9909
30	71.3845	72.7641	73.1140	74.1754	74.8932	75.6191	76.7237	77.0960	78.6070	80.1528	80.5448	81.7343

YEAR	5.75 %	5.80 %	5.875%	5.90 %	6.00 %	6.10 %	6.125%	6.20 %	6.25 %	6.30 %	6.375%	6.40 %
1	1.0592	1.0597	1.0605	1.0608	1.0618	1.0629	1.0632	1.0640	1.0645	1.0650	1.0658	1.0661
2	2.1810	2.1827	2.1852	2.1860	2.1893	2.1926	2.1935	2.1960	2.1976	2.1993	2.2018	2.2026
3	3.3693	3.3727	3.3779	3.3796	3.3865	3.3934	3.3952	3.4004	3.4038	3.4073	3.4125	3.4143
4	4.6279	4.6338	4.6428	4.6458	4.6577	4.6698	4.6728	4.6818	4.6878	4.6939	4.7030	4.7060
5	5.9609	5.9702	5.9842	5.9889	6.0076	6.0263	6.0310	6.0452	6.0546	6.0641	6.0783	6.0831
6	7.3729	7.3864	7.4068	7.4136	7.4409	7.4683	7.4751	7.4958	7.5096	7.5234	7.5442	7.5512
7	8.8684	8.8872	8.9154	8.9249	8.9628	9.0009	9.0104	9.0391	9.0584	9.0776	9.1066	9.1163
8	10.4524	10.4775	10.5154	10.5280	10.5788	10.6298	10.6427	10.6812	10.7070	10.7329	10.7718	10.7849
9	12.1302	12.1629	12.2121	12.2286	12.2947	12.3613	12.3780	12.4283	12.4620	12.4958	12.5467	12.5637
10	13.9072	13.9488	14.0115	14.0325	14.1167	14.2016	14.2229	14.2871	14.3301	14.3733	14.4383	14.4600
15	24.5001	24.6114	24.7795	24.8358	25.0627	25.2921	25.3499	25.5241	25.6411	25.7587	25.9363	25.9959
20	38.6211	38.8608	39.2238	39.3457	39.8378	40.3374	40.4634	40.8445	41.1009	41.3592	41.7503	41.8817
25	57.4451	57.9037	58.5996	58.8338	59.7817	60.7477	60.9920	61.7321	62.2314	62.7354	63.5005	63.7579
30	82.5388	83.3525	84.5907	85.0082	86.7024	88.4360	88.8757	90.2101	91.1126	92.0255	93.4149	93.8835

YEAR	6.50 %	6.60 %	6.625%	6.70 %	6.75 %	6.80 %	6.875%	6.90 %	7.00 %	7.10 %	7.125%	7.20 %
1	1.0672	1.0682	1.0685	1.0693	1.0698	1.0704	1.0712	1.0714	1.0725	1.0736	1.0738	1.0746
2	2.2060	2.2093	2.2102	2.2127	2.2143	2.2160	2.2185	2.2194	2.2228	2.2261	2.2270	2.2295
3	3.4213	3.4283	3.4300	3.4353	3.4388	3.4423	3.4476	3.4493	3.4564	3.4635	3.4653	3.4706
4	4.7182	4.7304	4.7334	4.7426	4.7487	4.7549	4.7641	4.7672	4.7795	4.7919	4.7950	4.8043
5	6.1021	6.1213	6.1261	6.1405	6.1501	6.1598	6.1743	6.1791	6.1985	6.2180	6.2229	6.2376
6	7.5791	7.6071	7.6141	7.6352	7.6494	7.6635	7.6848	7.6919	7.7204	7.7491	7.7563	7.7779
7	9.1552	9.1943	9.2041	9.2336	9.2533	9.2731	9.3028	9.3128	9.3527	9.3928	9.4028	9.4331
8	10.8371	10.8897	10.9029	10.9426	10.9692	10.9959	11.0360	11.0494	11.1032	11.1574	11.1710	11.2119
9	12.6320	12.7009	12.7181	12.7701	12.8049	12.8399	12.8925	12.9101	12.9807	13.0519	13.0697	13.1235
10	14.5475	14.6355	14.6576	14.7242	14.7689	14.8136	14.8811	14.9037	14.9944	15.0857	15.1087	15.1778
15	26.2357	26.4782	26.5393	26.7235	26.8471	26.9715	27.1593	27.2222	27.4758	27.7323	27.7968	27.9916
20	42.4121	42.9506	43.0864	43.4971	43.7736	44.0520	44.4737	44.6154	45.1873	45.7679	45.9144	46.3573
25	64.8001	65.8623	66.1311	66.9450	67.4942	68.0486	68.8903	69.1735	70.3202	71.4890	71.7848	72.6806
30	95.7849	97.7310	98.2246	99.7228	100.7362	101.7615	103.3220	103.8482	105.9842	108.1708	108.7254	110.4091

Description: This table shows what a series of $ 1 deposits grow to in the future. The deposit is made at the beginning of a period.

Example: At 8 % a regular one dollar deposit will grow to $ 6.40 by the end of the fifth year.

YEAR	7.25 %	7.30 %	7.375%	7.40 %	7.50 %	7.60 %	7.625%	7.70 %	7.75 %	7.80 %	7.875%	7.90 %
1	1.0752	1.0757	1.0765	1.0768	1.0779	1.0790	1.0792	1.0800	1.0806	1.0811	1.0819	1.0822
2	2.2312	2.2329	2.2354	2.2363	2.2397	2.2431	2.2439	2.2465	2.2482	2.2499	2.2525	2.2533
3	3.4741	3.4777	3.4831	3.4848	3.4920	3.4992	3.5009	3.5063	3.5099	3.5135	3.5189	3.5207
4	4.8105	4.8168	4.8261	4.8293	4.8418	4.8544	4.8575	4.8670	4.8733	4.8796	4.8892	4.8923
5	6.2474	6.2572	6.2720	6.2769	6.2967	6.3166	6.3216	6.3365	6.3465	6.3566	6.3716	6.3767
6	7.7923	7.8068	7.8285	7.8358	7.8650	7.8943	7.9016	7.9237	7.9385	7.9533	7.9755	7.9830
7	9.4533	9.4736	9.5042	9.5144	9.5553	9.5965	9.6068	9.6379	9.6587	9.6795	9.7109	9.7213
8	11.2393	11.2667	11.3081	11.3219	11.3774	11.4332	11.4472	11.4893	11.5175	11.5458	11.5883	11.6026
9	13.1595	13.1956	13.2500	13.2682	13.3412	13.4148	13.4333	13.4889	13.5261	13.5634	13.6196	13.6384
10	15.2241	15.2705	15.3405	15.3640	15.4581	15.5529	15.5767	15.6484	15.6965	15.7447	15.8173	15.8417
15	28.1224	28.2538	28.4525	28.5191	28.7873	29.0585	29.1268	29.3328	29.4711	29.6102	29.8203	29.8907
20	46.6554	46.9558	47.4106	47.5634	48.1803	48.8067	48.9648	49.4427	49.7643	50.0884	50.5793	50.7441
25	73.2850	73.8953	74.8218	75.1336	76.3960	77.6831	78.0087	78.9953	79.6610	80.3331	81.3537	81.6972
30	111.5481	112.7005	114.4547	115.0463	117.4480	119.9069	120.5307	122.4244	123.7056	125.0021	126.9758	127.6415

YEAR	8.00 %	8.10 %	8.125%	8.20 %	8.25 %	8.30 %	8.375%	8.40 %	8.50 %	8.60 %	8.625%	8.70 %
1	1.0833	1.0844	1.0846	1.0854	1.0860	1.0865	1.0873	1.0876	1.0887	1.0898	1.0901	1.0909
2	2.2568	2.2602	2.2611	2.2636	2.2654	2.2671	2.2697	2.2705	2.2740	2.2774	2.2783	2.2809
3	3.5280	3.5352	3.5370	3.5425	3.5461	3.5498	3.5553	3.5571	3.5644	3.5717	3.5736	3.5791
4	4.9051	4.9178	4.9210	4.9306	4.9371	4.9435	4.9532	4.9564	4.9693	4.9823	4.9855	4.9953
5	6.3968	6.4171	6.4221	6.4374	6.4476	6.4578	6.4731	6.4783	6.4988	6.5194	6.5246	6.5402
6	8.0128	8.0428	8.0503	8.0729	8.0880	8.1031	8.1259	8.1335	8.1640	8.1947	8.2023	8.2255
7	9.7634	9.8056	9.8162	9.8481	9.8694	9.8908	9.9230	9.9338	9.9769	10.0203	10.0312	10.0639
8	11.6597	11.7172	11.7316	11.7750	11.8041	11.8332	11.8771	11.8918	11.9506	12.0099	12.0247	12.0695
9	13.7140	13.7901	13.8091	13.8666	13.9051	13.9437	14.0019	14.0213	14.0994	14.1781	14.1978	14.2573
10	15.9393	16.0378	16.0625	16.1369	16.1868	16.2368	16.3122	16.3375	16.4389	16.5410	16.5667	16.6439
15	30.1745	30.4614	30.5337	30.7517	30.8980	31.0452	31.2675	31.3420	31.6423	31.9460	32.0224	32.2531
20	51.4099	52.0859	52.2566	52.7724	53.1196	53.4695	53.9994	54.1773	54.8962	55.6261	55.8104	56.3674
25	83.0880	84.5061	84.8650	85.9521	86.6858	87.4266	88.5515	88.9301	90.4633	92.0268	92.4225	93.6212
30	130.3441	133.1116	133.8138	135.9456	137.3881	138.8478	141.0702	141.8199	144.8638	147.9812	148.7723	151.1740

YEAR	8.75 %	8.80 %	8.875%	8.90 %	9.00 %	9.10 %	9.125%	9.20 %	9.25 %	9.30 %	9.375%	9.40 %
1	1.0914	1.0920	1.0928	1.0931	1.0942	1.0953	1.0955	1.0964	1.0969	1.0974	1.0983	1.0985
2	2.2827	2.2844	2.2870	2.2879	2.2914	2.2948	2.2957	2.2983	2.3001	2.3018	2.3045	2.3054
3	3.5828	3.5865	3.5920	3.5939	3.6013	3.6087	3.6106	3.6161	3.6199	3.6236	3.6292	3.6311
4	5.0018	5.0083	5.0181	5.0214	5.0345	5.0477	5.0510	5.0609	5.0675	5.0742	5.0841	5.0875
5	6.5505	6.5609	6.5766	6.5818	6.6028	6.6238	6.6291	6.6449	6.6555	6.6661	6.6820	6.6874
6	8.2409	8.2564	8.2797	8.2874	8.3187	8.3500	8.3579	8.3815	8.3973	8.4131	8.4370	8.4449
7	10.0858	10.1077	10.1408	10.1518	10.1961	10.2407	10.2518	10.2854	10.3079	10.3304	10.3643	10.3757
8	12.0994	12.1294	12.1746	12.1897	12.2504	12.3114	12.3267	12.3728	12.4036	12.4346	12.4811	12.4967
9	14.2971	14.3370	14.3971	14.4173	14.4981	14.5794	14.5998	14.6613	14.7025	14.7438	14.8060	14.8268
10	16.6957	16.7476	16.8259	16.8521	16.9574	17.0634	17.0901	17.1703	17.2240	17.2780	17.3592	17.3864
15	32.4080	32.5638	32.7991	32.8780	33.1958	33.5172	33.5982	33.8424	34.0063	34.1712	34.4204	34.5039
20	56.7424	57.1202	57.6925	57.8848	58.6612	59.4497	59.6488	60.2506	60.6557	61.0639	61.6823	61.8900
25	94.4303	95.2473	96.4879	96.9055	98.5967	100.3216	100.7581	102.0807	102.9734	103.8750	105.2441	105.7050
30	152.7993	154.4442	156.9488	157.7938	161.2247	164.7390	165.6309	168.3390	170.1717	172.0267	174.8515	175.8045

YEAR	9.50 %	9.75 %	10.00 %	10.25 %	10.50 %	10.75 %	11.00 %	12.00 %	13.00 %	14.00 %	15.00 %	16.00 %
1	1.0996	1.1024	1.1052	1.1079	1.1107	1.1135	1.1163	1.1275	1.1388	1.1502	1.1618	1.1735
2	2.3089	2.3177	2.3265	2.3354	2.3443	2.3533	2.3623	2.3987	2.4357	2.4733	2.5116	2.5505
3	3.6386	3.6574	3.6763	3.6954	3.7145	3.7338	3.7532	3.8319	3.9126	3.9951	4.0797	4.1664
4	5.1008	5.1343	5.1681	5.2021	5.2364	5.2710	5.3058	5.4479	5.5944	5.7456	5.9016	6.0626
5	6.7087	6.7624	6.8167	6.8714	6.9267	6.9826	7.0389	7.2698	7.5097	7.7591	8.0183	8.2878
6	8.4768	8.5573	8.6386	8.7209	8.8042	8.8884	8.9735	9.3240	9.6909	10.0751	10.4775	10.8989
7	10.4212	10.5359	10.6522	10.7700	10.8894	11.0104	11.1330	11.6400	12.1748	12.7391	13.3345	13.9630
8	12.5592	12.7172	12.8775	13.0403	13.2055	13.3733	13.5436	14.2513	15.0035	15.8033	16.6538	17.5587
9	14.9103	15.1218	15.3368	15.5555	15.7780	16.0043	16.2344	17.1955	18.2248	19.3278	20.5101	21.7780
10	17.4957	17.7726	18.0547	18.3422	18.6352	18.9338	19.2381	20.5149	21.8933	23.3819	24.9905	26.7293
15	34.8403	35.6986	36.5818	37.4908	38.4264	39.3894	40.3806	44.6468	49.4424	54.8382	60.9150	67.7645
20	62.7290	64.8846	67.1258	69.4564	71.8801	74.4009	77.0230	88.6135	102.2077	118.1749	136.9554	159.0741
25	107.5716	112.4032	117.4808	122.8177	128.4279	134.3262	140.5282	168.7183	203.2701	245.7022	297.9082	362.2515
30	179.6747	189.7700	200.4966	211.8959	224.0124	236.8934	250.5896	314.6642	396.8368	502.4762	638.5929	814.3521

SAVINGS GROWTH

Description: This table shows what a series of $ 1 deposits grow to in the future. The deposit is made at the beginning of a period.

Example: At 5 % a regular one dollar deposit will grow to $ 295.34 by the end of the fifth year.

YEAR	0.00 %	1.00 %	2.00 %	3.00 %	4.00 %	4.125%	4.25 %	4.375%	4.50 %	4.625%	4.75 %	4.875%
1	52.0000	52.2651	52.5317	52.7999	53.0697	53.1035	53.1374	53.1712	53.2051	53.2391	53.2730	53.3070
2	104.0000	105.0537	106.1207	107.2012	108.2954	108.4331	108.5711	108.7092	108.8476	108.9862	109.1251	109.2641
3	156.0000	158.3712	160.7884	163.2526	165.7648	166.0822	166.4004	166.7194	167.0391	167.3597	167.6809	168.0030
4	208.0000	212.2229	216.5565	221.0041	225.5689	226.1480	226.7289	227.3117	227.8964	228.4830	229.0716	229.6620
5	260.0000	266.6140	273.4471	280.5073	287.8028	288.7317	289.6645	290.6011	291.5416	292.4859	293.4341	294.3863
6	312.0000	321.5501	331.4828	341.8152	352.5651	353.9391	355.3199	356.7076	358.1023	359.5039	360.9126	362.3282
7	364.0000	377.0365	390.6867	404.9827	419.9584	421.8799	423.8127	425.7568	427.7122	429.6792	431.6577	433.6478
8	416.0000	433.0788	451.0823	470.0661	490.0897	492.6689	495.2654	497.8794	500.5110	503.1604	505.8276	508.5129
9	468.0000	489.6826	512.6935	537.1236	563.0703	566.4254	569.8060	573.2124	576.6448	580.1033	583.5882	587.0998
10	520.0000	546.8534	575.5448	606.2149	639.0158	643.2738	647.5680	651.8986	656.2662	660.6709	665.1132	669.5934
15	780.0000	841.4144	909.2950	984.4066	1067.6099	1078.6263	1089.7862	1101.0915	1112.5444	1124.1470	1135.9015	1147.8099
20	1040.0000	1151.0290	1278.0141	1423.5393	1590.6341	1613.2083	1636.1819	1659.5625	1683.3581	1707.5767	1732.2266	1757.3160
25	1300.0000	1476.4665	1685.3660	1933.4330	2228.8937	2269.6371	2311.2972	2353.8965	2397.4581	2442.0056	2487.5632	2534.1558
30	1560.0000	1818.5355	2135.3984	2525.4901	3007.7780	3075.6850	3145.4558	3217.1458	3290.8122	3366.5141	3444.3122	3524.2693

YEAR	5.00 %	5.10 %	5.125%	5.20 %	5.25 %	5.30 %	5.375%	5.40 %	5.50 %	5.60 %	5.625%	5.70 %
1	53.3410	53.3683	53.3751	53.3955	53.4091	53.4228	53.4432	53.4500	53.4773	53.5046	53.5115	53.5320
2	109.4034	109.5150	109.5429	109.6267	109.6826	109.7385	109.8225	109.8505	109.9626	110.0749	110.1030	110.1873
3	168.3259	168.5847	168.6495	168.8441	168.9739	169.1039	169.2991	169.3643	169.6251	169.8865	169.9519	170.1484
4	230.2544	230.7298	230.8488	231.2063	231.4451	231.6841	232.0433	232.1632	232.6435	233.1251	233.2457	233.6079
5	295.3424	296.1101	296.3025	296.8804	297.2665	297.6532	298.2345	298.4286	299.2065	299.9870	300.1826	300.7701
6	363.7510	364.8943	365.1809	366.0422	366.6179	367.1947	368.0621	368.3518	369.5136	370.6800	370.9723	371.8511
7	435.6496	437.2595	437.6632	438.8770	439.6886	440.5021	441.7259	442.1348	443.7753	445.4234	445.8367	447.0793
8	511.2163	513.3921	513.9380	515.5798	516.6780	517.7793	519.4367	519.9906	522.2140	524.4494	525.0101	526.6969
9	590.6382	593.4884	594.2036	596.3560	597.7964	599.2412	601.4167	602.1441	605.0647	608.0033	608.7408	610.9600
10	674.1119	677.7545	678.6690	681.4220	683.2651	685.1145	687.9005	688.8324	692.5757	696.3446	697.2909	700.1395
15	1159.8746	1169.6404	1172.0978	1179.5087	1184.4817	1189.4808	1197.0287	1199.5579	1209.7411	1220.0317	1222.6213	1230.4309
20	1782.8536	1803.6122	1808.8480	1824.6677	1835.3083	1846.0248	1862.2433	1867.6881	1889.6625	1911.9527	1917.5752	1934.5638
25	2581.8090	2620.7127	2630.5489	2660.3255	2680.4022	2700.6615	2731.3967	2741.7349	2783.5604	2826.1527	2836.9224	2869.5271
30	3606.4500	3673.8403	3690.9211	3742.7316	3777.7512	3813.1596	3867.0114	3885.1615	3958.7749	4034.0385	4053.1170	4110.9923

YEAR	5.75 %	5.80 %	5.875%	5.90 %	6.00 %	6.10 %	6.125%	6.20 %	6.25 %	6.30 %	6.375%	6.40 %
1	53.5456	53.5593	53.5798	53.5866	53.6140	53.6414	53.6483	53.6688	53.6825	53.6962	53.7168	53.7237
2	110.2436	110.2999	110.3844	110.4126	110.5254	110.6384	110.6667	110.7515	110.8082	110.8648	110.9499	110.9782
3	170.2795	170.4107	170.6079	170.6736	170.9370	171.2009	171.2670	171.4653	171.5977	171.7303	171.9293	171.9957
4	233.8498	234.0920	234.4559	234.5774	235.0641	235.5520	235.6742	236.0412	236.2863	236.5317	236.9004	237.0235
5	301.1627	301.5558	302.1468	302.3441	303.1351	303.9286	304.1274	304.7248	305.1238	305.5236	306.1244	306.3251
6	372.4384	373.0269	373.9118	374.2074	375.3926	376.5826	376.8808	377.7774	378.3766	378.9769	379.8798	380.1814
7	447.9102	448.7431	449.9960	450.4147	452.0941	453.7815	454.2046	455.4769	456.3276	457.1803	458.4631	458.8917
8	527.8253	528.9567	530.6595	531.2287	533.5130	535.8097	536.3859	538.1190	539.2783	540.4407	542.1904	542.7752
9	612.4451	613.9347	616.1778	616.9278	619.9393	622.9693	623.7297	626.0179	627.5493	629.0854	631.3983	632.1717
10	702.0466	703.9603	706.8432	707.8074	711.6810	715.5812	716.5604	719.5082	721.4819	723.4623	726.4458	727.4436
15	1235.6717	1240.9400	1248.8947	1251.5603	1262.2930	1273.1393	1275.8689	1284.1008	1289.6250	1295.1785	1303.5640	1306.3740
20	1945.9912	1957.5007	1974.9202	1980.7685	2004.3723	2028.3175	2034.3578	2052.6094	2064.8871	2077.2535	2095.9709	2102.2551
25	2891.5124	2913.6991	2947.3609	2958.6844	3004.4992	3051.1600	3062.9593	3098.6836	3122.7743	3147.0871	3183.9778	3196.3882
30	4150.1156	4189.6767	4249.8509	4270.1337	4352.4059	4436.5372	4457.8657	4522.5726	4566.3187	4610.5582	4677.8555	4700.5412

YEAR	6.50 %	6.60 %	6.625%	6.70 %	6.75 %	6.80 %	6.875%	6.90 %	7.00 %	7.10 %	7.125%	7.20 %
1	53.7511	53.7786	53.7855	53.8061	53.8198	53.8336	53.8542	53.8611	53.8886	53.9162	53.9231	53.9437
2	111.0918	111.2055	111.2339	111.3193	111.3763	111.4333	111.5189	111.5474	111.6617	111.7761	111.8047	111.8907
3	172.2617	172.5281	172.5948	172.7951	172.9288	173.0627	173.2636	173.3307	173.5992	173.8683	173.9357	174.1379
4	237.5165	238.0109	238.1347	238.5066	238.7549	239.0036	239.3771	239.5018	240.0014	240.5023	240.6278	241.0046
5	307.1292	307.9360	308.1381	308.7455	309.1512	309.5576	310.1685	310.3725	311.1901	312.0104	312.2159	312.8334
6	381.3906	382.6047	382.9090	383.8237	384.4351	385.0476	385.9688	386.2765	387.5103	388.7490	389.0595	389.9928
7	460.6112	462.3389	462.7721	464.0748	464.9458	465.8188	467.1323	467.5712	469.3318	471.1008	471.5444	472.8782
8	545.1223	547.4822	548.0742	549.8550	551.0463	552.2407	554.0386	554.6395	557.0513	559.4763	560.0847	561.9146
9	635.2771	638.4016	639.1857	641.5454	643.1246	644.7087	647.0939	647.8915	651.0939	654.3162	655.1249	657.5585
10	731.4524	735.4889	736.5023	739.5532	741.5958	743.6456	746.7334	747.7662	751.9154	756.0933	757.1423	760.3002
15	1317.6885	1329.1235	1332.0013	1340.6803	1346.5049	1352.3604	1361.2022	1364.1652	1376.0960	1388.1545	1391.1892	1400.3420
20	2127.6201	2153.3540	2159.8458	2179.4626	2192.6593	2205.9519	2226.0723	2232.8279	2260.0965	2287.7641	2294.7441	2315.8369
25	3246.6045	3297.7545	3310.6901	3349.8567	3376.2709	3402.9302	3443.3844	3456.9944	3512.0690	3568.1743	3582.3641	3625.3310
30	4792.5700	4886.6944	4910.5588	4982.9652	5031.9217	5081.4345	5156.7615	5182.1560	5285.1845	5390.5761	5417.3000	5498.3886

Description: This table shows what a series of $ 1 deposits grow to in the future. The deposit is made at the beginning of a period.

Example: At 8 % a regular one dollar deposit will grow to $ 319.52 by the end of the fifth year.

YEAR	7.25 %	7.30 %	7.375%	7.40 %	7.50 %	7.60 %	7.625%	7.70 %	7.75 %	7.80 %	7.875%	7.90 %
1	53.9575	53.9713	53.9920	53.9989	54.0265	54.0542	54.0611	54.0818	54.0956	54.1095	54.1302	54.1371
2	111.9480	112.0054	112.0915	112.1202	112.2352	112.3504	112.3792	112.4657	112.5234	112.5811	112.6678	112.6967
3	174.2729	174.4080	174.6110	174.6787	174.9498	175.2215	175.2895	175.4938	175.6301	175.7665	175.9714	176.0398
4	241.2562	241.5081	241.8866	242.0130	242.5192	243.0267	243.1538	243.5356	243.7905	244.0458	244.4293	244.5573
5	313.2460	313.6592	314.2803	314.4877	315.3190	316.1531	316.3620	316.9899	317.4094	317.8295	318.4611	318.6720
6	390.6165	391.2416	392.1815	392.4954	393.7543	395.0182	395.3350	396.2873	396.9238	397.5615	398.5206	398.8409
7	473.7701	474.6640	476.0090	476.4583	478.2612	480.0726	480.5268	481.8926	482.8058	483.7213	485.0985	485.5586
8	563.1387	564.3662	566.2137	566.8312	569.3097	571.8018	572.4269	574.3075	575.5655	576.8270	578.7256	579.3603
9	659.1871	660.8208	663.2808	664.1034	667.4063	670.7297	671.5638	674.0738	675.7536	677.4386	679.9759	680.8243
10	762.4145	764.5362	767.7324	768.8015	773.0965	777.4213	778.5072	781.7761	783.9649	786.1612	789.4701	790.5769
15	1406.4846	1412.6601	1421.9852	1425.1102	1437.6940	1450.4129	1453.6139	1463.2686	1469.7482	1476.2626	1486.0998	1489.3965
20	2330.0273	2344.3213	2365.9586	2373.2238	2402.5510	2432.3096	2439.8174	2462.5064	2477.7713	2493.1484	2516.4263	2524.2426
25	3654.3102	3683.5601	3727.9487	3742.8832	3803.3222	3864.8996	3880.4744	3927.6381	3959.4502	3991.5613	4040.2954	4056.6929
30	5553.2211	5608.6811	5693.0644	5721.5142	5836.9501	5955.0523	5985.0022	6075.8864	6137.3488	6199.5193	6294.1219	6326.0197

YEAR	8.00 %	8.10 %	8.125%	8.20 %	8.25 %	8.30 %	8.375%	8.40 %	8.50 %	8.60 %	8.625%	8.70 %
1	54.1648	54.1926	54.1995	54.2203	54.2342	54.2480	54.2688	54.2758	54.3036	54.3314	54.3383	54.3592
2	112.8124	112.9283	112.9572	113.0443	113.1023	113.1604	113.2477	113.2767	113.3932	113.5098	113.5390	113.6266
3	176.3136	176.5880	176.6566	176.8629	177.0005	177.1383	177.3452	177.4142	177.6907	177.9678	178.0371	178.2453
4	245.0703	245.5845	245.7133	246.1001	246.3584	246.6171	247.0057	247.1354	247.6551	248.1762	248.3067	248.6987
5	319.5172	320.3653	320.5777	321.2161	321.6427	322.0699	322.7121	322.9265	323.7859	324.6482	324.8643	325.5134
6	400.1254	401.4151	401.7384	402.7101	403.3595	404.0103	404.9889	405.3157	406.6265	407.9426	408.2724	409.2640
7	487.4048	489.2597	489.7248	491.1235	492.0587	492.9961	494.4065	494.8777	496.7683	498.6679	499.1442	500.5765
8	581.9074	584.4686	585.1111	587.0438	588.3367	589.6332	591.5846	592.2368	594.8547	597.4871	598.1474	600.1339
9	684.2311	687.6592	688.5195	691.1085	692.8412	694.5794	697.1967	698.0718	701.5861	705.1223	706.0098	708.6806
10	795.0232	799.5005	800.6247	804.0091	806.2751	808.5490	811.9748	813.1207	817.7243	822.3600	823.5240	827.0281
15	1502.6721	1516.0908	1519.4681	1529.6544	1536.4911	1543.3647	1553.7446	1557.2232	1571.2317	1585.3921	1588.9561	1599.7060
20	2555.7962	2587.8165	2595.8954	2620.3109	2636.7382	2653.2868	2678.3394	2686.7520	2720.7142	2755.1814	2763.8780	2790.1615
25	4123.0573	4190.6795	4207.7845	4259.5846	4294.5264	4329.7987	4383.3342	4401.3483	4474.2603	4548.5623	4567.3582	4624.2824
30	6455.4579	6587.9063	6621.4974	6723.4389	6792.3854	6862.1315	6968.2716	7004.0622	7149.3107	7297.9589	7335.6620	7450.0908

YEAR	8.75 %	8.80 %	8.875%	8.90 %	9.00 %	9.10 %	9.125%	9.20 %	9.25 %	9.30 %	9.375%	9.40 %
1	54.3731	54.3870	54.4079	54.4148	54.4427	54.4706	54.4775	54.4985	54.5124	54.5264	54.5473	54.5543
2	113.6850	113.7435	113.8312	113.8605	113.9777	114.0950	114.1244	114.2125	114.2713	114.3302	114.4185	114.4480
3	178.3843	178.5234	178.7324	178.8021	179.0813	179.3610	179.4311	179.6413	179.7817	179.9222	180.1331	180.2035
4	248.9604	249.2225	249.6163	249.7477	250.2744	250.8024	250.9346	251.3318	251.5970	251.8625	252.2616	252.3948
5	325.9471	326.3815	327.0345	327.2525	328.1265	329.0033	329.2230	329.8831	330.3241	330.7658	331.4298	331.6515
6	409.9267	410.5907	411.5893	411.9229	413.2604	414.6034	414.9400	415.9519	416.6282	417.3058	418.3249	418.6652
7	501.5343	502.4943	503.9387	504.4213	506.3574	508.3029	508.7907	510.2576	511.2385	512.2217	513.7010	514.1952
8	601.4628	602.7953	604.8010	605.4714	608.1623	610.8679	611.5467	613.5886	614.9545	616.3242	618.3859	619.0750
9	710.4680	712.2611	714.9611	715.8640	719.4894	723.1375	724.0531	726.8084	728.6525	730.5024	733.2880	734.2195
10	829.3744	831.7289	835.2761	836.4626	841.2295	846.0297	847.2351	850.8637	853.2933	855.7315	859.4048	860.6335
15	1606.9210	1614.1752	1625.1302	1628.8016	1643.5870	1658.5333	1662.2952	1673.6423	1681.2585	1688.9161	1700.4806	1704.3564
20	2807.8465	2825.6628	2852.6357	2861.6935	2898.2621	2935.3771	2944.7423	2973.0474	2992.0934	3011.2816	3040.3329	3050.0890
25	4662.6832	4701.4495	4760.2919	4780.0928	4860.2423	4941.9286	4962.5939	5025.1829	5067.4080	5110.0372	5174.7474	5196.5239
30	7527.4900	7605.7925	7724.9644	7765.1522	7928.2606	8095.2105	8137.5594	8266.0972	8353.0472	8441.0182	8574.9168	8620.0739

YEAR	9.50 %	9.75 %	10.00 %	10.25 %	10.50 %	10.75 %	11.00 %	12.00 %	13.00 %	14.00 %	15.00 %	16.00 %
1	54.5822	54.6522	54.7222	54.7923	54.8626	54.9329	55.0034	55.2862	55.5707	55.8568	56.1447	56.4343
2	114.5659	114.8614	115.1578	115.4552	115.7535	116.0528	116.3530	117.5633	118.7891	120.0305	121.2878	122.5612
3	180.4855	181.1927	181.9034	182.6175	183.3352	184.0563	184.7810	187.7154	190.7078	193.7594	196.8714	200.0453
4	252.9284	254.2686	255.6177	256.9757	258.3428	259.7190	261.1043	266.7383	272.5241	278.4662	284.5689	290.8372
5	332.5401	334.7748	337.0283	339.3008	341.5923	343.9032	346.2336	355.7537	365.6002	375.7854	386.3218	397.2227
6	420.0302	423.4670	426.9388	430.4462	433.9894	437.5689	441.1851	456.0251	471.4856	487.5950	504.3827	521.8797
7	516.1782	521.1774	526.2367	531.3570	536.5392	541.7839	547.0921	568.9759	591.9433	616.0526	641.3653	667.9466
8	621.8409	628.8229	635.9020	643.0796	650.3572	657.7363	665.2185	696.2093	728.9786	763.6369	800.3023	839.1004
9	737.9599	747.4140	757.0172	766.7723	776.6817	786.7481	796.9742	839.5315	884.8730	933.1959	984.7123	1039.6497
10	865.5699	878.0634	890.7778	903.7175	916.8868	930.2901	943.9318	1000.9769	1062.2219	1128.0015	1198.6778	1274.6433
15	1719.9652	1759.7379	1800.6080	1842.6081	1885.7719	1930.1339	1975.7297	2171.2050	2389.5784	2633.7256	2906.8969	3212.7678
20	3089.4786	3190.5612	3295.4913	3404.4248	3517.5246	3634.9600	3756.9078	4293.6237	4918.7490	5647.7596	6498.9334	7493.8691
25	5284.6764	5512.5695	5751.6378	6002.4607	6265.6491	6541.8463	6831.7302	8143.0111	9737.8795	11681.00	14052.25	16950.35
30	8803.3668	9280.8352	9787.1739	10324.22	10893.92	11498.36	12139.75	15124.57	18920.34	23757.85	29935.35	37838.65

SAVINGS GROWTH

Description: This table shows what a series of $ 1 deposits grow to in the future. The deposit is made at the beginning of a period.

Example: At 5 % a regular one dollar deposit will grow to $ 68.29 by the end of the fifth year.

YEAR	0.00 %	1.00 %	2.00 %	3.00 %	4.00 %	4.125%	4.25 %	4.375%	4.50 %	4.625%	4.75 %	4.875%
1	12.0000	12.0652	12.1308	12.1968	12.2632	12.2715	12.2799	12.2882	12.2966	12.3049	12.3133	12.3216
2	24.0000	24.2516	24.5064	24.7646	25.0260	25.0589	25.0919	25.1249	25.1580	25.1912	25.2243	25.2576
3	36.0000	36.5604	37.1319	37.7146	38.3088	38.3839	38.4592	38.5347	38.6103	38.6862	38.7622	38.8384
4	48.0000	48.9929	50.0122	51.0585	52.1328	52.2691	52.4058	52.5430	52.6806	52.8187	52.9573	53.0963
5	60.0000	61.5503	63.1524	64.8083	66.5200	66.7380	66.9568	67.1766	67.3973	67.6190	67.8415	68.0650
6	72.0000	74.2338	76.5579	78.9763	81.4933	81.8151	82.1385	82.4635	82.7901	83.1184	83.4484	83.7800
7	84.0000	87.0448	90.2340	93.5753	97.0767	97.5260	97.9780	98.4327	98.8901	99.3501	99.8129	100.2784
8	96.0000	99.9844	104.1861	108.6183	113.2949	113.8974	114.5040	115.1148	115.7296	116.3486	116.9719	117.5994
9	108.0000	113.0541	118.4198	124.1188	130.1739	130.9571	131.7463	132.5415	133.3428	134.1502	134.9639	135.7838
10	120.0000	126.2550	132.9409	140.0908	147.7406	148.7339	149.7357	150.7461	151.7651	152.7928	153.8294	154.8748
15	180.0000	194.2758	210.0626	227.5401	246.9108	249.4763	252.0754	254.7085	257.3762	260.0790	262.8173	265.5917
20	240.0000	265.7825	295.2882	329.1228	367.9972	373.2510	378.5981	384.0404	389.5798	395.2182	400.9574	406.7994
25	300.0000	340.9540	389.4692	447.1228	515.8433	525.3237	535.0184	544.9326	555.0718	565.4414	576.0472	586.8951
30	360.0000	419.9779	493.5466	584.1937	696.3629	712.1642	728.4011	745.0865	762.2338	779.8570	797.9703	816.5883

YEAR	5.00 %	5.10 %	5.125%	5.20 %	5.25 %	5.30 %	5.375%	5.40 %	5.50 %	5.60 %	5.625%	5.70 %
1	12.3300	12.3367	12.3384	12.3434	12.3468	12.3501	12.3552	12.3569	12.3636	12.3703	12.3720	12.3770
2	25.2909	25.3175	25.3242	25.3442	25.3576	25.3710	25.3911	25.3977	25.4246	25.4514	25.4581	25.4783
3	38.9148	38.9761	38.9914	39.0374	39.0682	39.0989	39.1451	39.1605	39.2223	39.2841	39.2996	39.3461
4	53.2358	53.3477	53.3757	53.4599	53.5161	53.5724	53.6570	53.6852	53.7983	53.9117	53.9401	54.0254
5	68.2894	68.4697	68.5148	68.6505	68.7411	68.8319	68.9683	69.0139	69.1965	69.3798	69.4257	69.5636
6	84.1133	84.3811	84.4482	84.6500	84.7849	84.9200	85.1233	85.1911	85.4633	85.7366	85.8051	86.0110
7	100.7467	101.1233	101.2177	101.5017	101.6916	101.8819	102.1682	102.2639	102.6477	103.0333	103.1300	103.4208
8	118.2311	118.7396	118.8671	119.2509	119.5075	119.7649	120.1523	120.2818	120.8014	121.3239	121.4550	121.8493
9	136.6100	137.2756	137.4426	137.9453	138.2817	138.6191	139.1271	139.2970	139.9792	140.6655	140.8378	141.3561
10	155.9293	156.7794	156.9928	157.6353	158.0655	158.4971	159.1474	159.3649	160.2387	161.1184	161.3393	162.0043
15	268.4026	270.6781	271.2507	272.9776	274.1365	275.3015	277.0604	277.6499	280.0231	282.4216	283.0251	284.8455
20	412.7463	417.5807	418.8001	422.4846	424.9629	427.4590	431.2368	432.5051	437.6240	442.8169	444.1268	448.0848
25	597.9910	607.0504	609.3411	616.2757	620.9516	625.6702	632.8291	635.2372	644.9801	654.9025	657.4115	665.0079
30	835.7264	851.4217	855.4001	867.4681	875.6256	883.8740	896.4196	900.6481	917.7993	935.3366	939.7823	953.2694

YEAR	5.75 %	5.80 %	5.875%	5.90 %	6.00 %	6.10 %	6.125%	6.20 %	6.25 %	6.30 %	6.375%	6.40 %
1	12.3804	12.3838	12.3888	12.3905	12.3972	12.4040	12.4057	12.4107	12.4141	12.4175	12.4226	12.4242
2	25.4917	25.5052	25.5254	25.5321	25.5591	25.5861	25.5929	25.6132	25.6267	25.6403	25.6606	25.6674
3	39.3772	39.4082	39.4549	39.4704	39.5328	39.5953	39.6109	39.6578	39.6892	39.7206	39.7677	39.7834
4	54.0824	54.1394	54.2251	54.2537	54.3683	54.4832	54.5120	54.5985	54.6562	54.7140	54.8008	54.8298
5	69.6558	69.7481	69.8868	69.9332	70.1189	70.3052	70.3519	70.4922	70.5859	70.6797	70.8208	70.8679
6	86.1486	86.2865	86.4939	86.5632	86.8409	87.1198	87.1897	87.3998	87.5402	87.6809	87.8925	87.9632
7	103.6152	103.8101	104.1033	104.2013	104.5943	104.9892	105.0882	105.3860	105.5850	105.7846	106.0849	106.1852
8	122.1131	122.3775	122.7756	122.9087	123.4427	123.9796	124.1143	124.5195	124.7906	125.0624	125.4715	125.6082
9	141.7030	142.0510	142.5749	142.7501	143.4536	144.1614	144.3391	144.8737	145.2314	145.5903	146.1307	146.3114
10	162.4495	162.8963	163.5693	163.7944	164.6987	165.6094	165.8380	166.5263	166.9871	167.4495	168.1462	168.3792
15	286.0670	287.2951	289.1494	289.7708	292.2728	294.8015	295.4379	297.3571	298.6452	299.9400	301.8953	302.5505
20	450.7473	453.4290	457.4880	458.8507	464.3511	469.9314	471.3391	475.5929	478.4545	481.3369	485.6997	487.1646
25	670.1303	675.2999	683.1437	685.7823	696.4589	707.3336	710.0836	718.4102	724.0255	729.6928	738.2925	741.1856
30	962.3871	971.6072	985.6323	990.3600	1009.5376	1029.1505	1034.1230	1049.2092	1059.4091	1069.7246	1085.4174	1090.7076

YEAR	6.50 %	6.60 %	6.625%	6.70 %	6.75 %	6.80 %	6.875%	6.90 %	7.00 %	7.10 %	7.125%	7.20 %
1	12.4310	12.4378	12.4395	12.4445	12.4479	12.4513	12.4564	12.4581	12.4649	12.4717	12.4734	12.4785
2	25.6945	25.7217	25.7285	25.7490	25.7626	25.7762	25.7967	25.8035	25.8308	25.8582	25.8650	25.8856
3	39.8464	39.9094	39.9252	39.9727	40.0043	40.0360	40.0836	40.0994	40.1630	40.2267	40.2427	40.2906
4	54.9459	55.0624	55.0916	55.1792	55.2376	55.2962	55.3842	55.4136	55.5313	55.6493	55.6788	55.7676
5	71.0568	71.2463	71.2937	71.4364	71.5317	71.6271	71.7706	71.8185	72.0105	72.2032	72.2515	72.3965
6	88.2466	88.5312	88.6025	88.8169	88.9602	89.1038	89.3197	89.3918	89.6810	89.9714	90.0442	90.2630
7	106.5876	106.9920	107.0934	107.3983	107.6022	107.8066	108.1141	108.2168	108.6290	109.0431	109.1470	109.4592
8	126.1570	126.7088	126.8473	127.2637	127.5423	127.8216	128.2421	128.3826	128.9466	129.5138	129.6561	130.0841
9	147.0370	147.7671	147.9503	148.5017	148.8707	149.2409	149.7983	149.9847	150.7331	151.4862	151.6752	152.2439
10	169.3153	170.2580	170.4946	171.2071	171.6842	172.1629	172.8841	173.1253	174.0945	175.0703	175.3154	176.0530
15	305.1890	307.8556	308.5267	310.5508	311.9093	313.2750	315.3372	316.0283	318.8112	321.6241	322.3320	324.4672
20	493.0774	499.0766	500.5901	505.1636	508.2405	511.3398	516.0313	517.6066	523.9654	530.4177	532.0455	536.9649
25	752.8927	764.8185	767.8346	776.9673	783.1267	789.3436	798.7779	801.9520	814.7971	827.8837	831.1937	841.2167
30	1112.1699	1134.1229	1139.6893	1156.5788	1167.9991	1179.5497	1197.1235	1203.0483	1227.0875	1251.6805	1257.9168	1276.8408

Description: This table shows what a series of $ 1 deposits grow to in the future. The deposit is made at the beginning of a period.

Example: At 8 % a regular one dollar deposit will grow to $ 73.97 by the end of the fifth year.

YEAR	7.25 %	7.30 %	7.375%	7.40 %	7.50 %	7.60 %	7.625%	7.70 %	7.75 %	7.80 %	7.875%	7.90 %
1	12.4818	12.4852	12.4903	12.4920	12.4988	12.5057	12.5074	12.5125	12.5159	12.5193	12.5244	12.5261
2	25.8993	25.9130	25.9336	25.9405	25.9680	25.9956	26.0024	26.0231	26.0369	26.0507	26.0715	26.0784
3	40.3225	40.3545	40.4026	40.4186	40.4828	40.5472	40.5633	40.6116	40.6439	40.6762	40.7248	40.7409
4	55.8269	55.8862	55.9754	56.0052	56.1245	56.2440	56.2740	56.3640	56.4240	56.4842	56.5746	56.6047
5	72.4934	72.5905	72.7364	72.7851	72.9804	73.1763	73.2254	73.3729	73.4715	73.5702	73.7186	73.7681
6	90.4093	90.5558	90.7761	90.8498	91.1449	91.4413	91.5155	91.7388	91.8881	92.0376	92.2625	92.3376
7	109.6680	109.8773	110.1922	110.2974	110.7196	111.1437	111.2501	111.5699	111.7837	111.9981	112.3206	112.4284
8	130.3704	130.6575	131.0897	131.2341	131.8139	132.3968	132.5431	132.9830	133.2773	133.5724	134.0166	134.1651
9	152.6246	153.0065	153.5815	153.7737	154.5458	155.3226	155.5176	156.1044	156.4971	156.8910	157.4842	157.6826
10	176.5469	177.0426	177.7892	178.0390	179.0424	180.0528	180.3065	181.0703	181.5817	182.0949	182.8681	183.1267
15	325.9002	327.3409	329.5166	330.2457	333.1817	336.1495	336.8964	339.1493	340.6614	342.1816	344.4774	345.2468
20	540.2746	543.6086	548.6556	550.3503	557.1915	564.1339	565.8855	571.1790	574.7406	578.3285	583.7601	585.5840
25	847.9771	854.8009	865.1571	868.6416	882.7438	897.1128	900.7473	911.7540	919.1784	926.6729	938.0478	941.8752
30	1289.6381	1302.5824	1322.2787	1328.9196	1355.8670	1383.4395	1390.4321	1411.6526	1426.0043	1440.5221	1462.6146	1470.0641

YEAR	8.00 %	8.10 %	8.125%	8.20 %	8.25 %	8.30 %	8.375%	8.40 %	8.50 %	8.60 %	8.625%	8.70 %
1	12.5329	12.5398	12.5415	12.5466	12.5500	12.5534	12.5586	12.5603	12.5671	12.5740	12.5757	12.5808
2	26.1061	26.1338	26.1407	26.1616	26.1754	26.1893	26.2102	26.2172	26.2450	26.2729	26.2799	26.3009
3	40.8058	40.8708	40.8870	40.9359	40.9685	41.0011	41.0501	41.0665	41.1320	41.1976	41.2140	41.2633
4	56.7256	56.8468	56.8771	56.9683	57.0292	57.0901	57.1817	57.2123	57.3348	57.4576	57.4883	57.5807
5	73.9667	74.1660	74.2159	74.3659	74.4661	74.5665	74.7174	74.7678	74.9697	75.1724	75.2231	75.3757
6	92.6388	92.9413	93.0171	93.2450	93.3973	93.5499	93.7794	93.8561	94.1635	94.4722	94.5495	94.7821
7	112.8607	113.2951	113.4041	113.7316	113.9507	114.1703	114.5006	114.6110	115.0538	115.4988	115.6103	115.9459
8	134.7610	135.3603	135.5106	135.9628	136.2654	136.5687	137.0254	137.1780	137.7906	138.4066	138.5612	139.0261
9	158.4791	159.2806	159.4817	160.0871	160.4922	160.8987	161.5107	161.7153	162.5372	163.3641	163.5717	164.1963
10	184.1657	185.2120	185.4747	186.2656	186.7952	187.3266	188.1273	188.3951	189.4711	190.5546	190.8267	191.6458
15	348.3451	351.4771	352.2654	354.6431	356.2389	357.8434	360.2665	361.0786	364.3490	367.6550	368.4871	370.9971
20	592.9472	600.4199	602.3053	608.0037	611.8379	615.7005	621.5483	623.5121	631.4402	639.4868	641.5172	647.6537
25	957.3666	973.1529	977.1462	989.2400	997.3984	1005.6342	1018.1351	1022.3417	1039.3687	1056.7219	1061.1119	1074.4078
30	1500.2952	1531.2324	1539.0791	1562.8932	1579.0005	1595.2955	1620.0947	1628.4575	1662.3982	1697.1368	1705.9485	1732.6932

YEAR	8.75 %	8.80 %	8.875%	8.90 %	9.00 %	9.10 %	9.125%	9.20 %	9.25 %	9.30 %	9.375%	9.40 %
1	12.5842	12.5877	12.5928	12.5945	12.6014	12.6083	12.6100	12.6151	12.6186	12.6220	12.6272	12.6289
2	26.3148	26.3288	26.3498	26.3568	26.3849	26.4130	26.4200	26.4411	26.4551	26.4692	26.4904	26.4974
3	41.2963	41.3292	41.3787	41.3952	41.4614	41.5279	41.5442	41.5940	41.6273	41.6606	41.7106	41.7272
4	57.6424	57.7042	57.7970	57.8280	57.9521	58.0766	58.1077	58.2014	58.2639	58.3265	58.4206	58.4520
5	75.4776	75.5797	75.7332	75.7844	75.9898	76.1959	76.2475	76.4027	76.5063	76.6102	76.7663	76.8184
6	94.9376	95.0933	95.3276	95.4058	95.7196	96.0346	96.1136	96.3510	96.5096	96.6686	96.9077	96.9876
7	116.1702	116.3951	116.7335	116.8465	117.3001	117.7559	117.8702	118.2139	118.4437	118.6741	119.0207	119.1365
8	139.3371	139.6489	140.1184	140.2753	140.9051	141.5384	141.6973	142.1752	142.4950	142.8156	143.2982	143.4595
9	164.6143	165.0337	165.6652	165.8764	166.7243	167.5777	167.7918	168.4364	168.8678	169.3005	169.9522	170.1701
10	192.1942	192.7446	193.5739	193.8512	194.9656	196.0879	196.3697	197.2181	197.7861	198.3562	199.2151	199.5024
15	372.6818	374.3756	376.9337	377.7910	381.2438	384.7344	385.6129	388.2631	390.0420	391.8305	394.5318	395.4371
20	651.7829	655.9429	662.2412	664.3564	672.8960	681.5639	683.7512	690.3621	694.8107	699.2927	706.0788	708.3578
25	1083.3776	1092.4332	1106.1792	1110.8050	1129.5304	1148.6164	1153.4451	1168.0705	1177.9379	1187.9002	1203.0236	1208.1132
30	1750.7843	1769.0875	1796.9457	1806.3407	1844.4741	1883.5095	1893.4119	1923.4695	1943.8034	1964.3771	1995.6938	2006.2558

YEAR	9.50 %	9.75 %	10.00 %	10.25 %	10.50 %	10.75 %	11.00 %	12.00 %	13.00 %	14.00 %	15.00 %	16.00 %
1	12.6358	12.6530	12.6703	12.6876	12.7049	12.7222	12.7396	12.8093	12.8795	12.9501	13.0211	13.0926
2	26.5256	26.5964	26.6673	26.7385	26.8099	26.8815	26.9534	27.2432	27.5368	27.8342	28.1354	28.4406
3	41.7940	41.9616	42.1300	42.2992	42.4693	42.6402	42.8120	43.5076	44.2172	44.9411	45.6794	46.4327
4	58.5778	58.8937	59.2118	59.5321	59.8545	60.1790	60.5057	61.8348	63.2001	64.6027	66.0437	67.5243
5	77.0273	77.5526	78.0824	78.6167	79.1555	79.6989	80.2470	82.4864	84.8033	87.2007	89.6817	92.2493
6	97.3078	98.1142	98.9289	99.7520	100.5836	101.4238	102.2727	105.7570	109.3884	113.1736	117.1195	121.2338
7	119.6012	120.7726	121.9583	123.1584	124.3732	125.6027	126.8471	131.9790	137.3671	143.0252	148.9682	155.2114
8	144.1071	145.7417	147.3993	149.0800	150.7844	152.5127	154.2653	161.5266	169.2077	177.3350	185.9366	195.0424
9	171.0451	173.2571	175.5042	177.7870	180.1062	182.4625	184.8563	194.8215	205.4433	216.7686	228.8478	241.7350
10	200.6567	203.5784	206.5520	209.5787	212.6594	215.7953	218.9873	232.3391	246.6807	262.0914	278.6573	296.4715
15	399.0832	408.3748	417.9243	427.7392	437.8276	448.1975	458.8576	504.5760	555.6813	612.8538	676.8631	748.5800
20	717.5596	741.1765	765.6969	791.1575	817.5968	845.0547	873.5731	999.1479	1145.5191	1316.3463	1515.9550	1749.4609
25	1228.7172	1281.9914	1337.8903	1396.5507	1458.1167	1522.7402	1590.5812	1897.6351	2271.4350	2727.2777	3284.0737	3965.2178
30	2049.1300	2160.8353	2279.3253	2405.0330	2538.4195	2679.9765	2830.2278	3529.9138	4420.6469	5557.0556	7009.8206	8870.4758

Description: This table shows what a series of $ 1 deposits grow to in the future. The deposit is made at the beginning of a period.

Example: At 5 % a regular one dollar deposit will grow to $ 22.86 by the end of the fifth year.

YEAR	0.00 %	1.00 %	2.00 %	3.00 %	4.00 %	4.125%	4.25 %	4.375%	4.50 %	4.625%	4.75 %	4.875%
1	4.0000	4.0251	4.0503	4.0758	4.1013	4.1046	4.1078	4.1110	4.1142	4.1174	4.1207	4.1239
2	8.0000	8.0906	8.1824	8.2755	8.3698	8.3817	8.3936	8.4055	8.4174	8.4294	8.4413	8.4533
3	12.0000	12.1970	12.3979	12.6029	12.8121	12.8386	12.8651	12.8917	12.9183	12.9450	12.9718	12.9987
4	16.0000	16.3446	16.6985	17.0620	17.4355	17.4829	17.5304	17.5781	17.6260	17.6740	17.7222	17.7706
5	20.0000	20.5339	21.0859	21.6567	22.2472	22.3224	22.3979	22.4738	22.5499	22.6264	22.7032	22.7804
6	24.0000	24.7652	25.5618	26.3912	27.2549	27.3653	27.4763	27.5879	27.7001	27.8128	27.9261	28.0400
7	28.0000	29.0391	30.1281	31.2697	32.4666	32.6203	32.7749	32.9304	33.0868	33.2442	33.4025	33.5617
8	32.0000	33.3559	34.7866	36.2965	37.8907	38.0962	38.3030	38.5113	38.7210	38.9322	39.1448	39.3588
9	36.0000	37.7161	39.5390	41.4763	43.5358	43.8022	44.0708	44.3414	44.6141	44.8889	45.1658	45.4449
10	40.0000	42.1201	44.3874	46.8136	49.4109	49.7482	50.0885	50.4317	50.7778	51.1270	51.4792	51.8344
15	60.0000	64.8125	70.1375	76.0362	82.5776	83.4443	84.3224	85.2120	86.1134	87.0267	87.9521	88.8897
20	80.0000	88.6680	98.5933	109.9816	123.0742	124.8442	126.6458	128.4796	130.3463	132.2465	134.1808	136.1499
25	100.0000	113.7460	130.0393	149.4132	172.5203	175.7092	178.9703	182.3056	185.7169	189.2060	192.7748	196.4254
30	120.0000	140.1093	164.7896	195.2177	232.8938	238.2032	243.6593	249.2665	255.0295	260.9529	267.0416	273.3004

YEAR	5.00 %	5.10 %	5.125%	5.20 %	5.25 %	5.30 %	5.375%	5.40 %	5.50 %	5.60 %	5.625%	5.70 %
1	4.1271	4.1297	4.1303	4.1323	4.1336	4.1349	4.1368	4.1375	4.1401	4.1426	4.1433	4.1452
2	8.4654	8.4750	8.4774	8.4846	8.4895	8.4943	8.5015	8.5040	8.5136	8.5233	8.5258	8.5330
3	13.0256	13.0472	13.0526	13.0688	13.0796	13.0905	13.1067	13.1122	13.1339	13.1557	13.1612	13.1776
4	17.8191	17.8580	17.8678	17.8971	17.9166	17.9362	17.9657	17.9755	18.0148	18.0543	18.0642	18.0939
5	22.8579	22.9201	22.9357	22.9825	23.0138	23.0451	23.0923	23.1080	23.1711	23.2343	23.2502	23.2978
6	28.1544	28.2464	28.2695	28.3388	28.3851	28.4315	28.5013	28.5246	28.6181	28.7120	28.7356	28.8063
7	33.7220	33.8508	33.8831	33.9803	34.0453	34.1104	34.2084	34.2411	34.3725	34.5045	34.5376	34.6371
8	39.5743	39.7478	39.7914	39.9223	40.0099	40.0977	40.2299	40.2741	40.4514	40.6297	40.6745	40.8091
9	45.7262	45.9527	46.0096	46.1807	46.2953	46.4101	46.5831	46.6410	46.8732	47.1070	47.1656	47.3422
10	52.1927	52.4816	52.5541	52.7725	52.9187	53.0654	53.2864	53.3603	53.6573	53.9564	54.0315	54.2575
15	89.8398	90.6090	90.8025	91.3863	91.7780	92.1719	92.7665	92.9658	93.7682	94.5792	94.7833	95.3988
20	138.1546	139.7843	140.1954	141.4376	142.2731	143.1147	144.3885	144.8162	146.5422	148.2934	148.7351	150.0699
25	200.1597	203.2089	203.9799	206.3141	207.8881	209.4765	211.8865	212.6971	215.9772	219.3180	220.1628	222.7206
30	279.7346	285.0117	286.3494	290.4072	293.1503	295.9240	300.1429	301.5650	307.3331	313.2316	314.7269	319.2634

YEAR	5.75 %	5.80 %	5.875%	5.90 %	6.00 %	6.10 %	6.125%	6.20 %	6.25 %	6.30 %	6.375%	6.40 %
1	4.1465	4.1478	4.1498	4.1504	4.1530	4.1556	4.1563	4.1582	4.1596	4.1609	4.1628	4.1635
2	8.5379	8.5428	8.5501	8.5525	8.5622	8.5720	8.5744	8.5818	8.5867	8.5915	8.5989	8.6013
3	13.1885	13.1995	13.2159	13.2214	13.2434	13.2654	13.2709	13.2875	13.2985	13.3096	13.3262	13.3317
4	18.1137	18.1336	18.1634	18.1733	18.2121	18.2532	18.2633	18.2934	18.3134	18.3336	18.3638	18.3739
5	23.3297	23.3616	23.4095	23.4255	23.4896	23.5540	23.5701	23.6186	23.6510	23.6834	23.7321	23.7484
6	28.8536	28.9010	28.9722	28.9960	29.0915	29.1873	29.2113	29.2835	29.3318	29.3801	29.4529	29.4772
7	34.7036	34.7704	34.8707	34.9043	35.0388	35.1740	35.2079	35.3098	35.3780	35.4463	35.5491	35.5835
8	40.8991	40.9894	41.1252	41.1707	41.3530	41.5363	41.5823	41.7206	41.8131	41.9059	42.0456	42.0923
9	47.4603	47.5788	47.7573	47.8169	48.0566	48.2977	48.3582	48.5403	48.6622	48.7844	48.9686	49.0301
10	54.4089	54.5608	54.7896	54.8661	55.1736	55.4833	55.5610	55.7951	55.9518	56.1090	56.3460	56.4252
15	95.8119	96.2272	96.8542	97.0644	97.9106	98.7658	98.9811	99.6303	100.0660	100.5040	101.1654	101.3871
20	150.9679	151.8724	153.2414	153.7010	155.5563	157.4387	157.9136	159.3486	160.3140	161.2865	162.7585	163.2527
25	224.4454	226.1862	228.8276	229.7162	233.3118	236.9744	237.9006	240.7052	242.5966	244.5057	247.4026	248.3772
30	322.3304	325.4319	330.1500	331.7404	338.1923	344.7911	346.4641	351.5403	354.9724	358.4436	363.7245	365.5048

YEAR	6.50 %	6.60 %	6.625%	6.70 %	6.75 %	6.80 %	6.875%	6.90 %	7.00 %	7.10 %	7.125%	7.20 %
1	4.1661	4.1687	4.1693	4.1713	4.1726	4.1739	4.1759	4.1765	4.1791	4.1818	4.1824	4.1844
2	8.6112	8.6210	8.6234	8.6308	8.6357	8.6407	8.6481	8.6505	8.6604	8.6703	8.6728	8.6802
3	13.3539	13.3762	13.3817	13.3985	13.4096	13.4208	13.4376	13.4432	13.4656	13.4881	13.4937	13.5106
4	18.4143	18.4549	18.4650	18.4956	18.5159	18.5363	18.5670	18.5772	18.6182	18.6593	18.6696	18.7005
5	23.8137	23.8791	23.8955	23.9448	23.9778	24.0107	24.0603	24.0769	24.1433	24.2099	24.2265	24.2767
6	29.5746	29.6724	29.6969	29.7706	29.8199	29.8692	29.9435	29.9683	30.0677	30.1676	30.1926	30.2678
7	35.7213	35.8598	35.8945	35.9990	36.0688	36.1388	36.2441	36.2793	36.4205	36.5623	36.5979	36.7049
8	42.2797	42.4682	42.5154	42.6576	42.7528	42.8482	42.9918	43.0398	43.2325	43.4262	43.4748	43.6210
9	49.2773	49.5261	49.5885	49.7764	49.9022	50.0283	50.2183	50.2818	50.5369	50.7936	50.8580	51.0519
10	56.7436	57.0642	57.1447	57.3871	57.5494	57.7122	57.9576	58.0396	58.3693	58.7014	58.7848	59.0357
15	102.2797	103.1819	103.4090	104.0938	104.5535	105.0156	105.7135	105.9473	106.8891	107.8411	108.0807	108.8034
20	165.2478	167.2722	167.7829	169.3263	170.3647	171.4106	172.9940	173.5257	175.6720	177.8499	178.3994	180.0601
25	252.3212	256.3391	257.3553	260.4324	262.5079	264.6027	267.7818	268.8515	273.1803	277.5908	278.7064	282.0846
30	372.7278	380.1164	381.9899	387.6748	391.5189	395.4071	401.3230	403.3175	411.4105	419.6905	421.7903	428.1622

Description: This table shows what a series of $ 1 deposits grow to in the future. The deposit is made at the beginning of a period.

Example: At 8 % a regular one dollar deposit will grow to $ 24.82 by the end of the fifth year.

YEAR	7.25 %	7.30 %	7.375%	7.40 %	7.50 %	7.60 %	7.625%	7.70 %	7.75 %	7.80 %	7.875%	7.90 %
1	4.1857	4.1870	4.1890	4.1896	4.1923	4.1949	4.1956	4.1975	4.1988	4.2002	4.2021	4.2028
2	8.6852	8.6901	8.6976	8.7000	8.7100	8.7199	8.7224	8.7299	8.7349	8.7399	8.7474	8.7499
3	13.5219	13.5332	13.5501	13.5558	13.5784	13.6011	13.6068	13.6239	13.6353	13.6467	13.6638	13.6695
4	18.7212	18.7418	18.7729	18.7833	18.8248	18.8665	18.8769	18.9083	18.9292	18.9502	18.9817	18.9922
5	24.3102	24.3437	24.3942	24.4110	24.4785	24.5463	24.5632	24.6142	24.6483	24.6825	24.7338	24.7509
6	30.3181	30.3685	30.4443	30.4696	30.5711	30.6731	30.6986	30.7754	30.8267	30.8782	30.9555	30.9814
7	36.7764	36.8481	36.9560	36.9921	37.1367	37.2820	37.3185	37.4281	37.5014	37.5748	37.6854	37.7223
8	43.7188	43.8169	43.9646	44.0139	44.2120	44.4112	44.4612	44.6115	44.7121	44.8129	44.9647	45.0155
9	51.1816	51.3118	51.5078	51.5733	51.8366	52.1014	52.1679	52.3680	52.5019	52.6362	52.8385	52.9061
10	59.2038	59.3725	59.6266	59.7116	60.0530	60.3969	60.4833	60.7432	60.9173	61.0920	61.3552	61.4432
15	109.2884	109.7761	110.5125	110.7593	111.7533	112.7580	113.0109	113.7736	114.2856	114.8003	115.5777	115.8382
20	181.1774	182.3030	184.0069	184.5791	186.8889	189.2331	189.8245	191.6121	192.8148	194.0265	195.8609	196.4769
25	284.3633	286.6635	290.1544	291.3291	296.0831	300.9275	302.1529	305.8640	308.3673	310.8944	314.7301	316.0208
30	432.4713	436.8301	443.4628	445.6993	454.7745	464.0609	466.4161	473.5638	478.3980	483.2884	490.7307	493.2403

YEAR	8.00 %	8.10 %	8.125%	8.20 %	8.25 %	8.30 %	8.375%	8.40 %	8.50 %	8.60 %	8.625%	8.70 %
1	4.2054	4.2081	4.2087	4.2107	4.2120	4.2133	4.2153	4.2160	4.2186	4.2213	4.2219	4.2239
2	8.7599	8.7699	8.7724	8.7800	8.7850	8.7900	8.7976	8.8001	8.8102	8.8203	8.8228	8.8304
3	13.6924	13.7153	13.7211	13.7383	13.7498	13.7613	13.7786	13.7844	13.8075	13.8307	13.8365	13.8539
4	19.0343	19.0765	19.0871	19.1189	19.1401	19.1614	19.1933	19.2039	19.2466	19.2895	19.3002	19.3324
5	24.8196	24.8885	24.9057	24.9576	24.9923	25.0270	25.0792	25.0966	25.1665	25.2366	25.2542	25.3070
6	31.0850	31.1891	31.2152	31.2936	31.3460	31.3985	31.4775	31.5038	31.6096	31.7159	31.7425	31.8225
7	37.8705	38.0194	38.0567	38.1690	38.2441	38.3194	38.4326	38.4705	38.6223	38.7748	38.8131	38.9281
8	45.2192	45.4240	45.4754	45.6299	45.7333	45.8371	45.9932	46.0453	46.2548	46.4654	46.5182	46.6772
9	53.1777	53.4511	53.5197	53.7262	53.8644	54.0030	54.2118	54.2816	54.5619	54.8440	54.9148	55.1279
10	61.7969	62.1531	62.2426	62.5118	62.6921	62.8731	63.1457	63.2369	63.6033	63.9723	64.0650	64.3440
15	116.8874	117.9481	118.2150	119.0203	119.5608	120.1043	120.9250	121.2001	122.3079	123.4279	123.7098	124.5601
20	198.9638	201.4879	202.1248	204.0496	205.3449	206.6498	208.6254	209.2888	211.9674	214.6863	215.3723	217.4460
25	321.2449	326.5690	327.9158	331.9948	334.7466	337.5246	341.7414	343.1605	348.9045	354.7590	356.2401	360.7261
30	503.4250	513.8483	516.4921	524.5162	529.9438	535.4347	543.7918	546.6100	558.0486	569.7569	572.7269	581.7416

YEAR	8.75 %	8.80 %	8.875%	8.90 %	9.00 %	9.10 %	9.125%	9.20 %	9.25 %	9.30 %	9.375%	9.40 %
1	4.2253	4.2266	4.2286	4.2292	4.2319	4.2345	4.2352	4.2372	4.2385	4.2399	4.2419	4.2425
2	8.8354	8.8405	8.8481	8.8506	8.8608	8.8709	8.8735	8.8811	8.8862	8.8913	8.8989	8.9015
3	13.8655	13.8772	13.8947	13.9005	13.9238	13.9473	13.9531	13.9707	13.9824	13.9942	14.0119	14.0177
4	19.3539	19.3754	19.4078	19.4186	19.4619	19.5053	19.5162	19.5488	19.5706	19.5925	19.6253	19.6362
5	25.3422	25.3775	25.4306	25.4484	25.5194	25.5908	25.6086	25.6623	25.6982	25.7341	25.7881	25.8062
6	31.8760	31.9297	32.0103	32.0372	32.1452	32.2537	32.2809	32.3626	32.4172	32.4720	32.5543	32.5818
7	39.0051	39.0822	39.1982	39.2370	39.3926	39.5489	39.5881	39.7060	39.7848	39.8638	39.9827	40.0224
8	46.7835	46.8902	47.0507	47.1044	47.3197	47.5363	47.5907	47.7542	47.8635	47.9732	48.1383	48.1935
9	55.2706	55.4137	55.6291	55.7012	55.9906	56.2818	56.3548	56.5748	56.7220	56.8697	57.0922	57.1665
10	64.5308	64.7182	65.0007	65.0951	65.4747	65.8570	65.9530	66.2421	66.4356	66.6298	66.9225	67.0204
15	125.1309	125.7048	126.5715	126.8620	128.0320	129.2148	129.5126	130.4107	131.0136	131.6198	132.5353	132.8422
20	218.8413	220.2471	222.3757	223.0905	225.9767	228.9065	229.6458	231.8805	233.3843	234.8994	237.1936	237.9640
25	363.7527	366.8083	371.4467	373.0077	379.3269	385.7682	387.3980	392.3343	395.6648	399.0275	404.1326	405.8507
30	587.8398	594.0097	603.4010	606.5682	619.4243	632.5856	635.9244	646.0595	652.9161	659.8539	670.4148	673.9768

YEAR	9.50 %	9.75 %	10.00 %	10.25 %	10.50 %	10.75 %	11.00 %	12.00 %	13.00 %	14.00 %	15.00 %	16.00 %
1	4.2452	4.2518	4.2585	4.2652	4.2719	4.2786	4.2853	4.3123	4.3395	4.3669	4.3944	4.4221
2	8.9117	8.9373	8.9630	8.9887	9.0146	9.0405	9.0666	9.1716	9.2780	9.3859	9.4952	9.6061
3	14.0413	14.1005	14.1600	14.2198	14.2799	14.3404	14.4011	14.6471	14.8982	15.1544	15.4160	15.6830
4	19.6801	19.7903	19.9013	20.0130	20.1256	20.2388	20.3529	20.8170	21.2941	21.7845	22.2886	22.8069
5	25.8785	26.0603	26.2438	26.4288	26.6154	26.8036	26.9934	27.7695	28.5729	29.4047	30.2660	31.1579
6	32.6920	32.9697	33.2503	33.5339	33.8204	34.1099	34.4024	35.6037	36.8564	38.1629	39.5258	40.9477
7	40.1818	40.5838	40.9906	41.4025	41.8194	42.2415	42.6688	44.4315	46.2833	48.2291	50.2742	52.4239
8	48.4150	48.9742	49.5414	50.1166	50.7000	51.2916	51.8917	54.3788	57.0114	59.7986	62.7504	65.8771
9	57.4652	58.2203	58.9875	59.7671	60.5592	61.3640	62.1819	65.5877	69.2203	73.0959	77.2322	81.6480
10	67.4137	68.4093	69.4228	70.4546	71.5049	72.5742	73.6628	78.2182	83.1145	88.3791	94.0420	100.1356
15	134.0781	137.2280	140.4658	143.7941	147.2158	150.7336	154.3503	169.8683	187.2265	206.6586	228.4295	252.8389
20	241.0751	249.0608	257.3533	265.9654	274.9100	284.2008	293.8521	336.3687	385.9614	443.8813	511.6085	590.8944
25	412.8063	430.7931	449.6695	469.4819	490.2793	512.1135	535.0390	638.8494	765.3178	919.6574	1108.3179	1339.2841
30	688.4365	726.1148	766.0890	808.5058	853.5220	901.3043	952.0308	1188.3651	1489.4548	1873.8786	2365.6928	2996.0744

SAVINGS GROWTH

Description: This table shows what a series of $ 1 deposits grow to in the future. The deposit is made at the beginning of a period.

Example: At 5 % a regular one dollar deposit will grow to $ 11.50 by the end of the fifth year.

YEAR	0.00 %	1.00 %	2.00 %	3.00 %	4.00 %	4.125%	4.25 %	4.375%	4.50 %	4.625%	4.75 %	4.875%
1	2.0000	2.0151	2.0302	2.0455	2.0609	2.0628	2.0648	2.0667	2.0687	2.0706	2.0725	2.0745
2	4.0000	4.0504	4.1014	4.1532	4.2058	4.2124	4.2190	4.2257	4.2323	4.2390	4.2457	4.2524
3	6.0000	6.1061	6.2144	6.3251	6.4380	6.4523	6.4667	6.4810	6.4954	6.5099	6.5243	6.5389
4	8.0000	8.1825	8.3701	8.5630	8.7612	8.7864	8.8117	8.8370	8.8625	8.8880	8.9136	8.9393
5	10.0000	10.2798	10.5693	10.8689	11.1791	11.2186	11.2583	11.2982	11.3383	11.3785	11.4189	11.4595
6	12.0000	12.3981	12.8128	13.2450	13.6955	13.7531	13.8110	13.8693	13.9278	13.9866	14.0458	14.1052
7	14.0000	14.5377	15.1017	15.6934	16.3143	16.3941	16.4743	16.5551	16.6363	16.7180	16.8002	16.8829
8	16.0000	16.6988	17.4367	18.2162	19.0399	19.1461	19.2531	19.3608	19.4692	19.5784	19.6884	19.7991
9	18.0000	18.8816	19.8189	20.8158	21.8766	22.0139	22.1522	22.2917	22.4323	22.5739	22.7167	22.8606
10	20.0000	21.0863	22.2492	23.4945	24.8287	25.0021	25.1770	25.3535	25.5315	25.7110	25.8921	26.0748
15	30.0000	32.4468	35.1563	38.1605	41.4949	41.9369	42.3848	42.8386	43.2984	43.7644	44.2366	44.7151
20	40.0000	44.3894	49.4198	55.1968	61.8443	62.7434	63.6687	64.5905	65.5391	66.5048	67.4880	68.4890
25	50.0000	56.9441	65.1821	74.9864	86.6907	88.3068	89.9597	91.6504	93.3798	95.1489	96.9586	98.8100
30	60.0000	70.1422	82.6006	97.9744	117.0282	119.7146	122.4757	125.3136	128.2307	131.1293	134.3120	137.4812

YEAR	5.00 %	5.10 %	5.125%	5.20 %	5.25 %	5.30 %	5.375%	5.40 %	5.50 %	5.60 %	5.625%	5.70 %
1	2.0764	2.0780	2.0784	2.0795	2.0803	2.0811	2.0823	2.0827	2.0842	2.0858	2.0862	2.0874
2	4.2591	4.2645	4.2658	4.2698	4.2725	4.2752	4.2793	4.2806	4.2860	4.2914	4.2928	4.2968
3	6.5534	6.5651	6.5680	6.5768	6.5826	6.5885	6.5973	6.6002	6.6120	6.6238	6.6268	6.6356
4	8.9651	8.9858	8.9910	9.0066	9.0170	9.0274	9.0430	9.0483	9.0692	9.0902	9.0954	9.1112
5	11.5002	11.5329	11.5411	11.5658	11.5822	11.5987	11.6235	11.6318	11.6650	11.6983	11.7066	11.7317
6	14.1650	14.2130	14.2251	14.2613	14.2855	14.3097	14.3462	14.3584	14.4072	14.4563	14.4686	14.5055
7	16.9661	17.0331	17.0499	17.1003	17.1341	17.1679	17.2189	17.2359	17.3041	17.3727	17.3899	17.4416
8	19.9106	20.0003	20.0229	20.0906	20.1359	20.1814	20.2498	20.2727	20.3644	20.4567	20.4799	20.5496
9	23.0057	23.1225	23.1519	23.2401	23.2992	23.3585	23.4477	23.4775	23.5974	23.7180	23.7482	23.8393
10	26.2591	26.4077	26.4450	26.5574	26.6326	26.7081	26.8218	26.8598	27.0127	27.1666	27.2052	27.3216
15	45.2001	45.5927	45.6915	45.9895	46.1895	46.3906	46.6942	46.7960	47.2057	47.6198	47.7241	48.0384
20	69.5081	70.3368	70.5458	71.1775	71.6024	72.0304	72.6782	72.8957	73.7737	74.6645	74.8892	75.5683
25	100.7041	102.2508	102.6419	103.8261	104.6247	105.4306	106.6534	107.0648	108.7293	110.4248	110.8536	112.1518
30	140.7396	143.4124	144.0899	146.1454	147.5349	148.9401	151.0775	151.7980	154.7206	157.7095	158.4673	160.7664

YEAR	5.75 %	5.80 %	5.875%	5.90 %	6.00 %	6.10 %	6.125%	6.20 %	6.25 %	6.30 %	6.375%	6.40 %
1	2.0881	2.0889	2.0901	2.0905	2.0921	2.0936	2.0940	2.0952	2.0960	2.0968	2.0979	2.0983
2	4.2996	4.3023	4.3063	4.3077	4.3131	4.3186	4.3200	4.3240	4.3268	4.3295	4.3336	4.3350
3	6.6415	6.6475	6.6564	6.6593	6.6712	6.6831	6.6861	6.6951	6.7011	6.7071	6.7160	6.7191
4	9.1218	9.1324	9.1482	9.1535	9.1747	9.1960	9.2014	9.2174	9.2281	9.2388	9.2549	9.2603
5	11.7485	11.7653	11.7905	11.7989	11.8327	11.8666	11.8751	11.9006	11.9176	11.9347	11.9604	11.9689
6	14.5302	14.5550	14.5922	14.6047	14.6545	14.7046	14.7172	14.7549	14.7802	14.8054	14.8435	14.8562
7	17.4762	17.5109	17.5631	17.5805	17.6505	17.7208	17.7384	17.7914	17.8268	17.8624	17.9158	17.9337
8	20.5962	20.6429	20.7133	20.7368	20.8312	20.9261	20.9499	21.0215	21.0695	21.1175	21.1899	21.2141
9	23.9003	23.9615	24.0536	24.0844	24.2080	24.3325	24.3637	24.4578	24.5207	24.5838	24.6789	24.7107
10	27.3995	27.4777	27.5955	27.6349	27.7932	27.9526	27.9927	28.1132	28.1939	28.2749	28.3969	28.4377
15	48.2494	48.4616	48.7819	48.8892	49.3215	49.7585	49.8685	50.2002	50.4228	50.6467	50.9847	51.0980
20	76.0252	76.4854	77.1820	77.4159	78.3600	79.3181	79.5598	80.2902	80.7816	81.2766	82.0260	82.2776
25	113.0274	113.9110	115.2520	115.7031	117.5286	119.3883	119.8587	121.2829	122.2435	123.2130	124.6844	125.1794
30	162.3208	163.8928	166.2843	167.0905	170.3612	173.7067	174.5550	177.1288	178.8692	180.6294	183.3076	184.2105

YEAR	6.50 %	6.60 %	6.625%	6.70 %	6.75 %	6.80 %	6.875%	6.90 %	7.00 %	7.10 %	7.125%	7.20 %
1	2.0999	2.1015	2.1019	2.1031	2.1039	2.1046	2.1058	2.1062	2.1078	2.1094	2.1098	2.1110
2	4.3405	4.3460	4.3473	4.3514	4.3542	4.3570	4.3611	4.3625	4.3680	4.3735	4.3749	4.3790
3	6.7311	6.7431	6.7461	6.7552	6.7612	6.7673	6.7764	6.7794	6.7915	6.8037	6.8068	6.8159
4	9.2818	9.3034	9.3088	9.3250	9.3359	9.3467	9.3630	9.3685	9.3903	9.4122	9.4177	9.4342
5	12.0033	12.0378	12.0464	12.0724	12.0897	12.1071	12.1333	12.1420	12.1769	12.2120	12.2208	12.2473
6	14.9071	14.9583	14.9711	15.0096	15.0354	15.0612	15.1000	15.1130	15.1650	15.2173	15.2304	15.2697
7	18.0054	18.0774	18.0955	18.1498	18.1861	18.2225	18.2773	18.2956	18.3691	18.4429	18.4614	18.5171
8	21.3111	21.4088	21.4333	21.5070	21.5562	21.6057	21.6801	21.7050	21.8048	21.9052	21.9304	22.0062
9	24.8383	24.9668	24.9990	25.0961	25.1610	25.2262	25.3243	25.3571	25.4889	25.6215	25.6548	25.7550
10	28.6017	28.7669	28.8083	28.9332	29.0168	29.1007	29.2271	29.2694	29.4393	29.6104	29.6534	29.7827
15	51.5542	52.0154	52.1315	52.4816	52.7166	52.9529	53.3097	53.4292	53.9108	54.3977	54.5202	54.8898
20	83.2934	84.3242	84.5842	85.3702	85.8990	86.4317	87.2382	87.5090	88.6023	89.7118	89.9918	90.8379
25	127.1829	129.2240	129.7403	131.3037	132.3583	133.4227	135.0382	135.5818	137.7818	140.0235	140.5906	142.3079
30	187.8740	191.6218	192.5723	195.4562	197.4065	199.3792	202.3810	203.3930	207.4999	211.7021	212.7678	216.0020

Description: This table shows what a series of $ 1 deposits grow to in the future. The deposit is made at the beginning of a period.

Example: At 8 % a regular one dollar deposit will grow to $ 12.53 by the end of the fifth year.

YEAR	7.25 %	7.30 %	7.375%	7.40 %	7.50 %	7.60 %	7.625%	7.70 %	7.75 %	7.80 %	7.875%	7.90 %
1	2.1118	2.1126	2.1137	2.1141	2.1157	2.1173	2.1177	2.1189	2.1197	2.1205	2.1217	2.1221
2	4.3818	4.3846	4.3887	4.3901	4.3957	4.4013	4.4027	4.4068	4.4096	4.4124	4.4166	4.4180
3	6.8220	6.8281	6.8373	6.8404	6.8527	6.8650	6.8680	6.8773	6.8835	6.8897	6.8989	6.9020
4	9.4452	9.4562	9.4727	9.4782	9.5004	9.5226	9.5281	9.5448	9.5560	9.5672	9.5840	9.5896
5	12.2649	12.2826	12.3092	12.3181	12.3536	12.3894	12.3983	12.4252	12.4432	12.4612	12.4882	12.4973
6	15.2960	15.3224	15.3620	15.3753	15.4284	15.4818	15.4951	15.5353	15.5622	15.5891	15.6296	15.6432
7	18.5544	18.5917	18.6478	18.6666	18.7419	18.8175	18.8365	18.8936	18.9317	18.9700	19.0276	19.0468
8	22.0569	22.1078	22.1843	22.2099	22.3126	22.4159	22.4418	22.5197	22.5719	22.6242	22.7029	22.7293
9	25.8220	25.8893	25.9906	26.0245	26.1605	26.2974	26.3318	26.4352	26.5044	26.5739	26.6784	26.7134
10	29.8694	29.9563	30.0873	30.1311	30.3071	30.4844	30.5290	30.6630	30.7528	30.8428	30.9786	31.0240
15	55.1379	55.3874	55.7641	55.8903	56.3988	56.9129	57.0423	57.4326	57.6946	57.9580	58.3558	58.4892
20	91.4072	91.9807	92.8490	93.1406	94.3177	95.5125	95.8140	96.7252	97.3383	97.9560	98.8913	99.2053
25	143.4663	144.6356	146.4105	147.0078	149.4251	151.8886	152.5118	154.3992	155.6725	156.9579	158.9090	159.5656
30	218.1893	220.4020	223.7692	224.9046	229.5123	234.2277	235.4237	239.0536	241.5087	243.9925	247.7727	249.0474

YEAR	8.00 %	8.10 %	8.125%	8.20 %	8.25 %	8.30 %	8.375%	8.40 %	8.50 %	8.60 %	8.625%	8.70 %
1	2.1237	2.1253	2.1257	2.1269	2.1277	2.1285	2.1297	2.1301	2.1317	2.1332	2.1336	2.1349
2	4.4236	4.4292	4.4306	4.4348	4.4376	4.4405	4.4447	4.4461	4.4517	4.4574	4.4588	4.4630
3	6.9144	6.9269	6.9300	6.9393	6.9456	6.9518	6.9612	6.9643	6.9769	6.9894	6.9926	7.0020
4	9.6120	9.6345	9.6402	9.6571	9.6684	9.6797	9.6968	9.7024	9.7252	9.7480	9.7538	9.7709
5	12.5335	12.5698	12.5789	12.6063	12.6246	12.6429	12.6704	12.6796	12.7165	12.7535	12.7627	12.7906
6	15.6974	15.7519	15.7656	15.8066	15.8341	15.8616	15.9029	15.9167	15.9721	16.0278	16.0417	16.0837
7	19.1240	19.2015	19.2210	19.2795	19.3186	19.3578	19.4168	19.4365	19.5156	19.5951	19.6150	19.6750
8	22.8349	22.9412	22.9678	23.0480	23.1017	23.1555	23.2365	23.2636	23.3722	23.4815	23.5090	23.5915
9	26.8539	26.9952	27.0307	27.1375	27.2090	27.2807	27.3886	27.4248	27.5698	27.7157	27.7524	27.8626
10	31.2064	31.3901	31.4363	31.5752	31.6682	31.7616	31.9022	31.9493	32.1384	32.3288	32.3766	32.5206
15	59.0262	59.5691	59.7058	60.1180	60.3948	60.6730	61.0933	61.2341	61.8014	62.3750	62.5193	62.9549
20	100.4734	101.7605	102.0853	103.0670	103.7276	104.3931	105.4009	105.7393	107.1058	108.4929	108.8430	109.9010
25	162.2233	164.9321	165.6174	167.6930	169.0934	170.5071	172.6532	173.3755	176.2992	179.2794	180.0335	182.3174
30	254.2212	259.5167	260.8600	264.9370	267.6950	270.4853	274.7323	276.1646	281.9784	287.9298	289.4396	294.0225

YEAR	8.75 %	8.80 %	8.875%	8.90 %	9.00 %	9.10 %	9.125%	9.20 %	9.25 %	9.30 %	9.375%	9.40 %
1	2.1357	2.1365	2.1377	2.1381	2.1397	2.1413	2.1417	2.1429	2.1437	2.1445	2.1457	2.1461
2	4.4659	4.4687	4.4729	4.4744	4.4800	4.4857	4.4871	4.4914	4.4943	4.4971	4.5014	4.5028
3	7.0083	7.0146	7.0241	7.0273	7.0400	7.0526	7.0558	7.0654	7.0717	7.0781	7.0877	7.0909
4	9.7824	9.7939	9.8112	9.8169	9.8400	9.8632	9.8690	9.8864	9.8980	9.9097	9.9272	9.9330
5	12.8092	12.8278	12.8559	12.8652	12.9027	12.9404	12.9498	12.9781	12.9971	13.0161	13.0446	13.0541
6	16.1117	16.1398	16.1820	16.1962	16.2527	16.3096	16.3238	16.3667	16.3953	16.4240	16.4671	16.4815
7	19.7151	19.7553	19.8157	19.8359	19.9170	19.9985	20.0190	20.0804	20.1215	20.1627	20.2247	20.2454
8	23.6467	23.7020	23.7854	23.8132	23.9250	24.0375	24.0657	24.1506	24.2074	24.2644	24.3501	24.3788
9	27.9364	28.0105	28.1220	28.1593	28.3090	28.4598	28.4976	28.6115	28.6877	28.7641	28.8793	28.9178
10	32.6170	32.7137	32.8595	32.9083	33.1043	33.3017	33.3512	33.5005	33.6004	33.7007	33.8518	33.9024
15	63.2472	63.5412	63.9852	64.1340	64.7335	65.3395	65.4921	65.9523	66.2613	66.5720	67.0412	67.1985
20	110.6131	111.3305	112.4167	112.7816	114.2547	115.7502	116.1276	117.2684	118.0362	118.8097	119.9811	120.3746
25	183.8583	185.4141	187.7761	188.5710	191.7891	195.0698	195.8999	198.4144	200.1110	201.8241	204.4249	205.3003
30	297.1229	300.2599	305.0350	306.6455	313.1833	319.8769	321.5751	326.7302	330.2181	333.7474	339.1202	340.9324

YEAR	9.50 %	9.75 %	10.00 %	10.25 %	10.50 %	10.75 %	11.00 %	12.00 %	13.00 %	14.00 %	15.00 %	16.00 %
1	2.1477	2.1517	2.1558	2.1598	2.1639	2.1679	2.1720	2.1883	2.2048	2.2214	2.2381	2.2550
2	4.5085	4.5229	4.5373	4.5517	4.5662	4.5807	4.5953	4.6542	4.7140	4.7746	4.8361	4.8984
3	7.1037	7.1358	7.1681	7.2006	7.2333	7.2661	7.2991	7.4328	7.5695	7.7090	7.8516	7.9973
4	9.9564	10.0153	10.0745	10.1342	10.1943	10.2548	10.3157	10.5639	10.8191	11.0817	11.3519	11.6300
5	13.0923	13.1883	13.2852	13.3830	13.4816	13.5811	13.6814	14.0920	14.5173	14.9581	15.4150	15.8885
6	16.5394	16.6850	16.8321	16.9808	17.1312	17.2831	17.4366	18.0675	18.7260	19.4134	20.1311	20.8806
7	20.3285	20.5382	20.7504	20.9653	21.1829	21.4033	21.6264	22.5473	23.5156	24.5341	25.6054	26.7327
8	24.4938	24.7843	25.0790	25.3780	25.6812	25.9889	26.3010	27.5952	28.9664	30.4195	31.9598	33.5929
9	29.0725	29.4635	29.8609	30.2648	30.6753	31.0925	31.5165	33.2833	35.1695	37.1838	39.3356	41.6350
10	34.1055	34.6198	35.1435	35.6767	36.2196	36.7725	37.3355	39.6928	42.2288	44.9583	47.8971	51.0624
15	67.8320	69.4468	71.1071	72.8143	74.5697	76.3749	78.2314	86.2017	95.1261	105.1269	116.3428	128.9308
20	121.9632	126.0419	130.2784	134.6792	139.2511	144.0013	148.9370	170.6944	196.0995	225.8017	260.5703	301.3163
25	208.8444	218.0110	227.6334	237.7356	248.3430	259.4820	271.1809	324.1919	388.8431	467.8283	564.4838	682.9447
30	348.2896	367.4641	387.8125	409.4101	432.3375	456.6805	482.5304	603.0504	756.7631	953.2392	1204.8847	1527.7960

SAVINGS GROWTH

MONTHLY COMPOUNDING
Annual Deposit

Description: This table shows what a series of $ 1 deposits grow to in the future. The deposit is made at the beginning of a period.

Example: At 5 % a regular one dollar deposit will grow to $ 5.82 by the end of the fifth year.

YEAR	0.00 %	1.00 %	2.00 %	3.00 %	4.00 %	4.125%	4.25 %	4.375%	4.50 %	4.625%	4.75 %	4.875%
1	1.0000	1.0100	1.0202	1.0304	1.0407	1.0420	1.0433	1.0446	1.0459	1.0472	1.0485	1.0499
2	2.0000	2.0302	2.0610	2.0922	2.1239	2.1279	2.1319	2.1359	2.1399	2.1440	2.1480	2.1520
3	3.0000	3.0607	3.1227	3.1862	3.2512	3.2594	3.2676	3.2759	3.2842	3.2925	3.3008	3.3092
4	4.0000	4.1015	4.2060	4.3136	4.4244	4.4384	4.4526	4.4668	4.4810	4.4953	4.5096	4.5240
5	5.0000	5.1527	5.3110	5.4752	5.6454	5.6671	5.6889	5.7108	5.7328	5.7549	5.7771	5.7994
6	6.0000	6.2145	6.4384	6.6721	6.9161	6.9473	6.9788	7.0103	7.0421	7.0740	7.1061	7.1384
7	7.0000	7.2870	7.5886	7.9055	8.2386	8.2814	8.3245	8.3679	8.4115	8.4555	8.4997	8.5441
8	8.0000	8.3703	8.7619	9.1763	9.6150	9.6716	9.7286	9.7861	9.8439	9.9022	9.9608	10.0199
9	9.0000	9.4644	9.9590	10.4859	11.0475	11.1202	11.1936	11.2675	11.3421	11.4172	11.4930	11.5693
10	10.0000	10.5695	11.1802	11.8352	12.5383	12.6298	12.7220	12.8151	12.9091	13.0038	13.0995	13.1960
15	15.0000	16.2639	17.6660	19.2232	20.9546	21.1843	21.4171	21.6531	21.8923	22.1347	22.3804	22.6295
20	20.0000	22.2502	24.8334	27.8051	31.2308	31.6947	32.1669	32.6478	33.1375	33.6361	34.1439	34.6610
25	25.0000	28.5432	32.7539	37.7741	43.7781	44.6079	45.4569	46.3255	47.2142	48.1234	49.0538	50.0059
30	30.0000	35.1587	41.5066	49.3541	59.0982	60.4735	61.8873	63.3408	64.8353	66.3718	67.9519	69.5766

YEAR	5.00 %	5.10 %	5.125%	5.20 %	5.25 %	5.30 %	5.375%	5.40 %	5.50 %	5.60 %	5.625%	5.70 %
1	1.0512	1.0522	1.0525	1.0533	1.0538	1.0543	1.0551	1.0554	1.0564	1.0575	1.0577	1.0585
2	2.1561	2.1594	2.1602	2.1626	2.1642	2.1659	2.1683	2.1691	2.1724	2.1757	2.1765	2.1790
3	3.3176	3.3243	3.3260	3.3310	3.3344	3.3378	3.3429	3.3446	3.3514	3.3582	3.3599	3.3650
4	4.5385	4.5501	4.5530	4.5617	4.5675	4.5734	4.5821	4.5851	4.5968	4.6086	4.6115	4.6204
5	5.8218	5.8398	5.8443	5.8579	5.8670	5.8760	5.8897	5.8942	5.9125	5.9308	5.9354	5.9492
6	7.1708	7.1969	7.2035	7.2231	7.2363	7.2495	7.2693	7.2759	7.3024	7.3291	7.3358	7.3559
7	8.5889	8.6249	8.6339	8.6611	8.6792	8.6975	8.7249	8.7340	8.7708	8.8077	8.8169	8.8448
8	10.0795	10.1274	10.1394	10.1756	10.1998	10.2241	10.2606	10.2729	10.3219	10.3712	10.3836	10.4208
9	11.6463	11.7084	11.7239	11.7708	11.8022	11.8336	11.8810	11.8969	11.9605	12.0246	12.0407	12.0891
10	13.2933	13.3718	13.3916	13.4509	13.4907	13.5306	13.5907	13.6108	13.6916	13.7730	13.7934	13.8550
15	22.8819	23.0864	23.1378	23.2930	23.3972	23.5019	23.6601	23.7131	23.9266	24.1425	24.1968	24.3607
20	35.1876	35.6158	35.7238	36.0504	36.2700	36.4913	36.8263	36.9388	37.3929	37.8537	37.9699	38.3213
25	50.9801	51.7758	51.9771	52.5864	52.9974	53.4122	54.0417	54.2534	55.1104	55.9835	56.2044	56.8731
30	71.2476	72.6185	72.9660	74.0205	74.7335	75.4545	76.5515	76.9213	78.4215	79.9561	80.3452	81.5259

YEAR	5.75 %	5.80 %	5.875%	5.90 %	6.00 %	6.10 %	6.125%	6.20 %	6.25 %	6.30 %	6.375%	6.40 %
1	1.0590	1.0596	1.0604	1.0606	1.0617	1.0627	1.0630	1.0638	1.0643	1.0649	1.0656	1.0659
2	2.1806	2.1822	2.1847	2.1855	2.1888	2.1921	2.1930	2.1954	2.1971	2.1988	2.2012	2.2021
3	3.3684	3.3718	3.3769	3.3787	3.3855	3.3924	3.3941	3.3993	3.4027	3.4062	3.4114	3.4131
4	4.6263	4.6322	4.6411	4.6441	4.6560	4.6680	4.6709	4.6799	4.6859	4.6920	4.7010	4.7040
5	5.9585	5.9677	5.9816	5.9863	6.0049	6.0235	6.0282	6.0423	6.0517	6.0611	6.0752	6.0800
6	7.3693	7.3828	7.4030	7.4098	7.4369	7.4641	7.4710	7.4915	7.5052	7.5190	7.5397	7.5466
7	8.8634	8.8821	8.9102	8.9196	8.9573	8.9951	9.0046	9.0332	9.0523	9.0715	9.1003	9.1099
8	10.4458	10.4707	10.5084	10.5209	10.5714	10.6222	10.6349	10.6733	10.6989	10.7246	10.7633	10.7763
9	12.1215	12.1540	12.2030	12.2194	12.2851	12.3513	12.3679	12.4179	12.4514	12.4850	12.5356	12.5525
10	13.8962	13.9376	13.9999	14.0207	14.1045	14.1889	14.2101	14.2739	14.3166	14.3595	14.4241	14.4457
15	24.4707	24.5813	24.7483	24.8043	25.0297	25.2577	25.3150	25.4881	25.6043	25.7211	25.8975	25.9567
20	38.5577	38.7958	39.1564	39.2774	39.7662	40.2623	40.3874	40.7657	41.0202	41.2766	41.6649	41.7952
25	57.3241	57.7793	58.4702	58.7027	59.6435	60.6021	60.8446	61.5789	62.0742	62.5742	63.3331	63.5884
30	82.3242	83.1317	84.3602	84.7744	86.4550	88.1744	88.6104	89.9335	90.8283	91.7333	93.1105	93.5749

YEAR	6.50 %	6.60 %	6.625%	6.70 %	6.75 %	6.80 %	6.875%	6.90 %	7.00 %	7.10 %	7.125%	7.20 %
1	1.0670	1.0680	1.0683	1.0691	1.0696	1.0702	1.0710	1.0712	1.0723	1.0734	1.0736	1.0744
2	2.2054	2.2087	2.2096	2.2121	2.2137	2.2154	2.2179	2.2187	2.2221	2.2255	2.2263	2.2288
3	3.4201	3.4270	3.4288	3.4340	3.4375	3.4410	3.4462	3.4480	3.4550	3.4621	3.4638	3.4691
4	4.7161	4.7282	4.7313	4.7404	4.7465	4.7526	4.7617	4.7648	4.7771	4.7894	4.7925	4.8017
5	6.0989	6.1179	6.1227	6.1370	6.1466	6.1562	6.1706	6.1754	6.1947	6.2141	6.2189	6.2335
6	7.5743	7.6022	7.6092	7.6302	7.6442	7.6583	7.6794	7.6865	7.7148	7.7433	7.7504	7.7719
7	9.1486	9.1874	9.1972	9.2265	9.2461	9.2657	9.2953	9.3052	9.3448	9.3846	9.3946	9.4247
8	10.8282	10.8805	10.8936	10.9331	10.9595	10.9860	11.0258	11.0391	11.0926	11.1464	11.1599	11.2005
9	12.6204	12.6888	12.7059	12.7576	12.7922	12.8269	12.8791	12.8966	12.9668	13.0375	13.0552	13.1086
10	14.5326	14.6201	14.6421	14.7082	14.7525	14.7970	14.8640	14.8864	14.9765	15.0672	15.0900	15.1586
15	26.1948	26.4356	26.4962	26.6791	26.8018	26.9252	27.1116	27.1741	27.4257	27.6801	27.7442	27.9374
20	42.3216	42.8558	42.9906	43.3980	43.6722	43.9484	44.3666	44.5070	45.0741	45.6497	45.7949	46.2339
25	64.6219	65.6751	65.9415	66.7484	67.2927	67.8421	68.6762	68.9568	70.0929	71.2507	71.5436	72.4307
30	95.4592	97.3873	97.8763	99.3604	100.3641	101.3794	102.9246	103.4456	105.5601	107.7242	108.2731	109.9390

Description: This table shows what a series of $ 1 deposits grow to in the future. The deposit is made at the beginning of a period.

Example: At 8 % a regular one dollar deposit will grow to $ 6.39 by the end of the fifth year.

YEAR	7.25 %	7.30 %	7.375%	7.40 %	7.50 %	7.60 %	7.625%	7.70 %	7.75 %	7.80 %	7.875%	7.90 %
1	1.0750	1.0755	1.0763	1.0766	1.0776	1.0787	1.0790	1.0798	1.0803	1.0808	1.0817	1.0819
2	2.2305	2.2322	2.2347	2.2355	2.2389	2.2423	2.2432	2.2457	2.2474	2.2491	2.2516	2.2525
3	3.4726	3.4762	3.4815	3.4833	3.4904	3.4975	3.4993	3.5046	3.5082	3.5118	3.5171	3.5189
4	4.8079	4.8141	4.8234	4.8265	4.8390	4.8515	4.8546	4.8640	4.8703	4.8766	4.8860	4.8892
5	6.2433	6.2530	6.2677	6.2726	6.2923	6.3120	6.3169	6.3318	6.3417	6.3517	6.3666	6.3716
6	7.7862	7.8006	7.8222	7.8294	7.8584	7.8875	7.8948	7.9167	7.9314	7.9460	7.9681	7.9755
7	9.4448	9.4650	9.4953	9.5054	9.5461	9.5870	9.5972	9.6280	9.6487	9.6693	9.7004	9.7108
8	11.2277	11.2550	11.2960	11.3097	11.3648	11.4202	11.4341	11.4759	11.5039	11.5319	11.5742	11.5883
9	13.1443	13.1801	13.2341	13.2522	13.3247	13.3977	13.4160	13.4712	13.5081	13.5452	13.6009	13.6196
10	15.2045	15.2506	15.3201	15.3434	15.4368	15.5309	15.5545	15.6257	15.6733	15.7211	15.7932	15.8173
15	28.0671	28.1975	28.3945	28.4605	28.7264	28.9953	29.0630	29.2672	29.4043	29.5422	29.7504	29.8202
20	46.5294	46.8270	47.2777	47.4291	48.0402	48.6607	48.8172	49.2905	49.6090	49.9299	50.4158	50.5790
25	73.0292	73.6335	74.5507	74.8594	76.1089	77.3825	77.7048	78.6808	79.3393	80.0041	81.0134	81.3531
30	111.0658	112.2059	113.9409	114.5260	116.9009	119.3318	119.9484	121.8200	123.0862	124.3672	126.3171	126.9747

YEAR	8.00 %	8.10 %	8.125%	8.20 %	8.25 %	8.30 %	8.375%	8.40 %	8.50 %	8.60 %	8.625%	8.70 %
1	1.0830	1.0841	1.0843	1.0852	1.0857	1.0862	1.0870	1.0873	1.0884	1.0895	1.0897	1.0906
2	2.2559	2.2593	2.2601	2.2627	2.2644	2.2661	2.2687	2.2696	2.2730	2.2764	2.2773	2.2799
3	3.5261	3.5333	3.5351	3.5405	3.5442	3.5478	3.5532	3.5550	3.5623	3.5696	3.5714	3.5769
4	4.9018	4.9145	4.9176	4.9272	4.9336	4.9399	4.9495	4.9527	4.9656	4.9784	4.9816	4.9913
5	6.3916	6.4117	6.4168	6.4319	6.4420	6.4521	6.4674	6.4725	6.4929	6.5133	6.5185	6.5339
6	8.0051	8.0349	8.0423	8.0647	8.0797	8.0948	8.1173	8.1249	8.1552	8.1856	8.1932	8.2161
7	9.7526	9.7945	9.8050	9.8366	9.8578	9.8790	9.9109	9.9216	9.9644	10.0074	10.0182	10.0506
8	11.6450	11.7020	11.7164	11.7594	11.7882	11.8171	11.8606	11.8752	11.9335	11.9923	12.0070	12.0513
9	13.6945	13.7700	13.7889	13.8459	13.8841	13.9224	13.9800	13.9993	14.0767	14.1547	14.1743	14.2332
10	15.9142	16.0118	16.0363	16.1101	16.1595	16.2091	16.2839	16.3089	16.4094	16.5106	16.5361	16.6126
15	30.1013	30.3856	30.4572	30.6730	30.8180	30.9637	31.1839	31.2577	31.5549	31.8555	31.9312	32.1595
20	51.2380	51.9070	52.0758	52.5862	52.9297	53.2758	53.7999	53.9759	54.6867	55.4084	55.5906	56.1412
25	82.7283	84.1302	84.4849	85.5593	86.2842	87.0162	88.1275	88.5016	90.0159	91.5598	91.9505	93.1339
30	129.6440	132.3768	133.0700	135.1745	136.5982	138.0389	140.2319	140.9715	143.9742	147.0487	147.8287	150.1967

YEAR	8.75 %	8.80 %	8.875%	8.90 %	9.00 %	9.10 %	9.125%	9.20 %	9.25 %	9.30 %	9.375%	9.40 %
1	1.0911	1.0916	1.0925	1.0927	1.0938	1.0949	1.0952	1.0960	1.0965	1.0971	1.0979	1.0982
2	2.2816	2.2833	2.2859	2.2868	2.2902	2.2937	2.2946	2.2972	2.2989	2.3006	2.3032	2.3041
3	3.5805	3.5842	3.5897	3.5915	3.5989	3.6062	3.6081	3.6136	3.6173	3.6210	3.6266	3.6284
4	4.9978	5.0043	5.0140	5.0173	5.0303	5.0433	5.0466	5.0564	5.0630	5.0696	5.0794	5.0827
5	6.5442	6.5545	6.5700	6.5752	6.5960	6.6168	6.6220	6.6377	6.6482	6.6587	6.6745	6.6798
6	8.2314	8.2468	8.2698	8.2776	8.3085	8.3396	8.3474	8.3708	8.3865	8.4022	8.4258	8.4336
7	10.0723	10.0941	10.1269	10.1378	10.1817	10.2258	10.2369	10.2702	10.2925	10.3148	10.3484	10.3596
8	12.0810	12.1107	12.1555	12.1705	12.2306	12.2911	12.3063	12.3519	12.3825	12.4131	12.4592	12.4747
9	14.2726	14.3122	14.3718	14.3917	14.4718	14.5523	14.5726	14.6334	14.6742	14.7151	14.7767	14.7973
10	16.6639	16.7154	16.7929	16.8188	16.9231	17.0281	17.0545	17.1339	17.1871	17.2405	17.3210	17.3479
15	32.3128	32.4669	32.6997	32.7778	33.0921	33.4101	33.4901	33.7316	33.8937	34.0568	34.3030	34.3856
20	56.5118	56.8852	57.4507	57.6406	58.4077	59.1866	59.3831	59.9774	60.3774	60.7805	61.3909	61.5959
25	93.9325	94.7389	95.9632	96.3753	98.0438	99.7451	100.1756	101.4798	102.3600	103.2488	104.5983	105.0526
30	151.7989	153.4202	155.8885	156.7211	160.1012	163.5627	164.4410	167.1075	168.9119	170.7379	173.5180	174.4558

YEAR	9.50 %	9.75 %	10.00 %	10.25 %	10.50 %	10.75 %	11.00 %	12.00 %	13.00 %	14.00 %	15.00 %	16.00 %
1	1.0992	1.1020	1.1047	1.1075	1.1102	1.1130	1.1157	1.1268	1.1380	1.1493	1.1608	1.1723
2	2.3076	2.3163	2.3251	2.3339	2.3428	2.3516	2.3605	2.3966	2.4332	2.4703	2.5081	2.5465
3	3.6359	3.6545	3.6733	3.6922	3.7111	3.7302	3.7494	3.8273	3.9070	3.9886	4.0720	4.1574
4	5.0960	5.1292	5.1626	5.1964	5.2303	5.2645	5.2990	5.4396	5.5844	5.7336	5.8874	6.0459
5	6.7010	6.7542	6.8079	6.8622	6.9169	6.9722	7.0279	7.2563	7.4932	7.7392	7.9946	8.2597
6	8.4653	8.5450	8.6255	8.7070	8.7894	8.8727	8.9569	9.3034	9.6656	10.0443	10.4405	10.8549
7	10.4047	10.5183	10.6335	10.7501	10.8682	10.9879	11.1091	11.6101	12.1378	12.6937	13.2796	13.8972
8	12.5366	12.6929	12.8516	13.0127	13.1761	13.3420	13.5104	14.2093	14.9512	15.7388	16.5751	17.4635
9	14.8800	15.0893	15.3021	15.5184	15.7384	15.9621	16.1895	17.1383	18.1530	19.2386	20.4004	21.6442
10	17.4561	17.7301	18.0091	18.2934	18.5830	18.8781	19.1787	20.4387	21.7967	23.2611	24.8406	26.5452
15	34.7182	35.5662	36.4385	37.3359	38.2591	39.2089	40.1862	44.3871	49.1000	54.3918	60.3383	67.0256
20	62.4240	64.5506	66.7606	69.0575	71.4449	73.9266	76.5065	87.8941	101.2181	116.8279	135.1383	156.6415
25	106.8920	111.6512	116.6497	121.9002	127.4161	133.2114	139.3013	166.9332	200.7041	242.0505	292.7555	355.0338
30	178.2637	188.1915	198.7328	209.9272	221.8172	234.4481	247.8681	310.5233	390.6085	493.1980	624.8835	794.2361

Description: This table shows what a series of $ 1 deposits grow to in the future. The deposit is made at the beginning of a period.

Example: At 5 % a regular one dollar deposit will grow to $ 295.29 by the end of the fifth year.

YEAR	0.00 %	1.00 %	2.00 %	3.00 %	4.00 %	4.125%	4.25 %	4.375%	4.50 %	4.625%	4.75 %	4.875%
1	52.0000	52.2654	52.5320	52.7997	53.0687	53.1024	53.1361	53.1698	53.2036	53.2374	53.2711	53.3050
2	104.0000	105.0554	106.1225	107.2013	108.2921	108.4293	108.5667	108.7043	108.8420	108.9800	109.1181	109.2564
3	156.0000	158.3753	160.7929	163.2535	165.7579	166.0741	166.3909	166.7085	167.0268	167.3457	167.6654	167.9858
4	208.0000	212.2304	216.5649	221.0062	225.5570	226.1337	226.7121	227.2923	227.8743	228.4581	229.0437	229.6310
5	260.0000	266.6261	273.4608	280.5110	287.7842	288.7093	289.6381	290.5705	291.5066	292.4463	293.3897	294.3368
6	312.0000	321.5677	331.5031	341.8212	352.5380	353.9065	355.2814	356.6629	358.0510	359.4457	360.8471	362.2551
7	364.0000	377.0609	390.7150	404.9915	419.9211	421.8348	423.7593	425.6946	427.6408	429.5980	431.5662	433.5455
8	416.0000	433.1111	451.1201	470.0784	490.0403	492.6089	495.1942	497.7964	500.4154	503.0515	505.7048	508.3753
9	468.0000	489.7238	512.7424	537.1399	563.0065	566.3479	569.7139	573.1047	576.5205	579.9616	583.4282	586.9203
10	520.0000	546.9049	575.6063	606.2360	638.9355	643.1760	647.4514	651.7622	656.1086	660.4910	664.9097	669.3650
15	780.0000	841.5355	909.4457	984.4627	1067.4069	1078.3770	1089.4870	1100.7390	1112.1348	1123.6766	1135.3663	1147.2059
20	1040.0000	1151.2528	1278.3032	1423.6535	1590.2235	1612.7006	1635.5691	1658.8363	1682.5098	1706.5972	1731.1064	1756.0453
25	1300.0000	1476.8294	1685.8524	1933.6349	2228.1590	2268.7234	2310.1883	2352.5753	2395.9066	2440.2049	2485.4933	2531.7959
30	1560.0000	1819.0772	2136.1516	2525.8173	3006.5616	3074.1639	3143.5998	3214.9227	3288.1881	3363.4526	3440.7751	3520.2159

YEAR	5.00 %	5.10 %	5.125%	5.20 %	5.25 %	5.30 %	5.375%	5.40 %	5.50 %	5.60 %	5.625%	5.70 %
1	53.3388	53.3659	53.3726	53.3930	53.4065	53.4201	53.4404	53.4472	53.4743	53.5014	53.5082	53.5286
2	109.3949	109.5059	109.5336	109.6170	109.6725	109.7282	109.8116	109.8395	109.9509	110.0625	110.0904	110.1741
3	168.3069	168.5643	168.6287	168.8221	168.9512	169.0804	169.2744	169.3392	169.5984	169.8581	169.9230	170.1182
4	230.2201	230.6927	230.8111	231.1665	231.4038	231.6414	231.9984	232.1175	232.5948	233.0732	233.1930	233.5527
5	295.2876	296.0509	296.2421	296.8166	297.2003	297.5847	298.1623	298.3551	299.1280	299.9034	300.0976	300.6811
6	363.6699	364.8066	365.0914	365.9476	366.5197	367.0929	367.9548	368.2427	369.3968	370.5554	370.8457	371.7184
7	435.5360	437.1364	437.5377	438.7441	439.5507	440.3590	441.5750	441.9813	443.6108	445.2478	445.6582	446.8921
8	511.0633	513.2263	513.7688	515.4005	516.4919	517.5861	519.2328	519.7831	521.9916	524.2116	524.7684	526.4432
9	590.4384	593.2715	593.9824	596.1215	597.5528	598.9883	601.1495	601.8721	604.7730	607.6911	608.4234	610.6266
10	673.8572	677.4778	678.3867	681.1225	682.9538	684.7913	687.5589	688.4845	692.2022	695.9446	696.8841	699.7120
15	1159.1976	1168.9019	1171.3435	1178.7059	1183.6457	1188.6108	1196.1064	1198.6177	1208.7277	1218.9420	1221.5120	1229.2618
20	1781.4221	1802.0444	1807.2451	1822.9566	1833.5227	1844.1630	1860.2637	1865.6682	1887.4767	1909.5930	1915.1708	1932.0219
25	2579.1370	2617.7745	2627.5418	2657.1058	2677.0358	2697.1444	2727.6456	2737.9037	2779.3979	2821.6411	2832.3206	2864.6478
30	3601.8373	3668.7475	3685.7034	3737.1280	3771.8804	3807.0135	3860.4365	3878.4393	3951.4418	4026.0580	4044.9687	4102.3261

YEAR	5.75 %	5.80 %	5.875%	5.90 %	6.00 %	6.10 %	6.125%	6.20 %	6.25 %	6.30 %	6.375%	6.40 %
1	53.5422	53.5558	53.5761	53.5829	53.6101	53.6373	53.6441	53.6645	53.6781	53.6917	53.7122	53.7190
2	110.2300	110.2860	110.3699	110.3979	110.5099	110.6221	110.6502	110.7344	110.7906	110.8468	110.9312	110.9594
3	170.2484	170.3788	170.5745	170.6398	170.9013	171.1633	171.2289	171.4257	171.5571	171.6886	171.8861	171.9520
4	233.7930	234.0335	234.3948	234.5154	234.9985	235.4828	235.6041	235.9683	236.2115	236.4550	236.8208	236.9428
5	301.0709	301.4613	302.0480	302.2439	303.0290	303.8165	304.0138	304.6066	305.0025	305.3990	305.9950	306.1940
6	372.3015	372.8858	373.7643	374.0577	375.2341	376.4149	376.7109	377.6003	378.1947	378.7903	379.6857	379.9847
7	447.7171	448.5439	449.7876	450.2031	451.8699	453.5441	453.9639	455.2260	456.0698	456.9155	458.1876	458.6127
8	527.5634	528.6865	530.3767	530.9415	533.2083	535.4870	536.0585	537.7776	538.9274	540.0802	541.8150	542.3948
9	612.1009	613.5795	615.8056	616.5499	619.5380	622.5438	623.2981	625.5675	627.0861	628.6093	630.9024	631.6691
10	701.6050	703.5044	706.3652	707.3220	711.1651	715.0339	716.0051	718.9284	720.8854	722.8489	725.8064	726.7955
15	1234.4615	1239.6881	1247.5785	1250.2222	1260.8653	1271.6187	1274.3244	1282.4834	1287.9580	1293.4609	1301.7686	1304.5522
20	1943.3551	1954.7681	1972.0389	1977.8364	2001.2318	2024.9591	2030.9435	2049.0236	2061.1838	2073.4302	2091.9628	2098.1842
25	2886.4421	2908.4327	2941.7913	2953.0110	2998.3981	3044.6095	3056.2930	3091.6613	3115.5075	3139.5699	3176.0736	3188.3519
30	4141.0918	4180.2851	4239.8880	4259.9749	4341.4364	4424.7117	4445.8189	4509.8435	4553.1194	4596.8760	4663.4247	4685.8541

YEAR	6.50 %	6.60 %	6.625%	6.70 %	6.75 %	6.80 %	6.875%	6.90 %	7.00 %	7.10 %	7.125%	7.20 %
1	53.7462	53.7735	53.7803	53.8007	53.8144	53.8280	53.8485	53.8553	53.8826	53.9099	53.9168	53.9373
2	111.0720	111.1848	111.2130	111.2977	111.3542	111.4108	111.4956	111.5239	111.6372	111.7506	111.7790	111.8642
3	172.2158	172.4801	172.5463	172.7449	172.8774	173.0101	173.2093	173.2758	173.5420	173.8086	173.8754	174.0757
4	237.4319	237.9221	238.0449	238.4136	238.6598	238.9062	239.2765	239.4001	239.8952	240.3915	240.5157	240.8890
5	306.9915	307.7914	307.9918	308.5939	308.9961	309.3989	310.0043	310.2064	311.0164	311.8290	312.0326	312.6442
6	381.1838	382.3875	382.6891	383.5957	384.2016	384.8086	385.7214	386.0262	387.2484	388.4753	388.7828	389.7069
7	460.3175	462.0300	462.4594	463.7504	464.6135	465.4785	466.7798	467.2145	468.9583	470.7101	471.1493	472.4698
8	544.7216	547.0606	547.6472	549.4118	550.5921	551.7754	553.5562	554.1514	556.5399	558.9409	559.5431	561.3545
9	634.7471	637.8435	638.6205	640.9584	642.5228	644.0918	646.4542	647.2440	650.4149	653.6048	654.4052	656.8137
10	730.7685	734.7681	735.7722	738.7944	740.8177	742.8477	745.9054	746.9280	751.0357	755.1709	756.2090	759.3338
15	1315.7588	1327.0819	1329.9310	1338.5228	1344.2878	1350.0828	1358.8317	1361.7632	1373.5654	1385.4908	1388.4915	1397.5406
20	2123.2910	2148.7558	2155.1786	2174.5842	2187.6365	2200.7817	2220.6755	2227.3540	2254.3068	2281.6459	2288.5417	2309.3772
25	3238.0243	3288.6043	3301.3933	3340.1098	3366.2152	3392.5587	3432.5255	3445.9693	3500.3605	3555.7515	3569.7577	3612.1617
30	4776.8242	4869.8335	4893.4101	4964.9305	5013.2773	5062.1648	5136.5237	5161.5873	5263.2502	5367.2069	5393.5608	5473.5120

SAVINGS GROWTH

Description: This table shows what a series of $ 1 deposits grow to in the future. The deposit is made at the beginning of a period.

Example: At 8 % a regular one dollar deposit will grow to $ 319.26 by the end of the fifth year.

YEAR	7.25 %	7.30 %	7.375%	7.40 %	7.50 %	7.60 %	7.625%	7.70 %	7.75 %	7.80 %	7.875%	7.90 %
1	53.9509	53.9646	53.9851	53.9920	54.0193	54.0467	54.0536	54.0741	54.0878	54.1015	54.1221	54.1289
2	111.9210	111.9778	112.0631	112.0916	112.2055	112.3195	112.3481	112.4337	112.4908	112.5480	112.6338	112.6624
3	174.2095	174.3433	174.5443	174.6114	174.8799	175.1489	175.2162	175.4184	175.5533	175.6884	175.8911	175.9588
4	241.1382	241.3877	241.7625	241.8876	242.3888	242.8912	243.0169	243.3948	243.6471	243.8996	244.2791	244.4057
5	313.0527	313.4619	314.0768	314.2821	315.1050	315.9304	316.1372	316.7584	317.1734	317.5890	318.2137	318.4223
6	390.3245	390.9433	391.8736	392.1844	393.4302	394.6808	394.9942	395.9363	396.5658	397.1965	398.1449	398.4616
7	473.3527	474.2375	475.5686	476.0133	477.7971	479.5891	480.0383	481.3891	482.2923	483.1974	484.5590	485.0139
8	562.5660	563.7808	565.6089	566.2199	568.6718	571.1366	571.7548	573.6143	574.8581	576.1051	577.9819	578.6091
9	658.4254	660.0418	662.4756	663.2892	666.5561	669.8425	670.6671	673.1485	674.8090	676.4744	678.9819	679.8202
10	761.4257	763.5246	766.6862	767.7436	771.9908	776.2666	777.3400	780.5710	782.7341	784.9045	788.1736	789.2670
15	1403.6127	1409.7165	1418.9318	1422.0196	1434.4515	1447.0136	1450.1747	1459.7074	1466.1041	1472.5343	1482.2427	1485.4958
20	2323.3918	2337.5068	2358.8690	2366.0407	2394.9851	2424.3464	2431.7526	2454.1309	2469.1838	2484.3451	2507.2917	2514.9956
25	3640.7552	3669.6110	3713.3922	3728.1199	3787.7089	3848.3993	3863.7465	3910.2127	3941.5473	3973.1710	4021.1546	4037.2967
30	5527.5628	5582.2218	5665.3665	5693.3935	5807.0860	5923.3597	5952.8387	6042.2764	6102.7455	6163.8993	6256.9314	6288.2933

YEAR	8.00 %	8.10 %	8.125%	8.20 %	8.25 %	8.30 %	8.375%	8.40 %	8.50 %	8.60 %	8.625%	8.70 %
1	54.1563	54.1838	54.1906	54.2112	54.2250	54.2387	54.2593	54.2662	54.2937	54.3212	54.3280	54.3487
2	112.7769	112.8916	112.9203	113.0064	113.0638	113.1213	113.2075	113.2363	113.3515	113.4668	113.4956	113.5822
3	176.2297	176.5011	176.5690	176.7730	176.9091	177.0453	177.2499	177.3182	177.5915	177.8653	177.9338	178.1396
4	244.9131	245.4216	245.5490	245.9315	246.1868	246.4425	246.8267	246.9549	247.4684	247.9833	248.1122	248.4994
5	319.2581	320.0966	320.3066	320.9377	321.3593	321.7815	322.4160	322.6279	323.4770	324.3287	324.5421	325.1831
6	399.7316	401.0065	401.3259	402.2862	402.9279	403.5709	404.5376	404.8605	406.1551	407.4546	407.7803	408.7592
7	486.8387	488.6718	489.1313	490.5132	491.4371	492.3630	493.7559	494.2213	496.0880	497.9632	498.4334	499.8470
8	581.1262	583.6566	584.2913	586.2003	587.4772	588.7575	590.6842	591.3281	593.9124	596.5102	597.1618	599.1218
9	683.1860	686.5721	687.4217	689.9784	691.6892	693.4052	695.9888	696.8526	700.3206	703.8095	704.6850	707.3194
10	793.6589	798.0803	799.1903	802.5316	804.7684	807.0128	810.3935	811.5242	816.0660	820.6384	821.7864	825.2418
15	1498.5935	1511.8288	1515.1593	1525.2034	1531.9433	1538.7187	1548.9485	1552.3764	1566.1780	1580.1252	1583.6350	1594.2197
20	2546.0892	2577.6326	2585.5896	2609.6328	2625.8064	2642.0968	2666.7534	2675.0317	2708.4447	2742.3434	2750.8948	2776.7350
25	4102.6127	4169.1425	4185.9673	4236.9098	4271.2651	4305.9389	4358.5538	4376.2547	4447.8826	4520.8482	4539.3018	4595.1781
30	6415.5248	6545.6621	6578.6585	6678.7748	6746.4692	6814.9344	6919.0978	6954.2143	7096.6895	7242.4369	7279.3942	7391.5353

YEAR	8.75 %	8.80 %	8.875%	8.90 %	9.00 %	9.10 %	9.125%	9.20 %	9.25 %	9.30 %	9.375%	9.40 %
1	54.3624	54.3762	54.3968	54.4037	54.4313	54.4588	54.4657	54.4864	54.5002	54.5140	54.5347	54.5416
2	113.6399	113.6977	113.7845	113.8134	113.9292	114.0451	114.0741	114.1612	114.2192	114.2773	114.3645	114.3936
3	178.2769	178.4144	178.6208	178.6896	178.9654	179.2416	179.3107	179.5183	179.6569	179.7955	180.0038	180.0732
4	248.7579	249.0168	249.4056	249.5354	250.0553	250.5765	250.7070	251.0990	251.3607	251.6227	252.0164	252.1478
5	325.6113	326.0402	326.6848	326.9001	327.7626	328.6278	328.8445	329.4958	329.9308	330.3665	331.0213	331.2399
6	409.4133	410.0688	411.0543	411.3834	412.7031	414.0278	414.3598	415.3577	416.0246	416.6927	417.6974	418.0329
7	500.7921	501.7394	503.1644	503.6404	505.5501	507.4685	507.9495	509.3957	510.3626	511.3317	512.7895	513.2765
8	600.4328	601.7472	603.7253	604.3865	607.0397	609.7069	610.3759	612.3883	613.7343	615.0838	617.1149	617.7937
9	709.0822	710.8504	713.5126	714.4026	717.9762	721.5713	722.4735	725.1881	727.0046	728.8267	731.5700	732.4872
10	827.5551	829.8762	833.3725	834.5419	839.2391	843.9681	845.1553	848.7290	851.1216	853.5222	857.1384	858.3479
15	1601.3226	1608.4630	1619.2441	1622.8568	1637.4029	1652.1029	1655.8022	1666.9587	1674.4454	1681.9718	1693.3361	1697.1442
20	2794.1181	2811.6273	2838.1297	2847.0280	2882.9449	2919.3859	2928.5790	2956.3592	2975.0481	2993.8731	3022.3682	3031.9358
25	4632.8630	4670.8991	4728.6192	4748.0386	4826.6246	4906.6856	4926.9348	4988.2509	5029.6068	5071.3501	5134.6993	5156.0135
30	7467.3663	7544.0655	7660.7651	7700.1104	7859.7546	8023.0851	8064.5042	8190.1911	8275.1882	8361.1636	8491.9867	8536.0963

YEAR	9.50 %	9.75 %	10.00 %	10.25 %	10.50 %	10.75 %	11.00 %	12.00 %	13.00 %	14.00 %	15.00 %	16.00 %
1	54.5692	54.6383	54.7074	54.7766	54.8459	54.9153	54.9847	55.2633	55.5431	55.8241	56.1063	56.3898
2	114.5101	114.8017	115.0941	115.3874	115.6814	115.9763	116.2719	117.4626	118.6665	119.8835	121.1139	122.3579
3	180.3514	181.0491	181.7498	182.4536	183.1606	183.8707	184.5839	187.4685	190.4047	193.3932	196.4350	199.5312
4	252.6741	253.9956	255.3252	256.6629	258.0090	259.3632	260.7259	266.2608	271.9334	277.7472	283.7058	289.8130
5	332.1161	334.3187	336.5386	338.7761	341.0313	343.3043	345.5954	354.9422	364.5889	374.5454	384.8222	395.4300
6	419.3782	422.7643	426.1831	429.6350	433.1203	436.6394	440.1927	454.7539	469.8895	485.6236	501.9807	518.9870
7	515.2303	520.1538	525.1338	530.1710	535.2661	540.4198	545.6329	567.0928	589.5612	613.0883	637.7265	663.5312
8	620.5178	627.3916	634.3568	641.4148	648.5669	655.8144	663.1587	693.5312	725.5652	759.3570	795.0084	832.6274
9	736.1697	745.4736	754.9186	764.5070	774.2410	784.1231	794.1556	835.8388	880.1305	927.2037	977.2432	1030.4461
10	863.2062	875.4965	887.9963	900.7094	913.6396	926.7910	940.1674	996.0073	1055.7902	1119.8117	1188.3895	1261.8660
15	1712.4776	1751.5275	1791.6240	1832.7970	1875.0772	1918.4960	1963.0861	2153.8421	2366.1960	2602.7342	2866.3601	3160.3337
20	3070.5558	3169.6014	3272.3232	3378.8654	3489.3780	3604.0169	3722.9445	4245.0206	4850.5130	5553.4369	6370.2179	7320.1104
25	5242.2722	5465.1065	5698.6211	5943.3533	6199.8684	6468.7605	6750.6549	8021.9216	9560.3753	11424.71	13686.81	16434.69
30	8715.0851	9180.9525	9674.3929	10197.11	10750.91	11337.73	11959.61	14843.42	18489.51	23107.31	28964.95	36405.87

Description: This table shows what a series of $ 1 deposits grow to in the future. The deposit is made at the beginning of a period.

Example: At 5 % a regular one dollar deposit will grow to $ 68.25 by the end of the fifth year.

YEAR	0.00 %	1.00 %	2.00 %	3.00 %	4.00 %	4.125%	4.25 %	4.375%	4.50 %	4.625%	4.75 %	4.875%
1	12.0000	12.0652	12.1306	12.1964	12.2624	12.2707	12.2790	12.2873	12.2956	12.3039	12.3122	12.3205
2	24.0000	24.2514	24.5056	24.7627	25.0227	25.0554	25.0882	25.1210	25.1538	25.1867	25.2196	25.2526
3	36.0000	36.5600	37.1300	37.7104	38.3012	38.3758	38.4505	38.5254	38.6005	38.6758	38.7512	38.8268
4	48.0000	48.9921	50.0088	51.0508	52.1188	52.2541	52.3899	52.5260	52.6626	52.7997	52.9371	53.0750
5	60.0000	61.5490	63.1471	64.7960	66.4974	66.7138	66.9311	67.1493	67.3683	67.5882	67.8089	68.0305
6	72.0000	74.2320	76.5502	78.9582	81.4599	81.7793	82.1003	82.4229	82.7470	83.0726	83.3998	83.7286
7	84.0000	87.0422	90.2233	93.5501	97.0299	97.4760	97.9246	98.3757	98.8295	99.2857	99.7446	100.2061
8	96.0000	99.9811	104.1720	108.5847	113.2321	113.8302	114.4322	115.0381	115.6479	116.2618	116.8797	117.5016
9	108.0000	113.0498	118.4017	124.0754	130.0922	130.8695	131.6526	132.4414	133.2361	134.0367	134.8433	135.6558
10	120.0000	126.2497	132.9181	140.0361	147.6368	148.6226	149.6166	150.6188	151.6293	152.6481	153.6755	154.7114
15	180.0000	194.2634	210.0078	227.4038	246.6424	249.1872	251.7645	254.3749	257.0187	259.6964	262.4085	265.1555
20	240.0000	265.7597	295.1838	328.8537	367.4480	372.6566	377.9561	383.3482	388.8345	394.4170	400.0974	405.8775
25	300.0000	340.9171	389.2944	446.6557	514.8538	524.2479	533.8508	543.6675	553.7033	563.9634	574.4531	585.1780
30	360.0000	419.9230	493.2768	583.4455	694.7168	710.3659	726.4400	742.9514	759.9130	777.3380	795.2400	813.6331

YEAR	5.00 %	5.10 %	5.125%	5.20 %	5.25 %	5.30 %	5.375%	5.40 %	5.50 %	5.60 %	5.625%	5.70 %
1	12.3288	12.3354	12.3371	12.3421	12.3454	12.3487	12.3537	12.3554	12.3621	12.3687	12.3704	12.3754
2	25.2856	25.3121	25.3187	25.3386	25.3518	25.3651	25.3850	25.3916	25.4182	25.4448	25.4515	25.4714
3	38.9026	38.9633	38.9785	39.0242	39.0546	39.0851	39.1309	39.1462	39.2074	39.2686	39.2840	39.3300
4	53.2133	53.3242	53.3520	53.4354	53.4911	53.5469	53.6307	53.6587	53.7707	53.8830	53.9112	53.9956
5	68.2530	68.4316	68.4764	68.6108	68.7006	68.7905	68.9257	68.9709	69.1517	69.3332	69.3786	69.5152
6	84.0590	84.3244	84.3909	84.5908	84.7244	84.8583	85.0596	85.1268	85.3963	85.6669	85.7347	85.9385
7	100.6701	101.0433	101.1368	101.4181	101.6062	101.7947	102.0782	102.1730	102.5529	102.9346	103.0303	103.3181
8	118.1276	118.6313	118.7577	119.1377	119.3919	119.6467	120.0303	120.1584	120.6728	121.1899	121.3196	121.7097
9	136.4744	137.1336	137.2991	137.7968	138.1299	138.4639	138.9668	139.1350	139.8100	140.4891	140.6595	141.1723
10	155.7559	156.5978	156.8091	157.4453	157.8711	158.2984	158.9419	159.1572	160.0217	160.8920	161.1105	161.7681
15	267.9379	270.1896	270.7561	272.4644	273.6107	274.7628	276.5021	277.0849	279.4309	281.8012	282.3976	284.1960
20	411.7594	416.5393	417.7448	421.3866	423.8358	426.3022	430.0343	431.2871	436.3425	441.4694	442.7624	446.6689
25	596.1438	605.0939	607.3564	614.2048	618.8216	623.4799	630.5457	632.9221	642.5348	652.3213	654.7955	662.2849
30	832.5316	848.0244	851.9505	863.8580	871.9051	880.0405	892.4112	896.5801	913.4852	930.7645	935.1438	948.4268

YEAR	5.75 %	5.80 %	5.875%	5.90 %	6.00 %	6.10 %	6.125%	6.20 %	6.25 %	6.30 %	6.375%	6.40 %
1	12.3787	12.3821	12.3871	12.3888	12.3954	12.4021	12.4038	12.4088	12.4122	12.4155	12.4205	12.4222
2	25.4848	25.4981	25.5181	25.5248	25.5515	25.5783	25.5849	25.6050	25.6184	25.6318	25.6520	25.6587
3	39.3608	39.3915	39.4377	39.4531	39.5149	39.5767	39.5922	39.6386	39.6697	39.7007	39.7473	39.7629
4	54.0520	54.1085	54.1933	54.2217	54.3351	54.4488	54.4773	54.5628	54.6199	54.6771	54.7629	54.7916
5	69.6064	69.6978	69.8351	69.8810	70.0647	70.2490	70.2952	70.4339	70.5266	70.6194	70.7589	70.8055
6	86.0747	86.2111	86.4163	86.4848	86.7596	87.0354	87.1045	87.3122	87.4511	87.5902	87.7993	87.8692
7	103.5104	103.7033	103.9933	104.0902	104.4789	104.8693	104.9672	105.2616	105.4584	105.6556	105.9523	106.0514
8	121.9706	122.2322	122.6259	122.7575	123.2855	123.8163	123.9495	124.3499	124.6178	124.8863	125.2905	125.4255
9	141.5153	141.8595	142.3775	142.5508	143.2462	143.9458	144.1213	144.6495	145.0030	145.3575	145.8912	146.0697
10	162.2084	162.6501	163.3154	163.5379	164.4317	165.3315	165.5574	166.2373	166.6924	167.1491	167.8370	168.0671
15	285.4027	286.6157	288.4468	289.0603	291.5304	294.0261	294.6540	296.5477	297.8183	299.0955	301.0238	301.6698
20	449.2962	451.9420	455.9459	457.2900	462.7139	468.2149	469.6023	473.7942	476.6136	479.4530	483.7499	485.1924
25	667.3342	672.4291	680.1578	682.7573	693.2732	703.9804	706.6875	714.8826	720.4080	725.9835	734.4420	737.2872
30	957.4044	966.4811	980.2847	984.9368	1003.8032	1023.0902	1027.9789	1042.8078	1052.8312	1062.9660	1078.3803	1083.5755

YEAR	6.50 %	6.60 %	6.625%	6.70 %	6.75 %	6.80 %	6.875%	6.90 %	7.00 %	7.10 %	7.125%	7.20 %
1	12.4289	12.4356	12.4373	12.4423	12.4456	12.4490	12.4540	12.4557	12.4624	12.4691	12.4708	12.4758
2	25.6856	25.7125	25.7192	25.7394	25.7529	25.7663	25.7866	25.7933	25.8204	25.8474	25.8542	25.8745
3	39.8251	39.8875	39.9031	39.9500	39.9813	40.0126	40.0597	40.0754	40.1382	40.2011	40.2169	40.2642
4	54.9064	55.0216	55.0504	55.1370	55.1948	55.2527	55.3396	55.3686	55.4849	55.6014	55.6306	55.7183
5	70.9922	71.1794	71.2263	71.3673	71.4614	71.5557	71.6974	71.7448	71.9344	72.1246	72.1723	72.3155
6	88.1493	88.4304	88.5009	88.7127	88.8542	88.9960	89.2092	89.2804	89.5659	89.8526	89.9244	90.1403
7	106.4490	106.8485	106.9486	107.2497	107.4510	107.6528	107.9563	108.0577	108.4645	108.8731	108.9755	109.2836
8	125.9676	126.5125	126.6492	127.0603	127.3353	127.6110	128.0259	128.1645	128.7210	129.2805	129.4208	129.8428
9	146.7861	147.5069	147.6877	148.2319	148.5961	148.9613	149.5112	149.6950	150.4332	151.1758	151.3621	151.9228
10	168.9912	169.9215	170.1551	170.8581	171.3287	171.8009	172.5122	172.7501	173.7056	174.6676	174.9091	175.6360
15	304.2710	306.8992	307.5605	309.5548	310.8930	312.2382	314.2691	314.9496	317.6893	320.4576	321.1543	323.2550
20	491.0138	496.9184	498.4077	502.9074	505.9340	508.9822	513.5954	515.1440	521.3943	527.7342	529.3334	534.1653
25	748.7974	760.5183	763.4819	772.4539	778.5036	784.6085	793.8707	796.9863	809.5916	822.4290	825.6751	835.5029
30	1104.6469	1126.1913	1131.6525	1148.2197	1159.4191	1170.7439	1187.9695	1193.7756	1217.3270	1241.4103	1247.5157	1266.0384

SAVINGS GROWTH

Description: This table shows what a series of $ 1 deposits grow to in the future. The deposit is made at the beginning of a period.

Example: At 8 % a regular one dollar deposit will grow to $ 73.86 by the end of the fifth year.

YEAR	7.25 %	7.30 %	7.375%	7.40 %	7.50 %	7.60 %	7.625%	7.70 %	7.75 %	7.80 %	7.875%	7.90 %
1	12.4792	12.4826	12.4876	12.4893	12.4960	12.5027	12.5044	12.5095	12.5128	12.5162	12.5213	12.5229
2	25.8880	25.9016	25.9220	25.9287	25.9559	25.9831	25.9899	26.0103	26.0240	26.0376	26.0581	26.0649
3	40.2958	40.3274	40.3748	40.3907	40.4541	40.5176	40.5335	40.5812	40.6130	40.6449	40.6928	40.7088
4	55.7768	55.8354	55.9234	55.9528	56.0705	56.1885	56.2181	56.3068	56.3661	56.4254	56.5145	56.5443
5	72.4111	72.5069	72.6509	72.6989	72.8916	73.0848	73.1332	73.2787	73.3759	73.4732	73.6195	73.6683
6	90.2846	90.4291	90.6465	90.7191	91.0101	91.3023	91.3756	91.5957	91.7428	91.8901	92.1117	92.1857
7	109.4895	109.6959	110.0064	110.1102	110.5263	110.9443	111.0491	111.3643	111.5750	111.7861	112.1038	112.2099
8	130.1251	130.4082	130.8342	130.9765	131.5479	132.1222	132.2663	132.6996	132.9894	133.2800	133.7174	133.8636
9	152.2980	152.6743	153.2409	153.4304	154.1909	154.9561	155.1481	155.7258	156.1124	156.5002	157.0840	157.2792
10	176.1227	176.6109	177.3465	177.5925	178.5806	179.5754	179.8251	180.5768	181.0801	181.5851	182.3457	182.6001
15	324.6646	326.0816	328.2210	328.9379	331.8241	334.7407	335.4746	337.6879	339.1730	340.6660	342.9202	343.6755
20	537.4154	540.6889	545.6432	547.3064	554.0193	560.8291	562.5469	567.7372	571.2286	574.7451	580.0676	581.8545
25	842.1300	848.8180	858.9655	862.3791	876.1908	890.2582	893.8156	904.5863	911.8497	919.1802	930.3031	934.0450
30	1278.5607	1291.2242	1310.4876	1316.9811	1343.3227	1370.2632	1377.0935	1397.8167	1411.8280	1425.9980	1447.5551	1454.8222

YEAR	8.00 %	8.10 %	8.125%	8.20 %	8.25 %	8.30 %	8.375%	8.40 %	8.50 %	8.60 %	8.625%	8.70 %
1	12.5297	12.5364	12.5381	12.5432	12.5466	12.5499	12.5550	12.5567	12.5634	12.5702	12.5719	12.5770
2	26.0922	26.1196	26.1264	26.1470	26.1607	26.1744	26.1950	26.2018	26.2293	26.2568	26.2637	26.2843
3	40.7728	40.8368	40.8529	40.9010	40.9332	40.9653	41.0137	41.0298	41.0943	41.1590	41.1752	41.2237
4	56.6634	56.7829	56.8128	56.9026	56.9626	57.0227	57.1129	57.1431	57.2637	57.3846	57.4149	57.5059
5	73.8640	74.0603	74.1095	74.2573	74.3560	74.4549	74.6035	74.6531	74.8519	75.0514	75.1013	75.2515
6	92.4825	92.7803	92.8550	93.0794	93.2293	93.3796	93.6055	93.6809	93.9835	94.2872	94.3633	94.5920
7	112.6357	113.0634	113.1706	113.4930	113.7086	113.9246	114.2496	114.3582	114.7938	115.2313	115.3410	115.6709
8	134.4502	135.0399	135.1878	135.6327	135.9303	136.2287	136.6777	136.8278	137.4301	138.0356	138.1875	138.6443
9	158.0629	158.8513	159.0491	159.6445	160.0428	160.4424	161.0440	161.2452	162.0528	162.8653	163.0691	163.6826
10	183.6220	184.6508	184.9091	185.6866	186.2071	186.7293	187.5160	187.7791	188.8360	189.9001	190.1672	190.9714
15	346.7167	349.7899	350.5632	352.8955	354.4606	356.0339	358.4094	359.2054	362.4104	365.6494	366.4644	368.9225
20	589.0668	596.3836	598.2293	603.8065	607.5583	611.3372	617.0570	618.9774	626.7287	634.5928	636.5767	642.5715
25	949.1862	964.6092	968.5096	980.3194	988.2840	996.3226	1008.5207	1012.6245	1029.2311	1046.1483	1050.4268	1063.3822
30	1484.3048	1514.4614	1522.1078	1545.3085	1560.9960	1576.8624	1601.0020	1609.1403	1642.1597	1675.9383	1684.5037	1710.4945

YEAR	8.75 %	8.80 %	8.875%	8.90 %	9.00 %	9.10 %	9.125%	9.20 %	9.25 %	9.30 %	9.375%	9.40 %
1	12.5803	12.5837	12.5888	12.5905	12.5973	12.6041	12.6057	12.6108	12.6142	12.6176	12.6227	12.6244
2	26.2981	26.3119	26.3326	26.3395	26.3671	26.3948	26.4017	26.4225	26.4364	26.4502	26.4710	26.4780
3	41.2562	41.2886	41.3374	41.3536	41.4188	41.4840	41.5003	41.5494	41.5821	41.6148	41.6640	41.6804
4	57.5666	57.6274	57.7188	57.7493	57.8714	57.9939	58.0245	58.1166	58.1781	58.2397	58.3322	58.3631
5	75.3518	75.4522	75.6032	75.6536	75.8556	76.0582	76.1090	76.2615	76.3634	76.4654	76.6188	76.6700
6	94.7449	94.8981	95.1284	95.2053	95.5137	95.8234	95.9010	96.1342	96.2901	96.4462	96.6810	96.7595
7	115.8914	116.1125	116.4450	116.5561	117.0018	117.4494	117.5617	117.8992	118.1248	118.3510	118.6912	118.8049
8	138.9499	139.2563	139.7174	139.8715	140.4899	141.1117	141.2676	141.7367	142.0505	142.3651	142.8386	142.9968
9	164.0932	164.5049	165.1249	165.3322	166.1645	167.0018	167.2119	167.8442	168.2673	168.6916	169.3306	169.5442
10	191.5097	192.0499	192.8636	193.1357	194.2289	195.3295	195.6058	196.4376	196.9945	197.5532	198.3949	198.6764
15	370.5721	372.2304	374.7342	375.5733	378.9516	382.3657	383.2249	385.8161	387.5551	389.3032	391.9428	392.8273
20	646.6044	650.6666	656.8153	658.8798	667.2130	675.6680	677.8011	684.2468	688.5832	692.9512	699.5631	701.7832
25	1072.1199	1080.9391	1094.3226	1098.8254	1117.0476	1135.6123	1140.3078	1154.5264	1164.1165	1173.7966	1188.4873	1193.4301
30	1728.0700	1745.8471	1772.8956	1782.0152	1819.0186	1856.8776	1866.4784	1895.6127	1915.3154	1935.2451	1965.5715	1975.7967

YEAR	9.50 %	9.75 %	10.00 %	10.25 %	10.50 %	10.75 %	11.00 %	12.00 %	13.00 %	14.00 %	15.00 %	16.00 %
1	12.6312	12.6482	12.6652	12.6822	12.6992	12.7163	12.7334	12.8019	12.8707	12.9399	13.0093	13.0791
2	26.5058	26.5754	26.6452	26.7151	26.7853	26.8557	26.9263	27.2105	27.4980	27.7887	28.0826	28.3798
3	41.7461	41.9109	42.0764	42.2427	42.4097	42.5775	42.7460	43.4276	44.1216	44.8280	45.5473	46.2795
4	58.4867	58.7972	59.1097	59.4241	59.7404	60.0587	60.3790	61.6801	63.0138	64.3811	65.7827	67.2196
5	76.8753	77.3912	77.9112	78.4354	78.9637	79.4963	80.0330	82.2233	84.4844	86.8186	89.2285	91.7165
6	97.0739	97.8654	98.6646	99.4715	100.2864	101.1091	101.9399	105.3450	108.8852	112.5662	116.3939	120.3744
7	119.2609	120.4100	121.5724	122.7482	123.9376	125.1407	126.3578	131.3686	136.6162	142.1122	147.8692	153.9002
8	143.6319	145.2344	146.8583	148.5040	150.1717	151.8617	153.5744	160.6584	168.1317	176.0169	184.3381	193.1205
9	170.4020	172.5691	174.7693	177.0030	179.2708	181.5732	183.9107	193.6244	203.9484	214.9233	226.5927	239.0028
10	199.8072	202.6680	205.5778	208.5374	211.5477	214.6096	217.7242	230.7279	244.6532	259.5694	275.5511	292.6786
15	396.3889	405.4598	414.7743	424.3396	434.1626	444.2509	454.6119	498.9435	548.3071	603.3068	664.6210	733.0113
20	710.7447	733.7287	757.5673	782.2941	807.9441	834.5536	862.1603	983.3708	1123.9859	1287.2718	1477.0580	1697.8345
25	1213.4341	1265.1135	1319.2734	1376.0389	1435.5415	1497.9195	1563.3182	1858.3005	2215.3794	2648.2178	3173.5502	3811.8810
30	2017.2897	2125.2919	2239.6943	2360.8928	2489.3085	2625.3889	2769.6101	3438.5207	4284.4847	5356.2129	6716.0836	8444.0172

Description: This table shows what a series of $ 1 deposits grow to in the future. The deposit is made at the beginning of a period.

Example: At 5 % a regular one dollar deposit will grow to $ 22.85 by the end of the fifth year.

YEAR	0.00 %	1.00 %	2.00 %	3.00 %	4.00 %	4.125%	4.25 %	4.375%	4.50 %	4.625%	4.75 %	4.875%
1	4.0000	4.0251	4.0503	4.0756	4.1010	4.1042	4.1074	4.1106	4.1138	4.1170	4.1202	4.1234
2	8.0000	8.0905	8.1821	8.2748	8.3685	8.3803	8.3921	8.4040	8.4158	8.4277	8.4396	8.4515
3	12.0000	12.1968	12.3972	12.6014	12.8093	12.8356	12.8619	12.8883	12.9147	12.9412	12.9678	12.9944
4	16.0000	16.3443	16.6973	17.0593	17.4304	17.4775	17.5247	17.5721	17.6196	17.6672	17.7150	17.7630
5	20.0000	20.5334	21.0840	21.6524	22.2392	22.3139	22.3888	22.4641	22.5397	22.6156	22.6917	22.7682
6	24.0000	24.7646	25.5591	26.3849	27.2432	27.3528	27.4630	27.5737	27.6850	27.7968	27.9091	28.0220
7	28.0000	29.0382	30.1244	31.2609	32.4504	32.6029	32.7563	32.9106	33.0658	33.2218	33.3788	33.5366
8	32.0000	33.3547	34.7817	36.2849	37.8690	38.0729	38.2782	38.4848	38.6928	38.9022	39.1129	39.3250
9	36.0000	37.7146	39.5328	41.4614	43.5076	43.7721	44.0385	44.3069	44.5774	44.8498	45.1243	45.4008
10	40.0000	42.1182	44.3796	46.7948	49.3752	49.7100	50.0476	50.3880	50.7312	51.0773	51.4263	51.7783
15	60.0000	64.8083	70.1189	75.9898	82.4864	83.3460	84.2166	85.0985	85.9918	86.8966	87.8130	88.7413
20	80.0000	88.6603	98.5581	109.8906	122.8882	124.6430	126.4284	128.2452	130.0939	131.9752	133.8896	135.8377
25	100.0000	113.7336	129.9804	149.2556	172.1862	175.3459	178.5761	181.8784	185.2547	188.7068	192.2364	195.8454
30	120.0000	140.0908	164.6987	194.9656	232.3391	237.5971	242.9982	248.5468	254.2472	260.1037	266.1210	272.3039

YEAR	5.00 %	5.10 %	5.125%	5.20 %	5.25 %	5.30 %	5.375%	5.40 %	5.50 %	5.60 %	5.625%	5.70 %
1	4.1266	4.1291	4.1298	4.1317	4.1330	4.1343	4.1362	4.1368	4.1394	4.1420	4.1426	4.1445
2	8.4634	8.4729	8.4753	8.4825	8.4873	8.4920	8.4992	8.5016	8.5112	8.5208	8.5232	8.5304
3	13.0211	13.0425	13.0479	13.0639	13.0747	13.0854	13.1015	13.1069	13.1285	13.1501	13.1555	13.1717
4	17.8111	17.8496	17.8593	17.8883	17.9077	17.9271	17.9563	17.9660	18.0050	18.0441	18.0538	18.0832
5	22.8450	22.9067	22.9221	22.9685	22.9995	23.0306	23.0772	23.0928	23.1553	23.2179	23.2336	23.2808
6	28.1354	28.2266	28.2494	28.3181	28.3640	28.4099	28.4791	28.5021	28.5947	28.6877	28.7109	28.7809
7	33.6954	33.8230	33.8550	33.9513	34.0156	34.0801	34.1771	34.2095	34.3396	34.4702	34.5029	34.6014
8	39.5386	39.7104	39.7535	39.8832	39.9699	40.0568	40.1877	40.2314	40.4070	40.5834	40.6277	40.7608
9	45.6794	45.9038	45.9602	46.1296	46.2430	46.3567	46.5279	46.5852	46.8150	47.0462	47.1042	47.2788
10	52.1332	52.4192	52.4911	52.7072	52.8519	52.9971	53.2158	53.2890	53.5828	53.8786	53.9529	54.1764
15	89.6817	90.4427	90.6342	91.2117	91.5991	91.9886	92.5765	92.7735	93.5667	94.3680	94.5697	95.1778
20	137.8203	139.4316	139.8379	141.0656	141.8913	142.7228	143.9811	144.4035	146.1081	147.8368	148.2729	149.5902
25	199.5357	202.5479	203.3094	205.6145	207.1685	208.7365	211.1150	211.9150	215.1510	218.4458	219.2788	221.8004
30	278.6573	283.8660	285.1861	289.1897	291.8955	294.6311	298.7910	300.1929	305.8780	311.6893	313.1622	317.6298

YEAR	5.75 %	5.80 %	5.875%	5.90 %	6.00 %	6.10 %	6.125%	6.20 %	6.25 %	6.30 %	6.375%	6.40 %
1	4.1458	4.1471	4.1490	4.1497	4.1523	4.1548	4.1555	4.1574	4.1587	4.1600	4.1619	4.1626
2	8.5352	8.5401	8.5473	8.5497	8.5593	8.5690	8.5714	8.5787	8.5835	8.5883	8.5956	8.5980
3	13.1825	13.1934	13.2096	13.2151	13.2368	13.2586	13.2641	13.2804	13.2914	13.3023	13.3187	13.3242
4	18.1029	18.1225	18.1520	18.1619	18.2014	18.2409	18.2508	18.2806	18.3005	18.3204	18.3503	18.3602
5	23.3123	23.3438	23.3912	23.4071	23.4705	23.5342	23.5501	23.5980	23.6301	23.6621	23.7103	23.7264
6	28.8277	28.8746	28.9451	28.9686	29.0630	29.1578	29.1815	29.2529	29.3006	29.3484	29.4203	29.4443
7	34.6672	34.7332	34.8325	34.8657	34.9987	35.1324	35.1659	35.2666	35.3340	35.4015	35.5031	35.5370
8	40.8498	40.9391	41.0735	41.1184	41.2986	41.4798	41.5252	41.6619	41.7534	41.8450	41.9830	42.0291
9	47.3957	47.5128	47.6893	47.7483	47.9851	48.2234	48.2832	48.4631	48.5835	48.7042	48.8860	48.9468
10	54.3261	54.4762	54.7024	54.7781	55.0819	55.3878	55.4646	55.6958	55.8506	56.0058	56.2398	56.3180
15	95.5858	95.9959	96.6151	96.8226	97.6579	98.5019	98.7143	99.3547	99.7845	100.2165	100.8687	101.0873
20	150.4762	151.3685	152.7188	153.1721	155.0015	156.8570	157.3250	158.7390	159.6901	160.6480	162.0976	162.5843
25	223.5005	225.2160	227.8185	228.6938	232.2351	235.8410	236.7527	239.5128	241.3738	243.2518	246.1009	247.0593
30	320.6495	323.7026	328.3458	329.9107	336.2575	342.7462	344.3909	349.3802	352.7527	356.1629	361.3496	363.0979

YEAR	6.50 %	6.60 %	6.625%	6.70 %	6.75 %	6.80 %	6.875%	6.90 %	7.00 %	7.10 %	7.125%	7.20 %
1	4.1652	4.1677	4.1684	4.1703	4.1716	4.1729	4.1749	4.1755	4.1781	4.1807	4.1813	4.1833
2	8.6077	8.6174	8.6199	8.6272	8.6320	8.6369	8.6442	8.6467	8.6564	8.6662	8.6686	8.6760
3	13.3462	13.3682	13.3737	13.3902	13.4012	13.4123	13.4289	13.4344	13.4565	13.4787	13.4843	13.5010
4	18.4002	18.4403	18.4503	18.4805	18.5006	18.5207	18.5510	18.5611	18.6016	18.6422	18.6524	18.6829
5	23.7909	23.8556	23.8718	23.9205	23.9530	23.9856	24.0345	24.0509	24.1164	24.1821	24.1986	24.2481
6	29.5405	29.6372	29.6614	29.7342	29.7828	29.8316	29.9048	29.9293	30.0275	30.1260	30.1507	30.2249
7	35.6731	35.8099	35.8442	35.9473	36.0162	36.0853	36.1893	36.2240	36.3633	36.5032	36.5383	36.6438
8	42.2142	42.4003	42.4469	42.5873	42.6812	42.7753	42.9170	42.9644	43.1544	43.3455	43.3934	43.5374
9	49.1909	49.4364	49.4981	49.6835	49.8075	49.9320	50.1194	50.1820	50.4335	50.6866	50.7501	50.9412
10	56.6323	56.9486	57.0281	57.2672	57.4272	57.5878	57.8298	57.9107	58.2357	58.5630	58.6451	58.8924
15	101.9671	102.8563	103.0800	103.7547	104.2075	104.6626	105.3497	105.5800	106.5070	107.4438	107.6796	108.3905
20	164.5483	166.5406	167.0431	168.5614	169.5828	170.6114	172.1682	172.6908	174.8002	176.9400	177.4798	179.1108
25	250.9366	254.8852	255.8836	258.9064	260.9446	263.0016	266.1225	267.1723	271.4199	275.7460	276.8400	280.1522
30	370.1888	377.4393	379.2773	384.8533	388.6228	392.4346	398.2328	400.1873	408.1154	416.2231	418.2786	424.5148

SAVINGS GROWTH

Description: This table shows what a series of $ 1 deposits grow to in the future. The deposit is made at the beginning of a period.

Example: At 8 % a regular one dollar deposit will grow to $ 24.78 by the end of the fifth year.

YEAR	7.25 %	7.30 %	7.375%	7.40 %	7.50 %	7.60 %	7.625%	7.70 %	7.75 %	7.80 %	7.875%	7.90 %
1	4.1846	4.1859	4.1878	4.1885	4.1910	4.1936	4.1943	4.1962	4.1975	4.1988	4.2008	4.2014
2	8.6809	8.6858	8.6931	8.6956	8.7054	8.7152	8.7177	8.7250	8.7300	8.7349	8.7423	8.7448
3	13.5121	13.5232	13.5400	13.5456	13.5679	13.5903	13.5959	13.6128	13.6240	13.6352	13.6521	13.6578
4	18.7033	18.7237	18.7543	18.7646	18.8055	18.8466	18.8569	18.8878	18.9085	18.9291	18.9602	18.9706
5	24.2811	24.3142	24.3640	24.3806	24.4472	24.5140	24.5307	24.5810	24.6146	24.6482	24.6988	24.7157
6	30.2745	30.3242	30.3989	30.4239	30.5240	30.6245	30.6496	30.7253	30.7759	30.8266	30.9028	30.9282
7	36.7144	36.7851	36.8914	36.9270	37.0695	37.2127	37.2486	37.3566	37.4288	37.5011	37.6100	37.6464
8	43.6340	43.7307	43.8762	43.9248	44.1200	44.3162	44.3654	44.5134	44.6125	44.7118	44.8612	44.9111
9	51.0691	51.1973	51.3904	51.4550	51.7142	51.9751	52.0405	52.2375	52.3693	52.5014	52.7005	52.7670
10	59.0580	59.2241	59.4744	59.5581	59.8943	60.2328	60.3178	60.5736	60.7449	60.9167	61.1756	61.2622
15	108.8676	109.3472	110.0712	110.3139	111.2908	112.2781	112.5265	113.2757	113.7785	114.2840	115.0471	115.3029
20	180.2079	181.3128	182.9853	183.5468	185.8131	188.1122	188.6922	190.4447	191.6236	192.8110	194.6083	195.2117
25	282.3857	284.6399	288.0602	289.2108	293.8665	298.6087	299.8079	303.4391	305.8879	308.3594	312.1097	313.3714
30	428.7310	432.9949	439.4813	441.6678	450.5383	459.6110	461.9113	468.8908	473.6099	478.3827	485.6439	488.0918

YEAR	8.00 %	8.10 %	8.125%	8.20 %	8.25 %	8.30 %	8.375%	8.40 %	8.50 %	8.60 %	8.625%	8.70 %
1	4.2040	4.2066	4.2073	4.2092	4.2105	4.2119	4.2138	4.2145	4.2171	4.2197	4.2203	4.2223
2	8.7546	8.7645	8.7670	8.7744	8.7794	8.7843	8.7918	8.7942	8.8042	8.8141	8.8166	8.8241
3	13.6803	13.7029	13.7086	13.7256	13.7369	13.7483	13.7653	13.7710	13.7938	13.8166	13.8223	13.8394
4	19.0121	19.0537	19.0641	19.0954	19.1163	19.1372	19.1687	19.1792	19.2212	19.2634	19.2739	19.3056
5	24.7833	24.8512	24.8682	24.9193	24.9534	24.9876	25.0390	25.0561	25.1249	25.1939	25.2112	25.2631
6	31.0303	31.1328	31.1584	31.2356	31.2872	31.3389	31.4166	31.4426	31.5466	31.6511	31.6773	31.7560
7	37.7922	37.9388	37.9755	38.0860	38.1599	38.2339	38.3453	38.3825	38.5318	38.6818	38.7194	38.8325
8	45.1116	45.3131	45.3636	45.5157	45.6174	45.7194	45.8728	45.9241	46.1300	46.3370	46.3889	46.5450
9	53.0343	53.3031	53.3706	53.5736	53.7094	53.8457	54.0508	54.1194	54.3949	54.6720	54.7415	54.9508
10	61.6100	61.9602	62.0481	62.3128	62.4900	62.6677	62.9356	63.0251	63.3850	63.7473	63.8382	64.1120
15	116.3326	117.3732	117.6350	118.4248	118.9548	119.4876	120.2921	120.5617	121.6472	122.7443	123.0204	123.8530
20	197.6474	200.1185	200.7419	202.6256	203.8929	205.1693	207.1014	207.7501	210.3687	213.0255	213.6957	215.7212
25	318.4770	323.6778	324.9932	328.9760	331.6621	334.3733	338.4875	339.8717	345.4732	351.1799	352.6232	356.9938
30	498.0233	508.1826	510.7587	518.5752	523.8608	529.2067	537.3406	540.0829	551.2097	562.5932	565.4798	574.2394

YEAR	8.75 %	8.80 %	8.875%	8.90 %	9.00 %	9.10 %	9.125%	9.20 %	9.25 %	9.30 %	9.375%	9.40 %
1	4.2236	4.2249	4.2269	4.2275	4.2301	4.2327	4.2334	4.2354	4.2367	4.2380	4.2399	4.2406
2	8.8290	8.8340	8.8415	8.8440	8.8540	8.8640	8.8665	8.8740	8.8790	8.8840	8.8916	8.8941
3	13.8509	13.8623	13.8795	13.8853	13.9083	13.9313	13.9371	13.9544	13.9659	13.9775	13.9948	14.0006
4	19.3268	19.3480	19.3798	19.3904	19.4330	19.4757	19.4864	19.5185	19.5399	19.5614	19.5936	19.6044
5	25.2978	25.3325	25.3847	25.4022	25.4720	25.5421	25.5597	25.6125	25.6477	25.6830	25.7361	25.7538
6	31.8086	31.8613	31.9406	31.9670	32.0732	32.1797	32.2064	32.2867	32.3403	32.3941	32.4749	32.5019
7	38.9081	38.9839	39.0979	39.1360	39.2888	39.4423	39.4808	39.5965	39.6739	39.7514	39.8681	39.9071
8	46.6495	46.7542	46.9119	46.9646	47.1760	47.3886	47.4419	47.6023	47.7096	47.8172	47.9791	48.0332
9	55.0908	55.2313	55.4428	55.5135	55.7974	56.0831	56.1548	56.3705	56.5149	56.6597	56.8777	56.9506
10	64.2954	64.4793	64.7564	64.8491	65.2214	65.5962	65.6903	65.9736	66.1633	66.3536	66.6403	66.7362
15	124.4118	124.9735	125.8218	126.1060	127.2506	128.4073	128.6985	129.5765	130.1657	130.7581	131.6526	131.9523
20	217.0838	218.4564	220.5341	221.2317	224.0477	226.9051	227.6260	229.8045	231.2701	232.7465	234.9815	235.7319
25	359.9417	362.9171	367.4327	368.9520	375.1005	381.3651	382.9497	387.7480	390.9846	394.2516	399.2098	400.8782
30	580.1631	586.1550	595.2722	598.3462	610.8199	623.5828	626.8196	636.6421	643.2850	650.0048	660.2304	663.6784

YEAR	9.50 %	9.75 %	10.00 %	10.25 %	10.50 %	10.75 %	11.00 %	12.00 %	13.00 %	14.00 %	15.00 %	16.00 %
1	4.2432	4.2498	4.2563	4.2629	4.2695	4.2761	4.2827	4.3091	4.3357	4.3625	4.3893	4.4163
2	8.9041	8.9293	8.9545	8.9798	9.0052	9.0307	9.0562	9.1591	9.2632	9.3685	9.4750	9.5828
3	14.0238	14.0820	14.1404	14.1992	14.2581	14.3174	14.3769	14.6178	14.8631	15.1130	15.3676	15.6268
4	19.6475	19.7558	19.8647	19.9744	20.0847	20.1957	20.3075	20.7616	21.2273	21.7050	22.1950	22.6975
5	25.8248	26.0033	26.1833	26.3647	26.5476	26.7320	26.9178	27.6765	28.4601	29.2695	30.1055	30.9692
6	32.6101	32.8826	33.1578	33.4356	33.7163	33.9997	34.2858	35.4593	36.6799	37.9499	39.2711	40.6459
7	40.0634	40.4576	40.8563	41.2597	41.6678	42.0807	42.4984	44.2189	46.0216	47.9108	49.8908	51.9663
8	48.2504	48.7985	49.3540	49.9171	50.4877	51.0661	51.6523	54.0778	56.6382	59.3412	62.1954	65.2095
9	57.2433	57.9829	58.7339	59.4965	60.2708	61.0570	61.8554	65.1742	68.7037	72.4579	76.4520	80.7022
10	67.1215	68.0961	69.0876	70.0962	71.1223	72.1661	73.2280	77.6633	82.4158	87.5095	92.9705	98.8265
15	133.1594	136.2338	139.3914	142.6344	145.9654	149.3869	152.9014	167.9450	184.7071	203.3950	224.2420	247.5103
20	238.7612	246.5316	254.5923	262.9547	271.6307	280.6327	289.9737	331.0039	378.6347	433.9825	498.3570	573.2948
25	407.6303	425.0760	443.3624	462.5317	482.6288	503.7007	525.7969	625.5064	746.2901	892.8031	1070.7507	1287.1287
30	677.6703	714.0946	752.6841	793.5734	836.9051	882.8314	931.5137	1157.4106	1443.3052	1805.7591	2265.9957	2851.2266

SAVINGS GROWTH

Description: This table shows what a series of $ 1 deposits grow to in the future. The deposit is made at the beginning of a period.

Example: At 5 % a regular one dollar deposit will grow to $ 11.49 by the end of the fifth year.

YEAR	0.00 %	1.00 %	2.00 %	3.00 %	4.00 %	4.125%	4.25 %	4.375%	4.50 %	4.625%	4.75 %	4.875%
1	2.0000	2.0150	2.0302	2.0454	2.0607	2.0626	2.0645	2.0665	2.0684	2.0703	2.0722	2.0742
2	4.0000	4.0503	4.1013	4.1528	4.2051	4.2117	4.2182	4.2248	4.2314	4.2381	4.2447	4.2513
3	6.0000	6.1060	6.2141	6.3242	6.4365	6.4507	6.4649	6.4792	6.4935	6.5078	6.5222	6.5366
4	8.0000	8.1823	8.3695	8.5615	8.7586	8.7836	8.8087	8.8338	8.8591	8.8844	8.9098	8.9353
5	10.0000	10.2795	10.5683	10.8666	11.1749	11.2142	11.2536	11.2931	11.3329	11.3728	11.4128	11.4531
6	12.0000	12.3977	12.8114	13.2417	13.6894	13.7466	13.8041	13.8619	13.9199	13.9783	14.0369	14.0959
7	14.0000	14.5372	15.0998	15.6889	16.3059	16.3851	16.4647	16.5448	16.6254	16.7064	16.7879	16.8699
8	16.0000	16.6982	17.4342	18.2103	19.0287	19.1341	19.2402	19.3471	19.4546	19.5629	19.6719	19.7816
9	18.0000	18.8808	19.8157	20.8081	21.8621	21.9983	22.1356	22.2740	22.4133	22.5538	22.6953	22.8379
10	20.0000	21.0854	22.2452	23.4848	24.8104	24.9825	25.1560	25.3310	25.5075	25.6855	25.8649	26.0459
15	30.0000	32.4446	35.1469	38.1369	41.4484	41.8868	42.3308	42.7807	43.2364	43.6980	44.1657	44.6394
20	40.0000	44.3855	49.4019	55.1506	61.7498	62.6412	63.5483	64.4714	65.4108	66.3669	67.3399	68.3302
25	50.0000	56.9378	65.1523	74.9066	86.5214	88.1227	89.7599	91.4338	93.1455	94.8957	96.6855	98.5158
30	60.0000	70.1328	82.5547	97.8470	116.7475	119.4079	122.1412	124.9493	127.8346	130.7994	133.8459	136.9766

YEAR	5.00 %	5.10 %	5.125%	5.20 %	5.25 %	5.30 %	5.375%	5.40 %	5.50 %	5.60 %	5.625%	5.70 %
1	2.0761	2.0776	2.0780	2.0792	2.0800	2.0807	2.0819	2.0823	2.0838	2.0854	2.0858	2.0869
2	4.2580	4.2633	4.2646	4.2686	4.2713	4.2740	4.2780	4.2793	4.2847	4.2900	4.2914	4.2954
3	6.5510	6.5626	6.5655	6.5742	6.5800	6.5858	6.5945	6.5974	6.6091	6.6207	6.6237	6.6324
4	8.9608	8.9814	8.9865	9.0019	9.0122	9.0226	9.0381	9.0432	9.0640	9.0847	9.0899	9.1056
5	11.4935	11.5259	11.5340	11.5584	11.5747	11.5911	11.6156	11.6238	11.6567	11.6897	11.6979	11.7227
6	14.1551	14.2027	14.2146	14.2505	14.2744	14.2985	14.3346	14.3466	14.3950	14.4435	14.4557	14.4923
7	16.9523	17.0186	17.0353	17.0853	17.1187	17.1522	17.2026	17.2195	17.2870	17.3549	17.3719	17.4231
8	19.8921	19.9810	20.0033	20.0704	20.1152	20.1602	20.2280	20.2506	20.3414	20.4328	20.4557	20.5246
9	22.9816	23.0973	23.1264	23.2138	23.2722	23.3309	23.4192	23.4488	23.5673	23.6866	23.7166	23.8067
10	26.2285	26.3756	26.4126	26.5238	26.5983	26.6730	26.7855	26.8231	26.9743	27.1266	27.1648	27.2799
15	45.1194	45.5078	45.6056	45.9004	46.0982	46.2970	46.5972	46.6978	47.1028	47.5120	47.6150	47.9255
20	69.3382	70.1574	70.3640	70.9883	71.4082	71.8311	72.4710	72.6859	73.5529	74.4323	74.6541	75.3242
25	100.3875	101.9155	102.3018	103.4712	104.2596	105.0551	106.2620	106.6679	108.3100	109.9821	110.4049	111.6848
30	140.1940	142.8321	143.5007	145.5287	146.8993	148.2851	150.3926	151.1028	153.9833	156.9280	157.6744	159.9385

YEAR	5.75 %	5.80 %	5.875%	5.90 %	6.00 %	6.10 %	6.125%	6.20 %	6.25 %	6.30 %	6.375%	6.40 %
1	2.0877	2.0885	2.0896	2.0900	2.0916	2.0931	2.0935	2.0947	2.0955	2.0963	2.0974	2.0978
2	4.2981	4.3008	4.3048	4.3061	4.3115	4.3169	4.3183	4.3223	4.3250	4.3277	4.3318	4.3331
3	6.6383	6.6442	6.6530	6.6559	6.6677	6.6795	6.6824	6.6913	6.6972	6.7031	6.7120	6.7150
4	9.1160	9.1265	9.1422	9.1474	9.1684	9.1895	9.1948	9.2106	9.2212	9.2318	9.2477	9.2530
5	11.7393	11.7559	11.7809	11.7892	11.8226	11.8561	11.8645	11.8898	11.9066	11.9235	11.9489	11.9573
6	14.5167	14.5412	14.5781	14.5904	14.6397	14.6892	14.7016	14.7389	14.7639	14.7889	14.8264	14.8390
7	17.4573	17.4916	17.5432	17.5605	17.6296	17.6991	17.7165	17.7689	17.8039	17.8391	17.8919	17.9095
8	20.5707	20.6169	20.6865	20.7097	20.8030	20.8968	20.9204	20.9912	21.0385	21.0860	21.1575	21.1813
9	23.8669	23.9274	24.0185	24.0489	24.1712	24.2941	24.3250	24.4179	24.4800	24.5424	24.6363	24.6676
10	27.3569	27.4342	27.5506	27.5895	27.7460	27.9035	27.9430	28.0621	28.1418	28.2217	28.3422	28.3825
15	48.1339	48.3434	48.6597	48.7657	49.1924	49.6236	49.7322	50.0594	50.2790	50.4998	50.8331	50.9448
20	75.7750	76.2290	76.9161	77.1468	78.0777	79.0220	79.2602	79.9799	80.4640	80.9516	81.6896	81.9373
25	112.5477	113.4185	114.7397	115.1841	116.9819	118.8128	119.2758	120.6774	121.6225	122.5762	124.0233	124.5100
30	161.4688	163.0163	165.3698	166.1630	169.3803	172.6699	173.5038	176.0335	177.7436	179.4729	182.1032	182.9898

YEAR	6.50 %	6.60 %	6.625%	6.70 %	6.75 %	6.80 %	6.875%	6.90 %	7.00 %	7.10 %	7.125%	7.20 %
1	2.0994	2.1009	2.1013	2.1025	2.1033	2.1040	2.1052	2.1056	2.1072	2.1087	2.1091	2.1103
2	4.3386	4.3440	4.3453	4.3494	4.3521	4.3549	4.3589	4.3603	4.3657	4.3712	4.3726	4.3767
3	6.7269	6.7388	6.7418	6.7507	6.7567	6.7627	6.7716	6.7746	6.7866	6.7987	6.8017	6.8107
4	9.2743	9.2956	9.3009	9.3170	9.3277	9.3384	9.3545	9.3599	9.3815	9.4031	9.4085	9.4248
5	11.9913	12.0254	12.0339	12.0596	12.0767	12.0939	12.1197	12.1283	12.1628	12.1974	12.2061	12.2322
6	14.8893	14.9398	14.9525	14.9906	15.0160	15.0415	15.0798	15.0926	15.1440	15.1955	15.2084	15.2473
7	17.9803	18.0515	18.0693	18.1229	18.1588	18.1947	18.2488	18.2669	18.3394	18.4122	18.4304	18.4853
8	21.2772	21.3736	21.3978	21.4705	21.5191	21.5679	21.6413	21.6659	21.7644	21.8634	21.8882	21.9629
9	24.7937	24.9205	24.9523	25.0481	25.1121	25.1764	25.2732	25.3056	25.4355	25.5662	25.5990	25.6978
10	28.5443	28.7073	28.7482	28.8714	28.9539	29.0366	29.1613	29.2029	29.3704	29.5391	29.5814	29.7089
15	51.3945	51.8489	51.9633	52.3082	52.5397	52.7724	53.1237	53.2414	53.7154	54.1945	54.3151	54.6787
20	82.9373	83.9516	84.2075	84.9807	85.5008	86.0247	86.8176	87.0838	88.1582	89.2483	89.5233	90.3542
25	126.4795	128.4854	128.9926	130.5284	131.5640	132.6091	134.1950	134.7285	136.8871	139.0859	139.6419	141.3255
30	186.5862	190.2638	191.1962	194.0248	195.9372	197.8711	200.8130	201.8047	205.8277	209.9423	210.9855	214.1507

Description: This table shows what a series of $ 1 deposits grow to in the future. The deposit is made at the beginning of a period.

Example: At 8 % a regular one dollar deposit will grow to $ 12.51 by the end of the fifth year.

YEAR	7.25 %	7.30 %	7.375%	7.40 %	7.50 %	7.60 %	7.625%	7.70 %	7.75 %	7.80 %	7.875%	7.90 %
1	2.1111	2.1119	2.1130	2.1134	2.1150	2.1166	2.1169	2.1181	2.1189	2.1197	2.1209	2.1213
2	4.3794	4.3821	4.3863	4.3876	4.3931	4.3986	4.4000	4.4041	4.4069	4.4096	4.4138	4.4151
3	6.8167	6.8228	6.8318	6.8349	6.8470	6.8591	6.8621	6.8713	6.8774	6.8835	6.8926	6.8957
4	9.4356	9.4465	9.4628	9.4683	9.4901	9.5120	9.5175	9.5340	9.5450	9.5560	9.5725	9.5780
5	12.2496	12.2670	12.2933	12.3020	12.3371	12.3723	12.3812	12.4077	12.4254	12.4431	12.4698	12.4787
6	15.2732	15.2992	15.3383	15.3514	15.4037	15.4563	15.4695	15.5091	15.5356	15.5621	15.6020	15.6153
7	18.5221	18.5589	18.6142	18.6327	18.7069	18.7815	18.8002	18.8564	18.8940	18.9316	18.9883	19.0072
8	22.0129	22.0630	22.1385	22.1637	22.2649	22.3666	22.3921	22.4689	22.5202	22.5717	22.6492	22.6751
9	25.7639	25.8301	25.9299	25.9633	26.0973	26.2321	26.2659	26.3677	26.4359	26.5042	26.6071	26.6415
10	29.7942	29.8798	30.0088	30.0520	30.2253	30.3998	30.4436	30.5755	30.6639	30.7525	30.8860	30.9306
15	54.9227	55.1680	55.5383	55.6625	56.1622	56.6673	56.7944	57.1778	57.4351	57.6937	58.0843	58.2152
20	90.9132	91.4762	92.3284	92.6145	93.7694	94.9412	95.2368	96.1301	96.7311	97.3364	98.2527	98.5603
25	142.4609	143.6069	145.3457	145.9307	148.2979	150.7094	151.3193	153.1659	154.4114	155.6684	157.5760	158.2178
30	216.2908	218.4551	221.7479	222.8579	227.3614	231.9681	233.1362	236.6804	239.0770	241.5009	245.1889	246.4323

YEAR	8.00 %	8.10 %	8.125%	8.20 %	8.25 %	8.30 %	8.375%	8.40 %	8.50 %	8.60 %	8.625%	8.70 %
1	2.1228	2.1244	2.1248	2.1260	2.1268	2.1275	2.1287	2.1291	2.1307	2.1323	2.1327	2.1339
2	4.4207	4.4262	4.4276	4.4317	4.4345	4.4373	4.4414	4.4428	4.4484	4.4539	4.4553	4.4595
3	6.9079	6.9201	6.9232	6.9324	6.9386	6.9447	6.9540	6.9570	6.9694	6.9818	6.9849	6.9942
4	9.6002	9.6223	9.6279	9.6446	9.6557	9.6669	9.6836	9.6892	9.7116	9.7341	9.7397	9.7567
5	12.5143	12.5501	12.5591	12.5861	12.6041	12.6221	12.6492	12.6583	12.6945	12.7309	12.7400	12.7674
6	15.6688	15.7224	15.7359	15.7763	15.8033	15.8303	15.8710	15.8846	15.9391	15.9939	16.0076	16.0488
7	19.0832	19.1595	19.1787	19.2362	19.2747	19.3133	19.3713	19.3907	19.4685	19.5466	19.5662	19.6251
8	22.7791	22.8836	22.9099	22.9887	23.0415	23.0944	23.1740	23.2007	23.3075	23.4149	23.4418	23.5229
9	26.7797	26.9187	26.9536	27.0586	27.1288	27.1993	27.3054	27.3409	27.4834	27.6267	27.6627	27.7710
10	31.1100	31.2906	31.3360	31.4725	31.5639	31.6556	31.7938	31.8400	32.0257	32.2126	32.2596	32.4009
15	58.7422	59.2748	59.4089	59.8132	60.0845	60.3573	60.7692	60.9072	61.4631	62.0249	62.1663	62.5927
20	99.8022	101.0622	101.3801	102.3407	102.9870	103.6380	104.6235	104.9544	106.2902	107.6456	107.9875	109.0210
25	160.8151	163.4611	164.1304	166.1569	167.5237	168.9034	170.0972	171.7016	174.5526	177.4575	178.1922	180.4172
30	251.4771	256.6382	257.9470	261.9183	264.6040	267.3204	271.4538	272.8474	278.5024	284.2884	285.7557	290.2086

YEAR	8.75 %	8.80 %	8.875%	8.90 %	9.00 %	9.10 %	9.125%	9.20 %	9.25 %	9.30 %	9.375%	9.40 %
1	2.1346	2.1354	2.1366	2.1370	2.1386	2.1402	2.1406	2.1418	2.1425	2.1433	2.1445	2.1449
2	4.4623	4.4651	4.4693	4.4707	4.4762	4.4818	4.4832	4.4874	4.4903	4.4931	4.4973	4.4987
3	7.0004	7.0066	7.0159	7.0190	7.0315	7.0440	7.0471	7.0565	7.0628	7.0690	7.0785	7.0816
4	9.7679	9.7792	9.7962	9.8019	9.8246	9.8474	9.8531	9.8702	9.8816	9.8931	9.9103	9.9160
5	12.7857	12.8041	12.8316	12.8408	12.8777	12.9147	12.9240	12.9518	12.9704	12.9891	13.0171	13.0264
6	16.0764	16.1040	16.1455	16.1594	16.2150	16.2708	16.2848	16.3269	16.3550	16.3832	16.4255	16.4397
7	19.6645	19.7040	19.7634	19.7833	19.8629	19.9429	19.9630	20.0233	20.0637	20.1041	20.1649	20.1853
8	23.5771	23.6315	23.7133	23.7406	23.8504	23.9608	23.9885	24.0718	24.1275	24.1833	24.2674	24.2955
9	27.8434	27.9161	28.0256	28.0621	28.2091	28.3569	28.3940	28.5057	28.5804	28.6554	28.7683	28.8060
10	32.4955	32.5904	32.7334	32.7813	32.9735	33.1670	33.2156	33.3618	33.4598	33.5581	33.7061	33.7556
15	62.8789	63.1666	63.6011	63.7468	64.3331	64.9258	65.0749	65.5248	65.8268	66.1303	66.5888	66.7424
20	109.7162	110.4166	111.4769	111.8329	113.2701	114.7286	115.0965	116.2086	116.9568	117.7106	118.8516	119.2348
25	181.9180	183.4329	185.7321	186.5057	189.6367	192.8272	193.6342	196.0782	197.7268	199.3910	201.9169	202.7669
30	293.2200	296.2663	300.9018	302.4648	308.8076	315.2982	316.9443	321.9401	325.3190	328.7371	333.9389	335.6930

YEAR	9.50 %	9.75 %	10.00 %	10.25 %	10.50 %	10.75 %	11.00 %	12.00 %	13.00 %	14.00 %	15.00 %	16.00 %
1	2.1465	2.1505	2.1544	2.1584	2.1624	2.1664	2.1704	2.1864	2.2025	2.2187	2.2351	2.2515
2	4.5043	4.5184	4.5325	4.5467	4.5609	4.5752	4.5895	4.6472	4.7057	4.7648	4.8247	4.8853
3	7.0942	7.1258	7.1575	7.1894	7.2214	7.2536	7.2860	7.4169	7.5504	7.6865	7.8252	7.9666
4	9.9390	9.9968	10.0550	10.1135	10.1725	10.2318	10.2915	10.5342	10.7834	11.0392	11.3017	11.5713
5	13.0639	13.1582	13.2533	13.3491	13.4458	13.5432	13.6415	14.0427	14.4576	14.8864	15.3298	15.7882
6	16.4964	16.6393	16.7836	16.9293	17.0765	17.2252	17.3754	17.9916	18.6332	19.3013	19.9970	20.7214
7	20.2668	20.4724	20.6803	20.8908	21.1038	21.3193	21.5374	22.4362	23.3787	24.3674	25.4045	26.4926
8	24.4083	24.6930	24.9817	25.2743	25.5709	25.8716	26.1764	27.4385	28.7719	30.1809	31.6700	33.2441
9	28.9576	29.3406	29.7295	30.1246	30.5258	30.9333	31.3472	33.0687	34.9011	36.8520	38.9296	41.1423
10	33.9546	34.4580	34.9703	35.4915	36.0218	36.5615	37.1106	39.4055	41.8668	44.5073	47.3408	50.3822
15	67.3610	68.9371	70.5561	72.2194	73.9282	75.6838	77.4876	85.2135	93.8303	103.4466	114.1846	126.1817
20	120.7816	124.7500	128.8677	133.1406	137.5748	142.1769	146.9534	167.9478	192.3446	220.7233	253.7646	292.2679
25	206.2070	215.0971	224.4180	234.1915	244.4406	255.1897	266.4643	317.3752	379.1117	454.0792	545.2289	656.1832
30	342.8116	361.3464	380.9883	401.8062	423.8736	447.2686	472.0741	587.2576	733.1919	918.4082	1153.8506	1453.5665

SAVINGS GROWTH

Description: This table shows what a series of $ 1 deposits grow to in the future. The deposit is made at the beginning of a period.

Example: At 5 % a regular one dollar deposit will grow to $ 5.82 by the end of the fifth year.

YEAR	0.00 %	1.00 %	2.00 %	3.00 %	4.00 %	4.125%	4.25 %	4.375%	4.50 %	4.625%	4.75 %	4.875%
1	1.0000	1.0100	1.0202	1.0303	1.0406	1.0419	1.0432	1.0445	1.0458	1.0471	1.0484	1.0496
2	2.0000	2.0302	2.0609	2.0919	2.1235	2.1274	2.1314	2.1354	2.1394	2.1434	2.1474	2.1514
3	3.0000	3.0606	3.1225	3.1857	3.2503	3.2584	3.2666	3.2748	3.2831	3.2913	3.2996	3.3079
4	4.0000	4.1014	4.2056	4.3127	4.4229	4.4368	4.4509	4.4650	4.4791	4.4933	4.5075	4.5218
5	5.0000	5.1526	5.3105	5.4739	5.6431	5.6646	5.6863	5.7080	5.7298	5.7518	5.7738	5.7959
6	6.0000	6.2144	6.4377	6.6703	6.9128	6.9438	6.9750	7.0063	7.0378	7.0695	7.1013	7.1333
7	7.0000	7.2868	7.5875	7.9030	8.2341	8.2766	8.3194	8.3624	8.4057	8.4492	8.4930	8.5371
8	8.0000	8.3699	8.7606	9.1732	9.6090	9.6652	9.7218	9.7788	9.8361	9.8939	9.9520	10.0106
9	9.0000	9.4640	9.9573	10.4818	11.0398	11.1120	11.1848	11.2581	11.3320	11.4065	11.4816	11.5573
10	10.0000	10.5690	11.1781	11.8302	12.5287	12.6194	12.7109	12.8033	12.8964	12.9904	13.0851	13.1807
15	15.0000	16.2628	17.6611	19.2109	20.9304	21.1582	21.3891	21.6230	21.8600	22.1002	22.3435	22.5901
20	20.0000	22.2482	24.8242	27.7813	31.1821	31.6419	32.1099	32.5863	33.0713	33.5649	34.0674	34.5790
25	25.0000	28.5400	32.7386	37.7331	43.6912	44.5134	45.3543	46.2142	47.0937	47.9933	48.9134	49.8546
30	30.0000	35.1540	41.4832	49.2891	58.9546	60.3165	61.7160	63.1542	64.6324	66.1515	67.7129	69.3179

YEAR	5.00 %	5.10 %	5.125%	5.20 %	5.25 %	5.30 %	5.375%	5.40 %	5.50 %	5.60 %	5.625%	5.70 %
1	1.0509	1.0520	1.0522	1.0530	1.0535	1.0541	1.0548	1.0551	1.0561	1.0572	1.0574	1.0582
2	2.1554	2.1587	2.1595	2.1619	2.1635	2.1651	2.1675	2.1683	2.1716	2.1748	2.1756	2.1781
3	3.3162	3.3229	3.3245	3.3295	3.3329	3.3362	3.3413	3.3429	3.3497	3.3564	3.3581	3.3631
4	4.5361	4.5476	4.5504	4.5591	4.5649	4.5707	4.5793	4.5822	4.5939	4.6055	4.6084	4.6172
5	5.8181	5.8360	5.8404	5.8539	5.8628	5.8718	5.8853	5.8898	5.9079	5.9261	5.9306	5.9443
6	7.1655	7.1913	7.1978	7.2173	7.2303	7.2433	7.2629	7.2695	7.2958	7.3222	7.3288	7.3487
7	8.5815	8.6171	8.6261	8.6530	8.6710	8.6890	8.7161	8.7252	8.7615	8.7981	8.8072	8.8348
8	10.0696	10.1171	10.1290	10.1648	10.1888	10.2128	10.2490	10.2611	10.3096	10.3584	10.3707	10.4075
9	11.6335	11.6950	11.7104	11.7568	11.7878	11.8190	11.8659	11.8816	11.9446	12.0080	12.0239	12.0717
10	13.2771	13.3549	13.3744	13.4332	13.4725	13.5120	13.5715	13.5914	13.6713	13.7518	13.7721	13.8329
15	22.8399	23.0422	23.0931	23.2466	23.3496	23.4532	23.6096	23.6620	23.8730	24.0863	24.1399	24.3018
20	35.0997	35.5231	35.6299	35.9526	36.1696	36.3883	36.7192	36.8302	37.2786	37.7335	37.8483	38.1950
25	50.8173	51.6033	51.8021	52.4038	52.8095	53.2189	53.8401	54.0491	54.8945	55.7556	55.9733	56.6325
30	70.9678	72.3208	72.6638	73.7041	74.4074	75.1184	76.1999	76.5645	78.0430	79.5548	79.9380	81.1007

YEAR	5.75 %	5.80 %	5.875%	5.90 %	6.00 %	6.10 %	6.125%	6.20 %	6.25 %	6.30 %	6.375%	6.40 %
1	1.0588	1.0593	1.0601	1.0603	1.0614	1.0624	1.0627	1.0635	1.0640	1.0645	1.0653	1.0656
2	2.1797	2.1813	2.1838	2.1846	2.1879	2.1911	2.1919	2.1944	2.1960	2.1977	2.2001	2.2010
3	3.3665	3.3699	3.3750	3.3767	3.3835	3.3903	3.3920	3.3971	3.4005	3.4039	3.4091	3.4108
4	4.6231	4.6289	4.6377	4.6407	4.6525	4.6643	4.6672	4.6761	4.6821	4.6880	4.6969	4.6999
5	5.9534	5.9626	5.9763	5.9809	5.9993	6.0178	6.0224	6.0363	6.0456	6.0549	6.0689	6.0736
6	7.3620	7.3753	7.3953	7.4020	7.4288	7.4558	7.4625	7.4828	7.4964	7.5100	7.5304	7.5373
7	8.8532	8.8717	8.8995	8.9088	8.9460	8.9835	8.9929	9.0211	9.0400	9.0589	9.0874	9.0969
8	10.4321	10.4568	10.4940	10.5065	10.5564	10.6065	10.6191	10.6570	10.6823	10.7077	10.7460	10.7588
9	12.1038	12.1359	12.1843	12.2005	12.2655	12.3309	12.3473	12.3967	12.4298	12.4629	12.5129	12.5296
10	13.8737	13.9145	13.9761	13.9967	14.0795	14.1629	14.1838	14.2468	14.2890	14.3314	14.3951	14.4165
15	24.4104	24.5197	24.6846	24.7398	24.9624	25.1873	25.2439	25.4147	25.5292	25.6444	25.8184	25.8767
20	38.4282	38.6632	39.0188	39.1381	39.6200	40.1089	40.2323	40.6050	40.8557	41.1083	41.4906	41.6189
25	57.0770	57.5256	58.2063	58.4352	59.3618	60.3055	60.5441	61.2667	61.7540	62.2458	62.9921	63.2431
30	81.8866	82.6814	83.8904	84.2979	85.9510	87.6415	88.0701	89.3704	90.2496	91.1387	92.4912	92.9471

YEAR	6.50 %	6.60 %	6.625%	6.70 %	6.75 %	6.80 %	6.875%	6.90 %	7.00 %	7.10 %	7.125%	7.20 %
1	1.0666	1.0677	1.0679	1.0687	1.0692	1.0698	1.0705	1.0708	1.0719	1.0729	1.0732	1.0740
2	2.2042	2.2075	2.2084	2.2108	2.2125	2.2141	2.2166	2.2174	2.2207	2.2241	2.2249	2.2274
3	3.4176	3.4245	3.4262	3.4314	3.4349	3.4383	3.4435	3.4452	3.4522	3.4591	3.4609	3.4661
4	4.7119	4.7239	4.7269	4.7359	4.7419	4.7479	4.7570	4.7600	4.7721	4.7843	4.7873	4.7964
5	6.0923	6.1111	6.1158	6.1299	6.1394	6.1489	6.1631	6.1678	6.1869	6.2060	6.2108	6.2252
6	7.5646	7.5922	7.5990	7.6198	7.6336	7.6475	7.6684	7.6754	7.7033	7.7314	7.7385	7.7596
7	9.1351	9.1734	9.1830	9.2120	9.2313	9.2507	9.2799	9.2896	9.3287	9.3680	9.3779	9.4075
8	10.8101	10.8617	10.8746	10.9136	10.9396	10.9657	11.0051	11.0182	11.0710	11.1240	11.1373	11.1774
9	12.5966	12.6641	12.6811	12.7320	12.7662	12.8004	12.8519	12.8692	12.9384	13.0080	13.0255	13.0781
10	14.5022	14.5885	14.6102	14.6755	14.7192	14.7630	14.8291	14.8512	14.9400	15.0294	15.0518	15.1194
15	26.1114	26.3487	26.4084	26.5885	26.7094	26.8309	27.0144	27.0760	27.3236	27.5740	27.6370	27.8270
20	42.1370	42.6627	42.7953	43.1961	43.4657	43.7373	44.1485	44.2865	44.8437	45.4092	45.5518	45.9830
25	64.2591	65.2940	65.5557	66.3482	66.8827	67.4222	68.2408	68.5162	69.6308	70.7664	71.0536	71.9232
30	94.7968	96.6887	97.1683	98.6238	99.6079	100.6032	102.1174	102.6279	104.6991	106.8179	107.3551	108.9854

SAVINGS GROWTH

Description: This table shows what a series of $ 1 deposits grow to in the future. The deposit is made at the beginning of a period.

Example: At 8 % a regular one dollar deposit will grow to $ 6.38 by the end of the fifth year.

YEAR	7.25 %	7.30 %	7.375%	7.40 %	7.50 %	7.60 %	7.625%	7.70 %	7.75 %	7.80 %	7.875%	7.90 %
1	1.0745	1.0750	1.0758	1.0761	1.0771	1.0782	1.0785	1.0793	1.0798	1.0803	1.0811	1.0814
2	2.2290	2.2307	2.2332	2.2340	2.2374	2.2407	2.2415	2.2440	2.2457	2.2474	2.2499	2.2507
3	3.4696	3.4731	3.4783	3.4801	3.4871	3.4941	3.4959	3.5011	3.5047	3.5082	3.5135	3.5153
4	4.8025	4.8087	4.8178	4.8209	4.8332	4.8455	4.8486	4.8579	4.8640	4.8702	4.8796	4.8827
5	6.2348	6.2444	6.2589	6.2638	6.2831	6.3026	6.3075	6.3221	6.3319	6.3417	6.3564	6.3613
6	7.7738	7.7879	7.8093	7.8164	7.8449	7.8736	7.8808	7.9024	7.9168	7.9313	7.9531	7.9603
7	9.4274	9.4472	9.4771	9.4871	9.5272	9.5675	9.5776	9.6079	9.6282	9.6486	9.6792	9.6895
8	11.2041	11.2310	11.2714	11.2850	11.3392	11.3938	11.4075	11.4486	11.4762	11.5038	11.5454	11.5593
9	13.1133	13.1486	13.2018	13.2196	13.2910	13.3629	13.3809	13.4352	13.4715	13.5080	13.5629	13.5812
10	15.1647	15.2101	15.2785	15.3014	15.3934	15.4860	15.5092	15.5792	15.6261	15.6732	15.7440	15.7677
15	27.9546	28.0828	28.2764	28.3413	28.6027	28.8669	28.9334	29.1339	29.2686	29.4039	29.6083	29.6768
20	46.2730	46.5652	47.0075	47.1560	47.7556	48.3640	48.5175	48.9814	49.2935	49.6080	50.0840	50.2438
25	72.5098	73.1019	74.0004	74.3027	75.5262	76.7728	77.0881	78.0430	78.6871	79.3372	80.3239	80.6559
30	110.0878	111.2028	112.8993	113.4713	115.7922	118.1668	118.7690	120.5963	121.8321	123.0822	124.9843	125.6256

YEAR	8.00 %	8.10 %	8.125%	8.20 %	8.25 %	8.30 %	8.375%	8.40 %	8.50 %	8.60 %	8.625%	8.70 %
1	1.0824	1.0835	1.0838	1.0846	1.0851	1.0856	1.0864	1.0867	1.0877	1.0888	1.0891	1.0899
2	2.2541	2.2575	2.2583	2.2608	2.2625	2.2642	2.2667	2.2676	2.2709	2.2743	2.2752	2.2777
3	3.5223	3.5294	3.5312	3.5365	3.5401	3.5437	3.5490	3.5508	3.5580	3.5651	3.5669	3.5723
4	4.8951	4.9076	4.9107	4.9201	4.9264	4.9327	4.9421	4.9453	4.9579	4.9706	4.9737	4.9833
5	6.3811	6.4009	6.4058	6.4207	6.4307	6.4406	6.4556	6.4606	6.4807	6.5008	6.5059	6.5211
6	7.9895	8.0188	8.0261	8.0482	8.0629	8.0777	8.0999	8.1074	8.1371	8.1670	8.1745	8.1970
7	9.7305	9.7718	9.7821	9.8133	9.8341	9.8549	9.8863	9.8968	9.9389	9.9812	9.9918	10.0237
8	11.6151	11.6712	11.6852	11.7276	11.7559	11.7843	11.8271	11.8414	11.8988	11.9565	11.9709	12.0145
9	13.6550	13.7291	13.7478	13.8038	13.8413	13.8789	13.9356	13.9545	14.0306	14.1072	14.1264	14.1842
10	15.8630	15.9589	15.9830	16.0555	16.1041	16.1528	16.2263	16.2508	16.3495	16.4489	16.4738	16.5490
15	29.9526	30.2315	30.3017	30.5134	30.6555	30.7984	31.0141	31.0864	31.3776	31.6720	31.7461	31.9696
20	50.8891	51.5440	51.7092	52.2086	52.5446	52.8831	53.3956	53.5677	54.2624	54.9675	55.1455	55.6832
25	81.9996	83.3688	83.7152	84.7641	85.4716	86.1859	87.2700	87.6348	89.1112	90.6159	90.9965	92.1493
30	128.2282	130.8913	131.5667	133.6163	135.0026	136.4049	138.5389	139.2585	142.1788	145.1674	145.9254	148.2260

YEAR	8.75 %	8.80 %	8.875%	8.90 %	9.00 %	9.10 %	9.125%	9.20 %	9.25 %	9.30 %	9.375%	9.40 %
1	1.0904	1.0909	1.0917	1.0920	1.0931	1.0942	1.0944	1.0952	1.0958	1.0963	1.0971	1.0974
2	2.2794	2.2811	2.2837	2.2845	2.2879	2.2913	2.2922	2.2947	2.2964	2.2982	2.3007	2.3016
3	3.5759	3.5795	3.5849	3.5867	3.5940	3.6012	3.6030	3.6085	3.6121	3.6157	3.6212	3.6230
4	4.9896	4.9960	5.0056	5.0088	5.0216	5.0344	5.0376	5.0473	5.0538	5.0602	5.0699	5.0732
5	6.5312	6.5413	6.5566	6.5617	6.5821	6.6026	6.6077	6.6231	6.6335	6.6438	6.6593	6.6645
6	8.2121	8.2272	8.2499	8.2575	8.2879	8.3184	8.3260	8.3490	8.3644	8.3798	8.4030	8.4107
7	10.0450	10.0664	10.0985	10.1093	10.1524	10.1957	10.2066	10.2393	10.2611	10.2830	10.3160	10.3270
8	12.0436	12.0728	12.1168	12.1315	12.1905	12.2499	12.2647	12.3095	12.3395	12.3695	12.4148	12.4299
9	14.2229	14.2618	14.3202	14.3398	14.4183	14.4974	14.5172	14.5769	14.6169	14.6569	14.7173	14.7375
10	16.5993	16.6498	16.7258	16.7513	16.8535	16.9565	16.9823	17.0602	17.1123	17.1646	17.2434	17.2698
15	32.1197	32.2705	32.4983	32.5747	32.8822	33.1930	33.2713	33.5073	33.6657	33.8250	34.0656	34.1462
20	56.0450	56.4095	56.9614	57.1468	57.8950	58.6545	58.8461	59.4253	59.8151	60.2078	60.8023	61.0019
25	92.9270	93.7120	94.9037	95.3046	96.9278	98.5821	99.0006	100.2681	101.1232	101.9865	103.2970	103.7380
30	149.7820	151.3562	153.7520	154.5599	157.8388	161.1948	162.0461	164.6298	166.3775	168.1457	170.8370	171.7446

YEAR	9.50 %	9.75 %	10.00 %	10.25 %	10.50 %	10.75 %	11.00 %	12.00 %	13.00 %	14.00 %	15.00 %	16.00 %
1	1.0984	1.1011	1.1038	1.1065	1.1092	1.1119	1.1146	1.1255	1.1365	1.1475	1.1587	1.1699
2	2.3050	2.3136	2.3222	2.3309	2.3395	2.3483	2.3570	2.3923	2.4281	2.4643	2.5011	2.5384
3	3.6303	3.6487	3.6671	3.6856	3.7043	3.7230	3.7418	3.8180	3.8959	3.9754	4.0566	4.1395
4	5.0861	5.1188	5.1516	5.1847	5.2180	5.2515	5.2853	5.4227	5.5641	5.7094	5.8588	6.0124
5	6.6853	6.7375	6.7902	6.8434	6.8970	6.9511	7.0057	7.2289	7.4599	7.6992	7.9470	8.2036
6	8.4418	8.5200	8.5990	8.6788	8.7595	8.8410	8.9233	9.2617	9.6145	9.9825	10.3664	10.7669
7	10.3712	10.4826	10.5954	10.7096	10.8253	10.9423	11.0608	11.5496	12.0631	12.6027	13.1697	13.7656
8	12.4906	12.6438	12.7992	12.9568	13.1167	13.2788	13.4432	14.1247	14.8459	15.6094	16.4177	17.2736
9	14.8186	15.0235	15.2317	15.4433	15.6583	15.8767	16.0987	17.0229	18.0085	19.0596	20.1810	21.3776
10	17.3757	17.6439	17.9168	18.1947	18.4775	18.7654	19.0586	20.2850	21.6027	23.0189	24.5414	26.1786
15	34.4709	35.2985	36.1490	37.0232	37.9217	38.8452	39.7946	43.8658	48.4151	53.5019	59.1931	65.5641
20	61.8081	63.8769	66.0246	68.2543	70.5694	72.9733	75.4695	86.4553	99.2471	114.1568	131.5512	151.8625
25	105.5232	110.1381	114.9792	120.0579	125.3865	130.9779	136.8457	163.3768	195.6164	234.8470	282.6459	340.9530
30	175.4284	185.0235	195.1970	205.9853	217.4271	229.5637	242.4389	302.3056	378.3168	474.9951	598.1546	755.2736

Description: This table shows what a series of $ 1 deposits grow to in the future. The deposit is made at the beginning of a period.

Example: At 5 % a regular one dollar deposit will grow to $ 295.06 by the end of the fifth year.

YEAR	0.00 %	1.00 %	2.00 %	3.00 %	4.00 %	4.125%	4.25 %	4.375%	4.50 %	4.625%	4.75 %	4.875%
1	52.0000	52.2650	52.5306	52.7969	53.0639	53.0973	53.1308	53.1642	53.1977	53.2311	53.2646	53.2981
2	104.0000	105.0539	106.1171	107.1896	108.2716	108.4075	108.5436	108.6798	108.8161	108.9526	109.0893	109.2261
3	156.0000	158.3720	160.7806	163.2264	165.7097	166.0228	166.3364	166.6507	166.9656	167.2811	167.5971	167.9138
4	208.0000	212.2247	216.5429	220.9568	225.4682	226.0391	226.6116	227.1856	227.7612	228.3384	228.9171	229.4975
5	260.0000	266.6172	273.4261	280.4321	287.6411	288.5567	289.4757	290.3979	291.3234	292.2523	293.1844	294.1199
6	312.0000	321.5550	331.4525	341.7051	352.3257	353.6798	355.0399	356.4060	357.7781	359.1563	360.5406	361.9311
7	364.0000	377.0435	390.6453	404.8301	419.6235	421.5169	423.4201	425.3335	427.2569	429.1905	431.1343	433.0883
8	416.0000	433.0884	451.0279	469.8630	489.6402	492.1811	494.7375	497.3096	499.8974	502.5012	505.1209	507.7567
9	468.0000	489.6951	512.6242	536.8615	562.4856	565.7902	569.1180	572.4690	575.8435	579.2417	582.6637	586.1096
10	520.0000	546.8692	575.4585	605.8851	638.2739	642.4671	646.6932	650.9527	655.2457	659.5725	663.9334	668.3288
15	780.0000	841.4534	909.0903	983.5865	1065.6934	1076.5326	1087.5053	1098.6134	1109.8586	1121.2427	1132.7675	1144.4349
20	1040.0000	1151.1026	1277.6273	1421.9244	1586.7154	1608.9071	1631.4743	1654.4238	1677.7626	1701.4975	1725.6359	1750.1851
25	1300.0000	1476.5873	1684.7214	1930.6334	2221.8383	2261.8562	2302.7407	2344.5118	2387.1902	2430.7967	2475.3531	2520.8813
30	1560.0000	1818.7174	2134.4066	2521.0110	2996.0496	3062.6880	3131.0939	3201.3172	3273.4096	3347.4239	3423.4148	3501.4385

YEAR	5.00 %	5.10 %	5.125%	5.20 %	5.25 %	5.30 %	5.375%	5.40 %	5.50 %	5.60 %	5.625%	5.70 %
1	53.3316	53.3584	53.3651	53.3852	53.3986	53.4120	53.4321	53.4388	53.4656	53.4925	53.4992	53.5193
2	109.3630	109.4727	109.5001	109.5825	109.6374	109.6923	109.7748	109.8023	109.9123	110.0225	110.0500	110.1327
3	168.2311	168.4854	168.5490	168.7400	168.8675	168.9951	169.1866	169.2505	169.5063	169.7625	169.8266	170.0191
4	230.0794	230.5460	230.6629	231.0137	231.2480	231.4825	231.8347	231.9522	232.4230	232.8948	233.0129	233.3676
5	295.0587	295.8122	296.0009	296.5678	296.9464	297.3256	297.8953	298.0855	298.8476	299.6119	299.8034	300.3784
6	363.3276	364.4493	364.7304	365.5750	366.1393	366.7046	367.5545	367.8383	368.9759	370.1176	370.4036	371.2633
7	435.0526	436.6316	437.0274	438.2172	439.0125	439.8095	441.0081	441.4085	443.0143	444.6268	445.0310	446.2462
8	510.4088	512.5421	513.0771	514.6859	515.7617	516.8402	518.4629	519.0052	521.1807	523.3670	523.9152	525.5640
9	589.5798	592.3734	593.0742	595.1827	596.5932	598.0077	600.1369	600.8486	603.7055	606.5784	607.2991	609.4674
10	672.7588	676.3280	677.2238	679.9197	681.7240	683.5341	686.2598	687.1713	690.8315	694.5148	695.4393	698.2214
15	1156.2468	1165.8017	1168.2051	1175.4511	1180.3117	1185.1962	1192.5685	1195.0380	1204.9775	1215.0156	1217.5407	1225.1535
20	1775.1524	1795.4325	1800.5456	1815.9890	1826.3722	1836.8260	1852.6402	1857.9475	1879.3576	1901.0605	1906.5325	1923.0606
25	2567.4039	2605.3535	2614.9440	2643.9663	2663.5253	2683.2548	2713.1720	2723.2314	2763.9090	2805.3005	2815.7615	2847.4193
30	3581.5528	3647.1893	3663.8171	3714.2331	3748.2927	3782.7161	3835.0426	3852.6712	3924.1317	3997.1320	4015.6268	4071.7072

YEAR	5.75 %	5.80 %	5.875%	5.90 %	6.00 %	6.10 %	6.125%	6.20 %	6.25 %	6.30 %	6.375%	6.40 %
1	53.5328	53.5462	53.5663	53.5730	53.5999	53.6268	53.6335	53.6536	53.6671	53.6805	53.7007	53.7074
2	110.1879	110.2431	110.3259	110.3535	110.4640	110.5747	110.6023	110.6854	110.7408	110.7962	110.8794	110.9071
3	170.1475	170.2761	170.4690	170.5334	170.7912	171.0493	171.1139	171.3079	171.4373	171.5668	171.7613	171.8262
4	233.6044	233.8414	234.1975	234.3163	234.7923	235.2692	235.3886	235.7472	235.9866	236.2263	236.5863	236.7064
5	300.7625	301.1471	301.7250	301.9179	302.6910	303.4663	303.6604	304.2438	304.6333	305.0235	305.6097	305.8054
6	371.8377	372.4131	373.2780	373.5669	374.7248	375.8868	376.1779	377.0529	377.6375	378.2231	379.1035	379.3975
7	447.0584	447.8724	449.0965	449.5055	451.1454	452.7923	453.2051	454.4462	455.2757	456.1070	457.3573	457.7749
8	526.6666	527.7718	529.4348	529.9905	532.2201	534.4606	535.0225	536.7122	537.8422	538.9749	540.6792	541.2487
9	610.9180	612.3726	614.5623	615.2942	618.2322	621.1867	621.9279	624.1578	625.6496	627.1456	629.3975	630.1502
10	700.0835	701.9514	704.7644	705.7051	709.4824	713.2837	714.2378	717.1090	719.0308	720.9586	723.8618	724.8325
15	1230.2601	1235.3921	1243.1379	1245.7326	1256.1761	1266.7235	1269.3767	1277.3760	1282.7420	1288.1347	1296.2741	1299.0007
20	1934.1733	1945.3620	1962.2885	1967.9692	1990.8866	2014.1187	2019.9765	2037.6701	2049.5670	2061.5455	2079.6674	2085.7495
25	2868.7557	2890.2790	2922.9182	2933.8932	2978.2761	3023.4420	3034.8575	3069.4055	3092.6910	3116.1814	3151.8057	3163.7850
30	4109.5965	4147.8931	4206.1117	4225.7265	4305.2451	4386.4872	4407.0716	4469.4923	4511.6685	4554.3006	4619.1150	4640.9534

YEAR	6.50 %	6.60 %	6.625%	6.70 %	6.75 %	6.80 %	6.875%	6.90 %	7.00 %	7.10 %	7.125%	7.20 %
1	53.7343	53.7612	53.7679	53.7881	53.8016	53.8150	53.8352	53.8420	53.8689	53.8958	53.9026	53.9228
2	111.0181	111.1292	111.1570	111.2404	111.2961	111.3517	111.4353	111.4631	111.5746	111.6862	111.7141	111.7979
3	172.0859	172.3460	172.4111	172.6065	172.7369	172.8674	173.0634	173.1287	173.3904	173.6525	173.7181	173.9150
4	237.1875	237.6697	237.7904	238.1530	238.3950	238.6373	239.0012	239.1226	239.6091	240.0965	240.2186	240.5851
5	306.5896	307.3760	307.5729	308.1646	308.5598	308.9555	309.5502	309.7487	310.5441	311.3418	311.5416	312.1418
6	380.5761	381.7587	382.0551	382.9456	383.5406	384.1367	385.0328	385.3320	386.5315	387.7353	388.0369	388.9433
7	459.4498	461.1318	461.5534	462.8209	463.6681	464.5171	465.7940	466.2205	467.9311	469.6490	470.0796	471.3741
8	543.5336	545.8299	546.4057	548.1374	549.2954	550.4563	552.2030	552.7866	555.1284	557.4818	558.0719	559.8467
9	633.1717	636.2103	636.9726	639.2659	640.8001	642.3387	644.6547	645.4288	648.5364	651.6614	652.4454	654.8040
10	728.7310	732.6542	733.6389	736.6023	738.5857	740.5753	743.5717	744.5736	748.5973	752.6464	753.6627	756.7213
15	1309.9752	1321.0592	1323.8475	1332.2540	1337.8933	1343.5607	1352.1148	1354.9805	1366.5145	1378.1640	1381.0946	1389.9302
20	2110.2869	2135.1626	2141.4350	2160.3815	2173.1212	2185.9486	2205.3555	2211.8690	2238.1478	2264.7902	2271.5082	2291.8016
25	3212.2316	3261.5371	3273.9995	3311.7174	3337.1407	3362.7889	3401.6874	3414.7683	3467.6726	3521.5190	3535.1299	3576.3253
30	4729.4930	4819.9624	4842.8865	4912.4059	4959.3821	5006.8688	5079.0689	5103.3973	5202.0388	5302.8418	5328.3861	5405.8559

Description: This table shows what a series of $ 1 deposits grow to in the future. The deposit is made at the beginning of a period.

Example: At 8 % a regular one dollar deposit will grow to $ 318.62 by the end of the fifth year.

YEAR	7.25 %	7.30 %	7.375%	7.40 %	7.50 %	7.60 %	7.625%	7.70 %	7.75 %	7.80 %	7.875%	7.90 %
1	53.9363	53.9497	53.9700	53.9767	54.0037	54.0306	54.0374	54.0576	54.0711	54.0846	54.1048	54.1116
2	111.8538	111.9097	111.9936	112.0216	112.1335	112.2456	112.2736	112.3578	112.4139	112.4700	112.5543	112.5824
3	174.0464	174.1779	174.3753	174.4412	174.7049	174.9690	175.0351	175.2335	175.3659	175.4984	175.6973	175.7637
4	240.8297	241.0747	241.4426	241.5654	242.0571	242.5499	242.6733	243.0438	243.2911	243.5388	243.9107	244.0348
5	312.5426	312.9440	313.5472	313.7486	314.5554	315.3646	315.5672	316.1760	316.5826	316.9898	317.6017	317.8059
6	389.5489	390.1556	391.0677	391.3722	392.5931	393.8183	394.1253	395.0478	395.6643	396.2817	397.2100	397.5200
7	472.2394	473.1065	474.4106	474.8462	476.5933	478.3478	478.7876	480.1097	480.9934	481.8791	483.2110	483.6559
8	561.0335	562.2233	564.0134	564.6116	567.0117	569.4236	570.0284	571.8474	573.0638	574.2832	576.1179	576.7309
9	656.3820	657.9644	660.3463	661.1425	664.3386	667.5527	668.3590	670.7849	672.4078	674.0353	676.4852	677.3041
10	758.7685	760.8221	763.9147	764.9489	769.1019	773.2812	774.3302	777.4872	779.6002	781.7199	784.9120	785.9795
15	1395.8575	1401.8144	1410.8056	1413.8177	1425.9414	1438.1868	1441.2673	1450.5552	1456.7859	1463.0479	1472.4997	1475.6661
20	2305.4473	2319.1872	2339.9754	2346.9527	2375.1034	2403.6451	2410.8423	2432.5835	2447.2032	2461.9242	2484.1974	2491.6733
25	3604.0939	3632.1093	3674.6000	3688.8894	3746.6843	3805.5129	3820.3839	3865.3947	3895.7367	3926.3494	3972.7817	3988.3972
30	5458.2080	5511.1319	5591.6045	5618.7218	5728.6788	5841.0573	5869.5368	5955.9131	6014.2877	6073.3031	6163.0438	6193.2857

YEAR	8.00 %	8.10 %	8.125%	8.20 %	8.25 %	8.30 %	8.375%	8.40 %	8.50 %	8.60 %	8.625%	8.70 %
1	54.1386	54.1656	54.1723	54.1926	54.2061	54.2196	54.2399	54.2466	54.2737	54.3007	54.3075	54.3278
2	112.6949	112.8074	112.8356	112.9201	112.9765	113.0328	113.1175	113.1457	113.2586	113.3717	113.4000	113.4848
3	176.0294	176.2955	176.3620	176.5620	176.6954	176.8289	177.0293	177.0962	177.3639	177.6320	177.6991	177.9005
4	244.5319	245.0301	245.1549	245.5294	245.7795	246.0298	246.4058	246.5313	247.0338	247.5375	247.6636	248.0422
5	318.6243	319.4451	319.6506	320.2682	320.6806	321.0936	321.7143	321.9214	322.7516	323.5841	323.7926	324.4190
6	398.7626	400.0097	400.3221	401.2611	401.8885	402.5170	403.4618	403.7773	405.0421	406.3114	406.6294	407.5851
7	485.4403	487.2322	487.6813	489.0317	489.9343	490.8388	492.1991	492.6535	494.4760	496.3061	496.7649	498.1440
8	579.1908	581.6627	582.2826	584.1469	585.3936	586.6434	588.5238	589.1521	591.6733	594.2069	594.8422	596.7530
9	680.5913	683.8971	684.7264	687.2215	688.8908	690.5647	693.0845	693.9268	697.3079	700.7080	701.5611	704.1274
10	790.2662	794.5801	795.6629	798.9215	801.1026	803.2905	806.5856	807.6874	812.1122	816.5653	817.6829	821.0467
15	1488.4113	1501.2847	1504.5232	1514.2876	1520.8382	1527.4216	1537.3588	1540.6879	1554.0879	1567.6231	1571.0282	1581.2948
20	2521.8366	2552.4202	2560.1325	2583.4303	2599.0973	2614.8731	2638.7430	2646.7549	2679.0822	2711.8613	2720.1275	2745.0991
25	4051.5585	4115.8544	4132.1081	4181.3060	4214.4720	4247.9351	4298.6929	4315.7638	4384.8147	4455.1108	4472.8822	4526.6755
30	6315.9207	6441.2691	6473.0375	6569.3936	6634.5168	6700.3582	6800.4847	6834.2283	6971.0711	7110.9553	7146.4097	7253.9510

YEAR	8.75 %	8.80 %	8.875%	8.90 %	9.00 %	9.10 %	9.125%	9.20 %	9.25 %	9.30 %	9.375%	9.40 %
1	54.3413	54.3548	54.3751	54.3819	54.4089	54.4360	54.4428	54.4631	54.4766	54.4902	54.5105	54.5173
2	113.5414	113.5981	113.6831	113.7114	113.8248	113.9384	113.9668	114.0520	114.1089	114.1657	114.2511	114.2796
3	178.0349	178.1694	178.3714	178.4388	178.7085	178.9787	179.0463	179.2492	179.3847	179.5202	179.7237	179.7916
4	248.2950	248.5481	248.9282	249.0550	249.5631	250.0723	250.1997	250.5825	250.8381	251.0939	251.4782	251.6064
5	324.8374	325.2563	325.8859	326.0960	326.9381	327.7826	327.9940	328.6294	329.0538	329.4787	330.1173	330.3305
6	408.2237	408.8634	409.8250	410.1462	411.4335	412.7254	413.0490	414.0218	414.6718	415.3228	416.3016	416.6285
7	499.0659	499.9897	501.3791	501.8432	503.7046	505.5738	506.0424	507.4510	508.3925	509.3361	510.7551	511.2292
8	598.0307	599.3116	601.2389	601.8829	604.4669	607.0637	607.7149	609.6733	610.9829	612.2958	614.2712	614.9313
9	705.8444	707.5661	710.1579	711.0243	714.5019	717.9993	718.8767	721.5164	723.2824	725.0534	727.7193	728.6104
10	823.2980	825.5566	828.9579	830.0953	834.6629	839.2597	840.4134	843.8857	846.2098	848.5413	852.0525	853.2266
15	1588.1824	1595.1046	1605.5534	1609.0539	1623.1441	1637.3767	1640.9573	1651.7533	1658.9960	1666.2753	1677.2632	1680.9443
20	2761.8920	2778.8021	2804.3887	2812.9771	2847.6312	2882.7712	2891.6330	2918.4044	2936.4081	2954.5378	2981.9707	2991.1789
25	4562.9411	4599.5327	4655.0384	4673.7067	4749.2222	4826.1046	4845.5418	4904.3797	4944.0476	4984.0735	5044.7911	5065.2130
30	7326.6381	7400.1301	7511.8979	7549.5664	7702.3350	7858.5130	7898.0995	8018.1795	8099.3460	8181.4150	8306.2336	8348.3023

YEAR	9.50 %	9.75 %	10.00 %	10.25 %	10.50 %	10.75 %	11.00 %	12.00 %	13.00 %	14.00 %	15.00 %	16.00 %
1	54.5444	54.6121	54.6800	54.7478	54.8157	54.8837	54.9517	55.2240	55.4971	55.7708	56.0452	56.3202
2	114.3935	114.6788	114.9646	115.2511	115.5382	115.8259	116.1142	117.2737	118.4432	119.6228	120.8124	122.0122
3	180.0634	180.7446	181.4284	182.1149	182.8039	183.4955	184.1897	186.9928	189.8384	192.7269	195.6590	198.6353
4	252.1200	253.4089	254.7048	256.0078	257.3179	258.6350	259.9594	265.3292	270.8165	276.4238	282.1536	288.0084
5	331.1846	333.3307	335.4920	337.6688	339.8612	342.0692	344.2930	353.3479	362.6639	372.2484	382.1090	392.2532
6	417.9387	421.2347	424.5599	427.9146	431.2991	434.7136	438.1583	452.2457	466.8395	481.9580	497.6198	513.8444
7	513.1303	517.9183	522.7573	527.6476	532.5900	537.5848	542.6328	563.3673	584.9981	607.5645	631.1071	655.6684
8	617.5797	624.2584	631.0198	637.8652	644.7956	651.8120	658.9156	688.2235	719.0166	751.3714	785.3683	821.0919
9	732.1876	741.2193	750.3793	759.6696	769.0921	778.6486	788.3411	828.5120	871.0237	916.0159	963.6365	1014.0418
10	857.9418	869.8619	881.9732	894.2789	906.7823	919.4865	932.3951	986.1401	1043.4339	1104.5174	1169.6476	1239.0986
15	1695.7619	1733.4660	1772.1334	1811.7896	1852.4611	1894.1748	1936.9584	2119.3745	2321.3328	2545.0013	2792.7895	3067.3742
20	3028.3351	3123.5290	3222.1106	3324.2056	3429.9441	3539.4615	3652.8977	4148.8249	4720.1246	5378.6512	6138.1363	7014.4840
25	5147.8253	5360.9834	5583.9706	5817.2575	6061.3373	6316.7274	6583.9700	7783.2613	9222.9866	10952.87	13033.00	15536.00
30	8518.9260	8962.4048	9431.1918	9926.7805	10450.75	11004.79	11590.66	14291.98	17675.48	21918.20	27243.54	33933.31

SAVINGS GROWTH

Description: This table shows what a series of $ 1 deposits grow to in the future. The deposit is made at the beginning of a period.

Example: At 5 % a regular one dollar deposit will grow to $ 68.20 by the end of the fifth year.

YEAR	0.00 %	1.00 %	2.00 %	3.00 %	4.00 %	4.125%	4.25 %	4.375%	4.50 %	4.625%	4.75 %	4.875%
1	12.0000	12.0651	12.1304	12.1958	12.2614	12.2696	12.2778	12.2860	12.2943	12.3025	12.3107	12.3190
2	24.0000	24.2511	24.5045	24.7602	25.0182	25.0506	25.0830	25.1155	25.1480	25.1806	25.2132	25.2458
3	36.0000	36.5593	37.1274	37.7044	38.2903	38.3642	38.4382	38.5124	38.5867	38.6611	38.7357	38.8105
4	48.0000	48.9909	50.0040	51.0398	52.0986	52.2326	52.3670	52.5018	52.6369	52.7724	52.9082	53.0445
5	60.0000	61.5471	63.1395	64.7782	66.4648	66.6791	66.8941	67.1099	67.3265	67.5438	67.7620	67.9809
6	72.0000	74.2292	76.5389	78.9319	81.4114	81.7275	82.0451	82.3641	82.6845	83.0063	83.3296	83.6543
7	84.0000	87.0385	90.2077	93.5134	96.9618	97.4032	97.8469	98.2930	98.7414	99.1923	99.6455	100.1011
8	96.0000	99.9761	104.1512	108.5357	113.1405	113.7321	114.3274	114.9264	115.5291	116.1354	116.7456	117.3594
9	108.0000	113.0435	118.3750	124.0119	129.9727	130.7416	131.5158	132.2955	133.0806	133.8713	134.6676	135.4694
10	120.0000	126.2418	132.8847	139.9560	147.4850	148.4599	149.4424	150.4328	151.4309	152.4369	153.4509	154.4730
15	180.0000	194.2450	209.9268	227.2029	246.2482	248.7628	251.3084	253.8855	256.4945	259.1357	261.8098	264.5169
20	240.0000	265.7259	295.0293	328.4564	366.6400	371.7827	377.0126	382.3312	387.7402	393.2412	398.8359	404.5259
25	300.0000	340.8623	389.0353	445.9653	513.3970	522.6648	532.1336	541.8080	551.6929	561.7930	572.1135	582.6594
30	360.0000	419.8412	492.8765	582.3392	692.2928	707.7192	723.5553	739.8126	756.5031	773.6391	791.2333	809.2987

YEAR	5.00 %	5.10 %	5.125%	5.20 %	5.25 %	5.30 %	5.375%	5.40 %	5.50 %	5.60 %	5.625%	5.70 %
1	12.3272	12.3338	12.3354	12.3404	12.3437	12.3470	12.3519	12.3536	12.3601	12.3667	12.3684	12.3733
2	25.2784	25.3046	25.3111	25.3308	25.3439	25.3570	25.3766	25.3832	25.4094	25.4357	25.4423	25.4620
3	38.8853	38.9454	38.9604	39.0055	39.0355	39.0657	39.1109	39.1259	39.1863	39.2468	39.2619	39.3074
4	53.1811	53.2907	53.3181	53.4005	53.4555	53.5105	53.5932	53.6208	53.7314	53.8421	53.8699	53.9532
5	68.2006	68.3769	68.4211	68.5538	68.6424	68.7311	68.8645	68.9090	69.0874	69.2663	69.3111	69.4457
6	83.9804	84.2424	84.3080	84.5053	84.6371	84.7691	84.9676	85.0339	85.2996	85.5662	85.6330	85.8338
7	100.5591	100.9273	101.0196	101.2970	101.4825	101.6683	101.9479	102.0412	102.4157	102.7918	102.8860	103.1694
8	117.9771	118.4740	118.5986	118.9733	119.2239	119.4751	119.8531	119.9794	120.4862	120.9954	121.1231	121.5072
9	136.2769	136.9270	137.0901	137.5807	137.9090	138.2382	138.7337	138.8993	139.5642	140.2328	140.4005	140.9052
10	155.5031	156.3331	156.5414	157.1683	157.5879	158.0088	158.6427	158.8547	159.7059	160.5625	160.7775	161.4245
15	267.2577	269.4748	270.0325	271.7139	272.8418	273.9753	275.6861	276.2592	278.5658	280.8953	281.4813	283.2480
20	410.3130	415.0139	416.1991	419.7789	422.1857	424.6090	428.2749	429.5052	434.4684	439.4997	440.7682	444.5999
25	593.4360	602.2269	604.4486	611.1717	615.7027	620.2733	627.2041	629.5345	638.9583	648.5478	650.9714	658.3060
30	827.8488	843.0471	846.8973	858.5716	866.4585	874.4297	886.5469	890.6292	907.1777	924.0832	928.3664	941.3539

YEAR	5.75 %	5.80 %	5.875%	5.90 %	6.00 %	6.10 %	6.125%	6.20 %	6.25 %	6.30 %	6.375%	6.40 %
1	12.3766	12.3799	12.3849	12.3865	12.3932	12.3998	12.4014	12.4064	12.4097	12.4130	12.4179	12.4196
2	25.4752	25.4883	25.5081	25.5147	25.5410	25.5674	25.5740	25.5938	25.6071	25.6203	25.6401	25.6467
3	39.3377	39.3680	39.4136	39.4288	39.4896	39.5506	39.5658	39.6116	39.6422	39.6728	39.7187	39.7340
4	54.0088	54.0644	54.1480	54.1760	54.2877	54.3997	54.4278	54.5120	54.5682	54.6245	54.7090	54.7372
5	69.5356	69.6256	69.7609	69.8060	69.9870	70.1685	70.2139	70.3505	70.4417	70.5330	70.6702	70.7160
6	85.9680	86.1024	86.3044	86.3719	86.6423	86.9138	86.9818	87.1862	87.3227	87.4595	87.6652	87.7339
7	103.3588	103.5487	103.8342	103.9295	104.3120	104.6961	104.7924	105.0819	105.2753	105.4692	105.7608	105.8583
8	121.7640	122.0215	122.4089	122.5384	123.0578	123.5797	123.7106	124.1043	124.3675	124.6314	125.0285	125.1612
9	141.2428	141.5813	142.0910	142.2613	142.9451	143.6328	143.8053	144.3244	144.6716	145.0198	145.5440	145.7192
10	161.8576	162.2921	162.9463	163.1651	164.0436	164.9278	165.1497	165.8175	166.2645	166.7130	167.3882	167.6141
15	284.4332	285.6242	287.4219	288.0241	290.4479	292.8959	293.5117	295.3684	296.6139	297.8656	299.7548	300.3877
20	447.1762	449.7701	453.6944	455.0114	460.3247	465.7111	467.0692	471.1717	473.9301	476.7075	480.9093	482.3196
25	663.2494	668.2361	675.7984	678.3413	688.6249	699.0901	701.7352	709.7404	715.1361	720.5793	728.8342	731.6102
30	950.1288	958.9981	972.4815	977.0243	995.4412	1014.2579	1019.0255	1033.4833	1043.2522	1053.1269	1068.1398	1073.1983

YEAR	6.50 %	6.60 %	6.625%	6.70 %	6.75 %	6.80 %	6.875%	6.90 %	7.00 %	7.10 %	7.125%	7.20 %
1	12.4262	12.4328	12.4345	12.4394	12.4427	12.4460	12.4510	12.4527	12.4593	12.4659	12.4676	12.4725
2	25.6732	25.6997	25.7064	25.7263	25.7395	25.7528	25.7727	25.7794	25.8060	25.8326	25.8393	25.8593
3	39.7953	39.8567	39.8721	39.9182	39.9490	39.9798	40.0261	40.0415	40.1033	40.1652	40.1807	40.2272
4	54.8502	54.9635	54.9918	55.0770	55.1338	55.1907	55.2762	55.3047	55.4190	55.5335	55.5621	55.6482
5	70.8996	71.0837	71.1298	71.2684	71.3609	71.4535	71.5927	71.6392	71.8255	72.0122	72.0590	72.1995
6	88.0092	88.2855	88.3547	88.5627	88.7018	88.8410	89.0504	89.1203	89.4005	89.6818	89.7522	89.9640
7	106.2489	106.6413	106.7396	107.0353	107.2329	107.4309	107.7288	107.8283	108.2273	108.6281	108.7285	109.0305
8	125.6935	126.2285	126.3627	126.7662	127.0360	127.3065	127.7135	127.8495	128.3951	128.9435	129.0810	129.4946
9	146.4226	147.1299	147.3073	147.8412	148.1984	148.5565	149.0957	149.2759	149.9994	150.7269	150.9094	151.4585
10	168.5209	169.4335	169.6626	170.3519	170.8133	171.2762	171.9732	172.2063	173.1424	174.0844	174.3208	175.0324
15	302.9351	305.5079	306.1552	308.1066	309.4157	310.7313	312.7170	313.3823	316.0598	318.7643	319.4446	321.4959
20	488.0092	493.7774	495.2318	499.6253	502.5795	505.5541	510.0545	511.5649	517.6591	523.8377	525.3957	530.1020
25	742.8367	754.2626	757.1506	765.8915	771.7832	777.7272	786.7420	789.7736	802.0347	814.5145	817.6691	827.2170
30	1093.7072	1114.6638	1119.9740	1136.0781	1146.9603	1157.9609	1174.6867	1180.3227	1203.1746	1226.5279	1232.4459	1250.3941

Description: This table shows what a series of $ 1 deposits grow to in the future. The deposit is made at the beginning of a period.

Example: At 8 % a regular one dollar deposit will grow to $ 73.72 by the end of the fifth year.

YEAR	7.25 %	7.30 %	7.375%	7.40 %	7.50 %	7.60 %	7.625%	7.70 %	7.75 %	7.80 %	7.875%	7.90 %
1	12.4758	12.4792	12.4841	12.4858	12.4924	12.4991	12.5007	12.5057	12.5090	12.5123	12.5173	12.5190
2	25.8726	25.8859	25.9059	25.9126	25.9393	25.9661	25.9728	25.9929	26.0062	26.0196	26.0397	26.0465
3	40.2582	40.2893	40.3359	40.3514	40.4137	40.4761	40.4917	40.5385	40.5698	40.6011	40.6481	40.6637
4	55.7057	55.7632	55.8496	55.8785	55.9940	56.1097	56.1387	56.2258	56.2839	56.3420	56.4294	56.4586
5	72.2934	72.3874	72.5286	72.5758	72.7647	72.9542	73.0016	73.1442	73.2394	73.3347	73.4780	73.5258
6	90.1055	90.2473	90.4604	90.5315	90.8168	91.1031	91.1748	91.3904	91.5344	91.6787	91.8956	91.9681
7	109.2324	109.4347	109.7389	109.8406	110.2482	110.6575	110.7601	111.0686	111.2748	111.4814	111.7922	111.8960
8	129.7711	130.0484	130.4655	130.6049	131.1642	131.7263	131.8673	132.2912	132.5747	132.8588	133.2864	133.4293
9	151.8259	152.1943	152.7489	152.9343	153.6784	154.4268	154.6145	155.1794	155.5573	155.9362	156.5067	156.6974
10	175.5087	175.9864	176.7060	176.9466	177.9129	178.8853	179.1293	179.8639	180.3556	180.8488	181.5915	181.8399
15	322.8720	324.2550	326.3424	327.0418	329.8566	332.6997	333.4150	335.5715	337.0182	338.4722	340.6668	341.4021
20	533.2667	536.4533	541.2746	542.8929	549.4219	556.0418	557.7112	562.7539	566.1449	569.5595	574.7259	576.4599
25	833.6531	840.1465	849.9952	853.3072	866.7035	880.3398	883.7868	894.2205	901.2540	908.3503	919.1139	922.7338
30	1262.5232	1274.7850	1293.4297	1299.7126	1325.1893	1351.2278	1357.8268	1377.8410	1391.3673	1405.0422	1425.8370	1432.8448

YEAR	8.00 %	8.10 %	8.125%	8.20 %	8.25 %	8.30 %	8.375%	8.40 %	8.50 %	8.60 %	8.625%	8.70 %
1	12.5256	12.5322	12.5339	12.5389	12.5422	12.5455	12.5505	12.5522	12.5588	12.5655	12.5671	12.5721
2	26.0733	26.1001	26.1069	26.1270	26.1405	26.1539	26.1741	26.1809	26.2078	26.2348	26.2416	26.2618
3	40.7265	40.7893	40.8050	40.8523	40.8838	40.9153	40.9626	40.9784	41.0417	41.1050	41.1208	41.1684
4	56.5753	56.6924	56.7217	56.8097	56.8684	56.9273	57.0156	57.0451	57.1631	57.2815	57.3111	57.4001
5	73.7175	73.9097	73.9578	74.1025	74.1991	74.2958	74.4411	74.4897	74.6841	74.8791	74.9279	75.0746
6	92.2584	92.5499	92.6229	92.8423	92.9889	93.1358	93.3566	93.4304	93.7260	94.0226	94.0969	94.3203
7	112.3123	112.7304	112.8353	113.1503	113.3610	113.5720	113.8895	113.9955	114.4208	114.8479	114.9549	115.2768
8	134.0026	134.5788	134.7232	135.1578	135.4483	135.7396	136.1779	136.3244	136.9120	137.5026	137.6507	138.0961
9	157.4628	158.2326	158.4258	159.0068	159.3955	159.7853	160.3721	160.5683	161.3557	162.1475	162.3462	162.9439
10	182.8374	183.8413	184.0932	184.8515	185.3591	185.8682	186.6350	186.8914	187.9212	188.9575	189.2176	190.0005
15	344.3615	347.3508	348.1028	350.3703	351.8914	353.4202	355.7279	356.5010	359.6129	362.7563	363.5471	365.9314
20	583.4567	590.5511	592.3401	597.7446	601.3790	605.0387	610.5761	612.4347	619.9344	627.5390	629.4568	635.2503
25	937.3759	952.2814	956.0494	967.4551	975.1442	982.9023	994.6702	998.6281	1014.6375	1030.9362	1035.0566	1047.5294
30	1461.2628	1490.3104	1497.6723	1520.0021	1535.0941	1550.3527	1573.5573	1581.3776	1613.0922	1645.5126	1653.7299	1678.6550

YEAR	8.75 %	8.80 %	8.875%	8.90 %	9.00 %	9.10 %	9.125%	9.20 %	9.25 %	9.30 %	9.375%	9.40 %
1	12.5754	12.5788	12.5838	12.5854	12.5921	12.5987	12.6004	12.6054	12.6087	12.6121	12.6171	12.6187
2	26.2753	26.2888	26.3091	26.3159	26.3430	26.3701	26.3768	26.3972	26.4108	26.4243	26.4447	26.4515
3	41.2002	41.2319	41.2796	41.2955	41.3593	41.4231	41.4390	41.4870	41.5190	41.5510	41.5991	41.6151
4	57.4595	57.5189	57.6083	57.6381	57.7574	57.8771	57.9070	57.9970	58.0570	58.1171	58.2074	58.2376
5	75.1726	75.2707	75.4182	75.4674	75.6646	75.8625	75.9120	76.0608	76.1602	76.2598	76.4094	76.4593
6	94.4695	94.6191	94.8438	94.9189	95.2198	95.5217	95.5974	95.8248	95.9767	96.1289	96.3577	96.4341
7	115.4919	115.7075	116.0317	116.1401	116.5745	117.0107	117.1201	117.4488	117.6686	117.8888	118.2200	118.3307
8	138.3940	138.6925	139.1418	139.2919	139.8943	140.4997	140.6515	141.1080	141.4134	141.7194	142.1800	142.3339
9	163.3438	163.7448	164.3484	164.5502	165.3602	166.1748	166.3791	166.9940	167.4053	167.8178	168.4388	168.6464
10	190.5244	191.0501	191.8417	192.1064	193.1695	194.2394	194.5080	195.3162	195.8571	196.3998	197.2171	197.4904
15	367.5310	369.1387	371.5655	372.3785	375.6510	378.9568	379.7884	382.2960	383.9783	385.6691	388.2214	389.0765
20	639.1464	643.0697	649.0061	650.9988	659.0392	667.1926	669.2488	675.4607	679.6382	683.8450	690.2106	692.3474
25	1055.9381	1064.4227	1077.2930	1081.6218	1099.1324	1116.9605	1121.4678	1135.1119	1144.3108	1153.5929	1167.6736	1172.4096
30	1695.5022	1712.5362	1738.4422	1747.1732	1782.5837	1818.7853	1827.9615	1855.7966	1874.6117	1893.6362	1922.5711	1932.3234

YEAR	9.50 %	9.75 %	10.00 %	10.25 %	10.50 %	10.75 %	11.00 %	12.00 %	13.00 %	14.00 %	15.00 %	16.00 %
1	12.6254	12.6421	12.6587	12.6754	12.6921	12.7089	12.7256	12.7926	12.8598	12.9272	12.9947	13.0624
2	26.4787	26.5468	26.6150	26.6834	26.7520	26.8206	26.8895	27.1664	27.4457	27.7274	28.0117	28.2984
3	41.6793	41.8403	42.0018	42.1640	42.3268	42.4902	42.6543	43.3167	43.9894	44.6723	45.3657	46.0696
4	58.3583	58.6612	58.9657	59.2720	59.5799	59.8895	60.2008	61.4633	62.7536	64.0725	65.4204	66.7980
5	76.6594	77.1621	77.6685	78.1785	78.6922	79.2095	79.7306	81.8527	84.0365	86.2837	88.5961	90.9756
6	96.7404	97.5109	98.2883	99.0726	99.8639	100.6623	101.4678	104.7623	108.1761	111.7134	115.3786	119.1764
7	118.7744	119.8920	121.0216	122.1632	123.3170	124.4831	125.6618	130.5036	135.5558	140.8278	146.3291	152.0697
8	142.9513	144.5085	146.0850	147.6812	149.2973	150.9336	152.5903	159.4264	166.6106	174.1609	182.0962	190.4365
9	169.4796	171.5835	173.7175	175.8819	178.0772	180.3039	182.5624	191.9241	201.8337	212.3240	223.4296	235.1875
10	198.5880	201.3628	204.1823	207.0472	209.9583	212.9163	215.9221	228.4385	241.7846	256.0168	271.1956	287.3851
15	392.5184	401.2770	410.2599	419.4731	428.9227	438.6151	448.5567	490.9513	537.8995	589.9076	647.5388	711.4186
20	700.9695	723.0602	745.9386	769.6339	794.1764	819.5976	845.9303	961.0718	1093.7478	1246.7213	1423.1940	1626.8749
25	1191.5684	1241.0046	1292.7239	1346.8356	1403.4547	1462.7013	1524.7017	1802.9860	2137.1514	2538.7732	3021.8438	3603.2766
30	1971.8779	2074.6913	2183.3795	2298.2895	2419.7893	2548.2689	2684.1414	3310.7260	4095.7635	5080.4348	6316.7116	7870.1795

Description: This table shows what a series of $ 1 deposits grow to in the future. The deposit is made at the beginning of a period.

Example: At 5 % a regular one dollar deposit will grow to $ 22.83 by the end of the fifth year.

YEAR	0.00 %	1.00 %	2.00 %	3.00 %	4.00 %	4.125%	4.25 %	4.375%	4.50 %	4.625%	4.75 %	4.875%
1	4.0000	4.0250	4.0502	4.0753	4.1006	4.1038	4.1069	4.1101	4.1133	4.1164	4.1196	4.1228
2	8.0000	8.0904	8.1817	8.2739	8.3669	8.3786	8.3903	8.4020	8.4137	8.4254	8.4372	8.4490
3	12.0000	12.1966	12.3963	12.5993	12.8055	12.8315	12.8576	12.8837	12.9098	12.9360	12.9623	12.9886
4	16.0000	16.3439	16.6956	17.0554	17.4234	17.4700	17.5167	17.5636	17.6106	17.6577	17.7049	17.7523
5	20.0000	20.5328	21.0814	21.6463	22.2279	22.3018	22.3760	22.4505	22.5252	22.6002	22.6755	22.7511
6	24.0000	24.7636	25.5552	26.3759	27.2265	27.3350	27.4440	27.5535	27.6635	27.7740	27.8850	27.9965
7	28.0000	29.0369	30.1191	31.2484	32.4271	32.5780	32.7297	32.8823	33.0356	33.1898	33.3448	33.5007
8	32.0000	33.3531	34.7746	36.2682	37.8377	38.0395	38.2425	38.4467	38.6522	38.8590	39.0671	39.2765
9	36.0000	37.7125	39.5237	41.4398	43.4670	43.7285	43.9920	44.2572	44.5244	44.7935	45.0644	45.3373
10	40.0000	42.1156	44.3683	46.7676	49.3237	49.6547	49.9884	50.3248	50.6638	51.0055	51.3500	51.6972
15	60.0000	64.8021	70.0916	75.9220	82.3532	83.2026	84.0625	84.9331	85.8146	86.7071	87.6106	88.5255
20	80.0000	88.6489	98.5060	109.7568	122.6160	124.3485	126.1105	127.9025	129.7251	131.5789	133.4643	135.3821
25	100.0000	113.7152	129.8933	149.0235	171.6962	174.8134	177.9984	181.2528	184.5783	187.9765	191.4491	194.9978
30	120.0000	140.0633	164.5644	194.5941	231.5246	236.7077	242.0288	247.4919	253.1011	258.8604	264.7742	270.8468

YEAR	5.00 %	5.10 %	5.125%	5.20 %	5.25 %	5.30 %	5.375%	5.40 %	5.50 %	5.60 %	5.625%	5.70 %
1	4.1259	4.1285	4.1291	4.1310	4.1323	4.1336	4.1355	4.1361	4.1386	4.1412	4.1418	4.1437
2	8.4608	8.4702	8.4725	8.4796	8.4844	8.4891	8.4962	8.4986	8.5080	8.5175	8.5199	8.5270
3	13.0150	13.0362	13.0414	13.0573	13.0679	13.0785	13.0944	13.0998	13.1210	13.1423	13.1477	13.1637
4	17.7998	17.8379	17.8475	17.8761	17.8953	17.9144	17.9432	17.9528	17.9912	18.0298	18.0394	18.0684
5	22.8269	22.8878	22.9030	22.9488	22.9794	23.0100	23.0561	23.0714	23.1330	23.1948	23.2102	23.2567
6	28.1084	28.1984	28.2209	28.2887	28.3339	28.3793	28.4474	28.4702	28.5615	28.6530	28.6760	28.7450
7	33.6574	33.7833	33.8149	33.9098	33.9733	34.0368	34.1325	34.1644	34.2926	34.4212	34.4535	34.5505
8	39.4872	39.6567	39.6992	39.8271	39.9126	39.9983	40.1272	40.1703	40.3432	40.5170	40.5606	40.6916
9	45.6122	45.8335	45.8890	46.0560	46.1677	46.2798	46.4485	46.5049	46.7312	46.9589	47.0160	47.1878
10	52.0472	52.3293	52.4000	52.6131	52.7556	52.8987	53.1141	53.1861	53.4754	53.7666	53.8397	54.0596
15	89.4518	90.2011	90.3896	90.9579	91.3392	91.7223	92.3006	92.4944	93.2741	94.0617	94.2598	94.8572
20	137.3327	138.9173	139.3168	140.5236	141.3350	142.1519	143.3879	143.8027	145.4761	147.1726	147.6003	148.8924
25	198.6244	201.5830	202.3307	204.5935	206.1186	207.6570	209.9900	210.7745	213.9469	217.1752	217.9912	220.4606
30	277.0829	282.1925	283.4870	287.4122	290.0640	292.7443	296.8189	298.1916	303.7567	309.4421	310.8826	315.2507

YEAR	5.75 %	5.80 %	5.875%	5.90 %	6.00 %	6.10 %	6.125%	6.20 %	6.25 %	6.30 %	6.375%	6.40 %
1	4.1450	4.1463	4.1482	4.1488	4.1514	4.1539	4.1545	4.1564	4.1577	4.1590	4.1609	4.1615
2	8.5317	8.5365	8.5436	8.5460	8.5555	8.5650	8.5674	8.5746	8.5793	8.5841	8.5913	8.5937
3	13.1744	13.1851	13.2011	13.2065	13.2279	13.2494	13.2547	13.2709	13.2816	13.2924	13.3086	13.3140
4	18.0878	18.1071	18.1362	18.1459	18.1848	18.2238	18.2336	18.2629	18.2824	18.3020	18.3314	18.3413
5	23.2878	23.3188	23.3655	23.3811	23.4436	23.5063	23.5220	23.5692	23.6007	23.6322	23.6796	23.6954
6	28.7910	28.8372	28.9066	28.9298	29.0227	29.1160	29.1393	29.2095	29.2565	29.3035	29.3741	29.3977
7	34.6153	34.6803	34.7780	34.8106	34.9415	35.0730	35.1060	35.2050	35.2713	35.3377	35.4375	35.4708
8	40.7793	40.8672	40.9994	41.0435	41.2208	41.3990	41.4437	41.5780	41.6679	41.7580	41.8935	41.9388
9	47.3028	47.4181	47.5916	47.6496	47.8825	48.1167	48.1755	48.3523	48.4705	48.5892	48.7677	48.8274
10	54.2068	54.3545	54.5769	54.6512	54.9499	55.2505	55.3259	55.5530	55.7050	55.8575	56.0871	56.1639
15	95.2579	95.6606	96.2685	96.4721	97.2917	98.1196	98.3279	98.9558	99.3770	99.8004	100.4394	100.6535
20	149.7612	150.6360	151.9594	152.4036	154.1956	156.0124	156.4705	157.8543	158.7848	159.7217	161.1392	161.6149
25	222.1250	223.8041	226.3504	227.2067	230.6696	234.1939	235.0847	237.7808	239.5980	241.4313	244.2118	245.1469
30	318.2021	321.1854	325.7208	327.2489	333.4443	339.7745	341.3785	346.2427	349.5295	352.8520	357.9036	359.6057

YEAR	6.50 %	6.60 %	6.625%	6.70 %	6.75 %	6.80 %	6.875%	6.90 %	7.00 %	7.10 %	7.125%	7.20 %
1	4.1641	4.1666	4.1673	4.1692	4.1705	4.1717	4.1736	4.1743	4.1768	4.1794	4.1800	4.1819
2	8.6032	8.6128	8.6152	8.6224	8.6272	8.6320	8.6392	8.6416	8.6512	8.6608	8.6632	8.6704
3	13.3356	13.3573	13.3627	13.3789	13.3898	13.4007	13.4170	13.4224	13.4442	13.4660	13.4715	13.4879
4	18.3806	18.4200	18.4299	18.4595	18.4793	18.4991	18.5289	18.5388	18.5786	18.6185	18.6284	18.6584
5	23.7588	23.8224	23.8384	23.8862	23.9182	23.9502	23.9983	24.0143	24.0787	24.1432	24.1594	24.2079
6	29.4923	29.5873	29.6111	29.6826	29.7304	29.7782	29.8502	29.8742	29.9705	30.0672	30.0914	30.1642
7	35.6046	35.7389	35.7726	35.8738	35.9415	36.0093	36.1113	36.1454	36.2820	36.4193	36.4537	36.5571
8	42.1206	42.3032	42.3490	42.4868	42.5789	42.6713	42.8103	42.8567	43.0430	43.2303	43.2773	43.4185
9	49.0670	49.3079	49.3684	49.5503	49.6720	49.7940	49.9777	50.0391	50.2856	50.5335	50.5957	50.7829
10	56.4722	56.7826	56.8605	57.0949	57.2519	57.4093	57.6464	57.7256	58.0440	58.3645	58.4449	58.6870
15	101.5151	102.3855	102.6045	103.2646	103.7075	104.1526	104.8245	105.0496	105.9555	106.8707	107.1009	107.7951
20	163.5345	165.4806	165.9714	167.4538	168.4506	169.4544	170.9731	171.4828	173.5394	175.6247	176.1506	177.7391
25	248.9285	252.7776	253.7505	256.6952	258.6802	260.6829	263.7203	264.7417	268.8732	273.0786	274.1417	277.3594
30	366.5071	373.5595	375.3467	380.7666	384.4291	388.1317	393.7615	395.6585	403.3509	411.2125	413.2049	419.2474

Description: This table shows what a series of $ 1 deposits grow to in the future. The deposit is made at the beginning of a period.

Example: At 8 % a regular one dollar deposit will grow to $ 24.73 by the end of the fifth year.

YEAR	7.25 %	7.30 %	7.375%	7.40 %	7.50 %	7.60 %	7.625%	7.70 %	7.75 %	7.80 %	7.875%	7.90 %
1	4.1832	4.1845	4.1864	4.1871	4.1896	4.1922	4.1928	4.1947	4.1960	4.1973	4.1992	4.1998
2	8.6752	8.6800	8.6873	8.6897	8.6993	8.7090	8.7114	8.7187	8.7235	8.7283	8.7356	8.7380
3	13.4988	13.5097	13.5262	13.5317	13.5536	13.5756	13.5811	13.5976	13.6087	13.6197	13.6363	13.6418
4	18.6784	18.6985	18.7285	18.7386	18.7788	18.8191	18.8292	18.8595	18.8798	18.9000	18.9305	18.9406
5	24.2404	24.2728	24.3217	24.3380	24.4032	24.4687	24.4851	24.5344	24.5673	24.6003	24.6498	24.6663
6	30.2129	30.2616	30.3349	30.3593	30.4574	30.5558	30.5805	30.6546	30.7042	30.7538	30.8284	30.8533
7	36.6262	36.6955	36.7997	36.8345	36.9742	37.1144	37.1495	37.2552	37.3258	37.3966	37.5031	37.5387
8	43.5130	43.6077	43.7502	43.7978	43.9888	44.1808	44.2290	44.3738	44.4707	44.5677	44.7138	44.7626
9	50.9081	51.0336	51.2226	51.2858	51.5395	51.7945	51.8585	52.0511	52.1799	52.3091	52.5036	52.5686
10	58.8490	59.0116	59.2564	59.3382	59.6670	59.9979	60.0809	60.3309	60.4982	60.6660	60.9188	61.0034
15	108.2608	108.7288	109.4353	109.6720	110.6247	111.5870	111.8291	112.5591	113.0489	113.5411	114.2841	114.5330
20	178.8073	179.8829	181.5104	182.0567	184.2608	186.4957	187.0593	188.7619	189.9068	191.0598	192.8043	193.3898
25	279.5285	281.7170	285.0364	286.1527	290.6682	295.2648	296.4268	299.9441	302.3153	304.7077	308.3367	309.5572
30	423.3310	427.4594	433.7372	435.8527	444.4315	453.2000	455.4223	462.1627	466.7182	471.3239	478.3280	480.6884

YEAR	8.00 %	8.10 %	8.125%	8.20 %	8.25 %	8.30 %	8.375%	8.40 %	8.50 %	8.60 %	8.625%	8.70 %
1	4.2024	4.2050	4.2056	4.2075	4.2088	4.2101	4.2120	4.2126	4.2152	4.2178	4.2184	4.2203
2	8.7477	8.7574	8.7598	8.7671	8.7720	8.7769	8.7842	8.7866	8.7963	8.8061	8.8085	8.8158
3	13.6639	13.6861	13.6916	13.7083	13.7194	13.7305	13.7472	13.7528	13.7751	13.7975	13.8030	13.8198
4	18.9813	19.0221	19.0323	19.0629	19.0834	19.1039	19.1347	19.1449	19.1861	19.2273	19.2376	19.2686
5	24.7326	24.7990	24.8157	24.8657	24.8991	24.9325	24.9828	24.9995	25.0668	25.1342	25.1511	25.2018
6	30.9532	31.0534	31.0785	31.1540	31.2044	31.2549	31.3309	31.3562	31.4579	31.5600	31.5856	31.6624
7	37.6813	37.8246	37.8605	37.9685	38.0407	38.1130	38.2218	38.2581	38.4039	38.5503	38.5870	38.6973
8	44.9585	45.1554	45.2048	45.3533	45.4526	45.5521	45.7019	45.7519	45.9528	46.1546	46.2053	46.3575
9	52.8296	53.0920	53.1579	53.3560	53.4885	53.6215	53.8216	53.8885	54.1570	54.4271	54.4948	54.6987
10	61.3428	61.6845	61.7703	62.0284	62.2012	62.3745	62.6355	62.7228	63.0734	63.4262	63.5148	63.7813
15	115.5350	116.5471	116.8017	117.5695	118.0846	118.6023	119.3838	119.6456	120.6995	121.7641	122.0320	122.8396
20	195.7526	198.1484	198.7526	200.5779	201.8054	203.0415	204.9119	205.5398	208.0731	210.6421	211.2900	213.2473
25	314.4942	319.5203	320.7909	324.6372	327.2303	329.8467	333.8156	335.1504	340.5502	346.0479	347.4378	351.6453
30	490.2608	500.0459	502.5260	510.0487	515.1333	520.2742	528.0925	530.7275	541.4140	552.3390	555.1081	563.5080

YEAR	8.75 %	8.80 %	8.875%	8.90 %	9.00 %	9.10 %	9.125%	9.20 %	9.25 %	9.30 %	9.375%	9.40 %
1	4.2216	4.2229	4.2248	4.2255	4.2280	4.2306	4.2312	4.2332	4.2345	4.2357	4.2377	4.2383
2	8.8207	8.8256	8.8329	8.8354	8.8452	8.8550	8.8574	8.8648	8.8697	8.8746	8.8819	8.8844
3	13.8310	13.8422	13.8591	13.8647	13.8872	13.9097	13.9153	13.9322	13.9435	13.9548	13.9718	13.9775
4	19.2893	19.3101	19.3412	19.3516	19.3932	19.4349	19.4453	19.4767	19.4976	19.5186	19.5500	19.5605
5	25.2357	25.2696	25.3206	25.3377	25.4059	25.4743	25.4914	25.5429	25.5773	25.6117	25.6635	25.6807
6	31.7137	31.7652	31.8425	31.8684	31.9719	32.0758	32.1018	32.1801	32.2324	32.2847	32.3635	32.3898
7	38.7710	38.8449	38.9561	38.9932	39.1421	39.2917	39.3292	39.4419	39.5173	39.5928	39.7063	39.7443
8	46.4593	46.5614	46.7150	46.7663	46.9722	47.1792	47.2311	47.3872	47.4916	47.5963	47.7537	47.8064
9	54.8351	54.9718	55.1777	55.2466	55.5229	55.8008	55.8705	56.0803	56.2206	56.3614	56.5732	56.6441
10	63.9597	64.1387	64.4082	64.4984	64.8604	65.2248	65.3162	65.5915	65.7757	65.9606	66.2390	66.3320
15	123.3814	123.9260	124.7481	125.0235	126.1321	127.2521	127.5338	128.3835	128.9535	129.5264	130.3912	130.6810
20	214.5636	215.8892	217.8950	218.5683	221.2852	224.0405	224.7353	226.8346	228.2465	229.6683	231.8198	232.5420
25	354.4820	357.3444	361.6865	363.1469	369.0550	375.0706	376.5915	381.1957	384.2999	387.4324	392.1844	393.7828
30	569.1859	574.9268	583.6583	586.6012	598.5370	610.7404	613.8338	623.2175	629.5607	635.9748	645.7305	649.0187

YEAR	9.50 %	9.75 %	10.00 %	10.25 %	10.50 %	10.75 %	11.00 %	12.00 %	13.00 %	14.00 %	15.00 %	16.00 %
1	4.2409	4.2473	4.2538	4.2602	4.2666	4.2731	4.2795	4.3054	4.3313	4.3574	4.3834	4.4096
2	8.8942	8.9188	8.9435	8.9682	8.9930	9.0179	9.0428	9.1429	9.2440	9.3461	9.4490	9.5530
3	14.0001	14.0569	14.1140	14.1712	14.2287	14.2864	14.3444	14.5784	14.8162	15.0577	15.3030	15.5522
4	19.6026	19.7082	19.8144	19.9212	20.0286	20.1366	20.2452	20.6857	21.1362	21.5969	22.0680	22.5497
5	25.7500	25.9239	26.0991	26.2756	26.4534	26.6325	26.8129	27.5479	28.3046	29.0836	29.8857	30.7115
6	32.4952	32.7604	33.0280	33.2981	33.5706	33.8455	34.1230	35.2582	36.4351	37.6552	38.9201	40.2315
7	39.8964	40.2797	40.6672	41.0588	41.4547	41.8548	42.2593	43.9215	45.6569	47.4688	49.3605	51.3356
8	48.0175	48.5500	49.0893	49.6353	50.1883	50.7482	51.3152	53.6556	56.1165	58.7044	61.4257	64.2875
9	56.9284	57.6464	58.3747	59.1135	59.8630	60.6233	61.3946	64.5928	67.9801	71.5680	75.3685	79.3945
10	66.7059	67.6512	68.6119	69.5881	70.5803	71.5886	72.6133	76.8819	81.4361	86.2955	91.4811	97.0154
15	131.8474	134.8157	137.8606	140.9840	144.1881	147.4750	150.8469	165.2316	181.1713	198.8400	218.4312	240.1604
20	235.4564	242.9242	250.6595	258.6723	266.9730	275.5722	284.4812	323.4525	368.3879	420.2319	480.0794	549.1998
25	400.2491	416.9363	434.3971	452.6686	471.7900	491.8021	512.7479	606.8020	719.8194	855.7434	1019.3445	1216.3927
30	662.3559	697.0274	733.6862	772.4503	813.4444	856.8010	902.6604	1114.2379	1379.5044	1712.4604	2130.7869	2656.8122

SAVINGS GROWTH

SEMIANNUAL COMPOUNDING
Semiannual Deposit

Description: This table shows what a series of $ 1 deposits grow to in the future. The deposit is made at the beginning of a period.

Example: At 5 % a regular one dollar deposit will grow to $ 11.48 by the end of the fifth year.

YEAR	0.00 %	1.00 %	2.00 %	3.00 %	4.00 %	4.125%	4.25 %	4.375%	4.50 %	4.625%	4.75 %	4.875%
1	2.0000	2.0150	2.0301	2.0452	2.0604	2.0623	2.0642	2.0661	2.0680	2.0699	2.0718	2.0737
2	4.0000	4.0503	4.1010	4.1523	4.2040	4.2105	4.2171	4.2236	4.2301	4.2367	4.2432	4.2498
3	6.0000	6.1059	6.2135	6.3230	6.4343	6.4483	6.4624	6.4765	6.4906	6.5048	6.5190	6.5332
4	8.0000	8.1821	8.3685	8.5593	8.7546	8.7794	8.8042	8.8290	8.8540	8.8790	8.9041	8.9293
5	10.0000	10.2792	10.5668	10.8633	11.1687	11.2075	11.2465	11.2856	11.3249	11.3643	11.4039	11.4436
6	12.0000	12.3972	12.8093	13.2368	13.6803	13.7369	13.7938	13.8509	13.9083	13.9659	14.0238	14.0820
7	14.0000	14.5365	15.0969	15.6821	16.2934	16.3717	16.4504	16.5296	16.6092	16.6892	16.7697	16.8506
8	16.0000	16.6973	17.4304	18.2014	19.0121	19.1163	19.2212	19.3268	19.4330	19.5399	19.6475	19.7558
9	18.0000	18.8797	19.8109	20.7967	21.8406	21.9753	22.1110	22.2477	22.3853	22.5240	22.6637	22.8043
10	20.0000	21.0840	22.2392	23.4705	24.7833	24.9534	25.1249	25.2978	25.4720	25.6477	25.8248	26.0033
15	30.0000	32.4414	35.1327	38.1018	41.3794	41.8125	42.2510	42.6951	43.1447	43.5999	44.0609	44.5276
20	40.0000	44.3796	49.3752	55.0819	61.6100	62.4900	63.3850	64.2954	65.2214	66.1633	67.1215	68.0961
25	50.0000	56.9284	65.1078	74.7881	86.2710	87.8505	89.4646	91.1140	92.7997	94.5223	96.2829	98.0823
30	60.0000	70.1189	82.4864	97.6579	116.3326	118.9548	121.6472	124.4118	127.2506	130.1657	133.1594	136.2338

YEAR	5.00 %	5.10 %	5.125%	5.20 %	5.25 %	5.30 %	5.375%	5.40 %	5.50 %	5.60 %	5.625%	5.70 %
1	2.0756	2.0772	2.0775	2.0787	2.0794	2.0802	2.0813	2.0817	2.0833	2.0848	2.0852	2.0863
2	4.2563	4.2616	4.2629	4.2668	4.2695	4.2721	4.2761	4.2774	4.2827	4.2880	4.2893	4.2932
3	6.5474	6.5588	6.5617	6.5703	6.5760	6.5817	6.5903	6.5932	6.6047	6.6162	6.6191	6.6278
4	8.9545	8.9748	8.9798	8.9951	9.0052	9.0154	9.0307	9.0358	9.0562	9.0767	9.0818	9.0972
5	11.4835	11.5155	11.5235	11.5476	11.5636	11.5797	11.6040	11.6120	11.6444	11.6769	11.6850	11.7095
6	14.1404	14.1874	14.1992	14.2345	14.2581	14.2818	14.3174	14.3293	14.3769	14.4247	14.4367	14.4727
7	16.9319	16.9973	17.0137	17.0630	17.0960	17.1290	17.1786	17.1952	17.2618	17.3286	17.3454	17.3958
8	19.8647	19.9524	19.9744	20.0405	20.0847	20.1290	20.1957	20.2180	20.3075	20.3974	20.4199	20.4878
9	22.9460	23.0601	23.0887	23.1748	23.2324	23.2902	23.3772	23.4063	23.5230	23.6404	23.6699	23.7585
10	26.1833	26.3283	26.3647	26.4743	26.5476	26.6212	26.7320	26.7690	26.9178	27.0676	27.1052	27.2184
15	45.0003	45.3827	45.4789	45.7689	45.9635	46.1591	46.4543	46.5532	46.9512	47.3533	47.4544	47.7594
20	69.0876	69.8931	70.0962	70.7098	71.1223	71.5377	72.1661	72.3770	73.2280	74.0908	74.3083	74.9655
25	99.9215	101.4220	101.8012	102.9490	103.7226	104.5030	105.6865	106.0845	107.6940	109.3321	109.7461	110.9993
30	139.3914	141.9789	142.6344	144.6223	145.9654	147.3230	149.3869	150.0822	152.9014	155.7818	156.5117	158.7250

YEAR	5.75 %	5.80 %	5.875%	5.90 %	6.00 %	6.10 %	6.125%	6.20 %	6.25 %	6.30 %	6.375%	6.40 %
1	2.0871	2.0878	2.0890	2.0894	2.0909	2.0924	2.0928	2.0940	2.0947	2.0955	2.0966	2.0970
2	4.2959	4.2985	4.3025	4.3038	4.3091	4.3144	4.3158	4.3198	4.3224	4.3251	4.3291	4.3304
3	6.6335	6.6393	6.6480	6.6509	6.6625	6.6741	6.6770	6.6857	6.6915	6.6973	6.7061	6.7090
4	9.1075	9.1178	9.1333	9.1384	9.1591	9.1798	9.1850	9.2006	9.2110	9.2214	9.2371	9.2423
5	11.7258	11.7421	11.7667	11.7749	11.8078	11.8408	11.8490	11.8738	11.8904	11.9070	11.9319	11.9403
6	14.4968	14.5209	14.5572	14.5693	14.6178	14.6665	14.6787	14.7154	14.7399	14.7645	14.8014	14.8137
7	17.4294	17.4632	17.5139	17.5309	17.5989	17.6672	17.6844	17.7358	17.7703	17.8048	17.8566	17.8740
8	20.5314	20.5786	20.6470	20.6698	20.7616	20.8538	20.8769	20.9465	20.9930	21.0396	21.1098	21.1332
9	23.8178	23.8773	23.9668	23.9967	24.1169	24.2377	24.2680	24.3592	24.4203	24.4815	24.5736	24.6044
10	27.2941	27.3701	27.4845	27.5228	27.6765	27.8312	27.8700	27.9869	28.0651	28.1436	28.2618	28.3013
15	47.9640	48.1697	48.4801	48.5841	49.0027	49.4255	49.5319	49.8526	50.0678	50.2841	50.6105	50.7199
20	75.4074	75.8524	76.5256	76.7516	77.6633	78.5877	78.8208	79.5249	79.9984	80.4752	81.1966	81.4388
25	111.8439	112.6961	113.9884	114.4230	116.1808	117.9698	118.4221	119.7908	120.7135	121.6444	123.0562	123.5310
30	160.2205	161.7322	164.0306	164.8051	167.9450	171.1537	171.9667	174.4326	176.0988	177.7833	180.3445	181.2076

YEAR	6.50 %	6.60 %	6.625%	6.70 %	6.75 %	6.80 %	6.875%	6.90 %	7.00 %	7.10 %	7.125%	7.20 %
1	2.0986	2.1001	2.1005	2.1016	2.1024	2.1032	2.1043	2.1047	2.1062	2.1078	2.1081	2.1093
2	4.3357	4.3411	4.3424	4.3464	4.3491	4.3518	4.3558	4.3571	4.3625	4.3678	4.3692	4.3732
3	6.7207	6.7324	6.7353	6.7441	6.7500	6.7559	6.7647	6.7676	6.7794	6.7912	6.7942	6.8030
4	9.2632	9.2842	9.2894	9.3052	9.3157	9.3262	9.3421	9.3473	9.3685	9.3897	9.3950	9.4110
5	11.9736	12.0071	12.0155	12.0407	12.0575	12.0743	12.0997	12.1081	12.1420	12.1760	12.1845	12.2100
6	14.8631	14.9127	14.9252	14.9625	14.9875	15.0125	15.0501	15.0627	15.1130	15.1636	15.1762	15.2143
7	17.9435	18.0133	18.0308	18.0834	18.1186	18.1539	18.2069	18.2246	18.2957	18.3670	18.3849	18.4387
8	21.2273	21.3219	21.3456	21.4170	21.4647	21.5125	21.5845	21.6085	21.7050	21.8020	21.8263	21.8995
9	24.7281	24.8525	24.8837	24.9775	25.0404	25.1034	25.1982	25.2299	25.3572	25.4852	25.5173	25.6139
10	28.4601	28.6199	28.6600	28.7807	28.8615	28.9426	29.0647	29.1055	29.2695	29.4345	29.4760	29.6006
15	51.1602	51.6049	51.7168	52.0541	52.2805	52.5079	52.8513	52.9664	53.4295	53.8973	54.0150	54.3699
20	82.4158	83.4064	83.6562	84.4109	84.9184	85.4295	86.2027	86.4623	87.5095	88.5715	88.8393	89.6483
25	125.4515	127.4063	127.9005	129.3962	130.4045	131.4218	132.9648	133.4838	135.5828	137.7197	138.2599	139.8950
30	184.7071	188.2835	189.1898	191.9387	193.7963	195.6744	198.5302	199.4925	203.3950	207.3837	208.3946	211.4607

Description: This table shows what a series of $ 1 deposits grow to in the future. The deposit is made at the beginning of a period.

Example: At 8 % a regular one dollar deposit will grow to $ 12.49 by the end of the fifth year.

YEAR	7.25 %	7.30 %	7.375%	7.40 %	7.50 %	7.60 %	7.625%	7.70 %	7.75 %	7.80 %	7.875%	7.90 %
1	2.1101	2.1108	2.1120	2.1124	2.1139	2.1154	2.1158	2.1170	2.1178	2.1185	2.1197	2.1201
2	4.3759	4.3786	4.3826	4.3839	4.3893	4.3947	4.3961	4.4001	4.4028	4.4055	4.4096	4.4109
3	6.8089	6.8149	6.8238	6.8267	6.8386	6.8505	6.8535	6.8624	6.8684	6.8744	6.8833	6.8863
4	9.4216	9.4323	9.4483	9.4536	9.4750	9.4965	9.5019	9.5180	9.5288	9.5395	9.5557	9.5611
5	12.2271	12.2442	12.2699	12.2785	12.3129	12.3474	12.3560	12.3820	12.3993	12.4167	12.4427	12.4514
6	15.2397	15.2652	15.3035	15.3163	15.3676	15.4190	15.4319	15.4707	15.4966	15.5226	15.5616	15.5746
7	18.4747	18.5107	18.5649	18.5830	18.6557	18.7286	18.7469	18.8019	18.8386	18.8754	18.9308	18.9494
8	21.9484	21.9975	22.0713	22.0960	22.1950	22.2945	22.3194	22.3945	22.4446	22.4950	22.5707	22.5960
9	25.6786	25.7435	25.8411	25.8737	26.0047	26.1365	26.1695	26.2690	26.3356	26.4023	26.5028	26.5364
10	29.6841	29.7679	29.8940	29.9361	30.1055	30.2760	30.3188	30.4476	30.5339	30.6204	30.7506	30.7942
15	54.6080	54.8473	55.2085	55.3295	55.8167	56.3089	56.4327	56.8061	57.0566	57.3083	57.6884	57.8157
20	90.1924	90.7403	91.5693	91.8476	92.9705	94.1092	94.3963	95.2639	95.8473	96.4348	97.3239	97.6223
25	140.9973	142.1096	143.7967	144.3641	146.6593	148.9960	149.5868	151.3750	152.5806	153.7971	155.6424	156.2631
30	213.5329	215.6280	218.8140	219.8878	224.2420	228.6931	229.8212	233.2431	235.5559	237.8944	241.4507	242.6493

YEAR	8.00 %	8.10 %	8.125%	8.20 %	8.25 %	8.30 %	8.375%	8.40 %	8.50 %	8.60 %	8.625%	8.70 %
1	2.1216	2.1231	2.1235	2.1247	2.1255	2.1262	2.1274	2.1278	2.1293	2.1308	2.1312	2.1324
2	4.4163	4.4217	4.4231	4.4272	4.4299	4.4326	4.4367	4.4380	4.4434	4.4489	4.4503	4.4543
3	6.8983	6.9103	6.9133	6.9223	6.9283	6.9343	6.9434	6.9464	6.9585	6.9706	6.9736	6.9827
4	9.5828	9.6045	9.6099	9.6263	9.6372	9.6481	9.6644	9.6699	9.6918	9.7138	9.7193	9.7358
5	12.4864	12.5214	12.5301	12.5565	12.5741	12.5917	12.6182	12.6270	12.6624	12.6980	12.7069	12.7336
6	15.6268	15.6793	15.6924	15.7319	15.7583	15.7847	15.8244	15.8377	15.8909	15.9443	15.9577	15.9979
7	19.0236	19.0981	19.1168	19.1730	19.2106	19.2482	19.3049	19.3238	19.3997	19.4759	19.4950	19.5524
8	22.6975	22.7996	22.8252	22.9021	22.9536	23.0052	23.0829	23.1088	23.2130	23.3177	23.3439	23.4229
9	26.6712	26.8069	26.8409	26.9433	27.0118	27.0805	27.1839	27.2185	27.3573	27.4969	27.5320	27.6374
10	30.9692	31.1453	31.1895	31.3226	31.4117	31.5010	31.6356	31.6806	31.8614	32.0434	32.0890	32.2265
15	58.3283	58.8462	58.9765	59.3693	59.6329	59.8978	60.2978	60.4318	60.9712	61.5161	61.6532	62.0666
20	98.8265	100.0478	100.3558	101.2863	101.9120	102.5422	103.4959	103.8160	105.1078	106.4179	106.7483	107.7465
25	158.7738	161.3300	161.9763	163.9327	165.2518	166.5828	168.6019	169.2810	172.0284	174.8259	175.5332	177.6743
30	247.5103	252.4798	253.7395	257.5604	260.1431	262.7545	266.7263	268.0650	273.4944	279.0455	280.4527	284.7213

YEAR	8.75 %	8.80 %	8.875%	8.90 %	9.00 %	9.10 %	9.125%	9.20 %	9.25 %	9.30 %	9.375%	9.40 %
1	2.1332	2.1339	2.1351	2.1355	2.1370	2.1386	2.1390	2.1401	2.1409	2.1417	2.1428	2.1432
2	4.4571	4.4598	4.4639	4.4652	4.4707	4.4762	4.4775	4.4817	4.4844	4.4871	4.4912	4.4926
3	6.9888	6.9948	7.0039	7.0070	7.0192	7.0313	7.0344	7.0436	7.0497	7.0558	7.0650	7.0681
4	9.7468	9.7578	9.7744	9.7800	9.8021	9.8243	9.8299	9.8466	9.8577	9.8689	9.8857	9.8913
5	12.7515	12.7694	12.7962	12.8052	12.8412	12.8772	12.8863	12.9134	12.9316	12.9497	12.9770	12.9861
6	16.0248	16.0517	16.0922	16.1057	16.1599	16.2143	16.2279	16.2689	16.2963	16.3237	16.3649	16.3787
7	19.5908	19.6293	19.6872	19.7065	19.7841	19.8619	19.8815	19.9402	19.9794	20.0188	20.0779	20.0977
8	23.4757	23.5286	23.6083	23.6349	23.7417	23.8491	23.8760	23.9570	24.0112	24.0655	24.1472	24.1745
9	27.7079	27.7786	27.8851	27.9207	28.0636	28.2073	28.2433	28.3518	28.4244	28.4972	28.6068	28.6435
10	32.3185	32.4108	32.5499	32.5964	32.7831	32.9711	33.0183	33.1603	33.2554	33.3508	33.4944	33.5425
15	62.3440	62.6228	63.0437	63.1847	63.7524	64.3259	64.4702	64.9053	65.1973	65.4907	65.9337	66.0821
20	108.4179	109.0940	110.1172	110.4607	111.8467	113.2524	113.6069	114.6781	115.3986	116.1241	117.2221	117.5907
25	179.1180	180.5748	182.7849	183.5282	186.5357	189.5981	190.3724	192.7166	194.2972	195.8922	198.3121	199.1261
30	287.6068	290.5245	294.9624	296.4582	302.5254	308.7292	310.3018	315.0728	318.2980	321.5594	326.5203	328.1925

YEAR	9.50 %	9.75 %	10.00 %	10.25 %	10.50 %	10.75 %	11.00 %	12.00 %	13.00 %	14.00 %	15.00 %	16.00 %
1	2.1448	2.1486	2.1525	2.1564	2.1603	2.1641	2.1680	2.1836	2.1992	2.2149	2.2306	2.2464
2	4.4981	4.5119	4.5256	4.5394	4.5533	4.5672	4.5811	4.6371	4.6936	4.7507	4.8084	4.8666
3	7.0803	7.1111	7.1420	7.1730	7.2042	7.2355	7.2669	7.3938	7.5229	7.6540	7.7873	7.9228
4	9.9137	9.9700	10.0266	10.0835	10.1407	10.1983	10.2563	10.4913	10.7319	10.9780	11.2298	11.4876
5	13.0226	13.1144	13.2068	13.2999	13.3937	13.4883	13.5835	13.9716	14.3716	14.7836	15.2081	15.6455
6	16.4339	16.5728	16.7130	16.8545	16.9972	17.1414	17.2868	17.8821	18.4998	19.1406	19.8055	20.4953
7	20.1770	20.3767	20.5786	20.7827	20.9891	21.1977	21.4087	22.2760	23.1822	24.1290	25.1184	26.1521
8	24.2840	24.5604	24.8404	25.1239	25.4110	25.7018	25.9964	27.2129	28.4930	29.8402	31.2580	32.7502
9	28.7906	29.1621	29.5390	29.9214	30.3095	30.7032	31.1027	32.7600	34.5167	36.3790	38.3532	40.4463
10	33.7354	34.2233	34.7193	35.2234	35.7358	36.2566	36.7861	38.9927	41.3490	43.8652	46.5525	49.4229
15	66.6796	68.2004	69.7608	71.3618	73.0044	74.6899	76.4194	83.8017	91.9892	101.0730	111.1544	122.3459
20	119.0781	122.8902	126.8398	130.9320	135.1721	139.5659	144.1189	164.0477	187.0480	213.6096	244.3008	279.7810
25	202.4193	210.9192	219.8154	229.1269	238.8738	249.0773	259.7594	307.7561	365.4864	434.9860	518.7197	619.6718
30	334.9754	352.6114	371.2629	390.9905	411.8582	433.9341	457.2901	565.1159	700.4397	870.4668	1084.3058	1353.4704

Description: This table shows what a series of $ 1 deposits grow to in the future. The deposit is made at the beginning of a period.

Example: At 5 % a regular one dollar deposit will grow to $ 5.81 by the end of the fifth year.

YEAR	0.00 %	1.00 %	2.00 %	3.00 %	4.00 %	4.125%	4.25 %	4.375%	4.50 %	4.625%	4.75 %	4.875%
1	1.0000	1.0100	1.0201	1.0302	1.0404	1.0417	1.0430	1.0442	1.0455	1.0468	1.0481	1.0493
2	2.0000	2.0302	2.0607	2.0916	2.1228	2.1268	2.1307	2.1346	2.1386	2.1425	2.1465	2.1505
3	3.0000	3.0606	3.1222	3.1850	3.2490	3.2571	3.2652	3.2733	3.2814	3.2896	3.2977	3.3059
4	4.0000	4.1013	4.2051	4.3115	4.4207	4.4345	4.4484	4.4623	4.4762	4.4903	4.5043	4.5184
5	5.0000	5.1524	5.3097	5.4721	5.6396	5.6610	5.6824	5.7039	5.7254	5.7471	5.7689	5.7907
6	6.0000	6.2141	6.4365	6.6677	6.9079	6.9386	6.9694	7.0004	7.0315	7.0628	7.0942	7.1258
7	7.0000	7.2864	7.5860	7.8994	8.2274	8.2694	8.3117	8.3542	8.3970	8.4400	8.4832	8.5267
8	8.0000	8.3695	8.7586	9.1684	9.6002	9.6557	9.7116	9.7679	9.8246	9.8816	9.9390	9.9968
9	9.0000	9.4634	9.9547	10.4758	11.0284	11.0998	11.1717	11.2442	11.3172	11.3907	11.4648	11.5395
10	10.0000	10.5683	11.1749	11.8226	12.5143	12.6041	12.6945	12.7857	12.8777	12.9704	13.0639	13.1582
15	15.0000	16.2612	17.6538	19.1927	20.8946	21.1197	21.3476	21.5785	21.8123	22.0491	22.2890	22.5319
20	20.0000	22.2452	24.8104	27.7460	31.1100	31.5639	32.0257	32.4955	32.9735	33.4598	33.9546	34.4580
25	25.0000	28.5352	32.7159	37.6724	43.5626	44.3736	45.2026	46.0499	46.9160	47.8014	48.7064	49.6317
30	30.0000	35.1469	41.4484	49.1924	58.7422	60.0845	61.4631	62.8789	64.3331	65.8268	67.3610	68.9371

YEAR	5.00 %	5.10 %	5.125%	5.20 %	5.25 %	5.30 %	5.375%	5.40 %	5.50 %	5.60 %	5.625%	5.70 %
1	1.0506	1.0517	1.0519	1.0527	1.0532	1.0537	1.0545	1.0547	1.0558	1.0568	1.0570	1.0578
2	2.1544	2.1576	2.1584	2.1608	2.1624	2.1640	2.1664	2.1672	2.1704	2.1736	2.1744	2.1768
3	3.3141	3.3207	3.3224	3.3273	3.3306	3.3339	3.3389	3.3405	3.3471	3.3538	3.3554	3.3604
4	4.5325	4.5439	4.5467	4.5552	4.5609	4.5666	4.5752	4.5781	4.5895	4.6010	4.6039	4.6125
5	5.8126	5.8302	5.8346	5.8479	5.8567	5.8656	5.8789	5.8834	5.9012	5.9191	5.9235	5.9370
6	7.1575	7.1830	7.1894	7.2086	7.2214	7.2343	7.2536	7.2601	7.2860	7.3119	7.3185	7.3380
7	8.5705	8.6057	8.6145	8.6410	8.6587	8.6765	8.7032	8.7121	8.7480	8.7839	8.7930	8.8201
8	10.0550	10.1018	10.1135	10.1488	10.1725	10.1961	10.2318	10.2437	10.2915	10.3395	10.3516	10.3878
9	11.6146	11.6752	11.6904	11.7361	11.7667	11.7974	11.8436	11.8590	11.9210	11.9834	11.9991	12.0462
10	13.2533	13.3299	13.3491	13.4070	13.4458	13.4846	13.5432	13.5628	13.6415	13.7207	13.7405	13.8004
15	22.7779	22.9770	23.0271	23.1781	23.2795	23.3813	23.5351	23.5866	23.7940	24.0035	24.0563	24.2152
20	34.9703	35.3865	35.4915	35.8086	36.0218	36.2366	36.5615	36.6706	37.1106	37.5569	37.6694	38.0094
25	50.5775	51.3494	51.5445	52.1351	52.5331	52.9348	53.5439	53.7488	54.5774	55.4208	55.6340	56.2794
30	70.5561	71.8831	72.2194	73.2391	73.9282	74.6247	75.6838	76.0407	77.4876	78.9663	79.3410	80.4775

YEAR	5.75 %	5.80 %	5.875%	5.90 %	6.00 %	6.10 %	6.125%	6.20 %	6.25 %	6.30 %	6.375%	6.40 %
1	1.0583	1.0588	1.0596	1.0599	1.0609	1.0619	1.0622	1.0630	1.0635	1.0640	1.0648	1.0650
2	2.1784	2.1800	2.1824	2.1832	2.1864	2.1896	2.1904	2.1928	2.1945	2.1961	2.1985	2.1993
3	3.3638	3.3671	3.3721	3.3738	3.3805	3.3872	3.3888	3.3939	3.3972	3.4006	3.4056	3.4073
4	4.6183	4.6241	4.6327	4.6356	4.6472	4.6589	4.6618	4.6705	4.6764	4.6822	4.6910	4.6939
5	5.9460	5.9550	5.9685	5.9730	5.9911	6.0093	6.0139	6.0275	6.0367	6.0458	6.0596	6.0642
6	7.3511	7.3642	7.3839	7.3905	7.4169	7.4434	7.4500	7.4700	7.4833	7.4967	7.5168	7.5235
7	8.8382	8.8564	8.8837	8.8929	8.9295	8.9663	8.9755	9.0033	9.0218	9.0404	9.0684	9.0777
8	10.4120	10.4363	10.4729	10.4851	10.5342	10.5835	10.5959	10.6331	10.6580	10.6829	10.7205	10.7330
9	12.0777	12.1093	12.1569	12.1728	12.2366	12.3009	12.3170	12.3655	12.3980	12.4305	12.4796	12.4959
10	13.8404	13.8806	13.9412	13.9614	14.0427	14.1246	14.1452	14.2070	14.2484	14.2900	14.3526	14.3735
15	24.3219	24.4291	24.5909	24.6451	24.8634	25.0840	25.1395	25.3068	25.4190	25.5319	25.7022	25.7593
20	38.2380	38.4683	38.8167	38.9336	39.4055	39.8841	40.0048	40.3694	40.6146	40.8615	41.2352	41.3606
25	56.7144	57.1534	57.8192	58.0431	58.9489	59.8709	60.1040	60.8096	61.2853	61.7653	62.4933	62.7382
30	81.2455	82.0219	83.2025	83.6003	85.2135	86.8623	87.2801	88.5475	89.4040	90.2700	91.5868	92.0306

YEAR	6.50 %	6.60 %	6.625%	6.70 %	6.75 %	6.80 %	6.875%	6.90 %	7.00 %	7.10 %	7.125%	7.20 %
1	1.0661	1.0671	1.0673	1.0681	1.0686	1.0692	1.0699	1.0702	1.0712	1.0723	1.0725	1.0733
2	2.2025	2.2058	2.2066	2.2090	2.2106	2.2123	2.2147	2.2155	2.2187	2.2220	2.2228	2.2253
3	3.4141	3.4208	3.4225	3.4276	3.4310	3.4344	3.4395	3.4412	3.4480	3.4548	3.4565	3.4617
4	4.7057	4.7174	4.7204	4.7292	4.7351	4.7411	4.7500	4.7529	4.7648	4.7767	4.7797	4.7887
5	6.0826	6.1010	6.1056	6.1195	6.1288	6.1381	6.1521	6.1567	6.1754	6.1942	6.1989	6.2130
6	7.5504	7.5774	7.5842	7.6045	7.6181	7.6317	7.6522	7.6591	7.6865	7.7140	7.7209	7.7416
7	9.1152	9.1529	9.1623	9.1907	9.2097	9.2287	9.2573	9.2668	9.3052	9.3437	9.3533	9.3824
8	10.7834	10.8340	10.8467	10.8849	10.9104	10.9360	10.9746	10.9875	11.0392	11.0911	11.1042	11.1434
9	12.5617	12.6279	12.6445	12.6945	12.7280	12.7615	12.8120	12.8289	12.8966	12.9648	12.9819	13.0334
10	14.4576	14.5422	14.5635	14.6274	14.6702	14.7132	14.7779	14.7995	14.8864	14.9739	14.9959	15.0620
15	25.9891	26.2213	26.2797	26.4558	26.5740	26.6928	26.8722	26.9323	27.1742	27.4186	27.4801	27.6656
20	41.8668	42.3801	42.5096	42.9008	43.1638	43.4287	43.8296	43.9642	44.5073	45.0581	45.1970	45.6167
25	63.7287	64.7372	64.9921	65.7639	66.2843	66.8093	67.6058	67.8737	68.9574	70.0608	70.3398	71.1843
30	93.8303	95.6699	96.1361	97.5503	98.5062	99.4726	100.9424	101.4377	103.4466	105.5003	106.0208	107.5998

SAVINGS GROWTH

Description: This table shows what a series of $ 1 deposits grow to in the future. The deposit is made at the beginning of a period.

Example: At 8 % a regular one dollar deposit will grow to $ 6.37 by the end of the fifth year.

YEAR	7.25 %	7.30 %	7.375%	7.40 %	7.50 %	7.60 %	7.625%	7.70 %	7.75 %	7.80 %	7.875%	7.90 %
1	1.0738	1.0743	1.0751	1.0754	1.0764	1.0774	1.0777	1.0785	1.0790	1.0795	1.0803	1.0806
2	2.2269	2.2285	2.2310	2.2318	2.2351	2.2383	2.2391	2.2416	2.2432	2.2449	2.2473	2.2482
3	3.4651	3.4685	3.4736	3.4754	3.4822	3.4891	3.4908	3.4960	3.4995	3.5029	3.5081	3.5098
4	4.7947	4.8007	4.8097	4.8127	4.8247	4.8368	4.8398	4.8489	4.8549	4.8610	4.8701	4.8732
5	6.2224	6.2318	6.2460	6.2508	6.2697	6.2888	6.2936	6.3079	6.3175	6.3271	6.3415	6.3463
6	7.7555	7.7694	7.7903	7.7972	7.8252	7.8533	7.8603	7.8814	7.8956	7.9097	7.9310	7.9381
7	9.4018	9.4212	9.4505	9.4603	9.4995	9.5389	9.5488	9.5785	9.5983	9.6182	9.6482	9.6582
8	11.1696	11.1959	11.2354	11.2487	11.3017	11.3551	11.3685	11.4087	11.4356	11.4626	11.5032	11.5168
9	13.0679	13.1024	13.1544	13.1718	13.2417	13.3119	13.3295	13.3826	13.4181	13.4537	13.5072	13.5252
10	15.1063	15.1507	15.2176	15.2400	15.3298	15.4203	15.4430	15.5113	15.5571	15.6030	15.6722	15.6953
15	27.7901	27.9151	28.1040	28.1673	28.4220	28.6794	28.7442	28.9395	29.0705	29.2022	29.4011	29.4677
20	45.8990	46.1833	46.6135	46.7580	47.3408	47.9319	48.0810	48.5315	48.8345	49.1397	49.6015	49.7565
25	71.7537	72.3283	73.2000	73.4932	74.6793	75.8871	76.1925	77.1170	77.7403	78.3694	79.3237	79.6447
30	108.6672	109.7464	111.3877	111.9409	114.1846	116.4786	117.0601	118.8241	120.0165	121.2223	123.0563	123.6744

YEAR	8.00 %	8.10 %	8.125%	8.20 %	8.25 %	8.30 %	8.375%	8.40 %	8.50 %	8.60 %	8.625%	8.70 %
1	1.0816	1.0826	1.0829	1.0837	1.0842	1.0847	1.0855	1.0858	1.0868	1.0878	1.0881	1.0889
2	2.2515	2.2548	2.2556	2.2580	2.2597	2.2613	2.2638	2.2646	2.2680	2.2713	2.2721	2.2746
3	3.5168	3.5237	3.5255	3.5307	3.5342	3.5377	3.5429	3.5446	3.5516	3.5586	3.5604	3.5657
4	4.8853	4.8976	4.9006	4.9098	4.9159	4.9221	4.9313	4.9344	4.9467	4.9591	4.9622	4.9715
5	6.3656	6.3849	6.3898	6.4044	6.4141	6.4238	6.4385	6.4434	6.4630	6.4826	6.4875	6.5023
6	7.9666	7.9952	8.0024	8.0240	8.0384	8.0528	8.0745	8.0817	8.1108	8.1400	8.1473	8.1692
7	9.6983	9.7386	9.7487	9.7791	9.7994	9.8198	9.8504	9.8606	9.9017	9.9429	9.9532	9.9843
8	11.5713	11.6260	11.6398	11.6811	11.7087	11.7364	11.7781	11.7921	11.8480	11.9042	11.9183	11.9607
9	13.5971	13.6695	13.6876	13.7423	13.7788	13.8155	13.8707	13.8892	13.9633	14.0378	14.0565	14.1128
10	15.7882	15.8818	15.9052	15.9759	16.0232	16.0707	16.1422	16.1661	16.2622	16.3589	16.3832	16.4563
15	29.7360	30.0071	30.0753	30.2810	30.4190	30.5577	30.7672	30.8374	31.1199	31.4054	31.4773	31.6939
20	50.3822	51.0168	51.1768	51.6605	51.9858	52.3134	52.8092	52.9757	53.6474	54.3289	54.5007	55.0201
25	80.9435	82.2661	82.6005	83.6129	84.2956	84.9845	86.0298	86.3814	87.8040	89.2527	89.6191	90.7282
30	126.1817	128.7455	129.3955	131.3671	132.7001	134.0479	136.0982	136.7893	139.5926	142.4594	143.1862	145.3911

YEAR	8.75 %	8.80 %	8.875%	8.90 %	9.00 %	9.10 %	9.125%	9.20 %	9.25 %	9.30 %	9.375%	9.40 %
1	1.0894	1.0899	1.0907	1.0910	1.0920	1.0931	1.0933	1.0941	1.0946	1.0952	1.0959	1.0962
2	2.2762	2.2779	2.2804	2.2812	2.2845	2.2879	2.2887	2.2912	2.2929	2.2945	2.2970	2.2979
3	3.5692	3.5727	3.5780	3.5797	3.5868	3.5939	3.5956	3.6010	3.6045	3.6081	3.6134	3.6152
4	4.9777	4.9839	4.9933	4.9964	5.0089	5.0214	5.0246	5.0340	5.0403	5.0466	5.0560	5.0592
5	6.5122	6.5221	6.5370	6.5420	6.5619	6.5818	6.5868	6.6019	6.6119	6.6220	6.6371	6.6421
6	8.1839	8.1986	8.2207	8.2281	8.2578	8.2875	8.2949	8.3173	8.3323	8.3473	8.3699	8.3774
7	10.0051	10.0259	10.0572	10.0677	10.1097	10.1519	10.1625	10.1942	10.2155	10.2368	10.2689	10.2796
8	11.9891	12.0175	12.0604	12.0747	12.1321	12.1898	12.2043	12.2478	12.2769	12.3061	12.3501	12.3648
9	14.1505	14.1883	14.2452	14.2642	14.3405	14.4174	14.4366	14.4946	14.5334	14.5724	14.6310	14.6506
10	16.5052	16.5543	16.6282	16.6529	16.7523	16.8523	16.8774	16.9529	17.0035	17.0543	17.1307	17.1563
15	31.8393	31.9854	32.2061	32.2800	32.5776	32.8784	32.9541	33.1823	33.3354	33.4894	33.7218	33.7997
20	55.3694	55.7212	56.2537	56.4325	57.1539	57.8858	58.0704	58.6282	59.0034	59.3813	59.9533	60.1453
25	91.4762	92.2310	93.3762	93.7614	95.3202	96.9078	97.3092	98.5247	99.3444	100.1716	101.4268	101.8491
30	146.8817	148.3892	150.6824	151.4554	154.5912	157.7983	158.6114	161.0783	162.7461	164.4329	166.9989	167.8640

YEAR	9.50 %	9.75 %	10.00 %	10.25 %	10.50 %	10.75 %	11.00 %	12.00 %	13.00 %	14.00 %	15.00 %	16.00 %
1	1.0973	1.0999	1.1025	1.1051	1.1078	1.1104	1.1130	1.1236	1.1342	1.1449	1.1556	1.1664
2	2.3012	2.3096	2.3180	2.3264	2.3349	2.3434	2.3518	2.3861	2.4207	2.4557	2.4911	2.5269
3	3.6223	3.6402	3.6581	3.6761	3.6942	3.7124	3.7307	3.8046	3.8798	3.9564	4.0344	4.1138
4	5.0718	5.1036	5.1356	5.1677	5.2001	5.2326	5.2654	5.3984	5.5348	5.6746	5.8179	5.9647
5	6.6624	6.7132	6.7645	6.8161	6.8682	6.9206	6.9735	7.1893	7.4120	7.6418	7.8789	8.1236
6	8.4076	8.4836	8.5603	8.6378	8.7160	8.7950	8.8747	9.2015	9.5411	9.8940	10.2607	10.6418
7	10.3225	10.4308	10.5402	10.6510	10.7630	10.8762	10.9908	11.4624	11.9559	12.4725	13.0131	13.5790
8	12.4237	12.5724	12.7231	12.8758	13.0305	13.1873	13.3461	14.0027	14.6949	15.4247	16.1939	17.0049
9	14.7292	14.9280	15.1297	15.3345	15.5424	15.7534	15.9676	16.8571	17.8016	18.8046	19.8697	21.0009
10	17.2590	17.5188	17.7830	18.0517	18.3249	18.6028	18.8853	20.0642	21.3252	22.6743	24.1176	25.6619
15	34.1132	34.9116	35.7311	36.5724	37.4359	38.3223	39.2324	43.1213	47.4424	52.2455	57.5860	63.5257
20	60.9203	62.9072	64.9667	67.1016	69.3148	71.6093	73.9881	84.4129	96.4678	110.4165	126.5655	145.2709
25	103.5576	107.9690	112.5884	117.4258	122.4919	127.7980	133.3558	158.3599	188.4954	224.8478	268.7343	321.7526
30	171.3733	180.5009	190.1590	200.3796	211.1965	222.6454	234.7645	290.7878	361.2437	449.9514	561.7488	702.7635

SAVINGS GROWTH

Description: This table shows what a series of $ 1 deposits grow to in the future. The deposit is made at the beginning of a period.

Example: At 5 % a regular one dollar deposit will grow to $ 294.63 by the end of the fifth year.

YEAR	0.00 %	1.00 %	2.00 %	3.00 %	4.00 %	4.125%	4.25 %	4.375%	4.50 %	4.625%	4.75 %	4.875%
1	52.0000	52.2643	52.5285	52.7928	53.0571	53.0901	53.1232	53.1562	53.1892	53.2223	53.2553	53.2883
2	104.0000	105.0512	106.1077	107.1694	108.2365	108.3702	108.5041	108.6380	108.7720	108.9061	109.0402	109.1745
3	156.0000	158.3660	160.7584	163.1773	165.6230	165.9306	166.2387	166.5471	166.8560	167.1652	167.4749	167.7851
4	208.0000	212.2139	216.5021	220.8655	225.3050	225.8654	226.4270	226.9897	227.5537	228.1189	228.6853	229.2529
5	260.0000	266.6003	273.3607	280.2843	287.3743	288.2725	289.1733	290.0767	290.9829	291.8917	292.8032	293.7173
6	312.0000	321.5306	331.3564	341.4856	351.9264	353.2538	354.5863	355.9238	357.2663	358.6139	359.9666	361.3244
7	364.0000	377.0102	390.5121	404.5230	419.0606	420.9157	422.7794	424.6516	426.5325	428.4221	430.3203	432.2273
8	416.0000	433.0446	450.8509	469.4515	488.8801	491.3686	493.8707	496.3864	498.9157	501.4589	504.0158	506.5867
9	468.0000	489.6393	512.3965	536.3279	561.4924	564.7277	567.9833	571.2595	574.5562	577.8736	581.2119	584.5712
10	520.0000	546.7999	575.1729	605.2105	637.0092	641.1128	645.2458	649.4083	653.6004	657.8225	662.0748	666.3573
15	780.0000	841.2926	908.3981	981.8891	1062.2934	1072.9831	1083.6945	1094.5289	1105.4789	1116.5729	1127.7853	1139.1267
20	1040.0000	1150.8073	1276.3056	1418.5629	1579.9384	1601.5846	1623.5768	1645.9206	1668.6219	1691.6866	1715.1208	1738.9305
25	1300.0000	1476.1103	1682.5051	1924.7874	2209.6109	2248.5834	2288.3590	2328.9551	2370.3893	2412.6797	2455.8447	2499.9032
30	1560.0000	1818.0071	2130.9823	2511.6404	2975.7039	3040.4984	3106.9364	3175.0618	3244.9192	3316.5549	3390.0161	3465.3513

YEAR	5.00 %	5.10 %	5.125%	5.20 %	5.25 %	5.30 %	5.375%	5.40 %	5.50 %	5.60 %	5.625%	5.70 %
1	53.3214	53.3478	53.3544	53.3742	53.3874	53.4007	53.4205	53.4271	53.4535	53.4799	53.4865	53.5064
2	109.3088	109.4163	109.4432	109.5239	109.5777	109.6315	109.7123	109.7392	109.8470	109.9547	109.9817	110.0626
3	168.0956	168.3444	168.4066	168.5934	168.7180	168.8427	169.0298	169.0922	169.3420	169.5921	169.6547	169.8425
4	229.8218	230.2777	230.3918	230.7345	230.9631	231.1920	231.5356	231.6503	232.1094	232.5692	232.6843	233.0299
5	294.6342	295.3697	295.5538	296.1069	296.4761	296.8458	297.4011	297.5865	298.3289	299.0731	299.2594	299.8190
6	362.6873	363.7813	364.0554	364.8787	365.4286	365.9793	366.8069	367.0832	368.1905	369.3011	369.5792	370.4150
7	434.1430	435.6820	436.0676	437.2266	438.0010	438.7768	439.9433	440.3328	441.8945	443.4619	443.8546	445.0350
8	509.1716	511.2496	511.7705	513.3366	514.3835	515.4327	517.0107	517.5378	519.6522	521.7757	522.3080	523.9084
9	587.9515	590.6711	591.3531	593.4043	594.7761	596.1512	598.2205	598.9120	601.6865	604.4750	605.1743	607.2775
10	670.6705	674.1431	675.0144	677.6356	679.3892	681.1479	683.7953	684.6803	688.2328	691.8056	692.7019	695.3987
15	1150.5986	1159.8710	1162.2024	1169.2288	1173.9399	1178.6726	1185.8124	1188.2033	1197.8216	1207.5285	1209.9692	1217.3248
20	1763.1220	1782.7543	1787.7016	1802.6383	1812.6757	1822.7773	1838.0509	1843.1747	1863.8339	1884.7583	1890.0313	1905.9515
25	2544.8743	2581.5215	2590.7778	2618.7757	2637.6337	2656.6473	2685.4625	2695.1468	2734.2852	2774.0734	2784.1233	2814.5225
30	3542.6104	3605.8372	3621.8445	3670.3549	3703.1064	3736.1909	3786.4498	3803.3732	3871.9303	3941.8916	3959.6048	4013.2867

YEAR	5.75 %	5.80 %	5.875%	5.90 %	6.00 %	6.10 %	6.125%	6.20 %	6.25 %	6.30 %	6.375%	6.40 %
1	53.5196	53.5328	53.5526	53.5592	53.5856	53.6121	53.6187	53.6385	53.6517	53.6649	53.6847	53.6914
2	110.1165	110.1705	110.2514	110.2784	110.3864	110.4945	110.5215	110.6026	110.6567	110.7107	110.7919	110.8190
3	169.9678	170.0932	170.2813	170.3441	170.5953	170.8467	170.9096	171.0984	171.2244	171.3504	171.5396	171.6027
4	233.2605	233.4913	233.8380	233.9536	234.4166	234.8804	234.9965	235.3450	235.5776	235.8104	236.1600	236.2766
5	300.1926	300.5666	301.1285	301.3161	302.0673	302.8202	303.0087	303.5749	303.9530	304.3314	304.9000	305.0897
6	370.9732	371.5323	372.3725	372.6529	373.7769	374.9043	375.1867	376.0351	376.6017	377.1692	378.0221	378.3068
7	445.8238	446.6140	447.8019	448.1987	449.7892	451.3856	451.7856	452.9878	453.7911	454.5958	455.8057	456.2098
8	524.9782	526.0504	527.6629	528.2016	530.3622	532.5321	533.0761	534.7115	535.8047	536.9003	538.5481	539.0986
9	608.6840	610.0941	612.2157	612.9247	615.7696	618.6287	619.3457	621.5021	622.9442	624.3899	626.5653	627.2922
10	697.2029	699.0123	701.7360	702.6465	706.3014	709.9771	710.8993	713.6737	715.5299	717.3914	720.1936	721.1303
15	1222.2566	1227.2111	1234.6856	1237.1886	1247.2578	1257.4198	1259.9749	1267.6754	1272.8386	1278.0255	1285.8505	1288.4708
20	1916.6500	1927.4171	1943.6971	1949.1585	1971.1796	1993.4839	1999.1047	2016.0752	2027.4797	2038.9573	2056.3121	2062.1341
25	2834.9985	2855.6439	2886.9332	2897.4492	2939.9502	2983.1588	2994.0729	3027.0871	3049.3250	3071.7475	3105.7309	3117.1527
30	4049.5316	4086.1463	4141.7707	4160.5014	4236.3838	4313.8260	4333.4341	4392.8610	4432.9865	4473.5229	4535.1076	4555.8461

YEAR	6.50 %	6.60 %	6.625%	6.70 %	6.75 %	6.80 %	6.875%	6.90 %	7.00 %	7.10 %	7.125%	7.20 %
1	53.7178	53.7442	53.7508	53.7706	53.7838	53.7971	53.8169	53.8235	53.8499	53.8763	53.8830	53.9028
2	110.9272	111.0355	111.0626	111.1439	111.1981	111.2523	111.3337	111.3608	111.4693	111.5779	111.6051	111.6865
3	171.8553	172.1081	172.1713	172.3612	172.4878	172.6145	172.8048	172.8682	173.1221	173.3763	173.4399	173.6307
4	236.7436	237.2114	237.3285	237.6800	237.9146	238.1494	238.5020	238.6196	239.0906	239.5623	239.6804	240.0349
5	305.8498	306.6116	306.8023	307.3752	307.7577	308.1406	308.7159	308.9078	309.6768	310.4476	310.6406	311.2202
6	379.4478	380.5922	380.8788	381.7400	382.3152	382.8912	383.7570	384.0460	385.2041	386.3657	386.6567	387.5309
7	457.8297	459.4555	459.8628	461.0872	461.9053	462.7249	463.9571	464.3686	466.0183	467.6741	468.0889	469.3358
8	541.3064	543.5237	544.0796	545.7507	546.8678	547.9873	549.6711	550.2335	552.4895	554.7553	555.3232	557.0308
9	630.2091	633.1405	633.8756	636.0866	637.5652	639.0475	641.2778	642.0231	645.0137	648.0192	648.7730	651.0398
10	724.8904	728.6720	729.6207	732.4750	734.3847	736.2998	739.1826	740.1462	744.0146	747.9049	748.8810	751.8174
15	1299.0125	1309.6512	1312.3262	1320.3880	1325.7935	1331.2238	1339.4160	1342.1594	1353.1958	1364.3339	1367.1345	1375.5748
20	2085.6094	2109.3872	2115.3794	2133.4715	2145.6298	2157.8663	2176.3686	2182.5757	2207.6039	2232.9551	2239.3438	2258.6335
25	3163.3154	3210.2487	3222.1039	3257.9657	3282.1224	3306.4800	3343.3972	3355.8053	3405.9555	3456.9447	3469.8248	3508.7875
30	4639.8660	4725.6187	4747.3319	4813.1409	4857.5774	4902.4704	4970.6766	4993.6455	5086.7056	5181.6906	5205.7424	5278.6415

SAVINGS GROWTH

Description: This table shows what a series of $ 1 deposits grow to in the future. The deposit is made at the beginning of a period.

Example: At 8 % a regular one dollar deposit will grow to $ 317.47 by the end of the fifth year.

YEAR	7.25 %	7.30 %	7.375%	7.40 %	7.50 %	7.60 %	7.625%	7.70 %	7.75 %	7.80 %	7.875%	7.90 %
1	53.9160	53.9292	53.9490	53.9556	53.9821	54.0085	54.0151	54.0349	54.0481	54.0613	54.0812	54.0878
2	111.7409	111.7952	111.8768	111.9040	112.0128	112.1216	112.1488	112.2305	112.2850	112.3395	112.4212	112.4485
3	173.7581	173.8855	174.0767	174.1405	174.3958	174.6513	174.7153	174.9072	175.0352	175.1633	175.3555	175.4197
4	240.2715	240.5083	240.8639	240.9825	241.4575	241.9333	242.0524	242.4099	242.6485	242.8873	243.2459	243.3656
5	311.6072	311.9946	312.5766	312.7708	313.5489	314.3287	314.5240	315.1104	315.5019	315.8939	316.4827	316.6792
6	388.1147	388.6994	389.5782	389.8715	391.0471	392.2262	392.5215	393.4088	394.0014	394.5950	395.4869	395.7846
7	470.1690	471.0037	472.2586	472.6776	474.3577	476.0439	476.4664	477.7362	478.5847	479.4347	480.7126	481.1394
8	558.1723	559.3162	561.0367	561.6114	563.9166	566.2317	566.8120	568.5568	569.7231	570.8919	572.6499	573.2372
9	652.5557	654.0754	656.3621	657.1263	660.1924	663.2738	664.0465	666.3706	667.9248	669.4829	671.8273	672.6107
10	753.7820	755.7522	758.7179	759.7093	763.6889	767.6911	768.6952	771.7160	773.7371	775.7639	778.8148	779.8347
15	1381.2340	1386.9192	1395.4962	1398.3683	1409.9230	1421.5842	1424.5163	1433.3530	1439.2780	1445.2303	1454.2102	1457.2172
20	2271.5968	2284.6435	2304.3712	2310.9894	2337.6757	2364.7068	2371.5190	2392.0874	2405.9101	2419.8219	2440.8579	2447.9151
25	3535.0335	3561.4984	3601.6103	3615.0924	3669.5846	3724.9906	3738.9866	3781.3258	3809.8470	3838.6064	3882.1970	3896.8486
30	5327.8672	5377.6001	5453.1623	5478.6092	5581.7122	5686.9538	5713.6036	5794.3794	5848.9256	5904.0354	5987.7696	6015.9692

YEAR	8.00 %	8.10 %	8.125%	8.20 %	8.25 %	8.30 %	8.375%	8.40 %	8.50 %	8.60 %	8.625%	8.70 %
1	54.1142	54.1406	54.1472	54.1670	54.1803	54.1935	54.2133	54.2199	54.2463	54.2728	54.2794	54.2992
2	112.5575	112.6666	112.6939	112.7758	112.8304	112.8850	112.9670	112.9943	113.1036	113.2130	113.2403	113.3224
3	175.6763	175.9332	175.9975	176.1905	176.3192	176.4479	176.6412	176.7057	176.9637	177.2220	177.2867	177.4806
4	243.8446	244.3245	244.4445	244.8051	245.0458	245.2866	245.6482	245.7689	246.2520	246.7359	246.8570	247.2206
5	317.4664	318.2554	318.4529	319.0462	319.4423	319.8388	320.4346	320.6334	321.4297	322.2279	322.4278	323.0280
6	396.9779	398.1747	398.4744	399.3750	399.9765	400.5789	401.4842	401.7865	402.9976	404.2123	404.5165	405.4306
7	482.8503	484.5674	484.9977	486.2908	487.1549	488.0205	489.3218	489.7564	491.4987	493.2473	493.6855	495.0023
8	575.5925	577.9580	578.5510	580.3337	581.5254	582.7196	584.5158	585.1159	587.5224	589.9393	590.5452	592.3667
9	675.7541	678.9132	679.7055	682.0881	683.6815	685.2789	687.6823	688.4855	691.7082	694.9469	695.7591	698.2017
10	783.9286	788.0458	789.0788	792.1864	794.2655	796.3505	799.4890	800.5382	804.7497	808.9851	810.0477	813.2445
15	1469.3147	1481.5238	1484.5936	1493.8455	1500.0489	1506.2809	1515.6827	1518.8310	1531.4970	1544.2798	1547.4939	1557.1805
20	2476.3717	2505.1965	2512.4608	2534.3943	2549.1346	2563.9701	2586.4029	2593.9287	2624.2754	2655.0151	2662.7620	2686.1530
25	3956.0689	4016.2840	4031.4952	4077.5110	4108.5094	4139.7673	4187.1457	4203.0707	4267.4389	4332.8904	4349.4247	4399.4437
30	6130.2294	6246.8653	6276.4014	6365.9275	6426.3845	6487.4675	6580.2802	6611.5380	6738.1928	6867.4868	6900.2293	6999.4762

YEAR	8.75 %	8.80 %	8.875%	8.90 %	9.00 %	9.10 %	9.125%	9.20 %	9.25 %	9.30 %	9.375%	9.40 %
1	54.3124	54.3256	54.3454	54.3520	54.3785	54.4049	54.4115	54.4313	54.4445	54.4577	54.4776	54.4842
2	113.3771	113.4319	113.5140	113.5414	113.6510	113.7606	113.7880	113.8703	113.9252	113.9801	114.0624	114.0899
3	177.6100	177.7395	177.9338	177.9986	178.2580	178.5177	178.5827	178.7777	178.9078	179.0380	179.2333	179.2985
4	247.4633	247.7062	248.0709	248.1925	248.6797	249.1677	249.2899	249.6566	249.9013	250.1462	250.5140	250.6367
5	323.4287	323.8299	324.4326	324.6337	325.4394	326.2469	326.4491	327.0563	327.4617	327.8676	328.4773	328.6807
6	406.0411	406.6526	407.5714	407.8782	409.1074	410.3403	410.6491	411.5768	412.1965	412.8170	413.7496	414.0609
7	495.8821	496.7636	498.0888	498.5314	500.3055	502.0861	502.5323	503.8732	504.7692	505.6668	507.0162	507.4668
8	593.5842	594.8044	596.6396	597.2527	599.7115	602.1809	602.7999	604.6609	605.9048	607.1515	609.0265	609.6529
9	699.8352	701.4728	703.9368	704.7602	708.0640	711.3842	712.2168	714.7210	716.3956	718.0743	720.6003	721.4444
10	815.3832	817.5280	820.7567	821.8359	826.1682	830.5251	831.6181	834.9066	837.1067	839.3130	842.6342	843.7444
15	1563.6755	1570.2004	1580.0440	1583.3403	1596.6016	1609.9852	1613.3504	1623.4924	1630.2926	1637.1242	1647.4305	1650.8818
20	2701.8729	2717.6944	2741.6184	2749.6445	2782.0088	2814.7927	2823.0549	2848.0017	2864.7674	2881.6414	2907.1572	2915.7174
25	4433.1394	4467.1176	4518.6201	4535.9315	4605.9048	4677.0574	4695.0322	4749.4096	4786.0420	4822.9819	4878.9744	4897.7952
30	7066.4994	7134.2181	7237.1160	7271.7710	7412.1948	7555.5504	7591.8546	7701.9000	7776.2174	7851.3073	7965.4084	8003.8372

YEAR	9.50 %	9.75 %	10.00 %	10.25 %	10.50 %	10.75 %	11.00 %	12.00 %	13.00 %	14.00 %	15.00 %	16.00 %
1	54.5106	54.5767	54.6427	54.7088	54.7749	54.8409	54.9070	55.1713	55.4356	55.6998	55.9641	56.2284
2	114.1997	114.4746	114.7498	115.0253	115.3011	115.5773	115.8538	116.9631	118.0777	119.1976	120.3228	121.4533
3	179.5593	180.2125	180.8675	181.5242	182.1826	182.8428	183.5047	186.1700	188.8634	191.5852	194.3354	197.1142
4	251.1280	252.3599	253.5970	254.8392	256.0867	257.3393	258.5973	263.6817	268.8512	274.1069	279.4498	284.8809
5	329.4958	331.5417	333.5994	335.6690	337.7506	339.8443	341.9500	350.4948	359.2374	368.1817	377.3314	386.6902
6	415.3085	418.4436	421.6021	424.7839	427.9893	431.2185	434.4715	447.7254	461.3739	475.4270	489.8952	504.7890
7	509.2734	513.8186	518.4050	523.0331	527.7031	532.4154	537.1704	556.6238	576.7880	597.6866	619.3436	641.7836
8	612.1650	618.4926	624.8883	631.3528	637.8868	644.4910	651.1661	678.5899	707.2060	737.0626	768.2092	800.6974
9	724.8313	733.3722	742.0198	750.7752	759.6398	768.6147	777.7014	815.1920	854.5784	895.9512	939.4047	985.0374
10	848.2008	859.4527	870.8645	882.4385	894.1768	906.0818	918.1556	968.1863	1021.1091	1077.0842	1136.2795	1198.8718
15	1664.7664	1700.0411	1736.1354	1773.0684	1810.8594	1849.5283	1889.0955	2056.7699	2240.5648	2442.0153	2662.7953	2904.7305
20	2950.2355	3038.5031	3129.6629	3223.8106	3321.0450	3421.4683	3525.1858	3975.2260	4487.3329	5070.0735	5733.1639	6487.6166
25	4973.8708	5169.7251	5373.9528	5586.9168	5808.9955	6040.5838	6282.0930	7356.2013	8626.8575	10130.18	11908.77	14012.90
30	8159.5560	8563.2523	8988.4041	9436.1677	9907.7615	10404.47	10927.64	13314.63	16253.66	19872.97	24330.13	29818.57

Description: This table shows what a series of $ 1 deposits grow to in the future. The deposit is made at the beginning of a period.

Example: At 5 % a regular one dollar deposit will grow to $ 68.10 by the end of the fifth year.

YEAR	0.00 %	1.00 %	2.00 %	3.00 %	4.00 %	4.125%	4.25 %	4.375%	4.50 %	4.625%	4.75 %	4.875%
1	12.0000	12.0650	12.1300	12.1950	12.2600	12.2681	12.2762	12.2844	12.2925	12.3006	12.3088	12.3169
2	24.0000	24.2507	24.5026	24.7559	25.0104	25.0423	25.0742	25.1062	25.1382	25.1702	25.2022	25.2342
3	36.0000	36.5582	37.1227	37.6935	38.2708	38.3434	38.4161	38.4890	38.5619	38.6349	38.7080	38.7812
4	48.0000	48.9887	49.9951	51.0193	52.0616	52.1932	52.3251	52.4572	52.5897	52.7224	52.8554	52.9887
5	60.0000	61.5436	63.1250	64.7449	66.4041	66.6143	66.8251	67.0366	67.2487	67.4614	67.6748	67.8888
6	72.0000	74.2241	76.5175	78.8823	81.3203	81.6303	81.9415	82.2538	82.5674	82.8821	83.1981	83.5152
7	84.0000	87.0313	90.1779	93.4437	96.8331	97.2657	97.7002	98.1368	98.5754	99.0161	99.4587	99.9035
8	96.0000	99.9666	104.1114	108.4420	112.9664	113.5460	114.1287	114.7147	115.3038	115.8962	116.4918	117.0906
9	108.0000	113.0313	118.3236	123.8903	129.7451	130.4979	131.2555	132.0178	132.7850	133.5570	134.3339	135.1157
10	120.0000	126.2266	132.8201	139.8020	147.1949	148.1491	149.1101	150.0780	151.0528	152.0346	153.0235	154.0194
15	180.0000	194.2090	209.7691	226.8138	245.4892	247.9461	250.4313	252.9452	255.4880	258.0601	260.6619	263.2937
20	240.0000	265.6593	294.7271	327.6842	365.0792	370.0959	375.1929	380.3716	385.6332	390.9793	396.4111	401.9302
25	300.0000	340.7542	388.5275	444.6207	510.5788	519.6051	528.8177	538.2205	547.8178	557.6138	567.6126	577.8187
30	360.0000	419.6797	492.0908	580.1822	687.6013	702.6017	717.9830	733.7554	749.9294	766.5156	783.5250	800.9689

YEAR	5.00 %	5.10 %	5.125%	5.20 %	5.25 %	5.30 %	5.375%	5.40 %	5.50 %	5.60 %	5.625%	5.70 %
1	12.3250	12.3315	12.3331	12.3380	12.3413	12.3445	12.3494	12.3510	12.3575	12.3640	12.3656	12.3705
2	25.2663	25.2919	25.2983	25.3176	25.3304	25.3433	25.3625	25.3690	25.3947	25.4204	25.4268	25.4461
3	38.8546	38.9133	38.9280	38.9721	39.0015	39.0310	39.0751	39.0899	39.1489	39.2079	39.2227	39.2670
4	53.1223	53.2294	53.2562	53.3366	53.3903	53.4441	53.5248	53.5517	53.6596	53.7676	53.7946	53.8758
5	68.1034	68.2756	68.3187	68.4481	68.5346	68.6211	68.7511	68.7945	68.9683	69.1426	69.1862	69.3172
6	83.8336	84.0891	84.1531	84.3454	84.4739	84.6025	84.7959	84.8604	85.1191	85.3785	85.4435	85.6388
7	100.3503	100.7092	100.7991	101.0694	101.2500	101.4310	101.7030	101.7939	102.1581	102.5237	102.6153	102.8907
8	117.6928	118.1768	118.2982	118.6630	118.9069	119.1513	119.5190	119.6418	120.1343	120.6291	120.7531	121.1259
9	135.9024	136.5354	136.6941	137.1715	137.4908	137.8108	138.2925	138.4534	139.0992	139.7483	139.9111	140.4006
10	155.0225	155.8302	156.0328	156.6424	157.0503	157.4593	158.0751	158.2809	159.1072	159.9382	160.1467	160.7740
15	265.9558	268.1076	268.6486	270.2792	271.3726	272.4709	274.1279	274.6828	276.9151	279.1679	279.7344	281.4416
20	407.5379	412.0889	413.2357	416.6983	419.0252	421.3670	424.9079	426.0957	430.8852	435.7364	436.9589	440.6499
25	588.2365	596.7263	598.8706	605.3569	609.7258	614.1307	620.8066	623.0503	632.1181	641.3367	643.6652	650.7086
30	818.8588	833.4999	837.2066	848.4402	856.0246	863.6862	875.3253	879.2444	895.1214	911.3240	915.4263	927.8591

YEAR	5.75 %	5.80 %	5.875%	5.90 %	6.00 %	6.10 %	6.125%	6.20 %	6.25 %	6.30 %	6.375%	6.40 %
1	12.3738	12.3770	12.3819	12.3835	12.3900	12.3965	12.3981	12.4030	12.4063	12.4095	12.4144	12.4160
2	25.4590	25.4719	25.4912	25.4976	25.5234	25.5492	25.5556	25.5750	25.5879	25.6008	25.6202	25.6266
3	39.2966	39.3262	39.3707	39.3855	39.4448	39.5042	39.5190	39.5636	39.5934	39.6231	39.6678	39.6827
4	53.9299	53.9842	54.0656	54.0927	54.2015	54.3104	54.3377	54.4196	54.4742	54.5289	54.6110	54.6384
5	69.4047	69.4922	69.6238	69.6677	69.8436	70.0199	70.0640	70.1966	70.2851	70.3737	70.5069	70.5513
6	85.7692	85.8998	86.0961	86.1616	86.4242	86.6876	86.7536	86.9518	87.0842	87.2168	87.4160	87.4826
7	103.0747	103.2590	103.5361	103.6286	103.9996	104.3720	104.4653	104.7458	104.9332	105.1209	105.4032	105.4974
8	121.3752	121.6250	122.0007	122.1262	122.6296	123.1352	123.2620	123.6430	123.8978	124.1530	124.5370	124.6653
9	140.7280	141.0562	141.5501	141.7152	142.3774	143.0430	143.2099	143.7119	144.0476	144.3842	144.8906	145.0599
10	161.1936	161.6145	162.2481	162.4599	163.3100	164.1651	164.3796	165.0250	165.4569	165.8899	166.5418	166.7597
15	282.5863	283.7362	285.4711	286.0521	288.3893	290.7480	291.3411	293.1286	294.3271	295.5311	297.3476	297.9559
20	443.1304	445.6267	449.4013	450.6676	455.7735	460.9451	462.2484	466.1835	468.8279	471.4894	475.5136	476.8637
25	655.4529	660.2366	667.4865	669.9232	679.7713	689.7836	692.3127	699.9629	705.1161	710.3122	718.1874	720.8343
30	936.2535	944.7338	957.6170	961.9552	979.5309	997.4683	1002.0101	1015.7752	1025.0696	1034.4593	1048.7248	1053.5288

YEAR	6.50 %	6.60 %	6.625%	6.70 %	6.75 %	6.80 %	6.875%	6.90 %	7.00 %	7.10 %	7.125%	7.20 %
1	12.4225	12.4290	12.4306	12.4355	12.4388	12.4420	12.4469	12.4485	12.4550	12.4615	12.4631	12.4680
2	25.6525	25.6783	25.6848	25.7042	25.7171	25.7301	25.7495	25.7559	25.7819	25.8078	25.8142	25.8337
3	39.7424	39.8021	39.8170	39.8619	39.8918	39.9217	39.9666	39.9816	40.0416	40.1016	40.1166	40.1617
4	54.7481	54.8580	54.8855	54.9681	55.0232	55.0784	55.1612	55.1888	55.2995	55.4103	55.4381	55.5214
5	70.7293	70.9076	70.9523	71.0865	71.1760	71.2657	71.4004	71.4454	71.6255	71.8060	71.8512	71.9869
6	87.7492	88.0166	88.0835	88.2848	88.4192	88.5538	88.7561	88.8236	89.0942	89.3657	89.4337	89.6380
7	105.8754	106.2546	106.3497	106.6353	106.8262	107.0174	107.3049	107.4009	107.7858	108.1722	108.2690	108.5599
8	125.1797	125.6965	125.8260	126.2154	126.4757	126.7366	127.1290	127.2601	127.7858	128.3139	128.4462	128.8442
9	145.7389	146.4214	146.5926	147.1073	147.4516	147.7967	148.3160	148.4895	149.1858	149.8857	150.0612	150.5890
10	167.6345	168.5142	168.7350	169.3990	169.8433	170.2889	170.9596	171.1838	172.0839	172.9890	173.2161	173.8994
15	300.4030	302.8727	303.4937	305.3653	306.6202	307.8809	309.7828	310.4197	312.9820	315.5679	316.2182	318.1778
20	482.3074	487.8214	489.2110	493.4066	496.2262	499.0639	503.3548	504.7943	510.5989	516.4784	517.9602	522.4340
25	731.5322	742.4089	745.1564	753.4676	759.0662	764.7113	773.2675	776.1433	787.7668	799.5850	802.5704	811.6013
30	1072.9917	1092.8566	1097.8867	1113.1320	1123.4263	1133.8265	1149.6279	1154.9492	1176.5091	1198.5155	1204.0880	1220.9781

SAVINGS GROWTH

ANNUAL COMPOUNDING
Monthly Deposit

Description: This table shows what a series of $ 1 deposits grow to in the future. The deposit is made at the beginning of a period.

Example: At 8 % a regular one dollar deposit will grow to $ 73.45 by the end of the fifth year.

YEAR	7.25 %	7.30 %	7.375%	7.40 %	7.50 %	7.60 %	7.625%	7.70 %	7.75 %	7.80 %	7.875%	7.90 %
1	12.4713	12.4745	12.4794	12.4810	12.4875	12.4940	12.4956	12.5005	12.5037	12.5070	12.5119	12.5135
2	25.8467	25.8596	25.8791	25.8856	25.9116	25.9375	25.9440	25.9635	25.9765	25.9895	26.0091	26.0156
3	40.1918	40.2219	40.2671	40.2821	40.3424	40.4028	40.4179	40.4632	40.4935	40.5237	40.5691	40.5843
4	55.5770	55.6326	55.7161	55.7440	55.8556	55.9674	55.9954	56.0794	56.1355	56.1916	56.2758	56.3040
5	72.0775	72.1683	72.3046	72.3501	72.5323	72.7149	72.7607	72.8980	72.9897	73.0815	73.2194	73.2655
6	89.7744	89.9111	90.1164	90.1850	90.4597	90.7353	90.8043	91.0117	91.1502	91.2889	91.4973	91.5669
7	108.7543	108.9491	109.2419	109.3397	109.7317	110.1251	110.2237	110.5201	110.7181	110.9164	111.2146	111.3142
8	129.1102	129.3768	129.7778	129.9118	130.4491	130.9887	131.1239	131.5306	131.8025	132.0749	132.4847	132.6216
9	150.9420	151.2959	151.8283	152.0063	152.7202	153.4378	153.6177	154.1590	154.5209	154.8837	155.4297	155.6122
10	174.3565	174.8149	175.5050	175.7357	176.6618	177.5931	177.8267	178.5297	179.0000	179.4717	180.1817	180.4190
15	319.4918	320.8118	322.8033	323.4702	326.1531	328.8608	329.5416	331.5936	332.9694	334.3516	336.4369	337.1352
20	525.4407	528.4667	533.0423	534.5774	540.7672	547.0372	548.6173	553.3883	556.5947	559.8218	564.7015	566.3385
25	817.6849	823.8192	833.1170	836.2421	848.8735	861.7171	864.9615	874.7764	881.3881	888.0552	898.1606	901.5572
30	1232.3834	1243.9063	1261.4141	1267.3103	1291.2000	1315.5860	1321.7612	1340.4786	1353.1183	1365.8887	1385.2926	1391.8274

YEAR	8.00 %	8.10 %	8.125%	8.20 %	8.25 %	8.30 %	8.375%	8.40 %	8.50 %	8.60 %	8.625%	8.70 %
1	12.5200	12.5265	12.5281	12.5330	12.5363	12.5395	12.5444	12.5460	12.5525	12.5590	12.5606	12.5655
2	26.0416	26.0676	26.0742	26.0937	26.1067	26.1198	26.1393	26.1459	26.1720	26.1981	26.2046	26.2242
3	40.6449	40.7056	40.7208	40.7664	40.7968	40.8272	40.8729	40.8881	40.9491	41.0101	41.0254	41.0712
4	56.4165	56.5293	56.5575	56.6422	56.6988	56.7554	56.8404	56.8687	56.9823	57.0960	57.1244	57.2099
5	73.4498	73.6347	73.6809	73.8199	73.9127	74.0056	74.1451	74.1917	74.3782	74.5652	74.6120	74.7527
6	91.8458	92.1256	92.1956	92.4061	92.5467	92.6875	92.8991	92.9698	93.2529	93.5368	93.6080	93.8216
7	111.7135	112.1142	112.2146	112.5164	112.7181	112.9201	113.2238	113.3253	113.7319	114.1400	114.2423	114.5496
8	133.1706	133.7220	133.8602	134.2758	134.5536	134.8320	135.2507	135.3906	135.9516	136.5151	136.6563	137.0809
9	156.3442	157.0800	157.2645	157.8194	158.1905	158.5625	159.1223	159.3094	160.0600	160.8143	161.0035	161.5725
10	181.3718	182.3299	182.5703	183.2936	183.7775	184.2627	184.9932	185.2374	186.2176	187.2034	187.4507	188.1948
15	339.9445	342.7797	343.4927	345.6412	347.0819	348.5292	350.7127	351.4439	354.3856	357.3544	358.1009	360.3508
20	572.9398	579.6266	581.3118	586.4001	589.8198	593.2615	598.4659	600.2119	607.2525	614.3844	616.1818	621.6089
25	915.2864	929.2465	932.7731	943.4416	950.6285	957.8757	968.8606	972.5529	987.4775	1002.6535	1006.4874	1018.0855
30	1418.3058	1445.3355	1452.1804	1472.9282	1486.9394	1501.0958	1522.6063	1529.8507	1559.2053	1589.1724	1596.7614	1619.7650

YEAR	8.75 %	8.80 %	8.875%	8.90 %	9.00 %	9.10 %	9.125%	9.20 %	9.25 %	9.30 %	9.375%	9.40 %
1	12.5688	12.5720	12.5769	12.5785	12.5850	12.5915	12.5931	12.5980	12.6012	12.6045	12.6094	12.6110
2	26.2373	26.2503	26.2699	26.2765	26.3027	26.3288	26.3354	26.3550	26.3681	26.3812	26.4009	26.4074
3	41.1018	41.1324	41.1783	41.1936	41.2549	41.3162	41.3316	41.3777	41.4084	41.4392	41.4853	41.5007
4	57.2669	57.3240	57.4097	57.4383	57.5528	57.6675	57.6962	57.7824	57.8399	57.8975	57.9840	58.0128
5	74.8465	74.9405	75.0817	75.1288	75.3176	75.5068	75.5541	75.6964	75.7914	75.8865	76.0293	76.0770
6	93.9644	94.1073	94.3221	94.3938	94.6812	94.9694	95.0416	95.2585	95.4033	95.5484	95.7665	95.8392
7	114.7550	114.9607	115.2701	115.3733	115.7875	116.2031	116.3072	116.6203	116.8294	117.0389	117.3539	117.4591
8	137.3648	137.6493	138.0771	138.2201	138.7933	139.3691	139.5134	139.9473	140.2374	140.5281	140.9652	141.1113
9	161.9530	162.3344	162.9084	163.1002	163.8697	164.6432	164.8371	165.4205	165.8106	166.2017	166.7901	166.9868
10	188.6926	189.1918	189.9434	190.1946	191.2030	192.2172	192.4716	193.2372	193.7493	194.2629	195.0361	195.2945
15	361.8593	363.3748	365.6612	366.4269	369.5071	372.6159	373.3976	375.7535	377.3331	378.9200	381.3142	382.1159
20	625.2562	628.9272	634.4782	636.3405	643.8501	651.4573	653.3744	659.1632	663.0537	666.9694	672.8904	674.8769
25	1025.8987	1033.7777	1045.7203	1049.7346	1065.9608	1082.4609	1086.6293	1099.2396	1107.7349	1116.3017	1129.2871	1133.6520
30	1635.3000	1650.9964	1674.8474	1682.8803	1715.4304	1748.6610	1757.0766	1782.5865	1799.8145	1817.2217	1843.6730	1852.5818

YEAR	9.50 %	9.75 %	10.00 %	10.25 %	10.50 %	10.75 %	11.00 %	12.00 %	13.00 %	14.00 %	15.00 %	16.00 %
1	12.6175	12.6337	12.6500	12.6663	12.6825	12.6988	12.7150	12.7800	12.8450	12.9100	12.9750	13.0400
2	26.4337	26.4993	26.5650	26.6308	26.6967	26.7626	26.8287	27.0936	27.3599	27.6274	27.8963	28.1664
3	41.5624	41.7167	41.8715	42.0267	42.1823	42.3383	42.4948	43.1248	43.7616	44.4052	45.0557	45.7130
4	58.1283	58.4179	58.7087	59.0007	59.2940	59.5885	59.8842	61.0798	62.2956	63.5320	64.7890	66.0671
5	76.2680	76.7473	77.2295	77.7145	78.2023	78.6930	79.1865	81.1894	83.2391	85.3364	87.4824	89.6778
6	96.1309	96.8640	97.6025	98.3465	99.0961	99.8512	100.6120	103.7121	106.9052	110.1935	113.5798	117.0663
7	117.8809	118.9419	120.0127	121.0933	122.1837	123.2840	124.3943	128.9376	133.6478	138.5306	143.5917	148.8369
8	141.6970	143.1725	144.6640	146.1716	147.6954	149.2358	150.7927	157.1901	163.8670	170.8349	178.1055	185.6908
9	167.7758	169.7656	171.7804	173.8204	175.8860	177.9774	180.0949	188.8329	198.0148	207.6618	217.7963	228.4413
10	196.3320	198.9515	201.6084	204.3032	207.0365	209.8087	212.6203	224.2728	236.6017	249.6445	263.4407	278.0320
15	385.3414	393.5362	401.9219	410.5030	419.2839	428.2694	437.4641	476.4348	519.1623	566.0056	617.3558	673.6400
20	682.8873	703.3718	724.5287	746.3806	768.9502	792.2615	816.3390	920.8302	1039.7620	1175.1318	1329.2055	1504.5519
25	1151.2956	1196.7204	1244.0903	1293.4898	1345.0069	1398.7334	1454.7652	1704.0069	1998.9332	2347.9524	2760.9894	3249.7509
30	1888.6821	1982.2753	2080.8494	2184.6731	2294.0296	2409.2172	2530.5505	3084.2317	3766.1439	4606.1182	5640.8183	6915.2650

SAVINGS GROWTH

ANNUAL COMPOUNDING
Quarterly Deposit

Description: This table shows what a series of $ 1 deposits grow to in the future. The deposit is made at the beginning of a period.

Example: At 5 % a regular one dollar deposit will grow to $ 22.79 by the end of the fifth year.

YEAR	0.00 %	1.00 %	2.00 %	3.00 %	4.00 %	4.125%	4.25 %	4.375%	4.50 %	4.625%	4.75 %	4.875%
1	4.0000	4.0250	4.0500	4.0750	4.1000	4.1031	4.1063	4.1094	4.1125	4.1156	4.1188	4.1219
2	8.0000	8.0903	8.1810	8.2722	8.3640	8.3755	8.3870	8.3985	8.4101	8.4216	8.4331	8.4447
3	12.0000	12.1962	12.3946	12.5954	12.7986	12.8241	12.8497	12.8753	12.9010	12.9267	12.9525	12.9782
4	16.0000	16.3431	16.6925	17.0483	17.4105	17.4562	17.5021	17.5480	17.5941	17.6402	17.6865	17.7328
5	20.0000	20.5315	21.0764	21.6347	22.2069	22.2794	22.3522	22.4251	22.4983	22.5717	22.6453	22.7192
6	24.0000	24.7619	25.5479	26.3588	27.1952	27.3016	27.4084	27.5156	27.6232	27.7313	27.8397	27.9486
7	28.0000	29.0345	30.1088	31.2245	32.3830	32.5309	32.6795	32.8288	32.9788	33.1295	33.2809	33.4330
8	32.0000	33.3498	34.7610	36.2363	37.7783	37.9759	38.1746	38.3744	38.5753	38.7773	38.9804	39.1847
9	36.0000	37.7083	39.5062	41.3984	43.3895	43.6456	43.9033	44.1627	44.4237	44.6864	44.9508	45.2168
10	40.0000	42.1104	44.3464	46.7153	49.2250	49.5491	49.8754	50.2042	50.5353	50.8688	51.2047	51.5430
15	60.0000	64.7900	70.0383	75.7906	82.0967	82.9266	83.7661	84.6153	85.4744	86.3435	87.2226	88.1119
20	80.0000	88.6265	98.4043	109.4968	122.0901	123.7801	125.4973	127.2421	129.0150	130.8164	132.6470	134.5070
25	100.0000	113.6789	129.7227	148.5715	170.7482	173.7841	176.8828	180.0458	183.2744	186.5701	189.9343	193.3686
30	120.0000	140.0092	164.3007	193.8698	229.9482	234.9880	240.1562	245.4562	250.8916	256.4659	262.1829	268.0464

YEAR	5.00 %	5.10 %	5.125%	5.20 %	5.25 %	5.30 %	5.375%	5.40 %	5.50 %	5.60 %	5.625%	5.70 %
1	4.1250	4.1275	4.1281	4.1300	4.1312	4.1325	4.1344	4.1350	4.1375	4.1400	4.1406	4.1425
2	8.4563	8.4655	8.4678	8.4748	8.4794	8.4840	8.4910	8.4933	8.5026	8.5118	8.5142	8.5211
3	13.0041	13.0247	13.0299	13.0454	13.0558	13.0662	13.0817	13.0869	13.1077	13.1285	13.1337	13.1493
4	17.7793	17.8165	17.8258	17.8538	17.8725	17.8912	17.9193	17.9286	17.9661	18.0037	18.0131	18.0413
5	22.7932	22.8526	22.8675	22.9122	22.9420	22.9719	23.0168	23.0318	23.0918	23.1519	23.1670	23.2122
6	28.0579	28.1456	28.1676	28.2336	28.2778	28.3219	28.3883	28.4105	28.4993	28.5884	28.6107	28.6778
7	33.5858	33.7086	33.7393	33.8318	33.8936	33.9555	34.0486	34.0796	34.2043	34.3294	34.3607	34.4549
8	39.3901	39.5552	39.5966	39.7210	39.8042	39.8876	40.0131	40.0549	40.2230	40.3918	40.4341	40.5614
9	45.4846	45.7000	45.7540	45.9165	46.0252	46.1342	46.2981	46.3529	46.5728	46.7937	46.8492	47.0159
10	51.8838	52.1582	52.2271	52.4342	52.5728	52.7118	52.9210	52.9910	53.2718	53.5542	53.6251	53.8383
15	89.0116	89.7388	89.9217	90.4728	90.8423	91.2136	91.7737	91.9612	92.7158	93.4775	93.6690	94.2461
20	136.3971	137.9311	138.3176	139.4849	140.2693	141.0587	142.2524	142.6529	144.2677	145.9033	146.3155	147.5601
25	196.8743	199.7314	200.4531	202.6361	204.1065	205.5892	207.8362	208.5915	211.6438	214.7472	215.5310	217.9023
30	274.0602	278.9823	280.2285	284.0054	286.5554	289.1315	293.0450	294.3629	299.7018	305.1505	306.5302	310.7115

YEAR	5.75 %	5.80 %	5.875%	5.90 %	6.00 %	6.10 %	6.125%	6.20 %	6.25 %	6.30 %	6.375%	6.40 %
1	4.1437	4.1450	4.1469	4.1475	4.1500	4.1525	4.1531	4.1550	4.1563	4.1575	4.1594	4.1600
2	8.5258	8.5304	8.5374	8.5397	8.5490	8.5583	8.5606	8.5676	8.5723	8.5769	8.5839	8.5862
3	13.1597	13.1702	13.1858	13.1910	13.2119	13.2329	13.2381	13.2538	13.2643	13.2748	13.2905	13.2958
4	18.0602	18.0790	18.1074	18.1168	18.1547	18.1926	18.2021	18.2305	18.2495	18.2686	18.2972	18.3067
5	23.2424	23.2726	23.3180	23.3332	23.3939	23.4548	23.4701	23.5158	23.5464	23.5770	23.6230	23.6383
6	28.7226	28.7674	28.8349	28.8574	28.9476	29.0381	29.0607	29.1288	29.1743	29.2199	29.2883	29.3112
7	34.5179	34.5810	34.6758	34.7075	34.8344	34.9619	34.9938	35.0898	35.1539	35.2182	35.3148	35.3471
8	40.6464	40.7316	40.8599	40.9027	41.0745	41.2470	41.2903	41.4204	41.5073	41.5944	41.7255	41.7693
9	47.1273	47.2391	47.4073	47.4635	47.6890	47.9156	47.9725	48.1434	48.2578	48.3724	48.5449	48.6025
10	53.9809	54.1240	54.3393	54.4113	54.7003	54.9910	55.0639	55.2833	55.4301	55.5774	55.7990	55.8731
15	94.6331	95.0220	95.6085	95.8050	96.5953	97.3929	97.5935	98.1980	98.6033	99.0105	99.6248	99.8306
20	148.3965	149.2383	150.5112	150.9383	152.6602	154.4044	154.8440	156.1713	157.0633	157.9610	159.3185	159.7739
25	219.4996	221.1102	223.5512	224.3717	227.6877	231.0593	231.9110	234.4873	236.2228	237.9728	240.6251	241.5166
30	313.5347	316.3870	320.7202	322.1795	328.0915	334.1255	335.6534	340.2843	343.4112	346.5703	351.3701	352.9864

YEAR	6.50 %	6.60 %	6.625%	6.70 %	6.75 %	6.80 %	6.875%	6.90 %	7.00 %	7.10 %	7.125%	7.20 %
1	4.1625	4.1650	4.1656	4.1675	4.1688	4.1700	4.1719	4.1725	4.1750	4.1775	4.1781	4.1800
2	8.5956	8.6049	8.6072	8.6142	8.6189	8.6236	8.6306	8.6329	8.6423	8.6516	8.6539	8.6610
3	13.3168	13.3378	13.3431	13.3589	13.3694	13.3800	13.3958	13.4011	13.4222	13.4434	13.4487	13.4645
4	18.3449	18.3831	18.3927	18.4214	18.4406	18.4598	18.4886	18.4982	18.5368	18.5753	18.5850	18.6140
5	23.6998	23.7614	23.7768	23.8232	23.8541	23.8851	23.9316	23.9471	24.0093	24.0717	24.0873	24.1342
6	29.4028	29.4946	29.5177	29.5868	29.6330	29.6793	29.7488	29.7720	29.8650	29.9583	29.9817	30.0519
7	35.4764	35.6063	35.6388	35.7366	35.8020	35.8674	35.9659	35.9987	36.1305	36.2628	36.2960	36.3956
8	41.9449	42.1213	42.1655	42.2985	42.3874	42.4764	42.6104	42.6552	42.8347	43.0150	43.0602	43.1961
9	48.8338	49.0663	49.1246	49.3000	49.4172	49.5348	49.7117	49.7709	50.0081	50.2465	50.3063	50.4862
10	56.1705	56.4697	56.5447	56.7706	56.9217	57.0732	57.3013	57.3776	57.6837	57.9916	58.0688	58.3012
15	100.6583	101.4937	101.7037	102.3368	102.7614	103.1878	103.8313	104.0468	104.9137	105.7886	106.0086	106.6717
20	161.6103	163.4706	163.9394	165.3550	166.3063	167.2638	168.7117	169.1974	171.1562	173.1404	173.6404	175.1503
25	245.1200	248.7838	249.7093	252.5090	254.3951	256.2969	259.1795	260.1485	264.0647	268.0469	269.0529	272.0961
30	359.5354	366.2200	367.9126	373.0431	376.5076	380.0078	385.3259	387.1170	394.3738	401.7814	403.6572	409.3430

Description: This table shows what a series of $ 1 deposits grow to in the future. The deposit is made at the beginning of a period.

Example: At 8 % a regular one dollar deposit will grow to $ 24.64 by the end of the fifth year.

YEAR	7.25 %	7.30 %	7.375%	7.40 %	7.50 %	7.60 %	7.625%	7.70 %	7.75 %	7.80 %	7.875%	7.90 %
1	4.1813	4.1825	4.1844	4.1850	4.1875	4.1900	4.1906	4.1925	4.1937	4.1950	4.1969	4.1975
2	8.6656	8.6703	8.6773	8.6797	8.6891	8.6984	8.7008	8.7078	8.7125	8.7172	8.7243	8.7266
3	13.4751	13.4858	13.5017	13.5070	13.5282	13.5495	13.5548	13.5708	13.5815	13.5922	13.6082	13.6135
4	18.6333	18.6527	18.6818	18.6915	18.7304	18.7693	18.7790	18.8083	18.8278	18.8473	18.8767	18.8865
5	24.1655	24.1969	24.2440	24.2597	24.3226	24.3858	24.4016	24.4490	24.4807	24.5124	24.5601	24.5760
6	30.0988	30.1457	30.2163	30.2399	30.3343	30.4291	30.4528	30.5241	30.5717	30.6194	30.6911	30.7150
7	36.4622	36.5289	36.6292	36.6626	36.7969	36.9317	36.9654	37.0669	37.1348	37.2027	37.3049	37.3390
8	43.2869	43.3780	43.5149	43.5607	43.7442	43.9285	43.9747	44.1136	44.2065	44.2995	44.4395	44.4863
9	50.6065	50.7271	50.9085	50.9692	51.2125	51.4570	51.5184	51.7028	51.8262	51.9499	52.1360	52.1982
10	58.4567	58.6127	58.8474	58.9259	59.2409	59.5578	59.6373	59.8765	60.0365	60.1970	60.4386	60.5193
15	107.1164	107.5631	108.2370	108.4627	109.3707	110.2871	110.5175	111.2120	111.6777	112.1456	112.8515	113.0879
20	176.1651	177.1864	178.7308	179.2490	181.3384	183.4549	183.9883	185.5990	186.6815	187.7710	189.4186	189.9713
25	274.1461	276.2134	279.3468	280.4001	284.6573	288.9863	290.0799	293.3883	295.6170	297.8645	301.2712	302.4163
30	413.1826	417.0619	422.9563	424.9414	432.9850	441.1962	443.2756	449.5785	453.8350	458.1357	464.6705	466.8714

YEAR	8.00 %	8.10 %	8.125%	8.20 %	8.25 %	8.30 %	8.375%	8.40 %	8.50 %	8.60 %	8.625%	8.70 %
1	4.2000	4.2025	4.2031	4.2050	4.2063	4.2075	4.2094	4.2100	4.2125	4.2150	4.2156	4.2175
2	8.7360	8.7454	8.7478	8.7548	8.7595	8.7642	8.7713	8.7736	8.7831	8.7925	8.7948	8.8019
3	13.6349	13.6563	13.6616	13.6777	13.6884	13.6992	13.7153	13.7206	13.7421	13.7636	13.7690	13.7852
4	18.9257	18.9649	18.9748	19.0043	19.0240	19.0437	19.0733	19.0832	19.1227	19.1623	19.1722	19.2020
5	24.6397	24.7036	24.7196	24.7676	24.7997	24.8318	24.8800	24.8961	24.9606	25.0253	25.0415	25.0901
6	30.8109	30.9071	30.9312	31.0036	31.0519	31.1003	31.1731	31.1974	31.2948	31.3925	31.4169	31.4904
7	37.4758	37.6131	37.6475	37.7509	37.8200	37.8892	37.9932	38.0280	38.1673	38.3072	38.3422	38.4476
8	44.6738	44.8622	44.9094	45.0514	45.1464	45.2415	45.3846	45.4324	45.6241	45.8166	45.8649	46.0100
9	52.4477	52.6986	52.7615	52.9507	53.0772	53.2040	53.3949	53.4587	53.7146	53.9719	54.0364	54.2304
10	60.8436	61.1696	61.2515	61.4976	61.6623	61.8275	62.0761	62.1592	62.4929	62.8284	62.9126	63.1659
15	114.0389	114.9988	115.2401	115.9676	116.4553	116.9454	117.6847	117.9323	118.9284	119.9338	120.1866	120.9486
20	192.2003	194.4582	195.0273	196.7456	197.9004	199.0628	200.8205	201.4102	203.7882	206.1972	206.8043	208.6376
25	307.0449	311.7518	312.9408	316.5381	318.9615	321.4053	325.1097	326.3548	331.3881	336.5065	337.7995	341.7115
30	475.7895	484.8938	487.1995	494.1884	498.9083	503.6772	510.9239	513.3645	523.2545	533.3515	535.9086	543.6599

YEAR	8.75 %	8.80 %	8.875%	8.90 %	9.00 %	9.10 %	9.125%	9.20 %	9.25 %	9.30 %	9.375%	9.40 %
1	4.2188	4.2200	4.2219	4.2225	4.2250	4.2275	4.2281	4.2300	4.2313	4.2325	4.2344	4.2350
2	8.8066	8.8114	8.8184	8.8208	8.8302	8.8397	8.8421	8.8492	8.8539	8.8586	8.8657	8.8681
3	13.7960	13.8068	13.8230	13.8284	13.8500	13.8716	13.8770	13.8933	13.9041	13.9150	13.9313	13.9367
4	19.2219	19.2418	19.2716	19.2816	19.3215	19.3614	19.3714	19.4015	19.4215	19.4416	19.4717	19.4817
5	25.1225	25.1550	25.2038	25.2201	25.2854	25.3508	25.3672	25.4164	25.4492	25.4821	25.5315	25.5480
6	31.5395	31.5887	31.6626	31.6872	31.7861	31.8852	31.9101	31.9847	32.0346	32.0845	32.1595	32.1845
7	38.5180	38.5885	38.6945	38.7299	38.8718	39.0143	39.0500	39.1573	39.2290	39.3008	39.4088	39.4449
8	46.1070	46.2043	46.3505	46.3994	46.5953	46.7921	46.8414	46.9898	47.0889	47.1883	47.3378	47.3877
9	54.3601	54.4902	54.6860	54.7514	55.0139	55.2777	55.3438	55.5428	55.6759	55.8093	56.0101	56.0771
10	63.3354	63.5054	63.7612	63.8468	64.1901	64.5355	64.6221	64.8828	65.0572	65.2321	65.4954	65.5834
15	121.4595	121.9728	122.7472	123.0065	124.0499	125.1029	125.3677	126.1658	126.7010	127.2386	128.0497	128.3214
20	209.8697	211.1098	212.9852	213.6143	216.1515	218.7218	219.3696	221.3256	222.6403	223.9635	225.9644	226.6358
25	344.3469	347.0046	351.0332	352.3873	357.8613	363.4280	364.8343	369.0890	371.9554	374.8460	379.2278	380.7007
30	548.8948	554.1843	562.2220	564.9292	575.8994	587.0996	589.9361	598.5348	604.3420	610.2099	619.1269	622.1302

YEAR	9.50 %	9.75 %	10.00 %	10.25 %	10.50 %	10.75 %	11.00 %	12.00 %	13.00 %	14.00 %	15.00 %	16.00 %
1	4.2375	4.2438	4.2500	4.2562	4.2625	4.2688	4.2750	4.3000	4.3250	4.3500	4.3750	4.4000
2	8.8776	8.9013	8.9250	8.9488	8.9726	8.9964	9.0203	9.1160	9.2123	9.3090	9.4063	9.5040
3	13.9584	14.0129	14.0675	14.1223	14.1772	14.2323	14.2875	14.5099	14.7348	14.9623	15.1922	15.4246
4	19.5220	19.6229	19.7243	19.8260	19.9283	20.0310	20.1341	20.5511	20.9754	21.4070	21.8460	22.2926
5	25.6141	25.7799	25.9467	26.1145	26.2833	26.4530	26.6239	27.3172	28.0272	28.7540	29.4979	30.2594
6	32.2849	32.5372	32.7913	33.0474	33.3055	33.5655	33.8275	34.8953	35.9957	37.1295	38.2976	39.5009
7	39.5895	39.9533	40.3205	40.6911	41.0651	41.4425	41.8235	43.3828	45.0001	46.6776	48.4172	50.2210
8	47.5880	48.0925	48.6025	49.1181	49.6394	50.1664	50.6991	52.8887	55.1752	57.5625	60.0548	62.6564
9	56.3463	57.0253	57.7128	58.4090	59.1140	59.8280	60.5510	63.5353	66.6729	69.9713	73.4381	77.0814
10	65.9367	66.8290	67.7341	68.6522	69.5835	70.5283	71.4866	75.4596	79.6654	84.1172	88.8288	93.8145
15	129.4142	132.1911	135.0330	137.9416	140.9184	143.9649	147.0829	160.3028	174.8055	190.7145	208.1643	227.3018
20	229.3430	236.2667	243.4187	250.8068	258.4388	266.3228	274.4671	309.8255	350.0950	395.9584	448.1907	507.6709
25	386.6546	401.9853	417.9750	434.6524	452.0475	470.1914	489.1169	573.3356	673.0546	791.1381	930.9695	1096.5417
30	634.3008	665.8578	699.0996	734.1174	771.0074	809.8707	850.8143	1037.7305	1268.0866	1552.0228	1902.0100	2333.3716

Description: This table shows what a series of $ 1 deposits grow to in the future. The deposit is made at the beginning of a period.

Example: At 5 % a regular one dollar deposit will grow to $ 11.47 by the end of the fifth year.

YEAR	0.00 %	1.00 %	2.00 %	3.00 %	4.00 %	4.125%	4.25 %	4.375%	4.50 %	4.625%	4.75 %	4.875%
1	2.0000	2.0150	2.0300	2.0450	2.0600	2.0619	2.0638	2.0656	2.0675	2.0694	2.0713	2.0731
2	4.0000	4.0502	4.1006	4.1514	4.2024	4.2088	4.2152	4.2216	4.2280	4.2345	4.2409	4.2473
3	6.0000	6.1057	6.2126	6.3209	6.4305	6.4443	6.4581	6.4719	6.4858	6.4997	6.5136	6.5275
4	8.0000	8.1817	8.3669	8.5555	8.7477	8.7720	8.7963	8.8207	8.8452	8.8697	8.8942	8.9188
5	10.0000	10.2785	10.5642	10.8572	11.1576	11.1957	11.2339	11.2722	11.3107	11.3493	11.3879	11.4268
6	12.0000	12.3963	12.8055	13.2279	13.6639	13.7194	13.7751	13.8310	13.8872	13.9435	14.0001	14.0569
7	14.0000	14.5353	15.0916	15.6697	16.2705	16.3472	16.4243	16.5018	16.5796	16.6578	16.7364	16.8153
8	16.0000	16.6956	17.4234	18.1848	18.9813	19.0834	19.1861	19.2893	19.3932	19.4976	19.6026	19.7082
9	18.0000	18.8776	19.8019	20.7754	21.8006	21.9325	22.0652	22.1989	22.3334	22.4687	22.6050	22.7421
10	20.0000	21.0814	22.2279	23.4436	24.7326	24.8991	25.0668	25.2357	25.4059	25.5773	25.7500	25.9239
15	30.0000	32.4352	35.1056	38.0348	41.2486	41.6717	42.0998	42.5329	42.9710	43.4143	43.8628	44.3165
20	40.0000	44.3683	49.3237	54.9499	61.3428	62.2012	63.0734	63.9597	64.8604	65.7757	66.7059	67.6512
25	50.0000	56.9100	65.0215	74.5592	85.7906	87.3288	88.8991	90.5021	92.1386	93.8092	95.5148	97.2560
30	60.0000	70.0916	82.3532	97.2917	115.5350	118.0846	120.6995	123.3814	126.1321	128.9535	131.8474	134.8157

YEAR	5.00 %	5.10 %	5.125%	5.20 %	5.25 %	5.30 %	5.375%	5.40 %	5.50 %	5.60 %	5.625%	5.70 %
1	2.0750	2.0765	2.0769	2.0780	2.0788	2.0795	2.0806	2.0810	2.0825	2.0840	2.0844	2.0855
2	4.2538	4.2589	4.2602	4.2641	4.2666	4.2692	4.2731	4.2744	4.2795	4.2847	4.2860	4.2899
3	6.5414	6.5526	6.5554	6.5638	6.5694	6.5750	6.5834	6.5862	6.5974	6.6086	6.6115	6.6199
4	8.9435	8.9633	8.9682	8.9831	8.9930	9.0030	9.0179	9.0228	9.0428	9.0627	9.0677	9.0827
5	11.4657	11.4969	11.5047	11.5282	11.5439	11.5596	11.5832	11.5911	11.6226	11.6542	11.6622	11.6859
6	14.1140	14.1598	14.1712	14.2057	14.2287	14.2518	14.2864	14.2980	14.3444	14.3909	14.4025	14.4375
7	16.8947	16.9584	16.9744	17.0224	17.0545	17.0866	17.1349	17.1511	17.2158	17.2808	17.2971	17.3460
8	19.8144	19.8998	19.9212	19.9856	20.0286	20.0717	20.1366	20.1582	20.2452	20.3325	20.3544	20.4202
9	22.8801	22.9912	23.0190	23.1028	23.1588	23.2150	23.2995	23.3278	23.4412	23.5551	23.5837	23.6697
10	26.0991	26.2402	26.2756	26.3821	26.4534	26.5249	26.6325	26.6685	26.8129	26.9582	26.9947	27.1043
15	44.7755	45.1466	45.2399	45.5212	45.7098	45.8992	46.1851	46.2809	46.6660	47.0548	47.1526	47.4473
20	68.6119	69.3916	69.5881	70.1815	70.5803	70.9816	71.5886	71.7922	72.6133	73.4450	73.6547	74.2877
25	99.0337	100.4827	100.8487	101.9559	102.7017	103.4538	104.5936	104.9767	106.5253	108.0998	108.4975	109.7007
30	137.8606	140.3530	140.9840	142.8966	144.1881	145.4928	147.4750	148.1425	150.8469	153.6072	154.3061	156.4246

YEAR	5.75 %	5.80 %	5.875%	5.90 %	6.00 %	6.10 %	6.125%	6.20 %	6.25 %	6.30 %	6.375%	6.40 %
1	2.0863	2.0870	2.0881	2.0885	2.0900	2.0915	2.0919	2.0930	2.0938	2.0945	2.0956	2.0960
2	4.2925	4.2950	4.2989	4.3002	4.3054	4.3106	4.3119	4.3158	4.3184	4.3210	4.3248	4.3261
3	6.6255	6.6312	6.6396	6.6424	6.6537	6.6650	6.6679	6.6763	6.6820	6.6877	6.6962	6.6990
4	9.0927	9.1028	9.1178	9.1228	9.1429	9.1631	9.1681	9.1833	9.1934	9.2035	9.2187	9.2238
5	11.7018	11.7177	11.7416	11.7496	11.7815	11.8135	11.8216	11.8456	11.8617	11.8778	11.9020	11.9101
6	14.4609	14.4844	14.5196	14.5313	14.5784	14.6257	14.6375	14.6731	14.6968	14.7206	14.7564	14.7683
7	17.3787	17.4114	17.4607	17.4772	17.5431	17.6093	17.6259	17.6758	17.7091	17.7425	17.7927	17.8095
8	20.4642	20.5083	20.5746	20.5968	20.6857	20.7750	20.7974	20.8647	20.9097	20.9548	21.0226	21.0453
9	23.7272	23.7848	23.8715	23.9005	24.0169	24.1338	24.1631	24.2513	24.3103	24.3694	24.4585	24.4882
10	27.1777	27.2513	27.3621	27.3992	27.5479	27.6974	27.7350	27.8479	27.9234	27.9992	28.1133	28.1514
15	47.6449	47.8434	48.1429	48.2432	48.6468	49.0541	49.1566	49.4653	49.6723	49.8803	50.1942	50.2993
20	74.7131	75.1412	75.7887	76.0059	76.8819	77.7693	77.9929	78.6682	79.1221	79.5789	80.2697	80.5015
25	110.5113	111.3286	112.5674	112.9838	114.6668	116.3782	116.8105	118.1184	118.9994	119.8879	121.2346	121.6872
30	157.8550	159.3003	161.4961	162.2355	165.2316	168.2898	169.0643	171.4115	172.9966	174.5981	177.0314	177.8509

YEAR	6.50 %	6.60 %	6.625%	6.70 %	6.75 %	6.80 %	6.875%	6.90 %	7.00 %	7.10 %	7.125%	7.20 %
1	2.0975	2.0990	2.0994	2.1005	2.1013	2.1020	2.1031	2.1035	2.1050	2.1065	2.1069	2.1080
2	4.3313	4.3365	4.3378	4.3417	4.3443	4.3469	4.3508	4.3521	4.3574	4.3626	4.3639	4.3678
3	6.7104	6.7217	6.7246	6.7331	6.7388	6.7445	6.7531	6.7559	6.7674	6.7788	6.7817	6.7903
4	9.2440	9.2644	9.2695	9.2847	9.2949	9.3052	9.3205	9.3256	9.3461	9.3666	9.3717	9.3872
5	11.9424	11.9748	11.9829	12.0073	12.0236	12.0399	12.0644	12.0726	12.1053	12.1381	12.1463	12.1710
6	14.8162	14.8642	14.8762	14.9123	14.9365	14.9606	14.9969	15.0091	15.0577	15.1064	15.1186	15.1553
7	17.8767	17.9442	17.9611	18.0119	18.0459	18.0799	18.1311	18.1482	18.2167	18.2855	18.3027	18.3545
8	21.1362	21.2275	21.2504	21.3192	21.3653	21.4114	21.4807	21.5039	21.5969	21.6903	21.7137	21.7841
9	24.6076	24.7275	24.7576	24.8481	24.9087	24.9694	25.0607	25.0912	25.2137	25.3368	25.3676	25.4605
10	28.3046	28.4586	28.4972	28.6135	28.6912	28.7693	28.8867	28.9260	29.0836	29.2422	29.2820	29.4017
15	50.7221	51.1489	51.2562	51.5797	51.7967	52.0146	52.3434	52.4535	52.8966	53.3438	53.4563	53.7952
20	81.4361	82.3829	82.6215	83.3421	83.8264	84.3138	85.0509	85.2982	86.2955	87.3058	87.5605	88.3294
25	123.5169	125.3775	125.8475	127.2694	128.2273	129.1933	130.6576	131.1497	133.1392	135.1624	135.6735	137.2197
30	181.1713	184.5608	185.4191	188.0209	189.7779	191.5531	194.2505	195.1589	198.8400	202.5978	203.5495	206.4342

SAVINGS GROWTH

Description: This table shows what a series of $ 1 deposits grow to in the future. The deposit is made at the beginning of a period.

Example: At 8 % a regular one dollar deposit will grow to $ 12.44 by the end of the fifth year.

YEAR	7.25 %	7.30 %	7.375%	7.40 %	7.50 %	7.60 %	7.625%	7.70 %	7.75 %	7.80 %	7.875%	7.90 %
1	2.1088	2.1095	2.1106	2.1110	2.1125	2.1140	2.1144	2.1155	2.1163	2.1170	2.1181	2.1185
2	4.3704	4.3730	4.3769	4.3782	4.3834	4.3887	4.3900	4.3939	4.3965	4.3991	4.4031	4.4044
3	6.7960	6.8017	6.8103	6.8132	6.8247	6.8362	6.8391	6.8477	6.8535	6.8593	6.8679	6.8708
4	9.3974	9.4077	9.4232	9.4284	9.4490	9.4698	9.4749	9.4905	9.5009	9.5113	9.5269	9.5321
5	12.1875	12.2040	12.2288	12.2371	12.2702	12.3035	12.3118	12.3368	12.3535	12.3702	12.3953	12.4036
6	15.1799	15.2044	15.2413	15.2536	15.3030	15.3525	15.3649	15.4022	15.4271	15.4520	15.4895	15.5020
7	18.3891	18.4238	18.4760	18.4934	18.5632	18.6333	18.6509	18.7037	18.7389	18.7743	18.8274	18.8452
8	21.8311	21.8783	21.9492	21.9729	22.0680	22.1634	22.1874	22.2593	22.3075	22.3557	22.4282	22.4525
9	25.5226	25.5849	25.6786	25.7099	25.8356	25.9619	25.9935	26.0888	26.1525	26.2164	26.3126	26.3447
10	29.4818	29.5621	29.6830	29.7234	29.8857	30.0490	30.0899	30.2132	30.2956	30.3783	30.5028	30.5444
15	54.0225	54.2509	54.5954	54.7108	55.1750	55.6436	55.7615	56.1167	56.3548	56.5941	56.9551	57.0760
20	88.8462	89.3663	90.1530	90.4169	91.4811	92.5594	92.8311	93.6517	94.2032	94.7583	95.5978	95.8795
25	138.2614	139.3119	140.9043	141.4396	143.6032	145.8036	146.3595	148.0412	149.1743	150.3168	152.0489	152.6311
30	208.3824	210.3507	213.3418	214.3492	218.4312	222.5987	223.6542	226.8535	229.0142	231.1974	234.5150	235.6324

YEAR	8.00 %	8.10 %	8.125%	8.20 %	8.25 %	8.30 %	8.375%	8.40 %	8.50 %	8.60 %	8.625%	8.70 %
1	2.1200	2.1215	2.1219	2.1230	2.1237	2.1245	2.1256	2.1260	2.1275	2.1290	2.1294	2.1305
2	4.4096	4.4148	4.4162	4.4201	4.4227	4.4253	4.4293	4.4306	4.4358	4.4411	4.4424	4.4464
3	6.8824	6.8939	6.8968	6.9055	6.9113	6.9171	6.9258	6.9288	6.9404	6.9520	6.9549	6.9637
4	9.5530	9.5739	9.5791	9.5948	9.6053	9.6158	9.6315	9.6368	9.6578	9.6789	9.6842	9.7000
5	12.4372	12.4708	12.4793	12.5046	12.5215	12.5384	12.5638	12.5723	12.6062	12.6403	12.6488	12.6744
6	15.5522	15.6025	15.6151	15.6529	15.6782	15.7036	15.7416	15.7543	15.8053	15.8564	15.8692	15.9076
7	18.9163	18.9878	19.0057	19.0595	19.0954	19.1314	19.1856	19.2037	19.2762	19.3490	19.3672	19.4221
8	22.5497	22.6473	22.6718	22.7454	22.7945	22.8439	22.9180	22.9428	23.0422	23.1420	23.1670	23.2423
9	26.4736	26.6032	26.6357	26.7335	26.7988	26.8644	26.9630	26.9960	27.1283	27.2612	27.2946	27.3949
10	30.7115	30.8796	30.9217	31.0486	31.1335	31.2186	31.3468	31.3897	31.5617	31.7347	31.7781	31.9087
15	57.5625	58.0535	58.1770	58.5491	58.7987	59.0494	59.4277	59.5544	60.0642	60.5787	60.7081	61.0980
20	97.0154	98.1661	98.4562	99.3320	99.9206	100.5131	101.4091	101.7097	102.9221	104.1504	104.4599	105.3948
25	154.9846	157.3781	157.9828	159.8122	161.0448	162.2877	164.1719	164.8053	167.3657	169.9697	170.6276	172.6180
30	240.1604	244.7834	245.9542	249.5034	251.9005	254.3226	258.0033	259.2430	264.2668	269.3963	270.6954	274.6337

YEAR	8.75 %	8.80 %	8.875%	8.90 %	9.00 %	9.10 %	9.125%	9.20 %	9.25 %	9.30 %	9.375%	9.40 %
1	2.1313	2.1320	2.1331	2.1335	2.1350	2.1365	2.1369	2.1380	2.1388	2.1395	2.1406	2.1410
2	4.4490	4.4516	4.4556	4.4569	4.4621	4.4674	4.4687	4.4727	4.4753	4.4780	4.4819	4.4833
3	6.9695	6.9754	6.9841	6.9870	6.9987	7.0105	7.0134	7.0222	7.0281	7.0339	7.0427	7.0457
4	9.7106	9.7212	9.7371	9.7424	9.7636	9.7849	9.7902	9.8062	9.8169	9.8276	9.8436	9.8490
5	12.6915	12.7087	12.7344	12.7430	12.7774	12.8118	12.8205	12.8464	12.8637	12.8810	12.9071	12.9158
6	15.9333	15.9590	15.9977	16.0106	16.0623	16.1142	16.1272	16.1663	16.1924	16.2185	16.2578	16.2709
7	19.4587	19.4954	19.5506	19.5690	19.6429	19.7171	19.7357	19.7916	19.8289	19.8663	19.9225	19.9413
8	23.2926	23.3430	23.4188	23.4442	23.5458	23.6479	23.6735	23.7504	23.8018	23.8534	23.9309	23.9568
9	27.4619	27.5292	27.6304	27.6642	27.7999	27.9363	27.9705	28.0734	28.1422	28.2112	28.3150	28.3497
10	31.9961	32.0838	32.2157	32.2598	32.4369	32.6150	32.6597	32.7942	32.8841	32.9744	33.1102	33.1556
15	61.3595	61.6223	62.0187	62.1514	62.6856	63.2247	63.3603	63.7689	64.0429	64.3183	64.7336	64.8727
20	106.0231	106.6555	107.6119	107.9328	109.2269	110.5379	110.8684	111.8662	112.5369	113.2120	114.2330	114.5755
25	173.9590	175.3113	177.3614	178.0505	180.8364	183.6698	184.3856	186.5514	188.0106	189.4821	191.7129	192.4628
30	277.2935	279.9813	284.0657	285.4414	291.0166	296.7092	298.1510	302.5218	305.4739	308.4570	312.9903	314.5173

YEAR	9.50 %	9.75 %	10.00 %	10.25 %	10.50 %	10.75 %	11.00 %	12.00 %	13.00 %	14.00 %	15.00 %	16.00 %
1	2.1425	2.1463	2.1500	2.1538	2.1575	2.1613	2.1650	2.1800	2.1950	2.2100	2.2250	2.2400
2	4.4885	4.5018	4.5150	4.5283	4.5415	4.5548	4.5682	4.6216	4.6754	4.7294	4.7837	4.8384
3	7.0574	7.0869	7.1165	7.1462	7.1759	7.2057	7.2356	7.3562	7.4781	7.6015	7.7263	7.8525
4	9.8704	9.9242	9.9782	10.0324	10.0869	10.1416	10.1966	10.4189	10.6453	10.8757	11.1103	11.3490
5	12.9506	13.0380	13.1260	13.2145	13.3035	13.3931	13.4832	13.8492	14.2242	14.6083	15.0018	15.4048
6	16.3234	16.4555	16.5886	16.7227	16.8579	16.9941	17.1313	17.6911	18.2683	18.8635	19.4771	20.1095
7	20.0166	20.2061	20.3974	20.5905	20.7854	20.9822	21.1808	21.9940	22.8382	23.7144	24.6236	25.5671
8	24.0607	24.3225	24.5872	24.8548	25.1254	25.3990	25.6757	26.8133	28.0022	29.2444	30.5422	31.8978
9	28.4890	28.8402	29.1959	29.5562	29.9211	30.2907	30.6650	32.2109	33.8375	35.5486	37.3485	39.2415
10	33.3379	33.7983	34.2655	34.7394	35.2203	35.7082	36.2031	38.2562	40.4313	42.7354	45.1758	47.7601
15	65.4324	66.8548	68.3108	69.8013	71.3270	72.8888	74.4876	81.2698	88.7163	96.8917	105.8664	115.7173
20	115.9569	119.4904	123.1412	126.9134	130.8110	134.8381	138.9991	157.0743	177.6783	201.1651	227.9370	258.4506
25	195.4944	203.3016	211.4462	219.9430	228.8076	238.0559	247.7048	290.6678	341.5849	401.9345	473.4645	558.2394
30	320.7055	336.7534	353.6621	371.4785	390.2518	410.0341	430.8802	526.1053	643.5723	788.4989	967.3080	1187.8983

SAVINGS GROWTH

Description: This table shows what a series of $ 1 deposits grow to in the future. The deposit is made at the beginning of a period.

Example: At 5 % a regular one dollar deposit will grow to $ 5.80 by the end of the fifth year.

YEAR	0.00 %	1.00 %	2.00 %	3.00 %	4.00 %	4.125%	4.25 %	4.375%	4.50 %	4.625%	4.75 %	4.875%
1	1.0000	1.0100	1.0200	1.0300	1.0400	1.0413	1.0425	1.0437	1.0450	1.0462	1.0475	1.0488
2	2.0000	2.0301	2.0604	2.0909	2.1216	2.1255	2.1293	2.1332	2.1370	2.1409	2.1448	2.1486
3	3.0000	3.0604	3.1216	3.1836	3.2465	3.2544	3.2623	3.2702	3.2782	3.2862	3.2941	3.3021
4	4.0000	4.1010	4.2040	4.3091	4.4163	4.4299	4.4434	4.4571	4.4707	4.4844	4.4981	4.5119
5	5.0000	5.1520	5.3081	5.4684	5.6330	5.6539	5.6748	5.6958	5.7169	5.7380	5.7593	5.7806
6	6.0000	6.2135	6.4343	6.6625	6.8983	6.9283	6.9585	6.9888	7.0192	7.0497	7.0803	7.1111
7	7.0000	7.2857	7.5830	7.8923	8.2142	8.2554	8.2967	8.3383	8.3800	8.4220	8.4641	8.5065
8	8.0000	8.3685	8.7546	9.1591	9.5828	9.6372	9.6918	9.7468	9.8021	9.8577	9.9137	9.9700
9	9.0000	9.4622	9.9497	10.4639	11.0061	11.0759	11.1462	11.2170	11.2882	11.3599	11.4321	11.5048
10	10.0000	10.5668	11.1687	11.8078	12.4864	12.5741	12.6624	12.7515	12.8412	12.9316	13.0226	13.1144
15	15.0000	16.2579	17.6393	19.1569	20.8245	21.0443	21.2666	21.4917	21.7193	21.9497	22.1829	22.4188
20	20.0000	22.2392	24.7833	27.6765	30.9692	31.4117	31.8614	32.3185	32.7831	33.2554	33.7354	34.2233
25	25.0000	28.5256	32.6709	37.5530	43.3117	44.1012	44.9072	45.7303	46.5706	47.4288	48.3050	49.1998
30	30.0000	35.1327	41.3794	49.0027	58.3283	59.6329	60.9712	62.3440	63.7524	65.1973	66.6796	68.2004

YEAR	5.00 %	5.10 %	5.125%	5.20 %	5.25 %	5.30 %	5.375%	5.40 %	5.50 %	5.60 %	5.625%	5.70 %
1	1.0500	1.0510	1.0513	1.0520	1.0525	1.0530	1.0537	1.0540	1.0550	1.0560	1.0562	1.0570
2	2.1525	2.1556	2.1564	2.1587	2.1603	2.1618	2.1641	2.1649	2.1680	2.1711	2.1719	2.1742
3	3.3101	3.3165	3.3181	3.3230	3.3262	3.3294	3.3342	3.3358	3.3423	3.3487	3.3503	3.3552
4	4.5256	4.5367	4.5394	4.5478	4.5533	4.5588	4.5672	4.5700	4.5811	4.5922	4.5950	4.6034
5	5.8019	5.8191	5.8233	5.8362	5.8448	5.8535	5.8664	5.8707	5.8881	5.9054	5.9098	5.9228
6	7.1420	7.1668	7.1730	7.1917	7.2042	7.2167	7.2355	7.2418	7.2669	7.2921	7.2984	7.3174
7	8.5491	8.5833	8.5919	8.6177	8.6349	8.6522	8.6781	8.6868	8.7216	8.7565	8.7652	8.7915
8	10.0266	10.0721	10.0835	10.1178	10.1407	10.1637	10.1983	10.2099	10.2563	10.3028	10.3145	10.3496
9	11.5779	11.6368	11.6515	11.6959	11.7256	11.7554	11.8002	11.8152	11.8754	11.9358	11.9510	11.9966
10	13.2068	13.2812	13.2999	13.3561	13.3937	13.4315	13.4883	13.5073	13.5835	13.6602	13.6794	13.7374
15	22.6575	22.8505	22.8991	23.0454	23.1435	23.2421	23.3908	23.4407	23.6411	23.8435	23.8944	24.0478
20	34.7193	35.1219	35.2234	35.5298	35.7358	35.9431	36.2566	36.3618	36.7861	37.2159	37.3243	37.6514
25	50.1135	50.8583	51.0465	51.6158	51.9993	52.3861	52.9723	53.1694	53.9660	54.7761	54.9808	55.5999
30	69.7608	71.0383	71.3618	72.3423	73.0044	73.6734	74.6899	75.0323	76.4194	77.8355	78.1941	79.2811

YEAR	5.75 %	5.80 %	5.875%	5.90 %	6.00 %	6.10 %	6.125%	6.20 %	6.25 %	6.30 %	6.375%	6.40 %
1	1.0575	1.0580	1.0588	1.0590	1.0600	1.0610	1.0613	1.0620	1.0625	1.0630	1.0637	1.0640
2	2.1758	2.1774	2.1797	2.1805	2.1836	2.1867	2.1875	2.1898	2.1914	2.1930	2.1953	2.1961
3	3.3584	3.3617	3.3665	3.3681	3.3746	3.3811	3.3827	3.3876	3.3909	3.3941	3.3990	3.4006
4	4.6090	4.6146	4.6230	4.6258	4.6371	4.6484	4.6512	4.6596	4.6653	4.6710	4.6795	4.6823
5	5.9315	5.9403	5.9534	5.9578	5.9753	5.9929	5.9973	6.0105	6.0194	6.0282	6.0415	6.0460
6	7.3301	7.3428	7.3619	7.3683	7.3938	7.4195	7.4259	7.4452	7.4581	7.4710	7.4904	7.4969
7	8.8091	8.8267	8.8532	8.8620	8.8975	8.9331	8.9420	8.9688	8.9867	9.0047	9.0317	9.0407
8	10.3731	10.3966	10.4320	10.4439	10.4913	10.5390	10.5509	10.5869	10.6109	10.6350	10.6712	10.6833
9	12.0271	12.0576	12.1037	12.1191	12.1808	12.2429	12.2584	12.3053	12.3366	12.3680	12.4152	12.4310
10	13.7761	13.8150	13.8735	13.8931	13.9716	14.0507	14.0705	14.1302	14.1701	14.2102	14.2705	14.2906
15	24.1507	24.2541	24.4101	24.4623	24.6725	24.8847	24.9381	25.0990	25.2069	25.3153	25.4788	25.5336
20	37.8713	38.0927	38.4274	38.5398	38.9927	39.4517	39.5674	39.9167	40.1515	40.3879	40.7453	40.8653
25	56.0171	56.4378	57.0755	57.2898	58.1564	59.0377	59.2603	59.9339	60.3878	60.8455	61.5393	61.7725
30	80.0152	80.7569	81.8840	82.2635	83.8017	85.3720	85.7697	86.9752	87.7893	88.6120	89.8620	90.2831

YEAR	6.50 %	6.60 %	6.625%	6.70 %	6.75 %	6.80 %	6.875%	6.90 %	7.00 %	7.10 %	7.125%	7.20 %
1	1.0650	1.0660	1.0662	1.0670	1.0675	1.0680	1.0688	1.0690	1.0700	1.0710	1.0713	1.0720
2	2.1992	2.2024	2.2031	2.2055	2.2071	2.2086	2.2110	2.2118	2.2149	2.2180	2.2188	2.2212
3	3.4072	3.4157	3.4153	3.4203	3.4235	3.4268	3.4317	3.4334	3.4399	3.4465	3.4482	3.4531
4	4.6936	4.7050	4.7079	4.7164	4.7221	4.7278	4.7364	4.7393	4.7507	4.7622	4.7651	4.7737
5	6.0637	6.0815	6.0860	6.0994	6.1084	6.1173	6.1308	6.1353	6.1533	6.1713	6.1759	6.1894
6	7.5229	7.5489	7.5555	7.5751	7.5882	7.6013	7.6210	7.6276	7.6540	7.6805	7.6871	7.7071
7	9.0769	9.1132	9.1223	9.1496	9.1679	9.1862	9.2137	9.2229	9.2598	9.2968	9.3061	9.3340
8	10.7319	10.7806	10.7929	10.8296	10.8542	10.8789	10.9159	10.9283	10.9780	11.0279	11.0404	11.0780
9	12.4944	12.5581	12.5741	12.6222	12.6544	12.6866	12.7351	12.7514	12.8164	12.8819	12.8983	12.9477
10	14.3716	14.4530	14.4734	14.5349	14.5760	14.6173	14.6794	14.7002	14.7836	14.8675	14.8885	14.9519
15	25.7540	25.9765	26.0325	26.2012	26.3143	26.4280	26.5995	26.6569	26.8881	27.1214	27.1801	27.3570
20	41.3490	41.8391	41.9626	42.3356	42.5864	42.8388	43.2205	43.3486	43.8652	44.3886	44.5205	44.9189
25	62.7154	63.6743	63.9166	64.6496	65.1435	65.6415	66.3966	66.6504	67.6765	68.7201	68.9838	69.7816
30	91.9892	93.7312	94.1724	95.5098	96.4130	97.3257	98.7127	99.1799	101.0730	103.0061	103.4957	104.9798

SAVINGS GROWTH

Description: This table shows what a series of $ 1 deposits grow to in the future. The deposit is made at the beginning of a period.

Example: At 8 % a regular one dollar deposit will grow to $ 6.34 by the end of the fifth year.

YEAR	7.25 %	7.30 %	7.375%	7.40 %	7.50 %	7.60 %	7.625%	7.70 %	7.75 %	7.80 %	7.875%	7.90 %
1	1.0725	1.0730	1.0737	1.0740	1.0750	1.0760	1.0762	1.0770	1.0775	1.0780	1.0788	1.0790
2	2.2228	2.2243	2.2267	2.2275	2.2306	2.2338	2.2346	2.2369	2.2385	2.2401	2.2425	2.2432
3	3.4564	3.4597	3.4647	3.4663	3.4729	3.4795	3.4812	3.4862	3.4895	3.4928	3.4978	3.4995
4	4.7795	4.7853	4.7939	4.7968	4.8084	4.8200	4.8229	4.8316	4.8374	4.8432	4.8520	4.8549
5	6.1985	6.2076	6.2212	6.2258	6.2440	6.2623	6.2669	6.2806	6.2898	6.2990	6.3128	6.3175
6	7.7204	7.7337	7.7538	7.7605	7.7873	7.8142	7.8210	7.8413	7.8548	7.8683	7.8887	7.8955
7	9.3526	9.3713	9.3994	9.4088	9.4464	9.4841	9.4936	9.5220	9.5410	9.5601	9.5887	9.5983
8	11.1032	11.1284	11.1663	11.1790	11.2298	11.2809	11.2937	11.3322	11.3580	11.3838	11.4226	11.4355
9	12.9807	13.0138	13.0636	13.0803	13.1471	13.2143	13.2311	13.2818	13.3157	13.3497	13.4009	13.4179
10	14.9943	15.0368	15.1008	15.1222	15.2081	15.2946	15.3162	15.3815	15.4252	15.4690	15.5349	15.5570
15	27.4756	27.5948	27.7746	27.8349	28.0772	28.3219	28.3835	28.5690	28.6934	28.8183	29.0069	29.0701
20	45.1867	45.4543	45.8640	46.0008	46.5525	47.1116	47.2525	47.6780	47.9641	48.2520	48.6875	48.8336
25	70.3191	70.8612	71.6830	71.9593	73.0762	74.2122	74.4993	75.3677	75.9529	76.5430	77.4377	77.7385
30	105.9823	106.9952	108.5346	109.0531	111.1544	113.3000	113.8435	115.4910	116.6038	117.7283	119.4373	120.0129

YEAR	8.00 %	8.10 %	8.125%	8.20 %	8.25 %	8.30 %	8.375%	8.40 %	8.50 %	8.60 %	8.625%	8.70 %
1	1.0800	1.0810	1.0813	1.0820	1.0825	1.0830	1.0837	1.0840	1.0850	1.0860	1.0862	1.0870
2	2.2464	2.2496	2.2504	2.2527	2.2543	2.2559	2.2583	2.2591	2.2622	2.2654	2.2662	2.2686
3	3.5061	3.5128	3.5144	3.5194	3.5228	3.5261	3.5311	3.5328	3.5395	3.5462	3.5479	3.5529
4	4.8666	4.8783	4.8812	4.8900	4.8959	4.9018	4.9106	4.9136	4.9254	4.9372	4.9402	4.9490
5	6.3359	6.3545	6.3591	6.3730	6.3823	6.3916	6.4056	6.4103	6.4290	6.4478	6.4525	6.4666
6	7.9228	7.9502	7.9570	7.9776	7.9914	8.0052	8.0259	8.0328	8.0605	8.0883	8.0953	8.1162
7	9.6366	9.6751	9.6848	9.7138	9.7332	9.7526	9.7818	9.7915	9.8306	9.8699	9.8797	9.9093
8	11.4876	11.5398	11.5529	11.5923	11.6186	11.6450	11.6848	11.6980	11.7512	11.8047	11.8181	11.8584
9	13.4866	13.5555	13.5728	13.6249	13.6597	13.6946	13.7471	13.7647	13.8351	13.9059	13.9237	13.9771
10	15.6455	15.7345	15.7569	15.8241	15.8691	15.9142	15.9822	16.0049	16.0961	16.1878	16.2108	16.2801
15	29.3243	29.5809	29.6454	29.8399	29.9704	30.1015	30.2992	30.3655	30.6320	30.9011	30.9688	31.1728
20	49.4229	50.0201	50.1706	50.6251	50.9307	51.2383	51.7034	51.8595	52.4891	53.1270	53.2878	53.7733
25	78.9544	80.1912	80.5037	81.4493	82.0864	82.7289	83.7031	84.0306	85.3546	86.7013	87.0416	88.0712
30	122.3459	124.7282	125.3316	127.1610	128.3966	129.6453	131.5430	132.1822	134.7730	137.4187	138.0888	140.1205

YEAR	8.75 %	8.80 %	8.875%	8.90 %	9.00 %	9.10 %	9.125%	9.20 %	9.25 %	9.30 %	9.375%	9.40 %
1	1.0875	1.0880	1.0888	1.0890	1.0900	1.0910	1.0913	1.0920	1.0925	1.0930	1.0938	1.0940
2	2.2702	2.2717	2.2741	2.2749	2.2781	2.2813	2.2821	2.2845	2.2861	2.2876	2.2900	2.2908
3	3.5563	3.5597	3.5647	3.5664	3.5731	3.5799	3.5816	3.5866	3.5900	3.5934	3.5985	3.6002
4	4.9550	4.9609	4.9698	4.9728	4.9847	4.9966	4.9996	5.0086	5.0146	5.0206	5.0296	5.0326
5	6.4760	6.4855	6.4996	6.5044	6.5233	6.5423	6.5471	6.5614	6.5709	6.5805	6.5949	6.5997
6	8.1302	8.1442	8.1652	8.1723	8.2004	8.2287	8.2358	8.2570	8.2713	8.2855	8.3069	8.3140
7	9.9291	9.9489	9.9787	9.9886	10.0285	10.0685	10.0785	10.1087	10.1288	10.1490	10.1794	10.1895
8	11.8854	11.9124	11.9530	11.9666	12.0210	12.0757	12.0895	12.1307	12.1583	12.1859	12.2275	12.2414
9	14.0128	14.0487	14.1026	14.1206	14.1929	14.2656	14.2839	14.3387	14.3754	14.4122	14.4675	14.4860
10	16.3265	16.3730	16.4429	16.4663	16.5603	16.6548	16.6785	16.7499	16.7976	16.8455	16.9176	16.9417
15	31.3096	31.4470	31.6544	31.7239	32.0034	32.2856	32.3566	32.5705	32.7139	32.8581	33.0756	33.1484
20	54.0997	54.4283	54.9253	55.0920	55.7645	56.4460	56.6178	57.1365	57.4853	57.8363	58.3672	58.5453
25	88.7650	89.4647	90.5255	90.8821	92.3240	93.7906	94.1612	95.2826	96.0381	96.8002	97.9555	98.3439
30	141.4929	142.8797	144.9875	145.6975	148.5752	151.5140	152.2585	154.5154	156.0399	157.5805	159.9221	160.7108

YEAR	9.50 %	9.75 %	10.00 %	10.25 %	10.50 %	10.75 %	11.00 %	12.00 %	13.00 %	14.00 %	15.00 %	16.00 %
1	1.0950	1.0975	1.1000	1.1025	1.1050	1.1075	1.1100	1.1200	1.1300	1.1400	1.1500	1.1600
2	2.2940	2.3020	2.3100	2.3180	2.3260	2.3341	2.3421	2.3744	2.4069	2.4396	2.4725	2.5056
3	3.6070	3.6240	3.6410	3.6581	3.6753	3.6925	3.7097	3.7793	3.8498	3.9211	3.9934	4.0665
4	5.0446	5.0748	5.1051	5.1356	5.1662	5.1969	5.2278	5.3528	5.4803	5.6101	5.7424	5.8771
5	6.6189	6.6671	6.7156	6.7645	6.8136	6.8631	6.9129	7.1152	7.3227	7.5355	7.7537	7.9775
6	8.3426	8.4146	8.4872	8.5603	8.6340	8.7084	8.7833	9.0890	9.4047	9.7305	10.0668	10.4139
7	10.2302	10.3325	10.4359	10.5402	10.6456	10.7520	10.8594	11.2997	11.7573	12.2328	12.7268	13.2401
8	12.2971	12.4375	12.5795	12.7231	12.8684	13.0153	13.1640	13.7757	14.4157	15.0853	15.7858	16.5185
9	14.5603	14.7476	14.9374	15.1297	15.3246	15.5220	15.7220	16.5487	17.4197	18.3373	19.3037	20.3215
10	17.0385	17.2830	17.5312	17.7830	18.0387	18.2981	18.5614	19.6546	20.8143	22.0445	23.3493	24.7329
15	33.4416	34.1867	34.9497	35.7311	36.5313	37.3508	38.1899	41.7533	45.6717	49.9804	54.7175	59.9250
20	59.2638	61.1022	63.0025	64.9667	66.9970	69.0957	71.2651	80.6987	91.4699	103.7684	117.8101	133.8405
25	99.9143	103.9597	108.1818	112.5884	117.1877	121.9882	126.9988	149.3339	175.8501	207.3327	244.7120	289.0883
30	163.9078	172.2012	180.9434	190.1590	199.8741	210.1158	220.9132	270.2926	331.3151	406.7370	499.9569	615.1616

TABLE **17**

Savings and Withdrawal

Interest Rates:	0, 1, 2, 3%; 4 to 10% by .25%; 10.50, 11, 12%.
Terms:	5, 10, 15, 25, 30 years.
Payment:	Monthly.

This table shows the amount to which a regular monthly savings will grow. It also shows how many full years a withdrawal may be taken from an amount at interest. Interest in the table is compounded monthly.

Example: At 5%, a regular monthly savings of $25 will grow to $10,319 in 20 years, as shown in the monthly savings section of the 5% table on page 17-6.

At 5%, an amount of $50,000 will support a monthly withdrawal of $700 for 7 years, as shown in the monthly withdrawal section on page 17-6.

How Much and How Long. At retirement, a person looks to a savings account to supplement retirement income. The questions to be asked are: How much can be withdrawn? How long will it last? This table answers these questions directly by showing the whole years that an amount may be withdrawn. If the actual payout period is 8 years and 3 months, then the table shows 8 years. When the payout period is longer than 30 years, a "greater than" symbol is printed next to the term, like this: > 30.

To have a certain sum of money in the future, 2 similar questions are asked with regard to savings: How much must be saved? How long must I save? Both questions are answered by the table.

Payout. The payout of a monthly withdrawal from a savings account is similar to a mortgage loan payment, only the process is in reverse. Instead of paying, there is receiving. A portion of each payout is interest on the amount; the balance is a return of principal. Page 5-18 shows the 5%, 18 year schedule. It provides approximate allocation, on an annual basis, of the payment to interest and principal from an amount of $100,000 with a monthly payment of $700. As this table shows, at 5% interest, the payout lasts 18 years.

Annual Withdrawal. The heading of each withdrawal table shows the monthly withdrawal amounts. The annual withdrawals are shown at the foot of the page.

SAVINGS & WITHDRAWAL

0.00 %

Description: This table shows the amount to which a regular monthly savings will grow. And then how many full years a withdrawal may be taken from an amount at interest.

Example: At 0.00 % a regular monthly saving of $ 25 will grow to $ 6000 in 20 years. An amount of $50000 will support a monthly withdrawal of $ 700 for 6 years.

MONTHLY SAVINGS, 0.00 %

AMOUNT SAVED

YEARS	25	50	75	100	200	300	400	500	600	700	800	900
5	1500	3000	4500	6000	12000	18000	24000	30000	36000	42000	48000	54000
10	3000	6000	9000	12000	24000	36000	48000	60000	72000	84000	96000	108000
15	4500	9000	13500	18000	36000	54000	72000	90000	108000	126000	144000	162000
20	6000	12000	18000	24000	48000	72000	96000	120000	144000	168000	192000	216000
25	7500	15000	22500	30000	60000	90000	120000	150000	180000	210000	240000	270000
30	9000	18000	27000	36000	72000	108000	144000	180000	216000	252000	288000	324000

MONTHLY WITHDRAWAL, 0.00 %

FULL YEARS TO WITHDRAW

AMOUNT	500	600	700	800	900	1000	1100	1200	1300	1400	1500	1600	1700	1800	1900	2000	2500	3000	4000	5000
50000	8	7	6	5	4	4	3	3	3	3	2	2	2	2	2	2	1	1	1	0
60000	10	8	7	6	5	5	4	4	3	3	3	3	3	2	2	2	2	1	1	1
70000	11	9	8	7	6	5	5	4	4	4	3	3	3	3	3	3	2	2	1	1
80000	13	11	9	8	7	6	6	5	5	4	4	4	3	3	3	3	2	2	1	1
90000	15	12	10	9	8	7	6	6	5	5	5	4	4	4	4	3	2	2	1	1
100000	16	13	11	10	9	8	7	7	6	6	5	5	4	4	4	4	3	2	2	1
110000	18	15	13	11	10	9	8	7	7	6	6	5	5	5	4	4	3	3	2	1
120000	20	16	14	12	11	10	9	8	7	7	6	6	5	5	5	5	4	3	2	1
130000	21	18	15	13	12	10	9	9	8	7	7	6	6	6	5	5	4	3	2	2
140000	23	19	16	14	13	11	10	9	9	8	7	7	6	6	6	5	4	3	2	2
150000	25	20	17	15	13	12	11	10	9	9	8	7	7	7	6	6	5	4	3	2
160000	26	22	19	16	14	13	12	11	10	9	9	8	7	7	7	6	5	4	3	2
170000	28	23	20	17	15	14	12	11	10	10	9	8	8	7	7	7	5	4	3	2
180000	30	25	21	18	16	15	13	12	11	10	10	9	8	8	7	7	5	4	3	2
190000	>30	26	22	19	17	15	14	13	12	11	10	10	9	8	8	8	6	5	4	3
200000	>30	27	23	20	18	16	15	13	12	11	11	10	9	9	8	8	6	5	4	3
225000	>30	>30	26	23	20	18	17	15	14	13	12	11	11	10	9	9	7	6	4	3
250000	>30	>30	29	26	23	20	19	17	16	14	13	13	12	11	11	10	8	7	5	4
275000	>30	>30	>30	28	25	23	20	19	17	16	15	14	13	12	12	11	9	7	5	4
300000	>30	>30	>30	>30	27	25	22	20	19	17	16	15	14	13	13	12	10	8	6	5
350000	>30	>30	>30	>30	>30	29	26	24	22	20	19	18	17	16	15	14	11	9	7	5
400000	>30	>30	>30	>30	>30	>30	>30	27	25	23	22	20	19	18	17	16	13	11	8	6
450000	>30	>30	>30	>30	>30	>30	>30	>30	28	26	25	23	22	20	19	18	15	12	9	7
500000	>30	>30	>30	>30	>30	>30	>30	>30	>30	29	27	26	24	23	22	20	16	13	10	8

MONTHLY SAVINGS, 1.00 %

AMOUNT SAVED

YEARS	25	50	75	100	200	300	400	500	600	700	800	900
5	1539	3078	4616	6155	12310	18465	24620	30775	36930	43085	49240	55395
10	3156	6313	9469	12625	25251	37876	50502	63127	75753	88378	101004	113629
15	4857	9714	14571	19428	38855	58283	77710	97138	116565	135993	155421	174848
20	6645	13289	19934	26578	53157	79735	106313	132891	159470	186048	212626	239204
25	8524	17048	25572	34095	68191	102286	136382	170477	204572	238668	272763	306859
30	10499	20999	31498	41998	83996	125993	167991	209989	251987	293985	335982	377980

MONTHLY WITHDRAWAL, 1.00 %

FULL YEARS TO WITHDRAW

AMOUNT	500	600	700	800	900	1000	1100	1200	1300	1400	1500	1600	1700	1800	1900	2000	2500	3000	4000	5000
50000	8	7	6	5	4	4	3	3	3	3	2	2	2	2	2	2	1	1	1	0
60000	10	8	7	6	5	5	4	4	4	3	3	3	3	2	2	2	2	1	1	1
70000	12	10	8	7	6	6	5	5	4	4	4	3	3	3	3	2	2	1	1	1
80000	14	11	10	8	7	6	6	5	5	4	4	4	3	3	3	3	2	2	1	1
90000	16	13	11	9	8	7	7	6	6	5	5	4	4	4	4	3	2	2	1	1
100000	18	15	12	11	9	8	7	7	6	6	5	5	5	4	4	4	3	2	2	1
110000	20	16	14	12	10	9	8	8	7	6	6	5	5	5	4	4	3	3	2	1
120000	22	18	15	13	11	10	9	8	8	7	6	6	6	5	5	4	3	3	2	2
130000	24	20	16	14	12	11	10	9	8	7	7	6	6	5	5	5	4	3	2	2
140000	26	21	18	15	13	12	11	10	9	8	8	7	6	6	5	5	4	3	2	2
150000	28	23	19	17	15	13	12	11	10	9	8	8	7	7	6	6	5	4	3	2
160000	>30	25	21	18	16	14	13	11	10	10	9	8	8	7	7	6	5	4	3	2
170000	>30	27	22	19	17	15	13	12	11	10	10	9	8	7	7	7	5	4	3	2
180000	>30	28	24	20	18	16	14	13	12	11	10	10	9	8	8	7	6	5	3	2
190000	>30	>30	25	22	19	17	15	14	13	12	11	10	9	9	8	8	6	5	3	3
200000	>30	>30	27	23	20	18	16	15	13	12	11	11	10	9	9	8	6	5	4	3
225000	>30	>30	>30	26	23	20	18	17	15	14	13	12	11	11	10	9	8	6	4	3
250000	>30	>30	>30	>30	26	23	21	19	17	16	15	14	13	12	11	11	8	7	5	4
275000	>30	>30	>30	>30	29	26	23	21	19	17	16	15	14	13	12	12	9	8	5	4
300000	>30	>30	>30	>30	>30	28	25	23	21	19	18	17	15	15	14	13	10	8	6	5
350000	>30	>30	>30	>30	>30	>30	>30	27	25	23	21	20	18	17	16	15	12	10	7	6
400000	>30	>30	>30	>30	>30	>30	>30	>30	29	27	25	23	21	20	19	18	14	11	8	6
450000	>30	>30	>30	>30	>30	>30	>30	>30	>30	>30	28	26	25	23	22	20	16	13	9	7
500000	>30	>30	>30	>30	>30	>30	>30	>30	>30	>30	>30	28	26	24	23	18	15	11	8	

| | 6000 | 7200 | 8400 | 9600 | 10800 | 12000 | 13200 | 14400 | 15600 | 16800 | 18000 | 19200 | 20400 | 21600 | 22800 | 24000 | 30000 | 36000 | 48000 | 60000 |

>30 = monthly withdrawal for more than 30 years

ANNUAL WITHDRAWAL

SAVINGS & WITHDRAWAL

Description: This table shows the amount to which a regular monthly savings will grow. And then how many full years a withdrawal may be taken from an amount at interest.

Example: At 2.00 % a regular monthly saving of $ 25 will grow to $ 7382 in 20 years. An amount of $50000 will support a monthly withdrawal of $ 700 for 6 years.

MONTHLY SAVINGS, 2.00 %
AMOUNT SAVED

YEARS	25	50	75	100	200	300	400	500	600	700	800	900
5	1579	3158	4736	6315	12630	18946	25261	31576	37891	44207	50522	56837
10	3324	6647	9971	13294	26588	39882	53176	66470	79765	93059	106353	119647
15	5252	10503	15755	21006	42013	63019	84025	105031	126038	147044	168050	189056
20	7382	14764	22147	29529	59058	88586	118115	147644	177173	206702	236231	265759
25	9737	19473	29210	38947	77894	116841	155788	194735	233681	272628	311575	350522
30	12339	24677	37016	49355	98709	148064	197419	246773	296128	345483	394837	444192

MONTHLY WITHDRAWAL, 2.00 %
FULL YEARS TO WITHDRAW

AMOUNT	500	600	700	800	900	1000	1100	1200	1300	1400	1500	1600	1700	1800	1900	2000	2500	3000	4000	5000
50000	9	7	6	5	4	4	4	3	3	3	2	2	2	2	2	2	1	1	1	0
60000	11	9	7	6	5	5	4	4	4	3	3	3	3	2	2	2	2	1	1	1
70000	13	10	9	7	7	6	5	5	4	4	4	3	3	3	3	2	2	1	1	1
80000	15	12	10	9	8	7	6	5	5	5	4	4	4	4	3	3	2	1	1	1
90000	17	14	12	10	9	8	7	6	6	5	5	5	4	4	4	3	3	2	2	1
100000	20	16	13	11	10	9	8	7	6	6	5	5	5	4	4	4	3	2	2	1
110000	22	18	15	13	11	10	9	8	7	7	6	6	5	5	5	4	3	3	2	2
120000	25	20	16	14	12	11	10	9	8	7	7	6	6	5	5	5	4	3	2	2
130000	28	22	18	15	13	12	11	10	9	8	7	7	6	6	6	5	4	3	3	2
140000	>30	24	20	17	15	13	12	11	10	9	8	7	7	7	6	6	4	4	3	2
150000	>30	27	22	18	16	14	12	11	10	9	9	8	8	7	7	6	5	4	3	2
160000	>30	29	24	20	17	15	13	12	11	10	10	9	9	8	8	7	6	5	3	3
170000	>30	>30	26	21	19	16	14	13	12	11	10	9	9	8	8	7	6	5	3	3
180000	>30	>30	28	23	20	17	16	14	13	12	11	10	9	9	8	8	6	5	4	3
190000	>30	>30	>30	25	21	19	17	15	14	12	11	11	10	9	9	8	6	5	4	3
200000	>30	>30	>30	27	23	20	18	16	14	13	12	11	11	10	9	9	7	5	4	3
225000	>30	>30	>30	>30	27	23	20	18	17	15	14	13	12	11	11	10	8	6	5	4
250000	>30	>30	>30	>30	>30	27	23	21	19	17	16	15	14	13	13	11	10	8	6	4
275000	>30	>30	>30	>30	>30	>30	27	24	21	19	18	16	15	14	13	13	10	8	6	5
300000	>30	>30	>30	>30	>30	>30	>30	27	24	22	20	18	17	16	15	14	11	9	7	5
350000	>30	>30	>30	>30	>30	>30	>30	>30	29	27	24	22	21	19	18	17	13	10	7	6
400000	>30	>30	>30	>30	>30	>30	>30	>30	>30	>30	29	27	24	23	21	20	15	12	9	7
450000	>30	>30	>30	>30	>30	>30	>30	>30	>30	>30	>30	>30	29	27	25	23	17	14	10	8
500000	>30	>30	>30	>30	>30	>30	>30	>30	>30	>30	>30	>30	>30	>30	28	27	20	16	11	9

MONTHLY SAVINGS, 3.00 %
AMOUNT SAVED

YEARS	25	50	75	100	200	300	400	500	600	700	800	900
5	1620	3240	4861	6481	12962	19442	25923	32404	38885	45366	51847	58327
10	3502	7005	10507	14009	28018	42027	56036	70045	84054	98064	112073	126082
15	5689	11377	17066	22754	45508	68262	91016	113770	136524	159278	182032	204786
20	8228	16456	24684	32912	65825	98737	131649	164561	197474	230386	263298	296210
25	11178	22356	33534	44712	89425	134137	178849	223561	268274	312986	357698	402411
30	14605	29210	43815	58419	116839	175258	233677	292097	350516	408936	467355	525774

MONTHLY WITHDRAWAL, 3.00 %
FULL YEARS TO WITHDRAW

AMOUNT	500	600	700	800	900	1000	1100	1200	1300	1400	1500	1600	1700	1800	1900	2000	2500	3000	4000	5000
50000	9	7	6	5	5	4	4	3	3	3	2	2	2	2	2	2	1	1	1	0
60000	11	9	8	7	6	5	4	4	4	3	3	3	3	2	2	2	2	1	1	1
70000	14	11	9	8	7	6	5	5	4	4	4	3	3	3	3	2	2	1	1	1
80000	17	13	11	9	8	7	6	6	5	5	4	4	4	4	3	3	2	2	1	1
90000	20	15	13	11	9	8	7	7	6	5	5	5	4	4	4	3	3	2	2	1
100000	23	18	14	12	10	9	8	7	7	6	6	5	5	5	4	4	3	2	2	1
110000	26	20	16	14	12	10	9	8	8	7	6	6	5	5	5	4	3	3	2	1
120000	>30	23	18	15	13	11	10	9	8	8	7	7	6	6	6	5	4	3	2	2
130000	>30	26	20	17	15	13	11	10	9	9	8	7	7	6	6	5	4	3	3	2
140000	>30	29	23	19	16	14	12	11	10	9	9	8	8	7	7	6	5	4	3	2
150000	>30	>30	25	21	18	15	13	12	11	10	9	9	8	8	7	7	5	4	3	2
160000	>30	>30	28	23	19	17	15	13	12	11	10	9	9	8	8	7	5	4	3	3
170000	>30	>30	>30	25	21	18	16	14	13	12	11	10	10	9	9	8	6	5	3	3
180000	>30	>30	>30	27	23	20	17	15	14	13	11	11	10	10	9	9	6	5	4	3
190000	>30	>30	>30	30	25	21	18	16	15	13	12	12	11	10	10	9	7	6	4	3
200000	>30	>30	>30	>30	27	23	20	18	16	14	13	12	11	11	10	9	7	5	4	3
225000	>30	>30	>30	>30	>30	27	23	21	19	17	15	14	13	12	11	11	8	7	5	4
250000	>30	>30	>30	>30	>30	>30	28	24	21	19	18	16	15	14	13	12	10	8	6	5
275000	>30	>30	>30	>30	>30	>30	>30	28	25	22	20	18	17	16	15	14	11	9	7	5
300000	>30	>30	>30	>30	>30	>30	>30	>30	28	25	23	21	19	18	16	15	11	9	7	5
350000	>30	>30	>30	>30	>30	>30	>30	>30	>30	>30	29	26	24	22	20	19	14	11	8	6
400000	>30	>30	>30	>30	>30	>30	>30	>30	>30	>30	29	27	25	23	21	20	15	13	9	7
450000	>30	>30	>30	>30	>30	>30	>30	>30	>30	>30	>30	>30	>30	>30	29	27	19	15	12	9
500000	>30	>30	>30	>30	>30	>30	>30	>30	>30	>30	>30	>30	>30	>30	>30	23	23	18	12	9

6000	7200	8400	9600	10800	12000	13200	14400	15600	16800	18000	19200	20400	21600	22800	24000	30000	36000	48000	60000

ANNUAL WITHDRAWAL

>30 = monthly withdrawal for more than 30 years

Description: This table shows the amount to which a regular monthly savings will grow. And then how many full years a withdrawal may be taken from an amount at interest.

Example: At 4.00 % a regular monthly saving of $ 25 will grow to $ 9200 in 20 years. An amount of $50000 will support a monthly withdrawal of $ 700 for 6 years.

MONTHLY SAVINGS, 4.00 %

YEARS	25	50	75	100	200	300	400	500	600	700	800	900
					AMOUNT SAVED							
5	1663	3326	4989	6652	13304	19956	26608	33260	39912	46564	53216	59868
10	3694	7387	11081	14774	29548	44322	59096	73870	88644	103418	118193	132967
15	6173	12346	18518	24691	49382	74073	98764	123455	148146	172838	197529	222220
20	9200	18400	27600	36800	73599	110399	147199	183999	220798	257598	294398	331197
25	12896	25792	38688	51584	103169	154753	206337	257922	309506	361090	412675	464259
30	17409	34818	52227	69636	139273	208909	278545	348181	417818	487454	557090	626727

MONTHLY WITHDRAWAL, 4.00 %
FULL YEARS TO WITHDRAW

AMOUNT	500	600	700	800	900	1000	1100	1200	1300	1400	1500	1600	1700	1800	1900	2000	2500	3000	4000	5000
50000	10	8	6	5	5	4	4	3	3	3	3		2	2	2	2	1	1	1	0
60000	12	10	8	7	6	5	5	4	4	3	3	3	3	3	2	2	2	1	1	1
70000	15	12	10	8	7	6	6	5	5	4	4	4	3	3	3	3	2	2	1	1
80000	19	14	12	10	8	7	7	6	5	5	4	4	4	3	3	3	2	2	1	1
90000	23	17	14	11	10	9	8	7	6	6	5	5	4	4	4	3	3	2	2	1
100000	27	20	16	13	11	10	9	8	7	6	6	5	5	5	4	4	3	3	2	1
110000	>30	23	18	15	13	11	10	9	8	7	7	6	6	5	4	4	3	3	2	1
120000	>30	27	21	17	14	12	11	10	9	8	7	7	6	5	5	5	4	3	2	1
130000	>30	>30	24	19	16	14	12	11	10	9	8	7	7	6	6	6	4	3	2	2
140000	>30	>30	27	22	18	15	13	12	11	10	9	8	8	7	7	6	5	4	3	2
150000	>30	>30	>30	24	20	17	15	13	12	11	10	9	8	8	7	7	5	4	3	2
160000	>30	>30	>30	27	22	19	16	14	13	12	11	10	9	8	8	7	6	4	3	2
170000	>30	>30	>30	>30	24	21	18	16	14	13	11	11	10	9	8	8	6	4	3	3
180000	>30	>30	>30	>30	27	23	19	17	15	14	12	11	10	10	9	8	6	5	3	3
190000	>30	>30	>30	>30	>30	25	21	18	16	15	13	12	11	10	10	9	7	6	4	3
200000	>30	>30	>30	>30	>30	27	23	20	18	16	14	13	12	11	10	10	7	6	4	3
225000	>30	>30	>30	>30	>30	>30	28	24	21	19	17	15	14	13	12	11	9	7	5	4
250000	>30	>30	>30	>30	>30	>30	>30	29	25	22	20	18	16	15	14	13	10	8	5	4
275000	>30	>30	>30	>30	>30	>30	>30	>30	>30	26	23	21	19	17	16	15	11	9	6	5
300000	>30	>30	>30	>30	>30	>30	>30	>30	>30	>30	27	24	22	20	18	17	12	10	7	5
350000	>30	>30	>30	>30	>30	>30	>30	>30	>30	>30	>30	>30	29	26	23	22	15	12	8	6
400000	>30	>30	>30	>30	>30	>30	>30	>30	>30	>30	>30	>30	>30	>30	27	23	19	14	10	7
450000	>30	>30	>30	>30	>30	>30	>30	>30	>30	>30	>30	>30	>30	>30	>30	27	23	17	11	9
500000	>30	>30	>30	>30	>30	>30	>30	>30	>30	>30	>30	>30	>30	>30	>30	>30	27	20	13	10

MONTHLY SAVINGS, 4.25 %

YEARS	25	50	75	100	200	300	400	500	600	700	800	900
					AMOUNT SAVED							
5	1674	3348	5022	6696	13391	20087	26783	33478	40174	46870	53565	60261
10	3743	7487	11230	14974	29947	44921	59894	74868	89841	104815	119789	134762
15	6302	12604	18906	25208	50415	75623	100830	126038	151245	176453	201660	226868
20	9465	18930	28395	37860	75720	113579	151439	189299	227159	265019	302878	340738
25	13375	26751	40126	53502	107004	160506	214007	267509	321011	374513	428015	481517
30	18210	36420	54630	72840	145680	218520	291360	364201	437041	509881	582721	655561

MONTHLY WITHDRAWAL, 4.25 %
FULL YEARS TO WITHDRAW

AMOUNT	500	600	700	800	900	1000	1100	1200	1300	1400	1500	1600	1700	1800	1900	2000	2500	3000	4000	5000
50000	10	8	6	5	5	4	4	3	3	3	3		2	2	2	2	1	1	1	0
60000	13	10	8	7	6	5	5	4	4	3	3	3	3	3	2	2	2	1	1	1
70000	16	12	10	8	7	6	6	5	5	4	4	4	3	3	3	3	2	1	1	1
80000	19	15	12	10	8	7	7	6	5	5	4	4	4	3	3	3	2	2	1	1
90000	24	17	14	12	10	9	8	7	6	6	5	5	4	4	4	3	2	2	1	1
100000	29	21	16	13	11	10	9	8	7	6	6	5	5	5	4	4	3	2	2	1
110000	>30	24	19	15	13	11	10	9	8	7	7	6	6	5	5	4	3	3	2	1
120000	>30	29	22	17	15	13	11	10	9	8	7	7	6	6	5	5	4	3	2	1
130000	>30	>30	25	20	16	14	12	11	10	9	8	7	7	6	6	5	4	3	2	2
140000	>30	>30	29	22	18	16	14	12	11	10	9	8	7	7	6	6	4	4	2	2
150000	>30	>30	>30	25	21	17	15	13	12	11	10	9	8	8	7	7	5	4	3	2
160000	>30	>30	>30	29	23	19	17	15	13	12	11	10	9	8	7	7	5	4	3	2
170000	>30	>30	>30	>30	26	21	18	16	14	13	12	11	10	9	8	7	6	5	3	2
180000	>30	>30	>30	>30	29	24	20	17	15	14	13	12	11	10	9	8	6	5	3	3
190000	>30	>30	>30	>30	>30	26	22	19	17	15	14	12	11	11	10	9	7	6	4	3
200000	>30	>30	>30	>30	>30	29	24	21	18	16	15	13	12	11	11	10	7	6	4	3
225000	>30	>30	>30	>30	>30	>30	>30	25	22	19	17	16	14	13	12	12	9	7	5	4
250000	>30	>30	>30	>30	>30	>30	>30	>30	27	23	21	19	17	16	14	13	10	8	5	4
275000	>30	>30	>30	>30	>30	>30	>30	>30	>30	28	24	22	20	18	17	15	11	9	6	5
300000	>30	>30	>30	>30	>30	>30	>30	>30	>30	>30	29	25	23	21	19	17	13	10	6	5
350000	>30	>30	>30	>30	>30	>30	>30	>30	>30	>30	>30	>30	>30	27	24	22	16	12	8	6
400000	>30	>30	>30	>30	>30	>30	>30	>30	>30	>30	>30	>30	>30	>30	29	23	19	15	10	7
450000	>30	>30	>30	>30	>30	>30	>30	>30	>30	>30	>30	>30	>30	>30	>30	29	24	17	12	9
500000	>30	>30	>30	>30	>30	>30	>30	>30	>30	>30	>30	>30	>30	>30	>30	>30	24	21	13	10

	6000	7200	8400	9600	10800	12000	13200	14400	15600	16800	18000	19200	20400	21600	22800	24000	30000	36000	48000	60000

>30 = monthly withdrawal for more than 30 years   ANNUAL WITHDRAWAL

SAVINGS & WITHDRAWAL

Description: This table shows the amount to which a regular monthly savings will grow. And then how many full years a withdrawal may be taken from an amount at interest.

Example: At 4.50 % a regular monthly saving of $ 25 will grow to $ 9739 in 20 years. An amount of $50000 will support a monthly withdrawal of $ 700 for 7 years.

MONTHLY SAVINGS, 4.50 %

YEARS	25	50	75	100	200	300	400	500	600	700	800	900
					AMOUNT SAVED							
5	1685	3370	5055	6740	13479	20219	26959	33699	40438	47178	53918	60658
10	3794	7588	11382	15177	30353	45530	60706	75883	91059	106236	121412	136589
15	6434	12869	19303	25738	51475	77213	102950	128688	154426	180163	205901	231639
20	9739	19479	29218	38958	77916	116874	155832	194790	233748	272706	311664	350622
25	13877	27754	41630	55507	111014	166522	222029	277536	333043	388550	444057	499565
30	19056	38112	57168	76223	152447	228670	304894	381117	457340	533564	609787	686010

MONTHLY WITHDRAWAL, 4.50 %

FULL YEARS TO WITHDRAW

AMOUNT	500	600	700	800	900	1000	1100	1200	1300	1400	1500	1600	1700	1800	1900	2000	2500	3000	4000	5000
50000	10	8	7	6	5	4	4	3	3	3	3	3	2	2	2	2	1	1	1	0
60000	13	10	8	7	6	5	5	4	4	3	3	3	3	3	2	2	2	1	1	1
70000	16	12	10	8	7	6	6	5	5	4	4	4	3	3	3	3	2	2	1	1
80000	20	15	12	10	9	8	7	6	5	5	5	5	4	4	3	3	3	2	2	1
90000	25	18	14	12	10	9	8	7	7	6	6	5	5	4	4	4	3	2	2	1
100000	>30	21	17	14	12	10	9	8	7	7	6	6	5	5	4	4	3	3	2	1
110000	>30	25	19	16	13	11	10	9	8	7	7	6	6	5	5	5	4	3	2	2
120000	>30	>30	23	18	15	13	11	10	9	8	8	7	6	6	6	5	4	3	2	2
130000	>30	>30	26	21	17	14	13	11	10	9	8	8	7	7	6	6	4	4	2	2
140000	>30	>30	>30	23	19	16	14	12	11	10	9	8	8	7	7	6	5	4	3	2
150000	>30	>30	>30	27	21	18	16	14	12	11	10	9	9	8	7	7	5	4	3	2
160000	>30	>30	>30	>30	24	20	17	15	13	12	11	10	9	9	8	8	6	5	3	3
170000	>30	>30	>30	>30	27	22	19	16	15	13	12	11	10	9	9	9	7	5	4	3
180000	>30	>30	>30	>30	>30	25	21	18	16	14	13	12	11	10	9	9	7	5	4	3
190000	>30	>30	>30	>30	>30	27	23	20	17	15	14	13	12	11	10	9	7	6	4	3
200000	>30	>30	>30	>30	>30	>30	25	21	19	17	15	14	13	12	11	10	8	6	4	3
225000	>30	>30	>30	>30	>30	>30	>30	27	23	20	18	16	15	14	13	12	9	7	5	4
250000	>30	>30	>30	>30	>30	>30	>30	>30	28	24	21	19	17	16	15	14	11	9	6	5
275000	>30	>30	>30	>30	>30	>30	>30	>30	>30	>30	29	25	23	20	18	16	13	10	7	5
300000	>30	>30	>30	>30	>30	>30	>30	>30	>30	>30	>30	>30	29	26	23	20	16	12	8	6
350000	>30	>30	>30	>30	>30	>30	>30	>30	>30	>30	>30	>30	>30	29	26	23	16	12	8	6
400000	>30	>30	>30	>30	>30	>30	>30	>30	>30	>30	>30	>30	>30	>30	>30	>30	20	15	10	8
450000	>30	>30	>30	>30	>30	>30	>30	>30	>30	>30	>30	>30	>30	>30	>30	>30	25	18	12	9
500000	>30	>30	>30	>30	>30	>30	>30	>30	>30	>30	>30	>30	>30	>30	>30	>30	>30	21	14	10

MONTHLY SAVINGS, 4.75 %

YEARS	25	50	75	100	200	300	400	500	600	700	800	900
					AMOUNT SAVED							
5	1696	3392	5088	6784	13568	20352	27137	33921	40705	47489	54273	61057
10	3846	7691	11537	15383	30766	46149	61532	76915	92298	107681	123063	138446
15	6570	13141	19711	26282	52563	78845	105127	131409	157690	183972	210254	236536
20	10024	20048	30072	40096	80191	120287	160383	200479	240574	280670	320766	360862
25	14401	28802	43204	57605	115209	172814	230419	288024	345628	403233	460838	518443
30	19949	39899	59848	79797	159594	239391	319188	398985	478782	558579	638376	718173

MONTHLY WITHDRAWAL, 4.75 %

FULL YEARS TO WITHDRAW

AMOUNT	500	600	700	800	900	1000	1100	1200	1300	1400	1500	1600	1700	1800	1900	2000	2500	3000	4000	5000
50000	10	8	7	6	5	4	4	3	3	3	3	3	2	2	2	2	1	1	1	0
60000	13	10	8	7	6	5	5	4	4	4	3	3	3	3	2	2	2	1	1	1
70000	17	13	10	9	7	6	6	5	5	5	4	4	3	3	3	3	2	2	1	1
80000	21	15	12	10	9	8	7	6	5	5	5	5	4	4	3	3	3	2	2	1
90000	26	19	15	12	10	9	8	7	7	6	6	5	5	4	4	4	3	2	2	1
100000	>30	22	17	14	12	10	9	8	7	7	6	6	5	5	4	4	3	3	2	1
110000	>30	27	20	16	14	12	10	9	8	7	7	6	6	5	5	5	4	3	2	2
120000	>30	>30	24	19	15	13	12	10	9	8	8	7	6	6	6	5	4	3	2	2
130000	>30	>30	28	21	17	15	13	11	10	9	8	8	7	7	6	6	4	4	3	2
140000	>30	>30	>30	24	20	17	14	13	11	10	9	9	8	7	7	6	5	4	3	2
150000	>30	>30	>30	28	22	19	16	14	12	11	10	9	9	8	7	7	5	4	3	2
160000	>30	>30	>30	>30	25	21	17	15	13	12	11	10	9	9	8	8	6	5	3	3
170000	>30	>30	>30	>30	29	23	20	17	15	13	12	11	10	9	9	9	7	5	4	3
180000	>30	>30	>30	>30	>30	26	22	19	16	15	13	12	11	10	10	9	7	6	4	3
190000	>30	>30	>30	>30	>30	29	24	20	18	16	14	13	12	11	10	10	7	6	4	3
200000	>30	>30	>30	>30	>30	>30	26	22	19	17	15	14	13	12	11	10	8	6	4	3
225000	>30	>30	>30	>30	>30	>30	>30	28	24	21	19	17	15	14	13	12	9	7	5	4
250000	>30	>30	>30	>30	>30	>30	>30	>30	>30	25	22	20	18	16	15	14	10	8	6	5
275000	>30	>30	>30	>30	>30	>30	>30	>30	>30	>30	27	24	21	19	18	16	12	9	6	5
300000	>30	>30	>30	>30	>30	>30	>30	>30	>30	>30	>30	28	25	22	20	19	13	10	7	5
350000	>30	>30	>30	>30	>30	>30	>30	>30	>30	>30	>30	>30	>30	>30	27	24	17	13	9	6
400000	>30	>30	>30	>30	>30	>30	>30	>30	>30	>30	>30	>30	>30	>30	>30	>30	21	15	10	8
450000	>30	>30	>30	>30	>30	>30	>30	>30	>30	>30	>30	>30	>30	>30	>30	>30	26	19	12	9
500000	>30	>30	>30	>30	>30	>30	>30	>30	>30	>30	>30	>30	>30	>30	>30	>30	>30	22	14	10

6000	7200	8400	9600	10800	12000	13200	14400	15600	16800	18000	19200	20400	21600	22800	24000	30000	36000	48000	60000

>30 = monthly withdrawal for more than 30 years   ANNUAL WITHDRAWAL

SAVINGS & WITHDRAWAL

Description: This table shows the amount to which a regular monthly savings will grow. And then how many full years a withdrawal may be taken from an amount at interest.

Example: At 5.00 % a regular monthly saving of $ 25 will grow to $10319 in 20 years. An amount of $50000 will support a monthly withdrawal of $ 700 for 7 years.

MONTHLY SAVINGS, 5.00 %

YEARS	25	50	75	100	200	300	400	500	600	700	800	900
					AMOUNT SAVED							
5	1707	3414	5122	6829	13658	20487	27316	34145	40974	47803	54632	61460
10	3898	7796	11695	15593	31186	46779	62372	77965	93558	109151	124743	140336
15	6710	13420	20130	26840	53681	80521	107361	134201	161042	187882	214722	241562
20	10319	20637	30956	41275	82549	123824	165099	206373	247648	288922	330197	371472
25	14950	29900	44849	59799	119598	179397	239196	298995	358795	418594	478393	538192
30	20893	41786	62679	83573	167145	250718	334291	417863	501436	585008	668581	752154

MONTHLY WITHDRAWAL, 5.00 %

AMOUNT	500	600	700	800	900	1000	1100	1200	1300	1400	1500	1600	1700	1800	1900	2000	2500	3000	4000	5000
								FULL YEARS TO WITHDRAW												
50000	10	8	7	6	5	4	4	3	3	3	3		2	2	2	2	1	1	1	0
60000	13	10	8	7	6	5	5	4	4	4	3	3	3	3	2	2	2	1	1	1
70000	17	13	10	9	7	6	6	5	5	4	4	4	3	3	3	3	2	2	1	1
80000	22	16	13	10	9	8	7	6	6	5	5	4	4	4	3	3	2	2	1	1
90000	27	19	15	12	10	9	8	7	6	6	5	5	5	4	4	4	3	2	2	1
100000	>30	23	18	14	12	10	9	8	7	7	6	6	5	5	5	4	3	3	2	1
110000	>30	29	21	17	14	12	10	9	8	7	7	6	6	5	5	5	4	3	2	2
120000	>30	>30	25	19	16	13	12	10	9	8	8	7	7	6	6	5	4	3	2	2
130000	>30	>30	29	22	18	15	13	12	10	9	9	8	7	7	6	6	4	4	2	2
140000	>30	>30	>30	26	21	17	15	13	12	10	9	9	8	7	7	6	5	4	3	2
150000	>30	>30	>30	>30	23	19	16	14	13	11	10	10	9	8	8	7	5	4	3	2
160000	>30	>30	>30	>30	27	22	18	16	14	13	11	10	10	9	8	8	6	5	3	2
170000	>30	>30	>30	>30	>30	24	20	17	15	14	12	11	10	10	9	8	6	5	3	3
180000	>30	>30	>30	>30	>30	27	23	19	17	15	13	12	11	10	10	9	7	5	4	3
190000	>30	>30	>30	>30	>30	>30	25	21	18	16	15	13	12	11	10	10	7	6	4	3
200000	>30	>30	>30	>30	>30	>30	28	23	20	18	16	14	13	12	11	10	8	6	4	3
225000	>30	>30	>30	>30	>30	>30	>30	>30	25	22	19	17	16	14	13	12	9	7	5	4
250000	>30	>30	>30	>30	>30	>30	>30	>30	27	23	21	19	17	16	14	10	8	6	4	
275000	>30	>30	>30	>30	>30	>30	>30	>30	>30	29	25	22	20	18	17	14	10	8	6	4
300000	>30	>30	>30	>30	>30	>30	>30	>30	>30	>30	29	25	22	20	18	17	12	9	6	5
350000	>30	>30	>30	>30	>30	>30	>30	>30	>30	>30	>30	>30	26	23	21	19	13	10	7	5
400000	>30	>30	>30	>30	>30	>30	>30	>30	>30	>30	>30	>30	>30	29	26	17	13	9	6	
450000	>30	>30	>30	>30	>30	>30	>30	>30	>30	>30	>30	>30	>30	>30	>30	22	16	10	8	
500000	>30	>30	>30	>30	>30	>30	>30	>30	>30	>30	>30	>30	>30	>30	>30	>30	23	14	10	

MONTHLY SAVINGS, 5.25 %

YEARS	25	50	75	100	200	300	400	500	600	700	800	900
					AMOUNT SAVED							
5	1719	3437	5156	6874	13748	20622	27496	34371	41245	48119	54993	61867
10	3952	7903	11855	15807	31613	47420	63226	79033	94839	110646	126452	142259
15	6853	13707	20560	27414	54827	82241	109655	137068	164482	191896	219309	246723
20	10624	21248	31872	42496	84993	127489	169985	212481	254978	297474	339970	382467
25	15524	31048	46571	62095	124190	186285	248381	310476	372571	434666	496761	558856
30	21891	43781	65672	87563	175125	262688	350250	437813	525375	612938	700500	788063

MONTHLY WITHDRAWAL, 5.25 %

AMOUNT	500	600	700	800	900	1000	1100	1200	1300	1400	1500	1600	1700	1800	1900	2000	2500	3000	4000	5000
								FULL YEARS TO WITHDRAW												
50000	11	8	7	6	5	4	4	3	3	3	3		2	2	2	2	1	1	1	0
60000	14	11	9	7	6	5	5	4	4	4	3	3	3	3	2	2	2	1	1	1
70000	18	13	11	9	8	7	6	5	5	4	4	4	3	3	3	2	2	1	1	1
80000	23	16	13	11	9	8	7	6	6	5	4	4	3	3	3	2	2	1	1	
90000	29	20	15	13	11	9	8	7	6	6	5	5	5	4	4	3	2	2	1	1
100000	>30	25	18	15	12	11	9	8	7	7	6	6	5	5	5	4	3	3	2	1
110000	>30	>30	22	17	14	12	11	9	8	8	7	6	6	6	5	5	4	3	2	1
120000	>30	>30	26	20	16	14	12	11	9	9	8	7	7	6	6	5	4	3	2	2
130000	>30	>30	>30	23	19	16	13	12	11	10	9	8	7	7	6	6	5	4	3	2
140000	>30	>30	>30	27	21	18	15	13	12	11	11	10	8	8	7	7	5	4	3	2
150000	>30	>30	>30	>30	25	20	17	15	13	12	11	10	9	8	8	7	5	4	3	2
160000	>30	>30	>30	>30	28	23	19	16	14	13	12	11	10	9	8	8	6	5	3	2
170000	>30	>30	>30	>30	>30	26	21	18	16	14	13	12	11	10	9	8	6	5	4	3
180000	>30	>30	>30	>30	>30	29	24	20	17	15	14	13	11	11	10	9	7	5	4	3
190000	>30	>30	>30	>30	>30	>30	26	22	19	17	15	14	12	11	11	10	7	6	4	3
200000	>30	>30	>30	>30	>30	>30	>30	25	21	18	16	15	13	12	11	11	8	6	4	3
225000	>30	>30	>30	>30	>30	>30	>30	>30	27	23	20	18	16	15	14	13	9	7	5	4
250000	>30	>30	>30	>30	>30	>30	>30	>30	>30	29	25	22	19	17	16	15	11	8	6	4
275000	>30	>30	>30	>30	>30	>30	>30	>30	>30	>30	>30	26	23	21	19	17	12	9	6	5
300000	>30	>30	>30	>30	>30	>30	>30	>30	>30	>30	>30	28	25	22	20	14	11	7	5	
350000	>30	>30	>30	>30	>30	>30	>30	>30	>30	>30	>30	>30	>30	>30	27	18	13	9	7	
400000	>30	>30	>30	>30	>30	>30	>30	>30	>30	>30	>30	>30	>30	>30	23	16	11	8		
450000	>30	>30	>30	>30	>30	>30	>30	>30	>30	>30	>30	>30	>30	>30	29	20	13	9		
500000	>30	>30	>30	>30	>30	>30	>30	>30	>30	>30	>30	>30	>30	>30	>30	25	15	11		

6000 7200 8400 9600 10800 12000 13200 14400 15600 16800 18000 19200 20400 21600 22800 24000 30000 36000 48000 60000

>30 = monthly withdrawal for more than 30 years   ANNUAL WITHDRAWAL

Description: This table shows the amount to which a regular monthly savings will grow. And then how many full years a withdrawal may be taken from an amount at interest.

Example: At 5.50 % a regular monthly saving of $ 25 will grow to $10941 in 20 years. An amount of $50000 will support a monthly withdrawal of $ 700 for 7 years.

MONTHLY SAVINGS, 5.50 %

YEARS	25	50	75	100	200	300	400	500	600	700	800	900
					AMOUNT SAVED							
5	1730	3460	5190	6920	13839	20759	27679	34598	41518	48438	55357	62277
10	4006	8012	12018	16024	32048	48072	64095	80119	96143	112167	128191	144215
15	7001	14001	21002	28002	56005	84007	112009	140012	168014	196016	224019	252021
20	10941	21881	32822	43762	87525	131287	175050	218812	262574	306337	350099	393862
25	16125	32249	48374	64498	128996	193494	257992	322490	386988	451486	515984	580482
30	22945	45890	68835	91780	183560	275340	367120	458900	550680	642459	734239	826019

MONTHLY WITHDRAWAL, 5.50 %

FULL YEARS TO WITHDRAW

AMOUNT	500	600	700	800	900	1000	1100	1200	1300	1400	1500	1600	1700	1800	1900	2000	2500	3000	4000	5000
50000	11	8	7	6	5	4	4	3	3	3	3	2	2	2	2	2	1	1	1	0
60000	14	11	9	7	6	5	5	4	4	4	3	3	3	3	2	2	2	1	1	1
70000	18	14	11	9	8	7	6	5	5	4	4	4	3	3	3	3	2	2	1	1
80000	24	17	13	11	9	8	7	6	6	5	5	4	4	4	3	3	2	2	1	1
90000	>30	21	16	13	11	9	8	7	7	6	5	5	5	4	4	4	3	2	2	1
100000	>30	26	19	15	13	11	9	8	8	7	6	6	5	5	5	4	3	3	2	1
110000	>30	>30	23	18	15	12	11	10	9	8	7	6	6	6	5	5	4	3	2	2
120000	>30	>30	28	21	17	14	12	11	10	9	8	7	7	6	6	5	4	3	2	2
130000	>30	>30	>30	24	19	16	14	12	11	10	9	8	7	7	6	6	5	4	3	2
140000	>30	>30	>30	29	22	18	16	14	12	11	10	9	8	8	7	7	5	4	3	2
150000	>30	>30	>30	>30	26	21	17	15	13	12	11	10	9	8	8	7	5	4	3	2
160000	>30	>30	>30	>30	>30	24	20	17	15	13	12	11	10	9	8	8	6	5	3	2
170000	>30	>30	>30	>30	>30	27	22	19	16	14	13	12	11	10	9	9	6	5	4	3
180000	>30	>30	>30	>30	>30	>30	25	21	18	16	14	13	12	11	10	9	7	5	4	3
190000	>30	>30	>30	>30	>30	>30	28	23	20	17	15	14	13	12	11	10	7	6	4	3
200000	>30	>30	>30	>30	>30	>30	>30	26	22	19	17	15	14	13	12	11	8	6	4	3
225000	>30	>30	>30	>30	>30	>30	>30	>30	28	24	21	18	17	15	14	13	9	7	5	4
250000	>30	>30	>30	>30	>30	>30	>30	>30	>30	>30	26	23	20	18	16	15	11	8	6	4
275000	>30	>30	>30	>30	>30	>30	>30	>30	>30	>30	>30	28	24	22	19	18	12	10	6	5
300000	>30	>30	>30	>30	>30	>30	>30	>30	>30	>30	>30	>30	>30	26	23	21	14	11	7	5
350000	>30	>30	>30	>30	>30	>30	>30	>30	>30	>30	>30	>30	>30	>30	>30	29	18	14	9	7
400000	>30	>30	>30	>30	>30	>30	>30	>30	>30	>30	>30	>30	>30	>30	>30	>30	24	17	11	8
450000	>30	>30	>30	>30	>30	>30	>30	>30	>30	>30	>30	>30	>30	>30	>30	>30	>30	21	13	9
500000	>30	>30	>30	>30	>30	>30	>30	>30	>30	>30	>30	>30	>30	>30	>30	>30	>30	26	15	11

MONTHLY SAVINGS, 5.75 %

YEARS	25	50	75	100	200	300	400	500	600	700	800	900
					AMOUNT SAVED							
5	1741	3483	5224	6966	13931	20897	27862	34828	41793	48759	55725	62690
10	4061	8122	12184	16245	32490	48735	64980	81225	97470	113715	129960	146205
15	7152	14303	21455	28607	57213	85820	114427	143034	171640	200247	228854	257460
20	11269	22537	33806	45075	90149	135224	180299	225374	270448	315523	360598	405673
25	16753	33507	50260	67013	134026	201039	268052	335065	402078	469091	536104	603117
30	24060	48119	72179	96239	192477	288716	384955	481194	577432	673671	769910	866148

MONTHLY WITHDRAWAL, 5.75 %

FULL YEARS TO WITHDRAW

AMOUNT	500	600	700	800	900	1000	1100	1200	1300	1400	1500	1600	1700	1800	1900	2000	2500	3000	4000	5000
50000	11	8	7	6	5	4	4	3	3	3	3	2	2	2	2	2	1	1	1	0
60000	15	11	9	7	6	5	5	4	4	4	3	3	3	3	2	2	2	1	1	1
70000	19	14	11	9	8	7	6	5	5	4	4	4	3	3	3	3	2	2	1	1
80000	25	17	13	11	9	8	7	6	6	5	5	4	4	4	3	3	2	2	1	1
90000	>30	22	16	13	11	9	8	7	7	6	5	5	5	4	4	4	3	2	2	1
100000	>30	28	20	16	13	11	10	8	8	7	6	6	5	5	5	4	3	3	2	1
110000	>30	>30	24	18	15	13	11	10	9	8	7	7	6	6	5	5	4	3	2	2
120000	>30	>30	30	22	17	15	12	11	10	9	8	7	7	6	6	5	4	3	2	2
130000	>30	>30	>30	26	20	17	14	12	11	10	9	8	8	7	7	6	5	4	3	2
140000	>30	>30	>30	>30	23	19	16	14	12	11	10	9	8	8	7	7	5	4	3	2
150000	>30	>30	>30	>30	28	22	18	16	14	12	11	10	9	8	8	7	5	4	3	2
160000	>30	>30	>30	>30	>30	25	20	17	15	13	12	11	10	9	9	8	6	5	3	2
170000	>30	>30	>30	>30	>30	29	23	19	17	15	13	12	11	10	9	9	6	5	4	3
180000	>30	>30	>30	>30	>30	>30	26	22	19	16	15	13	12	11	10	9	7	5	4	3
190000	>30	>30	>30	>30	>30	>30	>30	24	21	18	16	14	13	12	11	10	7	6	4	3
200000	>30	>30	>30	>30	>30	>30	>30	28	23	20	17	16	14	13	12	11	8	6	4	3
225000	>30	>30	>30	>30	>30	>30	>30	>30	>30	25	22	19	17	16	14	13	9	7	5	4
250000	>30	>30	>30	>30	>30	>30	>30	>30	>30	>30	28	24	21	19	17	16	11	8	6	4
275000	>30	>30	>30	>30	>30	>30	>30	>30	>30	>30	>30	>30	26	23	20	18	13	10	7	5
300000	>30	>30	>30	>30	>30	>30	>30	>30	>30	>30	>30	>30	>30	28	24	22	15	11	7	5
350000	>30	>30	>30	>30	>30	>30	>30	>30	>30	>30	>30	>30	>30	>30	>30	>30	19	14	9	7
400000	>30	>30	>30	>30	>30	>30	>30	>30	>30	>30	>30	>30	>30	>30	>30	>30	25	17	11	8
450000	>30	>30	>30	>30	>30	>30	>30	>30	>30	>30	>30	>30	>30	>30	>30	>30	>30	22	13	9
500000	>30	>30	>30	>30	>30	>30	>30	>30	>30	>30	>30	>30	>30	>30	>30	>30	>30	28	16	11

6000 7200 8400 9600 10800 12000 13200 14400 15600 16800 18000 19200 20400 21600 22800 24000 30000 36000 48000 60000

>30 = monthly withdrawal for more than 30 years   ANNUAL WITHDRAWAL

Description: This table shows the amount to which a regular monthly savings will grow. And then how many full years a withdrawal may be taken from an amount at interest.

Example: At 6.00 % a regular monthly saving of $ 25 will grow to $11609 in 20 years. An amount of $50000 will support a monthly withdrawal of $ 700 for 7 years.

MONTHLY SAVINGS, 6.00 %

YEARS	25	50	75	100	200	300	400	500	600	700	800	900
					AMOUNT SAVED							
5	1753	3506	5259	7012	14024	21036	28048	35059	42071	49083	56095	63107
10	4117	8235	12352	16470	32940	49410	65879	82349	98819	115289	131759	148229
15	7307	14614	21920	29227	58455	87682	116909	146136	175364	204591	233818	263046
20	11609	23218	34826	46435	92870	139305	185740	232176	278611	325046	371481	417916
25	17411	34823	52234	69646	139292	208938	278584	348229	417875	487521	557167	626813
30	25238	50477	75715	100954	201908	302861	403815	504769	605723	706676	807630	908584

MONTHLY WITHDRAWAL, 6.00 %

AMOUNT	500	600	700	800	900	1000	1100	1200	1300	1400	1500	1600	1700	1800	1900	2000	2500	3000	4000	5000
								FULL YEARS TO WITHDRAW												
50000	11	9	7	6	5	4	4	3	3	3	3	2	2	2	2	2	1	1	1	0
60000	15	11	9	7	6	6	5	4	4	4	3	3	3	3	2	2	2	1	1	1
70000	20	14	11	9	8	7	6	5	5	4	4	4	3	3	3	3	2	2	1	1
80000	26	18	14	11	9	8	7	6	6	5	5	4	4	4	4	3	2	2	1	1
90000	>30	23	17	13	11	10	8	7	7	6	6	5	5	4	4	4	3	2	2	1
100000	>30	30	21	16	13	11	10	9	8	7	6	6	5	5	5	4	3	3	2	1
110000	>30	>30	25	19	15	13	11	10	9	8	7	7	6	6	5	5	4	3	2	2
120000	>30	>30	>30	23	18	15	13	11	10	9	8	7	7	6	6	6	4	3	2	2
130000	>30	>30	>30	28	21	17	15	13	11	10	9	8	8	7	7	6	5	4	3	2
140000	>30	>30	>30	>30	25	20	16	14	13	11	10	9	8	8	7	7	5	4	3	2
150000	>30	>30	>30	>30	30	23	19	16	14	12	11	10	9	9	8	7	6	4	3	2
160000	>30	>30	>30	>30	>30	26	21	18	16	14	12	11	10	9	9	8	6	5	3	2
170000	>30	>30	>30	>30	>30	>30	24	20	17	15	14	12	11	10	9	9	7	5	4	3
180000	>30	>30	>30	>30	>30	>30	28	23	19	17	15	13	12	11	10	10	7	6	4	3
190000	>30	>30	>30	>30	>30	>30	>30	26	22	19	16	15	13	12	11	10	8	6	4	3
200000	>30	>30	>30	>30	>30	>30	>30	30	24	21	18	16	14	13	12	11	8	6	4	3
225000	>30	>30	>30	>30	>30	>30	>30	>30	>30	27	23	20	18	16	15	13	10	7	5	4
250000	>30	>30	>30	>30	>30	>30	>30	>30	>30	30	25	22	19	18	16	11	9	6	4	
275000	>30	>30	>30	>30	>30	>30	>30	>30	>30	>30	>30	27	24	21	19	13	10	7	5	
300000	>30	>30	>30	>30	>30	>30	>30	>30	>30	>30	>30	>30	30	26	23	15	11	7	6	
350000	>30	>30	>30	>30	>30	>30	>30	>30	>30	>30	>30	>30	>30	>30	>30	>30	20	14	9	7
400000	>30	>30	>30	>30	>30	>30	>30	>30	>30	>30	>30	>30	>30	>30	>30	>30	26	18	11	8
450000	>30	>30	>30	>30	>30	>30	>30	>30	>30	>30	>30	>30	>30	>30	>30	>30	>30	23	13	10
500000	>30	>30	>30	>30	>30	>30	>30	>30	>30	>30	>30	>30	>30	>30	>30	>30	>30	30	16	11

MONTHLY SAVINGS, 6.25 %

YEARS	25	50	75	100	200	300	400	500	600	700	800	900
					AMOUNT SAVED							
5	1765	3529	5294	7059	14117	21176	28234	35293	42352	49410	56469	63527
10	4175	8349	12524	16699	33397	50096	66795	83494	100192	116891	133590	150288
15	7466	14932	22398	29865	59729	89594	119458	149323	179187	209052	238916	268781
20	11961	23923	35884	47845	95691	143536	191382	239227	287073	334918	382764	430609
25	18101	36201	54302	72403	144805	217208	289610	362013	434415	506818	579220	651623
30	26485	52970	79456	105941	211882	317823	423764	529705	635645	741586	847527	953468

MONTHLY WITHDRAWAL, 6.25 %

AMOUNT	500	600	700	800	900	1000	1100	1200	1300	1400	1500	1600	1700	1800	1900	2000	2500	3000	4000	5000
								FULL YEARS TO WITHDRAW												
50000	11	9	7	6	5	4	4	4	3	3	3	2	2	2	2	2	1	1	1	0
60000	15	11	9	8	6	6	5	4	4	4	3	3	3	3	2	2	2	1	1	1
70000	21	15	11	9	8	7	6	5	5	4	4	4	3	3	3	3	2	1	1	1
80000	28	19	14	11	10	8	7	6	6	5	5	4	4	4	4	3	2	1	1	1
90000	>30	24	17	14	11	10	8	8	7	6	6	5	5	4	4	4	3	2	2	1
100000	>30	>30	21	16	13	11	10	9	8	7	6	6	5	5	5	4	3	3	2	1
110000	>30	>30	27	20	16	13	11	10	9	8	7	7	6	6	5	5	4	3	2	2
120000	>30	>30	>30	24	19	15	13	11	10	9	8	8	7	6	6	6	4	3	2	2
130000	>30	>30	>30	30	22	18	15	13	11	10	9	8	8	7	7	6	5	4	3	2
140000	>30	>30	>30	>30	26	21	17	15	13	11	10	9	8	8	7	7	5	4	3	2
150000	>30	>30	>30	>30	>30	24	19	16	14	13	11	11	10	9	9	8	6	4	3	2
160000	>30	>30	>30	>30	>30	28	22	19	16	14	13	11	10	10	9	8	6	5	3	2
170000	>30	>30	>30	>30	>30	>30	26	21	18	16	14	13	11	10	10	9	7	5	4	3
180000	>30	>30	>30	>30	>30	>30	>30	24	20	17	15	14	12	11	10	10	7	6	4	3
190000	>30	>30	>30	>30	>30	>30	>30	28	23	19	17	15	14	12	11	11	8	6	4	3
200000	>30	>30	>30	>30	>30	>30	>30	>30	26	21	19	16	15	13	12	11	8	6	4	3
225000	>30	>30	>30	>30	>30	>30	>30	>30	>30	29	24	21	18	16	15	14	10	8	5	4
250000	>30	>30	>30	>30	>30	>30	>30	>30	>30	>30	27	23	20	18	16	11	9	6	4	
275000	>30	>30	>30	>30	>30	>30	>30	>30	>30	>30	>30	29	25	22	20	13	10	7	5	
300000	>30	>30	>30	>30	>30	>30	>30	>30	>30	>30	>30	>30	>30	27	24	15	11	8	6	
350000	>30	>30	>30	>30	>30	>30	>30	>30	>30	>30	>30	>30	>30	>30	>30	>30	21	15	9	7
400000	>30	>30	>30	>30	>30	>30	>30	>30	>30	>30	>30	>30	>30	>30	>30	>30	28	19	11	8
450000	>30	>30	>30	>30	>30	>30	>30	>30	>30	>30	>30	>30	>30	>30	>30	>30	>30	24	14	10
500000	>30	>30	>30	>30	>30	>30	>30	>30	>30	>30	>30	>30	>30	>30	>30	>30	>30	16	11	

| | 6000 | 7200 | 8400 | 9600 | 10800 | 12000 | 13200 | 14400 | 15600 | 16800 | 18000 | 19200 | 20400 | 21600 | 22800 | 24000 | 30000 | 36000 | 48000 | 60000 |

>30 = monthly withdrawal for more than 30 years   ANNUAL WITHDRAWAL

SAVINGS & WITHDRAWAL

Description: This table shows the amount to which a regular monthly savings will grow. And then how many full years a withdrawal may be taken from an amount at interest.

Example: At 6.50 % a regular monthly saving of $ 25 will grow to $12327 in 20 years. An amount of $50000 will support a monthly withdrawal of $ 700 for 7 years.

MONTHLY SAVINGS, 6.50 %

YEARS	25	50	75	100	200	300	400	500	600	700	800	900
					AMOUNT SAVED							
5	1776	3553	5329	7106	14211	21317	28423	35528	42634	49740	56845	63951
10	4233	8466	12699	16932	33863	50795	67726	84658	101589	118521	135452	152384
15	7630	15259	22889	30519	61038	91557	122076	152594	183113	213632	244151	274670
20	12327	24654	36981	49308	98615	147923	197231	246539	295846	345154	394462	443770
25	18822	37645	56467	75289	150579	225868	301157	376446	451736	527025	602314	677603
30	27804	55608	83413	111217	222434	333651	444868	556085	667302	778519	889736	1000953

MONTHLY WITHDRAWAL, 6.50 %

FULL YEARS TO WITHDRAW

AMOUNT	500	600	700	800	900	1000	1100	1200	1300	1400	1500	1600	1700	1800	1900	2000	2500	3000	4000	5000
50000	12	9	7	6	5	4	4	4	3	3	3	2	2	2	2	2	1	1	1	0
60000	16	12	9	8	6	6	5	4	4	4	3	3	3	3	2	2	2	1	1	1
70000	21	15	12	9	8	7	6	5	5	4	4	4	3	3	3	3	2	1	1	1
80000	>30	19	14	12	10	8	7	6	6	5	5	5	5	4	4	4	3	2	2	1
90000	>30	25	18	14	12	10	9	8	7	6	6	5	5	4	4	4	3	2	2	1
100000	>30	>30	23	17	14	12	10	9	8	7	6	6	6	5	5	4	3	3	2	1
110000	>30	>30	29	21	16	14	12	10	9	8	7	7	6	6	5	5	4	3	2	2
120000	>30	>30	>30	25	19	16	13	12	10	9	8	8	7	6	6	6	4	3	2	2
130000	>30	>30	>30	>30	23	18	15	13	12	10	9	9	8	7	7	6	5	4	3	2
140000	>30	>30	>30	>30	28	21	18	15	13	12	10	10	9	8	7	7	5	4	3	2
150000	>30	>30	>30	>30	>30	25	20	17	15	13	12	11	10	9	8	8	6	4	3	2
160000	>30	>30	>30	>30	>30	>30	24	19	17	14	13	12	11	10	9	8	7	5	4	3
170000	>30	>30	>30	>30	>30	>30	28	22	19	16	14	13	12	11	10	10	7	6	4	3
180000	>30	>30	>30	>30	>30	>30	>30	25	21	18	16	14	13	12	11	11	7	6	4	3
190000	>30	>30	>30	>30	>30	>30	>30	30	24	20	17	15	14	13	12	11	8	6	4	3
200000	>30	>30	>30	>30	>30	>30	>30	>30	27	23	19	17	15	14	13	12	8	6	4	3
225000	>30	>30	>30	>30	>30	>30	>30	>30	>30	>30	25	22	19	17	15	14	9	6	5	4
250000	>30	>30	>30	>30	>30	>30	>30	>30	>30	>30	>30	28	24	21	19	17	12	10	7	5
275000	>30	>30	>30	>30	>30	>30	>30	>30	>30	>30	>30	>30	>30	29	25	21	14	10	7	5
300000	>30	>30	>30	>30	>30	>30	>30	>30	>30	>30	>30	>30	>30	>30	29	25	16	12	8	6
350000	>30	>30	>30	>30	>30	>30	>30	>30	>30	>30	>30	>30	>30	>30	>30	>30	21	15	9	7
400000	>30	>30	>30	>30	>30	>30	>30	>30	>30	>30	>30	>30	>30	>30	>30	>30	>30	19	12	8
450000	>30	>30	>30	>30	>30	>30	>30	>30	>30	>30	>30	>30	>30	>30	>30	>30	>30	>30	14	10
500000	>30	>30	>30	>30	>30	>30	>30	>30	>30	>30	>30	>30	>30	>30	>30	>30	>30	>30	17	12

MONTHLY SAVINGS, 6.75 %

YEARS	25	50	75	100	200	300	400	500	600	700	800	900
					AMOUNT SAVED							
5	1788	3577	5365	7153	14306	21459	28613	35766	42919	50072	57225	64378
10	4292	8584	12876	17168	34337	51505	68674	85842	103011	120179	137346	154516
15	7798	15595	23393	31191	62382	93573	124764	155955	187146	218336	249527	280718
20	12706	25412	38118	50824	101648	152472	203296	254120	304944	355768	406592	457416
25	19578	39156	58735	78313	156625	234938	313251	391563	469876	548189	626501	704814
30	29200	58400	87600	116800	233600	350400	467200	584000	700799	817599	934399	1051199

MONTHLY WITHDRAWAL, 6.75 %

FULL YEARS TO WITHDRAW

AMOUNT	500	600	700	800	900	1000	1100	1200	1300	1400	1500	1600	1700	1800	1900	2000	2500	3000	4000	5000
50000	12	9	7	6	5	4	4	4	3	3	3	2	2	2	2	2	1	1	1	0
60000	16	12	9	8	7	6	5	4	4	4	3	3	3	3	2	2	2	1	1	1
70000	23	15	12	10	8	7	6	5	5	4	4	4	3	3	3	3	2	1	1	1
80000	>30	20	15	12	10	8	7	7	6	5	5	4	4	4	3	3	2	2	1	1
90000	>30	27	19	14	12	10	9	8	7	6	6	5	5	4	4	4	3	2	2	1
100000	>30	>30	24	18	14	12	10	9	8	7	7	6	6	5	5	4	3	3	2	1
110000	>30	>30	>30	22	17	14	12	10	9	8	7	7	6	6	5	5	4	3	2	2
120000	>30	>30	>30	27	20	16	14	12	10	9	8	8	7	7	6	5	4	3	2	2
130000	>30	>30	>30	>30	24	19	16	14	12	11	10	9	9	8	7	7	5	4	3	2
140000	>30	>30	>30	>30	>30	23	18	15	13	12	11	10	9	8	8	7	5	4	3	2
150000	>30	>30	>30	>30	>30	27	21	18	15	13	12	11	10	9	8	8	6	4	3	2
160000	>30	>30	>30	>30	>30	>30	25	20	17	15	13	12	11	10	9	8	7	5	4	3
170000	>30	>30	>30	>30	>30	>30	>30	23	19	17	15	13	12	11	10	9	7	6	4	3
180000	>30	>30	>30	>30	>30	>30	>30	27	22	19	16	14	13	12	11	11	7	6	4	3
190000	>30	>30	>30	>30	>30	>30	>30	>30	25	21	18	16	14	13	12	11	8	6	4	3
200000	>30	>30	>30	>30	>30	>30	>30	>30	29	24	20	18	16	14	13	12	8	7	4	3
225000	>30	>30	>30	>30	>30	>30	>30	>30	>30	>30	27	23	20	18	16	14	10	8	5	4
250000	>30	>30	>30	>30	>30	>30	>30	>30	>30	>30	>30	29	25	22	20	18	12	10	7	5
275000	>30	>30	>30	>30	>30	>30	>30	>30	>30	>30	>30	>30	>30	29	25	22	14	10	7	6
300000	>30	>30	>30	>30	>30	>30	>30	>30	>30	>30	>30	>30	>30	>30	29	25	16	12	8	6
350000	>30	>30	>30	>30	>30	>30	>30	>30	>30	>30	>30	>30	>30	>30	>30	>30	23	15	10	7
400000	>30	>30	>30	>30	>30	>30	>30	>30	>30	>30	>30	>30	>30	>30	>30	>30	>30	20	12	8
450000	>30	>30	>30	>30	>30	>30	>30	>30	>30	>30	>30	>30	>30	>30	>30	>30	>30	>30	14	10
500000	>30	>30	>30	>30	>30	>30	>30	>30	>30	>30	>30	>30	>30	>30	>30	>30	>30	>30	18	12

6000	7200	8400	9600	10800	12000	13200	14400	15600	16800	18000	19200	20400	21600	22800	24000	30000	36000	48000	60000

ANNUAL WITHDRAWAL

>30 = monthly withdrawal for more than 30 years

Description: This table shows the amount to which a regular monthly savings will grow. And then how many full years a withdrawal may be taken from an amount at interest.

Example: At 7.00 % a regular monthly saving of $ 25 will grow to $13099 in 20 years. An amount of $50000 will support a monthly withdrawal of $ 700 for 7 years.

MONTHLY SAVINGS, 7.00 %

YEARS	25	50	75	100	200	300	400	500	600	700	800	900
						AMOUNT SAVED						
5	1800	3601	5401	7201	14402	21603	28804	36005	43206	50407	57608	64809
10	4352	8705	13057	17409	34819	52228	69638	87047	104457	121866	139276	156685
15	7970	15941	23911	31881	63762	95643	127524	159406	191287	223168	255049	286930
20	13099	26198	39297	52397	104793	157190	209586	261983	314379	366776	419172	471569
25	20370	40740	61110	81480	162959	244439	325919	407399	488878	570358	651838	733317
30	30677	61354	92032	122709	245417	368126	490835	613544	736252	858961	981670	1104379

MONTHLY WITHDRAWAL, 7.00 %
FULL YEARS TO WITHDRAW

AMOUNT	500	600	700	800	900	1000	1100	1200	1300	1400	1500	1600	1700	1800	1900	2000	2500	3000	4000	5000
50000	12	9	7	6	5	5	4	4	3	3	3	2	2	2	2	2	1	1	1	0
60000	17	12	10	8	7	6	5	5	4	4	3	3	3	3	3	2	1	1	1	1
70000	24	16	12	10	8	7	6	6	5	5	4	4	4	3	3	3	2	1	1	1
80000	>30	21	15	12	10	9	7	7	6	5	5	5	4	4	3	3	2	2	1	1
90000	>30	29	19	15	12	10	9	8	7	6	6	5	5	4	4	4	3	2	1	1
100000	>30	>30	25	18	15	12	10	9	8	7	7	6	6	5	5	4	3	2	2	1
110000	>30	>30	>30	23	17	14	12	11	9	8	8	7	6	6	5	5	3	3	2	1
120000	>30	>30	>30	29	21	17	14	12	11	10	9	8	7	7	6	5	4	3	2	2
130000	>30	>30	>30	>30	26	20	16	14	12	11	10	9	8	7	7	6	4	3	2	2
140000	>30	>30	>30	>30	>30	24	19	16	14	12	11	10	9	8	8	7	5	4	3	2
150000	>30	>30	>30	>30	>30	29	22	18	16	14	12	11	10	9	8	8	6	5	3	2
160000	>30	>30	>30	>30	>30	>30	27	21	18	15	14	12	11	10	9	9	6	5	3	3
170000	>30	>30	>30	>30	>30	>30	>30	25	20	17	15	13	12	11	10	9	6	5	3	3
180000	>30	>30	>30	>30	>30	>30	>30	29	23	19	17	15	13	12	11	10	7	6	4	3
190000	>30	>30	>30	>30	>30	>30	>30	>30	27	22	19	16	15	13	12	11	8	6	4	3
200000	>30	>30	>30	>30	>30	>30	>30	>30	>30	25	21	18	16	15	13	12	9	7	5	3
225000	>30	>30	>30	>30	>30	>30	>30	>30	>30	29	24	21	18	16	15	10	8	5	4	
250000	>30	>30	>30	>30	>30	>30	>30	>30	>30	>30	29	24	21	18	16	15	10	8	5	4
275000	>30	>30	>30	>30	>30	>30	>30	>30	>30	>30	>30	28	23	20	18	12	9	6	5	
300000	>30	>30	>30	>30	>30	>30	>30	>30	>30	>30	>30	>30	26	23	14	11	7	5		
350000	>30	>30	>30	>30	>30	>30	>30	>30	>30	>30	>30	>30	>30	29	17	12	8	6		
400000	>30	>30	>30	>30	>30	>30	>30	>30	>30	>30	>30	>30	>30	>30	24	16	10	7		
450000	>30	>30	>30	>30	>30	>30	>30	>30	>30	>30	>30	>30	>30	>30	>30	21	12	9		
500000	>30	>30	>30	>30	>30	>30	>30	>30	>30	>30	>30	>30	>30	>30	>30	>30	29	15	10	

MONTHLY SAVINGS, 7.25 %

YEARS	25	50	75	100	200	300	400	500	600	700	800	900
						AMOUNT SAVED						
5	1812	3625	5437	7249	14499	21748	28997	36247	43496	50745	57995	65244
10	4414	8827	13241	17655	35309	52964	70619	88273	105928	123583	141238	158892
15	8148	16295	24443	32590	65180	97770	130360	162950	195540	228130	260720	293310
20	13507	27014	40521	54027	108055	162082	216110	270137	324165	378192	432220	486247
25	21199	42399	63598	84798	169595	254393	339191	423989	508786	593584	678382	763179
30	32241	64482	96723	128964	257928	386891	515855	644819	773783	902747	1031710	1160674

MONTHLY WITHDRAWAL, 7.25 %
FULL YEARS TO WITHDRAW

AMOUNT	500	600	700	800	900	1000	1100	1200	1300	1400	1500	1600	1700	1800	1900	2000	2500	3000	4000	5000
50000	12	9	7	6	5	5	4	4	3	3	3	2	2	2	2	2	1	1	1	0
60000	17	12	10	8	7	6	5	5	4	4	3	3	3	3	2	2	1	1	1	1
70000	25	16	12	10	8	7	6	6	5	5	4	4	4	3	3	2	2	1	1	1
80000	>30	22	16	12	10	9	8	7	6	5	5	4	4	3	3	3	2	1	1	1
90000	>30	>30	20	15	12	10	9	8	7	6	5	5	4	4	4	3	3	2	1	1
100000	>30	>30	27	19	15	12	11	9	8	7	7	6	6	5	5	4	3	2	2	1
110000	>30	>30	>30	24	18	15	12	11	9	8	8	7	6	6	5	5	3	3	2	1
120000	>30	>30	>30	>30	22	17	14	12	11	10	9	8	7	7	6	5	4	3	2	2
130000	>30	>30	>30	>30	28	21	17	14	12	11	10	9	8	7	6	6	4	3	2	2
140000	>30	>30	>30	>30	>30	25	20	16	14	12	11	10	9	8	7	6	5	4	3	2
150000	>30	>30	>30	>30	>30	>30	24	19	16	14	12	11	10	9	9	8	6	5	3	2
160000	>30	>30	>30	>30	>30	>30	29	22	18	16	14	12	11	10	9	9	6	5	3	3
170000	>30	>30	>30	>30	>30	>30	>30	26	21	18	16	14	12	11	10	9	6	5	3	3
180000	>30	>30	>30	>30	>30	>30	>30	>30	25	20	17	15	14	12	11	10	7	5	4	3
190000	>30	>30	>30	>30	>30	>30	>30	>30	29	23	20	17	15	14	12	11	8	6	4	3
200000	>30	>30	>30	>30	>30	>30	>30	>30	>30	27	22	19	17	15	14	12	9	7	5	3
225000	>30	>30	>30	>30	>30	>30	>30	>30	>30	>30	26	22	19	17	15	10	8	5	4	
250000	>30	>30	>30	>30	>30	>30	>30	>30	>30	>30	>30	26	22	19	17	15	10	8	5	4
275000	>30	>30	>30	>30	>30	>30	>30	>30	>30	>30	>30	>30	25	22	19	12	9	6	5	
300000	>30	>30	>30	>30	>30	>30	>30	>30	>30	>30	>30	>30	>30	28	24	15	11	7	5	
350000	>30	>30	>30	>30	>30	>30	>30	>30	>30	>30	>30	>30	>30	>30	>30	17	12	8	6	
400000	>30	>30	>30	>30	>30	>30	>30	>30	>30	>30	>30	>30	>30	>30	>30	25	16	10	7	
450000	>30	>30	>30	>30	>30	>30	>30	>30	>30	>30	>30	>30	>30	>30	>30	>30	22	12	9	
500000	>30	>30	>30	>30	>30	>30	>30	>30	>30	>30	>30	>30	>30	>30	>30	>30	>30	15	10	

| 6000 | 7200 | 8400 | 9600 | 10800 | 12000 | 13200 | 14400 | 15600 | 16800 | 18000 | 19200 | 20400 | 21600 | 22800 | 24000 | 30000 | 36000 | 48000 | 60000 |

>30 = monthly withdrawal for more than 30 years

ANNUAL WITHDRAWAL

SAVINGS & WITHDRAWAL

Description: This table shows the amount to which a regular monthly savings will grow. And then how many full years a withdrawal may be taken from an amount at interest.

Example: At 7.50 % a regular monthly saving of $ 25 will grow to $13930 in 20 years. An amount of $50000 will support a monthly withdrawal of $ 700 for 7 years.

MONTHLY SAVINGS, 7.50 %

YEARS	25	50	75	100	200	300	400	500	600	700	800	900
					AMOUNT SAVED							
5	1825	3649	5474	7298	14596	21894	29192	36490	43788	51086	58384	65682
10	4476	8952	13428	17904	35808	53713	71617	89521	107425	125330	143234	161138
15	8330	16659	24989	33318	66636	99955	133273	166591	199909	233227	266545	299864
20	13930	27860	41789	55719	111438	167157	222877	278596	334315	390034	445753	501472
25	22069	44137	66206	88274	176549	264823	353098	441372	529646	617921	706195	794469
30	33897	67793	101690	135587	271173	406760	542347	677933	813520	949107	1084694	1220280

MONTHLY WITHDRAWAL, 7.50 %

AMOUNT	500	600	700	800	900	1000	1100	1200	1300	1400	1500	1600	1700	1800	1900	2000	2500	3000	4000	5000
						FULL YEARS TO WITHDRAW														
50000	13	9	7	6	5	5	4	4	3	3	3	2	2	2	2	2	1	1	1	0
60000	18	13	10	8	7	6	5	5	4	4	3	3	3	3	3	2	2	1	1	1
70000	27	17	13	10	8	7	6	6	5	5	4	4	4	3	3	3	2	2	1	1
80000	>30	24	16	13	10	9	8	7	6	5	5	5	4	4	4	3	2	2	2	1
90000	>30	>30	21	16	13	11	9	8	7	6	5	5	5	4	4	3	2	1		
100000	>30	>30	29	20	15	13	11	9	8	7	7	6	6	5	5	5	3	3	2	1
110000	>30	>30	>30	26	19	15	13	11	10	9	8	7	7	6	6	5	4	3	2	2
120000	>30	>30	>30	>30	24	18	15	13	11	10	9	8	7	7	6	6	4	3	2	2
130000	>30	>30	>30	>30	>30	22	18	15	13	11	10	9	8	8	7	7	5	4	3	2
140000	>30	>30	>30	>30	>30	27	21	17	15	13	11	10	9	8	8	7	5	4	3	2
150000	>30	>30	>30	>30	>30	>30	25	20	17	14	13	11	10	9	9	8	6	5	3	3
160000	>30	>30	>30	>30	>30	>30	>30	24	19	16	14	13	11	10	10	9	6	5	4	3
170000	>30	>30	>30	>30	>30	>30	>30	29	22	19	16	14	13	12	11	10	7	5	4	3
180000	>30	>30	>30	>30	>30	>30	>30	>30	26	21	18	16	14	13	12	11	8	6	4	3
190000	>30	>30	>30	>30	>30	>30	>30	>30	>30	25	21	18	16	14	13	12	8	6	4	3
200000	>30	>30	>30	>30	>30	>30	>30	>30	>30	29	24	20	17	15	14	13	9	7	5	3
225000	>30	>30	>30	>30	>30	>30	>30	>30	>30	>30	28	23	20	18	16	11	8	6	5	4
250000	>30	>30	>30	>30	>30	>30	>30	>30	>30	>30	>30	>30	23	20	13	9	6	5		
275000	>30	>30	>30	>30	>30	>30	>30	>30	>30	>30	>30	>30	>30	>30	26	15	11	7	8	6
300000	>30	>30	>30	>30	>30	>30	>30	>30	>30	>30	>30	>30	>30	>30	>30	18	13	8	6	
350000	>30	>30	>30	>30	>30	>30	>30	>30	>30	>30	>30	>30	>30	>30	>30	27	17	10	7	
400000	>30	>30	>30	>30	>30	>30	>30	>30	>30	>30	>30	>30	>30	>30	>30	>30	24	13	9	
450000	>30	>30	>30	>30	>30	>30	>30	>30	>30	>30	>30	>30	>30	>30	>30	>30	>30	16	11	
500000	>30	>30	>30	>30	>30	>30	>30	>30	>30	>30	>30	>30	>30	>30	>30	>30	>30	20	13	

MONTHLY SAVINGS, 7.75 %

YEARS	25	50	75	100	200	300	400	500	600	700	800	900
					AMOUNT SAVED							
5	1837	3674	5510	7347	14694	22041	29389	36736	44083	51430	58777	66124
10	4540	9079	13619	18158	36316	54475	72633	90791	108949	127107	145265	163424
15	8517	17033	25550	34066	68132	102198	136265	170331	204397	238463	272529	306595
20	14369	28737	43106	57474	114948	172422	229896	287370	344844	402318	459792	517267
25	22979	45959	68938	91918	183836	275754	367671	459589	551507	643425	735343	827261
30	35650	71300	106950	142600	285201	427801	570402	713002	855603	998203	1140803	1283404

MONTHLY WITHDRAWAL, 7.75 %

AMOUNT	500	600	700	800	900	1000	1100	1200	1300	1400	1500	1600	1700	1800	1900	2000	2500	3000	4000	5000
						FULL YEARS TO WITHDRAW														
50000	13	10	8	6	5	5	4	4	3	3	3	3	2	2	2	2	1	1	1	0
60000	19	13	10	8	7	6	5	5	4	4	3	3	3	3	3	2	2	1	1	1
70000	>30	18	13	10	9	7	6	6	5	5	4	4	4	3	3	3	2	2	1	1
80000	>30	25	17	13	11	9	8	7	6	6	5	5	4	4	4	3	2	2	2	1
90000	>30	>30	23	16	13	11	9	8	7	7	6	5	5	5	4	4	3	2	2	1
100000	>30	>30	>30	21	16	13	11	10	8	8	7	6	6	5	5	5	3	3	2	1
110000	>30	>30	>30	28	20	16	13	11	10	9	8	7	7	6	6	5	4	3	2	2
120000	>30	>30	>30	>30	25	19	15	13	11	10	9	8	7	7	6	6	4	3	2	2
130000	>30	>30	>30	>30	>30	23	18	15	13	11	10	9	8	8	7	7	5	4	3	2
140000	>30	>30	>30	>30	>30	>30	22	18	15	13	12	10	9	9	8	7	5	4	3	2
150000	>30	>30	>30	>30	>30	>30	27	21	17	15	13	12	11	10	9	8	6	5	3	2
160000	>30	>30	>30	>30	>30	>30	>30	25	20	17	15	13	12	11	10	9	6	5	3	3
170000	>30	>30	>30	>30	>30	>30	>30	>30	24	19	17	15	13	12	11	10	7	5	4	3
180000	>30	>30	>30	>30	>30	>30	>30	>30	29	23	19	16	14	13	12	11	8	6	4	3
190000	>30	>30	>30	>30	>30	>30	>30	>30	>30	27	22	18	16	14	13	12	8	6	4	3
200000	>30	>30	>30	>30	>30	>30	>30	>30	>30	>30	25	21	18	16	14	13	9	7	5	3
225000	>30	>30	>30	>30	>30	>30	>30	>30	>30	>30	>30	25	21	18	16	11	8	5	4	
250000	>30	>30	>30	>30	>30	>30	>30	>30	>30	>30	>30	>30	29	24	21	13	10	6	5	
275000	>30	>30	>30	>30	>30	>30	>30	>30	>30	>30	>30	>30	>30	28	16	11	7	5		
300000	>30	>30	>30	>30	>30	>30	>30	>30	>30	>30	>30	>30	>30	>30	19	13	8	6		
350000	>30	>30	>30	>30	>30	>30	>30	>30	>30	>30	>30	>30	>30	>30	18	10	7			
400000	>30	>30	>30	>30	>30	>30	>30	>30	>30	>30	>30	>30	>30	>30	25	13	9			
450000	>30	>30	>30	>30	>30	>30	>30	>30	>30	>30	>30	>30	>30	>30	>30	16	11			
500000	>30	>30	>30	>30	>30	>30	>30	>30	>30	>30	>30	>30	>30	>30	>30	21	13			

6000 7200 8400 9600 10800 12000 13200 14400 15600 16800 18000 19200 20400 21600 22800 24000 30000 36000 48000 60000

>30 = monthly withdrawal for more than 30 years

ANNUAL WITHDRAWAL

SAVINGS & WITHDRAWAL

Description: This table shows the amount to which a regular monthly savings will grow. And then how many full years a withdrawal may be taken from an amount at interest.

Example: At 8.00 % a regular monthly saving of $ 25 will grow to $14824 in 20 years. An amount of $50000 will support a monthly withdrawal of $ 700 for 8 years.

MONTHLY SAVINGS, 8.00 % — AMOUNT SAVED

YEARS	25	50	75	100	200	300	400	500	600	700	800	900
5	1849	3698	5548	7397	14793	22190	29587	36983	44380	51777	59173	66570
10	4604	9208	13812	18417	36833	55250	73666	92083	110499	128916	147333	165749
15	8709	17417	26126	34835	69669	104504	139338	174173	209007	243842	278676	313511
20	14824	29647	44471	59295	118589	177884	237179	296474	355768	415063	474358	533652
25	23934	47868	71802	95737	191473	287210	382947	478683	574420	670157	765893	861630
30	37507	75015	112522	150030	300059	450089	600118	750148	900177	1050207	1200236	1350266

MONTHLY WITHDRAWAL, 8.00 % — FULL YEARS TO WITHDRAW

AMOUNT	500	600	700	800	900	1000	1100	1200	1300	1400	1500	1600	1700	1800	1900	2000	2500	3000	4000	5000
50000	13	10	8	6	5	5	4	4	3	3	3	3	2	2	2	2	1	1	1	0
60000	20	13	10	8	7	6	5	5	4	4	3	3	3	3	3	2	2	1	1	0
70000	>30	18	13	11	9	7	7	6	5	5	4	4	4	3	3	3	2	2	1	1
80000	>30	27	18	13	11	9	8	7	6	6	5	5	4	4	3	3	2	2	1	1
90000	>30	>30	24	17	13	11	9	8	7	7	6	5	5	4	4	3	3	2	1	1
100000	>30	>30	>30	22	17	13	11	10	9	8	7	6	6	5	5	5	3	3	2	1
110000	>30	>30	>30	>30	21	16	13	11	10	9	8	7	7	6	6	5	3	3	2	1
120000	>30	>30	>30	>30	27	20	16	13	12	10	9	8	8	7	6	6	4	3	2	2
130000	>30	>30	>30	>30	>30	25	19	16	13	12	10	9	9	8	7	7	4	3	3	2
140000	>30	>30	>30	>30	>30	>30	23	18	15	13	12	11	10	9	8	7	5	4	3	2
150000	>30	>30	>30	>30	>30	>30	30	22	18	15	13	12	11	10	9	8	6	5	3	2
160000	>30	>30	>30	>30	>30	>30	>30	27	21	18	15	13	12	11	10	9	7	5	3	3
170000	>30	>30	>30	>30	>30	>30	>30	>30	25	20	17	15	13	12	11	10	7	5	3	3
180000	>30	>30	>30	>30	>30	>30	>30	>30	>30	24	20	17	15	13	12	11	7	6	4	3
190000	>30	>30	>30	>30	>30	>30	>30	>30	>30	29	23	19	17	15	13	12	8	6	4	3
200000	>30	>30	>30	>30	>30	>30	>30	>30	>30	>30	27	22	19	17	15	13	9	7	5	3
225000	>30	>30	>30	>30	>30	>30	>30	>30	>30	>30	>30	>30	26	22	19	17	11	8	5	3
250000	>30	>30	>30	>30	>30	>30	>30	>30	>30	>30	>30	>30	>30	26	22	19	13	10	6	5
275000	>30	>30	>30	>30	>30	>30	>30	>30	>30	>30	>30	>30	>30	>30	26	22	14	11	7	5
300000	>30	>30	>30	>30	>30	>30	>30	>30	>30	>30	>30	>30	>30	>30	>30	>30	16	11	7	5
350000	>30	>30	>30	>30	>30	>30	>30	>30	>30	>30	>30	>30	>30	>30	>30	>30	20	13	8	6
400000	>30	>30	>30	>30	>30	>30	>30	>30	>30	>30	>30	>30	>30	>30	>30	>30	>30	18	11	7
450000	>30	>30	>30	>30	>30	>30	>30	>30	>30	>30	>30	>30	>30	>30	>30	>30	>30	27	13	9
500000	>30	>30	>30	>30	>30	>30	>30	>30	>30	>30	>30	>30	>30	>30	>30	>30	>30	>30	22	13

MONTHLY SAVINGS, 8.25 % — AMOUNT SAVED

YEARS	25	50	75	100	200	300	400	500	600	700	800	900
5	1862	3723	5585	7447	14893	22340	29786	37233	44680	52126	59573	67019
10	4670	9340	14010	18680	37359	56039	74718	93398	112077	130757	149436	168116
15	8906	17812	26718	35624	71248	106872	142496	178119	213743	249367	284991	320615
20	15296	30592	45888	61184	122368	183551	244735	305919	367103	428287	489470	550654
25	24935	49870	74805	99740	199480	299220	398959	498699	598439	698179	797919	897659
30	39475	78950	118425	157900	315800	473700	631600	789500	947400	1105300	1263200	1421100

MONTHLY WITHDRAWAL, 8.25 % — FULL YEARS TO WITHDRAW

AMOUNT	500	600	700	800	900	1000	1100	1200	1300	1400	1500	1600	1700	1800	1900	2000	2500	3000	4000	5000
50000	14	10	8	6	5	5	4	4	3	3	3	3	2	2	2	2	1	1	1	0
60000	21	14	10	8	7	6	5	5	4	4	3	3	3	3	3	2	2	1	1	0
70000	>30	19	14	11	9	7	6	6	5	5	4	4	4	3	3	3	2	2	1	1
80000	>30	>30	18	14	11	9	8	7	6	6	5	5	4	4	3	3	2	2	1	1
90000	>30	>30	26	18	14	11	10	8	7	7	6	5	5	4	4	3	3	2	1	1
100000	>30	>30	>30	23	17	14	12	10	9	8	7	6	6	5	5	5	3	3	2	1
110000	>30	>30	>30	>30	22	17	14	12	10	9	8	7	7	6	6	5	3	3	2	1
120000	>30	>30	>30	>30	>30	21	16	14	12	10	9	8	8	7	7	6	4	3	2	2
130000	>30	>30	>30	>30	>30	27	20	16	14	12	10	9	9	8	7	7	4	3	3	2
140000	>30	>30	>30	>30	>30	>30	25	19	16	14	12	11	10	9	8	8	5	4	3	2
150000	>30	>30	>30	>30	>30	>30	>30	23	19	16	14	12	11	10	9	8	6	5	3	2
160000	>30	>30	>30	>30	>30	>30	>30	>30	22	18	16	14	12	11	10	9	7	5	3	3
170000	>30	>30	>30	>30	>30	>30	>30	>30	27	21	18	16	14	12	11	10	7	5	3	3
180000	>30	>30	>30	>30	>30	>30	>30	>30	>30	26	21	18	16	14	12	11	8	6	4	3
190000	>30	>30	>30	>30	>30	>30	>30	>30	>30	>30	24	20	17	15	14	12	9	7	4	3
200000	>30	>30	>30	>30	>30	>30	>30	>30	>30	>30	>30	24	20	17	15	14	9	7	4	3
225000	>30	>30	>30	>30	>30	>30	>30	>30	>30	>30	>30	>30	23	20	17	15	11	8	5	3
250000	>30	>30	>30	>30	>30	>30	>30	>30	>30	>30	>30	>30	29	23	20	18	11	8	6	4
275000	>30	>30	>30	>30	>30	>30	>30	>30	>30	>30	>30	>30	>30	>30	28	23	14	10	6	5
300000	>30	>30	>30	>30	>30	>30	>30	>30	>30	>30	>30	>30	>30	>30	>30	>30	17	12	7	5
350000	>30	>30	>30	>30	>30	>30	>30	>30	>30	>30	>30	>30	>30	>30	>30	>30	>30	19	11	8
400000	>30	>30	>30	>30	>30	>30	>30	>30	>30	>30	>30	>30	>30	>30	>30	>30	>30	>30	14	9
450000	>30	>30	>30	>30	>30	>30	>30	>30	>30	>30	>30	>30	>30	>30	>30	>30	>30	>30	18	11
500000	>30	>30	>30	>30	>30	>30	>30	>30	>30	>30	>30	>30	>30	>30	>30	>30	>30	>30	23	14

ANNUAL WITHDRAWAL: 6000 7200 8400 9600 10800 12000 13200 14400 15600 16800 18000 19200 20400 21600 22800 24000 30000 36000 48000 60000

>30 = monthly withdrawal for more than 30 years

SAVINGS & WITHDRAWAL

Description: This table shows the amount to which a regular monthly savings will grow. And then how many full years a withdrawal may be taken from an amount at interest.

Example: At 8.50 % a regular monthly saving of $ 25 will grow to $15786 in 20 years. An amount of $50000 will support a monthly withdrawal of $ 700 for 8 years.

MONTHLY SAVINGS, 8.50 %
AMOUNT SAVED

YEARS	25	50	75	100	200	300	400	500	600	700	800	900
5	1874	3748	5623	7497	14994	22491	29988	37485	44982	52479	59976	67473
10	4737	9474	14210	18947	37894	56841	75788	94736	113683	132630	151577	170524
15	9109	18217	27326	36435	72870	109305	145740	182175	218609	255044	291479	327914
20	15786	31572	47358	63144	126288	189432	252576	315720	378864	442008	505152	568296
25	25984	51968	77953	103937	207874	311811	415747	519684	623621	727558	831495	935432
30	41560	83120	124680	166240	332480	498719	664959	831199	997439	1163679	1329919	1496158

MONTHLY WITHDRAWAL, 8.50 %
FULL YEARS TO WITHDRAW

AMOUNT	500	600	700	800	900	1000	1100	1200	1300	1400	1500	1600	1700	1800	1900	2000	2500	3000	4000	5000
50000	14	10	8	6	5	5	4	4	3	3	3	3	2	2	2	2	1	1	1	0
60000	22	14	11	9	7	6	5	5	4	4	4	3	3	3	3	2	2	1	1	1
70000	>30	20	14	11	9	8	7	6	5	5	4	4	4	3	3	3	2	2	1	1
80000	>30	>30	19	14	11	9	8	7	6	6	5	5	4	4	4	3	2	2	2	1
90000	>30	>30	28	18	14	12	10	9	8	7	6	6	5	5	4	4	3	2	2	1
100000	>30	>30	>30	25	18	14	12	10	9	8	7	6	6	5	5	5	4	3	2	1
110000	>30	>30	>30	>30	23	17	14	12	10	9	8	7	7	6	6	5	4	3	2	2
120000	>30	>30	>30	>30	>30	22	17	14	12	11	9	9	8	7	7	6	4	4	2	2
130000	>30	>30	>30	>30	>30	30	21	17	14	12	11	10	9	8	7	7	5	4	3	2
140000	>30	>30	>30	>30	>30	>30	27	20	17	14	12	11	10	9	8	8	6	4	3	2
150000	>30	>30	>30	>30	>30	>30	>30	25	20	16	14	12	11	10	9	9	6	5	3	2
160000	>30	>30	>30	>30	>30	>30	>30	>30	24	19	16	14	13	11	10	9	7	5	4	3
170000	>30	>30	>30	>30	>30	>30	>30	>30	>30	23	19	16	14	13	11	10	7	6	4	3
180000	>30	>30	>30	>30	>30	>30	>30	>30	>30	28	22	18	16	14	13	12	8	6	4	3
190000	>30	>30	>30	>30	>30	>30	>30	>30	>30	>30	26	21	18	16	14	13	9	7	4	3
200000	>30	>30	>30	>30	>30	>30	>30	>30	>30	>30	>30	25	21	18	16	14	9	7	5	4
225000	>30	>30	>30	>30	>30	>30	>30	>30	>30	>30	>30	>30	25	21	18	12	9	6	6	5
250000	>30	>30	>30	>30	>30	>30	>30	>30	>30	>30	>30	>30	>30	>30	25	14	10	6	7	5
275000	>30	>30	>30	>30	>30	>30	>30	>30	>30	>30	>30	>30	>30	>30	>30	22	14	9	9	6
300000	>30	>30	>30	>30	>30	>30	>30	>30	>30	>30	>30	>30	>30	>30	>30	>30	22	14	9	6
350000	>30	>30	>30	>30	>30	>30	>30	>30	>30	>30	>30	>30	>30	>30	>30	>30	>30	20	11	8
400000	>30	>30	>30	>30	>30	>30	>30	>30	>30	>30	>30	>30	>30	>30	>30	>30	>30	>30	14	9
450000	>30	>30	>30	>30	>30	>30	>30	>30	>30	>30	>30	>30	>30	>30	>30	>30	>30	>30	18	12
500000	>30	>30	>30	>30	>30	>30	>30	>30	>30	>30	>30	>30	>30	>30	>30	>30	>30	>30	25	14

MONTHLY SAVINGS, 8.75 %
AMOUNT SAVED

YEARS	25	50	75	100	200	300	400	500	600	700	800	900
5	1887	3774	5661	7548	15096	22643	30191	37739	45287	52834	60382	67930
10	4805	9610	14415	19219	38439	57658	76878	96097	115317	134536	153755	172975
15	9317	18634	27951	37268	74536	111805	149073	186341	223609	260877	298145	335414
20	16295	32589	48884	65178	130357	195535	260713	325891	391070	456248	521426	586605
25	27084	54169	81253	108338	216676	325013	433351	541689	650027	758364	866702	975040
30	43770	87539	131309	175078	350157	525235	700314	875392	1050471	1225549	1400627	1575706

MONTHLY WITHDRAWAL, 8.75 %
FULL YEARS TO WITHDRAW

AMOUNT	500	600	700	800	900	1000	1100	1200	1300	1400	1500	1600	1700	1800	1900	2000	2500	3000	4000	5000
50000	15	10	8	7	6	5	4	4	3	3	3	3	2	2	2	2	1	1	1	0
60000	23	15	11	9	7	6	5	5	4	4	4	3	3	3	3	2	2	1	1	1
70000	>30	21	15	11	9	8	7	6	5	5	4	4	4	4	3	3	2	2	1	1
80000	>30	>30	20	15	12	10	8	7	6	6	5	5	4	4	4	3	2	2	2	1
90000	>30	>30	>30	19	15	12	10	9	8	7	6	6	5	5	4	4	3	2	2	1
100000	>30	>30	>30	27	19	15	12	10	9	8	7	7	6	6	5	5	4	3	2	1
110000	>30	>30	>30	>30	25	18	15	12	11	9	8	8	7	6	6	5	4	3	2	2
120000	>30	>30	>30	>30	>30	23	18	15	12	11	10	9	8	7	7	6	5	4	3	2
130000	>30	>30	>30	>30	>30	>30	22	17	15	13	11	10	9	8	8	6	4	4	3	2
140000	>30	>30	>30	>30	>30	>30	>30	21	17	15	13	11	10	9	8	8	6	4	3	2
150000	>30	>30	>30	>30	>30	>30	>30	27	21	17	15	13	11	10	9	9	6	5	3	2
160000	>30	>30	>30	>30	>30	>30	>30	>30	26	20	17	15	13	12	11	10	7	5	4	3
170000	>30	>30	>30	>30	>30	>30	>30	>30	>30	24	20	17	15	13	12	11	7	6	4	3
180000	>30	>30	>30	>30	>30	>30	>30	>30	>30	23	19	17	15	13	12	8	9	7	4	3
190000	>30	>30	>30	>30	>30	>30	>30	>30	>30	29	23	19	16	15	13	9	7	5	4
200000	>30	>30	>30	>30	>30	>30	>30	>30	>30	>30	27	22	19	16	15	10	7	5	4
225000	>30	>30	>30	>30	>30	>30	>30	>30	>30	>30	>30	27	22	19	12	9	7	5
250000	>30	>30	>30	>30	>30	>30	>30	>30	>30	>30	>30	>30	>30	27	15	10	8	5
275000	>30	>30	>30	>30	>30	>30	>30	>30	>30	>30	>30	>30	>30	>30	18	12	8	5
300000	>30	>30	>30	>30	>30	>30	>30	>30	>30	>30	>30	>30	>30	>30	23	15	9	6
350000	>30	>30	>30	>30	>30	>30	>30	>30	>30	>30	>30	>30	>30	>30	>30	21	11	8
400000	>30	>30	>30	>30	>30	>30	>30	>30	>30	>30	>30	>30	>30	>30	>30	>30	15	10	12
450000	>30	>30	>30	>30	>30	>30	>30	>30	>30	>30	>30	>30	>30	>30	>30	>30	27	15
500000	>30	>30	>30	>30	>30	>30	>30	>30	>30	>30	>30	>30	>30	>30	>30	>30	>30	15

| 6000 | 7200 | 8400 | 9600 | 10800 | 12000 | 13200 | 14400 | 15600 | 16800 | 18000 | 19200 | 20400 | 21600 | 22800 | 24000 | 30000 | 36000 | 48000 | 60000 |

>30 = monthly withdrawal for more than 30 years   ANNUAL WITHDRAWAL

Description: This table shows the amount to which a regular monthly savings will grow. And then how many full years a withdrawal may be taken from an amount at interest.

Example: At 9.00 % a regular monthly saving of $ 25 will grow to $16822 in 20 years. An amount of $50000 will support a monthly withdrawal of $ 700 for 8 years.

MONTHLY SAVINGS, 9.00 %

AMOUNT SAVED

YEARS	25	50	75	100	200	300	400	500	600	700	800	900
5	1900	3799	5699	7599	15198	22797	30396	37995	45594	53193	60792	68391
10	4874	9748	14622	19497	38993	58490	77986	97483	116979	136476	155973	175469
15	9531	19062	28593	38124	76249	114373	152498	190622	228746	266871	304995	343119
20	16822	33645	50467	67290	134579	201869	269158	336448	403738	471027	538317	605606
25	28238	56477	84715	112953	225906	338859	451812	564765	677718	790671	903624	1016577
30	46112	92224	138336	184447	368895	553342	737790	922237	1106684	1291132	1475579	1660027

MONTHLY WITHDRAWAL, 9.00 %

FULL YEARS TO WITHDRAW

AMOUNT	500	600	700	800	900	1000	1100	1200	1300	1400	1500	1600	1700	1800	1900	2000	2500	3000	4000	5000
50000	15	11	8	7	6	5	4	4	3	3	3	3	2	2	2	2	1	1	1	0
60000	25	15	11	9	7	6	5	5	4	4	4	3	3	3	3	2	2	1	1	1
70000	>30	23	15	11	9	8	7	6	5	5	4	4	4	3	3	3	2	1	1	1
80000	>30	>30	21	15	12	10	8	7	6	6	5	5	4	4	4	4	3	2	1	1
90000	>30	>30	>30	20	15	12	10	9	8	7	6	6	5	5	4	4	3	2	1	1
100000	>30	>30	>30	>30	20	15	12	11	9	8	7	7	6	6	5	5	4	3	2	1
110000	>30	>30	>30	>30	27	19	15	13	11	10	8	8	7	6	6	6	4	3	2	1
120000	>30	>30	>30	>30	>30	25	19	15	13	11	10	9	8	7	7	6	4	3	2	2
130000	>30	>30	>30	>30	>30	>30	24	18	15	13	11	10	9	8	8	7	5	4	2	2
140000	>30	>30	>30	>30	>30	>30	>30	23	18	15	13	11	10	9	9	8	6	4	3	2
150000	>30	>30	>30	>30	>30	>30	>30	>30	22	18	15	13	12	11	10	9	6	5	3	2
160000	>30	>30	>30	>30	>30	>30	>30	>30	28	21	18	15	13	12	11	10	7	5	4	3
170000	>30	>30	>30	>30	>30	>30	>30	>30	>30	27	21	17	15	13	12	11	8	6	4	3
180000	>30	>30	>30	>30	>30	>30	>30	>30	>30	>30	25	20	17	15	13	12	8	6	4	3
190000	>30	>30	>30	>30	>30	>30	>30	>30	>30	>30	>30	24	20	17	15	13	9	7	4	3
200000	>30	>30	>30	>30	>30	>30	>30	>30	>30	>30	>30	>30	23	20	17	15	10	7	5	4
225000	>30	>30	>30	>30	>30	>30	>30	>30	>30	>30	>30	>30	>30	>30	24	20	12	9	6	4
250000	>30	>30	>30	>30	>30	>30	>30	>30	>30	>30	>30	>30	>30	>30	>30	>30	15	11	7	5
275000	>30	>30	>30	>30	>30	>30	>30	>30	>30	>30	>30	>30	>30	>30	>30	>30	15	11	7	5
300000	>30	>30	>30	>30	>30	>30	>30	>30	>30	>30	>30	>30	>30	>30	>30	>30	19	13	8	6
350000	>30	>30	>30	>30	>30	>30	>30	>30	>30	>30	>30	>30	>30	>30	>30	>30	25	15	9	6
400000	>30	>30	>30	>30	>30	>30	>30	>30	>30	>30	>30	>30	>30	>30	>30	>30	>30	23	11	8
450000	>30	>30	>30	>30	>30	>30	>30	>30	>30	>30	>30	>30	>30	>30	>30	>30	>30	>30	15	10
500000	>30	>30	>30	>30	>30	>30	>30	>30	>30	>30	>30	>30	>30	>30	>30	>30	>30	>30	20	12

MONTHLY SAVINGS, 9.25 %

AMOUNT SAVED

YEARS	25	50	75	100	200	300	400	500	600	700	800	900
5	1913	3825	5738	7651	15301	22952	30603	38253	45904	53554	61205	68856
10	4945	9889	14834	19779	39557	59336	79114	98893	118672	138450	158229	178008
15	9751	19502	29253	39004	78008	117013	156017	195021	234025	273029	312034	351038
20	17370	34741	52111	69481	138962	208443	277924	347405	416886	486368	555849	625330
25	29448	58897	88345	117794	235588	353381	471175	588969	706763	824557	942350	1060144
30	48595	97190	145785	194380	388761	583141	777521	971902	1166282	1360662	1555043	1749423

MONTHLY WITHDRAWAL, 9.25 %

FULL YEARS TO WITHDRAW

AMOUNT	500	600	700	800	900	1000	1100	1200	1300	1400	1500	1600	1700	1800	1900	2000	2500	3000	4000	5000
50000	16	11	8	7	6	5	4	4	3	3	3	3	2	2	2	2	1	1	1	0
60000	28	16	11	9	7	6	6	5	4	4	4	3	3	3	3	2	2	1	1	1
70000	>30	24	16	12	10	8	7	6	5	5	4	4	4	3	3	3	2	2	1	1
80000	>30	>30	23	16	12	10	9	7	7	6	5	5	4	4	4	3	2	2	1	1
90000	>30	>30	>30	21	16	12	10	9	8	7	6	6	5	5	5	4	3	2	1	1
100000	>30	>30	>30	>30	21	16	13	11	9	8	7	7	6	6	5	5	4	3	2	1
110000	>30	>30	>30	>30	>30	20	16	13	11	10	9	8	7	6	6	5	4	3	2	1
120000	>30	>30	>30	>30	>30	28	20	16	13	11	10	9	8	7	7	6	4	3	2	2
130000	>30	>30	>30	>30	>30	>30	26	19	16	13	12	10	9	8	8	7	5	4	3	2
140000	>30	>30	>30	>30	>30	>30	>30	24	19	16	13	12	11	10	9	8	6	4	3	2
150000	>30	>30	>30	>30	>30	>30	>30	>30	23	19	16	14	12	11	10	9	6	5	3	2
160000	>30	>30	>30	>30	>30	>30	>30	>30	23	19	16	14	12	11	10	9	6	5	3	2
170000	>30	>30	>30	>30	>30	>30	>30	>30	>30	23	18	16	14	12	11	10	7	5	4	3
180000	>30	>30	>30	>30	>30	>30	>30	>30	>30	29	22	18	16	14	12	11	8	6	4	3
190000	>30	>30	>30	>30	>30	>30	>30	>30	>30	>30	26	21	18	16	14	12	9	7	5	3
200000	>30	>30	>30	>30	>30	>30	>30	>30	>30	>30	>30	25	21	18	16	14	10	7	5	4
225000	>30	>30	>30	>30	>30	>30	>30	>30	>30	>30	>30	>30	>30	26	21	18	12	9	6	4
250000	>30	>30	>30	>30	>30	>30	>30	>30	>30	>30	>30	>30	>30	>30	26	21	12	9	6	4
275000	>30	>30	>30	>30	>30	>30	>30	>30	>30	>30	>30	>30	>30	>30	>30	>30	16	11	7	5
300000	>30	>30	>30	>30	>30	>30	>30	>30	>30	>30	>30	>30	>30	>30	>30	>30	20	13	8	6
350000	>30	>30	>30	>30	>30	>30	>30	>30	>30	>30	>30	>30	>30	>30	>30	>30	28	16	9	6
400000	>30	>30	>30	>30	>30	>30	>30	>30	>30	>30	>30	>30	>30	>30	>30	>30	>30	24	12	8
450000	>30	>30	>30	>30	>30	>30	>30	>30	>30	>30	>30	>30	>30	>30	>30	>30	>30	>30	16	10
500000	>30	>30	>30	>30	>30	>30	>30	>30	>30	>30	>30	>30	>30	>30	>30	>30	>30	>30	21	12

ANNUAL WITHDRAWAL

6000 7200 8400 9600 10800 12000 13200 14400 15600 16800 18000 19200 20400 21600 22800 24000 30000 36000 48000 60000

>30 = monthly withdrawal for more than 30 years

Description: This table shows the amount to which a regular monthly savings will grow. And then how many full years a withdrawal may be taken from an amount at interest.

Example: At 9.50 % a regular monthly saving of $ 25 will grow to $17939 in 20 years. An amount of $50000 will support a monthly withdrawal of $ 700 for 8 years.

MONTHLY SAVINGS, 9.50 %

YEARS	25	50	75	100	200	300	400	500	600	700	800	900
					AMOUNT SAVED							
5	1926	3851	5777	7703	15405	23108	30811	38514	46216	53919	61622	69325
10	5016	10033	15049	20066	40131	60197	80263	100328	120394	140460	160525	180591
15	9977	19954	29931	39908	79817	119725	159633	199542	239450	279358	319267	359175
20	17939	35878	53817	71756	143512	215268	287024	358780	430536	502292	574048	645804
25	30718	61436	92154	122872	245743	368615	491487	614359	737230	860102	982974	1105846
30	51228	102457	153685	204913	409826	614739	819652	1024565	1229478	1434391	1639304	1844217

MONTHLY WITHDRAWAL, 9.50 %

AMOUNT	500	600	700	800	900	1000	1100	1200	1300	1400	1500	1600	1700	1800	1900	2000	2500	3000	4000	5000
							FULL YEARS TO WITHDRAW													
50000	16	11	8	7	6	5	4	4	3	3	3	3	2	2	2	2	1	1	1	0
60000	>30	16	12	9	8	6	6	5	4	4	4	3	3	3	3	2	2	1	1	1
70000	>30	27	16	12	10	8	7	6	5	5	4	4	4	3	3	3	2	2	1	1
80000	>30	>30	24	16	12	10	9	8	7	6	5	5	5	4	4	4	3	2	1	1
90000	>30	>30	>30	23	16	13	11	9	8	7	6	6	5	5	5	4	3	2	2	1
100000	>30	>30	>30	>30	22	16	13	11	10	8	8	7	6	6	5	5	4	3	2	1
110000	>30	>30	>30	>30	>30	21	16	13	11	10	9	8	7	7	6	6	4	3	2	2
120000	>30	>30	>30	>30	>30	>30	21	16	13	12	10	9	8	8	7	6	5	4	2	2
130000	>30	>30	>30	>30	>30	>30	29	20	16	14	12	10	9	9	8	7	5	4	3	2
140000	>30	>30	>30	>30	>30	>30	>30	27	20	16	14	12	11	10	9	8	6	4	3	2
150000	>30	>30	>30	>30	>30	>30	>30	>30	25	20	16	14	12	11	10	9	6	5	3	2
160000	>30	>30	>30	>30	>30	>30	>30	>30	>30	24	19	16	14	12	11	10	7	5	4	3
170000	>30	>30	>30	>30	>30	>30	>30	>30	>30	>30	24	19	16	14	13	11	8	6	4	3
180000	>30	>30	>30	>30	>30	>30	>30	>30	>30	>30	>30	23	19	16	14	13	9	6	4	3
190000	>30	>30	>30	>30	>30	>30	>30	>30	>30	>30	>30	29	22	19	16	14	9	7	5	3
200000	>30	>30	>30	>30	>30	>30	>30	>30	>30	>30	>30	>30	28	22	19	16	10	8	5	4
225000	>30	>30	>30	>30	>30	>30	>30	>30	>30	>30	>30	>30	>30	>30	29	23	13	9	6	4
250000	>30	>30	>30	>30	>30	>30	>30	>30	>30	>30	>30	>30	>30	>30	>30	>30	16	11	7	5
275000	>30	>30	>30	>30	>30	>30	>30	>30	>30	>30	>30	>30	>30	>30	>30	>30	21	13	8	6
300000	>30	>30	>30	>30	>30	>30	>30	>30	>30	>30	>30	>30	>30	>30	>30	>30	>30	16	9	6
350000	>30	>30	>30	>30	>30	>30	>30	>30	>30	>30	>30	>30	>30	>30	>30	>30	>30	27	12	8
400000	>30	>30	>30	>30	>30	>30	>30	>30	>30	>30	>30	>30	>30	>30	>30	>30	>30	>30	16	10
450000	>30	>30	>30	>30	>30	>30	>30	>30	>30	>30	>30	>30	>30	>30	>30	>30	>30	>30	23	13
500000	>30	>30	>30	>30	>30	>30	>30	>30	>30	>30	>30	>30	>30	>30	>30	>30	>30	>30	>30	16

MONTHLY SAVINGS, 9.75 %

YEARS	25	50	75	100	200	300	400	500	600	700	800	900
					AMOUNT SAVED							
5	1939	3878	5816	7755	15511	23266	31021	38776	46532	54287	62042	69797
10	5089	10179	15268	20358	40716	61074	81431	101789	122147	142505	162863	183221
15	10209	20419	30628	40837	81675	122512	163350	204187	245025	285862	326700	367537
20	18529	37059	55588	74118	148235	222353	296471	370588	444706	518824	592941	667059
25	32050	64100	96149	128199	256398	384597	512797	640996	769195	897394	1025593	1153792
30	54021	108042	162063	216084	432167	648251	864334	1080418	1296501	1512585	1728668	1944752

MONTHLY WITHDRAWAL, 9.75 %

AMOUNT	500	600	700	800	900	1000	1100	1200	1300	1400	1500	1600	1700	1800	1900	2000	2500	3000	4000	5000
							FULL YEARS TO WITHDRAW													
50000	17	11	9	7	6	5	4	4	3	3	3	3	2	2	2	2	1	1	1	0
60000	>30	17	12	9	8	6	6	5	4	4	4	3	3	3	3	2	2	1	1	1
70000	>30	>30	17	12	10	8	7	6	6	5	4	4	4	3	3	3	2	2	1	1
80000	>30	>30	>30	17	13	10	9	8	7	6	5	5	5	4	4	4	3	2	1	1
90000	>30	>30	>30	25	17	13	11	9	8	7	6	6	5	5	5	4	3	2	2	1
100000	>30	>30	>30	>30	24	17	13	11	10	9	8	7	6	6	5	5	4	3	2	1
110000	>30	>30	>30	>30	>30	23	17	14	12	10	9	8	7	7	6	6	4	3	2	2
120000	>30	>30	>30	>30	>30	>30	22	17	14	12	10	9	8	8	7	6	5	4	2	2
130000	>30	>30	>30	>30	>30	>30	>30	21	17	14	12	11	10	9	8	7	5	4	3	2
140000	>30	>30	>30	>30	>30	>30	>30	>30	21	17	14	12	11	10	9	8	6	4	3	2
150000	>30	>30	>30	>30	>30	>30	>30	>30	28	21	17	14	13	11	10	9	6	5	3	2
160000	>30	>30	>30	>30	>30	>30	>30	>30	>30	27	20	17	14	13	11	10	7	5	4	3
170000	>30	>30	>30	>30	>30	>30	>30	>30	>30	>30	26	20	17	15	13	12	8	6	4	3
180000	>30	>30	>30	>30	>30	>30	>30	>30	>30	>30	>30	25	20	17	15	13	9	6	4	3
190000	>30	>30	>30	>30	>30	>30	>30	>30	>30	>30	>30	>30	24	20	17	15	9	7	5	3
200000	>30	>30	>30	>30	>30	>30	>30	>30	>30	>30	>30	>30	>30	24	19	17	10	8	5	4
225000	>30	>30	>30	>30	>30	>30	>30	>30	>30	>30	>30	>30	>30	>30	>30	25	13	9	6	4
250000	>30	>30	>30	>30	>30	>30	>30	>30	>30	>30	>30	>30	>30	>30	>30	>30	17	11	7	5
275000	>30	>30	>30	>30	>30	>30	>30	>30	>30	>30	>30	>30	>30	>30	>30	>30	23	14	8	6
300000	>30	>30	>30	>30	>30	>30	>30	>30	>30	>30	>30	>30	>30	>30	>30	>30	>30	17	9	6
350000	>30	>30	>30	>30	>30	>30	>30	>30	>30	>30	>30	>30	>30	>30	>30	>30	>30	>30	12	8
400000	>30	>30	>30	>30	>30	>30	>30	>30	>30	>30	>30	>30	>30	>30	>30	>30	>30	>30	17	10
450000	>30	>30	>30	>30	>30	>30	>30	>30	>30	>30	>30	>30	>30	>30	>30	>30	>30	>30	25	13
500000	>30	>30	>30	>30	>30	>30	>30	>30	>30	>30	>30	>30	>30	>30	>30	>30	>30	>30	>30	17

6000	7200	8400	9600	10800	12000	13200	14400	15600	16800	18000	19200	20400	21600	22800	24000	30000	36000	48000	60000

>30 = monthly withdrawal for more than 30 years   ANNUAL WITHDRAWAL

Description: This table shows the amount to which a regular monthly savings will grow. And then how many full years a withdrawal may be taken from an amount at interest.

Example: At 10.00 % a regular monthly saving of $ 25 will grow to $19142 in 20 years. An amount of $50000 will support a monthly withdrawal of $ 700 for 9 years.

MONTHLY SAVINGS, 10.00 %

YEARS	25	50	75	100	200	300	400	500	600	700	800	900
					AMOUNT SAVED							
5	1952	3904	5856	7808	15616	23425	31233	39041	46849	54658	62466	70274
10	5164	10328	15491	20655	41310	61966	82621	103276	123931	144586	165242	185897
15	10448	20896	31344	41792	83585	125377	167170	208962	250755	292547	334339	376132
20	19142	38285	57427	76570	153139	229709	306279	382848	459418	535988	612558	689127
25	33447	66895	100342	133789	267578	401367	535156	668945	802734	936523	1070312	1204101
30	56983	113966	170949	227933	455865	683798	911730	1139663	1367595	1595528	1823460	2051393

MONTHLY WITHDRAWAL, 10.00 %

AMOUNT	500	600	700	800	900	1000	1100	1200	1300	1400	1500	1600	1700	1800	1900	2000	2500	3000	4000	5000
						FULL YEARS TO WITHDRAW														
50000	18	11	9	7	6	5	4	4	3	3	3	3	2	2	2	2	1	1	1	0
60000	>30	18	12	9	8	7	6	5	4	4	4	3	3	3	3	2	2	1	1	1
70000	>30	>30	18	13	10	8	7	6	6	5	5	4	4	4	3	3	2	2	1	1
80000	>30	>30	>30	18	13	11	9	8	7	6	5	5	5	4	4	4	3	2	1	1
90000	>30	>30	>30	27	18	14	11	9	8	7	7	6	5	5	5	4	3	2	2	1
100000	>30	>30	>30	>30	26	18	14	11	10	9	8	7	6	6	5	5	4	3	2	1
110000	>30	>30	>30	>30	>30	25	18	14	12	10	9	8	7	7	6	6	4	3	2	2
120000	>30	>30	>30	>30	>30	>30	24	18	14	12	11	9	8	8	7	7	5	4	2	2
130000	>30	>30	>30	>30	>30	>30	>30	23	18	15	12	11	10	9	8	7	5	4	3	2
140000	>30	>30	>30	>30	>30	>30	>30	>30	22	18	15	13	11	10	9	8	6	5	3	2
150000	>30	>30	>30	>30	>30	>30	>30	>30	>30	22	18	15	13	11	10	9	7	5	3	2
160000	>30	>30	>30	>30	>30	>30	>30	>30	>30	>30	22	18	15	13	12	11	7	5	4	3
170000	>30	>30	>30	>30	>30	>30	>30	>30	>30	>30	29	21	18	15	13	12	8	6	4	3
180000	>30	>30	>30	>30	>30	>30	>30	>30	>30	>30	>30	27	21	18	15	14	9	7	4	3
190000	>30	>30	>30	>30	>30	>30	>30	>30	>30	>30	>30	>30	26	21	18	15	10	7	5	3
200000	>30	>30	>30	>30	>30	>30	>30	>30	>30	>30	>30	>30	26	21	18	11	8	5	4	
225000	>30	>30	>30	>30	>30	>30	>30	>30	>30	>30	>30	>30	>30	>30	27	14	9	6	4	
250000	>30	>30	>30	>30	>30	>30	>30	>30	>30	>30	>30	>30	>30	>30	>30	18	11	7	5	
275000	>30	>30	>30	>30	>30	>30	>30	>30	>30	>30	>30	>30	>30	>30	>30	25	14	8	6	
300000	>30	>30	>30	>30	>30	>30	>30	>30	>30	>30	>30	>30	>30	>30	>30	>30	18	9	7	
350000	>30	>30	>30	>30	>30	>30	>30	>30	>30	>30	>30	>30	>30	>30	>30	>30	>30	18	13	8
400000	>30	>30	>30	>30	>30	>30	>30	>30	>30	>30	>30	>30	>30	>30	>30	>30	>30	>30	18	11
450000	>30	>30	>30	>30	>30	>30	>30	>30	>30	>30	>30	>30	>30	>30	>30	>30	>30	>30	27	14
500000	>30	>30	>30	>30	>30	>30	>30	>30	>30	>30	>30	>30	>30	>30	>30	>30	>30	>30	>30	18

MONTHLY SAVINGS, 10.50 %

YEARS	25	50	75	100	200	300	400	500	600	700	800	900
					AMOUNT SAVED							
5	1979	3958	5937	7916	15831	23747	31662	39578	47493	55409	63324	71240
10	5316	10633	15949	21266	42532	63798	85064	106330	127596	148862	170128	191393
15	10946	21891	32837	43783	87566	131348	175131	218914	262697	306479	350262	394045
20	20440	40880	61320	81760	163519	245279	327039	408798	490558	572318	654077	735837
25	36453	72906	109359	145812	291623	437435	583247	729058	874870	1020682	1166493	1312305
30	63460	126921	190381	253842	507684	761526	1015368	1269210	1523052	1776894	2030736	2284578

MONTHLY WITHDRAWAL, 10.50 %

AMOUNT	500	600	700	800	900	1000	1100	1200	1300	1400	1500	1600	1700	1800	1900	2000	2500	3000	4000	5000
						FULL YEARS TO WITHDRAW														
50000	19	12	9	7	6	5	4	4	4	3	3	3	2	2	2	1	1	1	0	
60000	>30	19	13	10	8	7	6	5	4	4	4	3	3	3	3	2	2	1	1	1
70000	>30	>30	19	13	10	9	7	6	6	5	5	4	4	4	3	3	2	2	1	1
80000	>30	>30	>30	19	14	11	9	8	7	6	6	5	5	4	4	4	3	2	1	1
90000	>30	>30	>30	>30	19	14	12	10	8	7	7	6	6	5	5	4	3	2	2	1
100000	>30	>30	>30	>30	>30	19	15	12	10	9	8	7	6	6	5	5	4	3	2	1
110000	>30	>30	>30	>30	>30	>30	19	15	12	11	9	8	8	7	6	6	4	3	2	2
120000	>30	>30	>30	>30	>30	>30	29	19	15	13	11	10	9	8	7	7	5	4	2	2
130000	>30	>30	>30	>30	>30	>30	>30	28	19	16	13	11	10	9	8	8	5	4	3	2
140000	>30	>30	>30	>30	>30	>30	>30	>30	27	19	16	13	12	10	9	9	6	5	3	2
150000	>30	>30	>30	>30	>30	>30	>30	>30	>30	26	19	16	14	12	11	10	7	5	3	2
160000	>30	>30	>30	>30	>30	>30	>30	>30	>30	>30	25	19	16	14	12	11	7	6	4	3
170000	>30	>30	>30	>30	>30	>30	>30	>30	>30	>30	>30	25	19	16	14	13	8	6	4	3
180000	>30	>30	>30	>30	>30	>30	>30	>30	>30	>30	>30	>30	25	19	16	14	9	7	4	3
190000	>30	>30	>30	>30	>30	>30	>30	>30	>30	>30	>30	>30	>30	24	19	17	10	7	5	3
200000	>30	>30	>30	>30	>30	>30	>30	>30	>30	>30	>30	>30	>30	24	19	11	8	5	4	
225000	>30	>30	>30	>30	>30	>30	>30	>30	>30	>30	>30	>30	>30	>30	14	10	6	4		
250000	>30	>30	>30	>30	>30	>30	>30	>30	>30	>30	>30	>30	>30	>30	19	12	7	5		
275000	>30	>30	>30	>30	>30	>30	>30	>30	>30	>30	>30	>30	>30	>30	>30	15	8	6		
300000	>30	>30	>30	>30	>30	>30	>30	>30	>30	>30	>30	>30	>30	>30	>30	19	10	7		
350000	>30	>30	>30	>30	>30	>30	>30	>30	>30	>30	>30	>30	>30	>30	>30	>30	13	9		
400000	>30	>30	>30	>30	>30	>30	>30	>30	>30	>30	>30	>30	>30	>30	>30	>30	19	11		
450000	>30	>30	>30	>30	>30	>30	>30	>30	>30	>30	>30	>30	>30	>30	>30	>30	>30	14		
500000	>30	>30	>30	>30	>30	>30	>30	>30	>30	>30	>30	>30	>30	>30	>30	>30	>30	19		

6000 7200 8400 9600 10800 12000 13200 14400 15600 16800 18000 19200 20400 21600 22800 24000 30000 36000 48000 60000
>30 = monthly withdrawal for more than 30 years   ANNUAL WITHDRAWAL

SAVINGS & WITHDRAWAL

Description: This table shows the amount to which a regular monthly savings will grow. And then how many full years a withdrawal may be taken from an amount at interest.

Example: At 11.00 % a regular monthly saving of $ 25 will grow to $21839 in 20 years. An amount of $50000 will support a monthly withdrawal of $ 700 for 9 years.

MONTHLY SAVINGS, 11.00 %

YEARS	25	50	75	100	200	300	400	500	600	700	800	900
					AMOUNT SAVED							
5	2006	4012	6019	8025	16049	24074	32099	40123	48148	56173	64198	72222
10	5475	10949	16424	21899	43797	65696	87595	109494	131392	153291	175190	197089
15	11471	22943	34414	45886	91772	137657	183543	229429	275315	321200	367086	412972
20	21839	43679	65518	87357	174715	262072	349429	436787	524144	611501	698858	786216
25	39765	79529	119294	159058	318116	477174	636232	795291	954349	1113407	1272465	1431523
30	70756	141511	212267	283023	566046	849068	1132091	1415114	1698137	1981159	2264182	2547205

MONTHLY WITHDRAWAL, 11.00 %

AMOUNT	500	600	700	800	900	1000	1100	1200	1300	1400	1500	1600	1700	1800	1900	2000	2500	3000	4000	5000
						FULL YEARS TO WITHDRAW														
50000	22	13	9	7	6	5	5	4	4	3	3	3	2	2	2	2	1	1	1	0
60000	>30	22	14	10	8	7	6	5	5	4	4	3	3	3	3	2	1	1	1	1
70000	>30	>30	22	14	11	9	8	7	6	5	5	4	4	4	3	3	2	2	1	1
80000	>30	>30	>30	22	15	12	10	8	7	6	6	5	5	4	4	4	3	2	1	1
90000	>30	>30	>30	>30	22	16	12	10	9	8	7	6	6	5	5	4	3	3	2	1
100000	>30	>30	>30	>30	>30	22	16	13	11	9	8	7	7	6	6	5	4	3	2	1
110000	>30	>30	>30	>30	>30	>30	22	16	13	11	10	9	8	7	6	6	4	3	2	2
120000	>30	>30	>30	>30	>30	>30	>30	22	17	14	12	10	9	8	7	7	5	4	3	2
130000	>30	>30	>30	>30	>30	>30	>30	>30	22	17	14	12	11	9	9	8	5	4	3	2
140000	>30	>30	>30	>30	>30	>30	>30	>30	>30	22	17	14	12	11	10	9	6	5	3	2
150000	>30	>30	>30	>30	>30	>30	>30	>30	>30	>30	22	17	15	13	11	10	7	5	3	3
160000	>30	>30	>30	>30	>30	>30	>30	>30	>30	>30	>30	22	18	15	13	12	8	6	4	3
170000	>30	>30	>30	>30	>30	>30	>30	>30	>30	>30	>30	>30	22	18	15	13	9	6	4	3
180000	>30	>30	>30	>30	>30	>30	>30	>30	>30	>30	>30	>30	>30	22	18	16	9	7	4	3
190000	>30	>30	>30	>30	>30	>30	>30	>30	>30	>30	>30	>30	>30	>30	22	18	10	8	5	3
200000	>30	>30	>30	>30	>30	>30	>30	>30	>30	>30	>30	>30	>30	>30	>30	22	12	8	5	4
225000	>30	>30	>30	>30	>30	>30	>30	>30	>30	>30	>30	>30	>30	>30	>30	>30	16	10	6	4
250000	>30	>30	>30	>30	>30	>30	>30	>30	>30	>30	>30	>30	>30	>30	>30	>30	22	13	7	5
275000	>30	>30	>30	>30	>30	>30	>30	>30	>30	>30	>30	>30	>30	>30	>30	>30	>30	16	9	6
300000	>30	>30	>30	>30	>30	>30	>30	>30	>30	>30	>30	>30	>30	>30	>30	>30	>30	22	10	7
350000	>30	>30	>30	>30	>30	>30	>30	>30	>30	>30	>30	>30	>30	>30	>30	>30	>30	>30	14	9
400000	>30	>30	>30	>30	>30	>30	>30	>30	>30	>30	>30	>30	>30	>30	>30	>30	>30	>30	22	12
450000	>30	>30	>30	>30	>30	>30	>30	>30	>30	>30	>30	>30	>30	>30	>30	>30	>30	>30	>30	16
500000	>30	>30	>30	>30	>30	>30	>30	>30	>30	>30	>30	>30	>30	>30	>30	>30	>30	>30	>30	22

MONTHLY SAVINGS, 12.00 %

YEARS	25	50	75	100	200	300	400	500	600	700	800	900
					AMOUNT SAVED							
5	2062	4124	6186	8249	16497	24746	32995	41243	49492	57740	65989	74238
10	5808	11617	17425	23234	46468	69702	92936	116170	139403	162637	185871	209105
15	12614	25229	37843	50458	100915	151373	201830	252288	302746	353203	403661	454118
20	24979	49957	74936	99915	199830	299744	399659	499574	599489	699404	799318	899233
25	47441	94882	142323	189764	379527	569291	759054	948818	1138581	1328345	1518108	1707872
30	88248	176496	264744	352991	705983	1058974	1411966	1764957	2117948	2470940	2823931	3176922

MONTHLY WITHDRAWAL, 12.00 %

AMOUNT	500	600	700	800	900	1000	1100	1200	1300	1400	1500	1600	1700	1800	1900	2000	2500	3000	4000	5000
						FULL YEARS TO WITHDRAW														
50000	>30	15	10	8	6	5	5	4	4	3	3	3	2	2	2	1	1	1	1	0
60000	>30	>30	16	11	9	7	6	5	5	4	4	4	3	3	3	2	1	1	1	1
70000	>30	>30	>30	17	12	10	8	7	6	6	5	5	4	4	3	3	2	2	1	1
80000	>30	>30	>30	>30	18	13	10	9	8	7	6	6	5	5	4	4	3	3	2	1
90000	>30	>30	>30	>30	>30	19	14	11	9	8	7	7	6	5	5	4	3	3	2	1
100000	>30	>30	>30	>30	>30	>30	20	15	12	10	9	8	7	6	6	5	4	3	2	1
110000	>30	>30	>30	>30	>30	>30	>30	20	15	12	11	9	8	7	7	6	4	3	2	2
120000	>30	>30	>30	>30	>30	>30	>30	>30	21	16	13	11	10	9	8	7	5	4	3	2
130000	>30	>30	>30	>30	>30	>30	>30	>30	22	16	14	12	10	9	8	6	4	3	2	2
140000	>30	>30	>30	>30	>30	>30	>30	>30	>30	22	17	14	12	11	10	6	5	3	2	2
150000	>30	>30	>30	>30	>30	>30	>30	>30	>30	>30	23	18	15	13	11	7	5	4	3	3
160000	>30	>30	>30	>30	>30	>30	>30	>30	>30	>30	>30	23	18	15	13	8	6	4	3	3
170000	>30	>30	>30	>30	>30	>30	>30	>30	>30	>30	>30	>30	24	18	15	9	7	4	3	3
180000	>30	>30	>30	>30	>30	>30	>30	>30	>30	>30	>30	>30	>30	24	19	10	7	5	3	3
190000	>30	>30	>30	>30	>30	>30	>30	>30	>30	>30	>30	>30	>30	>30	25	12	8	5	4	3
200000	>30	>30	>30	>30	>30	>30	>30	>30	>30	>30	>30	>30	>30	>30	>30	13	9	5	4	3
225000	>30	>30	>30	>30	>30	>30	>30	>30	>30	>30	>30	>30	>30	>30	>30	19	11	7	5	4
250000	>30	>30	>30	>30	>30	>30	>30	>30	>30	>30	>30	>30	>30	>30	>30	>30	15	8	6	5
275000	>30	>30	>30	>30	>30	>30	>30	>30	>30	>30	>30	>30	>30	>30	>30	>30	20	9	6	5
300000	>30	>30	>30	>30	>30	>30	>30	>30	>30	>30	>30	>30	>30	>30	>30	>30	>30	11	7	6
350000	>30	>30	>30	>30	>30	>30	>30	>30	>30	>30	>30	>30	>30	>30	>30	>30	>30	17	10	7
400000	>30	>30	>30	>30	>30	>30	>30	>30	>30	>30	>30	>30	>30	>30	>30	>30	>30	>30	13	9
450000	>30	>30	>30	>30	>30	>30	>30	>30	>30	>30	>30	>30	>30	>30	>30	>30	>30	>30	19	13
500000	>30	>30	>30	>30	>30	>30	>30	>30	>30	>30	>30	>30	>30	>30	>30	>30	>30	>30	>30	>30

6000	7200	8400	9600	10800	12000	13200	14400	15600	16800	18000	19200	20400	21600	22800	24000	30000	36000	48000	60000

>30 = monthly withdrawal for more than 30 years   **ANNUAL WITHDRAWAL**

TABLE **18**

Installment Loan Payments

Interest Rates: 0, 1, 2, 3%;
4 to 19% by .25%;
20, 25, 30%.

Terms: 1 to 30 years, each year.

Payments: Monthly, semimonthly, biweekly, weekly.

This table shows the payment to amortize a loan of $100 over the term. Payments, which include interest and principal, are shown for monthly, semimonthly, biweekly, and weekly periods: 12, 24, 26, and 52 payments per year.

Example: The monthly payment for an 8%, 10 year loan is 1.213276%. The payment for a $50,000 loan is $606.64. The payment is made 12 times per year.

The semimonthly payment for an 8%, 10 year loan is .605980%. The payment for a $50,000 loan is $303.00. The payment is made 24 times per year.

The biweekly payment for an 8%, 10 year loan is .559320%. The payment for a $50,000 loan is $279.67. The payment is made 26 times per year.

The weekly payment for an 8%, 10 year loan is .279520%. The payment for a $50,000 loan is $139.77. The payment is made 52 times per year.

Finance Charge. The finance charge can be computed from the payment by multiplying the payment by the term and subtracting the amount of loan. If there are no amounts deducted from the loan that could be considered as additional finance charge, then the rate in the index is the Annual Percentage Rate (APR).

Example: The weekly payment for a loan of $50,000 at 8% for 10 years is $139.77.

The note is:
$$139.77 \times 520 = 72,680.40.$$
The finance charge is:
$$72,680.40 - 50,000 = 22,680.40.$$

The APR is 8%.

Description: This table shows the payment to amortize a loan of $ 100 over the term. The payment, including interest and principal, is made monthly.

Example: The payment for an 8% 10 year loan is 1.213276 %. The payment of interest and principal for a $50,000 loan is $ 606.65. The payment is made 12 times per year.

RATE	1 yr	2 yr	3 yr	4 yr	5 yr	6 yr	7 yr	8 yr	9 yr	10 yr
0.00	8.333333	4.166667	2.777778	2.083333	1.666667	1.388889	1.190476	1.041667	.925926	.833333
1.00	8.378541	4.210208	2.820810	2.126146	1.709375	1.431551	1.233125	1.084323	.968603	.876041
2.00	8.423887	4.254026	2.864258	2.169512	1.752776	1.475044	1.276744	1.128087	1.012527	.920135
3.00	8.469370	4.298121	2.908121	2.213433	1.796869	1.519368	1.321330	1.172957	1.057694	.965607
4.00	8.514990	4.342492	2.952399	2.257905	1.841652	1.564518	1.366881	1.218928	1.104097	1.012451
4.25	8.526417	4.353628	2.963533	2.269110	1.852956	1.575935	1.378418	1.230591	1.115890	1.024375
4.50	8.537852	4.364781	2.974692	2.280349	1.864302	1.587403	1.390016	1.242323	1.127759	1.036384
4.75	8.549296	4.375951	2.985878	2.291622	1.875691	1.598922	1.401674	1.254124	1.139705	1.048477
5.00	8.560748	4.387139	2.997090	2.302929	1.887123	1.610493	1.413391	1.265992	1.151727	1.060655
5.25	8.572209	4.398344	3.008327	2.314271	1.898598	1.622115	1.425168	1.277928	1.163826	1.072917
5.50	8.583678	4.409566	3.019590	2.325648	1.910116	1.633789	1.437004	1.289932	1.176000	1.085263
5.75	8.595156	4.420805	3.030879	2.337058	1.921677	1.645513	1.448900	1.302004	1.188250	1.097692
6.00	8.606643	4.432061	3.042194	2.348503	1.933280	1.657289	1.460855	1.314143	1.200575	1.110205
6.25	8.618138	4.443334	3.053534	2.359982	1.944926	1.669115	1.472870	1.326350	1.212976	1.122801
6.50	8.629642	4.454625	3.064900	2.371495	1.956615	1.680993	1.484944	1.338623	1.225452	1.135480
6.75	8.641154	4.465933	3.076292	2.383043	1.968346	1.692921	1.497076	1.350964	1.238002	1.148241
7.00	8.652675	4.477258	3.087710	2.394624	1.980120	1.704901	1.509268	1.363372	1.250628	1.161085
7.25	8.664204	4.488600	3.099153	2.406240	1.991936	1.716931	1.521518	1.375846	1.263328	1.174010
7.50	8.675742	4.499959	3.110622	2.417890	2.003795	1.729011	1.533828	1.388387	1.276102	1.187018
7.75	8.687288	4.511336	3.122116	2.429574	2.015696	1.741142	1.546195	1.400994	1.288950	1.200106
8.00	8.698843	4.522729	3.133637	2.441292	2.027639	1.753324	1.558621	1.413668	1.301871	1.213276
8.25	8.710406	4.534140	3.145182	2.453044	2.039625	1.765556	1.571106	1.426407	1.314867	1.226526
8.50	8.721978	4.545567	3.156754	2.464830	2.051653	1.777838	1.583649	1.439213	1.327935	1.239857
8.75	8.733559	4.557012	3.168351	2.476650	2.063723	1.790171	1.596249	1.452084	1.341077	1.253268
9.00	8.745148	4.568474	3.179973	2.488504	2.075836	1.802554	1.608908	1.465020	1.354291	1.266758
9.25	8.756745	4.579953	3.191621	2.500392	2.087990	1.814986	1.621624	1.478022	1.367577	1.280327
9.50	8.768351	4.591449	3.203295	2.512314	2.100186	1.827469	1.634398	1.491089	1.380936	1.293976
9.75	8.779966	4.602962	3.214994	2.524269	2.112424	1.840002	1.647230	1.504220	1.394367	1.307702
10.00	8.791589	4.614493	3.226719	2.536258	2.124704	1.852584	1.660118	1.517416	1.407869	1.321507
10.25	8.803220	4.626040	3.238469	2.548281	2.137026	1.865216	1.673064	1.530677	1.421442	1.335390
10.50	8.814860	4.637604	3.250244	2.560338	2.149390	1.877897	1.686067	1.544002	1.435086	1.349350
10.75	8.826509	4.649185	3.262045	2.572428	2.161795	1.890628	1.699127	1.557390	1.448801	1.363387
11.00	8.838166	4.660784	3.273872	2.584552	2.174242	1.903408	1.712244	1.570843	1.462586	1.377500
11.25	8.849831	4.672399	3.285723	2.596710	2.186731	1.916237	1.725417	1.584358	1.476441	1.391689
11.50	8.861505	4.684032	3.297601	2.608901	2.199261	1.929116	1.738646	1.597937	1.490366	1.405954
11.75	8.873188	4.695681	3.309503	2.621125	2.211832	1.942043	1.751932	1.611579	1.504360	1.420295
12.00	8.884879	4.707347	3.321431	2.633384	2.224445	1.955019	1.765273	1.625284	1.518423	1.434709
12.25	8.896578	4.719031	3.333384	2.645675	2.237099	1.968044	1.778671	1.639051	1.532555	1.449199
12.50	8.908286	4.730731	3.345363	2.658000	2.249794	1.981118	1.792124	1.652881	1.546755	1.463762
12.75	8.920003	4.742448	3.357366	2.670358	2.262530	1.994240	1.805632	1.666772	1.561023	1.478398
13.00	8.931728	4.754182	3.369395	2.682750	2.275307	2.007411	1.819196	1.680726	1.575359	1.493107
13.25	8.943461	4.765933	3.381449	2.695174	2.288126	2.020629	1.832815	1.694740	1.589762	1.507889
13.50	8.955203	4.777701	3.393529	2.707632	2.300985	2.033896	1.846489	1.708816	1.604231	1.522743
13.75	8.966953	4.789486	3.405633	2.720123	2.313884	2.047211	1.860218	1.722953	1.618768	1.537668
14.00	8.978712	4.801288	3.417763	2.732648	2.326825	2.060574	1.874001	1.737150	1.633370	1.552664
14.25	8.990479	4.813107	3.429918	2.745205	2.339806	2.073985	1.887839	1.751408	1.648038	1.567731
14.50	9.002255	4.824943	3.442098	2.757795	2.352828	2.087443	1.901730	1.765726	1.662772	1.582868
14.75	9.014039	4.836795	3.454303	2.770419	2.365890	2.100948	1.915676	1.780103	1.677571	1.598074
15.00	9.025831	4.848665	3.466533	2.783075	2.378993	2.114501	1.929675	1.794541	1.692434	1.613350
15.25	9.037632	4.860551	3.478788	2.795764	2.392136	2.128102	1.943728	1.809037	1.707361	1.628693
15.50	9.049442	4.872454	3.491068	2.808486	2.405319	2.141749	1.957835	1.823592	1.722353	1.644105
15.75	9.061259	4.884374	3.503373	2.821241	2.418542	2.155443	1.971994	1.838206	1.737407	1.659585
16.00	9.073086	4.896311	3.515703	2.834028	2.431806	2.169184	1.986206	1.852879	1.752525	1.675131
16.25	9.084921	4.908265	3.528058	2.846848	2.445109	2.182972	2.000471	1.867609	1.767706	1.690744
16.50	9.096764	4.920235	3.540438	2.859701	2.458452	2.196806	2.014789	1.882397	1.782948	1.706423
16.75	9.108615	4.932222	3.552843	2.872586	2.471835	2.210686	2.029159	1.897243	1.798253	1.722167
17.00	9.120475	4.944226	3.565273	2.885504	2.485258	2.224613	2.043580	1.912145	1.813619	1.737977
17.25	9.132344	4.956247	3.577727	2.898455	2.498720	2.238586	2.058054	1.927105	1.829046	1.753850
17.50	9.144220	4.968285	3.590207	2.911437	2.512221	2.252605	2.072579	1.942121	1.844533	1.769788
17.75	9.156106	4.980339	3.602711	2.924453	2.525762	2.266669	2.087156	1.957193	1.860081	1.785788
18.00	9.167999	4.992410	3.615240	2.937500	2.539343	2.280779	2.101784	1.972321	1.875689	1.801852
18.25	9.179901	5.004498	3.627793	2.950580	2.552962	2.294935	2.116463	1.987505	1.891356	1.817978
18.50	9.191812	5.016603	3.640371	2.963692	2.566621	2.309135	2.131192	2.002744	1.907082	1.834165
18.75	9.203731	5.028724	3.652974	2.976836	2.580319	2.323381	2.145972	2.018038	1.922866	1.850414
19.00	9.215658	5.040862	3.665602	2.990012	2.594055	2.337672	2.160802	2.033386	1.938708	1.866724
20.00	9.263451	5.089580	3.716358	3.043036	2.649388	2.395283	2.220620	2.095320	2.002650	1.932557
25.00	9.504420	5.337152	3.975983	3.315713	2.935132	2.693718	2.531164	2.417267	2.335220	2.274930
30.00	9.748713	5.591282	4.245158	3.600599	3.235340	3.008417	2.859298	2.757662	2.686653	2.636179

INSTALLMENT LOAN PAYMENTS

MONTHLY PAYMENT

Description: This table shows the payment to amortize a loan of $ 100 over the term. The payment, including interest and principal, is made monthly.

Example: The payment for an 8% 20 year loan is .836440 %. The payment of interest and principal for a $50,000 loan is $ 418.23. The payment is made 12 times per year.

RATE	11 yr	12 yr	13 yr	14 yr	15 yr	16 yr	17 yr	18 yr	19 yr	20 yr
0.00	.757576	.694444	.641026	.595238	.555556	.520833	.490196	.462963	.438596	.416667
1.00	.800321	.737233	.683862	.638124	.598495	.563827	.533246	.506071	.481764	.459894
2.00	.844591	.781684	.728497	.682948	.643509	.609034	.578647	.551667	.527556	.505883
3.00	.890376	.827787	.774921	.729695	.690582	.656434	.626375	.599723	.575941	.554598
4.00	.937667	.875528	.823116	.778346	.739688	.705996	.676393	.650198	.626870	.605980
4.25	.949723	.887718	.835439	.790802	.752278	.718720	.689251	.663188	.639993	.619234
4.50	.961873	.900008	.847871	.803376	.764993	.731576	.702247	.676325	.653269	.632649
4.75	.974115	.912399	.860411	.816065	.777832	.744563	.715383	.689607	.666698	.646224
5.00	.986449	.924890	.873060	.828871	.790794	.757681	.728655	.703034	.680278	.659956
5.25	.998875	.937482	.885816	.841791	.803878	.770928	.742064	.716604	.694008	.673844
5.50	1.011393	.950172	.898679	.854826	.817083	.784304	.755609	.730316	.707886	.687887
5.75	1.024003	.962962	.911648	.867974	.830410	.797807	.769288	.744170	.721912	.702084
6.00	1.036703	.975850	.924723	.881236	.843857	.811438	.783101	.758162	.736083	.716431
6.25	1.049495	.988837	.937904	.894610	.857423	.825194	.797045	.772293	.750398	.730928
6.50	1.062377	1.001921	.951190	.908096	.871107	.839075	.811121	.786561	.764856	.745573
6.75	1.075349	1.015103	.964580	.921693	.884909	.853080	.825327	.800965	.779455	.760364
7.00	1.088410	1.028381	.978074	.935401	.898828	.867208	.839661	.815502	.794192	.775299
7.25	1.101561	1.041756	.991671	.949218	.912863	.881458	.854122	.830172	.809068	.790376
7.50	1.114801	1.055226	1.005370	.963143	.927012	.895828	.868709	.844973	.824079	.805593
7.75	1.128129	1.068792	1.019172	.977177	.941276	.910317	.883421	.859904	.839224	.820949
8.00	1.141545	1.082453	1.033074	.991318	.955652	.924925	.898257	.874963	.854501	.836440
8.25	1.155048	1.096207	1.047077	1.005566	.970140	.939650	.913214	.890148	.869909	.852066
8.50	1.168639	1.110056	1.061179	1.019919	.984740	.954491	.928292	.905457	.885446	.867823
8.75	1.182317	1.123997	1.075381	1.034376	.999449	.969447	.943489	.920890	.901109	.883711
9.00	1.196080	1.138031	1.089681	1.048938	1.014267	.984516	.958804	.936445	.916897	.899726
9.25	1.209930	1.152156	1.104078	1.063602	1.029192	.999697	.974235	.952119	.932808	.915867
9.50	1.223865	1.166373	1.118572	1.078368	1.044225	1.014990	.989781	.967911	.948840	.932131
9.75	1.237884	1.180681	1.133163	1.093235	1.059363	1.030392	1.005440	.983820	.964991	.948517
10.00	1.251988	1.195078	1.147848	1.108203	1.074605	1.045902	1.021210	.999844	.981259	.965022
10.25	1.266175	1.209565	1.162628	1.123269	1.089951	1.061519	1.037091	1.015980	.997642	.981643
10.50	1.280446	1.224141	1.177502	1.138434	1.105399	1.077242	1.053081	1.032228	1.014139	.998380
10.75	1.294799	1.238804	1.192469	1.153696	1.120948	1.093070	1.069178	1.048585	1.030747	1.015229
11.00	1.309235	1.253555	1.207527	1.169054	1.136597	1.109000	1.085381	1.065050	1.047464	1.032188
11.25	1.323752	1.268393	1.222677	1.184508	1.152345	1.125033	1.101687	1.081620	1.064288	1.049256
11.50	1.338350	1.283317	1.237918	1.200055	1.168190	1.141165	1.118096	1.098295	1.081218	1.066430
11.75	1.353029	1.298326	1.253248	1.215696	1.184131	1.157396	1.134606	1.115073	1.098251	1.083707
12.00	1.367788	1.313419	1.268666	1.231430	1.200168	1.173725	1.151216	1.131950	1.115386	1.101086
12.25	1.382626	1.328597	1.284173	1.247254	1.216299	1.190150	1.167923	1.148927	1.132620	1.118565
12.50	1.397543	1.343857	1.299766	1.263168	1.232522	1.206670	1.184726	1.166001	1.149951	1.136141
12.75	1.412538	1.359200	1.315446	1.279172	1.248837	1.223283	1.201624	1.183170	1.167378	1.153812
13.00	1.427611	1.374625	1.331210	1.295264	1.265242	1.239988	1.218614	1.200433	1.184898	1.171576
13.25	1.442761	1.390131	1.347059	1.311442	1.281736	1.256783	1.235697	1.217787	1.202510	1.189431
13.50	1.457987	1.405717	1.362992	1.327707	1.298319	1.273668	1.252869	1.235231	1.220211	1.207375
13.75	1.473289	1.421383	1.379007	1.344056	1.314987	1.290640	1.270129	1.252764	1.238001	1.225405
14.00	1.488666	1.437127	1.395103	1.360490	1.331741	1.307699	1.287476	1.270383	1.255876	1.243521
14.25	1.504118	1.452949	1.411280	1.377006	1.348580	1.324843	1.304908	1.288087	1.273835	1.261719
14.50	1.519644	1.468849	1.427538	1.393603	1.365501	1.342070	1.322424	1.305874	1.291876	1.279998
14.75	1.535243	1.484825	1.443874	1.410282	1.382504	1.359379	1.340022	1.323743	1.309998	1.298355
15.00	1.550915	1.500877	1.460287	1.427040	1.399587	1.376770	1.357700	1.341691	1.328198	1.316790
15.25	1.566659	1.517003	1.476778	1.443876	1.416750	1.394239	1.375458	1.359717	1.346475	1.335299
15.50	1.582474	1.533204	1.493346	1.460790	1.433990	1.411787	1.393292	1.377819	1.364826	1.353881
15.75	1.598361	1.549478	1.509988	1.477780	1.451308	1.429411	1.411203	1.395997	1.383250	1.372534
16.00	1.614317	1.565825	1.526704	1.494845	1.468701	1.447110	1.429188	1.414247	1.401746	1.391256
16.25	1.630343	1.582244	1.543494	1.511985	1.486168	1.464884	1.447246	1.432569	1.420312	1.410046
16.50	1.646438	1.598734	1.560357	1.529198	1.503709	1.482730	1.465376	1.450961	1.438945	1.428901
16.75	1.662601	1.615294	1.577291	1.546482	1.521321	1.500647	1.483575	1.469421	1.457644	1.447820
17.00	1.678832	1.631923	1.594295	1.563838	1.539004	1.518634	1.501843	1.487947	1.476409	1.466801
17.25	1.695130	1.648621	1.611369	1.581264	1.556757	1.536690	1.520179	1.506539	1.495236	1.485842
17.50	1.711494	1.665387	1.628512	1.598759	1.574578	1.554813	1.538579	1.525195	1.514124	1.504942
17.75	1.727923	1.682220	1.645723	1.616321	1.592467	1.573002	1.557045	1.543913	1.533072	1.524099
18.00	1.744418	1.699120	1.663001	1.633950	1.610421	1.591256	1.575573	1.562691	1.552078	1.543312
18.25	1.760977	1.716084	1.680345	1.651645	1.628440	1.609573	1.594163	1.581529	1.571141	1.562578
18.50	1.777599	1.733114	1.697753	1.669405	1.646523	1.627952	1.612812	1.600425	1.590259	1.581897
18.75	1.794285	1.750208	1.715226	1.687228	1.664669	1.646393	1.631521	1.619377	1.609431	1.601266
19.00	1.811033	1.767365	1.732762	1.705115	1.682876	1.664893	1.650288	1.638384	1.628655	1.620685
20.00	1.878634	1.836609	1.803522	1.777265	1.756297	1.739466	1.725903	1.714936	1.706046	1.698825
25.00	2.229976	2.196093	2.170344	2.150655	2.135529	2.123865	2.114846	2.107858	2.102433	2.098216
30.00	2.599862	2.573500	2.554242	2.540109	2.529701	2.522017	2.516334	2.512125	2.509005	2.506689

INSTALLMENT LOAN PAYMENTS

Description: This table shows the payment to amortize a loan of $ 100 over the term. The payment, including interest and principal, is made monthly.

Example: The payment for an 8% 30 year loan is .733765 %. The payment of interest and principal for a $50,000 loan is $ 366.89. The payment is made 12 times per year.

RATE	21 yr	22 yr	23 yr	24 yr	25 yr	26 yr	27 yr	28 yr	29 yr	30 yr
0.00	.396825	.378788	.362319	.347222	.333333	.320513	.308642	.297619	.287356	.277778
1.00	.440114	.422138	.405732	.390698	.376872	.364116	.352309	.341351	.331153	.321640
2.00	.486301	.468523	.452315	.437481	.423854	.411297	.399690	.388931	.378933	.369619
3.00	.535344	.517896	.502016	.487510	.474211	.461981	.450701	.440267	.430594	.421604
4.00	.587179	.570181	.554750	.540691	.527837	.516049	.505208	.495212	.485973	.477415
4.25	.600564	.583696	.568395	.554464	.541738	.530077	.519362	.509491	.500376	.491940
4.50	.614117	.597386	.582221	.568425	.555832	.544304	.533720	.523980	.514993	.506685
4.75	.627836	.611248	.596225	.582570	.570117	.558727	.548281	.538675	.529823	.521647
5.00	.641719	.625281	.610406	.596898	.584590	.573344	.563039	.553574	.544860	.536822
5.25	.655764	.639482	.624761	.611405	.599248	.588150	.577992	.568672	.560101	.552204
5.50	.669970	.653849	.639288	.626089	.614087	.603143	.593137	.583966	.575542	.567789
5.75	.684335	.668381	.653984	.640948	.629106	.618320	.608469	.599451	.591178	.583573
6.00	.698857	.683074	.668847	.655978	.644301	.633677	.623985	.615124	.607005	.599551
6.25	.713534	.697928	.683875	.671177	.659669	.649211	.639682	.630980	.623018	.615717
6.50	.728363	.712939	.699065	.686543	.675207	.664918	.655555	.647016	.639213	.632068
6.75	.743343	.728105	.714414	.702071	.690912	.680795	.671601	.663227	.655585	.648598
7.00	.758472	.743424	.729919	.717760	.706779	.696838	.687815	.679609	.672130	.665302
7.25	.773747	.758893	.745579	.733605	.722807	.713043	.704194	.696157	.688843	.682176
7.50	.789166	.774510	.761389	.749605	.738991	.729407	.720734	.712868	.705720	.699215
7.75	.804727	.790273	.777348	.765756	.755329	.745927	.737430	.729736	.722756	.716412
8.00	.820428	.806178	.793453	.782054	.771816	.762598	.754280	.746759	.739946	.733765
8.25	.836266	.822223	.809700	.798497	.788450	.779417	.771278	.763930	.757286	.751267
8.50	.852239	.838406	.826087	.815082	.805227	.796380	.788421	.781247	.774770	.768913
8.75	.868345	.854724	.842610	.831806	.822144	.813483	.805705	.798705	.792396	.786700
9.00	.884581	.871174	.859268	.848664	.839196	.830723	.823125	.816300	.810158	.804623
9.25	.900945	.887754	.876057	.865655	.856382	.848096	.840679	.834027	.828051	.822675
9.50	.917434	.904461	.892974	.882775	.873697	.865599	.858361	.851882	.846071	.840854
9.75	.934047	.921293	.910017	.900020	.891137	.883227	.876169	.869861	.864215	.859154
10.00	.950780	.938246	.927182	.917389	.908701	.900977	.894098	.887960	.882477	.877572
10.25	.967631	.955318	.944466	.934877	.926383	.918846	.912144	.906176	.900854	.896101
10.50	.984599	.972507	.961867	.952481	.944182	.936829	.930304	.924504	.919341	.914739
10.75	1.001679	.989810	.979382	.970199	.962093	.954924	.948574	.942940	.937934	.933481
11.00	1.018871	1.007223	.997008	.988027	.980113	.973127	.966950	.961480	.956629	.952323
11.25	1.036171	1.024746	1.014742	1.005962	.998240	.991435	.985429	.980121	.975423	.971261
11.50	1.053578	1.042374	1.032581	1.024002	1.016469	1.009844	1.004008	.998859	.994312	.990291
11.75	1.071088	1.060106	1.050523	1.042042	1.034798	1.028351	1.022682	1.017691	1.013292	1.009410
12.00	1.088700	1.077938	1.068565	1.060382	1.053224	1.046952	1.041449	1.036613	1.032359	1.028613
12.25	1.106410	1.095869	1.086704	1.078717	1.071744	1.065646	1.060305	1.055621	1.051510	1.047896
12.50	1.124218	1.113896	1.104937	1.097144	1.090354	1.084427	1.079247	1.074713	1.070741	1.067258
12.75	1.142120	1.132016	1.123262	1.115662	1.109052	1.103294	1.098272	1.093885	1.090049	1.086693
13.00	1.160114	1.150226	1.141676	1.134267	1.127835	1.122244	1.117376	1.113133	1.109432	1.106200
13.25	1.178198	1.168525	1.160177	1.152956	1.146700	1.141273	1.136557	1.132456	1.128885	1.125774
13.50	1.196370	1.186911	1.178761	1.171727	1.165645	1.160378	1.155812	1.151849	1.148406	1.145412
13.75	1.214627	1.205379	1.197428	1.190577	1.184666	1.179558	1.175138	1.171310	1.167992	1.165113
14.00	1.232967	1.223929	1.216173	1.209504	1.203761	1.198808	1.194532	1.190836	1.187639	1.184872
14.25	1.251388	1.242558	1.234995	1.228505	1.222928	1.218127	1.213992	1.210425	1.207346	1.204687
14.50	1.269889	1.261264	1.253892	1.247578	1.242163	1.237512	1.233514	1.230074	1.227110	1.224556
14.75	1.288465	1.280045	1.272860	1.266720	1.261465	1.256961	1.253097	1.249779	1.246928	1.244476
15.00	1.307117	1.298897	1.291899	1.285929	1.280831	1.276470	1.272738	1.269540	1.266797	1.264444
15.25	1.325841	1.317820	1.311004	1.305203	1.300258	1.296039	1.292434	1.289352	1.286716	1.284459
15.50	1.344636	1.336812	1.330176	1.324539	1.319745	1.315663	1.312183	1.309215	1.306681	1.304517
15.75	1.363500	1.355869	1.349410	1.343936	1.339290	1.335342	1.331984	1.329126	1.326692	1.324617
16.00	1.382430	1.374990	1.368706	1.363391	1.358889	1.355072	1.351833	1.349082	1.346745	1.344757
16.25	1.401426	1.394173	1.388061	1.382901	1.378541	1.374853	1.371729	1.369083	1.366838	1.364935
16.50	1.420484	1.413417	1.407473	1.402466	1.398245	1.394681	1.391670	1.389124	1.386971	1.385148
16.75	1.439603	1.432719	1.426940	1.422084	1.417997	1.414555	1.411654	1.409206	1.407140	1.405396
17.00	1.458782	1.452077	1.446461	1.441751	1.437797	1.434473	1.431678	1.429326	1.427344	1.425675
17.25	1.478018	1.471489	1.466033	1.461467	1.457641	1.454434	1.451742	1.449481	1.447582	1.445986
17.50	1.497310	1.490955	1.485655	1.481229	1.477530	1.474434	1.471843	1.469672	1.467852	1.466325
17.75	1.516656	1.510472	1.505325	1.501037	1.497460	1.494474	1.491980	1.489895	1.488151	1.486692
18.00	1.536055	1.530038	1.525041	1.520887	1.517430	1.514551	1.512151	1.510149	1.508479	1.507085
18.25	1.555504	1.549652	1.544802	1.540779	1.537439	1.534663	1.532354	1.530433	1.528835	1.527503
18.50	1.575003	1.569312	1.564606	1.560711	1.557484	1.554809	1.552589	1.550746	1.549216	1.547945
18.75	1.594550	1.589016	1.584452	1.580682	1.577565	1.574987	1.572853	1.571086	1.569622	1.568408
19.00	1.614143	1.608764	1.604337	1.600689	1.597680	1.595197	1.593146	1.591451	1.590051	1.588892
20.00	1.692948	1.688158	1.684251	1.681060	1.678452	1.676319	1.674574	1.673146	1.671977	1.671019
25.00	2.094936	2.092382	2.090391	2.088840	2.087631	2.086687	2.085951	2.085377	2.084928	2.084579
30.00	2.504970	2.503694	2.502746	2.502041	2.501517	2.501128	2.500839	2.500623	2.500464	2.500345

INSTALLMENT LOAN PAYMENTS

SEMIMONTHLY PAYMENT

Description: This table shows the payment to amortize a loan of $ 100 over the term. The payment, including interest and principal, is made twice a monthly.

Example: The payment for an 8% 10 year loan is .605980 %. The payment of interest and principal for a $50,000 loan is $ 303.00. The payment is made 24 times per year.

RATE	1 yr	2 yr	3 yr	4 yr	5 yr	6 yr	7 yr	8 yr	9 yr	10 yr
0.00	4.166667	2.083333	1.388889	1.041667	.833333	.694444	.595238	.520833	.462963	.416667
1.00	4.188403	2.104670	1.410116	1.062856	.854514	.715631	.616438	.542053	.484205	.437934
2.00	4.210208	2.126146	1.431551	1.084323	.876041	.737233	.638124	.563827	.506071	.459894
3.00	4.232083	2.147760	1.453194	1.106066	.897915	.759251	.660295	.586155	.528560	.482545
4.00	4.254026	2.169512	1.475044	1.128087	.920135	.781684	.682948	.609034	.551667	.505883
4.25	4.259523	2.174972	1.480539	1.133636	.925743	.787356	.688687	.614839	.557540	.511825
4.50	4.265024	2.180441	1.486047	1.139201	.931374	.793055	.694455	.620679	.563452	.517808
4.75	4.270530	2.185918	1.491568	1.144784	.937026	.798779	.700254	.626553	.569402	.523834
5.00	4.276039	2.191403	1.497102	1.150384	.942699	.804529	.706082	.632461	.575390	.529903
5.25	4.281553	2.196898	1.502649	1.156002	.948394	.810305	.711941	.638403	.581416	.536014
5.50	4.287072	2.202401	1.508209	1.161636	.954110	.816107	.717829	.644379	.587481	.542166
5.75	4.292594	2.207912	1.513782	1.167288	.959848	.821934	.723747	.650390	.593583	.548361
6.00	4.298121	2.213433	1.519368	1.172957	.965607	.827787	.729695	.656434	.599723	.554598
6.25	4.303652	2.218962	1.524966	1.178643	.971388	.833665	.735673	.662511	.605901	.560876
6.50	4.309188	2.224499	1.530578	1.184347	.977190	.839569	.741681	.668623	.612117	.567196
6.75	4.314728	2.230045	1.536202	1.190067	.983014	.845499	.747718	.674768	.618371	.573557
7.00	4.320272	2.235600	1.541840	1.195805	.988859	.851454	.753784	.680947	.624661	.579960
7.25	4.325821	2.241164	1.547490	1.201560	.994725	.857434	.759880	.687159	.630990	.586404
7.50	4.331374	2.246736	1.553153	1.207332	1.000612	.863440	.766006	.693405	.637355	.592888
7.75	4.336931	2.252316	1.558829	1.213121	1.006521	.869472	.772161	.699684	.643758	.599414
8.00	4.342492	2.257905	1.564518	1.218928	1.012451	.875528	.778346	.705996	.650198	.605980
8.25	4.348058	2.263503	1.570220	1.224751	1.018403	.881610	.784559	.712342	.656674	.612587
8.50	4.353628	2.269110	1.575935	1.230591	1.024375	.887718	.790802	.718720	.663188	.619234
8.75	4.359202	2.274725	1.581663	1.236449	1.030369	.893850	.797075	.725132	.669738	.625922
9.00	4.364781	2.280349	1.587403	1.242323	1.036384	.900008	.803376	.731576	.676325	.632649
9.25	4.370364	2.285981	1.593156	1.248215	1.042420	.906191	.809706	.738053	.682948	.639417
9.50	4.375951	2.291622	1.598922	1.254124	1.048477	.912399	.816065	.744563	.689607	.646224
9.75	4.381543	2.297271	1.604701	1.260049	1.054556	.918632	.822454	.751106	.696302	.653070
10.00	4.387139	2.302929	1.610493	1.265992	1.060655	.924890	.828871	.757681	.703034	.659956
10.25	4.392739	2.308596	1.616298	1.271952	1.066776	.931174	.835317	.764288	.709801	.666881
10.50	4.398344	2.314271	1.622115	1.277928	1.072917	.937482	.841791	.770928	.716604	.673844
10.75	4.403953	2.319955	1.627946	1.283922	1.079079	.943814	.848294	.777600	.723443	.680847
11.00	4.409566	2.325648	1.633789	1.289932	1.085263	.950172	.854826	.784304	.730316	.687887
11.25	4.415183	2.331349	1.639645	1.295960	1.091467	.956555	.861386	.791040	.737225	.694966
11.50	4.420805	2.337058	1.645513	1.302004	1.097692	.962962	.867974	.797807	.744170	.702084
11.75	4.426431	2.342776	1.651395	1.308065	1.103938	.969394	.874591	.804607	.751149	.709238
12.00	4.432061	2.348503	1.657289	1.314143	1.110205	.975850	.881236	.811438	.758162	.716431
12.25	4.437696	2.354238	1.663196	1.320238	1.116493	.982331	.887909	.818300	.765211	.723661
12.50	4.443334	2.359982	1.669115	1.326350	1.122801	.988837	.894610	.825194	.772293	.730928
12.75	4.448978	2.365734	1.675048	1.332478	1.129130	.995367	.901339	.832119	.779410	.738232
13.00	4.454625	2.371495	1.680993	1.338623	1.135480	1.001921	.908096	.839075	.786561	.745573
13.25	4.460277	2.377265	1.686951	1.344785	1.141850	1.008500	.914881	.846062	.793746	.752950
13.50	4.465933	2.383043	1.692921	1.350964	1.148241	1.015103	.921693	.853080	.800965	.760364
13.75	4.471593	2.388829	1.698905	1.357160	1.154653	1.021730	.928533	.860129	.808217	.767814
14.00	4.477258	2.394624	1.704901	1.363372	1.161085	1.028381	.935401	.867208	.815502	.775299
14.25	4.482927	2.400428	1.710909	1.369601	1.167537	1.035056	.942295	.874318	.822821	.782820
14.50	4.488600	2.406240	1.716931	1.375846	1.174010	1.041756	.949218	.881458	.830172	.790376
14.75	4.494277	2.412061	1.722965	1.382108	1.180504	1.048479	.956167	.888628	.837556	.797967
15.00	4.499959	2.417890	1.729011	1.388387	1.187018	1.055226	.963143	.895828	.844963	.805593
15.25	4.505645	2.423728	1.735071	1.394682	1.193552	1.061997	.970147	.903058	.852423	.813254
15.50	4.511336	2.429574	1.741142	1.400994	1.200106	1.068792	.977177	.910317	.859904	.820949
15.75	4.517030	2.435429	1.747227	1.407323	1.206681	1.075611	.984234	.917606	.867417	.828677
16.00	4.522729	2.441292	1.753324	1.413668	1.213276	1.082453	.991318	.924925	.874963	.836440
16.25	4.528432	2.447164	1.759434	1.420029	1.219891	1.089318	.998429	.932273	.882539	.844236
16.50	4.534140	2.453044	1.765556	1.426407	1.226526	1.096207	1.005566	.939650	.890148	.852066
16.75	4.539851	2.458933	1.771691	1.432802	1.233182	1.103120	1.012729	.947056	.897787	.859928
17.00	4.545567	2.464830	1.777838	1.439213	1.239857	1.110056	1.019919	.954491	.905457	.867823
17.25	4.551288	2.470736	1.783998	1.445640	1.246552	1.117015	1.027134	.961955	.913159	.875751
17.50	4.557012	2.476650	1.790171	1.452084	1.253268	1.123997	1.034376	.969447	.920890	.883711
17.75	4.562741	2.482573	1.796356	1.458544	1.260003	1.131002	1.041644	.976967	.928653	.891702
18.00	4.568474	2.488504	1.802554	1.465020	1.266758	1.138031	1.048938	.984516	.936445	.899726
18.25	4.574212	2.494444	1.808764	1.471513	1.273533	1.145082	1.056257	.992093	.944267	.907781
18.50	4.579953	2.500392	1.814986	1.478022	1.280327	1.152156	1.063602	.999697	.952119	.915867
18.75	4.585699	2.506349	1.821222	1.484547	1.287142	1.159253	1.070972	1.007330	.960001	.923984
19.00	4.591449	2.512314	1.827469	1.491089	1.293976	1.166373	1.078368	1.014990	.967911	.932131
20.00	4.614493	2.536258	1.852584	1.517416	1.321507	1.195078	1.108203	1.045902	.999844	.965022
25.00	4.730731	2.658000	1.981118	1.652881	1.463762	1.343857	1.263168	1.206670	1.166001	1.136141
30.00	4.848665	2.783075	2.114501	1.794541	1.613350	1.500877	1.427040	1.376770	1.341691	1.316790

INSTALLMENT LOAN PAYMENTS

Description: This table shows the payment to amortize a loan of $ 100 over the term. The payment, including interest and principal, is made twice a monthly.

Example: The payment for an 8% 20 year loan is .417938 %. The payment of interest and principal for a $50,000 loan is $ 208.98. The payment is made 24 times per year.

RATE	11 yr	12 yr	13 yr	14 yr	15 yr	16 yr	17 yr	18 yr	19 yr	20 yr
0.00	.378788	.347222	.320513	.297619	.277778	.260417	.245098	.231481	.219298	.208333
1.00	.400082	.368544	.341864	.319000	.299190	.281859	.266572	.252988	.240836	.229904
2.00	.422138	.390698	.364116	.341351	.321640	.304409	.289222	.275738	.263668	.252856
3.00	.444954	.413679	.387263	.364665	.345120	.328057	.313038	.299721	.287837	.277172
4.00	.468523	.437481	.411297	.388931	.369619	.352788	.338000	.324914	.313261	.302826
4.25	.474533	.443558	.417443	.395146	.375902	.359138	.344418	.331399	.319813	.309444
4.50	.480589	.449687	.423644	.401418	.382246	.365554	.350905	.337957	.326441	.316142
4.75	.486691	.455865	.429899	.407749	.388653	.372036	.357462	.344588	.333146	.322921
5.00	.492840	.462095	.436208	.414138	.395121	.378583	.364087	.351292	.339927	.329778
5.25	.499035	.468374	.442571	.420585	.401651	.385196	.370781	.358067	.346783	.336714
5.50	.505276	.474703	.448988	.427089	.408241	.391872	.377544	.364914	.353714	.343728
5.75	.511563	.481082	.455458	.433650	.414892	.398613	.384373	.371831	.360718	.350818
6.00	.517896	.487510	.461981	.440267	.421604	.405418	.391270	.378819	.367795	.357984
6.25	.524274	.493987	.468558	.446942	.428375	.412285	.398232	.385875	.374945	.365226
6.50	.530697	.500514	.475186	.453672	.435206	.419215	.405261	.393001	.382166	.372541
6.75	.537166	.507089	.481868	.460458	.442096	.426208	.412354	.400194	.389458	.379930
7.00	.543680	.513714	.488601	.467300	.449045	.433262	.419513	.407455	.396820	.387391
7.25	.550238	.520386	.495386	.474196	.456051	.440377	.426735	.414782	.404251	.394923
7.50	.556842	.527106	.502223	.481148	.463116	.447553	.434020	.422174	.411750	.402526
7.75	.563489	.533875	.509111	.488153	.470237	.454788	.441368	.429634	.419316	.410198
8.00	.570181	.540691	.516049	.495212	.477415	.462084	.448778	.437156	.426948	.417938
8.25	.576917	.547554	.523038	.502325	.484650	.469438	.456249	.444742	.434646	.425746
8.50	.583696	.554464	.530077	.509491	.491940	.476850	.463781	.452390	.442409	.433620
8.75	.590520	.561421	.537166	.516709	.499285	.484319	.471372	.460101	.450235	.441559
9.00	.597386	.568425	.544304	.523980	.506685	.491846	.479023	.467872	.458124	.449563
9.25	.604296	.575475	.551491	.531302	.514140	.499430	.486732	.475704	.466075	.457629
9.50	.611248	.582570	.558727	.538675	.521647	.507068	.494499	.483595	.474087	.465758
9.75	.618243	.589711	.566011	.546099	.529208	.514763	.502322	.491544	.482158	.473947
10.00	.625281	.596898	.573344	.553574	.536822	.522511	.510202	.499551	.490288	.482197
10.25	.632360	.604129	.580723	.561098	.544487	.530313	.518137	.507615	.498477	.490505
10.50	.639482	.611405	.588150	.568672	.552204	.538169	.526127	.515735	.506722	.498870
10.75	.646645	.618725	.595623	.576295	.559971	.546077	.534171	.523910	.515023	.507293
11.00	.653849	.626089	.603143	.583966	.567789	.554037	.542267	.532138	.523378	.515770
11.25	.661095	.633497	.610709	.591685	.575656	.562047	.550416	.540420	.531788	.524302
11.50	.668381	.640948	.618320	.599451	.583573	.570109	.558617	.548755	.540251	.532888
11.75	.675707	.648442	.625976	.607264	.591538	.578220	.566868	.557141	.548765	.541525
12.00	.683074	.655978	.633677	.615124	.599551	.586380	.575170	.565577	.557331	.550214
12.25	.690481	.663557	.641422	.623030	.607611	.594588	.583520	.574063	.565946	.558952
12.50	.697928	.671177	.649211	.630980	.615717	.602844	.591919	.582598	.574611	.567740
12.75	.705414	.678839	.657043	.638976	.623870	.611147	.600365	.591181	.583323	.576575
13.00	.712939	.686543	.664918	.647016	.632068	.619496	.608858	.599811	.592083	.585457
13.25	.720503	.694287	.672835	.655100	.640311	.627891	.617397	.608487	.600888	.594385
13.50	.728105	.702071	.680795	.663227	.648598	.636330	.625982	.617208	.609739	.603357
13.75	.735746	.709895	.688796	.671397	.656929	.644814	.634610	.625974	.618634	.612373
14.00	.743424	.717760	.696838	.679609	.665302	.653341	.643283	.634783	.627571	.621431
14.25	.751140	.725663	.704920	.687862	.673719	.661911	.651998	.643635	.636551	.630531
14.50	.758893	.733605	.713043	.696157	.682176	.670523	.660755	.652528	.645573	.639672
14.75	.766684	.741586	.721206	.704492	.690675	.679176	.669553	.661463	.654634	.648852
15.00	.774510	.749605	.729407	.712868	.699215	.687870	.678392	.670437	.663735	.658071
15.25	.782374	.757662	.737648	.721282	.707794	.696604	.687271	.679451	.672875	.667327
15.50	.790273	.765756	.745927	.729736	.716412	.705377	.696188	.688503	.682052	.676620
15.75	.798208	.773887	.754244	.738229	.725069	.714188	.705144	.697593	.691266	.685948
16.00	.806178	.782054	.762598	.746759	.733765	.723038	.714137	.706719	.700516	.695312
16.25	.814183	.790258	.770989	.755326	.742497	.731924	.723167	.715881	.709800	.704709
16.50	.822223	.798497	.779417	.763930	.751267	.740848	.732232	.725079	.719119	.714139
16.75	.830298	.806772	.787881	.772571	.760072	.749807	.741333	.734311	.728471	.723601
17.00	.838406	.815082	.796380	.781247	.768913	.758801	.750469	.743576	.737855	.733094
17.25	.846548	.823427	.804914	.789959	.777790	.767829	.759638	.752874	.747271	.742618
17.50	.854724	.831806	.813483	.798705	.786700	.776892	.768840	.762204	.756718	.752171
17.75	.862933	.840218	.822087	.807486	.795645	.785988	.778074	.771566	.766195	.761752
18.00	.871174	.848664	.830723	.816300	.804623	.795116	.787341	.780957	.775701	.771361
18.25	.879448	.857143	.839394	.825147	.813633	.804276	.796638	.790379	.785235	.780998
18.50	.887754	.865655	.848096	.834027	.822675	.813468	.805965	.799830	.794798	.790661
18.75	.896092	.874199	.856832	.842938	.831749	.822690	.815322	.809309	.804387	.800349
19.00	.904461	.882775	.865599	.851882	.840854	.831942	.824708	.818815	.814002	.810062
20.00	.938246	.917389	.900977	.887960	.877572	.869238	.862527	.857105	.852712	.849146
25.00	1.113896	1.097144	1.084427	1.074713	1.067258	1.061515	1.057080	1.053647	1.050986	1.048919
30.00	1.298897	1.285929	1.276470	1.269540	1.264444	1.260688	1.257916	1.255865	1.254348	1.253224

INSTALLMENT LOAN PAYMENTS

SEMIMONTHLY PAYMENT

Description: This table shows the payment to amortize a loan of $ 100 over the term. The payment, including interest and principal, is made twice a monthly.

Example: The payment for an 8% 30 year loan is .366736 %. The payment of interest and principal for a $50,000 loan is $ 183.38. The payment is made 24 times per year.

RATE	21 yr	22 yr	23 yr	24 yr	25 yr	26 yr	27 yr	28 yr	29 yr	30 yr
0.00	.198413	.189394	.181159	.173611	.166667	.160256	.154321	.148810	.143678	.138889
1.00	.220016	.211030	.202828	.195313	.188402	.182025	.176123	.170645	.165547	.160791
2.00	.243069	.234184	.226083	.218669	.211859	.205583	.199782	.194405	.189408	.184754
3.00	.267552	.258834	.250899	.243651	.237006	.230895	.225259	.220046	.215213	.210721
4.00	.293434	.284943	.277235	.270211	.263791	.257902	.252487	.247494	.242880	.238605
4.25	.300118	.291692	.284050	.277091	.270735	.264910	.259558	.254628	.250076	.245862
4.50	.306886	.298529	.290955	.284065	.277776	.272018	.266732	.261867	.257380	.253231
4.75	.313737	.305453	.297950	.291131	.284912	.279224	.274007	.269210	.264790	.260707
5.00	.320671	.312462	.305034	.298288	.292142	.286527	.281381	.276655	.272304	.268291
5.25	.327686	.319555	.312205	.305536	.299466	.293925	.288853	.284200	.279921	.275978
5.50	.334782	.326732	.319462	.312872	.306880	.301416	.296421	.291843	.287637	.283767
5.75	.341957	.333992	.326804	.320296	.314385	.309000	.304083	.299581	.295452	.291656
6.00	.349211	.341332	.334230	.327806	.321977	.316674	.311837	.307414	.303362	.299642
6.25	.356543	.348753	.341738	.335401	.329657	.324437	.319682	.315339	.311366	.307723
6.50	.363951	.356253	.349328	.343079	.337422	.332287	.327615	.323354	.319460	.315896
6.75	.371435	.363830	.356998	.350839	.345270	.340222	.335635	.331457	.327644	.324159
7.00	.378994	.371485	.364746	.358679	.353200	.348240	.343739	.339645	.335915	.332509
7.25	.386626	.379214	.372571	.366598	.361211	.356340	.351926	.347917	.344270	.340945
7.50	.394330	.387018	.380473	.374594	.369300	.364520	.360194	.356271	.352706	.349463
7.75	.402106	.394895	.388448	.382666	.377466	.372777	.368540	.364703	.361223	.358060
8.00	.409951	.402844	.396497	.390812	.385707	.381111	.376963	.373213	.369817	.366736
8.25	.417866	.410863	.404617	.399031	.394022	.389518	.385461	.381798	.378486	.375486
8.50	.425848	.418951	.412808	.407321	.402408	.397998	.394031	.390456	.387228	.384310
8.75	.433898	.427106	.421067	.415681	.410865	.406549	.402672	.399184	.396041	.393203
9.00	.442012	.435328	.429394	.424108	.419390	.415168	.411382	.407981	.404921	.402165
9.25	.450191	.443616	.437786	.432602	.427981	.423853	.420158	.416844	.413868	.411191
9.50	.458432	.451967	.446243	.441161	.436638	.432604	.428999	.425772	.422879	.420281
9.75	.466736	.460381	.454762	.449782	.445358	.441418	.437903	.434762	.431951	.429432
10.00	.475100	.468855	.463343	.458466	.454139	.450293	.446868	.443812	.441083	.438642
10.25	.483524	.477390	.471985	.467209	.462980	.459227	.455891	.452921	.450272	.447908
10.50	.492005	.485983	.480684	.476011	.471879	.468219	.464972	.462086	.459517	.457228
10.75	.500544	.494633	.489441	.484869	.480835	.477267	.474108	.471305	.468815	.466601
11.00	.509138	.503339	.498254	.493784	.489845	.486370	.483297	.480576	.478164	.476023
11.25	.517787	.512100	.507121	.502751	.498909	.495525	.492538	.489898	.487563	.485494
11.50	.526490	.520914	.516040	.511772	.508025	.504730	.501828	.499269	.497009	.495011
11.75	.535244	.529779	.525012	.520843	.517191	.513985	.511167	.508687	.506501	.504572
12.00	.544050	.538696	.534033	.529964	.526405	.523287	.520552	.518149	.516036	.514176
12.25	.552905	.547661	.543103	.539132	.535666	.532635	.529982	.527656	.525614	.523820
12.50	.561809	.556675	.552221	.548347	.544973	.542028	.539455	.537203	.535232	.533503
12.75	.570760	.565736	.561384	.557608	.554324	.551463	.548969	.546792	.544888	.543223
13.00	.579758	.574842	.570593	.566912	.563717	.560940	.558524	.556418	.554582	.552978
13.25	.588800	.583993	.579845	.576258	.573151	.570457	.568117	.566082	.564311	.562768
13.50	.597887	.593187	.589139	.585645	.582626	.580012	.577746	.575781	.574074	.572590
13.75	.607017	.602423	.598474	.595072	.592139	.589604	.587412	.585514	.583869	.582442
14.00	.616188	.611699	.607848	.604538	.601688	.599232	.597112	.595280	.593696	.592325
14.25	.625400	.621016	.617261	.614041	.611274	.608894	.606844	.605077	.603552	.602235
14.50	.634652	.630370	.626712	.623580	.620894	.618589	.616608	.614904	.613436	.612172
14.75	.643942	.639763	.636198	.633153	.630548	.628316	.626402	.624759	.623348	.622134
15.00	.653270	.649191	.645720	.642760	.640234	.638074	.636225	.634642	.633285	.632121
15.25	.662634	.658655	.655276	.652400	.649950	.647860	.646076	.644551	.643247	.642131
15.50	.672034	.668153	.664864	.662071	.659697	.657676	.655954	.654485	.653233	.652163
15.75	.681468	.677685	.674484	.671772	.669472	.667518	.665857	.664444	.663241	.662216
16.00	.690936	.687248	.684135	.681502	.679274	.677386	.675784	.674425	.673270	.672288
16.25	.700436	.696842	.693815	.691261	.689103	.687279	.685735	.684428	.683319	.682380
16.50	.709968	.706467	.703524	.701046	.698958	.697196	.695709	.694451	.693388	.692489
16.75	.719530	.716121	.713261	.710858	.708837	.707136	.705703	.704495	.703476	.702615
17.00	.729122	.725803	.723024	.720695	.718740	.717099	.715718	.714558	.713580	.712758
17.25	.738743	.735512	.732813	.730556	.728666	.727082	.725753	.724638	.723702	.722915
17.50	.748393	.745248	.742628	.740440	.738613	.737085	.735807	.734736	.733839	.733088
17.75	.758069	.755010	.752466	.750347	.748581	.747108	.745878	.744850	.743992	.743273
18.00	.767772	.764796	.762327	.760276	.758570	.757149	.755966	.754980	.754158	.753472
18.25	.777500	.774607	.772211	.770225	.768577	.767208	.766071	.765125	.764338	.763684
18.50	.787252	.784440	.782117	.780194	.778603	.777284	.776191	.775284	.774531	.773907
18.75	.797029	.794296	.792043	.790183	.788647	.787377	.786326	.785457	.784737	.784141
19.00	.806829	.804173	.801989	.800190	.798707	.797484	.796475	.795642	.794954	.794385
20.00	.846246	.843885	.841959	.840388	.839106	.838057	.837200	.836499	.835926	.835456
25.00	1.047314	1.046065	1.045093	1.044337	1.043748	1.043289	1.042931	1.042652	1.042435	1.042266
30.00	1.252391	1.251774	1.251316	1.250977	1.250725	1.250538	1.250399	1.250296	1.250220	1.250163

Description: This table shows the payment to amortize a loan of $ 100 over the term. The payment, including interest and principal, is made biweekly, every other week.

Example: The payment for an 8% 10 year loan is .559320 %. The payment of interest and principal for a $50,000 loan is $ 279.67. The payment is made 26 times per year.

RATE	1 yr	2 yr	3 yr	4 yr	5 yr	6 yr	7 yr	8 yr	9 yr	10 yr
0.00	3.846154	1.923077	1.282051	.961538	.769231	.641026	.549451	.480769	.427350	.384615
1.00	3.866156	1.942742	1.301625	.981082	.788770	.660572	.569011	.500349	.446952	.404241
2.00	3.886223	1.962534	1.321390	1.000882	.808629	.680502	.589020	.520440	.467129	.424506
3.00	3.906353	1.982455	1.341348	1.020938	.828808	.700817	.609476	.541043	.487881	.445408
4.00	3.926547	2.002504	1.361497	1.041250	.849306	.721513	.630378	.562154	.509204	.466945
4.25	3.931606	2.007536	1.366564	1.046368	.854480	.726747	.635673	.567512	.514624	.472428
4.50	3.936668	2.012576	1.371644	1.051501	.859674	.732005	.640996	.572900	.520079	.477950
4.75	3.941735	2.017624	1.376735	1.056651	.864888	.737286	.646347	.578321	.525570	.483511
5.00	3.946805	2.022680	1.381838	1.061816	.870122	.742592	.651725	.583772	.531096	.489111
5.25	3.951880	2.027744	1.386953	1.066998	.875376	.747921	.657130	.589256	.536657	.494750
5.50	3.956958	2.032816	1.392080	1.072195	.880650	.753273	.662564	.594770	.542253	.500428
5.75	3.962041	2.037896	1.397219	1.077409	.885943	.758650	.668025	.600316	.547884	.506145
6.00	3.967127	2.042984	1.402370	1.082638	.891257	.764050	.673513	.605893	.553551	.511900
6.25	3.972218	2.048080	1.407533	1.087883	.896590	.769474	.679029	.611502	.559252	.517694
6.50	3.977312	2.053184	1.412708	1.093144	.901942	.774921	.684572	.617141	.564988	.523527
6.75	3.982410	2.058296	1.417895	1.098420	.907315	.780392	.690143	.622812	.570759	.529397
7.00	3.987513	2.063416	1.423093	1.103713	.912707	.785886	.695740	.628514	.576564	.535306
7.25	3.992619	2.068543	1.428304	1.109022	.918119	.791405	.701366	.634246	.582404	.541253
7.50	3.997729	2.073679	1.433527	1.114346	.923551	.796946	.707018	.640010	.588279	.547237
7.75	4.002844	2.078823	1.438761	1.119686	.929002	.802511	.712698	.645804	.594187	.553260
8.00	4.007962	2.083975	1.444007	1.125042	.934473	.808099	.718404	.651629	.600130	.559320
8.25	4.013084	2.089134	1.449266	1.130413	.939964	.813711	.724138	.657485	.606107	.565417
8.50	4.018211	2.094302	1.454536	1.135801	.945474	.819346	.729899	.663371	.612118	.571552
8.75	4.023341	2.099477	1.459818	1.141204	.951004	.825005	.735687	.669288	.618163	.577724
9.00	4.028475	2.104661	1.465111	1.146623	.956553	.830687	.741501	.675235	.624241	.583932
9.25	4.033613	2.109852	1.470417	1.152058	.962122	.836392	.747343	.681212	.630353	.590178
9.50	4.038755	2.115052	1.475735	1.157508	.967711	.842120	.753211	.687220	.636499	.596460
9.75	4.043902	2.120259	1.481064	1.162974	.973318	.847871	.759106	.693257	.642678	.602778
10.00	4.049052	2.125474	1.486406	1.168456	.978946	.853645	.765027	.699325	.648890	.609133
10.25	4.054206	2.130697	1.491759	1.173954	.984592	.859443	.770975	.705422	.655136	.615524
10.50	4.059364	2.135928	1.497124	1.179467	.990259	.865263	.776950	.711550	.661414	.621951
10.75	4.064526	2.141167	1.502500	1.184996	.995944	.871107	.782950	.717707	.667725	.628414
11.00	4.069692	2.146414	1.507889	1.190540	1.001649	.876973	.788978	.723893	.674069	.634912
11.25	4.074862	2.151669	1.513289	1.196100	1.007373	.882862	.795031	.730110	.680445	.641445
11.50	4.080036	2.156932	1.518702	1.201676	1.013117	.888774	.801111	.736355	.686854	.648014
11.75	4.085214	2.162203	1.524126	1.207267	1.018879	.894709	.807217	.742630	.693295	.654617
12.00	4.090396	2.167481	1.529562	1.212874	1.024661	.900667	.813349	.748934	.699768	.661255
12.25	4.095582	2.172768	1.535009	1.218496	1.030462	.906647	.819507	.755267	.706272	.667928
12.50	4.100771	2.178062	1.540468	1.224134	1.036283	.912650	.825691	.761629	.712809	.674635
12.75	4.105965	2.183365	1.545940	1.229788	1.042122	.918675	.831900	.768020	.719377	.681377
13.00	4.111163	2.188675	1.551423	1.235457	1.047981	.924723	.838136	.774440	.725977	.688152
13.25	4.116365	2.193993	1.556917	1.241141	1.053858	.930794	.844397	.780888	.732608	.694961
13.50	4.121570	2.199319	1.562424	1.246841	1.059755	.936887	.850683	.787364	.739270	.701803
13.75	4.126780	2.204653	1.567942	1.252556	1.065671	.943002	.856995	.793869	.745963	.708679
14.00	4.131994	2.209995	1.573471	1.258287	1.071605	.949139	.863333	.800403	.752687	.715587
14.25	4.137211	2.215344	1.579013	1.264033	1.077559	.955299	.869696	.806964	.759442	.722529
14.50	4.142433	2.220702	1.584566	1.269795	1.083531	.961481	.876084	.813553	.766227	.729503
14.75	4.147658	2.226067	1.590131	1.275572	1.089522	.967685	.882497	.820170	.773042	.736509
15.00	4.152888	2.231441	1.595708	1.281364	1.095532	.973911	.888935	.826815	.779887	.743548
15.25	4.158121	2.236822	1.601296	1.287172	1.101561	.980159	.895398	.833488	.786762	.750618
15.50	4.163358	2.242211	1.606896	1.292995	1.107609	.986429	.901886	.840188	.793667	.757720
15.75	4.168600	2.247608	1.612508	1.298833	1.113675	.992721	.908399	.846915	.800602	.764854
16.00	4.173845	2.253013	1.618131	1.304686	1.119760	.999035	.914936	.853669	.807565	.772019
16.25	4.179094	2.258425	1.623766	1.310555	1.125864	1.005370	.921498	.860451	.814558	.779214
16.50	4.184347	2.263846	1.629413	1.316439	1.131986	1.011728	.928084	.867259	.821581	.786441
16.75	4.189604	2.269274	1.635071	1.322338	1.138127	1.018106	.934695	.874094	.828631	.793698
17.00	4.194865	2.274710	1.640741	1.328253	1.144286	1.024507	.941330	.880956	.835711	.800985
17.25	4.200131	2.280154	1.646422	1.334182	1.150464	1.030929	.947989	.887845	.842819	.808302
17.50	4.205399	2.285606	1.652115	1.340127	1.156660	1.037372	.954673	.894759	.849955	.815649
17.75	4.210672	2.291066	1.657819	1.346086	1.162875	1.043836	.961380	.901700	.857119	.823025
18.00	4.215949	2.296533	1.663536	1.352061	1.169108	1.050322	.968111	.908667	.864311	.830431
18.25	4.221230	2.302009	1.669263	1.358051	1.175359	1.056829	.974866	.915660	.871531	.837866
18.50	4.226515	2.307492	1.675002	1.364056	1.181628	1.063358	.981645	.922678	.878778	.845329
18.75	4.231804	2.312983	1.680753	1.370076	1.187916	1.069907	.988447	.929723	.886053	.852821
19.00	4.237096	2.318482	1.686515	1.376111	1.194222	1.076477	.995272	.936792	.893354	.860341
20.00	4.258306	2.340555	1.709679	1.400400	1.219626	1.102967	1.022807	.965323	.922827	.890700
25.00	4.365301	2.452786	1.828235	1.525382	1.350894	1.240270	1.165830	1.113710	1.076194	1.048651
30.00	4.473862	2.568098	1.951273	1.656089	1.488939	1.385188	1.317082	1.270718	1.238368	1.215406

INSTALLMENT LOAN PAYMENTS

Description: This table shows the payment to amortize a loan of $ 100 over the term. The payment, including interest and principal, is made biweekly, every other week.

Example: The payment for an 8% 20 year loan is .385769 %. The payment of interest and principal for a $50,000 loan is $ 192.89. The payment is made 26 times per year.

RATE	11 yr	12 yr	13 yr	14 yr	15 yr	16 yr	17 yr	18 yr	19 yr	20 yr
0.00	.349650	.320513	.295858	.274725	.256410	.240385	.226244	.213675	.202429	.192308
1.00	.369301	.340190	.315562	.294457	.276171	.260174	.246063	.233524	.222307	.212216
2.00	.389655	.360634	.336097	.315084	.296890	.280986	.266967	.254521	.243398	.233399
3.00	.410710	.381842	.357459	.336600	.318560	.302811	.288947	.276655	.265686	.255843
4.00	.432461	.403808	.379640	.358996	.341171	.325636	.311986	.299908	.289152	.279520
4.25	.438007	.409417	.385312	.364732	.346969	.331497	.317909	.305893	.295199	.285628
4.50	.443596	.415073	.391035	.370521	.352825	.337418	.323897	.311946	.301317	.291811
4.75	.449227	.420775	.396808	.376364	.358738	.343401	.329948	.318066	.307505	.298067
5.00	.454902	.426524	.402630	.382260	.364707	.349443	.336064	.324253	.313764	.304396
5.25	.460619	.432319	.408503	.388210	.370734	.355546	.342242	.330507	.320092	.310798
5.50	.466379	.438160	.414425	.394213	.376817	.361708	.348483	.336826	.326489	.317272
5.75	.472181	.444047	.420397	.400268	.382955	.367930	.354787	.343211	.332954	.323816
6.00	.478025	.449980	.426417	.406376	.389150	.374210	.361152	.349660	.339486	.330431
6.25	.483911	.455958	.432487	.412536	.395400	.380549	.367578	.356173	.346085	.337115
6.50	.489840	.461981	.438605	.418748	.401704	.386945	.374066	.362750	.352750	.343867
6.75	.495809	.468050	.444771	.425011	.408063	.393399	.380613	.369390	.359481	.350687
7.00	.501821	.474163	.450985	.431325	.414477	.399910	.387220	.376091	.366276	.357573
7.25	.507874	.480321	.457248	.437690	.420943	.406477	.393886	.382854	.373134	.364526
7.50	.513968	.486524	.463557	.444106	.427464	.413100	.400610	.389678	.380056	.371543
7.75	.520103	.492770	.469914	.450572	.434037	.419778	.407392	.396562	.387040	.378625
8.00	.526279	.499061	.476318	.457087	.440662	.426512	.414232	.403506	.394085	.385769
8.25	.532496	.505395	.482769	.463652	.447339	.433299	.421127	.410507	.401190	.392976
8.50	.538752	.511773	.489265	.470266	.454068	.440141	.428079	.417567	.408355	.400244
8.75	.545050	.518194	.495808	.476928	.460848	.447035	.435086	.424684	.415579	.407572
9.00	.551387	.524658	.502396	.483639	.467678	.453983	.442148	.431857	.422861	.414960
9.25	.557764	.531164	.509030	.490397	.474558	.460982	.449264	.439086	.430200	.422405
9.50	.564181	.537713	.515709	.497202	.481488	.468033	.456432	.446370	.437595	.429908
9.75	.570636	.544304	.522432	.504055	.488466	.475135	.463654	.453707	.445045	.437468
10.00	.577132	.550937	.529199	.510954	.495493	.482287	.470927	.461098	.452550	.445082
10.25	.583666	.557611	.536010	.517899	.502569	.489488	.478251	.468541	.460108	.452751
10.50	.590238	.564326	.542865	.524889	.509691	.496739	.485626	.476036	.467718	.460473
10.75	.596849	.571083	.549763	.531925	.516861	.504038	.493051	.483582	.475380	.468247
11.00	.603498	.577879	.556704	.539006	.524077	.511385	.500524	.491177	.483093	.476073
11.25	.610186	.584716	.563687	.546130	.531339	.518780	.508046	.498822	.490856	.483948
11.50	.616910	.591594	.570712	.553299	.538646	.526220	.515616	.506515	.498668	.491873
11.75	.623673	.598510	.577778	.560510	.545997	.533707	.523232	.514256	.506527	.499846
12.00	.630472	.605466	.584886	.567765	.553393	.541239	.530895	.522043	.514434	.507866
12.25	.637308	.612461	.592035	.575062	.560833	.548816	.538603	.529876	.522386	.515932
12.50	.644181	.619495	.599224	.582401	.568316	.556436	.546355	.537755	.530384	.524044
12.75	.651091	.626567	.606453	.589781	.575841	.564100	.554152	.545677	.538426	.532199
13.00	.658036	.633677	.613721	.597202	.583408	.571807	.561991	.553643	.546512	.540398
13.25	.665017	.640825	.621029	.604663	.591017	.579556	.569873	.561652	.554640	.548639
13.50	.672034	.648010	.628376	.612165	.598666	.587346	.577797	.569702	.562810	.556921
13.75	.679086	.655232	.635761	.619706	.606356	.595177	.585762	.577793	.571020	.565244
14.00	.686173	.662490	.643184	.627286	.614085	.603048	.593767	.585925	.579271	.573606
14.25	.693295	.669785	.650644	.634904	.621853	.610959	.601812	.594095	.587560	.582006
14.50	.700451	.677116	.658142	.642561	.629660	.618908	.609895	.602305	.595887	.590443
14.75	.707641	.684482	.665676	.650254	.637505	.626895	.618017	.610552	.604252	.598917
15.00	.714865	.691884	.673247	.657985	.645388	.634920	.626175	.618836	.612653	.607427
15.25	.722123	.699320	.680853	.665753	.653307	.642982	.634371	.627157	.621090	.615971
15.50	.729414	.706791	.688495	.673556	.661262	.651080	.642603	.635512	.629561	.624549
15.75	.736738	.714296	.696172	.681395	.669253	.659214	.650869	.643903	.638066	.633161
16.00	.744095	.721835	.703883	.689269	.677280	.667383	.659171	.652327	.646604	.641804
16.25	.751484	.729407	.711629	.697177	.685340	.675586	.667506	.660785	.655175	.650478
16.50	.758905	.737013	.719408	.705119	.693435	.683823	.675874	.669275	.663777	.659183
16.75	.766357	.744651	.727220	.713095	.701563	.692092	.684275	.677797	.672410	.667917
17.00	.773842	.752321	.735065	.721104	.709725	.700395	.692708	.686350	.681072	.676681
17.25	.781357	.760024	.742943	.729145	.717918	.708729	.701172	.694933	.689764	.685472
17.50	.788903	.767758	.750853	.737218	.726143	.717094	.709666	.703545	.698485	.694290
17.75	.796480	.775523	.758794	.745323	.734400	.725491	.718191	.712187	.707233	.703135
18.00	.804087	.783319	.766766	.753459	.742687	.733917	.726744	.720856	.716008	.712005
18.25	.811725	.791145	.774769	.761626	.751004	.742372	.735326	.729553	.724809	.720901
18.50	.819391	.799002	.782803	.769823	.759351	.750857	.743936	.738277	.733636	.729820
18.75	.827087	.806889	.790866	.778049	.767727	.759370	.752574	.747027	.742488	.738763
19.00	.834812	.814805	.798959	.786304	.776132	.767910	.761238	.755803	.751364	.747729
20.00	.865997	.846755	.831615	.819608	.810025	.802339	.796149	.791148	.787097	.783808
25.00	1.028134	1.012685	1.000957	.991999	.985125	.979831	.975742	.972578	.970124	.968220
30.00	1.198909	1.186954	1.178234	1.171846	1.167150	1.163690	1.161135	1.159246	1.157849	1.156814

INSTALLMENT LOAN PAYMENTS

BIWEEKLY PAYMENT

Description: This table shows the payment to amortize a loan of $ 100 over the term. The payment, including interest and principal, is made biweekly, every other week.

Example: The payment for an 8% 30 year loan is .338515 %. The payment of interest and principal for a $50,000 loan is $ 169.27. The payment is made 26 times per year.

RATE	21 yr	22 yr	23 yr	24 yr	25 yr	26 yr	27 yr	28 yr	29 yr	30 yr
0.00	.183150	.174825	.167224	.160256	.153846	.147929	.142450	.137363	.132626	.128205
1.00	.203089	.194794	.187223	.180286	.173907	.168020	.162572	.157516	.152810	.148420
2.00	.224366	.216164	.208687	.201844	.195557	.189765	.184410	.179447	.174834	.170538
3.00	.246963	.238915	.231592	.224901	.218768	.213127	.207925	.203113	.198652	.194506
4.00	.270851	.263013	.255899	.249416	.243490	.238055	.233057	.228448	.224189	.220243
4.25	.277020	.269243	.262189	.255766	.249899	.244523	.239584	.235033	.230831	.226942
4.50	.283267	.275554	.268563	.262203	.256398	.251084	.246205	.241715	.237573	.233743
4.75	.289591	.281944	.275020	.268725	.262985	.257735	.252920	.248493	.244413	.240645
5.00	.295990	.288414	.281558	.275332	.269659	.264476	.259727	.255365	.251349	.247644
5.25	.302465	.294961	.288177	.282021	.276419	.271304	.266623	.262329	.258379	.254740
5.50	.309015	.301585	.294875	.288793	.283263	.278220	.273609	.269383	.265502	.261930
5.75	.315638	.308286	.301652	.295645	.290189	.285220	.280681	.276526	.272715	.269212
6.00	.322333	.315061	.308506	.302577	.297198	.292303	.287839	.283757	.280016	.276583
6.25	.329100	.321911	.315437	.309587	.304286	.299469	.295079	.291072	.287404	.284042
6.50	.335938	.328833	.322442	.316674	.311453	.306714	.302402	.298470	.294876	.291586
6.75	.342846	.335828	.329522	.323837	.318698	.314039	.309805	.305949	.302430	.299213
7.00	.349823	.342893	.336673	.331074	.326017	.321440	.317286	.313507	.310064	.306921
7.25	.356868	.350028	.343896	.338383	.333412	.328916	.324843	.321143	.317777	.314708
7.50	.363979	.357231	.351190	.345764	.340878	.336467	.332474	.328854	.325564	.322571
7.75	.371156	.364501	.358552	.353215	.348416	.344089	.340178	.336638	.333426	.330507
8.00	.378398	.371838	.365981	.360735	.356023	.351781	.347953	.344493	.341359	.338515
8.25	.385704	.379240	.373476	.368321	.363698	.359542	.355797	.352417	.349361	.346592
8.50	.393072	.386706	.381037	.375973	.371439	.367369	.363708	.360409	.357430	.354737
8.75	.400501	.394234	.388660	.383690	.379245	.375262	.371684	.368466	.365565	.362946
9.00	.407991	.401823	.396346	.391469	.387114	.383218	.379724	.376586	.373762	.371218
9.25	.415541	.409473	.404093	.399309	.395045	.391235	.387825	.384767	.382021	.379551
9.50	.423148	.417182	.411899	.407209	.403035	.399313	.395986	.393008	.390339	.387942
9.75	.430813	.424948	.419763	.415168	.411084	.407449	.404205	.401307	.398713	.396389
10.00	.438533	.432771	.427684	.423183	.419190	.415641	.412480	.409661	.407143	.404890
10.25	.446309	.440648	.435660	.431254	.427351	.423888	.420810	.418069	.415625	.413443
10.50	.454138	.448580	.443691	.439378	.435566	.432189	.429192	.426529	.424159	.422047
10.75	.462020	.456565	.451774	.447555	.443833	.440541	.437625	.435039	.432742	.430699
11.00	.469953	.464601	.459909	.455784	.452150	.448943	.446108	.443597	.441372	.439396
11.25	.477937	.472688	.468094	.464062	.460517	.457394	.454638	.452202	.450047	.448139
11.50	.485969	.480824	.476327	.472389	.468931	.465891	.463214	.460852	.458767	.456924
11.75	.494050	.489008	.484609	.480762	.477392	.474434	.471834	.469546	.467529	.465750
12.00	.502178	.497238	.492936	.489181	.485897	.483021	.480497	.478281	.476331	.474615
12.25	.510353	.505514	.501308	.497644	.494446	.491650	.489202	.487056	.485172	.483517
12.50	.518571	.513835	.509725	.506151	.503037	.500320	.497946	.495869	.494050	.492455
12.75	.526834	.522199	.518184	.514699	.511669	.509030	.506729	.504720	.502964	.501428
13.00	.535140	.530604	.526684	.523287	.520340	.517778	.515549	.513606	.511912	.510433
13.25	.543487	.539051	.535224	.531915	.529049	.526563	.524404	.522527	.520893	.519470
13.50	.551875	.547538	.543803	.540580	.537794	.535383	.533293	.531480	.529905	.528536
13.75	.560302	.556063	.552420	.549282	.546576	.544238	.542215	.540464	.538947	.537631
14.00	.568768	.564627	.561074	.558020	.555391	.553125	.551169	.549479	.548018	.546753
14.25	.577272	.573226	.569763	.566792	.564240	.562044	.560153	.558523	.557116	.555901
14.50	.585812	.581862	.578487	.575597	.573120	.570993	.569166	.567594	.566240	.565074
14.75	.594387	.590532	.587244	.584435	.582031	.579972	.578207	.576691	.575390	.574271
15.00	.602998	.599235	.596033	.593303	.590972	.588980	.587275	.585814	.584563	.583489
15.25	.611642	.607971	.604854	.602201	.599941	.598014	.596368	.594961	.593759	.592730
15.50	.620319	.616739	.613705	.611128	.608938	.607074	.605486	.604132	.602976	.601990
15.75	.629027	.625537	.622585	.620084	.617962	.616159	.614627	.613324	.612215	.611269
16.00	.637767	.634365	.631493	.629066	.627010	.625269	.623792	.622538	.621473	.620567
16.25	.646537	.643222	.640429	.638074	.636084	.634401	.632977	.631771	.630749	.629883
16.50	.655335	.652106	.649392	.647107	.645181	.643556	.642184	.641024	.640044	.639215
16.75	.664162	.661018	.658380	.656164	.654300	.652731	.651410	.650295	.649355	.648562
17.00	.673017	.669955	.667392	.665244	.663441	.661927	.660655	.659584	.658683	.657924
17.25	.681898	.678918	.676429	.674347	.672604	.671143	.669918	.668890	.668026	.667301
17.50	.690805	.687905	.685488	.683471	.681786	.680377	.669918	.668890	.668026	.667301
17.75	.699738	.696916	.694570	.692616	.690988	.689629	.688495	.687547	.686756	.686093
18.00	.708694	.705950	.703673	.701781	.700208	.698898	.697807	.696898	.696140	.695508
18.25	.717674	.715006	.712797	.710965	.709446	.708184	.707135	.706263	.705538	.704934
18.50	.726677	.724083	.721941	.720168	.718701	.717485	.716477	.715641	.714947	.714371
18.75	.735702	.733181	.731103	.729389	.727972	.726801	.725832	.725031	.724367	.723818
19.00	.744748	.742299	.740285	.738626	.737259	.736131	.735201	.734433	.733798	.733274
20.00	.781134	.778957	.777182	.775733	.774550	.773584	.772794	.772148	.771619	.771187
25.00	.966740	.965590	.964694	.963997	.963455	.963032	.962703	.962446	.962246	.962090
30.00	1.156047	1.155479	1.155057	1.154745	1.154513	1.154341	1.154213	1.154118	1.154048	1.153996

INSTALLMENT LOAN PAYMENTS

Description: This table shows the payment to amortize a loan of $ 100 over the term. The payment, including interest and principal, is made weekly.

Example: The payment for an 8% 10 year loan is .279520 %. The payment of interest and principal for a $50,000 loan is $ 139.77. The payment is made 52 times per year.

RATE	1 yr	2 yr	3 yr	4 yr	5 yr	6 yr	7 yr	8 yr	9 yr	10 yr
0.00	1.923077	.961538	.641026	.480769	.384615	.320513	.274725	.240385	.213675	.192308
1.00	1.932893	.971278	.650751	.490495	.394348	.330255	.284479	.250151	.223455	.202102
2.00	1.942742	.981082	.660572	.500349	.404241	.340190	.294457	.260174	.233524	.212216
3.00	1.952622	.990950	.670489	.510331	.414293	.350316	.304659	.270453	.243879	.222649
4.00	1.962534	1.000882	.680502	.520440	.424506	.360634	.315084	.280986	.254521	.233399
4.25	1.965017	1.003375	.683021	.522988	.427084	.363243	.317725	.283659	.257226	.236136
4.50	1.967503	1.005872	.685545	.525543	.429672	.365865	.320380	.286347	.259948	.238893
4.75	1.969990	1.008373	.688075	.528107	.432269	.368498	.323049	.289052	.262689	.241669
5.00	1.972479	1.010878	.690612	.530678	.434877	.371143	.325732	.291772	.265447	.244465
5.25	1.974970	1.013387	.693154	.533257	.437495	.373800	.328428	.294508	.268222	.247280
5.50	1.977463	1.015900	.695702	.535845	.440123	.376469	.331138	.297260	.271016	.250115
5.75	1.979958	1.018417	.698256	.538440	.442761	.379150	.333863	.300028	.273827	.252969
6.00	1.982455	1.020938	.700817	.541043	.445408	.381842	.336600	.302811	.276655	.255843
6.25	1.984954	1.023463	.703383	.543654	.448066	.384547	.339352	.305610	.279501	.258735
6.50	1.987455	1.025992	.705955	.546273	.450733	.387263	.342117	.308424	.282364	.261647
6.75	1.989958	1.028525	.708533	.548900	.453410	.389991	.344896	.311254	.285245	.264579
7.00	1.992463	1.031062	.711117	.551535	.456098	.392731	.347689	.314099	.288143	.267529
7.25	1.994970	1.033603	.713707	.554178	.458795	.395482	.350496	.316960	.291058	.270498
7.50	1.997480	1.036148	.716303	.556829	.461502	.398246	.353316	.319837	.293991	.273486
7.75	1.999991	1.038697	.718905	.559488	.464218	.401021	.356149	.322729	.296941	.276494
8.00	2.002504	1.041250	.721513	.562154	.466945	.403808	.358996	.325636	.299908	.279520
8.25	2.005019	1.043807	.724127	.564829	.469681	.406607	.361857	.328559	.302892	.282564
8.50	2.007536	1.046368	.726747	.567512	.472428	.409417	.364732	.331497	.305893	.285628
8.75	2.010055	1.048932	.729373	.570202	.475184	.412239	.367619	.334450	.308911	.288710
9.00	2.012576	1.051501	.732005	.572900	.477950	.415073	.370521	.337418	.311946	.291811
9.25	2.015099	1.054074	.734643	.575606	.480725	.417918	.373435	.340402	.314997	.294930
9.50	2.017624	1.056651	.737286	.578321	.483511	.420775	.376364	.343401	.318066	.298067
9.75	2.020151	1.059232	.739936	.581043	.486306	.423644	.379305	.346415	.321151	.301223
10.00	2.022680	1.061816	.742592	.583772	.489111	.426524	.382260	.349443	.324253	.304396
10.25	2.025211	1.064405	.745253	.586510	.491926	.429416	.385228	.352487	.327372	.307588
10.50	2.027744	1.066998	.747921	.589256	.494750	.432319	.388210	.355546	.330507	.310798
10.75	2.030279	1.069595	.750594	.592009	.497584	.435234	.391205	.358620	.333658	.314026
11.00	2.032816	1.072195	.753273	.594770	.500428	.438160	.394213	.361708	.336826	.317272
11.25	2.035355	1.074800	.755959	.597539	.503282	.441098	.397234	.364812	.340010	.320535
11.50	2.037896	1.077409	.758650	.600316	.506145	.444047	.400268	.367930	.343211	.323816
11.75	2.040439	1.080021	.761347	.603101	.509018	.447008	.403315	.371063	.346427	.327115
12.00	2.042984	1.082638	.764050	.605893	.511900	.449980	.406376	.374210	.349660	.330431
12.25	2.045531	1.085258	.766759	.608694	.514793	.452963	.409449	.377372	.352909	.333764
12.50	2.048080	1.087883	.769474	.611502	.517694	.455958	.412536	.380549	.356173	.337115
12.75	2.050631	1.090511	.772194	.614318	.520606	.458964	.415635	.383740	.359454	.340482
13.00	2.053184	1.093144	.774921	.617141	.523527	.461981	.418748	.386945	.362750	.343867
13.25	2.055739	1.095780	.777654	.619973	.526457	.465010	.421873	.390165	.366062	.347268
13.50	2.058296	1.098420	.780392	.622812	.529397	.468050	.425011	.393399	.369390	.350687
13.75	2.060855	1.101065	.783136	.625659	.532347	.471101	.428162	.396647	.372733	.354122
14.00	2.063416	1.103713	.785886	.628514	.535306	.474163	.431325	.399910	.376091	.357573
14.25	2.065979	1.106365	.788643	.631376	.538275	.477237	.434502	.403186	.379465	.361041
14.50	2.068543	1.109022	.791405	.634246	.541253	.480321	.437690	.406477	.382854	.364526
14.75	2.071110	1.111682	.794172	.637124	.544240	.483417	.440892	.409781	.386259	.368026
15.00	2.073679	1.114346	.796946	.640010	.547237	.486524	.444106	.413100	.389678	.371543
15.25	2.076250	1.117014	.799726	.642903	.550244	.489642	.447333	.416432	.393113	.375076
15.50	2.078823	1.119686	.802511	.645804	.553260	.492770	.450572	.419778	.396562	.378625
15.75	2.081398	1.122362	.805302	.648713	.556285	.495910	.453823	.423138	.400027	.382189
16.00	2.083975	1.125042	.808099	.651629	.559320	.499061	.457087	.426512	.403506	.385769
16.25	2.086553	1.127726	.810902	.654553	.562364	.502223	.460364	.429899	.406999	.389365
16.50	2.089134	1.130413	.813711	.657485	.565417	.505395	.463652	.433299	.410507	.392976
16.75	2.091717	1.133105	.816526	.660424	.568480	.508579	.466953	.436713	.414030	.396603
17.00	2.094302	1.135801	.819346	.663371	.571552	.511773	.470266	.440141	.417567	.400244
17.25	2.096889	1.138501	.822173	.666326	.574633	.514978	.473591	.443582	.421119	.403901
17.50	2.099477	1.141204	.825005	.669288	.577724	.518194	.476928	.447035	.424684	.407572
17.75	2.102068	1.143912	.827843	.672257	.580823	.521421	.480277	.450503	.428264	.411259
18.00	2.104661	1.146623	.830687	.675235	.583932	.524658	.483639	.453983	.431857	.414960
18.25	2.107256	1.149338	.833536	.678220	.587050	.527906	.487012	.457476	.435465	.418675
18.50	2.109852	1.152058	.836392	.681212	.590178	.531164	.490397	.460982	.439086	.422405
18.75	2.112451	1.154781	.839253	.684212	.593314	.534434	.493794	.464501	.442721	.426150
19.00	2.115052	1.157508	.842120	.687220	.596460	.537713	.497202	.468033	.446370	.429908
20.00	2.125474	1.168456	.853645	.699325	.609133	.550937	.510954	.482287	.461098	.445082
25.00	2.178062	1.224134	.912650	.761629	.674635	.619495	.582401	.556436	.537755	.524044
30.00	2.231441	1.281364	.973911	.826815	.743548	.691884	.657985	.634920	.618836	.607427

Description: This table shows the payment to amortize a loan of $ 100 over the term. The payment, including interest and principal, is made weekly.

Example: The payment for an 8% 20 year loan is .192825 %. The payment of interest and principal for a $50,000 loan is $ 96.42. The payment is made 52 times per year.

RATE	11 yr	12 yr	13 yr	14 yr	15 yr	16 yr	17 yr	18 yr	19 yr	20 yr
0.00	.174825	.160256	.147929	.137363	.128205	.120192	.113122	.106838	.101215	.096154
1.00	.184634	.170079	.157767	.147215	.138073	.130076	.123021	.116752	.111144	.106099
2.00	.194794	.180286	.168020	.157516	.148420	.140470	.133462	.127240	.121680	.116682
3.00	.205305	.190875	.178688	.168261	.159244	.151371	.144442	.138297	.132815	.127894
4.00	.216164	.201844	.189765	.179447	.170538	.162773	.155951	.149914	.144539	.139725
4.25	.218933	.204644	.192597	.182311	.173434	.165701	.158910	.152905	.147560	.142777
4.50	.221724	.207469	.195455	.185203	.176359	.168659	.161902	.155929	.150617	.145866
4.75	.224536	.210316	.198338	.188121	.179313	.171648	.164925	.158987	.153709	.148993
5.00	.227369	.213187	.201247	.191067	.182295	.174667	.167981	.162079	.156837	.152156
5.25	.230224	.216081	.204180	.194039	.185305	.177716	.171068	.165203	.159999	.155355
5.50	.233100	.218998	.207138	.197037	.188344	.180795	.174186	.168361	.163195	.158590
5.75	.235997	.221938	.210120	.200062	.191411	.183903	.177336	.171551	.166426	.161860
6.00	.238915	.224901	.213127	.203113	.194506	.187041	.180516	.174774	.169691	.165166
6.25	.241855	.227887	.216159	.206190	.197628	.190208	.183727	.178029	.172988	.168506
6.50	.244815	.230895	.219215	.209294	.200778	.193404	.186969	.181315	.176319	.171881
6.75	.247796	.233926	.222295	.212423	.203955	.196629	.190241	.184633	.179683	.175290
7.00	.250799	.236980	.225400	.215577	.207160	.199882	.193542	.187983	.183079	.178732
7.25	.253821	.240056	.228528	.218757	.210391	.203164	.196873	.191363	.186507	.182206
7.50	.256865	.243154	.231680	.221963	.213649	.206473	.200234	.194773	.189966	.185714
7.75	.259929	.246274	.234856	.225193	.216933	.209810	.203623	.198213	.193457	.189254
8.00	.263013	.249416	.238055	.228448	.220243	.213175	.207041	.201683	.196978	.192825
8.25	.266118	.252581	.241278	.231729	.223580	.216567	.210487	.205183	.200529	.196427
8.50	.269243	.255766	.244523	.235033	.226942	.219986	.213962	.208712	.204111	.200060
8.75	.272389	.258974	.247792	.238362	.230330	.223432	.217464	.212269	.207722	.203723
9.00	.275554	.262203	.251084	.241715	.233743	.226904	.220993	.215854	.211362	.207416
9.25	.278739	.265454	.254398	.245092	.237182	.230402	.224550	.219467	.215030	.211138
9.50	.281944	.268725	.257735	.248493	.240645	.233926	.228133	.223108	.218727	.214889
9.75	.285169	.272018	.261094	.251917	.244132	.237475	.231742	.226776	.222451	.218668
10.00	.288414	.275332	.264476	.255365	.247644	.241050	.235378	.230470	.226202	.222474
10.25	.291678	.278666	.267879	.258835	.251180	.244649	.239039	.234191	.229980	.226308
10.50	.294961	.282021	.271304	.262329	.254740	.248273	.242725	.237937	.233785	.230168
10.75	.298264	.285397	.274751	.265845	.258323	.251922	.246436	.241709	.237616	.234055
11.00	.301585	.288793	.278220	.269383	.261930	.255594	.250172	.245506	.241471	.237967
11.25	.304926	.292209	.281709	.272944	.265559	.259290	.253932	.249328	.245352	.241905
11.50	.308286	.295645	.285220	.276526	.269212	.263009	.257716	.253174	.249257	.245867
11.75	.311664	.299101	.288751	.280131	.272886	.266752	.261524	.257044	.253187	.249853
12.00	.315061	.302577	.292303	.283757	.276583	.270517	.265354	.260937	.257140	.253863
12.25	.318477	.306073	.295876	.287404	.280302	.274304	.269207	.264853	.261116	.257896
12.50	.321911	.309587	.299469	.291072	.284042	.278114	.273083	.268792	.265114	.257896
12.75	.325363	.313121	.303081	.294760	.287804	.281945	.276981	.272753	.269135	.261952
13.00	.328833	.316674	.306714	.298470	.291586	.285798	.280900	.276735	.273178	.266029
13.25	.332322	.320246	.310367	.302199	.295390	.289671	.284841	.280739	.277242	.270129
13.50	.335828	.323837	.314039	.305949	.299213	.293566	.288802	.284764	.281327	.274249
13.75	.339351	.327446	.317730	.309718	.303058	.297481	.292784	.288810	.285432	.278390
14.00	.342893	.331074	.321440	.313507	.306921	.301416	.296787	.292875	.289557	.282552
14.25	.346452	.334720	.325169	.317316	.310805	.305371	.300809	.296961	.293702	.286733
14.50	.350028	.338383	.328916	.321143	.314708	.309345	.304850	.301065	.297866	.290933
14.75	.353621	.342065	.332682	.324989	.318630	.313338	.308911	.305189	.302048	.295152
15.00	.357231	.345764	.336467	.328854	.322571	.317351	.312990	.309331	.306249	.299389
15.25	.360858	.349481	.340269	.332737	.326530	.321381	.317088	.313492	.310468	.303645
15.50	.364501	.353215	.344089	.336638	.330507	.325430	.321204	.317670	.314704	.307917
15.75	.368162	.356966	.347926	.340556	.334502	.329497	.325337	.321865	.318957	.312207
16.00	.371838	.360735	.351781	.344493	.338515	.333581	.329488	.326078	.323226	.316513
16.25	.375531	.364520	.355653	.348447	.342545	.337683	.333656	.330307	.327512	.320835
16.50	.379240	.368321	.359542	.352417	.346592	.341801	.337840	.334552	.331813	.325172
16.75	.382965	.372139	.363447	.356405	.350656	.345936	.342041	.338813	.336130	.329525
17.00	.386706	.375973	.367369	.360409	.354737	.350088	.346258	.343090	.340462	.333893
17.25	.390462	.379824	.371308	.364429	.358834	.354255	.350490	.347382	.344809	.338275
17.50	.394234	.383690	.375262	.368466	.362946	.358438	.354738	.351689	.349169	.342671
17.75	.398021	.387571	.379232	.372518	.367075	.362636	.359000	.356010	.353544	.347081
18.00	.401823	.391469	.383218	.376586	.371218	.366850	.363277	.360346	.357932	.351504
18.25	.405641	.395381	.387219	.380669	.375377	.371078	.367569	.364695	.362333	.355940
18.50	.409473	.399309	.391235	.384767	.379551	.375320	.371874	.369057	.366747	.360388
18.75	.413320	.403252	.395267	.388881	.383739	.379577	.376194	.373433	.371174	.364849
19.00	.417182	.407209	.399313	.393008	.387942	.383848	.380526	.377821	.375613	.369321
20.00	.432771	.423183	.415641	.409661	.404890	.401064	.397984	.395497	.393482	.373805
25.00	.513835	.506151	.500320	.495869	.492455	.489827	.487799	.486229	.485013	.391848
30.00	.599235	.593303	.588980	.585814	.583489	.581777	.580515	.579582	.578892	.484070

INSTALLMENT LOAN PAYMENTS

WEEKLY PAYMENT

Description: This table shows the payment to amortize a loan of $ 100 over the term. The payment, including interest and principal, is made weekly.

Example: The payment for an 8% 30 year loan is .169226 %. The payment of interest and principal for a $50,000 loan is $ 84.62. The payment is made 52 times per year.

RATE	21 yr	22 yr	23 yr	24 yr	25 yr	26 yr	27 yr	28 yr	29 yr	30 yr
0.00	.091575	.087413	.083612	.080128	.076923	.073964	.071225	.068681	.066313	.064103
1.00	.101536	.097389	.093604	.090136	.086946	.084003	.081279	.078751	.076399	.074204
2.00	.112165	.108066	.104328	.100907	.097764	.094868	.092192	.089711	.087405	.085257
3.00	.123456	.119433	.115773	.112428	.109363	.106543	.103943	.101538	.099308	.097236
4.00	.135392	.131475	.127919	.124680	.121718	.119002	.116504	.114200	.112072	.110100
4.25	.138475	.134588	.131063	.127853	.124921	.122234	.119766	.117492	.115392	.113448
4.50	.141597	.137742	.134248	.131070	.128169	.125513	.123075	.120831	.118761	.116848
4.75	.144757	.140936	.137475	.134330	.131461	.128838	.126432	.124219	.122180	.120298
5.00	.147955	.144169	.140743	.137632	.134797	.132207	.129834	.127654	.125648	.123796
5.25	.151191	.147441	.144051	.140975	.138176	.135620	.133281	.131135	.129162	.127344
5.50	.154464	.150752	.147399	.144360	.141596	.139077	.136773	.134662	.132722	.130938
5.75	.157774	.154101	.150786	.147785	.145059	.142576	.140308	.138232	.136328	.134578
6.00	.161120	.157487	.154212	.151250	.148562	.146117	.143886	.141847	.139978	.138263
6.25	.164502	.160910	.157676	.154754	.152105	.149698	.147506	.145504	.143672	.141992
6.50	.167920	.164370	.161178	.158296	.155688	.153320	.151166	.149202	.147407	.145764
6.75	.171373	.167866	.164716	.161877	.159309	.156982	.154867	.152941	.151184	.149577
7.00	.174860	.171398	.168291	.165494	.162968	.160682	.158607	.156720	.155000	.153430
7.25	.178381	.174964	.171902	.169148	.166665	.164420	.162385	.160537	.158856	.157323
7.50	.181936	.178565	.175547	.172838	.170397	.168194	.166200	.164392	.162749	.161254
7.75	.185523	.182199	.179228	.176562	.174166	.172005	.170052	.168284	.166680	.165222
8.00	.189143	.185867	.182942	.180322	.177969	.175850	.173939	.172211	.170646	.169226
8.25	.192795	.189567	.186689	.184114	.181806	.179730	.177861	.176173	.174647	.173265
8.50	.196478	.193299	.190468	.187940	.185676	.183644	.181816	.180169	.178682	.177337
8.75	.200192	.197062	.194279	.191798	.189578	.187590	.185804	.184197	.182749	.181442
9.00	.203936	.200857	.198122	.195687	.193513	.191568	.189824	.188257	.186848	.185578
9.25	.207710	.204681	.201995	.199606	.197478	.195576	.193874	.192348	.190977	.189744
9.50	.211513	.208535	.205897	.203556	.201473	.199615	.197954	.196468	.195136	.193940
9.75	.215345	.212417	.209829	.207535	.205497	.203683	.202064	.200618	.199323	.198164
10.00	.219205	.216328	.213789	.211543	.209550	.207779	.206202	.204795	.203538	.202414
10.25	.223092	.220267	.217777	.215578	.213630	.211902	.210366	.208999	.207780	.206691
10.50	.227006	.224233	.221792	.219640	.217738	.216053	.214558	.213229	.212047	.210993
10.75	.230947	.228225	.225834	.223729	.221871	.220229	.218774	.217484	.216338	.215320
11.00	.234913	.232243	.229901	.227843	.226030	.224430	.223016	.221764	.220654	.219669
11.25	.238905	.236286	.233994	.231982	.230214	.228656	.227281	.226067	.224992	.224040
11.50	.242921	.240354	.238110	.236146	.234421	.232905	.231569	.230392	.229352	.228433
11.75	.246961	.244446	.242251	.240332	.238652	.237177	.235880	.234739	.233734	.232847
12.00	.251025	.248561	.246415	.244542	.242905	.241470	.240212	.239107	.238135	.237280
12.25	.255112	.252699	.250601	.248774	.247179	.245785	.244565	.243495	.242556	.241731
12.50	.259222	.256859	.254810	.253028	.251475	.250121	.248937	.247902	.246996	.246201
12.75	.263353	.261041	.259039	.257302	.255791	.254476	.253329	.252328	.251453	.250688
13.00	.267506	.265245	.263290	.261596	.260127	.258850	.257739	.256772	.255927	.255191
13.25	.271680	.269468	.267560	.265911	.264482	.263243	.262167	.261232	.260418	.259710
13.50	.275874	.273712	.271850	.270244	.268855	.267654	.266613	.265709	.264925	.264243
13.75	.280088	.277975	.276159	.274595	.273247	.272082	.271074	.270202	.269447	.268791
14.00	.284321	.282257	.280486	.278965	.277655	.276526	.275552	.274710	.273983	.273353
14.25	.288573	.286557	.284831	.283351	.282080	.280986	.280044	.279232	.278532	.277928
14.50	.292844	.290875	.289194	.287754	.286520	.285461	.284551	.283769	.283095	.282515
14.75	.297132	.295211	.293573	.292173	.290976	.289951	.289072	.288318	.287670	.287113
15.00	.301437	.299563	.297968	.296608	.295447	.294455	.293607	.292880	.292257	.291723
15.25	.305760	.303932	.302379	.301058	.299933	.298973	.298154	.297454	.296856	.296344
15.50	.310099	.308316	.306805	.305522	.304432	.303504	.302714	.302040	.301465	.300975
15.75	.314454	.312716	.311245	.310000	.308944	.308047	.307285	.306637	.306085	.305615
16.00	.318824	.317130	.315700	.314492	.313469	.312603	.311868	.311244	.310715	.310265
16.25	.323209	.321559	.320169	.318996	.318006	.317169	.316461	.315862	.315353	.314923
16.50	.327609	.326002	.324651	.323514	.322555	.321747	.321065	.320489	.320001	.319589
16.75	.332024	.330458	.329145	.328043	.327116	.326336	.325679	.325125	.324658	.324264
17.00	.336451	.334928	.333652	.332584	.331687	.330934	.330302	.329770	.329322	.328945
17.25	.340893	.339410	.338171	.337136	.336269	.335543	.334934	.334423	.333994	.333634
17.50	.345347	.343904	.342702	.341699	.340861	.340161	.339575	.339084	.338674	.338330
17.75	.349814	.348410	.347243	.346272	.345462	.344787	.344224	.343753	.343360	.343031
18.00	.354293	.352928	.351796	.350855	.350073	.349422	.348881	.348429	.348053	.347739
18.25	.358783	.357457	.356358	.355448	.354693	.354066	.353545	.353112	.352752	.352453
18.50	.363286	.361996	.360931	.360050	.359321	.358717	.358217	.357802	.357457	.357171
18.75	.367799	.366546	.365513	.364661	.363957	.363376	.362895	.362497	.362168	.361895
19.00	.372323	.371105	.370104	.369280	.368601	.368042	.367580	.367199	.366884	.366624
20.00	.390519	.389437	.388556	.387837	.387250	.386770	.386379	.386058	.385796	.385582
25.00	.483338	.482768	.482326	.481981	.481713	.481505	.481342	.481215	.481117	.481040
30.00	.578004	.577724	.577517	.577363	.577249	.577165	.577102	.577056	.577022	.576996

TABLE **19**

APR Scan Table

Interest Rates:	0, 1, 2, 3%; 4 to 19% by .25%; 20, 25, 30%.
Terms:	1 to 30 years, each year.
Payments:	Monthly, semimonthly, biweekly, weekly.

This table shows the finance charge per $100 of amount financed, at the Annual Percentage Rate (APR), for the term of the loan. The finance charge is shown for monthly, semimonthly, biweekly, and weekly periods: 12, 24, 26, and 52 periods.

Example: The finance charge for a 15 year monthly payment loan at an APR of 8% is 72.02%, as shown on page 19-2. The total interest for a $50,000 loan is $36,010.

The finance charge for a 15 year semimonthly payment loan at an APR of 8% is 71.87%, as shown on page 19-4. The total interest for a $50,000 loan is $35,935.

The finance charge for a 15 year biweekly payment loan at an APR of 8% is 71.86%, as shown on page 19-6. The total interest for a $50,000 loan is $35,930.

The finance charge for a 15 year weekly payment loan at an APR of 8% is 71.79%, as shown on page 19-8. The total interest for a $50,000 loan is $35,895.

Finding the APR. The APR Scan table can also be used to find the APR when an amount, payment, and term are given.

Compute the finance charge per $100 and enter the table. If the exact finance charge is not found, then interpolate between rates. The disclosed APR must be to the nearest .25%.

Example: A loan of $3,000 is repaid over 5 years by monthly payments of $70 each. There are 60 payments of $70 for a note of $4,200. The loan is $3,000 and the finance charge is $1,200. The finance charge per $100 is the charge divided by the loan, multiplied by 100.

Ratio of charge to loan:
1,200 ÷ 3,000 = .4

Finance charge per $100:
.4 × 100 = 40

Enter the table on page 19-2 in the 5 year column. The finance charge of 40 is exactly halfway between 14% and 14.25%. By interpolation, the actual APR for the loan is 14.125%. The disclosed rate could be either 14% or 14.25%. If the actual rate is 14.15%, then the disclosed rate is 14.25%. If 14.10%, then it is 14.00%.

APR SCAN TABLE

Description: This table shows the finance charge per $100 of amount financed, at the Annual Percentage Rate, for the term of the loan.

Example: The finance charge for a 15 year loan at an Annual Percentage Rate of 8 % is 72.02 %. The total interest for a $ 50,000 loan is $ 36010.00.

Finance Charge Per $100 of Amount Financed

RATE	1 yr	2 yr	3 yr	4 yr	5 yr	6 yr	7 yr	8 yr	9 yr	10 yr	11 yr	12 yr	13 yr	14 yr	15 yr
0.00	0.00	0.00	0.00	0.00	0.00	0.00	0.00	0.00	0.00	0.00	0.00	0.00	0.00	0.00	0.00
1.00	.54	1.04	1.55	2.05	2.56	3.07	3.58	4.09	4.61	5.12	5.64	6.16	6.68	7.20	7.73
2.00	1.09	2.10	3.11	4.14	5.17	6.20	7.25	8.30	9.35	10.42	11.49	12.56	13.65	14.74	15.83
3.00	1.63	3.15	4.69	6.24	7.81	9.39	10.99	12.60	14.23	15.87	17.53	19.20	20.89	22.59	24.30
4.00	2.18	4.22	6.29	8.38	10.50	12.65	14.82	17.02	19.24	21.49	23.77	26.08	28.41	30.76	33.14
4.25	2.32	4.49	6.69	8.92	11.18	13.47	15.79	18.14	20.52	22.93	25.36	27.83	30.33	32.85	35.41
4.50	2.45	4.75	7.09	9.46	11.86	14.29	16.76	19.26	21.80	24.37	26.97	29.60	32.27	34.97	37.70
4.75	2.59	5.02	7.49	10.00	12.54	15.12	17.74	20.40	23.09	25.82	28.58	31.39	34.22	37.10	40.01
5.00	2.73	5.29	7.90	10.54	13.23	15.96	18.72	21.54	24.39	27.28	30.21	33.18	36.20	39.25	42.34
5.25	2.87	5.56	8.30	11.09	13.92	16.79	19.71	22.68	25.69	28.75	31.85	35.00	38.19	41.42	44.70
5.50	3.00	5.83	8.71	11.63	14.61	17.63	20.71	23.83	27.01	30.23	33.50	36.82	40.19	43.61	47.08
5.75	3.14	6.10	9.11	12.18	15.30	18.48	21.71	24.99	28.33	31.72	35.17	38.67	42.22	45.82	49.47
6.00	3.28	6.37	9.52	12.73	16.00	19.32	22.71	26.16	29.66	33.22	36.84	40.52	44.26	48.05	51.89
6.25	3.42	6.64	9.93	13.28	16.70	20.18	23.72	27.33	31.00	34.74	38.53	42.39	46.31	50.29	54.34
6.50	3.56	6.91	10.34	13.83	17.40	21.03	24.74	28.51	32.35	36.26	40.23	44.28	48.39	52.56	56.80
6.75	3.69	7.18	10.75	14.39	18.10	21.89	25.75	29.69	33.70	37.79	41.95	46.17	50.47	54.84	59.28
7.00	3.83	7.45	11.16	14.94	18.81	22.75	26.78	30.88	35.07	39.33	43.67	48.09	52.58	57.15	61.79
7.25	3.97	7.73	11.57	15.50	19.52	23.62	27.81	32.08	36.44	40.88	45.41	50.01	54.70	59.47	64.32
7.50	4.11	8.00	11.98	16.06	20.23	24.49	28.84	33.29	37.82	42.44	47.15	51.95	56.84	61.81	66.86
7.75	4.25	8.27	12.40	16.62	20.94	25.36	29.88	34.50	39.21	44.01	48.91	53.91	58.99	64.17	69.43
8.00	4.39	8.55	12.81	17.18	21.66	26.24	30.92	35.71	40.60	45.59	50.68	55.87	61.16	66.54	72.02
8.25	4.52	8.82	13.23	17.75	22.38	27.12	31.97	36.94	42.01	47.18	52.47	57.85	63.34	68.94	74.63
8.50	4.66	9.09	13.64	18.31	23.10	28.00	33.03	38.16	43.42	48.78	54.26	59.85	65.54	71.35	77.25
8.75	4.80	9.37	14.06	18.88	23.82	28.89	34.08	39.40	44.84	50.39	56.07	61.86	67.76	73.78	79.90
9.00	4.94	9.64	14.48	19.45	24.55	29.78	35.15	40.64	46.26	52.01	57.88	63.88	69.99	76.22	82.57
9.25	5.08	9.92	14.90	20.02	25.28	30.68	36.22	41.89	47.70	53.64	59.71	65.91	72.24	78.69	85.25
9.50	5.22	10.19	15.32	20.59	26.01	31.58	37.29	43.14	49.14	55.28	61.55	67.96	74.50	81.17	87.96
9.75	5.36	10.47	15.74	21.16	26.75	32.48	38.37	44.41	50.59	56.92	63.40	70.02	76.77	83.66	90.69
10.00	5.50	10.75	16.16	21.74	27.48	33.39	39.45	45.67	52.05	58.58	65.26	72.09	79.06	86.18	93.43
10.25	5.64	11.02	16.58	22.32	28.22	34.30	40.54	46.94	53.52	60.25	67.14	74.18	81.37	88.71	96.19
10.50	5.78	11.30	17.01	22.90	28.96	35.21	41.63	48.22	54.99	61.92	69.02	76.28	83.69	91.26	98.97
10.75	5.92	11.58	17.43	23.48	29.71	36.13	42.73	49.51	56.47	63.61	70.91	78.39	86.03	93.82	101.77
11.00	6.06	11.86	17.86	24.06	30.45	37.05	43.83	50.80	57.96	65.30	72.82	80.51	88.37	96.40	104.59
11.25	6.20	12.14	18.29	24.64	31.20	37.97	44.94	52.10	59.46	67.00	74.74	82.65	90.74	99.00	107.42
11.50	6.34	12.42	18.71	25.23	31.96	38.90	46.05	53.40	60.96	68.71	76.66	84.80	93.12	101.61	110.27
11.75	6.48	12.70	19.14	25.81	32.71	39.83	47.16	54.71	62.47	70.44	78.60	86.96	95.51	104.24	113.14
12.00	6.62	12.98	19.57	26.40	33.47	40.76	48.28	56.03	63.99	72.17	80.55	89.13	97.91	106.88	116.03
12.25	6.76	13.26	20.00	26.99	34.23	41.70	49.41	57.35	65.52	73.90	82.51	91.32	100.33	109.54	118.93
12.50	6.90	13.54	20.43	27.58	34.99	42.64	50.54	58.68	67.05	75.65	84.48	93.52	102.76	112.21	121.85
12.75	7.04	13.82	20.87	28.18	35.75	43.59	51.67	60.01	68.59	77.41	86.46	95.72	105.21	114.90	124.79
13.00	7.18	14.10	21.30	28.77	36.52	44.53	52.81	61.35	70.14	79.17	88.44	97.95	107.67	117.60	127.74
13.25	7.32	14.38	21.73	29.37	37.29	45.49	53.96	62.70	71.69	80.95	90.44	100.18	110.14	120.32	130.71
13.50	7.46	14.66	22.17	29.97	38.06	46.44	55.11	64.05	73.26	82.73	92.45	102.42	112.63	123.05	133.70
13.75	7.60	14.95	22.60	30.57	38.83	47.40	56.26	65.40	74.83	84.52	94.47	104.68	115.13	125.80	136.70
14.00	7.74	15.23	23.04	31.17	39.61	48.36	57.42	66.77	76.40	86.32	96.50	106.95	117.64	128.56	139.71
14.25	7.89	15.51	23.48	31.77	40.39	49.33	58.58	68.14	77.99	88.13	98.54	109.22	120.16	131.34	142.74
14.50	8.03	15.80	23.92	32.37	41.17	50.30	59.75	69.51	79.58	89.94	100.59	111.51	122.70	134.13	145.79
14.75	8.17	16.08	24.35	32.98	41.95	51.27	60.92	70.89	81.18	91.77	102.65	113.81	125.24	136.93	148.85
15.00	8.31	16.37	24.80	33.59	42.74	52.24	62.09	72.28	82.78	93.60	104.72	116.13	127.80	139.74	151.92
15.25	8.45	16.65	25.24	34.20	43.53	53.22	63.27	73.67	84.40	95.44	106.80	118.45	130.38	142.57	155.01
15.50	8.59	16.94	25.68	34.81	44.32	54.21	64.46	75.06	86.01	97.29	108.89	120.78	132.96	145.41	158.12
15.75	8.74	17.22	26.12	35.42	45.11	55.19	65.65	76.47	87.64	99.15	110.98	123.12	135.56	148.27	161.24
16.00	8.88	17.51	26.57	36.03	45.91	56.18	66.84	77.88	89.27	101.02	113.09	125.48	138.17	151.13	164.37
16.25	9.02	17.80	27.01	36.65	46.71	57.17	68.04	79.29	90.91	102.89	115.21	127.84	140.79	154.01	167.51
16.50	9.16	18.09	27.46	37.27	47.51	58.17	69.24	80.71	92.56	104.77	117.33	130.22	143.42	156.91	170.67
16.75	9.30	18.37	27.90	37.88	48.31	59.17	70.45	82.14	94.21	106.66	119.46	132.60	146.06	159.81	173.84
17.00	9.45	18.66	28.35	38.50	49.12	60.17	71.66	83.57	95.87	108.56	121.61	135.00	148.71	162.72	177.02
17.25	9.59	18.95	28.80	39.13	49.92	61.18	72.88	85.00	97.54	110.46	123.76	137.40	151.37	165.65	180.22
17.50	9.73	19.24	29.25	39.75	50.73	62.19	74.10	86.44	99.21	112.37	125.92	139.82	154.05	168.59	183.42
17.75	9.87	19.53	29.70	40.37	51.55	63.20	75.32	87.89	100.89	114.29	128.09	142.24	156.73	171.54	186.64
18.00	10.02	19.82	30.15	41.00	52.36	64.22	76.55	89.34	102.57	116.22	130.26	144.67	159.43	174.50	189.88
18.25	10.16	20.11	30.60	41.63	53.18	65.24	77.78	90.80	104.27	118.16	132.45	147.12	162.13	177.48	193.12
18.50	10.30	20.40	31.05	42.26	54.00	66.26	79.02	92.26	105.96	120.10	134.64	149.57	164.85	180.46	196.37
18.75	10.44	20.69	31.51	42.89	54.82	67.28	80.26	93.73	107.67	122.05	136.85	152.03	167.58	183.45	199.64
19.00	10.59	20.98	31.96	43.52	55.64	68.31	81.51	95.21	109.38	124.01	139.06	154.50	170.31	186.46	202.92
20.00	11.16	22.15	33.79	46.07	58.96	72.46	86.53	101.15	116.29	131.91	147.98	164.47	181.35	198.58	216.13
25.00	14.05	28.09	43.14	59.15	76.11	93.95	112.62	132.06	152.20	172.99	194.36	216.24	238.57	261.31	284.40
30.00	16.98	34.19	52.83	72.83	94.12	116.61	140.18	164.74	190.16	216.34	243.18	270.58	298.46	326.74	355.35

APR SCAN TABLE

Description: This table shows the finance charge per $100 of amount financed, at the Annual Percentage Rate, for the term of the loan.

Example: The finance charge for a 30 year loan at an Annual Percentage Rate of 8 % is 164.16 %. The total interest for a $ 50,000 loan is $ 82080.00.

Finance Charge Per $100 of Amount Financed

RATE	16 yr	17 yr	18 yr	19 yr	20 yr	21 yr	22 yr	23 yr	24 yr	25 yr	26 yr	27 yr	28 yr	29 yr	30 yr
0.00	0.00	0.00	0.00	0.00	0.00	0.00	0.00	0.00	0.00	0.00	0.00	0.00	0.00	0.00	0.00
1.00	8.25	8.78	9.31	9.84	10.37	10.91	11.44	11.98	12.52	13.06	13.60	14.15	14.69	15.24	15.79
2.00	16.93	18.04	19.16	20.28	21.41	22.55	23.69	24.84	25.99	27.16	28.32	29.50	30.68	31.87	33.06
3.00	26.04	27.78	29.54	31.31	33.10	34.91	36.72	38.56	40.40	42.26	44.14	46.03	47.93	49.85	51.78
4.00	35.55	37.98	40.44	42.93	45.44	47.97	50.53	53.11	55.72	58.35	61.01	63.69	66.39	69.12	71.87
4.25	37.99	40.61	43.25	45.92	48.62	51.34	54.10	56.88	59.69	62.52	65.38	68.27	71.19	74.13	77.10
4.50	40.46	43.26	46.09	48.95	51.84	54.76	57.71	60.69	63.71	66.75	69.82	72.93	76.06	79.22	82.41
4.75	42.96	45.94	48.96	52.01	55.09	58.21	61.37	64.56	67.78	71.04	74.32	77.64	80.99	84.38	87.79
5.00	45.47	48.65	51.86	55.10	58.39	61.71	65.07	68.47	71.91	75.38	78.88	82.42	86.00	89.61	93.26
5.25	48.02	51.38	54.79	58.23	61.72	65.25	68.82	72.43	76.08	79.77	83.50	87.27	91.07	94.92	98.79
5.50	50.59	54.14	57.75	61.40	65.09	68.83	72.62	76.44	80.31	84.23	88.18	92.18	96.21	100.29	104.40
5.75	53.18	56.93	60.74	64.60	68.50	72.45	76.45	80.50	84.59	88.73	92.92	97.14	101.42	105.73	110.09
6.00	55.80	59.75	63.76	67.83	71.94	76.11	80.33	84.60	88.92	93.29	97.71	102.17	106.68	111.24	115.84
6.25	58.44	62.60	66.82	71.09	75.42	79.81	84.25	88.75	93.30	97.90	102.55	107.26	112.01	116.81	121.66
6.50	61.10	65.47	69.90	74.39	78.94	83.55	88.22	92.94	97.72	102.56	107.45	112.40	117.40	122.45	127.54
6.75	63.79	68.37	73.01	77.72	82.49	87.32	92.22	97.18	102.20	107.27	112.41	117.60	122.84	128.14	133.50
7.00	66.50	71.29	76.15	81.08	86.07	91.13	96.26	101.46	106.71	112.03	117.41	122.85	128.35	133.90	139.51
7.25	69.24	74.24	79.32	84.47	89.69	94.98	100.35	105.78	111.28	116.84	122.47	128.16	133.91	139.72	145.58
7.50	72.00	77.22	82.51	87.89	93.34	98.87	104.47	110.14	115.89	121.70	127.58	133.52	139.52	145.59	151.72
7.75	74.78	80.22	85.74	91.34	97.03	102.79	108.63	114.55	120.54	126.60	132.73	138.93	145.19	151.52	157.91
8.00	77.59	83.24	88.99	94.83	100.75	106.75	112.83	118.99	125.23	131.54	137.93	144.39	150.91	157.50	164.16
8.25	80.41	86.30	92.27	98.34	104.50	110.74	117.07	123.48	129.97	136.54	143.18	149.89	156.68	163.54	170.46
8.50	83.26	89.37	95.58	101.88	108.28	114.76	121.34	128.00	134.74	141.57	148.47	155.45	162.50	169.62	176.81
8.75	86.13	92.47	98.91	105.45	112.09	118.82	125.65	132.56	139.56	146.64	153.81	161.05	168.36	175.75	183.21
9.00	89.03	95.60	102.27	109.05	115.93	122.91	129.99	137.16	144.42	151.76	159.19	166.69	174.28	181.93	189.66
9.25	91.94	98.74	105.66	112.68	119.81	127.04	134.37	141.79	149.31	156.91	164.61	172.38	180.23	188.16	196.16
9.50	94.88	101.92	109.07	116.34	123.71	131.19	138.78	146.46	154.24	162.11	170.07	178.11	186.23	194.43	202.71
9.75	97.84	105.11	112.51	120.02	127.64	135.38	143.22	151.16	159.21	167.34	175.57	183.88	192.27	200.75	209.30
10.00	100.81	108.33	115.97	123.73	131.61	139.60	147.70	155.90	164.21	172.61	181.10	189.69	198.35	207.10	215.93
10.25	103.81	111.57	119.45	127.46	135.59	143.84	152.20	160.67	169.24	177.91	186.68	195.53	204.48	213.50	222.60
10.50	106.83	114.83	122.96	131.22	139.61	148.12	156.74	165.48	174.31	183.25	192.29	201.42	210.63	219.93	229.31
10.75	109.87	118.11	126.49	135.01	143.65	152.42	161.31	170.31	179.42	188.63	197.94	207.34	216.83	226.40	236.05
11.00	112.93	121.42	130.05	138.82	147.73	156.76	165.91	175.17	184.55	194.03	203.62	213.29	223.06	232.91	242.84
11.25	116.01	124.74	133.63	142.66	151.82	161.12	170.53	180.07	189.72	199.47	209.33	219.28	229.32	239.45	249.65
11.50	119.10	128.09	137.23	146.52	155.94	165.50	175.19	184.99	194.91	204.94	215.07	225.30	235.62	246.02	256.50
11.75	122.22	131.46	140.86	150.40	160.09	169.91	179.87	189.94	200.14	210.44	220.85	231.35	241.94	252.63	263.39
12.00	125.36	134.85	144.50	154.31	164.26	174.35	184.58	194.92	205.39	215.97	226.65	237.43	248.30	259.26	270.30
12.25	128.51	138.26	148.17	158.24	168.46	178.82	189.31	199.93	210.67	221.52	232.48	243.54	254.69	265.93	277.24
12.50	131.68	141.68	151.86	162.19	172.67	183.30	194.07	204.96	215.98	227.11	238.34	249.68	261.10	272.62	284.21
12.75	134.87	145.13	155.56	166.16	176.91	187.81	198.85	210.02	221.31	232.72	244.23	255.84	267.55	279.34	291.21
13.00	138.08	148.60	159.29	170.16	181.18	192.35	203.66	215.10	226.67	238.35	250.14	262.03	274.01	286.08	298.23
13.25	141.30	152.08	163.04	174.17	185.46	196.91	208.49	220.21	232.05	244.01	256.08	268.24	280.51	292.85	305.28
13.50	144.54	155.59	166.81	178.21	189.77	201.49	213.34	225.34	237.46	249.69	262.04	274.48	287.02	299.65	312.35
13.75	147.80	159.11	170.60	182.26	194.10	206.09	218.22	230.49	242.89	255.40	268.02	280.74	293.56	306.46	319.44
14.00	151.08	162.65	174.40	186.34	198.44	210.71	223.12	235.66	248.34	261.13	274.03	287.03	300.12	313.30	326.55
14.25	154.37	166.20	178.23	190.43	202.81	215.35	228.04	240.86	253.81	266.88	280.06	293.33	306.70	320.16	333.69
14.50	157.68	169.77	182.07	194.55	207.20	220.01	232.97	246.07	259.30	272.65	286.10	299.66	313.30	327.03	340.84
14.75	161.00	173.36	185.93	198.68	211.61	224.69	237.93	251.31	264.82	278.44	292.17	306.00	319.93	333.93	348.01
15.00	164.34	176.97	189.81	202.83	216.03	229.39	242.91	256.56	270.35	284.25	298.26	312.37	326.57	340.85	355.20
15.25	167.69	180.59	193.70	207.00	220.47	234.11	247.90	261.84	275.90	290.08	304.36	318.75	333.22	347.78	362.41
15.50	171.06	184.23	197.61	211.18	224.93	238.85	252.92	267.13	281.47	295.92	310.49	325.15	339.90	354.73	369.63
15.75	174.45	187.89	201.54	215.38	229.41	243.60	257.95	272.44	287.05	301.79	316.63	331.56	346.59	361.69	376.86
16.00	177.85	191.55	205.48	219.60	233.90	248.37	263.00	277.76	292.66	307.67	322.78	337.99	353.29	368.67	384.11
16.25	181.26	195.24	209.43	223.83	238.41	253.16	268.06	283.10	298.28	313.56	328.95	344.44	360.01	375.66	391.38
16.50	184.68	198.94	213.41	228.08	242.94	257.96	273.14	288.46	303.91	319.47	335.14	350.90	366.75	382.67	398.65
16.75	188.12	202.65	217.39	232.34	247.48	262.78	278.24	293.84	309.56	325.40	341.34	357.38	373.49	389.68	405.94
17.00	191.58	206.38	221.40	236.62	252.03	267.61	283.35	299.22	315.22	331.34	347.56	363.86	380.25	396.72	413.24
17.25	195.04	210.12	225.41	240.91	256.60	272.46	288.47	304.63	320.90	337.29	353.78	370.36	387.03	403.76	420.55
17.50	198.52	213.87	229.44	245.22	261.19	277.32	293.61	310.04	326.59	343.26	360.02	376.88	393.81	410.81	427.88
17.75	202.02	217.64	233.49	249.54	265.78	282.20	298.77	315.47	332.30	349.24	366.28	383.40	400.60	417.88	435.21
18.00	205.52	221.42	237.54	253.87	270.39	287.09	303.93	320.91	338.02	355.23	372.54	389.94	407.41	424.95	442.55
18.25	209.04	225.21	241.61	258.22	275.02	291.99	309.11	326.37	343.74	361.23	378.81	396.48	414.23	432.03	449.90
18.50	212.57	229.01	245.69	262.58	279.66	296.90	314.30	331.83	349.48	367.25	385.10	403.04	421.05	439.13	457.26
18.75	216.11	232.83	249.79	266.95	284.30	301.83	319.50	337.31	355.24	373.27	391.40	409.60	427.88	446.23	464.63
19.00	219.66	236.66	253.89	271.33	288.96	306.76	324.71	342.80	361.00	379.30	397.70	416.18	434.73	453.34	472.00
20.00	233.98	252.08	270.43	288.98	307.72	326.62	345.67	364.85	384.15	403.54	423.01	442.56	462.18	481.85	501.57
25.00	307.78	331.43	355.30	379.35	403.57	427.92	452.39	476.95	501.59	526.29	551.05	575.85	600.69	625.56	650.45
30.00	384.23	413.33	442.62	472.05	501.61	531.25	560.98	590.76	620.59	650.46	680.35	710.27	740.21	770.16	800.12

SEMIMONTHLY PAYMENT

Description: This table shows the finance charge per $100 of amount financed, at the Annual Percentage Rate, for the term of the loan. 24 payments are made each year.

Example: The finance charge for a 15 year loan at an Annual Percentage Rate of 8 % is 71.87 %. The total interest for a $ 50,000 loan is $ 35935.00.

Finance Charge Per $100 of Amount Financed

RATE	1 yr	2 yr	3 yr	4 yr	5 yr	6 yr	7 yr	8 yr	9 yr	10 yr	11 yr	12 yr	13 yr	14 yr	15 yr
0.00	0.00	0.00	0.00	0.00	0.00	0.00	0.00	0.00	0.00	0.00	0.00	0.00	0.00	0.00	0.00
1.00	.52	1.02	1.53	2.03	2.54	3.05	3.56	4.07	4.59	5.10	5.62	6.14	6.66	7.18	7.71
2.00	1.04	2.05	3.07	4.09	5.12	6.16	7.20	8.25	9.31	10.37	11.44	12.52	13.60	14.69	15.79
3.00	1.57	3.09	4.63	6.18	7.75	9.33	10.93	12.54	14.17	15.81	17.47	19.14	20.83	22.53	24.24
4.00	2.10	4.14	6.20	8.30	10.42	12.56	14.74	16.93	19.16	21.41	23.69	25.99	28.32	30.68	33.06
4.25	2.23	4.40	6.60	8.83	11.09	13.38	15.70	18.05	20.43	22.84	25.28	27.74	30.24	32.77	35.32
4.50	2.36	4.66	7.00	9.36	11.76	14.20	16.67	19.17	21.71	24.27	26.88	29.51	32.18	34.88	37.61
4.75	2.49	4.92	7.39	9.90	12.44	15.02	17.64	20.30	22.99	25.72	28.49	31.29	34.13	37.00	39.91
5.00	2.62	5.19	7.79	10.44	13.12	15.85	18.62	21.43	24.28	27.18	30.11	33.08	36.10	39.15	42.24
5.25	2.76	5.45	8.19	10.98	13.81	16.68	19.61	22.57	25.59	28.64	31.75	34.89	38.08	41.32	44.59
5.50	2.89	5.72	8.59	11.52	14.49	17.52	20.60	23.72	26.90	30.12	33.39	36.71	40.08	43.50	46.97
5.75	3.02	5.98	8.99	12.06	15.18	18.36	21.59	24.87	28.21	31.61	35.05	38.55	42.10	45.71	49.36
6.00	3.15	6.24	9.39	12.60	15.87	19.20	22.59	26.04	29.54	33.10	36.72	40.40	44.14	47.93	51.78
6.25	3.29	6.51	9.80	13.15	16.57	20.05	23.59	27.20	30.87	34.61	38.41	42.27	46.19	50.17	54.22
6.50	3.42	6.78	10.20	13.70	17.26	20.90	24.60	28.38	32.22	36.13	40.10	44.15	48.26	52.43	56.67
6.75	3.55	7.04	10.61	14.25	17.96	21.75	25.62	29.56	33.57	37.65	41.81	46.04	50.34	54.71	59.15
7.00	3.69	7.31	11.01	14.80	18.66	22.61	26.64	30.74	34.93	39.19	43.53	47.95	52.44	57.01	61.66
7.25	3.82	7.58	11.42	15.35	19.37	23.47	27.66	31.93	36.29	40.74	45.26	49.87	54.56	59.33	64.18
7.50	3.95	7.84	11.83	15.90	20.07	24.34	28.69	33.13	37.67	42.29	47.01	51.81	56.69	61.67	66.72
7.75	4.09	8.11	12.24	16.46	20.78	25.20	29.72	34.34	39.05	43.86	48.76	53.76	58.84	64.02	69.29
8.00	4.22	8.38	12.65	17.02	21.49	26.08	30.76	35.55	40.44	45.44	50.53	55.72	61.01	66.39	71.87
8.25	4.35	8.65	13.06	17.58	22.21	26.95	31.81	36.77	41.84	47.02	52.31	57.70	63.19	68.78	74.47
8.50	4.49	8.92	13.47	18.14	22.93	27.83	32.85	37.99	43.25	48.62	54.10	59.69	65.38	71.19	77.10
8.75	4.62	9.19	13.88	18.70	23.64	28.71	33.91	39.23	44.66	50.22	55.90	61.69	67.60	73.61	79.74
9.00	4.75	9.46	14.29	19.26	24.37	29.60	34.97	40.46	46.09	51.84	57.71	63.71	69.82	76.06	82.41
9.25	4.89	9.73	14.71	19.83	25.09	30.49	36.03	41.71	47.52	53.46	59.53	65.74	72.07	78.52	85.09
9.50	5.02	10.00	15.12	20.40	25.82	31.39	37.10	42.96	48.96	55.09	61.37	67.78	74.32	80.99	87.79
9.75	5.16	10.27	15.54	20.96	26.55	32.28	38.17	44.21	50.40	56.74	63.22	69.84	76.60	83.49	90.51
10.00	5.29	10.54	15.96	21.54	27.28	33.18	39.25	45.47	51.86	58.39	65.07	71.91	78.88	86.00	93.26
10.25	5.43	10.81	16.37	22.11	28.01	34.09	40.33	46.74	53.32	60.05	66.94	73.99	81.19	88.53	96.02
10.50	5.56	11.09	16.79	22.68	28.75	35.00	41.42	48.02	54.79	61.72	68.82	76.08	83.50	91.07	98.79
10.75	5.69	11.36	17.21	23.26	29.49	35.91	42.51	49.30	56.26	63.40	70.71	78.19	85.83	93.64	101.59
11.00	5.83	11.63	17.63	23.83	30.23	36.82	43.61	50.59	57.75	65.09	72.62	80.31	88.18	96.21	104.40
11.25	5.96	11.90	18.05	24.41	30.98	37.74	44.71	51.88	59.24	66.79	74.53	82.45	90.54	98.81	107.24
11.50	6.10	12.18	18.48	24.99	31.72	38.67	45.82	53.18	60.74	68.50	76.45	84.59	92.92	101.42	110.09
11.75	6.23	12.45	18.90	25.57	32.47	39.59	46.93	54.48	62.25	70.22	78.39	86.75	95.30	104.04	112.95
12.00	6.37	12.73	19.32	26.16	33.22	40.52	48.05	55.80	63.76	71.94	80.33	88.92	97.71	106.68	115.84
12.25	6.50	13.00	19.75	26.74	33.98	41.46	49.17	57.11	65.29	73.68	82.29	91.10	100.12	109.34	118.74
12.50	6.64	13.28	20.18	27.33	34.74	42.39	50.29	58.44	66.82	75.42	84.25	93.30	102.55	112.01	121.66
12.75	6.78	13.56	20.60	27.92	35.50	43.33	51.42	59.77	68.35	77.18	86.23	95.51	105.00	114.70	124.59
13.00	6.91	13.83	21.03	28.51	36.26	44.28	52.56	61.10	69.90	78.94	88.22	97.72	107.45	117.40	127.54
13.25	7.05	14.11	21.46	29.10	37.02	45.22	53.70	62.44	71.45	80.71	90.21	99.95	109.92	120.11	130.51
13.50	7.18	14.39	21.89	29.69	37.79	46.17	54.84	63.79	73.01	82.49	92.22	102.20	112.41	122.84	133.50
13.75	7.32	14.66	22.32	30.29	38.56	47.13	55.99	65.14	74.57	84.28	94.24	104.45	114.90	125.59	136.49
14.00	7.45	14.94	22.75	30.88	39.33	48.09	57.15	66.50	76.15	86.07	96.26	106.71	117.41	128.35	139.51
14.25	7.59	15.22	23.19	31.48	40.10	49.05	58.31	67.87	77.73	87.88	98.30	108.99	119.94	131.12	142.54
14.50	7.73	15.50	23.62	32.08	40.88	50.01	59.47	69.24	79.32	89.69	100.35	111.28	122.47	133.91	145.58
14.75	7.86	15.78	24.05	32.68	41.66	50.98	60.64	70.62	80.91	91.51	102.40	113.58	125.02	136.71	148.64
15.00	8.00	16.06	24.49	33.29	42.44	51.95	61.81	72.00	82.51	93.34	104.47	115.89	127.58	139.52	151.72
15.25	8.14	16.34	24.93	33.89	43.23	52.93	62.98	73.39	84.12	95.18	106.55	118.21	130.15	142.35	154.81
15.50	8.27	16.62	25.36	34.50	44.01	53.91	64.17	74.78	85.74	97.03	108.63	120.54	132.73	145.19	157.91
15.75	8.41	16.90	25.80	35.10	44.80	54.89	65.35	76.18	87.36	98.88	110.73	122.88	135.32	148.04	161.02
16.00	8.55	17.18	26.24	35.71	45.59	55.87	66.54	77.59	88.99	100.75	112.83	125.23	137.93	150.91	164.16
16.25	8.68	17.46	26.68	36.32	46.39	56.86	67.74	79.00	90.63	102.62	114.94	127.59	140.55	153.79	167.30
16.50	8.82	17.75	27.12	36.94	47.18	57.85	68.94	80.41	92.27	104.50	117.07	129.97	143.18	156.68	170.46
16.75	8.96	18.03	27.56	37.55	47.98	58.85	70.14	81.83	93.92	106.38	119.20	132.35	145.82	159.58	173.63
17.00	9.09	18.31	28.00	38.16	48.78	59.85	71.35	83.26	95.58	108.28	121.34	134.74	148.47	162.50	176.81
17.25	9.23	18.60	28.45	38.78	49.59	60.85	72.56	84.70	97.24	110.18	123.49	137.15	151.13	165.43	180.00
17.50	9.37	18.88	28.89	39.40	50.39	61.86	73.78	86.13	98.91	112.09	125.65	139.56	153.81	168.36	183.21
17.75	9.51	19.16	29.34	40.02	51.20	62.86	75.00	87.58	100.59	114.01	127.81	141.98	156.49	171.32	186.43
18.00	9.64	19.45	29.78	40.64	52.01	63.88	76.22	89.03	102.27	115.93	129.99	144.42	159.19	174.28	189.66
18.25	9.78	19.73	30.23	41.27	52.82	64.89	77.45	90.48	103.96	117.87	132.17	146.86	161.89	177.25	192.91
18.50	9.92	20.02	30.68	41.89	53.64	65.91	78.69	91.94	105.66	119.81	134.37	149.31	164.61	180.23	196.16
18.75	10.06	20.30	31.13	42.52	54.46	66.93	79.92	93.41	107.36	121.76	136.57	151.77	167.33	183.23	199.43
19.00	10.19	20.59	31.58	43.14	55.28	67.96	81.17	94.88	109.07	123.71	138.78	154.24	170.07	186.23	202.71
20.00	10.75	21.74	33.39	45.67	58.58	72.09	86.18	100.81	115.97	131.61	147.70	164.21	181.10	198.35	215.93
25.00	13.54	27.58	42.64	58.68	75.65	93.52	112.21	131.68	151.86	172.67	194.07	215.98	238.34	261.10	284.21
30.00	16.37	33.59	52.24	72.28	93.60	116.13	139.74	164.34	189.81	216.03	242.91	270.35	298.26	326.57	355.20

Description: This table shows the finance charge per $100 of amount financed, at the Annual Percentage Rate, for the term of the loan. 24 payments are made each year.

Example: The finance charge for a 30 year loan at an Annual Percentage Rate of 8 % is 164.05 %. The total interest for a $ 50,000 loan is $ 82025.00.

Finance Charge Per $100 of Amount Financed

RATE	16 yr	17 yr	18 yr	19 yr	20 yr	21 yr	22 yr	23 yr	24 yr	25 yr	26 yr	27 yr	28 yr	29 yr	30 yr
0.00	0.00	0.00	0.00	0.00	0.00	0.00	0.00	0.00	0.00	0.00	0.00	0.00	0.00	0.00	0.00
1.00	8.23	8.76	9.29	9.82	10.35	10.89	11.42	11.96	12.50	13.04	13.58	14.13	14.67	15.22	15.77
2.00	16.89	18.00	19.12	20.24	21.37	22.51	23.65	24.80	25.95	27.12	28.28	29.46	30.64	31.83	33.02
3.00	25.97	27.72	29.48	31.25	33.04	34.85	36.66	38.50	40.34	42.20	44.08	45.97	47.87	49.79	51.72
4.00	35.47	37.90	40.36	42.85	45.36	47.89	50.45	53.03	55.64	58.27	60.93	63.61	66.32	69.04	71.80
4.25	37.91	40.52	43.16	45.83	48.53	51.26	54.01	56.80	59.60	62.44	65.30	68.19	71.11	74.05	77.02
4.50	40.37	43.17	46.00	48.86	51.75	54.67	57.62	60.61	63.62	66.67	69.74	72.84	75.97	79.14	82.33
4.75	42.86	45.84	48.86	51.91	55.00	58.12	61.28	64.47	67.69	70.95	74.24	77.56	80.91	84.29	87.71
5.00	45.38	48.55	51.76	55.01	58.29	61.62	64.98	68.38	71.81	75.29	78.79	82.33	85.91	89.52	93.17
5.25	47.92	51.28	54.68	58.13	61.62	65.15	68.73	72.34	75.99	79.68	83.41	87.18	90.98	94.82	98.70
5.50	50.48	54.04	57.64	61.29	64.99	68.73	72.51	76.34	80.21	84.13	88.08	92.08	96.12	100.20	104.31
5.75	53.07	56.82	60.63	64.49	68.39	72.35	76.35	80.40	84.49	88.63	92.82	97.05	101.32	105.63	109.99
6.00	55.68	59.64	63.65	67.71	71.83	76.00	80.22	84.49	88.82	93.19	97.60	102.07	106.58	111.14	115.74
6.25	58.32	62.48	66.70	70.97	75.31	79.70	84.14	88.64	93.19	97.79	102.45	107.15	111.91	116.71	121.56
6.50	60.98	65.35	69.78	74.27	78.82	83.43	88.10	92.83	97.61	102.45	107.35	112.29	117.29	122.34	127.44
6.75	63.66	68.24	72.88	77.59	82.37	87.20	92.10	97.06	102.08	107.16	112.30	117.49	122.74	128.04	133.39
7.00	66.37	71.16	76.02	80.95	85.95	91.01	96.14	101.34	106.60	111.92	117.30	122.74	128.24	133.80	139.41
7.25	69.10	74.11	79.19	84.34	89.56	94.86	100.23	105.66	111.16	116.73	122.36	128.05	133.80	139.61	145.48
7.50	71.86	77.08	82.38	87.76	93.21	98.74	104.35	110.02	115.77	121.58	127.46	133.41	139.41	145.48	151.61
7.75	74.64	80.08	85.60	91.21	96.90	102.66	108.50	114.42	120.42	126.48	132.61	138.81	145.08	151.41	157.80
8.00	77.44	83.10	88.85	94.69	100.61	106.62	112.70	118.87	125.11	131.42	137.81	144.27	150.80	157.39	164.05
8.25	80.26	86.15	92.13	98.20	104.36	110.60	116.94	123.35	129.84	136.41	143.06	149.78	156.57	163.43	170.35
8.50	83.11	89.22	95.43	101.74	108.14	114.63	121.21	127.87	134.62	141.44	148.35	155.33	162.39	169.51	176.70
8.75	85.98	92.32	98.76	105.31	111.95	118.68	125.51	132.43	139.43	146.52	153.69	160.93	168.25	175.64	183.11
9.00	88.87	95.44	102.12	108.90	115.79	122.77	129.85	137.03	144.29	151.63	159.06	166.58	174.16	181.83	189.56
9.25	91.78	98.59	105.50	112.53	119.66	126.90	134.23	141.66	149.18	156.79	164.48	172.26	180.12	188.05	196.06
9.50	94.71	101.76	108.91	116.18	123.56	131.05	138.64	146.33	154.11	161.98	169.94	177.99	186.12	194.32	202.60
9.75	97.67	104.95	112.35	119.86	127.49	135.23	143.08	151.03	159.07	167.21	175.44	183.76	192.16	200.64	209.19
10.00	100.64	108.16	115.81	123.57	131.45	139.45	147.56	155.77	164.08	172.48	180.98	189.57	198.24	206.99	215.82
10.25	103.64	111.40	119.29	127.31	135.44	143.70	152.06	160.54	169.11	177.79	186.56	195.42	204.36	213.39	222.49
10.50	106.66	114.66	122.80	131.07	139.46	147.97	156.60	165.34	174.18	183.13	192.17	201.30	210.52	219.82	229.20
10.75	109.69	117.94	126.33	134.85	143.50	152.27	161.17	170.17	179.28	188.50	197.81	207.22	216.72	226.30	235.95
11.00	112.75	121.25	129.88	138.66	147.57	156.61	165.76	175.04	184.42	193.91	203.49	213.18	222.95	232.80	242.74
11.25	115.83	124.57	133.46	142.50	151.67	160.96	170.39	179.93	189.58	199.35	209.21	219.16	229.21	239.34	249.56
11.50	118.92	127.92	137.06	146.35	155.79	165.35	175.04	184.85	194.78	204.81	214.95	225.18	235.51	241.84	263.29
11.75	122.04	131.28	140.68	150.24	159.93	169.76	179.72	189.81	200.01	210.31	220.73	231.24	241.84	252.52	270.21
12.00	125.17	134.67	144.33	154.14	164.10	174.20	184.43	194.79	205.26	215.84	226.53	237.32	248.20	259.16	277.15
12.25	128.32	138.08	148.00	158.07	168.30	178.66	189.17	199.79	210.54	221.40	232.36	243.43	254.58	265.83	284.12
12.50	131.49	141.50	151.68	162.02	172.51	183.15	193.92	204.83	215.85	226.98	238.23	249.57	261.00	272.52	291.12
12.75	134.68	144.95	155.39	166.00	176.76	187.66	198.71	209.88	221.18	232.59	244.11	255.73	267.44	279.24	298.14
13.00	137.89	148.41	159.12	169.99	181.02	192.20	203.52	214.97	226.54	238.23	250.03	261.92	273.91	285.99	298.14
13.25	141.11	151.90	162.87	174.01	185.30	196.76	208.35	220.07	231.92	243.89	255.97	268.14	280.41	292.76	305.19
13.50	144.35	155.40	166.63	178.04	189.61	201.34	213.20	225.20	237.33	249.58	261.93	274.38	286.92	299.56	312.26
13.75	147.61	158.92	170.42	182.10	193.94	205.94	218.08	230.36	242.76	255.28	267.91	280.64	293.47	306.37	319.36
14.00	150.88	162.46	174.23	186.17	198.29	210.56	222.98	235.53	248.21	261.01	273.92	286.93	300.03	313.21	326.47
14.25	154.17	166.02	178.05	190.27	202.66	215.20	227.90	240.73	253.69	266.76	279.95	293.23	306.61	320.07	333.61
14.50	157.48	169.59	181.89	194.38	207.04	219.86	232.84	245.94	259.18	272.54	286.00	299.56	313.22	326.95	340.76
14.75	160.80	173.18	185.75	198.51	211.45	224.55	237.79	251.18	264.70	278.33	292.07	305.91	319.84	333.85	347.94
15.00	164.14	176.78	189.63	202.66	215.87	229.25	242.77	256.44	270.23	284.14	298.16	312.27	326.48	340.77	355.13
15.25	167.50	180.41	193.52	206.83	220.32	233.97	247.77	261.71	275.78	289.97	304.26	318.66	333.14	347.70	362.33
15.50	170.86	184.04	197.43	211.02	224.78	238.70	252.78	267.00	281.35	295.82	310.39	325.06	339.81	354.65	369.56
15.75	174.25	187.70	201.36	215.22	229.26	243.46	257.82	272.32	286.94	301.68	316.53	331.48	346.51	361.62	376.80
16.00	177.65	191.37	205.30	219.44	233.75	248.23	262.87	277.64	292.55	307.56	322.69	337.91	353.21	368.60	384.05
16.25	181.06	195.05	209.26	223.67	238.26	253.02	267.93	282.99	298.17	313.46	328.86	344.36	359.94	375.59	391.31
16.50	184.49	198.75	213.23	227.92	242.79	257.82	273.01	288.35	303.80	319.37	335.05	350.82	366.67	382.60	398.59
16.75	187.93	202.46	217.22	232.18	247.33	262.64	278.11	293.72	309.45	325.30	341.25	357.30	373.42	389.62	405.88
17.00	191.38	206.19	221.22	236.46	251.89	267.48	283.22	299.11	315.12	331.24	347.47	363.79	380.18	396.65	413.19
17.25	194.85	209.93	225.24	240.76	256.46	272.33	288.35	304.51	320.80	337.20	353.70	370.29	386.96	403.70	420.50
17.50	198.33	213.69	229.27	245.06	261.04	277.19	293.49	309.93	326.49	343.17	359.94	376.80	393.74	410.75	427.82
17.75	201.82	217.45	233.32	249.38	265.64	282.07	298.65	315.36	332.20	349.15	366.20	383.33	400.54	417.82	435.16
18.00	205.32	221.23	237.37	253.72	270.25	286.96	303.81	320.80	337.92	355.14	372.46	389.87	407.35	424.89	442.50
18.25	208.84	225.03	241.44	258.07	274.88	291.86	308.99	326.26	343.65	361.15	378.74	396.41	414.16	431.98	449.85
18.50	212.37	228.83	245.53	262.43	279.52	296.78	314.18	331.73	349.39	367.16	385.03	402.97	420.99	439.07	457.21
18.75	215.91	232.65	249.62	266.80	284.17	301.70	319.39	337.21	355.15	373.19	391.32	409.54	427.83	446.18	464.58
19.00	219.47	236.48	253.73	271.18	288.83	306.64	324.60	342.70	360.91	379.22	397.63	416.12	434.67	453.29	471.96
20.00	233.79	251.91	270.27	288.84	307.59	326.51	345.57	364.76	384.06	403.46	422.95	442.51	462.13	481.80	501.53
25.00	307.62	331.29	355.18	379.25	403.48	427.85	452.32	476.89	501.54	526.25	551.01	575.82	600.66	625.53	650.43
30.00	384.10	413.23	442.53	471.98	501.55	531.21	560.94	590.73	620.56	650.43	680.34	710.26	740.20	770.15	800.12

APR SCAN TABLE

Description: This table shows the finance charge per $100 of amount financed, at the Annual Percentage Rate, for the term of the loan. 26 payments are made each year.

Example: The finance charge for a 15 year loan at an Annual Percentage Rate of 8 % is 71.86 %. The total interest for a $ 50,000 loan is $ 35930.00.

Finance Charge Per $100 of Amount Financed

RATE	1 yr	2 yr	3 yr	4 yr	5 yr	6 yr	7 yr	8 yr	9 yr	10 yr	11 yr	12 yr	13 yr	14 yr	15 yr
0.00	0.00	0.00	0.00	0.00	0.00	0.00	0.00	0.00	0.00	0.00	0.00	0.00	0.00	0.00	0.00
1.00	.52	1.02	1.53	2.03	2.54	3.05	3.56	4.07	4.59	5.10	5.62	6.14	6.66	7.18	7.71
2.00	1.04	2.05	3.07	4.09	5.12	6.16	7.20	8.25	9.31	10.37	11.44	12.52	13.60	14.69	15.79
3.00	1.57	3.09	4.63	6.18	7.75	9.33	10.92	12.54	14.16	15.81	17.46	19.13	20.82	22.52	24.24
4.00	2.09	4.13	6.20	8.29	10.41	12.56	14.73	16.93	19.15	21.41	23.68	25.99	28.32	30.67	33.06
4.25	2.22	4.39	6.59	8.82	11.08	13.37	15.69	18.04	20.42	22.83	25.27	27.74	30.24	32.76	35.32
4.50	2.35	4.65	6.99	9.36	11.76	14.19	16.66	19.16	21.70	24.27	26.87	29.50	32.17	34.87	37.60
4.75	2.49	4.92	7.39	9.89	12.44	15.02	17.64	20.29	22.98	25.71	28.48	31.28	34.12	37.00	39.91
5.00	2.62	5.18	7.78	10.43	13.12	15.84	18.61	21.42	24.28	27.17	30.10	33.08	36.09	39.14	42.24
5.25	2.75	5.44	8.18	10.97	13.80	16.68	19.60	22.57	25.58	28.64	31.74	34.88	38.07	41.31	44.59
5.50	2.88	5.71	8.58	11.51	14.48	17.51	20.59	23.71	26.89	30.11	33.38	36.71	40.08	43.49	46.96
5.75	3.01	5.97	8.98	12.05	15.17	18.35	21.58	24.87	28.20	31.60	35.04	38.54	42.09	45.70	49.35
6.00	3.15	6.24	9.38	12.59	15.86	19.19	22.58	26.03	29.53	33.09	36.72	40.39	44.13	47.92	51.77
6.25	3.28	6.50	9.79	13.14	16.56	20.04	23.58	27.19	30.86	34.60	38.40	42.26	46.18	50.16	54.21
6.50	3.41	6.77	10.19	13.69	17.25	20.89	24.59	28.37	32.21	36.12	40.09	44.14	48.25	52.42	56.66
6.75	3.54	7.03	10.60	14.24	17.95	21.74	25.61	29.54	33.56	37.64	41.80	46.03	50.33	54.70	59.14
7.00	3.68	7.30	11.00	14.79	18.65	22.60	26.62	30.73	34.92	39.18	43.52	47.94	52.43	57.00	61.65
7.25	3.81	7.56	11.41	15.34	19.36	23.46	27.65	31.92	36.28	40.73	45.25	49.86	54.55	59.32	64.17
7.50	3.94	7.83	11.82	15.89	20.06	24.32	28.68	33.12	37.66	42.28	46.99	51.80	56.68	61.65	66.71
7.75	4.07	8.10	12.22	16.45	20.77	25.19	29.71	34.33	39.04	43.85	48.75	53.74	58.83	64.01	69.27
8.00	4.21	8.37	12.63	17.00	21.48	26.06	30.75	35.54	40.43	45.42	50.52	55.71	61.00	66.38	71.86
8.25	4.34	8.63	13.04	17.56	22.20	26.94	31.79	36.76	41.83	47.01	52.29	57.68	63.18	68.77	74.46
8.50	4.47	8.90	13.45	18.12	22.91	27.82	32.84	37.98	43.24	48.60	54.08	59.67	65.37	71.18	77.09
8.75	4.61	9.17	13.87	18.69	23.63	28.70	33.89	39.21	44.65	50.21	55.88	61.68	67.58	73.60	79.73
9.00	4.74	9.44	14.28	19.25	24.35	29.59	34.95	40.45	46.07	51.82	57.70	63.69	69.81	76.04	82.39
9.25	4.87	9.71	14.69	19.81	25.08	30.48	36.02	41.69	47.50	53.45	59.52	65.72	72.05	78.50	85.08
9.50	5.01	9.98	15.11	20.38	25.80	31.37	37.08	42.94	48.94	55.08	61.36	67.77	74.31	80.98	87.78
9.75	5.14	10.25	15.52	20.95	26.53	32.27	38.16	44.20	50.39	56.72	63.20	69.82	76.58	83.48	90.50
10.00	5.28	10.52	15.94	21.52	27.26	33.17	39.23	45.46	51.84	58.37	65.06	71.89	78.87	85.99	93.24
10.25	5.41	10.80	16.36	22.09	28.00	34.07	40.32	46.73	53.30	60.04	66.93	73.97	81.17	88.52	96.00
10.50	5.54	11.07	16.78	22.66	28.73	34.98	41.40	48.00	54.77	61.71	68.81	76.07	83.49	91.06	98.78
10.75	5.68	11.34	17.20	23.24	29.47	35.89	42.50	49.28	56.25	63.39	70.70	78.18	85.82	93.62	101.58
11.00	5.81	11.61	17.62	23.82	30.21	36.81	43.59	50.57	57.73	65.08	72.60	80.30	88.17	96.20	104.39
11.25	5.95	11.89	18.04	24.39	30.96	37.73	44.70	51.86	59.22	66.78	74.51	82.43	90.53	98.79	107.22
11.50	6.08	12.16	18.46	24.97	31.71	38.65	45.80	53.16	60.72	68.48	76.44	84.58	92.90	101.40	110.07
11.75	6.22	12.43	18.88	25.56	32.45	39.57	46.91	54.47	62.23	70.20	78.37	86.74	95.29	104.03	112.94
12.00	6.35	12.71	19.31	26.14	33.21	40.50	48.03	55.78	63.75	71.93	80.32	88.91	97.69	106.67	115.82
12.25	6.49	12.98	19.73	26.72	33.96	41.44	49.15	57.10	65.27	73.66	82.27	91.09	100.11	109.32	118.72
12.50	6.62	13.26	20.16	27.31	34.72	42.37	50.28	58.42	66.80	75.41	84.24	93.28	102.54	111.99	121.64
12.75	6.76	13.53	20.58	27.90	35.48	43.31	51.41	59.75	68.33	77.16	86.21	95.49	104.98	114.68	124.58
13.00	6.89	13.81	21.01	28.49	36.24	44.26	52.54	61.08	69.88	78.92	88.20	97.71	107.44	117.38	127.53
13.25	7.03	14.09	21.44	29.08	37.00	45.20	53.68	62.42	71.43	80.69	90.19	99.94	109.91	120.10	130.50
13.50	7.16	14.36	21.87	29.67	37.77	46.15	54.82	63.77	72.99	82.47	92.20	102.18	112.39	122.83	133.48
13.75	7.30	14.64	22.30	30.27	38.54	47.11	55.97	65.12	74.56	84.26	94.22	104.43	114.89	125.57	136.48
14.00	7.43	14.92	22.73	30.86	39.31	48.07	57.13	66.48	76.13	86.05	96.25	106.70	117.40	128.33	139.49
14.25	7.57	15.20	23.16	31.46	40.08	49.03	58.28	67.85	77.71	87.86	98.28	108.97	119.92	131.11	142.52
14.50	7.70	15.48	23.60	32.06	40.86	49.99	59.45	69.22	79.30	89.67	100.33	111.26	122.45	133.89	145.57
14.75	7.84	15.76	24.03	32.66	41.64	50.96	60.61	70.60	80.89	91.49	102.39	113.56	125.00	136.69	148.63
15.00	7.98	16.03	24.47	33.26	42.42	51.93	61.79	71.98	82.49	93.32	104.45	115.87	127.56	139.51	151.70
15.25	8.11	16.31	24.90	33.87	43.20	52.90	62.96	73.37	84.10	95.16	106.53	118.19	130.13	142.33	154.79
15.50	8.25	16.59	25.34	34.47	43.99	53.88	64.14	74.76	85.72	97.01	108.61	120.52	132.71	145.17	157.89
15.75	8.38	16.88	25.78	35.08	44.78	54.86	65.33	76.16	87.34	98.86	110.71	122.86	135.31	148.03	161.01
16.00	8.52	17.16	26.21	35.69	45.57	55.85	66.52	77.56	88.97	100.72	112.81	125.21	137.91	150.89	164.14
16.25	8.66	17.44	26.65	36.30	46.36	56.84	67.71	78.97	90.61	102.60	114.92	127.58	140.53	153.77	167.28
16.50	8.79	17.72	27.09	36.91	47.16	57.83	68.91	80.39	92.25	104.47	117.05	129.95	143.16	156.66	170.44
16.75	8.93	18.00	27.54	37.52	47.96	58.82	70.11	81.81	93.90	106.36	119.18	132.33	145.80	159.57	173.61
17.00	9.07	18.28	27.98	38.14	48.76	59.82	71.32	83.24	95.56	108.26	121.32	134.72	148.45	162.48	176.79
17.25	9.20	18.57	28.42	38.75	49.56	60.82	72.53	84.67	97.22	110.16	123.47	137.13	151.11	165.41	179.99
17.50	9.34	18.85	28.86	39.37	50.37	61.83	73.75	86.11	98.89	112.07	125.63	139.54	153.79	168.35	183.20
17.75	9.48	19.14	29.31	39.99	51.17	62.84	74.97	87.55	100.57	113.99	127.79	141.96	156.47	171.30	186.42
18.00	9.61	19.42	29.76	40.61	51.98	63.85	76.20	89.00	102.25	115.91	129.97	144.40	159.17	174.26	189.65
18.25	9.75	19.70	30.20	41.24	52.80	64.87	77.43	90.46	103.94	117.85	132.15	146.84	161.87	177.23	192.89
18.50	9.89	19.99	30.65	41.86	53.61	65.88	78.66	91.92	105.63	119.79	134.35	149.29	164.59	180.22	196.15
18.75	10.03	20.28	31.10	42.49	54.43	66.91	79.90	93.38	107.34	121.73	136.55	151.75	167.31	183.21	199.41
19.00	10.16	20.56	31.55	43.12	55.25	67.93	81.14	94.85	109.04	123.69	138.76	154.22	170.05	186.21	202.69
20.00	10.72	21.71	33.36	45.64	58.55	72.06	86.15	100.79	115.94	131.58	147.68	164.19	181.09	198.34	215.91
25.00	13.50	27.54	42.60	58.64	75.62	93.48	112.18	131.65	151.83	172.65	194.05	215.96	238.32	261.09	284.20
30.00	16.32	33.54	52.20	72.23	93.56	116.09	139.71	164.31	189.78	216.01	242.89	270.33	298.24	326.55	355.19

Description: This table shows the finance charge per $100 of amount financed, at the Annual Percentage Rate, for the term of the loan. 26 payments are made each year.

Example: The finance charge for a 30 year loan at an Annual Percentage Rate of 8 % is 164.04 %. The total interest for a $ 50,000 loan is $ 82020.00.

Finance Charge Per $100 of Amount Financed

RATE	16 yr	17 yr	18 yr	19 yr	20 yr	21 yr	22 yr	23 yr	24 yr	25 yr	26 yr	27 yr	28 yr	29 yr	30 yr
0.00	0.00	0.00	0.00	0.00	0.00	0.00	0.00	0.00	0.00	0.00	0.00	0.00	0.00	0.00	0.00
1.00	8.23	8.76	9.29	9.82	10.35	10.89	11.42	11.96	12.50	13.04	13.58	14.13	14.67	15.22	15.77
2.00	16.89	18.00	19.12	20.24	21.37	22.50	23.65	24.79	25.95	27.11	28.28	29.46	30.64	31.83	33.02
3.00	25.97	27.71	29.47	31.25	33.04	34.84	36.66	38.49	40.34	42.20	44.07	45.96	47.87	49.78	51.71
4.00	35.46	37.90	40.36	42.84	45.35	47.88	50.44	53.03	55.64	58.27	60.93	63.61	66.31	69.04	71.79
4.25	37.90	40.52	43.16	45.83	48.53	51.25	54.01	56.79	59.60	62.43	65.30	68.19	71.10	74.05	77.01
4.50	40.37	43.16	45.99	48.85	51.74	54.66	57.62	60.60	63.61	66.66	69.73	72.84	75.97	79.13	82.32
4.75	42.85	45.84	48.85	51.91	54.99	58.12	61.27	64.46	67.68	70.94	74.23	77.55	80.90	84.29	87.70
5.00	45.37	48.54	51.75	55.00	58.29	61.61	64.97	68.37	71.81	75.28	78.79	82.33	85.91	89.52	93.16
5.25	47.91	51.27	54.68	58.13	61.62	65.15	68.72	72.33	75.98	79.67	83.40	87.17	90.98	94.82	98.70
5.50	50.47	54.03	57.63	61.29	64.98	68.72	72.51	76.34	80.21	84.12	88.08	92.07	96.11	100.19	104.31
5.75	53.06	56.82	60.62	64.48	68.38	72.34	76.34	80.39	84.48	88.62	92.81	97.04	101.31	105.63	109.98
6.00	55.67	59.63	63.64	67.71	71.82	75.99	80.22	84.49	88.81	93.18	97.60	102.06	106.57	111.13	115.73
6.25	58.31	62.47	66.69	70.97	75.30	79.69	84.13	88.63	93.18	97.79	102.44	107.15	111.90	116.70	121.55
6.50	60.97	65.34	69.77	74.26	78.81	83.42	88.09	92.82	97.60	102.44	107.34	112.29	117.29	122.34	127.44
6.75	63.65	68.23	72.87	77.58	82.36	87.19	92.09	97.05	102.07	107.15	112.29	117.48	122.73	128.03	133.39
7.00	66.36	71.15	76.01	80.94	85.94	91.00	96.13	101.33	106.59	111.91	117.29	122.73	128.23	133.79	139.40
7.25	69.09	74.10	79.18	84.33	89.55	94.85	100.22	105.65	111.15	116.72	122.35	128.04	133.79	139.60	145.47
7.50	71.85	77.07	82.37	87.75	93.20	98.73	104.34	110.01	115.76	121.57	127.45	133.40	139.41	145.48	151.61
7.75	74.63	80.07	85.59	91.20	96.88	102.65	108.49	114.41	120.41	126.47	132.60	138.81	145.07	151.40	157.80
8.00	77.43	83.09	88.84	94.68	100.60	106.61	112.69	118.86	125.10	131.41	137.80	144.26	150.79	157.38	164.04
8.25	80.25	86.14	92.12	98.19	104.35	110.59	116.93	123.34	129.83	136.40	143.05	149.77	156.56	163.42	170.34
8.50	83.10	89.21	95.42	101.73	108.13	114.62	121.20	127.86	134.61	141.44	148.34	155.32	162.38	169.50	176.69
8.75	85.97	92.31	98.75	105.30	111.94	118.67	125.50	132.42	139.42	146.51	153.68	160.92	168.24	175.64	183.10
9.00	88.86	95.43	102.11	108.89	115.78	122.76	129.84	137.02	144.28	151.62	159.06	166.57	174.15	181.82	189.55
9.25	91.77	98.57	105.49	112.52	119.65	126.89	134.22	141.65	149.17	156.78	164.48	172.25	180.11	188.04	196.05
9.50	94.70	101.74	108.90	116.17	123.55	131.04	138.63	146.32	154.10	161.97	169.94	177.98	186.11	194.32	202.59
9.75	97.66	104.93	112.33	119.85	127.48	135.22	143.07	151.02	159.06	167.20	175.44	183.75	192.15	200.63	209.18
10.00	100.63	108.15	115.79	123.56	131.44	139.44	147.54	155.76	164.07	172.47	180.97	189.56	198.23	206.99	215.81
10.25	103.63	111.39	119.28	127.29	135.43	143.68	152.05	160.52	169.10	177.78	186.55	195.41	204.35	213.38	222.49
10.50	106.64	114.65	122.78	131.05	139.45	147.96	156.59	165.33	174.17	183.12	192.16	201.29	210.51	219.82	229.20
10.75	109.68	117.93	126.32	134.84	143.49	152.26	161.16	170.16	179.27	188.49	197.81	207.21	216.71	226.29	235.94
11.00	112.74	121.23	129.87	138.65	147.56	156.59	165.75	175.03	184.41	193.90	203.49	213.17	222.94	232.79	242.73
11.25	115.81	124.56	133.45	142.48	151.65	160.95	170.38	179.92	189.57	199.34	209.20	219.16	229.20	239.34	249.55
11.50	118.91	127.90	137.05	146.34	155.77	165.34	175.03	184.84	194.77	204.81	214.94	225.18	235.50	245.91	256.40
11.75	122.02	131.27	140.67	150.22	159.92	169.75	179.71	189.80	200.00	210.30	220.72	231.23	241.83	252.52	263.28
12.00	125.16	134.66	144.32	154.13	164.09	174.19	184.42	194.78	205.25	215.83	226.52	237.31	248.19	259.15	270.20
12.25	128.31	138.06	147.98	158.06	168.28	178.65	189.15	199.78	210.53	221.39	232.36	243.42	254.58	265.82	277.14
12.50	131.48	141.49	151.67	162.01	172.50	183.14	193.91	204.82	215.84	226.97	238.22	249.56	260.99	272.51	284.12
12.75	134.67	144.94	155.38	165.98	176.74	187.65	198.70	209.87	221.17	232.58	244.10	255.72	267.44	279.23	291.11
13.00	137.87	148.40	159.10	169.98	181.01	192.19	203.51	214.96	226.53	238.22	250.02	261.92	273.91	285.98	298.14
13.25	141.10	151.88	162.85	173.99	185.29	196.74	208.34	220.06	231.91	243.88	255.96	268.13	280.40	292.75	305.19
13.50	144.34	155.39	166.62	178.03	189.60	201.32	213.19	225.19	237.32	249.57	261.92	274.37	286.92	299.55	312.26
13.75	147.59	158.91	170.41	182.08	193.93	205.92	218.07	230.35	242.75	255.27	267.90	280.64	293.46	306.37	319.35
14.00	150.87	162.45	174.21	186.16	198.27	210.55	222.97	235.52	248.20	261.00	273.91	286.92	300.03	313.21	326.47
14.25	154.16	166.00	178.04	190.25	202.64	215.19	227.89	240.72	253.68	266.76	279.94	293.23	306.60	320.07	333.60
14.50	157.47	169.57	181.88	194.37	207.03	219.85	232.83	245.94	259.17	272.53	285.99	299.55	313.21	326.95	340.76
14.75	160.79	173.16	185.74	198.50	211.44	224.54	237.78	251.17	264.69	278.32	292.06	305.90	319.83	333.84	347.93
15.00	164.13	176.77	189.62	202.65	215.86	229.24	242.76	256.43	270.22	284.13	298.15	312.27	326.47	340.76	355.12
15.25	167.48	180.39	193.51	206.82	220.31	233.96	247.76	261.70	275.77	289.96	304.26	318.65	333.13	347.69	362.33
15.50	170.85	184.03	197.42	211.00	224.77	238.69	252.77	267.00	281.34	295.81	310.38	325.05	339.81	354.64	369.55
15.75	174.23	187.68	201.35	215.20	229.24	243.45	257.81	272.31	286.93	301.67	316.52	331.47	346.50	361.61	376.79
16.00	177.63	191.35	205.29	219.42	233.74	248.22	262.86	277.63	292.54	307.56	322.68	337.90	353.21	368.59	384.04
16.25	181.04	195.04	209.25	223.66	238.25	253.01	267.92	282.98	298.16	313.45	328.86	344.35	359.93	375.58	391.31
16.50	184.47	198.74	213.22	227.91	242.78	257.81	273.00	288.34	303.79	319.37	335.04	350.81	366.67	382.59	398.59
16.75	187.91	202.45	217.21	232.17	247.32	262.63	278.10	293.71	309.45	325.30	341.25	357.29	373.42	389.61	405.88
17.00	191.36	206.18	221.21	236.45	251.87	267.47	283.21	299.10	315.11	331.24	347.46	363.78	380.18	396.65	413.18
17.25	194.83	209.92	225.23	240.74	256.45	272.32	288.34	304.50	320.79	337.19	353.69	370.28	386.95	403.69	420.49
17.50	198.31	213.67	229.26	245.05	261.03	277.18	293.48	309.92	326.49	343.16	359.93	376.80	393.74	410.75	427.82
17.75	201.80	217.44	233.30	249.37	265.63	282.06	298.64	315.35	332.19	349.14	366.19	383.32	400.53	417.81	435.15
18.00	205.31	221.22	237.36	253.71	270.24	286.95	303.80	320.80	337.91	355.14	372.46	389.86	407.34	424.89	442.50
18.25	208.83	225.01	241.43	258.06	274.87	291.85	308.98	326.25	343.64	361.14	378.73	396.41	414.16	431.98	449.85
18.50	212.36	228.82	245.51	262.42	279.51	296.77	314.18	331.72	349.38	367.16	385.02	402.97	420.99	439.07	457.21
18.75	215.90	232.64	249.61	266.79	284.16	301.69	319.38	337.20	355.14	373.18	391.32	409.53	427.82	446.17	464.58
19.00	219.45	236.47	253.72	271.17	288.82	306.63	324.60	342.69	360.90	379.22	397.62	416.11	434.67	453.28	471.95
20.00	233.77	251.90	270.26	288.83	307.58	326.50	345.56	364.75	384.06	403.46	422.94	442.50	462.12	481.80	501.53
25.00	307.61	331.28	355.17	379.24	403.47	427.84	452.32	476.89	501.53	526.25	551.01	575.82	600.66	625.53	650.43
30.00	384.09	413.22	442.53	471.98	501.54	531.20	560.93	590.72	620.56	650.43	680.33	710.26	740.20	770.15	800.12

APR SCAN TABLE

Description: This table shows the finance charge per $100 of amount financed, at the Annual Percentage Rate, for the term of the loan. 52 payments are made each year.

Example: The finance charge for a 15 year loan at an Annual Percentage Rate of 8 % is 71.79 %. The total interest for a $ 50,000 loan is $ 35895.00.

Finance Charge Per $100 of Amount Financed

RATE	1 yr	2 yr	3 yr	4 yr	5 yr	6 yr	7 yr	8 yr	9 yr	10 yr	11 yr	12 yr	13 yr	14 yr	15 yr
0.00	0.00	0.00	0.00	0.00	0.00	0.00	0.00	0.00	0.00	0.00	0.00	0.00	0.00	0.00	0.00
1.00	.51	1.01	1.52	2.02	2.53	3.04	3.55	4.06	4.58	5.09	5.61	6.13	6.65	7.17	7.70
2.00	1.02	2.03	3.05	4.07	5.10	6.14	7.18	8.23	9.29	10.35	11.42	12.50	13.58	14.67	15.77
3.00	1.54	3.06	4.60	6.15	7.72	9.30	10.90	12.51	14.14	15.78	17.43	19.11	20.79	22.49	24.21
4.00	2.05	4.09	6.16	8.25	10.37	12.52	14.69	16.89	19.12	21.37	23.65	25.95	28.28	30.64	33.02
4.25	2.18	4.35	6.55	8.78	11.04	13.33	15.65	18.00	20.38	22.79	25.23	27.70	30.20	32.72	35.28
4.50	2.31	4.61	6.95	9.31	11.71	14.15	16.62	19.12	21.66	24.22	26.83	29.46	32.13	34.83	37.56
4.75	2.44	4.87	7.34	9.85	12.39	14.97	17.59	20.25	22.94	25.67	28.43	31.24	34.08	36.95	39.86
5.00	2.57	5.13	7.74	10.38	13.07	15.80	18.57	21.38	24.23	27.12	30.06	33.03	36.04	39.10	42.19
5.25	2.70	5.39	8.13	10.92	13.75	16.63	19.55	22.52	25.53	28.59	31.69	34.83	38.03	41.26	44.54
5.50	2.83	5.65	8.53	11.46	14.43	17.46	20.53	23.66	26.84	30.06	33.33	36.65	40.03	43.44	46.91
5.75	2.96	5.92	8.93	12.00	15.12	18.29	21.53	24.81	28.15	31.54	34.99	38.49	42.04	45.65	49.30
6.00	3.09	6.18	9.33	12.54	15.81	19.13	22.52	25.97	29.47	33.04	36.66	40.34	44.07	47.87	51.71
6.25	3.22	6.44	9.73	13.08	16.50	19.98	23.52	27.13	30.81	34.54	38.34	42.20	46.12	50.11	54.15
6.50	3.35	6.70	10.13	13.62	17.19	20.83	24.53	28.30	32.15	36.06	40.03	44.08	48.19	52.37	56.61
6.75	3.48	6.97	10.53	14.17	17.89	21.68	25.54	29.48	33.49	37.58	41.74	45.97	50.27	54.64	59.09
7.00	3.61	7.23	10.93	14.72	18.59	22.53	26.56	30.67	34.85	39.11	43.46	47.88	52.37	56.94	61.58
7.25	3.74	7.49	11.34	15.27	19.29	23.39	27.58	31.86	36.22	40.66	45.19	49.79	54.48	59.26	64.10
7.50	3.87	7.76	11.74	15.82	19.99	24.25	28.61	33.05	37.59	42.21	46.93	51.73	56.62	61.59	66.65
7.75	4.00	8.02	12.15	16.37	20.70	25.12	29.64	34.26	38.97	43.78	48.68	53.68	58.76	63.94	69.21
8.00	4.13	8.29	12.56	16.93	21.41	25.99	30.67	35.46	40.36	45.35	50.44	55.64	60.93	66.31	71.79
8.25	4.26	8.56	12.96	17.48	22.12	26.86	31.72	36.68	41.75	46.93	52.22	57.61	63.10	68.70	74.39
8.50	4.39	8.82	13.37	18.04	22.83	27.74	32.76	37.90	43.16	48.53	54.01	59.60	65.30	71.10	77.01
8.75	4.52	9.09	13.78	18.60	23.55	28.62	33.81	39.13	44.57	50.13	55.81	61.60	67.51	73.53	79.66
9.00	4.65	9.36	14.19	19.16	24.27	29.50	34.87	40.37	45.99	51.74	57.62	63.61	69.73	75.97	82.32
9.25	4.79	9.62	14.60	19.73	24.99	30.39	35.93	41.61	47.42	53.36	59.44	65.64	71.97	78.43	85.00
9.50	4.92	9.89	15.02	20.29	25.71	31.28	37.00	42.85	48.85	54.99	61.27	67.68	74.23	80.90	87.70
9.75	5.05	10.16	15.43	20.86	26.44	32.18	38.07	44.11	50.30	56.64	63.12	69.74	76.50	83.40	90.42
10.00	5.18	10.43	15.84	21.42	27.17	33.08	39.14	45.37	51.75	58.29	64.97	71.81	78.79	85.91	93.16
10.25	5.31	10.70	16.26	21.99	27.90	33.98	40.22	46.63	53.21	59.95	66.84	73.89	81.09	88.43	95.92
10.50	5.44	10.97	16.68	22.57	28.64	34.88	41.31	47.91	54.68	61.62	68.72	75.98	83.40	90.98	98.70
10.75	5.57	11.24	17.09	23.14	29.37	35.79	42.40	49.19	56.15	63.29	70.61	78.09	85.73	93.53	101.49
11.00	5.71	11.51	17.51	23.71	30.11	36.71	43.49	50.47	57.63	64.98	72.51	80.21	88.08	96.11	104.31
11.25	5.84	11.78	17.93	24.29	30.85	37.62	44.59	51.76	59.12	66.68	74.42	82.34	90.44	98.70	107.14
11.50	5.97	12.05	18.35	24.87	31.60	38.54	45.70	53.06	60.62	68.38	76.34	84.48	92.81	101.31	109.98
11.75	6.10	12.32	18.77	25.44	32.34	39.47	46.81	54.36	62.13	70.10	78.27	86.64	95.20	103.94	112.85
12.00	6.24	12.59	19.19	26.03	33.09	40.39	47.92	55.67	63.64	71.82	80.22	88.81	97.60	106.57	115.73
12.25	6.37	12.87	19.61	26.61	33.85	41.32	49.04	56.99	65.16	73.56	82.17	90.99	100.01	109.23	118.64
12.50	6.50	13.14	20.04	27.19	34.60	42.26	50.16	58.31	66.69	75.30	84.13	93.18	102.44	111.90	121.55
12.75	6.63	13.41	20.46	27.78	35.36	43.20	51.29	59.64	68.22	77.05	86.11	95.39	104.88	114.59	124.49
13.00	6.77	13.69	20.89	28.37	36.12	44.14	52.42	60.97	69.77	78.81	88.09	97.60	107.34	117.29	127.44
13.25	6.90	13.96	21.31	28.95	36.88	45.08	53.56	62.31	71.32	80.58	90.09	99.83	109.81	120.00	130.40
13.50	7.03	14.24	21.74	29.54	37.64	46.03	54.70	63.65	72.87	82.36	92.09	102.07	112.29	122.73	133.39
13.75	7.16	14.51	22.17	30.14	38.41	46.98	55.85	65.01	74.44	84.14	94.11	104.33	114.79	125.48	136.38
14.00	7.30	14.79	22.60	30.73	39.18	47.94	57.00	66.36	76.01	85.94	96.13	106.59	117.29	128.23	139.40
14.25	7.43	15.06	23.03	31.33	39.95	48.90	58.16	67.73	77.59	87.74	98.17	108.86	119.81	131.01	142.43
14.50	7.56	15.34	23.46	31.92	40.73	49.86	59.32	69.09	79.18	89.55	100.22	111.15	122.35	133.79	145.47
14.75	7.70	15.61	23.89	32.52	41.50	50.83	60.48	70.47	80.77	91.37	102.27	113.45	124.89	136.59	148.53
15.00	7.83	15.89	24.32	33.12	42.28	51.80	61.65	71.85	82.37	93.20	104.34	115.76	127.45	139.41	151.61
15.25	7.97	16.17	24.76	33.72	43.06	52.77	62.83	73.24	83.98	95.04	106.41	118.08	130.02	142.23	154.69
15.50	8.10	16.45	25.19	34.33	43.85	53.74	64.01	74.63	85.59	96.88	108.49	120.41	132.60	145.07	157.80
15.75	8.23	16.73	25.63	34.93	44.63	54.72	65.19	76.03	87.21	98.74	110.59	122.75	135.20	147.93	160.91
16.00	8.37	17.00	26.06	35.54	45.42	55.71	66.38	77.43	88.84	100.60	112.69	125.10	137.80	150.79	164.04
16.25	8.50	17.28	26.50	36.15	46.21	56.69	67.57	78.84	90.48	102.47	114.80	127.46	140.42	153.67	167.19
16.50	8.63	17.56	26.94	36.76	47.01	57.68	68.77	80.25	92.12	104.35	116.93	129.83	143.05	156.56	170.34
16.75	8.77	17.84	27.38	37.37	47.80	58.68	69.97	81.67	93.77	106.23	119.06	132.21	145.69	159.46	173.51
17.00	8.90	18.12	27.82	37.98	48.60	59.67	71.18	83.10	95.42	108.13	121.20	134.61	148.34	162.38	176.69
17.25	9.04	18.40	28.26	38.60	49.40	60.67	72.39	84.53	97.08	110.03	123.34	137.01	151.00	165.30	179.89
17.50	9.17	18.69	28.70	39.21	50.21	61.68	73.60	85.97	98.75	111.94	125.50	139.42	153.68	168.24	183.10
17.75	9.31	18.97	29.14	39.83	51.01	62.68	74.82	87.41	100.43	113.85	127.67	141.84	156.36	171.19	186.32
18.00	9.44	19.25	29.59	40.45	51.82	63.69	76.04	88.86	102.11	115.78	129.84	144.28	159.06	174.15	189.55
18.25	9.58	19.53	30.03	41.07	52.63	64.71	77.27	90.31	103.80	117.71	132.03	146.72	161.76	177.13	192.79
18.50	9.71	19.81	30.48	41.69	53.45	65.72	78.50	91.77	105.49	119.65	134.22	149.17	164.48	180.11	196.05
18.75	9.85	20.10	30.92	42.32	54.26	66.74	79.74	93.23	107.19	121.60	136.42	151.63	167.20	183.11	199.32
19.00	9.98	20.38	31.37	42.94	55.08	67.77	80.98	94.70	108.90	123.55	138.63	154.10	169.94	186.11	202.59
20.00	10.52	21.52	33.17	45.46	58.37	71.89	85.99	100.63	115.79	131.44	147.54	164.07	180.97	198.23	215.81
25.00	13.26	27.31	42.37	58.42	75.41	93.28	111.99	131.48	151.67	172.50	193.91	215.84	238.22	260.99	284.12
30.00	16.03	33.26	51.93	71.98	93.32	115.87	139.51	164.13	189.62	215.86	242.76	270.22	298.15	326.47	355.12

APR SCAN TABLE

Description: This table shows the finance charge per $100 of amount financed, at the Annual Percentage Rate, for the term of the loan. 52 payments are made each year.

Example: The finance charge for a 30 year loan at an Annual Percentage Rate of 8 % is 163.99 %. The total interest for a $ 50,000 loan is $ 81995.00.

Finance Charge Per $100 of Amount Financed

RATE	16 yr	17 yr	18 yr	19 yr	20 yr	21 yr	22 yr	23 yr	24 yr	25 yr	26 yr	27 yr	28 yr	29 yr	30 yr
0.00	0.00	0.00	0.00	0.00	0.00	0.00	0.00	0.00	0.00	0.00	0.00	0.00	0.00	0.00	0.00
1.00	8.22	8.75	9.28	9.81	10.34	10.88	11.41	11.95	12.49	13.03	13.57	14.12	14.66	15.21	15.76
2.00	16.87	17.98	19.10	20.22	21.35	22.48	23.63	24.78	25.93	27.09	28.26	29.44	30.62	31.81	33.00
3.00	25.94	27.69	29.45	31.22	33.01	34.81	36.63	38.46	40.31	42.17	44.05	45.94	47.84	49.76	51.69
4.00	35.43	37.86	40.32	42.80	45.31	47.85	50.41	52.99	55.60	58.23	60.89	63.57	66.28	69.00	71.76
4.25	37.86	40.48	43.12	45.79	48.49	51.21	53.97	56.75	59.56	62.40	65.26	68.15	71.07	74.01	76.98
4.50	40.32	43.12	45.95	48.81	51.70	54.62	57.58	60.56	63.58	66.62	69.69	72.80	75.93	79.09	82.28
4.75	42.81	45.79	48.81	51.86	54.95	58.07	61.23	64.42	67.64	70.90	74.19	77.51	80.86	84.25	87.66
5.00	45.32	48.49	51.71	54.95	58.24	61.57	64.93	68.33	71.76	75.24	78.74	82.29	85.86	89.48	93.12
5.25	47.86	51.22	54.63	58.08	61.57	65.10	68.67	72.28	75.94	79.63	83.36	87.13	90.93	94.78	98.66
5.50	50.42	53.98	57.59	61.24	64.93	68.67	72.46	76.29	80.16	84.08	88.03	92.03	96.07	100.15	104.26
5.75	53.01	56.76	60.57	64.43	68.33	72.29	76.29	80.34	84.44	88.58	92.76	96.99	101.27	105.58	109.94
6.00	55.62	59.58	63.59	67.65	71.77	75.94	80.17	84.44	88.76	93.13	97.55	102.02	106.53	111.09	115.69
6.25	58.25	62.41	66.64	70.91	75.25	79.64	84.08	88.58	93.13	97.74	102.39	107.10	111.85	116.66	121.51
6.50	60.91	65.28	69.71	74.20	78.76	83.37	88.04	92.77	97.55	102.39	107.29	112.24	117.24	122.29	127.39
6.75	63.60	68.17	72.82	77.53	82.30	87.14	92.04	97.00	102.02	107.10	112.24	117.43	122.68	127.98	133.34
7.00	66.30	71.09	75.95	80.88	85.88	90.95	96.08	101.28	106.54	111.86	117.24	122.68	128.18	133.74	139.35
7.25	69.03	74.04	79.12	84.27	89.49	94.79	100.16	105.59	111.10	116.66	122.30	127.99	133.74	139.55	145.42
7.50	71.79	77.01	82.31	87.69	93.14	98.67	104.28	109.95	115.70	121.52	127.40	133.35	139.35	145.43	151.56
7.75	74.56	80.00	85.53	91.14	96.82	102.59	108.44	114.36	120.35	126.42	132.55	138.75	145.02	151.35	157.75
8.00	77.36	83.02	88.78	94.61	100.54	106.54	112.63	118.80	125.04	131.36	137.75	144.21	150.74	157.33	163.99
8.25	80.18	86.07	92.05	98.12	104.28	110.53	116.86	123.28	129.77	136.35	143.00	149.72	156.51	163.37	170.29
8.50	83.03	89.14	95.35	101.66	108.06	114.55	121.13	127.80	134.55	141.38	148.29	155.27	162.33	169.45	176.65
8.75	85.90	92.24	98.68	105.23	111.87	118.61	125.44	132.36	139.36	146.45	153.62	160.87	168.19	175.59	183.05
9.00	88.78	95.36	102.04	108.83	115.71	122.70	129.78	136.95	144.22	151.57	159.00	166.51	174.10	181.77	189.50
9.25	91.69	98.50	105.42	112.45	119.58	126.82	134.15	141.59	149.11	156.72	164.42	172.20	180.06	187.99	196.00
9.50	94.63	101.67	108.83	116.10	123.48	130.97	138.56	146.25	154.04	161.91	169.88	177.93	186.06	194.27	202.55
9.75	97.58	104.86	112.26	119.78	127.41	135.16	143.01	150.96	159.00	167.15	175.38	183.70	192.10	200.58	209.14
10.00	100.55	108.07	115.72	123.49	131.37	139.37	147.48	155.69	164.01	172.41	180.92	189.51	198.18	206.94	215.77
10.25	103.55	111.31	119.20	127.22	135.36	143.62	151.99	160.46	169.04	177.72	186.49	195.35	204.30	213.33	222.44
10.50	106.56	114.57	122.71	130.98	139.38	147.89	156.52	165.26	174.11	183.06	192.10	201.24	210.46	219.77	229.15
10.75	109.60	117.85	126.24	134.76	143.42	152.19	161.09	170.10	179.21	188.43	197.75	207.16	216.66	226.24	235.90
11.00	112.65	121.15	129.79	138.57	147.49	156.53	165.69	174.96	184.35	193.84	203.43	213.11	222.89	232.75	242.68
11.25	115.73	124.48	133.37	142.41	151.58	160.88	170.31	179.86	189.51	199.28	209.14	219.10	229.15	239.29	249.50
11.50	118.82	127.82	136.97	146.27	155.70	165.27	174.96	184.78	194.71	204.75	214.89	225.12	235.45	245.86	256.36
11.75	121.94	131.19	140.59	150.15	159.85	169.68	179.65	189.73	199.93	210.25	220.66	231.18	241.78	252.47	263.24
12.00	125.07	134.57	144.24	154.05	164.02	174.12	184.35	194.71	205.19	215.78	226.47	237.26	248.14	259.11	270.16
12.25	128.22	137.98	147.90	157.98	168.21	178.58	189.09	199.72	210.47	221.33	232.30	243.37	254.53	265.77	277.10
12.50	131.39	141.41	151.59	161.93	172.43	183.07	193.85	204.75	215.78	226.92	238.16	249.51	260.95	272.47	284.07
12.75	134.58	144.85	155.30	165.91	176.67	187.58	198.63	209.81	221.11	232.53	244.05	255.67	267.39	279.19	291.07
13.00	137.78	148.32	159.02	169.90	180.93	192.12	203.44	214.89	226.47	238.17	249.97	261.87	273.86	285.94	298.10
13.25	141.01	151.80	162.77	173.92	185.22	196.67	208.27	220.00	231.86	243.83	255.90	268.08	280.35	292.71	305.15
13.50	144.25	155.30	166.54	177.95	189.53	201.25	213.13	225.13	237.26	249.51	261.87	274.32	286.87	299.51	312.22
13.75	147.50	158.82	170.33	182.01	193.85	205.86	218.00	230.29	242.69	255.22	267.85	280.59	293.41	306.33	319.31
14.00	150.78	162.36	174.13	186.08	198.20	210.48	222.90	235.46	248.15	260.95	273.86	286.87	299.98	313.17	326.43
14.25	154.07	165.91	177.96	190.18	202.57	215.12	227.82	240.66	253.62	266.70	279.89	293.18	306.56	320.03	333.57
14.50	157.37	169.49	181.80	194.29	206.96	219.79	232.76	245.88	259.12	272.48	285.94	299.51	313.17	326.91	340.72
14.75	160.70	173.08	185.66	198.42	211.36	224.47	237.72	251.11	264.63	278.27	292.01	305.86	319.79	333.81	347.90
15.00	164.04	176.68	189.53	202.57	215.79	229.17	242.70	256.37	270.17	284.08	298.10	312.22	326.43	340.72	355.09
15.25	167.39	180.31	193.43	206.74	220.23	233.89	247.70	261.64	275.72	289.91	304.21	318.61	333.09	347.66	362.30
15.50	170.76	183.94	197.34	210.93	224.69	238.63	252.71	266.94	281.29	295.76	310.34	325.01	339.77	354.61	369.52
15.75	174.14	187.60	201.27	215.13	229.17	243.38	257.75	272.25	286.88	301.63	316.48	331.43	346.46	361.58	376.76
16.00	177.54	191.27	205.21	219.35	233.67	248.16	262.80	277.58	292.49	307.51	322.64	337.86	353.17	368.56	384.01
16.25	180.95	194.95	209.17	223.58	238.18	252.94	267.86	282.92	298.11	313.41	328.81	344.31	359.89	375.55	391.28
16.50	184.38	198.65	213.14	227.83	242.71	257.75	272.95	288.28	303.75	319.32	335.00	350.78	366.63	382.56	398.56
16.75	187.82	202.36	217.13	232.10	247.25	262.57	278.04	293.66	309.40	325.25	341.21	357.25	373.38	389.58	405.85
17.00	191.27	206.09	221.13	236.38	251.81	267.41	283.16	299.05	315.06	331.19	347.42	363.74	380.14	396.62	413.15
17.25	194.74	209.83	225.15	240.67	256.38	272.25	288.28	304.45	320.75	337.15	353.65	370.25	386.92	403.66	420.47
17.50	198.22	213.59	229.18	244.98	260.96	277.12	293.43	309.87	326.44	343.12	359.90	376.76	393.71	410.72	427.79
17.75	201.71	217.36	233.23	249.30	265.56	282.00	298.58	315.30	332.15	349.10	366.15	383.29	400.50	417.79	435.13
18.00	205.22	221.14	237.28	253.64	270.18	286.89	303.75	320.75	337.87	355.10	372.42	389.83	407.31	424.86	442.47
18.25	208.74	224.93	241.35	257.99	274.80	291.79	308.93	326.20	343.60	361.10	378.70	396.38	414.13	431.95	449.83
18.50	212.27	228.74	245.44	262.35	279.44	296.71	314.12	331.67	349.34	367.12	384.99	402.94	420.96	439.05	457.19
18.75	215.81	232.56	249.53	266.72	284.09	301.64	319.33	337.15	355.10	373.14	391.28	409.50	427.80	446.15	464.56
19.00	219.36	236.39	253.64	271.11	288.76	306.58	324.54	342.64	360.86	379.18	397.59	416.08	434.64	453.26	471.93
20.00	233.69	251.82	270.18	288.76	307.52	326.45	345.52	364.71	384.02	403.42	422.91	442.48	462.10	481.78	501.51
25.00	307.54	331.21	355.11	379.19	403.43	427.80	452.29	476.86	501.51	526.23	550.99	575.80	600.65	625.52	650.42
30.00	384.04	413.17	442.49	471.95	501.52	531.18	560.92	590.71	620.55	650.42	680.33	710.25	740.19	770.15	800.11

TABLE *20*

Lease Payments

Interest Rates:	5 to 15%.
Terms:	2 to 10 years, each year; 12, 15, 20 years.
Payments:	Monthly, in arrears; monthly 1, 2, 3 payments, in advance.
Residual:	0, 5, 10, 15, 20%.

This table shows the Annual Percentage Rate (APR) for a monthly lease payment where the payment is expressed as a percent of the capital cost.

Example: An asset may be leased for 5 years at a monthly payment equal to 2.22% of the cost. If payments are in arrears, the APR is 11.92%, as shown on page 20-2.

If payments are in advance, the APR is 12.36%, as shown on page 20-12.

If there are 2 payments in advance and a 10% residual, the APR is 15.18%, as shown on page 20-26.

Annual Percentage Rate. The APR is the interest rate on the lease. It is the interest rate at which the monthly lease payment plus residual amortizes a loan in the amount of the capital cost.

Residual. The residual is the value of the asset at the end of the lease term. If the lessee purchases the asset for the residual, then that is an additional payment to the lessor at the end of the lease term. The effect of the purchase is to increase the APR.

Example: The APR is 9.66% on a 4 year lease with a 2.50% monthly payment made in advance.

If the asset is purchased for the 20% residual at the end of the lease term, then the APR is 15.99% on the 4 year financing. The effect of purchasing is to add the residual amount to the finance charge, thereby increasing the rate.

The following schedule illustrates the calculation of interest

at the APR and the allocation of the monthly payment to interest and principal:

| Loan: $1,000.00 | | Term: 4 years | |
Rate: 9.67%		Payment: $25.00, in advance	
Payment	Interest	Principal	Balance
1	.00	25.00	975.00
2	7.85	17.15	957.85
3	7.71	17.29	940.56
⋮	⋮	⋮	⋮
47	⋮	⋮	24.80
48	.20	24.80	.00

Since payments are in advance, the lease terminates 1 month after the last payment.

A second schedule illustrates the effect of the residual:

| Loan: $1,000.00 | | Term: 4 years | |
| Rate: 15.99% | | Payment: $25.00, in advance | |
		Residual: 20.00%	
Payment	Interest	Principal	Balance
1	.00	25.00	975.00
2	12.99	12.01	962.99
3	12.83	12.17	950.82
⋮	⋮	⋮	⋮
47	⋮	⋮	219.44
48	2.92	22.08	197.37
49	2.63	197.37	.00*

*Payment of $200 for the residual is made at the end of the lease term, i.e., at the end of month 48.

Description: This table shows the Annual Percentage Rate and finance charge per $100 for monthly lease payments.

Example: A 4.30% lease payment for 2 years is equivalent to an APR of 3.04%. The charge per $100 cost is $ 3.20.

2 yr PAYT	APR	CHARGE	3 yr PAYT	APR	CHARGE	4 yr PAYT	APR	CHARGE	5 yr PAYT	APR	CHARGE	6 yr PAYT	APR	CHARGE	7 yr PAYT	APR	CHARGE
4.30	3.04	3.20	3.00	5.06	8.00	2.30	4.94	10.40	1.90	5.28	14.00	1.70	6.90	22.40	1.50	6.81	26.00
4.31	3.27	3.44	3.01	5.29	8.36	2.31	5.16	10.88	1.91	5.50	14.60	1.71	7.11	23.12	1.51	7.01	26.84
4.32	3.49	3.68	3.02	5.51	8.72	2.32	5.38	11.36	1.92	5.71	15.20	1.72	7.31	23.84	1.52	7.22	27.68
4.33	3.72	3.92	3.03	5.73	9.08	2.33	5.60	11.84	1.93	5.93	15.80	1.73	7.52	24.56	1.53	7.42	28.52
4.34	3.94	4.16	3.04	5.95	9.44	2.34	5.81	12.32	1.94	6.14	16.40	1.74	7.73	25.28	1.54	7.62	29.36
4.35	4.17	4.40	3.05	6.17	9.80	2.35	6.03	12.80	1.95	6.36	17.00	1.75	7.93	26.00	1.55	7.83	30.20
4.36	4.39	4.64	3.06	6.39	10.16	2.36	6.25	13.28	1.96	6.57	17.60	1.76	8.14	26.72	1.56	8.03	31.04
4.37	4.62	4.88	3.07	6.61	10.52	2.37	6.47	13.76	1.97	6.79	18.20	1.77	8.34	27.44	1.57	8.23	31.88
4.38	4.84	5.12	3.08	6.83	10.88	2.38	6.68	14.24	1.98	7.00	18.80	1.78	8.54	28.16	1.58	8.43	32.72
4.39	5.06	5.36	3.09	7.05	11.24	2.39	6.90	14.72	1.99	7.21	19.40	1.79	8.75	28.88	1.59	8.63	33.56
4.40	5.29	5.60	3.10	7.27	11.60	2.40	7.12	15.20	2.00	7.42	20.00	1.80	8.95	29.60	1.60	8.82	34.40
4.41	5.51	5.84	3.11	7.49	11.96	2.41	7.33	15.68	2.01	7.63	20.60	1.81	9.15	30.32	1.61	9.02	35.24
4.42	5.73	6.08	3.12	7.70	12.32	2.42	7.55	16.16	2.02	7.84	21.20	1.82	9.35	31.04	1.62	9.22	36.08
4.43	5.95	6.32	3.13	7.92	12.68	2.43	7.76	16.64	2.03	8.05	21.80	1.83	9.55	31.76	1.63	9.41	36.92
4.44	6.18	6.56	3.14	8.14	13.04	2.44	7.97	17.12	2.04	8.26	22.40	1.84	9.75	32.48	1.64	9.61	37.76
4.45	6.40	6.80	3.15	8.35	13.40	2.45	8.19	17.60	2.05	8.47	23.00	1.85	9.95	33.20	1.65	9.80	38.60
4.46	6.62	7.04	3.16	8.57	13.76	2.46	8.40	18.08	2.06	8.67	23.60	1.86	10.15	33.92	1.66	10.00	39.44
4.47	6.84	7.28	3.17	8.79	14.12	2.47	8.61	18.56	2.07	8.88	24.20	1.87	10.34	34.64	1.67	10.19	40.28
4.48	7.06	7.52	3.18	9.00	14.48	2.48	8.82	19.04	2.08	9.09	24.80	1.88	10.54	35.36	1.68	10.38	41.12
4.49	7.28	7.76	3.19	9.22	14.84	2.49	9.03	19.52	2.09	9.29	25.40	1.89	10.74	36.08	1.69	10.58	41.96
4.50	7.50	8.00	3.20	9.43	15.20	2.50	9.24	20.00	2.10	9.50	26.00	1.90	10.93	36.80	1.70	10.77	42.80
4.51	7.72	8.24	3.21	9.64	15.56	2.51	9.45	20.48	2.11	9.70	26.60	1.91	11.13	37.52	1.71	10.96	43.64
4.52	7.94	8.48	3.22	9.86	15.92	2.52	9.66	20.96	2.12	9.90	27.20	1.92	11.32	38.24	1.72	11.15	44.48
4.53	8.16	8.72	3.23	10.07	16.28	2.53	9.87	21.44	2.13	10.11	27.80	1.93	11.52	38.96	1.73	11.34	45.32
4.54	8.38	8.96	3.24	10.28	16.64	2.54	10.08	21.92	2.14	10.31	28.40	1.94	11.71	39.68	1.74	11.53	46.16
4.55	8.60	9.20	3.25	10.49	17.00	2.55	10.29	22.40	2.15	10.51	29.00	1.95	11.90	40.40	1.75	11.71	47.00
4.56	8.82	9.44	3.26	10.71	17.36	2.56	10.49	22.88	2.16	10.71	29.60	1.96	12.10	41.12	1.76	11.90	47.84
4.57	9.03	9.68	3.27	10.92	17.72	2.57	10.70	23.36	2.17	10.91	30.20	1.97	12.29	41.84	1.77	12.09	48.68
4.58	9.25	9.92	3.28	11.13	18.08	2.58	10.91	23.84	2.18	11.12	30.80	1.98	12.48	42.56	1.78	12.27	49.52
4.59	9.47	10.16	3.29	11.34	18.44	2.59	11.11	24.32	2.19	11.32	31.40	1.99	12.67	43.28	1.79	12.46	50.36
4.60	9.69	10.40	3.30	11.55	18.80	2.60	11.32	24.80	2.20	11.51	32.00	2.00	12.86	44.00	1.80	12.65	51.20
4.61	9.90	10.64	3.31	11.76	19.16	2.61	11.52	25.28	2.21	11.71	32.60	2.01	13.05	44.72	1.81	12.83	52.04
4.62	10.12	10.88	3.32	11.97	19.52	2.62	11.73	25.76	2.22	11.91	33.20	2.02	13.24	45.44	1.82	13.01	52.88
4.63	10.34	11.12	3.33	12.18	19.88	2.63	11.93	26.24	2.23	12.11	33.80	2.03	13.43	46.16	1.83	13.20	53.72
4.64	10.55	11.36	3.34	12.39	20.24	2.64	12.13	26.72	2.24	12.31	34.40	2.04	13.61	46.88	1.84	13.38	54.56
4.65	10.77	11.60	3.35	12.60	20.60	2.65	12.34	27.20	2.25	12.50	35.00	2.05	13.80	47.60	1.85	13.56	55.40
4.66	10.98	11.84	3.36	12.80	20.96	2.66	12.54	27.68	2.26	12.70	35.60	2.06	13.99	48.32	1.86	13.75	56.24
4.67	11.20	12.08	3.37	13.01	21.32	2.67	12.74	28.16	2.27	12.90	36.20	2.07	14.18	49.04	1.87	13.93	57.08
4.68	11.41	12.32	3.38	13.22	21.68	2.68	12.94	28.64	2.28	13.09	36.80	2.08	14.36	49.76	1.88	14.11	57.92
4.69	11.63	12.56	3.39	13.43	22.04	2.69	13.15	29.12	2.29	13.29	37.40	2.09	14.55	50.48	1.89	14.29	58.76
4.70	11.84	12.80	3.40	13.63	22.40	2.70	13.35	29.60	2.30	13.48	38.00	2.10	14.73	51.20	1.90	14.47	59.60
4.71	12.06	13.04	3.41	13.84	22.76	2.71	13.55	30.08	2.31	13.67	38.60	2.11	14.92	51.92	1.91	14.65	60.44
4.72	12.27	13.28	3.42	14.05	23.12	2.72	13.75	30.56	2.32	13.87	39.20	2.12	15.10	52.64	1.92	14.83	61.28
4.73	12.48	13.52	3.43	14.25	23.48	2.73	13.95	31.04	2.33	14.06	39.80	2.13	15.28	53.36	1.93	15.01	62.12
4.74	12.70	13.76	3.44	14.46	23.84	2.74	14.15	31.52	2.34	14.25	40.40	2.14	15.47	54.08	1.94	15.18	62.96
4.75	12.91	14.00	3.45	14.66	24.20	2.75	14.35	32.00	2.35	14.45	41.00	2.15	15.65	54.80	1.95	15.36	63.80
4.76	13.12	14.24	3.46	14.87	24.56	2.76	14.54	32.48	2.36	14.64	41.60	2.16	15.83	55.52	1.96	15.54	64.64
4.77	13.34	14.48	3.47	15.07	24.92	2.77	14.74	32.96	2.37	14.83	42.20	2.17	16.01	56.24	1.97	15.71	65.48
4.78	13.55	14.72	3.48	15.27	25.28	2.78	14.94	33.44	2.38	15.02	42.80	2.18	16.20	56.96	1.98	15.89	66.32
4.79	13.76	14.96	3.49	15.48	25.64	2.79	15.14	33.92	2.39	15.21	43.40	2.19	16.38	57.68	1.99	16.07	67.16
4.80	13.97	15.20	3.50	15.68	26.00	2.80	15.33	34.40	2.40	15.40	44.00	2.20	16.56	58.40	2.00	16.24	68.00
4.81	14.18	15.44	3.51	15.88	26.36	2.81	15.53	34.88	2.41	15.59	44.60	2.21	16.74	59.12	2.01	16.42	68.84
4.82	14.40	15.68	3.52	16.09	26.72	2.82	15.73	35.36	2.42	15.78	45.20	2.22	16.92	59.84	2.02	16.59	69.68
4.83	14.61	15.92	3.53	16.29	27.08	2.83	15.92	35.84	2.43	15.97	45.80	2.23	17.10	60.56	2.03	16.76	70.52
4.84	14.82	16.16	3.54	16.49	27.44	2.84	16.12	36.32	2.44	16.15	46.40	2.24	17.28	61.28	2.04	16.94	71.36
4.85	15.03	16.40	3.55	16.69	27.80	2.85	16.31	36.80	2.45	16.34	47.00	2.25	17.45	62.00	2.05	17.11	72.20
4.86	15.24	16.64	3.56	16.89	28.16	2.86	16.51	37.28	2.46	16.53	47.60	2.26	17.63	62.72	2.06	17.28	73.04
4.87	15.45	16.88	3.57	17.09	28.52	2.87	16.70	37.76	2.47	16.72	48.20	2.27	17.81	63.44	2.07	17.46	73.88
4.88	15.66	17.12	3.58	17.30	28.88	2.88	16.89	38.24	2.48	16.90	48.80	2.28	17.99	64.16	2.08	17.63	74.72
4.89	15.87	17.36	3.59	17.50	29.24	2.89	17.09	38.72	2.49	17.09	49.40	2.29	18.16	64.88	2.09	17.80	75.56
4.90	16.08	17.60	3.60	17.70	29.60	2.90	17.28	39.20	2.50	17.27	50.00	2.30	18.34	65.60	2.10	17.97	76.40
4.91	16.29	17.84	3.61	17.90	29.96	2.91	17.47	39.68	2.51	17.46	50.60	2.31	18.52	66.32	2.11	18.14	77.24
4.92	16.50	18.08	3.62	18.09	30.32	2.92	17.66	40.16	2.52	17.64	51.20	2.32	18.69	67.04	2.12	18.31	78.08
4.93	16.70	18.32	3.63	18.29	30.68	2.93	17.86	40.64	2.53	17.83	51.80	2.33	18.87	67.76	2.13	18.48	78.92
4.94	16.91	18.56	3.64	18.49	31.04	2.94	18.05	41.12	2.54	18.01	52.40	2.34	19.04	68.48	2.14	18.65	79.76
4.95	17.12	18.80	3.65	18.69	31.40	2.95	18.24	41.60	2.55	18.20	53.00	2.35	19.22	69.20	2.15	18.82	80.60
4.96	17.33	19.04	3.66	18.89	31.76	2.96	18.43	42.08	2.56	18.38	53.60	2.36	19.39	69.92	2.16	18.99	81.44
4.97	17.54	19.28	3.67	19.09	32.12	2.97	18.62	42.56	2.57	18.56	54.20	2.37	19.56	70.64	2.17	19.15	82.28
4.98	17.74	19.52	3.68	19.28	32.48	2.98	18.81	43.04	2.58	18.74	54.80	2.38	19.74	71.36	2.18	19.32	83.12
4.99	17.95	19.76	3.69	19.48	32.84	2.99	19.00	43.52	2.59	18.93	55.40	2.39	19.91	72.08	2.19	19.49	83.96

LEASE PAYMENTS

Description: This table shows the Annual Percentage Rate and finance charge per $100 for monthly lease payments.

Example: A 1.30% lease payment for 8 years is equivalent to an APR of 5.71%. The charge per $100 cost is $ 24.80.

8 yr PAYT	APR	CHARGE	9 yr PAYT	APR	CHARGE	10 yr PAYT	APR	CHARGE	12 yr PAYT	APR	CHARGE	15 yr PAYT	APR	CHARGE	20 yr PAYT	APR	CHARGE
1.30	5.71	24.80	1.20	5.99	29.60	1.10	5.80	32.00	1.00	6.46	44.00	.80	5.18	44.00	.70	5.71	68.00
1.31	5.91	25.76	1.21	6.19	30.68	1.11	6.00	33.20	1.01	6.65	45.44	.81	5.37	45.80	.71	5.89	70.40
1.32	6.12	26.72	1.22	6.39	31.76	1.12	6.19	34.40	1.02	6.84	46.88	.82	5.55	47.60	.72	6.06	72.80
1.33	6.32	27.68	1.23	6.59	32.84	1.13	6.39	35.60	1.03	7.03	48.32	.83	5.74	49.40	.73	6.23	75.20
1.34	6.53	28.64	1.24	6.79	33.92	1.14	6.59	36.80	1.04	7.22	49.76	.84	5.93	51.20	.74	6.41	77.60
1.35	6.73	29.60	1.25	6.99	35.00	1.15	6.78	38.00	1.05	7.40	51.20	.85	6.11	53.00	.75	6.58	80.00
1.36	6.93	30.56	1.26	7.18	36.08	1.16	6.98	39.20	1.06	7.59	52.64	.86	6.30	54.80	.76	6.74	82.40
1.37	7.13	31.52	1.27	7.38	37.16	1.17	7.17	40.40	1.07	7.77	54.08	.87	6.48	56.60	.77	6.91	84.80
1.38	7.33	32.48	1.28	7.58	38.24	1.18	7.37	41.60	1.08	7.96	55.52	.88	6.66	58.40	.78	7.08	87.20
1.39	7.53	33.44	1.29	7.77	39.32	1.19	7.56	42.80	1.09	8.14	56.96	.89	6.84	60.20	.79	7.24	89.60
1.40	7.73	34.40	1.30	7.96	40.40	1.20	7.75	44.00	1.10	8.32	58.40	.90	7.02	62.00	.80	7.41	92.00
1.41	7.93	35.36	1.31	8.16	41.48	1.21	7.94	45.20	1.11	8.50	59.84	.91	7.20	63.80	.81	7.57	94.40
1.42	8.12	36.32	1.32	8.35	42.56	1.22	8.13	46.40	1.12	8.68	61.28	.92	7.38	65.60	.82	7.73	96.80
1.43	8.32	37.28	1.33	8.54	43.64	1.23	8.32	47.60	1.13	8.86	62.72	.93	7.55	67.40	.83	7.90	99.20
1.44	8.52	38.24	1.34	8.73	44.72	1.24	8.50	48.80	1.14	9.03	64.16	.94	7.73	69.20	.84	8.06	101.60
1.45	8.71	39.20	1.35	8.92	45.80	1.25	8.69	50.00	1.15	9.21	65.60	.95	7.90	71.00	.85	8.22	104.00
1.46	8.90	40.16	1.36	9.11	46.88	1.26	8.87	51.20	1.16	9.39	67.04	.96	8.08	72.80	.86	8.38	106.40
1.47	9.10	41.12	1.37	9.30	47.96	1.27	9.06	52.40	1.17	9.56	68.48	.97	8.25	74.60	.87	8.53	108.80
1.48	9.29	42.08	1.38	9.48	49.04	1.28	9.24	53.60	1.18	9.74	69.92	.98	8.42	76.40	.88	8.69	111.20
1.49	9.48	43.04	1.39	9.67	50.12	1.29	9.43	54.80	1.19	9.91	71.36	.99	8.59	78.20	.89	8.85	113.60
1.50	9.67	44.00	1.40	9.85	51.20	1.30	9.61	56.00	1.20	10.09	72.80	1.00	8.76	80.00	.90	9.00	116.00
1.51	9.86	44.96	1.41	10.04	52.28	1.31	9.79	57.20	1.21	10.26	74.24	1.01	8.93	81.80	.91	9.16	118.40
1.52	10.05	45.92	1.42	10.22	53.36	1.32	9.97	58.40	1.22	10.43	75.68	1.02	9.10	83.60	.92	9.31	120.80
1.53	10.24	46.88	1.43	10.41	54.44	1.33	10.15	59.60	1.23	10.60	77.12	1.03	9.26	85.40	.93	9.47	123.20
1.54	10.43	47.84	1.44	10.59	55.52	1.34	10.33	60.80	1.24	10.77	78.56	1.04	9.43	87.20	.94	9.62	125.60
1.55	10.61	48.80	1.45	10.77	56.60	1.35	10.51	62.00	1.25	10.94	80.00	1.05	9.60	89.00	.95	9.77	128.00
1.56	10.80	49.76	1.46	10.95	57.68	1.36	10.69	63.20	1.26	11.11	81.44	1.06	9.76	90.80	.96	9.92	130.40
1.57	10.98	50.72	1.47	11.13	58.76	1.37	10.87	64.40	1.27	11.28	82.88	1.07	9.92	92.60	.97	10.08	132.80
1.58	11.17	51.68	1.48	11.31	59.84	1.38	11.04	65.60	1.28	11.44	84.32	1.08	10.09	94.40	.98	10.23	135.20
1.59	11.35	52.64	1.49	11.49	60.92	1.39	11.22	66.80	1.29	11.61	85.76	1.09	10.25	96.20	.99	10.38	137.60
1.60	11.54	53.60	1.50	11.67	62.00	1.40	11.40	68.00	1.30	11.78	87.20	1.10	10.41	98.00	1.00	10.52	140.00
1.61	11.72	54.56	1.51	11.85	63.08	1.41	11.57	69.20	1.31	11.94	88.64	1.11	10.57	99.80	1.01	10.67	142.40
1.62	11.90	55.52	1.52	12.03	64.16	1.42	11.74	70.40	1.32	12.11	90.08	1.12	10.73	101.60	1.02	10.82	144.80
1.63	12.09	56.48	1.53	12.20	65.24	1.43	11.92	71.60	1.33	12.27	91.52	1.13	10.89	103.40	1.03	10.97	147.20
1.64	12.27	57.44	1.54	12.38	66.32	1.44	12.09	72.80	1.34	12.44	92.96	1.14	11.05	105.20	1.04	11.11	149.60
1.65	12.45	58.40	1.55	12.56	67.40	1.45	12.26	74.00	1.35	12.60	94.40	1.15	11.21	107.00	1.05	11.26	152.00
1.66	12.63	59.36	1.56	12.73	68.48	1.46	12.44	75.20	1.36	12.76	95.84	1.16	11.37	108.80	1.06	11.41	154.40
1.67	12.81	60.32	1.57	12.91	69.56	1.47	12.61	76.40	1.37	12.93	97.28	1.17	11.53	110.60	1.07	11.55	156.80
1.68	12.99	61.28	1.58	13.08	70.64	1.48	12.78	77.60	1.38	13.09	98.72	1.18	11.69	112.40	1.08	11.70	159.20
1.69	13.17	62.24	1.59	13.25	71.72	1.49	12.95	78.80	1.39	13.25	100.16	1.19	11.84	114.20	1.09	11.84	161.60
1.70	13.34	63.20	1.60	13.43	72.80	1.50	13.12	80.00	1.40	13.41	101.60	1.20	12.00	116.00	1.10	11.98	164.00
1.71	13.52	64.16	1.61	13.60	73.88	1.51	13.29	81.20	1.41	13.57	103.04	1.21	12.15	117.80	1.11	12.13	166.40
1.72	13.70	65.12	1.62	13.77	74.96	1.52	13.45	82.40	1.42	13.73	104.48	1.22	12.31	119.60	1.12	12.27	168.80
1.73	13.87	66.08	1.63	13.94	76.04	1.53	13.62	83.60	1.43	13.89	105.92	1.23	12.46	121.40	1.13	12.41	171.20
1.74	14.05	67.04	1.64	14.11	77.12	1.54	13.79	84.80	1.44	14.05	107.36	1.24	12.61	123.20	1.14	12.55	173.60
1.75	14.23	68.00	1.65	14.28	78.20	1.55	13.96	86.00	1.45	14.20	108.80	1.25	12.77	125.00	1.15	12.70	176.00
1.76	14.40	68.96	1.66	14.45	79.28	1.56	14.12	87.20	1.46	14.36	110.24	1.26	12.92	126.80	1.16	12.84	178.40
1.77	14.57	69.92	1.67	14.62	80.36	1.57	14.29	88.40	1.47	14.52	111.68	1.27	13.07	128.60	1.17	12.98	180.80
1.78	14.75	70.88	1.68	14.79	81.44	1.58	14.45	89.60	1.48	14.67	113.12	1.28	13.22	130.40	1.18	13.12	183.20
1.79	14.92	71.84	1.69	14.96	82.52	1.59	14.62	90.80	1.49	14.83	114.56	1.29	13.37	132.20	1.19	13.26	185.60
1.80	15.09	72.80	1.70	15.13	83.60	1.60	14.78	92.00	1.50	14.99	116.00	1.30	13.53	134.00	1.20	13.40	188.00
1.81	15.27	73.76	1.71	15.29	84.68	1.61	14.95	93.20	1.51	15.14	117.44	1.31	13.68	135.80	1.21	13.54	190.40
1.82	15.44	74.72	1.72	15.46	85.76	1.62	15.11	94.40	1.52	15.30	118.88	1.32	13.82	137.60	1.22	13.68	192.80
1.83	15.61	75.68	1.73	15.63	86.84	1.63	15.27	95.60	1.53	15.45	120.32	1.33	13.97	139.40	1.23	13.81	195.20
1.84	15.78	76.64	1.74	15.79	87.92	1.64	15.43	96.80	1.54	15.60	121.76	1.34	14.12	141.20	1.24	13.95	197.60
1.85	15.95	77.60	1.75	15.96	89.00	1.65	15.60	98.00	1.55	15.76	123.20	1.35	14.27	143.00	1.25	14.09	200.00
1.86	16.12	78.56	1.76	16.12	90.08	1.66	15.76	99.20	1.56	15.91	124.64	1.36	14.42	144.80	1.26	14.23	202.40
1.87	16.29	79.52	1.77	16.29	91.16	1.67	15.92	100.40	1.57	16.06	126.08	1.37	14.57	146.60	1.27	14.36	204.80
1.88	16.46	80.48	1.78	16.45	92.24	1.68	16.08	101.60	1.58	16.22	127.52	1.38	14.71	148.40	1.28	14.50	207.20
1.89	16.63	81.44	1.79	16.62	93.32	1.69	16.24	102.80	1.59	16.37	128.96	1.39	14.86	150.20	1.29	14.64	209.60
1.90	16.80	82.40	1.80	16.78	94.40	1.70	16.40	104.00	1.60	16.52	130.40	1.40	15.01	152.00	1.30	14.77	212.00
1.91	16.96	83.36	1.81	16.94	95.48	1.71	16.56	105.20	1.61	16.67	131.84	1.41	15.15	153.80	1.31	14.91	214.40
1.92	17.13	84.32	1.82	17.10	96.56	1.72	16.72	106.40	1.62	16.82	133.28	1.42	15.30	155.60	1.32	15.04	216.80
1.93	17.30	85.28	1.83	17.27	97.64	1.73	16.87	107.60	1.63	16.97	134.72	1.43	15.44	157.40	1.33	15.18	219.20
1.94	17.46	86.24	1.84	17.43	98.72	1.74	17.03	108.80	1.64	17.12	136.16	1.44	15.59	159.20	1.34	15.31	221.60
1.95	17.63	87.20	1.85	17.59	99.80	1.75	17.19	110.00	1.65	17.27	137.60	1.45	15.73	161.00	1.35	15.45	224.00
1.96	17.80	88.16	1.86	17.75	100.88	1.76	17.35	111.20	1.66	17.42	139.04	1.46	15.88	162.80	1.36	15.58	226.40
1.97	17.96	89.12	1.87	17.91	101.96	1.77	17.50	112.40	1.67	17.57	140.48	1.47	16.02	164.60	1.37	15.72	228.80
1.98	18.13	90.08	1.88	18.07	103.04	1.78	17.66	113.60	1.68	17.72	141.92	1.48	16.16	166.40	1.38	15.85	231.20
1.99	18.29	91.04	1.89	18.23	104.12	1.79	17.82	114.80	1.69	17.87	143.36	1.49	16.30	168.20	1.39	15.98	233.60

LEASE PAYMENTS

Description: This table shows the Annual Percentage Rate and finance charge per $100 for monthly lease payments.

Example: A 4.30% lease payment for 2 years is equivalent to an APR of 7.37%. The charge per $100 cost is $ 8.20.

2 yr PAYT	APR	CHARGE	3 yr PAYT	APR	CHARGE	4 yr PAYT	APR	CHARGE	5 yr PAYT	APR	CHARGE	6 yr PAYT	APR	CHARGE	7 yr PAYT	APR	CHARGE
4.30	7.37	8.20	3.00	7.79	13.00	2.30	6.92	15.40	1.90	6.79	19.00	1.70	8.02	27.40	1.50	7.73	31.00
4.31	7.58	8.44	3.01	7.99	13.36	2.31	7.12	15.88	1.91	6.99	19.60	1.71	8.22	28.12	1.51	7.92	31.84
4.32	7.79	8.68	3.02	8.20	13.72	2.32	7.33	16.36	1.92	7.20	20.20	1.72	8.41	28.84	1.52	8.12	32.68
4.33	8.00	8.92	3.03	8.41	14.08	2.33	7.54	16.84	1.93	7.40	20.80	1.73	8.61	29.56	1.53	8.31	33.52
4.34	8.21	9.16	3.04	8.62	14.44	2.34	7.74	17.32	1.94	7.60	21.40	1.74	8.81	30.28	1.54	8.50	34.36
4.35	8.42	9.40	3.05	8.82	14.80	2.35	7.95	17.80	1.95	7.81	22.00	1.75	9.00	31.00	1.55	8.69	35.20
4.36	8.63	9.64	3.06	9.03	15.16	2.36	8.15	18.28	1.96	8.01	22.60	1.76	9.20	31.72	1.56	8.89	36.04
4.37	8.84	9.88	3.07	9.24	15.52	2.37	8.36	18.76	1.97	8.21	23.20	1.77	9.39	32.44	1.57	9.08	36.88
4.38	9.05	10.12	3.08	9.44	15.88	2.38	8.56	19.24	1.98	8.41	23.80	1.78	9.58	33.16	1.58	9.27	37.72
4.39	9.26	10.36	3.09	9.65	16.24	2.39	8.76	19.72	1.99	8.61	24.40	1.79	9.78	33.88	1.59	9.46	38.56
4.40	9.47	10.60	3.10	9.86	16.60	2.40	8.97	20.20	2.00	8.81	25.00	1.80	9.97	34.60	1.60	9.65	39.40
4.41	9.68	10.84	3.11	10.06	16.96	2.41	9.17	20.68	2.01	9.01	25.60	1.81	10.16	35.32	1.61	9.83	40.24
4.42	9.89	11.08	3.12	10.27	17.32	2.42	9.37	21.16	2.02	9.21	26.20	1.82	10.35	36.04	1.62	10.02	41.08
4.43	10.10	11.32	3.13	10.47	17.68	2.43	9.58	21.64	2.03	9.41	26.80	1.83	10.54	36.76	1.63	10.21	41.92
4.44	10.30	11.56	3.14	10.67	18.04	2.44	9.78	22.12	2.04	9.60	27.40	1.84	10.73	37.48	1.64	10.40	42.76
4.45	10.51	11.80	3.15	10.88	18.40	2.45	9.98	22.60	2.05	9.80	28.00	1.85	10.92	38.20	1.65	10.58	43.60
4.46	10.72	12.04	3.16	11.08	18.76	2.46	10.18	23.08	2.06	10.00	28.60	1.86	11.11	38.92	1.66	10.77	44.44
4.47	10.93	12.28	3.17	11.28	19.12	2.47	10.38	23.56	2.07	10.19	29.20	1.87	11.30	39.64	1.67	10.95	45.28
4.48	11.13	12.52	3.18	11.49	19.48	2.48	10.58	24.04	2.08	10.39	29.80	1.88	11.49	40.36	1.68	11.14	46.12
4.49	11.34	12.76	3.19	11.69	19.84	2.49	10.78	24.52	2.09	10.58	30.40	1.89	11.68	41.08	1.69	11.32	46.96
4.50	11.55	13.00	3.20	11.89	20.20	2.50	10.98	25.00	2.10	10.78	31.00	1.90	11.86	41.80	1.70	11.51	47.80
4.51	11.75	13.24	3.21	12.09	20.56	2.51	11.18	25.48	2.11	10.97	31.60	1.91	12.05	42.52	1.71	11.69	48.64
4.52	11.96	13.48	3.22	12.30	20.92	2.52	11.37	25.96	2.12	11.17	32.20	1.92	12.24	43.24	1.72	11.87	49.48
4.53	12.17	13.72	3.23	12.50	21.28	2.53	11.57	26.44	2.13	11.36	32.80	1.93	12.42	43.96	1.73	12.05	50.32
4.54	12.37	13.96	3.24	12.70	21.64	2.54	11.77	26.92	2.14	11.55	33.40	1.94	12.61	44.68	1.74	12.24	51.16
4.55	12.58	14.20	3.25	12.90	22.00	2.55	11.97	27.40	2.15	11.75	34.00	1.95	12.79	45.40	1.75	12.42	52.00
4.56	12.78	14.44	3.26	13.10	22.36	2.56	12.16	27.88	2.16	11.94	34.60	1.96	12.98	46.12	1.76	12.60	52.84
4.57	12.99	14.68	3.27	13.30	22.72	2.57	12.36	28.36	2.17	12.13	35.20	1.97	13.16	46.84	1.77	12.78	53.68
4.58	13.19	14.92	3.28	13.50	23.08	2.58	12.56	28.84	2.18	12.32	35.80	1.98	13.35	47.56	1.78	12.96	54.52
4.59	13.40	15.16	3.29	13.70	23.44	2.59	12.75	29.32	2.19	12.51	36.40	1.99	13.53	48.28	1.79	13.14	55.36
4.60	13.60	15.40	3.30	13.90	23.80	2.60	12.95	29.80	2.20	12.70	37.00	2.00	13.71	49.00	1.80	13.31	56.20
4.61	13.81	15.64	3.31	14.10	24.16	2.61	13.14	30.28	2.21	12.89	37.60	2.01	13.89	49.72	1.81	13.49	57.04
4.62	14.01	15.88	3.32	14.29	24.52	2.62	13.34	30.76	2.22	13.08	38.20	2.02	14.07	50.44	1.82	13.67	57.88
4.63	14.21	16.12	3.33	14.49	24.88	2.63	13.53	31.24	2.23	13.27	38.80	2.03	14.26	51.16	1.83	13.85	58.72
4.64	14.42	16.36	3.34	14.69	25.24	2.64	13.72	31.72	2.24	13.46	39.40	2.04	14.44	51.88	1.84	14.02	59.56
4.65	14.62	16.60	3.35	14.89	25.60	2.65	13.92	32.20	2.25	13.65	40.00	2.05	14.62	52.60	1.85	14.20	60.40
4.66	14.82	16.84	3.36	15.08	25.96	2.66	14.11	32.68	2.26	13.83	40.60	2.06	14.80	53.32	1.86	14.38	61.24
4.67	15.03	17.08	3.37	15.28	26.32	2.67	14.30	33.16	2.27	14.02	41.20	2.07	14.98	54.04	1.87	14.55	62.08
4.68	15.23	17.32	3.38	15.48	26.68	2.68	14.49	33.64	2.28	14.21	41.80	2.08	15.16	54.76	1.88	14.73	62.92
4.69	15.43	17.56	3.39	15.67	27.04	2.69	14.69	34.12	2.29	14.40	42.40	2.09	15.34	55.48	1.89	14.90	63.76
4.70	15.63	17.80	3.40	15.87	27.40	2.70	14.88	34.60	2.30	14.58	43.00	2.10	15.51	56.20	1.90	15.07	64.60
4.71	15.84	18.04	3.41	16.07	27.76	2.71	15.07	35.08	2.31	14.77	43.60	2.11	15.69	56.92	1.91	15.25	65.44
4.72	16.04	18.28	3.42	16.26	28.12	2.72	15.26	35.56	2.32	14.95	44.20	2.12	15.87	57.64	1.92	15.42	66.28
4.73	16.24	18.52	3.43	16.46	28.48	2.73	15.45	36.04	2.33	15.14	44.80	2.13	16.05	58.36	1.93	15.59	67.12
4.74	16.44	18.76	3.44	16.65	28.84	2.74	15.64	36.52	2.34	15.32	45.40	2.14	16.22	59.08	1.94	15.77	67.96
4.75	16.64	19.00	3.45	16.85	29.20	2.75	15.83	37.00	2.35	15.51	46.00	2.15	16.40	59.80	1.95	15.94	68.80
4.76	16.84	19.24	3.46	17.04	29.56	2.76	16.02	37.48	2.36	15.69	46.60	2.16	16.58	60.52	1.96	16.11	69.64
4.77	17.04	19.48	3.47	17.24	29.92	2.77	16.21	37.96	2.37	15.87	47.20	2.17	16.75	61.24	1.97	16.28	70.48
4.78	17.24	19.72	3.48	17.43	30.28	2.78	16.40	38.44	2.38	16.06	47.80	2.18	16.93	61.96	1.98	16.45	71.32
4.79	17.44	19.96	3.49	17.62	30.64	2.79	16.59	38.92	2.39	16.24	48.40	2.19	17.10	62.68	1.99	16.62	72.16
4.80	17.64	20.20	3.50	17.82	31.00	2.80	16.77	39.40	2.40	16.42	49.00	2.20	17.28	63.40	2.00	16.79	73.00
4.81	17.84	20.44	3.51	18.01	31.36	2.81	16.96	39.88	2.41	16.60	49.60	2.21	17.45	64.12	2.01	16.96	73.84
4.82	18.04	20.68	3.52	18.20	31.72	2.82	17.15	40.36	2.42	16.79	50.20	2.22	17.62	64.84	2.02	17.13	74.68
4.83	18.24	20.92	3.53	18.40	32.08	2.83	17.34	40.84	2.43	16.97	50.80	2.23	17.80	65.56	2.03	17.30	75.52
4.84	18.44	21.16	3.54	18.59	32.44	2.84	17.52	41.32	2.44	17.15	51.40	2.24	17.97	66.28	2.04	17.47	76.36
4.85	18.64	21.40	3.55	18.78	32.80	2.85	17.71	41.80	2.45	17.33	52.00	2.25	18.14	67.00	2.05	17.64	77.20
4.86	18.84	21.64	3.56	18.97	33.16	2.86	17.90	42.28	2.46	17.51	52.60	2.26	18.31	67.72	2.06	17.81	78.04
4.87	19.04	21.88	3.57	19.16	33.52	2.87	18.08	42.76	2.47	17.69	53.20	2.27	18.49	68.44	2.07	17.97	78.88
4.88	19.24	22.12	3.58	19.35	33.88	2.88	18.27	43.24	2.48	17.87	53.80	2.28	18.66	69.16	2.08	18.14	79.72
4.89	19.44	22.36	3.59	19.54	34.24	2.89	18.45	43.72	2.49	18.05	54.40	2.29	18.83	69.88	2.09	18.31	80.56
4.90	19.64	22.60	3.60	19.74	34.60	2.90	18.64	44.20	2.50	18.23	55.00	2.30	19.00	70.60	2.10	18.47	81.40
4.91	19.83	22.84	3.61	19.93	34.96	2.91	18.82	44.68	2.51	18.40	55.60	2.31	19.17	71.32	2.11	18.64	82.24
4.92	20.03	23.08	3.62	20.12	35.32	2.92	19.01	45.16	2.52	18.58	56.20	2.32	19.34	72.04	2.12	18.80	83.08
4.93	20.23	23.32	3.63	20.31	35.68	2.93	19.19	45.64	2.53	18.76	56.80	2.33	19.51	72.76	2.13	18.97	83.92
4.94	20.43	23.56	3.64	20.50	36.04	2.94	19.37	46.12	2.54	18.94	57.40	2.34	19.68	73.48	2.14	19.13	84.76
4.95	20.62	23.80	3.65	20.69	36.40	2.95	19.56	46.60	2.55	19.11	58.00	2.35	19.85	74.20	2.15	19.30	85.60
4.96	20.82	24.04	3.66	20.87	36.76	2.96	19.74	47.08	2.56	19.29	58.60	2.36	20.02	74.92	2.16	19.46	86.44
4.97	21.02	24.28	3.67	21.06	37.12	2.97	19.92	47.56	2.57	19.47	59.20	2.37	20.19	75.64	2.17	19.63	87.28
4.98	21.21	24.52	3.68	21.25	37.48	2.98	20.11	48.04	2.58	19.64	59.80	2.38	20.36	76.36	2.18	19.79	88.12
4.99	21.41	24.76	3.69	21.44	37.84	2.99	20.29	48.52	2.59	19.82	60.40	2.39	20.52	77.08	2.19	19.95	88.96

LEASE PAYMENTS

Description: This table shows the Annual Percentage Rate and finance charge per $100 for monthly lease payments.

Example: A 1.30% lease payment for 8 years is equivalent to an APR of 6.52%. The charge per $100 cost is $ 29.80.

8 yr MONTHLY PAYT	APR	CHARGE	9 yr MONTHLY PAYT	APR	CHARGE	10 yr MONTHLY PAYT	APR	CHARGE	12 yr MONTHLY PAYT	APR	CHARGE	15 yr MONTHLY PAYT	APR	CHARGE	20 yr MONTHLY PAYT	APR	CHARGE
1.30	6.52	29.80	1.20	6.67	34.60	1.10	6.39	37.00	1.00	6.89	49.00	.80	5.52	49.00	.70	5.90	73.00
1.31	6.72	30.76	1.21	6.86	35.68	1.11	6.58	38.20	1.01	7.07	50.44	.81	5.70	50.80	.71	6.07	75.40
1.32	6.91	31.72	1.22	7.05	36.76	1.12	6.77	39.40	1.02	7.25	51.88	.82	5.88	52.60	.72	6.24	77.80
1.33	7.11	32.68	1.23	7.24	37.84	1.13	6.96	40.60	1.03	7.43	53.32	.83	6.06	54.40	.73	6.41	80.20
1.34	7.30	33.64	1.24	7.43	38.92	1.14	7.15	41.80	1.04	7.61	54.76	.84	6.24	56.20	.74	6.58	82.60
1.35	7.50	34.60	1.25	7.62	40.00	1.15	7.33	43.00	1.05	7.79	56.20	.85	6.42	58.00	.75	6.74	85.00
1.36	7.69	35.56	1.26	7.81	41.08	1.16	7.52	44.20	1.06	7.97	57.64	.86	6.59	59.80	.76	6.91	87.40
1.37	7.88	36.52	1.27	8.00	42.16	1.17	7.71	45.40	1.07	8.15	59.08	.87	6.77	61.60	.77	7.07	89.80
1.38	8.07	37.48	1.28	8.18	43.24	1.18	7.89	46.60	1.08	8.32	60.52	.88	6.95	63.40	.78	7.23	92.20
1.39	8.26	38.44	1.29	8.37	44.32	1.19	8.07	47.80	1.09	8.50	61.96	.89	7.12	65.20	.79	7.39	94.60
1.40	8.45	39.40	1.30	8.56	45.40	1.20	8.26	49.00	1.10	8.68	63.40	.90	7.29	67.00	.80	7.56	97.00
1.41	8.64	40.36	1.31	8.74	46.48	1.21	8.44	50.20	1.11	8.85	64.84	.91	7.47	68.80	.81	7.72	99.40
1.42	8.83	41.32	1.32	8.93	47.56	1.22	8.62	51.40	1.12	9.02	66.28	.92	7.64	70.60	.82	7.87	101.80
1.43	9.01	42.28	1.33	9.11	48.64	1.23	8.80	52.60	1.13	9.20	67.72	.93	7.81	72.40	.83	8.03	104.20
1.44	9.20	43.24	1.34	9.29	49.72	1.24	8.98	53.80	1.14	9.37	69.16	.94	7.98	74.20	.84	8.19	106.60
1.45	9.39	44.20	1.35	9.47	50.80	1.25	9.16	55.00	1.15	9.54	70.60	.95	8.15	76.00	.85	8.35	109.00
1.46	9.57	45.16	1.36	9.65	51.88	1.26	9.34	56.20	1.16	9.71	72.04	.96	8.32	77.80	.86	8.50	111.40
1.47	9.76	46.12	1.37	9.84	52.96	1.27	9.52	57.40	1.17	9.88	73.48	.97	8.48	79.60	.87	8.66	113.80
1.48	9.94	47.08	1.38	10.02	54.04	1.28	9.70	58.60	1.18	10.05	74.92	.98	8.65	81.40	.88	8.81	116.20
1.49	10.12	48.04	1.39	10.20	55.12	1.29	9.87	59.80	1.19	10.22	76.36	.99	8.82	83.20	.89	8.97	118.60
1.50	10.31	49.00	1.40	10.37	56.20	1.30	10.05	61.00	1.20	10.39	77.80	1.00	8.98	85.00	.90	9.12	121.00
1.51	10.49	49.96	1.41	10.55	57.28	1.31	10.23	62.20	1.21	10.56	79.24	1.01	9.15	86.80	.91	9.27	123.40
1.52	10.67	50.92	1.42	10.73	58.36	1.32	10.40	63.40	1.22	10.72	80.68	1.02	9.31	88.60	.92	9.42	125.80
1.53	10.85	51.88	1.43	10.91	59.44	1.33	10.58	64.60	1.23	10.89	82.12	1.03	9.47	90.40	.93	9.57	128.20
1.54	11.03	52.84	1.44	11.08	60.52	1.34	10.75	65.80	1.24	11.05	83.56	1.04	9.64	92.20	.94	9.72	130.60
1.55	11.21	53.80	1.45	11.26	61.60	1.35	10.92	67.00	1.25	11.22	85.00	1.05	9.80	94.00	.95	9.87	133.00
1.56	11.39	54.76	1.46	11.43	62.68	1.36	11.10	68.20	1.26	11.38	86.44	1.06	9.96	95.80	.96	10.02	135.40
1.57	11.57	55.72	1.47	11.61	63.76	1.37	11.27	69.40	1.27	11.55	87.88	1.07	10.12	97.60	.97	10.17	137.80
1.58	11.75	56.68	1.48	11.78	64.84	1.38	11.44	70.60	1.28	11.71	89.32	1.08	10.28	99.40	.98	10.32	140.20
1.59	11.93	57.64	1.49	11.96	65.92	1.39	11.61	71.80	1.29	11.87	90.76	1.09	10.44	101.20	.99	10.47	142.60
1.60	12.11	58.60	1.50	12.13	67.00	1.40	11.78	73.00	1.30	12.04	92.20	1.10	10.60	103.00	1.00	10.61	145.00
1.61	12.28	59.56	1.51	12.30	68.08	1.41	11.95	74.20	1.31	12.20	93.64	1.11	10.75	104.80	1.01	10.76	147.40
1.62	12.46	60.52	1.52	12.47	69.16	1.42	12.12	75.40	1.32	12.36	95.08	1.12	10.91	106.60	1.02	10.91	149.80
1.63	12.63	61.48	1.53	12.65	70.24	1.43	12.29	76.60	1.33	12.52	96.52	1.13	11.07	108.40	1.03	11.05	152.20
1.64	12.81	62.44	1.54	12.82	71.32	1.44	12.46	77.80	1.34	12.68	97.96	1.14	11.23	110.20	1.04	11.20	154.60
1.65	12.99	63.40	1.55	12.99	72.40	1.45	12.62	79.00	1.35	12.84	99.40	1.15	11.38	112.00	1.05	11.34	157.00
1.66	13.16	64.36	1.56	13.16	73.48	1.46	12.79	80.20	1.36	13.00	100.84	1.16	11.54	113.80	1.06	11.49	159.40
1.67	13.33	65.32	1.57	13.33	74.56	1.47	12.96	81.40	1.37	13.16	102.28	1.17	11.69	115.60	1.07	11.63	161.80
1.68	13.51	66.28	1.58	13.50	75.64	1.48	13.12	82.60	1.38	13.32	103.72	1.18	11.84	117.40	1.08	11.77	164.20
1.69	13.68	67.24	1.59	13.66	76.72	1.49	13.29	83.80	1.39	13.47	105.16	1.19	12.00	119.20	1.09	11.91	166.60
1.70	13.85	68.20	1.60	13.83	77.80	1.50	13.45	85.00	1.40	13.63	106.60	1.20	12.15	121.00	1.10	12.06	169.00
1.71	14.02	69.16	1.61	14.00	78.88	1.51	13.62	86.20	1.41	13.79	108.04	1.21	12.30	122.80	1.11	12.20	171.40
1.72	14.20	70.12	1.62	14.17	79.96	1.52	13.78	87.40	1.42	13.94	109.48	1.22	12.45	124.60	1.12	12.34	173.80
1.73	14.37	71.08	1.63	14.33	81.04	1.53	13.95	88.60	1.43	14.10	110.92	1.23	12.61	126.40	1.13	12.48	176.20
1.74	14.54	72.04	1.64	14.50	82.12	1.54	14.11	89.80	1.44	14.26	112.36	1.24	12.76	128.20	1.14	12.62	178.60
1.75	14.71	73.00	1.65	14.66	83.20	1.55	14.27	91.00	1.45	14.41	113.80	1.25	12.91	130.00	1.15	12.76	181.00
1.76	14.88	73.96	1.66	14.83	84.28	1.56	14.43	92.20	1.46	14.56	115.24	1.26	13.06	131.80	1.16	12.90	183.40
1.77	15.05	74.92	1.67	14.99	85.36	1.57	14.59	93.40	1.47	14.72	116.68	1.27	13.21	133.60	1.17	13.04	185.80
1.78	15.21	75.88	1.68	15.16	86.44	1.58	14.76	94.60	1.48	14.87	118.12	1.28	13.36	135.40	1.18	13.18	188.20
1.79	15.38	76.84	1.69	15.32	87.52	1.59	14.92	95.80	1.49	15.03	119.56	1.29	13.51	137.20	1.19	13.32	190.60
1.80	15.55	77.80	1.70	15.49	88.60	1.60	15.08	97.00	1.50	15.18	121.00	1.30	13.65	139.00	1.20	13.46	193.00
1.81	15.72	78.76	1.71	15.65	89.68	1.61	15.24	98.20	1.51	15.33	122.44	1.31	13.80	140.80	1.21	13.59	195.40
1.82	15.88	79.72	1.72	15.81	90.76	1.62	15.40	99.40	1.52	15.48	123.88	1.32	13.95	142.60	1.22	13.73	197.80
1.83	16.05	80.68	1.73	15.97	91.84	1.63	15.56	100.60	1.53	15.63	125.32	1.33	14.10	144.40	1.23	13.87	200.20
1.84	16.22	81.64	1.74	16.14	92.92	1.64	15.71	101.80	1.54	15.79	126.76	1.34	14.24	146.20	1.24	14.00	202.60
1.85	16.38	82.60	1.75	16.30	94.00	1.65	15.87	103.00	1.55	15.94	128.20	1.35	14.39	148.00	1.25	14.14	205.00
1.86	16.55	83.56	1.76	16.46	95.08	1.66	16.03	104.20	1.56	16.09	129.64	1.36	14.53	149.80	1.26	14.28	207.40
1.87	16.71	84.52	1.77	16.62	96.16	1.67	16.19	105.40	1.57	16.24	131.08	1.37	14.68	151.60	1.27	14.41	209.80
1.88	16.88	85.48	1.78	16.78	97.24	1.68	16.35	106.60	1.58	16.39	132.52	1.38	14.82	153.40	1.28	14.55	212.20
1.89	17.04	86.44	1.79	16.94	98.32	1.69	16.50	107.80	1.59	16.54	133.96	1.39	14.97	155.20	1.29	14.68	214.60
1.90	17.21	87.40	1.80	17.10	99.40	1.70	16.66	109.00	1.60	16.69	135.40	1.40	15.11	157.00	1.30	14.82	217.00
1.91	17.37	88.36	1.81	17.26	100.48	1.71	16.81	110.20	1.61	16.83	136.84	1.41	15.26	158.80	1.31	14.95	219.40
1.92	17.53	89.32	1.82	17.42	101.56	1.72	16.97	111.40	1.62	16.98	138.28	1.42	15.40	160.60	1.32	15.09	221.80
1.93	17.70	90.28	1.83	17.58	102.64	1.73	17.13	112.60	1.63	17.13	139.72	1.43	15.54	162.40	1.33	15.22	224.20
1.94	17.86	91.24	1.84	17.73	103.72	1.74	17.28	113.80	1.64	17.28	141.16	1.44	15.69	164.20	1.34	15.36	226.60
1.95	18.02	92.20	1.85	17.89	104.80	1.75	17.43	115.00	1.65	17.43	142.60	1.45	15.83	166.00	1.35	15.49	229.00
1.96	18.18	93.16	1.86	18.05	105.88	1.76	17.59	116.20	1.66	17.57	144.04	1.46	15.97	167.80	1.36	15.62	231.40
1.97	18.34	94.12	1.87	18.21	106.96	1.77	17.74	117.40	1.67	17.72	145.48	1.47	16.11	169.60	1.37	15.76	233.80
1.98	18.50	95.08	1.88	18.36	108.04	1.78	17.90	118.60	1.68	17.87	146.92	1.48	16.26	171.40	1.38	15.89	236.20
1.99	18.67	96.04	1.89	18.52	109.12	1.79	18.05	119.80	1.69	18.01	148.36	1.49	16.40	173.20	1.39	16.02	238.60

Description: This table shows the Annual Percentage Rate and finance charge per $100 for monthly lease payments.

Example: A 4.30% lease payment for 2 years is equivalent to an APR of 11.27%. The charge per $100 cost is $ 13.20.

2 yr MONTHLY PAYT	APR	CHARGE	3 yr MONTHLY PAYT	APR	CHARGE	4 yr MONTHLY PAYT	APR	CHARGE	5 yr MONTHLY PAYT	APR	CHARGE	6 yr MONTHLY PAYT	APR	CHARGE	7 yr MONTHLY PAYT	APR	CHARGE
4.30	11.27	13.20	3.00	10.25	18.00	2.30	8.71	20.40	1.90	8.16	24.00	1.70	9.05	32.40	1.50	8.57	36.00
4.31	11.47	13.44	3.01	10.45	18.36	2.31	8.91	20.88	1.91	8.36	24.60	1.71	9.24	33.12	1.51	8.76	36.84
4.32	11.67	13.68	3.02	10.64	18.72	2.32	9.10	21.36	1.92	8.55	25.20	1.72	9.43	33.84	1.52	8.94	37.68
4.33	11.87	13.92	3.03	10.84	19.08	2.33	9.30	21.84	1.93	8.74	25.80	1.73	9.61	34.56	1.53	9.13	38.52
4.34	12.07	14.16	3.04	11.04	19.44	2.34	9.50	22.32	1.94	8.94	26.40	1.74	9.80	35.28	1.54	9.31	39.36
4.35	12.27	14.40	3.05	11.23	19.80	2.35	9.69	22.80	1.95	9.13	27.00	1.75	9.99	36.00	1.55	9.50	40.20
4.36	12.46	14.64	3.06	11.43	20.16	2.36	9.88	23.28	1.96	9.32	27.60	1.76	10.17	36.72	1.56	9.68	41.04
4.37	12.66	14.88	3.07	11.62	20.52	2.37	10.08	23.76	1.97	9.51	28.20	1.77	10.36	37.44	1.57	9.86	41.88
4.38	12.86	15.12	3.08	11.82	20.88	2.38	10.27	24.24	1.98	9.70	28.80	1.78	10.54	38.16	1.58	10.05	42.72
4.39	13.06	15.36	3.09	12.01	21.24	2.39	10.47	24.72	1.99	9.89	29.40	1.79	10.73	38.88	1.59	10.23	43.56
4.40	13.25	15.60	3.10	12.21	21.60	2.40	10.66	25.20	2.00	10.08	30.00	1.80	10.91	39.60	1.60	10.41	44.40
4.41	13.45	15.84	3.11	12.40	21.96	2.41	10.85	25.68	2.01	10.27	30.60	1.81	11.10	40.32	1.61	10.59	45.24
4.42	13.65	16.08	3.12	12.60	22.32	2.42	11.04	26.16	2.02	10.46	31.20	1.82	11.28	41.04	1.62	10.77	46.08
4.43	13.85	16.32	3.13	12.79	22.68	2.43	11.23	26.64	2.03	10.65	31.80	1.83	11.46	41.76	1.63	10.95	46.92
4.44	14.04	16.56	3.14	12.98	23.04	2.44	11.43	27.12	2.04	10.84	32.40	1.84	11.65	42.48	1.64	11.13	47.76
4.45	14.24	16.80	3.15	13.18	23.40	2.45	11.62	27.60	2.05	11.03	33.00	1.85	11.83	43.20	1.65	11.31	48.60
4.46	14.44	17.04	3.16	13.37	23.76	2.46	11.81	28.08	2.06	11.22	33.60	1.86	12.01	43.92	1.66	11.49	49.44
4.47	14.63	17.28	3.17	13.56	24.12	2.47	12.00	28.56	2.07	11.40	34.20	1.87	12.19	44.64	1.67	11.67	50.28
4.48	14.83	17.52	3.18	13.76	24.48	2.48	12.19	29.04	2.08	11.59	34.80	1.88	12.37	45.36	1.68	11.84	51.12
4.49	15.02	17.76	3.19	13.95	24.84	2.49	12.38	29.52	2.09	11.78	35.40	1.89	12.55	46.08	1.69	12.02	51.96
4.50	15.22	18.00	3.20	14.14	25.20	2.50	12.57	30.00	2.10	11.96	36.00	1.90	12.73	46.80	1.70	12.20	52.80
4.51	15.41	18.24	3.21	14.33	25.56	2.51	12.76	30.48	2.11	12.15	36.60	1.91	12.91	47.52	1.71	12.38	53.64
4.52	15.61	18.48	3.22	14.52	25.92	2.52	12.95	30.96	2.12	12.33	37.20	1.92	13.09	48.24	1.72	12.55	54.48
4.53	15.80	18.72	3.23	14.72	26.28	2.53	13.14	31.44	2.13	12.52	37.80	1.93	13.27	48.96	1.73	12.73	55.32
4.54	16.00	18.96	3.24	14.91	26.64	2.54	13.32	31.92	2.14	12.70	38.40	1.94	13.45	49.68	1.74	12.90	56.16
4.55	16.19	19.20	3.25	15.10	27.00	2.55	13.51	32.40	2.15	12.89	39.00	1.95	13.62	50.40	1.75	13.08	57.00
4.56	16.39	19.44	3.26	15.29	27.36	2.56	13.70	32.88	2.16	13.07	39.60	1.96	13.80	51.12	1.76	13.25	57.84
4.57	16.58	19.68	3.27	15.48	27.72	2.57	13.89	33.36	2.17	13.25	40.20	1.97	13.98	51.84	1.77	13.42	58.68
4.58	16.78	19.92	3.28	15.67	28.08	2.58	14.07	33.84	2.18	13.44	40.80	1.98	14.16	52.56	1.78	13.60	59.52
4.59	16.97	20.16	3.29	15.86	28.44	2.59	14.26	34.32	2.19	13.62	41.40	1.99	14.33	53.28	1.79	13.77	60.36
4.60	17.17	20.40	3.30	16.05	28.80	2.60	14.45	34.80	2.20	13.80	42.00	2.00	14.51	54.00	1.80	13.94	61.20
4.61	17.36	20.64	3.31	16.24	29.16	2.61	14.63	35.28	2.21	13.99	42.60	2.01	14.68	54.72	1.81	14.12	62.04
4.62	17.55	20.88	3.32	16.43	29.52	2.62	14.82	35.76	2.22	14.17	43.20	2.02	14.86	55.44	1.82	14.29	62.88
4.63	17.75	21.12	3.33	16.62	29.88	2.63	15.00	36.24	2.23	14.35	43.80	2.03	15.03	56.16	1.83	14.46	63.72
4.64	17.94	21.36	3.34	16.80	30.24	2.64	15.19	36.72	2.24	14.53	44.40	2.04	15.21	56.88	1.84	14.63	64.56
4.65	18.13	21.60	3.35	16.99	30.60	2.65	15.37	37.20	2.25	14.71	45.00	2.05	15.38	57.60	1.85	14.80	65.40
4.66	18.32	21.84	3.36	17.18	30.96	2.66	15.56	37.68	2.26	14.89	45.60	2.06	15.56	58.32	1.86	14.97	66.24
4.67	18.52	22.08	3.37	17.37	31.32	2.67	15.74	38.16	2.27	15.07	46.20	2.07	15.73	59.04	1.87	15.14	67.08
4.68	18.71	22.32	3.38	17.56	31.68	2.68	15.93	38.64	2.28	15.25	46.80	2.08	15.90	59.76	1.88	15.31	67.92
4.69	18.90	22.56	3.39	17.74	32.04	2.69	16.11	39.12	2.29	15.43	47.40	2.09	16.08	60.48	1.89	15.48	68.76
4.70	19.09	22.80	3.40	17.93	32.40	2.70	16.29	39.60	2.30	15.61	48.00	2.10	16.25	61.20	1.90	15.65	69.60
4.71	19.29	23.04	3.41	18.12	32.76	2.71	16.48	40.08	2.31	15.79	48.60	2.11	16.42	61.92	1.91	15.82	70.44
4.72	19.48	23.28	3.42	18.30	33.12	2.72	16.66	40.56	2.32	15.97	49.20	2.12	16.59	62.64	1.92	15.98	71.28
4.73	19.67	23.52	3.43	18.49	33.48	2.73	16.84	41.04	2.33	16.14	49.80	2.13	16.76	63.36	1.93	16.15	72.12
4.74	19.86	23.76	3.44	18.68	33.84	2.74	17.03	41.52	2.34	16.32	50.40	2.14	16.93	64.08	1.94	16.32	72.96
4.75	20.05	24.00	3.45	18.86	34.20	2.75	17.21	42.00	2.35	16.50	51.00	2.15	17.11	64.80	1.95	16.49	73.80
4.76	20.24	24.24	3.46	19.05	34.56	2.76	17.39	42.48	2.36	16.68	51.60	2.16	17.28	65.52	1.96	16.65	74.64
4.77	20.43	24.48	3.47	19.23	34.92	2.77	17.57	42.96	2.37	16.85	52.20	2.17	17.45	66.24	1.97	16.82	75.48
4.78	20.62	24.72	3.48	19.42	35.28	2.78	17.75	43.44	2.38	17.03	52.80	2.18	17.62	66.96	1.98	16.99	76.32
4.79	20.82	24.96	3.49	19.60	35.64	2.79	17.93	43.92	2.39	17.20	53.40	2.19	17.79	67.68	1.99	17.15	77.16
4.80	21.01	25.20	3.50	19.79	36.00	2.80	18.11	44.40	2.40	17.38	54.00	2.20	17.95	68.40	2.00	17.32	78.00
4.81	21.20	25.44	3.51	19.97	36.36	2.81	18.29	44.88	2.41	17.56	54.60	2.21	18.12	69.12	2.01	17.48	78.84
4.82	21.39	25.68	3.52	20.16	36.72	2.82	18.47	45.36	2.42	17.73	55.20	2.22	18.29	69.84	2.02	17.65	79.68
4.83	21.58	25.92	3.53	20.34	37.08	2.83	18.65	45.84	2.43	17.91	55.80	2.23	18.46	70.56	2.03	17.81	80.52
4.84	21.77	26.16	3.54	20.53	37.44	2.84	18.83	46.32	2.44	18.08	56.40	2.24	18.63	71.28	2.04	17.97	81.36
4.85	21.96	26.40	3.55	20.71	37.80	2.85	19.01	46.80	2.45	18.25	57.00	2.25	18.80	72.00	2.05	18.14	82.20
4.86	22.14	26.64	3.56	20.89	38.16	2.86	19.19	47.28	2.46	18.43	57.60	2.26	18.96	72.72	2.06	18.30	83.04
4.87	22.33	26.88	3.57	21.08	38.52	2.87	19.37	47.76	2.47	18.60	58.20	2.27	19.13	73.44	2.07	18.46	83.88
4.88	22.52	27.12	3.58	21.26	38.88	2.88	19.55	48.24	2.48	18.78	58.80	2.28	19.30	74.16	2.08	18.63	84.72
4.89	22.71	27.36	3.59	21.44	39.24	2.89	19.73	48.72	2.49	18.95	59.40	2.29	19.46	74.88	2.09	18.79	85.56
4.90	22.90	27.60	3.60	21.63	39.60	2.90	19.90	49.20	2.50	19.12	60.00	2.30	19.63	75.60	2.10	18.95	86.40
4.91	23.09	27.84	3.61	21.81	39.96	2.91	20.08	49.68	2.51	19.30	60.60	2.31	19.79	76.32	2.11	19.11	87.24
4.92	23.28	28.08	3.62	21.99	40.32	2.92	20.26	50.16	2.52	19.47	61.20	2.32	19.96	77.04	2.12	19.27	88.08
4.93	23.47	28.32	3.63	22.17	40.68	2.93	20.44	50.64	2.53	19.64	61.80	2.33	20.13	77.76	2.13	19.43	88.92
4.94	23.65	28.56	3.64	22.36	41.04	2.94	20.61	51.12	2.54	19.81	62.40	2.34	20.29	78.48	2.14	19.60	89.76
4.95	23.84	28.80	3.65	22.54	41.40	2.95	20.79	51.60	2.55	19.98	63.00	2.35	20.45	79.20	2.15	19.76	90.60
4.96	24.03	29.04	3.66	22.72	41.76	2.96	20.97	52.08	2.56	20.15	63.60	2.36	20.62	79.92	2.16	19.92	91.44
4.97	24.22	29.28	3.67	22.90	42.12	2.97	21.14	52.56	2.57	20.32	64.20	2.37	20.78	80.64	2.17	20.08	92.28
4.98	24.41	29.52	3.68	23.08	42.48	2.98	21.32	53.04	2.58	20.49	64.80	2.38	20.95	81.36	2.18	20.24	93.12
4.99	24.59	29.76	3.69	23.26	42.84	2.99	21.49	53.52	2.59	20.66	65.40	2.39	21.11	82.08	2.19	20.40	93.96

LEASE PAYMENTS

PAYMENTS IN ARREARS
10 % RESIDUAL

Description: This table shows the Annual Percentage Rate and finance charge per $100 for monthly lease payments.

Example: A 1.30% lease payment for 8 years is equivalent to an APR of 7.27%. The charge per $100 cost is $ 34.80.

8 yr PAYT	APR	CHARGE	9 yr PAYT	APR	CHARGE	10 yr PAYT	APR	CHARGE	12 yr PAYT	APR	CHARGE	15 yr PAYT	APR	CHARGE	20 yr PAYT	APR	CHARGE
1.30	7.27	34.80	1.20	7.30	39.60	1.10	6.94	42.00	1.00	7.29	54.00	.80	5.83	54.00	.70	6.09	78.00
1.31	7.46	35.76	1.21	7.48	40.68	1.11	7.12	43.20	1.01	7.46	55.44	.81	6.01	55.80	.71	6.25	80.40
1.32	7.65	36.72	1.22	7.67	41.76	1.12	7.30	44.40	1.02	7.64	56.88	.82	6.18	57.60	.72	6.42	82.80
1.33	7.83	37.68	1.23	7.85	42.84	1.13	7.49	45.60	1.03	7.81	58.32	.83	6.36	59.40	.73	6.58	85.20
1.34	8.02	38.64	1.24	8.03	43.92	1.14	7.67	46.80	1.04	7.98	59.76	.84	6.53	61.20	.74	6.74	87.60
1.35	8.20	39.60	1.25	8.21	45.00	1.15	7.85	48.00	1.05	8.16	61.20	.85	6.70	63.00	.75	6.90	90.00
1.36	8.39	40.56	1.26	8.39	46.08	1.16	8.02	49.20	1.06	8.33	62.64	.86	6.88	64.80	.76	7.06	92.40
1.37	8.57	41.52	1.27	8.57	47.16	1.17	8.20	50.40	1.07	8.50	64.08	.87	7.05	66.60	.77	7.22	94.80
1.38	8.75	42.48	1.28	8.75	48.24	1.18	8.38	51.60	1.08	8.67	65.52	.88	7.22	68.40	.78	7.38	97.20
1.39	8.94	43.44	1.29	8.93	49.32	1.19	8.56	52.80	1.09	8.84	66.96	.89	7.39	70.20	.79	7.54	99.60
1.40	9.12	44.40	1.30	9.11	50.40	1.20	8.73	54.00	1.10	9.01	68.40	.90	7.55	72.00	.80	7.70	102.00
1.41	9.30	45.36	1.31	9.29	51.48	1.21	8.91	55.20	1.11	9.18	69.84	.91	7.72	73.80	.81	7.85	104.40
1.42	9.48	46.32	1.32	9.46	52.56	1.22	9.09	56.40	1.12	9.35	71.28	.92	7.89	75.60	.82	8.01	106.80
1.43	9.66	47.28	1.33	9.64	53.64	1.23	9.26	57.60	1.13	9.52	72.72	.93	8.05	77.40	.83	8.16	109.20
1.44	9.84	48.24	1.34	9.82	54.72	1.24	9.43	58.80	1.14	9.69	74.16	.94	8.22	79.20	.84	8.32	111.60
1.45	10.02	49.20	1.35	9.99	55.80	1.25	9.61	60.00	1.15	9.85	75.60	.95	8.38	81.00	.85	8.47	114.00
1.46	10.20	50.16	1.36	10.17	56.88	1.26	9.78	61.20	1.16	10.02	77.04	.96	8.55	82.80	.86	8.62	116.40
1.47	10.37	51.12	1.37	10.34	57.96	1.27	9.95	62.40	1.17	10.18	78.48	.97	8.71	84.60	.87	8.78	118.80
1.48	10.55	52.08	1.38	10.52	59.04	1.28	10.13	63.60	1.18	10.35	79.92	.98	8.87	86.40	.88	8.93	121.20
1.49	10.73	53.04	1.39	10.69	60.12	1.29	10.30	64.80	1.19	10.51	81.36	.99	9.03	88.20	.89	9.08	123.60
1.50	10.90	54.00	1.40	10.86	61.20	1.30	10.47	66.00	1.20	10.68	82.80	1.00	9.20	90.00	.90	9.23	126.00
1.51	11.08	54.96	1.41	11.03	62.28	1.31	10.64	67.20	1.21	10.84	84.24	1.01	9.36	91.80	.91	9.38	128.40
1.52	11.26	55.92	1.42	11.21	63.36	1.32	10.81	68.40	1.22	11.00	85.68	1.02	9.52	93.60	.92	9.53	130.80
1.53	11.43	56.88	1.43	11.38	64.44	1.33	10.98	69.60	1.23	11.16	87.12	1.03	9.68	95.40	.93	9.68	133.20
1.54	11.60	57.84	1.44	11.55	65.52	1.34	11.14	70.80	1.24	11.33	88.56	1.04	9.83	97.20	.94	9.83	135.60
1.55	11.78	58.80	1.45	11.72	66.60	1.35	11.31	72.00	1.25	11.49	90.00	1.05	9.99	99.00	.95	9.97	138.00
1.56	11.95	59.76	1.46	11.89	67.68	1.36	11.48	73.20	1.26	11.65	91.44	1.06	10.15	100.80	.96	10.12	140.40
1.57	12.13	60.72	1.47	12.06	68.76	1.37	11.65	74.40	1.27	11.81	92.88	1.07	10.31	102.60	.97	10.27	142.80
1.58	12.30	61.68	1.48	12.23	69.84	1.38	11.81	75.60	1.28	11.97	94.32	1.08	10.46	104.40	.98	10.41	145.20
1.59	12.47	62.64	1.49	12.40	70.92	1.39	11.98	76.80	1.29	12.13	95.76	1.09	10.62	106.20	.99	10.56	147.60
1.60	12.64	63.60	1.50	12.56	72.00	1.40	12.14	78.00	1.30	12.28	97.20	1.10	10.77	108.00	1.00	10.70	150.00
1.61	12.81	64.56	1.51	12.73	73.08	1.41	12.31	79.20	1.31	12.44	98.64	1.11	10.93	109.80	1.01	10.85	152.40
1.62	12.98	65.52	1.52	12.90	74.16	1.42	12.47	80.40	1.32	12.60	100.08	1.12	11.08	111.60	1.02	10.99	154.80
1.63	13.15	66.48	1.53	13.06	75.24	1.43	12.64	81.60	1.33	12.76	101.52	1.13	11.24	113.40	1.03	11.13	157.20
1.64	13.32	67.44	1.54	13.23	76.32	1.44	12.80	82.80	1.34	12.91	102.96	1.14	11.39	115.20	1.04	11.28	159.60
1.65	13.49	68.40	1.55	13.40	77.40	1.45	12.97	84.00	1.35	13.07	104.40	1.15	11.54	117.00	1.05	11.42	162.00
1.66	13.66	69.36	1.56	13.56	78.48	1.46	13.13	85.20	1.36	13.23	105.84	1.16	11.69	118.80	1.06	11.56	164.40
1.67	13.83	70.32	1.57	13.73	79.56	1.47	13.29	86.40	1.37	13.38	107.28	1.17	11.85	120.60	1.07	11.70	166.80
1.68	14.00	71.28	1.58	13.89	80.64	1.48	13.45	87.60	1.38	13.54	108.72	1.18	12.00	122.40	1.08	11.85	169.20
1.69	14.17	72.24	1.59	14.05	81.72	1.49	13.61	88.80	1.39	13.69	110.16	1.19	12.15	124.20	1.09	11.99	171.60
1.70	14.33	73.20	1.60	14.22	82.80	1.50	13.77	90.00	1.40	13.85	111.60	1.20	12.30	126.00	1.10	12.13	174.00
1.71	14.50	74.16	1.61	14.38	83.88	1.51	13.93	91.20	1.41	14.00	113.04	1.21	12.45	127.80	1.11	12.27	176.40
1.72	14.67	75.12	1.62	14.54	84.96	1.52	14.09	92.40	1.42	14.15	114.48	1.22	12.60	129.60	1.12	12.41	178.80
1.73	14.83	76.08	1.63	14.71	86.04	1.53	14.25	93.60	1.43	14.30	115.92	1.23	12.75	131.40	1.13	12.55	181.20
1.74	15.00	77.04	1.64	14.87	87.12	1.54	14.41	94.80	1.44	14.46	117.36	1.24	12.90	133.20	1.14	12.69	183.60
1.75	15.16	78.00	1.65	15.03	88.20	1.55	14.57	96.00	1.45	14.61	118.80	1.25	13.04	135.00	1.15	12.82	186.00
1.76	15.33	78.96	1.66	15.19	89.28	1.56	14.73	97.20	1.46	14.76	120.24	1.26	13.19	136.80	1.16	12.96	188.40
1.77	15.49	79.92	1.67	15.35	90.36	1.57	14.89	98.40	1.47	14.91	121.68	1.27	13.34	138.60	1.17	13.10	190.80
1.78	15.66	80.88	1.68	15.51	91.44	1.58	15.05	99.60	1.48	15.06	123.12	1.28	13.49	140.40	1.18	13.24	193.20
1.79	15.82	81.84	1.69	15.67	92.52	1.59	15.20	100.80	1.49	15.21	124.56	1.29	13.63	142.20	1.19	13.37	195.60
1.80	15.98	82.80	1.70	15.83	93.60	1.60	15.36	102.00	1.50	15.36	126.00	1.30	13.78	144.00	1.20	13.51	198.00
1.81	16.15	83.76	1.71	15.99	94.68	1.61	15.52	103.20	1.51	15.51	127.44	1.31	13.92	145.80	1.21	13.65	200.40
1.82	16.31	84.72	1.72	16.15	95.76	1.62	15.67	104.40	1.52	15.66	128.88	1.32	14.07	147.60	1.22	13.78	202.80
1.83	16.47	85.68	1.73	16.31	96.84	1.63	15.83	105.60	1.53	15.81	130.32	1.33	14.21	149.40	1.23	13.92	205.20
1.84	16.64	86.64	1.74	16.47	97.92	1.64	15.99	106.80	1.54	15.96	131.76	1.34	14.36	151.20	1.24	14.06	207.60
1.85	16.80	87.60	1.75	16.62	99.00	1.65	16.14	108.00	1.55	16.11	133.20	1.35	14.50	153.00	1.25	14.19	210.00
1.86	16.96	88.56	1.76	16.78	100.08	1.66	16.30	109.20	1.56	16.26	134.64	1.36	14.65	154.80	1.26	14.33	212.40
1.87	17.12	89.52	1.77	16.94	101.16	1.67	16.45	110.40	1.57	16.41	136.08	1.37	14.79	156.60	1.27	14.46	214.80
1.88	17.28	90.48	1.78	17.10	102.24	1.68	16.60	111.60	1.58	16.55	137.52	1.38	14.93	158.40	1.28	14.60	217.20
1.89	17.44	91.44	1.79	17.25	103.32	1.69	16.76	112.80	1.59	16.70	138.96	1.39	15.08	160.20	1.29	14.73	219.60
1.90	17.60	92.40	1.80	17.41	104.40	1.70	16.91	114.00	1.60	16.85	140.40	1.40	15.22	162.00	1.30	14.86	222.00
1.91	17.76	93.36	1.81	17.56	105.48	1.71	17.06	115.20	1.61	16.99	141.84	1.41	15.36	163.80	1.31	15.00	224.40
1.92	17.92	94.32	1.82	17.72	106.56	1.72	17.22	116.40	1.62	17.14	143.28	1.42	15.50	165.60	1.32	15.13	226.80
1.93	18.08	95.28	1.83	17.87	107.64	1.73	17.37	117.60	1.63	17.29	144.72	1.43	15.65	167.40	1.33	15.27	229.20
1.94	18.24	96.24	1.84	18.03	108.72	1.74	17.52	118.80	1.64	17.43	146.16	1.44	15.79	169.20	1.34	15.40	231.60
1.95	18.40	97.20	1.85	18.18	109.80	1.75	17.67	120.00	1.65	17.58	147.60	1.45	15.93	171.00	1.35	15.53	234.00
1.96	18.55	98.16	1.86	18.34	110.88	1.76	17.82	121.20	1.66	17.72	149.04	1.46	16.07	172.80	1.36	15.67	236.40
1.97	18.71	99.12	1.87	18.49	111.96	1.77	17.97	122.40	1.67	17.87	150.48	1.47	16.21	174.60	1.37	15.80	238.80
1.98	18.87	100.08	1.88	18.65	113.04	1.78	18.13	123.60	1.68	18.01	151.92	1.48	16.35	176.40	1.38	15.93	241.20
1.99	19.03	101.04	1.89	18.80	114.12	1.79	18.28	124.80	1.69	18.16	153.36	1.49	16.49	178.20	1.39	16.06	243.60

Description: This table shows the Annual Percentage Rate and finance charge per $100 for monthly lease payments.

Example: A 4.30% lease payment for 2 years is equivalent to an APR of 14.83%. The charge per $100 cost is $ 18.20.

2 yr PAYT	APR	CHARGE	3 yr PAYT	APR	CHARGE	4 yr PAYT	APR	CHARGE	5 yr PAYT	APR	CHARGE	6 yr PAYT	APR	CHARGE	7 yr PAYT	APR	CHARGE
4.30	14.83	18.20	3.00	12.50	23.00	2.30	10.36	25.40	1.90	9.43	29.00	1.70	10.01	37.40	1.50	9.36	41.00
4.31	15.02	18.44	3.01	12.69	23.36	2.31	10.55	25.88	1.91	9.61	29.60	1.71	10.19	38.12	1.51	9.54	41.84
4.32	15.21	18.68	3.02	12.88	23.72	2.32	10.73	26.36	1.92	9.80	30.20	1.72	10.37	38.84	1.52	9.71	42.68
4.33	15.40	18.92	3.03	13.07	24.08	2.33	10.92	26.84	1.93	9.98	30.80	1.73	10.55	39.56	1.53	9.89	43.52
4.34	15.59	19.16	3.04	13.25	24.44	2.34	11.10	27.32	1.94	10.17	31.40	1.74	10.72	40.28	1.54	10.07	44.36
4.35	15.78	19.40	3.05	13.44	24.80	2.35	11.29	27.80	1.95	10.35	32.00	1.75	10.90	41.00	1.55	10.25	45.20
4.36	15.96	19.64	3.06	13.63	25.16	2.36	11.48	28.28	1.96	10.53	32.60	1.76	11.08	41.72	1.56	10.42	46.04
4.37	16.15	19.88	3.07	13.81	25.52	2.37	11.66	28.76	1.97	10.72	33.20	1.77	11.26	42.44	1.57	10.60	46.88
4.38	16.34	20.12	3.08	14.00	25.88	2.38	11.85	29.24	1.98	10.90	33.80	1.78	11.44	43.16	1.58	10.77	47.72
4.39	16.53	20.36	3.09	14.18	26.24	2.39	12.03	29.72	1.99	11.08	34.40	1.79	11.62	43.88	1.59	10.95	48.56
4.40	16.72	20.60	3.10	14.37	26.60	2.40	12.21	30.20	2.00	11.26	35.00	1.80	11.79	44.60	1.60	11.12	49.40
4.41	16.90	20.84	3.11	14.55	26.96	2.41	12.40	30.68	2.01	11.44	35.60	1.81	11.97	45.32	1.61	11.30	50.24
4.42	17.09	21.08	3.12	14.74	27.32	2.42	12.58	31.16	2.02	11.62	36.20	1.82	12.15	46.04	1.62	11.47	51.08
4.43	17.28	21.32	3.13	14.93	27.68	2.43	12.77	31.64	2.03	11.81	36.80	1.83	12.32	46.76	1.63	11.65	51.92
4.44	17.47	21.56	3.14	15.11	28.04	2.44	12.95	32.12	2.04	11.99	37.40	1.84	12.50	47.48	1.64	11.82	52.76
4.45	17.65	21.80	3.15	15.29	28.40	2.45	13.13	32.60	2.05	12.17	38.00	1.85	12.67	48.20	1.65	11.99	53.60
4.46	17.84	22.04	3.16	15.48	28.76	2.46	13.31	33.08	2.06	12.35	38.60	1.86	12.85	48.92	1.66	12.16	54.44
4.47	18.03	22.28	3.17	15.66	29.12	2.47	13.50	33.56	2.07	12.53	39.20	1.87	13.02	49.64	1.67	12.34	55.28
4.48	18.21	22.52	3.18	15.85	29.48	2.48	13.68	34.04	2.08	12.70	39.80	1.88	13.20	50.36	1.68	12.51	56.12
4.49	18.40	22.76	3.19	16.03	29.84	2.49	13.86	34.52	2.09	12.88	40.40	1.89	13.37	51.08	1.69	12.68	56.96
4.50	18.59	23.00	3.20	16.21	30.20	2.50	14.04	35.00	2.10	13.06	41.00	1.90	13.54	51.80	1.70	12.85	57.80
4.51	18.77	23.24	3.21	16.40	30.56	2.51	14.22	35.48	2.11	13.24	41.60	1.91	13.72	52.52	1.71	13.02	58.64
4.52	18.96	23.48	3.22	16.58	30.92	2.52	14.40	35.96	2.12	13.42	42.20	1.92	13.89	53.24	1.72	13.19	59.48
4.53	19.14	23.72	3.23	16.76	31.28	2.53	14.58	36.44	2.13	13.60	42.80	1.93	14.06	53.96	1.73	13.36	60.32
4.54	19.33	23.96	3.24	16.95	31.64	2.54	14.76	36.92	2.14	13.77	43.40	1.94	14.23	54.68	1.74	13.53	61.16
4.55	19.52	24.20	3.25	17.13	32.00	2.55	14.94	37.40	2.15	13.95	44.00	1.95	14.40	55.40	1.75	13.70	62.00
4.56	19.70	24.44	3.26	17.31	32.36	2.56	15.12	37.88	2.16	14.13	44.60	1.96	14.58	56.12	1.76	13.87	62.84
4.57	19.89	24.68	3.27	17.49	32.72	2.57	15.30	38.36	2.17	14.30	45.20	1.97	14.75	56.84	1.77	14.04	63.68
4.58	20.07	24.92	3.28	17.67	33.08	2.58	15.48	38.84	2.18	14.48	45.80	1.98	14.92	57.56	1.78	14.20	64.52
4.59	20.26	25.16	3.29	17.86	33.44	2.59	15.66	39.32	2.19	14.66	46.40	1.99	15.09	58.28	1.79	14.37	65.36
4.60	20.44	25.40	3.30	18.04	33.80	2.60	15.84	39.80	2.20	14.83	47.00	2.00	15.26	59.00	1.80	14.54	66.20
4.61	20.63	25.64	3.31	18.22	34.16	2.61	16.02	40.28	2.21	15.01	47.60	2.01	15.43	59.72	1.81	14.70	67.04
4.62	20.81	25.88	3.32	18.40	34.52	2.62	16.20	40.76	2.22	15.18	48.20	2.02	15.60	60.44	1.82	14.87	67.88
4.63	20.99	26.12	3.33	18.58	34.88	2.63	16.38	41.24	2.23	15.36	48.80	2.03	15.77	61.16	1.83	15.04	68.72
4.64	21.18	26.36	3.34	18.76	35.24	2.64	16.55	41.72	2.24	15.53	49.40	2.04	15.94	61.88	1.84	15.20	69.56
4.65	21.36	26.60	3.35	18.94	35.60	2.65	16.73	42.20	2.25	15.70	50.00	2.05	16.10	62.60	1.85	15.37	70.40
4.66	21.55	26.84	3.36	19.12	35.96	2.66	16.91	42.68	2.26	15.88	50.60	2.06	16.27	63.32	1.86	15.53	71.24
4.67	21.73	27.08	3.37	19.30	36.32	2.67	17.09	43.16	2.27	16.05	51.20	2.07	16.44	64.04	1.87	15.70	72.08
4.68	21.91	27.32	3.38	19.48	36.68	2.68	17.26	43.64	2.28	16.22	51.80	2.08	16.61	64.76	1.88	15.86	72.92
4.69	22.10	27.56	3.39	19.66	37.04	2.69	17.44	44.12	2.29	16.40	52.40	2.09	16.78	65.48	1.89	16.03	73.76
4.70	22.28	27.80	3.40	19.84	37.40	2.70	17.62	44.60	2.30	16.57	53.00	2.10	16.94	66.20	1.90	16.19	74.60
4.71	22.47	28.04	3.41	20.02	37.76	2.71	17.79	45.08	2.31	16.74	53.60	2.11	17.11	66.92	1.91	16.36	75.44
4.72	22.65	28.28	3.42	20.20	38.12	2.72	17.97	45.56	2.32	16.91	54.20	2.12	17.28	67.64	1.92	16.52	76.28
4.73	22.83	28.52	3.43	20.38	38.48	2.73	18.14	46.04	2.33	17.09	54.80	2.13	17.44	68.36	1.93	16.68	77.12
4.74	23.01	28.76	3.44	20.56	38.84	2.74	18.32	46.52	2.34	17.26	55.40	2.14	17.61	69.08	1.94	16.84	77.96
4.75	23.20	29.00	3.45	20.73	39.20	2.75	18.49	47.00	2.35	17.43	56.00	2.15	17.77	69.80	1.95	17.01	78.80
4.76	23.38	29.24	3.46	20.91	39.56	2.76	18.67	47.48	2.36	17.60	56.60	2.16	17.94	70.52	1.96	17.17	79.64
4.77	23.56	29.48	3.47	21.09	39.92	2.77	18.84	47.96	2.37	17.77	57.20	2.17	18.10	71.24	1.97	17.33	80.48
4.78	23.74	29.72	3.48	21.27	40.28	2.78	19.02	48.44	2.38	17.94	57.80	2.18	18.27	71.96	1.98	17.49	81.32
4.79	23.93	29.96	3.49	21.45	40.64	2.79	19.19	48.92	2.39	18.11	58.40	2.19	18.43	72.68	1.99	17.65	82.16
4.80	24.11	30.20	3.50	21.62	41.00	2.80	19.37	49.40	2.40	18.28	59.00	2.20	18.60	73.40	2.00	17.82	83.00
4.81	24.29	30.44	3.51	21.80	41.36	2.81	19.54	49.88	2.41	18.45	59.60	2.21	18.76	74.12	2.01	17.98	83.84
4.82	24.47	30.68	3.52	21.98	41.72	2.82	19.71	50.36	2.42	18.62	60.20	2.22	18.93	74.84	2.02	18.14	84.68
4.83	24.65	30.92	3.53	22.16	42.08	2.83	19.89	50.84	2.43	18.79	60.80	2.23	19.09	75.56	2.03	18.30	85.52
4.84	24.84	31.16	3.54	22.33	42.44	2.84	20.06	51.32	2.44	18.96	61.40	2.24	19.25	76.28	2.04	18.46	86.36
4.85	25.02	31.40	3.55	22.51	42.80	2.85	20.23	51.80	2.45	19.13	62.00	2.25	19.42	77.00	2.05	18.62	87.20
4.86	25.20	31.64	3.56	22.69	43.16	2.86	20.40	52.28	2.46	19.30	62.60	2.26	19.58	77.72	2.06	18.77	88.04
4.87	25.38	31.88	3.57	22.86	43.52	2.87	20.58	52.76	2.47	19.46	63.20	2.27	19.74	78.44	2.07	18.93	88.88
4.88	25.56	32.12	3.58	23.04	43.88	2.88	20.75	53.24	2.48	19.63	63.80	2.28	19.90	79.16	2.08	19.09	89.72
4.89	25.74	32.36	3.59	23.21	44.24	2.89	20.92	53.72	2.49	19.80	64.40	2.29	20.06	79.88	2.09	19.25	90.56
4.90	25.92	32.60	3.60	23.39	44.60	2.90	21.09	54.20	2.50	19.97	65.00	2.30	20.23	80.60	2.10	19.41	91.40
4.91	26.10	32.84	3.61	23.57	44.96	2.91	21.26	54.68	2.51	20.13	65.60	2.31	20.39	81.32	2.11	19.57	92.24
4.92	26.28	33.08	3.62	23.74	45.32	2.92	21.44	55.16	2.52	20.30	66.20	2.32	20.55	82.04	2.12	19.72	93.08
4.93	26.46	33.32	3.63	23.92	45.68	2.93	21.61	55.64	2.53	20.47	66.80	2.33	20.71	82.76	2.13	19.88	93.92
4.94	26.64	33.56	3.64	24.09	46.04	2.94	21.78	56.12	2.54	20.63	67.40	2.34	20.87	83.48	2.14	20.04	94.76
4.95	26.82	33.80	3.65	24.27	46.40	2.95	21.95	56.60	2.55	20.80	68.00	2.35	21.03	84.20	2.15	20.20	95.60
4.96	27.00	34.04	3.66	24.44	46.76	2.96	22.12	57.08	2.56	20.97	68.60	2.36	21.19	84.92	2.16	20.35	96.44
4.97	27.18	34.28	3.67	24.62	47.12	2.97	22.29	57.56	2.57	21.13	69.20	2.37	21.35	85.64	2.17	20.51	97.28
4.98	27.36	34.52	3.68	24.79	47.48	2.98	22.46	58.04	2.58	21.30	69.80	2.38	21.51	86.36	2.18	20.66	98.12
4.99	27.54	34.76	3.69	24.96	47.84	2.99	22.63	58.52	2.59	21.46	70.40	2.39	21.67	87.08	2.19	20.82	98.96

Description: This table shows the Annual Percentage Rate and finance charge per $100 for monthly lease payments.

Example: A 1.30% lease payment for 8 years is equivalent to an APR of 7.97%. The charge per $100 cost is $ 39.80.

_8 yr_ MONTHLY PAYT	APR	CHARGE	_9 yr_ MONTHLY PAYT	APR	CHARGE	_10 yr_ MONTHLY PAYT	APR	CHARGE	_12 yr_ MONTHLY PAYT	APR	CHARGE	_15 yr_ MONTHLY PAYT	APR	CHARGE	_20 yr_ MONTHLY PAYT	APR	CHARGE
1.30	7.97	39.80	1.20	7.88	44.60	1.10	7.45	47.00	1.00	7.66	59.00	.80	6.13	59.00	.70	6.26	83.00
1.31	8.15	40.76	1.21	8.06	45.68	1.11	7.63	48.20	1.01	7.83	60.44	.81	6.30	60.80	.71	6.42	85.40
1.32	8.33	41.72	1.22	8.24	46.76	1.12	7.80	49.40	1.02	8.00	61.88	.82	6.47	62.60	.72	6.58	87.80
1.33	8.51	42.68	1.23	8.41	47.84	1.13	7.98	50.60	1.03	8.17	63.32	.83	6.64	64.40	.73	6.74	90.20
1.34	8.69	43.64	1.24	8.59	48.92	1.14	8.15	51.80	1.04	8.34	64.76	.84	6.81	66.20	.74	6.90	92.60
1.35	8.86	44.60	1.25	8.76	50.00	1.15	8.32	53.00	1.05	8.50	66.20	.85	6.97	68.00	.75	7.05	95.00
1.36	9.04	45.56	1.26	8.94	51.08	1.16	8.50	54.20	1.06	8.67	67.64	.86	7.14	69.80	.76	7.21	97.40
1.37	9.22	46.52	1.27	9.11	52.16	1.17	8.67	55.40	1.07	8.84	69.08	.87	7.31	71.60	.77	7.37	99.80
1.38	9.39	47.48	1.28	9.28	53.24	1.18	8.84	56.60	1.08	9.00	70.52	.88	7.47	73.40	.78	7.52	102.20
1.39	9.57	48.44	1.29	9.46	54.32	1.19	9.01	57.80	1.09	9.17	71.96	.89	7.64	75.20	.79	7.68	104.60
1.40	9.74	49.40	1.30	9.63	55.40	1.20	9.18	59.00	1.10	9.33	73.40	.90	7.80	77.00	.80	7.83	107.00
1.41	9.92	50.36	1.31	9.80	56.48	1.21	9.35	60.20	1.11	9.50	74.84	.91	7.96	78.80	.81	7.99	109.40
1.42	10.09	51.32	1.32	9.97	57.56	1.22	9.52	61.40	1.12	9.66	76.28	.92	8.12	80.60	.82	8.14	111.80
1.43	10.26	52.28	1.33	10.14	58.64	1.23	9.69	62.60	1.13	9.82	77.72	.93	8.29	82.40	.83	8.29	114.20
1.44	10.44	53.24	1.34	10.31	59.72	1.24	9.86	63.80	1.14	9.99	79.16	.94	8.45	84.20	.84	8.44	116.60
1.45	10.61	54.20	1.35	10.48	60.80	1.25	10.03	65.00	1.15	10.15	80.60	.95	8.61	86.00	.85	8.59	119.00
1.46	10.78	55.16	1.36	10.65	61.88	1.26	10.20	66.20	1.16	10.31	82.04	.96	8.77	87.80	.86	8.74	121.40
1.47	10.95	56.12	1.37	10.82	62.96	1.27	10.36	67.40	1.17	10.47	83.48	.97	8.93	89.60	.87	8.89	123.80
1.48	11.12	57.08	1.38	10.99	64.04	1.28	10.53	68.60	1.18	10.63	84.92	.98	9.09	91.40	.88	9.04	126.20
1.49	11.30	58.04	1.39	11.16	65.12	1.29	10.70	69.80	1.19	10.79	86.36	.99	9.24	93.20	.89	9.19	128.60
1.50	11.47	59.00	1.40	11.32	66.20	1.30	10.86	71.00	1.20	10.95	87.80	1.00	9.40	95.00	.90	9.33	131.00
1.51	11.64	59.96	1.41	11.49	67.28	1.31	11.03	72.20	1.21	11.11	89.24	1.01	9.56	96.80	.91	9.48	133.40
1.52	11.81	60.92	1.42	11.66	68.36	1.32	11.19	73.40	1.22	11.27	90.68	1.02	9.71	98.60	.92	9.63	135.80
1.53	11.97	61.88	1.43	11.82	69.44	1.33	11.36	74.60	1.23	11.43	92.12	1.03	9.87	100.40	.93	9.78	138.20
1.54	12.14	62.84	1.44	11.99	70.52	1.34	11.52	75.80	1.24	11.59	93.56	1.04	10.02	102.20	.94	9.92	140.60
1.55	12.31	63.80	1.45	12.15	71.60	1.35	11.68	77.00	1.25	11.74	95.00	1.05	10.18	104.00	.95	10.07	143.00
1.56	12.48	64.76	1.46	12.32	72.68	1.36	11.85	78.20	1.26	11.90	96.44	1.06	10.33	105.80	.96	10.21	145.40
1.57	12.65	65.72	1.47	12.48	73.76	1.37	12.01	79.40	1.27	12.06	97.88	1.07	10.49	107.60	.97	10.36	147.80
1.58	12.81	66.68	1.48	12.65	74.84	1.38	12.17	80.60	1.28	12.21	99.32	1.08	10.64	109.40	.98	10.50	150.20
1.59	12.98	67.64	1.49	12.81	75.92	1.39	12.33	81.80	1.29	12.37	100.76	1.09	10.79	111.20	.99	10.65	152.60
1.60	13.15	68.60	1.50	12.97	77.00	1.40	12.49	83.00	1.30	12.52	102.20	1.10	10.95	113.00	1.00	10.79	155.00
1.61	13.31	69.56	1.51	13.14	78.08	1.41	12.65	84.20	1.31	12.68	103.64	1.11	11.10	114.80	1.01	10.93	157.40
1.62	13.48	70.52	1.52	13.30	79.16	1.42	12.81	85.40	1.32	12.83	105.08	1.12	11.25	116.60	1.02	11.07	159.80
1.63	13.64	71.48	1.53	13.46	80.24	1.43	12.97	86.60	1.33	12.99	106.52	1.13	11.40	118.40	1.03	11.21	162.20
1.64	13.81	72.44	1.54	13.62	81.32	1.44	13.13	87.80	1.34	13.14	107.96	1.14	11.55	120.20	1.04	11.36	164.60
1.65	13.97	73.40	1.55	13.79	82.40	1.45	13.29	89.00	1.35	13.29	109.40	1.15	11.70	122.00	1.05	11.50	167.00
1.66	14.14	74.36	1.56	13.95	83.48	1.46	13.45	90.20	1.36	13.44	110.84	1.16	11.85	123.80	1.06	11.64	169.40
1.67	14.30	75.32	1.57	14.11	84.56	1.47	13.61	91.40	1.37	13.60	112.28	1.17	12.00	125.60	1.07	11.78	171.80
1.68	14.47	76.28	1.58	14.27	85.64	1.48	13.77	92.60	1.38	13.75	113.72	1.18	12.15	127.40	1.08	11.92	174.20
1.69	14.63	77.24	1.59	14.43	86.72	1.49	13.93	93.80	1.39	13.90	115.16	1.19	12.29	129.20	1.09	12.06	176.60
1.70	14.79	78.20	1.60	14.59	87.80	1.50	14.08	95.00	1.40	14.05	116.60	1.20	12.44	131.00	1.10	12.20	179.00
1.71	14.95	79.16	1.61	14.75	88.88	1.51	14.24	96.20	1.41	14.20	118.04	1.21	12.59	132.80	1.11	12.33	181.40
1.72	15.12	80.12	1.62	14.90	89.96	1.52	14.40	97.40	1.42	14.35	119.48	1.22	12.74	134.60	1.12	12.47	183.80
1.73	15.28	81.08	1.63	15.06	91.04	1.53	14.55	98.60	1.43	14.50	120.92	1.23	12.88	136.40	1.13	12.61	186.20
1.74	15.44	82.04	1.64	15.22	92.12	1.54	14.71	99.80	1.44	14.65	122.36	1.24	13.03	138.20	1.14	12.75	188.60
1.75	15.60	83.00	1.65	15.38	93.20	1.55	14.86	101.00	1.45	14.80	123.80	1.25	13.18	140.00	1.15	12.89	191.00
1.76	15.76	83.96	1.66	15.54	94.28	1.56	15.02	102.20	1.46	14.95	125.24	1.26	13.32	141.80	1.16	13.02	193.40
1.77	15.92	84.92	1.67	15.69	95.36	1.57	15.17	103.40	1.47	15.10	126.68	1.27	13.47	143.60	1.17	13.16	195.80
1.78	16.08	85.88	1.68	15.85	96.44	1.58	15.33	104.60	1.48	15.25	128.12	1.28	13.61	145.40	1.18	13.30	198.20
1.79	16.24	86.84	1.69	16.01	97.52	1.59	15.48	105.80	1.49	15.40	129.56	1.29	13.76	147.20	1.19	13.43	200.60
1.80	16.40	87.80	1.70	16.16	98.60	1.60	15.63	107.00	1.50	15.54	131.00	1.30	13.90	149.00	1.20	13.57	203.00
1.81	16.56	88.76	1.71	16.32	99.68	1.61	15.79	108.20	1.51	15.69	132.44	1.31	14.04	150.80	1.21	13.70	205.40
1.82	16.72	89.72	1.72	16.47	100.76	1.62	15.94	109.40	1.52	15.84	133.88	1.32	14.19	152.60	1.22	13.84	207.80
1.83	16.88	90.68	1.73	16.63	101.84	1.63	16.09	110.60	1.53	15.99	135.32	1.33	14.33	154.40	1.23	13.97	210.20
1.84	17.03	91.64	1.74	16.78	102.92	1.64	16.25	111.80	1.54	16.13	136.76	1.34	14.47	156.20	1.24	14.11	212.60
1.85	17.19	92.60	1.75	16.94	104.00	1.65	16.40	113.00	1.55	16.28	138.20	1.35	14.61	158.00	1.25	14.24	215.00
1.86	17.35	93.56	1.76	17.09	105.08	1.66	16.55	114.20	1.56	16.42	139.64	1.36	14.76	159.80	1.26	14.38	217.40
1.87	17.51	94.52	1.77	17.25	106.16	1.67	16.70	115.40	1.57	16.57	141.08	1.37	14.90	161.60	1.27	14.51	219.80
1.88	17.66	95.48	1.78	17.40	107.24	1.68	16.85	116.60	1.58	16.72	142.52	1.38	15.04	163.40	1.28	14.64	222.20
1.89	17.82	96.44	1.79	17.55	108.32	1.69	17.00	117.80	1.59	16.86	143.96	1.39	15.18	165.20	1.29	14.78	224.60
1.90	17.98	97.40	1.80	17.71	109.40	1.70	17.15	119.00	1.60	17.01	145.40	1.40	15.32	167.00	1.30	14.91	227.00
1.91	18.13	98.36	1.81	17.86	110.48	1.71	17.30	120.20	1.61	17.15	146.84	1.41	15.46	168.80	1.31	15.04	229.40
1.92	18.29	99.32	1.82	18.01	111.56	1.72	17.45	121.40	1.62	17.29	148.28	1.42	15.60	170.60	1.32	15.18	231.80
1.93	18.44	100.28	1.83	18.16	112.64	1.73	17.60	122.60	1.63	17.44	149.72	1.43	15.74	172.40	1.33	15.31	234.20
1.94	18.60	101.24	1.84	18.31	113.72	1.74	17.75	123.80	1.64	17.58	151.16	1.44	15.88	174.20	1.34	15.44	236.60
1.95	18.75	102.20	1.85	18.47	114.80	1.75	17.90	125.00	1.65	17.72	152.60	1.45	16.02	176.00	1.35	15.57	239.00
1.96	18.91	103.16	1.86	18.62	115.88	1.76	18.05	126.20	1.66	17.87	154.04	1.46	16.16	177.80	1.36	15.70	241.40
1.97	19.06	104.12	1.87	18.77	116.96	1.77	18.20	127.40	1.67	18.01	155.48	1.47	16.30	179.60	1.37	15.84	243.80
1.98	19.22	105.08	1.88	18.92	118.04	1.78	18.35	128.60	1.68	18.15	156.92	1.48	16.44	181.40	1.38	15.97	246.20
1.99	19.37	106.04	1.89	19.07	119.12	1.79	18.50	129.80	1.69	18.30	158.36	1.49	16.58	183.20	1.39	16.10	248.60

Description: This table shows the Annual Percentage Rate and finance charge per $100 for monthly lease payments.

Example: A 4.30% lease payment for 2 years is equivalent to an APR of 18.11%. The charge per $100 cost is $ 23.20.

2 yr PAYT	APR	CHARGE	3 yr PAYT	APR	CHARGE	4 yr PAYT	APR	CHARGE	5 yr PAYT	APR	CHARGE	6 yr PAYT	APR	CHARGE	7 yr PAYT	APR	CHARGE
4.30	18.11	23.20	3.00	14.58	28.00	2.30	11.88	30.40	1.90	10.60	34.00	1.70	10.89	42.40	1.50	10.09	46.00
4.31	18.29	23.44	3.01	14.76	28.36	2.31	12.06	30.88	1.91	10.77	34.60	1.71	11.07	43.12	1.51	10.26	46.84
4.32	18.47	23.68	3.02	14.94	28.72	2.32	12.24	31.36	1.92	10.95	35.20	1.72	11.24	43.84	1.52	10.43	47.68
4.33	18.65	23.92	3.03	15.12	29.08	2.33	12.42	31.84	1.93	11.13	35.80	1.73	11.41	44.56	1.53	10.61	48.52
4.34	18.83	24.16	3.04	15.30	29.44	2.34	12.59	32.32	1.94	11.30	36.40	1.74	11.59	45.28	1.54	10.78	49.36
4.35	19.01	24.40	3.05	15.48	29.80	2.35	12.77	32.80	1.95	11.48	37.00	1.75	11.76	46.00	1.55	10.95	50.20
4.36	19.19	24.64	3.06	15.66	30.16	2.36	12.95	33.28	1.96	11.66	37.60	1.76	11.93	46.72	1.56	11.12	51.04
4.37	19.37	24.88	3.07	15.84	30.52	2.37	13.13	33.76	1.97	11.83	38.20	1.77	12.10	47.44	1.57	11.29	51.88
4.38	19.55	25.12	3.08	16.01	30.88	2.38	13.30	34.24	1.98	12.01	38.80	1.78	12.27	48.16	1.58	11.46	52.72
4.39	19.73	25.36	3.09	16.19	31.24	2.39	13.48	34.72	1.99	12.18	39.40	1.79	12.44	48.88	1.59	11.63	53.56
4.40	19.91	25.60	3.10	16.37	31.60	2.40	13.66	35.20	2.00	12.36	40.00	1.80	12.62	49.60	1.60	11.79	54.40
4.41	20.09	25.84	3.11	16.55	31.96	2.41	13.83	35.68	2.01	12.53	40.60	1.81	12.79	50.32	1.61	11.96	55.24
4.42	20.27	26.08	3.12	16.72	32.32	2.42	14.01	36.16	2.02	12.71	41.20	1.82	12.96	51.04	1.62	12.13	56.08
4.43	20.45	26.32	3.13	16.90	32.68	2.43	14.19	36.64	2.03	12.88	41.80	1.83	13.13	51.76	1.63	12.30	56.92
4.44	20.63	26.56	3.14	17.08	33.04	2.44	14.36	37.12	2.04	13.05	42.40	1.84	13.30	52.48	1.64	12.47	57.76
4.45	20.81	26.80	3.15	17.26	33.40	2.45	14.54	37.60	2.05	13.23	43.00	1.85	13.46	53.20	1.65	12.63	58.60
4.46	20.98	27.04	3.16	17.43	33.76	2.46	14.71	38.08	2.06	13.40	43.60	1.86	13.63	53.92	1.66	12.80	59.44
4.47	21.16	27.28	3.17	17.61	34.12	2.47	14.89	38.56	2.07	13.57	44.20	1.87	13.80	54.64	1.67	12.97	60.28
4.48	21.34	27.52	3.18	17.79	34.48	2.48	15.06	39.04	2.08	13.75	44.80	1.88	13.97	55.36	1.68	13.13	61.12
4.49	21.52	27.76	3.19	17.96	34.84	2.49	15.24	39.52	2.09	13.92	45.40	1.89	14.14	56.08	1.69	13.30	61.96
4.50	21.70	28.00	3.20	18.14	35.20	2.50	15.41	40.00	2.10	14.09	46.00	1.90	14.31	56.80	1.70	13.46	62.80
4.51	21.88	28.24	3.21	18.31	35.56	2.51	15.58	40.48	2.11	14.26	46.60	1.91	14.47	57.52	1.71	13.63	63.64
4.52	22.05	28.48	3.22	18.49	35.92	2.52	15.76	40.96	2.12	14.43	47.20	1.92	14.64	58.24	1.72	13.79	64.48
4.53	22.23	28.72	3.23	18.66	36.28	2.53	15.93	41.44	2.13	14.60	47.80	1.93	14.81	58.96	1.73	13.96	65.32
4.54	22.41	28.96	3.24	18.84	36.64	2.54	16.11	41.92	2.14	14.77	48.40	1.94	14.97	59.68	1.74	14.12	66.16
4.55	22.59	29.20	3.25	19.01	37.00	2.55	16.28	42.40	2.15	14.95	49.00	1.95	15.14	60.40	1.75	14.29	67.00
4.56	22.77	29.44	3.26	19.19	37.36	2.56	16.45	42.88	2.16	15.12	49.60	1.96	15.31	61.12	1.76	14.45	67.84
4.57	22.94	29.68	3.27	19.36	37.72	2.57	16.63	43.36	2.17	15.29	50.20	1.97	15.47	61.84	1.77	14.61	68.68
4.58	23.12	29.92	3.28	19.54	38.08	2.58	16.80	43.84	2.18	15.46	50.80	1.98	15.64	62.56	1.78	14.78	69.52
4.59	23.30	30.16	3.29	19.71	38.44	2.59	16.97	44.32	2.19	15.63	51.40	1.99	15.80	63.28	1.79	14.94	70.36
4.60	23.47	30.40	3.30	19.89	38.80	2.60	17.14	44.80	2.20	15.80	52.00	2.00	15.97	64.00	1.80	15.10	71.20
4.61	23.65	30.64	3.31	20.06	39.16	2.61	17.31	45.28	2.21	15.96	52.60	2.01	16.13	64.72	1.81	15.26	72.04
4.62	23.83	30.88	3.32	20.24	39.52	2.62	17.49	45.76	2.22	16.13	53.20	2.02	16.30	65.44	1.82	15.43	72.88
4.63	24.01	31.12	3.33	20.41	39.88	2.63	17.66	46.24	2.23	16.30	53.80	2.03	16.46	66.16	1.83	15.59	73.72
4.64	24.18	31.36	3.34	20.58	40.24	2.64	17.83	46.72	2.24	16.47	54.40	2.04	16.62	66.88	1.84	15.75	74.56
4.65	24.36	31.60	3.35	20.76	40.60	2.65	18.00	47.20	2.25	16.64	55.00	2.05	16.79	67.60	1.85	15.91	75.40
4.66	24.54	31.84	3.36	20.93	40.96	2.66	18.17	47.68	2.26	16.81	55.60	2.06	16.95	68.32	1.86	16.07	76.24
4.67	24.71	32.08	3.37	21.10	41.32	2.67	18.34	48.16	2.27	16.97	56.20	2.07	17.11	69.04	1.87	16.23	77.08
4.68	24.89	32.32	3.38	21.28	41.68	2.68	18.51	48.64	2.28	17.14	56.80	2.08	17.28	69.76	1.88	16.39	77.92
4.69	25.06	32.56	3.39	21.45	42.04	2.69	18.68	49.12	2.29	17.31	57.40	2.09	17.44	70.48	1.89	16.55	78.76
4.70	25.24	32.80	3.40	21.62	42.40	2.70	18.85	49.60	2.30	17.48	58.00	2.10	17.60	71.20	1.90	16.71	79.60
4.71	25.42	33.04	3.41	21.79	42.76	2.71	19.02	50.08	2.31	17.64	58.60	2.11	17.76	71.92	1.91	16.87	80.44
4.72	25.59	33.28	3.42	21.97	43.12	2.72	19.19	50.56	2.32	17.81	59.20	2.12	17.93	72.64	1.92	17.03	81.28
4.73	25.77	33.52	3.43	22.14	43.48	2.73	19.36	51.04	2.33	17.98	59.80	2.13	18.09	73.36	1.93	17.19	82.12
4.74	25.94	33.76	3.44	22.31	43.84	2.74	19.53	51.52	2.34	18.14	60.40	2.14	18.25	74.08	1.94	17.35	82.96
4.75	26.12	34.00	3.45	22.48	44.20	2.75	19.70	52.00	2.35	18.31	61.00	2.15	18.41	74.80	1.95	17.50	83.80
4.76	26.29	34.24	3.46	22.66	44.56	2.76	19.87	52.48	2.36	18.47	61.60	2.16	18.57	75.52	1.96	17.66	84.64
4.77	26.47	34.48	3.47	22.83	44.92	2.77	20.04	52.96	2.37	18.64	62.20	2.17	18.73	76.24	1.97	17.82	85.48
4.78	26.64	34.72	3.48	23.00	45.28	2.78	20.21	53.44	2.38	18.80	62.80	2.18	18.89	76.96	1.98	17.98	86.32
4.79	26.82	34.96	3.49	23.17	45.64	2.79	20.37	53.92	2.39	18.97	63.40	2.19	19.05	77.68	1.99	18.13	87.16
4.80	26.99	35.20	3.50	23.34	46.00	2.80	20.54	54.40	2.40	19.13	64.00	2.20	19.21	78.40	2.00	18.29	88.00
4.81	27.17	35.44	3.51	23.51	46.36	2.81	20.71	54.88	2.41	19.30	64.60	2.21	19.37	79.12	2.01	18.45	88.84
4.82	27.34	35.68	3.52	23.68	46.72	2.82	20.88	55.36	2.42	19.46	65.20	2.22	19.53	79.84	2.02	18.61	89.68
4.83	27.52	35.92	3.53	23.85	47.08	2.83	21.05	55.84	2.43	19.63	65.80	2.23	19.69	80.56	2.03	18.76	90.52
4.84	27.69	36.16	3.54	24.02	47.44	2.84	21.21	56.32	2.44	19.79	66.40	2.24	19.85	81.28	2.04	18.92	91.36
4.85	27.87	36.40	3.55	24.19	47.80	2.85	21.38	56.80	2.45	19.95	67.00	2.25	20.01	82.00	2.05	19.07	92.20
4.86	28.04	36.64	3.56	24.36	48.16	2.86	21.55	57.28	2.46	20.12	67.60	2.26	20.17	82.72	2.06	19.23	93.04
4.87	28.21	36.88	3.57	24.53	48.52	2.87	21.71	57.76	2.47	20.28	68.20	2.27	20.32	83.44	2.07	19.38	93.88
4.88	28.39	37.12	3.58	24.70	48.88	2.88	21.88	58.24	2.48	20.44	68.80	2.28	20.48	84.16	2.08	19.54	94.72
4.89	28.56	37.36	3.59	24.87	49.24	2.89	22.05	58.72	2.49	20.61	69.40	2.29	20.64	84.88	2.09	19.69	95.56
4.90	28.73	37.60	3.60	25.04	49.60	2.90	22.21	59.20	2.50	20.77	70.00	2.30	20.80	85.60	2.10	19.85	96.40
4.91	28.91	37.84	3.61	25.21	49.96	2.91	22.38	59.68	2.51	20.93	70.60	2.31	20.95	86.32	2.11	20.00	97.24
4.92	29.08	38.08	3.62	25.38	50.32	2.92	22.55	60.16	2.52	21.09	71.20	2.32	21.11	87.04	2.12	20.16	98.08
4.93	29.26	38.32	3.63	25.55	50.68	2.93	22.71	60.64	2.53	21.25	71.80	2.33	21.27	87.76	2.13	20.31	98.92
4.94	29.43	38.56	3.64	25.72	51.04	2.94	22.88	61.12	2.54	21.42	72.40	2.34	21.43	88.48	2.14	20.46	99.76
4.95	29.60	38.80	3.65	25.89	51.40	2.95	23.04	61.60	2.55	21.58	73.00	2.35	21.58	89.20	2.15	20.62	100.60
4.96	29.77	39.04	3.66	26.06	51.76	2.96	23.21	62.08	2.56	21.74	73.60	2.36	21.74	89.92	2.16	20.77	101.44
4.97	29.95	39.28	3.67	26.23	52.12	2.97	23.37	62.56	2.57	21.90	74.20	2.37	21.89	90.64	2.17	20.92	102.28
4.98	30.12	39.52	3.68	26.39	52.48	2.98	23.54	63.04	2.58	22.06	74.80	2.38	22.05	91.36	2.18	21.08	103.12
4.99	30.29	39.76	3.69	26.56	52.84	2.99	23.70	63.52	2.59	22.22	75.40	2.39	22.21	92.08	2.19	21.23	103.96

Description: This table shows the Annual Percentage Rate and finance charge per $100 for monthly lease payments.

Example: A 1.30% lease payment for 8 years is equivalent to an APR of 8.62%. The charge per $100 cost is $ 44.80.

8 yr PAYT	APR	CHARGE	9 yr PAYT	APR	CHARGE	10 yr PAYT	APR	CHARGE	12 yr PAYT	APR	CHARGE	15 yr PAYT	APR	CHARGE	20 yr PAYT	APR	CHARGE
1.30	8.62	44.80	1.20	8.43	49.60	1.10	7.93	52.00	1.00	8.01	64.00	.80	6.41	64.00	.70	6.42	88.00
1.31	8.79	45.76	1.21	8.60	50.68	1.11	8.10	53.20	1.01	8.18	65.44	.81	6.58	65.80	.71	6.58	90.40
1.32	8.97	46.72	1.22	8.77	51.76	1.12	8.27	54.40	1.02	8.34	66.88	.82	6.74	67.60	.72	6.74	92.80
1.33	9.14	47.68	1.23	8.94	52.84	1.13	8.44	55.60	1.03	8.50	68.32	.83	6.91	69.40	.73	6.89	95.20
1.34	9.31	48.64	1.24	9.11	53.92	1.14	8.61	56.80	1.04	8.67	69.76	.84	7.07	71.20	.74	7.05	97.60
1.35	9.48	49.60	1.25	9.28	55.00	1.15	8.78	58.00	1.05	8.83	71.20	.85	7.23	73.00	.75	7.20	100.00
1.36	9.65	50.56	1.26	9.45	56.08	1.16	8.94	59.20	1.06	8.99	72.64	.86	7.39	74.80	.76	7.36	102.40
1.37	9.82	51.52	1.27	9.62	57.16	1.17	9.11	60.40	1.07	9.15	74.08	.87	7.55	76.60	.77	7.51	104.80
1.38	9.99	52.48	1.28	9.78	58.24	1.18	9.28	61.60	1.08	9.32	75.52	.88	7.71	78.40	.78	7.66	107.20
1.39	10.16	53.44	1.29	9.95	59.32	1.19	9.44	62.80	1.09	9.48	76.96	.89	7.87	80.20	.79	7.81	109.60
1.40	10.33	54.40	1.30	10.12	60.40	1.20	9.61	64.00	1.10	9.64	78.40	.90	8.03	82.00	.80	7.96	112.00
1.41	10.50	55.36	1.31	10.28	61.48	1.21	9.77	65.20	1.11	9.80	79.84	.91	8.19	83.80	.81	8.11	114.40
1.42	10.66	56.32	1.32	10.45	62.56	1.22	9.94	66.40	1.12	9.96	81.28	.92	8.35	85.60	.82	8.26	116.80
1.43	10.83	57.28	1.33	10.61	63.64	1.23	10.10	67.60	1.13	10.12	82.72	.93	8.51	87.40	.83	8.41	119.20
1.44	11.00	58.24	1.34	10.78	64.72	1.24	10.26	68.80	1.14	10.27	84.16	.94	8.67	89.20	.84	8.56	121.60
1.45	11.17	59.20	1.35	10.94	65.80	1.25	10.43	70.00	1.15	10.43	85.60	.95	8.82	91.00	.85	8.71	124.00
1.46	11.33	60.16	1.36	11.11	66.88	1.26	10.59	71.20	1.16	10.59	87.04	.96	8.98	92.80	.86	8.86	126.40
1.47	11.50	61.12	1.37	11.27	67.96	1.27	10.75	72.40	1.17	10.75	88.48	.97	9.13	94.60	.87	9.00	128.80
1.48	11.67	62.08	1.38	11.44	69.04	1.28	10.91	73.60	1.18	10.90	89.92	.98	9.29	96.40	.88	9.15	131.20
1.49	11.83	63.04	1.39	11.60	70.12	1.29	11.08	74.80	1.19	11.06	91.36	.99	9.44	98.20	.89	9.30	133.60
1.50	12.00	64.00	1.40	11.76	71.20	1.30	11.24	76.00	1.20	11.22	92.80	1.00	9.60	100.00	.90	9.44	136.00
1.51	12.16	64.96	1.41	11.92	72.28	1.31	11.40	77.20	1.21	11.37	94.24	1.01	9.75	101.80	.91	9.59	138.40
1.52	12.33	65.92	1.42	12.09	73.36	1.32	11.56	78.40	1.22	11.53	95.68	1.02	9.90	103.60	.92	9.73	140.80
1.53	12.49	66.88	1.43	12.25	74.44	1.33	11.72	79.60	1.23	11.68	97.12	1.03	10.06	105.40	.93	9.88	143.20
1.54	12.65	67.84	1.44	12.41	75.52	1.34	11.88	80.80	1.24	11.83	98.56	1.04	10.21	107.20	.94	10.02	145.60
1.55	12.82	68.80	1.45	12.57	76.60	1.35	12.04	82.00	1.25	11.99	100.00	1.05	10.36	109.00	.95	10.16	148.00
1.56	12.98	69.76	1.46	12.73	77.68	1.36	12.19	83.20	1.26	12.14	101.44	1.06	10.51	110.80	.96	10.30	150.40
1.57	13.14	70.72	1.47	12.89	78.76	1.37	12.35	84.40	1.27	12.30	102.88	1.07	10.66	112.60	.97	10.45	152.80
1.58	13.30	71.68	1.48	13.05	79.84	1.38	12.51	85.60	1.28	12.45	104.32	1.08	10.81	114.40	.98	10.59	155.20
1.59	13.47	72.64	1.49	13.21	80.92	1.39	12.67	86.80	1.29	12.60	105.76	1.09	10.96	116.20	.99	10.73	157.60
1.60	13.63	73.60	1.50	13.37	82.00	1.40	12.83	88.00	1.30	12.75	107.20	1.10	11.11	118.00	1.00	10.87	160.00
1.61	13.79	74.56	1.51	13.53	83.08	1.41	12.98	89.20	1.31	12.90	108.64	1.11	11.26	119.80	1.01	11.01	162.40
1.62	13.95	75.52	1.52	13.68	84.16	1.42	13.14	90.40	1.32	13.05	110.08	1.12	11.41	121.60	1.02	11.15	164.80
1.63	14.11	76.48	1.53	13.84	85.24	1.43	13.29	91.60	1.33	13.21	111.52	1.13	11.56	123.40	1.03	11.29	167.20
1.64	14.27	77.44	1.54	14.00	86.32	1.44	13.45	92.80	1.34	13.36	112.96	1.14	11.70	125.20	1.04	11.43	169.60
1.65	14.43	78.40	1.55	14.16	87.40	1.45	13.61	94.00	1.35	13.51	114.40	1.15	11.85	127.00	1.05	11.57	172.00
1.66	14.59	79.36	1.56	14.31	88.48	1.46	13.76	95.20	1.36	13.66	115.84	1.16	12.00	128.80	1.06	11.71	174.40
1.67	14.75	80.32	1.57	14.47	89.56	1.47	13.92	96.40	1.37	13.81	117.28	1.17	12.14	130.60	1.07	11.85	176.80
1.68	14.91	81.28	1.58	14.63	90.64	1.48	14.07	97.60	1.38	13.95	118.72	1.18	12.29	132.40	1.08	11.99	179.20
1.69	15.07	82.24	1.59	14.78	91.72	1.49	14.22	98.80	1.39	14.10	120.16	1.19	12.44	134.20	1.09	12.13	181.60
1.70	15.23	83.20	1.60	14.94	92.80	1.50	14.38	100.00	1.40	14.25	121.60	1.20	12.58	136.00	1.10	12.26	184.00
1.71	15.39	84.16	1.61	15.09	93.88	1.51	14.53	101.20	1.41	14.40	123.04	1.21	12.73	137.80	1.11	12.40	186.40
1.72	15.54	85.12	1.62	15.25	94.96	1.52	14.69	102.40	1.42	14.55	124.48	1.22	12.87	139.60	1.12	12.54	188.80
1.73	15.70	86.08	1.63	15.40	96.04	1.53	14.84	103.60	1.43	14.70	125.92	1.23	13.02	141.40	1.13	12.67	191.20
1.74	15.86	87.04	1.64	15.56	97.12	1.54	14.99	104.80	1.44	14.84	127.36	1.24	13.16	143.20	1.14	12.81	193.60
1.75	16.02	88.00	1.65	15.71	98.20	1.55	15.14	106.00	1.45	14.99	128.80	1.25	13.30	145.00	1.15	12.95	196.00
1.76	16.17	88.96	1.66	15.87	99.28	1.56	15.29	107.20	1.46	15.14	130.24	1.26	13.45	146.80	1.16	13.08	198.40
1.77	16.33	89.92	1.67	16.02	100.36	1.57	15.45	108.40	1.47	15.28	131.68	1.27	13.59	148.60	1.17	13.22	200.80
1.78	16.49	90.88	1.68	16.17	101.44	1.58	15.60	109.60	1.48	15.43	133.12	1.28	13.73	150.40	1.18	13.35	203.20
1.79	16.64	91.84	1.69	16.33	102.52	1.59	15.75	110.80	1.49	15.57	134.56	1.29	13.88	152.20	1.19	13.49	205.60
1.80	16.80	92.80	1.70	16.48	103.60	1.60	15.90	112.00	1.50	15.72	136.00	1.30	14.02	154.00	1.20	13.62	208.00
1.81	16.95	93.76	1.71	16.63	104.68	1.61	16.05	113.20	1.51	15.86	137.44	1.31	14.16	155.80	1.21	13.76	210.40
1.82	17.11	94.72	1.72	16.78	105.76	1.62	16.20	114.40	1.52	16.01	138.88	1.32	14.30	157.60	1.22	13.89	212.80
1.83	17.26	95.68	1.73	16.94	106.84	1.63	16.35	115.60	1.53	16.15	140.32	1.33	14.44	159.40	1.23	14.02	215.20
1.84	17.42	96.64	1.74	17.09	107.92	1.64	16.50	116.80	1.54	16.30	141.76	1.34	14.58	161.20	1.24	14.16	217.60
1.85	17.57	97.60	1.75	17.24	109.00	1.65	16.65	118.00	1.55	16.44	143.20	1.35	14.72	163.00	1.25	14.29	220.00
1.86	17.73	98.56	1.76	17.39	110.08	1.66	16.80	119.20	1.56	16.59	144.64	1.36	14.86	164.80	1.26	14.42	222.40
1.87	17.88	99.52	1.77	17.54	111.16	1.67	16.94	120.40	1.57	16.73	146.08	1.37	15.00	166.60	1.27	14.56	224.80
1.88	18.03	100.48	1.78	17.69	112.24	1.68	17.09	121.60	1.58	16.87	147.52	1.38	15.14	168.40	1.28	14.69	227.20
1.89	18.19	101.44	1.79	17.84	113.32	1.69	17.24	122.80	1.59	17.02	148.96	1.39	15.28	170.20	1.29	14.82	229.60
1.90	18.34	102.40	1.80	17.99	114.40	1.70	17.39	124.00	1.60	17.16	150.40	1.40	15.42	172.00	1.30	14.95	232.00
1.91	18.49	103.36	1.81	18.14	115.48	1.71	17.54	125.20	1.61	17.30	151.84	1.41	15.56	173.80	1.31	15.09	234.40
1.92	18.64	104.32	1.82	18.29	116.56	1.72	17.68	126.40	1.62	17.44	153.28	1.42	15.70	175.60	1.32	15.22	236.80
1.93	18.80	105.28	1.83	18.44	117.64	1.73	17.83	127.60	1.63	17.59	154.72	1.43	15.84	177.40	1.33	15.35	239.20
1.94	18.95	106.24	1.84	18.59	118.72	1.74	17.98	128.80	1.64	17.73	156.16	1.44	15.98	179.20	1.34	15.48	241.60
1.95	19.10	107.20	1.85	18.74	119.80	1.75	18.12	130.00	1.65	17.87	157.60	1.45	16.12	181.00	1.35	15.61	244.00
1.96	19.25	108.16	1.86	18.89	120.88	1.76	18.27	131.20	1.66	18.01	159.04	1.46	16.25	182.80	1.36	15.74	246.40
1.97	19.40	109.12	1.87	19.04	121.96	1.77	18.42	132.40	1.67	18.15	160.48	1.47	16.39	184.60	1.37	15.87	248.80
1.98	19.55	110.08	1.88	19.18	123.04	1.78	18.56	133.60	1.68	18.29	161.92	1.48	16.53	186.40	1.38	16.00	251.20
1.99	19.71	111.04	1.89	19.33	124.12	1.79	18.71	134.80	1.69	18.43	163.36	1.49	16.66	188.20	1.39	16.13	253.60

LEASE PAYMENTS

Description: This table shows the Annual Percentage Rate and finance charge per $100 for monthly lease payments.

Example: A 4.30% lease payment for 2 years is equivalent to an APR of 3.31%. The charge per $100 cost is $ 3.20.

2 yr MONTHLY PAYT	APR	CHARGE	3 yr MONTHLY PAYT	APR	CHARGE	4 yr MONTHLY PAYT	APR	CHARGE	5 yr MONTHLY PAYT	APR	CHARGE	6 yr MONTHLY PAYT	APR	CHARGE	7 yr MONTHLY PAYT	APR	CHARGE
4.30	3.31	3.20	3.00	5.36	8.00	2.30	5.15	10.40	1.90	5.47	14.00	1.70	7.11	22.40	1.50	6.99	26.00
4.31	3.56	3.44	3.01	5.60	8.36	2.31	5.38	10.88	1.91	5.69	14.60	1.71	7.32	23.12	1.51	7.20	26.84
4.32	3.80	3.68	3.02	5.83	8.72	2.32	5.61	11.36	1.92	5.92	15.20	1.72	7.54	23.84	1.52	7.41	27.68
4.33	4.05	3.92	3.03	6.07	9.08	2.33	5.84	11.84	1.93	6.14	15.80	1.73	7.75	24.56	1.53	7.62	28.52
4.34	4.29	4.16	3.04	6.30	9.44	2.34	6.07	12.32	1.94	6.36	16.40	1.74	7.96	25.28	1.54	7.83	29.36
4.35	4.54	4.40	3.05	6.54	9.80	2.35	6.30	12.80	1.95	6.59	17.00	1.75	8.18	26.00	1.55	8.04	30.20
4.36	4.78	4.64	3.06	6.77	10.16	2.36	6.53	13.28	1.96	6.81	17.60	1.76	8.39	26.72	1.56	8.24	31.04
4.37	5.03	4.88	3.07	7.00	10.52	2.37	6.76	13.76	1.97	7.03	18.20	1.77	8.60	27.44	1.57	8.45	31.88
4.38	5.27	5.12	3.08	7.24	10.88	2.38	6.98	14.24	1.98	7.25	18.80	1.78	8.81	28.16	1.58	8.65	32.72
4.39	5.51	5.36	3.09	7.47	11.24	2.39	7.21	14.72	1.99	7.47	19.40	1.79	9.02	28.88	1.59	8.86	33.56
4.40	5.76	5.60	3.10	7.70	11.60	2.40	7.44	15.20	2.00	7.69	20.00	1.80	9.23	29.60	1.60	9.06	34.40
4.41	6.00	5.84	3.11	7.93	11.96	2.41	7.66	15.68	2.01	7.91	20.60	1.81	9.44	30.32	1.61	9.27	35.24
4.42	6.24	6.08	3.12	8.16	12.32	2.42	7.89	16.16	2.02	8.13	21.20	1.82	9.64	31.04	1.62	9.47	36.08
4.43	6.48	6.32	3.13	8.40	12.68	2.43	8.11	16.64	2.03	8.34	21.80	1.83	9.85	31.76	1.63	9.67	36.92
4.44	6.73	6.56	3.14	8.63	13.04	2.44	8.33	17.12	2.04	8.56	22.40	1.84	10.06	32.48	1.64	9.87	37.76
4.45	6.97	6.80	3.15	8.86	13.40	2.45	8.56	17.60	2.05	8.78	23.00	1.85	10.26	33.20	1.65	10.07	38.60
4.46	7.21	7.04	3.16	9.08	13.76	2.46	8.78	18.08	2.06	8.99	23.60	1.86	10.47	33.92	1.66	10.27	39.44
4.47	7.45	7.28	3.17	9.31	14.12	2.47	9.00	18.56	2.07	9.21	24.20	1.87	10.67	34.64	1.67	10.47	40.28
4.48	7.69	7.52	3.18	9.54	14.48	2.48	9.22	19.04	2.08	9.42	24.80	1.88	10.88	35.36	1.68	10.67	41.12
4.49	7.93	7.76	3.19	9.77	14.84	2.49	9.44	19.52	2.09	9.63	25.40	1.89	11.08	36.08	1.69	10.87	41.96
4.50	8.17	8.00	3.20	10.00	15.20	2.50	9.66	20.00	2.10	9.85	26.00	1.90	11.28	36.80	1.70	11.07	42.80
4.51	8.41	8.24	3.21	10.23	15.56	2.51	9.88	20.48	2.11	10.06	26.60	1.91	11.48	37.52	1.71	11.26	43.64
4.52	8.65	8.48	3.22	10.45	15.92	2.52	10.10	20.96	2.12	10.27	27.20	1.92	11.69	38.24	1.72	11.46	44.48
4.53	8.89	8.72	3.23	10.68	16.28	2.53	10.32	21.44	2.13	10.48	27.80	1.93	11.89	38.96	1.73	11.65	45.32
4.54	9.13	8.96	3.24	10.91	16.64	2.54	10.54	21.92	2.14	10.70	28.40	1.94	12.09	39.68	1.74	11.85	46.16
4.55	9.37	9.20	3.25	11.13	17.00	2.55	10.76	22.40	2.15	10.91	29.00	1.95	12.29	40.40	1.75	12.04	47.00
4.56	9.61	9.44	3.26	11.36	17.36	2.56	10.98	22.88	2.16	11.12	29.60	1.96	12.49	41.12	1.76	12.24	47.84
4.57	9.85	9.68	3.27	11.58	17.72	2.57	11.19	23.36	2.17	11.32	30.20	1.97	12.69	41.84	1.77	12.43	48.68
4.58	10.09	9.92	3.28	11.81	18.08	2.58	11.41	23.84	2.18	11.53	30.80	1.98	12.88	42.56	1.78	12.62	49.52
4.59	10.32	10.16	3.29	12.03	18.44	2.59	11.63	24.32	2.19	11.74	31.40	1.99	13.08	43.28	1.79	12.81	50.36
4.60	10.56	10.40	3.30	12.26	18.80	2.60	11.84	24.80	2.20	11.95	32.00	2.00	13.28	44.00	1.80	13.01	51.20
4.61	10.80	10.64	3.31	12.48	19.16	2.61	12.06	25.28	2.21	12.16	32.60	2.01	13.48	44.72	1.81	13.20	52.04
4.62	11.04	10.88	3.32	12.70	19.52	2.62	12.27	25.76	2.22	12.36	33.20	2.02	13.67	45.44	1.82	13.39	52.88
4.63	11.27	11.12	3.33	12.93	19.88	2.63	12.49	26.24	2.23	12.57	33.80	2.03	13.87	46.16	1.83	13.58	53.72
4.64	11.51	11.36	3.34	13.15	20.24	2.64	12.70	26.72	2.24	12.78	34.40	2.04	14.06	46.88	1.84	13.77	54.56
4.65	11.75	11.60	3.35	13.37	20.60	2.65	12.91	27.20	2.25	12.98	35.00	2.05	14.26	47.60	1.85	13.95	55.40
4.66	11.98	11.84	3.36	13.59	20.96	2.66	13.13	27.68	2.26	13.19	35.60	2.06	14.45	48.32	1.86	14.14	56.24
4.67	12.22	12.08	3.37	13.82	21.32	2.67	13.34	28.16	2.27	13.39	36.20	2.07	14.64	49.04	1.87	14.33	57.08
4.68	12.45	12.32	3.38	14.04	21.68	2.68	13.55	28.64	2.28	13.59	36.80	2.08	14.84	49.76	1.88	14.52	57.92
4.69	12.69	12.56	3.39	14.26	22.04	2.69	13.76	29.12	2.29	13.80	37.40	2.09	15.03	50.48	1.89	14.70	58.76
4.70	12.92	12.80	3.40	14.48	22.40	2.70	13.98	29.60	2.30	14.00	38.00	2.10	15.22	51.20	1.90	14.89	59.60
4.71	13.16	13.04	3.41	14.70	22.76	2.71	14.19	30.08	2.31	14.20	38.60	2.11	15.42	51.92	1.91	15.08	60.44
4.72	13.39	13.28	3.42	14.92	23.12	2.72	14.40	30.56	2.32	14.40	39.20	2.12	15.61	52.64	1.92	15.26	61.28
4.73	13.63	13.52	3.43	15.14	23.48	2.73	14.61	31.04	2.33	14.61	39.80	2.13	15.80	53.36	1.93	15.45	62.12
4.74	13.86	13.76	3.44	15.36	23.84	2.74	14.82	31.52	2.34	14.81	40.40	2.14	15.99	54.08	1.94	15.63	62.96
4.75	14.10	14.00	3.45	15.58	24.20	2.75	15.03	32.00	2.35	15.01	41.00	2.15	16.18	54.80	1.95	15.82	63.80
4.76	14.33	14.24	3.46	15.79	24.56	2.76	15.24	32.48	2.36	15.21	41.60	2.16	16.37	55.52	1.96	16.00	64.64
4.77	14.56	14.48	3.47	16.01	24.92	2.77	15.44	32.96	2.37	15.41	42.20	2.17	16.56	56.24	1.97	16.18	65.48
4.78	14.80	14.72	3.48	16.23	25.28	2.78	15.65	33.44	2.38	15.61	42.80	2.18	16.75	56.96	1.98	16.36	66.32
4.79	15.03	14.96	3.49	16.45	25.64	2.79	15.86	33.92	2.39	15.81	43.40	2.19	16.93	57.68	1.99	16.55	67.16
4.80	15.26	15.20	3.50	16.66	26.00	2.80	16.07	34.40	2.40	16.00	44.00	2.20	17.12	58.40	2.00	16.73	68.00
4.81	15.49	15.44	3.51	16.88	26.36	2.81	16.27	34.88	2.41	16.20	44.60	2.21	17.31	59.12	2.01	16.91	68.84
4.82	15.72	15.68	3.52	17.10	26.72	2.82	16.48	35.36	2.42	16.40	45.20	2.22	17.50	59.84	2.02	17.09	69.68
4.83	15.96	15.92	3.53	17.31	27.08	2.83	16.69	35.84	2.43	16.60	45.80	2.23	17.68	60.56	2.03	17.27	70.52
4.84	16.19	16.16	3.54	17.53	27.44	2.84	16.89	36.32	2.44	16.79	46.40	2.24	17.87	61.28	2.04	17.45	71.36
4.85	16.42	16.40	3.55	17.75	27.80	2.85	17.10	36.80	2.45	16.99	47.00	2.25	18.05	62.00	2.05	17.63	72.20
4.86	16.65	16.64	3.56	17.96	28.16	2.86	17.30	37.28	2.46	17.19	47.60	2.26	18.24	62.72	2.06	17.81	73.04
4.87	16.88	16.88	3.57	18.18	28.52	2.87	17.51	37.76	2.47	17.38	48.20	2.27	18.42	63.44	2.07	17.99	73.88
4.88	17.11	17.12	3.58	18.39	28.88	2.88	17.71	38.24	2.48	17.58	48.80	2.28	18.61	64.16	2.08	18.17	74.72
4.89	17.34	17.36	3.59	18.60	29.24	2.89	17.92	38.72	2.49	17.77	49.40	2.29	18.79	64.88	2.09	18.34	75.56
4.90	17.57	17.60	3.60	18.82	29.60	2.90	18.12	39.20	2.50	17.97	50.00	2.30	18.98	65.60	2.10	18.52	76.40
4.91	17.80	17.84	3.61	19.03	29.96	2.91	18.32	39.68	2.51	18.16	50.60	2.31	19.16	66.32	2.11	18.70	77.24
4.92	18.03	18.08	3.62	19.25	30.32	2.92	18.53	40.16	2.52	18.35	51.20	2.32	19.34	67.04	2.12	18.87	78.08
4.93	18.26	18.32	3.63	19.46	30.68	2.93	18.73	40.64	2.53	18.55	51.80	2.33	19.53	67.76	2.13	19.05	78.92
4.94	18.49	18.56	3.64	19.67	31.04	2.94	18.93	41.12	2.54	18.74	52.40	2.34	19.71	68.48	2.14	19.23	79.76
4.95	18.72	18.80	3.65	19.88	31.40	2.95	19.13	41.60	2.55	18.93	53.00	2.35	19.89	69.20	2.15	19.40	80.60
4.96	18.95	19.04	3.66	20.10	31.76	2.96	19.33	42.08	2.56	19.12	53.60	2.36	20.07	69.92	2.16	19.58	81.44
4.97	19.18	19.28	3.67	20.31	32.12	2.97	19.54	42.56	2.57	19.31	54.20	2.37	20.25	70.64	2.17	19.75	82.28
4.98	19.40	19.52	3.68	20.52	32.48	2.98	19.74	43.04	2.58	19.51	54.80	2.38	20.43	71.36	2.18	19.93	83.12
4.99	19.63	19.76	3.69	20.73	32.84	2.99	19.94	43.52	2.59	19.70	55.40	2.39	20.61	72.08	2.19	20.10	83.96

Description: This table shows the Annual Percentage Rate and finance charge per $100 for monthly lease payments.

Example: A 1.30% lease payment for 8 years is equivalent to an APR of 5.84%. The charge per $100 cost is $ 24.80.

8 yr PAYT	APR	CHARGE	9 yr PAYT	APR	CHARGE	10 yr PAYT	APR	CHARGE	12 yr PAYT	APR	CHARGE	15 yr PAYT	APR	CHARGE	20 yr PAYT	APR	CHARGE
1.30	5.84	24.80	1.20	6.11	29.60	1.10	5.90	32.00	1.00	6.57	44.00	.80	5.24	44.00	.70	5.77	68.00
1.31	6.05	25.76	1.21	6.32	30.68	1.11	6.11	33.20	1.01	6.76	45.44	.81	5.44	45.80	.71	5.95	70.40
1.32	6.26	26.72	1.22	6.52	31.76	1.12	6.31	34.40	1.02	6.95	46.88	.82	5.63	47.60	.72	6.13	72.80
1.33	6.47	27.68	1.23	6.73	32.84	1.13	6.51	35.60	1.03	7.15	48.32	.83	5.82	49.40	.73	6.30	75.20
1.34	6.68	28.64	1.24	6.93	33.92	1.14	6.71	36.80	1.04	7.34	49.76	.84	6.01	51.20	.74	6.47	77.60
1.35	6.89	29.60	1.25	7.13	35.00	1.15	6.91	38.00	1.05	7.53	51.20	.85	6.19	53.00	.75	6.65	80.00
1.36	7.09	30.56	1.26	7.34	36.08	1.16	7.11	39.20	1.06	7.71	52.64	.86	6.38	54.80	.76	6.82	82.40
1.37	7.30	31.52	1.27	7.54	37.16	1.17	7.31	40.40	1.07	7.90	54.08	.87	6.57	56.60	.77	6.99	84.80
1.38	7.50	32.48	1.28	7.74	38.24	1.18	7.51	41.60	1.08	8.09	55.52	.88	6.75	58.40	.78	7.16	87.20
1.39	7.71	33.44	1.29	7.94	39.32	1.19	7.70	42.80	1.09	8.27	56.96	.89	6.93	60.20	.79	7.32	89.60
1.40	7.91	34.40	1.30	8.13	40.40	1.20	7.90	44.00	1.10	8.46	58.40	.90	7.12	62.00	.80	7.49	92.00
1.41	8.12	35.36	1.31	8.33	41.48	1.21	8.09	45.20	1.11	8.64	59.84	.91	7.30	63.80	.81	7.66	94.40
1.42	8.32	36.32	1.32	8.53	42.56	1.22	8.29	46.40	1.12	8.83	61.28	.92	7.48	65.60	.82	7.82	96.80
1.43	8.52	37.28	1.33	8.72	43.64	1.23	8.48	47.60	1.13	9.01	62.72	.93	7.66	67.40	.83	7.99	99.20
1.44	8.72	38.24	1.34	8.92	44.72	1.24	8.67	48.80	1.14	9.19	64.16	.94	7.83	69.20	.84	8.15	101.60
1.45	8.92	39.20	1.35	9.11	45.80	1.25	8.86	50.00	1.15	9.37	65.60	.95	8.01	71.00	.85	8.31	104.00
1.46	9.12	40.16	1.36	9.31	46.88	1.26	9.05	51.20	1.16	9.55	67.04	.96	8.19	72.80	.86	8.47	106.40
1.47	9.31	41.12	1.37	9.50	47.96	1.27	9.24	52.40	1.17	9.73	68.48	.97	8.36	74.60	.87	8.63	108.80
1.48	9.51	42.08	1.38	9.69	49.04	1.28	9.43	53.60	1.18	9.91	69.92	.98	8.54	76.40	.88	8.79	111.20
1.49	9.71	43.04	1.39	9.88	50.12	1.29	9.62	54.80	1.19	10.09	71.36	.99	8.71	78.20	.89	8.95	113.60
1.50	9.90	44.00	1.40	10.07	51.20	1.30	9.80	56.00	1.20	10.26	72.80	1.00	8.88	80.00	.90	9.11	116.00
1.51	10.10	44.96	1.41	10.26	52.28	1.31	9.99	57.20	1.21	10.44	74.24	1.01	9.06	81.80	.91	9.27	118.40
1.52	10.29	45.92	1.42	10.45	53.36	1.32	10.17	58.40	1.22	10.61	75.68	1.02	9.23	83.60	.92	9.42	120.80
1.53	10.49	46.88	1.43	10.64	54.44	1.33	10.36	59.60	1.23	10.79	77.12	1.03	9.40	85.40	.93	9.58	123.20
1.54	10.68	47.84	1.44	10.83	55.52	1.34	10.54	60.80	1.24	10.96	78.56	1.04	9.57	87.20	.94	9.74	125.60
1.55	10.87	48.80	1.45	11.01	56.60	1.35	10.73	62.00	1.25	11.14	80.00	1.05	9.74	89.00	.95	9.89	128.00
1.56	11.07	49.76	1.46	11.20	57.68	1.36	10.91	63.20	1.26	11.31	81.44	1.06	9.90	90.80	.96	10.05	130.40
1.57	11.26	50.72	1.47	11.38	58.76	1.37	11.09	64.40	1.27	11.48	82.88	1.07	10.07	92.60	.97	10.20	132.80
1.58	11.45	51.68	1.48	11.57	59.84	1.38	11.27	65.60	1.28	11.65	84.32	1.08	10.24	94.40	.98	10.35	135.20
1.59	11.64	52.64	1.49	11.75	60.92	1.39	11.45	66.80	1.29	11.82	85.76	1.09	10.40	96.20	.99	10.50	137.60
1.60	11.83	53.60	1.50	11.94	62.00	1.40	11.63	68.00	1.30	11.99	87.20	1.10	10.57	98.00	1.00	10.66	140.00
1.61	12.02	54.56	1.51	12.12	63.08	1.41	11.81	69.20	1.31	12.16	88.64	1.11	10.73	99.80	1.01	10.81	142.40
1.62	12.20	55.52	1.52	12.30	64.16	1.42	11.99	70.40	1.32	12.33	90.08	1.12	10.90	101.60	1.02	10.96	144.80
1.63	12.39	56.48	1.53	12.49	65.24	1.43	12.17	71.60	1.33	12.50	91.52	1.13	11.06	103.40	1.03	11.11	147.20
1.64	12.58	57.44	1.54	12.67	66.32	1.44	12.35	72.80	1.34	12.67	92.96	1.14	11.22	105.20	1.04	11.26	149.60
1.65	12.76	58.40	1.55	12.85	67.40	1.45	12.52	74.00	1.35	12.84	94.40	1.15	11.39	107.00	1.05	11.41	152.00
1.66	12.95	59.36	1.56	13.03	68.48	1.46	12.70	75.20	1.36	13.00	95.84	1.16	11.55	108.80	1.06	11.55	154.40
1.67	13.13	60.32	1.57	13.21	69.56	1.47	12.88	76.40	1.37	13.17	97.28	1.17	11.71	110.60	1.07	11.70	156.80
1.68	13.32	61.28	1.58	13.39	70.64	1.48	13.05	77.60	1.38	13.33	98.72	1.18	11.87	112.40	1.08	11.85	159.20
1.69	13.50	62.24	1.59	13.56	71.72	1.49	13.23	78.80	1.39	13.50	100.16	1.19	12.03	114.20	1.09	12.00	161.60
1.70	13.69	63.20	1.60	13.74	72.80	1.50	13.40	80.00	1.40	13.66	101.60	1.20	12.19	116.00	1.10	12.14	164.00
1.71	13.87	64.16	1.61	13.92	73.88	1.51	13.57	81.20	1.41	13.83	103.04	1.21	12.34	117.80	1.11	12.29	166.40
1.72	14.05	65.12	1.62	14.10	74.96	1.52	13.75	82.40	1.42	13.99	104.48	1.22	12.50	119.60	1.12	12.44	168.80
1.73	14.23	66.08	1.63	14.27	76.04	1.53	13.92	83.60	1.43	14.15	105.92	1.23	12.66	121.40	1.13	12.58	171.20
1.74	14.42	67.04	1.64	14.45	77.12	1.54	14.09	84.80	1.44	14.32	107.36	1.24	12.82	123.20	1.14	12.73	173.60
1.75	14.60	68.00	1.65	14.62	78.20	1.55	14.26	86.00	1.45	14.48	108.80	1.25	12.97	125.00	1.15	12.87	176.00
1.76	14.78	68.96	1.66	14.80	79.28	1.56	14.43	87.20	1.46	14.64	110.24	1.26	13.13	126.80	1.16	13.01	178.40
1.77	14.96	69.92	1.67	14.97	80.36	1.57	14.60	88.40	1.47	14.80	111.68	1.27	13.29	128.60	1.17	13.16	180.80
1.78	15.14	70.88	1.68	15.15	81.44	1.58	14.77	89.60	1.48	14.96	113.12	1.28	13.44	130.40	1.18	13.30	183.20
1.79	15.32	71.84	1.69	15.32	82.52	1.59	14.94	90.80	1.49	15.12	114.56	1.29	13.59	132.20	1.19	13.44	185.60
1.80	15.49	72.80	1.70	15.49	83.60	1.60	15.11	92.00	1.50	15.28	116.00	1.30	13.75	134.00	1.20	13.59	188.00
1.81	15.67	73.76	1.71	15.67	84.68	1.61	15.28	93.20	1.51	15.44	117.44	1.31	13.90	135.80	1.21	13.73	190.40
1.82	15.85	74.72	1.72	15.84	85.76	1.62	15.45	94.40	1.52	15.60	118.88	1.32	14.06	137.60	1.22	13.87	192.80
1.83	16.03	75.68	1.73	16.01	86.84	1.63	15.61	95.60	1.53	15.76	120.32	1.33	14.21	139.40	1.23	14.01	195.20
1.84	16.20	76.64	1.74	16.18	87.92	1.64	15.78	96.80	1.54	15.92	121.76	1.34	14.36	141.20	1.24	14.15	197.60
1.85	16.38	77.60	1.75	16.35	89.00	1.65	15.95	98.00	1.55	16.08	123.20	1.35	14.51	143.00	1.25	14.29	200.00
1.86	16.56	78.56	1.76	16.52	90.08	1.66	16.11	99.20	1.56	16.23	124.64	1.36	14.66	144.80	1.26	14.43	202.40
1.87	16.73	79.52	1.77	16.69	91.16	1.67	16.28	100.40	1.57	16.39	126.08	1.37	14.81	146.60	1.27	14.57	204.80
1.88	16.91	80.48	1.78	16.86	92.24	1.68	16.45	101.60	1.58	16.55	127.52	1.38	14.97	148.40	1.28	14.71	207.20
1.89	17.08	81.44	1.79	17.03	93.32	1.69	16.61	102.80	1.59	16.70	128.96	1.39	15.12	150.20	1.29	14.85	209.60
1.90	17.25	82.40	1.80	17.20	94.40	1.70	16.78	104.00	1.60	16.86	130.40	1.40	15.27	152.00	1.30	14.99	212.00
1.91	17.43	83.36	1.81	17.37	95.48	1.71	16.94	105.20	1.61	17.01	131.84	1.41	15.41	153.80	1.31	15.13	214.40
1.92	17.60	84.32	1.82	17.53	96.56	1.72	17.10	106.40	1.62	17.17	133.28	1.42	15.56	155.60	1.32	15.27	216.80
1.93	17.77	85.28	1.83	17.70	97.64	1.73	17.27	107.60	1.63	17.32	134.72	1.43	15.71	157.40	1.33	15.41	219.20
1.94	17.95	86.24	1.84	17.87	98.72	1.74	17.43	108.80	1.64	17.48	136.16	1.44	15.86	159.20	1.34	15.55	221.60
1.95	18.12	87.20	1.85	18.03	99.80	1.75	17.59	110.00	1.65	17.63	137.60	1.45	16.01	161.00	1.35	15.68	224.00
1.96	18.29	88.16	1.86	18.20	100.88	1.76	17.75	111.20	1.66	17.79	139.04	1.46	16.16	162.80	1.36	15.82	226.40
1.97	18.46	89.12	1.87	18.37	101.96	1.77	17.92	112.40	1.67	17.94	140.48	1.47	16.30	164.60	1.37	15.96	228.80
1.98	18.63	90.08	1.88	18.53	103.04	1.78	18.08	113.60	1.68	18.09	141.92	1.48	16.45	166.40	1.38	16.10	231.20
1.99	18.80	91.04	1.89	18.70	104.12	1.79	18.24	114.80	1.69	18.24	143.36	1.49	16.60	168.20	1.39	16.23	233.60

LEASE PAYMENTS

Description: This table shows the Annual Percentage Rate and finance charge per $100 for monthly lease payments.

Example: A 4.30% lease payment for 2 years is equivalent to an APR of 7.97%. The charge per $100 cost is $ 8.20.

2 yr MONTHLY PAYT	APR	CHARGE	3 yr MONTHLY PAYT	APR	CHARGE	4 yr MONTHLY PAYT	APR	CHARGE	5 yr MONTHLY PAYT	APR	CHARGE	6 yr MONTHLY PAYT	APR	CHARGE	7 yr MONTHLY PAYT	APR	CHARGE
4.30	7.97	8.20	3.00	8.21	13.00	2.30	7.20	15.40	1.90	7.02	19.00	1.70	8.25	27.40	1.50	7.92	31.00
4.31	8.20	8.44	3.01	8.43	13.36	2.31	7.42	15.88	1.91	7.23	19.60	1.71	8.45	28.12	1.51	8.12	31.84
4.32	8.43	8.68	3.02	8.65	13.72	2.32	7.63	16.36	1.92	7.44	20.20	1.72	8.66	28.84	1.52	8.32	32.68
4.33	8.66	8.92	3.03	8.87	14.08	2.33	7.85	16.84	1.93	7.65	20.80	1.73	8.86	29.56	1.53	8.52	33.52
4.34	8.89	9.16	3.04	9.09	14.44	2.34	8.06	17.32	1.94	7.86	21.40	1.74	9.06	30.28	1.54	8.72	34.36
4.35	9.11	9.40	3.05	9.31	14.80	2.35	8.28	17.80	1.95	8.07	22.00	1.75	9.26	31.00	1.55	8.92	35.20
4.36	9.34	9.64	3.06	9.53	15.16	2.36	8.49	18.28	1.96	8.28	22.60	1.76	9.47	31.72	1.56	9.11	36.04
4.37	9.57	9.88	3.07	9.75	15.52	2.37	8.71	18.76	1.97	8.49	23.20	1.77	9.67	32.44	1.57	9.31	36.88
4.38	9.80	10.12	3.08	9.97	15.88	2.38	8.92	19.24	1.98	8.70	23.80	1.78	9.87	33.16	1.58	9.50	37.72
4.39	10.03	10.36	3.09	10.19	16.24	2.39	9.13	19.72	1.99	8.90	24.40	1.79	10.07	33.88	1.59	9.70	38.56
4.40	10.25	10.60	3.10	10.41	16.60	2.40	9.35	20.20	2.00	9.11	25.00	1.80	10.26	34.60	1.60	9.90	39.40
4.41	10.48	10.84	3.11	10.62	16.96	2.41	9.56	20.68	2.01	9.32	25.60	1.81	10.46	35.32	1.61	10.09	40.24
4.42	10.71	11.08	3.12	10.84	17.32	2.42	9.77	21.16	2.02	9.53	26.20	1.82	10.66	36.04	1.62	10.28	41.08
4.43	10.93	11.32	3.13	11.06	17.68	2.43	9.98	21.64	2.03	9.73	26.80	1.83	10.86	36.76	1.63	10.48	41.92
4.44	11.16	11.56	3.14	11.27	18.04	2.44	10.19	22.12	2.04	9.94	27.40	1.84	11.05	37.48	1.64	10.67	42.76
4.45	11.39	11.80	3.15	11.49	18.40	2.45	10.40	22.60	2.05	10.14	28.00	1.85	11.25	38.20	1.65	10.86	43.60
4.46	11.61	12.04	3.16	11.71	18.76	2.46	10.61	23.08	2.06	10.35	28.60	1.86	11.45	38.92	1.66	11.05	44.44
4.47	11.84	12.28	3.17	11.92	19.12	2.47	10.82	23.56	2.07	10.55	29.20	1.87	11.64	39.64	1.67	11.24	45.28
4.48	12.06	12.52	3.18	12.14	19.48	2.48	11.03	24.04	2.08	10.75	29.80	1.88	11.84	40.36	1.68	11.43	46.12
4.49	12.29	12.76	3.19	12.35	19.84	2.49	11.24	24.52	2.09	10.96	30.40	1.89	12.03	41.08	1.69	11.62	46.96
4.50	12.51	13.00	3.20	12.57	20.20	2.50	11.45	25.00	2.10	11.16	31.00	1.90	12.23	41.80	1.70	11.81	47.80
4.51	12.74	13.24	3.21	12.78	20.56	2.51	11.66	25.48	2.11	11.36	31.60	1.91	12.42	42.52	1.71	12.00	48.64
4.52	12.96	13.48	3.22	13.00	20.92	2.52	11.87	25.96	2.12	11.56	32.20	1.92	12.61	43.24	1.72	12.19	49.48
4.53	13.19	13.72	3.23	13.21	21.28	2.53	12.07	26.44	2.13	11.76	32.80	1.93	12.80	43.96	1.73	12.38	50.32
4.54	13.41	13.96	3.24	13.42	21.64	2.54	12.28	26.92	2.14	11.96	33.40	1.94	13.00	44.68	1.74	12.57	51.16
4.55	13.64	14.20	3.25	13.64	22.00	2.55	12.49	27.40	2.15	12.16	34.00	1.95	13.19	45.40	1.75	12.75	52.00
4.56	13.86	14.44	3.26	13.85	22.36	2.56	12.69	27.88	2.16	12.36	34.60	1.96	13.38	46.12	1.76	12.94	52.84
4.57	14.08	14.68	3.27	14.06	22.72	2.57	12.90	28.36	2.17	12.56	35.20	1.97	13.57	46.84	1.77	13.12	53.68
4.58	14.31	14.92	3.28	14.27	23.08	2.58	13.11	28.84	2.18	12.76	35.80	1.98	13.76	47.56	1.78	13.31	54.52
4.59	14.53	15.16	3.29	14.49	23.44	2.59	13.31	29.32	2.19	12.96	36.40	1.99	13.95	48.28	1.79	13.49	55.36
4.60	14.75	15.40	3.30	14.70	23.80	2.60	13.52	29.80	2.20	13.16	37.00	2.00	14.14	49.00	1.80	13.68	56.20
4.61	14.98	15.64	3.31	14.91	24.16	2.61	13.72	30.28	2.21	13.36	37.60	2.01	14.33	49.72	1.81	13.86	57.04
4.62	15.20	15.88	3.32	15.12	24.52	2.62	13.92	30.76	2.22	13.55	38.20	2.02	14.52	50.44	1.82	14.05	57.88
4.63	15.42	16.12	3.33	15.33	24.88	2.63	14.13	31.24	2.23	13.75	38.80	2.03	14.71	51.16	1.83	14.23	58.72
4.64	15.64	16.36	3.34	15.54	25.24	2.64	14.33	31.72	2.24	13.95	39.40	2.04	14.89	51.88	1.84	14.41	59.56
4.65	15.87	16.60	3.35	15.75	25.60	2.65	14.53	32.20	2.25	14.14	40.00	2.05	15.08	52.60	1.85	14.60	60.40
4.66	16.09	16.84	3.36	15.96	25.96	2.66	14.74	32.68	2.26	14.34	40.60	2.06	15.27	53.32	1.86	14.78	61.24
4.67	16.31	17.08	3.37	16.17	26.32	2.67	14.94	33.16	2.27	14.54	41.20	2.07	15.45	54.04	1.87	14.96	62.08
4.68	16.53	17.32	3.38	16.38	26.68	2.68	15.14	33.64	2.28	14.73	41.80	2.08	15.64	54.76	1.88	15.14	62.92
4.69	16.75	17.56	3.39	16.59	27.04	2.69	15.34	34.12	2.29	14.92	42.40	2.09	15.83	55.48	1.89	15.32	63.76
4.70	16.97	17.80	3.40	16.80	27.40	2.70	15.54	34.60	2.30	15.12	43.00	2.10	16.01	56.20	1.90	15.50	64.60
4.71	17.19	18.04	3.41	17.01	27.76	2.71	15.75	35.08	2.31	15.31	43.60	2.11	16.20	56.92	1.91	15.68	65.44
4.72	17.41	18.28	3.42	17.22	28.12	2.72	15.95	35.56	2.32	15.51	44.20	2.12	16.38	57.64	1.92	15.86	66.28
4.73	17.63	18.52	3.43	17.43	28.48	2.73	16.15	36.04	2.33	15.70	44.80	2.13	16.56	58.36	1.93	16.04	67.12
4.74	17.85	18.76	3.44	17.63	28.84	2.74	16.35	36.52	2.34	15.89	45.40	2.14	16.75	59.08	1.94	16.22	67.96
4.75	18.08	19.00	3.45	17.84	29.20	2.75	16.55	37.00	2.35	16.08	46.00	2.15	16.93	59.80	1.95	16.39	68.80
4.76	18.29	19.24	3.46	18.05	29.56	2.76	16.75	37.48	2.36	16.28	46.60	2.16	17.12	60.52	1.96	16.57	69.64
4.77	18.51	19.48	3.47	18.26	29.92	2.77	16.94	37.96	2.37	16.47	47.20	2.17	17.30	61.24	1.97	16.75	70.48
4.78	18.73	19.72	3.48	18.46	30.28	2.78	17.14	38.44	2.38	16.66	47.80	2.18	17.48	61.96	1.98	16.93	71.32
4.79	18.95	19.96	3.49	18.67	30.64	2.79	17.34	38.92	2.39	16.85	48.40	2.19	17.66	62.68	1.99	17.10	72.16
4.80	19.17	20.20	3.50	18.88	31.00	2.80	17.54	39.40	2.40	17.04	49.00	2.20	17.84	63.40	2.00	17.28	73.00
4.81	19.39	20.44	3.51	19.08	31.36	2.81	17.74	39.88	2.41	17.23	49.60	2.21	18.03	64.12	2.01	17.46	73.84
4.82	19.61	20.68	3.52	19.29	31.72	2.82	17.94	40.36	2.42	17.42	50.20	2.22	18.21	64.84	2.02	17.63	74.68
4.83	19.83	20.92	3.53	19.49	32.08	2.83	18.13	40.84	2.43	17.61	50.80	2.23	18.39	65.56	2.03	17.81	75.52
4.84	20.05	21.16	3.54	19.70	32.44	2.84	18.33	41.32	2.44	17.80	51.40	2.24	18.57	66.28	2.04	17.98	76.36
4.85	20.27	21.40	3.55	19.91	32.80	2.85	18.53	41.80	2.45	17.99	52.00	2.25	18.75	67.00	2.05	18.16	77.20
4.86	20.48	21.64	3.56	20.11	33.16	2.86	18.72	42.28	2.46	18.18	52.60	2.26	18.93	67.72	2.06	18.33	78.04
4.87	20.70	21.88	3.57	20.31	33.52	2.87	18.92	42.76	2.47	18.37	53.20	2.27	19.11	68.44	2.07	18.50	78.88
4.88	20.92	22.12	3.58	20.52	33.88	2.88	19.11	43.24	2.48	18.55	53.80	2.28	19.28	69.16	2.08	18.68	79.72
4.89	21.14	22.36	3.59	20.72	34.24	2.89	19.31	43.72	2.49	18.74	54.40	2.29	19.46	69.88	2.09	18.85	80.56
4.90	21.36	22.60	3.60	20.93	34.60	2.90	19.50	44.20	2.50	18.93	55.00	2.30	19.64	70.60	2.10	19.02	81.40
4.91	21.57	22.84	3.61	21.13	34.96	2.91	19.70	44.68	2.51	19.11	55.60	2.31	19.82	71.32	2.11	19.19	82.24
4.92	21.79	23.08	3.62	21.33	35.32	2.92	19.89	45.16	2.52	19.30	56.20	2.32	20.00	72.04	2.12	19.37	83.08
4.93	22.01	23.32	3.63	21.54	35.68	2.93	20.09	45.64	2.53	19.49	56.80	2.33	20.17	72.76	2.13	19.54	83.92
4.94	22.22	23.56	3.64	21.74	36.04	2.94	20.28	46.12	2.54	19.67	57.40	2.34	20.35	73.48	2.14	19.71	84.76
4.95	22.44	23.80	3.65	21.94	36.40	2.95	20.48	46.60	2.55	19.86	58.00	2.35	20.53	74.20	2.15	19.88	85.60
4.96	22.66	24.04	3.66	22.15	36.76	2.96	20.67	47.08	2.56	20.04	58.60	2.36	20.70	74.92	2.16	20.05	86.44
4.97	22.87	24.28	3.67	22.35	37.12	2.97	20.87	47.56	2.57	20.23	59.20	2.37	20.88	75.64	2.17	20.22	87.28
4.98	23.09	24.52	3.68	22.55	37.48	2.98	21.06	48.04	2.58	20.41	59.80	2.38	21.06	76.36	2.18	20.39	88.12
4.99	23.30	24.76	3.69	22.75	37.84	2.99	21.25	48.52	2.59	20.60	60.40	2.39	21.23	77.08	2.19	20.56	88.96

Description: This table shows the Annual Percentage Rate and finance charge per $100 for monthly lease payments.

Example: A 1.30% lease payment for 8 years is equivalent to an APR of 6.67%. The charge per $100 cost is $ 29.80.

8 yr PAYT	APR	CHARGE	9 yr PAYT	APR	CHARGE	10 yr PAYT	APR	CHARGE	12 yr PAYT	APR	CHARGE	15 yr PAYT	APR	CHARGE	20 yr PAYT	APR	CHARGE
1.30	6.67	29.80	1.20	6.80	34.60	1.10	6.50	37.00	1.00	6.99	49.00	.80	5.58	49.00	.70	5.96	73.00
1.31	6.87	30.76	1.21	7.00	35.68	1.11	6.70	38.20	1.01	7.18	50.44	.81	5.77	50.80	.71	6.14	75.40
1.32	7.07	31.72	1.22	7.19	36.76	1.12	6.89	39.40	1.02	7.37	51.88	.82	5.95	52.60	.72	6.31	77.80
1.33	7.27	32.68	1.23	7.39	37.84	1.13	7.08	40.60	1.03	7.55	53.32	.83	6.14	54.40	.73	6.48	80.20
1.34	7.46	33.64	1.24	7.58	38.92	1.14	7.28	41.80	1.04	7.73	54.76	.84	6.32	56.20	.74	6.64	82.60
1.35	7.66	34.60	1.25	7.77	40.00	1.15	7.47	43.00	1.05	7.92	56.20	.85	6.50	58.00	.75	6.81	85.00
1.36	7.86	35.56	1.26	7.97	41.08	1.16	7.66	44.20	1.06	8.10	57.64	.86	6.68	59.80	.76	6.98	87.40
1.37	8.05	36.52	1.27	8.16	42.16	1.17	7.85	45.40	1.07	8.28	59.08	.87	6.86	61.60	.77	7.14	89.80
1.38	8.25	37.48	1.28	8.35	43.24	1.18	8.04	46.60	1.08	8.46	60.52	.88	7.04	63.40	.78	7.31	92.20
1.39	8.45	38.44	1.29	8.54	44.32	1.19	8.22	47.80	1.09	8.64	61.96	.89	7.21	65.20	.79	7.47	94.60
1.40	8.64	39.40	1.30	8.73	45.40	1.20	8.41	49.00	1.10	8.82	63.40	.90	7.39	67.00	.80	7.64	97.00
1.41	8.83	40.36	1.31	8.92	46.48	1.21	8.60	50.20	1.11	8.99	64.84	.91	7.57	68.80	.81	7.80	99.40
1.42	9.03	41.32	1.32	9.11	47.56	1.22	8.78	51.40	1.12	9.17	66.28	.92	7.74	70.60	.82	7.96	101.80
1.43	9.22	42.28	1.33	9.30	48.64	1.23	8.97	52.60	1.13	9.35	67.72	.93	7.91	72.40	.83	8.12	104.20
1.44	9.41	43.24	1.34	9.48	49.72	1.24	9.15	53.80	1.14	9.52	69.16	.94	8.09	74.20	.84	8.28	106.60
1.45	9.60	44.20	1.35	9.67	50.80	1.25	9.34	55.00	1.15	9.70	70.60	.95	8.26	76.00	.85	8.44	109.00
1.46	9.79	45.16	1.36	9.86	51.88	1.26	9.52	56.20	1.16	9.87	72.04	.96	8.43	77.80	.86	8.60	111.40
1.47	9.98	46.12	1.37	10.04	52.96	1.27	9.70	57.40	1.17	10.05	73.48	.97	8.60	79.60	.87	8.76	113.80
1.48	10.17	47.08	1.38	10.23	54.04	1.28	9.88	58.60	1.18	10.22	74.92	.98	8.77	81.40	.88	8.91	116.20
1.49	10.36	48.04	1.39	10.41	55.12	1.29	10.07	59.80	1.19	10.39	76.36	.99	8.94	83.20	.89	9.07	118.60
1.50	10.55	49.00	1.40	10.59	56.20	1.30	10.25	61.00	1.20	10.56	77.80	1.00	9.11	85.00	.90	9.22	121.00
1.51	10.74	49.96	1.41	10.78	57.28	1.31	10.43	62.20	1.21	10.74	79.24	1.01	9.28	86.80	.91	9.38	123.40
1.52	10.92	50.92	1.42	10.96	58.36	1.32	10.61	63.40	1.22	10.91	80.68	1.02	9.44	88.60	.92	9.53	125.80
1.53	11.11	51.88	1.43	11.14	59.44	1.33	10.78	64.60	1.23	11.08	82.12	1.03	9.61	90.40	.93	9.69	128.20
1.54	11.29	52.84	1.44	11.32	60.52	1.34	10.96	65.80	1.24	11.25	83.56	1.04	9.77	92.20	.94	9.84	130.60
1.55	11.48	53.80	1.45	11.50	61.60	1.35	11.14	67.00	1.25	11.42	85.00	1.05	9.94	94.00	.95	9.99	133.00
1.56	11.66	54.76	1.46	11.68	62.68	1.36	11.32	68.20	1.26	11.58	86.44	1.06	10.10	95.80	.96	10.14	135.40
1.57	11.85	55.72	1.47	11.86	63.76	1.37	11.49	69.40	1.27	11.75	87.88	1.07	10.27	97.60	.97	10.30	137.80
1.58	12.03	56.68	1.48	12.04	64.84	1.38	11.67	70.60	1.28	11.92	89.32	1.08	10.43	99.40	.98	10.45	140.20
1.59	12.22	57.64	1.49	12.22	65.92	1.39	11.84	71.80	1.29	12.08	90.76	1.09	10.59	101.20	.99	10.60	142.60
1.60	12.40	58.60	1.50	12.40	67.00	1.40	12.02	73.00	1.30	12.25	92.20	1.10	10.75	103.00	1.00	10.75	145.00
1.61	12.58	59.56	1.51	12.57	68.08	1.41	12.19	74.20	1.31	12.42	93.64	1.11	10.91	104.80	1.01	10.89	147.40
1.62	12.76	60.52	1.52	12.75	69.16	1.42	12.37	75.40	1.32	12.58	95.08	1.12	11.07	106.60	1.02	11.04	149.80
1.63	12.94	61.48	1.53	12.93	70.24	1.43	12.54	76.60	1.33	12.75	96.52	1.13	11.23	108.40	1.03	11.19	152.20
1.64	13.12	62.44	1.54	13.10	71.32	1.44	12.71	77.80	1.34	12.91	97.96	1.14	11.39	110.20	1.04	11.34	154.60
1.65	13.30	63.40	1.55	13.28	72.40	1.45	12.88	79.00	1.35	13.07	99.40	1.15	11.55	112.00	1.05	11.49	157.00
1.66	13.48	64.36	1.56	13.45	73.48	1.46	13.05	80.20	1.36	13.24	100.84	1.16	11.71	113.80	1.06	11.63	159.40
1.67	13.66	65.32	1.57	13.63	74.56	1.47	13.23	81.40	1.37	13.40	102.28	1.17	11.87	115.60	1.07	11.78	161.80
1.68	13.84	66.28	1.58	13.80	75.64	1.48	13.40	82.60	1.38	13.56	103.72	1.18	12.03	117.40	1.08	11.92	164.20
1.69	14.02	67.24	1.59	13.97	76.72	1.49	13.57	83.80	1.39	13.72	105.16	1.19	12.18	119.20	1.09	12.07	166.60
1.70	14.20	68.20	1.60	14.15	77.80	1.50	13.74	85.00	1.40	13.88	106.60	1.20	12.34	121.00	1.10	12.21	169.00
1.71	14.37	69.16	1.61	14.32	78.88	1.51	13.90	86.20	1.41	14.05	108.04	1.21	12.49	122.80	1.11	12.36	171.40
1.72	14.55	70.12	1.62	14.49	79.96	1.52	14.07	87.40	1.42	14.21	109.48	1.22	12.65	124.60	1.12	12.50	173.80
1.73	14.73	71.08	1.63	14.66	81.04	1.53	14.24	88.60	1.43	14.37	110.92	1.23	12.80	126.40	1.13	12.65	176.20
1.74	14.90	72.04	1.64	14.83	82.12	1.54	14.41	89.80	1.44	14.52	112.36	1.24	12.96	128.20	1.14	12.79	178.60
1.75	15.08	73.00	1.65	15.01	83.20	1.55	14.58	91.00	1.45	14.68	113.80	1.25	13.11	130.00	1.15	12.93	181.00
1.76	15.25	73.96	1.66	15.18	84.28	1.56	14.74	92.20	1.46	14.84	115.24	1.26	13.27	131.80	1.16	13.08	183.40
1.77	15.43	74.92	1.67	15.35	85.36	1.57	14.91	93.40	1.47	15.00	116.68	1.27	13.42	133.60	1.17	13.22	185.80
1.78	15.60	75.88	1.68	15.51	86.44	1.58	15.07	94.60	1.48	15.16	118.12	1.28	13.57	135.40	1.18	13.36	188.20
1.79	15.78	76.84	1.69	15.68	87.52	1.59	15.24	95.80	1.49	15.32	119.56	1.29	13.72	137.20	1.19	13.50	190.60
1.80	15.95	77.80	1.70	15.85	88.60	1.60	15.41	97.00	1.50	15.47	121.00	1.30	13.88	139.00	1.20	13.64	193.00
1.81	16.12	78.76	1.71	16.02	89.68	1.61	15.57	98.20	1.51	15.63	122.44	1.31	14.03	140.80	1.21	13.78	195.40
1.82	16.30	79.72	1.72	16.19	90.76	1.62	15.73	99.40	1.52	15.79	123.88	1.32	14.18	142.60	1.22	13.92	197.80
1.83	16.47	80.68	1.73	16.36	91.84	1.63	15.90	100.60	1.53	15.94	125.32	1.33	14.33	144.40	1.23	14.06	200.20
1.84	16.64	81.64	1.74	16.52	92.92	1.64	16.06	101.80	1.54	16.10	126.76	1.34	14.48	146.20	1.24	14.20	202.60
1.85	16.81	82.60	1.75	16.69	94.00	1.65	16.22	103.00	1.55	16.25	128.20	1.35	14.63	148.00	1.25	14.34	205.00
1.86	16.98	83.56	1.76	16.86	95.08	1.66	16.39	104.20	1.56	16.41	129.64	1.36	14.78	149.80	1.26	14.48	207.40
1.87	17.15	84.52	1.77	17.02	96.16	1.67	16.55	105.40	1.57	16.56	131.08	1.37	14.93	151.60	1.27	14.62	209.80
1.88	17.32	85.48	1.78	17.19	97.24	1.68	16.71	106.60	1.58	16.72	132.52	1.38	15.08	153.40	1.28	14.76	212.20
1.89	17.49	86.44	1.79	17.35	98.32	1.69	16.87	107.80	1.59	16.87	133.96	1.39	15.22	155.20	1.29	14.90	214.60
1.90	17.66	87.40	1.80	17.52	99.40	1.70	17.03	109.00	1.60	17.02	135.40	1.40	15.37	157.00	1.30	15.04	217.00
1.91	17.83	88.36	1.81	17.68	100.48	1.71	17.20	110.20	1.61	17.18	136.84	1.41	15.52	158.80	1.31	15.18	219.40
1.92	18.00	89.32	1.82	17.85	101.56	1.72	17.36	111.40	1.62	17.33	138.28	1.42	15.67	160.60	1.32	15.31	221.80
1.93	18.17	90.28	1.83	18.01	102.64	1.73	17.52	112.60	1.63	17.48	139.72	1.43	15.81	162.40	1.33	15.45	224.20
1.94	18.34	91.24	1.84	18.17	103.72	1.74	17.68	113.80	1.64	17.63	141.16	1.44	15.96	164.20	1.34	15.59	226.60
1.95	18.51	92.20	1.85	18.34	104.80	1.75	17.84	115.00	1.65	17.78	142.60	1.45	16.11	166.00	1.35	15.73	229.00
1.96	18.67	93.16	1.86	18.50	105.88	1.76	17.99	116.20	1.66	17.94	144.04	1.46	16.25	167.80	1.36	15.86	231.40
1.97	18.84	94.12	1.87	18.66	106.96	1.77	18.15	117.40	1.67	18.09	145.48	1.47	16.40	169.60	1.37	16.00	233.80
1.98	19.01	95.08	1.88	18.82	108.04	1.78	18.31	118.60	1.68	18.24	146.92	1.48	16.54	171.40	1.38	16.14	236.20
1.99	19.17	96.04	1.89	18.98	109.12	1.79	18.47	119.80	1.69	18.39	148.36	1.49	16.69	173.20	1.39	16.27	238.60

Description: This table shows the Annual Percentage Rate and finance charge per $100 for monthly lease payments.

Example: A 4.30% lease payment for 2 years is equivalent to an APR of 12.14%. The charge per $100 cost is $ 13.20.

2 yr MONTHLY PAYT	APR	CHARGE	3 yr MONTHLY PAYT	APR	CHARGE	4 yr MONTHLY PAYT	APR	CHARGE	5 yr MONTHLY PAYT	APR	CHARGE	6 yr MONTHLY PAYT	APR	CHARGE	7 yr MONTHLY PAYT	APR	CHARGE
4.30	12.14	13.20	3.00	10.78	18.00	2.30	9.05	20.40	1.90	8.42	24.00	1.70	9.30	32.40	1.50	8.78	36.00
4.31	12.35	13.44	3.01	10.99	18.36	2.31	9.26	20.88	1.91	8.62	24.60	1.71	9.49	33.12	1.51	8.97	36.84
4.32	12.57	13.68	3.02	11.20	18.72	2.32	9.46	21.36	1.92	8.82	25.20	1.72	9.69	33.84	1.52	9.16	37.68
4.33	12.78	13.92	3.03	11.40	19.08	2.33	9.67	21.84	1.93	9.02	25.80	1.73	9.88	34.56	1.53	9.35	38.52
4.34	13.00	14.16	3.04	11.61	19.44	2.34	9.87	22.32	1.94	9.22	26.40	1.74	10.07	35.28	1.54	9.54	39.36
4.35	13.21	14.40	3.05	11.82	19.80	2.35	10.07	22.80	1.95	9.42	27.00	1.75	10.27	36.00	1.55	9.73	40.20
4.36	13.43	14.64	3.06	12.03	20.16	2.36	10.28	23.28	1.96	9.62	27.60	1.76	10.46	36.72	1.56	9.92	41.04
4.37	13.64	14.88	3.07	12.23	20.52	2.37	10.48	23.76	1.97	9.82	28.20	1.77	10.65	37.44	1.57	10.11	41.88
4.38	13.86	15.12	3.08	12.44	20.88	2.38	10.68	24.24	1.98	10.02	28.80	1.78	10.84	38.16	1.58	10.29	42.72
4.39	14.07	15.36	3.09	12.65	21.24	2.39	10.88	24.72	1.99	10.22	29.40	1.79	11.03	38.88	1.59	10.48	43.56
4.40	14.29	15.60	3.10	12.85	21.60	2.40	11.08	25.20	2.00	10.41	30.00	1.80	11.22	39.60	1.60	10.67	44.40
4.41	14.50	15.84	3.11	13.06	21.96	2.41	11.29	25.68	2.01	10.61	30.60	1.81	11.41	40.32	1.61	10.85	45.24
4.42	14.71	16.08	3.12	13.26	22.32	2.42	11.49	26.16	2.02	10.81	31.20	1.82	11.60	41.04	1.62	11.04	46.08
4.43	14.93	16.32	3.13	13.47	22.68	2.43	11.69	26.64	2.03	11.00	31.80	1.83	11.79	41.76	1.63	11.23	46.92
4.44	15.14	16.56	3.14	13.68	23.04	2.44	11.89	27.12	2.04	11.20	32.40	1.84	11.98	42.48	1.64	11.41	47.76
4.45	15.35	16.80	3.15	13.88	23.40	2.45	12.09	27.60	2.05	11.39	33.00	1.85	12.17	43.20	1.65	11.59	48.60
4.46	15.57	17.04	3.16	14.09	23.76	2.46	12.29	28.08	2.06	11.59	33.60	1.86	12.36	43.92	1.66	11.78	49.44
4.47	15.78	17.28	3.17	14.29	24.12	2.47	12.49	28.56	2.07	11.78	34.20	1.87	12.54	44.64	1.67	11.96	50.28
4.48	15.99	17.52	3.18	14.49	24.48	2.48	12.69	29.04	2.08	11.98	34.80	1.88	12.73	45.36	1.68	12.15	51.12
4.49	16.21	17.76	3.19	14.70	24.84	2.49	12.89	29.52	2.09	12.17	35.40	1.89	12.92	46.08	1.69	12.33	51.96
4.50	16.42	18.00	3.20	14.90	25.20	2.50	13.08	30.00	2.10	12.36	36.00	1.90	13.10	46.80	1.70	12.51	52.80
4.51	16.63	18.24	3.21	15.11	25.56	2.51	13.28	30.48	2.11	12.56	36.60	1.91	13.29	47.52	1.71	12.69	53.64
4.52	16.84	18.48	3.22	15.31	25.92	2.52	13.48	30.96	2.12	12.75	37.20	1.92	13.47	48.24	1.72	12.87	54.48
4.53	17.06	18.72	3.23	15.51	26.28	2.53	13.68	31.44	2.13	12.94	37.80	1.93	13.66	48.96	1.73	13.06	55.32
4.54	17.27	18.96	3.24	15.71	26.64	2.54	13.88	31.92	2.14	13.13	38.40	1.94	13.84	49.68	1.74	13.24	56.16
4.55	17.48	19.20	3.25	15.92	27.00	2.55	14.07	32.40	2.15	13.33	39.00	1.95	14.03	50.40	1.75	13.42	57.00
4.56	17.69	19.44	3.26	16.12	27.36	2.56	14.27	32.88	2.16	13.52	39.60	1.96	14.21	51.12	1.76	13.60	57.84
4.57	17.90	19.68	3.27	16.32	27.72	2.57	14.47	33.36	2.17	13.71	40.20	1.97	14.40	51.84	1.77	13.78	58.68
4.58	18.12	19.92	3.28	16.52	28.08	2.58	14.66	33.84	2.18	13.90	40.80	1.98	14.58	52.56	1.78	13.96	59.52
4.59	18.33	20.16	3.29	16.73	28.44	2.59	14.86	34.32	2.19	14.09	41.40	1.99	14.76	53.28	1.79	14.13	60.36
4.60	18.54	20.40	3.30	16.93	28.80	2.60	15.05	34.80	2.20	14.28	42.00	2.00	14.95	54.00	1.80	14.31	61.20
4.61	18.75	20.64	3.31	17.13	29.16	2.61	15.25	35.28	2.21	14.47	42.60	2.01	15.13	54.72	1.81	14.49	62.04
4.62	18.96	20.88	3.32	17.33	29.52	2.62	15.44	35.76	2.22	14.66	43.20	2.02	15.31	55.44	1.82	14.67	62.88
4.63	19.17	21.12	3.33	17.53	29.88	2.63	15.64	36.24	2.23	14.85	43.80	2.03	15.49	56.16	1.83	14.85	63.72
4.64	19.38	21.36	3.34	17.73	30.24	2.64	15.83	36.72	2.24	15.04	44.40	2.04	15.67	56.88	1.84	15.02	64.56
4.65	19.59	21.60	3.35	17.93	30.60	2.65	16.03	37.20	2.25	15.22	45.00	2.05	15.85	57.60	1.85	15.20	65.40
4.66	19.80	21.84	3.36	18.13	30.96	2.66	16.22	37.68	2.26	15.41	45.60	2.06	16.03	58.32	1.86	15.38	66.24
4.67	20.01	22.08	3.37	18.33	31.32	2.67	16.41	38.16	2.27	15.60	46.20	2.07	16.21	59.04	1.87	15.55	67.08
4.68	20.22	22.32	3.38	18.53	31.68	2.68	16.61	38.64	2.28	15.79	46.80	2.08	16.39	59.76	1.88	15.73	67.92
4.69	20.43	22.56	3.39	18.73	32.04	2.69	16.80	39.12	2.29	15.97	47.40	2.09	16.57	60.48	1.89	15.90	68.76
4.70	20.64	22.80	3.40	18.93	32.40	2.70	16.99	39.60	2.30	16.16	48.00	2.10	16.75	61.20	1.90	16.08	69.60
4.71	20.85	23.04	3.41	19.13	32.76	2.71	17.19	40.08	2.31	16.35	48.60	2.11	16.93	61.92	1.91	16.25	70.44
4.72	21.06	23.28	3.42	19.33	33.12	2.72	17.38	40.56	2.32	16.53	49.20	2.12	17.11	62.64	1.92	16.42	71.28
4.73	21.27	23.52	3.43	19.53	33.48	2.73	17.57	41.04	2.33	16.72	49.80	2.13	17.29	63.36	1.93	16.60	72.12
4.74	21.48	23.76	3.44	19.73	33.84	2.74	17.76	41.52	2.34	16.90	50.40	2.14	17.47	64.08	1.94	16.77	72.96
4.75	21.69	24.00	3.45	19.92	34.20	2.75	17.95	42.00	2.35	17.09	51.00	2.15	17.64	64.80	1.95	16.94	73.80
4.76	21.90	24.24	3.46	20.12	34.56	2.76	18.14	42.48	2.36	17.27	51.60	2.16	17.82	65.52	1.96	17.12	74.64
4.77	22.10	24.48	3.47	20.32	34.92	2.77	18.34	42.96	2.37	17.46	52.20	2.17	18.00	66.24	1.97	17.29	75.48
4.78	22.31	24.72	3.48	20.52	35.28	2.78	18.53	43.44	2.38	17.64	52.80	2.18	18.17	66.96	1.98	17.46	76.32
4.79	22.52	24.96	3.49	20.72	35.64	2.79	18.72	43.92	2.39	17.83	53.40	2.19	18.35	67.68	1.99	17.63	77.16
4.80	22.73	25.20	3.50	20.91	36.00	2.80	18.91	44.40	2.40	18.01	54.00	2.20	18.53	68.40	2.00	17.80	78.00
4.81	22.94	25.44	3.51	21.11	36.36	2.81	19.10	44.88	2.41	18.19	54.60	2.21	18.70	69.12	2.01	17.98	78.84
4.82	23.15	25.68	3.52	21.31	36.72	2.82	19.29	45.36	2.42	18.38	55.20	2.22	18.88	69.84	2.02	18.15	79.68
4.83	23.35	25.92	3.53	21.50	37.08	2.83	19.48	45.84	2.43	18.56	55.80	2.23	19.05	70.56	2.03	18.32	80.52
4.84	23.56	26.16	3.54	21.70	37.44	2.84	19.66	46.32	2.44	18.74	56.40	2.24	19.23	71.28	2.04	18.49	81.36
4.85	23.77	26.40	3.55	21.90	37.80	2.85	19.85	46.80	2.45	18.92	57.00	2.25	19.40	72.00	2.05	18.66	82.20
4.86	23.98	26.64	3.56	22.09	38.16	2.86	20.04	47.28	2.46	19.11	57.60	2.26	19.58	72.72	2.06	18.83	83.04
4.87	24.18	26.88	3.57	22.29	38.52	2.87	20.23	47.76	2.47	19.29	58.20	2.27	19.75	73.44	2.07	19.00	83.88
4.88	24.39	27.12	3.58	22.48	38.88	2.88	20.42	48.24	2.48	19.47	58.80	2.28	19.92	74.16	2.08	19.16	84.72
4.89	24.60	27.36	3.59	22.68	39.24	2.89	20.61	48.72	2.49	19.65	59.40	2.29	20.10	74.88	2.09	19.33	85.56
4.90	24.80	27.60	3.60	22.87	39.60	2.90	20.79	49.20	2.50	19.83	60.00	2.30	20.27	75.60	2.10	19.50	86.40
4.91	25.01	27.84	3.61	23.07	39.96	2.91	20.98	49.68	2.51	20.01	60.60	2.31	20.44	76.32	2.11	19.67	87.24
4.92	25.22	28.08	3.62	23.26	40.32	2.92	21.17	50.16	2.52	20.19	61.20	2.32	20.62	77.04	2.12	19.84	88.08
4.93	25.42	28.32	3.63	23.46	40.68	2.93	21.36	50.64	2.53	20.37	61.80	2.33	20.79	77.76	2.13	20.00	88.92
4.94	25.63	28.56	3.64	23.65	41.04	2.94	21.54	51.12	2.54	20.55	62.40	2.34	20.96	78.48	2.14	20.17	89.76
4.95	25.84	28.80	3.65	23.85	41.40	2.95	21.73	51.60	2.55	20.73	63.00	2.35	21.13	79.20	2.15	20.34	90.60
4.96	26.04	29.04	3.66	24.04	41.76	2.96	21.92	52.08	2.56	20.91	63.60	2.36	21.30	79.92	2.16	20.51	91.44
4.97	26.25	29.28	3.67	24.24	42.12	2.97	22.10	52.56	2.57	21.09	64.20	2.37	21.48	80.64	2.17	20.67	92.28
4.98	26.45	29.52	3.68	24.43	42.48	2.98	22.29	53.04	2.58	21.27	64.80	2.38	21.65	81.36	2.18	20.84	93.12
4.99	26.66	29.76	3.69	24.62	42.84	2.99	22.47	53.52	2.59	21.45	65.40	2.39	21.82	82.08	2.19	21.00	93.96

Description: This table shows the Annual Percentage Rate and finance charge per $100 for monthly lease payments.

Example: A 1.30% lease payment for 8 years is equivalent to an APR of 7.43%. The charge per $100 cost is $ 34.80.

8 yr			9 yr			10 yr			12 yr			15 yr			20 yr		
MONTHLY PAYT	APR	CHARGE	MONTHLY PAYT	APR	CHARGE	MONTHLY PAYT	APR	CHARGE	MONTHLY PAYT	APR	CHARGE	MONTHLY PAYT	APR	CHARGE	MONTHLY PAYT	APR	CHARGE
1.30	7.43	34.80	1.20	7.43	39.60	1.10	7.06	42.00	1.00	7.39	54.00	.80	5.90	54.00	.70	6.15	78.00
1.31	7.62	35.76	1.21	7.62	40.68	1.11	7.24	43.20	1.01	7.57	55.44	.81	6.08	55.80	.71	6.31	80.40
1.32	7.81	36.72	1.22	7.81	41.76	1.12	7.43	44.40	1.02	7.75	56.88	.82	6.26	57.60	.72	6.48	82.80
1.33	8.00	37.68	1.23	8.00	42.84	1.13	7.61	45.60	1.03	7.93	58.32	.83	6.44	59.40	.73	6.64	85.20
1.34	8.19	38.64	1.24	8.18	43.92	1.14	7.80	46.80	1.04	8.11	59.76	.84	6.61	61.20	.74	6.81	87.60
1.35	8.38	39.60	1.25	8.37	45.00	1.15	7.98	48.00	1.05	8.28	61.20	.85	6.79	63.00	.75	6.97	90.00
1.36	8.57	40.56	1.26	8.55	46.08	1.16	8.17	49.20	1.06	8.46	62.64	.86	6.96	64.80	.76	7.13	92.40
1.37	8.75	41.52	1.27	8.74	47.16	1.17	8.35	50.40	1.07	8.63	64.08	.87	7.13	66.60	.77	7.30	94.80
1.38	8.94	42.48	1.28	8.92	48.24	1.18	8.53	51.60	1.08	8.81	65.52	.88	7.31	68.40	.78	7.46	97.20
1.39	9.13	43.44	1.29	9.11	49.32	1.19	8.71	52.80	1.09	8.98	66.96	.89	7.48	70.20	.79	7.62	99.60
1.40	9.31	44.40	1.30	9.29	50.40	1.20	8.89	54.00	1.10	9.16	68.40	.90	7.65	72.00	.80	7.78	102.00
1.41	9.50	45.36	1.31	9.47	51.48	1.21	9.07	55.20	1.11	9.33	69.84	.91	7.82	73.80	.81	7.94	104.40
1.42	9.69	46.32	1.32	9.65	52.56	1.22	9.25	56.40	1.12	9.50	71.28	.92	7.99	75.60	.82	8.09	106.80
1.43	9.87	47.28	1.33	9.83	53.64	1.23	9.43	57.60	1.13	9.67	72.72	.93	8.16	77.40	.83	8.25	109.20
1.44	10.05	48.24	1.34	10.01	54.72	1.24	9.61	58.80	1.14	9.84	74.16	.94	8.33	79.20	.84	8.41	111.60
1.45	10.24	49.20	1.35	10.19	55.80	1.25	9.78	60.00	1.15	10.01	75.60	.95	8.49	81.00	.85	8.56	114.00
1.46	10.42	50.16	1.36	10.37	56.88	1.26	9.96	61.20	1.16	10.18	77.04	.96	8.66	82.80	.86	8.72	116.40
1.47	10.60	51.12	1.37	10.55	57.96	1.27	10.14	62.40	1.17	10.35	78.48	.97	8.83	84.60	.87	8.87	118.80
1.48	10.79	52.08	1.38	10.73	59.04	1.28	10.31	63.60	1.18	10.52	79.92	.98	8.99	86.40	.88	9.03	121.20
1.49	10.97	53.04	1.39	10.91	60.12	1.29	10.49	64.80	1.19	10.69	81.36	.99	9.16	88.20	.89	9.18	123.60
1.50	11.15	54.00	1.40	11.08	61.20	1.30	10.66	66.00	1.20	10.85	82.80	1.00	9.32	90.00	.90	9.33	126.00
1.51	11.33	54.96	1.41	11.26	62.28	1.31	10.84	67.20	1.21	11.02	84.24	1.01	9.48	91.80	.91	9.49	128.40
1.52	11.51	55.92	1.42	11.44	63.36	1.32	11.01	68.40	1.22	11.19	85.68	1.02	9.65	93.60	.92	9.64	130.80
1.53	11.69	56.88	1.43	11.61	64.44	1.33	11.18	69.60	1.23	11.35	87.12	1.03	9.81	95.40	.93	9.79	133.20
1.54	11.87	57.84	1.44	11.79	65.52	1.34	11.36	70.80	1.24	11.52	88.56	1.04	9.97	97.20	.94	9.94	135.60
1.55	12.05	58.80	1.45	11.96	66.60	1.35	11.53	72.00	1.25	11.68	90.00	1.05	10.13	99.00	.95	10.09	138.00
1.56	12.23	59.76	1.46	12.14	67.68	1.36	11.70	73.20	1.26	11.85	91.44	1.06	10.29	100.80	.96	10.24	140.40
1.57	12.40	60.72	1.47	12.31	68.76	1.37	11.87	74.40	1.27	12.01	92.88	1.07	10.45	102.60	.97	10.39	142.80
1.58	12.58	61.68	1.48	12.49	69.84	1.38	12.04	75.60	1.28	12.17	94.32	1.08	10.61	104.40	.98	10.54	145.20
1.59	12.76	62.64	1.49	12.66	70.92	1.39	12.21	76.80	1.29	12.34	95.76	1.09	10.77	106.20	.99	10.69	147.60
1.60	12.94	63.60	1.50	12.83	72.00	1.40	12.38	78.00	1.30	12.50	97.20	1.10	10.93	108.00	1.00	10.83	150.00
1.61	13.11	64.56	1.51	13.00	73.08	1.41	12.55	79.20	1.31	12.66	98.64	1.11	11.09	109.80	1.01	10.98	152.40
1.62	13.29	65.52	1.52	13.18	74.16	1.42	12.72	80.40	1.32	12.82	100.08	1.12	11.24	111.60	1.02	11.13	154.80
1.63	13.46	66.48	1.53	13.35	75.24	1.43	12.89	81.60	1.33	12.98	101.52	1.13	11.40	113.40	1.03	11.27	157.20
1.64	13.64	67.44	1.54	13.52	76.32	1.44	13.06	82.80	1.34	13.14	102.96	1.14	11.56	115.20	1.04	11.42	159.60
1.65	13.81	68.40	1.55	13.69	77.40	1.45	13.23	84.00	1.35	13.30	104.40	1.15	11.71	117.00	1.05	11.56	162.00
1.66	13.99	69.36	1.56	13.86	78.48	1.46	13.39	85.20	1.36	13.46	105.84	1.16	11.87	118.80	1.06	11.71	164.40
1.67	14.16	70.32	1.57	14.03	79.56	1.47	13.56	86.40	1.37	13.62	107.28	1.17	12.02	120.60	1.07	11.85	166.80
1.68	14.33	71.28	1.58	14.20	80.64	1.48	13.72	87.60	1.38	13.78	108.72	1.18	12.18	122.40	1.08	12.00	169.20
1.69	14.51	72.24	1.59	14.36	81.72	1.49	13.89	88.80	1.39	13.94	110.16	1.19	12.33	124.20	1.09	12.14	171.60
1.70	14.68	73.20	1.60	14.53	82.80	1.50	14.06	90.00	1.40	14.10	111.60	1.20	12.49	126.00	1.10	12.28	174.00
1.71	14.85	74.16	1.61	14.70	83.88	1.51	14.22	91.20	1.41	14.26	113.04	1.21	12.64	127.80	1.11	12.43	176.40
1.72	15.02	75.12	1.62	14.87	84.96	1.52	14.39	92.40	1.42	14.41	114.48	1.22	12.79	129.60	1.12	12.57	178.80
1.73	15.20	76.08	1.63	15.04	86.04	1.53	14.55	93.60	1.43	14.57	115.92	1.23	12.94	131.40	1.13	12.71	181.20
1.74	15.37	77.04	1.64	15.21	87.12	1.54	14.71	94.80	1.44	14.73	117.36	1.24	13.10	133.20	1.14	12.85	183.60
1.75	15.54	78.00	1.65	15.37	88.20	1.55	14.88	96.00	1.45	14.88	118.80	1.25	13.25	135.00	1.15	13.00	186.00
1.76	15.71	78.96	1.66	15.54	89.28	1.56	15.04	97.20	1.46	15.04	120.24	1.26	13.40	136.80	1.16	13.14	188.40
1.77	15.88	79.92	1.67	15.70	90.36	1.57	15.20	98.40	1.47	15.19	121.68	1.27	13.55	138.60	1.17	13.28	190.80
1.78	16.05	80.88	1.68	15.87	91.44	1.58	15.36	99.60	1.48	15.35	123.12	1.28	13.70	140.40	1.18	13.42	193.20
1.79	16.22	81.84	1.69	16.03	92.52	1.59	15.53	100.80	1.49	15.50	124.56	1.29	13.85	142.20	1.19	13.56	195.60
1.80	16.39	82.80	1.70	16.20	93.60	1.60	15.69	102.00	1.50	15.66	126.00	1.30	14.00	144.00	1.20	13.70	198.00
1.81	16.55	83.76	1.71	16.36	94.68	1.61	15.85	103.20	1.51	15.81	127.44	1.31	14.15	145.80	1.21	13.84	200.40
1.82	16.72	84.72	1.72	16.52	95.76	1.62	16.01	104.40	1.52	15.97	128.88	1.32	14.30	147.60	1.22	13.98	202.80
1.83	16.89	85.68	1.73	16.69	96.84	1.63	16.17	105.60	1.53	16.12	130.32	1.33	14.45	149.40	1.23	14.12	205.20
1.84	17.06	86.64	1.74	16.85	97.92	1.64	16.33	106.80	1.54	16.27	131.76	1.34	14.59	151.20	1.24	14.26	207.60
1.85	17.22	87.60	1.75	17.01	99.00	1.65	16.49	108.00	1.55	16.42	133.20	1.35	14.74	153.00	1.25	14.39	210.00
1.86	17.39	88.56	1.76	17.18	100.08	1.66	16.65	109.20	1.56	16.58	134.64	1.36	14.89	154.80	1.26	14.53	212.40
1.87	17.56	89.52	1.77	17.34	101.16	1.67	16.81	110.40	1.57	16.73	136.08	1.37	15.04	156.60	1.27	14.67	214.80
1.88	17.72	90.48	1.78	17.50	102.24	1.68	16.97	111.60	1.58	16.88	137.52	1.38	15.18	158.40	1.28	14.81	217.20
1.89	17.89	91.44	1.79	17.66	103.32	1.69	17.13	112.80	1.59	17.03	138.96	1.39	15.33	160.20	1.29	14.95	219.60
1.90	18.06	92.40	1.80	17.82	104.40	1.70	17.28	114.00	1.60	17.18	140.40	1.40	15.48	162.00	1.30	15.08	222.00
1.91	18.22	93.36	1.81	17.98	105.48	1.71	17.44	115.20	1.61	17.33	141.84	1.41	15.62	163.80	1.31	15.22	224.40
1.92	18.39	94.32	1.82	18.15	106.56	1.72	17.60	116.40	1.62	17.48	143.28	1.42	15.77	165.60	1.32	15.36	226.80
1.93	18.55	95.28	1.83	18.31	107.64	1.73	17.76	117.60	1.63	17.63	144.72	1.43	15.91	167.40	1.33	15.49	229.20
1.94	18.71	96.24	1.84	18.47	108.72	1.74	17.91	118.80	1.64	17.78	146.16	1.44	16.06	169.20	1.34	15.63	231.60
1.95	18.88	97.20	1.85	18.63	109.80	1.75	18.07	120.00	1.65	17.93	147.60	1.45	16.20	171.00	1.35	15.77	234.00
1.96	19.04	98.16	1.86	18.79	110.88	1.76	18.23	121.20	1.66	18.08	149.04	1.46	16.35	172.80	1.36	15.90	236.40
1.97	19.21	99.12	1.87	18.94	111.96	1.77	18.38	122.40	1.67	18.23	150.48	1.47	16.49	174.60	1.37	16.04	238.80
1.98	19.37	100.08	1.88	19.10	113.04	1.78	18.54	123.60	1.68	18.38	151.92	1.48	16.64	176.40	1.38	16.17	241.20
1.99	19.53	101.04	1.89	19.26	114.12	1.79	18.69	124.80	1.69	18.53	153.36	1.49	16.78	178.20	1.39	16.31	243.60

LEASE PAYMENTS

Description: This table shows the Annual Percentage Rate and finance charge per $100 for monthly lease payments.

Example: A 4.30% lease payment for 2 years is equivalent to an APR of 15.91%. The charge per $100 cost is $ 18.20.

2 yr MONTHLY PAYT	APR	CHARGE	3 yr MONTHLY PAYT	APR	CHARGE	4 yr MONTHLY PAYT	APR	CHARGE	5 yr MONTHLY PAYT	APR	CHARGE	6 yr MONTHLY PAYT	APR	CHARGE	7 yr MONTHLY PAYT	APR	CHARGE
4.30	15.91	18.20	3.00	13.12	23.00	2.30	10.74	25.40	1.90	9.71	29.00	1.70	10.27	37.40	1.50	9.57	41.00
4.31	16.11	18.44	3.01	13.32	23.36	2.31	10.94	25.88	1.91	9.90	29.60	1.71	10.45	38.12	1.51	9.75	41.84
4.32	16.32	18.68	3.02	13.51	23.72	2.32	11.13	26.36	1.92	10.09	30.20	1.72	10.64	38.84	1.52	9.94	42.68
4.33	16.52	18.92	3.03	13.71	24.08	2.33	11.33	26.84	1.93	10.29	30.80	1.73	10.83	39.56	1.53	10.12	43.52
4.34	16.73	19.16	3.04	13.91	24.44	2.34	11.52	27.32	1.94	10.48	31.40	1.74	11.01	40.28	1.54	10.30	44.36
4.35	16.93	19.40	3.05	14.11	24.80	2.35	11.72	27.80	1.95	10.67	32.00	1.75	11.19	41.00	1.55	10.48	45.20
4.36	17.13	19.64	3.06	14.30	25.16	2.36	11.91	28.28	1.96	10.86	32.60	1.76	11.38	41.72	1.56	10.67	46.04
4.37	17.34	19.88	3.07	14.50	25.52	2.37	12.10	28.76	1.97	11.05	33.20	1.77	11.56	42.44	1.57	10.85	46.88
4.38	17.54	20.12	3.08	14.70	25.88	2.38	12.29	29.24	1.98	11.24	33.80	1.78	11.75	43.16	1.58	11.03	47.72
4.39	17.75	20.36	3.09	14.89	26.24	2.39	12.49	29.72	1.99	11.42	34.40	1.79	11.93	43.88	1.59	11.21	48.56
4.40	17.95	20.60	3.10	15.09	26.60	2.40	12.68	30.20	2.00	11.61	35.00	1.80	12.11	44.60	1.60	11.39	49.40
4.41	18.15	20.84	3.11	15.29	26.96	2.41	12.87	30.68	2.01	11.80	35.60	1.81	12.30	45.32	1.61	11.57	50.24
4.42	18.36	21.08	3.12	15.48	27.32	2.42	13.06	31.16	2.02	11.99	36.20	1.82	12.48	46.04	1.62	11.75	51.08
4.43	18.56	21.32	3.13	15.68	27.68	2.43	13.26	31.64	2.03	12.18	36.80	1.83	12.66	46.76	1.63	11.93	51.92
4.44	18.76	21.56	3.14	15.87	28.04	2.44	13.45	32.12	2.04	12.36	37.40	1.84	12.84	47.48	1.64	12.10	52.76
4.45	18.96	21.80	3.15	16.07	28.40	2.45	13.64	32.60	2.05	12.55	38.00	1.85	13.02	48.20	1.65	12.28	53.60
4.46	19.17	22.04	3.16	16.27	28.76	2.46	13.83	33.08	2.06	12.74	38.60	1.86	13.20	48.92	1.66	12.46	54.44
4.47	19.37	22.28	3.17	16.46	29.12	2.47	14.02	33.56	2.07	12.92	39.20	1.87	13.38	49.64	1.67	12.64	55.28
4.48	19.57	22.52	3.18	16.66	29.48	2.48	14.21	34.04	2.08	13.11	39.80	1.88	13.56	50.36	1.68	12.81	56.12
4.49	19.78	22.76	3.19	16.85	29.84	2.49	14.40	34.52	2.09	13.30	40.40	1.89	13.74	51.08	1.69	12.99	56.96
4.50	19.98	23.00	3.20	17.05	30.20	2.50	14.59	35.00	2.10	13.48	41.00	1.90	13.92	51.80	1.70	13.17	57.80
4.51	20.18	23.24	3.21	17.24	30.56	2.51	14.78	35.48	2.11	13.67	41.60	1.91	14.10	52.52	1.71	13.34	58.64
4.52	20.38	23.48	3.22	17.43	30.92	2.52	14.97	35.96	2.12	13.85	42.20	1.92	14.28	53.24	1.72	13.52	59.48
4.53	20.58	23.72	3.23	17.63	31.28	2.53	15.16	36.44	2.13	14.04	42.80	1.93	14.46	53.96	1.73	13.69	60.32
4.54	20.79	23.96	3.24	17.82	31.64	2.54	15.35	36.92	2.14	14.22	43.40	1.94	14.64	54.68	1.74	13.87	61.16
4.55	20.99	24.20	3.25	18.02	32.00	2.55	15.54	37.40	2.15	14.41	44.00	1.95	14.82	55.40	1.75	14.04	62.00
4.56	21.19	24.44	3.26	18.21	32.36	2.56	15.73	37.88	2.16	14.59	44.60	1.96	14.99	56.12	1.76	14.22	62.84
4.57	21.39	24.68	3.27	18.40	32.72	2.57	15.91	38.36	2.17	14.77	45.20	1.97	15.17	56.84	1.77	14.39	63.68
4.58	21.59	24.92	3.28	18.60	33.08	2.58	16.10	38.84	2.18	14.96	45.80	1.98	15.35	57.56	1.78	14.56	64.52
4.59	21.79	25.16	3.29	18.79	33.44	2.59	16.29	39.32	2.19	15.14	46.40	1.99	15.53	58.28	1.79	14.74	65.36
4.60	21.99	25.40	3.30	18.98	33.80	2.60	16.48	39.80	2.20	15.32	47.00	2.00	15.70	59.00	1.80	14.91	66.20
4.61	22.20	25.64	3.31	19.17	34.16	2.61	16.66	40.28	2.21	15.50	47.60	2.01	15.88	59.72	1.81	15.08	67.04
4.62	22.40	25.88	3.32	19.37	34.52	2.62	16.85	40.76	2.22	15.69	48.20	2.02	16.05	60.44	1.82	15.26	67.88
4.63	22.60	26.12	3.33	19.56	34.88	2.63	17.04	41.24	2.23	15.87	48.80	2.03	16.23	61.16	1.83	15.43	68.72
4.64	22.80	26.36	3.34	19.75	35.24	2.64	17.22	41.72	2.24	16.05	49.40	2.04	16.41	61.88	1.84	15.60	69.56
4.65	23.00	26.60	3.35	19.94	35.60	2.65	17.41	42.20	2.25	16.23	50.00	2.05	16.58	62.60	1.85	15.77	70.40
4.66	23.20	26.84	3.36	20.13	35.96	2.66	17.60	42.68	2.26	16.41	50.60	2.06	16.76	63.32	1.86	15.94	71.24
4.67	23.40	27.08	3.37	20.33	36.32	2.67	17.78	43.16	2.27	16.59	51.20	2.07	16.93	64.04	1.87	16.11	72.08
4.68	23.60	27.32	3.38	20.52	36.68	2.68	17.97	43.64	2.28	16.77	51.80	2.08	17.10	64.76	1.88	16.28	72.92
4.69	23.80	27.56	3.39	20.71	37.04	2.69	18.15	44.12	2.29	16.96	52.40	2.09	17.28	65.48	1.89	16.45	73.76
4.70	24.00	27.80	3.40	20.90	37.40	2.70	18.34	44.60	2.30	17.14	53.00	2.10	17.45	66.20	1.90	16.62	74.60
4.71	24.20	28.04	3.41	21.09	37.76	2.71	18.53	45.08	2.31	17.32	53.60	2.11	17.62	66.92	1.91	16.79	75.44
4.72	24.40	28.28	3.42	21.28	38.12	2.72	18.71	45.56	2.32	17.49	54.20	2.12	17.80	67.64	1.92	16.96	76.28
4.73	24.60	28.52	3.43	21.47	38.48	2.73	18.89	46.04	2.33	17.67	54.80	2.13	17.97	68.36	1.93	17.13	77.12
4.74	24.80	28.76	3.44	21.66	38.84	2.74	19.08	46.52	2.34	17.85	55.40	2.14	18.14	69.08	1.94	17.30	77.96
4.75	25.00	29.00	3.45	21.85	39.20	2.75	19.26	47.00	2.35	18.03	56.00	2.15	18.32	69.80	1.95	17.47	78.80
4.76	25.20	29.24	3.46	22.04	39.56	2.76	19.45	47.48	2.36	18.21	56.60	2.16	18.49	70.52	1.96	17.63	79.64
4.77	25.40	29.48	3.47	22.23	39.92	2.77	19.63	47.96	2.37	18.39	57.20	2.17	18.66	71.24	1.97	17.80	80.48
4.78	25.60	29.72	3.48	22.42	40.28	2.78	19.82	48.44	2.38	18.57	57.80	2.18	18.83	71.96	1.98	17.97	81.32
4.79	25.79	29.96	3.49	22.61	40.64	2.79	20.00	48.92	2.39	18.74	58.40	2.19	19.00	72.68	1.99	18.14	82.16
4.80	25.99	30.20	3.50	22.80	41.00	2.80	20.18	49.40	2.40	18.92	59.00	2.20	19.17	73.40	2.00	18.30	83.00
4.81	26.19	30.44	3.51	22.99	41.36	2.81	20.36	49.88	2.41	19.10	59.60	2.21	19.34	74.12	2.01	18.47	83.84
4.82	26.39	30.68	3.52	23.18	41.72	2.82	20.55	50.36	2.42	19.28	60.20	2.22	19.52	74.84	2.02	18.64	84.68
4.83	26.59	30.92	3.53	23.37	42.08	2.83	20.73	50.84	2.43	19.45	60.80	2.23	19.69	75.56	2.03	18.80	85.52
4.84	26.79	31.16	3.54	23.56	42.44	2.84	20.91	51.32	2.44	19.63	61.40	2.24	19.86	76.28	2.04	18.97	86.36
4.85	26.99	31.40	3.55	23.75	42.80	2.85	21.09	51.80	2.45	19.81	62.00	2.25	20.03	77.00	2.05	19.13	87.20
4.86	27.18	31.64	3.56	23.93	43.16	2.86	21.28	52.28	2.46	19.98	62.60	2.26	20.19	77.72	2.06	19.30	88.04
4.87	27.38	31.88	3.57	24.12	43.52	2.87	21.46	52.76	2.47	20.16	63.20	2.27	20.36	78.44	2.07	19.47	88.88
4.88	27.58	32.12	3.58	24.31	43.88	2.88	21.64	53.24	2.48	20.33	63.80	2.28	20.53	79.16	2.08	19.63	89.72
4.89	27.78	32.36	3.59	24.50	44.24	2.89	21.82	53.72	2.49	20.51	64.40	2.29	20.70	79.88	2.09	19.79	90.56
4.90	27.98	32.60	3.60	24.69	44.60	2.90	22.00	54.20	2.50	20.69	65.00	2.30	20.87	80.60	2.10	19.96	91.40
4.91	28.17	32.84	3.61	24.87	44.96	2.91	22.18	54.68	2.51	20.86	65.60	2.31	21.04	81.32	2.11	20.12	92.24
4.92	28.37	33.08	3.62	25.06	45.32	2.92	22.36	55.16	2.52	21.04	66.20	2.32	21.21	82.04	2.12	20.29	93.08
4.93	28.57	33.32	3.63	25.25	45.68	2.93	22.55	55.64	2.53	21.21	66.80	2.33	21.38	82.76	2.13	20.45	93.92
4.94	28.77	33.56	3.64	25.44	46.04	2.94	22.73	56.12	2.54	21.38	67.40	2.34	21.54	83.48	2.14	20.61	94.76
4.95	28.97	33.80	3.65	25.62	46.40	2.95	22.91	56.60	2.55	21.56	68.00	2.35	21.71	84.20	2.15	20.78	95.60
4.96	29.16	34.04	3.66	25.81	46.76	2.96	23.09	57.08	2.56	21.73	68.60	2.36	21.88	84.92	2.16	20.94	96.44
4.97	29.36	34.28	3.67	26.00	47.12	2.97	23.27	57.56	2.57	21.91	69.20	2.37	22.04	85.64	2.17	21.10	97.28
4.98	29.56	34.52	3.68	26.18	47.48	2.98	23.45	58.04	2.58	22.08	69.80	2.38	22.21	86.36	2.18	21.27	98.12
4.99	29.75	34.76	3.69	26.37	47.84	2.99	23.62	58.52	2.59	22.25	70.40	2.39	22.38	87.08	2.19	21.43	98.96

Description: This table shows the Annual Percentage Rate and finance charge per $100 for monthly lease payments.

Example: A 1.30% lease payment for 8 years is equivalent to an APR of 8.13%. The charge per $100 cost is $ 39.80.

8 yr MONTHLY PAYT	APR	CHARGE	9 yr MONTHLY PAYT	APR	CHARGE	10 yr MONTHLY PAYT	APR	CHARGE	12 yr MONTHLY PAYT	APR	CHARGE	15 yr MONTHLY PAYT	APR	CHARGE	20 yr MONTHLY PAYT	APR	CHARGE
1.30	8.13	39.80	1.20	8.03	44.60	1.10	7.57	47.00	1.00	7.77	59.00	.80	6.20	59.00	.70	6.32	83.00
1.31	8.31	40.76	1.21	8.21	45.68	1.11	7.75	48.20	1.01	7.94	60.44	.81	6.38	60.80	.71	6.48	85.40
1.32	8.50	41.72	1.22	8.39	46.76	1.12	7.93	49.40	1.02	8.12	61.88	.82	6.55	62.60	.72	6.64	87.80
1.33	8.68	42.68	1.23	8.57	47.84	1.13	8.11	50.60	1.03	8.29	63.32	.83	6.72	64.40	.73	6.80	90.20
1.34	8.86	43.64	1.24	8.75	48.92	1.14	8.29	51.80	1.04	8.46	64.76	.84	6.89	66.20	.74	6.97	92.60
1.35	9.04	44.60	1.25	8.92	50.00	1.15	8.47	53.00	1.05	8.63	66.20	.85	7.06	68.00	.75	7.12	95.00
1.36	9.22	45.56	1.26	9.10	51.08	1.16	8.64	54.20	1.06	8.80	67.64	.86	7.23	69.80	.76	7.28	97.40
1.37	9.40	46.52	1.27	9.28	52.16	1.17	8.82	55.40	1.07	8.97	69.08	.87	7.40	71.60	.77	7.44	99.80
1.38	9.58	47.48	1.28	9.46	53.24	1.18	8.99	56.60	1.08	9.14	70.52	.88	7.56	73.40	.78	7.60	102.20
1.39	9.76	48.44	1.29	9.63	54.32	1.19	9.17	57.80	1.09	9.31	71.96	.89	7.73	75.20	.79	7.76	104.60
1.40	9.94	49.40	1.30	9.81	55.40	1.20	9.34	59.00	1.10	9.48	73.40	.90	7.90	77.00	.80	7.91	107.00
1.41	10.12	50.36	1.31	9.99	56.48	1.21	9.52	60.20	1.11	9.64	74.84	.91	8.06	78.80	.81	8.07	109.40
1.42	10.30	51.32	1.32	10.16	57.56	1.22	9.69	61.40	1.12	9.81	76.28	.92	8.23	80.60	.82	8.22	111.80
1.43	10.48	52.28	1.33	10.34	58.64	1.23	9.86	62.60	1.13	9.98	77.72	.93	8.39	82.40	.83	8.38	114.20
1.44	10.66	53.24	1.34	10.51	59.72	1.24	10.04	63.80	1.14	10.14	79.16	.94	8.55	84.20	.84	8.53	116.60
1.45	10.83	54.20	1.35	10.69	60.80	1.25	10.21	65.00	1.15	10.31	80.60	.95	8.72	86.00	.85	8.68	119.00
1.46	11.01	55.16	1.36	10.86	61.88	1.26	10.38	66.20	1.16	10.47	82.04	.96	8.88	87.80	.86	8.84	121.40
1.47	11.19	56.12	1.37	11.03	62.96	1.27	10.55	67.40	1.17	10.64	83.48	.97	9.04	89.60	.87	8.99	123.80
1.48	11.36	57.08	1.38	11.20	64.04	1.28	10.72	68.60	1.18	10.80	84.92	.98	9.20	91.40	.88	9.14	126.20
1.49	11.54	58.04	1.39	11.38	65.12	1.29	10.89	69.80	1.19	10.97	86.36	.99	9.36	93.20	.89	9.29	128.60
1.50	11.71	59.00	1.40	11.55	66.20	1.30	11.06	71.00	1.20	11.13	87.80	1.00	9.53	95.00	.90	9.44	131.00
1.51	11.89	59.96	1.41	11.72	67.28	1.31	11.23	72.20	1.21	11.29	89.24	1.01	9.68	96.80	.91	9.59	133.40
1.52	12.06	60.92	1.42	11.89	68.36	1.32	11.40	73.40	1.22	11.45	90.68	1.02	9.84	98.60	.92	9.74	135.80
1.53	12.24	61.88	1.43	12.06	69.44	1.33	11.57	74.60	1.23	11.62	92.12	1.03	10.00	100.40	.93	9.89	138.20
1.54	12.41	62.84	1.44	12.23	70.52	1.34	11.73	75.80	1.24	11.78	93.56	1.04	10.16	102.20	.94	10.04	140.60
1.55	12.58	63.80	1.45	12.40	71.60	1.35	11.90	77.00	1.25	11.94	95.00	1.05	10.32	104.00	.95	10.19	143.00
1.56	12.76	64.76	1.46	12.57	72.68	1.36	12.07	78.20	1.26	12.10	96.44	1.06	10.48	105.80	.96	10.33	145.40
1.57	12.93	65.72	1.47	12.74	73.76	1.37	12.23	79.40	1.27	12.26	97.88	1.07	10.63	107.60	.97	10.48	147.80
1.58	13.10	66.68	1.48	12.91	74.84	1.38	12.40	80.60	1.28	12.42	99.32	1.08	10.79	109.40	.98	10.63	150.20
1.59	13.27	67.64	1.49	13.08	75.92	1.39	12.57	81.80	1.29	12.58	100.76	1.09	10.94	111.20	.99	10.77	152.60
1.60	13.45	68.60	1.50	13.24	77.00	1.40	12.73	83.00	1.30	12.74	102.20	1.10	11.10	113.00	1.00	10.92	155.00
1.61	13.62	69.56	1.51	13.41	78.08	1.41	12.90	84.20	1.31	12.89	103.64	1.11	11.25	114.80	1.01	11.06	157.40
1.62	13.79	70.52	1.52	13.58	79.16	1.42	13.06	85.40	1.32	13.05	105.08	1.12	11.41	116.60	1.02	11.21	159.80
1.63	13.96	71.48	1.53	13.75	80.24	1.43	13.23	86.60	1.33	13.21	106.52	1.13	11.56	118.40	1.03	11.35	162.20
1.64	14.13	72.44	1.54	13.91	81.32	1.44	13.39	87.80	1.34	13.37	107.96	1.14	11.72	120.20	1.04	11.50	164.60
1.65	14.30	73.40	1.55	14.08	82.40	1.45	13.55	89.00	1.35	13.52	109.40	1.15	11.87	122.00	1.05	11.64	167.00
1.66	14.47	74.36	1.56	14.24	83.48	1.46	13.72	90.20	1.36	13.68	110.84	1.16	12.02	123.80	1.06	11.78	169.40
1.67	14.63	75.32	1.57	14.41	84.56	1.47	13.88	91.40	1.37	13.84	112.28	1.17	12.17	125.60	1.07	11.93	171.80
1.68	14.80	76.28	1.58	14.57	85.64	1.48	14.04	92.60	1.38	13.99	113.72	1.18	12.33	127.40	1.08	12.07	174.20
1.69	14.97	77.24	1.59	14.74	86.72	1.49	14.20	93.80	1.39	14.15	115.16	1.19	12.48	129.20	1.09	12.21	176.60
1.70	15.14	78.20	1.60	14.90	87.80	1.50	14.36	95.00	1.40	14.30	116.60	1.20	12.63	131.00	1.10	12.35	179.00
1.71	15.31	79.16	1.61	15.07	88.88	1.51	14.52	96.20	1.41	14.46	118.04	1.21	12.78	132.80	1.11	12.49	181.40
1.72	15.47	80.12	1.62	15.23	89.96	1.52	14.69	97.40	1.42	14.61	119.48	1.22	12.93	134.60	1.12	12.64	183.80
1.73	15.64	81.08	1.63	15.39	91.04	1.53	14.85	98.60	1.43	14.77	120.92	1.23	13.08	136.40	1.13	12.78	186.20
1.74	15.81	82.04	1.64	15.56	92.12	1.54	15.01	99.80	1.44	14.92	122.36	1.24	13.23	138.20	1.14	12.92	188.60
1.75	15.97	83.00	1.65	15.72	93.20	1.55	15.17	101.00	1.45	15.07	123.80	1.25	13.38	140.00	1.15	13.06	191.00
1.76	16.14	83.96	1.66	15.88	94.28	1.56	15.33	102.20	1.46	15.23	125.24	1.26	13.53	141.80	1.16	13.20	193.40
1.77	16.31	84.92	1.67	16.04	95.36	1.57	15.48	103.40	1.47	15.38	126.68	1.27	13.68	143.60	1.17	13.34	195.80
1.78	16.47	85.88	1.68	16.20	96.44	1.58	15.64	104.60	1.48	15.53	128.12	1.28	13.82	145.40	1.18	13.48	198.20
1.79	16.64	86.84	1.69	16.36	97.52	1.59	15.80	105.80	1.49	15.68	129.56	1.29	13.97	147.20	1.19	13.62	200.60
1.80	16.80	87.80	1.70	16.53	98.60	1.60	15.96	107.00	1.50	15.84	131.00	1.30	14.12	149.00	1.20	13.75	203.00
1.81	16.96	88.76	1.71	16.69	99.68	1.61	16.12	108.20	1.51	15.99	132.44	1.31	14.27	150.80	1.21	13.89	205.40
1.82	17.13	89.72	1.72	16.85	100.76	1.62	16.28	109.40	1.52	16.14	133.88	1.32	14.41	152.60	1.22	14.03	207.80
1.83	17.29	90.68	1.73	17.01	101.84	1.63	16.43	110.60	1.53	16.29	135.32	1.33	14.56	154.40	1.23	14.17	210.20
1.84	17.46	91.64	1.74	17.17	102.92	1.64	16.59	111.80	1.54	16.44	136.76	1.34	14.71	156.20	1.24	14.31	212.60
1.85	17.62	92.60	1.75	17.33	104.00	1.65	16.75	113.00	1.55	16.59	138.20	1.35	14.85	158.00	1.25	14.44	215.00
1.86	17.78	93.56	1.76	17.49	105.08	1.66	16.90	114.20	1.56	16.74	139.64	1.36	15.00	159.80	1.26	14.58	217.40
1.87	17.95	94.52	1.77	17.64	106.16	1.67	17.06	115.40	1.57	16.89	141.08	1.37	15.14	161.60	1.27	14.72	219.80
1.88	18.11	95.48	1.78	17.80	107.24	1.68	17.22	116.60	1.58	17.04	142.52	1.38	15.29	163.40	1.28	14.85	222.20
1.89	18.27	96.44	1.79	17.96	108.32	1.69	17.37	117.80	1.59	17.19	143.96	1.39	15.43	165.20	1.29	14.99	224.60
1.90	18.43	97.40	1.80	18.12	109.40	1.70	17.53	119.00	1.60	17.34	145.40	1.40	15.58	167.00	1.30	15.13	227.00
1.91	18.59	98.36	1.81	18.28	110.48	1.71	17.68	120.20	1.61	17.49	146.84	1.41	15.72	168.80	1.31	15.26	229.40
1.92	18.75	99.32	1.82	18.43	111.56	1.72	17.84	121.40	1.62	17.64	148.28	1.42	15.87	170.60	1.32	15.40	231.80
1.93	18.92	100.28	1.83	18.59	112.64	1.73	17.99	122.60	1.63	17.78	149.72	1.43	16.01	172.40	1.33	15.54	234.20
1.94	19.08	101.24	1.84	18.75	113.72	1.74	18.14	123.80	1.64	17.93	151.16	1.44	16.15	174.20	1.34	15.67	236.60
1.95	19.24	102.20	1.85	18.91	114.80	1.75	18.30	125.00	1.65	18.08	152.60	1.45	16.30	176.00	1.35	15.81	239.00
1.96	19.40	103.16	1.86	19.06	115.88	1.76	18.45	126.20	1.66	18.23	154.04	1.46	16.44	177.80	1.36	15.94	241.40
1.97	19.56	104.12	1.87	19.22	116.96	1.77	18.61	127.40	1.67	18.37	155.48	1.47	16.58	179.60	1.37	16.08	243.80
1.98	19.72	105.08	1.88	19.37	118.04	1.78	18.76	128.60	1.68	18.52	156.92	1.48	16.72	181.40	1.38	16.21	246.20
1.99	19.88	106.04	1.89	19.53	119.12	1.79	18.91	129.80	1.69	18.67	158.36	1.49	16.87	183.20	1.39	16.34	248.60

Description: This table shows the Annual Percentage Rate and finance charge per $100 for monthly lease payments.

Example: A 4.30% lease payment for 2 years is equivalent to an APR of 19.36%. The charge per $100 cost is $ 23.20.

2 yr			3 yr			4 yr			5 yr			6 yr			7 yr		
MONTHLY PAYT	APR	CHARGE	MONTHLY PAYT	APR	CHARGE	MONTHLY PAYT	APR	CHARGE	MONTHLY PAYT	APR	CHARGE	MONTHLY PAYT	APR	CHARGE	MONTHLY PAYT	APR	CHARGE
4.30	19.36	23.20	3.00	15.27	28.00	2.30	12.30	30.40	1.90	10.90	34.00	1.70	11.17	42.40	1.50	10.31	46.00
4.31	19.56	23.44	3.01	15.46	28.36	2.31	12.49	30.88	1.91	11.09	34.60	1.71	11.35	43.12	1.51	10.49	46.84
4.32	19.75	23.68	3.02	15.65	28.72	2.32	12.67	31.36	1.92	11.27	35.20	1.72	11.53	43.84	1.52	10.67	47.68
4.33	19.95	23.92	3.03	15.84	29.08	2.33	12.86	31.84	1.93	11.45	35.80	1.73	11.71	44.56	1.53	10.84	48.52
4.34	20.14	24.16	3.04	16.02	29.44	2.34	13.05	32.32	1.94	11.64	36.40	1.74	11.88	45.28	1.54	11.02	49.36
4.35	20.34	24.40	3.05	16.21	29.80	2.35	13.23	32.80	1.95	11.82	37.00	1.75	12.06	46.00	1.55	11.19	50.20
4.36	20.53	24.64	3.06	16.40	30.16	2.36	13.42	33.28	1.96	12.00	37.60	1.76	12.24	46.72	1.56	11.37	51.04
4.37	20.73	24.88	3.07	16.59	30.52	2.37	13.60	33.76	1.97	12.18	38.20	1.77	12.42	47.44	1.57	11.54	51.88
4.38	20.92	25.12	3.08	16.78	30.88	2.38	13.79	34.24	1.98	12.36	38.80	1.78	12.59	48.16	1.58	11.72	52.72
4.39	21.11	25.36	3.09	16.97	31.24	2.39	13.97	34.72	1.99	12.55	39.40	1.79	12.77	48.88	1.59	11.89	53.56
4.40	21.31	25.60	3.10	17.16	31.60	2.40	14.16	35.20	2.00	12.73	40.00	1.80	12.95	49.60	1.60	12.07	54.40
4.41	21.50	25.84	3.11	17.34	31.96	2.41	14.34	35.68	2.01	12.91	40.60	1.81	13.12	50.32	1.61	12.24	55.24
4.42	21.70	26.08	3.12	17.53	32.32	2.42	14.52	36.16	2.02	13.09	41.20	1.82	13.30	51.04	1.62	12.41	56.08
4.43	21.89	26.32	3.13	17.72	32.68	2.43	14.71	36.64	2.03	13.27	41.80	1.83	13.47	51.76	1.63	12.58	56.92
4.44	22.09	26.56	3.14	17.91	33.04	2.44	14.89	37.12	2.04	13.45	42.40	1.84	13.65	52.48	1.64	12.76	57.76
4.45	22.28	26.80	3.15	18.09	33.40	2.45	15.08	37.60	2.05	13.63	43.00	1.85	13.82	53.20	1.65	12.93	58.60
4.46	22.47	27.04	3.16	18.28	33.76	2.46	15.26	38.08	2.06	13.81	43.60	1.86	14.00	53.92	1.66	13.10	59.44
4.47	22.67	27.28	3.17	18.47	34.12	2.47	15.44	38.56	2.07	13.99	44.20	1.87	14.17	54.64	1.67	13.27	60.28
4.48	22.86	27.52	3.18	18.65	34.48	2.48	15.62	39.04	2.08	14.17	44.80	1.88	14.35	55.36	1.68	13.44	61.12
4.49	23.05	27.76	3.19	18.84	34.84	2.49	15.81	39.52	2.09	14.35	45.40	1.89	14.52	56.08	1.69	13.62	61.96
4.50	23.25	28.00	3.20	19.03	35.20	2.50	15.99	40.00	2.10	14.53	46.00	1.90	14.69	56.80	1.70	13.79	62.80
4.51	23.44	28.24	3.21	19.21	35.56	2.51	16.17	40.48	2.11	14.70	46.60	1.91	14.87	57.52	1.71	13.96	63.64
4.52	23.63	28.48	3.22	19.40	35.92	2.52	16.35	40.96	2.12	14.88	47.20	1.92	15.04	58.24	1.72	14.13	64.48
4.53	23.83	28.72	3.23	19.59	36.28	2.53	16.54	41.44	2.13	15.06	47.80	1.93	15.21	58.96	1.73	14.30	65.32
4.54	24.02	28.96	3.24	19.77	36.64	2.54	16.72	41.92	2.14	15.24	48.40	1.94	15.39	59.68	1.74	14.47	66.16
4.55	24.21	29.20	3.25	19.96	37.00	2.55	16.90	42.40	2.15	15.42	49.00	1.95	15.56	60.40	1.75	14.64	67.00
4.56	24.41	29.44	3.26	20.14	37.36	2.56	17.08	42.88	2.16	15.59	49.60	1.96	15.73	61.12	1.76	14.80	67.84
4.57	24.60	29.68	3.27	20.33	37.72	2.57	17.26	43.36	2.17	15.77	50.20	1.97	15.90	61.84	1.77	14.97	68.68
4.58	24.79	29.92	3.28	20.52	38.08	2.58	17.44	43.84	2.18	15.95	50.80	1.98	16.07	62.56	1.78	15.14	69.52
4.59	24.99	30.16	3.29	20.70	38.44	2.59	17.62	44.32	2.19	16.12	51.40	1.99	16.25	63.28	1.79	15.31	70.36
4.60	25.18	30.40	3.30	20.89	38.80	2.60	17.80	44.80	2.20	16.30	52.00	2.00	16.42	64.00	1.80	15.48	71.20
4.61	25.37	30.64	3.31	21.07	39.16	2.61	17.98	45.28	2.21	16.48	52.60	2.01	16.59	64.72	1.81	15.65	72.04
4.62	25.56	30.88	3.32	21.26	39.52	2.62	18.17	45.76	2.22	16.65	53.20	2.02	16.76	65.44	1.82	15.81	72.88
4.63	25.76	31.12	3.33	21.44	39.88	2.63	18.35	46.24	2.23	16.83	53.80	2.03	16.93	66.16	1.83	15.98	73.72
4.64	25.95	31.36	3.34	21.63	40.24	2.64	18.53	46.72	2.24	17.00	54.40	2.04	17.10	66.88	1.84	16.15	74.56
4.65	26.14	31.60	3.35	21.81	40.60	2.65	18.70	47.20	2.25	17.18	55.00	2.05	17.27	67.60	1.85	16.31	75.40
4.66	26.33	31.84	3.36	21.99	40.96	2.66	18.88	47.68	2.26	17.35	55.60	2.06	17.44	68.32	1.86	16.48	76.24
4.67	26.52	32.08	3.37	22.18	41.32	2.67	19.06	48.16	2.27	17.53	56.20	2.07	17.61	69.04	1.87	16.65	77.08
4.68	26.72	32.32	3.38	22.36	41.68	2.68	19.24	48.64	2.28	17.70	56.80	2.08	17.78	69.76	1.88	16.81	77.92
4.69	26.91	32.56	3.39	22.55	42.04	2.69	19.42	49.12	2.29	17.88	57.40	2.09	17.95	70.48	1.89	16.98	78.76
4.70	27.10	32.80	3.40	22.73	42.40	2.70	19.60	49.60	2.30	18.05	58.00	2.10	18.11	71.20	1.90	17.14	79.60
4.71	27.29	33.04	3.41	22.91	42.76	2.71	19.78	50.08	2.31	18.23	58.60	2.11	18.28	71.92	1.91	17.31	80.44
4.72	27.48	33.28	3.42	23.10	43.12	2.72	19.96	50.56	2.32	18.40	59.20	2.12	18.45	72.64	1.92	17.47	81.28
4.73	27.67	33.52	3.43	23.28	43.48	2.73	20.14	51.04	2.33	18.57	59.80	2.13	18.62	73.36	1.93	17.64	82.12
4.74	27.87	33.76	3.44	23.46	43.84	2.74	20.31	51.52	2.34	18.75	60.40	2.14	18.79	74.08	1.94	17.80	82.96
4.75	28.06	34.00	3.45	23.65	44.20	2.75	20.49	52.00	2.35	18.92	61.00	2.15	18.95	74.80	1.95	17.96	83.80
4.76	28.25	34.24	3.46	23.83	44.56	2.76	20.67	52.48	2.36	19.09	61.60	2.16	19.12	75.52	1.96	18.13	84.64
4.77	28.44	34.48	3.47	24.01	44.92	2.77	20.85	52.96	2.37	19.27	62.20	2.17	19.29	76.24	1.97	18.29	85.48
4.78	28.63	34.72	3.48	24.20	45.28	2.78	21.02	53.44	2.38	19.44	62.80	2.18	19.46	76.96	1.98	18.46	86.32
4.79	28.82	34.96	3.49	24.38	45.64	2.79	21.20	53.92	2.39	19.61	63.40	2.19	19.62	77.68	1.99	18.62	87.16
4.80	29.01	35.20	3.50	24.56	46.00	2.80	21.38	54.40	2.40	19.78	64.00	2.20	19.79	78.40	2.00	18.78	88.00
4.81	29.20	35.44	3.51	24.74	46.36	2.81	21.56	54.88	2.41	19.95	64.60	2.21	19.96	79.12	2.01	18.94	88.84
4.82	29.40	35.68	3.52	24.93	46.72	2.82	21.73	55.36	2.42	20.12	65.20	2.22	20.12	79.84	2.02	19.11	89.68
4.83	29.59	35.92	3.53	25.11	47.08	2.83	21.91	55.84	2.43	20.30	65.80	2.23	20.29	80.56	2.03	19.27	90.52
4.84	29.78	36.16	3.54	25.29	47.44	2.84	22.09	56.32	2.44	20.47	66.40	2.24	20.45	81.28	2.04	19.43	91.36
4.85	29.97	36.40	3.55	25.47	47.80	2.85	22.26	56.80	2.45	20.64	67.00	2.25	20.62	82.00	2.05	19.59	92.20
4.86	30.16	36.64	3.56	25.65	48.16	2.86	22.44	57.28	2.46	20.81	67.60	2.26	20.78	82.72	2.06	19.75	93.04
4.87	30.35	36.88	3.57	25.84	48.52	2.87	22.61	57.76	2.47	20.98	68.20	2.27	20.95	83.44	2.07	19.92	93.88
4.88	30.54	37.12	3.58	26.02	48.88	2.88	22.79	58.24	2.48	21.15	68.80	2.28	21.11	84.16	2.08	20.08	94.72
4.89	30.73	37.36	3.59	26.20	49.24	2.89	22.96	58.72	2.49	21.32	69.40	2.29	21.28	84.88	2.09	20.24	95.56
4.90	30.92	37.60	3.60	26.38	49.60	2.90	23.14	59.20	2.50	21.49	70.00	2.30	21.44	85.60	2.10	20.40	96.40
4.91	31.11	37.84	3.61	26.56	49.96	2.91	23.32	59.68	2.51	21.66	70.60	2.31	21.61	86.32	2.11	20.56	97.24
4.92	31.30	38.08	3.62	26.74	50.32	2.92	23.49	60.16	2.52	21.83	71.20	2.32	21.77	87.04	2.12	20.72	98.08
4.93	31.49	38.32	3.63	26.92	50.68	2.93	23.67	60.64	2.53	22.00	71.80	2.33	21.94	87.76	2.13	20.88	98.92
4.94	31.68	38.56	3.64	27.10	51.04	2.94	23.84	61.12	2.54	22.17	72.40	2.34	22.10	88.48	2.14	21.04	99.76
4.95	31.87	38.80	3.65	27.28	51.40	2.95	24.01	61.60	2.55	22.34	73.00	2.35	22.26	89.20	2.15	21.20	100.60
4.96	32.06	39.04	3.66	27.47	51.76	2.96	24.19	62.08	2.56	22.51	73.60	2.36	22.43	89.92	2.16	21.36	101.44
4.97	32.25	39.28	3.67	27.65	52.12	2.97	24.36	62.56	2.57	22.68	74.20	2.37	22.59	90.64	2.17	21.52	102.28
4.98	32.44	39.52	3.68	27.83	52.48	2.98	24.54	63.04	2.58	22.85	74.80	2.38	22.75	91.36	2.18	21.68	103.12
4.99	32.63	39.76	3.69	28.01	52.84	2.99	24.71	63.52	2.59	23.02	75.40	2.39	22.91	92.08	2.19	21.84	103.96

Description: This table shows the Annual Percentage Rate and finance charge per $100 for monthly lease payments.

Example: A 1.30% lease payment for 8 years is equivalent to an APR of 8.78%. The charge per $100 cost is $ 44.80.

8 yr MONTHLY PAYT	APR	CHARGE	9 yr MONTHLY PAYT	APR	CHARGE	10 yr MONTHLY PAYT	APR	CHARGE	12 yr MONTHLY PAYT	APR	CHARGE	15 yr MONTHLY PAYT	APR	CHARGE	20 yr MONTHLY PAYT	APR	CHARGE
1.30	8.78	44.80	1.20	8.58	49.60	1.10	8.06	52.00	1.00	8.12	64.00	.80	6.49	64.00	.70	6.48	88.00
1.31	8.96	45.76	1.21	8.75	50.68	1.11	8.23	53.20	1.01	8.29	65.44	.81	6.65	65.80	.71	6.64	90.40
1.32	9.14	46.72	1.22	8.93	51.76	1.12	8.40	54.40	1.02	8.46	66.88	.82	6.82	67.60	.72	6.80	92.80
1.33	9.31	47.68	1.23	9.10	52.84	1.13	8.58	55.60	1.03	8.63	68.32	.83	6.99	69.40	.73	6.96	95.20
1.34	9.49	48.64	1.24	9.27	53.92	1.14	8.75	56.80	1.04	8.79	69.76	.84	7.15	71.20	.74	7.12	97.60
1.35	9.66	49.60	1.25	9.45	55.00	1.15	8.92	58.00	1.05	8.96	71.20	.85	7.32	73.00	.75	7.27	100.00
1.36	9.84	50.56	1.26	9.62	56.08	1.16	9.09	59.20	1.06	9.12	72.64	.86	7.48	74.80	.76	7.43	102.40
1.37	10.01	51.52	1.27	9.79	57.16	1.17	9.26	60.40	1.07	9.29	74.08	.87	7.64	76.60	.77	7.58	104.80
1.38	10.19	52.48	1.28	9.96	58.24	1.18	9.43	61.60	1.08	9.45	75.52	.88	7.81	78.40	.78	7.74	107.20
1.39	10.36	53.44	1.29	10.13	59.32	1.19	9.60	62.80	1.09	9.62	76.96	.89	7.97	80.20	.79	7.89	109.60
1.40	10.54	54.40	1.30	10.30	60.40	1.20	9.77	64.00	1.10	9.78	78.40	.90	8.13	82.00	.80	8.04	112.00
1.41	10.71	55.36	1.31	10.47	61.48	1.21	9.94	65.20	1.11	9.94	79.84	.91	8.29	83.80	.81	8.20	114.40
1.42	10.88	56.32	1.32	10.64	62.56	1.22	10.10	66.40	1.12	10.11	81.28	.92	8.45	85.60	.82	8.35	116.80
1.43	11.05	57.28	1.33	10.81	63.64	1.23	10.27	67.60	1.13	10.27	82.72	.93	8.61	87.40	.83	8.50	119.20
1.44	11.22	58.24	1.34	10.98	64.72	1.24	10.44	68.80	1.14	10.43	84.16	.94	8.77	89.20	.84	8.65	121.60
1.45	11.40	59.20	1.35	11.15	65.80	1.25	10.61	70.00	1.15	10.59	85.60	.95	8.93	91.00	.85	8.80	124.00
1.46	11.57	60.16	1.36	11.32	66.88	1.26	10.77	71.20	1.16	10.75	87.04	.96	9.09	92.80	.86	8.95	126.40
1.47	11.74	61.12	1.37	11.49	67.96	1.27	10.94	72.40	1.17	10.91	88.48	.97	9.25	94.60	.87	9.10	128.80
1.48	11.91	62.08	1.38	11.65	69.04	1.28	11.11	73.60	1.18	11.07	89.92	.98	9.41	96.40	.88	9.25	131.20
1.49	12.08	63.04	1.39	11.82	70.12	1.29	11.27	74.80	1.19	11.23	91.36	.99	9.56	98.20	.89	9.40	133.60
1.50	12.25	64.00	1.40	11.99	71.20	1.30	11.44	76.00	1.20	11.39	92.80	1.00	9.72	100.00	.90	9.55	136.00
1.51	12.42	64.96	1.41	12.15	72.28	1.31	11.60	77.20	1.21	11.55	94.24	1.01	9.88	101.80	.91	9.69	138.40
1.52	12.59	65.92	1.42	12.32	73.36	1.32	11.76	78.40	1.22	11.71	95.68	1.02	10.03	103.60	.92	9.84	140.80
1.53	12.76	66.88	1.43	12.49	74.44	1.33	11.93	79.60	1.23	11.87	97.12	1.03	10.19	105.40	.93	9.99	143.20
1.54	12.92	67.84	1.44	12.65	75.52	1.34	12.09	80.80	1.24	12.03	98.56	1.04	10.34	107.20	.94	10.13	145.60
1.55	13.09	68.80	1.45	12.82	76.60	1.35	12.25	82.00	1.25	12.18	100.00	1.05	10.50	109.00	.95	10.28	148.00
1.56	13.26	69.76	1.46	12.98	77.68	1.36	12.42	83.20	1.26	12.34	101.44	1.06	10.65	110.80	.96	10.42	150.40
1.57	13.43	70.72	1.47	13.15	78.76	1.37	12.58	84.40	1.27	12.50	102.88	1.07	10.81	112.60	.97	10.57	152.80
1.58	13.59	71.68	1.48	13.31	79.84	1.38	12.74	85.60	1.28	12.65	104.32	1.08	10.96	114.40	.98	10.71	155.20
1.59	13.76	72.64	1.49	13.47	80.92	1.39	12.90	86.80	1.29	12.81	105.76	1.09	11.11	116.20	.99	10.86	157.60
1.60	13.93	73.60	1.50	13.64	82.00	1.40	13.06	88.00	1.30	12.96	107.20	1.10	11.26	118.00	1.00	11.00	160.00
1.61	14.09	74.56	1.51	13.80	83.08	1.41	13.22	89.20	1.31	13.12	108.64	1.11	11.42	119.80	1.01	11.14	162.40
1.62	14.26	75.52	1.52	13.96	84.16	1.42	13.39	90.40	1.32	13.28	110.08	1.12	11.57	121.60	1.02	11.29	164.80
1.63	14.43	76.48	1.53	14.13	85.24	1.43	13.55	91.60	1.33	13.43	111.52	1.13	11.72	123.40	1.03	11.43	167.20
1.64	14.59	77.44	1.54	14.29	86.32	1.44	13.71	92.80	1.34	13.58	112.96	1.14	11.87	125.20	1.04	11.57	169.60
1.65	14.76	78.40	1.55	14.45	87.40	1.45	13.87	94.00	1.35	13.74	114.40	1.15	12.02	127.00	1.05	11.71	172.00
1.66	14.92	79.36	1.56	14.61	88.48	1.46	14.02	95.20	1.36	13.89	115.84	1.16	12.17	128.80	1.06	11.86	174.40
1.67	15.09	80.32	1.57	14.77	89.56	1.47	14.18	96.40	1.37	14.04	117.28	1.17	12.32	130.60	1.07	12.00	176.80
1.68	15.25	81.28	1.58	14.93	90.64	1.48	14.34	97.60	1.38	14.20	118.72	1.18	12.47	132.40	1.08	12.14	179.20
1.69	15.41	82.24	1.59	15.09	91.72	1.49	14.50	98.80	1.39	14.35	120.16	1.19	12.62	134.20	1.09	12.28	181.60
1.70	15.58	83.20	1.60	15.25	92.80	1.50	14.66	100.00	1.40	14.50	121.60	1.20	12.77	136.00	1.10	12.42	184.00
1.71	15.74	84.16	1.61	15.41	93.88	1.51	14.82	101.20	1.41	14.65	123.04	1.21	12.92	137.80	1.11	12.56	186.40
1.72	15.90	85.12	1.62	15.57	94.96	1.52	14.97	102.40	1.42	14.81	124.48	1.22	13.06	139.60	1.12	12.70	188.80
1.73	16.07	86.08	1.63	15.73	96.04	1.53	15.13	103.60	1.43	14.96	125.92	1.23	13.21	141.40	1.13	12.84	191.20
1.74	16.23	87.04	1.64	15.89	97.12	1.54	15.29	104.80	1.44	15.11	127.36	1.24	13.36	143.20	1.14	12.98	193.60
1.75	16.39	88.00	1.65	16.05	98.20	1.55	15.44	106.00	1.45	15.26	128.80	1.25	13.51	145.00	1.15	13.12	196.00
1.76	16.55	88.96	1.66	16.21	99.28	1.56	15.60	107.20	1.46	15.41	130.24	1.26	13.65	146.80	1.16	13.26	198.40
1.77	16.71	89.92	1.67	16.37	100.36	1.57	15.76	108.40	1.47	15.56	131.68	1.27	13.80	148.60	1.17	13.39	200.80
1.78	16.88	90.88	1.68	16.53	101.44	1.58	15.91	109.60	1.48	15.71	133.12	1.28	13.95	150.40	1.18	13.53	203.20
1.79	17.04	91.84	1.69	16.69	102.52	1.59	16.07	110.80	1.49	15.86	134.56	1.29	14.09	152.20	1.19	13.67	205.60
1.80	17.20	92.80	1.70	16.84	103.60	1.60	16.22	112.00	1.50	16.01	136.00	1.30	14.24	154.00	1.20	13.81	208.00
1.81	17.36	93.76	1.71	17.00	104.68	1.61	16.38	113.20	1.51	16.16	137.44	1.31	14.38	155.80	1.21	13.95	210.40
1.82	17.52	94.72	1.72	17.16	105.76	1.62	16.53	114.40	1.52	16.31	138.88	1.32	14.53	157.60	1.22	14.08	212.80
1.83	17.68	95.68	1.73	17.31	106.84	1.63	16.69	115.60	1.53	16.46	140.32	1.33	14.67	159.40	1.23	14.22	215.20
1.84	17.84	96.64	1.74	17.47	107.92	1.64	16.84	116.80	1.54	16.61	141.76	1.34	14.82	161.20	1.24	14.36	217.60
1.85	18.00	97.60	1.75	17.63	109.00	1.65	16.99	118.00	1.55	16.75	143.20	1.35	14.96	163.00	1.25	14.49	220.00
1.86	18.16	98.56	1.76	17.78	110.08	1.66	17.15	119.20	1.56	16.90	144.64	1.36	15.10	164.80	1.26	14.63	222.40
1.87	18.32	99.52	1.77	17.94	111.16	1.67	17.30	120.40	1.57	17.05	146.08	1.37	15.25	166.60	1.27	14.76	224.80
1.88	18.48	100.48	1.78	18.09	112.24	1.68	17.45	121.60	1.58	17.20	147.52	1.38	15.39	168.40	1.28	14.90	227.20
1.89	18.63	101.44	1.79	18.25	113.32	1.69	17.61	122.80	1.59	17.34	148.96	1.39	15.53	170.20	1.29	15.04	229.60
1.90	18.79	102.40	1.80	18.40	114.40	1.70	17.76	124.00	1.60	17.49	150.40	1.40	15.68	172.00	1.30	15.17	232.00
1.91	18.95	103.36	1.81	18.56	115.48	1.71	17.91	125.20	1.61	17.64	151.84	1.41	15.82	173.80	1.31	15.31	234.40
1.92	19.11	104.32	1.82	18.71	116.56	1.72	18.06	126.40	1.62	17.78	153.28	1.42	15.96	175.60	1.32	15.44	236.80
1.93	19.27	105.28	1.83	18.87	117.64	1.73	18.22	127.60	1.63	17.93	154.72	1.43	16.10	177.40	1.33	15.58	239.20
1.94	19.42	106.24	1.84	19.02	118.72	1.74	18.37	128.80	1.64	18.08	156.16	1.44	16.25	179.20	1.34	15.71	241.60
1.95	19.58	107.20	1.85	19.18	119.80	1.75	18.52	130.00	1.65	18.22	157.60	1.45	16.39	181.00	1.35	15.85	244.00
1.96	19.74	108.16	1.86	19.33	120.88	1.76	18.67	131.20	1.66	18.37	159.04	1.46	16.53	182.80	1.36	15.98	246.40
1.97	19.90	109.12	1.87	19.48	121.96	1.77	18.82	132.40	1.67	18.51	160.48	1.47	16.67	184.60	1.37	16.11	248.80
1.98	20.05	110.08	1.88	19.64	123.04	1.78	18.97	133.60	1.68	18.66	161.92	1.48	16.81	186.40	1.38	16.25	251.20
1.99	20.21	111.04	1.89	19.79	124.12	1.79	19.12	134.80	1.69	18.80	163.36	1.49	16.95	188.20	1.39	16.38	253.60

Description: This table shows the Annual Percentage Rate and finance charge per $100 for monthly lease payments.

Example: A 4.30% lease payment for 2 years is equivalent to an APR of 3.62%. The charge per $100 cost is $ 3.20.

2 yr

MONTHLY PAYT	APR	CHARGE
4.30	3.62	3.20
4.31	3.88	3.44
4.32	4.15	3.68
4.33	4.42	3.92
4.34	4.69	4.16
4.35	4.96	4.40
4.36	5.22	4.64
4.37	5.49	4.88
4.38	5.76	5.12
4.39	6.03	5.36
4.40	6.29	5.60
4.41	6.56	5.84
4.42	6.82	6.08
4.43	7.09	6.32
4.44	7.36	6.56
4.45	7.62	6.80
4.46	7.88	7.04
4.47	8.15	7.28
4.48	8.41	7.52
4.49	8.68	7.76
4.50	8.94	8.00
4.51	9.20	8.24
4.52	9.47	8.48
4.53	9.73	8.72
4.54	9.99	8.96
4.55	10.26	9.20
4.56	10.52	9.44
4.57	10.78	9.68
4.58	11.04	9.92
4.59	11.30	10.16
4.60	11.56	10.40
4.61	11.82	10.64
4.62	12.09	10.88
4.63	12.35	11.12
4.64	12.61	11.36
4.65	12.87	11.60
4.66	13.13	11.84
4.67	13.38	12.08
4.68	13.64	12.32
4.69	13.90	12.56
4.70	14.16	12.80
4.71	14.42	13.04
4.72	14.68	13.28
4.73	14.94	13.52
4.74	15.19	13.76
4.75	15.45	14.00
4.76	15.71	14.24
4.77	15.97	14.48
4.78	16.22	14.72
4.79	16.48	14.96
4.80	16.74	15.20
4.81	16.99	15.44
4.82	17.25	15.68
4.83	17.50	15.92
4.84	17.76	16.16
4.85	18.01	16.40
4.86	18.27	16.64
4.87	18.52	16.88
4.88	18.78	17.12
4.89	19.03	17.36
4.90	19.29	17.60
4.91	19.54	17.84
4.92	19.79	18.08
4.93	20.05	18.32
4.94	20.30	18.56
4.95	20.55	18.80
4.96	20.81	19.04
4.97	21.06	19.28
4.98	21.31	19.52
4.99	21.56	19.76

3 yr

MONTHLY PAYT	APR	CHARGE
3.00	5.69	8.00
3.01	5.94	8.36
3.02	6.19	8.72
3.03	6.44	9.08
3.04	6.69	9.44
3.05	6.94	9.80
3.06	7.19	10.16
3.07	7.43	10.52
3.08	7.68	10.88
3.09	7.93	11.24
3.10	8.18	11.60
3.11	8.42	11.96
3.12	8.67	12.32
3.13	8.91	12.68
3.14	9.16	13.04
3.15	9.40	13.40
3.16	9.65	13.76
3.17	9.89	14.12
3.18	10.14	14.48
3.19	10.38	14.84
3.20	10.62	15.20
3.21	10.86	15.56
3.22	11.11	15.92
3.23	11.35	16.28
3.24	11.59	16.64
3.25	11.83	17.00
3.26	12.07	17.36
3.27	12.31	17.72
3.28	12.55	18.08
3.29	12.79	18.44
3.30	13.03	18.80
3.31	13.27	19.16
3.32	13.51	19.52
3.33	13.75	19.88
3.34	13.98	20.24
3.35	14.22	20.60
3.36	14.46	20.96
3.37	14.70	21.32
3.38	14.93	21.68
3.39	15.17	22.04
3.40	15.40	22.40
3.41	15.64	22.76
3.42	15.87	23.12
3.43	16.11	23.48
3.44	16.34	23.84
3.45	16.58	24.20
3.46	16.81	24.56
3.47	17.05	24.92
3.48	17.28	25.28
3.49	17.51	25.64
3.50	17.75	26.00
3.51	17.98	26.36
3.52	18.21	26.72
3.53	18.44	27.08
3.54	18.67	27.44
3.55	18.90	27.80
3.56	19.13	28.16
3.57	19.36	28.52
3.58	19.59	28.88
3.59	19.82	29.24
3.60	20.05	29.60
3.61	20.28	29.96
3.62	20.51	30.32
3.63	20.74	30.68
3.64	20.97	31.04
3.65	21.20	31.40
3.66	21.43	31.76
3.67	21.65	32.12
3.68	21.88	32.48
3.69	22.11	32.84

4 yr

MONTHLY PAYT	APR	CHARGE
2.30	5.39	10.40
2.31	5.63	10.88
2.32	5.87	11.36
2.33	6.11	11.84
2.34	6.35	12.32
2.35	6.59	12.80
2.36	6.83	13.28
2.37	7.07	13.76
2.38	7.30	14.24
2.39	7.54	14.72
2.40	7.78	15.20
2.41	8.01	15.68
2.42	8.25	16.16
2.43	8.48	16.64
2.44	8.72	17.12
2.45	8.95	17.60
2.46	9.19	18.08
2.47	9.42	18.56
2.48	9.65	19.04
2.49	9.88	19.52
2.50	10.12	20.00
2.51	10.35	20.48
2.52	10.58	20.96
2.53	10.81	21.44
2.54	11.04	21.92
2.55	11.27	22.40
2.56	11.49	22.88
2.57	11.72	23.36
2.58	11.95	23.84
2.59	12.18	24.32
2.60	12.41	24.80
2.61	12.63	25.28
2.62	12.86	25.76
2.63	13.08	26.24
2.64	13.31	26.72
2.65	13.53	27.20
2.66	13.76	27.68
2.67	13.98	28.16
2.68	14.21	28.64
2.69	14.43	29.12
2.70	14.65	29.60
2.71	14.87	30.08
2.72	15.10	30.56
2.73	15.32	31.04
2.74	15.54	31.52
2.75	15.76	32.00
2.76	15.98	32.48
2.77	16.20	32.96
2.78	16.42	33.44
2.79	16.64	33.92
2.80	16.86	34.40
2.81	17.07	34.88
2.82	17.29	35.36
2.83	17.51	35.84
2.84	17.73	36.32
2.85	17.95	36.80
2.86	18.16	37.28
2.87	18.38	37.76
2.88	18.59	38.24
2.89	18.81	38.72
2.90	19.02	39.20
2.91	19.24	39.68
2.92	19.45	40.16
2.93	19.67	40.64
2.94	19.88	41.12
2.95	20.10	41.60
2.96	20.31	42.08
2.97	20.52	42.56
2.98	20.73	43.04
2.99	20.95	43.52

5 yr

MONTHLY PAYT	APR	CHARGE
1.90	5.67	14.00
1.91	5.90	14.60
1.92	6.13	15.20
1.93	6.37	15.80
1.94	6.60	16.40
1.95	6.83	17.00
1.96	7.06	17.60
1.97	7.29	18.20
1.98	7.52	18.80
1.99	7.75	19.40
2.00	7.97	20.00
2.01	8.20	20.60
2.02	8.43	21.20
2.03	8.65	21.80
2.04	8.88	22.40
2.05	9.10	23.00
2.06	9.33	23.60
2.07	9.55	24.20
2.08	9.78	24.80
2.09	10.00	25.40
2.10	10.22	26.00
2.11	10.44	26.60
2.12	10.66	27.20
2.13	10.88	27.80
2.14	11.10	28.40
2.15	11.32	29.00
2.16	11.54	29.60
2.17	11.76	30.20
2.18	11.98	30.80
2.19	12.19	31.40
2.20	12.41	32.00
2.21	12.63	32.60
2.22	12.84	33.20
2.23	13.06	33.80
2.24	13.27	34.40
2.25	13.49	35.00
2.26	13.70	35.60
2.27	13.91	36.20
2.28	14.13	36.80
2.29	14.34	37.40
2.30	14.55	38.00
2.31	14.76	38.60
2.32	14.97	39.20
2.33	15.18	39.80
2.34	15.39	40.40
2.35	15.60	41.00
2.36	15.81	41.60
2.37	16.02	42.20
2.38	16.23	42.80
2.39	16.44	43.40
2.40	16.65	44.00
2.41	16.85	44.60
2.42	17.06	45.20
2.43	17.27	45.80
2.44	17.47	46.40
2.45	17.68	47.00
2.46	17.88	47.60
2.47	18.09	48.20
2.48	18.29	48.80
2.49	18.50	49.40
2.50	18.70	50.00
2.51	18.90	50.60
2.52	19.11	51.20
2.53	19.31	51.80
2.54	19.51	52.40
2.55	19.71	53.00
2.56	19.91	53.60
2.57	20.11	54.20
2.58	20.31	54.80
2.59	20.52	55.40

6 yr

MONTHLY PAYT	APR	CHARGE
1.70	7.33	22.40
1.71	7.55	23.12
1.72	7.77	23.84
1.73	7.99	24.56
1.74	8.21	25.28
1.75	8.43	26.00
1.76	8.65	26.72
1.77	8.87	27.44
1.78	9.09	28.16
1.79	9.30	28.88
1.80	9.52	29.60
1.81	9.73	30.32
1.82	9.95	31.04
1.83	10.16	31.76
1.84	10.38	32.48
1.85	10.59	33.20
1.86	10.80	33.92
1.87	11.01	34.64
1.88	11.23	35.36
1.89	11.44	36.08
1.90	11.65	36.80
1.91	11.86	37.52
1.92	12.07	38.24
1.93	12.27	38.96
1.94	12.48	39.68
1.95	12.69	40.40
1.96	12.90	41.12
1.97	13.10	41.84
1.98	13.31	42.56
1.99	13.51	43.28
2.00	13.72	44.00
2.01	13.92	44.72
2.02	14.13	45.44
2.03	14.33	46.16
2.04	14.53	46.88
2.05	14.73	47.60
2.06	14.94	48.32
2.07	15.14	49.04
2.08	15.34	49.76
2.09	15.54	50.48
2.10	15.74	51.20
2.11	15.94	51.92
2.12	16.14	52.64
2.13	16.34	53.36
2.14	16.53	54.08
2.15	16.73	54.80
2.16	16.93	55.52
2.17	17.13	56.24
2.18	17.32	56.96
2.19	17.52	57.68
2.20	17.72	58.40
2.21	17.91	59.12
2.22	18.11	59.84
2.23	18.30	60.56
2.24	18.49	61.28
2.25	18.69	62.00
2.26	18.88	62.72
2.27	19.07	63.44
2.28	19.27	64.16
2.29	19.46	64.88
2.30	19.65	65.60
2.31	19.84	66.32
2.32	20.03	67.04
2.33	20.22	67.76
2.34	20.41	68.48
2.35	20.60	69.20
2.36	20.79	69.92
2.37	20.98	70.64
2.38	21.17	71.36
2.39	21.36	72.08

7 yr

MONTHLY PAYT	APR	CHARGE
1.50	7.18	26.00
1.51	7.39	26.84
1.52	7.61	27.68
1.53	7.82	28.52
1.54	8.04	29.36
1.55	8.25	30.20
1.56	8.47	31.04
1.57	8.68	31.88
1.58	8.89	32.72
1.59	9.10	33.56
1.60	9.31	34.40
1.61	9.52	35.24
1.62	9.73	36.08
1.63	9.94	36.92
1.64	10.14	37.76
1.65	10.35	38.60
1.66	10.56	39.44
1.67	10.76	40.28
1.68	10.97	41.12
1.69	11.17	41.96
1.70	11.38	42.80
1.71	11.58	43.64
1.72	11.78	44.48
1.73	11.98	45.32
1.74	12.19	46.16
1.75	12.39	47.00
1.76	12.59	47.84
1.77	12.79	48.68
1.78	12.98	49.52
1.79	13.18	50.36
1.80	13.38	51.20
1.81	13.58	52.04
1.82	13.78	52.88
1.83	13.97	53.72
1.84	14.17	54.56
1.85	14.36	55.40
1.86	14.56	56.24
1.87	14.75	57.08
1.88	14.95	57.92
1.89	15.14	58.76
1.90	15.33	59.60
1.91	15.53	60.44
1.92	15.72	61.28
1.93	15.91	62.12
1.94	16.10	62.96
1.95	16.29	63.80
1.96	16.48	64.64
1.97	16.67	65.48
1.98	16.86	66.32
1.99	17.05	67.16
2.00	17.24	68.00
2.01	17.42	68.84
2.02	17.61	69.68
2.03	17.80	70.52
2.04	17.99	71.36
2.05	18.17	72.20
2.06	18.36	73.04
2.07	18.54	73.88
2.08	18.73	74.72
2.09	18.91	75.56
2.10	19.10	76.40
2.11	19.29	77.24
2.12	19.47	78.08
2.13	19.65	78.92
2.14	19.83	79.76
2.15	20.01	80.60
2.16	20.20	81.44
2.17	20.38	82.28
2.18	20.56	83.12
2.19	20.74	83.96

LEASE PAYMENTS

Description: This table shows the Annual Percentage Rate and finance charge per $100 for monthly lease payments.

Example: A 1.30% lease payment for 8 years is equivalent to an APR of 5.97%. The charge per $100 cost is $ 24.80.

8 yr MONTHLY PAYT	APR	CHARGE	9 yr MONTHLY PAYT	APR	CHARGE	10 yr MONTHLY PAYT	APR	CHARGE	12 yr MONTHLY PAYT	APR	CHARGE	15 yr MONTHLY PAYT	APR	CHARGE	20 yr MONTHLY PAYT	APR	CHARGE
1.30	5.97	24.80	1.20	6.24	29.60	1.10	6.02	32.00	1.00	6.67	44.00	.80	5.31	44.00	.70	5.83	68.00
1.31	6.19	25.76	1.21	6.45	30.68	1.11	6.22	33.20	1.01	6.87	45.44	.81	5.51	45.80	.71	6.01	70.40
1.32	6.41	26.72	1.22	6.66	31.76	1.12	6.43	34.40	1.02	7.07	46.88	.82	5.70	47.60	.72	6.19	72.80
1.33	6.62	27.68	1.23	6.87	32.84	1.13	6.64	35.60	1.03	7.26	48.32	.83	5.89	49.40	.73	6.37	75.20
1.34	6.84	28.64	1.24	7.08	33.92	1.14	6.84	36.80	1.04	7.46	49.76	.84	6.09	51.20	.74	6.54	77.60
1.35	7.05	29.60	1.25	7.29	35.00	1.15	7.05	38.00	1.05	7.65	51.20	.85	6.28	53.00	.75	6.72	80.00
1.36	7.26	30.56	1.26	7.49	36.08	1.16	7.25	39.20	1.06	7.84	52.64	.86	6.47	54.80	.76	6.89	82.40
1.37	7.47	31.52	1.27	7.70	37.16	1.17	7.45	40.40	1.07	8.03	54.08	.87	6.65	56.60	.77	7.06	84.80
1.38	7.68	32.48	1.28	7.90	38.24	1.18	7.65	41.60	1.08	8.22	55.52	.88	6.84	58.40	.78	7.23	87.20
1.39	7.89	33.44	1.29	8.11	39.32	1.19	7.85	42.80	1.09	8.41	56.96	.89	7.03	60.20	.79	7.40	89.60
1.40	8.10	34.40	1.30	8.31	40.40	1.20	8.05	44.00	1.10	8.60	58.40	.90	7.21	62.00	.80	7.57	92.00
1.41	8.31	35.36	1.31	8.51	41.48	1.21	8.25	45.20	1.11	8.79	59.84	.91	7.40	63.80	.81	7.74	94.40
1.42	8.52	36.32	1.32	8.71	42.56	1.22	8.45	46.40	1.12	8.98	61.28	.92	7.58	65.60	.82	7.91	96.80
1.43	8.72	37.28	1.33	8.91	43.64	1.23	8.65	47.60	1.13	9.16	62.72	.93	7.76	67.40	.83	8.08	99.20
1.44	8.93	38.24	1.34	9.11	44.72	1.24	8.84	48.80	1.14	9.35	64.16	.94	7.94	69.20	.84	8.24	101.60
1.45	9.13	39.20	1.35	9.31	45.80	1.25	9.04	50.00	1.15	9.53	65.60	.95	8.12	71.00	.85	8.41	104.00
1.46	9.34	40.16	1.36	9.51	46.88	1.26	9.23	51.20	1.16	9.72	67.04	.96	8.30	72.80	.86	8.57	106.40
1.47	9.54	41.12	1.37	9.71	47.96	1.27	9.43	52.40	1.17	9.90	68.48	.97	8.48	74.60	.87	8.73	108.80
1.48	9.74	42.08	1.38	9.90	49.04	1.28	9.62	53.60	1.18	10.08	69.92	.98	8.66	76.40	.88	8.90	111.20
1.49	9.95	43.04	1.39	10.10	50.12	1.29	9.81	54.80	1.19	10.26	71.36	.99	8.84	78.20	.89	9.06	113.60
1.50	10.15	44.00	1.40	10.30	51.20	1.30	10.00	56.00	1.20	10.44	72.80	1.00	9.01	80.00	.90	9.22	116.00
1.51	10.35	44.96	1.41	10.49	52.28	1.31	10.19	57.20	1.21	10.62	74.24	1.01	9.19	81.80	.91	9.38	118.40
1.52	10.55	45.92	1.42	10.68	53.36	1.32	10.38	58.40	1.22	10.80	75.68	1.02	9.36	83.60	.92	9.54	120.80
1.53	10.75	46.88	1.43	10.88	54.44	1.33	10.57	59.60	1.23	10.98	77.12	1.03	9.54	85.40	.93	9.70	123.20
1.54	10.95	47.84	1.44	11.07	55.52	1.34	10.76	60.80	1.24	11.16	78.56	1.04	9.71	87.20	.94	9.85	125.60
1.55	11.15	48.80	1.45	11.26	56.60	1.35	10.95	62.00	1.25	11.34	80.00	1.05	9.88	89.00	.95	10.01	128.00
1.56	11.34	49.76	1.46	11.45	57.68	1.36	11.14	63.20	1.26	11.51	81.44	1.06	10.05	90.80	.96	10.17	130.40
1.57	11.54	50.72	1.47	11.64	58.76	1.37	11.32	64.40	1.27	11.69	82.88	1.07	10.22	92.60	.97	10.33	132.80
1.58	11.74	51.68	1.48	11.83	59.84	1.38	11.51	65.60	1.28	11.87	84.32	1.08	10.39	94.40	.98	10.48	135.20
1.59	11.93	52.64	1.49	12.02	60.92	1.39	11.69	66.80	1.29	12.04	85.76	1.09	10.56	96.20	.99	10.64	137.60
1.60	12.13	53.60	1.50	12.21	62.00	1.40	11.88	68.00	1.30	12.21	87.20	1.10	10.73	98.00	1.00	10.79	140.00
1.61	12.32	54.56	1.51	12.40	63.08	1.41	12.06	69.20	1.31	12.39	88.64	1.11	10.90	99.80	1.01	10.94	142.40
1.62	12.51	55.52	1.52	12.59	64.16	1.42	12.25	70.40	1.32	12.56	90.08	1.12	11.06	101.60	1.02	11.10	144.80
1.63	12.71	56.48	1.53	12.78	65.24	1.43	12.43	71.60	1.33	12.73	91.52	1.13	11.23	103.40	1.03	11.25	147.20
1.64	12.90	57.44	1.54	12.96	66.32	1.44	12.61	72.80	1.34	12.91	92.96	1.14	11.40	105.20	1.04	11.40	149.60
1.65	13.09	58.40	1.55	13.15	67.40	1.45	12.79	74.00	1.35	13.08	94.40	1.15	11.56	107.00	1.05	11.55	152.00
1.66	13.28	59.36	1.56	13.33	68.48	1.46	12.97	75.20	1.36	13.25	95.84	1.16	11.73	108.80	1.06	11.71	154.40
1.67	13.47	60.32	1.57	13.52	69.56	1.47	13.15	76.40	1.37	13.42	97.28	1.17	11.89	110.60	1.07	11.86	156.80
1.68	13.67	61.28	1.58	13.70	70.64	1.48	13.33	77.60	1.38	13.59	98.72	1.18	12.05	112.40	1.08	12.01	159.20
1.69	13.86	62.24	1.59	13.89	71.72	1.49	13.51	78.80	1.39	13.76	100.16	1.19	12.22	114.20	1.09	12.16	161.60
1.70	14.04	63.20	1.60	14.07	72.80	1.50	13.69	80.00	1.40	13.93	101.60	1.20	12.38	116.00	1.10	12.31	164.00
1.71	14.23	64.16	1.61	14.25	73.88	1.51	13.87	81.20	1.41	14.09	103.04	1.21	12.54	117.80	1.11	12.46	166.40
1.72	14.42	65.12	1.62	14.43	74.96	1.52	14.05	82.40	1.42	14.26	104.48	1.22	12.70	119.60	1.12	12.60	168.80
1.73	14.61	66.08	1.63	14.62	76.04	1.53	14.22	83.60	1.43	14.43	105.92	1.23	12.86	121.40	1.13	12.75	171.20
1.74	14.80	67.04	1.64	14.80	77.12	1.54	14.40	84.80	1.44	14.60	107.36	1.24	13.03	123.20	1.14	12.90	173.60
1.75	14.98	68.00	1.65	14.98	78.20	1.55	14.58	86.00	1.45	14.76	108.80	1.25	13.19	125.00	1.15	13.05	176.00
1.76	15.17	68.96	1.66	15.16	79.28	1.56	14.75	87.20	1.46	14.93	110.24	1.26	13.34	126.80	1.16	13.20	178.40
1.77	15.36	69.92	1.67	15.34	80.36	1.57	14.93	88.40	1.47	15.09	111.68	1.27	13.50	128.60	1.17	13.34	180.80
1.78	15.54	70.88	1.68	15.52	81.44	1.58	15.10	89.60	1.48	15.26	113.12	1.28	13.66	130.40	1.18	13.49	183.20
1.79	15.73	71.84	1.69	15.70	82.52	1.59	15.28	90.80	1.49	15.42	114.56	1.29	13.82	132.20	1.19	13.63	185.60
1.80	15.91	72.80	1.70	15.87	83.60	1.60	15.45	92.00	1.50	15.59	116.00	1.30	13.98	134.00	1.20	13.78	188.00
1.81	16.09	73.76	1.71	16.05	84.68	1.61	15.63	93.20	1.51	15.75	117.44	1.31	14.14	135.80	1.21	13.92	190.40
1.82	16.28	74.72	1.72	16.23	85.76	1.62	15.80	94.40	1.52	15.92	118.88	1.32	14.29	137.60	1.22	14.07	192.80
1.83	16.46	75.68	1.73	16.41	86.84	1.63	15.97	95.60	1.53	16.08	120.32	1.33	14.45	139.40	1.23	14.21	195.20
1.84	16.64	76.64	1.74	16.58	87.92	1.64	16.14	96.80	1.54	16.24	121.76	1.34	14.60	141.20	1.24	14.36	197.60
1.85	16.83	77.60	1.75	16.76	89.00	1.65	16.31	98.00	1.55	16.40	123.20	1.35	14.76	143.00	1.25	14.50	200.00
1.86	17.01	78.56	1.76	16.93	90.08	1.66	16.49	99.20	1.56	16.56	124.64	1.36	14.92	144.80	1.26	14.65	202.40
1.87	17.19	79.52	1.77	17.11	91.16	1.67	16.66	100.40	1.57	16.73	126.08	1.37	15.07	146.60	1.27	14.79	204.80
1.88	17.37	80.48	1.78	17.28	92.24	1.68	16.83	101.60	1.58	16.89	127.52	1.38	15.22	148.40	1.28	14.93	207.20
1.89	17.55	81.44	1.79	17.46	93.32	1.69	17.00	102.80	1.59	17.05	128.96	1.39	15.38	150.20	1.29	15.08	209.60
1.90	17.73	82.40	1.80	17.63	94.40	1.70	17.17	104.00	1.60	17.21	130.40	1.40	15.53	152.00	1.30	15.22	212.00
1.91	17.91	83.36	1.81	17.81	95.48	1.71	17.34	105.20	1.61	17.37	131.84	1.41	15.69	153.80	1.31	15.36	214.40
1.92	18.09	84.32	1.82	17.98	96.56	1.72	17.50	106.40	1.62	17.53	133.28	1.42	15.84	155.60	1.32	15.50	216.80
1.93	18.27	85.28	1.83	18.15	97.64	1.73	17.67	107.60	1.63	17.69	134.72	1.43	15.99	157.40	1.33	15.64	219.20
1.94	18.45	86.24	1.84	18.33	98.72	1.74	17.84	108.80	1.64	17.85	136.16	1.44	16.14	159.20	1.34	15.79	221.60
1.95	18.63	87.20	1.85	18.50	99.80	1.75	18.01	110.00	1.65	18.01	137.60	1.45	16.30	161.00	1.35	15.93	224.00
1.96	18.80	88.16	1.86	18.67	100.88	1.76	18.18	111.20	1.66	18.16	139.04	1.46	16.45	162.80	1.36	16.07	226.40
1.97	18.98	89.12	1.87	18.84	101.96	1.77	18.34	112.40	1.67	18.32	140.48	1.47	16.60	164.60	1.37	16.21	228.80
1.98	19.16	90.08	1.88	19.01	103.04	1.78	18.51	113.60	1.68	18.48	141.92	1.48	16.75	166.40	1.38	16.35	231.20
1.99	19.33	91.04	1.89	19.18	104.12	1.79	18.68	114.80	1.69	18.64	143.36	1.49	16.90	168.20	1.39	16.49	233.60

Description: This table shows the Annual Percentage Rate and finance charge per $100 for monthly lease payments.

Example: A 4.30% lease payment for 2 years is equivalent to an APR of 8.65%. The charge per $100 cost is $ 8.20.

2 yr MONTHLY PAYT	APR	CHARGE	3 yr MONTHLY PAYT	APR	CHARGE	4 yr MONTHLY PAYT	APR	CHARGE	5 yr MONTHLY PAYT	APR	CHARGE	6 yr MONTHLY PAYT	APR	CHARGE	7 yr MONTHLY PAYT	APR	CHARGE
4.30	8.65	8.20	3.00	8.68	13.00	2.30	7.51	15.40	1.90	7.26	19.00	1.70	8.49	27.40	1.50	8.12	31.00
4.31	8.90	8.44	3.01	8.91	13.36	2.31	7.73	15.88	1.91	7.48	19.60	1.71	8.70	28.12	1.51	8.33	31.84
4.32	9.15	8.68	3.02	9.14	13.72	2.32	7.96	16.36	1.92	7.69	20.20	1.72	8.91	28.84	1.52	8.53	32.68
4.33	9.40	8.92	3.03	9.38	14.08	2.33	8.18	16.84	1.93	7.91	20.80	1.73	9.12	29.56	1.53	8.74	33.52
4.34	9.65	9.16	3.04	9.61	14.44	2.34	8.41	17.32	1.94	8.13	21.40	1.74	9.33	30.28	1.54	8.94	34.36
4.35	9.89	9.40	3.05	9.84	14.80	2.35	8.63	17.80	1.95	8.35	22.00	1.75	9.54	31.00	1.55	9.14	35.20
4.36	10.14	9.64	3.06	10.08	15.16	2.36	8.86	18.28	1.96	8.57	22.60	1.76	9.75	31.72	1.56	9.35	36.04
4.37	10.39	9.88	3.07	10.31	15.52	2.37	9.08	18.76	1.97	8.78	23.20	1.77	9.95	32.44	1.57	9.55	36.88
4.38	10.64	10.12	3.08	10.54	15.88	2.38	9.30	19.24	1.98	9.00	23.80	1.78	10.16	33.16	1.58	9.75	37.72
4.39	10.89	10.36	3.09	10.77	16.24	2.39	9.53	19.72	1.99	9.21	24.40	1.79	10.37	33.88	1.59	9.95	38.56
4.40	11.14	10.60	3.10	11.00	16.60	2.40	9.75	20.20	2.00	9.43	25.00	1.80	10.57	34.60	1.60	10.15	39.40
4.41	11.38	10.84	3.11	11.23	16.96	2.41	9.97	20.68	2.01	9.64	25.60	1.81	10.78	35.32	1.61	10.35	40.24
4.42	11.63	11.08	3.12	11.47	17.32	2.42	10.19	21.16	2.02	9.86	26.20	1.82	10.98	36.04	1.62	10.55	41.08
4.43	11.88	11.32	3.13	11.70	17.68	2.43	10.42	21.64	2.03	10.07	26.80	1.83	11.19	36.76	1.63	10.75	41.92
4.44	12.13	11.56	3.14	11.93	18.04	2.44	10.64	22.12	2.04	10.29	27.40	1.84	11.39	37.48	1.64	10.95	42.76
4.45	12.37	11.80	3.15	12.16	18.40	2.45	10.86	22.60	2.05	10.50	28.00	1.85	11.59	38.20	1.65	11.15	43.60
4.46	12.62	12.04	3.16	12.39	18.76	2.46	11.08	23.08	2.06	10.71	28.60	1.86	11.80	38.92	1.66	11.35	44.44
4.47	12.87	12.28	3.17	12.61	19.12	2.47	11.30	23.56	2.07	10.92	29.20	1.87	12.00	39.64	1.67	11.54	45.28
4.48	13.11	12.52	3.18	12.84	19.48	2.48	11.52	24.04	2.08	11.14	29.80	1.88	12.20	40.36	1.68	11.74	46.12
4.49	13.36	12.76	3.19	13.07	19.84	2.49	11.74	24.52	2.09	11.35	30.40	1.89	12.40	41.08	1.69	11.94	46.96
4.50	13.60	13.00	3.20	13.30	20.20	2.50	11.95	25.00	2.10	11.56	31.00	1.90	12.60	41.80	1.70	12.13	47.80
4.51	13.85	13.24	3.21	13.53	20.56	2.51	12.17	25.48	2.11	11.77	31.60	1.91	12.80	42.52	1.71	12.33	48.64
4.52	14.10	13.48	3.22	13.76	20.92	2.52	12.39	25.96	2.12	11.98	32.20	1.92	13.00	43.24	1.72	12.52	49.48
4.53	14.34	13.72	3.23	13.98	21.28	2.53	12.61	26.44	2.13	12.19	32.80	1.93	13.20	43.96	1.73	12.71	50.32
4.54	14.59	13.96	3.24	14.21	21.64	2.54	12.83	26.92	2.14	12.40	33.40	1.94	13.40	44.68	1.74	12.91	51.16
4.55	14.83	14.20	3.25	14.44	22.00	2.55	13.04	27.40	2.15	12.60	34.00	1.95	13.60	45.40	1.75	13.10	52.00
4.56	15.08	14.44	3.26	14.67	22.36	2.56	13.26	27.88	2.16	12.81	34.60	1.96	13.80	46.12	1.76	13.29	52.84
4.57	15.32	14.68	3.27	14.89	22.72	2.57	13.48	28.36	2.17	13.02	35.20	1.97	14.00	46.84	1.77	13.49	53.68
4.58	15.57	14.92	3.28	15.12	23.08	2.58	13.69	28.84	2.18	13.23	35.80	1.98	14.20	47.56	1.78	13.68	54.52
4.59	15.81	15.16	3.29	15.34	23.44	2.59	13.91	29.32	2.19	13.44	36.40	1.99	14.39	48.28	1.79	13.87	55.36
4.60	16.06	15.40	3.30	15.57	23.80	2.60	14.12	29.80	2.20	13.64	37.00	2.00	14.59	49.00	1.80	14.06	56.20
4.61	16.30	15.64	3.31	15.80	24.16	2.61	14.34	30.28	2.21	13.85	37.60	2.01	14.79	49.72	1.81	14.25	57.04
4.62	16.54	15.88	3.32	16.02	24.52	2.62	14.55	30.76	2.22	14.05	38.20	2.02	14.98	50.44	1.82	14.44	57.88
4.63	16.79	16.12	3.33	16.25	24.88	2.63	14.77	31.24	2.23	14.26	38.80	2.03	15.18	51.16	1.83	14.63	58.72
4.64	17.03	16.36	3.34	16.47	25.24	2.64	14.98	31.72	2.24	14.46	39.40	2.04	15.37	51.88	1.84	14.82	59.56
4.65	17.27	16.60	3.35	16.70	25.60	2.65	15.19	32.20	2.25	14.67	40.00	2.05	15.57	52.60	1.85	15.01	60.40
4.66	17.52	16.84	3.36	16.92	25.96	2.66	15.41	32.68	2.26	14.87	40.60	2.06	15.76	53.32	1.86	15.20	61.24
4.67	17.76	17.08	3.37	17.14	26.32	2.67	15.62	33.16	2.27	15.08	41.20	2.07	15.95	54.04	1.87	15.38	62.08
4.68	18.00	17.32	3.38	17.37	26.68	2.68	15.83	33.64	2.28	15.28	41.80	2.08	16.15	54.76	1.88	15.57	62.92
4.69	18.25	17.56	3.39	17.59	27.04	2.69	16.05	34.12	2.29	15.48	42.40	2.09	16.34	55.48	1.89	15.76	63.76
4.70	18.49	17.80	3.40	17.81	27.40	2.70	16.26	34.60	2.30	15.69	43.00	2.10	16.53	56.20	1.90	15.94	64.60
4.71	18.73	18.04	3.41	18.04	27.76	2.71	16.47	35.08	2.31	15.89	43.60	2.11	16.73	56.92	1.91	16.13	65.44
4.72	18.97	18.28	3.42	18.26	28.12	2.72	16.68	35.56	2.32	16.09	44.20	2.12	16.92	57.64	1.92	16.32	66.28
4.73	19.22	18.52	3.43	18.48	28.48	2.73	16.89	36.04	2.33	16.29	44.80	2.13	17.11	58.36	1.93	16.50	67.12
4.74	19.46	18.76	3.44	18.71	28.84	2.74	17.10	36.52	2.34	16.49	45.40	2.14	17.30	59.08	1.94	16.69	67.96
4.75	19.70	19.00	3.45	18.93	29.20	2.75	17.31	37.00	2.35	16.70	46.00	2.15	17.49	59.80	1.95	16.87	68.80
4.76	19.94	19.24	3.46	19.15	29.56	2.76	17.52	37.48	2.36	16.90	46.60	2.16	17.68	60.52	1.96	17.06	69.64
4.77	20.18	19.48	3.47	19.37	29.92	2.77	17.73	37.96	2.37	17.10	47.20	2.17	17.87	61.24	1.97	17.24	70.48
4.78	20.42	19.72	3.48	19.59	30.28	2.78	17.94	38.44	2.38	17.30	47.80	2.18	18.06	61.96	1.98	17.42	71.32
4.79	20.67	19.96	3.49	19.81	30.64	2.79	18.15	38.92	2.39	17.50	48.40	2.19	18.25	62.68	1.99	17.61	72.16
4.80	20.91	20.20	3.50	20.03	31.00	2.80	18.36	39.40	2.40	17.70	49.00	2.20	18.44	63.40	2.00	17.79	73.00
4.81	21.15	20.44	3.51	20.25	31.36	2.81	18.57	39.88	2.41	17.89	49.60	2.21	18.63	64.12	2.01	17.97	73.84
4.82	21.39	20.68	3.52	20.48	31.72	2.82	18.78	40.36	2.42	18.09	50.20	2.22	18.82	64.84	2.02	18.15	74.68
4.83	21.63	20.92	3.53	20.70	32.08	2.83	18.99	40.84	2.43	18.29	50.80	2.23	19.01	65.56	2.03	18.34	75.52
4.84	21.87	21.16	3.54	20.92	32.44	2.84	19.19	41.32	2.44	18.49	51.40	2.24	19.20	66.28	2.04	18.52	76.36
4.85	22.11	21.40	3.55	21.14	32.80	2.85	19.40	41.80	2.45	18.69	52.00	2.25	19.38	67.00	2.05	18.70	77.20
4.86	22.35	21.64	3.56	21.35	33.16	2.86	19.61	42.28	2.46	18.89	52.60	2.26	19.57	67.72	2.06	18.88	78.04
4.87	22.59	21.88	3.57	21.57	33.52	2.87	19.82	42.76	2.47	19.08	53.20	2.27	19.76	68.44	2.07	19.06	78.88
4.88	22.83	22.12	3.58	21.79	33.88	2.88	20.02	43.24	2.48	19.28	53.80	2.28	19.94	69.16	2.08	19.24	79.72
4.89	23.07	22.36	3.59	22.01	34.24	2.89	20.23	43.72	2.49	19.48	54.40	2.29	20.13	69.88	2.09	19.42	80.56
4.90	23.31	22.60	3.60	22.23	34.60	2.90	20.44	44.20	2.50	19.67	55.00	2.30	20.32	70.60	2.10	19.60	81.40
4.91	23.55	22.84	3.61	22.45	34.96	2.91	20.64	44.68	2.51	19.87	55.60	2.31	20.50	71.32	2.11	19.78	82.24
4.92	23.79	23.08	3.62	22.67	35.32	2.92	20.85	45.16	2.52	20.06	56.20	2.32	20.69	72.04	2.12	19.96	83.08
4.93	24.03	23.32	3.63	22.89	35.68	2.93	21.05	45.64	2.53	20.26	56.80	2.33	20.87	72.76	2.13	20.14	83.92
4.94	24.27	23.56	3.64	23.10	36.04	2.94	21.26	46.12	2.54	20.45	57.40	2.34	21.06	73.48	2.14	20.31	84.76
4.95	24.51	23.80	3.65	23.32	36.40	2.95	21.46	46.60	2.55	20.65	58.00	2.35	21.24	74.20	2.15	20.49	85.60
4.96	24.74	24.04	3.66	23.54	36.76	2.96	21.67	47.08	2.56	20.84	58.60	2.36	21.43	74.92	2.16	20.67	86.44
4.97	24.98	24.28	3.67	23.76	37.12	2.97	21.87	47.56	2.57	21.04	59.20	2.37	21.61	75.64	2.17	20.85	87.28
4.98	25.22	24.52	3.68	23.97	37.48	2.98	22.07	48.04	2.58	21.23	59.80	2.38	21.79	76.36	2.18	21.02	88.12
4.99	25.46	24.76	3.69	24.19	37.84	2.99	22.28	48.52	2.59	21.42	60.40	2.39	21.98	77.08	2.19	21.20	88.96

Description: This table shows the Annual Percentage Rate and finance charge per $100 for monthly lease payments.

Example: A 1.30% lease payment for 8 years is equivalent to an APR of 6.81%. The charge per $100 cost is $ 29.80.

8 yr MONTHLY PAYT	APR	CHARGE	9 yr MONTHLY PAYT	APR	CHARGE	10 yr MONTHLY PAYT	APR	CHARGE	12 yr MONTHLY PAYT	APR	CHARGE	15 yr MONTHLY PAYT	APR	CHARGE	20 yr MONTHLY PAYT	APR	CHARGE
1.30	6.81	29.80	1.20	6.93	34.60	1.10	6.62	37.00	1.00	7.10	49.00	.80	5.65	49.00	.70	6.02	73.00
1.31	7.02	30.76	1.21	7.14	35.68	1.11	6.82	38.20	1.01	7.29	50.44	.81	5.84	50.80	.71	6.20	75.40
1.32	7.22	31.72	1.22	7.34	36.76	1.12	7.02	39.40	1.02	7.48	51.88	.82	6.03	52.60	.72	6.37	77.80
1.33	7.43	32.68	1.23	7.53	37.84	1.13	7.21	40.60	1.03	7.67	53.32	.83	6.21	54.40	.73	6.54	80.20
1.34	7.63	33.64	1.24	7.73	38.92	1.14	7.41	41.80	1.04	7.86	54.76	.84	6.40	56.20	.74	6.71	82.60
1.35	7.83	34.60	1.25	7.93	40.00	1.15	7.60	43.00	1.05	8.04	56.20	.85	6.58	58.00	.75	6.88	85.00
1.36	8.03	35.56	1.26	8.13	41.08	1.16	7.80	44.20	1.06	8.23	57.64	.86	6.77	59.80	.76	7.05	87.40
1.37	8.24	36.52	1.27	8.33	42.16	1.17	7.99	45.40	1.07	8.41	59.08	.87	6.95	61.60	.77	7.22	89.80
1.38	8.44	37.48	1.28	8.52	43.24	1.18	8.19	46.60	1.08	8.60	60.52	.88	7.13	63.40	.78	7.39	92.20
1.39	8.64	38.44	1.29	8.72	44.32	1.19	8.38	47.80	1.09	8.78	61.96	.89	7.31	65.20	.79	7.55	94.60
1.40	8.84	39.40	1.30	8.91	45.40	1.20	8.57	49.00	1.10	8.96	63.40	.90	7.49	67.00	.80	7.72	97.00
1.41	9.04	40.36	1.31	9.11	46.48	1.21	8.76	50.20	1.11	9.14	64.84	.91	7.67	68.80	.81	7.88	99.40
1.42	9.23	41.32	1.32	9.30	47.56	1.22	8.95	51.40	1.12	9.32	66.28	.92	7.84	70.60	.82	8.05	101.80
1.43	9.43	42.28	1.33	9.49	48.64	1.23	9.14	52.60	1.13	9.50	67.72	.93	8.02	72.40	.83	8.21	104.20
1.44	9.63	43.24	1.34	9.68	49.72	1.24	9.33	53.80	1.14	9.68	69.16	.94	8.20	74.20	.84	8.37	106.60
1.45	9.82	44.20	1.35	9.87	50.80	1.25	9.52	55.00	1.15	9.86	70.60	.95	8.37	76.00	.85	8.53	109.00
1.46	10.02	45.16	1.36	10.06	51.88	1.26	9.70	56.20	1.16	10.04	72.04	.96	8.55	77.80	.86	8.70	111.40
1.47	10.22	46.12	1.37	10.25	52.96	1.27	9.89	57.40	1.17	10.22	73.48	.97	8.72	79.60	.87	8.86	113.80
1.48	10.41	47.08	1.38	10.44	54.04	1.28	10.08	58.60	1.18	10.39	74.92	.98	8.89	81.40	.88	9.01	116.20
1.49	10.60	48.04	1.39	10.63	55.12	1.29	10.26	59.80	1.19	10.57	76.36	.99	9.06	83.20	.89	9.17	118.60
1.50	10.80	49.00	1.40	10.82	56.20	1.30	10.45	61.00	1.20	10.75	77.80	1.00	9.24	85.00	.90	9.33	121.00
1.51	10.99	49.96	1.41	11.01	57.28	1.31	10.63	62.20	1.21	10.92	79.24	1.01	9.41	86.80	.91	9.49	123.40
1.52	11.18	50.92	1.42	11.20	58.36	1.32	10.81	63.40	1.22	11.10	80.68	1.02	9.58	88.60	.92	9.65	125.80
1.53	11.37	51.88	1.43	11.38	59.44	1.33	11.00	64.60	1.23	11.27	82.12	1.03	9.74	90.40	.93	9.80	128.20
1.54	11.56	52.84	1.44	11.57	60.52	1.34	11.18	65.80	1.24	11.44	83.56	1.04	9.91	92.20	.94	9.96	130.60
1.55	11.76	53.80	1.45	11.75	61.60	1.35	11.36	67.00	1.25	11.62	85.00	1.05	10.08	94.00	.95	10.11	133.00
1.56	11.95	54.76	1.46	11.94	62.68	1.36	11.54	68.20	1.26	11.79	86.44	1.06	10.25	95.80	.96	10.27	135.40
1.57	12.14	55.72	1.47	12.12	63.76	1.37	11.72	69.40	1.27	11.96	87.88	1.07	10.42	97.60	.97	10.42	137.80
1.58	12.32	56.68	1.48	12.31	64.84	1.38	11.90	70.60	1.28	12.13	89.32	1.08	10.58	99.40	.98	10.57	140.20
1.59	12.51	57.64	1.49	12.49	65.92	1.39	12.08	71.80	1.29	12.30	90.76	1.09	10.75	101.20	.99	10.73	142.60
1.60	12.70	58.60	1.50	12.67	67.00	1.40	12.26	73.00	1.30	12.47	92.20	1.10	10.91	103.00	1.00	10.88	145.00
1.61	12.89	59.56	1.51	12.86	68.08	1.41	12.44	74.20	1.31	12.64	93.64	1.11	11.08	104.80	1.01	11.03	147.40
1.62	13.08	60.52	1.52	13.04	69.16	1.42	12.62	75.40	1.32	12.81	95.08	1.12	11.24	106.60	1.02	11.18	149.80
1.63	13.26	61.48	1.53	13.22	70.24	1.43	12.80	76.60	1.33	12.98	96.52	1.13	11.40	108.40	1.03	11.33	152.20
1.64	13.45	62.44	1.54	13.40	71.32	1.44	12.97	77.80	1.34	13.15	97.96	1.14	11.57	110.20	1.04	11.48	154.60
1.65	13.63	63.40	1.55	13.58	72.40	1.45	13.15	79.00	1.35	13.31	99.40	1.15	11.73	112.00	1.05	11.63	157.00
1.66	13.82	64.36	1.56	13.76	73.48	1.46	13.33	80.20	1.36	13.48	100.84	1.16	11.89	113.80	1.06	11.78	159.40
1.67	14.00	65.32	1.57	13.94	74.56	1.47	13.50	81.40	1.37	13.65	102.28	1.17	12.05	115.60	1.07	11.93	161.80
1.68	14.19	66.28	1.58	14.12	75.64	1.48	13.68	82.60	1.38	13.81	103.72	1.18	12.21	117.40	1.08	12.08	164.20
1.69	14.37	67.24	1.59	14.30	76.72	1.49	13.85	83.80	1.39	13.98	105.16	1.19	12.37	119.20	1.09	12.23	166.60
1.70	14.56	68.20	1.60	14.47	77.80	1.50	14.03	85.00	1.40	14.15	106.60	1.20	12.53	121.00	1.10	12.38	169.00
1.71	14.74	69.16	1.61	14.65	78.88	1.51	14.20	86.20	1.41	14.31	108.04	1.21	12.69	122.80	1.11	12.52	171.40
1.72	14.92	70.12	1.62	14.83	79.96	1.52	14.37	87.40	1.42	14.48	109.48	1.22	12.85	124.60	1.12	12.67	173.80
1.73	15.10	71.08	1.63	15.01	81.04	1.53	14.55	88.60	1.43	14.64	110.92	1.23	13.01	126.40	1.13	12.82	176.20
1.74	15.29	72.04	1.64	15.18	82.12	1.54	14.72	89.80	1.44	14.80	112.36	1.24	13.17	128.20	1.14	12.96	178.60
1.75	15.47	73.00	1.65	15.36	83.20	1.55	14.89	91.00	1.45	14.97	113.80	1.25	13.32	130.00	1.15	13.11	181.00
1.76	15.65	73.96	1.66	15.53	84.28	1.56	15.06	92.20	1.46	15.13	115.24	1.26	13.48	131.80	1.16	13.26	183.40
1.77	15.83	74.92	1.67	15.71	85.36	1.57	15.23	93.40	1.47	15.29	116.68	1.27	13.64	133.60	1.17	13.40	185.80
1.78	16.01	75.88	1.68	15.88	86.44	1.58	15.40	94.60	1.48	15.45	118.12	1.28	13.79	135.40	1.18	13.55	188.20
1.79	16.19	76.84	1.69	16.06	87.52	1.59	15.58	95.80	1.49	15.62	119.56	1.29	13.95	137.20	1.19	13.69	190.60
1.80	16.37	77.80	1.70	16.23	88.60	1.60	15.74	97.00	1.50	15.78	121.00	1.30	14.10	139.00	1.20	13.83	193.00
1.81	16.55	78.76	1.71	16.41	89.68	1.61	15.91	98.20	1.51	15.94	122.44	1.31	14.26	140.80	1.21	13.98	195.40
1.82	16.72	79.72	1.72	16.58	90.76	1.62	16.08	99.40	1.52	16.10	123.88	1.32	14.41	142.60	1.22	14.12	197.80
1.83	16.90	80.68	1.73	16.75	91.84	1.63	16.25	100.60	1.53	16.26	125.32	1.33	14.57	144.40	1.23	14.27	200.20
1.84	17.08	81.64	1.74	16.92	92.92	1.64	16.42	101.80	1.54	16.42	126.76	1.34	14.72	146.20	1.24	14.41	202.60
1.85	17.26	82.60	1.75	17.10	94.00	1.65	16.59	103.00	1.55	16.58	128.20	1.35	14.87	148.00	1.25	14.55	205.00
1.86	17.43	83.56	1.76	17.27	95.08	1.66	16.76	104.20	1.56	16.74	129.64	1.36	15.03	149.80	1.26	14.70	207.40
1.87	17.61	84.52	1.77	17.44	96.16	1.67	16.92	105.40	1.57	16.90	131.08	1.37	15.18	151.60	1.27	14.84	209.80
1.88	17.79	85.48	1.78	17.61	97.24	1.68	17.09	106.60	1.58	17.05	132.52	1.38	15.33	153.40	1.28	14.98	212.20
1.89	17.96	86.44	1.79	17.78	98.32	1.69	17.26	107.80	1.59	17.21	133.96	1.39	15.49	155.20	1.29	15.12	214.60
1.90	18.14	87.40	1.80	17.95	99.40	1.70	17.42	109.00	1.60	17.37	135.40	1.40	15.64	157.00	1.30	15.26	217.00
1.91	18.31	88.36	1.81	18.12	100.48	1.71	17.59	110.20	1.61	17.53	136.84	1.41	15.79	158.80	1.31	15.40	219.40
1.92	18.49	89.32	1.82	18.29	101.56	1.72	17.76	111.40	1.62	17.69	138.28	1.42	15.94	160.60	1.32	15.55	221.80
1.93	18.66	90.28	1.83	18.46	102.64	1.73	17.92	112.60	1.63	17.84	139.72	1.43	16.09	162.40	1.33	15.69	224.20
1.94	18.84	91.24	1.84	18.63	103.72	1.74	18.09	113.80	1.64	18.00	141.16	1.44	16.24	164.20	1.34	15.83	226.60
1.95	19.01	92.20	1.85	18.80	104.80	1.75	18.25	115.00	1.65	18.16	142.60	1.45	16.39	166.00	1.35	15.97	229.00
1.96	19.19	93.16	1.86	18.97	105.88	1.76	18.41	116.20	1.66	18.31	144.04	1.46	16.54	167.80	1.36	16.11	231.40
1.97	19.36	94.12	1.87	19.13	106.96	1.77	18.58	117.40	1.67	18.47	145.48	1.47	16.69	169.60	1.37	16.25	233.80
1.98	19.53	95.08	1.88	19.30	108.04	1.78	18.74	118.60	1.68	18.62	146.92	1.48	16.84	171.40	1.38	16.39	236.20
1.99	19.70	96.04	1.89	19.47	109.12	1.79	18.91	119.80	1.69	18.78	148.36	1.49	16.99	173.20	1.39	16.53	238.60

Description: This table shows the Annual Percentage Rate and finance charge per $100 for monthly lease payments.

Example: A 4.30% lease payment for 2 years is equivalent to an APR of 13.10%. The charge per $100 cost is $ 13.20.

2 yr MONTHLY PAYT	APR	CHARGE	3 yr MONTHLY PAYT	APR	CHARGE	4 yr MONTHLY PAYT	APR	CHARGE	5 yr MONTHLY PAYT	APR	CHARGE	6 yr MONTHLY PAYT	APR	CHARGE	7 yr MONTHLY PAYT	APR	CHARGE
4.30	13.10	13.20	3.00	11.35	18.00	2.30	9.41	20.40	1.90	8.69	24.00	1.70	9.56	32.40	1.50	8.99	36.00
4.31	13.33	13.44	3.01	11.57	18.36	2.31	9.63	20.88	1.91	8.90	24.60	1.71	9.76	33.12	1.51	9.18	36.84
4.32	13.57	13.68	3.02	11.79	18.72	2.32	9.84	21.36	1.92	9.11	25.20	1.72	9.96	33.84	1.52	9.38	37.68
4.33	13.80	13.92	3.03	12.01	19.08	2.33	10.05	21.84	1.93	9.32	25.80	1.73	10.16	34.56	1.53	9.58	38.52
4.34	14.04	14.16	3.04	12.23	19.44	2.34	10.27	22.32	1.94	9.52	26.40	1.74	10.36	35.28	1.54	9.77	39.36
4.35	14.27	14.40	3.05	12.45	19.80	2.35	10.48	22.80	1.95	9.73	27.00	1.75	10.56	36.00	1.55	9.97	40.20
4.36	14.50	14.64	3.06	12.67	20.16	2.36	10.69	23.28	1.96	9.94	27.60	1.76	10.75	36.72	1.56	10.16	41.04
4.37	14.74	14.88	3.07	12.89	20.52	2.37	10.90	23.76	1.97	10.14	28.20	1.77	10.95	37.44	1.57	10.36	41.88
4.38	14.97	15.12	3.08	13.11	20.88	2.38	11.11	24.24	1.98	10.35	28.80	1.78	11.15	38.16	1.58	10.55	42.72
4.39	15.20	15.36	3.09	13.33	21.24	2.39	11.33	24.72	1.99	10.55	29.40	1.79	11.35	38.88	1.59	10.74	43.56
4.40	15.44	15.60	3.10	13.55	21.60	2.40	11.54	25.20	2.00	10.76	30.00	1.80	11.54	39.60	1.60	10.93	44.40
4.41	15.67	15.84	3.11	13.77	21.96	2.41	11.75	25.68	2.01	10.96	30.60	1.81	11.74	40.32	1.61	11.13	45.24
4.42	15.90	16.08	3.12	13.99	22.32	2.42	11.96	26.16	2.02	11.17	31.20	1.82	11.94	41.04	1.62	11.32	46.08
4.43	16.14	16.32	3.13	14.20	22.68	2.43	12.17	26.64	2.03	11.37	31.80	1.83	12.13	41.76	1.63	11.51	46.92
4.44	16.37	16.56	3.14	14.42	23.04	2.44	12.38	27.12	2.04	11.57	32.40	1.84	12.33	42.48	1.64	11.70	47.76
4.45	16.60	16.80	3.15	14.64	23.40	2.45	12.59	27.60	2.05	11.78	33.00	1.85	12.52	43.20	1.65	11.89	48.60
4.46	16.83	17.04	3.16	14.86	23.76	2.46	12.80	28.08	2.06	11.98	33.60	1.86	12.72	43.92	1.66	12.08	49.44
4.47	17.07	17.28	3.17	15.07	24.12	2.47	13.01	28.56	2.07	12.18	34.20	1.87	12.91	44.64	1.67	12.27	50.28
4.48	17.30	17.52	3.18	15.29	24.48	2.48	13.21	29.04	2.08	12.38	34.80	1.88	13.11	45.36	1.68	12.46	51.12
4.49	17.53	17.76	3.19	15.51	24.84	2.49	13.42	29.52	2.09	12.58	35.40	1.89	13.30	46.08	1.69	12.65	51.96
4.50	17.76	18.00	3.20	15.72	25.20	2.50	13.63	30.00	2.10	12.79	36.00	1.90	13.49	46.80	1.70	12.84	52.80
4.51	17.99	18.24	3.21	15.94	25.56	2.51	13.84	30.48	2.11	12.99	36.60	1.91	13.68	47.52	1.71	13.02	53.64
4.52	18.23	18.48	3.22	16.16	25.92	2.52	14.05	30.96	2.12	13.19	37.20	1.92	13.88	48.24	1.72	13.21	54.48
4.53	18.46	18.72	3.23	16.37	26.28	2.53	14.25	31.44	2.13	13.39	37.80	1.93	14.07	48.96	1.73	13.40	55.32
4.54	18.69	18.96	3.24	16.59	26.64	2.54	14.46	31.92	2.14	13.59	38.40	1.94	14.26	49.68	1.74	13.59	56.16
4.55	18.92	19.20	3.25	16.80	27.00	2.55	14.67	32.40	2.15	13.79	39.00	1.95	14.45	50.40	1.75	13.77	57.00
4.56	19.15	19.44	3.26	17.02	27.36	2.56	14.87	32.88	2.16	13.99	39.60	1.96	14.64	51.12	1.76	13.96	57.84
4.57	19.38	19.68	3.27	17.24	27.72	2.57	15.08	33.36	2.17	14.19	40.20	1.97	14.83	51.84	1.77	14.14	58.68
4.58	19.61	19.92	3.28	17.45	28.08	2.58	15.29	33.84	2.18	14.38	40.80	1.98	15.02	52.56	1.78	14.33	59.52
4.59	19.85	20.16	3.29	17.67	28.44	2.59	15.49	34.32	2.19	14.58	41.40	1.99	15.21	53.28	1.79	14.51	60.36
4.60	20.08	20.40	3.30	17.88	28.80	2.60	15.70	34.80	2.20	14.78	42.00	2.00	15.40	54.00	1.80	14.70	61.20
4.61	20.31	20.64	3.31	18.09	29.16	2.61	15.90	35.28	2.21	14.98	42.60	2.01	15.59	54.72	1.81	14.88	62.04
4.62	20.54	20.88	3.32	18.31	29.52	2.62	16.11	35.76	2.22	15.18	43.20	2.02	15.78	55.44	1.82	15.07	62.88
4.63	20.77	21.12	3.33	18.52	29.88	2.63	16.31	36.24	2.23	15.37	43.80	2.03	15.97	56.16	1.83	15.25	63.72
4.64	21.00	21.36	3.34	18.74	30.24	2.64	16.52	36.72	2.24	15.57	44.40	2.04	16.16	56.88	1.84	15.43	64.56
4.65	21.23	21.60	3.35	18.95	30.60	2.65	16.72	37.20	2.25	15.77	45.00	2.05	16.35	57.60	1.85	15.61	65.40
4.66	21.46	21.84	3.36	19.16	30.96	2.66	16.92	37.68	2.26	15.96	45.60	2.06	16.53	58.32	1.86	15.79	66.24
4.67	21.69	22.08	3.37	19.38	31.32	2.67	17.13	38.16	2.27	16.16	46.20	2.07	16.72	59.04	1.87	15.98	67.08
4.68	21.92	22.32	3.38	19.59	31.68	2.68	17.33	38.64	2.28	16.35	46.80	2.08	16.91	59.76	1.88	16.16	67.92
4.69	22.15	22.56	3.39	19.80	32.04	2.69	17.53	39.12	2.29	16.55	47.40	2.09	17.09	60.48	1.89	16.34	68.76
4.70	22.38	22.80	3.40	20.02	32.40	2.70	17.74	39.60	2.30	16.74	48.00	2.10	17.28	61.20	1.90	16.52	69.60
4.71	22.61	23.04	3.41	20.23	32.76	2.71	17.94	40.08	2.31	16.94	48.60	2.11	17.47	61.92	1.91	16.70	70.44
4.72	22.84	23.28	3.42	20.44	33.12	2.72	18.14	40.56	2.32	17.13	49.20	2.12	17.65	62.64	1.92	16.88	71.28
4.73	23.07	23.52	3.43	20.65	33.48	2.73	18.34	41.04	2.33	17.33	49.80	2.13	17.84	63.36	1.93	17.06	72.12
4.74	23.30	23.76	3.44	20.87	33.84	2.74	18.55	41.52	2.34	17.52	50.40	2.14	18.02	64.08	1.94	17.24	72.96
4.75	23.53	24.00	3.45	21.08	34.20	2.75	18.75	42.00	2.35	17.71	51.00	2.15	18.21	64.80	1.95	17.42	73.80
4.76	23.75	24.24	3.46	21.29	34.56	2.76	18.95	42.48	2.36	17.91	51.60	2.16	18.39	65.52	1.96	17.60	74.64
4.77	23.98	24.48	3.47	21.50	34.92	2.77	19.15	42.96	2.37	18.10	52.20	2.17	18.58	66.24	1.97	17.78	75.48
4.78	24.21	24.72	3.48	21.71	35.28	2.78	19.35	43.44	2.38	18.29	52.80	2.18	18.76	66.96	1.98	17.96	76.32
4.79	24.44	24.96	3.49	21.92	35.64	2.79	19.55	43.92	2.39	18.48	53.40	2.19	18.94	67.68	1.99	18.14	77.16
4.80	24.67	25.20	3.50	22.13	36.00	2.80	19.75	44.40	2.40	18.68	54.00	2.20	19.13	68.40	2.00	18.31	78.00
4.81	24.90	25.44	3.51	22.34	36.36	2.81	19.95	44.88	2.41	18.87	54.60	2.21	19.31	69.12	2.01	18.49	78.84
4.82	25.13	25.68	3.52	22.56	36.72	2.82	20.15	45.36	2.42	19.06	55.20	2.22	19.49	69.84	2.02	18.67	79.68
4.83	25.36	25.92	3.53	22.77	37.08	2.83	20.35	45.84	2.43	19.25	55.80	2.23	19.68	70.56	2.03	18.85	80.52
4.84	25.58	26.16	3.54	22.98	37.44	2.84	20.55	46.32	2.44	19.44	56.40	2.24	19.86	71.28	2.04	19.02	81.36
4.85	25.81	26.40	3.55	23.19	37.80	2.85	20.75	46.80	2.45	19.63	57.00	2.25	20.04	72.00	2.05	19.20	82.20
4.86	26.04	26.64	3.56	23.40	38.16	2.86	20.95	47.28	2.46	19.82	57.60	2.26	20.22	72.72	2.06	19.38	83.04
4.87	26.27	26.88	3.57	23.61	38.52	2.87	21.15	47.76	2.47	20.01	58.20	2.27	20.40	73.44	2.07	19.55	83.88
4.88	26.50	27.12	3.58	23.82	38.88	2.88	21.35	48.24	2.48	20.21	58.80	2.28	20.59	74.16	2.08	19.73	84.72
4.89	26.72	27.36	3.59	24.03	39.24	2.89	21.55	48.72	2.49	20.39	59.40	2.29	20.77	74.88	2.09	19.90	85.56
4.90	26.95	27.60	3.60	24.23	39.60	2.90	21.75	49.20	2.50	20.58	60.00	2.30	20.95	75.60	2.10	20.08	86.40
4.91	27.18	27.84	3.61	24.44	39.96	2.91	21.94	49.68	2.51	20.77	60.60	2.31	21.13	76.32	2.11	20.25	87.24
4.92	27.41	28.08	3.62	24.65	40.32	2.92	22.14	50.16	2.52	20.96	61.20	2.32	21.31	77.04	2.12	20.43	88.08
4.93	27.63	28.32	3.63	24.86	40.68	2.93	22.34	50.64	2.53	21.15	61.80	2.33	21.49	77.76	2.13	20.60	88.92
4.94	27.86	28.56	3.64	25.07	41.04	2.94	22.54	51.12	2.54	21.34	62.40	2.34	21.67	78.48	2.14	20.78	89.76
4.95	28.09	28.80	3.65	25.28	41.40	2.95	22.74	51.60	2.55	21.53	63.00	2.35	21.85	79.20	2.15	20.95	90.60
4.96	28.32	29.04	3.66	25.49	41.76	2.96	22.93	52.08	2.56	21.72	63.60	2.36	22.03	79.92	2.16	21.12	91.44
4.97	28.54	29.28	3.67	25.70	42.12	2.97	23.13	52.56	2.57	21.91	64.20	2.37	22.21	80.64	2.17	21.30	92.28
4.98	28.77	29.52	3.68	25.90	42.48	2.98	23.33	53.04	2.58	22.09	64.80	2.38	22.38	81.36	2.18	21.47	93.12
4.99	29.00	29.76	3.69	26.11	42.84	2.99	23.52	53.52	2.59	22.28	65.40	2.39	22.56	82.08	2.19	21.64	93.96

Description: This table shows the Annual Percentage Rate and finance charge per $100 for monthly lease payments.

Example: A 1.30% lease payment for 8 years is equivalent to an APR of 7.58%. The charge per $100 cost is $ 34.80.

8 yr MONTHLY PAYT	APR	CHARGE	9 yr MONTHLY PAYT	APR	CHARGE	10 yr MONTHLY PAYT	APR	CHARGE	12 yr MONTHLY PAYT	APR	CHARGE	15 yr MONTHLY PAYT	APR	CHARGE	20 yr MONTHLY PAYT	APR	CHARGE
1.30	7.58	34.80	1.20	7.58	39.60	1.10	7.18	42.00	1.00	7.50	54.00	.80	5.97	54.00	.70	6.21	78.00
1.31	7.78	35.76	1.21	7.77	40.68	1.11	7.37	43.20	1.01	7.69	55.44	.81	6.15	55.80	.71	6.38	80.40
1.32	7.97	36.72	1.22	7.96	41.76	1.12	7.56	44.40	1.02	7.87	56.88	.82	6.33	57.60	.72	6.54	82.80
1.33	8.17	37.68	1.23	8.15	42.84	1.13	7.75	45.60	1.03	8.05	58.32	.83	6.51	59.40	.73	6.71	85.20
1.34	8.36	38.64	1.24	8.34	43.92	1.14	7.94	46.80	1.04	8.23	59.76	.84	6.69	61.20	.74	6.88	87.60
1.35	8.56	39.60	1.25	8.53	45.00	1.15	8.12	48.00	1.05	8.41	61.20	.85	6.87	63.00	.75	7.04	90.00
1.36	8.75	40.56	1.26	8.72	46.08	1.16	8.31	49.20	1.06	8.59	62.64	.86	7.05	64.80	.76	7.21	92.40
1.37	8.94	41.52	1.27	8.91	47.16	1.17	8.50	50.40	1.07	8.77	64.08	.87	7.22	66.60	.77	7.37	94.80
1.38	9.13	42.48	1.28	9.10	48.24	1.18	8.68	51.60	1.08	8.95	65.52	.88	7.40	68.40	.78	7.54	97.20
1.39	9.33	43.44	1.29	9.29	49.32	1.19	8.87	52.80	1.09	9.12	66.96	.89	7.57	70.20	.79	7.70	99.60
1.40	9.52	44.40	1.30	9.47	50.40	1.20	9.05	54.00	1.10	9.30	68.40	.90	7.75	72.00	.80	7.86	102.00
1.41	9.71	45.36	1.31	9.66	51.48	1.21	9.24	55.20	1.11	9.48	69.84	.91	7.92	73.80	.81	8.02	104.40
1.42	9.90	46.32	1.32	9.85	52.56	1.22	9.42	56.40	1.12	9.65	71.28	.92	8.09	75.60	.82	8.18	106.80
1.43	10.09	47.28	1.33	10.03	53.64	1.23	9.60	57.60	1.13	9.83	72.72	.93	8.27	77.40	.83	8.34	109.20
1.44	10.28	48.24	1.34	10.22	54.72	1.24	9.78	58.80	1.14	10.00	74.16	.94	8.44	79.20	.84	8.50	111.60
1.45	10.47	49.20	1.35	10.40	55.80	1.25	9.97	60.00	1.15	10.17	75.60	.95	8.61	81.00	.85	8.66	114.00
1.46	10.65	50.16	1.36	10.58	56.88	1.26	10.15	61.20	1.16	10.35	77.04	.96	8.78	82.80	.86	8.82	116.40
1.47	10.84	51.12	1.37	10.77	57.96	1.27	10.33	62.40	1.17	10.52	78.48	.97	8.95	84.60	.87	8.97	118.80
1.48	11.03	52.08	1.38	10.95	59.04	1.28	10.51	63.60	1.18	10.69	79.92	.98	9.11	86.40	.88	9.13	121.20
1.49	11.22	53.04	1.39	11.13	60.12	1.29	10.69	64.80	1.19	10.86	81.36	.99	9.28	88.20	.89	9.29	123.60
1.50	11.40	54.00	1.40	11.31	61.20	1.30	10.87	66.00	1.20	11.04	82.80	1.00	9.45	90.00	.90	9.44	126.00
1.51	11.59	54.96	1.41	11.50	62.28	1.31	11.04	67.20	1.21	11.21	84.24	1.01	9.61	91.80	.91	9.60	128.40
1.52	11.77	55.92	1.42	11.68	63.36	1.32	11.22	68.40	1.22	11.38	85.68	1.02	9.78	93.60	.92	9.75	130.80
1.53	11.96	56.88	1.43	11.86	64.44	1.33	11.40	69.60	1.23	11.55	87.12	1.03	9.95	95.40	.93	9.90	133.20
1.54	12.14	57.84	1.44	12.04	65.52	1.34	11.58	70.80	1.24	11.71	88.56	1.04	10.11	97.20	.94	10.06	135.60
1.55	12.33	58.80	1.45	12.22	66.60	1.35	11.75	72.00	1.25	11.88	90.00	1.05	10.27	99.00	.95	10.21	138.00
1.56	12.51	59.76	1.46	12.40	67.68	1.36	11.93	73.20	1.26	12.05	91.44	1.06	10.44	100.80	.96	10.36	140.40
1.57	12.69	60.72	1.47	12.58	68.76	1.37	12.10	74.40	1.27	12.22	92.88	1.07	10.60	102.60	.97	10.51	142.80
1.58	12.88	61.68	1.48	12.75	69.84	1.38	12.28	75.60	1.28	12.39	94.32	1.08	10.76	104.40	.98	10.66	145.20
1.59	13.06	62.64	1.49	12.93	70.92	1.39	12.45	76.80	1.29	12.55	95.76	1.09	10.93	106.20	.99	10.82	147.60
1.60	13.24	63.60	1.50	13.11	72.00	1.40	12.63	78.00	1.30	12.72	97.20	1.10	11.09	108.00	1.00	10.97	150.00
1.61	13.42	64.56	1.51	13.29	73.08	1.41	12.80	79.20	1.31	12.88	98.64	1.11	11.25	109.80	1.01	11.12	152.40
1.62	13.60	65.52	1.52	13.46	74.16	1.42	12.98	80.40	1.32	13.05	100.08	1.12	11.41	111.60	1.02	11.27	154.80
1.63	13.79	66.48	1.53	13.64	75.24	1.43	13.15	81.60	1.33	13.21	101.52	1.13	11.57	113.40	1.03	11.41	157.20
1.64	13.97	67.44	1.54	13.81	76.32	1.44	13.32	82.80	1.34	13.38	102.96	1.14	11.73	115.20	1.04	11.56	159.60
1.65	14.15	68.40	1.55	13.99	77.40	1.45	13.49	84.00	1.35	13.54	104.40	1.15	11.89	117.00	1.05	11.71	162.00
1.66	14.33	69.36	1.56	14.16	78.48	1.46	13.66	85.20	1.36	13.71	105.84	1.16	12.05	118.80	1.06	11.86	164.40
1.67	14.50	70.32	1.57	14.34	79.56	1.47	13.84	86.40	1.37	13.87	107.28	1.17	12.21	120.60	1.07	12.01	166.80
1.68	14.68	71.28	1.58	14.51	80.64	1.48	14.01	87.60	1.38	14.03	108.72	1.18	12.36	122.40	1.08	12.15	169.20
1.69	14.86	72.24	1.59	14.69	81.72	1.49	14.18	88.80	1.39	14.20	110.16	1.19	12.52	124.20	1.09	12.30	171.60
1.70	15.04	73.20	1.60	14.86	82.80	1.50	14.35	90.00	1.40	14.36	111.60	1.20	12.68	126.00	1.10	12.45	174.00
1.71	15.22	74.16	1.61	15.03	83.88	1.51	14.52	91.20	1.41	14.52	113.04	1.21	12.83	127.80	1.11	12.59	176.40
1.72	15.39	75.12	1.62	15.21	84.96	1.52	14.69	92.40	1.42	14.68	114.48	1.22	12.99	129.60	1.12	12.74	178.80
1.73	15.57	76.08	1.63	15.38	86.04	1.53	14.85	93.60	1.43	14.84	115.92	1.23	13.15	131.40	1.13	12.88	181.20
1.74	15.75	77.04	1.64	15.55	87.12	1.54	15.02	94.80	1.44	15.00	117.36	1.24	13.30	133.20	1.14	13.03	183.60
1.75	15.92	78.00	1.65	15.72	88.20	1.55	15.19	96.00	1.45	15.16	118.80	1.25	13.46	135.00	1.15	13.17	186.00
1.76	16.10	78.96	1.66	15.89	89.28	1.56	15.36	97.20	1.46	15.32	120.24	1.26	13.61	136.80	1.16	13.32	188.40
1.77	16.28	79.92	1.67	16.06	90.36	1.57	15.53	98.40	1.47	15.48	121.68	1.27	13.77	138.60	1.17	13.46	190.80
1.78	16.45	80.88	1.68	16.23	91.44	1.58	15.69	99.60	1.48	15.64	123.12	1.28	13.92	140.40	1.18	13.60	193.20
1.79	16.63	81.84	1.69	16.40	92.52	1.59	15.86	100.80	1.49	15.80	124.56	1.29	14.07	142.20	1.19	13.75	195.60
1.80	16.80	82.80	1.70	16.57	93.60	1.60	16.03	102.00	1.50	15.96	126.00	1.30	14.23	144.00	1.20	13.89	198.00
1.81	16.98	83.76	1.71	16.74	94.68	1.61	16.19	103.20	1.51	16.12	127.44	1.31	14.38	145.80	1.21	14.03	200.40
1.82	17.15	84.72	1.72	16.91	95.76	1.62	16.36	104.40	1.52	16.28	128.88	1.32	14.53	147.60	1.22	14.18	202.80
1.83	17.32	85.68	1.73	17.08	96.84	1.63	16.52	105.60	1.53	16.43	130.32	1.33	14.68	149.40	1.23	14.32	205.20
1.84	17.50	86.64	1.74	17.25	97.92	1.64	16.69	106.80	1.54	16.59	131.76	1.34	14.84	151.20	1.24	14.46	207.60
1.85	17.67	87.60	1.75	17.42	99.00	1.65	16.85	108.00	1.55	16.75	133.20	1.35	14.99	153.00	1.25	14.60	210.00
1.86	17.84	88.56	1.76	17.59	100.08	1.66	17.02	109.20	1.56	16.90	134.64	1.36	15.14	154.80	1.26	14.74	212.40
1.87	18.01	89.52	1.77	17.75	101.16	1.67	17.18	110.40	1.57	17.06	136.08	1.37	15.29	156.60	1.27	14.88	214.80
1.88	18.19	90.48	1.78	17.92	102.24	1.68	17.35	111.60	1.58	17.22	137.52	1.38	15.44	158.40	1.28	15.03	217.20
1.89	18.36	91.44	1.79	18.09	103.32	1.69	17.51	112.80	1.59	17.37	138.96	1.39	15.59	160.20	1.29	15.17	219.60
1.90	18.53	92.40	1.80	18.26	104.40	1.70	17.67	114.00	1.60	17.53	140.40	1.40	15.74	162.00	1.30	15.31	222.00
1.91	18.70	93.36	1.81	18.42	105.48	1.71	17.84	115.20	1.61	17.68	141.84	1.41	15.89	163.80	1.31	15.45	224.40
1.92	18.87	94.32	1.82	18.59	106.56	1.72	18.00	116.40	1.62	17.84	143.28	1.42	16.04	165.60	1.32	15.59	226.80
1.93	19.04	95.28	1.83	18.75	107.64	1.73	18.16	117.60	1.63	17.99	144.72	1.43	16.19	167.40	1.33	15.73	229.20
1.94	19.21	96.24	1.84	18.92	108.72	1.74	18.32	118.80	1.64	18.15	146.16	1.44	16.34	169.20	1.34	15.87	231.60
1.95	19.38	97.20	1.85	19.09	109.80	1.75	18.48	120.00	1.65	18.30	147.60	1.45	16.49	171.00	1.35	16.01	234.00
1.96	19.55	98.16	1.86	19.25	110.88	1.76	18.65	121.20	1.66	18.46	149.04	1.46	16.63	172.80	1.36	16.15	236.40
1.97	19.72	99.12	1.87	19.41	111.96	1.77	18.81	122.40	1.67	18.61	150.48	1.47	16.78	174.60	1.37	16.29	238.80
1.98	19.89	100.08	1.88	19.58	113.04	1.78	18.97	123.60	1.68	18.77	151.92	1.48	16.93	176.40	1.38	16.42	241.20
1.99	20.06	101.04	1.89	19.74	114.12	1.79	19.13	124.80	1.69	18.92	153.36	1.49	17.08	178.20	1.39	16.56	243.60

Description: This table shows the Annual Percentage Rate and finance charge per $100 for monthly lease payments.

Example: A 4.30% lease payment for 2 years is equivalent to an APR of 17.10%. The charge per $100 cost is $ 18.20.

2 yr PAYT	APR	CHARGE	3 yr PAYT	APR	CHARGE	4 yr PAYT	APR	CHARGE	5 yr PAYT	APR	CHARGE	6 yr PAYT	APR	CHARGE	7 yr PAYT	APR	CHARGE
4.30	17.10	18.20	3.00	13.78	23.00	2.30	11.15	25.40	1.90	10.01	29.00	1.70	10.54	37.40	1.50	9.79	41.00
4.31	17.32	18.44	3.01	13.99	23.36	2.31	11.35	25.88	1.91	10.21	29.60	1.71	10.73	38.12	1.51	9.98	41.84
4.32	17.54	18.68	3.02	14.20	23.72	2.32	11.56	26.36	1.92	10.41	30.20	1.72	10.92	38.84	1.52	10.17	42.68
4.33	17.76	18.92	3.03	14.41	24.08	2.33	11.76	26.84	1.93	10.60	30.80	1.73	11.12	39.56	1.53	10.36	43.52
4.34	17.99	19.16	3.04	14.61	24.44	2.34	11.96	27.32	1.94	10.80	31.40	1.74	11.31	40.28	1.54	10.54	44.36
4.35	18.21	19.40	3.05	14.82	24.80	2.35	12.16	27.80	1.95	11.00	32.00	1.75	11.50	41.00	1.55	10.73	45.20
4.36	18.43	19.64	3.06	15.03	25.16	2.36	12.37	28.28	1.96	11.20	32.60	1.76	11.69	41.72	1.56	10.92	46.04
4.37	18.65	19.88	3.07	15.24	25.52	2.37	12.57	28.76	1.97	11.39	33.20	1.77	11.88	42.44	1.57	11.11	46.88
4.38	18.87	20.12	3.08	15.45	25.88	2.38	12.77	29.24	1.98	11.59	33.80	1.78	12.07	43.16	1.58	11.29	47.72
4.39	19.09	20.36	3.09	15.66	26.24	2.39	12.97	29.72	1.99	11.78	34.40	1.79	12.26	43.88	1.59	11.48	48.56
4.40	19.32	20.60	3.10	15.87	26.60	2.40	13.17	30.20	2.00	11.98	35.00	1.80	12.45	44.60	1.60	11.66	49.40
4.41	19.54	20.84	3.11	16.07	26.96	2.41	13.37	30.68	2.01	12.18	35.60	1.81	12.64	45.32	1.61	11.85	50.24
4.42	19.76	21.08	3.12	16.28	27.32	2.42	13.57	31.16	2.02	12.37	36.20	1.82	12.82	46.04	1.62	12.03	51.08
4.43	19.98	21.32	3.13	16.49	27.68	2.43	13.77	31.64	2.03	12.57	36.80	1.83	13.01	46.76	1.63	12.22	51.92
4.44	20.20	21.56	3.14	16.70	28.04	2.44	13.98	32.12	2.04	12.76	37.40	1.84	13.20	47.48	1.64	12.40	52.76
4.45	20.42	21.80	3.15	16.91	28.40	2.45	14.18	32.60	2.05	12.96	38.00	1.85	13.39	48.20	1.65	12.58	53.60
4.46	20.64	22.04	3.16	17.11	28.76	2.46	14.38	33.08	2.06	13.15	38.60	1.86	13.58	48.92	1.66	12.77	54.44
4.47	20.86	22.28	3.17	17.32	29.12	2.47	14.58	33.56	2.07	13.34	39.20	1.87	13.76	49.64	1.67	12.95	55.28
4.48	21.08	22.52	3.18	17.53	29.48	2.48	14.77	34.04	2.08	13.54	39.80	1.88	13.95	50.36	1.68	13.13	56.12
4.49	21.30	22.76	3.19	17.73	29.84	2.49	14.97	34.52	2.09	13.73	40.40	1.89	14.14	51.08	1.69	13.32	56.96
4.50	21.52	23.00	3.20	17.94	30.20	2.50	15.17	35.00	2.10	13.92	41.00	1.90	14.32	51.80	1.70	13.50	57.80
4.51	21.74	23.24	3.21	18.15	30.56	2.51	15.37	35.48	2.11	14.12	41.60	1.91	14.51	52.52	1.71	13.68	58.64
4.52	21.96	23.48	3.22	18.35	30.92	2.52	15.57	35.96	2.12	14.31	42.20	1.92	14.69	53.24	1.72	13.86	59.48
4.53	22.18	23.72	3.23	18.56	31.28	2.53	15.77	36.44	2.13	14.50	42.80	1.93	14.88	53.96	1.73	14.04	60.32
4.54	22.40	23.96	3.24	18.77	31.64	2.54	15.97	36.92	2.14	14.69	43.40	1.94	15.06	54.68	1.74	14.22	61.16
4.55	22.62	24.20	3.25	18.97	32.00	2.55	16.17	37.40	2.15	14.88	44.00	1.95	15.25	55.40	1.75	14.40	62.00
4.56	22.84	24.44	3.26	19.18	32.36	2.56	16.36	37.88	2.16	15.08	44.60	1.96	15.43	56.12	1.76	14.58	62.84
4.57	23.06	24.68	3.27	19.38	32.72	2.57	16.56	38.36	2.17	15.27	45.20	1.97	15.62	56.84	1.77	14.76	63.68
4.58	23.28	24.92	3.28	19.59	33.08	2.58	16.76	38.84	2.18	15.46	45.80	1.98	15.80	57.56	1.78	14.94	64.52
4.59	23.50	25.16	3.29	19.79	33.44	2.59	16.96	39.32	2.19	15.65	46.40	1.99	15.98	58.28	1.79	15.12	65.36
4.60	23.72	25.40	3.30	20.00	33.80	2.60	17.15	39.80	2.20	15.84	47.00	2.00	16.17	59.00	1.80	15.30	66.20
4.61	23.94	25.64	3.31	20.20	34.16	2.61	17.35	40.28	2.21	16.03	47.60	2.01	16.35	59.72	1.81	15.48	67.04
4.62	24.16	25.88	3.32	20.41	34.52	2.62	17.55	40.76	2.22	16.22	48.20	2.02	16.53	60.44	1.82	15.66	67.88
4.63	24.38	26.12	3.33	20.61	34.88	2.63	17.74	41.24	2.23	16.41	48.80	2.03	16.71	61.16	1.83	15.83	68.72
4.64	24.60	26.36	3.34	20.82	35.24	2.64	17.94	41.72	2.24	16.60	49.40	2.04	16.90	61.88	1.84	16.01	69.56
4.65	24.82	26.60	3.35	21.02	35.60	2.65	18.13	42.20	2.25	16.79	50.00	2.05	17.08	62.60	1.85	16.19	70.40
4.66	25.04	26.84	3.36	21.23	35.96	2.66	18.33	42.68	2.26	16.98	50.60	2.06	17.26	63.32	1.86	16.37	71.24
4.67	25.26	27.08	3.37	21.43	36.32	2.67	18.53	43.16	2.27	17.17	51.20	2.07	17.44	64.04	1.87	16.54	72.08
4.68	25.48	27.32	3.38	21.64	36.68	2.68	18.72	43.64	2.28	17.35	51.80	2.08	17.62	64.76	1.88	16.72	72.92
4.69	25.70	27.56	3.39	21.84	37.04	2.69	18.92	44.12	2.29	17.54	52.40	2.09	17.80	65.48	1.89	16.90	73.76
4.70	25.92	27.80	3.40	22.04	37.40	2.70	19.11	44.60	2.30	17.73	53.00	2.10	17.98	66.20	1.90	17.07	74.60
4.71	26.14	28.04	3.41	22.25	37.76	2.71	19.31	45.08	2.31	17.92	53.60	2.11	18.16	66.92	1.91	17.25	75.44
4.72	26.35	28.28	3.42	22.45	38.12	2.72	19.50	45.56	2.32	18.11	54.20	2.12	18.34	67.64	1.92	17.42	76.28
4.73	26.57	28.52	3.43	22.65	38.48	2.73	19.70	46.04	2.33	18.29	54.80	2.13	18.52	68.36	1.93	17.60	77.12
4.74	26.79	28.76	3.44	22.86	38.84	2.74	19.89	46.52	2.34	18.48	55.40	2.14	18.70	69.08	1.94	17.77	77.96
4.75	27.01	29.00	3.45	23.06	39.20	2.75	20.08	47.00	2.35	18.67	56.00	2.15	18.88	69.80	1.95	17.95	78.80
4.76	27.23	29.24	3.46	23.26	39.56	2.76	20.28	47.48	2.36	18.85	56.60	2.16	19.06	70.52	1.96	18.12	79.64
4.77	27.45	29.48	3.47	23.47	39.92	2.77	20.47	47.96	2.37	19.04	57.20	2.17	19.24	71.24	1.97	18.29	80.48
4.78	27.67	29.72	3.48	23.67	40.28	2.78	20.66	48.44	2.38	19.23	57.80	2.18	19.42	71.96	1.98	18.47	81.32
4.79	27.88	29.96	3.49	23.87	40.64	2.79	20.86	48.92	2.39	19.41	58.40	2.19	19.60	72.68	1.99	18.64	82.16
4.80	28.10	30.20	3.50	24.08	41.00	2.80	21.05	49.40	2.40	19.60	59.00	2.20	19.78	73.40	2.00	18.81	83.00
4.81	28.32	30.44	3.51	24.28	41.36	2.81	21.24	49.88	2.41	19.78	59.60	2.21	19.96	74.12	2.01	18.99	83.84
4.82	28.54	30.68	3.52	24.48	41.72	2.82	21.44	50.36	2.42	19.97	60.20	2.22	20.13	74.84	2.02	19.16	84.68
4.83	28.76	30.92	3.53	24.68	42.08	2.83	21.63	50.84	2.43	20.15	60.80	2.23	20.31	75.56	2.03	19.33	85.52
4.84	28.98	31.16	3.54	24.88	42.44	2.84	21.82	51.32	2.44	20.34	61.40	2.24	20.49	76.28	2.04	19.51	86.36
4.85	29.19	31.40	3.55	25.09	42.80	2.85	22.01	51.80	2.45	20.52	62.00	2.25	20.67	77.00	2.05	19.68	87.20
4.86	29.41	31.64	3.56	25.29	43.16	2.86	22.21	52.28	2.46	20.71	62.60	2.26	20.84	77.72	2.06	19.85	88.04
4.87	29.63	31.88	3.57	25.49	43.52	2.87	22.40	52.76	2.47	20.89	63.20	2.27	21.02	78.44	2.07	20.02	88.88
4.88	29.85	32.12	3.58	25.69	43.88	2.88	22.59	53.24	2.48	21.08	63.80	2.28	21.20	79.16	2.08	20.19	89.72
4.89	30.07	32.36	3.59	25.89	44.24	2.89	22.78	53.72	2.49	21.26	64.40	2.29	21.37	79.88	2.09	20.36	90.56
4.90	30.28	32.60	3.60	26.09	44.60	2.90	22.97	54.20	2.50	21.45	65.00	2.30	21.55	80.60	2.10	20.53	91.40
4.91	30.50	32.84	3.61	26.29	44.96	2.91	23.17	54.68	2.51	21.63	65.60	2.31	21.72	81.32	2.11	20.71	92.24
4.92	30.72	33.08	3.62	26.50	45.32	2.92	23.36	55.16	2.52	21.81	66.20	2.32	21.90	82.04	2.12	20.88	93.08
4.93	30.94	33.32	3.63	26.70	45.68	2.93	23.55	55.64	2.53	22.00	66.80	2.33	22.07	82.76	2.13	21.05	93.92
4.94	31.15	33.56	3.64	26.90	46.04	2.94	23.74	56.12	2.54	22.18	67.40	2.34	22.25	83.48	2.14	21.22	94.76
4.95	31.37	33.80	3.65	27.10	46.40	2.95	23.93	56.60	2.55	22.36	68.00	2.35	22.43	84.20	2.15	21.39	95.60
4.96	31.59	34.04	3.66	27.30	46.76	2.96	24.12	57.08	2.56	22.54	68.60	2.36	22.60	84.92	2.16	21.56	96.44
4.97	31.80	34.28	3.67	27.50	47.12	2.97	24.31	57.56	2.57	22.73	69.20	2.37	22.77	85.64	2.17	21.73	97.28
4.98	32.02	34.52	3.68	27.70	47.48	2.98	24.50	58.04	2.58	22.91	69.80	2.38	22.95	86.36	2.18	21.89	98.12
4.99	32.24	34.76	3.69	27.90	47.84	2.99	24.69	58.52	2.59	23.09	70.40	2.39	23.12	87.08	2.19	22.06	98.96

Description: This table shows the Annual Percentage Rate and finance charge per $100 for monthly lease payments.

Example: A 1.30% lease payment for 8 years is equivalent to an APR of 8.29%. The charge per $100 cost is $ 39.80.

8 yr PAYT	APR	CHARGE	9 yr PAYT	APR	CHARGE	10 yr PAYT	APR	CHARGE	12 yr PAYT	APR	CHARGE	15 yr PAYT	APR	CHARGE	20 yr PAYT	APR	CHARGE
1.30	8.29	39.80	1.20	8.17	44.60	1.10	7.70	47.00	1.00	7.88	59.00	.80	6.27	59.00	.70	6.38	83.00
1.31	8.48	40.76	1.21	8.36	45.68	1.11	7.88	48.20	1.01	8.06	60.44	.81	6.45	60.80	.71	6.54	85.40
1.32	8.67	41.72	1.22	8.54	46.76	1.12	8.06	49.40	1.02	8.23	61.88	.82	6.62	62.60	.72	6.71	87.80
1.33	8.85	42.68	1.23	8.72	47.84	1.13	8.25	50.60	1.03	8.41	63.32	.83	6.80	64.40	.73	6.87	90.20
1.34	9.04	43.64	1.24	8.91	48.92	1.14	8.43	51.80	1.04	8.58	64.76	.84	6.97	66.20	.74	7.03	92.60
1.35	9.23	44.60	1.25	9.09	50.00	1.15	8.61	53.00	1.05	8.76	66.20	.85	7.14	68.00	.75	7.20	95.00
1.36	9.41	45.56	1.26	9.27	51.08	1.16	8.79	54.20	1.06	8.93	67.64	.86	7.31	69.80	.76	7.36	97.40
1.37	9.60	46.52	1.27	9.46	52.16	1.17	8.97	55.40	1.07	9.11	69.08	.87	7.49	71.60	.77	7.52	99.80
1.38	9.78	47.48	1.28	9.64	53.24	1.18	9.15	56.60	1.08	9.28	70.52	.88	7.66	73.40	.78	7.68	102.20
1.39	9.97	48.44	1.29	9.82	54.32	1.19	9.33	57.80	1.09	9.45	71.96	.89	7.83	75.20	.79	7.84	104.60
1.40	10.15	49.40	1.30	10.00	55.40	1.20	9.51	59.00	1.10	9.62	73.40	.90	7.99	77.00	.80	8.00	107.00
1.41	10.34	50.36	1.31	10.18	56.48	1.21	9.68	60.20	1.11	9.79	74.84	.91	8.16	78.80	.81	8.15	109.40
1.42	10.52	51.32	1.32	10.36	57.56	1.22	9.86	61.40	1.12	9.96	76.28	.92	8.33	80.60	.82	8.31	111.80
1.43	10.70	52.28	1.33	10.54	58.64	1.23	10.04	62.60	1.13	10.13	77.72	.93	8.50	82.40	.83	8.47	114.20
1.44	10.89	53.24	1.34	10.72	59.72	1.24	10.21	63.80	1.14	10.30	79.16	.94	8.66	84.20	.84	8.62	116.60
1.45	11.07	54.20	1.35	10.89	60.80	1.25	10.39	65.00	1.15	10.47	80.60	.95	8.83	86.00	.85	8.78	119.00
1.46	11.25	55.16	1.36	11.07	61.88	1.26	10.57	66.20	1.16	10.64	82.04	.96	9.00	87.80	.86	8.93	121.40
1.47	11.43	56.12	1.37	11.25	62.96	1.27	10.74	67.40	1.17	10.81	83.48	.97	9.16	89.60	.87	9.09	123.80
1.48	11.61	57.08	1.38	11.43	64.04	1.28	10.92	68.60	1.18	10.98	84.92	.98	9.33	91.40	.88	9.24	126.20
1.49	11.79	58.04	1.39	11.60	65.12	1.29	11.09	69.80	1.19	11.14	86.36	.99	9.49	93.20	.89	9.39	128.60
1.50	11.97	59.00	1.40	11.78	66.20	1.30	11.26	71.00	1.20	11.31	87.80	1.00	9.65	95.00	.90	9.55	131.00
1.51	12.15	59.96	1.41	11.96	67.28	1.31	11.44	72.20	1.21	11.48	89.24	1.01	9.81	96.80	.91	9.70	133.40
1.52	12.33	60.92	1.42	12.13	68.36	1.32	11.61	73.40	1.22	11.64	90.68	1.02	9.98	98.60	.92	9.85	135.80
1.53	12.51	61.88	1.43	12.31	69.44	1.33	11.78	74.60	1.23	11.81	92.12	1.03	10.14	100.40	.93	10.00	138.20
1.54	12.69	62.84	1.44	12.48	70.52	1.34	11.95	75.80	1.24	11.97	93.56	1.04	10.30	102.20	.94	10.15	140.60
1.55	12.87	63.80	1.45	12.66	71.60	1.35	12.13	77.00	1.25	12.14	95.00	1.05	10.46	104.00	.95	10.30	143.00
1.56	13.04	64.76	1.46	12.83	72.68	1.36	12.30	78.20	1.26	12.30	96.44	1.06	10.62	105.80	.96	10.45	145.40
1.57	13.22	65.72	1.47	13.00	73.76	1.37	12.47	79.40	1.27	12.47	97.88	1.07	10.78	107.60	.97	10.60	147.80
1.58	13.40	66.68	1.48	13.18	74.84	1.38	12.64	80.60	1.28	12.63	99.32	1.08	10.94	109.40	.98	10.75	150.20
1.59	13.58	67.64	1.49	13.35	75.92	1.39	12.81	81.80	1.29	12.79	100.76	1.09	11.10	111.20	.99	10.90	152.60
1.60	13.75	68.60	1.50	13.52	77.00	1.40	12.98	83.00	1.30	12.96	102.20	1.10	11.26	113.00	1.00	11.05	155.00
1.61	13.93	69.56	1.51	13.69	78.08	1.41	13.15	84.20	1.31	13.12	103.64	1.11	11.42	114.80	1.01	11.20	157.40
1.62	14.11	70.52	1.52	13.87	79.16	1.42	13.32	85.40	1.32	13.28	105.08	1.12	11.57	116.60	1.02	11.35	159.80
1.63	14.28	71.48	1.53	14.04	80.24	1.43	13.48	86.60	1.33	13.44	106.52	1.13	11.73	118.40	1.03	11.49	162.20
1.64	14.46	72.44	1.54	14.21	81.32	1.44	13.65	87.80	1.34	13.60	107.96	1.14	11.89	120.20	1.04	11.64	164.60
1.65	14.63	73.40	1.55	14.38	82.40	1.45	13.82	89.00	1.35	13.76	109.40	1.15	12.04	122.00	1.05	11.79	167.00
1.66	14.81	74.36	1.56	14.55	83.48	1.46	13.99	90.20	1.36	13.92	110.84	1.16	12.20	123.80	1.06	11.93	169.40
1.67	14.98	75.32	1.57	14.72	84.56	1.47	14.15	91.40	1.37	14.08	112.28	1.17	12.35	125.60	1.07	12.08	171.80
1.68	15.15	76.28	1.58	14.89	85.64	1.48	14.32	92.60	1.38	14.24	113.72	1.18	12.51	127.40	1.08	12.22	174.20
1.69	15.33	77.24	1.59	15.06	86.72	1.49	14.49	93.80	1.39	14.40	115.16	1.19	12.66	129.20	1.09	12.37	176.60
1.70	15.50	78.20	1.60	15.23	87.80	1.50	14.65	95.00	1.40	14.56	116.60	1.20	12.82	131.00	1.10	12.51	179.00
1.71	15.67	79.16	1.61	15.40	88.88	1.51	14.82	96.20	1.41	14.72	118.04	1.21	12.97	132.80	1.11	12.66	181.40
1.72	15.85	80.12	1.62	15.57	89.96	1.52	14.99	97.40	1.42	14.88	119.48	1.22	13.13	134.60	1.12	12.80	183.80
1.73	16.02	81.08	1.63	15.73	91.04	1.53	15.15	98.60	1.43	15.04	120.92	1.23	13.28	136.40	1.13	12.95	186.20
1.74	16.19	82.04	1.64	15.90	92.12	1.54	15.32	99.80	1.44	15.20	122.36	1.24	13.43	138.20	1.14	13.09	188.60
1.75	16.36	83.00	1.65	16.07	93.20	1.55	15.48	101.00	1.45	15.35	123.80	1.25	13.59	140.00	1.15	13.23	191.00
1.76	16.53	83.96	1.66	16.24	94.28	1.56	15.64	102.20	1.46	15.51	125.24	1.26	13.74	141.80	1.16	13.38	193.40
1.77	16.70	84.92	1.67	16.40	95.36	1.57	15.81	103.40	1.47	15.67	126.68	1.27	13.89	143.60	1.17	13.52	195.80
1.78	16.88	85.88	1.68	16.57	96.44	1.58	15.97	104.60	1.48	15.82	128.12	1.28	14.04	145.40	1.18	13.66	198.20
1.79	17.05	86.84	1.69	16.74	97.52	1.59	16.13	105.80	1.49	15.98	129.56	1.29	14.19	147.20	1.19	13.80	200.60
1.80	17.22	87.80	1.70	16.90	98.60	1.60	16.30	107.00	1.50	16.14	131.00	1.30	14.34	149.00	1.20	13.94	203.00
1.81	17.39	88.76	1.71	17.07	99.68	1.61	16.46	108.20	1.51	16.29	132.44	1.31	14.50	150.80	1.21	14.09	205.40
1.82	17.56	89.72	1.72	17.23	100.76	1.62	16.62	109.40	1.52	16.45	133.88	1.32	14.65	152.60	1.22	14.23	207.80
1.83	17.73	90.68	1.73	17.40	101.84	1.63	16.78	110.60	1.53	16.60	135.32	1.33	14.80	154.40	1.23	14.37	210.20
1.84	17.89	91.64	1.74	17.56	102.92	1.64	16.95	111.80	1.54	16.76	136.76	1.34	14.95	156.20	1.24	14.51	212.60
1.85	18.06	92.60	1.75	17.73	104.00	1.65	17.11	113.00	1.55	16.91	138.20	1.35	15.10	158.00	1.25	14.65	215.00
1.86	18.23	93.56	1.76	17.89	105.08	1.66	17.27	114.20	1.56	17.07	139.64	1.36	15.25	159.80	1.26	14.79	217.40
1.87	18.40	94.52	1.77	18.06	106.16	1.67	17.43	115.40	1.57	17.22	141.08	1.37	15.39	161.60	1.27	14.93	219.80
1.88	18.57	95.48	1.78	18.22	107.24	1.68	17.59	116.60	1.58	17.38	142.52	1.38	15.54	163.40	1.28	15.07	222.20
1.89	18.74	96.44	1.79	18.39	108.32	1.69	17.75	117.80	1.59	17.53	143.96	1.39	15.69	165.20	1.29	15.21	224.60
1.90	18.91	97.40	1.80	18.55	109.40	1.70	17.91	119.00	1.60	17.68	145.40	1.40	15.84	167.00	1.30	15.35	227.00
1.91	19.07	98.36	1.81	18.71	110.48	1.71	18.07	120.20	1.61	17.84	146.84	1.41	15.99	168.80	1.31	15.49	229.40
1.92	19.24	99.32	1.82	18.88	111.56	1.72	18.23	121.40	1.62	17.99	148.28	1.42	16.14	170.60	1.32	15.63	231.80
1.93	19.41	100.28	1.83	19.04	112.64	1.73	18.39	122.60	1.63	18.14	149.72	1.43	16.28	172.40	1.33	15.77	234.20
1.94	19.57	101.24	1.84	19.20	113.72	1.74	18.55	123.80	1.64	18.29	151.16	1.44	16.43	174.20	1.34	15.91	236.60
1.95	19.74	102.20	1.85	19.36	114.80	1.75	18.71	125.00	1.65	18.45	152.60	1.45	16.58	176.00	1.35	16.05	239.00
1.96	19.91	103.16	1.86	19.53	115.88	1.76	18.87	126.20	1.66	18.60	154.04	1.46	16.72	177.80	1.36	16.18	241.40
1.97	20.07	104.12	1.87	19.69	116.96	1.77	19.03	127.40	1.67	18.75	155.48	1.47	16.87	179.60	1.37	16.32	243.80
1.98	20.24	105.08	1.88	19.85	118.04	1.78	19.19	128.60	1.68	18.90	156.92	1.48	17.02	181.40	1.38	16.46	246.20
1.99	20.40	106.04	1.89	20.01	119.12	1.79	19.34	129.80	1.69	19.05	158.36	1.49	17.16	183.20	1.39	16.60	248.60

Description: This table shows the Annual Percentage Rate and finance charge per $100 for monthly lease payments.

Example: A 4.30% lease payment for 2 years is equivalent to an APR of 20.74%. The charge per $100 cost is $ 23.20.

2 yr MONTHLY PAYT	APR	CHARGE	3 yr MONTHLY PAYT	APR	CHARGE	4 yr MONTHLY PAYT	APR	CHARGE	5 yr MONTHLY PAYT	APR	CHARGE	6 yr MONTHLY PAYT	APR	CHARGE	7 yr MONTHLY PAYT	APR	CHARGE
4.30	20.74	23.20	3.00	16.00	28.00	2.30	12.74	30.40	1.90	11.22	34.00	1.70	11.45	42.40	1.50	10.54	46.00
4.31	20.95	23.44	3.01	16.20	28.36	2.31	12.94	30.88	1.91	11.41	34.60	1.71	11.64	43.12	1.51	10.72	46.84
4.32	21.16	23.68	3.02	16.40	28.72	2.32	13.13	31.36	1.92	11.60	35.20	1.72	11.82	43.84	1.52	10.90	47.68
4.33	21.37	23.92	3.03	16.60	29.08	2.33	13.33	31.84	1.93	11.79	35.80	1.73	12.01	44.56	1.53	11.09	48.52
4.34	21.58	24.16	3.04	16.80	29.44	2.34	13.52	32.32	1.94	11.98	36.40	1.74	12.19	45.28	1.54	11.27	49.36
4.35	21.79	24.40	3.05	17.00	29.80	2.35	13.72	32.80	1.95	12.17	37.00	1.75	12.38	46.00	1.55	11.45	50.20
4.36	22.01	24.64	3.06	17.20	30.16	2.36	13.91	33.28	1.96	12.36	37.60	1.76	12.56	46.72	1.56	11.63	51.04
4.37	22.22	24.88	3.07	17.40	30.52	2.37	14.10	33.76	1.97	12.55	38.20	1.77	12.74	47.44	1.57	11.81	51.88
4.38	22.43	25.12	3.08	17.60	30.88	2.38	14.30	34.24	1.98	12.74	38.80	1.78	12.92	48.16	1.58	11.99	52.72
4.39	22.64	25.36	3.09	17.80	31.24	2.39	14.49	34.72	1.99	12.93	39.40	1.79	13.11	48.88	1.59	12.17	53.56
4.40	22.85	25.60	3.10	18.00	31.60	2.40	14.68	35.20	2.00	13.11	40.00	1.80	13.29	49.60	1.60	12.35	54.40
4.41	23.06	25.84	3.11	18.20	31.96	2.41	14.87	35.68	2.01	13.30	40.60	1.81	13.47	50.32	1.61	12.52	55.24
4.42	23.27	26.08	3.12	18.39	32.32	2.42	15.07	36.16	2.02	13.49	41.20	1.82	13.65	51.04	1.62	12.70	56.08
4.43	23.48	26.32	3.13	18.59	32.68	2.43	15.26	36.64	2.03	13.68	41.80	1.83	13.84	51.76	1.63	12.88	56.92
4.44	23.70	26.56	3.14	18.79	33.04	2.44	15.45	37.12	2.04	13.86	42.40	1.84	14.02	52.48	1.64	13.06	57.76
4.45	23.91	26.80	3.15	18.99	33.40	2.45	15.64	37.60	2.05	14.05	43.00	1.85	14.20	53.20	1.65	13.24	58.60
4.46	24.12	27.04	3.16	19.19	33.76	2.46	15.84	38.08	2.06	14.24	43.60	1.86	14.38	53.92	1.66	13.41	59.44
4.47	24.33	27.28	3.17	19.39	34.12	2.47	16.03	38.56	2.07	14.42	44.20	1.87	14.56	54.64	1.67	13.59	60.28
4.48	24.54	27.52	3.18	19.59	34.48	2.48	16.22	39.04	2.08	14.61	44.80	1.88	14.74	55.36	1.68	13.77	61.12
4.49	24.75	27.76	3.19	19.79	34.84	2.49	16.41	39.52	2.09	14.80	45.40	1.89	14.92	56.08	1.69	13.94	61.96
4.50	24.96	28.00	3.20	19.98	35.20	2.50	16.60	40.00	2.10	14.98	46.00	1.90	15.10	56.80	1.70	14.12	62.80
4.51	25.17	28.24	3.21	20.18	35.56	2.51	16.79	40.48	2.11	15.17	46.60	1.91	15.28	57.52	1.71	14.30	63.64
4.52	25.38	28.48	3.22	20.38	35.92	2.52	16.98	40.96	2.12	15.35	47.20	1.92	15.46	58.24	1.72	14.47	64.48
4.53	25.59	28.72	3.23	20.58	36.28	2.53	17.17	41.44	2.13	15.54	47.80	1.93	15.64	58.96	1.73	14.65	65.32
4.54	25.80	28.96	3.24	20.78	36.64	2.54	17.37	41.92	2.14	15.72	48.40	1.94	15.82	59.68	1.74	14.82	66.16
4.55	26.01	29.20	3.25	20.97	37.00	2.55	17.56	42.40	2.15	15.91	49.00	1.95	16.00	60.40	1.75	15.00	67.00
4.56	26.22	29.44	3.26	21.17	37.36	2.56	17.75	42.88	2.16	16.09	49.60	1.96	16.17	61.12	1.76	15.17	67.84
4.57	26.44	29.68	3.27	21.37	37.72	2.57	17.94	43.36	2.17	16.28	50.20	1.97	16.35	61.84	1.77	15.35	68.68
4.58	26.65	29.92	3.28	21.57	38.08	2.58	18.13	43.84	2.18	16.46	50.80	1.98	16.53	62.56	1.78	15.52	69.52
4.59	26.86	30.16	3.29	21.76	38.44	2.59	18.32	44.32	2.19	16.65	51.40	1.99	16.71	63.28	1.79	15.69	70.36
4.60	27.07	30.40	3.30	21.96	38.80	2.60	18.51	44.80	2.20	16.83	52.00	2.00	16.89	64.00	1.80	15.87	71.20
4.61	27.28	30.64	3.31	22.16	39.16	2.61	18.70	45.28	2.21	17.01	52.60	2.01	17.06	64.72	1.81	16.04	72.04
4.62	27.49	30.88	3.32	22.35	39.52	2.62	18.88	45.76	2.22	17.20	53.20	2.02	17.24	65.44	1.82	16.21	72.88
4.63	27.70	31.12	3.33	22.55	39.88	2.63	19.07	46.24	2.23	17.38	53.80	2.03	17.42	66.16	1.83	16.39	73.72
4.64	27.91	31.36	3.34	22.75	40.24	2.64	19.26	46.72	2.24	17.56	54.40	2.04	17.59	66.88	1.84	16.56	74.56
4.65	28.12	31.60	3.35	22.94	40.60	2.65	19.45	47.20	2.25	17.75	55.00	2.05	17.77	67.60	1.85	16.73	75.40
4.66	28.33	31.84	3.36	23.14	40.96	2.66	19.64	47.68	2.26	17.93	55.60	2.06	17.95	68.32	1.86	16.91	76.24
4.67	28.54	32.08	3.37	23.34	41.32	2.67	19.83	48.16	2.27	18.11	56.20	2.07	18.12	69.04	1.87	17.08	77.08
4.68	28.75	32.32	3.38	23.53	41.68	2.68	20.02	48.64	2.28	18.29	56.80	2.08	18.30	69.76	1.88	17.25	77.92
4.69	28.96	32.56	3.39	23.73	42.04	2.69	20.21	49.12	2.29	18.48	57.40	2.09	18.48	70.48	1.89	17.42	78.76
4.70	29.17	32.80	3.40	23.93	42.40	2.70	20.39	49.60	2.30	18.66	58.00	2.10	18.65	71.20	1.90	17.59	79.60
4.71	29.38	33.04	3.41	24.12	42.76	2.71	20.58	50.08	2.31	18.84	58.60	2.11	18.83	71.92	1.91	17.76	80.44
4.72	29.59	33.28	3.42	24.32	43.12	2.72	20.77	50.56	2.32	19.02	59.20	2.12	19.00	72.64	1.92	17.93	81.28
4.73	29.80	33.52	3.43	24.51	43.48	2.73	20.96	51.04	2.33	19.20	59.80	2.13	19.18	73.36	1.93	18.10	82.12
4.74	30.01	33.76	3.44	24.71	43.84	2.74	21.15	51.52	2.34	19.38	60.40	2.14	19.35	74.08	1.94	18.27	82.96
4.75	30.22	34.00	3.45	24.90	44.20	2.75	21.33	52.00	2.35	19.56	61.00	2.15	19.53	74.80	1.95	18.44	83.80
4.76	30.43	34.24	3.46	25.10	44.56	2.76	21.52	52.48	2.36	19.75	61.60	2.16	19.70	75.52	1.96	18.61	84.64
4.77	30.64	34.48	3.47	25.30	44.92	2.77	21.71	52.96	2.37	19.93	62.20	2.17	19.87	76.24	1.97	18.78	85.48
4.78	30.84	34.72	3.48	25.49	45.28	2.78	21.89	53.44	2.38	20.11	62.80	2.18	20.05	76.96	1.98	18.95	86.32
4.79	31.05	34.96	3.49	25.69	45.64	2.79	22.08	53.92	2.39	20.29	63.40	2.19	20.22	77.68	1.99	19.12	87.16
4.80	31.26	35.20	3.50	25.88	46.00	2.80	22.27	54.40	2.40	20.47	64.00	2.20	20.40	78.40	2.00	19.29	88.00
4.81	31.47	35.44	3.51	26.08	46.36	2.81	22.45	54.88	2.41	20.65	64.60	2.21	20.57	79.12	2.01	19.46	88.84
4.82	31.68	35.68	3.52	26.27	46.72	2.82	22.64	55.36	2.42	20.83	65.20	2.22	20.74	79.84	2.02	19.63	89.68
4.83	31.89	35.92	3.53	26.47	47.08	2.83	22.83	55.84	2.43	21.01	65.80	2.23	20.91	80.56	2.03	19.80	90.52
4.84	32.10	36.16	3.54	26.66	47.44	2.84	23.01	56.32	2.44	21.19	66.40	2.24	21.09	81.28	2.04	19.97	91.36
4.85	32.31	36.40	3.55	26.86	47.80	2.85	23.20	56.80	2.45	21.37	67.00	2.25	21.26	82.00	2.05	20.14	92.20
4.86	32.52	36.64	3.56	27.05	48.16	2.86	23.38	57.28	2.46	21.54	67.60	2.26	21.43	82.72	2.06	20.30	93.04
4.87	32.73	36.88	3.57	27.25	48.52	2.87	23.57	57.76	2.47	21.72	68.20	2.27	21.60	83.44	2.07	20.47	93.88
4.88	32.94	37.12	3.58	27.44	48.88	2.88	23.76	58.24	2.48	21.90	68.80	2.28	21.78	84.16	2.08	20.64	94.72
4.89	33.15	37.36	3.59	27.63	49.24	2.89	23.94	58.72	2.49	22.08	69.40	2.29	21.95	84.88	2.09	20.81	95.56
4.90	33.36	37.60	3.60	27.83	49.60	2.90	24.13	59.20	2.50	22.26	70.00	2.30	22.12	85.60	2.10	20.97	96.40
4.91	33.57	37.84	3.61	28.02	49.96	2.91	24.31	59.68	2.51	22.44	70.60	2.31	22.29	86.32	2.11	21.14	97.24
4.92	33.77	38.08	3.62	28.22	50.32	2.92	24.50	60.16	2.52	22.62	71.20	2.32	22.46	87.04	2.12	21.31	98.08
4.93	33.98	38.32	3.63	28.41	50.68	2.93	24.68	60.64	2.53	22.79	71.80	2.33	22.64	87.76	2.13	21.47	98.92
4.94	34.19	38.56	3.64	28.60	51.04	2.94	24.87	61.12	2.54	22.97	72.40	2.34	22.81	88.48	2.14	21.64	99.76
4.95	34.40	38.80	3.65	28.80	51.40	2.95	25.05	61.60	2.55	23.15	73.00	2.35	22.98	89.20	2.15	21.81	100.60
4.96	34.61	39.04	3.66	28.99	51.76	2.96	25.24	62.08	2.56	23.33	73.60	2.36	23.15	89.92	2.16	21.97	101.44
4.97	34.82	39.28	3.67	29.19	52.12	2.97	25.42	62.56	2.57	23.50	74.20	2.37	23.32	90.64	2.17	22.14	102.28
4.98	35.03	39.52	3.68	29.38	52.48	2.98	25.61	63.04	2.58	23.68	74.80	2.38	23.49	91.36	2.18	22.30	103.12
4.99	35.24	39.76	3.69	29.57	52.84	2.99	25.79	63.52	2.59	23.86	75.40	2.39	23.66	92.08	2.19	22.47	103.96

Description: This table shows the Annual Percentage Rate and finance charge per $100 for monthly lease payments.

Example: A 1.30% lease payment for 8 years is equivalent to an APR of 8.95%. The charge per $100 cost is $ 44.80.

8 yr PAYT	APR	CHARGE	9 yr PAYT	APR	CHARGE	10 yr PAYT	APR	CHARGE	12 yr PAYT	APR	CHARGE	15 yr PAYT	APR	CHARGE	20 yr PAYT	APR	CHARGE
1.30	8.95	44.80	1.20	8.73	49.60	1.10	8.19	52.00	1.00	8.24	64.00	.80	6.56	64.00	.70	6.54	88.00
1.31	9.13	45.76	1.21	8.91	50.68	1.11	8.36	53.20	1.01	8.41	65.44	.81	6.73	65.80	.71	6.71	90.40
1.32	9.32	46.72	1.22	9.08	51.76	1.12	8.54	54.40	1.02	8.58	66.88	.82	6.90	67.60	.72	6.87	92.80
1.33	9.50	47.68	1.23	9.26	52.84	1.13	8.72	55.60	1.03	8.75	68.32	.83	7.07	69.40	.73	7.03	95.20
1.34	9.68	48.64	1.24	9.44	53.92	1.14	8.89	56.80	1.04	8.92	69.76	.84	7.23	71.20	.74	7.18	97.60
1.35	9.86	49.60	1.25	9.62	55.00	1.15	9.07	58.00	1.05	9.09	71.20	.85	7.40	73.00	.75	7.34	100.00
1.36	10.04	50.56	1.26	9.79	56.08	1.16	9.24	59.20	1.06	9.26	72.64	.86	7.57	74.80	.76	7.50	102.40
1.37	10.21	51.52	1.27	9.97	57.16	1.17	9.41	60.40	1.07	9.43	74.08	.87	7.73	76.60	.77	7.66	104.80
1.38	10.39	52.48	1.28	10.14	58.24	1.18	9.59	61.60	1.08	9.59	75.52	.88	7.90	78.40	.78	7.81	107.20
1.39	10.57	53.44	1.29	10.32	59.32	1.19	9.76	62.80	1.09	9.76	76.96	.89	8.07	80.20	.79	7.97	109.60
1.40	10.75	54.40	1.30	10.49	60.40	1.20	9.93	64.00	1.10	9.93	78.40	.90	8.23	82.00	.80	8.13	112.00
1.41	10.93	55.36	1.31	10.67	61.48	1.21	10.11	65.20	1.11	10.09	79.84	.91	8.39	83.80	.81	8.28	114.40
1.42	11.10	56.32	1.32	10.84	62.56	1.22	10.28	66.40	1.12	10.26	81.28	.92	8.56	85.60	.82	8.43	116.80
1.43	11.28	57.28	1.33	11.02	63.64	1.23	10.45	67.60	1.13	10.43	82.72	.93	8.72	87.40	.83	8.59	119.20
1.44	11.46	58.24	1.34	11.19	64.72	1.24	10.62	68.80	1.14	10.59	84.16	.94	8.88	89.20	.84	8.74	121.60
1.45	11.63	59.20	1.35	11.36	65.80	1.25	10.79	70.00	1.15	10.76	85.60	.95	9.04	91.00	.85	8.89	124.00
1.46	11.81	60.16	1.36	11.53	66.88	1.26	10.96	71.20	1.16	10.92	87.04	.96	9.21	92.80	.86	9.05	126.40
1.47	11.98	61.12	1.37	11.71	67.96	1.27	11.13	72.40	1.17	11.08	88.48	.97	9.37	94.60	.87	9.20	128.80
1.48	12.16	62.08	1.38	11.88	69.04	1.28	11.30	73.60	1.18	11.25	89.92	.98	9.53	96.40	.88	9.35	131.20
1.49	12.33	63.04	1.39	12.05	70.12	1.29	11.47	74.80	1.19	11.41	91.36	.99	9.69	98.20	.89	9.50	133.60
1.50	12.51	64.00	1.40	12.22	71.20	1.30	11.64	76.00	1.20	11.57	92.80	1.00	9.85	100.00	.90	9.65	136.00
1.51	12.68	64.96	1.41	12.39	72.28	1.31	11.81	77.20	1.21	11.74	94.24	1.01	10.01	101.80	.91	9.80	138.40
1.52	12.86	65.92	1.42	12.56	73.36	1.32	11.98	78.40	1.22	11.90	95.68	1.02	10.17	103.60	.92	9.95	140.80
1.53	13.03	66.88	1.43	12.73	74.44	1.33	12.14	79.60	1.23	12.06	97.12	1.03	10.32	105.40	.93	10.10	143.20
1.54	13.20	67.84	1.44	12.90	75.52	1.34	12.31	80.80	1.24	12.22	98.56	1.04	10.48	107.20	.94	10.25	145.60
1.55	13.38	68.80	1.45	13.07	76.60	1.35	12.48	82.00	1.25	12.38	100.00	1.05	10.64	109.00	.95	10.40	148.00
1.56	13.55	69.76	1.46	13.24	77.68	1.36	12.65	83.20	1.26	12.54	101.44	1.06	10.80	110.80	.96	10.54	150.40
1.57	13.72	70.72	1.47	13.41	78.76	1.37	12.81	84.40	1.27	12.70	102.88	1.07	10.95	112.60	.97	10.69	152.80
1.58	13.89	71.68	1.48	13.58	79.84	1.38	12.98	85.60	1.28	12.86	104.32	1.08	11.11	114.40	.98	10.84	155.20
1.59	14.07	72.64	1.49	13.75	80.92	1.39	13.14	86.80	1.29	13.02	105.76	1.09	11.27	116.20	.99	10.99	157.60
1.60	14.24	73.60	1.50	13.92	82.00	1.40	13.31	88.00	1.30	13.18	107.20	1.10	11.42	118.00	1.00	11.13	160.00
1.61	14.41	74.56	1.51	14.08	83.08	1.41	13.48	89.20	1.31	13.34	108.64	1.11	11.58	119.80	1.01	11.28	162.40
1.62	14.58	75.52	1.52	14.25	84.16	1.42	13.64	90.40	1.32	13.50	110.08	1.12	11.73	121.60	1.02	11.42	164.80
1.63	14.75	76.48	1.53	14.42	85.24	1.43	13.80	91.60	1.33	13.66	111.52	1.13	11.89	123.40	1.03	11.57	167.20
1.64	14.92	77.44	1.54	14.59	86.32	1.44	13.97	92.80	1.34	13.82	112.96	1.14	12.04	125.20	1.04	11.72	169.60
1.65	15.09	78.40	1.55	14.75	87.40	1.45	14.13	94.00	1.35	13.98	114.40	1.15	12.19	127.00	1.05	11.86	172.00
1.66	15.26	79.36	1.56	14.92	88.48	1.46	14.30	95.20	1.36	14.13	115.84	1.16	12.35	128.80	1.06	12.00	174.40
1.67	15.43	80.32	1.57	15.08	89.56	1.47	14.46	96.40	1.37	14.29	117.28	1.17	12.50	130.60	1.07	12.15	176.80
1.68	15.60	81.28	1.58	15.25	90.64	1.48	14.62	97.60	1.38	14.45	118.72	1.18	12.65	132.40	1.08	12.29	179.20
1.69	15.77	82.24	1.59	15.42	91.72	1.49	14.79	98.80	1.39	14.60	120.16	1.19	12.81	134.20	1.09	12.44	181.60
1.70	15.94	83.20	1.60	15.58	92.80	1.50	14.95	100.00	1.40	14.76	121.60	1.20	12.96	136.00	1.10	12.58	184.00
1.71	16.11	84.16	1.61	15.75	93.88	1.51	15.11	101.20	1.41	14.92	123.04	1.21	13.11	137.80	1.11	12.72	186.40
1.72	16.28	85.12	1.62	15.91	94.96	1.52	15.27	102.40	1.42	15.07	124.48	1.22	13.26	139.60	1.12	12.87	188.80
1.73	16.44	86.08	1.63	16.08	96.04	1.53	15.43	103.60	1.43	15.23	125.92	1.23	13.41	141.40	1.13	13.01	191.20
1.74	16.61	87.04	1.64	16.24	97.12	1.54	15.60	104.80	1.44	15.38	127.36	1.24	13.56	143.20	1.14	13.15	193.60
1.75	16.78	88.00	1.65	16.40	98.20	1.55	15.76	106.00	1.45	15.54	128.80	1.25	13.71	145.00	1.15	13.29	196.00
1.76	16.95	88.96	1.66	16.57	99.28	1.56	15.92	107.20	1.46	15.69	130.24	1.26	13.86	146.80	1.16	13.43	198.40
1.77	17.11	89.92	1.67	16.73	100.36	1.57	16.08	108.40	1.47	15.85	131.68	1.27	14.01	148.60	1.17	13.57	200.80
1.78	17.28	90.88	1.68	16.89	101.44	1.58	16.24	109.60	1.48	16.00	133.12	1.28	14.16	150.40	1.18	13.72	203.20
1.79	17.45	91.84	1.69	17.06	102.52	1.59	16.40	110.80	1.49	16.16	134.56	1.29	14.31	152.20	1.19	13.86	205.60
1.80	17.61	92.80	1.70	17.22	103.60	1.60	16.56	112.00	1.50	16.31	136.00	1.30	14.46	154.00	1.20	14.00	208.00
1.81	17.78	93.76	1.71	17.38	104.68	1.61	16.72	113.20	1.51	16.46	137.44	1.31	14.61	155.80	1.21	14.14	210.40
1.82	17.95	94.72	1.72	17.54	105.76	1.62	16.88	114.40	1.52	16.62	138.88	1.32	14.76	157.60	1.22	14.28	212.80
1.83	18.11	95.68	1.73	17.71	106.84	1.63	17.04	115.60	1.53	16.77	140.32	1.33	14.91	159.40	1.23	14.42	215.20
1.84	18.28	96.64	1.74	17.87	107.92	1.64	17.20	116.80	1.54	16.92	141.76	1.34	15.05	161.20	1.24	14.56	217.60
1.85	18.44	97.60	1.75	18.03	109.00	1.65	17.35	118.00	1.55	17.07	143.20	1.35	15.20	163.00	1.25	14.70	220.00
1.86	18.61	98.56	1.76	18.19	110.08	1.66	17.51	119.20	1.56	17.23	144.64	1.36	15.35	164.80	1.26	14.84	222.40
1.87	18.77	99.52	1.77	18.35	111.16	1.67	17.67	120.40	1.57	17.38	146.08	1.37	15.50	166.60	1.27	14.98	224.80
1.88	18.94	100.48	1.78	18.51	112.24	1.68	17.83	121.60	1.58	17.53	147.52	1.38	15.64	168.40	1.28	15.12	227.20
1.89	19.10	101.44	1.79	18.67	113.32	1.69	17.99	122.80	1.59	17.68	148.96	1.39	15.79	170.20	1.29	15.26	229.60
1.90	19.27	102.40	1.80	18.83	114.40	1.70	18.14	124.00	1.60	17.83	150.40	1.40	15.94	172.00	1.30	15.39	232.00
1.91	19.43	103.36	1.81	18.99	115.48	1.71	18.30	125.20	1.61	17.98	151.84	1.41	16.08	173.80	1.31	15.53	234.40
1.92	19.59	104.32	1.82	19.15	116.56	1.72	18.46	126.40	1.62	18.14	153.28	1.42	16.23	175.60	1.32	15.67	236.80
1.93	19.76	105.28	1.83	19.31	117.64	1.73	18.62	127.60	1.63	18.29	154.72	1.43	16.38	177.40	1.33	15.81	239.20
1.94	19.92	106.24	1.84	19.47	118.72	1.74	18.77	128.80	1.64	18.44	156.16	1.44	16.52	179.20	1.34	15.95	241.60
1.95	20.08	107.20	1.85	19.63	119.80	1.75	18.93	130.00	1.65	18.59	157.60	1.45	16.67	181.00	1.35	16.08	244.00
1.96	20.25	108.16	1.86	19.79	120.88	1.76	19.08	131.20	1.66	18.74	159.04	1.46	16.81	182.80	1.36	16.22	246.40
1.97	20.41	109.12	1.87	19.95	121.96	1.77	19.24	132.40	1.67	18.89	160.48	1.47	16.96	184.60	1.37	16.36	248.80
1.98	20.57	110.08	1.88	20.11	123.04	1.78	19.40	133.60	1.68	19.04	161.92	1.48	17.10	186.40	1.38	16.50	251.20
1.99	20.73	111.04	1.89	20.27	124.12	1.79	19.55	134.80	1.69	19.19	163.36	1.49	17.25	188.20	1.39	16.63	253.60

LEASE PAYMENTS

Description: This table shows the Annual Percentage Rate and finance charge per $100 for monthly lease payments.

Example: A 4.30% lease payment for 2 years is equivalent to an APR of 3.96%. The charge per $100 cost is $ 3.20.

2 yr			3 yr			4 yr			5 yr			6 yr			7 yr		
MONTHLY PAYT	APR	CHARGE	MONTHLY PAYT	APR	CHARGE	MONTHLY PAYT	APR	CHARGE	MONTHLY PAYT	APR	CHARGE	MONTHLY PAYT	APR	CHARGE	MONTHLY PAYT	APR	CHARGE
4.30	3.96	3.20	3.00	6.04	8.00	2.30	5.63	10.40	1.90	5.88	14.00	1.70	7.56	22.40	1.50	7.37	26.00
4.31	4.26	3.44	3.01	6.31	8.36	2.31	5.89	10.88	1.91	6.12	14.60	1.71	7.79	23.12	1.51	7.59	26.84
4.32	4.55	3.68	3.02	6.58	8.72	2.32	6.14	11.36	1.92	6.36	15.20	1.72	8.02	23.84	1.52	7.82	27.68
4.33	4.85	3.92	3.03	6.84	9.08	2.33	6.39	11.84	1.93	6.60	15.80	1.73	8.24	24.56	1.53	8.04	28.52
4.34	5.14	4.16	3.04	7.11	9.44	2.34	6.64	12.32	1.94	6.84	16.40	1.74	8.47	25.28	1.54	8.26	29.36
4.35	5.44	4.40	3.05	7.37	9.80	2.35	6.90	12.80	1.95	7.08	17.00	1.75	8.70	26.00	1.55	8.48	30.20
4.36	5.73	4.64	3.06	7.64	10.16	2.36	7.15	13.28	1.96	7.32	17.60	1.76	8.93	26.72	1.56	8.70	31.04
4.37	6.03	4.88	3.07	7.90	10.52	2.37	7.40	13.76	1.97	7.56	18.20	1.77	9.15	27.44	1.57	8.92	31.88
4.38	6.32	5.12	3.08	8.17	10.88	2.38	7.65	14.24	1.98	7.80	18.80	1.78	9.38	28.16	1.58	9.14	32.72
4.39	6.61	5.36	3.09	8.43	11.24	2.39	7.89	14.72	1.99	8.04	19.40	1.79	9.60	28.88	1.59	9.35	33.56
4.40	6.91	5.60	3.10	8.69	11.60	2.40	8.14	15.20	2.00	8.27	20.00	1.80	9.82	29.60	1.60	9.57	34.40
4.41	7.20	5.84	3.11	8.96	11.96	2.41	8.39	15.68	2.01	8.51	20.60	1.81	10.05	30.32	1.61	9.79	35.24
4.42	7.49	6.08	3.12	9.22	12.32	2.42	8.64	16.16	2.02	8.75	21.20	1.82	10.27	31.04	1.62	10.00	36.08
4.43	7.78	6.32	3.13	9.48	12.68	2.43	8.88	16.64	2.03	8.98	21.80	1.83	10.49	31.76	1.63	10.22	36.92
4.44	8.08	6.56	3.14	9.74	13.04	2.44	9.13	17.12	2.04	9.22	22.40	1.84	10.71	32.48	1.64	10.43	37.76
4.45	8.37	6.80	3.15	10.00	13.40	2.45	9.38	17.60	2.05	9.45	23.00	1.85	10.93	33.20	1.65	10.64	38.60
4.46	8.66	7.04	3.16	10.26	13.76	2.46	9.62	18.08	2.06	9.68	23.60	1.86	11.16	33.92	1.66	10.86	39.44
4.47	8.95	7.28	3.17	10.53	14.12	2.47	9.87	18.56	2.07	9.92	24.20	1.87	11.37	34.64	1.67	11.07	40.28
4.48	9.24	7.52	3.18	10.79	14.48	2.48	10.11	19.04	2.08	10.15	24.80	1.88	11.59	35.36	1.68	11.28	41.12
4.49	9.53	7.76	3.19	11.05	14.84	2.49	10.36	19.52	2.09	10.38	25.40	1.89	11.81	36.08	1.69	11.49	41.96
4.50	9.82	8.00	3.20	11.30	15.20	2.50	10.60	20.00	2.10	10.61	26.00	1.90	12.03	36.80	1.70	11.70	42.80
4.51	10.11	8.24	3.21	11.56	15.56	2.51	10.84	20.48	2.11	10.84	26.60	1.91	12.25	37.52	1.71	11.91	43.64
4.52	10.40	8.48	3.22	11.82	15.92	2.52	11.08	20.96	2.12	11.07	27.20	1.92	12.46	38.24	1.72	12.12	44.48
4.53	10.69	8.72	3.23	12.08	16.28	2.53	11.33	21.44	2.13	11.30	27.80	1.93	12.68	38.96	1.73	12.33	45.32
4.54	10.98	8.96	3.24	12.34	16.64	2.54	11.57	21.92	2.14	11.53	28.40	1.94	12.90	39.68	1.74	12.54	46.16
4.55	11.27	9.20	3.25	12.60	17.00	2.55	11.81	22.40	2.15	11.76	29.00	1.95	13.11	40.40	1.75	12.74	47.00
4.56	11.56	9.44	3.26	12.85	17.36	2.56	12.05	22.88	2.16	11.99	29.60	1.96	13.33	41.12	1.76	12.95	47.84
4.57	11.85	9.68	3.27	13.11	17.72	2.57	12.29	23.36	2.17	12.22	30.20	1.97	13.54	41.84	1.77	13.16	48.68
4.58	12.14	9.92	3.28	13.37	18.08	2.58	12.53	23.84	2.18	12.45	30.80	1.98	13.75	42.56	1.78	13.36	49.52
4.59	12.43	10.16	3.29	13.62	18.44	2.59	12.77	24.32	2.19	12.67	31.40	1.99	13.97	43.28	1.79	13.57	50.36
4.60	12.72	10.40	3.30	13.88	18.80	2.60	13.01	24.80	2.20	12.90	32.00	2.00	14.18	44.00	1.80	13.77	51.20
4.61	13.00	10.64	3.31	14.14	19.16	2.61	13.25	25.28	2.21	13.12	32.60	2.01	14.39	44.72	1.81	13.98	52.04
4.62	13.29	10.88	3.32	14.39	19.52	2.62	13.49	25.76	2.22	13.35	33.20	2.02	14.60	45.44	1.82	14.18	52.88
4.63	13.58	11.12	3.33	14.65	19.88	2.63	13.72	26.24	2.23	13.57	33.80	2.03	14.82	46.16	1.83	14.39	53.72
4.64	13.87	11.36	3.34	14.90	20.24	2.64	13.96	26.72	2.24	13.80	34.40	2.04	15.03	46.88	1.84	14.59	54.56
4.65	14.15	11.60	3.35	15.15	20.60	2.65	14.20	27.20	2.25	14.02	35.00	2.05	15.24	47.60	1.85	14.79	55.40
4.66	14.44	11.84	3.36	15.41	20.96	2.66	14.43	27.68	2.26	14.25	35.60	2.06	15.45	48.32	1.86	14.99	56.24
4.67	14.73	12.08	3.37	15.66	21.32	2.67	14.67	28.16	2.27	14.47	36.20	2.07	15.66	49.04	1.87	15.19	57.08
4.68	15.01	12.32	3.38	15.92	21.68	2.68	14.91	28.64	2.28	14.69	36.80	2.08	15.87	49.76	1.88	15.39	57.92
4.69	15.30	12.56	3.39	16.17	22.04	2.69	15.14	29.12	2.29	14.91	37.40	2.09	16.07	50.48	1.89	15.59	58.76
4.70	15.59	12.80	3.40	16.42	22.40	2.70	15.38	29.60	2.30	15.13	38.00	2.10	16.28	51.20	1.90	15.79	59.60
4.71	15.87	13.04	3.41	16.67	22.76	2.71	15.61	30.08	2.31	15.36	38.60	2.11	16.49	51.92	1.91	15.99	60.44
4.72	16.16	13.28	3.42	16.93	23.12	2.72	15.85	30.56	2.32	15.58	39.20	2.12	16.70	52.64	1.92	16.19	61.28
4.73	16.44	13.52	3.43	17.18	23.48	2.73	16.08	31.04	2.33	15.80	39.80	2.13	16.90	53.36	1.93	16.39	62.12
4.74	16.73	13.76	3.44	17.43	23.84	2.74	16.31	31.52	2.34	16.02	40.40	2.14	17.11	54.08	1.94	16.59	62.96
4.75	17.01	14.00	3.45	17.68	24.20	2.75	16.55	32.00	2.35	16.24	41.00	2.15	17.32	54.80	1.95	16.79	63.80
4.76	17.30	14.24	3.46	17.93	24.56	2.76	16.78	32.48	2.36	16.45	41.60	2.16	17.52	55.52	1.96	16.98	64.64
4.77	17.58	14.48	3.47	18.18	24.92	2.77	17.01	32.96	2.37	16.67	42.20	2.17	17.73	56.24	1.97	17.18	65.48
4.78	17.87	14.72	3.48	18.43	25.28	2.78	17.24	33.44	2.38	16.89	42.80	2.18	17.93	56.96	1.98	17.38	66.32
4.79	18.15	14.96	3.49	18.68	25.64	2.79	17.47	33.92	2.39	17.11	43.40	2.19	18.14	57.68	1.99	17.57	67.16
4.80	18.44	15.20	3.50	18.93	26.00	2.80	17.71	34.40	2.40	17.33	44.00	2.20	18.34	58.40	2.00	17.77	68.00
4.81	18.72	15.44	3.51	19.18	26.36	2.81	17.94	34.88	2.41	17.54	44.60	2.21	18.54	59.12	2.01	17.96	68.84
4.82	19.00	15.68	3.52	19.43	26.72	2.82	18.17	35.36	2.42	17.75	45.20	2.22	18.75	59.84	2.02	18.16	69.68
4.83	19.29	15.92	3.53	19.68	27.08	2.83	18.40	35.84	2.43	17.98	45.80	2.23	18.95	60.56	2.03	18.35	70.52
4.84	19.57	16.16	3.54	19.93	27.44	2.84	18.63	36.32	2.44	18.19	46.40	2.24	19.15	61.28	2.04	18.55	71.36
4.85	19.85	16.40	3.55	20.18	27.80	2.85	18.86	36.80	2.45	18.41	47.00	2.25	19.36	62.00	2.05	18.74	72.20
4.86	20.14	16.64	3.56	20.43	28.16	2.86	19.09	37.28	2.46	18.62	47.60	2.26	19.56	62.72	2.06	18.94	73.04
4.87	20.42	16.88	3.57	20.67	28.52	2.87	19.31	37.76	2.47	18.84	48.20	2.27	19.76	63.44	2.07	19.13	73.88
4.88	20.70	17.12	3.58	20.92	28.88	2.88	19.54	38.24	2.48	19.05	48.80	2.28	19.96	64.16	2.08	19.32	74.72
4.89	20.98	17.36	3.59	21.17	29.24	2.89	19.77	38.72	2.49	19.27	49.40	2.29	20.16	64.88	2.09	19.51	75.56
4.90	21.27	17.60	3.60	21.42	29.60	2.90	20.00	39.20	2.50	19.48	50.00	2.30	20.36	65.60	2.10	19.70	76.40
4.91	21.55	17.84	3.61	21.66	29.96	2.91	20.23	39.68	2.51	19.69	50.60	2.31	20.56	66.32	2.11	19.90	77.24
4.92	21.83	18.08	3.62	21.91	30.32	2.92	20.45	40.16	2.52	19.91	51.20	2.32	20.76	67.04	2.12	20.09	78.08
4.93	22.11	18.32	3.63	22.15	30.68	2.93	20.68	40.64	2.53	20.12	51.80	2.33	20.96	67.76	2.13	20.28	78.92
4.94	22.39	18.56	3.64	22.40	31.04	2.94	20.91	41.12	2.54	20.33	52.40	2.34	21.16	68.48	2.14	20.47	79.76
4.95	22.67	18.80	3.65	22.65	31.40	2.95	21.13	41.60	2.55	20.54	53.00	2.35	21.36	69.20	2.15	20.66	80.60
4.96	22.96	19.04	3.66	22.89	31.76	2.96	21.36	42.08	2.56	20.75	53.60	2.36	21.56	69.92	2.16	20.85	81.44
4.97	23.24	19.28	3.67	23.14	32.12	2.97	21.59	42.56	2.57	20.97	54.20	2.37	21.75	70.64	2.17	21.04	82.28
4.98	23.52	19.52	3.68	23.38	32.48	2.98	21.81	43.04	2.58	21.18	54.80	2.38	21.95	71.36	2.18	21.23	83.12
4.99	23.80	19.76	3.69	23.63	32.84	2.99	22.04	43.52	2.59	21.39	55.40	2.39	22.15	72.08	2.19	21.42	83.96

Description: This table shows the Annual Percentage Rate and finance charge per $100 for monthly lease payments.

Example: A 1.30% lease payment for 8 years is equivalent to an APR of 6.11%. The charge per $100 cost is $ 24.80.

8 yr MONTHLY PAYT	APR	CHARGE	9 yr MONTHLY PAYT	APR	CHARGE	10 yr MONTHLY PAYT	APR	CHARGE	12 yr MONTHLY PAYT	APR	CHARGE	15 yr MONTHLY PAYT	APR	CHARGE	20 yr MONTHLY PAYT	APR	CHARGE
1.30	6.11	24.80	1.20	6.37	29.60	1.10	6.13	32.00	1.00	6.78	44.00	.80	5.38	44.00	.70	5.89	68.00
1.31	6.34	25.76	1.21	6.59	30.68	1.11	6.34	33.20	1.01	6.98	45.44	.81	5.58	45.80	.71	6.07	70.40
1.32	6.56	26.72	1.22	6.80	31.76	1.12	6.55	34.40	1.02	7.18	46.88	.82	5.78	47.60	.72	6.26	72.80
1.33	6.78	27.68	1.23	7.02	32.84	1.13	6.76	35.60	1.03	7.38	48.32	.83	5.97	49.40	.73	6.43	75.20
1.34	7.00	28.64	1.24	7.23	33.92	1.14	6.97	36.80	1.04	7.58	49.76	.84	6.17	51.20	.74	6.61	77.60
1.35	7.22	29.60	1.25	7.44	35.00	1.15	7.18	38.00	1.05	7.78	51.20	.85	6.36	53.00	.75	6.79	80.00
1.36	7.43	30.56	1.26	7.65	36.08	1.16	7.39	39.20	1.06	7.97	52.64	.86	6.55	54.80	.76	6.97	82.40
1.37	7.65	31.52	1.27	7.86	37.16	1.17	7.60	40.40	1.07	8.17	54.08	.87	6.74	56.60	.77	7.14	84.80
1.38	7.87	32.48	1.28	8.07	38.24	1.18	7.80	41.60	1.08	8.36	55.52	.88	6.94	58.40	.78	7.31	87.20
1.39	8.08	33.44	1.29	8.28	39.32	1.19	8.01	42.80	1.09	8.56	56.96	.89	7.12	60.20	.79	7.49	89.60
1.40	8.30	34.40	1.30	8.49	40.40	1.20	8.21	44.00	1.10	8.75	58.40	.90	7.31	62.00	.80	7.66	92.00
1.41	8.51	35.36	1.31	8.70	41.48	1.21	8.42	45.20	1.11	8.94	59.84	.91	7.50	63.80	.81	7.83	94.40
1.42	8.72	36.32	1.32	8.90	42.56	1.22	8.62	46.40	1.12	9.13	61.28	.92	7.69	65.60	.82	8.00	96.80
1.43	8.94	37.28	1.33	9.11	43.64	1.23	8.82	47.60	1.13	9.32	62.72	.93	7.87	67.40	.83	8.17	99.20
1.44	9.15	38.24	1.34	9.31	44.72	1.24	9.02	48.80	1.14	9.51	64.16	.94	8.06	69.20	.84	8.34	101.60
1.45	9.36	39.20	1.35	9.52	45.80	1.25	9.22	50.00	1.15	9.70	65.60	.95	8.24	71.00	.85	8.50	104.00
1.46	9.57	40.16	1.36	9.72	46.88	1.26	9.42	51.20	1.16	9.89	67.04	.96	8.42	72.80	.86	8.67	106.40
1.47	9.78	41.12	1.37	9.92	47.96	1.27	9.62	52.40	1.17	10.07	68.48	.97	8.60	74.60	.87	8.84	108.80
1.48	9.99	42.08	1.38	10.13	49.04	1.28	9.81	53.60	1.18	10.26	69.92	.98	8.78	76.40	.88	9.00	111.20
1.49	10.19	43.04	1.39	10.33	50.12	1.29	10.01	54.80	1.19	10.45	71.36	.99	8.96	78.20	.89	9.16	113.60
1.50	10.40	44.00	1.40	10.53	51.20	1.30	10.21	56.00	1.20	10.63	72.80	1.00	9.14	80.00	.90	9.33	116.00
1.51	10.61	44.96	1.41	10.73	52.28	1.31	10.40	57.20	1.21	10.81	74.24	1.01	9.32	81.80	.91	9.49	118.40
1.52	10.81	45.92	1.42	10.93	53.36	1.32	10.60	58.40	1.22	11.00	75.68	1.02	9.50	83.60	.92	9.65	120.80
1.53	11.02	46.88	1.43	11.13	54.44	1.33	10.79	59.60	1.23	11.18	77.12	1.03	9.68	85.40	.93	9.81	123.20
1.54	11.22	47.84	1.44	11.32	55.52	1.34	10.98	60.80	1.24	11.36	78.56	1.04	9.85	87.20	.94	9.98	125.60
1.55	11.43	48.80	1.45	11.52	56.60	1.35	11.18	62.00	1.25	11.54	80.00	1.05	10.03	89.00	.95	10.14	128.00
1.56	11.63	49.76	1.46	11.72	57.68	1.36	11.37	63.20	1.26	11.72	81.44	1.06	10.20	90.80	.96	10.30	130.40
1.57	11.83	50.72	1.47	11.91	58.76	1.37	11.56	64.40	1.27	11.91	82.88	1.07	10.38	92.60	.97	10.45	132.80
1.58	12.04	51.68	1.48	12.11	59.84	1.38	11.75	65.60	1.28	12.08	84.32	1.08	10.55	94.40	.98	10.61	135.20
1.59	12.24	52.64	1.49	12.30	60.92	1.39	11.94	66.80	1.29	12.26	85.76	1.09	10.72	96.20	.99	10.77	137.60
1.60	12.44	53.60	1.50	12.50	62.00	1.40	12.13	68.00	1.30	12.44	87.20	1.10	10.89	98.00	1.00	10.93	140.00
1.61	12.64	54.56	1.51	12.69	63.08	1.41	12.32	69.20	1.31	12.62	88.64	1.11	11.06	99.80	1.01	11.08	142.40
1.62	12.84	55.52	1.52	12.88	64.16	1.42	12.51	70.40	1.32	12.80	90.08	1.12	11.23	101.60	1.02	11.24	144.80
1.63	13.04	56.48	1.53	13.08	65.24	1.43	12.70	71.60	1.33	12.97	91.52	1.13	11.40	103.40	1.03	11.40	147.20
1.64	13.24	57.44	1.54	13.27	66.32	1.44	12.88	72.80	1.34	13.15	92.96	1.14	11.57	105.20	1.04	11.55	149.60
1.65	13.43	58.40	1.55	13.46	67.40	1.45	13.07	74.00	1.35	13.33	94.40	1.15	11.74	107.00	1.05	11.71	152.00
1.66	13.63	59.36	1.56	13.65	68.48	1.46	13.25	75.20	1.36	13.50	95.84	1.16	11.91	108.80	1.06	11.86	154.40
1.67	13.83	60.32	1.57	13.84	69.56	1.47	13.44	76.40	1.37	13.68	97.28	1.17	12.08	110.60	1.07	12.01	156.80
1.68	14.02	61.28	1.58	14.03	70.64	1.48	13.63	77.60	1.38	13.85	98.72	1.18	12.25	112.40	1.08	12.17	159.20
1.69	14.22	62.24	1.59	14.22	71.72	1.49	13.81	78.80	1.39	14.02	100.16	1.19	12.41	114.20	1.09	12.32	161.60
1.70	14.42	63.20	1.60	14.41	72.80	1.50	13.99	80.00	1.40	14.20	101.60	1.20	12.58	116.00	1.10	12.47	164.00
1.71	14.61	64.16	1.61	14.60	73.88	1.51	14.18	81.20	1.41	14.37	103.04	1.21	12.74	117.80	1.11	12.63	166.40
1.72	14.81	65.12	1.62	14.78	74.96	1.52	14.36	82.40	1.42	14.54	104.48	1.22	12.91	119.60	1.12	12.78	168.80
1.73	15.00	66.08	1.63	14.97	76.04	1.53	14.54	83.60	1.43	14.71	105.92	1.23	13.07	121.40	1.13	12.93	171.20
1.74	15.19	67.04	1.64	15.16	77.12	1.54	14.72	84.80	1.44	14.88	107.36	1.24	13.24	123.20	1.14	13.08	173.60
1.75	15.39	68.00	1.65	15.34	78.20	1.55	14.91	86.00	1.45	15.06	108.80	1.25	13.40	125.00	1.15	13.23	176.00
1.76	15.58	68.96	1.66	15.53	79.28	1.56	15.09	87.20	1.46	15.23	110.24	1.26	13.57	126.80	1.16	13.38	178.40
1.77	15.77	69.92	1.67	15.72	80.36	1.57	15.27	88.40	1.47	15.40	111.68	1.27	13.73	128.60	1.17	13.53	180.80
1.78	15.96	70.88	1.68	15.90	81.44	1.58	15.45	89.60	1.48	15.57	113.12	1.28	13.89	130.40	1.18	13.68	183.20
1.79	16.15	71.84	1.69	16.08	82.52	1.59	15.63	90.80	1.49	15.73	114.56	1.29	14.05	132.20	1.19	13.83	185.60
1.80	16.34	72.80	1.70	16.27	83.60	1.60	15.81	92.00	1.50	15.90	116.00	1.30	14.21	134.00	1.20	13.98	188.00
1.81	16.53	73.76	1.71	16.45	84.68	1.61	15.98	93.20	1.51	16.07	117.44	1.31	14.37	135.80	1.21	14.13	190.40
1.82	16.72	74.72	1.72	16.64	85.76	1.62	16.16	94.40	1.52	16.24	118.88	1.32	14.54	137.60	1.22	14.27	192.80
1.83	16.91	75.68	1.73	16.82	86.84	1.63	16.34	95.60	1.53	16.41	120.32	1.33	14.70	139.40	1.23	14.42	195.20
1.84	17.10	76.64	1.74	17.00	87.92	1.64	16.52	96.80	1.54	16.57	121.76	1.34	14.86	141.20	1.24	14.57	197.60
1.85	17.29	77.60	1.75	17.18	89.00	1.65	16.69	98.00	1.55	16.74	123.20	1.35	15.01	143.00	1.25	14.72	200.00
1.86	17.48	78.56	1.76	17.36	90.08	1.66	16.87	99.20	1.56	16.91	124.64	1.36	15.17	144.80	1.26	14.86	202.40
1.87	17.67	79.52	1.77	17.55	91.16	1.67	17.05	100.40	1.57	17.07	126.08	1.37	15.33	146.60	1.27	15.01	204.80
1.88	17.85	80.48	1.78	17.73	92.24	1.68	17.22	101.60	1.58	17.24	127.52	1.38	15.49	148.40	1.28	15.16	207.20
1.89	18.04	81.44	1.79	17.91	93.32	1.69	17.40	102.80	1.59	17.41	128.96	1.39	15.65	150.20	1.29	15.30	209.60
1.90	18.23	82.40	1.80	18.09	94.40	1.70	17.57	104.00	1.60	17.57	130.40	1.40	15.81	152.00	1.30	15.45	212.00
1.91	18.41	83.36	1.81	18.27	95.48	1.71	17.75	105.20	1.61	17.74	131.84	1.41	15.96	153.80	1.31	15.60	214.40
1.92	18.60	84.32	1.82	18.44	96.56	1.72	17.92	106.40	1.62	17.90	133.28	1.42	16.12	155.60	1.32	15.74	216.80
1.93	18.79	85.28	1.83	18.62	97.64	1.73	18.10	107.60	1.63	18.06	134.72	1.43	16.28	157.40	1.33	15.89	219.20
1.94	18.97	86.24	1.84	18.80	98.72	1.74	18.27	108.80	1.64	18.23	136.16	1.44	16.43	159.20	1.34	16.03	221.60
1.95	19.16	87.20	1.85	18.98	99.80	1.75	18.44	110.00	1.65	18.39	137.60	1.45	16.59	161.00	1.35	16.18	224.00
1.96	19.34	88.16	1.86	19.16	100.88	1.76	18.62	111.20	1.66	18.55	139.04	1.46	16.75	162.80	1.36	16.32	226.40
1.97	19.52	89.12	1.87	19.34	101.96	1.77	18.79	112.40	1.67	18.72	140.48	1.47	16.90	164.60	1.37	16.47	228.80
1.98	19.71	90.08	1.88	19.51	103.04	1.78	18.96	113.60	1.68	18.88	141.92	1.48	17.06	166.40	1.38	16.61	231.20
1.99	19.89	91.04	1.89	19.69	104.12	1.79	19.13	114.80	1.69	19.04	143.36	1.49	17.21	168.20	1.39	16.75	233.60

Description: This table shows the Annual Percentage Rate and finance charge per $100 for monthly lease payments.

Example: A 4.30% lease payment for 2 years is equivalent to an APR of 9.41%. The charge per $100 cost is $ 8.20.

2 yr PAYT	APR	CHARGE	3 yr PAYT	APR	CHARGE	4 yr PAYT	APR	CHARGE	5 yr PAYT	APR	CHARGE	6 yr PAYT	APR	CHARGE	7 yr PAYT	APR	CHARGE
4.30	9.41	8.20	3.00	9.18	13.00	2.30	7.83	15.40	1.90	7.51	19.00	1.70	8.74	27.40	1.50	8.33	31.00
4.31	9.69	8.44	3.01	9.43	13.36	2.31	8.07	15.88	1.91	7.73	19.60	1.71	8.96	28.12	1.51	8.54	31.84
4.32	9.96	8.68	3.02	9.68	13.72	2.32	8.30	16.36	1.92	7.96	20.20	1.72	9.18	28.84	1.52	8.75	32.68
4.33	10.23	8.92	3.03	9.92	14.08	2.33	8.54	16.84	1.93	8.19	20.80	1.73	9.39	29.56	1.53	8.96	33.52
4.34	10.50	9.16	3.04	10.17	14.44	2.34	8.77	17.32	1.94	8.42	21.40	1.74	9.61	30.28	1.54	9.17	34.36
4.35	10.78	9.40	3.05	10.42	14.80	2.35	9.01	17.80	1.95	8.64	22.00	1.75	9.83	31.00	1.55	9.38	35.20
4.36	11.05	9.64	3.06	10.67	15.16	2.36	9.24	18.28	1.96	8.87	22.60	1.76	10.04	31.72	1.56	9.59	36.04
4.37	11.32	9.88	3.07	10.91	15.52	2.37	9.48	18.76	1.97	9.09	23.20	1.77	10.25	32.44	1.57	9.80	36.88
4.38	11.59	10.12	3.08	11.16	15.88	2.38	9.71	19.24	1.98	9.32	23.80	1.78	10.47	33.16	1.58	10.01	37.72
4.39	11.86	10.36	3.09	11.41	16.24	2.39	9.95	19.72	1.99	9.54	24.40	1.79	10.68	33.88	1.59	10.22	38.56
4.40	12.13	10.60	3.10	11.65	16.60	2.40	10.18	20.20	2.00	9.77	25.00	1.80	10.90	34.60	1.60	10.42	39.40
4.41	12.41	10.84	3.11	11.90	16.96	2.41	10.41	20.68	2.01	9.99	25.60	1.81	11.11	35.32	1.61	10.63	40.24
4.42	12.68	11.08	3.12	12.14	17.32	2.42	10.64	21.16	2.02	10.21	26.20	1.82	11.32	36.04	1.62	10.83	41.08
4.43	12.95	11.32	3.13	12.39	17.68	2.43	10.88	21.64	2.03	10.43	26.80	1.83	11.53	36.76	1.63	11.04	41.92
4.44	13.22	11.56	3.14	12.64	18.04	2.44	11.11	22.12	2.04	10.66	27.40	1.84	11.74	37.48	1.64	11.24	42.76
4.45	13.49	11.80	3.15	12.88	18.40	2.45	11.34	22.60	2.05	10.88	28.00	1.85	11.95	38.20	1.65	11.45	43.60
4.46	13.76	12.04	3.16	13.12	18.76	2.46	11.57	23.08	2.06	11.10	28.60	1.86	12.16	38.92	1.66	11.65	44.44
4.47	14.03	12.28	3.17	13.37	19.12	2.47	11.80	23.56	2.07	11.32	29.20	1.87	12.37	39.64	1.67	11.86	45.28
4.48	14.30	12.52	3.18	13.61	19.48	2.48	12.03	24.04	2.08	11.54	29.80	1.88	12.58	40.36	1.68	12.06	46.12
4.49	14.57	12.76	3.19	13.86	19.84	2.49	12.26	24.52	2.09	11.76	30.40	1.89	12.79	41.08	1.69	12.26	46.96
4.50	14.84	13.00	3.20	14.10	20.20	2.50	12.49	25.00	2.10	11.98	31.00	1.90	13.00	41.80	1.70	12.46	47.80
4.51	15.11	13.24	3.21	14.34	20.56	2.51	12.72	25.48	2.11	12.20	31.60	1.91	13.21	42.52	1.71	12.66	48.64
4.52	15.38	13.48	3.22	14.59	20.92	2.52	12.95	25.96	2.12	12.42	32.20	1.92	13.41	43.24	1.72	12.87	49.48
4.53	15.65	13.72	3.23	14.83	21.28	2.53	13.18	26.44	2.13	12.63	32.80	1.93	13.62	43.96	1.73	13.07	50.32
4.54	15.92	13.96	3.24	15.07	21.64	2.54	13.41	26.92	2.14	12.85	33.40	1.94	13.83	44.68	1.74	13.27	51.16
4.55	16.19	14.20	3.25	15.31	22.00	2.55	13.64	27.40	2.15	13.07	34.00	1.95	14.04	45.40	1.75	13.47	52.00
4.56	16.46	14.44	3.26	15.56	22.36	2.56	13.86	27.88	2.16	13.29	34.60	1.96	14.24	46.12	1.76	13.66	52.84
4.57	16.73	14.68	3.27	15.80	22.72	2.57	14.09	28.36	2.17	13.50	35.20	1.97	14.45	46.84	1.77	13.86	53.68
4.58	17.00	14.92	3.28	16.04	23.08	2.58	14.32	28.84	2.18	13.72	35.80	1.98	14.65	47.56	1.78	14.06	54.52
4.59	17.27	15.16	3.29	16.28	23.44	2.59	14.55	29.32	2.19	13.94	36.40	1.99	14.86	48.28	1.79	14.26	55.36
4.60	17.54	15.40	3.30	16.52	23.80	2.60	14.77	29.80	2.20	14.15	37.00	2.00	15.06	49.00	1.80	14.46	56.20
4.61	17.80	15.64	3.31	16.76	24.16	2.61	15.00	30.28	2.21	14.37	37.60	2.01	15.26	49.72	1.81	14.65	57.04
4.62	18.07	15.88	3.32	17.00	24.52	2.62	15.22	30.76	2.22	14.58	38.20	2.02	15.47	50.44	1.82	14.85	57.88
4.63	18.34	16.12	3.33	17.25	24.88	2.63	15.45	31.24	2.23	14.80	38.80	2.03	15.67	51.16	1.83	15.05	58.72
4.64	18.61	16.36	3.34	17.49	25.24	2.64	15.68	31.72	2.24	15.01	39.40	2.04	15.87	51.88	1.84	15.24	59.56
4.65	18.88	16.60	3.35	17.73	25.60	2.65	15.90	32.20	2.25	15.22	40.00	2.05	16.08	52.60	1.85	15.44	60.40
4.66	19.15	16.84	3.36	17.97	25.96	2.66	16.13	32.68	2.26	15.44	40.60	2.06	16.28	53.32	1.86	15.63	61.24
4.67	19.41	17.08	3.37	18.21	26.32	2.67	16.35	33.16	2.27	15.65	41.20	2.07	16.48	54.04	1.87	15.83	62.08
4.68	19.68	17.32	3.38	18.44	26.68	2.68	16.57	33.64	2.28	15.86	41.80	2.08	16.68	54.76	1.88	16.02	62.92
4.69	19.95	17.56	3.39	18.68	27.04	2.69	16.80	34.12	2.29	16.08	42.40	2.09	16.88	55.48	1.89	16.22	63.76
4.70	20.22	17.80	3.40	18.92	27.40	2.70	17.02	34.60	2.30	16.29	43.00	2.10	17.08	56.20	1.90	16.41	64.60
4.71	20.48	18.04	3.41	19.16	27.76	2.71	17.24	35.08	2.31	16.50	43.60	2.11	17.28	56.92	1.91	16.60	65.44
4.72	20.75	18.28	3.42	19.40	28.12	2.72	17.47	35.56	2.32	16.71	44.20	2.12	17.48	57.64	1.92	16.79	66.28
4.73	21.02	18.52	3.43	19.64	28.48	2.73	17.69	36.04	2.33	16.92	44.80	2.13	17.68	58.36	1.93	16.99	67.12
4.74	21.29	18.76	3.44	19.88	28.84	2.74	17.91	36.52	2.34	17.13	45.40	2.14	17.88	59.08	1.94	17.18	67.96
4.75	21.55	19.00	3.45	20.12	29.20	2.75	18.13	37.00	2.35	17.34	46.00	2.15	18.08	59.80	1.95	17.37	68.80
4.76	21.82	19.24	3.46	20.35	29.56	2.76	18.36	37.48	2.36	17.55	46.60	2.16	18.28	60.52	1.96	17.56	69.64
4.77	22.09	19.48	3.47	20.59	29.92	2.77	18.58	37.96	2.37	17.76	47.20	2.17	18.48	61.24	1.97	17.75	70.48
4.78	22.35	19.72	3.48	20.83	30.28	2.78	18.80	38.44	2.38	17.97	47.80	2.18	18.68	61.96	1.98	17.94	71.32
4.79	22.62	19.96	3.49	21.06	30.64	2.79	19.02	38.92	2.39	18.18	48.40	2.19	18.87	62.68	1.99	18.13	72.16
4.80	22.89	20.20	3.50	21.30	31.00	2.80	19.24	39.40	2.40	18.39	49.00	2.20	19.07	63.40	2.00	18.32	73.00
4.81	23.15	20.44	3.51	21.54	31.36	2.81	19.46	39.88	2.41	18.60	49.60	2.21	19.27	64.12	2.01	18.51	73.84
4.82	23.42	20.68	3.52	21.78	31.72	2.82	19.68	40.36	2.42	18.81	50.20	2.22	19.46	64.84	2.02	18.70	74.68
4.83	23.68	20.92	3.53	22.01	32.08	2.83	19.90	40.84	2.43	19.01	50.80	2.23	19.66	65.56	2.03	18.89	75.52
4.84	23.95	21.16	3.54	22.25	32.44	2.84	20.12	41.32	2.44	19.22	51.40	2.24	19.86	66.28	2.04	19.08	76.36
4.85	24.22	21.40	3.55	22.48	32.80	2.85	20.34	41.80	2.45	19.43	52.00	2.25	20.05	67.00	2.05	19.27	77.20
4.86	24.48	21.64	3.56	22.72	33.16	2.86	20.56	42.28	2.46	19.64	52.60	2.26	20.25	67.72	2.06	19.46	78.04
4.87	24.75	21.88	3.57	22.96	33.52	2.87	20.78	42.76	2.47	19.84	53.20	2.27	20.44	68.44	2.07	19.64	78.88
4.88	25.01	22.12	3.58	23.19	33.88	2.88	21.00	43.24	2.48	20.05	53.80	2.28	20.64	69.16	2.08	19.83	79.72
4.89	25.28	22.36	3.59	23.43	34.24	2.89	21.22	43.72	2.49	20.26	54.40	2.29	20.83	69.88	2.09	20.02	80.56
4.90	25.54	22.60	3.60	23.66	34.60	2.90	21.43	44.20	2.50	20.46	55.00	2.30	21.03	70.60	2.10	20.20	81.40
4.91	25.81	22.84	3.61	23.90	34.96	2.91	21.65	44.68	2.51	20.67	55.60	2.31	21.22	71.32	2.11	20.39	82.24
4.92	26.08	23.08	3.62	24.13	35.32	2.92	21.87	45.16	2.52	20.87	56.20	2.32	21.42	72.04	2.12	20.58	83.08
4.93	26.34	23.32	3.63	24.36	35.68	2.93	22.09	45.64	2.53	21.08	56.80	2.33	21.61	72.76	2.13	20.76	83.92
4.94	26.61	23.56	3.64	24.60	36.04	2.94	22.31	46.12	2.54	21.28	57.40	2.34	21.80	73.48	2.14	20.95	84.76
4.95	26.87	23.80	3.65	24.83	36.40	2.95	22.52	46.60	2.55	21.49	58.00	2.35	21.99	74.20	2.15	21.13	85.60
4.96	27.13	24.04	3.66	25.07	36.76	2.96	22.74	47.08	2.56	21.69	58.60	2.36	22.19	74.92	2.16	21.32	86.44
4.97	27.40	24.28	3.67	25.30	37.12	2.97	22.96	47.56	2.57	21.90	59.20	2.37	22.38	75.64	2.17	21.50	87.28
4.98	27.66	24.52	3.68	25.53	37.48	2.98	23.17	48.04	2.58	22.10	59.80	2.38	22.57	76.36	2.18	21.69	88.12
4.99	27.93	24.76	3.69	25.77	37.84	2.99	23.39	48.52	2.59	22.30	60.40	2.39	22.76	77.08	2.19	21.87	88.96

Description: This table shows the Annual Percentage Rate and finance charge per $100 for monthly lease payments.

Example: A 1.30% lease payment for 8 years is equivalent to an APR of 6.96%. The charge per $100 cost is $ 29.80.

8 yr PAYT	APR	CHARGE	9 yr PAYT	APR	CHARGE	10 yr PAYT	APR	CHARGE	12 yr PAYT	APR	CHARGE	15 yr PAYT	APR	CHARGE	20 yr PAYT	APR	CHARGE
1.30	6.96	29.80	1.20	7.07	34.60	1.10	6.74	37.00	1.00	7.22	49.00	.80	5.72	49.00	.70	6.08	73.00
1.31	7.17	30.76	1.21	7.28	35.68	1.11	6.94	38.20	1.01	7.41	50.44	.81	5.91	50.80	.71	6.26	75.40
1.32	7.38	31.72	1.22	7.48	36.76	1.12	7.14	39.40	1.02	7.60	51.88	.82	6.10	52.60	.72	6.44	77.80
1.33	7.59	32.68	1.23	7.69	37.84	1.13	7.35	40.60	1.03	7.79	53.32	.83	6.29	54.40	.73	6.61	80.20
1.34	7.80	33.64	1.24	7.89	38.92	1.14	7.55	41.80	1.04	7.98	54.76	.84	6.48	56.20	.74	6.78	82.60
1.35	8.01	34.60	1.25	8.09	40.00	1.15	7.75	43.00	1.05	8.17	56.20	.85	6.67	58.00	.75	6.96	85.00
1.36	8.22	35.56	1.26	8.30	41.08	1.16	7.94	44.20	1.06	8.36	57.64	.86	6.85	59.80	.76	7.13	87.40
1.37	8.42	36.52	1.27	8.50	42.16	1.17	8.14	45.40	1.07	8.55	59.08	.87	7.04	61.60	.77	7.30	89.80
1.38	8.63	37.48	1.28	8.70	43.24	1.18	8.34	46.60	1.08	8.74	60.52	.88	7.22	63.40	.78	7.47	92.20
1.39	8.84	38.44	1.29	8.90	44.32	1.19	8.54	47.80	1.09	8.92	61.96	.89	7.41	65.20	.79	7.64	94.60
1.40	9.04	39.40	1.30	9.10	45.40	1.20	8.73	49.00	1.10	9.11	63.40	.90	7.59	67.00	.80	7.80	97.00
1.41	9.24	40.36	1.31	9.30	46.48	1.21	8.93	50.20	1.11	9.29	64.84	.91	7.77	68.80	.81	7.97	99.40
1.42	9.45	41.32	1.32	9.49	47.56	1.22	9.12	51.40	1.12	9.48	66.28	.92	7.95	70.60	.82	8.14	101.80
1.43	9.65	42.28	1.33	9.69	48.64	1.23	9.32	52.60	1.13	9.66	67.72	.93	8.13	72.40	.83	8.30	104.20
1.44	9.85	43.24	1.34	9.89	49.72	1.24	9.51	53.80	1.14	9.85	69.16	.94	8.31	74.20	.84	8.47	106.60
1.45	10.05	44.20	1.35	10.08	50.80	1.25	9.70	55.00	1.15	10.03	70.60	.95	8.49	76.00	.85	8.63	109.00
1.46	10.26	45.16	1.36	10.28	51.88	1.26	9.89	56.20	1.16	10.21	72.04	.96	8.66	77.80	.86	8.79	111.40
1.47	10.46	46.12	1.37	10.47	52.96	1.27	10.08	57.40	1.17	10.39	73.48	.97	8.84	79.60	.87	8.96	113.80
1.48	10.66	47.08	1.38	10.67	54.04	1.28	10.27	58.60	1.18	10.57	74.92	.98	9.02	81.40	.88	9.12	116.20
1.49	10.86	48.04	1.39	10.86	55.12	1.29	10.46	59.80	1.19	10.75	76.36	.99	9.19	83.20	.89	9.28	118.60
1.50	11.06	49.00	1.40	11.06	56.20	1.30	10.65	61.00	1.20	10.93	77.80	1.00	9.37	85.00	.90	9.44	121.00
1.51	11.25	49.96	1.41	11.25	57.28	1.31	10.84	62.20	1.21	11.11	79.24	1.01	9.54	86.80	.91	9.60	123.40
1.52	11.45	50.92	1.42	11.44	58.36	1.32	11.03	63.40	1.22	11.29	80.68	1.02	9.71	88.60	.92	9.76	125.80
1.53	11.65	51.88	1.43	11.63	59.44	1.33	11.22	64.60	1.23	11.47	82.12	1.03	9.89	90.40	.93	9.92	128.20
1.54	11.85	52.84	1.44	11.82	60.52	1.34	11.41	65.80	1.24	11.65	83.56	1.04	10.06	92.20	.94	10.08	130.60
1.55	12.04	53.80	1.45	12.01	61.60	1.35	11.59	67.00	1.25	11.82	85.00	1.05	10.23	94.00	.95	10.24	133.00
1.56	12.24	54.76	1.46	12.20	62.68	1.36	11.78	68.20	1.26	12.00	86.44	1.06	10.40	95.80	.96	10.39	135.40
1.57	12.43	55.72	1.47	12.39	63.76	1.37	11.96	69.40	1.27	12.17	87.88	1.07	10.57	97.60	.97	10.55	137.80
1.58	12.63	56.68	1.48	12.58	64.84	1.38	12.15	70.60	1.28	12.35	89.32	1.08	10.74	99.40	.98	10.71	140.20
1.59	12.82	57.64	1.49	12.77	65.92	1.39	12.33	71.80	1.29	12.52	90.76	1.09	10.91	101.20	.99	10.86	142.60
1.60	13.02	58.60	1.50	12.96	67.00	1.40	12.52	73.00	1.30	12.70	92.20	1.10	11.07	103.00	1.00	11.02	145.00
1.61	13.21	59.56	1.51	13.15	68.08	1.41	12.70	74.20	1.31	12.87	93.64	1.11	11.24	104.80	1.01	11.17	147.40
1.62	13.40	60.52	1.52	13.33	69.16	1.42	12.88	75.40	1.32	13.05	95.08	1.12	11.41	106.60	1.02	11.32	149.80
1.63	13.59	61.48	1.53	13.52	70.24	1.43	13.06	76.60	1.33	13.22	96.52	1.13	11.58	108.40	1.03	11.48	152.20
1.64	13.79	62.44	1.54	13.71	71.32	1.44	13.25	77.80	1.34	13.39	97.96	1.14	11.74	110.20	1.04	11.63	154.60
1.65	13.98	63.40	1.55	13.89	72.40	1.45	13.43	79.00	1.35	13.56	99.40	1.15	11.91	112.00	1.05	11.78	157.00
1.66	14.17	64.36	1.56	14.08	73.48	1.46	13.61	80.20	1.36	13.73	100.84	1.16	12.07	113.80	1.06	11.94	159.40
1.67	14.36	65.32	1.57	14.26	74.56	1.47	13.79	81.40	1.37	13.90	102.28	1.17	12.24	115.60	1.07	12.09	161.80
1.68	14.55	66.28	1.58	14.45	75.64	1.48	13.97	82.60	1.38	14.08	103.72	1.18	12.40	117.40	1.08	12.24	164.20
1.69	14.74	67.24	1.59	14.63	76.72	1.49	14.15	83.80	1.39	14.25	105.16	1.19	12.57	119.20	1.09	12.39	166.60
1.70	14.93	68.20	1.60	14.81	77.80	1.50	14.33	85.00	1.40	14.41	106.60	1.20	12.73	121.00	1.10	12.54	169.00
1.71	15.12	69.16	1.61	15.00	78.88	1.51	14.51	86.20	1.41	14.58	108.04	1.21	12.89	122.80	1.11	12.69	171.40
1.72	15.31	70.12	1.62	15.18	79.96	1.52	14.68	87.40	1.42	14.75	109.48	1.22	13.05	124.60	1.12	12.84	173.80
1.73	15.49	71.08	1.63	15.36	81.04	1.53	14.86	88.60	1.43	14.92	110.92	1.23	13.22	126.40	1.13	12.99	176.20
1.74	15.68	72.04	1.64	15.54	82.12	1.54	15.04	89.80	1.44	15.09	112.36	1.24	13.38	128.20	1.14	13.14	178.60
1.75	15.87	73.00	1.65	15.72	83.20	1.55	15.22	91.00	1.45	15.26	113.80	1.25	13.54	130.00	1.15	13.29	181.00
1.76	16.06	73.96	1.66	15.91	84.28	1.56	15.39	92.20	1.46	15.42	115.24	1.26	13.70	131.80	1.16	13.44	183.40
1.77	16.24	74.92	1.67	16.09	85.36	1.57	15.57	93.40	1.47	15.59	116.68	1.27	13.86	133.60	1.17	13.59	185.80
1.78	16.43	75.88	1.68	16.27	86.44	1.58	15.75	94.60	1.48	15.76	118.12	1.28	14.02	135.40	1.18	13.74	188.20
1.79	16.61	76.84	1.69	16.45	87.52	1.59	15.92	95.80	1.49	15.92	119.56	1.29	14.18	137.20	1.19	13.89	190.60
1.80	16.80	77.80	1.70	16.63	88.60	1.60	16.10	97.00	1.50	16.09	121.00	1.30	14.34	139.00	1.20	14.03	193.00
1.81	16.99	78.76	1.71	16.80	89.68	1.61	16.27	98.20	1.51	16.26	122.44	1.31	14.50	140.80	1.21	14.18	195.40
1.82	17.17	79.72	1.72	16.98	90.76	1.62	16.45	99.40	1.52	16.42	123.88	1.32	14.65	142.60	1.22	14.33	197.80
1.83	17.35	80.68	1.73	17.16	91.84	1.63	16.62	100.60	1.53	16.59	125.32	1.33	14.81	144.40	1.23	14.47	200.20
1.84	17.54	81.64	1.74	17.34	92.92	1.64	16.79	101.80	1.54	16.75	126.76	1.34	14.97	146.20	1.24	14.62	202.60
1.85	17.72	82.60	1.75	17.52	94.00	1.65	16.97	103.00	1.55	16.91	128.20	1.35	15.13	148.00	1.25	14.77	205.00
1.86	17.91	83.56	1.76	17.70	95.08	1.66	17.14	104.20	1.56	17.08	129.64	1.36	15.29	149.80	1.26	14.91	207.40
1.87	18.09	84.52	1.77	17.87	96.16	1.67	17.31	105.40	1.57	17.24	131.08	1.37	15.44	151.60	1.27	15.06	209.80
1.88	18.27	85.48	1.78	18.05	97.24	1.68	17.48	106.60	1.58	17.41	132.52	1.38	15.60	153.40	1.28	15.20	212.20
1.89	18.45	86.44	1.79	18.23	98.32	1.69	17.66	107.80	1.59	17.57	133.96	1.39	15.75	155.20	1.29	15.35	214.60
1.90	18.64	87.40	1.80	18.40	99.40	1.70	17.83	109.00	1.60	17.73	135.40	1.40	15.91	157.00	1.30	15.49	217.00
1.91	18.82	88.36	1.81	18.58	100.48	1.71	18.00	110.20	1.61	17.89	136.84	1.41	16.07	158.80	1.31	15.64	219.40
1.92	19.00	89.32	1.82	18.75	101.56	1.72	18.17	111.40	1.62	18.06	138.28	1.42	16.22	160.60	1.32	15.78	221.80
1.93	19.18	90.28	1.83	18.93	102.64	1.73	18.34	112.60	1.63	18.22	139.72	1.43	16.38	162.40	1.33	15.93	224.20
1.94	19.36	91.24	1.84	19.10	103.72	1.74	18.51	113.80	1.64	18.38	141.16	1.44	16.53	164.20	1.34	16.07	226.60
1.95	19.54	92.20	1.85	19.28	104.80	1.75	18.68	115.00	1.65	18.54	142.60	1.45	16.68	166.00	1.35	16.22	229.00
1.96	19.72	93.16	1.86	19.45	105.88	1.76	18.85	116.20	1.66	18.70	144.04	1.46	16.84	167.80	1.36	16.36	231.40
1.97	19.90	94.12	1.87	19.63	106.96	1.77	19.02	117.40	1.67	18.86	145.48	1.47	16.99	169.60	1.37	16.50	233.80
1.98	20.08	95.08	1.88	19.80	108.04	1.78	19.19	118.60	1.68	19.02	146.92	1.48	17.15	171.40	1.38	16.65	236.20
1.99	20.26	96.04	1.89	19.97	109.12	1.79	19.36	119.80	1.69	19.18	148.36	1.49	17.30	173.20	1.39	16.79	238.60

Description: This table shows the Annual Percentage Rate and finance charge per $100 for monthly lease payments.

Example: A 4.30% lease payment for 2 years is equivalent to an APR of 14.18%. The charge per $100 cost is $ 13.20.

2 yr PAYT	APR	CHARGE	3 yr PAYT	APR	CHARGE	4 yr PAYT	APR	CHARGE	5 yr PAYT	APR	CHARGE	6 yr PAYT	APR	CHARGE	7 yr PAYT	APR	CHARGE
4.30	14.18	13.20	3.00	11.97	18.00	2.30	9.79	20.40	1.90	8.98	24.00	1.70	9.83	32.40	1.50	9.21	36.00
4.31	14.43	13.44	3.01	12.20	18.36	2.31	10.02	20.88	1.91	9.19	24.60	1.71	10.03	33.12	1.51	9.41	36.84
4.32	14.69	13.68	3.02	12.44	18.72	2.32	10.24	21.36	1.92	9.41	25.20	1.72	10.24	33.84	1.52	9.61	37.68
4.33	14.94	13.92	3.03	12.67	19.08	2.33	10.46	21.84	1.93	9.62	25.80	1.73	10.45	34.56	1.53	9.81	38.52
4.34	15.20	14.16	3.04	12.90	19.44	2.34	10.69	22.32	1.94	9.84	26.40	1.74	10.65	35.28	1.54	10.01	39.36
4.35	15.45	14.40	3.05	13.14	19.80	2.35	10.91	22.80	1.95	10.05	27.00	1.75	10.86	36.00	1.55	10.22	40.20
4.36	15.71	14.64	3.06	13.37	20.16	2.36	11.13	23.28	1.96	10.27	27.60	1.76	11.06	36.72	1.56	10.42	41.04
4.37	15.96	14.88	3.07	13.60	20.52	2.37	11.35	23.76	1.97	10.48	28.20	1.77	11.27	37.44	1.57	10.62	41.88
4.38	16.22	15.12	3.08	13.84	20.88	2.38	11.57	24.24	1.98	10.69	28.80	1.78	11.47	38.16	1.58	10.81	42.72
4.39	16.47	15.36	3.09	14.07	21.24	2.39	11.80	24.72	1.99	10.91	29.40	1.79	11.68	38.88	1.59	11.01	43.56
4.40	16.73	15.60	3.10	14.30	21.60	2.40	12.02	25.20	2.00	11.12	30.00	1.80	11.88	39.60	1.60	11.21	44.40
4.41	16.98	15.84	3.11	14.53	21.96	2.41	12.24	25.68	2.01	11.33	30.60	1.81	12.08	40.32	1.61	11.41	45.24
4.42	17.24	16.08	3.12	14.77	22.32	2.42	12.46	26.16	2.02	11.55	31.20	1.82	12.29	41.04	1.62	11.61	46.08
4.43	17.49	16.32	3.13	15.00	22.68	2.43	12.68	26.64	2.03	11.76	31.80	1.83	12.49	41.76	1.63	11.80	46.92
4.44	17.75	16.56	3.14	15.23	23.04	2.44	12.90	27.12	2.04	11.97	32.40	1.84	12.69	42.48	1.64	12.00	47.76
4.45	18.00	16.80	3.15	15.46	23.40	2.45	13.12	27.60	2.05	12.18	33.00	1.85	12.89	43.20	1.65	12.20	48.60
4.46	18.26	17.04	3.16	15.69	23.76	2.46	13.34	28.08	2.06	12.39	33.60	1.86	13.10	43.92	1.66	12.39	49.44
4.47	18.51	17.28	3.17	15.92	24.12	2.47	13.56	28.56	2.07	12.60	34.20	1.87	13.30	44.64	1.67	12.59	50.28
4.48	18.76	17.52	3.18	16.15	24.48	2.48	13.78	29.04	2.08	12.81	34.80	1.88	13.50	45.36	1.68	12.78	51.12
4.49	19.02	17.76	3.19	16.39	24.84	2.49	13.99	29.52	2.09	13.02	35.40	1.89	13.70	46.08	1.69	12.98	51.96
4.50	19.27	18.00	3.20	16.62	25.20	2.50	14.21	30.00	2.10	13.23	36.00	1.90	13.90	46.80	1.70	13.17	52.80
4.51	19.53	18.24	3.21	16.85	25.56	2.51	14.43	30.48	2.11	13.44	36.60	1.91	14.10	47.52	1.71	13.37	53.64
4.52	19.78	18.48	3.22	17.08	25.92	2.52	14.65	30.96	2.12	13.65	37.20	1.92	14.30	48.24	1.72	13.56	54.48
4.53	20.03	18.72	3.23	17.31	26.28	2.53	14.87	31.44	2.13	13.86	37.80	1.93	14.50	48.96	1.73	13.75	55.32
4.54	20.29	18.96	3.24	17.54	26.64	2.54	15.08	31.92	2.14	14.06	38.40	1.94	14.70	49.68	1.74	13.95	56.16
4.55	20.54	19.20	3.25	17.77	27.00	2.55	15.30	32.40	2.15	14.27	39.00	1.95	14.89	50.40	1.75	14.14	57.00
4.56	20.80	19.44	3.26	18.00	27.36	2.56	15.52	32.88	2.16	14.48	39.60	1.96	15.09	51.12	1.76	14.33	57.84
4.57	21.05	19.68	3.27	18.23	27.72	2.57	15.74	33.36	2.17	14.69	40.20	1.97	15.29	51.84	1.77	14.52	58.68
4.58	21.30	19.92	3.28	18.46	28.08	2.58	15.95	33.84	2.18	14.89	40.80	1.98	15.49	52.56	1.78	14.72	59.52
4.59	21.56	20.16	3.29	18.69	28.44	2.59	16.17	34.32	2.19	15.10	41.40	1.99	15.68	53.28	1.79	14.91	60.36
4.60	21.81	20.40	3.30	18.91	28.80	2.60	16.38	34.80	2.20	15.31	42.00	2.00	15.88	54.00	1.80	15.10	61.20
4.61	22.06	20.64	3.31	19.14	29.16	2.61	16.60	35.28	2.21	15.51	42.60	2.01	16.08	54.72	1.81	15.29	62.04
4.62	22.32	20.88	3.32	19.37	29.52	2.62	16.82	35.76	2.22	15.72	43.20	2.02	16.27	55.44	1.82	15.48	62.88
4.63	22.57	21.12	3.33	19.60	29.88	2.63	17.03	36.24	2.23	15.93	43.80	2.03	16.47	56.16	1.83	15.67	63.72
4.64	22.82	21.36	3.34	19.83	30.24	2.64	17.25	36.72	2.24	16.13	44.40	2.04	16.67	56.88	1.84	15.86	64.56
4.65	23.08	21.60	3.35	20.06	30.60	2.65	17.46	37.20	2.25	16.34	45.00	2.05	16.86	57.60	1.85	16.05	65.40
4.66	23.33	21.84	3.36	20.29	30.96	2.66	17.68	37.68	2.26	16.54	45.60	2.06	17.06	58.32	1.86	16.24	66.24
4.67	23.58	22.08	3.37	20.51	31.32	2.67	17.89	38.16	2.27	16.75	46.20	2.07	17.25	59.04	1.87	16.42	67.08
4.68	23.84	22.32	3.38	20.74	31.68	2.68	18.10	38.64	2.28	16.95	46.80	2.08	17.45	59.76	1.88	16.61	67.92
4.69	24.09	22.56	3.39	20.97	32.04	2.69	18.32	39.12	2.29	17.15	47.40	2.09	17.64	60.48	1.89	16.80	68.76
4.70	24.34	22.80	3.40	21.20	32.40	2.70	18.53	39.60	2.30	17.36	48.00	2.10	17.83	61.20	1.90	16.99	69.60
4.71	24.59	23.04	3.41	21.43	32.76	2.71	18.75	40.08	2.31	17.56	48.60	2.11	18.03	61.92	1.91	17.18	70.44
4.72	24.85	23.28	3.42	21.65	33.12	2.72	18.96	40.56	2.32	17.76	49.20	2.12	18.22	62.64	1.92	17.36	71.28
4.73	25.10	23.52	3.43	21.88	33.48	2.73	19.17	41.04	2.33	17.97	49.80	2.13	18.41	63.36	1.93	17.55	72.12
4.74	25.35	23.76	3.44	22.11	33.84	2.74	19.39	41.52	2.34	18.17	50.40	2.14	18.61	64.08	1.94	17.74	72.96
4.75	25.60	24.00	3.45	22.34	34.20	2.75	19.60	42.00	2.35	18.37	51.00	2.15	18.80	64.80	1.95	17.92	73.80
4.76	25.86	24.24	3.46	22.56	34.56	2.76	19.81	42.48	2.36	18.58	51.60	2.16	18.99	65.52	1.96	18.11	74.64
4.77	26.11	24.48	3.47	22.79	34.92	2.77	20.02	42.96	2.37	18.78	52.20	2.17	19.18	66.24	1.97	18.29	75.48
4.78	26.36	24.72	3.48	23.01	35.28	2.78	20.24	43.44	2.38	18.98	52.80	2.18	19.38	66.96	1.98	18.48	76.32
4.79	26.61	24.96	3.49	23.24	35.64	2.79	20.45	43.92	2.39	19.18	53.40	2.19	19.57	67.68	1.99	18.66	77.16
4.80	26.87	25.20	3.50	23.47	36.00	2.80	20.66	44.40	2.40	19.38	54.00	2.20	19.76	68.40	2.00	18.85	78.00
4.81	27.12	25.44	3.51	23.69	36.36	2.81	20.87	44.88	2.41	19.58	54.60	2.21	19.95	69.12	2.01	19.03	78.84
4.82	27.37	25.68	3.52	23.92	36.72	2.82	21.08	45.36	2.42	19.78	55.20	2.22	20.14	69.84	2.02	19.22	79.68
4.83	27.62	25.92	3.53	24.14	37.08	2.83	21.29	45.84	2.43	19.98	55.80	2.23	20.33	70.56	2.03	19.40	80.52
4.84	27.88	26.16	3.54	24.37	37.44	2.84	21.51	46.32	2.44	20.18	56.40	2.24	20.53	71.28	2.04	19.58	81.36
4.85	28.13	26.40	3.55	24.60	37.80	2.85	21.72	46.80	2.45	20.38	57.00	2.25	20.71	72.00	2.05	19.77	82.20
4.86	28.38	26.64	3.56	24.82	38.16	2.86	21.93	47.28	2.46	20.58	57.60	2.26	20.90	72.72	2.06	19.95	83.04
4.87	28.63	26.88	3.57	25.05	38.52	2.87	22.14	47.76	2.47	20.78	58.20	2.27	21.09	73.44	2.07	20.13	83.88
4.88	28.88	27.12	3.58	25.27	38.88	2.88	22.35	48.24	2.48	20.98	58.80	2.28	21.28	74.16	2.08	20.32	84.72
4.89	29.14	27.36	3.59	25.50	39.24	2.89	22.56	48.72	2.49	21.18	59.40	2.29	21.47	74.88	2.09	20.50	85.56
4.90	29.39	27.60	3.60	25.72	39.60	2.90	22.77	49.20	2.50	21.38	60.00	2.30	21.66	75.60	2.10	20.68	86.40
4.91	29.64	27.84	3.61	25.95	39.96	2.91	22.98	49.68	2.51	21.58	60.60	2.31	21.85	76.32	2.11	20.86	87.24
4.92	29.89	28.08	3.62	26.17	40.32	2.92	23.19	50.16	2.52	21.78	61.20	2.32	22.04	77.04	2.12	21.04	88.08
4.93	30.14	28.32	3.63	26.39	40.68	2.93	23.40	50.64	2.53	21.98	61.80	2.33	22.22	77.76	2.13	21.23	88.92
4.94	30.39	28.56	3.64	26.62	41.04	2.94	23.61	51.12	2.54	22.18	62.40	2.34	22.41	78.48	2.14	21.41	89.76
4.95	30.65	28.80	3.65	26.84	41.40	2.95	23.81	51.60	2.55	22.37	63.00	2.35	22.60	79.20	2.15	21.59	90.60
4.96	30.90	29.04	3.66	27.06	41.76	2.96	24.02	52.08	2.56	22.57	63.60	2.36	22.79	79.92	2.16	21.77	91.44
4.97	31.15	29.28	3.67	27.29	42.12	2.97	24.23	52.56	2.57	22.77	64.20	2.37	22.98	80.64	2.17	21.95	92.28
4.98	31.40	29.52	3.68	27.52	42.48	2.98	24.44	53.04	2.58	22.97	64.80	2.38	23.16	81.36	2.18	22.13	93.12
4.99	31.65	29.76	3.69	27.74	42.84	2.99	24.65	53.52	2.59	23.16	65.40	2.39	23.35	82.08	2.19	22.31	93.96

Description: This table shows the Annual Percentage Rate and finance charge per $100 for monthly lease payments.

Example: A 1.30% lease payment for 8 years is equivalent to an APR of 7.74%. The charge per $100 cost is $ 34.80.

8 yr PAYT	APR	CHARGE	9 yr PAYT	APR	CHARGE	10 yr PAYT	APR	CHARGE	12 yr PAYT	APR	CHARGE	15 yr PAYT	APR	CHARGE	20 yr PAYT	APR	CHARGE
1.30	7.74	34.80	1.20	7.72	39.60	1.10	7.30	42.00	1.00	7.62	54.00	.80	6.05	54.00	.70	6.27	78.00
1.31	7.94	35.76	1.21	7.92	40.68	1.11	7.50	43.20	1.01	7.80	55.44	.81	6.23	55.80	.71	6.44	80.40
1.32	8.14	36.72	1.22	8.11	41.76	1.12	7.69	44.40	1.02	7.99	56.88	.82	6.41	57.60	.72	6.61	82.80
1.33	8.34	37.68	1.23	8.31	42.84	1.13	7.88	45.60	1.03	8.17	58.32	.83	6.59	59.40	.73	6.78	85.20
1.34	8.54	38.64	1.24	8.50	43.92	1.14	8.08	46.80	1.04	8.36	59.76	.84	6.78	61.20	.74	6.95	87.60
1.35	8.74	39.60	1.25	8.70	45.00	1.15	8.27	48.00	1.05	8.54	61.20	.85	6.96	63.00	.75	7.12	90.00
1.36	8.94	40.56	1.26	8.89	46.08	1.16	8.46	49.20	1.06	8.72	62.64	.86	7.14	64.80	.76	7.28	92.40
1.37	9.14	41.52	1.27	9.09	47.16	1.17	8.65	50.40	1.07	8.91	64.08	.87	7.32	66.60	.77	7.45	94.80
1.38	9.33	42.48	1.28	9.28	48.24	1.18	8.84	51.60	1.08	9.09	65.52	.88	7.49	68.40	.78	7.61	97.20
1.39	9.53	43.44	1.29	9.47	49.32	1.19	9.03	52.80	1.09	9.27	66.96	.89	7.67	70.20	.79	7.78	99.60
1.40	9.73	44.40	1.30	9.66	50.40	1.20	9.22	54.00	1.10	9.45	68.40	.90	7.85	72.00	.80	7.94	102.00
1.41	9.92	45.36	1.31	9.85	51.48	1.21	9.41	55.20	1.11	9.63	69.84	.91	8.02	73.80	.81	8.11	104.40
1.42	10.12	46.32	1.32	10.04	52.56	1.22	9.59	56.40	1.12	9.81	71.28	.92	8.20	75.60	.82	8.27	106.80
1.43	10.31	47.28	1.33	10.23	53.64	1.23	9.78	57.60	1.13	9.99	72.72	.93	8.37	77.40	.83	8.43	109.20
1.44	10.51	48.24	1.34	10.42	54.72	1.24	9.97	58.80	1.14	10.16	74.16	.94	8.55	79.20	.84	8.59	111.60
1.45	10.70	49.20	1.35	10.61	55.80	1.25	10.15	60.00	1.15	10.34	75.60	.95	8.72	81.00	.85	8.75	114.00
1.46	10.90	50.16	1.36	10.80	56.88	1.26	10.34	61.20	1.16	10.52	77.04	.96	8.89	82.80	.86	8.92	116.40
1.47	11.09	51.12	1.37	10.99	57.96	1.27	10.52	62.40	1.17	10.70	78.48	.97	9.07	84.60	.87	9.07	118.80
1.48	11.28	52.08	1.38	11.18	59.04	1.28	10.71	63.60	1.18	10.87	79.92	.98	9.24	86.40	.88	9.23	121.20
1.49	11.47	53.04	1.39	11.37	60.12	1.29	10.89	64.80	1.19	11.05	81.36	.99	9.41	88.20	.89	9.39	123.60
1.50	11.67	54.00	1.40	11.55	61.20	1.30	11.07	66.00	1.20	11.22	82.80	1.00	9.58	90.00	.90	9.55	126.00
1.51	11.86	54.96	1.41	11.74	62.28	1.31	11.26	67.20	1.21	11.40	84.24	1.01	9.75	91.80	.91	9.71	128.40
1.52	12.05	55.92	1.42	11.92	63.36	1.32	11.44	68.40	1.22	11.57	85.68	1.02	9.92	93.60	.92	9.86	130.80
1.53	12.24	56.88	1.43	12.11	64.44	1.33	11.62	69.60	1.23	11.74	87.12	1.03	10.09	95.40	.93	10.02	133.20
1.54	12.43	57.84	1.44	12.29	65.52	1.34	11.80	70.80	1.24	11.92	88.56	1.04	10.25	97.20	.94	10.18	135.60
1.55	12.62	58.80	1.45	12.48	66.60	1.35	11.98	72.00	1.25	12.09	90.00	1.05	10.42	99.00	.95	10.33	138.00
1.56	12.81	59.76	1.46	12.66	67.68	1.36	12.16	73.20	1.26	12.26	91.44	1.06	10.59	100.80	.96	10.49	140.40
1.57	13.00	60.72	1.47	12.85	68.76	1.37	12.34	74.40	1.27	12.43	92.88	1.07	10.75	102.60	.97	10.64	142.80
1.58	13.18	61.68	1.48	13.03	69.84	1.38	12.52	75.60	1.28	12.60	94.32	1.08	10.92	104.40	.98	10.80	145.20
1.59	13.37	62.64	1.49	13.21	70.92	1.39	12.70	76.80	1.29	12.77	95.76	1.09	11.09	106.20	.99	10.95	147.60
1.60	13.56	63.60	1.50	13.40	72.00	1.40	12.88	78.00	1.30	12.94	97.20	1.10	11.25	108.00	1.00	11.10	150.00
1.61	13.75	64.56	1.51	13.58	73.08	1.41	13.06	79.20	1.31	13.11	98.64	1.11	11.41	109.80	1.01	11.25	152.40
1.62	13.93	65.52	1.52	13.76	74.16	1.42	13.24	80.40	1.32	13.28	100.08	1.12	11.58	111.60	1.02	11.41	154.80
1.63	14.12	66.48	1.53	13.94	75.24	1.43	13.42	81.60	1.33	13.45	101.52	1.13	11.74	113.40	1.03	11.56	157.20
1.64	14.31	67.44	1.54	14.12	76.32	1.44	13.59	82.80	1.34	13.62	102.96	1.14	11.90	115.20	1.04	11.71	159.60
1.65	14.49	68.40	1.55	14.30	77.40	1.45	13.77	84.00	1.35	13.79	104.40	1.15	12.07	117.00	1.05	11.86	162.00
1.66	14.68	69.36	1.56	14.48	78.48	1.46	13.95	85.20	1.36	13.96	105.84	1.16	12.23	118.80	1.06	12.01	164.40
1.67	14.86	70.32	1.57	14.66	79.56	1.47	14.12	86.40	1.37	14.13	107.28	1.17	12.39	120.60	1.07	12.16	166.80
1.68	15.05	71.28	1.58	14.84	80.64	1.48	14.30	87.60	1.38	14.29	108.72	1.18	12.55	122.40	1.08	12.31	169.20
1.69	15.23	72.24	1.59	15.02	81.72	1.49	14.47	88.80	1.39	14.46	110.16	1.19	12.71	124.20	1.09	12.46	171.60
1.70	15.41	73.20	1.60	15.20	82.80	1.50	14.65	90.00	1.40	14.63	111.60	1.20	12.87	126.00	1.10	12.61	174.00
1.71	15.60	74.16	1.61	15.38	83.88	1.51	14.82	91.20	1.41	14.79	113.04	1.21	13.03	127.80	1.11	12.76	176.40
1.72	15.78	75.12	1.62	15.56	84.96	1.52	15.00	92.40	1.42	14.96	114.48	1.22	13.19	129.60	1.12	12.91	178.80
1.73	15.96	76.08	1.63	15.73	86.04	1.53	15.17	93.60	1.43	15.12	115.92	1.23	13.35	131.40	1.13	13.06	181.20
1.74	16.15	77.04	1.64	15.91	87.12	1.54	15.34	94.80	1.44	15.29	117.36	1.24	13.51	133.20	1.14	13.20	183.60
1.75	16.33	78.00	1.65	16.09	88.20	1.55	15.52	96.00	1.45	15.45	118.80	1.25	13.67	135.00	1.15	13.35	186.00
1.76	16.51	78.96	1.66	16.26	89.28	1.56	15.69	97.20	1.46	15.62	120.24	1.26	13.83	136.80	1.16	13.50	188.40
1.77	16.69	79.92	1.67	16.44	90.36	1.57	15.86	98.40	1.47	15.78	121.68	1.27	13.99	138.60	1.17	13.65	190.80
1.78	16.87	80.88	1.68	16.62	91.44	1.58	16.03	99.60	1.48	15.94	123.12	1.28	14.14	140.40	1.18	13.79	193.20
1.79	17.05	81.84	1.69	16.79	92.52	1.59	16.21	100.80	1.49	16.11	124.56	1.29	14.30	142.20	1.19	13.94	195.60
1.80	17.23	82.80	1.70	16.97	93.60	1.60	16.38	102.00	1.50	16.27	126.00	1.30	14.46	144.00	1.20	14.09	198.00
1.81	17.41	83.76	1.71	17.14	94.68	1.61	16.55	103.20	1.51	16.43	127.44	1.31	14.62	145.80	1.21	14.23	200.40
1.82	17.59	84.72	1.72	17.32	95.76	1.62	16.72	104.40	1.52	16.60	128.88	1.32	14.77	147.60	1.22	14.38	202.80
1.83	17.77	85.68	1.73	17.49	96.84	1.63	16.89	105.60	1.53	16.76	130.32	1.33	14.93	149.40	1.23	14.52	205.20
1.84	17.95	86.64	1.74	17.67	97.92	1.64	17.06	106.80	1.54	16.92	131.76	1.34	15.08	151.20	1.24	14.67	207.60
1.85	18.13	87.60	1.75	17.84	99.00	1.65	17.23	108.00	1.55	17.08	133.20	1.35	15.24	153.00	1.25	14.81	210.00
1.86	18.31	88.56	1.76	18.01	100.08	1.66	17.40	109.20	1.56	17.24	134.64	1.36	15.39	154.80	1.26	14.96	212.40
1.87	18.49	89.52	1.77	18.19	101.16	1.67	17.57	110.40	1.57	17.41	136.08	1.37	15.55	156.60	1.27	15.10	214.80
1.88	18.67	90.48	1.78	18.36	102.24	1.68	17.74	111.60	1.58	17.57	137.52	1.38	15.70	158.40	1.28	15.25	217.20
1.89	18.85	91.44	1.79	18.53	103.32	1.69	17.91	112.80	1.59	17.73	138.96	1.39	15.86	160.20	1.29	15.39	219.60
1.90	19.02	92.40	1.80	18.70	104.40	1.70	18.07	114.00	1.60	17.89	140.40	1.40	16.01	162.00	1.30	15.54	222.00
1.91	19.20	93.36	1.81	18.88	105.48	1.71	18.24	115.20	1.61	18.05	141.84	1.41	16.16	163.80	1.31	15.68	224.40
1.92	19.38	94.32	1.82	19.05	106.56	1.72	18.41	116.40	1.62	18.21	143.28	1.42	16.32	165.60	1.32	15.82	226.80
1.93	19.56	95.28	1.83	19.22	107.64	1.73	18.58	117.60	1.63	18.37	144.72	1.43	16.47	167.40	1.33	15.97	229.20
1.94	19.73	96.24	1.84	19.39	108.72	1.74	18.75	118.80	1.64	18.53	146.16	1.44	16.62	169.20	1.34	16.11	231.60
1.95	19.91	97.20	1.85	19.56	109.80	1.75	18.91	120.00	1.65	18.69	147.60	1.45	16.78	171.00	1.35	16.25	234.00
1.96	20.09	98.16	1.86	19.73	110.88	1.76	19.08	121.20	1.66	18.84	149.04	1.46	16.93	172.80	1.36	16.40	236.40
1.97	20.26	99.12	1.87	19.90	111.96	1.77	19.25	122.40	1.67	19.00	150.48	1.47	17.08	174.60	1.37	16.54	238.80
1.98	20.44	100.08	1.88	20.08	113.04	1.78	19.41	123.60	1.68	19.16	151.92	1.48	17.23	176.40	1.38	16.68	241.20
1.99	20.61	101.04	1.89	20.25	114.12	1.79	19.58	124.80	1.69	19.32	153.36	1.49	17.39	178.20	1.39	16.83	243.60

LEASE PAYMENTS

Description: This table shows the Annual Percentage Rate and finance charge per $100 for monthly lease payments.

Example: A 4.30% lease payment for 2 years is equivalent to an APR of 18.42%. The charge per $100 cost is $ 18.20.

2 yr MONTHLY PAYT	APR	CHARGE	3 yr MONTHLY PAYT	APR	CHARGE	4 yr MONTHLY PAYT	APR	CHARGE	5 yr MONTHLY PAYT	APR	CHARGE	6 yr MONTHLY PAYT	APR	CHARGE	7 yr MONTHLY PAYT	APR	CHARGE
4.30	18.42	18.20	3.00	14.48	23.00	2.30	11.58	25.40	1.90	10.32	29.00	1.70	10.82	37.40	1.50	10.02	41.00
4.31	18.66	18.44	3.01	14.71	23.36	2.31	11.79	25.88	1.91	10.53	29.60	1.71	11.02	38.12	1.51	10.21	41.84
4.32	18.90	18.68	3.02	14.93	23.72	2.32	12.00	26.36	1.92	10.73	30.20	1.72	11.22	38.84	1.52	10.41	42.68
4.33	19.15	18.92	3.03	15.15	24.08	2.33	12.21	26.84	1.93	10.94	30.80	1.73	11.42	39.56	1.53	10.60	43.52
4.34	19.39	19.16	3.04	15.37	24.44	2.34	12.43	27.32	1.94	11.14	31.40	1.74	11.62	40.28	1.54	10.80	44.36
4.35	19.63	19.40	3.05	15.59	24.80	2.35	12.64	27.80	1.95	11.35	32.00	1.75	11.81	41.00	1.55	10.99	45.20
4.36	19.87	19.64	3.06	15.82	25.16	2.36	12.85	28.28	1.96	11.55	32.60	1.76	12.01	41.72	1.56	11.18	46.04
4.37	20.11	19.88	3.07	16.04	25.52	2.37	13.06	28.76	1.97	11.75	33.20	1.77	12.21	42.44	1.57	11.37	46.88
4.38	20.35	20.12	3.08	16.26	25.88	2.38	13.27	29.24	1.98	11.96	33.80	1.78	12.40	43.16	1.58	11.56	47.72
4.39	20.59	20.36	3.09	16.48	26.24	2.39	13.48	29.72	1.99	12.16	34.40	1.79	12.60	43.88	1.59	11.76	48.56
4.40	20.84	20.60	3.10	16.70	26.60	2.40	13.69	30.20	2.00	12.37	35.00	1.80	12.79	44.60	1.60	11.95	49.40
4.41	21.08	20.84	3.11	16.92	26.96	2.41	13.90	30.68	2.01	12.57	35.60	1.81	12.99	45.32	1.61	12.14	50.24
4.42	21.32	21.08	3.12	17.14	27.32	2.42	14.11	31.16	2.02	12.77	36.20	1.82	13.19	46.04	1.62	12.33	51.08
4.43	21.56	21.32	3.13	17.36	27.68	2.43	14.32	31.64	2.03	12.97	36.80	1.83	13.38	46.76	1.63	12.52	51.92
4.44	21.80	21.56	3.14	17.58	28.04	2.44	14.53	32.12	2.04	13.18	37.40	1.84	13.57	47.48	1.64	12.71	52.76
4.45	22.04	21.80	3.15	17.81	28.40	2.45	14.74	32.60	2.05	13.38	38.00	1.85	13.77	48.20	1.65	12.90	53.60
4.46	22.28	22.04	3.16	18.03	28.76	2.46	14.95	33.08	2.06	13.58	38.60	1.86	13.96	48.92	1.66	13.09	54.44
4.47	22.52	22.28	3.17	18.25	29.12	2.47	15.16	33.56	2.07	13.78	39.20	1.87	14.16	49.64	1.67	13.28	55.28
4.48	22.77	22.52	3.18	18.47	29.48	2.48	15.37	34.04	2.08	13.98	39.80	1.88	14.35	50.36	1.68	13.46	56.12
4.49	23.01	22.76	3.19	18.69	29.84	2.49	15.58	34.52	2.09	14.18	40.40	1.89	14.54	51.08	1.69	13.65	56.96
4.50	23.25	23.00	3.20	18.91	30.20	2.50	15.79	35.00	2.10	14.39	41.00	1.90	14.74	51.80	1.70	13.84	57.80
4.51	23.49	23.24	3.21	19.13	30.56	2.51	16.00	35.48	2.11	14.59	41.60	1.91	14.93	52.52	1.71	14.03	58.64
4.52	23.73	23.48	3.22	19.35	30.92	2.52	16.21	35.96	2.12	14.79	42.20	1.92	15.12	53.24	1.72	14.21	59.48
4.53	23.97	23.72	3.23	19.57	31.28	2.53	16.42	36.44	2.13	14.99	42.80	1.93	15.31	53.96	1.73	14.40	60.32
4.54	24.21	23.96	3.24	19.79	31.64	2.54	16.62	36.92	2.14	15.19	43.40	1.94	15.51	54.68	1.74	14.59	61.16
4.55	24.45	24.20	3.25	20.01	32.00	2.55	16.83	37.40	2.15	15.39	44.00	1.95	15.70	55.40	1.75	14.77	62.00
4.56	24.70	24.44	3.26	20.22	32.36	2.56	17.04	37.88	2.16	15.59	44.60	1.96	15.89	56.12	1.76	14.96	62.84
4.57	24.94	24.68	3.27	20.44	32.72	2.57	17.25	38.36	2.17	15.79	45.20	1.97	16.08	56.84	1.77	15.15	63.68
4.58	25.18	24.92	3.28	20.66	33.08	2.58	17.46	38.84	2.18	15.98	45.80	1.98	16.27	57.56	1.78	15.33	64.52
4.59	25.42	25.16	3.29	20.88	33.44	2.59	17.66	39.32	2.19	16.18	46.40	1.99	16.46	58.28	1.79	15.52	65.36
4.60	25.66	25.40	3.30	21.10	33.80	2.60	17.87	39.80	2.20	16.38	47.00	2.00	16.65	59.00	1.80	15.70	66.20
4.61	25.90	25.64	3.31	21.32	34.16	2.61	18.08	40.28	2.21	16.58	47.60	2.01	16.84	59.72	1.81	15.89	67.04
4.62	26.14	25.88	3.32	21.54	34.52	2.62	18.28	40.76	2.22	16.78	48.20	2.02	17.03	60.44	1.82	16.07	67.88
4.63	26.38	26.12	3.33	21.76	34.88	2.63	18.49	41.24	2.23	16.98	48.80	2.03	17.22	61.16	1.83	16.26	68.72
4.64	26.62	26.36	3.34	21.98	35.24	2.64	18.70	41.72	2.24	17.17	49.40	2.04	17.41	61.88	1.84	16.44	69.56
4.65	26.86	26.60	3.35	22.19	35.60	2.65	18.90	42.20	2.25	17.37	50.00	2.05	17.60	62.60	1.85	16.62	70.40
4.66	27.10	26.84	3.36	22.41	35.96	2.66	19.11	42.68	2.26	17.57	50.60	2.06	17.79	63.32	1.86	16.81	71.24
4.67	27.35	27.08	3.37	22.63	36.32	2.67	19.32	43.16	2.27	17.77	51.20	2.07	17.98	64.04	1.87	16.99	72.08
4.68	27.59	27.32	3.38	22.85	36.68	2.68	19.52	43.64	2.28	17.97	51.80	2.08	18.17	64.76	1.88	17.17	72.92
4.69	27.83	27.56	3.39	23.07	37.04	2.69	19.73	44.12	2.29	18.16	52.40	2.09	18.35	65.48	1.89	17.36	73.76
4.70	28.07	27.80	3.40	23.29	37.40	2.70	19.93	44.60	2.30	18.36	53.00	2.10	18.54	66.20	1.90	17.54	74.60
4.71	28.31	28.04	3.41	23.50	37.76	2.71	20.14	45.08	2.31	18.55	53.60	2.11	18.73	66.92	1.91	17.72	75.44
4.72	28.55	28.28	3.42	23.72	38.12	2.72	20.34	45.56	2.32	18.75	54.20	2.12	18.92	67.64	1.92	17.90	76.28
4.73	28.79	28.52	3.43	23.94	38.48	2.73	20.55	46.04	2.33	18.95	54.80	2.13	19.11	68.36	1.93	18.08	77.12
4.74	29.03	28.76	3.44	24.16	38.84	2.74	20.75	46.52	2.34	19.14	55.40	2.14	19.29	69.08	1.94	18.26	77.96
4.75	29.27	29.00	3.45	24.37	39.20	2.75	20.96	47.00	2.35	19.34	56.00	2.15	19.48	69.80	1.95	18.45	78.80
4.76	29.51	29.24	3.46	24.59	39.56	2.76	21.16	47.48	2.36	19.53	56.60	2.16	19.67	70.52	1.96	18.63	79.64
4.77	29.75	29.48	3.47	24.81	39.92	2.77	21.37	47.96	2.37	19.73	57.20	2.17	19.85	71.24	1.97	18.81	80.48
4.78	29.99	29.72	3.48	25.03	40.28	2.78	21.57	48.44	2.38	19.92	57.80	2.18	20.04	71.96	1.98	18.99	81.32
4.79	30.23	29.96	3.49	25.24	40.64	2.79	21.78	48.92	2.39	20.12	58.40	2.19	20.23	72.68	1.99	19.17	82.16
4.80	30.48	30.20	3.50	25.46	41.00	2.80	21.98	49.40	2.40	20.31	59.00	2.20	20.41	73.40	2.00	19.35	83.00
4.81	30.72	30.44	3.51	25.68	41.36	2.81	22.18	49.88	2.41	20.51	59.60	2.21	20.60	74.12	2.01	19.53	83.84
4.82	30.96	30.68	3.52	25.89	41.72	2.82	22.39	50.36	2.42	20.70	60.20	2.22	20.78	74.84	2.02	19.71	84.68
4.83	31.20	30.92	3.53	26.11	42.08	2.83	22.59	50.84	2.43	20.90	60.80	2.23	20.97	75.56	2.03	19.89	85.52
4.84	31.44	31.16	3.54	26.33	42.44	2.84	22.79	51.32	2.44	21.09	61.40	2.24	21.15	76.28	2.04	20.07	86.36
4.85	31.68	31.40	3.55	26.54	42.80	2.85	23.00	51.80	2.45	21.28	62.00	2.25	21.34	77.00	2.05	20.25	87.20
4.86	31.92	31.64	3.56	26.76	43.16	2.86	23.20	52.28	2.46	21.48	62.60	2.26	21.52	77.72	2.06	20.42	88.04
4.87	32.16	31.88	3.57	26.98	43.52	2.87	23.40	52.76	2.47	21.67	63.20	2.27	21.71	78.44	2.07	20.60	88.88
4.88	32.40	32.12	3.58	27.19	43.88	2.88	23.61	53.24	2.48	21.86	63.80	2.28	21.89	79.16	2.08	20.78	89.72
4.89	32.64	32.36	3.59	27.41	44.24	2.89	23.81	53.72	2.49	22.06	64.40	2.29	22.08	79.88	2.09	20.96	90.56
4.90	32.88	32.60	3.60	27.63	44.60	2.90	24.01	54.20	2.50	22.25	65.00	2.30	22.26	80.60	2.10	21.14	91.40
4.91	33.12	32.84	3.61	27.84	44.96	2.91	24.21	54.68	2.51	22.44	65.60	2.31	22.44	81.32	2.11	21.32	92.24
4.92	33.36	33.08	3.62	28.06	45.32	2.92	24.42	55.16	2.52	22.63	66.20	2.32	22.63	82.04	2.12	21.49	93.08
4.93	33.60	33.32	3.63	28.27	45.68	2.93	24.62	55.64	2.53	22.83	66.80	2.33	22.81	82.76	2.13	21.67	93.92
4.94	33.84	33.56	3.64	28.49	46.04	2.94	24.82	56.12	2.54	23.02	67.40	2.34	22.99	83.48	2.14	21.85	94.76
4.95	34.08	33.80	3.65	28.71	46.40	2.95	25.02	56.60	2.55	23.21	68.00	2.35	23.18	84.20	2.15	22.02	95.60
4.96	34.33	34.04	3.66	28.92	46.76	2.96	25.23	57.08	2.56	23.40	68.60	2.36	23.36	84.92	2.16	22.20	96.44
4.97	34.57	34.28	3.67	29.14	47.12	2.97	25.43	57.56	2.57	23.59	69.20	2.37	23.54	85.64	2.17	22.38	97.28
4.98	34.81	34.52	3.68	29.35	47.48	2.98	25.63	58.04	2.58	23.79	69.80	2.38	23.73	86.36	2.18	22.55	98.12
4.99	35.05	34.76	3.69	29.57	47.84	2.99	25.83	58.52	2.59	23.98	70.40	2.39	23.91	87.08	2.19	22.73	98.96

Description: This table shows the Annual Percentage Rate and finance charge per $100 for monthly lease payments.

Example: A 1.30% lease payment for 8 years is equivalent to an APR of 8.46%. The charge per $100 cost is $ 39.80.

8 yr PAYT	APR	CHARGE	9 yr PAYT	APR	CHARGE	10 yr PAYT	APR	CHARGE	12 yr PAYT	APR	CHARGE	15 yr PAYT	APR	CHARGE	20 yr PAYT	APR	CHARGE
1.30	8.46	39.80	1.20	8.32	44.60	1.10	7.83	47.00	1.00	8.00	59.00	.80	6.35	59.00	.70	6.44	83.00
1.31	8.65	40.76	1.21	8.51	45.68	1.11	8.01	48.20	1.01	8.18	60.44	.81	6.52	60.80	.71	6.61	85.40
1.32	8.84	41.72	1.22	8.70	46.76	1.12	8.20	49.40	1.02	8.36	61.88	.82	6.70	62.60	.72	6.77	87.80
1.33	9.04	42.68	1.23	8.89	47.84	1.13	8.39	50.60	1.03	8.54	63.32	.83	6.88	64.40	.73	6.94	90.20
1.34	9.23	43.64	1.24	9.07	48.92	1.14	8.57	51.80	1.04	8.71	64.76	.84	7.05	66.20	.74	7.10	92.60
1.35	9.42	44.60	1.25	9.26	50.00	1.15	8.76	53.00	1.05	8.89	66.20	.85	7.23	68.00	.75	7.27	95.00
1.36	9.61	45.56	1.26	9.45	51.08	1.16	8.94	54.20	1.06	9.07	67.64	.86	7.40	69.80	.76	7.43	97.40
1.37	9.80	46.52	1.27	9.64	52.16	1.17	9.12	55.40	1.07	9.24	69.08	.87	7.58	71.60	.77	7.59	99.80
1.38	9.99	47.48	1.28	9.82	53.24	1.18	9.31	56.60	1.08	9.42	70.52	.88	7.75	73.40	.78	7.76	102.20
1.39	10.18	48.44	1.29	10.01	54.32	1.19	9.49	57.80	1.09	9.60	71.96	.89	7.92	75.20	.79	7.92	104.60
1.40	10.37	49.40	1.30	10.19	55.40	1.20	9.67	59.00	1.10	9.77	73.40	.90	8.10	77.00	.80	8.08	107.00
1.41	10.56	50.36	1.31	10.38	56.48	1.21	9.86	60.20	1.11	9.95	74.84	.91	8.27	78.80	.81	8.24	109.40
1.42	10.75	51.32	1.32	10.56	57.56	1.22	10.04	61.40	1.12	10.12	76.28	.92	8.44	80.60	.82	8.40	111.80
1.43	10.93	52.28	1.33	10.74	58.64	1.23	10.22	62.60	1.13	10.29	77.72	.93	8.61	82.40	.83	8.56	114.20
1.44	11.12	53.24	1.34	10.93	59.72	1.24	10.40	63.80	1.14	10.47	79.16	.94	8.78	84.20	.84	8.72	116.60
1.45	11.31	54.20	1.35	11.11	60.80	1.25	10.58	65.00	1.15	10.64	80.60	.95	8.95	86.00	.85	8.87	119.00
1.46	11.49	55.16	1.36	11.29	61.88	1.26	10.76	66.20	1.16	10.81	82.04	.96	9.11	87.80	.86	9.03	121.40
1.47	11.68	56.12	1.37	11.48	62.96	1.27	10.94	67.40	1.17	10.98	83.48	.97	9.28	89.60	.87	9.19	123.80
1.48	11.87	57.08	1.38	11.66	64.04	1.28	11.12	68.60	1.18	11.16	84.92	.98	9.45	91.40	.88	9.34	126.20
1.49	12.05	58.04	1.39	11.84	65.12	1.29	11.29	69.80	1.19	11.33	86.36	.99	9.62	93.20	.89	9.50	128.60
1.50	12.24	59.00	1.40	12.02	66.20	1.30	11.47	71.00	1.20	11.50	87.80	1.00	9.78	95.00	.90	9.66	131.00
1.51	12.42	59.96	1.41	12.20	67.28	1.31	11.65	72.20	1.21	11.67	89.24	1.01	9.95	96.80	.91	9.81	133.40
1.52	12.61	60.92	1.42	12.38	68.36	1.32	11.83	73.40	1.22	11.84	90.68	1.02	10.11	98.60	.92	9.97	135.80
1.53	12.79	61.88	1.43	12.56	69.44	1.33	12.00	74.60	1.23	12.01	92.12	1.03	10.28	100.40	.93	10.12	138.20
1.54	12.98	62.84	1.44	12.74	70.52	1.34	12.18	75.80	1.24	12.18	93.56	1.04	10.44	102.20	.94	10.27	140.60
1.55	13.16	63.80	1.45	12.92	71.60	1.35	12.36	77.00	1.25	12.34	95.00	1.05	10.61	104.00	.95	10.43	143.00
1.56	13.34	64.76	1.46	13.10	72.68	1.36	12.53	78.20	1.26	12.51	96.44	1.06	10.77	105.80	.96	10.58	145.40
1.57	13.53	65.72	1.47	13.28	73.76	1.37	12.71	79.40	1.27	12.68	97.88	1.07	10.93	107.60	.97	10.73	147.80
1.58	13.71	66.68	1.48	13.45	74.84	1.38	12.88	80.60	1.28	12.85	99.32	1.08	11.10	109.40	.98	10.88	150.20
1.59	13.89	67.64	1.49	13.63	75.92	1.39	13.06	81.80	1.29	13.01	100.76	1.09	11.26	111.20	.99	11.03	152.60
1.60	14.07	68.60	1.50	13.81	77.00	1.40	13.23	83.00	1.30	13.18	102.20	1.10	11.42	113.00	1.00	11.19	155.00
1.61	14.25	69.56	1.51	13.99	78.08	1.41	13.40	84.20	1.31	13.35	103.64	1.11	11.58	114.80	1.01	11.34	157.40
1.62	14.43	70.52	1.52	14.16	79.16	1.42	13.58	85.40	1.32	13.51	105.08	1.12	11.74	116.60	1.02	11.49	159.80
1.63	14.62	71.48	1.53	14.34	80.24	1.43	13.75	86.60	1.33	13.68	106.52	1.13	11.90	118.40	1.03	11.64	162.20
1.64	14.80	72.44	1.54	14.52	81.32	1.44	13.92	87.80	1.34	13.84	107.96	1.14	12.06	120.20	1.04	11.79	164.60
1.65	14.98	73.40	1.55	14.69	82.40	1.45	14.10	89.00	1.35	14.01	109.40	1.15	12.22	122.00	1.05	11.94	167.00
1.66	15.16	74.36	1.56	14.87	83.48	1.46	14.27	90.20	1.36	14.17	110.84	1.16	12.38	123.80	1.06	12.08	169.40
1.67	15.34	75.32	1.57	15.04	84.56	1.47	14.44	91.40	1.37	14.34	112.28	1.17	12.54	125.60	1.07	12.23	171.80
1.68	15.52	76.28	1.58	15.22	85.64	1.48	14.61	92.60	1.38	14.50	113.72	1.18	12.70	127.40	1.08	12.38	174.20
1.69	15.70	77.24	1.59	15.39	86.72	1.49	14.78	93.80	1.39	14.67	115.16	1.19	12.86	129.20	1.09	12.53	176.60
1.70	15.87	78.20	1.60	15.57	87.80	1.50	14.95	95.00	1.40	14.83	116.60	1.20	13.01	131.00	1.10	12.68	179.00
1.71	16.05	79.16	1.61	15.74	88.88	1.51	15.12	96.20	1.41	14.99	118.04	1.21	13.17	132.80	1.11	12.82	181.40
1.72	16.23	80.12	1.62	15.91	89.96	1.52	15.29	97.40	1.42	15.15	119.48	1.22	13.33	134.60	1.12	12.97	183.80
1.73	16.41	81.08	1.63	16.09	91.04	1.53	15.46	98.60	1.43	15.32	120.92	1.23	13.49	136.40	1.13	13.12	186.20
1.74	16.59	82.04	1.64	16.26	92.12	1.54	15.63	99.80	1.44	15.48	122.36	1.24	13.64	138.20	1.14	13.27	188.60
1.75	16.77	83.00	1.65	16.43	93.20	1.55	15.80	101.00	1.45	15.64	123.80	1.25	13.80	140.00	1.15	13.41	191.00
1.76	16.94	83.96	1.66	16.61	94.28	1.56	15.97	102.20	1.46	15.80	125.24	1.26	13.96	141.80	1.16	13.56	193.40
1.77	17.12	84.92	1.67	16.78	95.36	1.57	16.14	103.40	1.47	15.96	126.68	1.27	14.11	143.60	1.17	13.70	195.80
1.78	17.30	85.88	1.68	16.95	96.44	1.58	16.31	104.60	1.48	16.13	128.12	1.28	14.27	145.40	1.18	13.85	198.20
1.79	17.47	86.84	1.69	17.12	97.52	1.59	16.48	105.80	1.49	16.29	129.56	1.29	14.42	147.20	1.19	13.99	200.60
1.80	17.65	87.80	1.70	17.29	98.60	1.60	16.65	107.00	1.50	16.45	131.00	1.30	14.58	149.00	1.20	14.14	203.00
1.81	17.82	88.76	1.71	17.47	99.68	1.61	16.81	108.20	1.51	16.61	132.44	1.31	14.73	150.80	1.21	14.28	205.40
1.82	18.00	89.72	1.72	17.64	100.76	1.62	16.98	109.40	1.52	16.77	133.88	1.32	14.89	152.60	1.22	14.43	207.80
1.83	18.18	90.68	1.73	17.81	101.84	1.63	17.15	110.60	1.53	16.93	135.32	1.33	15.04	154.40	1.23	14.57	210.20
1.84	18.35	91.64	1.74	17.98	102.92	1.64	17.32	111.80	1.54	17.09	136.76	1.34	15.19	156.20	1.24	14.72	212.60
1.85	18.53	92.60	1.75	18.15	104.00	1.65	17.48	113.00	1.55	17.25	138.20	1.35	15.35	158.00	1.25	14.86	215.00
1.86	18.70	93.56	1.76	18.32	105.08	1.66	17.65	114.20	1.56	17.41	139.64	1.36	15.50	159.80	1.26	15.01	217.40
1.87	18.88	94.52	1.77	18.49	106.16	1.67	17.81	115.40	1.57	17.56	141.08	1.37	15.65	161.60	1.27	15.15	219.80
1.88	19.05	95.48	1.78	18.66	107.24	1.68	17.98	116.60	1.58	17.72	142.52	1.38	15.81	163.40	1.28	15.29	222.20
1.89	19.22	96.44	1.79	18.83	108.32	1.69	18.15	117.80	1.59	17.88	143.96	1.39	15.96	165.20	1.29	15.44	224.60
1.90	19.40	97.40	1.80	19.00	109.40	1.70	18.31	119.00	1.60	18.04	145.40	1.40	16.11	167.00	1.30	15.58	227.00
1.91	19.57	98.36	1.81	19.17	110.48	1.71	18.48	120.20	1.61	18.20	146.84	1.41	16.26	168.80	1.31	15.72	229.40
1.92	19.75	99.32	1.82	19.33	111.56	1.72	18.64	121.40	1.62	18.36	148.28	1.42	16.41	170.60	1.32	15.87	231.80
1.93	19.92	100.28	1.83	19.50	112.64	1.73	18.81	122.60	1.63	18.51	149.72	1.43	16.57	172.40	1.33	16.01	234.20
1.94	20.09	101.24	1.84	19.67	113.72	1.74	18.97	123.80	1.64	18.67	151.16	1.44	16.72	174.20	1.34	16.15	236.60
1.95	20.26	102.20	1.85	19.84	114.80	1.75	19.14	125.00	1.65	18.83	152.60	1.45	16.87	176.00	1.35	16.29	239.00
1.96	20.44	103.16	1.86	20.01	115.88	1.76	19.30	126.20	1.66	18.98	154.04	1.46	17.02	177.80	1.36	16.44	241.40
1.97	20.61	104.12	1.87	20.17	116.96	1.77	19.46	127.40	1.67	19.14	155.48	1.47	17.17	179.60	1.37	16.58	243.80
1.98	20.78	105.08	1.88	20.34	118.04	1.78	19.63	128.60	1.68	19.30	156.92	1.48	17.32	181.40	1.38	16.72	246.20
1.99	20.95	106.04	1.89	20.51	119.12	1.79	19.79	129.80	1.69	19.45	158.36	1.49	17.47	183.20	1.39	16.86	248.60

Description: This table shows the Annual Percentage Rate and finance charge per $100 for monthly lease payments.

Example: A 4.30% lease payment for 2 years is equivalent to an APR of 22.25%. The charge per $100 cost is $ 23.20.

2 yr MONTHLY PAYT	APR	CHARGE	3 yr MONTHLY PAYT	APR	CHARGE	4 yr MONTHLY PAYT	APR	CHARGE	5 yr MONTHLY PAYT	APR	CHARGE	6 yr MONTHLY PAYT	APR	CHARGE	7 yr MONTHLY PAYT	APR	CHARGE
4.30	22.25	23.20	3.00	16.78	28.00	2.30	13.21	30.40	1.90	11.56	34.00	1.70	11.75	42.40	1.50	10.78	46.00
4.31	22.48	23.44	3.01	16.99	28.36	2.31	13.41	30.88	1.91	11.75	34.60	1.71	11.94	43.12	1.51	10.96	46.84
4.32	22.71	23.68	3.02	17.20	28.72	2.32	13.62	31.36	1.92	11.95	35.20	1.72	12.13	43.84	1.52	11.15	47.68
4.33	22.94	23.92	3.03	17.42	29.08	2.33	13.82	31.84	1.93	12.15	35.80	1.73	12.32	44.56	1.53	11.34	48.52
4.34	23.17	24.16	3.04	17.63	29.44	2.34	14.02	32.32	1.94	12.34	36.40	1.74	12.51	45.28	1.54	11.52	49.36
4.35	23.41	24.40	3.05	17.84	29.80	2.35	14.23	32.80	1.95	12.54	37.00	1.75	12.70	46.00	1.55	11.71	50.20
4.36	23.64	24.64	3.06	18.05	30.16	2.36	14.43	33.28	1.96	12.73	37.60	1.76	12.89	46.72	1.56	11.90	51.04
4.37	23.87	24.88	3.07	18.26	30.52	2.37	14.63	33.76	1.97	12.93	38.20	1.77	13.08	47.44	1.57	12.08	51.88
4.38	24.10	25.12	3.08	18.48	30.88	2.38	14.83	34.24	1.98	13.13	38.80	1.78	13.27	48.16	1.58	12.27	52.72
4.39	24.33	25.36	3.09	18.69	31.24	2.39	15.03	34.72	1.99	13.32	39.40	1.79	13.46	48.88	1.59	12.45	53.56
4.40	24.56	25.60	3.10	18.90	31.60	2.40	15.24	35.20	2.00	13.52	40.00	1.80	13.65	49.60	1.60	12.64	54.40
4.41	24.79	25.84	3.11	19.11	31.96	2.41	15.44	35.68	2.01	13.71	40.60	1.81	13.84	50.32	1.61	12.82	55.24
4.42	25.02	26.08	3.12	19.32	32.32	2.42	15.64	36.16	2.02	13.91	41.20	1.82	14.02	51.04	1.62	13.00	56.08
4.43	25.25	26.32	3.13	19.53	32.68	2.43	15.84	36.64	2.03	14.10	41.80	1.83	14.21	51.76	1.63	13.19	56.92
4.44	25.48	26.56	3.14	19.75	33.04	2.44	16.04	37.12	2.04	14.30	42.40	1.84	14.40	52.48	1.64	13.37	57.76
4.45	25.71	26.80	3.15	19.96	33.40	2.45	16.24	37.60	2.05	14.49	43.00	1.85	14.59	53.20	1.65	13.55	58.60
4.46	25.94	27.04	3.16	20.17	33.76	2.46	16.45	38.08	2.06	14.69	43.60	1.86	14.78	53.92	1.66	13.74	59.44
4.47	26.17	27.28	3.17	20.38	34.12	2.47	16.65	38.56	2.07	14.88	44.20	1.87	14.96	54.64	1.67	13.92	60.28
4.48	26.40	27.52	3.18	20.59	34.48	2.48	16.85	39.04	2.08	15.07	44.80	1.88	15.15	55.36	1.68	14.10	61.12
4.49	26.63	27.76	3.19	20.80	34.84	2.49	17.05	39.52	2.09	15.27	45.40	1.89	15.34	56.08	1.69	14.29	61.96
4.50	26.86	28.00	3.20	21.01	35.20	2.50	17.25	40.00	2.10	15.46	46.00	1.90	15.52	56.80	1.70	14.47	62.80
4.51	27.09	28.24	3.21	21.22	35.56	2.51	17.45	40.48	2.11	15.65	46.60	1.91	15.71	57.52	1.71	14.65	63.64
4.52	27.32	28.48	3.22	21.43	35.92	2.52	17.65	40.96	2.12	15.85	47.20	1.92	15.90	58.24	1.72	14.83	64.48
4.53	27.55	28.72	3.23	21.64	36.28	2.53	17.85	41.44	2.13	16.04	47.80	1.93	16.08	58.96	1.73	15.01	65.32
4.54	27.78	28.96	3.24	21.85	36.64	2.54	18.05	41.92	2.14	16.23	48.40	1.94	16.27	59.68	1.74	15.19	66.16
4.55	28.01	29.20	3.25	22.07	37.00	2.55	18.25	42.40	2.15	16.43	49.00	1.95	16.45	60.40	1.75	15.37	67.00
4.56	28.24	29.44	3.26	22.28	37.36	2.56	18.45	42.88	2.16	16.62	49.60	1.96	16.64	61.12	1.76	15.55	67.84
4.57	28.47	29.68	3.27	22.49	37.72	2.57	18.65	43.36	2.17	16.81	50.20	1.97	16.82	61.84	1.77	15.74	68.68
4.58	28.71	29.92	3.28	22.70	38.08	2.58	18.85	43.84	2.18	17.00	50.80	1.98	17.01	62.56	1.78	15.92	69.52
4.59	28.94	30.16	3.29	22.91	38.44	2.59	19.05	44.32	2.19	17.19	51.40	1.99	17.19	63.28	1.79	16.10	70.36
4.60	29.17	30.40	3.30	23.12	38.80	2.60	19.25	44.80	2.20	17.39	52.00	2.00	17.38	64.00	1.80	16.27	71.20
4.61	29.40	30.64	3.31	23.33	39.16	2.61	19.45	45.28	2.21	17.58	52.60	2.01	17.56	64.72	1.81	16.45	72.04
4.62	29.63	30.88	3.32	23.54	39.52	2.62	19.65	45.76	2.22	17.77	53.20	2.02	17.75	65.44	1.82	16.63	72.88
4.63	29.86	31.12	3.33	23.75	39.88	2.63	19.85	46.24	2.23	17.96	53.80	2.03	17.93	66.16	1.83	16.81	73.72
4.64	30.09	31.36	3.34	23.96	40.24	2.64	20.05	46.72	2.24	18.15	54.40	2.04	18.11	66.88	1.84	16.99	74.56
4.65	30.32	31.60	3.35	24.17	40.60	2.65	20.24	47.20	2.25	18.34	55.00	2.05	18.30	67.60	1.85	17.17	75.40
4.66	30.55	31.84	3.36	24.38	40.96	2.66	20.44	47.68	2.26	18.53	55.60	2.06	18.48	68.32	1.86	17.35	76.24
4.67	30.78	32.08	3.37	24.59	41.32	2.67	20.64	48.16	2.27	18.72	56.20	2.07	18.66	69.04	1.87	17.53	77.08
4.68	31.01	32.32	3.38	24.80	41.68	2.68	20.84	48.64	2.28	18.91	56.80	2.08	18.85	69.76	1.88	17.70	77.92
4.69	31.24	32.56	3.39	25.01	42.04	2.69	21.04	49.12	2.29	19.10	57.40	2.09	19.03	70.48	1.89	17.88	78.76
4.70	31.47	32.80	3.40	25.22	42.40	2.70	21.24	49.60	2.30	19.29	58.00	2.10	19.21	71.20	1.90	18.06	79.60
4.71	31.70	33.04	3.41	25.43	42.76	2.71	21.44	50.08	2.31	19.48	58.60	2.11	19.40	71.92	1.91	18.24	80.44
4.72	31.93	33.28	3.42	25.64	43.12	2.72	21.63	50.56	2.32	19.67	59.20	2.12	19.58	72.64	1.92	18.42	81.28
4.73	32.17	33.52	3.43	25.85	43.48	2.73	21.83	51.04	2.33	19.86	59.80	2.13	19.76	73.36	1.93	18.59	82.12
4.74	32.40	33.76	3.44	26.06	43.84	2.74	22.03	51.52	2.34	20.05	60.40	2.14	19.94	74.08	1.94	18.77	82.96
4.75	32.63	34.00	3.45	26.27	44.20	2.75	22.23	52.00	2.35	20.24	61.00	2.15	20.12	74.80	1.95	18.95	83.80
4.76	32.86	34.24	3.46	26.47	44.56	2.76	22.42	52.48	2.36	20.43	61.60	2.16	20.31	75.52	1.96	19.12	84.64
4.77	33.09	34.48	3.47	26.68	44.92	2.77	22.62	52.96	2.37	20.62	62.20	2.17	20.49	76.24	1.97	19.30	85.48
4.78	33.32	34.72	3.48	26.89	45.28	2.78	22.82	53.44	2.38	20.81	62.80	2.18	20.67	76.96	1.98	19.47	86.32
4.79	33.55	34.96	3.49	27.10	45.64	2.79	23.02	53.92	2.39	21.00	63.40	2.19	20.85	77.68	1.99	19.65	87.16
4.80	33.78	35.20	3.50	27.31	46.00	2.80	23.21	54.40	2.40	21.19	64.00	2.20	21.03	78.40	2.00	19.83	88.00
4.81	34.01	35.44	3.51	27.52	46.36	2.81	23.41	54.88	2.41	21.38	64.60	2.21	21.21	79.12	2.01	20.00	88.84
4.82	34.24	35.68	3.52	27.73	46.72	2.82	23.61	55.36	2.42	21.57	65.20	2.22	21.39	79.84	2.02	20.18	89.68
4.83	34.47	35.92	3.53	27.94	47.08	2.83	23.80	55.84	2.43	21.75	65.80	2.23	21.57	80.56	2.03	20.35	90.52
4.84	34.70	36.16	3.54	28.15	47.44	2.84	24.00	56.32	2.44	21.94	66.40	2.24	21.75	81.28	2.04	20.53	91.36
4.85	34.94	36.40	3.55	28.36	47.80	2.85	24.20	56.80	2.45	22.13	67.00	2.25	21.93	82.00	2.05	20.70	92.20
4.86	35.17	36.64	3.56	28.57	48.16	2.86	24.40	57.28	2.46	22.32	67.60	2.26	22.11	82.72	2.06	20.88	93.04
4.87	35.40	36.88	3.57	28.77	48.52	2.87	24.59	57.76	2.47	22.51	68.20	2.27	22.29	83.44	2.07	21.05	93.88
4.88	35.63	37.12	3.58	28.98	48.88	2.88	24.79	58.24	2.48	22.69	68.80	2.28	22.47	84.16	2.08	21.23	94.72
4.89	35.86	37.36	3.59	29.19	49.24	2.89	24.98	58.72	2.49	22.88	69.40	2.29	22.65	84.88	2.09	21.40	95.56
4.90	36.09	37.60	3.60	29.40	49.60	2.90	25.18	59.20	2.50	23.07	70.00	2.30	22.83	85.60	2.10	21.57	96.40
4.91	36.32	37.84	3.61	29.61	49.96	2.91	25.38	59.68	2.51	23.26	70.60	2.31	23.01	86.32	2.11	21.75	97.24
4.92	36.55	38.08	3.62	29.82	50.32	2.92	25.57	60.16	2.52	23.44	71.20	2.32	23.19	87.04	2.12	21.92	98.08
4.93	36.78	38.32	3.63	30.03	50.68	2.93	25.77	60.64	2.53	23.63	71.80	2.33	23.37	87.76	2.13	22.10	98.92
4.94	37.02	38.56	3.64	30.23	51.04	2.94	25.96	61.12	2.54	23.82	72.40	2.34	23.55	88.48	2.14	22.27	99.76
4.95	37.25	38.80	3.65	30.44	51.40	2.95	26.16	61.60	2.55	24.00	73.00	2.35	23.73	89.20	2.15	22.44	100.60
4.96	37.48	39.04	3.66	30.65	51.76	2.96	26.36	62.08	2.56	24.19	73.60	2.36	23.91	89.92	2.16	22.62	101.44
4.97	37.71	39.28	3.67	30.86	52.12	2.97	26.55	62.56	2.57	24.38	74.20	2.37	24.09	90.64	2.17	22.79	102.28
4.98	37.94	39.52	3.68	31.07	52.48	2.98	26.75	63.04	2.58	24.56	74.80	2.38	24.27	91.36	2.18	22.96	103.12
4.99	38.17	39.76	3.69	31.28	52.84	2.99	26.94	63.52	2.59	24.75	75.40	2.39	24.44	92.08	2.19	23.13	103.96

Description: This table shows the Annual Percentage Rate and finance charge per $100 for monthly lease payments.

Example: A 1.30% lease payment for 8 years is equivalent to an APR of 9.13%. The charge per $100 cost is $ 44.80.

8 yr MONTHLY PAYT	APR	CHARGE	9 yr MONTHLY PAYT	APR	CHARGE	10 yr MONTHLY PAYT	APR	CHARGE	12 yr MONTHLY PAYT	APR	CHARGE	15 yr MONTHLY PAYT	APR	CHARGE	20 yr MONTHLY PAYT	APR	CHARGE
1.30	9.13	44.80	1.20	8.88	49.60	1.10	8.32	52.00	1.00	8.35	64.00	.80	6.63	64.00	.70	6.61	88.00
1.31	9.31	45.76	1.21	9.06	50.68	1.11	8.50	53.20	1.01	8.53	65.44	.81	6.80	65.80	.71	6.77	90.40
1.32	9.50	46.72	1.22	9.25	51.76	1.12	8.68	54.40	1.02	8.70	66.88	.82	6.98	67.60	.72	6.93	92.80
1.33	9.68	47.68	1.23	9.43	52.84	1.13	8.86	55.60	1.03	8.88	68.32	.83	7.15	69.40	.73	7.09	95.20
1.34	9.87	48.64	1.24	9.61	53.92	1.14	9.04	56.80	1.04	9.05	69.76	.84	7.32	71.20	.74	7.25	97.60
1.35	10.05	49.60	1.25	9.79	55.00	1.15	9.22	58.00	1.05	9.22	71.20	.85	7.49	73.00	.75	7.41	100.00
1.36	10.24	50.56	1.26	9.97	56.08	1.16	9.39	59.20	1.06	9.39	72.64	.86	7.66	74.80	.76	7.57	102.40
1.37	10.42	51.52	1.27	10.15	57.16	1.17	9.57	60.40	1.07	9.57	74.08	.87	7.83	76.60	.77	7.73	104.80
1.38	10.60	52.48	1.28	10.33	58.24	1.18	9.75	61.60	1.08	9.74	75.52	.88	7.99	78.40	.78	7.89	107.20
1.39	10.79	53.44	1.29	10.51	59.32	1.19	9.93	62.80	1.09	9.91	76.96	.89	8.16	80.20	.79	8.05	109.60
1.40	10.97	54.40	1.30	10.69	60.40	1.20	10.10	64.00	1.10	10.08	78.40	.90	8.33	82.00	.80	8.21	112.00
1.41	11.15	55.36	1.31	10.87	61.48	1.21	10.28	65.20	1.11	10.25	79.84	.91	8.50	83.80	.81	8.37	114.40
1.42	11.33	56.32	1.32	11.05	62.56	1.22	10.46	66.40	1.12	10.42	81.28	.92	8.66	85.60	.82	8.52	116.80
1.43	11.51	57.28	1.33	11.22	63.64	1.23	10.63	67.60	1.13	10.59	82.72	.93	8.83	87.40	.83	8.68	119.20
1.44	11.70	58.24	1.34	11.40	64.72	1.24	10.81	68.80	1.14	10.76	84.16	.94	8.99	89.20	.84	8.83	121.60
1.45	11.88	59.20	1.35	11.58	65.80	1.25	10.98	70.00	1.15	10.92	85.60	.95	9.16	91.00	.85	8.99	124.00
1.46	12.06	60.16	1.36	11.76	66.88	1.26	11.16	71.20	1.16	11.09	87.04	.96	9.32	92.80	.86	9.14	126.40
1.47	12.24	61.12	1.37	11.93	67.96	1.27	11.33	72.40	1.17	11.26	88.48	.97	9.49	94.60	.87	9.30	128.80
1.48	12.42	62.08	1.38	12.11	69.04	1.28	11.50	73.60	1.18	11.43	89.92	.98	9.65	96.40	.88	9.45	131.20
1.49	12.60	63.04	1.39	12.29	70.12	1.29	11.68	74.80	1.19	11.59	91.36	.99	9.81	98.20	.89	9.61	133.60
1.50	12.78	64.00	1.40	12.46	71.20	1.30	11.85	76.00	1.20	11.76	92.80	1.00	9.98	100.00	.90	9.76	136.00
1.51	12.96	64.96	1.41	12.64	72.28	1.31	12.02	77.20	1.21	11.93	94.24	1.01	10.14	101.80	.91	9.91	138.40
1.52	13.14	65.92	1.42	12.81	73.36	1.32	12.20	78.40	1.22	12.09	95.68	1.02	10.30	103.60	.92	10.06	140.80
1.53	13.31	66.88	1.43	12.99	74.44	1.33	12.37	79.60	1.23	12.26	97.12	1.03	10.46	105.40	.93	10.22	143.20
1.54	13.49	67.84	1.44	13.16	75.52	1.34	12.54	80.80	1.24	12.42	98.56	1.04	10.62	107.20	.94	10.37	145.60
1.55	13.67	68.80	1.45	13.34	76.60	1.35	12.71	82.00	1.25	12.59	100.00	1.05	10.78	109.00	.95	10.52	148.00
1.56	13.85	69.76	1.46	13.51	77.68	1.36	12.88	83.20	1.26	12.75	101.44	1.06	10.95	110.80	.96	10.67	150.40
1.57	14.03	70.72	1.47	13.68	78.76	1.37	13.05	84.40	1.27	12.92	102.88	1.07	11.10	112.60	.97	10.82	152.80
1.58	14.20	71.68	1.48	13.86	79.84	1.38	13.22	85.60	1.28	13.08	104.32	1.08	11.26	114.40	.98	10.97	155.20
1.59	14.38	72.64	1.49	14.03	80.92	1.39	13.39	86.80	1.29	13.24	105.76	1.09	11.42	116.20	.99	11.12	157.60
1.60	14.56	73.60	1.50	14.20	82.00	1.40	13.56	88.00	1.30	13.41	107.20	1.10	11.58	118.00	1.00	11.27	160.00
1.61	14.74	74.56	1.51	14.38	83.08	1.41	13.73	89.20	1.31	13.57	108.64	1.11	11.74	119.80	1.01	11.42	162.40
1.62	14.91	75.52	1.52	14.55	84.16	1.42	13.90	90.40	1.32	13.73	110.08	1.12	11.90	121.60	1.02	11.56	164.80
1.63	15.09	76.48	1.53	14.72	85.24	1.43	14.07	91.60	1.33	13.90	111.52	1.13	12.06	123.40	1.03	11.71	167.20
1.64	15.26	77.44	1.54	14.89	86.32	1.44	14.24	92.80	1.34	14.06	112.96	1.14	12.21	125.20	1.04	11.86	169.60
1.65	15.44	78.40	1.55	15.06	87.40	1.45	14.41	94.00	1.35	14.22	114.40	1.15	12.37	127.00	1.05	12.01	172.00
1.66	15.61	79.36	1.56	15.24	88.48	1.46	14.58	95.20	1.36	14.38	115.84	1.16	12.53	128.80	1.06	12.16	174.40
1.67	15.79	80.32	1.57	15.41	89.56	1.47	14.75	96.40	1.37	14.54	117.28	1.17	12.68	130.60	1.07	12.30	176.80
1.68	15.96	81.28	1.58	15.58	90.64	1.48	14.91	97.60	1.38	14.70	118.72	1.18	12.84	132.40	1.08	12.45	179.20
1.69	16.14	82.24	1.59	15.75	91.72	1.49	15.08	98.80	1.39	14.87	120.16	1.19	13.00	134.20	1.09	12.60	181.60
1.70	16.31	83.20	1.60	15.92	92.80	1.50	15.25	100.00	1.40	15.03	121.60	1.20	13.15	136.00	1.10	12.74	184.00
1.71	16.49	84.16	1.61	16.09	93.88	1.51	15.41	101.20	1.41	15.19	123.04	1.21	13.31	137.80	1.11	12.89	186.40
1.72	16.66	85.12	1.62	16.26	94.96	1.52	15.58	102.40	1.42	15.35	124.48	1.22	13.46	139.60	1.12	13.03	188.80
1.73	16.84	86.08	1.63	16.43	96.04	1.53	15.75	103.60	1.43	15.51	125.92	1.23	13.62	141.40	1.13	13.18	191.20
1.74	17.01	87.04	1.64	16.60	97.12	1.54	15.91	104.80	1.44	15.67	127.36	1.24	13.77	143.20	1.14	13.33	193.60
1.75	17.18	88.00	1.65	16.77	98.20	1.55	16.08	106.00	1.45	15.82	128.80	1.25	13.92	145.00	1.15	13.47	196.00
1.76	17.36	88.96	1.66	16.94	99.28	1.56	16.25	107.20	1.46	15.98	130.24	1.26	14.08	146.80	1.16	13.62	198.40
1.77	17.53	89.92	1.67	17.10	100.36	1.57	16.41	108.40	1.47	16.14	131.68	1.27	14.23	148.60	1.17	13.76	200.80
1.78	17.70	90.88	1.68	17.27	101.44	1.58	16.58	109.60	1.48	16.30	133.12	1.28	14.39	150.40	1.18	13.90	203.20
1.79	17.87	91.84	1.69	17.44	102.52	1.59	16.74	110.80	1.49	16.46	134.56	1.29	14.54	152.20	1.19	14.05	205.60
1.80	18.05	92.80	1.70	17.61	103.60	1.60	16.91	112.00	1.50	16.62	136.00	1.30	14.69	154.00	1.20	14.19	208.00
1.81	18.22	93.76	1.71	17.78	104.68	1.61	17.07	113.20	1.51	16.78	137.44	1.31	14.84	155.80	1.21	14.34	210.40
1.82	18.39	94.72	1.72	17.94	105.76	1.62	17.24	114.40	1.52	16.93	138.88	1.32	15.00	157.60	1.22	14.48	212.80
1.83	18.56	95.68	1.73	18.11	106.84	1.63	17.40	115.60	1.53	17.09	140.32	1.33	15.15	159.40	1.23	14.62	215.20
1.84	18.73	96.64	1.74	18.28	107.92	1.64	17.56	116.80	1.54	17.25	141.76	1.34	15.30	161.20	1.24	14.77	217.60
1.85	18.90	97.60	1.75	18.45	109.00	1.65	17.73	118.00	1.55	17.41	143.20	1.35	15.45	163.00	1.25	14.91	220.00
1.86	19.07	98.56	1.76	18.61	110.08	1.66	17.89	119.20	1.56	17.56	144.64	1.36	15.60	164.80	1.26	15.05	222.40
1.87	19.25	99.52	1.77	18.78	111.16	1.67	18.05	120.40	1.57	17.72	146.08	1.37	15.75	166.60	1.27	15.19	224.80
1.88	19.42	100.48	1.78	18.95	112.24	1.68	18.22	121.60	1.58	17.88	147.52	1.38	15.91	168.40	1.28	15.34	227.20
1.89	19.59	101.44	1.79	19.11	113.32	1.69	18.38	122.80	1.59	18.03	148.96	1.39	16.06	170.20	1.29	15.48	229.60
1.90	19.76	102.40	1.80	19.28	114.40	1.70	18.54	124.00	1.60	18.19	150.40	1.40	16.21	172.00	1.30	15.62	232.00
1.91	19.93	103.36	1.81	19.44	115.48	1.71	18.70	125.20	1.61	18.34	151.84	1.41	16.36	173.80	1.31	15.76	234.40
1.92	20.10	104.32	1.82	19.61	116.56	1.72	18.87	126.40	1.62	18.50	153.28	1.42	16.51	175.60	1.32	15.91	236.80
1.93	20.27	105.28	1.83	19.78	117.64	1.73	19.03	127.60	1.63	18.65	154.72	1.43	16.66	177.40	1.33	16.05	239.20
1.94	20.44	106.24	1.84	19.94	118.72	1.74	19.19	128.80	1.64	18.81	156.16	1.44	16.81	179.20	1.34	16.19	241.60
1.95	20.61	107.20	1.85	20.11	119.80	1.75	19.35	130.00	1.65	18.97	157.60	1.45	16.96	181.00	1.35	16.33	244.00
1.96	20.78	108.16	1.86	20.27	120.88	1.76	19.51	131.20	1.66	19.12	159.04	1.46	17.11	182.80	1.36	16.47	246.40
1.97	20.94	109.12	1.87	20.44	121.96	1.77	19.68	132.40	1.67	19.28	160.48	1.47	17.26	184.60	1.37	16.61	248.80
1.98	21.11	110.08	1.88	20.60	123.04	1.78	19.84	133.60	1.68	19.43	161.92	1.48	17.41	186.40	1.38	16.75	251.20
1.99	21.28	111.04	1.89	20.76	124.12	1.79	20.00	134.80	1.69	19.58	163.36	1.49	17.55	188.20	1.39	16.90	253.60

TABLE **21**

Monthly Rebate and Earnings, Rule of 78

Terms: 1 to 10 years, each year.

Payment: Monthly.

This table shows the rebate of the unearned finance charge when an installment loan is prepaid in full prior to maturity. The table shows the cumulative earnings for each month during the term of the loan. The rebate and earnings are computed by the Rule of 78. The index corresponds to both the number of months to rebate and the number of months that have earned.

Example: An installment loan, written for 12 months, is prepaid in full after the fifth payment. What is the amount to be prepaid? The terms of the loan are:

Loan:	$1,000.00	Note:	1,095.00
Finance charge:	95.00	Term:	1 year
	Payment:	91.25 monthly	

The loan, prepaid at the end of the fifth month, leaves 7 months of unearned finance charge to rebate. On page 21-2, in the 1 year table, find line 7 in the index and read the corresponding rebate of 35.8974. This is the percent of the finance charge to rebate. The formula is:

$$\text{Rebate} = \text{Charge} \times \text{Factor}$$
$$= 95 \times .358974$$
$$= 34.10$$

To compute the total payments to prepay, multiply the monthly payment by the months rebated:

$$91.25 \times 7 = 638.75$$

Subtract the rebate:

$$638.75 - 34.10 = 604.65$$

The net to prepay in full is 604.65.

Minimum Charge. A lender may be entitled to a minimum charge. The rule is to compute the rebate first and see if the minimum charge has been earned. If the minimum has not been earned, then the rebate is reduced by an amount to satisfy the minimum charge. The minimum should not be subtracted from the finance charge before computing the rebate.

Rule of 78. The Rule of 78 is a method to compute rebates and to allocate earnings for installment loans. The results from the Rule of 78 are very close to the amounts calculated by the actuarial method, which is the absolutely precise method.

However, the Rule of 78 is much simpler to apply and in many states is the legally required method for rebate of unearned finance charge on a precomputed note for certain installment loans. The Rule of 78 derives its name from the following assumption:

1. A 1 year loan of $1,200 is paid off by 12 monthly payments of $100, as shown in the following schedule:

Payment	Payment Amount	Balance
		1,200
1	100	1,100
2	100	1,000
3	100	900
4	100	800
5	100	700
6	100	600
7	100	500
8	100	400
9	100	300
10	100	200
11	100	100
12	100	0

2. The monthly interest charge is proportionate to the balance oustanding during the month; that is, 12 units of the charge are earned in month 1, 11 in month 2, 10 in month 3, and so on, to 1 unit of the charge earned in month 12.

3. The sum of the numbers of these units, from 1 to 12, is 78, hence the name "Rule of 78." For a 1 year loan, there are 78 units in the finance charge.

4. Once the charge for each month is determined, the original schedule is discarded and a new schedule is computed to show the allocation of the monthly payment to interest and principal and the outstanding balance. The ratio to compute the monthly interest from the finance charge is $12 \div 78$ in month 1, $11 \div 78$ in month 2, and so on, to $1 \div 78$ in month 12.

Example: A loan of $1,100 for 1 year is paid off by monthly payments of $100 each. The finance charge of $100 is precomputed and included in the note of $1,200.

The unit charge is:
$$100 \div 78 = 1.282051$$

The charge in month 1 is:
$$1.282051 \times 12 = 15.384 = 15.38$$

The payment to principal is:
$$100 - 15.38 = 84.62$$

The charge in month 2 is:
$$1.1282051 \times 11 = 14.102 = 14.10$$

The process continues for the term of the loan. The following schedule illustrates the process:

Rule of 78 Loan Schedule for 1 Year

Payment	Monthly Payment	Interest Charge	Principal	Balance of Loan	Balance of Note
				1,100.00	1,200
1	100	15.38	84.62	1,015.38	1,100
2	100	14.10	85.90	929.48	1,000
3	100	12.82	87.18	842.30	900
4	100	11.54	88.46	753.84	800
5	100	10.26	89.74	664.10	700
6	100	8.97	91.03	573.07	600
7	100	7.69	92.31	480.76	500
8	100	6.41	93.59	387.17	400
9	100	5.13	94.87	292.30	300
10	100	3.85	96.15	196.15	200
11	100	2.56	97.44	98.71	100
12	100	1.29	98.71	.00	0
Total		100.00	1,100.00		

5. When a loan is prepaid prior to maturity, the lender rebates the unearned portion of the finance charge. The rebate is the finance charge less the cumulative earnings, as shown in the following schedule:

Rule of 78 Earnings and Rebate Schedule for 1 Year

Payment	Monthly Earnings	Cumulative Earnings	Rebate
			100.00
1	15.38	15.38	84.62
2	14.10	29.48	70.52
3	12.82	42.30	57.70
4	11.54	53.84	46.16
5	10.26	64.10	35.90
6	8.97	73.07	26.93
7	7.69	80.76	19.24
8	6.41	87.17	12.83
9	5.13	92.30	7.70
10	3.85	96.15	3.85
11	2.56	98.71	1.29
12	1.29	100.00	.00

6. When a loan is prepaid after payment 5, the balance of the note that is due equals 7 payments of $100 less a rebate of the unearned finance charge for the remaining 7 months.

Rebate:
$$100 \times .358974 = 35.90$$

Payment to prepay:
$$700 - 35.90 = 664.10$$

The payment to prepay is $664.10, which agrees with line 5 of the preceding loan schedule.

7. Compare the cumulative earnings and rebate of the schedule with the similar columns for 1 year in the table on page 21-2. The index corresponds to both the number of months to rebate and the number of months of earnings.

Sum of the Digits. The sum of the numbers from 1 to N is computed from a formula.

$$Sum = \frac{N \times (N + 1)}{2}$$

Example: For a 1 year loan, the sum of the numbers from 1 to 12 is 78.

$$Sum = \frac{12 \times (12 + 1)}{2}$$
$$= 78$$

For a 2 year loan, n = 24.

$$Sum = \frac{(24 \times (24 + 1))}{2}$$
$$= 300$$

The interest earned in the first months of a 24 month loan is $24 \div 300$ times the finance charge.

MONTHLY REBATE AND EARNINGS, RULE OF 78

1 YEAR

#	REBATE	EARN
1	1.2821	15.3846
2	3.8462	29.4872
3	7.6923	42.3077
4	12.8205	53.8462
5	19.2308	64.1026
6	26.9231	73.0769
7	35.8974	80.7692
8	46.1538	87.1795
9	57.6923	92.3077
10	70.5128	96.1538
11	84.6154	98.7179
12	100.0000	100.0000

2 YEARS

#	REBATE	EARN
1	.3333	8.0000
2	1.0000	15.6667
3	2.0000	23.0000
4	3.3333	30.0000
5	5.0000	36.6667
6	7.0000	43.0000
7	9.3333	49.0000
8	12.0000	54.6667
9	15.0000	60.0000
10	18.3333	65.0000
11	22.0000	69.6667
12	26.0000	74.0000
13	30.3333	78.0000
14	35.0000	81.6667
15	40.0000	85.0000
16	45.3333	88.0000
17	51.0000	90.6667
18	57.0000	93.0000
19	63.3333	95.0000
20	70.0000	96.6667
21	77.0000	98.0000
22	84.3333	99.0000
23	92.0000	99.6667
24	100.0000	100.0000

3 YEARS

#	REBATE	EARN
1	.1502	5.4054
2	.4505	10.6607
3	.9009	15.7658
4	1.5015	20.7207
5	2.2523	25.5255
6	3.1532	30.1802
7	4.2042	34.6847
8	5.4054	39.0390
9	6.7568	43.2432
10	8.2583	47.2973
11	9.9099	51.2012
12	11.7117	54.9550
13	13.6637	58.5586
14	15.7658	62.0120
15	18.0180	65.3153
16	20.4204	68.4685
17	22.9730	71.4715
18	25.6757	74.3243
19	28.5285	77.0270
20	31.5315	79.5796
21	34.6847	81.9820
22	37.9880	84.2342
23	41.4414	86.3363
24	45.0450	88.2883
25	48.7988	90.0901

4 YEARS

#	REBATE	EARN
1	.0850	4.0816
2	.2551	8.0782
3	.5102	11.9898
4	.8503	15.8163
5	1.2755	19.5578
6	1.7857	23.2143
7	2.3810	26.7857
8	3.0612	30.2721
9	3.8265	33.6735
10	4.6769	36.9898
11	5.6122	40.2211
12	6.6327	43.3673
13	7.7381	46.4286
14	8.9286	49.4048
15	10.2041	52.2959
16	11.5646	55.1020
17	13.0102	57.8231
18	14.5408	60.4592
19	16.1565	63.0102
20	17.8571	65.4762
21	19.6429	67.8571
22	21.5136	70.1531
23	23.4694	72.3639
24	25.5102	74.4898
25	27.6361	76.5306
26	29.8469	78.4864
27	32.1429	80.3571
28	34.5238	82.1429
29	36.9898	83.8435
30	39.5408	85.4592
31	42.1769	86.9898
32	44.8980	88.4354
33	47.7041	89.7959
34	50.5952	91.0714
35	53.5714	92.2619
36	56.6327	93.3673
37	59.7789	94.3878
38	63.0102	95.3231
39	66.3265	96.1735
40	69.7279	96.9388
41	73.2143	97.6190
42	76.7857	98.2143
43	80.4422	98.7245
44	84.1837	99.1497
45	88.0102	99.4898
46	91.9218	99.7449
47	95.9184	99.9150
48	100.0000	100.0000

5 YEARS

#	REBATE	EARN
1	.0546	3.2787
2	.1639	6.5027
3	.3279	9.6721
4	.5464	12.7869
5	.8197	15.8470
6	1.1475	18.8525
7	1.5301	21.8033
8	1.9672	24.6995
9	2.4590	27.5410
10	3.0055	30.3279
11	3.6066	33.0601
12	4.2623	35.7377
13	4.9727	38.3607
14	5.7377	40.9290
15	6.5574	43.4426
16	7.4317	45.9016
17	8.3607	48.3060
18	9.3443	50.6557
19	10.3825	52.9508
20	11.4754	55.1913
21	12.6230	57.3770
22	13.8251	59.5082
23	15.0820	61.5847
24	16.3934	63.6066
25	17.7596	65.5738
26	19.1803	67.4863
27	20.6557	69.3443
28	22.1858	71.1475
29	23.7705	72.8962
30	25.4098	74.5902
31	27.1038	76.2295
32	28.8525	77.8142
33	30.6557	79.3443
34	32.5137	80.8197
35	34.4262	82.2404
36	36.3934	83.6066
37	38.4153	84.9180
38	40.4918	86.1749
39	42.6230	87.3770
40	44.8087	88.5246
41	47.0492	89.6175
42	49.3443	90.6557
43	51.6940	91.6393
44	54.0984	92.5683
45	56.5574	93.4426
46	59.0710	94.2623
47	61.6393	95.0273
48	64.2623	95.7377
49	66.9399	96.3934
50	69.6721	96.9945
51	72.4590	97.5410
52	75.3005	98.0328
53	78.1967	98.4699
54	81.1475	98.8525
55	84.1530	99.1803
56	87.2131	99.4536
57	90.3279	99.6721
58	93.4973	99.8361
59	96.7213	99.9454
60	100.0000	100.0000

6 YEARS

#	REBATE	EARN
1	.0381	2.7397
2	.1142	5.4414
3	.2283	8.1050
4	.3805	10.7306
5	.5708	13.3181
6	.7991	15.8676
7	1.0654	18.3790
8	1.3699	20.8524
9	1.7123	23.2877
10	2.0928	25.6849
11	2.5114	28.0441
12	2.9680	30.3653
13	3.4627	32.6484
14	3.9954	34.8935
15	4.5662	37.1005
16	5.1750	39.2694
17	5.8219	41.4003
18	6.5068	43.4932
19	7.2298	45.5479
20	7.9909	47.5647
21	8.7900	49.5434
22	9.6271	51.4840
23	10.5023	53.3866
24	11.4155	55.2511
25	12.3668	57.0776
26	13.3562	58.8661
27	14.3836	60.6164
28	15.4490	62.3288
29	16.5525	64.0030
30	17.6941	65.6393
31	18.8737	67.2374
32	20.0913	68.7976
33	21.3470	70.3196
34	22.6408	71.8037
35	23.9726	73.2496
36	25.3425	74.6575
37	26.7504	76.0274
38	28.1963	77.3592
39	29.6804	78.6530
40	31.2024	79.9087
41	32.7626	81.1263
42	34.3607	82.3059
43	35.9970	83.4475
44	37.6712	84.5510
45	39.3836	85.6164
46	41.1339	86.6438
47	42.9224	87.6332
48	44.7489	88.5845
49	46.6134	89.4977
50	48.5160	90.3729
51	50.4566	91.2100
52	52.4353	92.0091
53	54.4521	92.7702
54	56.5068	93.4932
55	58.5997	94.1781
56	60.7306	94.8250
57	62.8995	95.4338
58	65.1065	96.0046
59	67.3516	96.5373
60	69.6347	97.0320
61	71.9559	97.4886
62	74.3151	97.9072
63	76.7123	98.2877
64	79.1476	98.6301
65	81.6210	98.9346
66	84.1324	99.2009
67	86.6819	99.4292
68	89.2694	99.6195
69	91.8950	99.7717
70	94.5586	99.8858
71	97.2603	99.9619
72	100.0000	100.0000

7 YEARS

#	REBATE	EARN
1	.0280	2.3529
2	.0840	4.6779
3	.1681	6.9748
4	.2801	9.2437
5	.4202	11.4846
6	.5882	13.6975
7	.7843	15.8824
8	1.0084	18.0392
9	1.2605	20.1681
10	1.5406	22.2689
11	1.8487	24.3417
12	2.1849	26.3866
13	2.5490	28.4034
14	2.9412	30.3922
15	3.3613	32.3529
16	3.8095	34.2857
17	4.2857	36.1905
18	4.7899	38.0672
19	5.3221	39.9160
20	5.8824	41.7367
21	6.4706	43.5294
22	7.0868	45.2941
23	7.7311	47.0308
24	8.4034	48.7395
25	9.1036	50.4202
26	9.8319	52.0728
27	10.5882	53.6975
28	11.3725	55.2941
29	12.1849	56.8627
30	13.0252	58.4034
31	13.8936	59.9160
32	14.7899	61.4006
33	15.7143	62.8571
34	16.6667	64.2857
35	17.6471	65.6863
36	18.6555	67.0588
37	19.6919	68.4034
38	20.7563	69.7199
39	21.8487	71.0084
40	22.9692	72.2689
41	24.1176	73.5014
42	25.2941	74.7059
43	26.4986	75.8824
44	27.7311	77.0308
45	28.9916	78.1513
46	30.2801	79.2437
47	31.5966	80.3081
48	32.9412	81.3445
49	34.3137	82.3529
50	35.7143	83.3333
51	37.1429	84.2857
52	38.5994	85.2101
53	40.0840	86.1064
54	41.5966	86.9748
55	43.1373	87.8151
56	44.7059	88.6275
57	46.3025	89.4118
58	47.9272	90.1681
59	49.5798	90.8964
60	51.2605	91.5966
61	52.9692	92.2689
62	54.7059	92.9132
63	56.4706	93.5294
64	58.2633	94.1176
65	60.0840	94.6779
66	61.9328	95.2101
67	63.8095	95.7143
68	65.7143	96.1905
69	67.6471	96.6387
70	69.6078	97.0588
71	71.5966	97.4510
72	73.6134	97.8151
73	75.6583	98.1513
74	77.7311	98.4594
75	79.8319	98.7395

#	REBATE	EARN
75	79.8319	98.7395
76	81.9608	98.9916
77	84.1176	99.2157
78	86.3025	99.4118
79	88.5154	99.5798
80	90.7563	99.7199
81	93.0252	99.8319
82	95.3221	99.9160
83	97.6471	99.9720
84	100.0000	100.0000

8 YEARS

#	REBATE	EARN
1	.0215	2.0619
2	.0644	4.1022
3	.1289	6.1211
4	.2148	8.1186
5	.3222	10.0945
6	.4510	12.0490
7	.6014	13.9820
8	.7732	15.8935
9	.9665	17.7835
10	1.1813	19.6521
11	1.4175	21.4991
12	1.6753	23.3247
13	1.9545	25.1289
14	2.2552	26.9115
15	2.5773	28.6727
16	2.9210	30.4124
17	3.2861	32.1306
18	3.6727	33.8273
19	4.0808	35.5026
20	4.5103	37.1564
21	4.9613	38.7887
22	5.4338	40.3995
23	5.9278	41.9888
24	6.4433	43.5567
25	6.9802	45.1031
26	7.5387	46.6280
27	8.1186	48.1314
28	8.7199	49.6134
29	9.3428	51.0739
30	9.9871	52.5129
31	10.6529	53.9304
32	11.3402	55.3265
33	12.0490	56.7010
34	12.7792	58.0541
35	13.5309	59.3857
36	14.3041	60.6959
37	15.0988	61.9845
38	15.9149	63.2517
39	16.7526	64.4974
40	17.6117	65.7216
41	18.4923	66.9244
42	19.3943	68.1057
43	20.3179	69.2655
44	21.2629	70.4038
45	22.2294	71.5206
46	23.2174	72.6160
47	24.2268	73.6899
48	25.2577	74.7423
49	26.3101	75.7732
50	27.3840	76.7826
51	28.4794	77.7706
52	29.5962	78.7371
53	30.7345	79.6821
54	31.8943	80.6057
55	33.0756	81.5077
56	34.2784	82.3883
57	35.5026	83.2474
58	36.7483	84.0851
59	38.0155	84.9012
60	39.3041	85.6959
61	40.6143	86.4691
62	41.9459	87.2208
63	43.2990	87.9510
64	44.6735	88.6598
65	46.0696	89.3471
66	47.4871	90.0129
67	48.9261	90.6572
68	50.3866	91.2801
69	51.8686	91.8814
70	53.3720	92.4613
71	54.8969	93.0198
72	56.4433	93.5567
73	58.0112	94.0722
74	59.6005	94.5662
75	61.2113	95.0387
76	62.8436	95.4897
77	64.4974	95.9192
78	66.1727	96.3273
79	67.8694	96.7139
80	69.5876	97.0790
81	71.3273	97.4227
82	73.0885	97.7448
83	74.8711	98.0455
84	76.6753	98.3247
85	78.5009	98.5825
86	80.3479	98.8187
87	82.2165	99.0335
88	84.1065	99.2268
89	86.0180	99.3986
90	87.9510	99.5490
91	89.9055	99.6778
92	91.8814	99.7852
93	93.8789	99.8711
94	95.8978	99.9356
95	97.9381	99.9785
96	100.0000	100.0000

9 YEARS

#	REBATE	EARN
1	.0170	1.8349
2	.0510	3.6527
3	.1019	5.4536
4	.1699	7.2375
5	.2548	9.0044
6	.3568	10.7543
7	.4757	12.4873
8	.6116	14.2032
9	.7645	15.9021
10	.9344	17.5841
11	1.1213	19.2491
12	1.3252	20.8970
13	1.5460	22.5280
14	1.7839	24.1420
15	2.0387	25.7390
16	2.3106	27.3191
17	2.5994	28.8821
18	2.9052	30.4281
19	3.2280	31.9572
20	3.5678	33.4692
21	3.9246	34.9643
22	4.2983	36.4424
23	4.6891	37.9035
24	5.0968	39.3476
25	5.5216	40.7747
26	5.9633	42.1848
27	6.4220	43.5780
28	6.8977	44.9541
29	7.3904	46.3133
30	7.9001	47.6555
31	8.4268	48.9806
32	8.9704	50.2888
33	9.5311	51.5800
34	10.1087	52.8542
35	10.7034	54.1115
36	11.3150	55.3517
37	11.9436	56.5749
38	12.5892	57.7812
39	13.2518	58.9704
40	13.9314	60.1427
41	14.6279	61.2980
42	15.3415	62.4363
43	16.0720	63.5576
44	16.8196	64.6619
45	17.5841	65.7492
46	18.3656	66.8196
47	19.1641	67.8729
48	19.9796	68.9093
49	20.8121	69.9286
50	21.6616	70.9310
51	22.5280	71.9164
52	23.4115	72.8848
53	24.3119	73.8362
54	25.2294	74.7706
55	26.1638	75.6881
56	27.1152	76.5885
57	28.0836	77.4720
58	29.0690	78.3384
59	30.0714	79.1879
60	31.0907	80.0204
61	32.1271	80.8359
62	33.1804	81.6344
63	34.2508	82.4159
64	35.3381	83.1804
65	36.4424	83.9280
66	37.5637	84.6585
67	38.7020	85.3721
68	39.8573	86.0686
69	41.0296	86.7482
70	42.2188	87.4108
71	43.4251	88.0564
72	44.6483	88.6850
73	45.8885	89.2966
74	47.1458	89.8913
75	48.4200	90.4689
76	49.7112	91.0296
77	51.0194	91.5732
78	52.3445	92.0999
79	53.6867	92.6096
80	55.0459	93.1023
81	56.4220	93.5780
82	57.8152	94.0367
83	59.2253	94.4784
84	60.6524	94.9032
85	62.0965	95.3109
86	63.5576	95.7017
87	65.0357	96.0754
88	66.5308	96.4322
89	68.0428	96.7720
90	69.5719	97.0948
91	71.1179	97.4006
92	72.6809	97.6894
93	74.2610	97.9613
94	75.8580	98.2161
95	77.4720	98.4540
96	79.1030	98.6748
97	80.7509	98.8787
98	82.4159	99.0656
99	84.0979	99.2355
100	85.7968	99.3884
101	87.5127	99.5243
102	89.2457	99.6432
103	90.9956	99.7452
104	92.7625	99.8301
105	94.5464	99.8981
106	96.3473	99.9490
107	98.1651	99.9830
108	100.0000	100.0000

10 YEARS

#	REBATE	EARN
1	.0138	1.6529
2	.0413	3.2920
3	.0826	4.9174
4	.1377	6.5289
5	.2066	8.1267
6	.2893	9.7107
7	.3857	11.2810
8	.4959	12.8375
9	.6198	14.3802
10	.7576	15.9091
11	.9091	17.4242
12	1.0744	18.9256
13	1.2534	20.4132
14	1.4463	21.8871
15	1.6529	23.3471
16	1.8733	24.7934
17	2.1074	26.2259
18	2.3554	27.6446
19	2.6171	29.0496
20	2.8926	30.4408
21	3.1818	31.8182
22	3.4848	33.1818
23	3.8017	34.5317
24	4.1322	35.8678
25	4.4766	37.1901
26	4.8347	38.4986
27	5.2066	39.7934
28	5.5923	41.0744
29	5.9917	42.3416
30	6.4050	43.5950
31	6.8320	44.8347
32	7.2727	46.0606
33	7.7273	47.2727
34	8.1956	48.4711
35	8.6777	49.6556
36	9.1736	50.8264
37	9.6832	51.9835
38	10.2066	53.1267
39	10.7438	54.2562
40	11.2948	55.3719
41	11.8595	56.4738
42	12.4380	57.5620
43	13.0303	58.6364
44	13.6364	59.6970
45	14.2562	60.7438
46	14.8898	61.7769
47	15.5372	62.7961
48	16.1983	63.8017
49	16.8733	64.7934
50	17.5620	65.7713
51	18.2645	66.7355
52	18.9807	67.6860
53	19.7107	68.6226
54	20.4545	69.5455
55	21.2121	70.4545
56	21.9835	71.3499
57	22.7686	72.2314
58	23.5675	73.0992
59	24.3802	73.9532
60	25.2066	74.7934
61	26.0468	75.6198
62	26.9008	76.4325
63	27.7686	77.2314
64	28.6501	78.0165
65	29.5455	78.7879
66	30.4545	79.5455
67	31.3774	80.2893
68	32.3140	81.0193
69	33.2645	81.7355
70	34.2287	82.4380
71	35.2066	83.1267
72	36.1983	83.8017
73	37.2039	84.4628
74	38.2231	85.1102
75	39.2562	85.7438
76	40.3030	86.3636
77	41.3636	86.9697
78	42.4380	87.5620
79	43.5262	88.1405
80	44.6281	88.7052
81	45.7438	89.2562
82	46.8733	89.7934
83	48.0165	90.3168
84	49.1736	90.8264
85	50.3444	91.3223
86	51.5289	91.8044
87	52.7273	92.2727
88	53.9394	92.7273
89	55.1653	93.1680
90	56.4050	93.5950
91	57.6584	94.0083
92	58.9256	94.4077
93	60.2066	94.7934
94	61.5014	95.1653
95	62.8099	95.5234
96	64.1322	95.8678
97	65.4683	96.1983
98	66.8182	96.5152
99	68.1818	96.8182
100	69.5592	97.1074
101	70.9504	97.3829
102	72.3554	97.6446
103	73.7741	97.8926
104	75.2066	98.1267
105	76.6529	98.3471
106	78.1129	98.5537
107	79.5868	98.7466
108	81.0744	98.9256
109	82.5758	99.0909
110	84.0909	99.2424
111	85.6198	99.3802
112	87.1625	99.5041
113	88.7190	99.6143
114	90.2893	99.7107
115	91.8733	99.7934
116	93.4711	99.8623
117	95.0826	99.9174
118	96.7080	99.9587
119	98.3471	99.9862
120	100.0000	100.0000

TABLE **22**

Actuarial Rebate and Earnings

Interest Rates: 10 to 18% by .25%.

Terms: 1 to 10 years, each year.

Payment: Monthly.

This table shows the rebate of the unearned finance charge when an installment loan is prepaid in full prior to maturity. The table shows the cumulative earnings for each month during the term of the loan. The rebate and earnings are computed by the actuarial method. The index shows both the number of months to rebate and the number of months that have earned.

Example: An installment loan, written for 12 months, is prepaid in full after the fifth payment. What is the amount to be prepaid? The terms of the loan are:

Loan:	$1,000.00	Payment:	87.92 monthly
Rate:	10%	Note:	1,054.99
Term:	1 year	Finance charge:	54.99

The loan, prepaid at the end of the fifth month, leaves 7 months of unearned finance charge to rebate. On page 22-2, in the 1 year table, find line 7 in the index and read the corresponding rebate of 36.3905. This is the percent of the finance charge to rebate. The formula is:

$$\text{Rebate} = \text{Charge} \times \text{Factor}$$

$$= 54.99 \times .363905$$

$$= 20.01$$

To compute the total payments to prepay, multiply the monthly payment by the months rebated:

$$87.92 \times 7 = 615.44$$

Subtract the rebate:

$$615.44 - 20.01 = 595.43$$

The net to prepay in full is $595.43.

Minimum Charge. A lender may be entitled to a minimum charge. The rule is to compute the rebate first and see if the minimum charge has been earned. If the minimum charge has not been earned, then the rebate is reduced by an amount sufficient to satisfy the minimum charge. The minimum charge should not be subtracted from the finance charge before computing the rebate.

Actuarial Method. The actuarial method for the calculation of interest is that the creditor shall calculate the interest for a period and add the interest to the balance outstanding at the beginning of the period. This greater balance then becomes the new outstanding balance. When a payment is made, it is applied to the new outstanding balance.

The following schedule is computed by the actuarial method at an interest rate of 10%. The interest for a month is the loan balance times the interest factor. For month 1, this is:

$$\text{Interest factor} = 10\% \div 100 \div 12 = .0083333333$$

$$\text{Interest} = 1,818.44 \times .0083333333$$

$$= 15.15.$$

Example: A loan of $1,818.44 at 10% for 1 year is paid off by monthly payments of $159.87 each. The precomputed note is the payment times the term: $159.87 \times 12 = 1,918.44$. The finance charge is $100.

Actuarial Loan Schedule for 1 Year at 10%

Payment	Monthly Payment	Interest Charge	Principal	Balance of Loan	Balance of Note
				1,818.44	1,918.44
1	159.87	15.15	144.72	1,673.72	1,758.57
2	159.87	13.95	145.92	1,527.80	1,598.70
3	159.87	12.73	147.14	1,380.66	1,438.83
4	159.87	11.51	148.36	1,232.30	1,278.96
5	159.87	10.27	149.60	1,082.70	1,119.09
6	159.87	9.02	150.85	931.85	959.22
7	159.87	7.77	152.10	779.75	799.35
8	159.87	6.50	153.37	626.38	639.48
9	159.87	5.22	154.65	471.73	479.61
10	159.87	3.93	155.94	315.79	319.74
11	159.87	2.63	157.24	158.55	159.87
12	159.87	1.32	158.55	.00	.00
Total		100.00	1,818.44		

ACTUARIAL REBATE AND EARNINGS

1. When a loan is prepaid prior to maturity, the lender rebates the unearned portion of the finance charge. The rebate is the finance charge less the cumulative earnings, as shown in the following schedule:

Actuarial Earnings and Rebate for 1 Year at 10%

Payment	Monthly Earnings	Cumulative Earnings	Rebate
			100.00
1	15.15	15.15	84.85
2	13.95	29.10	70.90
3	12.73	41.83	58.17
4	11.51	53.34	46.66
5	10.27	63.61	36.39
6	9.02	72.63	27.37
7	7.77	80.40	19.60
8	6.50	86.90	13.10
9	5.22	92.12	7.88
10	3.93	96.05	3.95
11	2.63	98.68	1.32
12	1.32	100.00	.00

2. When a loan is prepaid after payment 5, the balance of the note that is due equals 7 payments of $159.87 less a rebate of the unearned finance charge for the remaining 7 months.

Rebate:
$$100 \times .363905 = 36.39$$

Payment to prepay:
$$1,119.09 - 36.39 = 1,082.70$$

The payment to prepay is $1,082.70, which agrees with the balance of the loan on line 5 of the actuarial loan schedule.

3. Compare the cumulative earnings and rebate of the schedule with the similar columns for 1 year in the 10% table on page 22-2. The index corresponds to both the number of months to rebate and the number of months of earnings.

ACTUARIAL REBATE AND EARNINGS

1 YEAR

#	REBATE	EARN
1	1.3213	15.1541
2	3.9529	29.1022
3	7.8841	41.8342
4	13.1040	53.3401
5	19.6021	63.6095
6	27.3677	72.6323
7	36.3905	80.3979
8	46.6599	86.8960
9	58.1658	92.1159
10	70.8978	96.0471
11	84.8459	98.6787
12	100.0000	100.0000

2 YEARS

#	REBATE	EARN
1	.3548	7.7535
2	1.0616	15.2138
3	2.1173	22.3786
4	3.5191	29.2452
5	5.2641	35.8113
6	7.3496	42.0743
7	9.7727	48.0317
8	12.5305	53.6810
9	15.6204	59.0196
10	19.0396	64.0448
11	22.7854	68.7542
12	26.8550	73.1450
13	31.2458	77.2146
14	35.9552	80.9604
15	40.9804	84.4796
16	46.3190	87.4695
17	51.9683	90.2273
18	57.9257	92.6504
19	64.1887	94.7359
20	70.7548	96.4809
21	77.6214	97.8827
22	84.7862	98.9384
23	92.2465	99.6452
24	100.0000	100.0000

3 YEARS

#	REBATE	EARN
1	.1650	5.1562
2	.4936	10.1889
3	.9846	15.0973
4	1.6364	19.8801
5	2.4479	24.5364
6	3.4177	29.0652
7	4.5444	33.4653
8	5.8269	37.7358
9	7.2637	41.8754
10	8.8537	45.8831
11	10.5955	49.7579
12	12.4879	53.4986
13	14.5297	57.1041
14	16.7197	60.5733
15	19.0565	63.9050
16	21.5390	67.0980
17	24.1660	70.1514
18	26.9363	73.0637
19	29.8486	75.8340
20	32.9020	78.4610
21	36.0950	80.9435
22	39.4267	83.2803
23	42.8959	85.4703
24	46.5014	87.5121
25	50.2421	89.4045
26	54.1169	91.1463
27	58.1246	92.7363
28	62.2642	94.1731
29	66.5347	95.4556
30	70.9348	96.5823
31	75.4636	97.5521
32	80.1199	98.3636
33	84.9027	99.0154
34	89.8111	99.5064
35	94.8438	99.8350
36	100.0000	100.0000

4 YEARS

#	REBATE	EARN
1	.0964	3.8331
2	.2884	7.6009
3	.5753	11.3030
4	.9562	14.9386
5	1.4304	18.5073
6	1.9970	22.0086
7	2.6554	25.4418
8	3.4048	28.8064
9	4.2444	32.1018
10	5.1735	35.3275
11	6.1912	38.4828
12	7.2971	41.5672
13	8.4901	44.5801
14	9.7698	47.5209
15	11.1352	50.3890
16	12.5858	53.1837
17	14.1209	55.9045
18	15.7396	58.5508
19	17.4414	61.1219
20	19.2255	63.6173
21	21.0913	66.0362
22	23.0381	68.3780
23	25.0653	70.6422
24	27.1721	72.8279
25	29.3578	74.9347
26	31.6220	76.9619
27	33.9638	78.9087
28	36.3827	80.7745
29	38.8781	82.5586
30	41.4492	84.2604
31	44.0955	85.8791
32	46.8163	87.4142
33	49.6110	88.8648
34	52.4791	90.2302
35	55.4199	91.5099
36	58.4328	92.7029
37	61.5172	93.8088
38	64.6725	94.8265
39	67.8982	95.7556
40	71.1936	96.5952
41	74.5582	97.3446
42	77.9914	98.0030
43	81.4927	98.5696
44	85.0614	99.0438
45	88.6970	99.4247
46	92.3991	99.7116
47	96.1669	99.9036
48	100.0000	100.0000

5 YEARS

#	REBATE	EARN
1	.0639	3.0323
2	.1912	6.0254
3	.3813	8.9790
4	.6337	11.8928
5	.9479	14.7664
6	1.3234	17.5996
7	1.7598	20.3920
8	2.2564	23.1432
9	2.8128	25.8529
10	3.4285	28.5208
11	4.1030	31.1464
12	4.8358	33.7295
13	5.6264	36.2698
14	6.4745	38.7667
15	7.3794	41.2201
16	8.3407	43.6294
17	9.3580	45.9944
18	10.4307	48.3147
19	11.5585	50.5899
20	12.7408	52.8197
21	13.9773	55.0036
22	15.2675	57.1412
23	16.6109	59.2323
24	18.0070	61.2763
25	19.4556	63.2730
26	20.9560	65.2219
27	22.5080	67.1225
28	24.1110	68.9746
29	25.7647	70.7777
30	27.4686	72.5314
31	29.2223	74.2353
32	31.0254	75.8890
33	32.8775	77.4920
34	34.7781	79.0440
35	36.7270	80.5444
36	38.7237	81.9930
37	40.7677	83.3891
38	42.8588	84.7325
39	44.9964	86.0227
40	47.1803	87.2592
41	49.4101	88.4415
42	51.6853	89.5693
43	54.0056	90.6420
44	56.3706	91.6593
45	58.7799	92.6206
46	61.2333	93.5255
47	63.7302	94.3736
48	66.2705	95.1642
49	68.8536	95.8970
50	71.4792	96.5715
51	74.1471	97.1872
52	76.8568	97.7436
53	79.6080	98.2402
54	82.4004	98.6766
55	85.2336	99.0521
56	88.1072	99.3663
57	91.0210	99.6187
58	93.9746	99.8088
59	96.9677	99.9361
60	100.0000	100.0000

6 YEARS

#	REBATE	EARN
1	.0459	2.4961
2	.1372	4.9667
3	.2736	7.4116
4	.4548	9.8307
5	.6804	12.2237
6	.9499	14.5904
7	1.2631	16.9306
8	1.6195	19.2441
9	2.0188	21.5306
10	2.4607	23.7899
11	2.9449	26.0218
12	3.4708	28.2260
13	4.0383	30.4024
14	4.6470	32.5506
15	5.2965	34.6706
16	5.9864	36.7619
17	6.7166	38.8245
18	7.4865	40.8580
19	8.2960	42.8621
20	9.1446	44.8368
21	10.0321	46.7817
22	10.9581	48.6965
23	11.9223	50.5810
24	12.9244	52.4350
25	13.9640	54.2583
26	15.0410	56.0504
27	16.1549	57.8113
28	17.3054	59.5406
29	18.4923	61.2380
30	19.7153	62.9034
31	20.9740	64.5364
32	22.2681	66.1368
33	23.5975	67.7043
34	24.9617	69.2385
35	26.3604	70.7394
36	27.7935	72.2065
37	29.2606	73.6396
38	30.7615	75.0383
39	32.2957	76.4025
40	33.8632	77.7319
41	35.4636	79.0260
42	37.0966	80.2847
43	38.7620	81.5077
44	40.4594	82.6946
45	42.1887	83.8451
46	43.9496	84.9590
47	45.7417	86.0360
48	47.5650	87.0756
49	49.4190	88.0777
50	51.3035	89.0419
51	53.2183	89.9679
52	55.1632	90.8554
53	57.1379	91.7040
54	59.1420	92.5135
55	61.1755	93.2834
56	63.2381	94.0136
57	65.3294	94.7035
58	67.4494	95.3530
59	69.5976	95.9617
60	71.7740	96.5292
61	73.9782	97.0551
62	76.2101	97.5393
63	78.4694	97.9812
64	80.7559	98.3805
65	83.0694	98.7369
66	85.4096	99.0501
67	87.7763	99.3196
68	90.1693	99.5452
69	92.5884	99.7264
70	95.0333	99.8628
71	97.5039	99.9541
72	100.0000	100.0000

7 YEARS

#	REBATE	EARN
1	.0348	2.1124
2	.1040	4.2073
3	.2075	6.2846
4	.3449	8.3442
5	.5160	10.3858
6	.7204	12.4094
7	.9579	14.4148
8	1.2282	16.4018
9	1.5310	18.3703
10	1.8662	20.3202
11	2.2333	22.2512
12	2.6322	24.1633
13	3.0625	26.0562
14	3.5241	27.9298
15	4.0167	29.7840
16	4.5399	31.6186
17	5.0936	33.4333
18	5.6775	35.2282
19	6.2914	37.0029
20	6.9350	38.7574
21	7.6080	40.4914
22	8.3103	42.2047
23	9.0415	43.8973
24	9.8014	45.5690
25	10.5899	47.2194
26	11.4066	48.8486
27	12.2513	50.4563
28	13.1239	52.0423
29	14.0240	53.6065
30	14.9514	55.1486
31	15.9060	56.6685
32	16.8874	58.1660
33	17.8955	59.6410
34	18.9301	61.0931
35	19.9909	62.5223
36	21.0777	63.9283
37	22.1903	65.3110
38	23.3285	66.6701
39	24.4920	68.0055
40	25.6807	69.3169
41	26.8944	70.6042
42	28.1328	71.8672
43	29.3958	73.1056
44	30.6831	74.3193
45	31.9945	75.5080
46	33.3299	76.6715
47	34.6890	77.8097
48	36.0717	78.9223
49	37.4777	80.0091
50	38.9069	81.0699
51	40.3590	82.1045
52	41.8340	83.1126
53	43.3315	84.0940
54	44.8514	85.0486
55	46.3935	85.9760
56	47.9577	86.8761
57	49.5437	87.7487
58	51.1514	88.5934
59	52.7806	89.4101
60	54.4310	90.1986
61	56.1027	90.9585
62	57.7953	91.6897
63	59.5086	92.3920
64	61.2426	93.0650
65	62.9971	93.7086
66	64.7718	94.3225
67	66.5667	94.9064
68	68.3814	95.4601
69	70.2160	95.9833
70	72.0702	96.4759
71	73.9438	96.9375
72	75.8367	97.3678
73	77.7488	97.7667
74	79.6798	98.1338
75	81.6297	98.4690

#	REBATE	EARN
75	81.6297	98.4690
76	83.5982	98.7718
77	85.5852	99.0421
78	87.5906	99.2796
79	89.6142	99.4840
80	91.6558	99.6551
81	93.7154	99.7925
82	95.7927	99.8960
83	97.8876	99.9652
84	100.0000	100.0000

#	REBATE	EARN
57	39.1157	80.6631
58	40.3850	81.5817
59	41.6712	82.4803
60	42.9743	83.3588
61	44.2941	84.2168
62	45.6304	85.0543
63	46.9832	85.8711
64	48.3522	86.6671
65	49.7374	87.4419
66	51.1386	88.1956
67	52.5556	88.9278
68	53.9884	89.6385
69	55.4368	90.3273
70	56.9007	90.9943
71	58.3800	91.6391
72	59.8745	92.2616
73	61.3841	92.8616
74	62.9087	93.4389
75	64.4481	93.9933
76	66.0023	94.5247
77	67.5711	95.0328
78	69.1544	95.5175
79	70.7521	95.9785
80	72.3640	96.4156
81	73.9900	96.8288
82	75.6301	97.2176
83	77.2841	97.5821
84	78.9519	97.9219
85	80.6333	98.2368
86	82.3283	98.5266
87	84.0367	98.7912
88	85.7585	99.0303
89	87.4936	99.2438
90	89.2417	99.4313
91	91.0028	99.5926
92	92.7769	99.7277
93	94.5637	99.8362
94	96.3633	99.9179
95	98.1754	99.9725
96	100.0000	100.0000

#	REBATE	EARN
28	8.4355	41.0871
29	9.0141	42.3994
30	9.6102	43.7001
31	10.2238	44.9891
32	10.8546	46.2662
33	11.5026	47.5315
34	12.1676	48.7848
35	12.8494	50.0260
36	13.5479	51.2550
37	14.2631	52.4717
38	14.9947	53.6760
39	15.7426	54.8678
40	16.5066	56.0470
41	17.2867	57.2135
42	18.0827	58.3671
43	18.8945	59.5079
44	19.7219	60.6355
45	20.5649	61.7501
46	21.4232	62.8514
47	22.2968	63.9393
48	23.1855	65.0138
49	24.0893	66.0747
50	25.0079	67.1218
51	25.9413	68.1552
52	26.8893	69.1746
53	27.8518	70.1800
54	28.8288	71.1712
55	29.8200	72.1482
56	30.8254	73.1107
57	31.8448	74.0587
58	32.8782	74.9921
59	33.9253	75.9107
60	34.9862	76.8145
61	36.0607	77.7032
62	37.1486	78.5768
63	38.2499	79.4351
64	39.3645	80.2781
65	40.4921	81.1055
66	41.6329	81.9173
67	42.7865	82.7133
68	43.9530	83.4934
69	45.1322	84.2574
70	46.3240	85.0053
71	47.5283	85.7369
72	48.7450	86.4521
73	49.9740	87.1506
74	51.2152	87.8324
75	52.4685	88.4974
76	53.7338	89.1454
77	55.0109	89.7762
78	56.2999	90.3898
79	57.6006	90.9859
80	58.9129	91.5645
81	60.2367	92.1253
82	61.5719	92.6683
83	62.9185	93.1932
84	64.2762	93.7000
85	65.6451	94.1885
86	67.0250	94.6585
87	68.4159	95.1099
88	69.8177	95.5425
89	71.2302	95.9561
90	72.6534	96.3507
91	74.0872	96.7260
92	75.5314	97.0819
93	76.9861	97.4182
94	78.4512	97.7348
95	79.9265	98.0315
96	81.4119	98.3081

#	REBATE	EARN
97	82.9074	98.5645
98	84.4130	98.8005
99	85.9284	99.0159
100	87.4537	99.2106
101	88.9887	99.3843
102	90.5333	99.5370
103	92.0876	99.6684
104	93.6514	99.7783
105	95.2246	99.8666
106	96.8071	99.9331
107	98.3990	99.9776
108	100.0000	100.0000

#	REBATE	EARN
56	25.7086	67.1697
57	26.5589	68.0992
58	27.4207	69.0177
59	28.2940	69.9251
60	29.1788	70.8212
61	30.0749	71.7060
62	30.9823	72.5793
63	31.9008	73.4411
64	32.8303	74.2914
65	33.7708	75.1299
66	34.7222	75.9565
67	35.6843	76.7713
68	36.6572	77.5741
69	37.6406	78.3647
70	38.6346	79.1432
71	39.6390	79.9093
72	40.6538	80.6631
73	41.6787	81.4043
74	42.7139	82.1329
75	43.7592	82.8487
76	44.8144	83.5517
77	45.8796	84.2418
78	46.9546	84.9188
79	48.0394	85.5827
80	49.1339	86.2333
81	50.2380	86.8706
82	51.3515	87.4943
83	52.4746	88.1045
84	53.6069	88.7009
85	54.7486	89.2835
86	55.8995	89.8521
87	57.0595	90.4067
88	58.2286	90.9472
89	59.4066	91.4733
90	60.5936	91.9850
91	61.7893	92.4822
92	62.9939	92.9647
93	64.2071	93.4324
94	65.4290	93.8853
95	66.6594	94.3231
96	67.8983	94.7458
97	69.1455	95.1531
98	70.4012	95.5451
99	71.6650	95.9216
100	72.9371	96.2824
101	74.2173	96.6274
102	75.5056	96.9564
103	76.8019	97.2695
104	78.1061	97.5663
105	79.4181	97.8468
106	80.7380	98.1108
107	82.0656	98.3583
108	83.4009	98.5890
109	84.7438	98.8028
110	86.0942	98.9996
111	87.4521	99.1793
112	88.8174	99.3416
113	90.1901	99.4865
114	91.5701	99.6138
115	92.9574	99.7234
116	94.3518	99.8151
117	95.7533	99.8888
118	97.1619	99.9442
119	98.5775	99.9814
120	100.0000	100.0000

8 YEARS

#	REBATE	EARN
1	.0275	1.8246
2	.0821	3.6367
3	.1638	5.4363
4	.2723	7.2231
5	.4074	8.9972
6	.5687	10.7583
7	.7562	12.5064
8	.9697	14.2415
9	1.2088	15.9633
10	1.4734	17.6717
11	1.7632	19.3667
12	2.0781	21.0481
13	2.4179	22.7159
14	2.7824	24.3699
15	3.1712	26.0100
16	3.5844	27.6360
17	4.0215	29.2479
18	4.4825	30.8456
19	4.9672	32.4289
20	5.4753	33.9977
21	6.0067	35.5519
22	6.5611	37.0913
23	7.1384	38.6159
24	7.7384	40.1255
25	8.3609	41.6200
26	9.0057	43.0993
27	9.6727	44.5632
28	10.3615	46.0116
29	11.0722	47.4444
30	11.8044	48.8614
31	12.5581	50.2626
32	13.3329	51.6478
33	14.1289	53.0168
34	14.9457	54.3696
35	15.7832	55.7059
36	16.6412	57.0257
37	17.5197	58.3288
38	18.4183	59.6150
39	19.3369	60.8843
40	20.2754	62.1365
41	21.2336	63.3715
42	22.2114	64.5890
43	23.2085	65.7890
44	24.2249	66.9713
45	25.2603	68.1358
46	26.3146	69.2823
47	27.3876	70.4106
48	28.4793	71.5207
49	29.5894	72.6124
50	30.7177	73.6854
51	31.8642	74.7397
52	33.0287	75.7751
53	34.2110	76.7915
54	35.4110	77.7886
55	36.6285	78.7664
56	37.8635	79.7246

9 YEARS

#	REBATE	EARN
1	.0224	1.6010
2	.0669	3.1929
3	.1334	4.7754
4	.2217	6.3486
5	.3316	7.9124
6	.4630	9.4667
7	.6157	11.0113
8	.7894	12.5463
9	.9841	14.0716
10	1.1995	15.5870
11	1.4355	17.0926
12	1.6919	18.5881
13	1.9685	20.0735
14	2.2652	21.5488
15	2.5818	23.0139
16	2.9181	24.4686
17	3.2740	25.9128
18	3.6493	27.3466
19	4.0439	28.7698
20	4.4575	30.1823
21	4.8901	31.5841
22	5.3415	32.9750
23	5.8115	34.3549
24	6.3000	35.7238
25	6.8068	37.0815
26	7.3317	38.4281
27	7.8747	39.7633

10 YEARS

#	REBATE	EARN
1	.0186	1.4225
2	.0558	2.8381
3	.1112	4.2467
4	.1849	5.6482
5	.2766	7.0426
6	.3862	8.4299
7	.5135	9.8099
8	.6584	11.1826
9	.8207	12.5479
10	1.0004	13.9058
11	1.1972	15.2562
12	1.4110	16.5991
13	1.6417	17.9344
14	1.8892	19.2620
15	2.1532	20.5819
16	2.4337	21.8939
17	2.7305	23.1981
18	3.0436	24.4944
19	3.3726	25.7827
20	3.7176	27.0629
21	4.0784	28.3350
22	4.4549	29.5988
23	4.8469	30.8545
24	5.2542	32.1017
25	5.6769	33.3406
26	6.1147	34.5710
27	6.5676	35.7929
28	7.0353	37.0061
29	7.5178	38.2107
30	8.0150	39.4064
31	8.5267	40.5934
32	9.0528	41.7714
33	9.5933	42.9405
34	10.1479	44.1005
35	10.7165	45.2514
36	11.2991	46.3931
37	11.8955	47.5254
38	12.5057	48.6485
39	13.1294	49.7620
40	13.7667	50.8661
41	14.4173	51.9606
42	15.0812	53.0454
43	15.7582	54.1204
44	16.4483	55.1856
45	17.1513	56.2408
46	17.8671	57.2861
47	18.5957	58.3213
48	19.3369	59.3462
49	20.0907	60.3610
50	20.8568	61.3654
51	21.6353	62.3594
52	22.4259	63.3428
53	23.2287	64.3157
54	24.0435	65.2778
55	24.8701	66.2292

ACTUARIAL REBATE AND EARNINGS

10.25 %

1 YEAR

#	REBATE	EARN
1	1.3223	15.1484
2	3.9556	29.0927
3	7.8888	41.8226
4	13.1111	53.3276
5	19.6113	63.5973
6	27.3787	72.6213
7	36.4027	80.3887
8	46.6724	86.8889
9	58.1774	92.1112
10	70.9073	96.0444
11	84.8516	98.6777
12	100.0000	100.0000

2 YEARS

#	REBATE	EARN
1	.3554	7.7476
2	1.0631	15.2029
3	2.1202	22.3635
4	3.5237	29.2269
5	5.2707	35.7905
6	7.3583	42.0518
7	9.7836	48.0081
8	12.5437	53.6569
9	15.6358	58.9955
10	19.0571	64.0214
11	22.8047	68.7318
12	26.8761	73.1239
13	31.2682	77.1953
14	35.9786	80.9429
15	41.0045	84.3642
16	46.3431	87.4563
17	51.9919	90.2164
18	57.9482	92.6417
19	64.2095	94.7293
20	70.7731	96.4763
21	77.6365	97.8798
22	84.7971	98.9369
23	92.2524	99.6446
24	100.0000	100.0000

3 YEARS

#	REBATE	EARN
1	.1654	5.1503
2	.4947	10.1778
3	.9867	15.0814
4	1.6398	19.8601
5	2.4528	24.5129
6	3.4243	29.0386
7	4.5530	33.4361
8	5.8374	37.7045
9	7.2764	41.8425
10	8.8685	45.8491
11	10.6126	49.7231
12	12.5072	53.4634
13	14.5512	57.0688
14	16.7432	60.5383
15	19.0821	63.8706
16	21.5665	67.0646
17	24.1953	70.1191
18	26.9672	73.0328
19	29.8809	75.8047
20	32.9354	78.4335
21	36.1294	80.9179
22	39.4617	83.2568
23	42.9312	85.4488
24	46.5366	87.4928
25	50.2769	89.3874
26	54.1509	91.1315
27	58.1575	92.7236
28	62.2955	94.1626
29	66.5639	95.4470
30	70.9614	96.5757
31	75.4871	97.5472
32	80.1399	98.3602
33	84.9186	99.0133
34	89.8222	99.5053
35	94.8497	99.8346
36	100.0000	100.0000

4 YEARS

#	REBATE	EARN
1	.0967	3.8273
2	.2893	7.5898
3	.5770	11.2869
4	.9589	14.9181
5	1.4343	18.4827
6	2.0024	21.9803
7	2.6624	25.4102
8	3.4135	28.7719
9	4.2549	32.0647
10	5.1859	35.2882
11	6.2058	38.4416
12	7.3137	41.5245
13	8.5089	44.5361
14	9.7907	47.4759
15	11.1584	50.3434
16	12.6111	53.1378
17	14.1483	55.8585
18	15.7692	58.5049
19	17.4730	61.0764
20	19.2592	63.5724
21	21.1269	65.9921
22	23.0755	68.3349
23	25.1042	70.6003
24	27.2126	72.7874
25	29.3997	74.8958
26	31.6651	76.9245
27	34.0079	78.8731
28	36.4276	80.7408
29	38.9236	82.5270
30	41.4951	84.2308
31	44.1415	85.8517
32	46.8622	87.3889
33	49.6566	88.8416
34	52.5241	90.2093
35	55.4639	91.4911
36	58.4755	92.6863
37	61.5584	93.7942
38	64.7118	94.8141
39	67.9353	95.7451
40	71.2281	96.5865
41	74.5898	97.3376
42	78.0197	97.9976
43	81.5173	98.5657
44	85.0819	99.0411
45	88.7131	99.4230
46	92.4102	99.7107
47	96.1727	99.9033
48	100.0000	100.0000

5 YEARS

#	REBATE	EARN
1	.0641	3.0266
2	.1919	6.0145
3	.3826	8.9631
4	.6359	11.8723
5	.9512	14.7416
6	1.3279	17.5708
7	1.7656	20.3594
8	2.2637	23.1072
9	2.8217	25.8138
10	3.4392	28.4788
11	4.1155	31.1019
12	4.8502	33.6827
13	5.6429	36.2209
14	6.4929	38.7161
15	7.3999	41.1679
16	8.3634	43.5760
17	9.3828	45.9400
18	10.4577	48.2595
19	11.5876	50.5341
20	12.7722	52.7634
21	14.0108	54.9472
22	15.3030	57.0849
23	16.6485	59.1761
24	18.0466	61.2206
25	19.4971	63.2178
26	20.9994	65.1675
27	22.5531	67.0691
28	24.1578	68.9222
29	25.8131	70.7265
30	27.5184	72.4816
31	29.2735	74.1869
32	31.0778	75.8422
33	32.9309	77.4469
34	34.8325	79.0006
35	36.7822	80.5029
36	38.7794	81.9534
37	40.8239	83.3515
38	42.9151	84.6970
39	45.0528	85.9892
40	47.2366	87.2278
41	49.4659	88.4124
42	51.7405	89.5423
43	54.0600	90.6172
44	56.4240	91.6366
45	58.8321	92.6001
46	61.2839	93.5071
47	63.7791	94.3571
48	66.3173	95.1498
49	68.8981	95.8845
50	71.5212	96.5608
51	74.1862	97.1783
52	76.8928	97.7363
53	79.6406	98.2344
54	82.4292	98.6721
55	85.2584	99.0488
56	88.1277	99.3641
57	91.0369	99.6174
58	93.9855	99.8081
59	96.9734	99.9359
60	100.0000	100.0000

6 YEARS

#	REBATE	EARN
1	.0461	2.4906
2	.1378	4.9560
3	.2748	7.3961
4	.4567	9.8105
5	.6832	12.1991
6	.9538	14.5616
7	1.2681	16.8978
8	1.6259	19.2076
9	2.0267	21.4906
10	2.4701	23.7467
11	2.9559	25.9756
12	3.4836	28.1771
13	4.0529	30.3509
14	4.6634	32.4968
15	5.3148	34.6146
16	6.0068	36.7041
17	6.7390	38.7649
18	7.5110	40.7969
19	8.3226	42.7998
20	9.1733	44.7733
21	10.0629	46.7173
22	10.9911	48.6314
23	11.9574	50.5154
24	12.9616	52.3690
25	14.0034	54.1920
26	15.0824	55.9841
27	16.1983	57.7451
28	17.3509	59.4746
29	18.5397	61.1725
30	19.7645	62.8384
31	21.0251	64.4721
32	22.3210	66.0733
33	23.6520	67.6417
34	25.0177	69.1771
35	26.4180	70.6791
36	27.8525	72.1475
37	29.3209	73.5820
38	30.8229	74.9823
39	32.3583	76.3480
40	33.9267	77.6790
41	35.5279	78.9749
42	37.1616	80.2355
43	38.8275	81.4603
44	40.5254	82.6491
45	42.2549	83.8017
46	44.0159	84.9176
47	45.8080	85.9966
48	47.6310	87.0384
49	49.4846	88.0426
50	51.3686	89.0089
51	53.2827	89.9371
52	55.2267	90.8267
53	57.2002	91.6774
54	59.2031	92.4890
55	61.2351	93.2610
56	63.2959	93.9932
57	65.3854	94.6852
58	67.5032	95.3366
59	69.6491	95.9471
60	71.8229	96.5164
61	74.0244	97.0441
62	76.2533	97.5299
63	78.5094	97.9733
64	80.7924	98.3741
65	83.1022	98.7319
66	85.4384	99.0462
67	87.8009	99.3168
68	90.1895	99.5433
69	92.6039	99.7252
70	95.0440	99.8622
71	97.5094	99.9539
72	100.0000	100.0000

7 YEARS

#	REBATE	EARN
1	.0350	2.1071
2	.1046	4.1970
3	.2085	6.2694
4	.3466	8.3243
5	.5184	10.3615
6	.7238	12.3809
7	.9623	14.3822
8	1.2338	16.3654
9	1.5380	18.3302
10	1.8745	20.2766
11	2.2431	22.2044
12	2.6436	24.1134
13	3.0756	26.0034
14	3.5389	27.8744
15	4.0333	29.7260
16	4.5584	31.5582
17	5.1140	33.3709
18	5.6999	35.1637
19	6.3157	36.9366
20	6.9613	38.6894
21	7.6364	40.4219
22	8.3408	42.1340
23	9.0741	43.8254
24	9.8361	45.4960
25	10.6267	47.1457
26	11.4455	48.7741
27	12.2924	50.3813
28	13.1670	51.9669
29	14.0691	53.5308
30	14.9986	55.0728
31	15.9552	56.5927
32	16.9386	58.0904
33	17.9487	59.5656
34	18.9851	61.0181
35	20.0477	62.4478
36	21.1363	63.8544
37	22.2506	65.2379
38	23.3905	66.5978
39	24.5556	67.9342
40	25.7458	69.2467
41	26.9609	70.5351
42	28.2007	71.7993
43	29.4649	73.0391
44	30.7533	74.2542
45	32.0658	75.4444
46	33.4022	76.6095
47	34.7621	77.7494
48	36.1456	78.8637
49	37.5522	79.9523
50	38.9819	81.0149
51	40.4344	82.0513
52	41.9096	83.0614
53	43.4073	84.0448
54	44.9272	85.0014
55	46.4692	85.9309
56	48.0331	86.8330
57	49.6187	87.7076
58	51.2259	88.5545
59	52.8543	89.3733
60	54.5040	90.1639
61	56.1746	90.9259
62	57.8660	91.6592
63	59.5781	92.3636
64	61.3106	93.0387
65	63.0634	93.6843
66	64.8363	94.3001
67	66.6291	94.8860
68	68.4418	95.4416
69	70.2740	95.9667
70	72.1256	96.4611
71	73.9966	96.9244
72	75.8866	97.3564
73	77.7956	97.7569
74	79.7234	98.1255
75	81.6698	98.4620

ACTUARIAL REBATE AND EARNINGS

#	REBATE	EARN
75	81.6698	98.4620
76	83.6346	98.7662
77	85.6178	99.0377
78	87.6191	99.2762
79	89.6385	99.4816
80	91.6757	99.6534
81	93.7306	99.7915
82	95.8030	99.8954
83	97.8929	99.9650
84	100.0000	100.0000

8 YEARS

#	REBATE	EARN
1	.0276	1.8195
2	.0826	3.6267
3	.1648	5.4215
4	.2738	7.2037
5	.4096	8.9734
6	.5718	10.7303
7	.7603	12.4743
8	.9747	14.2054
9	1.2150	15.9235
10	1.4809	17.6283
11	1.7721	19.3199
12	2.0885	20.9981
13	2.4298	22.6627
14	2.7958	24.3138
15	3.1863	25.9510
16	3.6012	27.5744
17	4.0402	29.1839
18	4.5030	30.7792
19	4.9895	32.3603
20	5.4996	33.9270
21	6.0329	35.4793
22	6.5894	37.0170
23	7.1687	38.5400
24	7.7707	40.0481
25	8.3953	41.5413
26	9.0422	43.0194
27	9.7112	44.4822
28	10.4022	45.9297
29	11.1149	47.3617
30	11.8492	48.7781
31	12.6049	50.1787
32	13.3818	51.5634
33	14.1798	52.9322
34	14.9986	54.2847
35	15.8381	55.6210
36	16.6981	56.9408
37	17.5784	58.2441
38	18.4789	59.5306
39	19.3994	60.8003
40	20.3397	62.0529
41	21.2996	63.2884
42	22.2791	64.5066
43	23.2778	65.7074
44	24.2957	66.8906
45	25.3326	68.0560
46	26.3884	69.2036
47	27.4628	70.3330
48	28.5557	71.4443
49	29.6670	72.5372
50	30.7964	73.6116
51	31.9440	74.6674
52	33.1094	75.7043
53	34.2926	76.7222
54	35.4934	77.7209
55	36.7116	78.7004
56	37.9471	79.6603
57	39.1997	80.6006
58	40.4694	81.5211
59	41.7559	82.4216
60	43.0592	83.3019
61	44.3790	84.1619
62	45.7153	85.0014
63	47.0678	85.8202
64	48.4366	86.6182
65	49.8213	87.3951
66	51.2219	88.1508
67	52.6383	88.8851
68	54.0703	89.5978
69	55.5178	90.2888
70	56.9806	90.9578
71	58.4587	91.6047
72	59.9519	92.2293
73	61.4600	92.8313
74	62.9830	93.4106
75	64.5207	93.9671
76	66.0730	94.5004
77	67.6397	95.0105
78	69.2208	95.4970
79	70.8161	95.9598
80	72.4256	96.3988
81	74.0490	96.8137
82	75.6862	97.2042
83	77.3373	97.5702
84	79.0019	97.9115
85	80.6801	98.2279
86	82.3717	98.5191
87	84.0765	98.7850
88	85.7946	99.0253
89	87.5257	99.2397
90	89.2697	99.4282
91	91.0266	99.5904
92	92.7963	99.7262
93	94.5785	99.8352
94	96.3733	99.9174
95	98.1805	99.9724
96	100.0000	100.0000

9 YEARS

#	REBATE	EARN
1	.0225	1.5961
2	.0673	3.1832
3	.1342	4.7611
4	.2231	6.3298
5	.3336	7.8892
6	.4658	9.4393
7	.6193	10.9799
8	.7940	12.5109
9	.9898	14.0324
10	1.2063	15.5442
11	1.4436	17.0462
12	1.7013	18.5383
13	1.9793	20.0205
14	2.2775	21.4927
15	2.5957	22.9548
16	2.9336	24.4066
17	3.2912	25.8482
18	3.6682	27.2794
19	4.0646	28.7001
20	4.4801	30.1103
21	4.9145	31.5098
22	5.3678	32.8987
23	5.8397	34.2766
24	6.3302	35.6437
25	6.8389	36.9998
26	7.3659	38.3447
27	7.9109	39.6785
28	8.4738	41.0009
29	9.0544	42.3120
30	9.6526	43.6116
31	10.2682	44.8996
32	10.9011	46.1759
33	11.5511	47.4404
34	12.2181	48.6930
35	12.9020	49.9336
36	13.6025	51.1622
37	14.3197	52.3786
38	15.0532	53.5826
39	15.8031	54.7743
40	16.5690	55.9534
41	17.3510	57.1200
42	18.1489	58.2738
43	18.9625	59.4147
44	19.7917	60.5428
45	20.6364	61.6578
46	21.4964	62.7596
47	22.3716	63.8481
48	23.2619	64.9233
49	24.1672	65.9849
50	25.0873	67.0329
51	26.0221	68.0672
52	26.9715	69.0877
53	27.9353	70.0941
54	28.9135	71.0865
55	29.9059	72.0647
56	30.9123	73.0285
57	31.9328	73.9779
58	32.9671	74.9127
59	34.0151	75.8328
60	35.0767	76.7381
61	36.1519	77.6284
62	37.2404	78.5036
63	38.3422	79.3636
64	39.4572	80.2083
65	40.5853	81.0375
66	41.7262	81.8511
67	42.8800	82.6490
68	44.0466	83.4310
69	45.2257	84.1969
70	46.4174	84.9468
71	47.6214	85.6803
72	48.8378	86.3975
73	50.0664	87.0980
74	51.3070	87.7819
75	52.5596	88.4489
76	53.8241	89.0989
77	55.1004	89.7318
78	56.3884	90.3474
79	57.6880	90.9456
80	58.9991	91.5262
81	60.3215	92.0891
82	61.6553	92.6341
83	63.0002	93.1611
84	64.3563	93.6698
85	65.7234	94.1603
86	67.1013	94.6322
87	68.4902	95.0855
88	69.8897	95.5199
89	71.2999	95.9354
90	72.7206	96.3318
91	74.1518	96.7088
92	75.5934	97.0664
93	77.0452	97.4043
94	78.5073	97.7225
95	79.9795	98.0207
96	81.4617	98.2987
97	82.9538	98.5564
98	84.4558	98.7937
99	85.9676	99.0102
100	87.4891	99.2060
101	89.0201	99.3807
102	90.5607	99.5342
103	92.1108	99.6664
104	93.6702	99.7769
105	95.2389	99.8658
106	96.8168	99.9327
107	98.4039	99.9775
108	100.0000	100.0000

10 YEARS

#	REBATE	EARN
1	.0188	1.4178
2	.0562	2.8287
3	.1120	4.2328
4	.1861	5.6299
5	.2784	7.0201
6	.3887	8.4032
7	.5168	9.7791
8	.6626	11.1479
9	.8260	12.5094
10	1.0067	13.8637
11	1.2047	15.2105
12	1.4197	16.5500
13	1.6518	17.8819
14	1.9006	19.2063
15	2.1661	20.5231
16	2.4481	21.8322
17	2.7465	23.1335
18	3.0611	24.4270
19	3.3919	25.7127
20	3.7386	26.9904
21	4.1012	28.2600
22	4.4794	29.5216
23	4.8733	30.7750
24	5.2825	32.0202
25	5.7071	33.2571
26	6.1469	34.4856
27	6.6016	35.7057
28	7.0714	36.9173
29	7.5559	38.1203
30	8.0551	39.3146
31	8.5688	40.5002
32	9.0969	41.6770
33	9.6394	42.8450
34	10.1960	44.0039
35	10.7667	45.1538
36	11.3513	46.2947
37	11.9498	47.4263
38	12.5619	48.5487
39	13.1877	49.6617
40	13.8269	50.7653
41	14.4794	51.8593
42	15.1453	52.9438
43	15.8242	54.0187
44	16.5162	55.0837
45	17.2211	56.1390
46	17.9387	57.1843
47	18.6691	58.2196
48	19.4121	59.2448
49	20.1675	60.2599
50	20.9354	61.2647
51	21.7155	62.2591
52	22.5077	63.2431
53	23.3120	64.2166
54	24.1283	65.1794
55	24.9564	66.1316
56	25.7963	67.0729
57	26.6479	68.0034
58	27.5110	68.9229
59	28.3856	69.8312
60	29.2715	70.7285
61	30.1688	71.6144
62	31.0771	72.4890
63	31.9966	73.3521
64	32.9271	74.2037
65	33.8684	75.0436
66	34.8206	75.8717
67	35.7834	76.6880
68	36.7569	77.4923
69	37.7409	78.2845
70	38.7353	79.0646
71	39.7401	79.8325
72	40.7552	80.5879
73	41.7804	81.3309
74	42.8157	82.0613
75	43.8610	82.7789
76	44.9163	83.4838
77	45.9813	84.1758
78	47.0562	84.8547
79	48.1407	85.5206
80	49.2347	86.1731
81	50.3383	86.8123
82	51.4513	87.4381
83	52.5737	88.0502
84	53.7053	88.6487
85	54.8462	89.2333
86	55.9961	89.8040
87	57.1550	90.3606
88	58.3230	90.9031
89	59.4998	91.4312
90	60.6854	91.9449
91	61.8797	92.4441
92	63.0827	92.9286
93	64.2943	93.3984
94	65.5144	93.8531
95	66.7429	94.2929
96	67.9798	94.7175
97	69.2250	95.1267
98	70.4784	95.5206
99	71.7400	95.8988
100	73.0096	96.2614
101	74.2873	96.6081
102	75.5730	96.9389
103	76.8665	97.2535
104	78.1678	97.5519
105	79.4769	97.8339
106	80.7937	98.0994
107	82.1181	98.3482
108	83.4500	98.5803
109	84.7895	98.7953
110	86.1363	98.9933
111	87.4906	99.1740
112	88.8521	99.3374
113	90.2209	99.4832
114	91.5968	99.6113
115	92.9799	99.7216
116	94.3701	99.8139
117	95.7672	99.8880
118	97.1713	99.9438
119	98.5822	99.9812
120	100.0000	100.0000

ACTUARIAL REBATE AND EARNINGS

1 YEAR

#	REBATE	EARN
1	1.3232	15.1428
2	3.9582	29.0833
3	7.8936	41.8109
4	13.1181	53.3151
5	19.6205	63.5852
6	27.3897	72.6103
7	36.4148	80.3795
8	46.6849	86.8819
9	58.1891	92.1064
10	70.9167	96.0418
11	84.8572	98.6768
12	100.0000	100.0000

2 YEARS

#	REBATE	EARN
1	.3559	7.7417
2	1.0647	15.1920
3	2.1232	22.3485
4	3.5284	29.2087
5	5.2773	35.7698
6	7.3670	42.0293
7	9.7945	47.9845
8	12.5569	53.6328
9	15.6512	58.9716
10	19.0745	63.9980
11	22.8241	68.7093
12	26.8971	73.1029
13	31.2907	77.1759
14	36.0020	80.9255
15	41.0284	84.3488
16	46.3672	87.4431
17	52.0155	90.2055
18	57.9707	92.6330
19	64.2302	94.7227
20	70.7913	96.4716
21	77.6515	97.8768
22	84.8080	98.9353
23	92.2583	99.6441
24	100.0000	100.0000

3 YEARS

#	REBATE	EARN
1	.1658	5.1444
2	.4958	10.1666
3	.9888	15.0655
4	1.6432	19.8401
5	2.4578	24.4893
6	3.4310	29.0120
7	4.5615	33.4070
8	5.8480	37.6733
9	7.2890	41.8097
10	8.8834	45.8150
11	10.6296	49.6883
12	12.5265	53.4282
13	14.5726	57.0336
14	16.7668	60.5034
15	19.1077	63.8363
16	21.5940	67.0312
17	24.2246	70.0868
18	26.9980	73.0020
19	29.9132	75.7754
20	32.9688	78.4060
21	36.1637	80.8923
22	39.4966	83.2332
23	42.9664	85.4274
24	46.5718	87.4735
25	50.3117	89.3704
26	54.1850	91.1166
27	58.1903	92.7110
28	62.3267	94.1520
29	66.5930	95.4385
30	70.9880	96.5690
31	75.5107	97.5422
32	80.1599	98.3568
33	84.9345	99.0112
34	89.8334	99.5042
35	94.8556	99.8342
36	100.0000	100.0000

4 YEARS

#	REBATE	EARN
1	.0970	3.8216
2	.2901	7.5788
3	.5786	11.2710
4	.9616	14.8977
5	1.4382	18.4582
6	2.0077	21.9521
7	2.6693	25.3787
8	3.4221	28.7374
9	4.2654	32.0277
10	5.1984	35.2489
11	6.2203	38.4005
12	7.3303	41.4818
13	8.5276	44.4922
14	9.8116	47.4311
15	11.1815	50.2979
16	12.6364	53.0919
17	14.1758	55.8125
18	15.7988	58.4591
19	17.5047	61.0310
20	19.2928	63.5275
21	21.1624	65.9481
22	23.1127	68.2919
23	25.1432	70.5585
24	27.2530	72.7470
25	29.4415	74.8568
26	31.7081	76.8873
27	34.0519	78.8376
28	36.4725	80.7072
29	38.9690	82.4953
30	41.5409	84.2012
31	44.1875	85.8242
32	46.9081	87.3636
33	49.7021	88.8185
34	52.5689	90.1884
35	55.5078	91.4724
36	58.5182	92.6697
37	61.5995	93.7797
38	64.7511	94.8016
39	67.9723	95.7346
40	71.2626	96.5779
41	74.6213	97.3307
42	78.0479	97.9923
43	81.5418	98.5618
44	85.1023	99.0384
45	88.7290	99.4214
46	92.4212	99.7099
47	96.1784	99.9030
48	100.0000	100.0000

5 YEARS

#	REBATE	EARN
1	.0644	3.0211
2	.1926	6.0036
3	.3840	8.9473
4	.6382	11.8519
5	.9545	14.7169
6	1.3324	17.5420
7	1.7715	20.3270
8	2.2711	23.0714
9	2.8307	25.7748
10	3.4499	28.4370
11	4.1280	31.0575
12	4.8647	33.6361
13	5.6593	36.1722
14	6.5114	38.6656
15	7.4205	41.1159
16	8.3860	43.5227
17	9.4076	45.8857
18	10.4847	48.2043
19	11.6168	50.4784
20	12.8034	52.7073
21	14.0442	54.8909
22	15.3385	57.0286
23	16.6860	59.1201
24	18.0862	61.1650
25	19.5386	63.1628
26	21.0427	65.1132
27	22.5982	67.0157
28	24.2046	68.8699
29	25.8614	70.6754
30	27.5682	72.4318
31	29.3246	74.1386
32	31.1301	75.7954
33	32.9843	77.4018
34	34.8868	78.9573
35	36.8372	80.4614
36	38.8350	81.9138
37	40.8799	83.3140
38	42.9714	84.6615
39	45.1091	85.9558
40	47.2927	87.1966
41	49.5216	88.3832
42	51.7957	89.5153
43	54.1143	90.5924
44	56.4773	91.6140
45	58.8841	92.5795
46	61.3344	93.4886
47	63.8278	94.3407
48	66.3639	95.1353
49	68.9425	95.8720
50	71.5630	96.5501
51	74.2252	97.1693
52	76.9286	97.7289
53	79.6730	98.2285
54	82.4580	98.6676
55	85.2831	99.0455
56	88.1481	99.3618
57	91.0527	99.6160
58	93.9964	99.8074
59	96.9789	99.9356
60	100.0000	100.0000

6 YEARS

#	REBATE	EARN
1	.0463	2.4852
2	.1384	4.9455
3	.2760	7.3806
4	.4586	9.7903
5	.6860	12.1745
6	.9576	14.5329
7	1.2732	16.8652
8	1.6322	19.1713
9	2.0345	21.4509
10	2.4795	23.7037
11	2.9669	25.9296
12	3.4963	28.1284
13	4.0674	30.2996
14	4.6798	32.4433
15	5.3332	34.5589
16	6.0272	36.6465
17	6.7614	38.7056
18	7.5355	40.7361
19	8.3492	42.7377
20	9.2020	44.7101
21	10.0938	46.6531
22	11.0240	48.5665
23	11.9925	50.4499
24	12.9988	52.3031
25	14.0427	54.1259
26	15.1238	55.9180
27	16.2417	57.6791
28	17.3962	59.4089
29	18.5870	61.1071
30	19.8137	62.7736
31	21.0760	64.4080
32	22.3737	66.0100
33	23.7063	67.5794
34	25.0737	69.1158
35	26.4755	70.6190
36	27.9113	72.0887
37	29.3810	73.5245
38	30.8842	74.9263
39	32.4206	76.2937
40	33.9900	77.6263
41	35.5920	78.9240
42	37.2264	80.1863
43	38.8929	81.4130
44	40.5911	82.6038
45	42.3209	83.7583
46	44.0820	84.8762
47	45.8741	85.9573
48	47.6969	87.0012
49	49.5501	88.0075
50	51.4335	88.9760
51	53.3469	89.9062
52	55.2899	90.7980
53	57.2623	91.6508
54	59.2639	92.4645
55	61.2944	93.2386
56	63.3535	93.9728
57	65.4411	94.6668
58	67.5567	95.3202
59	69.7004	95.9326
60	71.8716	96.5037
61	74.0704	97.0331
62	76.2963	97.5205
63	78.5491	97.9655
64	80.8287	98.3678
65	83.1348	98.7268
66	85.4671	99.0424
67	87.8255	99.3140
68	90.2097	99.5414
69	92.6194	99.7240
70	95.0545	99.8616
71	97.5148	99.9537
72	100.0000	100.0000

7 YEARS

#	REBATE	EARN
1	.0351	2.1019
2	.1051	4.1867
3	.2096	6.2543
4	.3483	8.3046
5	.5209	10.3374
6	.7272	12.3525
7	.9668	14.3498
8	1.2395	16.3292
9	1.5449	18.2904
10	1.8828	20.2334
11	2.2529	22.1579
12	2.6550	24.0638
13	3.0886	25.9510
14	3.5537	27.8192
15	4.0498	29.6683
16	4.5768	31.4982
17	5.1344	33.3087
18	5.7222	35.0995
19	6.3400	36.8706
20	6.9877	38.6218
21	7.6648	40.3528
22	8.3712	42.0635
23	9.1066	43.7538
24	9.8708	45.4234
25	10.6635	47.0722
26	11.4844	48.7000
27	12.3333	50.3065
28	13.2100	51.8917
29	14.1143	53.4554
30	15.0458	54.9973
31	16.0043	56.5172
32	16.9897	58.0150
33	18.0017	59.4904
34	19.0400	60.9433
35	20.1045	62.3735
36	21.1948	63.7808
37	22.3108	65.1650
38	23.4523	66.5258
39	24.6190	67.8631
40	25.8107	69.1766
41	27.0272	70.4662
42	28.2683	71.7317
43	29.5338	72.9728
44	30.8234	74.1893
45	32.1369	75.3810
46	33.4742	76.5477
47	34.8350	77.6892
48	36.2192	78.8052
49	37.6265	79.8955
50	39.0567	80.9600
51	40.5096	81.9983
52	41.9850	83.0103
53	43.4828	83.9957
54	45.0027	84.9542
55	46.5446	85.8857
56	48.1083	86.7900
57	49.6935	87.6667
58	51.3000	88.5156
59	52.9278	89.3365
60	54.5766	90.1292
61	56.2462	90.8934
62	57.9365	91.6288
63	59.6472	92.3352
64	61.3782	93.0123
65	63.1294	93.6600
66	64.9005	94.2778
67	66.6913	94.8656
68	68.5018	95.4232
69	70.3317	95.9502
70	72.1808	96.4463
71	74.0490	96.9114
72	75.9362	97.3450
73	77.8421	97.7471
74	79.7666	98.1172
75	81.7096	98.4551

(7 YEARS continued)

#	REBATE	EARN
75	81.7096	98.4551
76	83.6708	98.7605
77	85.6502	99.0332
78	87.6475	99.2728
79	89.6626	99.4791
80	91.6954	99.6517
81	93.7457	99.7904
82	95.8133	99.8949
83	97.8981	99.9649
84	100.0000	100.0000

8 YEARS

#	REBATE	EARN
1	.0278	1.8144
2	.0831	3.6167
3	.1657	5.4068
4	.2753	7.1845
5	.4118	8.9498
6	.5749	10.7024
7	.7643	12.4424
8	.9798	14.1697
9	1.2213	15.8840
10	1.4884	17.5853
11	1.7810	19.2734
12	2.0988	20.9483
13	2.4416	22.6099
14	2.8093	24.2580
15	3.2015	25.8925
16	3.6180	27.5132
17	4.0588	29.1202
18	4.5235	30.7132
19	5.0119	32.2921
20	5.5239	33.8568
21	6.0592	35.4072
22	6.6176	36.9431
23	7.1990	38.4645
24	7.8030	39.9712
25	8.4297	41.4630
26	9.0786	42.9399
27	9.7497	44.4016
28	10.4428	45.8482
29	11.1576	47.2794
30	11.8939	48.6951
31	12.6517	50.0952
32	13.4307	51.4795
33	14.2306	52.8479
34	15.0515	54.2002
35	15.8929	55.5364
36	16.7549	56.8563
37	17.6371	58.1597
38	18.5394	59.4465
39	19.4617	60.7165
40	20.4038	61.9696
41	21.3655	63.2057
42	22.3466	64.4246
43	23.3469	65.6261
44	24.3664	66.8101
45	25.4048	67.9765
46	26.4619	69.1251
47	27.5377	70.2557
48	28.6319	71.3681
49	29.7443	72.4623
50	30.8749	73.5381
51	32.0235	74.5952
52	33.1899	75.6336
53	34.3739	76.6531
54	35.5754	77.6534
55	36.7943	78.6345
56	38.0304	79.5962
57	39.2835	80.5383
58	40.5535	81.4606
59	41.8403	82.3629
60	43.1437	83.2451
61	44.4636	84.1071
62	45.7998	84.9485
63	47.1521	85.7694
64	48.5205	86.5693
65	49.9048	87.3483
66	51.3049	88.1061
67	52.7206	88.8424
68	54.1518	89.5572
69	55.5984	90.2503
70	57.0601	90.9214
71	58.5370	91.5703
72	60.0288	92.1970
73	61.5355	92.8010
74	63.0569	93.3824
75	64.5928	93.9408
76	66.1432	94.4761
77	67.7079	94.9881
78	69.2868	95.4765
79	70.8798	95.9412
80	72.4868	96.3820
81	74.1075	96.7985
82	75.7420	97.1907
83	77.3901	97.5584
84	79.0517	97.9012
85	80.7266	98.2190
86	82.4147	98.5116
87	84.1160	98.7787
88	85.8303	99.0202
89	87.5576	99.2357
90	89.2976	99.4251
91	91.0502	99.5882
92	92.8155	99.7247
93	94.5932	99.8343
94	96.3833	99.9169
95	98.1856	99.9722
96	100.0000	100.0000

9 YEARS

#	REBATE	EARN
1	.0226	1.5912
2	.0677	3.1735
3	.1350	4.7468
4	.2244	6.3111
5	.3357	7.8662
6	.4686	9.4121
7	.6230	10.9486
8	.7987	12.4758
9	.9955	13.9935
10	1.2132	15.5016
11	1.4517	17.0001
12	1.7107	18.4889
13	1.9902	19.9679
14	2.2899	21.4370
15	2.6095	22.8961
16	2.9491	24.3451
17	3.3084	25.7840
18	3.6871	27.2126
19	4.0853	28.6309
20	4.5026	30.0388
21	4.9389	31.4361
22	5.3941	32.8228
23	5.8679	34.1989
24	6.3603	35.5641
25	6.8711	36.9185
26	7.4001	38.2619
27	7.9471	39.5942
28	8.5120	40.9153
29	9.0946	42.2251
30	9.6949	43.5236
31	10.3125	44.8106
32	10.9475	46.0860
33	11.5996	47.3497
34	12.2686	48.6017
35	12.9545	49.8418
36	13.6571	51.0698
37	14.3762	52.2859
38	15.1117	53.4897
39	15.8635	54.6812
40	16.6314	55.8603
41	17.4152	57.0269
42	18.2149	58.1808
43	19.0303	59.3220
44	19.8613	60.4504
45	20.7077	61.5658
46	21.5694	62.6681
47	22.4463	63.7573
48	23.3381	64.8331
49	24.2449	65.8955
50	25.1665	66.9444
51	26.1027	67.9796
52	27.0534	69.0010
53	28.0185	70.0086
54	28.9979	71.0021
55	29.9914	71.9815
56	30.9990	72.9466
57	32.0204	73.8973
58	33.0556	74.8335
59	34.1045	75.7551
60	35.1669	76.6619
61	36.2427	77.5537
62	37.3319	78.4306
63	38.4342	79.2923
64	39.5496	80.1387
65	40.6780	80.9697
66	41.8192	81.7851
67	42.9731	82.5848
68	44.1397	83.3686
69	45.3188	84.1365
70	46.5103	84.8883
71	47.7141	85.6238
72	48.9302	86.3429
73	50.1582	87.0455
74	51.3983	87.7314
75	52.6503	88.4004
76	53.9140	89.0525
77	55.1894	89.6875
78	56.4764	90.3051
79	57.7749	90.9054
80	59.0847	91.4880
81	60.4058	92.0529
82	61.7381	92.5999
83	63.0815	93.1289
84	64.4359	93.6397
85	65.8011	94.1321
86	67.1772	94.6059
87	68.5639	95.0611
88	69.9612	95.4974
89	71.3691	95.9147
90	72.7874	96.3129
91	74.2160	96.6916
92	75.6549	97.0509
93	77.1039	97.3905
94	78.5630	97.7101
95	80.0321	98.0098
96	81.5111	98.2893
97	82.9999	98.5483
98	84.4984	98.7868
99	86.0065	99.0045
100	87.5242	99.2013
101	89.0514	99.3770
102	90.5879	99.5314
103	92.1338	99.6643
104	93.6889	99.7756
105	95.2532	99.8650
106	96.8265	99.9323
107	98.4088	99.9774
108	100.0000	100.0000

10 YEARS

#	REBATE	EARN
1	.0189	1.4131
2	.0565	2.8194
3	.1128	4.2190
4	.1874	5.6118
5	.2803	6.9977
6	.3912	8.3767
7	.5202	9.7486
8	.6669	11.1135
9	.8312	12.4713
10	1.0130	13.8219
11	1.2121	15.1652
12	1.4285	16.5013
13	1.6618	17.8299
14	1.9120	19.1511
15	2.1789	20.4648
16	2.4625	21.7709
17	2.7624	23.0694
18	3.0787	24.3602
19	3.4111	25.6432
20	3.7596	26.9184
21	4.1239	28.1857
22	4.5040	29.4449
23	4.8997	30.6962
24	5.3108	31.9393
25	5.7373	33.1742
26	6.1790	34.4009
27	6.6357	35.6192
28	7.1074	36.8291
29	7.5939	38.0306
30	8.0951	39.2234
31	8.6108	40.4077
32	9.1410	41.5832
33	9.6855	42.7500
34	10.2441	43.9079
35	10.8168	45.0569
36	11.4035	46.1969
37	12.0039	47.3277
38	12.6181	48.4494
39	13.2458	49.5619
40	13.8870	50.6650
41	14.5415	51.7587
42	15.2092	52.8429
43	15.8901	53.9175
44	16.5839	54.9825
45	17.2907	56.0377
46	18.0102	57.0830
47	18.7423	58.1185
48	19.4871	59.1439
49	20.2442	60.1593
50	21.0137	61.1645
51	21.7954	62.1594
52	22.5893	63.1439
53	23.3951	64.1180
54	24.2129	65.0815
55	25.0425	66.0344
56	25.8837	66.9766
57	26.7366	67.9079
58	27.6010	68.8284
59	28.4768	69.7378
60	29.3639	70.6361
61	30.2622	71.5232
62	31.1716	72.3990
63	32.0921	73.2634
64	33.0234	74.1163
65	33.9656	74.9575
66	34.9185	75.7871
67	35.8820	76.6049
68	36.8561	77.4107
69	37.8406	78.2046
70	38.8355	78.9863
71	39.8407	79.7558
72	40.8561	80.5129
73	41.8815	81.2577
74	42.9170	81.9898
75	43.9623	82.7093
76	45.0175	83.4161
77	46.0825	84.1099
78	47.1571	84.7908
79	48.2413	85.4585
80	49.3350	86.1130
81	50.4381	86.7542
82	51.5506	87.3819
83	52.6723	87.9961
84	53.8031	88.5965
85	54.9431	89.1832
86	56.0921	89.7559
87	57.2500	90.3145
88	58.4168	90.8590
89	59.5923	91.3892
90	60.7766	91.9049
91	61.9694	92.4061
92	63.1709	92.8926
93	64.3808	93.3643
94	65.5991	93.8210
95	66.8258	94.2627
96	68.0607	94.6892
97	69.3038	95.1003
98	70.5551	95.4960
99	71.8143	95.8761
100	73.0816	96.2404
101	74.3568	96.5889
102	75.6398	96.9213
103	76.9306	97.2376
104	78.2291	97.5375
105	79.5352	97.8211
106	80.8489	98.0880
107	82.1701	98.3382
108	83.4987	98.5715
109	84.8348	98.7879
110	86.1781	98.9870
111	87.5287	99.1688
112	88.8865	99.3331
113	90.2514	99.4798
114	91.6233	99.6088
115	93.0023	99.7197
116	94.3882	99.8126
117	95.7810	99.8872
118	97.1806	99.9435
119	98.5869	99.9811
120	100.0000	100.0000

ACTUARIAL REBATE AND EARNINGS

1 YEAR

#	REBATE	EARN
1	1.3242	15.1372
2	3.9609	29.0738
3	7.8984	41.7993
4	13.1251	53.3027
5	19.6297	63.5730
6	27.4007	72.5993
7	36.4270	80.3703
8	46.6973	86.8749
9	58.2007	92.1016
10	70.9262	96.0391
11	84.8628	98.6758
12	100.0000	100.0000

2 YEARS

#	REBATE	EARN
1	.3565	7.7357
2	1.0662	15.1811
3	2.1261	22.3336
4	3.5330	29.1904
5	5.2840	35.7491
6	7.3758	42.0068
7	9.8055	47.9610
8	12.5701	53.6088
9	15.6666	58.9476
10	19.0920	63.9746
11	22.8435	68.6869
12	26.9181	73.0819
13	31.3131	77.1565
14	36.0254	80.9080
15	41.0524	84.3334
16	46.3912	87.4299
17	52.0390	90.1945
18	57.9932	92.6242
19	64.2509	94.7160
20	70.8096	96.4670
21	77.6664	97.8739
22	84.8189	98.9338
23	92.2643	99.6435
24	100.0000	100.0000

3 YEARS

#	REBATE	EARN
1	.1661	5.1385
2	.4969	10.1555
3	.9909	15.0498
4	1.6466	19.8202
5	2.4627	24.4658
6	3.4376	28.9855
7	4.5700	33.3779
8	5.8585	37.6421
9	7.3017	41.7769
10	8.8982	45.7811
11	10.6467	49.6535
12	12.5457	53.3930
13	14.5941	56.9984
14	16.7904	60.4685
15	19.1333	63.8020
16	21.6215	66.9978
17	24.2538	70.0546
18	27.0289	72.9711
19	29.9454	75.7462
20	33.0022	78.3785
21	36.1980	80.8667
22	39.5315	83.2096
23	43.0016	85.4059
24	46.6070	87.4543
25	50.3465	89.3533
26	54.2189	91.1018
27	58.2231	92.6983
28	62.3579	94.1415
29	66.6221	95.4300
30	71.0145	96.5624
31	75.5342	97.5373
32	80.1798	98.3534
33	84.9502	99.0091
34	89.8445	99.5031
35	94.8615	99.8339
36	100.0000	100.0000

4 YEARS

#	REBATE	EARN
1	.0973	3.8159
2	.2910	7.5677
3	.5803	11.2551
4	.9643	14.8773
5	1.4422	18.4338
6	2.0131	21.9240
7	2.6762	25.3473
8	3.4308	28.7031
9	4.2759	31.9908
10	5.2109	35.2098
11	6.2348	38.3595
12	7.3469	41.4392
13	8.5464	44.4484
14	9.8326	47.3864
15	11.2046	50.2525
16	12.6617	53.0461
17	14.2032	55.7666
18	15.8283	58.4133
19	17.5363	60.9856
20	19.3263	63.4827
21	21.1978	65.9041
22	23.1499	68.2490
23	25.1820	70.5167
24	27.2934	72.7066
25	29.4833	74.8180
26	31.7510	76.8501
27	34.0959	78.8022
28	36.5173	80.6737
29	39.0144	82.4637
30	41.5867	84.1717
31	44.2334	85.7968
32	46.9539	87.3383
33	49.7475	88.7954
34	52.6136	90.1674
35	55.5516	91.4536
36	58.5608	92.6531
37	61.6405	93.7652
38	64.7902	94.7891
39	68.0092	95.7241
40	71.2969	96.5692
41	74.6527	97.3238
42	78.0760	97.9869
43	81.5662	98.5578
44	85.1227	99.0357
45	88.7449	99.4197
46	92.4323	99.7090
47	96.1841	99.9027
48	100.0000	100.0000

5 YEARS

#	REBATE	EARN
1	.0646	3.0155
2	.1933	5.9928
3	.3854	8.9316
4	.6404	11.8315
5	.9578	14.6923
6	1.3369	17.5134
7	1.7773	20.2947
8	2.2784	23.0357
9	2.8397	25.7360
10	3.4606	28.3953
11	4.1405	31.0133
12	4.8791	33.5896
13	5.6757	36.1237
14	6.5298	38.6153
15	7.4410	41.0641
16	8.4087	43.4696
17	9.4324	45.8315
18	10.5116	48.1494
19	11.6459	50.4228
20	12.8347	52.6514
21	14.0776	54.8348
22	15.3740	56.9726
23	16.7235	59.0643
24	18.1257	61.1095
25	19.5800	63.1079
26	21.0860	65.0591
27	22.6432	66.9625
28	24.2513	68.8177
29	25.9096	70.6244
30	27.6179	72.3821
31	29.3756	74.0904
32	31.1823	75.7487
33	33.0375	77.3568
34	34.9409	78.9140
35	36.8921	80.4200
36	38.8905	81.8743
37	40.9357	83.2765
38	43.0274	84.6260
39	45.1652	85.9224
40	47.3486	87.1653
41	49.5772	88.3541
42	51.8506	89.4884
43	54.1685	90.5676
44	56.5304	91.5913
45	58.9359	92.5590
46	61.3847	93.4702
47	63.8763	94.3243
48	66.4104	95.1209
49	68.9867	95.8595
50	71.6047	96.5394
51	74.2640	97.1603
52	76.9643	97.7216
53	79.7053	98.2227
54	82.4866	98.6631
55	85.3077	99.0422
56	88.1685	99.3596
57	91.0684	99.6146
58	94.0072	99.8067
59	96.9845	99.9354
60	100.0000	100.0000

6 YEARS

#	REBATE	EARN
1	.0465	2.4798
2	.1390	4.9349
3	.2772	7.3652
4	.4606	9.7703
5	.6888	12.1501
6	.9615	14.5043
7	1.2782	16.8328
8	1.6386	19.1352
9	2.0423	21.4113
10	2.4888	23.6610
11	2.9779	25.8839
12	3.5090	28.0799
13	4.0820	30.2486
14	4.6963	32.3899
15	5.3516	34.5035
16	6.0476	36.5891
17	6.7838	38.6466
18	7.5600	40.6755
19	8.3758	42.6758
20	9.2307	44.6471
21	10.1246	46.5892
22	11.0570	48.5018
23	12.0276	50.3847
24	13.0360	52.2375
25	14.0819	54.0601
26	15.1651	55.8521
27	16.2850	57.6132
28	17.4415	59.3433
29	18.6342	61.0420
30	19.8628	62.7090
31	21.1270	64.3440
32	22.4263	65.9468
33	23.7606	67.5171
34	25.1296	69.0546
35	26.5328	70.5590
36	27.9701	72.0299
37	29.4410	73.4672
38	30.9454	74.8704
39	32.4829	76.2394
40	34.0532	77.5737
41	35.6560	78.8730
42	37.2910	80.1372
43	38.9580	81.3658
44	40.6567	82.5585
45	42.3868	83.7150
46	44.1479	84.8349
47	45.9399	85.9181
48	47.7625	86.9640
49	49.6153	87.9724
50	51.4982	88.9430
51	53.4108	89.8754
52	55.3529	90.7693
53	57.3242	91.6242
54	59.3245	92.4400
55	61.3534	93.2162
56	63.4109	93.9524
57	65.4965	94.6484
58	67.6101	95.3037
59	69.7514	95.9180
60	71.9201	96.4910
61	74.1161	97.0221
62	76.3390	97.5112
63	78.5887	97.9577
64	80.8648	98.3614
65	83.1672	98.7218
66	85.4957	99.0385
67	87.8499	99.3112
68	90.2297	99.5394
69	92.6348	99.7228
70	95.0651	99.8610
71	97.5202	99.9535
72	100.0000	100.0000

7 YEARS

#	REBATE	EARN
1	.0353	2.0967
2	.1056	4.1765
3	.2106	6.2393
4	.3500	8.2850
5	.5234	10.3134
6	.7306	12.3243
7	.9713	14.3176
8	1.2451	16.2932
9	1.5518	18.2508
10	1.8912	20.1903
11	2.2628	22.1116
12	2.6664	24.0145
13	3.1017	25.8987
14	3.5685	27.7643
15	4.0664	29.6109
16	4.5953	31.4385
17	5.1547	33.2468
18	5.7445	35.0356
19	6.3644	36.8049
20	7.0140	38.5544
21	7.6932	40.2840
22	8.4017	41.9934
23	9.1392	43.6825
24	9.9055	45.3511
25	10.7002	46.9990
26	11.5233	48.6261
27	12.3743	50.2321
28	13.2531	51.8169
29	14.1593	53.3803
30	15.0929	54.9220
31	16.0534	56.4419
32	17.0408	57.9398
33	18.0547	59.4155
34	19.0948	60.8688
35	20.1611	62.2995
36	21.2532	63.7074
37	22.3709	65.0923
38	23.5140	66.4539
39	24.6823	67.7922
40	25.8755	69.1068
41	27.0934	70.3975
42	28.3358	71.6642
43	29.6025	72.9066
44	30.8932	74.1245
45	32.2078	75.3177
46	33.5461	76.4860
47	34.9077	77.6291
48	36.2926	78.7468
49	37.7005	79.8389
50	39.1312	80.9052
51	40.5845	81.9453
52	42.0602	82.9592
53	43.5581	83.9466
54	45.0780	84.9071
55	46.6197	85.8407
56	48.1831	86.7469
57	49.7679	87.6257
58	51.3739	88.4767
59	53.0010	89.2998
60	54.6489	90.0945
61	56.3175	90.8608
62	58.0066	91.5983
63	59.7160	92.3068
64	61.4456	92.9860
65	63.1951	93.6356
66	64.9644	94.2555
67	66.7532	94.8453
68	68.5615	95.4047
69	70.3891	95.9336
70	72.2357	96.4315
71	74.1013	96.8983
72	75.9855	97.3336
73	77.8884	97.7372
74	79.8097	98.1088
75	81.7492	98.4482

(continued table)

#	REBATE	EARN
75	81.7492	98.4482
76	83.7068	98.7549
77	85.6824	99.0287
78	87.6757	99.2694
79	89.6866	99.4766
80	91.7150	99.6500
81	93.7607	99.7894
82	95.8235	99.8944
83	97.9033	99.9647
84	100.0000	100.0000

8 YEARS

#	REBATE	EARN
1	.0279	1.8094
2	.0835	3.6069
3	.1666	5.3922
4	.2768	7.1654
5	.4140	8.9263
6	.5779	10.6748
7	.7683	12.4108
8	.9849	14.1341
9	1.2275	15.8447
10	1.4959	17.5424
11	1.7899	19.2272
12	2.1091	20.8989
13	2.4535	22.5574
14	2.8227	24.2025
15	3.2166	25.8343
16	3.6349	27.4524
17	4.0774	29.0569
18	4.5440	30.6476
19	5.0343	32.2243
20	5.5482	33.7870
21	6.0854	35.3355
22	6.6458	36.8697
23	7.2292	38.3894
24	7.8353	39.8946
25	8.4640	41.3851
26	9.1150	42.8608
27	9.7882	44.3215
28	10.4833	45.7671
29	11.2002	47.1975
30	11.9386	48.6125
31	12.6984	50.0120
32	13.4794	51.3959
33	14.2814	52.7640
34	15.1042	54.1161
35	15.9477	55.4522
36	16.8115	56.7721
37	17.6957	58.0756
38	18.5999	59.3627
39	19.5240	60.6331
40	20.4678	61.8866
41	21.4312	63.1233
42	22.4139	64.3428
43	23.4159	65.5451
44	24.4369	66.7299
45	25.4767	67.8972
46	26.5353	69.0468
47	27.6124	70.1785
48	28.7078	71.2922
49	29.8215	72.3876
50	30.9532	73.4647
51	32.1028	74.5233
52	33.2701	75.5631
53	34.4549	76.5841
54	35.6572	77.5861
55	36.8767	78.5688
56	38.1134	79.5322
57	39.3669	80.4760
58	40.6373	81.4001
59	41.9244	82.3043
60	43.2279	83.1885
61	44.5478	84.0523
62	45.8839	84.8958
63	47.2360	85.7186
64	48.6041	86.5206
65	49.9880	87.3016
66	51.3875	88.0614
67	52.8025	88.7998
68	54.2329	89.5167
69	55.6785	90.2118
70	57.1392	90.8850
71	58.6149	91.5360
72	60.1054	92.1647
73	61.6106	92.7708
74	63.1303	93.3542
75	64.6645	93.9146
76	66.2130	94.4518
77	67.7757	94.9657
78	69.3524	95.4560
79	70.9431	95.9226
80	72.5476	96.3651
81	74.1657	96.7834
82	75.7975	97.1773
83	77.4426	97.5465
84	79.1011	97.8909
85	80.7728	98.2101
86	82.4576	98.5041
87	84.1553	98.7725
88	85.8659	99.0151
89	87.5892	99.2317
90	89.3252	99.4221
91	91.0737	99.5860
92	92.8346	99.7232
93	94.6078	99.8334
94	96.3931	99.9165
95	98.1906	99.9721
96	100.0000	100.0000

9 YEARS

#	REBATE	EARN
1	.0228	1.5864
2	.0681	3.1640
3	.1359	4.7327
4	.2258	6.2925
5	.3377	7.8434
6	.4713	9.3851
7	.6266	10.9176
8	.8033	12.4409
9	1.0012	13.9549
10	1.2201	15.4594
11	1.4598	16.9544
12	1.7202	18.4399
13	2.0011	19.9156
14	2.3022	21.3816
15	2.6235	22.8378
16	2.9646	24.2840
17	3.3256	25.7202
18	3.7061	27.1463
19	4.1060	28.5621
20	4.5251	29.9677
21	4.9633	31.3628
22	5.4204	32.7475
23	5.8962	34.1216
24	6.3905	35.4851
25	6.9033	36.8377
26	7.4342	38.1795
27	7.9833	39.5103
28	8.5502	40.8301
29	9.1349	42.1387
30	9.7372	43.4361
31	10.3569	44.7221
32	10.9938	45.9966
33	11.6480	47.2595
34	12.3190	48.5108
35	13.0069	49.7503
36	13.7115	50.9780
37	14.4326	52.1936
38	15.1701	53.3972
39	15.9238	54.5885
40	16.6936	55.7676
41	17.4793	56.9342
42	18.2808	58.0883
43	19.0980	59.2297
44	19.9307	60.3584
45	20.7789	61.4742
46	21.6422	62.5771
47	22.5207	63.6668
48	23.4141	64.7433
49	24.3224	65.8064
50	25.2455	66.8562
51	26.1830	67.8923
52	27.1351	68.9147
53	28.1015	69.9233
54	29.0821	70.9179
55	30.0767	71.8985
56	31.0853	72.8649
57	32.1077	73.8170
58	33.1438	74.7545
59	34.1936	75.6776
60	35.2567	76.5859
61	36.3332	77.4793
62	37.4229	78.3578
63	38.5258	79.2211
64	39.6416	80.0693
65	40.7703	80.9020
66	41.9117	81.7192
67	43.0658	82.5207
68	44.2324	83.3064
69	45.4115	84.0762
70	46.6028	84.8299
71	47.8064	85.5674
72	49.0220	86.2885
73	50.2497	86.9931
74	51.4892	87.6810
75	52.7405	88.3520
76	54.0034	89.0062
77	55.2779	89.6431
78	56.5639	90.2628
79	57.8613	90.8651
80	59.1699	91.4498
81	60.4897	92.0167
82	61.8205	92.5658
83	63.1623	93.0967
84	64.5149	93.6095
85	65.8784	94.1038
86	67.2525	94.5796
87	68.6372	95.0367
88	70.0323	95.4749
89	71.4379	95.8940
90	72.8537	96.2939
91	74.2798	96.6744
92	75.7160	97.0354
93	77.1622	97.3765
94	78.6184	97.6978
95	80.0844	97.9989
96	81.5601	98.2798
97	83.0456	98.5402
98	84.5406	98.7799
99	86.0451	98.9988
100	87.5591	99.1967
101	89.0824	99.3734
102	90.6149	99.5287
103	92.1566	99.6623
104	93.7075	99.7742
105	95.2673	99.8641
106	96.8360	99.9319
107	98.4136	99.9772
108	100.0000	100.0000

10 YEARS

#	REBATE	EARN
1	.0190	1.4084
2	.0569	2.8102
3	.1135	4.2054
4	.1886	5.5939
5	.2821	6.9756
6	.3938	8.3504
7	.5235	9.7184
8	.6711	11.0795
9	.8365	12.4335
10	1.0193	13.7805
11	1.2196	15.1203
12	1.4372	16.4530
13	1.6718	17.7783
14	1.9234	19.0964
15	2.1918	20.4070
16	2.4769	21.7102
17	2.7784	23.0058
18	3.0963	24.2939
19	3.4304	25.5743
20	3.7806	26.8470
21	4.1467	28.1118
22	4.5286	29.3688
23	4.9261	30.6179
24	5.3391	31.8589
25	5.7675	33.0919
26	6.2111	34.3167
27	6.6698	35.5333
28	7.1434	36.7415
29	7.6319	37.9414
30	8.1351	39.1329
31	8.6529	40.3158
32	9.1850	41.4901
33	9.7315	42.6557
34	10.2922	43.8125
35	10.8669	44.9606
36	11.4556	46.0997
37	12.0580	47.2298
38	12.6741	48.3508
39	13.3038	49.4627
40	13.9470	50.5653
41	14.6034	51.6586
42	15.2731	52.7425
43	15.9558	53.8169
44	16.6516	54.8817
45	17.3601	55.9369
46	18.0814	56.9823
47	18.8154	58.0179
48	19.5618	59.0435
49	20.3207	60.0592
50	21.0918	61.0647
51	21.8752	62.0601
52	22.6706	63.0451
53	23.4780	64.0198
54	24.2972	64.9840
55	25.1282	65.9376
56	25.9709	66.8806
57	26.8251	67.8129
58	27.6907	68.7342
59	28.5677	69.6447
60	29.4559	70.5441
61	30.3553	71.4323
62	31.2658	72.3093
63	32.1871	73.1749
64	33.1194	74.0291
65	34.0624	74.8718
66	35.0160	75.7028
67	35.9802	76.5220
68	36.9549	77.3294
69	37.9399	78.1248
70	38.9353	78.9082
71	39.9408	79.6793
72	40.9565	80.4382
73	41.9821	81.1846
74	43.0177	81.9186
75	44.0631	82.6399
76	45.1183	83.3484
77	46.1831	84.0442
78	47.2575	84.7269
79	48.3414	85.3966
80	49.4347	86.0530
81	50.5373	86.6962
82	51.6492	87.3259
83	52.7702	87.9420
84	53.9003	88.5444
85	55.0394	89.1331
86	56.1875	89.7078
87	57.3443	90.2685
88	58.5099	90.8150
89	59.6842	91.3471
90	60.8671	91.8649
91	62.0586	92.3681
92	63.2585	92.8566
93	64.4667	93.3302
94	65.6833	93.7889
95	66.9081	94.2325
96	68.1411	94.6609
97	69.3821	95.0739
98	70.6312	95.4714
99	71.8882	95.8533
100	73.1530	96.2194
101	74.4257	96.5696
102	75.7061	96.9037
103	76.9942	97.2216
104	78.2898	97.5231
105	79.5930	97.8082
106	80.9036	98.0766
107	82.2217	98.3282
108	83.5470	98.5628
109	84.8797	98.7804
110	86.2195	98.9807
111	87.5665	99.1635
112	88.9205	99.3289
113	90.2816	99.4765
114	91.6496	99.6062
115	93.0244	99.7179
116	94.4061	99.8114
117	95.7946	99.8865
118	97.1898	99.9431
119	98.5916	99.9810
120	100.0000	100.0000

1 YEAR

#	REBATE	EARN
1	1.3252	15.1315
2	3.9636	29.0644
3	7.9032	41.7877
4	13.1322	53.2902
5	19.6389	63.5608
6	27.4117	72.5883
7	36.4392	80.3611
8	46.7098	86.8678
9	58.2123	92.0968
10	70.9356	96.0364
11	84.8685	98.6748
12	100.0000	100.0000

2 YEARS

#	REBATE	EARN
1	.3570	7.7298
2	1.0678	15.1703
3	2.1290	22.3186
4	3.5377	29.1722
5	5.2906	35.7284
6	7.3845	41.9844
7	9.8164	47.9374
8	12.5832	53.5848
9	15.6819	58.9237
10	19.1095	63.9512
11	22.8629	68.6645
12	26.9392	73.0608
13	31.3355	77.1371
14	36.0488	80.8905
15	41.0763	84.3181
16	46.4152	87.4168
17	52.0626	90.1836
18	58.0156	92.6155
19	64.2716	94.7094
20	70.8278	96.4623
21	77.6814	97.8710
22	84.8297	98.9322
23	92.2702	99.6430
24	100.0000	100.0000

3 YEARS

#	REBATE	EARN
1	.1665	5.1327
2	.4980	10.1444
3	.9930	15.0340
4	1.6501	19.8004
5	2.4676	24.4424
6	3.4443	28.9590
7	4.5786	33.3489
8	5.8691	37.6110
9	7.3144	41.7442
10	8.9130	45.7472
11	10.6637	49.6189
12	12.5650	53.3580
13	14.6155	56.9633
14	16.8139	60.4337
15	19.1588	63.7678
16	21.6490	66.9645
17	24.2830	70.0224
18	27.0597	72.9403
19	29.9776	75.7170
20	33.0355	78.3510
21	36.2322	80.8412
22	39.5663	83.1861
23	43.0367	85.3845
24	46.6420	87.4350
25	50.3811	89.3363
26	54.2528	91.0870
27	58.2558	92.6856
28	62.3890	94.1309
29	66.6511	95.4214
30	71.0410	96.5557
31	75.5576	97.5324
32	80.1996	98.3499
33	84.9660	99.0070
34	89.8556	99.5020
35	94.8673	99.8335
36	100.0000	100.0000

4 YEARS

#	REBATE	EARN
1	.0976	3.8102
2	.2919	7.5568
3	.5819	11.2392
4	.9670	14.8570
5	1.4461	18.4094
6	2.0185	21.8960
7	2.6832	25.3160
8	3.4395	28.6689
9	4.2865	31.9540
10	5.2233	35.1708
11	6.2493	38.3186
12	7.3635	41.3968
13	8.5651	44.4047
14	9.8535	47.3417
15	11.2277	50.2072
16	12.6870	53.0005
17	14.2306	55.7208
18	15.8578	58.3677
19	17.5678	60.9403
20	19.3599	63.4381
21	21.2332	65.8602
22	23.1871	68.2061
23	25.2209	70.4750
24	27.3337	72.6663
25	29.5250	74.7791
26	31.7939	76.8129
27	34.1398	78.7668
28	36.5619	80.6401
29	39.0597	82.4322
30	41.6323	84.1422
31	44.2792	85.7694
32	46.9995	87.3130
33	49.7928	88.7723
34	52.6583	90.1465
35	55.5953	91.4349
36	58.6032	92.6365
37	61.6814	93.7507
38	64.8292	94.7767
39	68.0460	95.7135
40	71.3311	96.5605
41	74.6840	97.3168
42	78.1040	97.9815
43	81.5906	98.5539
44	85.1430	99.0330
45	88.7608	99.4181
46	92.4432	99.7081
47	96.1898	99.9024
48	100.0000	100.0000

5 YEARS

#	REBATE	EARN
1	.0648	3.0100
2	.1940	5.9820
3	.3867	8.9159
4	.6426	11.8113
5	.9610	14.6677
6	1.3414	17.4849
7	1.7832	20.2625
8	2.2858	23.0001
9	2.8486	25.6973
10	3.4713	28.3538
11	4.1531	30.9693
12	4.8935	33.5432
13	5.6921	36.0753
14	6.5483	38.5652
15	7.4616	41.0125
16	8.4314	43.4167
17	9.4572	45.7775
18	10.5386	48.0946
19	11.6750	50.3674
20	12.8659	52.5956
21	14.1109	54.7788
22	15.4094	56.9166
23	16.7610	59.0085
24	18.1651	61.0542
25	19.6213	63.0532
26	21.1292	65.0050
27	22.6882	66.9093
28	24.2979	68.7656
29	25.9578	70.5735
30	27.6675	72.3325
31	29.4265	74.0422
32	31.2344	75.7021
33	33.0907	77.3118
34	34.9950	78.8708
35	36.9468	80.3787
36	38.9458	81.8349
37	40.9915	83.2390
38	43.0834	84.5906
39	45.2212	85.8891
40	47.4044	87.1341
41	49.6326	88.3250
42	51.9054	89.4614
43	54.2225	90.5428
44	56.5833	91.5686
45	58.9875	92.5384
46	61.4348	93.4517
47	63.9247	94.3079
48	66.4568	95.1065
49	69.0307	95.8469
50	71.6462	96.5287
51	74.3027	97.1514
52	76.9999	97.7142
53	79.7375	98.2168
54	82.5151	98.6586
55	85.3323	99.0390
56	88.1887	99.3574
57	91.0841	99.6133
58	94.0180	99.8060
59	96.9900	99.9352
60	100.0000	100.0000

6 YEARS

#	REBATE	EARN
1	.0467	2.4744
2	.1396	4.9245
3	.2783	7.3499
4	.4625	9.7504
5	.6916	12.1258
6	.9654	14.4759
7	1.2833	16.8005
8	1.6450	19.0992
9	2.0501	21.3719
10	2.4982	23.6184
11	2.9889	25.8384
12	3.5218	28.0316
13	4.0965	30.1978
14	4.7127	32.3368
15	5.3700	34.4482
16	6.0679	36.5320
17	6.8062	38.5877
18	7.5845	40.6152
19	8.4023	42.6142
20	9.2594	44.5844
21	10.1554	46.5255
22	11.0899	48.4374
23	12.0626	50.3197
24	13.0731	52.1721
25	14.1212	53.9944
26	15.2063	55.7863
27	16.3283	57.5476
28	17.4868	59.2779
29	18.6814	60.9769
30	19.9119	62.6445
31	21.1778	64.2802
32	22.4789	65.8838
33	23.8149	67.4550
34	25.1853	68.9936
35	26.5901	70.4991
36	28.0287	71.9713
37	29.5009	73.4099
38	31.0064	74.8147
39	32.5450	76.1851
40	34.1162	77.5211
41	35.7198	78.8222
42	37.3555	80.0881
43	39.0231	81.3186
44	40.7221	82.5132
45	42.4524	83.6717
46	44.2137	84.7937
47	46.0056	85.8788
48	47.8279	86.9269
49	49.6803	87.9374
50	51.5626	88.9101
51	53.4745	89.8446
52	55.4156	90.7406
53	57.3858	91.5977
54	59.3848	92.4155
55	61.4123	93.1938
56	63.4680	93.9321
57	65.5518	94.6300
58	67.6632	95.2873
59	69.8022	95.9035
60	71.9684	96.4782
61	74.1616	97.0111
62	76.3816	97.5018
63	78.6281	97.9499
64	80.9008	98.3550
65	83.1995	98.7167
66	85.5241	99.0346
67	87.8742	99.3084
68	90.2496	99.5375
69	92.6501	99.7217
70	95.0755	99.8604
71	97.5256	99.9533
72	100.0000	100.0000

7 YEARS

#	REBATE	EARN
1	.0355	2.0915
2	.1061	4.1663
3	.2116	6.2244
4	.3517	8.2655
5	.5259	10.2895
6	.7340	12.2963
7	.9758	14.2856
8	1.2508	16.2574
9	1.5588	18.2114
10	1.8995	20.1475
11	2.2726	22.0656
12	2.6778	23.9654
13	3.1148	25.8468
14	3.5833	27.7097
15	4.0830	29.5538
16	4.6137	31.3790
17	5.1751	33.1852
18	5.7668	34.9721
19	6.3887	36.7395
20	7.0404	38.4874
21	7.7216	40.2155
22	8.4322	41.9235
23	9.1718	43.6115
24	9.9401	45.2791
25	10.7370	46.9262
26	11.5621	48.5525
27	12.4152	50.1580
28	13.2960	51.7423
29	14.2043	53.3054
30	15.1399	54.8470
31	16.1025	56.3669
32	17.0917	57.8649
33	18.1075	59.3409
34	19.1496	60.7946
35	20.2176	62.2257
36	21.3115	63.6342
37	22.4309	65.0198
38	23.5756	66.3823
39	24.7454	67.7215
40	25.9401	69.0371
41	27.1594	70.3290
42	28.4031	71.5969
43	29.6710	72.8406
44	30.9629	74.0599
45	32.2785	75.2546
46	33.6177	76.4244
47	34.9802	77.5691
48	36.3658	78.6885
49	37.7743	79.7824
50	39.2054	80.8504
51	40.6591	81.8925
52	42.1351	82.9083
53	43.6331	83.8975
54	45.1530	84.8601
55	46.6946	85.7957
56	48.2577	86.7040
57	49.8420	87.5848
58	51.4475	88.4379
59	53.0738	89.2630
60	54.7209	90.0599
61	56.3885	90.8282
62	58.0765	91.5678
63	59.7845	92.2784
64	61.5126	92.9596
65	63.2605	93.6113
66	65.0279	94.2332
67	66.8148	94.8249
68	68.6210	95.3863
69	70.4462	95.9170
70	72.2903	96.4167
71	74.1532	96.8852
72	76.0346	97.3222
73	77.9344	97.7274
74	79.8525	98.1005
75	81.7886	98.4412

7 YEARS (continued)

#	REBATE	EARN
75	81.7886	98.4412
76	83.7426	98.7492
77	85.7144	99.0242
78	87.7037	99.2660
79	89.7105	99.4741
80	91.7345	99.6483
81	93.7756	99.7884
82	95.8337	99.8939
83	97.9085	99.9645
84	100.0000	100.0000

8 YEARS

#	REBATE	EARN
1	.0281	1.8044
2	.0840	3.5971
3	.1675	5.3778
4	.2783	7.1465
5	.4162	8.9030
6	.5810	10.6473
7	.7723	12.3793
8	.9900	14.0988
9	1.2338	15.8057
10	1.5035	17.4999
11	1.7988	19.1813
12	2.1195	20.8498
13	2.4654	22.5052
14	2.8362	24.1475
15	3.2317	25.7764
16	3.6518	27.3919
17	4.0961	28.9940
18	4.5645	30.5823
19	5.0566	32.1569
20	5.5725	33.7175
21	6.1117	35.2641
22	6.6741	36.7966
23	7.2595	38.3147
24	7.8676	39.8184
25	8.4983	41.3076
26	9.1514	42.7821
27	9.8266	44.2417
28	10.5238	45.6864
29	11.2428	47.1159
30	11.9833	48.5303
31	12.7451	49.9292
32	13.5282	51.3126
33	14.3321	52.6804
34	15.1569	54.0324
35	16.0023	55.3684
36	16.8681	56.6883
37	17.7541	57.9919
38	18.6602	59.2792
39	19.5861	60.5499
40	20.5316	61.8040
41	21.4967	63.0411
42	22.4811	64.2613
43	23.4847	65.4643
44	24.5072	66.6500
45	25.5485	67.8182
46	26.6085	68.9688
47	27.6869	70.1016
48	28.7836	71.2164
49	29.8984	72.3131
50	31.0312	73.3915
51	32.1818	74.4515
52	33.3500	75.4928
53	34.5357	76.5153
54	35.7387	77.5189
55	36.9589	78.5033
56	38.1960	79.4684
57	39.4501	80.4139
58	40.7208	81.3398
59	42.0081	82.2459
60	43.3117	83.1319
61	44.6316	83.9977
62	45.9676	84.8431
63	47.3196	85.6679
64	48.6874	86.4718
65	50.0708	87.2549
66	51.4697	88.0167
67	52.8841	88.7572
68	54.3136	89.4762
69	55.7583	90.1734
70	57.2179	90.8486
71	58.6924	91.5017
72	60.1816	92.1324
73	61.6853	92.7405
74	63.2034	93.3259
75	64.7359	93.8883
76	66.2825	94.4275
77	67.8431	94.9434
78	69.4177	95.4355
79	71.0060	95.9039
80	72.6081	96.3482
81	74.2236	96.7683
82	75.8525	97.1638
83	77.4948	97.5346
84	79.1502	97.8805
85	80.8187	98.2012
86	82.5001	98.4965
87	84.1943	98.7662
88	85.9012	99.0100
89	87.6207	99.2277
90	89.3527	99.4190
91	91.0970	99.5838
92	92.8535	99.7217
93	94.6222	99.8325
94	96.4029	99.9160
95	98.1956	99.9719
96	100.0000	100.0000

9 YEARS

#	REBATE	EARN
1	.0229	1.5816
2	.0686	3.1545
3	.1367	4.7187
4	.2271	6.2742
5	.3397	7.8207
6	.4741	9.3583
7	.6303	10.8869
8	.8079	12.4063
9	1.0069	13.9166
10	1.2270	15.4175
11	1.4679	16.9091
12	1.7297	18.3912
13	2.0119	19.8638
14	2.3146	21.3267
15	2.6374	22.7799
16	2.9802	24.2234
17	3.3428	25.6569
18	3.7250	27.0804
19	4.1267	28.4938
20	4.5476	29.8971
21	4.9877	31.2901
22	5.4466	32.6727
23	5.9244	34.0449
24	6.4207	35.4065
25	6.9354	36.7574
26	7.4684	38.0977
27	8.0194	39.4270
28	8.5884	40.7454
29	9.1751	42.0528
30	9.7794	43.3491
31	10.4011	44.6340
32	11.0402	45.9077
33	11.6963	47.1698
34	12.3694	48.4204
35	13.0593	49.6594
36	13.7659	50.8866
37	14.4889	52.1018
38	15.2283	53.3051
39	15.9840	54.4963
40	16.7556	55.6753
41	17.5432	56.8420
42	18.3466	57.9962
43	19.1656	59.1378
44	20.0000	60.2668
45	20.8498	61.3831
46	21.7149	62.4864
47	22.5949	63.5767
48	23.4899	64.6538
49	24.3997	65.7177
50	25.3242	66.7683
51	26.2632	67.8053
52	27.2165	68.8287
53	28.1842	69.8383
54	29.1659	70.8341
55	30.1617	71.8158
56	31.1713	72.7835
57	32.1947	73.7368
58	33.2317	74.6758
59	34.2823	75.6003
60	35.3462	76.5101
61	36.4233	77.4051
62	37.5136	78.2851
63	38.6169	79.1502
64	39.7332	80.0000
65	40.8622	80.8344
66	42.0038	81.6534
67	43.1580	82.4568
68	44.3247	83.2444
69	45.5037	84.0160
70	46.6949	84.7717
71	47.8982	85.5111
72	49.1134	86.2341
73	50.3406	86.9407
74	51.5796	87.6306
75	52.8302	88.3037
76	54.0923	88.9598
77	55.3660	89.5989
78	56.6509	90.2206
79	57.9472	90.8249
80	59.2546	91.4116
81	60.5730	91.9806
82	61.9023	92.5316
83	63.2426	93.0646
84	64.5935	93.5793
85	65.9551	94.0756
86	67.3273	94.5534
87	68.7099	95.0123
88	70.1029	95.4524
89	71.5062	95.8733
90	72.9196	96.2750
91	74.3411	96.6572
92	75.7766	97.0198
93	77.2201	97.3626
94	78.6733	97.6854
95	80.1362	97.9881
96	81.6088	98.2703
97	83.0909	98.5321
98	84.5825	98.7730
99	86.0834	98.9931
100	87.5937	99.1921
101	89.1131	99.3697
102	90.6417	99.5259
103	92.1793	99.6603
104	93.7258	99.7729
105	95.2813	99.8633
106	96.8455	99.9314
107	98.4184	99.9771
108	100.0000	100.0000

10 YEARS

#	REBATE	EARN
1	.0192	1.4038
2	.0573	2.8011
3	.1143	4.1919
4	.1899	5.5761
5	.2840	6.9536
6	.3964	8.3244
7	.5269	9.6885
8	.6754	11.0457
9	.8417	12.3961
10	1.0257	13.7394
11	1.2271	15.0758
12	1.4459	16.4050
13	1.6819	17.7272
14	1.9349	19.0421
15	2.2047	20.3497
16	2.4913	21.6499
17	2.7944	22.9428
18	3.1139	24.2281
19	3.4497	25.5059
20	3.8016	26.7761
21	4.1694	28.0386
22	4.5531	29.2933
23	4.9525	30.5402
24	5.3674	31.7792
25	5.7976	33.0102
26	6.2432	34.2331
27	6.7038	35.4479
28	7.1794	36.6545
29	7.6699	37.8529
30	8.1751	39.0429
31	8.6948	40.2244
32	9.2290	41.3975
33	9.7775	42.5620
34	10.3402	43.7178
35	10.9169	44.8648
36	11.5076	46.0031
37	12.1120	47.1324
38	12.7301	48.2528
39	13.3618	49.3640
40	14.0069	50.4662
41	14.6652	51.5591
42	15.3368	52.6427
43	16.0214	53.7169
44	16.7190	54.7815
45	17.4294	55.8367
46	18.1525	56.8821
47	18.8882	57.9178
48	19.6364	58.9436
49	20.3969	59.9596
50	21.1697	60.9654
51	21.9547	61.9612
52	22.7516	62.9468
53	23.5605	63.9221
54	24.3812	64.8869
55	25.2136	65.8413
56	26.0577	66.7851
57	26.9132	67.7182
58	27.7801	68.6405
59	28.6582	69.5519
60	29.5476	70.4524
61	30.4481	71.3418
62	31.3595	72.2199
63	32.2818	73.0868
64	33.2149	73.9423
65	34.1587	74.7864
66	35.1131	75.6188
67	36.0779	76.4395
68	37.0532	77.2484
69	38.0388	78.0453
70	39.0346	78.8303
71	40.0404	79.6031
72	41.0564	80.3636
73	42.0822	81.1118
74	43.1179	81.8475
75	44.1633	82.5706
76	45.2185	83.2810
77	46.2831	83.9786
78	47.3573	84.6632
79	48.4409	85.3348
80	49.5338	85.9931
81	50.6360	86.6382
82	51.7472	87.2699
83	52.8676	87.8880
84	53.9969	88.4924
85	55.1352	89.0831
86	56.2822	89.6598
87	57.4380	90.2225
88	58.6025	90.7710
89	59.7756	91.3052
90	60.9571	91.8249
91	62.1471	92.3301
92	63.3455	92.8206
93	64.5521	93.2962
94	65.7669	93.7568
95	66.9898	94.2024
96	68.2208	94.6326
97	69.4598	95.0475
98	70.7067	95.4469
99	71.9614	95.8306
100	73.2239	96.1984
101	74.4941	96.5503
102	75.7719	96.8861
103	77.0572	97.2056
104	78.3501	97.5087
105	79.6503	97.7953
106	80.9579	98.0651
107	82.2728	98.3181
108	83.5950	98.5541
109	84.9242	98.7729
110	86.2606	98.9743
111	87.6039	99.1583
112	88.9543	99.3246
113	90.3115	99.4731
114	91.6756	99.6036
115	93.0464	99.7160
116	94.4239	99.8101
117	95.8081	99.8857
118	97.1989	99.9427
119	98.5962	99.9808
120	100.0000	100.0000

1 YEAR

#	REBATE	EARN
1	1.3262	15.1259
2	3.9662	29.0550
3	7.9079	41.7761
4	13.1392	53.2778
5	19.6481	63.5487
6	27.4227	72.5773
7	36.4513	80.3519
8	46.7222	86.8608
9	58.2239	92.0921
10	70.9450	96.0338
11	84.8741	98.6738
12	100.0000	100.0000

2 YEARS

#	REBATE	EARN
1	.3575	7.7239
2	1.0693	15.1594
3	2.1320	22.3037
4	3.5424	29.1540
5	5.2972	35.7077
6	7.3932	41.9620
7	9.8273	47.9140
8	12.5964	53.5608
9	15.6973	58.8998
10	19.1269	63.9279
11	22.8822	68.6422
12	26.9602	73.0398
13	31.3578	77.1178
14	36.0721	80.8731
15	41.1002	84.3027
16	46.4392	87.4036
17	52.0860	90.1727
18	58.0380	92.6068
19	64.2923	94.7028
20	70.8460	96.4576
21	77.6963	97.8680
22	84.8406	98.9307
23	92.2761	99.6425
24	100.0000	100.0000

3 YEARS

#	REBATE	EARN
1	.1669	5.1269
2	.4991	10.1333
3	.9952	15.0183
4	1.6535	19.7806
5	2.4726	24.4191
6	3.4509	28.9326
7	4.5871	33.3200
8	5.8796	37.5800
9	7.3270	41.7115
10	8.9279	45.7134
11	10.6807	49.5842
12	12.5842	53.3230
13	14.6369	56.9283
14	16.8374	60.3989
15	19.1844	63.7337
16	21.6764	66.9312
17	24.3122	69.9903
18	27.0904	72.9096
19	30.0097	75.6878
20	33.0688	78.3236
21	36.2663	80.8156
22	39.6011	83.1626
23	43.0717	85.3631
24	46.6770	87.4158
25	50.4158	89.3193
26	54.2866	91.0721
27	58.2885	92.6730
28	62.4200	94.1204
29	66.6800	95.4129
30	71.0674	96.5491
31	75.5809	97.5274
32	80.2194	98.3465
33	84.9817	99.0048
34	89.8667	99.5009
35	94.8731	99.8331
36	100.0000	100.0000

4 YEARS

#	REBATE	EARN
1	.0979	3.8045
2	.2927	7.5458
3	.5836	11.2234
4	.9697	14.8368
5	1.4500	18.3852
6	2.0238	21.8680
7	2.6901	25.2848
8	3.4481	28.6347
9	4.2970	31.9173
10	5.2358	35.1319
11	6.2638	38.2778
12	7.3801	41.3545
13	8.5839	44.3611
14	9.8744	47.2972
15	11.2508	50.1620
16	12.7123	52.9549
17	14.2580	55.6751
18	15.8873	58.3221
19	17.5994	60.8951
20	19.3934	63.3935
21	21.2686	65.8164
22	23.2243	68.1633
23	25.2597	70.4334
24	27.3740	72.6260
25	29.5666	74.7403
26	31.8367	76.7757
27	34.1836	78.7314
28	36.6065	80.6066
29	39.1049	82.4006
30	41.6779	84.1127
31	44.3249	85.7420
32	47.0451	87.2877
33	49.8380	88.7492
34	52.7028	90.1256
35	55.6389	91.4161
36	58.6455	92.6199
37	61.7222	93.7362
38	64.8681	94.7642
39	68.0827	95.7030
40	71.3653	96.5519
41	74.7152	97.3099
42	78.1320	97.9762
43	81.6148	98.5500
44	85.1632	99.0303
45	88.7766	99.4164
46	92.4542	99.7073
47	96.1955	99.9021
48	100.0000	100.0000

5 YEARS

#	REBATE	EARN
1	.0651	3.0044
2	.1947	5.9713
3	.3881	8.9004
4	.6449	11.7911
5	.9643	14.6433
6	1.3459	17.4566
7	1.7890	20.2304
8	2.2931	22.9647
9	2.8576	25.6588
10	3.4820	28.3125
11	4.1656	30.9254
12	4.9080	33.4970
13	5.7085	36.0271
14	6.5668	38.5152
15	7.4821	40.9610
16	8.4540	43.3639
17	9.4820	45.7237
18	10.5655	48.0399
19	11.7041	50.3122
20	12.8972	52.5400
21	14.1442	54.7230
22	15.4448	56.8608
23	16.7984	58.9529
24	18.2045	60.9990
25	19.6627	62.9985
26	21.1723	64.9511
27	22.7331	66.8563
28	24.3444	68.7136
29	26.0059	70.5227
30	27.7170	72.2830
31	29.4773	73.9941
32	31.2864	75.6556
33	33.1437	77.2669
34	35.0489	78.8277
35	37.0015	80.3373
36	39.0010	81.7955
37	41.0471	83.2016
38	43.1392	84.5552
39	45.2770	85.8558
40	47.4600	87.1028
41	49.6878	88.2959
42	51.9601	89.4345
43	54.2763	90.5180
44	56.6361	91.5460
45	59.0390	92.5179
46	61.4848	93.4332
47	63.9729	94.2915
48	66.5030	95.0920
49	69.0746	95.8344
50	71.6875	96.5180
51	74.3412	97.1424
52	77.0353	97.7069
53	79.7696	98.2110
54	82.5434	98.6541
55	85.3567	99.0357
56	88.2089	99.3551
57	91.0996	99.6119
58	94.0287	99.8053
59	96.9956	99.9349
60	100.0000	100.0000

6 YEARS

#	REBATE	EARN
1	.0469	2.4691
2	.1402	4.9141
3	.2795	7.3346
4	.4644	9.7306
5	.6945	12.1016
6	.9693	14.4476
7	1.2884	16.7683
8	1.6514	19.0634
9	2.0580	21.3327
10	2.5076	23.5760
11	2.9999	25.7930
12	3.5346	27.9835
13	4.1111	30.1472
14	4.7292	32.2838
15	5.3883	34.3932
16	6.0883	36.4751
17	6.8286	38.5291
18	7.6089	40.5551
19	8.4289	42.5528
20	9.2881	44.5218
21	10.1862	46.4621
22	11.1228	48.3732
23	12.0976	50.2549
24	13.1103	52.1069
25	14.1604	53.9290
26	15.2476	55.7208
27	16.3716	57.4822
28	17.5320	59.2127
29	18.7285	60.9121
30	19.9608	62.5802
31	21.2285	64.2166
32	22.5314	65.8210
33	23.8690	67.3931
34	25.2410	68.9327
35	26.6472	70.4393
36	28.0872	71.9128
37	29.5607	73.3528
38	31.0673	74.7590
39	32.6069	76.1310
40	34.1790	77.4686
41	35.7834	78.7715
42	37.4198	80.0392
43	39.0879	81.2715
44	40.7873	82.4680
45	42.5178	83.6284
46	44.2792	84.7524
47	46.0710	85.8396
48	47.8931	86.8897
49	49.7451	87.9024
50	51.6268	88.8772
51	53.5379	89.8138
52	55.4782	90.7119
53	57.4472	91.5711
54	59.4449	92.3911
55	61.4709	93.1714
56	63.5249	93.9117
57	65.6068	94.6117
58	67.7162	95.2708
59	69.8528	95.8889
60	72.0165	96.4654
61	74.2070	97.0001
62	76.4240	97.4924
63	78.6673	97.9420
64	80.9366	98.3486
65	83.2317	98.7116
66	85.5524	99.0307
67	87.8984	99.3055
68	90.2694	99.5356
69	92.6654	99.7205
70	95.0859	99.8598
71	97.5309	99.9531
72	100.0000	100.0000

7 YEARS

#	REBATE	EARN
1	.0357	2.0863
2	.1067	4.1563
3	.2127	6.2096
4	.3533	8.2461
5	.5284	10.2658
6	.7375	12.2684
7	.9803	14.2538
8	1.2565	16.2218
9	1.5658	18.1722
10	1.9079	20.1049
11	2.2824	22.0198
12	2.6892	23.9166
13	3.1279	25.7952
14	3.5981	27.6554
15	4.0996	29.4970
16	4.6322	31.3199
17	5.1954	33.1239
18	5.7891	34.9088
19	6.4130	36.6745
20	7.0667	38.4207
21	7.7500	40.1473
22	8.4626	41.8540
23	9.2043	43.5408
24	9.9747	45.2074
25	10.7737	46.8536
26	11.6009	48.4792
27	12.4561	50.0841
28	13.3390	51.6681
29	14.2493	53.2308
30	15.1869	54.7723
31	16.1514	56.2922
32	17.1426	57.7903
33	18.1603	59.2665
34	19.2042	60.7205
35	20.2741	62.1522
36	21.3697	63.5613
37	22.4908	64.9476
38	23.6371	66.3109
39	24.8084	67.6510
40	26.0046	68.9676
41	27.2253	70.2606
42	28.4703	71.5297
43	29.7394	72.7747
44	31.0324	73.9954
45	32.3490	75.1916
46	33.6891	76.3629
47	35.0524	77.5092
48	36.4387	78.6303
49	37.8478	79.7259
50	39.2795	80.7958
51	40.7335	81.8397
52	42.2097	82.8574
53	43.7078	83.8486
54	45.2277	84.8131
55	46.7692	85.7507
56	48.3319	86.6610
57	49.9159	87.5439
58	51.5208	88.3991
59	53.1464	89.2263
60	54.7926	90.0253
61	56.4592	90.7957
62	58.1460	91.5374
63	59.8527	92.2500
64	61.5793	92.9333
65	63.3255	93.5870
66	65.0912	94.2109
67	66.8761	94.8046
68	68.6801	95.3678
69	70.5030	95.9004
70	72.3446	96.4019
71	74.2048	96.8721
72	76.0834	97.3108
73	77.9802	97.7176
74	79.8951	98.0921
75	81.8278	98.4342

#	REBATE	EARN
75	81.8278	98.4342
76	83.7782	98.7435
77	85.7462	99.0197
78	87.7316	99.2625
79	89.7342	99.4716
80	91.7539	99.6467
81	93.7904	99.7873
82	95.8437	99.8933
83	97.9137	99.9643
84	100.0000	100.0000

8 YEARS

#	REBATE	EARN
1	.0282	1.7995
2	.0845	3.5873
3	.1684	5.3634
4	.2798	7.1276
5	.4185	8.8799
6	.5841	10.6201
7	.7763	12.3481
8	.9951	14.0637
9	1.2401	15.7670
10	1.5110	17.4577
11	1.8077	19.1357
12	2.1298	20.8010
13	2.4772	22.4534
14	2.8497	24.0927
15	3.2469	25.7189
16	3.6686	27.3318
17	4.1147	28.9314
18	4.5849	30.5174
19	5.0790	32.0898
20	5.5968	33.6485
21	6.1379	35.1932
22	6.7023	36.7239
23	7.2897	38.2404
24	7.8999	39.7427
25	8.5327	41.2305
26	9.1878	42.7038
27	9.8651	44.1623
28	10.5643	45.6061
29	11.2853	47.0348
30	12.0279	48.4484
31	12.7918	49.8468
32	13.5768	51.2298
33	14.3828	52.5972
34	15.2096	53.9490
35	16.0569	55.2849
36	16.9246	56.6048
37	17.8125	57.9086
38	18.7203	59.1961
39	19.6480	60.4671
40	20.5954	61.7216
41	21.5621	62.9593
42	22.5482	64.1801
43	23.5533	65.3838
44	24.5773	66.5703
45	25.6201	67.7395
46	26.6814	68.8911
47	27.7612	70.0249
48	28.8591	71.1409
49	29.9751	72.2388
50	31.1089	73.3186
51	32.2605	74.3799
52	33.4297	75.4227
53	34.6162	76.4467
54	35.8199	77.4518
55	37.0407	78.4379
56	38.2784	79.4046
57	39.5329	80.3520
58	40.8039	81.2797
59	42.0914	82.1875
60	43.3952	83.0754
61	44.7151	83.9431
62	46.0510	84.7904
63	47.4028	85.6172
64	48.7702	86.4232
65	50.1532	87.2082
66	51.5516	87.9721
67	52.9652	88.7147
68	54.3939	89.4357
69	55.8377	90.1349
70	57.2962	90.8122
71	58.7695	91.4673
72	60.2573	92.1001
73	61.7596	92.7103
74	63.2761	93.2977
75	64.8068	93.8621
76	66.3515	94.4032
77	67.9102	94.9210
78	69.4826	95.4151
79	71.0686	95.8853
80	72.6682	96.3314
81	74.2811	96.7531
82	75.9073	97.1503
83	77.5466	97.5228
84	79.1990	97.8702
85	80.8643	98.1923
86	82.5423	98.4890
87	84.2330	98.7599
88	85.9363	99.0049
89	87.6519	99.2237
90	89.3799	99.4159
91	91.1201	99.5815
92	92.8724	99.7202
93	94.6366	99.8316
94	96.4127	99.9155
95	98.2005	99.9718
96	100.0000	100.0000

9 YEARS

#	REBATE	EARN
1	.0231	1.5768
2	.0690	3.1451
3	.1375	4.7048
4	.2285	6.2559
5	.3417	7.7982
6	.4769	9.3318
7	.6339	10.8564
8	.8126	12.3720
9	1.0126	13.8785
10	1.2338	15.3759
11	1.4761	16.8641
12	1.7392	18.3429
13	2.0228	19.8123
14	2.3270	21.2722
15	2.6513	22.7225
16	2.9957	24.1631
17	3.3600	25.5940
18	3.7439	27.0149
19	4.1474	28.4260
20	4.5701	29.8269
21	5.0121	31.2177
22	5.4729	32.5983
23	5.9526	33.9686
24	6.4508	35.3284
25	6.9675	36.6776
26	7.5025	38.0163
27	8.0555	39.3442
28	8.6265	40.6613
29	9.2153	41.9674
30	9.8216	43.2625
31	10.4454	44.5465
32	11.0864	45.8193
33	11.7446	47.0806
34	12.4197	48.3306
35	13.1116	49.5689
36	13.8201	50.7956
37	14.5451	52.0105
38	15.2865	53.2135
39	16.0440	54.4046
40	16.8176	55.5835
41	17.6070	56.7501
42	18.4122	57.9045
43	19.2330	59.0464
44	20.0691	60.1757
45	20.9206	61.2923
46	21.7873	62.3961
47	22.6690	63.4869
48	23.5655	64.5647
49	24.4768	65.6294
50	25.4027	66.6807
51	26.3430	67.7186
52	27.2977	68.7429
53	28.2666	69.7536
54	29.2495	70.7505
55	30.2464	71.7334
56	31.2571	72.7023
57	32.2814	73.6570
58	33.3193	74.5973
59	34.3706	75.5232
60	35.4353	76.4345
61	36.5131	77.3310
62	37.6039	78.2127
63	38.7077	79.0794
64	39.8243	79.9309
65	40.9536	80.7670
66	42.0955	81.5878
67	43.2499	82.3930
68	44.4165	83.1824
69	45.5954	83.9560
70	46.7865	84.7135
71	47.9895	85.4549
72	49.2044	86.1799
73	50.4311	86.8884
74	51.6694	87.5803
75	52.9194	88.2554
76	54.1807	88.9136
77	55.4535	89.5546
78	56.7375	90.1784
79	58.0326	90.7847
80	59.3387	91.3735
81	60.6558	91.9445
82	61.9837	92.4975
83	63.3224	93.0325
84	64.6716	93.5492
85	66.0314	94.0474
86	67.4017	94.5271
87	68.7823	94.9879
88	70.1731	95.4299
89	71.5740	95.8526
90	72.9851	96.2561
91	74.4060	96.6400
92	75.8369	97.0043
93	77.2775	97.3487
94	78.7278	97.6730
95	80.1877	97.9772
96	81.6571	98.2608
97	83.1359	98.5239
98	84.6241	98.7662
99	86.1215	98.9874
100	87.6280	99.1874
101	89.1436	99.3661
102	90.6682	99.5231
103	92.2018	99.6583
104	93.7441	99.7715
105	95.2952	99.8625
106	96.8549	99.9310
107	98.4232	99.9769
108	100.0000	100.0000

10 YEARS

#	REBATE	EARN
1	.0193	1.3992
2	.0577	2.7920
3	.1150	4.1785
4	.1911	5.5584
5	.2858	6.9318
6	.3989	8.2987
7	.5302	9.6588
8	.6797	11.0123
9	.8470	12.3589
10	1.0320	13.6987
11	1.2346	15.0316
12	1.4547	16.3575
13	1.6920	17.6764
14	1.9463	18.9882
15	2.2176	20.2928
16	2.5057	21.5901
17	2.8104	22.8802
18	3.1315	24.1629
19	3.4690	25.4381
20	3.8226	26.7058
21	4.1922	27.9659
22	4.5777	29.2183
23	4.9789	30.4631
24	5.3956	31.7000
25	5.8278	32.9290
26	6.2753	34.1501
27	6.7378	35.3632
28	7.2154	36.5682
29	7.7079	37.7650
30	8.2150	38.9535
31	8.7368	40.1337
32	9.2730	41.3055
33	9.8235	42.4688
34	10.3881	43.6236
35	10.9668	44.7697
36	11.5595	45.9071
37	12.1659	47.0356
38	12.7860	48.1553
39	13.4196	49.2660
40	14.0666	50.3676
41	14.7269	51.4601
42	15.4004	52.5434
43	16.0869	53.6173
44	16.7863	54.6819
45	17.4985	55.7369
46	18.2234	56.7824
47	18.9609	57.8182
48	19.7108	58.8442
49	20.4730	59.8604
50	21.2474	60.8667
51	22.0339	61.8629
52	22.8325	62.8489
53	23.6428	63.8248
54	24.4650	64.7903
55	25.2988	65.7454
56	26.1442	66.6899
57	27.0010	67.6239
58	27.8691	68.5471
59	28.7485	69.4596
60	29.6389	70.3611
61	30.5404	71.2515
62	31.4529	72.1309
63	32.3761	72.9990
64	33.3101	73.8558
65	34.2546	74.7012
66	35.2097	75.5350
67	36.1752	76.3572
68	37.1511	77.1675
69	38.1371	77.9661
70	39.1333	78.7526
71	40.1396	79.5270
72	41.1558	80.2892
73	42.1818	81.0391
74	43.2176	81.7766
75	44.2631	82.5015
76	45.3181	83.2137
77	46.3827	83.9131
78	47.4566	84.5996
79	48.5399	85.2731
80	49.6324	85.9334
81	50.7340	86.5804
82	51.8447	87.2140
83	52.9644	87.8341
84	54.0929	88.4405
85	55.2303	89.0332
86	56.3764	89.6119
87	57.5312	90.1765
88	58.6945	90.7270
89	59.8663	91.2632
90	61.0465	91.7850
91	62.2350	92.2921
92	63.4318	92.7846
93	64.6368	93.2622
94	65.8499	93.7247
95	67.0710	94.1722
96	68.3000	94.6044
97	69.5369	95.0211
98	70.7817	95.4223
99	72.0341	95.8078
100	73.2942	96.1774
101	74.5619	96.5310
102	75.8371	96.8685
103	77.1198	97.1896
104	78.4099	97.4943
105	79.7072	97.7824
106	81.0118	98.0537
107	82.3236	98.3080
108	83.6425	98.5453
109	84.9684	98.7654
110	86.3013	98.9680
111	87.6411	99.1530
112	88.9877	99.3203
113	90.3412	99.4698
114	91.7013	99.6011
115	93.0682	99.7142
116	94.4416	99.8089
117	95.8215	99.8850
118	97.2080	99.9423
119	98.6008	99.9807
120	100.0000	100.0000

1 YEAR

#	REBATE	EARN
1	1.3272	15.1203
2	3.9689	29.0456
3	7.9127	41.7645
4	13.1463	53.2653
5	19.6573	63.5365
6	27.4337	72.5663
7	36.4635	80.3427
8	46.7347	86.8537
9	58.2355	92.0873
10	70.9544	96.0311
11	84.8797	98.6728
12	100.0000	100.0000

2 YEARS

#	REBATE	EARN
1	.3581	7.7181
2	1.0709	15.1486
3	2.1349	22.2888
4	3.5470	29.1359
5	5.3038	35.6871
6	7.4019	41.9396
7	9.8383	47.8905
8	12.6096	53.5369
9	15.7126	58.8759
10	19.1443	63.9045
11	22.9015	68.6198
12	26.9812	73.0188
13	31.3802	77.0985
14	36.0955	80.8557
15	41.1241	84.2874
16	46.4631	87.3904
17	52.1095	90.1617
18	58.0604	92.5981
19	64.3129	94.6962
20	70.8641	96.4530
21	77.7112	97.8651
22	84.8514	98.9291
23	92.2819	99.6419
24	100.0000	100.0000

3 YEARS

#	REBATE	EARN
1	.1673	5.1210
2	.5002	10.1223
3	.9973	15.0026
4	1.6569	19.7608
5	2.4775	24.3957
6	3.4576	28.9062
7	4.5957	33.2911
8	5.8902	37.5490
9	7.3397	41.6790
10	8.9427	45.6796
11	10.6978	49.5497
12	12.6034	53.2880
13	14.6583	56.8933
14	16.8609	60.3642
15	19.2099	63.6995
16	21.7039	66.8980
17	24.3414	69.9582
18	27.1212	72.8788
19	30.0418	75.6586
20	33.1020	78.2961
21	36.3005	80.7901
22	39.6358	83.1391
23	43.1067	85.3417
24	46.7120	87.3966
25	50.4503	89.3022
26	54.3204	91.0573
27	58.3210	92.6603
28	62.4510	94.1098
29	66.7089	95.4043
30	71.0938	96.5424
31	75.6043	97.5225
32	80.2392	98.3431
33	84.9974	99.0027
34	89.8777	99.4998
35	94.8790	99.8327
36	100.0000	100.0000

4 YEARS

#	REBATE	EARN
1	.0982	3.7988
2	.2936	7.5349
3	.5853	11.2077
4	.9724	14.8166
5	1.4540	18.3610
6	2.0292	21.8402
7	2.6971	25.2537
8	3.4568	28.6007
9	4.3075	31.8808
10	5.2483	35.0931
11	6.2783	38.2372
12	7.3967	41.3122
13	8.6026	44.3177
14	9.8953	47.2528
15	11.2739	50.1169
16	12.7375	52.9094
17	14.2854	55.6295
18	15.9168	58.2766
19	17.6309	60.8500
20	19.4269	63.3489
21	21.3039	65.7727
22	23.2614	68.1206
23	25.2984	70.3918
24	27.4142	72.5858
25	29.6082	74.7016
26	31.8794	76.7386
27	34.2273	78.6961
28	36.6511	80.5731
29	39.1500	82.3691
30	41.7234	84.0832
31	44.3705	85.7146
32	47.0906	87.2625
33	49.8831	88.7261
34	52.7472	90.1047
35	55.6823	91.3974
36	58.6878	92.6033
37	61.7628	93.7217
38	64.9069	94.7517
39	68.1192	95.6925
40	71.3993	96.5432
41	74.7463	97.3029
42	78.1598	97.9708
43	81.6390	98.5460
44	85.1834	99.0276
45	88.7923	99.4147
46	92.4651	99.7064
47	96.2012	99.9018
48	100.0000	100.0000

5 YEARS

#	REBATE	EARN
1	.0653	2.9989
2	.1954	5.9607
3	.3895	8.8848
4	.6471	11.7711
5	.9676	14.6190
6	1.3504	17.4283
7	1.7949	20.1985
8	2.3005	22.9294
9	2.8666	25.6204
10	3.4927	28.2713
11	4.1781	30.8816
12	4.9224	33.4510
13	5.7250	35.9791
14	6.5852	38.4654
15	7.5026	40.9096
16	8.4767	43.3113
17	9.5068	45.6701
18	10.5925	47.9854
19	11.7332	50.2571
20	12.9284	52.4845
21	14.1776	54.6673
22	15.4802	56.8051
23	16.8358	58.8975
24	18.2439	60.9439
25	19.7039	62.9440
26	21.2154	64.8973
27	22.7779	66.8033
28	24.3909	68.6617
29	26.0539	70.4719
30	27.7665	72.2335
31	29.5281	73.9461
32	31.3383	75.6091
33	33.1967	77.2221
34	35.1027	78.7846
35	37.0560	80.2961
36	39.0561	81.7561
37	41.1025	83.1642
38	43.1949	84.5198
39	45.3327	85.8224
40	47.5155	87.0716
41	49.7429	88.2668
42	52.0146	89.4075
43	54.3299	90.4932
44	56.6887	91.5233
45	59.0904	92.4974
46	61.5346	93.4148
47	64.0209	94.2750
48	66.5490	95.0776
49	69.1184	95.8219
50	71.7287	96.5073
51	74.3796	97.1334
52	77.0706	97.6995
53	79.8015	98.2051
54	82.5717	98.6496
55	85.3810	99.0324
56	88.2289	99.3529
57	91.1152	99.6105
58	94.0393	99.8046
59	97.0011	99.9347
60	100.0000	100.0000

6 YEARS

#	REBATE	EARN
1	.0471	2.4638
2	.1408	4.9037
3	.2807	7.3195
4	.4663	9.7108
5	.6973	12.0776
6	.9732	14.4195
7	1.2935	16.7363
8	1.6578	19.0278
9	2.0658	21.2937
10	2.5170	23.5339
11	3.0109	25.7479
12	3.5473	27.9356
13	4.1257	30.0968
14	4.7456	32.2312
15	5.4067	34.3384
16	6.1087	36.4184
17	6.8510	38.4707
18	7.6334	40.4952
19	8.4554	42.4916
20	9.3167	44.4595
21	10.2170	46.3988
22	11.1557	48.3092
23	12.1326	50.1903
24	13.1473	52.0419
25	14.1995	53.8637
26	15.2888	55.6555
27	16.4148	57.4169
28	17.5772	59.1477
29	18.7756	60.8475
30	20.0097	62.5160
31	21.2792	64.1531
32	22.5837	65.7583
33	23.9230	67.3313
34	25.2966	68.8719
35	26.7042	70.3797
36	28.1455	71.8545
37	29.6203	73.2958
38	31.1281	74.7034
39	32.6687	76.0770
40	34.2417	77.4163
41	35.8469	78.7208
42	37.4840	79.9903
43	39.1525	81.2244
44	40.8523	82.4228
45	42.5831	83.5852
46	44.3445	84.7112
47	46.1363	85.8005
48	47.9581	86.8527
49	49.8097	87.8674
50	51.6908	88.8443
51	53.6012	89.7830
52	55.5405	90.6833
53	57.5084	91.5446
54	59.5048	92.3666
55	61.5293	93.1490
56	63.5816	93.8913
57	65.6616	94.5933
58	67.7688	95.2544
59	69.9032	95.8743
60	72.0644	96.4527
61	74.2521	96.9891
62	76.4661	97.4830
63	78.7063	97.9342
64	80.9722	98.3422
65	83.2637	98.7065
66	85.5805	99.0268
67	87.9224	99.3027
68	90.2892	99.5337
69	92.6805	99.7193
70	95.0963	99.8592
71	97.5362	99.9529
72	100.0000	100.0000

7 YEARS

#	REBATE	EARN
1	.0358	2.0812
2	.1072	4.1462
3	.2137	6.1948
4	.3550	8.2269
5	.5309	10.2422
6	.7409	12.2407
7	.9847	14.2221
8	1.2621	16.1864
9	1.5727	18.1332
10	1.9162	20.0626
11	2.2923	21.9742
12	2.7006	23.8680
13	3.1409	25.7438
14	3.6129	27.6013
15	4.1162	29.4405
16	4.6506	31.2611
17	5.2158	33.0629
18	5.8115	34.8459
19	6.4373	36.6097
20	7.0930	38.3543
21	7.7784	40.0794
22	8.4931	41.7848
23	9.2368	43.4704
24	10.0093	45.1360
25	10.8104	46.7813
26	11.6396	48.4063
27	12.4969	50.0106
28	13.3818	51.5941
29	14.2942	53.1566
30	15.2338	54.6978
31	16.2003	56.2177
32	17.1935	57.7160
33	18.2130	59.1924
34	19.2588	60.6468
35	20.3304	62.0789
36	21.4277	63.4886
37	22.5505	64.8756
38	23.6984	66.2397
39	24.8713	67.5807
40	26.0689	68.8983
41	27.2910	70.1924
42	28.5373	71.4627
43	29.8076	72.7090
44	31.1017	73.9311
45	32.4193	75.1287
46	33.7603	76.3016
47	35.1244	77.4495
48	36.5114	78.5723
49	37.9211	79.6696
50	39.3532	80.7412
51	40.8076	81.7870
52	42.2840	82.8065
53	43.7823	83.7997
54	45.3022	84.7662
55	46.8434	85.7058
56	48.4059	86.6182
57	49.9894	87.5031
58	51.5937	88.3604
59	53.2187	89.1896
60	54.8640	89.9907
61	56.5296	90.7632
62	58.2152	91.5069
63	59.9206	92.2216
64	61.6457	92.9070
65	63.3903	93.5627
66	65.1541	94.1885
67	66.9371	94.7842
68	68.7389	95.3494
69	70.5595	95.8838
70	72.3987	96.3871
71	74.2562	96.8591
72	76.1320	97.2994
73	78.0258	97.7077
74	79.9374	98.0838
75	81.8668	98.4273

#	REBATE	EARN
75	81.8668	98.4273
76	83.8136	98.7379
77	85.7779	99.0153
78	87.7593	99.2591
79	89.7578	99.4691
80	91.7731	99.6450
81	93.8052	99.7863
82	95.8538	99.8928
83	97.9188	99.9642
84	100.0000	100.0000

8 YEARS

#	REBATE	EARN
1	.0284	1.7946
2	.0849	3.5777
3	.1693	5.3492
4	.2814	7.1089
5	.4207	8.8569
6	.5871	10.5930
7	.7804	12.3170
8	1.0002	14.0289
9	1.2463	15.7285
10	1.5186	17.4157
11	1.8166	19.0904
12	2.1402	20.7525
13	2.4891	22.4018
14	2.8631	24.0383
15	3.2620	25.6618
16	3.6855	27.2721
17	4.1334	28.8692
18	4.6054	30.4529
19	5.1014	32.0232
20	5.6210	33.5798
21	6.1642	35.1226
22	6.7305	36.6516
23	7.3199	38.1665
24	7.9321	39.6673
25	8.5669	41.1538
26	9.2241	42.6259
27	9.9035	44.0833
28	10.6048	45.5261
29	11.3278	46.9540
30	12.0724	48.3670
31	12.8383	49.7648
32	13.6254	51.1473
33	14.4334	52.5144
34	15.2621	53.8659
35	16.1114	55.2017
36	16.9810	56.5216
37	17.8707	57.8255
38	18.7804	59.1132
39	19.7099	60.3846
40	20.6590	61.6395
41	21.6274	62.8777
42	22.6151	64.0992
43	23.6218	65.3036
44	24.6473	66.4909
45	25.6915	67.6610
46	26.7542	68.8135
47	27.8352	69.9485
48	28.9344	71.0656
49	30.0515	72.1648
50	31.1865	73.2458
51	32.3390	74.3085
52	33.5091	75.3527
53	34.6964	76.3782
54	35.9008	77.3849
55	37.1223	78.3726
56	38.3605	79.3410
57	39.6154	80.2901
58	40.8868	81.2196
59	42.1745	82.1293
60	43.4784	83.0190
61	44.7983	83.8886
62	46.1341	84.7379
63	47.4856	85.5666
64	48.8527	86.3746
65	50.2352	87.1617
66	51.6330	87.9276
67	53.0460	88.6722
68	54.4739	89.3952
69	55.9167	90.0965
70	57.3741	90.7759
71	58.8462	91.4331
72	60.3327	92.0679
73	61.8335	92.6801
74	63.3484	93.2695
75	64.8774	93.8358
76	66.4202	94.3790
77	67.9768	94.8986
78	69.5471	95.3946
79	71.1308	95.8666
80	72.7279	96.3145
81	74.3382	96.7380
82	75.9617	97.1369
83	77.5982	97.5109
84	79.2475	97.8598
85	80.9096	98.1834
86	82.5843	98.4814
87	84.2715	98.7537
88	85.9711	98.9998
89	87.6830	99.2196
90	89.4070	99.4129
91	91.1431	99.5793
92	92.8911	99.7186
93	94.6508	99.8307
94	96.4223	99.9151
95	98.2054	99.9716
96	100.0000	100.0000

9 YEARS

#	REBATE	EARN
1	.0232	1.5721
2	.0694	3.1358
3	.1384	4.6911
4	.2299	6.2378
5	.3437	7.7760
6	.4797	9.3054
7	.6376	10.8261
8	.8172	12.3379
9	1.0183	13.8408
10	1.2407	15.3347
11	1.4842	16.8194
12	1.7486	18.2949
13	2.0337	19.7612
14	2.3393	21.2181
15	2.6652	22.6655
16	3.0113	24.1033
17	3.3772	25.5315
18	3.7629	26.9500
19	4.1681	28.3586
20	4.5927	29.7573
21	5.0364	31.1459
22	5.4992	32.5244
23	5.9808	33.8928
24	6.4810	35.2508
25	6.9996	36.5984
26	7.5366	37.9354
27	8.0916	39.2619
28	8.6646	40.5776
29	9.2554	41.8825
30	9.8638	43.1765
31	10.4896	44.4595
32	11.1326	45.7313
33	11.7928	46.9919
34	12.4699	48.2411
35	13.1638	49.4789
36	13.8743	50.7051
37	14.6013	51.9197
38	15.3446	53.1224
39	16.1040	54.3133
40	16.8794	55.4921
41	17.6707	56.6588
42	18.4777	57.8132
43	19.3002	58.9553
44	20.1381	60.0849
45	20.9913	61.2019
46	21.8596	62.3061
47	22.7428	63.3975
48	23.6409	64.4760
49	24.5536	65.5413
50	25.4809	66.5934
51	26.4226	67.6322
52	27.3786	68.6575
53	28.3487	69.6692
54	29.3328	70.6672
55	30.3308	71.6513
56	31.3425	72.6214
57	32.3678	73.5774
58	33.4066	74.5191
59	34.4587	75.4464
60	35.5240	76.3591
61	36.6025	77.2572
62	37.6939	78.1404
63	38.7981	79.0087
64	39.9151	79.8619
65	41.0447	80.6998
66	42.1868	81.5223
67	43.3412	82.3293
68	44.5079	83.1206
69	45.6867	83.8960
70	46.8776	84.6554
71	48.0803	85.3987
72	49.2949	86.1257
73	50.5211	86.8362
74	51.7589	87.5301
75	53.0081	88.2072
76	54.2687	88.8674
77	55.5405	89.5104
78	56.8235	90.1362
79	58.1175	90.7446
80	59.4224	91.3354
81	60.7381	91.9084
82	62.0646	92.4634
83	63.4016	93.0004
84	64.7492	93.5190
85	66.1072	94.0192
86	67.4756	94.5008
87	68.8541	94.9636
88	70.2427	95.4073
89	71.6414	95.8319
90	73.0500	96.2371
91	74.4685	96.6228
92	75.8967	96.9887
93	77.3345	97.3348
94	78.7819	97.6607
95	80.2388	97.9663
96	81.7051	98.2514
97	83.1806	98.5158
98	84.6653	98.7593
99	86.1592	98.9817
100	87.6621	99.1828
101	89.1739	99.3624
102	90.6946	99.5203
103	92.2240	99.6563
104	93.7622	99.7701
105	95.3089	99.8616
106	96.8642	99.9306
107	98.4279	99.9768
108	100.0000	100.0000

10 YEARS

#	REBATE	EARN
1	.0194	1.3947
2	.0581	2.7831
3	.1158	4.1652
4	.1924	5.5409
5	.2877	6.9103
6	.4015	8.2731
7	.5336	9.6294
8	.6839	10.9791
9	.8522	12.3221
10	1.0384	13.6584
11	1.2422	14.9878
12	1.4634	16.3104
13	1.7020	17.6261
14	1.9578	18.9348
15	2.2305	20.2364
16	2.5201	21.5308
17	2.8264	22.8181
18	3.1491	24.0981
19	3.4883	25.3707
20	3.8436	26.6360
21	4.2150	27.8937
22	4.6022	29.1439
23	5.0053	30.3865
24	5.4239	31.6214
25	5.8580	32.8485
26	6.3073	34.0677
27	6.7719	35.2791
28	7.2514	36.4824
29	7.7458	37.6776
30	8.2549	38.8647
31	8.7787	40.0436
32	9.3168	41.2141
33	9.8693	42.3763
34	10.4360	43.5300
35	11.0167	44.6751
36	11.6113	45.8116
37	12.2197	46.9394
38	12.8418	48.0584
39	13.4774	49.1685
40	14.1263	50.2697
41	14.7885	51.3617
42	15.4639	52.4447
43	16.1522	53.5184
44	16.8535	54.5828
45	17.5675	55.6378
46	18.2942	56.6832
47	19.0334	57.7191
48	19.7849	58.7453
49	20.5488	59.7618
50	21.3249	60.7684
51	22.1130	61.7650
52	22.9130	62.7515
53	23.7249	63.7279
54	24.5485	64.6941
55	25.3837	65.6499
56	26.2304	66.5952
57	27.0884	67.5300
58	27.9578	68.4542
59	28.8383	69.3676
60	29.7299	70.2701
61	30.6324	71.1617
62	31.5458	72.0422
63	32.4700	72.9116
64	33.4048	73.7696
65	34.3501	74.6163
66	35.3059	75.4515
67	36.2721	76.2751
68	37.2485	77.0870
69	38.2350	77.8870
70	39.2316	78.6751
71	40.2382	79.4512
72	41.2547	80.2151
73	42.2809	80.9666
74	43.3168	81.7058
75	44.3622	82.4325
76	45.4172	83.1465
77	46.4816	83.8478
78	47.5553	84.5361
79	48.6383	85.2115
80	49.7303	85.8737
81	50.8315	86.5226
82	51.9416	87.1582
83	53.0606	87.7803
84	54.1884	88.3887
85	55.3249	88.9833
86	56.4700	89.5640
87	57.6237	90.1307
88	58.7859	90.6832
89	59.9564	91.2213
90	61.1353	91.7451
91	62.3224	92.2542
92	63.5176	92.7486
93	64.7209	93.2281
94	65.9323	93.6927
95	67.1515	94.1420
96	68.3786	94.5761
97	69.6135	94.9947
98	70.8561	95.3978
99	72.1063	95.7850
100	73.3640	96.1564
101	74.6293	96.5117
102	75.9019	96.8509
103	77.1819	97.1736
104	78.4692	97.4799
105	79.7636	97.7695
106	81.0652	98.0422
107	82.3739	98.2980
108	83.6896	98.5366
109	85.0122	98.7578
110	86.3416	98.9616
111	87.6779	99.1478
112	89.0209	99.3161
113	90.3706	99.4664
114	91.7269	99.5985
115	93.0897	99.7123
116	94.4591	99.8076
117	95.8348	99.8842
118	97.2169	99.9419
119	98.6053	99.9806
120	100.0000	100.0000

11.75 %

1 YEAR

#	REBATE	EARN
1	1.3281	15.1147
2	3.9716	29.0362
3	7.9175	41.7529
4	13.1533	53.2529
5	19.6665	63.5244
6	27.4447	72.5553
7	36.4756	80.3335
8	46.7471	86.8467
9	58.2471	92.0825
10	70.9638	96.0284
11	84.8853	98.6719
12	100.0000	100.0000

2 YEARS

#	REBATE	EARN
1	.3586	7.7122
2	1.0724	15.1378
3	2.1379	22.2739
4	3.5517	29.1178
5	5.3104	35.6665
6	7.4107	41.9173
7	9.8492	47.8671
8	12.6227	53.5130
9	15.7280	58.8520
10	19.1618	63.8812
11	22.9209	68.5975
12	27.0021	72.9979
13	31.4025	77.0791
14	36.1188	80.8382
15	41.1480	84.2720
16	46.4870	87.3773
17	52.1329	90.1508
18	58.0827	92.5893
19	64.3335	94.6896
20	70.8822	96.4483
21	77.7261	97.8621
22	84.8622	98.9276
23	92.2878	99.6414
24	100.0000	100.0000

3 YEARS

#	REBATE	EARN
1	.1676	5.1152
2	.5013	10.1113
3	.9994	14.9870
4	1.6603	19.7411
5	2.4824	24.3725
6	3.4643	28.8799
7	4.6042	33.2622
8	5.9007	37.5181
9	7.3523	41.6464
10	8.9575	45.6459
11	10.7148	49.5152
12	12.6227	53.2531
13	14.6797	56.8583
14	16.8844	60.3295
15	19.2354	63.6655
16	21.7313	66.8648
17	24.3705	69.9261
18	27.1519	72.8481
19	30.0739	75.6295
20	33.1352	78.2687
21	36.3345	80.7646
22	39.6705	83.1156
23	43.1417	85.3203
24	46.7469	87.3773
25	50.4848	89.2852
26	54.3541	91.0425
27	58.3536	92.6477
28	62.4819	94.0993
29	66.7378	95.3958
30	71.1201	96.5357
31	75.6275	97.5176
32	80.2589	98.3397
33	85.0130	99.0006
34	89.8887	99.4987
35	94.8848	99.8324
36	100.0000	100.0000

4 YEARS

#	REBATE	EARN
1	.0985	3.7932
2	.2944	7.5240
3	.5869	11.1920
4	.9751	14.7965
5	1.4579	18.3368
6	2.0346	21.8124
7	2.7040	25.2226
8	3.4655	28.5668
9	4.3180	31.8443
10	5.2607	35.0544
11	6.2928	38.1966
12	7.4133	41.2701
13	8.6214	44.2743
14	9.9162	47.2085
15	11.2969	50.0719
16	12.7627	52.8640
17	14.3128	55.5840
18	15.9463	58.2313
19	17.6624	60.8050
20	19.4603	63.3045
21	21.3392	65.7290
22	23.2984	68.0779
23	25.3371	70.3503
24	27.4544	72.5456
25	29.6497	74.6629
26	31.9221	76.7016
27	34.2710	78.6608
28	36.6955	80.5397
29	39.1950	82.3376
30	41.7687	84.0537
31	44.4160	85.6872
32	47.1360	87.2373
33	49.9281	88.7031
34	52.7915	90.0838
35	55.7257	91.3786
36	58.7299	92.5867
37	61.8034	93.7072
38	64.9456	94.7393
39	68.1557	95.6820
40	71.4332	96.5345
41	74.7774	97.2960
42	78.1876	97.9654
43	81.6632	98.5421
44	85.2035	99.0249
45	88.8080	99.4131
46	92.4760	99.7056
47	96.2068	99.9015
48	100.0000	100.0000

5 YEARS

#	REBATE	EARN
1	.0656	2.9935
2	.1961	5.9501
3	.3909	8.8694
4	.6494	11.7511
5	.9709	14.5948
6	1.3549	17.4001
7	1.8008	20.1667
8	2.3078	22.8942
9	2.8756	25.5822
10	3.5034	28.2303
11	4.1907	30.8381
12	4.9369	33.4052
13	5.7414	35.9312
14	6.6037	38.4158
15	7.5232	40.8585
16	8.4993	43.2589
17	9.5316	45.6166
18	10.6194	47.9311
19	11.7622	50.2021
20	12.9596	52.4292
21	14.2108	54.6118
22	15.5155	56.7496
23	16.8732	58.8421
24	18.2832	60.8889
25	19.7452	62.8896
26	21.2585	64.8436
27	22.8227	66.7505
28	24.4373	68.6099
29	26.1019	70.4213
30	27.8158	72.1842
31	29.5787	73.8981
32	31.3901	75.5627
33	33.2495	77.1773
34	35.1564	78.7415
35	37.1104	80.2548
36	39.1111	81.7168
37	41.1579	83.1268
38	43.2504	84.4845
39	45.3882	85.7892
40	47.5708	87.0404
41	49.7979	88.2378
42	52.0689	89.3806
43	54.3834	90.4684
44	56.7411	91.5007
45	59.1415	92.4768
46	61.5842	93.3963
47	64.0688	94.2586
48	66.5948	95.0631
49	69.1619	95.8093
50	71.7697	96.4966
51	74.4178	97.1244
52	77.1058	97.6922
53	79.8333	98.1992
54	82.5999	98.6451
55	85.4052	99.0291
56	88.2489	99.3506
57	91.1306	99.6091
58	94.0499	99.8039
59	97.0065	99.9344
60	100.0000	100.0000

6 YEARS

#	REBATE	EARN
1	.0473	2.4585
2	.1414	4.8934
3	.2819	7.3044
4	.4683	9.6912
5	.7001	12.0537
6	.9771	14.3915
7	1.2986	16.7045
8	1.6642	18.9924
9	2.0736	21.2549
10	2.5264	23.4919
11	3.0220	25.7030
12	3.5601	27.8880
13	4.1402	30.0467
14	4.7620	32.1787
15	5.4251	34.2839
16	6.1290	36.3619
17	6.8734	38.4126
18	7.6579	40.4356
19	8.4820	42.4306
20	9.3454	44.3975
21	10.2477	46.3358
22	11.1886	48.2454
23	12.1676	50.1259
24	13.1844	51.9771
25	14.2386	53.7987
26	15.3299	55.5904
27	16.4579	57.3519
28	17.6222	59.0828
29	18.8226	60.7830
30	20.0585	62.4521
31	21.3298	64.0898
32	22.6360	65.6957
33	23.9769	67.2697
34	25.3520	68.8113
35	26.7611	70.3202
36	28.2038	71.7962
37	29.6798	73.2389
38	31.1887	74.6480
39	32.7303	76.0231
40	34.3043	77.3640
41	35.9102	78.6702
42	37.5479	79.9415
43	39.2170	81.1774
44	40.9172	82.3778
45	42.6481	83.5421
46	44.4096	84.6701
47	46.2013	85.7614
48	48.0229	86.8156
49	49.8741	87.8324
50	51.7546	88.8114
51	53.6642	89.7523
52	55.6025	90.6546
53	57.5694	91.5180
54	59.5644	92.3421
55	61.5874	93.1266
56	63.6381	93.8710
57	65.7161	94.5749
58	67.8213	95.2380
59	69.9533	95.8598
60	72.1120	96.4399
61	74.2970	96.9780
62	76.5081	97.4736
63	78.7451	97.9264
64	81.0076	98.3358
65	83.2955	98.7014
66	85.6085	99.0229
67	87.9463	99.2999
68	90.3088	99.5317
69	92.6956	99.7181
70	95.1066	99.8586
71	97.5415	99.9527
72	100.0000	100.0000

7 YEARS

#	REBATE	EARN
1	.0360	2.0762
2	.1077	4.1363
3	.2147	6.1802
4	.3567	8.2078
5	.5334	10.2188
6	.7443	12.2132
7	.9892	14.1907
8	1.2678	16.1512
9	1.5797	18.0945
10	1.9246	20.0205
11	2.3021	21.9290
12	2.7121	23.8198
13	3.1540	25.6927
14	3.6277	27.5476
15	4.1329	29.3843
16	4.6691	31.2025
17	5.2362	33.0023
18	5.8338	34.7832
19	6.4616	36.5453
20	7.1193	38.2882
21	7.8067	40.0118
22	8.5235	41.7159
23	9.2693	43.4003
24	10.0439	45.0649
25	10.8470	46.7094
26	11.6784	48.3336
27	12.5377	49.9373
28	13.4247	51.5204
29	14.3391	53.0826
30	15.2806	54.6237
31	16.2491	56.1435
32	17.2442	57.6419
33	18.2656	59.1185
34	19.3132	60.5732
35	20.3867	62.0058
36	21.4857	63.4161
37	22.6101	64.8037
38	23.7596	66.1687
39	24.9340	67.5105
40	26.1331	68.8292
41	27.3565	70.1244
42	28.6041	71.3959
43	29.8756	72.6435
44	31.1708	73.8669
45	32.4895	75.0660
46	33.8313	76.2404
47	35.1963	77.3899
48	36.5839	78.5143
49	37.9942	79.6133
50	39.4268	80.6868
51	40.8815	81.7344
52	42.3581	82.7558
53	43.8565	83.7509
54	45.3763	84.7194
55	46.9174	85.6609
56	48.4796	86.5753
57	50.0627	87.4623
58	51.6664	88.3216
59	53.2906	89.1530
60	54.9351	89.9561
61	56.5997	90.7307
62	58.2841	91.4765
63	59.9882	92.1933
64	61.7118	92.8807
65	63.4547	93.5384
66	65.2168	94.1662
67	66.9977	94.7638
68	68.7975	95.3309
69	70.6157	95.8671
70	72.4524	96.3723
71	74.3073	96.8460
72	76.1802	97.2879
73	78.0710	97.6979
74	79.9795	98.0754
75	81.9055	98.4203

#	REBATE	EARN
75	81.9055	98.4203
76	83.8488	98.7322
77	85.8093	99.0108
78	87.7868	99.2557
79	89.7812	99.4666
80	91.7922	99.6433
81	93.8198	99.7853
82	95.8637	99.8923
83	97.9238	99.9640
84	100.0000	100.0000

8 YEARS

#	REBATE	EARN
1	.0286	1.7897
2	.0854	3.5681
3	.1703	5.3350
4	.2829	7.0904
5	.4229	8.8341
6	.5902	10.5661
7	.7844	12.2862
8	1.0053	13.9943
9	1.2526	15.6903
10	1.5261	17.3740
11	1.8255	19.0454
12	2.1506	20.7043
13	2.5010	22.3506
14	2.8766	23.9842
15	3.2772	25.6050
16	3.7024	27.2127
17	4.1521	28.8074
18	4.6259	30.3888
19	5.1238	31.9569
20	5.6453	33.5115
21	6.1904	35.0525
22	6.7588	36.5797
23	7.3502	38.0930
24	7.9644	39.5924
25	8.6012	41.0775
26	9.2604	42.5484
27	9.9418	44.0048
28	10.6452	45.4466
29	11.3703	46.8737
30	12.1169	48.2859
31	12.8848	49.6831
32	13.6739	51.0652
33	14.4839	52.4319
34	15.3146	53.7832
35	16.1657	55.1189
36	17.0372	56.4388
37	17.9288	57.7428
38	18.8404	59.0308
39	19.7716	60.3024
40	20.7224	61.5577
41	21.6925	62.7965
42	22.6818	64.0185
43	23.6901	65.2237
44	24.7171	66.4118
45	25.7627	67.5827
46	26.8268	68.7363
47	27.9091	69.8722
48	29.0095	70.9905
49	30.1278	72.0909
50	31.2637	73.1732
51	32.4173	74.2373
52	33.5882	75.2829
53	34.7763	76.3099
54	35.9815	77.3182
55	37.2035	78.3075
56	38.4423	79.2776
57	39.6976	80.2284
58	40.9692	81.1596
59	42.2572	82.0712
60	43.5612	82.9628
61	44.8811	83.8343
62	46.2168	84.6854
63	47.5681	85.5161
64	48.9348	86.3261
65	50.3169	87.1152
66	51.7141	87.8831
67	53.1263	88.6297
68	54.5534	89.3548
69	55.9952	90.0582
70	57.4516	90.7396
71	58.9225	91.3988
72	60.4076	92.0356
73	61.9070	92.6498
74	63.4203	93.2412
75	64.9475	93.8096
76	66.4885	94.3547
77	68.0431	94.8762
78	69.6112	95.3741
79	71.1926	95.8479
80	72.7873	96.2976
81	74.3950	96.7228
82	76.0158	97.1234
83	77.6494	97.4990
84	79.2957	97.8494
85	80.9546	98.1745
86	82.6260	98.4739
87	84.3097	98.7474
88	86.0057	98.9947
89	87.7138	99.2156
90	89.4339	99.4098
91	91.1659	99.5771
92	92.9096	99.7171
93	94.6650	99.8297
94	96.4319	99.9146
95	98.2103	99.9714
96	100.0000	100.0000

9 YEARS

#	REBATE	EARN
1	.0234	1.5674
2	.0698	3.1266
3	.1392	4.6774
4	.2313	6.2199
5	.3458	7.7539
6	.4825	9.2793
7	.6413	10.7961
8	.8219	12.3041
9	1.0241	13.8034
10	1.2476	15.2937
11	1.4924	16.7750
12	1.7581	18.2473
13	2.0446	19.7104
14	2.3517	21.1643
15	2.6792	22.6088
16	3.0268	24.0439
17	3.3944	25.4695
18	3.7818	26.8854
19	4.1888	28.2916
20	4.6152	29.6880
21	5.0608	31.0745
22	5.5255	32.4511
23	6.0089	33.8175
24	6.5111	35.1737
25	7.0317	36.5196
26	7.5707	37.8551
27	8.1277	39.1801
28	8.7027	40.4945
29	9.2955	41.7981
30	9.9059	43.0910
31	10.5337	44.3730
32	11.1788	45.6439
33	11.8410	46.9037
34	12.5201	48.1522
35	13.2159	49.3894
36	13.9284	50.6151
37	14.6573	51.8293
38	15.4025	53.0317
39	16.1638	54.2224
40	16.9411	55.4011
41	17.7342	56.5678
42	18.5430	57.7224
43	19.3673	58.8646
44	20.2069	59.9945
45	21.0617	61.1118
46	21.9316	62.2166
47	22.8164	63.3085
48	23.7160	64.3876
49	24.6302	65.4536
50	25.5589	66.5065
51	26.5020	67.5462
52	27.4592	68.5724
53	28.4306	69.5851
54	29.4158	70.5842
55	30.4149	71.5694
56	31.4276	72.5408
57	32.4538	73.4980
58	33.4935	74.4411
59	34.5464	75.3698
60	35.6124	76.2840
61	36.6915	77.1836
62	37.7834	78.0684
63	38.8882	78.9383
64	40.0055	79.7931
65	41.1354	80.6327
66	42.2776	81.4570
67	43.4322	82.2658
68	44.5989	83.0589
69	45.7776	83.8362
70	46.9683	84.5975
71	48.1707	85.3427
72	49.3849	86.0716
73	50.6106	86.7841
74	51.8478	87.4799
75	53.0963	88.1590
76	54.3561	88.8212
77	55.6270	89.4663
78	56.9090	90.0941
79	58.2019	90.7045
80	59.5055	91.2973
81	60.8199	91.8723
82	62.1449	92.4293
83	63.4804	92.9683
84	64.8263	93.4889
85	66.1825	93.9911
86	67.5489	94.4745
87	68.9255	94.9392
88	70.3120	95.3848
89	71.7084	95.8112
90	73.1146	96.2182
91	74.5305	96.6056
92	75.9561	96.9732
93	77.3912	97.3208
94	78.8357	97.6483
95	80.2896	97.9554
96	81.7527	98.2419
97	83.2250	98.5076
98	84.7063	98.7524
99	86.1966	98.9759
100	87.6959	99.1781
101	89.2039	99.3587
102	90.7207	99.5175
103	92.2461	99.6542
104	93.7801	99.7687
105	95.3226	99.8608
106	96.8734	99.9302
107	98.4326	99.9766
108	100.0000	100.0000

10 YEARS

#	REBATE	EARN
1	.0196	1.3902
2	.0585	2.7742
3	.1166	4.1520
4	.1936	5.5236
5	.2895	6.8889
6	.4040	8.2478
7	.5370	9.6002
8	.6882	10.9462
9	.8575	12.2856
10	1.0447	13.6183
11	1.2497	14.9444
12	1.4722	16.2637
13	1.7121	17.5762
14	1.9693	18.8818
15	2.2434	20.1804
16	2.5345	21.4720
17	2.8424	22.7565
18	3.1668	24.0338
19	3.5076	25.3039
20	3.8646	26.5667
21	4.2377	27.8221
22	4.6268	29.0701
23	5.0317	30.3105
24	5.4521	31.5434
25	5.8881	32.7685
26	6.3394	33.9859
27	6.8058	35.1955
28	7.2873	36.3972
29	7.7837	37.5909
30	8.2948	38.7766
31	8.8205	39.9541
32	9.3607	41.1234
33	9.9152	42.2844
34	10.4838	43.4370
35	11.0665	44.5812
36	11.6631	45.7168
37	12.2735	46.8438
38	12.8975	47.9621
39	13.5350	49.0716
40	14.1859	50.1723
41	14.8500	51.2639
42	15.5272	52.3465
43	16.2174	53.4200
44	16.9205	54.4842
45	17.6363	55.5391
46	18.3647	56.5846
47	19.1056	57.6206
48	19.8589	58.6469
49	20.6244	59.6636
50	21.4021	60.6705
51	22.1918	61.6675
52	22.9933	62.6546
53	23.8067	63.6315
54	24.6317	64.5983
55	25.4683	65.5548
56	26.3163	66.5009
57	27.1756	67.4365
58	28.0462	68.3616
59	28.9278	69.2759
60	29.8205	70.1795
61	30.7241	71.0722
62	31.6384	71.9538
63	32.5635	72.8244
64	33.4991	73.6837
65	34.4452	74.5317
66	35.4017	75.3683
67	36.3685	76.1933
68	37.3454	77.0067
69	38.3325	77.8082
70	39.3295	78.5979
71	40.3364	79.3756
72	41.3531	80.1411
73	42.3794	80.8944
74	43.4154	81.6353
75	44.4609	82.3637
76	45.5158	83.0795
77	46.5800	83.7826
78	47.6535	84.4728
79	48.7361	85.1500
80	49.8277	85.8141
81	50.9284	86.4650
82	52.0379	87.1025
83	53.1562	87.7265
84	54.2832	88.3369
85	55.4188	88.9335
86	56.5630	89.5162
87	57.7156	90.0848
88	58.8766	90.6393
89	60.0459	91.1795
90	61.2234	91.7052
91	62.4091	92.2163
92	63.6028	92.7127
93	64.8045	93.1942
94	66.0141	93.6606
95	67.2315	94.1119
96	68.4566	94.5479
97	69.6895	94.9683
98	70.9299	95.3732
99	72.1779	95.7623
100	73.4333	96.1354
101	74.6961	96.4924
102	75.9662	96.8332
103	77.2435	97.1576
104	78.5280	97.4655
105	79.8196	97.7566
106	81.1182	98.0307
107	82.4238	98.2879
108	83.7363	98.5278
109	85.0556	98.7503
110	86.3817	98.9553
111	87.7144	99.1425
112	89.0538	99.3118
113	90.3998	99.4630
114	91.7522	99.5960
115	93.1111	99.7105
116	94.4764	99.8064
117	95.8480	99.8834
118	97.2258	99.9415
119	98.6098	99.9804
120	100.0000	100.0000

ACTUARIAL REBATE AND EARNINGS

1 YEAR

#	REBATE	EARN
1	1.3291	15.1091
2	3.9742	29.0268
3	7.9223	41.7413
4	13.1604	53.2405
5	19.6757	63.5122
6	27.4557	72.5443
7	36.4878	80.3243
8	46.7595	86.8396
9	58.2587	92.0777
10	70.9732	96.0258
11	84.8909	98.6709
12	100.0000	100.0000

2 YEARS

#	REBATE	EARN
1	.3592	7.7063
2	1.0740	15.1270
3	2.1408	22.2591
4	3.5563	29.0997
5	5.3170	35.6460
6	7.4194	41.8949
7	9.8601	47.8436
8	12.6359	53.4891
9	15.7433	58.8282
10	19.1792	63.8579
11	22.9402	68.5752
12	27.0231	72.9769
13	31.4248	77.0598
14	36.1421	80.8208
15	41.1718	84.2567
16	46.5109	87.3641
17	52.1564	90.1399
18	58.1051	92.5806
19	64.3540	94.6830
20	70.9003	96.4437
21	77.7409	97.8592
22	84.8730	98.9260
23	92.2937	99.6408
24	100.0000	100.0000

3 YEARS

#	REBATE	EARN
1	.1680	5.1095
2	.5024	10.1003
3	1.0015	14.9714
4	1.6637	19.7214
5	2.4874	24.3493
6	3.4709	28.8537
7	4.6127	33.2335
8	5.9113	37.4873
9	7.3650	41.6140
10	8.9724	45.6122
11	10.7318	49.4807
12	12.6419	53.2182
13	14.7011	56.8234
14	16.9079	60.2949
15	19.2609	63.6314
16	21.7586	66.8316
17	24.3997	69.8941
18	27.1826	72.8174
19	30.1059	75.6003
20	33.1684	78.2414
21	36.3686	80.7391
22	39.7051	83.0921
23	43.1766	85.2989
24	46.7818	87.3581
25	50.5193	89.2682
26	54.3878	91.0276
27	58.3860	92.6350
28	62.5127	94.0887
29	66.7665	95.3873
30	71.1463	96.5291
31	75.6507	97.5126
32	80.2786	98.3363
33	85.0286	98.9985
34	89.8997	99.4976
35	94.8905	99.8320
36	100.0000	100.0000

4 YEARS

#	REBATE	EARN
1	.0988	3.7875
2	.2953	7.5132
3	.5886	11.1764
4	.9778	14.7765
5	1.4619	18.3128
6	2.0399	21.7848
7	2.7110	25.1917
8	3.4742	28.5330
9	4.3286	31.8079
10	5.2732	35.0159
11	6.3073	38.1561
12	7.4299	41.2281
13	8.6401	44.2310
14	9.9371	47.1642
15	11.3200	50.0271
16	12.7880	52.8188
17	14.3401	55.5386
18	15.9757	58.1860
19	17.6938	60.7600
20	19.4937	63.2601
21	21.3745	65.6854
22	23.3354	68.0353
23	25.3757	70.3089
24	27.4945	72.5055
25	29.6911	74.6243
26	31.9647	76.6646
27	34.3146	78.6255
28	36.7399	80.5063
29	39.2400	82.3062
30	41.8140	84.0243
31	44.4614	85.6599
32	47.1812	87.2120
33	49.9729	88.6800
34	52.8358	90.0629
35	55.7690	91.3599
36	58.7719	92.5701
37	61.8439	93.6927
38	64.9841	94.7268
39	68.1921	95.6714
40	71.4670	96.5258
41	74.8083	97.2890
42	78.2152	97.9601
43	81.6872	98.5381
44	85.2235	99.0222
45	88.8236	99.4114
46	92.4868	99.7047
47	96.2125	99.9012
48	100.0000	100.0000

5 YEARS

#	REBATE	EARN
1	.0658	2.9880
2	.1968	5.9395
3	.3923	8.8540
4	.6516	11.7312
5	.9742	14.5707
6	1.3594	17.3721
7	1.8066	20.1351
8	2.3152	22.8592
9	2.8846	25.5441
10	3.5141	28.1894
11	4.2032	30.7946
12	4.9513	33.3595
13	5.7578	35.8835
14	6.6221	38.3663
15	7.5437	40.8075
16	8.5220	43.2066
17	9.5563	45.5632
18	10.6463	47.8770
19	11.7913	50.1474
20	12.9907	52.3740
21	14.2441	54.5564
22	15.5509	56.6942
23	16.9105	58.7869
24	18.3225	60.8341
25	19.7863	62.8353
26	21.3015	64.7900
27	22.8674	66.6978
28	24.4837	68.5582
29	26.1497	70.3707
30	27.8651	72.1349
31	29.6293	73.8503
32	31.4418	75.5163
33	33.3022	77.1326
34	35.2100	78.6985
35	37.1647	80.2137
36	39.1659	81.6775
37	41.2131	83.0895
38	43.3058	84.4491
39	45.4436	85.7559
40	47.6260	87.0093
41	49.8526	88.2087
42	52.1230	89.3537
43	54.4368	90.4437
44	56.7934	91.4780
45	59.1925	92.4563
46	61.6337	93.3779
47	64.1165	94.2422
48	66.6405	95.0487
49	69.2054	95.7968
50	71.8106	96.4859
51	74.4559	97.1154
52	77.1408	97.6848
53	79.8649	98.1934
54	82.6279	98.6406
55	85.4293	99.0258
56	88.2688	99.3484
57	91.1460	99.6077
58	94.0605	99.8032
59	97.0120	99.9342
60	100.0000	100.0000

6 YEARS

#	REBATE	EARN
1	.0475	2.4533
2	.1420	4.8832
3	.2830	7.2894
4	.4702	9.6717
5	.7030	12.0299
6	.9809	14.3636
7	1.3036	16.6728
8	1.6706	18.9571
9	2.0815	21.2163
10	2.5358	23.4501
11	3.0330	25.6583
12	3.5728	27.8406
13	4.1548	29.9967
14	4.7785	32.1265
15	5.4435	34.2296
16	6.1494	36.3057
17	6.8958	38.3547
18	7.6823	40.3762
19	8.5085	42.3699
20	9.3740	44.3356
21	10.2785	46.2730
22	11.2214	48.1818
23	12.2025	50.0618
24	13.2214	51.9126
25	14.2777	53.7339
26	15.3710	55.5255
27	16.5010	57.2870
28	17.6673	59.0182
29	18.8695	60.7187
30	20.1073	62.3883
31	21.3803	64.0266
32	22.6882	65.6333
33	24.0307	67.2082
34	25.4074	68.7508
35	26.8179	70.2609
36	28.2619	71.7381
37	29.7391	73.1821
38	31.2492	74.5926
39	32.7918	75.9693
40	34.3667	77.3118
41	35.9734	78.6197
42	37.6117	79.8927
43	39.2813	81.1305
44	40.9818	82.3327
45	42.7130	83.4990
46	44.4745	84.6290
47	46.2661	85.7223
48	48.0874	86.7786
49	49.9382	87.7975
50	51.8182	88.7786
51	53.7270	89.7215
52	55.6644	90.6260
53	57.6301	91.4915
54	59.6238	92.3177
55	61.6453	93.1042
56	63.6943	93.8506
57	65.7704	94.5565
58	67.8735	95.2215
59	70.0033	95.8452
60	72.1594	96.4272
61	74.3417	96.9670
62	76.5499	97.4642
63	78.7837	97.9185
64	81.0429	98.3294
65	83.3272	98.6964
66	85.6364	99.0191
67	87.9701	99.2970
68	90.3283	99.5298
69	92.7106	99.7170
70	95.1168	99.8580
71	97.5467	99.9525
72	100.0000	100.0000

7 YEARS

#	REBATE	EARN
1	.0362	2.0711
2	.1082	4.1264
3	.2158	6.1657
4	.3584	8.1888
5	.5359	10.1955
6	.7478	12.1858
7	.9937	14.1594
8	1.2735	16.1162
9	1.5867	18.0560
10	1.9330	19.9786
11	2.3120	21.8839
12	2.7235	23.7717
13	3.1671	25.6418
14	3.6426	27.4941
15	4.1495	29.3283
16	4.6876	31.1443
17	5.2566	32.9419
18	5.8561	34.7209
19	6.4859	36.4811
20	7.1457	38.2224
21	7.8351	39.9445
22	8.5539	41.6473
23	9.3018	43.3306
24	10.0785	44.9941
25	10.8836	46.6377
26	11.7171	48.2612
27	12.5784	49.8643
28	13.4675	51.4470
29	14.3839	53.0088
30	15.3274	54.5498
31	16.2979	56.0696
32	17.2949	57.5680
33	18.3182	59.0449
34	19.3676	60.4999
35	20.4428	61.9330
36	21.5436	63.3438
37	22.6696	64.7322
38	23.8207	66.0978
39	24.9966	67.4406
40	26.1971	68.7603
41	27.4219	70.0566
42	28.6707	71.3293
43	29.9434	72.5781
44	31.2397	73.8029
45	32.5594	75.0034
46	33.9022	76.1793
47	35.2678	77.3304
48	36.6562	78.4564
49	38.0670	79.5572
50	39.5001	80.6324
51	40.9551	81.6818
52	42.4320	82.7051
53	43.9304	83.7021
54	45.4502	84.6726
55	46.9912	85.6161
56	48.5530	86.5325
57	50.1357	87.4216
58	51.7388	88.2829
59	53.3623	89.1164
60	55.0059	89.9215
61	56.6694	90.6982
62	58.3527	91.4461
63	60.0555	92.1649
64	61.7776	92.8543
65	63.5189	93.5141
66	65.2791	94.1439
67	67.0581	94.7434
68	68.8557	95.3124
69	70.6717	95.8505
70	72.5059	96.3574
71	74.3582	96.8329
72	76.2283	97.2765
73	78.1161	97.6880
74	80.0214	98.0670
75	81.9440	98.4133

#	REBATE	EARN
75	81.9440	98.4133
76	83.8838	98.7265
77	85.8406	99.0063
78	87.8142	99.2522
79	89.8045	99.4641
80	91.8112	99.6416
81	93.8343	99.7842
82	95.8736	99.8918
83	97.9289	99.9638
84	100.0000	100.0000

8 YEARS

#	REBATE	EARN
1	.0287	1.7848
2	.0859	3.5585
3	.1712	5.3209
4	.2844	7.0720
5	.4252	8.8115
6	.5933	10.5394
7	.7885	12.2556
8	1.0104	13.9599
9	1.2589	15.6523
10	1.5337	17.3326
11	1.8344	19.0007
12	2.1609	20.6564
13	2.5129	22.2997
14	2.8901	23.9305
15	3.2923	25.5485
16	3.7193	27.1537
17	4.1707	28.7459
18	4.6464	30.3251
19	5.1461	31.8910
20	5.6696	33.4436
21	6.2166	34.9827
22	6.7870	36.5082
23	7.3804	38.0199
24	7.9966	39.5178
25	8.6355	41.0016
26	9.2967	42.4712
27	9.9802	43.9266
28	10.6856	45.3674
29	11.4127	46.7937
30	12.1613	48.2052
31	12.9313	49.6019
32	13.7224	50.9835
33	14.5343	52.3499
34	15.3669	53.7009
35	16.2200	55.0365
36	17.0934	56.3564
37	17.9869	57.6605
38	18.9002	58.9486
39	19.8332	60.2206
40	20.7857	61.4763
41	21.7575	62.7155
42	22.7484	63.9382
43	23.7582	65.1440
44	24.7867	66.3329
45	25.8338	67.5047
46	26.8992	68.6592
47	27.9828	69.7963
48	29.0843	70.9157
49	30.2037	72.0172
50	31.3408	73.1008
51	32.4953	74.1662
52	33.6671	75.2133
53	34.8560	76.2418
54	36.0618	77.2516
55	37.2845	78.2425
56	38.5237	79.2143
57	39.7794	80.1668
58	41.0514	81.0998
59	42.3395	82.0131
60	43.6436	82.9066
61	44.9635	83.7800
62	46.2991	84.6331
63	47.6501	85.4657
64	49.0165	86.2776
65	50.3981	87.0687
66	51.7948	87.8387
67	53.2063	88.5873
68	54.6326	89.3144
69	56.0734	90.0198
70	57.5288	90.7033
71	58.9984	91.3645
72	60.4822	92.0034
73	61.9801	92.6196
74	63.4918	93.2130
75	65.0173	93.7834
76	66.5564	94.3304
77	68.1090	94.8539
78	69.6749	95.3536
79	71.2541	95.8293
80	72.8463	96.2807
81	74.4515	96.7077
82	76.0695	97.1099
83	77.7003	97.4871
84	79.3436	97.8391
85	80.9993	98.1656
86	82.6674	98.4663
87	84.3477	98.7411
88	86.0401	98.9896
89	87.7444	99.2115
90	89.4606	99.4067
91	91.1885	99.5748
92	92.9280	99.7156
93	94.6791	99.8288
94	96.4415	99.9141
95	98.2152	99.9713
96	100.0000	100.0000

9 YEARS

#	REBATE	EARN
1	.0235	1.5628
2	.0703	3.1174
3	.1400	4.6639
4	.2326	6.2021
5	.3478	7.7319
6	.4853	9.2533
7	.6450	10.7663
8	.8265	12.2706
9	1.0298	13.7662
10	1.2546	15.2530
11	1.5006	16.7310
12	1.7676	18.2001
13	2.0556	19.6601
14	2.3641	21.1109
15	2.6931	22.5526
16	3.0424	23.9849
17	3.4117	25.4079
18	3.8008	26.8213
19	4.2095	28.2251
20	4.6377	29.6193
21	5.0852	31.0037
22	5.5517	32.3781
23	6.0371	33.7426
24	6.5412	35.0970
25	7.0638	36.4412
26	7.6047	37.7752
27	8.1638	39.0987
28	8.7408	40.4118
29	9.3356	41.7142
30	9.9480	43.0060
31	10.5778	44.2869
32	11.2249	45.5569
33	11.8890	46.8159
34	12.5701	48.0638
35	13.2680	49.3004
36	13.9824	50.5256
37	14.7133	51.7393
38	15.4604	52.9415
39	16.2236	54.1320
40	17.0027	55.3106
41	17.7976	56.4773
42	18.6082	57.6319
43	19.4342	58.7744
44	20.2755	59.9045
45	21.1320	61.0222
46	22.0035	62.1274
47	22.8899	63.2199
48	23.7910	64.2995
49	24.7066	65.3663
50	25.6367	66.4200
51	26.5811	67.4605
52	27.5396	68.4876
53	28.5121	69.5013
54	29.4985	70.5015
55	30.4987	71.4879
56	31.5124	72.4604
57	32.5395	73.4189
58	33.5800	74.3633
59	34.6337	75.2934
60	35.7005	76.2090
61	36.7801	77.1101
62	37.8726	77.9965
63	38.9778	78.8680
64	40.0955	79.7245
65	41.2256	80.5658
66	42.3681	81.3918
67	43.5227	82.2024
68	44.6894	82.9973
69	45.8680	83.7764
70	47.0585	84.5396
71	48.2607	85.2867
72	49.4744	86.0176
73	50.6996	86.7320
74	51.9362	87.4299
75	53.1841	88.1110
76	54.4431	88.7751
77	55.7131	89.4222
78	56.9940	90.0520
79	58.2858	90.6644
80	59.5882	91.2592
81	60.9013	91.8362
82	62.2248	92.3953
83	63.5588	92.9362
84	64.9030	93.4588
85	66.2574	93.9629
86	67.6219	94.4483
87	68.9963	94.9148
88	70.3807	95.3623
89	71.7749	95.7905
90	73.1787	96.1992
91	74.5921	96.5883
92	76.0151	96.9576
93	77.4474	97.3069
94	78.8891	97.6359
95	80.3399	97.9444
96	81.7999	98.2324
97	83.2690	98.4994
98	84.7470	98.7454
99	86.2338	98.9702
100	87.7294	99.1735
101	89.2337	99.3550
102	90.7467	99.5147
103	92.2681	99.6522
104	93.7979	99.7674
105	95.3361	99.8600
106	96.8826	99.9297
107	98.4372	99.9765
108	100.0000	100.0000

10 YEARS

#	REBATE	EARN
1	.0197	1.3857
2	.0589	2.7654
3	.1173	4.1390
4	.1949	5.5065
5	.2914	6.8677
6	.4066	8.2227
7	.5404	9.5713
8	.6925	10.9136
9	.8628	12.2494
10	1.0511	13.5787
11	1.2572	14.9014
12	1.4810	16.2174
13	1.7222	17.5267
14	1.9807	18.8292
15	2.2564	20.1249
16	2.5490	21.4137
17	2.8584	22.6954
18	3.1844	23.9701
19	3.5269	25.2377
20	3.8856	26.4980
21	4.2605	27.7511
22	4.6514	28.9968
23	5.0581	30.2351
24	5.4804	31.4659
25	5.9182	32.6891
26	6.3714	33.9047
27	6.8398	35.1126
28	7.3233	36.3126
29	7.8216	37.5048
30	8.3347	38.6890
31	8.8623	39.8652
32	9.4045	41.0332
33	9.9610	42.1931
34	10.5316	43.3446
35	11.1163	44.4878
36	11.7148	45.6226
37	12.3271	46.7488
38	12.9531	47.8664
39	13.5925	48.9753
40	14.2453	50.0754
41	14.9113	51.1667
42	15.5904	52.2489
43	16.2825	53.3221
44	16.9873	54.3862
45	17.7049	55.4410
46	18.4351	56.4865
47	19.1777	57.5225
48	19.9327	58.5491
49	20.6999	59.5660
50	21.4791	60.5732
51	22.2703	61.5706
52	23.0734	62.5581
53	23.8882	63.5355
54	24.7146	64.5029
55	25.5526	65.4601
56	26.4019	66.4070
57	27.2625	67.3434
58	28.1342	68.2693
59	29.0170	69.1846
60	29.9108	70.0892
61	30.8154	70.9830
62	31.7307	71.8658
63	32.6566	72.7375
64	33.5930	73.5981
65	34.5399	74.4474
66	35.4971	75.2854
67	36.4645	76.1118
68	37.4419	76.9266
69	38.4294	77.7297
70	39.4268	78.5209
71	40.4340	79.3001
72	41.4509	80.0673
73	42.4775	80.8223
74	43.5135	81.5649
75	44.5590	82.2951
76	45.6138	83.0127
77	46.6779	83.7175
78	47.7511	84.4096
79	48.8333	85.0887
80	49.9246	85.7547
81	51.0247	86.4075
82	52.1336	87.0469
83	53.2512	87.6729
84	54.3774	88.2852
85	55.5122	88.8837
86	56.6554	89.4684
87	57.8069	90.0390
88	58.9668	90.5955
89	60.1348	91.1377
90	61.3110	91.6653
91	62.4952	92.1784
92	63.6874	92.6767
93	64.8874	93.1602
94	66.0953	93.6286
95	67.3109	94.0818
96	68.5341	94.5196
97	69.7649	94.9419
98	71.0032	95.3486
99	72.2489	95.7395
100	73.5020	96.1144
101	74.7623	96.4731
102	76.0299	96.8156
103	77.3046	97.1416
104	78.5863	97.4510
105	79.8751	97.7436
106	81.1708	98.0193
107	82.4733	98.2778
108	83.7826	98.5190
109	85.0986	98.7428
110	86.4213	98.9489
111	87.7506	99.1372
112	89.0864	99.3075
113	90.4287	99.4596
114	91.7773	99.5934
115	93.1323	99.7086
116	94.4935	99.8051
117	95.8610	99.8827
118	97.2346	99.9411
119	98.6143	99.9803
120	100.0000	100.0000

1 YEAR

#	REBATE	EARN
1	1.3301	15.1035
2	3.9769	29.0174
3	7.9270	41.7297
4	13.1674	53.2281
5	19.6849	63.5001
6	27.4666	72.5334
7	36.4999	80.3151
8	46.7719	86.8326
9	58.2703	92.0730
10	70.9826	96.0231
11	84.8965	98.6699
12	100.0000	100.0000

2 YEARS

#	REBATE	EARN
1	.3597	7.7005
2	1.0755	15.1162
3	2.1438	22.2442
4	3.5610	29.0816
5	5.3236	35.6254
6	7.4281	41.8727
7	9.8710	47.8203
8	12.6490	53.4652
9	15.7587	58.8044
10	19.1966	63.8347
11	22.9595	68.5529
12	27.0441	72.9559
13	31.4471	77.0405
14	36.1653	80.8034
15	41.1956	84.2413
16	46.5348	87.3510
17	52.1797	90.1290
18	58.1273	92.5719
19	64.3746	94.6764
20	70.9184	96.4390
21	77.7558	97.8562
22	84.8838	98.9245
23	92.2995	99.6403
24	100.0000	100.0000

3 YEARS

#	REBATE	EARN
1	.1684	5.1037
2	.5035	10.0894
3	1.0037	14.9558
4	1.6671	19.7018
5	2.4923	24.3261
6	3.4776	28.8275
7	4.6213	33.2048
8	5.9218	37.4565
9	7.3777	41.5816
10	8.9872	45.5786
11	10.7488	49.4464
12	12.6611	53.1835
13	14.7224	56.7886
14	16.9314	60.2603
15	19.2864	63.5974
16	21.7860	66.7985
17	24.4287	69.8621
18	27.2132	72.7868
19	30.1379	75.5713
20	33.2015	78.2140
21	36.4026	80.7136
22	39.7397	83.0686
23	43.2114	85.2776
24	46.8165	87.3389
25	50.5536	89.2512
26	54.4214	91.0128
27	58.4184	92.6223
28	62.5435	94.0782
29	66.7952	95.3787
30	71.1725	96.5224
31	75.6739	97.5077
32	80.2982	98.3329
33	85.0442	98.9963
34	89.9106	99.4965
35	94.8963	99.8316
36	100.0000	100.0000

4 YEARS

#	REBATE	EARN
1	.0990	3.7819
2	.2961	7.5024
3	.5903	11.1608
4	.9805	14.7565
5	1.4658	18.2888
6	2.0453	21.7572
7	2.7180	25.1609
8	3.4829	28.4992
9	4.3391	31.7716
10	5.2857	34.9774
11	6.3218	38.1158
12	7.4465	41.1862
13	8.6588	44.1879
14	9.9580	47.1201
15	11.3430	49.9823
16	12.8132	52.7736
17	14.3675	55.4933
18	16.0051	58.1408
19	17.7253	60.7152
20	19.5271	63.2158
21	21.4097	65.6419
22	23.3724	67.9927
23	25.4143	70.2675
24	27.5346	72.4654
25	29.7325	74.5857
26	32.0073	76.6276
27	34.3581	78.5903
28	36.7842	80.4729
29	39.2848	82.2747
30	41.8592	83.9949
31	44.5067	85.6325
32	47.2264	87.1868
33	50.0177	88.6570
34	52.8799	90.0420
35	55.8121	91.3412
36	58.8138	92.5535
37	61.8842	93.6782
38	65.0226	94.7143
39	68.2284	95.6609
40	71.5008	96.5171
41	74.8391	97.2820
42	78.2428	97.9547
43	81.7112	98.5342
44	85.2435	99.0195
45	88.8392	99.4097
46	92.4976	99.7039
47	96.2181	99.9010
48	100.0000	100.0000

5 YEARS

#	REBATE	EARN
1	.0661	2.9826
2	.1975	5.9290
3	.3936	8.8387
4	.6539	11.7114
5	.9775	14.5467
6	1.3639	17.3442
7	1.8125	20.1035
8	2.3226	22.8243
9	2.8936	25.5061
10	3.5248	28.1486
11	4.2158	30.7514
12	4.9658	33.3139
13	5.7742	35.8360
14	6.6406	38.3170
15	7.5642	40.7566
16	8.5446	43.1545
17	9.5811	45.5100
18	10.6732	47.8229
19	11.8203	50.0927
20	13.0218	52.3190
21	14.2773	54.5012
22	15.5861	56.6390
23	16.9478	58.7319
24	18.3617	60.7794
25	19.8274	62.7811
26	21.3444	64.7365
27	22.9121	66.6452
28	24.5299	68.5066
29	26.1975	70.3202
30	27.9143	72.0857
31	29.6798	73.8025
32	31.4934	75.4701
33	33.3548	77.0879
34	35.2635	78.6556
35	37.2189	80.1726
36	39.2206	81.6383
37	41.2681	83.0522
38	43.3610	84.4139
39	45.4988	85.7227
40	47.6810	86.9782
41	49.9073	88.1797
42	52.1771	89.3268
43	54.4900	90.4189
44	56.8455	91.4554
45	59.2434	92.4358
46	61.6830	93.3594
47	64.1640	94.2258
48	66.6861	95.0342
49	69.2486	95.7842
50	71.8514	96.4752
51	74.4939	97.1064
52	77.1757	97.6774
53	79.8965	98.1875
54	82.6558	98.6361
55	85.4533	99.0225
56	88.2886	99.3461
57	91.1613	99.6064
58	94.0710	99.8025
59	97.0174	99.9339
60	100.0000	100.0000

6 YEARS

#	REBATE	EARN
1	.0477	2.4481
2	.1426	4.8730
3	.2842	7.2745
4	.4721	9.6523
5	.7058	12.0062
6	.9848	14.3359
7	1.3087	16.6413
8	1.6771	18.9220
9	2.0893	21.1778
10	2.5452	23.4085
11	3.0441	25.6137
12	3.5856	27.7933
13	4.1694	29.9470
14	4.7949	32.0745
15	5.4619	34.1755
16	6.1698	36.2497
17	6.9182	38.2970
18	7.7068	40.3170
19	8.5350	42.3094
20	9.4026	44.2740
21	10.3092	46.2105
22	11.2542	48.1185
23	12.2374	49.9979
24	13.2584	51.8482
25	14.3167	53.6693
26	15.4121	55.4608
27	16.5440	57.2224
28	17.7122	58.9537
29	18.9163	60.6546
30	20.1560	62.3247
31	21.4308	63.9636
32	22.7404	65.5711
33	24.0844	67.1468
34	25.4626	68.6905
35	26.8745	70.2017
36	28.3199	71.6801
37	29.7983	73.1255
38	31.3095	74.5374
39	32.8532	75.9156
40	34.4289	77.2596
41	36.0364	78.5692
42	37.6753	79.8440
43	39.3454	81.0837
44	41.0463	82.2878
45	42.7776	83.4560
46	44.5392	84.5879
47	46.3307	85.6833
48	48.1518	86.7416
49	50.0021	87.7626
50	51.8815	88.7458
51	53.7895	89.6908
52	55.7260	90.5974
53	57.6906	91.4650
54	59.6830	92.2932
55	61.7030	93.0818
56	63.7503	93.8302
57	65.8245	94.5381
58	67.9255	95.2051
59	70.0530	95.8306
60	72.2067	96.4144
61	74.3863	96.9559
62	76.5915	97.4548
63	78.8222	97.9107
64	81.0780	98.3229
65	83.3587	98.6913
66	85.6641	99.0152
67	87.9938	99.2942
68	90.3477	99.5279
69	92.7255	99.7158
70	95.1270	99.8574
71	97.5519	99.9523
72	100.0000	100.0000

7 YEARS

#	REBATE	EARN
1	.0364	2.0661
2	.1088	4.1166
3	.2168	6.1512
4	.3601	8.1699
5	.5384	10.1724
6	.7512	12.1586
7	.9983	14.1283
8	1.2792	16.0814
9	1.5937	18.0177
10	1.9413	19.9370
11	2.3219	21.8392
12	2.7350	23.7240
13	3.1802	25.5913
14	3.6574	27.4409
15	4.1661	29.2727
16	4.7061	31.0864
17	5.2769	32.8818
18	5.8784	34.6589
19	6.5102	36.4173
20	7.1720	38.1569
21	7.8634	39.8776
22	8.5843	41.5790
23	9.3342	43.2611
24	10.1130	44.9236
25	10.9202	46.5664
26	11.7557	48.1891
27	12.6191	49.7917
28	13.5102	51.3738
29	14.4286	52.9354
30	15.3742	54.4762
31	16.3465	55.9959
32	17.3454	57.4944
33	18.3706	58.9715
34	19.4219	60.4269
35	20.4988	61.8604
36	21.6013	63.2717
37	22.7290	64.6608
38	23.8817	66.0272
39	25.0591	67.3709
40	26.2610	68.6915
41	27.4871	69.9889
42	28.7372	71.2628
43	30.0111	72.5129
44	31.3085	73.7390
45	32.6291	74.9409
46	33.9728	76.1183
47	35.3392	77.2710
48	36.7283	78.3987
49	38.1396	79.5012
50	39.5731	80.5781
51	41.0285	81.6294
52	42.5056	82.6546
53	44.0041	83.6535
54	45.5238	84.6258
55	47.0646	85.5714
56	48.6262	86.4898
57	50.2083	87.3809
58	51.8109	88.2443
59	53.4336	89.0798
60	55.0764	89.8870
61	56.7389	90.6658
62	58.4210	91.4157
63	60.1224	92.1366
64	61.8431	92.8280
65	63.5827	93.4898
66	65.3411	94.1216
67	67.1182	94.7231
68	68.9136	95.2939
69	70.7273	95.8339
70	72.5591	96.3426
71	74.4087	96.8198
72	76.2760	97.2650
73	78.1608	97.6781
74	80.0630	98.0587
75	81.9823	98.4063

#	REBATE	EARN
75	81.9823	98.4063
76	83.9186	98.7208
77	85.8717	99.0017
78	87.8414	99.2488
79	89.8276	99.4616
80	91.8301	99.6399
81	93.8488	99.7832
82	95.8834	99.8912
83	97.9339	99.9636
84	100.0000	100.0000

8 YEARS

#	REBATE	EARN
1	.0289	1.7800
2	.0864	3.5491
3	.1721	5.3070
4	.2859	7.0537
5	.4274	8.7890
6	.5964	10.5129
7	.7925	12.2252
8	1.0156	13.9258
9	1.2652	15.6146
10	1.5413	17.2915
11	1.8434	18.9563
12	2.1713	20.6089
13	2.5248	22.2492
14	2.9036	23.8771
15	3.3075	25.4924
16	3.7362	27.0950
17	4.1894	28.6849
18	4.6669	30.2617
19	5.1685	31.8255
20	5.6939	33.3761
21	6.2429	34.9134
22	6.8152	36.4371
23	7.4105	37.9472
24	8.0288	39.4436
25	8.6697	40.9261
26	9.3330	42.3945
27	10.0185	43.8488
28	10.7259	45.2887
29	11.4551	46.7141
30	12.2057	48.1249
31	12.9777	49.5210
32	13.7707	50.9021
33	14.5847	52.2681
34	15.4192	53.6189
35	16.2742	54.9544
36	17.1495	56.2743
37	18.0448	57.5784
38	18.9599	58.8667
39	19.8947	60.1390
40	20.8489	61.3951
41	21.8223	62.6349
42	22.8148	63.8581
43	23.8261	65.0647
44	24.8561	66.2543
45	25.9046	67.4270
46	26.9713	68.5824
47	28.0562	69.7205
48	29.1590	70.8410
49	30.2795	71.9438
50	31.4176	73.0287
51	32.5730	74.0954
52	33.7457	75.1439
53	34.9353	76.1739
54	36.1419	77.1852
55	37.3651	78.1777
56	38.6049	79.1511
57	39.8610	80.1053
58	41.1333	81.0401
59	42.4216	81.9552
60	43.7257	82.8505
61	45.0456	83.7258
62	46.3811	84.5808
63	47.7319	85.4153
64	49.0979	86.2293
65	50.4790	87.0223
66	51.8751	87.7943
67	53.2859	88.5449
68	54.7113	89.2741
69	56.1512	89.9815
70	57.6055	90.6670
71	59.0739	91.3303
72	60.5564	91.9712
73	62.0528	92.5895
74	63.5629	93.1848
75	65.0866	93.7571
76	66.6239	94.3061
77	68.1745	94.8315
78	69.7383	95.3331
79	71.3151	95.8106
80	72.9050	96.2638
81	74.5076	96.6925
82	76.1229	97.0964
83	77.7508	97.4752
84	79.3911	97.8287
85	81.0437	98.1566
86	82.7085	98.4587
87	84.3854	98.7348
88	86.0742	98.9844
89	87.7748	99.2075
90	89.4871	99.4036
91	91.2110	99.5726
92	92.9463	99.7141
93	94.6930	99.8279
94	96.4509	99.9136
95	98.2200	99.9711
96	100.0000	100.0000

9 YEARS

#	REBATE	EARN
1	.0236	1.5581
2	.0707	3.1083
3	.1409	4.6504
4	.2340	6.1844
5	.3498	7.7102
6	.4881	9.2276
7	.6487	10.7367
8	.8312	12.2373
9	1.0356	13.7293
10	1.2615	15.2127
11	1.5087	16.6874
12	1.7772	18.1532
13	2.0665	19.6101
14	2.3765	21.0580
15	2.7071	22.4968
16	3.0580	23.9264
17	3.4289	25.3467
18	3.8197	26.7576
19	4.2303	28.1591
20	4.6603	29.5510
21	5.1096	30.9332
22	5.5780	32.3057
23	6.0653	33.6683
24	6.5713	35.0209
25	7.0959	36.3634
26	7.6388	37.6958
27	8.1998	39.0179
28	8.7788	40.3296
29	9.3756	41.6308
30	9.9900	42.9214
31	10.6218	44.2014
32	11.2709	45.4705
33	11.9371	46.7286
34	12.6201	47.9758
35	13.3200	49.2118
36	14.0363	50.4365
37	14.7691	51.6499
38	15.5181	52.8517
39	16.2832	54.0420
40	17.0642	55.2205
41	17.8609	56.3872
42	18.6732	57.5419
43	19.5009	58.6845
44	20.3440	59.8149
45	21.2021	60.9330
46	22.0752	62.0386
47	22.9631	63.1316
48	23.8657	64.2119
49	24.7828	65.2793
50	25.7143	66.3337
51	26.6600	67.3751
52	27.6197	68.4031
53	28.5935	69.4178
54	29.5810	70.4190
55	30.5822	71.4065
56	31.5969	72.3803
57	32.6249	73.3400
58	33.6663	74.2857
59	34.7207	75.2172
60	35.7881	76.1343
61	36.8684	77.0369
62	37.9614	77.9248
63	39.0670	78.7979
64	40.1851	79.6560
65	41.3155	80.4991
66	42.4581	81.3268
67	43.6128	82.1391
68	44.7795	82.9358
69	45.9580	83.7168
70	47.1483	84.4819
71	48.3501	85.2309
72	49.5635	85.9637
73	50.7882	86.6800
74	52.0242	87.3799
75	53.2714	88.0629
76	54.5295	88.7291
77	55.7986	89.3782
78	57.0786	90.0100
79	58.3692	90.6244
80	59.6704	91.2212
81	60.9821	91.8002
82	62.3042	92.3612
83	63.6366	92.9041
84	64.9791	93.4287
85	66.3317	93.9347
86	67.6943	94.4220
87	69.0668	94.8904
88	70.4490	95.3397
89	71.8409	95.7697
90	73.2424	96.1803
91	74.6533	96.5711
92	76.0736	96.9420
93	77.5032	97.2929
94	78.9420	97.6235
95	80.3899	97.9335
96	81.8468	98.2228
97	83.3126	98.4913
98	84.7873	98.7385
99	86.2707	98.9644
100	87.7627	99.1688
101	89.2633	99.3513
102	90.7724	99.5119
103	92.2898	99.6502
104	93.8156	99.7660
105	95.3496	99.8591
106	96.8917	99.9293
107	98.4419	99.9764
108	100.0000	100.0000

10 YEARS

#	REBATE	EARN
1	.0198	1.3813
2	.0592	2.7567
3	.1181	4.1261
4	.1962	5.4895
5	.2933	6.8467
6	.4092	8.1978
7	.5438	9.5427
8	.6968	10.8813
9	.8681	12.2135
10	1.0575	13.5393
11	1.2648	14.8587
12	1.4898	16.1715
13	1.7323	17.4776
14	1.9922	18.7771
15	2.2693	20.0699
16	2.5634	21.3558
17	2.8744	22.6348
18	3.2020	23.9069
19	3.5462	25.1719
20	3.9066	26.4298
21	4.2833	27.6806
22	4.6759	28.9241
23	5.0845	30.1602
24	5.5086	31.3890
25	5.9484	32.6103
26	6.4035	33.8241
27	6.8738	35.0302
28	7.3591	36.2286
29	7.8594	37.4192
30	8.3745	38.6020
31	8.9041	39.7768
32	9.4482	40.9436
33	10.0067	42.1023
34	10.5793	43.2529
35	11.1659	44.3951
36	11.7664	45.5290
37	12.3807	46.6544
38	13.0086	47.7713
39	13.6499	48.8796
40	14.3046	49.9792
41	14.9725	51.0700
42	15.6535	52.1519
43	16.3473	53.2248
44	17.0540	54.2887
45	17.7734	55.3434
46	18.5053	56.3889
47	19.2496	57.4250
48	20.0063	58.4517
49	20.7751	59.4688
50	21.5559	60.4763
51	22.3487	61.4741
52	23.1532	62.4620
53	23.9695	63.4400
54	24.7973	64.4080
55	25.6366	65.3658
56	26.4872	66.3134
57	27.3490	67.2507
58	28.2219	68.1775
59	29.1059	69.0937
60	30.0007	69.9993
61	30.9063	70.8941
62	31.8225	71.7781
63	32.7493	72.6510
64	33.6866	73.5128
65	34.6342	74.3634
66	35.5920	75.2027
67	36.5600	76.0305
68	37.5380	76.8468
69	38.5259	77.6513
70	39.5237	78.4441
71	40.5312	79.2249
72	41.5483	79.9937
73	42.5750	80.7504
74	43.6111	81.4947
75	44.6566	82.2266
76	45.7113	82.9460
77	46.7752	83.6527
78	47.8481	84.3465
79	48.9300	85.0275
80	50.0208	85.6954
81	51.1204	86.3501
82	52.2287	86.9914
83	53.3456	87.6193
84	54.4710	88.2336
85	55.6049	88.8341
86	56.7471	89.4207
87	57.8977	89.9933
88	59.0564	90.5518
89	60.2232	91.0959
90	61.3980	91.6255
91	62.5808	92.1406
92	63.7714	92.6409
93	64.9698	93.1262
94	66.1759	93.5965
95	67.3897	94.0516
96	68.6110	94.4914
97	69.8398	94.9155
98	71.0759	95.3241
99	72.3194	95.7167
100	73.5702	96.0934
101	74.8281	96.4538
102	76.0931	96.7980
103	77.3652	97.1256
104	78.6442	97.4366
105	79.9301	97.7307
106	81.2229	98.0078
107	82.5224	98.2677
108	83.8285	98.5102
109	85.1413	98.7352
110	86.4607	98.9425
111	87.7865	99.1319
112	89.1187	99.3032
113	90.4573	99.4562
114	91.8022	99.5908
115	93.1533	99.7067
116	94.5105	99.8038
117	95.8739	99.8819
118	97.2433	99.9408
119	98.6187	99.9802
120	100.0000	100.0000

ACTUARIAL REBATE AND EARNINGS

12.50 %

1 YEAR

#	REBATE	EARN
1	1.3311	15.0979
2	3.9796	29.0080
3	7.9318	41.7181
4	13.1744	53.2157
5	19.6941	63.4880
6	27.4776	72.5224
7	36.5120	80.3059
8	46.7843	86.8256
9	58.2819	92.0682
10	70.9920	96.0204
11	84.9021	98.6689
12	100.0000	100.0000

2 YEARS

#	REBATE	EARN
1	.3603	7.6947
2	1.0771	15.1054
3	2.1467	22.2294
4	3.5657	29.0636
5	5.3302	35.6049
6	7.4368	41.8504
7	9.8820	47.7969
8	12.6622	53.4414
9	15.7740	58.7806
10	19.2140	63.8114
11	22.9788	68.5306
12	27.0650	72.9350
13	31.4694	77.0212
14	36.1886	80.7860
15	41.2194	84.2260
16	46.5586	87.3378
17	52.2031	90.1180
18	58.1496	92.5632
19	64.3951	94.6698
20	70.9364	96.4343
21	77.7706	97.8533
22	84.8946	98.9229
23	92.3053	99.6397
24	100.0000	100.0000

3 YEARS

#	REBATE	EARN
1	.1688	5.0979
2	.5046	10.0785
3	1.0058	14.9403
4	1.6706	19.6822
5	2.4973	24.3030
6	3.4842	28.8014
7	4.6298	33.1761
8	5.9324	37.4258
9	7.3903	41.5493
10	9.0020	45.5451
11	10.7658	49.4121
12	12.6803	53.1487
13	14.7438	56.7538
14	16.9548	60.2258
15	19.3118	63.5635
16	21.8133	66.7654
17	24.4578	69.8301
18	27.2438	72.7562
19	30.1699	75.5422
20	33.2346	78.1867
21	36.4365	80.6882
22	39.7742	83.0452
23	43.2462	85.2562
24	46.8513	87.3197
25	50.5879	89.2342

4 YEARS

#	REBATE	EARN
1	.0993	3.7763
2	.2970	7.4917
3	.5920	11.1453
4	.9832	14.7366
5	1.4698	18.2649
6	2.0507	21.7297
7	2.7249	25.1301
8	3.4915	28.4656
9	4.3496	31.7355
10	5.2982	34.9390
11	6.3363	38.0756
12	7.4631	41.1444
13	8.6776	44.1448
14	9.9789	47.0761
15	11.3661	49.9376
16	12.8384	52.7285
17	14.3948	55.4481
18	16.0345	58.0956
19	17.7567	60.6704
20	19.5604	63.1716
21	21.4449	65.5985
22	23.4093	67.9503
23	25.4528	70.2262
24	27.5746	72.4254
25	29.7738	74.5472
26	32.0497	76.5907
27	34.4015	78.5551
28	36.8284	80.4396
29	39.3296	82.2433
30	41.9044	83.9655
31	44.5519	85.6052
32	47.2715	87.1616
33	50.0624	88.6339
34	52.9239	90.0211
35	55.8552	91.3224
36	58.8556	92.5369
37	61.9244	93.6637
38	65.0610	94.7018
39	68.2645	95.6504
40	71.5344	96.5085
41	74.8699	97.2751
42	78.2703	97.9493
43	81.7351	98.5302
44	85.2634	99.0168
45	88.8547	99.4080
46	92.5083	99.7030
47	96.2237	99.9007
48	100.0000	100.0000

5 YEARS

#	REBATE	EARN
1	.0663	2.9772
2	.1982	5.9185
3	.3950	8.8234
4	.6561	11.6917
5	.9808	14.5228
6	1.3684	17.3164
7	1.8184	20.0721
8	2.3300	22.7896
9	2.9026	25.4683
10	3.5355	28.1080
11	4.2283	30.7083
12	4.9802	33.2686
13	5.7907	35.7886
14	6.6590	38.2679
15	7.5848	40.7060
16	8.5672	43.1025
17	9.6059	45.4570
18	10.7001	47.7691
19	11.8493	50.0383
20	13.0530	52.2641
21	14.3105	54.4461
22	15.6214	56.5839
23	16.9850	58.6769
24	18.4009	60.7248
25	19.8685	62.7270
26	21.3873	64.6831
27	22.9566	66.5926
28	24.5761	68.4551
29	26.2452	70.2699
30	27.9634	72.0366
31	29.7301	73.7548
32	31.5449	75.4239
33	33.4074	77.0434
34	35.3169	78.6127
35	37.2730	80.1315
36	39.2752	81.5991
37	41.3231	83.0150
38	43.4161	84.3786
39	45.5539	85.6895
40	47.7359	86.9470
41	49.9617	88.1507
42	52.2309	89.2999
43	54.5430	90.3941
44	56.8975	91.4328
45	59.2940	92.4152
46	61.7321	93.3410
47	64.2114	94.2093
48	66.7314	95.0198
49	69.2917	95.7717
50	71.8920	96.4645
51	74.5317	97.0974
52	77.2104	97.6700
53	79.9279	98.1816
54	82.6836	98.6316
55	85.4772	99.0192
56	88.3083	99.3439
57	91.1766	99.6050
58	94.0815	99.8018
59	97.0228	99.9337
60	100.0000	100.0000

6 YEARS

#	REBATE	EARN
1	.0479	2.4429
2	.1432	4.8629
3	.2854	7.2596
4	.4741	9.6330
5	.7087	11.9826
6	.9888	14.3084
7	1.3138	16.6099
8	1.6835	18.8871
9	2.0972	21.1396
10	2.5546	23.3671
11	3.0551	25.5694
12	3.5984	27.7463
13	4.1840	29.8975
14	4.8114	32.0227
15	5.4803	34.1216
16	6.1901	36.1940
17	6.9406	38.2395
18	7.7312	40.2580
19	8.5615	42.2492
20	9.4312	44.2126
21	10.3399	46.1481
22	11.2870	48.0554
23	12.2723	49.9342
24	13.2953	51.7841
25	14.3557	53.6049
26	15.4531	55.3963
27	16.5870	57.1579
28	17.7572	58.8895
29	18.9631	60.5907
30	20.2046	62.2613
31	21.4811	63.9008
32	22.7924	65.5090
33	24.1380	67.0856
34	25.5177	68.6303
35	26.9311	70.1426
36	28.3778	71.6222
37	29.8574	73.0689
38	31.3697	74.4823
39	32.9144	75.8620
40	34.4910	77.2076
41	36.0992	78.5189
42	37.7387	79.7954
43	39.4093	81.0369
44	41.1105	82.2428
45	42.8421	83.4130
46	44.6037	84.5469
47	46.3951	85.6443
48	48.2159	86.7047
49	50.0658	87.7277
50	51.9446	88.7130
51	53.8519	89.6601
52	55.7874	90.5688
53	57.7508	91.4385
54	59.7420	92.2688
55	61.7605	93.0594
56	63.8060	93.8099
57	65.8784	94.5197
58	67.9773	95.1886
59	70.1025	95.8160
60	72.2537	96.4016
61	74.4306	96.9449
62	76.6329	97.4454
63	78.8604	97.9028
64	81.1129	98.3165
65	83.3901	98.6862
66	85.6916	99.0112
67	88.0174	99.2913
68	90.3670	99.5259
69	92.7404	99.7146
70	95.1371	99.8568
71	97.5571	99.9521
72	100.0000	100.0000

7 YEARS

#	REBATE	EARN
1	.0366	2.0611
2	.1093	4.1068
3	.2178	6.1369
4	.3618	8.1511
5	.5409	10.1494
6	.7546	12.1316
7	1.0028	14.0974
8	1.2849	16.0469
9	1.6007	17.9797
10	1.9497	19.8956
11	2.3318	21.7946
12	2.7464	23.6765
13	3.1933	25.5410
14	3.6722	27.3880
15	4.1827	29.2173
16	4.7245	31.0287
17	5.2973	32.8220
18	5.9007	34.5971
19	6.5345	36.3538
20	7.1983	38.0918
21	7.8918	39.8109
22	8.6147	41.5111
23	9.3667	43.1920
24	10.1475	44.8535
25	10.9568	46.4953
26	11.7943	48.1173
27	12.6598	49.7193
28	13.5529	51.3010
29	14.4733	52.8623
30	15.4208	54.4028
31	16.3951	55.9225
32	17.3959	57.4211
33	18.4230	58.8984
34	19.4760	60.3541
35	20.5547	61.7880
36	21.6589	63.1999
37	22.7882	64.5896
38	23.9425	65.9569
39	25.1214	67.3014
40	26.3247	68.6230
41	27.5522	69.9214
42	28.8035	71.1965
43	30.0786	72.4478
44	31.3770	73.6753
45	32.6986	74.8786
46	34.0431	76.0575
47	35.4104	77.2118
48	36.8001	78.3411
49	38.2120	79.4453
50	39.6459	80.5240
51	41.1016	81.5770
52	42.5789	82.6041
53	44.0775	83.6049
54	45.5972	84.5792
55	47.1377	85.5267
56	48.6990	86.4471
57	50.2807	87.3402
58	51.8827	88.2057
59	53.5047	89.0432
60	55.1465	89.8525
61	56.8080	90.6333
62	58.4889	91.3853
63	60.1891	92.1082
64	61.9082	92.8017
65	63.6462	93.4655
66	65.4029	94.0993
67	67.1780	94.7027
68	68.9713	95.2755
69	70.7827	95.8173
70	72.6120	96.3278
71	74.4590	96.8067
72	76.3235	97.2536
73	78.2054	97.6682
74	80.1044	98.0503
75	82.0203	98.3993

#	REBATE	EARN
75	82.0203	98.3993
76	83.9531	98.7151
77	85.9026	98.9972
78	87.8684	99.2454
79	89.8506	99.4591
80	91.8489	99.6382
81	93.8631	99.7822
82	95.8932	99.8907
83	97.9389	99.9634
84	100.0000	100.0000

8 YEARS

#	REBATE	EARN
1	.0290	1.7753
2	.0868	3.5397
3	.1730	5.2931
4	.2874	7.0355
5	.4297	8.7667
6	.5995	10.4866
7	.7966	12.1950
8	1.0207	13.8919
9	1.2715	15.5771
10	1.5488	17.2506
11	1.8523	18.9121
12	2.1817	20.5616
13	2.5367	22.1990
14	2.9172	23.8240
15	3.3227	25.4366
16	3.7531	27.0367
17	4.2081	28.6241
18	4.6874	30.1987
19	5.1909	31.7604
20	5.7182	33.3090
21	6.2691	34.8444
22	6.8433	36.3664
23	7.4407	37.8749
24	8.0610	39.3698
25	8.7039	40.8510
26	9.3692	42.3182
27	10.0567	43.7714
28	10.7662	45.2103
29	11.4974	46.6349
30	12.2501	48.0450
31	13.0240	49.4405
32	13.8191	50.8211
33	14.6349	52.1868
34	15.4714	53.5373
35	16.3284	54.8726
36	17.2055	56.1925
37	18.1026	57.4967
38	19.0195	58.7852
39	19.9560	60.0578
40	20.9119	61.3143
41	21.8870	62.5545
42	22.8811	63.7784
43	23.8939	64.9856
44	24.9254	66.1760
45	25.9752	67.3495
46	27.0433	68.5059
47	28.1294	69.6450
48	29.2334	70.7666
49	30.3550	71.8706
50	31.4941	72.9567
51	32.6505	74.0248
52	33.8240	75.0746
53	35.0144	76.1061
54	36.2216	77.1189
55	37.4455	78.1130
56	38.6857	79.0881
57	39.9422	80.0440
58	41.2148	80.9805
59	42.5033	81.8974
60	43.8075	82.7945
61	45.1274	83.6716
62	46.4627	84.5286
63	47.8132	85.3651
64	49.1789	86.1809
65	50.5595	86.9760
66	51.9550	87.7499
67	53.3651	88.5026
68	54.7897	89.2338
69	56.2286	89.9433
70	57.6818	90.6308
71	59.1490	91.2961
72	60.6302	91.9390
73	62.1251	92.5593
74	63.6336	93.1567
75	65.1556	93.7309
76	66.6910	94.2818
77	68.2396	94.8091
78	69.8013	95.3126
79	71.3759	95.7919
80	72.9633	96.2469
81	74.5634	96.6773
82	76.1760	97.0828
83	77.8010	97.4633
84	79.4384	97.8183
85	81.0879	98.1477
86	82.7494	98.4512
87	84.4229	98.7285
88	86.1081	98.9793
89	87.8050	99.2034
90	89.5134	99.4005
91	91.2333	99.5703
92	92.9645	99.7126
93	94.7069	99.8270
94	96.4603	99.9132
95	98.2247	99.9710
96	100.0000	100.0000

9 YEARS

#	REBATE	EARN
1	.0238	1.5536
2	.0711	3.0993
3	.1417	4.6371
4	.2354	6.1669
5	.3519	7.6886
6	.4909	9.2021
7	.6524	10.7074
8	.8359	12.2043
9	1.0413	13.6927
10	1.2684	15.1727
11	1.5169	16.6440
12	1.7867	18.1066
13	2.0774	19.5604
14	2.3890	21.0054
15	2.7211	22.4414
16	3.0735	23.8682
17	3.4461	25.2860
18	3.8387	26.6944
19	4.2510	28.0935
20	4.6828	29.4832
21	5.1340	30.8633
22	5.6042	32.2337
23	6.0935	33.5944
24	6.6014	34.9452
25	7.1279	36.2861
26	7.6728	37.6169
27	8.2358	38.9375
28	8.8168	40.2479
29	9.4156	41.5479
30	10.0320	42.8374
31	10.6658	44.1163
32	11.3169	45.3845
33	11.9850	46.6418
34	12.6701	47.8883
35	13.3718	49.1237
36	14.0902	50.3479
37	14.8248	51.5609
38	15.5757	52.7624
39	16.3427	53.9525
40	17.1255	55.1309
41	17.9240	56.2975
42	18.7381	57.4523
43	19.5675	58.5951
44	20.4122	59.7257
45	21.2720	60.8441
46	22.1467	61.9502
47	23.0361	63.0437
48	23.9402	64.1245
49	24.8587	65.1926
50	25.7916	66.2478
51	26.7386	67.2900
52	27.6996	68.3190
53	28.6745	69.3346
54	29.6631	70.3369
55	30.6654	71.3255
56	31.6810	72.3004
57	32.7100	73.2614
58	33.7522	74.2084
59	34.8074	75.1413
60	35.8755	76.0598
61	36.9563	76.9639
62	38.0498	77.8533
63	39.1559	78.7280
64	40.2743	79.5878
65	41.4049	80.4325
66	42.5477	81.2619
67	43.7025	82.0760
68	44.8691	82.8745
69	46.0475	83.6573
70	47.2376	84.4243
71	48.4391	85.1752
72	49.6521	85.9098
73	50.8763	86.6282
74	52.1117	87.3299
75	53.3582	88.0150
76	54.6155	88.6831
77	55.8837	89.3342
78	57.1626	89.9680
79	58.4521	90.5844
80	59.7521	91.1832
81	61.0625	91.7642
82	62.3831	92.3272
83	63.7139	92.8721
84	65.0548	93.3986
85	66.4056	93.9065
86	67.7663	94.3958
87	69.1367	94.8660
88	70.5168	95.3172
89	71.9065	95.7490
90	73.3056	96.1613
91	74.7140	96.5539
92	76.1318	96.9265
93	77.5586	97.2789
94	78.9946	97.6110
95	80.4396	97.9226
96	81.8934	98.2133
97	83.3560	98.4831
98	84.8273	98.7316
99	86.3073	98.9587
100	87.7957	99.1641
101	89.2926	99.3476
102	90.7979	99.5091
103	92.3114	99.6481
104	93.8331	99.7646
105	95.3629	99.8583
106	96.9007	99.9289
107	98.4464	99.9762
108	100.0000	100.0000

10 YEARS

#	REBATE	EARN
1	.0199	1.3769
2	.0596	2.7480
3	.1189	4.1133
4	.1974	5.4726
5	.2951	6.8259
6	.4118	8.1732
7	.5472	9.5143
8	.7011	10.8493
9	.8734	12.1780
10	1.0639	13.5004
11	1.2723	14.8164
12	1.4986	16.1259
13	1.7424	17.4290
14	2.0037	18.7254
15	2.2823	20.0153
16	2.5779	21.2984
17	2.8904	22.5747
18	3.2197	23.8441
19	3.5655	25.1066
20	3.9277	26.3621
21	4.3061	27.6106
22	4.7005	28.8519
23	5.1108	30.0859
24	5.5369	31.3127
25	5.9785	32.5321
26	6.4355	33.7440
27	6.9077	34.9484
28	7.3950	36.1452
29	7.8972	37.3343
30	8.4142	38.5156
31	8.9459	39.6891
32	9.4919	40.8547
33	10.0523	42.0122
34	10.6269	43.1617
35	11.2155	44.3029
36	11.8180	45.4359
37	12.4342	46.5606
38	13.0640	47.6768
39	13.7073	48.7844
40	14.3638	49.8835
41	15.0336	50.9738
42	15.7164	52.0554
43	16.4121	53.1281
44	17.1206	54.1917
45	17.8417	55.2463
46	18.5753	56.2918
47	19.3213	57.3280
48	20.0796	58.3548
49	20.8500	59.3721
50	21.6324	60.3799
51	22.4267	61.3781
52	23.2328	62.3664
53	24.0505	63.3450
54	24.8797	64.3135
55	25.7203	65.2720
56	26.5722	66.2203
57	27.4352	67.1584
58	28.3093	68.0861
59	29.1943	69.0032
60	30.0902	69.9098
61	30.9968	70.8057
62	31.9139	71.6907
63	32.8416	72.5648
64	33.7797	73.4278
65	34.7280	74.2797
66	35.6865	75.1203
67	36.6550	75.9495
68	37.6336	76.7672
69	38.6219	77.5733
70	39.6201	78.3676
71	40.6279	79.1500
72	41.6452	79.9204
73	42.6720	80.6787
74	43.7082	81.4247
75	44.7537	82.1583
76	45.8083	82.8794
77	46.8719	83.5879
78	47.9446	84.2836
79	49.0262	84.9664
80	50.1165	85.6362
81	51.2156	86.2927
82	52.3232	86.9360
83	53.4394	87.5658
84	54.5641	88.1820
85	55.6971	88.7845
86	56.8383	89.3731
87	57.9878	89.9477
88	59.1453	90.5081
89	60.3109	91.0541
90	61.4844	91.5858
91	62.6657	92.1028
92	63.8548	92.6050
93	65.0516	93.0923
94	66.2560	93.5645
95	67.4679	94.0215
96	68.6873	94.4631
97	69.9141	94.8892
98	71.1481	95.2995
99	72.3894	95.6939
100	73.6379	96.0723
101	74.8934	96.4345
102	76.1559	96.7803
103	77.4253	97.1096
104	78.7016	97.4221
105	79.9847	97.7177
106	81.2746	97.9963
107	82.5710	98.2576
108	83.8741	98.5014
109	85.1836	98.7277
110	86.4996	98.9361
111	87.8220	99.1266
112	89.1507	99.2989
113	90.4857	99.4528
114	91.8268	99.5882
115	93.1741	99.7049
116	94.5274	99.8026
117	95.8867	99.8811
118	97.2520	99.9404
119	98.6231	99.9801
120	100.0000	100.0000

1 YEAR

#	REBATE	EARN
1	1.3321	15.0923
2	3.9822	28.9986
3	7.9366	41.7066
4	13.1815	53.2033
5	19.7033	63.4759
6	27.4886	72.5114
7	36.5241	80.2967
8	46.7967	86.8185
9	58.2934	92.0634
10	71.0014	96.0178
11	84.9077	98.6679
12	100.0000	100.0000

2 YEARS

#	REBATE	EARN
1	.3608	7.6888
2	1.0786	15.0947
3	2.1497	22.2146
4	3.5703	29.0456
5	5.3368	35.5845
6	7.4455	41.8282
7	9.8929	47.7736
8	12.6753	53.4176
9	15.7893	58.7568
10	19.2314	63.7882
11	22.9980	68.5084
12	27.0859	72.9141
13	31.4916	77.0020
14	36.2118	80.7686
15	41.2432	84.2107
16	46.5824	87.3247
17	52.2264	90.1071
18	58.1718	92.5545
19	64.4155	94.6632
20	70.9544	96.4297
21	77.7854	97.8503
22	84.9053	98.9214
23	92.3112	99.6392
24	100.0000	100.0000

3 YEARS

#	REBATE	EARN
1	.1692	5.0922
2	.5057	10.0676
3	1.0079	14.9248
4	1.6740	19.6627
5	2.5022	24.2800
6	3.4909	28.7754
7	4.6384	33.1475
8	5.9429	37.3952
9	7.4030	41.5170
10	9.0168	45.5117
11	10.7828	49.3778
12	12.6995	53.1140
13	14.7651	56.7190
14	16.9782	60.1913
15	19.3373	63.5296
16	21.8406	66.7323
17	24.4868	69.7982
18	27.2744	72.7256
19	30.2018	75.5132
20	33.2677	78.1594
21	36.4704	80.6627
22	39.8087	83.0218
23	43.2810	85.2349
24	46.8860	87.3005
25	50.6222	89.2172
26	54.4883	90.9832
27	58.4830	92.5970
28	62.6048	94.0571
29	66.8525	95.3616
30	71.2246	96.5091
31	75.7200	97.4978
32	80.3373	98.3260
33	85.0752	98.9921
34	89.9324	99.4943
35	94.9078	99.8308
36	100.0000	100.0000

4 YEARS

#	REBATE	EARN
1	.0996	3.7708
2	.2979	7.4809
3	.5936	11.1298
4	.9859	14.7168
5	1.4737	18.2411
6	2.0561	21.7023
7	2.7319	25.0995
8	3.5002	28.4321
9	4.3601	31.6994
10	5.3107	34.9008
11	6.3508	38.0354
12	7.4797	41.1027
13	8.6963	44.1019
14	9.9997	47.0322
15	11.3891	49.8930
16	12.8635	52.6835
17	14.4221	55.4030
18	16.0639	58.0506
19	17.7881	60.6257
20	19.5938	63.1275
21	21.4801	65.5551
22	23.4462	67.9078
23	25.4913	70.1849
24	27.6146	72.3854
25	29.8151	74.5087
26	32.0922	76.5538
27	34.4449	78.5199
28	36.8725	80.4062
29	39.3743	82.2119
30	41.9494	83.9361
31	44.5970	85.5779
32	47.3165	87.1365
33	50.1070	88.6109
34	52.9678	90.0003
35	55.8981	91.3037
36	58.8973	92.5203
37	61.9646	93.6492
38	65.0992	94.6893
39	68.3006	95.6399
40	71.5679	96.4998
41	74.9005	97.2681
42	78.2977	97.9439
43	81.7589	98.5263
44	85.2832	99.0141
45	88.8702	99.4064
46	92.5191	99.7021
47	96.2292	99.9004
48	100.0000	100.0000

5 YEARS

#	REBATE	EARN
1	.0665	2.9719
2	.1989	5.9081
3	.3964	8.8083
4	.6584	11.6720
5	.9841	14.4989
6	1.3730	17.2887
7	1.8243	20.0408
8	2.3373	22.7549
9	2.9116	25.4307
10	3.5463	28.0676
11	4.2409	30.6653
12	4.9947	33.2234
13	5.8071	35.7414
14	6.6775	38.2135
15	7.6053	40.6555
16	8.5898	43.0507
17	9.6306	45.4042
18	10.7269	47.7154
19	11.8783	49.9839
20	13.0840	52.2093
21	14.3437	54.3912
22	15.6566	56.5289
23	17.0223	58.6221
24	18.4401	60.6704
25	19.9095	62.6731
26	21.4301	64.6299
27	23.0011	66.5402
28	24.6222	68.4036
29	26.2928	70.2196
30	28.0124	71.9876
31	29.7804	73.7072
32	31.5964	75.3778
33	33.4598	76.9989
34	35.3701	78.5699
35	37.3269	80.0905
36	39.3296	81.5599
37	41.3779	82.9777
38	43.4711	84.3434
39	45.6088	85.6563
40	47.7907	86.9160
41	50.0161	88.1217
42	52.2846	89.2731
43	54.5958	90.3694
44	56.9493	91.4102
45	59.3445	92.3947
46	61.7811	93.3225
47	64.2586	94.1929
48	66.7766	95.0053
49	69.3347	95.7591
50	71.9324	96.4537
51	74.5693	97.0884
52	77.2451	97.6627
53	79.9592	98.1757
54	82.7113	98.6270
55	85.5011	99.0159
56	88.3280	99.3416
57	91.1917	99.6036
58	94.0919	99.8011
59	97.0281	99.9335
60	100.0000	100.0000

6 YEARS

#	REBATE	EARN
1	.0481	2.4377
2	.1438	4.8528
3	.2866	7.2449
4	.4760	9.6137
5	.7115	11.9592
6	.9927	14.2809
7	1.3189	16.5787
8	1.6899	18.8523
9	2.1051	21.1015
10	2.5640	23.3259
11	3.0662	25.5253
12	3.6112	27.6995
13	4.1985	29.8482
14	4.8279	31.9711
15	5.4986	34.0679
16	6.2105	36.1384
17	6.9630	38.1823
18	7.7556	40.1993
19	8.5880	42.1891
20	9.4598	44.1515
21	10.3705	46.0860
22	11.3198	47.9925
23	12.3072	49.8707
24	13.3323	51.7202
25	14.3947	53.5407
26	15.4940	55.3320
27	16.6299	57.0936
28	17.8020	58.8254
29	19.0098	60.5270
30	20.2531	62.1980
31	21.5314	63.8382
32	22.8443	65.4471
33	24.1916	67.0246
34	25.5728	68.5702
35	26.9875	70.0836
36	28.4355	71.5645
37	29.9164	73.0125
38	31.4298	74.4272
39	32.9754	75.8084
40	34.5529	77.1557
41	36.1618	78.4686
42	37.8020	79.7469
43	39.4730	80.9902
44	41.1746	82.1980
45	42.9064	83.3701
46	44.6680	84.5060
47	46.4593	85.6053
48	48.2798	86.6677
49	50.1293	87.6928
50	52.0075	88.6802
51	53.9140	89.6295
52	55.8485	90.5402
53	57.8109	91.4120
54	59.8007	92.2444
55	61.8177	93.0370
56	63.8616	93.7895
57	65.9321	94.5014
58	68.0289	95.1721
59	70.1518	95.8015
60	72.3005	96.3888
61	74.4747	96.9338
62	76.6741	97.4360
63	78.8985	97.8949
64	81.1477	98.3101
65	83.4213	98.6811
66	85.7191	99.0073
67	88.0408	99.2885
68	90.3863	99.5240
69	92.7551	99.7134
70	95.1472	99.8562
71	97.5623	99.9519
72	100.0000	100.0000

7 YEARS

#	REBATE	EARN
1	.0367	2.0562
2	.1098	4.0971
3	.2189	6.1226
4	.3635	8.1324
5	.5434	10.1265
6	.7581	12.1047
7	1.0073	14.0667
8	1.2906	16.0125
9	1.6077	17.9418
10	1.9581	19.8545
11	2.3416	21.7504
12	2.7579	23.6293
13	3.2065	25.4910
14	3.6871	27.3354
15	4.1994	29.1622
16	4.7430	30.9713
17	5.3177	32.7626
18	5.9230	34.5357
19	6.5588	36.2906
20	7.2245	38.0269
21	7.9201	39.7446
22	8.6450	41.4434
23	9.3991	43.1231
24	10.1819	44.7836
25	10.9933	46.4245
26	11.8329	48.0458
27	12.7004	49.6472
28	13.5955	51.2285
29	14.5180	52.7894
30	15.4674	54.3298
31	16.4437	55.8494
32	17.4464	57.3480
33	18.4753	58.8255
34	19.5301	60.2815
35	20.6106	61.7159
36	21.7164	63.1283
37	22.8474	64.5187
38	24.0032	65.8867
39	25.1836	67.2321
40	26.3883	68.5547
41	27.6171	69.8541
42	28.8697	71.1303
43	30.1459	72.3829
44	31.4453	73.6117
45	32.7679	74.8164
46	34.1133	75.9968
47	35.4813	77.1526
48	36.8717	78.2836
49	38.2841	79.3894
50	39.7185	80.4699
51	41.1745	81.5247
52	42.6520	82.5536
53	44.1506	83.5563
54	45.6702	84.5326
55	47.2106	85.4820
56	48.7715	86.4045
57	50.3528	87.2996
58	51.9542	88.1671
59	53.5755	89.0067
60	55.2164	89.8181
61	56.8769	90.6009
62	58.5566	91.3550
63	60.2554	92.0799
64	61.9731	92.7755
65	63.7094	93.4412
66	65.4643	94.0770
67	67.2374	94.6823
68	69.0287	95.2570
69	70.8378	95.8006
70	72.6646	96.3129
71	74.5090	96.7935
72	76.3707	97.2421
73	78.2496	97.6584
74	80.1455	98.0419
75	82.0582	98.3923

#	REBATE	EARN
75	82.0582	98.3923
76	83.9875	98.7094
77	85.9333	98.9927
78	87.8953	99.2419
79	89.8735	99.4566
80	91.8676	99.6365
81	93.8774	99.7811
82	95.9029	99.8902
83	97.9438	99.9633
84	100.0000	100.0000

8 YEARS

#	REBATE	EARN
1	.0292	1.7705
2	.0873	3.5304
3	.1740	5.2794
4	.2890	7.0175
5	.4319	8.7445
6	.6026	10.4604
7	.8006	12.1650
8	1.0258	13.8583
9	1.2779	15.5399
10	1.5564	17.2100
11	1.8613	18.8683
12	2.1921	20.5147
13	2.5487	22.1490
14	2.9307	23.7713
15	3.3379	25.3812
16	3.7700	26.9788
17	4.2268	28.5638
18	4.7079	30.1361
19	5.2132	31.6957
20	5.7425	33.2423
21	6.2953	34.7758
22	6.8715	36.2961
23	7.4709	37.8030
24	8.0932	39.2965
25	8.7381	40.7763
26	9.4054	42.2423
27	10.0950	43.6943
28	10.8064	45.1323
29	11.5396	46.5561
30	12.2943	47.9655
31	13.0703	49.3603
32	13.8673	50.7405
33	14.6851	52.1058
34	15.5236	53.4561
35	16.3824	54.7912
36	17.2614	56.1110
37	18.1603	57.4154
38	19.0790	58.7040
39	20.0172	59.9769
40	20.9748	61.2338
41	21.9515	62.4745
42	22.9472	63.6989
43	23.9615	64.9067
44	24.9944	66.0980
45	26.0457	67.2723
46	27.1151	68.4296
47	28.2024	69.5697
48	29.3076	70.6924
49	30.4303	71.7976
50	31.5704	72.8849
51	32.7277	73.9543
52	33.9020	75.0056
53	35.0933	76.0385
54	36.3011	77.0528
55	37.5255	78.0485
56	38.7662	79.0252
57	40.0231	79.9828
58	41.2960	80.9210
59	42.5846	81.8397
60	43.8890	82.7386
61	45.2088	83.6176
62	46.5439	84.4764
63	47.8942	85.3149
64	49.2595	86.1327
65	50.6397	86.9297
66	52.0345	87.7057
67	53.4439	88.4604
68	54.8677	89.1936
69	56.3057	89.9050
70	57.7577	90.5946
71	59.2237	91.2619
72	60.7035	91.9068
73	62.1970	92.5291
74	63.7039	93.1285
75	65.2242	93.7047
76	66.7577	94.2575
77	68.3043	94.7868
78	69.8639	95.2921
79	71.4362	95.7732
80	73.0212	96.2300
81	74.6188	96.6621
82	76.2287	97.0693
83	77.8510	97.4513
84	79.4853	97.8079
85	81.1317	98.1387
86	82.7900	98.4436
87	84.4601	98.7221
88	86.1417	98.9742
89	87.8350	99.1994
90	89.5396	99.3974
91	91.2555	99.5681
92	92.9825	99.7110
93	94.7206	99.8260
94	96.4696	99.9127
95	98.2295	99.9708
96	100.0000	100.0000

9 YEARS

#	REBATE	EARN
1	.0239	1.5490
2	.0715	3.0904
3	.1426	4.6239
4	.2368	6.1495
5	.3539	7.6672
6	.4938	9.1768
7	.6560	10.6783
8	.8406	12.1715
9	1.0471	13.6564
10	1.2753	15.1329
11	1.5251	16.6010
12	1.7962	18.0604
13	2.0884	19.5112
14	2.4014	20.9532
15	2.7350	22.3863
16	3.0891	23.8105
17	3.4634	25.2257
18	3.8577	26.6316
19	4.2717	28.0284
20	4.7053	29.4158
21	5.1583	30.7938
22	5.6305	32.1622
23	6.1216	33.5210
24	6.6315	34.8700
25	7.1599	36.2092
26	7.7068	37.5385
27	8.2718	38.8577
28	8.8548	40.1667
29	9.4555	41.4655
30	10.0739	42.7538
31	10.7098	44.0317
32	11.3628	45.2990
33	12.0329	46.5555
34	12.7199	47.8013
35	13.4237	49.0360
36	14.1439	50.2598
37	14.8805	51.4723
38	15.6333	52.6736
39	16.4020	53.8634
40	17.1867	55.0417
41	17.9870	56.2083
42	18.8028	57.3631
43	19.6340	58.5061
44	20.4803	59.6370
45	21.3417	60.7557
46	22.2180	61.8621
47	23.1090	62.9561
48	24.0145	64.0376
49	24.9344	65.1063
50	25.8686	66.1623
51	26.8169	67.2052
52	27.7792	68.2351
53	28.7553	69.2517
54	29.7450	70.2550
55	30.7483	71.2447
56	31.7649	72.2208
57	32.7948	73.1831
58	33.8377	74.1314
59	34.8937	75.0656
60	35.9624	75.9855
61	37.0439	76.8910
62	38.1379	77.7820
63	39.2443	78.6583
64	40.3630	79.5197
65	41.4939	80.3660
66	42.6369	81.1972
67	43.7917	82.0130
68	44.9583	82.8133
69	46.1366	83.5980
70	47.3264	84.3667
71	48.5277	85.1195
72	49.7402	85.8561
73	50.9640	86.5763
74	52.1987	87.2801
75	53.4445	87.9671
76	54.7010	88.6372
77	55.9683	89.2902
78	57.2462	89.9261
79	58.5345	90.5445
80	59.8333	91.1452
81	61.1423	91.7282
82	62.4615	92.2932
83	63.7908	92.8401
84	65.1300	93.3685
85	66.4790	93.8784
86	67.8378	94.3695
87	69.2062	94.8417
88	70.5842	95.2947
89	71.9716	95.7283
90	73.3684	96.1423
91	74.7743	96.5366
92	76.1895	96.9109
93	77.6137	97.2650
94	79.0468	97.5986
95	80.4888	97.9116
96	81.9396	98.2038
97	83.3990	98.4749
98	84.8671	98.7247
99	86.3436	98.9529
100	87.8285	99.1594
101	89.3217	99.3440
102	90.8232	99.5062
103	92.3328	99.6461
104	93.8505	99.7632
105	95.3761	99.8574
106	96.9096	99.9285
107	98.4510	99.9761
108	100.0000	100.0000

10 YEARS

#	REBATE	EARN
1	.0201	1.3726
2	.0600	2.7395
3	.1196	4.1006
4	.1987	5.4559
5	.2970	6.8053
6	.4144	8.1488
7	.5505	9.4862
8	.7054	10.8175
9	.8787	12.1427
10	1.0702	13.4617
11	1.2799	14.7744
12	1.5074	16.0808
13	1.7525	17.3807
14	2.0152	18.6742
15	2.2952	19.9611
16	2.5924	21.2414
17	2.9065	22.5150
18	3.2373	23.7819
19	3.5848	25.0419
20	3.9487	26.2950
21	4.3288	27.5411
22	4.7251	28.7802
23	5.1372	30.0122
24	5.5651	31.2369
25	6.0086	32.4544
26	6.4675	33.6645
27	6.9416	34.8672
28	7.4308	36.0624
29	7.9350	37.2499
30	8.4540	38.4298
31	8.9875	39.6020
32	9.5356	40.7663
33	10.0979	41.9227
34	10.6745	43.0711
35	11.2650	44.2113
36	11.8694	45.3435
37	12.4876	46.4673
38	13.1193	47.5828
39	13.7645	48.6898
40	14.4229	49.7884
41	15.0945	50.8783
42	15.7792	51.9595
43	16.4767	53.0318
44	17.1869	54.0953
45	17.9098	55.1498
46	18.6452	56.1952
47	19.3929	57.2314
48	20.1528	58.2584
49	20.9248	59.2759
50	21.7088	60.2840
51	22.5046	61.2825
52	23.3121	62.2713
53	24.1312	63.2503
54	24.9618	64.2195
55	25.8037	65.1786
56	26.6568	66.1276
57	27.5211	67.0665
58	28.3964	67.9950
59	29.2825	68.9131
60	30.1794	69.8206
61	31.0869	70.7175
62	32.0050	71.6036
63	32.9335	72.4789
64	33.8724	73.3432
65	34.8214	74.1963
66	35.7805	75.0382
67	36.7497	75.8688
68	37.7287	76.6879
69	38.7175	77.4954
70	39.7160	78.2912
71	40.7241	79.0752
72	41.7416	79.8472
73	42.7686	80.6071
74	43.8048	81.3548
75	44.8502	82.0902
76	45.9047	82.8131
77	46.9682	83.5233
78	48.0405	84.2208
79	49.1217	84.9055
80	50.2116	85.5771
81	51.3102	86.2355
82	52.4172	86.8807
83	53.5327	87.5124
84	54.6565	88.1306
85	55.7887	88.7350
86	56.9289	89.3255
87	58.0773	89.9021
88	59.2337	90.4644
89	60.3980	91.0125
90	61.5702	91.5460
91	62.7501	92.0650
92	63.9376	92.5692
93	65.1328	93.0584
94	66.3355	93.5325
95	67.5456	93.9914
96	68.7631	94.4349
97	69.9878	94.8628
98	71.2198	95.2749
99	72.4589	95.6712
100	73.7050	96.0513
101	74.9581	96.4152
102	76.2181	96.7627
103	77.4850	97.0935
104	78.7586	97.4076
105	80.0389	97.7048
106	81.3258	97.9848
107	82.6193	98.2475
108	83.9192	98.4926
109	85.2256	98.7201
110	86.5383	98.9298
111	87.8573	99.1213
112	89.1825	99.2946
113	90.5138	99.4495
114	91.8512	99.5856
115	93.1947	99.7030
116	94.5441	99.8013
117	95.8994	99.8804
118	97.2605	99.9400
119	98.6274	99.9799
120	100.0000	100.0000

1 YEAR

#	REBATE	EARN
1	1.3331	15.0867
2	3.9849	28.9893
3	7.9414	41.6950
4	13.1885	53.1909
5	19.7124	63.4638
6	27.4995	72.5005
7	36.5362	80.2876
8	46.8091	86.8115
9	58.3050	92.0586
10	71.0107	96.0151
11	84.9133	98.6669
12	100.0000	100.0000

2 YEARS

#	REBATE	EARN
1	.3613	7.6830
2	1.0802	15.0840
3	2.1526	22.1999
4	3.5750	29.0276
5	5.3434	35.5640
6	7.4542	41.8060
7	9.9038	47.7503
8	12.6885	53.3938
9	15.8046	58.7331
10	19.2487	63.7650
11	23.0173	68.4862
12	27.1068	72.8932
13	31.5138	76.9827
14	36.2350	80.7513
15	41.2669	84.1954
16	46.6062	87.3115
17	52.2497	90.0962
18	58.1940	92.5458
19	64.4360	94.6566
20	70.9724	96.4250
21	77.8001	97.8474
22	84.9160	98.9198
23	92.3170	99.6387
24	100.0000	100.0000

3 YEARS

#	REBATE	EARN
1	.1695	5.0865
2	.5068	10.0567
3	1.0100	14.9094
4	1.6774	19.6432
5	2.5072	24.2570
6	3.4976	28.7494
7	4.6469	33.1190
8	5.9535	37.3646
9	7.4156	41.4848
10	9.0316	45.4783
11	10.7998	49.3436
12	12.7187	53.0794
13	14.7865	56.6843
14	17.0017	60.1569
15	19.3627	63.4957
16	21.8679	66.6993
17	24.5159	69.7663
18	27.3050	72.6950
19	30.2337	75.4841
20	33.3007	78.1321
21	36.5043	80.6373
22	39.8431	82.9983
23	43.3157	85.2135
24	46.9206	87.2813
25	50.6564	89.2002
26	54.5217	90.9684
27	58.5152	92.5844
28	62.6354	94.0465
29	66.8810	95.3531
30	71.2506	96.5024
31	75.7430	97.4928
32	80.3568	98.3226
33	85.0906	98.9900
34	89.9433	99.4932
35	94.9135	99.8305
36	100.0000	100.0000

4 YEARS

#	REBATE	EARN
1	.0999	3.7652
2	.2987	7.4703
3	.5953	11.1144
4	.9886	14.6970
5	1.4777	18.2174
6	2.0614	21.6749
7	2.7388	25.0689
8	3.5089	28.3987
9	4.3707	31.6634
10	5.3231	34.8626
11	6.3653	37.9954
12	7.4962	41.0611
13	8.7150	44.0590
14	10.0206	46.9884
15	11.4121	49.8485
16	12.8887	52.6386
17	14.4494	55.3579
18	16.0932	58.0057
19	17.8194	60.5811
20	19.6270	63.0834
21	21.5152	65.5118
22	23.4831	67.8655
23	25.5298	70.1437
24	27.6545	72.3455
25	29.8563	74.4702
26	32.1345	76.5169
27	34.4882	78.4848
28	36.9166	80.3730
29	39.4189	82.1806
30	41.9943	83.9068
31	44.6421	85.5506
32	47.3614	87.1113
33	50.1515	88.5879
34	53.0116	89.9794
35	55.9410	91.2850
36	58.9389	92.5038
37	62.0046	93.6347
38	65.1374	94.6769
39	68.3366	95.6293
40	71.6013	96.4911
41	74.9311	97.2612
42	78.3251	97.9386
43	81.7826	98.5223
44	85.3030	99.0114
45	88.8856	99.4047
46	92.5297	99.7013
47	96.2348	99.9001
48	100.0000	100.0000

5 YEARS

#	REBATE	EARN
1	.0668	2.9665
2	.1996	5.8977
3	.3978	8.7931
4	.6606	11.6525
5	.9874	14.4752
6	1.3775	17.2611
7	1.8301	20.0096
8	2.3447	22.7205
9	2.9206	25.3932
10	3.5570	28.0273
11	4.2534	30.6225
12	5.0091	33.1783
13	5.8235	35.6943
14	6.6959	38.1701
15	7.6258	40.6051
16	8.6124	42.9991
17	9.6553	45.3515
18	10.7538	47.6619
19	11.9072	49.9298
20	13.1151	52.1548
21	14.3768	54.3364
22	15.6918	56.4741
23	17.0594	58.5675
24	18.4792	60.6160
25	19.9505	62.6193
26	21.4728	64.5768
27	23.0456	66.4879
28	24.6683	68.3523
29	26.3404	70.1694
30	28.0613	71.9387
31	29.8306	73.6596
32	31.6477	75.3317
33	33.5121	76.9544
34	35.4232	78.5272
35	37.3807	80.0495
36	39.3840	81.5208
37	41.4325	82.9406
38	43.5259	84.3082
39	45.6636	85.6232
40	47.8452	86.8849
41	50.0702	88.0928
42	52.3381	89.2462
43	54.6485	90.3447
44	57.0009	91.3876
45	59.3949	92.3742
46	61.8299	93.3041
47	64.3057	94.1765
48	66.8217	94.9909
49	69.3775	95.7466
50	71.9727	96.4430
51	74.6068	97.0794
52	77.2795	97.6553
53	79.9904	98.1699
54	82.7389	98.6225
55	85.5248	99.0126
56	88.3475	99.3394
57	91.2069	99.6022
58	94.1023	99.8004
59	97.0335	99.9332
60	100.0000	100.0000

6 YEARS

#	REBATE	EARN
1	.0483	2.4326
2	.1444	4.8428
3	.2878	7.2302
4	.4779	9.5946
5	.7144	11.9359
6	.9966	14.2536
7	1.3241	16.5477
8	1.6963	18.8177
9	2.1129	21.0636
10	2.5734	23.2849
11	3.0772	25.4814
12	3.6239	27.6529
13	4.2131	29.7991
14	4.8443	31.9198
15	5.5170	34.0145
16	6.2309	36.0831
17	6.9853	38.1253
18	7.7800	40.1408
19	8.6145	42.1293
20	9.4884	44.0905
21	10.4012	46.0241
22	11.3525	47.9299
23	12.3420	49.8074
24	13.3691	51.6565
25	14.4336	53.4767
26	15.5350	55.2678
27	16.6728	57.0296
28	17.8468	58.7615
29	19.0565	60.4634
30	20.3015	62.1349
31	21.5816	63.7757
32	22.8962	65.3854
33	24.2450	66.9637
34	25.6277	68.5103
35	27.0438	70.0248
36	28.4931	71.5069
37	29.9752	72.9562
38	31.4897	74.3723
39	33.0363	75.7550
40	34.6146	77.1038
41	36.2243	78.4184
42	37.8651	79.6985
43	39.5366	80.9435
44	41.2385	82.1532
45	42.9704	83.3272
46	44.7322	84.4650
47	46.5233	85.5664
48	48.3435	86.6309
49	50.1926	87.6580
50	52.0701	88.6475
51	53.9759	89.5988
52	55.9095	90.5116
53	57.8707	91.3855
54	59.8592	92.2200
55	61.8747	93.0147
56	63.9169	93.7691
57	65.9855	94.4830
58	68.0802	95.1557
59	70.2009	95.7869
60	72.3471	96.3761
61	74.5186	96.9228
62	76.7151	97.4266
63	78.9364	97.8871
64	81.1823	98.3037
65	83.4523	98.6759
66	85.7464	99.0034
67	88.0641	99.2856
68	90.4054	99.5221
69	92.7698	99.7122
70	95.1572	99.8556
71	97.5674	99.9517
72	100.0000	100.0000

7 YEARS

#	REBATE	EARN
1	.0369	2.0513
2	.1104	4.0875
3	.2199	6.1084
4	.3652	8.1139
5	.5459	10.1038
6	.7616	12.0780
7	1.0118	14.0362
8	1.2963	15.9783
9	1.6147	17.9042
10	1.9665	19.8136
11	2.3515	21.7063
12	2.7693	23.5823
13	3.2196	25.4412
14	3.7019	27.2830
15	4.2160	29.1074
16	4.7615	30.9143
17	5.3380	32.7034
18	5.9453	34.4746
19	6.5830	36.2276
20	7.2508	37.9624
21	7.9484	39.6786
22	8.6754	41.3760
23	9.4315	43.0546
24	10.2164	44.7140
25	11.0298	46.3541
26	11.8715	47.9746
27	12.7410	49.5754
28	13.6381	51.1562
29	14.5625	52.7168
30	15.5140	54.2570
31	16.4921	55.7765
32	17.4967	57.2753
33	18.5275	58.7529
34	19.5841	60.2092
35	20.6663	61.6440
36	21.7738	63.0570
37	22.9064	64.4480
38	24.0637	65.8167
39	25.2456	67.1630
40	26.4517	68.4865
41	27.6818	69.7870
42	28.9357	71.0643
43	30.2130	72.3182
44	31.5135	73.5483
45	32.8370	74.7544
46	34.1833	75.9363
47	35.5520	77.0936
48	36.9430	78.2262
49	38.3560	79.3337
50	39.7908	80.4159
51	41.2471	81.4725
52	42.7247	82.5033
53	44.2235	83.5079
54	45.7430	84.4860
55	47.2832	85.4375
56	48.8438	86.3619
57	50.4246	87.2590
58	52.0254	88.1285
59	53.6459	88.9702
60	55.2860	89.7836
61	56.9454	90.5685
62	58.6240	91.3246
63	60.3214	92.0516
64	62.0376	92.7492
65	63.7724	93.4170
66	65.5254	94.0547
67	67.2966	94.6620
68	69.0857	95.2385
69	70.8926	95.7840
70	72.7170	96.2981
71	74.5588	96.7804
72	76.4177	97.2307
73	78.2937	97.6485
74	80.1864	98.0335
75	82.0958	98.3853

(continued)

#	REBATE	EARN
75	82.0958	98.3853
76	84.0217	98.7037
77	85.9638	98.9882
78	87.9220	99.2384
79	89.8962	99.4541
80	91.8861	99.6348
81	93.8916	99.7801
82	95.9125	99.8896
83	97.9487	99.9631
84	100.0000	100.0000

8 YEARS

#	REBATE	EARN
1	.0294	1.7658
2	.0878	3.5211
3	.1749	5.2657
4	.2905	6.9996
5	.4342	8.7225
6	.6057	10.4345
7	.8047	12.1353
8	1.0310	13.8248
9	1.2842	15.5030
10	1.5640	17.1697
11	1.8702	18.8247
12	2.2025	20.4680
13	2.5606	22.0994
14	2.9442	23.7189
15	3.3531	25.3262
16	3.7869	26.9212
17	4.2454	28.5038
18	4.7284	30.0739
19	5.2356	31.6313
20	5.7667	33.1759
21	6.3215	34.7076
22	6.8997	36.2261
23	7.5010	37.7315
24	8.1253	39.2235
25	8.7722	40.7019
26	9.4416	42.1667
27	10.1332	43.6177
28	10.8467	45.0548
29	11.5819	46.4777
30	12.3386	47.8863
31	13.1165	49.2806
32	13.9155	50.6602
33	14.7353	52.0252
34	15.5756	53.3752
35	16.4363	54.7102
36	17.3171	56.0300
37	18.2179	57.3343
38	19.1384	58.6232
39	20.0783	59.8963
40	21.0376	61.1535
41	22.0159	62.3947
42	23.0131	63.6197
43	24.0290	64.8282
44	25.0633	66.0202
45	26.1159	67.1953
46	27.1867	68.3536
47	28.2752	69.4947
48	29.3815	70.6185
49	30.5053	71.7248
50	31.6464	72.8133
51	32.8047	73.8841
52	33.9798	74.9367
53	35.1718	75.9710
54	36.3803	76.9869
55	37.6053	77.9841
56	38.8465	78.9624
57	40.1037	79.9217
58	41.3768	80.8616
59	42.6657	81.7821
60	43.9700	82.6829
61	45.2898	83.5637
62	46.6248	84.4244
63	47.9748	85.2647
64	49.3398	86.0845
65	50.7194	86.8835
66	52.1137	87.6614
67	53.5223	88.4181
68	54.9452	89.1533
69	56.3823	89.8668
70	57.8333	90.5584
71	59.2981	91.2278
72	60.7765	91.8747
73	62.2685	92.4990
74	63.7739	93.1003
75	65.2924	93.6785
76	66.8241	94.2333
77	68.3687	94.7644
78	69.9261	95.2716
79	71.4962	95.7546
80	73.0788	96.2131
81	74.6738	96.6469
82	76.2811	97.0558
83	77.9006	97.4394
84	79.5320	97.7975
85	81.1753	98.1298
86	82.8303	98.4360
87	84.4970	98.7158
88	86.1752	98.9690
89	87.8647	99.1953
90	89.5655	99.3943
91	91.2775	99.5658
92	93.0004	99.7095
93	94.7343	99.8251
94	96.4789	99.9122
95	98.2342	99.9706
96	100.0000	100.0000

9 YEARS

#	REBATE	EARN
1	.0241	1.5446
2	.0720	3.0815
3	.1434	4.6108
4	.2381	6.1323
5	.3560	7.6460
6	.4966	9.1517
7	.6597	10.6494
8	.8453	12.1390
9	1.0528	13.6204
10	1.2823	15.0935
11	1.5333	16.5583
12	1.8057	18.0146
13	2.0993	19.4623
14	2.4138	20.9014
15	2.7490	22.3317
16	3.1047	23.7532
17	3.4806	25.1658
18	3.8766	26.5693
19	4.2924	27.9637
20	4.7279	29.3489
21	5.1827	30.7248
22	5.6567	32.0912
23	6.1498	33.4481
24	6.6616	34.7954
25	7.1920	36.1329
26	7.7407	37.4606
27	8.3077	38.7783
28	8.8927	40.0860
29	9.4955	41.3835
30	10.1158	42.6708
31	10.7536	43.9476
32	11.4087	45.2140
33	12.0808	46.4697
34	12.7697	47.7147
35	13.4754	48.9489
36	14.1975	50.1721
37	14.9360	51.3842
38	15.6907	52.5851
39	16.4613	53.7747
40	17.2477	54.9529
41	18.0498	56.1195
42	18.8674	57.2744
43	19.7003	58.4175
44	20.5483	59.5486
45	21.4113	60.6676
46	22.2891	61.7745
47	23.1816	62.8689
48	24.0886	63.9510
49	25.0099	65.0204
50	25.9455	66.0770
51	26.8950	67.1208
52	27.8585	68.1516
53	28.8357	69.1692
54	29.8266	70.1734
55	30.8308	71.1643
56	31.8484	72.1415
57	32.8792	73.1050
58	33.9230	74.0545
59	34.9796	74.9901
60	36.0490	75.9114
61	37.1311	76.8184
62	38.2255	77.7109
63	39.3324	78.5887
64	40.4514	79.4517
65	41.5825	80.2997
66	42.7256	81.1326
67	43.8805	81.9502
68	45.0471	82.7523
69	46.2253	83.5387
70	47.4149	84.3093
71	48.6158	85.0640
72	49.8279	85.8025
73	51.0511	86.5246
74	52.2853	87.2303
75	53.5303	87.9192
76	54.7860	88.5913
77	56.0524	89.2464
78	57.3292	89.8842
79	58.6165	90.5045
80	59.9140	91.1073
81	61.2217	91.6923
82	62.5394	92.2593
83	63.8671	92.8080
84	65.2046	93.3384
85	66.5519	93.8502
86	67.9088	94.3433
87	69.2752	94.8173
88	70.6511	95.2721
89	72.0363	95.7076
90	73.4307	96.1234
91	74.8342	96.5194
92	76.2468	96.8953
93	77.6683	97.2510
94	79.0986	97.5862
95	80.5377	97.9007
96	81.9854	98.1943
97	83.4417	98.4667
98	84.9065	98.7177
99	86.3796	98.9472
100	87.8610	99.1547
101	89.3506	99.3403
102	90.8483	99.5034
103	92.3540	99.6440
104	93.8677	99.7619
105	95.3892	99.8566
106	96.9185	99.9280
107	98.4554	99.9759
108	100.0000	100.0000

10 YEARS

#	REBATE	EARN
1	.0202	1.3683
2	.0604	2.7310
3	.1204	4.0881
4	.2000	5.4394
5	.2989	6.7849
6	.4169	8.1246
7	.5540	9.4583
8	.7097	10.7861
9	.8840	12.1078
10	1.0766	13.4234
11	1.2874	14.7328
12	1.5162	16.0360
13	1.7627	17.3329
14	2.0267	18.6234
15	2.3082	19.9074
16	2.6068	21.1849
17	2.9225	22.4559
18	3.2550	23.7201
19	3.6041	24.9777
20	3.9697	26.2284
21	4.3516	27.4722
22	4.7496	28.7091
23	5.1636	29.9390
24	5.5933	31.1617
25	6.0387	32.3773
26	6.4994	33.5856
27	6.9755	34.7866
28	7.4667	35.9801
29	7.9728	37.1662
30	8.4937	38.3447
31	9.0292	39.5155
32	9.5792	40.6785
33	10.1435	41.8337
34	10.7220	42.9810
35	11.3145	44.1204
36	11.9208	45.2516
37	12.5409	46.3746
38	13.1745	47.4894
39	13.8216	48.5958
40	14.4819	49.6938
41	15.1554	50.7833
42	15.8418	51.8641
43	16.5411	52.9362
44	17.2532	53.9995
45	17.9778	55.0538
46	18.7148	56.0992
47	19.4642	57.1354
48	20.2257	58.1625
49	20.9993	59.1802
50	21.7848	60.1886
51	22.5822	61.1874
52	23.3911	62.1767
53	24.2116	63.1562
54	25.0436	64.1259
55	25.8868	65.0856
56	26.7412	66.0354
57	27.6067	66.9750
58	28.4831	67.9043
59	29.3703	68.8233
60	30.2682	69.7318
61	31.1767	70.6297
62	32.0957	71.5169
63	33.0250	72.3933
64	33.9646	73.2588
65	34.9144	74.1132
66	35.8741	74.9564
67	36.8438	75.7884
68	37.8233	76.6089
69	38.8126	77.4178
70	39.8114	78.2152
71	40.8198	79.0007
72	41.8375	79.7743
73	42.8646	80.5358
74	43.9008	81.2852
75	44.9462	82.0222
76	46.0005	82.7468
77	47.0638	83.4589
78	48.1359	84.1582
79	49.2167	84.8446
80	50.3062	85.5181
81	51.4042	86.1784
82	52.5106	86.8255
83	53.6254	87.4591
84	54.7484	88.0792
85	55.8796	88.6855
86	57.0190	89.2780
87	58.1663	89.8565
88	59.3215	90.4208
89	60.4845	90.9708
90	61.6553	91.5063
91	62.8338	92.0272
92	64.0199	92.5333
93	65.2134	93.0245
94	66.4144	93.5006
95	67.6227	93.9613
96	68.8383	94.4067
97	70.0610	94.8364
98	71.2909	95.2504
99	72.5278	95.6484
100	73.7716	96.0303
101	75.0223	96.3959
102	76.2799	96.7450
103	77.5441	97.0775
104	78.8151	97.3932
105	80.0926	97.6918
106	81.3766	97.9733
107	82.6671	98.2373
108	83.9640	98.4838
109	85.2672	98.7126
110	86.5766	98.9234
111	87.8922	99.1160
112	89.2139	99.2903
113	90.5417	99.4460
114	91.8754	99.5831
115	93.2151	99.7011
116	94.5606	99.8000
117	95.9119	99.8796
118	97.2690	99.9396
119	98.6317	99.9798
120	100.0000	100.0000

1 YEAR

#	REBATE	EARN
1	1.3340	15.0811
2	3.9876	28.9799
3	7.9461	41.6835
4	13.1955	53.1785
5	19.7216	63.4517
6	27.5105	72.4895
7	36.5483	80.2784
8	46.8215	86.8045
9	58.3165	92.0539
10	71.0201	96.0124
11	84.9189	98.6660
12	100.0000	100.0000

2 YEARS

#	REBATE	EARN
1	.3619	7.6772
2	1.0817	15.0733
3	2.1556	22.1852
4	3.5796	29.0096
5	5.3500	35.5436
6	7.4630	41.7838
7	9.9147	47.7270
8	12.7016	53.3700
9	15.8199	58.7094
10	19.2661	63.7418
11	23.0365	68.4639
12	27.1277	72.8723
13	31.5361	76.9635
14	36.2582	80.7339
15	41.2906	84.1801
16	46.6300	87.2984
17	52.2730	90.0853
18	58.2162	92.5370
19	64.4564	94.6500
20	70.9904	96.4204
21	77.8148	97.8444
22	84.9267	98.9183
23	92.3228	99.6381
24	100.0000	100.0000

3 YEARS

#	REBATE	EARN
1	.1699	5.0808
2	.5079	10.0459
3	1.0122	14.8940
4	1.6808	19.6238
5	2.5121	24.2341
6	3.5042	28.7234
7	4.6555	33.0905
8	5.9641	37.3341
9	7.4283	41.4527
10	9.0464	45.4449
11	10.8168	49.3095
12	12.7378	53.0449
13	14.8078	56.6497
14	17.0251	60.1226
15	19.3881	63.4619
16	21.8952	66.6664
17	24.5448	69.7344
18	27.3355	72.6645
19	30.2656	75.4552
20	33.3336	78.1048
21	36.5381	80.6119
22	39.8774	82.9749
23	43.3503	85.1922
24	46.9551	87.2622
25	50.6905	89.1832
26	54.5551	90.9536
27	58.5473	92.5717
28	62.6659	94.0359
29	66.9095	95.3445
30	71.2766	96.4958
31	75.7659	97.4879
32	80.3762	98.3192
33	85.1060	98.9878
34	89.9483	99.4921
35	94.9192	99.8301
36	100.0000	100.0000

4 YEARS

#	REBATE	EARN
1	.1002	3.7597
2	.2996	7.4596
3	.5970	11.0990
4	.9914	14.6773
5	1.4817	18.1938
6	2.0668	21.6477
7	2.7458	25.0385
8	3.5176	28.3653
9	4.3812	31.6276
10	5.3356	34.8246
11	6.3798	37.9555
12	7.5128	41.0196
13	8.7337	44.0163
14	10.0415	46.9447
15	11.4351	49.8042
16	12.9139	52.5938
17	14.4766	55.3130
18	16.1226	57.9608
19	17.8508	60.5366
20	19.6603	63.0394
21	21.5503	65.4686
22	23.5199	67.8232
23	25.5682	70.1025
24	27.6943	72.3057
25	29.8975	74.4318
26	32.1768	76.4801
27	34.5314	78.4497
28	36.9606	80.3397
29	39.4634	82.1492
30	42.0392	83.8774
31	44.6870	85.5234
32	47.4062	87.0861
33	50.1958	88.5649
34	53.0553	89.9585
35	55.9837	91.2663
36	58.9804	92.4872
37	62.0445	93.6202
38	65.1754	94.6644
39	68.3724	95.6188
40	71.6347	96.4824
41	74.9615	97.2542
42	78.3523	97.9332
43	81.8062	98.5183
44	85.3227	99.0086
45	88.9010	99.4030
46	92.5404	99.7004
47	96.2403	99.8998
48	100.0000	100.0000

5 YEARS

#	REBATE	EARN
1	.0670	2.9612
2	.2003	5.8874
3	.3992	8.7781
4	.6629	11.6330
5	.9907	14.4516
6	1.3820	17.2336
7	1.8360	19.9786
8	2.3521	22.6861
9	2.9296	25.3558
10	3.5677	27.9872
11	4.2660	30.5799
12	5.0236	33.1334
13	5.8399	35.6474
14	6.7144	38.1214
15	7.6463	40.5550
16	8.6351	42.9476
17	9.6800	45.2990
18	10.7806	47.6085
19	11.9362	49.8758
20	13.1462	52.1003
21	14.4099	54.2817
22	15.7269	56.4194
23	17.0966	58.5129
24	18.5182	60.5618
25	19.9914	62.5656
26	21.5155	64.5238
27	23.0900	66.4358
28	24.7143	68.3011
29	26.3879	70.1193
30	28.1102	71.8898
31	29.8807	73.6121
32	31.6989	75.2857
33	33.5642	76.9100
34	35.4762	78.4845
35	37.4344	80.0086
36	39.4382	81.4818
37	41.4871	82.9034
38	43.5806	84.2731
39	45.7183	85.5901
40	47.8997	86.8538
41	50.1242	88.0638
42	52.3915	89.2194
43	54.7010	90.3200
44	57.0524	91.3649
45	59.4450	92.3537
46	61.8786	93.2856
47	64.3526	94.1601
48	66.8666	94.9764
49	69.4201	95.7340
50	72.0128	96.4323
51	74.6442	97.0704
52	77.3139	97.6479
53	80.0214	98.1640
54	82.7664	98.6180
55	85.5484	99.0093
56	88.3670	99.3371
57	91.2219	99.6008
58	94.1126	99.7997
59	97.0388	99.9330
60	100.0000	100.0000

6 YEARS

#	REBATE	EARN
1	.0485	2.4275
2	.1450	4.8328
3	.2890	7.2156
4	.4799	9.5756
5	.7172	11.9127
6	1.0005	14.2265
7	1.3292	16.5168
8	1.7028	18.7833
9	2.1208	21.0258
10	2.5828	23.2441
11	3.0883	25.4377
12	3.6367	27.6066
13	4.2277	29.7503
14	4.8608	31.8686
15	5.5354	33.9613
16	6.2512	36.0281
17	7.0077	38.0686
18	7.8045	40.0826
19	8.6410	42.0698
20	9.5170	44.0298
21	10.4319	45.9625
22	11.3853	47.8674
23	12.3768	49.7444
24	13.4060	51.5930
25	14.4725	53.4129
26	15.5758	55.2039
27	16.7156	56.9657
28	17.8915	58.6978
29	19.1031	60.4000
30	20.3499	62.0720
31	21.6317	63.7133
32	22.9479	65.3238
33	24.2983	66.9029
34	25.6825	68.4505
35	27.1000	69.9661
36	28.5506	71.4494
37	30.0339	72.9000
38	31.5495	74.3175
39	33.0971	75.7017
40	34.6762	77.0521
41	36.2867	78.3683
42	37.9280	79.6501
43	39.6000	80.8969
44	41.3022	82.1085
45	43.0343	83.2844
46	44.7961	84.4242
47	46.5871	85.5275
48	48.4070	86.5940
49	50.2556	87.6232
50	52.1326	88.6147
51	54.0375	89.5681
52	55.9702	90.4830
53	57.9302	91.3590
54	59.9174	92.1955
55	61.9314	92.9923
56	63.9719	93.7488
57	66.0387	94.4646
58	68.1314	95.1392
59	70.2497	95.7723
60	72.3934	96.3633
61	74.5623	96.9117
62	76.7559	97.4172
63	78.9742	97.8792
64	81.2167	98.2972
65	83.4832	98.6708
66	85.7735	98.9995
67	88.0873	99.2828
68	90.4244	99.5201
69	92.7844	99.7110
70	95.1672	99.8550
71	97.5725	99.9515
72	100.0000	100.0000

7 YEARS

#	REBATE	EARN
1	.0371	2.0464
2	.1109	4.0779
3	.2210	6.0943
4	.3669	8.0955
5	.5484	10.0812
6	.7650	12.0514
7	1.0163	14.0059
8	1.3020	15.9444
9	1.6217	17.8668
10	1.9749	19.7729
11	2.3614	21.6625
12	2.7808	23.5356
13	3.2327	25.3917
14	3.7168	27.2309
15	4.2326	29.0529
16	4.7800	30.8575
17	5.3584	32.6445
18	5.9676	34.4138
19	6.6073	36.1650
20	7.2771	37.8981
21	7.9767	39.6128
22	8.7057	41.3090
23	9.4638	42.9864
24	10.2508	44.6448
25	11.0663	46.2839
26	11.9100	47.9037
27	12.7815	49.5039
28	13.6807	51.0842
29	14.6071	52.6445
30	15.5605	54.1845
31	16.5405	55.7040
32	17.5470	57.2027
33	18.5796	58.6805
34	19.6380	60.1371
35	20.7219	61.5723
36	21.8311	62.9858
37	22.9653	64.3775
38	24.1242	65.7469
39	25.3075	67.0940
40	26.5150	68.4185
41	27.7464	69.7201
42	29.0014	70.9986
43	30.2799	72.2536
44	31.5815	73.4850
45	32.9060	74.6925
46	34.2531	75.8758
47	35.6225	77.0347
48	37.0142	78.1689
49	38.4277	79.2781
50	39.8629	80.3620
51	41.3195	81.4204
52	42.7973	82.4530
53	44.2960	83.4595
54	45.8155	84.4395
55	47.3555	85.3929
56	48.9158	86.3193
57	50.4961	87.2185
58	52.0963	88.0900
59	53.7161	88.9337
60	55.3552	89.7492
61	57.0136	90.5362
62	58.6910	91.2943
63	60.3872	92.0233
64	62.1019	92.7229
65	63.8350	93.3927
66	65.5862	94.0324
67	67.3555	94.6416
68	69.1425	95.2200
69	70.9471	95.7674
70	72.7691	96.2832
71	74.6083	96.7673
72	76.4644	97.2192
73	78.3375	97.6386
74	80.2271	98.0251
75	82.1332	98.3783

(7 YEARS, continued)

#	REBATE	EARN
75	82.1332	98.3783
76	84.0556	98.6980
77	85.9941	98.9837
78	87.9486	99.2350
79	89.9188	99.4516
80	91.9045	99.6331
81	93.9057	99.7790
82	95.9221	99.8891
83	97.9536	99.9629
84	100.0000	100.0000

8 YEARS

#	REBATE	EARN
1	.0295	1.7612
2	.0882	3.5119
3	.1758	5.2522
4	.2920	6.9818
5	.4364	8.7007
6	.6088	10.4087
7	.8088	12.1057
8	1.0361	13.7916
9	1.2905	15.4663
10	1.5716	17.1296
11	1.8792	18.7814
12	2.2129	20.4217
13	2.5725	22.0502
14	2.9577	23.6668
15	3.3683	25.2714
16	3.8038	26.8639
17	4.2641	28.4442
18	4.7489	30.0120
19	5.2580	31.5673
20	5.7910	33.1099
21	6.3477	34.6397
22	6.9278	36.1566
23	7.5312	37.6604
24	8.1574	39.1509
25	8.8064	40.6280
26	9.4778	42.0916
27	10.1713	43.5415
28	10.8868	44.9776
29	11.6241	46.3996
30	12.3827	47.8076
31	13.1627	49.2012
32	13.9636	50.5804
33	14.7853	51.9449
34	15.6276	53.2947
35	16.4901	54.6295
36	17.3728	55.9492
37	18.2754	57.2537
38	19.1976	58.5427
39	20.1393	59.8160
40	21.1002	61.0736
41	22.0801	62.3153
42	23.0789	63.5408
43	24.0962	64.7499
44	25.1320	65.9426
45	26.1860	67.1186
46	27.2580	68.2778
47	28.3478	69.4199
48	29.4553	70.5447
49	30.5801	71.6522
50	31.7222	72.7420
51	32.8814	73.8140
52	34.0574	74.8680
53	35.2501	75.9038
54	36.4592	76.9211
55	37.6847	77.9199
56	38.9264	78.8998
57	40.1840	79.8607
58	41.4573	80.8024
59	42.7463	81.7246
60	44.0508	82.6272
61	45.3705	83.5099
62	46.7053	84.3724
63	48.0551	85.2147
64	49.4196	86.0364
65	50.7988	86.8373
66	52.1924	87.6173
67	53.6004	88.3759
68	55.0224	89.1132
69	56.4585	89.8287
70	57.9084	90.5222
71	59.3720	91.1936
72	60.8491	91.8426
73	62.3396	92.4688
74	63.8434	93.0722
75	65.3603	93.6523
76	66.8901	94.2090
77	68.4327	94.7420
78	69.9880	95.2511
79	71.5558	95.7359
80	73.1361	96.1962
81	74.7286	96.6317
82	76.3332	97.0423
83	77.9498	97.4275
84	79.5783	97.7871
85	81.2186	98.1208
86	82.8704	98.4284
87	84.5337	98.7095
88	86.2084	98.9639
89	87.8943	99.1912
90	89.5913	99.3912
91	91.2993	99.5636
92	93.0182	99.7080
93	94.7478	99.8242
94	96.4881	99.9118
95	98.2388	99.9705
96	100.0000	100.0000

9 YEARS

#	REBATE	EARN
1	.0242	1.5401
2	.0724	3.0727
3	.1442	4.5978
4	.2395	6.1152
5	.3580	7.6249
6	.4994	9.1268
7	.6635	10.6208
8	.8499	12.1067
9	1.0586	13.5847
10	1.2892	15.0544
11	1.5415	16.5159
12	1.8153	17.9690
13	2.1103	19.4137
14	2.4263	20.8499
15	2.7630	22.2775
16	3.1203	23.6963
17	3.4979	25.1063
18	3.8956	26.5074
19	4.3132	27.8995
20	4.7504	29.2824
21	5.2071	30.6562
22	5.6830	32.0206
23	6.1779	33.3756
24	6.6916	34.7211
25	7.2240	36.0570
26	7.7747	37.3831
27	8.3436	38.6994
28	8.9306	40.0058
29	9.5353	41.3021
30	10.1577	42.5882
31	10.7975	43.8640
32	11.4545	45.1294
33	12.1285	46.3843
34	12.8194	47.6286
35	13.5270	48.8622
36	14.2511	50.0849
37	14.9915	51.2966
38	15.7480	52.4972
39	16.5204	53.6865
40	17.3087	54.8646
41	18.1125	56.0311
42	18.9318	57.1860
43	19.7664	58.3292
44	20.6160	59.4606
45	21.4806	60.5799
46	22.3600	61.6872
47	23.2540	62.7821
48	24.1624	63.8647
49	25.0852	64.9348
50	26.0220	65.9921
51	26.9729	67.0367
52	27.9376	68.0683
53	28.9160	69.0869
54	29.9079	70.0921
55	30.9131	71.0840
56	31.9317	72.0624
57	32.9633	73.0271
58	34.0079	73.9780
59	35.0652	74.9148
60	36.1353	75.8376
61	37.2179	76.7460
62	38.3128	77.6400
63	39.4201	78.5194
64	40.5394	79.3840
65	41.6708	80.2336
66	42.8140	81.0682
67	43.9689	81.8875
68	45.1354	82.6913
69	46.3135	83.4796
70	47.5028	84.2520
71	48.7034	85.0085
72	49.9151	85.7489
73	51.1378	86.4730
74	52.3714	87.1806
75	53.6157	87.8715
76	54.8706	88.5455
77	56.1360	89.2025
78	57.4118	89.8423
79	58.6979	90.4647
80	59.9942	91.0694
81	61.3006	91.6564
82	62.6169	92.2253
83	63.9430	92.7760
84	65.2789	93.3084
85	66.6244	93.8221
86	67.9794	94.3170
87	69.3438	94.7929
88	70.7176	95.2496
89	72.1005	95.6868
90	73.4926	96.1044
91	74.8937	96.5021
92	76.3037	96.8797
93	77.7225	97.2370
94	79.1501	97.5737
95	80.5863	97.8897
96	82.0310	98.1847
97	83.4841	98.4585
98	84.9456	98.7108
99	86.4153	98.9414
100	87.8933	99.1501
101	89.3792	99.3365
102	90.8732	99.5006
103	92.3751	99.6420
104	93.8848	99.7605
105	95.4022	99.8558
106	96.9273	99.9276
107	98.4599	99.9758
108	100.0000	100.0000

10 YEARS

#	REBATE	EARN
1	.0203	1.3641
2	.0608	2.7226
3	.1212	4.0756
4	.2012	5.4230
5	.3008	6.7646
6	.4195	8.1006
7	.5574	9.4307
8	.7140	10.7549
9	.8893	12.0732
10	1.0830	13.3854
11	1.2950	14.6916
12	1.5250	15.9916
13	1.7728	17.2854
14	2.0383	18.5730
15	2.3212	19.8541
16	2.6213	21.1289
17	2.9385	22.3972
18	3.2726	23.6589
19	3.6234	24.9139
20	3.9907	26.1623
21	4.3744	27.4039
22	4.7742	28.6386
23	5.1899	29.8664
24	5.6215	31.0871
25	6.0687	32.3008
26	6.5314	33.5073
27	7.0093	34.7066
28	7.5024	35.8985
29	8.0105	37.0830
30	8.5333	38.2600
31	9.0708	39.4295
32	9.6227	40.5913
33	10.1890	41.7454
34	10.7694	42.8916
35	11.3638	44.0299
36	11.9721	45.1603
37	12.5941	46.2825
38	13.2296	47.3966
39	13.8786	48.5024
40	14.5407	49.5998
41	15.2160	50.6888
42	15.9043	51.7692
43	16.6054	52.8410
44	17.3192	53.9041
45	18.0455	54.9584
46	18.7843	56.0037
47	19.5353	57.0400
48	20.2985	58.0671
49	21.0736	59.0850
50	21.8607	60.0936
51	22.6595	61.0928
52	23.4699	62.0824
53	24.2918	63.0624
54	25.1251	64.0327
55	25.9696	64.9931
56	26.8253	65.9435
57	27.6919	66.8838
58	28.5695	67.8140
59	29.4577	68.7339
60	30.3567	69.6433
61	31.2661	70.5423
62	32.1860	71.4305
63	33.1162	72.3081
64	34.0565	73.1747
65	35.0069	74.0304
66	35.9673	74.8749
67	36.9376	75.7082
68	37.9176	76.5301
69	38.9072	77.3405
70	39.9064	78.1393
71	40.9150	78.9264
72	41.9329	79.7015
73	42.9600	80.4647
74	43.9963	81.2157
75	45.0416	81.9545
76	46.0959	82.6808
77	47.1590	83.3946
78	48.2308	84.0957
79	49.3112	84.7840
80	50.4002	85.4593
81	51.4976	86.1214
82	52.6034	86.7704
83	53.7175	87.4059
84	54.8397	88.0279
85	55.9701	88.6362
86	57.1084	89.2306
87	58.2546	89.8110
88	59.4087	90.3773
89	60.5705	90.9292
90	61.7400	91.4667
91	62.9170	91.9895
92	64.1015	92.4976
93	65.2934	92.9907
94	66.4927	93.4686
95	67.6992	93.9313
96	68.9129	94.3785
97	70.1336	94.8101
98	71.3614	95.2258
99	72.5961	95.6256
100	73.8377	96.0093
101	75.0861	96.3766
102	76.3411	96.7274
103	77.6028	97.0615
104	78.8711	97.3787
105	80.1459	97.6788
106	81.4270	97.9617
107	82.7146	98.2272
108	84.0084	98.4750
109	85.3084	98.7050
110	86.6146	98.9170
111	87.9268	99.1107
112	89.2451	99.2860
113	90.5693	99.4426
114	91.8994	99.5805
115	93.2354	99.6992
116	94.5770	99.7988
117	95.9244	99.8788
118	97.2774	99.9392
119	98.6359	99.9797
120	100.0000	100.0000

ACTUARIAL REBATE AND EARNINGS

1 YEAR

#	REBATE	EARN
1	1.3350	15.0755
2	3.9902	28.9706
3	7.9509	41.6719
4	13.2025	53.1661
5	19.7308	63.4396
6	27.5214	72.4786
7	36.5604	80.2692
8	46.8339	86.7975
9	58.3281	92.0491
10	71.0294	96.0098
11	84.9245	98.6650
12	100.0000	100.0000

2 YEARS

#	REBATE	EARN
1	.3624	7.6714
2	1.0833	15.0626
3	2.1586	22.1704
4	3.5843	28.9917
5	5.3566	35.5232
6	7.4717	41.7617
7	9.9256	47.7038
8	12.7147	53.3463
9	15.8352	58.6857
10	19.2835	63.7187
11	23.0558	68.4417
12	27.1486	72.8514
13	31.5583	76.9442
14	36.2813	80.7165
15	41.3143	84.1648
16	46.6537	87.2853
17	52.2962	90.0744
18	58.2383	92.5283
19	64.4768	94.6434
20	71.0083	96.4157
21	77.8296	97.8414
22	84.9374	98.9167
23	92.3286	99.6376
24	100.0000	100.0000

3 YEARS

#	REBATE	EARN
1	.1703	5.0751
2	.5090	10.0351
3	1.0143	14.8786
4	1.6842	19.6044
5	2.5171	24.2112
6	3.5109	28.6975
7	4.6640	33.0621
8	5.9746	37.3036
9	7.4409	41.4206
10	9.0612	45.4117
11	10.8338	49.2754
12	12.7570	53.0104
13	14.8291	56.6151
14	17.0485	60.0882
15	19.4134	63.4282
16	21.9224	66.6335
17	24.5738	69.7026
18	27.3660	72.6340
19	30.2974	75.4262
20	33.3665	78.0776
21	36.5718	80.5866
22	39.9118	82.9515
23	43.3849	85.1709
24	46.9896	87.2430
25	50.7246	89.1662
26	54.5883	90.9388
27	58.5794	92.5591
28	62.6964	94.0254
29	66.9379	95.3360
30	71.3025	96.4891
31	75.7888	97.4829
32	80.3956	98.3158
33	85.1214	98.9857
34	89.9649	99.4910
35	94.9249	99.8297
36	100.0000	100.0000

4 YEARS

#	REBATE	EARN
1	.1005	3.7542
2	.3004	7.4490
3	.5987	11.0837
4	.9941	14.6577
5	1.4856	18.1702
6	2.0722	21.6206
7	2.7528	25.0081
8	3.5263	28.3321
9	4.3918	31.5918
10	5.3481	34.7866
11	6.3943	37.9157
12	7.5294	40.9783
13	8.7524	43.9737
14	10.0623	46.9012
15	11.4581	49.7599
16	12.9390	52.5492
17	14.5039	55.2681
18	16.1519	57.9161
19	17.8821	60.4921
20	19.6935	62.9955
21	21.5853	65.4254
22	23.5566	67.7810
23	25.6065	70.0615
24	27.7341	72.2659
25	29.9385	74.3935
26	32.2190	76.4434
27	34.5746	78.4147
28	37.0045	80.3065
29	39.5079	82.1179
30	42.0839	83.8481
31	44.7319	85.4961
32	47.4508	87.0610
33	50.2401	88.5419
34	53.0988	89.9377
35	56.0263	91.2476
36	59.0217	92.4706
37	62.0843	93.6057
38	65.2134	94.6519
39	68.4082	95.6082
40	71.6679	96.4737
41	74.9919	97.2472
42	78.3794	97.9278
43	81.8298	98.5144
44	85.3423	99.0059
45	88.9163	99.4013
46	92.5510	99.6996
47	96.2458	99.8995
48	100.0000	100.0000

5 YEARS

#	REBATE	EARN
1	.0673	2.9559
2	.2010	5.8771
3	.4006	8.7631
4	.6651	11.6136
5	.9940	14.4281
6	1.3865	17.2063
7	1.8419	19.9477
8	2.3595	22.6519
9	2.9386	25.3186
10	3.5785	27.9472
11	4.2785	30.5374
12	5.0380	33.0887
13	5.8563	35.6007
14	6.7328	38.0729
15	7.6668	40.5049
16	8.6576	42.8963
17	9.7047	45.2466
18	10.8074	47.5553
19	11.9651	49.8219
20	13.1772	52.0461
21	14.4430	54.2272
22	15.7620	56.3649
23	17.1336	58.4585
24	18.5573	60.5078
25	20.0323	62.5121
26	21.5581	64.4709
27	23.1343	66.3837
28	24.7602	68.2500
29	26.4352	70.0693
30	28.1589	71.8411
31	29.9307	73.5648
32	31.7500	75.2398
33	33.6163	76.8657
34	35.5291	78.4419
35	37.4879	79.9677
36	39.4922	81.4427
37	41.5415	82.8664
38	43.6351	84.2380
39	45.7728	85.5570
40	47.9539	86.8228
41	50.1781	88.0349
42	52.4447	89.1926
43	54.7534	90.2953
44	57.1037	91.3424
45	59.4951	92.3332
46	61.9271	93.2672
47	64.3993	94.1437
48	66.9113	94.9620
49	69.4626	95.7215
50	72.0528	96.4215
51	74.6814	97.0614
52	77.3481	97.6405
53	80.0523	98.1581
54	82.7937	98.6135
55	85.5719	99.0060
56	88.3864	99.3349
57	91.2369	99.5994
58	94.1229	99.7990
59	97.0441	99.9327
60	100.0000	100.0000

6 YEARS

#	REBATE	EARN
1	.0487	2.4225
2	.1456	4.8229
3	.2902	7.2011
4	.4818	9.5567
5	.7201	11.8896
6	1.0044	14.1995
7	1.3343	16.4860
8	1.7092	18.7491
9	2.1287	20.9883
10	2.5922	23.2034
11	3.0993	25.3942
12	3.6495	27.5604
13	4.2423	29.7016
14	4.8772	31.8177
15	5.5538	33.9083
16	6.2716	35.9732
17	7.0301	38.0120
18	7.8289	40.0245
19	8.6675	42.0104
20	9.5455	43.9693
21	10.4625	45.9010
22	11.4180	47.8052
23	12.4115	49.6815
24	13.4428	51.5297
25	14.5113	53.3494
26	15.6166	55.1402
27	16.7584	56.9020
28	17.9362	58.6343
29	19.1496	60.3368
30	20.3982	62.0092
31	21.6817	63.6512
32	22.9996	65.2623
33	24.3515	66.8424
34	25.7372	68.3909
35	27.1561	69.9075
36	28.6080	71.3920
37	30.0925	72.8439
38	31.6091	74.2628
39	33.1576	75.6485
40	34.7377	77.0004
41	36.3488	78.3183
42	37.9908	79.6018
43	39.6632	80.8504
44	41.3657	82.0638
45	43.0980	83.2416
46	44.8598	84.3834
47	46.6506	85.4887
48	48.4703	86.5572
49	50.3185	87.5885
50	52.1948	88.5820
51	54.0990	89.5375
52	56.0307	90.4545
53	57.9896	91.3325
54	59.9755	92.1711
55	61.9880	92.9699
56	64.0268	93.7284
57	66.0917	94.4462
58	68.1823	95.1228
59	70.2984	95.7577
60	72.4396	96.3505
61	74.6058	96.9007
62	76.7966	97.4078
63	79.0117	97.8713
64	81.2509	98.2908
65	83.5140	98.6657
66	85.8005	98.9956
67	88.1104	99.2799
68	90.4433	99.5182
69	92.7989	99.7098
70	95.1771	99.8544
71	97.5775	99.9513
72	100.0000	100.0000

7 YEARS

#	REBATE	EARN
1	.0373	2.0416
2	.1114	4.0684
3	.2220	6.0803
4	.3687	8.0772
5	.5509	10.0588
6	.7685	12.0250
7	1.0209	13.9757
8	1.3077	15.9106
9	1.6287	17.8296
10	1.9833	19.7324
11	2.3713	21.6190
12	2.7923	23.4891
13	3.2458	25.3425
14	3.7316	27.1791
15	4.2493	28.9987
16	4.7984	30.8010
17	5.3788	32.5859
18	5.9899	34.3532
19	6.6316	36.1027
20	7.3034	37.8342
21	8.0049	39.5474
22	8.7360	41.2422
23	9.4962	42.9184
24	10.2852	44.5758
25	11.1027	46.2141
26	11.9484	47.8331
27	12.8220	49.4327
28	13.7231	51.0125
29	14.6515	52.5725
30	15.6069	54.1122
31	16.5888	55.6316
32	17.5972	57.1304
33	18.6316	58.6084
34	19.6917	60.0653
35	20.7774	61.5009
36	21.8883	62.9149
37	23.0240	64.3072
38	24.1844	65.6774
39	25.3692	67.0253
40	26.5781	68.3507
41	27.8108	69.6533
42	29.0671	70.9329
43	30.3467	72.1892
44	31.6493	73.4219
45	32.9747	74.6308
46	34.3226	75.8156
47	35.6928	76.9760
48	37.0851	78.1117
49	38.4991	79.2226
50	39.9347	80.3083
51	41.3916	81.3684
52	42.8696	82.4028
53	44.3684	83.4112
54	45.8878	84.3931
55	47.4275	85.3485
56	48.9875	86.2769
57	50.5673	87.1780
58	52.1669	88.0516
59	53.7859	88.8973
60	55.4242	89.7148
61	57.0816	90.5038
62	58.7578	91.2640
63	60.4526	91.9951
64	62.1658	92.6966
65	63.8973	93.3684
66	65.6468	94.0101
67	67.4141	94.6212
68	69.1990	95.2016
69	71.0013	95.7507
70	72.8209	96.2684
71	74.6575	96.7542
72	76.5109	97.2077
73	78.3810	97.6287
74	80.2676	98.0167
75	82.1704	98.3713

#	REBATE	EARN
75	82.1704	98.3713
76	84.0894	98.6923
77	86.0243	98.9791
78	87.9750	99.2315
79	89.9412	99.4491
80	91.9228	99.6313
81	93.9197	99.7780
82	95.9316	99.8886
83	97.9584	99.9627
84	100.0000	100.0000

8 YEARS

#	REBATE	EARN
1	.0297	1.7565
2	.0887	3.5028
3	.1768	5.2387
4	.2935	6.9642
5	.4387	8.6790
6	.6119	10.3831
7	.8129	12.0763
8	1.0413	13.7586
9	1.2968	15.4298
10	1.5792	17.0898
11	1.8882	18.7385
12	2.2233	20.3756
13	2.5845	22.0012
14	2.9713	23.6150
15	3.3834	25.2170
16	3.8207	26.8070
17	4.2828	28.3849
18	4.7694	29.9505
19	5.2803	31.5037
20	5.8152	33.0443
21	6.3739	34.5723
22	6.9560	36.0874
23	7.5613	37.5896
24	8.1895	39.0787
25	8.8405	40.5545
26	9.5139	42.0168
27	10.2094	43.4657
28	10.9270	44.9007
29	11.6662	46.3220
30	12.4269	47.7292
31	13.2088	49.1222
32	14.0116	50.5008
33	14.8353	51.8650
34	15.6794	53.2145
35	16.5439	54.5492
36	17.4284	55.8688
37	18.3327	57.1733
38	19.2567	58.4625
39	20.2001	59.7361
40	21.1626	60.9940
41	22.1442	62.2361
42	23.1445	63.4622
43	24.1633	64.6720
44	25.2005	65.8654
45	26.2559	67.0422
46	27.3292	68.2022
47	28.4202	69.3453
48	29.5288	70.4712
49	30.6547	71.5798
50	31.7978	72.6708
51	32.9578	73.7441
52	34.1346	74.7995
53	35.3280	75.8367
54	36.5378	76.8555
55	37.7639	77.8558
56	39.0060	78.8374
57	40.2639	79.7999
58	41.5375	80.7433
59	42.8267	81.6673
60	44.1312	82.5716
61	45.4508	83.4561
62	46.7855	84.3206
63	48.1350	85.1647
64	49.4992	85.9884
65	50.8778	86.7912
66	52.2708	87.5731
67	53.6780	88.3338
68	55.0993	89.0730
69	56.5343	89.7906
70	57.9832	90.4861
71	59.4455	91.1595
72	60.9213	91.8105
73	62.4104	92.4387
74	63.9126	93.0440
75	65.4277	93.6261
76	66.9557	94.1848
77	68.4963	94.7197
78	70.0495	95.2306
79	71.6151	95.7172
80	73.1930	96.1793
81	74.7830	96.6166
82	76.3850	97.0287
83	77.9988	97.4155
84	79.6244	97.7767
85	81.2615	98.1118
86	82.9102	98.4208
87	84.5702	98.7032
88	86.2414	98.9587
89	87.9237	99.1871
90	89.6169	99.3881
91	91.3210	99.5613
92	93.0358	99.7065
93	94.7613	99.8232
94	96.4972	99.9113
95	98.2435	99.9703
96	100.0000	100.0000

9 YEARS

#	REBATE	EARN
1	.0244	1.5357
2	.0728	3.0640
3	.1451	4.5849
4	.2409	6.0983
5	.3601	7.6040
6	.5022	9.1021
7	.6672	10.5923
8	.8546	12.0747
9	1.0644	13.5492
10	1.2962	15.0156
11	1.5497	16.4738
12	1.8248	17.9239
13	2.1212	19.3656
14	2.4387	20.7988
15	2.7770	22.2236
16	3.1359	23.6398
17	3.5152	25.0472
18	3.9146	26.4459
19	4.3339	27.8357
20	4.7729	29.2164
21	5.2314	30.5881
22	5.7092	31.9505
23	6.2060	33.3037
24	6.7217	34.6474
25	7.2559	35.9816
26	7.8086	37.3062
27	8.3795	38.6210
28	8.9684	39.9260
29	9.5752	41.2111
30	10.1995	42.5061
31	10.8412	43.7809
32	11.5002	45.0454
33	12.1762	46.2995
34	12.8691	47.5430
35	13.5786	48.7760
36	14.3045	49.9981
37	15.0468	51.2094
38	15.8052	52.4097
39	16.5794	53.5988
40	17.3695	54.7767
41	18.1751	55.9431
42	18.9961	57.0981
43	19.8323	58.2415
44	20.6836	59.3730
45	21.5498	60.4927
46	22.4307	61.6003
47	23.3262	62.6957
48	24.2361	63.7788
49	25.1602	64.8495
50	26.0984	65.9076
51	27.0505	66.9529
52	28.0164	67.9854
53	28.9959	69.0049
54	29.9889	70.0111
55	30.9951	71.0041
56	32.0146	71.9836
57	33.0471	72.9495
58	34.0924	73.9016
59	35.1505	74.8398
60	36.2212	75.7639
61	37.3043	76.6738
62	38.3997	77.5693
63	39.5073	78.4502
64	40.6270	79.3164
65	41.7585	80.1677
66	42.9019	81.0039
67	44.0569	81.8249
68	45.2233	82.6305
69	46.4012	83.4206
70	47.5903	84.1948
71	48.7906	84.9532
72	50.0019	85.6955
73	51.2240	86.4214
74	52.4570	87.1309
75	53.7005	87.8238
76	54.9546	88.4998
77	56.2191	89.1588
78	57.4939	89.8005
79	58.7789	90.4248
80	60.0740	91.0316
81	61.3790	91.6205
82	62.6938	92.1914
83	64.0184	92.7441
84	65.3526	93.2783
85	66.6963	93.7940
86	68.0495	94.2908
87	69.4119	94.7686
88	70.7836	95.2271
89	72.1643	95.6661
90	73.5541	96.0854
91	74.9528	96.4848
92	76.3602	96.8641
93	77.7764	97.2230
94	79.2012	97.5613
95	80.6344	97.8788
96	82.0761	98.1752
97	83.5262	98.4503
98	84.9844	98.7038
99	86.4508	98.9356
100	87.9253	99.1454
101	89.4077	99.3328
102	90.8979	99.4978
103	92.3960	99.6399
104	93.9017	99.7591
105	95.4151	99.8549
106	96.9360	99.9272
107	98.4643	99.9756
108	100.0000	100.0000

10 YEARS

#	REBATE	EARN
1	.0205	1.3599
2	.0612	2.7143
3	.1220	4.0633
4	.2025	5.4067
5	.3026	6.7446
6	.4221	8.0768
7	.5608	9.4033
8	.7183	10.7240
9	.8946	12.0388
10	1.0895	13.3478
11	1.3026	14.6507
12	1.5338	15.9476
13	1.7830	17.2384
14	2.0498	18.5230
15	2.3341	19.8013
16	2.6358	21.0733
17	2.9546	22.3390
18	3.2903	23.5981
19	3.6428	24.8507
20	4.0118	26.0967
21	4.3971	27.3360
22	4.7987	28.5686
23	5.2163	29.7943
24	5.6497	31.0130
25	6.0988	32.2248
26	6.5633	33.4295
27	7.0432	34.6271
28	7.5382	35.8174
29	8.0481	37.0004
30	8.5729	38.1760
31	9.1123	39.3441
32	9.6662	40.5047
33	10.2344	41.6576
34	10.8168	42.8028
35	11.4131	43.9401
36	12.0233	45.0696
37	12.6472	46.1910
38	13.2846	47.3043
39	13.9354	48.4095
40	14.5995	49.5064
41	15.2766	50.5949
42	15.9667	51.6750
43	16.6695	52.7465
44	17.3851	53.8093
45	18.1131	54.8634
46	18.8536	55.9087
47	19.6062	56.9450
48	20.3710	57.9722
49	21.1477	58.9903
50	21.9363	59.9992
51	22.7366	60.9987
52	23.5484	61.9887
53	24.3717	62.9692
54	25.2064	63.9399
55	26.0522	64.9009
56	26.9090	65.8520
57	27.7769	66.7931
58	28.6555	67.7241
59	29.5448	68.6448
60	30.4448	69.5552
61	31.3552	70.4552
62	32.2759	71.3445
63	33.2069	72.2231
64	34.1480	73.0910
65	35.0991	73.9478
66	36.0601	74.7936
67	37.0308	75.6283
68	38.0113	76.4516
69	39.0013	77.2634
70	40.0008	78.0637
71	41.0097	78.8523
72	42.0278	79.6290
73	43.0550	80.3938
74	44.0913	81.1464
75	45.1366	81.8869
76	46.1907	82.6149
77	47.2535	83.3305
78	48.3250	84.0333
79	49.4051	84.7234
80	50.4936	85.4005
81	51.5905	86.0646
82	52.6957	86.7154
83	53.8090	87.3528
84	54.9304	87.9767
85	56.0599	88.5869
86	57.1972	89.1832
87	58.3424	89.7656
88	59.4953	90.3338
89	60.6559	90.8877
90	61.8240	91.4271
91	62.9996	91.9519
92	64.1826	92.4618
93	65.3729	92.9568
94	66.5705	93.4367
95	67.7752	93.9012
96	68.9870	94.3503
97	70.2057	94.7837
98	71.4314	95.2013
99	72.6640	95.6029
100	73.9033	95.9882
101	75.1493	96.3572
102	76.4019	96.7097
103	77.6610	97.0454
104	78.9267	97.3642
105	80.1987	97.6659
106	81.4770	97.9502
107	82.7616	98.2170
108	84.0524	98.4662
109	85.3493	98.6974
110	86.6522	98.9105
111	87.9612	99.1054
112	89.2760	99.2817
113	90.5967	99.4392
114	91.9232	99.5779
115	93.2554	99.6974
116	94.5933	99.7975
117	95.9367	99.8780
118	97.2857	99.9388
119	98.6401	99.9795
120	100.0000	100.0000

ACTUARIAL REBATE AND EARNINGS   13.75 %

1 YEAR

#	REBATE	EARN
1	1.3360	15.0699
2	3.9929	28.9612
3	7.9557	41.6604
4	13.2096	53.1538
5	19.7400	63.4275
6	27.5324	72.4676
7	36.5725	80.2600
8	46.8462	86.7904
9	58.3396	92.0443
10	71.0388	96.0071
11	84.9301	98.6640
12	100.0000	100.0000

2 YEARS

#	REBATE	EARN
1	.3630	7.6656
2	1.0848	15.0519
3	2.1615	22.1558
4	3.5890	28.9738
5	5.3632	35.5029
6	7.4804	41.7396
7	9.9365	47.6806
8	12.7279	53.3226
9	15.8505	58.6620
10	19.3008	63.6955
11	23.0750	68.4196
12	27.1694	72.8306
13	31.5804	76.9250
14	36.3045	80.6992
15	41.1380	84.1495
16	46.6774	87.2721
17	52.3194	90.0635
18	58.2604	92.5196
19	64.4971	94.6368
20	71.0262	96.4110
21	77.8442	97.8385
22	84.9481	98.9152
23	92.3344	99.6370
24	100.0000	100.0000

3 YEARS

#	REBATE	EARN
1	.1707	5.0694
2	.5101	10.0243
3	1.0164	14.8633
4	1.6877	19.5851
5	2.5220	24.1884
6	3.5176	28.6717
7	4.6726	33.0338
8	5.9852	37.2732
9	7.4536	41.3886
10	9.0760	45.3784
11	10.8508	49.2414
12	12.7762	52.9759
13	14.8504	56.5806
14	17.0718	60.0540
15	19.4388	63.3945
16	21.9496	66.6006
17	24.6027	69.6708
18	27.3964	72.6036
19	30.3292	75.3973
20	33.3994	78.0504
21	36.6055	80.5612
22	39.9460	82.9282
23	43.4194	85.1496
24	47.0241	87.2238
25	50.7586	89.1492
26	54.6216	90.9240
27	58.6114	92.5464
28	62.7268	94.0148
29	66.9662	95.3274
30	71.3283	96.4824
31	75.8116	97.4780
32	80.4149	98.3123
33	85.1367	98.9836
34	89.9757	99.4899
35	94.9306	99.8293
36	100.0000	100.0000

4 YEARS

#	REBATE	EARN
1	.1008	3.7487
2	.3013	7.4384
3	.6003	11.0685
4	.9968	14.6381
5	1.4896	18.1467
6	2.0776	21.5935
7	2.7598	24.9778
8	3.5350	28.2990
9	4.4023	31.5562
10	5.3606	34.7488
11	6.4088	37.8760
12	7.5460	40.9370
13	8.7711	43.9312
14	10.0831	46.8577
15	11.4811	49.7157
16	12.9641	52.5046
17	14.5311	55.2234
18	16.1811	57.8714
19	17.9133	60.4478
20	19.7267	62.9517
21	21.6203	65.3823
22	23.5933	67.7389
23	25.6448	70.0204
24	27.7738	72.2262
25	29.9796	74.3552
26	32.2611	76.4067
27	34.6177	78.3797
28	37.0483	80.2733
29	39.5522	82.0867
30	42.1286	83.8189
31	44.7766	85.4689
32	47.4954	87.0359
33	50.2843	88.5189
34	53.1423	89.9169
35	56.0688	91.2289
36	59.0630	92.4540
37	62.1240	93.5912
38	65.2512	94.6394
39	68.4438	95.5977
40	71.7010	96.4650
41	75.0222	97.2402
42	78.4065	97.9224
43	81.8533	98.5104
44	85.3619	99.0032
45	88.9315	99.3997
46	92.5616	99.6987
47	96.2513	99.8992
48	100.0000	100.0000

5 YEARS

#	REBATE	EARN
1	.0675	2.9507
2	.2017	5.8669
3	.4020	8.7482
4	.6674	11.5943
5	.9974	14.4047
6	1.3911	17.1790
7	1.8478	19.9169
8	2.3669	22.6178
9	2.9476	25.2815
10	3.5892	27.9073
11	4.2911	30.4950
12	5.0525	33.0441
13	5.8728	35.5541
14	6.7513	38.0246
15	7.6873	40.4551
16	8.6802	42.8452
17	9.7294	45.1944
18	10.8342	47.5022
19	11.9940	49.7682
20	13.2082	51.9919
21	14.4761	54.1728
22	15.7971	56.3104
23	17.1707	58.4043
24	18.5962	60.4538
25	20.0731	62.4586
26	21.6007	64.4181
27	23.1786	66.3317
28	24.8060	68.1990
29	26.4826	70.0194
30	28.2076	71.7924
31	29.9806	73.5174
32	31.8010	75.1940
33	33.6683	76.8214
34	35.5819	78.3993
35	37.5414	79.9269
36	39.5462	81.4038
37	41.5957	82.8293
38	43.6896	84.2029
39	45.8272	85.5239
40	48.0081	86.7918
41	50.2318	88.0060
42	52.4978	89.1658
43	54.8056	90.2706
44	57.1548	91.3198
45	59.5449	92.3127
46	61.9754	93.2487
47	64.4459	94.1272
48	66.9559	94.9475
49	69.5050	95.7089
50	72.0927	96.4108
51	74.7185	97.0524
52	77.3822	97.6331
53	80.0831	98.1522
54	82.8210	98.6609
55	85.5953	99.0026
56	88.4057	99.3326
57	91.2518	99.5980
58	94.1331	99.7983
59	97.0493	99.9325
60	100.0000	100.0000

6 YEARS

#	REBATE	EARN
1	.0489	2.4174
2	.1462	4.8130
3	.2914	7.1866
4	.4838	9.5379
5	.7229	11.8666
6	1.0083	14.1726
7	1.3394	16.4554
8	1.7157	18.7150
9	2.1366	20.9509
10	2.6017	23.1630
11	3.1104	25.3509
12	3.6623	27.5144
13	4.2569	29.6532
14	4.8937	31.7670
15	5.5722	33.8556
16	6.2919	35.9186
17	7.0524	37.9557
18	7.8533	39.9667
19	8.6939	41.9513
20	9.5740	43.9091
21	10.4931	45.8398
22	11.4506	47.7432
23	12.4463	49.6189
24	13.4796	51.4666
25	14.5501	53.2860
26	15.6574	55.0767
27	16.8011	56.8385
28	17.9808	58.5710
29	19.1960	60.2738
30	20.4464	61.9467
31	21.7316	63.5892
32	23.0511	65.2011
33	24.4047	66.7819
34	25.7918	68.3314
35	27.2121	69.8491
36	28.6653	71.3347
37	30.1509	72.7879
38	31.6686	74.2082
39	33.2181	75.5953
40	34.7989	76.9489
41	36.4108	78.2684
42	38.0533	79.5536
43	39.7262	80.8040
44	41.4290	82.0192
45	43.1615	83.1989
46	44.9233	84.3426
47	46.7140	85.4499
48	48.5334	86.5204
49	50.3811	87.5537
50	52.2568	88.5494
51	54.1602	89.5069
52	56.0909	90.4260
53	58.0487	91.3061
54	60.0333	92.1467
55	62.0443	92.9476
56	64.0814	93.7081
57	66.1444	94.4278
58	68.2330	95.1063
59	70.3468	95.7431
60	72.4856	96.3377
61	74.6491	96.8896
62	76.8370	97.3983
63	79.0491	97.8634
64	81.2850	98.2843
65	83.5446	98.6606
66	85.8274	98.9917
67	88.1334	99.2771
68	90.4621	99.5162
69	92.8134	99.7086
70	95.1870	99.8538
71	97.5826	99.9511
72	100.0000	100.0000

7 YEARS

#	REBATE	EARN
1	.0375	2.0367
2	.1120	4.0589
3	.2231	6.0664
4	.3704	8.0590
5	.5535	10.0365
6	.7719	11.9988
7	1.0254	13.9457
8	1.3135	15.8770
9	1.6357	17.7926
10	1.9918	19.6922
11	2.3812	21.5757
12	2.8038	23.4429
13	3.2590	25.2936
14	3.7465	27.1276
15	4.2659	28.9447
16	4.8169	30.7448
17	5.3991	32.5276
18	6.0122	34.2930
19	6.6558	36.0407
20	7.3296	37.7705
21	8.0332	39.4823
22	8.7663	41.1758
23	9.5285	42.8508
24	10.3196	44.5071
25	11.1391	46.1445
26	11.9869	47.7628
27	12.8625	49.3618
28	13.7656	50.9411
29	14.6959	52.5007
30	15.6532	54.0403
31	16.6371	55.5596
32	17.6473	57.0584
33	18.6835	58.5365
34	19.7454	59.9937
35	20.8328	61.4297
36	21.9453	62.8442
37	23.0827	64.2371
38	24.2446	65.6081
39	25.4308	66.9568
40	26.6411	68.2831
41	27.8751	69.5868
42	29.1325	70.8675
43	30.4132	72.1249
44	31.7169	73.3589
45	33.0432	74.5692
46	34.3919	75.7554
47	35.7629	76.9173
48	37.1558	78.0547
49	38.5703	79.1672
50	40.0063	80.2546
51	41.4635	81.3165
52	42.9416	82.3527
53	44.4404	83.3629
54	45.9597	84.3468
55	47.4993	85.3041
56	49.0589	86.2344
57	50.6382	87.1375
58	52.2372	88.0131
59	53.8555	88.8609
60	55.4929	89.6804
61	57.1492	90.4715
62	58.8242	91.2337
63	60.5177	91.9668
64	62.2295	92.6704
65	63.9593	93.3442
66	65.7070	93.9878
67	67.4724	94.6009
68	69.2552	95.1831
69	71.0553	95.7341
70	72.8724	96.2535
71	74.7064	96.7410
72	76.5571	97.1962
73	78.4243	97.6188
74	80.3078	98.0082
75	82.2074	98.3643

#	REBATE	EARN
75	82.2074	98.3643
76	84.1230	98.6865
77	86.0543	98.9746
78	88.0012	99.2281
79	89.9635	99.4465
80	91.9410	99.6296
81	93.9336	99.7769
82	95.9411	99.8880
83	97.9633	99.9625
84	100.0000	100.0000

8 YEARS

#	REBATE	EARN
1	.0298	1.7519
2	.0892	3.4938
3	.1777	5.2254
4	.2951	6.9467
5	.4409	8.6575
6	.6150	10.3577
7	.8169	12.0472
8	1.0464	13.7259
9	1.3032	15.3936
10	1.5868	17.0503
11	1.8971	18.6958
12	2.2338	20.3299
13	2.5964	21.9526
14	2.9848	23.5636
15	3.3986	25.1630
16	3.8376	26.7505
17	4.3015	28.3260
18	4.7899	29.8893
19	5.3027	31.4404
20	5.8395	32.9791
21	6.4001	34.5052
22	6.9841	36.0187
23	7.5914	37.5193
24	8.2216	39.0069
25	8.8746	40.4813
26	9.5499	41.9425
27	10.2475	43.3902
28	10.9671	44.8243
29	11.7083	46.2447
30	12.4709	47.6512
31	13.2548	49.0435
32	14.0596	50.4217
33	14.8852	51.7855
34	15.7312	53.1347
35	16.5975	54.4692
36	17.4838	55.7888
37	18.3900	57.0933
38	19.3157	58.3826
39	20.2608	59.6565
40	21.2250	60.9147
41	22.2081	62.1573
42	23.2099	63.3838
43	24.2302	64.5943
44	25.2689	65.7884
45	26.3255	66.9660
46	27.4001	68.1269
47	28.4923	69.2710
48	29.6020	70.3980
49	30.7290	71.5077
50	31.8731	72.5999
51	33.0340	73.6745
52	34.2116	74.7311
53	35.4057	75.7698
54	36.6162	76.7901
55	37.8427	77.7919
56	39.0853	78.7750
57	40.3435	79.7392
58	41.6174	80.6843
59	42.9067	81.6100
60	44.2112	82.5162
61	45.5308	83.4025
62	46.8653	84.2688
63	48.2145	85.1148
64	49.5783	85.9404
65	50.9565	86.7452
66	52.3488	87.5291
67	53.7553	88.2917
68	55.1757	89.0329
69	56.6098	89.7525
70	58.0575	90.4501
71	59.5187	91.1254
72	60.9931	91.7784
73	62.4807	92.4086
74	63.9813	93.0159
75	65.4948	93.5999
76	67.0209	94.1605
77	68.5596	94.6973
78	70.1107	95.2101
79	71.6740	95.6985
80	73.2495	96.1624
81	74.8370	96.6014
82	76.4364	97.0152
83	78.0474	97.4036
84	79.6701	97.7662
85	81.3042	98.1029
86	82.9497	98.4132
87	84.6064	98.6968
88	86.2741	98.9536
89	87.9528	99.1831
90	89.6423	99.3850
91	91.3425	99.5591
92	93.0533	99.7049
93	94.7746	99.8223
94	96.5062	99.9108
95	98.2481	99.9702
96	100.0000	100.0000

9 YEARS

#	REBATE	EARN
1	.0245	1.5313
2	.0732	3.0554
3	.1459	4.5721
4	.2423	6.0815
5	.3621	7.5833
6	.5051	9.0776
7	.6709	10.5642
8	.8593	12.0430
9	1.0702	13.5140
10	1.3031	14.9771
11	1.5579	16.4321
12	1.8344	17.8790
13	2.1322	19.3177
14	2.4512	20.7482
15	2.7910	22.1702
16	3.1515	23.5837
17	3.5324	24.9886
18	3.9336	26.3849
19	4.3546	27.7723
20	4.7955	29.1509
21	5.2558	30.5204
22	5.7354	31.8809
23	6.2341	33.2322
24	6.7517	34.5741
25	7.2879	35.9067
26	7.8425	37.2297
27	8.4154	38.5431
28	9.0062	39.8468
29	9.6149	41.1406
30	10.2412	42.4244
31	10.8850	43.6982
32	11.5459	44.9618
33	12.2238	46.2151
34	12.9186	47.4579
35	13.6300	48.6902
36	14.3579	49.9118
37	15.1020	51.1227
38	15.8622	52.3226
39	16.6383	53.5115
40	17.4301	54.6892
41	18.2375	55.8556
42	19.0602	57.0106
43	19.8981	58.1541
44	20.7510	59.2858
45	21.6188	60.4058
46	22.5012	61.5138
47	23.3982	62.6096
48	24.3095	63.6933
49	25.2350	64.7646
50	26.1745	65.8234
51	27.1278	66.8695
52	28.0949	67.9028
53	29.0755	68.9232
54	30.0696	69.9304
55	31.0768	70.9245
56	32.0972	71.9051
57	33.1305	72.8722
58	34.1766	73.8255
59	35.2354	74.7650
60	36.3067	75.6905
61	37.3904	76.6018
62	38.4862	77.4988
63	39.5942	78.3812
64	40.7142	79.2490
65	41.8459	80.1019
66	42.9894	80.9398
67	44.1444	81.7625
68	45.3108	82.5699
69	46.4885	83.3617
70	47.6774	84.1378
71	48.8773	84.8980
72	50.0882	85.6421
73	51.3098	86.3700
74	52.5421	87.0814
75	53.7849	87.7762
76	55.0382	88.4541
77	56.3018	89.1150
78	57.5756	89.7588
79	58.8594	90.3851
80	60.1532	90.9938
81	61.4569	91.5846
82	62.7703	92.1575
83	64.0933	92.7121
84	65.4259	93.2483
85	66.7678	93.7659
86	68.1191	94.2646
87	69.4796	94.7442
88	70.8491	95.2045
89	72.2277	95.6454
90	73.6151	96.0664
91	75.0114	96.4676
92	76.4163	96.8485
93	77.8298	97.2090
94	79.2518	97.5488
95	80.6823	97.8678
96	82.1210	98.1656
97	83.5679	98.4421
98	85.0229	98.6969
99	86.4860	98.9298
100	87.9570	99.1407
101	89.4358	99.3291
102	90.9224	99.4949
103	92.4167	99.6379
104	93.9185	99.7577
105	95.4279	99.8541
106	96.9446	99.9268
107	98.4687	99.9755
108	100.0000	100.0000

10 YEARS

#	REBATE	EARN
1	.0206	1.3557
2	.0616	2.7061
3	.1227	4.0511
4	.2038	5.3907
5	.3045	6.7247
6	.4247	8.0532
7	.5642	9.3761
8	.7227	10.6933
9	.9000	12.0048
10	1.0959	13.3104
11	1.3102	14.6102
12	1.5426	15.9040
13	1.7931	17.1917
14	2.0613	18.4734
15	2.3471	19.7489
16	2.6503	21.0182
17	2.9706	22.2812
18	3.3080	23.5378
19	3.6621	24.7880
20	4.0328	26.0317
21	4.4199	27.2687
22	4.8233	28.4991
23	5.2426	29.7227
24	5.6779	30.9395
25	6.1288	32.1494
26	6.5952	33.3523
27	7.0770	34.5482
28	7.5739	35.7369
29	8.0858	36.9184
30	8.6125	38.0926
31	9.1538	39.2594
32	9.7096	40.4187
33	10.2798	41.5704
34	10.8641	42.7145
35	11.4623	43.8509
36	12.0744	44.9794
37	12.7002	46.1001
38	13.3395	47.2127
39	13.9922	48.3172
40	14.6581	49.4135
41	15.3370	50.5016
42	16.0289	51.5812
43	16.7335	52.6524
44	17.4508	53.7151
45	18.1805	54.7690
46	18.9226	55.8142
47	19.6769	56.8505
48	20.4433	57.8778
49	21.2216	58.8961
50	22.0117	59.9052
51	22.8134	60.9050
52	23.6267	61.8954
53	24.4514	62.8763
54	25.2873	63.8476
55	26.1344	64.8092
56	26.9925	65.7610
57	27.8614	66.7028
58	28.7412	67.6346
59	29.6316	68.5562
60	30.5325	69.4675
61	31.4438	70.3684
62	32.3654	71.2588
63	33.2972	72.1386
64	34.2390	73.0075
65	35.1908	73.8656
66	36.1524	74.7127
67	37.1237	75.5486
68	38.1046	76.3733
69	39.0950	77.1866
70	40.0948	77.9883
71	41.1039	78.7784
72	42.1222	79.5567
73	43.1495	80.3231
74	44.1858	81.0774
75	45.2310	81.8195
76	46.2849	82.5492
77	47.3476	83.2665
78	48.4188	83.9711
79	49.4984	84.6630
80	50.5865	85.3419
81	51.6828	86.0078
82	52.7873	86.6605
83	53.8999	87.2998
84	55.0206	87.9256
85	56.1491	88.5377
86	57.2855	89.1359
87	58.4296	89.7202
88	59.5813	90.2904
89	60.7406	90.8462
90	61.9074	91.3875
91	63.0816	91.9142
92	64.2631	92.4261
93	65.4518	92.9230
94	66.6477	93.4048
95	67.8506	93.8712
96	69.0605	94.3221
97	70.2773	94.7574
98	71.5009	95.1767
99	72.7313	95.5801
100	73.9683	95.9672
101	75.2120	96.3379
102	76.4622	96.6920
103	77.7188	97.0294
104	78.9818	97.3497
105	80.2511	97.6529
106	81.5266	97.9387
107	82.8083	98.2069
108	84.0960	98.4574
109	85.3898	98.6898
110	86.6896	98.9041
111	87.9952	99.1000
112	89.3067	99.2773
113	90.6239	99.4358
114	91.9468	99.5753
115	93.2753	99.6955
116	94.6093	99.7962
117	95.9489	99.8773
118	97.2939	99.9384
119	98.6443	99.9794
120	100.0000	100.0000

1 YEAR

#	REBATE	EARN
1	1.3370	15.0644
2	3.9955	28.9519
3	7.9604	41.6489
4	13.2166	53.1414
5	19.7491	63.4154
6	27.5433	72.4567
7	36.5846	80.2509
8	46.8586	86.7834
9	58.3511	92.0396
10	71.0481	96.0045
11	84.9356	98.6630
12	100.0000	100.0000

2 YEARS

#	REBATE	EARN
1	.3635	7.6599
2	1.0864	15.0413
3	2.1645	22.1411
4	3.5936	28.9560
5	5.3698	35.4825
6	7.4891	41.7175
7	9.9474	47.6574
8	12.7410	53.2989
9	15.8658	58.6384
10	19.3182	63.6724
11	23.0942	68.3974
12	27.1903	72.8097
13	31.6026	76.9058
14	36.3276	80.6818
15	41.3616	84.1342
16	46.7011	87.2590
17	52.3426	90.0526
18	58.2825	92.5109
19	64.5175	94.6302
20	71.0440	96.4064
21	77.8589	97.8355
22	84.9587	98.9136
23	92.3401	99.6365
24	100.0000	100.0000

3 YEARS

#	REBATE	EARN
1	.1711	5.0638
2	.5112	10.0136
3	1.0186	14.8480
4	1.6911	19.5658
5	2.5270	24.1656
6	3.5243	28.6460
7	4.6811	33.0055
8	5.9957	37.2429
9	7.4662	41.3566
10	9.0908	45.3453
11	10.8678	49.2074
12	12.7953	52.9415
13	14.8717	56.5461
14	17.0952	60.0197
15	19.4641	63.3608
16	21.9768	66.5678
17	24.6316	69.6391
18	27.4269	72.5731
19	30.3609	75.3684
20	33.4322	78.0232
21	36.6392	80.5359
22	39.9803	82.9048
23	43.4539	85.1283
24	47.0585	87.2047
25	50.7926	89.1322
26	54.6547	90.9092
27	58.6434	92.5338
28	62.7571	94.0043
29	66.9945	95.3189
30	71.3540	96.4757
31	75.8344	97.4730
32	80.4342	98.3089
33	85.1520	98.9814
34	89.9864	99.4888
35	94.9362	99.8289
36	100.0000	100.0000

4 YEARS

#	REBATE	EARN
1	.1011	3.7433
2	.3022	7.4279
3	.6020	11.0533
4	.9995	14.6186
5	1.4935	18.1233
6	2.0830	21.5665
7	2.7667	24.9476
8	3.5437	28.2659
9	4.4128	31.5206
10	5.3731	34.7110
11	6.4233	37.8364
12	7.5626	40.8959
13	8.7898	43.8888
14	10.1040	46.8143
15	11.5041	49.6717
16	12.9892	52.4601
17	14.5583	55.1787
18	16.2104	57.8268
19	17.9446	60.4035
20	19.7598	62.9080
21	21.6553	65.3393
22	23.6300	67.6968
23	25.6830	69.9795
24	27.8135	72.1865
25	30.0205	74.3170
26	32.3032	76.3700
27	34.6607	78.3447
28	37.0920	80.2402
29	39.5965	82.0554
30	42.1732	83.7896
31	44.8213	85.4417
32	47.5399	87.0108
33	50.3283	88.4959
34	53.1857	89.8960
35	56.1112	91.2102
36	59.1041	92.4374
37	62.1636	93.5767
38	65.2890	94.6269
39	68.4794	95.5872
40	71.7341	96.4563
41	75.0524	97.2333
42	78.4335	97.9170
43	81.8767	98.5065
44	85.3814	99.0005
45	88.9467	99.3980
46	92.5721	99.6978
47	96.2567	99.8989
48	100.0000	100.0000

5 YEARS

#	REBATE	EARN
1	.0677	2.9454
2	.2025	5.8567
3	.4034	8.7333
4	.6697	11.5751
5	1.0007	14.3814
6	1.3956	17.1519
7	1.8537	19.8862
8	2.3743	22.5839
9	2.9566	25.2445
10	3.6000	27.8677
11	4.3036	30.4529
12	5.0669	32.9997
13	5.8892	35.5077
14	6.7697	37.9764
15	7.7078	40.4054
16	8.7028	42.7942
17	9.7541	45.1423
18	10.8610	47.4493
19	12.0229	49.7147
20	13.2392	51.9379
21	14.5091	54.1186
22	15.8322	56.2562
23	17.2077	58.3502
24	18.6351	60.4000
25	20.1138	62.4053
26	21.6432	64.3654
27	23.2228	66.2798
28	24.8518	68.1481
29	26.5298	69.9696
30	28.2562	71.7438
31	30.0304	73.4702
32	31.8519	75.1482
33	33.7202	76.7772
34	35.6346	78.3568
35	37.5947	79.8862
36	39.6000	81.3649
37	41.6498	82.7923
38	43.7438	84.1678
39	45.8814	85.4909
40	48.0621	86.7608
41	50.2853	87.9771
42	52.5507	89.1390
43	54.8577	90.2459
44	57.2058	91.2972
45	59.5946	92.2922
46	62.0236	93.2303
47	64.4923	94.1108
48	67.0003	94.9331
49	69.5471	95.6964
50	72.1323	96.4000
51	74.7555	97.0434
52	77.4161	97.6257
53	80.1138	98.1463
54	82.8481	98.6044
55	85.6186	98.9993
56	88.4249	99.3303
57	91.2667	99.5966
58	94.1433	99.7975
59	97.0546	99.9323
60	100.0000	100.0000

6 YEARS

#	REBATE	EARN
1	.0491	2.4124
2	.1468	4.8032
3	.2926	7.1722
4	.4857	9.5192
5	.7258	11.8438
6	1.0122	14.1458
7	1.3445	16.4250
8	1.7221	18.6811
9	2.1445	20.9137
10	2.6111	23.1227
11	3.1215	25.3078
12	3.6751	27.4687
13	4.2715	29.6050
14	4.9102	31.7166
15	5.5906	33.8031
16	6.3123	35.8642
17	7.0748	37.8997
18	7.8776	39.9092
19	8.7204	41.8924
20	9.6025	43.8491
21	10.5237	45.7789
22	11.4833	47.6814
23	12.4810	49.5565
24	13.5163	51.4038
25	14.5888	53.2229
26	15.6981	55.0135
27	16.8438	56.7752
28	18.0253	58.5079
29	19.2424	60.2110
30	20.4946	61.8843
31	21.7815	63.5274
32	23.1026	65.1399
33	24.4577	66.7216
34	25.8463	68.2720
35	27.2679	69.7908
36	28.7224	71.2776
37	30.2092	72.7321
38	31.7280	74.1537
39	33.2784	75.5423
40	34.8601	76.8974
41	36.4726	78.2185
42	38.1157	79.5054
43	39.7890	80.7576
44	41.4921	81.9747
45	43.2248	83.1562
46	44.9865	84.3019
47	46.7771	85.4112
48	48.5962	86.4837
49	50.4435	87.5190
50	52.3186	88.5167
51	54.2211	89.4763
52	56.1509	90.3975
53	58.1076	91.2796
54	60.0908	92.1124
55	62.1003	92.9252
56	64.1358	93.6877
57	66.1969	94.4094
58	68.2834	95.0898
59	70.3950	95.7285
60	72.5313	96.3249
61	74.6922	96.8785
62	76.8773	97.3889
63	79.0863	97.8555
64	81.3189	98.2779
65	83.5750	98.6555
66	85.8542	98.9878
67	88.1562	99.2742
68	90.4808	99.5143
69	92.8278	99.7074
70	95.1968	99.8532
71	97.5876	99.9509
72	100.0000	100.0000

7 YEARS

#	REBATE	EARN
1	.0376	2.0320
2	.1125	4.0495
3	.2241	6.0526
4	.3721	8.0409
5	.5560	10.0143
6	.7754	11.9727
7	1.0299	13.9159
8	1.3192	15.8436
9	1.6427	17.7558
10	2.0002	19.6522
11	2.3912	21.5326
12	2.8153	23.3969
13	3.2721	25.2449
14	3.7613	27.0764
15	4.2825	28.8911
16	4.8354	30.6889
17	5.4195	32.4696
18	6.0345	34.2331
19	6.6801	35.9790
20	7.3558	37.7072
21	8.0614	39.4175
22	8.7965	41.1097
23	9.5608	42.7835
24	10.3539	44.4388
25	11.1755	46.0753
26	12.0253	47.6928
27	12.9028	49.2911
28	13.8080	50.8700
29	14.7403	52.4292
30	15.6995	53.9686
31	16.6853	55.4878
32	17.6973	56.9867
33	18.7353	58.4649
34	19.7990	59.9224
35	20.8881	61.3587
36	22.0022	62.7738
37	23.1412	64.1673
38	24.3046	65.5389
39	25.4923	66.8885
40	26.7039	68.2157
41	27.9391	69.5204
42	29.1978	70.8022
43	30.4796	72.0609
44	31.7843	73.2961
45	33.1115	74.5077
46	34.4611	75.6954
47	35.8327	76.8588
48	37.2262	77.9978
49	38.6413	79.1119
50	40.0776	80.2010
51	41.5351	81.2647
52	43.0133	82.3027
53	44.5122	83.3147
54	46.0314	84.3005
55	47.5708	85.2597
56	49.1300	86.1920
57	50.7089	87.0972
58	52.3072	87.9747
59	53.9247	88.8245
60	55.5612	89.6461
61	57.2165	90.4392
62	58.8903	91.2035
63	60.5825	91.9386
64	62.2928	92.6442
65	64.0210	93.3199
66	65.7669	93.9655
67	67.5304	94.5805
68	69.3111	95.1646
69	71.1089	95.7175
70	72.9236	96.2387
71	74.7551	96.7279
72	76.6031	97.1847
73	78.4674	97.6088
74	80.3478	97.9998
75	82.2442	98.3573

#	REBATE	EARN
75	82.2442	98.3573
76	84.1564	98.6808
77	86.0841	98.9701
78	88.0273	99.2246
79	89.9857	99.4440
80	91.9591	99.6279
81	93.9474	99.7759
82	95.9505	99.8875
83	97.9680	99.9624
84	100.0000	100.0000

8 YEARS

#	REBATE	EARN
1	.0300	1.7474
2	.0897	3.4848
3	.1786	5.2121
4	.2966	6.9293
5	.4432	8.6361
6	.6181	10.3324
7	.8210	12.0182
8	1.0516	13.6934
9	1.3095	15.3577
10	1.5945	17.0110
11	1.9061	18.6533
12	2.2442	20.2844
13	2.6084	21.9042
14	2.9984	23.5125
15	3.4139	25.1093
16	3.8546	26.6943
17	4.3202	28.2674
18	4.8105	29.8286
19	5.3251	31.3776
20	5.8637	32.9143
21	6.4262	34.4386
22	7.0122	35.9503
23	7.6215	37.4493
24	8.2537	38.9354
25	8.9086	40.4085
26	9.5860	41.8685
27	10.2856	43.3151
28	11.0071	44.7483
29	11.7503	46.1678
30	12.5149	47.5735
31	13.3007	48.9653
32	14.1075	50.3429
33	14.9350	51.7063
34	15.7829	53.0552
35	16.6511	54.3895
36	17.5392	55.7090
37	18.4471	57.0136
38	19.3746	58.3030
39	20.3213	59.5771
40	21.2871	60.8358
41	22.2718	62.0787
42	23.2752	63.3058
43	24.2970	64.5168
44	25.3370	65.7117
45	26.3950	66.8901
46	27.4708	68.0519
47	28.5643	69.1969
48	29.6751	70.3249
49	30.8031	71.4357
50	31.9481	72.5292
51	33.1099	73.6050
52	34.2883	74.6630
53	35.4832	75.7030
54	36.6942	76.7248
55	37.9213	77.7282
56	39.1642	78.7129
57	40.4229	79.6787
58	41.6970	80.6254
59	42.9864	81.5529
60	44.2910	82.4608
61	45.6105	83.3489
62	46.9448	84.2171
63	48.2937	85.0650
64	49.6571	85.8925
65	51.0347	86.6993
66	52.4265	87.4851
67	53.8322	88.2497
68	55.2517	88.9929
69	56.6849	89.7144
70	58.1315	90.4140
71	59.5915	91.0914
72	61.0646	91.7463
73	62.5507	92.3785
74	64.0497	92.9878
75	65.5614	93.5738
76	67.0857	94.1363
77	68.6224	94.6749
78	70.1714	95.1895
79	71.7326	95.6798
80	73.3057	96.1454
81	74.8907	96.5861
82	76.4875	97.0016
83	78.0958	97.3916
84	79.7156	97.7558
85	81.3467	98.0939
86	82.9890	98.4055
87	84.6423	98.6905
88	86.3066	98.9484
89	87.9818	99.1790
90	89.6676	99.3819
91	91.3639	99.5568
92	93.0707	99.7034
93	94.7879	99.8214
94	96.5152	99.9103
95	98.2526	99.9700
96	100.0000	100.0000

9 YEARS

#	REBATE	EARN
1	.0247	1.5270
2	.0737	3.0468
3	.1468	4.5595
4	.2437	6.0648
5	.3642	7.5628
6	.5079	9.0533
7	.6746	10.5362
8	.8641	12.0115
9	1.0760	13.4791
10	1.3101	14.9388
11	1.5662	16.3907
12	1.8440	17.8345
13	2.1432	19.2703
14	2.4636	20.6978
15	2.8050	22.1171
16	3.1671	23.5280
17	3.5497	24.9304
18	3.9525	26.3242
19	4.3754	27.7094
20	4.8180	29.0857
21	5.2801	30.4532
22	5.7616	31.8117
23	6.2622	33.1611
24	6.7817	34.5013
25	7.3198	35.8322
26	7.8764	37.1537
27	8.4512	38.4657
28	9.0440	39.7680
29	9.6547	41.0606
30	10.2830	42.3433
31	10.9286	43.6161
32	11.5915	44.8787
33	12.2714	46.1311
34	12.9681	47.3733
35	13.6814	48.6049
36	14.4112	49.8260
37	15.1572	51.0364
38	15.9192	52.2360
39	16.6971	53.4246
40	17.4907	54.6022
41	18.2998	55.7685
42	19.1242	56.9235
43	19.9637	58.0671
44	20.8183	59.1990
45	21.6876	60.3193
46	22.5715	61.4276
47	23.4700	62.5239
48	24.3827	63.6081
49	25.3095	64.6800
50	26.2503	65.7395
51	27.2049	66.7864
52	28.1732	67.8205
53	29.1549	68.8418
54	30.1500	69.8500
55	31.1582	70.8451
56	32.1795	71.8268
57	33.2136	72.7951
58	34.2605	73.7497
59	35.3200	74.6905
60	36.3919	75.6173
61	37.4761	76.5300
62	38.5724	77.4285
63	39.6807	78.3124
64	40.8010	79.1817
65	41.9329	80.0363
66	43.0765	80.8758
67	44.2315	81.7002
68	45.3978	82.5093
69	46.5754	83.3029
70	47.7640	84.0800
71	48.9636	84.8428
72	50.1740	85.5888
73	51.3951	86.3186
74	52.6267	87.0319
75	53.8689	87.7286
76	55.1213	88.4085
77	56.3839	89.0714
78	57.6567	89.7170
79	58.9394	90.3453
80	60.2320	90.9560
81	61.5343	91.5488
82	62.8463	92.1236
83	64.1678	92.6802
84	65.4987	93.2183
85	66.8389	93.7378
86	68.1883	94.2384
87	69.5468	94.7199
88	70.9143	95.1820
89	72.2906	95.6246
90	73.6758	96.0475
91	75.0696	96.4503
92	76.4720	96.8329
93	77.8829	97.1950
94	79.3022	97.5364
95	80.7297	97.8568
96	82.1655	98.1560
97	83.6093	98.4338
98	85.0612	98.6899
99	86.5209	98.9240
100	87.9885	99.1359
101	89.4638	99.3254
102	90.9467	99.4921
103	92.4372	99.6358
104	93.9352	99.7563
105	95.4405	99.8532
106	96.9532	99.9263
107	98.4730	99.9753
108	100.0000	100.0000

10 YEARS

#	REBATE	EARN
1	.0207	1.3516
2	.0620	2.6979
3	.1235	4.0390
4	.2051	5.3747
5	.3064	6.7050
6	.4273	8.0299
7	.5676	9.3492
8	.7270	10.6630
9	.9053	11.9711
10	1.1023	13.2734
11	1.3178	14.5700
12	1.5515	15.8607
13	1.8033	17.1455
14	2.0729	18.4243
15	2.3601	19.6970
16	2.6648	20.9636
17	2.9867	22.2240
18	3.3256	23.4780
19	3.6814	24.7258
20	4.0538	25.9671
21	4.4427	27.2019
22	4.8478	28.4301
23	5.2690	29.6517
24	5.7061	30.8666
25	6.1588	32.0746
26	6.6271	33.2757
27	7.1108	34.4699
28	7.6096	35.6570
29	8.1234	36.8370
30	8.6520	38.0097
31	9.1953	39.1752
32	9.7530	40.3332
33	10.3251	41.4838
34	10.9113	42.6269
35	11.5114	43.7622
36	12.1255	44.8899
37	12.7531	46.0097
38	13.3943	47.1216
39	14.0488	48.2255
40	14.7165	49.3212
41	15.3973	50.4088
42	16.0909	51.4881
43	16.7973	52.5589
44	17.5163	53.6213
45	18.2478	54.6751
46	18.9915	55.7202
47	19.7475	56.7565
48	20.5154	57.7840
49	21.2952	58.8024
50	22.0868	59.8117
51	22.8900	60.8118
52	23.7047	61.8026
53	24.5307	62.7839
54	25.3680	63.7558
55	26.2163	64.7179
56	27.0756	65.6704
57	27.9457	66.6129
58	28.8266	67.5455
59	29.7180	68.4679
60	30.6199	69.3801
61	31.5321	70.2820
62	32.4545	71.1734
63	33.3871	72.0543
64	34.3296	72.9244
65	35.2821	73.7837
66	36.2442	74.6320
67	37.2161	75.4693
68	38.1974	76.2953
69	39.1882	77.1100
70	40.1883	77.9132
71	41.1976	78.7048
72	42.2160	79.4846
73	43.2435	80.2525
74	44.2798	81.0085
75	45.3249	81.7522
76	46.3787	82.4837
77	47.4411	83.2027
78	48.5119	83.9091
79	49.5912	84.6027
80	50.6788	85.2835
81	51.7745	85.9512
82	52.8784	86.6057
83	53.9903	87.2469
84	55.1101	87.8745
85	56.2378	88.4886
86	57.3731	89.0887
87	58.5162	89.6749
88	59.6668	90.2470
89	60.8248	90.8047
90	61.9903	91.3480
91	63.1630	91.8766
92	64.3430	92.3904
93	65.5301	92.8892
94	66.7243	93.3729
95	67.9254	93.8412
96	69.1334	94.2939
97	70.3483	94.7310
98	71.5699	95.1522
99	72.7981	95.5573
100	74.0329	95.9462
101	75.2742	96.3186
102	76.5220	96.6744
103	77.7760	97.0133
104	79.0364	97.3352
105	80.3030	97.6399
106	81.5757	97.9271
107	82.8545	98.1967
108	84.1393	98.4485
109	85.4300	98.6822
110	86.7266	98.8977
111	88.0289	99.0947
112	89.3370	99.2730
113	90.6508	99.4324
114	91.9701	99.5727
115	93.2950	99.6936
116	94.6253	99.7949
117	95.9610	99.8765
118	97.3021	99.9380
119	98.6484	99.9793
120	100.0000	100.0000

1 YEAR

#	REBATE	EARN
1	1.3380	15.0588
2	3.9982	28.9426
3	7.9652	41.6374
4	13.2236	53.1291
5	19.7583	63.4033
6	27.5542	72.4458
7	36.5967	80.2417
8	46.8709	86.7764
9	58.3626	92.0348
10	71.0574	96.0018
11	84.9412	98.6620
12	100.0000	100.0000

2 YEARS

#	REBATE	EARN
1	.3641	7.6541
2	1.0880	15.0307
3	2.1674	22.1265
4	3.5983	28.9381
5	5.3764	35.4623
6	7.4978	41.6955
7	9.9583	47.6343
8	12.7541	53.2752
9	15.8811	58.6148
10	19.3355	63.6493
11	23.1134	68.3753
12	27.2111	72.7889
13	31.6247	76.8866
14	36.3507	80.6645
15	41.3852	84.1189
16	46.7248	87.2459
17	52.3657	90.0417
18	58.3045	92.5022
19	64.5377	94.6236
20	71.0619	96.4017
21	77.8735	97.8326
22	84.9693	98.9120
23	92.3459	99.6359
24	100.0000	100.0000

3 YEARS

#	REBATE	EARN
1	.1715	5.0581
2	.5123	10.0028
3	1.0207	14.8328
4	1.6945	19.5466
5	2.5319	24.1429
6	3.5309	28.6203
7	4.6897	32.9773
8	6.0063	37.2126
9	7.4789	41.3247
10	9.1056	45.3122
11	10.8848	49.1735
12	12.8145	52.9072
13	14.8930	56.5117
14	17.1186	59.9856
15	19.4895	63.3272
16	22.0040	66.5350
17	24.6605	69.6074
18	27.4572	72.5428
19	30.3926	75.3395
20	33.4650	77.9960
21	36.6728	80.5105
22	40.0144	82.8814
23	43.4883	85.1070
24	47.0928	87.1855
25	50.8265	89.1152
26	54.6878	90.8944
27	58.6753	92.5211
28	62.7874	93.9937
29	67.0227	95.3103
30	71.3797	96.4691
31	75.8571	97.4681
32	80.4534	98.3055
33	85.1672	98.9793
34	89.9972	99.4877
35	94.9419	99.8285
36	100.0000	100.0000

4 YEARS

#	REBATE	EARN
1	.1014	3.7378
2	.3030	7.4174
3	.6037	11.0381
4	1.0022	14.5992
5	1.4975	18.0999
6	2.0884	21.5396
7	2.7737	24.9176
8	3.5524	28.2330
9	4.4234	31.4852
10	5.3855	34.6734
11	6.4378	37.7969
12	7.5791	40.8548
13	8.8085	43.8465
14	10.1248	46.7710
15	11.5271	49.6277
16	13.0143	52.4157
17	14.5855	55.1342
18	16.2396	57.7823
19	17.9758	60.3593
20	19.7930	62.8643
21	21.6902	65.2964
22	23.6666	67.6548
23	25.7212	69.9386
24	27.8531	72.1469
25	30.0614	74.2788
26	32.3452	76.3334
27	34.7036	78.3098
28	37.1357	80.2070
29	39.6407	82.0242
30	42.2177	83.7604
31	44.8658	85.4145
32	47.5843	86.9857
33	50.3723	88.4729
34	53.2290	89.8752
35	56.1535	91.1915
36	59.1452	92.4209
37	62.2031	93.5622
38	65.3266	94.6145
39	68.5148	95.5766
40	71.7670	96.4476
41	75.0824	97.2263
42	78.4604	97.9116
43	81.9001	98.5025
44	85.4008	98.9978
45	88.9619	99.3963
46	92.5826	99.6970
47	96.2622	99.8986
48	100.0000	100.0000

5 YEARS

#	REBATE	EARN
1	.0680	2.9402
2	.2032	5.8465
3	.4047	8.7186
4	.6719	11.5559
5	1.0040	14.3582
6	1.4001	17.1249
7	1.8596	19.8557
8	2.3817	22.5501
9	2.9656	25.2077
10	3.6107	27.8281
11	4.3162	30.4108
12	5.0814	32.9554
13	5.9056	35.4614
14	6.7881	37.9284
15	7.7283	40.3559
16	8.7254	42.7434
17	9.7788	45.0904
18	10.8878	47.3966
19	12.0518	49.6613
20	13.2701	51.8841
21	14.5421	54.0645
22	15.8672	56.2021
23	17.2447	58.2962
24	18.6740	60.3464
25	20.1546	62.3521
26	21.6857	64.3128
27	23.2669	66.2281
28	24.8975	68.0973
29	26.5769	69.9199
30	28.3047	71.6953
31	30.0801	73.4231
32	31.9027	75.1025
33	33.7719	76.7331
34	35.6872	78.3143
35	37.6479	79.8454
36	39.6536	81.3260
37	41.7038	82.7553
38	43.7979	84.1328
39	45.9355	85.4579
40	48.1159	86.7299
41	50.3387	87.9482
42	52.6034	89.1122
43	54.9096	90.2212
44	57.2566	91.2746
45	59.6441	92.2717
46	62.0716	93.2119
47	64.5386	94.0944
48	67.0446	94.9186
49	69.5892	95.6838
50	72.1719	96.3893
51	74.7923	97.0344
52	77.4499	97.6183
53	80.1443	98.1404
54	82.8751	98.5999
55	85.6418	98.9960
56	88.4441	99.3281
57	91.2814	99.5953
58	94.1535	99.7968
59	97.0598	99.9320
60	100.0000	100.0000

6 YEARS

#	REBATE	EARN
1	.0493	2.4074
2	.1475	4.7935
3	.2938	7.1580
4	.4877	9.5006
5	.7287	11.8211
6	1.0162	14.1192
7	1.3497	16.3947
8	1.7286	18.6473
9	2.1524	20.8767
10	2.6205	23.0827
11	3.1326	25.2649
12	3.6879	27.4231
13	4.2861	29.5570
14	4.9266	31.6663
15	5.6089	33.7508
16	6.3326	35.8100
17	7.0971	37.8438
18	7.9020	39.8518
19	8.7468	41.8337
20	9.6310	43.7893
21	10.5542	45.7181
22	11.5159	47.6199
23	12.5157	49.4943
24	13.5530	51.3411
25	14.6275	53.1599
26	15.7388	54.9504
27	16.8864	56.7121
28	18.0698	58.4449
29	19.2887	60.1483
30	20.5427	61.8221
31	21.8312	63.4657
32	23.1540	65.0790
33	24.5106	66.6615
34	25.9006	68.2128
35	27.3237	69.7327
36	28.7794	71.2206
37	30.2673	72.6763
38	31.7872	74.0994
39	33.3385	75.4894
40	34.9210	76.8460
41	36.5343	78.1688
42	38.1779	79.4573
43	39.8517	80.7113
44	41.5551	81.9302
45	43.2879	83.1136
46	45.0496	84.2612
47	46.8401	85.3725
48	48.6589	86.4470
49	50.5057	87.4843
50	52.3801	88.4841
51	54.2819	89.4458
52	56.2107	90.3690
53	58.1663	91.2532
54	60.1482	92.0980
55	62.1562	92.9029
56	64.1900	93.6674
57	66.2492	94.3911
58	68.3337	95.0734
59	70.4430	95.7139
60	72.5769	96.3121
61	74.7351	96.8674
62	76.9173	97.3795
63	79.1233	97.8476
64	81.3527	98.2714
65	83.6053	98.6503
66	85.8808	98.9838
67	88.1789	99.2713
68	90.4994	99.5123
69	92.8420	99.7062
70	95.2065	99.8525
71	97.5926	99.9507
72	100.0000	100.0000

7 YEARS

#	REBATE	EARN
1	.0378	2.0272
2	.1130	4.0402
3	.2252	6.0388
4	.3738	8.0229
5	.5585	9.9923
6	.7789	11.9468
7	1.0345	13.8863
8	1.3249	15.8105
9	1.6498	17.7192
10	2.0086	19.6124
11	2.4011	21.4898
12	2.8267	23.3512
13	3.2852	25.1965
14	3.7762	27.0254
15	4.2992	28.8377
16	4.8539	30.6333
17	5.4399	32.4119
18	6.0568	34.1734
19	6.7043	35.9176
20	7.3821	37.6442
21	8.0897	39.3530
22	8.8268	41.0438
23	9.5931	42.7165
24	10.3882	44.3707
25	11.2118	46.0063
26	12.0636	47.6231
27	12.9432	49.2208
28	13.8503	50.7992
29	14.7846	52.3581
30	15.7457	53.8972
31	16.7334	55.4163
32	17.7473	56.9152
33	18.7871	58.3936
34	19.8525	59.8513
35	20.9433	61.2880
36	22.0590	62.7036
37	23.1995	64.0976
38	24.3645	65.4700
39	25.5536	66.8204
40	26.7665	68.1485
41	28.0031	69.4542
42	29.2629	70.7371
43	30.5458	71.9969
44	31.8515	73.2335
45	33.1796	74.4464
46	34.5300	75.6355
47	35.9024	76.8005
48	37.2964	77.9410
49	38.7120	79.0567
50	40.1487	80.1475
51	41.6064	81.2129
52	43.0848	82.2527
53	44.5837	83.2666
54	46.1028	84.2543
55	47.6419	85.2154
56	49.2008	86.1497
57	50.7792	87.0568
58	52.3769	87.9364
59	53.9937	88.7882
60	55.6293	89.6118
61	57.2835	90.4069
62	58.9562	91.1732
63	60.6470	91.9103
64	62.3558	92.6179
65	64.0824	93.2957
66	65.8266	93.9432
67	67.5881	94.5601
68	69.3667	95.1461
69	71.1623	95.7008
70	72.9746	96.2238
71	74.8035	96.7148
72	76.6488	97.1733
73	78.5102	97.5989
74	80.3876	97.9914
75	82.2808	98.3502

#	REBATE	EARN
75	82.2808	98.3502
76	84.1895	98.6751
77	86.1137	98.9655
78	88.0532	99.2211
79	90.0077	99.4415
80	91.9771	99.6262
81	93.9612	99.7748
82	95.9598	99.8870
83	97.9728	99.9622
84	100.0000	100.0000

8 YEARS

#	REBATE	EARN
1	.0302	1.7429
2	.0901	3.4759
3	.1796	5.1990
4	.2981	6.9120
5	.4455	8.6148
6	.6212	10.3074
7	.8251	11.9895
8	1.0568	13.6611
9	1.3159	15.3219
10	1.6021	16.9720
11	1.9151	18.6112
12	2.2546	20.2393
13	2.6203	21.8562
14	3.0119	23.4618
15	3.4291	25.0559
16	3.8715	26.6384
17	4.3389	28.2092
18	4.8310	29.7681
19	5.3474	31.3151
20	5.8880	32.8498
21	6.4524	34.3723
22	7.0403	35.8823
23	7.6515	37.3797
24	8.2857	38.8644
25	8.9426	40.3362
26	9.6220	41.7949
27	10.3236	43.2404
28	11.0471	44.6726
29	11.7923	46.0913
30	12.5589	47.4963
31	13.3466	48.8874
32	14.1553	50.2645
33	14.9847	51.6275
34	15.8345	52.9761
35	16.7045	54.3102
36	17.5944	55.6297
37	18.5041	56.9343
38	19.4333	58.2238
39	20.3817	59.4981
40	21.3492	60.7571
41	22.3354	62.0004
42	23.3403	63.2280
43	24.3636	64.4397
44	25.4050	65.6352
45	26.4643	66.8144
46	27.5414	67.9771
47	28.6360	69.1231
48	29.7479	70.2521
49	30.8769	71.3640
50	32.0229	72.4586
51	33.1856	73.5357
52	34.3648	74.5950
53	35.5603	75.6364
54	36.7720	76.6597
55	37.9996	77.6646
56	39.2429	78.6508

#	REBATE	EARN
57	40.5019	79.6183
58	41.7762	80.5667
59	43.0657	81.4959
60	44.3703	82.4056
61	45.6898	83.2955
62	47.0239	84.1655
63	48.3725	85.0153
64	49.7355	85.8447
65	51.1126	86.6534
66	52.5037	87.4411
67	53.9087	88.2077
68	55.3274	88.9529
69	56.7596	89.6764
70	58.2051	90.3780
71	59.6638	91.0574
72	61.1356	91.7143
73	62.6203	92.3485
74	64.1177	92.9597
75	65.6277	93.5476
76	67.1502	94.1120
77	68.6849	94.6526
78	70.2319	95.1690
79	71.7908	95.6611
80	73.3616	96.1285
81	74.9441	96.5709
82	76.5382	96.9881
83	78.1438	97.3797
84	79.7607	97.7454
85	81.3888	98.0849
86	83.0280	98.3979
87	84.6781	98.6841
88	86.3389	98.9432
89	88.0105	99.1749
90	89.6926	99.3788
91	91.3852	99.5545
92	93.0880	99.7019
93	94.8010	99.8204
94	96.5241	99.9099
95	98.2571	99.9698
96	100.0000	100.0000

9 YEARS

#	REBATE	EARN
1	.0248	1.5227
2	.0741	3.0383
3	.1476	4.5469
4	.2451	6.0483
5	.3662	7.5424
6	.5107	9.0291
7	.6783	10.5085
8	.8688	11.9803
9	1.0818	13.4444
10	1.3171	14.9009
11	1.5744	16.3496
12	1.8535	17.7904
13	2.1542	19.2232
14	2.4761	20.6479
15	2.8190	22.0644
16	3.1827	23.4727
17	3.5670	24.8726
18	3.9715	26.2640
19	4.3961	27.6469
20	4.8405	29.0211
21	5.3045	30.3865
22	5.7878	31.7430
23	6.2903	33.0906
24	6.8117	34.4290
25	7.3517	35.7583
26	7.9102	37.0782
27	8.4870	38.3887

#	REBATE	EARN
28	9.0818	39.6897
29	9.6944	40.9811
30	10.3246	42.2627
31	10.9722	43.5344
32	11.6370	44.7961
33	12.3189	46.0477
34	13.0175	47.2891
35	13.7327	48.5201
36	14.4643	49.7406
37	15.2122	50.9506
38	15.9760	52.1498
39	16.7557	53.3382
40	17.5511	54.5156
41	18.3619	55.6818
42	19.1880	56.8369
43	20.0292	57.9805
44	20.8853	59.1127
45	21.7562	60.2332
46	22.6417	61.3419
47	23.5415	62.4386
48	24.4556	63.5233
49	25.3838	64.5958
50	26.3259	65.6559
51	27.2817	66.7036
52	28.2511	67.7385
53	29.2340	68.7607
54	30.2301	69.7699
55	31.2393	70.7660
56	32.2615	71.7489
57	33.2964	72.7183
58	34.3441	73.6741
59	35.4042	74.6162
60	36.4767	75.5444
61	37.5614	76.4585
62	38.6581	77.3583
63	39.7668	78.2438
64	40.8873	79.1147
65	42.0195	79.9708
66	43.1631	80.8120
67	44.3182	81.6381
68	45.4844	82.4489
69	46.6618	83.2443
70	47.8502	84.0240
71	49.0494	84.7878
72	50.2594	85.5357
73	51.4799	86.2673
74	52.7109	86.9825
75	53.9523	87.6811
76	55.2039	88.3630
77	56.4656	89.0278
78	57.7373	89.6754
79	59.0189	90.3056
80	60.3103	90.9182
81	61.6113	91.5130
82	62.9218	92.0898
83	64.2417	92.6483
84	65.5710	93.1883
85	66.9094	93.7097
86	68.2570	94.2122
87	69.6135	94.6955
88	70.9789	95.1595
89	72.3531	95.6039
90	73.7360	96.0285
91	75.1274	96.4330
92	76.5273	96.8173
93	77.9356	97.1810
94	79.3521	97.5239
95	80.7768	97.8458
96	82.2096	98.1465

#	REBATE	EARN
97	83.6504	98.4256
98	85.0991	98.6829
99	86.5556	98.9182
100	88.0197	99.1312
101	89.4915	99.3217
102	90.9709	99.4893
103	92.4576	99.6338
104	93.9517	99.7549
105	95.4531	99.8524
106	96.9617	99.9259
107	98.4773	99.9752
108	100.0000	100.0000

10 YEARS

#	REBATE	EARN
1	.0209	1.3475
2	.0624	2.6898
3	.1243	4.0270
4	.2063	5.3589
5	.3083	6.6855
6	.4299	8.0068
7	.5710	9.3226
8	.7313	10.6329
9	.9107	11.9376
10	1.1087	13.2367
11	1.3254	14.5302
12	1.5603	15.8178
13	1.8134	17.0996
14	2.0844	18.3755
15	2.3731	19.6455
16	2.6793	20.9094
17	3.0028	22.1671
18	3.3433	23.4187
19	3.7007	24.6641
20	4.0748	25.9031
21	4.4654	27.1356
22	4.8723	28.3617
23	5.2953	29.5812
24	5.7342	30.7941
25	6.1888	32.0003
26	6.6590	33.1997
27	7.1445	34.3921
28	7.6452	35.5776
29	8.1609	36.7561
30	8.6915	37.9274
31	9.2367	39.0916
32	9.7963	40.2484
33	10.3703	41.3978
34	10.9584	42.5398
35	11.5605	43.6742
36	12.1764	44.8009
37	12.8059	45.9199
38	13.4490	47.0311
39	14.1053	48.1343
40	14.7749	49.2295
41	15.4574	50.3166
42	16.1529	51.3954
43	16.8610	52.4660
44	17.5817	53.5281
45	18.3148	54.5818
46	19.0602	55.6268
47	19.8178	56.6631
48	20.5873	57.6906
49	21.3687	58.7091
50	22.1617	59.7187
51	22.9664	60.7191
52	23.7824	61.7102
53	24.6098	62.6920
54	25.4483	63.6643
55	26.2979	64.6271

#	REBATE	EARN
56	27.1584	65.5801
57	28.0297	66.5234
58	28.9116	67.4567
59	29.8040	68.3800
60	30.7069	69.2931
61	31.6200	70.1960
62	32.5433	71.0884
63	33.4766	71.9703
64	34.4199	72.8416
65	35.3729	73.7021
66	36.3357	74.5517
67	37.3080	75.3902
68	38.2898	76.2176
69	39.2809	77.0336
70	40.2813	77.8383
71	41.2909	78.6313
72	42.3094	79.4127
73	43.3369	80.1822
74	44.3732	80.9398
75	45.4182	81.6852
76	46.4719	82.4183
77	47.5340	83.1390
78	48.6046	83.8471
79	49.6834	84.5426
80	50.7705	85.2251
81	51.8657	85.8947
82	52.9689	86.5510
83	54.0801	87.1941
84	55.1991	87.8236
85	56.3258	88.4395
86	57.4602	89.0416
87	58.6022	89.6297
88	59.7516	90.2037
89	60.9084	90.7633
90	62.0726	91.3085
91	63.2439	91.8391
92	64.4224	92.3548
93	65.6079	92.8555
94	66.8003	93.3410
95	67.9997	93.8112
96	69.2059	94.2658
97	70.4188	94.7047
98	71.6383	95.1277
99	72.8644	95.5346
100	74.0969	95.9252
101	75.3359	96.2993
102	76.5813	96.6567
103	77.8329	96.9972
104	79.0906	97.3207
105	80.3545	97.6269
106	81.6245	97.9156
107	82.9004	98.1866
108	84.1822	98.4397
109	85.4698	98.6746
110	86.7633	98.8913
111	88.0624	99.0893
112	89.3671	99.2687
113	90.6774	99.4290
114	91.9932	99.5701
115	93.3145	99.6917
116	94.6411	99.7937
117	95.9730	99.8757
118	97.3102	99.9376
119	98.6525	99.9791
120	100.0000	100.0000

1 YEAR

#	REBATE	EARN
1	1.3390	15.0533
2	4.0009	28.9333
3	7.9700	41.6259
4	13.2306	53.1167
5	19.7674	63.3913
6	27.5652	72.4348
7	36.6087	80.2326
8	46.8833	86.7694
9	58.3741	92.0300
10	71.0667	95.9991
11	84.9467	98.6610
12	100.0000	100.0000

2 YEARS

#	REBATE	EARN
1	.3646	7.6483
2	1.0895	15.0201
3	2.1704	22.1119
4	3.6030	28.9203
5	5.3830	35.4420
6	7.5065	41.6734
7	9.9692	47.6112
8	12.7672	53.2516
9	15.8964	58.5912
10	19.3528	63.6263
11	23.1326	68.3531
12	27.2319	72.7681
13	31.6469	76.8674
14	36.3737	80.6472
15	41.4088	84.1036
16	46.7484	87.2328
17	52.3888	90.0308
18	58.3266	92.4935
19	64.5580	94.6170
20	71.0797	96.3970
21	77.8881	97.8296
22	84.9799	98.9105
23	92.3517	99.6354
24	100.0000	100.0000

3 YEARS

#	REBATE	EARN
1	.1718	5.0525
2	.5135	9.9922
3	1.0228	14.8176
4	1.6980	19.5274
5	2.5369	24.1202
6	3.5376	28.5946
7	4.6982	32.9492
8	6.0168	37.1824
9	7.4915	41.2929
10	9.1204	45.2792
11	10.9017	49.1397
12	12.8336	52.8729
13	14.9142	56.4774
14	17.1419	59.9514
15	19.5148	63.2936
16	22.0311	66.5022
17	24.6893	69.5757
18	27.4876	72.5124
19	30.4243	75.3107
20	33.4978	77.9689
21	36.7064	80.4852
22	40.0486	82.8581
23	43.5226	85.0858
24	47.1271	87.1664
25	50.8603	89.0983
26	54.7208	90.8796
27	58.7071	92.5085
28	62.8176	93.9832
29	67.0508	95.3018
30	71.4054	96.4624
31	75.8798	97.4631
32	80.4726	98.3020
33	85.1824	98.9772
34	90.0078	99.4865
35	94.9475	99.8282
36	100.0000	100.0000

4 YEARS

#	REBATE	EARN
1	.1017	3.7324
2	.3039	7.4070
3	.6054	11.0230
4	1.0050	14.5798
5	1.5015	18.0766
6	2.0938	21.5128
7	2.7807	24.8876
8	3.5611	28.2002
9	4.4339	31.4499
10	5.3980	34.6359
11	6.4523	37.7575
12	7.5957	40.8139
13	8.8272	43.8043
14	10.1456	46.7278
15	11.5500	49.5838
16	13.0394	52.3714
17	14.6127	55.0897
18	16.2688	57.7379
19	18.0070	60.3152
20	19.8260	62.8207
21	21.7251	65.2535
22	23.7032	67.6129
23	25.7594	69.8977
24	27.8927	72.1073
25	30.1023	74.2406
26	32.3871	76.2968
27	34.7465	78.2749
28	37.1793	80.1740
29	39.6848	81.9930
30	42.2621	83.7312
31	44.9103	85.3873
32	47.6286	86.9606
33	50.4162	88.4500
34	53.2722	89.8544
35	56.1957	91.1728
36	59.1861	92.4043
37	62.2425	93.5477
38	65.3641	94.6020
39	68.5501	95.5661
40	71.7998	96.4389
41	75.1124	97.2193
42	78.4872	97.9062
43	81.9234	98.4985
44	85.4202	98.9950
45	88.9770	99.3946
46	92.5930	99.6961
47	96.2676	99.8983
48	100.0000	100.0000

5 YEARS

#	REBATE	EARN
1	.0682	2.9350
2	.2039	5.8364
3	.4061	8.7038
4	.6742	11.5369
5	1.0073	14.3350
6	1.4047	17.0980
7	1.8655	19.8253
8	2.3891	22.5164
9	2.9747	25.1711
10	3.6215	27.7887
11	4.3288	30.3690
12	5.0959	32.9113
13	5.9220	35.4153
14	6.8066	37.8805
15	7.7488	40.3065
16	8.7480	42.6927
17	9.8034	45.0387
18	10.9146	47.3440
19	12.0806	49.6081
20	13.3010	51.8304
21	14.5751	54.0106
22	15.9022	56.1481
23	17.2816	58.2423
24	18.7128	60.2928
25	20.1952	62.2990
26	21.7281	64.2604
27	23.3109	66.1764
28	24.9431	68.0466
29	26.6240	69.8703
30	28.3531	71.6469
31	30.1297	73.3760
32	31.9534	75.0569
33	33.8236	76.6891
34	35.7396	78.2719
35	37.7010	79.8048
36	39.7072	81.2872
37	41.7577	82.7184
38	43.8519	84.0978
39	45.9894	85.4249
40	48.1696	86.6990
41	50.3919	87.9194
42	52.6560	89.0854
43	54.9613	90.1966
44	57.3073	91.2520
45	59.6935	92.2512
46	62.1195	93.1934
47	64.5847	94.0780
48	67.0887	94.9041
49	69.6310	95.6712
50	72.2113	96.3785
51	74.8289	97.0253
52	77.4836	97.6109
53	80.1747	98.1345
54	82.9020	98.5953
55	85.6650	98.9927
56	88.4631	99.3258
57	91.2962	99.5939
58	94.1636	99.7961
59	97.0650	99.9318
60	100.0000	100.0000

6 YEARS

#	REBATE	EARN
1	.0496	2.4025
2	.1481	4.7838
3	.2949	7.1437
4	.4896	9.4821
5	.7315	11.7985
6	1.0201	14.0927
7	1.3548	16.3646
8	1.7350	18.6137
9	2.1603	20.8399
10	2.6300	23.0428
11	3.1436	25.2222
12	3.7007	27.3778
13	4.3007	29.5092
14	4.9431	31.6163
15	5.6273	33.6987
16	6.3530	35.7561
17	7.1195	37.7882
18	7.9264	39.7947
19	8.7732	41.7753
20	9.6595	43.7297
21	10.5848	45.6576
22	11.5485	47.5586
23	12.5503	49.4324
24	13.5897	51.2787
25	14.6662	53.0972
26	15.7794	54.8875
27	16.9289	56.6492
28	18.1142	58.3822
29	19.3350	60.0859
30	20.5906	61.7600
31	21.8809	63.4042
32	23.2053	65.0182
33	24.5634	66.6015
34	25.9549	68.1538
35	27.3793	69.6746
36	28.8363	71.1637
37	30.3254	72.6207
38	31.8462	74.0451
39	33.3985	75.4366
40	34.9818	76.7947
41	36.5958	78.1191
42	38.2400	79.4094
43	39.9141	80.6650
44	41.6178	81.8858
45	43.3508	83.0711
46	45.1125	84.2206
47	46.9028	85.3338
48	48.7213	86.4103
49	50.5676	87.4497
50	52.4414	88.4515
51	54.3424	89.4152
52	56.2703	90.3405
53	58.2247	91.2268
54	60.2053	92.0736
55	62.2118	92.8805
56	64.2439	93.6470
57	66.3013	94.3727
58	68.3837	95.0569
59	70.4908	95.6993
60	72.6222	96.2993
61	74.7778	96.8564
62	76.9572	97.3700
63	79.1601	97.8397
64	81.3863	98.2650
65	83.6354	98.6452
66	85.9073	98.9799
67	88.2015	99.2685
68	90.5179	99.5104
69	92.8563	99.7051
70	95.2162	99.8519
71	97.5975	99.9504
72	100.0000	100.0000

7 YEARS

#	REBATE	EARN
1	.0380	2.0225
2	.1136	4.0309
3	.2262	6.0252
4	.3755	8.0051
5	.5610	9.9704
6	.7824	11.9211
7	1.0390	13.8568
8	1.3307	15.7775
9	1.6568	17.6829
10	2.0170	19.5729
11	2.4110	21.4472
12	2.8382	23.3058
13	3.2984	25.1483
14	3.7911	26.9747
15	4.3158	28.7846
16	4.8724	30.5780
17	5.4602	32.3545
18	6.0791	34.1141
19	6.7286	35.8565
20	7.4083	37.5814
21	8.1179	39.2888
22	8.8570	40.9783
23	9.6254	42.6498
24	10.4225	44.3030
25	11.2481	45.9377
26	12.1019	47.5537
27	12.9835	49.1507
28	13.8926	50.7286
29	14.8288	52.2871
30	15.7918	53.8260
31	16.7814	55.3450
32	17.7971	56.8439
33	18.8387	58.3225
34	19.9059	59.7805
35	20.9983	61.2176
36	22.1157	62.6336
37	23.2578	64.0282
38	24.4242	65.4013
39	25.6147	66.7525
40	26.8290	68.0815
41	28.0668	69.3882
42	29.3279	70.6721
43	30.6118	71.9332
44	31.9185	73.1710
45	33.2475	74.3853
46	34.5987	75.5758
47	35.9718	76.7422
48	37.3664	77.8843
49	38.7824	79.0017
50	40.2195	80.0941
51	41.6775	81.1613
52	43.1561	82.2029
53	44.6550	83.2186
54	46.1740	84.2082
55	47.7129	85.1712
56	49.2714	86.1074
57	50.8493	87.0165
58	52.4463	87.8981
59	54.0623	88.7519
60	55.6970	89.5775
61	57.3502	90.3746
62	59.0217	91.1430
63	60.7112	91.8821
64	62.4186	92.5917
65	64.1435	93.2714
66	65.8859	93.9209
67	67.6455	94.5398
68	69.4220	95.1276
69	71.2154	95.6842
70	73.0253	96.2089
71	74.8517	96.7016
72	76.6942	97.1618
73	78.5528	97.5890
74	80.4271	97.9830
75	82.3171	98.3432

#	REBATE	EARN
75	82.3171	98.3432
76	84.2225	98.6693
77	86.1432	98.9610
78	88.0789	99.2176
79	90.0296	99.4390
80	91.9949	99.6245
81	93.9748	99.7738
82	95.9691	99.8864
83	97.9775	99.9620
84	100.0000	100.0000

8 YEARS

#	REBATE	EARN
1	.0303	1.7384
2	.0906	3.4670
3	.1805	5.1859
4	.2997	6.8949
5	.4477	8.5938
6	.6244	10.2825
7	.8292	11.9609
8	1.0619	13.6290
9	1.3222	15.2865
10	1.6097	16.9333
11	1.9241	18.5693
12	2.2651	20.1944
13	2.6323	21.8085
14	3.0255	23.4113
15	3.4443	25.0029
16	3.8884	26.5829
17	4.3576	28.1514
18	4.8514	29.7081
19	5.3698	31.2529
20	5.9122	32.7857
21	6.4785	34.3064
22	7.0684	35.8147
23	7.6816	37.3105
24	8.3177	38.7937
25	8.9766	40.2642
26	9.6580	41.7217
27	10.3616	43.1662
28	11.0870	44.5974
29	11.8342	46.0152
30	12.6028	47.4194
31	13.3925	48.8099
32	14.2031	50.1865
33	15.0343	51.5491
34	15.8860	52.8974
35	16.7578	54.2313
36	17.6496	55.5507
37	18.5610	56.8552
38	19.4919	58.1449
39	20.4420	59.4195
40	21.4111	60.6787
41	22.3989	61.9225
42	23.4053	63.1506
43	24.4299	64.3629
44	25.4727	65.5591
45	26.5334	66.7390
46	27.6117	67.9026
47	28.7075	69.0495
48	29.8205	70.1795
49	30.9505	71.2925
50	32.0974	72.3883
51	33.2610	73.4666
52	34.4409	74.5273
53	35.6371	75.5701
54	36.8494	76.5947
55	38.0775	77.6011
56	39.3213	78.5889
57	40.5805	79.5580
58	41.8551	80.5081
59	43.1448	81.4390
60	44.4493	82.3504
61	45.7687	83.2422
62	47.1026	84.1140
63	48.4509	84.9657
64	49.8135	85.7969
65	51.1901	86.6075
66	52.5806	87.3972
67	53.9848	88.1658
68	55.4026	88.9130
69	56.8338	89.6384
70	58.2783	90.3420
71	59.7358	91.0234
72	61.2063	91.6823
73	62.6895	92.3184
74	64.1853	92.9316
75	65.6936	93.5215
76	67.2143	94.0878
77	68.7471	94.6302
78	70.2919	95.1486
79	71.8486	95.6424
80	73.4171	96.1116
81	74.9971	96.5557
82	76.5887	96.9745
83	78.1915	97.3677
84	79.8056	97.7349
85	81.4307	98.0759
86	83.0667	98.3903
87	84.7135	98.6778
88	86.3710	98.9381
89	88.0391	99.1708
90	89.7175	99.3756
91	91.4062	99.5523
92	93.1051	99.7003
93	94.8141	99.8195
94	96.5330	99.9094
95	98.2616	99.9697
96	100.0000	100.0000

9 YEARS

#	REBATE	EARN
1	.0249	1.5184
2	.0745	3.0299
3	.1485	4.5344
4	.2465	6.0319
5	.3683	7.5222
6	.5136	9.0052
7	.6821	10.4809
8	.8735	11.9493
9	1.0876	13.4101
10	1.3240	14.8633
11	1.5826	16.3088
12	1.8631	17.7465
13	2.1652	19.1764
14	2.4886	20.5983
15	2.8330	22.0121
16	3.1983	23.4178
17	3.5842	24.8152
18	3.9905	26.2042
19	4.4168	27.5848
20	4.8630	28.9568
21	5.3288	30.3202
22	5.8140	31.6748
23	6.3184	33.0204
24	6.8416	34.3572
25	7.3836	35.6848
26	7.9440	37.0032
27	8.5227	38.3123
28	9.1195	39.6119
29	9.7340	40.9020
30	10.3662	42.1825
31	11.0158	43.4532
32	11.6825	44.7139
33	12.3663	45.9647
34	13.0668	47.2054
35	13.7839	48.4357
36	14.5174	49.6557
37	15.2671	50.8652
38	16.0328	52.0641
39	16.8142	53.2522
40	17.6113	54.4294
41	18.4239	55.5956
42	19.2516	56.7506
43	20.0945	57.8944
44	20.9522	59.0267
45	21.8246	60.1474
46	22.7116	61.2565
47	23.6129	62.3537
48	24.5284	63.4389
49	25.4579	64.5119
50	26.4013	65.5727
51	27.3583	66.6211
52	28.3289	67.6569
53	29.3128	68.6799
54	30.3099	69.6901
55	31.3201	70.6872
56	32.3431	71.6711
57	33.3789	72.6417
58	34.4273	73.5987
59	35.4881	74.5421
60	36.5611	75.4716
61	37.6463	76.3871
62	38.7435	77.2884
63	39.8526	78.1754
64	40.9733	79.0478
65	42.1056	79.9055
66	43.2494	80.7484
67	44.4044	81.5761
68	45.5706	82.3887
69	46.7478	83.1858
70	47.9359	83.9672
71	49.1348	84.7329
72	50.3443	85.4826
73	51.5643	86.2161
74	52.7946	86.9332
75	54.0353	87.6337
76	55.2861	88.3175
77	56.5468	88.9842
78	57.8175	89.6338
79	59.0980	90.2660
80	60.3881	90.8805
81	61.6877	91.4773
82	62.9968	92.0560
83	64.3152	92.6164
84	65.6428	93.1584
85	66.9796	93.6816
86	68.3252	94.1860
87	69.6798	94.6712
88	71.0432	95.1370
89	72.4152	95.5832
90	73.7958	96.0095
91	75.1848	96.4158
92	76.5822	96.8017
93	77.9879	97.1670
94	79.4017	97.5114
95	80.8236	97.8348
96	82.2535	98.1369
97	83.6912	98.4174
98	85.1367	98.6760
99	86.5899	98.9124
100	88.0507	99.1265
101	89.5191	99.3179
102	90.9948	99.4864
103	92.4778	99.6317
104	93.9681	99.7535
105	95.4656	99.8515
106	96.9701	99.9255
107	98.4816	99.9751
108	100.0000	100.0000

10 YEARS

#	REBATE	EARN
1	.0210	1.3434
2	.0628	2.6818
3	.1251	4.0151
4	.2076	5.3433
5	.3102	6.6662
6	.4326	7.9839
7	.5745	9.2962
8	.7357	10.6031
9	.9160	11.9045
10	1.1152	13.2004
11	1.3330	14.4907
12	1.5692	15.7753
13	1.8236	17.0542
14	2.0960	18.3272
15	2.3861	19.5944
16	2.6938	20.8556
17	3.0188	22.1108
18	3.3610	23.3599
19	3.7201	24.6028
20	4.0959	25.8395
21	4.4882	27.0699
22	4.8968	28.2938
23	5.3216	29.5113
24	5.7623	30.7223
25	6.2188	31.9266
26	6.6908	33.1241
27	7.1783	34.3149
28	7.6809	35.4989
29	8.1985	36.6758
30	8.7309	37.8457
31	9.2780	39.0085
32	9.8396	40.1641
33	10.4155	41.3124
34	11.0055	42.4533
35	11.6095	43.5867
36	12.2272	44.7125
37	12.8587	45.8307
38	13.5035	46.9411
39	14.1617	48.0437
40	14.8331	49.1383
41	15.5174	50.2249
42	16.2146	51.3034
43	16.9245	52.3736
44	17.6469	53.4355
45	18.3817	54.4889
46	19.1288	55.5339
47	19.8879	56.5701
48	20.6590	57.5977
49	21.4418	58.6164
50	22.2364	59.6261
51	23.0425	60.6268
52	23.8599	61.6183
53	24.6886	62.6005
54	25.5284	63.5733
55	26.3792	64.5367
56	27.2409	65.4903
57	28.1133	66.4343
58	28.9963	67.3684
59	29.8897	68.2925
60	30.7935	69.2065
61	31.7075	70.1103
62	32.6316	71.0037
63	33.5657	71.8867
64	34.5097	72.7591
65	35.4633	73.6208
66	36.4267	74.4716
67	37.3995	75.3114
68	38.3817	76.1401
69	39.3732	76.9575
70	40.3739	77.7636
71	41.3836	78.5582
72	42.4023	79.3410
73	43.4299	80.1121
74	44.4661	80.8712
75	45.5111	81.6183
76	46.5645	82.3531
77	47.6264	83.0755
78	48.6966	83.7854
79	49.7751	84.4826
80	50.8617	85.1669
81	51.9563	85.8383
82	53.0589	86.4965
83	54.1693	87.1413
84	55.2875	87.7728
85	56.4133	88.3905
86	57.5467	88.9945
87	58.6876	89.5845
88	59.8359	90.1604
89	60.9915	90.7220
90	62.1543	91.2691
91	63.3242	91.8015
92	64.5011	92.3191
93	65.6851	92.8217
94	66.8759	93.3092
95	68.0734	93.7812
96	69.2777	94.2377
97	70.4887	94.6784
98	71.7062	95.1032
99	72.9301	95.5118
100	74.1605	95.9041
101	75.3972	96.2799
102	76.6401	96.6390
103	77.8892	96.9812
104	79.1444	97.3062
105	80.4056	97.6139
106	81.6728	97.9040
107	82.9458	98.1764
108	84.2247	98.4308
109	85.5093	98.6670
110	86.7996	98.8848
111	88.0955	99.0840
112	89.3969	99.2643
113	90.7038	99.4255
114	92.0161	99.5674
115	93.3338	99.6898
116	94.6567	99.7924
117	95.9849	99.8749
118	97.3182	99.9372
119	98.6566	99.9790
120	100.0000	100.0000

1 YEAR

#	REBATE	EARN
1	1.3399	15.0477
2	4.0035	28.9240
3	7.9747	41.6144
4	13.2376	53.1044
5	19.7766	63.3792
6	27.5761	72.4239
7	36.6208	80.2234
8	46.8956	86.7624
9	58.3856	92.0253
10	71.0760	95.9965
11	84.9523	98.6601
12	100.0000	100.0000

2 YEARS

#	REBATE	EARN
1	.3652	7.6426
2	1.0911	15.0095
3	2.1733	22.0973
4	3.6076	28.9025
5	5.3897	35.4217
6	7.5152	41.6515
7	9.9801	47.5881
8	12.7803	53.2280
9	15.9116	58.5676
10	19.3701	63.6032
11	23.1518	68.3310
12	27.2527	72.7473
13	31.6690	76.8482
14	36.3968	80.6299
15	41.4324	84.0884
16	46.7720	87.2197
17	52.4119	90.0199
18	58.3485	92.4848
19	64.5783	94.6103
20	71.0975	96.3924
21	77.9027	97.8267
22	84.9905	98.9089
23	92.3574	99.6348
24	100.0000	100.0000

3 YEARS

#	REBATE	EARN
1	.1722	5.0469
2	.5146	9.9815
3	1.0250	14.8024
4	1.7014	19.5082
5	2.5418	24.0976
6	3.5443	28.5690
7	4.7068	32.9211
8	6.0274	37.1523
9	7.5041	41.2611
10	9.1352	45.2462
11	10.9187	49.1059
12	12.8527	52.8387
13	14.9355	56.4430
14	17.1652	59.9174
15	19.5400	63.2601
16	22.0583	66.4695
17	24.7181	69.5441
18	27.5179	72.4821
19	30.4559	75.2819
20	33.5305	77.9417
21	36.7399	80.4600
22	40.0826	82.8348
23	43.5570	85.0645
24	47.1613	87.1473
25	50.8941	89.0813
26	54.7538	90.8648
27	58.7389	92.4959
28	62.8477	93.9726
29	67.0789	95.2932
30	71.4310	96.4557
31	75.9024	97.4582
32	80.4918	98.2986
33	85.1976	98.9750
34	90.0185	99.4854
35	94.9531	99.8278
36	100.0000	100.0000

4 YEARS

#	REBATE	EARN
1	.1020	3.7270
2	.3048	7.3965
3	.6071	11.0080
4	1.0077	14.5605
5	1.5054	18.0535
6	2.0992	21.4861
7	2.7877	24.8577
8	3.5698	28.1674
9	4.4445	31.4146
10	5.4105	34.5985
11	6.4668	37.7182
12	7.6123	40.7730
13	8.8458	43.7622
14	10.1664	46.6848
15	11.5730	49.5401
16	13.0644	52.3272
17	14.6398	55.0453
18	16.2980	57.6936
19	18.0381	60.2712
20	19.8591	62.7772
21	21.7600	65.2108
22	23.7397	67.5710
23	25.7975	69.8570
24	27.9322	72.0678
25	30.1430	74.2025
26	32.4290	76.2603
27	34.7892	78.2400
28	37.2228	80.1409
29	39.7288	81.9619
30	42.3064	83.7020
31	44.9547	85.3602
32	47.6728	86.9356
33	50.4599	88.4270
34	53.3152	89.8336
35	56.2378	91.1542
36	59.2270	92.3877
37	62.2818	93.5332
38	65.4015	94.5895
39	68.5854	95.5555
40	71.8326	96.4302
41	75.1423	97.2123
42	78.5139	97.9008
43	81.9465	98.4946
44	85.4395	98.9923
45	88.9920	99.3929
46	92.6035	99.6952
47	96.2730	99.8980
48	100.0000	100.0000

5 YEARS

#	REBATE	EARN
1	.0685	2.9298
2	.2046	5.8264
3	.4075	8.6892
4	.6765	11.5179
5	1.0106	14.3120
6	1.4092	17.0712
7	1.8714	19.7950
8	2.3965	22.4829
9	2.9837	25.1346
10	3.6322	27.7495
11	4.3413	30.3272
12	5.1103	32.8674
13	5.9384	35.3694
14	6.8250	37.8329
15	7.7692	40.2573
16	8.7705	42.6422
17	9.8281	44.9871
18	10.9413	47.2915
19	12.1095	49.5550
20	13.3319	51.7769
21	14.6080	53.9568
22	15.9371	56.0942
23	17.3185	58.1886
24	18.7516	60.2394
25	20.2358	62.2461
26	21.7705	64.2081
27	23.3549	66.1249
28	24.9886	67.9960
29	26.6710	69.8207
30	28.4014	71.5986
31	30.1793	73.3290
32	32.0040	75.0114
33	33.8751	76.6451
34	35.7919	78.2295
35	37.7539	79.7642
36	39.7606	81.2484
37	41.8114	82.6815
38	43.9058	84.0629
39	46.0432	85.3920
40	48.2231	86.6681
41	50.4450	87.8905
42	52.7085	89.0587
43	55.0129	90.1719
44	57.3578	91.2295
45	59.7427	92.2308
46	62.1671	93.1750
47	64.6306	94.0616
48	67.1326	94.8897
49	69.6728	95.6587
50	72.2505	96.3678
51	74.8654	97.0163
52	77.5171	97.6035
53	80.2050	98.1286
54	82.9288	98.5908
55	85.6880	98.9894
56	88.4821	99.3235
57	91.3108	99.5925
58	94.1736	99.7954
59	97.0702	99.9315
60	100.0000	100.0000

6 YEARS

#	REBATE	EARN
1	.0498	2.3975
2	.1487	4.7741
3	.2961	7.1296
4	.4916	9.4636
5	.7344	11.7760
6	1.0240	14.0664
7	1.3599	16.3346
8	1.7415	18.5803
9	2.1682	20.8032
10	2.6394	23.0031
11	3.1547	25.1797
12	3.7135	27.3326
13	4.3153	29.4617
14	4.9595	31.5665
15	5.6457	33.6468
16	6.3733	35.7024
17	7.1418	37.7328
18	7.9508	39.7378
19	8.7996	41.7171
20	9.6880	43.6704
21	10.6153	45.5973
22	11.5811	47.4975
23	12.5849	49.3706
24	13.6263	51.2165
25	14.7048	53.0346
26	15.8200	54.8248
27	16.9714	56.5866
28	18.1586	58.3196
29	19.3811	60.0236
30	20.6386	61.6982
31	21.9305	63.3429
32	23.2565	64.9575
33	24.6161	66.5416
34	26.0090	68.0948
35	27.4348	69.6168
36	28.8930	71.1070
37	30.3832	72.5652
38	31.9052	73.9910
39	33.4584	75.3839
40	35.0425	76.7435
41	36.6571	78.0695
42	38.3018	79.3614
43	39.9764	80.6189
44	41.6804	81.8414
45	43.4134	83.0286
46	45.1752	84.1800
47	46.9654	85.2952
48	48.7835	86.3737
49	50.6294	87.4151
50	52.5025	88.4189
51	54.4027	89.3847
52	56.3296	90.3120
53	58.2829	91.2004
54	60.2622	92.0492
55	62.2672	92.8582
56	64.2976	93.6267
57	66.3532	94.3543
58	68.4335	95.0405
59	70.5383	95.6847
60	72.6674	96.2865
61	74.8203	96.8453
62	76.9969	97.3606
63	79.1968	97.8318
64	81.4197	98.2585
65	83.6654	98.6401
66	85.9336	98.9760
67	88.2240	99.2656
68	90.5364	99.5084
69	92.8704	99.7039
70	95.2259	99.8513
71	97.6025	99.9502
72	100.0000	100.0000

7 YEARS

#	REBATE	EARN
1	.0382	2.0178
2	.1141	4.0217
3	.2273	6.0116
4	.3772	7.9873
5	.5636	9.9487
6	.7858	11.8955
7	1.0436	13.8275
8	1.3364	15.7447
9	1.6638	17.6468
10	2.0255	19.5336
11	2.4209	21.4049
12	2.8497	23.2606
13	3.3115	25.1004
14	3.8059	26.9242
15	4.3325	28.7318
16	4.8908	30.5229
17	5.4806	32.2974
18	6.1014	34.0551
19	6.7528	35.7957
20	7.4345	37.5190
21	8.1461	39.2249
22	8.8872	40.9131
23	9.6576	42.5833
24	10.4568	44.2355
25	11.2844	45.8693
26	12.1402	47.4845
27	13.0238	49.0810
28	13.9348	50.6584
29	14.8730	52.2165
30	15.8379	53.7552
31	16.8293	55.2741
32	17.8469	56.7730
33	18.8903	58.2517
34	19.9592	59.7099
35	21.0533	61.1473
36	22.1723	62.5638
37	23.3159	63.9591
38	24.4838	65.3328
39	25.6757	66.6848
40	26.8914	68.0147
41	28.1304	69.3223
42	29.3926	70.6074
43	30.6777	71.8696
44	31.9853	73.1086
45	33.3152	74.3243
46	34.6672	75.5162
47	36.0409	76.6841
48	37.4362	77.8277
49	38.8527	78.9467
50	40.2901	80.0408
51	41.7483	81.1097
52	43.2270	82.1531
53	44.7259	83.1707
54	46.2448	84.1621
55	47.7835	85.1270
56	49.3416	86.0652
57	50.9190	86.9762
58	52.5155	87.8598
59	54.1307	88.7156
60	55.7645	89.5432
61	57.4167	90.3424
62	59.0869	91.1128
63	60.7751	91.8539
64	62.4810	92.5655
65	64.2043	93.2472
66	65.9449	93.8986
67	67.7026	94.5194
68	69.4771	95.1092
69	71.2682	95.6675
70	73.0758	96.1941
71	74.8996	96.6885
72	76.7394	97.1503
73	78.5951	97.5791
74	80.4664	97.9745
75	82.3532	98.3362

14.75 %

#	REBATE	EARN
75	82.3532	98.3362
76	84.2553	98.6636
77	86.1725	98.9564
78	88.1045	99.2142
79	90.0513	99.4364
80	92.0127	99.6228
81	93.9884	99.7727
82	95.9783	99.8859
83	97.9822	99.9618
84	100.0000	100.0000

8 YEARS

#	REBATE	EARN
1	.0305	1.7339
2	.0911	3.4583
3	.1815	5.1730
4	.3012	6.8778
5	.4500	8.5728
6	.6275	10.2578
7	.8333	11.9326
8	1.0671	13.5971
9	1.3286	15.2512
10	1.6174	16.8948
11	1.9331	18.5277
12	2.2755	20.1499
13	2.6443	21.7611
14	3.0390	23.3612
15	3.4595	24.9501
16	3.9053	26.5278
17	4.3763	28.0939
18	4.8719	29.6484
19	5.3921	31.1912
20	5.9364	32.7220
21	6.5047	34.2408
22	7.0965	35.7474
23	7.7116	37.2417
24	8.3497	38.7235
25	9.0106	40.1926
26	9.6940	41.6489
27	10.3995	43.0922
28	11.1270	44.5225
29	11.8761	45.9394
30	12.6466	47.3429
31	13.4382	48.7328
32	14.2508	50.1088
33	15.0839	51.4710
34	15.9374	52.8190
35	16.8111	54.1527
36	17.7046	55.4720
37	18.6178	56.7766
38	19.5504	58.0663
39	20.5021	59.3411
40	21.4728	60.6007
41	22.4622	61.8448
42	23.4700	63.0734
43	24.4962	64.2863
44	25.5403	65.4832
45	26.6023	66.6639
46	27.6818	67.8283
47	28.7787	68.9761
48	29.8928	70.1072
49	31.0239	71.2213
50	32.1717	72.3182
51	33.3361	73.3977
52	34.5168	74.4597
53	35.7137	75.5038
54	36.9266	76.5300
55	38.1552	77.5378
56	39.3993	78.5272
57	40.6589	79.4979
58	41.9337	80.4496
59	43.2234	81.3822
60	44.5280	82.2954
61	45.8473	83.1889
62	47.1810	84.0626
63	48.5290	84.9161
64	49.8912	85.7492
65	51.2672	86.5618
66	52.6571	87.3534
67	54.0606	88.1239
68	55.4775	88.8730
69	56.9078	89.6005
70	58.3511	90.3060
71	59.8074	90.9894
72	61.2765	91.6503
73	62.7583	92.2884
74	64.2526	92.9035
75	65.7592	93.4953
76	67.2780	94.0636
77	68.8088	94.6079
78	70.3516	95.1281
79	71.9061	95.6237
80	73.4722	96.0947
81	75.0499	96.5405
82	76.6388	96.9610
83	78.2389	97.3557
84	79.8501	97.7245
85	81.4723	98.0669
86	83.1052	98.3826
87	84.7488	98.6714
88	86.4029	98.9329
89	88.0674	99.1667
90	89.7422	99.3725
91	91.4272	99.5500
92	93.1222	99.6988
93	94.8270	99.8185
94	96.5417	99.9089
95	98.2661	99.9695
96	100.0000	100.0000

9 YEARS

#	REBATE	EARN
1	.0251	1.5142
2	.0750	3.0215
3	.1493	4.5221
4	.2479	6.0156
5	.3704	7.5021
6	.5164	8.9815
7	.6858	10.4536
8	.8782	11.9185
9	1.0934	13.3760
10	1.3310	14.8259
11	1.5909	16.2683
12	1.8727	17.7030
13	2.1762	19.1300
14	2.5010	20.5491
15	2.8471	21.9602
16	3.2140	23.3633
17	3.6015	24.7582
18	4.0095	26.1449
19	4.4375	27.5232
20	4.8855	28.8931
21	5.3531	30.2543
22	5.8402	31.6070
23	6.3464	32.9508
24	6.8716	34.2858
25	7.4155	35.6117
26	7.9778	36.9286
27	8.5585	38.2363
28	9.1571	39.5346
29	9.7736	40.8235
30	10.4078	42.1028
31	11.0593	43.3724
32	11.7279	44.6323
33	12.4136	45.8822
34	13.1160	47.1221
35	13.8350	48.3518
36	14.5704	49.5713
37	15.3219	50.7803
38	16.0894	51.9788
39	16.8726	53.1667
40	17.6715	54.3437
41	18.4857	55.5098
42	19.3151	56.6648
43	20.1596	57.8086
44	21.0189	58.9411
45	21.8928	60.0621
46	22.7813	61.1715
47	23.6840	62.2691
48	24.6009	63.3548
49	25.5317	64.4284
50	26.4764	65.4899
51	27.4346	66.5390
52	28.4063	67.5755
53	29.3913	68.5995
54	30.3894	69.6106
55	31.4005	70.6087
56	32.4245	71.5937
57	33.4610	72.5654
58	34.5101	73.5236
59	35.5716	74.4683
60	36.6452	75.3991
61	37.7309	76.3160
62	38.8285	77.2187
63	39.9379	78.1072
64	41.0589	78.9811
65	42.1914	79.8404
66	43.3352	80.6849
67	44.4902	81.5143
68	45.6563	82.3285
69	46.8333	83.1274
70	48.0212	83.9106
71	49.2197	84.6781
72	50.4287	85.4296
73	51.6482	86.1650
74	52.8779	86.8840
75	54.1178	87.5864
76	55.3677	88.2721
77	56.6276	88.9407
78	57.8972	89.5922
79	59.1765	90.2264
80	60.4654	90.8429
81	61.7637	91.4415
82	63.0714	92.0222
83	64.3883	92.5845
84	65.7142	93.1284
85	67.0492	93.6536
86	68.3930	94.1598
87	69.7457	94.6469
88	71.1069	95.1145
89	72.4768	95.5625
90	73.8551	95.9905
91	75.2418	96.3985
92	76.6367	96.7860
93	78.0398	97.1529
94	79.4509	97.4990
95	80.8700	97.8238
96	82.2970	98.1273
97	83.7317	98.4091
98	85.1741	98.6690
99	86.6240	98.9066
100	88.0815	99.1218
101	89.5464	99.3142
102	91.0185	99.4836
103	92.4979	99.6296
104	93.9844	99.7521
105	95.4779	99.8507
106	96.9785	99.9250
107	98.4858	99.9749
108	100.0000	100.0000

10 YEARS

#	REBATE	EARN
1	.0211	1.3394
2	.0632	2.6739
3	.1258	4.0034
4	.2089	5.3278
5	.3121	6.6471
6	.4352	7.9611
7	.5779	9.2700
8	.7400	10.5735
9	.9214	11.8717
10	1.1216	13.1644
11	1.3406	14.4515
12	1.5781	15.7331
13	1.8338	17.0091
14	2.1075	18.2793
15	2.3991	19.5437
16	2.7083	20.8023
17	3.0349	22.0549
18	3.3786	23.3015
19	3.7394	24.5421
20	4.1169	25.7765
21	4.5109	27.0046
22	4.9213	28.2265
23	5.3479	29.4419
24	5.7905	30.6509
25	6.2488	31.8534
26	6.7227	33.0492
27	7.2120	34.2383
28	7.7164	35.4206
29	8.2359	36.5961
30	8.7703	37.7646
31	9.3193	38.9261
32	9.8828	40.0804
33	10.4606	41.2275
34	11.0525	42.3673
35	11.6583	43.4997
36	12.2780	44.6247
37	12.9113	45.7420
38	13.5580	46.8517
39	14.2180	47.9536
40	14.8912	49.0477
41	15.5773	50.1338
42	16.2763	51.2118
43	16.9879	52.2817
44	17.7120	53.3433
45	18.4484	54.3966
46	19.1971	55.4414
47	19.9578	56.4777
48	20.7304	57.5053
49	21.5148	58.5241
50	22.3108	59.5341
51	23.1183	60.5350
52	23.9371	61.5268
53	24.7671	62.5095
54	25.6082	63.4828
55	26.4603	64.4466
56	27.3231	65.4009
57	28.1966	66.3456
58	29.0806	67.2804
59	29.9751	68.2053
60	30.8798	69.1202
61	31.7947	70.0249
62	32.7196	70.9194
63	33.6544	71.8034
64	34.5991	72.6769
65	35.5534	73.5397
66	36.5172	74.3918
67	37.4905	75.2329
68	38.4732	76.0629
69	39.4650	76.8817
70	40.4659	77.6892
71	41.4759	78.4852
72	42.4947	79.2696
73	43.5223	80.0422
74	44.5586	80.8029
75	45.6034	81.5516
76	46.6567	82.2880
77	47.7183	83.0121
78	48.7882	83.7237
79	49.8662	84.4227
80	50.9523	85.1088
81	52.0464	85.7820
82	53.1483	86.4420
83	54.2580	87.0887
84	55.3753	87.7220
85	56.5003	88.3417
86	57.6327	88.9475
87	58.7725	89.5394
88	59.9196	90.1172
89	61.0739	90.6807
90	62.2354	91.2297
91	63.4039	91.7641
92	64.5794	92.2836
93	65.7617	92.7880
94	66.9508	93.2773
95	68.1466	93.7512
96	69.3491	94.2095
97	70.5581	94.6521
98	71.7735	95.0787
99	72.9954	95.4891
100	74.2235	95.8831
101	75.4579	96.2606
102	76.6985	96.6214
103	77.9451	96.9651
104	79.1977	97.2917
105	80.4563	97.6009
106	81.7207	97.8925
107	82.9909	98.1662
108	84.2669	98.4219
109	85.5485	98.6594
110	86.8356	98.8784
111	88.1283	99.0786
112	89.4265	99.2600
113	90.7300	99.4221
114	92.0389	99.5648
115	93.3529	99.6879
116	94.6722	99.7911
117	95.9966	99.8742
118	97.3261	99.9368
119	98.6606	99.9789
120	100.0000	100.0000

1 YEAR

#	REBATE	EARN
1	1.3409	15.0422
2	4.0062	28.9147
3	7.9795	41.6029
4	13.2447	53.0921
5	19.7857	63.3672
6	27.5870	72.4130
7	36.6328	80.2143
8	46.9079	86.7553
9	58.3971	92.0205
10	71.0853	95.9938
11	84.9578	98.6591
12	100.0000	100.0000

2 YEARS

#	REBATE	EARN
1	.3657	7.6369
2	1.0926	14.9989
3	2.1763	22.0827
4	3.6123	28.8848
5	5.3963	35.4015
6	7.5239	41.6295
7	9.9910	47.5650
8	12.7934	53.2045
9	15.9269	58.5441
10	19.3874	63.5802
11	23.1709	68.3090
12	27.2735	72.7265
13	31.6910	76.8291
14	36.4198	80.6126
15	41.4559	84.0731
16	46.7955	87.2066
17	52.4350	90.0090
18	58.3705	92.4761
19	64.5985	94.6037
20	71.1152	96.3877
21	77.9173	97.8237
22	85.0011	98.9074
23	92.3631	99.6343
24	100.0000	100.0000

3 YEARS

#	REBATE	EARN
1	.1726	5.0413
2	.5157	9.9709
3	1.0271	14.7873
4	1.7048	19.4892
5	2.5468	24.0750
6	3.5510	28.5435
7	4.7153	32.8930
8	6.0379	37.1222
9	7.5168	41.2294
10	9.1500	45.2133
11	10.9356	49.0722
12	12.8718	52.8045
13	14.9567	56.4088
14	17.1885	59.8833
15	19.5653	63.2266
16	22.0854	66.4368
17	24.7469	69.5125
18	27.5482	72.4518
19	30.4875	75.2531
20	33.5632	77.9146
21	36.7734	80.4347
22	40.1167	82.8115
23	43.5912	85.0433
24	47.1955	87.1282
25	50.9278	89.0644
26	54.7867	90.8500
27	58.7706	92.4832
28	62.8778	93.9621
29	67.1070	95.2847
30	71.4565	96.4490
31	75.9250	97.4532
32	80.5108	98.2952
33	85.2127	98.9729
34	90.0291	99.4843
35	94.9587	99.8274
36	100.0000	100.0000

4 YEARS

#	REBATE	EARN
1	.1023	3.7216
2	.3056	7.3862
3	.6087	10.9930
4	1.0104	14.5413
5	1.5094	18.0303
6	2.1046	21.4595
7	2.7947	24.8279
8	3.5785	28.1348
9	4.4550	31.3795
10	5.4230	34.5612
11	6.4813	37.6790
12	7.6288	40.7323
13	8.8645	43.7202
14	10.1872	46.6418
15	11.5959	49.4964
16	13.0895	52.2831
17	14.6669	55.0010
18	16.3272	57.6494
19	18.0693	60.2272
20	19.8921	62.7338
21	21.7948	65.1680
22	23.7762	67.5292
23	25.8355	69.8163
24	27.9717	72.0283
25	30.1837	74.1645
26	32.4708	76.2238
27	34.8320	78.2052
28	37.2662	80.1079
29	39.7728	81.9307
30	42.3506	83.6728
31	44.9990	85.3331
32	47.7169	86.9105
33	50.5036	88.4041
34	53.3582	89.8128
35	56.2798	91.1355
36	59.2677	92.3712
37	62.3210	93.5187
38	65.4388	94.5770
39	68.6205	95.5450
40	71.8652	96.4215
41	75.1721	97.2053
42	78.5405	97.8954
43	81.9697	98.4906
44	85.4587	98.9896
45	89.0070	99.3913
46	92.6138	99.6944
47	96.2784	99.8977
48	100.0000	100.0000

5 YEARS

#	REBATE	EARN
1	.0687	2.9247
2	.2053	5.8164
3	.4089	8.6746
4	.6788	11.4990
5	1.0140	14.2891
6	1.4138	17.0445
7	1.8774	19.7648
8	2.4039	22.4495
9	2.9927	25.0982
10	3.6430	27.7104
11	4.3539	30.2857
12	5.1248	32.8236
13	5.9549	35.3236
14	6.8434	37.7853
15	7.7897	40.2083
16	8.7931	42.5919
17	9.8527	44.9357
18	10.9680	47.2393
19	12.1383	49.5020
20	13.3628	51.7235
21	14.6409	53.9032
22	15.9720	56.0405
23	17.3554	58.1350
24	18.7904	60.1861
25	20.2764	62.1932
26	21.8127	64.1559
27	23.3989	66.0735
28	25.0341	67.9455
29	26.7179	69.7713
30	28.4496	71.5504
31	30.2287	73.2821
32	32.0545	74.9659
33	33.9265	76.6011
34	35.8441	78.1873
35	37.8068	79.7236
36	39.8139	81.2096
37	41.8650	82.6446
38	43.9595	84.0280
39	46.0968	85.3591
40	48.2765	86.6372
41	50.4980	87.8617
42	52.7607	89.0320
43	55.0643	90.1473
44	57.4081	91.2069
45	59.7917	92.2103
46	62.2147	93.1566
47	64.6764	94.0451
48	67.1764	94.8752
49	69.7143	95.6461
50	72.2896	96.3570
51	74.9018	97.0073
52	77.5505	97.5961
53	80.2352	98.1226
54	82.9555	98.5862
55	85.7109	98.9860
56	88.5010	99.3212
57	91.3254	99.5911
58	94.1836	99.7947
59	97.0753	99.9313
60	100.0000	100.0000

6 YEARS

#	REBATE	EARN
1	.0500	2.3926
2	.1493	4.7645
3	.2973	7.1155
4	.4935	9.4453
5	.7373	11.7536
6	1.0280	14.0402
7	1.3651	16.3048
8	1.7480	18.5471
9	2.1761	20.7668
10	2.6489	22.9636
11	3.1658	25.1374
12	3.7263	27.2877
13	4.3299	29.4143
14	4.9760	31.5169
15	5.6641	33.5952
16	6.3936	35.6489
17	7.1641	37.6776
18	7.9751	39.6812
19	8.8260	41.6591
20	9.7164	43.6112
21	10.6458	45.5372
22	11.6136	47.4366
23	12.6195	49.3091
24	13.6629	51.1545
25	14.7434	52.9723
26	15.8605	54.7623
27	17.0138	56.5240
28	18.2029	58.2572
29	19.4272	59.9615
30	20.6864	61.6365
31	21.9800	63.2818
32	23.3076	64.8971
33	24.6688	66.4820
34	26.0631	68.0361
35	27.4902	69.5590
36	28.9496	71.0504
37	30.4410	72.5098
38	31.9639	73.9369
39	33.5180	75.3312
40	35.1029	76.6924
41	36.7182	78.0200
42	38.3635	79.3136
43	40.0385	80.5728
44	41.7428	81.7971
45	43.4760	82.9862
46	45.2377	84.1395
47	47.0277	85.2566
48	48.8455	86.3371
49	50.6909	87.3805
50	52.5634	88.3864
51	54.4628	89.3542
52	56.3888	90.2836
53	58.3409	91.1740
54	60.3188	92.0249
55	62.3224	92.8359
56	64.3511	93.6064
57	66.4048	94.3359
58	68.4831	95.0240
59	70.5857	95.6701
60	72.7123	96.2737
61	74.8626	96.8342
62	77.0364	97.3511
63	79.2332	97.8239
64	81.4529	98.2520
65	83.6952	98.6349
66	85.9598	98.9720
67	88.2464	99.2627
68	90.5547	99.5065
69	92.8845	99.7027
70	95.2355	99.8507
71	97.6074	99.9500
72	100.0000	100.0000

7 YEARS

#	REBATE	EARN
1	.0384	2.0131
2	.1146	4.0126
3	.2283	5.9981
4	.3790	7.9697
5	.5661	9.9270
6	.7893	11.8700
7	1.0482	13.7984
8	1.3422	15.7121
9	1.6709	17.6108
10	2.0339	19.4945
11	2.4309	21.3628
12	2.8613	23.2157
13	3.3247	25.0528
14	3.8208	26.8741
15	4.3491	28.6793
16	4.9093	30.4682
17	5.5009	32.2406
18	6.1236	33.9963
19	6.7770	35.7352
20	7.4607	37.4569
21	8.1743	39.1613
22	8.9174	40.8481
23	9.6898	42.5172
24	10.4910	44.1683
25	11.3206	45.8012
26	12.1784	47.4157
27	13.0640	49.0115
28	13.9770	50.5884
29	14.9171	52.1462
30	15.8839	53.6846
31	16.8772	55.2033
32	17.8966	56.7023
33	18.9417	58.1811
34	20.0124	59.6395
35	21.1082	61.0773
36	22.2288	62.4943
37	23.3739	63.8901
38	24.5433	65.2645
39	25.7366	66.6173
40	26.9536	67.9481
41	28.1938	69.2567
42	29.4572	70.5428
43	30.7433	71.8062
44	32.0519	73.0464
45	33.3827	74.2634
46	34.7355	75.4567
47	36.1099	76.6261
48	37.5057	77.7712
49	38.9227	78.8918
50	40.3605	79.9876
51	41.8189	81.0583
52	43.2977	82.1034
53	44.7967	83.1228
54	46.3154	84.1161
55	47.8538	85.0829
56	49.4116	86.0230
57	50.9885	86.9360
58	52.5843	87.8216
59	54.1988	88.6794
60	55.8317	89.5090
61	57.4828	90.3102
62	59.1519	91.0826
63	60.8387	91.8257
64	62.5431	92.5393
65	64.2648	93.2230
66	66.0037	93.8764
67	67.7594	94.4991
68	69.5318	95.0907
69	71.3207	95.6509
70	73.1259	96.1792
71	74.9472	96.6753
72	76.7843	97.1387
73	78.6372	97.5691
74	80.5055	97.9661
75	82.3892	98.3291

#	REBATE	EARN
75	82.3892	98.3291
76	84.2879	98.6578
77	86.2016	98.9518
78	88.1300	99.2107
79	90.0730	99.4339
80	92.0303	99.6210
81	94.0019	99.7717
82	95.9874	99.8854
83	97.9869	99.9616
84	100.0000	100.0000

8 YEARS

#	REBATE	EARN
1	.0307	1.7295
2	.0916	3.4496
3	.1824	5.1601
4	.3028	6.8610
5	.4523	8.5521
6	.6306	10.2333
7	.8374	11.9044
8	1.0723	13.5655
9	1.3349	15.2162
10	1.6250	16.8566
11	1.9421	18.4864
12	2.2860	20.1056
13	2.6562	21.7140
14	3.0526	23.3114
15	3.4747	24.8978
16	3.9223	26.4729
17	4.3949	28.0367
18	4.8924	29.5891
19	5.4144	31.1298
20	5.9607	32.6587
21	6.5308	34.1757
22	7.1245	35.6806
23	7.7416	37.1733
24	8.3817	38.6536
25	9.0445	40.1214
26	9.7299	41.5765
27	10.4374	43.0187
28	11.1668	44.4480
29	11.9179	45.8640
30	12.6904	47.2668
31	13.4839	48.6560
32	14.2984	50.0316
33	15.1334	51.3933
34	15.9888	52.7410
35	16.8642	54.0745
36	17.7595	55.3936
37	18.6745	56.6982
38	19.6087	57.9881
39	20.5621	59.2631
40	21.5344	60.5229
41	22.5253	61.7675
42	23.5346	62.9966
43	24.5622	64.2100
44	25.6077	65.4075
45	26.6709	66.5890
46	27.7517	67.7542
47	28.8498	68.9030
48	29.9650	70.0350
49	31.0970	71.1502
50	32.2458	72.2483
51	33.4110	73.3291
52	34.5925	74.3923
53	35.7900	75.4378
54	37.0034	76.4654
55	38.2325	77.4747
56	39.4771	78.4656
57	40.7369	79.4379
58	42.0119	80.3913
59	43.3018	81.3255
60	44.6064	82.2405
61	45.9255	83.1358
62	47.2590	84.0112
63	48.6067	84.8666
64	49.9684	85.7016
65	51.3440	86.5161
66	52.7332	87.3096
67	54.1360	88.0821
68	55.5520	88.8332
69	56.9813	89.5626
70	58.4235	90.2701
71	59.8786	90.9555
72	61.3464	91.6183
73	62.8267	92.2584
74	64.3194	92.8755
75	65.8243	93.4692
76	67.3413	94.0393
77	68.8702	94.5856
78	70.4109	95.1076
79	71.9633	95.6051
80	73.5271	96.0777
81	75.1022	96.5253
82	76.6886	96.9474
83	78.2860	97.3438
84	79.8944	97.7140
85	81.5136	98.0579
86	83.1434	98.3750
87	84.7838	98.6651
88	86.4345	98.9277
89	88.0956	99.1626
90	89.7667	99.3694
91	91.4479	99.5477
92	93.1390	99.6972
93	94.8399	99.8176
94	96.5504	99.9084
95	98.2705	99.9693
96	100.0000	100.0000

9 YEARS

#	REBATE	EARN
1	.0252	1.5100
2	.0754	3.0133
3	.1502	4.5098
4	.2493	5.9995
5	.3724	7.4822
6	.5193	8.9580
7	.6895	10.4266
8	.8829	11.8880
9	1.0992	13.3421
10	1.3380	14.7889
11	1.5991	16.2282
12	1.8823	17.6599
13	2.1872	19.0839
14	2.5135	20.5002
15	2.8611	21.9087
16	3.2296	23.3092
17	3.6188	24.7017
18	4.0284	26.0860
19	4.4583	27.4620
20	4.9080	28.8297
21	5.3775	30.1889
22	5.8664	31.5396
23	6.3744	32.8816
24	6.9015	34.2148
25	7.4473	35.5392
26	8.0116	36.8545
27	8.5942	38.1607
28	9.1948	39.4577
29	9.8132	40.7454
30	10.4493	42.0236
31	11.1027	43.2922
32	11.7733	44.5511
33	12.4609	45.8002
34	13.1652	47.0393
35	13.8860	48.2684
36	14.6232	49.4873
37	15.3766	50.6959
38	16.1458	51.8940
39	16.9309	53.0815
40	17.7314	54.2584
41	18.5474	55.4244
42	19.3785	56.5794
43	20.2245	57.7233
44	21.0854	58.8559
45	21.9609	59.9772
46	22.8508	61.0869
47	23.7550	62.1849
48	24.6732	63.2711
49	25.6053	64.3453
50	26.5512	65.4073
51	27.5106	66.4571
52	28.4835	67.4945
53	29.4695	68.5193
54	30.4687	69.5313
55	31.4807	70.5305
56	32.5055	71.5165
57	33.5429	72.4894
58	34.5927	73.4488
59	35.6547	74.3947
60	36.7289	75.3268
61	37.8151	76.2450
62	38.9131	77.1492
63	40.0228	78.0391
64	41.1441	78.9146
65	42.2767	79.7755
66	43.4206	80.6215
67	44.5756	81.4526
68	45.7416	82.2686
69	46.9185	83.0691
70	48.1060	83.8542
71	49.3041	84.6234
72	50.5127	85.3768
73	51.7316	86.1140
74	52.9607	86.8348
75	54.1998	87.5391
76	55.4489	88.2267
77	56.7078	88.8973
78	57.9764	89.5507
79	59.2546	90.1868
80	60.5423	90.8052
81	61.8393	91.4058
82	63.1455	91.9884
83	64.4608	92.5527
84	65.7852	93.0985
85	67.1184	93.6256
86	68.4604	94.1336
87	69.8111	94.6225
88	71.1703	95.0920
89	72.5380	95.5417
90	73.9140	95.9716
91	75.2983	96.3812
92	76.6908	96.7704
93	78.0913	97.1389
94	79.4998	97.4865
95	80.9161	97.8128
96	82.3401	98.1177
97	83.7718	98.4009
98	85.2111	98.6620
99	86.6579	98.9008
100	88.1120	99.1171
101	89.5734	99.3105
102	91.0420	99.4807
103	92.5178	99.6276
104	94.0005	99.7507
105	95.4902	99.8498
106	96.9867	99.9246
107	98.4900	99.9748
108	100.0000	100.0000

10 YEARS

#	REBATE	EARN
1	.0213	1.3354
2	.0636	2.6660
3	.1266	3.9917
4	.2102	5.3124
5	.3140	6.6281
6	.4378	7.9386
7	.5813	9.2440
8	.7444	10.5442
9	.9267	11.8391
10	1.1281	13.1286
11	1.3482	14.4127
12	1.5869	15.6913
13	1.8440	16.9644
14	2.1191	18.2318
15	2.4121	19.4935
16	2.7228	20.7494
17	3.0510	21.9995
18	3.3963	23.2437
19	3.7587	24.4818
20	4.1379	25.7139
21	4.5337	26.9399
22	4.9458	28.1596
23	5.3742	29.3731
24	5.8186	30.5801
25	6.2787	31.7807
26	6.7545	32.9748
27	7.2456	34.1623
28	7.7520	35.3430
29	8.2734	36.5170
30	8.8096	37.6841
31	9.3605	38.8442
32	9.9259	39.9973
33	10.5056	41.1432
34	11.0994	42.2820
35	11.7071	43.4134
36	12.3287	44.5374
37	12.9638	45.6539
38	13.6124	46.7629
39	14.2742	47.8641
40	14.9491	48.9576
41	15.6370	50.0432
42	16.3377	51.1208
43	17.0510	52.1904
44	17.7768	53.2517
45	18.5149	54.3048
46	19.2652	55.3496
47	20.0275	56.3858
48	20.8016	57.4134
49	21.5875	58.4323
50	22.3850	59.4425
51	23.1939	60.4437
52	24.0140	61.4359
53	24.8454	62.4189
54	25.6877	63.3927
55	26.5410	64.3571
56	27.4049	65.3120
57	28.2795	66.2573
58	29.1646	67.1928
59	30.0600	68.1186
60	30.9657	69.0343
61	31.8814	69.9400
62	32.8072	70.8354
63	33.7427	71.7205
64	34.6880	72.5951
65	35.6429	73.4590
66	36.6073	74.3123
67	37.5811	75.1546
68	38.5641	75.9860
69	39.5563	76.8061
70	40.5575	77.6150
71	41.5677	78.4125
72	42.5866	79.1984
73	43.6142	79.9725
74	44.6504	80.7348
75	45.6952	81.4851
76	46.7483	82.2232
77	47.8096	82.9490
78	48.8792	83.6623
79	49.9568	84.3630
80	51.0424	85.0509
81	52.1359	85.7258
82	53.2371	86.3876
83	54.3461	87.0362
84	55.4626	87.6713
85	56.5866	88.2929
86	57.7180	88.9006
87	58.8568	89.4944
88	60.0027	90.0741
89	61.1558	90.6395
90	62.3159	91.1904
91	63.4830	91.7266
92	64.6570	92.2480
93	65.8377	92.7544
94	67.0252	93.2455
95	68.2193	93.7213
96	69.4199	94.1814
97	70.6269	94.6258
98	71.8404	95.0542
99	73.0601	95.4663
100	74.2861	95.8621
101	75.5182	96.2413
102	76.7563	96.6037
103	78.0005	96.9490
104	79.2506	97.2772
105	80.5065	97.5879
106	81.7682	97.8809
107	83.0356	98.1560
108	84.3087	98.4131
109	85.5873	98.6518
110	86.8714	98.8719
111	88.1609	99.0733
112	89.4558	99.2556
113	90.7560	99.4187
114	92.0614	99.5622
115	93.3719	99.6860
116	94.6876	99.7898
117	96.0083	99.8734
118	97.3340	99.9364
119	98.6646	99.9787
120	100.0000	100.0000

1 YEAR

#	REBATE	EARN
1	1.3419	15.0366
2	4.0089	28.9054
3	7.9843	41.5914
4	13.2517	53.0798
5	19.7949	63.3551
6	27.5979	72.4021
7	36.6449	80.2051
8	46.9202	86.7483
9	58.4086	92.0157
10	71.0946	95.9911
11	84.9634	98.6581
12	100.0000	100.0000
26	54.8196	90.8352
27	58.8022	92.4706
28	62.9078	93.9515
29	67.1349	95.2761
30	71.4820	96.4424
31	75.9475	97.4483
32	80.5299	98.2917
33	85.2278	98.9708
34	90.0397	99.4832
35	94.9643	99.8270
36	100.0000	100.0000

2 YEARS

#	REBATE	EARN
1	.3663	7.6312
2	1.0942	14.9884
3	2.1792	22.0682
4	3.6169	28.8670
5	5.4029	35.3814
6	7.5326	41.6076
7	10.0019	47.5420
8	12.8065	53.1809
9	15.9422	58.5206
10	19.4047	63.5572
11	23.1901	68.2869
12	27.2942	72.7058
13	31.7131	76.8099
14	36.4428	80.5953
15	41.4794	84.0578
16	46.8191	87.1935
17	52.4580	89.9981
18	58.3924	92.4674
19	64.6186	94.5971
20	71.1330	96.3831
21	77.9318	97.8208
22	85.0116	98.9058
23	92.3688	99.6337
24	100.0000	100.0000

3 YEARS

#	REBATE	EARN
1	.1730	5.0357
2	.5168	9.9603
3	1.0292	14.7722
4	1.7083	19.4701
5	2.5517	24.0525
6	3.5576	28.5180
7	4.7239	32.8651
8	6.0485	37.0922
9	7.5294	41.1978
10	9.1648	45.1804
11	10.9526	49.0385
12	12.8909	52.7704
13	14.9780	56.3746
14	17.2118	59.8494
15	19.5906	63.1931
16	22.1125	66.4042
17	24.7757	69.4809
18	27.5785	72.4215
19	30.5191	75.2243
20	33.5958	77.8875
21	36.8069	80.4094
22	40.1506	82.7882
23	43.6254	85.0220
24	47.2296	87.1091
25	50.9615	89.0474

4 YEARS

#	REBATE	EARN
1	.1026	3.7162
2	.3065	7.3758
3	.6104	10.9780
4	1.0131	14.5221
5	1.5134	18.0073
6	2.1100	21.4329
7	2.8016	24.7981
8	3.5872	28.1022
9	4.4656	31.3444
10	5.4355	34.5240
11	6.4958	37.6400
12	7.6454	40.6917
13	8.8832	43.6783
14	10.2080	46.5989
15	11.6188	49.4528
16	13.1145	52.2391
17	14.6940	54.9568
18	16.3563	57.6052
19	18.1004	60.1834
20	19.9251	62.6904
21	21.8295	65.1254
22	23.8127	67.4874
23	25.8735	69.7756
24	28.0111	71.9889
25	30.2244	74.1265
26	32.5126	76.1873
27	34.8746	78.1705
28	37.3096	80.0749
29	39.8166	81.8996
30	42.3948	83.6437
31	45.0432	85.3060
32	47.7609	86.8855
33	50.5472	88.3812
34	53.4011	89.7920
35	56.3217	91.1168
36	59.3083	92.3546
37	62.3600	93.5042
38	65.4760	94.5645
39	68.6556	95.5344
40	71.8978	96.4128
41	75.2019	97.1984
42	78.5671	97.8900
43	81.9927	98.4866
44	85.4779	98.9869
45	89.0220	99.3896
46	92.6242	99.6935
47	96.2838	99.8974
48	100.0000	100.0000

5 YEARS

#	REBATE	EARN
1	.0690	2.9196
2	.2060	5.8064
3	.4103	8.6601
4	.6810	11.4802
5	1.0173	14.2663
6	1.4183	17.0179
7	1.8833	19.7347
8	2.4113	22.4162
9	3.0018	25.0619
10	3.6537	27.6714
11	4.3665	30.2443
12	5.1392	32.7799
13	5.9713	35.2780
14	6.8618	37.7380
15	7.8102	40.1594
16	8.8156	42.5417
17	9.8773	44.8845
18	10.9947	47.1871
19	12.1671	49.4493
20	13.3937	51.6703
21	14.6738	53.8497
22	16.0069	55.9870
23	17.3922	58.0816
24	18.8291	60.1329
25	20.3169	62.1405
26	21.8550	64.1038
27	23.4427	66.0222
28	25.0795	67.8951
29	26.7647	69.7220
30	28.4978	71.5022
31	30.2780	73.2353
32	32.1049	74.9205
33	33.9778	76.5573
34	35.8962	78.1450
35	37.8595	79.6831
36	39.8671	81.1709
37	41.9184	82.6078
38	44.0130	83.9931
39	46.1503	85.3262
40	48.3297	86.6063
41	50.5507	87.8329
42	52.8129	89.0053
43	55.1155	90.1227
44	57.4583	91.1844
45	59.8406	92.1898
46	62.2620	93.1382
47	64.7220	94.0287
48	67.2201	94.8608
49	69.7557	95.6335
50	72.3286	96.3463
51	74.9381	96.9982
52	77.5838	97.5887
53	80.2653	98.1167
54	82.9821	98.5817
55	85.7337	98.9827
56	88.5198	99.3190
57	91.3399	99.5897
58	94.1936	99.7940
59	97.0804	99.9310
60	100.0000	100.0000

6 YEARS

#	REBATE	EARN
1	.0502	2.3877
2	.1499	4.7550
3	.2985	7.1015
4	.4955	9.4271
5	.7402	11.7314
6	1.0319	14.0141
7	1.3702	16.2751
8	1.7544	18.5140
9	2.1840	20.7305
10	2.6583	22.9243
11	3.1769	25.0953
12	3.7392	27.2430
13	4.3445	29.3672
14	4.9925	31.4675
15	5.6825	33.5438
16	6.4140	35.5956
17	7.1865	37.6227
18	7.9994	39.6247
19	8.8524	41.6014
20	9.7448	43.5524
21	10.6762	45.4773
22	11.6461	47.3759
23	12.6540	49.2478
24	13.6995	51.0927
25	14.7819	52.9102
26	15.9010	54.7000
27	17.0562	56.4617
28	18.2471	58.1951
29	19.4732	59.8996
30	20.7341	61.5749
31	22.0294	63.2208
32	23.3586	64.8367
33	24.7213	66.4224
34	26.1170	67.9774
35	27.5454	69.5014
36	29.0061	70.9939
37	30.4986	72.4546
38	32.0226	73.8830
39	33.5776	75.2787
40	35.1633	76.6414
41	36.7792	77.9706
42	38.4251	79.2659
43	40.1004	80.5268
44	41.8049	81.7529
45	43.5383	82.9438
46	45.3000	84.0990
47	47.0898	85.2181
48	48.9073	86.3005
49	50.7522	87.3460
50	52.6241	88.3539
51	54.5227	89.3238
52	56.4476	90.2552
53	58.3986	91.1476
54	60.3753	92.0006
55	62.3773	92.8135
56	64.4044	93.5860
57	66.4562	94.3175
58	68.5325	95.0075
59	70.6328	95.6555
60	72.7570	96.2608
61	74.9047	96.8231
62	77.0757	97.3417
63	79.2695	97.8160
64	81.4860	98.2456
65	83.7249	98.6298
66	85.9859	98.9681
67	88.2686	99.2598
68	90.5729	99.5045
69	92.8985	99.7015
70	95.2450	99.8501
71	97.6123	99.9498
72	100.0000	100.0000

7 YEARS

#	REBATE	EARN
1	.0385	2.0085
2	.1152	4.0035
3	.2294	5.9847
4	.3807	7.9522
5	.5687	9.9056
6	.7928	11.8447
7	1.0527	13.7695
8	1.3479	15.6797
9	1.6779	17.5751
10	2.0424	19.4556
11	2.4408	21.3210
12	2.8728	23.1710
13	3.3379	25.0054
14	3.8357	26.8242
15	4.3658	28.6270
16	4.9278	30.4137
17	5.5213	32.1841
18	6.1459	33.9379
19	6.8012	35.6750
20	7.4869	37.3951
21	8.2025	39.0980
22	8.9476	40.7835
23	9.7220	42.4514
24	10.5252	44.1015
25	11.3568	45.7335
26	12.2166	47.3472
27	13.1041	48.9423
28	14.0191	50.5187
29	14.9611	52.0761
30	15.9298	53.6143
31	16.9250	55.1329
32	17.9462	56.6318
33	18.9931	58.1107
34	20.0655	59.5694
35	21.1629	61.0076
36	22.2851	62.4250
37	23.4318	63.8214
38	24.6026	65.1965
39	25.7973	66.5500
40	27.0156	67.8817
41	28.2571	69.1912
42	29.5216	70.4784
43	30.8088	71.7429
44	32.1183	72.9844
45	33.4500	74.2027
46	34.8035	75.3974
47	36.1786	76.5682
48	37.5750	77.7149
49	38.9924	78.8371
50	40.4306	79.9345
51	41.8893	81.0069
52	43.3682	82.0538
53	44.8671	83.0750
54	46.3857	84.0702
55	47.9239	85.0389
56	49.4813	85.9809
57	51.0577	86.8959
58	52.6528	87.7834
59	54.2665	88.6432
60	55.8985	89.4748
61	57.5486	90.2780
62	59.2165	91.0524
63	60.9020	91.7975
64	62.6049	92.5131
65	64.3250	93.1988
66	66.0621	93.8541
67	67.8159	94.4787
68	69.5863	95.0722
69	71.3730	95.6342
70	73.1758	96.1643
71	74.9946	96.6621
72	76.8290	97.1272
73	78.6790	97.5592
74	80.5444	97.9576
75	82.4249	98.3221

#	REBATE	EARN
75	82.4249	98.3221
76	84.3203	98.6521
77	86.2305	98.9473
78	88.1553	99.2072
79	90.0944	99.4313
80	92.0478	99.6193
81	94.0153	99.7706
82	95.9965	99.8848
83	97.9915	99.9615
84	100.0000	100.0000

8 YEARS

#	REBATE	EARN
1	.0308	1.7251
2	.0921	3.4409
3	.1834	5.1473
4	.3043	6.8442
5	.4546	8.5314
6	.6338	10.2089
7	.8415	11.8765
8	1.0775	13.5341
9	1.3413	15.1815
10	1.6326	16.8186
11	1.9511	18.4454
12	2.2964	20.0616
13	2.6682	21.6672
14	3.0662	23.2619
15	3.4899	24.8457
16	3.9392	26.4185
17	4.4136	27.9800
18	4.9129	29.5301
19	5.4368	31.0687
20	5.9849	32.5957
21	6.5569	34.1109
22	7.1526	35.6141
23	7.7716	37.1052
24	8.4136	38.5841
25	9.0785	40.0506
26	9.7658	41.5044
27	10.4752	42.9456
28	11.2066	44.3738
29	11.9597	45.7890
30	12.7341	47.1910
31	13.5296	48.5796
32	14.3459	49.9546
33	15.1828	51.3159
34	16.0400	52.6633
35	16.9173	53.9966
36	17.8144	55.3156
37	18.7310	56.6202
38	19.6669	57.9102
39	20.6220	59.1853
40	21.5958	60.4455
41	22.5883	61.6904
42	23.5991	62.9200
43	24.6280	64.1340
44	25.6749	65.3322
45	26.7394	66.5144
46	27.8214	67.6804
47	28.9206	68.8301
48	30.0369	69.9631
49	31.1699	71.0794
50	32.3196	72.1786
51	33.4856	73.2606
52	34.6678	74.3251
53	35.8660	75.3720
54	37.0800	76.4009
55	38.3096	77.4117
56	39.5545	78.4042
57	40.8147	79.3780
58	42.0898	80.3331
59	43.3798	81.2690
60	44.6844	82.1856
61	46.0034	83.0827
62	47.3367	83.9600
63	48.6841	84.8172
64	50.0454	85.6541
65	51.4204	86.4704
66	52.8090	87.2659
67	54.2110	88.0403
68	55.6262	88.7934
69	57.0544	89.5248
70	58.4956	90.2342
71	59.9494	90.9215
72	61.4159	91.5864
73	62.8948	92.2284
74	64.3859	92.8474
75	65.8891	93.4431
76	67.4043	94.0151
77	68.9313	94.5632
78	70.4699	95.0871
79	72.0200	95.5864
80	73.5815	96.0608
81	75.1543	96.5101
82	76.7381	96.9338
83	78.3328	97.3318
84	79.9384	97.7036
85	81.5546	98.0489
86	83.1814	98.3674
87	84.8185	98.6587
88	86.4659	98.9225
89	88.1235	99.1585
90	89.7911	99.3662
91	91.4686	99.5454
92	93.1558	99.6957
93	94.8527	99.8166
94	96.5591	99.9079
95	98.2749	99.9692
96	100.0000	100.0000

9 YEARS

#	REBATE	EARN
1	.0254	1.5058
2	.0758	3.0051
3	.1511	4.4976
4	.2507	5.9835
5	.3745	7.4625
6	.5221	8.9346
7	.6933	10.3997
8	.8877	11.8577
9	1.1050	13.3086
10	1.3450	14.7521
11	1.6074	16.1883
12	1.8919	17.6170
13	2.1982	19.0382
14	2.5260	20.4518
15	2.8751	21.8575
16	3.2452	23.2555
17	3.6361	24.6455
18	4.0474	26.0274
19	4.4790	27.4012
20	4.9305	28.7668
21	5.4018	30.1240
22	5.8925	31.4727
23	6.4025	32.8129
24	6.9314	34.1444
25	7.4791	35.4671
26	8.0453	36.7809
27	8.6298	38.0857
28	9.2324	39.3813
29	9.8527	40.6678
30	10.4907	41.9448
31	11.1460	43.2124
32	11.8186	44.4704
33	12.5080	45.7186
34	13.2142	46.9570
35	13.9370	48.1854
36	14.6760	49.4038
37	15.4311	50.6119
38	16.2022	51.8096
39	16.9890	52.9969
40	17.7913	54.1735
41	18.6089	55.3394
42	19.4416	56.4944
43	20.2893	57.6383
44	21.1517	58.7711
45	22.0287	59.8926
46	22.9201	61.0026
47	23.8257	62.1010
48	24.7453	63.1877
49	25.6787	64.2625
50	26.6258	65.3252
51	27.5864	66.3757
52	28.5604	67.4138
53	29.5475	68.4394
54	30.5476	69.4524
55	31.5606	70.4525
56	32.5862	71.4396
57	33.6243	72.4136
58	34.6748	73.3742
59	35.7375	74.3213
60	36.8123	75.2547
61	37.8990	76.1743
62	38.9974	77.0799
63	40.1074	77.9713
64	41.2289	78.8483
65	42.3617	79.7107
66	43.5056	80.5584
67	44.6606	81.3911
68	45.8265	82.2087
69	47.0031	83.0110
70	48.1904	83.7978
71	49.3881	84.5689
72	50.5962	85.3240
73	51.8146	86.0630
74	53.0430	86.7858
75	54.2814	87.4920
76	55.5296	88.1814
77	56.7876	88.8540
78	58.0552	89.5093
79	59.3322	90.1473
80	60.6187	90.7676
81	61.9143	91.3702
82	63.2191	91.9547
83	64.5329	92.5209
84	65.8556	93.0686
85	67.1871	93.5975
86	68.5273	94.1075
87	69.8760	94.5982
88	71.2332	95.0695
89	72.5988	95.5210
90	73.9726	95.9526
91	75.3545	96.3639
92	76.7445	96.7548
93	78.1425	97.1249
94	79.5482	97.4740
95	80.9618	97.8018
96	82.3830	98.1081
97	83.8117	98.3926
98	85.2479	98.6550
99	86.6914	98.8950
100	88.1423	99.1123
101	89.6003	99.3067
102	91.0654	99.4779
103	92.5375	99.6255
104	94.0165	99.7493
105	95.5024	99.8489
106	96.9949	99.9242
107	98.4942	99.9746
108	100.0000	100.0000

10 YEARS

#	REBATE	EARN
1	.0214	1.3315
2	.0640	2.6582
3	.1274	3.9802
4	.2115	5.2972
5	.3159	6.6093
6	.4404	7.9163
7	.5848	9.2183
8	.7488	10.5152
9	.9321	11.8068
10	1.1345	13.0932
11	1.3558	14.3743
12	1.5958	15.6499
13	1.8542	16.9200
14	2.1307	18.1847
15	2.4252	19.4437
16	2.7373	20.6970
17	3.0670	21.9445
18	3.4140	23.1862
19	3.7780	24.4221
20	4.1589	25.6519
21	4.5564	26.8757
22	4.9703	28.0933
23	5.4005	29.3047
24	5.8467	30.5099
25	6.3086	31.7086
26	6.7862	32.9010
27	7.2793	34.0867
28	7.7875	35.2659
29	8.3108	36.4384
30	8.8489	37.6041
31	9.4017	38.7629
32	9.9690	39.9147
33	10.5505	41.0595
34	11.1462	42.1972
35	11.7558	43.3276
36	12.3792	44.4507
37	13.0162	45.5664
38	13.6666	46.6746
39	14.3302	47.7752
40	15.0070	48.8681
41	15.6966	49.9532
42	16.3990	51.0304
43	17.1141	52.0996
44	17.8415	53.1607
45	18.5812	54.2136
46	19.3331	55.2582
47	20.0970	56.2944
48	20.8727	57.3220
49	21.6600	58.3411
50	22.4589	59.3514
51	23.2692	60.3528
52	24.0907	61.3453
53	24.9233	62.3287
54	25.7669	63.3030
55	26.6214	64.2679
56	27.4865	65.2234
57	28.3622	66.1694
58	29.2483	67.1057
59	30.1447	68.0322
60	31.0512	68.9488
61	31.9678	69.8553
62	32.8943	70.7517
63	33.8306	71.6378
64	34.7766	72.5135
65	35.7321	73.3786
66	36.6970	74.2331
67	37.6713	75.0767
68	38.6547	75.9093
69	39.6472	76.7308
70	40.6486	77.5411
71	41.6589	78.3400
72	42.6780	79.1273
73	43.7056	79.9030
74	44.7418	80.6669
75	45.7864	81.4188
76	46.8393	82.1585
77	47.9004	82.8859
78	48.9696	83.6010
79	50.0468	84.3034
80	51.1319	84.9930
81	52.2248	85.6698
82	53.3254	86.3334
83	54.4336	86.9838
84	55.5493	87.6208
85	56.6724	88.2442
86	57.8028	88.8538
87	58.9405	89.4495
88	60.0853	90.0310
89	61.2371	90.5983
90	62.3959	91.1511
91	63.5616	91.6892
92	64.7341	92.2125
93	65.9133	92.7207
94	67.0990	93.2138
95	68.2914	93.6914
96	69.4901	94.1533
97	70.6953	94.5995
98	71.9067	95.0297
99	73.1243	95.4436
100	74.3481	95.8411
101	75.5779	96.2220
102	76.8138	96.5860
103	78.0555	96.9330
104	79.3030	97.2627
105	80.5563	97.5748
106	81.8153	97.8693
107	83.0800	98.1458
108	84.3501	98.4042
109	85.6257	98.6442
110	86.9068	98.8655
111	88.1932	99.0679
112	89.4848	99.2512
113	90.7817	99.4152
114	92.0837	99.5596
115	93.3907	99.6841
116	94.7028	99.7885
117	96.0198	99.8726
118	97.3418	99.9360
119	98.6685	99.9786
120	100.0000	100.0000

1 YEAR

#	REBATE	EARN
1	1.3429	15.0311
2	4.0115	28.8961
3	7.9890	41.5800
4	13.2587	53.0675
5	19.8040	63.3431
6	27.6088	72.3912
7	36.6569	80.1960
8	46.9325	86.7413
9	58.4200	92.0110
10	71.1039	95.9885
11	84.9689	98.6571
12	100.0000	100.0000

2 YEARS

#	REBATE	EARN
1	.3668	7.6254
2	1.0957	14.9778
3	2.1822	22.0537
4	3.6216	28.8493
5	5.4095	35.3612
6	7.5413	41.5857
7	10.0128	47.5190
8	12.8196	53.1574
9	15.9574	58.4971
10	19.4220	63.5342
11	23.2092	68.2648
12	27.3150	72.6850
13	31.7352	76.7908
14	36.4658	80.5780
15	41.5029	84.0426
16	46.8426	87.1804
17	52.4810	89.9872
18	58.4143	92.4587
19	64.6388	94.5905
20	71.1507	96.3784
21	77.9463	97.8178
22	85.0222	98.9043
23	92.3746	99.6332
24	100.0000	100.0000

3 YEARS

#	REBATE	EARN
1	.1734	5.0302
2	.5179	9.9497
3	1.0314	14.7571
4	1.7117	19.4511
5	2.5567	24.0301
6	3.5643	28.4926
7	4.7324	32.8371
8	6.0590	37.0622
9	7.5420	41.1662
10	9.1795	45.1477
11	10.9695	49.0049
12	12.9100	52.7364
13	14.9992	56.3404
14	17.2351	59.8154
15	19.6158	63.1597
16	22.1395	66.3716
17	24.8044	69.4494
18	27.6087	72.3913
19	30.5506	75.1956
20	33.6284	77.8605
21	36.8403	80.3842
22	40.1846	82.7649
23	43.6596	85.0008
24	47.2636	87.0900
25	50.9951	89.0305

1 YEAR (continued)

#	REBATE	EARN
26	54.8523	90.8205
27	58.8338	92.4580
28	62.9378	93.9410
29	67.1629	95.2676
30	71.5074	96.4357
31	75.9699	97.4433
32	80.5489	98.2883
33	85.2429	98.9686
34	90.0503	99.4821
35	94.9698	99.8266
36	100.0000	100.0000

4 YEARS

#	REBATE	EARN
1	.1029	3.7109
2	.3074	7.3655
3	.6121	10.9631
4	1.0159	14.5030
5	1.5174	17.9843
6	2.1154	21.4064
7	2.8086	24.7685
8	3.5960	28.0698
9	4.4761	31.3095
10	5.4480	34.4869
11	6.5103	37.6010
12	7.6620	40.6512
13	8.9018	43.6365
14	10.2288	46.5562
15	11.6417	49.4094
16	13.1395	52.1952
17	14.7211	54.9127
18	16.3855	57.5612
19	18.1314	60.1396
20	19.9581	62.6472
21	21.8643	65.0828
22	23.8491	67.4458
23	25.9114	69.7350
24	28.0504	71.9496
25	30.2650	74.0886
26	32.5542	76.1509
27	34.9172	78.1357
28	37.3528	80.0419
29	39.8604	81.8686
30	42.4388	83.6145
31	45.0873	85.2789
32	47.8048	86.8605
33	50.5906	88.3583
34	53.4438	89.7712
35	56.3635	91.0982
36	59.3488	92.3380
37	62.3990	93.4897
38	65.5131	94.5520
39	68.6905	95.5239
40	71.9302	96.4040
41	75.2315	97.1914
42	78.5936	97.8846
43	82.0157	98.4826
44	85.4970	98.9841
45	89.0369	99.3879
46	92.6345	99.6926
47	96.2891	99.8971
48	100.0000	100.0000

5 YEARS

#	REBATE	EARN
1	.0692	2.9145
2	.2067	5.7965
3	.4117	8.6456
4	.6833	11.4614
5	1.0206	14.2435
6	1.4229	16.9915
7	1.8892	19.7048
8	2.4188	22.3831
9	3.0108	25.0258
10	3.6645	27.6326
11	4.3790	30.2030
12	5.1537	32.7365
13	5.9877	35.2326
14	6.8803	37.6908
15	7.8306	40.1107
16	8.8381	42.4917
17	9.9020	44.8334
18	11.0214	47.1352
19	12.1958	49.3966
20	13.4245	51.6172
21	14.7067	53.7964
22	16.0417	55.9335
23	17.4289	58.0282
24	18.8677	60.0799
25	20.3573	62.0879
26	21.8971	64.0518
27	23.4865	65.9710
28	25.1248	67.8448
29	26.8115	69.6727
30	28.5458	71.4542
31	30.3273	73.1885
32	32.1552	74.8752
33	34.0290	76.5135
34	35.9482	78.1029
35	37.9121	79.6427
36	39.9201	81.1323
37	41.9718	82.5711
38	44.0665	83.9583
39	46.2036	85.2933
40	48.3828	86.5755
41	50.6034	87.8042
42	52.8648	88.9786
43	55.1666	90.0980
44	57.5083	91.1619
45	59.8893	92.1694
46	62.3092	93.1197
47	64.7674	94.0123
48	67.2635	94.8463
49	69.7970	95.6210
50	72.3674	96.3355
51	74.9742	96.9892
52	77.6169	97.5812
53	80.2952	98.1108
54	83.0085	98.5771
55	85.7565	98.9794
56	88.5386	99.3167
57	91.3544	99.5883
58	94.2035	99.7933
59	97.0855	99.9308
60	100.0000	100.0000

6 YEARS

#	REBATE	EARN
1	.0504	2.3829
2	.1505	4.7455
3	.2997	7.0876
4	.4975	9.4090
5	.7430	11.7092
6	1.0359	13.9882
7	1.3754	16.2456
8	1.7609	18.4810
9	2.1919	20.6944
10	2.6678	22.8852
11	3.1880	25.0534
12	3.7520	27.1985
13	4.3591	29.3202
14	5.0089	31.4184
15	5.7008	33.4926
16	6.4343	35.5426
17	7.2088	37.5680
18	8.0238	39.5685
19	8.8788	41.5439
20	9.7732	43.4937
21	10.7067	45.4177
22	11.6786	47.3154
23	12.6885	49.1867
24	13.7360	51.0311
25	14.8204	52.8483
26	15.9414	54.6379
27	17.0985	56.3996
28	18.2913	58.1331
29	19.5192	59.8378
30	20.7818	61.5136
31	22.0787	63.1600
32	23.4095	64.7766
33	24.7737	66.3630
34	26.1708	67.9189
35	27.6006	69.4439
36	29.0625	70.9375
37	30.5561	72.3994
38	32.0811	73.8292
39	33.6370	75.2263
40	35.2234	76.5905
41	36.8400	77.9213
42	38.4864	79.2182
43	40.1622	80.4808
44	41.8669	81.7087
45	43.6004	82.9015
46	45.3621	84.0586
47	47.1517	85.1796
48	48.9689	86.2640
49	50.8133	87.3115
50	52.6846	88.3214
51	54.5823	89.2933
52	56.5063	90.2268
53	58.4561	91.1212
54	60.4315	91.9762
55	62.4320	92.7912
56	64.4574	93.5657
57	66.5074	94.2992
58	68.5816	94.9911
59	70.6798	95.6409
60	72.8015	96.2480
61	74.9466	96.8120
62	77.1148	97.3322
63	79.3056	97.8081
64	81.5190	98.2391
65	83.7544	98.6246
66	86.0118	98.9641
67	88.2908	99.2570
68	90.5910	99.5025
69	92.9124	99.7003
70	95.2545	99.8495
71	97.6171	99.9496
72	100.0000	100.0000

7 YEARS

#	REBATE	EARN
1	.0387	2.0039
2	.1157	3.9944
3	.2304	5.9714
4	.3824	7.9348
5	.5712	9.8842
6	.7963	11.8196
7	1.0573	13.7407
8	1.3537	15.6475
9	1.6850	17.5396
10	2.0508	19.4170
11	2.4507	21.2793
12	2.8843	23.1265
13	3.3510	24.9583
14	3.8505	26.7746
15	4.3824	28.5750
16	4.9463	30.3595
17	5.5416	32.1278
18	6.1682	33.8797
19	6.8254	35.6150
20	7.5130	37.3335
21	8.2306	39.0350
22	8.9778	40.7192
23	9.7541	42.3859
24	10.5593	44.0349
25	11.3930	45.6660
26	12.2547	47.2289
27	13.1442	48.8734
28	14.0611	50.4493
29	15.0051	52.0063
30	15.9757	53.5442
31	16.9727	55.0627
32	17.9957	56.5616
33	19.0444	58.0407
34	20.1184	59.4995
35	21.2175	60.9381
36	22.3413	62.3559
37	23.4895	63.7528
38	24.6618	65.1286
39	25.8579	66.4829
40	27.0775	67.8154
41	28.3202	69.1259
42	29.5858	70.4142
43	30.8741	71.6798
44	32.1846	72.9225
45	33.5171	74.1421
46	34.8714	75.3382
47	36.2472	76.5105
48	37.6441	77.6587
49	39.0619	78.7825
50	40.5005	79.8816
51	41.9593	80.9556
52	43.4384	82.0043
53	44.9373	83.0273
54	46.4558	84.0243
55	47.9937	84.9949
56	49.5507	85.9389
57	51.1266	86.8558
58	52.7211	87.7453
59	54.3340	88.6070
60	55.9651	89.4407
61	57.6141	90.2459
62	59.2808	91.0222
63	60.9650	91.7694
64	62.6665	92.4870
65	64.3850	93.1746
66	66.1203	93.8318
67	67.8722	94.4584
68	69.6405	95.0537
69	71.4250	95.6176
70	73.2254	96.1495
71	75.0417	96.6490
72	76.8735	97.1157
73	78.7207	97.5493
74	80.5830	97.9492
75	82.4604	98.3150

#	REBATE	EARN
75	82.4604	98.3150
76	84.3525	98.6463
77	86.2593	98.9427
78	88.1804	99.2037
79	90.1158	99.4288
80	92.0652	99.6176
81	94.0286	99.7696
82	96.0056	99.8843
83	97.9961	99.9613
84	100.0000	100.0000

8 YEARS

#	REBATE	EARN
1	.0310	1.7207
2	.0925	3.4323
3	.1843	5.1346
4	.3059	6.8275
5	.4569	8.5110
6	.6369	10.1847
7	.8456	11.8487
8	1.0827	13.5029
9	1.3477	15.1470
10	1.6403	16.7809
11	1.9601	18.4046
12	2.3069	20.0179
13	2.6802	21.6207
14	3.0797	23.2127
15	3.5052	24.7940
16	3.9561	26.3643
17	4.4323	27.9235
18	4.9334	29.4715
19	5.4591	31.0081
20	6.0091	32.5331
21	6.5830	34.0465
22	7.1806	35.5480
23	7.8016	37.0376
24	8.4456	38.5150
25	9.1123	39.9801
26	9.8016	41.4328
27	10.5130	42.8728
28	11.2464	44.3001
29	12.0014	45.7144
30	12.7777	47.1156
31	13.5751	48.5036
32	14.3933	49.8781
33	15.2321	51.2389
34	16.0911	52.5860
35	16.9702	53.9191
36	17.8691	55.2380
37	18.7874	56.5425
38	19.7250	57.8326
39	20.6817	59.1079
40	21.6571	60.3683
41	22.6511	61.6137
42	23.6634	62.8437
43	24.6937	64.0582
44	25.7419	65.2571
45	26.8077	66.4400
46	27.8909	67.6069
47	28.9912	68.7574
48	30.1085	69.8915
49	31.2426	71.0088
50	32.3931	72.1091
51	33.5600	73.1923
52	34.7429	74.2581
53	35.9418	75.3063
54	37.1563	76.3366
55	38.3863	77.3489
56	39.6317	78.3429
57	40.8921	79.3183
58	42.1674	80.2750
59	43.4575	81.2126
60	44.7620	82.1309
61	46.0809	83.0298
62	47.4140	83.9089
63	48.7611	84.7679
64	50.1219	85.6067
65	51.4964	86.4249
66	52.8844	87.2223
67	54.2856	87.9986
68	55.6999	88.7536
69	57.1272	89.4870
70	58.5672	90.1984
71	60.0199	90.8877
72	61.4850	91.5544
73	62.9624	92.1984
74	64.4520	92.8194
75	65.9535	93.4170
76	67.4669	93.9909
77	68.9919	94.5409
78	70.5285	95.0666
79	72.0765	95.5677
80	73.6357	96.0439
81	75.2060	96.4948
82	76.7873	96.9203
83	78.3793	97.3198
84	79.9821	97.6931
85	81.5954	98.0399
86	83.2191	98.3597
87	84.8530	98.6523
88	86.4971	98.9173
89	88.1513	99.1544
90	89.8153	99.3631
91	91.4890	99.5431
92	93.1725	99.6941
93	94.8654	99.8157
94	96.5677	99.9075
95	98.2793	99.9690
96	100.0000	100.0000

9 YEARS

#	REBATE	EARN
1	.0255	1.5017
2	.0763	2.9969
3	.1519	4.4856
4	.2521	5.9676
5	.3766	7.4429
6	.5250	8.9115
7	.6970	10.3731
8	.8924	11.8277
9	1.1108	13.2752
10	1.3520	14.7156
11	1.6157	16.1488
12	1.9015	17.5745
13	2.2092	18.9928
14	2.5385	20.4036
15	2.8891	21.8068
16	3.2609	23.2022
17	3.6534	24.5897
18	4.0664	25.9693
19	4.4997	27.3409
20	4.9530	28.7043
21	5.4261	30.0595
22	5.9186	31.4063
23	6.4305	32.7446
24	6.9613	34.0744
25	7.5109	35.3955
26	8.0790	36.7077
27	8.6654	38.0111
28	9.2699	39.3054
29	9.8922	40.5906
30	10.5321	41.8665
31	11.1893	43.1331
32	11.8638	44.3901
33	12.5551	45.6375
34	13.2632	46.8752
35	13.9878	48.1029
36	14.7287	49.3207
37	15.4856	50.5283
38	16.2585	51.7257
39	17.0470	52.9127
40	17.8510	54.0891
41	18.6703	55.2549
42	19.5046	56.4098
43	20.3539	57.5538
44	21.2179	58.6868
45	22.0964	59.8084
46	22.9892	60.9188
47	23.8962	62.0176
48	24.8171	63.1047
49	25.7518	64.1800
50	26.7002	65.2433
51	27.6620	66.2945
52	28.6370	67.3334
53	29.6252	68.3599
54	30.6263	69.3737
55	31.6401	70.3748
56	32.6666	71.3630
57	33.7055	72.3380
58	34.7567	73.2998
59	35.8200	74.2482
60	36.8953	75.1829
61	37.9824	76.1038
62	39.0812	77.0108
63	40.1916	77.9036
64	41.3132	78.7821
65	42.4462	79.6461
66	43.5902	80.4954
67	44.7451	81.3297
68	45.9109	82.1490
69	47.0873	82.9530
70	48.2743	83.7415
71	49.4717	84.5144
72	50.6793	85.2713
73	51.8971	86.0122
74	53.1248	86.7368
75	54.3625	87.4449
76	55.6099	88.1362
77	56.8669	88.8107
78	58.1335	89.4679
79	59.4094	90.1078
80	60.6946	90.7301
81	61.9889	91.3346
82	63.2923	91.9210
83	64.6045	92.4891
84	65.9256	93.0387
85	67.2554	93.5695
86	68.5937	94.0814
87	69.9405	94.5739
88	71.2957	95.0470
89	72.6591	95.5003
90	74.0307	95.9336
91	75.4103	96.3466
92	76.7978	96.7391
93	78.1932	97.1109
94	79.5964	97.4615
95	81.0072	97.7908
96	82.4255	98.0985
97	83.8512	98.3843
98	85.2844	98.6480
99	86.7248	98.8892
100	88.1723	99.1076
101	89.6269	99.3030
102	91.0885	99.4750
103	92.5571	99.6234
104	94.0324	99.7479
105	95.5144	99.8481
106	97.0031	99.9237
107	98.4983	99.9745
108	100.0000	100.0000

10 YEARS

#	REBATE	EARN
1	.0215	1.3276
2	.0644	2.6505
3	.1282	3.9687
4	.2128	5.2821
5	.3178	6.5907
6	.4430	7.8943
7	.5882	9.1929
8	.7531	10.4864
9	.9375	11.7749
10	1.1410	13.0581
11	1.3635	14.3361
12	1.6047	15.6088
13	1.8644	16.8761
14	2.1423	18.1379
15	2.4382	19.3943
16	2.7519	20.6450
17	3.0831	21.8900
18	3.4317	23.1293
19	3.7973	24.3628
20	4.1799	25.5903
21	4.5791	26.8119
22	4.9948	28.0275
23	5.4267	29.2369
24	5.8747	30.4402
25	6.3385	31.6371
26	6.8180	32.8277
27	7.3129	34.0118
28	7.8230	35.1894
29	8.3481	36.3604
30	8.8881	37.5246
31	9.4428	38.6821
32	10.0120	39.8327
33	10.5954	40.9764
34	11.1930	42.1130
35	11.8045	43.2424
36	12.4297	44.3646
37	13.0685	45.4795
38	13.7207	46.5869
39	14.3862	47.6868
40	15.0647	48.7791
41	15.7561	49.8637
42	16.4602	50.9405
43	17.1769	52.0093
44	17.9060	53.0701
45	18.6474	54.1228
46	19.4008	55.1673
47	20.1662	56.2034
48	20.9434	57.2311
49	21.7323	58.2503
50	22.5326	59.2607
51	23.3443	60.2624
52	24.1671	61.2552
53	25.0010	62.2390
54	25.8459	63.2137
55	26.7015	64.1792
56	27.5677	65.1353
57	28.4445	66.0819
58	29.3316	67.0189
59	30.2289	67.9462
60	31.1364	68.8636
61	32.0538	69.7711
62	32.9811	70.6684
63	33.9181	71.5555
64	34.8647	72.4323
65	35.8208	73.2985
66	36.7863	74.1541
67	37.7610	74.9990
68	38.7448	75.8329
69	39.7376	76.6557
70	40.7393	77.4674
71	41.7497	78.2677
72	42.7689	79.0566
73	43.7966	79.8338
74	44.8327	80.5992
75	45.8772	81.3526
76	46.9299	82.0940
77	47.9907	82.8231
78	49.0595	83.5398
79	50.1363	84.2439
80	51.2209	84.9353
81	52.3132	85.6138
82	53.4131	86.2793
83	54.5205	86.9315
84	55.6354	87.5703
85	56.7576	88.1955
86	57.8870	88.8070
87	59.0236	89.4046
88	60.1673	89.9880
89	61.3179	90.5572
90	62.4754	91.1119
91	63.6396	91.6519
92	64.8106	92.1770
93	65.9882	92.6871
94	67.1723	93.1820
95	68.3629	93.6615
96	69.5598	94.1253
97	70.7631	94.5733
98	71.9725	95.0052
99	73.1881	95.4209
100	74.4097	95.8201
101	75.6372	96.2027
102	76.8707	96.5683
103	78.1100	96.9169
104	79.3550	97.2481
105	80.6057	97.5618
106	81.8621	97.8577
107	83.1239	98.1356
108	84.3912	98.3953
109	85.6639	98.6365
110	86.9419	98.8590
111	88.2251	99.0625
112	89.5136	99.2469
113	90.8071	99.4118
114	92.1057	99.5570
115	93.4093	99.6822
116	94.7179	99.7872
117	96.0313	99.8718
118	97.3495	99.9356
119	98.6724	99.9785
120	100.0000	100.0000

1 YEAR

#	REBATE	EARN
1	1.3439	15.0256
2	4.0142	28.8868
3	7.9938	41.5685
4	13.2657	53.0552
5	19.8132	63.3310
6	27.6197	72.3803
7	36.6690	80.1868
8	46.9448	86.7343
9	58.4315	92.0062
10	71.1132	95.9858
11	84.9744	98.6561
12	100.0000	100.0000

2 YEARS

#	REBATE	EARN
1	.3674	7.6197
2	1.0973	14.9673
3	2.1852	22.0392
4	3.6263	28.8316
5	5.4161	35.3411
6	7.5500	41.5638
7	10.0237	47.4960
8	12.8327	53.1339
9	15.9727	58.4736
10	19.4393	63.5113
11	23.2284	68.2428
12	27.3357	72.6643
13	31.7572	76.7716
14	36.4887	80.5607
15	41.5264	84.0273
16	46.8661	87.1673
17	52.5040	89.9763
18	58.4362	92.4500
19	64.6589	94.5839
20	71.1684	96.3737
21	77.9608	97.8148
22	85.0327	98.9027
23	92.3803	99.6326
24	100.0000	100.0000

3 YEARS

#	REBATE	EARN
1	.1738	5.0246
2	.5190	9.9391
3	1.0335	14.7421
4	1.7151	19.4321
5	2.5617	24.0077
6	3.5710	28.4672
7	4.7410	32.8093
8	6.0696	37.0323
9	7.5547	41.1347
10	9.1943	45.1149
11	10.9865	48.9714
12	12.9291	52.7024
13	15.0204	56.3063
14	17.2583	59.7816
15	19.6410	63.1264
16	22.1665	66.3391
17	24.8331	69.4179
18	27.6389	72.3611
19	30.5821	75.1669
20	33.6609	77.8335
21	36.8736	80.3590
22	40.2184	82.7417
23	43.6937	84.9796
24	47.2976	87.0709
25	51.0286	89.0135
26	54.8851	90.8057
27	58.8653	92.4453
28	62.9677	93.9304
29	67.1907	95.2590
30	71.5328	96.4290
31	75.9923	97.4383
32	80.5679	98.2849
33	85.2579	98.9665
34	90.0609	99.4810
35	94.9754	99.8262
36	100.0000	100.0000

4 YEARS

#	REBATE	EARN
1	.1032	3.7056
2	.3082	7.3553
3	.6138	10.9483
4	1.0186	14.4839
5	1.5214	17.9614
6	2.1208	21.3800
7	2.8156	24.7390
8	3.6047	28.0375
9	4.4867	31.2747
10	5.4604	34.4499
11	6.5248	37.5622
12	7.6785	40.6108
13	8.9205	43.5948
14	10.2496	46.5135
15	11.6646	49.3660
16	13.1645	52.1514
17	14.7482	54.8687
18	16.4145	57.5172
19	18.1625	60.0959
20	19.9910	62.6040
21	21.8990	65.0404
22	23.8854	67.4042
23	25.9493	69.6945
24	28.0897	71.9103
25	30.3055	74.0507
26	32.5958	76.1146
27	34.9596	78.1010
28	37.3960	80.0090
29	39.9041	81.8375
30	42.4828	83.5855
31	45.1313	85.2518
32	47.8486	86.8355
33	50.6340	88.3354
34	53.4865	89.7504
35	56.4052	91.0795
36	59.3892	92.3215
37	62.4378	93.4752
38	65.5501	94.5396
39	68.7253	95.5133
40	71.9625	96.3953
41	75.2610	97.1844
42	78.6200	97.8792
43	82.0386	98.4786
44	85.5161	98.9814
45	89.0517	99.3862
46	92.6447	99.6918
47	96.2944	99.8968
48	100.0000	100.0000

5 YEARS

#	REBATE	EARN
1	.0695	2.9094
2	.2075	5.7866
3	.4131	8.6312
4	.6856	11.4428
5	1.0240	14.2209
6	1.4274	16.9651
7	1.8951	19.6750
8	2.4262	22.3501
9	3.0198	24.9899
10	3.6752	27.5940
11	4.3916	30.1619
12	5.1682	32.6931
13	6.0041	35.1873
14	6.8987	37.6437
15	7.8511	40.0621
16	8.8606	42.4418
17	9.9266	44.7824
18	11.0481	47.0834
19	12.2246	49.3442
20	13.4553	51.5643
21	14.7395	53.7432
22	16.0765	55.8803
23	17.4657	57.9751
24	18.9063	60.0270
25	20.3977	62.0355
26	21.9392	63.9999
27	23.5302	65.9199
28	25.1701	67.7946
29	26.8582	69.6236
30	28.5938	71.4062
31	30.3764	73.1418
32	32.2054	74.8299
33	34.0801	76.4698
34	36.0001	78.0608
35	37.9645	79.6023
36	39.9730	81.0937
37	42.0249	82.5343
38	44.1197	83.9235
39	46.2568	85.2605
40	48.4357	86.5447
41	50.6558	87.7754
42	52.9166	88.9519
43	55.2176	90.0734
44	57.5582	91.1394
45	59.9379	92.1489
46	62.3563	93.1013
47	64.8127	93.9959
48	67.3069	94.8318
49	69.8381	95.6084
50	72.4060	96.3248
51	75.0101	96.9802
52	77.6499	97.5738
53	80.3250	98.1049
54	83.0349	98.5726
55	85.7791	98.9760
56	88.5572	99.3144
57	91.3688	99.5869
58	94.2134	99.7925
59	97.0906	99.9305
60	100.0000	100.0000

6 YEARS

#	REBATE	EARN
1	.0506	2.3781
2	.1511	4.7361
3	.3009	7.0738
4	.4994	9.3909
5	.7459	11.6872
6	1.0398	13.9624
7	1.3805	16.2162
8	1.7674	18.4483
9	2.1998	20.6584
10	2.6773	22.8463
11	3.1991	25.0116
12	3.7648	27.1541
13	4.3737	29.2735
14	5.0254	31.3694
15	5.7192	33.4416
16	6.4546	35.4897
17	7.2311	37.5135
18	8.0481	39.5125
19	8.9051	41.4866
20	9.8016	43.4352
21	10.7371	45.3582
22	11.7111	47.2552
23	12.7230	49.1258
24	13.7724	50.9697
25	14.8589	52.7866
26	15.9818	54.5760
27	17.1408	56.3377
28	18.3354	58.0713
29	19.5651	59.7763
30	20.8294	61.4524
31	22.1280	63.0993
32	23.4603	64.7166
33	24.8260	66.3038
34	26.2245	67.8606
35	27.6556	69.3866
36	29.1187	70.8813
37	30.6134	72.3444
38	32.1394	73.7755
39	33.6962	75.1740
40	35.2834	76.5397
41	36.9007	77.8720
42	38.5476	79.1706
43	40.2237	80.4349
44	41.9287	81.6646
45	43.6623	82.8592
46	45.4240	84.0182
47	47.2134	85.1411
48	49.0303	86.2276
49	50.8742	87.2770
50	52.7448	88.2889
51	54.6418	89.2629
52	56.5648	90.1984
53	58.5134	91.0949
54	60.4875	91.9519
55	62.4865	92.7689
56	64.5103	93.5454
57	66.5584	94.2808
58	68.6306	94.9746
59	70.7265	95.6263
60	72.8459	96.2352
61	74.9884	96.8009
62	77.1537	97.3227
63	79.3416	97.8002
64	81.5517	98.2326
65	83.7838	98.6195
66	86.0376	98.9602
67	88.3128	99.2541
68	90.6091	99.5006
69	92.9262	99.6991
70	95.2639	99.8489
71	97.6219	99.9494
72	100.0000	100.0000

7 YEARS

#	REBATE	EARN
1	.0389	1.9993
2	.1162	3.9854
3	.2315	5.9582
4	.3841	7.9175
5	.5737	9.8630
6	.7998	11.7946
7	1.0619	13.7122
8	1.3594	15.6155
9	1.6921	17.5043
10	2.0593	19.3786
11	2.4607	21.2379
12	2.8958	23.0823
13	3.3642	24.9115
14	3.8654	26.7252
15	4.3991	28.5233
16	4.9647	30.3056
17	5.5620	32.0719
18	6.1904	33.8219
19	6.8496	35.5554
20	7.5392	37.2723
21	8.2587	38.9723
22	9.0079	40.6552
23	9.7863	42.3207
24	10.5934	43.9687
25	11.4291	45.5988
26	12.2928	47.2110
27	13.1843	48.8048
28	14.1031	50.3802
29	15.0490	51.9368
30	16.0215	53.4744
31	17.0203	54.9928
32	18.0451	56.4917
33	19.0956	57.9708
34	20.1713	59.4299
35	21.2720	60.8688
36	22.3974	62.2871
37	23.5471	63.6846
38	24.7209	65.0609
39	25.9183	66.4160
40	27.1392	67.7494
41	28.3831	69.0609
42	29.6499	70.3501
43	30.9391	71.6169
44	32.2506	72.8608
45	33.5840	74.0817
46	34.9391	75.2791
47	36.3154	76.4529
48	37.7129	77.6026
49	39.1312	78.7280
50	40.5701	79.8287
51	42.0292	80.9044
52	43.5083	81.9549
53	45.0072	82.9797
54	46.5256	83.9785
55	48.0632	84.9510
56	49.6198	85.8969
57	51.1952	86.8157
58	52.7890	87.7072
59	54.4012	88.5709
60	56.0313	89.4066
61	57.6793	90.2137
62	59.3448	90.9921
63	61.0277	91.7413
64	62.7277	92.4608
65	64.4446	93.1504
66	66.1781	93.8096
67	67.9281	94.4380
68	69.6944	95.0353
69	71.4767	95.6009
70	73.2748	96.1346
71	75.0885	96.6358
72	76.9177	97.1042
73	78.7621	97.5393
74	80.6214	97.9407
75	82.4957	98.3079

ACTUARIAL REBATE AND EARNINGS

#	REBATE	EARN
75	82.4957	98.3079
76	84.3845	98.6406
77	86.2878	98.9381
78	88.2054	99.2002
79	90.1370	99.4263
80	92.0825	99.6159
81	94.0418	99.7685
82	96.0146	99.8838
83	98.0007	99.9611
84	100.0000	100.0000

8 YEARS

#	REBATE	EARN
1	.0311	1.7164
2	.0930	3.4238
3	.1852	5.1220
4	.3074	6.8110
5	.4591	8.4906
6	.6401	10.1607
7	.8498	11.8212
8	1.0879	13.4719
9	1.3541	15.1127
10	1.6480	16.7435
11	1.9692	18.3642
12	2.3174	19.9745
13	2.6922	21.5745
14	3.0933	23.1639
15	3.5204	24.7426
16	3.9731	26.3105
17	4.4510	27.8674
18	4.9539	29.4132
19	5.4814	30.9478
20	6.0333	32.4709
21	6.6091	33.9825
22	7.2086	35.4823
23	7.8315	36.9703
24	8.4775	38.4463
25	9.1462	39.9101
26	9.8374	41.3615
27	10.5508	42.8004
28	11.2861	44.2267
29	12.0430	45.6402
30	12.8213	47.0406
31	13.6206	48.4279
32	14.4407	49.8019
33	15.2813	51.1623
34	16.1422	52.5090
35	17.0230	53.8419
36	17.9236	55.1607
37	18.8437	56.4652
38	19.7830	57.7553
39	20.7413	59.0308
40	21.7183	60.2915
41	22.7137	61.5372
42	23.7275	62.7677
43	24.7592	63.9828
44	25.8087	65.1823
45	26.8758	66.3660
46	27.9601	67.5336
47	29.0616	68.6851
48	30.1800	69.8200
49	31.3149	70.9384
50	32.4664	72.0399
51	33.6340	73.1242
52	34.8177	74.1913
53	36.0172	75.2408
54	37.2323	76.2725
55	38.4628	77.2863
56	39.7085	78.2817
57	40.9692	79.2587
58	42.2447	80.2170
59	43.5348	81.1563
60	44.8393	82.0764
61	46.1581	82.9770
62	47.4910	83.8578
63	48.8377	84.7187
64	50.1981	85.5593
65	51.5721	86.3794
66	52.9594	87.1787
67	54.3598	87.9570
68	55.7733	88.7139
69	57.1996	89.4492
70	58.6385	90.1626
71	60.0899	90.8538
72	61.5537	91.5225
73	63.0297	92.1685
74	64.5177	92.7914
75	66.0175	93.3909
76	67.5291	93.9667
77	69.0522	94.5186
78	70.5868	95.0461
79	72.1326	95.5490
80	73.6895	96.0269
81	75.2574	96.4796
82	76.8361	96.9067
83	78.4255	97.3078
84	80.0255	97.6826
85	81.6358	98.0308
86	83.2565	98.3520
87	84.8873	98.6459
88	86.5281	98.9121
89	88.1788	99.1502
90	89.8393	99.3599
91	91.5094	99.5409
92	93.1890	99.6926
93	94.8780	99.8148
94	96.5762	99.9070
95	98.2836	99.9689
96	100.0000	100.0000

9 YEARS

#	REBATE	EARN
1	.0257	1.4976
2	.0767	2.9888
3	.1528	4.4736
4	.2535	5.9519
5	.3786	7.4235
6	.5278	8.8885
7	.7008	10.3466
8	.8972	11.7979
9	1.1167	13.2422
10	1.3590	14.6794
11	1.6239	16.1095
12	1.9111	17.5323
13	2.2202	18.9478
14	2.5510	20.3559
15	2.9032	21.7564
16	3.2765	23.1492
17	3.6706	24.5343
18	4.0854	25.9116
19	4.5204	27.2810
20	4.9755	28.6423
21	5.4504	29.9954
22	5.9448	31.3403
23	6.4585	32.6768
24	6.9912	34.0049
25	7.5426	35.3243
26	8.1127	36.6351
27	8.7010	37.9370
28	9.3074	39.2300
29	9.9316	40.5139
30	10.5734	41.7887
31	11.2326	43.0542
32	11.9089	44.3103
33	12.6021	45.5569
34	13.3121	46.7938
35	14.0385	48.0209
36	14.7812	49.2381
37	15.5400	50.4452
38	16.3146	51.6422
39	17.1048	52.8289
40	17.9105	54.0051
41	18.7315	55.1707
42	19.5675	56.3257
43	20.4183	57.4697
44	21.2838	58.6028
45	22.1638	59.7247
46	23.0581	60.8353
47	23.9664	61.9345
48	24.8887	63.0220
49	25.8247	64.0979
50	26.7743	65.1618
51	27.7372	66.2137
52	28.7134	67.2534
53	29.7025	68.2806
54	30.7046	69.2954
55	31.7194	70.2975
56	32.7466	71.2866
57	33.7863	72.2628
58	34.8382	73.2257
59	35.9021	74.1753
60	36.9780	75.1113
61	38.0655	76.0336
62	39.1647	76.9419
63	40.2753	77.8362
64	41.3972	78.7162
65	42.5303	79.5817
66	43.6743	80.4325
67	44.8293	81.2685
68	45.9949	82.0895
69	47.1711	82.8952
70	48.3578	83.6854
71	49.5548	84.4600
72	50.7619	85.2188
73	51.9791	85.9615
74	53.2062	86.6879
75	54.4431	87.3979
76	55.6897	88.0911
77	56.9458	88.7674
78	58.2113	89.4266
79	59.4861	90.0684
80	60.7700	90.6926
81	62.0630	91.2990
82	63.3649	91.8873
83	64.6757	92.4574
84	65.9951	93.0088
85	67.3232	93.5415
86	68.6597	94.0552
87	70.0046	94.5496
88	71.3577	95.0245
89	72.7190	95.4796
90	74.0884	95.9146
91	75.4657	96.3294
92	76.8508	96.7235
93	78.2436	97.0968
94	79.6441	97.4490
95	81.0522	97.7798
96	82.4677	98.0889
97	83.8905	98.3761
98	85.3206	98.6410
99	86.7578	98.8833
100	88.2021	99.1028
101	89.6534	99.2992
102	91.1115	99.4722
103	92.5765	99.6214
104	94.0481	99.7465
105	95.5264	99.8472
106	97.0112	99.9233
107	98.5024	99.9743
108	100.0000	100.0000

10 YEARS

#	REBATE	EARN
1	.0217	1.3237
2	.0648	2.6429
3	.1290	3.9574
4	.2141	5.2672
5	.3197	6.5722
6	.4457	7.8724
7	.5917	9.1676
8	.7575	10.4579
9	.9428	11.7432
10	1.1475	13.0233
11	1.3711	14.2983
12	1.6136	15.5681
13	1.8746	16.8325
14	2.1538	18.0916
15	2.4512	19.3453
16	2.7664	20.5934
17	3.0992	21.8359
18	3.4494	23.0728
19	3.8167	24.3040
20	4.2009	25.5293
21	4.6018	26.7487
22	5.0193	27.9622
23	5.4530	29.1697
24	5.9028	30.3710
25	6.3684	31.5661
26	6.8497	32.7549
27	7.3464	33.9374
28	7.8584	35.1134
29	8.3854	36.2829
30	8.9273	37.4458
31	9.4839	38.6019
32	10.0549	39.7513
33	10.6402	40.8938
34	11.2396	42.0293
35	11.8530	43.1578
36	12.4801	44.2790
37	13.1207	45.3931
38	13.7747	46.4998
39	14.4419	47.5990
40	15.1222	48.6907
41	15.8154	49.7748
42	16.5212	50.8511
43	17.2396	51.9196
44	17.9704	52.9801
45	18.7133	54.0326
46	19.4684	55.0770
47	20.2353	56.1130
48	21.0140	57.1407
49	21.8043	58.1600
50	22.6060	59.1706
51	23.4191	60.1725
52	24.2432	61.1656
53	25.0784	62.1498
54	25.9245	63.1249
55	26.7813	64.0909
56	27.6486	65.0475
57	28.5264	65.9948
58	29.4146	66.9325
59	30.3129	67.8605
60	31.2212	68.7788
61	32.1395	69.6871
62	33.0675	70.5854
63	34.0052	71.4736
64	34.9525	72.3514
65	35.9091	73.2187
66	36.8751	74.0755
67	37.8502	74.9216
68	38.8344	75.7568
69	39.8275	76.5809
70	40.8294	77.3940
71	41.8400	78.1957
72	42.8593	78.9860
73	43.8870	79.7647
74	44.9230	80.5316
75	45.9674	81.2867
76	47.0199	82.0296
77	48.0804	82.7604
78	49.1489	83.4788
79	50.2252	84.1846
80	51.3093	84.8778
81	52.4010	85.5581
82	53.5002	86.2253
83	54.6069	86.8793
84	55.7210	87.5199
85	56.8422	88.1470
86	57.9707	88.7604
87	59.1062	89.3598
88	60.2487	89.9451
89	61.3981	90.5161
90	62.5542	91.0727
91	63.7171	91.6146
92	64.8866	92.1416
93	66.0626	92.6536
94	67.2451	93.1503
95	68.4339	93.6316
96	69.6290	94.0972
97	70.8303	94.5470
98	72.0378	94.9807
99	73.2513	95.3982
100	74.4707	95.7991
101	75.6960	96.1833
102	76.9272	96.5506
103	78.1641	96.9008
104	79.4066	97.2336
105	80.6547	97.5488
106	81.9084	97.8462
107	83.1675	98.1254
108	84.4319	98.3864
109	85.7017	98.6289
110	86.9767	98.8525
111	88.2568	99.0572
112	89.5421	99.2425
113	90.8324	99.4083
114	92.1276	99.5543
115	93.4278	99.6803
116	94.7328	99.7859
117	96.0426	99.8710
118	97.3571	99.9352
119	98.6763	99.9783
120	100.0000	100.0000

1 YEAR

#	REBATE	EARN
1	1.3448	15.0200
2	4.0169	28.8776
3	7.9985	41.5571
4	13.2727	53.0429
5	19.8223	63.3190
6	27.6306	72.3694
7	36.6810	80.1777
8	46.9571	86.7273
9	58.4429	92.0015
10	71.1224	95.9831
11	84.9800	98.6552
12	100.0000	100.0000

2 YEARS

#	REBATE	EARN
1	.3679	7.6141
2	1.0989	14.9568
3	2.1881	22.0247
4	3.6309	28.8140
5	5.4227	35.3210
6	7.5587	41.5420
7	10.0346	47.4731
8	12.8458	53.1105
9	15.9879	58.4502
10	19.4565	63.4883
11	23.2475	68.2208
12	27.3564	72.6436
13	31.7792	76.7525
14	36.5117	80.5435
15	41.5498	84.0121
16	46.8895	87.1542
17	52.5269	89.9654
18	58.4580	92.4413
19	64.6790	94.5773
20	71.1860	96.3691
21	77.9753	97.8119
22	85.0432	98.9011
23	92.3859	99.6321
24	100.0000	100.0000

3 YEARS

#	REBATE	EARN
1	.1741	5.0191
2	.5201	9.9286
3	1.0357	14.7272
4	1.7186	19.4132
5	2.5666	23.9853
6	3.5777	28.4419
7	4.7495	32.7815
8	6.0801	37.0025
9	7.5673	41.1033
10	9.2091	45.0823
11	11.0034	48.9379
12	12.9482	52.6685
13	15.0416	56.2723
14	17.2815	59.7478
15	19.6662	63.0931
16	22.1935	66.3066
17	24.8618	69.3864
18	27.6691	72.3309
19	30.6136	75.1382
20	33.6934	77.8065
21	36.9069	80.3338
22	40.2522	82.7185
23	43.7277	84.9584
24	47.3315	87.0518
25	51.0621	88.9966
26	54.9177	90.7909
27	58.8967	92.4327
28	62.9975	93.9199
29	67.2185	95.2505
30	71.5581	96.4223
31	76.0147	97.4334
32	80.5868	98.2814
33	85.2728	98.9643
34	90.0714	99.4799
35	94.9809	99.8259
36	100.0000	100.0000

4 YEARS

#	REBATE	EARN
1	.1035	3.7003
2	.3091	7.3450
3	.6155	10.9335
4	1.0213	14.4650
5	1.5253	17.9386
6	2.1627	21.3538
7	2.8226	24.7095
8	3.6134	28.0052
9	4.4972	31.2400
10	5.4729	34.4130
11	6.5393	37.5234
12	7.6951	40.5705
13	8.9391	43.5533
14	10.2703	46.4710
15	11.6875	49.3227
16	13.1895	52.1077
17	14.7753	54.8248
18	16.4436	57.4734
19	18.1935	60.0524
20	20.0239	62.5609
21	21.9336	64.9979
22	23.9217	67.3627
23	25.9872	69.6540
24	28.1289	71.8711
25	30.3460	74.0128
26	32.6373	76.0783
27	35.0021	78.0664
28	37.4391	79.9761
29	39.9476	81.8065
30	42.5266	83.5564
31	45.1752	85.2247
32	47.8923	86.8105
33	50.6773	88.3125
34	53.5290	89.7297
35	56.4467	91.0609
36	59.4295	92.3049
37	62.4766	93.4607
38	65.5870	94.5271
39	68.7600	95.5028
40	71.9948	96.3866
41	75.2905	97.1774
42	78.6462	97.8738
43	82.0614	98.4747
44	85.5350	98.9787
45	89.0665	99.3845
46	92.6550	99.6909
47	96.2997	99.8965
48	100.0000	100.0000

5 YEARS

#	REBATE	EARN
1	.0697	2.9043
2	.2082	5.7768
3	.4145	8.6169
4	.6879	11.4242
5	1.0273	14.1984
6	1.4320	16.9389
7	1.9010	19.6453
8	2.4336	22.3172
9	3.0289	24.9541
10	3.6860	27.5555
11	4.4042	30.1209
12	5.1826	32.6500
13	6.0205	35.1421
14	6.9171	37.5969
15	7.8715	40.0137
16	8.8831	42.3921
17	9.9511	44.7317
18	11.0748	47.0317
19	12.2533	49.2919
20	13.4861	51.5115
21	14.7723	53.6901
22	16.1113	55.8271
23	17.5024	57.9220
24	18.9448	59.9742
25	20.4380	61.9831
26	21.9813	63.9482
27	23.5739	65.8689
28	25.2153	67.7445
29	26.9047	69.5745
30	28.6417	71.3583
31	30.4255	73.0953
32	32.2555	74.7847
33	34.1311	76.4261
34	36.0518	78.0187
35	38.0169	79.5620
36	40.0258	81.0552
37	42.0780	82.4976
38	44.1729	83.8887
39	46.3099	85.2277
40	48.4885	86.5139
41	50.7081	87.7467
42	52.9683	88.9252
43	55.2683	90.0489
44	57.6079	91.1169
45	59.9863	92.1285
46	62.4031	93.0829
47	64.8579	93.9795
48	67.3500	94.8174
49	69.8791	95.5958
50	72.4445	96.3140
51	75.0459	96.9711
52	77.6828	97.5664
53	80.3547	98.0990
54	83.0611	98.5680
55	85.8016	98.9727
56	88.5758	99.3121
57	91.3831	99.5855
58	94.2232	99.7918
59	97.0957	99.9303
60	100.0000	100.0000

6 YEARS

#	REBATE	EARN
1	.0508	2.3733
2	.1517	4.7267
3	.3022	7.0600
4	.5014	9.3730
5	.7488	11.6653
6	1.0438	13.9367
7	1.3857	16.1869
8	1.7739	18.4157
9	2.2077	20.6226
10	2.6867	22.8076
11	3.2102	24.9701
12	3.7776	27.1100
13	4.3884	29.2270
14	5.0419	31.3207
15	5.7376	33.3909
16	6.4749	35.4371
17	7.2534	37.4592
18	8.0724	39.4568
19	8.9314	41.4295
20	9.8300	43.3770
21	10.7675	45.2990
22	11.7435	47.1952
23	12.7575	49.0652
24	13.8089	50.9086
25	14.8973	52.7251
26	16.0221	54.5144
27	17.1830	56.2760
28	18.3794	58.0096
29	19.6109	59.7149
30	20.8769	61.3915
31	22.1771	63.0389
32	23.5110	64.6567
33	24.8782	66.2447
34	26.2781	67.8024
35	27.7105	69.3294
36	29.1748	70.8252
37	30.6706	72.2895
38	32.1976	73.7219
39	33.7553	75.1218
40	35.3433	76.4890
41	36.9611	77.8229
42	38.6085	79.1231
43	40.2851	80.3891
44	41.9904	81.6206
45	43.7240	82.8170
46	45.4856	83.9779
47	47.2749	85.1027
48	49.0914	86.1911
49	50.9348	87.2425
50	52.8048	88.2565
51	54.7010	89.2325
52	56.6230	90.1700
53	58.5705	91.0686
54	60.5432	91.9276
55	62.5408	92.7466
56	64.5629	93.5251
57	66.6091	94.2624
58	68.6793	94.9581
59	70.7730	95.6116
60	72.8900	96.2224
61	75.0299	96.7898
62	77.1924	97.3133
63	79.3774	97.7923
64	81.5843	98.2261
65	83.8131	98.6143
66	86.0633	98.9562
67	88.3347	99.2512
68	90.6270	99.4986
69	92.9400	99.6978
70	95.2733	99.8483
71	97.6267	99.9492
72	100.0000	100.0000

7 YEARS

#	REBATE	EARN
1	.0391	1.9948
2	.1168	3.9765
3	.2325	5.9451
4	.3859	7.9003
5	.5763	9.8419
6	.8033	11.7698
7	1.0664	13.6838
8	1.3652	15.5836
9	1.6991	17.4692
10	2.0678	19.3404
11	2.4706	21.1968
12	2.9073	23.0384
13	3.3773	24.8649
14	3.8803	26.6761
15	4.4157	28.4719
16	4.9832	30.2520
17	5.5823	32.0162
18	6.2126	33.7643
19	6.8738	35.4961
20	7.5653	37.2114
21	8.2869	38.9099
22	9.0380	40.5914
23	9.8184	42.2558
24	10.6275	43.9027
25	11.4652	45.5320
26	12.3309	47.1433
27	13.2243	48.7365
28	14.1451	50.3114
29	15.0928	51.8676
30	16.0672	53.4050
31	17.0679	54.9232
32	18.0945	56.4220
33	19.1466	57.9013
34	20.2241	59.3606
35	21.3264	60.7997
36	22.4534	62.2185
37	23.6046	63.6165
38	24.7798	64.9935
39	25.9786	66.3493
40	27.2007	67.6835
41	28.4459	68.9959
42	29.7138	70.2862
43	31.0041	71.5541
44	32.3165	72.7993
45	33.6507	74.0214
46	35.0065	75.2202
47	36.3835	76.3954
48	37.7815	77.5466
49	39.2003	78.6736
50	40.6394	79.7759
51	42.0987	80.8534
52	43.5780	81.9055
53	45.0768	82.9321
54	46.5950	83.9328
55	48.1324	84.9072
56	49.6886	85.8549
57	51.2635	86.7757
58	52.8567	87.6691
59	54.4680	88.5348
60	56.0973	89.3725
61	57.7442	90.1816
62	59.4086	90.9620
63	61.0901	91.7131
64	62.7886	92.4347
65	64.5039	93.1262
66	66.2357	93.7874
67	67.9838	94.4177
68	69.7480	95.0168
69	71.5281	95.5843
70	73.3239	96.1197
71	75.1351	96.6227
72	76.9616	97.0927
73	78.8032	97.5294
74	80.6596	97.9322
75	82.5308	98.3009

#	REBATE	EARN
75	82.5308	98.3009
76	84.4164	98.6348
77	86.3162	98.9336
78	88.2302	99.1967
79	90.1581	99.4237
80	92.0997	99.6141
81	94.0549	99.7675
82	96.0235	99.8832
83	98.0052	99.9609
84	100.0000	100.0000

8 YEARS

#	REBATE	EARN
1	.0313	1.7121
2	.0935	3.4153
3	.1862	5.1095
4	.3090	6.7946
5	.4614	8.4704
6	.6432	10.1369
7	.8539	11.7938
8	1.0931	13.4411
9	1.3605	15.0787
10	1.6556	16.7063
11	1.9782	18.3239
12	2.3278	19.9314
13	2.7042	21.5286
14	3.1069	23.1154
15	3.5356	24.6916
16	3.9900	26.2570
17	4.4697	27.8117
18	4.9744	29.3553
19	5.5037	30.8878
20	6.0574	32.4090
21	6.6352	33.9188
22	7.2366	35.4170
23	7.8614	36.9034
24	8.5093	38.3779
25	9.1800	39.8404
26	9.8732	41.2906
27	10.5885	42.7285
28	11.3258	44.1538
29	12.0846	45.5663
30	12.8648	46.9660
31	13.6660	48.3526
32	14.4880	49.7260
33	15.3305	51.0860
34	16.1931	52.4324
35	17.0758	53.7650
36	17.9781	55.0837
37	18.8999	56.3882
38	19.8408	57.6784
39	20.8007	58.9541
40	21.7793	60.2150
41	22.7762	61.4611
42	23.7914	62.6920
43	24.8245	63.9076
44	25.8753	65.1077
45	26.9436	66.2921
46	28.0292	67.4606
47	29.1318	68.6129
48	30.2511	69.7489
49	31.3871	70.8682
50	32.5394	71.9708
51	33.7079	73.0564
52	34.8923	74.1247
53	36.0924	75.1755
54	37.3080	76.2086
55	38.5389	77.2238
56	39.7850	78.2207

#	REBATE	EARN
57	41.0459	79.1993
58	42.3216	80.1592
59	43.6118	81.1001
60	44.9163	82.0219
61	46.2350	82.9242
62	47.5676	83.8069
63	48.9140	84.6695
64	50.2740	85.5120
65	51.6474	86.3340
66	53.0340	87.1352
67	54.4337	87.9154
68	55.8462	88.6742
69	57.2715	89.4115
70	58.7094	90.1268
71	60.1596	90.8200
72	61.6221	91.4907
73	63.0966	92.1386
74	64.5830	92.7634
75	66.0812	93.3648
76	67.5910	93.9426
77	69.1122	94.4963
78	70.6447	95.0256
79	72.1883	95.5303
80	73.7430	96.0100
81	75.3084	96.4644
82	76.8846	96.8931
83	78.4714	97.2958
84	80.0686	97.6722
85	81.6761	98.0218
86	83.2937	98.3444
87	84.9213	98.6395
88	86.5589	98.9069
89	88.2062	99.1461
90	89.8631	99.3568
91	91.5296	99.5386
92	93.2054	99.6910
93	94.8905	99.8138
94	96.5847	99.9065
95	98.2879	99.9687
96	100.0000	100.0000

9 YEARS

#	REBATE	EARN
1	.0258	1.4936
2	.0772	2.9808
3	.1536	4.4618
4	.2549	5.9363
5	.3807	7.4043
6	.5307	8.8657
7	.7045	10.3204
8	.9019	11.7684
9	1.1225	13.2094
10	1.3660	14.6435
11	1.6322	16.0706
12	1.9207	17.4905
13	2.2312	18.9031
14	2.5635	20.3084
15	2.9172	21.7063
16	3.2921	23.0967
17	3.6879	24.4794
18	4.1043	25.8544
19	4.5411	27.2215
20	4.9980	28.5807
21	5.4746	29.9318
22	5.9709	31.2748
23	6.4864	32.6095
24	7.0210	33.9358
25	7.5744	35.2536
26	8.1463	36.5628
27	8.7365	37.8634

#	REBATE	EARN
28	9.3448	39.1550
29	9.9710	40.4377
30	10.6147	41.7114
31	11.2758	42.9759
32	11.9540	44.2310
33	12.6491	45.4767
34	13.3609	46.7128
35	14.0891	47.9393
36	14.8337	49.1559
37	15.5942	50.3626
38	16.3706	51.5592
39	17.1626	52.7455
40	17.9700	53.9215
41	18.7926	55.0870
42	19.6302	56.2419
43	20.4826	57.3860
44	21.3496	58.5192
45	22.2311	59.6413
46	23.1268	60.7522
47	24.0365	61.8517
48	24.9601	62.9398
49	25.8974	64.0161
50	26.8481	65.0806
51	27.8122	66.1332
52	28.7894	67.1736
53	29.7796	68.2017
54	30.7827	69.2173
55	31.7983	70.2204
56	32.8264	71.2106
57	33.8668	72.1878
58	34.9194	73.1519
59	35.9839	74.1026
60	37.0602	75.0399
61	38.1483	75.9635
62	39.2478	76.8732
63	40.3587	77.7689
64	41.4808	78.6504
65	42.6140	79.5174
66	43.7581	80.3698
67	44.9130	81.2074
68	46.0785	82.0300
69	47.2545	82.8374
70	48.4408	83.6294
71	49.6374	84.4058
72	50.8441	85.1663
73	52.0607	85.9109
74	53.2872	86.6391
75	54.5233	87.3509
76	55.7690	88.0460
77	57.0241	88.7242
78	58.2886	89.3853
79	59.5623	90.0290
80	60.8450	90.6552
81	62.1366	91.2635
82	63.4372	91.8537
83	64.7464	92.4256
84	66.0642	92.9790
85	67.3905	93.5136
86	68.7252	94.0291
87	70.0682	94.5254
88	71.4193	95.0020
89	72.7785	95.4589
90	74.1456	95.8957
91	75.5206	96.3121
92	76.9033	96.7079
93	78.2937	97.0828
94	79.6916	97.4365
95	81.0969	97.7688
96	82.5095	98.0793

#	REBATE	EARN
97	83.9294	98.3678
98	85.3565	98.6340
99	86.7906	98.8775
100	88.2316	99.0981
101	89.6796	99.2955
102	91.1343	99.4693
103	92.5957	99.6193
104	94.0637	99.7451
105	95.5382	99.8464
106	97.0192	99.9228
107	98.5064	99.9742
108	100.0000	100.0000

10 YEARS

#	REBATE	EARN
1	.0218	1.3199
2	.0652	2.6353
3	.1298	3.9462
4	.2153	5.2524
5	.3216	6.5539
6	.4483	7.8507
7	.5951	9.1426
8	.7619	10.4297
9	.9482	11.7118
10	1.1539	12.9889
11	1.3788	14.2609
12	1.6225	15.5277
13	1.8848	16.7894
14	2.1654	18.0457
15	2.4642	19.2967
16	2.7809	20.5422
17	3.1153	21.7823
18	3.4670	23.0168
19	3.8360	24.2456
20	4.2219	25.4687
21	4.6246	26.6860
22	5.0437	27.8974
23	5.4792	29.1029
24	5.9308	30.3023
25	6.3983	31.4956
26	6.8814	32.6827
27	7.3800	33.8635
28	7.8938	35.0380
29	8.4227	36.2060
30	8.9665	37.3675
31	9.5249	38.5223
32	10.0978	39.6705
33	10.6850	40.8118
34	11.2862	41.9462
35	11.9014	43.0737
36	12.5303	44.1940
37	13.1728	45.3073
38	13.8286	46.4132
39	14.4976	47.5118
40	15.1796	48.6029
41	15.8745	49.6864
42	16.5821	50.7623
43	17.3021	51.8304
44	18.0345	52.8907
45	18.7791	53.9429
46	19.5357	54.9871
47	20.3042	56.0231
48	21.0844	57.0508
49	21.8761	58.0701
50	22.6792	59.0809
51	23.4936	60.0831
52	24.3191	61.0765
53	25.1555	62.0610
54	26.0028	63.0365
55	26.8607	64.0030

#	REBATE	EARN
56	27.7292	64.9602
57	28.6081	65.9081
58	29.4972	66.8465
59	30.3964	67.7753
60	31.3056	68.6944
61	32.2247	69.6036
62	33.1535	70.5028
63	34.0919	71.3919
64	35.0398	72.2708
65	35.9970	73.1393
66	36.9635	73.9972
67	37.9390	74.8445
68	38.9235	75.6809
69	39.9169	76.5064
70	40.9191	77.3208
71	41.9299	78.1239
72	42.9492	78.9156
73	43.9769	79.6958
74	45.0129	80.4643
75	46.0571	81.2209
76	47.1093	81.9655
77	48.1696	82.6979
78	49.2377	83.4179
79	50.3136	84.1255
80	51.3971	84.8204
81	52.4882	85.5024
82	53.5868	86.1714
83	54.6927	86.8272
84	55.8060	87.4697
85	56.9263	88.0986
86	58.0538	88.7138
87	59.1882	89.3150
88	60.3295	89.9022
89	61.4777	90.4751
90	62.6325	91.0335
91	63.7940	91.5773
92	64.9620	92.1062
93	66.1365	92.6200
94	67.3173	93.1186
95	68.5044	93.6017
96	69.6977	94.0692
97	70.8971	94.5208
98	72.1026	94.9563
99	73.3140	95.3754
100	74.5313	95.7781
101	75.7544	96.1640
102	76.9832	96.5330
103	78.2177	96.8847
104	79.4578	97.2191
105	80.7033	97.5358
106	81.9543	97.8346
107	83.2106	98.1152
108	84.4723	98.3775
109	85.7391	98.6212
110	87.0111	98.8461
111	88.2882	99.0518
112	89.5703	99.2381
113	90.8574	99.4049
114	92.1493	99.5517
115	93.4461	99.6784
116	94.7476	99.7847
117	96.0538	99.8702
118	97.3647	99.9348
119	98.6801	99.9782
120	100.0000	100.0000

1 YEAR

#	REBATE	EARN
1	1.3458	15.0145
2	4.0195	28.8683
3	8.0033	41.5456
4	13.2797	53.0306
5	19.8314	63.3070
6	27.6415	72.3585
7	36.6930	80.1686
8	46.9694	86.7203
9	58.4544	91.9967
10	71.1317	95.9805
11	84.9855	98.6542
12	100.0000	100.0000

2 YEARS

#	REBATE	EARN
1	.3685	7.6084
2	1.1004	14.9464
3	2.1911	22.0103
4	3.6356	28.7964
5	5.4293	35.3010
6	7.5674	41.5202
7	10.0455	47.4502
8	12.8589	53.0870
9	16.0031	58.4268
10	19.4738	63.4654
11	23.2666	68.1988
12	27.3771	72.6229
13	31.8012	76.7334
14	36.5346	80.5262
15	41.5732	83.9969
16	46.9130	87.1411
17	52.5498	89.9545
18	58.4798	92.4326
19	64.6990	94.5707
20	71.2036	96.3644
21	77.9897	97.8089
22	85.0536	98.8996
23	92.3916	99.6315
24	100.0000	100.0000

3 YEARS

#	REBATE	EARN
1	.1745	5.0136
2	.5212	9.9181
3	1.0378	14.7122
4	1.7220	19.3944
5	2.5716	23.9630
6	3.5843	28.4167
7	4.7581	32.7538
8	6.0907	36.9727
9	7.5799	41.0719
10	9.2238	45.0497
11	11.0203	48.9045
12	12.9673	52.6346
13	15.0628	56.2383
14	17.3048	59.7140
15	19.6913	63.0598
16	22.2205	66.2741
17	24.8905	69.3550
18	27.6992	72.3008
19	30.6450	75.1095
20	33.7259	77.7795
21	36.9402	80.3087
22	40.2860	82.6952
23	43.7617	84.9372
24	47.3654	87.0327
25	51.0955	88.9797
26	54.9503	90.7762
27	58.9281	92.4201
28	63.0273	93.9093
29	67.2462	95.2419
30	71.5833	96.4157
31	76.0370	97.4284
32	80.6056	98.2780
33	85.2878	98.9622
34	90.0819	99.4788
35	94.9864	99.8255
36	100.0000	100.0000

4 YEARS

#	REBATE	EARN
1	.1038	3.6950
2	.3100	7.3348
3	.6172	10.9188
4	1.0241	14.4460
5	1.5293	17.9159
6	2.1316	21.3275
7	2.8296	24.6802
8	3.6221	27.9731
9	4.5078	31.2053
10	5.4854	34.3762
11	6.5537	37.4848
12	7.7116	40.5303
13	8.9578	43.5118
14	10.2911	46.4285
15	11.7104	49.2796
16	13.2145	52.0640
17	14.8023	54.7810
18	16.4727	57.4296
19	18.2245	60.0088
20	20.0567	62.5178
21	21.9682	64.9556
22	23.9580	67.3212
23	26.0250	69.6136
24	28.1681	71.8319
25	30.3864	73.9750
26	32.6788	76.0420
27	35.0444	78.0318
28	37.4822	79.9433
29	39.9912	81.7755
30	42.5704	83.5273
31	45.2190	85.1977
32	47.9360	86.7855
33	50.7204	88.2896
34	53.5715	89.7089
35	56.4882	91.0422
36	59.4697	92.2884
37	62.5152	93.4463
38	65.6238	94.5146
39	68.7947	95.4922
40	72.0269	96.3779
41	75.3198	97.1704
42	78.6725	97.8684
43	82.0841	98.4707
44	85.5540	98.9759
45	89.0812	99.3828
46	92.6652	99.6900
47	96.3050	99.8962
48	100.0000	100.0000

5 YEARS

#	REBATE	EARN
1	.0699	2.8993
2	.2089	5.7670
3	.4159	8.6026
4	.6902	11.4057
5	1.0307	14.1759
6	1.4366	16.9128
7	1.9070	19.6157
8	2.4410	22.2844
9	3.0379	24.9184
10	3.6968	27.5171
11	4.4168	30.0801
12	5.1971	32.6070
13	6.0369	35.0971
14	6.9355	37.5501
15	7.8920	39.9655
16	8.9056	42.3426
17	9.9757	44.6810
18	11.1014	46.9802
19	12.2820	49.2397
20	13.5168	51.4589
21	14.8050	53.6372
22	16.1460	55.7741
23	17.5390	57.8691
24	18.9833	59.9215
25	20.4783	61.9309
26	22.0232	63.8966
27	23.6175	65.8180
28	25.2604	67.6945
29	26.9513	69.5256
30	28.6895	71.3105
31	30.4744	73.0487
32	32.3055	74.7396
33	34.1820	76.3825
34	36.1034	77.9768
35	38.0691	79.5217
36	40.0785	81.0167
37	42.1309	82.4610
38	44.2259	83.8540
39	46.3628	85.1950
40	48.5411	86.4832
41	50.7603	87.7180
42	53.0198	88.8986
43	55.3190	90.0243
44	57.6574	91.0944
45	60.0345	92.1080
46	62.4499	93.0645
47	64.9029	93.9631
48	67.3930	94.8029
49	69.9199	95.5832
50	72.4829	96.3032
51	75.0816	96.9621
52	77.7156	97.5590
53	80.3843	98.0930
54	83.0872	98.5634
55	85.8241	98.9693
56	88.5943	99.3098
57	91.3974	99.5841
58	94.2330	99.7911
59	97.1007	99.9301
60	100.0000	100.0000

6 YEARS

#	REBATE	EARN
1	.0510	2.3685
2	.1524	4.7174
3	.3034	7.0464
4	.5034	9.3552
5	.7517	11.6435
6	1.0477	13.9112
7	1.3908	16.1578
8	1.7803	18.3832
9	2.2157	20.5870
10	2.6962	22.7690
11	3.2213	24.9288
12	3.7904	27.0661
13	4.4030	29.1807
14	5.0583	31.2722
15	5.7559	33.3403
16	6.4952	35.3848
17	7.2757	37.4052
18	8.0967	39.4013
19	8.9578	41.3726
20	9.8583	43.3190
21	10.7979	45.2401
22	11.7759	47.1354
23	12.7919	49.0047
24	13.8453	50.8477
25	14.9356	52.6638
26	16.0624	54.4529
27	17.2251	56.2145
28	18.4234	57.9482
29	19.6566	59.6537
30	20.9244	61.3306
31	22.2262	62.9785
32	23.5616	64.5971
33	24.9303	66.1858
34	26.3316	67.7444
35	27.7653	69.2723
36	29.2308	70.7692
37	30.7277	72.2347
38	32.2556	73.6684
39	33.8142	75.0697
40	35.4029	76.4384
41	37.0215	77.7738
42	38.6694	79.0756
43	40.3463	80.3434
44	42.0518	81.5766
45	43.7855	82.7749
46	45.5471	83.9376
47	47.3362	85.0644
48	49.1523	86.1547
49	50.9953	87.2081
50	52.8646	88.2241
51	54.7599	89.2021
52	56.6810	90.1417
53	58.6274	91.0422
54	60.5987	91.9033
55	62.5948	92.7243
56	64.6152	93.5048
57	66.6597	94.2441
58	68.7278	94.9417
59	70.8193	95.5970
60	72.9339	96.2096
61	75.0712	96.7787
62	77.2310	97.3038
63	79.4130	97.7843
64	81.6168	98.2197
65	83.8422	98.6092
66	86.0888	98.9523
67	88.3565	99.2483
68	90.6448	99.4966
69	92.9536	99.6966
70	95.2826	99.8476
71	97.6315	99.9490
72	100.0000	100.0000

7 YEARS

#	REBATE	EARN
1	.0393	1.9903
2	.1173	3.9677
3	.2336	5.9320
4	.3876	7.8832
5	.5788	9.8209
6	.8068	11.7451
7	1.0710	13.6555
8	1.3710	15.5520
9	1.7062	17.4344
10	2.0762	19.3024
11	2.4806	21.1559
12	2.9188	22.9947
13	3.3905	24.8185
14	3.8952	26.6273
15	4.4324	28.4207
16	5.0017	30.1986
17	5.6027	31.9608
18	6.2349	33.7070
19	6.8980	35.4371
20	7.5914	37.1507
21	8.3150	38.8478
22	9.0681	40.5280
23	9.8504	42.1912
24	10.6616	43.8370
25	11.5012	45.4654
26	12.3689	47.0759
27	13.2643	48.6685
28	14.1870	50.2428
29	15.1366	51.7987
30	16.1129	53.3357
31	17.1154	54.8538
32	18.1437	56.3526
33	19.1976	57.8319
34	20.2768	59.2915
35	21.3807	60.7309
36	22.5093	62.1501
37	23.6620	63.5486
38	24.8386	64.9263
39	26.0387	66.2828
40	27.2621	67.6179
41	28.5085	68.9312
42	29.7775	70.2225
43	31.0688	71.4915
44	32.3821	72.7379
45	33.7172	73.9613
46	35.0737	75.1614
47	36.4514	76.3380
48	37.8499	77.4907
49	39.2691	78.6193
50	40.7085	79.7232
51	42.1681	80.8024
52	43.6474	81.8563
53	45.1462	82.8846
54	46.6643	83.8871
55	48.2013	84.8634
56	49.7572	85.8130
57	51.3315	86.7357
58	52.9241	87.6311
59	54.5346	88.4988
60	56.1630	89.3384
61	57.8088	90.1496
62	59.4720	90.9319
63	61.1522	91.6850
64	62.8493	92.4086
65	64.5629	93.1020
66	66.2930	93.7651
67	68.0392	94.3973
68	69.8014	94.9983
69	71.5793	95.5676
70	73.3727	96.1048
71	75.1815	96.6095
72	77.0053	97.0812
73	78.8441	97.5194
74	80.6976	97.9238
75	82.5656	98.2938

ACTUARIAL REBATE AND EARNINGS

	REBATE	EARN
75	82.5656	98.2938
76	84.4480	98.6290
77	86.3445	98.9290
78	88.2549	99.1932
79	90.1791	99.4212
80	92.1168	99.6124
81	94.0680	99.7664
82	96.0323	99.8827
83	98.0097	99.9607
84	100.0000	100.0000

8 YEARS

#	REBATE	EARN
1	.0315	1.7079
2	.0940	3.4069
3	.1871	5.0971
4	.3105	6.7783
5	.4637	8.4504
6	.6463	10.1132
7	.8580	11.7666
8	1.0983	13.4106
9	1.3669	15.0448
10	1.6633	16.6694
11	1.9872	18.2840
12	2.3383	19.8886
13	2.7162	21.4830
14	3.1205	23.0671
15	3.5508	24.6408
16	4.0069	26.2039
17	4.4884	27.7563
18	4.9949	29.2978
19	5.5260	30.8282
20	6.0816	32.3475
21	6.6612	33.8555
22	7.2646	35.3520
23	7.8913	36.8369
24	8.5412	38.3099
25	9.2138	39.7711
26	9.9089	41.2201
27	10.6262	42.6568
28	11.3654	44.0811
29	12.1262	45.4928
30	12.9082	46.8918
31	13.7114	48.2777
32	14.5352	49.6506
33	15.3795	51.0101
34	16.2440	52.3561
35	17.1284	53.6885
36	18.0325	55.0071
37	18.9559	56.3115
38	19.8985	57.6018
39	20.8600	58.8776
40	21.8401	60.1388
41	22.8386	61.3852
42	23.8552	62.6166
43	24.8896	63.8327
44	25.9418	65.0335
45	27.0113	66.2186
46	28.0980	67.3878
47	29.2017	68.5410
48	30.3221	69.6779
49	31.4590	70.7983
50	32.6122	71.9020
51	33.7814	72.9887
52	34.9665	74.0582
53	36.1673	75.1104
54	37.3834	76.1448
55	38.6148	77.1614
56	39.8612	78.1599

	REBATE	EARN
57	41.1224	79.1400
58	42.3982	80.1015
59	43.6885	81.0441
60	44.9929	81.9675
61	46.3115	82.8716
62	47.6439	83.7560
63	48.9899	84.6205
64	50.3494	85.4648
65	51.7223	86.2886
66	53.1082	87.0918
67	54.5072	87.8738
68	55.9189	88.6346
69	57.3432	89.3738
70	58.7799	90.0911
71	60.2289	90.7862
72	61.6901	91.4588
73	63.1631	92.1087
74	64.6480	92.7354
75	66.1445	93.3388
76	67.6525	93.9184
77	69.1718	94.4740
78	70.7022	95.0051
79	72.2437	95.5116
80	73.7961	95.9931
81	75.3592	96.4492
82	76.9329	96.8795
83	78.5170	97.2838
84	80.1114	97.6617
85	81.7160	98.0128
86	83.3306	98.3367
87	84.9552	98.6331
88	86.5894	98.9017
89	88.2334	99.1420
90	89.8868	99.3537
91	91.5496	99.5363
92	93.2217	99.6895
93	94.9029	99.8129
94	96.5931	99.9060
95	98.2921	99.9685
96	100.0000	100.0000

9 YEARS

#	REBATE	EARN
1	.0260	1.4895
2	.0776	2.9729
3	.1545	4.4500
4	.2563	5.9208
5	.3828	7.3852
6	.5336	8.8431
7	.7083	10.2944
8	.9067	11.7390
9	1.1284	13.1769
10	1.3731	14.6079
11	1.6405	16.0319
12	1.9303	17.4489
13	2.2422	18.8588
14	2.5760	20.2614
15	2.9313	21.6567
16	3.3077	23.0445
17	3.7052	24.4248
18	4.1233	25.7975
19	4.5618	27.1624
20	5.0204	28.5195
21	5.4989	29.8686
22	5.9970	31.2097
23	6.5144	32.5426
24	7.0508	33.8672
25	7.6061	35.1834
26	8.1799	36.4911
27	8.7720	37.7902

	REBATE	EARN
28	9.3822	39.0805
29	10.0103	40.3620
30	10.6559	41.6345
31	11.3189	42.8980
32	11.9990	44.1521
33	12.6959	45.3970
34	13.4096	46.6324
35	14.1397	47.8581
36	14.8860	49.0742
37	15.6483	50.2804
38	16.4265	51.4766
39	17.2202	52.6626
40	18.0292	53.8384
41	18.8535	55.0038
42	19.6927	56.1586
43	20.5467	57.3027
44	21.4152	58.4360
45	22.2981	59.5583
46	23.1952	60.6695
47	24.1063	61.7694
48	25.0312	62.8578
49	25.9698	63.9347
50	26.9217	64.9998
51	27.8869	66.0530
52	28.8652	67.0942
53	29.8565	68.1231
54	30.8604	69.1396
55	31.8769	70.1435
56	32.9058	71.1348
57	33.9470	72.1131
58	35.0002	73.0783
59	36.0653	74.0302
60	37.1422	74.9688
61	38.2306	75.8937
62	39.3305	76.8048
63	40.4417	77.7019
64	41.5640	78.5848
65	42.6973	79.4533
66	43.8414	80.3073
67	44.9962	81.1465
68	46.1616	81.9708
69	47.3374	82.7798
70	48.5234	83.5735
71	49.7196	84.3517
72	50.9258	85.1140
73	52.1419	85.8603
74	53.3676	86.5904
75	54.6030	87.3041
76	55.8479	88.0010
77	57.1020	88.6811
78	58.3655	89.3441
79	59.6380	89.9897
80	60.9195	90.6178
81	62.2098	91.2280
82	63.5089	91.8201
83	64.8166	92.3939
84	66.1328	92.9492
85	67.4574	93.4856
86	68.7903	94.0030
87	70.1314	94.5011
88	71.4805	94.9796
89	72.8376	95.4382
90	74.2025	95.8767
91	75.5752	96.2948
92	76.9555	96.6923
93	78.3433	97.0687
94	79.7386	97.4240
95	81.1412	97.7578
96	82.5511	98.0697

	REBATE	EARN
97	83.9681	98.3595
98	85.3921	98.6269
99	86.8231	98.8716
100	88.2610	99.0933
101	89.7056	99.2917
102	91.1569	99.4664
103	92.6148	99.6172
104	94.0792	99.7437
105	95.5500	99.8455
106	97.0271	99.9224
107	98.5105	99.9740
108	100.0000	100.0000

10 YEARS

#	REBATE	EARN
1	.0220	1.3161
2	.0656	2.6278
3	.1306	3.9351
4	.2166	5.2377
5	.3235	6.5358
6	.4509	7.8292
7	.5986	9.1178
8	.7662	10.4017
9	.9536	11.6806
10	1.1604	12.9547
11	1.3864	14.2237
12	1.6314	15.4877
13	1.8950	16.7465
14	2.1770	18.0002
15	2.4773	19.2485
16	2.7955	20.4915
17	3.1313	21.7291
18	3.4847	22.9612
19	3.8553	24.1877
20	4.2429	25.4086
21	4.6473	26.6238
22	5.0682	27.8332
23	5.5054	29.0366
24	5.9588	30.2342
25	6.4281	31.4257
26	6.9130	32.6111
27	7.4135	33.7902
28	7.9292	34.9631
29	8.4599	36.1297
30	9.0055	37.2897
31	9.5658	38.4433
32	10.1406	39.5902
33	10.7296	40.7303
34	11.3328	41.8637
35	11.9498	42.9902
36	12.5805	44.1096
37	13.2248	45.2220
38	13.8824	46.3272
39	14.5531	47.4250
40	15.2369	48.5156
41	15.9335	49.5986
42	16.6427	50.6740
43	17.3645	51.7417
44	18.0985	52.8017
45	18.8447	53.8537
46	19.6028	54.8978
47	20.3728	55.9337
48	21.1545	56.9614
49	21.9476	57.9808
50	22.7522	58.9917
51	23.5679	59.9941
52	24.3947	60.9878
53	25.2324	61.9726
54	26.0808	62.9486
55	26.9399	63.9155

	REBATE	EARN
56	27.8095	64.8733
57	28.6894	65.8218
58	29.5795	66.7609
59	30.4796	67.6904
60	31.3897	68.6103
61	32.3096	69.5204
62	33.2391	70.4205
63	34.1782	71.3106
64	35.1267	72.1905
65	36.0845	73.0601
66	37.0514	73.9192
67	38.0274	74.7676
68	39.0122	75.6053
69	40.0059	76.4321
70	41.0083	77.2478
71	42.0192	78.0524
72	43.0386	78.8455
73	44.0663	79.6272
74	45.1022	80.3972
75	46.1463	81.1553
76	47.1983	81.9015
77	48.2583	82.6355
78	49.3260	83.3573
79	50.4014	84.0665
80	51.4844	84.7631
81	52.5750	85.4469
82	53.6728	86.1176
83	54.7780	86.7752
84	55.8904	87.4195
85	57.0098	88.0502
86	58.1363	88.6672
87	59.2697	89.2704
88	60.4098	89.8594
89	61.5567	90.4342
90	62.7103	90.9945
91	63.8703	91.5401
92	65.0369	92.0708
93	66.2098	92.5865
94	67.3889	93.0870
95	68.5743	93.5719
96	69.7658	94.0412
97	70.9634	94.4946
98	72.1668	94.9318
99	73.3762	95.3527
100	74.5914	95.7571
101	75.8123	96.1447
102	77.0388	96.5153
103	78.2709	96.8687
104	79.5085	97.2045
105	80.7515	97.5227
106	81.9998	97.8230
107	83.2535	98.1050
108	84.5123	98.3686
109	85.7763	98.6136
110	87.0453	98.8396
111	88.3194	99.0464
112	89.5983	99.2338
113	90.8822	99.4014
114	92.1708	99.5491
115	93.4642	99.6765
116	94.7623	99.7834
117	96.0649	99.8694
118	97.3722	99.9344
119	98.6839	99.9780
120	100.0000	100.0000

1 YEAR

#	REBATE	EARN
1	1.3468	15.0090
2	4.0222	28.8591
3	8.0081	41.5342
4	13.2867	53.0183
5	19.8406	63.2950
6	27.6524	72.3476
7	36.7050	80.1594
8	46.9817	86.7133
9	58.4658	91.9919
10	71.1409	95.9778
11	84.9910	98.6532
12	100.0000	100.0000

2 YEARS

#	REBATE	EARN
1	.3690	7.6027
2	1.1020	14.9359
3	2.1940	21.9958
4	3.6403	28.7788
5	5.4359	35.2809
6	7.5761	41.4984
7	10.0564	47.4273
8	12.8719	53.0636
9	16.0183	58.4034
10	19.4911	63.4425
11	23.2857	68.1768
12	27.3978	72.6022
13	31.8232	76.7143
14	36.5575	80.5089
15	41.5966	83.9817
16	46.9364	87.1281
17	52.5727	89.9436
18	58.5016	92.4239
19	64.7191	94.5641
20	71.2212	96.3597
21	78.0042	97.8060
22	85.0641	98.8980
23	92.3973	99.6310
24	100.0000	100.0000

3 YEARS

#	REBATE	EARN
1	.1749	5.0081
2	.5223	9.9077
3	1.0400	14.6973
4	1.7255	19.3756
5	2.5766	23.9408
6	3.5910	28.3915
7	4.7666	32.7261
8	6.1012	36.9430
9	7.5926	41.0405
10	9.2386	45.0171
11	11.0372	48.8711
12	12.9863	52.6008
13	15.0839	56.2044
14	17.3280	59.6803
15	19.7165	63.0266
16	22.2475	66.2417
17	24.9191	69.3236
18	27.7293	72.2707
19	30.6764	75.0809
20	33.7583	77.7525
21	36.9734	80.2835
22	40.3197	82.6720
23	43.7956	84.9161
24	47.3992	87.0137
25	51.1289	88.9628
26	54.9829	90.7614
27	58.9595	92.4074
28	63.0570	93.8988
29	67.2739	95.2334
30	71.6085	96.4090
31	76.0592	97.4234
32	80.6244	98.2745
33	85.3027	98.9600
34	90.0923	99.4777
35	94.9919	99.8251
36	100.0000	100.0000

4 YEARS

#	REBATE	EARN
1	.1041	3.6897
2	.3108	7.3247
3	.6189	10.9041
4	1.0268	14.4272
5	1.5333	17.8932
6	2.1370	21.3014
7	2.8366	24.6509
8	3.6308	27.9410
9	4.5183	31.1708
10	5.4979	34.3395
11	6.5682	37.4462
12	7.7282	40.4902
13	8.9764	43.4705
14	10.3118	46.3862
15	11.7332	49.2365
16	13.2394	52.0205
17	14.8293	54.7373
18	16.5017	57.3859
19	18.2554	59.9654
20	20.0895	62.4749
21	22.0028	64.9133
22	23.9942	67.2798
23	26.0627	69.5733
24	28.2072	71.7928
25	30.4267	73.9373
26	32.7202	76.0058
27	35.0867	77.9972
28	37.5251	79.9105
29	40.0346	81.7446
30	42.6141	83.4983
31	45.2627	85.1707
32	47.9795	86.7606
33	50.7635	88.2668
34	53.6138	89.6882
35	56.5295	91.0236
36	59.5098	92.2718
37	62.5538	93.4318
38	65.6605	94.5021
39	68.8292	95.4817
40	72.0590	96.3692
41	75.3491	97.1634
42	78.6986	97.8630
43	82.1068	98.4667
44	85.5728	98.9732
45	89.0959	99.3811
46	92.6753	99.6892
47	96.3103	99.8959
48	100.0000	100.0000

5 YEARS

#	REBATE	EARN
1	.0702	2.8943
2	.2096	5.7572
3	.4173	8.5884
4	.6924	11.3873
5	1.0340	14.1536
6	1.4411	16.8867
7	1.9129	19.5863
8	2.4485	22.2518
9	3.0470	24.8828
10	3.7075	27.4789
11	4.4293	30.0395
12	5.2115	32.5641
13	6.0533	35.0523
14	6.9539	37.5036
15	7.9124	39.9174
16	8.9281	42.2932
17	10.0003	44.6306
18	11.1280	46.9289
19	12.3107	49.1877
20	13.5475	51.4064
21	14.8378	53.5844
22	16.1807	55.7213
23	17.5756	57.8163
24	19.0218	59.8690
25	20.5185	61.8788
26	22.0652	63.8451
27	23.6610	65.7672
28	25.3054	67.6446
29	26.9977	69.4767
30	28.7372	71.2628
31	30.5233	73.0023
32	32.3554	74.6946
33	34.2328	76.3390
34	36.1549	77.9348
35	38.1212	79.4815
36	40.1310	80.9782
37	42.1837	82.4244
38	44.2787	83.8193
39	46.4156	85.1622
40	48.5936	86.4525
41	50.8123	87.6893
42	53.0711	88.8720
43	55.3694	89.9997
44	57.7068	91.0719
45	60.0826	92.0876
46	62.4964	93.0461
47	64.9477	93.9467
48	67.4359	94.7885
49	69.9605	95.5707
50	72.5211	96.2925
51	75.1172	96.9530
52	77.7482	97.5515
53	80.4137	98.0871
54	83.1133	98.5589
55	85.8464	98.9660
56	88.6127	99.3076
57	91.4116	99.5827
58	94.2428	99.7904
59	97.1057	99.9298
60	100.0000	100.0000

6 YEARS

#	REBATE	EARN
1	.0512	2.3638
2	.1530	4.7081
3	.3046	7.0327
4	.5053	9.3374
5	.7546	11.6219
6	1.0517	13.8858
7	1.3960	16.1289
8	1.7868	18.3510
9	2.2236	20.5516
10	2.7057	22.7306
11	3.2324	24.8877
12	3.8033	27.0224
13	4.4176	29.1346
14	5.0748	31.2239
15	5.7743	33.2900
16	6.5155	35.3326
17	7.2980	37.3514
18	8.1210	39.3459
19	8.9841	41.3160
20	9.8867	43.2613
21	10.8283	45.1813
22	11.8083	47.0759
23	12.8263	48.9445
24	13.8816	50.7869
25	14.9739	52.6028
26	16.1026	54.3916
27	17.2672	56.1532
28	18.4673	57.8870
29	19.7023	59.5927
30	20.9717	61.2700
31	22.2752	62.9184
32	23.6122	64.5376
33	24.9823	66.1270
34	26.3850	67.6864
35	27.8199	69.2154
36	29.2866	70.7134
37	30.7846	72.1801
38	32.3136	73.6150
39	33.8730	75.0177
40	35.4624	76.3878
41	37.0816	77.7248
42	38.7300	79.0283
43	40.4073	80.2977
44	42.1130	81.5327
45	43.8468	82.7328
46	45.6084	83.8974
47	47.3972	85.0261
48	49.2131	86.1184
49	51.0555	87.1737
50	52.9241	88.1917
51	54.8187	89.1717
52	56.7387	90.1133
53	58.6840	91.0159
54	60.6541	91.8790
55	62.6486	92.7020
56	64.6674	93.4845
57	66.7100	94.2257
58	68.7761	94.9252
59	70.8654	95.5824
60	72.9776	96.1967
61	75.1123	96.7676
62	77.2694	97.2943
63	79.4484	97.7764
64	81.6490	98.2132
65	83.8711	98.6040
66	86.1142	98.9483
67	88.3781	99.2454
68	90.6626	99.4947
69	92.9673	99.6954
70	95.2919	99.8470
71	97.6362	99.9488
72	100.0000	100.0000

7 YEARS

#	REBATE	EARN
1	.0395	1.9858
2	.1179	3.9589
3	.2347	5.9191
4	.3893	7.8662
5	.5814	9.8001
6	.8103	11.7206
7	1.0756	13.6275
8	1.3767	15.5206
9	1.7133	17.3997
10	2.0847	19.2646
11	2.4905	21.1152
12	2.9304	22.9512
13	3.4037	24.7725
14	3.9101	26.5787
15	4.4490	28.3698
16	5.0201	30.1456
17	5.6230	31.9057
18	6.2571	33.6500
19	6.9221	35.3783
20	7.6176	37.0904
21	8.3430	38.7860
22	9.0981	40.4649
23	9.8825	42.1268
24	10.6956	43.7717
25	11.5372	45.3991
26	12.4069	47.0089
27	13.3042	48.6008
28	14.2288	50.1746
29	15.1803	51.7300
30	16.1584	53.2668
31	17.1627	54.7847
32	18.1929	56.2835
33	19.2485	57.7629
34	20.3293	59.2226
35	21.4349	60.6624
36	22.5650	62.0819
37	23.7192	63.4810
38	24.8972	64.8593
39	26.0987	66.2165
40	27.3234	67.5524
41	28.5709	68.8667
42	29.8410	70.1590
43	31.1333	71.4291
44	32.4476	72.6766
45	33.7835	73.9013
46	35.1407	75.1028
47	36.5190	76.2808
48	37.9181	77.4350
49	39.3376	78.5651
50	40.7774	79.6707
51	42.2371	80.7515
52	43.7165	81.8071
53	45.2153	82.8373
54	46.7332	83.8416
55	48.2700	84.8197
56	49.8254	85.7712
57	51.3992	86.6958
58	52.9911	87.5931
59	54.6009	88.4628
60	56.2283	89.3044
61	57.8732	90.1175
62	59.5351	90.9019
63	61.2140	91.6570
64	62.9096	92.3824
65	64.6217	93.0779
66	66.3500	93.7429
67	68.0943	94.3770
68	69.8544	94.9799
69	71.6302	95.5510
70	73.4213	96.0899
71	75.2275	96.5963
72	77.0488	97.0696
73	78.8848	97.5095
74	80.7354	97.9153
75	82.6003	98.2867

#	REBATE	EARN
75	82.6003	98.2867
76	84.4794	98.6233
77	86.3725	98.9244
78	88.2794	99.1897
79	90.1999	99.4186
80	92.1338	99.6107
81	94.0809	99.7653
82	96.0411	99.8821
83	98.0142	99.9605
84	100.0000	100.0000

8 YEARS

#	REBATE	EARN
1	.0316	1.7036
2	.0945	3.3986
3	.1881	5.0848
4	.3121	6.7622
5	.4660	8.4305
6	.6495	10.0897
7	.8621	11.7396
8	1.1035	13.3802
9	1.3732	15.0113
10	1.6710	16.6327
11	1.9963	18.2443
12	2.3488	19.8460
13	2.7282	21.4377
14	3.1341	23.0192
15	3.5661	24.5904
16	4.0238	26.1511
17	4.5070	27.7012
18	5.0153	29.2406
19	5.5483	30.7690
20	6.1058	32.2864
21	6.6873	33.7926
22	7.2925	35.2874
23	7.9212	36.7707
24	8.5730	38.2423
25	9.2475	39.7021
26	9.9446	41.1500
27	10.6638	42.5856
28	11.4050	44.0089
29	12.1676	45.4197
30	12.9516	46.8179
31	13.7566	48.2032
32	14.5823	49.5755
33	15.4285	50.9345
34	16.2948	52.2802
35	17.1809	53.6124
36	18.0867	54.9308
37	19.0119	56.2352
38	19.9561	57.5255
39	20.9191	58.8015
40	21.9008	60.0629
41	22.9007	61.3097
42	23.9187	62.5415
43	24.9546	63.7582
44	26.0080	64.9595
45	27.0788	66.1453
46	28.1667	67.3153
47	29.2714	68.4693
48	30.3928	69.6072
49	31.5307	70.7286
50	32.6847	71.8333
51	33.8547	72.9212
52	35.0405	73.9920
53	36.2418	75.0454
54	37.4585	76.0813
55	38.6903	77.0993
56	39.9371	78.0992

#	REBATE	EARN
57	41.1985	79.0809
58	42.4745	80.0439
59	43.7648	80.9881
60	45.0692	81.9133
61	46.3876	82.8191
62	47.7198	83.7052
63	49.0655	84.5715
64	50.4245	85.4177
65	51.7968	86.2434
66	53.1821	87.0484
67	54.5803	87.8324
68	55.9911	88.5950
69	57.4144	89.3362
70	58.8500	90.0554
71	60.2979	90.7525
72	61.7577	91.4270
73	63.2293	92.0788
74	64.7126	92.7075
75	66.2074	93.3127
76	67.7136	93.8942
77	69.2310	94.4517
78	70.7594	94.9847
79	72.2988	95.4930
80	73.8489	95.9762
81	75.4096	96.4339
82	76.9808	96.8659
83	78.5623	97.2718
84	80.1540	97.6512
85	81.7557	98.0037
86	83.3673	98.3290
87	84.9887	98.6268
88	86.6198	98.8965
89	88.2604	99.1379
90	89.9103	99.3505
91	91.5695	99.5340
92	93.2378	99.6879
93	94.9152	99.8119
94	96.6014	99.9055
95	98.2964	99.9684
96	100.0000	100.0000

9 YEARS

#	REBATE	EARN
1	.0261	1.4855
2	.0780	2.9650
3	.1554	4.4384
4	.2578	5.9055
5	.3849	7.3663
6	.5364	8.8207
7	.7121	10.2686
8	.9114	11.7100
9	1.1342	13.1446
10	1.3801	14.5725
11	1.6488	15.9936
12	1.9399	17.4077
13	2.2533	18.8148
14	2.5885	20.2147
15	2.9453	21.6074
16	3.3234	22.9927
17	3.7225	24.3706
18	4.1423	25.7410
19	4.5825	27.1037
20	5.0429	28.4587
21	5.5232	29.8058
22	6.0231	31.1450
23	6.5423	32.4761
24	7.0806	33.7990
25	7.6378	35.1136
26	8.2135	36.4198
27	8.8075	37.7175

#	REBATE	EARN
28	9.4196	39.0065
29	10.0495	40.2868
30	10.6971	41.5581
31	11.3619	42.8205
32	12.0439	44.0738
33	12.7427	45.3178
34	13.4582	46.5524
35	14.1901	47.7775
36	14.9382	48.9929
37	15.7023	50.1986
38	16.4822	51.3944
39	17.2776	52.5801
40	18.0884	53.7557
41	18.9142	54.9209
42	19.7550	56.0757
43	20.6106	57.2198
44	21.4806	58.3532
45	22.3650	59.4757
46	23.2635	60.5872
47	24.1759	61.6874
48	25.1021	62.7763
49	26.0419	63.8536
50	26.9951	64.9193
51	27.9614	65.9732
52	28.9408	67.0151
53	29.9330	68.0448
54	30.9379	69.0621
55	31.9552	70.0670
56	32.9849	71.0592
57	34.0268	72.0386
58	35.0807	73.0049
59	36.1464	73.9581
60	37.2237	74.8979
61	38.3126	75.8241
62	39.4128	76.7365
63	40.5243	77.6350
64	41.6468	78.5194
65	42.7802	79.3894
66	43.9243	80.2450
67	45.0791	81.0858
68	46.2443	81.9116
69	47.4199	82.7224
70	48.6056	83.5178
71	49.8014	84.2977
72	51.0071	85.0618
73	52.2225	85.8099
74	53.4476	86.5418
75	54.6822	87.2573
76	55.9262	87.9561
77	57.1795	88.6381
78	58.4419	89.3029
79	59.7132	89.9505
80	60.9935	90.5804
81	62.2825	91.1925
82	63.5802	91.7865
83	64.8864	92.3622
84	66.2010	92.9194
85	67.5239	93.4577
86	68.8550	93.9769
87	70.1942	94.4768
88	71.5413	94.9571
89	72.8963	95.4175
90	74.2590	95.8577
91	75.6294	96.2775
92	77.0073	96.6766
93	78.3926	97.0547
94	79.7853	97.4115
95	81.1852	97.7467
96	82.5923	98.0601

#	REBATE	EARN
97	84.0064	98.3512
98	85.4275	98.6199
99	86.8554	98.8658
100	88.2900	99.0886
101	89.7314	99.2879
102	91.1793	99.4636
103	92.6337	99.6151
104	94.0945	99.7422
105	95.5616	99.8446
106	97.0350	99.9220
107	98.5145	99.9739
108	100.0000	100.0000

10 YEARS

#	REBATE	EARN
1	.0221	1.3124
2	.0660	2.6204
3	.1314	3.9241
4	.2179	5.2232
5	.3254	6.5178
6	.4536	7.8079
7	.6021	9.0933
8	.7706	10.3739
9	.9590	11.6498
10	1.1669	12.9208
11	1.3941	14.1869
12	1.6403	15.4480
13	1.9052	16.7041
14	2.1886	17.9550
15	2.4903	19.2008
16	2.8100	20.4412
17	3.1474	21.6764
18	3.5024	22.9061
19	3.8746	24.1303
20	4.2639	25.3490
21	4.6700	26.5621
22	5.0926	27.7694
23	5.5316	28.9709
24	5.9868	30.1666
25	6.4579	31.3563
26	6.9447	32.5399
27	7.4469	33.7175
28	7.9645	34.8888
29	8.4971	36.0539
30	9.0446	37.2126
31	9.6067	38.3648
32	10.1833	39.5104
33	10.7742	40.6495
34	11.3792	41.7817
35	11.9980	42.9072
36	12.6306	44.0257
37	13.2766	45.1373
38	13.9360	46.2417
39	14.6086	47.3389
40	15.2941	48.4288
41	15.9924	49.5113
42	16.7033	50.5863
43	17.4266	51.6536
44	18.1623	52.7133
45	18.9100	53.7651
46	19.6697	54.8090
47	20.4412	55.8448
48	21.2244	56.8725
49	22.0190	57.8919
50	22.8249	58.9030
51	23.6419	59.9056
52	24.4700	60.8995
53	25.3089	61.8847
54	26.1586	62.8611
55	27.0188	63.8285

#	REBATE	EARN
56	27.8894	64.7868
57	28.7703	65.7359
58	29.6614	66.6757
59	30.5625	67.6059
60	31.4734	68.5266
61	32.3941	69.4375
62	33.3243	70.3386
63	34.2641	71.2297
64	35.2132	72.1106
65	36.1715	72.9812
66	37.1389	73.8414
67	38.1153	74.6911
68	39.1005	75.5300
69	40.0944	76.3581
70	41.0970	77.1751
71	42.1081	77.9810
72	43.1275	78.7756
73	44.1552	79.5588
74	45.1910	80.3303
75	46.2349	81.0900
76	47.2867	81.8377
77	48.3464	82.5734
78	49.4137	83.2967
79	50.4887	84.0076
80	51.5712	84.7059
81	52.6611	85.3914
82	53.7583	86.0640
83	54.8627	86.7234
84	55.9743	87.3694
85	57.0928	88.0020
86	58.2183	88.6208
87	59.3505	89.2258
88	60.4896	89.8167
89	61.6352	90.3933
90	62.7874	90.9554
91	63.9461	91.5029
92	65.1112	92.0355
93	66.2825	92.5531
94	67.4601	93.0553
95	68.6437	93.5421
96	69.8334	94.0132
97	71.0291	94.4684
98	72.2306	94.9074
99	73.4379	95.3300
100	74.6510	95.7361
101	75.8697	96.1254
102	77.0939	96.4976
103	78.3236	96.8526
104	79.5588	97.1900
105	80.7992	97.5097
106	82.0450	97.8114
107	83.2959	98.0948
108	84.5520	98.3597
109	85.8131	98.6059
110	87.0792	98.8331
111	88.3502	99.0410
112	89.6261	99.2294
113	90.9067	99.3979
114	92.1921	99.5464
115	93.4822	99.6746
116	94.7768	99.7821
117	96.0759	99.8686
118	97.3796	99.9340
119	98.6876	99.9779
120	100.0000	100.0000

1 YEAR

#	REBATE	EARN
1	1.3478	15.0035
2	4.0248	28.8498
3	8.0128	41.5228
4	13.2937	53.0061
5	19.8497	63.2830
6	27.6632	72.3368
7	36.7170	80.1503
8	46.9939	86.7063
9	58.4772	91.9872
10	71.1502	95.9752
11	84.9965	98.6522
12	100.0000	100.0000

2 YEARS

#	REBATE	EARN
1	.3695	7.5971
2	1.1035	14.9255
3	2.1970	21.9814
4	3.6449	28.7612
5	5.4425	35.2609
6	7.5848	41.4766
7	10.0672	47.4044
8	12.8850	53.0402
9	16.0336	58.3800
10	19.5083	63.4196
11	23.3047	68.1549
12	27.4185	72.5815
13	31.8451	76.6953
14	36.5804	80.4917
15	41.6200	83.9664
16	46.9598	87.1150
17	52.5956	89.9328
18	58.5234	92.4152
19	64.7391	94.5575
20	71.2388	96.3551
21	78.0186	97.8030
22	85.0745	98.8965
23	92.4029	99.6305
24	100.0000	100.0000

3 YEARS

#	REBATE	EARN
1	.1753	5.0026
2	.5234	9.8972
3	1.0421	14.6825
4	1.7289	19.3568
5	2.5815	23.9186
6	3.5977	28.3664
7	4.7752	32.6985
8	6.1118	36.9133
9	7.6052	41.0093
10	9.2534	44.9847
11	11.0541	48.8378
12	13.0054	52.5670
13	15.1051	56.1705
14	17.3512	59.6466
15	19.7416	62.9935
16	22.2744	66.2093
17	24.9477	69.2923
18	27.7594	72.2406
19	30.7077	75.0523
20	33.7907	77.7256
21	37.0065	80.2584
22	40.3534	82.6488
23	43.8295	84.8949
24	47.4330	86.9946
25	51.1622	88.9459
26	55.0153	90.7466
27	58.9907	92.3948
28	63.0867	93.8882
29	67.3015	95.2248
30	71.6336	96.4023
31	76.0814	97.4185
32	80.6432	98.2711
33	85.3175	98.9579
34	90.1028	99.4766
35	94.9974	99.8247
36	100.0000	100.0000

4 YEARS

#	REBATE	EARN
1	.1044	3.6845
2	.3117	7.3145
3	.6206	10.8894
4	1.0296	14.4084
5	1.5373	17.8706
6	2.1424	21.2754
7	2.8436	24.6218
8	3.6395	27.9091
9	4.5289	31.1364
10	5.5104	34.3029
11	6.5827	37.4078
12	7.7447	40.4502
13	8.9951	43.4292
14	10.3326	46.3440
15	11.7561	49.1936
16	13.2644	51.9771
17	14.8563	54.6937
18	16.5307	57.3423
19	18.2864	59.9221
20	20.1223	62.4320
21	22.0373	64.8711
22	24.0304	67.2385
23	26.1004	69.5330
24	28.2463	71.7537
25	30.4670	73.8996
26	32.7615	75.9696
27	35.1289	77.9627
28	37.5680	79.8777
29	40.0779	81.7136
30	42.6577	83.4693
31	45.3063	85.1437
32	48.0229	86.7356
33	50.8064	88.2439
34	53.6560	89.6674
35	56.5708	91.0049
36	59.5498	92.2553
37	62.5922	93.4173
38	65.6971	94.4896
39	68.8636	95.4711
40	72.0909	96.3605
41	75.3782	97.1564
42	78.7246	97.8576
43	82.1294	98.4627
44	85.5916	98.9704
45	89.1106	99.3794
46	92.6855	99.6883
47	96.3155	99.8956
48	100.0000	100.0000

5 YEARS

#	REBATE	EARN
1	.0704	2.8893
2	.2103	5.7360
3	.4188	8.5743
4	.6947	11.3690
5	1.0373	14.1313
6	1.4457	16.8608
7	1.9188	19.5570
8	2.4559	22.2193
9	3.0560	24.8474
10	3.7183	27.4408
11	4.4419	29.9990
12	5.2260	32.5214
13	6.0697	35.0077
14	6.9723	37.4572
15	7.9328	39.8695
16	8.9506	42.2440
17	10.0248	44.5803
18	11.1547	46.8777
19	12.3394	49.1358
20	13.5782	51.3541
21	14.8705	53.5318
22	16.2154	55.6685
23	17.6122	57.7637
24	19.0602	59.8166
25	20.5587	61.8268
26	22.1070	63.7937
27	23.7045	65.7165
28	25.3503	67.5948
29	27.0440	69.4279
30	28.7848	71.2152
31	30.5721	72.9560
32	32.4052	74.6497
33	34.2835	76.2955
34	36.2063	77.8930
35	38.1732	79.4413
36	40.1834	80.9398
37	42.2363	82.3878
38	44.3315	83.7846
39	46.4682	85.1295
40	48.6459	86.4218
41	50.8642	87.6606
42	53.1223	88.8453
43	55.4197	89.9752
44	57.7560	91.0494
45	60.1305	92.0672
46	62.5428	93.0277
47	64.9923	93.9303
48	67.4786	94.7740
49	70.0010	95.5581
50	72.5592	96.2817
51	75.1526	96.9440
52	77.7807	97.5441
53	80.4430	98.0812
54	83.1392	98.5543
55	85.8687	98.9627
56	88.6310	99.3053
57	91.4257	99.5812
58	94.2524	99.7897
59	97.1107	99.9296
60	100.0000	100.0000

6 YEARS

#	REBATE	EARN
1	.0514	2.3590
2	.1536	4.6989
3	.3058	7.0192
4	.5073	9.3198
5	.7575	11.6003
6	1.0557	13.8605
7	1.4012	16.1001
8	1.7933	18.3188
9	2.2315	20.5164
10	2.7152	22.6924
11	3.2435	24.8467
12	3.8161	26.9789
13	4.4322	29.0887
14	5.0912	31.1758
15	5.7926	33.2399
16	6.5358	35.2807
17	7.3202	37.2978
18	8.1453	39.2909
19	9.0104	41.2596
20	9.9150	43.2037
21	10.8586	45.1228
22	11.8406	47.0165
23	12.8606	48.8845
24	13.9179	50.7264
25	15.0122	52.5419
26	16.1428	54.3305
27	17.3093	56.0920
28	18.5111	57.8259
29	19.7478	59.5319
30	21.0190	61.2095
31	22.3241	62.8584
32	23.6626	64.4782
33	25.0342	66.0684
34	26.4383	67.6287
35	27.8745	69.1586
36	29.3423	70.6577
37	30.8414	72.1255
38	32.3713	73.5617
39	33.9316	74.9658
40	35.5218	76.3374
41	37.1416	77.6759
42	38.7905	78.9810
43	40.4681	80.2522
44	42.1741	81.4889
45	43.9080	82.6907
46	45.6695	83.8572
47	47.4581	84.9878
48	49.2736	86.0821
49	51.1155	87.1394
50	52.9835	88.1594
51	54.8772	89.1414
52	56.7963	90.0850
53	58.7404	90.9896
54	60.7091	91.8547
55	62.7022	92.6798
56	64.7193	93.4642
57	66.7601	94.2074
58	68.8242	94.9088
59	70.9113	95.5678
60	73.0211	96.1839
61	75.1533	96.7565
62	77.3076	97.2848
63	79.4836	97.7685
64	81.6812	98.2067
65	83.8999	98.5988
66	86.1395	98.9443
67	88.3997	99.2425
68	90.6802	99.4927
69	92.9808	99.6942
70	95.3011	99.8464
71	97.6410	99.9486
72	100.0000	100.0000

7 YEARS

#	REBATE	EARN
1	.0397	1.9813
2	.1184	3.9501
3	.2357	5.9062
4	.3911	7.8493
5	.5840	9.7794
6	.8138	11.6962
7	1.0802	13.5996
8	1.3825	15.4893
9	1.7203	17.3652
10	2.0932	19.2271
11	2.5005	21.0747
12	2.9419	22.9080
13	3.4169	24.7266
14	3.9249	26.5304
15	4.4657	28.3192
16	5.0386	30.0928
17	5.6433	31.8509
18	6.2793	33.5933
19	6.9463	35.3199
20	7.6437	37.0304
21	8.3711	38.7245
22	9.1282	40.4020
23	9.9145	42.0628
24	10.7296	43.7066
25	11.5732	45.3331
26	12.4448	46.9421
27	13.3441	48.5333
28	14.2706	50.1066
29	15.2240	51.6616
30	16.2040	53.1981
31	17.2101	54.7159
32	18.2420	56.2146
33	19.2993	57.6941
34	20.3818	59.1540
35	21.4890	60.5940
36	22.6206	62.0140
37	23.7763	63.4136
38	24.9557	64.7925
39	26.1585	66.1505
40	27.3845	67.4872
41	28.6332	68.8023
42	29.9043	70.0957
43	31.1977	71.3668
44	32.5128	72.6155
45	33.8495	73.8415
46	35.2075	75.0443
47	36.5864	76.2237
48	37.9860	77.3794
49	39.4060	78.5110
50	40.8460	79.6182
51	42.3059	80.7007
52	43.7854	81.7580
53	45.2841	82.7899
54	46.8019	83.7960
55	48.3384	84.7760
56	49.8934	85.7294
57	51.4667	86.6559
58	53.0579	87.5552
59	54.6669	88.4268
60	56.2934	89.2704
61	57.9372	90.0855
62	59.5980	90.8718
63	61.2755	91.6289
64	62.9696	92.3563
65	64.6801	93.0537
66	66.4067	93.7207
67	68.1491	94.3567
68	69.9072	94.9614
69	71.6808	95.5343
70	73.4696	96.0751
71	75.2734	96.5831
72	77.0920	97.0581
73	78.9253	97.4995
74	80.7729	97.9068
75	82.6348	98.2797

ACTUARIAL REBATE AND EARNINGS

#	REBATE	EARN
75	82.6348	98.2797
76	84.5107	98.6175
77	86.4004	98.9198
78	88.3038	99.1862
79	90.2206	99.4160
80	92.1507	99.6089
81	94.0938	99.7643
82	96.0499	99.8816
83	98.0187	99.9603
84	100.0000	100.0000

8 YEARS

#	REBATE	EARN
1	.0318	1.6994
2	.0950	3.3903
3	.1890	5.0726
4	.3136	6.7461
5	.4683	8.4107
6	.6527	10.0664
7	.8663	11.7129
8	1.1087	13.3501
9	1.3796	14.9779
10	1.6786	16.5962
11	2.0053	18.2049
12	2.3593	19.8038
13	2.7402	21.3927
14	3.1477	22.9716
15	3.5813	24.5403
16	4.0408	26.0986
17	4.5257	27.6465
18	5.0358	29.1837
19	5.5706	30.7101
20	6.1299	32.2256
21	6.7133	33.7300
22	7.3205	35.2232
23	7.9510	36.7049
24	8.6048	38.1751
25	9.2813	39.6336
26	9.9803	41.0802
27	10.7014	42.5147
28	11.4445	43.9371
29	12.2091	45.3470
30	12.9950	46.7444
31	13.8018	48.1290
32	14.6294	49.5007
33	15.4773	50.8593
34	16.3454	52.2047
35	17.2333	53.5366
36	18.1409	54.8548
37	19.0677	56.1592
38	20.0135	57.4496
39	20.9782	58.7257
40	21.9613	59.9874
41	22.9627	61.2344
42	23.9821	62.4667
43	25.0193	63.6838
44	26.0741	64.8858
45	27.1460	66.0722
46	28.2351	67.2430
47	29.3409	68.3979
48	30.4633	69.5367
49	31.6021	70.6591
50	32.7570	71.7649
51	33.9278	72.8540
52	35.1142	73.9259
53	36.3162	74.9807
54	37.5333	76.0179
55	38.7656	77.0373
56	40.0126	78.0387
57	41.2743	79.0218
58	42.5504	79.9865
59	43.8408	80.9323
60	45.1452	81.8591
61	46.4634	82.7667
62	47.7953	83.6546
63	49.1407	84.5227
64	50.4993	85.3706
65	51.8710	86.1982
66	53.2556	87.0050
67	54.6530	87.7909
68	56.0629	88.5555
69	57.4853	89.2986
70	58.9198	90.0197
71	60.3664	90.7187
72	61.8249	91.3952
73	63.2951	92.0490
74	64.7768	92.6795
75	66.2700	93.2867
76	67.7744	93.8701
77	69.2899	94.4294
78	70.8163	94.9642
79	72.3535	95.4743
80	73.9014	95.9592
81	75.4597	96.4187
82	77.0284	96.8523
83	78.6073	97.2598
84	80.1962	97.6407
85	81.7951	97.9947
86	83.4038	98.3214
87	85.0221	98.6204
88	86.6499	98.8913
89	88.2871	99.1337
90	89.9336	99.3473
91	91.5893	99.5317
92	93.2539	99.6864
93	94.9274	99.8110
94	96.6097	99.9050
95	98.3006	99.9682
96	100.0000	100.0000

9 YEARS

#	REBATE	EARN
1	.0263	1.4816
2	.0785	2.9572
3	.1562	4.4268
4	.2592	5.8903
5	.3870	7.3475
6	.5393	8.7985
7	.7158	10.2430
8	.9162	11.6811
9	1.1400	13.1126
10	1.3871	14.5375
11	1.6571	15.9555
12	1.9496	17.3668
13	2.2643	18.7711
14	2.6010	20.1683
15	2.9593	21.5584
16	3.3390	22.9413
17	3.7397	24.3169
18	4.1612	25.6849
19	4.6032	27.0455
20	5.0654	28.3984
21	5.5474	29.7435
22	6.0491	31.0808
23	6.5702	32.4101
24	7.1104	33.7313
25	7.6694	35.0443
26	8.2470	36.3490
27	8.8429	37.6452
28	9.4569	38.9329
29	10.0888	40.2120
30	10.7382	41.4822
31	11.4049	42.7435
32	12.0887	43.9958
33	12.7894	45.2390
34	13.5067	46.4728
35	14.2405	47.6972
36	14.9904	48.9121
37	15.7562	50.1173
38	16.5378	51.3127
39	17.3349	52.4981
40	18.1473	53.6734
41	18.9748	54.8385
42	19.8172	55.9932
43	20.6743	57.1373
44	21.5458	58.2708
45	22.4317	59.3935
46	23.3316	60.5052
47	24.2453	61.6058
48	25.1728	62.6951
49	26.1138	63.7729
50	27.0681	64.8392
51	28.0356	65.8937
52	29.0160	66.9363
53	30.0092	67.9668
54	31.0150	68.9850
55	32.0332	69.9908
56	33.0637	70.9840
57	34.1063	71.9644
58	35.1608	72.9319
59	36.2271	73.8862
60	37.3049	74.8272
61	38.3942	75.7547
62	39.4948	76.6684
63	40.6065	77.5683
64	41.7292	78.4542
65	42.8627	79.3257
66	44.0068	80.1828
67	45.1615	81.0252
68	46.3266	81.8527
69	47.5019	82.6651
70	48.6873	83.4622
71	49.8827	84.2438
72	51.0879	85.0096
73	52.3028	85.7595
74	53.5272	86.4933
75	54.7610	87.2106
76	56.0042	87.9113
77	57.2565	88.5951
78	58.5178	89.2618
79	59.7880	89.9112
80	61.0671	90.5431
81	62.3548	91.1571
82	63.6510	91.7530
83	64.9557	92.3306
84	66.2687	92.8896
85	67.5899	93.4298
86	68.9192	93.9509
87	70.2565	94.4526
88	71.6016	94.9346
89	72.9545	95.3968
90	74.3151	95.8388
91	75.6831	96.2603
92	77.0587	96.6610
93	78.4416	97.0407
94	79.8317	97.3990
95	81.2289	97.7357
96	82.6332	98.0504
97	84.0445	98.3429
98	85.4625	98.6129
99	86.8874	98.8600
100	88.3189	99.0838
101	89.7570	99.2842
102	91.2015	99.4607
103	92.6525	99.6130
104	94.1097	99.7408
105	95.5732	99.8438
106	97.0428	99.9215
107	98.5184	99.9737
108	100.0000	100.0000

10 YEARS

#	REBATE	EARN
1	.0222	1.3087
2	.0664	2.6131
3	.1321	3.9132
4	.2192	5.2088
5	.3274	6.5001
6	.4562	7.7868
7	.6055	9.0689
8	.7750	10.3464
9	.9644	11.6192
10	1.1734	12.8872
11	1.4017	14.1504
12	1.6492	15.4087
13	1.9154	16.6620
14	2.2002	17.9103
15	2.5033	19.1534
16	2.8245	20.3914
17	3.1635	21.6241
18	3.5200	22.8514
19	3.8939	24.0734
20	4.2848	25.2899
21	4.6926	26.5008
22	5.1170	27.7061
23	5.5578	28.9057
24	6.0148	30.0995
25	6.4876	31.2874
26	6.9762	32.4693
27	7.4804	33.6453
28	7.9997	34.8151
29	8.5342	35.9786
30	9.0835	37.1359
31	9.6475	38.2868
32	10.2260	39.4313
33	10.8187	40.5691
34	11.4255	41.7003
35	12.0462	42.8248
36	12.6806	43.9424
37	13.3284	45.0531
38	13.9896	46.1568
39	14.6638	47.2533
40	15.3511	48.3426
41	16.0511	49.4245
42	16.7636	50.4990
43	17.4886	51.5660
44	18.2259	52.6254
45	18.9752	53.6769
46	19.7365	54.7207
47	20.5095	55.7564
48	21.2940	56.7841
49	22.0900	57.8036
50	22.8973	58.8148
51	23.7157	59.8175
52	24.5450	60.8117
53	25.3852	61.7973
54	26.2360	62.7740
55	27.0973	63.7419
56	27.9690	64.7007
57	28.8510	65.6504
58	29.7430	66.5908
59	30.6449	67.5218
60	31.5567	68.4433
61	32.4782	69.3551
62	33.4092	70.2570
63	34.3496	71.1490
64	35.2993	72.0310
65	36.2581	72.9027
66	37.2260	73.7640
67	38.2027	74.6148
68	39.1883	75.4550
69	40.1825	76.2843
70	41.1852	77.1027
71	42.1964	77.9100
72	43.2159	78.7060
73	44.2436	79.4905
74	45.2793	80.2635
75	46.3231	81.0248
76	47.3746	81.7741
77	48.4340	82.5114
78	49.5010	83.2364
79	50.5755	83.9489
80	51.6574	84.6489
81	52.7467	85.3362
82	53.8432	86.0104
83	54.9469	86.6716
84	56.0576	87.3194
85	57.1752	87.9538
86	58.2997	88.5745
87	59.4309	89.1813
88	60.5687	89.7740
89	61.7132	90.3525
90	62.8641	90.9165
91	64.0214	91.4658
92	65.1849	92.0003
93	66.3547	92.5196
94	67.5307	93.0238
95	68.7126	93.5124
96	69.9005	93.9852
97	71.0943	94.4422
98	72.2939	94.8830
99	73.4992	95.3074
100	74.7101	95.7152
101	75.9266	96.1061
102	77.1486	96.4800
103	78.3759	96.8365
104	79.6086	97.1755
105	80.8466	97.4967
106	82.0897	97.7998
107	83.3380	98.0846
108	84.5913	98.3508
109	85.8496	98.5983
110	87.1128	98.8266
111	88.3808	99.0356
112	89.6536	99.2250
113	90.9311	99.3945
114	92.2132	99.5438
115	93.4999	99.6726
116	94.7912	99.7808
117	96.0868	99.8679
118	97.3869	99.9336
119	98.6913	99.9778
120	100.0000	100.0000

1 YEAR

#	REBATE	EARN
1	1.3488	14.9980
2	4.0275	28.8406
3	8.0176	41.5114
4	13.3007	52.9938
5	19.8588	63.2710
6	27.6741	72.3259
7	36.7290	80.1412
8	47.0062	86.6993
9	58.4886	91.9824
10	71.1594	95.9725
11	85.0020	98.6512
12	100.0000	100.0000

2 YEARS

#	REBATE	EARN
1	.3701	7.5914
2	1.1051	14.9150
3	2.2000	21.9671
4	3.6496	28.7437
5	5.4491	35.2409
6	7.5935	41.4549
7	10.0781	47.3816
8	12.8981	53.0169
9	16.0488	58.3567
10	19.5255	63.3968
11	23.3238	68.1330
12	27.4391	72.5609
13	31.8670	76.6762
14	36.6032	80.4745
15	41.6433	83.9512
16	46.9831	87.1019
17	52.6184	89.9219
18	58.5451	92.4065
19	64.7591	94.5509
20	71.2563	96.3504
21	78.0329	97.8000
22	85.0850	98.8949
23	92.4086	99.6299
24	100.0000	100.0000

3 YEARS

#	REBATE	EARN
1	.1757	4.9971
2	.5246	9.8868
3	1.0442	14.6677
4	1.7323	19.3381
5	2.5865	23.8965
6	3.6044	28.3413
7	4.7838	32.6709
8	6.1223	36.8837
9	7.6178	40.9781
10	9.2681	44.9522
11	11.0710	48.8046
12	13.0244	52.5333
13	15.1262	56.1367
14	17.3743	59.6130
15	19.7667	62.9603
16	22.3013	66.1770
17	24.9762	69.2610
18	27.7894	72.2106
19	30.7390	75.0238
20	33.8230	77.6987
21	37.0397	80.2333
22	40.3870	82.6257
23	43.8633	84.8738
24	47.4667	86.9756
25	51.1954	88.9290
26	55.0478	90.7319
27	59.0219	92.3822
28	63.1163	93.8777
29	67.3291	95.2162
30	71.6587	96.3956
31	76.1035	97.4135
32	80.6619	98.2677
33	85.3323	98.9558
34	90.1132	99.4754
35	95.0029	99.8243
36	100.0000	100.0000

4 YEARS

#	REBATE	EARN
1	.1047	3.6793
2	.3126	7.3045
3	.6223	10.8749
4	1.0323	14.3897
5	1.5413	17.8481
6	2.1479	21.2494
7	2.8506	24.5927
8	3.6483	27.8772
9	4.5394	31.1021
10	5.5228	34.2664
11	6.5972	37.3695
12	7.7612	40.4103
13	9.0137	43.3881
14	10.3533	46.3018
15	11.7789	49.1507
16	13.2893	51.9338
17	14.8833	54.6501
18	16.5596	57.2988
19	18.3173	59.8788
20	20.1550	62.3892
21	22.0718	64.8290
22	24.0665	67.1972
23	26.1380	69.4928
24	28.2853	71.7147
25	30.5072	73.8620
26	32.8028	75.9335
27	35.1710	77.9282
28	37.6108	79.8450
29	40.1212	81.6827
30	42.7012	83.4404
31	45.3499	85.1167
32	48.0662	86.7107
33	50.8493	88.2211
34	53.6982	89.6467
35	56.6119	90.9863
36	59.5897	92.2388
37	62.6305	93.4028
38	65.7336	94.4772
39	68.8979	95.4606
40	72.1228	96.3517
41	75.4073	97.1494
42	78.7506	97.8521
43	82.1519	98.4587
44	85.6103	98.9677
45	89.1251	99.3777
46	92.6955	99.6874
47	96.3207	99.8953
48	100.0000	100.0000

5 YEARS

#	REBATE	EARN
1	.0707	2.8844
2	.2111	5.7379
3	.4202	8.5602
4	.6970	11.3508
5	1.0407	14.1092
6	1.4503	16.8350
7	1.9248	19.5278
8	2.4633	22.1870
9	3.0651	24.8122
10	3.7291	27.4029
11	4.4545	29.9586
12	5.2405	32.4789
13	6.0861	34.9631
14	6.9907	37.4109
15	7.9533	39.8217
16	8.9731	42.1950
17	10.0493	44.5301
18	11.1812	46.8267
19	12.3680	49.0841
20	13.6089	51.3019
21	14.9031	53.4793
22	16.2500	55.6160
23	17.6487	57.7112
24	19.0985	59.7644
25	20.5988	61.7750
26	22.1488	63.7424
27	23.7478	65.6660
28	25.3952	67.5452
29	27.0903	69.3793
30	28.8323	71.1677
31	30.6207	72.9097
32	32.4548	74.6048
33	34.3340	76.2522
34	36.2576	77.8512
35	38.2250	79.4012
36	40.2356	80.9015
37	42.2888	82.3513
38	44.3840	83.7500
39	46.5207	85.0969
40	48.6981	86.3911
41	50.9159	87.6320
42	53.1733	88.8188
43	55.4699	89.9507
44	57.8050	91.0269
45	60.1783	92.0467
46	62.5891	93.0093
47	65.0369	93.9139
48	67.5211	94.7595
49	70.0414	95.5455
50	72.5971	96.2709
51	75.1878	96.9349
52	77.8130	97.5367
53	80.4722	98.0752
54	83.1650	98.5497
55	85.8908	98.9593
56	88.6492	99.3030
57	91.4398	99.5798
58	94.2621	99.7889
59	97.1156	99.9293
60	100.0000	100.0000

6 YEARS

#	REBATE	EARN
1	.0516	2.3544
2	.1542	4.6897
3	.3070	7.0057
4	.5093	9.3022
5	.7604	11.5788
6	1.0596	13.8354
7	1.4063	16.0715
8	1.7998	18.2869
9	2.2395	20.4813
10	2.7246	22.6544
11	3.2547	24.8060
12	3.8289	26.9356
13	4.4468	29.0430
14	5.1077	31.1280
15	5.8110	33.1901
16	6.5561	35.2290
17	7.3425	37.2444
18	8.1695	39.2360
19	9.0366	41.2034
20	9.9433	43.1464
21	10.8889	45.0645
22	11.8729	46.9574
23	12.8949	48.8247
24	13.9542	50.6661
25	15.0504	52.4812
26	16.1829	54.2697
27	17.3512	56.0311
28	18.5549	57.7651
29	19.7933	59.4713
30	21.0662	61.1493
31	22.3729	62.7986
32	23.7129	64.4190
33	25.0859	66.0100
34	26.4914	67.5711
35	27.9289	69.1019
36	29.3979	70.6021
37	30.8981	72.0711
38	32.4289	73.5086
39	33.9900	74.9141
40	35.5810	76.2871
41	37.2014	77.6271
42	38.8507	78.9338
43	40.5287	80.2067
44	42.2349	81.4451
45	43.9689	82.6488
46	45.7303	83.8171
47	47.5188	84.9496
48	49.3339	86.0458
49	51.1753	87.1051
50	53.0426	88.1271
51	54.9355	89.1111
52	56.8536	90.0567
53	58.7966	90.9634
54	60.7640	91.8305
55	62.7556	92.6575
56	64.7710	93.4439
57	66.8099	94.1890
58	68.8720	94.8923
59	70.9570	95.5532
60	73.0644	96.1711
61	75.1940	96.7453
62	77.3456	97.2754
63	79.5187	97.7605
64	81.7131	98.2002
65	83.9285	98.5937
66	86.1646	98.9404
67	88.4212	99.2396
68	90.6978	99.4907
69	92.9943	99.6930
70	95.3103	99.8458
71	97.6456	99.9484
72	100.0000	100.0000

7 YEARS

#	REBATE	EARN
1	.0398	1.9769
2	.1189	3.9414
3	.2368	5.8934
4	.3928	7.8326
5	.5865	9.7588
6	.8173	11.6720
7	1.0848	13.5719
8	1.3883	15.4582
9	1.7274	17.3309
10	2.1016	19.1898
11	2.5105	21.0345
12	2.9534	22.8650
13	3.4300	24.6811
14	3.9398	26.4824
15	4.4823	28.2689
16	5.0571	30.0403
17	5.6636	31.7964
18	6.3015	33.5369
19	6.9704	35.2617
20	7.6697	36.9706
21	8.3991	38.6633
22	9.1582	40.3395
23	9.9465	41.9991
24	10.7636	43.6418
25	11.6091	45.2674
26	12.4827	46.8756
27	13.3839	48.4662
28	14.3123	50.0389
29	15.2676	51.5935
30	16.2494	53.1297
31	17.2573	54.6473
32	18.2910	56.1460
33	19.3500	57.6255
34	20.4341	59.0856
35	21.5429	60.5259
36	22.6761	61.9463
37	23.8332	63.3464
38	25.0140	64.7259
39	26.2182	66.0846
40	27.4454	67.4221
41	28.6953	68.7382
42	29.9675	70.0325
43	31.2618	71.3047
44	32.5779	72.5546
45	33.9154	73.7818
46	35.2741	74.9860
47	36.6536	76.1668
48	38.0537	77.3239
49	39.4741	78.4571
50	40.9144	79.5659
51	42.3745	80.6500
52	43.8540	81.7090
53	45.3527	82.7427
54	46.8703	83.7506
55	48.4065	84.7324
56	49.9611	85.6877
57	51.5338	86.6161
58	53.1244	87.5173
59	54.7326	88.3909
60	56.3582	89.2364
61	58.0009	90.0535
62	59.6605	90.8418
63	61.3367	91.6009
64	63.0294	92.3303
65	64.7383	93.0296
66	66.4631	93.6985
67	68.2036	94.3364
68	69.9597	94.9429
69	71.7311	95.5177
70	73.5176	96.0602
71	75.3189	96.5700
72	77.1350	97.0466
73	78.9655	97.4895
74	80.8102	97.8984
75	82.6691	98.2726

#	REBATE	EARN
75	82.6691	98.2726
76	84.5418	98.6117
77	86.4281	98.9152
78	88.3280	99.1827
79	90.2412	99.4135
80	92.1674	99.6072
81	94.1066	99.7632
82	96.0586	99.8811
83	98.0231	99.9602
84	100.0000	100.0000

8 YEARS

#	REBATE	EARN
1	.0320	1.6953
2	.0954	3.3821
3	.1900	5.0605
4	.3152	6.7302
5	.4706	8.3911
6	.6558	10.0432
7	.8704	11.6863
8	1.1139	13.3202
9	1.3861	14.9448
10	1.6863	16.5601
11	2.0144	18.1658
12	2.3698	19.7618
13	2.7522	21.3480
14	3.1612	22.9243
15	3.5965	24.4905
16	4.0577	26.0465
17	4.5444	27.5921
18	5.0563	29.1272
19	5.5929	30.6516
20	6.1541	32.1652
21	6.7393	33.6678
22	7.3484	35.1593
23	7.9809	36.6395
24	8.6365	38.1083
25	9.3149	39.5654
26	10.0159	41.0108
27	10.7390	42.4443
28	11.4839	43.8656
29	12.2504	45.2746
30	13.0382	46.6712
31	13.8469	48.0552
32	14.6763	49.4263
33	15.5261	50.7845
34	16.3960	52.1295
35	17.2857	53.4611
36	18.1949	54.7792
37	19.1234	56.0835
38	20.0708	57.3739
39	21.0370	58.6502
40	22.0217	59.9121
41	23.0246	61.1595
42	24.0454	62.3921
43	25.0839	63.6098
44	26.1399	64.8123
45	27.2131	65.9995
46	28.3033	67.1710
47	29.4102	68.3267
48	30.5336	69.4664
49	31.6733	70.5898
50	32.8290	71.6967
51	34.0005	72.7869
52	35.1877	73.8601
53	36.3902	74.9161
54	37.6079	75.9546
55	38.8405	76.9754
56	40.0879	77.9783
57	41.3498	78.9630
58	42.6261	79.9292
59	43.9165	80.8766
60	45.2208	81.8051
61	46.5389	82.7143
62	47.8705	83.6040
63	49.2155	84.4739
64	50.5737	85.3237
65	51.9448	86.1531
66	53.3288	86.9618
67	54.7254	87.7496
68	56.1344	88.5161
69	57.5557	89.2610
70	58.9892	89.9841
71	60.4346	90.6851
72	61.8917	91.3635
73	63.3605	92.0191
74	64.8407	92.6516
75	66.3322	93.2607
76	67.8348	93.8459
77	69.3484	94.4071
78	70.8728	94.9437
79	72.4079	95.4556
80	73.9535	95.9423
81	75.5095	96.4035
82	77.0757	96.8388
83	78.6520	97.2478
84	80.2382	97.6302
85	81.8342	97.9856
86	83.4399	98.3137
87	85.0552	98.6139
88	86.6798	98.8861
89	88.3137	99.1296
90	89.9568	99.3442
91	91.6089	99.5294
92	93.2698	99.6848
93	94.9395	99.8100
94	96.6179	99.9046
95	98.3047	99.9680
96	100.0000	100.0000

9 YEARS

#	REBATE	EARN
1	.0264	1.4777
2	.0789	2.9495
3	.1571	4.4154
4	.2606	5.8752
5	.3891	7.3289
6	.5422	8.7764
7	.7196	10.2176
8	.9209	11.6525
9	1.1459	13.0808
10	1.3941	14.5026
11	1.6653	15.9178
12	1.9592	17.3262
13	2.2753	18.7277
14	2.6135	20.1223
15	2.9734	21.5099
16	3.3547	22.8903
17	3.7570	24.2635
18	4.1802	25.6293
19	4.6239	26.9877
20	5.0878	28.3385
21	5.5717	29.6816
22	6.0752	31.0170
23	6.5981	32.3445
24	7.1401	33.6640
25	7.7010	34.9754
26	8.2805	36.2786
27	8.8783	37.5734
28	9.4942	38.8598
29	10.1279	40.1376
30	10.7792	41.4067
31	11.4478	42.6670
32	12.1335	43.9184
33	12.8360	45.1607
34	13.5552	46.3937
35	14.2907	47.6175
36	15.0424	48.8318
37	15.8100	50.0364
38	16.5933	51.2314
39	17.3921	52.4165
40	18.2062	53.5915
41	19.0353	54.7564
42	19.8792	55.9111
43	20.7378	57.0552
44	21.6109	58.1888
45	22.4981	59.3117
46	23.3994	60.4236
47	24.3145	61.5245
48	25.2433	62.6142
49	26.1855	63.6926
50	27.1410	64.7594
51	28.1095	65.8145
52	29.0910	66.8578
53	30.0852	67.8891
54	31.0919	68.9081
55	32.1109	69.9148
56	33.1422	70.9090
57	34.1855	71.8905
58	35.2406	72.8590
59	36.3074	73.8145
60	37.3858	74.7567
61	38.4755	75.6855
62	39.5764	76.6006
63	40.6883	77.5019
64	41.8112	78.3891
65	42.9448	79.2622
66	44.0889	80.1208
67	45.2436	80.9647
68	46.4085	81.7938
69	47.5835	82.6079
70	48.7686	83.4067
71	49.9636	84.1900
72	51.1682	84.9576
73	52.3825	85.7093
74	53.6063	86.4448
75	54.8393	87.1640
76	56.0816	87.8665
77	57.3330	88.5522
78	58.5933	89.2208
79	59.8624	89.8721
80	61.1402	90.5058
81	62.4266	91.1217
82	63.7214	91.7195
83	65.0246	92.2990
84	66.3360	92.8599
85	67.6555	93.4019
86	68.9830	93.9248
87	70.3184	94.4283
88	71.6615	94.9122
89	73.0123	95.3761
90	74.3707	95.8198
91	75.7365	96.2430
92	77.1097	96.6453
93	78.4901	97.0266
94	79.8777	97.3865
95	81.2723	97.7247
96	82.6738	98.0408
97	84.0822	98.3347
98	85.4974	98.6059
99	86.9192	98.8541
100	88.3475	99.0791
101	89.7824	99.2804
102	91.2236	99.4578
103	92.6711	99.6109
104	94.1248	99.7394
105	95.5846	99.8429
106	97.0505	99.9211
107	98.5223	99.9736
108	100.0000	100.0000

10 YEARS

#	REBATE	EARN
1	.0224	1.3050
2	.0668	2.6058
3	.1329	3.9023
4	.2205	5.1946
5	.3293	6.4824
6	.4589	7.7659
7	.6090	9.0448
8	.7794	10.3192
9	.9698	11.5889
10	1.1799	12.8540
11	1.4094	14.1142
12	1.6581	15.3697
13	1.9256	16.6203
14	2.2118	17.8659
15	2.5164	19.1065
16	2.8391	20.3419
17	3.1796	21.5722
18	3.5377	22.7972
19	3.9132	24.0169
20	4.3058	25.2312
21	4.7153	26.4401
22	5.1414	27.6433
23	5.5840	28.8410
24	6.0427	30.0329
25	6.5174	31.2190
26	7.0078	32.3993
27	7.5137	33.5736
28	8.0350	34.7418
29	8.5713	35.9039
30	9.1225	37.0598
31	9.6883	38.2094
32	10.2686	39.3526
33	10.8632	40.4894
34	11.4718	41.6195
35	12.0943	42.7430
36	12.7304	43.8597
37	13.3801	44.9695
38	14.0430	46.0724
39	14.7190	47.1682
40	15.4079	48.2569
41	16.1096	49.3383
42	16.8239	50.4124
43	17.5505	51.4789
44	18.2893	52.5380
45	19.0402	53.5893
46	19.8030	54.6329
47	20.5775	55.6685
48	21.3635	56.6962
49	22.1609	57.7157
50	22.9695	58.7270
51	23.7892	59.7299
52	24.6198	60.7244
53	25.4612	61.7103
54	26.3131	62.6874
55	27.1756	63.6557
56	28.0483	64.6151
57	28.9313	65.5654
58	29.8242	66.5064
59	30.7271	67.4381
60	31.6397	68.3603
61	32.5619	69.2729
62	33.4936	70.1758
63	34.4346	71.0687
64	35.3849	71.9517
65	36.3443	72.8244
66	37.3126	73.6869
67	38.2897	74.5388
68	39.2756	75.3802
69	40.2701	76.2108
70	41.2730	77.0305
71	42.2843	77.8391
72	43.3038	78.6365
73	44.3315	79.4225
74	45.3671	80.1970
75	46.4107	80.9598
76	47.4620	81.7107
77	48.5211	82.4495
78	49.5876	83.1761
79	50.6617	83.8904
80	51.7431	84.5921
81	52.8318	85.2810
82	53.9276	85.9570
83	55.0305	86.6199
84	56.1403	87.2696
85	57.2570	87.9057
86	58.3805	88.5282
87	59.5106	89.1368
88	60.6474	89.7314
89	61.7906	90.3117
90	62.9402	90.8775
91	64.0961	91.4287
92	65.2582	91.9650
93	66.4264	92.4863
94	67.6007	92.9922
95	68.7810	93.4826
96	69.9671	93.9573
97	71.1590	94.4160
98	72.3567	94.8586
99	73.5599	95.2847
100	74.7688	95.6942
101	75.9831	96.0868
102	77.2028	96.4623
103	78.4278	96.8204
104	79.6581	97.1609
105	80.8935	97.4836
106	82.1341	97.7882
107	83.3797	98.0744
108	84.6303	98.3419
109	85.8858	98.5906
110	87.1460	98.8201
111	88.4111	99.0302
112	89.6808	99.2206
113	90.9552	99.3910
114	92.2341	99.5411
115	93.5176	99.6707
116	94.8054	99.7795
117	96.0977	99.8671
118	97.3942	99.9332
119	98.6950	99.9776
120	100.0000	100.0000

1 YEAR

#	REBATE	EARN
1	1.3498	14.9925
2	4.0302	28.8314
3	8.0223	41.5000
4	13.3077	52.9816
5	19.8680	63.2590
6	27.6850	72.3150
7	36.7410	80.1320
8	47.0184	86.6923
9	58.5000	91.9777
10	71.1686	95.9698
11	85.0075	98.6502
12	100.0000	100.0000
26	55.0801	90.7171
27	59.0531	92.3696
28	63.1458	93.8672
29	67.3566	95.2077
30	71.6837	96.3889
31	76.1256	97.4085
32	80.6806	98.2642
33	85.3471	98.9536
34	90.1236	99.4743
35	95.0084	99.8239
36	100.0000	100.0000

2 YEARS

#	REBATE	EARN
1	.3706	7.5858
2	1.1067	14.9046
3	2.2029	21.9527
4	3.6543	28.7262
5	5.4557	35.2210
6	7.6022	41.4332
7	10.0890	47.3588
8	12.9112	52.9936
9	16.0640	58.3334
10	19.5427	63.3740
11	23.3428	68.1110
12	27.4598	72.5402
13	31.8890	76.6572
14	36.6260	80.4573
15	41.6666	83.9360
16	47.0064	87.0888
17	52.6412	89.9110
18	58.5668	92.3978
19	64.7790	94.5443
20	71.2738	96.3457
21	78.0473	97.7971
22	85.0954	98.8933
23	92.4142	99.6294
24	100.0000	100.0000

3 YEARS

#	REBATE	EARN
1	.1761	4.9916
2	.5257	9.8764
3	1.0464	14.6529
4	1.7358	19.3194
5	2.5915	23.8744
6	3.6111	28.3163
7	4.7923	32.6434
8	6.1328	36.8542
9	7.6304	40.9469
10	9.2829	44.9199
11	11.0879	48.7714
12	13.0435	52.4996
13	15.1474	56.1029
14	17.3975	59.5794
15	19.7918	62.9273
16	22.3282	66.1447
17	25.0048	69.2297
18	27.8194	72.1806
19	30.7703	74.9952
20	33.8553	77.6718
21	37.0727	80.2082
22	40.4206	82.6025
23	43.8971	84.8526
24	47.5004	86.9565
25	51.2286	88.9121

4 YEARS

#	REBATE	EARN
1	.1050	3.6740
2	.3135	7.2944
3	.6240	10.8603
4	1.0350	14.3710
5	1.5453	17.8257
6	2.1533	21.2235
7	2.8576	24.5637
8	3.6570	27.8454
9	4.5500	31.0678
10	5.5353	34.2301
11	6.6117	37.3313
12	7.7778	40.3705
13	9.0323	43.3470
14	10.3740	46.2598
15	11.8017	49.1080
16	13.3142	51.8906
17	14.9102	54.6067
18	16.5886	57.2554
19	18.3481	59.8356
20	20.1877	62.3465
21	22.1063	64.7870
22	24.1026	67.1560
23	26.1756	69.4526
24	28.3242	71.6758
25	30.5474	73.8244
26	32.8440	75.8974
27	35.2130	77.8937
28	37.6535	79.8123
29	40.1644	81.6519
30	42.7446	83.4114
31	45.3933	85.0898
32	48.1094	86.6858
33	50.8920	88.1983
34	53.7402	89.6260
35	56.6530	90.9677
36	59.6295	92.2222
37	62.6687	93.3883
38	65.7699	94.4647
39	68.9322	95.4500
40	72.1546	96.3430
41	75.4363	97.1424
42	78.7765	97.8467
43	82.1743	98.4547
44	85.6290	98.9650
45	89.1397	99.3760
46	92.7056	99.6865
47	96.3260	99.8950
48	100.0000	100.0000

5 YEARS

#	REBATE	EARN
1	.0709	2.8794
2	.2118	5.7283
3	.4216	8.5462
4	.6993	11.3326
5	1.0440	14.0871
6	1.4548	16.8093
7	1.9307	19.4987
8	2.4708	22.1547
9	3.0741	24.7771
10	3.7399	27.3651
11	4.4671	29.9184
12	5.2549	32.4365
13	6.1025	34.9188
14	7.0091	37.3648
15	7.9737	39.7741
16	8.9955	42.1461
17	10.0739	44.4801
18	11.2078	46.7758
19	12.3966	49.0326
20	13.6396	51.2498
21	14.9358	53.4270
22	16.2846	55.5635
23	17.6852	57.6588
24	19.1368	59.7122
25	20.6389	61.7233
26	22.1905	63.6912
27	23.7912	65.6156
28	25.4400	67.4956
29	27.1365	69.3307
30	28.8798	71.1202
31	30.6693	72.8635
32	32.5044	74.5600
33	34.3844	76.2088
34	36.3088	77.8095
35	38.2767	79.3611
36	40.2878	80.8632
37	42.3412	82.3148
38	44.4365	83.7154
39	46.5730	85.0642
40	48.7502	86.3604
41	50.9674	87.6034
42	53.2242	88.7922
43	55.5199	89.9261
44	57.8539	91.0045
45	60.2259	92.0263
46	62.6352	92.9909
47	65.0812	93.8975
48	67.5635	94.7451
49	70.0816	95.5329
50	72.6349	96.2601
51	75.2229	96.9259
52	77.8453	97.5292
53	80.5013	98.0693
54	83.1907	98.5452
55	85.9129	98.9560
56	88.6674	99.3007
57	91.4538	99.5784
58	94.2717	99.7882
59	97.1206	99.9291
60	100.0000	100.0000

6 YEARS

#	REBATE	EARN
1	.0519	2.3497
2	.1548	4.6806
3	.3082	6.9923
4	.5112	9.2848
5	.7633	11.5575
6	1.0636	13.8103
7	1.4115	16.0430
8	1.8063	18.2551
9	2.2474	20.4464
10	2.7341	22.6166
11	3.2658	24.7654
12	3.8417	26.8925
13	4.4614	28.9976
14	5.1242	31.0803
15	5.8294	33.1404
16	6.5764	35.1775
17	7.3647	37.1912
18	8.1938	39.1814
19	9.0629	41.1475
20	9.9715	43.0893
21	10.9192	45.0064
22	11.9052	46.8985
23	12.9292	48.7651
24	13.9905	50.6060
25	15.0886	52.4208
26	16.2229	54.2090
27	17.3931	55.9704
28	18.5986	57.7044
29	19.8388	59.4108
30	21.1133	61.0892
31	22.4216	62.7390
32	23.7632	64.3600
33	25.1376	65.9516
34	26.5444	67.5136
35	27.9832	69.0454
36	29.4534	70.5466
37	30.9546	72.0168
38	32.4864	73.4556
39	34.0484	74.8624
40	35.6400	76.2368
41	37.2610	77.5784
42	38.9108	78.8867
43	40.5892	80.1612
44	42.2956	81.4014
45	44.0296	82.6069
46	45.7910	83.7771
47	47.5792	84.9114
48	49.3940	86.0095
49	51.2349	87.0708
50	53.1015	88.0948
51	54.9936	89.0808
52	56.9107	90.0285
53	58.8525	90.9371
54	60.8186	91.8062
55	62.8088	92.6353
56	64.8225	93.4236
57	66.8596	94.1706
58	68.9197	94.8758
59	71.0024	95.5386
60	73.1075	96.1583
61	75.2346	96.7342
62	77.3834	97.2659
63	79.5536	97.7526
64	81.7449	98.1937
65	83.9570	98.5885
66	86.1897	98.9364
67	88.4425	99.2367
68	90.7152	99.4888
69	93.0077	99.6918
70	95.3194	99.8452
71	97.6503	99.9481
72	100.0000	100.0000

7 YEARS

#	REBATE	EARN
1	.0400	1.9725
2	.1195	3.9328
3	.2379	5.8806
4	.3946	7.8159
5	.5891	9.7384
6	.8209	11.6479
7	1.0894	13.5443
8	1.3941	15.4273
9	1.7345	17.2969
10	2.1101	19.1527
11	2.5204	20.9945
12	2.9650	22.8223
13	3.4432	24.6357
14	3.9547	26.4347
15	4.4990	28.2188
16	5.0755	29.9881
17	5.6839	31.7421
18	6.3238	33.4808
19	6.9945	35.2039
20	7.6958	36.9111
21	8.4272	38.6024
22	9.1882	40.2773
23	9.9784	41.9357
24	10.7975	43.5773
25	11.6450	45.2020
26	12.5205	46.8094
27	13.4236	48.3993
28	14.3539	49.9715
29	15.3111	51.5257
30	16.2947	53.0616
31	17.3044	54.5790
32	18.3399	56.0776
33	19.4006	57.5572
34	20.4864	59.0174
35	21.5968	60.4581
36	22.7314	61.8789
37	23.8900	63.2794
38	25.0723	64.6596
39	26.2777	66.0189
40	27.5062	67.3573
41	28.7572	68.6742
42	30.0305	69.9695
43	31.3258	71.2428
44	32.6427	72.4938
45	33.9811	73.7223
46	35.3404	74.9277
47	36.7206	76.1100
48	38.1211	77.2686
49	39.5419	78.4032
50	40.9826	79.5136
51	42.4428	80.5994
52	43.9224	81.6601
53	45.4210	82.6956
54	46.9384	83.7053
55	48.4743	84.6889
56	50.0285	85.6461
57	51.6007	86.5764
58	53.1906	87.4795
59	54.7980	88.3550
60	56.4227	89.2025
61	58.0643	90.0216
62	59.7227	90.8118
63	61.3976	91.5728
64	63.0889	92.3042
65	64.7961	93.0055
66	66.5192	93.6762
67	68.2579	94.3161
68	70.0119	94.9245
69	71.7812	95.5010
70	73.5653	96.0453
71	75.3643	96.5568
72	77.1777	97.0350
73	79.0055	97.4796
74	80.8473	97.8899
75	82.7031	98.2655

#	REBATE	EARN
75	82.7031	98.2655
76	84.5727	98.6059
77	86.4557	98.9106
78	88.3521	99.1791
79	90.2616	99.4109
80	92.1841	99.6054
81	94.1194	99.7621
82	96.0672	99.8805
83	98.0275	99.9600
84	100.0000	100.0000

8 YEARS

#	REBATE	EARN
1	.0321	1.6911
2	.0959	3.3740
3	.1910	5.0484
4	.3168	6.7144
5	.4729	8.3717
6	.6590	10.0202
7	.8745	11.6598
8	1.1192	13.2905
9	1.3925	14.9119
10	1.6940	16.5241
11	2.0234	18.1269
12	2.3803	19.7201
13	2.7642	21.3036
14	3.1748	22.8773
15	3.6118	24.4411
16	4.0746	25.9947
17	4.5631	27.5381
18	5.0767	29.0710
19	5.6152	30.5934
20	6.1782	32.1052
21	6.7653	33.6060
22	7.3763	35.0958
23	8.0107	36.5745
24	8.6682	38.0418
25	9.3486	39.4976
26	10.0514	40.9418
27	10.7765	42.3741
28	11.5233	43.7945
29	12.2917	45.2026
30	13.0814	46.5985
31	13.8920	47.9817
32	14.7232	49.3523
33	15.5748	50.7100
34	16.4464	52.0547
35	17.3379	53.3860
36	18.2488	54.7039
37	19.1789	56.0082
38	20.1280	57.2986
39	21.0957	58.5750
40	22.0819	59.8371
41	23.0862	61.0848
42	24.1085	62.3179
43	25.1483	63.5361
44	26.2056	64.7392
45	27.2800	65.9270
46	28.3713	67.0992
47	29.4792	68.2558
48	30.6036	69.3964
49	31.7442	70.5208
50	32.9008	71.6289
51	34.0730	72.7200
52	35.2608	73.7944
53	36.4639	74.8517
54	37.6821	75.8915
55	38.9152	76.9138
56	40.1629	77.9181
57	41.4250	78.9043
58	42.7014	79.8720
59	43.9918	80.8211
60	45.2961	81.7512
61	46.6140	82.6621
62	47.9453	83.5536
63	49.2900	84.4252
64	50.6477	85.2768
65	52.0183	86.1080
66	53.4015	86.9186
67	54.7974	87.7083
68	56.2055	88.4767
69	57.6259	89.2235
70	59.0582	89.9486
71	60.5024	90.6514
72	61.9582	91.3318
73	63.4255	91.9893
74	64.9042	92.6237
75	66.3940	93.2347
76	67.8948	93.8218
77	69.4066	94.3848
78	70.9290	94.9233
79	72.4619	95.4369
80	74.0053	95.9254
81	75.5589	96.3882
82	77.1227	96.8252
83	78.6964	97.2358
84	80.2799	97.6197
85	81.8731	97.9766
86	83.4759	98.3060
87	85.0881	98.6075
88	86.7095	98.8808
89	88.3402	99.1255
90	89.9798	99.3410
91	91.6283	99.5271
92	93.2856	99.6832
93	94.9516	99.8090
94	96.6260	99.9041
95	98.3089	99.9679
96	100.0000	100.0000

9 YEARS

#	REBATE	EARN
1	.0266	1.4738
2	.0793	2.9418
3	.1579	4.4040
4	.2620	5.8602
5	.3912	7.3105
6	.5451	8.7546
7	.7234	10.1925
8	.9257	11.6241
9	1.1518	13.0493
10	1.4012	14.4681
11	1.6736	15.8803
12	1.9688	17.2859
13	2.2864	18.6847
14	2.6260	20.0767
15	2.9874	21.4617
16	3.3703	22.8396
17	3.7743	24.2105
18	4.1992	25.5740
19	4.6446	26.9302
20	5.1102	28.2790
21	5.5959	29.6202
22	6.1012	30.9537
23	6.6260	32.2794
24	7.1699	33.5972
25	7.7326	34.9070
26	8.3140	36.2087
27	8.9137	37.5021
28	9.5314	38.7872
29	10.1670	40.0638
30	10.8202	41.3317
31	11.4906	42.5910
32	12.1782	43.8414
33	12.8826	45.0828
34	13.6035	46.3151
35	14.3409	47.5382
36	15.0943	48.7518
37	15.8637	49.9560
38	16.6487	51.1505
39	17.4492	52.3353
40	18.2649	53.5101
41	19.0956	54.6749
42	19.9411	55.8294
43	20.8012	56.9736
44	21.6757	58.1072
45	22.5644	59.2302
46	23.4670	60.3424
47	24.3835	61.4437
48	25.3135	62.5338
49	26.2569	63.6126
50	27.2136	64.6799
51	28.1832	65.7357
52	29.1657	66.7797
53	30.1608	67.8117
54	31.1684	68.8316
55	32.1883	69.8392
56	33.2203	70.8343
57	34.2643	71.8168
58	35.3201	72.7864
59	36.3874	73.7431
60	37.4662	74.6865
61	38.5563	75.6165
62	39.6576	76.5330
63	40.7698	77.4356
64	41.8928	78.3243
65	43.0264	79.1988
66	44.1706	80.0589
67	45.3251	80.9044
68	46.4899	81.7351
69	47.6647	82.5508
70	48.8495	83.3513
71	50.0440	84.1363
72	51.2482	84.9057
73	52.4618	85.6591
74	53.6849	86.3965
75	54.9172	87.1174
76	56.1586	87.8218
77	57.4090	88.5094
78	58.6683	89.1798
79	59.9362	89.8330
80	61.2128	90.4686
81	62.4979	91.0863
82	63.7913	91.6860
83	65.0930	92.2674
84	66.4028	92.8301
85	67.7206	93.3740
86	69.0463	93.8988
87	70.3798	94.4041
88	71.7210	94.8898
89	73.0698	95.3554
90	74.4260	95.8008
91	75.7895	96.2257
92	77.1604	96.6297
93	78.5383	97.0126
94	79.9233	97.3740
95	81.3153	97.7136
96	82.7141	98.0312
97	84.1197	98.3264
98	85.5319	98.5988
99	86.9507	98.8482
100	88.3759	99.0743
101	89.8075	99.2766
102	91.2454	99.4549
103	92.6895	99.6088
104	94.1398	99.7380
105	95.5960	99.8421
106	97.0582	99.9207
107	98.5262	99.9734
108	100.0000	100.0000

10 YEARS

#	REBATE	EARN
1	.0225	1.3014
2	.0672	2.5986
3	.1337	3.8916
4	.2218	5.1805
5	.3312	6.4650
6	.4615	7.7452
7	.6125	9.0209
8	.7838	10.2922
9	.9752	11.5589
10	1.1864	12.8210
11	1.4171	14.0784
12	1.6670	15.3311
13	1.9359	16.5789
14	2.2234	17.8219
15	2.5294	19.0599
16	2.8536	20.2929
17	3.1957	21.5208
18	3.5554	22.7435
19	3.9325	23.9609
20	4.3268	25.1731
21	4.7380	26.3798
22	5.1658	27.5811
23	5.6101	28.7768
24	6.0706	29.9668
25	6.5471	31.1512
26	7.0393	32.3298
27	7.5471	33.5024
28	8.0702	34.6691
29	8.6083	35.8298
30	9.1613	36.9843
31	9.7290	38.1326
32	10.3111	39.2746
33	10.9075	40.4101
34	11.5180	41.5392
35	12.1423	42.6617
36	12.7802	43.7775
37	13.4316	44.8865
38	14.0963	45.9886
39	14.7740	47.0837
40	15.4647	48.1718
41	16.1680	49.2526
42	16.8839	50.3262
43	17.6122	51.3924
44	18.3526	52.4511
45	19.1050	53.5022
46	19.8693	54.5456
47	20.6452	55.5811
48	21.4327	56.6087
49	22.2315	57.6283
50	23.0414	58.6397
51	23.8624	59.6428
52	24.6943	60.6375
53	25.5368	61.6237
54	26.3900	62.6012
55	27.2535	63.5700
56	28.1273	64.5298
57	29.0112	65.4807
58	29.9051	66.4224
59	30.8089	67.3548
60	31.7223	68.2777
61	32.6452	69.1911
62	33.5776	70.0949
63	34.5193	70.9888
64	35.4702	71.8727
65	36.4300	72.7465
66	37.3988	73.6100
67	38.3763	74.4632
68	39.3625	75.3057
69	40.3572	76.1376
70	41.3603	76.9586
71	42.3717	77.7685
72	43.3913	78.5673
73	44.4189	79.3548
74	45.4544	80.1307
75	46.4978	80.8950
76	47.5489	81.6474
77	48.6076	82.3878
78	49.6738	83.1161
79	50.7474	83.8320
80	51.8282	84.5353
81	52.9163	85.2260
82	54.0114	85.9037
83	55.1135	86.5684
84	56.2225	87.2198
85	57.3383	87.8577
86	58.4608	88.4820
87	59.5899	89.0925
88	60.7254	89.6889
89	61.8674	90.2710
90	63.0157	90.8387
91	64.1702	91.3917
92	65.3309	91.9298
93	66.4976	92.4529
94	67.6702	92.9607
95	68.8488	93.4529
96	70.0332	93.9294
97	71.2232	94.3899
98	72.4189	94.8342
99	73.6202	95.2620
100	74.8269	95.6732
101	76.0391	96.0675
102	77.2565	96.4446
103	78.4792	96.8043
104	79.7071	97.1464
105	80.9401	97.4706
106	82.1781	97.7766
107	83.4211	98.0641
108	84.6689	98.3330
109	85.9216	98.5829
110	87.1790	98.8136
111	88.4411	99.0248
112	89.7078	99.2162
113	90.9791	99.3875
114	92.2548	99.5385
115	93.5350	99.6688
116	94.8195	99.7782
117	96.1084	99.8663
118	97.4014	99.9328
119	98.6986	99.9775
120	100.0000	100.0000

ACTUARIAL REBATE AND EARNINGS

17.50 %

1 YEAR

#	REBATE	EARN
1	1.3507	14.9870
2	4.0328	28.8221
3	8.0271	41.4886
4	13.3147	52.9693
5	19.8771	63.2470
6	27.6958	72.3042
7	36.7530	80.1229
8	47.0307	86.6853
9	58.5114	91.9729
10	71.1779	95.9672
11	85.0130	98.6493
12	100.0000	100.0000

2 YEARS

#	REBATE	EARN
1	.3712	7.5802
2	1.1082	14.8942
3	2.2059	21.9384
4	3.6589	28.7087
5	5.4623	35.2011
6	7.6109	41.4116
7	10.0999	47.3360
8	12.9242	52.9703
9	16.0792	58.3101
10	19.5599	63.3512
11	23.3619	68.0891
12	27.4804	72.5196
13	31.9109	76.6381
14	36.6488	80.4401
15	41.6899	83.9208
16	47.0297	87.0758
17	52.6640	89.9001
18	58.5884	92.3891
19	64.7989	94.5377
20	71.2913	96.3411
21	78.0616	97.7941
22	85.1058	98.8918
23	92.4198	99.6288
24	100.0000	100.0000

3 YEARS

#	REBATE	EARN
1	.1764	4.9862
2	.5268	9.8661
3	1.0485	14.6381
4	1.7392	19.3007
5	2.5964	23.8524
6	3.6178	28.2913
7	4.8009	32.6160
8	6.1434	36.8247
9	7.6431	40.9158
10	9.2976	44.8876
11	11.1048	48.7383
12	13.0625	52.4660
13	15.1685	56.0692
14	17.4206	59.5459
15	19.8169	62.8942
16	22.3551	66.1124
17	25.0333	69.1985
18	27.8494	72.1506
19	30.8015	74.9667
20	33.8876	77.6449
21	37.1058	80.1831
22	40.4541	82.5794
23	43.9308	84.8315
24	47.5340	86.9375
25	51.2617	88.8952
26	55.1124	90.7024
27	59.0842	92.3569
28	63.1753	93.8566
29	67.3840	95.1991
30	71.7087	96.3822
31	76.1476	97.4036
32	80.6993	98.2608
33	85.3619	98.9515
34	90.1339	99.4732
35	95.0138	99.8236
36	100.0000	100.0000

4 YEARS

#	REBATE	EARN
1	.1053	3.6689
2	.3143	7.2844
3	.6257	10.8459
4	1.0378	14.3524
5	1.5493	17.8033
6	2.1587	21.1977
7	2.8646	24.5348
8	3.6657	27.8138
9	4.5605	31.0337
10	5.5478	34.1938
11	6.6262	37.2931
12	7.7943	40.3309
13	9.0509	43.3061
14	10.3947	46.2179
15	11.8246	49.0653
16	13.3391	51.8475
17	14.9371	54.5634
18	16.6175	57.2121
19	18.3790	59.7926
20	20.2204	62.3039
21	22.1407	64.7450
22	24.1386	67.1149
23	26.2131	69.4126
24	28.3631	71.6369
25	30.5874	73.7869
26	32.8851	75.8614
27	35.2550	77.8593
28	37.6961	79.7796
29	40.2074	81.6210
30	42.7879	83.3825
31	45.4366	85.0629
32	48.1525	86.6609
33	50.9347	88.1754
34	53.7821	89.6053
35	56.6939	90.9491
36	59.6691	92.2057
37	62.7069	93.3738
38	65.8062	94.4522
39	68.9663	95.4395
40	72.1862	96.3343
41	75.4652	97.1354
42	78.8023	97.8413
43	82.1967	98.4507
44	85.6476	98.9622
45	89.1541	99.3743
46	92.7156	99.6857
47	96.3311	99.8947
48	100.0000	100.0000

5 YEARS

#	REBATE	EARN
1	.0712	2.8745
2	.2125	5.7187
3	.4230	8.5322
4	.7016	11.3145
5	1.0474	14.0652
6	1.4594	16.7837
7	1.9367	19.4697
8	2.4782	22.1226
9	3.0832	24.7421
10	3.7506	27.3275
11	4.4797	29.8784
12	5.2694	32.3943
13	6.1189	34.8746
14	7.0274	37.3189
15	7.9941	39.7267
16	9.0180	42.0973
17	10.0984	44.4303
18	11.2344	46.7251
19	12.4252	48.9812
20	13.6702	51.1980
21	14.9684	53.3748
22	16.3191	55.5112
23	17.7216	57.6066
24	19.1751	59.6602
25	20.6789	61.6717
26	22.2322	63.6402
27	23.8344	65.5652
28	25.4847	67.4461
29	27.1825	69.2822
30	28.9271	71.0729
31	30.7178	72.8175
32	32.5539	74.5153
33	34.4348	76.1656
34	36.3598	77.7678
35	38.3283	79.3211
36	40.3398	80.8249
37	42.3934	82.2784
38	44.4888	83.6809
39	46.6252	85.0316
40	48.8020	86.3298
41	51.0188	87.5748
42	53.2749	88.7656
43	55.5697	89.9016
44	57.9027	90.9820
45	60.2733	92.0059
46	62.6811	92.9726
47	65.1254	93.8811
48	67.6057	94.7306
49	70.1216	95.5203
50	72.6725	96.2494
51	75.2579	96.9168
52	77.8774	97.5218
53	80.5303	98.0633
54	83.2163	98.5406
55	85.9348	98.9526
56	88.6855	99.2984
57	91.4678	99.5770
58	94.2813	99.7875
59	97.1255	99.9288
60	100.0000	100.0000

6 YEARS

#	REBATE	EARN
1	.0521	2.3451
2	.1554	4.6715
3	.3094	6.9790
4	.5132	9.2674
5	.7662	11.5363
6	1.0676	13.7855
7	1.4167	16.0146
8	1.8128	18.2234
9	2.2554	20.4117
10	2.7436	22.5790
11	3.2769	24.7250
12	3.8546	26.8496
13	4.4760	28.9523
14	5.1406	31.0329
15	5.8477	33.0909
16	6.5967	35.1262
17	7.3870	37.1383
18	8.2180	39.1270
19	9.0891	41.0918
20	9.9998	43.0324
21	10.9494	44.9485
22	11.9375	46.8398
23	12.9634	48.7057
24	14.0266	50.5461
25	15.1267	52.3605
26	16.2630	54.1485
27	17.4350	55.9098
28	18.6422	57.6440
29	19.8841	59.3506
30	21.1603	61.0292
31	22.4702	62.6795
32	23.8133	64.3011
33	25.1892	65.8935
34	26.5973	67.4563
35	28.0373	68.9890
36	29.5087	70.4913
37	31.0110	71.9627
38	32.5437	73.4027
39	34.1065	74.8108
40	35.6989	76.1867
41	37.3205	77.5298
42	38.9708	78.8397
43	40.6494	80.1159
44	42.3560	81.3578
45	44.0902	82.5650
46	45.8515	83.7370
47	47.6395	84.8733
48	49.4539	85.9734
49	51.2943	87.0366
50	53.1602	88.0625
51	55.0515	89.0506
52	56.9676	90.0002
53	58.9082	90.9109
54	60.8730	91.7820
55	62.8617	92.6130
56	64.8738	93.4033
57	66.9091	94.1523
58	68.9671	94.8594
59	71.0477	95.5240
60	73.1504	96.1454
61	75.2750	96.7231
62	77.4210	97.2564
63	79.5883	97.7446
64	81.7766	98.1872
65	83.9854	98.5833
66	86.2145	98.9324
67	88.4637	99.2338
68	90.7326	99.4868
69	93.0210	99.6906
70	95.3285	99.8446
71	97.6549	99.9479
72	100.0000	100.0000

7 YEARS

#	REBATE	EARN
1	.0402	1.9681
2	.1200	3.9242
3	.2389	5.8680
4	.3963	7.7994
5	.5916	9.7181
6	.8244	11.6240
7	1.0940	13.5169
8	1.3999	15.3966
9	1.7416	17.2630
10	2.1186	19.1158
11	2.5304	20.9548
12	2.9765	22.7798
13	3.4564	24.5907
14	3.9696	26.3871
15	4.5156	28.1690
16	5.0940	29.9361
17	5.7042	31.6882
18	6.3459	33.4250
19	7.0186	35.1463
20	7.7219	36.8520
21	8.4552	38.5417
22	9.2181	40.2153
23	10.0104	41.8725
24	10.8314	43.5131
25	11.6808	45.1368
26	12.5583	46.7435
27	13.4633	48.3327
28	14.3955	49.9043
29	15.3546	51.4581
30	16.3400	52.9937
31	17.3515	54.5110
32	18.3887	56.0095
33	19.4511	57.4891
34	20.5385	58.9496
35	21.6505	60.3905
36	22.7867	61.8116
37	23.9467	63.2127
38	25.1303	64.5934
39	26.3371	65.9535
40	27.5668	67.2926
41	28.8189	68.6104
42	30.0933	69.9067
43	31.3896	71.1811
44	32.7074	72.4332
45	34.0465	73.6629
46	35.4066	74.8697
47	36.7873	76.0533
48	38.1884	77.2133
49	39.6095	78.3495
50	41.0504	79.4615
51	42.5109	80.5489
52	43.9905	81.6113
53	45.4890	82.6485
54	47.0063	83.6600
55	48.5419	84.6454
56	50.0957	85.6045
57	51.6673	86.5367
58	53.2565	87.4417
59	54.8632	88.3192
60	56.4869	89.1686
61	58.1275	89.9896
62	59.7847	90.7819
63	61.4583	91.5448
64	63.1480	92.2781
65	64.8537	92.9814
66	66.5750	93.6541
67	68.3118	94.2958
68	70.0639	94.9060
69	71.8310	95.4844
70	73.6129	96.0304
71	75.4093	96.5436
72	77.2202	97.0235
73	79.0452	97.4696
74	80.8842	97.8814
75	82.7370	98.2584

#	REBATE	EARN
75	82.7370	98.2584
76	84.6034	98.6001
77	86.4831	98.9060
78	88.3760	99.1756
79	90.2819	99.4084
80	92.2006	99.6037
81	94.1320	99.7611
82	96.0758	99.8800
83	98.0319	99.9598
84	100.0000	100.0000

8 YEARS

#	REBATE	EARN
1	.0323	1.6870
2	.0964	3.3659
3	.1919	5.0365
4	.3183	6.6987
5	.4752	8.3524
6	.6621	9.9974
7	.8787	11.6336
8	1.1244	13.2610
9	1.3989	14.8793
10	1.7017	16.4884
11	2.0325	18.0883
12	2.3908	19.6787
13	2.7762	21.2595
14	3.1884	22.8307
15	3.6270	24.3919
16	4.0916	25.9432
17	4.5817	27.4844
18	5.0972	29.0152
19	5.6375	30.5356
20	6.2023	32.0455
21	6.7913	33.5445
22	7.4041	35.0327
23	8.0405	36.5098
24	8.6999	37.9757
25	9.3822	39.4302
26	10.0870	40.8732
27	10.8139	42.3044
28	11.5627	43.7238
29	12.3330	45.1310
30	13.1245	46.5261
31	13.9370	47.9087
32	14.7700	49.2787
33	15.6234	50.6359
34	16.4968	51.9802
35	17.3900	53.3113
36	18.3026	54.6290
37	19.2343	55.9332
38	20.1850	57.2236
39	21.1543	58.5001
40	22.1420	59.7625
41	23.1477	61.0105
42	24.1713	62.2439
43	25.2125	63.4626
44	26.2710	64.6663
45	27.3466	65.8547
46	28.4390	67.0277
47	29.5460	68.1851
48	30.6734	69.3266
49	31.8149	70.4520
50	32.9723	71.5610
51	34.1453	72.6534
52	35.3337	73.7290
53	36.5374	74.7875
54	37.7561	75.8287
55	38.9895	76.8523
56	40.2375	77.8580
57	41.4999	78.8457
58	42.7764	79.8150
59	44.0668	80.7657
60	45.3710	81.6974
61	46.6887	82.6100
62	48.0198	83.5032
63	49.3641	84.3766
64	50.7213	85.2300
65	52.0913	86.0630
66	53.4739	86.8755
67	54.8690	87.6670
68	56.2762	88.4373
69	57.6956	89.1861
70	59.1268	89.9130
71	60.5698	90.6178
72	62.0243	91.3001
73	63.4902	91.9595
74	64.9673	92.5959
75	66.4555	93.2087
76	67.9545	93.7977
77	69.4644	94.3625
78	70.9848	94.9028
79	72.5156	95.4183
80	74.0568	95.9084
81	75.6081	96.3730
82	77.1693	96.8116
83	78.7405	97.2238
84	80.3213	97.6092
85	81.9117	97.9675
86	83.5116	98.2983
87	85.1207	98.6011
88	86.7390	98.8756
89	88.3664	99.1213
90	90.0026	99.3379
91	91.6476	99.5248
92	93.3013	99.6817
93	94.9635	99.8081
94	96.6341	99.9036
95	98.3130	99.9677
96	100.0000	100.0000

9 YEARS

#	REBATE	EARN
1	.0267	1.4700
2	.0798	2.9342
3	.1588	4.3927
4	.2634	5.8454
5	.3933	7.2922
6	.5480	8.7329
7	.7271	10.1675
8	.9305	11.5959
9	1.1576	13.0181
10	1.4082	14.4339
11	1.6819	15.8432
12	1.9785	17.2459
13	2.2974	18.6420
14	2.6386	20.0313
15	3.0015	21.4138
16	3.3859	22.7894
17	3.7916	24.1578
18	4.2181	25.5192
19	4.6652	26.8732
20	5.1327	28.2199
21	5.6201	29.5591
22	6.1272	30.8908
23	6.6538	32.2147
24	7.1995	33.5308
25	7.7642	34.8390
26	8.3474	36.1392
27	8.9490	37.4312
28	9.5686	38.7150
29	10.2061	39.9904
30	10.8611	41.2572
31	11.5334	42.5154
32	12.2228	43.7648
33	12.9290	45.0054
34	13.6518	46.2369
35	14.3909	47.4593
36	15.1461	48.6724
37	15.9172	49.8760
38	16.7039	51.0701
39	17.5061	52.2545
40	18.3234	53.4291
41	19.1557	54.5937
42	20.0028	55.7481
43	20.8644	56.8923
44	21.7403	58.0260
45	22.6304	59.1492
46	23.5345	60.2616
47	24.4522	61.3632
48	25.3835	62.4536
49	26.3281	63.5329
50	27.2859	64.6008
51	28.2566	65.6572
52	29.2401	66.7018
53	30.2362	67.7346
54	31.2447	68.7553
55	32.2654	69.7638
56	33.2982	70.7599
57	34.3428	71.7434
58	35.3992	72.7141
59	36.4671	73.6719
60	37.5464	74.6165
61	38.6368	75.5478
62	39.7384	76.4655
63	40.8508	77.3696
64	41.9740	78.2597
65	43.1077	79.1356
66	44.2519	79.9972
67	45.4063	80.8443
68	46.5709	81.6766
69	47.7455	82.4939
70	48.9299	83.2961
71	50.1240	84.0828
72	51.3276	84.8539
73	52.5407	85.6091
74	53.7631	86.3482
75	54.9946	87.0710
76	56.2352	87.7772
77	57.4846	88.4666
78	58.7428	89.1389
79	60.0096	89.7939
80	61.2850	90.4314
81	62.5688	91.0510
82	63.8608	91.6526
83	65.1610	92.2358
84	66.4692	92.8005
85	67.7853	93.3462
86	69.1092	93.8728
87	70.4409	94.3799
88	71.7801	94.8673
89	73.1268	95.3348
90	74.4808	95.7819
91	75.8422	96.2084
92	77.2106	96.6141
93	78.5862	96.9985
94	79.9687	97.3614
95	81.3580	97.7026
96	82.7541	98.0215
97	84.1568	98.3181
98	85.5661	98.5918
99	86.9819	98.8424
100	88.4041	99.0695
101	89.8325	99.2729
102	91.2671	99.4520
103	92.7078	99.6067
104	94.1546	99.7366
105	95.6073	99.8412
106	97.0658	99.9202
107	98.5300	99.9733
108	100.0000	100.0000

10 YEARS

#	REBATE	EARN
1	.0226	1.2977
2	.0676	2.5914
3	.1345	3.8810
4	.2231	5.1665
5	.3331	6.4477
6	.4642	7.7246
7	.6159	8.9972
8	.7882	10.2654
9	.9806	11.5291
10	1.1929	12.7883
11	1.4247	14.0429
12	1.6759	15.2928
13	1.9461	16.5379
14	2.2350	17.7783
15	2.5425	19.0137
16	2.8681	20.2442
17	3.2117	21.4697
18	3.5730	22.6901
19	3.9518	23.9054
20	4.3477	25.1154
21	4.7606	26.3200
22	5.1902	27.5193
23	5.6363	28.7131
24	6.0985	29.9013
25	6.5768	31.0839
26	7.0708	32.2608
27	7.5804	33.4318
28	8.1053	34.5970
29	8.6453	35.7562
30	9.2001	36.9093
31	9.7696	38.0563
32	10.3536	39.1971
33	10.9518	40.3315
34	11.5640	41.4595
35	12.1901	42.5809
36	12.8299	43.6958
37	13.4830	44.8039
38	14.1494	45.9053
39	14.8289	46.9997
40	15.5212	48.0872
41	16.2263	49.1675
42	16.9438	50.2406
43	17.6737	51.3064
44	18.4157	52.3648
45	19.1696	53.4156
46	19.9354	54.4588
47	20.7128	55.4942
48	21.5017	56.5218
49	22.3018	57.5414
50	23.1131	58.5529
51	23.9354	59.5561
52	24.7685	60.5511
53	25.6122	61.5376
54	26.4665	62.5155
55	27.3311	63.4847
56	28.2060	64.4450
57	29.0909	65.3964
58	29.9857	66.3387
59	30.8903	67.2718
60	31.8045	68.1955
61	32.7282	69.1097
62	33.6613	70.0143
63	34.6036	70.9091
64	35.5550	71.7940
65	36.5153	72.6689
66	37.4845	73.5335
67	38.4624	74.3878
68	39.4489	75.2315
69	40.4439	76.0646
70	41.4471	76.8869
71	42.4586	77.6982
72	43.4782	78.4983
73	44.5058	79.2872
74	45.5412	80.0646
75	46.5844	80.8304
76	47.6352	81.5843
77	48.6936	82.3263
78	49.7594	83.0562
79	50.8325	83.7737
80	51.9128	84.4788
81	53.0003	85.1711
82	54.0947	85.8506
83	55.1961	86.5170
84	56.3042	87.1701
85	57.4191	87.8099
86	58.5405	88.4360
87	59.6685	89.0482
88	60.8029	89.6464
89	61.9437	90.2304
90	63.0907	90.7999
91	64.2438	91.3547
92	65.4030	91.8947
93	66.5682	92.4196
94	67.7392	92.9292
95	68.9161	93.4232
96	70.0987	93.9015
97	71.2869	94.3637
98	72.4807	94.8098
99	73.6800	95.2394
100	74.8846	95.6523
101	76.0946	96.0482
102	77.3099	96.4270
103	78.5303	96.7883
104	79.7558	97.1319
105	80.9863	97.4575
106	82.2217	97.7650
107	83.4621	98.0539
108	84.7072	98.3241
109	85.9571	98.5753
110	87.2117	98.8071
111	88.4709	99.0194
112	89.7346	99.2118
113	91.0028	99.3841
114	92.2754	99.5358
115	93.5523	99.6669
116	94.8335	99.7769
117	96.1190	99.8655
118	97.4086	99.9324
119	98.7023	99.9774
120	100.0000	100.0000

ACTUARIAL REBATE AND EARNINGS

1 YEAR

#	REBATE	EARN
1	1.3517	14.9815
2	4.0355	28.8129
3	8.0319	41.4772
4	13.3217	52.9571
5	19.8862	63.2350
6	27.7067	72.2933
7	36.7650	80.1138
8	47.0429	86.6783
9	58.5228	91.9681
10	71.1871	95.9645
11	85.0185	98.6483
12	100.0000	100.0000

2 YEARS

#	REBATE	EARN
1	.3717	7.5745
2	1.1098	14.8839
3	2.2088	21.9241
4	3.6636	28.6912
5	5.4689	35.1812
6	7.6196	41.3899
7	10.1107	47.3133
8	12.9373	52.9470
9	16.0943	58.2868
10	19.5771	63.3284
11	23.3809	68.0673
12	27.5010	72.4990
13	31.9327	76.6191
14	36.6716	80.4229
15	41.7132	83.9057
16	47.0530	87.0627
17	52.6867	89.8893
18	58.6101	92.3804
19	64.8188	94.5311
20	71.3088	96.3364
21	78.0759	97.7912
22	85.1161	98.8902
23	92.4255	99.6283
24	100.0000	100.0000

3 YEARS

#	REBATE	EARN
1	.1768	4.9808
2	.5279	9.8558
3	1.0507	14.6234
4	1.7427	19.2822
5	2.6014	23.8304
6	3.6245	28.2664
7	4.8094	32.5886
8	6.1539	36.7953
9	7.6557	40.8848
10	9.3124	44.8554
11	11.1217	48.7052
12	13.0815	52.4325
13	15.1896	56.0355
14	17.4438	59.5124
15	19.8419	62.8613
16	22.3819	66.0802
17	25.0617	69.1673
18	27.8793	72.1207
19	30.8327	74.9383
20	33.9198	77.6181
21	37.1387	80.1581
22	40.4876	82.5562
23	43.9645	84.8104
24	47.5675	86.9185
25	51.2948	88.8783
26	55.1446	90.6876
27	59.1152	92.3443
28	63.2047	93.8461
29	67.4114	95.1906
30	71.7336	96.3755
31	76.1696	97.3986
32	80.7178	98.2573
33	85.3766	98.9493
34	90.1442	99.4721
35	95.0192	99.8232
36	100.0000	100.0000

4 YEARS

#	REBATE	EARN
1	.1056	3.6637
2	.3152	7.2744
3	.6274	10.8314
4	1.0405	14.3339
5	1.5533	17.7810
6	2.1641	21.1720
7	2.8716	24.5060
8	3.6744	27.7822
9	4.5711	30.9997
10	5.5603	34.1576
11	6.6406	37.2551
12	7.8108	40.2913
13	9.0695	43.2653
14	10.4154	46.1761
15	11.8473	49.0228
16	13.3640	51.8044
17	14.9640	54.5201
18	16.6464	57.1688
19	18.4098	59.7496
20	20.2531	62.2613
21	22.1751	64.7031
22	24.1746	67.0739
23	26.2506	69.3725
24	28.4019	71.5981
25	30.6275	73.7494
26	32.9261	75.8254
27	35.2969	77.8249
28	37.7387	79.7469
29	40.2504	81.5902
30	42.8312	83.3536
31	45.4799	85.0360
32	48.1956	86.6360
33	50.9772	88.1527
34	53.8239	89.5846
35	56.7347	90.9305
36	59.7087	92.1892
37	62.7449	93.3594
38	65.8424	94.4397
39	69.0003	95.4289
40	72.2178	96.3256
41	75.4940	97.1284
42	78.8280	97.8359
43	82.2190	98.4467
44	85.6661	98.9595
45	89.1686	99.3726
46	92.7256	99.6848
47	96.3363	99.8944
48	100.0000	100.0000

5 YEARS

#	REBATE	EARN
1	.0714	2.8696
2	.2132	5.7092
3	.4244	8.5183
4	.7039	11.2965
5	1.0508	14.0433
6	1.4640	16.7582
7	1.9426	19.4409
8	2.4857	22.0907
9	3.0923	24.7072
10	3.7614	27.2900
11	4.4922	29.8385
12	5.2838	32.3522
13	6.1353	34.8306
14	7.0458	37.2732
15	8.0145	39.6794
16	9.0404	42.0487
17	10.1228	44.3807
18	11.2609	46.6746
19	12.4538	48.9300
20	13.7008	51.1462
21	15.0009	53.3228
22	16.3536	55.4591
23	17.7580	57.5545
24	19.2133	59.6084
25	20.7188	61.6202
26	22.2738	63.5893
27	23.8776	65.5150
28	25.5294	67.3967
29	27.2286	69.2338
30	28.9744	71.0256
31	30.7662	72.7714
32	32.6033	74.4706
33	34.4850	76.1224
34	36.4107	77.7262
35	38.3798	79.2812
36	40.3916	80.7867
37	42.4455	82.2420
38	44.5409	83.6464
39	46.6772	84.9991
40	48.8538	86.2992
41	51.0700	87.5462
42	53.3254	88.7391
43	55.6193	89.8772
44	57.9513	90.9596
45	60.3206	91.9855
46	62.7268	92.9542
47	65.1694	93.8647
48	67.6478	94.7162
49	70.1615	95.5078
50	72.7100	96.2386
51	75.2928	96.9077
52	77.9093	97.5143
53	80.5591	98.0574
54	83.2418	98.5360
55	85.9567	98.9492
56	88.7035	99.2961
57	91.4817	99.5756
58	94.2908	99.7868
59	97.1304	99.9286
60	100.0000	100.0000

6 YEARS

#	REBATE	EARN
1	.0523	2.3404
2	.1561	4.6625
3	.3106	6.9658
4	.5152	9.2501
5	.7691	11.5152
6	1.0715	13.7607
7	1.4219	15.9864
8	1.8193	18.1920
9	2.2633	20.3771
10	2.7531	22.5415
11	3.2880	24.6849
12	3.8674	26.8069
13	4.4906	28.9073
14	5.1571	30.9856
15	5.8660	33.0417
16	6.6170	35.0751
17	7.4092	37.0856
18	8.2422	39.0728
19	9.1153	41.0363
20	10.0280	42.9757
21	10.9797	44.8909
22	11.9697	46.7813
23	12.9976	48.6466
24	14.0628	50.4865
25	15.1647	52.3005
26	16.3029	54.0883
27	17.4767	55.8495
28	18.6858	57.5837
29	19.9294	59.2905
30	21.2072	60.9695
31	22.5187	62.6203
32	23.8633	64.2424
33	25.2406	65.8355
34	26.6501	67.3991
35	28.0914	68.9328
36	29.5639	70.4361
37	31.0672	71.9086
38	32.6009	73.3499
39	34.1645	74.7594
40	35.7576	76.1367
41	37.3797	77.4813
42	39.0305	78.7928
43	40.7095	80.0706
44	42.4163	81.3142
45	44.1505	82.5233
46	45.9117	83.6971
47	47.6995	84.8353
48	49.5135	85.9372
49	51.3534	87.0024
50	53.2187	88.0303
51	55.1091	89.0203
52	57.0243	89.9720
53	58.9637	90.8847
54	60.9272	91.7578
55	62.9144	92.5908
56	64.9249	93.3830
57	66.9583	94.1340
58	69.0144	94.8429
59	71.0927	95.5094
60	73.1931	96.1326
61	75.3151	96.7120
62	77.4585	97.2469
63	79.6229	97.7367
64	81.8080	98.1807
65	84.0136	98.5781
66	86.2393	98.9285
67	88.4848	99.2309
68	90.7499	99.4848
69	93.0342	99.6894
70	95.3375	99.8439
71	97.6596	99.9477
72	100.0000	100.0000

7 YEARS

#	REBATE	EARN
1	.0404	1.9638
2	.1206	3.9157
3	.2400	5.8554
4	.3981	7.7829
5	.5942	9.6979
6	.8279	11.6002
7	1.0986	13.4897
8	1.4057	15.3661
9	1.7487	17.2293
10	2.1271	19.0791
11	2.5404	20.9152
12	2.9881	22.7376
13	3.4696	24.5459
14	3.9845	26.3399
15	4.5322	28.1195
16	5.1124	29.8844
17	5.7245	31.6345
18	6.3681	33.3694
19	7.0427	35.0890
20	7.7479	36.7931
21	8.4832	38.4814
22	9.2481	40.1537
23	10.0423	41.8097
24	10.8653	43.4492
25	11.7166	45.0720
26	12.5960	46.6778
27	13.5030	48.2664
28	14.4371	49.8375
29	15.3980	51.3908
30	16.3852	52.9261
31	17.3985	54.4432
32	18.4374	55.9417
33	19.5015	57.4213
34	20.5906	58.8819
35	21.7041	60.3231
36	22.8418	61.7446
37	24.0033	63.1462
38	25.1882	64.5275
39	26.3963	65.8882
40	27.6272	67.2281
41	28.8805	68.5468
42	30.1559	69.8441
43	31.4532	71.1195
44	32.7719	72.3728
45	34.1118	73.6037
46	35.4725	74.8118
47	36.8538	75.9967
48	38.2554	77.1582
49	39.6769	78.2959
50	41.1181	79.4094
51	42.5787	80.4985
52	44.0583	81.5626
53	45.5568	82.6015
54	47.0739	83.6148
55	48.6092	84.6020
56	50.1625	85.5629
57	51.7336	86.4970
58	53.3222	87.4040
59	54.9280	88.2834
60	56.5508	89.1347
61	58.1903	89.9577
62	59.8463	90.7519
63	61.5186	91.5168
64	63.2069	92.2521
65	64.9110	92.9573
66	66.6306	93.6319
67	68.3655	94.2755
68	70.1156	94.8876
69	71.8805	95.4678
70	73.6601	96.0155
71	75.4541	96.5304
72	77.2624	97.0119
73	79.0848	97.4596
74	80.9209	97.8729
75	82.7707	98.2513

#	REBATE	EARN
75	82.7707	98.2513
76	84.6339	98.5943
77	86.5103	98.9014
78	88.3998	99.1721
79	90.3021	99.4058
80	92.2171	99.6019
81	94.1446	99.7600
82	96.0843	99.8794
83	98.0362	99.9596
84	100.0000	100.0000

8 YEARS

#	REBATE	EARN
1	.0325	1.6830
2	.0969	3.3579
3	.1929	5.0246
4	.3199	6.6831
5	.4775	8.3332
6	.6653	9.9747
7	.8828	11.6076
8	1.1296	13.2317
9	1.4053	14.8468
10	1.7094	16.4530
11	2.0415	18.0499
12	2.4013	19.6375
13	2.7882	21.2157
14	3.2020	22.7843
15	3.6422	24.3431
16	4.1085	25.8921
17	4.6004	27.4310
18	5.1176	28.9598
19	5.6597	30.4782
20	6.2264	31.9861
21	6.8173	33.4834
22	7.4320	34.9700
23	8.0702	36.4455
24	8.7316	37.9100
25	9.4158	39.3632
26	10.1225	40.8049
27	10.8513	42.2351
28	11.6020	43.6534
29	12.3742	45.0598
30	13.1676	46.4540
31	13.9819	47.8360
32	14.8167	49.2054
33	15.6719	50.5621
34	16.5471	51.9060
35	17.4419	53.2368
36	18.3562	54.5544
37	19.2896	55.8585
38	20.2419	57.1490
39	21.2127	58.4256
40	22.2019	59.6882
41	23.2091	60.9365
42	24.2341	62.1703
43	25.2765	63.3894
44	26.3363	64.5936
45	27.4131	65.7827
46	28.5066	66.9565
47	29.6166	68.1147
48	30.7430	69.2570
49	31.8853	70.3834
50	33.0435	71.4934
51	34.2173	72.5869
52	35.4064	73.6637
53	36.6106	74.7235
54	37.8294	75.7659
55	39.0635	76.7909
56	40.3118	77.7981
57	41.5744	78.7873
58	42.8510	79.7581
59	44.1415	80.7104
60	45.4456	81.6438
61	46.7632	82.5581
62	48.0940	83.4529
63	49.4379	84.3281
64	50.7946	85.1833
65	52.1640	86.0181
66	53.5460	86.8324
67	54.9402	87.6258
68	56.3466	88.3980
69	57.7649	89.1487
70	59.1951	89.8775
71	60.6368	90.5842
72	62.0900	91.2684
73	63.5545	91.9298
74	65.0300	92.5680
75	66.5166	93.1827
76	68.0139	93.7736
77	69.5218	94.3403
78	71.0402	94.8824
79	72.5690	95.3996
80	74.1079	95.8915
81	75.6569	96.3578
82	77.2157	96.7980
83	78.7843	97.2118
84	80.3625	97.5987
85	81.9501	97.9585
86	83.5470	98.2906
87	85.1532	98.5947
88	86.7683	98.8704
89	88.3924	99.1172
90	90.0253	99.3347
91	91.6668	99.5225
92	93.3169	99.6801
93	94.9754	99.8071
94	96.6421	99.9031
95	98.3170	99.9675
96	100.0000	100.0000

9 YEARS

#	REBATE	EARN
1	.0269	1.4661
2	.0802	2.9267
3	.1597	4.3816
4	.2648	5.8307
5	.3954	7.2740
6	.5508	8.7114
7	.7309	10.1427
8	.9353	11.5680
9	1.1635	12.9871
10	1.4153	14.3999
11	1.6903	15.8063
12	1.9881	17.2062
13	2.3085	18.5996
14	2.6511	19.9864
15	3.0155	21.3663
16	3.4016	22.7394
17	3.8088	24.1056
18	4.2370	25.4647
19	4.6859	26.8166
20	5.1551	28.1612
21	5.6443	29.4985
22	6.1532	30.8283
23	6.6816	32.1504
24	7.2292	33.4649
25	7.7957	34.7715
26	8.3808	36.0702
27	8.9842	37.3608
28	9.6057	38.6433
29	10.2450	39.9174
30	10.9019	41.1831
31	11.5761	42.4403
32	12.2673	43.6888
33	12.9754	44.9284
34	13.6999	46.1592
35	14.4408	47.3809
36	15.1978	48.5934
37	15.9706	49.7965
38	16.7590	50.9902
39	17.5628	52.1742
40	18.3818	53.3485
41	19.2157	54.5129
42	20.0643	55.6673
43	20.9274	56.8114
44	21.8048	57.9452
45	22.6963	59.0685
46	23.6017	60.1812
47	24.5207	61.2830
48	25.4533	62.3739
49	26.3991	63.4536
50	27.3580	64.5220
51	28.3297	65.5790
52	29.3143	66.6243
53	30.3113	67.6578
54	31.3206	68.6794
55	32.3422	69.6887
56	33.3757	70.6857
57	34.4210	71.6703
58	35.4780	72.6420
59	36.5464	73.6009
60	37.6261	74.5467
61	38.7170	75.4793
62	39.8188	76.3983
63	40.9315	77.3037
64	42.0548	78.1952
65	43.1886	79.0726
66	44.3327	79.9357
67	45.4871	80.7843
68	46.6515	81.6182
69	47.8258	82.4372
70	49.0098	83.2410
71	50.2035	84.0294
72	51.4066	84.8022
73	52.6191	85.5592
74	53.8408	86.3001
75	55.0716	87.0246
76	56.3112	87.7327
77	57.5597	88.4239
78	58.8169	89.0981
79	60.0826	89.7550
80	61.3567	90.3943
81	62.6392	91.0158
82	63.9298	91.6192
83	65.2285	92.2043
84	66.5351	92.7708
85	67.8496	93.3184
86	69.1717	93.8468
87	70.5015	94.3557
88	71.8388	94.8449
89	73.1834	95.3141
90	74.5353	95.7630
91	75.8944	96.1912
92	77.2606	96.5984
93	78.6337	96.9845
94	80.0136	97.3489
95	81.4004	97.6915
96	82.7938	98.0119
97	84.1937	98.3097
98	85.6001	98.5847
99	87.0129	98.8365
100	88.4320	99.0647
101	89.8573	99.2691
102	91.2886	99.4492
103	92.7260	99.6046
104	94.1693	99.7352
105	95.6184	99.8403
106	97.0733	99.9198
107	98.5339	99.9731
108	100.0000	100.0000

10 YEARS

#	REBATE	EARN
1	.0228	1.2942
2	.0680	2.5844
3	.1353	3.8705
4	.2244	5.1526
5	.3350	6.4306
6	.4668	7.7043
7	.6194	8.9738
8	.7926	10.2389
9	.9860	11.4996
10	1.1994	12.7559
11	1.4324	14.0076
12	1.6848	15.2548
13	1.9563	16.4973
14	2.2467	17.7350
15	2.5555	18.9680
16	2.8827	20.1960
17	3.2278	21.4192
18	3.5907	22.6373
19	3.9711	23.8503
20	4.3687	25.0581
21	4.7833	26.2607
22	5.2146	27.4580
23	5.6624	28.6499
24	6.1264	29.8363
25	6.6065	31.0171
26	7.1023	32.1923
27	7.6137	33.3617
28	8.1404	34.5254
29	8.6822	35.6831
30	9.2389	36.8349
31	9.8102	37.9806
32	10.3960	39.1201
33	10.9960	40.2534
34	11.6100	41.3803
35	12.2379	42.5007
36	12.8794	43.6147
37	13.5343	44.7220
38	14.2025	45.8226
39	14.8837	46.9163
40	15.5777	48.0031
41	16.2844	49.0829
42	17.0035	50.1555
43	17.7350	51.2209
44	18.4785	52.2789
45	19.2340	53.3295
46	20.0013	54.3725
47	20.7801	55.4078
48	21.5704	56.4353
49	22.3719	57.4549
50	23.1846	58.4665
51	24.0081	59.47C0
52	24.8424	60.4651
53	25.6874	61.4519
54	26.5427	62.4301
55	27.4084	63.3998
56	28.2843	64.3606
57	29.1702	65.3125
58	30.0659	66.2555
59	30.9713	67.1892
60	31.8863	68.1137
61	32.8108	69.0287
62	33.7445	69.9341
63	34.6875	70.8298
64	35.6394	71.7157
65	36.6002	72.5916
66	37.5699	73.4573
67	38.5481	74.3126
68	39.5349	75.1576
69	40.5300	75.9919
70	41.5335	76.8154
71	42.5451	77.6281
72	43.5647	78.4296
73	44.5922	79.2199
74	45.6275	79.9987
75	46.6705	80.7660
76	47.7211	81.5215
77	48.7791	82.2650
78	49.8445	82.9965
79	50.9171	83.7156
80	51.9969	84.4223
81	53.0837	85.1163
82	54.1774	85.7975
83	55.2780	86.4657
84	56.3853	87.1206
85	57.4993	87.7621
86	58.6197	88.3900
87	59.7466	89.0040
88	60.8799	89.6040
89	62.0194	90.1898
90	63.1651	90.7611
91	64.3169	91.3178
92	65.4746	91.8596
93	66.6383	92.3863
94	67.8077	92.8977
95	68.9829	93.3935
96	70.1637	93.8736
97	71.3501	94.3376
98	72.5420	94.7854
99	73.7393	95.2167
100	74.9419	95.6313
101	76.1497	96.0289
102	77.3627	96.4093
103	78.5808	96.7722
104	79.8040	97.1173
105	81.0320	97.4445
106	82.2650	97.7533
107	83.5027	98.0437
108	84.7452	98.3152
109	85.9924	98.5676
110	87.2441	98.8006
111	88.5004	99.0140
112	89.7611	99.2074
113	91.0262	99.3806
114	92.2957	99.5332
115	93.5694	99.6650
116	94.8474	99.7756
117	96.1295	99.8647
118	97.4156	99.9320
119	98.7058	99.9772
120	100.0000	100.0000

1 YEAR

#	REBATE	EARN
1	1.3527	14.9761
2	4.0381	28.8037
3	8.0366	41.4658
4	13.3287	52.9449
5	19.8953	63.2231
6	27.7176	72.2824
7	36.7769	80.1047
8	47.0551	86.6713
9	58.5342	91.9634
10	71.1963	95.9619
11	85.0239	98.6473
12	100.0000	100.0000

2 YEARS

#	REBATE	EARN
1	.3723	7.5689
2	1.1114	14.8735
3	2.2118	21.9098
4	3.6683	28.6738
5	5.4755	35.1613
6	7.6283	41.3683
7	10.1216	47.2906
8	12.9503	52.9238
9	16.1095	58.2636
10	19.5943	63.3056
11	23.3999	68.0454
12	27.5216	72.4784
13	31.9546	76.6001
14	36.6944	80.4057
15	41.7364	83.8905
16	47.0762	87.0497
17	52.7094	89.8784
18	58.6137	92.3717
19	64.8387	94.5245
20	71.3262	96.3317
21	78.0902	97.7882
22	85.1265	98.8886
23	92.4311	99.6277
24	100.0000	100.0000

3 YEARS

#	REBATE	EARN
1	.1772	4.9754
2	.5290	9.8455
3	1.0528	14.6088
4	1.7461	19.2636
5	2.6064	23.8084
6	3.6311	28.2416
7	4.8180	32.5613
8	6.1645	36.7660
9	7.6683	40.8539
10	9.3271	44.8232
11	11.1386	48.6722
12	13.1005	52.3990
13	15.2107	56.0019
14	17.4669	59.4790
15	19.8669	62.8283
16	22.4087	66.0480
17	25.0902	69.1362
18	27.9092	72.0908
19	30.8638	74.9098
20	33.9520	77.5913
21	37.1717	80.1331
22	40.5210	82.5331
23	43.9981	84.7893
24	47.6010	86.8995
25	51.3278	88.8614
26	55.1768	90.6729
27	59.1461	92.3317
28	63.2340	93.8355
29	67.4387	95.1820
30	71.7584	96.3689
31	76.1916	97.3936
32	80.7364	98.2539
33	85.3912	98.9472
34	90.1545	99.4710
35	95.0246	99.8228
36	100.0000	100.0000

4 YEARS

#	REBATE	EARN
1	.1059	3.6585
2	.3161	7.2645
3	.6291	10.8170
4	1.0433	14.3154
5	1.5573	17.7588
6	2.1695	21.1464
7	2.8787	24.4773
8	3.6832	27.7507
9	4.5817	30.9658
10	5.5728	34.1216
11	6.6551	37.2172
12	7.8273	40.2519
13	9.0881	43.2245
14	10.4361	46.1343
15	11.8701	48.9803
16	13.3888	51.7615
17	14.9909	54.4770
18	16.6753	57.1257
19	18.4406	59.7066
20	20.2857	62.2189
21	22.2094	64.6613
22	24.2106	67.0329
23	26.2880	69.3326
24	28.4407	71.5593
25	30.6674	73.7120
26	32.9671	75.7894
27	35.3387	77.7906
28	37.7811	79.7143
29	40.2934	81.5594
30	42.8743	83.3247
31	45.5230	85.0091
32	48.2385	86.6112
33	51.0197	88.1299
34	53.8657	89.5639
35	56.7755	90.9119
36	59.7481	92.1727
37	62.7828	93.3449
38	65.8784	94.4272
39	69.0342	95.4183
40	72.2493	96.3168
41	75.5227	97.1213
42	78.8536	97.8305
43	82.2412	98.4427
44	85.6846	98.9567
45	89.1830	99.3709
46	92.7355	99.6839
47	96.3415	99.8941
48	100.0000	100.0000

5 YEARS

#	REBATE	EARN
1	.0717	2.8648
2	.2140	5.6997
3	.4258	8.5045
4	.7062	11.2786
5	1.0541	14.0215
6	1.4686	16.7329
7	1.9486	19.4121
8	2.4931	22.0588
9	3.1013	24.6725
10	3.7722	27.2526
11	4.5048	29.7987
12	5.2983	32.3102
13	6.1517	34.7867
14	7.0642	37.2276
15	8.0349	39.6323
16	9.0629	42.0003
17	10.1473	44.3311
18	11.2874	46.6242
19	12.4824	48.8789
20	13.7313	51.0946
21	15.0335	53.2709
22	16.3881	55.4070
23	17.7943	57.5025
24	19.2514	59.5566
25	20.7587	61.5688
26	22.3154	63.5385
27	23.9207	65.4649
28	25.5740	67.3475
29	27.2745	69.1856
30	29.0215	70.9785
31	30.8144	72.7255
32	32.6525	74.4260
33	34.5351	76.0793
34	36.4615	77.6846
35	38.4312	79.2413
36	40.4434	80.7486
37	42.4975	82.2057
38	44.5930	83.6119
39	46.7291	84.9665
40	48.9054	86.2687
41	51.1211	87.5176
42	53.3758	88.7126
43	55.6689	89.8527
44	57.9997	90.9371
45	60.3677	91.9651
46	62.7724	92.9358
47	65.2133	93.8483
48	67.6898	94.7017
49	70.2013	95.4952
50	72.7474	96.2278
51	75.3275	96.8987
52	77.9412	97.5069
53	80.5879	98.0514
54	83.2671	98.5314
55	85.9785	98.9459
56	88.7214	99.2938
57	91.4955	99.5742
58	94.3003	99.7860
59	97.1352	99.9283
60	100.0000	100.0000

6 YEARS

#	REBATE	EARN
1	.0525	2.3359
2	.1567	4.6535
3	.3118	6.9526
4	.5172	9.2329
5	.7720	11.4942
6	1.0755	13.7361
7	1.4270	15.9583
8	1.8259	18.1606
9	2.2713	20.3427
10	2.7626	22.5042
11	3.2991	24.6449
12	3.8802	26.7644
13	4.5052	28.8624
14	5.1735	30.9386
15	5.8844	32.9927
16	6.6372	35.0243
17	7.4315	37.0331
18	8.2664	39.0188
19	9.1415	40.9810
20	10.0562	42.9193
21	11.0099	44.8334
22	12.0019	46.7230
23	13.0318	48.5877
24	14.0989	50.4270
25	15.2028	52.2406
26	16.3428	54.0282
27	17.5185	55.7893
28	18.7293	57.5236
29	19.9746	59.2306
30	21.2541	60.9099
31	22.5671	62.5611
32	23.9133	64.1839
33	25.2920	65.7776
34	26.7028	67.3421
35	28.1453	68.8767
36	29.6190	70.3810
37	31.1233	71.8547
38	32.6579	73.2972
39	34.2224	74.7080
40	35.8161	76.0867
41	37.4389	77.4329
42	39.0901	78.7459
43	40.7694	80.0254
44	42.4764	81.2707
45	44.2107	82.4815
46	45.9718	83.6572
47	47.7594	84.7972
48	49.5730	85.9011
49	51.4123	86.9682
50	53.2770	87.9981
51	55.1666	88.9901
52	57.0807	89.9438
53	59.0190	90.8585
54	60.9812	91.7336
55	62.9669	92.5685
56	64.9757	93.3628
57	67.0073	94.1156
58	69.0614	94.8265
59	71.1376	95.4948
60	73.2356	96.1198
61	75.3551	96.7009
62	77.4958	97.2374
63	79.6573	97.7287
64	81.8394	98.1741
65	84.0417	98.5730
66	86.2639	98.9245
67	88.5058	99.2280
68	90.7671	99.4828
69	93.0474	99.6882
70	95.3465	99.8433
71	97.6641	99.9475
72	100.0000	100.0000

7 YEARS

#	REBATE	EARN
1	.0406	1.9595
2	.1211	3.9072
3	.2411	5.8430
4	.3998	7.7666
5	.5968	9.6778
6	.8314	11.5766
7	1.1032	13.4626
8	1.4115	15.3358
9	1.7558	17.1959
10	2.1356	19.0426
11	2.5504	20.8759
12	2.9996	22.6956
13	3.4828	24.5013
14	3.9994	26.2929
15	4.5489	28.0702
16	5.1309	29.8330
17	5.7448	31.5811
18	6.3903	33.3142
19	7.0668	35.0321
20	7.7739	36.7345
21	8.5111	38.4214
22	9.2780	40.0923
23	10.0741	41.7472
24	10.8991	43.3856
25	11.7524	45.0075
26	12.6337	46.6125
27	13.5426	48.2004
28	14.4785	49.7709
29	15.4413	51.3238
30	16.4304	52.8588
31	17.4454	54.3757
32	18.4860	55.8741
33	19.5518	57.3538
34	20.6425	58.8145
35	21.7576	60.2560
36	22.8968	61.6779
37	24.0597	63.0799
38	25.2460	64.4618
39	26.4554	65.8232
40	27.6875	67.1638
41	28.9419	68.4834
42	30.2184	69.7816
43	31.5166	71.0581
44	32.8362	72.3125
45	34.1768	73.5446
46	35.5382	74.7540
47	36.9201	75.9403
48	38.3221	77.1032
49	39.7440	78.2424
50	41.1855	79.3575
51	42.6462	80.4482
52	44.1259	81.5140
53	45.6243	82.5546
54	47.1412	83.5696
55	48.6762	84.5587
56	50.2291	85.5215
57	51.7996	86.4574
58	53.3875	87.3663
59	54.9925	88.2476
60	56.6144	89.1009
61	58.2528	89.9259
62	59.9077	90.7220
63	61.5786	91.4889
64	63.2655	92.2261
65	64.9679	92.9332
66	66.6858	93.6097
67	68.4189	94.2552
68	70.1670	94.8691
69	71.9298	95.4511
70	73.7071	96.0006
71	75.4987	96.5172
72	77.3044	97.0004
73	79.1241	97.4496
74	80.9574	97.8644
75	82.8041	98.2442

#	REBATE	EARN
75	82.8041	98.2442
76	84.6642	98.5885
77	86.5374	98.8968
78	88.4234	99.1686
79	90.3222	99.4032
80	92.2334	99.6002
81	94.1570	99.7589
82	96.0928	99.8789
83	98.0405	99.9594
84	100.0000	100.0000

8 YEARS

#	REBATE	EARN
1	.0326	1.6789
2	.0974	3.3499
3	.1938	5.0129
4	.3215	6.6676
5	.4798	8.3141
6	.6685	9.9522
7	.8870	11.5817
8	1.1349	13.2026
9	1.4117	14.8146
10	1.7171	16.4178
11	2.0506	18.0118
12	2.4118	19.5967
13	2.8003	21.1722
14	3.2156	22.7382
15	3.6575	24.2946
16	4.1254	25.8412
17	4.6190	27.3780
18	5.1380	28.9046
19	5.6820	30.4211
20	6.2505	31.9271
21	6.8432	33.4227
22	7.4598	34.9076
23	8.0999	36.3816
24	8.7632	37.8446
25	9.4493	39.2965
26	10.1579	40.7370
27	10.8887	42.1661
28	11.6412	43.5834
29	12.4153	44.9889
30	13.2106	46.3824
31	14.0267	47.7636
32	14.8634	49.1325
33	15.7203	50.4887
34	16.5972	51.8322
35	17.4938	53.1628
36	18.4098	54.4801
37	19.3448	55.7842
38	20.2987	57.0747
39	21.2710	58.3514
40	22.2617	59.6141
41	23.2703	60.8627
42	24.2966	62.0969
43	25.3404	63.3165
44	26.4014	64.5213
45	27.4793	65.7110
46	28.5739	66.8855
47	29.6850	68.0445
48	30.8123	69.1877
49	31.9555	70.3150
50	33.1145	71.4261
51	34.2890	72.5207
52	35.4787	73.5986
53	36.6835	74.6596
54	37.9031	75.7034
55	39.1373	76.7297
56	40.3859	77.7383
57	41.6486	78.7290
58	42.9253	79.7013
59	44.2158	80.6552
60	45.5199	81.5902
61	46.8372	82.5062
62	48.1678	83.4028
63	49.5113	84.2797
64	50.8675	85.1366
65	52.2364	85.9733
66	53.6176	86.7894
67	55.0111	87.5847
68	56.4166	88.3588
69	57.8339	89.1113
70	59.2630	89.8421
71	60.7035	90.5507
72	62.1554	91.2368
73	63.6184	91.9001
74	65.0924	92.5402
75	66.5773	93.1568
76	68.0729	93.7495
77	69.5789	94.3180
78	71.0954	94.8620
79	72.6220	95.3810
80	74.1588	95.8746
81	75.7054	96.3425
82	77.2618	96.7844
83	78.8278	97.1997
84	80.4033	97.5882
85	81.9882	97.9494
86	83.5822	98.2829
87	85.1854	98.5883
88	86.7974	98.8651
89	88.4183	99.1130
90	90.0478	99.3315
91	91.6859	99.5202
92	93.3324	99.6785
93	94.9871	99.8062
94	96.6501	99.9026
95	98.3211	99.9674
96	100.0000	100.0000

9 YEARS

#	REBATE	EARN
1	.0270	1.4624
2	.0807	2.9192
3	.1606	4.3705
4	.2663	5.8161
5	.3975	7.2560
6	.5537	8.6900
7	.7347	10.1182
8	.9400	11.5403
9	1.1694	12.9563
10	1.4223	14.3662
11	1.6986	15.7697
12	1.9978	17.1669
13	2.3195	18.5576
14	2.6636	19.9417
15	3.0296	21.3192
16	3.4172	22.6899
17	3.8261	24.0537
18	4.2560	25.4106
19	4.7065	26.7604
20	5.1775	28.1030
21	5.6685	29.4383
22	6.1792	30.7662
23	6.7094	32.0866
24	7.2589	33.3994
25	7.8272	34.7045
26	8.4141	36.0016
27	9.0194	37.2909
28	9.6428	38.5720
29	10.2840	39.8449
30	10.9427	41.1095
31	11.6187	42.3656
32	12.3118	43.6131
33	13.0216	44.8520
34	13.7480	46.0819
35	14.4907	47.3029
36	15.2494	48.5148
37	16.0239	49.7174
38	16.8140	50.9106
39	17.6195	52.0943
40	18.4400	53.2684
41	19.2755	54.4326
42	20.1256	55.5868
43	20.9902	56.7310
44	21.8691	57.8648
45	22.7620	58.9883
46	23.6687	60.1011
47	24.5890	61.2033
48	25.5228	62.2945
49	26.4698	63.3747
50	27.4298	64.4436
51	28.4026	65.5011
52	29.3881	66.5471
53	30.3861	67.5814
54	31.3963	68.6037
55	32.4186	69.6139
56	33.4529	70.6119
57	34.4989	71.5974
58	35.5564	72.5702
59	36.6253	73.5302
60	37.7055	74.4772
61	38.7967	75.4110
62	39.8989	76.3313
63	41.0117	77.2380
64	42.1352	78.1309
65	43.2690	79.0098
66	44.4132	79.8744
67	45.5674	80.7245
68	46.7316	81.5600
69	47.9057	82.3805
70	49.0894	83.1860
71	50.2826	83.9761
72	51.4852	84.7506
73	52.6971	85.5093
74	53.9181	86.2520
75	55.1480	86.9784
76	56.3869	87.6882
77	57.6344	88.3813
78	58.8905	89.0573
79	60.1551	89.7160
80	61.4280	90.3572
81	62.7091	90.9806
82	63.9984	91.5859
83	65.2955	92.1728
84	66.6006	92.7411
85	67.9134	93.2906
86	69.2338	93.8208
87	70.5617	94.3315
88	71.8970	94.8225
89	73.2396	95.2935
90	74.5894	95.7440
91	75.9463	96.1739
92	77.3101	96.5828
93	78.6808	96.9704
94	80.0583	97.3364
95	81.4424	97.6805
96	82.8331	98.0022
97	84.2303	98.3014
98	85.6338	98.5777
99	87.0437	98.8306
100	88.4597	99.0600
101	89.8818	99.2653
102	91.3100	99.4463
103	92.7440	99.6025
104	94.1839	99.7337
105	95.6295	99.8394
106	97.0808	99.9193
107	98.5376	99.9730
108	100.0000	100.0000

10 YEARS

#	REBATE	EARN
1	.0229	1.2906
2	.0684	2.5774
3	.1361	3.8601
4	.2258	5.1389
5	.3370	6.4136
6	.4695	7.6842
7	.6229	8.9505
8	.7970	10.2126
9	.9914	11.4704
10	1.2059	12.7238
11	1.4401	13.9727
12	1.6937	15.2171
13	1.9666	16.4570
14	2.2583	17.6921
15	2.5686	18.9226
16	2.8972	20.1482
17	3.2439	21.3690
18	3.6083	22.5848
19	3.9903	23.7956
20	4.3896	25.0013
21	4.8059	26.2019
22	5.2389	27.3972
23	5.6885	28.5872
24	6.1543	29.7717
25	6.6361	30.9508
26	7.1337	32.1243
27	7.6469	33.2922
28	8.1754	34.4543
29	8.7191	35.6106
30	9.2775	36.7610
31	9.8507	37.9054
32	10.4383	39.0437
33	11.0401	40.1758
34	11.6560	41.3016
35	12.2856	42.4211
36	12.9289	43.5341
37	13.5855	44.6406
38	14.2554	45.7404
39	14.9383	46.8334
40	15.6340	47.9196
41	16.3423	48.9988
42	17.0631	50.0709
43	17.7961	51.1359
44	18.5412	52.1936
45	19.2982	53.2439
46	20.0670	54.2867
47	20.8473	55.3219
48	21.6389	56.3494
49	22.4418	57.3690
50	23.2557	58.3806
51	24.0806	59.3842
52	24.9161	60.3796
53	25.7622	61.3666
54	26.6187	62.3453
55	27.4854	63.3153
56	28.3623	64.2766
57	29.2491	65.2291
58	30.1457	66.1726
59	31.0520	67.1070
60	31.9678	68.0322
61	32.8930	68.9480
62	33.8274	69.8543
63	34.7709	70.7509
64	35.7234	71.6377
65	36.6847	72.5146
66	37.6547	73.3813
67	38.6334	74.2378
68	39.6204	75.0839
69	40.6158	75.9194
70	41.6194	76.7443
71	42.6310	77.5582
72	43.6506	78.3611
73	44.6781	79.1527
74	45.7133	79.9330
75	46.7561	80.7018
76	47.8064	81.4588
77	48.8641	82.2039
78	49.9291	82.9369
79	51.0012	83.6577
80	52.0804	84.3660
81	53.1666	85.0617
82	54.2596	85.7446
83	55.3594	86.4145
84	56.4659	87.0711
85	57.5789	87.7144
86	58.6984	88.3440
87	59.8242	88.9599
88	60.9563	89.5617
89	62.0946	90.1493
90	63.2390	90.7225
91	64.3894	91.2809
92	65.5457	91.8246
93	66.7078	92.3531
94	67.8757	92.8663
95	69.0492	93.3639
96	70.2283	93.8457
97	71.4128	94.3115
98	72.6028	94.7611
99	73.7981	95.1941
100	74.9987	95.6104
101	76.2044	96.0097
102	77.4152	96.3917
103	78.6310	96.7561
104	79.8518	97.1028
105	81.0774	97.4314
106	82.3079	97.7417
107	83.5430	98.0334
108	84.7829	98.3063
109	86.0273	98.5599
110	87.2762	98.7941
111	88.5296	99.0086
112	89.7874	99.2030
113	91.0495	99.3771
114	92.3158	99.5305
115	93.5864	99.6630
116	94.8611	99.7742
117	96.1399	99.8639
118	97.4226	99.9316
119	98.7094	99.9771
120	100.0000	100.0000

TABLE **23**

Daily Rebate

Method: Pro rata.

Terms: 1 to 366 days, each day.

Basis: 365 and 366 day years.

This table shows the daily rebate for an original amount of $100. The amount is prorated over the year. The rebate is proportional to the number of days remaining in the year.

Example: A house is sold on June 1. The seller has paid the real estate tax of $1,245 for the year. What portion of the tax should the buyer rebate to the seller?

Turn to Table 10, Days Between Dates, to find the number of days from June 1 to December 31. The number of days is 213.

Turn next to the Daily Rebate table for a 365 day year. Read the factor 58.356164 next to day 213. This is the factor per $100. Move the decimal point 2 places to the left and multiply by the tax, as follows:

$$.58356164 \times 1,245 = 726.534$$

The rebate is $726.53.

Description: This table shows the prorata rebate per $100 for each day of the year.

Example: The rebate for 85 days of a prepaid tax bill is 23.287671%. The tax is $1,260. The rebate is $293.42.

Rebate per $100

DAY	REBATE	DAY	REBATE	DAY	REBATE	DAY	REBATE	DAY	REBATE	DAY	REBATE
1	.273973	66	18.082192	131	35.890411	196	53.698630	261	71.506849	326	89.315068
2	.547945	67	18.356164	132	36.164384	197	53.972603	262	71.780822	327	89.589041
3	.821918	68	18.630137	133	36.438356	198	54.246575	263	72.054795	328	89.863014
4	1.095890	69	18.904110	134	36.712329	199	54.520548	264	72.328767	329	90.136986
5	1.369863	70	19.178082	135	36.986301	200	54.794521	265	72.602740	330	90.410959
6	1.643836	71	19.452055	136	37.260274	201	55.068493	266	72.876712	331	90.684932
7	1.917808	72	19.726027	137	37.534247	202	55.342466	267	73.150685	332	90.958904
8	2.191781	73	20.000000	138	37.808219	203	55.616438	268	73.424658	333	91.232877
9	2.465753	74	20.273973	139	38.082192	204	55.890411	269	73.698630	334	91.506849
10	2.739726	75	20.547945	140	38.356164	205	56.164384	270	73.972603	335	91.780822
11	3.013699	76	20.821918	141	38.630137	206	56.438356	271	74.246575	336	92.054795
12	3.287671	77	21.095890	142	38.904110	207	56.712329	272	74.520548	337	92.328767
13	3.561644	78	21.369863	143	39.178082	208	56.986301	273	74.794521	338	92.602740
14	3.835616	79	21.643836	144	39.452055	209	57.260274	274	75.068493	339	92.876712
15	4.109589	80	21.917808	145	39.726027	210	57.534247	275	75.342466	340	93.150685
16	4.383562	81	22.191781	146	40.000000	211	57.808219	276	75.616438	341	93.424658
17	4.657534	82	22.465753	147	40.273973	212	58.082192	277	75.890411	342	93.698630
18	4.931507	83	22.739726	148	40.547945	213	58.356164	278	76.164384	343	93.972603
19	5.205479	84	23.013699	149	40.821918	214	58.630137	279	76.438356	344	94.246575
20	5.479452	85	23.287671	150	41.095890	215	58.904110	280	76.712329	345	94.520548
21	5.753425	86	23.561644	151	41.369863	216	59.178082	281	76.986301	346	94.794521
22	6.027397	87	23.835616	152	41.643836	217	59.452055	282	77.260274	347	95.068493
23	6.301370	88	24.109589	153	41.917808	218	59.726027	283	77.534247	348	95.342466
24	6.575342	89	24.383562	154	42.191781	219	60.000000	284	77.808219	349	95.616438
25	6.849315	90	24.657534	155	42.465753	220	60.273973	285	78.082192	350	95.890411
26	7.123288	91	24.931507	156	42.739726	221	60.547945	286	78.356164	351	96.164384
27	7.397260	92	25.205479	157	43.013699	222	60.821918	287	78.630137	352	96.438356
28	7.671233	93	25.479452	158	43.287671	223	61.095890	288	78.904110	353	96.712329
29	7.945205	94	25.753425	159	43.561644	224	61.369863	289	79.178082	354	96.986301
30	8.219178	95	26.027397	160	43.835616	225	61.643836	290	79.452055	355	97.260274
31	8.493151	96	26.301370	161	44.109589	226	61.917808	291	79.726027	356	97.534247
32	8.767123	97	26.575342	162	44.383562	227	62.191781	292	80.000000	357	97.808219
33	9.041096	98	26.849315	163	44.657534	228	62.465753	293	80.273973	358	98.082192
34	9.315068	99	27.123288	164	44.931507	229	62.739726	294	80.547945	359	98.356164
35	9.589041	100	27.397260	165	45.205479	230	63.013699	295	80.821918	360	98.630137
36	9.863014	101	27.671233	166	45.479452	231	63.287671	296	81.095890	361	98.904110
37	10.136986	102	27.945205	167	45.753425	232	63.561644	297	81.369863	362	99.178082
38	10.410959	103	28.219178	168	46.027397	233	63.835616	298	81.643836	363	99.452055
39	10.684932	104	28.493151	169	46.301370	234	64.109589	299	81.917808	364	99.726027
40	10.958904	105	28.767123	170	46.575342	235	64.383562	300	82.191781	365	100.000000
41	11.232877	106	29.041096	171	46.849315	236	64.657534	301	82.465753		
42	11.506849	107	29.315068	172	47.123288	237	64.931507	302	82.739726		
43	11.780822	108	29.589041	173	47.397260	238	65.205479	303	83.013699		
44	12.054795	109	29.863014	174	47.671233	239	65.479452	304	83.287671		
45	12.328767	110	30.136986	175	47.945205	240	65.753425	305	83.561644		
46	12.602740	111	30.410959	176	48.219178	241	66.027397	306	83.835616		
47	12.876712	112	30.684932	177	48.493151	242	66.301370	307	84.109589		
48	13.150685	113	30.958904	178	48.767123	243	66.575342	308	84.383562		
49	13.424658	114	31.232877	179	49.041096	244	66.849315	309	84.657534		
50	13.698630	115	31.506849	180	49.315068	245	67.123288	310	84.931507		
51	13.972603	116	31.780822	181	49.589041	246	67.397260	311	85.205479		
52	14.246575	117	32.054795	182	49.863014	247	67.671233	312	85.479452		
53	14.520548	118	32.328767	183	50.136986	248	67.945205	313	85.753425		
54	14.794521	119	32.602740	184	50.410959	249	68.219178	314	86.027397		
55	15.068493	120	32.876712	185	50.684932	250	68.493151	315	86.301370		
56	15.342466	121	33.150685	186	50.958904	251	68.767123	316	86.575342		
57	15.616438	122	33.424658	187	51.232877	252	69.041096	317	86.849315		
58	15.890411	123	33.698630	188	51.506849	253	69.315068	318	87.123288		
59	16.164384	124	33.972603	189	51.780822	254	69.589041	319	87.397260		
60	16.438356	125	34.246575	190	52.054795	255	69.863014	320	87.671233		
61	16.712329	126	34.520548	191	52.328767	256	70.136986	321	87.945205		
62	16.986301	127	34.794521	192	52.602740	257	70.410959	322	88.219178		
63	17.260274	128	35.068493	193	52.876712	258	70.684932	323	88.493151		
64	17.534247	129	35.342466	194	53.150685	259	70.958904	324	88.767123		
65	17.808219	130	35.616438	195	53.424658	260	71.232877	325	89.041096		

Description: This table shows the prorata rebate per $100 for each day of the year.

Example: The rebate for 85 days of a prepaid tax bill is 23.224044%. The tax is $1,260. The rebate is $292.62.

Rebate per $100

DAY	REBATE	DAY	REBATE	DAY	REBATE	DAY	REBATE	DAY	REBATE	DAY	REBATE
1	.273224	66	18.032787	131	35.792350	196	53.551913	261	71.311475	326	89.071038
2	.546448	67	18.306011	132	36.065574	197	53.825137	262	71.584699	327	89.344262
3	.819672	68	18.579235	133	36.338798	198	54.098361	263	71.857923	328	89.617486
4	1.092896	69	18.852459	134	36.612022	199	54.371585	264	72.131148	329	89.890710
5	1.366120	70	19.125683	135	36.885246	200	54.644809	265	72.404372	330	90.163934
6	1.639344	71	19.398907	136	37.158470	201	54.918033	266	72.677596	331	90.437158
7	1.912568	72	19.672131	137	37.431694	202	55.191257	267	72.950820	332	90.710383
8	2.185792	73	19.945355	138	37.704918	203	55.464481	268	73.224044	333	90.983607
9	2.459016	74	20.218579	139	37.978142	204	55.737705	269	73.497268	334	91.256831
10	2.732240	75	20.491803	140	38.251366	205	56.010929	270	73.770492	335	91.530055
11	3.005464	76	20.765027	141	38.524590	206	56.284153	271	74.043716	336	91.803279
12	3.278689	77	21.038251	142	38.797814	207	56.557377	272	74.316940	337	92.076503
13	3.551913	78	21.311475	143	39.071038	208	56.830601	273	74.590164	338	92.349727
14	3.825137	79	21.584699	144	39.344262	209	57.103825	274	74.863388	339	92.622951
15	4.098361	80	21.857923	145	39.617486	210	57.377049	275	75.136612	340	92.896175
16	4.371585	81	22.131148	146	39.890710	211	57.650273	276	75.409836	341	93.169399
17	4.644809	82	22.404372	147	40.163934	212	57.923497	277	75.683060	342	93.442623
18	4.918033	83	22.677596	148	40.437158	213	58.196721	278	75.956284	343	93.715847
19	5.191257	84	22.950820	149	40.710383	214	58.469945	279	76.229508	344	93.989071
20	5.464481	85	23.224044	150	40.983607	215	58.743169	280	76.502732	345	94.262295
21	5.737705	86	23.497268	151	41.256831	216	59.016393	281	76.775956	346	94.535519
22	6.010929	87	23.770492	152	41.530055	217	59.289617	282	77.049180	347	94.808743
23	6.284153	88	24.043716	153	41.803279	218	59.562842	283	77.322404	348	95.081967
24	6.557377	89	24.316940	154	42.076503	219	59.836066	284	77.595628	349	95.355191
25	6.830601	90	24.590164	155	42.349727	220	60.109290	285	77.868852	350	95.628415
26	7.103825	91	24.863388	156	42.622951	221	60.382514	286	78.142077	351	95.901639
27	7.377049	92	25.136612	157	42.896175	222	60.655738	287	78.415301	352	96.174863
28	7.650273	93	25.409836	158	43.169399	223	60.928962	288	78.688525	353	96.448087
29	7.923497	94	25.683060	159	43.442623	224	61.202186	289	78.961749	354	96.721311
30	8.196721	95	25.956284	160	43.715847	225	61.475410	290	79.234973	355	96.994536
31	8.469945	96	26.229508	161	43.989071	226	61.748634	291	79.508197	356	97.267760
32	8.743169	97	26.502732	162	44.262295	227	62.021858	292	79.781421	357	97.540984
33	9.016393	98	26.775956	163	44.535519	228	62.295082	293	80.054645	358	97.814208
34	9.289617	99	27.049180	164	44.808743	229	62.568306	294	80.327869	359	98.087432
35	9.562842	100	27.322404	165	45.081967	230	62.841530	295	80.601093	360	98.360656
36	9.836066	101	27.595628	166	45.355191	231	63.114754	296	80.874317	361	98.633880
37	10.109290	102	27.868852	167	45.628415	232	63.387978	297	81.147541	362	98.907104
38	10.382514	103	28.142077	168	45.901639	233	63.661202	298	81.420765	363	99.180328
39	10.655738	104	28.415301	169	46.174863	234	63.934426	299	81.693989	364	99.453552
40	10.928962	105	28.688525	170	46.448087	235	64.207650	300	81.967213	365	99.726776
41	11.202186	106	28.961749	171	46.721311	236	64.480874	301	82.240437	366	100.000000
42	11.475410	107	29.234973	172	46.994536	237	64.754098	302	82.513661		
43	11.748634	108	29.508197	173	47.267760	238	65.027322	303	82.786885		
44	12.021858	109	29.781421	174	47.540984	239	65.300546	304	83.060109		
45	12.295082	110	30.054645	175	47.814208	240	65.573770	305	83.333333		
46	12.568306	111	30.327869	176	48.087432	241	65.846995	306	83.606557		
47	12.841530	112	30.601093	177	48.360656	242	66.120219	307	83.879781		
48	13.114754	113	30.874317	178	48.633880	243	66.393443	308	84.153005		
49	13.387978	114	31.147541	179	48.907104	244	66.666667	309	84.426230		
50	13.661202	115	31.420765	180	49.180328	245	66.939891	310	84.699454		
51	13.934426	116	31.693989	181	49.453552	246	67.213115	311	84.972678		
52	14.207650	117	31.967213	182	49.726776	247	67.486339	312	85.245902		
53	14.480874	118	32.240437	183	50.000000	248	67.759563	313	85.519126		
54	14.754098	119	32.513661	184	50.273224	249	68.032787	314	85.792350		
55	15.027322	120	32.786885	185	50.546448	250	68.306011	315	86.065574		
56	15.300546	121	33.060109	186	50.819672	251	68.579235	316	86.338798		
57	15.573770	122	33.333333	187	51.092896	252	68.852459	317	86.612022		
58	15.846995	123	33.606557	188	51.366120	253	69.125683	318	86.885246		
59	16.120219	124	33.879781	189	51.639344	254	69.398907	319	87.158470		
60	16.393443	125	34.153005	190	51.912568	255	69.672131	320	87.431694		
61	16.666667	126	34.426230	191	52.185792	256	69.945355	321	87.704918		
62	16.939891	127	34.699454	192	52.459016	257	70.218579	322	87.978142		
63	17.213115	128	34.972678	193	52.732240	258	70.491803	323	88.251366		
64	17.486339	129	35.245902	194	53.005464	259	70.765027	324	88.524590		
65	17.759563	130	35.519126	195	53.278689	260	71.038251	325	88.797814		

TABLE **24**

Discount Price

Discount Rates: 0, 1, 2, 3%;
4 to 20% by .25%;
20, 25, 30%.

Terms: 30 to 360 days, each 30 days;
89, 91, 92, 181, 182, 183, 184, 365, 366 days.

This table shows the Coupon Issue Yield Equivalent (CIYE) and the price at a discount rate.

Example: Commercial paper that matures in 30 days is purchased at a 7% discount rate. In the table on page 24-2, find the rate in the index. The CIYE is 7.14, and the price is 99.4167.
A 91 day Treasury bill sells at a discount rate of 6.25%. The CIYE is 6.44% and the price is 98.4201.

CIYE. The CIYE enables an investor to compare the yield of a Treasury bill with that of a government bond on a comparable basis. These 2 types of securities are different. The bill is noninterest bearing and issued for terms of 91 days, 6 months, and 1 year. A government bond is interest bearing, with coupons payable each 6 months. The method of computing a price from an interest rate is also different for each type of security. In order to be able to compare the 2 on a yield basis, the U.S. Treasury Department has defined 3 formulas for computing a CIYE, which converts the discount price to a yield that is the equivalent of a semiannual-coupon bond yield. Each formula applies to issues that mature within a specific time period: 1 to 182 days, 183 to 364 days, or 365 days. P, n, and i are equivalent for all 3 formulas.

Time period 1. Matures in 1 to 182 days. The formula is:

$$i = (\frac{100}{P} - 1) \times \frac{365}{n}$$

where:
  i = CIYE
  P = discount price
  n = number of days to maturity

Time period 2. Matures in 183 to 364 days. The formula is:

$$100 = P(1 + \frac{i}{2}) \times \left(1 + (\frac{2n - 365}{365}) \times \frac{i}{2} \right)$$

This formula cannot be solved for i directly, as can the formulae for time periods 1 and 3. Rather, it is solved by an iterative process. There is a description in the Appendix of how to calculate a rate by iteration.

Time period 3. Matures in 365 days. The formula is:

$$i = 2 \left(\sqrt{\frac{100}{P}} - 1 \right)$$

Bank Discount. The price of a Treasury bill is computed by using the bank discount formula. The bank discount formula computes interest by using the exact days on a 360 day basis. Bank discount at 8% for 91 days is computed as follows:

$$\text{Bank discount} = (.08 \times \frac{91}{360}) \times \text{Face amount}$$

$$= .02022222$$

$$\text{Per } \$100 = 2.022222$$

Price. The price of a Treasury bill is the face amount less the bank discount, as follows:

$$\text{Price} = \$100 - 2.022222$$

$$= \$97.9778$$

Description: This table shows, for the discount rate, the Coupon Issue Yield Equivalent and the price.

Example: At a discount rate of 8.00 % the price of a bill with 91 days to maturity is 97.9778. The CIYE is 8.28 %.

RATE	30 DAYS CIYE	PRICE	RATE	60 DAYS CIYE	PRICE	RATE	89 DAYS CIYE	PRICE	RATE	90 DAYS CIYE	PRICE	RATE	91 DAYS CIYE	PRICE
0.00	0.00	100.0000	0.00	0.00	100.0000	0.00	0.00	100.0000	0.00	0.00	100.0000	0.00	0.00	100.0000
1.00	1.01	99.9167	1.00	1.02	99.8333	1.00	1.02	99.7528	1.00	1.02	99.7500	1.00	1.02	99.7472
2.00	2.03	99.8333	2.00	2.03	99.6667	2.00	2.04	99.5056	2.00	2.04	99.5000	2.00	2.04	99.4944
3.00	3.05	99.7500	3.00	3.06	99.5000	3.00	3.06	99.2583	3.00	3.06	99.2500	3.00	3.06	99.2417
4.00	4.07	99.6667	4.00	4.08	99.3333	4.00	4.10	99.0111	4.00	4.10	99.0000	4.00	4.10	98.9889
4.25	4.32	99.6458	4.25	4.34	99.2917	4.25	4.35	98.9493	4.25	4.36	98.9375	4.25	4.36	98.9257
4.50	4.58	99.6250	4.50	4.60	99.2500	4.50	4.61	98.8875	4.50	4.61	98.8750	4.50	4.61	98.8625
4.75	4.84	99.6042	4.75	4.85	99.2083	4.75	4.87	98.8257	4.75	4.87	98.8125	4.75	4.87	98.7993
5.00	5.09	99.5833	5.00	5.11	99.1667	5.00	5.13	98.7639	5.00	5.13	98.7500	5.00	5.13	98.7361
5.25	5.35	99.5625	5.25	5.37	99.1250	5.25	5.39	98.7021	5.25	5.39	98.6875	5.25	5.39	98.6729
5.50	5.60	99.5417	5.50	5.63	99.0833	5.50	5.65	98.6403	5.50	5.65	98.6250	5.50	5.66	98.6097
5.75	5.86	99.5208	5.75	5.89	99.0417	5.75	5.91	98.5785	5.75	5.91	98.5625	5.75	5.92	98.5465
6.00	6.11	99.5000	6.00	6.14	99.0000	6.00	6.17	98.5167	6.00	6.18	98.5000	6.00	6.18	98.4833
6.25	6.37	99.4792	6.25	6.40	98.9583	6.25	6.44	98.4549	6.25	6.44	98.4375	6.25	6.44	98.4201
6.50	6.63	99.4583	6.50	6.66	98.9167	6.50	6.70	98.3931	6.50	6.70	98.3750	6.50	6.70	98.3569
6.75	6.88	99.4375	6.75	6.92	98.8750	6.75	6.96	98.3313	6.75	6.96	98.3125	6.75	6.96	98.2938
7.00	7.14	99.4167	7.00	7.18	98.8333	7.00	7.22	98.2694	7.00	7.22	98.2500	7.00	7.23	98.2306
7.25	7.40	99.3958	7.25	7.44	98.7917	7.25	7.48	98.2076	7.25	7.49	98.1875	7.25	7.49	98.1674
7.50	7.65	99.3750	7.50	7.70	98.7500	7.50	7.75	98.1458	7.50	7.75	98.1250	7.50	7.75	98.1042
7.75	7.91	99.3542	7.75	7.96	98.7083	7.75	8.01	98.0840	7.75	8.01	98.0625	7.75	8.01	98.0410
8.00	8.17	99.3333	8.00	8.22	98.6667	8.00	8.27	98.0222	8.00	8.28	98.0000	8.00	8.28	97.9778
8.25	8.42	99.3125	8.25	8.48	98.6250	8.25	8.54	97.9604	8.25	8.54	97.9375	8.25	8.54	97.9146
8.50	8.68	99.2917	8.50	8.74	98.5833	8.50	8.80	97.8986	8.50	8.81	97.8750	8.50	8.81	97.8514
8.75	8.94	99.2708	8.75	9.00	98.5417	8.75	9.07	97.8368	8.75	9.07	97.8125	8.75	9.07	97.7882
9.00	9.19	99.2500	9.00	9.26	98.5000	9.00	9.33	97.7750	9.00	9.34	97.7500	9.00	9.34	97.7250
9.25	9.45	99.2292	9.25	9.53	98.4583	9.25	9.60	97.7132	9.25	9.60	97.6875	9.25	9.60	97.6618
9.50	9.71	99.2083	9.50	9.79	98.4167	9.50	9.86	97.6514	9.50	9.87	97.6250	9.50	9.87	97.5986
9.75	9.97	99.1875	9.75	10.05	98.3750	9.75	10.13	97.5896	9.75	10.13	97.5625	9.75	10.14	97.5354
10.00	10.22	99.1667	10.00	10.31	98.3333	10.00	10.40	97.5278	10.00	10.40	97.5000	10.00	10.40	97.4722
10.25	10.48	99.1458	10.25	10.57	98.2917	10.25	10.66	97.4660	10.25	10.67	97.4375	10.25	10.67	97.4090
10.50	10.74	99.1250	10.50	10.84	98.2500	10.50	10.93	97.4042	10.50	10.93	97.3750	10.50	10.94	97.3458
10.75	11.00	99.1042	10.75	11.10	98.2083	10.75	11.20	97.3424	10.75	11.20	97.3125	10.75	11.20	97.2826
11.00	11.26	99.0833	11.00	11.36	98.1667	11.00	11.46	97.2806	11.00	11.47	97.2500	11.00	11.47	97.2194
11.25	11.51	99.0625	11.25	11.62	98.1250	11.25	11.73	97.2187	11.25	11.74	97.1875	11.25	11.74	97.1562
11.50	11.77	99.0417	11.50	11.89	98.0833	11.50	12.00	97.1569	11.50	12.00	97.1250	11.50	12.01	97.0931
11.75	12.03	99.0208	11.75	12.15	98.0417	11.75	12.27	97.0951	11.75	12.27	97.0625	11.75	12.28	97.0299
12.00	12.29	99.0000	12.00	12.41	98.0000	12.00	12.54	97.0333	12.00	12.54	97.0000	12.00	12.55	96.9667
12.25	12.55	98.9792	12.25	12.68	97.9583	12.25	12.81	96.9715	12.25	12.81	96.9375	12.25	12.82	96.9035
12.50	12.81	98.9583	12.50	12.94	97.9167	12.50	13.08	96.9097	12.50	13.08	96.8750	12.50	13.09	96.8403
12.75	13.07	98.9375	12.75	13.21	97.8750	12.75	13.35	96.8479	12.75	13.35	96.8125	12.75	13.36	96.7771
13.00	13.32	98.9167	13.00	13.47	97.8333	13.00	13.62	96.7861	13.00	13.62	96.7500	13.00	13.63	96.7139
13.25	13.58	98.8958	13.25	13.74	97.7917	13.25	13.89	96.7243	13.25	13.89	96.6875	13.25	13.90	96.6507
13.50	13.84	98.8750	13.50	14.00	97.7500	13.50	14.16	96.6625	13.50	14.17	96.6250	13.50	14.17	96.5875
13.75	14.10	98.8542	13.75	14.27	97.7083	13.75	14.43	96.6007	13.75	14.44	96.5625	13.75	14.44	96.5243
14.00	14.36	98.8333	14.00	14.53	97.6667	14.00	14.70	96.5389	14.00	14.71	96.5000	14.00	14.72	96.4611
14.25	14.62	98.8125	14.25	14.80	97.6250	14.25	14.98	96.4771	14.25	14.98	96.4375	14.25	14.99	96.3979
14.50	14.88	98.7917	14.50	15.07	97.5833	14.50	15.25	96.4153	14.50	15.25	96.3750	14.50	15.26	96.3347
14.75	15.14	98.7708	14.75	15.33	97.5417	14.75	15.52	96.3535	14.75	15.53	96.3125	14.75	15.53	96.2715
15.00	15.40	98.7500	15.00	15.60	97.5000	15.00	15.79	96.2917	15.00	15.80	96.2500	15.00	15.81	96.2083
15.25	15.66	98.7292	15.25	15.87	97.4583	15.25	16.07	96.2299	15.25	16.07	96.1875	15.25	16.08	96.1451
15.50	15.92	98.7083	15.50	16.13	97.4167	15.50	16.34	96.1681	15.50	16.35	96.1250	15.50	16.36	96.0819
15.75	16.18	98.6875	15.75	16.40	97.3750	15.75	16.62	96.1063	15.75	16.62	96.0625	15.75	16.63	96.0187
16.00	16.44	98.6667	16.00	16.67	97.3333	16.00	16.89	96.0444	16.00	16.90	96.0000	16.00	16.91	95.9556
16.25	16.70	98.6458	16.25	16.93	97.2917	16.25	17.17	95.9826	16.25	17.17	95.9375	16.25	17.18	95.8924
16.50	16.96	98.6250	16.50	17.20	97.2500	16.50	17.44	95.9208	16.50	17.45	95.8750	16.50	17.46	95.8292
16.75	17.22	98.6042	16.75	17.47	97.2083	16.75	17.72	95.8590	16.75	17.72	95.8125	16.75	17.73	95.7660
17.00	17.48	98.5833	17.00	17.74	97.1667	17.00	17.99	95.7972	17.00	18.00	95.7500	17.00	18.01	95.7028
17.25	17.74	98.5625	17.25	18.01	97.1250	17.25	18.27	95.7354	17.25	18.28	95.6875	17.25	18.29	95.6396
17.50	18.01	98.5417	17.50	18.28	97.0833	17.50	18.55	95.6736	17.50	18.55	95.6250	17.50	18.56	95.5764
17.75	18.27	98.5208	17.75	18.55	97.0417	17.75	18.82	95.6118	17.75	18.83	95.5625	17.75	18.84	95.5132
18.00	18.53	98.5000	18.00	18.81	97.0000	18.00	19.10	95.5500	18.00	19.11	95.5000	18.00	19.12	95.4500
18.25	18.79	98.4792	18.25	19.08	96.9583	18.25	19.38	95.4882	18.25	19.39	95.4375	18.25	19.40	95.3868
18.50	19.05	98.4583	18.50	19.35	96.9167	18.50	19.66	95.4264	18.50	19.67	95.3750	18.50	19.68	95.3236
18.75	19.31	98.4375	18.75	19.62	96.8750	18.75	19.93	95.3646	18.75	19.95	95.3125	18.75	19.96	95.2604
19.00	19.57	98.4167	19.00	19.89	96.8333	19.00	20.21	95.3028	19.00	20.22	95.2500	19.00	20.24	95.1972
20.00	20.62	98.3333	20.00	20.98	96.6667	20.00	21.33	95.0556	20.00	21.35	95.0000	20.00	21.36	94.9444
25.00	25.89	97.9167	25.00	26.45	95.8333	25.00	27.02	93.8194	25.00	27.04	93.7500	25.00	27.06	93.6806
30.00	31.20	97.5000	30.00	32.02	95.0000	30.00	32.85	92.5833	30.00	32.88	92.5000	30.00	32.91	92.4167

Description: This table shows, for the discount rate, the Coupon Issue Yield Equivalent and the price.

Example: At a discount rate of 8.00 % the price of a bill with 181 days to maturity is 95.9778. The CIYE is 8.45 %.

___ 92 DAYS ___			___ 120 DAYS ___			___ 150 DAYS ___			___ 180 DAYS ___			___ 181 DAYS ___		
RATE	CIYE	PRICE	RATE	CIYE	PRICE	RATE	CIYE	PRICE	RATE	CIYE	PRICE	RATE	CIYE	PRICE
0.00	0.00	100.0000	0.00	0.00	100.0000	0.00	0.00	100.0000	0.00	0.00	100.0000	0.00	0.00	100.0000
1.00	1.02	99.7444	1.00	1.02	99.6667	1.00	1.02	99.5833	1.00	1.02	99.5000	1.00	1.02	99.4972
2.00	2.04	99.4889	2.00	2.04	99.3333	2.00	2.04	99.1667	2.00	2.05	99.0000	2.00	2.05	98.9944
3.00	3.07	99.2333	3.00	3.07	99.0000	3.00	3.08	98.7500	3.00	3.09	98.5000	3.00	3.09	98.4917
4.00	4.10	98.9778	4.00	4.11	98.6667	4.00	4.12	98.3333	4.00	4.14	98.0000	4.00	4.14	97.9889
4.25	4.36	98.9139	4.25	4.37	98.5833	4.25	4.39	98.2292	4.25	4.40	97.8750	4.25	4.40	97.8632
4.50	4.62	98.8500	4.50	4.63	98.5000	4.50	4.65	98.1250	4.50	4.67	97.7500	4.50	4.67	97.7375
4.75	4.88	98.7861	4.75	4.89	98.4167	4.75	4.91	98.0208	4.75	4.93	97.6250	4.75	4.93	97.6118
5.00	5.14	98.7222	5.00	5.16	98.3333	5.00	5.18	97.9167	5.00	5.20	97.5000	5.00	5.20	97.4861
5.25	5.40	98.6583	5.25	5.42	98.2500	5.25	5.44	97.8125	5.25	5.47	97.3750	5.25	5.47	97.3604
5.50	5.66	98.5944	5.50	5.68	98.1667	5.50	5.71	97.7083	5.50	5.73	97.2500	5.50	5.73	97.2347
5.75	5.92	98.5306	5.75	5.94	98.0833	5.75	5.97	97.6042	5.75	6.00	97.1250	5.75	6.00	97.1090
6.00	6.18	98.4667	6.00	6.21	98.0000	6.00	6.24	97.5000	6.00	6.27	97.0000	6.00	6.27	96.9833
6.25	6.44	98.4028	6.25	6.47	97.9167	6.25	6.51	97.3958	6.25	6.54	96.8750	6.25	6.54	96.8576
6.50	6.70	98.3389	6.50	6.74	97.8333	6.50	6.77	97.2917	6.50	6.81	96.7500	6.50	6.81	96.7319
6.75	6.96	98.2750	6.75	7.00	97.7500	6.75	7.04	97.1875	6.75	7.08	96.6250	6.75	7.08	96.6063
7.00	7.23	98.2111	7.00	7.27	97.6667	7.00	7.31	97.0833	7.00	7.35	96.5000	7.00	7.36	96.4806
7.25	7.49	98.1472	7.25	7.53	97.5833	7.25	7.58	96.9792	7.25	7.63	96.3750	7.25	7.63	96.3549
7.50	7.75	98.0833	7.50	7.80	97.5000	7.50	7.85	96.8750	7.50	7.90	96.2500	7.50	7.90	96.2292
7.75	8.02	98.0194	7.75	8.07	97.4167	7.75	8.12	96.7708	7.75	8.17	96.1250	7.75	8.18	96.1035
8.00	8.28	97.9556	8.00	8.33	97.3333	8.00	8.39	96.6667	8.00	8.45	96.0000	8.00	8.45	95.9778
8.25	8.54	97.8917	8.25	8.60	97.2500	8.25	8.66	96.5625	8.25	8.72	95.8750	8.25	8.73	95.8521
8.50	8.81	97.8278	8.50	8.87	97.1667	8.50	8.93	96.4583	8.50	9.00	95.7500	8.50	9.00	95.7264
8.75	9.07	97.7639	8.75	9.14	97.0833	8.75	9.21	96.3542	8.75	9.28	95.6250	8.75	9.28	95.6007
9.00	9.34	97.7000	9.00	9.41	97.0000	9.00	9.48	96.2500	9.00	9.55	95.5000	9.00	9.56	95.4750
9.25	9.61	97.6361	9.25	9.68	96.9167	9.25	9.75	96.1458	9.25	9.83	95.3750	9.25	9.84	95.3493
9.50	9.87	97.5722	9.50	9.95	96.8333	9.50	10.03	96.0417	9.50	10.11	95.2500	9.50	10.12	95.2236
9.75	10.14	97.5083	9.75	10.22	96.7500	9.75	10.30	95.9375	9.75	10.39	95.1250	9.75	10.39	95.0979
10.00	10.40	97.4444	10.00	10.49	96.6667	10.00	10.58	95.8333	10.00	10.67	95.0000	10.00	10.68	94.9722
10.25	10.67	97.3806	10.25	10.76	96.5833	10.25	10.86	95.7292	10.25	10.95	94.8750	10.25	10.96	94.8465
10.50	10.94	97.3167	10.50	11.03	96.5000	10.50	11.13	95.6250	10.50	11.24	94.7500	10.50	11.24	94.7208
10.75	11.21	97.2528	10.75	11.30	96.4167	10.75	11.41	95.5208	10.75	11.52	94.6250	10.75	11.52	94.5951
11.00	11.48	97.1889	11.00	11.58	96.3333	11.00	11.69	95.4167	11.00	11.80	94.5000	11.00	11.81	94.4694
11.25	11.74	97.1250	11.25	11.85	96.2500	11.25	11.97	95.3125	11.25	12.09	94.3750	11.25	12.09	94.3438
11.50	12.01	97.0611	11.50	12.12	96.1667	11.50	12.25	95.2083	11.50	12.37	94.2500	11.50	12.38	94.2181
11.75	12.28	96.9972	11.75	12.40	96.0833	11.75	12.53	95.1042	11.75	12.66	94.1250	11.75	12.66	94.0924
12.00	12.55	96.9333	12.00	12.67	96.0000	12.00	12.81	95.0000	12.00	12.94	94.0000	12.00	12.95	93.9667
12.25	12.82	96.8694	12.25	12.95	95.9167	12.25	13.09	94.8958	12.25	13.23	93.8750	12.25	13.24	93.8410
12.50	13.09	96.8056	12.50	13.22	95.8333	12.50	13.37	94.7917	12.50	13.52	93.7500	12.50	13.52	93.7153
12.75	13.36	96.7417	12.75	13.50	95.7500	12.75	13.65	94.6875	12.75	13.81	93.6250	12.75	13.81	93.5896
13.00	13.63	96.6778	13.00	13.78	95.6667	13.00	13.94	94.5833	13.00	14.10	93.5000	13.00	14.10	93.4639
13.25	13.90	96.6139	13.25	14.05	95.5833	13.25	14.22	94.4792	13.25	14.39	93.3750	13.25	14.39	93.3382
13.50	14.18	96.5500	13.50	14.33	95.5000	13.50	14.50	94.3750	13.50	14.68	93.2500	13.50	14.68	93.2125
13.75	14.45	96.4861	13.75	14.61	95.4167	13.75	14.79	94.2708	13.75	14.97	93.1250	13.75	14.98	93.0868
14.00	14.72	96.4222	14.00	14.89	95.3333	14.00	15.07	94.1667	14.00	15.26	93.0000	14.00	15.27	92.9611
14.25	14.99	96.3583	14.25	15.17	95.2500	14.25	15.36	94.0625	14.25	15.56	92.8750	14.25	15.56	92.8354
14.50	15.27	96.2944	14.50	15.45	95.1667	14.50	15.65	93.9583	14.50	15.85	92.7500	14.50	15.86	92.7097
14.75	15.54	96.2306	14.75	15.73	95.0833	14.75	15.93	93.8542	14.75	16.15	92.6250	14.75	16.15	92.5840
15.00	15.81	96.1667	15.00	16.01	95.0000	15.00	16.22	93.7500	15.00	16.44	92.5000	15.00	16.45	92.4583
15.25	16.09	96.1028	15.25	16.29	94.9167	15.25	16.51	93.6458	15.25	16.74	92.3750	15.25	16.75	92.3326
15.50	16.36	96.0389	15.50	16.57	94.8333	15.50	16.80	93.5417	15.50	17.04	92.2500	15.50	17.04	92.2069
15.75	16.64	95.9750	15.75	16.85	94.7500	15.75	17.09	93.4375	15.75	17.33	92.1250	15.75	17.34	92.0813
16.00	16.91	95.9111	16.00	17.14	94.6667	16.00	17.38	93.3333	16.00	17.63	92.0000	16.00	17.64	91.9556
16.25	17.19	95.8472	16.25	17.42	94.5833	16.25	17.67	93.2292	16.25	17.93	91.8750	16.25	17.94	91.8299
16.50	17.47	95.7833	16.50	17.70	94.5000	16.50	17.96	93.1250	16.50	18.23	91.7500	16.50	18.24	91.7042
16.75	17.74	95.7194	16.75	17.99	94.4167	16.75	18.26	93.0208	16.75	18.53	91.6250	16.75	18.54	91.5785
17.00	18.02	95.6556	17.00	18.27	94.3333	17.00	18.55	92.9167	17.00	18.84	91.5000	17.00	18.85	91.4528
17.25	18.30	95.5917	17.25	18.56	94.2500	17.25	18.84	92.8125	17.25	19.14	91.3750	17.25	19.15	91.3271
17.50	18.57	95.5278	17.50	18.84	94.1667	17.50	19.14	92.7083	17.50	19.44	91.2500	17.50	19.45	91.2014
17.75	18.85	95.4639	17.75	19.13	94.0833	17.75	19.43	92.6042	17.75	19.75	91.1250	17.75	19.76	91.0757
18.00	19.13	95.4000	18.00	19.41	94.0000	18.00	19.73	92.5000	18.00	20.05	91.0000	18.00	20.07	90.9500
18.25	19.41	95.3361	18.25	19.70	93.9167	18.25	20.03	92.3958	18.25	20.36	90.8750	18.25	20.37	90.8243
18.50	19.69	95.2722	18.50	19.99	93.8333	18.50	20.32	92.2917	18.50	20.67	90.7500	18.50	20.68	90.6986
18.75	19.97	95.2083	18.75	20.28	93.7500	18.75	20.62	92.1875	18.75	20.98	90.6250	18.75	20.99	90.5729
19.00	20.25	95.1444	19.00	20.57	93.6667	19.00	20.92	92.0833	19.00	21.29	90.5000	19.00	21.30	90.4472
20.00	21.37	94.8889	20.00	21.73	93.3333	20.00	22.12	91.6667	20.00	22.53	90.0000	20.00	22.54	89.9444
25.00	27.08	93.6111	25.00	27.65	91.6667	25.00	28.29	89.5833	25.00	28.97	87.5000	25.00	28.99	87.4306
30.00	32.94	92.3333	30.00	33.80	90.0000	30.00	34.76	87.5000	30.00	35.78	85.0000	30.00	35.82	84.9167

Description: This table shows, for the discount rate, the Coupon Issue Yield Equivalent and the price.

Example: At a discount rate of 8.00 % the price of a bill with 240 days to maturity is 94.6667. The CIYE is 8.48 %.

RATE	182 DAYS CIYE	PRICE	RATE	183 DAYS CIYE	PRICE	RATE	184 DAYS CIYE	PRICE	RATE	210 DAYS CIYE	PRICE	RATE	240 DAYS CIYE	PRICE
0.00	0.00	100.0000	0.00	0.00	100.0000	0.00	0.00	100.0000	0.00	0.00	100.0000	0.00	0.00	100.0000
1.00	1.02	99.4944	1.00	1.02	99.4917	1.00	1.02	99.4889	1.00	1.02	99.4167	1.00	1.02	99.3333
2.00	2.05	98.9889	2.00	2.05	98.9833	2.00	2.05	98.9778	2.00	2.05	98.8333	2.00	2.05	98.6667
3.00	3.09	98.4833	3.00	3.09	98.4750	3.00	3.09	98.4667	3.00	3.09	98.2500	3.00	3.09	98.0000
4.00	4.14	97.9778	4.00	4.14	97.9667	4.00	4.14	97.9556	4.00	4.14	97.6667	4.00	4.15	97.3333
4.25	4.40	97.8514	4.25	4.40	97.8396	4.25	4.40	97.8278	4.25	4.41	97.5208	4.25	4.41	97.1667
4.50	4.67	97.7250	4.50	4.67	97.7125	4.50	4.67	97.7000	4.50	4.67	97.3750	4.50	4.68	97.0000
4.75	4.93	97.5986	4.75	4.93	97.5854	4.75	4.93	97.5722	4.75	4.94	97.2292	4.75	4.94	96.8333
5.00	5.20	97.4722	5.00	5.20	97.4583	5.00	5.20	97.4444	5.00	5.20	97.0833	5.00	5.21	96.6667
5.25	5.47	97.3458	5.25	5.47	97.3313	5.25	5.47	97.3167	5.25	5.47	96.9375	5.25	5.48	96.5000
5.50	5.74	97.2194	5.50	5.74	97.2042	5.50	5.74	97.1889	5.50	5.74	96.7917	5.50	5.75	96.3333
5.75	6.00	97.0931	5.75	6.01	97.0771	5.75	6.01	97.0611	5.75	6.01	96.6458	5.75	6.02	96.1667
6.00	6.27	96.9667	6.00	6.27	96.9500	6.00	6.27	96.9333	6.00	6.28	96.5000	6.00	6.29	96.0000
6.25	6.54	96.8403	6.25	6.54	96.8229	6.25	6.54	96.8056	6.25	6.55	96.3542	6.25	6.56	95.8333
6.50	6.81	96.7139	6.50	6.81	96.6958	6.50	6.81	96.6778	6.50	6.82	96.2083	6.50	6.83	95.6667
6.75	7.09	96.5875	6.75	7.09	96.5687	6.75	7.09	96.5500	6.75	7.09	96.0625	6.75	7.11	95.5000
7.00	7.36	96.4611	7.00	7.36	96.4417	7.00	7.36	96.4222	7.00	7.36	95.9167	7.00	7.38	95.3333
7.25	7.63	96.3347	7.25	7.63	96.3146	7.25	7.63	96.2944	7.25	7.64	95.7708	7.25	7.65	95.1667
7.50	7.90	96.2083	7.50	7.90	96.1875	7.50	7.90	96.1667	7.50	7.91	95.6250	7.50	7.93	95.0000
7.75	8.18	96.0819	7.75	8.18	96.0604	7.75	8.18	96.0389	7.75	8.19	95.4792	7.75	8.21	94.8333
8.00	8.45	95.9556	8.00	8.45	95.9333	8.00	8.45	95.9111	8.00	8.46	95.3333	8.00	8.48	94.6667
8.25	8.73	95.8292	8.25	8.73	95.8063	8.25	8.73	95.7833	8.25	8.74	95.1875	8.25	8.76	94.5000
8.50	9.01	95.7028	8.50	9.01	95.6792	8.50	9.01	95.6556	8.50	9.01	95.0417	8.50	9.04	94.3333
8.75	9.28	95.5764	8.75	9.28	95.5521	8.75	9.28	95.5278	8.75	9.29	94.8958	8.75	9.32	94.1667
9.00	9.56	95.4500	9.00	9.56	95.4250	9.00	9.56	95.4000	9.00	9.57	94.7500	9.00	9.60	94.0000
9.25	9.84	95.3236	9.25	9.84	95.2979	9.25	9.84	95.2722	9.25	9.85	94.6042	9.25	9.88	93.8333
9.50	10.12	95.1972	9.50	10.12	95.1708	9.50	10.12	95.1444	9.50	10.13	94.4583	9.50	10.16	93.6667
9.75	10.40	95.0708	9.75	10.40	95.0438	9.75	10.40	95.0167	9.75	10.41	94.3125	9.75	10.44	93.5000
10.00	10.68	94.9444	10.00	10.68	94.9167	10.00	10.68	94.8889	10.00	10.69	94.1667	10.00	10.73	93.3333
10.25	10.96	94.8181	10.25	10.96	94.7896	10.25	10.96	94.7611	10.25	10.97	94.0208	10.25	11.01	93.1667
10.50	11.24	94.6917	10.50	11.24	94.6625	10.50	11.24	94.6333	10.50	11.26	93.8750	10.50	11.29	93.0000
10.75	11.53	94.5653	10.75	11.53	94.5354	10.75	11.53	94.5056	10.75	11.54	93.7292	10.75	11.58	92.8333
11.00	11.81	94.4389	11.00	11.81	94.4083	11.00	11.81	94.3778	11.00	11.83	93.5833	11.00	11.87	92.6667
11.25	12.09	94.3125	11.25	12.10	94.2813	11.25	12.10	94.2500	11.25	12.11	93.4375	11.25	12.15	92.5000
11.50	12.38	94.1861	11.50	12.38	94.1542	11.50	12.38	94.1222	11.50	12.40	93.2917	11.50	12.44	92.3333
11.75	12.67	94.0597	11.75	12.67	94.0271	11.75	12.67	93.9944	11.75	12.68	93.1458	11.75	12.73	92.1667
12.00	12.95	93.9333	12.00	12.95	93.9000	12.00	12.95	93.8667	12.00	12.97	93.0000	12.00	13.02	92.0000
12.25	13.24	93.8069	12.25	13.24	93.7729	12.25	13.24	93.7389	12.25	13.26	92.8542	12.25	13.31	91.8333
12.50	13.53	93.6806	12.50	13.53	93.6458	12.50	13.53	93.6111	12.50	13.55	92.7083	12.50	13.60	91.6667
12.75	13.82	93.5542	12.75	13.82	93.5187	12.75	13.82	93.4833	12.75	13.84	92.5625	12.75	13.90	91.5000
13.00	14.11	93.4278	13.00	14.11	93.3917	13.00	14.11	93.3556	13.00	14.13	92.4167	13.00	14.19	91.3333
13.25	14.40	93.3014	13.25	14.40	93.2646	13.25	14.40	93.2278	13.25	14.42	92.2708	13.25	14.48	91.1667
13.50	14.69	93.1750	13.50	14.69	93.1375	13.50	14.69	93.1000	13.50	14.72	92.1250	13.50	14.78	91.0000
13.75	14.98	93.0486	13.75	14.99	93.0104	13.75	14.99	92.9722	13.75	15.01	91.9792	13.75	15.08	90.8333
14.00	15.28	92.9222	14.00	15.28	92.8833	14.00	15.28	92.8444	14.00	15.30	91.8333	14.00	15.37	90.6667
14.25	15.57	92.7958	14.25	15.57	92.7562	14.25	15.57	92.7167	14.25	15.60	91.6875	14.25	15.67	90.5000
14.50	15.86	92.6694	14.50	15.87	92.6292	14.50	15.87	92.5889	14.50	15.89	91.5417	14.50	15.97	90.3333
14.75	16.16	92.5431	14.75	16.16	92.5021	14.75	16.16	92.4611	14.75	16.19	91.3958	14.75	16.27	90.1667
15.00	16.46	92.4167	15.00	16.46	92.3750	15.00	16.46	92.3333	15.00	16.49	91.2500	15.00	16.57	90.0000
15.25	16.75	92.2903	15.25	16.76	92.2479	15.25	16.76	92.2056	15.25	16.79	91.1042	15.25	16.87	89.8333
15.50	17.05	92.1639	15.50	17.06	92.1208	15.50	17.06	92.0778	15.50	17.09	90.9583	15.50	17.17	89.6667
15.75	17.35	92.0375	15.75	17.35	91.9938	15.75	17.35	91.9500	15.75	17.39	90.8125	15.75	17.48	89.5000
16.00	17.65	91.9111	16.00	17.65	91.8667	16.00	17.65	91.8222	16.00	17.69	90.6667	16.00	17.78	89.3333
16.25	17.95	91.7847	16.25	17.96	91.7396	16.25	17.96	91.6944	16.25	17.99	90.5208	16.25	18.09	89.1667
16.50	18.25	91.6583	16.50	18.26	91.6125	16.50	18.26	91.5667	16.50	18.29	90.3750	16.50	18.39	89.0000
16.75	18.55	91.5319	16.75	18.56	91.4854	16.75	18.56	91.4389	16.75	18.60	90.2292	16.75	18.70	88.8333
17.00	18.86	91.4056	17.00	18.86	91.3583	17.00	18.86	91.3111	17.00	18.90	90.0833	17.00	19.01	88.6667
17.25	19.16	91.2792	17.25	19.17	91.2313	17.25	19.17	91.1833	17.25	19.21	89.9375	17.25	19.32	88.5000
17.50	19.47	91.1528	17.50	19.47	91.1042	17.50	19.47	91.0556	17.50	19.51	89.7917	17.50	19.63	88.3333
17.75	19.77	91.0264	17.75	19.78	90.9771	17.75	19.78	90.9278	17.75	19.82	89.6458	17.75	19.94	88.1667
18.00	20.08	90.9000	18.00	20.08	90.8500	18.00	20.08	90.8000	18.00	20.13	89.5000	18.00	20.25	88.0000
18.25	20.38	90.7736	18.25	20.39	90.7229	18.25	20.39	90.6722	18.25	20.43	89.3542	18.25	20.56	87.8333
18.50	20.69	90.6472	18.50	20.70	90.5958	18.50	20.70	90.5444	18.50	20.74	89.2083	18.50	20.87	87.6667
18.75	21.00	90.5208	18.75	21.01	90.4687	18.75	21.01	90.4167	18.75	21.05	89.0625	18.75	21.19	87.5000
19.00	21.31	90.3944	19.00	21.32	90.3417	19.00	21.32	90.2889	19.00	21.37	88.9167	19.00	21.50	87.3333
20.00	22.56	89.8889	20.00	22.57	89.8333	20.00	22.57	89.7778	20.00	22.62	88.3333	20.00	22.78	86.6667
25.00	29.01	87.3611	25.00	29.03	87.2917	25.00	29.03	87.2222	25.00	29.12	85.4167	25.00	29.38	83.3333
30.00	35.85	84.8333	30.00	35.87	84.7500	30.00	35.87	84.6667	30.00	36.02	82.5000	30.00	36.43	80.0000

Description: This table shows, for the discount rate, the Coupon Issue Yield Equivalent and the price.

Example: At a discount rate of 8.00 % the price of a bill with 366 days to maturity is 91.8667. The CIYE is 8.67 %.

	270 DAYS			300 DAYS			360 DAYS			365 DAYS			366 DAYS	
RATE	CIYE	PRICE	RATE	CIYE	PRICE	RATE	CIYE	PRICE	RATE	CIYE	PRICE	RATE	CIYE	PRICE
0.00	0.00	100.0000	0.00	0.00	100.0000	0.00	0.00	100.0000	0.00	0.00	100.0000	0.00	0.00	100.0000
1.00	1.02	99.2500	1.00	1.02	99.1667	1.00	1.02	99.0000	1.00	1.02	98.9861	1.00	1.02	98.9833
2.00	2.05	98.5000	2.00	2.05	98.3333	2.00	2.06	98.0000	2.00	2.06	97.9722	2.00	2.06	97.9667
3.00	3.10	97.7500	3.00	3.10	97.5000	3.00	3.11	97.0000	3.00	3.11	96.9583	3.00	3.12	96.9500
4.00	4.15	97.0000	4.00	4.16	96.6667	4.00	4.18	96.0000	4.00	4.18	95.9444	4.00	4.20	95.9333
4.25	4.42	96.8125	4.25	4.43	96.4583	4.25	4.45	95.7500	4.25	4.45	95.6910	4.25	4.47	95.6792
4.50	4.69	96.6250	4.50	4.70	96.2500	4.50	4.72	95.5000	4.50	4.72	95.4375	4.50	4.74	95.4250
4.75	4.95	96.4375	4.75	4.97	96.0417	4.75	4.99	95.2500	4.75	5.00	95.1840	4.75	5.01	95.1708
5.00	5.22	96.2500	5.00	5.24	95.8333	5.00	5.27	95.0000	5.00	5.27	94.9306	5.00	5.29	94.9167
5.25	5.49	96.0625	5.25	5.51	95.6250	5.25	5.54	94.7500	5.25	5.55	94.6771	5.25	5.56	94.6625
5.50	5.76	95.8750	5.50	5.78	95.4167	5.50	5.82	94.5000	5.50	5.82	94.4236	5.50	5.84	94.4083
5.75	6.03	95.6875	5.75	6.05	95.2083	5.75	6.09	94.2500	5.75	6.10	94.1701	5.75	6.12	94.1542
6.00	6.31	95.5000	6.00	6.33	95.0000	6.00	6.37	94.0000	6.00	6.38	93.9167	6.00	6.39	93.9000
6.25	6.58	95.3125	6.25	6.60	94.7917	6.25	6.65	93.7500	6.25	6.65	93.6632	6.25	6.67	93.6458
6.50	6.85	95.1250	6.50	6.88	94.5833	6.50	6.93	93.5000	6.50	6.94	93.4097	6.50	6.96	93.3917
6.75	7.13	94.9375	6.75	7.15	94.3750	6.75	7.21	93.2500	6.75	7.22	93.1563	6.75	7.24	93.1375
7.00	7.40	94.7500	7.00	7.43	94.1667	7.00	7.49	93.0000	7.00	7.50	92.9028	7.00	7.52	92.8833
7.25	7.68	94.5625	7.25	7.71	93.9583	7.25	7.78	92.7500	7.25	7.78	92.6493	7.25	7.81	92.6292
7.50	7.95	94.3750	7.50	7.99	93.7500	7.50	8.06	92.5000	7.50	8.07	92.3958	7.50	8.09	92.3750
7.75	8.23	94.1875	7.75	8.27	93.5417	7.75	8.35	92.2500	7.75	8.35	92.1424	7.75	8.38	92.1208
8.00	8.51	94.0000	8.00	8.55	93.3333	8.00	8.63	92.0000	8.00	8.64	91.8889	8.00	8.67	91.8667
8.25	8.79	93.8125	8.25	8.83	93.1250	8.25	8.92	91.7500	8.25	8.93	91.6354	8.25	8.95	91.6125
8.50	9.07	93.6250	8.50	9.11	92.9167	8.50	9.21	91.5000	8.50	9.22	91.3819	8.50	9.25	91.3583
8.75	9.35	93.4375	8.75	9.40	92.7083	8.75	9.50	91.2500	8.75	9.51	91.1285	8.75	9.54	91.1042
9.00	9.64	93.2500	9.00	9.68	92.5000	9.00	9.79	91.0000	9.00	9.80	90.8750	9.00	9.83	90.8500
9.25	9.92	93.0625	9.25	9.97	92.2917	9.25	10.08	90.7500	9.25	10.09	90.6215	9.25	10.12	90.5958
9.50	10.20	92.8750	9.50	10.25	92.0833	9.50	10.38	90.5000	9.50	10.39	90.3681	9.50	10.42	90.3417
9.75	10.49	92.6875	9.75	10.54	91.8750	9.75	10.67	90.2500	9.75	10.68	90.1146	9.75	10.72	90.0875
10.00	10.77	92.5000	10.00	10.83	91.6667	10.00	10.97	90.0000	10.00	10.98	89.8611	10.00	11.01	89.8333
10.25	11.06	92.3125	10.25	11.12	91.4583	10.25	11.27	89.7500	10.25	11.28	89.6076	10.25	11.31	89.5792
10.50	11.35	92.1250	10.50	11.41	91.2500	10.50	11.57	89.5000	10.50	11.58	89.3542	10.50	11.61	89.3250
10.75	11.64	91.9375	10.75	11.70	91.0417	10.75	11.87	89.2500	10.75	11.88	89.1007	10.75	11.92	89.0708
11.00	11.93	91.7500	11.00	12.00	90.8333	11.00	12.17	89.0000	11.00	12.18	88.8472	11.00	12.22	88.8167
11.25	12.22	91.5625	11.25	12.29	90.6250	11.25	12.47	88.7500	11.25	12.49	88.5938	11.25	12.52	88.5625
11.50	12.51	91.3750	11.50	12.59	90.4167	11.50	12.77	88.5000	11.50	12.79	88.3403	11.50	12.83	88.3083
11.75	12.80	91.1875	11.75	12.88	90.2083	11.75	13.08	88.2500	11.75	13.10	88.0868	11.75	13.14	88.0542
12.00	13.09	91.0000	12.00	13.18	90.0000	12.00	13.38	88.0000	12.00	13.40	87.8333	12.00	13.44	87.8000
12.25	13.39	90.8125	12.25	13.48	89.7917	12.25	13.69	87.7500	12.25	13.71	87.5799	12.25	13.75	87.5458
12.50	13.68	90.6250	12.50	13.78	89.5833	12.50	14.00	87.5000	12.50	14.02	87.3264	12.50	14.06	87.2917
12.75	13.98	90.4375	12.75	14.08	89.3750	12.75	14.31	87.2500	12.75	14.33	87.0729	12.75	14.38	87.0375
13.00	14.27	90.2500	13.00	14.38	89.1667	13.00	14.62	87.0000	13.00	14.65	86.8194	13.00	14.69	86.7833
13.25	14.57	90.0625	13.25	14.68	88.9583	13.25	14.94	86.7500	13.25	14.96	86.5660	13.25	15.01	86.5292
13.50	14.87	89.8750	13.50	14.98	88.7500	13.50	15.25	86.5000	13.50	15.27	86.3125	13.50	15.32	86.2750
13.75	15.17	89.6875	13.75	15.29	88.5417	13.75	15.57	86.2500	13.75	15.59	86.0590	13.75	15.64	86.0208
14.00	15.47	89.5000	14.00	15.59	88.3333	14.00	15.88	86.0000	14.00	15.91	85.8056	14.00	15.96	85.7667
14.25	15.77	89.3125	14.25	15.90	88.1250	14.25	16.20	85.7500	14.25	16.23	85.5521	14.25	16.28	85.5125
14.50	16.08	89.1250	14.50	16.21	87.9167	14.50	16.52	85.5000	14.50	16.55	85.2986	14.50	16.60	85.2583
14.75	16.38	88.9375	14.75	16.52	87.7083	14.75	16.84	85.2500	14.75	16.87	85.0451	14.75	16.93	85.0042
15.00	16.69	88.7500	15.00	16.83	87.5000	15.00	17.17	85.0000	15.00	17.20	84.7917	15.00	17.25	84.7500
15.25	16.99	88.5625	15.25	17.14	87.2917	15.25	17.49	84.7500	15.25	17.52	84.5382	15.25	17.58	84.4958
15.50	17.30	88.3750	15.50	17.45	87.0833	15.50	17.82	84.5000	15.50	17.85	84.2847	15.50	17.90	84.2417
15.75	17.61	88.1875	15.75	17.76	86.8750	15.75	18.14	84.2500	15.75	18.18	84.0313	15.75	18.23	83.9875
16.00	17.91	88.0000	16.00	18.08	86.6667	16.00	18.47	84.0000	16.00	18.51	83.7778	16.00	18.57	83.7333
16.25	18.22	87.8125	16.25	18.39	86.4583	16.25	18.80	83.7500	16.25	18.84	83.5243	16.25	18.90	83.4792
16.50	18.54	87.6250	16.50	18.71	86.2500	16.50	19.13	83.5000	16.50	19.17	83.2708	16.50	19.23	83.2250
16.75	18.85	87.4375	16.75	19.03	86.0417	16.75	19.47	83.2500	16.75	19.51	83.0174	16.75	19.57	82.9708
17.00	19.16	87.2500	17.00	19.35	85.8333	17.00	19.80	83.0000	17.00	19.84	82.7639	17.00	19.90	82.7167
17.25	19.47	87.0625	17.25	19.67	85.6250	17.25	20.14	82.7500	17.25	20.18	82.5104	17.25	20.24	82.4625
17.50	19.79	86.8750	17.50	19.99	85.4167	17.50	20.47	82.5000	17.50	20.52	82.2569	17.50	20.58	82.2083
17.75	20.11	86.6875	17.75	20.31	85.2083	17.75	20.81	82.2500	17.75	20.86	82.0035	17.75	20.92	81.9542
18.00	20.42	86.5000	18.00	20.64	85.0000	18.00	21.15	82.0000	18.00	21.20	81.7500	18.00	21.27	81.7000
18.25	20.74	86.3125	18.25	20.96	84.7917	18.25	21.50	81.7500	18.25	21.54	81.4965	18.25	21.61	81.4458
18.50	21.06	86.1250	18.50	21.29	84.5833	18.50	21.84	81.5000	18.50	21.89	81.2431	18.50	21.96	81.1917
18.75	21.38	85.9375	18.75	21.62	84.3750	18.75	22.18	81.2500	18.75	22.24	80.9896	18.75	22.31	80.9375
19.00	21.70	85.7500	19.00	21.94	84.1667	19.00	22.53	81.0000	19.00	22.59	80.7361	19.00	22.66	80.6833
20.00	23.00	85.0000	20.00	23.27	83.3333	20.00	23.94	80.0000	20.00	24.00	79.7222	20.00	24.07	79.6667
25.00	29.76	81.2500	25.00	30.23	79.1667	25.00	31.37	75.0000	25.00	31.48	74.6528	25.00	31.58	74.5833
30.00	37.03	77.5000	30.00	37.76	75.0000	30.00	39.59	70.0000	30.00	39.76	69.5833	30.00	39.90	69.5000

TABLE **25**

Mortgage Price and Yield

Interest Rates: 0, 1, 2, 3%; 4 to 15% by .25%.

Terms: 1 to 30 years, each year.

Payment: Monthly.

This table shows the price of a mortgage at a yield rate and the yield of a mortgage at a price, when the term and the interest rate are the same for both. In each case, the yield is to maturity.

Example: An 8%, 30 year mortgage is for sale. To yield 9% to maturity, the price is $91.19. This means that for every $100 of face amount, the purchaser will pay $91.19. A $100,000 mortgage will sell for $91,190.

To yield 7% to maturity, the price is $110.29.

If the 8% mortgage is sold at a price of 91, the yield is 9.02% to maturity.

An 8%, 30 year mortgage is held for 5 years before it is sold. It then is a 25 year mortgage and the balance is no longer 100 but the amortized balance, which is 95.0699% of the original amount. The price read from the table is applied to the amortized balance.

The prices and yields in the example are shown in the table beginning on page 25-178.

Mortgage. A mortgage is evidence of a loan that has been made to a borrower who has agreed to make regular periodic payments for a specified time to amortize the loan. The mortgage document states, among other things, the amount of the loan, the interest rate on the loan, the term, and the payment.

Once a mortgage has been signed, it is a document that represents a specific stream of payments in the future. As such it has value and may be held by the issuer or sold to an investor. The value is determined by the market and prevailing interest rate.

This table shows the price-yield relationship of a mortgage purchased for investment. The yield is the return on the investment. Notice on the price page that for an interest rate, as the yield goes up, the price goes down, and on the facing yield page, as the price goes down, the yield goes up.

Mortgage Price. The mortgage price is a function of yield. The yield creates the price. The price is the present value of all future payments at the yield rate. The price is computed directly from this formula:

$$\text{Price} = \text{Payment} \times A_{\overline{n}|}$$

where:

$A_{\overline{n}|}$ = Present Worth of 1 Per Period at the yield rate

Example: The monthly payment per 100 for an 8%, 30 year mortgage is .73376457. The 30 year mortgage has 360 periods.

At 8%, the Present Worth of 1 Per Period is 136.283494. Multiply the 2 factors for the price:

$$\text{Price} = .733765 \times 136.2835 = 100$$

The price of an 8% mortgage to yield 8% is par.

At 9% the Present Worth of 1 Per Period is 124.281866. Multiply the 2 factors:

$$\text{Price} = .733765 \times 124.2819 = 91.19$$

To yield 9%, the price is below par.

At 7%, the Present Worth of 1 Per Period is 150.307568. Multiply the 2 factors:

$$\text{Price} = .733765 \times 150.3077 = 110.29$$

To yield 7%, the price is above par.

Mortgage Yield. There is no direct way to compute a yield for a given price. In practice, the process is by trial and error, that is, a price is computed at a trial rate. If the computed price is too high, a greater yield rate is used. The process is continued until the yield is found that computes the price exactly. The process is called iteration. A program for computing a yield is described in the Appendix.

Premium and Discount. A premium price is higher than par and the yield is less than the interest rate on the mortgage.

MORTGAGE PRICE AND YIELD

The $110.29 in the example is a premium price and the yield is 7% on the 8% mortgage.

A discount price is less than par and the yield is greater than the interest rate. The $91.19 in the example is a discount price and the yield is 9%.

For all fixed-rate securities, price up, yield down and yield up, price down. The yield is that rate at which the investment is amortized over the term.

Example: The underlying security of a mortgage is the borrower's loan. The first few lines and the final lines of the 8%, 30 year schedule look like this:

Loan: 100.0000   Term: 30 years
Rate: 8%   Payment: .7338

Payment	Interest	Principal	Balance
1	.6667	.0671	99.9329
2	.6662	.0676	99.8653
3	.6658	.0680	99.7973
⋮	⋮	⋮	⋮
359	—	—	.6782
360	.0045	.6782	.0000

If the investor buys at a premium price to yield 7%, the first few lines and the final lines of the 30 year schedule look like this:

Loan: 110.2900   Term: 10 years
Rate: 7%   Payment: .7338

Payment	Interest	Principal	Balance
1	.6434	.0904	110.1996
2	.6428	.0910	110.1086
3	.6423	.0915	110.0171
⋮	⋮	⋮	⋮
359	—	—	.6831
360	.0040	.6831	.0000

If the investor buys at a discount price to yield 9%, the first few lines and the final lines of the 30 year schedule look like this:

Loan: 91.1900   Term: 30 years
Rate: 9%   Payment: .7338

Payment	Interest	Principal	Balance
1	.6839	.0499	91.1401
2	.6836	.0502	91.0899
3	.6832	.0506	91.0393
⋮	⋮	⋮	⋮
359	—	—	.6088
360	.0046	.6088	.0000

Each schedule has the same payment and term. The lender creates the stream of payments by making the original loan. The investor buys the stream of payments at a yield rate and allocates the payment to amortize the investment over the term of the original loan.

The Mortgage Price and Yield table shows prices and yields for mortgages that run to maturity. Table 26 shows prices and yields for 30 year mortgages that are prepaid.

If a discount mortgage is purchased with the expectation that it will run to maturity and it is then prepaid prior to maturity, the yield will be greater than shown in Table 25. Table 25 sets a floor on the yield.

If a premium mortgage is purchased with the expectation that it will run to maturity and it is then prepaid prior to maturity, the yield will be less than shown in Table 25. Table 25 sets a ceiling on the yield.

MORTGAGE PRICE AND YIELD

MORTGAGE PRICE

Description: This table shows the price to pay for a monthly payment mortgage loan at the yield rate.

Example: The price of a 6.75 %, 1 year mortgage loan to yield 8.00 % to maturity is $ 99.34.

INTEREST RATE, %

YIELD	0.00%	1.00%	2.00%	3.00%	4.00%	4.25%	4.50%	4.75%	5.00%	5.25%	5.50%	5.75%	6.00%	6.25%	6.50%	6.75%
0.00	100.00	100.54	101.09	101.63	102.18	102.32	102.45	102.59	102.73	102.87	103.00	103.14	103.28	103.42	103.56	103.69
1.00	99.46	100.00	100.54	101.08	101.63	101.76	101.90	102.04	102.17	102.31	102.45	102.59	102.72	102.86	103.00	103.13
2.00	98.93	99.46	100.00	100.54	101.08	101.22	101.35	101.49	101.62	101.76	101.90	102.03	102.17	102.31	102.44	102.58
3.00	98.39	98.93	99.46	100.00	100.54	100.67	100.81	100.94	101.08	101.21	101.35	101.49	101.62	101.76	101.89	102.03
4.00	97.87	98.40	98.93	99.46	100.00	100.13	100.27	100.40	100.54	100.67	100.81	100.94	101.08	101.21	101.35	101.48
4.25	97.74	98.27	98.80	99.33	99.87	100.00	100.13	100.27	100.40	100.54	100.67	100.81	100.94	101.08	101.21	101.35
4.50	97.60	98.13	98.67	99.20	99.73	99.87	100.00	100.13	100.27	100.40	100.54	100.67	100.81	100.94	101.08	101.21
4.75	97.47	98.00	98.53	99.07	99.60	99.73	99.87	100.00	100.13	100.27	100.40	100.54	100.67	100.81	100.94	101.07
5.00	97.34	97.87	98.40	98.93	99.47	99.60	99.73	99.87	100.00	100.13	100.27	100.40	100.54	100.67	100.80	100.94
5.25	97.21	97.74	98.27	98.80	99.33	99.47	99.60	99.73	99.87	100.00	100.13	100.27	100.40	100.54	100.67	100.80
5.50	97.08	97.61	98.14	98.67	99.20	99.33	99.47	99.60	99.73	99.87	100.00	100.13	100.27	100.40	100.54	100.67
5.75	96.95	97.48	98.01	98.54	99.07	99.20	99.33	99.47	99.60	99.73	99.87	100.00	100.13	100.27	100.40	100.54
6.00	96.82	97.35	97.88	98.41	98.94	99.07	99.20	99.33	99.47	99.60	99.73	99.87	100.00	100.13	100.27	100.40
6.25	96.70	97.22	97.75	98.27	98.80	98.94	99.07	99.20	99.33	99.47	99.60	99.73	99.87	100.00	100.13	100.27
6.50	96.57	97.09	97.62	98.14	98.67	98.80	98.94	99.07	99.20	99.33	99.47	99.60	99.73	99.87	100.00	100.13
6.75	96.44	96.96	97.49	98.01	98.54	98.67	98.80	98.94	99.07	99.20	99.33	99.47	99.60	99.73	99.87	100.00
7.00	96.31	96.83	97.36	97.88	98.41	98.54	98.67	98.81	98.94	99.07	99.20	99.34	99.47	99.60	99.73	99.87
7.25	96.18	96.70	97.23	97.75	98.28	98.41	98.54	98.67	98.81	98.94	99.07	99.20	99.34	99.47	99.60	99.73
7.50	96.05	96.57	97.10	97.62	98.15	98.28	98.41	98.54	98.67	98.81	98.94	99.07	99.20	99.34	99.47	99.60
7.75	95.93	96.45	96.97	97.49	98.02	98.15	98.28	98.41	98.54	98.68	98.81	98.94	99.07	99.20	99.34	99.47
8.00	95.80	96.32	96.84	97.36	97.89	98.02	98.15	98.28	98.41	98.54	98.68	98.81	98.94	99.07	99.20	99.34
8.25	95.67	96.19	96.71	97.23	97.76	97.89	98.02	98.15	98.28	98.41	98.55	98.68	98.81	98.94	99.07	99.20
8.50	95.54	96.06	96.58	97.10	97.63	97.76	97.89	98.02	98.15	98.28	98.41	98.55	98.68	98.81	98.94	99.07
8.75	95.42	95.94	96.45	96.98	97.50	97.63	97.76	97.89	98.02	98.15	98.28	98.42	98.55	98.68	98.81	98.94
9.00	95.29	95.81	96.33	96.85	97.37	97.50	97.63	97.76	97.89	98.02	98.15	98.28	98.42	98.55	98.68	98.81
9.25	95.16	95.68	96.20	96.72	97.24	97.37	97.50	97.63	97.76	97.89	98.02	98.15	98.29	98.42	98.55	98.68
9.50	95.04	95.55	96.07	96.59	97.11	97.24	97.37	97.50	97.63	97.76	97.89	98.02	98.15	98.29	98.42	98.55
9.75	94.91	95.43	95.94	96.46	96.98	97.11	97.24	97.37	97.50	97.63	97.76	97.89	98.02	98.16	98.29	98.42
10.00	94.79	95.30	95.82	96.33	96.85	96.98	97.11	97.24	97.37	97.50	97.63	97.64	97.77	97.90	98.03	98.16
10.00	94.79	95.30	95.82	96.33	96.85	96.98	97.11	97.24	97.37	97.50	97.64	97.77	97.90	98.03	98.16	98.29
10.25	94.66	95.18	95.69	96.21	96.73	96.86	96.99	97.12	97.25	97.38	97.51	97.64	97.77	97.90	98.03	98.16
10.50	94.54	95.05	95.56	96.08	96.60	96.73	96.86	96.99	97.12	97.25	97.38	97.51	97.64	97.77	97.90	98.03
10.75	94.41	94.92	95.44	95.95	96.47	96.60	96.73	96.86	96.99	97.12	97.25	97.38	97.51	97.64	97.77	97.90
11.00	94.29	94.80	95.31	95.83	96.34	96.47	96.60	96.73	96.86	96.99	97.12	97.25	97.38	97.51	97.64	97.77
11.25	94.16	94.67	95.19	95.70	96.22	96.35	96.47	96.60	96.73	96.86	96.99	97.12	97.25	97.38	97.51	97.64
11.50	94.04	94.55	95.06	95.57	96.09	96.22	96.35	96.48	96.61	96.74	96.86	96.99	97.12	97.25	97.38	97.51
11.75	93.92	94.43	94.94	95.45	95.96	96.09	96.22	96.35	96.48	96.61	96.74	96.86	96.99	97.12	97.25	97.38
12.00	93.79	94.30	94.81	95.32	95.84	95.97	96.09	96.22	96.35	96.48	96.61	96.74	96.87	97.00	97.13	97.26
12.25	93.67	94.18	94.69	95.20	95.71	95.84	95.97	96.10	96.23	96.35	96.48	96.61	96.74	96.87	97.00	97.13
12.50	93.55	94.05	94.56	95.07	95.59	95.71	95.84	95.97	96.10	96.23	96.36	96.48	96.61	96.74	96.87	97.00
12.75	93.42	93.93	94.44	94.95	95.46	95.59	95.72	95.84	95.97	96.10	96.23	96.36	96.49	96.62	96.74	96.87
13.00	93.30	93.81	94.31	94.82	95.33	95.46	95.59	95.72	95.85	95.97	96.10	96.23	96.36	96.49	96.62	96.75
13.25	93.18	93.68	94.19	94.70	95.21	95.34	95.46	95.59	95.72	95.85	95.98	96.11	96.23	96.36	96.49	96.62
13.50	93.06	93.56	94.07	94.57	95.08	95.21	95.34	95.47	95.60	95.72	95.85	95.98	96.11	96.24	96.36	96.49
13.75	92.93	93.44	93.94	94.45	94.96	95.09	95.21	95.34	95.47	95.60	95.73	95.85	95.98	96.11	96.24	96.37
14.00	92.81	93.32	93.82	94.33	94.84	94.96	95.09	95.22	95.34	95.47	95.60	95.73	95.86	95.98	96.11	96.24
14.25	92.69	93.19	93.70	94.20	94.71	94.84	94.97	95.09	95.22	95.35	95.48	95.60	95.73	95.86	95.98	96.11
14.50	92.57	93.07	93.58	94.08	94.59	94.71	94.84	94.97	95.10	95.22	95.35	95.48	95.61	95.73	95.86	95.99
14.75	92.45	92.95	93.45	93.96	94.46	94.59	94.72	94.84	94.97	95.10	95.23	95.35	95.48	95.61	95.73	95.86
15.00	92.33	92.83	93.33	93.83	94.34	94.47	94.59	94.72	94.85	94.97	95.10	95.23	95.36	95.48	95.61	95.74
15.25	92.21	92.71	93.21	93.71	94.22	94.34	94.47	94.60	94.72	94.85	94.98	95.10	95.23	95.36	95.49	95.61
15.50	92.09	92.59	93.09	93.59	94.09	94.22	94.35	94.47	94.60	94.73	94.85	94.98	95.11	95.23	95.36	95.49
15.75	91.97	92.47	92.97	93.47	93.97	94.10	94.22	94.35	94.48	94.60	94.73	94.86	94.98	95.11	95.23	95.36
16.00	91.85	92.35	92.84	93.35	93.85	93.97	94.10	94.23	94.35	94.48	94.61	94.73	94.86	94.99	95.11	95.24
16.25	91.73	92.22	92.72	93.22	93.73	93.85	93.98	94.10	94.23	94.36	94.48	94.61	94.73	94.86	94.99	95.11
16.50	91.61	92.10	92.60	93.10	93.60	93.73	93.86	93.98	94.11	94.23	94.36	94.48	94.61	94.74	94.86	94.99
16.75	91.49	91.98	92.48	92.98	93.48	93.61	93.73	93.86	93.99	94.11	94.24	94.36	94.49	94.61	94.74	94.87
17.00	91.37	91.87	92.36	92.86	93.36	93.49	93.61	93.74	93.86	93.99	94.11	94.24	94.37	94.49	94.62	94.74
17.25	91.25	91.75	92.24	92.74	93.24	93.37	93.49	93.62	93.74	93.87	93.99	94.12	94.24	94.37	94.50	94.62
17.50	91.13	91.63	92.12	92.62	93.12	93.24	93.37	93.49	93.62	93.74	93.87	93.99	94.12	94.24	94.37	94.50
17.75	91.01	91.51	92.00	92.50	93.00	93.12	93.25	93.37	93.50	93.62	93.74	93.87	94.00	94.12	94.25	94.37
18.00	90.90	91.39	91.88	92.38	92.88	93.00	93.13	93.25	93.38	93.50	93.63	93.75	93.88	94.00	94.13	94.25
18.25	90.78	91.27	91.76	92.26	92.76	92.88	93.01	93.13	93.26	93.38	93.51	93.63	93.76	93.88	94.01	94.13
18.50	90.66	91.15	91.65	92.14	92.64	92.76	92.89	93.01	93.13	93.26	93.38	93.51	93.63	93.76	93.88	94.01
18.75	90.54	91.03	91.53	92.02	92.52	92.64	92.77	92.89	93.01	93.14	93.26	93.39	93.51	93.63	93.76	93.89
19.00	90.43	90.92	91.41	91.90	92.40	92.52	92.65	92.77	92.89	93.02	93.14	93.27	93.39	93.52	93.64	93.77
20.00	89.96	90.45	90.94	91.43	91.92	92.04	92.17	92.29	92.41	92.54	92.66	92.79	92.91	93.03	93.16	93.28
25.00	87.68	88.15	88.63	89.11	89.59	89.71	89.83	89.95	90.07	90.19	90.31	90.43	90.55	90.68	90.80	90.92
30.00	85.48	85.95	86.41	86.88	87.34	87.46	87.58	87.70	87.81	87.93	88.05	88.17	88.28	88.40	88.52	88.64

MORTGAGE YIELD

Description: This table shows the yield to maturity of a mortgage purchased at the price shown in the index.

Example: The yield to maturity of a 6.75 %, 1 year mortgage at a price of 95.00 is 16.48 %.

INTEREST RATE, %

PRICE	0.00%	1.00%	2.00%	3.00%	4.00%	4.25%	4.50%	4.75%	5.00%	5.25%	5.50%	5.75%	6.00%	6.25%	6.50%	6.75%
100	0.00	1.00	2.00	3.00	4.00	4.25	4.50	4.75	5.00	5.25	5.50	5.75	6.00	6.25	6.50	6.75
99.75	.46	1.46	2.46	3.46	4.46	4.71	4.96	5.21	5.46	5.71	5.96	6.21	6.46	6.71	6.96	7.21
99.50	.92	1.92	2.93	3.93	4.93	5.18	5.43	5.68	5.93	6.18	6.43	6.68	6.93	7.19	7.44	7.69
99.25	1.39	2.39	3.39	4.40	5.40	5.65	5.90	6.15	6.40	6.65	6.91	7.16	7.41	7.66	7.91	8.16
99.00	1.85	2.86	3.86	4.87	5.87	6.12	6.37	6.63	6.88	7.13	7.38	7.63	7.88	8.13	8.38	8.63
98.75	2.32	3.33	4.33	5.34	6.35	6.60	6.85	7.10	7.35	7.60	7.85	8.11	8.36	8.61	8.86	9.11
98.50	2.79	3.80	4.81	5.81	6.82	7.07	7.32	7.58	7.83	8.08	8.33	8.58	8.83	9.09	9.34	9.59
98.25	3.27	4.27	5.28	6.29	7.30	7.55	7.80	8.05	8.31	8.56	8.81	9.06	9.31	9.57	9.82	10.07
98.00	3.74	4.75	5.76	6.77	7.78	8.03	8.28	8.53	8.79	9.04	9.29	9.54	9.80	10.05	10.30	10.55
97.75	4.22	5.23	6.24	7.25	8.26	8.51	8.76	9.02	9.27	9.52	9.77	10.03	10.28	10.53	10.78	11.04
97.50	4.70	5.71	6.72	7.73	8.74	8.99	9.25	9.50	9.75	10.00	10.26	10.51	10.76	11.02	11.27	11.52
97.25	5.17	6.19	7.20	8.21	9.22	9.48	9.73	9.98	10.24	10.49	10.74	11.00	11.25	11.50	11.76	12.01
97.00	5.66	6.67	7.68	8.70	9.71	9.96	10.22	10.47	10.72	10.98	11.23	11.48	11.74	11.99	12.24	12.50
96.75	6.14	7.15	8.17	9.18	10.20	10.45	10.71	10.96	11.21	11.47	11.72	11.97	12.23	12.48	12.74	12.99
96.50	6.62	7.64	8.66	9.67	10.69	10.94	11.20	11.45	11.70	11.96	12.21	12.47	12.72	12.97	13.23	13.48
96.25	7.11	8.13	9.14	10.16	11.18	11.43	11.69	11.94	12.20	12.45	12.70	12.96	13.21	13.47	13.72	13.98
96.00	7.60	8.62	9.64	10.65	11.67	11.93	12.18	12.44	12.69	12.95	13.20	13.45	13.71	13.96	14.22	14.47
95.75	8.09	9.11	10.13	11.15	12.17	12.42	12.68	12.93	13.19	13.44	13.70	13.95	14.21	14.46	14.72	14.97
95.50	8.58	9.60	10.62	11.64	12.66	12.92	13.17	13.43	13.69	13.94	14.20	14.45	14.71	14.96	15.22	15.47
95.25	9.08	10.10	11.12	12.14	13.16	13.42	13.67	13.93	14.19	14.44	14.70	14.95	15.21	15.46	15.72	15.97
95.00	9.57	10.60	11.62	12.64	13.66	13.92	14.18	14.43	14.69	14.94	15.20	15.45	15.71	15.97	16.22	16.48
94.75	10.07	11.09	12.12	13.14	14.17	14.42	14.68	14.94	15.19	15.45	15.70	15.96	16.22	16.47	16.73	16.98
94.50	10.57	11.60	12.62	13.65	14.67	14.93	15.18	15.44	15.70	15.95	16.21	16.47	16.72	16.98	17.24	17.49
94.25	11.07	12.10	13.12	14.15	15.18	15.43	15.69	15.95	16.21	16.46	16.72	16.98	17.23	17.49	17.75	18.00
94.00	11.58	12.60	13.63	14.66	15.69	15.94	16.20	16.46	16.71	16.97	17.23	17.49	17.74	18.00	18.26	18.51
93.75	12.08	13.11	14.14	15.17	16.20	16.45	16.71	16.97	17.23	17.48	17.74	18.00	18.26	18.51	18.77	19.03
93.50	12.59	13.62	14.65	15.68	16.71	16.97	17.23	17.48	17.74	18.00	18.26	18.51	18.77	19.03	19.29	19.54
93.25	13.10	14.13	15.16	16.19	17.22	17.48	17.74	18.00	18.26	18.51	18.77	19.03	19.29	19.55	19.80	20.06
93.00	13.61	14.64	15.68	16.71	17.74	18.00	18.26	18.52	18.77	19.03	19.29	19.55	19.81	20.07	20.32	20.58
92.75	14.12	15.16	16.19	17.23	18.26	18.52	18.78	19.04	19.29	19.55	19.81	20.07	20.33	20.59	20.85	21.10
92.50	14.64	15.67	16.71	17.74	18.78	19.04	19.30	19.56	19.82	20.07	20.33	20.59	20.85	21.11	21.37	21.63
92.25	15.16	16.19	17.23	18.27	19.30	19.56	19.82	20.08	20.34	20.60	20.86	21.12	21.38	21.64	21.90	22.15
92.00	15.68	16.71	17.75	18.79	19.83	20.09	20.35	20.61	20.87	21.13	21.38	21.64	21.90	22.16	22.42	22.68
91.75	16.20	17.24	18.28	19.31	20.35	20.61	20.87	21.13	21.39	21.65	21.91	22.17	22.43	22.69	22.95	23.21
91	17.77	18.82	19.86	20.90	21.95	22.21	22.47	22.73	22.99	23.25	23.51	23.77	24.03	24.30	24.56	24.82
90	19.91	20.96	22.00	23.05	24.10	24.36	24.63	24.89	25.15	25.41	25.67	25.94	26.20	26.46	26.72	26.99
89	22.08	23.13	24.18	25.24	26.29	26.55	26.82	27.08	27.35	27.61	27.87	28.14	28.40	28.66	28.93	29.19
88	24.28	25.34	26.40	27.46	28.52	28.78	29.05	29.31	29.58	29.84	30.11	30.37	30.64	30.90	31.17	31.43
87	26.52	27.58	28.65	29.71	30.78	31.05	31.31	31.58	31.85	32.11	32.38	32.64	32.91	33.18	33.44	33.71
86	28.80	29.87	30.94	32.01	33.08	33.35	33.62	33.89	34.15	34.42	34.69	34.96	35.22	35.49	35.76	36.03
85	31.12	32.19	33.27	34.35	35.42	35.69	35.96	36.23	36.50	36.77	37.04	37.31	37.58	37.85	38.12	38.39
84	33.47	34.56	35.64	36.72	37.81	38.08	38.35	38.62	38.89	39.16	39.43	39.70	39.97	40.24	40.51	40.79
83	35.87	36.96	38.05	39.14	40.23	40.50	40.78	41.05	41.32	41.59	41.86	42.14	42.41	42.68	42.95	43.23
82	38.32	39.41	40.51	41.60	42.70	42.97	43.25	43.52	43.79	44.07	44.34	44.62	44.89	45.17	45.44	45.71
81	40.80	41.91	43.01	44.11	45.21	45.49	45.76	46.04	46.31	46.59	46.87	47.14	47.42	47.69	47.97	48.25
80	43.34	44.45	45.55	46.66	47.77	48.05	48.33	48.60	48.88	49.16	49.44	49.71	49.99	50.27	50.55	50.82
79	45.92	47.03	48.15	49.26	50.38	50.66	50.94	51.22	51.50	51.78	52.05	52.33	52.61	52.89	53.17	53.45
78	48.55	49.67	50.79	51.92	53.04	53.32	53.60	53.88	54.16	54.44	54.72	55.00	55.29	55.57	55.85	56.13
77	51.23	52.36	53.49	54.62	55.75	56.03	56.31	56.60	56.88	57.16	57.44	57.73	58.01	58.29	58.57	58.86
76	53.96	55.10	56.24	57.37	58.51	58.79	59.08	59.36	59.65	59.93	60.22	60.50	60.79	61.07	61.36	61.64
75	56.75	57.89	59.04	60.18	61.33	61.61	61.90	62.19	62.47	62.76	63.05	63.33	63.62	63.91	64.19	64.48
74	59.59	60.75	61.90	63.05	64.20	64.49	64.78	65.07	65.36	65.64	65.93	66.22	66.51	66.80	67.09	67.38
73	62.50	63.66	64.82	65.98	67.14	67.43	67.72	68.01	68.30	68.59	68.88	69.17	69.46	69.75	70.04	70.33
72	65.46	66.63	67.79	68.96	70.13	70.42	70.72	71.01	71.30	71.59	71.89	72.18	72.47	72.76	73.06	73.35
71	68.48	69.66	70.84	72.01	73.19	73.49	73.78	74.07	74.37	74.66	74.96	75.25	75.55	75.84	76.14	76.43
70	71.57	72.76	73.94	75.13	76.32	76.61	76.91	77.21	77.50	77.80	78.10	78.39	78.69	78.99	79.28	79.58
69	74.73	75.93	77.12	78.31	79.51	79.81	80.11	80.41	80.71	81.00	81.30	81.60	81.90	82.20	82.50	82.80
68	77.96	79.16	80.37	81.57	82.77	83.08	83.38	83.68	83.98	84.28	84.58	84.88	85.19	85.49	85.79	86.09
67	81.26	82.47	83.69	84.90	86.11	86.42	86.72	87.03	87.33	87.63	87.94	88.24	88.54	88.85	89.15	89.46
66	84.64	85.86	87.08	88.31	89.53	89.84	90.14	90.45	90.76	91.06	91.37	91.67	91.98	92.29	92.59	92.90
65	88.10	89.33	90.56	91.79	93.03	93.34	93.65	93.95	94.26	94.57	94.88	95.19	95.50	95.81	96.12	96.42
64	91.64	92.88	94.12	95.36	96.61	96.92	97.23	97.54	97.85	98.17	98.48	98.79	99.10	99.41	99.72	100.03
63	95.26	96.51	97.77	99.02	100.28	100.59	100.90	101.22	101.53	101.85	102.16	102.48	102.79	103.10	103.42	103.73
62	98.98	100.24	101.51	102.77	104.04	104.35	104.67	104.99	105.30	105.62	105.94	106.25	106.57	106.89	107.21	107.52
61	102.79	104.06	105.34	106.61	107.89	108.21	108.53	108.85	109.17	109.49	109.81	110.13	110.45	110.77	111.09	111.41
60	106.69	107.98	109.27	110.56	111.85	112.17	112.49	112.81	113.14	113.46	113.78	114.10	114.43	114.75	115.07	115.40
59	110.70	112.00	113.30	114.60	115.91	116.23	116.56	116.88	117.21	117.53	117.86	118.19	118.51	118.84	119.16	119.49
58	114.82	116.13	117.45	118.76	120.07	120.40	120.73	121.06	121.39	121.72	122.05	122.38	122.70	123.03	123.36	123.69

MORTGAGE PRICE

Description: This table shows the price to pay for a monthly payment mortgage loan at the yield rate.

Example: The price of a 10.75 %, 1 year mortgage loan to yield 8.00 % to maturity is $ 101.47.

INTEREST RATE, %

YIELD	7.00%	7.25%	7.50%	7.75%	8.00%	8.25%	8.50%	8.75%	9.00%	9.25%	9.50%	9.75%	10.00%	10.25%	10.50%	10.75%
0.00	103.83	103.97	104.11	104.25	104.39	104.52	104.66	104.80	104.94	105.08	105.22	105.36	105.50	105.64	105.78	105.92
1.00	103.27	103.41	103.55	103.68	103.82	103.96	104.10	104.24	104.38	104.51	104.65	104.79	104.93	105.07	105.21	105.35
2.00	102.72	102.85	102.99	103.13	103.26	103.40	103.54	103.68	103.81	103.95	104.09	104.23	104.36	104.50	104.64	104.78
3.00	102.16	102.30	102.44	102.57	102.71	102.85	102.98	103.12	103.26	103.39	103.53	103.67	103.80	103.94	104.08	104.22
4.00	101.62	101.75	101.89	102.02	102.16	102.29	102.43	102.57	102.70	102.84	102.98	103.11	103.25	103.38	103.52	103.66
4.25	101.48	101.62	101.75	101.89	102.02	102.16	102.29	102.43	102.57	102.70	102.84	102.97	103.11	103.25	103.38	103.52
4.50	101.34	101.48	101.62	101.75	101.89	102.02	102.16	102.29	102.43	102.56	102.70	102.84	102.97	103.11	103.24	103.38
4.75	101.21	101.34	101.48	101.61	101.75	101.88	102.02	102.16	102.29	102.43	102.56	102.70	102.83	102.97	103.11	103.24
5.00	101.07	101.21	101.34	101.48	101.61	101.75	101.88	102.02	102.15	102.29	102.43	102.56	102.70	102.83	102.97	103.10
5.25	100.94	101.07	101.21	101.34	101.48	101.61	101.75	101.88	102.02	102.15	102.29	102.42	102.56	102.69	102.83	102.97
5.50	100.80	100.94	101.07	101.21	101.34	101.48	101.61	101.75	101.88	102.02	102.15	102.29	102.42	102.56	102.69	102.83
5.75	100.67	100.80	100.94	101.07	101.21	101.34	101.48	101.61	101.75	101.88	102.02	102.15	102.29	102.42	102.56	102.69
6.00	100.53	100.67	100.80	100.94	101.07	101.21	101.34	101.47	101.61	101.74	101.88	102.01	102.15	102.28	102.42	102.55
6.25	100.40	100.53	100.67	100.80	100.94	101.07	101.20	101.34	101.47	101.61	101.74	101.88	102.01	102.15	102.28	102.42
6.50	100.27	100.40	100.53	100.67	100.80	100.94	101.07	101.20	101.34	101.47	101.61	101.74	101.88	102.01	102.15	102.28
6.75	100.13	100.27	100.40	100.53	100.67	100.80	100.94	101.07	101.20	101.34	101.47	101.61	101.74	101.88	102.01	102.15
7.00	100.00	100.13	100.27	100.40	100.53	100.67	100.80	100.93	101.07	101.20	101.34	101.47	101.61	101.74	101.87	102.01
7.25	99.87	100.00	100.13	100.27	100.40	100.53	100.67	100.80	100.93	101.07	101.20	101.34	101.47	101.60	101.74	101.87
7.50	99.73	99.87	100.00	100.13	100.27	100.40	100.53	100.67	100.80	100.93	101.07	101.20	101.34	101.47	101.60	101.74
7.75	99.60	99.73	99.87	100.00	100.13	100.27	100.40	100.53	100.67	100.80	100.93	101.07	101.20	101.34	101.47	101.60
8.00	99.47	99.60	99.73	99.87	100.00	100.13	100.27	100.40	100.53	100.67	100.80	100.93	101.07	101.20	101.33	101.47
8.25	99.34	99.47	99.60	99.73	99.87	100.00	100.13	100.27	100.40	100.53	100.67	100.80	100.93	101.07	101.20	101.33
8.50	99.21	99.34	99.47	99.60	99.73	99.87	100.00	100.13	100.27	100.40	100.53	100.67	100.80	100.93	101.06	101.20
8.75	99.07	99.21	99.34	99.47	99.60	99.73	99.87	100.00	100.13	100.27	100.40	100.53	100.66	100.80	100.93	101.06
9.00	98.94	99.07	99.21	99.34	99.47	99.60	99.74	99.87	100.00	100.13	100.27	100.40	100.53	100.66	100.80	100.93
9.25	98.81	98.94	99.07	99.21	99.34	99.47	99.60	99.74	99.87	100.00	100.13	100.27	100.40	100.53	100.66	100.80
9.50	98.68	98.81	98.94	99.08	99.21	99.34	99.47	99.60	99.74	99.87	100.00	100.13	100.27	100.40	100.53	100.66
9.75	98.55	98.68	98.81	98.94	99.08	99.21	99.34	99.47	99.60	99.74	99.87	100.00	100.13	100.27	100.40	100.53
10.00	98.42	98.55	98.68	98.81	98.95	99.08	99.21	99.34	99.47	99.60	99.74	99.87	100.00	100.13	100.26	100.40
10.25	98.29	98.42	98.55	98.68	98.81	98.95	99.08	99.21	99.34	99.47	99.60	99.74	99.87	100.00	100.13	100.26
10.50	98.16	98.29	98.42	98.55	98.68	98.82	98.95	99.08	99.21	99.34	99.47	99.60	99.74	99.87	100.00	100.13
10.75	98.03	98.16	98.29	98.42	98.55	98.68	98.82	98.95	99.08	99.21	99.34	99.47	99.60	99.74	99.87	100.00
11.00	97.90	98.03	98.16	98.29	98.42	98.55	98.69	98.82	98.95	99.08	99.21	99.34	99.47	99.60	99.74	99.87
11.25	97.77	97.90	98.03	98.16	98.29	98.42	98.56	98.69	98.82	98.95	99.08	99.21	99.34	99.47	99.60	99.74
11.50	97.64	97.77	97.90	98.03	98.16	98.29	98.43	98.56	98.69	98.82	98.95	99.08	99.21	99.34	99.47	99.61
11.75	97.51	97.64	97.77	97.90	98.04	98.17	98.30	98.43	98.56	98.69	98.82	98.95	99.08	99.21	99.34	99.47
12.00	97.39	97.52	97.65	97.78	97.91	98.04	98.17	98.30	98.43	98.56	98.69	98.82	98.95	99.08	99.21	99.34
12.25	97.26	97.39	97.52	97.65	97.78	97.91	98.04	98.17	98.30	98.43	98.56	98.69	98.82	98.95	99.08	99.21
12.50	97.13	97.26	97.39	97.52	97.65	97.78	97.91	98.04	98.17	98.30	98.43	98.56	98.69	98.82	98.95	99.08
12.75	97.00	97.13	97.26	97.39	97.52	97.65	97.78	97.91	98.04	98.17	98.30	98.43	98.56	98.69	98.82	98.95
13.00	96.88	97.00	97.13	97.26	97.39	97.52	97.65	97.78	97.91	98.04	98.17	98.30	98.43	98.56	98.69	98.82
13.25	96.75	96.88	97.01	97.14	97.26	97.39	97.52	97.65	97.78	97.91	98.04	98.17	98.30	98.43	98.56	98.69
13.50	96.62	96.75	96.88	97.01	97.14	97.27	97.40	97.52	97.65	97.78	97.91	98.04	98.17	98.30	98.43	98.56
13.75	96.50	96.62	96.75	96.88	97.01	97.14	97.27	97.40	97.53	97.66	97.79	97.91	98.04	98.17	98.30	98.43
14.00	96.37	96.50	96.63	96.75	96.88	97.01	97.14	97.27	97.40	97.53	97.66	97.79	97.92	98.05	98.18	98.30
14.25	96.24	96.37	96.50	96.63	96.76	96.88	97.01	97.14	97.27	97.40	97.53	97.66	97.79	97.92	98.05	98.18
14.50	96.12	96.24	96.37	96.50	96.63	96.76	96.89	97.02	97.14	97.27	97.40	97.53	97.66	97.79	97.92	98.05
14.75	95.99	96.12	96.25	96.38	96.50	96.63	96.76	96.89	97.02	97.15	97.27	97.40	97.53	97.66	97.79	97.92
15.00	95.87	95.99	96.12	96.25	96.38	96.51	96.63	96.76	96.89	97.02	97.15	97.28	97.40	97.53	97.66	97.79
15.25	95.74	95.87	96.00	96.12	96.25	96.38	96.51	96.64	96.76	96.89	97.02	97.15	97.28	97.41	97.54	97.66
15.50	95.62	95.74	95.87	96.00	96.13	96.25	96.38	96.51	96.64	96.77	96.89	97.02	97.15	97.28	97.41	97.54
15.75	95.49	95.62	95.75	95.87	96.00	96.13	96.26	96.38	96.51	96.64	96.77	96.90	97.02	97.15	97.28	97.41
16.00	95.37	95.49	95.62	95.75	95.88	96.00	96.13	96.26	96.39	96.51	96.64	96.77	96.90	97.03	97.15	97.28
16.25	95.24	95.37	95.50	95.62	95.75	95.88	96.01	96.13	96.26	96.39	96.52	96.64	96.77	96.90	97.03	97.16
16.50	95.12	95.24	95.37	95.50	95.63	95.75	95.88	96.01	96.13	96.26	96.39	96.52	96.64	96.77	96.90	97.03
16.75	94.99	95.12	95.25	95.37	95.50	95.63	95.76	95.88	96.01	96.14	96.26	96.39	96.52	96.65	96.77	96.90
17.00	94.87	95.00	95.12	95.25	95.38	95.50	95.63	95.76	95.88	96.01	96.14	96.27	96.39	96.52	96.65	96.78
17.25	94.75	94.87	95.00	95.13	95.25	95.38	95.51	95.63	95.76	95.89	96.01	96.14	96.27	96.40	96.52	96.65
17.50	94.62	94.75	94.88	95.00	95.13	95.26	95.38	95.51	95.64	95.76	95.89	96.02	96.14	96.27	96.40	96.53
17.75	94.50	94.63	94.75	94.88	95.01	95.13	95.26	95.39	95.51	95.64	95.77	95.89	96.02	96.15	96.27	96.40
18.00	94.38	94.50	94.63	94.76	94.88	95.01	95.14	95.26	95.39	95.51	95.64	95.77	95.89	96.02	96.15	96.28
18.25	94.26	94.38	94.51	94.63	94.76	94.89	95.01	95.14	95.26	95.39	95.52	95.64	95.77	95.90	96.02	96.15
18.50	94.13	94.26	94.39	94.51	94.64	94.76	94.89	95.01	95.14	95.27	95.39	95.52	95.65	95.77	95.90	96.03
18.75	94.01	94.14	94.26	94.39	94.51	94.64	94.77	94.89	95.02	95.14	95.27	95.40	95.52	95.65	95.77	95.90
19.00	93.89	94.02	94.14	94.27	94.39	94.52	94.64	94.77	94.89	95.02	95.15	95.27	95.40	95.52	95.65	95.78
20.00	93.41	93.53	93.66	93.78	93.90	94.03	94.15	94.28	94.40	94.53	94.66	94.78	94.91	95.03	95.16	95.28
25.00	91.04	91.16	91.28	91.40	91.52	91.65	91.77	91.89	92.01	92.13	92.26	92.38	92.50	92.62	92.74	92.87
30.00	88.76	88.88	88.99	89.11	89.23	89.35	89.47	89.59	89.71	89.82	89.94	90.06	90.18	90.30	90.42	90.54

Description: This table shows the yield to maturity of a mortgage purchased at the price shown in the index.

Example: The yield to maturity of a 10.75 %, 1 year mortgage at a price of 100.00 is 10.75 %.

INTEREST RATE, %

PRICE	7.00%	7.25%	7.50%	7.75%	8.00%	8.25%	8.50%	8.75%	9.00%	9.25%	9.50%	9.75%	10.00%	10.25%	10.50%	10.75%
105	–	–	–	–	–	–	–	–	–	.14	.38	.63	.87	1.12	1.36	1.61
104.75	–	–	–	–	–	–	–	.09	.33	.58	.82	1.07	1.31	1.56	1.80	2.05
104.50	–	–	–	–	–	–	.28	.53	.77	1.02	1.27	1.51	1.76	2.00	2.25	2.49
104.25	–	–	–	–	.24	.48	.73	.97	1.22	1.46	1.71	1.95	2.20	2.45	2.69	2.94
104.00	–	–	.19	.43	.68	.93	1.17	1.42	1.66	1.91	2.15	2.40	2.65	2.89	3.14	3.38
103.75	–	.39	.63	.88	1.13	1.37	1.62	1.86	2.11	2.35	2.60	2.85	3.09	3.34	3.58	3.83
103.50	.59	.83	1.08	1.33	1.57	1.82	2.06	2.31	2.56	2.80	3.05	3.30	3.54	3.79	4.03	4.28
103.25	1.03	1.28	1.53	1.77	2.02	2.27	2.51	2.76	3.01	3.25	3.50	3.75	3.99	4.24	4.49	4.73
103.00	1.48	1.73	1.98	2.22	2.47	2.72	2.96	3.21	3.46	3.70	3.95	4.20	4.44	4.69	4.94	5.18
102.75	1.93	2.18	2.43	2.67	2.92	3.17	3.42	3.66	3.91	4.16	4.40	4.65	4.90	5.14	5.39	5.64
102.50	2.39	2.63	2.88	3.13	3.37	3.62	3.87	4.12	4.36	4.61	4.86	5.11	5.35	5.60	5.85	6.09
102.25	2.84	3.09	3.33	3.58	3.83	4.08	4.32	4.57	4.82	5.07	5.31	5.56	5.81	6.06	6.31	6.55
102.00	3.29	3.54	3.79	4.04	4.29	4.53	4.78	5.03	5.28	5.52	5.77	6.02	6.27	6.52	6.76	7.01
101.75	3.75	4.00	4.25	4.50	4.74	4.99	5.24	5.49	5.74	5.98	6.23	6.48	6.73	6.98	7.22	7.47
101.50	4.21	4.46	4.71	4.95	5.20	5.45	5.70	5.95	6.20	6.45	6.69	6.94	7.19	7.44	7.69	7.94
101.25	4.67	4.92	5.17	5.42	5.66	5.91	6.16	6.41	6.66	6.91	7.16	7.40	7.65	7.90	8.15	8.40
101.00	5.13	5.38	5.63	5.88	6.13	6.38	6.63	6.87	7.12	7.37	7.62	7.87	8.12	8.37	8.62	8.87
100.75	5.60	5.84	6.09	6.34	6.59	6.84	7.09	7.34	7.59	7.84	8.09	8.34	8.59	8.83	9.08	9.33
100.50	6.06	6.31	6.56	6.81	7.06	7.31	7.56	7.81	8.06	8.31	8.55	8.80	9.05	9.30	9.55	9.80
100.25	6.53	6.78	7.03	7.28	7.53	7.78	8.03	8.27	8.52	8.77	9.02	9.27	9.52	9.77	10.02	10.27
100.00	7.00	7.25	7.50	7.75	8.00	8.25	8.50	8.75	9.00	9.25	9.50	9.75	10.00	10.25	10.50	10.75
99.75	7.47	7.72	7.97	8.22	8.47	8.72	8.97	9.22	9.47	9.72	9.97	10.22	10.47	10.72	10.97	11.22
99.50	7.94	8.19	8.44	8.69	8.94	9.19	9.44	9.69	9.94	10.19	10.44	10.69	10.94	11.19	11.44	11.70
99.25	8.41	8.66	8.91	9.16	9.41	9.66	9.92	10.17	10.42	10.67	10.92	11.17	11.42	11.67	11.92	12.17
99.00	8.89	9.14	9.39	9.64	9.89	10.14	10.39	10.64	10.89	11.15	11.40	11.65	11.90	12.15	12.40	12.65
98.75	9.36	9.61	9.87	10.12	10.37	10.62	10.87	11.12	11.37	11.63	11.88	12.13	12.38	12.63	12.88	13.13
98.50	9.84	10.09	10.34	10.60	10.85	11.10	11.35	11.60	11.86	12.11	12.36	12.61	12.86	13.11	13.37	13.62
98.25	10.32	10.57	10.83	11.08	11.33	11.58	11.83	12.09	12.34	12.59	12.84	13.09	13.35	13.60	13.85	14.10
98.00	10.80	11.06	11.31	11.56	11.81	12.07	12.32	12.57	12.82	13.07	13.33	13.58	13.83	14.08	14.34	14.59
97.75	11.29	11.54	11.79	12.05	12.30	12.55	12.80	13.06	13.31	13.56	13.81	14.07	14.32	14.57	14.82	15.08
97.50	11.77	12.03	12.28	12.53	12.79	13.04	13.29	13.54	13.80	14.05	14.30	14.56	14.81	15.06	15.31	15.57
97.25	12.26	12.51	12.77	13.02	13.27	13.53	13.78	14.03	14.29	14.54	14.79	15.05	15.30	15.55	15.81	16.06
97.00	12.75	13.00	13.26	13.51	13.76	14.02	14.27	14.53	14.78	15.03	15.29	15.54	15.79	16.05	16.30	16.55
96.75	13.24	13.50	13.75	14.00	14.26	14.51	14.76	15.02	15.27	15.53	15.78	16.03	16.29	16.54	16.79	17.05
96.50	13.74	13.99	14.24	14.50	14.75	15.01	15.26	15.51	15.77	16.02	16.28	16.53	16.78	17.04	17.29	17.55
96.25	14.23	14.48	14.74	14.99	15.25	15.50	15.76	16.01	16.27	16.52	16.77	17.03	17.28	17.54	17.79	18.05
96.00	14.73	14.98	15.24	15.49	15.75	16.00	16.26	16.51	16.76	17.02	17.27	17.53	17.78	18.04	18.29	18.55
95.75	15.23	15.48	15.74	15.99	16.25	16.50	16.76	17.01	17.27	17.52	17.78	18.03	18.29	18.54	18.80	19.05
95.50	15.73	15.98	16.24	16.49	16.75	17.00	17.26	17.51	17.77	18.02	18.28	18.53	18.79	19.04	19.30	19.56
95.25	16.23	16.48	16.74	17.00	17.25	17.51	17.76	18.02	18.27	18.53	18.78	19.04	19.30	19.55	19.81	20.06
95.00	16.73	16.99	17.25	17.50	17.76	18.01	18.27	18.52	18.78	19.04	19.29	19.55	19.80	20.06	20.32	20.57
94.75	17.24	17.50	17.75	18.01	18.26	18.52	18.78	19.03	19.29	19.55	19.80	20.06	20.31	20.57	20.83	21.08
94	18.77	19.03	19.29	19.54	19.80	20.06	20.31	20.57	20.83	21.08	21.34	21.60	21.86	22.11	22.37	22.63
93	20.84	21.10	21.36	21.62	21.87	22.13	22.39	22.65	22.91	23.17	23.42	23.68	23.94	24.20	24.46	24.72
92	22.94	23.20	23.46	23.72	23.98	24.24	24.50	24.76	25.02	25.28	25.54	25.80	26.06	26.32	26.58	26.84
91	25.08	25.34	25.60	25.86	26.12	26.38	26.64	26.90	27.17	27.43	27.69	27.95	28.21	28.47	28.73	28.99
90	27.25	27.51	27.77	28.03	28.30	28.56	28.82	29.08	29.35	29.61	29.87	30.13	30.40	30.66	30.92	31.18
89	29.45	29.72	29.98	30.24	30.51	30.77	31.04	31.30	31.56	31.83	32.09	32.35	32.62	32.88	33.15	33.41
88	31.70	31.96	32.23	32.49	32.76	33.02	33.29	33.55	33.82	34.08	34.35	34.61	34.88	35.14	35.41	35.67
87	33.98	34.24	34.51	34.78	35.04	35.31	35.58	35.84	36.11	36.38	36.64	36.91	37.18	37.44	37.71	37.98
86	36.30	36.56	36.83	37.10	37.37	37.64	37.90	38.17	38.44	38.71	38.98	39.24	39.51	39.78	40.05	40.32
85	38.66	38.92	39.19	39.46	39.73	40.00	40.27	40.54	40.81	41.08	41.35	41.62	41.89	42.16	42.43	42.70
84	41.06	41.33	41.60	41.87	42.14	42.41	42.68	42.95	43.22	43.50	43.77	44.04	44.31	44.58	44.85	45.12
83	43.50	43.77	44.05	44.32	44.59	44.86	45.14	45.41	45.68	45.95	46.23	46.50	46.77	47.04	47.32	47.59
82	45.99	46.26	46.54	46.81	47.08	47.36	47.63	47.91	48.18	48.46	48.73	49.00	49.28	49.55	49.83	50.10
81	48.52	48.80	49.07	49.35	49.62	49.90	50.18	50.45	50.73	51.00	51.28	51.56	51.83	52.11	52.38	52.66
80	51.10	51.38	51.66	51.93	52.21	52.49	52.77	53.04	53.32	53.60	53.88	54.15	54.43	54.71	54.99	55.27
79	53.73	54.01	54.29	54.57	54.85	55.13	55.41	55.69	55.96	56.24	56.52	56.80	57.08	57.36	57.64	57.92
78	56.41	56.69	56.97	57.25	57.53	57.81	58.10	58.38	58.66	58.94	59.22	59.50	59.78	60.06	60.35	60.63
77	59.14	59.42	59.71	59.99	60.27	60.55	60.84	61.12	61.40	61.69	61.97	62.25	62.54	62.82	63.10	63.39
76	61.92	62.21	62.49	62.78	63.06	63.35	63.63	63.92	64.20	64.49	64.77	65.06	65.34	65.63	65.91	66.20
75	64.77	65.05	65.34	65.63	65.91	66.20	66.49	66.77	67.06	67.35	67.63	67.92	68.21	68.49	68.78	69.07
74	67.66	67.95	68.24	68.53	68.82	69.11	69.40	69.68	69.97	70.26	70.55	70.84	71.13	71.42	71.71	72.00
73	70.62	70.91	71.20	71.49	71.78	72.08	72.37	72.66	72.95	73.24	73.53	73.82	74.11	74.40	74.69	74.98
72	73.64	73.93	74.23	74.52	74.81	75.11	75.40	75.69	75.98	76.28	76.57	76.86	77.16	77.45	77.74	78.04
71	76.73	77.02	77.32	77.61	77.91	78.20	78.50	78.79	79.09	79.38	79.68	79.97	80.27	80.56	80.86	81.15
70	79.88	80.17	80.47	80.77	81.07	81.36	81.66	81.96	82.26	82.55	82.85	83.15	83.44	83.74	84.04	84.34
69	83.10	83.40	83.70	84.00	84.30	84.60	84.89	85.19	85.49	85.79	86.09	86.39	86.69	86.99	87.29	87.59

MORTGAGE PRICE

Description: This table shows the price to pay for a monthly payment mortgage loan at the yield rate.

Example: The price of a 15.00 %, 1 year mortgage loan to yield 8.00 % to maturity is $ 103.76.

INTEREST RATE, %

YIELD	11.00%	11.25%	11.50%	11.75%	12.00%	12.25%	12.50%	12.75%	13.00%	13.25%	13.50%	13.75%	14.00%	14.25%	14.50%	15.00%
0.00	106.06	106.20	106.34	106.48	106.62	106.76	106.90	107.04	107.18	107.32	107.46	107.60	107.74	107.89	108.03	108.31
1.00	105.49	105.62	105.76	105.90	106.04	106.18	106.32	106.46	106.60	106.74	106.88	107.02	107.16	107.30	107.44	107.73
2.00	104.92	105.06	105.19	105.33	105.47	105.61	105.75	105.89	106.03	106.17	106.31	106.45	106.59	106.73	106.87	107.15
3.00	104.35	104.49	104.63	104.77	104.91	105.04	105.18	105.32	105.46	105.60	105.74	105.88	106.01	106.15	106.29	106.57
4.00	103.80	103.93	104.07	104.21	104.34	104.48	104.62	104.76	104.89	105.03	105.17	105.31	105.45	105.58	105.72	106.00
4.25	103.66	103.79	103.93	104.07	104.20	104.34	104.48	104.62	104.75	104.89	105.03	105.17	105.30	105.44	105.58	105.86
4.50	103.52	103.65	103.79	103.93	104.06	104.20	104.34	104.48	104.61	104.75	104.89	105.03	105.16	105.30	105.44	105.72
4.75	103.38	103.52	103.65	103.79	103.93	104.06	104.20	104.34	104.47	104.61	104.75	104.89	105.02	105.16	105.30	105.57
5.00	103.24	103.38	103.51	103.65	103.79	103.92	104.06	104.20	104.33	104.47	104.61	104.74	104.88	105.02	105.16	105.43
5.25	103.10	103.24	103.37	103.51	103.65	103.78	103.92	104.06	104.19	104.33	104.47	104.60	104.74	104.88	105.02	105.29
5.50	102.96	103.10	103.24	103.37	103.51	103.65	103.78	103.92	104.05	104.19	104.33	104.47	104.60	104.74	104.88	105.15
5.75	102.83	102.96	103.10	103.23	103.37	103.51	103.64	103.78	103.92	104.05	104.19	104.33	104.47	104.60	104.74	105.01
6.00	102.69	102.83	102.96	103.10	103.23	103.37	103.50	103.64	103.78	103.91	104.05	104.19	104.32	104.46	104.60	104.87
6.25	102.55	102.69	102.82	102.96	103.10	103.23	103.37	103.50	103.64	103.77	103.91	104.05	104.18	104.32	104.46	104.73
6.50	102.42	102.55	102.69	102.82	102.96	103.09	103.23	103.36	103.50	103.64	103.77	103.91	104.05	104.18	104.32	104.59
6.75	102.28	102.41	102.55	102.69	102.82	102.96	103.09	103.23	103.36	103.50	103.63	103.77	103.91	104.04	104.18	104.45
7.00	102.14	102.28	102.41	102.55	102.68	102.82	102.95	103.09	103.23	103.36	103.50	103.63	103.77	103.90	104.04	104.31
7.25	102.01	102.14	102.28	102.41	102.55	102.68	102.82	102.95	103.09	103.22	103.36	103.49	103.63	103.77	103.90	104.17
7.50	101.87	102.01	102.14	102.28	102.41	102.55	102.68	102.82	102.95	103.09	103.22	103.36	103.49	103.63	103.77	104.04
7.75	101.74	101.87	102.01	102.14	102.27	102.41	102.54	102.68	102.81	102.95	103.09	103.22	103.36	103.49	103.63	103.90
8.00	101.60	101.74	101.87	102.00	102.14	102.27	102.41	102.54	102.68	102.81	102.95	103.08	103.22	103.35	103.49	103.76
8.25	101.47	101.60	101.73	101.87	102.00	102.14	102.27	102.41	102.54	102.68	102.81	102.95	103.08	103.22	103.35	103.62
8.50	101.33	101.47	101.60	101.73	101.87	102.00	102.14	102.27	102.40	102.54	102.67	102.81	102.94	103.08	103.22	103.48
8.75	101.20	101.33	101.47	101.60	101.73	101.87	102.00	102.13	102.27	102.40	102.54	102.67	102.81	102.94	103.08	103.35
9.00	101.06	101.20	101.33	101.46	101.60	101.73	101.87	102.00	102.13	102.27	102.40	102.54	102.67	102.81	102.94	103.21
9.25	100.93	101.06	101.20	101.33	101.46	101.60	101.73	101.86	102.00	102.13	102.27	102.40	102.53	102.67	102.80	103.07
9.50	100.80	100.93	101.06	101.20	101.33	101.46	101.60	101.73	101.86	102.00	102.13	102.27	102.40	102.53	102.67	102.94
9.75	100.66	100.80	100.93	101.06	101.19	101.33	101.46	101.60	101.73	101.86	102.00	102.13	102.26	102.40	102.53	102.80
10.00	100.53	100.66	100.80	100.93	101.06	101.19	101.33	101.46	101.59	101.73	101.86	101.99	102.13	102.26	102.40	102.66
10.25	100.40	100.53	100.66	100.79	100.93	101.06	101.19	101.33	101.46	101.59	101.73	101.86	101.99	102.13	102.26	102.53
10.50	100.26	100.40	100.53	100.66	100.79	100.93	101.06	101.19	101.33	101.46	101.59	101.73	101.86	101.99	102.13	102.39
10.75	100.13	100.26	100.40	100.53	100.66	100.79	100.93	101.06	101.19	101.33	101.46	101.59	101.72	101.86	101.99	102.26
11.00	100.00	100.13	100.26	100.40	100.53	100.66	100.79	100.93	101.06	101.19	101.32	101.46	101.59	101.72	101.86	102.12
11.25	99.87	100.00	100.13	100.26	100.40	100.53	100.66	100.79	100.93	101.06	101.19	101.32	101.46	101.59	101.72	101.99
11.50	99.74	99.87	100.00	100.13	100.26	100.40	100.53	100.66	100.79	100.92	101.06	101.19	101.32	101.46	101.59	101.85
11.75	99.61	99.74	99.87	100.00	100.13	100.26	100.40	100.53	100.66	100.79	100.92	101.06	101.19	101.32	101.46	101.72
12.00	99.47	99.61	99.74	99.87	100.00	100.13	100.26	100.40	100.53	100.66	100.79	100.92	101.06	101.19	101.32	101.59
12.25	99.34	99.47	99.61	99.74	99.87	100.00	100.13	100.26	100.40	100.53	100.66	100.79	100.92	101.06	101.19	101.45
12.50	99.21	99.34	99.47	99.61	99.74	99.87	100.00	100.13	100.26	100.39	100.53	100.66	100.79	100.92	101.05	101.32
12.75	99.08	99.21	99.34	99.48	99.61	99.74	99.87	100.00	100.13	100.26	100.39	100.53	100.66	100.79	100.92	101.19
13.00	98.95	99.08	99.21	99.34	99.48	99.61	99.74	99.87	100.00	100.13	100.26	100.39	100.53	100.66	100.79	101.05
13.25	98.82	98.95	99.08	99.21	99.34	99.48	99.61	99.74	99.87	100.00	100.13	100.26	100.39	100.53	100.66	100.92
13.50	98.69	98.82	98.95	99.08	99.21	99.35	99.48	99.61	99.74	99.87	100.00	100.13	100.26	100.39	100.53	100.79
13.75	98.56	98.69	98.82	98.95	99.08	99.22	99.35	99.48	99.61	99.74	99.87	100.00	100.13	100.26	100.39	100.66
14.00	98.43	98.56	98.69	98.82	98.95	99.09	99.22	99.35	99.48	99.61	99.74	99.87	100.00	100.13	100.26	100.52
14.25	98.31	98.44	98.57	98.70	98.83	98.96	99.09	99.22	99.35	99.48	99.61	99.74	99.87	100.00	100.13	100.39
14.50	98.18	98.31	98.44	98.57	98.70	98.83	98.96	99.09	99.22	99.35	99.48	99.61	99.74	99.87	100.00	100.26
14.75	98.05	98.18	98.31	98.44	98.57	98.70	98.83	98.96	99.09	99.22	99.35	99.48	99.61	99.74	99.87	100.13
15.00	97.92	98.05	98.18	98.31	98.44	98.57	98.70	98.83	98.96	99.09	99.22	99.35	99.48	99.61	99.74	100.00
15.25	97.79	97.92	98.05	98.18	98.31	98.44	98.57	98.70	98.83	98.96	99.09	99.22	99.35	99.48	99.61	99.87
15.50	97.67	97.79	97.92	98.05	98.18	98.31	98.44	98.57	98.70	98.83	98.96	99.09	99.22	99.35	99.48	99.74
15.75	97.54	97.67	97.80	97.92	98.05	98.18	98.31	98.44	98.57	98.70	98.83	98.96	99.09	99.22	99.35	99.61
16.00	97.41	97.54	97.67	97.80	97.93	98.05	98.18	98.31	98.44	98.57	98.70	98.83	98.96	99.09	99.22	99.48
16.25	97.28	97.41	97.54	97.67	97.80	97.93	98.06	98.18	98.31	98.44	98.57	98.70	98.83	98.96	99.09	99.35
16.50	97.16	97.29	97.41	97.54	97.67	97.80	97.93	98.06	98.19	98.31	98.44	98.57	98.70	98.83	98.96	99.22
16.75	97.03	97.16	97.29	97.42	97.54	97.67	97.80	97.93	98.06	98.19	98.32	98.44	98.57	98.70	98.83	99.09
17.00	96.90	97.03	97.16	97.29	97.42	97.55	97.67	97.80	97.93	98.06	98.19	98.32	98.45	98.57	98.70	98.96
17.25	96.78	96.91	97.03	97.16	97.29	97.42	97.55	97.67	97.80	97.93	98.06	98.19	98.32	98.45	98.58	98.83
17.50	96.65	96.78	96.91	97.04	97.16	97.29	97.42	97.55	97.68	97.80	97.93	98.06	98.19	98.32	98.45	98.71
17.75	96.53	96.65	96.78	96.91	97.04	97.17	97.29	97.42	97.55	97.68	97.80	97.93	98.06	98.19	98.32	98.58
18.00	96.40	96.53	96.66	96.78	96.91	97.04	97.17	97.29	97.42	97.55	97.68	97.81	97.93	98.06	98.19	98.45
18.25	96.28	96.40	96.53	96.66	96.79	96.91	97.04	97.17	97.30	97.42	97.55	97.68	97.81	97.94	98.06	98.32
18.50	96.15	96.28	96.41	96.53	96.66	96.79	96.92	97.04	97.17	97.30	97.43	97.55	97.68	97.81	97.94	98.19
18.75	96.03	96.15	96.28	96.41	96.54	96.66	96.79	96.92	97.04	97.17	97.30	97.43	97.56	97.68	97.81	98.07
19.00	95.90	96.03	96.16	96.28	96.41	96.54	96.66	96.79	96.92	97.05	97.17	97.30	97.43	97.56	97.68	97.94
20.00	95.41	95.53	95.66	95.79	95.91	96.04	96.17	96.29	96.42	96.55	96.67	96.80	96.93	97.05	97.18	97.43
25.00	92.99	93.11	93.24	93.36	93.48	93.60	93.73	93.85	93.97	94.10	94.22	94.35	94.47	94.59	94.72	94.96
30.00	90.66	90.78	90.90	91.02	91.14	91.26	91.38	91.50	91.62	91.74	91.86	91.98	92.10	92.22	92.34	92.58

Description: This table shows the yield to maturity of a mortgage purchased at the price shown in the index.

Example: The yield to maturity of a 15.00 %, 1 year mortgage at a price of 102.00 is 11.22 %.

INTEREST RATE, %

PRICE	11.00%	11.25%	11.50%	11.75%	12.00%	12.25%	12.50%	12.75%	13.00%	13.25%	13.50%	13.75%	14.00%	14.25%	14.50%	15.00%
110	—	—	—	—	—	—	—	—	—	—	—	—	—	—	—	—
109	—	—	—	—	—	—	—	—	—	—	—	—	—	—	—	—
108	—	—	—	—	—	—	—	—	—	—	—	—	—	—	—	.52
107	—	—	—	—	—	—	—	.06	.31	.55	.79	1.03	1.28	1.52	1.76	2.25
106	.10	.34	.58	.83	1.07	1.31	1.56	1.80	2.05	2.29	2.53	2.78	3.02	3.26	3.51	3.99
105.75	.53	.78	1.02	1.26	1.51	1.75	2.00	2.24	2.48	2.73	2.97	3.22	3.46	3.70	3.95	4.43
105.50	.97	1.21	1.46	1.70	1.95	2.19	2.43	2.68	2.92	3.17	3.41	3.66	3.90	4.14	4.39	4.88
105.25	1.41	1.65	1.90	2.14	2.39	2.63	2.88	3.12	3.36	3.61	3.85	4.10	4.34	4.59	4.83	5.32
105.00	1.85	2.09	2.34	2.58	2.83	3.07	3.32	3.56	3.81	4.05	4.30	4.54	4.79	5.03	5.27	5.76
104.75	2.29	2.54	2.78	3.03	3.27	3.52	3.76	4.01	4.25	4.50	4.74	4.99	5.23	5.48	5.72	6.21
104.50	2.74	2.98	3.23	3.47	3.72	3.96	4.21	4.45	4.70	4.94	5.19	5.43	5.68	5.92	6.17	6.66
104.25	3.18	3.43	3.67	3.92	4.16	4.41	4.65	4.90	5.14	5.39	5.64	5.88	6.13	6.37	6.62	7.11
104.00	3.63	3.87	4.12	4.37	4.61	4.86	5.10	5.35	5.59	5.84	6.08	6.33	6.58	6.82	7.07	7.56
103.75	4.08	4.32	4.57	4.81	5.06	5.31	5.55	5.80	6.04	6.29	6.54	6.78	7.03	7.27	7.52	8.01
103.50	4.53	4.77	5.02	5.27	5.51	5.76	6.00	6.25	6.50	6.74	6.99	7.23	7.48	7.73	7.97	8.47
103.25	4.98	5.22	5.47	5.72	5.96	6.21	6.46	6.70	6.95	7.20	7.44	7.69	7.94	8.18	8.43	8.92
103.00	5.43	5.68	5.92	6.17	6.42	6.66	6.91	7.16	7.41	7.65	7.90	8.15	8.39	8.64	8.89	9.38
102.75	5.89	6.13	6.38	6.63	6.87	7.12	7.37	7.61	7.86	8.11	8.36	8.60	8.85	9.10	9.34	9.84
102.50	6.34	6.59	6.84	7.08	7.33	7.58	7.83	8.07	8.32	8.57	8.81	9.06	9.31	9.56	9.80	10.30
102.25	6.80	7.05	7.30	7.54	7.79	8.04	8.29	8.53	8.78	9.03	9.28	9.52	9.77	10.02	10.27	10.76
102.00	7.26	7.51	7.76	8.00	8.25	8.50	8.75	8.99	9.24	9.49	9.74	9.99	10.23	10.48	10.73	11.22
101.75	7.72	7.97	8.22	8.46	8.71	8.96	9.21	9.46	9.71	9.95	10.20	10.45	10.70	10.95	11.19	11.69
101.50	8.18	8.43	8.68	8.93	9.18	9.43	9.67	9.92	10.17	10.42	10.67	10.92	11.16	11.41	11.66	12.16
101.25	8.65	8.90	9.15	9.39	9.64	9.89	10.14	10.39	10.64	10.89	11.13	11.38	11.63	11.88	12.13	12.63
101.00	9.11	9.36	9.61	9.86	10.11	10.36	10.61	10.86	11.11	11.35	11.60	11.85	12.10	12.35	12.60	13.10
100.75	9.58	9.83	10.08	10.33	10.58	10.83	11.08	11.33	11.58	11.82	12.07	12.32	12.57	12.82	13.07	13.57
100.50	10.05	10.30	10.55	10.80	11.05	11.30	11.55	11.80	12.05	12.30	12.55	12.80	13.04	13.29	13.54	14.04
100.25	10.52	10.77	11.02	11.27	11.52	11.77	12.02	12.27	12.52	12.77	13.02	13.27	13.52	13.77	14.02	14.52
100.00	11.00	11.25	11.50	11.75	12.00	12.25	12.50	12.75	13.00	13.25	13.50	13.75	14.00	14.25	14.50	15.00
99.75	11.47	11.72	11.97	12.22	12.47	12.72	12.97	13.22	13.47	13.72	13.97	14.22	14.47	14.72	14.97	15.47
99.50	11.95	12.20	12.45	12.70	12.95	13.20	13.45	13.70	13.95	14.20	14.45	14.70	14.95	15.20	15.45	15.96
99.25	12.42	12.67	12.93	13.18	13.43	13.68	13.93	14.18	14.43	14.68	14.93	15.18	15.43	15.69	15.94	16.44
99.00	12.90	13.15	13.41	13.66	13.91	14.16	14.41	14.66	14.91	15.16	15.42	15.67	15.92	16.17	16.42	16.92
98.75	13.39	13.64	13.89	14.14	14.39	14.64	14.89	15.15	15.40	15.65	15.90	16.15	16.40	16.65	16.91	17.41
98.50	13.87	14.12	14.37	14.62	14.88	15.13	15.38	15.63	15.88	16.13	16.39	16.64	16.89	17.14	17.39	17.90
98.25	14.35	14.61	14.86	15.11	15.36	15.61	15.87	16.12	16.37	16.62	16.87	17.13	17.38	17.63	17.88	18.39
98.00	14.84	15.09	15.35	15.60	15.85	16.10	16.35	16.61	16.86	17.11	17.36	17.62	17.87	18.12	18.37	18.88
97.75	15.33	15.58	15.83	16.09	16.34	16.59	16.84	17.10	17.35	17.60	17.86	18.11	18.36	18.61	18.87	19.37
97.50	15.82	16.07	16.33	16.58	16.83	17.08	17.34	17.59	17.84	18.10	18.35	18.60	18.85	19.11	19.36	19.87
97.25	16.31	16.57	16.82	17.07	17.32	17.58	17.83	18.08	18.34	18.59	18.84	19.10	19.35	19.60	19.86	20.36
97.00	16.81	17.06	17.31	17.57	17.82	18.07	18.33	18.58	18.83	19.09	19.34	19.59	19.85	20.10	20.35	20.86
96.75	17.30	17.56	17.81	18.06	18.32	18.57	18.82	19.08	19.33	19.59	19.84	20.09	20.35	20.60	20.86	21.36
96.50	17.80	18.05	18.31	18.56	18.82	19.07	19.32	19.58	19.83	20.08	20.33	20.84	20.59	21.10	21.36	21.87
96.25	18.30	18.55	18.81	19.06	19.32	19.57	19.83	20.08	20.33	20.59	20.84	21.10	21.35	21.61	21.86	22.37
96.00	18.80	19.06	19.31	19.57	19.82	20.07	20.33	20.58	20.84	21.09	21.35	21.60	21.86	22.11	22.37	22.88
95.75	19.31	19.56	19.82	20.07	20.33	20.58	20.84	21.09	21.35	21.60	21.86	22.11	22.37	22.62	22.88	23.39
95.50	19.81	20.07	20.32	20.58	20.83	21.09	21.34	21.60	21.85	22.11	22.36	22.62	22.87	23.13	23.38	23.90
95.25	20.32	20.57	20.83	21.08	21.34	21.60	21.85	22.11	22.36	22.62	22.87	23.13	23.39	23.64	23.90	24.41
95.00	20.83	21.08	21.34	21.60	21.85	22.11	22.36	22.62	22.87	23.13	23.39	23.64	23.90	24.15	24.41	24.92
94.75	21.34	21.60	21.85	22.11	22.36	22.62	22.88	23.13	23.39	23.64	23.90	24.16	24.41	24.67	24.93	25.44
94.50	21.85	22.11	22.37	22.62	22.88	23.13	23.39	23.65	23.90	24.16	24.42	24.67	24.93	25.19	25.44	25.96
94.25	22.37	22.62	22.88	23.14	23.39	23.65	23.91	24.17	24.42	24.68	24.94	25.19	25.45	25.71	25.96	26.48
94.00	22.88	23.14	23.40	23.66	23.91	24.17	24.43	24.68	24.94	25.20	25.46	25.71	25.97	26.23	26.49	27.00
93.75	23.40	23.66	23.92	24.18	24.43	24.69	24.95	25.21	25.46	25.72	25.98	26.24	26.49	26.75	27.01	27.52
93	24.97	25.23	25.49	25.75	26.01	26.27	26.52	26.78	27.04	27.30	27.56	27.82	28.08	28.33	28.59	29.11
92	27.10	27.36	27.62	27.88	28.14	28.40	28.66	28.91	29.17	29.43	29.69	29.95	30.21	30.47	30.73	31.25
91	29.25	29.51	29.78	30.04	30.30	30.56	30.82	31.08	31.34	31.60	31.86	32.13	32.39	32.65	32.91	33.43
90	31.45	31.71	31.97	32.23	32.50	32.76	33.02	33.28	33.54	33.81	34.07	34.33	34.59	34.86	35.12	35.64
89	33.67	33.94	34.20	34.46	34.73	34.99	35.26	35.52	35.78	36.05	36.31	36.58	36.84	37.10	37.37	37.89
88	35.94	36.20	36.47	36.73	37.00	37.26	37.53	37.80	38.06	38.33	38.59	38.86	39.12	39.39	39.65	40.18
87	38.24	38.51	38.78	39.04	39.31	39.58	39.84	40.11	40.38	40.64	40.91	41.18	41.44	41.71	41.98	42.51
86	40.58	40.85	41.12	41.39	41.66	41.93	42.19	42.46	42.73	43.00	43.27	43.53	43.80	44.07	44.34	44.88
85	42.97	43.24	43.51	43.78	44.05	44.32	44.59	44.86	45.13	45.40	45.67	45.94	46.21	46.47	46.74	47.28
84	45.39	45.67	45.94	46.21	46.48	46.75	47.02	47.29	47.56	47.84	48.11	48.38	48.65	48.92	49.19	49.73
83	47.86	48.14	48.41	48.68	48.95	49.23	49.50	49.77	50.05	50.32	50.59	50.86	51.14	51.41	51.68	52.23
82	50.38	50.65	50.93	51.20	51.47	51.75	52.02	52.30	52.57	52.85	53.12	53.40	53.67	53.95	54.22	54.77
81	52.94	53.21	53.49	53.76	54.04	54.32	54.59	54.87	55.15	55.42	55.70	55.97	56.25	56.53	56.80	57.36
80	55.54	55.82	56.10	56.38	56.65	56.93	57.21	57.49	57.77	58.04	58.32	58.60	58.88	59.16	59.43	59.99

MORTGAGE PRICE

Description: This table shows the price to pay for a monthly payment mortgage loan at the yield rate.

Example: The price of a 6.75 %, 2 year mortgage loan to yield 8.00 % to maturity is $ 98.74.

INTEREST RATE, %

YIELD	0.00%	1.00%	2.00%	3.00%	4.00%	4.25%	4.50%	4.75%	5.00%	5.25%	5.50%	5.75%	6.00%	6.25%	6.50%	6.75%
0.00	100.00	101.04	102.10	103.15	104.22	104.49	104.75	105.02	105.29	105.56	105.83	106.10	106.37	106.64	106.91	107.18
1.00	98.97	100.00	101.04	102.09	103.14	103.41	103.67	103.94	104.20	104.47	104.74	105.00	105.27	105.54	105.81	106.07
2.00	97.95	98.97	100.00	101.04	102.08	102.34	102.60	102.87	103.13	103.39	103.66	103.92	104.19	104.45	104.72	104.98
3.00	96.94	97.95	98.97	100.00	101.03	101.29	101.55	101.81	102.07	102.33	102.59	102.85	103.12	103.38	103.64	103.90
4.00	95.95	96.95	97.96	98.98	100.00	100.26	100.51	100.77	101.03	101.29	101.54	101.80	102.06	102.32	102.58	102.84
4.25	95.71	96.71	97.71	98.73	99.74	100.00	100.26	100.51	100.77	101.03	101.28	101.54	101.80	102.06	102.32	102.58
4.50	95.46	96.46	97.46	98.47	99.49	99.74	100.00	100.26	100.51	100.77	101.03	101.28	101.54	101.80	102.06	102.32
4.75	95.22	96.21	97.21	98.22	99.24	99.49	99.74	100.00	100.26	100.51	100.77	101.02	101.28	101.54	101.80	102.06
5.00	94.97	95.97	96.97	97.97	98.98	99.24	99.49	99.74	100.00	100.26	100.51	100.77	101.02	101.28	101.54	101.80
5.25	94.73	95.72	96.72	97.72	98.73	98.98	99.24	99.49	99.75	100.00	100.26	100.51	100.77	101.02	101.28	101.54
5.50	94.49	95.48	96.47	97.47	98.48	98.73	98.98	99.24	99.49	99.75	100.00	100.26	100.51	100.77	101.02	101.28
5.75	94.25	95.24	96.23	97.22	98.23	98.48	98.73	98.99	99.24	99.49	99.75	100.00	100.25	100.51	100.77	101.02
6.00	94.01	94.99	95.98	96.98	97.98	98.23	98.48	98.73	98.99	99.24	99.49	99.75	100.00	100.25	100.51	100.76
6.25	93.77	94.75	95.74	96.73	97.73	97.98	98.23	98.48	98.74	98.99	99.24	99.49	99.75	100.00	100.25	100.51
6.50	93.54	94.51	95.50	96.49	97.48	97.73	97.98	98.23	98.49	98.74	98.99	99.24	99.49	99.75	100.00	100.25
6.75	93.30	94.27	95.26	96.24	97.24	97.49	97.74	97.99	98.24	98.49	98.74	98.99	99.24	99.49	99.75	100.00
7.00	93.06	94.04	95.01	96.00	96.99	97.24	97.49	97.74	97.99	98.24	98.49	98.74	98.99	99.24	99.49	99.75
7.25	92.83	93.80	94.77	95.76	96.74	96.99	97.24	97.49	97.74	97.99	98.24	98.49	98.74	98.99	99.24	99.50
7.50	92.59	93.56	94.53	95.51	96.50	96.75	97.00	97.24	97.49	97.74	97.99	98.24	98.49	98.74	98.99	99.24
7.75	92.36	93.33	94.30	95.27	96.26	96.50	96.75	97.00	97.25	97.50	97.74	97.99	98.24	98.49	98.74	98.99
8.00	92.13	93.09	94.06	95.03	96.01	96.26	96.51	96.75	97.00	97.25	97.50	97.75	98.00	98.24	98.49	98.74
8.25	91.90	92.86	93.82	94.79	95.77	96.02	96.26	96.51	96.76	97.01	97.25	97.50	97.75	98.00	98.25	98.50
8.50	91.66	92.62	93.59	94.56	95.53	95.78	96.02	96.27	96.51	96.76	97.01	97.26	97.50	97.75	98.00	98.25
8.75	91.43	92.39	93.35	94.32	95.29	95.54	95.78	96.03	96.27	96.52	96.76	97.01	97.26	97.51	97.75	98.00
9.00	91.20	92.16	93.12	94.08	95.05	95.30	95.54	95.79	96.03	96.28	96.52	96.77	97.01	97.26	97.51	97.76
9.25	90.98	91.93	92.88	93.85	94.82	95.06	95.30	95.55	95.79	96.03	96.28	96.52	96.77	97.02	97.26	97.51
9.50	90.75	91.70	92.65	93.61	94.58	94.82	95.06	95.31	95.55	95.79	96.04	96.28	96.53	96.77	97.02	97.26
9.75	90.52	91.47	92.42	93.38	94.34	94.58	94.83	95.07	95.31	95.55	95.79	96.04	96.28	96.53	96.77	97.02
10.00	90.30	91.24	92.19	93.14	94.11	94.35	94.59	94.83	95.07	95.32	95.56	95.80	96.05	96.29	96.54	96.78
10.25	90.07	91.01	91.96	92.91	93.87	94.11	94.35	94.59	94.84	95.08	95.32	95.56	95.80	96.05	96.29	96.54
10.50	89.85	90.78	91.73	92.68	93.64	93.88	94.12	94.36	94.60	94.84	95.08	95.33	95.57	95.81	96.05	96.30
10.75	89.62	90.56	91.50	92.45	93.40	93.64	93.88	94.12	94.36	94.60	94.85	95.09	95.33	95.57	95.82	96.06
11.00	89.40	90.33	91.27	92.22	93.17	93.41	93.65	93.89	94.13	94.37	94.61	94.85	95.09	95.33	95.58	95.82
11.25	89.18	90.11	91.05	91.99	92.94	93.18	93.42	93.66	93.89	94.13	94.37	94.62	94.86	95.10	95.34	95.58
11.50	88.95	89.88	90.82	91.76	92.71	92.95	93.18	93.42	93.66	93.90	94.14	94.38	94.62	94.86	95.10	95.34
11.75	88.73	89.66	90.59	91.53	92.48	92.72	92.95	93.19	93.43	93.67	93.91	94.15	94.39	94.63	94.86	95.11
12.00	88.51	89.44	90.37	91.31	92.25	92.49	92.72	92.96	93.20	93.44	93.67	93.91	94.15	94.39	94.63	94.87
12.25	88.29	89.22	90.15	91.08	92.02	92.26	92.49	92.73	92.97	93.20	93.44	93.68	93.92	94.16	94.40	94.64
12.50	88.08	89.00	89.92	90.86	91.79	92.03	92.26	92.50	92.74	92.97	93.21	93.45	93.69	93.92	94.16	94.40
12.75	87.86	88.78	89.70	90.63	91.57	91.80	92.04	92.27	92.51	92.74	92.98	93.22	93.46	93.69	93.93	94.17
13.00	87.64	88.56	89.48	90.41	91.34	91.57	91.81	92.04	92.28	92.52	92.75	92.99	93.22	93.46	93.70	93.94
13.25	87.43	88.34	89.26	90.18	91.12	91.35	91.58	91.82	92.05	92.29	92.52	92.76	92.99	93.23	93.47	93.71
13.50	87.21	88.12	89.04	89.96	90.89	91.12	91.36	91.59	91.83	92.06	92.29	92.53	92.77	93.00	93.24	93.47
13.75	87.00	87.91	88.82	89.74	90.67	90.90	91.13	91.37	91.60	91.83	92.07	92.30	92.54	92.77	93.00	93.24
14.00	86.78	87.69	88.60	89.52	90.44	90.68	90.91	91.14	91.37	91.61	91.84	92.08	92.31	92.54	92.78	93.02
14.25	86.57	87.47	88.38	89.30	90.22	90.45	90.69	90.92	91.15	91.38	91.62	91.85	92.08	92.32	92.55	92.79
14.50	86.36	87.26	88.17	89.08	90.00	90.23	90.46	90.69	90.93	91.16	91.39	91.62	91.86	92.09	92.32	92.56
14.75	86.15	87.05	87.95	88.86	89.78	90.01	90.24	90.47	90.70	90.94	91.17	91.40	91.63	91.87	92.10	92.33
15.00	85.93	86.83	87.74	88.65	89.56	89.79	90.02	90.25	90.48	90.71	90.94	91.18	91.41	91.64	91.87	92.11
15.25	85.72	86.62	87.52	88.43	89.34	89.57	89.80	90.03	90.26	90.49	90.72	90.95	91.18	91.42	91.65	91.88
15.50	85.51	86.41	87.31	88.21	89.12	89.35	89.58	89.81	90.04	90.27	90.50	90.73	90.96	91.19	91.42	91.66
15.75	85.31	86.20	87.09	88.00	88.91	89.13	89.36	89.59	89.82	90.05	90.28	90.51	90.74	90.97	91.19	91.43
16.00	85.10	85.99	86.88	87.78	88.69	88.92	89.14	89.37	89.60	89.83	90.06	90.29	90.52	90.75	90.98	91.21
16.25	84.89	85.78	86.67	87.57	88.47	88.70	88.93	89.15	89.38	89.61	89.84	90.07	90.30	90.53	90.76	90.99
16.50	84.68	85.57	86.46	87.36	88.26	88.48	88.71	88.94	89.17	89.39	89.62	89.85	90.08	90.31	90.54	90.77
16.75	84.48	85.36	86.25	87.14	88.04	88.27	88.50	88.72	88.95	89.18	89.40	89.63	89.86	90.09	90.32	90.55
17.00	84.27	85.15	86.04	86.93	87.83	88.05	88.28	88.51	88.73	88.96	89.19	89.41	89.64	89.87	90.10	90.33
17.25	84.07	84.95	85.83	86.72	87.62	87.84	88.07	88.29	88.52	88.74	88.97	89.20	89.42	89.65	89.88	90.11
17.50	83.87	84.74	85.62	86.51	87.40	87.63	87.85	88.08	88.30	88.53	88.75	88.98	89.21	89.43	89.66	89.89
17.75	83.66	84.54	85.42	86.30	87.19	87.42	87.64	87.86	88.09	88.31	88.54	88.77	88.99	89.21	89.43	89.67
18.00	83.46	84.33	85.21	86.09	86.98	87.20	87.43	87.65	87.88	88.10	88.33	88.55	88.78	89.00	89.23	89.45
18.25	83.26	84.13	85.00	85.89	86.77	86.99	87.22	87.44	87.66	87.89	88.11	88.34	88.56	88.79	89.01	89.23
18.50	83.06	83.93	84.80	85.68	86.56	86.78	87.01	87.23	87.45	87.68	87.90	88.12	88.34	88.57	88.79	89.02
18.75	82.86	83.72	84.59	85.47	86.35	86.58	86.80	87.02	87.24	87.46	87.69	87.91	88.13	88.36	88.58	88.81
19.00	82.66	83.52	84.39	85.27	86.15	86.37	86.59	86.81	87.03	87.25	87.48	87.70	87.92	88.15	88.37	88.59
20.00	81.87	82.72	83.58	84.45	85.32	85.54	85.76	85.98	86.20	86.42	86.64	86.86	87.08	87.30	87.52	87.75
25.00	78.07	78.88	79.71	80.53	81.36	81.57	81.78	81.99	82.20	82.41	82.62	82.83	83.04	83.25	83.46	83.68
30.00	74.52	75.30	76.08	76.87	77.67	77.86	78.06	78.26	78.46	78.66	78.87	79.07	79.27	79.47	79.67	79.87

Description: This table shows the yield to maturity of a mortgage purchased at the price shown in the index.

Example: The yield to maturity of a 6.75 %, 2 year mortgage at a price of 95.00 is 11.86 %.

INTEREST RATE, %

PRICE	0.00%	1.00%	2.00%	3.00%	4.00%	4.25%	4.50%	4.75%	5.00%	5.25%	5.50%	5.75%	6.00%	6.25%	6.50%	6.75%
100	0.00	1.00	2.00	3.00	4.00	4.25	4.50	4.75	5.00	5.25	5.50	5.75	6.00	6.25	6.50	6.75
99.75	.24	1.24	2.24	3.24	4.24	4.49	4.74	4.99	5.24	5.49	5.74	5.99	6.24	6.49	6.74	6.99
99.50	.48	1.48	2.48	3.48	4.48	4.74	4.99	5.24	5.49	5.74	5.99	6.24	6.49	6.74	6.99	7.24
99.25	.72	1.72	2.72	3.73	4.73	4.98	5.23	5.48	5.73	5.98	6.24	6.49	6.74	6.99	7.24	7.49
99.00	.96	1.97	2.97	3.97	4.98	5.23	5.48	5.73	5.98	6.23	6.48	6.73	6.99	7.24	7.49	7.74
98.75	1.21	2.21	3.22	4.22	5.23	5.48	5.73	5.98	6.23	6.48	6.73	6.98	7.24	7.49	7.74	7.99
98.50	1.45	2.46	3.46	4.47	5.47	5.73	5.98	6.23	6.48	6.73	6.98	7.23	7.49	7.74	7.99	8.24
98.25	1.70	2.70	3.71	4.72	5.72	5.98	6.23	6.48	6.73	6.98	7.23	7.49	7.74	7.99	8.24	8.49
98.00	1.94	2.95	3.96	4.97	5.97	6.23	6.48	6.73	6.98	7.23	7.49	7.74	7.99	8.24	8.49	8.75
97.75	2.19	3.20	4.21	5.22	6.23	6.48	6.73	6.98	7.23	7.49	7.74	7.99	8.24	8.50	8.75	9.00
97.50	2.44	3.45	4.46	5.47	6.48	6.73	6.98	7.24	7.49	7.74	7.99	8.25	8.50	8.75	9.00	9.26
97.25	2.69	3.70	4.71	5.72	6.73	6.98	7.24	7.49	7.74	7.99	8.25	8.50	8.75	9.01	9.26	9.51
97.00	2.94	3.95	4.96	5.97	6.98	7.24	7.49	7.74	8.00	8.25	8.50	8.76	9.01	9.26	9.52	9.77
96.75	3.19	4.20	5.21	6.23	7.24	7.49	7.75	8.00	8.25	8.51	8.76	9.01	9.27	9.52	9.77	10.03
96.50	3.44	4.45	5.47	6.48	7.50	7.75	8.00	8.26	8.51	8.76	9.02	9.27	9.52	9.78	10.03	10.29
96.25	3.69	4.71	5.72	6.74	7.75	8.01	8.26	8.51	8.77	9.02	9.28	9.53	9.78	10.04	10.29	10.55
96.00	3.95	4.96	5.98	6.99	8.01	8.26	8.52	8.77	9.03	9.28	9.54	9.79	10.04	10.30	10.55	10.81
95.75	4.20	5.22	6.23	7.25	8.27	8.52	8.78	9.03	9.29	9.54	9.80	10.05	10.30	10.56	10.81	11.07
95.50	4.46	5.47	6.49	7.51	8.53	8.78	9.04	9.29	9.55	9.80	10.06	10.31	10.57	10.82	11.08	11.33
95.25	4.71	5.73	6.75	7.77	8.79	9.04	9.30	9.55	9.81	10.06	10.32	10.57	10.83	11.08	11.34	11.59
95.00	4.97	5.99	7.01	8.03	9.05	9.31	9.56	9.82	10.07	10.33	10.58	10.84	11.09	11.35	11.60	11.86
94.75	5.23	6.25	7.27	8.29	9.31	9.57	9.82	10.08	10.34	10.59	10.85	11.10	11.36	11.61	11.87	12.12
94.50	5.49	6.51	7.53	8.55	9.58	9.83	10.09	10.34	10.60	10.86	11.11	11.37	11.62	11.88	12.14	12.39
94.25	5.75	6.77	7.79	8.82	9.84	10.10	10.35	10.61	10.87	11.12	11.38	11.63	11.89	12.15	12.40	12.66
94.00	6.01	7.03	8.06	9.08	10.11	10.36	10.62	10.88	11.13	11.39	11.65	11.90	12.16	12.41	12.67	12.93
93.75	6.27	7.30	8.32	9.35	10.37	10.63	10.89	11.14	11.40	11.66	11.91	12.17	12.43	12.68	12.94	13.20
93.50	6.53	7.56	8.59	9.61	10.64	10.90	11.16	11.41	11.67	11.93	12.18	12.44	12.70	12.95	13.21	13.47
93.25	6.80	7.82	8.85	9.88	10.91	11.17	11.42	11.68	11.94	12.20	12.45	12.71	12.97	13.22	13.48	13.74
93.00	7.06	8.09	9.12	10.15	11.18	11.44	11.69	11.95	12.21	12.47	12.72	12.98	13.24	13.50	13.75	14.01
92.75	7.33	8.36	9.39	10.42	11.45	11.71	11.97	12.22	12.48	12.74	13.00	13.25	13.51	13.77	14.03	14.29
92.50	7.60	8.63	9.66	10.69	11.72	11.98	12.24	12.50	12.75	13.01	13.27	13.53	13.79	14.04	14.30	14.56
92.25	7.86	8.90	9.93	10.96	11.99	12.25	12.51	12.77	13.03	13.29	13.54	13.80	14.06	14.32	14.58	14.84
92.00	8.13	9.17	10.20	11.23	12.27	12.53	12.79	13.04	13.30	13.56	13.82	14.08	14.34	14.60	14.85	15.11
91.75	8.40	9.44	10.47	11.51	12.54	12.80	13.06	13.32	13.58	13.84	14.10	14.36	14.61	14.87	15.13	15.39
91	9.22	10.26	11.30	12.33	13.37	13.63	13.89	14.15	14.41	14.67	14.93	15.19	15.45	15.71	15.97	16.23
90	10.32	11.37	12.41	13.45	14.50	14.76	15.02	15.28	15.54	15.80	16.06	16.32	16.58	16.85	17.11	17.37
89	11.44	12.49	13.54	14.59	15.64	15.90	16.16	16.42	16.69	16.95	17.21	17.47	17.73	18.00	18.26	18.52
88	12.58	13.64	14.69	15.74	16.80	17.06	17.32	17.59	17.85	18.11	18.38	18.64	18.90	19.17	19.43	19.69
87	13.74	14.80	15.86	16.91	17.97	18.24	18.50	18.77	19.03	19.30	19.56	19.83	20.09	20.36	20.62	20.89
86	14.92	15.98	17.04	18.11	19.17	19.44	19.70	19.97	20.24	20.50	20.77	21.03	21.30	21.57	21.83	22.10
85	16.11	17.18	18.25	19.32	20.39	20.66	20.92	21.19	21.46	21.73	21.99	22.26	22.53	22.80	23.06	23.33
84	17.33	18.40	19.48	20.55	21.63	21.90	22.16	22.43	22.70	22.97	23.24	23.51	23.78	24.05	24.32	24.58
83	18.57	19.65	20.73	21.81	22.89	23.16	23.43	23.70	23.97	24.24	24.51	24.78	25.05	25.32	25.59	25.86
82	19.83	20.91	22.00	23.08	24.17	24.44	24.71	24.98	25.25	25.53	25.80	26.07	26.34	26.61	26.89	27.16
81	21.11	22.20	23.29	24.38	25.47	25.75	26.02	26.29	26.56	26.84	27.11	27.38	27.66	27.93	28.20	28.48
80	22.41	23.51	24.60	25.70	26.80	27.07	27.35	27.62	27.90	28.17	28.45	28.72	29.00	29.27	29.55	29.82
79	23.74	24.84	25.94	27.05	28.15	28.43	28.70	28.98	29.26	29.53	29.81	30.09	30.36	30.64	30.92	31.19
78	25.09	26.20	27.31	28.42	29.53	29.81	30.08	30.36	30.64	30.92	31.20	31.47	31.75	32.03	32.31	32.59
77	26.47	27.58	28.70	29.81	30.93	31.21	31.49	31.77	32.05	32.33	32.61	32.89	33.17	33.45	33.73	34.01
76	27.87	28.99	30.11	31.24	32.36	32.64	32.92	33.20	33.49	33.77	34.05	34.33	34.61	34.89	35.17	35.46
75	29.30	30.43	31.56	32.69	33.82	34.10	34.38	34.67	34.95	35.23	35.52	35.80	36.08	36.37	36.65	36.93
74	30.76	31.89	33.03	34.17	35.31	35.59	35.87	36.16	36.44	36.73	37.01	37.30	37.58	37.87	38.15	38.44
73	32.25	33.39	34.53	35.68	36.82	37.11	37.39	37.68	37.97	38.25	38.54	38.83	39.11	39.40	39.69	39.98
72	33.76	34.91	36.06	37.22	38.37	38.66	38.95	39.23	39.52	39.81	40.10	40.39	40.68	40.97	41.25	41.54
71	35.31	36.47	37.63	38.79	39.95	40.24	40.53	40.82	41.11	41.40	41.69	41.98	42.27	42.56	42.85	43.14
70	36.89	38.06	39.22	40.39	41.56	41.85	42.14	42.44	42.73	43.02	43.31	43.61	43.90	44.19	44.49	44.78
69	38.51	39.68	40.85	42.03	43.21	43.50	43.79	44.09	44.38	44.68	44.97	45.27	45.56	45.86	46.15	46.45
68	40.16	41.34	42.52	43.70	44.89	45.19	45.48	45.78	46.07	46.37	46.67	46.97	47.26	47.56	47.86	48.15
67	41.84	43.03	44.22	45.42	46.61	46.91	47.21	47.50	47.80	48.10	48.40	48.70	49.00	49.30	49.60	49.90
66	43.56	44.76	45.96	47.16	48.37	48.67	48.97	49.27	49.57	49.87	50.17	50.48	50.78	51.08	51.38	51.68
65	45.33	46.54	47.74	48.95	50.17	50.47	50.77	51.08	51.38	51.68	51.99	52.29	52.59	52.90	53.20	53.51
64	47.13	48.35	49.57	50.79	52.01	52.31	52.62	52.92	53.23	53.54	53.84	54.15	54.45	54.76	55.07	55.37
63	48.98	50.20	51.43	52.66	53.89	54.20	54.51	54.82	55.13	55.43	55.74	56.05	56.36	56.67	56.98	57.29
62	50.87	52.10	53.34	54.58	55.82	56.13	56.45	56.76	57.07	57.38	57.69	58.00	58.31	58.62	58.93	59.25
61	52.81	54.05	55.30	56.55	57.80	58.12	58.43	58.74	59.06	59.37	59.68	60.00	60.31	60.63	60.94	61.25
60	54.79	56.05	57.31	58.57	59.83	60.15	60.46	60.78	61.10	61.41	61.73	62.05	62.36	62.68	63.00	63.31
59	56.83	58.10	59.37	60.64	61.91	62.23	62.55	62.87	63.19	63.51	63.83	64.15	64.47	64.79	65.11	65.43
58	58.92	60.20	61.48	62.76	64.05	64.37	64.69	65.01	65.34	65.66	65.98	66.30	66.63	66.95	67.27	67.59

Description: This table shows the price to pay for a monthly payment mortgage loan at the yield rate.

Example: The price of a 10.75 %, 2 year mortgage loan to yield 8.00 % to maturity is $ 102.80.

INTEREST RATE, %

YIELD	7.00%	7.25%	7.50%	7.75%	8.00%	8.25%	8.50%	8.75%	9.00%	9.25%	9.50%	9.75%	10.00%	10.25%	10.50%	10.75%
0.00	107.45	107.73	108.00	108.27	108.55	108.82	109.09	109.37	109.64	109.92	110.19	110.47	110.75	111.02	111.30	111.58
1.00	106.34	106.61	106.88	107.15	107.42	107.69	107.97	108.24	108.51	108.78	109.06	109.33	109.60	109.88	110.15	110.43
2.00	105.25	105.51	105.78	106.05	106.32	106.58	106.85	107.12	107.39	107.66	107.93	108.20	108.47	108.74	109.02	109.29
3.00	104.17	104.43	104.70	104.96	105.23	105.49	105.76	106.02	106.29	106.56	106.82	107.09	107.36	107.63	107.90	108.17
4.00	103.10	103.36	103.63	103.89	104.15	104.41	104.68	104.94	105.20	105.47	105.73	106.00	106.26	106.53	106.80	107.06
4.25	102.84	103.10	103.36	103.62	103.88	104.15	104.41	104.67	104.93	105.20	105.46	105.73	105.99	106.26	106.52	106.79
4.50	102.58	102.84	103.10	103.36	103.62	103.88	104.14	104.40	104.67	104.93	105.19	105.46	105.72	105.99	106.25	106.52
4.75	102.32	102.57	102.83	103.09	103.35	103.61	103.88	104.14	104.40	104.66	104.92	105.19	105.45	105.72	105.98	106.24
5.00	102.05	102.31	102.57	102.83	103.09	103.35	103.61	103.87	104.13	104.39	104.66	104.92	105.18	105.45	105.71	105.97
5.25	101.79	102.05	102.31	102.57	102.83	103.09	103.35	103.61	103.87	104.13	104.39	104.65	104.91	105.18	105.44	105.70
5.50	101.54	101.79	102.05	102.31	102.57	102.83	103.08	103.34	103.60	103.86	104.12	104.39	104.65	104.91	105.17	105.43
5.75	101.28	101.53	101.79	102.05	102.31	102.56	102.82	103.08	103.34	103.60	103.86	104.12	104.38	104.64	104.90	105.17
6.00	101.02	101.28	101.53	101.79	102.05	102.30	102.56	102.82	103.08	103.34	103.60	103.86	104.12	104.38	104.64	104.90
6.25	100.76	101.02	101.27	101.53	101.79	102.04	102.30	102.56	102.82	103.07	103.33	103.59	103.85	104.11	104.37	104.63
6.50	100.51	100.76	101.02	101.27	101.53	101.78	102.04	102.30	102.56	102.81	103.07	103.33	103.59	103.85	104.11	104.37
6.75	100.25	100.51	100.76	101.02	101.27	101.53	101.78	102.04	102.30	102.55	102.81	103.07	103.33	103.59	103.84	104.10
7.00	100.00	100.25	100.51	100.76	101.02	101.27	101.53	101.78	102.04	102.29	102.55	102.81	103.07	103.32	103.58	103.84
7.25	99.75	100.00	100.25	100.51	100.76	101.01	101.27	101.52	101.78	102.04	102.29	102.55	102.80	103.06	103.32	103.58
7.50	99.50	99.75	100.00	100.25	100.51	100.76	101.01	101.27	101.52	101.78	102.03	102.29	102.55	102.80	103.06	103.32
7.75	99.24	99.50	99.75	100.00	100.25	100.51	100.76	101.01	101.27	101.52	101.78	102.03	102.29	102.54	102.80	103.06
8.00	98.99	99.25	99.50	99.75	100.00	100.25	100.50	100.76	101.01	101.27	101.52	101.77	102.03	102.28	102.54	102.80
8.25	98.75	99.00	99.25	99.50	99.75	100.00	100.25	100.50	100.76	101.01	101.27	101.52	101.77	102.03	102.28	102.54
8.50	98.50	98.75	99.00	99.25	99.50	99.75	100.00	100.25	100.50	100.76	101.01	101.26	101.52	101.77	102.03	102.28
8.75	98.25	98.50	98.75	99.00	99.25	99.50	99.75	100.00	100.25	100.50	100.76	101.01	101.26	101.52	101.77	102.02
9.00	98.00	98.25	98.50	98.75	99.00	99.25	99.50	99.75	100.00	100.25	100.50	100.75	101.01	101.26	101.51	101.77
9.25	97.76	98.01	98.25	98.50	98.75	99.00	99.25	99.50	99.75	100.00	100.25	100.50	100.75	101.01	101.26	101.51
9.50	97.51	97.76	98.01	98.26	98.50	98.75	99.00	99.25	99.50	99.75	100.00	100.25	100.50	100.75	101.01	101.26
9.75	97.27	97.52	97.76	98.01	98.26	98.50	98.75	99.00	99.25	99.50	99.75	100.00	100.25	100.50	100.75	101.00
10.00	97.03	97.27	97.52	97.76	98.01	98.26	98.51	98.75	99.00	99.25	99.50	99.75	100.00	100.25	100.50	100.75
10.25	96.78	97.03	97.27	97.52	97.77	98.01	98.26	98.51	98.76	99.00	99.25	99.50	99.75	100.00	100.25	100.50
10.50	96.54	96.79	97.03	97.28	97.52	97.77	98.02	98.26	98.51	98.76	99.00	99.25	99.50	99.75	100.00	100.25
10.75	96.30	96.55	96.79	97.03	97.28	97.53	97.77	98.02	98.26	98.51	98.76	99.00	99.25	99.50	99.75	100.00
11.00	96.06	96.31	96.55	96.79	97.04	97.28	97.53	97.77	98.02	98.27	98.51	98.76	99.01	99.25	99.50	99.75
11.25	95.82	96.07	96.31	96.55	96.80	97.04	97.29	97.53	97.78	98.02	98.27	98.51	98.76	99.01	99.26	99.50
11.50	95.59	95.83	96.07	96.31	96.56	96.80	97.04	97.29	97.53	97.78	98.02	98.27	98.52	98.76	99.01	99.26
11.75	95.35	95.59	95.83	96.07	96.32	96.56	96.80	97.05	97.29	97.54	97.78	98.03	98.27	98.52	98.76	99.01
12.00	95.11	95.35	95.59	95.84	96.08	96.32	96.56	96.81	97.05	97.29	97.54	97.78	98.03	98.27	98.52	98.76
12.25	94.88	95.12	95.36	95.60	95.84	96.08	96.32	96.57	96.81	97.05	97.30	97.54	97.78	98.03	98.27	98.52
12.50	94.64	94.88	95.12	95.36	95.60	95.84	96.09	96.33	96.57	96.81	97.06	97.30	97.54	97.78	98.03	98.28
12.75	94.41	94.65	94.89	95.13	95.37	95.61	95.85	96.09	96.33	96.57	96.82	97.06	97.30	97.54	97.79	98.03
13.00	94.18	94.41	94.65	94.89	95.13	95.37	95.61	95.85	96.09	96.34	96.58	96.82	97.06	97.30	97.55	97.79
13.25	93.94	94.18	94.42	94.66	94.90	95.14	95.38	95.62	95.86	96.10	96.34	96.58	96.82	97.06	97.31	97.55
13.50	93.71	93.95	94.19	94.42	94.66	94.90	95.14	95.38	95.62	95.86	96.10	96.34	96.58	96.83	97.07	97.31
13.75	93.48	93.72	93.95	94.19	94.43	94.67	94.91	95.15	95.39	95.63	95.87	96.11	96.35	96.59	96.83	97.07
14.00	93.25	93.49	93.72	93.96	94.20	94.44	94.67	94.91	95.15	95.39	95.63	95.87	96.11	96.35	96.59	96.83
14.25	93.02	93.26	93.49	93.73	93.97	94.20	94.44	94.68	94.92	95.16	95.39	95.63	95.87	96.11	96.35	96.59
14.50	92.79	93.03	93.26	93.50	93.74	93.97	94.21	94.45	94.68	94.92	95.16	95.40	95.64	95.88	96.12	96.36
14.75	92.57	92.80	93.04	93.27	93.51	93.74	93.98	94.22	94.45	94.69	94.93	95.17	95.40	95.64	95.88	96.12
15.00	92.34	92.57	92.81	93.04	93.28	93.51	93.75	93.98	94.22	94.46	94.70	94.93	95.17	95.41	95.65	95.89
15.25	92.11	92.35	92.58	92.82	93.05	93.28	93.52	93.76	93.99	94.23	94.46	94.70	94.94	95.18	95.41	95.65
15.50	91.89	92.12	92.36	92.59	92.82	93.06	93.29	93.53	93.76	94.00	94.23	94.47	94.71	94.94	95.18	95.42
15.75	91.66	91.90	92.13	92.36	92.60	92.83	93.06	93.30	93.53	93.77	94.00	94.24	94.47	94.71	94.95	95.18
16.00	91.44	91.67	91.91	92.14	92.37	92.60	92.84	93.07	93.30	93.54	93.77	94.01	94.24	94.48	94.72	94.95
16.25	91.22	91.45	91.68	91.91	92.15	92.38	92.61	92.84	93.08	93.31	93.55	93.78	94.01	94.25	94.49	94.72
16.50	91.00	91.23	91.46	91.69	91.92	92.15	92.39	92.62	92.85	93.08	93.32	93.55	93.79	94.02	94.26	94.49
16.75	90.78	91.01	91.24	91.47	91.70	91.93	92.16	92.39	92.63	92.86	93.09	93.32	93.56	93.79	94.02	94.26
17.00	90.56	90.78	91.01	91.24	91.47	91.71	91.94	92.17	92.40	92.63	92.86	93.10	93.33	93.56	93.80	94.03
17.25	90.34	90.56	90.79	91.02	91.25	91.48	91.71	91.94	92.18	92.41	92.64	92.87	93.10	93.34	93.57	93.80
17.50	90.12	90.35	90.57	90.80	91.03	91.26	91.49	91.72	91.95	92.18	92.42	92.65	92.88	93.11	93.34	93.58
17.75	89.90	90.13	90.35	90.58	90.81	91.04	91.27	91.50	91.73	91.96	92.19	92.42	92.65	92.89	93.12	93.35
18.00	89.68	89.91	90.14	90.36	90.59	90.82	91.05	91.28	91.51	91.74	91.97	92.20	92.43	92.66	92.89	93.13
18.25	89.46	89.69	89.92	90.15	90.37	90.60	90.83	91.06	91.29	91.52	91.75	91.98	92.21	92.44	92.67	92.90
18.50	89.25	89.47	89.70	89.93	90.16	90.38	90.61	90.84	91.07	91.30	91.53	91.75	91.98	92.21	92.45	92.68
18.75	89.03	89.26	89.49	89.71	89.94	90.16	90.39	90.62	90.85	91.08	91.30	91.53	91.76	91.99	92.21	92.45
19.00	88.82	89.04	89.27	89.50	89.72	89.95	90.17	90.40	90.63	90.86	91.08	91.31	91.54	91.77	92.00	92.23
20.00	87.97	88.19	88.42	88.64	88.86	89.09	89.31	89.54	89.76	89.99	90.21	90.44	90.67	90.89	91.12	91.35
25.00	83.89	84.10	84.31	84.53	84.74	84.95	85.17	85.38	85.60	85.81	86.03	86.24	86.46	86.68	86.89	87.11
30.00	80.08	80.28	80.48	80.69	80.89	81.09	81.30	81.50	81.71	81.91	82.12	82.32	82.53	82.74	82.94	83.15

Description: This table shows the yield to maturity of a mortgage purchased at the price shown in the index.

Example: The yield to maturity of a 10.75 %, 2 year mortgage at a price of 100.00 is 10.75 %.

INTEREST RATE, %

PRICE	7.00%	7.25%	7.50%	7.75%	8.00%	8.25%	8.50%	8.75%	9.00%	9.25%	9.50%	9.75%	10.00%	10.25%	10.50%	10.75%
105	2.22	2.47	2.71	2.96	3.20	3.45	3.69	3.94	4.18	4.43	4.67	4.92	5.17	5.41	5.66	5.90
104.75	2.45	2.70	2.94	3.19	3.44	3.68	3.93	4.17	4.42	4.66	4.91	5.15	5.40	5.64	5.89	6.13
104.50	2.69	2.93	3.18	3.42	3.67	3.91	4.16	4.41	4.65	4.90	5.14	5.39	5.63	5.88	6.12	6.37
104.25	2.92	3.16	3.41	3.66	3.90	4.15	4.39	4.64	4.89	5.13	5.38	5.62	5.87	6.11	6.36	6.61
104.00	3.15	3.40	3.64	3.89	4.14	4.38	4.63	4.87	5.12	5.37	5.61	5.86	6.10	6.35	6.60	6.84
103.75	3.39	3.63	3.88	4.12	4.37	4.62	4.86	5.11	5.36	5.60	5.85	6.10	6.34	6.59	6.83	7.08
103.50	3.62	3.87	4.11	4.36	4.61	4.85	5.10	5.35	5.59	5.84	6.09	6.33	6.58	6.83	7.07	7.32
103.25	3.86	4.10	4.35	4.60	4.84	5.09	5.34	5.58	5.83	6.08	6.32	6.57	6.82	7.06	7.31	7.56
103.00	4.09	4.34	4.59	4.83	5.08	5.33	5.58	5.82	6.07	6.32	6.56	6.81	7.06	7.30	7.55	7.80
102.75	4.33	4.58	4.82	5.07	5.32	5.57	5.81	6.06	6.31	6.56	6.80	7.05	7.30	7.54	7.79	8.04
102.50	4.57	4.82	5.06	5.31	5.56	5.81	6.05	6.30	6.55	6.80	7.04	7.29	7.54	7.79	8.03	8.28
102.25	4.81	5.06	5.30	5.55	5.80	6.05	6.29	6.54	6.79	7.04	7.29	7.53	7.78	8.03	8.28	8.52
102.00	5.05	5.30	5.54	5.79	6.04	6.29	6.54	6.78	7.03	7.28	7.53	7.78	8.02	8.27	8.52	8.77
101.75	5.29	5.54	5.78	6.03	6.28	6.53	6.78	7.03	7.27	7.52	7.77	8.02	8.27	8.51	8.76	9.01
101.50	5.53	5.78	6.03	6.27	6.52	6.77	7.02	7.27	7.52	7.77	8.01	8.26	8.51	8.76	9.01	9.26
101.25	5.77	6.02	6.27	6.52	6.77	7.02	7.26	7.51	7.76	8.01	8.26	8.51	8.76	9.00	9.25	9.50
101.00	6.01	6.26	6.51	6.76	7.01	7.26	7.51	7.76	8.01	8.26	8.50	8.75	9.00	9.25	9.50	9.75
100.75	6.26	6.51	6.76	7.01	7.26	7.50	7.75	8.00	8.25	8.50	8.75	9.00	9.25	9.50	9.75	10.00
100.50	6.50	6.75	7.00	7.25	7.50	7.75	8.00	8.25	8.50	8.75	9.00	9.25	9.50	9.75	10.00	10.25
100.25	6.75	7.00	7.25	7.50	7.75	8.00	8.25	8.50	8.75	9.00	9.25	9.50	9.75	10.00	10.25	10.49
100.00	7.00	7.25	7.50	7.75	8.00	8.25	8.50	8.75	9.00	9.25	9.50	9.75	10.00	10.25	10.50	10.75
99.75	7.24	7.49	7.74	7.99	8.24	8.49	8.74	8.99	9.24	9.49	9.74	10.00	10.25	10.50	10.75	11.00
99.50	7.49	7.74	7.99	8.24	8.49	8.74	8.99	9.24	9.49	9.75	10.00	10.25	10.50	10.75	11.00	11.25
99.25	7.74	7.99	8.24	8.49	8.74	8.99	9.24	9.50	9.75	10.00	10.25	10.50	10.75	11.00	11.25	11.50
99.00	7.99	8.24	8.49	8.74	8.99	9.24	9.50	9.75	10.00	10.25	10.50	10.75	11.00	11.25	11.50	11.76
98.75	8.24	8.49	8.74	8.99	9.25	9.50	9.75	10.00	10.25	10.50	10.75	11.00	11.26	11.51	11.76	12.01
98.50	8.49	8.74	9.00	9.25	9.50	9.75	10.00	10.25	10.50	10.76	11.01	11.26	11.51	11.76	12.01	12.27
98.25	8.74	9.00	9.25	9.50	9.75	10.00	10.26	10.51	10.76	11.01	11.26	11.51	11.77	12.02	12.27	12.52
98.00	9.00	9.25	9.50	9.75	10.01	10.26	10.51	10.76	11.02	11.27	11.52	11.77	12.02	12.28	12.53	12.78
97.75	9.25	9.51	9.76	10.01	10.26	10.51	10.77	11.02	11.27	11.52	11.78	12.03	12.28	12.53	12.79	13.04
97.50	9.51	9.76	10.01	10.27	10.52	10.77	11.02	11.28	11.53	11.78	12.03	12.29	12.54	12.79	13.04	13.30
97.25	9.76	10.02	10.27	10.52	10.78	11.03	11.28	11.53	11.79	12.04	12.29	12.55	12.80	13.05	13.30	13.56
97.00	10.02	10.28	10.53	10.78	11.03	11.29	11.54	11.79	12.05	12.30	12.55	12.81	13.06	13.31	13.57	13.82
96.75	10.28	10.53	10.79	11.04	11.29	11.55	11.80	12.05	12.31	12.56	12.81	13.07	13.32	13.57	13.83	14.08
96.50	10.54	10.79	11.05	11.30	11.55	11.81	12.06	12.31	12.57	12.82	13.08	13.33	13.58	13.84	14.09	14.34
96.25	10.80	11.05	11.31	11.56	11.81	12.07	12.32	12.58	12.83	13.08	13.34	13.59	13.85	14.10	14.35	14.61
96.00	11.06	11.31	11.57	11.82	12.08	12.33	12.59	12.84	13.09	13.35	13.60	13.86	14.11	14.37	14.62	14.87
95.75	11.32	11.58	11.83	12.09	12.34	12.59	12.85	13.10	13.36	13.61	13.87	14.12	14.38	14.63	14.89	15.14
95.50	11.59	11.84	12.09	12.35	12.60	12.86	13.11	13.37	13.62	13.88	14.13	14.39	14.64	14.90	15.15	15.41
95.25	11.85	12.10	12.36	12.61	12.87	13.12	13.38	13.63	13.89	14.14	14.40	14.65	14.91	15.16	15.42	15.68
95.00	12.11	12.37	12.62	12.88	13.14	13.39	13.65	13.90	14.16	14.41	14.67	14.92	15.18	15.43	15.69	15.94
94.75	12.38	12.64	12.89	13.15	13.40	13.66	13.91	14.17	14.42	14.68	14.94	15.19	15.45	15.70	15.96	16.21
94	13.18	13.44	13.70	13.95	14.21	14.47	14.72	14.98	15.24	15.49	15.75	16.00	16.26	16.52	16.77	17.03
93	14.27	14.53	14.78	15.04	15.30	15.56	15.81	16.07	16.33	16.59	16.85	17.10	17.36	17.62	17.88	18.13
92	15.37	15.63	15.89	16.15	16.41	16.67	16.92	17.18	17.44	17.70	17.96	18.22	18.48	18.74	19.00	19.25
91	16.49	16.75	17.01	17.27	17.53	17.79	18.05	18.31	18.57	18.83	19.09	19.35	19.61	19.87	20.13	20.39
90	17.63	17.89	18.15	18.41	18.67	18.93	19.20	19.46	19.72	19.98	20.24	20.50	20.76	21.03	21.29	21.55
89	18.78	19.05	19.31	19.57	19.83	20.10	20.36	20.62	20.88	21.15	21.41	21.67	21.93	22.20	22.46	22.72
88	19.96	20.22	20.49	20.75	21.01	21.28	21.54	21.80	22.07	22.33	22.60	22.86	23.12	23.39	23.65	23.92
87	21.15	21.42	21.68	21.95	22.21	22.48	22.74	23.01	23.27	23.54	23.80	24.07	24.33	24.60	24.86	25.13
86	22.37	22.63	22.90	23.16	23.43	23.70	23.96	24.23	24.50	24.76	25.03	25.30	25.56	25.83	26.10	26.36
85	23.60	23.87	24.13	24.40	24.67	24.94	25.21	25.47	25.74	26.01	26.28	26.55	26.81	27.08	27.35	27.62
84	24.85	25.12	25.39	25.66	25.93	26.20	26.47	26.74	27.01	27.28	27.55	27.82	28.09	28.35	28.62	28.89
83	26.13	26.40	26.67	26.94	27.21	27.48	27.75	28.03	28.30	28.57	28.84	29.11	29.38	29.65	29.92	30.19
82	27.43	27.70	27.97	28.25	28.52	28.79	29.06	29.33	29.61	29.88	30.15	30.42	30.70	30.97	31.24	31.51
81	28.75	29.03	29.30	29.57	29.85	30.12	30.39	30.67	30.94	31.21	31.49	31.76	32.04	32.31	32.58	32.86
80	30.10	30.37	30.65	30.92	31.20	31.47	31.75	32.02	32.30	32.58	32.85	33.13	33.40	33.68	33.95	34.23
79	31.47	31.75	32.02	32.30	32.58	32.85	33.13	33.41	33.68	33.96	34.24	34.51	34.79	35.07	35.35	35.62
78	32.87	33.14	33.42	33.70	33.98	34.26	34.54	34.81	35.09	35.37	35.65	35.93	36.21	36.49	36.77	37.04
77	34.29	34.57	34.85	35.13	35.41	35.69	35.97	36.25	36.53	36.81	37.09	37.37	37.65	37.93	38.21	38.49
76	35.74	36.02	36.30	36.58	36.87	37.15	37.43	37.71	37.99	38.28	38.56	38.84	39.12	39.40	39.69	39.97
75	37.22	37.50	37.78	38.07	38.35	38.63	38.92	39.20	39.49	39.77	40.05	40.34	40.62	40.91	41.19	41.47
74	38.72	39.01	39.30	39.58	39.87	40.15	40.44	40.72	41.01	41.29	41.58	41.87	42.15	42.44	42.72	43.01
73	40.26	40.55	40.84	41.12	41.41	41.70	41.99	42.27	42.56	42.85	43.14	43.42	43.71	44.00	44.29	44.58
72	41.83	42.12	42.41	42.70	42.99	43.28	43.57	43.86	44.15	44.44	44.73	45.02	45.31	45.59	45.88	46.17
71	43.43	43.73	44.02	44.31	44.60	44.89	45.18	45.47	45.76	46.06	46.35	46.64	46.93	47.22	47.51	47.81
70	45.07	45.36	45.66	45.95	46.24	46.54	46.83	47.12	47.42	47.71	48.00	48.30	48.59	48.89	49.18	49.47
69	46.74	47.04	47.33	47.63	47.92	48.22	48.51	48.81	49.11	49.40	49.70	49.99	50.29	50.58	50.88	51.18

MORTGAGE PRICE

Description: This table shows the price to pay for a monthly payment mortgage loan at the yield rate.

Example: The price of a 15.00 %, 2 year mortgage loan to yield 8.00 % to maturity is $ 107.21.

INTEREST RATE, %

YIELD	11.00%	11.25%	11.50%	11.75%	12.00%	12.25%	12.50%	12.75%	13.00%	13.25%	13.50%	13.75%	14.00%	14.25%	14.50%	15.00%
0.00	111.86	112.14	112.42	112.70	112.98	113.26	113.54	113.82	114.10	114.38	114.66	114.95	115.23	115.51	115.80	116.37
1.00	110.70	110.98	111.25	111.53	111.81	112.09	112.36	112.64	112.92	113.20	113.48	113.76	114.04	114.32	114.60	115.16
2.00	109.56	109.83	110.11	110.38	110.66	110.93	111.21	111.48	111.76	112.03	112.31	112.59	112.86	113.14	113.42	113.98
3.00	108.44	108.71	108.98	109.25	109.52	109.79	110.07	110.34	110.61	110.88	111.16	111.43	111.71	111.98	112.26	112.81
4.00	107.33	107.60	107.87	108.13	108.40	108.67	108.94	109.21	109.48	109.75	110.02	110.29	110.57	110.84	111.11	111.66
4.25	107.06	107.32	107.59	107.86	108.12	108.39	108.66	108.93	109.20	109.47	109.74	110.01	110.28	110.55	110.83	111.37
4.50	106.78	107.05	107.31	107.58	107.85	108.12	108.38	108.65	108.92	109.19	109.46	109.73	110.00	110.27	110.54	111.09
4.75	106.51	106.77	107.04	107.31	107.57	107.84	108.11	108.38	108.64	108.91	109.18	109.45	109.72	109.99	110.26	110.80
5.00	106.24	106.50	106.77	107.03	107.30	107.57	107.83	108.10	108.37	108.63	108.90	109.17	109.44	109.71	109.98	110.52
5.25	105.97	106.23	106.50	106.76	107.03	107.29	107.56	107.82	108.09	108.36	108.63	108.89	109.16	109.43	109.70	110.24
5.50	105.70	105.96	106.22	106.49	106.75	107.02	107.28	107.55	107.82	108.08	108.35	108.62	108.88	109.15	109.42	109.96
5.75	105.43	105.69	105.95	106.22	106.48	106.75	107.01	107.28	107.54	107.81	108.07	108.34	108.61	108.87	109.14	109.68
6.00	105.16	105.42	105.69	105.95	106.21	106.47	106.74	107.00	107.27	107.53	107.80	108.06	108.33	108.60	108.86	109.40
6.25	104.89	105.16	105.42	105.68	105.94	106.20	106.47	106.73	107.00	107.26	107.53	107.79	108.06	108.32	108.59	109.12
6.50	104.63	104.89	105.15	105.41	105.67	105.94	106.20	106.46	106.72	106.99	107.25	107.52	107.78	108.05	108.31	108.85
6.75	104.36	104.62	104.88	105.14	105.41	105.67	105.93	106.19	106.45	106.72	106.98	107.24	107.51	107.77	108.04	108.57
7.00	104.10	104.36	104.62	104.88	105.14	105.40	105.66	105.92	106.19	106.45	106.71	106.97	107.24	107.50	107.77	108.30
7.25	103.84	104.09	104.35	104.61	104.87	105.13	105.39	105.66	105.92	106.18	106.44	106.70	106.97	107.23	107.49	108.02
7.50	103.57	103.83	104.09	104.35	104.61	104.87	105.13	105.39	105.65	105.91	106.18	106.44	106.70	106.97	107.23	108.02
7.75	103.31	103.57	103.83	104.09	104.34	104.60	104.86	105.12	105.38	105.64	105.90	106.17	106.43	106.70	106.96	107.22	107.75
8.00	103.05	103.31	103.57	103.82	104.08	104.34	104.60	104.86	105.12	105.38	105.64	105.90	106.16	106.42	106.69	106.95	107.48
8.25	102.79	103.05	103.31	103.56	103.82	104.08	104.34	104.59	104.85	105.11	105.37	105.63	105.89	106.16	106.42	106.68	107.21
8.50	102.53	102.79	103.05	103.30	103.56	103.82	104.07	104.33	104.59	104.85	105.11	105.37	105.63	105.89	106.15	106.41	106.94
8.75	102.28	102.53	102.79	103.04	103.30	103.56	103.81	104.07	104.33	104.58	104.84	105.10	105.36	105.62	105.88	106.15	106.67
9.00	102.02	102.27	102.53	102.78	103.04	103.30	103.55	103.81	104.06	104.32	104.58	104.84	105.10	105.35	105.61	106.13
9.25	101.76	102.02	102.27	102.53	102.78	103.04	103.29	103.55	103.80	104.06	104.32	104.58	104.83	105.09	105.35	105.87
9.50	101.51	101.76	102.02	102.27	102.52	102.78	103.03	103.29	103.54	103.80	104.06	104.31	104.57	104.83	105.09	105.60
9.75	101.26	101.51	101.76	102.01	102.27	102.52	102.78	103.03	103.29	103.54	103.80	104.05	104.31	104.57	104.82	105.34
10.00	101.00	101.25	101.51	101.76	102.01	102.27	102.52	102.77	103.03	103.28	103.54	103.79	104.05	104.30	104.56	105.07
10.25	100.75	101.00	101.25	101.51	101.76	102.01	102.26	102.52	102.77	103.02	103.28	103.53	103.79	104.04	104.30	104.81
10.50	100.50	100.75	101.00	101.25	101.50	101.76	102.01	102.26	102.51	102.77	103.02	103.28	103.53	103.78	104.04	104.55
10.75	100.25	100.50	100.75	101.00	101.25	101.50	101.75	102.01	102.26	102.51	102.76	103.02	103.27	103.53	103.78	104.29
11.00	100.00	100.25	100.50	100.75	101.00	101.25	101.50	101.75	102.00	102.26	102.51	102.76	103.01	103.27	103.52	104.03
11.25	99.75	100.00	100.25	100.50	100.75	101.00	101.25	101.50	101.75	102.00	102.26	102.51	102.76	103.01	103.26	103.77
11.50	99.50	99.75	100.00	100.25	100.50	100.75	101.00	101.25	101.50	101.75	102.00	102.25	102.51	102.76	103.01	103.26	103.51
11.75	99.26	99.50	99.75	100.00	100.25	100.50	100.75	101.00	101.25	101.50	101.75	102.00	102.25	102.50	102.76	103.01	103.51
12.00	99.01	99.26	99.50	99.75	100.00	100.25	100.50	100.75	101.00	100.99	101.24	101.49	101.74	102.00	102.25	102.50	102.75	103.26
12.25	98.77	99.01	99.26	99.51	99.75	100.00	100.25	100.50	100.74	100.99	101.24	101.49	101.74	102.00	102.25	102.50	103.00
12.50	98.52	98.77	99.01	99.26	99.51	99.75	100.00	100.25	100.50	100.74	100.99	101.24	101.49	101.74	101.99	102.24	102.75
12.75	98.28	98.52	98.77	99.01	99.26	99.51	99.75	100.00	100.25	100.50	100.74	100.99	101.24	101.49	101.74	101.99	102.49
13.00	98.04	98.28	98.52	98.77	99.01	99.26	99.51	99.75	100.00	100.25	100.49	100.74	100.99	101.24	101.49	101.99
13.25	97.79	98.04	98.28	98.53	98.77	99.02	99.26	99.51	99.75	100.00	100.25	100.49	100.74	100.99	101.24	101.74
13.50	97.55	97.80	98.04	98.28	98.53	98.77	99.02	99.26	99.51	99.75	100.00	100.25	100.49	100.74	100.99	101.24	101.74
13.75	97.31	97.56	97.80	98.04	98.29	98.53	98.77	99.02	99.26	99.51	99.75	100.00	100.25	100.49	100.74	100.99	101.49
14.00	97.07	97.32	97.56	97.80	98.04	98.29	98.53	98.77	99.02	99.26	99.51	99.75	100.00	100.25	100.49	100.74	101.24
14.25	96.84	97.08	97.32	97.56	97.80	98.05	98.29	98.53	98.78	99.02	99.26	99.51	99.75	100.00	100.25	100.49	100.99
14.50	96.60	96.84	97.08	97.32	97.56	97.80	98.05	98.29	98.53	98.78	99.02	99.27	99.51	99.75	100.00	100.25	100.74
14.75	96.36	96.60	96.84	97.08	97.32	97.57	97.81	98.05	98.29	98.53	98.78	99.02	99.27	99.51	99.75	100.49
15.00	96.13	96.36	96.60	96.84	97.09	97.33	97.57	97.81	98.05	98.29	98.54	98.78	99.02	99.27	99.51	100.00
15.25	95.89	96.13	96.37	96.61	96.85	97.09	97.33	97.57	97.81	98.05	98.30	98.54	98.78	99.02	99.27	99.76
15.50	95.66	95.89	96.13	96.37	96.61	96.85	97.09	97.33	97.57	97.81	98.06	98.30	98.54	98.78	99.02	99.51
15.75	95.42	95.66	95.90	96.14	96.38	96.61	96.85	97.09	97.33	97.58	97.82	98.06	98.30	98.54	98.78	99.27
16.00	95.19	95.43	95.66	95.90	96.14	96.38	96.62	96.86	97.10	97.34	97.58	97.82	98.06	98.30	98.54	99.03
16.25	94.96	95.19	95.43	95.67	95.91	96.14	96.38	96.62	96.86	97.10	97.34	97.58	97.82	98.06	98.30	98.54	99.03
16.50	94.73	94.96	95.20	95.44	95.67	95.91	96.15	96.39	96.63	96.86	97.10	97.34	97.58	97.82	98.06	98.79
16.75	94.50	94.73	94.97	95.20	95.44	95.68	95.91	96.15	96.39	96.63	96.87	97.11	97.35	97.58	97.82	98.55
17.00	94.27	94.50	94.74	94.97	95.21	95.45	95.68	95.92	96.16	96.39	96.63	96.87	97.11	97.35	97.59	98.07
17.25	94.04	94.27	94.51	94.74	94.98	95.21	95.45	95.69	95.92	96.16	96.40	96.64	96.87	97.11	97.35	97.83
17.50	93.81	94.04	94.28	94.51	94.75	94.98	95.22	95.45	95.69	95.93	96.16	96.40	96.64	96.87	97.11	97.35	97.83
17.75	93.58	93.82	94.05	94.28	94.52	94.75	94.99	95.22	95.46	95.69	95.93	96.17	96.40	96.64	96.88	97.11	97.59
18.00	93.36	93.59	93.82	94.06	94.29	94.52	94.76	94.99	95.23	95.46	95.70	95.94	96.17	96.40	96.64	96.88	97.36
18.25	93.13	93.36	93.60	93.83	94.06	94.30	94.53	94.76	95.00	95.23	95.46	95.70	95.94	96.17	96.41	96.65	97.12
18.50	92.91	93.14	93.37	93.60	93.84	94.07	94.30	94.54	94.77	95.00	95.24	95.47	95.70	95.94	96.18	96.41	96.89
18.75	92.68	92.91	93.15	93.38	93.61	93.84	94.07	94.31	94.54	94.77	95.01	95.24	95.47	95.71	95.94	96.18	96.65
19.00	92.46	92.69	92.92	93.15	93.38	93.62	93.85	94.08	94.31	94.55	94.78	95.01	95.25	95.48	95.72	96.19
20.00	91.58	91.80	92.03	92.26	92.49	92.72	92.95	93.18	93.41	93.64	93.87	94.10	94.34	94.57	94.80	95.27
25.00	87.33	87.54	87.76	87.98	88.20	88.42	88.64	88.86	89.08	89.30	89.52	89.74	89.96	90.18	90.40	90.85
30.00	83.36	83.57	83.77	83.98	84.19	84.40	84.61	84.82	85.03	85.24	85.45	85.66	85.87	86.08	86.29	86.72

Description: This table shows the yield to maturity of a mortgage purchased at the price shown in the index.

Example: The yield to maturity of a 15.00 %, 2 year mortgage at a price of 102.00 is 12.98 %.

INTEREST RATE, %

PRICE	11.00%	11.25%	11.50%	11.75%	12.00%	12.25%	12.50%	12.75%	13.00%	13.25%	13.50%	13.75%	14.00%	14.25%	14.50%	15.00%
110	1.61	1.85	2.09	2.33	2.57	2.81	3.05	3.29	3.53	3.77	4.01	4.26	4.50	4.74	4.98	5.46
109	2.49	2.73	2.98	3.22	3.46	3.70	3.94	4.18	4.42	4.67	4.91	5.15	5.39	5.63	5.87	6.36
108	3.39	3.63	3.87	4.12	4.36	4.60	4.84	5.08	5.33	5.57	5.81	6.05	6.30	6.54	6.78	7.27
107	4.30	4.54	4.78	5.03	5.27	5.51	5.75	6.00	6.24	6.48	6.73	6.97	7.21	7.46	7.70	8.19
106	5.21	5.46	5.70	5.95	6.19	6.44	6.68	6.92	7.17	7.41	7.66	7.90	8.14	8.39	8.63	9.12
105.75	5.45	5.69	5.93	6.18	6.42	6.67	6.91	7.16	7.40	7.65	7.89	8.13	8.38	8.62	8.87	9.36
105.50	5.68	5.92	6.17	6.41	6.66	6.90	7.15	7.39	7.64	7.88	8.12	8.37	8.61	8.86	9.10	9.59
105.25	5.91	6.16	6.40	6.65	6.89	7.14	7.38	7.63	7.87	8.12	8.36	8.60	8.85	9.09	9.34	9.83
105.00	6.15	6.39	6.64	6.88	7.13	7.37	7.62	7.86	8.11	8.35	8.60	8.84	9.09	9.33	9.58	10.07
104.75	6.38	6.63	6.87	7.12	7.36	7.61	7.85	8.10	8.34	8.59	8.83	9.08	9.32	9.57	9.81	10.30
104.50	6.62	6.86	7.11	7.35	7.60	7.84	8.09	8.33	8.58	8.83	9.07	9.32	9.56	9.81	10.05	10.54
104.25	6.85	7.10	7.34	7.59	7.84	8.08	8.33	8.57	8.82	9.06	9.31	9.56	9.80	10.05	10.29	10.78
104.00	7.09	7.34	7.58	7.83	8.07	8.32	8.57	8.81	9.06	9.30	9.55	9.80	10.04	10.29	10.53	11.03
103.75	7.33	7.57	7.82	8.07	8.31	8.56	8.80	9.05	9.30	9.54	9.79	10.04	10.28	10.53	10.77	11.27
103.50	7.57	7.81	8.06	8.31	8.55	8.80	9.04	9.29	9.54	9.78	10.03	10.28	10.52	10.77	11.01	11.51
103.25	7.81	8.05	8.30	8.55	8.79	9.04	9.29	9.53	9.78	10.03	10.27	10.52	10.77	11.01	11.26	11.75
103.00	8.05	8.29	8.54	8.79	9.03	9.28	9.53	9.77	10.02	10.27	10.52	10.76	11.01	11.26	11.50	12.00
102.75	8.29	8.53	8.78	9.03	9.28	9.52	9.77	10.02	10.26	10.51	10.76	11.01	11.25	11.50	11.75	12.24
102.50	8.53	8.78	9.02	9.27	9.52	9.77	10.01	10.26	10.51	10.76	11.00	11.25	11.50	11.75	11.99	12.49
102.25	8.77	9.02	9.27	9.51	9.76	10.01	10.26	10.51	10.75	11.00	11.25	11.50	11.74	11.99	12.24	12.73
102.00	9.02	9.26	9.51	9.76	10.01	10.26	10.50	10.75	11.00	11.25	11.49	11.74	11.99	12.24	12.49	12.98
101.75	9.26	9.51	9.76	10.00	10.25	10.50	10.75	11.00	11.25	11.49	11.74	11.99	12.24	12.49	12.73	13.23
101.50	9.51	9.75	10.00	10.25	10.50	10.75	11.00	11.24	11.49	11.74	11.99	12.24	12.49	12.74	12.98	13.48
101.25	9.75	10.00	10.25	10.50	10.75	10.99	11.24	11.49	11.74	11.99	12.24	12.49	12.74	12.98	13.23	13.73
101.00	10.00	10.25	10.50	10.75	10.99	11.24	11.49	11.74	11.99	12.24	12.49	12.74	12.99	13.23	13.48	13.98
100.75	10.25	10.50	10.74	10.99	11.24	11.49	11.74	11.99	12.24	12.49	12.74	12.99	13.24	13.49	13.74	14.23
100.50	10.49	10.74	10.99	11.24	11.49	11.74	11.99	12.24	12.49	12.74	12.99	13.24	13.49	13.74	13.99	14.49
100.25	10.74	10.99	11.24	11.49	11.74	11.99	12.24	12.49	12.74	12.99	13.24	13.49	13.74	13.99	14.24	14.74
100.00	11.00	11.25	11.50	11.75	12.00	12.25	12.50	12.75	13.00	13.25	13.50	13.75	14.00	14.25	14.50	15.00
99.75	11.25	11.50	11.75	12.00	12.25	12.50	12.75	13.00	13.25	13.50	13.75	14.00	14.25	14.50	14.75	15.25
99.50	11.50	11.75	12.00	12.25	12.50	12.75	13.00	13.25	13.50	13.75	14.00	14.25	14.51	14.76	15.01	15.51
99.25	11.75	12.00	12.25	12.50	12.76	13.01	13.26	13.51	13.76	14.01	14.26	14.51	14.76	15.01	15.26	15.76
99.00	12.01	12.26	12.51	12.76	13.01	13.26	13.51	13.76	14.01	14.27	14.52	14.77	15.02	15.27	15.52	16.02
98.75	12.26	12.51	12.76	13.02	13.27	13.52	13.77	14.02	14.27	14.52	14.77	15.03	15.28	15.53	15.78	16.28
98.50	12.52	12.77	13.02	13.27	13.52	13.77	14.03	14.28	14.53	14.78	15.03	15.28	15.54	15.79	16.04	16.54
98.25	12.77	13.03	13.28	13.53	13.78	14.03	14.28	14.54	14.79	15.04	15.29	15.54	15.80	16.05	16.30	16.80
98.00	13.03	13.28	13.54	13.79	14.04	14.29	14.54	14.80	15.05	15.30	15.55	15.80	16.06	16.31	16.56	17.07
97.75	13.29	13.54	13.80	14.05	14.30	14.55	14.80	15.06	15.31	15.56	15.81	16.07	16.32	16.57	16.82	17.33
97.50	13.55	13.80	14.06	14.31	14.56	14.81	15.07	15.32	15.57	15.82	16.08	16.33	16.58	16.85	17.10	17.59
97.25	13.81	14.06	14.32	14.57	14.82	15.08	15.33	15.58	15.83	16.09	16.34	16.59	16.85	17.11	17.35	17.86
97.00	14.07	14.33	14.58	14.83	15.08	15.34	15.59	15.84	16.10	16.35	16.60	16.86	17.11	17.36	17.62	18.12
96.75	14.33	14.59	14.84	15.10	15.35	15.60	15.86	16.11	16.36	16.62	16.87	17.12	17.38	17.63	17.88	18.39
96.50	14.60	14.85	15.11	15.36	15.61	15.87	16.12	16.37	16.63	16.88	17.14	17.39	17.64	17.90	18.15	18.66
96.25	14.86	15.12	15.37	15.62	15.88	16.13	16.39	16.64	16.89	17.15	17.40	17.66	17.91	18.17	18.42	18.93
96.00	15.13	15.38	15.64	15.89	16.15	16.40	16.65	16.91	17.16	17.42	17.67	17.93	18.18	18.43	18.69	19.20
95.75	15.39	15.65	15.90	16.16	16.41	16.67	16.92	17.18	17.43	17.69	17.94	18.20	18.45	18.70	18.96	19.47
95.50	15.66	15.92	16.17	16.43	16.68	16.94	17.19	17.45	17.70	17.96	18.21	18.47	18.72	18.98	19.23	19.74
95.25	15.93	16.19	16.44	16.70	16.95	17.21	17.46	17.72	17.97	18.23	18.48	18.74	18.99	19.25	19.50	20.01
95.00	16.20	16.46	16.71	16.97	17.22	17.48	17.73	17.99	18.24	18.50	18.75	19.01	19.27	19.52	19.78	20.29
94.75	16.47	16.73	16.98	17.24	17.49	17.75	18.00	18.26	18.52	18.77	19.03	19.28	19.54	19.79	20.05	20.56
94.50	16.74	17.00	17.25	17.51	17.77	18.02	18.28	18.53	18.79	19.05	19.30	19.56	19.81	20.07	20.33	20.84
94.25	17.01	17.27	17.53	17.78	18.04	18.30	18.55	18.81	19.06	19.32	19.58	19.83	20.09	20.35	20.60	21.12
94.00	17.29	17.54	17.80	18.06	18.31	18.57	18.83	19.08	19.34	19.60	19.85	20.11	20.37	20.62	20.88	21.39
93.75	17.56	17.82	18.08	18.33	18.59	18.85	19.10	19.36	19.62	19.87	20.13	20.39	20.64	20.90	21.16	21.67
93	18.39	18.65	18.91	19.16	19.42	19.68	19.94	20.20	20.45	20.71	20.97	21.23	21.49	21.74	22.00	22.52
92	19.51	19.77	20.03	20.29	20.55	20.81	21.07	21.33	21.59	21.84	22.10	22.36	22.62	22.88	23.14	23.66
91	20.65	20.91	21.17	21.43	21.69	21.95	22.21	22.47	22.73	22.99	23.25	23.51	23.78	24.04	24.30	24.82
90	21.81	22.07	22.33	22.59	22.86	23.12	23.38	23.64	23.90	24.16	24.42	24.69	24.95	25.21	25.47	25.99
89	22.99	23.25	23.51	23.77	24.04	24.30	24.56	24.82	25.09	25.35	25.61	25.88	26.14	26.40	26.66	27.19
88	24.18	24.44	24.71	24.97	25.24	25.50	25.76	26.03	26.29	26.56	26.82	27.09	27.35	27.61	27.88	28.41
87	25.39	25.66	25.93	26.19	26.46	26.72	26.99	27.25	27.52	27.78	28.05	28.31	28.58	28.85	29.11	29.64
86	26.63	26.90	27.16	27.43	27.70	27.96	28.23	28.50	28.76	29.03	29.30	29.57	29.83	30.10	30.37	30.90
85	27.89	28.15	28.42	28.69	28.96	29.23	29.49	29.76	30.03	30.30	30.57	30.84	31.11	31.37	31.64	32.18
84	29.16	29.43	29.70	29.97	30.24	30.51	30.78	31.05	31.32	31.59	31.86	32.13	32.40	32.67	32.94	33.48
83	30.46	30.73	31.01	31.28	31.55	31.82	32.09	32.36	32.63	32.90	33.18	33.45	33.72	33.99	34.26	34.80
82	31.79	32.06	32.33	32.60	32.88	33.15	33.42	33.69	33.97	34.24	34.51	34.79	35.06	35.33	35.60	36.15
81	33.13	33.41	33.68	33.96	34.23	34.50	34.78	35.05	35.33	35.60	35.88	36.15	36.42	36.70	36.97	37.52
80	34.50	34.78	35.06	35.33	35.61	35.88	36.16	36.43	36.71	36.99	37.26	37.54	37.81	38.09	38.37	38.92

MORTGAGE PRICE

Description: This table shows the price to pay for a monthly payment mortgage loan at the yield rate.

Example: The price of a 6.75 %, 3 year mortgage loan to yield 8.00 % to maturity is $ 98.17.

INTEREST RATE, %

YIELD	0.00%	1.00%	2.00%	3.00%	4.00%	4.25%	4.50%	4.75%	5.00%	5.25%	5.50%	5.75%	6.00%	6.25%	6.50%	6.75%
0.00	100.00	101.55	103.11	104.69	106.29	106.69	107.09	107.49	107.90	108.30	108.71	109.11	109.52	109.93	110.34	110.75
1.00	98.47	100.00	101.54	103.10	104.66	105.06	105.46	105.85	106.25	106.65	107.05	107.45	107.85	108.25	108.65	109.06
2.00	96.98	98.48	100.00	101.53	103.08	103.47	103.86	104.25	104.64	105.03	105.42	105.82	106.21	106.61	107.01	107.40
3.00	95.52	97.00	98.49	100.00	101.52	101.91	102.29	102.67	103.06	103.45	103.83	104.22	104.61	105.00	105.39	105.78
4.00	94.09	95.54	97.01	98.50	100.00	100.38	100.76	101.13	101.51	101.89	102.28	102.66	103.04	103.43	103.81	104.20
4.25	93.73	95.18	96.65	98.13	99.62	100.00	100.38	100.75	101.13	101.51	101.89	102.27	102.65	103.04	103.42	103.80
4.50	93.38	94.83	96.29	97.76	99.25	99.62	100.00	100.38	100.75	101.13	101.51	101.89	102.27	102.65	103.03	103.42
4.75	93.03	94.47	95.93	97.40	98.88	99.25	99.63	100.00	100.38	100.75	101.13	101.51	101.89	102.27	102.65	103.03
5.00	92.68	94.12	95.57	97.03	98.51	98.88	99.25	99.63	100.00	100.37	100.75	101.13	101.50	101.88	102.26	102.64
5.25	92.34	93.77	95.21	96.67	98.14	98.51	98.88	99.25	99.63	100.00	100.37	100.75	101.13	101.50	101.88	102.26
5.50	91.99	93.42	94.86	96.31	97.77	98.14	98.51	98.88	99.25	99.63	100.00	100.37	100.75	101.13	101.50	101.88
5.75	91.65	93.07	94.50	95.95	97.41	97.78	98.15	98.52	98.89	99.26	99.63	100.00	100.37	100.75	101.12	101.50
6.00	91.31	92.72	94.15	95.59	97.05	97.41	97.78	98.15	98.52	98.89	99.26	99.63	100.00	100.37	100.75	101.12
6.25	90.97	92.38	93.80	95.24	96.69	97.05	97.42	97.78	98.15	98.52	98.89	99.26	99.63	100.00	100.37	100.75
6.50	90.63	92.04	93.45	94.88	96.33	96.69	97.06	97.42	97.79	98.15	98.52	98.89	99.26	99.63	100.00	100.37
6.75	90.30	91.70	93.11	94.53	95.97	96.33	96.70	97.06	97.43	97.79	98.16	98.52	98.89	99.26	99.63	100.00
7.00	89.96	91.36	92.76	94.18	95.62	95.98	96.34	96.70	97.07	97.43	97.79	98.16	98.53	98.89	99.26	99.63
7.25	89.63	91.02	92.42	93.84	95.26	95.62	95.98	96.34	96.71	97.07	97.43	97.80	98.16	98.53	98.89	99.26
7.50	89.30	90.68	92.08	93.49	94.91	95.27	95.63	95.99	96.35	96.71	97.07	97.44	97.80	98.16	98.53	98.90
7.75	88.97	90.35	91.74	93.15	94.56	94.92	95.28	95.64	96.00	96.36	96.72	97.08	97.44	97.80	98.16	98.53
8.00	88.64	90.02	91.40	92.80	94.22	94.57	94.93	95.28	95.64	96.00	96.36	96.72	97.08	97.44	97.80	98.17
8.25	88.32	89.69	91.07	92.46	93.87	94.22	94.58	94.93	95.29	95.65	96.01	96.37	96.73	97.09	97.45	97.81
8.50	87.99	89.36	90.73	92.12	93.53	93.88	94.23	94.59	94.94	95.30	95.65	96.01	96.37	96.73	97.09	97.45
8.75	87.67	89.03	90.40	91.79	93.18	93.54	93.89	94.24	94.59	94.95	95.30	95.66	96.02	96.38	96.73	97.09
9.00	87.35	88.71	90.07	91.45	92.84	93.19	93.54	93.90	94.25	94.60	94.96	95.31	95.67	96.02	96.38	96.74
9.25	87.03	88.38	89.74	91.12	92.50	92.85	93.20	93.55	93.90	94.26	94.61	94.96	95.32	95.67	96.03	96.39
9.50	86.72	88.06	89.42	90.79	92.17	92.52	92.86	93.21	93.56	93.91	94.27	94.62	94.97	95.32	95.68	96.04
9.75	86.40	87.74	89.09	90.45	91.83	92.18	92.53	92.87	93.22	93.57	93.92	94.27	94.63	94.98	95.33	95.69
10.00	86.09	87.42	88.77	90.13	91.50	91.84	92.19	92.54	92.88	93.23	93.58	93.93	94.28	94.63	94.99	95.34
10.25	85.77	87.10	88.44	89.80	91.17	91.51	91.85	92.20	92.55	92.89	93.24	93.59	93.94	94.29	94.64	94.99
10.50	85.46	86.79	88.12	89.47	90.84	91.18	91.52	91.87	92.21	92.56	92.90	93.25	93.60	93.95	94.30	94.65
10.75	85.15	86.47	87.81	89.15	90.51	90.85	91.19	91.53	91.88	92.22	92.57	92.91	93.26	93.61	93.96	94.31
11.00	84.85	86.16	87.49	88.83	90.18	90.52	90.86	91.20	91.55	91.89	92.23	92.58	92.92	93.27	93.62	93.96
11.25	84.54	85.85	87.17	88.51	89.86	90.19	90.53	90.87	91.22	91.56	91.90	92.24	92.59	92.93	93.28	93.63
11.50	84.24	85.54	86.86	88.19	89.53	89.87	90.21	90.55	90.89	91.23	91.57	91.91	92.25	92.60	92.94	93.29
11.75	83.93	85.23	86.55	87.87	89.21	89.55	89.88	90.22	90.56	90.90	91.24	91.58	91.92	92.27	92.61	92.95
12.00	83.63	84.93	86.24	87.56	88.89	89.22	89.56	89.90	90.23	90.57	90.91	91.25	91.59	91.93	92.28	92.62
12.25	83.33	84.62	85.93	87.24	88.57	88.90	89.24	89.57	89.91	90.25	90.59	90.92	91.26	91.60	91.95	92.29
12.50	83.03	84.32	85.62	86.93	88.25	88.59	88.92	89.25	89.59	89.93	90.26	90.60	90.94	91.28	91.62	91.96
12.75	82.74	84.02	85.31	86.62	87.94	88.27	88.60	88.94	89.27	89.60	89.94	90.28	90.61	90.95	91.29	91.63
13.00	82.44	83.72	85.01	86.31	87.62	87.95	88.29	88.62	88.95	89.28	89.62	89.95	90.29	90.63	90.96	91.30
13.25	82.15	83.42	84.71	86.00	87.31	87.64	87.97	88.30	88.63	88.97	89.30	89.63	89.97	90.30	90.64	90.98
13.50	81.86	83.12	84.40	85.70	87.00	87.33	87.66	87.99	88.32	88.65	88.98	89.31	89.65	89.98	90.32	90.65
13.75	81.56	82.83	84.10	85.39	86.69	87.02	87.35	87.67	88.00	88.33	88.66	89.00	89.33	89.66	90.00	90.33
14.00	81.27	82.53	83.81	85.09	86.38	86.71	87.04	87.36	87.69	88.02	88.35	88.68	89.01	89.34	89.68	90.01
14.25	80.99	82.24	83.51	84.79	86.08	86.40	86.73	87.05	87.38	87.71	88.04	88.37	88.70	89.03	89.36	89.69
14.50	80.70	81.95	83.21	84.49	85.77	86.10	86.42	86.75	87.07	87.40	87.73	88.05	88.38	88.71	89.04	89.37
14.75	80.42	81.66	82.92	84.19	85.47	85.79	86.12	86.44	86.76	87.09	87.42	87.74	88.07	88.40	88.73	89.06
15.00	80.13	81.37	82.63	83.89	85.17	85.49	85.81	86.13	86.46	86.78	87.11	87.43	87.76	88.09	88.41	88.74
15.25	79.85	81.09	82.33	83.60	84.87	85.19	85.51	85.83	86.15	86.48	86.80	87.12	87.45	87.78	88.10	88.43
15.50	79.57	80.80	82.05	83.30	84.57	84.89	85.21	85.53	85.85	86.17	86.49	86.82	87.14	87.47	87.79	88.12
15.75	79.29	80.52	81.76	83.01	84.27	84.59	84.91	85.23	85.55	85.87	86.19	86.51	86.84	87.16	87.48	87.81
16.00	79.01	80.23	81.47	82.72	83.98	84.29	84.61	84.93	85.25	85.57	85.89	86.21	86.53	86.85	87.18	87.50
16.25	78.73	79.95	81.19	82.43	83.68	84.00	84.32	84.63	84.95	85.27	85.59	85.91	86.23	86.55	86.87	87.20
16.50	78.46	79.67	80.90	82.14	83.39	83.71	84.02	84.34	84.65	84.97	85.29	85.61	85.93	86.25	86.57	86.89
16.75	78.18	79.40	80.62	81.85	83.10	83.41	83.73	84.04	84.36	84.67	84.99	85.31	85.63	85.95	86.27	86.59
17.00	77.91	79.12	80.34	81.57	82.81	83.12	83.44	83.75	84.06	84.38	84.69	85.01	85.33	85.65	85.97	86.28
17.25	77.64	78.84	80.06	81.28	82.52	82.83	83.14	83.46	83.77	84.08	84.40	84.72	85.03	85.35	85.67	85.98
17.50	77.37	78.57	79.78	81.00	82.23	82.54	82.86	83.17	83.48	83.79	84.11	84.42	84.74	85.05	85.37	85.69
17.75	77.10	78.30	79.50	80.72	81.95	82.26	82.57	82.88	83.19	83.50	83.81	84.13	84.44	84.76	85.07	85.39
18.00	76.84	78.03	79.23	80.44	81.67	81.97	82.28	82.59	82.90	83.21	83.52	83.84	84.15	84.46	84.78	85.09
18.25	76.57	77.76	78.95	80.16	81.38	81.69	82.00	82.31	82.61	82.92	83.23	83.55	83.86	84.15	84.46	84.80
18.50	76.30	77.49	78.68	79.89	81.10	81.41	81.71	82.02	82.33	82.64	82.95	83.26	83.57	83.88	84.19	84.50
18.75	76.04	77.22	78.41	79.61	80.82	81.13	81.43	81.74	82.05	82.35	82.66	82.97	83.28	83.59	83.90	84.21
19.00	75.78	76.95	78.14	79.34	80.54	80.85	81.15	81.46	81.76	82.07	82.38	82.68	82.99	83.30	83.61	83.92
20.00	74.74	75.90	77.07	78.25	79.44	79.74	80.04	80.34	80.65	80.95	81.25	81.56	81.86	82.16	82.47	82.78
25.00	69.86	70.95	72.04	73.14	74.26	74.54	74.82	75.10	75.38	75.66	75.95	76.23	76.51	76.80	77.09	77.37
30.00	65.43	66.45	67.47	68.50	69.55	69.81	70.07	70.34	70.60	70.86	71.13	71.40	71.66	71.93	72.20	72.47

MORTGAGE YIELD

Description: This table shows the yield to maturity of a mortgage purchased at the price shown in the index.

Example: The yield to maturity of a 6.75 %, 3 year mortgage at a price of 95.00 is 10.24 %.

INTEREST RATE, %

PRICE	0.00%	1.00%	2.00%	3.00%	4.00%	4.25%	4.50%	4.75%	5.00%	5.25%	5.50%	5.75%	6.00%	6.25%	6.50%	6.75%
100	0.00	1.00	2.00	3.00	4.00	4.25	4.50	4.75	5.00	5.25	5.50	5.75	6.00	6.25	6.50	6.75
99.75	.16	1.16	2.16	3.16	4.16	4.41	4.66	4.91	5.16	5.41	5.66	5.91	6.16	6.41	6.66	6.91
99.50	.32	1.32	2.32	3.33	4.33	4.58	4.83	5.08	5.33	5.58	5.83	6.08	6.33	6.58	6.83	7.08
99.25	.48	1.49	2.49	3.49	4.50	4.75	5.00	5.25	5.50	5.75	6.00	6.25	6.50	6.75	7.00	7.25
99.00	.65	1.65	2.66	3.66	4.66	4.91	5.17	5.42	5.67	5.92	6.17	6.42	6.67	6.92	7.17	7.42
98.75	.81	1.82	2.82	3.83	4.83	5.08	5.33	5.59	5.84	6.09	6.34	6.59	6.84	7.09	7.34	7.60
98.50	.98	1.98	2.99	4.00	5.00	5.25	5.50	5.76	6.01	6.26	6.51	6.76	7.01	7.26	7.52	7.77
98.25	1.14	2.15	3.16	4.16	5.17	5.42	5.67	5.93	6.18	6.43	6.68	6.93	7.18	7.44	7.69	7.94
98.00	1.31	2.32	3.33	4.33	5.34	5.59	5.85	6.10	6.35	6.60	6.85	7.10	7.36	7.61	7.86	8.11
97.75	1.48	2.49	3.49	4.50	5.51	5.76	6.02	6.27	6.52	6.77	7.03	7.28	7.53	7.78	8.03	8.29
97.50	1.65	2.65	3.66	4.67	5.68	5.94	6.19	6.44	6.69	6.95	7.20	7.45	7.70	7.96	8.21	8.46
97.25	1.81	2.82	3.83	4.84	5.86	6.11	6.36	6.61	6.87	7.12	7.37	7.62	7.88	8.13	8.38	8.64
97.00	1.98	2.99	4.01	5.02	6.03	6.28	6.53	6.79	7.04	7.29	7.55	7.80	8.05	8.31	8.56	8.81
96.75	2.15	3.16	4.18	5.19	6.20	6.46	6.71	6.96	7.21	7.47	7.72	7.97	8.23	8.48	8.73	8.99
96.50	2.32	3.33	4.35	5.36	6.38	6.63	6.88	7.14	7.39	7.64	7.90	8.15	8.40	8.66	8.91	9.16
96.25	2.49	3.51	4.52	5.54	6.55	6.80	7.06	7.31	7.57	7.82	8.07	8.33	8.58	8.83	9.09	9.34
96.00	2.66	3.68	4.69	5.71	6.73	6.98	7.23	7.49	7.74	8.00	8.25	8.50	8.76	9.01	9.27	9.52
95.75	2.84	3.85	4.87	5.88	6.90	7.16	7.41	7.66	7.92	8.17	8.43	8.68	8.94	9.19	9.44	9.70
95.50	3.01	4.02	5.04	6.06	7.08	7.33	7.59	7.84	8.10	8.35	8.61	8.86	9.11	9.37	9.62	9.88
95.25	3.18	4.20	5.22	6.24	7.26	7.51	7.77	8.02	8.27	8.53	8.78	9.04	9.29	9.55	9.80	10.06
95.00	3.35	4.37	5.39	6.41	7.43	7.69	7.94	8.20	8.45	8.71	8.96	9.22	9.47	9.73	9.98	10.24
94.75	3.53	4.55	5.57	6.59	7.61	7.87	8.12	8.38	8.63	8.89	9.14	9.40	9.65	9.91	10.17	10.42
94.50	3.70	4.73	5.75	6.77	7.79	8.05	8.30	8.56	8.81	9.07	9.32	9.58	9.84	10.09	10.35	10.60
94.25	3.88	4.90	5.92	6.95	7.97	8.23	8.48	8.74	8.99	9.25	9.51	9.76	10.02	10.27	10.53	10.79
94.00	4.06	5.08	6.10	7.13	8.15	8.41	8.66	8.92	9.18	9.43	9.69	9.94	10.20	10.46	10.71	10.97
93.75	4.23	5.26	6.28	7.31	8.33	8.59	8.85	9.10	9.36	9.61	9.87	10.13	10.38	10.64	10.90	11.15
93.50	4.41	5.44	6.46	7.49	8.51	8.77	9.03	9.28	9.54	9.80	10.05	10.31	10.57	10.82	11.08	11.34
93.25	4.59	5.61	6.64	7.67	8.70	8.95	9.21	9.47	9.72	9.98	10.24	10.50	10.75	11.01	11.27	11.52
93.00	4.77	5.79	6.82	7.85	8.88	9.14	9.39	9.65	9.91	10.17	10.42	10.68	10.94	11.20	11.45	11.71
92.75	4.95	5.98	7.00	8.03	9.06	9.32	9.58	9.84	10.09	10.35	10.61	10.87	11.12	11.38	11.64	11.90
92.50	5.13	6.16	7.19	8.22	9.25	9.51	9.76	10.02	10.28	10.54	10.80	11.24	11.24	11.50	11.76	12.27
92.25	5.31	6.34	7.37	8.40	9.43	9.69	9.95	10.21	10.47	10.72	10.98	11.24	11.50	11.76	12.02	12.27
92.00	5.49	6.52	7.55	8.59	9.62	9.88	10.14	10.39	10.65	10.91	11.17	11.43	11.69	11.95	12.20	12.46
91.75	5.67	6.70	7.74	8.77	9.81	10.07	10.32	10.58	10.84	11.10	11.36	11.62	11.88	12.13	12.39	12.65
91	6.22	7.26	8.30	9.33	10.37	10.63	10.89	11.15	11.41	11.67	11.93	12.19	12.45	12.71	12.97	13.23
90	6.97	8.01	9.05	10.09	11.13	11.39	11.66	11.92	12.18	12.44	12.70	12.96	13.22	13.48	13.74	14.00
89	7.72	8.77	9.81	10.86	11.91	12.17	12.43	12.69	12.96	13.22	13.48	13.74	14.00	14.27	14.53	14.79
88	8.49	9.54	10.59	11.64	12.70	12.96	13.22	13.49	13.75	14.01	14.27	14.54	14.80	15.06	15.33	15.59
87	9.27	10.33	11.38	12.44	13.50	13.76	14.02	14.29	14.55	14.82	15.08	15.35	15.61	15.88	16.14	16.40
86	10.06	11.12	12.19	13.25	14.31	14.57	14.84	15.11	15.37	15.64	15.90	16.17	16.43	16.70	16.97	17.23
85	10.87	11.94	13.00	14.07	15.14	15.40	15.67	15.94	16.20	16.47	16.74	17.00	17.27	17.54	17.81	18.07
84	11.69	12.76	13.83	14.90	15.98	16.24	16.51	16.78	17.05	17.32	17.59	17.85	18.12	18.39	18.66	18.93
83	12.52	13.60	14.68	15.75	16.83	17.10	17.37	17.64	17.91	18.18	18.45	18.72	18.99	19.26	19.53	19.80
82	13.37	14.45	15.53	16.62	17.70	17.97	18.24	18.51	18.78	19.06	19.33	19.60	19.87	20.14	20.41	20.68
81	14.23	15.32	16.41	17.50	18.59	18.86	19.13	19.40	19.68	19.95	20.22	20.49	20.77	21.04	21.31	21.59
80	15.11	16.20	17.30	18.39	19.49	19.76	20.03	20.31	20.58	20.86	21.13	21.41	21.68	21.95	22.23	22.50
79	16.00	17.10	18.20	19.30	20.40	20.68	20.95	21.23	21.51	21.78	22.06	22.33	22.61	22.88	23.16	23.44
78	16.91	18.02	19.12	20.23	21.34	21.61	21.89	22.17	22.45	22.72	23.00	23.28	23.56	23.83	24.11	24.39
77	17.84	18.95	20.06	21.18	22.29	22.57	22.85	23.13	23.40	23.68	23.96	24.24	24.52	24.80	25.08	25.36
76	18.78	19.90	21.02	22.14	23.26	23.54	23.82	24.10	24.38	24.66	24.94	25.22	25.50	25.78	26.06	26.35
75	19.75	20.87	21.99	23.12	24.25	24.53	24.81	25.09	25.38	25.66	25.94	26.22	26.50	26.79	27.07	27.35
74	20.73	21.86	22.99	24.12	25.25	25.54	25.82	26.11	26.39	26.67	26.96	27.24	27.53	27.81	28.09	28.38
73	21.73	22.86	24.00	25.14	26.28	26.57	26.85	27.14	27.42	27.71	28.00	28.28	28.57	28.85	29.14	29.43
72	22.75	23.89	25.04	26.18	27.33	27.62	27.91	28.19	28.48	28.77	29.06	29.34	29.63	29.92	30.21	30.50
71	23.79	24.94	26.09	27.25	28.40	28.69	28.98	29.27	29.56	29.85	30.14	30.43	30.72	31.01	31.30	31.59
70	24.85	26.01	27.17	28.33	29.49	29.78	30.08	30.37	30.66	30.95	31.24	31.53	31.82	32.12	32.41	32.70
69	25.93	27.10	28.27	29.44	30.61	30.90	31.20	31.49	31.78	32.08	32.37	32.66	32.96	33.25	33.54	33.84
68	27.04	28.22	29.39	30.57	31.75	32.04	32.34	32.63	32.93	33.23	33.52	33.82	34.11	34.41	34.71	35.00
67	28.17	29.35	30.54	31.73	32.91	33.21	33.51	33.81	34.10	34.40	34.70	35.00	35.29	35.59	35.89	36.19
66	29.33	30.52	31.71	32.91	34.10	34.40	34.70	35.00	35.30	35.60	35.90	36.20	36.50	36.80	37.10	37.41
65	30.51	31.71	32.91	34.12	35.32	35.62	35.93	36.23	36.53	36.83	37.13	37.44	37.74	38.04	38.35	38.65
64	31.72	32.93	34.14	35.35	36.57	36.87	37.18	37.48	37.79	38.09	38.40	38.70	39.01	39.31	39.62	39.92
63	32.96	34.18	35.40	36.62	37.85	38.15	38.46	38.76	39.07	39.38	39.69	39.99	40.30	40.61	40.92	41.22
62	34.23	35.46	36.69	37.92	39.15	39.46	39.77	40.08	40.39	40.70	41.01	41.32	41.63	41.94	42.25	42.56
61	35.53	36.76	38.00	39.25	40.49	40.80	41.11	41.43	41.74	42.05	42.36	42.68	42.99	43.30	43.61	43.93
60	36.86	38.11	39.36	40.61	41.86	42.18	42.49	42.81	43.12	43.44	43.75	44.07	44.38	44.70	45.01	45.33
59	38.22	39.48	40.74	42.01	43.27	43.59	43.91	44.22	44.54	44.86	45.18	45.49	45.81	46.13	46.45	46.77
58	39.62	40.89	42.16	43.44	44.72	45.04	45.36	45.68	46.00	46.32	46.64	46.96	47.28	47.60	47.92	48.25

MORTGAGE PRICE

Description: This table shows the price to pay for a monthly payment mortgage loan at the yield rate.

Example: The price of a 10.75 %, 3 year mortgage loan to yield 8.00 % to maturity is $ 104.10.

YIELD	INTEREST RATE, %															
	7.00%	7.25%	7.50%	7.75%	8.00%	8.25%	8.50%	8.75%	9.00%	9.25%	9.50%	9.75%	10.00%	10.25%	10.50%	10.75%
0.00	111.16	111.57	111.98	112.40	112.81	113.23	113.64	114.06	114.48	114.90	115.32	115.74	116.16	116.58	117.01	117.43
1.00	109.46	109.87	110.27	110.68	111.09	111.50	111.91	112.32	112.73	113.15	113.56	113.97	114.39	114.81	115.22	115.64
2.00	107.80	108.20	108.60	109.00	109.40	109.81	110.21	110.62	111.02	111.43	111.84	112.25	112.65	113.06	113.48	113.89
3.00	106.18	106.57	106.96	107.36	107.75	108.15	108.55	108.95	109.35	109.75	110.15	110.55	110.96	111.36	111.76	112.17
4.00	104.58	104.97	105.36	105.75	106.14	106.53	106.92	107.31	107.71	108.10	108.50	108.89	109.29	109.69	110.09	110.49
4.25	104.19	104.58	104.96	105.35	105.74	106.13	106.52	106.91	107.30	107.70	108.09	108.49	108.88	109.28	109.67	110.07
4.50	103.80	104.18	104.57	104.96	105.34	105.73	106.12	106.51	106.90	107.29	107.68	108.08	108.47	108.87	109.26	109.66
4.75	103.41	103.79	104.18	104.56	104.95	105.34	105.72	106.11	106.50	106.89	107.28	107.67	108.07	108.46	108.85	109.25
5.00	103.02	103.41	103.79	104.17	104.56	104.94	105.33	105.71	106.10	106.49	106.88	107.27	107.66	108.05	108.45	108.84
5.25	102.64	103.02	103.40	103.78	104.17	104.55	104.93	105.32	105.71	106.09	106.48	106.87	107.26	107.65	108.05	108.43
5.50	102.26	102.63	103.01	103.40	103.78	104.16	104.54	104.93	105.31	105.70	106.08	106.47	106.86	107.26	107.64	108.03
5.75	101.88	102.25	102.63	103.01	103.39	103.77	104.15	104.54	104.92	105.30	105.69	106.07	106.46	106.85	107.25	107.63
6.00	101.50	101.87	102.25	102.63	103.01	103.39	103.77	104.15	104.53	104.91	105.30	105.68	106.07	106.46	106.85	107.24
6.25	101.12	101.49	101.87	102.25	102.62	103.00	103.38	103.76	104.14	104.52	104.90	105.29	105.67	106.06	106.45	106.84
6.50	100.74	101.12	101.49	101.87	102.24	102.62	103.00	103.38	103.75	104.13	104.52	104.90	105.28	105.66	106.04	106.43
6.75	100.37	100.74	101.12	101.49	101.86	102.24	102.62	102.99	103.37	103.75	104.13	104.52	104.90	105.28	105.66	106.04
7.00	100.00	100.37	100.74	101.11	101.49	101.86	102.24	102.61	102.99	103.37	103.75	104.13	104.51	104.89	105.27	105.65
7.25	99.63	100.00	100.37	100.74	101.11	101.49	101.86	102.23	102.61	102.99	103.37	103.74	104.12	104.50	104.88	105.26
7.50	99.26	99.63	100.00	100.37	100.74	101.11	101.48	101.86	102.23	102.61	102.98	103.36	103.74	104.12	104.50	104.88
7.75	98.90	99.26	99.63	100.00	100.37	100.74	101.11	101.48	101.85	102.23	102.60	102.98	103.36	103.73	104.11	104.49
8.00	98.53	98.90	99.27	99.63	100.00	100.37	100.74	101.11	101.48	101.85	102.22	102.60	102.97	103.35	103.73	104.10
8.25	98.17	98.54	98.90	99.27	99.63	100.00	100.37	100.74	101.11	101.48	101.85	102.22	102.59	102.97	103.34	103.72
8.50	97.81	98.18	98.54	98.90	99.27	99.63	100.00	100.37	100.74	101.10	101.47	101.84	102.22	102.59	102.96	103.34
8.75	97.45	97.82	98.18	98.54	98.90	99.27	99.63	100.00	100.37	100.74	101.10	101.47	101.84	102.22	102.59	102.96
9.00	97.10	97.46	97.82	98.18	98.54	98.91	99.27	99.63	100.00	100.37	100.73	101.10	101.47	101.84	102.21	102.58
9.25	96.74	97.10	97.46	97.82	98.18	98.54	98.91	99.27	99.64	100.00	100.37	100.73	101.10	101.47	101.84	102.21
9.50	96.39	96.75	97.11	97.47	97.83	98.19	98.55	98.91	99.27	99.64	100.00	100.37	100.73	101.10	101.47	101.84
9.75	96.04	96.40	96.75	97.11	97.47	97.83	98.19	98.55	98.91	99.27	99.64	100.00	100.37	100.73	101.10	101.47
10.00	95.69	96.05	96.40	96.76	97.12	97.47	97.83	98.19	98.55	98.91	99.27	99.64	100.00	100.36	100.73	101.10
10.25	95.34	95.70	96.05	96.41	96.76	97.12	97.48	97.83	98.19	98.55	98.91	99.28	99.64	100.00	100.36	100.73
10.50	95.00	95.35	95.70	96.06	96.41	96.77	97.12	97.48	97.84	98.20	98.56	98.92	99.28	99.64	100.00	100.36
10.75	94.66	95.01	95.36	95.71	96.06	96.42	96.77	97.13	97.48	97.84	98.20	98.56	98.92	99.28	99.64	100.00
11.00	94.31	94.66	95.01	95.36	95.72	96.07	96.42	96.78	97.13	97.49	97.84	98.20	98.56	98.92	99.28	99.64
11.25	93.97	94.32	94.67	95.02	95.37	95.72	96.07	96.43	96.78	97.14	97.49	97.84	98.20	98.56	98.92	99.28
11.50	93.64	93.98	94.33	94.68	95.03	95.38	95.73	96.08	96.43	96.79	97.14	97.49	97.85	98.20	98.56	98.92
11.75	93.30	93.64	93.99	94.34	94.69	95.03	95.38	95.73	96.09	96.44	96.79	97.14	97.50	97.85	98.21	98.57
12.00	92.96	93.31	93.65	94.00	94.35	94.69	95.04	95.39	95.74	96.09	96.44	96.80	97.15	97.50	97.86	98.21
12.25	92.63	92.97	93.32	93.66	94.01	94.35	94.70	95.05	95.40	95.75	96.10	96.45	96.80	97.15	97.50	97.86
12.50	92.30	92.64	92.98	93.33	93.67	94.02	94.36	94.71	95.06	95.40	95.75	96.10	96.45	96.80	97.16	97.51
12.75	91.97	92.31	92.65	92.99	93.34	93.68	94.02	94.37	94.72	95.06	95.41	95.76	96.11	96.45	96.80	97.16
13.00	91.64	91.98	92.32	92.66	93.00	93.35	93.69	94.03	94.38	94.72	95.07	95.42	95.77	96.11	96.46	96.81
13.25	91.31	91.65	91.99	92.33	92.67	93.01	93.36	93.70	94.04	94.39	94.73	95.08	95.42	95.77	96.11	96.46
13.50	90.99	91.33	91.66	92.00	92.34	92.68	93.02	93.36	93.70	94.04	94.39	94.73	95.08	95.42	95.77	96.12
13.75	90.66	91.00	91.34	91.68	92.01	92.35	92.69	93.03	93.37	93.71	94.05	94.39	94.74	95.08	95.43	96.13
14.00	90.34	90.68	91.01	91.35	91.69	92.02	92.36	92.70	93.04	93.38	93.72	94.07	94.41	94.75	95.09	95.44
14.25	90.02	90.36	90.69	91.03	91.36	91.70	92.04	92.37	92.71	93.05	93.39	93.73	94.08	94.42	94.76	95.10
14.50	89.70	90.04	90.37	90.70	91.04	91.37	91.71	92.05	92.38	92.72	93.06	93.40	93.74	94.08	94.43	94.77
14.75	89.39	89.72	90.05	90.38	90.72	91.05	91.39	91.72	92.06	92.40	92.73	93.07	93.41	93.75	94.09	94.43
15.00	89.07	89.40	89.73	90.06	90.40	90.73	91.06	91.40	91.73	92.07	92.41	92.74	93.08	93.42	93.76	94.10
15.25	88.76	89.09	89.42	89.75	90.08	90.41	90.74	91.08	91.41	91.75	92.08	92.42	92.75	93.09	93.43	93.77
15.50	88.45	88.77	89.10	89.43	89.76	90.09	90.42	90.76	91.09	91.42	91.76	92.09	92.43	92.76	93.10	93.44
15.75	88.14	88.46	88.79	89.12	89.45	89.78	90.11	90.44	90.77	91.10	91.43	91.77	92.10	92.44	92.77	93.11
16.00	87.83	88.15	88.48	88.80	89.13	89.46	89.79	90.12	90.45	90.78	91.11	91.45	91.78	92.11	92.44	92.79
16.25	87.52	87.84	88.17	88.49	88.82	89.15	89.48	89.80	90.13	90.46	90.79	91.13	91.46	91.79	92.11	92.46
16.50	87.21	87.54	87.86	88.18	88.51	88.84	89.16	89.49	89.82	90.15	90.48	90.81	91.14	91.47	91.80	92.14
16.75	86.91	87.23	87.55	87.88	88.20	88.53	88.85	89.18	89.51	89.83	90.16	90.49	90.82	91.15	91.48	91.82
17.00	86.61	86.93	87.25	87.57	87.89	88.22	88.54	88.87	89.19	89.52	89.85	90.18	90.50	90.83	91.16	91.49
17.25	86.30	86.62	86.94	87.27	87.59	87.91	88.23	88.56	88.88	89.21	89.53	89.86	90.19	90.52	90.85	91.18
17.50	86.00	86.32	86.64	86.96	87.28	87.60	87.93	88.25	88.57	88.90	89.22	89.55	89.88	90.20	90.53	90.86
17.75	85.71	86.02	86.34	86.66	86.98	87.30	87.62	87.94	88.27	88.59	88.91	89.24	89.56	89.89	90.22	90.54
18.00	85.41	85.72	86.04	86.36	86.68	87.00	87.32	87.64	87.96	88.28	88.61	88.93	89.25	89.58	89.90	90.23
18.25	85.11	85.43	85.74	86.06	86.38	86.70	87.02	87.34	87.66	87.98	88.30	88.62	88.94	89.27	89.59	89.92
18.50	84.82	85.13	85.45	85.76	86.08	86.40	86.72	87.03	87.35	87.67	87.99	88.32	88.64	88.96	89.28	89.61
18.75	84.53	84.84	85.15	85.47	85.78	86.10	86.42	86.73	87.05	87.37	87.69	88.01	88.33	88.65	88.96	89.30
19.00	84.23	84.55	84.86	85.17	85.49	85.80	86.12	86.43	86.75	87.07	87.39	87.71	88.03	88.35	88.67	88.99
20.00	83.08	83.39	83.70	84.01	84.32	84.63	84.94	85.25	85.57	85.88	86.19	86.51	86.82	87.14	87.46	87.78
25.00	77.66	77.95	78.24	78.52	78.81	79.10	79.40	79.69	79.98	80.27	80.57	80.86	81.16	81.45	81.75	82.04
30.00	72.73	73.00	73.27	73.55	73.82	74.09	74.36	74.63	74.91	75.18	75.46	75.73	76.01	76.29	76.56	76.84

Description: This table shows the yield to maturity of a mortgage purchased at the price shown in the index.

Example: The yield to maturity of a 10.75 %, 3 year mortgage at a price of 100.00 is 10.75 %.

INTEREST RATE, %

PRICE	7.00%	7.25%	7.50%	7.75%	8.00%	8.25%	8.50%	8.75%	9.00%	9.25%	9.50%	9.75%	10.00%	10.25%	10.50%	10.75%
105	3.73	3.98	4.22	4.47	4.71	4.96	5.20	5.45	5.69	5.94	6.18	6.43	6.67	6.92	7.16	7.41
104.75	3.89	4.13	4.38	4.63	4.87	5.12	5.36	5.61	5.85	6.10	6.34	6.59	6.84	7.08	7.33	7.57
104.50	4.05	4.29	4.54	4.79	5.03	5.28	5.52	5.77	6.01	6.26	6.51	6.75	7.00	7.24	7.49	7.73
104.25	4.21	4.45	4.70	4.94	5.19	5.44	5.68	5.93	6.17	6.42	6.67	6.91	7.16	7.40	7.65	7.90
104.00	4.37	4.61	4.86	5.11	5.35	5.60	5.84	6.09	6.34	6.58	6.83	7.07	7.32	7.57	7.81	8.06
103.75	4.53	4.77	5.02	5.27	5.51	5.76	6.01	6.25	6.50	6.74	6.99	7.24	7.48	7.73	7.98	8.22
103.50	4.69	4.93	5.18	5.43	5.67	5.92	6.17	6.41	6.66	6.91	7.15	7.40	7.65	7.89	8.14	8.39
103.25	4.85	5.10	5.34	5.59	5.84	6.08	6.33	6.58	6.82	7.07	7.32	7.56	7.81	8.06	8.30	8.55
103.00	5.01	5.26	5.50	5.75	6.00	6.25	6.49	6.74	6.99	7.23	7.48	7.73	7.98	8.22	8.47	8.72
102.75	5.17	5.42	5.67	5.91	6.16	6.41	6.66	6.90	7.15	7.40	7.65	7.89	8.14	8.39	8.64	8.88
102.50	5.34	5.58	5.83	6.08	6.33	6.57	6.82	7.07	7.32	7.56	7.81	8.06	8.31	8.55	8.80	9.05
102.25	5.50	5.75	5.99	6.24	6.49	6.74	6.99	7.23	7.48	7.73	7.98	8.22	8.47	8.72	8.97	9.22
102.00	5.66	5.91	6.16	6.41	6.66	6.90	7.15	7.40	7.65	7.90	8.14	8.39	8.64	8.89	9.14	9.38
101.75	5.83	6.08	6.32	6.57	6.82	7.07	7.32	7.57	7.81	8.06	8.31	8.56	8.81	9.06	9.30	9.55
101.50	5.99	6.24	6.49	6.74	6.99	7.24	7.48	7.73	7.98	8.23	8.48	8.73	8.97	9.22	9.47	9.72
101.25	6.16	6.41	6.66	6.90	7.15	7.40	7.65	7.90	8.15	8.40	8.65	8.89	9.14	9.39	9.64	9.89
101.00	6.32	6.57	6.82	7.07	7.32	7.57	7.82	8.07	8.32	8.57	8.81	9.06	9.31	9.56	9.81	10.06
100.75	6.49	6.74	6.99	7.24	7.49	7.74	7.99	8.24	8.49	8.73	8.98	9.23	9.48	9.73	9.98	10.23
100.50	6.66	6.91	7.16	7.41	7.66	7.91	8.16	8.41	8.65	8.90	9.15	9.40	9.65	9.90	10.15	10.40
100.25	6.83	7.08	7.33	7.58	7.83	8.08	8.33	8.57	8.82	9.07	9.32	9.57	9.82	10.07	10.32	10.57
100.00	7.00	7.25	7.50	7.75	8.00	8.25	8.50	8.75	9.00	9.25	9.50	9.75	10.00	10.25	10.50	10.75
99.75	7.16	7.41	7.66	7.91	8.17	8.42	8.67	8.92	9.17	9.42	9.67	9.92	10.17	10.42	10.67	10.92
99.50	7.33	7.58	7.83	8.09	8.34	8.59	8.84	9.09	9.34	9.59	9.84	10.09	10.34	10.59	10.84	11.09
99.25	7.50	7.75	8.01	8.26	8.51	8.76	9.01	9.26	9.51	9.76	10.01	10.26	10.51	10.76	11.01	11.27
99.00	7.68	7.93	8.18	8.43	8.68	8.93	9.18	9.43	9.68	9.93	10.19	10.44	10.69	10.94	11.19	11.44
98.75	7.85	8.10	8.35	8.60	8.85	9.10	9.35	9.61	9.86	10.11	10.36	10.61	10.86	11.11	11.36	11.62
98.50	8.02	8.27	8.52	8.77	9.02	9.28	9.53	9.78	10.03	10.28	10.53	10.79	11.04	11.29	11.54	11.79
98.25	8.19	8.44	8.70	8.95	9.20	9.45	9.70	9.95	10.21	10.46	10.71	10.96	11.21	11.46	11.72	11.97
98.00	8.36	8.62	8.87	9.12	9.37	9.62	9.88	10.13	10.38	10.63	10.89	11.14	11.39	11.64	11.89	12.15
97.75	8.54	8.79	9.04	9.30	9.55	9.80	10.05	10.30	10.56	10.81	11.06	11.31	11.57	11.82	12.07	12.32
97.50	8.71	8.97	9.22	9.47	9.72	9.98	10.23	10.48	10.73	10.99	11.24	11.49	11.74	12.00	12.25	12.50
97.25	8.89	9.14	9.39	9.65	9.90	10.15	10.41	10.66	10.91	11.16	11.42	11.67	11.92	12.18	12.43	12.68
97.00	9.06	9.32	9.57	9.82	10.08	10.33	10.58	10.84	11.09	11.34	11.60	11.85	12.10	12.35	12.61	12.86
96.75	9.24	9.49	9.75	10.00	10.25	10.51	10.76	11.01	11.27	11.52	11.77	12.03	12.28	12.53	12.79	13.04
96.50	9.42	9.67	9.93	10.18	10.43	10.69	10.94	11.19	11.45	11.70	11.95	12.21	12.46	12.72	12.97	13.22
96.25	9.60	9.85	10.10	10.36	10.61	10.87	11.12	11.37	11.63	11.88	12.13	12.39	12.64	12.90	13.15	13.40
96.00	9.77	10.03	10.28	10.54	10.79	11.04	11.30	11.55	11.81	12.06	12.32	12.57	12.82	13.08	13.33	13.59
95.75	9.95	10.21	10.46	10.72	10.97	11.23	11.48	11.73	11.99	12.24	12.50	12.75	13.01	13.26	13.52	13.77
95.50	10.13	10.39	10.64	10.90	11.15	11.41	11.66	11.92	12.17	12.43	12.68	12.93	13.19	13.44	13.70	13.95
95.25	10.31	10.57	10.82	11.08	11.33	11.59	11.84	12.10	12.35	12.61	12.86	13.12	13.37	13.63	13.88	14.14
95.00	10.49	10.75	11.00	11.26	11.52	11.77	12.03	12.28	12.54	12.79	13.05	13.30	13.56	13.81	14.07	14.32
94.75	10.68	10.93	11.19	11.44	11.70	11.95	12.21	12.46	12.72	12.98	13.23	13.49	13.74	14.00	14.25	14.51
94	11.23	11.48	11.74	11.99	12.25	12.51	12.76	13.02	13.28	13.53	13.79	14.05	14.30	14.56	14.81	15.07
93	11.97	12.22	12.48	12.74	13.00	13.25	13.51	13.77	14.03	14.28	14.54	14.80	15.06	15.32	15.57	15.83
92	12.72	12.98	13.24	13.50	13.76	14.01	14.27	14.53	14.79	15.05	15.31	15.57	15.82	16.08	16.34	16.60
91	13.49	13.75	14.01	14.27	14.52	14.78	15.04	15.30	15.56	15.82	16.08	16.34	16.60	16.86	17.12	17.38
90	14.26	14.52	14.78	15.05	15.31	15.57	15.83	16.09	16.35	16.61	16.87	17.13	17.40	17.66	17.92	18.18
89	15.05	15.31	15.58	15.84	16.10	16.36	16.63	16.89	17.15	17.41	17.68	17.94	18.20	18.46	18.72	18.99
88	15.85	16.12	16.38	16.64	16.91	17.17	17.44	17.70	17.96	18.23	18.49	18.75	19.02	19.28	19.54	19.81
87	16.67	16.93	17.20	17.46	17.73	17.99	18.26	18.52	18.79	19.05	19.32	19.58	19.85	20.11	20.38	20.64
86	17.50	17.76	18.03	18.30	18.56	18.83	19.09	19.36	19.63	19.89	20.16	20.43	20.69	20.96	21.23	21.49
85	18.34	18.61	18.88	19.14	19.41	19.68	19.95	20.21	20.48	20.75	21.02	21.28	21.55	21.82	22.09	22.36
84	19.20	19.47	19.74	20.00	20.27	20.54	20.81	21.08	21.35	21.62	21.89	22.16	22.43	22.69	22.96	23.23
83	20.07	20.34	20.61	20.88	21.15	21.42	21.69	21.96	22.23	22.50	22.77	23.04	23.31	23.58	23.86	24.13
82	20.96	21.23	21.50	21.77	22.04	22.31	22.59	22.86	23.13	23.40	23.67	23.95	24.22	24.49	24.76	25.04
81	21.86	22.13	22.40	22.68	22.95	23.22	23.50	23.77	24.04	24.32	24.59	24.87	25.14	25.41	25.69	25.96
80	22.78	23.05	23.33	23.60	23.88	24.15	24.43	24.70	24.98	25.25	25.53	25.80	26.08	26.35	26.63	26.90
79	23.71	23.99	24.27	24.54	24.82	25.09	25.37	25.65	25.92	26.20	26.48	26.75	27.03	27.31	27.58	27.86
78	24.67	24.94	25.22	25.50	25.78	26.06	26.33	26.61	26.89	27.17	27.45	27.73	28.00	28.28	28.56	28.84
77	25.64	25.92	26.20	26.48	26.76	27.03	27.31	27.59	27.87	28.15	28.43	28.71	28.99	29.27	29.56	29.84
76	26.63	26.91	27.19	27.47	27.75	28.03	28.31	28.60	28.88	29.16	29.44	29.72	30.00	30.29	30.57	30.85
75	27.64	27.92	28.20	28.48	28.77	29.05	29.33	29.62	29.90	30.18	30.47	30.75	31.03	31.32	31.60	31.89
74	28.66	28.95	29.23	29.52	29.80	30.09	30.37	30.66	30.94	31.23	31.51	31.80	32.08	32.37	32.66	32.94
73	29.71	30.00	30.29	30.57	30.86	31.15	31.43	31.72	32.01	32.29	32.58	32.87	33.16	33.44	33.73	34.02
72	30.78	31.07	31.36	31.65	31.94	32.23	32.52	32.80	33.09	33.38	33.67	33.96	34.25	34.54	34.83	35.12
71	31.88	32.17	32.46	32.75	33.04	33.33	33.62	33.91	34.20	34.49	34.78	35.08	35.37	35.66	35.95	36.24
70	32.99	33.29	33.58	33.87	34.16	34.46	34.75	35.04	35.33	35.63	35.92	36.21	36.51	36.80	37.09	37.39
69	34.13	34.43	34.72	35.02	35.31	35.61	35.90	36.20	36.49	36.79	37.08	37.38	37.67	37.97	38.26	38.56

MORTGAGE PRICE

Description: This table shows the price to pay for a monthly payment mortgage loan at the yield rate.

Example: The price of a 15.00 %, 3 year mortgage loan to yield 8.00 % to maturity is $ 110.62.

INTEREST RATE, %

YIELD	11.00%	11.25%	11.50%	11.75%	12.00%	12.25%	12.50%	12.75%	13.00%	13.25%	13.50%	13.75%	14.00%	14.25%	14.50%	15.00%
0.00	117.86	118.29	118.71	119.14	119.57	120.00	120.43	120.87	121.30	121.73	122.17	122.60	123.04	123.48	123.92	124.80
1.00	116.06	116.48	116.90	117.32	117.75	118.17	118.60	119.02	119.45	119.88	120.30	120.73	121.16	121.59	122.03	122.89
2.00	114.30	114.71	115.13	115.54	115.96	116.38	116.80	117.22	117.64	118.06	118.48	118.90	119.32	119.75	120.17	121.03
3.00	112.58	112.98	113.39	113.80	114.21	114.62	115.04	115.45	115.86	116.28	116.69	117.11	117.52	117.94	118.36	119.20
4.00	110.89	111.29	111.69	112.10	112.50	112.90	113.31	113.72	114.12	114.53	114.94	115.35	115.76	116.17	116.59	117.41
4.25	110.47	110.87	111.27	111.67	112.08	112.48	112.88	113.29	113.70	114.10	114.51	114.92	115.33	115.74	116.15	116.97
4.50	110.06	110.46	110.86	111.26	111.66	112.06	112.46	112.86	113.27	113.67	114.08	114.49	114.89	115.30	115.71	116.53
4.75	109.65	110.04	110.44	110.84	111.24	111.64	112.04	112.44	112.84	113.25	113.65	114.06	114.46	114.87	115.28	116.10
5.00	109.24	109.63	110.03	110.42	110.82	111.22	111.62	112.02	112.42	112.82	113.23	113.63	114.04	114.44	114.85	115.66
5.25	108.83	109.22	109.62	110.01	110.41	110.81	111.20	111.60	112.00	112.40	112.80	113.21	113.61	114.01	114.42	115.23
5.50	108.42	108.81	109.21	109.60	110.00	110.39	110.79	111.19	111.58	111.98	112.38	112.78	113.19	113.59	113.99	114.80
5.75	108.02	108.41	108.80	109.19	109.59	109.98	110.38	110.77	111.17	111.57	111.97	112.36	112.76	113.17	113.57	114.37
6.00	107.62	108.01	108.40	108.79	109.18	109.57	109.97	110.36	110.76	111.15	111.55	111.95	112.35	112.74	113.15	113.95
6.25	107.22	107.60	107.99	108.38	108.77	109.16	109.56	109.95	110.34	110.74	111.13	111.53	111.93	112.33	112.73	113.53
6.50	106.82	107.20	107.59	107.98	108.37	108.76	109.15	109.54	109.93	110.33	110.72	111.12	111.51	111.91	112.31	113.10
6.75	106.42	106.81	107.19	107.58	107.97	108.36	108.75	109.14	109.53	109.92	110.31	110.71	111.10	111.50	111.89	112.69
7.00	106.03	106.41	106.80	107.18	107.57	107.96	108.34	108.73	109.12	109.51	109.90	110.30	110.69	111.08	111.48	112.27
7.25	105.64	106.02	106.40	106.79	107.17	107.56	107.94	108.33	108.72	109.11	109.50	109.89	110.28	110.67	111.07	111.85
7.50	105.25	105.63	106.01	106.39	106.78	107.16	107.55	107.93	108.32	108.71	109.09	109.48	109.87	110.26	110.66	111.44
7.75	104.86	105.24	105.62	106.00	106.38	106.77	107.15	107.53	107.92	108.31	108.69	109.08	109.47	109.86	110.25	111.03
8.00	104.48	104.85	105.23	105.61	105.99	106.37	106.76	107.14	107.52	107.91	108.29	108.68	109.07	109.45	109.84	110.62
8.25	104.09	104.47	104.85	105.22	105.60	105.98	106.36	106.75	107.13	107.51	107.90	108.28	108.67	109.05	109.44	110.22
8.50	103.71	104.09	104.46	104.84	105.22	105.60	105.97	106.36	106.74	107.12	107.50	107.88	108.27	108.65	109.04	109.81
8.75	103.33	103.70	104.08	104.46	104.83	105.21	105.59	105.97	106.35	106.73	107.11	107.49	107.87	108.26	108.64	109.41
9.00	102.95	103.33	103.70	104.07	104.45	104.82	105.20	105.58	105.96	106.34	106.72	107.10	107.48	107.86	108.24	109.01
9.25	102.58	102.95	103.32	103.69	104.07	104.44	104.82	105.19	105.57	105.95	106.33	106.71	107.09	107.47	107.85	108.61
9.50	102.20	102.57	102.94	103.32	103.69	104.06	104.44	104.81	105.19	105.56	105.94	106.32	106.70	107.09	107.47	108.22
9.75	101.83	102.20	102.57	102.94	103.31	103.68	104.06	104.43	104.80	105.18	105.55	105.93	106.31	106.69	107.06	107.82
10.00	101.46	101.83	102.20	102.57	102.94	103.31	103.68	104.05	104.42	104.80	105.17	105.54	105.92	106.30	106.67	107.43
10.25	101.09	101.46	101.83	102.19	102.56	102.93	103.30	103.67	104.04	104.42	104.79	105.16	105.54	105.91	106.29	107.04
10.50	100.73	101.09	101.46	101.82	102.19	102.56	102.93	103.30	103.67	104.04	104.41	104.78	105.15	105.53	105.90	106.65
10.75	100.36	100.73	101.09	101.45	101.82	102.19	102.55	102.92	103.29	103.66	104.03	104.40	104.77	105.15	105.52	106.27
11.00	100.00	100.36	100.72	101.09	101.45	101.82	102.18	102.55	102.92	103.29	103.65	104.02	104.40	104.77	105.14	105.88
11.25	99.64	100.00	100.36	100.72	101.09	101.45	101.82	102.18	102.55	102.92	103.29	103.65	104.02	104.40	104.77	105.50
11.50	99.28	99.64	100.00	100.36	100.72	101.09	101.45	101.81	102.18	102.55	102.91	103.28	103.65	104.02	104.39	104.76	105.50
11.75	98.92	99.28	99.64	100.00	100.36	100.72	101.08	101.45	101.81	102.17	102.54	102.91	103.28	103.64	104.01	104.38	105.12
12.00	98.57	98.92	99.28	99.64	100.00	100.36	100.72	101.08	101.44	101.81	102.17	102.54	102.90	103.27	103.64	104.01	104.74
12.25	98.21	98.57	98.93	99.28	99.64	100.00	100.36	100.72	101.08	101.44	101.80	102.17	102.53	102.90	103.26	103.63	104.37
12.50	97.86	98.22	98.57	98.93	99.28	99.64	100.00	100.36	100.72	101.08	101.44	101.80	102.16	102.53	102.90	103.26	103.99
12.75	97.51	97.87	98.22	98.57	98.93	99.29	99.64	100.00	100.36	100.72	101.08	101.44	101.80	102.16	102.52	102.89	103.62
13.00	97.16	97.52	97.87	98.22	98.58	98.93	99.29	99.64	100.00	100.36	100.72	101.08	101.44	101.80	102.16	102.88	103.25
13.25	96.82	97.17	97.52	97.87	98.23	98.58	98.93	99.29	99.64	100.00	100.36	100.72	101.08	101.44	101.80	102.16	102.88
13.50	96.47	96.82	97.17	97.52	97.88	98.23	98.58	98.93	99.29	99.64	100.00	100.36	100.72	101.07	101.43	101.79	102.52
13.75	96.13	96.48	96.83	97.18	97.53	97.88	98.23	98.58	98.94	99.29	99.64	100.00	100.36	100.71	101.07	101.43	102.15
14.00	95.79	96.14	96.48	96.83	97.18	97.53	97.88	98.23	98.58	98.94	99.29	99.64	100.00	100.36	100.71	101.07	101.79
14.25	95.45	95.80	96.14	96.49	96.84	97.19	97.53	97.88	98.24	98.59	98.94	99.29	99.65	100.00	100.36	100.71	101.43
14.50	95.11	95.46	95.80	96.15	96.49	96.84	97.19	97.54	97.89	98.24	98.59	98.94	99.29	99.65	100.00	100.36	101.07
14.75	94.78	95.12	95.46	95.81	96.15	96.50	96.85	97.19	97.54	97.89	98.24	98.59	98.94	99.29	99.65	100.00	100.71
15.00	94.44	94.78	95.13	95.47	95.81	96.16	96.50	96.85	97.20	97.55	97.89	98.24	98.59	98.94	99.30	100.00	100.35
15.25	94.11	94.45	94.79	95.13	95.48	95.82	96.16	96.51	96.86	97.20	97.55	97.90	98.25	98.60	98.95	99.65	100.00
15.50	93.78	94.12	94.46	94.80	95.14	95.48	95.83	96.17	96.51	96.86	97.21	97.55	97.90	98.25	98.60	98.95	99.65
15.75	93.45	93.79	94.13	94.47	94.81	95.15	95.49	95.83	96.18	96.52	96.86	97.21	97.56	97.90	98.25	99.30
16.00	93.12	93.46	93.80	94.13	94.47	94.81	95.15	95.50	95.84	96.18	96.52	96.87	97.21	97.56	97.91	98.95
16.25	92.80	93.13	93.47	93.81	94.14	94.48	94.82	95.16	95.50	95.84	96.19	96.53	96.87	97.22	97.56	98.60
16.50	92.47	92.81	93.14	93.48	93.81	94.15	94.49	94.83	95.17	95.51	95.85	96.19	96.54	96.88	97.22	98.26
16.75	92.15	92.48	92.82	93.15	93.49	93.82	94.16	94.50	94.84	95.18	95.52	95.86	96.20	96.54	96.88	97.91
17.00	91.83	92.16	92.49	92.83	93.16	93.50	93.83	94.17	94.51	94.84	95.18	95.52	95.86	96.20	96.55	97.23
17.25	91.51	91.84	92.17	92.50	92.84	93.17	93.51	93.84	94.18	94.51	94.85	95.19	95.53	95.87	96.21	96.89
17.50	91.19	91.52	91.85	92.18	92.51	92.85	93.18	93.51	93.85	94.19	94.52	94.86	95.20	95.54	95.87	96.56
17.75	90.87	91.20	91.53	91.86	92.19	92.52	92.86	93.19	93.52	93.86	94.19	94.53	94.87	95.20	95.54	96.22
18.00	90.56	90.89	91.21	91.54	91.87	92.20	92.54	92.87	93.20	93.53	93.87	94.20	94.54	94.87	95.21	95.89
18.25	90.24	90.57	90.90	91.23	91.56	91.88	92.21	92.55	92.88	93.21	93.54	93.88	94.21	94.55	94.88	95.55
18.50	89.93	90.26	90.58	90.91	91.24	91.57	91.90	92.23	92.56	92.89	93.22	93.55	93.89	94.22	94.55	95.22
18.75	89.62	89.95	90.27	90.60	90.92	91.25	91.58	91.91	92.24	92.57	92.90	93.23	93.56	93.89	94.23	94.90
19.00	89.31	89.64	89.96	90.29	90.61	90.94	91.26	91.59	91.92	92.25	92.58	92.91	93.24	93.57	93.90	94.57
20.00	88.09	88.41	88.73	89.05	89.37	89.69	90.02	90.34	90.66	90.99	91.31	91.64	91.97	92.29	92.62	93.28
25.00	82.34	82.64	82.94	83.24	83.54	83.84	84.14	84.44	84.74	85.05	85.35	85.66	85.96	86.27	86.57	87.19
30.00	77.12	77.40	77.68	77.96	78.24	78.52	78.80	79.09	79.37	79.65	79.94	80.22	80.51	80.80	81.08	81.66

MORTGAGE YIELD

Description: This table shows the yield to maturity of a mortgage purchased at the price shown in the index.

Example: The yield to maturity of a 15.00 %, 3 year mortgage at a price of 102.00 is 13.60 %.

INTEREST RATE, %

PRICE	11.00%	11.25%	11.50%	11.75%	12.00%	12.25%	12.50%	12.75%	13.00%	13.25%	13.50%	13.75%	14.00%	14.25%	14.50%	15.00%
110	4.53	4.77	5.01	5.25	5.49	5.73	5.97	6.21	6.46	6.70	6.94	7.18	7.42	7.66	7.90	8.38
109	5.14	5.38	5.62	5.86	6.11	6.35	6.59	6.83	7.07	7.31	7.55	7.80	8.04	8.28	8.52	9.00
108	5.76	6.00	6.24	6.48	6.73	6.97	7.21	7.45	7.69	7.94	8.18	8.42	8.66	8.91	9.15	9.63
107	6.38	6.62	6.87	7.11	7.35	7.60	7.84	8.08	8.33	8.57	8.81	9.06	9.30	9.54	9.79	10.27
106	7.01	7.26	7.50	7.75	7.99	8.23	8.48	8.72	8.97	9.21	9.46	9.70	9.94	10.19	10.43	10.92
105.75	7.17	7.42	7.66	7.91	8.15	8.40	8.64	8.88	9.13	9.37	9.62	9.86	10.11	10.35	10.59	11.08
105.50	7.33	7.58	7.82	8.07	8.31	8.56	8.80	9.05	9.29	9.54	9.78	10.02	10.27	10.51	10.76	11.25
105.25	7.49	7.74	7.98	8.23	8.47	8.72	8.96	9.21	9.45	9.70	9.94	10.19	10.43	10.68	10.92	11.41
105.00	7.66	7.90	8.15	8.39	8.64	8.88	9.13	9.37	9.62	9.86	10.11	10.35	10.60	10.84	11.09	11.58
104.75	7.82	8.06	8.31	8.55	8.80	9.04	9.29	9.53	9.78	10.02	10.27	10.52	10.76	11.01	11.25	11.74
104.50	7.98	8.22	8.47	8.72	8.96	9.21	9.45	9.70	9.94	10.19	10.43	10.68	10.93	11.17	11.42	11.91
104.25	8.14	8.39	8.63	8.88	9.13	9.37	9.62	9.86	10.11	10.35	10.60	10.85	11.09	11.34	11.58	12.07
104.00	8.30	8.55	8.80	9.04	9.29	9.54	9.78	10.03	10.27	10.52	10.77	11.01	11.26	11.50	11.75	12.24
103.75	8.47	8.72	8.96	9.21	9.45	9.70	9.95	10.19	10.44	10.69	10.93	11.18	11.42	11.67	11.92	12.41
103.50	8.63	8.88	9.13	9.37	9.62	9.87	10.11	10.36	10.61	10.85	11.10	11.34	11.59	11.84	12.08	12.58
103.25	8.80	9.05	9.29	9.54	9.79	10.03	10.28	10.53	10.77	11.02	11.27	11.51	11.76	12.01	12.25	12.75
103.00	8.96	9.21	9.46	9.70	9.95	10.20	10.45	10.69	10.94	11.19	11.43	11.68	11.93	12.17	12.42	12.92
102.75	9.13	9.38	9.62	9.87	10.12	10.37	10.61	10.86	11.11	11.36	11.60	11.85	12.10	12.34	12.59	13.09
102.50	9.30	9.54	9.79	10.04	10.29	10.53	10.78	11.03	11.28	11.52	11.77	12.02	12.27	12.51	12.76	13.26
102.25	9.46	9.71	9.96	10.21	10.45	10.70	10.95	11.20	11.45	11.69	11.94	12.19	12.44	12.68	12.93	13.43
102.00	9.63	9.88	10.13	10.38	10.62	10.87	11.12	11.37	11.62	11.86	12.11	12.36	12.61	12.86	13.10	13.60
101.75	9.80	10.05	10.30	10.54	10.79	11.04	11.29	11.54	11.79	12.03	12.28	12.53	12.78	12.95	13.28	13.77
101.50	9.97	10.22	10.47	10.71	10.96	11.21	11.46	11.71	11.96	12.21	12.45	12.70	12.95	13.20	13.45	13.94
101.25	10.14	10.39	10.64	10.88	11.13	11.38	11.63	11.88	12.13	12.38	12.63	12.87	13.12	13.37	13.62	14.12
101.00	10.31	10.56	10.81	11.06	11.30	11.55	11.80	12.05	12.30	12.55	12.80	13.05	13.30	13.55	13.79	14.29
100.75	10.48	10.73	10.98	11.23	11.48	11.73	11.97	12.22	12.47	12.72	12.97	13.22	13.47	13.72	13.97	14.47
100.50	10.65	10.90	11.15	11.40	11.65	11.90	12.15	12.40	12.65	12.90	13.15	13.39	13.64	13.89	14.14	14.64
100.25	10.82	11.07	11.32	11.57	11.82	12.07	12.32	12.57	12.82	13.07	13.32	13.57	13.82	14.07	14.32	14.82
100.00	11.00	11.25	11.50	11.75	12.00	12.25	12.50	12.75	13.00	13.25	13.50	13.75	14.00	14.25	14.50	15.00
99.75	11.17	11.42	11.67	11.92	12.17	12.42	12.67	12.92	13.17	13.42	13.67	13.92	14.17	14.42	14.67	15.17
99.50	11.34	11.59	11.84	12.09	12.34	12.59	12.85	13.10	13.35	13.60	13.85	14.10	14.35	14.60	14.85	15.35
99.25	11.52	11.77	12.02	12.27	12.52	12.77	13.02	13.27	13.52	13.77	14.02	14.27	14.53	14.78	15.03	15.53
99.00	11.69	11.94	12.19	12.44	12.70	12.95	13.20	13.45	13.70	13.95	14.20	14.45	14.70	14.95	15.21	15.71
98.75	11.87	12.12	12.37	12.62	12.87	13.12	13.37	13.63	13.88	14.13	14.38	14.63	14.88	15.13	15.39	15.89
98.50	12.04	12.29	12.55	12.80	13.05	13.30	13.55	13.80	14.06	14.31	14.56	14.81	15.06	15.31	15.57	16.07
98.25	12.22	12.47	12.72	12.98	13.23	13.48	13.73	13.98	14.23	14.49	14.74	14.99	15.24	15.49	15.75	16.25
98.00	12.40	12.65	12.90	13.15	13.41	13.66	13.91	14.16	14.41	14.67	14.92	15.17	15.42	15.67	15.93	16.43
97.75	12.58	12.83	13.08	13.33	13.59	13.84	14.09	14.34	14.59	14.85	15.10	15.35	15.60	15.86	16.11	16.61
97.50	12.75	13.01	13.26	13.51	13.76	14.02	14.27	14.52	14.78	15.03	15.28	15.53	15.79	16.04	16.29	16.80
97.25	12.93	13.19	13.44	13.69	13.95	14.20	14.45	14.70	14.96	15.21	15.46	15.72	15.97	16.22	16.47	16.98
97.00	13.11	13.37	13.62	13.87	14.13	14.38	14.63	14.89	15.14	15.39	15.65	15.90	16.15	16.41	16.66	17.17
96.75	13.29	13.55	13.80	14.06	14.31	14.56	14.82	15.07	15.32	15.58	15.83	16.08	16.34	16.59	16.84	17.35
96.50	13.48	13.73	13.98	14.24	14.49	14.74	15.00	15.25	15.51	15.76	16.01	16.27	16.52	16.77	17.03	17.54
96.25	13.66	13.91	14.17	14.42	14.67	14.93	15.18	15.44	15.69	15.94	16.20	16.45	16.71	16.96	17.21	17.72
96.00	13.84	14.10	14.35	14.60	14.86	15.11	15.37	15.62	15.88	16.13	16.38	16.64	16.89	17.15	17.40	17.91
95.75	14.02	14.28	14.53	14.79	15.04	15.30	15.55	15.81	16.06	16.32	16.57	16.82	17.08	17.33	17.59	18.10
95.50	14.21	14.46	14.72	14.97	15.23	15.48	15.74	15.99	16.25	16.50	16.76	17.01	17.27	17.52	17.78	18.29
95.25	14.39	14.65	14.90	15.16	15.41	15.67	15.92	16.18	16.43	16.69	16.94	17.20	17.45	17.71	17.97	18.48
95.00	14.58	14.83	15.09	15.34	15.60	15.86	16.11	16.37	16.62	16.88	17.13	17.39	17.64	17.90	18.15	18.67
94.75	14.76	15.02	15.28	15.53	15.79	16.04	16.30	16.55	16.81	17.07	17.32	17.58	17.83	18.09	18.35	18.86
94.50	14.95	15.21	15.46	15.72	15.98	16.23	16.49	16.74	17.00	17.26	17.51	17.77	18.02	18.28	18.54	19.05
94.25	15.14	15.40	15.65	15.91	16.16	16.42	16.68	16.93	17.19	17.45	17.70	17.96	18.21	18.47	18.73	19.24
94.00	15.33	15.58	15.84	16.10	16.35	16.61	16.87	17.12	17.38	17.64	17.89	18.15	18.41	18.66	18.92	19.43
93.75	15.52	15.77	16.03	16.29	16.54	16.80	17.06	17.31	17.57	17.83	18.09	18.34	18.60	18.86	19.11	19.63
93	16.09	16.35	16.60	16.86	17.12	17.38	17.63	17.89	18.15	18.41	18.67	18.92	19.18	19.44	19.70	20.21
92	16.86	17.12	17.38	17.64	17.90	18.15	18.41	18.67	18.93	19.19	19.45	19.71	19.97	20.23	20.49	21.00
91	17.64	17.90	18.16	18.42	18.68	18.94	19.20	19.47	19.73	19.99	20.25	20.51	20.77	21.03	21.29	21.81
90	18.44	18.70	18.96	19.22	19.49	19.75	20.01	20.27	20.53	20.79	21.06	21.32	21.58	21.84	22.10	22.62
89	19.25	19.51	19.78	20.04	20.30	20.56	20.83	21.09	21.35	21.61	21.88	22.14	22.40	22.67	22.93	23.45
88	20.07	20.34	20.60	20.86	21.13	21.39	21.66	21.92	22.18	22.45	22.71	22.98	23.24	23.51	23.77	24.30
87	20.91	21.17	21.44	21.70	21.97	22.24	22.50	22.77	23.03	23.30	23.56	23.83	24.09	24.36	24.62	25.16
86	21.76	22.03	22.29	22.56	22.83	23.09	23.36	23.63	23.89	24.16	24.43	24.69	24.96	25.23	25.49	26.03
85	22.62	22.89	23.16	23.43	23.70	23.96	24.23	24.50	24.77	25.04	25.30	25.57	25.84	26.11	26.38	26.92
84	23.50	23.77	24.04	24.31	24.58	24.85	25.12	25.39	25.66	25.93	26.20	26.47	26.74	27.01	27.28	27.82
83	24.40	24.67	24.94	25.21	25.48	25.75	26.02	26.29	26.57	26.84	27.11	27.38	27.65	27.92	28.19	28.74
82	25.31	25.58	25.85	26.12	26.40	26.67	26.94	27.22	27.49	27.76	28.03	28.31	28.58	28.85	29.13	29.67
81	26.23	26.51	26.78	27.06	27.33	27.60	27.88	28.15	28.43	28.70	28.98	29.25	29.53	29.80	30.07	30.62
80	27.18	27.45	27.73	28.00	28.28	28.56	28.83	29.11	29.38	29.66	29.94	30.21	30.49	30.76	31.04	31.59

MORTGAGE PRICE

Description: This table shows the price to pay for a monthly payment mortgage loan at the yield rate.

Example: The price of a 6.75 %, 4 year mortgage loan to yield 8.00 % to maturity is $ 97.61.

INTEREST RATE, %

YIELD	0.00%	1.00%	2.00%	3.00%	4.00%	4.25%	4.50%	4.75%	5.00%	5.25%	5.50%	5.75%	6.00%	6.25%	6.50%	6.75%
0.00	100.00	102.05	104.14	106.24	108.38	108.92	109.46	110.00	110.54	111.09	111.63	112.18	112.73	113.28	113.83	114.39
1.00	97.99	100.00	102.04	104.11	106.20	106.72	107.25	107.78	108.31	108.85	109.38	109.92	110.46	111.00	111.54	112.08
2.00	96.03	98.00	100.00	102.02	104.07	104.59	105.11	105.63	106.15	106.67	107.20	107.72	108.25	108.78	109.31	109.84
3.00	94.12	96.06	98.02	100.00	102.01	102.52	103.02	103.53	104.04	104.56	105.07	105.59	106.10	106.62	107.14	107.66
4.00	92.27	94.16	96.09	98.03	100.00	100.50	100.99	101.49	101.99	102.50	103.00	103.51	104.01	104.52	105.03	105.54
4.25	91.81	93.70	95.61	97.55	99.51	100.00	100.50	100.99	101.49	101.99	102.49	102.99	103.50	104.01	104.52	105.03
4.50	91.36	93.24	95.14	97.07	99.02	99.51	100.00	100.49	100.99	101.49	101.99	102.49	102.99	103.49	104.00	104.51
4.75	90.91	92.78	94.67	96.59	98.53	99.02	99.51	100.00	100.49	100.99	101.49	101.99	102.49	102.99	103.49	104.00
5.00	90.46	92.32	94.21	96.11	98.04	98.53	99.02	99.51	100.00	100.49	100.99	101.48	101.98	102.48	102.98	103.49
5.25	90.02	91.87	93.74	95.64	97.56	98.05	98.53	99.02	99.51	100.00	100.49	100.99	101.48	101.98	102.48	102.98
5.50	89.58	91.42	93.29	95.17	97.09	97.57	98.05	98.54	99.02	99.51	100.00	100.49	100.98	101.48	101.98	102.47
5.75	89.14	90.98	92.83	94.71	96.61	97.09	97.57	98.06	98.54	99.02	99.51	100.00	100.49	100.98	101.48	101.97
6.00	88.71	90.53	92.38	94.25	96.14	96.62	97.10	97.58	98.06	98.54	99.03	99.51	100.00	100.49	100.98	101.47
6.25	88.28	90.09	91.93	93.79	95.67	96.15	96.63	97.10	97.58	98.06	98.55	99.03	99.51	100.00	100.49	100.98
6.50	87.85	89.65	91.48	93.33	95.21	95.68	96.16	96.63	97.11	97.59	98.07	98.55	99.03	99.51	100.00	100.49
6.75	87.42	89.22	91.04	92.88	94.75	95.22	95.69	96.16	96.64	97.11	97.59	98.07	98.55	99.03	99.51	100.00
7.00	87.00	88.79	90.60	92.43	94.29	94.76	95.23	95.70	96.17	96.64	97.12	97.60	98.07	98.55	99.03	99.52
7.25	86.58	88.36	90.16	91.99	93.84	94.30	94.77	95.24	95.71	96.18	96.65	97.12	97.60	98.08	98.56	99.04
7.50	86.16	87.93	89.73	91.54	93.38	93.85	94.31	94.78	95.25	95.71	96.18	96.66	97.13	97.61	98.08	98.56
7.75	85.75	87.51	89.30	91.10	92.93	93.40	93.86	94.32	94.79	95.25	95.72	96.19	96.66	97.13	97.61	98.08
8.00	85.34	87.09	88.87	90.67	92.49	92.95	93.41	93.87	94.33	94.80	95.26	95.73	96.20	96.66	97.14	97.61
8.25	84.93	86.67	88.44	90.23	92.05	92.50	92.96	93.42	93.88	94.34	94.81	95.27	95.74	96.20	96.67	97.14
8.50	84.52	86.26	88.02	89.80	91.60	92.06	92.52	92.97	93.43	93.89	94.35	94.82	95.28	95.74	96.21	96.68
8.75	84.12	85.85	87.60	89.37	91.17	91.62	92.07	92.53	92.99	93.44	93.90	94.36	94.83	95.29	95.75	96.22
9.00	83.72	85.44	87.18	88.95	90.73	91.18	91.64	92.09	92.54	93.00	93.46	93.91	94.37	94.84	95.30	95.76
9.25	83.32	85.03	86.77	88.52	90.30	90.75	91.20	91.65	92.10	92.56	93.01	93.47	93.93	94.38	94.84	95.31
9.50	82.92	84.63	86.36	88.10	89.87	90.32	90.77	91.22	91.67	92.12	92.57	93.02	93.48	93.93	94.38	94.85
9.75	82.53	84.23	85.95	87.69	89.45	89.89	90.34	90.78	91.23	91.68	92.13	92.58	93.04	93.48	93.94	94.41
10.00	82.14	83.83	85.54	87.27	89.03	89.47	89.91	90.35	90.80	91.25	91.70	92.15	92.60	93.05	93.50	93.96
10.25	81.75	83.43	85.14	86.86	88.61	89.04	89.49	89.93	90.37	90.82	91.26	91.71	92.16	92.61	93.06	93.52
10.50	81.37	83.04	84.74	86.45	88.19	88.63	89.06	89.50	89.95	90.39	90.83	91.28	91.73	92.17	92.62	93.08
10.75	80.99	82.65	84.34	86.04	87.77	88.21	88.65	89.08	89.52	89.96	90.41	90.85	91.30	91.74	92.19	92.64
11.00	80.61	82.26	83.94	85.64	87.36	87.80	88.23	88.67	89.10	89.54	89.98	90.42	90.87	91.31	91.76	92.20
11.25	80.23	81.88	83.55	85.24	86.95	87.38	87.82	88.25	88.69	89.12	89.56	90.00	90.44	90.88	91.33	91.77
11.50	79.85	81.50	83.16	84.84	86.55	86.98	87.41	87.84	88.27	88.71	89.14	89.58	90.00	90.46	90.88	91.34
11.75	79.48	81.12	82.77	84.45	86.14	86.57	87.00	87.43	87.86	88.29	88.73	89.16	89.60	90.02	90.46	90.92
12.00	79.11	80.74	82.38	84.05	85.74	86.17	86.59	87.02	87.45	87.88	88.31	88.75	89.18	89.62	90.04	90.49
12.25	78.74	80.36	82.00	83.66	85.34	85.77	86.19	86.62	87.05	87.47	87.90	88.34	88.77	89.20	89.64	90.07
12.50	78.38	79.99	81.62	83.27	84.95	85.37	85.79	86.22	86.64	87.07	87.50	87.93	88.36	88.79	89.22	89.66
12.75	78.02	79.62	81.24	82.89	84.55	84.97	85.39	85.82	86.24	86.67	87.09	87.52	87.95	88.38	88.81	89.24
13.00	77.66	79.25	80.87	82.51	84.16	84.58	85.00	85.42	85.84	86.26	86.69	87.11	87.54	87.97	88.40	88.83
13.25	77.30	78.89	80.50	82.13	83.78	84.19	84.61	85.03	85.45	85.87	86.29	86.71	87.14	87.56	87.99	88.42
13.50	76.94	78.52	80.13	81.75	83.39	83.80	84.22	84.64	85.05	85.47	85.89	86.31	86.71	87.14	87.56	87.99
13.75	76.59	78.16	79.76	81.37	83.01	83.42	83.83	84.25	84.66	85.08	85.50	85.92	86.34	86.74	87.16	87.59
14.00	76.24	77.81	79.39	81.00	82.63	83.04	83.45	83.86	84.27	84.69	85.11	85.52	85.94	86.34	86.76	87.18
14.25	75.89	77.45	79.03	80.63	82.25	82.66	83.07	83.48	83.89	84.30	84.72	85.13	85.55	85.94	86.36	86.78
14.50	75.54	77.10	78.67	80.26	81.87	82.28	82.69	83.10	83.51	83.92	84.33	84.74	85.16	85.55	85.97	86.39
14.75	75.20	76.74	78.31	79.90	81.50	81.90	82.31	82.72	83.13	83.54	83.95	84.36	84.77	85.19	85.60	86.02
15.00	74.86	76.40	77.95	79.53	81.13	81.53	81.94	82.34	82.75	83.16	83.56	83.97	84.39	84.80	85.21	85.63
15.25	74.52	76.05	77.60	79.17	80.76	81.16	81.56	81.97	82.37	82.78	83.18	83.59	84.00	84.41	84.82	85.24
15.50	74.18	75.70	77.25	78.81	80.40	80.79	81.19	81.60	82.00	82.40	82.81	83.21	83.62	84.03	84.44	84.85
15.75	73.84	75.36	76.90	78.46	80.03	80.43	80.83	81.23	81.63	82.03	82.43	82.84	83.24	83.65	84.06	84.47
16.00	73.51	75.02	76.55	78.10	79.67	80.07	80.46	80.86	81.26	81.66	82.06	82.46	82.87	83.27	83.68	84.09
16.25	73.18	74.68	76.21	77.75	79.31	79.71	80.10	80.50	80.89	81.29	81.69	82.09	82.49	82.90	83.30	83.71
16.50	72.85	74.35	75.87	77.40	78.96	79.35	79.74	80.14	80.53	80.93	81.32	81.72	82.12	82.53	82.93	83.33
16.75	72.52	74.02	75.52	77.05	78.60	78.99	79.38	79.78	80.17	80.56	80.96	81.36	81.76	82.16	82.56	82.96
17.00	72.20	73.68	75.19	76.71	78.25	78.64	79.03	79.42	79.81	80.20	80.60	80.99	81.39	81.79	82.19	82.59
17.25	71.88	73.35	74.85	76.37	77.90	78.29	78.67	79.06	79.45	79.85	80.24	80.63	81.03	81.42	81.82	82.22
17.50	71.56	73.03	74.52	76.03	77.55	77.94	78.32	78.71	79.10	79.49	79.88	80.27	80.66	81.06	81.45	81.85
17.75	71.24	72.70	74.19	75.69	77.21	77.59	77.98	78.36	78.75	79.14	79.52	79.91	80.31	80.70	81.09	81.49
18.00	70.92	72.38	73.86	75.35	76.86	77.25	77.63	78.01	78.40	78.78	79.17	79.56	79.95	80.34	80.73	81.12
18.25	70.61	72.06	73.53	75.02	76.52	76.90	77.28	77.67	78.05	78.43	78.82	79.21	79.59	79.98	80.37	80.77
18.50	70.30	71.74	73.20	74.68	76.19	76.56	76.94	77.32	77.70	78.09	78.47	78.86	79.24	79.63	80.02	80.41
18.75	69.98	71.42	72.88	74.36	75.85	76.23	76.60	76.98	77.36	77.74	78.12	78.51	78.89	79.28	79.66	80.05
19.00	69.68	71.11	72.56	74.03	75.51	75.89	76.27	76.64	77.02	77.40	77.78	78.16	78.54	78.93	79.31	79.70
20.00	68.46	69.87	71.29	72.74	74.20	74.57	74.94	75.31	75.68	76.05	76.43	76.80	77.18	77.55	77.93	78.31
25.00	62.83	64.12	65.43	66.76	68.10	68.44	68.77	69.11	69.46	69.80	70.14	70.48	70.83	71.18	71.52	71.87
30.00	57.86	59.05	60.25	61.47	62.71	63.02	63.33	63.65	63.96	64.27	64.59	64.91	65.23	65.54	65.86	66.18

Description: This table shows the yield to maturity of a mortgage purchased at the price shown in the index.

Example: The yield to maturity of a 6.75 %, 4 year mortgage at a price of 95.00 is 9.41 %.

INTEREST RATE, %

PRICE	0.00%	1.00%	2.00%	3.00%	4.00%	4.25%	4.50%	4.75%	5.00%	5.25%	5.50%	5.75%	6.00%	6.25%	6.50%	6.75%
100	0.00	1.00	2.00	3.00	4.00	4.25	4.50	4.75	5.00	5.25	5.50	5.75	6.00	6.25	6.50	6.75
99.75	.12	1.12	2.12	3.12	4.12	4.37	4.62	4.87	5.12	5.37	5.62	5.87	6.12	6.37	6.62	6.87
99.50	.24	1.24	2.24	3.25	4.25	4.50	4.75	5.00	5.25	5.50	5.75	6.00	6.25	6.50	6.75	7.00
99.25	.36	1.37	2.37	3.37	4.38	4.63	4.88	5.13	5.38	5.63	5.88	6.13	6.38	6.63	6.88	7.13
99.00	.49	1.49	2.50	3.50	4.50	4.75	5.01	5.26	5.51	5.76	6.01	6.26	6.51	6.76	7.01	7.26
98.75	.61	1.62	2.62	3.63	4.63	4.88	5.13	5.38	5.64	5.89	6.14	6.39	6.64	6.89	7.14	7.39
98.50	.74	1.74	2.75	3.75	4.76	5.01	5.26	5.51	5.77	6.02	6.27	6.52	6.77	7.02	7.27	7.53
98.25	.86	1.87	2.88	3.88	4.89	5.14	5.39	5.64	5.90	6.15	6.40	6.65	6.90	7.15	7.41	7.66
98.00	.99	2.00	3.00	4.01	5.02	5.27	5.52	5.77	6.03	6.28	6.53	6.78	7.03	7.29	7.54	7.79
97.75	1.11	2.12	3.13	4.14	5.15	5.40	5.65	5.90	6.16	6.41	6.66	6.91	7.17	7.42	7.67	7.92
97.50	1.24	2.25	3.26	4.27	5.28	5.53	5.78	6.04	6.29	6.54	6.79	7.05	7.30	7.55	7.80	8.06
97.25	1.37	2.38	3.39	4.40	5.41	5.66	5.91	6.17	6.42	6.67	6.93	7.18	7.43	7.68	7.94	8.19
97.00	1.50	2.51	3.52	4.53	5.54	5.79	6.05	6.30	6.55	6.81	7.06	7.31	7.56	7.82	8.07	8.32
96.75	1.62	2.64	3.65	4.66	5.67	5.93	6.18	6.43	6.69	6.94	7.19	7.45	7.70	7.95	8.20	8.46
96.50	1.75	2.76	3.78	4.79	5.80	6.06	6.31	6.57	6.82	7.07	7.33	7.58	7.83	8.09	8.34	8.59
96.25	1.88	2.89	3.91	4.92	5.94	6.19	6.45	6.70	6.95	7.21	7.46	7.71	7.97	8.22	8.48	8.73
96.00	2.01	3.02	4.04	5.06	6.07	6.32	6.58	6.83	7.09	7.34	7.59	7.85	8.10	8.36	8.61	8.87
95.75	2.14	3.16	4.17	5.19	6.20	6.46	6.71	6.97	7.22	7.48	7.73	7.98	8.24	8.49	8.75	9.00
95.50	2.27	3.29	4.30	5.32	6.34	6.59	6.85	7.10	7.36	7.61	7.87	8.12	8.37	8.63	8.88	9.14
95.25	2.40	3.42	4.44	5.45	6.47	6.73	6.98	7.24	7.49	7.75	8.00	8.26	8.51	8.77	9.02	9.28
95.00	2.53	3.55	4.57	5.59	6.61	6.86	7.12	7.37	7.63	7.88	8.14	8.39	8.65	8.90	9.16	9.41
94.75	2.66	3.68	4.70	5.72	6.74	7.00	7.25	7.51	7.77	8.02	8.28	8.53	8.79	9.04	9.30	9.55
94.50	2.79	3.82	4.84	5.86	6.88	7.14	7.39	7.65	7.90	8.16	8.41	8.67	8.93	9.18	9.44	9.69
94.25	2.93	3.95	4.97	5.99	7.02	7.27	7.53	7.78	8.04	8.30	8.55	8.81	9.06	9.32	9.58	9.83
94.00	3.06	4.08	5.11	6.13	7.15	7.41	7.67	7.92	8.18	8.43	8.69	8.95	9.20	9.46	9.72	9.97
93.75	3.19	4.22	5.24	6.27	7.29	7.55	7.80	8.06	8.32	8.57	8.83	9.09	9.34	9.60	9.86	10.11
93.50	3.33	4.35	5.38	6.40	7.43	7.69	7.94	8.20	8.46	8.71	8.97	9.23	9.48	9.74	10.00	10.25
93.25	3.46	4.49	5.51	6.54	7.57	7.83	8.08	8.34	8.60	8.85	9.11	9.37	9.62	9.88	10.14	10.40
93.00	3.60	4.62	5.65	6.68	7.71	7.97	8.22	8.48	8.74	8.99	9.25	9.51	9.77	10.02	10.28	10.54
92.75	3.73	4.76	5.79	6.82	7.85	8.11	8.36	8.62	8.88	9.14	9.39	9.65	9.91	10.17	10.42	10.68
92.50	3.87	4.90	5.93	6.96	7.99	8.25	8.50	8.76	9.02	9.28	9.53	9.79	10.05	10.31	10.57	10.82
92.25	4.01	5.04	6.07	7.10	8.13	8.39	8.65	8.90	9.16	9.42	9.68	9.94	10.19	10.45	10.71	10.97
92.00	4.14	5.17	6.21	7.24	8.27	8.53	8.79	9.05	9.30	9.56	9.82	10.08	10.34	10.60	10.85	11.11
91.75	4.28	5.31	6.35	7.38	8.41	8.67	8.93	9.19	9.45	9.71	9.96	10.22	10.48	10.74	11.00	11.26
91	4.70	5.73	6.77	7.80	8.84	9.10	9.36	9.62	9.88	10.14	10.40	10.66	10.92	11.18	11.44	11.70
90	5.26	6.30	7.34	8.38	9.42	9.68	9.94	10.20	10.46	10.72	10.98	11.25	11.51	11.77	12.03	12.29
89	5.83	6.87	7.92	8.96	10.01	10.27	10.53	10.80	11.06	11.32	11.58	11.84	12.10	12.37	12.63	12.89
88	6.41	7.46	8.51	9.56	10.61	10.87	11.13	11.40	11.66	11.92	12.19	12.45	12.71	12.98	13.24	13.50
87	7.00	8.05	9.10	10.16	11.22	11.48	11.74	12.01	12.27	12.54	12.80	13.07	13.33	13.60	13.86	14.12
86	7.59	8.65	9.71	10.77	11.83	12.10	12.36	12.63	12.90	13.16	13.43	13.69	13.96	14.22	14.49	14.76
85	8.20	9.27	10.33	11.40	12.46	12.73	13.00	13.26	13.53	13.80	14.06	14.33	14.60	14.86	15.13	15.40
84	8.82	9.89	10.96	12.03	13.10	13.37	13.64	13.90	14.17	14.44	14.71	14.98	15.25	15.52	15.78	16.05
83	9.45	10.52	11.60	12.67	13.75	14.02	14.29	14.56	14.83	15.10	15.37	15.64	15.91	16.18	16.45	16.72
82	10.09	11.17	12.25	13.33	14.41	14.68	14.95	15.22	15.49	15.77	16.04	16.31	16.58	16.85	17.12	17.39
81	10.74	11.82	12.91	13.99	15.08	15.36	15.63	15.90	16.17	16.45	16.72	16.99	17.26	17.54	17.81	18.08
80	11.40	12.49	13.58	14.67	15.77	16.04	16.31	16.59	16.86	17.14	17.41	17.69	17.96	18.23	18.51	18.78
79	12.07	13.17	14.27	15.36	16.46	16.74	17.01	17.29	17.57	17.84	18.12	18.39	18.67	18.94	19.22	19.50
78	12.76	13.86	14.96	16.07	17.17	17.45	17.73	18.00	18.28	18.56	18.84	19.11	19.39	19.67	19.95	20.22
77	13.45	14.56	15.67	16.78	17.90	18.17	18.45	18.73	19.01	19.29	19.57	19.85	20.13	20.40	20.68	20.96
76	14.17	15.28	16.40	17.51	18.63	18.91	19.19	19.47	19.75	20.03	20.31	20.59	20.88	21.16	21.44	21.72
75	14.89	16.01	17.13	18.26	19.38	19.67	19.95	20.23	20.51	20.79	21.07	21.36	21.64	21.92	22.20	22.49
74	15.63	16.76	17.89	19.02	20.15	20.43	20.72	21.00	21.28	21.57	21.85	22.13	22.42	22.70	22.99	23.27
73	16.38	17.52	18.65	19.79	20.93	21.21	21.50	21.78	22.07	22.36	22.64	22.93	23.21	23.50	23.79	24.07
72	17.15	18.29	19.43	20.58	21.73	22.01	22.30	22.59	22.87	23.16	23.45	23.74	24.02	24.31	24.60	24.89
71	17.93	19.08	20.23	21.38	22.54	22.83	23.12	23.40	23.69	23.98	24.27	24.56	24.85	25.14	25.43	25.72
70	18.73	19.89	21.05	22.21	23.37	23.66	23.95	24.24	24.53	24.82	25.11	25.41	25.70	25.99	26.28	26.57
69	19.55	20.71	21.88	23.04	24.21	24.51	24.80	25.09	25.39	25.68	25.97	26.27	26.56	26.85	27.15	27.44
68	20.38	21.55	22.73	23.90	25.08	25.37	25.67	25.96	26.26	26.56	26.85	27.15	27.44	27.74	28.03	28.33
67	21.23	22.41	23.59	24.78	25.96	26.26	26.56	26.86	27.15	27.45	27.75	28.05	28.34	28.64	28.94	29.24
66	22.10	23.29	24.48	25.67	26.87	27.17	27.47	27.77	28.07	28.37	28.67	28.97	29.27	29.57	29.87	30.17
65	22.99	24.19	25.39	26.59	27.79	28.10	28.40	28.70	29.00	29.30	29.60	29.91	30.21	30.51	30.82	31.12
64	23.91	25.11	26.32	27.53	28.74	29.04	29.35	29.65	29.96	30.26	30.57	30.87	31.17	31.48	31.79	32.09
63	24.84	26.05	27.27	28.49	29.71	30.02	30.32	30.63	30.93	31.24	31.55	31.86	32.16	32.47	32.78	33.09
62	25.79	27.01	28.24	29.47	30.70	31.01	31.32	31.63	31.94	32.25	32.56	32.87	33.18	33.49	33.80	34.11
61	26.77	28.00	29.24	30.48	31.72	32.03	32.34	32.65	32.96	33.28	33.59	33.90	34.21	34.53	34.84	35.15
60	27.77	29.01	30.26	31.51	32.76	33.07	33.39	33.70	34.02	34.33	34.65	34.96	35.28	35.59	35.91	36.22
59	28.79	30.05	31.30	32.56	33.83	34.15	34.46	34.78	35.10	35.41	35.73	36.05	36.37	36.69	37.01	37.32
58	29.85	31.11	32.38	33.65	34.93	35.25	35.56	35.88	36.21	36.53	36.85	37.17	37.49	37.81	38.13	38.45

MORTGAGE PRICE

Description: This table shows the price to pay for a monthly payment mortgage loan at the yield rate.

Example: The price of a 10.75 %, 4 year mortgage loan to yield 8.00 % to maturity is $ 105.37.

INTEREST RATE, %

YIELD	7.00%	7.25%	7.50%	7.75%	8.00%	8.25%	8.50%	8.75%	9.00%	9.25%	9.50%	9.75%	10.00%	10.25%	10.50%	10.75%
0.00	114.94	115.50	116.06	116.62	117.18	117.75	118.31	118.88	119.45	120.02	120.59	121.16	121.74	122.32	122.90	123.48
1.00	112.63	113.17	113.72	114.27	114.82	115.38	115.93	116.49	117.04	117.60	118.16	118.73	119.29	119.85	120.42	120.99
2.00	110.38	110.91	111.45	111.99	112.53	113.07	113.61	114.16	114.70	115.25	115.80	116.35	116.90	117.46	118.01	118.57
3.00	108.19	108.71	109.24	109.76	110.29	110.83	111.36	111.89	112.43	112.96	113.50	114.04	114.58	115.13	115.67	116.22
4.00	106.06	106.57	107.09	107.60	108.12	108.64	109.16	109.69	110.21	110.74	111.27	111.80	112.33	112.86	113.39	113.93
4.25	105.53	106.04	106.56	107.07	107.59	108.11	108.63	109.15	109.67	110.19	110.72	111.24	111.77	112.30	112.83	113.37
4.50	105.01	105.52	106.03	106.54	107.06	107.57	108.09	108.61	109.13	109.65	110.17	110.70	111.22	111.75	112.28	112.81
4.75	104.49	105.00	105.51	106.02	106.53	107.04	107.56	108.07	108.59	109.11	109.63	110.15	110.68	111.20	111.73	112.25
5.00	103.98	104.49	104.99	105.50	106.01	106.52	107.03	107.54	108.06	108.57	109.09	109.61	110.13	110.65	111.18	111.70
5.25	103.47	103.97	104.48	104.98	105.49	106.00	106.51	107.02	107.53	108.04	108.56	109.07	109.59	110.11	110.63	111.16
5.50	102.97	103.47	103.97	104.47	104.97	105.48	105.98	106.49	107.00	107.51	108.03	108.54	109.06	109.57	110.09	110.61
5.75	102.46	102.96	103.46	103.96	104.46	104.96	105.47	105.97	106.48	106.99	107.50	108.01	108.52	109.04	109.55	110.07
6.00	101.96	102.46	102.95	103.45	103.95	104.45	104.95	105.46	105.96	106.47	106.98	107.48	107.99	108.51	109.02	109.53
6.25	101.47	101.96	102.45	102.95	103.45	103.94	104.44	104.94	105.45	105.95	106.45	106.96	107.47	107.98	108.49	109.00
6.50	100.98	101.47	101.96	102.45	102.94	103.44	103.94	104.43	104.93	105.44	105.94	106.44	106.95	107.45	107.96	108.47
6.75	100.49	100.97	101.46	101.95	102.44	102.94	103.43	103.93	104.43	104.92	105.42	105.93	106.43	106.93	107.44	107.95
7.00	100.00	100.49	100.97	101.46	101.95	102.44	102.93	103.43	103.92	104.42	104.91	105.41	105.91	106.42	106.92	107.43
7.25	99.52	100.00	100.48	100.97	101.46	101.95	102.43	102.93	103.42	103.91	104.41	104.91	105.40	105.90	106.40	106.91
7.50	99.04	99.52	100.00	100.48	100.97	101.45	101.94	102.43	102.92	103.41	103.91	104.40	104.90	105.39	105.89	106.39
7.75	98.56	99.04	99.52	100.00	100.48	100.97	101.45	101.94	102.43	102.91	103.41	103.90	104.39	104.89	105.38	105.88
8.00	98.09	98.56	99.04	99.52	100.00	100.48	100.96	101.45	101.93	102.42	102.91	103.40	103.89	104.38	104.88	105.37
8.25	97.62	98.09	98.57	99.04	99.52	100.00	100.48	100.96	101.45	101.93	102.42	102.90	103.39	103.88	104.37	104.87
8.50	97.15	97.62	98.10	98.57	99.05	99.52	100.00	100.48	100.96	101.44	101.93	102.41	102.90	103.39	103.87	104.37
8.75	96.69	97.16	97.63	98.10	98.57	99.05	99.52	100.00	100.48	100.96	101.44	101.92	102.41	102.89	103.38	103.87
9.00	96.23	96.69	97.16	97.63	98.10	98.58	99.05	99.52	100.00	100.48	100.96	101.44	101.92	102.40	102.89	103.37
9.25	95.77	96.23	96.70	97.17	97.64	98.11	98.58	99.05	99.52	100.00	100.48	100.95	101.43	101.92	102.40	102.88
9.50	95.32	95.78	96.24	96.71	97.17	97.64	98.11	98.58	99.05	99.52	100.00	100.48	100.95	101.43	101.92	102.40
9.75	94.86	95.32	95.79	96.25	96.71	97.18	97.65	98.11	98.58	99.05	99.53	100.00	100.48	100.95	101.43	101.91
10.00	94.42	94.87	95.33	95.79	96.26	96.72	97.18	97.65	98.12	98.59	99.06	99.53	100.00	100.47	100.95	101.43
10.25	93.97	94.43	94.88	95.34	95.80	96.26	96.73	97.19	97.65	98.12	98.59	99.06	99.53	100.00	100.47	100.95
10.50	93.53	93.98	94.44	94.89	95.35	95.81	96.27	96.73	97.19	97.66	98.12	98.59	99.06	99.53	100.00	100.47
10.75	93.09	93.54	93.99	94.45	94.90	95.36	95.82	96.28	96.74	97.20	97.66	98.13	98.59	99.06	99.53	100.00
11.00	92.65	93.10	93.55	94.00	94.46	94.91	95.37	95.83	96.28	96.74	97.20	97.67	98.13	98.60	99.06	99.53
11.25	92.22	92.66	93.11	93.56	94.01	94.47	94.92	95.38	95.83	96.29	96.75	97.21	97.67	98.14	98.60	99.06
11.50	91.79	92.23	92.68	93.13	93.58	94.03	94.48	94.93	95.39	95.84	96.30	96.76	97.22	97.68	98.14	98.60
11.75	91.36	91.80	92.25	92.69	93.14	93.59	94.04	94.49	94.94	95.39	95.85	96.30	96.76	97.22	97.68	98.14
12.00	90.93	91.37	91.82	92.26	92.71	93.15	93.60	94.05	94.50	94.95	95.40	95.86	96.31	96.77	97.23	97.69
12.25	90.51	90.95	91.39	91.83	92.27	92.72	93.16	93.61	94.06	94.51	94.96	95.41	95.86	96.32	96.77	97.23
12.50	90.09	90.53	90.97	91.41	91.85	92.29	92.73	93.18	93.62	94.07	94.52	94.97	95.42	95.87	96.33	96.78
12.75	89.67	90.11	90.55	90.98	91.42	91.86	92.30	92.75	93.19	93.64	94.08	94.53	94.98	95.43	95.88	96.33
13.00	89.26	89.69	90.13	90.56	91.00	91.44	91.88	92.32	92.76	93.20	93.65	94.09	94.54	94.99	95.44	95.89
13.25	88.85	89.28	89.71	90.15	90.58	91.02	91.45	91.89	92.33	92.77	93.22	93.66	94.10	94.55	95.00	95.45
13.50	88.44	88.87	89.30	89.73	90.16	90.60	91.03	91.47	91.91	92.35	92.79	93.23	93.67	94.11	94.56	95.01
13.75	88.03	88.46	88.89	89.32	89.75	90.18	90.61	91.05	91.48	91.92	92.36	92.80	93.24	93.68	94.13	94.57
14.00	87.63	88.06	88.48	88.91	89.34	89.77	90.20	90.63	91.07	91.50	91.94	92.37	92.81	93.25	93.69	94.14
14.25	87.23	87.65	88.08	88.50	88.93	89.36	89.79	90.22	90.65	91.08	91.52	91.95	92.39	92.83	93.27	93.71
14.50	86.83	87.25	87.67	88.10	88.52	88.95	89.38	89.81	90.24	90.67	91.10	91.53	91.97	92.40	92.84	93.28
14.75	86.44	86.85	87.28	87.70	88.12	88.54	88.97	89.40	89.82	90.25	90.68	91.12	91.55	91.98	92.42	92.85
15.00	86.04	86.46	86.88	87.30	87.72	88.14	88.57	88.99	89.42	89.84	90.27	90.70	91.13	91.56	92.00	92.43
15.25	85.65	86.07	86.48	86.90	87.32	87.74	88.16	88.59	89.01	89.44	89.86	90.29	90.72	91.15	91.58	92.01
15.50	85.26	85.68	86.09	86.51	86.93	87.34	87.76	88.18	88.61	89.03	89.45	89.88	90.31	90.74	91.16	91.59
15.75	84.88	85.29	85.70	86.12	86.53	86.95	87.37	87.79	88.21	88.63	89.05	89.47	89.90	90.32	90.75	91.18
16.00	84.50	84.91	85.32	85.73	86.14	86.56	86.97	87.39	87.81	88.23	88.65	89.07	89.49	89.92	90.34	90.77
16.25	84.11	84.52	84.93	85.34	85.75	86.17	86.58	87.00	87.41	87.83	88.25	88.67	89.09	89.51	89.94	90.36
16.50	83.74	84.14	84.55	84.96	85.37	85.78	86.19	86.61	87.02	87.44	87.85	88.27	88.69	89.11	89.53	89.95
16.75	83.36	83.77	84.17	84.58	84.99	85.39	85.81	86.22	86.63	87.04	87.46	87.87	88.29	88.71	89.13	89.55
17.00	82.99	83.39	83.79	84.20	84.61	85.01	85.42	85.83	86.24	86.65	87.07	87.48	87.90	88.31	88.73	89.15
17.25	82.62	83.02	83.42	83.82	84.23	84.63	85.04	85.45	85.86	86.27	86.68	87.09	87.50	87.92	88.33	88.75
17.50	82.25	82.65	83.05	83.45	83.85	84.26	84.66	85.07	85.47	85.88	86.29	86.70	87.11	87.53	87.94	88.36
17.75	81.88	82.28	82.68	83.08	83.48	83.88	84.28	84.69	85.09	85.50	85.91	86.32	86.73	87.14	87.55	87.96
18.00	81.52	81.91	82.31	82.71	83.11	83.51	83.91	84.31	84.72	85.12	85.53	85.93	86.34	86.75	87.16	87.57
18.25	81.16	81.55	81.95	82.34	82.74	83.14	83.54	83.94	84.34	84.74	85.15	85.55	85.96	86.37	86.77	87.18
18.50	80.80	81.19	81.58	81.98	82.37	82.77	83.17	83.57	83.97	84.37	84.77	85.17	85.58	85.98	86.39	86.80
18.75	80.44	80.83	81.22	81.62	82.01	82.40	82.80	83.20	83.60	83.99	84.40	84.80	85.20	85.60	86.01	86.41
19.00	80.09	80.48	80.87	81.26	81.65	82.04	82.44	82.83	83.23	83.62	84.02	84.42	84.82	85.23	85.63	86.03
20.00	78.69	79.07	79.46	79.84	80.23	80.61	81.00	81.39	81.78	82.17	82.56	82.95	83.35	83.74	84.14	84.53
25.00	72.22	72.57	72.92	73.27	73.63	73.98	74.34	74.69	75.05	75.41	75.77	76.13	76.49	76.85	77.22	77.58
30.00	66.51	66.83	67.15	67.48	67.80	68.13	68.46	68.78	69.11	69.44	69.77	70.11	70.44	70.77	71.11	71.44

Description: This table shows the yield to maturity of a mortgage purchased at the price shown in the index.

Example: The yield to maturity of a 10.75 %, 4 year mortgage at a price of 100.00 is 10.75 %.

INTEREST RATE, %

PRICE	7.00%	7.25%	7.50%	7.75%	8.00%	8.25%	8.50%	8.75%	9.00%	9.25%	9.50%	9.75%	10.00%	10.25%	10.50%	10.75%
105	4.50	4.75	4.99	5.24	5.48	5.73	5.97	6.22	6.46	6.71	6.95	7.20	7.44	7.69	7.93	8.18
104.75	4.62	4.87	5.11	5.36	5.60	5.85	6.09	6.34	6.59	6.83	7.08	7.32	7.57	7.81	8.06	8.30
104.50	4.74	4.99	5.23	5.48	5.73	5.97	6.22	6.46	6.71	6.95	7.20	7.45	7.69	7.94	8.18	8.43
104.25	4.86	5.11	5.36	5.60	5.85	6.09	6.34	6.59	6.83	7.08	7.32	7.57	7.82	8.06	8.31	8.55
104.00	4.99	5.23	5.48	5.72	5.97	6.22	6.46	6.71	6.96	7.20	7.45	7.69	7.94	8.19	8.43	8.68
103.75	5.11	5.35	5.60	5.85	6.09	6.34	6.59	6.83	7.08	7.33	7.57	7.82	8.07	8.31	8.56	8.80
103.50	5.23	5.48	5.72	5.97	6.22	6.46	6.71	6.96	7.20	7.45	7.70	7.94	8.19	8.44	8.68	8.93
103.25	5.35	5.60	5.85	6.10	6.34	6.59	6.84	7.08	7.33	7.58	7.82	8.07	8.32	8.56	8.81	9.06
103.00	5.48	5.73	5.97	6.22	6.47	6.71	6.96	7.21	7.46	7.70	7.95	8.20	8.44	8.69	8.94	9.18
102.75	5.60	5.85	6.10	6.34	6.59	6.84	7.09	7.33	7.58	7.83	8.08	8.32	8.57	8.82	9.06	9.31
102.50	5.73	5.97	6.22	6.47	6.72	6.96	7.21	7.46	7.71	7.95	8.20	8.45	8.70	8.94	9.19	9.44
102.25	5.85	6.10	6.35	6.60	6.84	7.09	7.34	7.59	7.83	8.08	8.33	8.58	8.83	9.07	9.32	9.57
102.00	5.98	6.22	6.47	6.72	6.97	7.22	7.47	7.71	7.96	8.21	8.46	8.71	8.95	9.20	9.45	9.70
101.75	6.10	6.35	6.60	6.85	7.10	7.34	7.59	7.84	8.09	8.34	8.59	8.83	9.08	9.33	9.58	9.83
101.50	6.23	6.48	6.73	6.97	7.22	7.47	7.72	7.97	8.22	8.47	8.71	8.96	9.21	9.46	9.71	9.96
101.25	6.36	6.60	6.85	7.10	7.35	7.60	7.85	8.10	8.35	8.59	8.84	9.09	9.34	9.59	9.84	10.09
101.00	6.48	6.73	6.98	7.23	7.48	7.73	7.98	8.23	8.47	8.72	8.97	9.22	9.47	9.72	9.97	10.22
100.75	6.61	6.86	7.11	7.36	7.61	7.86	8.11	8.35	8.60	8.85	9.10	9.35	9.60	9.85	10.10	10.35
100.50	6.74	6.99	7.24	7.49	7.74	7.99	8.23	8.48	8.73	8.98	9.23	9.48	9.73	9.98	10.23	10.48
100.25	6.87	7.12	7.37	7.62	7.87	8.12	8.36	8.61	8.86	9.11	9.36	9.61	9.86	10.11	10.36	10.61
100.00	7.00	7.25	7.50	7.75	8.00	8.25	8.50	8.75	9.00	9.25	9.50	9.75	10.00	10.25	10.50	10.75
99.75	7.12	7.37	7.62	7.88	8.13	8.38	8.63	8.88	9.13	9.38	9.63	9.88	10.13	10.38	10.63	10.88
99.50	7.25	7.50	7.76	8.01	8.26	8.51	8.76	9.01	9.26	9.51	9.76	10.01	10.26	10.51	10.76	11.01
99.25	7.38	7.63	7.89	8.14	8.39	8.64	8.89	9.14	9.39	9.64	9.89	10.14	10.39	10.64	10.89	11.15
99.00	7.51	7.77	8.02	8.27	8.52	8.77	9.02	9.27	9.52	9.77	10.02	10.28	10.53	10.78	11.03	11.28
98.75	7.65	7.90	8.15	8.40	8.65	8.90	9.15	9.40	9.66	9.91	10.16	10.41	10.66	10.91	11.16	11.41
98.50	7.78	8.03	8.28	8.53	8.78	9.03	9.29	9.54	9.79	10.04	10.29	10.54	10.80	11.05	11.30	11.55
98.25	7.91	8.16	8.41	8.66	8.92	9.17	9.42	9.67	9.92	10.18	10.43	10.68	10.93	11.18	11.43	11.69
98.00	8.04	8.29	8.55	8.80	9.05	9.30	9.55	9.81	10.06	10.31	10.56	10.81	11.07	11.32	11.57	11.82
97.75	8.17	8.43	8.68	8.93	9.18	9.44	9.69	9.94	10.19	10.45	10.70	10.95	11.20	11.45	11.71	11.96
97.50	8.31	8.56	8.81	9.07	9.32	9.57	9.82	10.08	10.33	10.58	10.83	11.09	11.34	11.59	11.84	12.10
97.25	8.44	8.70	8.95	9.20	9.45	9.71	9.96	10.21	10.46	10.72	10.97	11.22	11.48	11.73	11.98	12.23
97.00	8.58	8.83	9.08	9.34	9.59	9.84	10.10	10.35	10.60	10.85	11.11	11.36	11.61	11.87	12.12	12.37
96.75	8.71	8.96	9.22	9.47	9.72	9.98	10.23	10.48	10.74	10.99	11.24	11.50	11.75	12.01	12.26	12.51
96.50	8.85	9.10	9.35	9.61	9.86	10.11	10.37	10.62	10.88	11.13	11.38	11.64	11.89	12.14	12.40	12.65
96.25	8.98	9.24	9.49	9.74	10.00	10.25	10.51	10.76	11.01	11.27	11.52	11.78	12.03	12.28	12.54	12.79
96.00	9.12	9.37	9.63	9.88	10.14	10.39	10.64	10.90	11.15	11.41	11.66	11.91	12.17	12.42	12.68	12.93
95.75	9.26	9.51	9.76	10.02	10.27	10.53	10.78	11.04	11.29	11.55	11.80	12.05	12.31	12.56	12.82	13.07
95.50	9.39	9.65	9.90	10.16	10.41	10.67	10.92	11.18	11.43	11.69	11.94	12.20	12.45	12.70	12.96	13.21
95.25	9.53	9.79	10.04	10.30	10.55	10.81	11.06	11.32	11.57	11.83	12.08	12.34	12.59	12.85	13.10	13.36
95.00	9.67	9.92	10.18	10.44	10.69	10.95	11.20	11.46	11.71	11.97	12.22	12.48	12.73	12.99	13.24	13.50
94.75	9.81	10.06	10.32	10.57	10.83	11.09	11.34	11.60	11.85	12.11	12.36	12.62	12.87	13.13	13.39	13.64
94	10.23	10.48	10.74	11.00	11.25	11.51	11.77	12.02	12.28	12.54	12.79	13.05	13.30	13.56	13.82	14.07
93	10.80	11.05	11.31	11.57	11.83	12.08	12.34	12.60	12.86	13.11	13.37	13.63	13.89	14.14	14.40	14.66
92	11.37	11.63	11.89	12.15	12.41	12.66	12.92	13.18	13.44	13.70	13.96	14.22	14.48	14.73	14.99	15.25
91	11.96	12.22	12.48	12.74	12.99	13.25	13.51	13.77	14.03	14.29	14.55	14.81	15.07	15.33	15.59	15.85
90	12.55	12.81	13.07	13.33	13.59	13.85	14.12	14.38	14.64	14.90	15.16	15.42	15.68	15.94	16.21	16.47
89	13.15	13.42	13.68	13.94	14.20	14.46	14.73	14.99	15.25	15.51	15.78	16.04	16.30	16.56	16.83	17.09
88	13.77	14.03	14.29	14.56	14.82	15.08	15.35	15.61	15.87	16.14	16.40	16.67	16.93	17.19	17.46	17.72
87	14.39	14.65	14.92	15.18	15.45	15.71	15.98	16.24	16.51	16.77	17.04	17.30	17.57	17.83	18.10	18.36
86	15.02	15.29	15.55	15.82	16.09	16.35	16.62	16.89	17.15	17.42	17.68	17.95	18.22	18.48	18.75	19.02
85	15.67	15.93	16.20	16.47	16.74	17.00	17.27	17.54	17.81	18.07	18.34	18.61	18.88	19.15	19.41	19.68
84	16.32	16.59	16.86	17.13	17.40	17.67	17.93	18.20	18.47	18.74	19.01	19.28	19.55	19.82	20.09	20.36
83	16.99	17.26	17.53	17.80	18.07	18.34	18.61	18.88	19.15	19.42	19.69	19.96	20.23	20.50	20.77	21.05
82	17.66	17.94	18.21	18.48	18.75	19.02	19.30	19.57	19.84	20.11	20.38	20.66	20.93	21.20	21.47	21.75
81	18.35	18.63	18.90	19.17	19.45	19.72	19.99	20.27	20.54	20.82	21.09	21.36	21.64	21.91	22.18	22.46
80	19.06	19.33	19.61	19.88	20.16	20.43	20.71	20.98	21.26	21.53	21.81	22.08	22.36	22.63	22.91	23.18
79	19.77	20.05	20.32	20.60	20.88	21.15	21.43	21.71	21.98	22.26	22.54	22.81	23.09	23.37	23.65	23.92
78	20.50	20.78	21.06	21.33	21.61	21.89	22.17	22.45	22.73	23.00	23.28	23.56	23.84	24.12	24.40	24.68
77	21.24	21.52	21.80	22.08	22.36	22.64	22.92	23.20	23.48	23.76	24.04	24.32	24.60	24.88	25.16	25.44
76	22.00	22.28	22.56	22.84	23.12	23.41	23.69	23.97	24.25	24.53	24.81	25.10	25.38	25.66	25.94	26.23
75	22.77	23.05	23.34	23.62	23.90	24.19	24.47	24.75	25.04	25.32	25.60	25.89	26.17	26.46	26.74	27.02
74	23.56	23.84	24.13	24.41	24.70	24.98	25.27	25.55	25.84	26.12	26.41	26.69	26.98	27.27	27.55	27.84
73	24.36	24.65	24.93	25.22	25.51	25.79	26.08	26.37	26.65	26.94	27.23	27.52	27.80	28.09	28.38	28.67
72	25.18	25.47	25.75	26.04	26.33	26.62	26.91	27.20	27.49	27.78	28.07	28.36	28.65	28.94	29.23	29.52
71	26.01	26.30	26.59	26.88	27.17	27.47	27.76	28.05	28.34	28.63	28.92	29.21	29.51	29.80	30.09	30.38
70	26.87	27.16	27.45	27.74	28.04	28.33	28.62	28.92	29.21	29.50	29.80	30.09	30.38	30.68	30.97	31.27
69	27.74	28.03	28.33	28.62	28.92	29.21	29.51	29.80	30.10	30.39	30.69	30.98	31.28	31.58	31.87	32.17

Description: This table shows the price to pay for a monthly payment mortgage loan at the yield rate.

Example: The price of a 15.00 %, 4 year mortgage loan to yield 8.00 % to maturity is $ 114.00.

INTEREST RATE, %

YIELD	11.00%	11.25%	11.50%	11.75%	12.00%	12.25%	12.50%	12.75%	13.00%	13.25%	13.50%	13.75%	14.00%	14.25%	14.50%	15.00%
0.00	124.06	124.64	125.23	125.81	126.40	126.99	127.58	128.18	128.77	129.37	129.97	130.57	131.17	131.77	132.37	133.59
1.00	121.56	122.13	122.71	123.28	123.86	124.44	125.01	125.60	126.18	126.76	127.35	127.94	128.53	129.12	129.71	130.90
2.00	119.13	119.69	120.25	120.82	121.38	121.95	122.52	123.09	123.66	124.23	124.80	125.38	125.96	126.54	127.12	128.28
3.00	116.77	117.32	117.87	118.42	118.97	119.53	120.08	120.64	121.20	121.76	122.33	122.89	123.46	124.02	124.59	125.74
4.00	114.47	115.01	115.55	116.09	116.63	117.17	117.72	118.27	118.82	119.37	119.92	120.47	121.03	121.58	122.14	123.26
4.25	113.90	114.44	114.97	115.51	116.05	116.60	117.14	117.68	118.23	118.78	119.33	119.88	120.43	120.98	121.54	122.65
4.50	113.34	113.87	114.41	114.94	115.48	116.02	116.56	117.10	117.65	118.19	118.74	119.29	119.83	120.39	120.94	122.05
4.75	112.78	113.31	113.85	114.38	114.91	115.45	115.99	116.53	117.07	117.61	118.15	118.70	119.25	119.79	120.34	121.45
5.00	112.23	112.76	113.29	113.82	114.35	114.88	115.42	115.95	116.49	117.03	117.57	118.12	118.66	119.20	119.75	120.85
5.25	111.68	112.20	112.73	113.26	113.79	114.32	114.85	115.39	115.92	116.46	117.00	117.54	118.08	118.62	119.16	120.26
5.50	111.13	111.66	112.18	112.71	113.23	113.76	114.29	114.82	115.35	115.89	116.42	116.96	117.50	118.04	118.58	119.67
5.75	110.59	111.11	111.63	112.15	112.68	113.21	113.73	114.26	114.79	115.32	115.86	116.39	116.93	117.46	118.00	119.08
6.00	110.05	110.57	111.09	111.61	112.13	112.65	113.18	113.70	114.23	114.76	115.29	115.82	116.36	116.89	117.43	118.50
6.25	109.52	110.03	110.55	111.07	111.58	112.11	112.63	113.15	113.68	114.20	114.73	115.26	115.79	116.32	116.86	117.93
6.50	108.98	109.50	110.01	110.53	111.04	111.56	112.08	112.60	113.12	113.65	114.17	114.70	115.23	115.76	116.29	117.36
6.75	108.46	108.97	109.48	109.99	110.51	111.02	111.54	112.06	112.58	113.10	113.62	114.14	114.67	115.20	115.73	116.79
7.00	107.93	108.44	108.95	109.46	109.97	110.48	111.00	111.51	112.03	112.55	113.07	113.59	114.12	114.64	115.17	116.22
7.25	107.41	107.92	108.42	108.93	109.44	109.95	110.46	110.98	111.49	112.01	112.53	113.04	113.57	114.09	114.61	115.66
7.50	106.89	107.40	107.90	108.41	108.91	109.42	109.93	110.44	110.95	111.47	111.98	112.50	113.02	113.54	114.06	115.10
7.75	106.38	106.88	107.38	107.88	108.39	108.89	109.40	109.91	110.42	110.93	111.44	111.96	112.47	112.99	113.51	114.55
8.00	105.87	106.37	106.87	107.37	107.87	108.37	108.88	109.38	109.89	110.40	110.91	111.42	111.93	112.45	112.96	114.00
8.25	105.36	105.86	106.35	106.85	107.35	107.85	108.36	108.86	109.36	109.87	110.38	110.89	111.40	111.91	112.42	113.45
8.50	104.86	105.35	105.85	106.34	106.84	107.34	107.84	108.34	108.84	109.35	109.85	110.36	110.87	111.38	111.89	112.91
8.75	104.36	104.85	105.34	105.83	106.33	106.82	107.32	107.82	108.32	108.82	109.33	109.83	110.34	110.84	111.35	112.37
9.00	103.86	104.35	104.84	105.33	105.82	106.32	106.81	107.31	107.81	108.30	108.81	109.31	109.81	110.32	110.82	111.84
9.25	103.37	103.85	104.34	104.83	105.32	105.81	106.30	106.80	107.29	107.79	108.29	108.79	109.29	109.79	110.29	111.31
9.50	102.88	103.36	103.84	104.33	104.82	105.31	105.80	106.29	106.78	107.28	107.77	108.27	108.77	109.27	109.77	110.78
9.75	102.39	102.87	103.35	103.84	104.32	104.81	105.30	105.79	106.28	106.77	107.26	107.76	108.26	108.75	109.25	110.25
10.00	101.90	102.38	102.86	103.35	103.83	104.31	104.80	105.29	105.78	106.27	106.76	107.25	107.74	108.24	108.73	109.73
10.25	101.42	101.90	102.38	102.86	103.34	103.82	104.31	104.79	105.28	105.76	106.25	106.74	107.23	107.73	108.22	109.21
10.50	100.95	101.42	101.90	102.37	102.85	103.33	103.81	104.30	104.78	105.27	105.75	106.24	106.73	107.22	107.71	108.70
10.75	100.47	100.94	101.42	101.89	102.37	102.85	103.33	103.81	104.29	104.77	105.26	105.74	106.23	106.72	107.21	108.19
11.00	100.00	100.47	100.94	101.42	101.89	102.36	102.84	103.32	103.80	104.28	104.76	105.25	105.73	106.22	106.70	107.68
11.25	99.53	100.00	100.47	100.94	101.41	101.89	102.36	102.84	103.31	103.79	104.27	104.75	105.24	105.72	106.20	107.18
11.50	99.07	99.53	100.00	100.47	100.94	101.41	101.88	102.36	102.83	103.31	103.78	104.26	104.74	105.22	105.71	106.68
11.75	98.60	99.07	99.53	100.00	100.47	100.94	101.41	101.88	102.35	102.83	103.31	103.78	104.25	104.73	105.21	106.18
12.00	98.15	98.61	99.07	99.53	100.00	100.47	100.93	101.40	101.87	102.35	102.83	103.30	103.78	104.25	104.73	105.68
12.25	97.69	98.15	98.61	99.07	99.54	100.00	100.47	100.93	101.40	101.87	102.34	102.82	103.29	103.77	104.25	104.72 105.68
12.50	97.24	97.69	98.15	98.61	99.07	99.54	100.00	100.46	100.93	101.40	101.87	102.34	102.81	103.29	103.76	104.24 105.19
12.75	96.79	97.24	97.70	98.16	98.62	99.08	99.54	100.00	100.46	100.93	101.40	101.87	102.34	102.81	103.28	103.75 104.71
13.00	96.34	96.79	97.25	97.70	98.16	98.62	99.08	99.54	100.00	100.46	100.93	101.39	101.86	102.33	102.80	103.27 104.22
13.25	95.90	96.35	96.80	97.25	97.71	98.16	98.62	99.08	99.54	100.00	100.46	100.93	101.39	101.86	102.33	102.80 103.74
13.50	95.45	95.90	96.35	96.81	97.26	97.71	98.17	98.62	99.08	99.54	100.00	100.46	100.93	101.39	101.86	102.32 103.26
13.75	95.02	95.46	95.91	96.36	96.81	97.26	97.72	98.17	98.62	99.08	99.54	100.00	100.46	100.92	101.39	101.85 102.79
14.00	94.58	95.03	95.47	95.92	96.37	96.82	97.27	97.72	98.17	98.63	99.08	99.54	100.00	100.46	100.92	101.38 102.31
14.25	94.15	94.59	95.03	95.48	95.93	96.37	96.82	97.27	97.72	98.17	98.63	99.08	99.54	100.00	100.46	100.92 101.85
14.50	93.72	94.16	94.60	95.04	95.49	95.93	96.38	96.83	97.28	97.73	98.18	98.63	99.09	99.54	100.00	100.46 101.38
14.75	93.29	93.73	94.17	94.61	95.05	95.50	95.94	96.39	96.84	97.28	97.73	98.18	98.63	99.09	99.54	100.00 100.92
15.00	92.87	93.30	93.74	94.18	94.62	95.06	95.51	95.95	96.40	96.84	97.29	97.74	98.19	98.64	99.09	99.54 100.46
15.25	92.45	92.88	93.32	93.75	94.19	94.63	95.07	95.51	95.96	96.40	96.85	97.29	97.74	98.64	99.09	100.00
15.50	92.03	92.46	92.89	93.33	93.77	94.20	94.64	95.08	95.52	95.97	96.41	96.85	97.30	97.75	98.64	99.55
15.75	91.61	92.04	92.47	92.91	93.34	93.78	94.21	94.65	95.09	95.53	95.97	96.42	96.86	97.30	98.20	99.10
16.00	91.20	91.63	92.06	92.49	92.92	93.35	93.79	94.22	94.66	95.10	95.54	95.98	96.42	96.87	97.75	98.65
16.25	90.79	91.21	91.64	92.07	92.50	92.93	93.37	93.80	94.24	94.67	95.11	95.55	95.99	96.43	97.31	98.20
16.50	90.38	90.80	91.23	91.66	92.09	92.52	92.95	93.38	93.81	94.25	94.68	95.12	95.56	96.00	96.87	97.76
16.75	89.97	90.40	90.82	91.25	91.67	92.10	92.53	92.96	93.39	93.82	94.26	94.69	95.13	95.57	96.44	97.32
17.00	89.57	89.99	90.41	90.84	91.26	91.69	92.12	92.54	92.97	93.40	93.84	94.27	94.70	95.14	96.00	96.88
17.25	89.17	89.59	90.01	90.43	90.85	91.28	91.70	92.13	92.56	92.99	93.42	93.85	94.28	94.71	95.57	96.45
17.50	88.77	89.19	89.61	90.03	90.45	90.87	91.30	91.72	92.15	92.57	93.00	93.43	93.86	94.29	95.15	96.02
17.75	88.38	88.79	89.21	89.63	90.05	90.47	90.89	91.31	91.74	92.16	92.59	93.01	93.44	93.87	94.72	95.59
18.00	87.98	88.40	88.81	89.23	89.65	90.07	90.49	90.91	91.33	91.75	92.17	92.60	93.03	93.45	94.30	95.17
18.25	87.59	88.01	88.42	88.83	89.25	89.67	90.08	90.50	90.92	91.34	91.77	92.19	92.61	93.04	93.88	94.74
18.50	87.21	87.62	88.03	88.44	88.85	89.27	89.69	90.10	90.52	90.94	91.36	91.78	92.20	92.63	93.47	94.32
18.75	86.82	87.23	87.64	88.05	88.46	88.88	89.29	89.70	90.12	90.54	90.96	91.38	91.80	92.22	93.05	93.91
19.00	86.44	86.85	87.25	87.66	88.07	88.48	88.90	89.31	89.72	90.14	90.56	90.97	91.39	91.81	92.64	93.49
20.00	84.93	85.33	85.73	86.14	86.54	86.94	87.35	87.75	88.16	88.57	88.98	89.39	89.80	90.21	91.03	93.08
25.00	77.95	78.32	78.68	79.05	79.42	79.79	80.16	80.54	80.91	81.28	81.66	82.04	82.42	82.79	90.63	91.46
30.00	71.78	72.12	72.46	72.80	73.14	73.48	73.82	74.16	74.51	74.85	75.20	75.55	75.89	76.24	76.59	77.29

Description: This table shows the yield to maturity of a mortgage purchased at the price shown in the index.

Example: The yield to maturity of a 15.00 %, 4 year mortgage at a price of 102.00 is 13.91 %.

INTEREST RATE, %

PRICE	11.00%	11.25%	11.50%	11.75%	12.00%	12.25%	12.50%	12.75%	13.00%	13.25%	13.50%	13.75%	14.00%	14.25%	14.50%	15.00%
110	6.02	6.26	6.50	6.74	6.98	7.22	7.46	7.70	7.94	8.18	8.42	8.66	8.90	9.15	9.39	9.87
109	6.49	6.73	6.97	7.21	7.45	7.69	7.94	8.18	8.42	8.66	8.90	9.14	9.38	9.63	9.87	10.35
108	6.96	7.20	7.45	7.69	7.93	8.17	8.42	8.66	8.90	9.14	9.39	9.63	9.87	10.11	10.35	10.84
107	7.44	7.69	7.93	8.17	8.42	8.66	8.90	9.15	9.39	9.63	9.88	10.12	10.36	10.60	10.85	11.33
106	7.93	8.17	8.42	8.66	8.91	9.15	9.40	9.64	9.88	10.13	10.37	10.62	10.86	11.10	11.35	11.84
105.75	8.05	8.30	8.54	8.79	9.03	9.28	9.52	9.76	10.01	10.25	10.50	10.74	10.98	11.23	11.47	11.96
105.50	8.18	8.42	8.67	8.91	9.15	9.40	9.64	9.89	10.13	10.38	10.62	10.87	11.11	11.36	11.60	12.09
105.25	8.30	8.54	8.79	9.03	9.28	9.52	9.77	10.01	10.26	10.50	10.75	10.99	11.24	11.48	11.73	12.22
105.00	8.42	8.67	8.91	9.16	9.40	9.65	9.89	10.14	10.38	10.63	10.87	11.12	11.36	11.61	11.85	12.34
104.75	8.55	8.79	9.04	9.28	9.53	9.78	10.02	10.27	10.51	10.76	11.00	11.25	11.49	11.74	11.98	12.47
104.50	8.67	8.92	9.16	9.41	9.66	9.90	10.15	10.39	10.64	10.88	11.13	11.37	11.62	11.86	12.11	12.60
104.25	8.80	9.04	9.29	9.54	9.78	10.03	10.27	10.52	10.76	11.01	11.26	11.50	11.75	11.99	12.24	12.73
104.00	8.92	9.17	9.42	9.66	9.91	10.15	10.40	10.65	10.89	11.14	11.38	11.63	11.88	12.12	12.37	12.86
103.75	9.05	9.30	9.54	9.79	10.04	10.28	10.53	10.77	11.02	11.27	11.51	11.76	12.01	12.25	12.50	12.99
103.50	9.18	9.42	9.67	9.92	10.16	10.41	10.66	10.90	11.15	11.40	11.64	11.89	12.13	12.38	12.63	13.12
103.25	9.30	9.55	9.80	10.04	10.29	10.54	10.78	11.03	11.28	11.52	11.77	12.02	12.26	12.51	12.76	13.25
103.00	9.43	9.68	9.93	10.17	10.42	10.67	10.91	11.16	11.41	11.65	11.90	12.15	12.39	12.64	12.89	13.38
102.75	9.56	9.81	10.05	10.30	10.55	10.80	11.04	11.29	11.54	11.78	12.03	12.28	12.53	12.77	13.02	13.51
102.50	9.69	9.94	10.18	10.43	10.68	10.92	11.17	11.42	11.67	11.91	12.16	12.41	12.66	12.90	13.15	13.65
102.25	9.82	10.06	10.31	10.56	10.81	11.05	11.30	11.55	11.80	12.05	12.29	12.54	12.79	13.04	13.28	13.78
102.00	9.95	10.19	10.44	10.69	10.94	11.19	11.43	11.68	11.93	12.18	12.42	12.67	12.92	13.17	13.42	13.91
101.75	10.08	10.32	10.57	10.82	11.07	11.32	11.56	11.81	12.06	12.31	12.56	12.81	13.05	13.30	13.55	14.05
101.50	10.21	10.45	10.70	10.95	11.20	11.45	11.70	11.94	12.19	12.44	12.69	12.94	13.19	13.43	13.68	14.18
101.25	10.34	10.58	10.83	11.08	11.33	11.58	11.83	12.08	12.33	12.57	12.82	13.07	13.32	13.57	13.82	14.31
101.00	10.47	10.72	10.96	11.21	11.46	11.71	11.96	12.21	12.46	12.71	12.96	13.21	13.45	13.70	13.95	14.45
100.75	10.60	10.85	11.10	11.35	11.59	11.84	12.09	12.34	12.59	12.84	13.09	13.34	13.59	13.84	14.09	14.59
100.50	10.73	10.98	11.23	11.48	11.73	11.98	12.23	12.48	12.73	12.98	13.22	13.47	13.72	13.97	14.22	14.72
100.25	10.86	11.11	11.36	11.61	11.86	12.11	12.36	12.61	12.86	13.11	13.36	13.61	13.86	14.11	14.36	14.86
100.00	11.00	11.25	11.50	11.75	12.00	12.25	12.50	12.75	13.00	13.25	13.50	13.75	14.00	14.25	14.50	15.00
99.75	11.13	11.38	11.63	11.88	12.13	12.38	12.63	12.88	13.13	13.38	13.63	13.88	14.13	14.38	14.63	15.13
99.50	11.26	11.51	11.76	12.01	12.26	12.51	12.77	13.02	13.27	13.52	13.77	14.02	14.27	14.52	14.77	15.27
99.25	11.40	11.65	11.90	12.15	12.40	12.65	12.90	13.15	13.40	13.65	13.90	14.16	14.41	14.66	14.91	15.41
99.00	11.53	11.78	12.03	12.28	12.54	12.79	13.04	13.29	13.54	13.79	14.04	14.29	14.54	14.79	15.05	15.55
98.75	11.67	11.92	12.17	12.42	12.67	12.92	13.17	13.43	13.68	13.93	14.18	14.43	14.68	14.93	15.18	15.69
98.50	11.80	12.05	12.31	12.56	12.81	13.06	13.31	13.56	13.81	14.07	14.32	14.57	14.82	15.07	15.32	15.83
98.25	11.94	12.19	12.44	12.69	12.95	13.20	13.45	13.70	13.95	14.20	14.46	14.71	14.96	15.21	15.46	15.97
98.00	12.07	12.33	12.58	12.83	13.08	13.34	13.59	13.84	14.09	14.34	14.60	14.85	15.10	15.35	15.60	16.11
97.75	12.21	12.46	12.72	12.97	13.22	13.47	13.73	13.98	14.23	14.48	14.74	14.99	15.24	15.49	15.75	16.25
97.50	12.35	12.60	12.85	13.11	13.36	13.61	13.87	14.12	14.37	14.62	14.88	15.13	15.38	15.63	15.89	16.39
97.25	12.49	12.74	12.99	13.25	13.50	13.75	14.01	14.26	14.51	14.76	15.02	15.27	15.52	15.78	16.03	16.54
97.00	12.63	12.88	13.13	13.39	13.64	13.89	14.15	14.40	14.65	14.91	15.16	15.41	15.67	15.92	16.17	16.68
96.75	12.77	13.02	13.27	13.53	13.78	14.03	14.29	14.54	14.79	15.05	15.30	15.55	15.81	16.06	16.31	16.82
96.50	12.91	13.16	13.41	13.67	13.92	14.17	14.43	14.68	14.94	15.19	15.44	15.70	15.95	16.20	16.46	16.97
96.25	13.05	13.30	13.55	13.81	14.06	14.32	14.57	14.82	15.08	15.33	15.59	15.84	16.09	16.35	16.60	17.11
96.00	13.19	13.44	13.69	13.95	14.20	14.46	14.71	14.97	15.22	15.48	15.73	15.98	16.24	16.49	16.75	17.26
95.75	13.33	13.58	13.84	14.09	14.35	14.60	14.85	15.11	15.36	15.62	15.87	16.13	16.38	16.64	16.89	17.40
95.50	13.47	13.72	13.98	14.23	14.49	14.74	15.00	15.25	15.51	15.76	16.02	16.27	16.53	16.78	17.04	17.55
95.25	13.61	13.87	14.12	14.38	14.63	14.89	15.14	15.40	15.65	15.91	16.16	16.42	16.67	16.93	17.18	17.70
95.00	13.75	14.01	14.27	14.52	14.78	15.03	15.29	15.54	15.80	16.05	16.31	16.56	16.82	17.08	17.33	17.84
94.75	13.90	14.15	14.41	14.66	14.92	15.18	15.43	15.69	15.94	16.20	16.46	16.71	16.97	17.22	17.48	17.99
94.50	14.04	14.30	14.55	14.81	15.07	15.32	15.58	15.83	16.09	16.35	16.60	16.86	17.11	17.37	17.63	18.14
94.25	14.19	14.44	14.70	14.95	15.21	15.47	15.72	15.98	16.24	16.49	16.75	17.01	17.26	17.52	17.78	18.29
94.00	14.33	14.59	14.84	15.10	15.36	15.61	15.87	16.13	16.38	16.64	16.90	17.15	17.41	17.67	17.92	18.44
93.75	14.48	14.73	14.99	15.25	15.50	15.76	16.02	16.27	16.53	16.79	17.05	17.30	17.56	17.82	18.07	18.59
93	14.92	15.17	15.43	15.69	15.95	16.21	16.46	16.72	16.98	17.24	17.49	17.75	18.01	18.27	18.53	19.04
92	15.51	15.77	16.03	16.29	16.55	16.81	17.07	17.32	17.58	17.84	18.10	18.36	18.62	18.88	19.14	19.66
91	16.11	16.38	16.64	16.90	17.16	17.42	17.68	17.94	18.20	18.46	18.72	18.98	19.24	19.50	19.76	20.28
90	16.73	16.99	17.25	17.51	17.77	18.04	18.30	18.56	18.82	19.08	19.34	19.61	19.87	20.13	20.39	20.92
89	17.35	17.61	17.88	18.14	18.40	18.67	18.93	19.19	19.45	19.72	19.98	20.24	20.51	20.77	21.03	21.56
88	17.99	18.25	18.51	18.78	19.04	19.31	19.57	19.83	20.10	20.36	20.63	20.89	21.16	21.42	21.69	22.22
87	18.63	18.89	19.16	19.43	19.69	19.96	20.22	20.49	20.75	21.02	21.29	21.55	21.82	22.08	22.35	22.88
86	19.28	19.55	19.82	20.08	20.35	20.62	20.89	21.15	21.42	21.69	21.95	22.22	22.49	22.76	23.02	23.56
85	19.95	20.22	20.49	20.76	21.02	21.29	21.56	21.83	22.10	22.37	22.63	22.90	23.17	23.44	23.71	24.25
84	20.63	20.90	21.17	21.44	21.71	21.98	22.25	22.52	22.79	23.06	23.33	23.60	23.87	24.14	24.41	24.95
83	21.32	21.59	21.86	22.13	22.40	22.67	22.95	23.22	23.49	23.76	24.03	24.30	24.58	24.85	25.12	25.66
82	22.02	22.29	22.56	22.84	23.11	23.38	23.66	23.93	24.20	24.48	24.75	25.02	25.30	25.57	25.84	26.39
81	22.73	23.01	23.28	23.56	23.83	24.11	24.38	24.65	24.93	25.20	25.48	25.75	26.03	26.30	26.58	27.13
80	23.46	23.74	24.01	24.29	24.56	24.84	25.12	25.39	25.67	25.95	26.22	26.50	26.78	27.05	27.33	27.88

MORTGAGE PRICE

Description: This table shows the price to pay for a monthly payment mortgage loan at the yield rate.

Example: The price of a 6.75 %, 5 year mortgage loan to yield 8.00 % to maturity is $ 97.08.

INTEREST RATE, %

YIELD	0.00%	1.00%	2.00%	3.00%	4.00%	4.25%	4.50%	4.75%	5.00%	5.25%	5.50%	5.75%	6.00%	6.25%	6.50%	6.75%
0.00	100.00	102.56	105.17	107.81	110.50	111.18	111.86	112.54	113.23	113.92	114.61	115.30	116.00	116.70	117.40	118.10
1.00	97.50	100.00	102.54	105.12	107.74	108.40	109.06	109.73	110.40	111.07	111.74	112.42	113.10	113.78	114.46	115.15
2.00	95.09	97.52	100.00	102.52	105.07	105.72	106.36	107.01	107.66	108.32	108.98	109.64	110.30	110.96	111.63	112.30
3.00	92.75	95.13	97.55	100.00	102.49	103.12	103.75	104.39	105.02	105.66	106.30	106.95	107.59	108.24	108.89	109.54
4.00	90.50	92.82	95.17	97.57	100.00	100.61	101.23	101.85	102.47	103.09	103.72	104.35	104.98	105.61	106.24	106.88
4.25	89.95	92.25	94.59	96.97	99.39	100.00	100.61	101.23	101.84	102.46	103.08	103.71	104.33	104.96	105.59	106.23
4.50	89.40	91.69	94.02	96.38	98.79	99.39	100.00	100.61	101.22	101.84	102.46	103.08	103.70	104.32	104.95	105.58
4.75	88.86	91.13	93.45	95.80	98.19	98.79	99.39	100.00	100.61	101.22	101.84	102.46	103.08	103.70	104.32	104.94
5.00	88.32	90.58	92.88	95.22	97.59	98.19	98.79	99.39	100.00	100.61	101.22	101.84	102.45	103.07	103.69	104.31
5.25	87.78	90.03	92.32	94.64	97.00	97.60	98.19	98.79	99.40	100.00	100.61	101.22	101.83	102.45	103.06	103.68
5.50	87.25	89.49	91.76	94.07	96.42	97.01	97.60	98.20	98.80	99.40	100.00	100.61	101.22	101.83	102.44	103.06
5.75	86.73	88.95	91.21	93.51	95.84	96.42	97.01	97.61	98.20	98.80	99.40	100.00	100.60	101.21	101.82	102.43
6.00	86.21	88.42	90.66	92.94	95.26	95.85	96.43	97.02	97.61	98.21	98.80	99.40	100.00	100.60	101.21	101.81
6.25	85.69	87.89	90.12	92.39	94.69	95.27	95.85	96.44	97.03	97.62	98.21	98.80	99.40	100.00	100.60	101.20
6.50	85.18	87.36	89.58	91.84	94.12	94.70	95.28	95.86	96.45	97.03	97.62	98.21	98.80	99.40	100.00	100.60
6.75	84.67	86.84	89.05	91.29	93.56	94.14	94.71	95.29	95.87	96.46	97.04	97.63	98.22	98.81	99.40	100.00
7.00	84.17	86.33	88.52	90.75	93.01	93.58	94.15	94.73	95.30	95.88	96.46	97.05	97.63	98.22	98.81	99.41
7.25	83.67	85.81	87.99	90.21	92.46	93.02	93.59	94.16	94.74	95.31	95.89	96.47	97.06	97.64	98.23	98.82
7.50	83.18	85.31	87.47	89.67	91.91	92.47	93.04	93.61	94.18	94.75	95.32	95.90	96.48	97.06	97.65	98.23
7.75	82.68	84.80	86.96	89.14	91.37	91.93	92.49	93.05	93.62	94.19	94.76	95.34	95.91	96.49	97.07	97.65
8.00	82.20	84.30	86.44	88.62	90.83	91.38	91.94	92.51	93.07	93.64	94.20	94.77	95.35	95.92	96.50	97.08
8.25	81.71	83.81	85.94	88.10	90.29	90.85	91.40	91.96	92.52	93.09	93.65	94.22	94.79	95.36	95.93	96.51
8.50	81.24	83.32	85.43	87.58	89.76	90.32	90.87	91.42	91.98	92.54	93.10	93.66	94.23	94.80	95.37	95.94
8.75	80.76	82.83	84.93	87.07	89.24	89.79	90.34	90.89	91.44	92.00	92.56	93.12	93.68	94.24	94.81	95.38
9.00	80.29	82.35	84.44	86.56	88.72	89.26	89.81	90.36	90.91	91.46	92.02	92.57	93.13	93.69	94.26	94.82
9.25	79.82	81.87	83.95	86.06	88.20	88.74	89.29	89.83	90.38	90.93	91.48	92.03	92.59	93.15	93.71	94.27
9.50	79.36	81.39	83.46	85.56	87.69	88.23	88.77	89.31	89.86	90.40	90.95	91.50	92.05	92.61	93.16	93.72
9.75	78.90	80.92	82.97	85.06	87.18	87.72	88.25	88.79	89.33	89.88	90.42	90.97	91.52	92.07	92.62	93.18
10.00	78.44	80.45	82.50	84.57	86.68	87.21	87.74	88.28	88.82	89.36	89.90	90.44	90.99	91.54	92.09	92.64
10.25	77.99	79.99	82.02	84.08	86.18	86.71	87.24	87.77	88.31	88.84	89.38	89.92	90.47	91.01	91.56	92.11
10.50	77.54	79.53	81.55	83.60	85.68	86.21	86.74	87.27	87.80	88.33	88.87	89.41	89.95	90.49	91.03	91.58
10.75	77.10	79.07	81.08	83.12	85.19	85.71	86.24	86.77	87.29	87.83	88.36	88.89	89.43	89.97	90.51	91.05
11.00	76.66	78.62	80.62	82.64	84.70	85.22	85.74	86.27	86.79	87.32	87.85	88.38	88.92	89.45	89.99	90.53
11.25	76.22	78.17	80.16	82.17	84.22	84.74	85.26	85.78	86.30	86.82	87.35	87.88	88.41	88.94	89.48	90.01
11.50	75.78	77.72	79.70	81.70	83.74	84.25	84.77	85.29	85.81	86.33	86.85	87.38	87.91	88.44	88.97	89.50
11.75	75.35	77.28	79.25	81.24	83.26	83.77	84.29	84.80	85.32	85.84	86.36	86.88	87.41	87.93	88.46	88.99
12.00	74.93	76.85	78.80	80.78	82.79	83.30	83.81	84.32	84.84	85.35	85.87	86.39	86.91	87.43	87.96	88.49
12.25	74.50	76.41	78.35	80.32	82.32	82.83	83.34	83.84	84.36	84.87	85.38	85.90	86.42	86.94	87.46	87.99
12.50	74.08	75.98	77.91	79.87	81.86	82.36	82.87	83.37	83.88	84.39	84.90	85.42	85.93	86.45	86.97	87.49
12.75	73.66	75.55	77.47	79.42	81.40	81.90	82.40	82.90	83.41	83.91	84.42	84.93	85.45	85.96	86.48	87.00
13.00	73.25	75.13	77.03	78.97	80.94	81.44	81.94	82.44	82.94	83.44	83.95	84.46	84.97	85.48	85.99	86.51
13.25	72.84	74.71	76.60	78.53	80.49	80.98	81.48	81.98	82.47	82.98	83.48	83.98	84.49	85.00	85.51	86.02
13.50	72.43	74.29	76.18	78.09	80.04	80.53	81.02	81.52	82.01	82.51	83.01	83.52	84.02	84.53	85.03	85.54
13.75	72.03	73.87	75.75	77.66	79.59	80.08	80.57	81.06	81.56	82.05	82.55	83.05	83.55	84.05	84.56	85.07
14.00	71.63	73.46	75.33	77.22	79.15	79.63	80.12	80.61	81.10	81.60	82.09	82.59	83.09	83.59	84.09	84.59
14.25	71.23	73.06	74.91	76.80	78.71	79.19	79.68	80.16	80.65	81.14	81.64	82.13	82.63	83.12	83.62	84.12
14.50	70.84	72.65	74.50	76.37	78.27	78.75	79.24	79.72	80.21	80.69	81.18	81.68	82.17	82.66	83.16	83.66
14.75	70.45	72.25	74.09	75.95	77.84	78.32	78.80	79.28	79.76	80.25	80.74	81.22	81.71	82.21	82.70	83.20
15.00	70.06	71.85	73.68	75.53	77.41	77.89	78.37	78.84	79.32	79.81	80.29	80.78	81.26	81.75	82.25	82.74
15.25	69.67	71.46	73.27	75.12	76.99	77.46	77.93	78.41	78.89	79.37	79.85	80.33	80.82	81.31	81.79	82.28
15.50	69.29	71.07	72.87	74.70	76.57	77.04	77.51	77.98	78.46	78.93	79.41	79.89	80.38	80.86	81.35	81.83
15.75	68.91	70.68	72.47	74.30	76.15	76.61	77.08	77.55	78.03	78.50	78.98	79.46	79.94	80.42	80.90	81.39
16.00	68.54	70.29	72.08	73.89	75.73	76.20	76.66	77.13	77.60	78.07	78.55	79.02	79.50	79.98	80.46	80.94
16.25	68.16	69.91	71.68	73.49	75.32	75.78	76.25	76.71	77.18	77.65	78.12	78.59	79.07	79.54	80.02	80.50
16.50	67.79	69.53	71.30	73.09	74.91	75.37	75.83	76.30	76.76	77.23	77.70	78.17	78.64	79.11	79.59	80.06
16.75	67.43	69.15	70.91	72.69	74.51	74.96	75.42	75.88	76.35	76.81	77.28	77.74	78.21	78.68	79.16	79.63
17.00	67.06	68.78	70.53	72.30	74.10	74.56	75.01	75.47	75.93	76.39	76.86	77.32	77.79	78.26	78.73	79.20
17.25	66.70	68.41	70.15	71.91	73.70	74.16	74.61	75.07	75.52	75.98	76.44	76.91	77.37	77.84	78.30	78.77
17.50	66.34	68.04	69.77	71.53	73.31	73.76	74.21	74.66	75.12	75.57	76.03	76.49	76.96	77.42	77.88	78.35
17.75	65.99	67.68	69.40	71.14	72.91	73.36	73.81	74.26	74.71	75.17	75.63	76.08	76.54	77.00	77.47	77.93
18.00	65.63	67.32	69.02	70.76	72.52	72.97	73.42	73.87	74.32	74.77	75.22	75.68	76.13	76.59	77.05	77.51
18.25	65.28	66.96	68.66	70.38	72.14	72.58	73.03	73.47	73.92	74.37	74.82	75.27	75.73	76.18	76.64	77.10
18.50	64.94	66.60	68.29	70.01	71.75	72.19	72.64	73.08	73.53	73.97	74.42	74.87	75.32	75.78	76.23	76.69
18.75	64.59	66.25	67.93	69.64	71.37	71.81	72.25	72.69	73.14	73.58	74.03	74.47	74.92	75.38	75.83	76.28
19.00	64.25	65.90	67.57	69.27	71.00	71.43	71.87	72.31	72.75	73.19	73.63	74.08	74.53	74.98	75.43	75.88
20.00	62.91	64.52	66.16	67.82	69.51	69.94	70.37	70.80	71.23	71.66	72.10	72.53	72.97	73.41	73.85	74.29
25.00	56.78	58.24	59.72	61.22	62.75	63.13	63.52	63.90	64.29	64.69	65.08	65.47	65.87	66.26	66.66	67.06
30.00	51.51	52.83	54.18	55.54	56.92	57.27	57.62	57.98	58.33	58.68	59.04	59.40	59.76	60.12	60.48	60.84

MORTGAGE YIELD

Description: This table shows the yield to maturity of a mortgage purchased at the price shown in the index.

Example: The yield to maturity of a 6.75 %, 5 year mortgage at a price of 95.00 is 8.91 %.

INTEREST RATE, %

PRICE	0.00%	1.00%	2.00%	3.00%	4.00%	4.25%	4.50%	4.75%	5.00%	5.25%	5.50%	5.75%	6.00%	6.25%	6.50%	6.75%
100	0.00	1.00	2.00	3.00	4.00	4.25	4.50	4.75	5.00	5.25	5.50	5.75	6.00	6.25	6.50	6.75
99.75	.09	1.09	2.10	3.10	4.10	4.35	4.60	4.85	5.10	5.35	5.60	5.85	6.10	6.35	6.60	6.85
99.50	.19	1.19	2.20	3.20	4.20	4.45	4.70	4.95	5.20	5.45	5.70	5.95	6.20	6.45	6.70	6.96
99.25	.29	1.29	2.30	3.30	4.30	4.55	4.80	5.05	5.31	5.56	5.81	6.06	6.31	6.56	6.81	7.06
99.00	.39	1.39	2.40	3.40	4.41	4.66	4.91	5.16	5.41	5.66	5.91	6.16	6.41	6.66	6.92	7.17
98.75	.49	1.50	2.50	3.50	4.51	4.76	5.01	5.26	5.51	5.77	6.02	6.27	6.52	6.77	7.02	7.27
98.50	.59	1.60	2.60	3.61	4.61	4.87	5.12	5.37	5.62	5.87	6.12	6.37	6.63	6.88	7.13	7.38
98.25	.69	1.70	2.70	3.71	4.72	4.97	5.22	5.47	5.72	5.98	6.23	6.48	6.73	6.98	7.24	7.49
98.00	.79	1.80	2.81	3.82	4.82	5.07	5.33	5.58	5.83	6.08	6.33	6.59	6.84	7.09	7.34	7.59
97.75	.89	1.90	2.91	3.92	4.93	5.18	5.43	5.68	5.94	6.19	6.44	6.69	6.95	7.20	7.45	7.70
97.50	1.00	2.00	3.01	4.02	5.03	5.29	5.54	5.79	6.04	6.30	6.55	6.80	7.05	7.31	7.56	7.81
97.25	1.10	2.11	3.12	4.13	5.14	5.39	5.64	5.90	6.15	6.40	6.66	6.91	7.16	7.41	7.67	7.92
97.00	1.20	2.21	3.22	4.23	5.25	5.50	5.75	6.00	6.26	6.51	6.76	7.02	7.27	7.52	7.78	8.03
96.75	1.30	2.31	3.33	4.34	5.35	5.61	5.86	6.11	6.36	6.62	6.87	7.12	7.38	7.63	7.88	8.14
96.50	1.41	2.42	3.43	4.45	5.46	5.71	5.97	6.22	6.47	6.73	6.98	7.23	7.49	7.74	7.99	8.25
96.25	1.51	2.52	3.54	4.55	5.57	5.82	6.07	6.33	6.58	6.83	7.09	7.34	7.60	7.85	8.10	8.36
96.00	1.61	2.63	3.64	4.66	5.67	5.93	6.18	6.44	6.69	6.94	7.20	7.45	7.71	7.96	8.21	8.47
95.75	1.72	2.73	3.75	4.77	5.78	6.04	6.29	6.54	6.80	7.05	7.31	7.56	7.82	8.07	8.32	8.58
95.50	1.82	2.84	3.86	4.87	5.89	6.15	6.40	6.65	6.91	7.16	7.42	7.67	7.93	8.18	8.44	8.69
95.25	1.93	2.94	3.96	4.98	6.00	6.25	6.51	6.76	7.02	7.27	7.53	7.78	8.04	8.29	8.55	8.80
95.00	2.03	3.05	4.07	5.09	6.11	6.36	6.62	6.87	7.13	7.38	7.64	7.89	8.15	8.40	8.66	8.91
94.75	2.14	3.16	4.18	5.20	6.22	6.47	6.73	6.98	7.24	7.50	7.75	8.01	8.26	8.52	8.77	9.03
94.50	2.24	3.26	4.29	5.31	6.33	6.58	6.84	7.10	7.35	7.61	7.86	8.12	8.37	8.63	8.88	9.14
94.25	2.35	3.37	4.39	5.42	6.44	6.70	6.95	7.21	7.46	7.72	7.97	8.23	8.49	8.74	9.00	9.25
94.00	2.46	3.48	4.50	5.53	6.55	6.81	7.06	7.32	7.57	7.83	8.09	8.34	8.60	8.86	9.11	9.37
93.75	2.56	3.59	4.61	5.64	6.66	6.92	7.17	7.43	7.69	7.94	8.20	8.46	8.71	8.97	9.23	9.48
93.50	2.67	3.70	4.72	5.75	6.77	7.03	7.29	7.54	7.80	8.06	8.31	8.57	8.83	9.08	9.34	9.60
93.25	2.78	3.81	4.83	5.86	6.89	7.14	7.40	7.66	7.91	8.17	8.43	8.68	8.94	9.20	9.46	9.71
93.00	2.89	3.91	4.94	5.97	7.00	7.26	7.51	7.77	8.03	8.28	8.54	8.80	9.06	9.31	9.57	9.83
92.75	3.00	4.02	5.05	6.08	7.11	7.37	7.63	7.88	8.14	8.40	8.66	8.91	9.17	9.43	9.69	9.94
92.50	3.11	4.13	5.16	6.19	7.22	7.48	7.74	8.00	8.26	8.51	8.77	9.03	9.29	9.54	9.80	10.06
92.25	3.22	4.25	5.28	6.31	7.34	7.60	7.85	8.11	8.37	8.63	8.89	9.14	9.40	9.66	9.92	10.18
92.00	3.33	4.36	5.39	6.42	7.45	7.71	7.97	8.23	8.49	8.74	9.00	9.26	9.52	9.78	10.04	10.30
91.75	3.44	4.47	5.50	6.53	7.57	7.83	8.08	8.34	8.60	8.86	9.12	9.38	9.64	9.90	10.15	10.41
91	3.77	4.81	5.84	6.88	7.91	8.17	8.43	8.69	8.95	9.21	9.47	9.73	9.99	10.25	10.51	10.77
90	4.22	5.26	6.30	7.34	8.38	8.64	8.90	9.17	9.43	9.69	9.95	10.21	10.47	10.73	10.99	11.25
89	4.68	5.72	6.77	7.81	8.86	9.12	9.38	9.64	9.91	10.17	10.43	10.69	10.95	11.22	11.48	11.74
88	5.14	6.19	7.24	8.29	9.34	9.61	9.87	10.13	10.40	10.66	10.92	11.18	11.45	11.71	11.97	12.24
87	5.62	6.67	7.72	8.78	9.84	10.10	10.36	10.63	10.89	11.16	11.42	11.69	11.95	12.21	12.48	12.74
86	6.10	7.15	8.21	9.27	10.33	10.60	10.87	11.13	11.40	11.66	11.93	12.19	12.46	12.73	12.99	13.26
85	6.58	7.65	8.71	9.78	10.84	11.11	11.38	11.64	11.91	12.18	12.44	12.71	12.98	13.25	13.51	13.78
84	7.08	8.15	9.22	10.29	11.36	11.63	11.90	12.16	12.43	12.70	12.97	13.24	13.51	13.77	14.04	14.31
83	7.58	8.66	9.73	10.81	11.88	12.15	12.42	12.69	12.96	13.23	13.50	13.77	14.04	14.31	14.58	14.85
82	8.10	9.18	10.26	11.34	12.42	12.69	12.96	13.23	13.50	13.77	14.04	14.32	14.59	14.86	15.13	15.40
81	8.62	9.70	10.79	11.87	12.96	13.23	13.51	13.78	14.05	14.32	14.60	14.87	15.14	15.42	15.69	15.96
80	9.15	10.24	11.33	12.42	13.52	13.79	14.06	14.34	14.61	14.89	15.16	15.43	15.71	15.98	16.26	16.53
79	9.69	10.78	11.88	12.98	14.08	14.35	14.63	14.91	15.18	15.46	15.73	16.01	16.28	16.56	16.84	17.11
78	10.24	11.34	12.44	13.55	14.65	14.93	15.21	15.48	15.76	16.04	16.32	16.59	16.87	17.15	17.43	17.70
77	10.80	11.91	13.02	14.13	15.24	15.52	15.79	16.07	16.35	16.63	16.91	17.19	17.47	17.75	18.03	18.31
76	11.37	12.48	13.60	14.71	15.83	16.11	16.39	16.67	16.95	17.23	17.52	17.80	18.08	18.36	18.64	18.92
75	11.95	13.07	14.19	15.32	16.44	16.72	17.00	17.29	17.57	17.85	18.13	18.41	18.70	18.98	19.26	19.55
74	12.54	13.67	14.80	15.93	17.06	17.34	17.63	17.91	18.19	18.48	18.76	19.05	19.33	19.61	19.90	20.18
73	13.15	14.28	15.41	16.55	17.69	17.98	18.26	18.55	18.83	19.12	19.40	19.69	19.98	20.26	20.55	20.84
72	13.76	14.90	16.04	17.19	18.33	18.62	18.91	19.20	19.48	19.77	20.06	20.35	20.63	20.92	21.21	21.50
71	14.39	15.54	16.69	17.84	18.99	19.28	19.57	19.86	20.15	20.44	20.73	21.02	21.31	21.60	21.89	22.18
70	15.03	16.19	17.34	18.50	19.66	19.95	20.24	20.54	20.83	21.12	21.41	21.70	21.99	22.29	22.58	22.87
69	15.69	16.85	18.01	19.18	20.35	20.64	20.93	21.23	21.52	21.81	22.11	22.40	22.70	22.99	23.28	23.58
68	16.36	17.52	18.70	19.87	21.05	21.34	21.64	21.93	22.23	22.52	22.82	23.12	23.41	23.71	24.01	24.30
67	17.04	18.21	19.39	20.58	21.76	22.06	22.36	22.65	22.95	23.25	23.55	23.85	24.14	24.44	24.74	25.04
66	17.74	18.92	20.11	21.30	22.49	22.79	23.09	23.39	23.69	23.99	24.29	24.59	24.89	25.19	25.50	25.80
65	18.45	19.64	20.84	22.04	23.24	23.54	23.85	24.15	24.45	24.75	25.05	25.36	25.66	25.96	26.27	26.57
64	19.18	20.38	21.59	22.80	24.01	24.31	24.62	24.92	25.23	25.53	25.83	26.14	26.45	26.75	27.06	27.36
63	19.93	21.14	22.35	23.57	24.79	25.10	25.40	25.71	26.02	26.33	26.63	26.94	27.25	27.56	27.86	28.17
62	20.69	21.91	23.13	24.36	25.59	25.90	26.21	26.52	26.83	27.14	27.45	27.76	28.07	28.38	28.69	29.00
61	21.47	22.70	23.94	25.17	26.42	26.73	27.04	27.35	27.66	27.98	28.29	28.60	28.91	29.23	29.54	29.86
60	22.27	23.51	24.76	26.01	27.26	27.57	27.89	28.20	28.52	28.83	29.15	29.46	29.78	30.10	30.41	30.73
59	23.10	24.35	25.60	26.86	28.13	28.44	28.76	29.08	29.39	29.71	30.03	30.35	30.67	30.99	31.31	31.63
58	23.94	25.20	26.47	27.74	29.01	29.33	29.65	29.97	30.29	30.61	30.93	31.26	31.58	31.90	32.22	32.55

Description: This table shows the price to pay for a monthly payment mortgage loan at the yield rate.

Example: The price of a 10.75 %, 5 year mortgage loan to yield 8.00 % to maturity is $ 106.62.

YIELD	7.00%	7.25%	7.50%	7.75%	8.00%	8.25%	8.50%	8.75%	9.00%	9.25%	9.50%	9.75%	10.00%	10.25%	10.50%	10.75%
0.00	118.81	119.52	120.23	120.94	121.66	122.38	123.10	123.82	124.55	125.28	126.01	126.75	127.48	128.22	128.96	129.71
1.00	115.84	116.53	117.22	117.92	118.62	119.32	120.02	120.73	121.44	122.15	122.86	123.58	124.30	125.02	125.74	126.47
2.00	112.97	113.64	114.32	115.00	115.68	116.37	117.05	117.74	118.43	119.12	119.82	120.52	121.22	121.92	122.63	123.34
3.00	110.20	110.86	111.52	112.18	112.84	113.51	114.18	114.85	115.53	116.20	116.88	117.56	118.24	118.93	119.62	120.31
4.00	107.52	108.16	108.80	109.45	110.10	110.75	111.40	112.06	112.72	113.38	114.04	114.70	115.37	116.04	116.71	117.38
4.25	106.86	107.50	108.14	108.78	109.43	110.07	110.72	111.37	112.03	112.68	113.34	114.00	114.67	115.33	116.00	116.67
4.50	106.21	106.85	107.48	108.12	108.76	109.40	110.05	110.70	111.35	112.00	112.65	113.31	113.97	114.63	115.29	115.96
4.75	105.57	106.20	106.83	107.46	108.10	108.74	109.38	110.02	110.67	111.32	111.97	112.62	113.28	113.93	114.59	115.25
5.00	104.93	105.55	106.18	106.81	107.45	108.08	108.72	109.36	110.00	110.64	111.29	111.94	112.59	113.24	113.90	114.56
5.25	104.29	104.92	105.54	106.17	106.80	107.43	108.06	108.70	109.34	109.98	110.62	111.26	111.91	112.56	113.21	113.86
5.50	103.66	104.28	104.90	105.53	106.15	106.78	107.41	108.04	108.68	109.31	109.95	110.59	111.23	111.88	112.53	113.18
5.75	103.04	103.66	104.27	104.89	105.51	106.14	106.76	107.39	108.02	108.65	109.29	109.93	110.57	111.21	111.85	112.50
6.00	102.42	103.03	103.65	104.26	104.88	105.50	106.12	106.75	107.37	108.00	108.63	109.27	109.90	110.54	111.18	111.82
6.25	101.81	102.42	103.03	103.64	104.25	104.87	105.49	106.11	106.73	107.36	107.98	108.61	109.24	109.88	110.51	111.15
6.50	101.20	101.81	102.41	103.02	103.63	104.24	104.86	105.47	106.09	106.71	107.34	107.96	108.59	109.22	109.85	110.49
6.75	100.60	101.20	101.80	102.41	103.01	103.62	104.23	104.85	105.46	106.08	106.70	107.32	107.94	108.57	109.20	109.83
7.00	100.00	100.60	101.20	101.80	102.40	103.01	103.61	104.22	104.83	105.45	106.06	106.68	107.30	107.92	108.55	109.17
7.25	99.41	100.00	100.60	101.19	101.79	102.39	103.00	103.60	104.21	104.82	105.43	106.05	106.67	107.28	107.90	108.53
7.50	98.82	99.41	100.00	100.59	101.19	101.79	102.39	102.99	103.60	104.20	104.81	105.42	106.03	106.65	107.27	107.89
7.75	98.24	98.82	99.41	100.00	100.59	101.19	101.78	102.38	102.98	103.59	104.19	104.80	105.41	106.02	106.63	107.25
8.00	97.66	98.24	98.82	99.41	100.00	100.59	101.18	101.78	102.38	102.98	103.58	104.18	104.79	105.39	106.00	106.62
8.25	97.08	97.66	98.24	98.83	99.41	100.00	100.59	101.18	101.78	102.37	102.97	103.57	104.17	104.78	105.38	105.99
8.50	96.51	97.09	97.67	98.25	98.83	99.41	100.00	100.59	101.18	101.77	102.37	102.96	103.56	104.16	104.76	105.37
8.75	95.95	96.52	97.10	97.67	98.25	98.83	99.42	100.00	100.59	101.18	101.77	102.36	102.95	103.55	104.15	104.75
9.00	95.39	95.96	96.53	97.10	97.68	98.26	98.84	99.42	100.00	100.59	101.17	101.76	102.35	102.95	103.54	104.14
9.25	94.83	95.40	95.97	96.54	97.11	97.68	98.26	98.84	99.42	100.00	100.58	101.17	101.76	102.35	102.94	103.53
9.50	94.28	94.85	95.41	95.98	96.55	97.12	97.69	98.26	98.84	99.42	100.00	100.58	101.17	101.76	102.35	102.94
9.75	93.74	94.30	94.86	95.42	95.99	96.55	97.12	97.69	98.27	98.84	99.42	100.00	100.58	101.17	101.75	102.93
10.00	93.20	93.75	94.31	94.87	95.43	96.00	96.56	97.13	97.70	98.27	98.85	99.42	100.00	100.58	101.16	102.34
10.25	92.66	93.21	93.77	94.32	94.88	95.44	96.01	96.57	97.14	97.71	98.28	98.85	99.42	100.00	100.58	101.75
10.50	92.12	92.67	93.23	93.78	94.34	94.89	95.45	96.01	96.58	97.14	97.71	98.28	98.85	99.42	100.00	101.16
10.75	91.60	92.14	92.69	93.24	93.79	94.35	94.91	95.46	96.02	96.59	97.15	97.72	98.28	98.85	99.42	100.58
11.00	91.07	91.62	92.16	92.71	93.26	93.81	94.36	94.92	95.47	96.03	96.59	97.16	97.72	98.29	98.86	100.00
11.25	90.55	91.09	91.63	92.18	92.72	93.27	93.82	94.37	94.93	95.48	96.04	96.60	97.16	97.73	98.29	99.43
11.50	90.04	90.57	91.11	91.65	92.20	92.74	93.29	93.84	94.39	94.94	95.50	96.05	96.61	97.17	97.73	98.86
11.75	89.52	90.06	90.59	91.13	91.67	92.21	92.76	93.30	93.85	94.40	94.95	95.51	96.06	96.62	97.18	98.30
12.00	89.02	89.55	90.08	90.62	91.15	91.69	92.23	92.77	93.32	93.87	94.41	94.96	95.52	96.07	96.63	97.74
12.25	88.51	89.04	89.57	90.10	90.64	91.17	91.71	92.25	92.79	93.33	93.88	94.43	94.98	95.53	96.08	97.18
12.50	88.01	88.54	89.07	89.59	90.13	90.66	91.19	91.73	92.27	92.81	93.35	93.89	94.44	94.99	95.54	96.63
12.75	87.52	88.04	88.56	89.09	89.62	90.15	90.68	91.21	91.75	92.29	92.82	93.37	93.91	94.45	95.00	96.09
13.00	87.03	87.55	88.07	88.59	89.11	89.64	90.17	90.70	91.23	91.77	92.30	92.84	93.38	93.92	94.47	95.55
13.25	86.54	87.06	87.57	88.09	88.62	89.14	89.67	90.19	90.72	91.25	91.79	92.32	92.86	93.40	93.94	95.01
13.50	86.06	86.57	87.08	87.60	88.12	88.64	89.16	89.69	90.22	90.74	91.27	91.81	92.34	92.87	93.41	94.48
13.75	85.58	86.09	86.60	87.11	87.63	88.15	88.67	89.19	89.71	90.24	90.76	91.29	91.82	92.36	92.89	93.95
14.00	85.10	85.61	86.12	86.63	87.14	87.66	88.17	88.69	89.21	89.74	90.26	90.79	91.31	91.84	92.37	93.43
14.25	84.63	85.13	85.64	86.15	86.66	87.17	87.68	88.20	88.72	89.24	89.76	90.28	90.81	91.33	91.86	92.91
14.50	84.16	84.66	85.17	85.67	86.18	86.69	87.20	87.71	88.23	88.74	89.26	89.78	90.30	90.83	91.35	92.39
14.75	83.69	84.19	84.70	85.20	85.70	86.21	86.72	87.23	87.74	88.25	88.77	89.29	89.81	90.33	90.85	91.88
15.00	83.23	83.73	84.23	84.73	85.23	85.73	86.24	86.75	87.26	87.77	88.28	88.79	89.31	89.83	90.35	91.37
15.25	82.78	83.27	83.77	84.26	84.76	85.26	85.77	86.27	86.78	87.29	87.80	88.31	88.82	89.34	89.85	90.87
15.50	82.32	82.81	83.31	83.80	84.30	84.80	85.30	85.80	86.30	86.81	87.31	87.82	88.33	88.85	89.36	90.37
15.75	81.87	82.36	82.85	83.34	83.84	84.33	84.83	85.33	85.83	86.33	86.84	87.34	87.85	88.36	88.87	89.88
16.00	81.43	81.91	82.40	82.89	83.38	83.87	84.37	84.86	85.36	85.86	86.36	86.87	87.37	87.88	88.39	89.38
16.25	80.98	81.47	81.95	82.44	82.93	83.42	83.91	84.40	84.90	85.39	85.89	86.39	86.90	87.40	87.91	88.90
16.50	80.54	81.02	81.51	81.99	82.48	82.96	83.45	83.94	84.44	84.93	85.43	85.92	86.42	86.93	87.43	88.41
16.75	80.11	80.59	81.07	81.55	82.03	82.51	83.00	83.49	83.98	84.47	84.96	85.46	85.96	86.46	86.96	87.93
17.00	79.67	80.15	80.63	81.11	81.59	82.07	82.55	83.04	83.53	84.02	84.51	85.00	85.49	85.99	86.49	87.46
17.25	79.25	79.72	80.19	80.67	81.15	81.63	82.11	82.59	83.08	83.56	84.05	84.54	85.03	85.52	86.02	86.98
17.50	78.82	79.29	79.76	80.24	80.71	81.19	81.67	82.15	82.63	83.11	83.60	84.09	84.57	85.07	85.56	86.52
17.75	78.40	78.86	79.33	79.81	80.28	80.75	81.23	81.71	82.19	82.67	83.15	83.64	84.12	84.61	85.10	86.05
18.00	77.98	78.44	78.91	79.38	79.85	80.32	80.79	81.27	81.75	82.23	82.71	83.19	83.67	84.16	84.64	85.59
18.25	77.56	78.02	78.49	78.96	79.42	79.89	80.36	80.84	81.31	81.79	82.26	82.74	83.23	83.71	84.19	85.13
18.50	77.15	77.61	78.07	78.54	79.00	79.47	79.94	80.41	80.88	81.35	81.83	82.30	82.78	83.26	83.74	84.68
18.75	76.74	77.20	77.66	78.12	78.58	79.05	79.51	79.98	80.45	80.92	81.39	81.87	82.34	82.82	83.30	84.23
19.00	76.33	76.79	77.25	77.70	78.16	78.63	79.09	79.56	80.02	80.49	80.96	81.43	81.91	82.38	82.86	83.78
20.00	74.74	75.18	75.63	76.08	76.53	76.98	77.44	77.89	78.35	78.81	79.27	79.73	80.20	80.66	81.13	83.34
25.00	67.46	67.87	68.27	68.67	69.08	69.49	69.90	70.31	70.72	71.14	71.55	71.97	72.39	72.81	73.23	81.60
30.00	61.20	61.57	61.93	62.30	62.67	63.04	63.41	63.79	64.16	64.54	64.91	65.29	65.67	66.05	66.43	73.65

Description: This table shows the yield to maturity of a mortgage purchased at the price shown in the index.

Example: The yield to maturity of a 10.75 %, 5 year mortgage at a price of 100.00 is 10.75 %.

INTEREST RATE, %

PRICE	7.00%	7.25%	7.50%	7.75%	8.00%	8.25%	8.50%	8.75%	9.00%	9.25%	9.50%	9.75%	10.00%	10.25%	10.50%	10.75%
105	4.97	5.21	5.46	5.70	5.95	6.19	6.44	6.68	6.93	7.17	7.42	7.66	7.91	8.15	8.40	8.64
104.75	5.06	5.31	5.56	5.80	6.05	6.29	6.54	6.78	7.03	7.27	7.52	7.76	8.01	8.26	8.50	8.75
104.50	5.16	5.41	5.65	5.90	6.15	6.39	6.64	6.88	7.13	7.37	7.62	7.87	8.11	8.36	8.60	8.85
104.25	5.26	5.51	5.75	6.00	6.25	6.49	6.74	6.98	7.23	7.48	7.72	7.97	8.21	8.46	8.70	8.95
104.00	5.36	5.61	5.85	6.10	6.35	6.59	6.84	7.08	7.33	7.58	7.82	8.07	8.31	8.56	8.81	9.05
103.75	5.46	5.71	5.95	6.20	6.45	6.69	6.94	7.19	7.43	7.68	7.92	8.17	8.42	8.66	8.91	9.16
103.50	5.56	5.81	6.05	6.30	6.55	6.79	7.04	7.29	7.53	7.78	8.03	8.27	8.52	8.77	9.01	9.26
103.25	5.66	5.91	6.15	6.40	6.65	6.90	7.14	7.39	7.64	7.88	8.13	8.38	8.62	8.87	9.12	9.36
103.00	5.76	6.01	6.26	6.50	6.75	7.00	7.24	7.49	7.74	7.99	8.23	8.48	8.73	8.97	9.22	9.47
102.75	5.86	6.11	6.36	6.60	6.85	7.10	7.35	7.59	7.84	8.09	8.34	8.58	8.83	9.08	9.32	9.57
102.50	5.96	6.21	6.46	6.71	6.95	7.20	7.45	7.70	7.94	8.19	8.44	8.69	8.93	9.18	9.43	9.68
102.25	6.07	6.31	6.56	6.81	7.06	7.30	7.55	7.80	8.05	8.30	8.54	8.79	9.04	9.29	9.53	9.78
102.00	6.17	6.42	6.66	6.91	7.16	7.41	7.66	7.90	8.15	8.40	8.65	8.90	9.14	9.39	9.64	9.89
101.75	6.27	6.52	6.77	7.01	7.26	7.51	7.76	8.01	8.26	8.50	8.75	9.00	9.25	9.50	9.75	9.99
101.50	6.37	6.62	6.87	7.12	7.37	7.61	7.86	8.11	8.36	8.61	8.86	9.11	9.35	9.60	9.85	10.10
101.25	6.47	6.72	6.97	7.22	7.47	7.72	7.97	8.22	8.47	8.71	8.96	9.21	9.46	9.71	9.96	10.21
101.00	6.58	6.83	7.08	7.33	7.57	7.82	8.07	8.32	8.57	8.82	9.07	9.32	9.57	9.82	10.06	10.31
100.75	6.68	6.93	7.18	7.43	7.68	7.93	8.18	8.43	8.68	8.93	9.17	9.42	9.67	9.92	10.17	10.42
100.50	6.79	7.04	7.28	7.53	7.78	8.03	8.28	8.53	8.78	9.03	9.28	9.53	9.78	10.03	10.28	10.53
100.25	6.89	7.14	7.39	7.64	7.89	8.14	8.39	8.64	8.89	9.14	9.39	9.64	9.89	10.14	10.39	10.64
100.00	7.00	7.25	7.50	7.75	8.00	8.25	8.50	8.75	9.00	9.25	9.50	9.75	10.00	10.25	10.50	10.75
99.75	7.10	7.35	7.60	7.85	8.10	8.35	8.60	8.85	9.10	9.35	9.60	9.85	10.10	10.35	10.60	10.85
99.50	7.21	7.46	7.71	7.96	8.21	8.46	8.71	8.96	9.21	9.46	9.71	9.96	10.21	10.46	10.71	10.96
99.25	7.31	7.56	7.81	8.06	8.31	8.57	8.82	9.07	9.32	9.57	9.82	10.07	10.32	10.57	10.82	11.07
99.00	7.42	7.67	7.92	8.17	8.42	8.67	8.92	9.17	9.43	9.68	9.93	10.18	10.43	10.68	10.93	11.18
98.75	7.52	7.78	8.03	8.28	8.53	8.78	9.03	9.28	9.53	9.79	10.04	10.29	10.54	10.79	11.04	11.29
98.50	7.63	7.88	8.13	8.39	8.64	8.89	9.14	9.39	9.64	9.90	10.15	10.40	10.65	10.90	11.15	11.40
98.25	7.74	7.99	8.24	8.49	8.75	9.00	9.25	9.50	9.75	10.00	10.26	10.51	10.76	11.01	11.26	11.52
98.00	7.85	8.10	8.35	8.60	8.85	9.11	9.36	9.61	9.86	10.11	10.37	10.62	10.87	11.12	11.38	11.63
97.75	7.95	8.21	8.46	8.71	8.96	9.22	9.47	9.72	9.97	10.23	10.48	10.73	10.98	11.23	11.49	11.74
97.50	8.06	8.32	8.57	8.82	9.07	9.33	9.58	9.83	10.08	10.34	10.59	10.84	11.09	11.35	11.60	11.85
97.25	8.17	8.42	8.68	8.93	9.18	9.44	9.69	9.94	10.19	10.45	10.70	10.95	11.21	11.46	11.71	11.96
97.00	8.28	8.53	8.79	9.04	9.29	9.55	9.80	10.05	10.31	10.56	10.81	11.07	11.32	11.57	11.83	12.08
96.75	8.39	8.64	8.90	9.15	9.40	9.66	9.91	10.16	10.42	10.67	10.92	11.18	11.43	11.69	11.94	12.19
96.50	8.50	8.75	9.01	9.26	9.52	9.77	10.02	10.28	10.53	10.78	11.04	11.29	11.54	11.80	12.05	12.31
96.25	8.61	8.87	9.12	9.37	9.63	9.88	10.13	10.39	10.64	10.90	11.15	11.40	11.66	11.91	12.17	12.42
96.00	8.72	8.98	9.23	9.48	9.74	9.99	10.25	10.50	10.76	11.01	11.26	11.52	11.77	12.03	12.28	12.54
95.75	8.83	9.09	9.34	9.60	9.85	10.11	10.36	10.61	10.87	11.12	11.38	11.63	11.89	12.14	12.40	12.65
95.50	8.95	9.20	9.45	9.71	9.96	10.22	10.47	10.73	10.98	11.24	11.49	11.75	12.00	12.26	12.51	12.77
95.25	9.06	9.31	9.57	9.82	10.08	10.33	10.59	10.84	11.10	11.35	11.61	11.86	12.12	12.37	12.63	12.88
95.00	9.17	9.43	9.68	9.94	10.19	10.45	10.70	10.96	11.21	11.47	11.72	11.98	12.23	12.49	12.74	13.00
94.75	9.28	9.54	9.79	10.05	10.31	10.56	10.82	11.07	11.33	11.58	11.84	12.09	12.35	12.61	12.86	13.12
94	9.62	9.88	10.14	10.39	10.65	10.91	11.16	11.42	11.68	11.93	12.19	12.45	12.70	12.96	13.22	13.47
93	10.09	10.34	10.60	10.86	11.12	11.37	11.63	11.89	12.15	12.40	12.66	12.92	13.18	13.43	13.69	13.95
92	10.55	10.81	11.07	11.33	11.59	11.85	12.11	12.36	12.62	12.88	13.14	13.40	13.66	13.92	14.18	14.44
91	11.03	11.29	11.55	11.81	12.07	12.33	12.59	12.85	13.11	13.37	13.63	13.89	14.15	14.41	14.67	14.93
90	11.51	11.77	12.03	12.30	12.56	12.82	13.08	13.34	13.60	13.86	14.12	14.39	14.65	14.91	15.17	15.43
89	12.00	12.27	12.53	12.79	13.05	13.31	13.58	13.84	14.10	14.37	14.63	14.89	15.15	15.42	15.68	15.94
88	12.50	12.77	13.03	13.29	13.56	13.82	14.08	14.35	14.61	14.88	15.14	15.40	15.67	15.93	16.20	16.46
87	13.01	13.27	13.54	13.80	14.07	14.33	14.60	14.86	15.13	15.39	15.66	15.92	16.19	16.46	16.72	16.99
86	13.52	13.79	14.06	14.32	14.59	14.86	15.12	15.39	15.65	15.92	16.19	16.45	16.72	16.99	17.26	17.52
85	14.05	14.32	14.58	14.85	15.12	15.39	15.65	15.92	16.19	16.46	16.73	16.99	17.26	17.53	17.80	18.07
84	14.58	14.85	15.12	15.39	15.66	15.93	16.20	16.46	16.73	17.00	17.27	17.54	17.81	18.08	18.35	18.62
83	15.12	15.39	15.66	15.93	16.20	16.47	16.75	17.02	17.29	17.56	17.83	18.10	18.37	18.64	18.91	19.19
82	15.67	15.95	16.22	16.49	16.76	17.03	17.31	17.58	17.85	18.12	18.40	18.67	18.94	19.21	19.49	19.76
81	16.24	16.51	16.78	17.06	17.33	17.60	17.88	18.15	18.42	18.70	18.97	19.25	19.52	19.80	20.07	20.34
80	16.81	17.08	17.36	17.63	17.91	18.18	18.46	18.73	19.01	19.28	19.56	19.84	20.11	20.39	20.66	20.94
79	17.39	17.67	17.94	18.22	18.50	18.77	19.05	19.33	19.60	19.88	20.16	20.44	20.71	20.99	21.27	21.55
78	17.98	18.26	18.54	18.82	19.09	19.37	19.65	19.93	20.21	20.49	20.77	21.05	21.33	21.61	21.88	22.16
77	18.59	18.87	19.15	19.43	19.71	19.99	20.27	20.55	20.83	21.11	21.39	21.67	21.95	22.23	22.51	22.79
76	19.20	19.48	19.76	20.05	20.33	20.61	20.89	21.17	21.46	21.74	22.02	22.30	22.59	22.87	23.15	23.44
75	19.83	20.11	20.40	20.68	20.96	21.25	21.53	21.81	22.10	22.38	22.67	22.95	23.24	23.52	23.81	24.09
74	20.47	20.75	21.04	21.32	21.61	21.90	22.18	22.47	22.75	23.04	23.33	23.61	23.90	24.19	24.47	24.76
73	21.12	21.41	21.70	21.98	22.27	22.56	22.85	23.13	23.42	23.71	24.00	24.29	24.57	24.86	25.15	25.44
72	21.79	22.08	22.37	22.66	22.94	23.23	23.52	23.81	24.10	24.39	24.68	24.97	25.26	25.56	25.85	26.14
71	22.47	22.76	23.05	23.34	23.63	23.92	24.22	24.51	24.80	25.09	25.38	25.68	25.97	26.26	26.56	26.85
70	23.16	23.46	23.75	24.04	24.34	24.63	24.92	25.22	25.51	25.81	26.10	26.39	26.69	26.98	27.28	27.57
69	23.87	24.17	24.46	24.76	25.05	25.35	25.65	25.94	26.24	26.53	26.83	27.13	27.43	27.72	28.02	28.32

MORTGAGE PRICE

Description: This table shows the price to pay for a monthly payment mortgage loan at the yield rate.

Example: The price of a 15.00 %, 5 year mortgage loan to yield 8.00 % to maturity is $ 117.33.

INTEREST RATE, %

YIELD	11.00%	11.25%	11.50%	11.75%	12.00%	12.25%	12.50%	12.75%	13.00%	13.25%	13.50%	13.75%	14.00%	14.25%	14.50%	15.00%
0.00	130.45	131.20	131.96	132.71	133.47	134.23	134.99	135.75	136.52	137.29	138.06	138.83	139.61	140.39	141.17	142.74
1.00	127.20	127.93	128.66	129.39	130.13	130.87	131.62	132.36	133.11	133.86	134.61	135.36	136.12	136.88	137.64	139.17
2.00	124.05	124.76	125.47	126.19	126.91	127.63	128.36	129.08	129.81	130.54	131.28	132.01	132.75	133.49	134.23	135.73
3.00	121.00	121.70	122.39	123.09	123.80	124.50	125.21	125.92	126.63	127.34	128.06	128.77	129.49	130.22	130.94	132.40
4.00	118.06	118.74	119.42	120.10	120.79	121.47	122.16	122.85	123.55	124.24	124.94	125.64	126.34	127.05	127.76	129.18
4.25	117.34	118.01	118.69	119.37	120.05	120.73	121.42	122.10	122.79	123.49	124.18	124.88	125.57	126.27	126.98	128.39
4.50	116.63	117.29	117.97	118.64	119.32	120.00	120.68	121.36	122.05	122.73	123.42	124.12	124.81	125.51	126.20	127.61
4.75	115.92	116.58	117.25	117.92	118.59	119.27	119.94	120.62	121.31	121.99	122.67	123.36	124.05	124.74	125.44	126.83
5.00	115.21	115.88	116.54	117.21	117.87	118.55	119.22	119.89	120.57	121.25	121.93	122.61	123.30	123.99	124.68	126.06
5.25	114.52	115.18	115.84	116.50	117.16	117.83	118.50	119.17	119.84	120.52	121.19	121.87	122.55	123.24	123.92	125.30
5.50	113.83	114.48	115.14	115.80	116.46	117.12	117.78	118.45	119.12	119.79	120.46	121.14	121.82	122.50	123.18	124.55
5.75	113.14	113.79	114.44	115.10	115.76	116.41	117.07	117.74	118.40	119.07	119.74	120.41	121.08	121.76	122.44	123.80
6.00	112.46	113.11	113.76	114.41	115.06	115.72	116.37	117.03	117.69	118.35	119.02	119.69	120.36	121.03	121.70	123.05
6.25	111.79	112.43	113.08	113.72	114.37	115.02	115.68	116.33	116.99	117.65	118.31	118.97	119.64	120.30	120.97	122.32
6.50	111.12	111.76	112.40	113.04	113.69	114.34	114.98	115.63	116.29	116.94	117.60	118.26	118.92	119.58	120.25	121.59
6.75	110.46	111.09	111.73	112.37	113.01	113.65	114.30	114.95	115.59	116.25	116.90	117.55	118.21	118.87	119.53	120.86
7.00	109.80	110.43	111.07	111.70	112.34	112.98	113.62	114.26	114.91	115.55	116.20	116.86	117.51	118.16	118.82	120.14
7.25	109.15	109.78	110.41	111.04	111.67	112.31	112.95	113.58	114.23	114.87	115.51	116.16	116.81	117.46	118.12	119.43
7.50	108.51	109.13	109.75	110.38	111.01	111.64	112.28	112.91	113.55	114.19	114.83	115.48	116.12	116.77	117.42	118.72
7.75	107.87	108.49	109.11	109.73	110.36	110.98	111.61	112.25	112.88	113.52	114.15	114.79	115.44	116.08	116.73	118.02
8.00	107.23	107.85	108.46	109.08	109.71	110.33	110.96	111.58	112.21	112.85	113.48	114.12	114.76	115.40	116.04	117.33
8.25	106.60	107.21	107.83	108.44	109.06	109.68	110.30	110.93	111.56	112.18	112.81	113.45	114.08	114.72	115.36	116.64
8.50	105.98	106.58	107.19	107.81	108.42	109.04	109.66	110.28	110.90	111.53	112.15	112.78	113.41	114.04	114.68	115.95
8.75	105.36	105.96	106.57	107.18	107.79	108.40	109.02	109.63	110.25	110.87	111.50	112.12	112.75	113.38	114.01	115.28
9.00	104.74	105.34	105.95	106.55	107.16	107.77	108.38	108.99	109.61	110.23	110.85	111.47	112.09	112.72	113.34	114.60
9.25	104.13	104.73	105.33	105.93	106.54	107.14	107.75	108.36	108.97	109.59	110.20	110.82	111.44	112.06	112.68	113.94
9.50	103.53	104.12	104.72	105.32	105.92	106.52	107.12	107.73	108.34	108.95	109.56	110.18	110.79	111.41	112.03	113.28
9.75	102.93	103.52	104.11	104.71	105.30	105.90	106.50	107.11	107.71	108.32	108.93	109.54	110.15	110.76	111.38	112.62
10.00	102.33	102.92	103.51	104.10	104.69	105.29	105.89	106.49	107.09	107.69	108.30	108.90	109.51	110.12	110.74	111.97
10.25	101.74	102.33	102.91	103.50	104.09	104.68	105.28	105.87	106.47	107.07	107.67	108.28	108.88	109.49	110.10	111.32
10.50	101.16	101.74	102.32	102.91	103.49	104.08	104.67	105.26	105.86	106.45	107.05	107.65	108.26	108.86	109.46	110.68
10.75	100.58	101.15	101.73	102.31	102.90	103.48	104.07	104.66	105.25	105.84	106.44	107.04	107.63	108.23	108.84	110.05
11.00	100.00	100.57	101.15	101.73	102.31	102.89	103.47	104.06	104.65	105.24	105.83	106.42	107.02	107.61	108.21	109.42
11.25	99.43	100.00	100.57	101.15	101.72	102.30	102.88	103.47	104.05	104.64	105.22	105.81	106.41	107.00	107.60	108.79
11.50	98.86	99.43	100.00	100.57	101.15	101.72	102.30	102.88	103.46	104.04	104.63	105.21	105.80	106.39	106.98	108.17
11.75	98.30	98.87	99.43	100.00	100.57	101.14	101.72	102.29	102.87	103.45	104.03	104.61	105.20	105.79	106.37	107.56
12.00	97.74	98.30	98.87	99.43	100.00	100.57	101.14	101.71	102.29	102.86	103.44	104.02	104.60	105.19	105.77	106.95
12.25	97.19	97.75	98.31	98.87	99.43	100.00	100.57	101.14	101.71	102.28	102.86	103.44	104.01	104.60	105.19	106.34
12.50	96.64	97.20	97.75	98.31	98.87	99.44	100.00	100.57	101.13	101.70	102.28	102.85	103.42	104.00	104.58	105.74
12.75	96.10	96.65	97.20	97.76	98.32	98.88	99.44	100.00	100.56	101.13	101.70	102.27	102.84	103.42	103.99	105.15
13.00	95.56	96.11	96.66	97.21	97.76	98.32	98.88	99.44	100.00	100.56	101.13	101.70	102.26	102.83	103.41	104.56
13.25	95.02	95.57	96.12	96.67	97.22	97.77	98.32	98.88	99.44	100.00	100.56	101.13	101.69	102.26	102.83	103.97
13.50	94.49	95.03	95.58	96.13	96.67	97.22	97.78	98.33	98.88	99.44	100.00	100.56	101.13	101.69	102.26	103.97
13.75	93.97	94.50	95.05	95.59	96.13	96.68	97.23	97.78	98.33	98.88	99.44	100.00	100.56	101.12	101.69	103.39
14.00	93.44	93.98	94.52	95.06	95.60	96.14	96.69	97.24	97.79	98.34	98.89	99.44	100.00	100.56	101.12	102.81
14.25	92.92	93.46	93.99	94.53	95.07	95.61	96.15	96.70	97.24	97.79	98.34	98.89	99.44	100.00	100.56	102.24
14.50	92.41	92.94	93.47	94.01	94.54	95.08	95.62	96.16	96.71	97.25	97.80	98.34	98.89	99.45	100.00	101.67
14.75	91.90	92.43	92.96	93.49	94.02	94.56	95.09	95.63	96.17	96.71	97.26	97.80	98.35	98.89	99.45	101.11
15.00	91.39	91.92	92.45	92.97	93.50	94.04	94.57	95.10	95.64	96.18	96.72	97.26	97.81	98.35	98.90	100.55
15.25	90.89	91.41	91.94	92.46	92.99	93.52	94.05	94.58	95.12	95.65	96.19	96.73	97.27	97.81	98.36	100.00
15.50	90.39	90.91	91.43	91.96	92.48	93.01	93.53	94.06	94.59	95.13	95.66	96.20	96.74	97.28	97.82	99.45
15.75	89.90	90.42	90.93	91.45	91.97	92.50	93.02	93.55	94.08	94.61	95.14	95.67	96.21	96.74	97.28	98.91
16.00	89.41	89.92	90.44	90.95	91.47	91.99	92.52	93.04	93.56	94.09	94.62	95.15	95.68	96.22	96.75	98.36
16.25	88.92	89.43	89.95	90.46	90.98	91.49	92.01	92.53	93.06	93.58	94.11	94.63	95.16	95.69	96.23	97.83
16.50	88.44	88.95	89.46	89.97	90.48	91.00	91.51	92.03	92.55	93.07	93.59	94.12	94.65	95.17	95.70	97.30
16.75	87.96	88.47	88.97	89.48	89.99	90.50	91.02	91.53	92.05	92.57	93.09	93.61	94.13	94.66	95.19	96.77
17.00	87.49	87.99	88.49	89.00	89.51	90.01	90.53	91.04	91.55	92.07	92.59	93.10	93.63	94.15	94.67	96.24
17.25	87.01	87.51	88.02	88.52	89.02	89.53	90.04	90.55	91.06	91.57	92.09	92.60	93.12	93.64	94.16	95.72
17.50	86.55	87.04	87.54	88.04	88.54	89.05	89.55	90.06	90.57	91.08	91.59	92.11	92.62	93.14	93.66	95.21
17.75	86.08	86.58	87.07	87.57	88.07	88.57	89.07	89.58	90.08	90.59	91.10	91.61	92.12	92.64	93.15	94.70
18.00	85.62	86.11	86.61	87.10	87.60	88.10	88.60	89.10	89.60	90.11	90.61	91.12	91.63	92.14	92.66	94.19
18.25	85.17	85.65	86.15	86.64	87.13	87.63	88.12	88.62	89.12	89.63	90.13	90.64	91.14	91.65	92.16	93.69
18.50	84.71	85.20	85.69	86.18	86.67	87.16	87.66	88.15	88.65	89.15	89.65	90.15	90.66	91.16	91.67	93.19
18.75	84.26	84.75	85.23	85.72	86.21	86.70	87.19	87.68	88.18	88.68	89.17	89.67	90.18	90.68	91.18	92.69
19.00	83.82	84.30	84.78	85.27	85.75	86.24	86.73	87.22	87.71	88.21	88.70	89.20	89.70	90.20	90.70	92.20
20.00	82.07	82.54	83.01	83.48	83.96	84.44	84.92	85.40	85.88	86.36	86.85	87.34	87.82	88.31	88.81	91.71
25.00	74.08	74.50	74.93	75.36	75.79	76.22	76.65	77.08	77.52	77.96	78.39	78.83	79.27	79.72	80.16	89.79
30.00	67.20	67.59	67.98	68.36	68.75	69.15	69.54	69.93	70.33	70.72	71.12	71.52	71.92	72.32	72.72	81.05

MORTGAGE YIELD

Description: This table shows the yield to maturity of a mortgage purchased at the price shown in the index.

Example: The yield to maturity of a 15.00 %, 5 year mortgage at a price of 102.00 is 14.10 %.

INTEREST RATE, %

PRICE	11.00%	11.25%	11.50%	11.75%	12.00%	12.25%	12.50%	12.75%	13.00%	13.25%	13.50%	13.75%	14.00%	14.25%	14.50%	15.00%
110	6.92	7.16	7.40	7.64	7.88	8.12	8.36	8.60	8.84	9.08	9.32	9.56	9.80	10.04	10.28	10.76
109	7.30	7.55	7.79	8.03	8.27	8.51	8.75	8.99	9.23	9.47	9.72	9.96	10.20	10.44	10.68	11.16
108	7.69	7.93	8.18	8.42	8.66	8.90	9.15	9.39	9.63	9.87	10.11	10.36	10.60	10.84	11.08	11.56
107	8.09	8.33	8.57	8.82	9.06	9.30	9.54	9.79	10.03	10.27	10.52	10.76	11.00	11.25	11.49	11.97
106	8.49	8.73	8.97	9.22	9.46	9.71	9.95	10.19	10.44	10.68	10.92	11.17	11.41	11.66	11.90	12.39
105.75	8.59	8.83	9.07	9.32	9.56	9.81	10.05	10.30	10.54	10.78	11.03	11.27	11.52	11.76	12.00	12.49
105.50	8.69	8.93	9.18	9.42	9.66	9.91	10.15	10.40	10.64	10.89	11.13	11.38	11.62	11.86	12.11	12.60
105.25	8.79	9.03	9.28	9.52	9.77	10.01	10.26	10.50	10.75	10.99	11.23	11.48	11.72	11.97	12.21	12.70
105.00	8.89	9.13	9.38	9.62	9.87	10.11	10.36	10.60	10.85	11.09	11.34	11.58	11.83	12.07	12.32	12.81
104.75	8.99	9.24	9.48	9.73	9.97	10.22	10.46	10.71	10.95	11.20	11.44	11.69	11.93	12.18	12.42	12.91
104.50	9.09	9.34	9.58	9.83	10.08	10.32	10.57	10.81	11.06	11.30	11.55	11.79	12.04	12.28	12.53	13.02
104.25	9.20	9.44	9.69	9.93	10.18	10.42	10.67	10.92	11.16	11.41	11.65	11.90	12.14	12.39	12.63	13.13
104.00	9.30	9.54	9.79	10.04	10.28	10.53	10.77	11.02	11.27	11.51	11.76	12.00	12.25	12.50	12.74	13.23
103.75	9.40	9.65	9.89	10.14	10.39	10.63	10.88	11.13	11.37	11.62	11.86	12.11	12.36	12.60	12.85	13.34
103.50	9.51	9.75	10.00	10.25	10.49	10.74	10.98	11.23	11.48	11.72	11.97	12.22	12.46	12.71	12.96	13.45
103.25	9.61	9.86	10.10	10.35	10.60	10.84	11.09	11.34	11.58	11.83	12.08	12.32	12.57	12.82	13.06	13.56
103.00	9.71	9.96	10.21	10.46	10.70	10.95	11.20	11.44	11.69	11.94	12.18	12.43	12.68	12.92	13.17	13.66
102.75	9.82	10.07	10.31	10.56	10.81	11.05	11.30	11.55	11.80	12.04	12.29	12.54	12.78	13.03	13.28	13.77
102.50	9.92	10.17	10.42	10.67	10.91	11.16	11.41	11.66	11.90	12.15	12.40	12.65	12.89	13.14	13.39	13.88
102.25	10.03	10.28	10.52	10.77	11.02	11.27	11.52	11.76	12.01	12.26	12.51	12.75	13.00	13.25	13.50	13.99
102.00	10.14	10.38	10.63	10.88	11.13	11.37	11.62	11.87	12.12	12.37	12.61	12.86	13.11	13.36	13.61	14.10
101.75	10.24	10.49	10.74	10.99	11.23	11.48	11.73	11.98	12.23	12.47	12.72	12.97	13.22	13.47	13.72	14.21
101.50	10.35	10.60	10.84	11.09	11.34	11.59	11.84	12.09	12.34	12.58	12.83	13.08	13.33	13.58	13.83	14.32
101.25	10.45	10.70	10.95	11.20	11.45	11.70	11.95	12.20	12.44	12.69	12.94	13.19	13.44	13.69	13.94	14.43
101.00	10.56	10.81	11.06	11.31	11.56	11.81	12.06	12.30	12.55	12.80	13.05	13.30	13.55	13.80	14.05	14.55
100.75	10.67	10.92	11.17	11.42	11.67	11.92	12.17	12.41	12.66	12.91	13.16	13.41	13.66	13.91	14.16	14.66
100.50	10.78	11.03	11.28	11.53	11.78	12.03	12.27	12.52	12.77	13.02	13.27	13.52	13.77	14.02	14.27	14.77
100.25	10.89	11.14	11.39	11.64	11.89	12.13	12.38	12.63	12.88	13.13	13.38	13.63	13.88	14.13	14.38	14.88
100.00	11.00	11.25	11.50	11.75	12.00	12.25	12.50	12.75	13.00	13.25	13.50	13.75	14.00	14.25	14.50	15.00
99.75	11.10	11.35	11.60	11.86	12.11	12.36	12.61	12.86	13.11	13.36	13.61	13.86	14.11	14.36	14.61	15.11
99.50	11.21	11.46	11.71	11.97	12.22	12.47	12.72	12.97	13.22	13.47	13.72	13.97	14.22	14.47	14.72	15.22
99.25	11.32	11.57	11.83	12.08	12.33	12.58	12.83	13.08	13.33	13.58	13.83	14.08	14.33	14.58	14.84	15.34
99.00	11.43	11.69	11.94	12.19	12.44	12.69	12.94	13.19	13.44	13.69	13.94	14.20	14.45	14.70	14.95	15.45
98.75	11.54	11.80	12.05	12.30	12.55	12.80	13.05	13.30	13.56	13.81	14.06	14.31	14.56	14.81	15.06	15.57
98.50	11.66	11.91	12.16	12.41	12.66	12.91	13.17	13.42	13.67	13.92	14.17	14.42	14.68	14.93	15.18	15.68
98.25	11.77	12.02	12.27	12.52	12.78	13.03	13.28	13.53	13.78	14.03	14.29	14.54	14.79	15.04	15.29	15.80
98.00	11.88	12.13	12.38	12.64	12.89	13.14	13.39	13.64	13.90	14.15	14.40	14.65	14.91	15.16	15.41	15.91
97.75	11.99	12.24	12.50	12.75	13.00	13.25	13.51	13.76	14.01	14.26	14.52	14.77	15.02	15.27	15.53	16.03
97.50	12.10	12.36	12.61	12.86	13.12	13.37	13.62	13.87	14.13	14.38	14.63	14.88	15.14	15.39	15.64	16.15
97.25	12.22	12.47	12.72	12.98	13.23	13.48	13.74	13.99	14.24	14.50	14.75	15.00	15.25	15.51	15.76	16.27
97.00	12.33	12.58	12.84	13.09	13.34	13.60	13.85	14.10	14.36	14.61	14.86	15.12	15.37	15.62	15.88	16.38
96.75	12.45	12.70	12.95	13.21	13.46	13.71	13.97	14.22	14.47	14.73	14.98	15.24	15.49	15.74	16.00	16.50
96.50	12.56	12.81	13.07	13.32	13.58	13.83	14.08	14.34	14.59	14.84	15.10	15.35	15.61	15.86	16.11	16.62
96.25	12.67	12.93	13.18	13.44	13.69	13.95	14.20	14.45	14.71	14.96	15.22	15.47	15.73	15.98	16.23	16.74
96.00	12.79	13.04	13.30	13.55	13.81	14.06	14.32	14.57	14.83	15.08	15.33	15.59	15.84	16.10	16.35	16.86
95.75	12.91	13.16	13.42	13.67	13.92	14.18	14.43	14.69	14.94	15.20	15.45	15.71	15.96	16.22	16.47	16.98
95.50	13.02	13.28	13.53	13.79	14.04	14.30	14.55	14.81	15.06	15.32	15.57	15.83	16.08	16.34	16.59	17.10
95.25	13.14	13.39	13.65	13.90	14.16	14.42	14.67	14.93	15.18	15.44	15.69	15.95	16.20	16.46	16.71	17.22
95.00	13.26	13.51	13.77	14.02	14.28	14.53	14.79	15.04	15.30	15.56	15.81	16.07	16.32	16.58	16.84	17.35
94.75	13.37	13.63	13.88	14.14	14.40	14.65	14.91	15.16	15.42	15.68	15.93	16.19	16.44	16.70	16.96	17.47
94.50	13.49	13.75	14.00	14.26	14.52	14.77	15.03	15.28	15.54	15.80	16.05	16.31	16.57	16.82	17.08	17.59
94.25	13.61	13.87	14.12	14.38	14.64	14.89	15.15	15.40	15.66	15.92	16.17	16.43	16.69	16.94	17.20	17.71
94.00	13.73	13.99	14.24	14.50	14.76	15.01	15.27	15.53	15.78	16.04	16.30	16.55	16.81	17.07	17.32	17.84
93.75	13.85	14.10	14.36	14.62	14.88	15.13	15.39	15.65	15.90	16.16	16.42	16.68	16.93	17.19	17.45	17.96
93	14.21	14.47	14.72	14.98	15.24	15.50	15.76	16.01	16.27	16.53	16.79	17.05	17.31	17.56	17.82	18.34
92	14.70	14.95	15.21	15.47	15.73	15.99	16.25	16.51	16.77	17.03	17.29	17.55	17.81	18.07	18.33	18.85
91	15.19	15.45	15.71	15.97	16.23	16.49	16.75	17.01	17.28	17.54	17.80	18.06	18.32	18.58	18.84	19.36
90	15.69	15.96	16.22	16.48	16.74	17.00	17.26	17.53	17.79	18.05	18.31	18.57	18.84	19.10	19.36	19.89
89	16.20	16.47	16.73	16.99	17.26	17.52	17.78	18.05	18.31	18.57	18.84	19.10	19.36	19.63	19.89	20.42
88	16.72	16.99	17.25	17.52	17.78	18.05	18.31	18.58	18.84	19.11	19.37	19.64	19.90	20.17	20.43	20.96
87	17.25	17.52	17.78	18.05	18.32	18.58	18.85	19.11	19.38	19.65	19.91	20.18	20.45	20.71	20.98	21.51
86	17.79	18.06	18.32	18.59	18.86	19.13	19.39	19.66	19.93	20.20	20.46	20.73	21.00	21.27	21.54	22.07
85	18.34	18.60	18.87	19.14	19.41	19.68	19.95	20.22	20.49	20.76	21.03	21.29	21.56	21.83	22.10	22.64
84	18.89	19.16	19.43	19.70	19.97	20.24	20.51	20.78	21.05	21.33	21.60	21.87	22.14	22.41	22.68	23.22
83	19.46	19.73	20.00	20.27	20.54	20.82	21.09	21.36	21.63	21.91	22.18	22.45	22.72	23.00	23.27	23.81
82	20.03	20.31	20.58	20.85	21.13	21.40	21.67	21.95	22.22	22.50	22.77	23.04	23.32	23.59	23.87	24.41
81	20.62	20.89	21.17	21.44	21.72	21.99	22.27	22.54	22.82	23.10	23.37	23.65	23.92	24.20	24.48	25.03
80	21.22	21.49	21.77	22.05	22.32	22.60	22.88	23.15	23.43	23.71	23.99	24.26	24.54	24.82	25.10	25.65

MORTGAGE PRICE

Description: This table shows the price to pay for a monthly payment mortgage loan at the yield rate.

Example: The price of a 6.75 %, 6 year mortgage loan to yield 8.00 % to maturity is $ 96.55.

INTEREST RATE, %

YIELD	0.00%	1.00%	2.00%	3.00%	4.00%	4.25%	4.50%	4.75%	5.00%	5.25%	5.50%	5.75%	6.00%	6.25%	6.50%	6.75%
0.00	100.00	103.07	106.20	109.39	112.65	113.47	114.29	115.12	115.96	116.79	117.63	118.48	119.32	120.18	121.03	121.89
1.00	97.02	100.00	103.04	106.13	109.29	110.09	110.89	111.69	112.50	113.31	114.13	114.95	115.77	116.59	117.42	118.26
2.00	94.16	97.05	100.00	103.00	106.07	106.84	107.62	108.40	109.18	109.97	110.76	111.56	112.36	113.16	113.96	114.77
3.00	91.41	94.22	97.08	100.00	102.97	103.72	104.48	105.24	106.00	106.76	107.53	108.30	109.08	109.86	110.64	111.42
4.00	88.77	91.50	94.28	97.11	100.00	100.73	101.46	102.20	102.94	103.68	104.43	105.18	105.93	106.69	107.44	108.21
4.25	88.13	90.84	93.60	96.41	99.28	100.00	100.73	101.46	102.19	102.93	103.67	104.42	105.16	105.91	106.67	107.42
4.50	87.49	90.18	92.92	95.71	98.56	99.28	100.00	100.73	101.45	102.19	102.92	103.66	104.40	105.15	105.90	106.65
4.75	86.86	89.53	92.25	95.02	97.85	98.56	99.28	100.00	100.72	101.45	102.18	102.91	103.65	104.39	105.13	105.88
5.00	86.24	88.89	91.59	94.34	97.15	97.85	98.57	99.28	100.00	100.72	101.45	102.17	102.91	103.64	104.38	105.12
5.25	85.62	88.25	90.93	93.67	96.45	97.15	97.86	98.57	99.28	100.00	100.72	101.44	102.17	102.90	103.63	104.37
5.50	85.01	87.62	90.28	93.00	95.76	96.46	97.16	97.87	98.57	99.29	100.00	100.72	101.44	102.17	102.90	104.37
5.75	84.40	87.00	89.64	92.33	95.08	95.77	96.47	97.17	97.87	98.58	99.29	100.00	100.72	101.44	102.16	102.89	103.62
6.00	83.80	86.38	89.00	91.68	94.40	95.09	95.78	96.48	97.18	97.88	98.58	99.29	100.00	100.72	101.43	102.16	102.88
6.25	83.21	85.77	88.37	91.03	93.73	94.42	95.10	95.79	96.49	97.18	97.88	98.59	99.29	100.00	100.71	101.43	102.15
6.50	82.62	85.16	87.75	90.39	93.07	93.75	94.43	95.12	95.81	96.50	97.19	97.89	98.59	99.29	100.00	100.71	101.43
6.75	82.04	84.56	87.13	89.75	92.42	93.09	93.77	94.45	95.13	95.82	96.51	97.20	97.90	98.59	99.30	100.00
7.00	81.46	83.97	86.52	89.12	91.77	92.44	93.11	93.78	94.46	95.14	95.83	96.52	97.21	97.90	98.60	99.30
7.25	80.89	83.38	85.91	88.49	91.12	91.79	92.46	93.13	93.80	94.48	95.16	95.84	96.53	97.22	97.91	98.60
7.50	80.33	82.80	85.31	87.87	90.49	91.15	91.81	92.48	93.15	93.82	94.49	95.17	95.85	96.54	97.22	97.91
7.75	79.77	82.22	84.72	87.26	89.86	90.51	91.17	91.83	92.50	93.16	93.83	94.51	95.18	95.86	96.54	97.23
8.00	79.21	81.65	84.13	86.66	89.23	89.88	90.54	91.19	91.85	92.52	93.18	93.85	94.52	95.20	95.87	96.55
8.25	78.67	81.08	83.55	86.06	88.61	89.26	89.91	90.56	91.22	91.88	92.54	93.20	93.87	94.54	95.21	95.89
8.50	78.12	80.52	82.97	85.46	88.00	88.64	89.29	89.94	90.59	91.24	91.90	92.56	93.22	93.88	94.55	95.22
8.75	77.58	79.97	82.40	84.87	87.39	88.03	88.67	89.32	89.96	90.61	91.26	91.92	92.58	93.24	93.90	94.57
9.00	77.05	79.42	81.83	84.29	86.79	87.43	88.06	88.70	89.35	89.99	90.64	91.29	91.94	92.60	93.26	93.92
9.25	76.52	78.87	81.27	83.71	86.20	86.83	87.46	88.10	88.73	89.37	90.02	90.66	91.31	91.96	92.62	93.27
9.50	76.00	78.34	80.72	83.14	85.61	86.24	86.86	87.49	88.13	88.76	89.40	90.04	90.69	91.33	91.98	93.27
9.75	75.48	77.80	80.17	82.57	85.03	85.65	86.27	86.90	87.53	88.16	88.79	89.43	90.07	90.71	91.36	92.64
10.00	74.97	77.27	79.62	82.01	84.45	85.07	85.69	86.31	86.93	87.56	88.19	88.82	89.46	90.10	90.74	92.01
10.25	74.46	76.75	79.08	81.46	83.88	84.49	85.11	85.72	86.34	86.97	87.59	88.22	88.85	89.49	90.12	91.38
10.50	73.96	76.23	78.55	80.91	83.31	83.92	84.53	85.14	85.76	86.38	87.00	87.63	88.25	88.88	89.51	90.76
10.75	73.46	75.72	78.02	80.36	82.75	83.36	83.96	84.57	85.18	85.80	86.42	87.04	87.66	88.28	88.91	90.15
11.00	72.97	75.21	77.49	79.82	82.20	82.80	83.40	84.00	84.61	85.22	85.83	86.45	87.07	87.69	88.31	89.54
11.25	72.48	74.71	76.98	79.29	81.65	82.24	82.84	83.44	84.04	84.65	85.26	85.87	86.49	87.10	87.72	88.94
11.50	72.00	74.21	76.46	78.76	81.10	81.69	82.29	82.88	83.48	84.09	84.69	85.30	85.91	86.52	87.14	88.35
11.75	71.52	73.71	75.95	78.24	80.56	81.15	81.74	82.33	82.93	83.53	84.13	84.73	85.34	85.95	86.56	87.76
12.00	71.04	73.22	75.45	77.72	80.03	80.61	81.20	81.79	82.38	82.97	83.57	84.17	84.77	85.38	85.98	87.17
12.25	70.57	72.74	74.95	77.20	79.50	80.08	80.66	81.24	81.83	82.42	83.02	83.61	84.21	84.81	85.41	86.59
12.50	70.11	72.26	74.46	76.69	78.97	79.55	80.13	80.71	81.29	81.88	82.47	83.06	83.65	84.25	84.85	86.02
12.75	69.65	71.78	73.97	76.19	78.45	79.02	79.60	80.18	80.76	81.34	81.93	82.51	83.10	83.70	84.29	85.45
13.00	69.19	71.31	73.48	75.69	77.94	78.51	79.08	79.65	80.23	80.81	81.39	81.97	82.56	83.15	83.74	84.89
13.25	68.74	70.85	73.00	75.19	77.43	77.99	78.56	79.13	79.70	80.28	80.86	81.44	82.02	82.60	83.19	84.33
13.50	68.29	70.38	72.52	74.70	76.92	77.48	78.05	78.61	79.18	79.75	80.33	80.90	81.48	82.06	82.65	83.78
13.75	67.84	69.93	72.05	74.22	76.42	76.98	77.54	78.10	78.67	79.24	79.81	80.38	80.95	81.53	82.11	83.24
14.00	67.40	69.47	71.58	73.74	75.93	76.48	77.04	77.60	78.16	78.72	79.29	79.86	80.43	81.00	81.58	82.69
14.25	66.97	69.02	71.12	73.26	75.44	75.99	76.54	77.09	77.65	78.21	78.78	79.34	79.91	80.48	81.05	82.16
14.50	66.54	68.58	70.66	72.79	74.95	75.50	76.05	76.60	77.15	77.71	78.27	78.83	79.39	79.96	80.53	81.63
14.75	66.11	68.14	70.21	72.32	74.47	75.01	75.56	76.10	76.66	77.21	77.76	78.32	78.88	79.45	80.01	81.10
15.00	65.68	67.70	69.76	71.85	73.99	74.53	75.07	75.62	76.16	76.71	77.27	77.82	78.38	78.94	79.50	80.58
15.25	65.26	67.27	69.31	71.40	73.52	74.05	74.59	75.13	75.68	76.22	76.77	77.32	77.88	78.43	78.99	80.06
15.50	64.85	66.84	68.87	70.94	73.05	73.58	74.12	74.65	75.20	75.74	76.28	76.83	77.38	77.93	78.49	79.55
15.75	64.44	66.42	68.43	70.49	72.58	73.11	73.65	74.18	74.72	75.26	75.80	76.34	76.89	77.44	77.99	79.04
16.00	64.03	65.99	68.00	70.04	72.12	72.65	73.18	73.71	74.24	74.78	75.32	75.86	76.40	76.95	77.49	78.54
16.25	63.62	65.58	67.57	69.60	71.67	72.19	72.72	73.25	73.78	74.31	74.84	75.38	75.92	76.46	77.00	78.04
16.50	63.22	65.17	67.14	69.16	71.22	71.74	72.26	72.78	73.31	73.84	74.37	74.90	75.44	75.98	76.52	77.55
16.75	62.83	64.76	66.72	68.73	70.77	71.29	71.81	72.33	72.85	73.38	73.90	74.43	74.97	75.50	76.04	77.06
17.00	62.43	64.35	66.31	68.30	70.33	70.84	71.36	71.87	72.39	72.92	73.44	73.97	74.50	75.03	75.56	76.10
17.25	62.04	63.95	65.89	67.87	69.89	70.40	70.91	71.43	71.94	72.46	72.98	73.51	74.03	74.56	75.09	75.62
17.50	61.66	63.55	65.48	67.45	69.45	69.96	70.47	70.98	71.49	72.01	72.53	73.05	73.57	74.10	74.62	75.15
17.75	61.27	63.16	65.08	67.03	69.02	69.53	70.03	70.54	71.05	71.56	72.08	72.60	73.12	73.64	74.16	74.69
18.00	60.90	62.77	64.67	66.62	68.60	69.10	69.60	70.10	70.61	71.12	71.63	72.15	72.66	73.18	73.70	74.23
18.25	60.52	62.38	64.27	66.21	68.17	68.67	69.17	69.67	70.18	70.68	71.19	71.70	72.22	72.73	73.25	73.77
18.50	60.15	62.00	63.88	65.80	67.75	68.25	68.74	69.24	69.74	70.25	70.75	71.26	71.77	72.28	72.80	73.31
18.75	59.78	61.61	63.49	65.39	67.34	67.83	68.32	68.82	69.32	69.82	70.32	70.82	71.33	71.84	72.35	72.86
19.00	59.41	61.24	63.10	64.99	66.93	67.41	67.91	68.40	68.89	69.39	69.89	70.39	70.89	71.40	71.91	72.42
20.00	57.98	59.77	61.58	63.43	65.32	65.79	66.27	66.75	67.24	67.72	68.21	68.70	69.19	69.68	70.18	70.68
25.00	51.56	53.14	54.76	56.40	58.08	58.50	58.93	59.36	59.79	60.22	60.65	61.09	61.52	61.96	62.40	62.85
30.00	46.17	47.58	49.03	50.50	52.00	52.38	52.77	53.15	53.53	53.92	54.31	54.70	55.09	55.48	55.88	56.27

Description: This table shows the yield to maturity of a mortgage purchased at the price shown in the index.

Example: The yield to maturity of a 6.75 %, 6 year mortgage at a price of 80.00 is 15.03 %.

							INTEREST RATE, %									
PRICE	0.00%	1.00%	2.00%	3.00%	4.00%	4.25%	4.50%	4.75%	5.00%	5.25%	5.50%	5.75%	6.00%	6.25%	6.50%	6.75%
100	0.00	1.00	2.00	3.00	4.00	4.25	4.50	4.75	5.00	5.25	5.50	5.75	6.00	6.25	6.50	6.75
99	.33	1.33	2.33	3.34	4.34	4.59	4.84	5.09	5.34	5.60	5.85	6.10	6.35	6.60	6.85	7.10
98	.66	1.67	2.68	3.68	4.69	4.94	5.20	5.45	5.70	5.95	6.20	6.46	6.71	6.96	7.21	7.46
97	1.00	2.01	3.02	4.04	5.05	5.30	5.55	5.81	6.06	6.31	6.56	6.82	7.07	7.32	7.58	7.83
96	1.35	2.36	3.38	4.39	5.41	5.66	5.92	6.17	6.42	6.68	6.93	7.19	7.44	7.69	7.95	8.20
95	1.70	2.72	3.73	4.75	5.77	6.03	6.28	6.54	6.79	7.05	7.30	7.56	7.81	8.07	8.32	8.58
94	2.05	3.07	4.10	5.12	6.15	6.40	6.66	6.91	7.17	7.43	7.68	7.94	8.19	8.45	8.71	8.96
93	2.41	3.44	4.47	5.49	6.52	6.78	7.04	7.29	7.55	7.81	8.07	8.32	8.58	8.84	9.10	9.35
92	2.78	3.81	4.84	5.87	6.90	7.16	7.42	7.68	7.94	8.20	8.45	8.71	8.97	9.23	9.49	9.75
91	3.15	4.18	5.22	6.26	7.29	7.55	7.81	8.07	8.33	8.59	8.85	9.11	9.37	9.63	9.89	10.15
90	3.53	4.56	5.60	6.65	7.69	7.95	8.21	8.47	8.73	8.99	9.25	9.51	9.77	10.03	10.30	10.56
89	3.91	4.95	6.00	7.04	8.09	8.35	8.61	8.87	9.14	9.40	9.66	9.92	10.18	10.45	10.71	10.97
88	4.30	5.34	6.39	7.44	8.50	8.76	9.02	9.28	9.55	9.81	10.07	10.34	10.60	10.86	11.13	11.39
87	4.69	5.74	6.80	7.85	8.91	9.17	9.44	9.70	9.97	10.23	10.50	10.76	11.02	11.29	11.55	11.82
86	5.09	6.15	7.21	8.27	9.33	9.60	9.86	10.13	10.39	10.66	10.92	11.19	11.46	11.72	11.99	12.25
85	5.50	6.56	7.63	8.69	9.76	10.02	10.29	10.56	10.82	11.09	11.36	11.63	11.89	12.16	12.43	12.70
84	5.91	6.98	8.05	9.12	10.19	10.46	10.73	11.00	11.26	11.53	11.80	12.07	12.34	12.61	12.88	13.15
83	6.33	7.41	8.48	9.56	10.63	10.90	11.17	11.44	11.71	11.98	12.25	12.52	12.79	13.06	13.33	13.60
82	6.76	7.84	8.92	10.00	11.08	11.35	11.63	11.90	12.17	12.44	12.71	12.98	13.25	13.53	13.80	14.07
81	7.20	8.28	9.37	10.45	11.54	11.81	12.09	12.36	12.63	12.90	13.18	13.45	13.72	14.00	14.27	14.54
80	7.64	8.73	9.82	10.91	12.01	12.28	12.55	12.83	13.10	13.38	13.65	13.93	14.20	14.48	14.75	15.03
79	8.09	9.19	10.28	11.38	12.48	12.76	13.03	13.31	13.58	13.86	14.14	14.41	14.69	14.96	15.24	15.52
78	8.55	9.65	10.75	11.86	12.96	13.24	13.52	13.80	14.07	14.35	14.63	14.91	15.18	15.46	15.74	16.02
77	9.02	10.13	11.23	12.34	13.46	13.73	14.01	14.29	14.57	14.85	15.13	15.41	15.69	15.97	16.25	16.53
76	9.50	10.61	11.72	12.84	13.96	14.24	14.52	14.80	15.08	15.36	15.64	15.92	16.20	16.48	16.77	17.05
75	9.98	11.10	12.22	13.34	14.47	14.75	15.03	15.31	15.60	15.88	16.16	16.44	16.73	17.01	17.29	17.58
74	10.47	11.60	12.73	13.86	14.99	15.27	15.56	15.84	16.12	16.41	16.69	16.98	17.26	17.55	17.83	18.12
73	10.98	12.11	13.24	14.38	15.52	15.81	16.09	16.38	16.66	16.95	17.24	17.52	17.81	18.10	18.38	18.67
72	11.49	12.63	13.77	14.92	16.06	16.35	16.64	16.93	17.21	17.50	17.79	18.08	18.37	18.65	18.94	19.23
71	12.02	13.16	14.31	15.46	16.62	16.91	17.19	17.48	17.77	18.06	18.35	18.64	18.93	19.23	19.52	19.81
70	12.55	13.70	14.86	16.02	17.18	17.47	17.76	18.06	18.35	18.64	18.93	19.22	19.52	19.81	20.10	20.39
69	13.10	14.26	15.42	16.59	17.76	18.05	18.34	18.64	18.93	19.23	19.52	19.81	20.11	20.40	20.70	20.99
68	13.66	14.82	16.00	17.17	18.35	18.64	18.94	19.23	19.53	19.83	20.12	20.42	20.71	21.01	21.31	21.61
67	14.23	15.40	16.58	17.76	18.95	19.25	19.54	19.84	20.14	20.44	20.74	21.04	21.33	21.63	21.93	22.23
66	14.81	15.99	17.18	18.37	19.57	19.87	20.17	20.47	20.77	21.07	21.37	21.67	21.97	22.27	22.57	22.87
65	15.40	16.60	17.79	18.99	20.20	20.50	20.80	21.10	21.40	21.71	22.01	22.31	22.62	22.92	23.23	23.53
64	16.01	17.21	18.42	19.63	20.84	21.14	21.45	21.75	22.06	22.36	22.67	22.98	23.28	23.59	23.89	24.20
63	16.64	17.84	19.06	20.28	21.50	21.81	22.11	22.42	22.73	23.04	23.34	23.65	23.96	24.27	24.58	24.89
62	17.27	18.49	19.72	20.94	22.18	22.49	22.80	23.10	23.41	23.73	24.04	24.35	24.66	24.97	25.28	25.59
61	17.93	19.15	20.39	21.63	22.87	23.18	23.49	23.81	24.12	24.43	24.74	25.06	25.37	25.69	26.00	26.32
60	18.59	19.83	21.08	22.33	23.58	23.89	24.21	24.52	24.84	25.15	25.47	25.79	26.10	26.42	26.74	27.06
59	19.28	20.53	21.78	23.04	24.31	24.63	24.94	25.26	25.58	25.90	26.22	26.54	26.86	27.18	27.50	27.82
58	19.98	21.24	22.51	23.78	25.06	25.38	25.70	26.02	26.34	26.66	26.98	27.30	27.63	27.95	28.27	28.60
57	20.71	21.98	23.25	24.54	25.82	26.15	26.47	26.79	27.12	27.44	27.77	28.09	28.42	28.74	29.07	29.40
56	21.45	22.73	24.02	25.31	26.61	26.94	27.26	27.59	27.92	28.25	28.58	28.90	29.23	29.56	29.89	30.22
55	22.21	23.50	24.80	26.11	27.42	27.75	28.08	28.41	28.74	29.07	29.41	29.74	30.07	30.40	30.74	31.07
54	22.99	24.30	25.61	26.93	28.26	28.59	28.92	29.26	29.59	29.93	30.26	30.60	30.93	31.27	31.60	31.94
53	23.79	25.11	26.44	27.77	29.12	29.45	29.79	30.13	30.46	30.80	31.14	31.48	31.82	32.16	32.50	32.84
52	24.62	25.96	27.30	28.64	30.00	30.34	30.68	31.02	31.36	31.70	32.05	32.39	32.73	33.08	33.42	33.77
51	25.48	26.82	28.18	29.54	30.91	31.25	31.60	31.94	32.29	32.63	32.98	33.33	33.68	34.02	34.37	34.72
50	26.36	27.72	29.09	30.46	31.85	32.20	32.55	32.90	33.25	33.60	33.95	34.30	34.65	35.00	35.35	35.71
49	27.26	28.64	30.02	31.42	32.82	33.17	33.53	33.88	34.23	34.59	34.94	35.30	35.65	36.01	36.37	36.72
48	28.20	29.59	30.99	32.40	33.82	34.18	34.54	34.89	35.25	35.61	35.97	36.33	36.69	37.05	37.41	37.78
47	29.16	30.57	31.99	33.42	34.86	35.22	35.58	35.94	36.31	36.67	37.03	37.40	37.76	38.13	38.50	38.86
46	30.16	31.59	33.03	34.48	35.93	36.30	36.66	37.03	37.40	37.77	38.14	38.51	38.88	39.25	39.62	39.99
45	31.20	32.64	34.10	35.57	37.04	37.41	37.79	38.16	38.53	38.90	39.28	39.65	40.03	40.40	40.78	41.16
44	32.27	33.73	35.21	36.70	38.19	38.57	38.95	39.33	39.70	40.08	40.46	40.84	41.22	41.61	41.99	42.37
43	33.38	34.87	36.36	37.87	39.39	39.77	40.15	40.54	40.92	41.31	41.69	42.08	42.46	42.85	43.24	43.63
42	34.53	36.04	37.56	39.09	40.63	41.02	41.41	41.80	42.19	42.58	42.97	43.36	43.75	44.15	44.54	44.94
41	35.73	37.26	38.80	40.36	41.92	42.32	42.71	43.11	43.50	43.90	44.30	44.70	45.10	45.50	45.90	46.30
40	36.98	38.53	40.10	41.68	43.27	43.67	44.07	44.47	44.87	45.28	45.68	46.09	46.49	46.90	47.31	47.72
39	38.27	39.85	41.44	43.05	44.67	45.08	45.49	45.90	46.31	46.72	47.13	47.54	47.95	48.37	48.78	49.20
38	39.63	41.23	42.85	44.49	46.13	46.55	46.96	47.38	47.80	48.22	48.64	49.06	49.48	49.90	50.32	50.75
37	41.04	42.67	44.32	45.99	47.67	48.09	48.51	48.94	49.36	49.79	50.21	50.64	51.07	51.50	51.93	52.37
36	42.52	44.18	45.86	47.56	49.27	49.70	50.13	50.56	51.00	51.43	51.87	52.30	52.74	53.18	53.62	54.06
35	44.07	45.76	47.47	49.20	50.95	51.39	51.83	52.27	52.71	53.16	53.60	54.05	54.50	54.94	55.39	55.84
30	53.09	54.98	56.90	58.83	60.79	61.29	61.78	62.28	62.78	63.28	63.78	64.28	64.78	65.29	65.79	66.30
25	65.18	67.36	69.57	71.81	74.09	74.66	75.23	75.81	76.39	76.97	77.55	78.14	78.73	79.31	79.91	80.50

Description: This table shows the price to pay for a monthly payment mortgage loan at the yield rate.

Example: The price of a 10.75 %, 6 year mortgage loan to yield 8.00 % to maturity is $ 107.83.

YIELD	7.00%	7.25%	7.50%	7.75%	8.00%	8.25%	8.50%	8.75%	9.00%	9.25%	9.50%	9.75%	10.00%	10.25%	10.50%	10.75%
0.00	122.75	123.62	124.49	125.36	126.24	127.12	128.00	128.89	129.78	130.68	131.58	132.48	133.39	134.30	135.21	136.13
1.00	119.09	119.94	120.78	121.63	122.48	123.33	124.19	125.05	125.92	126.78	127.66	128.53	129.41	130.29	131.18	132.07
2.00	115.58	116.40	117.22	118.04	118.87	119.70	120.53	121.36	122.20	123.05	123.89	124.74	125.60	126.45	127.31	128.17
3.00	112.21	113.00	113.80	114.60	115.40	116.20	117.01	117.82	118.64	119.46	120.28	121.10	121.93	122.76	123.60	124.44
4.00	108.97	109.74	110.51	111.29	112.07	112.85	113.63	114.42	115.21	116.01	116.81	117.61	118.41	119.22	120.03	120.84
4.25	108.18	108.95	109.71	110.48	111.26	112.03	112.81	113.59	114.38	115.17	115.96	116.76	117.55	118.36	119.16	119.97
4.50	107.40	108.16	108.92	109.68	110.45	111.22	112.00	112.77	113.55	114.34	115.12	115.91	116.71	117.50	118.30	119.10
4.75	106.63	107.38	108.14	108.89	109.66	110.42	111.19	111.96	112.74	113.51	114.29	115.08	115.86	116.65	117.45	118.24
5.00	105.86	106.61	107.36	108.11	108.87	109.63	110.39	111.16	111.93	112.70	113.47	114.25	115.03	115.82	116.60	117.39
5.25	105.10	105.85	106.59	107.34	108.09	108.84	109.60	110.36	111.12	111.89	112.66	113.43	114.21	114.99	115.77	116.55
5.50	104.35	105.09	105.83	106.57	107.32	108.07	108.82	109.57	110.33	111.09	111.85	112.62	113.39	114.17	114.94	115.72
5.75	103.61	104.34	105.07	105.81	106.55	107.30	108.04	108.79	109.54	110.30	111.06	111.82	112.58	113.35	114.12	114.90
6.00	102.87	103.60	104.33	105.06	105.79	106.53	107.27	108.02	108.77	109.52	110.27	111.02	111.78	112.55	113.31	114.08
6.25	102.14	102.86	103.59	104.32	105.05	105.78	106.51	107.25	107.99	108.74	109.49	110.24	110.99	111.75	112.51	113.27
6.50	101.42	102.14	102.86	103.58	104.30	105.03	105.76	106.49	107.23	107.97	108.71	109.46	110.21	110.96	111.71	112.47
6.75	100.71	101.42	102.13	102.85	103.57	104.29	105.02	105.74	106.48	107.21	107.95	108.69	109.43	110.18	110.93	111.68
7.00	100.00	100.71	101.41	102.13	102.84	103.56	104.28	105.00	105.73	106.46	107.19	107.92	108.66	109.40	110.15	110.89
7.25	99.30	100.00	100.70	101.41	102.12	102.83	103.55	104.27	104.99	105.71	106.44	107.17	107.90	108.64	109.38	110.12
7.50	98.61	99.30	100.00	100.70	101.41	102.11	102.82	103.54	104.25	104.97	105.69	106.42	107.15	107.88	108.61	109.35
7.75	97.92	98.61	99.30	100.00	100.70	101.40	102.11	102.82	103.53	104.24	104.96	105.68	106.40	107.13	107.85	108.59
8.00	97.24	97.92	98.61	99.31	100.00	100.70	101.40	102.10	102.81	103.52	104.23	104.94	105.66	106.38	107.10	107.83
8.25	96.56	97.25	97.93	98.62	99.31	100.00	100.70	101.39	102.10	102.80	103.51	104.22	104.93	105.64	106.36	107.08
8.50	95.90	96.57	97.25	97.94	98.62	99.31	100.00	100.69	101.39	102.09	102.79	103.50	104.20	104.91	105.63	106.34
8.75	95.24	95.91	96.58	97.26	97.94	98.62	99.31	100.00	100.69	101.39	102.08	102.78	103.49	104.19	104.90	105.61
9.00	94.58	95.25	95.92	96.59	97.27	97.95	98.63	99.31	100.00	100.69	101.38	102.08	102.78	103.48	104.18	104.89
9.25	93.93	94.60	95.26	95.93	96.60	97.28	97.95	98.63	99.31	100.00	100.69	101.38	102.07	102.77	103.47	104.17
9.50	93.29	93.95	94.61	95.28	95.94	96.61	97.28	97.96	98.64	99.32	100.00	100.69	101.38	102.07	102.76	103.46
9.75	92.66	93.31	93.97	94.63	95.29	95.95	96.62	97.29	97.96	98.64	99.32	100.00	100.69	101.37	102.07	102.75
10.00	92.03	92.68	93.33	93.98	94.64	95.30	95.97	96.63	97.30	97.97	98.64	99.32	100.00	100.68	101.37	102.05
10.25	91.41	92.05	92.70	93.35	94.00	94.66	95.32	95.98	96.64	97.31	97.98	98.65	99.32	100.00	100.68	101.36
10.50	90.79	91.43	92.07	92.72	93.37	94.02	94.67	95.33	95.99	96.65	97.31	97.98	98.65	99.32	100.00	100.68
10.75	90.18	90.81	91.45	92.09	92.74	93.38	94.03	94.69	95.34	96.00	96.66	97.32	97.99	98.66	99.33	100.00
11.00	89.57	90.20	90.84	91.48	92.11	92.76	93.40	94.05	94.70	95.35	96.01	96.67	97.33	97.99	98.66	99.33
11.25	88.97	89.60	90.23	90.86	91.50	92.14	92.78	93.42	94.07	94.72	95.37	96.02	96.68	97.34	98.00	98.66
11.50	88.38	89.00	89.63	90.26	90.89	91.52	92.16	92.80	93.44	94.08	94.73	95.38	96.03	96.69	97.34	98.00
11.75	87.79	88.41	89.03	89.66	90.28	90.91	91.54	92.18	92.82	93.46	94.10	94.75	95.39	96.04	96.70	97.35
12.00	87.21	87.82	88.44	89.06	89.68	90.31	90.94	91.57	92.20	92.84	93.48	94.12	94.76	95.41	96.06	96.71
12.25	86.63	87.24	87.85	88.47	89.09	89.71	90.34	90.96	91.59	92.22	92.86	93.49	94.13	94.78	95.42	96.07
12.50	86.06	86.66	87.27	87.89	88.50	89.12	89.74	90.36	90.99	91.61	92.24	92.88	93.51	94.15	94.79	95.43
12.75	85.49	86.09	86.70	87.31	87.92	88.53	89.15	89.77	90.39	91.01	91.64	92.27	92.90	93.53	94.17	94.80
13.00	84.93	85.53	86.13	86.74	87.34	87.95	88.56	89.18	89.79	90.41	91.04	91.66	92.29	92.92	93.55	94.18
13.25	84.37	84.97	85.57	86.17	86.77	87.38	87.98	88.59	89.21	89.82	90.44	91.06	91.68	92.31	92.94	93.57
13.50	83.82	84.42	85.01	85.61	86.21	86.81	87.41	88.02	88.63	89.24	89.85	90.47	91.09	91.71	92.33	92.96
13.75	83.28	83.87	84.46	85.05	85.64	86.24	86.84	87.44	88.05	88.66	89.27	89.88	90.49	91.11	91.73	92.35
14.00	82.74	83.32	83.91	84.50	85.09	85.68	86.28	86.88	87.48	88.08	88.69	89.30	89.91	90.52	91.13	91.75
14.25	82.20	82.78	83.37	83.95	84.54	85.13	85.72	86.32	86.91	87.51	88.11	88.72	89.32	89.93	90.55	91.16
14.50	81.67	82.25	82.83	83.41	83.99	84.58	85.17	85.76	86.35	86.95	87.55	88.15	88.75	89.35	89.96	90.57
14.75	81.15	81.72	82.30	82.87	83.45	84.04	84.62	85.21	85.80	86.39	86.98	87.58	88.18	88.78	89.38	89.99
15.00	80.63	81.20	81.77	82.34	82.92	83.50	84.08	84.66	85.25	85.84	86.43	87.02	87.61	88.21	88.81	89.41
15.25	80.11	80.68	81.25	81.82	82.39	82.96	83.54	84.12	84.70	85.29	85.87	86.46	87.05	87.65	88.24	88.84
15.50	79.60	80.16	80.73	81.30	81.86	82.44	83.01	83.58	84.16	84.74	85.33	85.91	86.50	87.09	87.68	88.27
15.75	79.10	79.66	80.22	80.78	81.34	81.91	82.48	83.05	83.63	84.20	84.78	85.37	85.95	86.54	87.12	87.71
16.00	78.60	79.15	79.71	80.27	80.83	81.39	81.96	82.53	83.10	83.67	84.25	84.82	85.40	85.99	86.57	87.16
16.25	78.10	78.65	79.20	79.76	80.32	80.88	81.44	82.01	82.57	83.14	83.71	84.29	84.87	85.44	86.02	86.61
16.50	77.61	78.16	78.71	79.26	79.81	80.37	80.93	81.49	82.05	82.62	83.19	83.76	84.33	84.91	85.48	86.06
16.75	77.12	77.67	78.21	78.76	79.31	79.86	80.42	80.98	81.54	82.10	82.67	83.23	83.80	84.37	84.95	85.52
17.00	76.64	77.18	77.72	78.27	78.81	79.36	79.92	80.47	81.03	81.59	82.15	82.71	83.28	83.84	84.41	84.99
17.25	76.16	76.70	77.24	77.78	78.32	78.87	79.42	79.97	80.52	81.08	81.63	82.19	82.76	83.32	83.89	84.46
17.50	75.69	76.22	76.76	77.29	77.84	78.38	78.92	79.47	80.02	80.57	81.13	81.68	82.24	82.80	83.37	83.93
17.75	75.22	75.75	76.28	76.82	77.35	77.89	78.43	78.98	79.52	80.07	80.62	81.18	81.73	82.29	82.85	83.41
18.00	74.75	75.28	75.81	76.34	76.87	77.41	77.95	78.49	79.03	79.58	80.12	80.67	81.23	81.78	82.34	82.89
18.25	74.29	74.81	75.34	75.87	76.40	76.93	77.47	78.01	78.54	79.09	79.63	80.18	80.72	81.28	81.83	82.38
18.50	73.83	74.35	74.88	75.40	75.93	76.46	76.99	77.53	78.06	78.60	79.14	79.68	80.23	80.78	81.32	81.88
18.75	73.38	73.90	74.42	74.94	75.46	75.99	76.52	77.05	77.58	78.12	78.66	79.19	79.74	80.28	80.83	81.37
19.00	72.93	73.45	73.96	74.48	75.00	75.53	76.05	76.58	77.11	77.64	78.17	78.71	79.25	79.79	80.33	80.88
20.00	71.18	71.68	72.18	72.69	73.20	73.71	74.22	74.74	75.25	75.77	76.29	76.82	77.34	77.87	78.40	78.93
25.00	63.29	63.74	64.19	64.64	65.09	65.54	66.00	66.46	66.92	67.38	67.84	68.31	68.77	69.24	69.71	70.19
30.00	56.67	57.07	57.47	57.88	58.28	58.69	59.10	59.51	59.92	60.33	60.75	61.16	61.58	62.00	62.42	62.84

Description: This table shows the yield to maturity of a mortgage purchased at the price shown in the index.

Example: The yield to maturity of a 10.75 %, 6 year mortgage at a price of 105.00 is 8.96 %.

INTEREST RATE, %

PRICE	7.00%	7.25%	7.50%	7.75%	8.00%	8.25%	8.50%	8.75%	9.00%	9.25%	9.50%	9.75%	10.00%	10.25%	10.50%	10.75%
125	–	–	–	.09	.32	.55	.78	1.01	1.24	1.47	1.70	1.93	2.15	2.38	2.61	2.84
124	–	–	.12	.35	.59	.82	1.05	1.28	1.51	1.74	1.97	2.20	2.43	2.66	2.88	3.11
123	–	.16	.39	.62	.85	1.08	1.32	1.55	1.78	2.01	2.24	2.47	2.70	2.93	3.16	3.39
122	.20	.43	.66	.89	1.12	1.36	1.59	1.82	2.05	2.28	2.51	2.74	2.98	3.21	3.44	3.67
121	.47	.70	.93	1.17	1.40	1.63	1.86	2.10	2.33	2.56	2.79	3.02	3.26	3.49	3.72	3.95
120	.74	.98	1.21	1.44	1.68	1.91	2.14	2.38	2.61	2.84	3.07	3.31	3.54	3.77	4.00	4.24
119	1.02	1.26	1.49	1.72	1.96	2.19	2.42	2.66	2.89	3.13	3.36	3.59	3.83	4.06	4.29	4.52
118	1.30	1.54	1.77	2.01	2.24	2.48	2.71	2.94	3.18	3.41	3.65	3.88	4.11	4.35	4.58	4.82
117	1.59	1.82	2.06	2.29	2.53	2.76	3.00	3.23	3.47	3.70	3.94	4.17	4.41	4.64	4.88	5.11
116	1.87	2.11	2.35	2.58	2.82	3.05	3.29	3.53	3.76	4.00	4.23	4.47	4.70	4.94	5.18	5.41
115	2.17	2.40	2.64	2.88	3.11	3.35	3.59	3.82	4.06	4.30	4.53	4.77	5.00	5.24	5.48	5.71
114	2.46	2.70	2.93	3.17	3.41	3.65	3.88	4.12	4.36	4.60	4.83	5.07	5.31	5.55	5.78	6.02
113	2.76	3.00	3.23	3.47	3.71	3.95	4.19	4.43	4.66	4.90	5.14	5.38	5.62	5.85	6.09	6.33
112	3.06	3.30	3.54	3.78	4.02	4.25	4.49	4.73	4.97	5.21	5.45	5.69	5.93	6.17	6.40	6.64
111	3.36	3.60	3.84	4.08	4.32	4.56	4.80	5.04	5.28	5.52	5.76	6.00	6.24	6.48	6.72	6.96
110	3.67	3.91	4.16	4.40	4.64	4.88	5.12	5.36	5.60	5.84	6.08	6.32	6.56	6.80	7.04	7.28
109	3.99	4.23	4.47	4.71	4.95	5.19	5.44	5.68	5.92	6.16	6.40	6.64	6.88	7.13	7.37	7.61
108	4.30	4.55	4.79	5.03	5.27	5.52	5.76	6.00	6.24	6.49	6.73	6.97	7.21	7.45	7.70	7.94
107	4.62	4.87	5.11	5.35	5.60	5.84	6.08	6.33	6.57	6.81	7.06	7.30	7.54	7.79	8.03	8.27
106	4.95	5.19	5.44	5.68	5.93	6.17	6.42	6.66	6.90	7.15	7.39	7.64	7.88	8.12	8.37	8.61
105	5.28	5.52	5.77	6.01	6.26	6.51	6.75	7.00	7.24	7.49	7.73	7.98	8.22	8.47	8.71	8.96
104	5.61	5.86	6.11	6.35	6.60	6.84	7.09	7.34	7.58	7.83	8.07	8.32	8.57	8.81	9.06	9.30
103	5.95	6.20	6.45	6.69	6.94	7.19	7.43	7.68	7.93	8.17	8.42	8.67	8.92	9.16	9.41	9.66
102	6.29	6.54	6.79	7.04	7.29	7.53	7.78	8.03	8.28	8.53	8.77	9.02	9.27	9.52	9.77	10.01
101	6.64	6.89	7.14	7.39	7.64	7.89	8.14	8.39	8.63	8.88	9.13	9.38	9.63	9.88	10.13	10.38
100	7.00	7.25	7.50	7.75	8.00	8.25	8.50	8.75	9.00	9.25	9.50	9.75	10.00	10.25	10.50	10.75
99	7.35	7.60	7.85	8.11	8.36	8.61	8.86	9.11	9.36	9.61	9.86	10.11	10.37	10.62	10.87	11.12
98	7.72	7.97	8.22	8.47	8.72	8.98	9.23	9.48	9.73	9.98	10.24	10.49	10.74	10.99	11.24	11.50
97	8.08	8.34	8.59	8.84	9.10	9.35	9.60	9.86	10.11	10.36	10.61	10.87	11.12	11.37	11.63	11.88
96	8.46	8.71	8.96	9.22	9.47	9.73	9.98	10.24	10.49	10.74	11.00	11.25	11.51	11.76	12.02	12.27
95	8.84	9.09	9.35	9.60	9.86	10.11	10.37	10.62	10.88	11.13	11.39	11.64	11.90	12.16	12.41	12.67
94	9.22	9.48	9.73	9.99	10.25	10.50	10.76	11.02	11.27	11.53	11.79	12.04	12.30	12.56	12.81	13.07
93	9.61	9.87	10.13	10.38	10.64	10.90	11.16	11.41	11.67	11.93	12.19	12.44	12.70	12.96	13.22	13.48
92	10.01	10.27	10.52	10.78	11.04	11.30	11.56	11.82	12.08	12.34	12.60	12.85	13.11	13.37	13.63	13.89
91	10.41	10.67	10.93	11.19	11.45	11.71	11.97	12.23	12.49	12.75	13.01	13.27	13.53	13.79	14.05	14.31
90	10.82	11.08	11.34	11.60	11.86	12.12	12.39	12.65	12.91	13.17	13.43	13.69	13.95	14.22	14.48	14.74
89	11.23	11.50	11.76	12.02	12.28	12.55	12.81	13.07	13.33	13.60	13.86	14.12	14.39	14.65	14.91	15.18
88	11.66	11.92	12.18	12.45	12.71	12.97	13.24	13.50	13.77	14.03	14.29	14.56	14.82	15.09	15.35	15.62
87	12.08	12.35	12.61	12.88	13.14	13.41	13.68	13.94	14.21	14.47	14.74	15.00	15.27	15.53	15.80	16.07
86	12.52	12.79	13.05	13.32	13.59	13.85	14.12	14.39	14.65	14.92	15.19	15.45	15.72	15.99	16.26	16.52
85	12.96	13.23	13.50	13.77	14.04	14.30	14.57	14.84	15.11	15.38	15.65	15.91	16.18	16.45	16.72	16.99
84	13.42	13.68	13.95	14.22	14.49	14.76	15.03	15.30	15.57	15.84	16.11	16.38	16.65	16.92	17.19	17.46
83	13.87	14.14	14.42	14.69	14.96	15.23	15.50	15.77	16.04	16.31	16.58	16.86	17.13	17.40	17.67	17.94
82	14.34	14.61	14.89	15.16	15.43	15.70	15.98	16.25	16.52	16.79	17.07	17.34	17.61	17.89	18.16	18.43
81	14.82	15.09	15.36	15.64	15.91	16.19	16.46	16.73	17.01	17.28	17.56	17.83	18.11	18.38	18.66	18.93
80	15.30	15.58	15.85	16.13	16.40	16.68	16.95	17.23	17.51	17.78	18.06	18.33	18.61	18.89	19.16	19.44
79	15.79	16.07	16.35	16.62	16.90	17.18	17.46	17.73	18.01	18.29	18.57	18.85	19.12	19.40	19.68	19.96
78	16.30	16.57	16.85	17.13	17.41	17.69	17.97	18.25	18.53	18.81	19.09	19.37	19.65	19.93	20.21	20.49
77	16.81	17.09	17.37	17.65	17.93	18.21	18.49	18.77	19.05	19.33	19.62	19.90	20.18	20.46	20.74	21.03
76	17.33	17.61	17.89	18.18	18.46	18.74	19.02	19.31	19.59	19.87	20.16	20.44	20.72	21.01	21.29	21.57
75	17.86	18.14	18.43	18.71	19.00	19.28	19.57	19.85	20.14	20.42	20.71	20.99	21.28	21.56	21.85	22.13
74	18.40	18.69	18.97	19.26	19.55	19.83	20.12	20.41	20.69	20.98	21.27	21.55	21.84	22.13	22.42	22.70
73	18.96	19.24	19.53	19.82	20.11	20.40	20.68	20.97	21.26	21.55	21.84	22.13	22.42	22.71	23.00	23.29
72	19.52	19.81	20.10	20.39	20.68	20.97	21.26	21.55	21.84	22.13	22.42	22.72	23.01	23.30	23.59	23.88
71	20.10	20.39	20.68	20.97	21.27	21.56	21.85	22.14	22.44	22.73	23.02	23.31	23.61	23.90	24.20	24.49
70	20.69	20.98	21.27	21.57	21.86	22.16	22.45	22.75	23.04	23.34	23.63	23.93	24.22	24.52	24.82	25.11
69	21.29	21.58	21.88	22.18	22.47	22.77	23.07	23.36	23.66	23.96	24.26	24.55	24.85	25.15	25.45	25.75
68	21.90	22.20	22.50	22.80	23.10	23.40	23.69	23.99	24.29	24.59	24.89	25.19	25.49	25.79	26.10	26.40
67	22.53	22.83	23.13	23.43	23.73	24.04	24.34	24.64	24.94	25.24	25.55	25.85	26.15	26.45	26.76	27.06
66	23.18	23.48	23.78	24.08	24.39	24.69	24.99	25.30	25.60	25.91	26.21	26.52	26.82	27.13	27.43	27.74
65	23.83	24.14	24.44	24.75	25.06	25.36	25.67	25.97	26.28	26.59	26.90	27.20	27.51	27.82	28.13	28.44
64	24.51	24.82	25.12	25.43	25.74	26.05	26.36	26.67	26.98	27.29	27.60	27.91	28.22	28.53	28.84	29.15
63	25.20	25.51	25.82	26.13	26.44	26.75	27.06	27.37	27.69	28.00	28.31	28.62	28.94	29.25	29.57	29.88
62	25.91	26.22	26.53	26.84	27.16	27.47	27.79	28.10	28.42	28.73	29.05	29.36	29.68	30.00	30.31	30.63
60	27.37	27.69	28.01	28.33	28.65	28.97	29.29	29.61	29.93	30.25	30.57	30.89	31.22	31.54	31.86	32.19
55	31.40	31.74	32.07	32.41	32.74	33.08	33.42	33.75	34.09	34.43	34.77	35.11	35.45	35.79	36.13	36.47
50	36.06	36.41	36.77	37.12	37.48	37.84	38.19	38.55	38.91	39.27	39.63	39.99	40.35	40.71	41.07	41.43
45	41.54	41.92	42.30	42.68	43.06	43.44	43.82	44.20	44.59	44.97	45.36	45.74	46.13	46.52	46.91	47.29

Description: This table shows the price to pay for a monthly payment mortgage loan at the yield rate.

Example: The price of a 15.00 %, 6 year mortgage loan to yield 8.00 % to maturity is $ 120.60.

INTEREST RATE, %

YIELD	11.00%	11.25%	11.50%	11.75%	12.00%	12.25%	12.50%	12.75%	13.00%	13.25%	13.50%	13.75%	14.00%	14.25%	14.50%	15.00%
0.00	137.05	137.97	138.90	139.83	140.76	141.70	142.64	143.59	144.53	145.49	146.44	147.40	148.36	149.33	150.30	152.24
1.00	132.96	133.86	134.76	135.66	136.57	137.48	138.39	139.31	140.23	141.15	142.08	143.01	143.94	144.88	145.82	147.71
2.00	129.04	129.91	130.78	131.66	132.54	133.42	134.31	135.20	136.09	136.99	137.89	138.79	139.70	140.60	141.52	143.35
3.00	125.28	126.12	126.97	127.82	128.67	129.53	130.39	131.25	132.12	132.99	133.86	134.74	135.62	136.50	137.39	139.17
4.00	121.66	122.48	123.30	124.13	124.96	125.79	126.63	127.47	128.31	129.15	130.00	130.85	131.71	132.56	133.42	135.15
4.25	120.78	121.59	122.41	123.23	124.05	124.88	125.71	126.54	127.38	128.22	129.06	129.90	130.75	131.60	132.46	134.17
4.50	119.91	120.72	121.53	122.34	123.16	123.98	124.80	125.63	126.46	127.29	128.13	128.97	129.81	130.65	131.50	133.21
4.75	119.04	119.85	120.65	121.46	122.27	123.09	123.90	124.72	125.55	126.37	127.20	128.04	128.87	129.71	130.55	132.25
5.00	118.19	118.98	119.78	120.59	121.39	122.20	123.01	123.83	124.65	125.47	126.29	127.12	127.95	128.78	129.62	131.30
5.25	117.34	118.13	118.93	119.72	120.52	121.33	122.13	122.94	123.75	124.57	125.39	126.21	127.03	127.86	128.69	130.35
5.50	116.50	117.29	118.08	118.87	119.66	120.46	121.26	122.06	122.87	123.68	124.49	125.30	126.12	126.94	127.77	129.42
5.75	115.67	116.45	117.23	118.02	118.81	119.60	120.40	121.19	121.99	122.80	123.60	124.41	125.22	126.04	126.86	128.50
6.00	114.85	115.62	116.40	117.18	117.96	118.75	119.54	120.33	121.13	121.92	122.72	123.53	124.33	125.14	125.96	127.59
6.25	114.04	114.81	115.58	116.35	117.13	117.91	118.69	119.48	120.27	121.06	121.85	122.65	123.45	124.26	125.06	126.68
6.50	113.23	113.99	114.76	115.53	116.30	117.08	117.85	118.63	119.42	120.20	120.99	121.79	122.58	123.38	124.18	125.79
6.75	112.43	113.19	113.95	114.72	115.48	116.25	117.02	117.80	118.58	119.36	120.14	120.93	121.72	122.51	123.30	124.90
7.00	111.64	112.40	113.15	113.91	114.67	115.43	116.20	116.97	117.74	118.52	119.30	120.08	120.86	121.65	122.44	124.02
7.25	110.86	111.61	112.36	113.11	113.87	114.63	115.39	116.15	116.92	117.69	118.46	119.24	120.01	120.80	121.58	123.16
7.50	110.09	110.83	111.57	112.32	113.07	113.82	114.58	115.34	116.10	116.87	117.63	118.40	119.18	119.95	120.73	122.30
7.75	109.32	110.06	110.80	111.54	112.28	113.03	113.78	114.54	115.29	116.05	116.81	117.58	118.35	119.12	119.89	121.44
8.00	108.56	109.29	110.03	110.76	111.50	112.25	112.99	113.74	114.49	115.25	116.00	116.76	117.52	118.29	119.06	120.60
8.25	107.81	108.53	109.26	110.00	110.73	111.47	112.21	112.95	113.70	114.45	115.20	115.95	116.71	117.47	118.23	119.76
8.50	107.06	107.78	108.51	109.24	109.97	110.70	111.43	112.17	112.91	113.66	114.40	115.15	115.90	116.66	117.41	118.94
8.75	106.33	107.04	107.76	108.48	109.21	109.94	110.67	111.40	112.14	112.87	113.61	114.36	115.10	115.85	116.61	118.12
9.00	105.60	106.31	107.02	107.74	108.46	109.18	109.91	110.63	111.36	112.10	112.83	113.57	114.31	115.06	115.80	117.31
9.25	104.87	105.58	106.29	107.00	107.72	108.43	109.15	109.88	110.60	111.33	112.06	112.79	113.53	114.27	115.01	116.50
9.50	104.16	104.86	105.56	106.27	106.98	107.69	108.41	109.13	109.85	110.57	111.30	112.02	112.76	113.49	114.23	115.71
9.75	103.45	104.14	104.84	105.55	106.25	106.96	107.67	108.38	109.10	109.82	110.54	111.26	111.99	112.72	113.45	114.92
10.00	102.74	103.44	104.13	104.83	105.53	106.23	106.94	107.65	108.36	109.07	109.79	110.51	111.23	111.95	112.68	114.14
10.25	102.05	102.74	103.43	104.12	104.81	105.51	106.21	106.92	107.62	108.33	109.04	109.76	110.47	111.19	111.91	113.36
10.50	101.36	102.04	102.73	103.42	104.11	104.80	105.50	106.20	106.90	107.60	108.31	109.02	109.73	110.44	111.16	112.60
10.75	100.68	101.35	102.04	102.72	103.41	104.09	104.79	105.48	106.18	106.88	107.58	108.28	108.99	109.70	110.41	111.84
11.00	100.00	100.67	101.35	102.03	102.71	103.40	104.08	104.77	105.46	106.16	106.86	107.56	108.26	108.96	109.67	111.09
11.25	99.33	100.00	100.67	101.35	102.02	102.70	103.39	104.07	104.76	105.45	106.14	106.83	107.53	108.23	108.93	110.35
11.50	98.67	99.33	100.00	100.67	101.34	102.02	102.70	103.38	104.06	104.74	105.43	106.12	106.81	107.51	108.21	109.61
11.75	98.01	98.67	99.33	100.00	100.67	101.34	102.01	102.69	103.37	104.05	104.73	105.42	106.10	106.79	107.49	108.88
12.00	97.36	98.02	98.68	99.34	100.00	100.67	101.33	102.01	102.68	103.36	104.03	104.72	105.40	106.09	106.77	108.16
12.25	96.72	97.37	98.02	98.68	99.34	100.00	100.66	101.33	102.00	102.67	103.35	104.02	104.70	105.38	106.07	107.44
12.50	96.08	96.73	97.38	98.03	98.68	99.34	100.00	100.66	101.33	101.99	102.66	103.34	104.01	104.69	105.37	106.73
12.75	95.45	96.09	96.73	97.38	98.03	98.69	99.34	100.00	100.66	101.32	101.99	102.66	103.33	104.00	104.67	106.03
13.00	94.82	95.46	96.10	96.74	97.39	98.04	98.69	99.34	100.00	100.66	101.32	101.98	102.65	103.32	103.99	105.33
13.25	94.20	94.83	95.47	96.11	96.75	97.40	98.04	98.69	99.35	100.00	100.66	101.32	101.98	102.64	103.31	104.65
13.50	93.58	94.22	94.85	95.48	96.12	96.76	97.41	98.05	98.70	99.35	100.00	100.66	101.32	101.98	102.64	103.96
13.75	92.98	93.60	94.23	94.86	95.50	96.13	96.77	97.41	98.06	98.70	99.35	100.00	100.65	101.31	101.97	103.29
14.00	92.37	93.00	93.62	94.25	94.88	95.51	96.14	96.78	97.42	98.06	98.70	99.35	100.00	100.65	101.31	102.62
14.25	91.78	92.39	93.01	93.64	94.26	94.89	95.52	96.16	96.79	97.43	98.07	98.71	99.35	100.00	100.65	101.95
14.50	91.18	91.80	92.42	93.03	93.66	94.28	94.91	95.54	96.17	96.80	97.43	98.07	98.71	99.36	100.00	101.30
14.75	90.60	91.21	91.82	92.44	93.05	93.67	94.30	94.92	95.55	96.18	96.81	97.44	98.08	98.72	99.36	100.65
15.00	90.02	90.62	91.23	91.84	92.46	93.07	93.69	94.31	94.94	95.56	96.19	96.82	97.45	98.08	98.72	100.00
15.25	89.44	90.04	90.65	91.26	91.87	92.48	93.09	93.71	94.33	94.95	95.57	96.20	96.83	97.46	98.09	99.36
15.50	88.87	89.47	90.07	90.68	91.28	91.89	92.50	93.11	93.73	94.34	94.96	95.59	96.21	96.84	97.46	98.73
15.75	88.31	88.90	89.50	90.10	90.70	91.31	91.91	92.52	93.13	93.75	94.36	94.98	95.60	96.22	96.85	98.10
16.00	87.75	88.34	88.93	89.53	90.13	90.73	91.33	91.94	92.54	93.15	93.76	94.38	94.99	95.61	96.23	97.48
16.25	87.19	87.78	88.37	88.96	89.56	90.15	90.75	91.35	91.96	92.56	93.17	93.78	94.39	95.01	95.62	96.86
16.50	86.64	87.23	87.81	88.40	88.99	89.59	90.18	90.78	91.38	91.98	92.58	93.19	93.80	94.41	95.02	96.25
16.75	86.10	86.68	87.26	87.85	88.43	89.02	89.62	90.21	90.80	91.40	92.00	92.61	93.21	93.82	94.43	95.65
17.00	85.56	86.14	86.72	87.30	87.88	88.47	89.05	89.64	90.24	90.83	91.43	92.03	92.63	93.23	93.83	95.05
17.25	85.03	85.60	86.18	86.75	87.33	87.91	88.50	89.08	89.67	90.26	90.86	91.45	92.05	92.65	93.25	94.46
17.50	84.50	85.07	85.64	86.21	86.79	87.37	87.95	88.53	89.12	89.70	90.29	90.88	91.48	92.07	92.67	93.87
17.75	83.97	84.54	85.11	85.68	86.25	86.83	87.40	87.98	88.56	89.15	89.73	90.32	90.91	91.50	92.09	93.29
18.00	83.45	84.02	84.58	85.15	85.72	86.29	86.86	87.44	88.01	88.59	89.18	89.76	90.35	90.93	91.52	92.71
18.25	82.94	83.50	84.06	84.62	85.19	85.76	86.33	86.90	87.47	88.05	88.63	89.21	89.79	90.37	90.96	92.14
18.50	82.43	82.99	83.54	84.10	84.66	85.23	85.79	86.36	86.93	87.51	88.08	88.66	89.24	89.82	90.40	91.57
18.75	81.92	82.48	83.03	83.59	84.15	84.71	85.27	85.83	86.40	86.97	87.54	88.11	88.69	89.27	89.85	91.01
19.00	81.42	81.97	82.52	83.08	83.63	84.19	84.75	85.31	85.87	86.44	87.01	87.57	88.15	88.72	89.30	90.45
20.00	79.46	80.00	80.54	81.08	81.62	82.16	82.71	83.26	83.81	84.36	84.91	85.47	86.03	86.59	87.15	88.28
25.00	70.66	71.14	71.62	72.10	72.58	73.06	73.55	74.03	74.52	75.01	75.51	76.00	76.50	76.99	77.49	78.50
30.00	63.27	63.70	64.12	64.55	64.98	65.42	65.85	66.29	66.73	67.17	67.61	68.05	68.49	68.94	69.39	70.29

Description: This table shows the yield to maturity of a mortgage purchased at the price shown in the index.

Example: The yield to maturity of a 15.00 %, 6 year mortgage at a price of 116.00 is 9.40 %.

INTEREST RATE, %

PRICE	11.00%	11.25%	11.50%	11.75%	12.00%	12.25%	12.50%	12.75%	13.00%	13.25%	13.50%	13.75%	14.00%	14.25%	14.50%	15.00%
160	–	–	–	–	–	–	–	–	–	–	–	–	–	–	–	–
155	–	–	–	–	–	–	–	–	–	–	–	–	–	–	–	.48
150	–	–	–	–	–	–	–	–	–	.10	.32	.54	.75	.97	1.18	1.61
145	–	–	–	–	–	–	–	–	–							
140	–	–	–	–	.17	.39	.61	.83	1.05	1.27	1.49	1.70	1.92	2.14	2.36	2.79
135	.49	.71	.94	1.16	1.38	1.60	1.82	2.04	2.27	2.49	2.71	2.93	3.15	3.37	3.59	4.03
130	1.75	1.97	2.20	2.42	2.65	2.87	3.10	3.32	3.55	3.77	4.00	4.22	4.44	4.67	4.89	5.34
129	2.01	2.23	2.46	2.68	2.91	3.13	3.36	3.59	3.81	4.04	4.26	4.49	4.71	4.94	5.16	5.61
128	2.27	2.49	2.72	2.95	3.17	3.40	3.63	3.85	4.08	4.30	4.53	4.76	4.98	5.21	5.43	5.88
127	2.53	2.76	2.99	3.21	3.44	3.67	3.89	4.12	4.35	4.57	4.80	5.03	5.25	5.48	5.71	6.16
126	2.80	3.03	3.26	3.48	3.71	3.94	4.17	4.39	4.62	4.85	5.07	5.30	5.53	5.76	5.98	6.44
125	3.07	3.30	3.53	3.76	3.98	4.21	4.44	4.67	4.90	5.12	5.35	5.58	5.81	6.04	6.26	6.72
124	3.34	3.57	3.80	4.03	4.26	4.49	4.72	4.95	5.18	5.40	5.63	5.86	6.09	6.32	6.55	7.00
123	3.62	3.85	4.08	4.31	4.54	4.77	5.00	5.23	5.46	5.69	5.92	6.15	6.37	6.60	6.83	7.29
122	3.90	4.13	4.36	4.59	4.82	5.05	5.28	5.51	5.74	5.97	6.20	6.43	6.66	6.89	7.12	7.58
121	4.18	4.41	4.65	4.88	5.11	5.34	5.57	5.80	6.03	6.26	6.49	6.72	6.95	7.18	7.42	7.88
120	4.47	4.70	4.93	5.16	5.40	5.63	5.86	6.09	6.32	6.56	6.79	7.02	7.25	7.48	7.71	8.17
119	4.76	4.99	5.22	5.46	5.69	5.92	6.15	6.39	6.62	6.85	7.08	7.32	7.55	7.78	8.01	8.48
118	5.05	5.28	5.52	5.75	5.98	6.22	6.45	6.68	6.92	7.15	7.38	7.62	7.85	8.08	8.32	8.78
117	5.35	5.58	5.82	6.05	6.28	6.52	6.75	6.99	7.22	7.45	7.69	7.92	8.16	8.39	8.62	9.09
116	5.65	5.88	6.12	6.35	6.59	6.82	7.06	7.29	7.53	7.76	8.00	8.23	8.46	8.70	8.93	9.40
115	5.95	6.19	6.42	6.66	6.89	7.13	7.36	7.60	7.84	8.07	8.31	8.54	8.78	9.01	9.25	9.72
114	6.26	6.49	6.73	6.97	7.20	7.44	7.68	7.91	8.15	8.39	8.62	8.86	9.10	9.33	9.57	10.04
113	6.57	6.80	7.04	7.28	7.52	7.76	7.99	8.23	8.47	8.70	8.94	9.18	9.42	9.65	9.89	10.36
112	6.88	7.12	7.36	7.60	7.84	8.07	8.31	8.55	8.79	9.03	9.26	9.50	9.74	9.98	10.22	10.69
111	7.20	7.44	7.68	7.92	8.16	8.40	8.64	8.88	9.11	9.35	9.59	9.83	10.07	10.31	10.55	11.03
110	7.52	7.76	8.00	8.24	8.48	8.72	8.96	9.20	9.44	9.68	9.92	10.16	10.40	10.64	10.88	11.36
109	7.85	8.09	8.33	8.57	8.81	9.06	9.30	9.54	9.78	10.02	10.26	10.50	10.74	10.98	11.22	11.70
108	8.18	8.42	8.67	8.91	9.15	9.39	9.63	9.87	10.12	10.36	10.60	10.84	11.08	11.33	11.57	12.05
107	8.52	8.76	9.00	9.25	9.49	9.73	9.97	10.22	10.46	10.70	10.94	11.19	11.43	11.67	11.92	12.40
106	8.86	9.10	9.34	9.59	9.83	10.08	10.32	10.56	10.81	11.05	11.29	11.54	11.78	12.03	12.27	12.76
105	9.20	9.45	9.69	9.94	10.18	10.42	10.67	10.91	11.16	11.40	11.65	11.89	12.14	12.38	12.63	13.12
104	9.55	9.80	10.04	10.29	10.53	10.78	11.02	11.27	11.52	11.76	12.01	12.25	12.50	12.74	12.99	13.48
103	9.90	10.15	10.40	10.64	10.89	11.14	11.38	11.63	11.88	12.12	12.37	12.62	12.87	13.11	13.36	13.85
102	10.26	10.51	10.76	11.01	11.25	11.50	11.75	12.00	12.25	12.49	12.74	12.99	13.24	13.48	13.73	14.23
101	10.63	10.87	11.12	11.37	11.62	11.87	12.12	12.37	12.62	12.87	13.12	13.36	13.61	13.86	14.11	14.61
100	11.00	11.25	11.50	11.75	12.00	12.25	12.50	12.75	13.00	13.25	13.50	13.75	14.00	14.25	14.50	15.00
99	11.37	11.62	11.87	12.12	12.37	12.62	12.88	13.13	13.38	13.63	13.88	14.13	14.38	14.63	14.88	15.39
98	11.75	12.00	12.25	12.51	12.76	13.01	13.26	13.51	13.77	14.02	14.27	14.52	14.78	15.03	15.28	15.79
97	12.13	12.39	12.64	12.89	13.15	13.40	13.65	13.91	14.16	14.41	14.67	14.92	15.18	15.43	15.68	16.19
96	12.53	12.78	13.03	13.29	13.54	13.80	14.05	14.31	14.56	14.82	15.07	15.33	15.58	15.84	16.09	16.60
95	12.92	13.18	13.43	13.69	13.95	14.20	14.46	14.71	14.97	15.22	15.48	15.74	15.99	16.25	16.50	17.02
94	13.33	13.58	13.84	14.10	14.35	14.61	14.87	15.12	15.38	15.64	15.90	16.15	16.41	16.67	16.92	17.44
93	13.73	13.99	14.25	14.51	14.77	15.03	15.28	15.54	15.80	16.06	16.32	16.58	16.83	17.09	17.35	17.87
92	14.15	14.41	14.67	14.93	15.19	15.45	15.71	15.97	16.23	16.49	16.75	17.01	17.27	17.53	17.79	18.31
91	14.57	14.83	15.09	15.36	15.62	15.88	16.14	16.40	16.66	16.92	17.18	17.44	17.70	17.97	18.23	18.75
90	15.00	15.26	15.53	15.79	16.05	16.31	16.58	16.84	17.10	17.36	17.62	17.89	18.15	18.41	18.67	19.20
89	15.44	15.70	15.97	16.23	16.49	16.76	17.02	17.28	17.55	17.81	18.07	18.34	18.60	18.87	19.13	19.66
88	15.88	16.15	16.41	16.68	16.94	17.21	17.47	17.74	18.00	18.27	18.53	18.80	19.06	19.33	19.59	20.13
87	16.33	16.60	16.87	17.13	17.40	17.66	17.93	18.20	18.46	18.73	19.00	19.26	19.53	19.80	20.07	20.60
86	16.79	17.06	17.33	17.59	17.86	18.13	18.40	18.67	18.93	19.20	19.47	19.74	20.01	20.28	20.54	21.08
85	17.26	17.53	17.80	18.07	18.33	18.60	18.87	19.14	19.41	19.68	19.95	20.22	20.49	20.76	21.03	21.57
84	17.73	18.00	18.27	18.54	18.82	19.09	19.36	19.63	19.90	20.17	20.44	20.71	20.99	21.26	21.53	22.07
83	18.22	18.49	18.76	19.03	19.30	19.58	19.85	20.12	20.40	20.67	20.94	21.21	21.49	21.76	22.04	22.58
82	18.71	18.98	19.26	19.53	19.80	20.08	20.35	20.63	20.90	21.18	21.45	21.72	22.00	22.27	22.55	23.10
81	19.21	19.48	19.76	20.03	20.31	20.59	20.86	21.14	21.41	21.69	21.97	22.24	22.52	22.80	23.07	23.63
80	19.72	20.00	20.27	20.55	20.83	21.11	21.38	21.66	21.94	22.22	22.49	22.77	23.05	23.33	23.61	24.17
79	20.24	20.52	20.80	21.07	21.35	21.63	21.91	22.19	22.47	22.75	23.03	23.31	23.59	23.87	24.15	24.72
78	20.77	21.05	21.33	21.61	21.89	22.17	22.45	22.73	23.02	23.30	23.58	23.86	24.14	24.43	24.71	25.27
77	21.31	21.59	21.87	22.16	22.44	22.72	23.00	23.29	23.57	23.86	24.14	24.42	24.71	24.99	25.28	25.84
76	21.86	22.14	22.43	22.71	23.00	23.28	23.57	23.85	24.14	24.42	24.71	24.99	25.28	25.57	25.85	26.43
75	22.42	22.71	22.99	23.28	23.57	23.85	24.14	24.43	24.71	25.00	25.29	25.58	25.87	26.15	26.44	27.02
74	22.99	23.28	23.57	23.86	24.15	24.44	24.73	25.01	25.30	25.59	25.88	26.17	26.46	26.75	27.05	27.63
73	23.58	23.87	24.16	24.45	24.74	25.03	25.32	25.61	25.91	26.20	26.49	26.78	27.07	27.37	27.66	28.25
72	24.18	24.47	24.76	25.05	25.35	25.64	25.93	26.23	26.52	26.81	27.11	27.40	27.70	27.99	28.29	28.88
71	24.79	25.08	25.37	25.67	25.97	26.26	26.56	26.85	27.15	27.44	27.74	28.04	28.33	28.63	28.93	29.52
70	25.41	25.71	26.00	26.30	26.60	26.90	27.19	27.49	27.79	28.09	28.39	28.69	28.99	29.29	29.59	30.19
65	28.75	29.05	29.36	29.67	29.98	30.29	30.61	30.92	31.23	31.54	31.85	32.16	32.48	32.79	33.10	33.73

Description: This table shows the price to pay for a monthly payment mortgage loan at the yield rate.

Example: The price of a 6.75 %, 7 year mortgage loan to yield 8.00 % to maturity is $ 96.05.

INTEREST RATE, %

YIELD	0.00%	1.00%	2.00%	3.00%	4.00%	4.25%	4.50%	4.75%	5.00%	5.25%	5.50%	5.75%	6.00%	6.25%	6.50%	6.75%
0.00	100.00	103.58	107.25	110.99	114.82	115.79	116.76	117.74	118.72	119.71	120.71	121.71	122.71	123.72	124.74	125.75
1.00	96.54	100.00	103.54	107.15	110.85	111.78	112.72	113.67	114.62	115.57	116.53	117.50	118.47	119.44	120.42	121.41
2.00	93.24	96.58	100.00	103.49	107.06	107.96	108.87	109.79	110.70	111.63	112.55	113.48	114.42	115.36	116.31	117.26
3.00	90.10	93.32	96.63	100.00	103.45	104.32	105.20	106.08	106.97	107.86	108.75	109.65	110.56	111.47	112.38	113.30
4.00	87.09	90.21	93.41	96.67	100.00	100.84	101.69	102.55	103.40	104.26	105.13	106.00	106.88	107.75	108.64	109.53
4.25	86.37	89.46	92.62	95.86	99.16	100.00	100.84	101.69	102.54	103.39	104.25	105.11	105.98	106.85	107.73	108.61
4.50	85.64	88.71	91.85	95.06	98.34	99.17	100.00	100.84	101.68	102.53	103.38	104.24	105.10	105.96	106.83	107.70
4.75	84.93	87.98	91.09	94.27	97.52	98.34	99.17	100.00	100.84	101.68	102.52	103.37	104.22	105.08	105.94	106.81
5.00	84.23	87.25	90.33	93.49	96.71	97.53	98.35	99.17	100.00	100.83	101.67	102.51	103.36	104.21	105.06	105.92
5.25	83.53	86.52	89.59	92.71	95.91	96.72	97.53	98.35	99.17	100.00	100.83	101.67	102.50	103.35	104.19	105.05
5.50	82.84	85.81	88.85	91.95	95.12	95.92	96.73	97.54	98.36	99.18	100.00	100.83	101.66	102.50	103.34	104.18
5.75	82.16	85.11	88.12	91.20	94.34	95.14	95.94	96.74	97.55	98.36	99.18	100.00	100.83	101.65	102.49	103.33
6.00	81.49	84.41	87.40	90.45	93.57	94.36	95.15	95.95	96.75	97.56	98.37	99.18	100.00	100.82	101.65	102.48
6.25	80.83	83.72	86.68	89.71	92.80	93.59	94.37	95.17	95.96	96.76	97.56	98.37	99.18	100.00	100.82	101.64
6.50	80.17	83.04	85.98	88.98	92.05	92.83	93.61	94.39	95.18	95.97	96.77	97.57	98.38	99.19	100.00	100.82
6.75	79.52	82.37	85.28	88.26	91.30	92.07	92.85	93.63	94.41	95.20	95.99	96.78	97.58	98.38	99.19	100.00
7.00	78.88	81.70	84.59	87.55	90.57	91.33	92.10	92.87	93.65	94.43	95.21	96.00	96.79	97.59	98.39	99.19
7.25	78.24	81.05	83.91	86.84	89.84	90.59	91.36	92.12	92.89	93.67	94.45	95.23	96.01	96.80	97.60	98.39
7.50	77.61	80.40	83.24	86.15	89.12	89.87	90.62	91.38	92.15	92.92	93.69	94.46	95.24	96.03	96.81	97.60
7.75	76.99	79.75	82.57	85.46	88.40	89.15	89.90	90.65	91.41	92.17	92.94	93.71	94.48	95.26	96.04	96.82
8.00	76.38	79.12	81.91	84.78	87.70	88.44	89.18	89.93	90.68	91.44	92.20	92.96	93.73	94.50	95.27	96.05
8.25	75.77	78.49	81.26	84.10	87.00	87.74	88.47	89.22	89.96	90.71	91.46	92.22	92.98	93.75	94.52	95.29
8.50	75.17	77.87	80.62	83.44	86.31	87.04	87.77	88.51	89.25	89.99	90.74	91.49	92.25	93.00	93.77	94.53
8.75	74.58	77.25	79.98	82.78	85.63	86.35	87.08	87.81	88.54	89.28	90.02	90.77	91.52	92.27	93.03	93.79
9.00	73.99	76.64	79.35	82.13	84.96	85.67	86.40	87.12	87.85	88.58	89.32	90.05	90.80	91.54	92.30	93.05
9.25	73.41	76.04	78.73	81.48	84.29	85.00	85.72	86.44	87.16	87.89	88.62	89.35	90.09	90.83	91.57	92.32
9.50	72.84	75.45	78.12	80.85	83.63	84.34	85.05	85.76	86.48	87.20	87.92	88.65	89.38	90.12	90.86	91.60
9.75	72.27	74.86	77.51	80.22	82.98	83.68	84.39	85.09	85.80	86.52	87.24	87.96	88.69	89.41	90.15	90.88
10.00	71.71	74.28	76.91	79.59	82.34	83.03	83.73	84.43	85.14	85.85	86.56	87.28	88.00	88.72	89.45	90.18
10.25	71.16	73.70	76.31	78.98	81.70	82.39	83.08	83.78	84.48	85.18	85.89	86.60	87.32	88.03	88.76	89.48
10.50	70.61	73.14	75.72	78.37	81.07	81.75	82.44	83.13	83.83	84.53	85.23	85.93	86.64	87.36	88.07	88.79
10.75	70.06	72.57	75.14	77.77	80.45	81.13	81.81	82.49	83.18	83.88	84.57	85.27	85.98	86.68	87.39	88.11
11.00	69.53	72.02	74.57	77.17	79.83	80.50	81.18	81.86	82.55	83.23	83.93	84.62	85.32	86.02	86.73	87.43
11.25	69.00	71.47	74.00	76.58	79.22	79.89	80.56	81.24	81.92	82.60	83.28	83.97	84.67	85.36	86.06	86.77
11.50	68.47	70.92	73.43	76.00	78.62	79.28	79.95	80.62	81.29	81.97	82.65	83.33	84.02	84.71	85.41	86.11
11.75	67.95	70.39	72.88	75.42	78.02	78.68	79.34	80.01	80.68	81.35	82.02	82.70	83.39	84.07	84.76	85.45
12.00	67.44	69.85	72.33	74.85	77.43	78.09	78.74	79.40	80.07	80.73	81.40	82.08	82.76	83.44	84.12	84.81
12.25	66.93	69.33	71.78	74.29	76.85	77.50	78.15	78.80	79.46	80.13	80.79	81.46	82.13	82.81	83.49	84.17
12.50	66.43	68.81	71.24	73.73	76.27	76.92	77.56	78.21	78.87	79.52	80.18	80.85	81.52	82.19	82.86	83.54
12.75	65.93	68.29	70.71	73.18	75.70	76.34	76.98	77.63	78.28	78.93	79.58	80.24	80.91	81.57	82.24	82.91
13.00	65.44	67.78	70.18	72.63	75.14	75.77	76.41	77.05	77.69	78.34	78.99	79.65	80.30	80.96	81.63	82.29
13.25	64.95	67.28	69.66	72.09	74.58	75.21	75.84	76.48	77.12	77.76	78.40	79.05	79.71	80.36	81.02	81.68
13.50	64.47	66.78	69.14	71.56	74.03	74.65	75.28	75.91	76.54	77.18	77.82	78.47	79.12	79.77	80.42	81.08
13.75	64.00	66.29	68.63	71.03	73.48	74.10	74.72	75.35	75.98	76.61	77.25	77.89	78.53	79.18	79.83	80.48
14.00	63.53	65.80	68.13	70.51	72.94	73.55	74.17	74.80	75.42	76.05	76.68	77.32	77.95	78.59	79.24	79.89
14.25	63.06	65.32	67.63	69.99	72.40	73.02	73.63	74.25	74.87	75.49	76.12	76.75	77.38	78.02	78.66	79.30
14.50	62.60	64.84	67.14	69.48	71.88	72.48	73.09	73.71	74.32	74.94	75.56	76.19	76.82	77.45	78.08	78.72
14.75	62.14	64.37	66.65	68.97	71.35	71.95	72.56	73.17	73.78	74.40	75.01	75.63	76.26	76.89	77.52	78.15
15.00	61.69	63.90	66.16	68.47	70.83	71.43	72.03	72.64	73.25	73.86	74.47	75.09	75.70	76.33	76.95	77.58
15.25	61.25	63.44	65.69	67.98	70.32	70.92	71.51	72.11	72.72	73.32	73.93	74.54	75.16	75.78	76.40	77.02
15.50	60.81	62.98	65.21	67.49	69.82	70.41	71.00	71.59	72.19	72.79	73.40	74.01	74.62	75.23	75.85	76.47
15.75	60.37	62.53	64.74	67.00	69.31	69.90	70.49	71.08	71.67	72.27	72.87	73.47	74.08	74.69	75.30	75.92
16.00	59.94	62.08	64.28	66.53	68.82	69.40	69.98	70.57	71.16	71.75	72.35	72.95	73.55	74.15	74.76	75.37
16.25	59.51	61.64	63.82	66.05	68.33	68.90	69.48	70.07	70.65	71.24	71.83	72.43	73.03	73.63	74.23	74.84
16.50	59.09	61.20	63.37	65.58	67.84	68.42	68.99	69.57	70.15	70.74	71.32	71.91	72.51	73.10	73.70	74.30
16.75	58.67	60.77	62.92	65.12	67.36	67.93	68.50	69.08	69.65	70.23	70.82	71.40	71.99	72.59	73.18	73.78
17.00	58.25	60.34	62.48	64.66	66.89	67.45	68.02	68.59	69.16	69.74	70.32	70.90	71.49	72.07	72.66	73.26
17.25	57.84	59.92	62.04	64.20	66.42	66.98	67.54	68.11	68.68	69.25	69.82	70.40	70.98	71.57	72.15	72.74
17.50	57.44	59.50	61.60	63.75	65.95	66.51	67.07	67.63	68.19	68.76	69.33	69.91	70.48	71.06	71.65	72.23
17.75	57.04	59.08	61.17	63.31	65.49	66.04	66.60	67.16	67.72	68.28	68.85	69.42	69.99	70.57	71.15	71.73
18.00	56.64	58.67	60.75	62.87	65.03	65.58	66.14	66.69	67.25	67.81	68.37	68.94	69.51	70.08	70.65	71.23
18.25	56.25	58.26	60.32	62.43	64.58	65.13	65.68	66.23	66.78	67.34	67.90	68.46	69.02	69.59	70.16	70.73
18.50	55.86	57.86	59.91	62.00	64.14	64.68	65.22	65.77	66.32	66.87	67.43	67.99	68.55	69.11	69.68	70.25
18.75	55.47	57.46	59.49	61.57	63.70	64.23	64.77	65.32	65.86	66.41	66.96	67.52	68.07	68.63	69.20	69.76
19.00	55.09	57.07	59.09	61.15	63.26	63.79	64.33	64.87	65.41	65.96	66.50	67.05	67.61	68.16	68.72	69.28
20.00	53.61	55.53	57.49	59.50	61.55	62.07	62.60	63.12	63.65	64.18	64.71	65.25	65.79	66.33	66.87	67.42
25.00	47.03	48.72	50.44	52.20	54.00	54.46	54.92	55.38	55.84	56.30	56.77	57.24	57.71	58.19	58.67	59.15
30.00	41.64	43.13	44.65	46.21	47.80	48.21	48.61	49.02	49.43	49.84	50.26	50.67	51.09	51.51	51.93	52.36

Description: This table shows the yield to maturity of a mortgage purchased at the price shown in the index.

Example: The yield to maturity of a 6.75 %, 7 year mortgage at a price of 80.00 is 13.95 %.

INTEREST RATE, %

PRICE	0.00%	1.00%	2.00%	3.00%	4.00%	4.25%	4.50%	4.75%	5.00%	5.25%	5.50%	5.75%	6.00%	6.25%	6.50%	6.75%
100	0.00	1.00	2.00	3.00	4.00	4.25	4.50	4.75	5.00	5.25	5.50	5.75	6.00	6.25	6.50	6.75
99	.28	1.28	2.29	3.29	4.29	4.55	4.80	5.05	5.30	5.55	5.80	6.05	6.30	6.55	6.80	7.05
98	.57	1.57	2.58	3.59	4.60	4.85	5.10	5.35	5.61	5.86	6.11	6.36	6.61	6.87	7.12	7.37
97	.86	1.87	2.88	3.89	4.90	5.16	5.41	5.66	5.92	6.17	6.42	6.68	6.93	7.18	7.44	7.69
96	1.16	2.17	3.19	4.20	5.22	5.47	5.72	5.98	6.23	6.49	6.74	7.00	7.25	7.50	7.76	8.01
95	1.46	2.48	3.49	4.51	5.53	5.79	6.04	6.30	6.55	6.81	7.06	7.32	7.57	7.83	8.08	8.34
94	1.76	2.78	3.81	4.83	5.85	6.11	6.37	6.62	6.88	7.14	7.39	7.65	7.90	8.16	8.42	8.67
93	2.07	3.10	4.12	5.15	6.18	6.44	6.69	6.95	7.21	7.47	7.72	7.98	8.24	8.50	8.75	9.01
92	2.38	3.42	4.45	5.48	6.51	6.77	7.03	7.29	7.54	7.80	8.06	8.32	8.58	8.84	9.10	9.36
91	2.70	3.74	4.77	5.81	6.85	7.11	7.37	7.63	7.89	8.15	8.41	8.66	8.92	9.18	9.44	9.70
90	3.03	4.07	5.11	6.15	7.19	7.45	7.71	7.97	8.23	8.49	8.75	9.01	9.28	9.54	9.80	10.06
89	3.35	4.40	5.44	6.49	7.54	7.80	8.06	8.32	8.58	8.85	9.11	9.37	9.63	9.89	10.16	10.42
88	3.69	4.74	5.79	6.84	7.89	8.15	8.41	8.68	8.94	9.20	9.47	9.73	9.99	10.26	10.52	10.79
87	4.03	5.08	6.13	7.19	8.25	8.51	8.77	9.04	9.30	9.57	9.83	10.10	10.36	10.63	10.89	11.16
86	4.37	5.43	6.49	7.55	8.61	8.87	9.14	9.41	9.67	9.94	10.20	10.47	10.74	11.00	11.27	11.54
85	4.72	5.78	6.85	7.91	8.98	9.25	9.51	9.78	10.05	10.31	10.58	10.85	11.12	11.38	11.65	11.92
84	5.08	6.14	7.21	8.28	9.36	9.62	9.89	10.16	10.43	10.70	10.97	11.23	11.50	11.77	12.04	12.31
83	5.44	6.51	7.58	8.66	9.74	10.01	10.28	10.55	10.82	11.09	11.36	11.63	11.90	12.17	12.44	12.71
82	5.81	6.88	7.96	9.04	10.13	10.40	10.67	10.94	11.21	11.48	11.75	12.03	12.30	12.57	12.84	13.11
81	6.18	7.26	8.35	9.43	10.52	10.80	11.07	11.34	11.61	11.89	12.16	12.43	12.71	12.98	13.25	13.53
80	6.56	7.65	8.74	9.83	10.93	11.20	11.47	11.75	12.02	12.30	12.57	12.85	13.12	13.40	13.67	13.95
79	6.95	8.04	9.14	10.24	11.34	11.61	11.89	12.16	12.44	12.72	12.99	13.27	13.54	13.82	14.10	14.37
78	7.34	8.44	9.54	10.65	11.75	12.03	12.31	12.59	12.86	13.14	13.42	13.70	13.97	14.25	14.53	14.81
77	7.74	8.85	9.96	11.07	12.18	12.46	12.74	13.02	13.30	13.57	13.85	14.13	14.41	14.69	14.97	15.25
76	8.15	9.26	10.38	11.49	12.61	12.89	13.17	13.46	13.74	14.02	14.30	14.58	14.86	15.14	15.42	15.71
75	8.57	9.69	10.81	11.93	13.06	13.34	13.62	13.90	14.19	14.47	14.75	15.03	15.32	15.60	15.88	16.17
74	8.99	10.12	11.24	12.37	13.51	13.79	14.07	14.36	14.64	14.93	15.21	15.50	15.78	16.07	16.35	16.64
73	9.42	10.56	11.69	12.83	13.97	14.25	14.54	14.82	15.11	15.40	15.68	15.97	16.26	16.54	16.83	17.12
72	9.87	11.00	12.14	13.29	14.44	14.72	15.01	15.30	15.59	15.88	16.16	16.45	16.74	17.03	17.32	17.61
71	10.32	11.46	12.61	13.76	14.91	15.20	15.49	15.78	16.07	16.36	16.65	16.95	17.24	17.53	17.82	18.11
70	10.77	11.93	13.08	14.24	15.40	15.70	15.99	16.28	16.57	16.86	17.16	17.45	17.74	18.03	18.33	18.62
69	11.24	12.40	13.57	14.73	15.90	16.20	16.49	16.78	17.08	17.37	17.67	17.96	18.26	18.55	18.85	19.14
68	11.72	12.89	14.06	15.23	16.41	16.71	17.00	17.30	17.60	17.89	18.19	18.49	18.78	19.08	19.38	19.68
67	12.21	13.39	14.56	15.75	16.94	17.23	17.53	17.83	18.13	18.43	18.72	19.02	19.32	19.62	19.92	20.22
66	12.71	13.89	15.08	16.27	17.47	17.77	18.07	18.37	18.67	18.97	19.27	19.57	19.88	20.18	20.48	20.78
65	13.22	14.41	15.61	16.81	18.01	18.32	18.62	18.92	19.22	19.53	19.83	20.14	20.44	20.74	21.05	21.35
64	13.74	14.94	16.15	17.36	18.57	18.88	19.18	19.49	19.79	20.10	20.40	20.71	21.02	21.32	21.63	21.94
63	14.28	15.49	16.70	17.92	19.14	19.45	19.76	20.07	20.37	20.68	20.99	21.30	21.61	21.92	22.23	22.54
62	14.82	16.04	17.27	18.49	19.73	20.04	20.35	20.66	20.97	21.28	21.59	21.90	22.22	22.53	22.84	23.15
61	15.38	16.61	17.85	19.08	20.33	20.64	20.95	21.27	21.58	21.89	22.21	22.52	22.84	23.15	23.47	23.78
60	15.96	17.20	18.44	19.69	20.94	21.26	21.57	21.89	22.21	22.52	22.84	23.16	23.47	23.79	24.11	24.43
59	16.55	17.79	19.05	20.31	21.58	21.89	22.21	22.53	22.85	23.17	23.49	23.81	24.13	24.45	24.77	25.09
58	17.15	18.41	19.67	20.94	22.22	22.54	22.86	23.19	23.51	23.83	24.15	24.48	24.80	25.12	25.45	25.77
57	17.77	19.04	20.31	21.60	22.89	23.21	23.54	23.86	24.19	24.51	24.84	25.16	25.49	25.82	26.15	26.47
56	18.40	19.69	20.97	22.27	23.57	23.90	24.23	24.55	24.88	25.21	25.54	25.87	26.20	26.53	26.86	27.19
55	19.06	20.35	21.65	22.96	24.27	24.60	24.93	25.26	25.60	25.93	26.26	26.60	26.93	27.26	27.60	27.93
54	19.73	21.03	22.35	23.67	25.00	25.33	25.66	26.00	26.33	26.67	27.01	27.34	27.68	28.02	28.36	28.69
53	20.42	21.74	23.06	24.40	25.74	26.08	26.42	26.75	27.09	27.43	27.77	28.11	28.45	28.79	29.14	29.48
52	21.13	22.46	23.80	25.15	26.51	26.85	27.19	27.53	27.87	28.22	28.56	28.90	29.25	29.59	29.94	30.29
51	21.86	23.21	24.56	25.92	27.30	27.64	27.99	28.33	28.68	29.03	29.37	29.72	30.07	30.42	30.77	31.12
50	22.61	23.97	25.34	26.72	28.11	28.46	28.81	29.16	29.51	29.86	30.21	30.57	30.92	31.27	31.63	31.98
49	23.39	24.77	26.15	27.55	28.95	29.31	29.66	30.01	30.37	30.72	31.08	31.44	31.80	32.15	32.51	32.87
48	24.19	25.59	26.99	28.40	29.82	30.18	30.54	30.90	31.26	31.62	31.98	32.34	32.70	33.06	33.43	33.79
47	25.02	26.43	27.85	29.28	30.72	31.08	31.45	31.81	32.17	32.54	32.90	33.27	33.64	34.01	34.37	34.74
46	25.88	27.31	28.74	30.19	31.65	32.02	32.39	32.75	33.12	33.49	33.86	34.24	34.61	34.98	35.35	35.73
45	26.77	28.21	29.67	31.13	32.61	32.99	33.36	33.73	34.11	34.48	34.86	35.24	35.61	35.99	36.37	36.75
44	27.68	29.15	30.62	32.11	33.61	33.99	34.37	34.75	35.13	35.51	35.89	36.27	36.66	37.04	37.43	37.81
43	28.64	30.12	31.62	33.13	34.65	35.03	35.42	35.80	36.19	36.57	36.96	37.35	37.74	38.13	38.52	38.91
42	29.63	31.13	32.65	34.18	35.73	36.12	36.51	36.90	37.29	37.68	38.08	38.47	38.87	39.26	39.66	40.06
41	30.65	32.18	33.72	35.28	36.85	37.24	37.64	38.04	38.44	38.84	39.24	39.64	40.04	40.44	40.85	41.25
40	31.72	33.27	34.84	36.42	38.02	38.42	38.82	39.23	39.63	40.04	40.44	40.85	41.26	41.67	42.08	42.49
39	32.83	34.41	36.00	37.61	39.23	39.64	40.05	40.46	40.88	41.29	41.70	42.12	42.54	42.95	43.37	43.79
38	33.99	35.59	37.21	38.85	40.51	40.92	41.34	41.76	42.18	42.60	43.02	43.44	43.87	44.29	44.72	45.15
37	35.20	36.83	38.48	40.15	41.84	42.26	42.68	43.11	43.54	43.97	44.40	44.83	45.26	45.70	46.13	46.57
36	36.47	38.13	39.81	41.51	43.23	43.66	44.09	44.53	44.97	45.40	45.84	46.28	46.72	47.17	47.61	48.05
35	37.80	39.49	41.20	42.93	44.69	45.13	45.57	46.02	46.46	46.91	47.36	47.81	48.26	48.71	49.16	49.62
30	45.53	47.42	49.33	51.28	53.25	53.74	54.24	54.74	55.24	55.75	56.25	56.76	57.27	57.78	58.29	58.80
25	55.89	58.07	60.28	62.53	64.82	65.39	65.97	66.55	67.14	67.72	68.31	68.90	69.50	70.09	70.69	71.29

Description: This table shows the price to pay for a monthly payment mortgage loan at the yield rate.

Example: The price of a 10.75 %, 7 year mortgage loan to yield 8.00 % to maturity is $ 109.01.

INTEREST RATE, %

YIELD	7.00%	7.25%	7.50%	7.75%	8.00%	8.25%	8.50%	8.75%	9.00%	9.25%	9.50%	9.75%	10.00%	10.25%	10.50%	10.75%
0.00	126.78	127.81	128.84	129.88	130.92	131.97	133.03	134.08	135.15	136.22	137.29	138.37	139.45	140.54	141.63	142.73
1.00	122.39	123.39	124.39	125.39	126.40	127.41	128.43	129.45	130.47	131.51	132.54	133.58	134.63	135.68	136.73	137.79
2.00	118.21	119.17	120.14	121.10	122.08	123.06	124.04	125.03	126.02	127.01	128.01	129.02	130.03	131.04	132.06	133.08
3.00	114.22	115.15	116.08	117.02	117.96	118.90	119.85	120.81	121.76	122.73	123.69	124.66	125.64	126.62	127.60	128.59
4.00	110.42	111.31	112.21	113.12	114.03	114.94	115.86	116.78	117.71	118.64	119.57	120.51	121.45	122.40	123.35	124.31
4.25	109.49	110.38	111.27	112.17	113.07	113.98	114.89	115.80	116.72	117.64	118.57	119.50	120.44	121.38	122.32	123.27
4.50	108.58	109.46	110.35	111.24	112.13	113.03	113.93	114.84	115.75	116.66	117.58	118.50	119.43	120.36	121.30	122.24
4.75	107.68	108.55	109.43	110.31	111.20	112.09	112.98	113.88	114.78	115.69	116.60	117.52	118.44	119.36	120.29	121.22
5.00	106.78	107.65	108.52	109.40	110.28	111.16	112.05	112.94	113.83	114.73	115.64	116.54	117.46	118.37	119.29	120.22
5.25	105.90	106.76	107.62	108.49	109.36	110.24	111.12	112.00	112.89	113.78	114.68	115.58	116.49	117.39	118.31	119.22
5.50	105.03	105.88	106.74	107.60	108.46	109.33	110.20	111.08	111.96	112.85	113.74	114.63	115.53	116.43	117.33	118.24
5.75	104.17	105.01	105.86	106.72	107.57	108.43	109.30	110.17	111.04	111.92	112.80	113.69	114.58	115.47	116.37	117.27
6.00	103.31	104.15	105.00	105.84	106.69	107.55	108.41	109.27	110.13	111.01	111.88	112.76	113.64	114.53	115.42	116.31
6.25	102.47	103.30	104.14	104.98	105.82	106.67	107.52	108.38	109.24	110.10	110.97	111.84	112.71	113.59	114.47	115.36
6.50	101.64	102.46	103.29	104.12	104.96	105.80	106.65	107.50	108.35	109.20	110.06	110.93	111.80	112.67	113.54	114.42
6.75	100.81	101.63	102.45	103.28	104.11	104.94	105.78	106.62	107.47	108.32	109.17	110.03	110.89	111.76	112.62	113.50
7.00	100.00	100.81	101.63	102.45	103.27	104.10	104.93	105.76	106.60	107.44	108.29	109.14	109.99	110.85	111.71	112.58
7.25	99.19	100.00	100.81	101.62	102.44	103.26	104.08	104.91	105.74	106.58	107.42	108.26	109.11	109.96	110.81	111.67
7.50	98.40	99.20	100.00	100.81	101.62	102.43	103.25	104.07	104.89	105.72	106.56	107.39	108.23	109.08	109.93	110.78
7.75	97.61	98.40	99.20	100.00	100.80	101.61	102.42	103.24	104.06	104.88	105.70	106.53	107.37	108.21	109.05	109.89
8.00	96.83	97.62	98.41	99.20	100.00	100.80	101.61	102.41	103.23	104.04	104.86	105.69	106.51	107.34	108.18	109.01
8.25	96.06	96.84	97.63	98.41	99.21	100.00	100.80	101.60	102.41	103.22	104.03	104.85	105.67	106.49	107.32	108.15
8.50	95.30	96.08	96.85	97.64	98.42	99.21	100.00	100.80	101.60	102.40	103.20	104.01	104.83	105.65	106.47	107.29
8.75	94.55	95.32	96.09	96.86	97.64	98.42	99.21	100.00	100.79	101.59	102.39	103.19	104.00	104.81	105.63	106.44
9.00	93.81	94.57	95.33	96.10	96.87	97.65	98.43	99.21	100.00	100.79	101.58	102.38	103.18	103.99	104.80	105.61
9.25	93.07	93.83	94.59	95.35	96.11	96.88	97.66	98.44	99.22	100.00	100.79	101.58	102.37	103.17	103.97	104.78
9.50	92.34	93.09	93.85	94.60	95.36	96.13	96.89	97.67	98.44	99.22	100.00	100.79	101.57	102.37	103.16	103.96
9.75	91.62	92.37	93.12	93.87	94.62	95.38	96.14	96.91	97.67	98.45	99.22	100.00	100.78	101.57	102.37	103.15
10.00	90.91	91.65	92.39	93.14	93.89	94.64	95.39	96.15	96.92	97.68	98.45	99.22	100.00	100.78	101.56	102.35
10.25	90.21	90.94	91.68	92.42	93.16	93.91	94.66	95.41	96.17	96.93	97.69	98.46	99.23	100.00	100.78	101.56
10.50	89.51	90.24	90.97	91.70	92.44	93.18	93.93	94.67	95.42	96.18	96.94	97.70	98.46	99.23	100.00	100.77
10.75	88.83	89.55	90.27	91.00	91.73	92.47	93.20	93.95	94.69	95.44	96.19	96.95	97.70	98.47	99.23	100.00
11.00	88.15	88.86	89.58	90.30	91.03	91.76	92.49	93.23	93.96	94.71	95.45	96.20	96.96	97.71	98.47	99.23
11.25	87.47	88.18	88.90	89.61	90.33	91.06	91.78	92.51	93.25	93.98	94.72	95.47	96.22	96.97	97.72	98.48
11.50	86.81	87.51	88.22	88.93	89.65	90.36	91.09	91.81	92.54	93.27	94.00	94.74	95.48	96.23	96.98	97.73
11.75	86.15	86.85	87.55	88.26	88.97	89.68	90.39	91.11	91.84	92.56	93.29	94.02	94.76	95.50	96.24	96.99
12.00	85.50	86.19	86.89	87.59	88.29	89.00	89.71	90.43	91.14	91.86	92.59	93.31	94.04	94.78	95.51	96.25
12.25	84.85	85.54	86.23	86.93	87.63	88.33	89.04	89.74	90.46	91.17	91.89	92.61	93.33	94.06	94.79	95.53
12.50	84.22	84.90	85.59	86.28	86.97	87.67	88.37	89.07	89.78	90.49	91.20	91.91	92.63	93.36	94.08	94.81
12.75	83.59	84.27	84.95	85.63	86.32	87.01	87.71	88.40	89.10	89.81	90.52	91.23	91.94	92.66	93.38	94.10
13.00	82.96	83.64	84.31	84.99	85.68	86.36	87.05	87.74	88.44	89.14	89.84	90.55	91.26	91.97	92.68	93.40
13.25	82.35	83.02	83.69	84.36	85.04	85.72	86.41	87.09	87.78	88.48	89.17	89.87	90.58	91.28	91.99	92.71
13.50	81.74	82.40	83.07	83.74	84.41	85.09	85.77	86.45	87.13	87.82	88.51	89.21	89.91	90.61	91.31	92.02
13.75	81.13	81.79	82.45	83.12	83.79	84.46	85.13	85.81	86.49	87.17	87.86	88.55	89.24	89.94	90.64	91.34
14.00	80.54	81.19	81.85	82.51	83.17	83.84	84.51	85.18	85.85	86.53	87.21	87.90	88.59	89.28	89.97	90.67
14.25	79.95	80.60	81.25	81.90	82.56	83.22	83.89	84.55	85.22	85.90	86.58	87.25	87.94	88.62	89.31	90.00
14.50	79.36	80.01	80.65	81.30	81.96	82.61	83.27	83.94	84.60	85.27	85.94	86.62	87.30	87.98	88.66	89.35
14.75	78.79	79.42	80.07	80.71	81.36	82.01	82.67	83.33	83.99	84.65	85.32	85.99	86.66	87.34	88.01	88.70
15.00	78.21	78.85	79.49	80.13	80.77	81.42	82.07	82.72	83.38	84.04	84.70	85.36	86.03	86.70	87.38	88.05
15.25	77.65	78.28	78.91	79.55	80.19	80.83	81.47	82.12	82.77	83.43	84.09	84.75	85.41	86.08	86.74	87.42
15.50	77.09	77.71	78.34	78.97	79.61	80.25	80.89	81.53	82.18	82.83	83.48	84.14	84.79	85.45	86.12	86.79
15.75	76.54	77.16	77.78	78.41	79.04	79.67	80.31	80.95	81.59	82.23	82.88	83.53	84.18	84.84	85.50	86.16
16.00	75.99	76.60	77.22	77.85	78.47	79.10	79.73	80.37	81.00	81.64	82.29	82.93	83.58	84.23	84.89	85.55
16.25	75.45	76.06	76.67	77.29	77.91	78.54	79.16	79.79	80.43	81.06	81.70	82.34	82.99	83.63	84.28	84.94
16.50	74.91	75.52	76.13	76.74	77.36	77.98	78.60	79.23	79.85	80.49	81.12	81.76	82.40	83.04	83.68	84.33
16.75	74.38	74.98	75.59	76.20	76.81	77.43	78.04	78.67	79.29	79.92	80.55	81.18	81.81	82.45	83.09	83.74
17.00	73.85	74.45	75.06	75.66	76.27	76.88	77.49	78.11	78.73	79.35	79.98	80.61	81.24	81.87	82.51	83.14
17.25	73.33	73.93	74.53	75.13	75.73	76.34	76.95	77.56	78.18	78.79	79.41	80.04	80.66	81.29	81.93	82.56
17.50	72.82	73.41	74.01	74.60	75.20	75.80	76.41	77.02	77.63	78.24	78.86	79.48	80.10	80.72	81.35	81.98
17.75	72.31	72.90	73.49	74.08	74.68	75.27	75.88	76.48	77.09	77.70	78.31	78.92	79.54	80.16	80.78	81.41
18.00	71.81	72.39	72.98	73.57	74.16	74.75	75.35	75.95	76.55	77.15	77.76	78.37	78.99	79.60	80.22	80.84
18.25	71.31	71.89	72.47	73.06	73.64	74.23	74.83	75.42	76.02	76.62	77.22	77.83	78.44	79.05	79.66	80.28
18.50	70.82	71.39	71.97	72.55	73.13	73.72	74.31	74.90	75.49	76.09	76.69	77.29	77.90	78.50	79.11	79.73
18.75	70.33	70.90	71.47	72.05	72.63	73.21	73.80	74.38	74.97	75.57	76.16	76.76	77.36	77.96	78.57	79.18
19.00	69.85	70.41	70.98	71.56	72.13	72.71	73.29	73.87	74.46	75.05	75.64	76.23	76.83	77.43	78.03	78.63
20.00	67.97	68.52	69.07	69.63	70.19	70.75	71.32	71.88	72.45	73.03	73.60	74.18	74.76	75.34	75.93	76.52
25.00	59.63	60.11	60.60	61.09	61.58	62.07	62.57	63.06	63.56	64.07	64.57	65.08	65.59	66.10	66.61	67.13
30.00	52.78	53.21	53.64	54.08	54.51	54.95	55.39	55.83	56.27	56.71	57.16	57.61	58.06	58.51	58.97	59.42

Description: This table shows the yield to maturity of a mortgage purchased at the price shown in the index.

Example: The yield to maturity of a 10.75 %, 7 year mortgage at a price of 105.00 is 9.18 %.

INTEREST RATE, %

PRICE	7.00%	7.25%	7.50%	7.75%	8.00%	8.25%	8.50%	8.75%	9.00%	9.25%	9.50%	9.75%	10.00%	10.25%	10.50%	10.75%
125	.39	.62	.85	1.08	1.31	1.54	1.77	2.00	2.23	2.46	2.69	2.92	3.14	3.37	3.60	3.83
124	.62	.85	1.08	1.31	1.54	1.77	2.00	2.23	2.46	2.69	2.92	3.15	3.38	3.61	3.84	4.07
123	.85	1.08	1.32	1.55	1.78	2.01	2.24	2.47	2.70	2.93	3.16	3.39	3.62	3.85	4.08	4.31
122	1.09	1.32	1.55	1.78	2.01	2.24	2.48	2.71	2.94	3.17	3.40	3.63	3.86	4.09	4.32	4.55
121	1.32	1.56	1.79	2.02	2.25	2.48	2.72	2.95	3.18	3.41	3.64	3.87	4.11	4.34	4.57	4.80
120	1.56	1.79	2.03	2.26	2.49	2.73	2.96	3.19	3.42	3.66	3.89	4.12	4.35	4.59	4.82	5.05
119	1.80	2.04	2.27	2.50	2.74	2.97	3.20	3.44	3.67	3.90	4.14	4.37	4.60	4.84	5.07	5.30
118	2.05	2.28	2.52	2.75	2.98	3.22	3.45	3.69	3.92	4.16	4.39	4.62	4.86	5.09	5.32	5.56
117	2.29	2.53	2.76	3.00	3.23	3.47	3.70	3.94	4.17	4.41	4.64	4.88	5.11	5.35	5.58	5.82
116	2.54	2.78	3.02	3.25	3.49	3.72	3.96	4.19	4.43	4.67	4.90	5.14	5.37	5.61	5.84	6.08
115	2.80	3.03	3.27	3.51	3.74	3.98	4.22	4.45	4.69	4.93	5.16	5.40	5.63	5.87	6.11	6.34
114	3.05	3.29	3.53	3.76	4.00	4.24	4.48	4.71	4.95	5.19	5.42	5.66	5.90	6.14	6.37	6.61
113	3.31	3.55	3.79	4.03	4.26	4.50	4.74	4.98	5.22	5.45	5.69	5.93	6.17	6.40	6.64	6.88
112	3.57	3.81	4.05	4.29	4.53	4.77	5.01	5.25	5.48	5.72	5.96	6.20	6.44	6.68	6.92	7.15
111	3.84	4.08	4.32	4.56	4.80	5.04	5.28	5.52	5.76	6.00	6.24	6.48	6.71	6.95	7.19	7.43
110	4.11	4.35	4.59	4.83	5.07	5.31	5.55	5.79	6.03	6.27	6.51	6.75	6.99	7.23	7.47	7.71
109	4.38	4.62	4.86	5.10	5.35	5.59	5.83	6.07	6.31	6.55	6.79	7.03	7.28	7.52	7.76	8.00
108	4.66	4.90	5.14	5.38	5.62	5.87	6.11	6.35	6.59	6.84	7.08	7.32	7.56	7.80	8.05	8.29
107	4.93	5.18	5.42	5.66	5.91	6.15	6.39	6.64	6.88	7.12	7.37	7.61	7.85	8.10	8.34	8.58
106	5.22	5.46	5.71	5.95	6.19	6.44	6.68	6.93	7.17	7.41	7.66	7.90	8.15	8.39	8.63	8.88
105	5.50	5.75	5.99	6.24	6.48	6.73	6.97	7.22	7.46	7.71	7.95	8.20	8.44	8.69	8.93	9.18
104	5.79	6.04	6.29	6.53	6.78	7.02	7.27	7.52	7.76	8.01	8.25	8.50	8.75	8.99	9.24	9.48
103	6.09	6.33	6.58	6.83	7.08	7.32	7.57	7.82	8.06	8.31	8.56	8.80	9.05	9.30	9.55	9.79
102	6.39	6.63	6.88	7.13	7.38	7.63	7.87	8.12	8.37	8.62	8.87	9.11	9.36	9.61	9.86	10.11
101	6.69	6.94	7.19	7.44	7.68	7.93	8.18	8.43	8.68	8.93	9.18	9.43	9.68	9.92	10.17	10.42
100	7.00	7.25	7.50	7.75	8.00	8.25	8.50	8.75	9.00	9.25	9.50	9.75	10.00	10.25	10.50	10.75
99	7.31	7.56	7.81	8.06	8.31	8.56	8.81	9.06	9.31	9.57	9.82	10.07	10.32	10.57	10.82	11.07
98	7.62	7.87	8.13	8.38	8.63	8.88	9.13	9.39	9.64	9.89	10.14	10.39	10.65	10.90	11.15	11.40
97	7.94	8.19	8.45	8.70	8.95	9.21	9.46	9.71	9.97	10.22	10.47	10.73	10.98	11.23	11.49	11.74
96	8.27	8.52	8.77	9.03	9.28	9.54	9.79	10.05	10.30	10.55	10.81	11.06	11.32	11.57	11.83	12.08
95	8.60	8.85	9.11	9.36	9.62	9.87	10.13	10.38	10.64	10.89	11.15	11.41	11.66	11.92	12.17	12.43
94	8.93	9.19	9.44	9.70	9.96	10.21	10.47	10.73	10.98	11.24	11.50	11.75	12.01	12.27	12.52	12.78
93	9.27	9.53	9.78	10.04	10.30	10.56	10.82	11.07	11.33	11.59	11.85	12.11	12.36	12.62	12.88	13.14
92	9.61	9.87	10.13	10.39	10.65	10.91	11.17	11.43	11.69	11.95	12.20	12.46	12.72	12.98	13.24	13.50
91	9.96	10.22	10.48	10.74	11.01	11.27	11.53	11.79	12.05	12.31	12.57	12.83	13.09	13.35	13.61	13.87
90	10.32	10.58	10.84	11.10	11.37	11.63	11.89	12.15	12.41	12.67	12.94	13.20	13.46	13.72	13.98	14.25
89	10.68	10.94	11.21	11.47	11.73	12.00	12.26	12.52	12.78	13.05	13.31	13.57	13.84	14.10	14.36	14.63
88	11.05	11.31	11.58	11.84	12.11	12.37	12.63	12.90	13.16	13.43	13.69	13.96	14.22	14.49	14.75	15.02
87	11.42	11.69	11.95	12.22	12.48	12.75	13.02	13.28	13.55	13.81	14.08	14.34	14.61	14.88	15.14	15.41
86	11.80	12.07	12.34	12.60	12.87	13.14	13.40	13.67	13.94	14.20	14.47	14.74	15.01	15.28	15.54	15.81
85	12.19	12.46	12.72	12.99	13.26	13.53	13.80	14.07	14.34	14.60	14.87	15.14	15.41	15.68	15.95	16.22
84	12.58	12.85	13.12	13.39	13.66	13.93	14.20	14.47	14.74	15.01	15.28	15.55	15.82	16.09	16.36	16.63
83	12.98	13.25	13.52	13.79	14.06	14.34	14.61	14.88	15.15	15.42	15.69	15.97	16.24	16.51	16.78	17.06
82	13.39	13.66	13.93	14.20	14.48	14.75	15.02	15.30	15.57	15.84	16.12	16.39	16.66	16.94	17.21	17.49
81	13.80	14.07	14.35	14.62	14.90	15.17	15.45	15.72	16.00	16.27	16.55	16.82	17.10	17.37	17.65	17.93
80	14.22	14.50	14.77	15.05	15.33	15.60	15.88	16.15	16.43	16.71	16.98	17.26	17.54	17.82	18.09	18.37
79	14.65	14.93	15.21	15.48	15.76	16.04	16.32	16.60	16.87	17.15	17.43	17.71	17.99	18.27	18.55	18.83
78	15.09	15.37	15.65	15.93	16.21	16.49	16.77	17.05	17.33	17.61	17.89	18.17	18.45	18.73	19.01	19.29
77	15.53	15.82	16.10	16.38	16.66	16.94	17.22	17.50	17.79	18.07	18.35	18.63	18.91	19.20	19.48	19.76
76	15.99	16.27	16.55	16.84	17.12	17.40	17.69	17.97	18.25	18.54	18.82	19.11	19.39	19.68	19.96	20.24
75	16.45	16.74	17.02	17.31	17.59	17.88	18.16	18.45	18.73	19.02	19.30	19.59	19.88	20.16	20.45	20.74
74	16.93	17.21	17.50	17.78	18.07	18.36	18.65	18.93	19.22	19.51	19.80	20.08	20.37	20.66	20.95	21.24
73	17.41	17.70	17.98	18.27	18.56	18.85	19.14	19.43	19.72	20.01	20.30	20.59	20.88	21.17	21.46	21.75
72	17.90	18.19	18.48	18.77	19.06	19.35	19.64	19.94	20.23	20.52	20.81	21.10	21.40	21.69	21.98	22.27
71	18.40	18.69	18.99	19.28	19.57	19.87	20.16	20.45	20.75	21.04	21.33	21.63	21.92	22.22	22.51	22.81
70	18.92	19.21	19.50	19.80	20.09	20.39	20.69	20.98	21.28	21.57	21.87	22.17	22.46	22.76	23.06	23.36
69	19.44	19.74	20.03	20.33	20.63	20.93	21.22	21.52	21.82	22.12	22.42	22.72	23.02	23.31	23.61	23.91
68	19.98	20.28	20.57	20.87	21.17	21.47	21.77	22.07	22.37	22.67	22.98	23.28	23.58	23.88	24.18	24.49
67	20.52	20.83	21.13	21.43	21.73	22.03	22.34	22.64	22.94	23.24	23.55	23.85	24.16	24.46	24.77	25.07
66	21.09	21.39	21.69	22.00	22.30	22.61	22.91	23.22	23.52	23.83	24.13	24.44	24.75	25.05	25.36	25.67
65	21.66	21.97	22.27	22.58	22.89	23.19	23.50	23.81	24.12	24.42	24.73	25.04	25.35	25.66	25.97	26.28
64	22.25	22.56	22.87	23.17	23.48	23.79	24.10	24.41	24.72	25.04	25.35	25.66	25.97	26.28	26.60	26.91
63	22.85	23.16	23.47	23.78	24.10	24.41	24.72	25.04	25.35	25.66	25.98	26.29	26.61	26.92	27.24	27.55
62	23.47	23.78	24.10	24.41	24.72	25.04	25.36	25.67	25.99	26.31	26.62	26.94	27.26	27.58	27.89	28.21
60	24.75	25.07	25.39	25.71	26.03	26.35	26.67	26.99	27.32	27.64	27.96	28.29	28.61	28.94	29.26	29.59
55	28.27	28.60	28.94	29.28	29.62	29.95	30.29	30.63	30.97	31.31	31.65	31.99	32.34	32.68	33.02	33.37
50	32.34	32.69	33.05	33.41	33.77	34.13	34.49	34.85	35.21	35.57	35.93	36.29	36.66	37.02	37.39	37.75
45	37.13	37.51	37.90	38.28	38.66	39.05	39.43	39.82	40.21	40.60	40.98	41.37	41.77	42.16	42.55	42.94

Description: This table shows the price to pay for a monthly payment mortgage loan at the yield rate.

Example: The price of a 15.00 %, 7 year mortgage loan to yield 8.00 % to maturity is $ 123.81.

INTEREST RATE, %

YIELD	11.00%	11.25%	11.50%	11.75%	12.00%	12.25%	12.50%	12.75%	13.00%	13.25%	13.50%	13.75%	14.00%	14.25%	14.50%	15.00%
0.00	143.83	144.94	146.05	147.16	148.28	149.41	150.54	151.67	152.81	153.96	155.11	156.26	157.42	158.58	159.75	162.09
1.00	138.85	139.92	141.00	142.07	143.15	144.24	145.33	146.43	147.53	148.63	149.74	150.85	151.97	153.09	154.22	156.49
2.00	134.11	135.14	136.18	137.22	138.26	139.31	140.37	141.42	142.49	143.55	144.62	145.70	146.78	147.86	148.95	151.14
3.00	129.58	130.58	131.58	132.59	133.60	134.61	135.63	136.65	137.68	138.71	139.74	140.78	141.83	142.87	143.93	146.04
4.00	125.27	126.23	127.20	128.17	129.15	130.13	131.11	132.10	133.09	134.09	135.09	136.09	137.10	138.11	139.13	141.17
4.25	124.22	125.17	126.13	127.10	128.07	129.04	130.01	130.99	131.98	132.97	133.96	134.95	135.95	136.96	137.96	139.99
4.50	123.18	124.13	125.08	126.04	127.00	127.96	128.93	129.90	130.88	131.86	132.84	133.83	134.82	135.81	136.81	138.82
4.75	122.16	123.10	124.04	124.99	125.94	126.90	127.86	128.82	129.79	130.76	131.73	132.71	133.70	134.68	135.68	137.67
5.00	121.14	122.08	123.01	123.95	124.90	125.84	126.80	127.75	128.71	129.68	130.64	131.61	132.59	133.57	134.55	136.53
5.25	120.14	121.07	122.00	122.93	123.86	124.80	125.75	126.70	127.65	128.60	129.56	130.53	131.49	132.46	133.44	135.40
5.50	119.15	120.07	120.99	121.92	122.84	123.78	124.71	125.65	126.60	127.54	128.50	129.45	130.41	131.37	132.34	134.28
5.75	118.18	119.08	120.00	120.91	121.84	122.76	123.69	124.62	125.56	126.50	127.44	128.39	129.34	130.29	131.25	133.18
6.00	117.21	118.11	119.02	119.93	120.84	121.76	122.68	123.60	124.53	125.46	126.40	127.34	128.28	129.23	130.18	132.09
6.25	116.25	117.15	118.04	118.95	119.85	120.76	121.68	122.59	123.51	124.44	125.37	126.30	127.23	128.17	129.12	131.01
6.50	115.31	116.19	117.08	117.98	118.88	119.78	120.69	121.60	122.51	123.43	124.35	125.27	126.20	127.13	128.07	129.95
6.75	114.37	115.25	116.14	117.02	117.91	118.81	119.71	120.61	121.52	122.43	123.34	124.26	125.18	126.10	127.03	128.90
7.00	113.45	114.32	115.20	116.08	116.96	117.85	118.74	119.64	120.54	121.44	122.34	123.25	124.17	125.08	126.00	127.86
7.25	112.54	113.40	114.27	115.14	116.02	116.90	117.79	118.67	119.56	120.46	121.36	122.26	123.17	124.08	124.99	126.83
7.50	111.63	112.49	113.35	114.22	115.09	115.96	116.84	117.72	118.61	119.49	120.38	121.28	122.18	123.08	123.99	125.81
7.75	110.74	111.59	112.45	113.31	114.17	115.04	115.91	116.78	117.66	118.54	119.42	120.31	121.20	122.10	122.99	124.80
8.00	109.86	110.70	111.55	112.40	113.26	114.12	114.98	115.85	116.72	117.59	118.47	119.35	120.23	121.12	122.01	123.81
8.25	108.98	109.82	110.66	111.51	112.36	113.21	114.07	114.93	115.79	116.66	117.53	118.40	119.28	120.16	121.04	122.82
8.50	108.12	108.95	109.79	110.63	111.47	112.31	113.16	114.02	114.87	115.73	116.60	117.46	118.33	119.21	120.09	121.85
8.75	107.27	108.09	108.92	109.75	110.59	111.43	112.27	113.12	113.97	114.82	115.68	116.54	117.40	118.27	119.14	120.89
9.00	106.42	107.24	108.06	108.89	109.72	110.55	111.39	112.23	113.07	113.92	114.77	115.62	116.48	117.34	118.20	119.94
9.25	105.59	106.40	107.22	108.04	108.86	109.68	110.51	111.35	112.18	113.02	113.87	114.71	115.56	116.42	117.27	119.00
9.50	104.76	105.57	106.38	107.19	108.01	108.83	109.65	110.48	111.31	112.14	112.98	113.82	114.66	115.51	116.36	118.07
9.75	103.95	104.75	105.55	106.36	107.17	107.98	108.80	109.62	110.44	111.27	112.10	112.93	113.77	114.61	115.45	117.15
10.00	103.14	103.93	104.73	105.53	106.33	107.14	107.95	108.77	109.58	110.40	111.23	112.05	112.88	113.72	114.55	116.24
10.25	102.34	103.13	103.92	104.71	105.51	106.31	107.12	107.92	108.73	109.55	110.37	111.19	112.01	112.84	113.67	115.34
10.50	101.55	102.33	103.12	103.91	104.70	105.49	106.29	107.09	107.90	108.70	109.51	110.33	111.15	111.97	112.79	114.45
10.75	100.77	101.55	102.33	103.11	103.89	104.68	105.47	106.27	107.07	107.87	108.67	109.48	110.29	111.11	111.92	113.57
11.00	100.00	100.77	101.54	102.32	103.10	103.88	104.67	105.45	106.25	107.04	107.84	108.64	109.45	110.26	111.07	112.70
11.25	99.24	100.00	100.77	101.54	102.31	103.09	103.87	104.65	105.44	106.22	107.02	107.81	108.61	109.41	110.22	111.84
11.50	98.48	99.24	100.00	100.76	101.53	102.30	103.08	103.85	104.63	105.42	106.20	106.99	107.79	108.58	109.38	110.99
11.75	97.73	98.49	99.24	100.00	100.76	101.53	102.29	103.07	103.84	104.62	105.40	106.18	106.97	107.76	108.55	110.15
12.00	97.00	97.74	98.49	99.24	100.00	100.76	101.52	102.29	103.05	103.83	104.60	105.38	106.16	106.94	107.73	109.31
12.25	96.27	97.01	97.75	98.50	99.25	100.00	100.76	101.52	102.28	103.04	103.81	104.58	105.36	106.14	106.92	108.49
12.50	95.54	96.28	97.02	97.76	98.50	99.25	100.00	100.75	101.51	102.27	103.03	103.80	104.57	105.34	106.12	107.68
12.75	94.83	95.56	96.29	97.03	97.76	98.51	99.25	100.00	100.75	101.51	102.26	103.02	103.79	104.55	105.32	106.87
13.00	94.12	94.84	95.57	96.30	97.04	97.77	98.51	99.25	100.00	100.75	101.50	102.25	103.01	103.77	104.54	106.07
13.25	93.42	94.14	94.86	95.59	96.31	97.05	97.78	98.52	99.26	100.00	100.75	101.50	102.25	103.00	103.76	105.28
13.50	92.73	93.44	94.16	94.88	95.60	96.33	97.06	97.79	98.52	99.26	100.00	100.74	101.49	102.24	102.99	104.51
13.75	92.05	92.75	93.46	94.18	94.90	95.62	96.34	97.07	97.79	98.53	99.26	100.00	100.74	101.48	102.23	103.73
14.00	91.37	92.07	92.78	93.49	94.20	94.91	95.63	96.35	97.08	97.80	98.53	99.26	100.00	100.74	101.48	102.97
14.25	90.70	91.40	92.10	92.80	93.51	94.22	94.93	95.65	96.36	97.09	97.81	98.54	99.27	100.00	100.74	102.22
14.50	90.04	90.73	91.42	92.12	92.82	93.53	94.24	94.95	95.66	96.38	97.10	97.82	98.54	99.27	100.00	101.47
14.75	89.38	90.07	90.76	91.45	92.15	92.85	93.55	94.26	94.96	95.67	96.39	97.11	97.82	98.55	99.27	100.73
15.00	88.73	89.41	90.10	90.79	91.48	92.17	92.87	93.57	94.27	94.98	95.69	96.40	97.11	97.83	98.55	100.00
15.25	88.09	88.77	89.45	90.13	90.82	91.51	92.20	92.90	93.59	94.29	95.00	95.70	96.41	97.12	97.84	99.28
15.50	87.46	88.13	88.80	89.48	90.16	90.85	91.54	92.23	92.92	93.61	94.31	95.01	95.72	96.42	97.13	98.56
15.75	86.83	87.50	88.17	88.84	89.52	90.20	90.88	91.56	92.25	92.94	93.64	94.33	95.03	95.73	96.44	97.85
16.00	86.21	86.87	87.54	88.20	88.88	89.55	90.23	90.91	91.59	92.28	92.97	93.66	94.35	95.05	95.75	97.15
16.25	85.59	86.25	86.91	87.58	88.24	88.91	89.59	90.26	90.94	91.62	92.30	92.99	93.68	94.37	95.06	96.46
16.50	84.98	85.64	86.29	86.95	87.62	88.28	88.95	89.62	90.29	90.97	91.65	92.33	93.01	93.70	94.39	95.78
16.75	84.38	85.03	85.68	86.34	87.00	87.66	88.32	88.98	89.65	90.32	91.00	91.67	92.35	93.04	93.72	95.10
17.00	83.79	84.43	85.08	85.73	86.38	87.04	87.70	88.36	89.02	89.69	90.36	91.03	91.70	92.38	93.06	94.43
17.25	83.20	83.84	84.48	85.13	85.77	86.42	87.08	87.73	88.39	89.06	89.72	90.39	91.06	91.73	92.40	93.76
17.50	82.61	83.25	83.89	84.53	85.17	85.82	86.47	87.12	87.77	88.43	89.09	89.75	90.42	91.09	91.76	93.11
17.75	82.04	82.67	83.30	83.94	84.58	85.22	85.86	86.51	87.16	87.81	88.47	89.13	89.79	90.45	91.12	92.45
18.00	81.47	82.09	82.72	83.35	83.99	84.63	85.27	85.91	86.55	87.20	87.85	88.51	89.16	89.82	90.48	91.81
18.25	80.90	81.52	82.15	82.78	83.41	84.04	84.68	85.31	85.95	86.60	87.24	87.89	88.54	89.20	89.85	91.17
18.50	80.34	80.96	81.58	82.20	82.83	83.46	84.09	84.72	85.36	86.00	86.64	87.29	87.93	88.58	89.23	90.54
18.75	79.79	80.40	81.02	81.64	82.26	82.88	83.51	84.14	84.77	85.41	86.04	86.68	87.33	87.97	88.62	89.92
19.00	79.24	79.85	80.46	81.08	81.70	82.32	82.94	83.56	84.19	84.82	85.45	86.09	86.73	87.37	88.01	89.30
20.00	77.11	77.70	78.30	78.89	79.49	80.10	80.70	81.31	81.92	82.54	83.15	83.77	84.39	85.01	85.64	86.90
25.00	67.65	68.17	68.69	69.21	69.74	70.27	70.80	71.34	71.87	72.41	72.95	73.49	74.04	74.58	75.13	76.24
30.00	59.88	60.34	60.81	61.27	61.74	62.21	62.68	63.15	63.62	64.10	64.58	65.06	65.54	66.02	66.51	67.49

Description: This table shows the yield to maturity of a mortgage purchased at the price shown in the index.

Example: The yield to maturity of a 15.00 %, 7 year mortgage at a price of 116.00 is 10.06 %.

INTEREST RATE, %

PRICE	11.00%	11.25%	11.50%	11.75%	12.00%	12.25%	12.50%	12.75%	13.00%	13.25%	13.50%	13.75%	14.00%	14.25%	14.50%	15.00%
160	–	–	–	–	–	–	–	–	–	–	–	–	–	–	–	.36
155	–	–	–	–	–	–	–	–	–	–	–	–	.22	.43	.64	.85	1.27
150	–	–	–	–	–	–	.10	.31	.52	–	.95	1.16	1.37	1.58	1.79	2.21
145	–	–	.20	.41	.63	.85	1.06	1.28	1.49	1.71	1.92	2.13	2.35	2.56	2.78	3.20
140	.76	.98	1.20	1.42	1.63	1.85	2.07	2.29	2.51	2.72	2.94	3.16	3.38	3.59	3.81	4.24
135	1.80	2.03	2.25	2.47	2.69	2.91	3.13	3.35	3.57	3.79	4.01	4.23	4.45	4.67	4.89	5.33
130	2.90	3.13	3.35	3.58	3.80	4.02	4.25	4.47	4.70	4.92	5.14	5.37	5.59	5.81	6.04	6.48
129	3.13	3.35	3.58	3.80	4.03	4.25	4.48	4.70	4.93	5.15	5.38	5.60	5.82	6.05	6.27	6.72
128	3.36	3.58	3.81	4.03	4.26	4.49	4.71	4.94	5.16	5.39	5.61	5.84	6.06	6.29	6.51	6.96
127	3.59	3.81	4.04	4.27	4.49	4.72	4.95	5.17	5.40	5.62	5.85	6.08	6.30	6.53	6.75	7.20
126	3.82	4.05	4.28	4.50	4.73	4.96	5.18	5.41	5.64	5.86	6.09	6.32	6.54	6.77	7.00	7.45
125	4.06	4.29	4.51	4.74	4.97	5.20	5.43	5.65	5.88	6.11	6.33	6.56	6.79	7.02	7.24	7.70
124	4.30	4.53	4.75	4.98	5.21	5.44	5.67	5.90	6.12	6.35	6.58	6.81	7.04	7.26	7.49	7.95
123	4.54	4.77	5.00	5.23	5.46	5.69	5.91	6.14	6.37	6.60	6.83	7.06	7.29	7.52	7.74	8.20
122	4.78	5.01	5.24	5.47	5.70	5.93	6.16	6.39	6.62	6.85	7.08	7.31	7.54	7.77	8.00	8.46
121	5.03	5.26	5.49	5.72	5.95	6.18	6.42	6.65	6.88	7.11	7.34	7.57	7.80	8.03	8.26	8.72
120	5.28	5.51	5.74	5.98	6.21	6.44	6.67	6.90	7.13	7.36	7.59	7.83	8.06	8.29	8.52	8.98
119	5.53	5.77	6.00	6.23	6.46	6.70	6.93	7.16	7.39	7.62	7.86	8.09	8.32	8.55	8.78	9.24
118	5.79	6.02	6.26	6.49	6.72	6.96	7.19	7.42	7.65	7.89	8.12	8.35	8.58	8.82	9.05	9.51
117	6.05	6.28	6.52	6.75	6.99	7.22	7.45	7.69	7.92	8.15	8.39	8.62	8.85	9.09	9.32	9.51
116	6.31	6.55	6.78	7.02	7.25	7.49	7.72	7.95	8.19	8.42	8.66	8.89	9.13	9.36	9.59	10.06
115	6.58	6.81	7.05	7.28	7.52	7.75	7.99	8.23	8.46	8.70	8.93	9.17	9.40	9.64	9.87	10.34
114	6.85	7.08	7.32	7.55	7.79	8.03	8.26	8.50	8.74	8.97	9.21	9.44	9.68	9.92	10.15	10.62
113	7.12	7.35	7.59	7.83	8.07	8.30	8.54	8.78	9.01	9.25	9.49	9.73	9.96	10.20	10.44	10.91
112	7.39	7.63	7.87	8.11	8.35	8.58	8.82	9.06	9.30	9.53	9.77	10.01	10.25	10.49	10.72	11.20
111	7.67	7.91	8.15	8.39	8.63	8.87	9.11	9.34	9.58	9.82	10.06	10.30	10.54	10.78	11.01	11.49
110	7.95	8.19	8.43	8.67	8.91	9.15	9.39	9.63	9.87	10.11	10.35	10.59	10.83	11.07	11.31	11.79
109	8.24	8.48	8.72	8.96	9.20	9.44	9.69	9.93	10.17	10.41	10.65	10.89	11.13	11.37	11.61	12.09
108	8.53	8.77	9.01	9.26	9.50	9.74	9.98	10.22	10.46	10.71	10.95	11.19	11.43	11.67	11.91	12.40
107	8.82	9.07	9.31	9.55	9.79	10.04	10.28	10.52	10.77	11.01	11.25	11.49	11.74	11.98	12.22	12.70
106	9.12	9.37	9.61	9.85	10.10	10.34	10.58	10.83	11.07	11.31	11.56	11.80	12.04	12.29	12.53	13.02
105	9.42	9.67	9.91	10.16	10.40	10.65	10.89	11.14	11.38	11.62	11.87	12.11	12.36	12.60	12.85	13.34
104	9.73	9.97	10.22	10.47	10.71	10.96	11.20	11.45	11.69	11.94	12.19	12.43	12.68	12.92	13.17	13.66
103	10.04	10.29	10.53	10.78	11.03	11.27	11.52	11.77	12.01	12.26	12.51	12.75	13.00	13.25	13.49	13.99
102	10.35	10.60	10.85	11.10	11.34	11.59	11.84	12.09	12.34	12.58	12.83	13.08	13.33	13.57	13.82	14.32
101	10.67	10.92	11.17	11.42	11.67	11.92	12.17	12.41	12.66	12.91	13.16	13.41	13.66	13.91	14.16	14.65
100	11.00	11.25	11.50	11.75	12.00	12.25	12.50	12.75	13.00	13.25	13.50	13.75	14.00	14.25	14.50	15.00
99	11.32	11.57	11.83	12.08	12.33	12.58	12.83	13.08	13.33	13.58	13.83	14.09	14.34	14.59	14.84	15.34
98	11.66	11.91	12.16	12.41	12.66	12.92	13.17	13.42	13.67	13.93	14.18	14.43	14.68	14.94	15.19	15.69
97	11.99	12.25	12.50	12.75	13.01	13.26	13.51	13.77	14.02	14.27	14.53	14.78	15.04	15.29	15.54	16.05
96	12.34	12.59	12.85	13.10	13.36	13.61	13.86	14.12	14.37	14.63	14.88	15.14	15.39	15.65	15.90	16.41
95	12.68	12.94	13.20	13.45	13.71	13.96	14.22	14.48	14.73	14.99	15.24	15.50	15.76	16.01	16.27	16.78
94	13.04	13.30	13.55	13.81	14.07	14.32	14.58	14.84	15.10	15.35	15.61	15.87	16.13	16.38	16.64	17.16
93	13.40	13.66	13.91	14.17	14.43	14.69	14.95	15.21	15.46	15.72	15.98	16.24	16.50	16.76	17.02	17.54
92	13.76	14.02	14.28	14.54	14.80	15.06	15.32	15.58	15.84	16.10	16.36	16.62	16.88	17.14	17.40	17.92
91	14.13	14.39	14.65	14.92	15.18	15.44	15.70	15.96	16.22	16.48	16.74	17.01	17.27	17.53	17.79	18.31
90	14.51	14.77	15.03	15.30	15.56	15.82	16.08	16.35	16.61	16.87	17.13	17.40	17.66	17.92	18.19	18.71
89	14.89	15.16	15.42	15.68	15.95	16.21	16.47	16.74	17.00	17.27	17.53	17.80	18.06	18.32	18.59	19.12
88	15.28	15.55	15.81	16.08	16.34	16.61	16.87	17.14	17.40	17.67	17.94	18.20	18.47	18.73	19.00	19.53
87	15.68	15.94	16.21	16.48	16.74	17.01	17.28	17.54	17.81	18.08	18.35	18.61	18.88	19.15	19.42	19.95
86	16.08	16.35	16.62	16.88	17.15	17.42	17.69	17.96	18.23	18.49	18.76	19.03	19.30	19.57	19.84	20.38
85	16.49	16.76	17.03	17.30	17.57	17.84	18.11	18.38	18.65	18.92	19.19	19.46	19.73	20.00	20.27	20.81
84	16.91	17.18	17.45	17.72	17.99	18.26	18.53	18.81	19.08	19.35	19.62	19.89	20.17	20.44	20.71	21.26
83	17.33	17.60	17.88	18.15	18.42	18.69	18.97	19.24	19.51	19.79	20.06	20.34	20.61	20.88	21.16	21.71
82	17.76	18.04	18.31	18.58	18.86	19.13	19.41	19.69	19.96	20.24	20.51	20.79	21.06	21.34	21.62	22.17
81	18.20	18.48	18.75	19.03	19.31	19.58	19.86	20.14	20.41	20.69	20.97	21.25	21.52	21.80	22.08	22.64
80	18.65	18.93	19.21	19.48	19.76	20.04	20.32	20.60	20.88	21.16	21.43	21.71	21.99	22.27	22.55	23.11
79	19.11	19.39	19.67	19.95	20.23	20.51	20.79	21.07	21.35	21.63	21.91	22.19	22.47	22.75	23.04	23.60
78	19.57	19.85	20.13	20.42	20.70	20.98	21.26	21.55	21.83	22.11	22.39	22.68	22.96	23.24	23.53	24.10
77	20.05	20.33	20.61	20.90	21.18	21.46	21.75	22.03	22.32	22.60	22.89	23.17	23.46	23.74	24.03	24.60
76	20.53	20.82	21.10	21.39	21.67	21.96	22.25	22.53	22.82	23.11	23.39	23.68	23.97	24.25	24.54	25.12
75	21.02	21.31	21.60	21.89	22.17	22.46	22.75	23.04	23.33	23.62	23.91	24.20	24.49	24.78	25.07	25.65
74	21.53	21.82	22.11	22.40	22.69	22.98	23.27	23.56	23.85	24.14	24.43	24.72	25.01	25.31	25.60	26.18
73	22.04	22.33	22.63	22.92	23.21	23.50	23.80	24.09	24.38	24.67	24.97	25.26	25.56	25.85	26.14	26.73
72	22.57	22.86	23.16	23.45	23.74	24.04	24.33	24.63	24.92	25.22	25.52	25.81	26.11	26.40	26.70	27.30
71	23.11	23.40	23.70	23.99	24.29	24.59	24.88	25.18	25.48	25.78	26.08	26.37	26.67	26.97	27.27	27.87
70	23.65	23.95	24.25	24.55	24.85	25.15	25.45	25.75	26.05	26.35	26.65	26.95	27.25	27.55	27.85	28.46
65	26.59	26.90	27.22	27.53	27.84	28.15	28.46	28.78	29.09	29.40	29.72	30.03	30.35	30.66	30.98	31.61

Description: This table shows the price to pay for a monthly payment mortgage loan at the yield rate.

Example: The price of a 6.75 %, 8 year mortgage loan to yield 8.00 % to maturity is $ 95.56.

INTEREST RATE, %

YIELD	0.00%	1.00%	2.00%	3.00%	4.00%	4.25%	4.50%	4.75%	5.00%	5.25%	5.50%	5.75%	6.00%	6.25%	6.50%	6.75%
0.00	100.00	104.09	108.30	112.60	117.02	118.14	119.26	120.40	121.54	122.68	123.83	124.99	126.16	127.33	128.51	129.69
1.00	96.07	100.00	104.04	108.17	112.41	113.49	114.57	115.66	116.75	117.85	118.96	120.08	121.19	122.32	123.45	124.59
2.00	92.34	96.12	100.00	103.98	108.05	109.09	110.13	111.17	112.22	113.28	114.35	115.42	116.49	117.58	118.66	119.76
3.00	88.81	92.44	96.17	100.00	103.92	104.91	105.91	106.92	107.93	108.95	109.97	111.00	112.04	113.08	114.12	115.18
4.00	85.46	88.96	92.55	96.23	100.00	100.96	101.92	102.89	103.86	104.84	105.83	106.82	107.81	108.81	109.82	110.83
4.25	84.65	88.11	91.67	95.32	99.05	100.00	100.95	101.91	102.88	103.85	104.82	105.80	106.79	107.78	108.78	109.78
4.50	83.85	87.28	90.80	94.42	98.12	99.06	100.00	100.95	101.91	102.87	103.83	104.80	105.78	106.76	107.75	108.74
4.75	83.06	86.46	89.95	93.53	97.19	98.12	99.06	100.00	100.95	101.90	102.86	103.82	104.79	105.76	106.74	107.72
5.00	82.28	85.65	89.11	92.65	96.28	97.20	98.13	99.06	100.00	100.94	101.89	102.84	103.80	104.77	105.74	106.71
5.25	81.51	84.85	88.27	91.79	95.38	96.30	97.21	98.14	99.07	100.00	100.94	101.88	102.83	103.79	104.75	105.72
5.50	80.75	84.06	87.45	90.93	94.50	95.40	96.31	97.22	98.14	99.07	100.00	100.94	101.88	102.82	103.77	104.73
5.75	80.00	83.28	86.64	90.09	93.62	94.52	95.42	96.32	97.23	98.15	99.07	100.00	100.93	101.87	102.81	103.76
6.00	79.27	82.51	85.84	89.26	92.75	93.64	94.53	95.43	96.34	97.24	98.16	99.08	100.00	100.93	101.86	102.80
6.25	78.54	81.75	85.05	88.43	91.90	92.78	93.66	94.55	95.45	96.35	97.25	98.16	99.08	100.00	100.93	101.86
6.50	77.82	81.00	84.27	87.62	91.06	91.93	92.81	93.69	94.57	95.47	96.36	97.26	98.17	99.08	100.00	100.92
6.75	77.11	80.26	83.50	86.82	90.23	91.09	91.96	92.83	93.71	94.59	95.48	96.38	97.27	98.18	99.09	100.00
7.00	76.40	79.53	82.74	86.03	89.41	90.26	91.12	91.99	92.86	93.73	94.61	95.50	96.39	97.28	98.18	99.09
7.25	75.71	78.81	81.99	85.25	88.59	89.44	90.30	91.15	92.02	92.88	93.76	94.63	95.52	96.40	97.29	98.19
7.50	75.03	78.10	81.25	84.48	87.79	88.63	89.48	90.33	91.18	92.04	92.91	93.78	94.65	95.53	96.42	97.30
7.75	74.35	77.40	80.52	83.72	87.00	87.84	88.67	89.52	90.36	91.22	92.07	92.93	93.80	94.67	95.55	96.43
8.00	73.69	76.70	79.80	82.97	86.22	87.05	87.88	88.71	89.55	90.40	91.25	92.10	92.96	93.82	94.69	95.56
8.25	73.03	76.02	79.09	82.23	85.45	86.27	87.09	87.92	88.75	89.59	90.43	91.28	92.13	92.99	93.85	94.71
8.50	72.38	75.34	78.38	81.50	84.69	85.50	86.32	87.14	87.96	88.79	89.63	90.47	91.31	92.16	93.01	93.87
8.75	71.74	74.67	77.69	80.78	83.94	84.75	85.55	86.37	87.18	88.01	88.83	89.66	90.50	91.34	92.19	93.04
9.00	71.10	74.01	77.00	80.06	83.20	84.00	84.80	85.60	86.41	87.23	88.05	88.87	89.70	90.53	91.37	92.21
9.25	70.48	73.36	76.32	79.36	82.47	83.26	84.05	84.85	85.65	86.46	87.27	88.09	88.91	89.74	90.57	91.40
9.50	69.86	72.72	75.66	78.66	81.75	82.53	83.32	84.11	84.90	85.70	86.51	87.32	88.13	88.95	89.77	90.60
9.75	69.25	72.09	74.99	77.98	81.03	81.81	82.59	83.37	84.16	84.96	85.75	86.56	87.36	88.18	88.99	89.81
10.00	68.65	71.46	74.34	77.30	80.33	81.10	81.87	82.65	83.43	84.22	85.01	85.80	86.60	87.41	88.22	89.03
10.25	68.05	70.84	73.70	76.63	79.63	80.40	81.16	81.93	82.71	83.49	84.27	85.06	85.85	86.65	87.45	88.26
10.50	67.47	70.23	73.06	75.97	78.95	79.70	80.46	81.23	81.99	82.77	83.54	84.33	85.11	85.90	86.70	87.50
10.75	66.89	69.62	72.43	75.32	78.27	79.02	79.77	80.53	81.29	82.06	82.83	83.60	84.38	85.16	85.95	86.75
11.00	66.31	69.03	71.81	74.67	77.60	78.34	79.09	79.84	80.59	81.35	82.12	82.89	83.66	84.44	85.22	86.00
11.25	65.75	68.44	71.20	74.03	76.94	77.67	78.41	79.16	79.91	80.66	81.42	82.18	82.94	83.72	84.49	85.27
11.50	65.19	67.86	70.60	73.40	76.28	77.01	77.75	78.48	79.23	79.97	80.72	81.48	82.24	83.00	83.77	84.54
11.75	64.64	67.28	70.00	72.78	75.64	76.36	77.09	77.82	78.56	79.30	80.04	80.79	81.54	82.30	83.06	83.83
12.00	64.09	66.72	69.41	72.17	75.00	75.72	76.44	77.16	77.89	78.63	79.37	80.11	80.86	81.61	82.36	83.12
12.25	63.55	66.16	68.83	71.56	74.37	75.08	75.80	76.52	77.24	77.97	78.70	79.44	80.18	80.92	81.67	82.42
12.50	63.02	65.60	68.25	70.96	73.75	74.45	75.16	75.88	76.59	77.32	78.04	78.77	79.51	80.24	80.99	81.73
12.75	62.50	65.06	67.68	70.37	73.13	73.83	74.53	75.24	75.95	76.67	77.39	78.12	78.84	79.58	80.31	81.05
13.00	61.98	64.52	67.12	69.79	72.52	73.22	73.92	74.62	75.32	76.03	76.75	77.47	78.19	78.92	79.65	80.38
13.25	61.46	63.98	66.56	69.21	71.92	72.61	73.30	74.00	74.70	75.41	76.11	76.83	77.54	78.26	78.99	79.72
13.50	60.96	63.45	66.02	68.64	71.33	72.01	72.70	73.39	74.09	74.78	75.49	76.19	76.90	77.62	78.34	79.06
13.75	60.46	62.93	65.47	68.08	70.75	71.42	72.10	72.79	73.48	74.17	74.87	75.57	76.27	76.98	77.69	78.41
14.00	59.96	62.42	64.94	67.52	70.17	70.84	71.52	72.19	72.88	73.56	74.26	74.95	75.65	76.35	77.06	77.77
14.25	59.48	61.91	64.41	66.97	69.60	70.26	70.93	71.61	72.28	72.97	73.65	74.34	75.03	75.73	76.43	77.14
14.50	58.99	61.41	63.89	66.43	69.03	69.69	70.36	71.03	71.70	72.37	73.05	73.74	74.43	75.12	75.81	76.51
14.75	58.52	60.91	63.37	65.89	68.48	69.13	69.79	70.45	71.12	71.79	72.46	73.14	73.82	74.51	75.20	75.89
15.00	58.05	60.42	62.86	65.36	67.92	68.57	69.23	69.89	70.55	71.21	71.88	72.55	73.23	73.91	74.59	75.28
15.25	57.58	59.94	62.36	64.84	67.38	68.02	68.67	69.33	69.98	70.64	71.30	71.97	72.64	73.32	74.00	74.68
15.50	57.12	59.46	61.86	64.32	66.84	67.48	68.13	68.77	69.42	70.08	70.74	71.40	72.06	72.73	73.41	74.08
15.75	56.67	58.99	61.37	63.81	66.31	66.95	67.58	68.23	68.87	69.52	70.17	70.83	71.49	72.15	72.82	73.49
16.00	56.22	58.52	60.88	63.30	65.79	66.42	67.05	67.69	68.33	68.97	69.62	70.27	70.92	71.58	72.25	72.91
16.25	55.78	58.06	60.40	62.81	65.27	65.89	66.52	67.15	67.79	68.43	69.07	69.72	70.36	71.02	71.68	72.34
16.50	55.34	57.60	59.93	62.31	64.75	65.37	66.00	66.62	67.25	67.89	68.53	69.17	69.81	70.46	71.11	71.77
16.75	54.90	57.15	59.46	61.82	64.25	64.86	65.48	66.10	66.73	67.36	67.99	68.63	69.27	69.91	70.56	71.21
17.00	54.48	56.71	59.00	61.34	63.75	64.36	64.97	65.59	66.21	66.83	67.46	68.09	68.73	69.36	70.01	70.65
17.25	54.05	56.27	58.54	60.87	63.25	63.86	64.47	65.08	65.69	66.31	66.94	67.56	68.19	68.83	69.46	70.10
17.50	53.64	55.83	58.09	60.40	62.76	63.36	63.97	64.57	65.19	65.80	66.42	67.04	67.67	68.29	68.93	69.56
17.75	53.22	55.40	57.64	59.93	62.28	62.88	63.47	64.08	64.68	65.29	65.91	66.52	67.14	67.77	68.40	69.03
18.00	52.81	54.98	57.20	59.47	61.80	62.39	62.99	63.59	64.19	64.79	65.40	66.01	66.63	67.25	67.87	68.50
18.25	52.41	54.56	56.76	59.02	61.33	61.92	62.51	63.10	63.70	64.30	64.90	65.51	66.12	66.73	67.35	67.97
18.50	52.01	54.14	56.33	58.57	60.86	61.45	62.03	62.62	63.21	63.81	64.41	65.01	65.62	66.23	66.84	67.46
18.75	51.62	53.73	55.90	58.12	60.40	60.98	61.56	62.15	62.73	63.33	63.92	64.52	65.12	65.72	66.33	66.94
19.00	51.23	53.33	55.48	57.68	59.95	60.52	61.10	61.68	62.26	62.85	63.44	64.03	64.63	65.23	65.83	66.44
20.00	49.71	51.75	53.84	55.98	58.17	58.73	59.29	59.85	60.42	60.99	61.56	62.14	62.72	63.30	63.89	64.48
25.00	43.09	44.86	46.67	48.52	50.43	50.91	51.39	51.88	52.37	52.87	53.36	53.86	54.36	54.87	55.38	55.89
30.00	37.77	39.32	40.91	42.53	44.20	44.62	45.05	45.48	45.91	46.34	46.78	47.21	47.65	48.10	48.54	48.99

Description: This table shows the yield to maturity of a mortgage purchased at the price shown in the index.

Example: The yield to maturity of a 6.75 %, 8 year mortgage at a price of 80.00 is 13.14 %.

INTEREST RATE, %

PRICE	0.00%	1.00%	2.00%	3.00%	4.00%	4.25%	4.50%	4.75%	5.00%	5.25%	5.50%	5.75%	6.00%	6.25%	6.50%	6.75%
100	0.00	1.00	2.00	3.00	4.00	4.25	4.50	4.75	5.00	5.25	5.50	5.75	6.00	6.25	6.50	6.75
99	.24	1.25	2.25	3.26	4.26	4.51	4.76	5.01	5.26	5.51	5.76	6.02	6.27	6.52	6.77	7.02
98	.50	1.50	2.51	3.52	4.53	4.78	5.03	5.28	5.53	5.79	6.04	6.29	6.54	6.79	7.05	7.30
97	.75	1.76	2.77	3.79	4.80	5.05	5.30	5.56	5.81	6.06	6.32	6.57	6.82	7.08	7.33	7.58
96	1.01	2.03	3.04	4.06	5.07	5.33	5.58	5.84	6.09	6.34	6.60	6.85	7.11	7.36	7.61	7.87
95	1.28	2.29	3.31	4.33	5.35	5.61	5.86	6.12	6.37	6.63	6.88	7.14	7.39	7.65	7.90	8.16
94	1.54	2.57	3.59	4.61	5.64	5.89	6.15	6.40	6.66	6.92	7.17	7.43	7.69	7.94	8.20	8.46
93	1.81	2.84	3.87	4.90	5.92	6.18	6.44	6.70	6.95	7.21	7.47	7.73	7.98	8.24	8.50	8.76
92	2.09	3.12	4.15	5.18	6.22	6.47	6.73	6.99	7.25	7.51	7.77	8.03	8.28	8.54	8.80	9.06
91	2.37	3.40	4.44	5.47	6.51	6.77	7.03	7.29	7.55	7.81	8.07	8.33	8.59	8.85	9.11	9.37
90	2.65	3.69	4.73	5.77	6.81	7.07	7.34	7.60	7.86	8.12	8.38	8.64	8.90	9.16	9.42	9.69
89	2.94	3.98	5.03	6.07	7.12	7.38	7.64	7.91	8.17	8.43	8.69	8.95	9.22	9.48	9.74	10.00
88	3.23	4.28	5.33	6.38	7.43	7.69	7.96	8.22	8.48	8.75	9.01	9.27	9.54	9.80	10.07	10.33
87	3.53	4.58	5.63	6.69	7.75	8.01	8.28	8.54	8.80	9.07	9.33	9.60	9.86	10.13	10.39	10.66
86	3.83	4.89	5.95	7.01	8.07	8.33	8.60	8.86	9.13	9.40	9.66	9.93	10.20	10.46	10.73	11.00
85	4.14	5.20	6.26	7.33	8.39	8.66	8.93	9.20	9.46	9.73	10.00	10.27	10.53	10.80	11.07	11.34
84	4.45	5.51	6.58	7.65	8.73	8.99	9.26	9.53	9.80	10.07	10.34	10.61	10.88	11.15	11.42	11.68
83	4.76	5.84	6.91	7.99	9.06	9.33	9.60	9.87	10.14	10.41	10.68	10.95	11.23	11.50	11.77	12.04
82	5.09	6.16	7.24	8.32	9.41	9.68	9.95	10.22	10.49	10.76	11.04	11.31	11.58	11.85	12.13	12.40
81	5.41	6.50	7.58	8.67	9.76	10.03	10.30	10.58	10.85	11.12	11.40	11.67	11.94	12.22	12.49	12.76
80	5.75	6.83	7.92	9.02	10.11	10.39	10.66	10.94	11.21	11.49	11.76	12.04	12.31	12.59	12.86	13.14
79	6.09	7.18	8.28	9.37	10.48	10.75	11.03	11.30	11.58	11.86	12.13	12.41	12.69	12.96	13.24	13.52
78	6.43	7.53	8.63	9.74	10.84	11.12	11.40	11.68	11.95	12.23	12.51	12.79	13.07	13.35	13.63	13.90
77	6.78	7.89	9.00	10.11	11.22	11.50	11.78	12.06	12.34	12.62	12.90	13.18	13.46	13.74	14.02	14.30
76	7.14	8.25	9.37	10.48	11.60	11.88	12.16	12.45	12.73	13.01	13.29	13.57	13.85	14.14	14.42	14.70
75	7.51	8.62	9.74	10.87	11.99	12.28	12.56	12.84	13.12	13.41	13.69	13.97	14.26	14.54	14.83	15.11
74	7.88	9.00	10.13	11.26	12.39	12.68	12.96	13.25	13.53	13.82	14.10	14.39	14.67	14.96	15.24	15.53
73	8.26	9.39	10.52	11.66	12.80	13.08	13.37	13.66	13.94	14.23	14.52	14.81	15.09	15.38	15.67	15.96
72	8.64	9.78	10.92	12.06	13.21	13.50	13.79	14.08	14.37	14.65	14.94	15.23	15.52	15.81	16.10	16.39
71	9.04	10.18	11.33	12.48	13.64	13.93	14.22	14.51	14.80	15.09	15.38	15.67	15.96	16.25	16.55	16.84
70	9.44	10.59	11.74	12.90	14.07	14.36	14.65	14.94	15.24	15.53	15.82	16.12	16.41	16.70	17.00	17.29
69	9.85	11.01	12.17	13.34	14.51	14.80	15.10	15.39	15.69	15.98	16.28	16.57	16.87	17.16	17.46	17.76
68	10.27	11.43	12.60	13.78	14.96	15.26	15.55	15.85	16.15	16.44	16.74	17.04	17.34	17.63	17.93	18.23
67	10.70	11.87	13.05	14.23	15.42	15.72	16.02	16.32	16.62	16.91	17.21	17.51	17.81	18.12	18.42	18.72
66	11.13	12.31	13.50	14.69	15.89	16.19	16.49	16.79	17.10	17.40	17.70	18.00	18.30	18.61	18.91	19.21
65	11.58	12.77	13.97	15.17	16.37	16.68	16.98	17.28	17.59	17.89	18.20	18.50	18.81	19.11	19.42	19.72
64	12.04	13.24	14.44	15.65	16.87	17.17	17.48	17.78	18.09	18.40	18.70	19.01	19.32	19.63	19.94	20.24
63	12.51	13.71	14.93	16.15	17.37	17.68	17.99	18.30	18.61	18.91	19.22	19.53	19.84	20.16	20.47	20.78
62	12.98	14.20	15.42	16.65	17.89	18.20	18.51	18.82	19.13	19.45	19.76	20.07	20.38	20.70	21.01	21.32
61	13.47	14.70	15.93	17.17	18.42	18.73	19.05	19.36	19.67	19.99	20.30	20.62	20.94	21.25	21.57	21.89
60	13.98	15.21	16.46	17.71	18.97	19.28	19.60	19.91	20.23	20.55	20.86	21.18	21.50	21.82	22.14	22.46
59	14.49	15.74	16.99	18.25	19.52	19.84	20.16	20.48	20.80	21.12	21.44	21.76	22.08	22.41	22.73	23.05
58	15.02	16.28	17.54	18.82	20.10	20.42	20.74	21.06	21.38	21.71	22.03	22.36	22.68	23.01	23.33	23.66
57	15.56	16.83	18.11	19.39	20.68	21.01	21.33	21.66	21.98	22.31	22.64	22.97	23.29	23.62	23.95	24.28
56	16.12	17.40	18.69	19.98	21.29	21.62	21.94	22.27	22.60	22.93	23.26	23.59	23.92	24.26	24.59	24.92
55	16.69	17.98	19.28	20.59	21.91	22.24	22.57	22.90	23.24	23.57	23.90	24.24	24.57	24.91	25.24	25.58
54	17.28	18.58	19.89	21.22	22.55	22.88	23.22	23.55	23.89	24.23	24.56	24.90	25.24	25.58	25.92	26.26
53	17.88	19.20	20.52	21.86	23.21	23.54	23.88	24.22	24.56	24.90	25.24	25.59	25.93	26.27	26.62	26.96
52	18.50	19.83	21.17	22.52	23.88	24.23	24.57	24.91	25.26	25.60	25.95	26.29	26.64	26.98	27.33	27.68
51	19.14	20.49	21.84	23.21	24.58	24.93	25.28	25.62	25.97	26.32	26.67	27.02	27.37	27.72	28.07	28.42
50	19.80	21.16	22.53	23.91	25.30	25.65	26.01	26.36	26.71	27.06	27.41	27.77	28.12	28.48	28.84	29.19
49	20.48	21.86	23.24	24.64	26.05	26.40	26.76	27.11	27.47	27.83	28.19	28.54	28.90	29.26	29.62	29.99
48	21.19	22.58	23.98	25.39	26.82	27.18	27.54	27.90	28.26	28.62	28.98	29.35	29.71	30.07	30.44	30.81
47	21.91	23.32	24.74	26.17	27.61	27.98	28.34	28.71	29.07	29.44	29.81	30.18	30.54	30.91	31.29	31.66
46	22.66	24.09	25.52	26.97	28.44	28.81	29.18	29.55	29.92	30.29	30.66	31.03	31.41	31.78	32.16	32.54
45	23.44	24.88	26.34	27.81	29.29	29.66	30.04	30.41	30.79	31.17	31.55	31.92	32.30	32.68	33.07	33.45
44	24.24	25.70	27.18	28.67	30.18	30.55	30.93	31.32	31.70	32.08	32.46	32.85	33.23	33.62	34.01	34.40
43	25.07	26.56	28.05	29.57	31.09	31.48	31.86	32.25	32.64	33.03	33.42	33.81	34.20	34.59	34.99	35.38
42	25.94	27.44	28.96	30.50	32.05	32.44	32.83	33.22	33.62	34.01	34.41	34.81	35.20	35.60	36.00	36.40
41	26.84	28.36	29.91	31.47	33.04	33.44	33.84	34.24	34.64	35.04	35.44	35.84	36.25	36.66	37.06	37.47
40	27.77	29.32	30.89	32.47	34.08	34.48	34.89	35.29	35.70	36.11	36.52	36.93	37.34	37.75	38.17	38.58
39	28.74	30.32	31.91	33.52	35.16	35.57	35.98	36.39	36.81	37.22	37.64	38.06	38.48	38.90	39.32	39.74
38	29.76	31.36	32.98	34.62	36.28	36.70	37.12	37.54	37.96	38.39	38.81	39.24	39.67	40.09	40.52	40.96
37	30.82	32.45	34.10	35.77	37.46	37.89	38.32	38.75	39.18	39.61	40.04	40.47	40.91	41.35	41.79	42.23
36	31.93	33.59	35.27	36.97	38.70	39.13	39.57	40.01	40.44	40.89	41.33	41.77	42.22	42.66	43.11	43.56
35	33.09	34.78	36.49	38.23	39.99	40.44	40.88	41.33	41.78	42.23	42.68	43.13	43.59	44.04	44.50	44.96
30	39.85	41.74	43.66	45.61	47.59	48.09	48.59	49.09	49.60	50.11	50.62	51.13	51.64	52.16	52.67	53.19
25	48.92	51.09	53.31	55.57	57.87	58.45	59.03	59.62	60.21	60.80	61.40	62.00	62.60	63.20	63.80	64.41

Description: This table shows the price to pay for a monthly payment mortgage loan at the yield rate.

Example: The price of a 10.75 %, 8 year mortgage loan to yield 8.00 % to maturity is $ 110.17.

INTEREST RATE, %

YIELD	7.00%	7.25%	7.50%	7.75%	8.00%	8.25%	8.50%	8.75%	9.00%	9.25%	9.50%	9.75%	10.00%	10.25%	10.50%	10.75%
0.00	130.88	132.08	133.29	134.50	135.71	136.94	138.16	139.40	140.64	141.89	143.14	144.41	145.67	146.94	148.22	149.51
1.00	125.73	126.89	128.04	129.20	130.37	131.55	132.73	133.92	135.11	136.31	137.51	138.72	139.94	141.16	142.39	143.63
2.00	120.86	121.96	123.07	124.19	125.32	126.44	127.58	128.72	129.87	131.02	132.18	133.34	134.51	135.69	136.87	138.06
3.00	116.23	117.30	118.37	119.44	120.52	121.61	122.70	123.80	124.90	126.01	127.12	128.24	129.37	130.50	131.63	132.77
4.00	111.85	112.87	113.90	114.94	115.98	117.02	118.07	119.13	120.19	121.26	122.33	123.41	124.49	125.58	126.67	127.77
4.25	110.79	111.80	112.82	113.85	114.88	115.91	116.95	118.00	119.05	120.11	121.17	122.24	123.31	124.39	125.47	126.56
4.50	109.74	110.75	111.76	112.77	113.79	114.82	115.85	116.88	117.93	118.97	120.02	121.08	122.14	123.21	124.28	125.36
4.75	108.71	109.71	110.71	111.71	112.72	113.74	114.76	115.78	116.82	117.85	118.89	119.94	120.99	122.05	123.11	124.18
5.00	107.69	108.68	109.67	110.66	111.66	112.67	113.68	114.70	115.72	116.75	117.78	118.82	119.86	120.91	121.96	123.02
5.25	106.69	107.66	108.64	109.63	110.62	111.62	112.62	113.63	114.64	115.66	116.68	117.71	118.74	119.78	120.82	121.87
5.50	105.69	106.66	107.63	108.61	109.59	110.58	111.57	112.57	113.57	114.58	115.59	116.61	117.64	118.66	119.70	120.73
5.75	104.71	105.67	106.63	107.60	108.58	109.55	110.54	111.53	112.52	113.52	114.52	115.53	116.54	117.56	118.59	119.61
6.00	103.75	104.70	105.65	106.61	107.57	108.54	109.52	110.50	111.48	112.47	113.46	114.46	115.47	116.48	117.49	118.51
6.25	102.79	103.73	104.68	105.63	106.58	107.54	108.51	109.48	110.46	111.44	112.42	113.41	114.41	115.41	116.41	117.42
6.50	101.85	102.78	103.72	104.66	105.61	106.56	107.51	108.48	109.44	110.41	111.39	112.37	113.36	114.35	115.34	116.34
6.75	100.92	101.84	102.77	103.70	104.64	105.58	106.53	107.49	108.44	109.40	110.37	111.34	112.32	113.30	114.29	115.28
7.00	100.00	100.91	101.83	102.76	103.69	104.62	105.56	106.51	107.46	108.41	109.37	110.33	111.30	112.27	113.25	114.23
7.25	99.09	100.00	100.91	101.83	102.75	103.67	104.61	105.54	106.48	107.43	108.38	109.33	110.29	111.25	112.22	113.20
7.50	98.20	99.10	100.00	100.91	101.82	102.74	103.66	104.59	105.52	106.46	107.40	108.34	109.29	110.25	111.21	112.17
7.75	97.31	98.20	99.10	100.00	100.90	101.81	102.73	103.65	104.57	105.50	106.43	107.37	108.31	109.26	110.21	111.16
8.00	96.44	97.32	98.21	99.10	100.00	100.90	101.81	102.72	103.63	104.55	105.48	106.41	107.34	108.28	109.22	110.17
8.25	95.58	96.46	97.33	98.22	99.11	100.00	100.90	101.80	102.71	103.62	104.53	105.46	106.38	107.31	108.24	109.18
8.50	94.73	95.60	96.47	97.34	98.23	99.11	100.00	100.89	101.79	102.70	103.60	104.52	105.43	106.36	107.28	108.21
8.75	93.89	94.75	95.61	96.48	97.35	98.23	99.11	100.00	100.89	101.79	102.69	103.59	104.50	105.41	106.33	107.25
9.00	93.06	93.91	94.77	95.63	96.49	97.36	98.24	99.12	100.00	100.89	101.78	102.68	103.58	104.48	105.39	106.31
9.25	92.24	93.09	93.94	94.79	95.65	96.51	97.37	98.25	99.12	100.00	100.88	101.77	102.67	103.56	104.46	105.37
9.50	91.43	92.27	93.11	93.96	94.81	95.66	96.52	97.38	98.25	99.12	100.00	100.88	101.77	102.65	103.55	104.45
9.75	90.64	91.47	92.30	93.14	93.98	94.83	95.68	96.53	97.39	98.25	99.12	100.00	100.88	101.76	102.64	103.53
10.00	89.85	90.67	91.50	92.33	93.16	94.00	94.85	95.69	96.55	97.40	98.26	99.13	100.00	100.87	101.75	102.63
10.25	89.07	89.88	90.70	91.53	92.36	93.19	94.02	94.87	95.71	96.56	97.41	98.27	99.13	100.00	100.87	101.75
10.50	88.30	89.11	89.92	90.74	91.56	92.38	93.21	94.05	94.88	95.73	96.57	97.42	98.28	99.14	100.00	100.87
10.75	87.54	88.34	89.15	89.96	90.77	91.59	92.41	93.24	94.07	94.90	95.74	96.59	97.43	98.28	99.14	100.00
11.00	86.79	87.59	88.38	89.19	89.99	90.81	91.62	92.44	93.26	94.09	94.92	95.76	96.60	97.44	98.29	99.14
11.25	86.05	86.84	87.63	88.43	89.23	90.03	90.84	91.65	92.47	93.29	94.11	94.94	95.77	96.61	97.45	98.30
11.50	85.32	86.10	86.89	87.68	88.47	89.27	90.07	90.87	91.68	92.50	93.31	94.14	94.96	95.79	96.62	97.46
11.75	84.60	85.37	86.15	86.93	87.72	88.51	89.30	90.10	90.91	91.71	92.52	93.34	94.16	94.98	95.81	96.64
12.00	83.89	84.65	85.42	86.20	86.98	87.76	88.55	89.34	90.14	90.94	91.74	92.55	93.36	94.18	95.00	95.82
12.25	83.18	83.94	84.71	85.48	86.25	87.03	87.81	88.59	89.38	90.18	90.97	91.77	92.58	93.39	94.20	95.02
12.50	82.48	83.24	84.00	84.76	85.53	86.30	87.07	87.85	88.63	89.42	90.21	91.01	91.80	92.61	93.41	94.22
12.75	81.80	82.55	83.30	84.05	84.81	85.58	86.35	87.12	87.90	88.68	89.46	90.25	91.04	91.83	92.63	93.44
13.00	81.12	81.86	82.61	83.36	84.11	84.87	85.63	86.40	87.17	87.94	88.72	89.50	90.28	91.07	91.87	92.66
13.25	80.45	81.18	81.92	82.67	83.42	84.17	84.92	85.68	86.45	87.21	87.98	88.76	89.54	90.32	91.11	91.90
13.50	79.78	80.51	81.25	81.99	82.73	83.47	84.22	84.98	85.73	86.49	87.26	88.03	88.80	89.58	90.36	91.14
13.75	79.13	79.85	80.58	81.31	82.05	82.79	83.53	84.28	85.03	85.78	86.54	87.30	88.07	88.84	89.61	90.39
14.00	78.48	79.20	79.92	80.65	81.38	82.11	82.85	83.59	84.33	85.08	85.84	86.59	87.35	88.11	88.88	89.65
14.25	77.84	78.56	79.27	79.99	80.72	81.44	82.17	82.91	83.65	84.39	85.14	85.89	86.64	87.40	88.16	88.92
14.50	77.21	77.92	78.63	79.34	80.06	80.78	81.51	82.24	82.97	83.71	84.45	85.19	85.94	86.69	87.44	88.20
14.75	76.59	77.29	77.99	78.70	79.41	80.13	80.85	81.57	82.30	83.03	83.76	84.50	85.24	85.99	86.74	87.49
15.00	75.97	76.67	77.37	78.07	78.78	79.49	80.20	80.92	81.64	82.36	83.09	83.82	84.56	85.30	86.04	86.78
15.25	75.36	76.05	76.75	77.44	78.14	78.85	79.56	80.27	80.98	81.70	82.42	83.15	83.88	84.61	85.35	86.09
15.50	74.76	75.45	76.13	76.83	77.52	78.22	78.92	79.63	80.34	81.05	81.77	82.49	83.21	83.94	84.67	85.40
15.75	74.17	74.85	75.53	76.22	76.90	77.60	78.29	78.99	79.70	80.41	81.12	81.83	82.55	83.27	84.00	84.72
16.00	73.58	74.25	74.93	75.61	76.30	76.98	77.67	78.37	79.07	79.77	80.47	81.18	81.90	82.61	83.33	84.05
16.25	73.00	73.67	74.34	75.02	75.69	76.38	77.06	77.75	78.44	79.14	79.84	80.54	81.25	81.96	82.67	83.39
16.50	72.43	73.09	73.76	74.43	75.10	75.78	76.46	77.14	77.83	78.52	79.21	79.91	80.61	81.32	82.02	82.74
16.75	71.86	72.52	73.18	73.84	74.51	75.18	75.86	76.54	77.22	77.90	78.59	79.28	79.98	80.68	81.38	82.09
17.00	71.30	71.95	72.61	73.27	73.93	74.60	75.27	75.94	76.62	77.30	77.98	78.67	79.36	80.05	80.75	81.45
17.25	70.75	71.39	72.05	72.70	73.36	74.02	74.68	75.35	76.02	76.70	77.37	78.06	78.74	79.43	80.12	80.82
17.50	70.20	70.84	71.49	72.14	72.79	73.45	74.11	74.77	75.43	76.10	76.78	77.45	78.13	78.81	79.50	80.19
17.75	69.66	70.30	70.94	71.58	72.23	72.88	73.53	74.19	74.85	75.52	76.19	76.86	77.53	78.21	78.89	79.57
18.00	69.13	69.76	70.39	71.03	71.68	72.32	72.97	73.62	74.28	74.94	75.60	76.27	76.94	77.61	78.28	78.96
18.25	68.60	69.22	69.86	70.49	71.13	71.77	72.41	73.06	73.71	74.37	75.02	75.68	76.35	77.01	77.69	78.36
18.50	68.08	68.70	69.32	69.95	70.59	71.22	71.86	72.50	73.15	73.80	74.45	75.11	75.77	76.43	77.09	77.76
18.75	67.56	68.18	68.80	69.42	70.05	70.68	71.32	71.96	72.60	73.24	73.89	74.54	75.19	75.85	76.51	77.17
19.00	67.05	67.66	68.28	68.90	69.52	70.15	70.78	71.41	72.05	72.69	73.33	73.98	74.63	75.28	75.93	76.59
20.00	65.07	65.66	66.26	66.86	67.47	68.08	68.69	69.30	69.92	70.54	71.16	71.79	72.42	73.05	73.69	74.33
25.00	56.40	56.92	57.44	57.96	58.48	59.01	59.54	60.07	60.61	61.14	61.68	62.23	62.77	63.32	63.87	64.43
30.00	49.44	49.89	50.35	50.80	51.26	51.73	52.19	52.66	53.13	53.60	54.07	54.55	55.03	55.51	55.99	56.48

MORTGAGE YIELD

Description: This table shows the yield to maturity of a mortgage purchased at the price shown in the index.

Example: The yield to maturity of a 10.75 %, 8 year mortgage at a price of 105.00 is 9.34 %.

INTEREST RATE, %

PRICE	7.00%	7.25%	7.50%	7.75%	8.00%	8.25%	8.50%	8.75%	9.00%	9.25%	9.50%	9.75%	10.00%	10.25%	10.50%	10.75%
125	1.14	1.37	1.60	1.83	2.06	2.29	2.52	2.75	2.97	3.20	3.43	3.66	3.89	4.12	4.34	4.57
124	1.34	1.57	1.80	2.03	2.26	2.49	2.72	2.95	3.18	3.41	3.64	3.87	4.10	4.33	4.56	4.78
123	1.55	1.78	2.01	2.24	2.47	2.70	2.93	3.16	3.39	3.62	3.85	4.08	4.31	4.54	4.77	5.00
122	1.76	1.99	2.22	2.45	2.68	2.91	3.14	3.37	3.60	3.83	4.07	4.30	4.53	4.76	4.99	5.22
121	1.96	2.20	2.43	2.66	2.89	3.12	3.36	3.59	3.82	4.05	4.28	4.51	4.74	4.97	5.21	5.44
120	2.18	2.41	2.64	2.87	3.11	3.34	3.57	3.80	4.04	4.27	4.50	4.73	4.96	5.20	5.43	5.66
119	2.39	2.62	2.86	3.09	3.32	3.56	3.79	4.02	4.26	4.49	4.72	4.95	5.19	5.42	5.65	5.88
118	2.61	2.84	3.08	3.31	3.54	3.78	4.01	4.24	4.48	4.71	4.95	5.18	5.41	5.65	5.88	6.11
117	2.83	3.06	3.30	3.53	3.77	4.00	4.23	4.47	4.70	4.94	5.17	5.41	5.64	5.87	6.11	6.34
116	3.05	3.28	3.52	3.75	3.99	4.23	4.46	4.70	4.93	5.17	5.40	5.64	5.87	6.11	6.34	6.58
115	3.27	3.51	3.74	3.98	4.22	4.45	4.69	4.93	5.16	5.40	5.63	5.87	6.10	6.34	6.58	6.81
114	3.50	3.74	3.97	4.21	4.45	4.68	4.92	5.16	5.39	5.63	5.87	6.10	6.34	6.58	6.81	7.05
113	3.73	3.97	4.20	4.44	4.68	4.92	5.16	5.39	5.63	5.87	6.11	6.34	6.58	6.82	7.06	7.29
112	3.96	4.20	4.44	4.68	4.92	5.15	5.39	5.63	5.87	6.11	6.35	6.58	6.82	7.06	7.30	7.54
111	4.20	4.44	4.67	4.91	5.15	5.39	5.63	5.87	6.11	6.35	6.59	6.83	7.07	7.31	7.55	7.79
110	4.43	4.67	4.91	5.16	5.40	5.64	5.88	6.12	6.36	6.60	6.84	7.08	7.32	7.56	7.80	8.04
109	4.67	4.92	5.16	5.40	5.64	5.88	6.12	6.36	6.61	6.85	7.09	7.33	7.57	7.81	8.05	8.29
108	4.92	5.16	5.40	5.65	5.89	6.13	6.37	6.61	6.86	7.10	7.34	7.58	7.82	8.07	8.31	8.55
107	5.17	5.41	5.65	5.90	6.14	6.38	6.63	6.87	7.11	7.35	7.60	7.84	8.08	8.33	8.57	8.81
106	5.42	5.66	5.91	6.15	6.39	6.64	6.88	7.13	7.37	7.61	7.86	8.10	8.35	8.59	8.83	9.08
105	5.67	5.92	6.16	6.41	6.65	6.90	7.14	7.39	7.63	7.88	8.12	8.37	8.61	8.86	9.10	9.34
104	5.93	6.18	6.42	6.67	6.91	7.16	7.40	7.65	7.90	8.14	8.39	8.63	8.88	9.13	9.37	9.62
103	6.19	6.44	6.68	6.93	7.18	7.42	7.67	7.92	8.17	8.41	8.66	8.91	9.15	9.40	9.65	9.89
102	6.45	6.70	6.95	7.20	7.45	7.69	7.94	8.19	8.44	8.69	8.93	9.18	9.43	9.68	9.93	10.17
101	6.72	6.97	7.22	7.47	7.72	7.97	8.22	8.47	8.71	8.96	9.21	9.46	9.71	9.96	10.21	10.46
100	7.00	7.25	7.50	7.75	8.00	8.25	8.50	8.75	9.00	9.25	9.50	9.75	10.00	10.25	10.50	10.75
99	7.27	7.52	7.77	8.02	8.28	8.53	8.78	9.03	9.28	9.53	9.78	10.03	10.28	10.54	10.79	11.04
98	7.55	7.80	8.06	8.31	8.56	8.81	9.06	9.32	9.57	9.82	10.07	10.32	10.58	10.83	11.08	11.33
97	7.83	8.09	8.34	8.59	8.85	9.10	9.35	9.61	9.86	10.11	10.37	10.62	10.87	11.13	11.38	11.63
96	8.12	8.38	8.63	8.89	9.14	9.39	9.65	9.90	10.16	10.41	10.67	10.92	11.18	11.43	11.69	11.94
95	8.42	8.67	8.93	9.18	9.44	9.69	9.95	10.20	10.46	10.72	10.97	11.23	11.48	11.74	11.99	12.25
94	8.71	8.97	9.23	9.48	9.74	10.00	10.25	10.51	10.77	11.02	11.28	11.54	11.79	12.05	12.31	12.57
93	9.01	9.27	9.53	9.79	10.05	10.30	10.56	10.82	11.08	11.34	11.59	11.85	12.11	12.37	12.63	12.89
92	9.32	9.58	9.84	10.10	10.36	10.62	10.87	11.13	11.39	11.65	11.91	12.17	12.43	12.69	12.95	13.21
91	9.63	9.89	10.15	10.41	10.67	10.93	11.19	11.45	11.71	11.98	12.24	12.50	12.76	13.02	13.28	13.54
90	9.95	10.21	10.47	10.73	10.99	11.25	11.52	11.78	12.04	12.30	12.57	12.83	13.09	13.35	13.61	13.88
89	10.27	10.53	10.79	11.06	11.32	11.58	11.85	12.11	12.37	12.64	12.90	13.16	13.43	13.69	13.95	14.22
88	10.59	10.86	11.12	11.39	11.65	11.92	12.18	12.44	12.71	12.97	13.24	13.50	13.77	14.03	14.30	14.57
87	10.93	11.19	11.46	11.72	11.99	12.25	12.52	12.79	13.05	13.32	13.58	13.85	14.12	14.38	14.65	14.92
86	11.26	11.53	11.80	12.06	12.33	12.60	12.87	13.13	13.40	13.67	13.94	14.20	14.47	14.74	15.01	15.28
85	11.61	11.87	12.14	12.41	12.68	12.95	13.22	13.49	13.76	14.02	14.29	14.56	14.83	15.10	15.37	15.64
84	11.95	12.22	12.49	12.76	13.03	13.30	13.58	13.85	14.12	14.39	14.66	14.93	15.20	15.47	15.74	16.01
83	12.31	12.58	12.85	13.12	13.40	13.67	13.94	14.21	14.48	14.76	15.03	15.30	15.57	15.85	16.12	16.39
82	12.67	12.94	13.22	13.49	13.76	14.04	14.31	14.58	14.86	15.13	15.41	15.68	15.95	16.23	16.50	16.78
81	13.04	13.31	13.59	13.86	14.14	14.41	14.69	14.96	15.24	15.51	15.79	16.07	16.34	16.62	16.89	17.17
80	13.41	13.69	13.97	14.24	14.52	14.80	15.07	15.35	15.63	15.90	16.18	16.46	16.74	17.02	17.29	17.57
79	13.80	14.07	14.35	14.63	14.91	15.19	15.46	15.74	16.02	16.30	16.58	16.86	17.14	17.42	17.70	17.98
78	14.18	14.46	14.74	15.02	15.30	15.58	15.86	16.14	16.42	16.71	16.99	17.27	17.55	17.83	18.11	18.40
77	14.58	14.86	15.14	15.42	15.71	15.99	16.27	16.55	16.84	17.12	17.40	17.68	17.97	18.25	18.54	18.82
76	14.98	15.27	15.55	15.83	16.12	16.40	16.69	16.97	17.25	17.54	17.82	18.11	18.39	18.68	18.97	19.25
75	15.40	15.68	15.97	16.25	16.54	16.82	17.11	17.40	17.68	17.97	18.26	18.54	18.83	19.12	19.40	19.69
74	15.82	16.10	16.39	16.68	16.97	17.25	17.54	17.83	18.12	18.41	18.70	18.98	19.27	19.56	19.85	20.14
73	16.25	16.53	16.82	17.11	17.40	17.69	17.98	18.27	18.56	18.85	19.14	19.44	19.73	20.02	20.31	20.60
72	16.68	16.97	17.27	17.56	17.85	18.14	18.43	18.72	19.02	19.31	19.60	19.90	20.19	20.48	20.78	21.07
71	17.13	17.42	17.72	18.01	18.30	18.60	18.89	19.19	19.48	19.78	20.07	20.37	20.66	20.96	21.26	21.55
70	17.59	17.88	18.18	18.47	18.77	19.07	19.36	19.66	19.96	20.25	20.55	20.85	21.15	21.45	21.74	22.04
69	18.05	18.35	18.65	18.95	19.25	19.54	19.84	20.14	20.44	20.74	21.04	21.34	21.64	21.94	22.24	22.55
68	18.53	18.83	19.13	19.43	19.73	20.03	20.33	20.64	20.94	21.24	21.54	21.84	22.15	22.45	22.76	23.06
67	19.02	19.32	19.62	19.93	20.23	20.53	20.84	21.14	21.44	21.75	22.05	22.36	22.67	22.97	23.28	23.58
66	19.52	19.82	20.13	20.43	20.74	21.04	21.35	21.66	21.96	22.27	22.58	22.89	23.20	23.50	23.81	24.12
65	20.03	20.34	20.64	20.95	21.26	21.57	21.88	22.19	22.50	22.81	23.12	23.43	23.74	24.05	24.36	24.67
64	20.55	20.86	21.17	21.48	21.79	22.11	22.42	22.73	23.04	23.35	23.67	23.98	24.29	24.61	24.92	25.24
63	21.09	21.40	21.71	22.03	22.34	22.66	22.97	23.28	23.60	23.92	24.23	24.55	24.86	25.18	25.50	25.82
62	21.64	21.95	22.27	22.59	22.90	23.22	23.54	23.85	24.17	24.49	24.81	25.13	25.45	25.77	26.09	26.41
60	22.78	23.10	23.42	23.75	24.07	24.39	24.71	25.04	25.36	25.69	26.01	26.34	26.66	26.99	27.32	27.65
55	25.92	26.26	26.60	26.93	27.27	27.61	27.96	28.30	28.64	28.98	29.32	29.67	30.01	30.36	30.70	31.05
50	29.55	29.91	30.27	30.63	30.99	31.35	31.71	32.08	32.44	32.81	33.17	33.54	33.90	34.27	34.64	35.01
45	33.83	34.22	34.60	34.99	35.38	35.76	36.15	36.54	36.94	37.33	37.72	38.11	38.51	38.91	39.30	39.70

MORTGAGE PRICE

Description: This table shows the price to pay for a monthly payment mortgage loan at the yield rate.

Example: The price of a 15.00 %, 8 year mortgage loan to yield 8.00 % to maturity is $ 126.94.

INTEREST RATE, %

YIELD	11.00%	11.25%	11.50%	11.75%	12.00%	12.25%	12.50%	12.75%	13.00%	13.25%	13.50%	13.75%	14.00%	14.25%	14.50%	15.00%
0.00	150.80	152.10	153.40	154.71	156.03	157.35	158.68	160.01	161.35	162.70	164.05	165.40	166.77	168.14	169.51	172.28
1.00	144.87	146.12	147.37	148.63	149.89	151.16	152.43	153.72	155.00	156.29	157.59	158.90	160.21	161.52	162.84	165.50
2.00	139.25	140.45	141.65	142.86	144.07	145.29	146.52	147.75	148.99	150.23	151.48	152.73	153.99	155.25	156.52	159.08
3.00	133.92	135.07	136.23	137.39	138.56	139.74	140.92	142.10	143.29	144.48	145.68	146.89	148.10	149.32	150.54	152.99
4.00	128.87	129.98	131.09	132.21	133.34	134.47	135.60	136.74	137.89	139.04	140.19	141.35	142.51	143.68	144.86	147.22
4.25	127.65	128.75	129.85	130.96	132.07	133.19	134.32	135.44	136.58	137.72	138.86	140.01	141.16	142.32	143.49	145.83
4.50	126.44	127.53	128.62	129.72	130.83	131.93	133.05	134.17	135.29	136.42	137.55	138.69	139.83	140.98	142.13	144.45
4.75	125.25	126.33	127.41	128.50	129.60	130.69	131.80	132.90	134.02	135.13	136.26	137.38	138.52	139.65	140.79	143.09
5.00	124.08	125.15	126.22	127.30	128.38	129.47	130.56	131.66	132.76	133.87	134.98	136.10	137.22	138.34	139.47	141.75
5.25	122.92	123.98	125.04	126.11	127.18	128.26	129.34	130.43	131.52	132.62	133.72	134.82	135.93	137.05	138.17	140.43
5.50	121.78	122.82	123.88	124.94	126.00	127.06	128.14	129.21	130.30	131.38	132.47	133.57	134.67	135.78	136.89	139.12
5.75	120.65	121.69	122.73	123.78	124.83	125.89	126.95	128.02	129.09	130.16	131.25	132.33	133.42	134.52	135.62	137.83
6.00	119.53	120.56	121.60	122.63	123.68	124.72	125.78	126.83	127.90	128.96	130.03	131.11	132.19	133.27	134.36	136.56
6.25	118.43	119.45	120.48	121.50	122.54	123.58	124.62	125.67	126.72	127.77	128.84	129.90	130.97	132.05	133.13	135.30
6.50	117.35	118.36	119.37	120.39	121.41	122.44	123.48	124.51	125.56	126.60	127.65	128.71	129.77	130.84	131.91	134.06
6.75	116.28	117.28	118.28	119.29	120.31	121.32	122.35	123.38	124.41	125.45	126.49	127.54	128.59	129.64	130.70	132.83
7.00	115.22	116.21	117.20	118.21	119.21	120.22	121.23	122.25	123.28	124.31	125.34	126.37	127.42	128.46	129.51	131.63
7.25	114.17	115.16	116.14	117.13	118.13	119.13	120.14	121.15	122.16	123.18	124.20	125.23	126.26	127.30	128.34	130.43
7.50	113.14	114.12	115.09	116.08	117.06	118.05	119.05	120.05	121.06	122.07	123.08	124.10	125.12	126.15	127.18	129.25
7.75	112.12	113.09	114.06	115.03	116.01	116.99	117.98	118.97	119.97	120.97	121.97	122.98	123.99	125.01	126.03	128.09
8.00	111.12	112.07	113.03	114.00	114.97	115.94	116.92	117.90	118.89	119.88	120.88	121.88	122.88	123.89	124.90	126.94
8.25	110.13	111.07	112.03	112.98	113.94	114.91	115.88	116.85	117.83	118.81	119.80	120.79	121.78	122.78	123.79	125.81
8.50	109.15	110.09	111.03	111.98	112.93	113.89	114.85	115.81	116.78	117.75	118.73	119.71	120.70	121.69	122.69	124.69
8.75	108.18	109.11	110.04	110.98	111.93	112.88	113.83	114.78	115.75	116.71	117.68	118.65	119.63	120.61	121.60	123.58
9.00	107.22	108.15	109.07	110.00	110.94	111.88	112.82	113.77	114.72	115.68	116.64	117.61	118.58	119.55	120.53	122.49
9.25	106.28	107.19	108.11	109.04	109.96	110.89	111.83	112.77	113.71	114.66	115.62	116.57	117.53	118.50	119.47	121.42
9.50	105.35	106.26	107.17	108.08	109.00	109.92	110.85	111.78	112.72	113.66	114.60	115.55	116.50	117.46	118.42	120.35
9.75	104.43	105.33	106.23	107.14	108.05	108.96	109.88	110.81	111.73	112.67	113.60	114.54	115.49	116.43	117.38	119.30
10.00	103.52	104.41	105.31	106.21	107.11	108.02	108.93	109.84	110.76	111.69	112.61	113.55	114.48	115.42	116.36	118.26
10.25	102.62	103.51	104.39	105.29	106.18	107.08	107.98	108.89	109.80	110.72	111.64	112.56	113.49	114.42	115.36	117.24
10.50	101.74	102.61	103.49	104.38	105.26	106.16	107.05	107.95	108.86	109.76	110.67	111.59	112.51	113.43	114.36	116.23
10.75	100.86	101.73	102.60	103.48	104.36	105.24	106.13	107.02	107.92	108.82	109.72	110.63	111.54	112.46	113.36	115.23
11.00	100.00	100.86	101.72	102.59	103.47	104.34	105.22	106.11	107.00	107.89	108.78	109.68	110.59	111.49	112.41	114.24
11.25	99.15	100.00	100.86	101.72	102.58	103.45	104.32	105.20	106.08	106.97	107.86	108.75	109.64	110.54	111.45	113.27
11.50	98.30	99.15	100.00	100.85	101.71	102.57	103.44	104.31	105.18	106.06	106.94	107.82	108.71	109.60	110.50	112.30
11.75	97.47	98.31	99.15	100.00	100.85	101.70	102.56	103.42	104.29	105.16	106.03	106.91	107.79	108.68	109.56	111.35
12.00	96.65	97.48	98.32	99.16	100.00	100.85	101.70	102.55	103.41	104.27	105.14	106.01	106.88	107.76	108.64	110.41
12.25	95.84	96.66	97.49	98.32	99.16	100.00	100.84	101.69	102.54	103.40	104.26	105.12	105.99	106.85	107.73	109.49
12.50	95.04	95.85	96.68	97.50	98.33	99.16	100.00	100.84	101.68	102.53	103.38	104.24	105.10	105.96	106.83	108.57
12.75	94.24	95.06	95.87	96.69	97.51	98.34	99.17	100.00	100.84	101.68	102.52	103.37	104.22	105.08	105.94	107.67
13.00	93.46	94.27	95.07	95.89	96.70	97.52	98.34	99.17	100.00	100.83	101.67	102.51	103.36	104.21	105.06	106.77
13.25	92.69	93.49	94.29	95.09	95.90	96.71	97.53	98.35	99.17	100.00	100.83	101.66	102.50	103.34	104.19	105.89
13.50	91.93	92.72	93.51	94.31	95.11	95.92	96.73	97.54	98.36	99.18	100.00	100.83	101.66	102.49	103.33	105.02
13.75	91.17	91.96	92.74	93.54	94.33	95.13	95.93	96.74	97.55	98.36	99.18	100.00	100.82	101.65	102.48	104.15
14.00	90.43	91.20	91.99	92.77	93.56	94.35	95.15	95.95	96.75	97.56	98.37	99.18	100.00	100.82	101.64	103.30
14.25	89.69	90.46	91.24	92.02	92.80	93.58	94.37	95.17	95.96	96.76	97.57	98.38	99.19	100.00	100.82	102.46
14.50	88.96	89.73	90.50	91.27	92.05	92.83	93.61	94.40	95.19	95.98	96.78	97.58	98.38	99.19	100.00	101.63
14.75	88.24	89.00	89.77	90.53	91.30	92.08	92.85	93.63	94.42	95.20	96.00	96.79	97.59	98.39	99.19	100.81
15.00	87.53	88.29	89.04	89.80	90.57	91.34	92.11	92.88	93.66	94.44	95.22	96.01	96.80	97.60	98.39	100.00
15.25	86.83	87.58	88.33	89.08	89.84	90.60	91.37	92.14	92.91	93.68	94.46	95.24	96.03	96.81	97.61	99.20
15.50	86.14	86.88	87.63	88.37	89.13	89.88	90.64	91.40	92.17	92.93	93.71	94.48	95.26	96.04	96.83	98.41
15.75	85.46	86.19	86.93	87.67	88.42	89.17	89.92	90.67	91.43	92.20	92.96	93.73	94.50	95.28	96.06	97.62
16.00	84.78	85.51	86.24	86.98	87.72	88.46	89.21	89.96	90.71	91.47	92.22	92.99	93.75	94.52	95.30	96.85
16.25	84.11	84.83	85.56	86.29	87.02	87.76	88.50	89.25	89.99	90.74	91.50	92.25	93.01	93.78	94.54	96.09
16.50	83.45	84.17	84.89	85.61	86.34	87.07	87.81	88.55	89.29	90.03	90.78	91.53	92.28	93.04	93.80	95.33
16.75	82.80	83.51	84.22	84.94	85.67	86.39	87.12	87.85	88.59	89.33	90.07	90.81	91.56	92.31	93.07	94.59
17.00	82.15	82.86	83.57	84.28	85.00	85.72	86.44	87.17	87.90	88.63	89.37	90.11	90.85	91.59	92.34	93.85
17.25	81.51	82.21	82.92	83.63	84.34	85.05	85.77	86.49	87.22	87.94	88.67	89.41	90.14	90.88	91.63	93.12
17.50	80.88	81.58	82.28	82.98	83.69	84.39	85.11	85.82	86.54	87.26	87.99	88.72	89.45	90.18	90.92	92.40
17.75	80.26	80.95	81.64	82.34	83.04	83.74	84.45	85.16	85.87	86.59	87.31	88.03	88.76	89.49	90.22	91.69
18.00	79.64	80.33	81.02	81.71	82.40	83.10	83.80	84.51	85.22	85.93	86.64	87.36	88.08	88.80	89.53	90.99
18.25	79.04	79.72	80.40	81.09	81.78	82.47	83.16	83.86	84.56	85.27	85.98	86.69	87.40	88.12	88.84	90.29
18.50	78.43	79.11	79.79	80.47	81.15	81.84	82.53	83.22	83.92	84.62	85.32	86.03	86.74	87.45	88.17	89.60
18.75	77.84	78.51	79.18	79.86	80.54	81.22	81.91	82.59	83.29	83.98	84.68	85.38	86.08	86.79	87.50	88.93
19.00	77.25	77.92	78.59	79.26	79.93	80.61	81.29	81.97	82.66	83.35	84.04	84.73	85.43	86.13	86.84	88.25
20.00	74.97	75.61	76.26	76.91	77.57	78.22	78.88	79.55	80.21	80.88	81.55	82.23	82.91	83.59	84.27	85.65
25.00	64.98	65.54	66.11	66.67	67.24	67.81	68.38	68.95	69.53	70.11	70.69	71.28	71.86	72.45	73.05	74.24
30.00	56.96	57.45	57.95	58.44	58.94	59.44	59.94	60.44	60.95	61.46	61.97	62.48	62.99	63.51	64.03	65.07

MORTGAGE YIELD

Description: This table shows the yield to maturity of a mortgage purchased at the price shown in the index.

Example: The yield to maturity of a 15.00 %, 8 year mortgage at a price of 116.00 is 10.55 %.

INTEREST RATE, %

PRICE	11.00%	11.25%	11.50%	11.75%	12.00%	12.25%	12.50%	12.75%	13.00%	13.25%	13.50%	13.75%	14.00%	14.25%	14.50%	15.00%
160	–	–	–	–				0.00	.20	.41	.62	.82	1.03	1.23	1.44	1.85
155	–	–	–	–	.16	.37	.58	.79	1.00	1.20	1.41	1.62	1.83	2.04	2.24	2.66
150	.13	.34	.55	.76	.98	1.19	1.40	1.61	1.82	2.03	2.25	2.46	2.67	2.88	3.09	3.51
145	.97	1.19	1.40	1.62	1.83	2.05	2.26	2.48	2.69	2.90	3.12	3.33	3.54	3.76	3.97	4.39
140	1.86	2.08	2.29	2.51	2.73	2.95	3.16	3.38	3.60	3.81	4.03	4.25	4.46	4.68	4.89	5.33
135	2.79	3.01	3.23	3.45	3.67	3.89	4.11	4.33	4.55	4.77	4.99	5.21	5.43	5.65	5.87	6.31
130	3.77	3.99	4.21	4.44	4.66	4.89	5.11	5.33	5.56	5.78	6.00	6.22	6.45	6.67	6.89	7.34
129	3.97	4.19	4.42	4.64	4.87	5.09	5.32	5.54	5.76	5.99	6.21	6.43	6.66	6.88	7.10	7.55
128	4.17	4.40	4.62	4.85	5.07	5.30	5.52	5.75	5.97	6.20	6.42	6.65	6.87	7.09	7.32	7.76
127	4.38	4.61	4.83	5.06	5.28	5.51	5.73	5.96	6.18	6.41	6.63	6.86	7.08	7.31	7.53	7.98
126	4.59	4.81	5.04	5.27	5.49	5.72	5.95	6.17	6.40	6.63	6.85	7.08	7.30	7.53	7.75	8.20
125	4.80	5.03	5.25	5.48	5.71	5.94	6.16	6.39	6.62	6.84	7.07	7.30	7.52	7.75	7.97	8.43
124	5.01	5.24	5.47	5.70	5.92	6.15	6.38	6.61	6.84	7.06	7.29	7.52	7.74	7.97	8.20	8.65
123	5.23	5.46	5.69	5.91	6.14	6.37	6.60	6.83	7.06	7.28	7.51	7.74	7.97	8.20	8.42	8.88
122	5.45	5.68	5.91	6.13	6.36	6.59	6.82	7.05	7.28	7.51	7.74	7.97	8.20	8.43	8.66	9.11
121	5.67	5.90	6.13	6.36	6.59	6.82	7.05	7.28	7.51	7.74	7.97	8.20	8.43	8.66	8.88	9.34
120	5.89	6.12	6.35	6.58	6.81	7.05	7.28	7.51	7.74	7.97	8.20	8.43	8.66	8.89	9.12	9.58
119	6.12	6.35	6.58	6.81	7.04	7.28	7.51	7.74	7.97	8.20	8.43	8.66	8.89	9.12	9.36	9.82
118	6.34	6.58	6.81	7.04	7.28	7.51	7.74	7.97	8.20	8.44	8.67	8.90	9.13	9.36	9.60	10.06
117	6.58	6.81	7.04	7.28	7.51	7.74	7.98	8.21	8.44	8.68	8.91	9.14	9.37	9.61	9.84	10.30
116	6.81	7.04	7.28	7.51	7.75	7.98	8.22	8.45	8.68	8.92	9.15	9.38	9.62	9.85	10.08	10.55
115	7.05	7.28	7.52	7.75	7.99	8.22	8.46	8.69	8.93	9.16	9.40	9.63	9.87	10.10	10.33	10.80
114	7.29	7.52	7.76	7.99	8.23	8.47	8.70	8.94	9.17	9.41	9.65	9.88	10.12	10.35	10.59	11.06
113	7.53	7.77	8.00	8.24	8.48	8.71	8.95	9.19	9.42	9.66	9.90	10.13	10.37	10.61	10.84	11.31
112	7.78	8.01	8.25	8.49	8.73	8.96	9.20	9.44	9.68	9.91	10.15	10.39	10.63	10.86	11.10	11.57
111	8.02	8.26	8.50	8.74	8.98	9.22	9.46	9.70	9.93	10.17	10.41	10.65	10.89	11.12	11.36	11.84
110	8.28	8.52	8.76	9.00	9.24	9.48	9.71	9.95	10.19	10.43	10.67	10.91	11.15	11.39	11.63	12.11
109	8.53	8.77	9.01	9.25	9.49	9.74	9.98	10.22	10.46	10.70	10.94	11.18	11.42	11.66	11.90	12.38
108	8.79	9.03	9.27	9.52	9.76	10.00	10.24	10.48	10.72	10.96	11.21	11.45	11.69	11.93	12.17	12.65
107	9.05	9.30	9.54	9.78	10.02	10.27	10.51	10.75	10.99	11.24	11.48	11.72	11.96	12.20	12.45	12.93
106	9.32	9.56	9.81	10.05	10.29	10.54	10.78	11.02	11.27	11.51	11.75	12.00	12.24	12.48	12.73	13.21
105	9.59	9.83	10.08	10.32	10.57	10.81	11.06	11.30	11.55	11.79	12.03	12.28	12.52	12.77	13.01	13.50
104	9.86	10.11	10.35	10.60	10.85	11.09	11.34	11.58	11.83	12.07	12.32	12.56	12.81	13.05	13.30	13.79
103	10.14	10.39	10.63	10.88	11.13	11.37	11.62	11.87	12.11	12.36	12.61	12.85	13.10	13.35	13.59	14.08
102	10.42	10.67	10.92	11.16	11.41	11.66	11.91	12.16	12.40	12.65	12.90	13.15	13.39	13.64	13.89	14.38
101	10.71	10.95	11.20	11.45	11.70	11.95	12.20	12.45	12.70	12.95	13.19	13.44	13.69	13.94	14.19	14.69
100	11.00	11.25	11.50	11.75	12.00	12.25	12.50	12.75	13.00	13.25	13.50	13.75	14.00	14.25	14.50	15.00
99	11.29	11.54	11.79	12.04	12.29	12.54	12.80	13.05	13.30	13.55	13.80	14.05	14.30	14.55	14.81	15.31
98	11.59	11.84	12.09	12.34	12.60	12.85	13.10	13.35	13.60	13.86	14.11	14.36	14.61	14.87	15.12	15.62
97	11.89	12.14	12.40	12.65	12.90	13.16	13.41	13.66	13.92	14.17	14.42	14.68	14.93	15.19	15.44	15.95
96	12.20	12.45	12.70	12.96	13.21	13.47	13.72	13.98	14.23	14.49	14.74	15.00	15.25	15.51	15.76	16.27
95	12.51	12.76	13.02	13.27	13.53	13.79	14.04	14.30	14.56	14.81	15.07	15.32	15.58	15.84	16.09	16.61
94	12.82	13.08	13.34	13.59	13.85	14.11	14.37	14.62	14.88	15.14	15.40	15.65	15.91	16.17	16.43	16.94
93	13.14	13.40	13.66	13.92	14.18	14.44	14.70	14.96	15.21	15.47	15.73	15.99	16.25	16.51	16.77	17.29
92	13.47	13.73	13.99	14.25	14.51	14.77	15.03	15.29	15.55	15.81	16.07	16.33	16.59	16.85	17.11	17.64
91	13.80	14.06	14.32	14.59	14.85	15.11	15.37	15.63	15.89	16.16	16.42	16.68	16.94	17.20	17.47	17.99
90	14.14	14.40	14.66	14.93	15.19	15.45	15.72	15.98	16.24	16.51	16.77	17.03	17.30	17.56	17.82	18.35
89	14.48	14.75	15.01	15.27	15.54	15.80	16.07	16.33	16.60	16.86	17.13	17.39	17.66	17.92	18.19	18.72
88	14.83	15.10	15.36	15.63	15.89	16.16	16.43	16.69	16.96	17.22	17.49	17.76	18.02	18.29	18.56	19.09
87	15.19	15.45	15.72	15.99	16.25	16.52	16.79	17.06	17.32	17.59	17.86	18.13	18.40	18.66	18.93	19.47
86	15.55	15.81	16.08	16.35	16.62	16.89	17.16	17.43	17.70	17.97	18.24	18.51	18.78	19.05	19.32	19.86
85	15.91	16.18	16.45	16.72	16.99	17.26	17.54	17.81	18.08	18.35	18.62	18.89	19.16	19.43	19.71	20.25
84	16.29	16.56	16.83	17.10	17.37	17.65	17.92	18.19	18.46	18.74	19.01	19.28	19.56	19.83	20.10	20.65
83	16.67	16.94	17.21	17.49	17.76	18.04	18.31	18.58	18.86	19.13	19.41	19.68	19.96	20.23	20.51	21.06
82	17.05	17.33	17.60	17.88	18.16	18.43	18.71	18.98	19.26	19.54	19.81	20.09	20.37	20.64	20.92	21.47
81	17.45	17.73	18.00	18.28	18.56	18.83	19.11	19.39	19.67	19.95	20.22	20.50	20.78	21.06	21.34	21.90
80	17.85	18.13	18.41	18.69	18.97	19.25	19.52	19.80	20.08	20.36	20.64	20.93	21.21	21.49	21.77	22.33
79	18.26	18.54	18.82	19.10	19.38	19.66	19.95	20.23	20.51	20.79	21.07	21.36	21.64	21.92	22.20	22.77
78	18.68	18.96	19.24	19.53	19.81	20.09	20.38	20.66	20.94	21.23	21.51	21.79	22.08	22.36	22.65	23.22
77	19.10	19.39	19.67	19.96	20.24	20.53	20.81	21.10	21.38	21.67	21.96	22.24	22.53	22.82	23.10	23.68
76	19.54	19.82	20.11	20.40	20.68	20.97	21.26	21.55	21.84	22.12	22.41	22.70	22.99	23.28	23.57	24.15
75	19.98	20.27	20.56	20.85	21.14	21.43	21.72	22.01	22.30	22.59	22.88	23.17	23.46	23.75	24.04	24.62
74	20.43	20.72	21.02	21.31	21.60	21.89	22.18	22.47	22.77	23.06	23.35	23.64	23.94	24.23	24.52	25.11
73	20.90	21.19	21.48	21.78	22.07	22.36	22.66	22.95	23.25	23.54	23.84	24.13	24.43	24.72	25.02	25.61
72	21.37	21.66	21.96	22.25	22.55	22.85	23.14	23.44	23.74	24.03	24.33	24.63	24.93	25.22	25.52	26.12
71	21.85	22.15	22.45	22.74	23.04	23.34	23.64	23.94	24.24	24.54	24.84	25.14	25.44	25.74	26.04	26.64
70	22.34	22.64	22.94	23.24	23.54	23.85	24.15	24.45	24.75	25.05	25.35	25.66	25.96	26.26	26.57	27.18
65	24.99	25.30	25.61	25.93	26.24	26.56	26.87	27.19	27.50	27.82	28.13	28.45	28.77	29.09	29.40	30.04

MORTGAGE PRICE

Description: This table shows the price to pay for a monthly payment mortgage loan at the yield rate.

Example: The price of a 6.75 %, 9 year mortgage loan to yield 8.00 % to maturity is $ 95.09.

INTEREST RATE, %

YIELD	0.00%	1.00%	2.00%	3.00%	4.00%	4.25%	4.50%	4.75%	5.00%	5.25%	5.50%	5.75%	6.00%	6.25%	6.50%	6.75%
0.00	100.00	104.61	109.35	114.23	119.24	120.52	121.80	123.09	124.39	125.69	127.01	128.33	129.66	131.00	132.35	133.70
1.00	95.59	100.00	104.53	109.20	113.99	115.21	116.43	117.66	118.91	120.16	121.41	122.68	123.95	125.23	126.52	127.81
2.00	91.45	95.66	100.00	104.46	109.04	110.21	111.38	112.56	113.75	114.94	116.14	117.35	118.57	119.80	121.03	122.27
3.00	87.54	91.58	95.73	100.00	104.39	105.50	106.62	107.75	108.89	110.03	111.19	112.34	113.51	114.68	115.86	117.05
4.00	83.86	87.73	91.71	95.80	100.00	101.07	102.14	103.23	104.31	105.41	106.51	107.62	108.74	109.86	110.99	112.13
4.25	82.98	86.80	90.74	94.78	98.94	100.00	101.06	102.13	103.21	104.30	105.39	106.48	107.59	108.70	109.82	110.94
4.50	82.10	85.89	89.78	93.79	97.90	98.95	100.00	101.06	102.13	103.20	104.28	105.36	106.46	107.56	108.66	109.78
4.75	81.24	84.99	88.84	92.80	96.88	97.91	98.95	100.00	101.05	102.12	103.18	104.26	105.34	106.43	107.52	108.62
5.00	80.39	84.10	87.91	91.84	95.86	96.89	97.92	98.96	100.00	101.05	102.11	103.17	104.24	105.32	106.40	107.49
5.25	79.56	83.23	87.00	90.88	94.87	95.88	96.90	97.93	98.96	100.00	101.05	102.10	103.16	104.22	105.30	106.37
5.50	78.74	82.36	86.10	89.94	93.89	94.89	95.90	96.91	97.94	98.96	100.00	101.04	102.09	103.14	104.21	105.27
5.75	77.92	81.52	85.21	89.01	92.92	93.91	94.91	95.91	96.93	97.94	98.97	100.00	101.04	102.08	103.13	104.19
6.00	77.12	80.68	84.34	88.10	91.96	92.95	93.93	94.93	95.93	96.94	97.95	98.97	100.00	101.03	102.07	103.12
6.25	76.34	79.85	83.47	87.20	91.02	92.00	92.97	93.96	94.95	95.95	96.95	97.96	98.98	100.00	101.03	102.06
6.50	75.56	79.04	82.62	86.31	90.10	91.06	92.03	93.00	93.98	94.97	95.96	96.96	97.97	98.98	100.00	101.02
6.75	74.79	78.24	81.79	85.44	89.18	90.14	91.10	92.06	93.03	94.01	94.99	95.98	96.98	97.98	98.99	100.00
7.00	74.04	77.45	80.96	84.57	88.28	89.23	90.18	91.13	92.09	93.06	94.03	95.01	96.00	96.99	97.99	98.99
7.25	73.29	76.67	80.15	83.72	87.40	88.33	89.27	90.21	91.17	92.12	93.09	94.06	95.03	96.01	97.00	98.00
7.50	72.56	75.90	79.35	82.88	86.52	87.45	88.38	89.31	90.25	91.20	92.16	93.12	94.08	95.05	96.03	97.01
7.75	71.84	75.15	78.55	82.06	85.66	86.57	87.49	88.42	89.35	90.29	91.24	92.19	93.14	94.11	95.07	96.05
8.00	71.12	74.40	77.77	81.24	84.81	85.71	86.63	87.54	88.47	89.40	90.33	91.27	92.22	93.17	94.13	95.09
8.25	70.42	73.67	77.01	80.44	83.97	84.87	85.77	86.68	87.59	88.51	89.44	90.37	91.31	92.25	93.20	94.15
8.50	69.73	72.94	76.25	79.65	83.14	84.03	84.93	85.83	86.73	87.64	88.56	89.48	90.41	91.34	92.28	93.23
8.75	69.04	72.23	75.50	78.87	82.33	83.21	84.09	84.98	85.88	86.78	87.69	88.60	89.52	90.45	91.38	92.31
9.00	68.37	71.52	74.76	78.10	81.53	82.40	83.27	84.16	85.04	85.94	86.84	87.74	88.65	89.57	90.49	91.41
9.25	67.71	70.83	74.04	77.34	80.73	81.60	82.46	83.34	84.22	85.10	85.99	86.89	87.79	88.70	89.61	90.53
9.50	67.05	70.14	73.32	76.59	79.95	80.81	81.67	82.53	83.40	84.28	85.16	86.05	86.94	87.84	88.74	89.65
9.75	66.40	69.47	72.62	75.85	79.18	80.03	80.88	81.74	82.60	83.47	84.34	85.22	86.10	86.99	87.89	88.79
10.00	65.77	68.80	71.92	75.13	78.42	79.26	80.10	80.95	81.81	82.67	83.53	84.40	85.28	86.16	87.04	87.93
10.25	65.14	68.14	71.23	74.41	77.67	78.50	79.34	80.18	81.03	81.88	82.73	83.59	84.46	85.33	86.21	87.09
10.50	64.52	67.49	70.56	73.70	76.94	77.76	78.58	79.42	80.25	81.10	81.95	82.80	83.66	84.52	85.39	86.27
10.75	63.91	66.86	69.89	73.00	76.21	77.02	77.84	78.67	79.50	80.33	81.17	82.02	82.87	83.72	84.58	85.45
11.00	63.31	66.23	69.23	72.32	75.49	76.30	77.11	77.92	78.75	79.57	80.41	81.24	82.09	82.93	83.79	84.64
11.25	62.71	65.60	68.58	71.64	74.78	75.58	76.38	77.19	78.01	78.83	79.65	80.48	81.32	82.16	83.00	83.85
11.50	62.13	64.99	67.94	70.97	74.08	74.87	75.67	76.47	77.28	78.09	78.91	79.73	80.56	81.39	82.22	83.07
11.75	61.55	64.39	67.31	70.31	73.39	74.18	74.97	75.76	76.56	77.36	78.17	78.99	79.81	80.63	81.46	82.29
12.00	60.98	63.79	66.68	69.66	72.71	73.49	74.27	75.06	75.85	76.65	77.45	78.26	79.07	79.88	80.71	81.53
12.25	60.42	63.20	66.07	69.02	72.04	72.81	73.59	74.37	75.15	75.94	76.73	77.53	78.34	79.15	79.96	80.78
12.50	59.86	62.62	65.46	68.38	71.38	72.14	72.91	73.68	74.46	75.24	76.03	76.82	77.62	78.42	79.23	80.04
12.75	59.32	62.05	64.86	67.76	70.73	71.48	72.24	73.01	73.78	74.56	75.34	76.12	76.91	77.70	78.50	79.31
13.00	58.78	61.48	64.27	67.14	70.09	70.83	71.59	72.35	73.11	73.88	74.65	75.43	76.21	77.00	77.79	78.59
13.25	58.24	60.93	63.69	66.53	69.45	70.19	70.94	71.69	72.45	73.21	73.97	74.74	75.52	76.30	77.08	77.87
13.50	57.72	60.38	63.12	65.93	68.82	69.56	70.30	71.04	71.79	72.55	73.31	74.07	74.84	75.61	76.39	77.17
13.75	57.20	59.84	62.55	65.34	68.21	68.93	69.67	70.41	71.15	71.90	72.65	73.40	74.17	74.93	75.70	76.48
14.00	56.69	59.30	61.99	64.76	67.60	68.32	69.04	69.78	70.51	71.25	72.00	72.75	73.50	74.26	75.03	75.79
14.25	56.18	58.77	61.44	64.18	66.99	67.71	68.43	69.16	69.88	70.62	71.36	72.10	72.85	73.60	74.36	75.12
14.50	55.69	58.25	60.89	63.61	66.40	67.11	67.82	68.54	69.27	69.99	70.73	71.46	72.20	72.95	73.70	74.45
14.75	55.19	57.74	60.36	63.05	65.82	66.52	67.23	67.94	68.65	69.38	70.10	70.83	71.57	72.31	73.05	73.80
15.00	54.71	57.23	59.83	62.50	65.24	65.93	66.64	67.34	68.05	68.77	69.49	70.21	70.94	71.67	72.41	73.15
15.25	54.23	56.73	59.30	61.95	64.67	65.36	66.05	66.75	67.46	68.17	68.88	69.60	70.32	71.04	71.77	72.51
15.50	53.76	56.24	58.79	61.41	64.10	64.79	65.48	66.17	66.87	67.57	68.28	68.99	69.71	70.43	71.15	71.88
15.75	53.29	55.75	58.28	60.88	63.55	64.23	64.91	65.60	66.29	66.99	67.69	68.39	69.10	69.82	70.53	71.26
16.00	52.83	55.27	57.78	60.35	63.00	63.67	64.35	65.03	65.72	66.41	67.10	67.80	68.51	69.21	69.92	70.64
16.25	52.38	54.79	57.28	59.83	62.46	63.13	63.80	64.47	65.15	65.84	66.53	67.22	67.92	68.62	69.32	70.03
16.50	51.93	54.33	56.79	59.32	61.93	62.59	63.25	63.92	64.60	65.28	65.96	66.65	67.34	68.03	68.73	69.44
16.75	51.49	53.86	56.31	58.82	61.40	62.05	62.71	63.38	64.05	64.72	65.40	66.08	66.76	67.45	68.15	68.84
17.00	51.05	53.41	55.83	58.32	60.88	61.53	62.18	62.84	63.50	64.17	64.84	65.52	66.20	66.88	67.57	68.26
17.25	50.62	52.96	55.36	57.83	60.36	61.01	61.66	62.31	62.97	63.63	64.30	64.97	65.64	66.32	67.00	67.69
17.50	50.20	52.51	54.89	57.34	59.86	60.50	61.14	61.79	62.44	63.10	63.76	64.42	65.09	65.76	66.44	67.12
17.75	49.78	52.07	54.43	56.86	59.36	59.99	60.63	61.27	61.92	62.57	63.22	63.88	64.54	65.21	65.88	66.56
18.00	49.36	51.64	53.98	56.39	58.86	59.49	60.13	60.76	61.40	62.05	62.70	63.35	64.01	64.67	65.33	66.00
18.25	48.96	51.21	53.53	55.92	58.38	59.00	59.63	60.26	60.89	61.53	62.18	62.83	63.48	64.13	64.79	65.46
18.50	48.55	50.79	53.09	55.46	57.89	58.51	59.14	59.76	60.39	61.03	61.66	62.31	62.95	63.60	64.26	64.92
18.75	48.15	50.37	52.66	55.01	57.42	58.03	58.65	59.27	59.90	60.53	61.16	61.80	62.44	63.08	63.73	64.38
19.00	47.76	49.96	52.23	54.56	56.95	57.56	58.17	58.79	59.41	60.03	60.66	61.29	61.93	62.57	63.21	63.86
20.00	46.24	48.37	50.56	52.81	55.13	55.72	56.31	56.91	57.51	58.11	58.72	59.33	59.95	60.57	61.19	61.82
25.00	39.65	41.48	43.36	45.29	47.28	47.79	48.29	48.81	49.32	49.84	50.36	50.88	51.41	51.94	52.48	53.01
30.00	34.46	36.05	37.69	39.37	41.10	41.53	41.98	42.42	42.87	43.32	43.77	44.23	44.69	45.15	45.61	46.08

Description: This table shows the yield to maturity of a mortgage purchased at the price shown in the index.

Example: The yield to maturity of a 6.75 %, 9 year mortgage at a price of 80.00 is 12.51 %.

INTEREST RATE, %

PRICE	0.00%	1.00%	2.00%	3.00%	4.00%	4.25%	4.50%	4.75%	5.00%	5.25%	5.50%	5.75%	6.00%	6.25%	6.50%	6.75%
100	0.00	1.00	2.00	3.00	4.00	4.25	4.50	4.75	5.00	5.25	5.50	5.75	6.00	6.25	6.50	6.75
99	.22	1.22	2.22	3.23	4.23	4.48	4.73	4.98	5.24	5.49	5.74	5.99	6.24	6.49	6.74	6.99
98	.44	1.45	2.46	3.46	4.47	4.72	4.98	5.23	5.48	5.73	5.98	6.24	6.24	6.49	6.74	7.24
97	.67	1.68	2.69	3.70	4.71	4.97	5.22	5.47	5.73	5.98	6.23	6.49	6.49	6.74	7.25	7.50
96	.90	1.91	2.93	3.95	4.96	5.22	5.47	5.72	5.98	6.23	6.49	6.74	6.99	7.25	7.50	7.76
95	1.13	2.15	3.17	4.19	5.21	5.47	5.72	5.98	6.23	6.49	6.74	7.00	7.25	7.51	7.76	8.02
94	1.37	2.39	3.42	4.44	5.47	5.72	5.98	6.23	6.49	6.75	7.00	7.26	7.52	7.77	8.03	8.29
93	1.61	2.64	3.67	4.69	5.72	5.98	6.24	6.50	6.75	7.01	7.27	7.53	7.78	8.04	8.30	8.56
92	1.86	2.89	3.92	4.95	5.99	6.24	6.50	6.76	7.02	7.28	7.54	7.80	8.05	8.31	8.57	8.83
91	2.11	3.14	4.18	5.21	6.25	6.51	6.77	7.03	7.29	7.55	7.81	8.07	8.33	8.59	8.85	9.11
90	2.36	3.40	4.44	5.48	6.52	6.78	7.04	7.30	7.57	7.83	8.09	8.35	8.61	8.87	9.13	9.39
89	2.61	3.66	4.70	5.75	6.80	7.06	7.32	7.58	7.84	8.11	8.37	8.63	8.89	9.16	9.42	9.68
88	2.87	3.92	4.97	6.02	7.07	7.34	7.60	7.86	8.13	8.39	8.66	8.92	9.18	9.45	9.71	9.98
87	3.14	4.19	5.25	6.30	7.36	7.62	7.89	8.15	8.42	8.68	8.95	9.21	9.48	9.74	10.01	10.27
86	3.41	4.46	5.52	6.58	7.65	7.91	8.18	8.44	8.71	8.98	9.24	9.51	9.78	10.04	10.31	10.58
85	3.68	4.74	5.81	6.87	7.94	8.21	8.47	8.74	9.01	9.28	9.54	9.81	10.08	10.35	10.62	10.88
84	3.96	5.02	6.09	7.16	8.24	8.50	8.77	9.04	9.31	9.58	9.85	10.12	10.39	10.66	10.93	11.20
83	4.24	5.31	6.38	7.46	8.54	8.81	9.08	9.35	9.62	9.89	10.16	10.43	10.70	10.97	11.25	11.52
82	4.52	5.60	6.68	7.76	8.85	9.12	9.39	9.66	9.93	10.21	10.48	10.75	11.02	11.30	11.57	11.84
81	4.82	5.90	6.98	8.07	9.16	9.43	9.71	9.98	10.25	10.53	10.80	11.07	11.35	11.62	11.90	12.17
80	5.11	6.20	7.29	8.38	9.48	9.75	10.03	10.30	10.58	10.85	11.13	11.40	11.68	11.96	12.23	12.51
79	5.41	6.51	7.60	8.70	9.80	10.08	10.36	10.63	10.91	11.19	11.46	11.74	12.02	12.30	12.57	12.85
78	5.72	6.82	7.92	9.03	10.14	10.41	10.69	10.97	11.25	11.53	11.80	12.08	12.36	12.64	12.92	13.20
77	6.03	7.14	8.25	9.36	10.47	10.75	11.03	11.31	11.59	11.87	12.15	12.43	12.71	12.99	13.28	13.56
76	6.35	7.46	8.58	9.70	10.82	11.10	11.38	11.66	11.94	12.22	12.51	12.79	13.07	13.35	13.64	13.92
75	6.68	7.79	8.91	10.04	11.17	11.45	11.73	12.02	12.30	12.58	12.87	13.15	13.44	13.72	14.00	14.29
74	7.01	8.13	9.26	10.39	11.52	11.81	12.09	12.38	12.66	12.95	13.24	13.52	13.81	14.09	14.38	14.67
73	7.34	8.47	9.61	10.75	11.89	12.18	12.46	12.75	13.04	13.32	13.61	13.90	14.19	14.48	14.76	15.05
72	7.69	8.82	9.97	11.11	12.26	12.55	12.84	13.13	13.42	13.70	13.99	14.28	14.57	14.86	15.16	15.45
71	8.04	9.18	10.33	11.48	12.64	12.93	13.22	13.51	13.80	14.09	14.39	14.68	14.97	15.26	15.56	15.85
70	8.40	9.55	10.70	11.86	13.03	13.32	13.61	13.91	14.20	14.49	14.79	15.08	15.37	15.67	15.96	16.26
69	8.76	9.92	11.08	12.25	13.42	13.72	14.01	14.31	14.60	14.90	15.19	15.49	15.79	16.08	16.38	16.68
68	9.13	10.30	11.47	12.65	13.83	14.13	14.42	14.72	15.02	15.31	15.61	15.91	16.21	16.51	16.81	17.11
67	9.51	10.69	11.87	13.05	14.24	14.54	14.84	15.14	15.44	15.74	16.04	16.34	16.64	16.94	17.24	17.55
66	9.90	11.09	12.27	13.47	14.67	14.97	15.27	15.57	15.87	16.17	16.48	16.78	17.08	17.39	17.69	18.00
65	10.30	11.49	12.69	13.89	15.10	15.40	15.71	16.01	16.31	16.62	16.92	17.23	17.54	17.84	18.15	18.46
64	10.71	11.91	13.11	14.32	15.54	15.85	16.15	16.46	16.77	17.07	17.38	17.69	18.00	18.31	18.62	18.93
63	11.12	12.33	13.55	14.77	16.00	16.30	16.61	16.92	17.23	17.54	17.85	18.16	18.47	18.78	19.10	19.41
62	11.55	12.77	13.99	15.22	16.46	16.77	17.08	17.39	17.71	18.02	18.33	18.64	18.96	19.27	19.59	19.90
61	11.99	13.21	14.45	15.69	16.94	17.25	17.56	17.88	18.19	18.51	18.82	19.14	19.46	19.77	20.09	20.41
60	12.43	13.67	14.91	16.16	17.42	17.74	18.06	18.37	18.69	19.01	19.33	19.65	19.97	20.29	20.61	20.93
59	12.89	14.14	15.39	16.65	17.93	18.24	18.56	18.88	19.21	19.53	19.85	20.17	20.49	20.82	21.14	21.47
58	13.36	14.62	15.88	17.16	18.44	18.76	19.08	19.41	19.73	20.06	20.38	20.71	21.03	21.36	21.69	22.01
57	13.84	15.11	16.39	17.67	18.97	19.29	19.62	19.95	20.27	20.60	20.93	21.26	21.59	21.92	22.25	22.58
56	14.34	15.62	16.91	18.20	19.51	19.84	20.17	20.50	20.83	21.16	21.49	21.82	22.16	22.49	22.82	23.16
55	14.84	16.14	17.44	18.75	20.07	20.40	20.73	21.07	21.40	21.74	22.07	22.41	22.74	23.08	23.42	23.76
54	15.37	16.67	17.98	19.31	20.64	20.98	21.32	21.65	21.99	22.33	22.67	23.01	23.35	23.69	24.03	24.37
53	15.90	17.22	18.55	19.89	21.24	21.57	21.91	22.25	22.60	22.94	23.28	23.62	23.97	24.31	24.66	25.00
52	16.46	17.79	19.13	20.48	21.84	22.19	22.53	22.88	23.22	23.57	23.91	24.26	24.61	24.96	25.31	25.66
51	17.03	18.37	19.73	21.09	22.47	22.82	23.17	23.52	23.87	24.22	24.57	24.92	25.27	25.62	25.98	26.33
50	17.61	18.97	20.34	21.73	23.12	23.47	23.82	24.18	24.53	24.88	25.24	25.60	25.95	26.31	26.67	27.03
49	18.22	19.59	20.98	22.38	23.79	24.15	24.50	24.86	25.22	25.58	25.94	26.30	26.66	27.02	27.38	27.75
48	18.84	20.23	21.63	23.05	24.48	24.84	25.20	25.56	25.93	26.29	26.66	27.02	27.39	27.75	28.12	28.49
47	19.49	20.89	22.31	23.75	25.20	25.56	25.93	26.29	26.66	27.03	27.40	27.77	28.14	28.51	28.89	29.26
46	20.15	21.58	23.02	24.47	25.94	26.31	26.68	27.05	27.42	27.80	28.17	28.55	28.92	29.30	29.68	30.06
45	20.84	22.29	23.74	25.22	26.71	27.08	27.46	27.83	28.21	28.59	28.97	29.35	29.73	30.12	30.50	30.89
44	21.56	23.02	24.50	25.99	27.50	27.88	28.26	28.65	29.03	29.42	29.80	30.19	30.58	30.97	31.36	31.75
43	22.30	23.78	25.28	26.80	28.33	28.72	29.10	29.49	29.88	30.27	30.66	31.06	31.45	31.85	32.24	32.64
42	23.07	24.57	26.09	27.63	29.19	29.58	29.97	30.37	30.76	31.16	31.56	31.96	32.36	32.76	33.17	33.57
41	23.87	25.39	26.94	28.50	30.08	30.48	30.88	31.28	31.69	32.09	32.49	32.90	33.31	33.72	34.13	34.54
40	24.70	26.25	27.81	29.40	31.01	31.42	31.83	32.23	32.64	33.06	33.47	33.88	34.30	34.71	35.13	35.55
39	25.56	27.14	28.73	30.35	31.99	32.40	32.81	33.23	33.65	34.06	34.48	34.90	35.33	35.75	36.18	36.60
38	26.46	28.06	29.69	31.33	33.00	33.42	33.84	34.27	34.69	35.12	35.55	35.97	36.41	36.84	37.27	37.71
37	27.41	29.03	30.69	32.36	34.06	34.49	34.92	35.35	35.79	36.22	36.66	37.09	37.53	37.98	38.42	38.86
36	28.39	30.05	31.73	33.44	35.17	35.61	36.05	36.49	36.93	37.38	37.82	38.27	38.72	39.17	39.62	40.07
35	29.42	31.11	32.83	34.57	36.34	36.79	37.24	37.69	38.14	38.59	39.05	39.50	39.96	40.42	40.88	41.35
30	35.43	37.32	39.24	41.20	43.19	43.69	44.20	44.71	45.22	45.73	46.24	46.76	47.28	47.80	48.32	48.85
25	43.49	45.67	47.89	50.16	52.47	53.06	53.65	54.24	54.83	55.43	56.04	56.64	57.25	57.86	58.47	59.09

Description: This table shows the price to pay for a monthly payment mortgage loan at the yield rate.

Example: The price of a 10.75 %, 9 year mortgage loan to yield 8.00 % to maturity is $ 111.29.

YIELD	7.00%	7.25%	7.50%	7.75%	8.00%	8.25%	8.50%	8.75%	9.00%	9.25%	9.50%	9.75%	10.00%	10.25%	10.50%	10.75%
0.00	135.07	136.44	137.82	139.21	140.60	142.01	143.42	144.84	146.26	147.70	149.14	150.59	152.05	153.52	154.99	156.47
1.00	129.12	130.43	131.75	133.07	134.41	135.75	137.10	138.45	139.82	141.19	142.57	143.96	145.35	146.75	148.16	149.58
2.00	123.52	124.77	126.03	127.30	128.58	129.86	131.15	132.45	133.75	135.07	136.39	137.71	139.05	140.39	141.73	143.09
3.00	118.24	119.44	120.65	121.86	123.09	124.31	125.55	126.79	128.04	129.30	130.56	131.83	133.11	134.39	135.68	136.98
4.00	113.27	114.42	115.58	116.74	117.91	119.09	120.27	121.46	122.66	123.86	125.07	126.29	127.51	128.74	129.98	131.22
4.25	112.07	113.21	114.36	115.51	116.67	117.83	119.00	120.18	121.36	122.55	123.75	124.96	126.17	127.38	128.60	129.83
4.50	110.89	112.02	113.15	114.29	115.44	116.59	117.75	118.92	120.09	121.27	122.45	123.64	124.84	126.04	127.25	128.47
4.75	109.73	110.85	111.97	113.10	114.23	115.37	116.52	117.67	118.83	119.99	121.17	122.34	123.53	124.72	125.92	127.12
5.00	108.59	109.69	110.80	111.91	113.04	114.16	115.30	116.44	117.59	118.74	119.90	121.07	122.24	123.42	124.60	125.79
5.25	107.46	108.55	109.65	110.75	111.86	112.98	114.10	115.23	116.37	117.51	118.65	119.81	120.97	122.14	123.31	124.49
5.50	106.35	107.43	108.51	109.60	110.70	111.81	112.92	114.04	115.16	116.29	117.43	118.57	119.72	120.87	122.03	123.20
5.75	105.25	106.32	107.39	108.47	109.56	110.66	111.76	112.86	113.97	115.09	116.22	117.35	118.48	119.62	120.77	121.93
6.00	104.17	105.23	106.29	107.36	108.44	109.52	110.61	111.70	112.80	113.91	115.02	116.14	117.27	118.40	119.53	120.68
6.25	103.10	104.15	105.20	106.26	107.33	108.40	109.48	110.56	111.65	112.75	113.85	114.95	116.07	117.19	118.31	119.44
6.50	102.05	103.09	104.13	105.18	106.24	107.30	108.36	109.44	110.51	111.60	112.69	113.78	114.89	115.99	117.11	118.23
6.75	101.02	102.05	103.08	104.12	105.16	106.21	107.26	108.33	109.39	110.47	111.55	112.63	113.72	114.82	115.92	117.03
7.00	100.00	101.02	102.04	103.06	104.10	105.14	106.18	107.23	108.29	109.35	110.42	111.49	112.57	113.66	114.75	115.85
7.25	98.99	100.00	101.01	102.03	103.05	104.08	105.11	106.15	107.20	108.25	109.31	110.37	111.44	112.52	113.60	114.68
7.50	98.00	99.00	100.00	101.01	102.02	103.04	104.06	105.09	106.13	107.17	108.22	109.27	110.33	111.39	112.46	113.53
7.75	97.03	98.01	99.00	100.00	101.00	102.01	103.02	104.04	105.07	106.10	107.14	108.18	109.23	110.28	111.34	112.40
8.00	96.06	97.04	98.02	99.01	100.00	101.00	102.00	103.01	104.03	105.05	106.07	107.10	108.14	109.18	110.23	111.29
8.25	95.11	96.08	97.05	98.03	99.01	100.00	100.99	101.99	103.00	104.01	105.02	106.05	107.07	108.11	109.14	110.19
8.50	94.18	95.13	96.10	97.06	98.04	99.02	100.00	100.99	101.98	102.99	103.99	105.00	106.02	107.04	108.07	109.10
8.75	93.26	94.20	95.16	96.11	97.08	98.05	99.02	100.00	100.99	101.98	102.97	103.97	104.98	105.99	107.01	108.03
9.00	92.35	93.28	94.23	95.18	96.13	97.09	98.05	99.02	100.00	100.98	101.97	102.96	103.96	104.96	105.97	106.98
9.25	91.45	92.38	93.31	94.25	95.20	96.15	97.10	98.06	99.03	100.00	100.98	101.96	102.95	103.94	104.94	105.94
9.50	90.56	91.48	92.41	93.34	94.27	95.22	96.16	97.11	98.07	99.03	100.00	100.97	101.95	102.93	103.92	104.91
9.75	89.69	90.60	91.52	92.44	93.37	94.30	95.24	96.18	97.13	98.08	99.04	100.00	100.97	101.94	102.92	103.90
10.00	88.83	89.73	90.64	91.55	92.47	93.39	94.32	95.26	96.19	97.14	98.09	99.04	100.00	100.96	101.93	102.91
10.25	87.98	88.88	89.78	90.68	91.59	92.50	93.42	94.35	95.28	96.21	97.15	98.10	99.05	100.00	100.96	101.92
10.50	87.15	88.03	88.92	89.82	90.72	91.62	92.53	93.45	94.37	95.30	96.23	97.16	98.10	99.05	100.00	100.96
10.75	86.32	87.20	88.08	88.97	89.86	90.76	91.66	92.56	93.48	94.39	95.32	96.24	97.17	98.11	99.05	100.00
11.00	85.51	86.38	87.25	88.13	89.01	89.90	90.79	91.69	92.60	93.50	94.42	95.34	96.26	97.19	98.12	99.06
11.25	84.71	85.57	86.43	87.30	88.18	89.06	89.94	90.83	91.73	92.63	93.53	94.44	95.36	96.27	97.20	98.13
11.50	83.91	84.77	85.62	86.49	87.35	88.22	89.10	89.98	90.87	91.76	92.66	93.56	94.46	95.38	96.29	97.21
11.75	83.13	83.98	84.83	85.68	86.54	87.40	88.27	89.15	90.02	90.91	91.80	92.69	93.59	94.49	95.40	96.31
12.00	82.36	83.20	84.04	84.89	85.74	86.59	87.45	88.32	89.19	90.07	90.95	91.83	92.72	93.61	94.51	95.41
12.25	81.60	82.43	83.27	84.10	84.95	85.80	86.65	87.51	88.37	89.24	90.11	90.98	91.86	92.75	93.64	94.54
12.50	80.85	81.68	82.50	83.33	84.17	85.01	85.85	86.70	87.56	88.42	89.28	90.15	91.02	91.90	92.78	93.67
12.75	80.12	80.93	81.75	82.57	83.40	84.23	85.07	85.91	86.76	87.61	88.46	89.32	90.19	91.06	91.93	92.81
13.00	79.39	80.19	81.00	81.82	82.64	83.46	84.29	85.13	85.97	86.81	87.66	88.51	89.37	90.23	91.10	91.97
13.25	78.67	79.47	80.27	81.08	81.89	82.71	83.53	84.36	85.19	86.02	86.86	87.71	88.56	89.41	90.27	91.13
13.50	77.96	78.75	79.55	80.35	81.15	81.96	82.78	83.60	84.42	85.25	86.08	86.92	87.76	88.61	89.46	90.31
13.75	77.26	78.04	78.83	79.63	80.42	81.23	82.03	82.85	83.66	84.48	85.31	86.14	86.97	87.81	88.65	89.50
14.00	76.57	77.34	78.13	78.91	79.70	80.50	81.30	82.10	82.91	83.73	84.55	85.37	86.19	87.03	87.86	88.70
14.25	75.89	76.66	77.43	78.21	79.00	79.78	80.58	81.37	82.18	82.98	83.79	84.61	85.43	86.25	87.08	87.91
14.50	75.21	75.98	76.75	77.52	78.30	79.08	79.86	80.65	81.45	82.25	83.05	83.86	84.67	85.49	86.31	87.13
14.75	74.55	75.31	76.07	76.83	77.60	78.38	79.16	79.94	80.73	81.52	82.32	83.12	83.92	84.73	85.55	86.36
15.00	73.90	74.65	75.40	76.16	76.92	77.69	78.46	79.24	80.02	80.81	81.59	82.39	83.19	83.99	84.79	85.60
15.25	73.25	73.99	74.74	75.49	76.25	77.01	77.78	78.55	79.32	80.10	80.88	81.67	82.46	83.25	84.05	84.86
15.50	72.61	73.35	74.09	74.84	75.59	76.34	77.10	77.86	78.63	79.40	80.18	80.96	81.74	82.53	83.32	84.12
15.75	71.98	72.71	73.45	74.19	74.93	75.68	76.43	77.19	77.95	78.71	79.48	80.26	81.03	81.81	82.60	83.39
16.00	71.36	72.09	72.82	73.55	74.29	75.03	75.77	76.52	77.28	78.03	78.80	79.56	80.33	81.11	81.89	82.67
16.25	70.75	71.47	72.19	72.92	73.65	74.38	75.12	75.87	76.61	77.36	78.12	78.88	79.64	80.41	81.18	81.96
16.50	70.14	70.86	71.57	72.29	73.02	73.75	74.48	75.22	75.96	76.70	77.45	78.21	78.96	79.72	80.49	81.26
16.75	69.55	70.25	70.96	71.68	72.40	73.12	73.85	74.58	75.31	76.05	76.79	77.54	78.29	79.05	79.80	80.57
17.00	68.96	69.66	70.36	71.07	71.78	72.50	73.22	73.94	74.67	75.41	76.14	76.88	77.63	78.38	79.13	79.88
17.25	68.38	69.07	69.77	70.47	71.18	71.89	72.60	73.32	74.04	74.77	75.50	76.23	76.97	77.71	78.46	79.21
17.50	67.80	68.49	69.18	69.88	70.58	71.28	71.99	72.71	73.42	74.14	74.87	75.59	76.33	77.06	77.80	78.55
17.75	67.24	67.92	68.60	69.30	69.99	70.69	71.39	72.10	72.81	73.52	74.24	74.96	75.69	76.42	77.15	77.89
18.00	66.68	67.35	68.03	68.72	69.41	70.10	70.80	71.50	72.20	72.91	73.62	74.34	75.06	75.78	76.51	77.24
18.25	66.12	66.79	67.47	68.15	68.83	69.52	70.21	70.91	71.60	72.31	73.01	73.72	74.44	75.15	75.88	76.60
18.50	65.58	66.24	66.91	67.59	68.27	68.95	69.63	70.32	71.01	71.71	72.41	73.12	73.82	74.53	75.25	75.97
18.75	65.04	65.70	66.36	67.03	67.70	68.38	69.06	69.74	70.43	71.12	71.82	72.52	73.22	73.92	74.63	75.35
19.00	64.51	65.16	65.82	66.48	67.15	67.82	68.50	69.17	69.86	70.54	71.23	71.92	72.62	73.32	74.02	74.73
20.00	62.45	63.08	63.72	64.36	65.01	65.66	66.31	66.97	67.62	68.29	68.96	69.63	70.30	70.98	71.66	72.34
25.00	53.56	54.10	54.65	55.20	55.75	56.31	56.87	57.43	57.99	58.56	59.14	59.71	60.29	60.87	61.45	62.04
30.00	46.55	47.02	47.50	47.98	48.46	48.94	49.43	49.92	50.41	50.90	51.40	51.90	52.40	52.91	53.42	53.93

Description: This table shows the yield to maturity of a mortgage purchased at the price shown in the index.

Example: The yield to maturity of a 10.75 %, 9 year mortgage at a price of 105.00 is 9.47 %.

INTEREST RATE, %

PRICE	7.00%	7.25%	7.50%	7.75%	8.00%	8.25%	8.50%	8.75%	9.00%	9.25%	9.50%	9.75%	10.00%	10.25%	10.50%	10.75%
125	1.72	1.95	2.18	2.41	2.64	2.87	3.10	3.32	3.55	3.78	4.01	4.24	4.46	4.69	4.92	5.15
124	1.91	2.14	2.37	2.59	2.82	3.05	3.28	3.51	3.74	3.97	4.20	4.43	4.65	4.88	5.11	5.34
123	2.09	2.32	2.55	2.78	3.01	3.24	3.47	3.70	3.93	4.16	4.39	4.62	4.85	5.04	5.30	5.53
122	2.28	2.51	2.74	2.97	3.20	3.43	3.66	3.89	4.12	4.35	4.58	4.81	5.04	5.27	5.50	5.73
121	2.46	2.70	2.93	3.16	3.39	3.62	3.85	4.08	4.32	4.55	4.78	5.01	5.24	5.47	5.70	5.93
120	2.65	2.89	3.12	3.35	3.58	3.82	4.05	4.28	4.51	4.74	4.98	5.21	5.44	5.67	5.90	6.13
119	2.85	3.08	3.31	3.55	3.78	4.01	4.25	4.48	4.71	4.94	5.18	5.41	5.64	5.87	6.10	6.34
118	3.04	3.28	3.51	3.74	3.98	4.21	4.44	4.68	4.91	5.14	5.38	5.61	5.84	6.08	6.31	6.54
117	3.24	3.47	3.71	3.94	4.18	4.41	4.65	4.88	5.11	5.35	5.58	5.82	6.05	6.28	6.52	6.75
116	3.44	3.67	3.91	4.15	4.38	4.62	4.85	5.09	5.32	5.56	5.79	6.02	6.26	6.49	6.73	6.96
115	3.64	3.88	4.11	4.35	4.59	4.82	5.06	5.29	5.53	5.76	6.00	6.24	6.47	6.71	6.94	7.18
114	3.84	4.08	4.32	4.56	4.79	5.03	5.27	5.50	5.74	5.98	6.21	6.45	6.68	6.92	7.16	7.39
113	4.05	4.29	4.53	4.77	5.00	5.24	5.48	5.72	5.95	6.19	6.43	6.66	6.90	7.14	7.38	7.61
112	4.26	4.50	4.74	4.98	5.22	5.45	5.69	5.93	6.17	6.41	6.65	6.88	7.12	7.36	7.60	7.83
111	4.47	4.71	4.95	5.19	5.43	5.67	5.91	6.15	6.39	6.63	6.87	7.10	7.34	7.58	7.82	8.06
110	4.69	4.93	5.17	5.41	5.65	5.89	6.13	6.37	6.61	6.85	7.09	7.33	7.57	7.81	8.05	8.29
109	4.90	5.15	5.39	5.63	5.87	6.11	6.35	6.59	6.83	7.07	7.32	7.56	7.80	8.04	8.28	8.52
108	5.12	5.37	5.61	5.85	6.09	6.34	6.58	6.82	7.06	7.30	7.54	7.79	8.03	8.27	8.51	8.75
107	5.35	5.59	5.83	6.08	6.32	6.56	6.81	7.05	7.29	7.53	7.78	8.02	8.26	8.50	8.75	8.99
106	5.57	5.82	6.06	6.31	6.55	6.79	7.04	7.28	7.52	7.77	8.01	8.26	8.50	8.74	8.99	9.23
105	5.80	6.05	6.29	6.54	6.78	7.03	7.27	7.52	7.76	8.01	8.25	8.50	8.74	8.98	9.23	9.47
104	6.03	6.28	6.53	6.77	7.02	7.26	7.51	7.76	8.00	8.25	8.49	8.74	8.98	9.23	9.48	9.72
103	6.27	6.52	6.76	7.01	7.26	7.50	7.75	8.00	8.24	8.49	8.74	8.98	9.23	9.48	9.72	9.97
102	6.51	6.76	7.00	7.25	7.50	7.75	8.00	8.24	8.49	8.74	8.99	9.23	9.48	9.73	9.98	10.23
101	6.75	7.00	7.25	7.50	7.75	7.99	8.24	8.49	8.74	8.99	9.24	9.49	9.74	9.99	10.23	10.48
100	7.00	7.25	7.50	7.75	8.00	8.25	8.50	8.75	9.00	9.25	9.50	9.75	10.00	10.25	10.50	10.75
99	7.24	7.49	7.75	8.00	8.25	8.50	8.75	9.00	9.25	9.50	9.75	10.01	10.26	10.51	10.76	11.01
98	7.50	7.75	8.00	8.25	8.50	8.76	9.01	9.26	9.51	9.77	10.02	10.27	10.52	10.78	11.03	11.28
97	7.75	8.01	8.26	8.51	8.77	9.02	9.27	9.53	9.78	10.03	10.29	10.54	10.79	11.05	11.30	11.55
96	8.01	8.27	8.52	8.77	9.03	9.28	9.54	9.79	10.05	10.30	10.56	10.81	11.07	11.32	11.58	11.83
95	8.28	8.53	8.79	9.04	9.30	9.55	9.81	10.06	10.32	10.58	10.83	11.09	11.34	11.60	11.86	12.11
94	8.54	8.80	9.06	9.31	9.57	9.83	10.08	10.34	10.60	10.86	11.11	11.37	11.63	11.88	12.14	12.40
93	8.81	9.07	9.33	9.59	9.85	10.11	10.36	10.62	10.88	11.14	11.40	11.66	11.91	12.17	12.43	12.69
92	9.09	9.35	9.61	9.87	10.13	10.39	10.65	10.91	11.17	11.43	11.69	11.95	12.21	12.46	12.72	12.99
91	9.37	9.63	9.89	10.15	10.41	10.67	10.93	11.20	11.46	11.72	11.98	12.24	12.50	12.76	13.02	13.29
90	9.66	9.92	10.18	10.44	10.70	10.97	11.23	11.49	11.75	12.01	12.28	12.54	12.80	13.06	13.33	13.59
89	9.95	10.21	10.47	10.74	11.00	11.26	11.53	11.79	12.05	12.32	12.58	12.84	13.11	13.37	13.64	13.90
88	10.24	10.50	10.77	11.03	11.30	11.56	11.83	12.09	12.36	12.62	12.89	13.15	13.42	13.69	13.95	14.22
87	10.54	10.80	11.07	11.34	11.60	11.87	12.14	12.40	12.67	12.94	13.20	13.47	13.74	14.00	14.27	14.54
86	10.84	11.11	11.38	11.65	11.91	12.18	12.45	12.72	12.98	13.25	13.52	13.79	14.06	14.33	14.60	14.86
85	11.15	11.42	11.69	11.96	12.23	12.50	12.77	13.04	13.31	13.58	13.85	14.12	14.39	14.66	14.93	15.20
84	11.47	11.74	12.01	12.28	12.55	12.82	13.09	13.36	13.63	13.90	14.18	14.45	14.72	14.99	15.26	15.54
83	11.79	12.06	12.33	12.60	12.88	13.15	13.42	13.69	13.97	14.24	14.51	14.79	15.06	15.33	15.61	15.88
82	12.11	12.39	12.66	12.93	13.21	13.48	13.76	14.03	14.31	14.58	14.85	15.13	15.40	15.68	15.96	16.23
81	12.45	12.72	13.00	13.27	13.55	13.82	14.10	14.37	14.65	14.93	15.20	15.48	15.76	16.03	16.31	16.59
80	12.78	13.06	13.34	13.61	13.89	14.17	14.45	14.72	15.00	15.28	15.56	15.84	16.12	16.39	16.67	16.95
79	13.13	13.41	13.69	13.96	14.24	14.52	14.80	15.08	15.36	15.64	15.92	16.20	16.48	16.76	17.04	17.32
78	13.48	13.76	14.04	14.32	14.60	14.88	15.16	15.44	15.73	16.01	16.29	16.57	16.85	17.14	17.42	17.70
77	13.84	14.12	14.40	14.68	14.97	15.25	15.53	15.82	16.10	16.38	16.67	16.95	17.23	17.52	17.80	18.09
76	14.20	14.49	14.77	15.05	15.34	15.62	15.91	16.19	16.48	16.76	17.05	17.34	17.62	17.91	18.20	18.48
75	14.58	14.86	15.15	15.43	15.72	16.01	16.29	16.58	16.87	17.15	17.44	17.73	18.02	18.31	18.60	18.89
74	14.95	15.24	15.53	15.82	16.11	16.40	16.68	16.97	17.26	17.55	17.84	18.13	18.42	18.71	19.00	19.30
73	15.34	15.63	15.92	16.21	16.50	16.79	17.08	17.38	17.67	17.96	18.25	18.54	18.84	19.13	19.42	19.72
72	15.74	16.03	16.32	16.61	16.91	17.20	17.49	17.79	18.08	18.37	18.67	18.96	19.26	19.55	19.85	20.14
71	16.14	16.44	16.73	17.02	17.32	17.61	17.91	18.20	18.50	18.80	19.09	19.39	19.69	19.99	20.28	20.58
70	16.55	16.85	17.15	17.44	17.74	18.04	18.34	18.63	18.93	19.23	19.53	19.83	20.13	20.43	20.73	21.03
69	16.98	17.28	17.57	17.87	18.17	18.47	18.77	19.07	19.37	19.67	19.97	20.28	20.58	20.88	21.18	21.49
68	17.41	17.71	18.01	18.31	18.61	18.91	19.22	19.52	19.82	20.13	20.43	20.73	21.04	21.34	21.65	21.96
67	17.85	18.15	18.46	18.76	19.06	19.37	19.67	19.98	20.28	20.59	20.90	21.20	21.51	21.82	22.13	22.44
66	18.30	18.61	18.91	19.22	19.53	19.83	20.14	20.45	20.76	21.07	21.37	21.68	21.99	22.30	22.62	22.93
65	18.76	19.07	19.38	19.69	20.00	20.31	20.62	20.93	21.24	21.55	21.86	22.18	22.49	22.80	23.12	23.43
64	19.24	19.55	19.86	20.17	20.48	20.80	21.11	21.42	21.74	22.05	22.37	22.68	23.00	23.31	23.63	23.95
63	19.72	20.04	20.35	20.66	20.98	21.29	21.61	21.93	22.24	22.56	22.88	23.20	23.52	23.84	24.15	24.47
62	20.22	20.54	20.85	21.17	21.49	21.81	22.13	22.44	22.76	23.09	23.41	23.73	24.05	24.37	24.69	25.02
60	21.25	21.58	21.90	22.22	22.55	22.87	23.20	23.52	23.85	24.18	24.50	24.83	25.16	25.49	25.82	26.15
55	24.10	24.43	24.78	25.12	25.46	25.80	26.14	26.49	26.83	27.18	27.52	27.87	28.22	28.57	28.91	29.26
50	27.39	27.75	28.11	28.47	28.84	29.20	29.57	29.93	30.30	30.67	31.04	31.41	31.78	32.15	32.52	32.89
45	31.27	31.66	32.05	32.44	32.83	33.22	33.62	34.01	34.40	34.80	35.20	35.60	36.00	36.40	36.80	37.20

Description: This table shows the price to pay for a monthly payment mortgage loan at the yield rate.

Example: The price of a 15.00 %, 9 year mortgage loan to yield 8.00 % to maturity is $ 130.00.

INTEREST RATE, %

YIELD	11.00%	11.25%	11.50%	11.75%	12.00%	12.25%	12.50%	12.75%	13.00%	13.25%	13.50%	13.75%	14.00%	14.25%	14.50%	15.00%
0.00	157.96	159.46	160.96	162.47	163.99	165.52	167.05	168.59	170.14	171.69	173.26	174.83	176.40	177.99	179.58	182.78
1.00	151.00	152.43	153.87	155.31	156.76	158.22	159.69	161.16	162.64	164.13	165.62	167.12	168.63	170.15	171.67	174.73
2.00	144.45	145.82	147.19	148.57	149.96	151.36	152.76	154.17	155.59	157.01	158.44	159.87	161.32	162.76	164.22	167.15
3.00	138.28	139.59	140.91	142.23	143.56	144.90	146.24	147.59	148.94	150.30	151.67	153.05	154.43	155.81	157.21	160.01
4.00	132.47	133.72	134.99	136.25	137.53	138.81	140.09	141.38	142.68	143.99	145.30	146.61	147.94	149.27	150.60	153.29
4.25	131.07	132.31	133.56	134.81	136.07	137.34	138.61	139.89	141.18	142.47	143.76	145.07	146.37	147.69	149.01	151.67
4.50	129.69	130.92	132.15	133.39	134.64	135.89	137.15	138.42	139.69	140.97	142.25	143.54	144.83	146.13	147.44	150.07
4.75	128.33	129.55	130.77	132.00	133.23	134.47	135.72	136.97	138.23	139.49	140.76	142.03	143.32	144.60	145.89	148.50
5.00	126.99	128.19	129.40	130.62	131.84	133.07	134.30	135.54	136.78	138.03	139.29	140.55	141.82	143.09	144.37	146.95
5.25	125.67	126.86	128.06	129.26	130.47	131.68	132.90	134.13	135.36	136.60	137.84	139.09	140.34	141.61	142.87	145.42
5.50	124.37	125.55	126.73	127.92	129.12	130.32	131.53	132.74	133.96	135.18	136.41	137.65	138.89	140.14	141.39	143.91
5.75	123.09	124.25	125.43	126.60	127.79	128.98	130.17	131.37	132.58	133.79	135.01	136.23	137.46	138.69	139.93	142.43
6.00	121.82	122.98	124.14	125.30	126.47	127.65	128.83	130.02	131.22	132.42	133.62	134.83	136.05	137.27	138.50	140.97
6.25	120.58	121.72	122.87	124.02	125.18	126.35	127.52	128.69	129.88	131.06	132.26	133.45	134.66	135.87	137.08	139.53
6.50	119.35	120.48	121.62	122.76	123.91	125.06	126.22	127.38	128.55	129.73	130.91	132.10	133.29	134.48	135.69	138.11
6.75	118.14	119.26	120.38	121.52	122.65	123.79	124.94	126.09	127.25	128.41	129.58	130.76	131.94	133.12	134.31	136.71
7.00	116.95	118.06	119.17	120.29	121.41	122.54	123.68	124.82	125.97	127.12	128.27	129.44	130.60	131.78	132.95	135.33
7.25	115.77	116.87	117.97	119.08	120.19	121.31	122.44	123.56	124.70	125.84	126.98	128.14	129.29	130.45	131.62	133.97
7.50	114.61	115.70	116.79	117.89	118.99	120.10	121.21	122.33	123.45	124.58	125.71	126.85	128.00	129.15	130.30	132.63
7.75	113.47	114.55	115.63	116.71	117.80	118.90	120.00	121.11	122.22	123.34	124.46	125.59	126.72	127.86	129.00	131.30
8.00	112.34	113.41	114.48	115.55	116.63	117.72	118.81	119.91	121.01	122.11	123.23	124.34	125.46	126.59	127.72	130.00
8.25	111.23	112.29	113.35	114.41	115.48	116.56	117.64	118.72	119.81	120.91	122.01	123.11	124.22	125.34	126.46	128.72
8.50	110.14	111.18	112.23	113.29	114.34	115.41	116.48	117.55	118.63	119.72	120.81	121.90	123.00	124.11	125.21	127.45
8.75	109.06	110.09	111.13	112.18	113.22	114.28	115.34	116.40	117.47	118.54	119.62	120.71	121.80	122.89	123.99	126.20
9.00	108.00	109.02	110.05	111.08	112.12	113.16	114.21	115.26	116.32	117.39	118.46	119.53	120.61	121.69	122.78	124.97
9.25	106.95	107.96	108.98	110.00	111.03	112.06	113.10	114.15	115.19	116.25	117.30	118.37	119.44	120.51	121.59	123.75
9.50	105.91	106.92	107.92	108.94	109.96	110.98	112.01	113.04	114.08	115.12	116.17	117.22	118.28	119.34	120.41	122.56
9.75	104.89	105.89	106.88	107.89	108.90	109.91	110.93	111.95	112.98	114.01	115.05	116.09	117.14	118.19	119.25	121.38
10.00	103.89	104.87	105.86	106.85	107.85	108.86	109.87	110.88	111.90	112.92	113.95	114.98	116.02	117.06	118.11	120.21
10.25	102.89	103.87	104.85	105.83	106.82	107.82	108.82	109.82	110.83	111.84	112.86	113.88	114.91	115.94	116.98	119.06
10.50	101.92	102.88	103.85	104.83	105.81	106.79	107.78	108.78	109.77	110.78	111.79	112.80	113.82	114.84	115.87	117.93
10.75	100.95	101.91	102.87	103.83	104.81	105.78	106.76	107.75	108.74	109.73	110.73	111.73	112.74	113.75	114.77	116.82
11.00	100.00	100.95	101.90	102.86	103.82	104.78	105.75	106.73	107.71	108.70	109.68	110.68	111.68	112.68	113.69	115.72
11.25	99.06	100.00	100.94	101.89	102.84	103.80	104.76	105.73	106.70	107.68	108.66	109.64	110.63	111.62	112.62	114.63
11.50	98.14	99.07	100.00	100.94	101.88	102.83	103.78	104.74	105.70	106.67	107.64	108.62	109.60	110.58	111.57	113.56
11.75	97.22	98.14	99.07	100.00	100.93	101.87	102.82	103.77	104.72	105.68	106.64	107.61	108.58	109.55	110.53	112.50
12.00	96.32	97.24	98.15	99.07	100.00	100.93	101.87	102.81	103.75	104.70	105.65	106.61	107.57	108.54	109.51	111.46
12.25	95.43	96.34	97.25	98.16	99.08	100.00	100.93	101.86	102.79	103.73	104.68	105.63	106.58	107.54	108.50	110.43
12.50	94.56	95.45	96.35	97.26	98.17	99.08	100.00	100.92	101.85	102.78	103.72	104.66	105.60	106.55	107.50	109.42
12.75	93.69	94.58	95.47	96.37	97.27	98.18	99.09	100.00	100.92	101.84	102.77	103.70	104.63	105.57	106.52	108.42
13.00	92.84	93.72	94.60	95.49	96.39	97.28	98.18	99.09	100.00	100.91	101.83	102.76	103.68	104.61	105.55	107.43
13.25	92.00	92.87	93.75	94.63	95.51	96.40	97.29	98.19	99.09	100.00	100.91	101.82	102.74	103.67	104.59	106.46
13.50	91.17	92.03	92.90	93.77	94.65	95.53	96.42	97.31	98.20	99.10	100.00	100.91	101.82	102.73	103.65	105.50
13.75	90.35	91.21	92.07	92.93	93.80	94.67	95.55	96.43	97.32	98.21	99.10	100.00	100.90	101.81	102.72	104.55
14.00	89.54	90.39	91.24	92.10	92.96	93.83	94.70	95.57	96.45	97.33	98.22	99.11	100.00	100.90	101.80	103.62
14.25	88.75	89.59	90.43	91.28	92.14	92.99	93.85	94.72	95.59	96.46	97.34	98.22	99.11	100.00	100.89	102.69
14.50	87.96	88.79	89.63	90.47	91.32	92.17	93.02	93.88	94.74	95.61	96.48	97.35	98.23	99.11	100.00	101.78
14.75	87.18	88.01	88.84	89.67	90.51	91.36	92.20	93.05	93.91	94.77	95.63	96.49	97.37	98.24	99.12	100.89
15.00	86.42	87.24	88.06	88.89	89.72	90.55	91.39	92.24	93.08	93.93	94.79	95.65	96.51	97.38	98.25	100.00
15.25	85.66	86.48	87.29	88.11	88.93	89.76	90.59	91.43	92.27	93.11	93.96	94.81	95.67	96.53	97.39	99.13
15.50	84.92	85.72	86.53	87.34	88.16	88.98	89.80	90.63	91.47	92.30	93.14	93.99	94.83	95.69	96.54	98.26
15.75	84.18	84.98	85.78	86.59	87.40	88.21	89.03	89.85	90.67	91.50	92.33	93.17	94.01	94.86	95.70	97.41
16.00	83.46	84.25	85.04	85.84	86.64	87.45	88.26	89.07	89.89	90.71	91.54	92.37	93.20	94.04	94.88	96.57
16.25	82.74	83.52	84.31	85.10	85.90	86.70	87.50	88.31	89.12	89.93	90.75	91.57	92.40	93.23	94.06	95.74
16.50	82.03	82.81	83.59	84.37	85.16	85.96	86.75	87.55	88.36	89.16	89.98	90.79	91.61	92.43	93.26	94.92
16.75	81.33	82.10	82.88	83.66	84.44	85.22	86.01	86.81	87.60	88.41	89.21	90.02	90.83	91.65	92.47	94.12
17.00	80.64	81.41	82.18	82.95	83.72	84.50	85.29	86.07	86.86	87.66	88.45	89.26	90.06	90.87	91.68	93.32
17.25	79.96	80.72	81.48	82.25	83.02	83.79	84.57	85.35	86.13	86.92	87.71	88.50	89.30	90.10	90.91	92.53
17.50	79.29	80.04	80.80	81.56	82.32	83.09	83.86	84.63	85.41	86.19	86.97	87.76	88.55	89.35	90.15	91.75
17.75	78.63	79.38	80.12	80.88	81.63	82.39	83.16	83.92	84.69	85.47	86.25	87.03	87.81	88.60	89.39	90.99
18.00	77.98	78.71	79.46	80.20	80.95	81.71	82.46	83.22	83.99	84.76	85.53	86.30	87.08	87.86	88.65	90.23
18.25	77.33	78.06	78.80	79.54	80.28	81.03	81.78	82.53	83.29	84.05	84.82	85.59	86.36	87.14	87.91	89.48
18.50	76.69	77.42	78.15	78.88	79.62	80.36	81.11	81.85	82.61	83.36	84.12	84.88	85.65	86.42	87.19	88.74
18.75	76.06	76.78	77.51	78.24	78.97	79.70	80.44	81.18	81.93	82.68	83.43	84.19	84.94	85.71	86.47	88.02
19.00	75.44	76.16	76.87	77.60	78.32	79.05	79.78	80.52	81.26	82.00	82.75	83.50	84.25	85.01	85.77	87.30
20.00	73.03	73.72	74.42	75.12	75.82	76.53	77.24	77.95	78.66	79.38	80.11	80.83	81.56	82.29	83.03	84.51
25.00	62.63	63.22	63.82	64.42	65.02	65.63	66.24	66.85	67.46	68.08	68.70	69.32	69.95	70.57	71.20	72.47
30.00	54.44	54.95	55.47	55.99	56.52	57.04	57.57	58.10	58.64	59.17	59.71	60.25	60.80	61.34	61.89	62.99

MORTGAGE YIELD

Description: This table shows the yield to maturity of a mortgage purchased at the price shown in the index.

Example: The yield to maturity of a 15.00 %, 9 year mortgage at a price of 116.00 is 10.93 %.

INTEREST RATE, %

PRICE	11.00%	11.25%	11.50%	11.75%	12.00%	12.25%	12.50%	12.75%	13.00%	13.25%	13.50%	13.75%	14.00%	14.25%	14.50%	15.00%
160	–	–	.13	.33	.54	.75	.95	1.16	1.36	1.57	1.77	1.98	2.18	2.39	2.59	3.00
155	.41	.62	.83	1.04	1.25	1.46	1.67	1.87	2.08	2.29	2.50	2.70	2.91	3.12	3.32	3.73
150	.14	1.36	1.57	1.78	1.99	2.20	2.41	2.62	2.83	3.04	3.25	3.46	3.67	3.88	4.09	4.51
145	1.91	2.12	2.34	2.55	2.76	2.98	3.19	3.40	3.62	3.83	4.04	4.26	4.47	4.68	4.89	5.31
140	2.71	2.93	3.14	3.36	3.58	3.79	4.01	4.23	4.44	4.66	4.87	5.09	5.30	5.52	5.73	6.16
135	3.55	3.77	3.99	4.21	4.43	4.65	4.87	5.09	5.31	5.53	5.75	5.96	6.18	6.40	6.62	7.05
130	4.44	4.66	4.89	5.11	5.33	5.55	5.78	6.00	6.22	6.44	6.67	6.89	7.11	7.33	7.55	8.00
129	4.62	4.85	5.07	5.29	5.52	5.74	5.96	6.19	6.41	6.63	6.86	7.08	7.30	7.52	7.75	8.19
128	4.81	5.03	5.26	5.48	5.70	5.93	6.15	6.38	6.60	6.82	7.05	7.27	7.49	7.72	7.94	8.39
127	4.99	5.22	5.44	5.67	5.89	6.12	6.34	6.57	6.79	7.02	7.24	7.47	7.69	7.91	8.14	8.58
126	5.18	5.41	5.63	5.86	6.09	6.31	6.54	6.76	6.99	7.21	7.44	7.66	7.89	8.11	8.34	8.79
125	5.37	5.60	5.83	6.05	6.28	6.51	6.73	6.96	7.19	7.41	7.64	7.86	8.09	8.31	8.54	8.99
124	5.57	5.79	6.02	6.25	6.48	6.70	6.93	7.16	7.38	7.61	7.84	8.06	8.29	8.52	8.74	9.19
123	5.76	5.99	6.22	6.45	6.68	6.90	7.13	7.36	7.59	7.81	8.04	8.27	8.50	8.72	8.95	9.40
122	5.96	6.19	6.42	6.65	6.88	7.10	7.33	7.56	7.79	8.02	8.25	8.47	8.70	8.93	9.16	9.61
121	6.16	6.39	6.62	6.85	7.08	7.31	7.54	7.77	8.00	8.23	8.45	8.68	8.91	9.14	9.37	9.83
120	6.36	6.59	6.82	7.05	7.28	7.52	7.75	7.98	8.21	8.44	8.66	8.89	9.12	9.35	9.58	10.04
119	6.57	6.80	7.03	7.26	7.49	7.72	7.95	8.19	8.42	8.65	8.88	9.11	9.34	9.57	9.80	10.26
118	6.77	7.01	7.24	7.47	7.70	7.94	8.17	8.40	8.63	8.86	9.09	9.32	9.56	9.79	10.02	10.48
117	6.98	7.22	7.45	7.68	7.92	8.15	8.38	8.61	8.85	9.08	9.31	9.54	9.78	10.01	10.24	10.70
116	7.20	7.43	7.66	7.90	8.13	8.37	8.60	8.83	9.07	9.30	9.53	9.77	10.00	10.23	10.46	10.93
115	7.41	7.65	7.88	8.12	8.35	8.58	8.82	9.05	9.29	9.52	9.76	9.99	10.22	10.46	10.69	11.16
114	7.63	7.86	8.10	8.34	8.57	8.81	9.04	9.28	9.51	9.75	9.98	10.22	10.45	10.69	10.92	11.39
113	7.85	8.09	8.32	8.56	8.80	9.03	9.27	9.50	9.74	9.98	10.21	10.45	10.68	10.92	11.16	11.63
112	8.07	8.31	8.55	8.78	9.02	9.26	9.50	9.73	9.97	10.21	10.44	10.68	10.92	11.16	11.39	11.87
111	8.30	8.54	8.78	9.01	9.25	9.49	9.73	9.97	10.20	10.44	10.68	10.92	11.16	11.39	11.63	12.11
110	8.53	8.77	9.01	9.25	9.48	9.72	9.96	10.20	10.44	10.68	10.92	11.16	11.40	11.64	11.88	12.35
109	8.76	9.00	9.24	9.48	9.72	9.96	10.20	10.44	10.68	10.92	11.16	11.40	11.64	11.88	12.12	12.60
108	8.99	9.24	9.48	9.72	9.96	10.20	10.44	10.68	10.92	11.17	11.41	11.65	11.89	12.13	12.37	12.85
107	9.23	9.47	9.72	9.96	10.20	10.44	10.69	10.93	11.17	11.41	11.65	11.90	12.14	12.38	12.62	13.11
106	9.47	9.72	9.96	10.20	10.45	10.69	10.93	11.18	11.42	11.66	11.91	12.15	12.39	12.64	12.88	13.36
105	9.72	9.96	10.21	10.45	10.70	10.94	11.18	11.43	11.67	11.92	12.16	12.41	12.65	12.89	13.14	13.63
104	9.97	10.21	10.46	10.70	10.95	11.19	11.44	11.68	11.93	12.18	12.42	12.67	12.91	13.16	13.40	13.89
103	10.22	10.46	10.71	10.96	11.20	11.45	11.70	11.94	12.19	12.44	12.68	12.93	13.18	13.42	13.67	14.16
102	10.47	10.72	10.97	11.22	11.46	11.71	11.96	12.21	12.45	12.70	12.95	13.20	13.45	13.69	13.94	14.44
101	10.73	10.98	11.23	11.48	11.73	11.98	12.23	12.47	12.72	12.97	13.22	13.47	13.72	13.97	14.22	14.71
100	11.00	11.25	11.50	11.75	12.00	12.25	12.50	12.75	13.00	13.25	13.50	13.75	14.00	14.25	14.50	15.00
99	11.26	11.51	11.76	12.02	12.27	12.52	12.77	13.02	13.27	13.52	13.77	14.02	14.28	14.53	14.78	15.28
98	11.53	11.78	12.04	12.29	12.54	12.79	13.05	13.30	13.55	13.80	14.06	14.31	14.56	14.81	15.07	15.57
97	11.81	12.06	12.31	12.57	12.82	13.07	13.33	13.58	13.84	14.09	14.34	14.60	14.85	15.11	15.36	15.87
96	12.09	12.34	12.60	12.85	13.11	13.36	13.62	13.87	14.13	14.38	14.64	14.89	15.15	15.40	15.66	16.17
95	12.37	12.62	12.88	13.14	13.39	13.65	13.91	14.16	14.42	14.68	14.93	15.19	15.44	15.70	15.96	16.47
94	12.66	12.91	13.17	13.43	13.69	13.94	14.20	14.46	14.72	14.97	15.23	15.49	15.75	16.01	16.26	16.78
93	12.95	13.21	13.47	13.72	13.98	14.24	14.50	14.76	15.02	15.28	15.54	15.80	16.06	16.32	16.58	17.10
92	13.25	13.51	13.77	14.03	14.29	14.55	14.81	15.07	15.33	15.59	15.85	16.11	16.37	16.63	16.89	17.42
91	13.55	13.81	14.07	14.33	14.59	14.86	15.12	15.38	15.64	15.90	16.17	16.43	16.69	16.95	17.22	17.74
90	13.85	14.12	14.38	14.64	14.91	15.17	15.43	15.70	15.96	16.22	16.49	16.75	17.02	17.28	17.54	18.07
89	14.17	14.43	14.69	14.96	15.22	15.49	15.75	16.02	16.28	16.55	16.81	17.08	17.35	17.61	17.88	18.41
88	14.48	14.75	15.01	15.28	15.55	15.81	16.08	16.35	16.61	16.88	17.15	17.41	17.68	17.95	18.22	18.75
87	14.81	15.07	15.34	15.61	15.88	16.14	16.41	16.68	16.95	17.22	17.49	17.75	18.02	18.29	18.56	19.10
86	15.13	15.40	15.67	15.94	16.21	16.48	16.75	17.02	17.29	17.56	17.83	18.10	18.37	18.64	18.91	19.45
85	15.47	15.74	16.01	16.28	16.55	16.82	17.09	17.37	17.64	17.91	18.18	18.45	18.73	19.00	19.27	19.82
84	15.81	16.08	16.35	16.63	16.90	17.17	17.44	17.72	17.99	18.26	18.54	18.81	19.09	19.36	19.63	20.18
83	16.15	16.43	16.70	16.98	17.25	17.53	17.80	18.08	18.35	18.63	18.90	19.18	19.45	19.73	20.01	20.56
82	16.51	16.78	17.06	17.33	17.61	17.89	18.16	18.44	18.72	19.00	19.27	19.55	19.83	20.11	20.38	20.94
81	16.87	17.14	17.42	17.70	17.98	18.26	18.53	18.81	19.09	19.37	19.65	19.93	20.21	20.49	20.77	21.33
80	17.23	17.51	17.79	18.07	18.35	18.63	18.91	19.19	19.47	19.75	20.04	20.32	20.60	20.88	21.16	21.73
79	17.61	17.89	18.17	18.45	18.73	19.01	19.30	19.58	19.86	20.15	20.43	20.71	21.00	21.28	21.56	22.13
78	17.99	18.27	18.55	18.84	19.12	19.41	19.69	19.97	20.26	20.54	20.83	21.12	21.40	21.69	21.97	22.55
77	18.37	18.66	18.95	19.23	19.52	19.80	20.09	20.38	20.66	20.95	21.24	21.53	21.81	22.10	22.39	22.97
76	18.77	19.06	19.35	19.63	19.92	20.21	20.50	20.79	21.08	21.37	21.66	21.95	22.24	22.53	22.82	23.40
75	19.17	19.46	19.75	20.04	20.33	20.63	20.92	21.21	21.50	21.79	22.08	22.37	22.67	22.96	23.25	23.84
74	19.59	19.88	20.17	20.46	20.76	21.05	21.34	21.64	21.93	22.22	22.52	22.81	23.11	23.40	23.70	24.29
73	20.01	20.30	20.60	20.89	21.19	21.48	21.78	22.07	22.37	22.67	22.96	23.26	23.56	23.85	24.15	24.75
72	20.44	20.74	21.03	21.33	21.63	21.92	22.22	22.52	22.82	23.12	23.42	23.72	24.02	24.32	24.62	25.22
71	20.88	21.18	21.48	21.78	22.08	22.38	22.68	22.98	23.28	23.58	23.88	24.18	24.49	24.79	25.09	25.70
70	21.33	21.63	21.93	22.24	22.54	22.84	23.14	23.45	23.75	24.05	24.36	24.66	24.97	25.27	25.58	26.19
65	23.74	24.06	24.37	24.69	25.01	25.32	25.64	25.96	26.28	26.59	26.91	27.23	27.55	27.87	28.19	28.84

MORTGAGE PRICE

Description: This table shows the price to pay for a monthly payment mortgage loan at the yield rate.

Example: The price of a 6.75 %, 10 year mortgage loan to yield 8.00 % to maturity is $ 94.64.

							INTEREST RATE, %									
YIELD	0.00%	1.00%	2.00%	3.00%	4.00%	4.25%	4.50%	4.75%	5.00%	5.25%	5.50%	5.75%	6.00%	6.25%	6.50%	6.75%
0.00	100.00	105.12	110.42	115.87	121.49	122.93	124.37	125.82	127.28	128.75	130.23	131.72	133.22	134.74	136.26	137.79
1.00	95.12	100.00	105.03	110.22	115.57	116.93	118.30	119.68	121.07	122.47	123.88	125.30	126.73	128.17	129.61	131.07
2.00	90.57	95.21	100.00	104.94	110.03	111.33	112.63	113.95	115.27	116.60	117.95	119.30	120.66	122.03	123.40	124.79
3.00	86.30	90.72	95.29	100.00	104.85	106.09	107.33	108.58	109.84	111.11	112.39	113.68	114.97	116.28	117.59	118.91
4.00	82.31	86.53	90.88	95.37	100.00	101.18	102.36	103.56	104.76	105.97	107.19	108.42	109.66	110.90	112.15	113.41
4.25	81.35	85.52	89.82	94.26	98.84	100.00	101.17	102.35	103.54	104.74	105.94	107.16	108.38	109.61	110.85	112.09
4.50	80.41	84.53	88.78	93.17	97.69	98.84	100.00	101.17	102.34	103.53	104.72	105.92	107.12	108.34	109.56	110.79
4.75	79.48	83.55	87.76	92.10	96.56	97.70	98.85	100.00	101.16	102.33	103.51	104.69	105.89	107.09	108.30	109.52
5.00	78.57	82.59	86.75	91.04	95.46	96.58	97.71	98.85	100.00	101.16	102.32	103.49	104.67	105.86	107.05	108.26
5.25	77.67	81.65	85.76	90.00	94.36	95.48	96.59	97.72	98.86	100.00	101.15	102.31	103.48	104.65	105.83	107.02
5.50	76.79	80.72	84.78	88.97	93.29	94.39	95.50	96.61	97.73	98.86	100.00	101.15	102.30	103.46	104.63	105.80
5.75	75.92	79.81	83.82	87.97	92.23	93.32	94.41	95.52	96.63	97.74	98.87	100.00	101.14	102.29	103.44	104.61
6.00	75.06	78.91	82.88	86.98	91.19	92.27	93.35	94.44	95.54	96.64	97.75	98.87	100.00	101.13	102.28	103.43
6.25	74.22	78.02	81.95	86.00	90.17	91.23	92.30	93.38	94.47	95.56	96.66	97.76	98.88	100.00	101.13	102.27
6.50	73.39	77.15	81.03	85.04	89.17	90.22	91.27	92.34	93.41	94.49	95.58	96.67	97.77	98.88	100.00	101.12
6.75	72.57	76.29	80.13	84.09	88.17	89.21	90.26	91.31	92.37	93.44	94.52	95.60	96.69	97.78	98.89	100.00
7.00	71.77	75.45	79.25	83.16	87.20	88.23	89.26	90.30	91.35	92.41	93.47	94.54	95.62	96.70	97.79	98.89
7.25	70.98	74.62	78.38	82.25	86.24	87.25	88.28	89.31	90.34	91.39	92.44	93.50	94.57	95.64	96.72	97.81
7.50	70.20	73.80	77.52	81.35	85.29	86.30	87.31	88.33	89.35	90.39	91.43	92.47	93.53	94.59	95.66	96.73
7.75	69.44	73.00	76.67	80.46	84.36	85.36	86.36	87.37	88.38	89.40	90.43	91.47	92.51	93.56	94.61	95.68
8.00	68.68	72.20	75.84	79.59	83.45	84.43	85.42	86.42	87.42	88.43	89.45	90.47	91.50	92.54	93.59	94.64
8.25	67.94	71.42	75.02	78.73	82.55	83.52	84.50	85.48	86.48	87.48	88.48	89.50	90.52	91.54	92.58	93.62
8.50	67.21	70.66	74.21	77.88	81.66	82.62	83.59	84.56	85.55	86.54	87.53	88.53	89.54	90.56	91.58	92.61
8.75	66.49	69.90	73.42	77.05	80.78	81.74	82.69	83.66	84.63	85.61	86.59	87.59	88.58	89.59	90.60	91.62
9.00	65.78	69.16	72.64	76.23	79.92	80.87	81.81	82.77	83.73	84.70	85.67	86.65	87.64	88.64	89.64	90.64
9.25	65.09	68.42	71.87	75.42	79.08	80.01	80.95	81.89	82.84	83.80	84.76	85.74	86.71	87.70	88.69	89.68
9.50	64.40	67.70	71.11	74.62	78.24	79.16	80.09	81.03	81.97	82.92	83.87	84.83	85.80	86.77	87.75	88.74
9.75	63.72	66.99	70.36	73.84	77.42	78.33	79.25	80.18	81.11	82.05	82.99	83.94	84.90	85.86	86.83	87.81
10.00	63.06	66.29	69.63	73.07	76.61	77.52	78.42	79.34	80.26	81.19	82.12	83.06	84.01	84.96	85.92	86.89
10.25	62.40	65.60	68.90	72.31	75.82	76.71	77.61	78.51	79.43	80.34	81.27	82.20	83.14	84.08	85.03	85.99
10.50	61.76	64.92	68.19	71.56	75.03	75.92	76.81	77.70	78.60	79.51	80.43	81.35	82.28	83.21	84.15	85.10
10.75	61.12	64.25	67.49	70.82	74.26	75.13	76.02	76.90	77.80	78.69	79.60	80.51	81.43	82.35	83.28	84.22
11.00	60.50	63.60	66.80	70.10	73.50	74.36	75.24	76.11	77.00	77.89	78.78	79.69	80.60	81.51	82.43	83.36
11.25	59.88	62.95	66.12	69.38	72.75	73.61	74.47	75.34	76.21	77.09	77.98	78.87	79.77	80.68	81.59	82.51
11.50	59.27	62.31	65.45	68.68	72.01	72.86	73.71	74.57	75.44	76.31	77.19	78.07	78.96	79.86	80.76	81.67
11.75	58.67	61.68	64.78	67.99	71.28	72.12	72.97	73.82	74.68	75.54	76.41	77.29	78.17	79.05	79.95	80.85
12.00	58.08	61.06	64.13	67.30	70.57	71.40	72.24	73.08	73.93	74.78	75.64	76.51	77.38	78.26	79.14	80.03
12.25	57.50	60.45	63.49	66.63	69.86	70.69	71.51	72.35	73.19	74.04	74.89	75.74	76.61	77.48	78.35	79.23
12.50	56.93	59.85	62.86	65.97	69.17	69.98	70.80	71.63	72.46	73.30	74.14	74.99	75.85	76.71	77.57	78.44
12.75	56.37	59.26	62.24	65.31	68.48	69.29	70.10	70.92	71.74	72.57	73.41	74.25	75.10	75.95	76.80	77.67
13.00	55.81	58.67	61.63	64.67	67.81	68.61	69.41	70.22	71.04	71.86	72.68	73.52	74.36	75.20	76.05	76.90
13.25	55.26	58.10	61.02	64.04	67.14	67.93	68.73	69.53	70.34	71.15	71.97	72.80	73.63	74.46	75.30	76.15
13.50	54.73	57.53	60.43	63.41	66.49	67.27	68.06	68.85	69.65	70.46	71.27	72.09	72.91	73.74	74.57	75.41
13.75	54.19	56.97	59.84	62.80	65.84	66.62	67.40	68.19	68.98	69.78	70.58	71.39	72.20	73.02	73.84	74.67
14.00	53.67	56.42	59.26	62.19	65.21	65.98	66.75	67.53	68.31	69.10	69.90	70.70	71.50	72.31	73.13	73.95
14.25	53.16	55.88	58.69	61.59	64.58	65.34	66.11	66.88	67.66	68.44	69.23	70.02	70.82	71.62	72.43	73.24
14.50	52.65	55.35	58.13	61.00	63.96	64.72	65.48	66.24	67.01	67.78	68.56	69.35	70.14	70.93	71.74	72.54
14.75	52.15	54.82	57.58	60.42	63.35	64.10	64.85	65.61	66.37	67.14	67.91	68.69	69.47	70.26	71.05	71.85
15.00	51.65	54.30	57.03	59.85	62.75	63.49	64.24	64.99	65.74	66.50	67.27	68.04	68.81	69.59	70.38	71.17
15.25	51.17	53.79	56.50	59.29	62.16	62.90	63.63	64.38	65.12	65.88	66.63	67.40	68.17	68.94	69.72	70.50
15.50	50.69	53.28	55.97	58.73	61.58	62.31	63.04	63.77	64.51	65.26	66.01	66.77	67.53	68.29	69.06	69.84
15.75	50.21	52.79	55.44	58.18	61.01	61.72	62.45	63.18	63.91	64.65	65.39	66.14	66.90	67.66	68.42	69.19
16.00	49.75	52.30	54.93	57.64	60.44	61.15	61.87	62.59	63.32	64.05	64.79	65.53	66.28	67.03	67.78	68.55
16.25	49.29	51.81	54.42	57.11	59.88	60.59	61.30	62.01	62.73	63.46	64.19	64.92	65.66	66.41	67.16	67.91
16.50	48.84	51.34	53.92	56.59	59.33	60.03	60.73	61.44	62.16	62.88	63.60	64.33	65.06	65.80	66.54	67.29
16.75	48.39	50.87	53.43	56.07	58.79	59.48	60.18	60.88	61.59	62.30	63.02	63.74	64.47	65.20	65.93	66.67
17.00	47.95	50.41	52.94	55.56	58.25	58.94	59.63	60.33	61.03	61.73	62.44	63.16	63.88	64.60	65.33	66.07
17.25	47.51	49.95	52.46	55.06	57.73	58.41	59.09	59.78	60.48	61.17	61.88	62.59	63.30	64.02	64.74	65.47
17.50	47.09	49.50	51.99	54.56	57.21	57.88	58.56	59.24	59.93	60.62	61.32	62.02	62.73	63.44	64.16	64.88
17.75	46.66	49.06	51.53	54.07	56.69	57.36	58.04	58.71	59.39	60.08	60.77	61.47	62.17	62.87	63.58	64.30
18.00	46.25	48.62	51.07	53.59	56.19	56.85	57.52	58.19	58.86	59.55	60.23	60.92	61.61	62.31	63.02	63.73
18.25	45.84	48.19	50.61	53.11	55.69	56.35	57.01	57.67	58.34	59.02	59.70	60.38	61.07	61.76	62.46	63.16
18.50	45.43	47.76	50.17	52.65	55.20	55.85	56.50	57.16	57.83	58.50	59.17	59.85	60.53	61.22	61.91	62.60
18.75	45.03	47.34	49.73	52.18	54.71	55.36	56.01	56.66	57.32	57.98	58.65	59.32	60.00	60.68	61.36	62.05
19.00	44.64	46.93	49.29	51.73	54.24	54.88	55.52	56.17	56.82	57.48	58.14	58.80	59.47	60.15	60.83	61.51
20.00	43.12	45.33	47.61	49.97	52.39	53.01	53.63	54.25	54.88	55.52	56.16	56.80	57.45	58.10	58.76	59.42
25.00	36.63	38.51	40.45	42.45	44.50	45.03	45.56	46.09	46.62	47.16	47.71	48.25	48.80	49.36	49.91	50.47
30.00	31.61	33.23	34.90	36.63	38.41	38.86	39.31	39.77	40.23	40.70	41.17	41.64	42.11	42.59	43.07	43.56

Description: This table shows the yield to maturity of a mortgage purchased at the price shown in the index.

Example: The yield to maturity of a 6.75 %, 10 year mortgage at a price of 80.00 is 12.01 %.

INTEREST RATE, %

PRICE	0.00%	1.00%	2.00%	3.00%	4.00%	4.25%	4.50%	4.75%	5.00%	5.25%	5.50%	5.75%	6.00%	6.25%	6.50%	6.75%
100	0.00	1.00	2.00	3.00	4.00	4.25	4.50	4.75	5.00	5.25	5.50	5.75	6.00	6.25	6.50	6.75
99	.19	1.20	2.20	3.21	4.21	4.46	4.71	4.96	5.21	5.46	5.72	5.97	6.22	6.47	6.72	6.97
98	.40	1.40	2.41	3.42	4.43	4.68	4.93	5.18	5.44	5.69	5.94	6.19	6.44	6.70	6.95	7.20
97	.60	1.61	2.62	3.64	4.65	4.90	5.15	5.41	5.66	5.91	6.17	6.42	6.67	6.93	7.18	7.43
96	.81	1.83	2.84	3.86	4.87	5.13	5.38	5.63	5.89	6.14	6.40	6.65	6.91	7.16	7.41	7.67
95	1.02	2.04	3.06	4.08	5.10	5.35	5.61	5.86	6.12	6.38	6.63	6.89	7.14	7.40	7.65	7.91
94	1.24	2.26	3.28	4.30	5.33	5.59	5.84	6.10	6.35	6.61	6.87	7.12	7.38	7.64	7.89	8.15
93	1.45	2.48	3.51	4.53	5.56	5.82	6.08	6.34	6.59	6.85	7.11	7.37	7.62	7.88	8.14	8.40
92	1.67	2.70	3.74	4.77	5.80	6.06	6.32	6.58	6.84	7.09	7.35	7.61	7.87	8.13	8.39	8.65
91	1.90	2.93	3.97	5.00	6.04	6.30	6.56	6.82	7.08	7.34	7.60	7.86	8.12	8.38	8.64	8.90
90	2.12	3.16	4.20	5.24	6.29	6.55	6.81	7.07	7.33	7.59	7.85	8.11	8.37	8.64	8.90	9.16
89	2.35	3.40	4.44	5.49	6.54	6.80	7.06	7.32	7.59	7.85	8.11	8.37	8.64	8.90	9.16	9.43
88	2.59	3.64	4.69	5.74	6.79	7.05	7.32	7.58	7.84	8.11	8.37	8.64	8.90	9.16	9.43	9.69
87	2.83	3.88	4.93	5.99	7.05	7.31	7.58	7.84	8.11	8.37	8.64	8.90	9.17	9.43	9.70	9.96
86	3.07	4.13	5.18	6.24	7.31	7.57	7.84	8.11	8.37	8.64	8.91	9.17	9.44	9.71	9.97	10.24
85	3.31	4.38	5.44	6.51	7.57	7.84	8.11	8.38	8.64	8.91	9.18	9.45	9.72	9.98	10.25	10.52
84	3.56	4.63	5.70	6.77	7.84	8.11	8.38	8.65	8.92	9.19	9.46	9.73	10.00	10.27	10.54	10.81
83	3.82	4.89	5.96	7.04	8.12	8.39	8.66	8.93	9.20	9.47	9.74	10.01	10.28	10.56	10.83	11.10
82	4.08	5.15	6.23	7.31	8.40	8.67	8.94	9.21	9.49	9.76	10.03	10.30	10.58	10.85	11.12	11.40
81	4.34	5.42	6.50	7.59	8.68	8.96	9.23	9.50	9.78	10.05	10.32	10.60	10.87	11.15	11.42	11.70
80	4.60	5.69	6.78	7.88	8.97	9.25	9.52	9.80	10.07	10.35	10.62	10.90	11.18	11.45	11.73	12.01
79	4.88	5.97	7.07	8.17	9.27	9.54	9.82	10.10	10.37	10.65	10.93	11.21	11.48	11.76	12.04	12.32
78	5.15	6.25	7.35	8.46	9.57	9.85	10.12	10.40	10.68	10.96	11.24	11.52	11.80	12.08	12.36	12.64
77	5.43	6.54	7.65	8.76	9.88	10.15	10.43	10.71	10.99	11.28	11.56	11.84	12.12	12.40	12.68	12.96
76	5.72	6.83	7.95	9.06	10.19	10.47	10.75	11.03	11.31	11.60	11.88	12.16	12.44	12.73	13.01	13.29
75	6.01	7.13	8.25	9.38	10.51	10.79	11.07	11.36	11.64	11.92	12.21	12.49	12.78	13.06	13.35	13.63
74	6.31	7.43	8.56	9.69	10.83	11.11	11.40	11.69	11.97	12.26	12.54	12.83	13.12	13.40	13.69	13.98
73	6.61	7.74	8.88	10.02	11.16	11.45	11.73	12.02	12.31	12.60	12.89	13.17	13.46	13.75	14.04	14.33
72	6.92	8.06	9.20	10.35	11.50	11.79	12.08	12.37	12.66	12.95	13.24	13.53	13.82	14.11	14.40	14.69
71	7.24	8.38	9.53	10.69	11.84	12.13	12.43	12.72	13.01	13.30	13.59	13.88	14.18	14.47	14.76	15.06
70	7.56	8.71	9.87	11.03	12.20	12.49	12.78	13.07	13.37	13.66	13.96	14.25	14.55	14.84	15.14	15.43
69	7.89	9.05	10.21	11.38	12.56	12.85	13.15	13.44	13.74	14.03	14.33	14.63	14.92	15.22	15.52	15.82
68	8.23	9.39	10.56	11.74	12.92	13.22	13.52	13.82	14.11	14.41	14.71	15.01	15.31	15.61	15.91	16.21
67	8.57	9.74	10.92	12.11	13.30	13.60	13.90	14.20	14.50	14.80	15.10	15.40	15.70	16.01	16.31	16.61
66	8.92	10.10	11.29	12.48	13.68	13.99	14.29	14.59	14.89	15.20	15.50	15.80	16.11	16.41	16.72	17.02
65	9.28	10.47	11.66	12.87	14.08	14.38	14.69	14.99	15.30	15.60	15.91	16.21	16.52	16.83	17.14	17.44
64	9.64	10.84	12.05	13.26	14.48	14.79	15.09	15.40	15.71	16.02	16.32	16.63	16.94	17.25	17.56	17.87
63	10.02	11.22	12.44	13.66	14.89	15.20	15.51	15.82	16.13	16.44	16.75	17.06	17.38	17.69	18.00	18.32
62	10.40	11.62	12.84	14.07	15.31	15.63	15.94	16.25	16.56	16.88	17.19	17.51	17.82	18.14	18.45	18.77
61	10.79	12.02	13.25	14.50	15.75	16.06	16.38	16.69	17.01	17.32	17.64	17.96	18.28	18.60	18.91	19.23
60	11.20	12.43	13.68	14.93	16.19	16.51	16.83	17.14	17.46	17.78	18.10	18.42	18.74	19.07	19.39	19.71
59	11.61	12.85	14.11	15.37	16.65	16.97	17.29	17.61	17.93	18.25	18.58	18.90	19.22	19.55	19.87	20.20
58	12.03	13.29	14.55	15.83	17.12	17.44	17.76	18.09	18.41	18.74	19.06	19.39	19.72	20.04	20.37	20.70
57	12.46	13.73	15.01	16.30	17.60	17.92	18.25	18.58	18.90	19.23	19.56	19.89	20.22	20.55	20.89	21.22
56	12.91	14.19	15.48	16.78	18.09	18.42	18.75	19.08	19.41	19.74	20.08	20.41	20.74	21.08	21.42	21.75
55	13.37	14.66	15.96	17.27	18.60	18.93	19.26	19.60	19.93	20.27	20.61	20.94	21.28	21.62	21.96	22.30
54	13.84	15.14	16.46	17.78	19.12	19.46	19.79	20.13	20.47	20.81	21.15	21.49	21.83	22.18	22.52	22.86
53	14.32	15.64	16.97	18.31	19.66	20.00	20.34	20.68	21.02	21.37	21.71	22.06	22.40	22.75	23.10	23.44
52	14.82	16.15	17.49	18.85	20.21	20.56	20.90	21.25	21.59	21.94	22.29	22.64	22.99	23.34	23.69	24.04
51	15.33	16.67	18.03	19.40	20.78	21.13	21.48	21.83	22.18	22.53	22.89	23.24	23.59	23.95	24.30	24.66
50	15.86	17.22	18.59	19.97	21.37	21.73	22.08	22.43	22.79	23.15	23.50	23.86	24.22	24.58	24.94	25.30
49	16.40	17.78	19.16	20.57	21.98	22.34	22.70	23.06	23.42	23.78	24.14	24.50	24.86	25.23	25.59	25.96
48	16.97	18.35	19.76	21.18	22.61	22.98	23.34	23.70	24.07	24.43	24.80	25.16	25.53	25.90	26.27	26.64
47	17.55	18.95	20.37	21.81	23.27	23.63	24.00	24.37	24.74	25.11	25.48	25.85	26.22	26.60	26.97	27.35
46	18.15	19.57	21.01	22.47	23.94	24.31	24.68	25.06	25.43	25.81	26.18	26.56	26.94	27.32	27.70	28.08
45	18.77	20.21	21.67	23.14	24.64	25.02	25.39	25.77	26.15	26.53	26.92	27.30	27.68	28.07	28.46	28.85
44	19.41	20.87	22.35	23.85	25.36	25.75	26.13	26.51	26.90	27.29	27.68	28.06	28.46	28.85	29.24	29.64
43	20.08	21.56	23.06	24.58	26.12	26.51	26.89	27.29	27.68	28.07	28.46	28.86	29.26	29.66	30.06	30.46
42	20.77	22.27	23.79	25.34	26.90	27.29	27.69	28.09	28.49	28.89	29.29	29.69	30.09	30.50	30.90	31.31
41	21.49	23.01	24.56	26.13	27.72	28.12	28.52	28.92	29.33	29.73	30.14	30.55	30.96	31.37	31.79	32.20
40	22.24	23.78	25.35	26.95	28.56	28.97	29.38	29.79	30.20	30.62	31.03	31.45	31.87	32.29	32.71	33.13
39	23.01	24.59	26.18	27.81	29.45	29.87	30.28	30.70	31.12	31.54	31.96	32.39	32.81	33.24	33.67	34.10
38	23.83	25.43	27.05	28.70	30.38	30.80	31.22	31.65	32.08	32.51	32.94	33.37	33.80	34.24	34.68	35.12
37	24.67	26.30	27.96	29.64	31.34	31.78	32.21	32.64	33.08	33.52	33.96	34.40	34.84	35.29	35.73	36.18
36	25.56	27.22	28.90	30.62	32.36	32.80	33.24	33.68	34.13	34.58	35.03	35.48	35.93	36.38	36.84	37.30
35	26.49	28.18	29.90	31.65	33.42	33.87	34.32	34.78	35.23	35.69	36.15	36.61	37.07	37.54	38.00	38.47
30	31.90	33.79	35.71	37.67	39.68	40.18	40.69	41.20	41.72	42.24	42.76	43.28	43.80	44.33	44.86	45.39
25	39.15	41.32	43.55	45.83	48.16	48.75	49.35	49.95	50.55	51.15	51.76	52.37	52.99	53.61	54.23	54.85

MORTGAGE PRICE

Description: This table shows the price to pay for a monthly payment mortgage loan at the yield rate.

Example: The price of a 10.75 %, 10 year mortgage loan to yield 8.00 % to maturity is $ 112.37.

INTEREST RATE, %

YIELD	7.00%	7.25%	7.50%	7.75%	8.00%	8.25%	8.50%	8.75%	9.00%	9.25%	9.50%	9.75%	10.00%	10.25%	10.50%	10.75%
0.00	139.33	140.88	142.44	144.01	145.59	147.18	148.78	150.39	152.01	153.64	155.28	156.92	158.58	160.25	161.92	163.61
1.00	132.54	134.01	135.50	136.99	138.50	140.01	141.53	143.06	144.60	146.15	147.71	149.27	150.85	152.43	154.03	155.63
2.00	126.19	127.59	129.00	130.43	131.86	133.30	134.75	136.20	137.67	139.15	140.63	142.12	143.62	145.13	146.65	148.17
3.00	120.24	121.58	122.93	124.29	125.65	127.02	128.40	129.79	131.19	132.59	134.01	135.43	136.86	138.30	139.74	141.19
4.00	114.68	115.96	117.24	118.53	119.84	121.14	122.46	123.79	125.12	126.46	127.81	129.16	130.53	131.90	133.28	134.66
4.25	113.35	114.61	115.88	117.15	118.44	119.73	121.04	122.34	123.66	124.99	126.32	127.66	129.01	130.36	131.72	133.09
4.50	112.03	113.28	114.53	115.80	117.07	118.35	119.63	120.93	122.23	123.54	124.85	126.18	127.51	128.85	130.20	131.55
4.75	110.74	111.97	113.21	114.46	115.72	116.98	118.25	119.53	120.82	122.11	123.41	124.72	126.04	127.36	128.70	130.03
5.00	109.47	110.69	111.91	113.15	114.39	115.64	116.90	118.16	119.43	120.71	122.00	123.29	124.59	125.90	127.22	128.54
5.25	108.22	109.42	110.63	111.85	113.08	114.32	115.56	116.81	118.07	119.33	120.60	121.88	123.17	124.46	125.76	127.07
5.50	106.99	108.18	109.38	110.58	111.80	113.02	114.24	115.48	116.72	117.97	119.23	120.50	121.77	123.05	124.33	125.63
5.75	105.78	106.95	108.14	109.33	110.53	111.74	112.95	114.17	115.40	116.64	117.88	119.13	120.39	121.65	122.93	124.20
6.00	104.58	105.75	106.92	108.10	109.28	110.48	111.68	112.89	114.10	115.32	116.55	117.79	119.03	120.28	121.54	122.80
6.25	103.41	104.56	105.72	106.89	108.06	109.24	110.43	111.62	112.82	114.03	115.25	116.47	117.70	118.93	120.18	121.43
6.50	102.25	103.39	104.54	105.69	106.85	108.02	109.19	110.37	111.56	112.76	113.96	115.17	116.38	117.61	118.84	120.07
6.75	101.12	102.24	103.38	104.52	105.66	106.82	107.98	109.15	110.32	111.50	112.69	113.89	115.09	116.30	117.51	118.74
7.00	100.00	101.11	102.23	103.36	104.50	105.64	106.78	107.94	109.10	110.27	111.45	112.63	113.82	115.01	116.21	117.42
7.25	98.90	100.00	101.11	102.22	103.34	104.47	105.61	106.75	107.90	109.06	110.22	111.39	112.56	113.75	114.94	116.13
7.50	97.82	98.90	100.00	101.10	102.21	103.33	104.45	105.58	106.72	107.86	109.01	110.17	111.33	112.50	113.68	114.86
7.75	96.75	97.83	98.91	100.00	101.10	102.20	103.31	104.43	105.55	106.68	107.82	108.97	110.12	111.27	112.44	113.61
8.00	95.70	96.76	97.84	98.91	100.00	101.09	102.19	103.30	104.41	105.53	106.65	107.78	108.92	110.06	111.22	112.37
8.25	94.66	95.72	96.78	97.85	98.92	100.00	101.09	102.18	103.28	104.39	105.50	106.62	107.74	108.88	110.01	111.16
8.50	93.65	94.69	95.74	96.79	97.86	98.92	100.00	101.08	102.17	103.26	104.36	105.47	106.59	107.71	108.83	109.96
8.75	92.64	93.68	94.71	95.76	96.81	97.87	98.93	100.00	101.08	102.16	103.25	104.34	105.44	106.55	107.67	108.79
9.00	91.66	92.68	93.71	94.74	95.78	96.82	97.88	98.94	100.00	101.07	102.15	103.23	104.32	105.42	106.52	107.63
9.25	90.69	91.70	92.71	93.73	94.76	95.80	96.84	97.89	98.94	100.00	101.07	102.14	103.22	104.30	105.39	106.49
9.50	89.73	90.73	91.73	92.75	93.76	94.79	95.82	96.85	97.90	98.95	100.00	101.06	102.13	103.20	104.28	105.36
9.75	88.79	89.78	90.77	91.77	92.78	93.79	94.81	95.84	96.87	97.91	98.95	100.00	101.06	102.12	103.18	104.26
10.00	87.86	88.84	89.82	90.81	91.81	92.81	93.82	94.84	95.86	96.88	97.92	98.96	100.00	101.05	102.11	103.17
10.25	86.95	87.92	88.89	89.87	90.86	91.85	92.85	93.85	94.86	95.88	96.90	97.93	98.96	100.00	101.05	102.10
10.50	86.05	87.01	87.97	88.94	89.92	90.90	91.89	92.88	93.88	94.88	95.90	96.91	97.94	98.97	100.00	101.04
10.75	85.16	86.11	87.06	88.02	88.99	89.96	90.94	91.92	92.91	93.91	94.91	95.92	96.93	97.95	98.97	100.00
11.00	84.29	85.23	86.17	87.12	88.08	89.04	90.01	90.98	91.96	92.95	93.94	94.93	95.94	96.94	97.96	98.98
11.25	83.43	84.36	85.29	86.23	87.18	88.13	89.09	90.05	91.02	92.00	92.98	93.97	94.96	95.95	96.96	97.97
11.50	82.58	83.50	84.43	85.36	86.30	87.24	88.19	89.14	90.10	91.06	92.04	93.01	93.99	94.98	95.97	96.97
11.75	81.75	82.66	83.58	84.50	85.42	86.36	87.30	88.24	89.19	90.15	91.11	92.07	93.04	94.02	95.00	95.99
12.00	80.93	81.83	82.74	83.65	84.57	85.49	86.42	87.35	88.29	89.24	90.19	91.15	92.11	93.08	94.05	95.03
12.25	80.12	81.01	81.91	82.81	83.72	84.63	85.55	86.48	87.41	88.35	89.29	90.24	91.19	92.15	93.11	94.08
12.50	79.32	80.21	81.09	81.99	82.89	83.79	84.70	85.62	86.54	87.47	88.40	89.34	90.28	91.23	92.18	93.14
12.75	78.54	79.41	80.29	81.18	82.07	82.96	83.86	84.77	85.68	86.60	87.53	88.45	89.39	90.33	91.27	92.22
13.00	77.76	78.63	79.50	80.38	81.26	82.15	83.04	83.94	84.84	85.75	86.66	87.58	88.51	89.44	90.37	91.31
13.25	77.00	77.86	78.72	79.59	80.46	81.34	82.22	83.11	84.01	84.91	85.81	86.72	87.64	88.56	89.49	90.42
13.50	76.25	77.10	77.95	78.81	79.68	80.55	81.42	82.30	83.19	84.08	84.98	85.88	86.78	87.70	88.61	89.53
13.75	75.51	76.35	77.20	78.05	78.90	79.77	80.63	81.50	82.38	83.26	84.15	85.04	85.94	86.85	87.75	88.67
14.00	74.78	75.61	76.45	77.29	78.14	78.99	79.85	80.72	81.59	82.46	83.34	84.22	85.11	86.01	86.91	87.81
14.25	74.06	74.89	75.72	76.55	77.39	78.24	79.09	79.94	80.80	81.67	82.54	83.41	84.29	85.18	86.07	86.97
14.50	73.35	74.17	74.99	75.82	76.65	77.49	78.33	79.18	80.03	80.89	81.75	82.62	83.49	84.37	85.25	86.13
14.75	72.66	73.46	74.28	75.10	75.92	76.75	77.58	78.42	79.27	80.12	80.97	81.83	82.69	83.56	84.44	85.31
15.00	71.97	72.77	73.57	74.39	75.20	76.02	76.85	77.68	78.52	79.36	80.20	81.06	81.91	82.77	83.64	84.51
15.25	71.29	72.08	72.88	73.69	74.49	75.31	76.13	76.95	77.78	78.61	79.45	80.29	81.14	81.99	82.85	83.71
15.50	70.62	71.41	72.20	72.99	73.80	74.60	75.41	76.23	77.05	77.87	78.70	79.54	80.38	81.22	82.07	82.93
15.75	69.96	70.74	71.52	72.31	73.11	73.91	74.71	75.52	76.33	77.15	77.97	78.80	79.63	80.47	81.31	82.15
16.00	69.31	70.08	70.86	71.64	72.43	73.22	74.02	74.82	75.62	76.43	77.25	78.07	78.89	79.72	80.55	81.39
16.25	68.67	69.44	70.21	70.98	71.76	72.54	73.33	74.13	74.92	75.73	76.53	77.34	78.16	78.98	79.81	80.64
16.50	68.04	68.80	69.56	70.33	71.10	71.88	72.66	73.44	74.23	75.03	75.83	76.63	77.44	78.26	79.07	79.90
16.75	67.42	68.17	68.93	69.69	70.45	71.22	71.99	72.77	73.56	74.34	75.14	75.93	76.74	77.54	78.35	79.17
17.00	66.81	67.55	68.30	69.05	69.81	70.57	71.34	72.11	72.89	73.67	74.45	75.24	76.04	76.84	77.64	78.45
17.25	66.20	66.94	67.68	68.43	69.18	69.93	70.69	71.46	72.23	73.00	73.78	74.56	75.35	76.14	76.94	77.74
17.50	65.61	66.34	67.07	67.81	68.55	69.30	70.06	70.81	71.58	72.34	73.11	73.89	74.67	75.45	76.24	77.04
17.75	65.02	65.74	66.47	67.20	67.94	68.68	69.43	70.18	70.94	71.70	72.46	73.23	74.00	74.78	75.56	76.35
18.00	64.44	65.16	65.88	66.60	67.33	68.07	68.81	69.55	70.30	71.06	71.81	72.58	73.34	74.11	74.89	75.67
18.25	63.87	64.58	65.29	66.01	66.74	67.47	68.20	68.94	69.68	70.43	71.18	71.93	72.69	73.45	74.22	74.99
18.50	63.30	64.01	64.72	65.43	66.15	66.87	67.60	68.33	69.06	69.80	70.55	71.30	72.05	72.81	73.57	74.33
18.75	62.75	63.45	64.15	64.86	65.57	66.28	67.00	67.73	68.45	69.19	69.93	70.67	71.42	72.17	72.92	73.68
19.00	62.20	62.89	63.59	64.29	64.99	65.70	66.42	67.14	67.86	68.59	69.32	70.05	70.79	71.54	72.28	73.04
20.00	60.08	60.75	61.42	62.10	62.78	63.47	64.16	64.85	65.55	66.25	66.96	67.67	68.38	69.10	69.82	70.55
25.00	51.04	51.61	52.18	52.75	53.33	53.91	54.50	55.09	55.68	56.28	56.88	57.48	58.09	58.70	59.31	59.93
30.00	44.04	44.53	45.03	45.52	46.02	46.53	47.03	47.54	48.05	48.57	49.09	49.61	50.13	50.66	51.19	51.72

Description: This table shows the yield to maturity of a mortgage purchased at the price shown in the index.

Example: The yield to maturity of a 10.75 %, 10 year mortgage at a price of 105.00 is 9.58 %.

INTEREST RATE, %

PRICE	7.00%	7.25%	7.50%	7.75%	8.00%	8.25%	8.50%	8.75%	9.00%	9.25%	9.50%	9.75%	10.00%	10.25%	10.50%	10.75%
125	2.19	2.42	2.65	2.88	3.10	3.33	3.56	3.79	4.02	4.24	4.47	4.70	4.92	5.15	5.38	5.60
124	2.36	2.58	2.81	3.04	3.27	3.50	3.73	3.96	4.19	4.41	4.64	4.87	5.10	5.33	5.55	5.78
123	2.52	2.75	2.98	3.21	3.44	3.67	3.90	4.13	4.36	4.59	4.82	5.05	5.28	5.50	5.73	5.96
122	2.69	2.92	3.15	3.38	3.61	3.85	4.08	4.31	4.54	4.77	4.99	5.22	5.45	5.68	5.91	6.14
121	2.86	3.10	3.33	3.56	3.79	4.02	4.25	4.48	4.71	4.94	5.17	5.40	5.63	5.86	6.09	6.32
120	3.04	3.27	3.50	3.73	3.97	4.20	4.43	4.66	4.89	5.12	5.35	5.59	5.82	6.05	6.28	6.51
119	3.21	3.45	3.68	3.91	4.14	4.38	4.61	4.84	5.07	5.31	5.54	5.77	6.00	6.23	6.46	6.70
118	3.39	3.62	3.86	4.09	4.32	4.56	4.79	5.02	5.26	5.49	5.72	5.96	6.19	6.42	6.65	6.88
117	3.57	3.80	4.04	4.27	4.51	4.74	4.98	5.21	5.44	5.68	5.91	6.14	6.38	6.61	6.84	7.08
116	3.75	3.99	4.22	4.46	4.69	4.93	5.16	5.40	5.63	5.87	6.10	6.33	6.57	6.80	7.04	7.27
115	3.94	4.17	4.41	4.64	4.88	5.12	5.35	5.59	5.82	6.06	6.29	6.53	6.76	7.00	7.23	7.47
114	4.12	4.36	4.60	4.83	5.07	5.31	5.54	5.78	6.01	6.25	6.49	6.72	6.96	7.19	7.43	7.67
113	4.31	4.55	4.79	5.02	5.26	5.50	5.74	5.97	6.21	6.45	6.68	6.92	7.16	7.39	7.63	7.87
112	4.50	4.74	4.98	5.22	5.46	5.69	5.93	6.17	6.41	6.65	6.88	7.12	7.36	7.60	7.83	8.07
111	4.69	4.93	5.17	5.41	5.65	5.89	6.13	6.37	6.61	6.85	7.09	7.32	7.56	7.80	8.04	8.28
110	4.89	5.13	5.37	5.61	5.85	6.09	6.33	6.57	6.81	7.05	7.29	7.53	7.77	8.01	8.25	8.49
109	5.09	5.33	5.57	5.81	6.05	6.29	6.53	6.78	7.02	7.26	7.50	7.74	7.98	8.22	8.46	8.70
108	5.29	5.53	5.77	6.02	6.26	6.50	6.74	6.98	7.22	7.47	7.71	7.95	8.19	8.43	8.67	8.91
107	5.49	5.74	5.98	6.22	6.46	6.71	6.95	7.19	7.43	7.68	7.92	8.16	8.41	8.65	8.89	9.13
106	5.70	5.94	6.19	6.43	6.67	6.92	7.16	7.41	7.65	7.89	8.14	8.38	8.62	8.87	9.11	9.35
105	5.91	6.15	6.40	6.64	6.89	7.13	7.38	7.62	7.87	8.11	8.35	8.60	8.84	9.09	9.33	9.58
104	6.12	6.36	6.61	6.86	7.10	7.35	7.59	7.84	8.09	8.33	8.58	8.82	9.07	9.31	9.56	9.80
103	6.33	6.58	6.83	7.07	7.32	7.57	7.81	8.06	8.31	8.55	8.80	9.05	9.29	9.54	9.79	10.03
102	6.55	6.80	7.05	7.29	7.54	7.79	8.04	8.29	8.53	8.78	9.03	9.28	9.52	9.77	10.02	10.27
101	6.77	7.02	7.27	7.52	7.77	8.02	8.26	8.51	8.76	9.01	9.26	9.51	9.76	10.01	10.26	10.50
100	7.00	7.25	7.50	7.75	8.00	8.25	8.50	8.75	9.00	9.25	9.50	9.75	10.00	10.25	10.50	10.75
99	7.22	7.47	7.72	7.98	8.23	8.48	8.73	8.98	9.23	9.48	9.72	9.97	10.24	10.49	10.74	10.99
98	7.45	7.70	7.96	8.21	8.46	8.71	8.97	9.22	9.47	9.72	9.97	10.23	10.48	10.73	10.98	11.24
97	7.69	7.94	8.19	8.45	8.70	8.95	9.21	9.46	9.71	9.97	10.22	10.47	10.73	10.98	11.23	11.49
96	7.92	8.18	8.43	8.69	8.94	9.20	9.45	9.70	9.96	10.21	10.47	10.72	10.98	11.23	11.49	11.74
95	8.16	8.42	8.67	8.93	9.19	9.44	9.70	9.95	10.21	10.47	10.72	10.98	11.23	11.49	11.75	12.00
94	8.41	8.66	8.92	9.18	9.44	9.69	9.95	10.21	10.46	10.72	10.98	11.24	11.49	11.75	12.01	12.27
93	8.66	8.91	9.17	9.43	9.69	9.95	10.21	10.46	10.72	10.98	11.24	11.50	11.76	12.02	12.27	12.53
92	8.91	9.17	9.43	9.69	9.95	10.21	10.47	10.72	10.98	11.24	11.50	11.76	12.02	12.28	12.55	12.81
91	9.16	9.42	9.69	9.95	10.21	10.47	10.73	10.99	11.25	11.51	11.77	12.04	12.30	12.56	12.82	13.08
90	9.42	9.69	9.95	10.21	10.47	10.73	11.00	11.26	11.52	11.78	12.05	12.31	12.57	12.84	13.10	13.36
89	9.69	9.95	10.22	10.48	10.74	11.01	11.27	11.53	11.80	12.06	12.33	12.59	12.85	13.12	13.38	13.65
88	9.96	10.22	10.49	10.75	11.02	11.28	11.55	11.81	12.08	12.34	12.61	12.87	13.14	13.41	13.67	13.94
87	10.23	10.50	10.76	11.03	11.30	11.56	11.83	12.10	12.36	12.63	12.90	13.16	13.43	13.70	13.97	14.23
86	10.51	10.78	11.04	11.31	11.58	11.85	12.12	12.38	12.65	12.92	13.19	13.46	13.73	14.00	14.27	14.54
85	10.79	11.06	11.33	11.60	11.87	12.14	12.41	12.68	12.95	13.22	13.49	13.76	14.03	14.30	14.57	14.84
84	11.08	11.35	11.62	11.89	12.16	12.43	12.70	12.98	13.25	13.52	13.79	14.06	14.34	14.61	14.88	15.15
83	11.37	11.64	11.92	12.19	12.46	12.73	13.01	13.28	13.55	13.83	14.10	14.37	14.65	14.92	15.20	15.47
82	11.67	11.94	12.22	12.49	12.77	13.04	13.31	13.59	13.86	14.14	14.42	14.69	14.97	15.24	15.52	15.79
81	11.97	12.25	12.52	12.80	13.08	13.35	13.63	13.90	14.18	14.46	14.74	15.01	15.29	15.57	15.85	16.12
80	12.28	12.56	12.84	13.11	13.39	13.67	13.95	14.23	14.50	14.78	15.06	15.34	15.62	15.90	16.18	16.46
79	12.60	12.88	13.15	13.43	13.71	13.99	14.27	14.55	14.83	15.11	15.40	15.68	15.96	16.24	16.52	16.80
78	12.92	13.20	13.48	13.76	14.04	14.32	14.61	14.89	15.17	15.45	15.73	16.02	16.30	16.58	16.87	17.15
77	13.25	13.53	13.81	14.09	14.38	14.66	14.94	15.23	15.51	15.80	16.08	16.37	16.65	16.94	17.22	17.51
76	13.58	13.86	14.15	14.43	14.72	15.00	15.29	15.57	15.86	16.15	16.43	16.72	17.01	17.30	17.58	17.87
75	13.92	14.21	14.49	14.78	15.07	15.35	15.64	15.93	16.22	16.51	16.79	17.08	17.37	17.66	17.95	18.24
74	14.27	14.55	14.84	15.13	15.42	15.71	16.00	16.29	16.58	16.87	17.16	17.45	17.75	18.04	18.33	18.62
73	14.62	14.91	15.20	15.49	15.78	16.08	16.37	16.66	16.95	17.25	17.54	17.83	18.13	18.42	18.71	19.01
72	14.98	15.28	15.57	15.86	16.15	16.45	16.74	17.04	17.33	17.63	17.92	18.22	18.51	18.81	19.11	19.40
71	15.35	15.65	15.94	16.24	16.53	16.83	17.13	17.42	17.72	18.02	18.31	18.61	18.91	19.21	19.51	19.81
70	15.73	16.03	16.32	16.62	16.92	17.22	17.52	17.82	18.12	18.42	18.72	19.02	19.32	19.62	19.92	20.22
69	16.12	16.42	16.72	17.02	17.32	17.62	17.92	18.22	18.52	18.82	19.13	19.43	19.73	20.04	20.34	20.65
68	16.51	16.81	17.12	17.42	17.72	18.02	18.33	18.63	18.94	19.24	19.55	19.85	20.16	20.46	20.77	21.08
67	16.92	17.22	17.52	17.83	18.13	18.44	18.75	19.05	19.36	19.67	19.98	20.28	20.59	20.90	21.21	21.52
66	17.33	17.64	17.94	18.25	18.56	18.87	19.18	19.49	19.80	20.11	20.42	20.73	21.04	21.35	21.66	21.98
65	17.75	18.06	18.37	18.68	18.99	19.30	19.62	19.93	20.24	20.55	20.87	21.18	21.50	21.81	22.13	22.44
64	18.19	18.50	18.81	19.12	19.44	19.75	20.07	20.38	20.70	21.01	21.33	21.65	21.96	22.28	22.60	22.92
63	18.63	18.95	19.26	19.58	19.89	20.21	20.53	20.85	21.16	21.48	21.80	22.12	22.44	22.77	23.09	23.41
62	19.09	19.40	19.72	20.04	20.36	20.68	21.00	21.32	21.64	21.97	22.29	22.61	22.94	23.26	23.59	23.91
60	20.03	20.36	20.68	21.01	21.33	21.66	21.99	22.31	22.64	22.97	23.30	23.63	23.96	24.29	24.63	24.96
55	22.64	22.98	23.32	23.67	24.01	24.36	24.70	25.05	25.40	25.74	26.09	26.44	26.79	27.14	27.49	27.85
50	25.66	26.03	26.39	26.76	27.12	27.49	27.86	28.23	28.60	28.97	29.34	29.71	30.09	30.46	30.84	31.22
45	29.23	29.63	30.02	30.41	30.80	31.20	31.60	31.99	32.39	32.79	33.20	33.60	34.00	34.41	34.82	35.22

Description: This table shows the price to pay for a monthly payment mortgage loan at the yield rate.

Example: The price of a 15.00 %, 10 year mortgage loan to yield 8.00 % to maturity is $ 132.97.

INTEREST RATE, %

YIELD	11.00%	11.25%	11.50%	11.75%	12.00%	12.25%	12.50%	12.75%	13.00%	13.25%	13.50%	13.75%	14.00%	14.25%	14.50%	15.00%
0.00	165.30	167.00	168.71	170.44	172.17	173.90	175.65	177.41	179.17	180.95	182.73	184.52	186.32	188.13	189.94	193.60
1.00	157.24	158.86	160.49	162.13	163.77	165.43	167.09	168.76	170.44	172.13	173.82	175.52	177.24	178.96	180.68	184.16
2.00	149.71	151.25	152.80	154.36	155.92	157.50	159.08	160.67	162.27	163.88	165.49	167.11	168.74	170.38	172.03	175.34
3.00	142.66	144.13	145.60	147.09	148.58	150.08	151.59	153.11	154.63	156.16	157.70	159.24	160.80	162.36	163.92	167.08
4.00	136.06	137.46	138.87	140.28	141.71	143.14	144.58	146.02	147.47	148.93	150.40	151.88	153.36	154.85	156.34	159.35
4.25	134.47	135.86	137.25	138.65	140.06	141.47	142.89	144.32	145.76	147.20	148.65	150.11	151.57	153.04	154.52	157.50
4.50	132.91	134.28	135.66	137.04	138.43	139.83	141.24	142.65	144.07	145.50	146.93	148.37	149.82	151.27	152.73	155.67
4.75	131.38	132.73	134.09	135.46	136.84	138.22	139.61	141.00	142.41	143.82	145.23	146.66	148.09	149.52	150.97	153.88
5.00	129.87	131.21	132.56	133.91	135.27	136.63	138.01	139.39	140.77	142.17	143.57	144.97	146.39	147.81	149.23	152.11
5.25	128.39	129.71	131.04	132.38	133.72	135.07	136.43	137.79	139.16	140.54	141.93	143.32	144.71	146.12	147.53	150.37
5.50	126.93	128.24	129.55	130.87	132.20	133.53	134.88	136.22	137.58	138.94	140.31	141.69	143.07	144.46	145.85	148.66
5.75	125.49	126.78	128.08	129.39	130.70	132.02	133.35	134.68	136.02	137.37	138.72	140.08	141.45	142.82	144.20	146.98
6.00	124.08	125.35	126.64	127.93	129.23	130.53	131.85	133.16	134.49	135.82	137.16	138.50	139.85	141.21	142.57	145.32
6.25	122.68	123.95	125.22	126.50	127.78	129.07	130.37	131.67	132.98	134.30	135.62	136.95	138.28	139.63	140.97	143.69
6.50	121.31	122.56	123.82	125.08	126.35	127.63	128.91	130.20	131.50	132.80	134.11	135.42	136.74	138.07	139.40	142.09
6.75	119.97	121.20	122.44	123.69	124.95	126.21	127.48	128.75	130.03	131.32	132.62	133.92	135.22	136.53	137.85	140.51
7.00	118.64	119.86	121.09	122.32	123.57	124.81	126.07	127.33	128.60	129.87	131.15	132.43	133.73	135.02	136.33	138.95
7.25	117.33	118.54	119.76	120.98	122.21	123.44	124.68	125.93	127.18	128.44	129.70	130.98	132.25	133.54	134.83	137.42
7.50	116.05	117.24	118.44	119.65	120.87	122.09	123.31	124.55	125.79	127.03	128.28	129.54	130.80	132.07	133.35	135.92
7.75	114.78	115.96	117.15	118.35	119.55	120.76	121.97	123.19	124.41	125.65	126.88	128.13	129.38	130.63	131.89	134.43
8.00	113.54	114.71	115.88	117.06	118.25	119.45	120.65	121.85	123.06	124.28	125.51	126.74	127.97	129.21	130.46	132.97
8.25	112.31	113.47	114.63	115.80	116.97	118.15	119.34	120.54	121.73	122.94	124.15	125.37	126.59	127.82	129.05	131.54
8.50	111.10	112.25	113.40	114.55	115.72	116.88	118.06	119.24	120.43	121.62	122.82	124.02	125.23	126.44	127.67	130.12
8.75	109.91	111.04	112.18	113.33	114.48	115.63	116.80	117.96	119.14	120.32	121.50	122.69	123.89	125.09	126.30	128.73
9.00	108.74	109.86	110.99	112.12	113.26	114.40	115.55	116.71	117.87	119.04	120.21	121.39	122.57	123.76	124.95	127.36
9.25	107.59	108.70	109.81	110.93	112.06	113.19	114.33	115.47	116.62	117.77	118.93	120.10	121.27	122.45	123.63	126.01
9.50	106.45	107.55	108.65	109.76	110.88	112.00	113.12	114.25	115.39	116.53	117.68	118.83	119.99	121.16	122.33	124.68
9.75	105.34	106.42	107.51	108.61	109.71	110.82	111.93	113.05	114.18	115.31	116.44	117.59	118.73	119.88	121.04	123.37
10.00	104.24	105.31	106.39	107.48	108.57	109.66	110.76	111.87	112.99	114.10	115.23	116.36	117.49	118.63	119.78	122.08
10.25	103.15	104.22	105.28	106.36	107.44	108.52	109.61	110.71	111.81	112.92	114.03	115.15	116.27	117.40	118.53	120.81
10.50	102.09	103.14	104.19	105.26	106.33	107.40	108.48	109.56	110.65	111.75	112.85	113.96	115.07	116.18	117.31	119.56
10.75	101.04	102.08	103.12	104.17	105.23	106.29	107.36	108.44	109.51	110.60	111.69	112.78	113.88	114.99	116.10	118.33
11.00	100.00	101.03	102.07	103.11	104.15	105.20	106.26	107.32	108.39	109.47	110.54	111.63	112.72	113.81	114.91	117.12
11.25	98.98	100.00	101.03	102.06	103.09	104.13	105.18	106.23	107.29	108.35	109.42	110.49	111.57	112.65	113.74	115.93
11.50	97.98	98.99	100.00	101.02	102.05	103.08	104.11	105.15	106.20	107.25	108.31	109.37	110.43	111.51	112.58	114.75
11.75	96.99	97.99	98.99	100.00	101.01	102.04	103.06	104.09	105.13	106.17	107.21	108.26	109.32	110.38	111.45	113.59
12.00	96.01	97.00	98.00	99.00	100.00	101.01	102.02	103.05	104.07	105.10	106.14	107.18	108.22	109.27	110.33	112.45
12.25	95.05	96.03	97.02	98.01	99.00	100.00	101.00	102.01	103.03	104.05	105.07	106.10	107.14	108.18	109.22	111.33
12.50	94.11	95.08	96.05	97.03	98.02	99.01	100.00	101.00	102.00	103.01	104.03	105.05	106.07	107.10	108.14	110.22
12.75	93.18	94.13	95.10	96.07	97.04	98.02	99.01	100.00	100.99	101.99	103.00	104.01	105.02	106.04	107.07	109.13
13.00	92.26	93.21	94.16	95.12	96.09	97.06	98.03	99.01	100.00	100.99	101.98	102.98	103.99	105.00	106.01	108.05
13.25	91.35	92.29	93.24	94.19	95.15	96.11	97.07	98.04	99.02	100.00	100.99	101.97	102.97	103.97	104.97	106.99
13.50	90.46	91.39	92.33	93.27	94.22	95.17	96.13	97.09	98.05	99.02	100.00	100.98	101.96	102.95	103.95	105.95
13.75	89.58	90.51	91.43	92.37	93.30	94.25	95.19	96.15	97.10	98.06	99.03	100.00	100.98	101.96	102.94	104.92
14.00	88.72	89.63	90.55	91.47	92.40	93.34	94.27	95.22	96.16	97.12	98.07	99.03	100.00	100.97	101.95	103.91
14.25	87.87	88.77	89.68	90.60	91.52	92.44	93.37	94.30	95.24	96.18	97.13	98.08	99.04	100.00	100.97	102.91
14.50	87.03	87.92	88.82	89.73	90.64	91.56	92.48	93.40	94.33	95.26	96.20	97.14	98.09	99.04	100.00	101.93
14.75	86.20	87.09	87.98	88.88	89.78	90.68	91.60	92.51	93.43	94.36	95.29	96.22	97.16	98.10	99.05	100.96
15.00	85.38	86.26	87.15	88.03	88.93	89.83	90.73	91.64	92.55	93.46	94.38	95.31	96.24	97.17	98.11	100.00
15.25	84.58	85.45	86.32	87.20	88.09	88.98	89.87	90.77	91.68	92.58	93.49	94.41	95.33	96.26	97.19	99.06
15.50	83.78	84.65	85.51	86.39	87.26	88.15	89.03	89.92	90.82	91.71	92.62	93.53	94.44	95.35	96.28	98.13
15.75	83.00	83.86	84.72	85.58	86.45	87.32	88.20	89.08	89.97	90.86	91.75	92.65	93.56	94.47	95.38	97.21
16.00	82.23	83.08	83.93	84.79	85.65	86.51	87.38	88.26	89.13	90.02	90.90	91.79	92.69	93.59	94.49	96.31
16.25	81.47	82.31	83.16	84.00	84.86	85.71	86.57	87.44	88.31	89.18	90.06	90.95	91.83	92.72	93.62	95.42
16.50	80.72	81.56	82.39	83.23	84.08	84.93	85.78	86.64	87.50	88.37	89.24	90.11	90.99	91.87	92.76	94.55
16.75	79.99	80.81	81.64	82.47	83.31	84.15	85.00	85.85	86.70	87.56	88.42	89.29	90.16	91.03	91.91	93.68
17.00	79.26	80.08	80.90	81.72	82.55	83.38	84.22	85.06	85.91	86.76	87.62	88.47	89.34	90.20	91.08	92.83
17.25	78.54	79.35	80.16	80.98	81.80	82.63	83.46	84.29	85.13	85.98	86.82	87.67	88.53	89.39	90.25	91.99
17.50	77.83	78.64	79.44	80.25	81.07	81.89	82.71	83.54	84.37	85.20	86.04	86.88	87.73	88.58	89.44	91.16
17.75	77.14	77.93	78.73	79.53	80.34	81.15	81.97	82.79	83.61	84.44	85.27	86.11	86.95	87.79	88.64	90.34
18.00	76.45	77.24	78.03	78.82	79.62	80.43	81.24	82.05	82.87	83.69	84.51	85.34	86.17	87.01	87.85	89.54
18.25	75.77	76.55	77.34	78.12	78.92	79.71	80.52	81.32	82.13	82.94	83.76	84.58	85.41	86.23	87.07	88.74
18.50	75.10	75.88	76.65	77.44	78.22	79.01	79.81	80.60	81.41	82.21	83.02	83.83	84.65	85.47	86.30	87.96
18.75	74.44	75.21	75.98	76.76	77.53	78.32	79.10	79.90	80.69	81.49	82.29	83.10	83.91	84.72	85.54	87.19
19.00	73.79	74.55	75.32	76.08	76.86	77.63	78.41	79.20	79.99	80.78	81.57	82.37	83.18	83.98	84.79	86.43
20.00	71.28	72.01	72.75	73.49	74.24	74.99	75.74	76.50	77.26	78.03	78.79	79.57	80.34	81.12	81.91	83.48
25.00	60.55	61.18	61.80	62.43	63.07	63.70	64.34	64.99	65.63	66.28	66.94	67.59	68.25	68.91	69.58	70.92
30.00	52.25	52.79	53.33	53.88	54.42	54.97	55.53	56.08	56.64	57.20	57.76	58.33	58.90	59.47	60.04	61.20

Description: This table shows the yield to maturity of a mortgage purchased at the price shown in the index.

Example: The yield to maturity of a 15.00 %, 10 year mortgage at a price of 116.00 is 11.23 %.

INTEREST RATE, %

PRICE	11.00%	11.25%	11.50%	11.75%	12.00%	12.25%	12.50%	12.75%	13.00%	13.25%	13.50%	13.75%	14.00%	14.25%	14.50%	15.00%
160	.65	.85	1.06	1.26	1.47	1.67	1.88	2.08	2.29	2.49	2.69	2.90	3.10	3.30	3.50	3.91
155	1.29	1.49	1.70	1.91	2.12	2.32	2.53	2.74	2.94	3.15	3.36	3.56	3.77	3.97	4.18	4.59
150	1.95	2.17	2.38	2.59	2.80	3.01	3.22	3.43	3.63	3.84	4.05	4.26	4.47	4.68	4.88	5.30
145	2.66	2.87	3.08	3.29	3.51	3.72	3.93	4.14	4.36	4.57	4.78	4.99	5.20	5.41	5.62	6.04
140	3.39	3.61	3.82	4.04	4.25	4.47	4.68	4.90	5.11	5.33	5.54	5.76	5.97	6.19	6.40	6.83
135	4.16	4.38	4.60	4.82	5.04	5.26	5.47	5.69	5.91	6.13	6.35	6.56	6.78	7.00	7.22	7.65
130	4.97	5.20	5.42	5.64	5.86	6.09	6.31	6.53	6.75	6.97	7.19	7.41	7.64	7.86	8.08	8.52
129	5.14	5.36	5.59	5.81	6.03	6.26	6.48	6.70	6.92	7.15	7.37	7.59	7.81	8.03	8.25	8.70
128	5.31	5.54	5.76	5.98	6.21	6.43	6.65	6.88	7.10	7.32	7.55	7.77	7.99	8.21	8.43	8.88
127	5.48	5.71	5.93	6.16	6.38	6.61	6.83	7.05	7.28	7.50	7.72	7.95	8.17	8.39	8.62	9.06
126	5.66	5.88	6.11	6.33	6.56	6.78	7.01	7.23	7.46	7.68	7.91	8.13	8.35	8.58	8.80	9.25
125	5.83	6.06	6.28	6.51	6.74	6.96	7.19	7.41	7.64	7.86	8.09	8.31	8.54	8.76	8.99	9.43
124	6.01	6.24	6.46	6.69	6.92	7.14	7.37	7.60	7.82	8.05	8.27	8.50	8.72	8.95	9.17	9.62
123	6.19	6.42	6.64	6.87	7.10	7.33	7.55	7.78	8.01	8.23	8.46	8.69	8.91	9.14	9.37	9.82
122	6.37	6.60	6.83	7.05	7.28	7.51	7.74	7.97	8.19	8.42	8.65	8.88	9.10	9.33	9.56	10.01
121	6.55	6.78	7.01	7.24	7.47	7.70	7.93	8.16	8.38	8.61	8.84	9.07	9.30	9.53	9.75	10.21
120	6.74	6.97	7.20	7.43	7.66	7.89	8.12	8.35	8.58	8.81	9.04	9.26	9.49	9.72	9.95	10.41
119	6.93	7.16	7.39	7.62	7.85	8.08	8.31	8.54	8.77	9.00	9.23	9.46	9.69	9.92	10.15	10.61
118	7.12	7.35	7.58	7.81	8.04	8.28	8.51	8.74	8.97	9.20	9.43	9.66	9.89	10.12	10.35	10.81
117	7.31	7.54	7.77	8.01	8.24	8.47	8.70	8.94	9.17	9.40	9.63	9.86	10.10	10.33	10.56	11.02
116	7.50	7.74	7.97	8.20	8.44	8.67	8.90	9.14	9.37	9.60	9.84	10.07	10.30	10.53	10.77	11.23
115	7.70	7.94	8.17	8.40	8.64	8.87	9.11	9.34	9.57	9.81	10.04	10.28	10.51	10.74	10.98	11.44
114	7.90	8.14	8.37	8.61	8.84	9.08	9.31	9.55	9.78	10.02	10.25	10.49	10.72	10.95	11.19	11.66
113	8.10	8.34	8.58	8.81	9.05	9.28	9.52	9.76	9.99	10.23	10.46	10.70	10.93	11.17	11.40	11.87
112	8.31	8.55	8.78	9.02	9.26	9.49	9.73	9.97	10.20	10.44	10.68	10.91	11.15	11.39	11.62	12.09
111	8.52	8.75	8.99	9.23	9.47	9.71	9.94	10.18	10.42	10.66	10.89	11.13	11.37	11.61	11.84	12.32
110	8.73	8.97	9.20	9.44	9.68	9.92	10.16	10.40	10.64	10.88	11.12	11.35	11.59	11.83	12.07	12.54
109	8.94	9.18	9.42	9.66	9.90	10.14	10.38	10.62	10.86	11.10	11.34	11.58	11.82	12.06	12.30	12.77
108	9.16	9.40	9.64	9.88	10.12	10.36	10.60	10.84	11.08	11.32	11.56	11.81	12.05	12.29	12.53	13.01
107	9.37	9.62	9.86	10.10	10.34	10.58	10.83	11.07	11.31	11.55	11.79	12.04	12.28	12.52	12.76	13.24
106	9.60	9.84	10.08	10.33	10.57	10.81	11.06	11.30	11.54	11.78	12.03	12.27	12.51	12.76	13.00	13.48
105	9.82	10.07	10.31	10.55	10.80	11.04	11.29	11.53	11.77	12.02	12.26	12.51	12.75	12.99	13.24	13.73
104	10.05	10.29	10.54	10.79	11.03	11.28	11.52	11.77	12.01	12.26	12.50	12.75	12.99	13.24	13.48	13.97
103	10.28	10.53	10.77	11.02	11.27	11.51	11.76	12.01	12.25	12.50	12.74	12.99	13.24	13.48	13.73	14.22
102	10.52	10.76	11.01	11.26	11.51	11.75	12.00	12.25	12.50	12.74	12.99	13.24	13.49	13.74	13.99	14.48
101	10.75	11.00	11.25	11.50	11.75	12.00	12.25	12.50	12.74	12.99	13.24	13.49	13.74	13.99	14.24	14.73
100	11.00	11.25	11.50	11.75	12.00	12.25	12.50	12.75	13.00	13.25	13.50	13.75	14.00	14.25	14.50	15.00
99	11.24	11.49	11.74	11.99	12.25	12.50	12.75	13.00	13.25	13.50	13.75	14.00	14.26	14.51	14.76	15.26
98	11.49	11.74	11.99	12.25	12.50	12.75	13.00	13.26	13.51	13.76	14.01	14.27	14.52	14.77	15.02	15.53
97	11.74	12.00	12.25	12.50	12.76	13.01	13.26	13.52	13.77	14.03	14.28	14.53	14.79	15.04	15.30	15.80
96	12.00	12.25	12.51	12.76	13.02	13.27	13.53	13.78	14.04	14.29	14.55	14.81	15.06	15.32	15.57	16.08
95	12.26	12.52	12.77	13.03	13.28	13.54	13.80	14.05	14.31	14.57	14.82	15.08	15.34	15.59	15.85	16.37
94	12.52	12.78	13.04	13.30	13.55	13.81	14.07	14.33	14.59	14.84	15.10	15.36	15.62	15.88	16.14	16.65
93	12.79	13.05	13.31	13.57	13.83	14.09	14.35	14.61	14.87	15.13	15.39	15.65	15.91	16.16	16.42	16.94
92	13.07	13.33	13.59	13.85	14.11	14.37	14.63	14.89	15.15	15.41	15.67	15.93	16.20	16.46	16.72	17.24
91	13.34	13.61	13.87	14.13	14.39	14.65	14.92	15.18	15.44	15.70	15.97	16.23	16.49	16.75	17.02	17.54
90	13.63	13.89	14.15	14.42	14.68	14.94	15.21	15.47	15.74	16.00	16.26	16.53	16.79	17.06	17.32	17.85
89	13.91	14.18	14.44	14.71	14.97	15.24	15.50	15.77	16.04	16.30	16.57	16.83	17.10	17.37	17.63	18.16
88	14.21	14.47	14.74	15.01	15.27	15.54	15.81	16.07	16.34	16.61	16.88	17.14	17.41	17.68	17.95	18.48
87	14.50	14.77	15.04	15.31	15.58	15.84	16.11	16.38	16.65	16.92	17.19	17.46	17.73	18.00	18.27	18.81
86	14.81	15.07	15.34	15.61	15.88	16.16	16.43	16.70	16.97	17.24	17.51	17.78	18.05	18.32	18.59	19.14
85	15.11	15.38	15.66	15.93	16.20	16.47	16.74	17.02	17.29	17.56	17.83	18.11	18.38	18.65	18.93	19.47
84	15.43	15.70	15.97	16.25	16.52	16.79	17.07	17.34	17.62	17.89	18.16	18.44	18.71	18.99	19.26	19.82
83	15.75	16.02	16.30	16.57	16.85	17.12	17.40	17.67	17.95	18.23	18.50	18.78	19.06	19.33	19.61	20.16
82	16.07	16.35	16.62	16.90	17.18	17.46	17.73	18.01	18.29	18.57	18.85	19.12	19.40	19.68	19.96	20.52
81	16.40	16.68	16.96	17.24	17.52	17.80	18.08	18.36	18.64	18.92	19.20	19.48	19.76	20.04	20.32	20.88
80	16.74	17.02	17.30	17.58	17.86	18.14	18.43	18.71	18.99	19.27	19.55	19.84	20.12	20.40	20.69	21.25
79	17.08	17.37	17.65	17.93	18.22	18.50	18.78	19.07	19.35	19.63	19.92	20.20	20.49	20.77	21.06	21.63
78	17.44	17.72	18.01	18.29	18.58	18.86	19.15	19.43	19.72	20.00	20.29	20.58	20.87	21.15	21.44	22.02
77	17.79	18.08	18.37	18.65	18.94	19.23	19.52	19.81	20.09	20.38	20.67	20.96	21.25	21.54	21.83	22.41
76	18.16	18.45	18.74	19.03	19.32	19.61	19.90	20.19	20.48	20.77	21.06	21.35	21.64	21.93	22.23	22.81
75	18.53	18.82	19.12	19.41	19.70	19.99	20.28	20.58	20.87	21.16	21.45	21.75	22.04	22.34	22.63	23.22
74	18.91	19.21	19.50	19.80	20.09	20.38	20.68	20.97	21.27	21.56	21.86	22.16	22.45	22.75	23.05	23.64
73	19.30	19.60	19.90	20.19	20.49	20.78	21.08	21.38	21.68	21.97	22.27	22.57	22.87	23.17	23.47	24.07
72	19.70	20.00	20.30	20.60	20.90	21.20	21.49	21.79	22.09	22.40	22.70	23.00	23.30	23.60	23.90	24.51
71	20.11	20.41	20.71	21.01	21.31	21.61	21.92	22.22	22.52	22.83	23.13	23.43	23.74	24.04	24.35	24.96
70	20.53	20.83	21.13	21.44	21.74	22.04	22.35	22.65	22.96	23.27	23.57	23.88	24.19	24.49	24.80	25.42
65	22.76	23.08	23.39	23.71	24.03	24.35	24.67	24.99	25.31	25.63	25.95	26.27	26.60	26.92	27.24	27.89

MORTGAGE PRICE

Description: This table shows the price to pay for a monthly payment mortgage loan at the yield rate.

Example: The price of a 6.75 %, 11 year mortgage loan to yield 8.00 % to maturity is $ 94.20.

INTEREST RATE, %

YIELD	0.00%	1.00%	2.00%	3.00%	4.00%	4.25%	4.50%	4.75%	5.00%	5.25%	5.50%	5.75%	6.00%	6.25%	6.50%	6.75%
0.00	100.00	105.64	111.49	117.53	123.77	125.36	126.97	128.58	130.21	131.85	133.50	135.17	136.84	138.53	140.23	141.95
1.00	94.66	100.00	105.53	111.25	117.16	118.67	120.19	121.72	123.26	124.81	126.37	127.95	129.54	131.13	132.74	134.36
2.00	89.70	94.76	100.00	105.42	111.02	112.45	113.89	115.34	116.80	118.27	119.75	121.24	122.75	124.26	125.79	127.32
3.00	85.08	89.89	94.86	100.00	105.31	106.67	108.03	109.40	110.79	112.19	113.59	115.01	116.43	117.87	119.32	120.77
4.00	80.79	85.35	90.07	94.96	100.00	101.29	102.58	103.89	105.20	106.53	107.86	109.21	110.56	111.93	113.30	114.68
4.25	79.77	84.27	88.93	93.75	98.73	100.00	101.28	102.57	103.87	105.18	106.49	107.82	109.16	110.51	111.86	113.23
4.50	78.76	83.20	87.81	92.57	97.48	98.74	100.00	101.27	102.56	103.85	105.15	106.46	107.78	109.11	110.45	111.80
4.75	77.77	82.16	86.70	91.40	96.26	97.50	98.74	100.00	101.27	102.54	103.83	105.12	106.43	107.74	109.06	110.39
5.00	76.80	81.13	85.62	90.26	95.05	96.28	97.51	98.75	100.00	101.26	102.53	103.81	105.09	106.39	107.70	109.01
5.25	75.84	80.12	84.55	89.14	93.87	95.08	96.30	97.52	98.76	100.00	101.25	102.52	103.79	105.07	106.36	107.66
5.50	74.90	79.13	83.51	88.03	92.71	93.90	95.10	96.31	97.53	98.76	100.00	101.25	102.50	103.77	105.04	106.32
5.75	73.98	78.16	82.48	86.95	91.57	92.75	93.93	95.13	96.33	97.55	98.77	100.00	101.24	102.49	103.75	105.01
6.00	73.08	77.20	81.47	85.89	90.45	91.61	92.78	93.96	95.15	96.35	97.56	98.77	100.00	101.23	102.48	103.73
6.25	72.18	76.26	80.48	84.84	89.34	90.49	91.65	92.82	93.99	95.18	96.37	97.57	98.78	100.00	101.23	102.46
6.50	71.31	75.33	79.50	83.81	88.26	89.40	90.54	91.69	92.85	94.02	95.20	96.39	97.58	98.79	100.00	101.22
6.75	70.45	74.42	78.54	82.80	87.20	88.32	89.45	90.59	91.73	92.89	94.05	95.23	96.41	97.60	98.79	100.00
7.00	69.60	73.53	77.60	81.81	86.15	87.26	88.37	89.50	90.63	91.77	92.92	94.08	95.25	96.42	97.61	98.80
7.25	68.77	72.65	76.67	80.83	85.12	86.22	87.32	88.43	89.55	90.68	91.81	92.96	94.11	95.27	96.44	97.62
7.50	67.96	71.79	75.76	79.87	84.11	85.19	86.28	87.38	88.49	89.60	90.72	91.86	92.99	94.14	95.30	96.46
7.75	67.15	70.94	74.87	78.93	83.12	84.19	85.26	86.35	87.44	88.54	89.65	90.77	91.90	93.03	94.17	95.32
8.00	66.36	70.11	73.99	78.00	82.14	83.20	84.26	85.33	86.41	87.50	88.60	89.70	90.82	91.94	93.06	94.20
8.25	65.59	69.29	73.12	77.09	81.18	82.22	83.28	84.34	85.40	86.48	87.56	88.65	89.75	90.86	91.98	93.10
8.50	64.83	68.48	72.27	76.19	80.24	81.27	82.31	83.35	84.41	85.47	86.54	87.62	88.71	89.80	90.91	92.02
8.75	64.08	67.69	71.44	75.31	79.31	80.33	81.35	82.39	83.43	84.48	85.54	86.61	87.68	88.77	89.86	90.95
9.00	63.34	66.91	70.61	74.44	78.39	79.40	80.42	81.44	82.47	83.51	84.56	85.61	86.68	87.74	88.82	89.91
9.25	62.61	66.15	69.80	73.59	77.50	78.49	79.50	80.51	81.53	82.56	83.59	84.63	85.68	86.74	87.80	88.88
9.50	61.90	65.39	69.01	72.75	76.62	77.60	78.59	79.59	80.60	81.62	82.64	83.67	84.71	85.75	86.81	87.86
9.75	61.20	64.65	68.23	71.93	75.75	76.72	77.70	78.69	79.69	80.69	81.70	82.72	83.75	84.78	85.82	86.87
10.00	60.51	63.92	67.46	71.12	74.89	75.86	76.83	77.81	78.79	79.78	80.78	81.79	82.80	83.83	84.86	85.89
10.25	59.83	63.21	66.70	70.32	74.06	75.01	75.97	76.93	77.91	78.89	79.88	80.87	81.88	82.89	83.90	84.93
10.50	59.16	62.50	65.96	69.54	73.23	74.17	75.12	76.08	77.04	78.01	78.99	79.97	80.96	81.96	82.97	83.98
10.75	58.51	61.81	65.23	68.77	72.42	73.35	74.29	75.23	76.19	77.15	78.11	79.09	80.07	81.05	82.05	83.05
11.00	57.86	61.13	64.51	68.01	71.62	72.54	73.47	74.40	75.35	76.29	77.25	78.21	79.18	80.16	81.14	82.14
11.25	57.23	60.46	63.80	67.26	70.83	71.74	72.66	73.59	74.52	75.46	76.40	77.36	78.32	79.28	80.25	81.23
11.50	56.61	59.80	63.11	66.53	70.06	70.96	71.87	72.78	73.71	74.63	75.57	76.51	77.46	78.42	79.38	80.35
11.75	55.99	59.15	62.42	65.81	69.30	70.19	71.09	72.00	72.91	73.83	74.75	75.68	76.62	77.57	78.52	79.48
12.00	55.39	58.51	61.75	65.10	68.55	69.43	70.32	71.22	72.12	73.03	73.94	74.87	75.79	76.73	77.67	78.62
12.25	54.79	57.88	61.09	64.40	67.82	68.69	69.57	70.45	71.35	72.24	73.15	74.06	74.98	75.91	76.84	77.78
12.50	54.21	57.27	60.43	63.71	67.09	67.96	68.83	69.70	70.58	71.47	72.37	73.27	74.18	75.10	76.02	76.95
12.75	53.63	56.66	59.79	63.03	66.38	67.24	68.10	68.96	69.84	70.71	71.60	72.49	73.39	74.30	75.21	76.13
13.00	53.07	56.06	59.16	62.37	65.68	66.53	67.38	68.23	69.10	69.97	70.85	71.73	72.62	73.51	74.42	75.33
13.25	52.51	55.47	58.54	61.71	64.99	65.83	66.67	67.52	68.37	69.23	70.10	70.98	71.86	72.74	73.63	74.53
13.50	51.96	54.89	57.93	61.07	64.31	65.14	65.97	66.81	67.66	68.51	69.37	70.23	71.11	71.98	72.87	73.76
13.75	51.42	54.32	57.33	60.43	63.64	64.46	65.29	66.12	66.96	67.80	68.65	69.50	70.37	71.23	72.11	72.99
14.00	50.89	53.76	56.73	59.81	62.99	63.80	64.61	65.44	66.26	67.10	67.94	68.79	69.64	70.50	71.36	72.24
14.25	50.37	53.21	56.15	59.20	62.34	63.14	63.95	64.76	65.58	66.41	67.24	68.08	68.92	69.77	70.63	71.49
14.50	49.85	52.67	55.58	58.59	61.70	62.50	63.30	64.10	64.91	65.73	66.55	67.38	68.22	69.06	69.91	70.76
14.75	49.35	52.13	55.01	58.00	61.08	61.86	62.65	63.45	64.25	65.06	65.88	66.70	67.53	68.36	69.20	70.04
15.00	48.85	51.60	54.46	57.41	60.46	61.24	62.02	62.81	63.60	64.41	65.21	66.03	66.84	67.67	68.50	69.34
15.25	48.36	51.08	53.91	56.83	59.85	60.62	61.40	62.18	62.97	63.76	64.56	65.36	66.17	66.99	67.81	68.64
15.50	47.87	50.57	53.37	56.26	59.25	60.02	60.78	61.56	62.34	63.12	63.91	64.71	65.51	66.32	67.13	67.95
15.75	47.40	50.07	52.84	55.71	58.66	59.42	60.18	60.94	61.72	62.49	63.28	64.07	64.86	65.66	66.47	67.28
16.00	46.93	49.58	52.32	55.15	58.08	58.83	59.58	60.34	61.11	61.88	62.65	63.43	64.22	65.01	65.81	66.61
16.25	46.47	49.09	51.80	54.61	57.51	58.25	59.00	59.75	60.51	61.27	62.04	62.81	63.59	64.37	65.16	65.96
16.50	46.01	48.61	51.30	54.08	56.95	57.68	58.42	59.16	59.91	60.67	61.43	62.20	62.97	63.74	64.53	65.31
16.75	45.57	48.14	50.80	53.55	56.40	57.12	57.85	58.59	59.33	60.08	60.83	61.59	62.35	63.12	63.90	64.68
17.00	45.13	47.67	50.31	53.04	55.85	56.57	57.29	58.02	58.76	59.50	60.24	60.99	61.75	62.51	63.28	64.05
17.25	44.69	47.21	49.82	52.53	55.32	56.03	56.74	57.47	58.19	58.93	59.66	60.41	61.16	61.91	62.67	63.44
17.50	44.26	46.76	49.35	52.02	54.79	55.49	56.20	56.92	57.64	58.36	59.09	59.83	60.57	61.32	62.07	62.83
17.75	43.84	46.32	48.88	51.53	54.27	54.96	55.67	56.37	57.09	57.81	58.53	59.26	60.00	60.74	61.48	62.23
18.00	43.43	45.88	48.42	51.04	53.75	54.44	55.14	55.84	56.55	57.26	57.98	58.70	59.43	60.16	60.90	61.65
18.25	43.02	45.45	47.96	50.56	53.25	53.93	54.62	55.32	56.02	56.72	57.43	58.15	58.87	59.60	60.33	61.07
18.50	42.62	45.02	47.51	50.09	52.75	53.43	54.11	54.80	55.49	56.19	56.90	57.61	58.32	59.04	59.76	60.49
18.75	42.22	44.60	47.07	49.62	52.26	52.93	53.61	54.29	54.98	55.67	56.37	57.07	57.78	58.49	59.21	59.93
19.00	41.83	44.19	46.64	49.16	51.78	52.44	53.11	53.79	54.47	55.16	55.85	56.54	57.24	57.95	58.66	59.38
20.00	40.33	42.60	44.96	47.39	49.91	50.55	51.20	51.85	52.51	53.17	53.84	54.51	55.18	55.86	56.55	57.24
25.00	33.97	35.89	37.87	39.93	42.05	42.59	43.13	43.68	44.24	44.79	45.35	45.92	46.49	47.06	47.64	48.22
30.00	29.14	30.78	32.49	34.25	36.07	36.53	37.00	37.47	37.94	38.42	38.90	39.39	39.88	40.37	40.86	41.36

Description: This table shows the yield to maturity of a mortgage purchased at the price shown in the index.

Example: The yield to maturity of a 6.75 %, 11 year mortgage at a price of 80.00 is 11.59 %.

INTEREST RATE, %

PRICE	0.00%	1.00%	2.00%	3.00%	4.00%	4.25%	4.50%	4.75%	5.00%	5.25%	5.50%	5.75%	6.00%	6.25%	6.50%	6.75%
100	0.00	1.00	2.00	3.00	4.00	4.25	4.50	4.75	5.00	5.25	5.50	5.75	6.00	6.25	6.50	6.75
99	.18	1.18	2.18	3.19	4.19	4.44	4.69	4.94	5.20	5.45	5.70	5.95	6.20	6.45	6.70	6.95
98	.36	1.37	2.38	3.38	4.39	4.64	4.89	5.15	5.40	5.65	5.90	6.16	6.41	6.66	6.91	7.16
97	.55	1.56	2.57	3.58	4.59	4.85	5.10	5.35	5.61	5.86	6.11	6.37	6.62	6.87	7.12	7.38
96	.74	1.75	2.77	3.78	4.80	5.05	5.31	5.56	5.82	6.07	6.32	6.58	6.83	7.09	7.34	7.60
95	.93	1.95	2.97	3.99	5.01	5.26	5.52	5.77	6.03	6.28	6.54	6.79	7.05	7.31	7.56	7.82
94	1.12	2.15	3.17	4.19	5.22	5.47	5.73	5.99	6.24	6.50	6.76	7.01	7.27	7.53	7.78	8.04
93	1.32	2.35	3.37	4.40	5.43	5.69	5.95	6.20	6.46	6.72	6.98	7.24	7.49	7.75	8.01	8.27
92	1.52	2.55	3.58	4.62	5.65	5.91	6.17	6.43	6.69	6.94	7.20	7.46	7.72	7.98	8.24	8.50
91	1.73	2.76	3.80	4.83	5.87	6.13	6.39	6.65	6.91	7.17	7.43	7.69	7.95	8.21	8.47	8.73
90	1.93	2.97	4.01	5.05	6.10	6.36	6.62	6.88	7.14	7.40	7.66	7.93	8.19	8.45	8.71	8.97
89	2.14	3.18	4.23	5.28	6.32	6.59	6.85	7.11	7.37	7.64	7.90	8.16	8.43	8.69	8.95	9.21
88	2.35	3.40	4.45	5.50	6.56	6.82	7.08	7.35	7.61	7.87	8.14	8.40	8.67	8.93	9.20	9.46
87	2.57	3.62	4.68	5.73	6.79	7.06	7.32	7.59	7.85	8.12	8.38	8.65	8.91	9.18	9.45	9.71
86	2.79	3.85	4.91	5.97	7.03	7.30	7.56	7.83	8.10	8.36	8.63	8.90	9.16	9.43	9.70	9.97
85	3.01	4.08	5.14	6.21	7.27	7.54	7.81	8.08	8.35	8.61	8.88	9.15	9.42	9.69	9.96	10.23
84	3.24	4.31	5.38	6.45	7.52	7.79	8.06	8.33	8.60	8.87	9.14	9.41	9.68	9.95	10.22	10.49
83	3.47	4.54	5.62	6.69	7.77	8.05	8.32	8.59	8.86	9.13	9.40	9.67	9.94	10.21	10.49	10.76
82	3.71	4.78	5.86	6.95	8.03	8.30	8.58	8.85	9.12	9.39	9.67	9.94	10.21	10.49	10.76	11.03
81	3.95	5.03	6.11	7.20	8.29	8.57	8.84	9.11	9.39	9.66	9.94	10.21	10.49	10.76	11.04	11.31
80	4.19	5.28	6.37	7.46	8.56	8.83	9.11	9.38	9.66	9.94	10.21	10.49	10.76	11.04	11.32	11.59
79	4.44	5.53	6.62	7.73	8.83	9.11	9.38	9.66	9.94	10.21	10.49	10.77	11.05	11.33	11.60	11.88
78	4.69	5.79	6.89	7.99	9.10	9.38	9.66	9.94	10.22	10.50	10.78	11.06	11.34	11.62	11.90	12.18
77	4.94	6.05	7.16	8.27	9.39	9.67	9.95	10.23	10.51	10.79	11.07	11.35	11.63	11.91	12.20	12.48
76	5.20	6.31	7.43	8.55	9.67	9.95	10.24	10.52	10.80	11.08	11.37	11.65	11.93	12.22	12.50	12.78
75	5.47	6.59	7.71	8.83	9.96	10.25	10.53	10.81	11.10	11.38	11.67	11.95	12.24	12.52	12.81	13.10
74	5.74	6.86	7.99	9.12	10.26	10.55	10.83	11.12	11.40	11.69	11.98	12.26	12.55	12.84	13.13	13.42
73	6.02	7.15	8.28	9.42	10.57	10.85	11.14	11.43	11.72	12.00	12.29	12.58	12.87	13.16	13.45	13.74
72	6.30	7.43	8.58	9.72	10.88	11.16	11.45	11.74	12.03	12.32	12.61	12.91	13.20	13.49	13.78	14.07
71	6.58	7.73	8.88	10.03	11.19	11.48	11.77	12.07	12.36	12.65	12.94	13.24	13.53	13.82	14.12	14.41
70	6.88	8.03	9.18	10.35	11.52	11.81	12.10	12.40	12.69	12.98	13.28	13.57	13.87	14.17	14.46	14.76
69	7.18	8.33	9.50	10.67	11.85	12.14	12.44	12.73	13.03	13.33	13.62	13.92	14.22	14.52	14.82	15.12
68	7.48	8.65	9.82	11.00	12.18	12.48	12.78	13.08	13.37	13.67	13.97	14.27	14.57	14.87	15.18	15.48
67	7.79	8.97	10.15	11.33	12.53	12.83	13.13	13.43	13.73	14.03	14.33	14.63	14.94	15.24	15.54	15.85
66	8.11	9.29	10.48	11.68	12.88	13.18	13.49	13.79	14.09	14.40	14.70	15.00	15.31	15.62	15.92	16.23
65	8.44	9.63	10.82	12.03	13.24	13.55	13.85	14.16	14.46	14.77	15.08	15.38	15.69	16.00	16.31	16.62
64	8.77	9.97	11.17	12.39	13.61	13.92	14.23	14.53	14.84	15.15	15.46	15.77	16.08	16.39	16.70	17.02
63	9.11	10.32	11.53	12.76	13.99	14.30	14.61	14.92	15.23	15.54	15.86	16.17	16.48	16.80	17.11	17.43
62	9.46	10.68	11.90	13.14	14.38	14.69	15.00	15.32	15.63	15.94	16.26	16.58	16.89	17.21	17.53	17.84
61	9.82	11.04	12.28	13.52	14.78	15.09	15.41	15.72	16.04	16.36	16.67	16.99	17.31	17.63	17.95	18.27
60	10.18	11.42	12.66	13.92	15.18	15.50	15.82	16.14	16.46	16.78	17.10	17.42	17.74	18.07	18.39	18.71
59	10.56	11.80	13.06	14.33	15.60	15.92	16.24	16.57	16.89	17.21	17.54	17.86	18.19	18.51	18.84	19.17
58	10.94	12.20	13.47	14.74	16.03	16.36	16.68	17.01	17.33	17.66	17.99	18.31	18.64	18.97	19.30	19.63
57	11.34	12.60	13.88	15.17	16.47	16.80	17.13	17.46	17.79	18.12	18.45	18.78	19.11	19.44	19.78	20.11
56	11.74	13.02	14.31	15.61	16.93	17.26	17.59	17.92	18.25	18.59	18.92	19.26	19.59	19.93	20.27	20.60
55	12.16	13.45	14.75	16.07	17.39	17.73	18.06	18.40	18.73	19.07	19.41	19.75	20.09	20.43	20.77	21.11
54	12.58	13.89	15.20	16.53	17.87	18.21	18.55	18.89	19.23	19.57	19.91	20.25	20.60	20.94	21.29	21.63
53	13.02	14.34	15.67	17.01	18.37	18.71	19.05	19.39	19.74	20.08	20.43	20.78	21.12	21.47	21.82	22.17
52	13.48	14.81	16.15	17.51	18.88	19.22	19.57	19.92	20.26	20.61	20.96	21.31	21.67	22.02	22.37	22.73
51	13.94	15.29	16.64	18.02	19.40	19.75	20.10	20.45	20.81	21.16	21.51	21.87	22.23	22.58	22.94	23.30
50	14.42	15.78	17.15	18.54	19.95	20.30	20.65	21.01	21.37	21.72	22.08	22.44	22.80	23.17	23.77	23.89
49	14.92	16.29	17.68	19.09	20.51	20.86	21.22	21.58	21.95	22.31	22.67	23.04	23.40	23.77	24.14	24.50
48	15.43	16.82	18.22	19.65	21.09	21.45	21.81	22.18	22.54	22.91	23.28	23.65	24.02	24.39	24.76	25.14
47	15.96	17.36	18.79	20.23	21.69	22.05	22.42	22.79	23.16	23.54	23.91	24.28	24.66	25.04	25.41	25.79
46	16.50	17.93	19.37	20.83	22.31	22.68	23.05	23.43	23.80	24.18	24.56	24.94	25.32	25.71	26.09	26.47
45	17.07	18.51	19.97	21.45	22.95	23.33	23.71	24.09	24.47	24.85	25.24	25.62	26.01	26.40	26.79	27.18
44	17.65	19.11	20.59	22.09	23.62	24.00	24.39	24.77	25.16	25.55	25.94	26.33	26.73	27.12	27.52	27.91
43	18.26	19.74	21.24	22.76	24.31	24.70	25.09	25.48	25.88	26.27	26.67	27.07	27.47	27.87	28.27	28.68
42	18.89	20.39	21.91	23.46	25.03	25.43	25.82	26.22	26.62	27.03	27.43	27.84	28.24	28.65	29.06	29.47
41	19.54	21.06	22.61	24.18	25.78	26.18	26.59	26.99	27.40	27.81	28.22	28.63	29.05	29.46	29.88	30.30
40	20.22	21.77	23.34	24.94	26.56	26.97	27.38	27.80	28.21	28.63	29.05	29.47	29.89	30.31	30.74	31.16
39	20.93	22.50	24.10	25.73	27.38	27.80	28.21	28.64	29.06	29.48	29.91	30.34	30.77	31.20	31.63	32.06
35	24.09	25.78	27.50	29.25	31.04	31.49	31.95	32.40	32.86	33.32	33.78	34.25	34.72	35.18	35.66	36.13
30	29.00	30.89	32.82	34.79	36.81	37.32	37.83	38.35	38.87	39.39	39.91	40.44	40.97	41.50	42.04	42.58
25	35.59	37.77	40.00	42.29	44.64	45.24	45.84	46.44	47.05	47.66	48.28	48.90	49.52	50.14	50.77	51.41
20	45.10	47.74	50.45	53.24	56.12	56.85	57.59	58.33	59.08	59.83	60.59	61.35	62.12	62.89	63.67	64.45
15	60.51	63.95	67.51	71.19	74.98	75.95	76.92	77.91	78.89	79.89	80.89	81.90	82.92	83.94	84.98	86.01
10	90.90	96.03	101.34	106.84	112.52	113.96	115.42	116.89	118.37	119.86	121.36	122.88	124.40	125.94	127.48	129.04

Description: This table shows the price to pay for a monthly payment mortgage loan at the yield rate.

Example: The price of a 10.75 %, 11 year mortgage loan to yield 8.00 % to maturity is $ 113.43.

YIELD	7.00%	7.25%	7.50%	7.75%	8.00%	8.25%	8.50%	8.75%	9.00%	9.25%	9.50%	9.75%	10.00%	10.25%	10.50%	10.75%
0.00	143.67	145.41	147.15	148.91	150.68	152.47	154.26	156.07	157.88	159.71	161.55	163.40	165.26	167.14	169.02	170.91
1.00	136.00	137.64	139.29	140.96	142.64	144.32	146.02	147.73	149.45	151.18	152.92	154.67	156.44	158.21	159.99	161.78
2.00	128.87	130.43	131.99	133.57	135.16	136.76	138.37	139.99	141.62	143.26	144.91	146.57	148.24	149.92	151.61	153.30
3.00	122.24	123.72	125.21	126.70	128.21	129.73	131.25	132.79	134.33	135.89	137.45	139.03	140.61	142.21	143.81	145.42
4.00	116.08	117.48	118.89	120.31	121.74	123.18	124.63	126.09	127.56	129.04	130.52	132.02	133.52	135.03	136.56	138.09
4.25	114.60	115.99	117.38	118.78	120.20	121.62	123.05	124.49	125.94	127.40	128.87	130.34	131.83	133.32	134.82	136.33
4.50	113.16	114.52	115.90	117.28	118.68	120.08	121.50	122.92	124.35	125.79	127.24	128.70	130.16	131.64	133.12	134.61
4.75	111.73	113.08	114.44	115.81	117.19	118.57	119.97	121.37	122.79	124.21	125.64	127.08	128.53	129.98	131.45	132.92
5.00	110.34	111.67	113.01	114.36	115.72	117.09	118.47	119.86	121.25	122.66	124.07	125.49	126.92	128.36	129.80	131.26
5.25	108.96	110.28	111.61	112.94	114.28	115.63	117.00	118.36	119.74	121.13	122.52	123.93	125.34	126.76	128.19	129.63
5.50	107.61	108.92	110.22	111.54	112.87	114.20	115.55	116.90	118.26	119.63	121.01	122.39	123.79	125.19	126.60	128.02
5.75	106.29	107.57	108.87	110.17	111.48	112.80	114.12	115.46	116.80	118.16	119.52	120.89	122.26	123.65	125.04	126.44
6.00	104.99	106.26	107.53	108.82	110.11	111.42	112.73	114.05	115.37	116.71	118.05	119.41	120.77	122.13	123.51	124.90
6.25	103.71	104.96	106.22	107.49	108.77	110.06	111.35	112.66	113.97	115.29	116.61	117.95	119.29	120.65	122.01	123.37
6.50	102.45	103.69	104.93	106.19	107.45	108.72	110.00	111.29	112.59	113.89	115.20	116.52	117.85	119.18	120.53	121.88
6.75	101.21	102.44	103.67	104.91	106.16	107.41	108.68	109.95	111.23	112.52	113.81	115.11	116.43	117.75	119.07	120.41
7.00	100.00	101.21	102.42	103.65	104.88	106.12	107.37	108.63	109.89	111.16	112.45	113.73	115.03	116.33	117.64	118.96
7.25	98.81	100.00	101.20	102.41	103.63	104.86	106.09	107.33	108.58	109.84	111.10	112.38	113.66	114.94	116.24	117.54
7.50	97.63	98.81	100.00	101.20	102.40	103.61	104.83	106.06	107.29	108.53	109.78	111.04	112.31	113.58	114.86	116.15
7.75	96.48	97.64	98.82	100.00	101.19	102.39	103.59	104.80	106.02	107.25	108.49	109.73	110.98	112.24	113.50	114.77
8.00	95.35	96.50	97.66	98.82	100.00	101.18	102.37	103.57	104.78	105.99	107.21	108.44	109.67	110.92	112.17	113.43
8.25	94.23	95.37	96.52	97.67	98.83	100.00	101.18	102.36	103.55	104.75	105.96	107.17	108.39	109.62	110.86	112.10
8.50	93.13	94.26	95.39	96.53	97.68	98.84	100.00	101.17	102.35	103.53	104.73	105.93	107.13	108.35	109.57	110.80
8.75	92.06	93.17	94.29	95.42	96.55	97.69	98.84	100.00	101.16	102.34	103.51	104.70	105.89	107.09	108.30	109.51
9.00	91.00	92.10	93.20	94.32	95.44	96.57	97.71	98.85	100.00	101.16	102.32	103.50	104.67	105.86	107.05	108.25
9.25	89.96	91.04	92.14	93.24	94.35	95.46	96.59	97.72	98.86	100.00	101.15	102.31	103.48	104.65	105.83	107.01
9.50	88.93	90.01	91.09	92.18	93.27	94.38	95.49	96.61	97.73	98.86	100.00	101.15	102.30	103.46	104.62	105.80
9.75	87.93	88.99	90.06	91.13	92.22	93.31	94.41	95.51	96.62	97.74	98.87	100.00	101.14	102.29	103.44	104.60
10.00	86.93	87.98	89.04	90.11	91.18	92.26	93.34	94.44	95.54	96.64	97.75	98.87	100.00	101.13	102.27	103.42
10.25	85.96	87.00	88.04	89.10	90.16	91.22	92.30	93.38	94.46	95.56	96.66	97.77	98.88	100.00	101.13	102.26
10.50	85.00	86.03	87.06	88.10	89.15	90.21	91.27	92.34	93.41	94.49	95.58	96.68	97.78	98.89	100.00	101.12
10.75	84.06	85.08	86.10	87.13	88.16	89.21	90.26	91.31	92.38	93.45	94.52	95.60	96.69	97.79	98.89	100.00
11.00	83.13	84.14	85.15	86.17	87.19	88.22	89.26	90.31	91.36	92.42	93.48	94.55	95.63	96.71	97.80	98.90
11.25	82.22	83.22	84.22	85.22	86.24	87.26	88.28	89.32	90.36	91.40	92.45	93.51	94.58	95.65	96.73	97.81
11.50	81.32	82.31	83.30	84.29	85.29	86.30	87.32	88.34	89.37	90.40	91.45	92.49	93.55	94.61	95.67	96.75
11.75	80.44	81.41	82.39	83.38	84.37	85.37	86.37	87.38	88.40	89.42	90.45	91.49	92.53	93.58	94.64	95.70
12.00	79.57	80.54	81.50	82.48	83.46	84.45	85.44	86.44	87.45	88.46	89.48	90.50	91.53	92.57	93.61	94.66
12.25	78.72	79.67	80.63	81.59	82.56	83.54	84.52	85.51	86.51	87.51	88.52	89.53	90.55	91.58	92.61	93.65
12.50	77.88	78.82	79.77	80.72	81.68	82.65	83.62	84.60	85.58	86.58	87.57	88.58	89.58	90.60	91.62	92.65
12.75	77.05	77.98	78.92	79.87	80.82	81.77	82.73	83.70	84.68	85.66	86.64	87.64	88.63	89.64	90.65	91.66
13.00	76.24	77.16	78.09	79.02	79.96	80.91	81.86	82.82	83.78	84.75	85.73	86.71	87.70	88.69	89.69	90.70
13.25	75.44	76.35	77.27	78.19	79.12	80.06	81.00	81.95	82.90	83.86	84.83	85.80	86.78	87.76	88.75	89.74
13.50	74.65	75.55	76.46	77.38	78.30	79.22	80.15	81.09	82.04	82.99	83.94	84.90	85.87	86.84	87.82	88.81
13.75	73.88	74.77	75.67	76.57	77.48	78.40	79.32	80.25	81.18	82.12	83.07	84.02	84.98	85.94	86.91	87.88
14.00	73.11	74.00	74.89	75.78	76.68	77.59	78.50	79.42	80.35	81.28	82.21	83.15	84.10	85.05	86.01	86.98
14.25	72.36	73.24	74.12	75.00	75.89	76.79	77.70	78.61	79.52	80.44	81.37	82.30	83.24	84.18	85.13	86.08
14.50	71.62	72.49	73.36	74.24	75.12	76.01	76.90	77.80	78.71	79.62	80.54	81.46	82.39	83.32	84.26	85.20
14.75	70.89	71.75	72.61	73.48	74.36	75.24	76.12	77.01	77.91	78.81	79.72	80.63	81.55	82.47	83.40	84.34
15.00	70.18	71.03	71.88	72.74	73.60	74.48	75.35	76.23	77.12	78.01	78.91	79.82	80.73	81.64	82.56	83.49
15.25	69.47	70.31	71.16	72.01	72.86	73.73	74.59	75.47	76.35	77.23	78.12	79.01	79.91	80.82	81.73	82.65
15.50	68.78	69.61	70.45	71.29	72.14	72.99	73.85	74.71	75.58	76.46	77.34	78.22	79.12	80.01	80.91	81.82
15.75	68.10	68.92	69.75	70.58	71.42	72.26	73.11	73.97	74.83	75.70	76.57	77.45	78.33	79.22	80.11	81.01
16.00	67.42	68.24	69.06	69.88	70.71	71.55	72.39	73.24	74.09	74.95	75.81	76.68	77.56	78.43	79.32	80.21
16.25	66.76	67.57	68.38	69.20	70.02	70.85	71.68	72.52	73.36	74.21	75.07	75.93	76.79	77.66	78.54	79.42
16.50	66.11	66.91	67.71	68.52	69.33	70.15	70.98	71.81	72.65	73.49	74.33	75.19	76.04	76.90	77.77	78.64
16.75	65.46	66.26	67.05	67.85	68.66	69.47	70.29	71.11	71.94	72.77	73.61	74.45	75.30	76.16	77.01	77.88
17.00	64.83	65.61	66.40	67.20	68.00	68.80	69.61	70.42	71.24	72.07	72.90	73.73	74.57	75.42	76.27	77.13
17.25	64.21	64.98	65.76	66.55	67.34	68.14	68.94	69.75	70.56	71.38	72.20	73.03	73.86	74.69	75.54	76.38
17.50	63.59	64.36	65.14	65.91	66.70	67.49	68.28	69.08	69.89	70.69	71.51	72.33	73.15	73.98	74.81	75.65
17.75	62.99	63.75	64.52	65.29	66.06	66.85	67.63	68.42	69.22	70.02	70.83	71.64	72.46	73.28	74.10	74.93
18.00	62.39	63.15	63.91	64.67	65.44	66.21	66.99	67.78	68.57	69.36	70.16	70.96	71.77	72.58	73.40	74.23
18.25	61.81	62.55	63.31	64.06	64.82	65.59	66.36	67.14	67.92	68.71	69.50	70.30	71.10	71.90	72.71	73.53
18.50	61.23	61.97	62.71	63.46	64.22	64.98	65.74	66.51	67.29	68.07	68.85	69.64	70.43	71.23	72.03	72.84
18.75	60.66	61.39	62.13	62.87	63.62	64.37	65.13	65.89	66.66	67.43	68.21	68.99	69.78	70.57	71.36	72.16
19.00	60.10	60.83	61.56	62.29	63.03	63.78	64.53	65.28	66.04	66.81	67.58	68.35	69.13	69.91	70.70	71.50
20.00	57.94	58.64	59.34	60.05	60.76	61.48	62.21	62.93	63.67	64.40	65.15	65.89	66.64	67.40	68.16	68.92
25.00	48.81	49.40	49.99	50.59	51.19	51.80	52.41	53.02	53.64	54.26	54.88	55.51	56.14	56.78	57.42	58.06
30.00	41.86	42.37	42.88	43.39	43.91	44.43	44.95	45.48	46.01	46.54	47.07	47.61	48.16	48.70	49.25	49.80

Description: This table shows the yield to maturity of a mortgage purchased at the price shown in the index.

Example: The yield to maturity of a 10.75 %, 11 year mortgage at a price of 113.00 is 8.07 %.

INTEREST RATE, %

PRICE	7.00%	7.25%	7.50%	7.75%	8.00%	8.25%	8.50%	8.75%	9.00%	9.25%	9.50%	9.75%	10.00%	10.25%	10.50%	10.75%
145	–	.05	.26	.48	.69	.91	1.12	1.34	1.55	1.77	1.98	2.20	2.41	2.62	2.84	3.05
140	.46	.68	.90	1.12	1.34	1.56	1.78	1.99	2.21	2.43	2.65	2.86	3.08	3.30	3.51	3.73
135	1.13	1.35	1.57	1.80	2.02	2.24	2.46	2.68	2.90	3.12	3.34	3.56	3.78	4.00	4.22	4.44
130	1.83	2.06	2.28	2.51	2.73	2.95	3.18	3.40	3.63	3.85	4.07	4.30	4.52	4.74	4.96	5.19
129	1.98	2.20	2.43	2.65	2.88	3.10	3.33	3.55	3.78	4.00	4.22	4.45	4.67	4.90	5.12	5.34
128	2.12	2.35	2.57	2.80	3.03	3.25	3.48	3.70	3.93	4.15	4.38	4.60	4.83	5.05	5.27	5.50
127	2.27	2.50	2.72	2.95	3.18	3.40	3.63	3.86	4.08	4.31	4.53	4.76	4.98	5.21	5.43	5.66
126	2.42	2.65	2.87	3.10	3.33	3.56	3.78	4.01	4.24	4.46	4.69	4.91	5.14	5.37	5.59	5.82
125	2.57	2.80	3.03	3.25	3.48	3.71	3.94	4.16	4.39	4.62	4.85	5.07	5.30	5.53	5.75	5.98
124	2.72	2.95	3.18	3.41	3.64	3.87	4.09	4.32	4.55	4.78	5.01	5.23	5.46	5.69	5.91	6.14
123	2.88	3.11	3.34	3.57	3.79	4.02	4.25	4.48	4.71	4.94	5.17	5.40	5.62	5.85	6.08	6.31
122	3.03	3.26	3.49	3.72	3.95	4.18	4.41	4.64	4.87	5.10	5.33	5.56	5.79	6.02	6.25	6.47
121	3.19	3.42	3.65	3.88	4.11	4.35	4.58	4.81	5.04	5.27	5.50	5.73	5.96	6.19	6.41	6.64
120	3.35	3.58	3.81	4.05	4.28	4.51	4.74	4.97	5.20	5.43	5.66	5.89	6.12	6.35	6.59	6.82
119	3.51	3.74	3.98	4.21	4.44	4.67	4.91	5.14	5.37	5.60	5.83	6.06	6.30	6.53	6.76	6.99
118	3.68	3.91	4.14	4.38	4.61	4.84	5.07	5.31	5.54	5.77	6.00	6.24	6.47	6.70	6.93	7.16
117	3.84	4.07	4.31	4.54	4.78	5.01	5.24	5.48	5.71	5.94	6.18	6.41	6.64	6.88	7.11	7.34
116	4.01	4.24	4.48	4.71	4.95	5.18	5.42	5.65	5.89	6.12	6.35	6.59	6.82	7.05	7.29	7.52
115	4.18	4.41	4.65	4.88	5.12	5.36	5.59	5.83	6.06	6.30	6.53	6.77	7.00	7.23	7.47	7.70
114	4.35	4.59	4.82	5.06	5.29	5.53	5.77	6.00	6.24	6.48	6.71	6.95	7.18	7.42	7.65	7.89
113	4.52	4.76	5.00	5.23	5.47	5.71	5.95	6.18	6.42	6.66	6.89	7.13	7.37	7.60	7.84	8.07
112	4.70	4.94	5.17	5.41	5.65	5.89	6.13	6.36	6.60	6.84	7.08	7.31	7.55	7.79	8.03	8.26
111	4.88	5.11	5.35	5.59	5.83	6.07	6.31	6.55	6.79	7.03	7.26	7.50	7.74	7.98	8.22	8.46
110	5.06	5.30	5.54	5.78	6.02	6.26	6.50	6.74	6.97	7.21	7.45	7.69	7.93	8.17	8.41	8.65
109	5.24	5.48	5.72	5.96	6.20	6.44	6.68	6.92	7.16	7.41	7.65	7.89	8.13	8.37	8.61	8.85
108	5.42	5.67	5.91	6.15	6.39	6.63	6.87	7.12	7.36	7.60	7.84	8.08	8.32	8.56	8.80	9.05
107	5.61	5.85	6.10	6.34	6.58	6.82	7.07	7.31	7.55	7.79	8.04	8.28	8.52	8.76	9.01	9.25
106	5.80	6.04	6.29	6.53	6.78	7.02	7.26	7.51	7.75	7.99	8.24	8.48	8.72	8.97	9.21	9.45
105	5.99	6.24	6.48	6.73	6.97	7.22	7.46	7.71	7.95	8.19	8.44	8.68	8.93	9.17	9.42	9.66
104	6.19	6.43	6.68	6.92	7.17	7.42	7.66	7.91	8.15	8.40	8.64	8.89	9.14	9.38	9.63	9.87
103	6.39	6.63	6.88	7.13	7.37	7.62	7.87	8.11	8.36	8.61	8.85	9.10	9.35	9.59	9.84	10.09
102	6.59	6.83	7.08	7.33	7.58	7.82	8.07	8.32	8.57	8.82	9.06	9.31	9.56	9.81	10.05	10.30
101	6.79	7.04	7.29	7.54	7.78	8.03	8.28	8.53	8.78	9.03	9.28	9.53	9.78	10.02	10.27	10.52
100	7.00	7.25	7.50	7.75	8.00	8.25	8.50	8.75	9.00	9.25	9.50	9.75	10.00	10.25	10.50	10.75
99	7.20	7.46	7.71	7.96	8.21	8.46	8.71	8.96	9.21	9.46	9.72	9.97	10.22	10.47	10.72	10.97
98	7.42	7.67	7.92	8.17	8.43	8.68	8.93	9.18	9.43	9.69	9.94	10.19	10.44	10.70	10.95	11.20
97	7.63	7.89	8.14	8.39	8.65	8.90	9.15	9.41	9.66	9.91	10.17	10.42	10.67	10.93	11.18	11.44
96	7.85	8.10	8.36	8.61	8.87	9.12	9.38	9.63	9.89	10.14	10.40	10.65	10.91	11.16	11.42	11.67
95	8.07	8.33	8.58	8.84	9.10	9.35	9.61	9.86	10.12	10.38	10.63	10.89	11.14	11.40	11.66	11.91
94	8.30	8.55	8.81	9.07	9.33	9.58	9.84	10.10	10.35	10.61	10.87	11.13	11.38	11.64	11.90	12.16
93	8.53	8.78	9.04	9.30	9.56	9.82	10.08	10.34	10.59	10.85	11.11	11.37	11.63	11.89	12.15	12.41
92	8.76	9.02	9.28	9.54	9.80	10.06	10.32	10.58	10.84	11.10	11.36	11.62	11.88	12.14	12.40	12.66
91	8.99	9.26	9.52	9.78	10.04	10.30	10.56	10.82	11.08	11.35	11.61	11.87	12.13	12.39	12.65	12.92
90	9.23	9.50	9.76	10.02	10.28	10.55	10.81	11.07	11.33	11.60	11.86	12.12	12.39	12.65	12.91	13.18
89	9.48	9.74	10.01	10.27	10.53	10.80	11.06	11.33	11.59	11.85	12.12	12.38	12.65	12.91	13.18	13.44
88	9.73	9.99	10.26	10.52	10.79	11.05	11.32	11.58	11.85	12.12	12.38	12.65	12.91	13.18	13.45	13.71
87	9.98	10.24	10.51	10.78	11.04	11.31	11.58	11.85	12.11	12.38	12.65	12.92	13.18	13.45	13.72	13.99
86	10.23	10.50	10.77	11.04	11.31	11.58	11.84	12.11	12.38	12.65	12.92	13.19	13.46	13.73	14.00	14.27
85	10.50	10.77	11.03	11.30	11.57	11.84	12.11	12.38	12.66	12.93	13.20	13.47	13.74	14.01	14.28	14.55
84	10.76	11.03	11.30	11.57	11.85	12.12	12.39	12.66	12.93	13.21	13.48	13.75	14.02	14.30	14.57	14.84
83	11.03	11.30	11.58	11.85	12.12	12.40	12.67	12.94	13.22	13.49	13.77	14.04	14.31	14.59	14.86	15.14
82	11.31	11.58	11.86	12.13	12.40	12.68	12.95	13.23	13.51	13.78	14.06	14.33	14.61	14.89	15.16	15.44
81	11.59	11.86	12.14	12.41	12.69	12.97	13.25	13.52	13.80	14.08	14.36	14.63	14.91	15.19	15.47	15.75
80	11.87	12.15	12.43	12.71	12.98	13.26	13.54	13.82	14.10	14.38	14.66	14.94	15.22	15.50	15.78	16.06
79	12.16	12.44	12.72	13.00	13.28	13.56	13.84	14.12	14.40	14.69	14.97	15.25	15.53	15.81	16.10	16.38
78	12.46	12.74	13.02	13.30	13.59	13.87	14.15	14.43	14.72	15.00	15.28	15.57	15.85	16.14	16.42	16.70
77	12.76	13.04	13.33	13.61	13.90	14.18	14.46	14.75	15.03	15.32	15.60	15.89	16.18	16.46	16.75	17.04
76	13.07	13.35	13.64	13.93	14.21	14.50	14.78	15.07	15.36	15.65	15.93	16.22	16.51	16.80	17.09	17.38
75	13.38	13.67	13.96	14.25	14.53	14.82	15.11	15.40	15.69	15.98	16.27	16.56	16.85	17.14	17.43	17.72
74	13.70	13.99	14.28	14.57	14.86	15.15	15.44	15.74	16.03	16.32	16.61	16.90	17.20	17.49	17.78	18.08
70	15.06	15.36	15.65	15.95	16.25	16.55	16.85	17.15	17.45	17.75	18.05	18.36	18.66	18.96	19.27	19.57
65	16.93	17.24	17.55	17.86	18.17	18.49	18.80	19.11	19.43	19.74	20.06	20.37	20.69	21.01	21.32	21.64
60	19.04	19.37	19.69	20.02	20.35	20.67	21.00	21.33	21.66	21.99	22.33	22.66	22.99	23.32	23.66	23.99
55	21.45	21.80	22.14	22.49	22.83	23.18	23.53	23.88	24.23	24.58	24.93	25.28	25.63	25.99	26.34	26.70
50	24.26	24.62	24.99	25.36	25.73	26.10	26.47	26.84	27.21	27.59	27.96	28.34	28.72	29.10	29.48	29.86
45	27.57	27.97	28.36	28.76	29.16	29.56	29.96	30.36	30.76	31.17	31.57	31.98	32.39	32.80	33.21	33.62
40	31.59	32.02	32.45	32.89	33.32	33.76	34.20	34.64	35.08	35.52	35.97	36.41	36.86	37.31	37.77	38.22
35	36.61	37.08	37.56	38.05	38.53	39.02	39.51	40.00	40.49	40.99	41.48	41.98	42.49	42.99	43.50	44.01

MORTGAGE PRICE

Description: This table shows the price to pay for a monthly payment mortgage loan at the yield rate.

Example: The price of a 15.00 %, 11 year mortgage loan to yield 8.00 % to maturity is $ 135.86.

INTEREST RATE, %

YIELD	11.00%	11.25%	11.50%	11.75%	12.00%	12.25%	12.50%	12.75%	13.00%	13.25%	13.50%	13.75%	14.00%	14.25%	14.50%	15.00%
0.00	172.82	174.74	176.66	178.60	180.55	182.51	184.48	186.46	188.44	190.44	192.45	194.47	196.50	198.54	200.59	204.72
1.00	163.59	165.40	167.23	169.06	170.90	172.76	174.62	176.50	178.38	180.27	182.18	184.09	186.01	187.94	189.88	193.79
2.00	155.01	156.73	158.46	160.20	161.95	163.70	165.47	167.25	169.03	170.82	172.63	174.44	176.26	178.09	179.93	183.63
3.00	147.04	148.67	150.31	151.96	153.62	155.29	156.96	158.65	160.34	162.04	163.75	165.47	167.20	168.93	170.67	174.19
4.00	139.63	141.18	142.73	144.30	145.87	147.45	149.04	150.64	152.25	153.87	155.49	157.12	158.76	160.41	162.07	165.40
4.25	137.85	139.38	140.92	142.47	144.02	145.58	147.15	148.73	150.32	151.91	153.52	155.13	156.75	158.37	160.01	163.30
4.50	136.11	137.62	139.14	140.67	142.20	143.74	145.29	146.85	148.42	149.99	151.58	153.17	154.77	156.37	157.99	161.24
4.75	134.40	135.89	137.39	138.90	140.41	141.94	143.47	145.01	146.55	148.11	149.67	151.24	152.82	154.41	156.00	159.21
5.00	132.72	134.19	135.67	137.16	138.66	140.16	141.67	143.19	144.72	146.26	147.80	149.35	150.91	152.48	154.05	157.22
5.25	131.07	132.52	133.99	135.46	136.93	138.42	139.91	141.41	142.92	144.44	145.96	147.49	149.03	150.58	152.14	155.27
5.50	129.45	130.88	132.33	133.78	135.24	136.71	138.18	139.66	141.15	142.65	144.16	145.67	147.19	148.72	150.25	153.34
5.75	127.85	129.27	130.70	132.13	133.57	135.02	136.48	137.94	139.41	140.89	142.38	143.88	145.38	146.89	148.40	151.46
6.00	126.29	127.69	129.10	130.51	131.94	133.37	134.81	136.25	137.71	139.17	140.64	142.11	143.60	145.09	146.58	149.60
6.25	124.75	126.13	127.52	128.92	130.33	131.74	133.16	134.59	136.03	137.47	138.92	140.38	141.85	143.32	144.80	147.78
6.50	123.24	124.60	125.98	127.36	128.75	130.14	131.55	132.96	134.38	135.80	137.24	138.68	140.13	141.58	143.04	145.99
6.75	121.75	123.10	124.46	125.82	127.19	128.57	129.96	131.36	132.76	134.17	135.58	137.01	138.44	139.87	141.32	144.22
7.00	120.29	121.62	122.96	124.31	125.67	127.03	128.40	129.78	131.16	132.56	133.96	135.36	136.77	138.19	139.62	142.49
7.25	118.85	120.17	121.50	122.83	124.17	125.52	126.87	128.23	129.60	130.97	132.36	133.75	135.14	136.54	137.95	140.79
7.50	117.44	118.74	120.05	121.37	122.69	124.02	125.36	126.71	128.06	129.42	130.78	132.16	133.54	134.92	136.32	139.12
7.75	116.05	117.34	118.63	119.94	121.24	122.56	123.88	125.21	126.55	127.89	129.24	130.60	131.96	133.33	134.70	137.48
8.00	114.69	115.96	117.24	118.53	119.82	121.12	122.43	123.74	125.06	126.39	127.72	129.06	130.41	131.76	133.12	135.86
8.25	113.35	114.61	115.87	117.14	118.42	119.70	120.99	122.29	123.60	124.91	126.23	127.55	128.88	130.22	131.57	134.27
8.50	112.03	113.27	114.52	115.78	117.04	118.31	119.59	120.87	122.16	123.46	124.76	126.07	127.38	128.71	130.04	132.71
8.75	110.73	111.96	113.20	114.44	115.69	116.94	118.20	119.47	120.75	122.03	123.32	124.61	125.91	127.22	128.53	131.18
9.00	109.46	110.67	111.89	113.12	114.36	115.60	116.84	118.10	119.36	120.62	121.90	123.18	124.46	125.75	127.05	129.67
9.25	108.21	109.41	110.61	111.83	113.05	114.27	115.51	116.75	117.99	119.24	120.50	121.77	123.04	124.31	125.60	128.18
9.50	106.98	108.16	109.35	110.55	111.76	112.97	114.19	115.42	116.65	117.89	119.13	120.38	121.64	122.90	124.17	126.72
9.75	105.76	106.94	108.12	109.30	110.49	111.69	112.90	114.11	115.33	116.55	117.78	119.02	120.26	121.51	122.76	125.29
10.00	104.57	105.73	106.90	108.07	109.25	110.43	111.63	112.82	114.03	115.24	116.45	117.68	118.90	120.14	121.38	123.88
10.25	103.40	104.55	105.70	106.86	108.03	109.20	110.38	111.56	112.75	113.95	115.15	116.36	117.57	118.79	120.02	122.49
10.50	102.25	103.38	104.52	105.67	106.82	107.98	109.15	110.32	111.49	112.68	113.87	115.06	116.26	117.47	118.68	121.12
10.75	101.11	102.24	103.36	104.50	105.64	106.78	107.94	109.09	110.26	111.43	112.60	113.79	114.97	116.17	117.37	119.78
11.00	100.00	101.11	102.22	103.35	104.47	105.61	106.75	107.89	109.04	110.20	111.36	112.53	113.71	114.89	116.07	118.46
11.25	98.90	100.00	101.10	102.21	103.33	104.45	105.57	106.71	107.85	108.99	110.14	111.30	112.46	113.63	114.80	117.16
11.50	97.82	98.91	100.00	101.10	102.20	103.31	104.42	105.54	106.67	107.80	108.94	110.08	111.23	112.39	113.55	115.88
11.75	96.76	97.84	98.92	100.00	101.09	102.19	103.29	104.40	105.51	106.63	107.76	108.89	110.02	111.17	112.31	114.63
12.00	95.72	96.78	97.85	98.92	100.00	101.08	102.18	103.27	104.37	105.48	106.59	107.71	108.84	109.97	111.10	113.39
12.25	94.69	95.74	96.80	97.86	98.93	100.00	101.08	102.16	103.25	104.35	105.45	106.56	107.67	108.79	109.91	112.17
12.50	93.68	94.72	95.76	96.81	97.87	98.93	100.00	101.07	102.15	103.24	104.33	105.42	106.52	107.63	108.74	110.97
12.75	92.69	93.71	94.75	95.79	96.83	97.88	98.94	100.00	101.07	102.14	103.22	104.30	105.39	106.48	107.58	109.80
13.00	91.71	92.72	93.75	94.78	95.81	96.85	97.89	98.94	100.00	101.06	102.13	103.20	104.28	105.36	106.45	108.64
13.25	90.75	91.75	92.76	93.78	94.80	95.83	96.87	97.91	98.95	100.00	101.06	102.12	103.18	104.25	105.33	107.50
13.50	89.80	90.79	91.79	92.80	93.81	94.83	95.85	96.88	97.92	98.96	100.00	101.05	102.10	103.16	104.23	106.37
13.75	88.86	89.85	90.84	91.84	92.84	93.85	94.86	95.88	96.90	97.93	98.96	100.00	101.04	102.09	103.15	105.27
14.00	87.95	88.92	89.90	90.89	91.88	92.88	93.88	94.89	95.90	96.92	97.94	98.97	100.00	101.04	102.08	104.18
14.25	87.04	88.01	88.98	89.95	90.94	91.92	92.91	93.91	94.91	95.92	96.93	97.95	98.97	100.00	101.03	103.11
14.50	86.15	87.11	88.07	89.04	90.01	90.99	91.97	92.95	93.94	94.94	95.94	96.95	97.96	98.98	100.00	102.06
14.75	85.28	86.22	87.18	88.13	89.09	90.06	91.03	92.01	92.99	93.98	94.97	95.96	96.97	97.97	98.98	101.02
15.00	84.42	85.35	86.29	87.24	88.19	89.15	90.11	91.08	92.05	93.03	94.01	94.99	95.99	96.98	97.98	100.00
15.25	83.57	84.50	85.43	86.36	87.31	88.25	89.21	90.16	91.12	92.09	93.06	94.04	95.02	96.01	97.00	99.00
15.50	82.73	83.65	84.57	85.50	86.43	87.37	88.31	89.26	90.21	91.17	92.13	93.10	94.07	95.05	96.03	98.01
15.75	81.91	82.82	83.73	84.65	85.57	86.50	87.44	88.37	89.32	90.27	91.22	92.17	93.14	94.10	95.08	97.03
16.00	81.10	82.00	82.91	83.81	84.73	85.65	86.57	87.50	88.43	89.37	90.32	91.26	92.22	93.17	94.14	96.07
16.25	80.30	81.19	82.09	82.99	83.90	84.81	85.72	86.64	87.57	88.49	89.43	90.37	91.31	92.26	93.21	95.13
16.50	79.52	80.40	81.29	82.18	83.08	83.98	84.88	85.79	86.71	87.63	88.55	89.48	90.42	91.36	92.30	94.20
16.75	78.75	79.62	80.50	81.38	82.27	83.16	84.06	84.96	85.87	86.78	87.69	88.61	89.54	90.47	91.40	93.28
17.00	77.98	78.85	79.72	80.59	81.47	82.36	83.24	84.14	85.04	85.94	86.85	87.76	88.67	89.59	90.52	92.38
17.25	77.24	78.09	78.95	79.82	80.69	81.56	82.44	83.33	84.22	85.11	86.01	86.91	87.82	88.73	89.65	91.49
17.50	76.50	77.34	78.20	79.06	79.92	80.78	81.66	82.53	83.41	84.30	85.19	86.08	86.98	87.88	88.79	90.62
17.75	75.77	76.61	77.45	78.30	79.16	80.02	80.88	81.75	82.62	83.50	84.38	85.26	86.15	87.05	87.95	89.76
18.00	75.05	75.89	76.72	77.56	78.41	79.26	80.12	80.97	81.84	82.71	83.58	84.46	85.34	86.22	87.11	88.91
18.25	74.35	75.17	76.00	76.83	77.67	78.51	79.36	80.21	81.07	81.93	82.79	83.66	84.54	85.41	86.30	88.07
18.50	73.65	74.47	75.29	76.12	76.95	77.78	78.62	79.46	80.31	81.16	82.02	82.88	83.75	84.62	85.49	87.25
18.75	72.97	73.78	74.59	75.41	76.23	77.06	77.89	78.72	79.56	80.41	81.26	82.11	82.97	83.83	84.69	86.44
19.00	72.29	73.09	73.90	74.71	75.53	76.34	77.17	78.00	78.83	79.67	80.51	81.35	82.20	83.05	83.91	85.64
20.00	69.69	70.46	71.24	72.02	72.81	73.60	74.39	75.19	75.99	76.80	77.61	78.42	79.24	80.06	80.89	82.56
25.00	58.71	59.36	60.02	60.67	61.34	62.00	62.67	63.34	64.02	64.70	65.38	66.07	66.76	67.45	68.15	69.55
30.00	50.36	50.92	51.48	52.04	52.61	53.18	53.75	54.33	54.91	55.49	56.08	56.67	57.26	57.85	58.45	59.65

Description: This table shows the yield to maturity of a mortgage purchased at the price shown in the index.

Example: The yield to maturity of a 15.00 %, 11 year mortgage at a price of 117.00 is 11.28 %.

INTEREST RATE, %

PRICE	11.00%	11.25%	11.50%	11.75%	12.00%	12.25%	12.50%	12.75%	13.00%	13.25%	13.50%	13.75%	14.00%	14.25%	14.50%	15.00%
190	–	–	–	–	–	–	–	–	–	.04	.23	.42	.61	.79	.98	1.36
185	–	–	–	–	–	–	–	.14	.33	.52	.71	.90	1.10	1.29	1.48	1.86
180	–	–	–	–	–	.25	.44	.63	.83	1.02	1.22	1.41	1.60	1.80	1.99	2.37
175	–	–	.17	.36	.56	.76	.96	1.15	1.35	1.54	1.74	1.93	2.13	2.32	2.52	2.91
170	.29	.49	.69	.89	1.09	1.29	1.49	1.69	1.89	2.09	2.28	2.48	2.68	2.87	3.07	3.46
165	.84	1.04	1.24	1.44	1.65	1.85	2.05	2.25	2.45	2.65	2.85	3.05	3.25	3.45	3.65	4.04
160	1.40	1.61	1.81	2.02	2.22	2.43	2.63	2.83	3.04	3.24	3.44	3.64	3.84	4.05	4.25	4.65
155	2.00	2.20	2.41	2.62	2.82	3.03	3.24	3.44	3.65	3.85	4.06	4.26	4.47	4.67	4.87	5.28
150	2.62	2.83	3.03	3.24	3.45	3.66	3.87	4.08	4.29	4.49	4.70	4.91	5.12	5.32	5.53	5.94
145	3.26	3.48	3.69	3.90	4.11	4.32	4.53	4.75	4.96	5.17	5.38	5.59	5.80	6.01	6.22	6.63
140	3.94	4.16	4.37	4.59	4.80	5.02	5.23	5.45	5.66	5.87	6.09	6.30	6.51	6.73	6.94	7.36
135	4.66	4.88	5.09	5.31	5.53	5.75	5.97	6.18	6.40	6.62	6.83	7.05	7.27	7.48	7.70	8.13
130	5.41	5.63	5.85	6.08	6.30	6.52	6.74	6.96	7.18	7.40	7.62	7.84	8.06	8.28	8.50	8.94
125	6.20	6.43	6.66	6.88	7.11	7.33	7.56	7.78	8.01	8.23	8.45	8.68	8.90	9.13	9.35	9.80
123	6.53	6.76	6.99	7.22	7.44	7.67	7.90	8.12	8.35	8.57	8.80	9.03	9.25	9.48	9.70	10.15
122	6.70	6.93	7.16	7.39	7.61	7.84	8.07	8.30	8.52	8.75	8.98	9.20	9.43	9.66	9.88	10.33
121	6.87	7.10	7.33	7.56	7.79	8.02	8.24	8.47	8.70	8.93	9.16	9.38	9.61	9.84	10.06	10.52
120	7.04	7.27	7.50	7.73	7.96	8.19	8.42	8.65	8.88	9.11	9.34	9.56	9.79	10.02	10.25	10.70
119	7.22	7.45	7.68	7.91	8.14	8.37	8.60	8.83	9.06	9.29	9.52	9.75	9.98	10.21	10.43	10.89
118	7.40	7.63	7.86	8.09	8.32	8.55	8.78	9.01	9.24	9.47	9.70	9.93	10.16	10.39	10.62	11.08
117	7.57	7.81	8.04	8.27	8.50	8.73	8.97	9.20	9.43	9.66	9.89	10.12	10.35	10.58	10.82	11.28
116	7.75	7.99	8.22	8.45	8.69	8.92	9.15	9.38	9.62	9.85	10.08	10.31	10.55	10.78	11.01	11.47
115	7.94	8.17	8.41	8.64	8.87	9.11	9.34	9.57	9.81	10.04	10.27	10.51	10.74	10.97	11.21	11.67
114	8.12	8.36	8.59	8.83	9.06	9.30	9.53	9.77	10.00	10.23	10.47	10.70	10.94	11.17	11.40	11.87
113	8.31	8.55	8.78	9.02	9.25	9.49	9.73	9.96	10.20	10.43	10.67	10.90	11.14	11.37	11.61	12.07
112	8.50	8.74	8.97	9.21	9.45	9.68	9.92	10.16	10.39	10.63	10.87	11.10	11.34	11.57	11.81	12.28
111	8.69	8.93	9.17	9.41	9.64	9.88	10.12	10.36	10.59	10.83	11.07	11.31	11.54	11.78	12.02	12.49
110	8.89	9.13	9.37	9.61	9.84	10.08	10.32	10.56	10.80	11.04	11.27	11.51	11.75	11.99	12.23	12.70
109	9.09	9.33	9.57	9.81	10.05	10.29	10.52	10.76	11.00	11.24	11.48	11.72	11.96	12.20	12.44	12.92
108	9.29	9.53	9.77	10.01	10.25	10.49	10.73	10.97	11.21	11.45	11.69	11.93	12.17	12.41	12.65	13.13
107	9.49	9.73	9.97	10.22	10.46	10.70	10.94	11.18	11.42	11.67	11.91	12.15	12.39	12.63	12.87	13.36
106	9.70	9.94	10.18	10.43	10.67	10.91	11.15	11.40	11.64	11.88	12.12	12.37	12.61	12.85	13.09	13.58
105	9.90	10.15	10.39	10.64	10.88	11.13	11.37	11.61	11.86	12.10	12.34	12.59	12.83	13.08	13.32	13.81
104	10.12	10.36	10.61	10.85	11.10	11.34	11.59	11.83	12.08	12.32	12.57	12.81	13.06	13.30	13.55	14.04
103	10.33	10.58	10.82	11.07	11.32	11.56	11.81	12.06	12.30	12.55	12.79	13.04	13.29	13.53	13.78	14.27
102	10.55	10.80	11.04	11.29	11.54	11.79	12.03	12.28	12.53	12.78	13.02	13.27	13.52	13.77	14.01	14.51
101	10.77	11.02	11.27	11.52	11.77	12.01	12.26	12.51	12.76	13.01	13.26	13.51	13.76	14.00	14.25	14.75
100	11.00	11.25	11.50	11.75	12.00	12.25	12.50	12.75	13.00	13.25	13.50	13.75	14.00	14.25	14.50	15.00
99	11.22	11.47	11.73	11.98	12.23	12.48	12.73	12.98	13.23	13.48	13.74	13.99	14.24	14.49	14.74	15.24
98	11.45	11.71	11.96	12.21	12.46	12.72	12.97	13.22	13.47	13.73	13.98	14.23	14.49	14.74	14.99	15.50
97	11.69	11.94	12.20	12.45	12.70	12.96	13.21	13.47	13.72	13.97	14.23	14.48	14.74	14.99	15.24	15.75
96	11.93	12.18	12.44	12.69	12.95	13.20	13.46	13.71	13.97	14.22	14.48	14.74	14.99	15.25	15.50	16.01
95	12.17	12.43	12.68	12.94	13.20	13.45	13.71	13.97	14.22	14.48	14.74	14.99	15.25	15.51	15.76	16.28
94	12.42	12.67	12.93	13.19	13.45	13.71	13.96	14.22	14.48	14.74	15.00	15.26	15.51	15.77	16.03	16.55
93	12.67	12.93	13.18	13.44	13.70	13.96	14.22	14.48	14.74	15.00	15.26	15.52	15.78	16.04	16.30	16.82
92	12.92	13.18	13.44	13.70	13.96	14.22	14.49	14.75	15.01	15.27	15.53	15.79	16.05	16.32	16.58	17.10
91	13.18	13.44	13.70	13.97	14.23	14.49	14.75	15.02	15.28	15.54	15.81	16.07	16.33	16.59	16.86	17.39
90	13.44	13.71	13.97	14.23	14.50	14.76	15.03	15.29	15.55	15.82	16.08	16.35	16.61	16.88	17.14	17.67
89	13.71	13.97	14.24	14.50	14.77	15.04	15.30	15.57	15.83	16.10	16.37	16.63	16.90	17.17	17.43	17.97
88	13.98	14.25	14.51	14.78	15.05	15.32	15.58	15.85	16.12	16.39	16.66	16.92	17.19	17.46	17.73	18.27
87	14.26	14.53	14.79	15.06	15.33	15.60	15.87	16.14	16.41	16.68	16.95	17.22	17.49	17.76	18.03	18.57
86	14.54	14.81	15.08	15.35	15.62	15.89	16.16	16.43	16.71	16.98	17.25	17.52	17.79	18.06	18.34	18.88
85	14.83	15.10	15.37	15.64	15.91	16.19	16.46	16.73	17.01	17.28	17.55	17.83	18.10	18.37	18.65	19.20
84	15.12	15.39	15.67	15.94	16.21	16.49	16.76	17.04	17.31	17.59	17.86	18.14	18.41	18.69	18.97	19.52
83	15.41	15.69	15.97	16.24	16.52	16.79	17.07	17.35	17.62	17.90	18.18	18.46	18.73	19.01	19.29	19.85
82	15.72	16.00	16.27	16.55	16.83	17.11	17.39	17.66	17.94	18.22	18.50	18.78	19.06	19.34	19.62	20.18
81	16.03	16.31	16.59	16.87	17.15	17.43	17.71	17.99	18.27	18.55	18.83	19.11	19.39	19.68	19.96	20.52
80	16.34	16.62	16.90	17.19	17.47	17.75	18.03	18.32	18.60	18.88	19.17	19.45	19.73	20.02	20.30	20.87
79	16.66	16.95	17.23	17.51	17.80	18.08	18.37	18.65	18.94	19.22	19.51	19.79	20.08	20.37	20.65	21.23
78	16.99	17.28	17.56	17.85	18.13	18.42	18.71	18.99	19.28	19.57	19.86	20.14	20.43	20.72	21.01	21.59
77	17.32	17.61	17.90	18.19	18.48	18.76	19.05	19.34	19.63	19.92	20.21	20.50	20.79	21.09	21.38	21.96
76	17.67	17.96	18.25	18.54	18.83	19.12	19.41	19.70	19.99	20.28	20.58	20.87	21.16	21.46	21.75	22.34
75	18.01	18.31	18.60	18.89	19.18	19.48	19.77	20.06	20.36	20.65	20.95	21.24	21.54	21.84	22.13	22.73
74	18.37	18.66	18.96	19.25	19.55	19.84	20.14	20.44	20.73	21.03	21.33	21.63	21.92	22.22	22.52	23.12
73	18.73	19.03	19.33	19.62	19.92	20.22	20.52	20.82	21.12	21.42	21.72	22.02	22.32	22.62	22.92	23.53
70	19.87	20.18	20.48	20.79	21.09	21.40	21.71	22.01	22.32	22.63	22.94	23.25	23.55	23.86	24.17	24.80
65	21.96	22.28	22.60	22.92	23.24	23.56	23.88	24.21	24.53	24.85	25.18	25.50	25.83	26.15	26.48	27.13
60	24.33	24.67	25.00	25.34	25.68	26.02	26.36	26.70	27.04	27.38	27.73	28.07	28.41	28.76	29.10	29.80

Description: This table shows the price to pay for a monthly payment mortgage loan at the yield rate.

Example: The price of a 6.75 %, 12 year mortgage loan to yield 8.00 % to maturity is $ 93.78.

INTEREST RATE, %

YIELD	0.00%	1.00%	2.00%	3.00%	4.00%	4.25%	4.50%	4.75%	5.00%	5.25%	5.50%	5.75%	6.00%	6.25%	6.50%	6.75%
0.00	100.00	106.16	112.56	119.20	126.08	127.83	129.60	131.39	133.18	135.00	136.82	138.67	140.52	142.39	144.28	146.17
1.00	94.20	100.00	106.03	112.28	118.76	120.41	122.08	123.76	125.45	127.16	128.88	130.62	132.37	134.13	135.90	137.69
2.00	88.84	94.31	100.00	105.90	112.01	113.56	115.14	116.72	118.32	119.93	121.55	123.19	124.84	126.50	128.17	129.86
3.00	83.89	89.06	94.43	100.00	105.77	107.24	108.72	110.22	111.73	113.25	114.78	116.33	117.89	119.46	121.04	122.63
4.00	79.32	84.20	89.28	94.55	100.00	101.39	102.80	104.21	105.64	107.08	108.53	109.99	111.46	112.94	114.44	115.94
4.25	78.23	83.05	88.06	93.25	98.63	100.00	101.38	102.78	104.19	105.61	107.04	108.48	109.93	111.39	112.86	114.35
4.50	77.16	81.91	86.85	91.98	97.28	98.63	100.00	101.38	102.76	104.16	105.57	106.99	108.43	109.87	111.32	114.35
4.75	76.11	80.80	85.67	90.73	95.96	97.29	98.64	100.00	101.37	102.75	104.14	105.54	106.95	108.38	109.81	111.26
5.00	75.08	79.71	84.52	89.50	94.66	95.98	97.31	98.65	100.00	101.36	102.73	104.12	105.51	106.91	108.33	109.75
5.25	74.08	78.64	83.38	88.30	93.39	94.69	96.00	97.32	98.66	100.00	101.35	102.72	104.09	105.48	106.87	108.28
5.50	73.09	77.59	82.27	87.12	92.14	93.43	94.72	96.02	97.34	98.66	100.00	101.35	102.70	104.07	105.45	106.83
5.75	72.12	76.56	81.17	85.96	90.92	92.19	93.46	94.75	96.05	97.35	98.67	100.00	101.34	102.69	104.05	105.41
6.00	71.16	75.55	80.10	84.83	89.72	90.97	92.23	93.50	94.78	96.07	97.37	98.68	100.00	101.33	102.67	104.02
6.25	70.23	74.56	79.05	83.71	88.54	89.77	91.02	92.27	93.53	94.81	96.09	97.38	98.69	100.00	101.33	102.66
6.50	69.31	73.58	78.02	82.62	87.38	88.60	89.83	91.06	92.31	93.57	94.84	96.11	97.40	98.69	100.00	101.32
6.75	68.41	72.63	77.01	81.55	86.25	87.45	88.66	89.88	91.11	92.35	93.60	94.86	96.13	97.41	98.70	100.00
7.00	67.53	71.69	76.01	80.49	85.14	86.32	87.52	88.72	89.94	91.16	92.39	93.64	94.89	96.15	97.43	98.71
7.25	66.66	70.77	75.04	79.46	84.04	85.21	86.39	87.58	88.78	89.99	91.21	92.44	93.67	94.92	96.18	97.44
7.50	65.81	69.86	74.08	78.45	82.97	84.13	85.29	86.46	87.65	88.84	90.04	91.26	92.48	93.71	94.95	96.20
7.75	64.97	68.98	73.14	77.45	81.92	83.06	84.21	85.37	86.54	87.71	88.90	90.10	91.30	92.52	93.74	94.98
8.00	64.15	68.11	72.21	76.47	80.88	82.01	83.15	84.29	85.44	86.61	87.78	88.96	90.15	91.35	92.56	93.78
8.25	63.35	67.25	71.31	75.51	79.87	80.98	82.10	83.23	84.37	85.52	86.68	87.84	89.02	90.21	91.40	92.60
8.50	62.56	66.41	70.42	74.57	78.87	79.97	81.08	82.19	83.32	84.45	85.60	86.75	87.91	89.08	90.26	91.45
8.75	61.78	65.59	69.55	73.65	77.89	78.98	80.07	81.17	82.29	83.41	84.54	85.67	86.82	87.98	89.14	90.31
9.00	61.02	64.78	68.69	72.74	76.93	78.00	79.08	80.17	81.27	82.38	83.49	84.62	85.75	86.89	88.04	89.20
9.25	60.27	63.99	67.85	71.85	75.99	77.05	78.12	79.19	80.27	81.37	82.47	83.58	84.70	85.82	86.96	88.10
9.50	59.54	63.21	67.02	70.97	75.06	76.11	77.16	78.23	79.30	80.38	81.46	82.56	83.67	84.78	85.90	87.03
9.75	58.82	62.44	66.21	70.11	74.15	75.19	76.23	77.28	78.34	79.40	80.48	81.56	82.65	83.75	84.86	85.98
10.00	58.11	61.69	65.41	69.27	73.26	74.28	75.31	76.35	77.39	78.45	79.51	80.58	81.66	82.74	83.84	84.94
10.25	57.41	60.95	64.63	68.44	72.38	73.39	74.41	75.43	76.46	77.51	78.55	79.61	80.68	81.75	82.83	83.92
10.50	56.73	60.22	63.86	67.62	71.52	72.52	73.52	74.53	75.55	76.58	77.62	78.66	79.72	80.78	81.85	82.92
10.75	56.06	59.51	63.10	66.82	70.68	71.66	72.65	73.65	74.66	75.68	76.70	77.73	78.77	79.82	80.88	81.94
11.00	55.40	58.81	62.36	66.04	69.84	70.82	71.80	72.78	73.78	74.79	75.80	76.82	77.85	78.88	79.93	80.98
11.25	54.75	58.12	61.63	65.26	69.03	69.99	70.96	71.93	72.92	73.91	74.91	75.92	76.94	77.96	78.99	80.03
11.50	54.11	57.45	60.91	64.50	68.22	69.17	70.13	71.10	72.07	73.05	74.04	75.04	76.04	77.05	78.07	79.10
11.75	53.49	56.78	60.21	63.76	67.44	68.37	69.32	70.28	71.24	72.21	73.18	74.17	75.16	76.16	77.17	78.19
12.00	52.87	56.13	59.52	63.03	66.66	67.59	68.52	69.47	70.42	71.38	72.34	73.32	74.30	75.29	76.28	77.29
12.25	52.27	55.49	58.84	62.31	65.90	66.82	67.74	68.67	69.61	70.56	71.52	72.48	73.45	74.43	75.41	76.40
12.50	51.68	54.86	58.17	61.60	65.15	66.06	66.97	67.89	68.82	69.76	70.70	71.66	72.62	73.58	74.56	75.54
12.75	51.09	54.24	57.51	60.90	64.41	65.31	66.22	67.13	68.05	68.97	69.91	70.85	71.80	72.75	73.71	74.68
13.00	50.52	53.63	56.87	60.22	63.69	64.58	65.47	66.37	67.28	68.20	69.12	70.05	70.99	71.94	72.89	73.85
13.25	49.96	53.03	56.23	59.55	62.98	63.86	64.74	65.63	66.53	67.44	68.35	69.27	70.20	71.13	72.07	73.02
13.50	49.40	52.45	55.61	58.89	62.28	63.15	64.02	64.91	65.79	66.69	67.59	68.50	69.42	70.34	71.27	72.21
13.75	48.86	51.87	54.99	58.24	61.60	62.45	63.32	64.19	65.07	65.96	66.85	67.75	68.65	69.57	70.49	71.42
14.00	48.32	51.30	54.39	57.60	60.92	61.77	62.63	63.49	64.36	65.23	66.12	67.01	67.90	68.81	69.72	70.63
14.25	47.80	50.74	53.80	56.97	60.26	61.10	61.94	62.80	63.66	64.52	65.40	66.28	67.16	68.06	68.96	69.86
14.50	47.28	50.19	53.22	56.36	59.61	60.44	61.27	62.12	62.97	63.82	64.69	65.56	66.44	67.32	68.21	69.11
14.75	46.77	49.65	52.64	55.75	58.97	59.79	60.61	61.45	62.29	63.14	63.99	64.85	65.72	66.60	67.48	68.37
15.00	46.27	49.12	52.08	55.15	58.33	59.15	59.97	60.79	61.62	62.46	63.31	64.16	65.02	65.88	66.76	67.63
15.25	45.78	48.60	51.53	54.57	57.71	58.52	59.33	60.14	60.97	61.80	62.63	63.48	64.33	65.18	66.05	66.91
15.50	45.29	48.08	50.98	53.99	57.10	57.90	58.70	59.51	60.32	61.15	61.97	62.81	63.65	64.49	65.35	66.21
15.75	44.82	47.58	50.45	53.42	56.50	57.29	58.08	58.88	59.69	60.50	61.32	62.15	62.98	63.82	64.66	65.51
16.00	44.35	47.08	49.92	52.87	55.91	56.69	57.48	58.27	59.07	59.87	60.68	61.50	62.32	63.15	63.99	64.83
16.25	43.89	46.59	49.40	52.32	55.33	56.10	56.88	57.66	58.45	59.25	60.05	60.86	61.68	62.50	63.32	64.16
16.50	43.44	46.11	48.89	51.78	54.76	55.53	56.30	57.07	57.85	58.64	59.43	60.23	61.04	61.85	62.67	63.49
16.75	42.99	45.64	48.39	51.25	54.20	54.96	55.72	56.49	57.26	58.04	58.82	59.62	60.41	61.22	62.03	62.84
17.00	42.55	45.18	47.90	50.72	53.65	54.40	55.15	55.91	56.67	57.45	58.22	59.01	59.80	60.59	61.40	62.20
17.25	42.12	44.72	47.41	50.21	53.11	53.85	54.59	55.34	56.10	56.86	57.63	58.41	59.19	59.98	60.77	61.57
17.50	41.70	44.27	46.94	49.71	52.57	53.30	54.04	54.79	55.54	56.29	57.05	57.82	58.60	59.38	60.16	60.95
17.75	41.28	43.83	46.47	49.21	52.05	52.77	53.50	54.24	54.98	55.73	56.48	57.24	58.01	58.78	59.56	60.34
18.00	40.87	43.39	46.01	48.72	51.53	52.25	52.97	53.70	54.43	55.17	55.92	56.67	57.43	58.20	58.97	59.74
18.25	40.47	42.96	45.55	48.24	51.02	51.73	52.45	53.17	53.90	54.63	55.37	56.11	56.86	57.62	58.38	59.15
18.50	40.07	42.54	45.10	47.76	50.52	51.22	51.93	52.65	53.37	54.09	54.82	55.56	56.31	57.06	57.81	58.57
18.75	39.68	42.12	44.66	47.30	50.02	50.72	51.42	52.13	52.84	53.56	54.29	55.02	55.76	56.50	57.25	58.00
19.00	39.29	41.71	44.23	46.84	49.54	50.23	50.92	51.62	52.33	53.04	53.76	54.49	55.21	55.95	56.69	57.44
20.00	37.81	40.14	42.56	45.07	47.67	48.33	49.00	49.68	50.36	51.04	51.74	52.43	53.13	53.84	54.55	55.27
25.00	31.62	33.57	35.59	37.69	39.87	40.42	40.98	41.55	42.12	42.69	43.27	43.85	44.44	45.03	45.62	46.22
30.00	26.98	28.65	30.37	32.17	34.02	34.49	34.97	35.45	35.94	36.43	36.92	37.42	37.92	38.42	38.93	39.44

MORTGAGE YIELD

12 YEARS

Description: This table shows the yield to maturity of a mortgage purchased at the price shown in the index.

Example: The yield to maturity of a 6.75 %, 12 year mortgage at a price of 80.00 is 11.25 %.

INTEREST RATE, %

PRICE	0.00%	1.00%	2.00%	3.00%	4.00%	4.25%	4.50%	4.75%	5.00%	5.25%	5.50%	5.75%	6.00%	6.25%	6.50%	6.75%
100	0.00	1.00	2.00	3.00	4.00	4.25	4.50	4.75	5.00	5.25	5.50	5.75	6.00	6.25	6.50	6.75
99	.16	1.17	2.17	3.17	4.18	4.43	4.68	4.93	5.18	5.43	5.68	5.93	6.18	6.44	6.69	6.94
98	.33	1.34	2.35	3.35	4.36	4.61	4.86	5.12	5.37	5.62	5.87	6.13	6.38	6.63	6.88	7.13
97	.50	1.51	2.52	3.54	4.55	4.80	5.05	5.31	5.56	5.81	6.07	6.32	6.57	6.83	7.08	7.33
96	.68	1.69	2.71	3.72	4.74	4.99	5.25	5.50	5.75	6.01	6.26	6.52	6.77	7.03	7.28	7.54
95	.85	1.87	2.89	3.91	4.93	5.18	5.44	5.70	5.95	6.21	6.46	6.72	6.97	7.23	7.48	7.74
94	1.03	2.05	3.08	4.10	5.12	5.38	5.64	5.89	6.15	6.41	6.66	6.92	7.18	7.43	7.69	7.95
93	1.21	2.24	3.27	4.29	5.32	5.58	5.84	6.10	6.35	6.61	6.87	7.13	7.39	7.64	7.90	8.16
92	1.40	2.43	3.46	4.49	5.52	5.78	6.04	6.30	6.56	6.82	7.08	7.34	7.60	7.86	8.12	8.37
91	1.58	2.62	3.65	4.69	5.73	5.99	6.25	6.51	6.77	7.03	7.29	7.55	7.81	8.07	8.33	8.59
90	1.77	2.81	3.85	4.89	5.94	6.20	6.46	6.72	6.98	7.24	7.50	7.77	8.03	8.29	8.55	8.81
89	1.96	3.01	4.05	5.10	6.15	6.41	6.67	6.93	7.20	7.46	7.72	7.99	8.25	8.51	8.78	9.04
88	2.16	3.21	4.26	5.31	6.36	6.63	6.89	7.15	7.42	7.68	7.95	8.21	8.47	8.74	9.00	9.27
87	2.36	3.41	4.46	5.52	6.58	6.84	7.11	7.37	7.64	7.91	8.17	8.44	8.70	8.97	9.24	9.50
86	2.56	3.62	4.68	5.74	6.80	7.07	7.33	7.60	7.87	8.13	8.40	8.67	8.94	9.20	9.47	9.74
85	2.76	3.83	4.89	5.96	7.03	7.29	7.56	7.83	8.10	8.37	8.63	8.90	9.17	9.44	9.71	9.98
84	2.97	4.04	5.11	6.18	7.26	7.52	7.79	8.06	8.33	8.60	8.87	9.14	9.41	9.68	9.95	10.23
83	3.18	4.26	5.33	6.41	7.49	7.76	8.03	8.30	8.57	8.84	9.11	9.39	9.66	9.93	10.20	10.48
82	3.40	4.48	5.56	6.64	7.73	8.00	8.27	8.54	8.81	9.09	9.36	9.63	9.91	10.18	10.46	10.73
81	3.62	4.70	5.79	6.87	7.97	8.24	8.51	8.79	9.06	9.34	9.61	9.89	10.16	10.44	10.71	10.99
80	3.84	4.93	6.02	7.11	8.21	8.49	8.76	9.04	9.31	9.59	9.87	10.14	10.42	10.70	10.98	11.25
79	4.07	5.16	6.26	7.36	8.46	8.74	9.02	9.29	9.57	9.85	10.13	10.41	10.68	10.96	11.24	11.52
78	4.30	5.40	6.50	7.61	8.72	9.00	9.28	9.55	9.83	10.11	10.39	10.67	10.95	11.23	11.52	11.80
77	4.53	5.64	6.75	7.86	8.98	9.26	9.54	9.82	10.10	10.38	10.66	10.95	11.23	11.51	11.79	12.08
76	4.77	5.88	7.00	8.12	9.24	9.52	9.81	10.09	10.37	10.66	10.94	11.22	11.51	11.79	12.08	12.36
75	5.02	6.13	7.25	8.38	9.51	9.80	10.08	10.36	10.65	10.93	11.22	11.51	11.79	12.08	12.36	12.65
74	5.26	6.39	7.52	8.65	9.79	10.07	10.36	10.65	10.93	11.22	11.51	11.79	12.08	12.37	12.66	12.95
73	5.52	6.65	7.78	8.92	10.07	10.36	10.64	10.93	11.22	11.51	11.80	12.09	12.38	12.67	12.96	13.25
72	5.78	6.91	8.05	9.20	10.36	10.65	10.94	11.23	11.52	11.81	12.10	12.39	12.68	12.97	13.27	13.56
71	6.04	7.18	8.33	9.49	10.65	10.94	11.23	11.52	11.82	12.11	12.40	12.70	12.99	13.29	13.58	13.88
70	6.31	7.46	8.61	9.78	10.95	11.24	11.54	11.83	12.12	12.42	12.72	13.01	13.31	13.61	13.90	14.20
69	6.58	7.74	8.90	10.07	11.25	11.55	11.85	12.14	12.44	12.74	13.03	13.33	13.63	13.93	14.23	14.53
68	6.86	8.03	9.20	10.38	11.57	11.86	12.16	12.46	12.76	13.06	13.36	13.66	13.96	14.26	14.57	14.87
67	7.15	8.32	9.50	10.69	11.88	12.19	12.49	12.79	13.09	13.39	13.69	14.00	14.30	14.61	14.91	15.22
66	7.44	8.62	9.81	11.01	12.21	12.51	12.82	13.12	13.43	13.73	14.04	14.34	14.65	14.95	15.26	15.57
65	7.74	8.93	10.12	11.33	12.55	12.85	13.16	13.46	13.77	14.08	14.38	14.69	15.00	15.31	15.62	15.93
64	8.04	9.24	10.45	11.66	12.89	13.20	13.50	13.81	14.12	14.43	14.74	15.05	15.36	15.68	15.99	16.30
63	8.36	9.56	10.78	12.00	13.24	13.55	13.86	14.17	14.48	14.80	15.11	15.42	15.74	16.05	16.37	16.68
62	8.67	9.89	11.12	12.35	13.60	13.91	14.22	14.54	14.85	15.17	15.48	15.80	16.12	16.44	16.76	17.08
61	9.00	10.23	11.46	12.71	13.97	14.28	14.60	14.92	15.23	15.55	15.87	16.19	16.51	16.83	17.15	17.48
60	9.34	10.57	11.82	13.08	14.34	14.66	14.98	15.30	15.62	15.94	16.27	16.59	16.91	17.24	17.56	17.89
59	9.68	10.93	12.18	13.45	14.73	15.05	15.38	15.70	16.02	16.35	16.67	17.00	17.33	17.65	17.98	18.31
58	10.03	11.29	12.56	13.84	15.13	15.45	15.78	16.11	16.43	16.76	17.09	17.42	17.75	18.08	18.41	18.74
57	10.40	11.66	12.94	14.23	15.54	15.87	16.20	16.52	16.86	17.19	17.52	17.85	18.19	18.52	18.86	19.19
56	10.77	12.05	13.34	14.64	15.96	16.29	16.62	16.96	17.29	17.62	17.96	18.30	18.63	18.97	19.31	19.65
55	11.15	12.44	13.74	15.06	16.39	16.73	17.06	17.40	17.74	18.07	18.41	18.75	19.10	19.44	19.78	20.12
54	11.54	12.84	14.16	15.49	16.84	17.17	17.51	17.85	18.20	18.54	18.88	19.23	19.57	19.92	20.26	20.61
53	11.94	13.26	14.59	15.93	17.29	17.64	17.98	18.32	18.67	19.02	19.36	19.71	20.06	20.41	20.76	21.12
52	12.36	13.69	15.03	16.39	17.77	18.11	18.46	18.81	19.16	19.51	19.86	20.21	20.57	20.92	21.28	21.63
51	12.78	14.13	15.49	16.86	18.25	18.60	18.96	19.31	19.66	20.02	20.37	20.73	21.09	21.45	21.81	22.17
50	13.23	14.58	15.96	17.35	18.76	19.11	19.47	19.83	20.18	20.54	20.90	21.27	21.63	21.99	22.36	22.72
49	13.68	15.05	16.44	17.85	19.28	19.64	20.00	20.36	20.72	21.09	21.45	21.82	22.19	22.55	22.92	23.30
48	14.15	15.54	16.94	18.37	19.81	20.18	20.54	20.91	21.28	21.65	22.02	22.39	22.76	23.14	23.51	23.89
47	14.63	16.04	17.46	18.91	20.37	20.74	21.11	21.48	21.85	22.23	22.60	22.98	23.36	23.74	24.12	24.50
46	15.13	16.55	18.00	19.46	20.95	21.32	21.70	22.07	22.45	22.83	23.21	23.60	23.98	24.36	24.75	25.14
45	15.65	17.09	18.55	20.04	21.54	21.92	22.30	22.69	23.07	23.46	23.84	24.23	24.62	25.01	25.41	25.80
44	16.18	17.65	19.13	20.63	22.16	22.55	22.93	23.32	23.71	24.11	24.50	24.89	25.29	25.69	26.09	26.49
43	16.74	18.22	19.73	21.25	22.81	23.20	23.59	23.99	24.38	24.78	25.18	25.58	25.98	26.39	26.79	27.20
42	17.32	18.82	20.35	21.90	23.47	23.87	24.27	24.67	25.08	25.48	25.89	26.30	26.71	27.12	27.53	27.94
41	17.92	19.44	20.99	22.57	24.17	24.58	24.98	25.39	25.80	26.21	26.63	27.04	27.46	27.88	28.30	28.72
40	18.54	20.09	21.66	23.27	24.90	25.31	25.72	26.14	26.56	26.98	27.40	27.82	28.24	28.67	29.10	29.53
39	19.19	20.76	22.36	23.99	25.65	26.07	26.50	26.92	27.34	27.77	28.20	28.63	29.06	29.50	29.93	30.38
35	22.08	23.77	25.50	27.26	29.06	29.51	29.97	30.43	30.89	31.35	31.82	32.29	32.76	33.24	33.71	34.19
30	26.59	28.48	30.41	32.39	34.42	34.93	35.45	35.97	36.50	37.02	37.55	38.09	38.62	39.16	39.70	40.25
25	32.63	34.81	37.05	39.35	41.71	42.32	42.92	43.53	44.15	44.76	45.39	46.01	46.64	47.28	47.92	48.56
20	41.34	43.98	46.70	49.52	52.42	53.15	53.90	54.65	55.41	56.17	56.93	57.71	58.48	59.27	60.06	60.85
15	55.47	58.91	62.49	66.19	70.02	70.99	71.98	72.97	73.97	74.98	76.00	77.02	78.05	79.09	80.14	81.20
10	83.32	88.46	93.80	99.33	105.06	106.52	108.00	109.48	110.98	112.49	114.02	115.55	117.10	118.66	120.23	121.81

Description: This table shows the price to pay for a monthly payment mortgage loan at the yield rate.

Example: The price of a 10.75 %, 12 year mortgage loan to yield 8.00 % to maturity is $ 114.44.

INTEREST RATE, %

YIELD	7.00%	7.25%	7.50%	7.75%	8.00%	8.25%	8.50%	8.75%	9.00%	9.25%	9.50%	9.75%	10.00%	10.25%	10.50%	10.75%
0.00	148.09	150.01	151.95	153.91	155.87	157.85	159.85	161.86	163.88	165.91	167.96	170.02	172.09	174.18	176.28	178.39
1.00	139.49	141.31	143.13	144.97	146.83	148.69	150.57	152.46	154.37	156.28	158.21	160.15	162.10	164.07	166.05	168.03
2.00	131.56	133.27	134.99	136.73	138.48	140.24	142.01	143.79	145.59	147.39	149.21	151.04	152.89	154.74	156.60	158.48
3.00	124.23	125.85	127.48	129.11	130.76	132.43	134.10	135.78	137.48	139.19	140.90	142.63	144.37	146.12	147.88	149.65
4.00	117.46	118.99	120.52	122.07	123.63	125.21	126.79	128.38	129.98	131.60	133.22	134.85	136.50	138.15	139.82	141.49
4.25	115.85	117.35	118.87	120.40	121.94	123.49	125.05	126.62	128.20	129.79	131.39	133.00	134.62	136.26	137.90	139.55
4.50	114.26	115.75	117.25	118.75	120.27	121.80	123.34	124.89	126.45	128.02	129.60	131.19	132.79	134.39	136.01	137.64
4.75	112.71	114.18	115.65	117.14	118.64	120.15	121.66	123.19	124.73	126.28	127.84	129.40	130.98	132.57	134.17	135.77
5.00	111.19	112.64	114.09	115.56	117.04	118.52	120.02	121.53	123.04	124.57	126.11	127.66	129.21	130.78	132.36	133.94
5.25	109.70	111.12	112.56	114.01	115.46	116.93	118.41	119.90	121.39	122.90	124.42	125.94	127.48	129.02	130.58	132.14
5.50	108.23	109.64	111.06	112.48	113.92	115.37	116.83	118.29	119.77	121.26	122.75	124.26	125.77	127.30	128.83	130.38
5.75	106.79	108.18	109.58	110.99	112.41	113.84	115.28	116.72	118.18	119.65	121.12	122.61	124.10	125.61	127.12	128.65
6.00	105.38	106.75	108.13	109.52	110.92	112.33	113.75	115.18	116.62	118.07	119.52	120.99	122.47	123.95	125.44	126.95
6.25	104.00	105.35	106.71	108.09	109.47	110.86	112.26	113.67	115.09	116.52	117.95	119.40	120.86	122.32	123.80	125.28
6.50	102.64	103.98	105.32	106.67	108.04	109.41	110.79	112.18	113.58	114.99	116.41	117.84	119.28	120.72	122.18	123.64
6.75	101.31	102.63	103.95	105.29	106.63	107.99	109.35	110.73	112.11	113.50	114.90	116.31	117.73	119.16	120.59	122.04
7.00	100.00	101.30	102.61	103.93	105.26	106.60	107.94	109.30	110.66	112.04	113.42	114.81	116.21	117.62	119.04	120.46
7.25	98.72	100.00	101.29	102.60	103.91	105.23	106.56	107.89	109.24	110.60	111.96	113.34	114.72	116.11	117.51	118.92
7.50	97.46	98.72	100.00	101.29	102.58	103.88	105.20	106.52	107.85	109.19	110.53	111.89	113.25	114.63	116.01	117.40
7.75	96.22	97.47	98.73	100.00	101.28	102.57	103.86	105.17	106.48	107.80	109.13	110.47	111.82	113.17	114.53	115.91
8.00	95.00	96.24	97.48	98.74	100.00	101.27	102.55	103.84	105.13	106.44	107.75	109.07	110.40	111.74	113.09	114.44
8.25	93.81	95.03	96.26	97.50	98.75	100.00	101.26	102.54	103.82	105.10	106.40	107.71	109.02	110.34	111.67	113.01
8.50	92.64	93.85	95.06	96.28	97.51	98.75	100.00	101.26	102.52	103.79	105.07	106.36	107.66	108.96	110.28	111.60
8.75	91.49	92.68	93.88	95.09	96.30	97.53	98.76	100.00	101.25	102.51	103.77	105.04	106.32	107.61	108.91	110.21
9.00	90.36	91.54	92.72	93.92	95.12	96.32	97.54	98.77	100.00	101.24	102.49	103.75	105.01	106.29	107.57	108.86
9.25	89.26	90.42	91.59	92.76	93.95	95.14	96.35	97.56	98.77	100.00	101.23	102.48	103.73	104.98	106.25	107.52
9.50	88.17	89.32	90.47	91.63	92.80	93.98	95.17	96.37	97.57	98.78	100.00	101.23	102.46	103.70	104.95	106.21
9.75	87.10	88.23	89.37	90.52	91.68	92.85	94.02	95.20	96.39	97.58	98.79	100.00	101.22	102.45	103.68	104.92
10.00	86.05	87.17	88.30	89.43	90.58	91.73	92.89	94.05	95.23	96.41	97.60	98.80	100.00	101.21	102.43	103.66
10.25	85.02	86.13	87.24	88.36	89.49	90.63	91.77	92.93	94.09	95.25	96.43	97.61	98.80	100.00	101.21	102.42
10.50	84.01	85.10	86.20	87.31	88.43	89.55	90.68	91.82	92.97	94.12	95.28	96.45	97.63	98.81	100.00	101.20
10.75	83.01	84.09	85.18	86.28	87.38	88.49	89.61	90.73	91.87	93.01	94.15	95.31	96.47	97.64	98.82	100.00
11.00	82.04	83.10	84.18	85.26	86.35	87.45	88.55	89.66	90.78	91.91	93.05	94.19	95.34	96.49	97.65	98.82
11.25	81.08	82.13	83.19	84.26	85.34	86.42	87.52	88.62	89.72	90.84	91.96	93.08	94.22	95.36	96.51	97.67
11.50	80.13	81.18	82.23	83.28	84.35	85.42	86.50	87.59	88.68	89.78	90.89	92.00	93.12	94.25	95.39	96.53
11.75	79.21	80.24	81.28	82.32	83.37	84.43	85.50	86.57	87.65	88.74	89.84	90.94	92.05	93.16	94.29	95.42
12.00	78.30	79.32	80.34	81.37	82.41	83.46	84.52	85.58	86.65	87.72	88.80	89.89	90.99	92.09	93.20	94.32
12.25	77.40	78.41	79.42	80.45	81.47	82.51	83.55	84.60	85.66	86.72	87.79	88.87	89.95	91.04	92.14	93.24
12.50	76.52	77.52	78.52	79.53	80.55	81.57	82.60	83.64	84.68	85.74	86.79	87.86	88.93	90.01	91.09	92.18
12.75	75.66	76.64	77.64	78.63	79.64	80.65	81.67	82.70	83.73	84.77	85.81	86.87	87.93	88.99	90.06	91.14
13.00	74.81	75.78	76.76	77.75	78.75	79.75	80.75	81.77	82.79	83.82	84.85	85.89	86.94	87.99	89.05	90.12
13.25	73.98	74.94	75.91	76.88	77.87	78.86	79.85	80.86	81.86	82.88	83.90	84.93	85.97	87.01	88.06	89.11
13.50	73.16	74.11	75.07	76.03	77.00	77.98	78.97	79.96	80.96	81.96	82.97	83.99	85.02	86.05	87.08	88.13
13.75	72.35	73.29	74.24	75.19	76.15	77.12	78.10	79.08	80.07	81.06	82.06	83.07	84.08	85.10	86.12	87.15
14.00	71.56	72.49	73.43	74.37	75.32	76.28	77.24	78.21	79.19	80.17	81.16	82.16	83.16	84.17	85.18	86.20
14.25	70.78	71.70	72.63	73.56	74.50	75.45	76.40	77.36	78.33	79.30	80.28	81.26	82.25	83.25	84.25	85.26
14.50	70.01	70.92	71.84	72.76	73.69	74.63	75.57	76.52	77.48	78.44	79.41	80.38	81.36	82.35	83.34	84.34
14.75	69.26	70.16	71.07	71.98	72.90	73.83	74.76	75.70	76.64	77.60	78.55	79.52	80.49	81.46	82.44	83.43
15.00	68.52	69.41	70.31	71.21	72.12	73.04	73.96	74.89	75.82	76.77	77.71	78.67	79.63	80.59	81.56	82.54
15.25	67.79	68.67	69.56	70.45	71.35	72.26	73.17	74.09	75.02	75.95	76.89	77.83	78.78	79.73	80.69	81.66
15.50	67.07	67.95	68.82	69.71	70.60	71.50	72.40	73.31	74.23	75.15	76.07	77.01	77.95	78.89	79.84	80.80
15.75	66.37	67.23	68.10	68.98	69.86	70.75	71.64	72.54	73.45	74.36	75.28	76.20	77.13	78.06	79.00	79.95
16.00	65.68	66.53	67.39	68.26	69.13	70.01	70.89	71.78	72.68	73.58	74.49	75.40	76.32	77.25	78.18	79.12
16.25	65.00	65.84	66.69	67.55	68.41	69.28	70.16	71.04	71.93	72.82	73.72	74.62	75.53	76.45	77.37	78.29
16.50	64.32	65.16	66.00	66.85	67.71	68.57	69.43	70.31	71.18	72.07	72.96	73.85	74.75	75.66	76.57	77.49
16.75	63.67	64.49	65.33	66.17	67.01	67.86	68.72	69.58	70.45	71.33	72.21	73.09	73.99	74.88	75.78	76.69
17.00	63.02	63.84	64.66	65.49	66.33	67.17	68.02	68.88	69.74	70.60	71.47	72.35	73.23	74.12	75.01	75.91
17.25	62.38	63.19	64.01	64.83	65.66	66.49	67.33	68.18	69.03	69.89	70.75	71.62	72.49	73.37	74.25	75.14
17.50	61.75	62.55	63.36	64.18	65.00	65.82	66.65	67.49	68.33	69.18	70.04	70.90	71.76	72.63	73.50	74.39
17.75	61.13	61.93	62.73	63.53	64.35	65.16	65.99	66.82	67.65	68.49	69.34	70.19	71.04	71.90	72.77	73.64
18.00	60.52	61.31	62.10	62.90	63.71	64.52	65.33	66.15	66.98	67.81	68.65	69.49	70.34	71.19	72.05	72.91
18.25	59.93	60.71	61.49	62.28	63.08	63.88	64.69	65.50	66.32	67.14	67.97	68.80	69.64	70.48	71.33	72.19
18.50	59.34	60.11	60.89	61.67	62.46	63.25	64.05	64.85	65.66	66.48	67.30	68.12	68.96	69.79	70.63	71.48
18.75	58.76	59.52	60.29	61.07	61.85	62.63	63.42	64.21	65.02	65.83	66.64	67.46	68.28	69.11	69.94	70.78
19.00	58.19	58.94	59.71	60.47	61.25	62.02	62.81	63.60	64.39	65.19	66.00	66.80	67.62	68.44	69.26	70.09
20.00	55.99	56.72	57.46	58.19	58.94	59.69	60.44	61.20	61.96	62.73	63.51	64.29	65.07	65.86	66.65	67.45
25.00	46.83	47.44	48.05	48.67	49.29	49.92	50.55	51.18	51.82	52.46	53.11	53.76	54.42	55.08	55.74	56.41
30.00	39.96	40.48	41.00	41.53	42.06	42.60	43.13	43.68	44.22	44.77	45.32	45.88	46.44	47.00	47.57	48.14

MORTGAGE YIELD

Description: This table shows the yield to maturity of a mortgage purchased at the price shown in the index.

Example: The yield to maturity of a 10.75 %, 12 year mortgage at a price of 113.00 is 8.25 %.

INTEREST RATE, %

PRICE	7.00%	7.25%	7.50%	7.75%	8.00%	8.25%	8.50%	8.75%	9.00%	9.25%	9.50%	9.75%	10.00%	10.25%	10.50%	10.75%
145	.34	.56	.78	.99	1.21	1.42	1.64	1.85	2.06	2.28	2.49	2.71	2.92	3.13	3.34	3.56
140	.93	1.15	1.37	1.59	1.81	2.02	2.24	2.46	2.68	2.89	3.11	3.32	3.54	3.76	3.97	4.19
135	1.55	1.77	1.99	2.22	2.44	2.66	2.88	3.10	3.32	3.54	3.76	3.98	4.19	4.41	4.63	4.85
130	2.20	2.43	2.65	2.87	3.10	3.32	3.55	3.77	3.99	4.22	4.44	4.66	4.88	5.11	5.33	5.55
129	2.34	2.56	2.79	3.01	3.24	3.46	3.68	3.91	4.13	4.36	4.58	4.80	5.03	5.25	5.47	5.69
128	2.47	2.70	2.92	3.15	3.37	3.60	3.82	4.05	4.27	4.50	4.72	4.95	5.17	5.39	5.62	5.84
127	2.61	2.83	3.06	3.29	3.51	3.74	3.96	4.19	4.42	4.64	4.87	5.09	5.31	5.54	5.76	5.99
126	2.75	2.97	3.20	3.43	3.65	3.88	4.11	4.33	4.56	4.79	5.01	5.24	5.46	5.69	5.91	6.14
125	2.89	3.11	3.34	3.57	3.80	4.02	4.25	4.48	4.71	4.93	5.16	5.38	5.61	5.84	6.06	6.29
124	3.03	3.26	3.49	3.71	3.94	4.17	4.40	4.63	4.85	5.08	5.31	5.53	5.76	5.99	6.21	6.44
123	3.17	3.40	3.63	3.86	4.09	4.32	4.55	4.77	5.00	5.23	5.46	5.69	5.91	6.14	6.37	6.59
122	3.32	3.55	3.78	4.01	4.24	4.47	4.69	4.92	5.15	5.38	5.61	5.84	6.07	6.30	6.52	6.75
121	3.46	3.69	3.92	4.15	4.39	4.62	4.85	5.08	5.31	5.53	5.76	5.99	6.22	6.45	6.68	6.91
120	3.61	3.84	4.07	4.31	4.54	4.77	5.00	5.23	5.46	5.69	5.92	6.15	6.38	6.61	6.84	7.07
119	3.76	3.99	4.23	4.46	4.69	4.92	5.15	5.38	5.62	5.85	6.08	6.31	6.54	6.77	7.00	7.23
118	3.91	4.15	4.38	4.61	4.84	5.08	5.31	5.54	5.77	6.01	6.24	6.47	6.70	6.93	7.16	7.40
117	4.07	4.30	4.53	4.77	5.00	5.23	5.47	5.70	5.93	6.17	6.40	6.63	6.86	7.10	7.33	7.56
116	4.22	4.46	4.69	4.92	5.16	5.39	5.63	5.86	6.10	6.33	6.56	6.80	7.03	7.26	7.50	7.73
115	4.38	4.61	4.85	5.08	5.32	5.55	5.79	6.02	6.26	6.49	6.73	6.96	7.20	7.43	7.67	7.90
114	4.54	4.77	5.01	5.25	5.48	5.72	5.95	6.19	6.43	6.66	6.90	7.13	7.37	7.60	7.84	8.07
113	4.70	4.94	5.17	5.41	5.65	5.88	6.12	6.36	6.59	6.83	7.07	7.30	7.54	7.77	8.01	8.25
112	4.86	5.10	5.34	5.58	5.81	6.05	6.29	6.53	6.76	7.00	7.24	7.48	7.71	7.95	8.19	8.42
111	5.03	5.27	5.50	5.74	5.98	6.22	6.46	6.70	6.94	7.17	7.41	7.65	7.89	8.13	8.36	8.60
110	5.19	5.43	5.67	5.91	6.15	6.39	6.63	6.87	7.11	7.35	7.59	7.83	8.07	8.31	8.55	8.78
109	5.36	5.60	5.84	6.09	6.33	6.57	6.81	7.05	7.29	7.53	7.77	8.01	8.25	8.49	8.73	8.97
108	5.53	5.78	6.02	6.26	6.50	6.74	6.98	7.23	7.47	7.71	7.95	8.19	8.43	8.67	8.91	9.15
107	5.71	5.95	6.19	6.44	6.68	6.92	7.16	7.41	7.65	7.89	8.13	8.38	8.62	8.86	9.10	9.34
106	5.89	6.13	6.37	6.62	6.86	7.10	7.35	7.59	7.83	8.08	8.32	8.56	8.81	9.05	9.29	9.54
105	6.06	6.31	6.55	6.80	7.04	7.29	7.53	7.78	8.02	8.26	8.51	8.75	9.00	9.24	9.49	9.73
104	6.24	6.49	6.74	6.98	7.23	7.47	7.72	7.96	8.21	8.46	8.70	8.95	9.19	9.44	9.68	9.93
103	6.43	6.68	6.92	7.17	7.42	7.66	7.91	8.16	8.40	8.65	8.89	9.14	9.39	9.63	9.88	10.13
102	6.61	6.86	7.11	7.36	7.61	7.85	8.10	8.35	8.60	8.84	9.09	9.34	9.59	9.83	10.08	10.33
101	6.80	7.05	7.30	7.55	7.80	8.05	8.30	8.55	8.79	9.04	9.29	9.54	9.79	10.04	10.29	10.54
100	7.00	7.25	7.50	7.75	8.00	8.25	8.50	8.75	9.00	9.25	9.50	9.75	10.00	10.25	10.50	10.75
99	7.19	7.44	7.69	7.94	8.19	8.45	8.70	8.95	9.20	9.45	9.70	9.95	10.20	10.45	10.71	10.96
98	7.39	7.64	7.89	8.14	8.40	8.65	8.90	9.15	9.41	9.66	9.91	10.16	10.42	10.67	10.92	11.17
97	7.59	7.84	8.09	8.35	8.60	8.85	9.11	9.36	9.61	9.87	10.12	10.38	10.63	10.88	11.14	11.39
96	7.79	8.04	8.30	8.55	8.81	9.06	9.32	9.57	9.83	10.08	10.34	10.59	10.85	11.10	11.36	11.61
95	8.00	8.25	8.51	8.76	9.02	9.28	9.53	9.79	10.04	10.30	10.56	10.81	11.07	11.33	11.58	11.84
94	8.21	8.46	8.72	8.98	9.23	9.49	9.75	10.01	10.26	10.52	10.78	11.04	11.29	11.55	11.81	12.07
93	8.42	8.68	8.93	9.19	9.45	9.71	9.97	10.23	10.49	10.75	11.01	11.26	11.52	11.78	12.04	12.30
92	8.63	8.89	9.15	9.41	9.67	9.93	10.19	10.45	10.71	10.97	11.24	11.50	11.76	12.02	12.28	12.54
91	8.85	9.11	9.38	9.64	9.90	10.16	10.42	10.68	10.94	11.21	11.47	11.73	11.99	12.25	12.52	12.78
90	9.08	9.34	9.60	9.86	10.13	10.39	10.65	10.92	11.18	11.44	11.71	11.97	12.23	12.50	12.76	13.02
89	9.30	9.57	9.83	10.10	10.36	10.62	10.89	11.15	11.42	11.68	11.95	12.21	12.48	12.74	13.01	13.27
88	9.53	9.80	10.06	10.33	10.60	10.86	11.13	11.39	11.66	11.93	12.19	12.46	12.73	12.99	13.26	13.53
87	9.77	10.04	10.30	10.57	10.84	11.10	11.37	11.64	11.91	12.17	12.44	12.71	12.98	13.25	13.52	13.79
86	10.01	10.28	10.54	10.81	11.08	11.35	11.62	11.89	12.16	12.43	12.70	12.97	13.24	13.51	13.78	14.05
85	10.25	10.52	10.79	11.06	11.33	11.60	11.87	12.14	12.41	12.68	12.96	13.23	13.50	13.77	14.04	14.32
84	10.50	10.77	11.04	11.31	11.58	11.86	12.13	12.40	12.67	12.95	13.22	13.49	13.77	14.04	14.31	14.59
83	10.75	11.02	11.29	11.57	11.84	12.12	12.39	12.66	12.94	13.21	13.49	13.76	14.04	14.31	14.59	14.87
82	11.00	11.28	11.55	11.83	12.10	12.38	12.66	12.93	13.21	13.48	13.76	14.04	14.32	14.59	14.87	15.15
81	11.27	11.54	11.82	12.10	12.37	12.65	12.93	13.21	13.48	13.76	14.04	14.32	14.60	14.88	15.16	15.44
80	11.53	11.81	12.09	12.37	12.65	12.92	13.20	13.48	13.76	14.04	14.32	14.60	14.89	15.17	15.45	15.73
79	11.80	12.08	12.36	12.64	12.92	13.20	13.49	13.77	14.05	14.33	14.61	14.90	15.18	15.46	15.75	16.03
78	12.08	12.36	12.64	12.92	13.21	13.49	13.77	14.06	14.34	14.62	14.91	15.19	15.48	15.76	16.05	16.34
77	12.36	12.64	12.93	13.21	13.50	13.78	14.07	14.35	14.64	14.92	15.21	15.50	15.78	16.07	16.36	16.65
76	12.65	12.93	13.22	13.50	13.79	14.08	14.37	14.65	14.94	15.23	15.52	15.81	16.10	16.39	16.68	16.97
75	12.94	13.23	13.52	13.80	14.09	14.38	14.67	14.96	15.25	15.54	15.83	16.12	16.41	16.71	17.00	17.29
74	13.24	13.53	13.82	14.11	14.40	14.69	14.98	15.27	15.57	15.86	16.15	16.45	16.74	17.03	17.33	17.62
70	14.50	14.80	15.10	15.40	15.70	16.00	16.30	16.60	16.90	17.20	17.51	17.81	18.12	18.42	18.72	19.03
65	16.24	16.56	16.87	17.18	17.49	17.81	18.12	18.44	18.75	19.07	19.39	19.71	20.02	20.34	20.66	20.98
60	18.21	18.54	18.87	19.20	19.53	19.86	20.19	20.52	20.85	21.19	21.52	21.85	22.19	22.53	22.86	23.20
55	20.47	20.82	21.16	21.51	21.86	22.21	22.56	22.91	23.26	23.61	23.97	24.32	24.68	25.04	25.40	25.75
50	23.09	23.46	23.83	24.20	24.57	24.95	25.32	25.70	26.07	26.45	26.83	27.21	27.59	27.97	28.36	28.74
45	26.20	26.59	26.99	27.39	27.79	28.20	28.60	29.01	29.41	29.82	30.23	30.65	31.06	31.48	31.89	32.31
40	29.96	30.40	30.83	31.27	31.71	32.15	32.60	33.04	33.49	33.94	34.39	34.84	35.30	35.75	36.21	36.67
35	34.67	35.15	35.64	36.13	36.62	37.11	37.61	38.10	38.61	39.11	39.61	40.12	40.63	41.14	41.66	42.17

Description: This table shows the price to pay for a monthly payment mortgage loan at the yield rate.

Example: The price of a 15.00 %, 12 year mortgage loan to yield 8.00 % to maturity is $ 138.66.

INTEREST RATE, %

YIELD	11.00%	11.25%	11.50%	11.75%	12.00%	12.25%	12.50%	12.75%	13.00%	13.25%	13.50%	13.75%	14.00%	14.25%	14.50%	15.00%
0.00	180.51	182.65	184.80	186.96	189.13	191.32	193.52	195.72	197.95	200.18	202.42	204.68	206.95	209.22	211.51	216.13
1.00	170.04	172.05	174.07	176.11	178.16	180.21	182.28	184.37	186.46	188.56	190.67	192.80	194.94	197.08	199.24	203.58
2.00	160.37	162.26	164.17	166.09	168.02	169.97	171.92	173.88	175.85	177.84	179.83	181.84	183.85	185.87	187.91	192.01
3.00	151.43	153.23	155.03	156.84	158.67	160.50	162.34	164.20	166.06	167.93	169.82	171.71	173.61	175.52	177.44	181.31
4.00	143.18	144.87	146.58	148.29	150.01	151.75	153.49	155.24	157.01	158.78	160.56	162.35	164.14	165.95	167.77	171.43
4.25	141.21	142.88	144.56	146.25	147.95	149.66	151.38	153.11	154.85	156.60	158.35	160.12	161.89	163.67	165.46	169.07
4.50	139.28	140.93	142.59	144.26	145.93	147.62	149.32	151.02	152.73	154.46	156.19	157.93	159.68	161.44	163.20	166.76
4.75	137.39	139.02	140.65	142.30	143.95	145.62	147.29	148.97	150.66	152.36	154.07	155.79	157.51	159.24	160.99	164.50
5.00	135.54	137.14	138.75	140.38	142.01	143.65	145.30	146.96	148.63	150.30	151.99	153.68	155.38	157.09	158.81	162.28
5.25	133.72	135.30	136.89	138.49	140.10	141.72	143.35	144.98	146.63	148.28	149.95	151.62	153.30	154.98	156.68	160.10
5.50	131.93	133.49	135.06	136.64	138.23	139.83	141.43	143.05	144.67	146.30	147.94	149.59	151.25	152.91	154.59	157.96
5.75	130.18	131.72	133.27	134.83	136.39	137.97	139.55	141.15	142.75	144.36	145.98	147.61	149.24	150.88	152.53	155.86
6.00	128.46	129.98	131.51	133.05	134.59	136.15	137.71	139.28	140.86	142.45	144.05	145.66	147.27	148.89	150.52	153.80
6.25	126.77	128.27	129.78	131.30	132.82	134.36	135.90	137.45	139.01	140.58	142.16	143.74	145.34	146.94	148.54	151.78
6.50	125.12	126.60	128.09	129.58	131.09	132.60	134.13	135.66	137.20	138.75	140.30	141.87	143.44	145.02	146.60	149.80
6.75	123.49	124.95	126.42	127.90	129.39	130.88	132.39	133.90	135.42	136.94	138.48	140.02	141.57	143.13	144.70	147.85
7.00	121.90	123.34	124.79	126.25	127.72	129.19	130.68	132.17	133.67	135.18	136.69	138.22	139.75	141.29	142.83	145.95
7.25	120.33	121.76	123.19	124.63	126.08	127.53	129.00	130.47	131.95	133.44	134.94	136.44	137.95	139.47	141.00	144.07
7.50	118.79	120.20	121.62	123.04	124.47	125.91	127.35	128.81	130.27	131.74	133.21	134.70	136.19	137.69	139.20	142.23
7.75	117.29	118.68	120.07	121.48	122.89	124.31	125.74	127.17	128.61	130.07	131.52	132.99	134.46	135.94	137.43	140.43
8.00	115.81	117.18	118.56	119.94	121.34	122.74	124.15	125.57	126.99	128.42	129.86	131.31	132.77	134.23	135.70	138.66
8.25	114.35	115.71	117.07	118.44	119.81	121.20	122.59	123.99	125.40	126.81	128.23	129.66	131.10	132.54	133.99	136.92
8.50	112.93	114.26	115.61	116.96	118.32	119.69	121.06	122.44	123.83	125.23	126.63	128.05	129.46	130.89	132.32	135.21
8.75	111.53	112.85	114.17	115.51	116.85	118.20	119.56	120.93	122.30	123.68	125.06	126.46	127.86	129.27	130.68	133.53
9.00	110.15	111.46	112.77	114.09	115.41	116.75	118.09	119.43	120.79	122.15	123.52	124.90	126.28	127.67	129.07	131.88
9.25	108.80	110.09	111.38	112.69	114.00	115.31	116.64	117.97	119.31	120.65	122.01	123.37	124.73	126.11	127.49	130.27
9.50	107.47	108.75	110.03	111.31	112.61	113.91	115.22	116.53	117.85	119.18	120.52	121.86	123.21	124.57	125.93	128.68
9.75	106.17	107.43	108.69	109.96	111.24	112.53	113.82	115.12	116.43	117.74	119.06	120.39	121.72	123.06	124.41	127.12
10.00	104.89	106.13	107.38	108.64	109.90	111.17	112.45	113.73	115.02	116.32	117.63	118.94	120.25	121.58	122.91	125.59
10.25	103.64	104.86	106.10	107.34	108.59	109.84	111.10	112.37	113.65	114.93	116.22	117.51	118.81	120.12	121.44	124.08
10.50	102.40	103.61	104.83	106.06	107.29	108.53	109.78	111.03	112.29	113.56	114.83	116.11	117.40	118.69	119.99	122.61
10.75	101.19	102.39	103.59	104.80	106.02	107.25	108.48	109.72	110.96	112.22	113.47	114.74	116.01	117.29	118.57	121.16
11.00	100.00	101.18	102.37	103.57	104.78	105.99	107.20	108.43	109.66	110.90	112.14	113.39	114.64	115.91	117.17	119.73
11.25	98.83	100.00	101.18	102.36	103.55	104.75	105.95	107.16	108.38	109.60	110.83	112.06	113.30	114.55	115.80	118.33
11.50	97.68	98.84	100.00	101.17	102.35	103.53	104.72	105.91	107.12	108.32	109.54	110.76	111.99	113.22	114.46	116.95
11.75	96.55	97.69	98.84	100.00	101.16	102.33	103.51	104.69	105.88	107.07	108.27	109.48	110.69	111.91	113.13	115.60
12.00	95.44	96.57	97.71	98.85	100.00	101.16	102.32	103.49	104.66	105.84	107.03	108.22	109.42	110.62	111.83	114.27
12.25	94.35	95.47	96.59	97.72	98.86	100.00	101.15	102.30	103.46	104.63	105.80	106.98	108.17	109.36	110.56	112.97
12.50	93.28	94.38	95.50	96.61	97.74	98.86	100.00	101.14	102.29	103.44	104.60	105.77	106.94	108.12	109.30	111.68
12.75	92.23	93.32	94.42	95.52	96.63	97.75	98.87	100.00	101.13	102.28	103.42	104.57	105.73	106.90	108.07	110.42
13.00	91.19	92.27	93.36	94.45	95.55	96.65	97.76	98.88	100.00	101.13	102.26	103.40	104.55	105.70	106.85	109.18
13.25	90.18	91.24	92.32	93.40	94.48	95.57	96.67	97.77	98.88	100.00	101.12	102.25	103.38	104.52	105.66	107.97
13.50	89.18	90.23	91.29	92.36	93.43	94.51	95.60	96.69	97.79	98.89	100.00	101.11	102.23	103.36	104.49	106.77
13.75	88.19	89.24	90.29	91.34	92.40	93.47	94.55	95.63	96.71	97.80	98.90	100.00	101.11	102.22	103.34	105.59
14.00	87.23	88.26	89.30	90.34	91.39	92.45	93.51	94.58	95.65	96.73	97.81	98.90	100.00	101.10	102.21	104.44
14.25	86.28	87.30	88.32	89.36	90.40	91.44	92.49	93.55	94.61	95.68	96.75	97.83	98.91	100.00	101.09	103.30
14.50	85.34	86.35	87.37	88.39	89.42	90.45	91.49	92.54	93.59	94.64	95.70	96.77	97.84	98.92	100.00	102.18
14.75	84.42	85.42	86.43	87.44	88.46	89.48	90.51	91.54	92.58	93.62	94.67	95.73	96.79	97.85	98.92	101.08
15.00	83.52	84.51	85.50	86.50	87.51	88.52	89.54	90.56	91.59	92.62	93.66	94.70	95.75	96.81	97.87	100.00
15.25	82.63	83.61	84.60	85.58	86.58	87.58	88.59	89.60	90.61	91.64	92.66	93.70	94.73	95.78	96.83	98.94
15.50	81.76	82.73	83.70	84.68	85.66	86.65	87.65	88.65	89.66	90.67	91.68	92.71	93.73	94.77	95.80	97.89
15.75	80.90	81.86	82.82	83.79	84.77	85.74	86.73	87.72	88.72	89.72	90.72	91.73	92.75	93.77	94.80	96.86
16.00	80.06	81.00	81.96	82.92	83.88	84.85	85.82	86.80	87.79	88.78	89.77	90.78	91.78	92.79	93.81	95.85
16.25	79.23	80.16	81.11	82.06	83.01	83.97	84.93	85.90	86.88	87.86	88.84	89.83	90.83	91.83	92.83	94.86
16.50	78.41	79.34	80.27	81.21	82.15	83.10	84.06	85.02	85.98	86.95	87.93	88.91	89.89	90.88	91.88	93.88
16.75	77.61	78.52	79.45	80.38	81.31	82.25	83.20	84.15	85.10	86.06	87.03	88.00	88.97	89.95	90.93	92.92
17.00	76.81	77.72	78.64	79.56	80.48	81.41	82.35	83.29	84.23	85.18	86.14	87.10	88.06	89.03	90.01	91.97
17.25	76.04	76.94	77.84	78.75	79.67	80.59	81.51	82.44	83.38	84.32	85.27	86.22	87.17	88.13	89.10	91.04
17.50	75.27	76.16	77.06	77.96	78.87	79.78	80.69	81.61	82.54	83.47	84.41	85.35	86.29	87.24	88.20	90.12
17.75	74.52	75.40	76.29	77.18	78.08	78.98	79.89	80.80	81.71	82.64	83.56	84.49	85.43	86.37	87.32	89.22
18.00	73.78	74.65	75.53	76.41	77.30	78.19	79.09	79.99	80.90	81.81	82.73	83.65	84.58	85.51	86.45	88.33
18.25	73.05	73.91	74.78	75.66	76.54	77.42	78.31	79.20	80.10	81.01	81.91	82.83	83.74	84.67	85.59	87.46
18.50	72.33	73.19	74.05	74.91	75.78	76.66	77.54	78.43	79.32	80.21	81.11	82.01	82.92	83.83	84.75	86.60
18.75	71.62	72.47	73.32	74.18	75.04	75.91	76.78	77.66	78.54	79.43	80.32	81.21	82.11	83.02	83.92	85.75
19.00	70.93	71.77	72.61	73.46	74.32	75.17	76.04	76.91	77.78	78.66	79.54	80.42	81.31	82.21	83.11	84.92
20.00	68.25	69.06	69.87	70.69	71.51	72.34	73.17	74.01	74.85	75.69	76.54	77.39	78.25	79.11	79.98	81.72
25.00	57.08	57.76	58.44	59.12	59.81	60.50	61.19	61.89	62.59	63.30	64.01	64.72	65.44	66.16	66.88	68.34
30.00	48.71	49.29	49.87	50.45	51.04	51.63	52.22	52.82	53.41	54.02	54.62	55.23	55.84	56.46	57.08	58.32

MORTGAGE YIELD

Description: This table shows the yield to maturity of a mortgage purchased at the price shown in the index.

Example: The yield to maturity of a 15.00 %, 12 year mortgage at a price of 117.00 is 11.49 %.

INTEREST RATE, %

PRICE	11.00%	11.25%	11.50%	11.75%	12.00%	12.25%	12.50%	12.75%	13.00%	13.25%	13.50%	13.75%	14.00%	14.25%	14.50%	15.00%
190	–	–	–	–	–	.11	.30	.49	.68	.87	1.05	1.24	1.43	1.62	1.80	2.18
185	–	–	–	.17	.36	.55	.75	.94	1.13	1.32	1.51	1.70	1.89	2.08	2.27	2.64
180	–	.24	.43	.63	.82	1.02	1.21	1.40	1.59	1.79	1.98	2.17	2.36	2.55	2.74	3.12
175	.51	.71	.91	1.10	1.30	1.49	1.69	1.88	2.08	2.27	2.47	2.66	2.85	3.05	3.24	3.62
170	1.00	1.20	1.40	1.60	1.79	1.99	2.19	2.39	2.58	2.78	2.98	3.17	3.37	3.56	3.76	4.15
165	1.51	1.71	1.91	2.11	2.31	2.51	2.71	2.91	3.11	3.31	3.51	3.70	3.90	4.10	4.30	4.69
160	2.03	2.24	2.44	2.64	2.85	3.05	3.25	3.45	3.66	3.86	4.06	4.26	4.46	4.66	4.86	5.26
155	2.59	2.79	3.00	3.20	3.41	3.61	3.82	4.02	4.23	4.43	4.63	4.84	5.04	5.24	5.45	5.85
150	3.16	3.37	3.58	3.79	4.00	4.20	4.41	4.62	4.83	5.03	5.24	5.44	5.65	5.86	6.06	6.47
145	3.77	3.98	4.19	4.40	4.61	4.82	5.03	5.24	5.45	5.66	5.87	6.08	6.29	6.50	6.71	7.12
140	4.40	4.62	4.83	5.04	5.26	5.47	5.69	5.90	6.11	6.32	6.54	6.75	6.96	7.17	7.38	7.80
135	5.07	5.29	5.50	5.72	5.94	6.15	6.37	6.59	6.80	7.02	7.24	7.45	7.67	7.88	8.10	8.53
130	5.77	5.99	6.21	6.43	6.65	6.88	7.10	7.32	7.54	7.75	7.97	8.19	8.41	8.63	8.85	9.29
125	6.51	6.74	6.96	7.19	7.41	7.64	7.86	8.08	8.31	8.53	8.76	8.98	9.20	9.42	9.65	10.09
123	6.82	7.05	7.27	7.50	7.73	7.95	8.18	8.40	8.63	8.86	9.08	9.31	9.53	9.76	9.98	10.43
122	6.98	7.21	7.43	7.66	7.89	8.11	8.34	8.57	8.79	9.02	9.25	9.47	9.70	9.92	10.15	10.60
121	7.14	7.37	7.59	7.82	8.05	8.28	8.51	8.73	8.96	9.19	9.41	9.64	9.87	10.09	10.32	10.77
120	7.30	7.53	7.76	7.99	8.21	8.44	8.67	8.90	9.13	9.36	9.58	9.81	10.04	10.27	10.49	10.95
119	7.46	7.69	7.92	8.15	8.38	8.61	8.84	9.07	9.30	9.53	9.76	9.98	10.21	10.44	10.67	11.12
118	7.63	7.86	8.09	8.32	8.55	8.78	9.01	9.24	9.47	9.70	9.93	10.16	10.39	10.62	10.85	11.30
117	7.79	8.02	8.26	8.49	8.72	8.95	9.18	9.41	9.64	9.87	10.11	10.34	10.57	10.80	11.03	11.49
116	7.96	8.19	8.43	8.66	8.89	9.12	9.36	9.59	9.82	10.05	10.28	10.52	10.75	10.98	11.21	11.67
115	8.13	8.37	8.60	8.83	9.07	9.30	9.53	9.77	10.00	10.23	10.46	10.70	10.93	11.16	11.39	11.86
114	8.31	8.54	8.78	9.01	9.24	9.48	9.71	9.95	10.18	10.41	10.65	10.88	11.11	11.35	11.58	12.05
113	8.48	8.72	8.95	9.19	9.42	9.66	9.89	10.13	10.36	10.60	10.83	11.07	11.30	11.54	11.77	12.24
112	8.66	8.90	9.13	9.37	9.61	9.84	10.08	10.31	10.55	10.79	11.02	11.26	11.49	11.73	11.96	12.43
111	8.84	9.08	9.32	9.55	9.79	10.03	10.26	10.50	10.74	10.97	11.21	11.45	11.68	11.92	12.16	12.63
110	9.02	9.26	9.50	9.74	9.98	10.21	10.45	10.69	10.93	11.17	11.40	11.64	11.88	12.12	12.36	12.83
109	9.21	9.45	9.69	9.93	10.17	10.41	10.64	10.88	11.12	11.36	11.60	11.84	12.08	12.32	12.56	13.03
108	9.40	9.64	9.88	10.12	10.36	10.60	10.84	11.08	11.32	11.56	11.80	12.04	12.28	12.52	12.76	13.24
107	9.59	9.83	10.07	10.31	10.55	10.79	11.04	11.28	11.52	11.76	12.00	12.24	12.48	12.72	12.96	13.45
106	9.78	10.02	10.26	10.51	10.75	10.99	11.23	11.48	11.72	11.96	12.20	12.45	12.69	12.93	13.17	13.66
105	9.97	10.22	10.46	10.71	10.95	11.19	11.44	11.68	11.92	12.17	12.41	12.66	12.90	13.14	13.39	13.87
104	10.17	10.42	10.66	10.91	11.15	11.40	11.64	11.89	12.13	12.38	12.62	12.87	13.11	13.36	13.60	14.09
103	10.37	10.62	10.87	11.11	11.36	11.60	11.85	12.10	12.34	12.59	12.84	13.08	13.33	13.57	13.82	14.31
102	10.58	10.83	11.07	11.32	11.57	11.82	12.06	12.31	12.56	12.80	13.05	13.30	13.55	13.79	14.04	14.54
101	10.78	11.03	11.28	11.53	11.78	12.03	12.28	12.53	12.77	13.02	13.27	13.52	13.77	14.02	14.27	14.76
100	11.00	11.25	11.50	11.75	12.00	12.25	12.50	12.75	13.00	13.25	13.50	13.75	14.00	14.25	14.50	15.00
99	11.21	11.46	11.71	11.96	12.21	12.46	12.72	12.97	13.22	13.47	13.72	13.97	14.22	14.48	14.73	15.23
98	11.43	11.68	11.93	12.18	12.44	12.69	12.94	13.19	13.45	13.70	13.95	14.20	14.46	14.71	14.96	15.47
97	11.65	11.90	12.15	12.41	12.66	12.92	13.17	13.42	13.68	13.93	14.19	14.44	14.69	14.95	15.20	15.71
96	11.87	12.12	12.38	12.63	12.89	13.15	13.40	13.66	13.91	14.17	14.42	14.68	14.93	15.19	15.45	15.96
95	12.10	12.35	12.61	12.87	13.12	13.38	13.64	13.89	14.15	14.41	14.66	14.92	15.18	15.44	15.69	16.21
94	12.33	12.58	12.84	13.10	13.36	13.62	13.88	14.13	14.39	14.65	14.91	15.17	15.43	15.69	15.95	16.46
93	12.56	12.82	13.08	13.34	13.60	13.86	14.12	14.38	14.64	14.90	15.16	15.42	15.68	15.94	16.20	16.72
92	12.80	13.06	13.32	13.58	13.84	14.11	14.37	14.63	14.89	15.15	15.41	15.68	15.94	16.20	16.46	16.99
91	13.04	13.30	13.57	13.83	14.09	14.36	14.62	14.88	15.15	15.41	15.67	15.94	16.20	16.46	16.73	17.26
90	13.29	13.55	13.82	14.08	14.35	14.61	14.88	15.14	15.40	15.67	15.94	16.20	16.47	16.73	17.00	17.53
89	13.54	13.81	14.07	14.34	14.60	14.87	15.14	15.40	15.67	15.94	16.20	16.47	16.74	17.00	17.27	17.81
88	13.79	14.06	14.33	14.60	14.87	15.13	15.40	15.67	15.94	16.21	16.47	16.74	17.01	17.28	17.55	18.09
87	14.05	14.32	14.59	14.86	15.13	15.40	15.67	15.95	16.22	16.49	16.76	17.03	17.31	17.58	17.85	18.38
86	14.32	14.59	14.86	15.13	15.40	15.67	15.95	16.22	16.49	16.76	17.05	17.32	17.60	17.87	18.13	18.67
85	14.59	14.86	15.13	15.41	15.68	15.95	16.23	16.50	16.77	17.05	17.32	17.60	17.87	18.15	18.42	18.97
84	14.86	15.14	15.41	15.69	15.96	16.24	16.51	16.79	17.06	17.34	17.62	17.89	18.17	18.45	18.72	19.28
83	15.14	15.42	15.69	15.97	16.25	16.53	16.80	17.08	17.36	17.64	17.91	18.19	18.47	18.75	19.03	19.59
82	15.43	15.70	15.98	16.26	16.54	16.82	17.10	17.38	17.66	17.94	18.22	18.50	18.78	19.06	19.34	19.91
81	15.72	16.00	16.28	16.56	16.84	17.12	17.40	17.68	17.96	18.25	18.53	18.81	19.09	19.38	19.66	20.23
80	16.01	16.29	16.58	16.86	17.14	17.43	17.71	17.99	18.28	18.56	18.85	19.13	19.42	19.70	19.99	20.56
79	16.31	16.60	16.88	17.17	17.45	17.74	18.02	18.31	18.60	18.88	19.17	19.46	19.74	20.03	20.32	20.90
78	16.62	16.91	17.20	17.48	17.77	18.06	18.35	18.63	18.92	19.21	19.50	19.79	20.08	20.37	20.66	21.24
77	16.94	17.22	17.51	17.80	18.09	18.38	18.67	18.96	19.25	19.55	19.84	20.13	20.42	20.71	21.01	21.59
76	17.26	17.55	17.84	18.13	18.42	18.72	19.01	19.30	19.59	19.89	20.18	20.48	20.77	21.07	21.36	21.95
75	17.58	17.88	18.17	18.47	18.76	19.05	19.35	19.65	19.94	20.24	20.53	20.83	21.13	21.43	21.72	22.32
74	17.92	18.22	18.51	18.81	19.10	19.40	19.70	20.00	20.30	20.59	20.89	21.19	21.49	21.79	22.09	22.70
73	18.26	18.56	18.86	19.16	19.46	19.76	20.06	20.36	20.66	20.96	21.26	21.56	21.87	22.17	22.47	23.08
70	19.33	19.64	19.95	20.25	20.56	20.87	21.18	21.49	21.80	22.11	22.42	22.73	23.04	23.35	23.66	24.29
65	21.30	21.62	21.95	22.27	22.59	22.91	23.24	23.56	23.89	24.21	24.54	24.87	25.20	25.52	25.85	26.51
60	23.54	23.88	24.22	24.56	24.90	25.24	25.58	25.93	26.27	26.62	26.96	27.31	27.66	28.01	28.36	29.06

13 YEARS

Description: This table shows the price to pay for a monthly payment mortgage loan at the yield rate.

Example: The price of a 6.75 %, 13 year mortgage loan to yield 8.00 % to maturity is $ 93.37.

INTEREST RATE, %

YIELD	0.00%	1.00%	2.00%	3.00%	4.00%	4.25%	4.50%	4.75%	5.00%	5.25%	5.50%	5.75%	6.00%	6.25%	6.50%	6.75%
0.00	100.00	106.68	113.65	120.89	128.41	130.33	132.27	134.22	136.20	138.19	140.19	142.22	144.26	146.31	148.39	150.47
1.00	93.74	100.00	106.53	113.32	120.36	122.16	123.98	125.82	127.67	129.53	131.41	133.31	135.22	137.15	139.09	141.05
2.00	87.99	93.87	100.00	106.37	112.99	114.68	116.39	118.11	119.84	121.59	123.36	125.14	126.94	128.75	130.57	132.41
3.00	82.72	88.25	94.01	100.00	106.22	107.81	109.41	111.03	112.66	114.31	115.97	117.64	119.33	121.03	122.75	124.47
4.00	77.88	83.08	88.50	94.14	100.00	101.50	103.01	104.53	106.07	107.62	109.18	110.76	112.34	113.95	115.56	117.19
4.25	76.73	81.86	87.20	92.76	98.52	100.00	101.49	102.99	104.50	106.03	107.57	109.12	110.69	112.26	113.86	115.46
4.50	75.60	80.66	85.92	91.40	97.08	98.53	100.00	101.48	102.97	104.48	105.99	107.52	109.06	110.62	112.19	113.76
4.75	74.50	79.48	84.67	90.06	95.67	97.10	98.54	100.00	101.47	102.95	104.45	105.95	107.47	109.01	110.55	112.11
5.00	73.42	78.33	83.44	88.76	94.28	95.69	97.11	98.55	100.00	101.46	102.93	104.42	105.92	107.43	108.95	110.48
5.25	72.37	77.20	82.24	87.48	92.92	94.31	95.72	97.13	98.56	100.00	101.45	102.92	104.39	105.88	107.38	108.89
5.50	71.33	76.10	81.06	86.23	91.59	92.96	94.35	95.74	97.15	98.57	100.00	101.44	102.90	104.36	105.84	107.33
5.75	70.32	75.01	79.91	85.00	90.29	91.64	93.00	94.38	95.77	97.17	98.58	100.00	101.43	102.88	104.34	105.81
6.00	69.32	73.95	78.78	83.80	89.01	90.34	91.69	93.05	94.41	95.79	97.18	98.59	100.00	101.43	102.86	104.31
6.25	68.35	72.91	77.67	82.62	87.76	89.08	90.40	91.74	93.09	94.45	95.82	97.20	98.59	100.00	101.42	102.84
6.50	67.39	71.90	76.59	81.47	86.54	87.83	89.14	90.46	91.79	93.13	94.48	95.84	97.22	98.60	100.00	101.41
6.75	66.46	70.90	75.52	80.34	85.33	86.61	87.90	89.20	90.51	91.83	93.17	94.51	95.87	97.23	98.61	100.00
7.00	65.54	69.92	74.48	79.23	84.16	85.42	86.69	87.97	89.26	90.57	91.88	93.21	94.55	95.89	97.25	98.62
7.25	64.64	68.96	73.46	78.14	83.00	84.25	85.50	86.76	88.04	89.33	90.62	91.93	93.25	94.58	95.92	97.27
7.50	63.76	68.02	72.46	77.08	81.87	83.10	84.33	85.58	86.84	88.11	89.39	90.68	91.98	93.29	94.61	95.94
7.75	62.90	67.10	71.48	76.03	80.76	81.97	83.19	84.42	85.66	86.92	88.18	89.45	90.73	92.03	93.33	94.64
8.00	62.05	66.20	70.52	75.01	79.68	80.87	82.07	83.29	84.51	85.75	86.99	88.25	89.51	90.79	92.07	93.37
8.25	61.22	65.31	69.57	74.01	78.61	79.79	80.98	82.17	83.38	84.60	85.83	87.07	88.31	89.57	90.84	92.12
8.50	60.41	64.44	68.65	73.02	77.57	78.73	79.90	81.08	82.27	83.47	84.69	85.91	87.14	88.38	89.64	90.90
8.75	59.61	63.59	67.74	72.06	76.54	77.69	78.84	80.01	81.19	82.37	83.57	84.77	85.99	87.22	88.45	89.70
9.00	58.83	62.76	66.85	71.11	75.54	76.67	77.81	78.96	80.12	81.29	82.47	83.66	84.86	86.07	87.29	88.52
9.25	58.06	61.94	65.98	70.19	74.55	75.67	76.79	77.93	79.08	80.23	81.40	82.57	83.76	84.95	86.15	87.37
9.50	57.31	61.14	65.13	69.28	73.59	74.69	75.80	76.92	78.05	79.19	80.34	81.50	82.67	83.85	85.04	86.23
9.75	56.57	60.35	64.29	68.39	72.64	73.73	74.82	75.93	77.05	78.17	79.31	80.45	81.61	82.77	83.94	85.12
10.00	55.85	59.58	63.47	67.51	71.71	72.78	73.87	74.96	76.06	77.17	78.29	79.42	80.56	81.71	82.87	84.03
10.25	55.14	58.82	62.66	66.65	70.80	71.86	72.93	74.01	75.09	76.19	77.30	78.41	79.54	80.67	81.81	82.97
10.50	54.44	58.08	61.87	65.81	69.90	70.95	72.01	73.07	74.15	75.23	76.32	77.42	78.53	79.65	80.78	81.92
10.75	53.76	57.35	61.09	64.98	69.03	70.06	71.10	72.15	73.21	74.28	75.36	76.45	77.55	78.65	79.77	80.89
11.00	53.09	56.63	60.33	64.17	68.17	69.19	70.22	71.25	72.30	73.36	74.42	75.50	76.58	77.67	78.77	79.88
11.25	52.43	55.93	59.58	63.38	67.32	68.33	69.35	70.37	71.41	72.45	73.50	74.56	75.63	76.71	77.80	78.89
11.50	51.78	55.24	58.85	62.60	66.49	67.49	68.49	69.50	70.53	71.56	72.60	73.64	74.70	75.76	76.84	77.92
11.75	51.15	54.57	58.13	61.83	65.68	66.66	67.65	68.65	69.66	70.68	71.71	72.74	73.79	74.84	75.90	76.97
12.00	50.53	53.90	57.42	61.08	64.88	65.85	66.83	67.82	68.82	69.82	70.84	71.86	72.89	73.93	74.98	76.03
12.25	49.92	53.25	56.73	60.34	64.10	65.06	66.02	67.00	67.99	68.98	69.98	70.99	72.01	73.04	74.07	75.11
12.50	49.32	52.61	56.05	59.62	63.33	64.28	65.23	66.20	67.17	68.15	69.14	70.14	71.15	72.16	73.18	74.21
12.75	48.73	51.99	55.38	58.91	62.57	63.51	64.46	65.41	66.37	67.34	68.32	69.30	70.30	71.30	72.31	73.33
13.00	48.15	51.37	54.72	58.21	61.83	62.76	63.69	64.63	65.58	66.54	67.51	68.48	69.46	70.46	71.45	72.46
13.25	47.59	50.77	54.08	57.53	61.10	62.02	62.94	63.87	64.81	65.76	66.71	67.68	68.65	69.63	70.61	71.61
13.50	47.03	50.17	53.45	56.85	60.39	61.29	62.21	63.13	64.05	64.99	65.93	66.89	67.85	68.81	69.79	70.77
13.75	46.48	49.59	52.83	56.19	59.69	60.58	61.48	62.39	63.31	64.24	65.17	66.11	67.06	68.01	68.98	69.95
14.00	45.95	49.02	52.22	55.55	59.00	59.88	60.77	61.67	62.58	63.49	64.42	65.35	66.28	67.23	68.18	69.14
14.25	45.42	48.46	51.62	54.91	58.32	59.20	60.08	60.97	61.86	62.77	63.68	64.60	65.52	66.46	67.40	68.35
14.50	44.90	47.90	51.03	54.28	57.66	58.52	59.39	60.27	61.16	62.05	62.95	63.86	64.78	65.70	66.63	67.57
14.75	44.40	47.36	50.45	53.67	57.01	57.86	58.72	59.59	60.47	61.35	62.24	63.14	64.04	64.96	65.88	66.81
15.00	43.90	46.83	49.89	53.07	56.37	57.21	58.06	58.92	59.79	60.66	61.54	62.43	63.32	64.23	65.14	66.05
15.25	43.41	46.31	49.33	52.47	55.74	56.57	57.41	58.26	59.12	59.98	60.85	61.73	62.62	63.51	64.41	65.32
15.50	42.93	45.79	48.78	51.89	55.12	55.94	56.78	57.62	58.46	59.32	60.18	61.05	61.92	62.81	63.70	64.59
15.75	42.45	45.29	48.25	51.32	54.51	55.33	56.15	56.98	57.82	58.66	59.52	60.37	61.24	62.11	62.99	63.88
16.00	41.99	44.79	47.72	50.76	53.91	54.72	55.54	56.36	57.19	58.02	58.86	59.71	60.57	61.43	62.30	63.18
16.25	41.53	44.31	47.20	50.21	53.33	54.13	54.93	55.74	56.56	57.39	58.22	59.06	59.91	60.76	61.63	62.49
16.50	41.08	43.83	46.69	49.66	52.75	53.54	54.34	55.14	55.95	56.77	57.59	58.43	59.26	60.11	60.96	61.82
16.75	40.64	43.36	46.19	49.13	52.19	52.97	53.75	54.55	55.35	56.16	56.98	57.80	58.63	59.46	60.31	61.15
17.00	40.21	42.89	45.69	48.61	51.63	52.40	53.18	53.97	54.76	55.56	56.37	57.18	58.00	58.83	59.66	60.50
17.25	39.78	42.44	45.21	48.09	51.08	51.85	52.62	53.40	54.18	54.97	55.77	56.58	57.39	58.21	59.03	59.86
17.50	39.36	41.99	44.73	47.58	50.54	51.30	52.06	52.83	53.61	54.39	55.18	55.98	56.78	57.59	58.41	59.23
17.75	38.95	41.55	44.27	47.09	50.02	50.76	51.52	52.28	53.05	53.83	54.61	55.39	56.19	56.99	57.80	58.61
18.00	38.55	41.12	43.81	46.60	49.50	50.24	50.98	51.74	52.50	53.27	54.04	54.82	55.61	56.40	57.20	58.00
18.25	38.15	40.70	43.35	46.12	48.98	49.72	50.46	51.20	51.96	52.72	53.48	54.25	55.03	55.82	56.61	57.40
18.50	37.76	40.28	42.91	45.64	48.48	49.21	49.94	50.68	51.42	52.18	52.93	53.70	54.47	55.24	56.03	56.82
18.75	37.37	39.87	42.47	45.18	47.99	48.71	49.43	50.16	50.90	51.64	52.39	53.15	53.91	54.68	55.46	56.24
19.00	36.99	39.47	42.04	44.72	47.50	48.21	48.93	49.66	50.39	51.12	51.86	52.61	53.37	54.13	54.89	55.67
20.00	35.54	37.92	40.39	42.97	45.64	46.32	47.01	47.71	48.41	49.12	49.83	50.55	51.27	52.00	52.74	53.48
25.00	29.54	31.51	33.57	35.70	37.93	38.49	39.07	39.64	40.23	40.81	41.41	42.00	42.61	43.21	43.83	44.44
30.00	25.10	26.77	28.52	30.34	32.23	32.71	33.19	33.69	34.18	34.68	35.18	35.69	36.20	36.72	37.24	37.76

Description: This table shows the yield to maturity of a mortgage purchased at the price shown in the index.

Example: The yield to maturity of a 6.75 %, 13 year mortgage at a price of 80.00 is 10.97 %.

INTEREST RATE, %

PRICE	0.00%	1.00%	2.00%	3.00%	4.00%	4.25%	4.50%	4.75%	5.00%	5.25%	5.50%	5.75%	6.00%	6.25%	6.50%	6.75%
100	0.00	1.00	2.00	3.00	4.00	4.25	4.50	4.75	5.00	5.25	5.50	5.75	6.00	6.25	6.50	6.75
99	.15	1.15	2.16	3.16	4.16	4.41	4.67	4.92	5.17	5.42	5.67	5.92	6.17	6.42	6.67	6.93
98	.30	1.31	2.32	3.33	4.34	4.59	4.84	5.09	5.34	5.60	5.85	6.10	6.35	6.60	6.86	7.11
97	.46	1.47	2.49	3.50	4.51	4.76	5.02	5.27	5.52	5.78	6.03	6.28	6.53	6.79	7.04	7.30
96	.62	1.64	2.65	3.67	4.69	4.94	5.19	5.45	5.70	5.96	6.21	6.47	6.72	6.97	7.23	7.48
95	.79	1.80	2.82	3.84	4.86	5.12	5.38	5.63	5.89	6.14	6.40	6.65	6.91	7.16	7.42	7.68
94	.95	1.97	3.00	4.02	5.05	5.30	5.56	5.82	6.07	6.33	6.59	6.84	7.10	7.36	7.61	7.87
93	1.12	2.14	3.17	4.20	5.23	5.49	5.75	6.00	6.26	6.52	6.78	7.04	7.29	7.55	7.81	8.07
92	1.29	2.32	3.35	4.38	5.42	5.68	5.94	6.19	6.45	6.71	6.97	7.23	7.49	7.75	8.01	8.27
91	1.46	2.50	3.53	4.57	5.61	5.87	6.13	6.39	6.65	6.91	7.17	7.43	7.69	7.95	8.21	8.47
90	1.64	2.67	3.71	4.76	5.80	6.06	6.32	6.59	6.85	7.11	7.37	7.63	7.89	8.16	8.42	8.68
89	1.81	2.86	3.90	4.95	6.00	6.26	6.52	6.79	7.05	7.31	7.57	7.84	8.10	8.36	8.63	8.89
88	1.99	3.04	4.09	5.14	6.20	6.46	6.72	6.99	7.25	7.52	7.78	8.05	8.31	8.58	8.84	9.11
87	2.18	3.23	4.28	5.34	6.40	6.66	6.93	7.20	7.46	7.73	7.99	8.26	8.53	8.79	9.06	9.33
86	2.36	3.42	4.48	5.54	6.61	6.87	7.14	7.41	7.67	7.94	8.21	8.48	8.74	9.01	9.28	9.55
85	2.55	3.61	4.68	5.75	6.82	7.08	7.35	7.62	7.89	8.16	8.43	8.69	8.96	9.23	9.50	9.77
84	2.74	3.81	4.88	5.95	7.03	7.30	7.57	7.84	8.11	8.38	8.65	8.92	9.19	9.46	9.73	10.00
83	2.94	4.01	5.09	6.16	7.25	7.52	7.79	8.06	8.33	8.60	8.87	9.15	9.42	9.69	9.96	10.24
82	3.14	4.22	5.30	6.38	7.47	7.74	8.01	8.28	8.56	8.83	9.10	9.38	9.65	9.93	10.20	10.48
81	3.34	4.42	5.51	6.60	7.69	7.97	8.24	8.51	8.79	9.06	9.34	9.61	9.89	10.17	10.44	10.72
80	3.55	4.63	5.73	6.82	7.92	8.20	8.47	8.75	9.02	9.30	9.58	9.85	10.13	10.41	10.69	10.97
79	3.76	4.85	5.95	7.05	8.15	8.43	8.71	8.99	9.26	9.54	9.82	10.10	10.38	10.66	10.94	11.22
78	3.97	5.07	6.17	7.28	8.39	8.67	8.95	9.23	9.51	9.79	10.07	10.35	10.63	10.91	11.19	11.47
77	4.19	5.29	6.40	7.51	8.63	8.91	9.19	9.48	9.76	10.04	10.32	10.60	10.89	11.17	11.45	11.74
76	4.41	5.52	6.63	7.75	8.88	9.16	9.44	9.73	10.01	10.29	10.58	10.86	11.15	11.43	11.72	12.00
75	4.63	5.75	6.87	8.00	9.13	9.41	9.70	9.98	10.27	10.56	10.84	11.13	11.41	11.70	11.99	12.28
74	4.86	5.98	7.11	8.25	9.39	9.67	9.96	10.25	10.53	10.82	11.11	11.40	11.69	11.98	12.26	12.55
73	5.09	6.22	7.36	8.50	9.65	9.94	10.23	10.51	10.80	11.09	11.38	11.67	11.96	12.26	12.55	12.84
72	5.33	6.47	7.61	8.76	9.92	10.21	10.50	10.79	11.08	11.37	11.66	11.95	12.25	12.54	12.83	13.13
71	5.58	6.72	7.87	9.03	10.19	10.48	10.77	11.07	11.36	11.65	11.95	12.24	12.54	12.83	13.13	13.43
70	5.82	6.97	8.13	9.30	10.47	10.76	11.06	11.35	11.65	11.94	12.24	12.54	12.83	13.13	13.43	13.73
69	6.08	7.23	8.40	9.57	10.75	11.05	11.35	11.64	11.94	12.24	12.54	12.84	13.14	13.44	13.74	14.04
68	6.34	7.50	8.67	9.85	11.04	11.34	11.64	11.94	12.24	12.54	12.84	13.14	13.45	13.75	14.05	14.36
67	6.60	7.77	8.95	10.14	11.34	11.64	11.94	12.25	12.55	12.85	13.15	13.46	13.76	14.07	14.37	14.68
66	6.87	8.05	9.24	10.44	11.65	11.95	12.25	12.56	12.86	13.17	13.47	13.78	14.09	14.40	14.70	15.01
65	7.14	8.33	9.53	10.74	11.96	12.26	12.57	12.88	13.18	13.49	13.80	14.11	14.42	14.73	15.04	15.35
64	7.43	8.62	9.83	11.05	12.28	12.58	12.89	13.20	13.51	13.82	14.14	14.45	14.76	15.07	15.39	15.70
63	7.71	8.92	10.14	11.37	12.60	12.91	13.23	13.54	13.85	14.16	14.48	14.79	15.11	15.43	15.74	16.06
62	8.01	9.23	10.45	11.69	12.94	13.25	13.57	13.88	14.20	14.51	14.83	15.15	15.47	15.79	16.11	16.43
61	8.31	9.54	10.77	12.02	13.28	13.60	13.92	14.23	14.55	14.87	15.19	15.51	15.83	16.16	16.48	16.80
60	8.62	9.86	11.10	12.36	13.63	13.95	14.27	14.59	14.92	15.24	15.56	15.89	16.21	16.54	16.86	17.19
59	8.94	10.19	11.44	12.71	14.00	14.32	14.64	14.97	15.29	15.62	15.94	16.27	16.60	16.93	17.26	17.59
58	9.26	10.52	11.79	13.07	14.37	14.69	15.02	15.35	15.67	16.00	16.33	16.66	17.00	17.33	17.66	18.00
57	9.60	10.87	12.15	13.44	14.75	15.08	15.41	15.74	16.07	16.40	16.74	17.07	17.40	17.74	18.08	18.42
56	9.94	11.22	12.51	13.82	15.14	15.47	15.81	16.14	16.48	16.81	17.15	17.49	17.83	18.17	18.51	18.85
55	10.29	11.58	12.89	14.21	15.54	15.88	16.22	16.55	16.89	17.23	17.57	17.92	18.26	18.60	18.95	19.29
54	10.66	11.96	13.28	14.61	15.96	16.30	16.64	16.98	17.32	17.67	18.01	18.36	18.71	19.05	19.40	19.75
53	11.03	12.34	13.68	15.02	16.39	16.73	17.08	17.42	17.77	18.12	18.46	18.81	19.17	19.52	19.87	20.23
52	11.41	12.74	14.09	15.45	16.83	17.18	17.52	17.87	18.23	18.58	18.93	19.28	19.64	20.00	20.35	20.71
51	11.80	13.15	14.51	15.89	17.28	17.63	17.99	18.34	18.70	19.05	19.41	19.77	20.13	20.49	20.85	21.22
50	12.21	13.57	14.94	16.34	17.75	18.11	18.47	18.82	19.18	19.55	19.91	20.27	20.64	21.00	21.37	21.74
49	12.63	14.00	15.40	16.81	18.24	18.60	18.96	19.32	19.69	20.05	20.42	20.79	21.16	21.53	21.90	22.28
48	13.06	14.45	15.86	17.29	18.74	19.11	19.47	19.84	20.21	20.58	20.95	21.33	21.70	22.08	22.46	22.84
47	13.51	14.92	16.34	17.79	19.26	19.63	20.00	20.38	20.75	21.13	21.50	21.88	22.26	22.65	23.03	23.42
46	13.97	15.39	16.84	18.31	19.80	20.17	20.55	20.93	21.31	21.69	22.08	22.46	22.85	23.23	23.62	24.02
45	14.45	15.89	17.35	18.84	20.35	20.74	21.12	21.50	21.89	22.28	22.67	23.06	23.45	23.84	24.24	24.64
44	14.94	16.40	17.89	19.40	20.93	21.32	21.71	22.10	22.49	22.89	23.28	23.68	24.08	24.48	24.88	25.29
43	15.46	16.94	18.44	19.98	21.53	21.93	22.32	22.72	23.12	23.52	23.92	24.33	24.73	25.14	25.55	25.96
42	15.99	17.49	19.02	20.58	22.16	22.56	22.96	23.37	23.77	24.18	24.59	25.00	25.41	25.83	26.24	26.66
41	16.54	18.07	19.62	21.20	22.81	23.22	23.63	24.04	24.45	24.86	25.28	25.70	26.12	26.54	26.97	27.39
40	17.12	18.67	20.24	21.85	23.49	23.90	24.32	24.74	25.16	25.58	26.00	26.43	26.86	27.29	27.72	28.16
39	17.72	19.29	20.89	22.53	24.20	24.62	25.04	25.47	25.90	26.33	26.76	27.20	27.63	28.07	28.51	28.96
35	20.39	22.08	23.81	25.57	27.38	27.84	28.30	28.76	29.23	29.70	30.17	30.64	31.12	31.59	32.08	32.56
30	24.55	26.44	28.37	30.36	32.40	32.92	33.44	33.97	34.50	35.03	35.57	36.10	36.65	37.19	37.74	38.29
25	30.12	32.30	34.55	36.86	39.24	39.85	40.46	41.08	41.70	42.32	42.95	43.59	44.23	44.87	45.52	46.17
20	38.17	40.80	43.54	46.36	49.29	50.04	50.79	51.55	52.31	53.08	53.86	54.64	55.43	56.23	57.03	57.83
15	51.20	54.65	58.24	61.97	65.83	66.82	67.81	68.82	69.83	70.85	71.88	72.92	73.97	75.02	76.09	77.16
10	76.91	82.06	87.41	92.99	98.77	100.25	101.74	103.25	104.76	106.29	107.84	109.39	110.96	112.54	114.14	115.75

Description: This table shows the price to pay for a monthly payment mortgage loan at the yield rate.

Example: The price of a 10.75 %, 13 year mortgage loan to yield 8.00 % to maturity is $ 115.43.

INTEREST RATE, %

YIELD	7.00%	7.25%	7.50%	7.75%	8.00%	8.25%	8.50%	8.75%	9.00%	9.25%	9.50%	9.75%	10.00%	10.25%	10.50%	10.75%
0.00	152.58	154.70	156.84	158.99	161.16	163.34	165.54	167.76	169.99	172.24	174.50	176.77	179.06	181.37	183.69	186.03
1.00	143.02	145.01	147.01	149.03	151.06	153.11	155.17	157.25	159.34	161.45	163.57	165.70	167.85	170.01	172.18	174.37
2.00	134.26	136.13	138.01	139.90	141.81	143.73	145.67	147.62	149.58	151.56	153.55	155.55	157.56	159.59	161.63	163.69
3.00	126.22	127.97	129.74	131.52	133.31	135.12	136.94	138.77	140.62	142.48	144.35	146.23	148.12	150.03	151.95	153.88
4.00	118.83	120.48	122.14	123.82	125.51	127.21	128.92	130.65	132.38	134.13	135.89	137.67	139.45	141.25	143.05	144.87
4.25	117.07	118.70	120.34	121.99	123.66	125.33	127.02	128.72	130.43	132.16	133.89	135.64	137.39	139.16	140.94	142.74
4.50	115.36	116.96	118.58	120.20	121.84	123.49	125.16	126.83	128.52	130.22	131.93	133.65	135.38	137.12	138.88	140.64
4.75	113.68	115.26	116.85	118.45	120.07	121.69	123.33	124.98	126.65	128.32	130.00	131.70	133.41	135.12	136.85	138.59
5.00	112.03	113.59	115.15	116.74	118.33	119.93	121.55	123.17	124.81	126.46	128.12	129.79	131.47	133.17	134.87	136.59
5.25	110.42	111.95	113.50	115.05	116.62	118.20	119.80	121.40	123.01	124.64	126.28	127.92	129.58	131.25	132.93	134.62
5.50	108.83	110.35	111.87	113.41	114.95	116.51	118.08	119.66	121.25	122.86	124.47	126.09	127.73	129.37	131.03	132.69
5.75	107.29	108.78	110.28	111.79	113.32	114.86	116.40	117.96	119.53	121.11	122.70	124.30	125.91	127.53	129.16	130.80
6.00	105.77	107.24	108.72	110.21	111.72	113.23	114.76	116.29	117.84	119.40	120.96	122.54	124.13	125.73	127.34	128.95
6.25	104.28	105.73	107.19	108.66	110.15	111.64	113.14	114.66	116.18	117.72	119.26	120.82	122.38	123.96	125.55	127.14
6.50	102.83	104.26	105.70	107.15	108.61	110.08	111.56	113.06	114.56	116.07	117.60	119.13	120.67	122.23	123.79	125.37
6.75	101.40	102.81	104.23	105.66	107.10	108.55	110.01	111.49	112.97	114.46	115.96	117.48	119.00	120.53	122.07	123.63
7.00	100.00	101.39	102.79	104.20	105.62	107.05	108.50	109.95	111.41	112.88	114.36	115.86	117.36	118.87	120.39	121.92
7.25	98.63	100.00	101.38	102.77	104.18	105.59	107.01	108.44	109.88	111.34	112.80	114.27	115.75	117.24	118.74	120.25
7.50	97.28	98.64	100.00	101.37	102.76	104.15	105.55	106.96	108.39	109.82	111.26	112.71	114.17	115.64	117.12	118.61
7.75	95.97	97.30	98.65	100.00	101.36	102.74	104.12	105.52	106.92	108.33	109.75	111.18	112.63	114.08	115.54	117.00
8.00	94.68	95.99	97.32	98.65	100.00	101.36	102.72	104.10	105.48	106.87	108.28	109.69	111.11	112.54	113.98	115.43
8.25	93.41	94.71	96.02	97.33	98.66	100.00	101.35	102.70	104.07	105.44	106.83	108.22	109.62	111.04	112.46	113.89
8.50	92.17	93.45	94.74	96.04	97.35	98.67	100.00	101.34	102.69	104.04	105.41	106.78	108.17	109.56	110.96	112.37
8.75	90.95	92.22	93.49	94.77	96.07	97.37	98.68	100.00	101.33	102.67	104.02	105.37	106.74	108.11	109.50	110.89
9.00	89.76	91.01	92.26	93.53	94.81	96.09	97.38	98.69	100.00	101.32	102.65	103.99	105.34	106.69	108.06	109.43
9.25	88.59	89.82	91.06	92.31	93.57	94.84	96.11	97.40	98.70	100.00	101.31	102.63	103.96	105.30	106.65	108.01
9.50	87.44	88.66	89.88	91.11	92.36	93.61	94.87	96.14	97.42	98.70	100.00	101.30	102.62	103.94	105.27	106.61
9.75	86.31	87.51	88.72	89.94	91.17	92.40	93.65	94.90	96.16	97.43	98.71	100.00	101.30	102.60	103.91	105.23
10.00	85.21	86.39	87.59	88.79	90.00	91.22	92.45	93.69	94.93	96.19	97.45	98.72	100.00	101.29	102.58	103.89
10.25	84.13	85.30	86.47	87.66	88.86	90.06	91.27	92.50	93.73	94.96	96.21	97.47	98.73	100.00	101.28	102.57
10.50	83.06	84.22	85.38	86.55	87.73	88.92	90.12	91.33	92.54	93.76	95.00	96.23	97.48	98.74	100.00	101.27
10.75	82.02	83.16	84.31	85.47	86.63	87.81	88.99	90.18	91.38	92.59	93.80	95.03	96.26	97.50	98.74	100.00
11.00	81.00	82.12	83.26	84.40	85.55	86.71	87.88	89.06	90.24	91.43	92.63	93.84	95.06	96.28	97.51	98.75
11.25	79.99	81.11	82.23	83.36	84.49	85.64	86.79	87.95	89.12	90.30	91.49	92.68	93.88	95.09	96.31	97.53
11.50	79.01	80.11	81.21	82.33	83.45	84.58	85.72	86.87	88.03	89.19	90.36	91.54	92.72	93.92	95.12	96.33
11.75	78.04	79.13	80.22	81.32	82.43	83.55	84.67	85.81	86.95	88.10	89.25	90.42	91.59	92.77	93.96	95.15
12.00	77.09	78.17	79.25	80.33	81.43	82.53	83.65	84.76	85.89	87.03	88.17	89.32	90.48	91.64	92.81	93.99
12.25	76.16	77.22	78.29	79.36	80.45	81.54	82.64	83.74	84.85	85.98	87.10	88.24	89.38	90.54	91.69	92.86
12.50	75.25	76.30	77.35	78.41	79.48	80.56	81.64	82.74	83.84	84.94	86.06	87.18	88.31	89.45	90.59	91.74
12.75	74.35	75.39	76.43	77.48	78.53	79.60	80.67	81.75	82.84	83.93	85.03	86.14	87.26	88.38	89.51	90.65
13.00	73.47	74.49	75.52	76.56	77.60	78.66	79.72	80.78	81.86	82.94	84.03	85.12	86.23	87.34	88.45	89.58
13.25	72.61	73.62	74.63	75.66	76.69	77.73	78.78	79.83	80.89	81.96	83.04	84.12	85.21	86.31	87.41	88.52
13.50	71.76	72.76	73.76	74.77	75.79	76.82	77.86	78.90	79.95	81.00	82.07	83.14	84.22	85.30	86.39	87.49
13.75	70.93	71.91	72.91	73.91	74.91	75.93	76.95	77.98	79.02	80.06	81.11	82.17	83.24	84.31	85.39	86.47
14.00	70.11	71.08	72.06	73.05	74.05	75.05	76.06	77.08	78.11	79.14	80.18	81.22	82.28	83.34	84.40	85.48
14.25	69.30	70.27	71.24	72.22	73.20	74.19	75.19	76.20	77.21	78.23	79.26	80.29	81.33	82.38	83.44	84.50
14.50	68.51	69.47	70.43	71.39	72.37	73.35	74.34	75.33	76.33	77.34	78.36	79.38	80.41	81.44	82.48	83.53
14.75	67.74	68.68	69.63	70.59	71.55	72.52	73.50	74.48	75.47	76.47	77.47	78.48	79.50	80.52	81.55	82.59
15.00	66.98	67.91	68.85	69.79	70.74	71.70	72.67	73.64	74.62	75.61	76.60	77.60	78.60	79.62	80.63	81.66
15.25	66.23	67.15	68.08	69.01	69.95	70.90	71.86	72.82	73.79	74.76	75.74	76.73	77.73	78.73	79.73	80.75
15.50	65.50	66.41	67.32	68.25	69.18	70.12	71.06	72.01	72.97	73.93	74.90	75.88	76.86	77.85	78.85	79.85
15.75	64.77	65.67	66.58	67.50	68.42	69.34	70.28	71.22	72.16	73.12	74.08	75.04	76.02	77.00	77.98	78.97
16.00	64.06	64.96	65.85	66.76	67.67	68.58	69.51	70.44	71.37	72.32	73.27	74.22	75.18	76.15	77.13	78.11
16.25	63.37	64.25	65.14	66.03	66.93	67.84	68.75	69.67	70.60	71.53	72.47	73.42	74.37	75.32	76.29	77.26
16.50	62.68	63.55	64.43	65.32	66.21	67.10	68.01	68.92	69.84	70.76	71.69	72.62	73.56	74.51	75.46	76.42
16.75	62.01	62.87	63.74	64.62	65.50	66.38	67.28	68.18	69.09	70.00	70.92	71.84	72.77	73.71	74.65	75.60
17.00	61.35	62.20	63.06	63.93	64.80	65.68	66.56	67.45	68.35	69.25	70.16	71.08	72.00	72.92	73.86	74.80
17.25	60.70	61.54	62.39	63.25	64.11	64.98	65.86	66.74	67.62	68.52	69.42	70.32	71.23	72.15	73.07	74.00
17.50	60.06	60.89	61.74	62.58	63.44	64.30	65.16	66.03	66.91	67.80	68.69	69.58	70.48	71.39	72.31	73.22
17.75	59.43	60.26	61.09	61.93	62.77	63.62	64.48	65.34	66.21	67.09	67.97	68.85	69.75	70.65	71.55	72.46
18.00	58.81	59.63	60.46	61.29	62.12	62.96	63.81	64.67	65.52	66.39	67.26	68.14	69.02	69.91	70.81	71.71
18.25	58.21	59.02	59.83	60.65	61.48	62.31	63.15	64.00	64.85	65.71	66.57	67.44	68.31	69.19	70.08	70.97
18.50	57.61	58.41	59.22	60.03	60.85	61.67	62.50	63.34	64.18	65.03	65.89	66.74	67.61	68.48	69.36	70.24
18.75	57.02	57.82	58.61	59.42	60.23	61.05	61.87	62.70	63.53	64.37	65.21	66.06	66.92	67.78	68.65	69.52
19.00	56.45	57.23	58.02	58.82	59.62	60.43	61.24	62.06	62.89	63.72	64.55	65.40	66.24	67.10	67.96	68.82
20.00	54.23	54.99	55.74	56.51	57.28	58.06	58.84	59.63	60.42	61.22	62.02	62.83	63.64	64.46	65.29	66.12
25.00	45.07	45.69	46.32	46.96	47.60	48.24	48.89	49.55	50.21	50.87	51.54	52.21	52.89	53.57	54.25	54.94
30.00	38.29	38.82	39.36	39.90	40.45	40.99	41.55	42.10	42.66	43.23	43.79	44.36	44.94	45.52	46.10	46.69

Description: This table shows the yield to maturity of a mortgage purchased at the price shown in the index.

Example: The yield to maturity of a 10.75 %, 13 year mortgage at a price of 113.00 is 8.39 %.

INTEREST RATE, %

PRICE	7.00%	7.25%	7.50%	7.75%	8.00%	8.25%	8.50%	8.75%	9.00%	9.25%	9.50%	9.75%	10.00%	10.25%	10.50%	10.75%
145	.78	1.00	1.21	1.43	1.64	1.85	2.07	2.28	2.50	2.71	2.92	3.13	3.35	3.56	3.77	3.98
140	1.33	1.55	1.77	1.98	2.20	2.42	2.63	2.85	3.07	3.28	3.50	3.71	3.93	4.14	4.36	4.57
135	1.91	2.13	2.35	2.57	2.79	3.01	3.23	3.45	3.67	3.89	4.11	4.32	4.54	4.76	4.98	5.20
130	2.51	2.74	2.96	3.19	3.41	3.63	3.86	4.08	4.30	4.52	4.75	4.97	5.19	5.41	5.63	5.85
129	2.64	2.86	3.09	3.31	3.54	3.76	3.98	4.21	4.43	4.65	4.88	5.10	5.32	5.54	5.77	5.99
128	2.77	2.99	3.22	3.44	3.67	3.89	4.12	4.34	4.56	4.79	5.01	5.23	5.46	5.68	5.90	6.13
127	2.89	3.12	3.35	3.57	3.80	4.02	4.25	4.47	4.70	4.92	5.15	5.37	5.59	5.82	6.04	6.26
126	3.02	3.25	3.48	3.70	3.93	4.16	4.38	4.61	4.83	5.06	5.28	5.51	5.73	5.96	6.18	6.41
125	3.15	3.38	3.61	3.84	4.06	4.29	4.52	4.74	4.97	5.20	5.42	5.65	5.87	6.10	6.32	6.55
124	3.29	3.51	3.74	3.97	4.20	4.43	4.65	4.88	5.11	5.33	5.56	5.79	6.01	6.24	6.47	6.69
123	3.42	3.65	3.88	4.11	4.33	4.56	4.79	5.02	5.25	5.47	5.70	5.93	6.16	6.38	6.61	6.84
122	3.56	3.78	4.01	4.24	4.47	4.70	4.93	5.16	5.39	5.62	5.84	6.07	6.30	6.53	6.76	6.98
121	3.69	3.92	4.15	4.38	4.61	4.84	5.07	5.30	5.53	5.76	5.99	6.22	6.45	6.68	6.90	7.13
120	3.83	4.06	4.29	4.52	4.75	4.99	5.22	5.45	5.68	5.91	6.14	6.37	6.60	6.82	7.05	7.28
119	3.97	4.20	4.43	4.67	4.90	5.13	5.36	5.59	5.82	6.05	6.28	6.51	6.74	6.98	7.21	7.44
118	4.11	4.35	4.58	4.81	5.04	5.28	5.51	5.74	5.97	6.20	6.43	6.67	6.90	7.13	7.36	7.59
117	4.26	4.49	4.72	4.96	5.19	5.42	5.66	5.89	6.12	6.35	6.59	6.82	7.05	7.28	7.51	7.75
116	4.40	4.64	4.87	5.10	5.34	5.57	5.81	6.04	6.27	6.51	6.74	6.97	7.21	7.44	7.67	7.90
115	4.55	4.78	5.02	5.25	5.49	5.72	5.96	6.19	6.43	6.66	6.90	7.13	7.36	7.60	7.83	8.06
114	4.70	4.93	5.17	5.40	5.64	5.88	6.11	6.35	6.58	6.82	7.05	7.29	7.52	7.76	7.99	8.23
113	4.85	5.08	5.32	5.56	5.79	6.03	6.27	6.50	6.74	6.98	7.21	7.45	7.68	7.92	8.16	8.39
112	5.00	5.24	5.48	5.71	5.95	6.19	6.43	6.66	6.90	7.14	7.37	7.61	7.85	8.08	8.32	8.56
111	5.15	5.39	5.63	5.87	6.11	6.35	6.59	6.82	7.06	7.30	7.54	7.78	8.01	8.25	8.49	8.73
110	5.31	5.55	5.79	6.03	6.27	6.51	6.75	6.99	7.23	7.46	7.70	7.94	8.18	8.42	8.66	8.90
109	5.47	5.71	5.95	6.19	6.43	6.67	6.91	7.15	7.39	7.63	7.87	8.11	8.35	8.59	8.83	9.07
108	5.63	5.87	6.11	6.35	6.60	6.84	7.08	7.32	7.56	7.80	8.04	8.28	8.52	8.76	9.01	9.25
107	5.79	6.03	6.28	6.52	6.76	7.00	7.25	7.49	7.73	7.97	8.22	8.46	8.70	8.94	9.18	9.42
106	5.96	6.20	6.44	6.69	6.93	7.17	7.42	7.66	7.90	8.15	8.39	8.63	8.88	9.12	9.36	9.60
105	6.12	6.37	6.61	6.86	7.10	7.35	7.59	7.84	8.08	8.32	8.57	8.81	9.06	9.30	9.54	9.79
104	6.29	6.54	6.78	7.03	7.28	7.52	7.77	8.01	8.26	8.50	8.75	8.99	9.24	9.48	9.73	9.97
103	6.46	6.71	6.96	7.20	7.45	7.70	7.94	8.19	8.44	8.68	8.93	9.18	9.42	9.67	9.92	10.16
102	6.64	6.89	7.13	7.38	7.63	7.88	8.13	8.37	8.62	8.87	9.12	9.36	9.61	9.86	10.11	10.35
101	6.82	7.06	7.31	7.56	7.81	8.06	8.31	8.56	8.81	9.06	9.30	9.55	9.80	10.05	10.30	10.55
100	7.00	7.25	7.50	7.75	8.00	8.25	8.50	8.75	9.00	9.25	9.50	9.75	10.00	10.25	10.50	10.75
99	7.18	7.43	7.68	7.93	8.18	8.43	8.68	8.94	9.19	9.44	9.69	9.94	10.19	10.44	10.69	10.95
98	7.36	7.61	7.87	8.12	8.37	8.62	8.88	9.13	9.38	9.63	9.89	10.14	10.39	10.64	10.90	11.15
97	7.55	7.80	8.06	8.31	8.56	8.82	9.07	9.32	9.58	9.83	10.09	10.34	10.59	10.85	11.10	11.35
96	7.74	7.99	8.25	8.50	8.76	9.01	9.27	9.52	9.78	10.03	10.29	10.54	10.80	11.05	11.31	11.56
95	7.93	8.19	8.44	8.70	8.96	9.21	9.47	9.72	9.98	10.24	10.49	10.75	11.01	11.26	11.52	11.78
94	8.13	8.39	8.64	8.90	9.16	9.41	9.67	9.93	10.19	10.45	10.70	10.96	11.22	11.48	11.74	11.99
93	8.33	8.59	8.84	9.10	9.36	9.62	9.88	10.14	10.40	10.66	10.92	11.18	11.43	11.69	11.95	12.21
92	8.53	8.79	9.05	9.31	9.57	9.83	10.09	10.35	10.61	10.87	11.13	11.39	11.65	11.92	12.18	12.44
91	8.73	9.00	9.26	9.52	9.78	10.04	10.30	10.57	10.83	11.09	11.35	11.61	11.88	12.14	12.40	12.66
90	8.94	9.21	9.47	9.73	10.00	10.26	10.52	10.78	11.05	11.31	11.58	11.84	12.10	12.37	12.63	12.90
89	9.16	9.42	9.68	9.95	10.21	10.48	10.74	11.01	11.27	11.54	11.80	12.07	12.33	12.60	12.87	13.13
88	9.37	9.64	9.90	10.17	10.44	10.70	10.97	11.23	11.50	11.77	12.03	12.30	12.57	12.84	13.10	13.37
87	9.59	9.86	10.13	10.39	10.66	10.93	11.20	11.46	11.73	12.00	12.27	12.54	12.81	13.08	13.35	13.61
86	9.82	10.08	10.35	10.62	10.89	11.16	11.43	11.70	11.97	12.24	12.51	12.78	13.05	13.32	13.59	13.86
85	10.04	10.31	10.58	10.85	11.12	11.40	11.67	11.94	12.21	12.48	12.75	13.03	13.30	13.57	13.84	14.12
84	10.27	10.55	10.82	11.09	11.36	11.64	11.91	12.18	12.45	12.73	13.00	13.28	13.55	13.82	14.10	14.37
83	10.51	10.78	11.06	11.33	11.61	11.88	12.15	12.43	12.70	12.98	13.25	13.53	13.81	14.08	14.36	14.64
82	10.75	11.03	11.30	11.58	11.85	12.13	12.40	12.68	12.96	13.24	13.51	13.79	14.07	14.35	14.62	14.90
81	10.99	11.27	11.55	11.83	12.10	12.38	12.66	12.94	13.22	13.50	13.78	14.05	14.33	14.61	14.89	15.18
80	11.24	11.52	11.80	12.08	12.36	12.64	12.92	13.20	13.48	13.76	14.04	14.32	14.61	14.89	15.17	15.45
79	11.50	11.78	12.06	12.34	12.62	12.90	13.19	13.47	13.75	14.03	14.32	14.60	14.88	15.17	15.45	15.74
78	11.76	12.04	12.32	12.60	12.89	13.17	13.46	13.74	14.02	14.31	14.60	14.88	15.17	15.45	15.74	16.03
77	12.02	12.30	12.59	12.87	13.16	13.45	13.73	14.02	14.30	14.59	14.88	15.17	15.46	15.74	16.03	16.32
76	12.29	12.58	12.86	13.15	13.44	13.73	14.01	14.30	14.59	14.88	15.17	15.46	15.75	16.04	16.33	16.62
75	12.56	12.85	13.14	13.43	13.72	14.01	14.30	14.59	14.88	15.18	15.47	15.76	16.06	16.34	16.64	16.93
74	12.84	13.14	13.43	13.72	14.01	14.30	14.59	14.89	15.18	15.47	15.77	16.06	16.36	16.65	16.95	17.25
70	14.03	14.33	14.63	14.93	15.23	15.53	15.83	16.14	16.44	16.74	17.05	17.35	17.66	17.96	18.27	18.58
65	15.67	15.98	16.29	16.61	16.92	17.24	17.55	17.87	18.19	18.51	18.83	19.15	19.47	19.79	20.11	20.43
60	17.52	17.85	18.18	18.51	18.84	19.17	19.50	19.84	20.17	20.51	20.84	21.18	21.52	21.86	22.20	22.54
55	19.64	19.99	20.34	20.69	21.04	21.39	21.74	22.10	22.45	22.81	23.16	23.52	23.88	24.24	24.60	24.97
50	22.11	22.48	22.85	23.23	23.60	23.98	24.36	24.73	25.11	25.50	25.88	26.26	26.65	27.04	27.42	27.81
45	25.04	25.44	25.84	26.24	26.65	27.06	27.46	27.87	28.29	28.70	29.12	29.53	29.95	30.37	30.79	31.22
40	28.59	29.03	29.47	29.91	30.36	30.81	31.25	31.70	32.16	32.61	33.07	33.53	33.99	34.45	34.92	35.39
35	33.05	33.53	34.03	34.52	35.02	35.52	36.02	36.52	37.03	37.54	38.05	38.57	39.08	39.61	40.13	40.65

Description: This table shows the price to pay for a monthly payment mortgage loan at the yield rate.

Example: The price of a 15.00 %, 13 year mortgage loan to yield 8.00 % to maturity is $ 141.35.

INTEREST RATE, %

YIELD	11.00%	11.25%	11.50%	11.75%	12.00%	12.25%	12.50%	12.75%	13.00%	13.25%	13.50%	13.75%	14.00%	14.25%	14.50%	15.00%
0.00	188.37	190.74	193.12	195.51	197.91	200.33	202.76	205.21	207.67	210.14	212.63	215.13	217.64	220.16	222.70	227.80
1.00	176.57	178.79	181.02	183.26	185.52	187.78	190.06	192.36	194.66	196.98	199.31	201.65	204.00	206.37	208.75	213.54
2.00	165.76	167.84	169.93	172.03	174.15	176.28	178.42	180.57	182.73	184.91	187.10	189.29	191.50	193.72	195.96	200.45
3.00	155.83	157.78	159.75	161.73	163.72	165.72	167.73	169.75	171.79	173.83	175.89	177.95	180.03	182.12	184.22	188.44
4.00	146.70	148.54	150.39	152.26	154.13	156.01	157.91	159.81	161.73	163.65	165.59	167.53	169.49	171.46	173.43	177.41
4.25	144.54	146.35	148.18	150.01	151.86	153.71	155.58	157.46	159.34	161.24	163.15	165.06	166.99	168.93	170.87	174.79
4.50	142.42	144.21	146.00	147.81	149.63	151.46	153.30	155.15	157.01	158.88	160.75	162.64	164.54	166.45	168.37	172.23
4.75	140.34	142.10	143.88	145.66	147.45	149.25	151.06	152.89	154.72	156.56	158.41	160.27	162.14	164.02	165.91	169.72
5.00	138.31	140.05	141.79	143.55	145.31	147.09	148.87	150.67	152.48	154.29	156.12	157.95	159.79	161.65	163.51	167.26
5.25	136.32	138.03	139.75	141.48	143.22	144.97	146.73	148.50	150.28	152.07	153.87	155.68	157.49	159.32	161.16	164.85
5.50	134.37	136.05	137.75	139.45	141.17	142.90	144.63	146.38	148.13	149.89	151.67	153.45	155.24	157.04	158.85	162.49
5.75	132.46	134.12	135.79	137.47	139.16	140.86	142.57	144.29	146.02	147.76	149.51	151.27	153.03	154.81	156.59	160.18
6.00	130.58	132.22	133.87	135.53	137.19	138.87	140.56	142.25	143.96	145.67	147.39	149.13	150.87	152.62	154.37	157.92
6.25	128.75	130.36	131.99	133.62	135.27	136.92	138.58	140.25	141.93	143.62	145.32	147.03	148.75	150.47	152.21	155.70
6.50	126.95	128.54	130.14	131.76	133.38	135.01	136.65	138.29	139.95	141.62	143.29	144.98	146.67	148.37	150.08	153.52
6.75	125.19	126.76	128.34	129.93	131.53	133.13	134.75	136.37	138.01	139.65	141.30	142.96	144.63	146.31	148.00	151.39
7.00	123.46	125.01	126.57	128.13	129.71	131.30	132.89	134.49	136.11	137.73	139.35	140.99	142.64	144.29	145.95	149.30
7.25	121.77	123.29	124.83	126.38	127.93	129.50	131.07	132.65	134.24	135.84	137.44	139.06	140.68	142.31	143.95	147.26
7.50	120.11	121.61	123.13	124.66	126.19	127.73	129.28	130.84	132.41	133.99	135.57	137.16	138.77	140.37	141.99	145.25
7.75	118.48	119.97	121.46	122.97	124.48	126.00	127.53	129.07	130.62	132.17	133.74	135.31	136.89	138.47	140.07	143.28
8.00	116.89	118.35	119.83	121.31	122.80	124.31	125.82	127.33	128.86	130.39	131.94	133.49	135.04	136.61	138.18	141.35
8.25	115.32	116.77	118.23	119.69	121.16	122.64	124.13	125.63	127.14	128.65	130.17	131.70	133.24	134.78	136.34	139.46
8.50	113.79	115.22	116.65	118.10	119.55	121.01	122.48	123.96	125.45	126.94	128.44	129.95	131.47	132.99	134.52	137.61
8.75	112.29	113.70	115.11	116.54	117.97	119.42	120.87	122.32	123.79	125.26	126.75	128.23	129.73	131.24	132.75	135.79
9.00	110.81	112.21	113.60	115.01	116.43	117.85	119.28	120.72	122.17	123.62	125.08	126.55	128.03	129.51	131.01	134.01
9.25	109.37	110.74	112.12	113.51	114.91	116.31	117.72	119.14	120.57	122.01	123.45	124.90	126.36	127.82	129.30	132.26
9.50	107.95	109.31	110.67	112.04	113.42	114.80	116.20	117.60	119.01	120.43	121.85	123.28	124.72	126.17	127.62	130.55
9.75	106.56	107.90	109.24	110.60	111.96	113.33	114.70	116.09	117.48	118.88	120.28	121.70	123.12	124.54	125.98	128.87
10.00	105.20	106.52	107.85	109.18	110.53	111.88	113.24	114.60	115.97	117.36	118.74	120.14	121.54	122.95	124.37	127.22
10.25	103.86	105.16	106.48	107.79	109.12	110.45	111.80	113.14	114.50	115.86	117.23	118.61	120.00	121.39	122.79	125.60
10.50	102.55	103.84	105.13	106.43	107.74	109.06	110.38	111.71	113.05	114.40	115.75	117.11	118.48	119.85	121.23	124.02
10.75	101.26	102.53	103.81	105.10	106.39	107.69	109.00	110.31	111.63	112.96	114.30	115.64	116.99	118.35	119.71	122.46
11.00	100.00	101.25	102.52	103.79	105.06	106.35	107.64	108.94	110.24	111.56	112.87	114.20	115.53	116.87	118.22	120.93
11.25	98.76	100.00	101.25	102.50	103.76	105.03	106.30	107.59	108.88	110.17	111.48	112.79	114.10	115.43	116.76	119.43
11.50	97.55	98.77	100.00	101.24	102.48	103.74	105.00	106.26	107.54	108.82	110.10	111.40	112.70	114.00	115.32	117.96
11.75	96.35	97.56	98.78	100.00	101.23	102.47	103.71	104.96	106.22	107.49	108.76	110.03	111.32	112.61	113.91	116.52
12.00	95.18	96.38	97.58	98.78	100.00	101.22	102.45	103.69	104.93	106.18	107.44	108.70	109.97	111.24	112.52	115.10
12.25	94.03	95.21	96.40	97.59	98.79	100.00	101.21	102.44	103.66	104.90	106.14	107.38	108.64	109.90	111.16	113.71
12.50	92.90	94.07	95.24	96.42	97.61	98.80	100.00	101.21	102.42	103.64	104.86	106.10	107.33	108.58	109.83	112.35
12.75	91.80	92.95	94.11	95.27	96.44	97.62	98.81	100.00	101.20	102.40	103.61	104.83	106.06	107.29	108.52	111.01
13.00	90.71	91.85	92.99	94.14	95.30	96.47	97.64	98.82	100.00	101.19	102.39	103.59	104.80	106.01	107.24	109.70
13.25	89.64	90.77	91.90	93.04	94.18	95.33	96.49	97.65	98.82	100.00	101.18	102.37	103.57	104.77	105.97	108.41
13.50	88.59	89.71	90.82	91.95	93.08	94.22	95.36	96.51	97.67	98.83	100.00	101.17	102.36	103.54	104.74	107.14
13.75	87.57	88.66	89.77	90.88	92.00	93.12	94.25	95.39	96.53	97.68	98.84	100.00	101.17	102.34	103.52	105.89
14.00	86.55	87.64	88.73	89.83	90.94	92.05	93.17	94.29	95.42	96.56	97.70	98.85	100.00	101.16	102.32	104.67
14.25	85.56	86.64	87.72	88.80	89.89	90.99	92.10	93.21	94.33	95.45	96.58	97.71	98.85	100.00	101.15	103.47
14.50	84.59	85.65	86.72	87.79	88.87	89.96	91.05	92.15	93.25	94.36	95.48	96.60	97.73	98.86	100.00	102.29
14.75	83.63	84.68	85.74	86.80	87.87	88.94	90.02	91.11	92.20	93.29	94.40	95.51	96.62	97.74	98.87	101.14
15.00	82.69	83.73	84.77	85.82	86.88	87.94	89.01	90.08	91.16	92.25	93.34	94.43	95.54	96.64	97.76	100.00
15.25	81.77	82.79	83.83	84.86	85.91	86.96	88.01	89.08	90.14	91.22	92.29	93.38	94.47	95.56	96.67	98.88
15.50	80.86	81.88	82.90	83.92	84.95	85.99	87.04	88.09	89.14	90.20	91.27	92.34	93.42	94.50	95.59	97.79
15.75	79.97	80.97	81.98	83.00	84.02	85.05	86.08	87.12	88.16	89.21	90.27	91.33	92.39	93.46	94.54	96.71
16.00	79.09	80.09	81.08	82.09	83.10	84.11	85.14	86.16	87.20	88.23	89.28	90.33	91.38	92.44	93.50	95.65
16.25	78.23	79.21	80.20	81.20	82.19	83.20	84.21	85.23	86.25	87.27	88.31	89.34	90.39	91.43	92.49	94.61
16.50	77.39	78.36	79.34	80.32	81.31	82.30	83.30	84.30	85.31	86.33	87.35	88.38	89.41	90.45	91.49	93.59
16.75	76.56	77.52	78.48	79.46	80.43	81.42	82.40	83.40	84.40	85.40	86.41	87.43	88.45	89.47	90.51	92.58
17.00	75.74	76.69	77.65	78.61	79.58	80.55	81.53	82.51	83.50	84.49	85.49	86.50	87.51	88.52	89.54	91.59
17.25	74.94	75.88	76.82	77.78	78.73	79.69	80.66	81.64	82.61	83.60	84.59	85.58	86.58	87.58	88.59	90.62
17.50	74.15	75.08	76.02	76.96	77.90	78.86	79.81	80.78	81.74	82.72	83.70	84.68	85.67	86.66	87.66	89.67
17.75	73.37	74.29	75.22	76.15	77.09	78.03	78.98	79.93	80.89	81.85	82.82	83.79	84.77	85.75	86.74	88.73
18.00	72.61	73.52	74.44	75.36	76.29	77.22	78.16	79.10	80.05	81.00	81.96	82.92	83.89	84.86	85.84	87.81
18.25	71.86	72.76	73.67	74.58	75.50	76.42	77.35	78.28	79.22	80.17	81.11	82.07	83.02	83.99	84.96	86.90
18.50	71.13	72.02	72.92	73.82	74.73	75.64	76.56	77.48	78.41	79.34	80.28	81.23	82.17	83.13	84.08	86.01
18.75	70.40	71.28	72.17	73.07	73.96	74.87	75.78	76.69	77.61	78.54	79.46	80.40	81.34	82.28	83.23	85.14
19.00	69.69	70.56	71.44	72.33	73.22	74.11	75.01	75.92	76.83	77.74	78.66	79.58	80.51	81.45	82.39	84.28
20.00	66.95	67.79	68.64	69.49	70.34	71.20	72.07	72.94	73.81	74.69	75.57	76.46	77.35	78.25	79.15	80.97
25.00	55.64	56.34	57.04	57.74	58.45	59.17	59.89	60.61	61.34	62.07	62.80	63.54	64.28	65.03	65.77	67.28
30.00	47.28	47.87	48.47	49.07	49.67	50.28	50.89	51.50	52.12	52.74	53.36	53.99	54.62	55.25	55.89	57.17

Description: This table shows the yield to maturity of a mortgage purchased at the price shown in the index.

Example: The yield to maturity of a 15.00 %, 13 year mortgage at a price of 117.00 is 11.66 %.

INTEREST RATE, %

PRICE	11.00%	11.25%	11.50%	11.75%	12.00%	12.25%	12.50%	12.75%	13.00%	13.25%	13.50%	13.75%	14.00%	14.25%	14.50%	15.00%
190	–	.05	.24	.43	.62	.81	1.00	1.19	1.38	1.56	1.75	1.94	2.12	2.31	2.49	2.86
185	.27	.46	.66	.85	1.04	1.23	1.42	1.61	1.80	1.99	2.18	2.36	2.55	2.74	2.93	3.30
180	.70	.89	1.08	1.28	1.47	1.66	1.85	2.05	2.24	2.43	2.62	2.81	3.00	3.19	3.38	3.75
175	1.14	1.33	1.53	1.72	1.92	2.11	2.31	2.50	2.69	2.89	3.08	3.27	3.46	3.65	3.84	4.23
170	1.59	1.79	1.99	2.19	2.38	2.58	2.78	2.97	3.17	3.36	3.56	3.75	3.94	4.14	4.33	4.72
165	2.07	2.27	2.47	2.67	2.87	3.07	3.26	3.46	3.66	3.86	4.05	4.25	4.45	4.64	4.84	5.23
160	2.56	2.77	2.97	3.17	3.37	3.57	3.77	3.98	4.18	4.38	4.57	4.77	4.97	5.17	5.37	5.76
155	3.08	3.29	3.49	3.70	3.90	4.10	4.31	4.51	4.71	4.92	5.12	5.32	5.52	5.72	5.92	6.32
150	3.62	3.83	4.04	4.25	4.45	4.66	4.87	5.07	5.28	5.48	5.69	5.89	6.10	6.30	6.50	6.91
145	4.19	4.40	4.61	4.82	5.03	5.24	5.45	5.66	5.87	6.08	6.28	6.49	6.70	6.91	7.11	7.53
140	4.79	5.00	5.21	5.43	5.64	5.85	6.07	6.28	6.49	6.70	6.91	7.12	7.33	7.54	7.75	8.17
135	5.41	5.63	5.85	6.06	6.28	6.50	6.71	6.93	7.14	7.36	7.57	7.79	8.00	8.22	8.43	8.86
130	6.07	6.29	6.51	6.73	6.95	7.17	7.39	7.61	7.83	8.05	8.27	8.49	8.71	8.92	9.14	9.58
125	6.77	7.00	7.22	7.44	7.67	7.89	8.12	8.34	8.56	8.78	9.01	9.23	9.45	9.67	9.90	10.34
123	7.06	7.29	7.51	7.74	7.97	8.19	8.42	8.64	8.87	9.09	9.31	9.54	9.76	9.99	10.21	10.66
122	7.21	7.44	7.66	7.89	8.12	8.34	8.57	8.80	9.02	9.25	9.47	9.70	9.92	10.15	10.37	10.82
121	7.36	7.59	7.82	8.04	8.27	8.50	8.72	8.95	9.18	9.40	9.63	9.86	10.08	10.31	10.53	10.98
120	7.51	7.74	7.97	8.20	8.43	8.65	8.88	9.11	9.34	9.56	9.79	10.02	10.24	10.47	10.70	11.15
119	7.66	7.89	8.12	8.35	8.58	8.81	9.04	9.27	9.50	9.72	9.95	10.18	10.41	10.64	10.86	11.32
118	7.82	8.05	8.28	8.51	8.74	8.97	9.20	9.43	9.66	9.89	10.12	10.35	10.58	10.80	11.03	11.49
117	7.98	8.21	8.44	8.67	8.90	9.13	9.36	9.59	9.82	10.05	10.28	10.51	10.74	10.97	11.20	11.66
116	8.14	8.37	8.60	8.83	9.06	9.30	9.53	9.76	9.99	10.22	10.45	10.68	10.91	11.15	11.38	11.84
115	8.30	8.53	8.76	9.00	9.23	9.46	9.69	9.93	10.16	10.39	10.62	10.86	11.09	11.32	11.55	12.01
114	8.46	8.69	8.93	9.16	9.40	9.63	9.86	10.10	10.33	10.56	10.80	11.03	11.26	11.50	11.73	12.19
113	8.63	8.86	9.10	9.33	9.57	9.80	10.04	10.27	10.50	10.74	10.97	11.21	11.44	11.67	11.91	12.38
112	8.79	9.03	9.27	9.50	9.74	9.97	10.21	10.44	10.68	10.92	11.15	11.39	11.62	11.86	12.09	12.56
111	8.96	9.20	9.44	9.67	9.91	10.15	10.39	10.62	10.86	11.09	11.33	11.57	11.80	12.04	12.28	12.75
110	9.14	9.37	9.61	9.85	10.09	10.33	10.56	10.80	11.04	11.28	11.51	11.75	11.99	12.23	12.46	12.94
109	9.31	9.55	9.79	10.03	10.27	10.51	10.74	10.98	11.22	11.46	11.70	11.94	12.18	12.41	12.65	13.13
108	9.49	9.73	9.97	10.21	10.45	10.69	10.93	11.17	11.41	11.65	11.89	12.13	12.37	12.61	12.85	13.32
107	9.67	9.91	10.15	10.39	10.63	10.87	11.11	11.36	11.60	11.84	12.08	12.32	12.56	12.80	13.04	13.52
106	9.85	10.09	10.33	10.58	10.82	11.06	11.30	11.55	11.79	12.03	12.27	12.51	12.76	13.00	13.24	13.72
105	10.03	10.28	10.52	10.76	11.01	11.25	11.49	11.74	11.98	12.22	12.47	12.71	12.95	13.20	13.44	13.93
104	10.22	10.46	10.71	10.95	11.20	11.44	11.69	11.93	12.18	12.42	12.67	12.91	13.16	13.40	13.65	14.13
103	10.41	10.65	10.90	11.15	11.39	11.64	11.89	12.13	12.38	12.62	12.87	13.12	13.36	13.61	13.85	14.34
102	10.60	10.85	11.10	11.34	11.59	11.84	12.09	12.33	12.58	12.83	13.07	13.32	13.57	13.82	14.06	14.56
101	10.80	11.05	11.29	11.54	11.79	12.04	12.29	12.54	12.79	13.03	13.28	13.53	13.78	14.03	14.28	14.77
100	11.00	11.25	11.50	11.75	12.00	12.25	12.50	12.75	13.00	13.25	13.50	13.75	14.00	14.25	14.50	15.00
99	11.20	11.45	11.70	11.95	12.20	12.45	12.70	12.96	13.21	13.46	13.71	13.96	14.21	14.46	14.72	15.22
98	11.40	11.65	11.91	12.16	12.41	12.66	12.92	13.17	13.42	13.68	13.93	14.18	14.43	14.69	14.94	15.45
97	11.61	11.86	12.12	12.37	12.62	12.88	13.13	13.39	13.64	13.90	14.15	14.40	14.66	14.91	15.17	15.68
96	11.82	12.08	12.33	12.59	12.84	13.10	13.35	13.61	13.86	14.12	14.38	14.63	14.89	15.14	15.40	15.91
95	12.03	12.29	12.55	12.80	13.06	13.32	13.58	13.83	14.09	14.35	14.61	14.86	15.12	15.38	15.64	16.15
94	12.25	12.51	12.77	13.03	13.29	13.54	13.80	14.06	14.32	14.58	14.84	15.10	15.36	15.62	15.87	16.39
93	12.47	12.73	12.99	13.25	13.51	13.77	14.03	14.29	14.55	14.81	15.08	15.34	15.60	15.86	16.12	16.64
92	12.70	12.96	13.22	13.48	13.74	14.01	14.27	14.53	14.79	15.05	15.32	15.58	15.84	16.10	16.37	16.89
91	12.93	13.19	13.45	13.72	13.98	14.24	14.51	14.77	15.03	15.30	15.56	15.83	16.09	16.35	16.62	17.15
90	13.16	13.43	13.69	13.95	14.22	14.48	14.75	15.02	15.28	15.55	15.81	16.08	16.34	16.61	16.88	17.41
89	13.40	13.66	13.93	14.20	14.46	14.73	15.00	15.26	15.53	15.80	16.07	16.33	16.60	16.87	17.14	17.67
88	13.64	13.91	14.17	14.44	14.71	14.98	15.25	15.52	15.79	16.06	16.32	16.59	16.86	17.13	17.40	17.94
87	13.88	14.15	14.42	14.69	14.96	15.23	15.50	15.78	16.05	16.32	16.59	16.86	17.13	17.40	17.67	18.22
86	14.13	14.41	14.68	14.95	15.22	15.49	15.77	16.04	16.31	16.58	16.86	17.13	17.40	17.68	17.95	18.50
85	14.39	14.66	14.94	15.21	15.48	15.76	16.03	16.31	16.58	16.86	17.13	17.41	17.68	17.96	18.23	18.78
84	14.65	14.92	15.20	15.47	15.75	16.03	16.30	16.58	16.86	17.13	17.41	17.69	17.96	18.24	18.52	19.08
83	14.91	15.19	15.47	15.74	16.02	16.30	16.58	16.86	17.14	17.41	17.69	17.97	18.25	18.53	18.81	19.37
82	15.18	15.46	15.74	16.02	16.30	16.58	16.86	17.14	17.42	17.70	17.98	18.26	18.55	18.83	19.11	19.68
81	15.46	15.74	16.02	16.30	16.58	16.86	17.15	17.43	17.71	18.00	18.28	18.56	18.85	19.13	19.42	19.99
80	15.74	16.02	16.30	16.59	16.87	17.16	17.44	17.72	18.01	18.30	18.58	18.87	19.15	19.44	19.73	20.30
79	16.02	16.31	16.59	16.88	17.17	17.45	17.74	18.03	18.31	18.60	18.89	19.18	19.47	19.75	20.04	20.62
78	16.31	16.60	16.89	17.18	17.47	17.75	18.04	18.33	18.62	18.91	19.20	19.49	19.79	20.08	20.37	20.95
77	16.61	16.90	17.19	17.48	17.77	18.06	18.36	18.65	18.94	19.23	19.52	19.82	20.11	20.41	20.70	21.29
76	16.92	17.21	17.50	17.79	18.09	18.38	18.67	18.97	19.26	19.56	19.85	20.15	20.44	20.74	21.04	21.63
75	17.23	17.52	17.82	18.11	18.41	18.70	19.00	19.30	19.59	19.89	20.19	20.49	20.79	21.08	21.38	21.98
74	17.54	17.84	18.14	18.44	18.73	19.03	19.33	19.63	19.93	20.23	20.53	20.83	21.13	21.44	21.74	22.34
73	17.87	18.17	18.47	18.77	19.07	19.37	19.67	19.97	20.28	20.58	20.88	21.19	21.49	21.80	22.10	22.71
70	18.89	19.19	19.50	19.81	20.12	20.43	20.74	21.05	21.36	21.67	21.99	22.30	22.61	22.93	23.24	23.87
65	20.75	21.08	21.40	21.72	22.05	22.38	22.70	23.03	23.36	23.69	24.02	24.34	24.68	25.01	25.34	26.00
60	22.88	23.22	23.56	23.91	24.25	24.60	24.94	25.29	25.64	25.98	26.33	26.68	27.03	27.39	27.74	28.45

Description: This table shows the price to pay for a monthly payment mortgage loan at the yield rate.

Example: The price of a 6.75 %, 14 year mortgage loan to yield 8.00 % to maturity is $ 92.98.

INTEREST RATE, %

YIELD	0.00%	1.00%	2.00%	3.00%	4.00%	4.25%	4.50%	4.75%	5.00%	5.25%	5.50%	5.75%	6.00%	6.25%	6.50%	6.75%
0.00	100.00	107.20	114.74	122.59	130.76	132.85	134.97	137.10	139.25	141.42	143.61	145.82	148.05	150.29	152.56	154.84
1.00	93.28	100.00	107.02	114.35	121.97	123.93	125.90	127.89	129.89	131.92	133.96	136.02	138.10	140.19	142.31	144.44
2.00	87.16	93.44	100.00	106.84	113.97	115.79	117.63	119.49	121.37	123.26	125.17	127.09	129.03	130.99	132.97	134.96
3.00	81.57	87.45	93.59	100.00	106.67	108.37	110.10	111.84	113.59	115.36	117.15	118.95	120.77	122.60	124.45	126.31
4.00	76.47	81.98	87.74	93.75	100.00	101.60	103.22	104.85	106.49	108.15	109.83	111.52	113.22	114.94	116.67	118.42
4.25	75.27	80.69	86.36	92.27	98.42	100.00	101.59	103.19	104.81	106.45	108.10	109.76	111.44	113.13	114.83	116.55
4.50	74.09	79.43	85.01	90.83	96.88	98.43	100.00	101.58	103.17	104.78	106.40	108.04	109.69	111.36	113.04	114.73
4.75	72.94	78.20	83.69	89.42	95.38	96.90	98.45	100.00	101.57	103.15	104.75	106.36	107.99	109.62	111.28	112.94
5.00	71.81	76.99	82.39	88.03	93.90	95.41	96.92	98.46	100.00	101.56	103.13	104.72	106.32	107.93	109.56	111.20
5.25	70.71	75.81	81.13	86.68	92.46	93.94	95.44	96.94	98.47	100.00	101.55	103.11	104.69	106.27	107.88	109.49
5.50	69.63	74.65	79.89	85.36	91.05	92.51	93.98	95.47	96.96	98.48	100.00	101.54	103.09	104.65	106.23	107.82
5.75	68.58	73.52	78.68	84.07	89.67	91.11	92.56	94.02	95.49	96.98	98.49	100.00	101.53	103.07	104.62	106.19
6.00	67.55	72.41	77.50	82.80	88.32	89.74	91.16	92.60	94.06	95.52	97.00	98.50	100.00	101.52	103.05	104.59
6.25	66.54	71.33	76.34	81.57	87.00	88.40	89.80	91.22	92.65	94.10	95.55	97.02	98.51	100.00	101.51	103.03
6.50	65.55	70.27	75.21	80.35	85.71	87.08	88.47	89.87	91.28	92.70	94.13	95.58	97.04	98.51	100.00	101.50
6.75	64.58	69.23	74.10	79.17	84.45	85.80	87.16	88.54	89.93	91.33	92.75	94.17	95.61	97.06	98.52	100.00
7.00	63.63	68.22	73.01	78.01	83.21	84.54	85.89	87.24	88.61	89.99	91.39	92.79	94.21	95.64	97.08	98.53
7.25	62.71	67.23	71.95	76.87	82.00	83.31	84.64	85.97	87.32	88.68	90.06	91.44	92.84	94.25	95.67	97.10
7.50	61.80	66.25	70.91	75.76	80.81	82.11	83.41	84.73	86.06	87.40	88.75	90.12	91.50	92.88	94.28	95.70
7.75	60.91	65.30	69.89	74.67	79.65	80.93	82.21	83.51	84.82	86.15	87.48	88.82	90.18	91.55	92.93	94.32
8.00	60.05	64.37	68.89	73.61	78.52	79.77	81.04	82.32	83.61	84.92	86.23	87.56	88.90	90.24	91.60	92.98
8.25	59.19	63.46	67.92	72.57	77.40	78.64	79.89	81.15	82.43	83.71	85.01	86.32	87.64	88.97	90.31	91.66
8.50	58.36	62.57	66.96	71.54	76.31	77.54	78.77	80.01	81.27	82.54	83.81	85.10	86.40	87.71	89.04	90.37
8.75	57.55	61.69	66.03	70.54	75.25	76.45	77.67	78.89	80.13	81.38	82.64	83.91	85.19	86.49	87.79	89.11
9.00	56.75	60.84	65.11	69.57	74.20	75.39	76.59	77.80	79.02	80.25	81.49	82.75	84.01	85.29	86.57	87.87
9.25	55.96	60.00	64.21	68.61	73.18	74.35	75.53	76.73	77.93	79.15	80.37	81.61	82.85	84.11	85.38	86.66
9.50	55.20	59.17	63.33	67.67	72.18	73.33	74.50	75.68	76.86	78.06	79.27	80.49	81.72	82.96	84.21	85.47
9.75	54.45	58.37	62.47	66.75	71.20	72.34	73.49	74.65	75.82	77.00	78.19	79.40	80.61	81.83	83.07	84.31
10.00	53.71	57.58	61.63	65.84	70.23	71.36	72.49	73.64	74.79	75.96	77.14	78.32	79.52	80.73	81.94	83.17
10.25	52.99	56.81	60.80	64.96	69.29	70.40	71.52	72.65	73.79	74.94	76.10	77.27	78.45	79.64	80.84	82.05
10.50	52.29	56.05	59.99	64.10	68.37	69.46	70.57	71.68	72.81	73.94	75.09	76.24	77.41	78.58	79.77	80.96
10.75	51.59	55.31	59.20	63.25	67.47	68.55	69.63	70.73	71.84	72.96	74.09	75.23	76.38	77.54	78.71	79.89
11.00	50.92	54.58	58.42	62.42	66.58	67.64	68.72	69.81	70.90	72.01	73.12	74.25	75.38	76.52	77.68	78.84
11.25	50.25	53.87	57.66	61.60	65.71	66.76	67.82	68.89	69.98	71.07	72.17	73.28	74.40	75.53	76.66	77.81
11.50	49.60	53.17	56.91	60.81	64.86	65.90	66.94	68.00	69.07	70.15	71.23	72.33	73.43	74.55	75.67	76.80
11.75	48.96	52.49	56.18	60.02	64.02	65.05	66.08	67.13	68.18	69.24	70.32	71.40	72.49	73.59	74.70	75.82
12.00	48.34	51.82	55.46	59.26	63.21	64.22	65.24	66.27	67.31	68.36	69.42	70.49	71.56	72.65	73.74	74.85
12.25	47.72	51.16	54.76	58.50	62.40	63.40	64.41	65.43	66.46	67.49	68.54	69.59	70.65	71.73	72.81	73.90
12.50	47.12	50.52	54.07	57.77	61.62	62.60	63.60	64.60	65.62	66.64	67.67	68.71	69.76	70.82	71.89	72.97
12.75	46.53	49.89	53.39	57.04	60.85	61.82	62.80	63.80	64.80	65.81	66.83	67.85	68.89	69.94	70.99	72.05
13.00	45.95	49.27	52.73	56.34	60.09	61.05	62.02	63.00	63.99	64.99	66.00	67.01	68.04	69.07	70.11	71.16
13.25	45.39	48.66	52.08	55.64	59.35	60.30	61.26	62.23	63.20	64.19	65.18	66.18	67.20	68.22	69.24	70.28
13.50	44.83	48.06	51.44	54.96	58.62	59.56	60.51	61.46	62.43	63.40	64.38	65.37	66.37	67.38	68.40	69.42
13.75	44.29	47.48	50.81	54.29	57.91	58.84	59.77	60.72	61.67	62.63	63.60	64.58	65.57	66.56	67.56	68.58
14.00	43.75	46.90	50.20	53.63	57.21	58.13	59.05	59.98	60.92	61.87	62.83	63.80	64.77	65.76	66.75	67.75
14.25	43.23	46.34	49.60	52.99	56.52	57.43	58.34	59.26	60.19	61.13	62.08	63.03	64.00	64.97	65.95	66.93
14.50	42.71	45.79	49.01	52.36	55.85	56.75	57.65	58.56	59.48	60.40	61.34	62.28	63.23	64.19	65.16	66.14
14.75	42.21	45.25	48.43	51.74	55.19	56.07	56.97	57.87	58.77	59.69	60.61	61.55	62.49	63.43	64.39	65.36
15.00	41.71	44.72	47.86	51.13	54.54	55.42	56.30	57.19	58.08	58.99	59.90	60.82	61.75	62.69	63.63	64.59
15.25	41.23	44.20	47.30	50.54	53.91	54.77	55.64	56.52	57.41	58.30	59.20	60.11	61.03	61.96	62.89	63.83
15.50	40.75	43.68	46.75	49.95	53.28	54.14	55.00	55.86	56.74	57.63	58.52	59.42	60.33	61.24	62.16	63.10
15.75	40.28	43.18	46.21	49.38	52.67	53.51	54.36	55.22	56.09	56.96	57.85	58.74	59.63	60.54	61.45	62.37
16.00	39.82	42.69	45.69	48.81	52.07	52.90	53.74	54.59	55.45	56.31	57.18	58.06	58.95	59.85	60.75	61.66
16.25	39.37	42.20	45.17	48.26	51.48	52.30	53.13	53.97	54.82	55.67	56.54	57.41	58.28	59.17	60.06	60.96
16.50	38.92	41.73	44.66	47.72	50.90	51.71	52.54	53.37	54.20	55.05	55.90	56.76	57.63	58.50	59.38	60.27
16.75	38.49	41.26	44.16	47.18	50.33	51.14	51.95	52.77	53.60	54.43	55.28	56.13	56.98	57.85	58.72	59.60
17.00	38.06	40.81	43.67	46.66	49.77	50.57	51.37	52.18	53.00	53.83	54.66	55.50	56.35	57.21	58.07	58.94
17.25	37.64	40.36	43.19	46.15	49.22	50.01	50.81	51.61	52.42	53.24	54.06	54.89	55.73	56.58	57.43	58.29
17.50	37.23	39.91	42.72	45.64	48.68	49.46	50.25	51.04	51.84	52.65	53.47	54.29	55.12	55.96	56.80	57.65
17.75	36.83	39.48	42.25	45.15	48.16	48.93	49.70	50.49	51.28	52.08	52.89	53.70	54.52	55.35	56.18	57.02
18.00	36.43	39.05	41.80	44.66	47.64	48.40	49.17	49.94	50.73	51.52	52.32	53.12	53.93	54.75	55.58	56.41
18.25	36.04	38.64	41.35	44.18	47.13	47.88	48.64	49.41	50.18	50.97	51.76	52.55	53.36	54.16	54.98	55.80
18.50	35.66	38.22	40.91	43.71	46.62	47.37	48.12	48.88	49.65	50.42	51.21	51.99	52.79	53.59	54.40	55.21
18.75	35.28	37.82	40.48	43.25	46.13	46.87	47.62	48.37	49.13	49.89	50.66	51.44	52.23	53.02	53.82	54.63
19.00	34.91	37.42	40.05	42.79	45.65	46.38	47.12	47.86	48.61	49.37	50.13	50.90	51.68	52.47	53.26	54.05
20.00	33.49	35.90	38.43	41.06	43.79	44.50	45.20	45.92	46.64	47.36	48.10	48.84	49.58	50.34	51.10	51.86
25.00	27.68	29.67	31.76	33.93	36.19	36.77	37.35	37.94	38.54	39.14	39.75	40.36	40.98	41.60	42.22	42.86
30.00	23.43	25.12	26.89	28.73	30.64	31.13	31.63	32.13	32.63	33.14	33.65	34.17	34.69	35.22	35.75	36.29

Description: This table shows the yield to maturity of a mortgage purchased at the price shown in the index.

Example: The yield to maturity of a 6.75 %, 14 year mortgage at a price of 80.00 is 10.72 %.

INTEREST RATE, %

PRICE	0.00%	1.00%	2.00%	3.00%	4.00%	4.25%	4.50%	4.75%	5.00%	5.25%	5.50%	5.75%	6.00%	6.25%	6.50%	6.75%
100	0.00	1.00	2.00	3.00	4.00	4.25	4.50	4.75	5.00	5.25	5.50	5.75	6.00	6.25	6.50	6.75
99	.14	1.14	2.15	3.15	4.15	4.40	4.66	4.91	5.16	5.41	5.66	5.91	6.16	6.41	6.66	6.92
98	.28	1.29	2.30	3.31	4.31	4.57	4.82	5.07	5.32	5.57	5.83	6.08	6.33	6.58	6.84	7.09
97	.43	1.44	2.45	3.46	4.48	4.73	4.98	5.24	5.49	5.74	6.00	6.25	6.50	6.76	7.01	7.26
96	.58	1.59	2.61	3.62	4.64	4.90	5.15	5.40	5.66	5.91	6.17	6.42	6.68	6.93	7.19	7.44
95	.73	1.75	2.77	3.79	4.81	5.06	5.32	5.57	5.83	6.09	6.34	6.60	6.85	7.11	7.37	7.62
94	.88	1.91	2.93	3.95	4.98	5.24	5.49	5.75	6.01	6.26	6.52	6.78	7.03	7.29	7.55	7.80
93	1.04	2.06	3.09	4.12	5.15	5.41	5.67	5.92	6.18	6.44	6.70	6.96	7.22	7.47	7.73	7.99
92	1.20	2.23	3.26	4.29	5.33	5.59	5.84	6.10	6.36	6.62	6.88	7.14	7.40	7.66	7.92	8.18
91	1.36	2.39	3.43	4.47	5.50	5.76	6.02	6.29	6.55	6.81	7.07	7.33	7.59	7.85	8.11	8.37
90	1.52	2.56	3.60	4.64	5.69	5.95	6.21	6.47	6.73	6.99	7.26	7.52	7.78	8.04	8.30	8.57
89	1.68	2.73	3.77	4.82	5.87	6.13	6.39	6.66	6.92	7.18	7.45	7.71	7.97	8.24	8.50	8.77
88	1.85	2.90	3.95	5.00	6.06	6.32	6.58	6.85	7.11	7.38	7.64	7.91	8.17	8.44	8.70	8.97
87	2.02	3.07	4.13	5.19	6.25	6.51	6.78	7.04	7.31	7.57	7.84	8.11	8.37	8.64	8.91	9.17
86	2.19	3.25	4.31	5.37	6.44	6.71	6.97	7.24	7.51	7.77	8.04	8.31	8.58	8.85	9.11	9.38
85	2.37	3.43	4.50	5.56	6.64	6.90	7.17	7.44	7.71	7.98	8.25	8.52	8.79	9.06	9.33	9.60
84	2.55	3.62	4.69	5.76	6.83	7.10	7.37	7.64	7.91	8.18	8.46	8.73	9.00	9.27	9.54	9.81
83	2.73	3.80	4.88	5.96	7.04	7.31	7.58	7.85	8.12	8.40	8.67	8.94	9.21	9.49	9.76	10.03
82	2.92	3.99	5.07	6.16	7.24	7.52	7.79	8.06	8.34	8.61	8.88	9.16	9.43	9.71	9.98	10.26
81	3.10	4.19	5.27	6.36	7.46	7.73	8.00	8.28	8.55	8.83	9.10	9.38	9.66	9.93	10.21	10.49
80	3.29	4.38	5.47	6.57	7.67	7.95	8.22	8.50	8.77	9.05	9.33	9.61	9.88	10.16	10.44	10.72
79	3.49	4.58	5.68	6.78	7.89	8.17	8.44	8.72	9.00	9.28	9.56	9.84	10.12	10.40	10.68	10.96
78	3.69	4.79	5.89	7.00	8.11	8.39	8.67	8.95	9.23	9.51	9.79	10.07	10.35	10.63	10.92	11.20
77	3.89	4.99	6.10	7.22	8.34	8.62	8.90	9.18	9.46	9.75	10.03	10.31	10.59	10.88	11.16	11.45
76	4.09	5.20	6.32	7.44	8.57	8.85	9.13	9.42	9.70	9.99	10.27	10.55	10.84	11.13	11.41	11.70
75	4.30	5.42	6.54	7.67	8.80	9.09	9.37	9.66	9.94	10.23	10.52	10.80	11.09	11.38	11.67	11.96
74	4.51	5.64	6.77	7.90	9.04	9.33	9.62	9.90	10.19	10.48	10.77	11.06	11.35	11.64	11.93	12.22
73	4.73	5.86	7.00	8.14	9.29	9.58	9.87	10.16	10.45	10.74	11.03	11.32	11.61	11.90	12.19	12.49
72	4.95	6.09	7.23	8.38	9.54	9.83	10.12	10.41	10.70	11.00	11.29	11.58	11.88	12.17	12.46	12.76
71	5.18	6.32	7.47	8.63	9.80	10.09	10.38	10.67	10.97	11.26	11.56	11.85	12.15	12.45	12.74	13.04
70	5.41	6.56	7.72	8.88	10.06	10.35	10.65	10.94	11.24	11.54	11.83	12.13	12.43	12.73	13.03	13.33
69	5.64	6.80	7.97	9.14	10.32	10.62	10.92	11.22	11.51	11.81	12.11	12.41	12.71	13.01	13.32	13.62
68	5.88	7.05	8.22	9.41	10.60	10.90	11.20	11.50	11.80	12.10	12.40	12.70	13.01	13.31	13.61	13.92
67	6.13	7.30	8.48	9.68	10.88	11.18	11.48	11.78	12.09	12.39	12.69	13.00	13.30	13.61	13.92	14.22
66	6.38	7.56	8.75	9.95	11.16	11.47	11.77	12.07	12.38	12.69	12.99	13.30	13.61	13.92	14.23	14.54
65	6.64	7.83	9.02	10.23	11.45	11.76	12.07	12.37	12.68	12.99	13.30	13.61	13.92	14.23	14.55	14.86
64	6.90	8.10	9.30	10.52	11.75	12.06	12.37	12.68	12.99	13.30	13.62	13.93	14.24	14.56	14.87	15.19
63	7.17	8.37	9.59	10.82	12.06	12.37	12.68	13.00	13.31	13.62	13.94	14.26	14.57	14.89	15.21	15.53
62	7.44	8.66	9.88	11.12	12.37	12.69	13.00	13.32	13.64	13.95	14.27	14.59	14.91	15.23	15.55	15.87
61	7.72	8.95	10.18	11.43	12.70	13.01	13.33	13.65	13.97	14.29	14.61	14.93	15.26	15.58	15.90	16.23
60	8.01	9.24	10.49	11.75	13.03	13.35	13.67	13.99	14.31	14.64	14.96	15.29	15.61	15.94	16.27	16.60
59	8.30	9.55	10.81	12.08	13.36	13.69	14.01	14.34	14.66	14.99	15.32	15.65	15.98	16.31	16.64	16.97
58	8.61	9.86	11.13	12.42	13.71	14.04	14.37	14.70	15.03	15.36	15.69	16.02	16.35	16.69	17.02	17.36
57	8.92	10.18	11.46	12.76	14.07	14.40	14.73	15.06	15.40	15.73	16.07	16.40	16.74	17.08	17.42	17.75
56	9.23	10.51	11.81	13.12	14.44	14.77	15.11	15.44	15.78	16.12	16.46	16.80	17.14	17.48	17.82	18.16
55	9.56	10.85	12.16	13.48	14.82	15.16	15.49	15.83	16.17	16.51	16.86	17.20	17.54	17.89	18.24	18.58
54	9.90	11.20	12.52	13.86	15.21	15.55	15.89	16.23	16.58	16.92	17.27	17.62	17.97	18.32	18.67	19.02
53	10.24	11.56	12.89	14.24	15.61	15.95	16.30	16.65	17.00	17.35	17.70	18.05	18.40	18.76	19.11	19.47
52	10.60	11.93	13.27	14.64	16.02	16.37	16.72	17.07	17.43	17.78	18.14	18.49	18.85	19.21	19.57	19.93
51	10.96	12.31	13.67	15.05	16.45	16.80	17.16	17.51	17.87	18.23	18.59	18.95	19.31	19.68	20.04	20.41
50	11.34	12.70	14.08	15.47	16.89	17.25	17.61	17.97	18.33	18.69	19.06	19.42	19.79	20.16	20.53	20.90
49	11.73	13.10	14.50	15.91	17.35	17.71	18.07	18.44	18.81	19.17	19.54	19.91	20.29	20.66	21.03	21.41
48	12.13	13.52	14.93	16.36	17.82	18.19	18.56	18.93	19.30	19.67	20.04	20.42	20.80	21.18	21.56	21.94
47	12.55	13.95	15.38	16.83	18.31	18.68	19.05	19.43	19.81	20.18	20.56	20.95	21.33	21.71	22.10	22.49
46	12.98	14.40	15.85	17.32	18.81	19.19	19.57	19.95	20.33	20.72	21.10	21.49	21.88	22.27	22.66	23.06
45	13.42	14.86	16.33	17.82	19.34	19.72	20.11	20.49	20.88	21.27	21.66	22.06	22.45	22.85	23.25	23.65
44	13.88	15.34	16.83	18.34	19.88	20.27	20.66	21.05	21.45	21.85	22.24	22.64	23.05	23.45	23.85	24.26
43	14.35	15.84	17.35	18.88	20.45	20.84	21.24	21.64	22.04	22.44	22.85	23.25	23.66	24.07	24.49	24.90
42	14.85	16.35	17.88	19.44	21.03	21.44	21.84	22.25	22.65	23.07	23.48	23.89	24.31	24.73	25.15	25.57
41	15.36	16.89	18.44	20.03	21.65	22.06	22.47	22.88	23.30	23.71	24.13	24.55	24.98	25.40	25.83	26.26
40	15.90	17.45	19.03	20.64	22.29	22.70	23.12	23.54	23.96	24.39	24.82	25.25	25.68	26.11	26.55	26.99
39	16.45	18.03	19.63	21.28	22.95	23.38	23.80	24.23	24.66	25.10	25.53	25.97	26.41	26.85	27.30	27.75
35	18.93	20.63	22.36	24.13	25.95	26.41	26.87	27.34	27.81	28.28	28.76	29.23	29.71	30.20	30.68	31.17
30	22.80	24.69	26.63	28.63	30.68	31.20	31.73	32.26	32.79	33.33	33.87	34.41	34.96	35.51	36.07	36.63
25	27.97	30.15	32.40	34.73	37.13	37.75	38.36	38.98	39.61	40.24	40.88	41.52	42.17	42.82	43.47	44.13
20	35.44	38.08	40.82	43.67	46.62	47.37	48.13	48.90	49.67	50.45	51.24	52.03	52.83	53.64	54.45	55.27
15	47.54	51.00	54.60	58.35	62.25	63.25	64.26	65.27	66.30	67.33	68.38	69.43	70.49	71.56	72.64	73.73
10	71.42	76.57	81.95	87.56	93.40	94.89	96.40	97.92	99.46	101.01	102.58	104.15	105.74	107.35	108.97	110.60

Description: This table shows the price to pay for a monthly payment mortgage loan at the yield rate.

Example: The price of a 10.75 %, 14 year mortgage loan to yield 8.00 % to maturity is $ 116.38.

INTEREST RATE, %

YIELD	7.00%	7.25%	7.50%	7.75%	8.00%	8.25%	8.50%	8.75%	9.00%	9.25%	9.50%	9.75%	10.00%	10.25%	10.50%	10.75%
0.00	157.15	159.47	161.81	164.17	166.54	168.94	171.35	173.78	176.22	178.69	181.17	183.66	186.18	188.71	191.26	193.82
1.00	146.59	148.75	150.93	153.13	155.35	157.58	159.83	162.10	164.38	166.68	168.99	171.32	173.67	176.03	178.40	180.79
2.00	136.97	138.99	141.03	143.08	145.15	147.24	149.34	151.46	153.59	155.74	157.90	160.08	162.27	164.47	166.69	168.93
3.00	128.19	130.08	131.99	133.92	135.85	137.81	139.77	141.75	143.75	145.76	147.78	149.82	151.87	153.94	156.01	158.11
4.00	120.18	121.95	123.74	125.55	127.36	129.19	131.04	132.89	134.76	136.65	138.55	140.46	142.38	144.31	146.26	148.22
4.25	118.28	120.03	121.79	123.57	125.36	127.16	128.97	130.80	132.64	134.50	136.36	138.24	140.14	142.04	143.96	145.89
4.50	116.43	118.15	119.89	121.63	123.39	125.17	126.95	128.75	130.57	132.39	134.23	136.08	137.94	139.82	141.71	143.61
4.75	114.62	116.32	118.02	119.74	121.48	123.22	124.98	126.75	128.54	130.33	132.14	133.96	135.80	137.64	139.50	141.37
5.00	112.85	114.52	116.20	117.89	119.60	121.32	123.05	124.79	126.55	128.32	130.10	131.89	133.70	135.52	137.35	139.19
5.25	111.12	112.76	114.42	116.08	117.76	119.46	121.16	122.88	124.61	126.35	128.10	129.87	131.65	133.44	135.24	137.05
5.50	109.43	111.04	112.67	114.31	115.97	117.63	119.31	121.00	122.71	124.42	126.15	127.89	129.64	131.40	133.18	134.96
5.75	107.77	109.36	110.96	112.58	114.21	115.85	117.51	119.17	120.85	122.54	124.24	125.95	127.68	129.41	131.16	132.92
6.00	106.15	107.71	109.29	110.89	112.49	114.11	115.74	117.38	119.03	120.69	122.37	124.06	125.76	127.47	129.19	130.92
6.25	104.56	106.10	107.66	109.23	110.81	112.40	114.01	115.62	117.25	118.89	120.54	122.20	123.88	125.56	127.25	128.96
6.50	103.01	104.53	106.06	107.61	109.16	110.73	112.31	113.91	115.51	117.12	118.75	120.39	122.04	123.69	125.36	127.05
6.75	101.49	102.99	104.50	106.02	107.55	109.10	110.66	112.23	113.81	115.40	117.00	118.61	120.24	121.87	123.52	125.17
7.00	100.00	101.48	102.97	104.47	105.98	107.50	109.04	110.58	112.14	113.71	115.28	116.87	118.47	120.08	121.71	123.34
7.25	98.54	100.00	101.47	102.95	104.44	105.94	107.45	108.97	110.51	112.05	113.61	115.17	116.75	118.34	119.93	121.54
7.50	97.12	98.55	100.00	101.46	102.93	104.40	105.89	107.40	108.91	110.43	111.96	113.51	115.06	116.63	118.20	119.78
7.75	95.72	97.14	98.56	100.00	101.45	102.91	104.37	105.85	107.34	108.84	110.36	111.88	113.41	114.95	116.50	118.06
8.00	94.36	95.75	97.16	98.57	100.00	101.44	102.89	104.34	105.81	107.29	108.78	110.28	111.79	113.31	114.84	116.38
8.25	93.02	94.40	95.78	97.18	98.58	100.00	101.43	102.87	104.31	105.77	107.24	108.72	110.21	111.71	113.21	114.73
8.50	91.71	93.07	94.43	95.81	97.20	98.59	100.00	101.42	102.85	104.28	105.73	107.19	108.66	110.13	111.62	113.12
8.75	90.43	91.77	93.11	94.47	95.84	97.21	98.60	100.00	101.41	102.83	104.25	105.69	107.14	108.59	110.06	111.54
9.00	89.18	90.49	91.82	93.16	94.51	95.87	97.23	98.61	100.00	101.40	102.81	104.22	105.65	107.09	108.53	109.99
9.25	87.95	89.25	90.55	91.87	93.20	94.54	95.89	97.25	98.62	100.00	101.39	102.79	104.19	105.61	107.04	108.47
9.50	86.74	88.02	89.31	90.62	91.93	93.25	94.58	95.92	97.27	98.63	100.00	101.38	102.77	104.16	105.57	106.99
9.75	85.56	86.83	88.10	89.38	90.68	91.98	93.29	94.62	95.95	97.29	98.64	100.00	101.37	102.75	104.13	105.53
10.00	84.41	85.65	86.91	88.18	89.45	90.74	92.03	93.34	94.65	95.98	97.31	98.65	100.00	101.36	102.73	104.11
10.25	83.27	84.50	85.74	86.99	88.25	89.52	90.80	92.09	93.38	94.69	96.00	97.33	98.66	100.00	101.35	102.71
10.50	82.17	83.38	84.60	85.84	87.08	88.33	89.59	90.86	92.14	93.43	94.72	96.03	97.34	98.67	100.00	101.34
10.75	81.08	82.28	83.48	84.70	85.93	87.16	88.40	89.66	90.92	92.19	93.47	94.76	96.06	97.36	98.68	100.00
11.00	80.01	81.20	82.39	83.59	84.80	86.02	87.24	88.48	89.73	90.98	92.24	93.51	94.79	96.08	97.38	98.69
11.25	78.97	80.14	81.31	82.50	83.69	84.89	86.10	87.33	88.55	89.79	91.04	92.29	93.56	94.83	96.11	97.40
11.50	77.95	79.10	80.26	81.43	82.61	83.79	84.99	86.19	87.41	88.63	89.86	91.10	92.35	93.60	94.87	96.14
11.75	76.94	78.08	79.23	80.38	81.54	82.72	83.90	85.09	86.28	87.49	88.70	89.93	91.16	92.40	93.64	94.90
12.00	75.96	77.08	78.21	79.35	80.50	81.66	82.82	84.00	85.18	86.37	87.57	88.78	89.99	91.22	92.45	93.69
12.25	75.00	76.10	77.22	78.35	79.48	80.62	81.77	82.93	84.10	85.28	86.46	87.65	88.85	90.06	91.28	92.50
12.50	74.05	75.15	76.25	77.36	78.48	79.61	80.74	81.89	83.04	84.20	85.37	86.55	87.73	88.92	90.13	91.33
12.75	73.13	74.21	75.29	76.39	77.50	78.61	79.73	80.86	82.00	83.15	84.30	85.46	86.63	87.81	89.00	90.19
13.00	72.22	73.28	74.36	75.44	76.53	77.63	78.74	79.86	80.98	82.11	83.25	84.40	85.56	86.72	87.89	89.07
13.25	71.33	72.38	73.44	74.51	75.59	76.68	77.77	78.87	79.98	81.10	82.23	83.36	84.50	85.65	86.81	87.97
13.50	70.45	71.49	72.54	73.60	74.66	75.74	76.82	77.91	79.00	80.11	81.22	82.34	83.47	84.60	85.74	86.89
13.75	69.60	70.62	71.66	72.70	73.76	74.82	75.88	76.96	78.04	79.13	80.23	81.34	82.45	83.57	84.70	85.84
14.00	68.75	69.77	70.79	71.83	72.86	73.91	74.97	76.03	77.10	78.18	79.26	80.36	81.46	82.56	83.68	84.80
14.25	67.93	68.93	69.94	70.96	71.99	73.03	74.07	75.12	76.18	77.24	78.31	79.39	80.48	81.57	82.67	83.78
14.50	67.12	68.11	69.11	70.12	71.13	72.16	73.19	74.22	75.27	76.32	77.38	78.45	79.52	80.60	81.69	82.79
14.75	66.33	67.31	68.29	69.29	70.29	71.30	72.32	73.35	74.38	75.42	76.46	77.52	78.58	79.65	80.72	81.81
15.00	65.55	66.52	67.49	68.48	69.47	70.47	71.47	72.48	73.50	74.53	75.57	76.61	77.66	78.71	79.78	80.85
15.25	64.78	65.74	66.71	67.68	68.66	69.64	70.64	71.64	72.65	73.66	74.69	75.72	76.75	77.80	78.85	79.90
15.50	64.03	64.98	65.93	66.89	67.86	68.84	69.82	70.81	71.81	72.81	73.82	74.84	75.86	76.89	77.93	78.98
15.75	63.30	64.23	65.18	66.12	67.08	68.05	69.02	70.00	70.98	71.97	72.97	73.98	74.99	76.01	77.04	78.07
16.00	62.58	63.50	64.43	65.37	66.32	67.27	68.23	69.20	70.17	71.15	72.14	73.13	74.13	75.14	76.16	77.18
16.25	61.87	62.78	63.70	64.63	65.56	66.51	67.46	68.41	69.37	70.34	71.32	72.30	73.29	74.29	75.29	76.30
16.50	61.17	62.07	62.98	63.90	64.83	65.76	66.70	67.64	68.59	69.55	70.52	71.49	72.47	73.45	74.45	75.44
16.75	60.49	61.38	62.28	63.19	64.10	65.02	65.95	66.89	67.83	68.78	69.73	70.69	71.66	72.63	73.61	74.60
17.00	59.81	60.70	61.59	62.49	63.39	64.30	65.22	66.14	67.07	68.01	68.96	69.91	70.86	71.83	72.80	73.77
17.25	59.16	60.03	60.91	61.80	62.69	63.59	64.50	65.41	66.34	67.26	68.20	69.14	70.08	71.04	72.00	72.96
17.50	58.51	59.37	60.24	61.12	62.01	62.90	63.79	64.70	65.61	66.53	67.45	68.38	69.32	70.26	71.21	72.16
17.75	57.87	58.73	59.59	60.46	61.33	62.21	63.10	64.00	64.90	65.80	66.72	67.64	68.56	69.50	70.43	71.38
18.00	57.25	58.09	58.95	59.80	60.67	61.54	62.42	63.31	64.20	65.09	66.00	66.91	67.82	68.75	69.67	70.61
18.25	56.63	57.47	58.31	59.16	60.02	60.88	61.75	62.63	63.51	64.40	65.29	66.19	67.10	68.01	68.93	69.85
18.50	56.03	56.86	57.69	58.53	59.38	60.23	61.09	61.96	62.83	63.71	64.60	65.49	66.38	67.29	68.19	69.11
18.75	55.44	56.26	57.08	57.92	58.75	59.60	60.45	61.31	62.17	63.04	63.91	64.79	65.68	66.57	67.47	68.38
19.00	54.86	55.67	56.49	57.31	58.14	58.97	59.82	60.66	61.52	62.38	63.24	64.12	64.99	65.88	66.77	67.66
20.00	52.63	53.41	54.19	54.98	55.78	56.58	57.39	58.20	59.02	59.84	60.68	61.51	62.35	63.20	64.06	64.91
25.00	43.49	44.14	44.78	45.44	46.09	46.76	47.42	48.10	48.77	49.45	50.14	50.83	51.53	52.23	52.93	53.64
30.00	36.83	37.37	37.92	38.47	39.03	39.59	40.15	40.72	41.29	41.87	42.45	43.04	43.63	44.22	44.82	45.42

Description: This table shows the yield to maturity of a mortgage purchased at the price shown in the index.

Example: The yield to maturity of a 10.75 %, 14 year mortgage at a price of 113.00 is 8.51 %.

PRICE	7.00%	7.25%	7.50%	7.75%	8.00%	8.25%	8.50%	8.75%	9.00%	9.25%	9.50%	9.75%	10.00%	10.25%	10.50%	10.75%
145	1.15	1.37	1.58	1.80	2.01	2.22	2.44	2.65	2.86	3.08	3.29	3.50	3.71	3.92	4.13	4.34
140	1.67	1.89	2.10	2.32	2.54	2.75	2.97	3.19	3.40	3.62	3.83	4.05	4.26	4.47	4.69	4.90
135	2.21	2.43	2.65	2.87	3.09	3.31	3.53	3.75	3.97	4.19	4.40	4.62	4.84	5.06	5.27	5.49
130	2.78	3.00	3.23	3.45	3.67	3.90	4.12	4.34	4.56	4.79	5.01	5.23	5.45	5.67	5.89	6.11
129	2.90	3.12	3.35	3.57	3.79	4.02	4.24	4.46	4.69	4.91	5.13	5.35	5.58	5.80	6.02	6.24
128	3.02	3.24	3.47	3.69	3.92	4.14	4.36	4.59	4.81	5.04	5.26	5.48	5.70	5.93	6.15	6.37
127	3.14	3.36	3.59	3.81	4.04	4.26	4.49	4.71	4.94	5.16	5.39	5.61	5.83	6.06	6.28	6.50
126	3.26	3.49	3.71	3.94	4.16	4.39	4.62	4.84	5.07	5.29	5.51	5.74	5.96	6.19	6.41	6.63
125	3.38	3.61	3.84	4.06	4.29	4.52	4.74	4.97	5.19	5.42	5.64	5.87	6.09	6.32	6.54	6.77
124	3.51	3.73	3.96	4.19	4.42	4.64	4.87	5.10	5.32	5.55	5.78	6.00	6.23	6.45	6.68	6.90
123	3.63	3.86	4.09	4.32	4.55	4.77	5.00	5.23	5.46	5.68	5.91	6.14	6.36	6.59	6.82	7.04
122	3.76	3.99	4.22	4.45	4.68	4.90	5.13	5.36	5.59	5.82	6.05	6.27	6.50	6.73	6.95	7.18
121	3.89	4.12	4.35	4.58	4.81	5.04	5.27	5.50	5.72	5.95	6.18	6.41	6.64	6.87	7.09	7.32
120	4.02	4.25	4.48	4.71	4.94	5.17	5.40	5.63	5.86	6.09	6.32	6.55	6.78	7.01	7.24	7.46
119	4.15	4.38	4.61	4.84	5.08	5.31	5.54	5.77	6.00	6.23	6.46	6.69	6.92	7.15	7.38	7.61
118	4.28	4.52	4.75	4.98	5.21	5.44	5.68	5.91	6.14	6.37	6.60	6.83	7.06	7.29	7.52	7.75
117	4.42	4.65	4.88	5.12	5.35	5.58	5.82	6.05	6.28	6.51	6.74	6.98	7.21	7.44	7.67	7.90
116	4.55	4.79	5.02	5.26	5.49	5.72	5.96	6.19	6.42	6.66	6.89	7.12	7.36	7.59	7.82	8.05
115	4.69	4.93	5.16	5.40	5.63	5.87	6.10	6.34	6.57	6.80	7.04	7.27	7.50	7.74	7.97	8.20
114	4.83	5.07	5.30	5.54	5.78	6.01	6.25	6.48	6.72	6.95	7.19	7.42	7.65	7.89	8.12	8.36
113	4.97	5.21	5.45	5.68	5.92	6.16	6.39	6.63	6.87	7.10	7.34	7.57	7.81	8.04	8.28	8.51
112	5.12	5.36	5.59	5.83	6.07	6.30	6.54	6.78	7.02	7.25	7.49	7.73	7.96	8.20	8.43	8.67
111	5.26	5.50	5.74	5.98	6.22	6.45	6.69	6.93	7.17	7.41	7.64	7.88	8.12	8.36	8.59	8.83
110	5.41	5.65	5.89	6.13	6.37	6.61	6.85	7.08	7.32	7.56	7.80	8.04	8.28	8.52	8.75	8.99
109	5.56	5.80	6.04	6.28	6.52	6.76	7.00	7.24	7.48	7.72	7.96	8.20	8.44	8.68	8.92	9.16
108	5.71	5.95	6.19	6.43	6.68	6.92	7.16	7.40	7.64	7.88	8.12	8.36	8.60	8.84	9.08	9.32
107	5.86	6.11	6.35	6.59	6.83	7.07	7.32	7.56	7.80	8.04	8.28	8.53	8.77	9.01	9.25	9.49
106	6.02	6.26	6.50	6.75	6.99	7.23	7.48	7.72	7.96	8.21	8.45	8.69	8.94	9.18	9.42	9.66
105	6.18	6.42	6.66	6.91	7.15	7.40	7.64	7.89	8.13	8.37	8.62	8.86	9.11	9.35	9.59	9.84
104	6.33	6.58	6.83	7.07	7.32	7.56	7.81	8.05	8.30	8.54	8.79	9.03	9.28	9.52	9.77	10.01
103	6.50	6.74	6.99	7.24	7.48	7.73	7.98	8.22	8.47	8.71	8.96	9.21	9.45	9.70	9.95	10.19
102	6.66	6.91	7.16	7.40	7.65	7.90	8.15	8.39	8.64	8.89	9.14	9.38	9.63	9.88	10.13	10.37
101	6.83	7.08	7.32	7.57	7.82	8.07	8.32	8.57	8.82	9.07	9.31	9.56	9.81	10.06	10.31	10.56
100	7.00	7.25	7.50	7.75	8.00	8.25	8.50	8.75	9.00	9.25	9.50	9.75	10.00	10.25	10.50	10.75
99	7.17	7.42	7.67	7.92	8.17	8.42	8.67	8.92	9.18	9.43	9.68	9.93	10.18	10.43	10.68	10.93
98	7.34	7.59	7.84	8.10	8.35	8.60	8.85	9.11	9.36	9.61	9.86	10.12	10.37	10.62	10.87	11.13
97	7.52	7.77	8.02	8.28	8.53	8.78	9.04	9.29	9.55	9.80	10.05	10.31	10.56	10.82	11.07	11.32
96	7.70	7.95	8.20	8.46	8.71	8.97	9.22	9.48	9.74	9.99	10.25	10.50	10.76	11.01	11.27	11.52
95	7.88	8.13	8.39	8.65	8.90	9.16	9.41	9.67	9.93	10.18	10.44	10.70	10.95	11.21	11.47	11.72
94	8.06	8.32	8.58	8.83	9.09	9.35	9.61	9.86	10.12	10.38	10.64	10.90	11.16	11.41	11.67	11.93
93	8.25	8.51	8.77	9.03	9.28	9.54	9.80	10.06	10.32	10.58	10.84	11.10	11.36	11.62	11.88	12.14
92	8.44	8.70	8.96	9.22	9.48	9.74	10.00	10.26	10.52	10.78	11.05	11.31	11.57	11.83	12.09	12.35
91	8.63	8.89	9.16	9.42	9.68	9.94	10.20	10.47	10.73	10.99	11.25	11.52	11.78	12.04	12.30	12.57
90	8.83	9.09	9.36	9.62	9.88	10.15	10.41	10.67	10.94	11.20	11.47	11.73	11.99	12.26	12.52	12.79
89	9.03	9.29	9.56	9.82	10.09	10.35	10.62	10.88	11.15	11.41	11.68	11.95	12.21	12.48	12.74	13.01
88	9.23	9.50	9.77	10.03	10.30	10.56	10.83	11.10	11.37	11.63	11.90	12.17	12.43	12.70	12.97	13.24
87	9.44	9.71	9.98	10.24	10.51	10.78	11.05	11.32	11.59	11.85	12.12	12.39	12.66	12.93	13.20	13.47
86	9.65	9.92	10.19	10.46	10.73	11.00	11.27	11.54	11.81	12.08	12.35	12.62	12.89	13.16	13.43	13.71
85	9.87	10.14	10.41	10.68	10.95	11.22	11.49	11.76	12.04	12.31	12.58	12.85	13.13	13.40	13.67	13.95
84	10.08	10.36	10.63	10.90	11.17	11.45	11.72	11.99	12.27	12.54	12.82	13.09	13.37	13.64	13.92	14.19
83	10.31	10.58	10.85	11.13	11.40	11.68	11.95	12.23	12.50	12.78	13.06	13.33	13.61	13.89	14.16	14.44
82	10.53	10.81	11.08	11.36	11.64	11.91	12.19	12.47	12.75	13.02	13.30	13.58	13.86	14.14	14.42	14.70
81	10.76	11.04	11.32	11.60	11.87	12.15	12.43	12.71	12.99	13.27	13.55	13.83	14.11	14.39	14.67	14.95
80	11.00	11.28	11.56	11.84	12.12	12.40	12.68	12.96	13.24	13.52	13.80	14.09	14.37	14.65	14.94	15.22
79	11.24	11.52	11.80	12.08	12.36	12.65	12.93	13.21	13.50	13.78	14.06	14.35	14.63	14.92	15.20	15.49
78	11.48	11.76	12.05	12.33	12.62	12.90	13.19	13.47	13.76	14.04	14.33	14.61	14.90	15.19	15.48	15.76
77	11.73	12.02	12.30	12.59	12.87	13.16	13.45	13.73	14.02	14.31	14.60	14.89	15.18	15.47	15.76	16.05
76	11.98	12.27	12.56	12.85	13.14	13.42	13.71	14.00	14.29	14.58	14.87	15.16	15.46	15.75	16.04	16.33
75	12.24	12.53	12.82	13.11	13.40	13.69	13.99	14.28	14.57	14.86	15.16	15.45	15.74	16.04	16.33	16.63
74	12.51	12.80	13.09	13.38	13.68	13.97	14.26	14.56	14.85	15.15	15.44	15.74	16.03	16.33	16.63	16.93
70	13.63	13.93	14.23	14.53	14.83	15.14	15.44	15.74	16.05	16.35	16.66	16.97	17.27	17.58	17.89	18.20
65	15.17	15.49	15.80	16.12	16.44	16.75	17.07	17.39	17.71	18.03	18.35	18.67	18.99	19.32	19.64	19.96
60	16.93	17.26	17.59	17.92	18.25	18.59	18.92	19.26	19.59	19.93	20.27	20.61	20.95	21.29	21.63	21.98
55	18.93	19.28	19.63	19.99	20.34	20.69	21.05	21.41	21.76	22.12	22.48	22.84	23.21	23.57	23.93	24.30
50	21.27	21.65	22.02	22.40	22.78	23.16	23.54	23.92	24.30	24.69	25.07	25.46	25.85	26.24	26.63	27.03
45	24.05	24.45	24.86	25.27	25.68	26.09	26.50	26.91	27.33	27.75	28.17	28.59	29.01	29.44	29.87	30.29
40	27.43	27.87	28.32	28.76	29.21	29.66	30.12	30.57	31.03	31.49	31.96	32.42	32.89	33.36	33.83	34.30
35	31.66	32.16	32.65	33.15	33.66	34.16	34.67	35.18	35.70	36.21	36.73	37.26	37.78	38.31	38.84	39.38

Description: This table shows the price to pay for a monthly payment mortgage loan at the yield rate.

Example: The price of a 15.00 %, 14 year mortgage loan to yield 8.00 % to maturity is $ 143.95.

INTEREST RATE, %

YIELD	11.00%	11.25%	11.50%	11.75%	12.00%	12.25%	12.50%	12.75%	13.00%	13.25%	13.50%	13.75%	14.00%	14.25%	14.50%	15.00%
0.00	196.40	199.00	201.61	204.24	206.88	209.54	212.21	214.90	217.60	220.32	223.05	225.80	228.56	231.34	234.13	239.74
1.00	183.20	185.62	188.06	190.51	192.98	195.46	197.95	200.46	202.98	205.52	208.06	210.63	213.20	215.79	218.39	223.63
2.00	171.18	173.44	175.72	178.01	180.31	182.63	184.96	187.30	189.66	192.03	194.41	196.80	199.21	201.63	204.06	208.95
3.00	160.21	162.33	164.46	166.60	168.76	170.93	173.11	175.30	177.51	179.72	181.95	184.19	186.45	188.71	190.98	195.57
4.00	150.20	152.18	154.18	156.19	158.21	160.24	162.29	164.34	166.41	168.49	170.58	172.68	174.79	176.91	179.05	183.34
4.25	147.83	149.79	151.75	153.73	155.72	157.72	159.73	161.76	163.79	165.84	167.89	169.96	172.04	174.13	176.23	180.45
4.50	145.52	147.44	149.38	151.32	153.28	155.25	157.23	159.22	161.23	163.24	165.27	167.30	169.35	171.40	173.47	177.63
4.75	143.25	145.15	147.05	148.97	150.90	152.84	154.79	156.75	158.72	160.70	162.70	164.70	166.71	168.74	170.77	174.87
5.00	141.04	142.91	144.78	146.67	148.57	150.48	152.40	154.33	156.27	158.22	160.18	162.16	164.14	166.13	168.13	172.17
5.25	138.88	140.71	142.56	144.42	146.29	148.17	150.06	151.96	153.87	155.79	157.72	159.67	161.62	163.58	165.55	169.52
5.50	136.76	138.57	140.39	142.22	144.06	145.91	147.77	149.64	151.52	153.42	155.32	157.23	159.15	161.09	163.03	166.94
5.75	134.69	136.47	138.26	140.06	141.87	143.70	145.53	147.37	149.23	151.09	152.97	154.85	156.74	158.65	160.56	164.41
6.00	132.66	134.41	136.18	137.95	139.74	141.53	143.34	145.16	146.98	148.82	150.66	152.52	154.38	156.26	158.14	161.94
6.25	130.68	132.40	134.14	135.89	137.65	139.42	141.20	142.99	144.79	146.59	148.41	150.24	152.08	153.92	155.78	159.52
6.50	128.74	130.44	132.15	133.87	135.61	137.35	139.10	140.86	142.64	144.42	146.21	148.01	149.82	151.64	153.46	157.15
6.75	126.84	128.51	130.20	131.90	133.61	135.32	137.05	138.79	140.53	142.29	144.05	145.82	147.61	149.40	151.20	154.83
7.00	124.98	126.63	128.29	129.97	131.65	133.34	135.04	136.75	138.47	140.20	141.94	143.69	145.44	147.21	148.98	152.56
7.25	123.16	124.79	126.43	128.07	129.73	131.40	133.07	134.76	136.46	138.16	139.87	141.60	143.33	145.07	146.82	150.34
7.50	121.38	122.98	124.60	126.22	127.86	129.50	131.15	132.81	134.48	136.16	137.85	139.55	141.26	142.97	144.69	148.16
7.75	119.64	121.22	122.81	124.41	126.02	127.64	129.27	130.90	132.55	134.21	135.87	137.54	139.23	140.92	142.62	146.04
8.00	117.93	119.49	121.06	122.63	124.22	125.82	127.42	129.04	130.66	132.29	133.93	135.58	137.24	138.91	140.58	143.95
8.25	116.26	117.80	119.34	120.90	122.46	124.04	125.62	127.21	128.81	130.42	132.04	133.66	135.30	136.94	138.59	141.91
8.50	114.62	116.14	117.66	119.20	120.74	122.29	123.85	125.42	127.00	128.58	130.18	131.78	133.39	135.01	136.64	139.92
8.75	113.02	114.51	116.02	117.53	119.05	120.58	122.12	123.67	125.22	126.79	128.36	129.94	131.53	133.12	134.73	137.96
9.00	111.45	112.92	114.41	115.90	117.40	118.91	120.42	121.95	123.48	125.03	126.58	128.14	129.70	131.28	132.86	136.05
9.25	109.91	111.37	112.83	114.30	115.78	117.27	118.76	120.27	121.78	123.30	124.83	126.37	127.91	129.47	131.03	134.17
9.50	108.41	109.84	111.28	112.73	114.19	115.66	117.14	118.62	120.11	121.61	123.12	124.64	126.16	127.69	129.23	132.33
9.75	106.94	108.35	109.77	111.20	112.64	114.09	115.54	117.01	118.48	119.96	121.45	122.94	124.45	125.96	127.48	130.53
10.00	105.49	106.89	108.29	109.70	111.12	112.55	113.98	115.43	116.88	118.34	119.81	121.28	122.77	124.26	125.75	128.77
10.25	104.08	105.45	106.84	108.23	109.63	111.04	112.45	113.88	115.31	116.75	118.20	119.66	121.12	122.59	124.07	127.04
10.50	102.69	104.05	105.41	106.79	108.17	109.56	110.96	112.36	113.78	115.20	116.63	118.06	119.51	120.96	122.41	125.35
10.75	101.33	102.67	104.02	105.37	106.74	108.11	109.49	110.88	112.27	113.67	115.08	116.50	117.92	119.36	120.79	123.69
11.00	100.00	101.32	102.65	103.99	105.34	106.69	108.05	109.42	110.80	112.18	113.57	114.97	116.38	117.79	119.21	122.07
11.25	98.70	100.00	101.31	102.63	103.96	105.30	106.64	107.99	109.35	110.72	112.09	113.47	114.86	116.25	117.65	120.48
11.50	97.42	98.70	100.00	101.30	102.61	103.93	105.26	106.59	107.93	109.28	110.64	112.00	113.37	114.75	116.13	118.91
11.75	96.16	97.43	98.71	100.00	101.29	102.60	103.90	105.22	106.54	107.88	109.21	110.56	111.91	113.27	114.63	117.38
12.00	94.93	96.19	97.45	98.72	100.00	101.29	102.58	103.88	105.18	106.50	107.82	109.15	110.48	111.82	113.17	115.88
12.25	93.73	94.97	96.22	97.47	98.73	100.00	101.28	102.56	103.85	105.15	106.45	107.76	109.08	110.40	111.73	114.41
12.50	92.55	93.77	95.00	96.24	97.49	98.74	100.00	101.27	102.54	103.82	105.11	106.40	107.70	109.01	110.33	112.97
12.75	91.39	92.60	93.82	95.04	96.27	97.50	98.75	100.00	101.26	102.52	103.79	105.07	106.36	107.65	108.95	111.56
13.00	90.26	91.45	92.65	93.86	95.07	96.29	97.52	98.76	100.00	101.25	102.50	103.77	105.04	106.31	107.59	110.17
13.25	89.14	90.32	91.51	92.70	93.90	95.11	96.32	97.54	98.77	100.00	101.24	102.49	103.74	105.00	106.26	108.81
13.50	88.05	89.21	90.39	91.56	92.75	93.94	95.14	96.34	97.56	98.77	100.00	101.23	102.47	103.71	104.96	107.48
13.75	86.98	88.13	89.29	90.45	91.62	92.80	93.98	95.17	96.37	97.57	98.78	100.00	101.22	102.45	103.69	106.17
14.00	85.93	87.06	88.21	89.36	90.51	91.68	92.85	94.02	95.21	96.39	97.59	98.79	100.00	101.21	102.43	104.89
14.25	84.90	86.02	87.15	88.29	89.43	90.58	91.73	92.90	94.06	95.24	96.42	97.61	98.80	100.00	101.21	103.63
14.50	83.89	85.00	86.11	87.23	88.36	89.50	90.64	91.79	92.94	94.10	95.27	96.44	97.62	98.81	100.00	102.40
14.75	82.90	83.99	85.09	86.20	87.32	88.44	89.57	90.70	91.84	92.99	94.14	95.30	96.47	97.64	98.82	101.19
15.00	81.92	83.00	84.09	85.19	86.29	87.40	88.52	89.64	90.77	91.90	93.04	94.18	95.34	96.49	97.66	100.00
15.25	80.97	82.04	83.11	84.20	85.29	86.38	87.48	88.59	89.71	90.83	91.95	93.09	94.22	95.37	96.52	98.83
15.50	80.03	81.09	82.15	83.22	84.30	85.38	86.47	87.57	88.67	89.78	90.89	92.01	93.13	94.26	95.40	97.69
15.75	79.11	80.15	81.21	82.27	83.33	84.40	85.48	86.56	87.65	88.74	89.84	90.95	92.06	93.18	94.30	96.57
16.00	78.21	79.24	80.28	81.33	82.38	83.44	84.50	85.57	86.65	87.73	88.82	89.91	91.01	92.12	93.23	95.46
16.25	77.32	78.34	79.37	80.40	81.44	82.49	83.54	84.60	85.67	86.74	87.81	88.89	89.98	91.07	92.17	94.38
16.50	76.45	77.46	78.48	79.50	80.53	81.56	82.60	83.65	84.70	85.76	86.82	87.89	88.97	90.05	91.13	93.32
16.75	75.59	76.59	77.60	78.61	79.63	80.65	81.68	82.71	83.76	84.80	85.85	86.91	87.97	89.04	90.11	92.28
17.00	74.76	75.74	76.74	77.74	78.74	79.76	80.77	81.80	82.83	83.86	84.90	85.95	87.00	88.05	89.11	91.25
17.25	73.93	74.91	75.89	76.88	77.88	78.88	79.88	80.90	81.91	82.94	83.96	85.00	86.04	87.08	88.13	90.25
17.50	73.12	74.09	75.06	76.04	77.02	78.01	79.01	80.01	81.02	82.03	83.05	84.07	85.10	86.13	87.17	89.26
17.75	72.33	73.28	74.25	75.21	76.19	77.17	78.15	79.14	80.14	81.14	82.14	83.16	84.17	85.19	86.22	88.29
18.00	71.55	72.49	73.45	74.40	75.37	76.33	77.31	78.29	79.27	80.26	81.26	82.26	83.26	84.27	85.29	87.34
18.25	70.78	71.72	72.66	73.61	74.56	75.52	76.48	77.45	78.42	79.40	80.39	81.38	82.37	83.37	84.38	86.40
18.50	70.03	70.95	71.89	72.82	73.76	74.71	75.67	76.62	77.59	78.56	79.53	80.51	81.50	82.48	83.48	85.48
18.75	69.29	70.20	71.13	72.05	72.99	73.92	74.87	75.81	76.77	77.73	78.69	79.66	80.63	81.61	82.60	84.58
19.00	68.56	69.47	70.38	71.30	72.22	73.15	74.08	75.02	75.96	76.91	77.87	78.82	79.79	80.76	81.73	83.69
20.00	65.78	66.65	67.52	68.40	69.29	70.18	71.07	71.97	72.88	73.79	74.71	75.62	76.55	77.48	78.41	80.29
25.00	54.36	55.08	55.80	56.53	57.26	57.99	58.73	59.48	60.23	60.98	61.73	62.50	63.26	64.03	64.80	66.35
30.00	46.02	46.63	47.24	47.86	48.48	49.10	49.73	50.36	50.99	51.63	52.27	52.91	53.56	54.21	54.86	56.18

MORTGAGE YIELD

14 YEARS

Description: This table shows the yield to maturity of a mortgage purchased at the price shown in the index.

Example: The yield to maturity of a 15.00 %, 14 year mortgage at a price of 117.00 is 11.81 %.

INTEREST RATE, %

PRICE	11.00%	11.25%	11.50%	11.75%	12.00%	12.25%	12.50%	12.75%	13.00%	13.25%	13.50%	13.75%	14.00%	14.25%	14.50%	15.00%
190	.47	.66	.85	1.03	1.22	1.41	1.60	1.78	1.97	2.15	2.34	2.52	2.71	2.89	3.07	3.44
185	.85	1.04	1.23	1.42	1.61	1.80	1.99	2.18	2.37	2.55	2.74	2.93	3.11	3.30	3.49	3.85
180	1.25	1.45	1.64	1.83	2.02	2.21	2.40	2.59	2.78	2.97	3.16	3.35	3.54	3.72	3.91	4.28
175	1.67	1.86	2.06	2.25	2.44	2.64	2.83	3.02	3.21	3.40	3.60	3.79	3.98	4.17	4.36	4.73
170	2.10	2.29	2.49	2.69	2.88	3.08	3.27	3.47	3.66	3.86	4.05	4.24	4.43	4.63	4.82	5.20
165	2.55	2.75	2.94	3.14	3.34	3.54	3.74	3.93	4.13	4.33	4.52	4.72	4.91	5.11	5.30	5.69
160	3.02	3.22	3.42	3.62	3.82	4.02	4.22	4.42	4.62	4.82	5.01	5.21	5.41	5.61	5.80	6.19
155	3.50	3.71	3.91	4.12	4.32	4.52	4.72	4.92	5.13	5.33	5.53	5.73	5.93	6.13	6.33	6.73
150	4.02	4.22	4.43	4.63	4.84	5.05	5.25	5.46	5.66	5.86	6.07	6.27	6.47	6.68	6.88	7.28
145	4.55	4.76	4.97	5.18	5.39	5.60	5.81	6.01	6.22	6.43	6.63	6.84	7.05	7.25	7.46	7.87
140	5.11	5.33	5.54	5.75	5.96	6.18	6.39	6.60	6.81	7.02	7.23	7.44	7.65	7.86	8.07	8.48
135	5.71	5.92	6.14	6.35	6.57	6.79	7.00	7.21	7.43	7.64	7.86	8.07	8.28	8.50	8.71	9.13
130	6.33	6.55	6.77	6.99	7.21	7.43	7.65	7.87	8.08	8.30	8.52	8.74	8.95	9.17	9.39	9.82
125	6.99	7.22	7.44	7.66	7.89	8.11	8.33	8.55	8.78	9.00	9.22	9.44	9.66	9.89	10.11	10.55
123	7.27	7.49	7.72	7.94	8.17	8.39	8.62	8.84	9.07	9.29	9.51	9.74	9.96	10.18	10.41	10.85
122	7.41	7.63	7.86	8.09	8.31	8.54	8.76	8.99	9.21	9.44	9.66	9.89	10.11	10.33	10.56	11.01
121	7.55	7.78	8.00	8.23	8.46	8.68	8.91	9.14	9.36	9.59	9.81	10.04	10.26	10.49	10.71	11.16
120	7.69	7.92	8.15	8.38	8.60	8.83	9.06	9.29	9.51	9.74	9.97	10.19	10.42	10.64	10.87	11.32
119	7.84	8.07	8.30	8.52	8.75	8.98	9.21	9.44	9.66	9.89	10.12	10.35	10.57	10.80	11.03	11.48
118	7.98	8.21	8.44	8.67	8.90	9.13	9.36	9.59	9.82	10.05	10.28	10.50	10.73	10.96	11.19	11.64
117	8.13	8.36	8.60	8.83	9.06	9.29	9.52	9.75	9.98	10.21	10.44	10.66	10.89	11.12	11.35	11.81
116	8.28	8.52	8.75	8.98	9.21	9.44	9.67	9.90	10.13	10.37	10.60	10.83	11.06	11.29	11.52	11.98
115	8.44	8.67	8.90	9.13	9.37	9.60	9.83	10.06	10.30	10.53	10.76	10.99	11.22	11.45	11.68	12.14
114	8.59	8.83	9.06	9.29	9.53	9.76	9.99	10.23	10.46	10.69	10.92	11.16	11.39	11.62	11.85	12.32
113	8.75	8.98	9.22	9.45	9.69	9.92	10.16	10.39	10.62	10.86	11.09	11.32	11.56	11.79	12.02	12.49
112	8.91	9.14	9.38	9.61	9.85	10.09	10.32	10.56	10.79	11.03	11.26	11.49	11.73	11.96	12.20	12.67
111	9.07	9.30	9.54	9.78	10.01	10.25	10.49	10.72	10.96	11.20	11.43	11.67	11.90	12.14	12.37	12.85
110	9.23	9.47	9.71	9.94	10.18	10.42	10.66	10.89	11.13	11.37	11.61	11.84	12.08	12.32	12.55	13.03
109	9.40	9.64	9.87	10.11	10.35	10.59	10.83	11.07	11.31	11.54	11.78	12.02	12.26	12.50	12.74	13.21
108	9.56	9.80	10.04	10.28	10.52	10.76	11.00	11.24	11.48	11.72	11.96	12.20	12.44	12.68	12.92	13.40
107	9.73	9.98	10.22	10.46	10.70	10.94	11.18	11.42	11.66	11.90	12.14	12.38	12.63	12.87	13.11	13.59
106	9.91	10.15	10.39	10.63	10.88	11.12	11.36	11.60	11.84	12.09	12.33	12.57	12.81	13.05	13.30	13.78
105	10.08	10.32	10.57	10.81	11.06	11.30	11.54	11.79	12.03	12.27	12.52	12.76	13.00	13.24	13.49	13.97
104	10.26	10.50	10.75	10.99	11.24	11.48	11.73	11.97	12.22	12.46	12.71	12.95	13.19	13.44	13.68	14.17
103	10.44	10.68	10.93	11.18	11.42	11.67	11.91	12.16	12.41	12.65	12.90	13.14	13.39	13.64	13.88	14.37
102	10.62	10.87	11.12	11.36	11.61	11.86	12.11	12.35	12.60	12.85	13.09	13.34	13.59	13.84	14.08	14.58
101	10.81	11.06	11.30	11.55	11.80	12.05	12.30	12.55	12.80	13.04	13.29	13.54	13.79	14.04	14.29	14.78
100	11.00	11.25	11.50	11.75	12.00	12.25	12.50	12.75	13.00	13.25	13.50	13.75	14.00	14.25	14.50	15.00
99	11.19	11.44	11.69	11.94	12.19	12.44	12.69	12.95	13.20	13.45	13.70	13.95	14.20	14.45	14.71	15.21
98	11.38	11.63	11.89	12.14	12.39	12.64	12.90	13.15	13.40	13.66	13.91	14.16	14.41	14.67	14.92	15.43
97	11.58	11.83	12.09	12.34	12.59	12.85	13.10	13.36	13.61	13.87	14.12	14.38	14.63	14.88	15.14	15.65
96	11.78	12.03	12.29	12.54	12.80	13.06	13.31	13.57	13.82	14.08	14.34	14.59	14.85	15.10	15.36	15.87
95	11.98	12.24	12.50	12.75	13.01	13.27	13.52	13.78	14.04	14.30	14.55	14.81	15.07	15.33	15.59	16.10
94	12.19	12.45	12.71	12.96	13.22	13.48	13.74	14.00	14.26	14.52	14.78	15.04	15.30	15.56	15.82	16.33
93	12.40	12.66	12.92	13.18	13.44	13.70	13.96	14.22	14.48	14.74	15.00	15.26	15.53	15.79	16.05	16.57
92	12.61	12.87	13.14	13.40	13.66	13.92	14.18	14.45	14.71	14.97	15.23	15.50	15.76	16.02	16.29	16.81
91	12.83	13.09	13.36	13.62	13.88	14.15	14.41	14.68	14.94	15.20	15.47	15.73	16.00	16.26	16.53	17.06
90	13.05	13.32	13.58	13.85	14.11	14.38	14.64	14.91	15.18	15.44	15.71	15.97	16.24	16.51	16.77	17.31
89	13.28	13.54	13.81	14.08	14.34	14.61	14.88	15.15	15.41	15.68	15.95	16.22	16.49	16.76	17.02	17.56
88	13.51	13.78	14.04	14.31	14.58	14.85	15.12	15.39	15.66	15.93	16.20	16.47	16.74	17.01	17.28	17.82
87	13.74	14.01	14.28	14.55	14.82	15.09	15.36	15.64	15.91	16.18	16.45	16.72	16.99	17.27	17.54	18.08
86	13.98	14.25	14.52	14.79	15.07	15.34	15.61	15.89	16.16	16.43	16.71	16.98	17.26	17.53	17.80	18.35
85	14.22	14.49	14.77	15.04	15.32	15.59	15.87	16.14	16.42	16.69	16.97	17.24	17.52	17.80	18.07	18.63
84	14.47	14.74	15.02	15.30	15.57	15.85	16.13	16.40	16.68	16.96	17.24	17.51	17.79	18.07	18.35	18.91
83	14.72	15.00	15.27	15.55	15.83	16.11	16.39	16.67	16.95	17.23	17.51	17.79	18.07	18.35	18.63	19.19
82	14.97	15.25	15.53	15.82	16.10	16.38	16.66	16.94	17.22	17.50	17.79	18.07	18.35	18.63	18.92	19.48
81	15.24	15.52	15.80	16.08	16.37	16.65	16.93	17.22	17.50	17.78	18.07	18.35	18.64	18.92	19.21	19.78
80	15.50	15.79	16.07	16.36	16.64	16.93	17.21	17.50	17.78	18.07	18.36	18.64	18.93	19.22	19.51	20.08
79	15.77	16.06	16.35	16.63	16.92	17.21	17.50	17.79	18.07	18.36	18.65	18.94	19.23	19.52	19.81	20.39
78	16.05	16.34	16.63	16.92	17.21	17.50	17.79	18.08	18.37	18.66	18.95	19.25	19.54	19.83	20.12	20.71
77	16.34	16.63	16.92	17.21	17.50	17.79	18.09	18.38	18.67	18.97	19.26	19.56	19.85	20.15	20.44	21.04
76	16.63	16.92	17.21	17.51	17.80	18.10	18.39	18.69	18.98	19.28	19.58	19.87	20.17	20.47	20.77	21.37
75	16.92	17.22	17.51	17.81	18.11	18.41	18.70	19.00	19.30	19.60	19.90	20.20	20.50	20.80	21.10	21.70
74	17.22	17.52	17.82	18.12	18.42	18.72	19.02	19.32	19.62	19.93	20.23	20.53	20.83	21.14	21.44	22.05
73	17.53	17.83	18.14	18.44	18.74	19.04	19.35	19.65	19.95	20.26	20.56	20.87	21.18	21.48	21.79	22.41
70	18.50	18.81	19.12	19.43	19.75	20.06	20.37	20.68	21.00	21.31	21.62	21.94	22.25	22.57	22.89	23.52
65	20.29	20.61	20.94	21.27	21.59	21.92	22.25	22.58	22.91	23.24	23.57	23.91	24.24	24.57	24.91	25.58
60	22.32	22.66	23.01	23.36	23.70	24.05	24.40	24.75	25.10	25.45	25.81	26.16	26.51	26.87	27.22	27.94

MORTGAGE PRICE

15 YEARS

Description: This table shows the price to pay for a monthly payment mortgage loan at the yield rate.

Example: The price of a 6.75 %, 15 year mortgage loan to yield 8.00 % to maturity is $ 92.60.

INTEREST RATE, %

YIELD	0.00%	1.00%	2.00%	3.00%	4.00%	4.25%	4.50%	4.75%	5.00%	5.25%	5.50%	5.75%	6.00%	6.25%	6.50%	6.75%
0.00	100.00	107.73	115.83	124.30	133.14	135.41	137.70	140.01	142.34	144.70	147.08	149.47	151.89	154.34	156.80	159.28
1.00	92.83	100.00	107.52	115.39	123.59	125.70	127.82	129.96	132.13	134.32	136.52	138.75	141.00	143.26	145.55	147.86
2.00	86.33	93.00	100.00	107.32	114.95	116.90	118.88	120.87	122.89	124.92	126.97	129.04	131.13	133.24	135.37	137.51
3.00	80.45	86.67	93.18	100.00	107.11	108.93	110.78	112.63	114.51	116.41	118.32	120.25	122.20	124.16	126.14	128.14
4.00	75.11	80.91	87.00	93.36	100.00	101.70	103.42	105.16	106.91	108.68	110.46	112.26	114.08	115.92	117.77	119.63
4.25	73.85	79.56	85.54	91.80	98.33	100.00	101.69	103.40	105.12	106.86	108.61	110.39	112.17	113.98	115.80	117.63
4.50	72.62	78.24	84.12	90.27	96.69	98.34	100.00	101.68	103.37	105.08	106.81	108.55	110.31	112.08	113.87	115.68
4.75	71.42	76.94	82.73	88.78	95.10	96.71	98.35	100.00	101.67	103.35	105.05	106.76	108.49	110.23	111.99	113.77
5.00	70.25	75.68	81.38	87.33	93.54	95.13	96.74	98.36	100.00	101.65	103.32	105.01	106.71	108.43	110.16	111.90
5.25	69.11	74.45	80.05	85.91	92.01	93.58	95.16	96.76	98.37	100.00	101.64	103.30	104.97	106.66	108.36	110.08
5.50	67.99	73.25	78.76	84.52	90.53	92.07	93.62	95.20	96.78	98.38	100.00	101.63	103.28	104.94	106.61	108.30
5.75	66.90	72.07	77.49	83.16	89.08	90.59	92.12	93.67	95.23	96.80	98.40	100.00	101.62	103.25	104.90	106.56
6.00	65.84	70.92	76.26	81.84	87.66	89.15	90.65	92.18	93.71	95.26	96.83	98.41	100.00	101.61	103.23	104.86
6.25	64.79	69.80	75.05	80.54	86.27	87.74	89.22	90.72	92.23	93.76	95.30	96.85	98.42	100.00	101.60	103.21
6.50	63.78	68.71	73.87	79.28	84.91	86.36	87.82	89.29	90.78	92.28	93.80	95.33	96.87	98.43	100.00	101.58
6.75	62.78	67.63	72.72	78.04	83.59	85.01	86.45	87.90	89.36	90.84	92.34	93.84	95.36	96.89	98.44	100.00
7.00	61.81	66.59	71.59	76.83	82.29	83.70	85.11	86.54	87.98	89.44	90.91	92.39	93.88	95.39	96.92	98.45
7.25	60.86	65.56	70.49	75.65	81.03	82.41	83.80	85.21	86.63	88.06	89.51	90.97	92.44	93.93	95.43	96.94
7.50	59.93	64.56	69.42	74.50	79.79	81.15	82.52	83.91	85.31	86.72	88.14	89.58	91.03	92.49	93.97	95.46
7.75	59.02	63.58	68.37	73.37	78.58	79.92	81.27	82.64	84.01	85.40	86.81	88.22	89.65	91.09	92.55	94.01
8.00	58.13	62.63	67.34	72.26	77.40	78.72	80.05	81.39	82.75	84.12	85.50	86.89	88.30	89.72	91.15	92.60
8.25	57.27	61.69	66.33	71.18	76.25	77.54	78.85	80.18	81.51	82.86	84.22	85.60	86.98	88.38	89.79	91.21
8.50	56.42	60.78	65.35	70.13	75.12	76.39	77.68	78.99	80.30	81.63	82.97	84.33	85.69	87.07	88.46	89.86
8.75	55.59	59.88	64.39	69.10	74.01	75.27	76.54	77.83	79.12	80.43	81.75	83.09	84.43	85.79	87.16	88.54
9.00	54.77	59.01	63.45	68.09	72.93	74.17	75.42	76.69	77.97	79.26	80.56	81.87	83.20	84.54	85.89	87.25
9.25	53.98	58.15	62.53	67.10	71.87	73.09	74.33	75.58	76.84	78.11	79.39	80.69	81.99	83.31	84.64	85.98
9.50	53.20	57.31	61.63	66.13	70.84	72.04	73.26	74.49	75.73	76.98	78.25	79.52	80.81	82.11	83.42	84.74
9.75	52.44	56.50	60.74	65.19	69.82	71.01	72.21	73.42	74.65	75.88	77.13	78.39	79.66	80.94	82.23	83.53
10.00	51.70	55.69	59.88	64.26	68.83	70.01	71.19	72.38	73.59	74.81	76.04	77.28	78.53	79.79	81.06	82.35
10.25	50.97	54.91	59.04	63.36	67.86	69.02	70.19	71.36	72.55	73.75	74.97	76.19	77.42	78.67	79.92	81.19
10.50	50.26	54.14	58.22	62.47	66.92	68.05	69.21	70.37	71.54	72.72	73.92	75.12	76.34	77.57	78.80	80.05
10.75	49.56	53.39	57.41	61.61	65.99	67.11	68.25	69.39	70.55	71.71	72.89	74.08	75.28	76.49	77.71	78.94
11.00	48.88	52.66	56.62	60.76	65.08	66.19	67.31	68.44	69.58	70.73	71.89	73.06	74.24	75.44	76.64	77.86
11.25	48.21	51.94	55.84	59.93	64.19	65.28	66.39	67.50	68.62	69.76	70.91	72.06	73.23	74.41	75.59	76.79
11.50	47.56	51.23	55.09	59.12	63.32	64.40	65.49	66.58	67.69	68.81	69.94	71.09	72.24	73.40	74.57	75.75
11.75	46.92	50.54	54.34	58.32	62.47	63.53	64.60	65.69	66.78	67.89	69.00	70.13	71.26	72.41	73.57	74.73
12.00	46.29	49.87	53.62	57.54	61.63	62.68	63.74	64.81	65.89	66.98	68.08	69.19	70.31	71.44	72.58	73.73
12.25	45.68	49.21	52.91	56.78	60.81	61.85	62.90	63.95	65.02	66.09	67.18	68.27	69.38	70.49	71.62	72.75
12.50	45.07	48.56	52.21	56.03	60.01	61.04	62.07	63.11	64.16	65.22	66.29	67.37	68.47	69.57	70.68	71.80
12.75	44.49	47.92	51.53	55.30	59.23	60.24	61.26	62.28	63.32	64.37	65.43	66.49	67.57	68.66	69.75	70.86
13.00	43.91	47.30	50.86	54.58	58.46	59.46	60.46	61.48	62.50	63.54	64.58	65.63	66.70	67.77	68.85	69.94
13.25	43.34	46.69	50.21	53.88	57.71	58.69	59.68	60.69	61.70	62.72	63.75	64.79	65.84	66.90	67.96	69.04
13.50	42.79	46.10	49.56	53.19	56.97	57.94	58.92	59.91	60.91	61.92	62.93	63.96	65.00	66.04	67.10	68.16
13.75	42.25	45.51	48.94	52.52	56.25	57.21	58.17	59.15	60.14	61.13	62.14	63.15	64.17	65.20	66.24	67.29
14.00	41.72	44.94	48.32	51.86	55.54	56.49	57.44	58.41	59.38	60.36	61.35	62.36	63.36	64.38	65.41	66.45
14.25	41.20	44.38	47.72	51.21	54.85	55.78	56.73	57.68	58.64	59.61	60.59	61.58	62.57	63.58	64.59	65.62
14.50	40.69	43.83	47.13	50.57	54.17	55.09	56.02	56.96	57.91	58.87	59.84	60.81	61.80	62.79	63.79	64.80
14.75	40.18	43.29	46.55	49.95	53.50	54.41	55.33	56.26	57.20	58.15	59.10	60.07	61.04	62.02	63.01	64.01
15.00	39.69	42.76	45.98	49.34	52.85	53.75	54.66	55.58	56.50	57.44	58.38	59.33	60.29	61.26	62.24	63.23
15.25	39.21	42.24	45.42	48.74	52.21	53.10	54.00	54.90	55.82	56.74	57.67	58.61	59.56	60.52	61.49	62.46
15.50	38.74	41.74	44.88	48.16	51.58	52.46	53.35	54.24	55.15	56.06	56.98	57.91	58.85	59.79	60.75	61.71
15.75	38.28	41.24	44.34	47.58	50.97	51.83	52.71	53.60	54.49	55.39	56.30	57.22	58.14	59.08	60.02	60.97
16.00	37.83	40.75	43.81	47.02	50.36	51.22	52.09	52.96	53.84	54.73	55.63	56.54	57.46	58.38	59.31	60.25
16.25	37.38	40.27	43.30	46.47	49.77	50.62	51.47	52.34	53.21	54.09	54.98	55.88	56.78	57.69	58.61	59.54
16.50	36.95	39.80	42.79	45.93	49.19	50.03	50.87	51.73	52.59	53.46	54.34	55.22	56.12	57.02	57.93	58.85
16.75	36.52	39.34	42.30	45.39	48.62	49.45	50.28	51.13	51.98	52.84	53.71	54.58	55.47	56.36	57.26	58.17
17.00	36.10	38.89	41.81	44.87	48.06	48.88	49.71	50.54	51.38	52.23	53.09	53.96	54.83	55.71	56.60	57.50
17.25	35.69	38.44	41.34	44.36	47.51	48.32	49.14	49.96	50.80	51.64	52.49	53.34	54.21	55.08	55.96	56.84
17.50	35.28	38.01	40.87	43.86	46.98	47.78	48.58	49.40	50.22	51.05	51.89	52.74	53.59	54.45	55.32	56.20
17.75	34.89	37.58	40.41	43.37	46.45	47.24	48.04	48.84	49.66	50.48	51.31	52.15	52.99	53.84	54.70	55.57
18.00	34.50	37.16	39.96	42.88	45.93	46.71	47.50	48.30	49.10	49.92	50.74	51.56	52.40	53.24	54.09	54.95
18.25	34.12	36.75	39.52	42.41	45.42	46.20	46.98	47.77	48.56	49.36	50.18	50.99	51.82	52.65	53.49	54.34
18.50	33.74	36.35	39.08	41.94	44.92	45.69	46.46	47.24	48.03	48.82	49.62	50.43	51.25	52.07	52.91	53.74
18.75	33.37	35.95	38.66	41.48	44.43	45.19	45.95	46.73	47.50	48.29	49.08	49.88	50.69	51.51	52.33	53.16
19.00	33.01	35.56	38.24	41.04	43.95	44.70	45.46	46.22	46.99	47.77	48.55	49.34	50.14	50.95	51.76	52.58
20.00	31.63	34.08	36.64	39.32	42.12	42.83	43.56	44.29	45.03	45.77	46.52	47.28	48.05	48.82	49.60	50.38
25.00	26.01	28.03	30.13	32.34	34.64	35.23	35.82	36.42	37.03	37.64	38.26	38.89	39.52	40.15	40.79	41.44
30.00	21.96	23.66	25.44	27.30	29.24	29.74	30.24	30.75	31.26	31.78	32.30	32.83	33.36	33.89	34.44	34.98

Description: This table shows the yield to maturity of a mortgage purchased at the price shown in the index.

Example: The yield to maturity of a 6.75 %, 15 year mortgage at a price of 80.00 is 10.51 %.

INTEREST RATE, %

PRICE	0.00%	1.00%	2.00%	3.00%	4.00%	4.25%	4.50%	4.75%	5.00%	5.25%	5.50%	5.75%	6.00%	6.25%	6.50%	6.75%
100	0.00	1.00	2.00	3.00	4.00	4.25	4.50	4.75	5.00	5.25	5.50	5.75	6.00	6.25	6.50	6.75
99	.13	1.13	2.14	3.14	4.14	4.39	4.65	4.90	5.15	5.40	5.65	5.90	6.15	6.40	6.65	6.91
98	.26	1.27	2.28	3.29	4.29	4.55	4.80	5.05	5.30	5.56	5.81	6.06	6.31	6.56	6.82	7.07
97	.40	1.41	2.42	3.44	4.45	4.70	4.95	5.21	5.46	5.71	5.97	6.22	6.47	6.73	6.98	7.23
96	.54	1.55	2.57	3.59	4.60	4.86	5.11	5.37	5.62	5.87	6.13	6.38	6.64	6.89	7.15	7.40
95	.68	1.70	2.72	3.74	4.76	5.02	5.27	5.53	5.78	6.04	6.29	6.55	6.81	7.06	7.32	7.57
94	.82	1.85	2.87	3.89	4.92	5.18	5.43	5.69	5.95	6.20	6.46	6.72	6.98	7.23	7.49	7.75
93	.97	2.00	3.02	4.05	5.08	5.34	5.60	5.86	6.11	6.37	6.63	6.89	7.15	7.41	7.66	7.92
92	1.12	2.15	3.18	4.21	5.25	5.51	5.77	6.02	6.28	6.54	6.80	7.06	7.32	7.58	7.84	8.10
91	1.27	2.30	3.34	4.38	5.42	5.68	5.94	6.20	6.46	6.72	6.98	7.24	7.50	7.76	8.02	8.28
90	1.42	2.46	3.50	4.54	5.59	5.85	6.11	6.37	6.63	6.89	7.16	7.42	7.68	7.94	8.21	8.47
89	1.57	2.62	3.66	4.71	5.76	6.02	6.28	6.55	6.81	7.07	7.34	7.60	7.86	8.13	8.39	8.66
88	1.73	2.78	3.83	4.88	5.93	6.20	6.46	6.73	6.99	7.26	7.52	7.79	8.05	8.32	8.58	8.85
87	1.89	2.94	3.99	5.05	6.11	6.38	6.64	6.91	7.18	7.44	7.71	7.97	8.24	8.51	8.78	9.04
86	2.05	3.11	4.17	5.23	6.29	6.56	6.83	7.10	7.36	7.63	7.90	8.17	8.44	8.70	8.97	9.24
85	2.21	3.27	4.34	5.41	6.48	6.75	7.02	7.28	7.55	7.82	8.09	8.36	8.63	8.90	9.17	9.44
84	2.38	3.45	4.52	5.59	6.67	6.94	7.21	7.48	7.75	8.02	8.29	8.56	8.83	9.10	9.38	9.65
83	2.55	3.62	4.70	5.78	6.86	7.13	7.40	7.67	7.94	8.22	8.49	8.76	9.04	9.31	9.58	9.86
82	2.72	3.80	4.88	5.96	7.05	7.33	7.60	7.87	8.15	8.42	8.69	8.97	9.24	9.52	9.79	10.07
81	2.90	3.98	5.07	6.16	7.25	7.53	7.80	8.08	8.35	8.63	8.90	9.18	9.45	9.73	10.01	10.29
80	3.08	4.16	5.25	6.35	7.45	7.73	8.01	8.28	8.56	8.84	9.11	9.39	9.67	9.95	10.23	10.51
79	3.26	4.35	5.45	6.55	7.66	7.94	8.21	8.49	8.77	9.05	9.33	9.61	9.89	10.17	10.45	10.73
78	3.44	4.54	5.64	6.75	7.87	8.15	8.43	8.71	8.99	9.27	9.55	9.83	10.11	10.40	10.68	10.96
77	3.63	4.73	5.84	6.96	8.08	8.36	8.64	8.93	9.21	9.49	9.77	10.06	10.34	10.63	10.91	11.20
76	3.82	4.93	6.05	7.17	8.30	8.58	8.87	9.15	9.43	9.72	10.00	10.29	10.57	10.86	11.15	11.43
75	4.02	5.13	6.26	7.39	8.52	8.81	9.09	9.38	9.66	9.95	10.24	10.52	10.81	11.10	11.39	11.68
74	4.21	5.34	6.47	7.60	8.75	9.03	9.32	9.61	9.90	10.19	10.48	10.76	11.05	11.35	11.64	11.93
73	4.42	5.55	6.68	7.83	8.98	9.27	9.56	9.85	10.14	10.43	10.72	11.01	11.30	11.59	11.89	12.18
72	4.62	5.76	6.90	8.06	9.21	9.51	9.80	10.09	10.38	10.67	10.97	11.26	11.56	11.85	12.15	12.44
71	4.83	5.98	7.13	8.29	9.46	9.75	10.04	10.34	10.63	10.93	11.22	11.52	11.81	12.11	12.41	12.71
70	5.05	6.20	7.36	8.53	9.70	10.00	10.29	10.59	10.89	11.18	11.48	11.78	12.08	12.38	12.68	12.98
69	5.27	6.43	7.59	8.77	9.95	10.25	10.55	10.85	11.15	11.45	11.75	12.05	12.35	12.65	12.95	13.26
68	5.49	6.66	7.83	9.02	10.21	10.51	10.81	11.11	11.41	11.71	12.02	12.32	12.62	12.93	13.23	13.54
67	5.72	6.90	8.08	9.27	10.47	10.77	11.08	11.38	11.68	11.99	12.29	12.60	12.91	13.21	13.52	13.83
66	5.96	7.14	8.33	9.53	10.74	11.05	11.35	11.66	11.96	12.27	12.58	12.89	13.20	13.51	13.82	14.13
65	6.20	7.38	8.58	9.80	11.02	11.32	11.63	11.94	12.25	12.56	12.87	13.18	13.49	13.81	14.12	14.43
64	6.44	7.64	8.85	10.07	11.30	11.61	11.92	12.23	12.54	12.86	13.17	13.48	13.80	14.11	14.43	14.75
63	6.69	7.90	9.12	10.35	11.59	11.90	12.21	12.53	12.84	13.16	13.47	13.79	14.11	14.43	14.75	15.07
62	6.95	8.16	9.39	10.63	11.88	12.20	12.52	12.83	13.15	13.47	13.79	14.11	14.43	14.75	15.07	15.40
61	7.21	8.43	9.67	10.92	12.19	12.51	12.83	13.15	13.47	13.79	14.11	14.43	14.76	15.08	15.41	15.74
60	7.48	8.71	9.96	11.22	12.50	12.82	13.14	13.47	13.79	14.11	14.44	14.77	15.09	15.42	15.75	16.08
59	7.75	9.00	10.26	11.53	12.82	13.14	13.47	13.80	14.12	14.45	14.78	15.11	15.44	15.77	16.11	16.44
58	8.03	9.29	10.56	11.85	13.15	13.48	13.80	14.13	14.46	14.80	15.13	15.46	15.80	16.13	16.47	16.81
57	8.32	9.59	10.87	12.17	13.49	13.82	14.15	14.48	14.82	15.15	15.49	15.82	16.16	16.50	16.84	17.18
56	8.62	9.90	11.19	12.51	13.83	14.17	14.50	14.84	15.18	15.52	15.86	16.20	16.54	16.88	17.23	17.57
55	8.92	10.22	11.52	12.85	14.19	14.53	14.87	15.21	15.55	15.89	16.24	16.58	16.93	17.28	17.62	17.97
54	9.24	10.54	11.86	13.20	14.56	14.90	15.24	15.59	15.93	16.28	16.63	16.98	17.33	17.68	18.03	18.39
53	9.56	10.88	12.21	13.57	14.94	15.28	15.63	15.98	16.33	16.68	17.03	17.39	17.74	18.10	18.45	18.81
52	9.89	11.22	12.57	13.94	15.33	15.68	16.03	16.38	16.74	17.09	17.45	17.81	18.17	18.53	18.89	19.25
51	10.23	11.58	12.94	14.33	15.73	16.09	16.44	16.80	17.16	17.52	17.88	18.24	18.61	18.97	19.34	19.71
50	10.59	11.95	13.32	14.73	16.15	16.51	16.87	17.23	17.59	17.96	18.32	18.69	19.06	19.43	19.80	20.18
49	10.95	12.32	13.72	15.14	16.58	16.94	17.31	17.67	18.04	18.41	18.78	19.16	19.53	19.91	20.29	20.66
48	11.33	12.71	14.13	15.56	17.02	17.39	17.76	18.13	18.51	18.88	19.26	19.64	20.02	20.40	20.78	21.17
47	11.71	13.12	14.55	16.00	17.48	17.86	18.23	18.61	18.99	19.37	19.75	20.14	20.52	20.91	21.30	21.69
46	12.11	13.54	14.99	16.46	17.96	18.34	18.72	19.11	19.49	19.88	20.26	20.65	21.05	21.44	21.84	22.23
45	12.53	13.97	15.44	16.93	18.46	18.84	19.23	19.62	20.01	20.40	20.80	21.19	21.59	21.99	22.39	22.80
44	12.96	14.42	15.91	17.42	18.97	19.36	19.76	20.15	20.55	20.95	21.35	21.75	22.16	22.56	22.97	23.38
43	13.40	14.88	16.39	17.93	19.51	19.90	20.30	20.70	21.11	21.51	21.92	22.33	22.74	23.16	23.57	23.99
42	13.86	15.36	16.90	18.46	20.06	20.47	20.87	21.28	21.69	22.10	22.52	22.94	23.36	23.78	24.20	24.63
41	14.34	15.87	17.42	19.02	20.64	21.05	21.47	21.88	22.30	22.72	23.14	23.57	23.99	24.42	24.85	25.29
40	14.84	16.39	17.97	19.59	21.24	21.66	22.08	22.51	22.93	23.36	23.79	24.23	24.66	25.10	25.54	25.98
39	15.36	16.93	18.54	20.19	21.87	22.30	22.73	23.16	23.60	24.03	24.47	24.91	25.36	25.80	26.25	26.71
35	17.67	19.37	21.10	22.88	24.71	25.17	25.64	26.11	26.58	27.06	27.54	28.02	28.50	28.99	29.48	29.98
30	21.28	23.17	25.12	27.12	29.19	29.72	30.25	30.78	31.32	31.86	32.41	32.96	33.51	34.07	34.63	35.20
25	26.11	28.29	30.55	32.89	35.31	35.93	36.55	37.18	37.81	38.45	39.09	39.74	40.40	41.05	41.72	42.39
20	33.08	35.72	38.47	41.34	44.31	45.07	45.84	46.62	47.40	48.19	48.98	49.79	50.60	51.41	52.24	53.07
15	44.38	47.83	51.45	55.23	59.16	60.17	61.19	62.22	63.25	64.30	65.36	66.42	67.50	68.59	69.68	70.79
10	66.66	71.81	77.22	82.87	88.76	90.27	91.79	93.34	94.89	96.46	98.05	99.65	101.26	102.89	104.53	106.19

MORTGAGE PRICE

15 YEARS

Description: This table shows the price to pay for a monthly payment mortgage loan at the yield rate.

Example: The price of a 10.75 %, 15 year mortgage loan to yield 8.00 % to maturity is $ 117.30.

YIELD	7.00%	7.25%	7.50%	7.75%	8.00%	8.25%	8.50%	8.75%	9.00%	9.25%	9.50%	9.75%	10.00%	10.25%	10.50%	10.75%
0.00	161.79	164.32	166.86	169.43	172.02	174.63	177.25	179.90	182.57	185.25	187.96	190.69	193.43	196.19	198.97	201.77
1.00	150.18	152.53	154.89	157.27	159.68	162.10	164.54	166.99	169.47	171.96	174.48	177.00	179.55	182.12	184.70	187.29
2.00	139.68	141.86	144.06	146.27	148.51	150.76	153.03	155.31	157.62	159.93	162.27	164.62	166.99	169.38	171.78	174.19
3.00	130.16	132.19	134.24	136.30	138.38	140.48	142.60	144.73	146.87	149.03	151.21	153.40	155.61	157.83	160.07	162.32
4.00	121.51	123.41	125.32	127.25	129.20	131.16	133.13	135.12	137.12	139.14	141.17	143.22	145.28	147.35	149.44	151.54
4.25	119.48	121.35	123.23	125.12	127.03	128.96	130.90	132.86	134.83	136.81	138.81	140.82	142.85	144.89	146.94	149.01
4.50	117.49	119.33	121.18	123.04	124.92	126.82	128.73	130.65	132.59	134.54	136.50	138.48	140.47	142.48	144.50	146.53
4.75	115.56	117.36	119.18	121.01	122.86	124.72	126.60	128.49	130.40	132.32	134.25	136.19	138.15	140.13	142.11	144.11
5.00	113.66	115.44	117.23	119.03	120.85	122.68	124.53	126.39	128.26	130.15	132.05	133.96	135.89	137.83	139.78	141.75
5.25	111.81	113.56	115.32	117.09	118.88	120.68	122.50	124.33	126.17	128.03	129.90	131.78	133.68	135.59	137.51	139.44
5.50	110.00	111.72	113.45	115.20	116.96	118.73	120.52	122.32	124.13	125.96	127.80	129.65	131.52	133.40	135.29	137.19
5.75	108.24	109.93	111.63	113.35	115.08	116.83	118.58	120.36	122.14	123.94	125.75	127.57	129.41	131.25	133.11	134.99
6.00	106.51	108.18	109.85	111.54	113.25	114.97	116.70	118.44	120.19	121.96	123.74	125.54	127.34	129.16	130.99	132.84
6.25	104.83	106.47	108.12	109.78	111.46	113.15	114.85	116.56	118.29	120.03	121.79	123.55	125.33	127.12	128.92	130.73
6.50	103.18	104.79	106.42	108.06	109.71	111.37	113.04	114.73	116.43	118.15	119.87	121.61	123.36	125.12	126.90	128.68
6.75	101.57	103.16	104.76	106.37	107.99	109.63	111.28	112.94	114.62	116.30	118.00	119.71	121.44	123.17	124.92	126.67
7.00	100.00	101.56	103.14	104.72	106.32	107.93	109.56	111.19	112.84	114.50	116.18	117.86	119.56	121.26	122.98	124.71
7.25	98.46	100.00	101.55	103.11	104.69	106.27	107.87	109.49	111.11	112.74	114.39	116.05	117.72	119.40	121.09	122.79
7.50	96.96	98.47	100.00	101.54	103.09	104.65	106.23	107.81	109.41	111.02	112.64	114.28	115.92	117.58	119.24	120.92
7.75	95.49	96.98	98.48	100.00	101.53	103.07	104.62	106.18	107.75	109.34	110.94	112.55	114.16	115.80	117.44	119.09
8.00	94.05	95.52	97.00	98.50	100.00	101.52	103.04	104.58	106.13	107.70	109.27	110.85	112.45	114.05	115.67	117.30
8.25	92.65	94.10	95.55	97.02	98.51	100.00	101.50	103.02	104.55	106.09	107.64	109.20	110.77	112.35	113.94	115.54
8.50	91.28	92.70	94.14	95.59	97.05	98.52	100.00	101.49	103.00	104.51	106.04	107.58	109.13	110.68	112.25	113.83
8.75	89.93	91.34	92.75	94.18	95.62	97.07	98.53	100.00	101.48	102.98	104.48	105.99	107.52	109.06	110.60	112.16
9.00	88.62	90.00	91.40	92.80	94.22	95.65	97.09	98.54	100.00	101.47	102.95	104.45	105.95	107.46	108.99	110.52
9.25	87.33	88.70	90.07	91.46	92.85	94.26	95.68	97.11	98.55	100.00	101.46	102.93	104.41	105.90	107.40	108.92
9.50	86.08	87.42	88.78	90.14	91.52	92.91	94.30	95.71	97.13	98.56	100.00	101.45	102.91	104.38	105.86	107.35
9.75	84.85	86.17	87.51	88.85	90.21	91.58	92.96	94.34	95.74	97.15	98.57	100.00	101.44	102.89	104.35	105.81
10.00	83.64	84.95	86.27	87.59	88.93	90.28	91.64	93.01	94.39	95.77	97.17	98.58	100.00	101.43	102.87	104.31
10.25	82.47	83.75	85.05	86.36	87.68	89.01	90.35	91.70	93.06	94.43	95.80	97.19	98.59	100.00	101.42	102.84
10.50	81.31	82.58	83.86	85.15	86.45	87.76	89.08	90.42	91.76	93.11	94.47	95.84	97.21	98.60	100.00	101.41
10.75	80.18	81.44	82.70	83.97	85.25	86.55	87.85	89.16	90.48	91.81	93.16	94.51	95.87	97.23	98.61	100.00
11.00	79.08	80.32	81.56	82.82	84.08	85.35	86.64	87.93	89.24	90.55	91.87	93.20	94.55	95.90	97.26	98.62
11.25	78.00	79.22	80.45	81.68	82.93	84.19	85.46	86.73	88.02	89.31	90.62	91.93	93.25	94.59	95.93	97.28
11.50	76.94	78.14	79.35	80.58	81.81	83.05	84.30	85.56	86.82	88.10	89.39	90.68	91.99	93.30	94.62	95.96
11.75	75.91	77.09	78.29	79.49	80.70	81.93	83.16	84.40	85.65	86.92	88.18	89.46	90.75	92.05	93.35	94.66
12.00	74.89	76.06	77.24	78.43	79.63	80.83	82.05	83.28	84.51	85.75	87.01	88.27	89.54	90.82	92.10	93.40
12.25	73.90	75.05	76.22	77.39	78.57	79.76	80.96	82.17	83.39	84.62	85.85	87.10	88.35	89.61	90.88	92.16
12.50	72.93	74.06	75.21	76.37	77.54	78.71	79.90	81.09	82.29	83.50	84.72	85.95	87.19	88.43	89.69	90.95
12.75	71.97	73.10	74.23	75.37	76.52	77.68	78.85	80.03	81.22	82.41	83.62	84.83	86.05	87.28	88.51	89.76
13.00	71.04	72.15	73.27	74.39	75.53	76.68	77.83	78.99	80.16	81.34	82.53	83.73	84.93	86.15	87.37	88.60
13.25	70.13	71.22	72.32	73.44	74.56	75.69	76.83	77.98	79.13	80.30	81.47	82.65	83.84	85.04	86.24	87.46
13.50	69.23	70.31	71.40	72.50	73.61	74.72	75.85	76.98	78.12	79.27	80.43	81.59	82.77	83.95	85.14	86.34
13.75	68.35	69.42	70.50	71.58	72.67	73.78	74.89	76.00	77.13	78.27	79.41	80.56	81.72	82.89	84.06	85.24
14.00	67.49	68.55	69.61	70.68	71.76	72.85	73.94	75.05	76.16	77.28	78.41	79.55	80.69	81.84	83.00	84.17
14.25	66.65	67.69	68.74	69.80	70.86	71.94	73.02	74.11	75.21	76.32	77.43	78.55	79.68	80.82	81.97	83.12
14.50	65.82	66.85	67.89	68.93	69.99	71.05	72.12	73.19	74.28	75.37	76.47	77.58	78.70	79.82	80.95	82.09
14.75	65.01	66.03	67.05	68.08	69.12	70.17	71.23	72.29	73.36	74.44	75.53	76.63	77.73	78.84	79.96	81.08
15.00	64.22	65.22	66.23	67.25	68.28	69.32	70.36	71.41	72.47	73.54	74.61	75.69	76.78	77.88	78.98	80.09
15.25	63.44	64.43	65.43	66.44	67.45	68.48	69.51	70.55	71.59	72.64	73.71	74.77	75.85	76.93	78.02	79.12
15.50	62.68	63.66	64.65	65.64	66.64	67.65	68.67	69.70	70.73	71.77	72.82	73.88	74.94	76.01	77.09	78.17
15.75	61.93	62.90	63.87	64.86	65.85	66.85	67.85	68.87	69.89	70.91	71.95	72.99	74.04	75.10	76.17	77.24
16.00	61.20	62.15	63.12	64.09	65.07	66.05	67.05	68.05	69.06	70.08	71.10	72.13	73.17	74.21	75.26	76.32
16.25	60.48	61.42	62.38	63.34	64.30	65.28	66.26	67.25	68.25	69.25	70.26	71.28	72.31	73.34	74.38	75.43
16.50	59.77	60.71	61.65	62.60	63.55	64.52	65.49	66.47	67.45	68.44	69.44	70.45	71.46	72.48	73.51	74.55
16.75	59.08	60.00	60.93	61.87	62.82	63.77	64.73	65.70	66.67	67.65	68.64	69.63	70.64	71.65	72.66	73.68
17.00	58.40	59.32	60.23	61.16	62.10	63.04	63.99	64.94	65.90	66.87	67.85	68.83	69.82	70.82	71.83	72.84
17.25	57.74	58.64	59.55	60.46	61.39	62.32	63.26	64.20	65.15	66.11	67.08	68.05	69.03	70.01	71.01	72.01
17.50	57.08	57.98	58.87	59.78	60.69	61.61	62.54	63.47	64.42	65.36	66.32	67.28	68.25	69.22	70.20	71.19
17.75	56.44	57.32	58.21	59.11	60.01	60.92	61.84	62.76	63.69	64.63	65.57	66.52	67.48	68.44	69.41	70.39
18.00	55.81	56.68	57.56	58.45	59.34	60.24	61.15	62.06	62.98	63.91	64.84	65.78	66.73	67.68	68.64	69.61
18.25	55.20	56.06	56.93	57.80	58.69	59.57	60.47	61.37	62.28	63.20	64.12	65.05	65.99	66.93	67.88	68.84
18.50	54.59	55.44	56.30	57.17	58.04	58.92	59.81	60.70	61.60	62.51	63.42	64.34	65.27	66.20	67.14	68.08
18.75	53.99	54.84	55.69	56.54	57.41	58.28	59.16	60.04	60.93	61.83	62.73	63.64	64.55	65.48	66.40	67.34
19.00	53.41	54.24	55.09	55.93	56.79	57.65	58.52	59.39	60.27	61.16	62.05	62.95	63.86	64.77	65.69	66.61
20.00	51.18	51.98	52.78	53.59	54.41	55.24	56.07	56.91	57.75	58.60	59.46	60.32	61.19	62.06	62.94	63.82
25.00	42.09	42.75	43.41	44.08	44.75	45.43	46.11	46.80	47.49	48.19	48.90	49.61	50.32	51.04	51.76	52.49
30.00	35.53	36.09	36.65	37.21	37.78	38.35	38.93	39.51	40.09	40.68	41.28	41.88	42.48	43.09	43.70	44.31

Description: This table shows the yield to maturity of a mortgage purchased at the price shown in the index.

Example: The yield to maturity of a 10.75 %, 15 year mortgage at a price of 113.00 is 8.62 %.

INTEREST RATE, %

PRICE	7.00%	7.25%	7.50%	7.75%	8.00%	8.25%	8.50%	8.75%	9.00%	9.25%	9.50%	9.75%	10.00%	10.25%	10.50%	10.75%
145	1.48	1.69	1.90	2.12	2.33	2.54	2.76	2.97	3.18	3.39	3.60	3.81	4.02	4.23	4.44	4.65
140	1.96	2.18	2.40	2.61	2.83	3.04	3.26	3.47	3.69	3.90	4.12	4.33	4.55	4.76	4.97	5.18
135	2.47	2.69	2.91	3.13	3.35	3.57	3.79	4.01	4.23	4.44	4.66	4.88	5.09	5.31	5.53	5.74
130	3.01	3.24	3.46	3.68	3.90	4.13	4.35	4.57	4.79	5.01	5.23	5.45	5.67	5.89	6.11	6.33
129	3.12	3.35	3.57	3.79	4.02	4.24	4.46	4.69	4.91	5.13	5.35	5.57	5.79	6.01	6.24	6.46
128	3.24	3.46	3.68	3.91	4.13	4.36	4.58	4.80	5.03	5.25	5.47	5.69	5.91	6.14	6.36	6.58
127	3.35	3.57	3.80	4.02	4.25	4.47	4.70	4.92	5.15	5.37	5.59	5.81	6.04	6.26	6.48	6.70
126	3.46	3.69	3.92	4.14	4.37	4.59	4.82	5.04	5.27	5.49	5.71	5.94	6.16	6.38	6.61	6.83
125	3.58	3.81	4.03	4.26	4.49	4.71	4.94	5.16	5.39	5.61	5.84	6.06	6.29	6.51	6.73	6.96
124	3.70	3.92	4.15	4.38	4.61	4.83	5.06	5.29	5.51	5.74	5.96	6.19	6.41	6.64	6.86	7.09
123	3.82	4.04	4.27	4.50	4.73	4.96	5.18	5.41	5.64	5.86	6.09	6.32	6.54	6.77	6.99	7.22
122	3.94	4.17	4.39	4.62	4.85	5.08	5.31	5.54	5.76	5.99	6.22	6.44	6.67	6.90	7.12	7.35
121	4.06	4.29	4.52	4.75	4.98	5.20	5.43	5.66	5.89	6.12	6.35	6.57	6.80	7.03	7.26	7.48
120	4.18	4.41	4.64	4.87	5.10	5.33	5.56	5.79	6.02	6.25	6.48	6.71	6.94	7.16	7.39	7.62
119	4.30	4.54	4.77	5.00	5.23	5.46	5.69	5.92	6.15	6.38	6.61	6.84	7.07	7.30	7.53	7.76
118	4.43	4.66	4.90	5.13	5.36	5.59	5.82	6.05	6.28	6.51	6.75	6.98	7.21	7.44	7.67	7.90
117	4.56	4.79	5.02	5.26	5.49	5.72	5.95	6.19	6.42	6.65	6.88	7.11	7.34	7.58	7.81	8.04
116	4.69	4.92	5.15	5.39	5.62	5.86	6.09	6.32	6.55	6.79	7.02	7.25	7.48	7.72	7.95	8.18
115	4.82	5.05	5.29	5.52	5.76	5.99	6.22	6.46	6.69	6.93	7.16	7.39	7.63	7.86	8.09	8.32
114	4.95	5.19	5.42	5.66	5.89	6.13	6.36	6.60	6.83	7.07	7.30	7.53	7.77	8.00	8.24	8.47
113	5.08	5.32	5.56	5.79	6.03	6.27	6.50	6.74	6.97	7.21	7.44	7.68	7.91	8.15	8.38	8.62
112	5.22	5.46	5.69	5.93	6.17	6.41	6.64	6.88	7.12	7.35	7.59	7.82	8.06	8.30	8.53	8.77
111	5.36	5.60	5.83	6.07	6.31	6.55	6.79	7.02	7.26	7.50	7.74	7.97	8.21	8.45	8.68	8.92
110	5.50	5.74	5.97	6.21	6.45	6.69	6.93	7.17	7.41	7.65	7.88	8.12	8.36	8.60	8.84	9.08
109	5.64	5.88	6.12	6.36	6.60	6.84	7.08	7.32	7.56	7.80	8.04	8.28	8.51	8.75	8.99	9.23
108	5.78	6.02	6.26	6.50	6.74	6.99	7.23	7.47	7.71	7.95	8.19	8.43	8.67	8.91	9.15	9.39
107	5.92	6.17	6.41	6.65	6.89	7.14	7.38	7.62	7.86	8.10	8.34	8.59	8.83	9.07	9.31	9.55
106	6.07	6.31	6.56	6.80	7.04	7.29	7.53	7.77	8.02	8.26	8.50	8.74	8.99	9.23	9.47	9.71
105	6.22	6.46	6.71	6.95	7.20	7.44	7.69	7.93	8.17	8.42	8.66	8.90	9.15	9.39	9.64	9.88
104	6.37	6.62	6.86	7.11	7.35	7.60	7.84	8.09	8.33	8.58	8.82	9.07	9.31	9.56	9.80	10.05
103	6.52	6.77	7.02	7.26	7.51	7.76	8.00	8.25	8.49	8.74	8.99	9.23	9.48	9.73	9.97	10.22
102	6.68	6.93	7.17	7.42	7.67	7.92	8.16	8.41	8.66	8.91	9.15	9.40	9.65	9.90	10.14	10.39
101	6.84	7.08	7.33	7.58	7.83	8.08	8.33	8.58	8.83	9.07	9.32	9.57	9.82	10.07	10.32	10.57
100	7.00	7.25	7.50	7.75	8.00	8.25	8.50	8.75	9.00	9.25	9.50	9.75	10.00	10.25	10.50	10.75
99	7.16	7.41	7.66	7.91	8.16	8.41	8.66	8.92	9.17	9.42	9.67	9.92	10.17	10.42	10.67	10.93
98	7.32	7.57	7.83	8.08	8.33	8.58	8.84	9.09	9.34	9.59	9.85	10.10	10.35	10.60	10.86	11.11
97	7.49	7.74	8.00	8.25	8.50	8.76	9.01	9.26	9.52	9.77	10.03	10.28	10.53	10.79	11.04	11.30
96	7.66	7.91	8.17	8.42	8.68	8.93	9.19	9.44	9.70	9.95	10.21	10.46	10.72	10.98	11.23	11.49
95	7.83	8.09	8.34	8.60	8.85	9.11	9.37	9.62	9.88	10.14	10.39	10.65	10.91	11.17	11.42	11.68
94	8.00	8.26	8.52	8.78	9.04	9.29	9.55	9.81	10.07	10.33	10.58	10.84	11.10	11.36	11.62	11.88
93	8.18	8.44	8.70	8.96	9.22	9.48	9.74	10.00	10.26	10.52	10.78	11.03	11.29	11.55	11.81	12.08
92	8.36	8.62	8.88	9.14	9.40	9.66	9.93	10.19	10.45	10.71	10.97	11.23	11.49	11.75	12.02	12.28
91	8.55	8.81	9.07	9.33	9.59	9.86	10.12	10.38	10.64	10.91	11.17	11.43	11.69	11.96	12.22	12.48
90	8.73	9.00	9.26	9.52	9.79	10.05	10.31	10.58	10.84	11.11	11.37	11.63	11.90	12.16	12.43	12.69
89	8.92	9.19	9.45	9.72	9.98	10.25	10.51	10.78	11.04	11.31	11.58	11.84	12.11	12.37	12.64	12.91
88	9.11	9.38	9.65	9.91	10.18	10.45	10.71	10.98	11.25	11.52	11.78	12.05	12.32	12.59	12.86	13.12
87	9.31	9.58	9.85	10.11	10.38	10.65	10.92	11.19	11.46	11.73	12.00	12.27	12.54	12.81	13.08	13.35
86	9.51	9.78	10.05	10.32	10.59	10.86	11.13	11.40	11.67	11.94	12.21	12.48	12.76	13.03	13.30	13.57
85	9.71	9.98	10.26	10.53	10.80	11.07	11.34	11.61	11.89	12.16	12.43	12.71	12.98	13.25	13.53	13.80
84	9.92	10.19	10.47	10.74	11.01	11.29	11.56	11.83	12.11	12.38	12.66	12.93	13.21	13.48	13.76	14.04
83	10.13	10.41	10.68	10.95	11.23	11.51	11.78	12.06	12.33	12.61	12.89	13.16	13.44	13.72	14.00	14.27
82	10.35	10.62	10.90	11.17	11.45	11.73	12.01	12.28	12.56	12.84	13.12	13.40	13.68	13.96	14.24	14.52
81	10.56	10.84	11.12	11.40	11.68	11.96	12.24	12.52	12.80	13.08	13.36	13.64	13.92	14.20	14.48	14.77
80	10.79	11.07	11.35	11.63	11.91	12.19	12.47	12.75	13.03	13.32	13.60	13.88	14.17	14.45	14.73	15.02
79	11.01	11.30	11.58	11.86	12.14	12.43	12.71	12.99	13.28	13.56	13.85	14.13	14.42	14.70	14.99	15.28
78	11.25	11.53	11.81	12.10	12.38	12.67	12.95	13.24	13.53	13.81	14.10	14.39	14.67	14.96	15.25	15.54
77	11.48	11.77	12.05	12.34	12.63	12.91	13.20	13.49	13.78	14.07	14.36	14.65	14.94	15.23	15.52	15.81
76	11.72	12.01	12.30	12.59	12.88	13.17	13.46	13.75	14.04	14.33	14.62	14.91	15.20	15.50	15.79	16.08
75	11.97	12.26	12.55	12.84	13.13	13.42	13.72	14.01	14.30	14.59	14.89	15.18	15.48	15.77	16.07	16.37
74	12.22	12.51	12.80	13.10	13.39	13.69	13.98	14.28	14.57	14.87	15.16	15.46	15.76	16.06	16.35	16.65
70	13.28	13.58	13.88	14.19	14.49	14.80	15.10	15.41	15.71	16.02	16.32	16.63	16.94	17.25	17.56	17.87
65	14.75	15.07	15.38	15.70	16.02	16.34	16.66	16.98	17.30	17.62	17.94	18.26	18.59	18.91	19.24	19.56
60	16.41	16.75	17.08	17.41	17.75	18.09	18.42	18.76	19.10	19.44	19.78	20.12	20.46	20.81	21.15	21.50
55	18.33	18.68	19.03	19.39	19.74	20.10	20.46	20.82	21.18	21.54	21.90	22.26	22.63	23.00	23.36	23.73
50	20.55	20.93	21.31	21.69	22.07	22.45	22.84	23.22	23.61	24.00	24.39	24.78	25.17	25.57	25.96	26.36
45	23.20	23.61	24.02	24.43	24.84	25.26	25.67	26.09	26.51	26.94	27.36	27.79	28.21	28.64	29.08	29.51
40	26.43	26.87	27.32	27.77	28.23	28.69	29.14	29.61	30.07	30.54	31.00	31.48	31.95	32.42	32.90	33.38
35	30.47	30.97	31.48	31.98	32.49	33.01	33.52	34.04	34.56	35.08	35.61	36.14	36.68	37.21	37.75	38.29

Description: This table shows the price to pay for a monthly payment mortgage loan at the yield rate.

Example: The price of a 15.00 %, 15 year mortgage loan to yield 8.00 % to maturity is $ 146.45.

INTEREST RATE, %

YIELD	11.00%	11.25%	11.50%	11.75%	12.00%	12.25%	12.50%	12.75%	13.00%	13.25%	13.50%	13.75%	14.00%	14.25%	14.50%	15.00%
0.00	204.59	207.42	210.27	213.14	216.03	218.93	221.85	224.79	227.74	230.71	233.70	236.70	239.71	242.74	245.79	251.93
1.00	189.91	192.54	195.19	197.85	200.53	203.23	205.94	208.66	211.40	214.16	216.93	219.72	222.52	225.33	228.16	233.85
2.00	176.62	179.07	181.53	184.01	186.50	189.01	191.53	194.07	196.62	199.18	201.76	204.35	206.95	209.57	212.20	217.49
3.00	164.59	166.87	169.16	171.47	173.79	176.13	178.48	180.84	183.21	185.60	188.00	190.42	192.84	195.28	197.73	202.67
4.00	153.66	155.79	157.93	160.09	162.25	164.43	166.63	168.83	171.05	173.28	175.52	177.78	180.04	182.32	184.60	189.21
4.25	151.09	153.18	155.29	157.41	159.54	161.68	163.84	166.01	168.19	170.38	172.58	174.80	177.03	179.27	181.52	186.05
4.50	148.58	150.63	152.71	154.79	156.89	158.99	161.12	163.25	165.39	167.55	169.72	171.90	174.09	176.29	178.50	182.95
4.75	146.12	148.15	150.19	152.23	154.30	156.37	158.46	160.55	162.66	164.78	166.92	169.06	171.21	173.38	175.55	179.93
5.00	143.73	145.72	147.72	149.74	151.77	153.81	155.86	157.92	160.00	162.08	164.18	166.29	168.41	170.53	172.67	176.99
5.25	141.39	143.35	145.32	147.30	149.30	151.30	153.32	155.35	157.39	159.44	161.51	163.58	165.66	167.76	169.86	174.10
5.50	139.10	141.03	142.97	144.92	146.88	148.86	150.84	152.84	154.85	156.87	158.90	160.94	162.99	165.05	167.12	171.29
5.75	136.87	138.77	140.68	142.60	144.53	146.47	148.42	150.39	152.36	154.35	156.35	158.35	160.37	162.40	164.44	168.54
6.00	134.69	136.56	138.43	140.32	142.22	144.14	146.06	147.99	149.94	151.89	153.86	155.83	157.82	159.81	161.82	165.86
6.25	132.56	134.40	136.24	138.10	139.97	141.86	143.75	145.65	147.56	149.49	151.42	153.37	155.32	157.28	159.26	163.23
6.50	130.48	132.29	134.10	135.93	137.77	139.63	141.49	143.36	145.25	147.14	149.04	150.96	152.88	154.81	156.75	160.67
6.75	128.44	130.22	132.01	133.81	135.63	137.45	139.28	141.13	142.98	144.84	146.72	148.60	150.49	152.40	154.31	158.16
7.00	126.45	128.21	129.97	131.74	133.53	135.32	137.13	138.94	140.77	142.60	144.45	146.30	148.16	150.04	151.92	155.71
7.25	124.51	126.23	127.97	129.72	131.47	133.24	135.02	136.80	138.60	140.41	142.22	144.05	145.89	147.73	149.58	153.32
7.50	122.61	124.31	126.02	127.74	129.47	131.21	132.96	134.72	136.49	138.27	140.05	141.85	143.66	145.48	147.30	150.98
7.75	120.75	122.42	124.11	125.80	127.50	129.22	130.94	132.67	134.42	136.17	137.93	139.70	141.48	143.27	145.07	148.69
8.00	118.93	120.58	122.24	123.91	125.59	127.27	128.97	130.68	132.40	134.12	135.86	137.60	139.35	141.12	142.89	146.45
8.25	117.16	118.78	120.41	122.06	123.71	125.37	127.05	128.73	130.42	132.12	133.83	135.55	137.27	139.01	140.75	144.27
8.50	115.42	117.02	118.63	120.25	121.88	123.51	125.16	126.82	128.48	130.16	131.84	133.54	135.24	136.95	138.67	142.13
8.75	113.72	115.30	116.88	118.48	120.08	121.70	123.32	124.95	126.59	128.24	129.90	131.57	133.25	134.93	136.63	140.04
9.00	112.06	113.61	115.18	116.75	118.33	119.92	121.52	123.13	124.74	126.37	128.01	129.65	131.30	132.96	134.63	137.99
9.25	110.44	111.97	113.51	115.05	116.61	118.18	119.76	121.34	122.94	124.54	126.15	127.77	129.40	131.03	132.68	135.99
9.50	108.85	110.35	111.87	113.40	114.93	116.48	118.03	119.59	121.17	122.75	124.33	125.93	127.53	129.15	130.77	134.03
9.75	107.29	108.78	110.27	111.78	113.29	114.81	116.35	117.89	119.43	120.99	122.56	124.13	125.71	127.30	128.90	132.12
10.00	105.77	107.23	108.71	110.19	111.68	113.19	114.70	116.21	117.74	119.28	120.82	122.37	123.93	125.50	127.07	130.24
10.25	104.28	105.72	107.18	108.64	110.11	111.59	113.08	114.58	116.08	117.60	119.12	120.65	122.18	123.73	125.28	128.41
10.50	102.82	104.25	105.68	107.12	108.57	110.03	111.50	112.98	114.46	115.95	117.45	118.96	120.48	122.00	123.53	126.61
10.75	101.40	102.80	104.21	105.64	107.07	108.51	109.95	111.41	112.87	114.34	115.82	117.31	118.80	120.31	121.82	124.86
11.00	100.00	101.39	102.78	104.18	105.59	107.01	108.44	109.88	111.32	112.77	114.23	115.70	117.17	118.65	120.14	123.14
11.25	98.63	100.00	101.38	102.76	104.15	105.55	106.96	108.37	109.80	111.23	112.67	114.11	115.57	117.03	118.50	121.46
11.50	97.30	98.64	100.00	101.36	102.74	104.12	105.51	106.90	108.31	109.72	111.14	112.57	114.00	115.44	116.89	119.81
11.75	95.99	97.32	98.65	100.00	101.35	102.72	104.09	105.46	106.85	108.24	109.64	111.05	112.47	113.89	115.32	118.20
12.00	94.70	96.02	97.34	98.66	100.00	101.34	102.70	104.06	105.42	106.80	108.18	109.57	110.96	112.37	113.78	116.62
12.25	93.45	94.74	96.04	97.36	98.67	100.00	101.33	102.68	104.02	105.38	106.74	108.11	109.49	110.88	112.27	115.07
12.50	92.22	93.49	94.78	96.07	97.37	98.68	100.00	101.32	102.65	103.99	105.34	106.69	108.05	109.42	110.79	113.55
12.75	91.01	92.27	93.54	94.82	96.10	97.39	98.69	100.00	101.31	102.63	103.96	105.30	106.64	107.99	109.34	112.07
13.00	89.83	91.08	92.33	93.59	94.86	96.13	97.41	98.70	100.00	101.30	102.61	103.93	105.26	106.59	107.92	110.62
13.25	88.68	89.90	91.14	92.38	93.64	94.89	96.16	97.43	98.71	100.00	101.29	102.59	103.90	105.22	106.54	109.19
13.50	87.54	88.76	89.98	91.20	92.44	93.68	94.93	96.19	97.45	98.72	100.00	101.28	102.57	103.87	105.17	107.80
13.75	86.43	87.63	88.84	90.05	91.27	92.50	93.73	94.97	96.22	97.47	98.73	100.00	101.27	102.55	103.84	106.43
14.00	85.35	86.53	87.72	88.92	90.12	91.33	92.55	93.77	95.01	96.25	97.49	98.74	100.00	101.26	102.53	105.09
14.25	84.28	85.45	86.62	87.81	88.99	90.19	91.39	92.60	93.82	95.04	96.27	97.51	98.75	100.00	101.25	103.78
14.50	83.24	84.39	85.55	86.72	87.89	89.07	90.26	91.46	92.66	93.87	95.08	96.30	97.53	98.76	100.00	102.50
14.75	82.21	83.35	84.50	85.65	86.81	87.98	89.15	90.33	91.52	92.71	93.91	95.12	96.33	97.55	98.77	101.24
15.00	81.21	82.33	83.47	84.61	85.75	86.90	88.06	89.23	90.40	91.58	92.76	93.96	95.15	96.36	97.56	100.00
15.25	80.23	81.34	82.46	83.58	84.71	85.85	87.00	88.15	89.31	90.47	91.64	92.82	94.00	95.19	96.38	98.79
15.50	79.26	80.36	81.46	82.58	83.69	84.82	85.95	87.09	88.23	89.38	90.54	91.70	92.87	94.04	95.22	97.60
15.75	78.32	79.40	80.49	81.59	82.70	83.81	84.92	86.05	87.18	88.32	89.46	90.61	91.76	92.92	94.09	96.44
16.00	77.39	78.46	79.54	80.62	81.72	82.81	83.92	85.03	86.15	87.27	88.40	89.53	90.67	91.82	92.97	95.29
16.25	76.48	77.54	78.60	79.68	80.76	81.84	82.93	84.03	85.13	86.24	87.36	88.48	89.61	90.74	91.88	94.17
16.50	75.59	76.63	77.69	78.75	79.81	80.89	81.97	83.05	84.14	85.24	86.34	87.45	88.56	89.68	90.81	93.08
16.75	74.71	75.75	76.79	77.84	78.89	79.95	81.02	82.09	83.17	84.25	85.34	86.44	87.54	88.65	89.76	92.00
17.00	73.85	74.88	75.91	76.94	77.98	79.03	80.09	81.15	82.21	83.28	84.36	85.44	86.53	87.63	88.73	90.94
17.25	73.01	74.02	75.04	76.06	77.09	78.13	79.17	80.22	81.27	82.33	83.40	84.47	85.55	86.63	87.71	89.90
17.50	72.18	73.18	74.19	75.20	76.22	77.25	78.28	79.31	80.35	81.40	82.46	83.51	84.58	85.65	86.72	88.89
17.75	71.37	72.36	73.36	74.36	75.37	76.38	77.40	78.42	79.45	80.49	81.53	82.58	83.63	84.68	85.75	87.89
18.00	70.58	71.56	72.54	73.53	74.53	75.53	76.53	77.55	78.57	79.59	80.62	81.65	82.70	83.74	84.79	86.91
18.25	69.80	70.76	71.74	72.72	73.70	74.69	75.69	76.69	77.70	78.71	79.73	80.75	81.78	82.81	83.85	85.95
18.50	69.03	69.99	70.95	71.92	72.89	73.87	74.86	75.85	76.84	77.85	78.85	79.86	80.88	81.90	82.93	85.00
18.75	68.28	69.22	70.18	71.13	72.10	73.07	74.04	75.02	76.01	77.00	77.99	78.99	80.00	81.01	82.03	84.08
19.00	67.54	68.47	69.42	70.36	71.32	72.28	73.24	74.21	75.18	76.16	77.15	78.14	79.13	80.14	81.14	83.17
20.00	64.72	65.61	66.51	67.42	68.34	69.25	70.18	71.11	72.04	72.98	73.92	74.87	75.83	76.79	77.75	79.69
25.00	53.22	53.96	54.70	55.45	56.20	56.96	57.72	58.48	59.25	60.02	60.80	61.58	62.36	63.15	63.94	65.54
30.00	44.93	45.55	46.18	46.81	47.44	48.08	48.72	49.37	50.02	50.67	51.32	51.98	52.64	53.31	53.98	55.33

Description: This table shows the yield to maturity of a mortgage purchased at the price shown in the index.

Example: The yield to maturity of a 15.00 %, 15 year mortgage at a price of 117.00 is 11.93 %.

INTEREST RATE, %

PRICE	11.00%	11.25%	11.50%	11.75%	12.00%	12.25%	12.50%	12.75%	13.00%	13.25%	13.50%	13.75%	14.00%	14.25%	14.50%	15.00%
190	.99	1.18	1.36	1.55	1.74	1.92	2.11	2.29	2.48	2.66	2.84	3.03	3.21	3.39	3.57	3.93
185	1.35	1.54	1.73	1.92	2.11	2.30	2.48	2.67	2.86	3.04	3.23	3.41	3.60	3.78	3.96	4.33
180	1.73	1.92	2.11	2.30	2.49	2.68	2.87	3.06	3.25	3.44	3.63	3.81	4.00	4.18	4.37	4.74
175	2.12	2.32	2.51	2.70	2.90	3.09	3.28	3.47	3.66	3.85	4.04	4.23	4.42	4.60	4.79	5.17
170	2.53	2.73	2.92	3.12	3.31	3.51	3.70	3.89	4.09	4.28	4.47	4.66	4.85	5.04	5.23	5.61
165	2.96	3.16	3.35	3.55	3.75	3.94	4.14	4.34	4.53	4.73	4.92	5.11	5.31	5.50	5.69	6.08
160	3.40	3.60	3.80	4.00	4.20	4.40	4.60	4.80	4.99	5.19	5.39	5.59	5.78	5.98	6.17	6.56
155	3.87	4.07	4.27	4.47	4.68	4.88	5.08	5.28	5.48	5.68	5.88	6.08	6.28	6.48	6.67	7.07
150	4.35	4.56	4.76	4.97	5.17	5.38	5.58	5.79	5.99	6.19	6.39	6.60	6.80	7.00	7.20	7.60
145	4.86	5.07	5.28	5.49	5.69	5.90	6.11	6.32	6.52	6.73	6.93	7.14	7.34	7.55	7.75	8.16
140	5.40	5.61	5.82	6.03	6.24	6.45	6.66	6.87	7.08	7.29	7.50	7.71	7.92	8.13	8.33	8.75
135	5.96	6.17	6.39	6.60	6.82	7.03	7.25	7.46	7.67	7.89	8.10	8.31	8.52	8.74	8.95	9.37
130	6.55	6.77	6.99	7.21	7.43	7.65	7.86	8.08	8.30	8.52	8.73	8.95	9.17	9.38	9.60	10.03
125	7.18	7.40	7.63	7.85	8.07	8.29	8.52	8.74	8.96	9.18	9.40	9.62	9.84	10.06	10.28	10.72
123	7.44	7.67	7.89	8.12	8.34	8.57	8.79	9.01	9.24	9.46	9.68	9.90	10.13	10.35	10.57	11.02
122	7.58	7.80	8.03	8.25	8.48	8.70	8.93	9.15	9.38	9.60	9.82	10.05	10.27	10.49	10.72	11.16
121	7.71	7.94	8.16	8.39	8.62	8.84	9.07	9.29	9.52	9.74	9.97	10.19	10.42	10.64	10.87	11.31
120	7.85	8.08	8.30	8.53	8.76	8.98	9.21	9.44	9.66	9.89	10.11	10.34	10.57	10.79	11.02	11.47
119	7.99	8.21	8.44	8.67	8.90	9.13	9.35	9.58	9.81	10.04	10.26	10.49	10.72	10.94	11.17	11.62
118	8.13	8.36	8.58	8.81	9.04	9.27	9.50	9.73	9.96	10.18	10.41	10.64	10.87	11.09	11.32	11.78
117	8.27	8.50	8.73	8.96	9.19	9.42	9.65	9.88	10.11	10.34	10.56	10.79	11.02	11.25	11.48	11.93
116	8.41	8.64	8.87	9.10	9.34	9.57	9.80	10.03	10.26	10.49	10.72	10.95	11.18	11.41	11.64	12.09
115	8.56	8.79	9.02	9.25	9.49	9.72	9.95	10.18	10.41	10.64	10.87	11.10	11.33	11.57	11.80	12.26
114	8.70	8.94	9.17	9.40	9.64	9.87	10.10	10.33	10.57	10.80	11.03	11.26	11.50	11.73	11.96	12.42
113	8.85	9.09	9.32	9.56	9.79	10.02	10.26	10.49	10.72	10.96	11.19	11.42	11.66	11.89	12.12	12.59
112	9.00	9.24	9.48	9.71	9.95	10.18	10.42	10.65	10.88	11.12	11.35	11.59	11.82	12.06	12.29	12.76
111	9.16	9.39	9.63	9.87	10.10	10.34	10.58	10.81	11.05	11.28	11.52	11.75	11.99	12.22	12.46	12.93
110	9.31	9.55	9.79	10.03	10.26	10.50	10.74	10.97	11.21	11.45	11.68	11.92	12.16	12.39	12.63	13.10
109	9.47	9.71	9.95	10.19	10.43	10.66	10.90	11.14	11.38	11.62	11.85	12.09	12.33	12.57	12.80	13.28
108	9.63	9.87	10.11	10.35	10.59	10.83	11.07	11.31	11.55	11.79	12.03	12.26	12.50	12.74	12.98	13.46
107	9.79	10.03	10.27	10.52	10.76	11.00	11.24	11.48	11.72	11.96	12.20	12.44	12.68	12.92	13.16	13.64
106	9.96	10.20	10.44	10.68	10.93	11.17	11.41	11.65	11.89	12.13	12.38	12.62	12.86	13.10	13.34	13.83
105	10.12	10.37	10.61	10.85	11.10	11.34	11.58	11.83	12.07	12.31	12.56	12.80	13.04	13.28	13.53	14.01
104	10.29	10.54	10.78	11.03	11.27	11.52	11.76	12.00	12.25	12.49	12.74	12.98	13.23	13.47	13.72	14.20
103	10.46	10.71	10.96	11.20	11.45	11.69	11.94	12.19	12.43	12.68	12.92	13.17	13.41	13.66	13.91	14.40
102	10.64	10.89	11.13	11.38	11.63	11.87	12.12	12.37	12.62	12.86	13.11	13.36	13.60	13.85	14.10	14.59
101	10.82	11.06	11.31	11.56	11.81	12.06	12.31	12.56	12.80	13.05	13.30	13.55	13.80	14.05	14.30	14.79
100	11.00	11.25	11.50	11.75	12.00	12.25	12.50	12.75	13.00	13.25	13.50	13.75	14.00	14.25	14.50	15.00
99	11.18	11.43	11.68	11.93	12.18	12.43	12.69	12.94	13.19	13.44	13.69	13.94	14.19	14.45	14.70	15.20
98	11.36	11.62	11.87	12.12	12.37	12.63	12.88	13.13	13.39	13.64	13.89	14.14	14.40	14.65	14.90	15.41
97	11.55	11.81	12.06	12.31	12.57	12.82	13.08	13.33	13.59	13.84	14.10	14.35	14.60	14.86	15.11	15.62
96	11.74	12.00	12.25	12.51	12.77	13.02	13.28	13.53	13.79	14.05	14.30	14.56	14.81	15.07	15.33	15.84
95	11.94	12.19	12.45	12.71	12.97	13.22	13.48	13.74	14.00	14.25	14.51	14.77	15.03	15.29	15.54	16.06
94	12.13	12.39	12.65	12.91	13.17	13.43	13.69	13.95	14.21	14.47	14.73	14.99	15.24	15.50	15.76	16.28
93	12.34	12.60	12.86	13.12	13.38	13.64	13.90	14.16	14.42	14.68	14.94	15.20	15.47	15.73	15.99	16.51
92	12.54	12.80	13.06	13.33	13.59	13.85	14.11	14.38	14.64	14.90	15.16	15.43	15.69	15.95	16.22	16.74
91	12.75	13.01	13.28	13.54	13.80	14.07	14.33	14.60	14.86	15.13	15.39	15.65	15.92	16.18	16.45	16.98
90	12.96	13.22	13.49	13.76	14.02	14.29	14.55	14.82	15.09	15.35	15.62	15.89	16.15	16.42	16.69	17.22
89	13.17	13.44	13.71	13.98	14.24	14.51	14.78	15.05	15.32	15.58	15.85	16.12	16.39	16.66	16.93	17.47
88	13.39	13.66	13.93	14.20	14.47	14.74	15.01	15.28	15.55	15.82	16.09	16.36	16.63	16.90	17.17	17.72
87	13.62	13.89	14.16	14.43	14.70	14.97	15.24	15.52	15.79	16.06	16.33	16.61	16.88	17.15	17.42	17.97
86	13.84	14.12	14.39	14.66	14.94	15.21	15.48	15.76	16.03	16.31	16.58	16.85	17.13	17.40	17.68	18.23
85	14.08	14.35	14.63	14.90	15.18	15.45	15.73	16.00	16.28	16.55	16.83	17.11	17.39	17.66	17.94	18.50
84	14.31	14.59	14.87	15.14	15.42	15.70	15.97	16.25	16.53	16.81	17.09	17.37	17.65	17.93	18.21	18.77
83	14.55	14.83	15.11	15.39	15.67	15.95	16.23	16.51	16.79	17.07	17.35	17.63	17.91	18.19	18.48	19.04
82	14.80	15.08	15.36	15.64	15.92	16.20	16.49	16.77	17.05	17.33	17.62	17.90	18.18	18.47	18.75	19.32
81	15.05	15.33	15.61	15.90	16.18	16.47	16.75	17.03	17.32	17.60	17.89	18.18	18.46	18.75	19.04	19.61
80	15.30	15.59	15.87	16.16	16.45	16.73	17.02	17.31	17.59	17.88	18.17	18.46	18.75	19.03	19.32	19.90
79	15.56	15.85	16.14	16.43	16.71	17.00	17.29	17.58	17.87	18.16	18.45	18.74	19.03	19.33	19.62	20.20
78	15.83	16.12	16.41	16.70	16.99	17.28	17.57	17.86	18.16	18.45	18.74	19.04	19.33	19.62	19.92	20.51
77	16.10	16.39	16.69	16.98	17.27	17.57	17.86	18.15	18.45	18.74	19.04	19.34	19.63	19.93	20.23	20.82
76	16.38	16.67	16.97	17.26	17.56	17.86	18.15	18.45	18.75	19.04	19.34	19.64	19.94	20.24	20.54	21.14
75	16.66	16.96	17.26	17.55	17.85	18.15	18.45	18.75	19.05	19.35	19.65	19.95	20.26	20.56	20.86	21.47
74	16.95	17.25	17.55	17.85	18.15	18.46	18.76	19.06	19.36	19.67	19.97	20.27	20.58	20.89	21.19	21.80
73	17.25	17.55	17.85	18.16	18.46	18.77	19.07	19.38	19.68	19.99	20.30	20.60	20.91	21.22	21.53	22.15
70	18.18	18.49	18.80	19.11	19.43	19.74	20.06	20.37	20.69	21.00	21.32	21.63	21.95	22.27	22.59	23.23
65	19.89	20.22	20.55	20.88	21.21	21.54	21.87	22.20	22.53	22.87	23.20	23.54	23.87	24.21	24.55	25.22
60	21.84	22.19	22.54	22.89	23.24	23.59	23.94	24.30	24.65	25.00	25.36	25.72	26.07	26.43	26.79	27.51

Description: This table shows the price to pay for a monthly payment mortgage loan at the yield rate.

Example: The price of a 6.75 %, 16 year mortgage loan to yield 8.00 % to maturity is $ 92.23.

INTEREST RATE, %

YIELD	0.00%	1.00%	2.00%	3.00%	4.00%	4.25%	4.50%	4.75%	5.00%	5.25%	5.50%	5.75%	6.00%	6.25%	6.50%	6.75%
0.00	100.00	108.25	116.93	126.04	135.55	137.99	140.46	142.96	145.47	148.02	150.59	153.18	155.80	158.44	161.10	163.79
1.00	92.37	100.00	108.02	116.42	125.22	127.47	129.75	132.06	134.38	136.73	139.10	141.50	143.92	146.36	148.82	151.30
2.00	85.52	92.58	100.00	107.78	115.92	118.01	120.12	122.25	124.41	126.58	128.78	131.00	133.23	135.49	137.77	140.07
3.00	79.34	85.89	92.78	100.00	107.55	109.49	111.45	113.43	115.42	117.44	119.48	121.54	123.61	125.71	127.82	129.96
4.00	73.77	79.86	86.27	92.98	100.00	101.80	103.62	105.46	107.32	109.20	111.09	113.00	114.94	116.88	118.85	120.83
4.25	72.47	78.45	84.74	91.33	98.23	100.00	101.79	103.60	105.42	107.26	109.13	111.00	112.90	114.81	116.75	118.69
4.50	71.19	77.07	83.25	89.73	96.50	98.24	100.00	101.78	103.57	105.38	107.21	109.05	110.92	112.80	114.69	116.61
4.75	69.95	75.73	81.80	88.16	94.82	96.53	98.26	100.00	101.76	103.54	105.34	107.15	108.98	110.83	112.69	114.57
5.00	68.74	74.41	80.38	86.64	93.18	94.86	96.55	98.27	100.00	101.75	103.51	105.30	107.09	108.91	110.74	112.59
5.25	67.56	73.14	79.00	85.15	91.58	93.23	94.90	96.58	98.28	100.00	101.74	103.49	105.25	107.04	108.84	110.66
5.50	66.41	71.89	77.65	83.70	90.02	91.64	93.28	94.93	96.61	98.29	100.00	101.72	103.46	105.21	106.98	108.77
5.75	65.28	70.67	76.34	82.28	88.49	90.09	91.70	93.33	94.97	96.63	98.31	100.00	101.71	103.43	105.17	106.93
6.00	64.19	69.48	75.06	80.90	87.01	88.57	90.16	91.76	93.38	95.01	96.66	98.32	100.00	101.70	103.41	105.13
6.25	63.12	68.33	73.80	79.55	85.56	87.10	88.66	90.23	91.82	93.42	95.04	96.66	98.33	100.00	101.68	103.38
6.50	62.07	67.20	72.58	78.23	84.14	85.66	87.19	88.74	90.30	91.88	93.47	95.08	96.71	98.35	100.00	101.67
6.75	61.05	66.09	71.39	76.95	82.76	84.25	85.76	87.28	88.82	90.37	91.94	93.52	95.12	96.73	98.36	100.00
7.00	60.06	65.02	70.23	75.70	81.41	82.88	84.36	85.86	87.37	88.90	90.44	92.00	93.57	95.16	96.76	98.37
7.25	59.09	63.97	69.09	74.47	80.09	81.54	83.00	84.47	85.96	87.46	88.98	90.51	92.06	93.62	95.19	96.78
7.50	58.14	62.94	67.99	73.28	78.81	80.23	81.66	83.11	84.58	86.06	87.55	89.06	90.58	92.12	93.66	95.23
7.75	57.21	61.94	66.90	72.11	77.55	78.95	80.36	81.79	83.23	84.69	86.16	87.64	89.14	90.65	92.17	93.71
8.00	56.31	60.96	65.85	70.97	76.33	77.71	79.10	80.50	81.92	83.35	84.80	86.26	87.73	89.22	90.72	92.23
8.25	55.43	60.00	64.81	69.86	75.13	76.49	77.86	79.24	80.63	82.04	83.47	84.90	86.36	87.82	89.30	90.79
8.50	54.57	59.07	63.81	68.77	73.97	75.30	76.65	78.01	79.38	80.77	82.17	83.58	85.01	86.45	87.91	89.38
8.75	53.72	58.16	62.82	67.71	72.82	74.14	75.46	76.80	78.16	79.52	80.90	82.30	83.70	85.12	86.55	88.00
9.00	52.90	57.27	61.86	66.68	71.71	73.00	74.31	75.63	76.96	78.31	79.66	81.04	82.42	83.82	85.23	86.65
9.25	52.10	56.40	60.92	65.66	70.62	71.89	73.18	74.48	75.79	77.12	78.45	79.80	81.17	82.54	83.93	85.33
9.50	51.31	55.55	60.00	64.67	69.56	70.81	72.08	73.36	74.65	75.95	77.27	78.60	79.95	81.30	82.67	84.05
9.75	50.55	54.72	59.11	63.71	68.52	69.75	71.00	72.26	73.53	74.82	76.12	77.43	78.75	80.09	81.43	82.79
10.00	49.80	53.91	58.23	62.76	67.50	68.72	69.95	71.19	72.44	73.71	74.99	76.28	77.58	78.90	80.23	81.56
10.25	49.06	53.12	57.37	61.84	66.51	67.71	68.92	70.14	71.38	72.62	73.89	75.16	76.44	77.74	79.04	80.36
10.50	48.35	52.34	56.54	60.94	65.54	66.72	67.91	69.12	70.34	71.56	72.81	74.06	75.33	76.60	77.89	79.19
10.75	47.65	51.58	55.72	60.05	64.59	65.75	66.93	68.12	69.32	70.53	71.75	72.99	74.23	75.49	76.76	78.04
11.00	46.96	50.84	54.92	59.19	63.66	64.81	65.97	67.14	68.32	69.52	70.72	71.94	73.17	74.41	75.66	76.92
11.25	46.29	50.12	54.13	58.35	62.75	63.88	65.03	66.18	67.35	68.52	69.71	70.91	72.13	73.35	74.58	75.83
11.50	45.64	49.41	53.37	57.52	61.87	62.98	64.11	65.25	66.40	67.56	68.73	69.91	71.11	72.31	73.53	74.76
11.75	45.00	48.72	52.62	56.72	61.00	62.10	63.21	64.33	65.46	66.61	67.76	68.93	70.11	71.30	72.50	73.71
12.00	44.37	48.04	51.89	55.93	60.15	61.23	62.33	63.44	64.55	65.68	66.82	67.97	69.13	70.31	71.49	72.68
12.25	43.76	47.37	51.17	55.16	59.32	60.39	61.47	62.56	63.66	64.78	65.90	67.03	68.18	69.34	70.50	71.68
12.50	43.16	46.73	50.47	54.40	58.51	59.56	60.63	61.70	62.79	63.89	65.00	66.12	67.25	68.39	69.54	70.70
12.75	42.58	46.09	49.79	53.66	57.71	58.75	59.80	60.87	61.94	63.02	64.11	65.22	66.33	67.46	68.59	69.74
13.00	42.00	45.47	49.12	52.94	56.94	57.96	59.00	60.05	61.10	62.17	63.25	64.34	65.44	66.55	67.67	68.80
13.25	41.44	44.86	48.46	52.23	56.17	57.19	58.21	59.24	60.29	61.34	62.41	63.48	64.56	65.66	66.76	67.88
13.50	40.89	44.27	47.82	51.54	55.43	56.43	57.44	58.46	59.49	60.53	61.58	62.64	63.71	64.79	65.88	66.98
13.75	40.35	43.69	47.19	50.86	54.70	55.69	56.68	57.69	58.71	59.73	60.77	61.81	62.87	63.94	65.01	66.10
14.00	39.83	43.12	46.57	50.20	53.99	54.96	55.94	56.94	57.94	58.95	59.98	61.01	62.05	63.10	64.16	65.24
14.25	39.31	42.56	45.97	49.55	53.29	54.25	55.22	56.20	57.19	58.19	59.20	60.22	61.25	62.29	63.33	64.39
14.50	38.81	42.01	45.38	48.91	52.61	53.55	54.51	55.48	56.46	57.44	58.44	59.45	60.46	61.49	62.52	63.56
14.75	38.31	41.48	44.80	48.29	51.94	52.87	53.82	54.77	55.74	56.71	57.70	58.69	59.69	60.70	61.72	62.76
15.00	37.83	40.95	44.24	47.68	51.28	52.20	53.14	54.08	55.03	56.00	56.97	57.95	58.94	59.94	60.95	61.96
15.25	37.36	40.44	43.68	47.08	50.64	51.55	52.47	53.40	54.34	55.29	56.25	57.22	58.20	59.19	60.18	61.19
15.50	36.89	39.94	43.14	46.50	50.01	50.91	51.82	52.74	53.67	54.61	55.55	56.51	57.48	58.45	59.43	60.43
15.75	36.44	39.44	42.61	45.92	49.39	50.28	51.18	52.09	53.01	53.93	54.87	55.81	56.77	57.73	58.70	59.68
16.00	35.99	38.96	42.09	45.36	48.79	49.67	50.55	51.45	52.36	53.27	54.20	55.13	56.07	57.02	57.98	58.95
16.25	35.55	38.49	41.58	44.81	48.19	49.06	49.94	50.83	51.72	52.63	53.54	54.46	55.39	56.33	57.28	58.24
16.50	35.13	38.03	41.08	44.27	47.61	48.47	49.34	50.22	51.10	51.99	52.90	53.81	54.73	55.65	56.59	57.53
16.75	34.71	37.57	40.58	43.74	47.05	47.89	48.75	49.62	50.49	51.37	52.26	53.16	54.07	54.99	55.91	56.85
17.00	34.30	37.13	40.10	43.23	46.49	47.33	48.17	49.03	49.89	50.76	51.65	52.53	53.43	54.34	55.25	56.17
17.25	33.89	36.69	39.63	42.72	45.94	46.77	47.61	48.45	49.31	50.17	51.04	51.92	52.80	53.70	54.60	55.51
17.50	33.50	36.26	39.17	42.22	45.41	46.23	47.05	47.89	48.73	49.58	50.44	51.31	52.19	53.07	53.97	54.87
17.75	33.11	35.84	38.72	41.73	44.88	45.69	46.51	47.33	48.17	49.01	49.86	50.72	51.59	52.46	53.34	54.23
18.00	32.73	35.43	38.27	41.25	44.37	45.17	45.97	46.79	47.62	48.45	49.29	50.14	50.99	51.86	52.73	53.61
18.25	32.36	35.03	37.84	40.78	43.86	44.65	45.45	46.26	47.07	47.90	48.73	49.57	50.41	51.27	52.13	53.00
18.50	31.99	34.63	37.41	40.32	43.37	44.15	44.94	45.74	46.54	47.36	48.18	49.01	49.84	50.69	51.54	52.40
18.75	31.63	34.25	36.99	39.87	42.88	43.65	44.44	45.22	46.02	46.83	47.64	48.46	49.29	50.12	50.96	51.82
19.00	31.28	33.87	36.58	39.43	42.40	43.17	43.94	44.72	45.51	46.30	47.11	47.92	48.74	49.56	50.40	51.24
20.00	29.94	32.41	35.01	37.74	40.59	41.32	42.06	42.80	43.56	44.32	45.09	45.87	46.65	47.44	48.24	49.04
25.00	24.52	26.55	28.68	30.91	33.24	33.84	34.45	35.06	35.67	36.30	36.93	37.56	38.21	38.85	39.51	40.17
30.00	20.65	22.36	24.15	26.03	27.99	28.50	29.01	29.52	30.04	30.57	31.10	31.63	32.17	32.72	33.27	33.83

MORTGAGE YIELD

Description: This table shows the yield to maturity of a mortgage purchased at the price shown in the index.

Example: The yield to maturity of a 6.75 %, 16 year mortgage at a price of 80.00 is 10.32 %.

PRICE	0.00%	1.00%	2.00%	3.00%	4.00%	4.25%	4.50%	4.75%	5.00%	5.25%	5.50%	5.75%	6.00%	6.25%	6.50%	6.75%
100	0.00	1.00	2.00	3.00	4.00	4.25	4.50	4.75	5.00	5.25	5.50	5.75	6.00	6.25	6.50	6.75
99	.12	1.12	2.13	3.13	4.14	4.39	4.64	4.89	5.14	5.39	5.64	5.89	6.14	6.40	6.65	6.90
98	.25	1.25	2.26	3.27	4.28	4.53	4.78	5.03	5.29	5.54	5.79	6.04	6.30	6.55	6.80	7.05
97	.38	1.39	2.40	3.41	4.42	4.68	4.93	5.18	5.44	5.69	5.94	6.20	6.45	6.70	6.96	7.21
96	.51	1.52	2.54	3.55	4.57	4.82	5.08	5.33	5.59	5.84	6.10	6.35	6.61	6.86	7.12	7.37
95	.64	1.66	2.68	3.70	4.72	4.97	5.23	5.48	5.74	6.00	6.25	6.51	6.76	7.02	7.28	7.53
94	.77	1.80	2.82	3.84	4.87	5.13	5.38	5.64	5.90	6.15	6.41	6.67	6.92	7.18	7.44	7.70
93	.91	1.94	2.96	3.99	5.02	5.28	5.54	5.80	6.05	6.31	6.57	6.83	7.09	7.35	7.61	7.86
92	1.05	2.08	3.11	4.14	5.18	5.44	5.70	5.96	6.22	6.48	6.73	6.99	7.25	7.51	7.77	8.03
91	1.19	2.22	3.26	4.30	5.34	5.60	5.86	6.12	6.38	6.64	6.90	7.16	7.42	7.68	7.95	8.21
90	1.33	2.37	3.41	4.45	5.50	5.76	6.02	6.28	6.55	6.81	7.07	7.33	7.59	7.86	8.12	8.38
89	1.47	2.52	3.56	4.61	5.66	5.92	6.19	6.45	6.71	6.98	7.24	7.51	7.77	8.03	8.30	8.56
88	1.62	2.67	3.72	4.77	5.83	6.09	6.36	6.62	6.89	7.15	7.42	7.68	7.95	8.21	8.48	8.74
87	1.77	2.82	3.88	4.94	6.00	6.26	6.53	6.79	7.06	7.33	7.59	7.86	8.13	8.39	8.66	8.93
86	1.92	2.98	4.04	5.10	6.17	6.43	6.70	6.97	7.24	7.51	7.77	8.04	8.31	8.58	8.85	9.12
85	2.08	3.14	4.20	5.27	6.34	6.61	6.88	7.15	7.42	7.69	7.96	8.23	8.50	8.77	9.04	9.31
84	2.23	3.30	4.37	5.44	6.52	6.79	7.06	7.33	7.60	7.87	8.14	8.42	8.69	8.96	9.23	9.50
83	2.39	3.46	4.54	5.62	6.70	6.97	7.24	7.52	7.79	8.06	8.33	8.61	8.88	9.15	9.43	9.70
82	2.55	3.63	4.71	5.80	6.88	7.16	7.43	7.71	7.98	8.25	8.53	8.80	9.08	9.35	9.63	9.91
81	2.72	3.80	4.89	5.98	7.07	7.35	7.62	7.90	8.17	8.45	8.73	9.00	9.28	9.56	9.83	10.11
80	2.88	3.97	5.06	6.16	7.26	7.54	7.82	8.09	8.37	8.65	8.93	9.20	9.48	9.76	10.04	10.32
79	3.05	4.15	5.25	6.35	7.46	7.74	8.01	8.29	8.57	8.85	9.13	9.41	9.69	9.97	10.25	10.54
78	3.23	4.33	5.43	6.54	7.66	7.94	8.22	8.50	8.78	9.06	9.34	9.62	9.91	10.19	10.47	10.75
77	3.40	4.51	5.62	6.73	7.86	8.14	8.42	8.70	8.99	9.27	9.55	9.84	10.12	10.41	10.69	10.98
76	3.58	4.69	5.81	6.93	8.06	8.35	8.63	8.92	9.20	9.49	9.77	10.06	10.34	10.63	10.92	11.21
75	3.77	4.88	6.01	7.14	8.27	8.56	8.84	9.13	9.42	9.70	9.99	10.28	10.57	10.86	11.15	11.44
74	3.95	5.08	6.21	7.34	8.49	8.77	9.06	9.35	9.64	9.93	10.22	10.51	10.80	11.09	11.38	11.67
73	4.14	5.27	6.41	7.55	8.71	9.00	9.29	9.58	9.87	10.16	10.45	10.74	11.04	11.33	11.62	11.92
72	4.34	5.47	6.62	7.77	8.93	9.22	9.51	9.81	10.10	10.39	10.69	10.98	11.28	11.57	11.87	12.16
71	4.53	5.68	6.83	7.99	9.16	9.45	9.74	10.04	10.33	10.63	10.93	11.22	11.52	11.82	12.12	12.42
70	4.74	5.89	7.05	8.21	9.39	9.69	9.98	10.28	10.58	10.87	11.17	11.47	11.77	12.07	12.37	12.68
69	4.94	6.10	7.27	8.44	9.63	9.93	10.22	10.52	10.82	11.12	11.43	11.73	12.03	12.33	12.64	12.94
68	5.15	6.32	7.49	8.68	9.87	10.17	10.47	10.77	11.08	11.38	11.68	11.99	12.29	12.60	12.90	13.21
67	5.37	6.54	7.72	8.92	10.12	10.42	10.73	11.03	11.34	11.64	11.95	12.25	12.56	12.87	13.18	13.49
66	5.58	6.77	7.96	9.16	10.38	10.68	10.99	11.29	11.60	11.91	12.22	12.53	12.84	13.15	13.46	13.77
65	5.81	7.00	8.20	9.41	10.64	10.94	11.25	11.56	11.87	12.18	12.49	12.81	13.12	13.43	13.75	14.06
64	6.04	7.24	8.45	9.67	10.90	11.21	11.52	11.84	12.15	12.46	12.78	13.09	13.41	13.73	14.04	14.36
63	6.27	7.48	8.70	9.93	11.18	11.49	11.80	12.12	12.43	12.75	13.07	13.39	13.71	14.03	14.35	14.67
62	6.51	7.73	8.96	10.20	11.46	11.77	12.09	12.41	12.73	13.05	13.37	13.69	14.01	14.33	14.66	14.98
61	6.76	7.98	9.22	10.48	11.74	12.06	12.38	12.70	13.03	13.35	13.67	14.00	14.32	14.65	14.98	15.31
60	7.01	8.25	9.50	10.76	12.04	12.36	12.69	13.01	13.33	13.66	13.99	14.32	14.64	14.97	15.31	15.64
59	7.27	8.51	9.78	11.05	12.34	12.67	12.99	13.32	13.65	13.98	14.31	14.64	14.97	15.31	15.64	15.98
58	7.53	8.79	10.06	11.35	12.65	12.98	13.31	13.64	13.98	14.31	14.64	14.98	15.31	15.65	15.99	16.33
57	7.80	9.07	10.36	11.66	12.97	13.31	13.64	13.97	14.31	14.65	14.98	15.32	15.66	16.00	16.35	16.69
56	8.08	9.36	10.66	11.97	13.30	13.64	13.98	14.31	14.65	14.99	15.33	15.68	16.02	16.37	16.71	17.06
55	8.37	9.66	10.97	12.30	13.64	13.98	14.32	14.66	15.01	15.35	15.70	16.04	16.39	16.74	17.09	17.44
54	8.66	9.97	11.29	12.63	13.99	14.33	14.68	15.02	15.37	15.72	16.07	16.42	16.77	17.13	17.48	17.84
53	8.97	10.28	11.62	12.97	14.35	14.70	15.05	15.40	15.75	16.10	16.45	16.81	17.17	17.52	17.88	18.25
52	9.28	10.61	11.96	13.33	14.72	15.07	15.43	15.78	16.14	16.49	16.85	17.21	17.57	17.94	18.30	18.67
51	9.60	10.94	12.31	13.69	15.10	15.46	15.82	16.18	16.54	16.90	17.26	17.63	17.99	18.36	18.73	19.10
50	9.93	11.29	12.67	14.07	15.50	15.86	16.22	16.58	16.95	17.32	17.68	18.05	18.43	18.80	19.17	19.55
49	10.27	11.64	13.04	14.46	15.91	16.27	16.64	17.01	17.38	17.75	18.12	18.50	18.87	19.25	19.63	20.02
48	10.62	12.01	13.42	14.86	16.33	16.70	17.07	17.44	17.82	18.20	18.58	18.96	19.34	19.72	20.11	20.50
47	10.98	12.39	13.82	15.28	16.77	17.14	17.52	17.90	18.28	18.66	19.05	19.43	19.82	20.21	20.60	21.00
46	11.36	12.78	14.23	15.71	17.22	17.60	17.98	18.37	18.76	19.14	19.53	19.93	20.32	20.72	21.12	21.52
45	11.75	13.19	14.66	16.16	17.69	18.08	18.46	18.86	19.25	19.64	20.04	20.44	20.84	21.24	21.65	22.06
44	12.15	13.61	15.10	16.62	18.18	18.57	18.97	19.36	19.76	20.16	20.57	20.97	21.38	21.79	22.20	22.62
43	12.56	14.05	15.56	17.11	18.68	19.08	19.49	19.89	20.30	20.70	21.11	21.53	21.94	22.36	22.78	23.20
42	13.00	14.50	16.04	17.61	19.21	19.62	20.03	20.44	20.85	21.27	21.68	22.10	22.53	22.95	23.38	23.81
41	13.45	14.97	16.53	18.13	19.76	20.17	20.59	21.01	21.43	21.85	22.28	22.71	23.14	23.57	24.01	24.44
40	13.91	15.46	17.05	18.67	20.33	20.76	21.18	21.61	22.04	22.47	22.90	23.34	23.78	24.22	24.66	25.11
39	14.40	15.98	17.59	19.24	20.93	21.36	21.80	22.23	22.67	23.11	23.55	23.99	24.44	24.89	25.35	25.80
35	16.57	18.26	20.00	21.79	23.63	24.10	24.57	25.04	25.52	26.00	26.48	26.97	27.45	27.95	28.44	28.94
30	19.95	21.84	23.80	25.81	27.89	28.42	28.96	29.50	30.04	30.59	31.14	31.69	32.25	32.82	33.39	33.96
25	24.48	26.66	28.93	31.28	33.72	34.34	34.97	35.60	36.24	36.89	37.54	38.20	38.86	39.53	40.20	40.88
20	31.01	33.66	36.42	39.30	42.30	43.07	43.85	44.63	45.42	46.22	47.02	47.84	48.66	49.49	50.32	51.16
15	41.60	45.06	48.69	52.50	56.47	57.49	58.52	59.56	60.61	61.67	62.74	63.82	64.91	66.01	67.12	68.24
10	62.49	67.65	73.08	78.77	84.72	86.24	87.78	89.34	90.92	92.51	94.11	95.73	97.37	99.02	100.69	102.37

Description: This table shows the price to pay for a monthly payment mortgage loan at the yield rate.

Example: The price of a 10.75 %, 16 year mortgage loan to yield 8.00 % to maturity is $ 118.18.

INTEREST RATE, %

YIELD	7.00%	7.25%	7.50%	7.75%	8.00%	8.25%	8.50%	8.75%	9.00%	9.25%	9.50%	9.75%	10.00%	10.25%	10.50%	10.75%
0.00	166.50	169.24	172.00	174.78	177.59	180.41	183.26	186.13	189.03	191.94	194.88	197.84	200.81	203.81	206.83	209.87
1.00	153.81	156.33	158.88	161.45	164.04	166.66	169.29	171.94	174.61	177.31	180.02	182.75	185.50	188.27	191.06	193.87
2.00	142.39	144.73	147.09	149.47	151.87	154.29	156.72	159.18	161.65	164.14	166.66	169.18	171.73	174.30	176.88	179.48
3.00	132.11	134.28	136.47	138.68	140.90	143.14	145.41	147.68	149.98	152.29	154.62	156.97	159.33	161.71	164.11	166.52
4.00	122.83	124.85	126.89	128.94	131.01	133.10	135.20	137.32	139.45	141.60	143.77	145.95	148.15	150.36	152.58	154.83
4.25	120.66	122.64	124.64	126.66	128.69	130.74	132.80	134.89	136.98	139.09	141.22	143.36	145.52	147.70	149.88	152.09
4.50	118.54	120.49	122.45	124.43	126.43	128.44	130.47	132.51	134.57	136.65	138.74	140.85	142.97	145.10	147.25	149.41
4.75	116.47	118.39	120.32	122.26	124.22	126.20	128.19	130.20	132.23	134.27	136.32	138.39	140.47	142.57	144.68	146.81
5.00	114.46	116.34	118.23	120.15	122.07	124.02	125.98	127.95	129.94	131.94	133.96	135.99	138.04	140.10	142.18	144.27
5.25	112.49	114.34	116.20	118.08	119.98	121.89	123.81	125.75	127.71	129.67	131.66	133.66	135.67	137.69	139.73	141.79
5.50	110.57	112.39	114.22	116.07	117.93	119.81	121.70	123.61	125.53	127.46	129.41	131.38	133.35	135.35	137.35	139.37
5.75	108.70	110.48	112.29	114.10	115.93	117.78	119.64	121.51	123.40	125.31	127.22	129.15	131.10	133.05	135.03	137.01
6.00	106.87	108.63	110.40	112.19	113.99	115.80	117.63	119.47	121.33	123.20	125.09	126.98	128.89	130.82	132.76	134.71
6.25	105.09	106.82	108.56	110.32	112.09	113.87	115.67	117.48	119.31	121.15	123.00	124.87	126.75	128.64	130.54	132.46
6.50	103.35	105.05	106.76	108.49	110.23	111.99	113.76	115.54	117.33	119.14	120.97	122.80	124.65	126.51	128.38	130.27
6.75	101.66	103.33	105.01	106.71	108.42	110.15	111.89	113.64	115.41	117.19	118.98	120.78	122.60	124.43	126.28	128.13
7.00	100.00	101.64	103.30	104.97	106.66	108.35	110.06	111.79	113.53	115.28	117.04	118.82	120.61	122.41	124.22	126.04
7.25	98.38	100.00	101.63	103.27	104.93	106.60	108.29	109.98	111.69	113.41	115.15	116.90	118.66	120.43	122.21	124.01
7.50	96.81	98.40	100.00	101.62	103.25	104.89	106.55	108.22	109.90	111.59	113.30	115.02	116.75	118.50	120.25	122.02
7.75	95.26	96.83	98.41	100.00	101.60	103.22	104.85	106.50	108.15	109.82	111.50	113.19	114.89	116.61	118.34	120.08
8.00	93.76	95.30	96.85	98.42	100.00	101.59	103.20	104.81	106.44	108.08	109.74	111.40	113.08	114.77	116.47	118.18
8.25	92.29	93.81	95.34	96.88	98.43	100.00	101.58	103.17	104.77	106.39	108.02	109.66	111.31	112.97	114.64	116.33
8.50	90.86	92.35	93.85	95.37	96.90	98.45	100.00	101.57	103.15	104.74	106.34	107.95	109.58	111.21	112.86	114.52
8.75	89.45	90.92	92.41	93.90	95.41	96.93	98.46	100.00	101.55	103.12	104.70	106.29	107.89	109.50	111.12	112.75
9.00	88.08	89.53	90.99	92.46	93.95	95.44	96.95	98.47	100.00	101.54	103.10	104.66	106.24	107.82	109.42	111.03
9.25	86.75	88.17	89.61	91.06	92.52	93.99	95.48	96.97	98.48	100.00	101.53	103.07	104.62	106.18	107.76	109.34
9.50	85.44	86.84	88.26	89.69	91.13	92.58	94.04	95.51	97.00	98.49	100.00	101.52	103.05	104.58	106.13	107.69
9.75	84.16	85.55	86.94	88.35	89.76	91.19	92.63	94.09	95.55	97.02	98.51	100.00	101.51	103.02	104.55	106.08
10.00	82.91	84.28	85.65	87.04	88.43	89.84	91.26	92.69	94.13	95.58	97.04	98.52	100.00	101.49	103.00	104.51
10.25	81.69	83.04	84.39	85.76	87.13	88.52	89.92	91.33	92.75	94.18	95.62	97.07	98.53	100.00	101.48	102.97
10.50	80.50	81.83	83.16	84.50	85.86	87.23	88.61	89.99	91.39	92.80	94.22	95.65	97.09	98.54	100.00	101.47
10.75	79.34	80.64	81.96	83.28	84.62	85.96	87.32	88.69	90.07	91.46	92.86	94.27	95.68	97.11	98.55	100.00
11.00	78.20	79.48	80.78	82.08	83.40	84.73	86.07	87.42	88.78	90.14	91.52	92.91	94.31	95.72	97.14	98.56
11.25	77.08	78.35	79.63	80.91	82.21	83.52	84.84	86.17	87.51	88.86	90.22	91.59	92.97	94.35	95.75	97.16
11.50	75.99	77.24	78.50	79.77	81.05	82.34	83.64	84.95	86.27	87.60	88.94	90.29	91.65	93.02	94.40	95.79
11.75	74.93	76.16	77.40	78.65	79.91	81.19	82.47	83.76	85.06	86.37	87.70	89.03	90.37	91.72	93.07	94.44
12.00	73.89	75.10	76.32	77.56	78.80	80.06	81.32	82.60	83.88	85.17	86.48	87.79	89.11	90.44	91.78	93.13
12.25	72.87	74.06	75.27	76.49	77.71	78.95	80.20	81.46	82.72	84.00	85.28	86.58	87.88	89.19	90.51	91.84
12.50	71.87	73.05	74.24	75.44	76.65	77.87	79.10	80.34	81.59	82.85	84.11	85.39	86.68	87.97	89.27	90.59
12.75	70.89	72.06	73.23	74.42	75.61	76.81	78.03	79.25	80.48	81.72	82.97	84.23	85.50	86.78	88.06	89.36
13.00	69.94	71.09	72.24	73.41	74.59	75.78	76.98	78.18	79.40	80.62	81.85	83.10	84.35	85.61	86.88	88.15
13.25	69.00	70.14	71.28	72.43	73.59	74.77	75.95	77.14	78.34	79.54	80.76	81.99	83.22	84.46	85.71	86.97
13.50	68.09	69.21	70.33	71.47	72.62	73.78	74.94	76.11	77.30	78.49	79.69	80.90	82.12	83.34	84.58	85.82
13.75	67.19	68.30	69.41	70.53	71.66	72.80	73.95	75.11	76.28	77.46	78.64	79.84	81.04	82.25	83.47	84.69
14.00	66.32	67.41	68.50	69.61	70.73	71.86	72.99	74.13	75.29	76.45	77.62	78.79	79.98	81.17	82.38	83.59
14.25	65.46	66.53	67.62	68.71	69.81	70.93	72.05	73.17	74.31	75.46	76.61	77.77	78.95	80.12	81.31	82.51
14.50	64.62	65.68	66.75	67.83	68.92	70.01	71.12	72.24	73.36	74.49	75.63	76.78	77.93	79.10	80.27	81.45
14.75	63.79	64.84	65.90	66.97	68.04	69.12	70.22	71.32	72.42	73.54	74.67	75.80	76.94	78.09	79.25	80.41
15.00	62.99	64.02	65.07	66.12	67.18	68.25	69.33	70.41	71.51	72.61	73.72	74.84	75.97	77.10	78.24	79.39
15.25	62.20	63.22	64.25	65.29	66.34	67.40	68.46	69.53	70.61	71.70	72.80	73.90	75.02	76.14	77.26	78.40
15.50	61.43	62.44	63.45	64.48	65.51	66.56	67.61	68.67	69.74	70.81	71.89	72.98	74.08	75.19	76.30	77.42
15.75	60.67	61.67	62.67	63.68	64.71	65.74	66.78	67.82	68.88	69.94	71.01	72.09	73.17	74.26	75.36	76.47
16.00	59.93	60.91	61.90	62.91	63.92	64.93	65.96	66.99	68.03	69.08	70.14	71.20	72.28	73.35	74.44	75.53
16.25	59.20	60.17	61.15	62.14	63.14	64.15	65.16	66.18	67.21	68.24	69.29	70.34	71.40	72.46	73.54	74.62
16.50	58.49	59.45	60.42	61.39	62.38	63.37	64.37	65.38	66.40	67.42	68.45	69.49	70.54	71.59	72.65	73.72
16.75	57.79	58.74	59.70	60.66	61.64	62.62	63.61	64.60	65.61	66.62	67.64	68.66	69.70	70.74	71.79	72.84
17.00	57.10	58.04	58.99	59.94	60.91	61.87	62.85	63.84	64.83	65.83	66.84	67.85	68.87	69.90	70.93	71.98
17.25	56.43	57.36	58.30	59.24	60.19	61.15	62.11	63.09	64.07	65.06	66.05	67.05	68.06	69.08	70.10	71.13
17.50	55.78	56.69	57.62	58.55	59.49	60.43	61.39	62.35	63.32	64.30	65.28	66.27	67.27	68.27	69.28	70.30
17.75	55.13	56.04	56.95	57.87	58.80	59.74	60.68	61.63	62.59	63.55	64.53	65.50	66.49	67.48	68.48	69.49
18.00	54.50	55.39	56.30	57.21	58.13	59.05	59.98	60.92	61.87	62.82	63.79	64.75	65.73	66.71	67.70	68.69
18.25	53.88	54.76	55.66	56.56	57.46	58.38	59.30	60.23	61.17	62.11	63.06	64.02	64.98	65.95	66.93	67.91
18.50	53.27	54.15	55.03	55.92	56.82	57.72	58.63	59.55	60.48	61.41	62.35	63.29	64.25	65.21	66.17	67.14
18.75	52.67	53.54	54.41	55.29	56.18	57.07	57.97	58.88	59.80	60.72	61.65	62.58	63.53	64.48	65.43	66.39
19.00	52.09	52.94	53.81	54.68	55.55	56.44	57.33	58.23	59.13	60.05	60.96	61.89	62.82	63.76	64.70	65.65
20.00	49.85	50.67	51.50	52.33	53.17	54.02	54.87	55.73	56.60	57.47	58.35	59.24	60.13	61.03	61.93	62.84
25.00	40.83	41.50	42.18	42.86	43.55	44.24	44.94	45.65	46.35	47.07	47.79	48.51	49.25	49.98	50.72	51.47
30.00	34.39	34.95	35.52	36.09	36.67	37.26	37.85	38.44	39.04	39.64	40.25	40.86	41.47	42.09	42.71	43.34

Description: This table shows the yield to maturity of a mortgage purchased at the price shown in the index.

Example: The yield to maturity of a 10.75 %, 16 year mortgage at a price of 111.00 is 9.00 %.

INTEREST RATE, %

PRICE	7.00%	7.25%	7.50%	7.75%	8.00%	8.25%	8.50%	8.75%	9.00%	9.25%	9.50%	9.75%	10.00%	10.25%	10.50%	10.75%
155	.90	1.10	1.31	1.52	1.73	1.93	2.14	2.35	2.55	2.76	2.96	3.17	3.37	3.57	3.78	3.98
150	1.32	1.53	1.74	1.95	2.16	2.37	2.58	2.78	2.99	3.20	3.41	3.62	3.82	4.03	4.23	4.44
145	1.76	1.97	2.18	2.40	2.61	2.82	3.03	3.24	3.46	3.67	3.88	4.09	4.30	4.50	4.71	4.92
140	2.22	2.43	2.65	2.87	3.08	3.30	3.51	3.73	3.94	4.15	4.37	4.58	4.79	5.01	5.22	5.43
135	2.70	2.92	3.14	3.36	3.58	3.80	4.02	4.23	4.45	4.67	4.88	5.10	5.32	5.53	5.75	5.96
130	3.21	3.44	3.66	3.88	4.10	4.32	4.55	4.77	4.99	5.21	5.43	5.65	5.87	6.09	6.31	6.53
125	3.75	3.98	4.20	4.43	4.66	4.88	5.11	5.33	5.56	5.78	6.01	6.23	6.45	6.68	6.90	7.12
124	3.86	4.09	4.32	4.54	4.77	5.00	5.22	5.45	5.67	5.90	6.12	6.35	6.57	6.80	7.02	7.25
123	3.98	4.20	4.43	4.66	4.89	5.11	5.34	5.57	5.79	6.02	6.25	6.47	6.70	6.92	7.15	7.37
122	4.09	4.32	4.55	4.78	5.00	5.23	5.46	5.69	5.91	6.14	6.37	6.59	6.82	7.05	7.27	7.50
121	4.21	4.43	4.66	4.89	5.12	5.35	5.58	5.81	6.04	6.26	6.49	6.72	6.95	7.17	7.40	7.63
120	4.32	4.55	4.78	5.01	5.24	5.47	5.70	5.93	6.16	6.39	6.62	6.84	7.07	7.30	7.53	7.75
119	4.44	4.67	4.90	5.13	5.36	5.59	5.82	6.05	6.28	6.51	6.74	6.97	7.20	7.43	7.66	7.89
118	4.56	4.79	5.02	5.25	5.49	5.72	5.95	6.18	6.41	6.64	6.87	7.10	7.33	7.56	7.79	8.02
117	4.68	4.91	5.15	5.38	5.61	5.84	6.07	6.31	6.54	6.77	7.00	7.23	7.46	7.69	7.92	8.15
116	4.80	5.04	5.27	5.50	5.74	5.97	6.20	6.43	6.67	6.90	7.13	7.36	7.60	7.83	8.06	8.29
115	4.93	5.16	5.40	5.63	5.86	6.10	6.33	6.57	6.80	7.03	7.26	7.50	7.73	7.96	8.20	8.43
114	5.05	5.29	5.52	5.76	5.99	6.23	6.46	6.70	6.93	7.17	7.40	7.63	7.87	8.10	8.33	8.57
113	5.18	5.42	5.65	5.89	6.12	6.36	6.60	6.83	7.07	7.30	7.54	7.77	8.01	8.24	8.48	8.71
112	5.31	5.55	5.78	6.02	6.26	6.49	6.73	6.97	7.20	7.44	7.67	7.91	8.15	8.38	8.62	8.85
111	5.44	5.68	5.91	6.15	6.39	6.63	6.87	7.10	7.34	7.58	7.82	8.05	8.29	8.53	8.76	9.00
110	5.57	5.81	6.05	6.29	6.53	6.77	7.00	7.24	7.48	7.72	7.96	8.20	8.43	8.67	8.91	9.15
109	5.70	5.94	6.18	6.42	6.66	6.90	7.14	7.38	7.62	7.86	8.10	8.34	8.58	8.82	9.06	9.30
108	5.84	6.08	6.32	6.56	6.80	7.04	7.29	7.53	7.77	8.01	8.25	8.49	8.73	8.97	9.21	9.45
107	5.98	6.22	6.46	6.70	6.95	7.19	7.43	7.67	7.91	8.15	8.40	8.64	8.88	9.12	9.36	9.60
106	6.12	6.36	6.60	6.85	7.09	7.33	7.58	7.82	8.06	8.30	8.55	8.79	9.03	9.27	9.52	9.76
105	6.26	6.50	6.75	6.99	7.23	7.48	7.72	7.97	8.21	8.45	8.70	8.94	9.19	9.43	9.67	9.92
104	6.40	6.65	6.89	7.14	7.38	7.63	7.87	8.12	8.36	8.61	8.85	9.10	9.34	9.59	9.83	10.08
103	6.55	6.79	7.04	7.29	7.53	7.78	8.03	8.27	8.52	8.76	9.01	9.26	9.50	9.75	9.99	10.24
102	6.69	6.94	7.19	7.44	7.68	7.93	8.18	8.43	8.67	8.92	9.17	9.42	9.66	9.91	10.16	10.41
101	6.84	7.09	7.34	7.59	7.84	8.09	8.34	8.58	8.83	9.08	9.33	9.58	9.83	10.08	10.33	10.57
100	7.00	7.25	7.50	7.75	8.00	8.25	8.50	8.75	9.00	9.25	9.50	9.75	10.00	10.25	10.50	10.75
99	7.15	7.40	7.65	7.90	8.15	8.41	8.66	8.91	9.16	9.41	9.66	9.91	10.16	10.42	10.67	10.92
98	7.31	7.56	7.81	8.06	8.32	8.57	8.82	9.07	9.33	9.58	9.83	10.08	10.34	10.59	10.84	11.09
97	7.46	7.72	7.97	8.23	8.48	8.73	8.99	9.24	9.49	9.75	10.00	10.26	10.51	10.77	11.02	11.27
96	7.62	7.88	8.13	8.39	8.65	8.90	9.16	9.41	9.67	9.92	10.18	10.43	10.69	10.94	11.20	11.46
95	7.79	8.04	8.30	8.56	8.81	9.07	9.33	9.58	9.84	10.10	10.35	10.61	10.87	11.13	11.38	11.64
94	7.95	8.21	8.47	8.73	8.99	9.24	9.50	9.76	10.02	10.28	10.54	10.79	11.05	11.31	11.57	11.83
93	8.12	8.38	8.64	8.90	9.16	9.42	9.68	9.94	10.20	10.46	10.72	10.98	11.24	11.50	11.76	12.02
92	8.30	8.56	8.82	9.08	9.34	9.60	9.86	10.12	10.38	10.64	10.90	11.17	11.43	11.69	11.95	12.21
91	8.47	8.73	8.99	9.26	9.52	9.78	10.04	10.31	10.57	10.83	11.09	11.36	11.62	11.88	12.15	12.41
90	8.65	8.91	9.17	9.44	9.70	9.97	10.23	10.49	10.76	11.02	11.29	11.55	11.82	12.08	12.35	12.61
89	8.83	9.09	9.36	9.62	9.89	10.15	10.42	10.69	10.95	11.22	11.48	11.75	12.02	12.28	12.55	12.82
88	9.01	9.28	9.54	9.81	10.08	10.34	10.61	10.88	11.15	11.42	11.68	11.95	12.22	12.49	12.76	13.03
87	9.20	9.47	9.73	10.00	10.27	10.54	10.81	11.08	11.35	11.62	11.89	12.16	12.43	12.70	12.97	13.24
86	9.39	9.66	9.93	10.20	10.47	10.74	11.01	11.28	11.55	11.82	12.09	12.37	12.64	12.91	13.18	13.46
85	9.58	9.85	10.12	10.40	10.67	10.94	11.21	11.49	11.76	12.03	12.31	12.58	12.85	13.13	13.40	13.68
84	9.78	10.05	10.32	10.60	10.87	11.15	11.42	11.69	11.97	12.24	12.52	12.80	13.07	13.35	13.62	13.90
83	9.98	10.25	10.53	10.80	11.08	11.35	11.63	11.91	12.18	12.46	12.74	13.02	13.29	13.57	13.85	14.13
82	10.18	10.46	10.74	11.01	11.29	11.57	11.85	12.12	12.40	12.68	12.96	13.24	13.52	13.80	14.08	14.36
81	10.39	10.67	10.95	11.23	11.51	11.79	12.07	12.35	12.63	12.91	13.19	13.47	13.75	14.04	14.32	14.60
80	10.60	10.88	11.16	11.44	11.73	12.01	12.29	12.57	12.86	13.14	13.42	13.71	13.99	14.27	14.56	14.85
79	10.82	11.10	11.38	11.67	11.95	12.23	12.52	12.80	13.09	13.37	13.66	13.95	14.23	14.52	14.81	15.09
78	11.04	11.32	11.61	11.89	12.18	12.46	12.75	13.04	13.33	13.61	13.90	14.19	14.48	14.77	15.06	15.35
77	11.26	11.55	11.84	12.12	12.41	12.70	12.99	13.28	13.57	13.86	14.15	14.44	14.73	15.02	15.31	15.61
76	11.49	11.78	12.07	12.36	12.65	12.94	13.23	13.52	13.82	14.11	14.40	14.69	14.99	15.28	15.57	15.87
75	11.73	12.02	12.31	12.60	12.89	13.19	13.48	13.77	14.07	14.36	14.66	14.95	15.25	15.55	15.84	16.14
74	11.97	12.26	12.55	12.85	13.14	13.44	13.73	14.03	14.33	14.62	14.92	15.22	15.52	15.82	16.12	16.42
73	12.21	12.51	12.80	13.10	13.40	13.69	13.99	14.29	14.59	14.89	15.19	15.49	15.79	16.09	16.40	16.70
70	12.98	13.28	13.58	13.89	14.19	14.50	14.81	15.11	15.42	15.73	16.04	16.34	16.65	16.96	17.28	17.59
65	14.38	14.70	15.02	15.33	15.65	15.97	16.30	16.62	16.94	17.26	17.59	17.91	18.24	18.56	18.89	19.22
60	15.97	16.30	16.64	16.98	17.31	17.65	17.99	18.33	18.67	19.01	19.36	19.70	20.04	20.39	20.74	21.09
55	17.80	18.15	18.51	18.86	19.22	19.58	19.94	20.30	20.67	21.03	21.40	21.76	22.13	22.50	22.87	23.24
50	19.93	20.31	20.69	21.07	21.45	21.84	22.23	22.62	23.01	23.40	23.79	24.19	24.59	24.98	25.38	25.79
45	22.46	22.88	23.29	23.70	24.12	24.54	24.96	25.38	25.81	26.23	26.66	27.09	27.53	27.96	28.40	28.84
40	25.56	26.01	26.46	26.92	27.38	27.84	28.30	28.77	29.24	29.71	30.19	30.66	31.14	31.63	32.11	32.60
35	29.45	29.95	30.46	30.97	31.49	32.01	32.53	33.05	33.58	34.11	34.65	35.19	35.73	36.27	36.82	37.37
30	34.53	35.11	35.70	36.29	36.88	37.48	38.08	38.69	39.29	39.91	40.53	41.15	41.77	42.40	43.04	43.67

Description: This table shows the price to pay for a monthly payment mortgage loan at the yield rate.

Example: The price of a 15.00 %, 16 year mortgage loan to yield 8.00 % to maturity is $ 148.85.

INTEREST RATE, %

YIELD	11.00%	11.25%	11.50%	11.75%	12.00%	12.25%	12.50%	12.75%	13.00%	13.25%	13.50%	13.75%	14.00%	14.25%	14.50%	15.00%
0.00	212.93	216.01	219.10	222.22	225.36	228.51	231.68	234.87	238.08	241.30	244.54	247.80	251.08	254.37	257.68	264.34
1.00	196.69	199.54	202.40	205.28	208.17	211.08	214.01	216.96	219.92	222.90	225.90	228.91	231.93	234.97	238.03	244.18
2.00	182.09	184.72	187.37	190.04	192.72	195.42	198.13	200.86	203.60	206.36	209.13	211.92	214.72	217.53	220.36	226.06
3.00	168.94	171.39	173.84	176.32	178.80	181.31	183.82	186.35	188.90	191.46	194.03	196.61	199.21	201.82	204.45	209.73
4.00	157.08	159.35	161.64	163.94	166.25	168.58	170.92	173.27	175.64	178.02	180.41	182.81	185.23	187.66	190.10	195.01
4.25	154.30	156.53	158.78	161.04	163.31	165.59	167.89	170.20	172.53	174.86	177.21	179.57	181.95	184.33	186.73	191.56
4.50	151.59	153.78	155.99	158.21	160.44	162.68	164.94	167.21	169.50	171.79	174.10	176.42	178.75	181.09	183.45	188.19
4.75	148.95	151.10	153.27	155.45	157.64	159.85	162.06	164.30	166.54	168.79	171.06	173.34	175.63	177.94	180.25	184.91
5.00	146.37	148.48	150.61	152.76	154.91	157.08	159.26	161.45	163.66	165.87	168.10	170.34	172.59	174.85	177.13	181.71
5.25	143.85	145.93	148.02	150.13	152.25	154.38	156.52	158.68	160.84	163.02	165.21	167.41	169.63	171.85	174.08	178.59
5.50	141.40	143.44	145.50	147.57	149.65	151.75	153.85	155.97	158.10	160.24	162.39	164.56	166.73	168.92	171.12	175.54
5.75	139.01	141.02	143.04	145.07	147.12	149.18	151.25	153.33	155.42	157.53	159.65	161.77	163.91	166.06	168.22	172.57
6.00	136.67	138.65	140.63	142.64	144.65	146.67	148.71	150.75	152.81	154.88	156.96	159.06	161.16	163.27	165.39	169.67
6.25	134.39	136.34	138.29	140.26	142.24	144.23	146.23	148.24	150.27	152.30	154.35	156.40	158.47	160.55	162.64	166.84
6.50	132.17	134.08	136.00	137.94	139.88	141.84	143.81	145.79	147.78	149.78	151.79	153.82	155.85	157.89	159.95	164.08
6.75	130.00	131.88	133.77	135.67	137.59	139.51	141.45	143.40	145.35	147.32	149.30	151.29	153.29	155.30	157.32	161.39
7.00	127.88	129.73	131.59	133.46	135.35	137.24	139.14	141.06	142.99	144.92	146.87	148.83	150.79	152.77	154.76	158.76
7.25	125.81	127.63	129.46	131.30	133.16	135.02	136.89	138.78	140.67	142.58	144.50	146.42	148.36	150.30	152.26	156.19
7.50	123.80	125.59	127.39	129.20	131.02	132.85	134.70	136.55	138.42	140.29	142.18	144.07	145.98	147.89	149.81	153.69
7.75	121.83	123.59	125.36	127.14	128.94	130.74	132.55	134.38	136.21	138.06	139.91	141.78	143.65	145.54	147.43	151.24
8.00	119.90	121.63	123.38	125.13	126.90	128.68	130.46	132.26	134.06	135.88	137.71	139.54	141.38	143.24	145.10	148.85
8.25	118.02	119.73	121.45	123.17	124.91	126.66	128.42	130.18	131.96	133.75	135.55	137.35	139.17	140.99	142.83	146.52
8.50	116.19	117.87	119.56	121.26	122.97	124.69	126.42	128.16	129.91	131.67	133.44	135.22	137.00	138.80	140.61	144.24
8.75	114.40	116.05	117.71	119.39	121.07	122.77	124.47	126.18	127.91	129.64	131.38	133.13	134.89	136.66	138.44	142.02
9.00	112.64	114.27	115.91	117.56	119.22	120.89	122.56	124.25	125.95	127.65	129.37	131.09	132.83	134.57	136.32	139.84
9.25	110.93	112.54	114.15	115.77	117.41	119.05	120.70	122.37	124.04	125.72	127.41	129.10	130.81	132.52	134.25	137.72
9.50	109.26	110.84	112.43	114.03	115.64	117.26	118.88	120.52	122.17	123.82	125.49	127.16	128.84	130.53	132.23	135.64
9.75	107.63	109.18	110.75	112.33	113.91	115.50	117.11	118.72	120.34	121.97	123.61	125.26	126.91	128.58	130.25	133.62
10.00	106.03	107.57	109.11	110.66	112.22	113.79	115.37	116.96	118.56	120.16	121.78	123.40	125.03	126.67	128.32	131.63
10.25	104.47	105.98	107.50	109.03	110.57	112.12	113.67	115.24	116.81	118.39	119.99	121.58	123.19	124.81	126.43	129.70
10.50	102.95	104.44	105.93	107.44	108.96	110.48	112.01	113.56	115.11	116.67	118.23	119.81	121.39	122.98	124.58	127.80
10.75	101.46	102.92	104.40	105.88	107.38	108.88	110.39	111.91	113.44	114.98	116.52	118.07	119.64	121.20	122.78	125.95
11.00	100.00	101.45	102.90	104.36	105.84	107.32	108.81	110.30	111.81	113.33	114.85	116.38	117.92	119.46	121.02	124.15
11.25	98.57	100.00	101.43	102.88	104.33	105.79	107.26	108.73	110.22	111.71	113.21	114.72	116.24	117.76	119.29	122.38
11.50	97.18	98.59	100.00	101.42	102.85	104.29	105.74	107.20	108.66	110.13	111.61	113.10	114.59	116.10	117.61	120.65
11.75	95.82	97.20	98.60	100.00	101.41	102.83	104.26	105.69	107.14	108.59	110.05	111.51	112.99	114.47	115.96	118.95
12.00	94.49	95.85	97.23	98.61	100.00	101.40	102.81	104.22	105.65	107.08	108.52	109.96	111.41	112.88	114.34	117.30
12.25	93.18	94.53	95.88	97.25	98.62	100.00	101.39	102.78	104.19	105.60	107.02	108.44	109.88	111.32	112.76	115.68
12.50	91.91	93.23	94.57	95.92	97.27	98.63	100.00	101.38	102.76	104.15	105.55	106.96	108.37	109.79	111.22	114.10
12.75	90.66	91.97	93.29	94.61	95.95	97.29	98.64	100.00	101.37	102.74	104.12	105.51	106.90	108.30	109.71	112.55
13.00	89.44	90.73	92.03	93.34	94.66	95.98	97.31	98.65	100.00	101.35	102.72	104.08	105.46	106.84	108.23	111.03
13.25	88.24	89.52	90.80	92.09	93.39	94.70	96.01	97.33	98.66	100.00	101.34	102.69	104.05	105.42	106.79	109.55
13.50	87.07	88.33	89.60	90.87	92.15	93.44	94.74	96.04	97.36	98.67	100.00	101.33	102.67	104.02	105.37	108.09
13.75	85.93	87.17	88.42	89.68	90.94	92.21	93.49	94.78	96.08	97.38	98.68	100.00	101.32	102.65	103.98	106.67
14.00	84.81	86.03	87.27	88.51	89.75	91.01	92.27	93.54	94.82	96.11	97.40	98.70	100.00	101.31	102.63	105.28
14.25	83.71	84.92	86.14	87.36	88.59	89.83	91.08	92.33	93.60	94.86	96.14	97.42	98.71	100.00	101.30	103.92
14.50	82.63	83.83	85.03	86.24	87.46	88.68	89.91	91.15	92.39	93.65	94.90	96.17	97.44	98.72	100.00	102.59
14.75	81.58	82.76	83.95	85.14	86.34	87.55	88.77	89.99	91.22	92.45	93.69	94.94	96.20	97.46	98.73	101.28
15.00	80.55	81.72	82.89	84.07	85.25	86.45	87.65	88.85	90.07	91.28	92.51	93.74	94.98	96.23	97.48	100.00
15.25	79.54	80.69	81.85	83.01	84.18	85.36	86.55	87.74	88.94	90.14	91.35	92.57	93.79	95.02	96.26	98.75
15.50	78.55	79.69	80.83	81.98	83.14	84.30	85.47	86.65	87.83	89.02	90.22	91.42	92.63	93.84	95.06	97.52
15.75	77.58	78.71	79.83	80.97	82.11	83.26	84.42	85.58	86.75	87.92	89.10	90.29	91.49	92.68	93.89	96.32
16.00	76.64	77.74	78.86	79.98	81.11	82.24	83.38	84.53	85.69	86.85	88.01	89.19	90.37	91.55	92.74	95.14
16.25	75.71	76.80	77.90	79.01	80.12	81.25	82.37	83.51	84.65	85.79	86.95	88.11	89.27	90.44	91.62	93.98
16.50	74.79	75.88	76.96	78.06	79.16	80.27	81.38	82.50	83.63	84.76	85.90	87.04	88.20	89.35	90.51	92.85
16.75	73.90	74.97	76.04	77.13	78.21	79.31	80.41	81.52	82.63	83.75	84.87	86.01	87.14	88.28	89.43	91.75
17.00	73.03	74.08	75.14	76.21	77.29	78.37	79.46	80.55	81.65	82.76	83.87	84.99	86.11	87.24	88.37	90.66
17.25	72.17	73.21	74.26	75.32	76.38	77.45	78.52	79.61	80.69	81.79	82.88	83.99	85.10	86.21	87.34	89.59
17.50	71.33	72.36	73.40	74.44	75.49	76.55	77.61	78.68	79.75	80.83	81.92	83.01	84.11	85.21	86.32	88.55
17.75	70.50	71.52	72.55	73.58	74.62	75.66	76.71	77.77	78.83	79.90	80.97	82.05	83.13	84.22	85.32	87.52
18.00	69.69	70.70	71.71	72.73	73.76	74.79	75.83	76.88	77.93	78.98	80.04	81.11	82.18	83.26	84.34	86.52
18.25	68.90	69.90	70.90	71.91	72.92	73.94	74.97	76.00	77.04	78.08	79.13	80.19	81.25	82.31	83.38	85.54
18.50	68.12	69.11	70.10	71.10	72.10	73.11	74.12	75.14	76.17	77.20	78.24	79.28	80.33	81.38	82.44	84.57
18.75	67.36	68.33	69.31	70.30	71.29	72.29	73.29	74.30	75.32	76.34	77.36	78.39	79.43	80.47	81.52	83.62
19.00	66.61	67.57	68.54	69.52	70.50	71.49	72.48	73.48	74.48	75.49	76.50	77.52	78.55	79.58	80.61	82.69
20.00	63.76	64.68	65.60	66.54	67.48	68.42	69.37	70.33	71.29	72.25	73.22	74.20	75.18	76.16	77.15	79.15
25.00	52.22	52.97	53.73	54.49	55.26	56.04	56.81	57.60	58.38	59.17	59.97	60.77	61.57	62.38	63.19	64.82
30.00	43.97	44.61	45.25	45.89	46.54	47.19	47.85	48.50	49.17	49.83	50.50	51.17	51.85	52.53	53.21	54.59

Description: This table shows the yield to maturity of a mortgage purchased at the price shown in the index.

Example: The yield to maturity of a 15.00 %, 16 year mortgage at a price of 125.00 is 10.88 %.

INTEREST RATE, %

PRICE	11.00%	11.25%	11.50%	11.75%	12.00%	12.25%	12.50%	12.75%	13.00%	13.25%	13.50%	13.75%	14.00%	14.25%	14.50%	15.00%
250	–	–	–	–	–	–	–	–	–	–	–	–	.05	.21	.37	.70
240	–	–	–	–	–	–	–	–	–	–	.23	.40	.56	.73	.89	1.22
230	–	–	–	–	–	–	.09	.26	–	.60	.77	.93	1.10	1.27	1.44	1.77
220	–	–	–	.12	.30	.47	.64	.82	.99	1.16	1.33	1.51	1.68	1.85	2.02	2.35
210	.17	.35	.53	.71	.88	1.06	1.24	1.41	1.59	1.77	1.94	2.11	2.29	2.46	2.63	2.98
200	.78	.97	1.15	1.33	1.51	1.69	1.87	2.05	2.23	2.41	2.59	2.76	2.94	3.12	3.29	3.64
195	1.11	1.29	1.47	1.66	1.84	2.02	2.20	2.39	2.57	2.75	2.93	3.11	3.29	3.46	3.64	4.00
190	1.44	1.63	1.81	2.00	2.18	2.37	2.55	2.73	2.92	3.10	3.28	3.46	3.64	3.82	4.00	4.36
185	1.79	1.98	2.16	2.35	2.54	2.72	2.91	3.09	3.28	3.46	3.65	3.83	4.01	4.19	4.38	4.74
180	2.15	2.34	2.53	2.72	2.90	3.09	3.28	3.47	3.65	3.84	4.03	4.21	4.40	4.58	4.76	5.13
175	2.52	2.71	2.91	3.10	3.29	3.48	3.67	3.86	4.05	4.23	4.42	4.61	4.80	4.98	5.17	5.54
170	2.91	3.11	3.30	3.49	3.69	3.88	4.07	4.26	4.45	4.64	4.83	5.02	5.21	5.40	5.59	5.97
165	3.32	3.51	3.71	3.91	4.10	4.30	4.49	4.68	4.88	5.07	5.26	5.46	5.65	5.84	6.03	6.41
160	3.74	3.94	4.14	4.34	4.53	4.73	4.93	5.12	5.32	5.52	5.71	5.91	6.10	6.30	6.49	6.88
155	4.18	4.38	4.58	4.79	4.99	5.19	5.39	5.59	5.79	5.98	6.18	6.38	6.58	6.77	6.97	7.36
150	4.64	4.85	5.05	5.26	5.46	5.66	5.87	6.07	6.27	6.47	6.67	6.88	7.08	7.28	7.48	7.87
145	5.13	5.34	5.55	5.75	5.96	6.17	6.37	6.58	6.78	6.99	7.19	7.40	7.60	7.80	8.01	8.41
140	5.64	5.85	6.06	6.27	6.48	6.69	6.90	7.11	7.32	7.53	7.74	7.94	8.15	8.36	8.56	8.98
135	6.18	6.39	6.61	6.82	7.03	7.25	7.46	7.67	7.89	8.10	8.31	8.52	8.73	8.94	9.15	9.57
130	6.74	6.96	7.18	7.40	7.62	7.83	8.05	8.27	8.48	8.70	8.92	9.13	9.35	9.56	9.78	10.21
125	7.35	7.57	7.79	8.01	8.23	8.46	8.68	8.90	9.12	9.34	9.56	9.78	10.00	10.22	10.44	10.88
120	7.98	8.21	8.44	8.66	8.89	9.12	9.34	9.57	9.79	10.02	10.24	10.47	10.69	10.92	11.14	11.59
115	8.66	8.89	9.12	9.36	9.59	9.82	10.05	10.28	10.51	10.74	10.97	11.20	11.43	11.66	11.89	12.35
113	8.94	9.18	9.41	9.65	9.88	10.11	10.35	10.58	10.81	11.04	11.28	11.51	11.74	11.98	12.21	12.67
112	9.09	9.32	9.56	9.79	10.03	10.26	10.50	10.73	10.97	11.20	11.43	11.67	11.90	12.13	12.37	12.83
111	9.24	9.47	9.71	9.94	10.18	10.42	10.65	10.89	11.12	11.36	11.59	11.83	12.06	12.30	12.53	13.00
110	9.38	9.62	9.86	10.10	10.33	10.57	10.81	11.04	11.28	11.52	11.75	11.99	12.22	12.46	12.70	13.17
109	9.53	9.77	10.01	10.25	10.49	10.73	10.96	11.20	11.44	11.68	11.92	12.15	12.39	12.63	12.86	13.34
108	9.69	9.93	10.17	10.41	10.65	10.89	11.12	11.36	11.60	11.84	12.08	12.32	12.56	12.80	13.03	13.51
107	9.84	10.08	10.32	10.57	10.81	11.05	11.29	11.53	11.77	12.01	12.25	12.49	12.73	12.97	13.21	13.69
106	10.00	10.24	10.48	10.73	10.97	11.21	11.45	11.69	11.94	12.18	12.42	12.66	12.90	13.14	13.38	13.87
105	10.16	10.40	10.65	10.89	11.13	11.38	11.62	11.86	12.11	12.35	12.59	12.83	13.08	13.32	13.56	14.05
104	10.32	10.57	10.81	11.06	11.30	11.54	11.79	12.03	12.28	12.52	12.77	13.01	13.25	13.50	13.74	14.23
103	10.49	10.73	10.98	11.22	11.47	11.72	11.96	12.21	12.45	12.70	12.94	13.19	13.44	13.68	13.93	14.42
102	10.65	10.90	11.15	11.40	11.64	11.89	12.14	12.38	12.63	12.88	13.12	13.37	13.62	13.87	14.11	14.61
101	10.82	11.07	11.32	11.57	11.82	12.07	12.31	12.56	12.81	13.06	13.31	13.56	13.81	14.05	14.30	14.80
100	11.00	11.25	11.50	11.75	12.00	12.25	12.50	12.75	13.00	13.25	13.50	13.75	14.00	14.25	14.50	15.00
99	11.17	11.42	11.67	11.92	12.18	12.43	12.68	12.93	13.18	13.43	13.68	13.94	14.19	14.44	14.69	15.19
98	11.35	11.60	11.85	12.11	12.36	12.61	12.87	13.12	13.37	13.62	13.88	14.13	14.38	14.64	14.89	15.40
97	11.53	11.78	12.04	12.29	12.55	12.80	13.05	13.31	13.56	13.82	14.07	14.33	14.58	14.84	15.09	15.60
96	11.71	11.97	12.22	12.48	12.74	12.99	13.25	13.50	13.76	14.02	14.27	14.53	14.79	15.04	15.30	15.81
95	11.90	12.16	12.41	12.67	12.93	13.19	13.44	13.70	13.96	14.22	14.48	14.73	14.99	15.25	15.51	16.02
94	12.09	12.35	12.61	12.86	13.12	13.38	13.64	13.90	14.16	14.42	14.68	14.94	15.20	15.46	15.72	16.24
93	12.28	12.54	12.80	13.06	13.32	13.58	13.85	14.11	14.37	14.63	14.89	15.15	15.41	15.68	15.94	16.46
92	12.48	12.74	13.00	13.26	13.53	13.79	14.05	14.31	14.58	14.84	15.10	15.37	15.63	15.90	16.16	16.69
91	12.68	12.94	13.20	13.47	13.73	14.00	14.26	14.53	14.79	15.06	15.32	15.59	15.85	16.12	16.38	16.92
90	12.88	13.14	13.41	13.68	13.94	14.21	14.48	14.74	15.01	15.28	15.54	15.81	16.08	16.35	16.61	17.15
89	13.09	13.35	13.62	13.89	14.16	14.43	14.69	14.96	15.23	15.50	15.77	16.04	16.31	16.58	16.85	17.39
88	13.30	13.57	13.84	14.10	14.37	14.64	14.92	15.19	15.46	15.73	16.00	16.27	16.54	16.81	17.08	17.63
87	13.51	13.78	14.05	14.32	14.60	14.87	15.14	15.41	15.69	15.96	16.23	16.51	16.78	17.05	17.33	17.88
86	13.73	14.00	14.28	14.55	14.82	15.10	15.37	15.65	15.92	16.20	16.47	16.75	17.02	17.30	17.57	18.13
85	13.95	14.23	14.50	14.78	15.05	15.33	15.61	15.88	16.16	16.44	16.71	16.99	17.27	17.55	17.83	18.38
84	14.18	14.46	14.73	15.01	15.29	15.57	15.85	16.12	16.40	16.68	16.96	17.24	17.52	17.80	18.08	18.65
83	14.41	14.69	14.97	15.25	15.53	15.81	16.09	16.37	16.65	16.93	17.22	17.50	17.78	18.06	18.35	18.91
82	14.64	14.93	15.21	15.49	15.77	16.06	16.34	16.62	16.91	17.19	17.47	17.76	18.04	18.33	18.61	19.18
81	14.89	15.17	15.45	15.74	16.02	16.31	16.59	16.88	17.16	17.45	17.74	18.02	18.31	18.60	18.89	19.46
80	15.13	15.42	15.70	15.99	16.28	16.56	16.85	17.14	17.43	17.72	18.01	18.30	18.59	18.88	19.17	19.75
79	15.38	15.67	15.96	16.25	16.54	16.83	17.12	17.41	17.70	17.99	18.28	18.57	18.87	19.16	19.45	20.04
78	15.64	15.93	16.22	16.51	16.80	17.09	17.39	17.68	17.97	18.27	18.56	18.86	19.15	19.44	19.74	20.34
77	15.90	16.19	16.49	16.78	17.07	17.37	17.66	17.96	18.26	18.55	18.85	19.15	19.44	19.74	20.04	20.64
76	16.17	16.46	16.76	17.05	17.35	17.65	17.95	18.25	18.54	18.84	19.14	19.44	19.74	20.04	20.35	20.95
75	16.44	16.74	17.04	17.33	17.63	17.93	18.24	18.54	18.84	19.14	19.44	19.75	20.05	20.35	20.66	21.27
74	16.72	17.02	17.32	17.62	17.92	18.23	18.53	18.84	19.14	19.45	19.75	20.06	20.36	20.67	20.98	21.59
73	17.00	17.31	17.61	17.92	18.22	18.53	18.83	19.14	19.45	19.76	20.07	20.37	20.68	20.99	21.31	21.93
70	17.90	18.21	18.53	18.84	19.15	19.47	19.79	20.10	20.42	20.74	21.06	21.37	21.69	22.01	22.34	22.98
65	19.55	19.88	20.21	20.54	20.87	21.21	21.54	21.88	22.21	22.55	22.88	23.22	23.56	23.90	24.24	24.92
60	21.43	21.79	22.14	22.49	22.84	23.20	23.55	23.91	24.26	24.62	24.98	25.34	25.70	26.06	26.43	27.16
55	23.62	23.99	24.37	24.75	25.12	25.50	25.89	26.27	26.65	27.04	27.42	27.81	28.20	28.59	28.98	29.76

Description: This table shows the price to pay for a monthly payment mortgage loan at the yield rate.

Example: The price of a 6.75 %, 17 year mortgage loan to yield 8.00 % to maturity is $ 91.88.

INTEREST RATE, %

YIELD	0.00%	1.00%	2.00%	3.00%	4.00%	4.25%	4.50%	4.75%	5.00%	5.25%	5.50%	5.75%	6.00%	6.25%	6.50%	6.75%
0.00	100.00	108.78	118.04	127.78	137.98	140.61	143.26	145.94	148.65	151.38	154.14	156.93	159.75	162.60	165.47	168.37
1.00	91.93	100.00	108.51	117.46	126.84	129.26	131.69	134.16	136.65	139.16	141.70	144.27	146.86	149.47	152.11	154.77
2.00	84.71	92.15	100.00	108.25	116.89	119.11	121.36	123.63	125.92	128.24	130.58	132.95	135.33	137.74	140.18	142.63
3.00	78.26	85.13	92.38	100.00	107.99	110.04	112.11	114.21	116.33	118.47	120.63	122.82	125.02	127.25	129.49	131.76
4.00	72.47	78.84	85.55	92.61	100.00	101.90	103.82	105.76	107.73	109.71	111.71	113.73	115.78	117.84	119.92	122.02
4.25	71.12	77.37	83.95	90.88	98.13	100.00	101.89	103.79	105.72	107.66	109.63	111.61	113.62	115.64	117.68	119.74
4.50	69.80	75.93	82.40	89.20	96.32	98.15	100.00	101.87	103.76	105.67	107.60	109.55	111.51	113.50	115.50	117.53
4.75	68.52	74.54	80.89	87.56	94.55	96.35	98.16	100.00	101.86	103.73	105.62	107.54	109.47	111.42	113.38	115.37
5.00	67.27	73.18	79.41	85.96	92.83	94.59	96.38	98.18	100.00	101.84	103.70	105.58	107.47	109.39	111.32	113.27
5.25	66.06	71.86	77.98	84.41	91.15	92.88	94.63	96.40	98.19	100.00	101.83	103.67	105.53	107.41	109.31	111.22
5.50	64.87	70.57	76.58	82.90	89.52	91.22	92.94	94.68	96.43	98.21	100.00	101.81	103.64	105.48	107.35	109.23
5.75	63.72	69.32	75.22	81.42	87.92	89.60	91.29	92.99	94.72	96.46	98.22	100.00	101.80	103.61	105.44	107.28
6.00	62.60	68.09	73.89	79.99	86.37	88.02	89.68	91.35	93.05	94.76	96.49	98.24	100.00	101.78	103.58	105.39
6.25	61.50	66.90	72.60	78.59	84.86	86.48	88.11	89.75	91.42	93.10	94.80	96.52	98.25	100.00	101.77	103.55
6.50	60.43	65.74	71.34	77.22	83.39	84.98	86.58	88.20	89.83	91.49	93.16	94.84	96.55	98.26	100.00	101.75
6.75	59.39	64.61	70.11	75.89	81.95	83.51	85.09	86.68	88.29	89.91	91.55	93.21	94.88	96.57	98.28	100.00
7.00	58.38	63.51	68.91	74.60	80.56	82.09	83.63	85.20	86.78	88.38	89.99	91.62	93.26	94.92	96.60	98.29
7.25	57.39	62.43	67.75	73.34	79.19	80.70	82.22	83.76	85.31	86.88	88.47	90.07	91.68	93.32	94.97	96.63
7.50	56.43	61.38	66.61	72.10	77.86	79.34	80.84	82.35	83.88	85.42	86.98	88.56	90.15	91.75	93.37	95.01
7.75	55.49	60.36	65.50	70.90	76.57	78.02	79.49	80.98	82.48	84.00	85.53	87.08	88.64	90.22	91.82	93.42
8.00	54.57	59.36	64.42	69.73	75.30	76.73	78.18	79.64	81.12	82.61	84.12	85.64	87.18	88.73	90.30	91.88
8.25	53.68	58.39	63.36	68.59	74.07	75.48	76.90	78.34	79.79	81.26	82.74	84.24	85.75	87.28	88.82	90.38
8.50	52.81	57.44	62.33	67.48	72.86	74.25	75.65	77.06	78.49	79.94	81.40	82.87	84.36	85.86	87.38	88.91
8.75	51.96	56.52	61.33	66.39	71.69	73.05	74.43	75.82	77.23	78.65	80.09	81.54	83.00	84.48	85.97	87.48
9.00	51.13	55.62	60.35	65.33	70.55	71.89	73.24	74.61	76.00	77.39	78.81	80.23	81.67	83.13	84.60	86.08
9.25	50.32	54.73	59.40	64.29	69.43	70.75	72.08	73.43	74.79	76.17	77.56	78.96	80.38	81.81	83.26	84.72
9.50	49.53	53.88	58.46	63.28	68.34	69.64	70.95	72.28	73.62	74.97	76.34	77.72	79.12	80.53	81.95	83.38
9.75	48.75	53.04	57.55	62.30	67.27	68.55	69.84	71.15	72.47	73.80	75.15	76.51	77.89	79.27	80.67	82.09
10.00	48.00	52.22	56.66	61.34	66.23	67.49	68.77	70.05	71.35	72.67	73.99	75.33	76.68	78.05	79.43	80.82
10.25	47.27	51.42	55.80	60.40	65.22	66.46	67.71	68.98	70.26	71.55	72.86	74.18	75.51	76.85	78.21	79.58
10.50	46.55	50.64	54.95	59.48	64.23	65.45	66.69	67.93	69.19	70.47	71.75	73.05	74.36	75.69	77.02	78.37
10.75	45.85	49.87	54.12	58.58	63.26	64.47	65.68	66.91	68.15	69.41	70.67	71.95	73.24	74.55	75.86	77.19
11.00	45.16	49.13	53.31	57.71	62.32	63.50	64.70	65.91	67.13	68.37	69.62	70.88	72.15	73.43	74.73	76.04
11.25	44.50	48.40	52.52	56.86	61.40	62.56	63.74	64.94	66.14	67.36	68.59	69.83	71.08	72.35	73.63	74.91
11.50	43.84	47.69	51.75	56.02	60.50	61.65	62.81	63.98	65.17	66.37	67.58	68.80	70.04	71.29	72.54	73.82
11.75	43.20	47.00	51.00	55.21	59.61	60.75	61.89	63.05	64.22	65.40	66.60	67.80	69.02	70.25	71.49	72.74
12.00	42.58	46.32	50.26	54.41	58.75	59.87	61.00	62.14	63.29	64.46	65.64	66.82	68.02	69.24	70.46	71.69
12.25	41.97	45.66	49.54	53.63	57.91	59.02	60.13	61.25	62.39	63.54	64.70	65.87	67.05	68.24	69.45	70.67
12.50	41.38	45.01	48.84	52.87	57.09	58.18	59.28	60.38	61.50	62.64	63.78	64.93	66.10	67.28	68.46	69.66
12.75	40.79	44.38	48.16	52.13	56.29	57.36	58.44	59.53	60.64	61.76	62.88	64.02	65.17	66.33	67.50	68.68
13.00	40.23	43.76	47.48	51.40	55.51	56.56	57.63	58.70	59.79	60.89	62.01	63.13	64.26	65.41	66.56	67.73
13.25	39.67	43.15	46.83	50.69	54.74	55.78	56.83	57.89	58.97	60.05	61.15	62.26	63.37	64.50	65.64	66.79
13.50	39.13	42.56	46.19	50.00	53.99	55.01	56.05	57.10	58.16	59.23	60.31	61.40	62.50	63.62	64.74	65.87
13.75	38.59	41.98	45.56	49.32	53.25	54.27	55.29	56.32	57.37	58.42	59.49	60.57	61.66	62.75	63.86	64.98
14.00	38.07	41.42	44.94	48.65	52.54	53.54	54.54	55.56	56.60	57.64	58.69	59.75	60.82	61.91	63.00	64.10
14.25	37.57	40.86	44.34	48.00	51.83	52.82	53.82	54.82	55.84	56.87	57.91	58.95	60.01	61.08	62.16	63.25
14.50	37.07	40.32	43.76	47.37	51.15	52.12	53.10	54.10	55.10	56.11	57.14	58.17	59.22	60.27	61.34	62.41
14.75	36.58	39.79	43.18	46.74	50.48	51.44	52.41	53.39	54.38	55.38	56.39	57.41	58.44	59.48	60.53	61.59
15.00	36.10	39.28	42.62	46.13	49.82	50.77	51.72	52.69	53.67	54.66	55.65	56.66	57.68	58.71	59.74	60.79
15.25	35.64	38.77	42.07	45.54	49.18	50.11	51.06	52.01	52.98	53.95	54.94	55.93	56.93	57.95	58.97	60.00
15.50	35.18	38.27	41.53	44.96	48.55	49.47	50.40	51.34	52.30	53.26	54.23	55.21	56.21	57.21	58.22	59.24
15.75	34.74	37.79	41.00	44.39	47.93	48.84	49.76	50.69	51.63	52.58	53.54	54.51	55.49	56.48	57.48	58.48
16.00	34.30	37.31	40.49	43.83	47.33	48.23	49.14	50.06	50.98	51.92	52.87	53.83	54.79	55.77	56.75	57.75
16.25	33.87	36.85	39.98	43.28	46.74	47.62	48.52	49.43	50.35	51.27	52.21	53.16	54.11	55.07	56.05	57.03
16.50	33.45	36.39	39.49	42.74	46.16	47.04	47.92	48.82	49.72	50.64	51.56	52.50	53.44	54.39	55.35	56.32
16.75	33.04	35.94	39.00	42.22	45.59	46.46	47.33	48.22	49.11	50.02	50.93	51.85	52.78	53.72	54.67	55.63
17.00	32.64	35.51	38.53	41.71	45.04	45.89	46.76	47.63	48.52	49.41	50.31	51.22	52.14	53.07	54.01	54.95
17.25	32.25	35.08	38.06	41.20	44.49	45.34	46.20	47.06	47.93	48.81	49.71	50.61	51.51	52.43	53.36	54.29
17.50	31.86	34.66	37.61	40.71	43.96	44.80	45.64	46.50	47.36	48.23	49.11	50.00	50.90	51.80	52.72	53.64
17.75	31.48	34.25	37.16	40.23	43.44	44.27	45.10	45.94	46.80	47.66	48.53	49.41	50.29	51.19	52.09	53.01
18.00	31.11	33.84	36.73	39.76	42.93	43.75	44.57	45.40	46.25	47.10	47.96	48.83	49.70	50.59	51.48	52.38
18.25	30.75	33.45	36.30	39.29	42.43	43.24	44.05	44.88	45.71	46.55	47.40	48.26	49.12	50.00	50.88	51.77
18.50	30.39	33.06	35.88	38.84	41.94	42.74	43.54	44.36	45.18	46.01	46.85	47.70	48.55	49.42	50.29	51.17
18.75	30.05	32.68	35.47	38.39	41.46	42.25	43.04	43.85	44.66	45.48	46.31	47.15	48.00	48.85	49.72	50.59
19.00	29.70	32.31	35.06	37.96	40.99	41.77	42.55	43.35	44.15	44.97	45.79	46.62	47.45	48.30	49.15	50.01
20.00	28.40	30.90	33.53	36.29	39.19	39.94	40.69	41.45	42.22	43.00	43.78	44.57	45.37	46.18	47.00	47.82
25.00	23.18	25.21	27.36	29.62	31.98	32.59	33.21	33.83	34.45	35.09	35.73	36.38	37.03	37.69	38.35	39.03
30.00	19.48	21.19	23.00	24.89	26.88	27.39	27.91	28.43	28.96	29.49	30.03	30.57	31.12	31.67	32.23	32.80

Description: This table shows the yield to maturity of a mortgage purchased at the price shown in the index.

Example: The yield to maturity of a 6.75 %, 17 year mortgage at a price of 80.00 is 10.16 %.

INTEREST RATE, %

PRICE	0.00%	1.00%	2.00%	3.00%	4.00%	4.25%	4.50%	4.75%	5.00%	5.25%	5.50%	5.75%	6.00%	6.25%	6.50%	6.75%
100	0.00	1.00	2.00	3.00	4.00	4.25	4.50	4.75	5.00	5.25	5.50	5.75	6.00	6.25	6.50	6.75
99	.11	1.12	2.12	3.12	4.13	4.38	4.63	4.88	5.13	5.38	5.63	5.89	6.14	6.39	6.64	6.89
98	.23	1.24	2.25	3.25	4.26	4.52	4.77	5.02	5.27	5.52	5.78	6.03	6.28	6.53	6.79	7.04
97	.35	1.36	2.38	3.39	4.40	4.65	4.91	5.16	5.41	5.67	5.92	6.17	6.43	6.68	6.93	7.19
96	.48	1.49	2.51	3.52	4.54	4.79	5.05	5.30	5.56	5.81	6.07	6.32	6.58	6.83	7.09	7.34
95	.60	1.62	2.64	3.66	4.68	4.94	5.19	5.45	5.70	5.96	6.22	6.47	6.73	6.98	7.24	7.50
94	.73	1.75	2.77	3.80	4.82	5.08	5.34	5.59	5.85	6.11	6.37	6.62	6.88	7.14	7.40	7.65
93	.86	1.88	2.91	3.94	4.97	5.23	5.49	5.74	6.00	6.26	6.52	6.78	7.04	7.30	7.55	7.81
92	.99	2.02	3.05	4.08	5.12	5.38	5.64	5.90	6.16	6.41	6.67	6.93	7.19	7.45	7.72	7.98
91	1.12	2.15	3.19	4.23	5.27	5.53	5.79	6.05	6.31	6.57	6.83	7.09	7.36	7.62	7.88	8.14
90	1.25	2.29	3.33	4.37	5.42	5.68	5.94	6.21	6.47	6.73	6.99	7.26	7.52	7.78	8.05	8.31
89	1.39	2.43	3.48	4.52	5.58	5.84	6.10	6.37	6.63	6.89	7.16	7.42	7.69	7.95	8.21	8.48
88	1.53	2.57	3.62	4.68	5.73	6.00	6.26	6.53	6.79	7.06	7.32	7.59	7.85	8.12	8.39	8.65
87	1.67	2.72	3.77	4.83	5.89	6.16	6.43	6.69	6.96	7.22	7.49	7.76	8.03	8.29	8.56	8.83
86	1.81	2.87	3.93	4.99	6.06	6.32	6.59	6.86	7.13	7.40	7.66	7.93	8.20	8.47	8.74	9.01
85	1.95	3.01	4.08	5.15	6.22	6.49	6.76	7.03	7.30	7.57	7.84	8.11	8.38	8.65	8.92	9.19
84	2.10	3.17	4.24	5.31	6.39	6.66	6.93	7.20	7.47	7.74	8.02	8.29	8.56	8.83	9.11	9.38
83	2.25	3.32	4.40	5.48	6.56	6.83	7.11	7.38	7.65	7.92	8.20	8.47	8.75	9.02	9.29	9.57
82	2.40	3.48	4.56	5.65	6.74	7.01	7.28	7.56	7.83	8.11	8.38	8.66	8.93	9.21	9.49	9.76
81	2.56	3.64	4.73	5.82	6.91	7.19	7.47	7.74	8.02	8.29	8.57	8.85	9.12	9.40	9.68	9.96
80	2.71	3.80	4.89	5.99	7.10	7.37	7.65	7.93	8.21	8.48	8.76	9.04	9.32	9.60	9.88	10.16
79	2.87	3.97	5.07	6.17	7.28	7.56	7.84	8.12	8.40	8.68	8.96	9.24	9.52	9.80	10.08	10.36
78	3.04	4.14	5.24	6.35	7.47	7.75	8.03	8.31	8.59	8.87	9.16	9.44	9.72	10.01	10.29	10.57
77	3.20	4.31	5.42	6.54	7.66	7.94	8.22	8.51	8.79	9.07	9.36	9.64	9.93	10.21	10.50	10.79
76	3.37	4.48	5.60	6.72	7.86	8.14	8.42	8.71	8.99	9.28	9.57	9.85	10.14	10.43	10.72	11.00
75	3.54	4.66	5.79	6.92	8.06	8.34	8.63	8.91	9.20	9.49	9.78	10.07	10.36	10.65	10.94	11.23
74	3.72	4.84	5.97	7.11	8.26	8.55	8.83	9.12	9.41	9.70	9.99	10.28	10.58	10.87	11.16	11.45
73	3.90	5.03	6.17	7.31	8.47	8.76	9.05	9.34	9.63	9.92	10.21	10.51	10.80	11.09	11.39	11.68
72	4.08	5.22	6.36	7.52	8.68	8.97	9.26	9.56	9.85	10.14	10.44	10.73	11.03	11.33	11.62	11.92
71	4.27	5.41	6.56	7.72	8.90	9.19	9.48	9.78	10.07	10.37	10.67	10.97	11.26	11.56	11.86	12.16
70	4.46	5.61	6.77	7.94	9.12	9.41	9.71	10.01	10.31	10.60	10.90	11.20	11.50	11.81	12.11	12.41
69	4.65	5.81	6.98	8.15	9.34	9.64	9.94	10.24	10.54	10.84	11.14	11.45	11.75	12.05	12.36	12.66
68	4.85	6.01	7.19	8.38	9.57	9.87	10.18	10.48	10.78	11.09	11.39	11.70	12.00	12.31	12.62	12.92
67	5.05	6.22	7.41	8.60	9.81	10.11	10.42	10.72	11.03	11.33	11.64	11.95	12.26	12.57	12.88	13.19
66	5.26	6.44	7.63	8.84	10.05	10.36	10.66	10.97	11.28	11.59	11.90	12.21	12.52	12.83	13.15	13.46
65	5.47	6.66	7.86	9.07	10.30	10.61	10.92	11.23	11.54	11.85	12.16	12.48	12.79	13.11	13.42	13.74
64	5.68	6.88	8.09	9.32	10.55	10.87	11.18	11.49	11.80	12.12	12.43	12.75	13.07	13.39	13.71	14.03
63	5.90	7.11	8.33	9.57	10.81	11.13	11.44	11.76	12.08	12.39	12.71	13.03	13.35	13.67	14.00	14.32
62	6.13	7.35	8.58	9.82	11.08	11.40	11.72	12.03	12.35	12.67	13.00	13.32	13.64	13.97	14.29	14.62
61	6.36	7.59	8.83	10.08	11.35	11.67	12.00	12.32	12.64	12.96	13.29	13.61	13.94	14.27	14.60	14.93
60	6.60	7.83	9.09	10.35	11.63	11.96	12.28	12.61	12.93	13.26	13.59	13.92	14.25	14.58	14.91	15.25
59	6.84	8.09	9.35	10.63	11.92	12.25	12.58	12.91	13.23	13.57	13.90	14.23	14.56	14.90	15.24	15.57
58	7.09	8.35	9.62	10.91	12.22	12.55	12.88	13.21	13.54	13.88	14.21	14.55	14.89	15.23	15.57	15.91
57	7.35	8.61	9.90	11.20	12.52	12.86	13.19	13.53	13.86	14.20	14.54	14.88	15.22	15.57	15.91	16.25
56	7.61	8.89	10.19	11.50	12.84	13.17	13.51	13.85	14.19	14.53	14.88	15.22	15.57	15.91	16.26	16.61
55	7.88	9.17	10.48	11.81	13.16	13.50	13.84	14.18	14.53	14.88	15.22	15.57	15.92	16.27	16.62	16.98
54	8.15	9.46	10.78	12.13	13.49	13.84	14.18	14.53	14.88	15.23	15.58	15.93	16.29	16.64	17.00	17.36
53	8.44	9.76	11.09	12.45	13.83	14.18	14.53	14.88	15.24	15.59	15.95	16.30	16.66	17.02	17.38	17.75
52	8.73	10.06	11.41	12.79	14.19	14.54	14.89	15.25	15.61	15.97	16.33	16.69	17.05	17.42	17.78	18.15
51	9.03	10.38	11.74	13.14	14.55	14.91	15.27	15.63	15.99	16.35	16.72	17.08	17.45	17.82	18.19	18.57
50	9.34	10.70	12.09	13.49	14.93	15.29	15.65	16.02	16.38	16.75	17.12	17.50	17.87	18.24	18.62	19.00
49	9.66	11.04	12.44	13.86	15.31	15.68	16.05	16.42	16.79	17.17	17.54	17.92	18.30	18.68	19.06	19.45
48	10.00	11.39	12.80	14.25	15.72	16.09	16.46	16.84	17.22	17.60	17.98	18.36	18.74	19.13	19.52	19.91
47	10.34	11.74	13.18	14.64	16.13	16.51	16.89	17.27	17.65	18.04	18.43	18.82	19.21	19.60	19.99	20.39
46	10.69	12.12	13.57	15.05	16.56	16.95	17.33	17.72	18.11	18.50	18.89	19.29	19.69	20.08	20.49	20.89
45	11.06	12.50	13.97	15.48	17.01	17.40	17.79	18.19	18.58	18.98	19.38	19.78	20.18	20.59	21.00	21.41
44	11.43	12.90	14.39	15.92	17.48	17.87	18.27	18.67	19.07	19.48	19.88	20.29	20.70	21.11	21.53	21.95
43	11.83	13.31	14.83	16.38	17.96	18.36	18.77	19.17	19.58	19.99	20.41	20.82	21.24	21.66	22.08	22.51
42	12.23	13.74	15.28	16.85	18.46	18.87	19.28	19.70	20.11	20.53	20.95	21.38	21.80	22.23	22.66	23.09
41	12.66	14.18	15.75	17.35	18.99	19.40	19.82	20.24	20.67	21.09	21.52	21.95	22.39	22.82	23.26	23.70
40	13.10	14.65	16.24	17.87	19.53	19.96	20.39	20.81	21.25	21.68	22.12	22.56	23.00	23.45	23.89	24.34
39	13.55	15.13	16.75	18.41	20.11	20.54	20.97	21.41	21.85	22.29	22.74	23.19	23.64	24.09	24.55	25.01
35	15.60	17.29	19.03	20.83	22.68	23.15	23.62	24.10	24.58	25.06	25.55	26.04	26.53	27.03	27.53	28.04
30	18.78	20.67	22.63	24.65	26.75	27.28	27.82	28.37	28.91	29.47	30.02	30.59	31.15	31.72	32.30	32.88
25	23.04	25.22	27.50	29.86	32.32	32.95	33.58	34.22	34.87	35.52	36.18	36.84	37.51	38.19	38.87	39.56
20	29.19	31.84	34.61	37.51	40.53	41.31	42.09	42.88	43.68	44.49	45.31	46.13	46.96	47.80	48.65	49.50
15	39.15	42.62	46.27	50.09	54.10	55.13	56.17	57.22	58.28	59.36	60.44	61.54	62.64	63.76	64.88	66.02
10	58.82	63.98	69.43	75.16	81.16	82.71	84.27	85.84	87.43	89.04	90.67	92.31	93.97	95.64	97.33	99.04

Description: This table shows the price to pay for a monthly payment mortgage loan at the yield rate.

Example: The price of a 10.75 %, 17 year mortgage loan to yield 8.00 % to maturity is $ 119.03.

INTEREST RATE, %

YIELD	7.00%	7.25%	7.50%	7.75%	8.00%	8.25%	8.50%	8.75%	9.00%	9.25%	9.50%	9.75%	10.00%	10.25%	10.50%	10.75%
0.00	171.29	174.24	177.22	180.22	183.24	186.30	189.37	192.47	195.60	198.74	201.92	205.11	208.33	211.57	214.83	218.11
1.00	157.46	160.17	162.91	165.67	168.45	171.26	174.08	176.93	179.81	182.70	185.61	188.55	191.51	194.49	197.48	200.50
2.00	145.11	147.61	150.13	152.67	155.23	157.82	160.42	163.05	165.70	168.36	171.05	173.76	176.48	179.23	181.99	184.77
3.00	134.05	136.36	138.69	141.04	143.41	145.79	148.20	150.63	153.07	155.54	158.02	160.52	163.04	165.57	168.12	170.69
4.00	124.14	126.28	128.43	130.61	132.80	135.01	137.24	139.49	141.75	144.03	146.33	148.65	150.98	153.33	155.69	158.07
4.25	121.82	123.92	126.04	128.17	130.32	132.49	134.68	136.89	139.11	141.35	143.60	145.87	148.16	150.47	152.79	155.12
4.50	119.57	121.63	123.70	125.80	127.91	130.04	132.19	134.35	136.53	138.73	140.94	143.17	145.42	147.68	149.96	152.25
4.75	117.37	119.39	121.43	123.49	125.56	127.65	129.76	131.89	134.03	136.18	138.36	140.55	142.75	144.97	147.21	149.46
5.00	115.23	117.22	119.22	121.24	123.28	125.33	127.40	129.48	131.59	133.70	135.84	137.99	140.15	142.33	144.52	146.73
5.25	113.15	115.10	117.07	119.05	121.05	123.06	125.10	127.14	129.21	131.29	133.38	135.49	137.62	139.76	141.91	144.08
5.50	111.12	113.04	114.97	116.92	118.88	120.86	122.85	124.86	126.89	128.93	130.99	133.06	135.15	137.25	139.37	141.50
5.75	109.15	111.03	112.92	114.84	116.76	118.71	120.67	122.64	124.64	126.64	128.66	130.70	132.75	134.81	136.89	138.98
6.00	107.22	109.07	110.93	112.81	114.71	116.62	118.54	120.48	122.44	124.41	126.39	128.39	130.41	132.43	134.48	136.53
6.25	105.35	107.16	108.99	110.84	112.70	114.57	116.47	118.37	120.29	122.23	124.18	126.15	128.12	130.12	132.12	134.14
6.50	103.52	105.30	107.10	108.91	110.74	112.59	114.45	116.32	118.21	120.11	122.03	123.96	125.90	127.86	129.83	131.81
6.75	101.74	103.49	105.26	107.04	108.84	110.65	112.48	114.32	116.17	118.04	119.93	121.82	123.73	125.66	127.60	129.55
7.00	100.00	101.72	103.46	105.21	106.98	108.76	110.56	112.37	114.19	116.03	117.88	119.74	121.62	123.51	125.42	127.33
7.25	98.31	100.00	101.71	103.43	105.17	106.92	108.68	110.46	112.26	114.06	115.88	117.72	119.56	121.42	123.29	125.18
7.50	96.66	98.32	100.00	101.69	103.40	105.12	106.86	108.61	110.37	112.15	113.94	115.74	117.55	119.38	121.22	123.08
7.75	95.05	96.68	98.33	100.00	101.68	103.37	105.08	106.80	108.53	110.28	112.04	113.81	115.60	117.39	119.20	121.03
8.00	93.48	95.09	96.71	98.35	100.00	101.67	103.34	105.04	106.74	108.46	110.19	111.93	113.69	115.46	117.24	119.03
8.25	91.95	93.53	95.13	96.74	98.36	100.00	101.65	103.32	104.99	106.68	108.38	110.10	111.83	113.56	115.32	117.08
8.50	90.45	92.01	93.58	95.17	96.76	98.38	100.00	101.64	103.29	104.95	106.62	108.31	110.01	111.72	113.44	115.18
8.75	89.00	90.53	92.07	93.63	95.21	96.79	98.39	100.00	101.62	103.26	104.91	106.57	108.24	109.92	111.62	113.32
9.00	87.57	89.08	90.60	92.14	93.69	95.25	96.82	98.40	100.00	101.61	103.23	104.86	106.51	108.17	109.83	111.51
9.25	86.19	87.67	89.17	90.68	92.20	93.74	95.28	96.84	98.42	100.00	101.60	103.20	104.82	106.45	108.09	109.75
9.50	84.83	86.29	87.77	89.25	90.75	92.26	93.79	95.32	96.87	98.43	100.00	101.58	103.18	104.78	106.40	108.02
9.75	83.51	84.95	86.40	87.86	89.34	90.83	92.33	93.84	95.36	96.90	98.44	100.00	101.57	103.15	104.74	106.34
10.00	82.22	83.64	85.07	86.51	87.96	89.42	90.90	92.39	93.89	95.40	96.92	98.46	100.00	101.56	103.12	104.70
10.25	80.96	82.36	83.76	85.18	86.61	88.06	89.51	90.97	92.45	93.94	95.44	96.95	98.47	100.00	101.54	103.09
10.50	79.73	81.11	82.49	83.89	85.30	86.72	88.15	89.59	91.05	92.51	93.99	95.48	96.97	98.48	100.00	101.53
10.75	78.53	79.89	81.25	82.63	84.01	85.41	86.82	88.24	89.68	91.12	92.57	94.04	95.51	97.00	98.49	100.00
11.00	77.36	78.69	80.04	81.39	82.76	84.14	85.53	86.93	88.34	89.76	91.19	92.63	94.09	95.55	97.02	98.51
11.25	76.22	77.53	78.85	80.19	81.53	82.89	84.26	85.64	87.03	88.43	89.84	91.26	92.70	94.14	95.59	97.05
11.50	75.10	76.39	77.70	79.01	80.34	81.68	83.02	84.38	85.75	87.13	88.52	89.92	91.33	92.76	94.19	95.62
11.75	74.00	75.28	76.56	77.86	79.17	80.49	81.82	83.16	84.51	85.87	87.24	88.62	90.01	91.41	92.81	94.23
12.00	72.94	74.19	75.46	76.74	78.03	79.33	80.64	81.96	83.29	84.63	85.98	87.34	88.71	90.09	91.48	92.87
12.25	71.89	73.13	74.38	75.64	76.91	78.19	79.48	80.78	82.09	83.42	84.75	86.09	87.44	88.80	90.17	91.55
12.50	70.87	72.09	73.33	74.57	75.82	77.08	78.36	79.64	80.93	82.23	83.55	84.87	86.20	87.54	88.89	90.25
12.75	69.88	71.08	72.29	73.52	74.75	76.00	77.25	78.52	79.79	81.08	82.37	83.67	84.99	86.31	87.64	88.98
13.00	68.90	70.09	71.29	72.49	73.71	74.94	76.18	77.42	78.68	79.95	81.22	82.51	83.80	85.10	86.42	87.74
13.25	67.95	69.12	70.30	71.49	72.69	73.90	75.12	76.35	77.59	78.84	80.10	81.37	82.64	83.93	85.22	86.52
13.50	67.02	68.17	69.34	70.51	71.70	72.89	74.09	75.31	76.53	77.76	79.00	80.25	81.51	82.78	84.05	85.34
13.75	66.11	67.25	68.40	69.55	70.72	71.90	73.09	74.28	75.49	76.70	77.93	79.16	80.40	81.65	82.91	84.18
14.00	65.22	66.34	67.47	68.62	69.77	70.93	72.10	73.28	74.47	75.67	76.88	78.09	79.32	80.55	81.79	83.04
14.25	64.35	65.45	66.57	67.70	68.84	69.98	71.14	72.30	73.48	74.66	75.85	77.05	78.26	79.48	80.70	81.94
14.50	63.49	64.59	65.69	66.80	67.93	69.06	70.20	71.35	72.50	73.67	74.85	76.03	77.22	78.42	79.63	80.85
14.75	62.66	63.74	64.83	65.93	67.03	68.15	69.27	70.41	71.55	72.70	73.86	75.03	76.21	77.39	78.59	79.79
15.00	61.84	62.91	63.98	65.07	66.16	67.26	68.37	69.49	70.62	71.76	72.90	74.05	75.22	76.39	77.56	78.75
15.25	61.05	62.10	63.16	64.23	65.31	66.39	67.49	68.59	69.71	70.83	71.96	73.10	74.25	75.40	76.56	77.73
15.50	60.26	61.30	62.35	63.41	64.47	65.54	66.63	67.72	68.82	69.92	71.04	72.16	73.29	74.43	75.58	76.74
15.75	59.50	60.52	61.56	62.60	63.65	64.71	65.78	66.86	67.94	69.04	70.14	71.25	72.36	73.49	74.62	75.76
16.00	58.75	59.76	60.78	61.81	62.85	63.90	64.95	66.02	67.09	68.17	69.25	70.35	71.45	72.57	73.68	74.81
16.25	58.02	59.02	60.02	61.04	62.07	63.10	64.14	65.19	66.25	67.32	68.39	69.47	70.56	71.66	72.76	73.88
16.50	57.30	58.29	59.28	60.29	61.30	62.32	63.35	64.39	65.43	66.48	67.54	68.61	69.69	70.77	71.86	72.96
16.75	56.60	57.57	58.56	59.55	60.55	61.55	62.57	63.60	64.63	65.67	66.72	67.77	68.83	69.90	70.98	72.07
17.00	55.91	56.87	57.84	58.82	59.81	60.81	61.81	62.82	63.84	64.87	65.90	66.95	68.00	69.05	70.12	71.19
17.25	55.23	56.19	57.15	58.11	59.09	60.07	61.06	62.06	63.07	64.09	65.11	66.14	67.18	68.22	69.27	70.33
17.50	54.57	55.51	56.46	57.42	58.38	59.35	60.33	61.32	62.32	63.32	64.33	65.35	66.37	67.41	68.45	69.49
17.75	53.93	54.86	55.79	56.74	57.69	58.65	59.62	60.59	61.58	62.57	63.57	64.57	65.59	66.61	67.63	68.67
18.00	53.29	54.21	55.14	56.07	57.01	57.96	58.92	59.88	60.85	61.83	62.82	63.81	64.82	65.82	66.84	67.86
18.25	52.67	53.58	54.49	55.42	56.35	57.28	58.23	59.18	60.14	61.11	62.09	63.07	64.06	65.06	66.06	67.07
18.50	52.06	52.96	53.86	54.78	55.70	56.62	57.56	58.50	59.45	60.41	61.37	62.34	63.32	64.30	65.29	66.29
18.75	51.46	52.35	53.25	54.15	55.06	55.97	56.90	57.83	58.77	59.71	60.67	61.63	62.59	63.57	64.55	65.53
19.00	50.88	51.76	52.64	53.53	54.43	55.34	56.25	57.17	58.10	59.03	59.98	60.93	61.88	62.84	63.81	64.79
20.00	48.65	49.49	50.33	51.19	52.05	52.91	53.79	54.67	55.55	56.45	57.35	58.26	59.17	60.09	61.02	61.95
25.00	39.70	40.39	41.08	41.77	42.47	43.18	43.89	44.61	45.34	46.07	46.80	47.54	48.29	49.04	49.79	50.56
30.00	33.37	33.94	34.52	35.11	35.70	36.29	36.89	37.49	38.10	38.72	39.33	39.96	40.58	41.21	41.85	42.49

Description: This table shows the yield to maturity of a mortgage purchased at the price shown in the index.

Example: The yield to maturity of a 10.75 %, 17 year mortgage at a price of 111.00 is 9.07 %.

INTEREST RATE, %

PRICE	7.00%	7.25%	7.50%	7.75%	8.00%	8.25%	8.50%	8.75%	9.00%	9.25%	9.50%	9.75%	10.00%	10.25%	10.50%	10.75%
155	1.19	1.39	1.60	1.81	2.01	2.22	2.43	2.63	2.84	3.04	3.24	3.45	3.65	3.85	4.05	4.26
150	1.59	1.80	2.01	2.21	2.42	2.63	2.84	3.05	3.26	3.46	3.67	3.88	4.08	4.29	4.49	4.70
145	2.00	2.22	2.43	2.64	2.85	3.07	3.28	3.49	3.70	3.91	4.12	4.33	4.53	4.74	4.95	5.16
140	2.44	2.66	2.87	3.09	3.30	3.52	3.73	3.95	4.16	4.37	4.59	4.80	5.01	5.22	5.43	5.64
135	2.90	3.12	3.34	3.56	3.78	4.00	4.21	4.43	4.65	4.86	5.08	5.30	5.51	5.73	5.94	6.15
130	3.39	3.61	3.84	4.06	4.28	4.50	4.72	4.94	5.16	5.38	5.60	5.82	6.04	6.26	6.48	6.69
125	3.90	4.13	4.36	4.58	4.81	5.03	5.26	5.48	5.70	5.93	6.15	6.38	6.60	6.82	7.04	7.27
124	4.01	4.24	4.46	4.69	4.92	5.14	5.37	5.59	5.82	6.04	6.27	6.49	6.71	6.94	7.16	7.38
123	4.12	4.34	4.57	4.80	5.03	5.25	5.48	5.70	5.93	6.16	6.38	6.61	6.83	7.06	7.28	7.50
122	4.23	4.45	4.68	4.91	5.14	5.36	5.59	5.82	6.05	6.27	6.50	6.72	6.95	7.18	7.40	7.63
121	4.34	4.56	4.79	5.02	5.25	5.48	5.71	5.93	6.16	6.39	6.62	6.84	7.07	7.30	7.52	7.75
120	4.45	4.68	4.91	5.14	5.36	5.59	5.82	6.05	6.28	6.51	6.74	6.96	7.19	7.42	7.65	7.87
119	4.56	4.79	5.02	5.25	5.48	5.71	5.94	6.17	6.40	6.63	6.86	7.09	7.31	7.54	7.77	8.00
118	4.67	4.90	5.14	5.37	5.60	5.83	6.06	6.29	6.52	6.75	6.98	7.21	7.44	7.67	7.90	8.13
117	4.79	5.02	5.25	5.48	5.72	5.95	6.18	6.41	6.64	6.87	7.10	7.33	7.57	7.80	8.03	8.26
116	4.90	5.14	5.37	5.60	5.84	6.07	6.30	6.53	6.77	7.00	7.23	7.46	7.69	7.92	8.16	8.39
115	5.02	5.26	5.49	5.73	5.96	6.19	6.43	6.66	6.89	7.12	7.36	7.59	7.82	8.05	8.29	8.52
114	5.14	5.38	5.61	5.85	6.08	6.32	6.55	6.79	7.02	7.25	7.49	7.72	7.95	8.19	8.42	8.65
113	5.26	5.50	5.74	5.97	6.21	6.44	6.68	6.91	7.15	7.38	7.62	7.85	8.09	8.32	8.56	8.79
112	5.39	5.62	5.86	6.10	6.33	6.57	6.81	7.04	7.28	7.51	7.75	7.99	8.22	8.46	8.69	8.93
111	5.51	5.75	5.99	6.22	6.46	6.70	6.94	7.17	7.41	7.65	7.88	8.12	8.36	8.59	8.83	9.07
110	5.64	5.88	6.11	6.35	6.59	6.83	7.07	7.31	7.54	7.78	8.02	8.26	8.50	8.73	8.97	9.21
109	5.76	6.00	6.24	6.48	6.72	6.96	7.20	7.44	7.68	7.92	8.16	8.40	8.64	8.88	9.11	9.35
108	5.89	6.13	6.38	6.62	6.86	7.10	7.34	7.58	7.82	8.06	8.30	8.54	8.78	9.02	9.26	9.50
107	6.02	6.27	6.51	6.75	6.99	7.23	7.48	7.72	7.96	8.20	8.44	8.68	8.92	9.16	9.41	9.65
106	6.16	6.40	6.64	6.89	7.13	7.37	7.61	7.86	8.10	8.34	8.59	8.83	9.07	9.31	9.55	9.80
105	6.29	6.54	6.78	7.02	7.27	7.51	7.76	8.00	8.24	8.49	8.73	8.97	9.22	9.46	9.71	9.95
104	6.43	6.67	6.92	7.16	7.41	7.65	7.90	8.14	8.39	8.63	8.88	9.12	9.37	9.61	9.86	10.10
103	6.57	6.81	7.06	7.31	7.55	7.80	8.05	8.29	8.54	8.78	9.03	9.28	9.52	9.77	10.01	10.26
102	6.71	6.96	7.20	7.45	7.70	7.95	8.19	8.44	8.69	8.94	9.18	9.43	9.68	9.92	10.17	10.42
101	6.85	7.10	7.35	7.60	7.85	8.09	8.34	8.59	8.84	9.09	9.34	9.59	9.83	10.08	10.33	10.58
100	7.00	7.25	7.50	7.75	8.00	8.25	8.50	8.75	9.00	9.25	9.50	9.75	10.00	10.25	10.50	10.75
99	7.14	7.39	7.64	7.90	8.15	8.40	8.65	8.90	9.15	9.40	9.65	9.91	10.16	10.41	10.66	10.91
98	7.29	7.54	7.80	8.05	8.30	8.55	8.81	9.06	9.31	9.56	9.82	10.07	10.32	10.58	10.83	11.08
97	7.44	7.70	7.95	8.20	8.46	8.71	8.97	9.22	9.47	9.73	9.98	10.24	10.49	10.74	11.00	11.25
96	7.60	7.85	8.11	8.36	8.62	8.87	9.13	9.38	9.64	9.89	10.15	10.41	10.66	10.92	11.17	11.43
95	7.75	8.01	8.27	8.52	8.78	9.04	9.29	9.55	9.81	10.06	10.32	10.58	10.83	11.09	11.35	11.61
94	7.91	8.17	8.43	8.68	8.94	9.20	9.46	9.72	9.98	10.23	10.49	10.75	11.01	11.27	11.53	11.79
93	8.07	8.33	8.59	8.85	9.11	9.37	9.63	9.89	10.15	10.41	10.67	10.93	11.19	11.45	11.71	11.97
92	8.24	8.50	8.76	9.02	9.28	9.54	9.80	10.06	10.32	10.59	10.85	11.11	11.37	11.63	11.90	12.16
91	8.40	8.66	8.93	9.19	9.45	9.71	9.98	10.24	10.50	10.77	11.03	11.29	11.56	11.82	12.09	12.35
90	8.57	8.84	9.10	9.36	9.63	9.89	10.16	10.42	10.69	10.95	11.22	11.48	11.75	12.01	12.28	12.54
89	8.74	9.01	9.27	9.54	9.81	10.07	10.34	10.60	10.87	11.14	11.40	11.67	11.94	12.21	12.47	12.74
88	8.92	9.19	9.45	9.72	9.99	10.26	10.52	10.79	11.06	11.33	11.60	11.86	12.13	12.40	12.67	12.94
87	9.10	9.37	9.63	9.90	10.17	10.44	10.71	10.98	11.25	11.52	11.79	12.06	12.33	12.60	12.87	13.15
86	9.28	9.55	9.82	10.09	10.36	10.63	10.90	11.17	11.45	11.72	11.99	12.26	12.54	12.81	13.08	13.35
85	9.46	9.74	10.01	10.28	10.55	10.83	11.10	11.37	11.65	11.92	12.19	12.47	12.74	13.02	13.29	13.57
84	9.65	9.93	10.20	10.47	10.75	11.02	11.30	11.57	11.85	12.12	12.40	12.68	12.95	13.23	13.51	13.78
83	9.84	10.12	10.39	10.67	10.95	11.22	11.50	11.78	12.05	12.33	12.61	12.89	13.17	13.45	13.73	14.00
82	10.04	10.32	10.59	10.87	11.15	11.43	11.71	11.99	12.27	12.54	12.83	13.11	13.39	13.67	13.95	14.23
81	10.24	10.52	10.80	11.08	11.36	11.64	11.92	12.20	12.48	12.76	13.04	13.33	13.61	13.89	14.18	14.46
80	10.44	10.72	11.00	11.28	11.57	11.85	12.13	12.42	12.70	12.98	13.27	13.55	13.84	14.12	14.41	14.69
79	10.65	10.93	11.21	11.50	11.78	12.07	12.35	12.64	12.92	13.21	13.50	13.78	14.07	14.36	14.65	14.93
78	10.86	11.14	11.43	11.71	12.00	12.29	12.57	12.86	13.15	13.44	13.73	14.02	14.31	14.60	14.89	15.18
77	11.07	11.36	11.65	11.94	12.22	12.51	12.80	13.09	13.38	13.67	13.97	14.26	14.55	14.84	15.14	15.43
76	11.29	11.58	11.87	12.16	12.45	12.74	13.04	13.33	13.62	13.91	14.21	14.50	14.80	15.09	15.39	15.68
75	11.52	11.81	12.10	12.39	12.69	12.98	13.27	13.57	13.86	14.16	14.46	14.75	15.05	15.35	15.65	15.94
74	11.75	12.04	12.33	12.63	12.93	13.22	13.52	13.82	14.11	14.41	14.71	15.01	15.31	15.61	15.91	16.21
73	11.98	12.28	12.57	12.87	13.17	13.47	13.77	14.07	14.37	14.67	14.97	15.27	15.57	15.88	16.18	16.48
70	12.71	13.02	13.32	13.63	13.93	14.24	14.55	14.86	15.16	15.47	15.78	16.09	16.41	16.72	17.03	17.34
65	14.06	14.38	14.69	15.01	15.34	15.66	15.98	16.30	16.63	16.95	17.28	17.61	17.93	18.26	18.59	18.92
60	15.58	15.92	16.25	16.59	16.93	17.27	17.61	17.95	18.30	18.64	18.99	19.33	19.68	20.03	20.38	20.73
55	17.33	17.69	18.05	18.41	18.77	19.13	19.49	19.86	20.22	20.59	20.96	21.33	21.70	22.07	22.45	22.82
50	19.38	19.76	20.15	20.53	20.92	21.31	21.70	22.09	22.49	22.88	23.28	23.68	24.08	24.48	24.89	25.29
45	21.82	22.23	22.65	23.07	23.49	23.91	24.34	24.77	25.19	25.63	26.06	26.50	26.93	27.37	27.82	28.26
40	24.80	25.25	25.71	26.17	26.64	27.10	27.57	28.05	28.52	29.00	29.48	29.96	30.45	30.94	31.43	31.92
35	28.55	29.06	29.57	30.09	30.61	31.14	31.67	32.20	32.73	33.27	33.81	34.36	34.91	35.46	36.01	36.57
30	33.46	34.05	34.64	35.24	35.84	36.44	37.05	37.67	38.28	38.91	39.53	40.16	40.80	41.44	42.08	42.73

MORTGAGE PRICE

17 YEARS

Description: This table shows the price to pay for a monthly payment mortgage loan at the yield rate.

Example: The price of a 15.00 %, 17 year mortgage loan to yield 8.00 % to maturity is $ 151.15.

INTEREST RATE, %

YIELD	11.00%	11.25%	11.50%	11.75%	12.00%	12.25%	12.50%	12.75%	13.00%	13.25%	13.50%	13.75%	14.00%	14.25%	14.50%	15.00%
0.00	221.42	224.74	228.09	231.46	234.85	238.26	241.68	245.13	248.60	252.08	255.59	259.11	262.65	266.20	269.77	276.97
1.00	203.54	206.60	209.68	212.77	215.89	219.02	222.17	225.34	228.53	231.73	234.95	238.19	241.44	244.71	247.99	254.61
2.00	187.57	190.39	193.23	196.08	198.95	201.84	204.74	207.66	210.60	213.55	216.52	219.50	222.50	225.51	228.54	234.63
3.00	173.28	175.88	178.50	181.14	183.79	186.46	189.14	191.84	194.55	197.28	200.02	202.77	205.54	208.33	211.12	216.76
4.00	160.47	162.88	165.30	167.74	170.20	172.67	175.15	177.65	180.16	182.69	185.23	187.78	190.34	192.92	195.51	200.73
4.25	157.47	159.84	162.22	164.61	167.02	169.45	171.89	174.34	176.80	179.28	181.77	184.28	186.79	189.32	191.86	196.98
4.50	154.56	156.88	159.22	161.57	163.93	166.31	168.70	171.11	173.53	175.96	178.41	180.87	183.34	185.82	188.31	193.34
4.75	151.72	154.00	156.29	158.60	160.92	163.26	165.61	167.97	170.34	172.73	175.13	177.55	179.97	182.41	184.86	189.79
5.00	148.96	151.19	153.45	155.71	157.99	160.28	162.59	164.91	167.24	169.59	171.94	174.31	176.69	179.08	181.49	186.33
5.25	146.27	148.46	150.67	152.90	155.14	157.39	159.65	161.93	164.22	166.52	168.84	171.16	173.50	175.85	178.21	182.96
5.50	143.64	145.80	147.97	150.16	152.36	154.57	156.79	159.03	161.28	163.54	165.81	168.09	170.39	172.70	175.01	179.68
5.75	141.09	143.21	145.34	147.49	149.65	151.82	154.00	156.20	158.41	160.63	162.86	165.10	167.36	169.63	171.90	176.49
6.00	138.60	140.68	142.78	144.89	147.01	149.14	151.29	153.44	155.61	157.80	159.99	162.19	164.41	166.63	168.87	173.37
6.25	136.18	138.22	140.28	142.35	144.44	146.53	148.64	150.76	152.89	155.03	157.19	159.35	161.53	163.72	165.92	170.34
6.50	133.81	135.82	137.85	139.88	141.93	143.99	146.06	148.14	150.24	152.34	154.46	156.59	158.73	160.88	163.04	167.39
6.75	131.51	133.49	135.47	137.47	139.49	141.51	143.55	145.59	147.65	149.72	151.80	153.89	156.00	158.11	160.23	164.50
7.00	129.26	131.21	133.16	135.13	137.10	139.09	141.10	143.11	145.13	147.17	149.21	151.27	153.33	155.41	157.50	161.70
7.25	127.08	128.98	130.91	132.84	134.78	136.74	138.71	140.69	142.67	144.67	146.68	148.71	150.74	152.78	154.83	158.96
7.50	124.94	126.82	128.71	130.61	132.52	134.44	136.38	138.32	140.28	142.25	144.22	146.21	148.21	150.21	152.23	156.29
7.75	122.86	124.71	126.56	128.43	130.31	132.20	134.11	136.02	137.94	139.88	141.82	143.77	145.74	147.71	149.69	153.69
8.00	120.83	122.65	124.47	126.31	128.16	130.02	131.89	133.77	135.66	137.57	139.48	141.40	143.33	145.27	147.22	151.15
8.25	118.85	120.64	122.44	124.24	126.06	127.89	129.73	131.58	133.44	135.31	137.19	139.08	140.98	142.89	144.81	148.67
8.50	116.92	118.68	120.45	122.23	124.01	125.81	127.62	129.44	131.27	133.12	134.96	136.82	138.69	140.57	142.46	146.26
8.75	115.04	116.77	118.51	120.26	122.02	123.79	125.57	127.36	129.16	130.97	132.79	134.62	136.46	138.31	140.16	143.90
9.00	113.20	114.90	116.61	118.34	120.07	121.81	123.56	125.33	127.10	128.88	130.67	132.47	134.28	136.10	137.92	141.60
9.25	111.41	113.08	114.77	116.46	118.17	119.88	121.61	123.34	125.08	126.84	128.60	130.37	132.15	133.94	135.74	139.36
9.50	109.66	111.31	112.96	114.63	116.31	118.00	119.70	121.40	123.12	124.85	126.58	128.32	130.08	131.84	133.61	137.17
9.75	107.95	109.57	111.20	112.85	114.50	116.16	117.83	119.51	121.20	122.90	124.61	126.33	128.05	129.78	131.53	135.04
10.00	106.28	107.88	109.49	111.10	112.73	114.37	116.01	117.67	119.33	121.00	122.68	124.37	126.07	127.78	129.50	132.95
10.25	104.66	106.23	107.81	109.40	111.00	112.62	114.24	115.86	117.50	119.15	120.81	122.47	124.14	125.82	127.51	130.91
10.50	103.07	104.62	106.17	107.74	109.32	110.91	112.50	114.11	115.72	117.34	118.97	120.61	122.26	123.91	125.58	128.93
10.75	101.52	103.04	104.58	106.12	107.67	109.24	110.81	112.39	113.98	115.57	117.18	118.79	120.42	122.05	123.69	126.99
11.00	100.00	101.50	103.01	104.54	106.07	107.60	109.15	110.71	112.28	113.85	115.43	117.02	118.62	120.23	121.84	125.09
11.25	98.52	100.00	101.49	102.99	104.50	106.01	107.54	109.07	110.61	112.16	113.72	115.29	116.86	118.45	120.04	123.24
11.50	97.07	98.53	100.00	101.48	102.96	104.46	105.96	107.47	108.99	110.52	112.05	113.60	115.15	116.71	118.27	121.43
11.75	95.66	97.10	98.54	100.00	101.46	102.94	104.42	105.91	107.40	108.91	110.42	111.94	113.47	115.01	116.55	119.66
12.00	94.28	95.70	97.12	98.56	100.00	101.45	102.91	104.38	105.85	107.34	108.83	110.33	111.84	113.35	114.87	117.94
12.25	92.93	94.33	95.73	97.15	98.57	100.00	101.44	102.89	104.34	105.80	107.27	108.75	110.24	111.73	113.23	116.25
12.50	91.61	92.99	94.38	95.77	97.17	98.58	100.00	101.43	102.86	104.30	105.75	107.21	108.67	110.14	111.62	114.60
12.75	90.33	91.68	93.05	94.42	95.81	97.20	98.59	100.00	101.41	102.84	104.26	105.70	107.14	108.60	110.05	112.99
13.00	89.07	90.40	91.75	93.11	94.47	95.84	97.22	98.61	100.00	101.40	102.81	104.23	105.65	107.08	108.52	111.41
13.25	87.84	89.16	90.48	91.82	93.16	94.52	95.88	97.24	98.62	100.00	101.39	102.79	104.19	105.60	107.02	109.87
13.50	86.63	87.93	89.24	90.56	91.89	93.22	94.56	95.91	97.27	98.63	100.00	101.38	102.76	104.15	105.55	108.37
13.75	85.45	86.74	88.03	89.33	90.64	91.95	93.28	94.61	95.94	97.29	98.64	100.00	101.37	102.74	104.12	106.89
14.00	84.30	85.57	86.84	88.13	89.42	90.71	92.02	93.33	94.65	95.98	97.31	98.65	100.00	101.35	102.71	105.45
14.25	83.18	84.43	85.68	86.95	88.22	89.50	90.79	92.08	93.39	94.70	96.01	97.33	98.66	100.00	101.34	104.05
14.50	82.08	83.31	84.55	85.80	87.05	88.32	89.59	90.87	92.15	93.44	94.74	96.05	97.36	98.68	100.00	102.67
14.75	81.00	82.21	83.44	84.67	85.91	87.16	88.41	89.67	90.94	92.21	93.50	94.78	96.08	97.38	98.69	101.32
15.00	79.94	81.14	82.35	83.57	84.79	86.02	87.26	88.50	89.76	91.01	92.28	93.55	94.83	96.11	97.40	100.00
15.25	78.91	80.10	81.29	82.49	83.70	84.91	86.13	87.36	88.60	89.84	91.09	92.34	93.60	94.87	96.14	98.71
15.50	77.90	79.07	80.25	81.43	82.63	83.82	85.03	86.24	87.46	88.69	89.92	91.16	92.41	93.66	94.91	97.45
15.75	76.91	78.07	79.23	80.40	81.58	82.76	83.95	85.15	86.35	87.56	88.78	90.00	91.23	92.47	93.71	96.21
16.00	75.94	77.08	78.23	79.39	80.55	81.72	82.90	84.08	85.27	86.46	87.66	88.87	90.08	91.30	92.53	95.00
16.25	75.00	76.12	77.26	78.40	79.55	80.70	81.86	83.03	84.20	85.38	86.57	87.76	88.96	90.16	91.38	93.81
16.50	74.07	75.18	76.30	77.43	78.56	79.70	80.85	82.00	83.16	84.33	85.50	86.68	87.86	89.05	90.24	92.65
16.75	73.16	74.26	75.36	76.48	77.60	78.72	79.86	81.00	82.14	83.29	84.45	85.61	86.78	87.96	89.14	91.52
17.00	72.27	73.36	74.45	75.55	76.65	77.77	78.88	80.01	81.14	82.28	83.42	84.57	85.73	86.89	88.05	90.40
17.25	71.40	72.47	73.55	74.64	75.73	76.83	77.93	79.04	80.16	81.29	82.42	83.55	84.69	85.84	86.99	89.31
17.50	70.54	71.60	72.67	73.74	74.82	75.91	77.00	78.10	79.20	80.31	81.43	82.55	83.68	84.81	85.95	88.24
17.75	69.71	70.76	71.81	72.87	73.94	75.01	76.09	77.17	78.26	79.36	80.46	81.57	82.69	83.81	84.93	87.20
18.00	68.89	69.92	70.96	72.01	73.07	74.13	75.19	76.27	77.34	78.43	79.52	80.61	81.71	82.82	83.93	86.17
18.25	68.08	69.11	70.14	71.17	72.21	73.26	74.32	75.38	76.44	77.51	78.59	79.67	80.76	81.86	82.95	85.17
18.50	67.30	68.31	69.33	70.35	71.38	72.42	73.46	74.50	75.56	76.62	77.68	78.75	79.83	80.91	81.99	84.18
18.75	66.53	67.53	68.53	69.54	70.56	71.58	72.61	73.65	74.69	75.74	76.79	77.85	78.91	79.98	81.05	83.22
19.00	65.77	66.76	67.75	68.75	69.76	70.77	71.79	72.81	73.84	74.88	75.92	76.96	78.02	79.07	80.13	82.27
20.00	62.89	63.83	64.78	65.74	66.70	67.67	68.64	69.62	70.61	71.60	72.59	73.59	74.60	75.61	76.62	78.67
25.00	51.32	52.09	52.87	53.65	54.43	55.22	56.02	56.82	57.62	58.43	59.24	60.06	60.88	61.70	62.53	64.20
30.00	43.13	43.78	44.43	45.09	45.75	46.41	47.08	47.75	48.43	49.11	49.79	50.48	51.16	51.86	52.55	53.96

Description: This table shows the yield to maturity of a mortgage purchased at the price shown in the index.

Example: The yield to maturity of a 15.00 %, 17 year mortgage at a price of 125.00 is 11.01 %.

INTEREST RATE, %

PRICE	11.00%	11.25%	11.50%	11.75%	12.00%	12.25%	12.50%	12.75%	13.00%	13.25%	13.50%	13.75%	14.00%	14.25%	14.50%	15.00%
250	–	–	–	–	–	–	–	–	–	.09	.25	.42	.58	.74	.90	1.22
240	–	–	–	–	–	–	–	.24	.41	.57	.74	.90	1.07	1.23	1.39	1.72
230	–	–	–	.07	.24	.41	.58	.75	.92	1.09	1.25	1.42	1.59	1.75	1.92	2.24
220	.07	.25	–	.59	.77	.94	1.11	1.29	1.46	1.63	1.80	1.97	2.14	2.30	2.47	2.81
210	.62	.80	.98	1.15	1.33	1.51	1.68	1.86	2.03	2.20	2.38	2.55	2.72	2.89	3.06	3.40
200	1.21	1.39	1.57	1.75	1.93	2.11	2.29	2.47	2.64	2.82	3.00	3.17	3.35	3.52	3.70	4.04
195	1.52	1.70	1.88	2.06	2.25	2.43	2.61	2.79	2.97	3.14	3.32	3.50	3.68	3.85	4.03	4.38
190	1.84	2.02	2.20	2.39	2.57	2.75	2.94	3.12	3.30	3.48	3.66	3.84	4.02	4.20	4.38	4.73
185	2.17	2.35	2.54	2.73	2.91	3.10	3.28	3.46	3.65	3.83	4.01	4.19	4.37	4.55	4.73	5.09
180	2.51	2.70	2.89	3.08	3.26	3.45	3.64	3.82	4.01	4.19	4.38	4.56	4.74	4.93	5.11	5.47
175	2.87	3.06	3.25	3.44	3.63	3.82	4.01	4.19	4.38	4.57	4.76	4.94	5.13	5.31	5.50	5.86
170	3.24	3.43	3.63	3.82	4.01	4.20	4.39	4.58	4.77	4.96	5.15	5.34	5.53	5.71	5.90	6.27
165	3.63	3.82	4.02	4.21	4.41	4.60	4.79	4.99	5.18	5.37	5.56	5.75	5.94	6.13	6.32	6.70
160	4.03	4.23	4.43	4.63	4.82	5.02	5.22	5.41	5.61	5.80	5.99	6.19	6.38	6.57	6.77	7.15
155	4.46	4.66	4.86	5.06	5.26	5.46	5.65	5.85	6.05	6.25	6.45	6.64	6.84	7.03	7.23	7.62
150	4.90	5.10	5.31	5.51	5.71	5.91	6.12	6.32	6.52	6.72	6.92	7.12	7.32	7.52	7.71	8.11
145	5.36	5.57	5.78	5.98	6.19	6.39	6.60	6.80	7.01	7.21	7.42	7.62	7.82	8.02	8.23	8.63
140	5.85	6.06	6.27	6.48	6.69	6.90	7.11	7.32	7.52	7.73	7.94	8.15	8.35	8.56	8.76	9.17
135	6.37	6.58	6.80	7.01	7.22	7.43	7.65	7.86	8.07	8.28	8.49	8.70	8.91	9.12	9.33	9.75
130	6.91	7.13	7.35	7.56	7.78	8.00	8.21	8.43	8.65	8.86	9.08	9.29	9.50	9.72	9.93	10.36
125	7.49	7.71	7.93	8.15	8.37	8.59	8.82	9.04	9.26	9.48	9.69	9.91	10.13	10.35	10.57	11.01
120	8.10	8.33	8.55	8.78	9.00	9.23	9.45	9.68	9.90	10.13	10.35	10.58	10.80	11.03	11.25	11.70
115	8.75	8.98	9.21	9.44	9.68	9.91	10.14	10.37	10.60	10.83	11.06	11.29	11.52	11.75	11.98	12.43
113	9.02	9.26	9.49	9.72	9.96	10.19	10.42	10.66	10.89	11.12	11.35	11.58	11.82	12.05	12.28	12.74
112	9.16	9.40	9.63	9.87	10.10	10.33	10.57	10.80	11.04	11.27	11.50	11.74	11.97	12.20	12.44	12.90
111	9.30	9.54	9.77	10.01	10.25	10.48	10.72	10.95	11.19	11.42	11.66	11.89	12.12	12.36	12.59	13.06
110	9.45	9.68	9.92	10.16	10.39	10.63	10.87	11.10	11.34	11.57	11.81	12.05	12.28	12.52	12.75	13.22
109	9.59	9.83	10.07	10.31	10.54	10.78	11.02	11.26	11.49	11.73	11.97	12.21	12.44	12.68	12.92	13.39
108	9.74	9.98	10.22	10.46	10.69	10.93	11.17	11.41	11.65	11.89	12.13	12.37	12.60	12.84	13.08	13.56
107	9.89	10.13	10.37	10.61	10.85	11.09	11.33	11.57	11.81	12.05	12.29	12.53	12.77	13.01	13.25	13.73
106	10.04	10.28	10.52	10.76	11.01	11.25	11.49	11.73	11.97	12.21	12.45	12.69	12.94	13.18	13.42	13.90
105	10.19	10.43	10.68	10.92	11.16	11.41	11.65	11.89	12.14	12.38	12.62	12.86	13.11	13.35	13.59	14.08
104	10.35	10.59	10.84	11.08	11.33	11.57	11.81	12.06	12.30	12.55	12.79	13.03	13.28	13.52	13.77	14.25
103	10.51	10.75	11.00	11.24	11.49	11.73	11.98	12.23	12.47	12.72	12.96	13.21	13.45	13.70	13.94	14.43
102	10.67	10.91	11.16	11.41	11.65	11.90	12.15	12.40	12.64	12.89	13.14	13.38	13.63	13.88	14.12	14.62
101	10.83	11.08	11.33	11.58	11.82	12.07	12.32	12.57	12.82	13.07	13.31	13.56	13.81	14.06	14.31	14.81
100	11.00	11.25	11.50	11.75	12.00	12.25	12.50	12.75	13.00	13.25	13.50	13.75	14.00	14.25	14.50	15.00
99	11.16	11.41	11.67	11.92	12.17	12.42	12.67	12.92	13.18	13.43	13.68	13.93	14.18	14.43	14.68	15.19
98	11.33	11.59	11.84	12.09	12.35	12.60	12.85	13.11	13.36	13.61	13.86	14.12	14.37	14.62	14.88	15.38
97	11.51	11.76	12.02	12.27	12.53	12.78	13.04	13.29	13.54	13.80	14.05	14.31	14.56	14.82	15.07	15.58
96	11.68	11.94	12.20	12.45	12.71	12.97	13.22	13.48	13.73	13.99	14.25	14.50	14.76	15.02	15.27	15.79
95	11.86	12.12	12.38	12.64	12.90	13.15	13.41	13.67	13.93	14.19	14.44	14.70	14.96	15.22	15.48	15.99
94	12.05	12.31	12.57	12.82	13.08	13.34	13.60	13.86	14.12	14.38	14.64	14.90	15.16	15.42	15.68	16.21
93	12.23	12.49	12.75	13.02	13.28	13.54	13.80	14.06	14.32	14.58	14.85	15.11	15.37	15.63	15.89	16.42
92	12.42	12.68	12.95	13.21	13.47	13.74	14.00	14.26	14.53	14.79	15.05	15.32	15.58	15.84	16.11	16.64
91	12.61	12.88	13.14	13.41	13.67	13.94	14.20	14.47	14.73	15.00	15.26	15.53	15.80	16.06	16.33	16.86
90	12.81	13.08	13.34	13.61	13.87	14.14	14.41	14.68	14.94	15.21	15.48	15.75	16.01	16.28	16.55	17.09
89	13.01	13.28	13.54	13.81	14.08	14.35	14.62	14.89	15.16	15.43	15.70	15.97	16.24	16.51	16.78	17.32
88	13.21	13.48	13.75	14.02	14.29	14.56	14.83	15.10	15.38	15.65	15.92	16.19	16.46	16.74	17.01	17.55
87	13.42	13.69	13.96	14.23	14.51	14.78	15.05	15.33	15.60	15.87	16.15	16.42	16.69	16.97	17.24	17.79
86	13.63	13.90	14.18	14.45	14.73	15.00	15.27	15.55	15.83	16.10	16.38	16.65	16.93	17.21	17.48	18.04
85	13.84	14.12	14.40	14.67	14.95	15.22	15.50	15.78	16.06	16.33	16.61	16.89	17.17	17.45	17.73	18.29
84	14.06	14.34	14.62	14.90	15.18	15.45	15.73	16.01	16.29	16.57	16.85	17.13	17.42	17.70	17.98	18.54
83	14.28	14.56	14.85	15.13	15.41	15.69	15.97	16.25	16.53	16.82	17.10	17.38	17.67	17.95	18.23	18.80
82	14.51	14.79	15.08	15.36	15.64	15.93	16.21	16.50	16.78	17.06	17.35	17.64	17.92	18.21	18.49	19.07
81	14.74	15.03	15.31	15.60	15.88	16.17	16.46	16.74	17.03	17.32	17.61	17.89	18.18	18.47	18.76	19.34
80	14.98	15.27	15.56	15.84	16.13	16.42	16.71	17.00	17.29	17.58	17.87	18.16	18.45	18.74	19.03	19.62
79	15.22	15.51	15.80	16.09	16.38	16.67	16.97	17.26	17.55	17.84	18.13	18.43	18.72	19.01	19.31	19.90
78	15.47	15.76	16.05	16.35	16.64	16.93	17.23	17.52	17.82	18.11	18.41	18.70	19.00	19.30	19.59	20.19
77	15.72	16.02	16.31	16.61	16.90	17.20	17.50	17.79	18.09	18.39	18.69	18.98	19.28	19.58	19.88	20.48
76	15.98	16.28	16.57	16.87	17.17	17.47	17.77	18.07	18.37	18.67	18.97	19.27	19.58	19.88	20.18	20.79
75	16.24	16.54	16.84	17.14	17.45	17.75	18.05	18.35	18.66	18.96	19.26	19.57	19.87	20.18	20.48	21.10
74	16.51	16.82	17.12	17.42	17.73	18.03	18.34	18.64	18.95	19.25	19.56	19.87	20.18	20.49	20.80	21.42
73	16.79	17.09	17.40	17.71	18.01	18.32	18.63	18.94	19.25	19.56	19.87	20.18	20.49	20.80	21.11	21.74
70	17.66	17.97	18.29	18.60	18.92	19.24	19.55	19.87	20.19	20.51	20.83	21.15	21.47	21.80	22.12	22.77
65	19.25	19.59	19.92	20.25	20.59	20.92	21.26	21.60	21.93	22.27	22.61	22.95	23.29	23.64	23.98	24.67
60	21.08	21.43	21.79	22.14	22.50	22.86	23.21	23.57	23.93	24.30	24.66	25.02	25.39	25.75	26.12	26.85
55	23.20	23.58	23.96	24.34	24.72	25.10	25.49	25.87	26.26	26.65	27.04	27.43	27.82	28.22	28.61	29.41

Description: This table shows the price to pay for a monthly payment mortgage loan at the yield rate.

Example: The price of a 6.75 %, 18 year mortgage loan to yield 8.00 % to maturity is $ 91.54.

INTEREST RATE, %

YIELD	0.00%	1.00%	2.00%	3.00%	4.00%	4.25%	4.50%	4.75%	5.00%	5.25%	5.50%	5.75%	6.00%	6.25%	6.50%	6.75%
0.00	100.00	109.31	119.16	129.54	140.44	143.25	146.09	148.96	151.86	154.79	157.75	160.74	163.76	166.82	169.90	173.01
1.00	91.48	100.00	109.01	118.51	128.48	131.05	133.64	136.27	138.92	141.60	144.31	147.05	149.81	152.61	155.42	158.27
2.00	83.92	91.73	100.00	108.71	117.86	120.22	122.60	125.00	127.44	129.90	132.38	134.89	137.43	139.99	142.58	145.19
3.00	77.20	84.38	91.99	100.00	108.42	110.58	112.77	114.99	117.23	119.49	121.78	124.09	126.42	128.77	131.15	133.56
4.00	71.20	77.83	84.85	92.24	100.00	102.00	104.02	106.06	108.13	110.21	112.32	114.45	116.60	118.78	120.97	123.19
4.25	69.81	76.31	83.18	90.43	98.04	100.00	101.98	103.98	106.01	108.05	110.12	112.21	114.32	116.45	118.60	120.77
4.50	68.45	74.83	81.57	88.67	96.14	98.06	100.00	101.96	103.95	105.96	107.98	110.03	112.10	114.19	116.30	118.43
4.75	67.13	73.39	80.00	86.97	94.29	96.17	98.07	100.00	101.95	103.91	105.90	107.91	109.94	111.99	114.06	116.15
5.00	65.85	71.98	78.47	85.31	92.48	94.33	96.20	98.09	100.00	101.93	103.88	105.85	107.84	109.85	111.88	113.93
5.25	64.61	70.62	76.98	83.69	90.73	92.55	94.38	96.23	98.11	100.00	101.91	103.85	105.80	107.77	109.76	111.77
5.50	63.39	69.29	75.54	82.12	89.03	90.81	92.61	94.43	96.26	98.12	100.00	101.90	103.81	105.75	107.70	109.67
5.75	62.21	68.00	74.13	80.59	87.37	89.12	90.88	92.67	94.47	96.30	98.14	100.00	101.88	103.78	105.70	107.63
6.00	61.06	66.75	72.76	79.10	85.76	87.47	89.21	90.96	92.73	94.52	96.33	98.15	100.00	101.86	103.75	105.65
6.25	59.95	65.53	71.43	77.65	84.19	85.87	87.57	89.29	91.03	92.79	94.56	96.36	98.17	100.00	101.85	103.71
6.50	58.86	64.34	70.14	76.25	82.66	84.31	85.98	87.67	89.38	91.11	92.85	94.61	96.39	98.19	100.00	101.83
6.75	57.80	63.18	68.88	74.88	81.18	82.80	84.44	86.10	87.77	89.47	91.18	92.91	94.66	96.42	98.20	100.00
7.00	56.77	62.06	67.65	73.54	79.73	81.32	82.93	84.56	86.21	87.87	89.55	91.25	92.97	94.70	96.45	98.22
7.25	55.77	60.96	66.45	72.24	78.32	79.89	81.47	83.07	84.69	86.32	87.97	89.64	91.33	93.03	94.75	96.48
7.50	54.79	59.89	65.29	70.98	76.95	78.49	80.04	81.61	83.20	84.81	86.43	88.07	89.73	91.40	93.09	94.79
7.75	53.84	58.85	64.15	69.74	75.61	77.12	78.65	80.20	81.76	83.34	84.93	86.54	88.17	89.81	91.47	93.15
8.00	52.91	57.84	63.05	68.54	74.31	75.80	77.30	78.82	80.35	81.90	83.47	85.05	86.65	88.27	89.90	91.54
8.25	52.01	56.85	61.97	67.37	73.04	74.50	75.98	77.47	78.98	80.50	82.04	83.60	85.17	86.76	88.36	89.98
8.50	51.13	55.89	60.93	66.23	71.81	73.24	74.69	76.16	77.64	79.14	80.66	82.19	83.73	85.29	86.87	88.46
8.75	50.27	54.95	59.91	65.12	70.61	72.02	73.44	74.88	76.34	77.82	79.31	80.81	82.33	83.86	85.41	86.98
9.00	49.44	54.04	58.91	64.04	69.43	70.82	72.22	73.64	75.07	76.52	77.99	79.47	80.96	82.47	83.99	85.53
9.25	48.62	53.15	57.94	62.99	68.29	69.65	71.03	72.43	73.84	75.26	76.70	78.16	79.63	81.11	82.61	84.12
9.50	47.83	52.28	57.00	61.96	67.18	68.52	69.87	71.25	72.63	74.04	75.45	76.88	78.33	79.79	81.26	82.75
9.75	47.06	51.44	56.07	60.96	66.09	67.41	68.74	70.09	71.46	72.84	74.23	75.64	77.06	78.50	79.95	81.41
10.00	46.30	50.62	55.18	59.98	65.03	66.33	67.64	68.97	70.31	71.67	73.04	74.43	75.83	77.24	78.67	80.11
10.25	45.57	49.81	54.30	59.03	64.00	65.28	66.57	67.88	69.20	70.53	71.88	73.25	74.62	76.01	77.42	78.84
10.50	44.85	49.03	53.44	58.10	62.99	64.25	65.52	66.81	68.11	69.42	70.75	72.09	73.45	74.82	76.20	77.60
10.75	44.15	48.26	52.61	57.19	62.01	63.25	64.50	65.77	67.05	68.34	69.65	70.97	72.30	73.65	75.01	76.39
11.00	43.47	47.52	51.80	56.31	61.05	62.27	63.50	64.75	66.01	67.28	68.57	69.87	71.19	72.51	73.85	75.20
11.25	42.80	46.79	51.00	55.45	60.11	61.31	62.53	63.76	65.00	66.25	67.52	68.80	70.10	71.40	72.72	74.05
11.50	42.15	46.08	50.23	54.60	59.20	60.38	61.58	62.79	64.01	65.25	66.50	67.76	69.03	70.32	71.62	72.93
11.75	41.52	45.38	49.47	53.78	58.31	59.47	60.65	61.84	63.05	64.27	65.49	66.74	67.99	69.26	70.54	71.83
12.00	40.90	44.71	48.74	52.98	57.44	58.59	59.75	60.92	62.11	63.31	64.52	65.74	66.98	68.23	69.49	70.76
12.25	40.30	44.05	48.02	52.20	56.59	57.72	58.87	60.02	61.19	62.37	63.57	64.77	65.99	67.22	68.46	69.71
12.50	39.71	43.40	47.31	51.43	55.76	56.88	58.00	59.14	60.29	61.46	62.63	63.82	65.02	66.23	67.46	68.69
12.75	39.13	42.77	46.63	50.69	54.95	56.05	57.16	58.28	59.42	60.57	61.73	62.90	64.08	65.27	66.48	67.70
13.00	38.57	42.16	45.96	49.96	54.16	55.25	56.34	57.45	58.57	59.70	60.84	61.99	63.16	64.33	65.52	66.72
13.25	38.02	41.56	45.30	49.25	53.39	54.46	55.54	56.63	57.73	58.84	59.97	61.11	62.26	63.42	64.59	65.77
13.50	37.48	40.97	44.66	48.55	52.64	53.69	54.75	55.83	56.92	58.01	59.12	60.25	61.38	62.52	63.68	64.84
13.75	36.96	40.40	44.04	47.87	51.90	52.94	53.99	55.05	56.12	57.20	58.30	59.40	60.52	61.65	62.79	63.94
14.00	36.44	39.84	43.43	47.21	51.18	52.20	53.24	54.28	55.34	56.41	57.49	58.58	59.68	60.79	61.92	63.05
14.25	35.94	39.29	42.83	46.56	50.48	51.49	52.51	53.54	54.58	55.63	56.70	57.77	58.86	59.96	61.06	62.18
14.50	35.45	38.75	42.25	45.93	49.79	50.78	51.79	52.81	53.84	54.88	55.93	56.99	58.06	59.14	60.23	61.34
14.75	34.97	38.23	41.67	45.31	49.12	50.10	51.09	52.10	53.11	54.13	55.17	56.22	57.27	58.34	59.42	60.51
15.00	34.51	37.72	41.12	44.70	48.46	49.43	50.41	51.40	52.40	53.41	54.43	55.47	56.51	57.56	58.62	59.70
15.25	34.05	37.22	40.57	44.11	47.82	48.77	49.74	50.72	51.70	52.70	53.71	54.73	55.76	56.80	57.85	58.91
15.50	33.60	36.73	40.04	43.53	47.19	48.13	49.09	50.05	51.03	52.01	53.01	54.01	55.03	56.05	57.09	58.13
15.75	33.16	36.25	39.52	42.96	46.58	47.51	48.45	49.40	50.36	51.33	52.32	53.31	54.31	55.32	56.34	57.38
16.00	32.74	35.78	39.01	42.41	45.97	46.89	47.82	48.76	49.71	50.67	51.64	52.62	53.61	54.61	55.62	56.64
16.25	32.32	35.33	38.51	41.86	45.39	46.29	47.21	48.14	49.08	50.02	50.98	51.95	52.92	53.91	54.91	55.91
16.50	31.91	34.88	38.02	41.33	44.81	45.71	46.61	47.53	48.45	49.39	50.33	51.29	52.25	53.23	54.21	55.20
16.75	31.51	34.44	37.54	40.81	44.25	45.13	46.03	46.93	47.84	48.77	49.70	50.64	51.60	52.56	53.53	54.51
17.00	31.11	34.01	37.08	40.31	43.70	44.57	45.45	46.35	47.25	48.16	49.08	50.01	50.95	51.90	52.86	53.83
17.25	30.73	33.59	36.62	39.81	43.16	44.02	44.89	45.77	46.67	47.57	48.48	49.40	50.32	51.26	52.21	53.17
17.50	30.35	33.18	36.17	39.32	42.63	43.48	44.34	45.21	46.09	46.98	47.88	48.79	49.71	50.64	51.57	52.52
17.75	29.99	32.78	35.73	38.84	42.11	42.96	43.81	44.67	45.54	46.41	47.30	48.20	49.11	50.02	50.95	51.88
18.00	29.63	32.38	35.30	38.38	41.61	42.44	43.28	44.13	44.99	45.86	46.73	47.62	48.52	49.42	50.33	51.26
18.25	29.27	32.00	34.88	37.92	41.11	41.93	42.76	43.60	44.45	45.31	46.18	47.05	47.94	48.83	49.73	50.64
18.50	28.93	31.62	34.47	37.47	40.63	41.44	42.26	43.09	43.93	44.78	45.63	46.50	47.37	48.26	49.15	50.05
18.75	28.59	31.25	34.07	37.03	40.15	40.95	41.76	42.58	43.41	44.25	45.10	45.95	46.82	47.69	48.57	49.46
19.00	28.26	30.89	33.67	36.60	39.69	40.48	41.28	42.09	42.91	43.74	44.58	45.42	46.28	47.14	48.01	48.89
20.00	27.00	29.51	32.17	34.97	37.91	38.67	39.44	40.21	40.99	41.79	42.59	43.39	44.21	45.03	45.87	46.71
25.00	21.96	24.01	26.17	28.45	30.85	31.46	32.09	32.72	33.35	34.00	34.65	35.30	35.97	36.64	37.32	38.00
30.00	18.43	20.15	21.96	23.87	25.88	26.40	26.92	27.45	27.99	28.53	29.07	29.62	30.18	30.74	31.31	31.88

Description: This table shows the yield to maturity of a mortgage purchased at the price shown in the index.

Example: The yield to maturity of a 6.75 %, 18 year mortgage at a price of 80.00 is 10.02 %.

INTEREST RATE, %

PRICE	0.00%	1.00%	2.00%	3.00%	4.00%	4.25%	4.50%	4.75%	5.00%	5.25%	5.50%	5.75%	6.00%	6.25%	6.50%	6.75%
100	0.00	1.00	2.00	3.00	4.00	4.25	4.50	4.75	5.00	5.25	5.50	5.75	6.00	6.25	6.50	6.75
99	.11	1.11	2.11	3.12	4.12	4.37	4.62	4.88	5.13	5.38	5.63	5.88	6.13	6.38	6.63	6.88
98	.22	1.23	2.23	3.24	4.25	4.50	4.75	5.01	5.26	5.51	5.76	6.02	6.27	6.52	6.77	7.03
97	.33	1.34	2.36	3.37	4.38	4.63	4.89	5.14	5.39	5.65	5.90	6.15	6.41	6.66	6.92	7.17
96	.45	1.46	2.48	3.50	4.51	4.77	5.02	5.28	5.53	5.79	6.04	6.30	6.55	6.81	7.06	7.32
95	.57	1.59	2.61	3.63	4.65	4.90	5.16	5.41	5.67	5.93	6.18	6.44	6.69	6.95	7.21	7.46
94	.69	1.71	2.73	3.76	4.78	5.04	5.30	5.55	5.81	6.07	6.33	6.58	6.84	7.10	7.36	7.61
93	.81	1.83	2.86	3.89	4.92	5.18	5.44	5.70	5.96	6.21	6.47	6.73	6.99	7.25	7.51	7.77
92	.93	1.96	2.99	4.03	5.06	5.32	5.58	5.84	6.10	6.36	6.62	6.88	7.14	7.40	7.66	7.92
91	1.06	2.09	3.13	4.17	5.21	5.47	5.73	5.99	6.25	6.51	6.77	7.03	7.30	7.56	7.82	8.08
90	1.18	2.22	3.26	4.31	5.35	5.61	5.88	6.14	6.40	6.66	6.93	7.19	7.45	7.71	7.98	8.24
89	1.31	2.35	3.40	4.45	5.50	5.76	6.03	6.29	6.55	6.82	7.08	7.35	7.61	7.88	8.14	8.41
88	1.44	2.49	3.54	4.59	5.65	5.91	6.18	6.44	6.71	6.97	7.24	7.51	7.77	8.04	8.31	8.57
87	1.57	2.63	3.68	4.74	5.80	6.07	6.33	6.60	6.87	7.13	7.40	7.67	7.94	8.20	8.47	8.74
86	1.71	2.77	3.83	4.89	5.96	6.22	6.49	6.76	7.03	7.30	7.57	7.84	8.10	8.37	8.64	8.91
85	1.84	2.91	3.97	5.04	6.12	6.38	6.65	6.92	7.19	7.46	7.73	8.00	8.27	8.55	8.82	9.09
84	1.98	3.05	4.12	5.20	6.28	6.55	6.82	7.09	7.36	7.63	7.90	8.18	8.45	8.72	8.99	9.27
83	2.13	3.20	4.27	5.35	6.44	6.71	6.98	7.26	7.53	7.80	8.08	8.35	8.62	8.90	9.17	9.45
82	2.27	3.35	4.43	5.51	6.61	6.88	7.15	7.43	7.70	7.98	8.25	8.53	8.80	9.08	9.36	9.63
81	2.42	3.50	4.58	5.68	6.78	7.05	7.33	7.60	7.88	8.16	8.43	8.71	8.99	9.27	9.54	9.82
80	2.56	3.65	4.74	5.84	6.95	7.22	7.50	7.78	8.06	8.34	8.62	8.90	9.17	9.45	9.74	10.02
79	2.72	3.81	4.91	6.01	7.12	7.40	7.68	7.96	8.24	8.52	8.80	9.08	9.37	9.65	9.93	10.21
78	2.87	3.97	5.07	6.18	7.30	7.58	7.86	8.15	8.43	8.71	8.99	9.28	9.56	9.84	10.13	10.41
77	3.03	4.13	5.24	6.36	7.49	7.77	8.05	8.33	8.62	8.90	9.19	9.47	9.76	10.04	10.33	10.62
76	3.19	4.30	5.41	6.54	7.67	7.96	8.24	8.53	8.81	9.10	9.38	9.67	9.96	10.25	10.54	10.83
75	3.35	4.47	5.59	6.72	7.86	8.15	8.43	8.72	9.01	9.30	9.59	9.88	10.17	10.46	10.75	11.04
74	3.51	4.64	5.77	6.91	8.06	8.34	8.63	8.92	9.21	9.50	9.79	10.08	10.38	10.67	10.96	11.26
73	3.68	4.81	5.95	7.10	8.25	8.54	8.83	9.13	9.42	9.71	10.00	10.30	10.59	10.89	11.18	11.48
72	3.86	4.99	6.14	7.29	8.46	8.75	9.04	9.33	9.63	9.92	10.22	10.52	10.81	11.11	11.41	11.71
71	4.03	5.17	6.33	7.49	8.66	8.96	9.25	9.55	9.84	10.14	10.44	10.74	11.04	11.34	11.64	11.94
70	4.21	5.36	6.52	7.69	8.87	9.17	9.47	9.77	10.06	10.36	10.66	10.97	11.27	11.57	11.87	12.18
69	4.39	5.55	6.72	7.90	9.09	9.39	9.69	9.99	10.29	10.59	10.89	11.20	11.50	11.81	12.11	12.42
68	4.58	5.75	6.92	8.11	9.31	9.61	9.91	10.22	10.52	10.82	11.13	11.44	11.74	12.05	12.36	12.67
67	4.77	5.94	7.13	8.33	9.53	9.84	10.14	10.45	10.76	11.06	11.37	11.68	11.99	12.30	12.61	12.92
66	4.97	6.15	7.34	8.55	9.77	10.07	10.38	10.69	11.00	11.31	11.62	11.93	12.24	12.56	12.87	13.18
65	5.17	6.36	7.56	8.77	10.00	10.31	10.62	10.93	11.24	11.56	11.87	12.19	12.50	12.82	13.13	13.45
64	5.37	6.57	7.78	9.00	10.24	10.56	10.87	11.18	11.50	11.81	12.13	12.45	12.77	13.09	13.41	13.73
63	5.58	6.79	8.01	9.24	10.49	10.81	11.12	11.44	11.76	12.08	12.40	12.72	13.04	13.36	13.68	14.01
62	5.79	7.01	8.24	9.49	10.75	11.06	11.38	11.70	12.02	12.35	12.67	12.99	13.32	13.64	13.97	14.30
61	6.01	7.24	8.48	9.73	11.01	11.33	11.65	11.97	12.30	12.62	12.95	13.28	13.60	13.93	14.26	14.60
60	6.23	7.47	8.72	9.99	11.28	11.60	11.92	12.25	12.58	12.91	13.24	13.57	13.90	14.23	14.57	14.90
59	6.46	7.71	8.97	10.25	11.55	11.88	12.21	12.54	12.87	13.20	13.53	13.87	14.20	14.54	14.88	15.22
58	6.70	7.95	9.23	10.52	11.83	12.16	12.50	12.83	13.16	13.50	13.84	14.17	14.51	14.85	15.20	15.54
57	6.94	8.21	9.49	10.80	12.12	12.46	12.79	13.13	13.47	13.81	14.15	14.49	14.83	15.18	15.52	15.87
56	7.19	8.47	9.77	11.08	12.42	12.76	13.10	13.44	13.78	14.13	14.47	14.82	15.16	15.51	15.86	16.21
55	7.44	8.73	10.04	11.38	12.73	13.07	13.42	13.76	14.11	14.45	14.80	15.15	15.50	15.86	16.21	16.57
54	7.70	9.01	10.33	11.68	13.05	13.39	13.74	14.09	14.44	14.79	15.14	15.50	15.85	16.21	16.57	16.93
53	7.97	9.29	10.63	11.99	13.37	13.72	14.08	14.43	14.78	15.14	15.50	15.86	16.22	16.58	16.94	17.31
52	8.25	9.58	10.93	12.31	13.71	14.07	14.42	14.78	15.14	15.50	15.86	16.22	16.59	16.96	17.33	17.70
51	8.53	9.88	11.25	12.64	14.06	14.42	14.78	15.14	15.50	15.87	16.24	16.61	16.98	17.35	17.72	18.10
50	8.83	10.19	11.57	12.98	14.42	14.78	15.15	15.51	15.88	16.25	16.63	17.00	17.38	17.75	18.13	18.51
49	9.13	10.50	11.90	13.33	14.79	15.16	15.53	15.90	16.27	16.65	17.03	17.41	17.79	18.17	18.56	18.95
48	9.44	10.83	12.25	13.70	15.17	15.55	15.92	16.30	16.68	17.06	17.45	17.83	18.22	18.61	19.00	19.39
47	9.76	11.17	12.61	14.07	15.57	15.95	16.33	16.72	17.10	17.49	17.88	18.27	18.66	19.06	19.46	19.86
46	10.10	11.52	12.98	14.47	15.98	16.37	16.76	17.15	17.54	17.93	18.33	18.72	19.12	19.53	19.93	20.34
45	10.44	11.89	13.36	14.87	16.41	16.80	17.20	17.59	17.99	18.39	18.79	19.20	19.60	20.01	20.42	20.84
44	10.80	12.26	13.76	15.29	16.86	17.25	17.65	18.06	18.46	18.87	19.28	19.69	20.10	20.52	20.94	21.36
43	11.17	12.65	14.17	15.73	17.32	17.72	18.13	18.54	18.95	19.36	19.78	20.20	20.62	21.04	21.47	21.90
42	11.55	13.06	14.60	16.18	17.80	18.21	18.63	19.04	19.46	19.88	20.31	20.73	21.16	21.59	22.03	22.46
41	11.95	13.48	15.05	16.65	18.30	18.72	19.14	19.57	19.99	20.42	20.85	21.29	21.73	22.17	22.61	23.05
40	12.37	13.92	15.51	17.15	18.83	19.25	19.68	20.11	20.55	20.99	21.43	21.87	22.32	22.76	23.22	23.67
39	12.80	14.38	16.00	17.66	19.37	19.81	20.24	20.69	21.13	21.58	22.02	22.48	22.93	23.39	23.85	24.32
35	14.73	16.43	18.17	19.98	21.83	22.31	22.78	23.27	23.75	24.24	24.73	25.22	25.72	26.23	26.73	27.24
30	17.74	19.63	21.59	23.63	25.74	26.28	26.82	27.37	27.92	28.48	29.04	29.61	30.18	30.76	31.34	31.92
25	21.76	23.95	26.23	28.60	31.08	31.71	32.36	33.00	33.66	34.31	34.98	35.65	36.33	37.01	37.70	38.40
20	27.57	30.22	33.00	35.92	38.97	39.75	40.54	41.34	42.15	42.97	43.80	44.63	45.47	46.32	47.18	48.04
15	36.98	40.45	44.11	47.96	52.01	53.05	54.10	55.16	56.24	57.32	58.42	59.53	60.65	61.78	62.92	64.07
10	55.55	60.72	66.20	71.96	78.02	79.58	81.15	82.75	84.36	85.99	87.63	89.30	90.98	92.67	94.38	96.11

Description: This table shows the price to pay for a monthly payment mortgage loan at the yield rate.

Example: The price of a 10.75 %, 18 year mortgage loan to yield 8.00 % to maturity is $ 119.84.

INTEREST RATE, %

YIELD	7.00%	7.25%	7.50%	7.75%	8.00%	8.25%	8.50%	8.75%	9.00%	9.25%	9.50%	9.75%	10.00%	10.25%	10.50%	10.75%
0.00	176.15	179.32	182.51	185.74	188.99	192.27	195.58	198.91	202.27	205.66	209.07	212.51	215.97	219.45	222.96	226.49
1.00	161.14	164.04	166.97	169.92	172.89	175.89	178.92	181.97	185.04	188.14	191.26	194.40	197.57	200.76	203.97	207.20
2.00	147.83	150.48	153.17	155.87	158.60	161.36	164.13	166.93	169.75	172.59	175.45	178.34	181.24	184.17	187.11	190.08
3.00	135.98	138.43	140.89	143.38	145.89	148.43	150.98	153.55	156.15	158.76	161.39	164.05	166.72	169.41	172.12	174.84
4.00	125.42	127.68	129.96	132.25	134.57	136.90	139.26	141.63	144.02	146.44	148.86	151.31	153.78	156.26	158.76	161.27
4.25	122.97	125.18	127.41	129.66	131.93	134.22	136.53	138.86	141.20	143.57	145.95	148.35	150.76	153.20	155.65	158.11
4.50	120.58	122.75	124.94	127.14	129.37	131.62	133.88	136.16	138.46	140.78	143.11	145.47	147.83	150.22	152.62	155.04
4.75	118.26	120.38	122.53	124.69	126.88	129.08	131.30	133.54	135.79	138.07	140.36	142.66	144.99	147.33	149.68	152.06
5.00	116.00	118.08	120.19	122.31	124.46	126.62	128.79	130.99	133.20	135.43	137.68	139.94	142.22	144.51	146.82	149.15
5.25	113.80	115.85	117.91	120.00	122.10	124.22	126.35	128.51	130.68	132.87	135.07	137.29	139.53	141.78	144.04	146.33
5.50	111.66	113.67	115.70	117.74	119.81	121.89	123.98	126.09	128.22	130.37	132.53	134.71	136.91	139.12	141.34	143.58
5.75	109.59	111.56	113.55	115.55	117.58	119.62	121.67	123.75	125.84	127.94	130.07	132.20	134.36	136.53	138.71	140.91
6.00	107.56	109.50	111.45	113.42	115.41	117.41	119.43	121.46	123.52	125.58	127.67	129.76	131.88	134.01	136.15	138.31
6.25	105.59	107.49	109.41	111.34	113.29	115.26	117.24	119.24	121.26	123.28	125.33	127.39	129.46	131.55	133.66	135.78
6.50	103.68	105.54	107.43	109.32	111.24	113.17	115.12	117.08	119.06	121.05	123.06	125.08	127.12	129.17	131.23	133.31
6.75	101.81	103.65	105.49	107.36	109.24	111.13	113.05	114.97	116.91	118.87	120.84	122.83	124.83	126.84	128.87	130.92
7.00	100.00	101.80	103.61	105.44	107.29	109.15	111.03	112.92	114.83	116.75	118.69	120.64	122.60	124.58	126.58	128.58
7.25	98.23	100.00	101.78	103.58	105.40	107.22	109.07	110.93	112.80	114.69	116.59	118.51	120.44	122.38	124.34	126.31
7.50	96.51	98.25	100.00	101.77	103.55	105.35	107.16	108.98	110.83	112.68	114.55	116.43	118.33	120.24	122.16	124.10
7.75	94.84	96.54	98.26	100.00	101.75	103.52	105.30	107.10	108.90	110.72	112.56	114.41	116.27	118.15	120.04	121.94
8.00	93.20	94.88	96.57	98.28	100.00	101.74	103.49	105.25	107.03	108.82	110.62	112.44	114.27	116.12	117.97	119.84
8.25	91.61	93.26	94.93	96.60	98.29	100.00	101.72	103.45	105.20	106.96	108.74	110.52	112.32	114.14	115.96	117.80
8.50	90.07	91.69	93.32	94.97	96.63	98.31	100.00	101.70	103.42	105.15	106.90	108.65	110.42	112.21	114.00	115.81
8.75	88.56	90.15	91.76	93.38	95.01	96.66	98.32	100.00	101.69	103.39	105.11	106.83	108.57	110.33	112.09	113.87
9.00	87.08	88.65	90.23	91.83	93.43	95.06	96.69	98.34	100.00	101.67	103.36	105.06	106.77	108.49	110.23	111.98
9.25	85.65	87.19	88.75	90.31	91.90	93.49	95.10	96.72	98.35	100.00	101.66	103.33	105.01	106.71	108.41	110.13
9.50	84.25	85.77	87.30	88.84	90.40	91.97	93.55	95.14	96.75	98.37	100.00	101.64	103.30	104.97	106.64	108.33
9.75	82.89	84.38	85.89	87.40	88.94	90.48	92.03	93.60	95.18	96.78	98.38	100.00	101.63	103.27	104.92	106.58
10.00	81.56	83.03	84.51	86.00	87.51	89.03	90.56	92.10	93.66	95.23	96.81	98.40	100.00	101.61	103.24	104.87
10.25	80.27	81.71	83.17	84.64	86.12	87.61	89.12	90.64	92.17	93.71	95.27	96.83	98.41	100.00	101.60	103.21
10.50	79.00	80.43	81.86	83.31	84.76	86.24	87.72	89.21	90.72	92.24	93.77	95.31	96.86	98.43	100.00	101.58
10.75	77.77	79.17	80.58	82.01	83.44	84.89	86.35	87.82	89.31	90.80	92.31	93.82	95.35	96.89	98.44	100.00
11.00	76.57	77.95	79.34	80.74	82.15	83.58	85.02	86.46	87.92	89.40	90.88	92.37	93.88	95.39	96.92	98.45
11.25	75.40	76.75	78.12	79.50	80.89	82.30	83.71	85.14	86.58	88.03	89.49	90.96	92.44	93.93	95.43	96.95
11.50	74.25	75.59	76.93	78.29	79.67	81.05	82.44	83.85	85.26	86.69	88.13	89.58	91.04	92.51	93.98	95.47
11.75	73.13	74.45	75.78	77.12	78.47	79.83	81.20	82.58	83.98	85.39	86.80	88.23	89.67	91.11	92.57	94.04
12.00	72.04	73.34	74.65	75.97	77.30	78.64	79.99	81.35	82.73	84.11	85.51	86.91	88.33	89.75	91.19	92.64
12.25	70.98	72.26	73.54	74.84	76.15	77.48	78.81	80.15	81.51	82.87	84.24	85.63	87.02	88.43	89.84	91.27
12.50	69.94	71.20	72.47	73.75	75.04	76.34	77.65	78.98	80.31	81.66	83.01	84.38	85.76	87.13	88.53	89.93
12.75	68.93	70.17	71.42	72.68	73.95	75.23	76.53	77.83	79.15	80.47	81.81	83.15	84.51	85.87	87.24	88.63
13.00	67.93	69.16	70.39	71.63	72.89	74.15	75.43	76.71	78.01	79.31	80.63	81.96	83.29	84.63	85.99	87.35
13.25	66.97	68.17	69.39	70.61	71.85	73.10	74.35	75.62	76.90	78.18	79.48	80.79	82.10	83.43	84.76	86.11
13.50	66.02	67.21	68.41	69.61	70.83	72.06	73.30	74.55	75.81	77.08	78.36	79.65	80.94	82.25	83.57	84.89
13.75	65.10	66.27	67.45	68.64	69.84	71.05	72.28	73.51	74.75	76.00	77.26	78.53	79.81	81.10	82.40	83.70
14.00	64.19	65.35	66.51	67.69	68.87	70.07	71.27	72.49	73.71	74.95	76.19	77.44	78.70	79.97	81.25	82.54
14.25	63.31	64.45	65.60	66.76	67.93	69.11	70.29	71.49	72.70	73.92	75.14	76.38	77.62	78.88	80.14	81.41
14.50	62.45	63.57	64.71	65.85	67.00	68.16	69.34	70.52	71.71	72.91	74.12	75.34	76.57	77.80	79.04	80.30
14.75	61.61	62.71	63.83	64.96	66.10	67.24	68.40	69.57	70.74	71.93	73.12	74.32	75.53	76.75	77.98	79.21
15.00	60.78	61.88	62.98	64.09	65.21	66.35	67.49	68.64	69.80	70.96	72.14	73.33	74.52	75.72	76.93	78.15
15.25	59.98	61.05	62.14	63.24	64.35	65.47	66.59	67.73	68.87	70.02	71.18	72.35	73.53	74.72	75.91	77.12
15.50	59.19	60.25	61.33	62.41	63.50	64.61	65.72	66.84	67.97	69.10	70.25	71.40	72.57	73.74	74.92	76.10
15.75	58.42	59.47	60.53	61.60	62.68	63.76	64.86	65.97	67.08	68.20	69.33	70.47	71.62	72.78	73.94	75.11
16.00	57.66	58.70	59.75	60.80	61.87	62.94	64.02	65.12	66.22	67.32	68.44	69.56	70.70	71.84	72.99	74.14
16.25	56.93	57.95	58.98	60.03	61.08	62.14	63.21	64.28	65.37	66.46	67.56	68.68	69.79	70.92	72.05	73.20
16.50	56.20	57.22	58.24	59.26	60.30	61.35	62.40	63.47	64.54	65.62	66.71	67.80	68.91	70.02	71.14	72.27
16.75	55.50	56.50	57.50	58.52	59.54	60.58	61.62	62.67	63.73	64.80	65.87	66.95	68.04	69.14	70.25	71.36
17.00	54.81	55.79	56.79	57.79	58.80	59.82	60.85	61.89	62.94	63.99	65.05	66.12	67.20	68.28	69.37	70.47
17.25	54.13	55.10	56.09	57.08	58.08	59.09	60.10	61.13	62.16	63.20	64.25	65.30	66.37	67.44	68.52	69.60
17.50	53.47	54.43	55.40	56.38	57.37	58.36	59.37	60.38	61.40	62.43	63.46	64.50	65.56	66.61	67.68	68.75
17.75	52.82	53.77	54.73	55.70	56.67	57.66	58.65	59.65	60.65	61.67	62.69	63.72	64.76	65.81	66.86	67.92
18.00	52.19	53.12	54.07	55.03	55.99	56.96	57.94	58.93	59.93	60.93	61.94	62.96	63.98	65.01	66.05	67.10
18.25	51.56	52.49	53.43	54.37	55.32	56.28	57.25	58.23	59.21	60.20	61.20	62.21	63.22	64.24	65.27	66.30
18.50	50.96	51.87	52.80	53.73	54.67	55.62	56.58	57.54	58.51	59.49	60.48	61.47	62.47	63.48	64.50	65.52
18.75	50.36	51.26	52.18	53.10	54.03	54.97	55.91	56.87	57.83	58.80	59.77	60.75	61.74	62.74	63.74	64.75
19.00	49.77	50.67	51.57	52.48	53.40	54.33	55.27	56.21	57.16	58.11	59.08	60.05	61.03	62.01	63.00	64.00
20.00	47.55	48.41	49.27	50.14	51.02	51.91	52.80	53.70	54.61	55.52	56.44	57.37	58.30	59.24	60.19	61.14
25.00	38.69	39.38	40.09	40.80	41.51	42.23	42.96	43.69	44.43	45.17	45.92	46.67	47.43	48.20	48.97	49.75
30.00	32.46	33.05	33.64	34.23	34.83	35.43	36.04	36.66	37.28	37.90	38.53	39.16	39.80	40.44	41.09	41.74

Description: This table shows the yield to maturity of a mortgage purchased at the price shown in the index.

Example: The yield to maturity of a 10.75 %, 18 year mortgage at a price of 111.00 is 9.13 %.

INTEREST RATE, %

PRICE	7.00%	7.25%	7.50%	7.75%	8.00%	8.25%	8.50%	8.75%	9.00%	9.25%	9.50%	9.75%	10.00%	10.25%	10.50%	10.75%
155	1.44	1.65	1.86	2.06	2.27	2.47	2.68	2.88	3.08	3.29	3.49	3.69	3.90	4.10	4.30	4.50
150	1.82	2.03	2.24	2.45	2.66	2.87	3.07	3.28	3.49	3.69	3.90	4.10	4.31	4.51	4.72	4.92
145	2.22	2.44	2.65	2.86	3.07	3.28	3.49	3.70	3.91	4.12	4.33	4.54	4.74	4.95	5.16	5.36
140	2.64	2.86	3.07	3.29	3.50	3.71	3.93	4.14	4.35	4.57	4.78	4.99	5.20	5.41	5.62	5.83
135	3.08	3.30	3.52	3.74	3.95	4.17	4.39	4.60	4.82	5.04	5.25	5.47	5.68	5.90	6.11	6.32
130	3.55	3.77	3.99	4.21	4.43	4.65	4.87	5.09	5.31	5.53	5.75	5.97	6.19	6.41	6.62	6.84
125	4.04	4.26	4.49	4.71	4.94	5.16	5.39	5.61	5.83	6.06	6.28	6.50	6.73	6.95	7.17	7.39
124	4.14	4.37	4.59	4.82	5.04	5.27	5.49	5.72	5.94	6.17	6.39	6.61	6.84	7.06	7.28	7.51
123	4.24	4.47	4.70	4.92	5.15	5.37	5.60	5.83	6.05	6.28	6.50	6.73	6.95	7.17	7.40	7.62
122	4.35	4.57	4.80	5.03	5.26	5.48	5.71	5.94	6.16	6.39	6.61	6.84	7.06	7.29	7.51	7.74
121	4.45	4.68	4.91	5.14	5.36	5.59	5.82	6.05	6.27	6.50	6.73	6.95	7.18	7.41	7.63	7.86
120	4.56	4.79	5.02	5.24	5.47	5.70	5.93	6.16	6.39	6.61	6.84	7.07	7.30	7.52	7.75	7.98
119	4.66	4.89	5.12	5.35	5.58	5.81	6.04	6.27	6.50	6.73	6.96	7.19	7.41	7.64	7.87	8.10
118	4.77	5.00	5.24	5.47	5.70	5.93	6.16	6.39	6.62	6.85	7.08	7.31	7.53	7.76	7.99	8.22
117	4.88	5.12	5.35	5.58	5.81	6.04	6.27	6.50	6.73	6.97	7.20	7.43	7.66	7.89	8.12	8.34
116	4.99	5.23	5.46	5.69	5.93	6.16	6.39	6.62	6.85	7.09	7.32	7.55	7.78	8.01	8.24	8.47
115	5.11	5.34	5.58	5.81	6.04	6.28	6.51	6.74	6.97	7.21	7.44	7.67	7.90	8.14	8.37	8.60
114	5.22	5.46	5.69	5.93	6.16	6.39	6.63	6.86	7.10	7.33	7.56	7.80	8.03	8.26	8.50	8.73
113	5.34	5.57	5.81	6.05	6.28	6.52	6.75	6.99	7.22	7.45	7.69	7.92	8.16	8.39	8.63	8.86
112	5.46	5.69	5.93	6.17	6.40	6.64	6.87	7.11	7.35	7.58	7.82	8.05	8.29	8.52	8.76	8.99
111	5.57	5.81	6.05	6.29	6.52	6.76	7.00	7.24	7.47	7.71	7.95	8.18	8.42	8.65	8.89	9.13
110	5.69	5.93	6.17	6.41	6.65	6.89	7.13	7.36	7.60	7.84	8.08	8.31	8.55	8.79	9.03	9.26
109	5.82	6.06	6.30	6.54	6.78	7.01	7.25	7.49	7.73	7.97	8.21	8.45	8.69	8.93	9.16	9.40
108	5.94	6.18	6.42	6.66	6.90	7.14	7.38	7.62	7.86	8.10	8.34	8.58	8.82	9.06	9.30	9.54
107	6.07	6.31	6.55	6.79	7.03	7.27	7.52	7.76	8.00	8.24	8.48	8.72	8.96	9.20	9.44	9.68
106	6.19	6.44	6.68	6.92	7.16	7.41	7.65	7.89	8.13	8.38	8.62	8.86	9.10	9.35	9.59	9.83
105	6.32	6.57	6.81	7.05	7.30	7.54	7.79	8.03	8.27	8.52	8.76	9.00	9.25	9.49	9.73	9.98
104	6.45	6.70	6.94	7.19	7.43	7.68	7.92	8.17	8.41	8.66	8.90	9.15	9.39	9.64	9.88	10.13
103	6.59	6.83	7.08	7.32	7.57	7.82	8.06	8.31	8.56	8.80	9.05	9.29	9.54	9.79	10.03	10.28
102	6.72	6.97	7.22	7.46	7.71	7.96	8.20	8.45	8.70	8.95	9.19	9.44	9.69	9.94	10.18	10.43
101	6.86	7.11	7.35	7.60	7.85	8.10	8.35	8.60	8.85	9.09	9.34	9.59	9.84	10.09	10.34	10.59
100	7.00	7.25	7.50	7.75	8.00	8.25	8.50	8.75	9.00	9.25	9.50	9.75	10.00	10.25	10.50	10.75
99	7.14	7.39	7.64	7.89	8.14	8.39	8.64	8.89	9.15	9.40	9.65	9.90	10.15	10.40	10.65	10.91
98	7.28	7.53	7.78	8.04	8.29	8.54	8.79	9.05	9.30	9.55	9.81	10.06	10.31	10.56	10.82	11.07
97	7.42	7.68	7.93	8.19	8.44	8.69	8.95	9.20	9.46	9.71	9.96	10.22	10.47	10.73	10.98	11.24
96	7.57	7.83	8.08	8.34	8.59	8.85	9.10	9.36	9.61	9.87	10.13	10.38	10.64	10.89	11.15	11.40
95	7.72	7.98	8.23	8.49	8.75	9.00	9.26	9.52	9.77	10.03	10.29	10.55	10.80	11.06	11.32	11.58
94	7.87	8.13	8.39	8.65	8.90	9.16	9.42	9.68	9.94	10.20	10.46	10.72	10.97	11.23	11.49	11.75
93	8.03	8.29	8.55	8.81	9.06	9.32	9.58	9.84	10.11	10.37	10.63	10.89	11.15	11.41	11.67	11.93
92	8.18	8.44	8.71	8.97	9.23	9.49	9.75	10.01	10.27	10.54	10.80	11.06	11.32	11.59	11.85	12.11
91	8.34	8.61	8.87	9.13	9.39	9.66	9.92	10.18	10.45	10.71	10.97	11.24	11.50	11.77	12.03	12.29
90	8.51	8.77	9.03	9.30	9.56	9.83	10.09	10.36	10.62	10.89	11.15	11.42	11.68	11.95	12.22	12.48
89	8.67	8.94	9.20	9.47	9.73	10.00	10.27	10.53	10.80	11.07	11.33	11.60	11.87	12.14	12.40	12.67
88	8.84	9.11	9.37	9.64	9.91	10.18	10.44	10.71	10.98	11.25	11.52	11.79	12.06	12.33	12.60	12.87
87	9.01	9.28	9.55	9.82	10.09	10.36	10.63	10.90	11.17	11.44	11.71	11.98	12.25	12.52	12.79	13.06
86	9.18	9.45	9.72	10.00	10.27	10.54	10.81	11.08	11.35	11.63	11.90	12.17	12.45	12.72	12.99	13.27
85	9.36	9.63	9.91	10.18	10.45	10.72	11.00	11.27	11.55	11.82	12.09	12.37	12.64	12.92	13.20	13.47
84	9.54	9.82	10.09	10.36	10.64	10.91	11.19	11.47	11.74	12.02	12.29	12.57	12.85	13.13	13.40	13.68
83	9.72	10.00	10.28	10.55	10.83	11.11	11.38	11.66	11.94	12.22	12.50	12.78	13.06	13.34	13.62	13.90
82	9.91	10.19	10.47	10.75	11.02	11.30	11.58	11.86	12.14	12.42	12.70	12.99	13.27	13.55	13.83	14.11
81	10.10	10.38	10.66	10.94	11.22	11.50	11.79	12.07	12.35	12.63	12.92	13.20	13.48	13.77	14.05	14.34
80	10.30	10.58	10.86	11.14	11.43	11.71	11.99	12.28	12.56	12.85	13.13	13.42	13.70	13.99	14.28	14.56
79	10.50	10.78	11.06	11.35	11.63	11.92	12.20	12.49	12.78	13.06	13.35	13.64	13.93	14.22	14.51	14.79
78	10.70	10.98	11.27	11.56	11.84	12.13	12.42	12.71	13.00	13.29	13.58	13.87	14.16	14.45	14.74	15.03
77	10.90	11.19	11.48	11.77	12.06	12.35	12.64	12.93	13.22	13.51	13.81	14.10	14.39	14.69	14.98	15.27
76	11.12	11.41	11.70	11.99	12.28	12.57	12.86	13.16	13.45	13.75	14.04	14.34	14.63	14.93	15.22	15.52
75	11.33	11.62	11.92	12.21	12.50	12.80	13.09	13.39	13.69	13.98	14.28	14.58	14.88	15.17	15.47	15.77
74	11.55	11.85	12.14	12.44	12.73	13.03	13.33	13.63	13.93	14.22	14.52	14.83	15.13	15.43	15.73	16.03
73	11.78	12.07	12.37	12.67	12.97	13.27	13.57	13.87	14.17	14.47	14.78	15.08	15.38	15.69	15.99	16.30
70	12.48	12.79	13.09	13.40	13.70	14.01	14.32	14.63	14.94	15.25	15.56	15.87	16.19	16.50	16.82	17.13
65	13.77	14.09	14.41	14.73	15.06	15.38	15.70	16.03	16.36	16.68	17.01	17.34	17.67	18.00	18.33	18.66
60	15.24	15.57	15.91	16.25	16.59	16.94	17.28	17.62	17.97	18.32	18.66	19.01	19.36	19.71	20.07	20.42
55	16.92	17.28	17.64	18.01	18.37	18.73	19.10	19.47	19.83	20.21	20.58	20.95	21.32	21.70	22.08	22.46
50	18.90	19.28	19.67	20.06	20.45	20.84	21.23	21.63	22.03	22.43	22.83	23.23	23.64	24.04	24.45	24.86
45	21.25	21.67	22.09	22.51	22.94	23.36	23.79	24.22	24.66	25.09	25.53	25.97	26.42	26.86	27.31	27.76
40	24.13	24.59	25.05	25.52	25.99	26.46	26.93	27.41	27.89	28.38	28.86	29.35	29.84	30.34	30.83	31.33
35	27.76	28.27	28.79	29.32	29.85	30.38	30.91	31.45	31.99	32.54	33.09	33.64	34.20	34.76	35.32	35.88
30	32.51	33.11	33.71	34.31	34.92	35.54	36.15	36.78	37.40	38.03	38.67	39.31	39.96	40.60	41.26	41.91

Description: This table shows the price to pay for a monthly payment mortgage loan at the yield rate.

Example: The price of a 15.00 %, 18 year mortgage loan to yield 8.00 % to maturity is $ 153.34.

INTEREST RATE, %

YIELD	11.00%	11.25%	11.50%	11.75%	12.00%	12.25%	12.50%	12.75%	13.00%	13.25%	13.50%	13.75%	14.00%	14.25%	14.50%	15.00%
0.00	230.05	233.63	237.23	240.86	244.50	248.17	251.86	255.56	259.29	263.04	266.81	270.60	274.40	278.23	282.07	289.81
1.00	210.45	213.73	217.02	220.34	223.67	227.03	230.40	233.80	237.21	240.64	244.08	247.55	251.03	254.53	258.04	265.12
2.00	193.06	196.06	199.09	202.13	205.19	208.26	211.36	214.47	217.60	220.75	223.91	227.09	230.28	233.49	236.71	243.21
3.00	177.59	180.35	183.13	185.93	188.75	191.58	194.42	197.29	200.16	203.06	205.97	208.89	211.83	214.78	217.75	223.72
4.00	163.80	166.35	168.92	171.50	174.09	176.70	179.33	181.97	184.63	187.29	189.98	192.67	195.38	198.11	200.84	206.35
4.25	160.60	163.09	165.61	168.14	170.68	173.24	175.82	178.41	181.01	183.63	186.26	188.90	191.56	194.23	196.91	202.31
4.50	157.48	159.93	162.39	164.87	167.37	169.88	172.40	174.94	177.49	180.06	182.64	185.23	187.84	190.45	193.08	198.38
4.75	154.44	156.85	159.26	161.70	164.14	166.61	169.08	171.57	174.07	176.59	179.12	181.66	184.22	186.79	189.36	194.56
5.00	151.49	153.85	156.22	158.61	161.01	163.42	165.85	168.29	170.75	173.22	175.70	178.19	180.70	183.22	185.75	190.84
5.25	148.62	150.94	153.26	155.61	157.96	160.33	162.71	165.11	167.52	169.94	172.37	174.82	177.28	179.75	182.23	187.23
5.50	145.83	148.10	150.39	152.68	154.99	157.32	159.66	162.01	164.37	166.75	169.14	171.54	173.95	176.37	178.81	183.71
5.75	143.12	145.35	147.59	149.84	152.11	154.39	156.68	158.99	161.31	163.64	165.99	168.34	170.71	173.09	175.48	180.29
6.00	140.48	142.66	144.86	147.08	149.30	151.54	153.79	156.06	158.33	160.62	162.92	165.24	167.56	169.90	172.24	176.97
6.25	137.91	140.05	142.21	144.38	146.57	148.77	150.98	153.20	155.44	157.68	159.94	162.21	164.49	166.79	169.09	173.73
6.50	135.41	137.51	139.63	141.77	143.91	146.07	148.24	150.42	152.62	154.82	157.04	159.27	161.51	163.76	166.02	170.58
6.75	132.97	135.04	137.12	139.22	141.32	143.44	145.57	147.72	149.87	152.04	154.22	156.41	158.61	160.82	163.04	167.51
7.00	130.60	132.63	134.68	136.73	138.80	140.89	142.98	145.08	147.20	149.33	151.47	153.62	155.78	157.95	160.13	164.52
7.25	128.29	130.29	132.30	134.32	136.35	138.40	140.45	142.52	144.60	146.69	148.79	150.90	153.03	155.16	157.30	161.62
7.50	126.05	128.01	129.98	131.97	133.96	135.97	137.99	140.02	142.07	144.12	146.19	148.26	150.35	152.44	154.55	158.78
7.75	123.86	125.78	127.72	129.67	131.64	133.61	135.60	137.59	139.60	141.62	143.65	145.69	147.74	149.79	151.86	156.03
8.00	121.73	123.62	125.52	127.44	129.37	131.31	133.26	135.23	137.20	139.18	141.18	143.18	145.19	147.22	149.25	153.34
8.25	119.65	121.51	123.38	125.27	127.16	129.07	130.99	132.92	134.86	136.81	138.77	140.74	142.72	144.70	146.70	150.73
8.50	117.63	119.46	121.30	123.15	125.01	126.89	128.77	130.67	132.58	134.49	136.42	138.36	140.30	142.26	144.22	148.18
8.75	115.65	117.45	119.26	121.09	122.92	124.76	126.62	128.48	130.36	132.24	134.13	136.04	137.95	139.87	141.81	145.69
9.00	113.73	115.50	117.28	119.08	120.88	122.69	124.51	126.35	128.19	130.04	131.91	133.78	135.66	137.55	139.45	143.27
9.25	111.86	113.60	115.35	117.11	118.89	120.67	122.46	124.27	126.08	127.90	129.73	131.58	133.43	135.29	137.15	140.92
9.50	110.04	111.75	113.47	115.20	116.95	118.70	120.47	122.24	124.02	125.82	127.62	129.43	131.25	133.08	134.92	138.62
9.75	108.26	109.94	111.64	113.34	115.06	116.78	118.52	120.26	122.02	123.78	125.55	127.34	129.13	130.93	132.74	136.38
10.00	106.52	108.18	109.85	111.52	113.21	114.91	116.62	118.34	120.06	121.80	123.54	125.30	127.06	128.83	130.61	134.19
10.25	104.83	106.46	108.10	109.75	111.41	113.09	114.77	116.46	118.16	119.86	121.58	123.31	125.04	126.78	128.53	132.06
10.50	103.18	104.79	106.40	108.03	109.66	111.31	112.96	114.62	116.30	117.98	119.67	121.37	123.07	124.79	126.51	129.98
10.75	101.57	103.15	104.74	106.34	107.95	109.57	111.20	112.83	114.48	116.14	117.80	119.47	121.15	122.84	124.54	127.95
11.00	100.00	101.56	103.12	104.70	106.28	107.88	109.48	111.09	112.71	114.34	115.98	117.62	119.28	120.94	122.61	125.97
11.25	98.47	100.00	101.54	103.09	104.65	106.22	107.80	109.39	110.98	112.59	114.20	115.82	117.45	119.09	120.73	124.04
11.50	96.97	98.48	100.00	101.53	103.06	104.61	106.16	107.73	109.30	110.88	112.47	114.06	115.67	117.28	118.90	122.16
11.75	95.51	97.00	98.50	100.00	101.51	103.04	104.57	106.11	107.66	109.21	110.78	112.35	113.93	115.52	117.11	120.32
12.00	94.09	95.55	97.03	98.51	100.00	101.50	103.01	104.52	106.05	107.58	109.12	110.67	112.23	113.79	115.36	118.53
12.25	92.70	94.14	95.59	97.05	98.52	100.00	101.49	102.98	104.48	105.99	107.51	109.04	110.57	112.11	113.66	116.78
12.50	91.34	92.76	94.19	95.63	97.08	98.54	100.00	101.47	102.95	104.44	105.94	107.44	108.95	110.47	112.00	115.07
12.75	90.02	91.42	92.83	94.24	95.67	97.11	98.55	100.00	101.46	102.93	104.40	105.88	107.37	108.87	110.37	113.40
13.00	88.72	90.10	91.49	92.89	94.30	95.71	97.13	98.56	100.00	101.45	102.90	104.36	105.83	107.30	108.78	111.77
13.25	87.46	88.82	90.19	91.57	92.95	94.35	95.75	97.16	98.57	100.00	101.43	102.87	104.32	105.77	107.23	110.17
13.50	86.22	87.56	88.91	90.27	91.64	93.01	94.40	95.79	97.18	98.59	100.00	101.42	102.85	104.28	105.72	108.62
13.75	85.02	86.34	87.67	89.01	90.36	91.71	93.07	94.44	95.82	97.21	98.60	100.00	101.41	102.82	104.24	107.10
14.00	83.84	85.14	86.45	87.77	89.10	90.44	91.78	93.13	94.49	95.86	97.23	98.61	100.00	101.39	102.79	105.61
14.25	82.68	83.97	85.27	86.57	87.88	89.20	90.52	91.85	93.19	94.54	95.90	97.26	98.63	100.00	101.38	104.16
14.50	81.56	82.83	84.10	85.39	86.68	87.98	89.29	90.60	91.93	93.25	94.59	95.93	97.28	98.64	100.00	102.74
14.75	80.46	81.71	82.97	84.24	85.51	86.79	88.08	89.38	90.68	92.00	93.31	94.64	95.97	97.31	98.65	101.36
15.00	79.38	80.62	81.86	83.11	84.37	85.63	86.91	88.18	89.47	90.77	92.07	93.37	94.69	96.00	97.33	100.00
15.25	78.33	79.55	80.77	82.01	83.25	84.50	85.75	87.02	88.29	89.56	90.84	92.13	93.43	94.73	96.04	98.67
15.50	77.30	78.50	79.71	80.93	82.16	83.39	84.63	85.87	87.13	88.39	89.65	90.92	92.20	93.49	94.78	97.38
15.75	76.29	77.48	78.67	79.88	81.09	82.30	83.52	84.75	85.99	87.23	88.48	89.74	91.00	92.27	93.54	96.11
16.00	75.31	76.48	77.66	78.85	80.04	81.24	82.45	83.66	84.88	86.11	87.34	88.58	89.83	91.08	92.34	94.87
16.25	74.35	75.50	76.67	77.84	79.02	80.20	81.39	82.59	83.80	85.01	86.22	87.45	88.68	89.91	91.16	93.66
16.50	73.40	74.55	75.69	76.85	78.01	79.18	80.36	81.54	82.73	83.93	85.13	86.34	87.55	88.77	90.00	92.47
16.75	72.48	73.61	74.74	75.89	77.03	78.19	79.35	80.52	81.69	82.88	84.06	85.26	86.45	87.66	88.87	91.31
17.00	71.58	72.69	73.81	74.94	76.07	77.22	78.36	79.52	80.68	81.84	83.02	84.19	85.38	86.57	87.76	90.17
17.25	70.70	71.80	72.90	74.02	75.14	76.26	77.40	78.54	79.68	80.83	81.99	83.16	84.32	85.50	86.68	89.06
17.50	69.83	70.92	72.01	73.11	74.22	75.33	76.45	77.57	78.71	79.84	80.99	82.14	83.29	84.45	85.62	87.97
17.75	68.98	70.06	71.14	72.22	73.32	74.42	75.52	76.63	77.75	78.88	80.01	81.14	82.28	83.43	84.58	86.90
18.00	68.15	69.22	70.28	71.36	72.44	73.52	74.61	75.71	76.82	77.93	79.05	80.17	81.29	82.43	83.57	85.86
18.25	67.34	68.39	69.45	70.51	71.57	72.65	73.73	74.81	75.90	77.00	78.10	79.21	80.33	81.45	82.57	84.84
18.50	66.55	67.58	68.63	69.67	70.73	71.79	72.86	73.93	75.01	76.09	77.18	78.28	79.38	80.48	81.60	83.83
18.75	65.77	66.79	67.82	68.86	69.90	70.95	72.00	73.06	74.13	75.20	76.28	77.36	78.45	79.54	80.64	82.85
19.00	65.01	66.02	67.04	68.06	69.09	70.13	71.17	72.22	73.27	74.33	75.39	76.46	77.54	78.62	79.70	81.89
20.00	62.10	63.07	64.04	65.02	66.01	67.00	67.99	68.99	70.00	71.01	72.03	73.05	74.08	75.11	76.15	78.24
25.00	50.53	51.31	52.10	52.90	53.70	54.51	55.32	56.13	56.95	57.77	58.60	59.43	60.27	61.11	61.95	63.65
30.00	42.40	43.06	43.72	44.39	45.06	45.74	46.41	47.10	47.79	48.48	49.17	49.87	50.57	51.27	51.98	53.41

Description: This table shows the yield to maturity of a mortgage purchased at the price shown in the index.

Example: The yield to maturity of a 15.00 %, 18 year mortgage at a price of 125.00 is 11.12 %.

INTEREST RATE, %

PRICE	11.00%	11.25%	11.50%	11.75%	12.00%	12.25%	12.50%	12.75%	13.00%	13.25%	13.50%	13.75%	14.00%	14.25%	14.50%	15.00%
250	—	—	—	—	—	—	.08	.24	.40	.56	.72	.88	1.04	1.20	1.36	1.67
240	—	—	—	—	.20	.37	.53	.70	.86	1.03	1.19	1.35	1.51	1.67	1.83	2.15
230	—	—	.34	.51	.68	.85	1.01	1.18	1.35	1.52	1.68	1.85	2.01	2.17	2.34	2.66
220	.49	.67	.84	1.01	1.18	1.36	1.53	1.70	1.87	2.03	2.20	2.37	2.54	2.70	2.87	3.20
210	1.02	1.20	1.37	1.55	1.72	1.90	2.07	2.24	2.42	2.59	2.76	2.93	3.10	3.27	3.44	3.78
200	1.58	1.76	1.94	2.12	2.30	2.48	2.65	2.83	3.01	3.18	3.35	3.53	3.70	3.88	4.05	4.39
195	1.88	2.06	2.24	2.42	2.60	2.78	2.96	3.14	3.31	3.49	3.67	3.84	4.02	4.19	4.37	4.72
190	2.18	2.37	2.55	2.73	2.91	3.10	3.28	3.46	3.64	3.82	3.99	4.17	4.35	4.53	4.70	5.05
185	2.50	2.69	2.87	3.06	3.24	3.42	3.61	3.79	3.97	4.15	4.33	4.51	4.69	4.87	5.05	5.40
180	2.83	3.02	3.21	3.39	3.58	3.76	3.95	4.13	4.32	4.50	4.68	4.86	5.05	5.23	5.41	5.77
175	3.17	3.36	3.55	3.74	3.93	4.12	4.30	4.49	4.68	4.86	5.05	5.23	5.42	5.60	5.78	6.15
170	3.53	3.72	3.91	4.11	4.30	4.49	4.68	4.86	5.05	5.24	5.43	5.61	5.80	5.99	6.17	6.54
165	3.90	4.10	4.29	4.49	4.68	4.87	5.06	5.25	5.44	5.63	5.82	6.01	6.20	6.39	6.58	6.95
160	4.29	4.49	4.69	4.88	5.08	5.27	5.47	5.66	5.85	6.05	6.24	6.43	6.62	6.82	7.01	7.39
155	4.70	4.90	5.10	5.30	5.49	5.69	5.89	6.09	6.28	6.48	6.68	6.87	7.07	7.26	7.45	7.84
150	5.12	5.33	5.53	5.73	5.93	6.13	6.33	6.53	6.73	6.93	7.13	7.33	7.53	7.73	7.92	8.32
145	5.57	5.78	5.98	6.19	6.39	6.60	6.80	7.00	7.21	7.41	7.61	7.81	8.01	8.22	8.42	8.82
140	6.04	6.25	6.46	6.67	6.88	7.08	7.29	7.50	7.70	7.91	8.12	8.32	8.53	8.73	8.94	9.34
135	6.54	6.75	6.96	7.17	7.39	7.60	7.81	8.02	8.23	8.44	8.65	8.86	9.07	9.28	9.49	9.90
130	7.06	7.28	7.49	7.71	7.92	8.14	8.36	8.57	8.79	9.00	9.21	9.43	9.64	9.85	10.07	10.49
125	7.61	7.83	8.06	8.28	8.50	8.72	8.94	9.16	9.38	9.59	9.81	10.03	10.25	10.47	10.69	11.12
120	8.20	8.43	8.65	8.88	9.10	9.33	9.55	9.78	10.00	10.23	10.45	10.67	10.90	11.12	11.34	11.79
115	8.83	9.06	9.29	9.52	9.75	9.98	10.21	10.44	10.67	10.90	11.13	11.36	11.59	11.82	12.05	12.51
113	9.09	9.33	9.56	9.79	10.02	10.26	10.49	10.72	10.95	11.19	11.42	11.65	11.88	12.11	12.34	12.81
112	9.23	9.46	9.69	9.93	10.16	10.40	10.63	10.86	11.10	11.33	11.56	11.80	12.03	12.26	12.49	12.96
111	9.36	9.60	9.83	10.07	10.30	10.54	10.77	11.01	11.24	11.48	11.71	11.95	12.18	12.41	12.65	13.11
110	9.50	9.74	9.97	10.21	10.45	10.68	10.92	11.15	11.39	11.63	11.86	12.10	12.33	12.57	12.80	13.27
109	9.64	9.88	10.12	10.35	10.59	10.83	11.07	11.30	11.54	11.78	12.01	12.25	12.49	12.72	12.96	13.43
108	9.78	10.02	10.26	10.50	10.74	10.98	11.22	11.45	11.69	11.93	12.17	12.41	12.64	12.88	13.12	13.60
107	9.93	10.17	10.41	10.65	10.89	11.13	11.37	11.61	11.85	12.09	12.33	12.57	12.80	13.04	13.28	13.76
106	10.07	10.31	10.55	10.80	11.04	11.28	11.52	11.76	12.00	12.24	12.48	12.73	12.97	13.21	13.45	13.93
105	10.22	10.46	10.71	10.95	11.19	11.43	11.68	11.92	12.16	12.40	12.65	12.89	13.13	13.37	13.62	14.10
104	10.37	10.61	10.86	11.10	11.35	11.59	11.84	12.08	12.32	12.57	12.81	13.05	13.30	13.54	13.79	14.27
103	10.52	10.77	11.01	11.26	11.51	11.75	12.00	12.24	12.49	12.73	12.98	13.22	13.47	13.71	13.96	14.45
102	10.68	10.92	11.17	11.42	11.67	11.91	12.16	12.41	12.65	12.90	13.15	13.39	13.64	13.89	14.13	14.63
101	10.84	11.08	11.33	11.58	11.83	12.08	12.33	12.57	12.82	13.07	13.32	13.57	13.82	14.07	14.31	14.81
100	11.00	11.25	11.50	11.75	12.00	12.25	12.50	12.75	13.00	13.25	13.50	13.75	14.00	14.25	14.50	15.00
99	11.16	11.41	11.66	11.91	12.16	12.42	12.67	12.92	13.17	13.42	13.67	13.92	14.18	14.43	14.68	15.18
98	11.32	11.58	11.83	12.08	12.33	12.59	12.84	13.09	13.35	13.60	13.85	14.11	14.36	14.61	14.87	15.37
97	11.49	11.75	12.00	12.25	12.51	12.76	13.02	13.27	13.53	13.78	14.04	14.29	14.55	14.80	15.06	15.57
96	11.66	11.92	12.17	12.43	12.69	12.94	13.20	13.46	13.71	13.97	14.23	14.48	14.74	15.00	15.25	15.77
95	11.83	12.09	12.35	12.61	12.87	13.12	13.38	13.64	13.90	14.16	14.42	14.67	14.93	15.19	15.45	15.97
94	12.01	12.27	12.53	12.79	13.05	13.31	13.57	13.83	14.09	14.35	14.61	14.87	15.13	15.39	15.65	16.17
93	12.19	12.45	12.71	12.97	13.24	13.50	13.76	14.02	14.28	14.55	14.81	15.07	15.33	15.59	15.86	16.38
92	12.37	12.64	12.90	13.16	13.43	13.69	13.95	14.22	14.48	14.74	15.01	15.27	15.54	15.80	16.07	16.60
91	12.56	12.82	13.09	13.35	13.62	13.88	14.15	14.42	14.68	14.95	15.21	15.48	15.75	16.01	16.28	16.81
90	12.75	13.01	13.28	13.55	13.82	14.08	14.35	14.62	14.89	15.15	15.42	15.69	15.96	16.23	16.50	17.03
89	12.94	13.21	13.48	13.75	14.02	14.29	14.55	14.82	15.09	15.36	15.63	15.90	16.17	16.45	16.72	17.26
88	13.14	13.41	13.68	13.95	14.22	14.49	14.76	15.03	15.31	15.58	15.85	16.12	16.40	16.67	16.94	17.49
87	13.34	13.61	13.88	14.15	14.43	14.70	14.97	15.25	15.52	15.80	16.07	16.35	16.62	16.90	17.17	17.72
86	13.54	13.82	14.09	14.36	14.64	14.92	15.19	15.47	15.74	16.02	16.30	16.57	16.85	17.13	17.40	17.96
85	13.75	14.02	14.30	14.58	14.86	15.13	15.41	15.69	15.97	16.25	16.53	16.80	17.08	17.36	17.64	18.20
84	13.96	14.24	14.52	14.80	15.08	15.36	15.64	15.92	16.20	16.48	16.76	17.04	17.32	17.61	17.89	18.45
83	14.18	14.46	14.74	15.02	15.30	15.58	15.87	16.15	16.43	16.72	17.00	17.28	17.57	17.85	18.14	18.71
82	14.40	14.68	14.96	15.25	15.53	15.82	16.10	16.39	16.67	16.96	17.24	17.53	17.82	18.10	18.39	18.97
81	14.62	14.91	15.19	15.48	15.77	16.05	16.34	16.63	16.92	17.20	17.49	17.78	18.07	18.36	18.65	19.23
80	14.85	15.14	15.43	15.72	16.00	16.29	16.58	16.87	17.16	17.46	17.75	18.04	18.33	18.62	18.92	19.50
79	15.08	15.38	15.67	15.96	16.25	16.54	16.83	17.13	17.42	17.71	18.01	18.30	18.60	18.89	19.19	19.78
78	15.32	15.62	15.91	16.20	16.50	16.79	17.09	17.38	17.68	17.98	18.27	18.57	18.87	19.17	19.46	20.06
77	15.57	15.86	16.16	16.46	16.75	17.05	17.35	17.65	17.95	18.25	18.54	18.84	19.15	19.45	19.75	20.35
76	15.82	16.12	16.42	16.72	17.01	17.31	17.62	17.92	18.22	18.52	18.82	19.13	19.43	19.73	20.04	20.65
75	16.07	16.38	16.68	16.98	17.28	17.58	17.89	18.19	18.50	18.80	19.11	19.41	19.72	20.03	20.34	20.95
74	16.34	16.64	16.94	17.25	17.55	17.86	18.17	18.47	18.78	19.09	19.40	19.71	20.02	20.33	20.64	21.26
73	16.60	16.91	17.22	17.53	17.83	18.14	18.45	18.76	19.07	19.39	19.70	20.01	20.32	20.64	20.95	21.58
70	17.45	17.76	18.08	18.40	18.71	19.03	19.35	19.67	19.99	20.32	20.64	20.96	21.29	21.61	21.93	22.59
65	19.00	19.33	19.67	20.00	20.34	20.68	21.02	21.35	21.70	22.04	22.38	22.72	23.06	23.41	23.75	24.45
60	20.77	21.13	21.49	21.84	22.20	22.56	22.92	23.29	23.65	24.01	24.38	24.75	25.11	25.48	25.85	26.59
55	22.84	23.22	23.60	23.99	24.37	24.76	25.15	25.54	25.93	26.32	26.71	27.11	27.51	27.90	28.30	29.10

Description: This table shows the price to pay for a monthly payment mortgage loan at the yield rate.

Example: The price of a 6.75 %, 19 year mortgage loan to yield 8.00 % to maturity is $ 91.22.

INTEREST RATE, %

YIELD	0.00%	1.00%	2.00%	3.00%	4.00%	4.25%	4.50%	4.75%	5.00%	5.25%	5.50%	5.75%	6.00%	6.25%	6.50%	6.75%
0.00	100.00	109.84	120.28	131.31	142.93	145.92	148.95	152.01	155.10	158.23	161.40	164.60	167.83	171.09	174.39	177.72
1.00	91.04	100.00	109.51	119.55	130.12	132.84	135.60	138.39	141.21	144.06	146.94	149.85	152.79	155.76	158.76	161.79
2.00	83.14	91.32	100.00	109.17	118.83	121.31	123.83	126.37	128.95	131.55	134.18	136.84	139.53	142.24	144.98	147.75
3.00	76.15	83.65	91.60	100.00	108.84	111.12	113.43	115.76	118.12	120.50	122.91	125.34	127.81	130.29	132.80	135.34
4.00	69.97	76.85	84.16	91.88	100.00	102.09	104.21	106.35	108.52	110.71	112.92	115.16	117.42	119.71	122.01	124.34
4.25	68.53	75.28	82.43	89.99	97.95	100.00	102.07	104.17	106.29	108.44	110.61	112.80	115.01	117.25	119.51	121.79
4.50	67.14	73.75	80.76	88.16	95.96	97.97	100.00	102.06	104.13	106.24	108.36	110.51	112.68	114.87	117.08	119.32
4.75	65.79	72.26	79.13	86.39	94.03	95.99	97.99	100.00	102.04	104.10	106.18	108.28	110.41	112.55	114.72	116.91
5.00	64.47	70.82	77.55	84.66	92.15	94.08	96.03	98.00	100.00	102.02	104.06	106.12	108.20	110.31	112.43	114.58
5.25	63.20	69.42	76.02	82.99	90.33	92.22	94.13	96.06	98.02	100.00	102.00	104.02	106.06	108.13	110.21	112.31
5.50	61.96	68.06	74.53	81.36	88.56	90.41	92.28	94.18	96.10	98.04	100.00	101.98	103.98	106.01	108.05	110.11
5.75	60.75	66.73	73.08	79.78	86.83	88.65	90.49	92.35	94.23	96.13	98.06	100.00	101.96	103.95	105.95	107.97
6.00	59.59	65.45	71.67	78.24	85.16	86.95	88.75	90.57	92.42	94.28	96.17	98.07	100.00	101.94	103.91	105.89
6.25	58.45	64.20	70.30	76.75	83.54	85.29	87.06	88.85	90.66	92.49	94.33	96.20	98.09	100.00	101.93	103.87
6.50	57.34	62.99	68.97	75.30	81.96	83.67	85.41	87.17	88.94	90.74	92.55	94.39	96.24	98.11	100.00	101.91
6.75	56.27	61.81	67.68	73.89	80.42	82.11	83.81	85.53	87.28	89.04	90.82	92.62	94.44	96.27	98.13	100.00
7.00	55.23	60.66	66.43	72.52	78.93	80.58	82.26	83.95	85.66	87.39	89.13	90.90	92.68	94.49	96.31	98.14
7.25	54.21	59.55	65.21	71.19	77.48	79.10	80.74	82.40	84.08	85.78	87.49	89.23	90.98	92.75	94.54	96.34
7.50	53.22	58.46	64.02	69.89	76.07	77.66	79.27	80.90	82.55	84.22	85.90	87.60	89.32	91.06	92.81	94.58
7.75	52.26	57.41	62.86	68.63	74.70	76.26	77.84	79.44	81.06	82.70	84.35	86.02	87.71	89.42	91.14	92.88
8.00	51.33	56.38	61.74	67.40	73.36	74.90	76.45	78.02	79.61	81.22	82.84	84.48	86.14	87.82	89.51	91.22
8.25	50.42	55.38	60.64	66.21	72.06	73.57	75.10	76.64	78.20	79.78	81.37	82.99	84.62	86.26	87.92	89.60
8.50	49.53	54.41	59.58	65.05	70.80	72.28	73.78	75.30	76.83	78.38	79.95	81.53	83.13	84.75	86.38	88.03
8.75	48.67	53.46	58.55	63.91	69.57	71.02	72.50	73.99	75.49	77.02	78.56	80.11	81.69	83.27	84.88	86.50
9.00	47.83	52.54	57.54	62.81	68.37	69.80	71.25	72.71	74.19	75.69	77.20	78.73	80.28	81.84	83.42	85.01
9.25	47.02	51.65	56.56	61.74	67.20	68.61	70.03	71.47	72.93	74.40	75.89	77.39	78.91	80.45	82.00	83.56
9.50	46.22	50.77	55.60	60.70	66.07	67.45	68.85	70.26	71.70	73.14	74.61	76.08	77.58	79.09	80.61	82.15
9.75	45.45	49.92	54.67	59.68	64.96	66.32	67.70	69.09	70.50	71.92	73.36	74.81	76.28	77.76	79.26	80.77
10.00	44.70	49.10	53.76	58.69	63.88	65.22	66.57	67.94	69.33	70.73	72.14	73.57	75.01	76.47	77.95	79.43
10.25	43.96	48.29	52.88	57.73	62.84	64.15	65.48	66.83	68.19	69.56	70.96	72.36	73.78	75.22	76.67	78.13
10.50	43.25	47.50	52.02	56.79	61.81	63.11	64.42	65.74	67.08	68.43	69.80	71.18	72.58	73.99	75.42	76.86
10.75	42.55	46.74	51.18	55.88	60.82	62.09	63.38	64.68	66.00	67.33	68.68	70.04	71.41	72.80	74.20	75.62
11.00	41.87	45.99	50.37	54.98	59.85	61.10	62.37	63.65	64.95	66.26	67.58	68.92	70.27	71.64	73.02	74.41
11.25	41.21	45.27	49.57	54.12	58.90	60.13	61.38	62.64	63.92	65.21	66.51	67.83	69.16	70.51	71.87	73.24
11.50	40.57	44.56	48.79	53.27	57.98	59.19	60.42	61.66	62.92	64.19	65.47	66.77	68.08	69.40	70.74	72.09
11.75	39.94	43.87	48.04	52.44	57.08	58.27	59.48	60.71	61.94	63.19	64.46	65.73	67.02	68.33	69.64	70.97
12.00	39.32	43.19	47.30	51.64	56.20	57.38	58.57	59.77	60.99	62.22	63.47	64.72	65.99	67.28	68.57	69.88
12.25	38.72	42.54	46.58	50.85	55.35	56.51	57.68	58.86	60.06	61.27	62.50	63.74	64.99	66.25	67.53	68.82
12.50	38.14	41.89	45.88	50.08	54.51	55.65	56.81	57.98	59.16	60.35	61.56	62.78	64.01	65.25	66.51	67.78
12.75	37.57	41.27	45.19	49.34	53.70	54.82	55.96	57.11	58.27	59.45	60.64	61.84	63.05	64.28	65.52	66.77
13.00	37.02	40.66	44.52	48.61	52.91	54.01	55.13	56.27	57.41	58.57	59.74	60.93	62.12	63.33	64.55	65.78
13.25	36.47	40.06	43.87	47.89	52.13	53.22	54.33	55.44	56.57	57.71	58.87	60.03	61.21	62.40	63.60	64.82
13.50	35.94	39.48	43.23	47.20	51.37	52.45	53.54	54.64	55.75	56.88	58.01	59.16	60.32	61.50	62.68	63.88
13.75	35.43	38.91	42.61	46.52	50.64	51.70	52.77	53.85	54.95	56.06	57.18	58.31	59.46	60.61	61.78	62.96
14.00	34.92	38.36	42.01	45.86	49.91	50.96	52.02	53.09	54.17	55.26	56.37	57.48	58.61	59.75	60.90	62.06
14.25	34.43	37.82	41.41	45.21	49.21	50.24	51.28	52.34	53.40	54.48	55.57	56.67	57.78	58.91	60.04	61.19
14.50	33.95	37.29	40.84	44.58	48.52	49.54	50.57	51.61	52.66	53.72	54.80	55.88	56.98	58.09	59.21	60.34
14.75	33.48	36.78	40.27	43.97	47.85	48.85	49.87	50.89	51.93	52.98	54.04	55.11	56.19	57.28	58.39	59.50
15.00	33.02	36.27	39.72	43.36	47.20	48.19	49.18	50.20	51.22	52.25	53.30	54.35	55.42	56.50	57.59	58.69
15.25	32.57	35.78	39.18	42.77	46.56	47.53	48.52	49.51	50.52	51.54	52.57	53.61	54.67	55.73	56.80	57.89
15.50	32.14	35.30	38.65	42.20	45.93	46.89	47.86	48.85	49.84	50.85	51.87	52.89	53.93	54.98	56.04	57.11
15.75	31.71	34.83	38.14	41.64	45.32	46.27	47.23	48.20	49.18	50.17	51.18	52.19	53.21	54.25	55.29	56.35
16.00	31.29	34.37	37.64	41.09	44.72	45.66	46.60	47.56	48.53	49.51	50.50	51.50	52.51	53.53	54.56	55.61
16.25	30.88	33.92	37.14	40.55	44.14	45.06	45.99	46.94	47.90	48.86	49.84	50.83	51.83	52.83	53.85	54.88
16.50	30.48	33.48	36.66	40.03	43.56	44.48	45.40	46.33	47.28	48.23	49.19	50.17	51.15	52.15	53.15	54.17
16.75	30.09	33.05	36.19	39.51	43.01	43.91	44.82	45.74	46.67	47.61	48.56	49.53	50.50	51.48	52.47	53.47
17.00	29.71	32.63	35.73	39.01	42.46	43.35	44.25	45.16	46.08	47.01	47.95	48.90	49.86	50.83	51.81	52.79
17.25	29.33	32.22	35.28	38.52	41.92	42.80	43.69	44.59	45.50	46.41	47.34	48.28	49.23	50.19	51.15	52.13
17.50	28.97	31.82	34.84	38.04	41.40	42.27	43.15	44.03	44.93	45.84	46.75	47.68	48.61	49.56	50.51	51.48
17.75	28.61	31.42	34.41	37.57	40.89	41.75	42.61	43.49	44.37	45.27	46.17	47.09	48.01	48.95	49.89	50.84
18.00	28.26	31.04	33.99	37.11	40.39	41.23	42.09	42.96	43.83	44.71	45.61	46.51	47.43	48.35	49.28	50.22
18.25	27.92	30.66	33.58	36.66	39.90	40.73	41.58	42.43	43.30	44.17	45.06	45.95	46.85	47.76	48.68	49.61
18.50	27.58	30.29	33.17	36.22	39.42	40.24	41.08	41.92	42.78	43.64	44.51	45.40	46.29	47.19	48.10	49.01
18.75	27.25	29.93	32.78	35.79	38.95	39.77	40.59	41.42	42.27	43.12	43.98	44.86	45.74	46.63	47.52	48.43
19.00	26.93	29.58	32.39	35.36	38.49	39.30	40.11	40.94	41.77	42.61	43.46	44.33	45.20	46.07	46.96	47.86
20.00	25.71	28.24	30.92	33.76	36.74	37.51	38.29	39.08	39.87	40.68	41.49	42.31	43.15	43.98	44.83	45.69
25.00	20.86	22.91	25.09	27.39	29.82	30.44	31.07	31.71	32.36	33.01	33.67	34.34	35.01	35.69	36.38	37.07
30.00	17.48	19.20	21.03	22.95	24.98	25.51	26.04	26.57	27.11	27.66	28.21	28.77	29.34	29.91	30.48	31.07

Description: This table shows the yield to maturity of a mortgage purchased at the price shown in the index.

Example: The yield to maturity of a 6.75 %, 19 year mortgage at a price of 80.00 is 9.89 %.

INTEREST RATE, %

PRICE	0.00%	1.00%	2.00%	3.00%	4.00%	4.25%	4.50%	4.75%	5.00%	5.25%	5.50%	5.75%	6.00%	6.25%	6.50%	6.75%
100	0.00	1.00	2.00	3.00	4.00	4.25	4.50	4.75	5.00	5.25	5.50	5.75	6.00	6.25	6.50	6.75
99	.10	1.10	2.11	3.11	4.12	4.37	4.62	4.87	5.12	5.37	5.62	5.87	6.13	6.38	6.63	6.88
98	.21	1.21	2.22	3.23	4.24	4.49	4.74	5.00	5.25	5.50	5.75	6.00	6.26	6.51	6.76	7.01
97	.32	1.33	2.34	3.35	4.36	4.62	4.87	5.12	5.38	5.63	5.88	6.14	6.39	6.65	6.90	7.15
96	.43	1.44	2.46	3.47	4.49	4.74	5.00	5.25	5.51	5.76	6.02	6.27	6.53	6.78	7.04	7.29
95	.54	1.56	2.58	3.60	4.62	4.87	5.13	5.39	5.64	5.90	6.15	6.41	6.67	6.92	7.18	7.44
94	.65	1.67	2.70	3.72	4.75	5.01	5.26	5.52	5.78	6.03	6.29	6.55	6.81	7.06	7.32	7.58
93	.77	1.79	2.82	3.85	4.88	5.14	5.40	5.66	5.91	6.17	6.43	6.69	6.95	7.21	7.47	7.73
92	.88	1.91	2.94	3.98	5.02	5.27	5.53	5.79	6.05	6.31	6.57	6.83	7.09	7.35	7.62	7.88
91	1.00	2.03	3.07	4.11	5.15	5.41	5.67	5.93	6.20	6.46	6.72	6.98	7.24	7.50	7.77	8.03
90	1.12	2.16	3.20	4.24	5.29	5.55	5.81	6.08	6.34	6.60	6.87	7.13	7.39	7.66	7.92	8.18
89	1.24	2.28	3.33	4.38	5.43	5.69	5.96	6.22	6.49	6.75	7.02	7.28	7.54	7.81	8.07	8.34
88	1.37	2.41	3.46	4.52	5.57	5.84	6.10	6.37	6.64	6.90	7.17	7.43	7.70	7.97	8.23	8.50
87	1.49	2.54	3.60	4.66	5.72	5.99	6.25	6.52	6.79	7.05	7.32	7.59	7.86	8.13	8.39	8.66
86	1.62	2.68	3.74	4.80	5.87	6.14	6.40	6.67	6.94	7.21	7.48	7.75	8.02	8.29	8.56	8.83
85	1.75	2.81	3.88	4.95	6.02	6.29	6.56	6.83	7.10	7.37	7.64	7.91	8.18	8.45	8.72	9.00
84	1.88	2.95	4.02	5.09	6.17	6.44	6.72	6.99	7.26	7.53	7.80	8.08	8.35	8.62	8.89	9.17
83	2.01	3.09	4.16	5.24	6.33	6.60	6.87	7.15	7.42	7.69	7.97	8.24	8.52	8.79	9.07	9.34
82	2.15	3.23	4.31	5.40	6.49	6.76	7.04	7.31	7.59	7.86	8.14	8.41	8.69	8.97	9.24	9.52
81	2.29	3.37	4.46	5.55	6.65	6.93	7.20	7.48	7.76	8.03	8.31	8.59	8.87	9.14	9.42	9.70
80	2.43	3.52	4.61	5.71	6.82	7.09	7.37	7.65	7.93	8.21	8.49	8.77	9.05	9.33	9.61	9.89
79	2.57	3.67	4.77	5.87	6.98	7.26	7.54	7.82	8.10	8.38	8.66	8.95	9.23	9.51	9.79	10.08
78	2.72	3.82	4.92	6.04	7.15	7.44	7.72	8.00	8.28	8.56	8.85	9.13	9.42	9.70	9.98	10.27
77	2.87	3.97	5.08	6.20	7.33	7.61	7.90	8.18	8.46	8.75	9.03	9.32	9.61	9.89	10.18	10.47
76	3.02	4.13	5.25	6.37	7.51	7.79	8.08	8.36	8.65	8.94	9.22	9.51	9.80	10.09	10.38	10.67
75	3.17	4.29	5.41	6.55	7.69	7.98	8.26	8.55	8.84	9.13	9.42	9.71	10.00	10.29	10.58	10.87
74	3.33	4.45	5.58	6.73	7.87	8.16	8.45	8.74	9.03	9.32	9.62	9.91	10.20	10.49	10.79	11.08
73	3.49	4.62	5.76	6.91	8.06	8.35	8.65	8.94	9.23	9.52	9.82	10.11	10.41	10.70	11.00	11.30
72	3.65	4.79	5.94	7.09	8.26	8.55	8.84	9.14	9.43	9.73	10.02	10.32	10.62	10.92	11.22	11.52
71	3.82	4.96	6.12	7.28	8.45	8.75	9.05	9.34	9.64	9.94	10.24	10.53	10.83	11.14	11.44	11.74
70	3.99	5.14	6.30	7.47	8.66	8.95	9.25	9.55	9.85	10.15	10.45	10.75	11.06	11.36	11.66	11.97
69	4.16	5.32	6.49	7.67	8.86	9.16	9.46	9.76	10.07	10.37	10.67	10.98	11.28	11.59	11.89	12.20
68	4.34	5.51	6.68	7.87	9.07	9.38	9.68	9.98	10.29	10.59	10.90	11.21	11.51	11.82	12.13	12.44
67	4.52	5.69	6.88	8.08	9.29	9.59	9.90	10.21	10.51	10.82	11.13	11.44	11.75	12.06	12.37	12.69
66	4.71	5.89	7.08	8.29	9.51	9.82	10.13	10.43	10.74	11.06	11.37	11.68	11.99	12.31	12.62	12.94
65	4.89	6.08	7.29	8.50	9.74	10.05	10.36	10.67	10.98	11.30	11.61	11.93	12.24	12.56	12.88	13.20
64	5.09	6.29	7.50	8.73	9.97	10.28	10.59	10.91	11.22	11.54	11.86	12.18	12.50	12.82	13.14	13.46
63	5.28	6.49	7.71	8.95	10.21	10.52	10.84	11.16	11.47	11.79	12.11	12.44	12.76	13.08	13.41	13.73
62	5.49	6.70	7.94	9.18	10.45	10.77	11.09	11.41	11.73	12.05	12.38	12.70	13.03	13.36	13.68	14.01
61	5.69	6.92	8.16	9.42	10.70	11.02	11.34	11.67	11.99	12.32	12.65	12.97	13.30	13.64	13.97	14.30
60	5.91	7.14	8.40	9.67	10.96	11.28	11.61	11.93	12.26	12.59	12.92	13.25	13.59	13.92	14.26	14.59
59	6.12	7.37	8.63	9.92	11.22	11.55	11.88	12.21	12.54	12.87	13.21	13.54	13.88	14.22	14.56	14.90
58	6.35	7.60	8.88	10.17	11.49	11.82	12.15	12.49	12.82	13.16	13.50	13.84	14.18	14.52	14.86	15.21
57	6.57	7.84	9.13	10.44	11.77	12.10	12.44	12.78	13.12	13.46	13.80	14.14	14.49	14.83	15.18	15.53
56	6.81	8.09	9.39	10.71	12.05	12.39	12.73	13.08	13.42	13.76	14.11	14.46	14.81	15.16	15.51	15.86
55	7.05	8.34	9.66	10.99	12.35	12.69	13.04	13.38	13.73	14.08	14.43	14.78	15.13	15.49	15.85	16.20
54	7.30	8.60	9.93	11.28	12.65	13.00	13.35	13.70	14.05	14.40	14.76	15.11	15.47	15.83	16.19	16.56
53	7.55	8.87	10.21	11.58	12.96	13.32	13.67	14.02	14.38	14.74	15.10	15.46	15.82	16.18	16.55	16.92
52	7.81	9.15	10.50	11.88	13.29	13.64	14.00	14.36	14.72	15.08	15.45	15.81	16.18	16.55	16.92	17.29
51	8.08	9.43	10.80	12.20	13.62	13.98	14.34	14.71	15.07	15.44	15.81	16.18	16.56	16.94	17.32	17.68
50	8.36	9.72	11.11	12.52	13.97	14.33	14.70	15.07	15.44	15.81	16.19	16.57	16.95	17.34	17.72	18.08
49	8.65	10.02	11.43	12.86	14.32	14.69	15.06	15.44	15.81	16.19	16.57	16.95	17.34	17.72	18.11	18.50
48	8.95	10.34	11.76	13.21	14.69	15.07	15.44	15.82	16.20	16.59	16.97	17.36	17.75	18.14	18.54	18.93
47	9.25	10.66	12.10	13.57	15.07	15.45	15.84	16.22	16.61	17.00	17.39	17.78	18.18	18.58	18.98	19.38
46	9.57	10.99	12.45	13.94	15.47	15.85	16.24	16.63	17.03	17.42	17.82	18.22	18.62	19.03	19.44	19.85
45	9.89	11.34	12.82	14.33	15.88	16.27	16.67	17.06	17.46	17.87	18.27	18.68	19.09	19.50	19.91	20.33
44	10.23	11.70	13.20	14.73	16.30	16.70	17.11	17.51	17.92	18.33	18.74	19.15	19.57	19.99	20.41	20.83
43	10.58	12.07	13.59	15.15	16.75	17.15	17.56	17.97	18.39	18.80	19.22	19.64	20.07	20.50	20.93	21.36
42	10.95	12.45	14.00	15.58	17.21	17.62	18.04	18.46	18.88	19.30	19.73	20.16	20.59	21.03	21.46	21.91
41	11.33	12.85	14.42	16.04	17.69	18.11	18.54	18.96	19.39	19.82	20.26	20.70	21.14	21.58	22.03	22.48
40	11.72	13.27	14.87	16.51	18.19	18.62	19.05	19.49	19.93	20.37	20.81	21.26	21.71	22.16	22.62	23.07
39	12.13	13.71	15.33	17.00	18.72	19.16	19.60	20.04	20.49	20.94	21.39	21.84	22.30	22.77	23.23	23.70
35	13.96	15.65	17.40	19.21	21.08	21.56	22.04	22.52	23.01	23.50	24.00	24.50	25.00	25.51	26.02	26.54
30	16.80	18.70	20.67	22.71	24.84	25.38	25.93	26.48	27.04	27.60	28.17	28.74	29.32	29.90	30.49	31.08
25	20.61	22.80	25.09	27.48	29.98	30.62	31.26	31.92	32.58	33.24	33.91	34.59	35.28	35.97	36.67	37.37
20	26.12	28.77	31.56	34.50	37.57	38.37	39.17	39.97	40.79	41.62	42.45	43.30	44.15	45.01	45.88	46.75
15	35.03	38.51	42.18	46.06	50.14	51.19	52.25	53.33	54.42	55.51	56.62	57.75	58.88	60.03	61.18	62.35
10	52.62	57.81	63.30	69.11	75.22	76.79	78.39	80.00	81.63	83.28	84.94	86.63	88.33	90.04	91.78	93.53

Description: This table shows the price to pay for a monthly payment mortgage loan at the yield rate.

Example: The price of a 10.75 %, 19 year mortgage loan to yield 8.00 % to maturity is $ 120.63.

INTEREST RATE, %

YIELD	7.00%	7.25%	7.50%	7.75%	8.00%	8.25%	8.50%	8.75%	9.00%	9.25%	9.50%	9.75%	10.00%	10.25%	10.50%	10.75%
0.00	181.08	184.47	187.89	191.34	194.83	198.34	201.88	205.45	209.05	212.68	216.34	220.02	223.73	227.46	231.22	235.01
1.00	164.85	167.94	171.05	174.20	177.37	180.57	183.79	187.04	190.32	193.62	196.95	200.30	203.68	207.08	210.51	213.95
2.00	150.54	153.36	156.21	159.08	161.97	164.89	167.84	170.81	173.80	176.82	179.86	182.92	186.00	189.11	192.23	195.38
3.00	137.89	140.48	143.08	145.71	148.37	151.04	153.74	156.46	159.20	161.96	164.75	167.55	170.37	173.22	176.08	178.97
4.00	126.69	129.06	131.46	133.88	136.31	138.77	141.25	143.75	146.27	148.80	151.36	153.94	156.53	159.15	161.78	164.43
4.25	124.09	126.42	128.76	131.13	133.52	135.92	138.35	140.80	143.27	145.75	148.26	150.78	153.32	155.88	158.46	161.06
4.50	121.57	123.85	126.15	128.47	130.80	133.16	135.54	137.94	140.36	142.79	145.24	147.72	150.21	152.72	155.24	157.78
4.75	119.12	121.35	123.61	125.88	128.17	130.48	132.81	135.16	137.53	139.91	142.32	144.74	147.18	149.64	152.11	154.60
5.00	116.75	118.93	121.14	123.36	125.61	127.88	130.16	132.46	134.78	137.12	139.48	141.85	144.24	146.65	149.08	151.52
5.25	114.44	116.58	118.74	120.92	123.13	125.35	127.58	129.84	132.12	134.41	136.72	139.05	141.39	143.75	146.13	148.52
5.50	112.19	114.29	116.41	118.55	120.71	122.89	125.08	127.30	129.53	131.77	134.04	136.32	138.62	140.93	143.26	145.61
5.75	110.01	112.07	114.15	116.25	118.37	120.50	122.65	124.82	127.01	129.21	131.43	133.67	135.93	138.19	140.48	142.78
6.00	107.89	109.92	111.95	114.01	116.09	118.18	120.29	122.42	124.56	126.73	128.90	131.10	133.31	135.53	137.78	140.03
6.25	105.84	107.82	109.82	111.84	113.87	115.93	118.00	120.08	122.19	124.31	126.44	128.60	130.77	132.95	135.15	137.36
6.50	103.84	105.78	107.74	109.72	111.72	113.74	115.77	117.81	119.88	121.96	124.05	126.17	128.29	130.44	132.59	134.76
6.75	101.89	103.80	105.73	107.67	109.63	111.60	113.60	115.61	117.63	119.67	121.73	123.80	125.89	127.99	130.11	132.24
7.00	100.00	101.87	103.76	105.67	107.59	109.53	111.49	113.46	115.45	117.45	119.47	121.51	123.55	125.62	127.69	129.79
7.25	98.16	100.00	101.86	103.73	105.62	107.52	109.44	111.38	113.33	115.29	117.28	119.27	121.28	123.31	125.35	127.40
7.50	96.37	98.18	100.00	101.84	103.69	105.56	107.45	109.35	111.26	113.19	115.14	117.10	119.07	121.06	123.06	125.08
7.75	94.63	96.41	98.20	100.00	101.82	103.66	105.51	107.37	109.26	111.15	113.06	114.99	116.92	118.88	120.84	122.82
8.00	92.94	94.68	96.44	98.21	100.00	101.80	103.62	105.45	107.30	109.16	111.04	112.93	114.83	116.75	118.68	120.63
8.25	91.30	93.01	94.73	96.47	98.23	100.00	101.79	103.59	105.40	107.23	109.07	110.93	112.80	114.68	116.58	118.49
8.50	89.69	91.37	93.07	94.78	96.51	98.25	100.00	101.77	103.55	105.35	107.16	108.98	110.82	112.67	114.53	116.41
8.75	88.14	89.79	91.45	93.13	94.83	96.54	98.26	100.00	101.75	103.52	105.30	107.09	108.89	110.71	112.54	114.39
9.00	86.62	88.24	89.88	91.53	93.19	94.88	96.57	98.28	100.00	101.74	103.48	105.25	107.02	108.81	110.61	112.42
9.25	85.14	86.73	88.34	89.97	91.61	93.26	94.92	96.60	98.29	100.00	101.72	103.45	105.19	106.95	108.72	110.50
9.50	83.70	85.27	86.85	88.45	90.06	91.68	93.32	94.97	96.63	98.31	100.00	101.70	103.42	105.14	106.88	108.63
9.75	82.30	83.84	85.40	86.97	88.55	90.15	91.76	93.38	95.02	96.66	98.33	100.00	101.69	103.38	105.09	106.81
10.00	80.94	82.45	83.98	85.53	87.08	88.65	90.24	91.83	93.44	95.06	96.70	98.34	100.00	101.67	103.35	105.04
10.25	79.61	81.10	82.60	84.12	85.65	87.20	88.75	90.32	91.91	93.50	95.11	96.73	98.36	100.00	101.65	103.32
10.50	78.31	79.78	81.26	82.75	84.26	85.78	87.31	88.85	90.41	91.98	93.56	95.15	96.76	98.37	100.00	101.64
10.75	77.05	78.49	79.95	81.42	82.90	84.40	85.90	87.42	88.95	90.50	92.05	93.62	95.20	96.79	98.39	100.00
11.00	75.82	77.24	78.67	80.12	81.58	83.05	84.53	86.03	87.53	89.05	90.58	92.13	93.68	95.24	96.82	98.40
11.25	74.62	76.02	77.43	78.85	80.29	81.74	83.20	34.67	86.15	87.65	89.15	90.67	92.20	93.74	95.29	96.85
11.50	73.45	74.83	76.22	77.62	79.03	80.46	81.89	83.34	84.80	86.27	87.76	89.25	90.75	92.27	93.80	95.33
11.75	72.31	73.67	75.04	76.41	77.81	79.21	80.62	82.05	83.49	84.94	86.40	87.87	89.35	90.84	92.34	93.85
12.00	71.20	72.54	73.88	75.24	76.61	77.99	79.38	80.79	82.20	83.63	85.07	86.52	87.97	89.44	90.92	92.41
12.25	70.12	71.43	72.76	74.10	75.44	76.81	78.18	79.56	80.95	82.36	83.77	85.20	86.64	88.08	89.54	91.01
12.50	69.06	70.36	71.66	72.98	74.31	75.65	77.00	78.36	79.73	81.12	82.51	83.92	85.33	86.76	88.19	89.63
12.75	68.03	69.31	70.59	71.89	73.20	74.52	75.85	77.19	78.54	79.91	81.28	82.66	84.06	85.46	86.87	88.30
13.00	67.03	68.28	69.55	70.83	72.12	73.42	74.73	76.05	77.38	78.72	80.08	81.44	82.81	84.20	85.59	86.99
13.25	66.04	67.28	68.53	69.79	71.06	72.34	73.63	74.94	76.25	77.57	78.90	80.25	81.60	82.96	84.34	85.72
13.50	65.09	66.31	67.54	68.78	70.03	71.29	72.56	73.85	75.14	76.45	77.76	79.08	80.42	81.76	83.11	84.47
13.75	64.15	65.35	66.57	67.79	69.02	70.27	71.52	72.79	74.06	75.35	76.64	77.95	79.26	80.58	81.92	83.26
14.00	63.24	64.42	65.62	66.82	68.04	69.27	70.50	71.75	73.01	74.28	75.55	76.84	78.13	79.44	80.75	82.07
14.25	62.35	63.51	64.69	65.88	67.08	68.29	69.51	70.74	71.98	73.23	74.49	75.75	77.03	78.32	79.61	80.92
14.50	61.48	62.63	63.79	64.96	66.14	67.34	68.54	69.75	70.97	72.21	73.45	74.70	75.96	77.22	78.50	79.79
14.75	60.63	61.76	62.91	64.06	65.23	66.41	67.59	68.79	69.99	71.21	72.43	73.66	74.91	76.16	77.42	78.68
15.00	59.79	60.91	62.04	63.19	64.34	65.50	66.67	67.84	69.03	70.23	71.44	72.65	73.88	75.11	76.35	77.60
15.25	58.98	60.09	61.20	62.33	63.46	64.61	65.76	66.92	68.10	69.28	70.47	71.67	72.88	74.09	75.32	76.55
15.50	58.19	59.28	60.38	61.49	62.61	63.74	64.88	66.02	67.18	68.35	69.52	70.70	71.90	73.10	74.31	75.52
15.75	57.41	58.49	59.58	60.67	61.77	62.89	64.01	65.14	66.29	67.44	68.59	69.76	70.94	72.12	73.32	74.52
16.00	56.66	57.72	58.79	59.87	60.96	62.06	63.17	64.28	65.41	66.55	67.69	68.84	70.00	71.17	72.35	73.53
16.25	55.92	56.96	58.02	59.09	60.16	61.25	62.34	63.44	64.56	65.68	66.81	67.94	69.09	70.24	71.40	72.57
16.50	55.19	56.23	57.27	58.32	59.38	60.45	61.53	62.62	63.72	64.83	65.94	67.06	68.19	69.33	70.48	71.63
16.75	54.48	55.51	56.53	57.57	58.62	59.68	60.74	61.82	62.90	63.99	65.09	66.20	67.32	68.44	69.57	70.71
17.00	53.79	54.80	55.82	56.84	57.88	58.92	59.97	61.03	62.10	63.18	64.27	65.36	66.46	67.57	68.69	69.81
17.25	53.11	54.11	55.11	56.13	57.15	58.18	59.22	60.27	61.32	62.39	63.46	64.54	65.63	66.72	67.82	68.94
17.50	52.45	53.43	54.43	55.43	56.44	57.45	58.48	59.51	60.56	61.61	62.67	63.73	64.81	65.89	66.98	68.08
17.75	51.80	52.77	53.75	54.74	55.74	56.74	57.76	58.78	59.81	60.85	61.89	62.94	64.01	65.07	66.15	67.23
18.00	51.17	52.13	53.10	54.07	55.06	56.05	57.05	58.06	59.08	60.10	61.13	62.17	63.22	64.28	65.34	66.41
18.25	50.55	51.50	52.45	53.41	54.39	55.37	56.36	57.35	58.36	59.37	60.39	61.42	62.46	63.50	64.55	65.60
18.50	49.94	50.88	51.82	52.77	53.73	54.70	55.68	56.66	57.66	58.66	59.67	60.68	61.70	62.73	63.77	64.82
18.75	49.35	50.27	51.20	52.14	53.09	54.05	55.02	55.99	56.97	57.96	58.95	59.96	60.97	61.99	63.01	64.04
19.00	48.76	49.68	50.60	51.53	52.47	53.41	54.37	55.33	56.30	57.27	58.26	59.25	60.25	61.26	62.27	63.29
20.00	46.55	47.42	48.30	49.19	50.09	50.99	51.90	52.82	53.74	54.68	55.62	56.56	57.52	58.48	59.44	60.42
25.00	37.77	38.48	39.20	39.92	40.64	41.38	42.12	42.86	43.61	44.37	45.13	45.90	46.67	47.45	48.24	49.03
30.00	31.65	32.25	32.84	33.45	34.06	34.67	35.29	35.91	36.54	37.18	37.82	38.46	39.11	39.76	40.42	41.08

Description: This table shows the yield to maturity of a mortgage purchased at the price shown in the index.

Example: The yield to maturity of a 10.75 %, 19 year mortgage at a price of 111.00 is 9.18 %.

INTEREST RATE, %

PRICE	7.00%	7.25%	7.50%	7.75%	8.00%	8.25%	8.50%	8.75%	9.00%	9.25%	9.50%	9.75%	10.00%	10.25%	10.50%	10.75%
155	1.67	1.88	2.08	2.29	2.49	2.70	2.90	3.10	3.31	3.51	3.71	3.91	4.11	4.31	4.51	4.71
150	2.04	2.24	2.45	2.66	2.87	3.08	3.28	3.49	3.69	3.90	4.10	4.31	4.51	4.72	4.92	5.12
145	2.42	2.63	2.84	3.05	3.26	3.47	3.68	3.89	4.10	4.31	4.52	4.72	4.93	5.14	5.34	5.55
140	2.82	3.03	3.25	3.46	3.68	3.89	4.10	4.31	4.53	4.74	4.95	5.16	5.37	5.58	5.79	6.00
135	3.24	3.46	3.68	3.89	4.11	4.33	4.54	4.76	4.97	5.19	5.40	5.62	5.83	6.05	6.26	6.47
130	3.69	3.91	4.13	4.35	4.57	4.79	5.01	5.23	5.45	5.67	5.89	6.10	6.32	6.54	6.76	6.97
125	4.16	4.38	4.61	4.83	5.06	5.28	5.50	5.73	5.95	6.17	6.40	6.62	6.84	7.06	7.28	7.50
124	4.25	4.48	4.71	4.93	5.16	5.38	5.61	5.83	6.05	6.28	6.50	6.72	6.95	7.17	7.39	7.61
123	4.35	4.58	4.81	5.03	5.26	5.48	5.71	5.93	6.16	6.38	6.61	6.83	7.06	7.28	7.50	7.72
122	4.45	4.68	4.91	5.13	5.36	5.59	5.81	6.04	6.27	6.49	6.72	6.94	7.17	7.39	7.61	7.84
121	4.55	4.78	5.01	5.24	5.46	5.69	5.92	6.15	6.37	6.60	6.83	7.05	7.28	7.50	7.73	7.95
120	4.65	4.88	5.11	5.34	5.57	5.80	6.03	6.25	6.48	6.71	6.94	7.16	7.39	7.62	7.84	8.07
119	4.76	4.99	5.22	5.45	5.68	5.91	6.13	6.36	6.59	6.82	7.05	7.28	7.50	7.73	7.96	8.18
118	4.86	5.09	5.32	5.55	5.78	6.01	6.24	6.47	6.70	6.93	7.16	7.39	7.62	7.85	8.08	8.30
117	4.97	5.20	5.43	5.66	5.89	6.13	6.36	6.59	6.82	7.05	7.28	7.51	7.74	7.97	8.19	8.42
116	5.07	5.31	5.54	5.77	6.00	6.24	6.47	6.70	6.93	7.16	7.39	7.62	7.85	8.09	8.32	8.55
115	5.18	5.42	5.65	5.88	6.12	6.35	6.58	6.82	7.05	7.28	7.51	7.74	7.97	8.21	8.44	8.67
114	5.29	5.53	5.76	6.00	6.23	6.46	6.70	6.93	7.17	7.40	7.63	7.86	8.10	8.33	8.56	8.79
113	5.40	5.64	5.88	6.11	6.35	6.58	6.82	7.05	7.28	7.52	7.75	7.99	8.22	8.45	8.69	8.92
112	5.52	5.75	5.99	6.23	6.46	6.70	6.93	7.17	7.40	7.64	7.88	8.11	8.35	8.58	8.81	9.05
111	5.63	5.87	6.11	6.34	6.58	6.82	7.05	7.29	7.53	7.76	8.00	8.24	8.47	8.71	8.94	9.18
110	5.75	5.99	6.22	6.46	6.70	6.94	7.18	7.41	7.65	7.89	8.13	8.36	8.60	8.84	9.07	9.31
109	5.86	6.10	6.34	6.58	6.82	7.06	7.30	7.54	7.78	8.02	8.25	8.49	8.73	8.97	9.21	9.45
108	5.98	6.22	6.46	6.70	6.94	7.18	7.42	7.66	7.90	8.14	8.38	8.62	8.86	9.10	9.34	9.58
107	6.10	6.34	6.59	6.83	7.07	7.31	7.55	7.79	8.03	8.28	8.52	8.76	9.00	9.24	9.48	9.72
106	6.22	6.47	6.71	6.95	7.20	7.44	7.68	7.92	8.17	8.41	8.65	8.89	9.13	9.38	9.62	9.86
105	6.35	6.59	6.84	7.08	7.32	7.57	7.81	8.06	8.30	8.54	8.79	9.03	9.27	9.52	9.76	10.00
104	6.47	6.72	6.96	7.21	7.45	7.70	7.94	8.19	8.43	8.68	8.92	9.17	9.41	9.66	9.90	10.15
103	6.60	6.85	7.09	7.34	7.59	7.83	8.08	8.32	8.57	8.82	9.06	9.31	9.55	9.80	10.05	10.29
102	6.73	6.98	7.23	7.47	7.72	7.97	8.22	8.46	8.71	8.96	9.20	9.45	9.70	9.95	10.19	10.44
101	6.86	7.11	7.36	7.61	7.86	8.11	8.35	8.60	8.85	9.10	9.35	9.60	9.85	10.09	10.34	10.59
100	7.00	7.25	7.50	7.75	8.00	8.25	8.50	8.75	9.00	9.25	9.50	9.75	10.00	10.25	10.50	10.75
99	7.13	7.38	7.63	7.88	8.14	8.39	8.64	8.89	9.14	9.39	9.64	9.90	10.15	10.40	10.65	10.90
98	7.27	7.52	7.77	8.03	8.28	8.53	8.78	9.04	9.29	9.54	9.79	10.05	10.30	10.55	10.81	11.06
97	7.41	7.66	7.91	8.17	8.42	8.68	8.93	9.19	9.44	9.69	9.95	10.20	10.46	10.71	10.97	11.22
96	7.55	7.80	8.06	8.31	8.57	8.83	9.08	9.34	9.59	9.85	10.10	10.36	10.62	10.87	11.13	11.38
95	7.69	7.95	8.21	8.46	8.72	8.98	9.23	9.49	9.75	10.00	10.26	10.52	10.78	11.04	11.29	11.55
94	7.84	8.10	8.35	8.61	8.87	9.13	9.39	9.65	9.91	10.16	10.42	10.68	10.94	11.20	11.46	11.72
93	7.99	8.25	8.51	8.77	9.03	9.29	9.55	9.81	10.07	10.33	10.59	10.85	11.11	11.37	11.63	11.89
92	8.14	8.40	8.66	8.92	9.18	9.44	9.71	9.97	10.23	10.49	10.75	11.02	11.28	11.54	11.80	12.07
91	8.29	8.55	8.82	9.08	9.34	9.61	9.87	10.13	10.40	10.66	10.92	11.19	11.45	11.72	11.98	12.25
90	8.45	8.71	8.98	9.24	9.50	9.77	10.03	10.30	10.56	10.83	11.10	11.36	11.63	11.89	12.16	12.43
89	8.61	8.87	9.14	9.40	9.67	9.94	10.20	10.47	10.74	11.00	11.27	11.54	11.81	12.08	12.34	12.61
88	8.77	9.03	9.30	9.57	9.84	10.11	10.37	10.64	10.91	11.18	11.45	11.72	11.99	12.26	12.53	12.80
87	8.93	9.20	9.47	9.74	10.01	10.28	10.55	10.82	11.09	11.36	11.63	11.90	12.18	12.45	12.72	12.99
86	9.10	9.37	9.64	9.91	10.18	10.46	10.73	11.00	11.27	11.55	11.82	12.09	12.37	12.64	12.91	13.19
85	9.27	9.54	9.81	10.09	10.36	10.63	10.91	11.18	11.46	11.73	12.01	12.28	12.56	12.84	13.11	13.39
84	9.44	9.72	9.99	10.27	10.54	10.82	11.09	11.37	11.65	11.92	12.20	12.48	12.76	13.03	13.31	13.59
83	9.62	9.90	10.17	10.45	10.73	11.00	11.28	11.56	11.84	12.12	12.40	12.68	12.96	13.24	13.52	13.80
82	9.80	10.08	10.36	10.64	10.91	11.19	11.47	11.75	12.04	12.32	12.60	12.88	13.16	13.44	13.73	14.01
81	9.98	10.26	10.54	10.82	11.11	11.39	11.67	11.95	12.24	12.52	12.80	13.09	13.37	13.66	13.94	14.23
80	10.17	10.45	10.74	11.02	11.30	11.59	11.87	12.15	12.44	12.73	13.01	13.30	13.58	13.87	14.16	14.45
79	10.36	10.65	10.93	11.22	11.50	11.79	12.07	12.36	12.65	12.94	13.22	13.51	13.80	14.09	14.38	14.67
78	10.56	10.84	11.13	11.42	11.70	11.99	12.28	12.57	12.86	13.15	13.44	13.73	14.02	14.32	14.61	14.90
77	10.76	11.04	11.33	11.62	11.91	12.20	12.49	12.79	13.08	13.37	13.66	13.96	14.25	14.55	14.84	15.14
76	10.96	11.25	11.54	11.83	12.13	12.42	12.71	13.01	13.30	13.60	13.89	14.19	14.48	14.78	15.08	15.38
75	11.17	11.46	11.75	12.05	12.34	12.64	12.93	13.23	13.53	13.83	14.12	14.42	14.72	15.02	15.32	15.62
74	11.38	11.67	11.97	12.27	12.56	12.86	13.16	13.46	13.76	14.06	14.36	14.66	14.97	15.27	15.57	15.88
73	11.59	11.89	12.19	12.49	12.79	13.09	13.39	13.69	14.00	14.30	14.60	14.91	15.21	15.52	15.83	16.13
70	12.27	12.58	12.89	13.19	13.50	13.81	14.12	14.43	14.74	15.06	15.37	15.68	16.00	16.31	16.63	16.94
65	13.52	13.84	14.16	14.48	14.81	15.13	15.46	15.79	16.11	16.44	16.77	17.10	17.44	17.77	18.10	18.44
60	14.93	15.27	15.61	15.95	16.30	16.64	16.99	17.33	17.68	18.03	18.38	18.73	19.08	19.44	19.79	20.15
55	16.56	16.92	17.29	17.65	18.02	18.38	18.75	19.12	19.49	19.87	20.24	20.62	20.99	21.37	21.75	22.14
50	18.47	18.86	19.25	19.64	20.03	20.43	20.83	21.22	21.63	22.03	22.43	22.84	23.25	23.66	24.07	24.49
45	20.75	21.17	21.59	22.02	22.45	22.88	23.31	23.75	24.19	24.63	25.07	25.52	25.96	26.41	26.87	27.32
40	23.54	24.00	24.47	24.94	25.41	25.89	26.37	26.85	27.34	27.83	28.32	28.82	29.31	29.81	30.32	30.82
35	27.06	27.58	28.11	28.64	29.17	29.71	30.25	30.79	31.34	31.90	32.45	33.01	33.58	34.14	34.71	35.29
30	31.68	32.28	32.89	33.50	34.12	34.74	35.37	36.00	36.63	37.27	37.92	38.57	39.22	39.88	40.54	41.21

Description: This table shows the price to pay for a monthly payment mortgage loan at the yield rate.

Example: The price of a 15.00 %, 19 year mortgage loan to yield 8.00 % to maturity is $ 155.44.

INTEREST RATE, %

YIELD	11.00%	11.25%	11.50%	11.75%	12.00%	12.25%	12.50%	12.75%	13.00%	13.25%	13.50%	13.75%	14.00%	14.25%	14.50%	15.00%
0.00	238.82	242.66	246.52	250.40	254.31	258.24	262.19	266.16	270.16	274.17	278.21	282.26	286.34	290.43	294.55	302.83
1.00	217.42	220.91	224.43	227.96	231.52	235.10	238.70	242.31	245.95	249.61	253.28	256.97	260.68	264.41	268.16	275.69
2.00	198.55	201.74	204.95	208.18	211.43	214.69	217.98	221.28	224.60	227.94	231.30	234.67	238.06	241.46	244.88	251.76
3.00	181.87	184.79	187.73	190.69	193.66	196.66	199.66	202.69	205.73	208.79	211.86	214.95	218.06	221.17	224.31	230.61
4.00	167.09	169.78	172.48	175.20	177.93	180.68	183.44	186.22	189.02	191.83	194.65	197.49	200.34	203.21	206.08	211.88
4.25	163.67	166.30	168.94	171.60	174.28	176.97	179.68	182.40	185.14	187.89	190.66	193.44	196.23	199.04	201.86	207.53
4.50	160.34	162.92	165.51	168.12	170.74	173.38	176.03	178.70	181.38	184.08	186.79	189.51	192.24	194.99	197.76	203.32
4.75	157.11	159.64	162.18	164.73	167.30	169.89	172.48	175.10	177.73	180.37	183.02	185.69	188.37	191.07	193.77	199.22
5.00	153.98	156.45	158.94	161.44	163.96	166.49	169.04	171.60	174.18	176.77	179.37	181.98	184.61	187.25	189.90	195.24
5.25	150.93	153.35	155.79	158.25	160.72	163.20	165.70	168.21	170.73	173.27	175.82	178.38	180.96	183.55	186.15	191.38
5.50	147.97	150.35	152.74	155.15	157.57	160.00	162.45	164.91	167.39	169.87	172.37	174.89	177.41	179.95	182.50	187.63
5.75	145.10	147.43	149.77	152.13	154.50	156.89	159.29	161.71	164.13	166.57	169.03	171.49	173.97	176.45	178.95	183.98
6.00	142.30	144.59	146.89	149.20	151.53	153.87	156.23	158.59	160.97	163.37	165.77	168.19	170.62	173.06	175.51	180.44
6.25	139.59	141.83	144.09	146.36	148.64	150.94	153.25	155.57	157.90	160.25	162.61	164.98	167.36	169.75	172.16	177.00
6.50	136.95	139.15	141.36	143.59	145.83	148.08	150.35	152.63	154.92	157.22	159.53	161.86	164.20	166.55	168.90	173.65
6.75	134.38	136.54	138.71	140.90	143.10	145.31	147.53	149.77	152.02	154.28	156.55	158.83	161.12	163.43	165.74	170.40
7.00	131.89	134.01	136.14	138.29	140.44	142.61	144.79	146.99	149.20	151.41	153.64	155.88	158.13	160.39	162.67	167.24
7.25	129.47	131.55	133.64	135.74	137.86	139.99	142.13	144.29	146.45	148.63	150.82	153.02	155.23	157.44	159.67	164.16
7.50	127.11	129.15	131.20	133.27	135.35	137.44	139.54	141.66	143.78	145.92	148.07	150.23	152.40	154.58	156.77	161.17
7.75	124.81	126.82	128.84	130.87	132.91	134.96	137.03	139.10	141.19	143.29	145.40	147.52	149.65	151.79	153.94	158.27
8.00	122.58	124.55	126.53	128.53	130.53	132.55	134.58	136.62	138.67	140.73	142.80	144.88	146.97	149.07	151.18	155.44
8.25	120.41	122.34	124.29	126.25	128.22	130.20	132.19	134.20	136.21	138.23	140.27	142.31	144.37	146.43	148.51	152.68
8.50	118.30	120.20	122.11	124.03	125.97	127.92	129.87	131.84	133.82	135.81	137.81	139.82	141.84	143.86	145.90	150.00
8.75	116.24	118.11	119.99	121.88	123.78	125.69	127.62	129.55	131.49	133.45	135.41	137.39	139.37	141.36	143.37	147.40
9.00	114.24	116.08	117.92	119.78	121.65	123.53	125.42	127.32	129.23	131.15	133.08	135.02	136.97	138.93	140.90	144.86
9.25	112.29	114.10	115.91	117.74	119.57	121.42	123.28	125.15	127.02	128.91	130.81	132.72	134.63	136.56	138.49	142.39
9.50	110.39	112.17	113.95	115.75	117.55	119.37	121.20	123.03	124.88	126.73	128.60	130.48	132.36	134.25	136.15	139.98
9.75	108.55	110.29	112.04	113.81	115.59	117.37	119.17	120.97	122.79	124.61	126.45	128.29	130.14	132.00	133.87	137.64
10.00	106.75	108.46	110.19	111.92	113.67	115.43	117.19	118.97	120.75	122.55	124.35	126.16	127.99	129.82	131.66	135.36
10.25	104.99	106.68	108.38	110.08	111.80	113.53	115.27	117.01	118.77	120.54	122.31	124.09	125.88	127.68	129.49	133.13
10.50	103.29	104.95	106.61	108.29	109.98	111.68	113.39	115.11	116.84	118.57	120.32	122.07	123.84	125.61	127.39	130.97
10.75	101.62	103.25	104.90	106.55	108.21	109.88	111.56	113.26	114.96	116.66	118.38	120.11	121.84	123.58	125.33	128.86
11.00	100.00	101.61	103.22	104.85	106.48	108.13	109.78	111.45	113.12	114.80	116.49	118.19	119.90	121.61	123.33	126.80
11.25	98.42	100.00	101.59	103.19	104.80	106.42	108.05	109.69	111.33	112.99	114.65	116.32	118.00	119.69	121.38	124.80
11.50	96.88	98.43	100.00	101.58	103.16	104.75	106.36	107.97	109.59	111.22	112.86	114.50	116.15	117.81	119.48	122.84
11.75	95.38	96.91	98.45	100.00	101.56	103.13	104.71	106.29	107.89	109.49	111.10	112.72	114.35	115.99	117.63	120.94
12.00	93.91	95.42	96.94	98.46	100.00	101.55	103.10	104.66	106.23	107.81	109.40	110.99	112.60	114.21	115.82	119.08
12.25	92.48	93.97	95.46	96.97	98.48	100.00	101.53	103.07	104.62	106.17	107.73	109.30	110.88	112.47	114.06	117.27
12.50	91.09	92.55	94.02	95.50	96.99	98.49	100.00	101.52	103.04	104.57	106.11	107.66	109.21	110.77	112.34	115.50
12.75	89.73	91.17	92.62	94.08	95.55	97.02	98.51	100.00	101.50	103.01	104.53	106.05	107.58	109.12	110.66	113.78
13.00	88.40	89.82	91.25	92.69	94.13	95.59	97.05	98.52	100.00	101.49	102.98	104.48	105.99	107.51	109.03	112.09
13.25	87.11	88.51	89.91	91.33	92.75	94.19	95.63	97.08	98.54	100.00	101.47	102.95	104.44	105.93	107.43	110.45
13.50	85.84	87.22	88.61	90.00	91.41	92.82	94.24	95.67	97.11	98.55	100.00	101.46	102.92	104.39	105.87	108.85
13.75	84.61	85.97	87.34	88.71	90.10	91.49	92.89	94.30	95.71	97.13	98.56	100.00	101.44	102.89	104.35	107.29
14.00	83.41	84.74	86.09	87.45	88.81	90.19	91.57	92.95	94.35	95.75	97.16	98.58	100.00	101.43	102.87	105.76
14.25	82.23	83.55	84.88	86.22	87.56	88.91	90.27	91.64	93.02	94.40	95.79	97.19	98.59	100.00	101.42	104.27
14.50	81.08	82.38	83.69	85.01	86.34	87.67	89.01	90.36	91.72	93.08	94.45	95.83	97.21	98.60	100.00	102.81
14.75	79.96	81.24	82.54	83.84	85.14	86.46	87.78	89.11	90.45	91.79	93.15	94.50	95.87	97.24	98.62	101.39
15.00	78.86	80.13	81.40	82.69	83.98	85.27	86.58	87.89	89.21	90.54	91.87	93.21	94.55	95.91	97.27	100.00
15.25	77.79	79.04	80.30	81.56	82.84	84.12	85.40	86.70	88.00	89.31	90.62	91.94	93.27	94.61	95.95	98.64
15.50	76.75	77.98	79.22	80.47	81.72	82.99	84.26	85.53	86.82	88.11	89.40	90.71	92.02	93.33	94.66	97.32
15.75	75.72	76.94	78.17	79.40	80.64	81.88	83.13	84.39	85.66	86.93	88.21	89.50	90.79	92.09	93.39	96.02
16.00	74.73	75.93	77.13	78.35	79.57	80.80	82.04	83.28	84.53	85.79	87.05	88.32	89.59	90.87	92.16	94.75
16.25	73.75	74.93	76.13	77.32	78.53	79.74	80.96	82.19	83.43	84.67	85.91	87.16	88.42	89.69	90.96	93.51
16.50	72.79	73.96	75.14	76.32	77.51	78.71	79.92	81.13	82.34	83.57	84.80	86.04	87.28	88.53	89.78	92.30
16.75	71.86	73.01	74.18	75.34	76.52	77.70	78.89	80.09	81.29	82.50	83.71	84.93	86.16	87.39	88.63	91.12
17.00	70.95	72.09	73.23	74.39	75.55	76.71	77.89	79.07	80.26	81.45	82.65	83.85	85.06	86.28	87.50	89.96
17.25	70.05	71.18	72.31	73.45	74.60	75.75	76.91	78.07	79.24	80.42	81.61	82.80	83.99	85.19	86.40	88.83
17.50	69.18	70.29	71.41	72.53	73.67	74.80	75.95	77.10	78.26	79.42	80.59	81.76	82.94	84.13	85.32	87.72
17.75	68.32	69.42	70.53	71.64	72.75	73.88	75.01	76.15	77.29	78.44	79.59	80.75	81.92	83.09	84.27	86.64
18.00	67.49	68.57	69.66	70.76	71.86	72.97	74.09	75.21	76.34	77.48	78.62	79.76	80.92	82.07	83.24	85.58
18.25	66.67	67.74	68.82	69.90	70.99	72.09	73.19	74.30	75.42	76.54	77.66	78.80	79.93	81.08	82.23	84.54
18.50	65.87	66.93	67.99	69.06	70.14	71.22	72.31	73.41	74.51	75.62	76.73	77.85	78.97	80.10	81.24	83.52
18.75	65.08	66.13	67.18	68.24	69.30	70.37	71.45	72.53	73.62	74.72	75.82	76.92	78.03	79.15	80.27	82.53
19.00	64.31	65.35	66.39	67.43	68.49	69.54	70.61	71.68	72.75	73.83	74.92	76.01	77.11	78.21	79.32	81.55
20.00	61.40	62.38	63.38	64.37	65.38	66.39	67.40	68.43	69.45	70.49	71.52	72.57	73.61	74.67	75.72	77.85
25.00	49.82	50.62	51.43	52.24	53.05	53.87	54.70	55.53	56.36	57.20	58.04	58.88	59.73	60.59	61.45	63.17
30.00	41.75	42.42	43.09	43.77	44.46	45.14	45.83	46.53	47.23	47.93	48.63	49.34	50.05	50.77	51.49	52.94

Description: This table shows the yield to maturity of a mortgage purchased at the price shown in the index.

Example: The yield to maturity of a 15.00 %, 19 year mortgage at a price of 125.00 is 11.22 %.

INTEREST RATE, %

PRICE	11.00%	11.25%	11.50%	11.75%	12.00%	12.25%	12.50%	12.75%	13.00%	13.25%	13.50%	13.75%	14.00%	14.25%	14.50%	15.00%
250	–	–	–	.01	.17	.34	.50	.66	.82	.98	1.14	1.29	1.45	1.61	1.76	2.07
240	–	.11	.28	.44	.61	.77	.94	1.10	1.26	1.42	1.58	1.74	1.90	2.06	2.22	2.54
230	.39	.56	.73	.90	1.07	1.23	1.40	1.57	1.73	1.89	2.06	2.22	2.38	2.54	2.71	3.03
220	.87	1.04	1.21	1.38	1.55	1.72	1.89	2.06	2.23	2.39	2.56	2.73	2.89	3.06	3.22	3.55
210	1.37	1.55	1.72	1.90	2.07	2.24	2.42	2.59	2.76	2.93	3.10	3.27	3.43	3.60	3.77	4.10
200	1.91	2.09	2.27	2.45	2.62	2.80	2.98	3.15	3.32	3.50	3.67	3.84	4.02	4.19	4.36	4.70
195	2.20	2.38	2.56	2.74	2.92	3.09	3.27	3.45	3.62	3.80	3.97	4.15	4.32	4.49	4.67	5.01
190	2.49	2.67	2.86	3.04	3.22	3.40	3.58	3.75	3.93	4.11	4.29	4.46	4.64	4.81	4.99	5.34
185	2.80	2.98	3.17	3.35	3.53	3.71	3.89	4.07	4.25	4.43	4.61	4.79	4.97	5.15	5.32	5.67
180	3.12	3.30	3.49	3.67	3.86	4.04	4.22	4.41	4.59	4.77	4.95	5.13	5.31	5.49	5.67	6.03
175	3.45	3.63	3.82	4.01	4.20	4.38	4.57	4.75	4.94	5.12	5.30	5.49	5.67	5.85	6.03	6.39
170	3.79	3.98	4.17	4.36	4.55	4.74	4.92	5.11	5.30	5.49	5.67	5.86	6.04	6.23	6.41	6.78
165	4.15	4.34	4.53	4.72	4.92	5.11	5.30	5.49	5.68	5.87	6.06	6.24	6.43	6.62	6.80	7.18
160	4.52	4.72	4.91	5.11	5.30	5.50	5.69	5.88	6.07	6.27	6.46	6.65	6.84	7.03	7.22	7.60
155	4.91	5.11	5.31	5.51	5.70	5.90	6.10	6.29	6.49	6.68	6.88	7.07	7.26	7.46	7.65	8.03
150	5.32	5.52	5.73	5.93	6.13	6.33	6.53	6.72	6.92	7.12	7.32	7.52	7.71	7.91	8.10	8.50
145	5.75	5.96	6.16	6.37	6.57	6.77	6.98	7.18	7.38	7.58	7.78	7.98	8.18	8.38	8.58	8.98
140	6.21	6.41	6.62	6.83	7.04	7.24	7.45	7.66	7.86	8.07	8.27	8.48	8.68	8.88	9.09	9.49
135	6.68	6.90	7.11	7.32	7.53	7.74	7.95	8.16	8.37	8.58	8.79	9.00	9.21	9.41	9.62	10.03
130	7.19	7.41	7.62	7.84	8.05	8.27	8.48	8.70	8.91	9.12	9.34	9.55	9.76	9.97	10.19	10.61
125	7.72	7.94	8.17	8.39	8.60	8.82	9.04	9.26	9.48	9.70	9.92	10.13	10.35	10.57	10.79	11.22
120	8.29	8.52	8.74	8.97	9.19	9.42	9.64	9.87	10.09	10.31	10.54	10.76	10.98	11.20	11.43	11.87
115	8.90	9.13	9.36	9.59	9.82	10.05	10.28	10.51	10.74	10.97	11.20	11.43	11.65	11.88	12.11	12.57
113	9.15	9.39	9.62	9.85	10.08	10.32	10.55	10.78	11.01	11.24	11.47	11.71	11.94	12.17	12.40	12.86
112	9.28	9.52	9.75	9.98	10.22	10.45	10.68	10.92	11.15	11.38	11.62	11.85	12.08	12.31	12.55	13.01
111	9.41	9.65	9.88	10.12	10.35	10.59	10.82	11.06	11.29	11.53	11.76	11.99	12.23	12.46	12.69	13.16
110	9.55	9.78	10.02	10.26	10.49	10.73	10.96	11.20	11.44	11.67	11.91	12.14	12.38	12.61	12.85	13.31
109	9.68	9.92	10.16	10.40	10.63	10.87	11.11	11.34	11.58	11.82	12.05	12.29	12.53	12.76	13.00	13.47
108	9.82	10.06	10.30	10.54	10.78	11.01	11.25	11.49	11.73	11.97	12.20	12.44	12.68	12.92	13.16	13.63
107	9.96	10.20	10.44	10.68	10.92	11.16	11.40	11.64	11.88	12.12	12.36	12.60	12.84	13.07	13.31	13.79
106	10.10	10.34	10.58	10.83	11.07	11.31	11.55	11.79	12.03	12.27	12.51	12.75	12.99	13.23	13.47	13.96
105	10.24	10.49	10.73	10.97	11.22	11.46	11.70	11.94	12.19	12.43	12.67	12.91	13.15	13.40	13.64	14.12
104	10.39	10.63	10.88	11.12	11.37	11.61	11.85	12.10	12.34	12.59	12.83	13.07	13.32	13.56	13.80	14.29
103	10.54	10.78	11.03	11.27	11.52	11.77	12.01	12.26	12.50	12.75	12.99	13.24	13.48	13.73	13.97	14.46
102	10.69	10.93	11.18	11.43	11.68	11.92	12.17	12.42	12.66	12.91	13.16	13.40	13.65	13.90	14.14	14.64
101	10.84	11.09	11.34	11.59	11.83	12.08	12.33	12.58	12.83	13.08	13.32	13.57	13.82	14.07	14.32	14.81
100	11.00	11.25	11.50	11.75	12.00	12.25	12.50	12.75	13.00	13.25	13.50	13.75	14.00	14.25	14.50	15.00
99	11.15	11.40	11.66	11.91	12.16	12.41	12.66	12.91	13.17	13.42	13.67	13.92	14.17	14.42	14.68	15.18
98	11.31	11.57	11.82	12.07	12.32	12.58	12.83	13.08	13.34	13.59	13.84	14.10	14.35	14.60	14.86	15.37
97	11.48	11.73	11.98	12.24	12.49	12.75	13.00	13.26	13.51	13.77	14.02	14.28	14.53	14.79	15.04	15.56
96	11.64	11.90	12.15	12.41	12.67	12.92	13.18	13.44	13.69	13.95	14.21	14.46	14.72	14.98	15.23	15.75
95	11.81	12.07	12.32	12.58	12.84	13.10	13.36	13.62	13.87	14.13	14.39	14.65	14.91	15.17	15.43	15.95
94	11.98	12.24	12.50	12.76	13.02	13.28	13.54	13.80	14.06	14.32	14.58	14.84	15.10	15.36	15.62	16.15
93	12.15	12.42	12.68	12.94	13.20	13.46	13.72	13.99	14.25	14.51	14.77	15.04	15.30	15.56	15.82	16.35
92	12.33	12.59	12.86	13.12	13.38	13.65	13.91	14.18	14.44	14.70	14.97	15.23	15.50	15.76	16.03	16.56
91	12.51	12.78	13.04	13.31	13.57	13.84	14.10	14.37	14.64	14.90	15.17	15.44	15.70	15.97	16.24	16.77
90	12.69	12.96	13.23	13.50	13.76	14.03	14.30	14.57	14.84	15.10	15.37	15.64	15.91	16.18	16.45	16.99
89	12.88	13.15	13.42	13.69	13.96	14.23	14.50	14.77	15.04	15.31	15.58	15.85	16.12	16.39	16.66	17.21
88	13.07	13.34	13.61	13.89	14.16	14.43	14.70	14.97	15.25	15.52	15.79	16.06	16.34	16.61	16.88	17.43
87	13.27	13.54	13.81	14.09	14.36	14.63	14.91	15.18	15.46	15.73	16.01	16.28	16.56	16.83	17.11	17.66
86	13.46	13.74	14.01	14.29	14.57	14.84	15.12	15.39	15.67	15.95	16.23	16.50	16.78	17.06	17.34	17.89
85	13.67	13.94	14.22	14.50	14.78	15.05	15.33	15.61	15.89	16.17	16.45	16.73	17.01	17.29	17.57	18.13
84	13.87	14.15	14.43	14.71	14.99	15.27	15.55	15.83	16.11	16.40	16.68	16.96	17.24	17.53	17.81	18.38
83	14.08	14.36	14.64	14.93	15.21	15.49	15.78	16.06	16.34	16.63	16.91	17.20	17.48	17.77	18.05	18.63
82	14.29	14.58	14.86	15.15	15.43	15.72	16.00	16.29	16.58	16.86	17.15	17.44	17.73	18.01	18.30	18.88
81	14.51	14.80	15.09	15.37	15.66	15.95	16.24	16.53	16.81	17.10	17.39	17.68	17.97	18.26	18.56	19.14
80	14.74	15.02	15.31	15.60	15.89	16.18	16.47	16.77	17.06	17.35	17.64	17.93	18.23	18.52	18.82	19.40
79	14.96	15.25	15.55	15.84	16.13	16.42	16.72	17.01	17.31	17.60	17.90	18.19	18.49	18.78	19.08	19.68
78	15.20	15.49	15.78	16.08	16.37	16.67	16.97	17.26	17.56	17.86	18.16	18.45	18.75	19.05	19.35	19.95
77	15.43	15.73	16.03	16.33	16.62	16.92	17.22	17.52	17.82	18.12	18.42	18.72	19.03	19.33	19.63	20.24
76	15.68	15.98	16.28	16.58	16.88	17.18	17.48	17.78	18.09	18.39	18.69	19.00	19.30	19.61	19.92	20.53
75	15.93	16.23	16.53	16.83	17.14	17.44	17.75	18.05	18.36	18.67	18.97	19.28	19.59	19.90	20.21	20.83
74	16.18	16.49	16.79	17.10	17.40	17.71	18.02	18.33	18.64	18.95	19.26	19.57	19.88	20.19	20.50	21.13
73	16.44	16.75	17.06	17.37	17.68	17.99	18.30	18.61	18.92	19.24	19.55	19.86	20.18	20.49	20.81	21.44
70	17.26	17.58	17.90	18.22	18.54	18.86	19.18	19.50	19.82	20.15	20.47	20.80	21.12	21.45	21.77	22.43
65	18.77	19.11	19.45	19.78	20.12	20.46	20.80	21.15	21.49	21.83	22.18	22.52	22.87	23.21	23.56	24.26
60	20.50	20.86	21.22	21.58	21.94	22.31	22.67	23.04	23.40	23.77	24.14	24.51	24.88	25.25	25.62	26.37
55	22.52	22.90	23.29	23.68	24.07	24.46	24.85	25.24	25.64	26.04	26.43	26.83	27.23	27.63	28.04	28.85

MORTGAGE PRICE

20 YEARS

Description: This table shows the price to pay for a monthly payment mortgage loan at the yield rate.

Example: The price of a 6.75 %, 20 year mortgage loan to yield 8.00 % to maturity is $ 90.90.

YIELD	0.00%	1.00%	2.00%	3.00%	4.00%	4.25%	4.50%	4.75%	5.00%	5.25%	5.50%	5.75%	6.00%	6.25%	6.50%	6.75%
0.00	100.00	110.37	121.41	133.10	145.44	148.62	151.84	155.09	158.39	161.72	165.09	168.50	171.94	175.42	178.94	182.49
1.00	90.60	100.00	110.00	120.59	131.77	134.65	137.56	140.52	143.50	146.52	149.58	152.66	155.78	158.93	162.12	165.33
2.00	82.36	90.91	100.00	109.63	119.79	122.41	125.06	127.74	130.46	133.20	135.98	138.78	141.62	144.49	147.38	150.30
3.00	75.13	82.92	91.22	100.00	109.26	111.65	114.07	116.52	119.00	121.50	124.03	126.59	129.18	131.79	134.43	137.10
4.00	68.76	75.89	83.48	91.52	100.00	102.19	104.40	106.64	108.91	111.20	113.52	115.86	118.23	120.62	123.04	125.48
4.25	67.29	74.27	81.69	89.56	97.86	100.00	102.17	104.36	106.58	108.82	111.09	113.38	115.70	118.04	120.40	122.79
4.50	65.86	72.69	79.96	87.66	95.78	97.88	100.00	102.15	104.32	106.51	108.73	110.98	113.24	115.53	117.85	120.19
4.75	64.48	71.17	78.28	85.82	93.77	95.82	97.90	100.00	102.12	104.27	106.45	108.64	110.86	113.11	115.37	117.66
5.00	63.14	69.69	76.65	84.04	91.82	93.83	95.86	97.92	100.00	102.10	104.23	106.38	108.56	110.75	112.97	115.21
5.25	61.83	68.25	75.07	82.30	89.93	91.90	93.89	95.90	97.94	100.00	102.08	104.19	106.32	108.47	110.64	112.84
5.50	60.57	66.86	73.54	80.62	88.09	90.02	91.97	93.94	95.94	97.96	100.00	102.06	104.15	106.26	108.39	110.54
5.75	59.35	65.50	72.05	78.99	86.31	88.20	90.11	92.04	94.00	95.98	97.98	100.00	102.04	104.11	106.19	108.30
6.00	58.16	64.19	70.61	77.41	84.58	86.43	88.31	90.20	92.12	94.06	96.02	98.00	100.00	102.02	104.07	106.13
6.25	57.01	62.92	69.21	75.88	82.91	84.72	86.55	88.41	90.29	92.19	94.11	96.05	98.02	100.00	102.00	104.03
6.50	55.89	61.68	67.85	74.39	81.28	83.05	84.85	86.67	88.52	90.38	92.26	94.17	96.09	98.04	100.00	101.98
6.75	54.80	60.48	66.53	72.94	79.70	81.44	83.20	84.99	86.79	88.62	90.47	92.34	94.22	96.13	98.05	100.00
7.00	53.74	59.32	65.25	71.53	78.16	79.87	81.60	83.35	85.12	86.91	88.73	90.56	92.41	94.28	96.17	98.07
7.25	52.72	58.19	64.01	70.17	76.67	78.35	80.04	81.76	83.50	85.26	87.03	88.83	90.64	92.48	94.33	96.20
7.50	51.72	57.09	62.80	68.84	75.22	76.87	78.53	80.22	81.92	83.65	85.39	87.15	88.93	90.73	92.55	94.39
7.75	50.75	56.02	61.62	67.56	73.81	75.43	77.06	78.72	80.39	82.08	83.79	85.52	87.27	89.03	90.82	92.62
8.00	49.81	54.98	60.48	66.30	72.45	74.03	75.64	77.26	78.90	80.56	82.24	83.94	85.65	87.39	89.14	90.90
8.25	48.90	53.97	59.37	65.09	71.12	72.67	74.25	75.84	77.45	79.08	80.73	82.40	84.08	85.78	87.50	89.24
8.50	48.01	52.99	58.29	63.91	69.83	71.35	72.90	74.46	76.05	77.65	79.27	80.90	82.55	84.23	85.91	87.62
8.75	47.15	52.04	57.25	62.76	68.57	70.07	71.59	73.13	74.68	76.25	77.84	79.45	81.07	82.71	84.37	86.04
9.00	46.31	51.11	56.23	61.64	67.35	68.82	70.32	71.82	73.35	74.89	76.46	78.03	79.63	81.24	82.87	84.51
9.25	45.49	50.21	55.24	60.55	66.16	67.61	69.08	70.56	72.06	73.57	75.11	76.66	78.22	79.81	81.41	83.02
9.50	44.70	49.34	54.27	59.50	65.01	66.43	67.87	69.33	70.80	72.29	73.80	75.32	76.86	78.41	79.99	81.57
9.75	43.93	48.49	53.33	58.47	63.89	65.28	66.70	68.13	69.58	71.04	72.52	74.02	75.53	77.06	78.60	80.16
10.00	43.18	47.66	52.42	57.47	62.79	64.17	65.56	66.96	68.39	69.83	71.28	72.75	74.24	75.74	77.26	78.79
10.25	42.45	46.85	51.53	56.50	61.73	63.08	64.45	65.83	67.23	68.64	70.08	71.52	72.98	74.46	75.95	77.46
10.50	41.73	46.06	50.67	55.55	60.70	62.02	63.37	64.73	66.10	67.49	68.90	70.32	71.76	73.21	74.68	76.16
10.75	41.04	45.30	49.83	54.63	59.69	60.99	62.32	63.65	65.01	66.37	67.76	69.16	70.57	72.00	73.44	74.90
11.00	40.37	44.56	49.01	53.73	58.71	59.99	61.29	62.61	63.94	65.28	66.64	68.02	69.41	70.81	72.23	73.67
11.25	39.71	43.83	48.21	52.86	57.75	59.02	60.30	61.59	62.90	64.22	65.56	66.91	68.28	69.66	71.06	72.47
11.50	39.07	43.12	47.44	52.01	56.82	58.07	59.32	60.60	61.88	63.19	64.50	65.83	67.18	68.54	69.91	71.30
11.75	38.45	42.44	46.68	51.18	55.92	57.14	58.38	59.63	60.90	62.18	63.48	64.79	66.11	67.45	68.80	70.16
12.00	37.84	41.77	45.94	50.37	55.03	56.24	57.46	58.69	59.94	61.20	62.47	63.76	65.07	66.38	67.71	69.06
12.25	37.25	41.11	45.23	49.58	54.17	55.36	56.56	57.77	59.00	60.24	61.50	62.77	64.05	65.35	66.65	67.98
12.50	36.67	40.48	44.53	48.81	53.34	54.50	55.68	56.88	58.09	59.31	60.55	61.80	63.06	64.33	65.62	66.93
12.75	36.11	39.86	43.84	48.07	52.52	53.67	54.83	56.01	57.20	58.40	59.62	60.85	62.09	63.35	64.62	65.90
13.00	35.56	39.25	43.18	47.34	51.72	52.85	54.00	55.16	56.33	57.52	58.71	59.93	61.15	62.39	63.64	64.90
13.25	35.03	38.67	42.53	46.63	50.95	52.06	53.19	54.33	55.49	56.65	57.83	59.03	60.23	61.45	62.68	63.93
13.50	34.51	38.09	41.90	45.93	50.19	51.29	52.40	53.52	54.66	55.81	56.97	58.15	59.34	60.54	61.75	62.98
13.75	34.00	37.53	41.28	45.26	49.45	50.53	51.63	52.74	53.86	54.99	56.14	57.29	58.46	59.65	60.84	62.05
14.00	33.51	36.98	40.68	44.60	48.73	49.80	50.88	51.97	53.07	54.19	55.32	56.46	57.61	58.78	59.96	61.15
14.25	33.02	36.45	40.09	43.96	48.03	49.08	50.14	51.22	52.31	53.41	54.52	55.65	56.78	57.93	59.09	60.26
14.50	32.55	35.93	39.52	43.33	47.34	48.38	49.43	50.49	51.56	52.64	53.74	54.85	55.97	57.10	58.25	59.40
14.75	32.09	35.42	38.96	42.72	46.67	47.69	48.73	49.77	50.83	51.90	52.98	54.07	55.18	56.30	57.42	58.56
15.00	31.64	34.93	38.42	42.12	46.02	47.03	48.04	49.08	50.12	51.17	52.24	53.32	54.41	55.51	56.62	57.74
15.25	31.20	34.44	37.89	41.53	45.38	46.37	47.38	48.40	49.42	50.46	51.52	52.58	53.65	54.74	55.84	56.94
15.50	30.78	33.97	37.37	40.96	44.76	45.74	46.73	47.73	48.75	49.77	50.81	51.86	52.92	53.99	55.07	56.16
15.75	30.36	33.51	36.86	40.41	44.15	45.12	46.09	47.08	48.08	49.09	50.12	51.15	52.20	53.25	54.32	55.40
16.00	29.95	33.06	36.36	39.86	43.56	44.51	45.47	46.45	47.44	48.43	49.44	50.46	51.50	52.54	53.59	54.65
16.25	29.55	32.62	35.88	39.33	42.98	43.92	44.87	45.83	46.80	47.79	48.78	49.79	50.81	51.84	52.88	53.92
16.50	29.16	32.19	35.40	38.81	42.41	43.34	44.28	45.23	46.19	47.16	48.14	49.13	50.14	51.15	52.18	53.21
16.75	28.78	31.76	34.94	38.31	41.85	42.77	43.70	44.63	45.58	46.54	47.51	48.49	49.48	50.48	51.50	52.52
17.00	28.41	31.35	34.49	37.81	41.31	42.22	43.13	44.06	44.99	45.94	46.90	47.86	48.84	49.83	50.83	51.84
17.25	28.04	30.95	34.05	37.33	40.78	41.68	42.58	43.49	44.42	45.35	46.30	47.25	48.22	49.19	50.18	51.17
17.50	27.69	30.56	33.61	36.85	40.27	41.15	42.04	42.94	43.85	44.78	45.71	46.65	47.61	48.57	49.54	50.52
17.75	27.34	30.17	33.19	36.39	39.76	40.63	41.51	42.40	43.30	44.21	45.13	46.07	47.01	47.96	48.92	49.89
18.00	27.00	29.80	32.78	35.94	39.26	40.12	40.99	41.87	42.76	43.66	44.57	45.49	46.42	47.36	48.31	49.27
18.25	26.67	29.43	32.37	35.49	38.78	39.63	40.49	41.36	42.24	43.12	44.02	44.93	45.85	46.78	47.71	48.66
18.50	26.34	29.07	31.98	35.06	38.31	39.15	39.99	40.85	41.72	42.60	43.48	44.38	45.29	46.21	47.13	48.07
18.75	26.02	28.72	31.59	34.63	37.84	38.67	39.51	40.36	41.21	42.08	42.96	43.85	44.74	45.65	46.56	47.49
19.00	25.71	28.38	31.21	34.22	37.39	38.21	39.04	39.87	40.72	41.58	42.44	43.32	44.21	45.10	46.00	46.92
20.00	24.53	27.07	29.78	32.65	35.67	36.45	37.24	38.04	38.85	39.67	40.49	41.33	42.17	43.03	43.89	44.76
25.00	19.86	21.92	24.11	26.43	28.88	29.51	30.15	30.80	31.45	32.12	32.78	33.46	34.14	34.84	35.53	36.24
30.00	16.62	18.35	20.18	22.12	24.17	24.70	25.24	25.78	26.33	26.88	27.44	28.01	28.58	29.16	29.74	30.33

Description: This table shows the yield to maturity of a mortgage purchased at the price shown in the index.

Example: The yield to maturity of a 6.75 %, 20 year mortgage at a price of 80.00 is 9.77 %.

INTEREST RATE, %

PRICE	0.00%	1.00%	2.00%	3.00%	4.00%	4.25%	4.50%	4.75%	5.00%	5.25%	5.50%	5.75%	6.00%	6.25%	6.50%	6.75%
100	0.00	1.00	2.00	3.00	4.00	4.25	4.50	4.75	5.00	5.25	5.50	5.75	6.00	6.25	6.50	6.75
99	.10	1.10	2.10	3.11	4.11	4.36	4.61	4.86	5.12	5.37	5.62	5.87	6.12	6.37	6.62	6.87
98	.20	1.20	2.21	3.22	4.23	4.48	4.73	4.99	5.24	5.49	5.74	5.99	6.25	6.50	6.75	7.00
97	.30	1.31	2.32	3.33	4.35	4.60	4.85	5.11	5.36	5.62	5.87	6.12	6.38	6.63	6.88	7.14
96	.40	1.42	2.43	3.45	4.47	4.72	4.98	5.23	5.49	5.74	6.00	6.25	6.51	6.76	7.02	7.27
95	.51	1.53	2.55	3.57	4.59	4.85	5.10	5.36	5.62	5.87	6.13	6.38	6.64	6.90	7.15	7.41
94	.62	1.64	2.66	3.69	4.72	4.97	5.23	5.49	5.74	6.00	6.26	6.52	6.78	7.03	7.29	7.55
93	.73	1.75	2.78	3.81	4.84	5.10	5.36	5.62	5.88	6.14	6.39	6.65	6.91	7.17	7.43	7.69
92	.84	1.87	2.90	3.94	4.97	5.23	5.49	5.75	6.01	6.27	6.53	6.79	7.05	7.31	7.57	7.83
91	.95	1.98	3.02	4.06	5.10	5.36	5.62	5.89	6.15	6.41	6.67	6.93	7.19	7.46	7.72	7.98
90	1.06	2.10	3.14	4.19	5.24	5.50	5.76	6.02	6.29	6.55	6.81	7.07	7.34	7.60	7.87	8.13
89	1.18	2.22	3.27	4.32	5.37	5.63	5.90	6.16	6.43	6.69	6.96	7.22	7.48	7.75	8.02	8.28
88	1.30	2.34	3.40	4.45	5.51	5.77	6.04	6.30	6.57	6.84	7.10	7.37	7.63	7.90	8.17	8.44
87	1.42	2.47	3.52	4.58	5.65	5.91	6.18	6.45	6.71	6.98	7.25	7.52	7.79	8.05	8.32	8.59
86	1.54	2.59	3.66	4.72	5.79	6.06	6.33	6.59	6.86	7.13	7.40	7.67	7.94	8.21	8.48	8.75
85	1.66	2.72	3.79	4.86	5.93	6.20	6.47	6.74	7.01	7.28	7.56	7.83	8.10	8.37	8.64	8.91
84	1.79	2.85	3.92	5.00	6.08	6.35	6.62	6.90	7.17	7.44	7.71	7.98	8.26	8.53	8.81	9.08
83	1.91	2.98	4.06	5.14	6.23	6.50	6.78	7.05	7.32	7.60	7.87	8.15	8.42	8.70	8.97	9.25
82	2.04	3.12	4.20	5.29	6.38	6.66	6.93	7.21	7.48	7.76	8.03	8.31	8.59	8.86	9.14	9.42
81	2.17	3.26	4.34	5.44	6.54	6.81	7.09	7.37	7.64	7.92	8.20	8.48	8.76	9.04	9.32	9.60
80	2.31	3.40	4.49	5.59	6.70	6.97	7.25	7.53	7.81	8.09	8.37	8.65	8.93	9.21	9.49	9.77
79	2.44	3.54	4.64	5.74	6.86	7.14	7.42	7.70	7.98	8.26	8.54	8.82	9.11	9.39	9.67	9.96
78	2.58	3.68	4.79	5.90	7.02	7.30	7.58	7.87	8.15	8.43	8.72	9.00	9.29	9.57	9.86	10.14
77	2.72	3.83	4.94	6.06	7.19	7.47	7.76	8.04	8.32	8.61	8.90	9.18	9.47	9.76	10.04	10.33
76	2.87	3.98	5.10	6.22	7.36	7.64	7.93	8.22	8.50	8.79	9.08	9.37	9.66	9.95	10.24	10.53
75	3.01	4.13	5.26	6.39	7.53	7.82	8.11	8.40	8.69	8.98	9.27	9.56	9.85	10.14	10.43	10.72
74	3.16	4.29	5.42	6.56	7.71	8.00	8.29	8.58	8.87	9.16	9.46	9.75	10.04	10.34	10.63	10.93
73	3.32	4.45	5.59	6.73	7.89	8.18	8.48	8.77	9.06	9.36	9.65	9.95	10.24	10.54	10.84	11.13
72	3.47	4.61	5.75	6.91	8.08	8.37	8.67	8.96	9.26	9.55	9.85	10.15	10.45	10.74	11.04	11.34
71	3.63	4.77	5.93	7.09	8.27	8.56	8.86	9.16	9.45	9.75	10.05	10.35	10.65	10.96	11.26	11.56
70	3.79	4.94	6.10	7.28	8.46	8.76	9.06	9.36	9.66	9.96	10.26	10.56	10.87	11.17	11.48	11.78
69	3.95	5.11	6.28	7.47	8.66	8.96	9.26	9.56	9.87	10.17	10.47	10.78	11.08	11.39	11.70	12.01
68	4.12	5.29	6.47	7.66	8.86	9.16	9.47	9.77	10.08	10.38	10.69	11.00	11.31	11.62	11.93	12.24
67	4.29	5.47	6.66	7.86	9.07	9.37	9.68	9.99	10.30	10.60	10.91	11.23	11.54	11.85	12.16	12.48
66	4.47	5.65	6.85	8.06	9.28	9.59	9.90	10.21	10.52	10.83	11.14	11.46	11.77	12.09	12.40	12.72
65	4.65	5.84	7.04	8.26	9.50	9.81	10.12	10.43	10.75	11.06	11.38	11.69	12.01	12.33	12.65	12.97
64	4.83	6.03	7.25	8.48	9.72	10.03	10.35	10.66	10.98	11.30	11.62	11.94	12.26	12.58	12.90	13.23
63	5.02	6.23	7.45	8.69	9.95	10.26	10.58	10.90	11.22	11.54	11.86	12.19	12.51	12.84	13.16	13.49
62	5.21	6.43	7.66	8.91	10.18	10.50	10.82	11.14	11.47	11.79	12.12	12.44	12.77	13.10	13.43	13.76
61	5.41	6.64	7.88	9.14	10.42	10.74	11.07	11.39	11.72	12.05	12.37	12.70	13.04	13.37	13.70	14.04
60	5.61	6.85	8.10	9.38	10.67	10.99	11.32	11.65	11.98	12.31	12.64	12.97	13.31	13.65	13.98	14.32
59	5.82	7.06	8.33	9.62	10.92	11.25	11.58	11.91	12.25	12.58	12.92	13.25	13.59	13.93	14.27	14.61
58	6.03	7.29	8.56	9.86	11.18	11.51	11.85	12.18	12.52	12.86	13.20	13.54	13.88	14.22	14.57	14.92
57	6.25	7.52	8.80	10.11	11.45	11.78	12.12	12.46	12.80	13.14	13.49	13.83	14.18	14.53	14.88	15.23
56	6.47	7.75	9.05	10.38	11.72	12.06	12.40	12.75	13.09	13.44	13.79	14.14	14.49	14.84	15.19	15.55
55	6.70	7.99	9.31	10.64	12.01	12.35	12.70	13.04	13.39	13.74	14.09	14.45	14.80	15.16	15.52	15.88
54	6.93	8.24	9.57	10.92	12.30	12.65	12.99	13.35	13.70	14.05	14.41	14.77	15.13	15.49	15.85	16.22
53	7.18	8.49	9.84	11.20	12.60	12.95	13.30	13.66	14.02	14.38	14.74	15.10	15.47	15.83	16.20	16.57
52	7.42	8.76	10.11	11.50	12.91	13.26	13.62	13.98	14.35	14.71	15.08	15.45	15.81	16.19	16.56	16.94
51	7.68	9.03	10.40	11.80	13.23	13.59	13.95	14.32	14.69	15.06	15.43	15.80	16.17	16.55	16.93	17.31
50	7.95	9.31	10.69	12.11	13.56	13.93	14.29	14.66	15.04	15.41	15.79	16.17	16.55	16.93	17.31	17.70
49	8.22	9.59	11.00	12.43	13.90	14.27	14.65	15.02	15.40	15.78	16.16	16.55	16.93	17.32	17.71	18.10
48	8.50	9.89	11.31	12.77	14.26	14.63	15.01	15.39	15.78	16.16	16.55	16.94	17.33	17.73	18.12	18.52
47	8.79	10.20	11.64	13.11	14.62	15.00	15.39	15.78	16.17	16.56	16.95	17.35	17.75	18.15	18.55	18.96
46	9.09	10.52	11.98	13.47	15.00	15.39	15.78	16.18	16.57	16.97	17.37	17.77	18.18	18.59	19.00	19.41
45	9.40	10.84	12.33	13.84	15.40	15.79	16.19	16.59	16.99	17.40	17.80	18.21	18.63	19.04	19.46	19.88
44	9.72	11.19	12.69	14.23	15.81	16.21	16.61	17.02	17.43	17.84	18.26	18.67	19.09	19.51	19.94	20.37
43	10.05	11.54	13.06	14.63	16.23	16.64	17.05	17.47	17.88	18.30	18.73	19.15	19.58	20.01	20.44	20.88
42	10.40	11.91	13.45	15.04	16.68	17.09	17.51	17.93	18.36	18.79	19.22	19.65	20.08	20.52	20.96	21.41
41	10.76	12.29	13.86	15.48	17.14	17.57	17.99	18.42	18.85	19.29	19.73	20.17	20.61	21.06	21.51	21.96
40	11.13	12.69	14.29	15.93	17.63	18.06	18.49	18.93	19.37	19.81	20.26	20.71	21.16	21.62	22.08	22.54
39	11.52	13.10	14.73	16.40	18.13	18.57	19.01	19.46	19.91	20.36	20.82	21.28	21.74	22.21	22.68	23.15
35	13.26	14.96	16.71	18.53	20.41	20.89	21.37	21.86	22.35	22.85	23.35	23.85	24.36	24.87	25.39	25.91
30	15.96	17.86	19.84	21.89	24.03	24.57	25.13	25.68	26.25	26.81	27.39	27.97	28.55	29.14	29.73	30.33
25	19.58	21.78	24.07	26.47	28.99	29.63	30.29	30.95	31.61	32.28	32.96	33.65	34.34	35.04	35.75	36.46
20	24.81	27.47	30.27	33.22	36.33	37.12	37.93	38.75	39.58	40.41	41.26	42.11	42.97	43.84	44.72	45.61
15	33.28	36.76	40.45	44.36	48.47	49.53	50.60	51.69	52.79	53.90	55.03	56.16	57.31	58.47	59.64	60.82
10	49.99	55.18	60.70	66.55	72.71	74.30	75.91	77.54	79.19	80.86	82.54	84.25	85.97	87.71	89.46	91.24

Description: This table shows the price to pay for a monthly payment mortgage loan at the yield rate.

Example: The price of a 10.75 %, 20 year mortgage loan to yield 8.00 % to maturity is $ 121.37.

INTEREST RATE, %

YIELD	7.00%	7.25%	7.50%	7.75%	8.00%	8.25%	8.50%	8.75%	9.00%	9.25%	9.50%	9.75%	10.00%	10.25%	10.50%	10.75%
0.00	186.07	189.69	193.34	197.03	200.75	204.50	208.28	212.09	215.93	219.81	223.71	227.64	231.61	235.59	239.61	243.65
1.00	168.58	171.86	175.17	178.51	181.88	185.27	188.70	192.16	195.64	199.15	202.68	206.25	209.84	213.45	217.09	220.75
2.00	153.26	156.24	159.24	162.28	165.34	168.43	171.55	174.69	177.85	181.04	184.26	187.50	190.76	194.05	197.35	200.68
3.00	139.79	142.51	145.26	148.03	150.82	153.64	156.48	159.34	162.23	165.14	168.07	171.03	174.00	177.00	180.02	183.06
4.00	127.94	130.43	132.94	135.47	138.03	140.61	143.21	145.83	148.47	151.14	153.82	156.53	159.25	161.99	164.75	167.53
4.25	125.20	127.64	130.10	132.57	135.08	137.60	140.14	142.71	145.30	147.90	150.53	153.18	155.84	158.53	161.23	163.95
4.50	122.55	124.93	127.34	129.76	132.21	134.68	137.17	139.68	142.22	144.77	147.34	149.93	152.54	155.16	157.81	160.47
4.75	119.97	122.31	124.66	127.04	129.44	131.85	134.29	136.75	139.23	141.73	144.24	146.78	149.33	151.90	154.49	157.10
5.00	117.48	119.76	122.07	124.39	126.74	129.11	131.50	133.90	136.33	138.78	141.24	143.72	146.23	148.74	151.28	153.83
5.25	115.06	117.29	119.55	121.83	124.13	126.45	128.79	131.14	133.52	135.92	138.33	140.76	143.21	145.68	148.16	150.66
5.50	112.71	114.90	117.11	119.34	121.60	123.87	126.16	128.47	130.80	133.14	135.51	137.89	140.29	142.70	145.14	147.59
5.75	110.43	112.58	114.74	116.93	119.14	121.36	123.61	125.87	128.15	130.45	132.77	135.10	137.45	139.82	142.20	144.60
6.00	108.22	110.32	112.45	114.59	116.75	118.93	121.13	123.35	125.58	127.84	130.11	132.39	134.70	137.02	139.35	141.71
6.25	106.07	108.13	110.22	112.32	114.44	116.57	118.73	120.90	123.09	125.30	127.53	129.77	132.03	134.30	136.59	138.90
6.50	103.99	106.01	108.05	110.11	112.19	114.28	116.40	118.53	120.68	122.84	125.02	127.22	129.43	131.66	133.91	136.17
6.75	101.96	103.95	105.95	107.97	110.01	112.06	114.13	116.22	118.33	120.45	122.59	124.75	126.92	129.10	131.30	133.52
7.00	100.00	101.94	103.91	105.89	107.89	109.90	111.93	113.98	116.05	118.13	120.23	122.34	124.47	126.61	128.77	130.95
7.25	98.09	100.00	101.93	103.87	105.83	107.81	109.80	111.81	113.84	115.88	117.94	120.01	122.10	124.20	126.32	128.45
7.50	96.24	98.11	100.00	101.91	103.83	105.77	107.72	109.70	111.68	113.69	115.71	117.74	119.79	121.85	123.93	126.02
7.75	94.44	96.28	98.13	100.00	101.89	103.79	105.71	107.65	109.60	111.56	113.54	115.54	117.55	119.57	121.61	123.67
8.00	92.69	94.49	96.31	98.15	100.00	101.87	103.75	105.65	107.57	109.50	111.44	113.40	115.37	117.36	119.36	121.37
8.25	90.99	92.76	94.55	96.35	98.17	100.00	101.85	103.71	105.59	107.49	109.40	111.32	113.26	115.21	117.17	119.15
8.50	89.34	91.08	92.83	94.60	96.38	98.18	100.00	101.83	103.68	105.54	107.41	109.30	111.20	113.12	115.04	116.99
8.75	87.73	89.44	91.16	92.90	94.65	96.42	98.20	100.00	101.81	103.64	105.48	107.33	109.20	111.08	112.98	114.88
9.00	86.17	87.85	89.54	91.24	92.97	94.70	96.45	98.22	100.00	101.79	103.60	105.42	107.26	109.10	110.96	112.84
9.25	84.65	86.30	87.96	89.64	91.33	93.03	94.75	96.49	98.24	100.00	101.78	103.56	105.37	107.18	109.01	110.85
9.50	83.17	84.79	86.42	88.07	89.73	91.41	93.10	94.81	96.52	98.26	100.00	101.76	103.53	105.31	107.11	108.91
9.75	81.74	83.33	84.93	86.55	88.18	89.83	91.49	93.17	94.86	96.56	98.27	100.00	101.74	103.49	105.26	107.03
10.00	80.34	81.90	83.48	85.07	86.68	88.29	89.93	91.57	93.23	94.91	96.59	98.29	100.00	101.72	103.46	105.20
10.25	78.98	80.52	82.07	83.63	85.21	86.80	88.41	90.02	91.66	93.30	94.96	96.63	98.31	100.00	101.70	103.42
10.50	77.66	79.17	80.69	82.23	83.78	85.34	86.92	88.51	90.12	91.74	93.36	95.01	96.66	98.32	100.00	101.69
10.75	76.37	77.85	79.35	80.86	82.39	83.93	85.48	87.05	88.62	90.21	91.81	93.43	95.05	96.69	98.34	100.00
11.00	75.11	76.57	78.05	79.53	81.04	82.55	84.08	85.62	87.17	88.73	90.31	91.89	93.49	95.10	96.72	98.36
11.25	73.89	75.33	76.78	78.24	79.72	81.21	82.71	84.22	85.75	87.29	88.84	90.40	91.97	93.56	95.15	96.76
11.50	72.70	74.11	75.54	76.98	78.43	79.90	81.38	82.87	84.37	85.88	87.41	88.94	90.49	92.05	93.62	95.20
11.75	71.54	72.93	74.34	75.75	77.18	78.63	80.08	81.55	83.02	84.51	86.01	87.53	89.05	90.58	92.13	93.68
12.00	70.41	71.78	73.16	74.56	75.96	77.38	78.82	80.26	81.71	83.18	84.66	86.14	87.64	89.15	90.67	92.20
12.25	69.31	70.66	72.02	73.39	74.78	76.17	77.58	79.00	80.44	81.88	83.33	84.80	86.27	87.76	89.26	90.76
12.50	68.24	69.57	70.91	72.26	73.62	75.00	76.38	77.78	79.19	80.61	82.04	83.49	84.94	86.40	87.87	89.36
12.75	67.19	68.50	69.82	71.15	72.49	73.85	75.21	76.59	77.98	79.38	80.79	82.21	83.64	85.08	86.53	87.99
13.00	66.18	67.46	68.76	70.07	71.39	72.73	74.07	75.43	76.80	78.17	79.56	80.96	82.37	83.79	85.22	86.66
13.25	65.18	66.45	67.73	69.02	70.32	71.64	72.96	74.30	75.64	77.00	78.37	79.75	81.13	82.53	83.94	85.35
13.50	64.21	65.46	66.72	67.99	69.28	70.57	71.88	73.19	74.52	75.86	77.20	78.56	79.93	81.30	82.69	84.09
13.75	63.27	64.50	65.74	66.99	68.26	69.53	70.82	72.12	73.42	74.74	76.07	77.40	78.75	80.11	81.47	82.85
14.00	62.35	63.56	64.78	66.02	67.26	68.52	69.79	71.07	72.35	73.65	74.96	76.28	77.60	78.94	80.29	81.64
14.25	61.45	62.64	63.85	65.07	66.29	67.53	68.78	70.04	71.31	72.59	73.88	75.18	76.48	77.80	79.13	80.46
14.50	60.57	61.75	62.94	64.14	65.35	66.57	67.80	69.04	70.29	71.55	72.82	74.10	75.39	76.69	78.00	79.31
14.75	59.71	60.88	62.05	63.23	64.42	65.63	66.84	68.06	69.30	70.54	71.79	73.06	74.33	75.61	76.90	78.19
15.00	58.88	60.02	61.18	62.34	63.52	64.71	65.90	67.11	68.33	69.55	70.79	72.03	73.29	74.55	75.82	77.10
15.25	58.06	59.19	60.33	61.48	62.64	63.81	64.99	66.18	67.38	68.59	69.81	71.03	72.27	73.51	74.77	76.03
15.50	57.26	58.38	59.50	60.64	61.78	62.94	64.10	65.27	66.46	67.65	68.85	70.06	71.28	72.51	73.74	74.99
15.75	56.49	57.59	58.69	59.81	60.94	62.08	63.23	64.39	65.55	66.73	67.91	69.11	70.31	71.52	72.74	73.97
16.00	55.73	56.81	57.90	59.01	60.12	61.24	62.38	63.52	64.67	65.83	67.00	68.18	69.36	70.56	71.76	72.97
16.25	54.98	56.05	57.13	58.22	59.32	60.43	61.55	62.67	63.81	64.95	66.11	67.27	68.44	69.62	70.80	72.00
16.50	54.26	55.31	56.38	57.45	58.54	59.63	60.73	61.85	62.97	64.10	65.23	66.38	67.54	68.70	69.87	71.05
16.75	53.55	54.59	55.64	56.70	57.77	58.85	59.94	61.04	62.14	63.26	64.38	65.51	66.65	67.80	68.96	70.12
17.00	52.86	53.88	54.92	55.97	57.02	58.09	59.16	60.25	61.34	62.44	63.55	64.67	65.79	66.92	68.07	69.21
17.25	52.18	53.19	54.22	55.25	56.29	57.35	58.41	59.48	60.55	61.64	62.73	63.84	64.95	66.07	67.19	68.33
17.50	51.52	52.52	53.53	54.55	55.58	56.62	57.66	58.72	59.78	60.86	61.94	63.03	64.12	65.23	66.34	67.46
17.75	50.87	51.86	52.86	53.86	54.88	55.91	56.94	57.98	59.03	60.09	61.16	62.23	63.32	64.41	65.51	66.61
18.00	50.24	51.21	52.20	53.19	54.20	55.21	56.23	57.26	58.30	59.34	60.40	61.46	62.53	63.61	64.69	65.78
18.25	49.62	50.58	51.56	52.54	53.53	54.53	55.54	56.55	57.58	58.61	59.65	60.70	61.76	62.82	63.89	64.97
18.50	49.01	49.96	50.93	51.90	52.88	53.86	54.86	55.86	56.88	57.90	58.92	59.96	61.00	62.05	63.11	64.18
18.75	48.42	49.36	50.31	51.27	52.24	53.21	54.20	55.19	56.19	57.20	58.21	59.24	60.27	61.30	62.35	63.40
19.00	47.84	48.77	49.71	50.65	51.61	52.57	53.55	54.53	55.52	56.51	57.51	58.53	59.54	60.57	61.60	62.64
20.00	45.64	46.52	47.42	48.32	49.24	50.16	51.08	52.02	52.96	53.91	54.87	55.83	56.81	57.78	58.77	59.76
25.00	36.95	37.67	38.39	39.13	39.86	40.61	41.36	42.12	42.88	43.65	44.42	45.21	45.99	46.78	47.58	48.39
30.00	30.93	31.53	32.14	32.75	33.37	33.99	34.62	35.25	35.89	36.54	37.19	37.84	38.50	39.16	39.83	40.50

Description: This table shows the yield to maturity of a mortgage purchased at the price shown in the index.

Example: The yield to maturity of a 10.75 %, 20 year mortgage at a price of 111.00 is 9.23 %.

INTEREST RATE, %

PRICE	7.00%	7.25%	7.50%	7.75%	8.00%	8.25%	8.50%	8.75%	9.00%	9.25%	9.50%	9.75%	10.00%	10.25%	10.50%	10.75%
155	1.87	2.08	2.29	2.49	2.69	2.90	3.10	3.30	3.50	3.71	3.91	4.11	4.31	4.51	4.71	4.90
150	2.23	2.43	2.64	2.85	3.06	3.26	3.47	3.67	3.88	4.08	4.29	4.49	4.69	4.89	5.10	5.30
145	2.59	2.80	3.01	3.22	3.43	3.64	3.85	4.06	4.27	4.48	4.68	4.89	5.10	5.30	5.51	5.71
140	2.98	3.19	3.41	3.62	3.83	4.05	4.26	4.47	4.68	4.89	5.10	5.31	5.52	5.73	5.94	6.15
135	3.38	3.60	3.82	4.04	4.25	4.47	4.68	4.90	5.11	5.33	5.54	5.75	5.97	6.18	6.39	6.60
130	3.81	4.03	4.25	4.47	4.69	4.91	5.13	5.35	5.57	5.79	6.01	6.22	6.44	6.66	6.87	7.09
125	4.26	4.49	4.71	4.94	5.16	5.38	5.61	5.83	6.05	6.28	6.50	6.72	6.94	7.16	7.38	7.60
124	4.36	4.58	4.81	5.03	5.26	5.48	5.71	5.93	6.15	6.38	6.60	6.82	7.04	7.27	7.49	7.71
123	4.45	4.68	4.90	5.13	5.36	5.58	5.81	6.03	6.25	6.48	6.70	6.93	7.15	7.37	7.59	7.82
122	4.55	4.77	5.00	5.23	5.45	5.68	5.91	6.13	6.36	6.58	6.81	7.03	7.26	7.48	7.70	7.93
121	4.64	4.87	5.10	5.33	5.55	5.78	6.01	6.23	6.46	6.69	6.91	7.14	7.36	7.59	7.81	8.04
120	4.74	4.97	5.20	5.43	5.66	5.88	6.11	6.34	6.57	6.79	7.02	7.25	7.47	7.70	7.92	8.15
119	4.84	5.07	5.30	5.53	5.76	5.99	6.22	6.44	6.67	6.90	7.13	7.36	7.58	7.81	8.04	8.26
118	4.94	5.17	5.40	5.63	5.86	6.09	6.32	6.55	6.78	7.01	7.24	7.47	7.69	7.92	8.15	8.38
117	5.04	5.28	5.51	5.74	5.97	6.20	6.43	6.66	6.89	7.12	7.35	7.58	7.81	8.04	8.26	8.49
116	5.15	5.38	5.61	5.84	6.08	6.31	6.54	6.77	7.00	7.23	7.46	7.69	7.92	8.15	8.38	8.61
115	5.25	5.48	5.72	5.95	6.18	6.42	6.65	6.88	7.11	7.34	7.58	7.81	8.04	8.27	8.50	8.73
114	5.36	5.59	5.83	6.06	6.29	6.53	6.76	6.99	7.23	7.46	7.69	7.92	8.16	8.39	8.62	8.85
113	5.46	5.70	5.93	6.17	6.40	6.64	6.87	7.11	7.34	7.58	7.81	8.04	8.28	8.51	8.74	8.97
112	5.57	5.81	6.04	6.28	6.52	6.75	6.99	7.22	7.46	7.69	7.93	8.16	8.40	8.63	8.87	9.10
111	5.68	5.92	6.16	6.39	6.63	6.87	7.10	7.34	7.58	7.81	8.05	8.28	8.52	8.76	8.99	9.23
110	5.79	6.03	6.27	6.51	6.75	6.98	7.22	7.46	7.70	7.93	8.17	8.41	8.64	8.88	9.12	9.35
109	5.91	6.15	6.38	6.62	6.86	7.10	7.34	7.58	7.82	8.06	8.29	8.53	8.77	9.01	9.25	9.48
108	6.02	6.26	6.50	6.74	6.98	7.22	7.46	7.70	7.94	8.18	8.42	8.66	8.90	9.14	9.38	9.62
107	6.14	6.38	6.62	6.86	7.10	7.34	7.58	7.83	8.07	8.31	8.55	8.79	9.03	9.27	9.51	9.75
106	6.25	6.50	6.74	6.98	7.22	7.47	7.71	7.95	8.19	8.43	8.68	8.92	9.16	9.40	9.64	9.89
105	6.37	6.62	6.86	7.10	7.35	7.59	7.83	8.08	8.32	8.56	8.81	9.05	9.29	9.54	9.78	10.02
104	6.49	6.74	6.98	7.23	7.47	7.72	7.96	8.21	8.45	8.70	8.94	9.19	9.43	9.67	9.92	10.16
103	6.62	6.86	7.11	7.35	7.60	7.85	8.09	8.34	8.58	8.83	9.08	9.32	9.57	9.81	10.06	10.31
102	6.74	6.99	7.24	7.48	7.73	7.98	8.22	8.47	8.72	8.97	9.21	9.46	9.71	9.96	10.20	10.45
101	6.87	7.12	7.36	7.61	7.86	8.11	8.36	8.61	8.86	9.10	9.35	9.60	9.85	10.10	10.35	10.60
100	7.00	7.25	7.50	7.75	8.00	8.25	8.50	8.75	9.00	9.25	9.50	9.75	10.00	10.25	10.50	10.75
99	7.13	7.38	7.63	7.88	8.13	8.38	8.63	8.88	9.14	9.39	9.64	9.89	10.14	10.39	10.64	10.90
98	7.26	7.51	7.76	8.02	8.27	8.52	8.77	9.03	9.28	9.53	9.79	10.04	10.29	10.54	10.80	11.05
97	7.39	7.65	7.90	8.15	8.41	8.66	8.92	9.17	9.42	9.68	9.93	10.19	10.44	10.70	10.95	11.21
96	7.53	7.78	8.04	8.29	8.55	8.81	9.06	9.32	9.57	9.83	10.08	10.34	10.60	10.85	11.11	11.37
95	7.67	7.92	8.18	8.44	8.69	8.95	9.21	9.47	9.72	9.98	10.24	10.50	10.75	11.01	11.27	11.53
94	7.81	8.07	8.32	8.58	8.84	9.10	9.36	9.62	9.88	10.14	10.39	10.65	10.91	11.17	11.43	11.69
93	7.95	8.21	8.47	8.73	8.99	9.25	9.51	9.77	10.03	10.29	10.55	10.81	11.08	11.34	11.60	11.86
92	8.10	8.36	8.62	8.88	9.14	9.40	9.67	9.93	10.19	10.45	10.71	10.98	11.24	11.50	11.77	12.03
91	8.24	8.51	8.77	9.03	9.30	9.56	9.82	10.09	10.35	10.61	10.88	11.14	11.41	11.67	11.94	12.20
90	8.39	8.66	8.92	9.19	9.45	9.72	9.98	10.25	10.51	10.78	11.05	11.31	11.58	11.85	12.11	12.38
89	8.55	8.81	9.08	9.35	9.61	9.88	10.15	10.41	10.68	10.95	11.22	11.49	11.75	12.02	12.29	12.56
88	8.70	8.97	9.24	9.51	9.78	10.04	10.31	10.58	10.85	11.12	11.39	11.66	11.93	12.20	12.47	12.74
87	8.86	9.13	9.40	9.67	9.94	10.21	10.48	10.75	11.02	11.30	11.57	11.84	12.11	12.38	12.66	12.93
86	9.02	9.29	9.57	9.84	10.11	10.38	10.65	10.93	11.20	11.47	11.75	12.02	12.30	12.57	12.85	13.12
85	9.19	9.46	9.73	10.01	10.28	10.56	10.83	11.10	11.38	11.66	11.93	12.21	12.48	12.76	13.04	13.31
84	9.35	9.63	9.90	10.18	10.46	10.73	11.01	11.29	11.56	11.84	12.12	12.40	12.67	12.95	13.23	13.51
83	9.53	9.80	10.08	10.36	10.63	10.91	11.19	11.47	11.75	12.03	12.31	12.59	12.87	13.15	13.43	13.71
82	9.70	9.98	10.26	10.54	10.82	11.10	11.38	11.66	11.94	12.22	12.50	12.79	13.07	13.35	13.64	13.92
81	9.88	10.16	10.44	10.72	11.00	11.28	11.57	11.85	12.13	12.42	12.70	12.99	13.27	13.56	13.84	14.13
80	10.06	10.34	10.62	10.91	11.19	11.48	11.76	12.05	12.33	12.62	12.90	13.19	13.48	13.77	14.06	14.35
79	10.24	10.53	10.81	11.10	11.38	11.67	11.96	12.25	12.53	12.82	13.11	13.40	13.69	13.98	14.27	14.56
78	10.43	10.72	11.00	11.29	11.58	11.87	12.16	12.45	12.74	13.03	13.32	13.62	13.91	14.20	14.49	14.79
77	10.62	10.91	11.20	11.49	11.78	12.07	12.37	12.66	12.95	13.25	13.54	13.83	14.13	14.42	14.72	15.02
76	10.82	11.11	11.40	11.69	11.99	12.28	12.58	12.87	13.17	13.46	13.76	14.06	14.36	14.65	14.95	15.25
75	11.02	11.31	11.61	11.90	12.20	12.49	12.79	13.09	13.39	13.69	13.99	14.29	14.59	14.89	15.19	15.49
74	11.22	11.52	11.82	12.11	12.41	12.71	13.01	13.31	13.61	13.91	14.22	14.52	14.82	15.13	15.43	15.74
73	11.43	11.73	12.03	12.33	12.63	12.93	13.24	13.54	13.84	14.15	14.45	14.76	15.06	15.37	15.68	15.99
70	12.09	12.40	12.70	13.01	13.32	13.63	13.94	14.25	14.57	14.88	15.20	15.51	15.83	16.14	16.46	16.78
65	13.29	13.61	13.94	14.26	14.59	14.91	15.24	15.57	15.90	16.23	16.56	16.90	17.23	17.56	17.90	18.24
60	14.66	15.00	15.34	15.69	16.03	16.38	16.73	17.07	17.42	17.78	18.13	18.48	18.84	19.19	19.55	19.91
55	16.24	16.60	16.97	17.33	17.70	18.07	18.44	18.82	19.19	19.57	19.94	20.32	20.70	21.09	21.47	21.85
50	18.09	18.48	18.87	19.27	19.66	20.06	20.46	20.87	21.27	21.68	22.09	22.50	22.91	23.32	23.74	24.16
45	20.30	20.73	21.15	21.58	22.02	22.45	22.89	23.33	23.77	24.22	24.66	25.11	25.57	26.02	26.48	26.94
40	23.01	23.48	23.95	24.43	24.91	25.39	25.87	26.36	26.85	27.35	27.85	28.35	28.85	29.36	29.86	30.38
35	26.43	26.96	27.50	28.03	28.57	29.12	29.66	30.22	30.77	31.33	31.89	32.46	33.03	33.61	34.18	34.77
30	30.94	31.55	32.16	32.78	33.41	34.04	34.67	35.31	35.95	36.60	37.26	37.91	38.58	39.24	39.91	40.59

Description: This table shows the price to pay for a monthly payment mortgage loan at the yield rate.

Example: The price of a 15.00 %, 20 year mortgage loan to yield 8.00 % to maturity is $ 157.43.

INTEREST RATE, %

YIELD	11.00%	11.25%	11.50%	11.75%	12.00%	12.25%	12.50%	12.75%	13.00%	13.25%	13.50%	13.75%	14.00%	14.25%	14.50%	15.00%
0.00	247.73	251.82	255.94	260.09	264.26	268.46	272.67	276.91	281.18	285.46	289.77	294.10	298.44	302.81	307.20	316.03
1.00	224.44	228.15	231.89	235.64	239.42	243.22	247.04	250.89	254.75	258.63	262.53	266.45	270.39	274.35	278.32	286.32
2.00	204.04	207.41	210.81	214.22	217.66	221.11	224.59	228.08	231.59	235.12	238.67	242.23	245.81	249.41	253.02	260.30
3.00	186.11	189.19	192.29	195.40	198.54	201.69	204.86	208.04	211.25	214.47	217.70	220.95	224.22	227.50	230.80	237.43
4.00	170.33	173.15	175.98	178.84	181.70	184.59	187.49	190.40	193.34	196.28	199.24	202.22	205.21	208.21	211.23	217.30
4.25	166.69	169.44	172.22	175.01	177.81	180.64	183.48	186.33	189.20	192.08	194.98	197.89	200.82	203.75	206.71	212.65
4.50	163.15	165.85	168.57	171.30	174.04	176.81	179.58	182.38	185.19	188.01	190.84	193.69	196.56	199.43	202.32	208.14
4.75	159.73	162.37	165.02	167.70	170.39	173.09	175.81	178.55	181.30	184.06	186.84	189.63	192.43	195.24	198.07	203.77
5.00	156.40	158.99	161.59	164.21	166.84	169.49	172.15	174.83	177.52	180.23	182.95	185.68	188.42	191.18	193.95	199.53
5.25	153.18	155.71	158.26	160.82	163.40	166.00	168.61	171.23	173.86	176.51	179.18	181.85	184.54	187.24	189.95	195.41
5.50	150.05	152.53	155.03	157.54	160.07	162.61	165.16	167.73	170.32	172.91	175.52	178.14	180.77	183.42	186.08	191.43
5.75	147.02	149.45	151.89	154.36	156.83	159.32	161.82	164.34	166.87	169.41	171.97	174.54	177.12	179.71	182.31	187.55
6.00	144.07	146.46	148.85	151.26	153.69	156.13	158.58	161.05	163.53	166.02	168.53	171.04	173.57	176.11	178.66	183.80
6.25	141.22	143.55	145.90	148.26	150.64	153.03	155.44	157.86	160.29	162.73	165.18	167.65	170.13	172.62	175.12	180.15
6.50	138.44	140.73	143.03	145.35	147.68	150.03	152.38	154.75	157.14	159.53	161.94	164.36	166.79	169.23	171.68	176.61
6.75	135.75	137.99	140.25	142.52	144.81	147.11	149.42	151.74	154.08	156.43	158.79	161.16	163.54	165.94	168.34	173.18
7.00	133.13	135.34	137.55	139.78	142.02	144.28	146.54	148.82	151.11	153.42	155.73	158.06	160.39	162.74	165.10	169.84
7.25	130.59	132.75	134.93	137.11	139.31	141.52	143.75	145.98	148.23	150.49	152.76	155.04	157.33	159.64	161.95	166.60
7.50	128.13	130.25	132.38	134.52	136.68	138.85	141.03	143.23	145.43	147.65	149.87	152.11	154.36	156.62	158.89	163.46
7.75	125.73	127.81	129.90	132.01	134.12	136.25	138.39	140.55	142.71	144.88	147.07	149.27	151.47	153.69	155.92	160.40
8.00	123.40	125.44	127.50	129.56	131.64	133.73	135.83	137.94	140.07	142.20	144.35	146.50	148.67	150.84	153.03	157.43
8.25	121.14	123.14	125.16	127.19	129.23	131.28	133.34	135.41	137.50	139.59	141.70	143.82	145.94	148.08	150.22	154.54
8.50	118.94	120.91	122.89	124.88	126.88	128.89	130.92	132.95	135.00	137.06	139.13	141.20	143.29	145.39	147.50	151.73
8.75	116.80	118.73	120.68	122.63	124.60	126.58	128.56	130.56	132.57	134.60	136.63	138.67	140.72	142.78	144.84	149.01
9.00	114.72	116.62	118.53	120.45	122.38	124.32	126.28	128.24	130.21	132.20	134.19	136.20	138.21	140.23	142.27	146.35
9.25	112.70	114.56	116.44	118.33	120.22	122.13	124.05	125.98	127.92	129.87	131.83	133.80	135.78	137.76	139.76	143.78
9.50	110.73	112.57	114.41	116.26	118.13	120.00	121.89	123.78	125.69	127.60	129.53	131.46	133.41	135.36	137.32	141.27
9.75	108.82	110.62	112.43	114.25	116.09	117.93	119.78	121.64	123.52	125.40	127.29	129.19	131.10	133.02	134.95	138.83
10.00	106.96	108.73	110.51	112.30	114.10	115.91	117.73	119.56	121.40	123.25	125.11	126.98	128.86	130.75	132.64	136.45
10.25	105.15	106.89	108.64	110.40	112.17	113.95	115.74	117.54	119.35	121.17	123.00	124.83	126.68	128.53	130.39	134.14
10.50	103.39	105.10	106.82	108.55	110.29	112.04	113.80	115.57	117.35	119.14	120.93	122.74	124.55	126.38	128.21	131.89
10.75	101.67	103.35	105.04	106.75	108.46	110.18	111.91	113.65	115.40	117.16	118.93	120.70	122.49	124.28	126.08	129.70
11.00	100.00	101.65	103.32	104.99	106.67	108.37	110.07	111.78	113.50	115.23	116.97	118.72	120.47	122.24	124.01	127.57
11.25	98.37	100.00	101.64	103.28	104.94	106.61	108.28	109.96	111.66	113.36	115.07	116.79	118.51	120.25	121.99	125.50
11.50	96.79	98.39	100.00	101.62	103.25	104.89	106.54	108.19	109.86	111.53	113.22	114.91	116.61	118.31	120.03	123.48
11.75	95.25	96.82	98.41	100.00	101.60	103.22	104.84	106.47	108.11	109.76	111.41	113.08	114.75	116.43	118.11	121.51
12.00	93.74	95.29	96.85	98.42	100.00	101.59	103.18	104.79	106.40	108.02	109.65	111.29	112.94	114.59	116.25	119.59
12.25	92.28	93.80	95.34	96.88	98.44	100.00	101.57	103.15	104.74	106.34	107.94	109.55	111.17	112.80	114.43	117.72
12.50	90.85	92.35	93.86	95.38	96.91	98.45	100.00	101.56	103.12	104.69	106.27	107.86	109.45	111.05	112.66	115.90
12.75	89.46	90.94	92.43	93.92	95.43	96.95	98.47	100.00	101.54	103.09	104.64	106.20	107.78	109.35	110.94	114.13
13.00	88.10	89.56	91.03	92.50	93.98	95.48	96.98	98.48	100.00	101.52	103.06	104.59	106.14	107.69	109.25	112.39
13.25	86.78	88.21	89.66	91.11	92.57	94.04	95.52	97.01	98.50	100.00	101.51	103.02	104.55	106.08	107.61	110.71
13.50	85.49	86.90	88.33	89.76	91.20	92.64	94.10	95.56	97.03	98.51	100.00	101.49	102.99	104.50	106.01	109.06
13.75	84.23	85.63	87.03	88.44	89.85	91.28	92.72	94.16	95.61	97.06	98.53	100.00	101.48	102.96	104.46	107.46
14.00	83.01	84.38	85.76	87.15	88.55	89.95	91.36	92.79	94.21	95.65	97.09	98.54	100.00	101.46	102.93	105.89
14.25	81.81	83.16	84.52	85.89	87.27	88.65	90.05	91.45	92.86	94.27	95.69	97.12	98.56	100.00	101.45	104.36
14.50	80.64	81.97	83.31	84.66	86.02	87.39	88.76	90.14	91.53	92.92	94.33	95.73	97.15	98.57	100.00	102.87
14.75	79.50	80.81	82.14	83.47	84.81	86.15	87.51	88.87	90.24	91.61	92.99	94.38	95.78	97.18	98.59	101.42
15.00	78.39	79.68	80.99	82.30	83.62	84.95	86.28	87.62	88.97	90.33	91.69	93.06	94.44	95.82	97.21	100.00
15.25	77.30	78.58	79.86	81.16	82.46	83.77	85.09	86.41	87.74	89.08	90.42	91.77	93.13	94.49	95.86	98.61
15.50	76.24	77.50	78.77	80.04	81.33	82.62	83.92	85.22	86.53	87.85	89.18	90.51	91.85	93.19	94.54	97.26
15.75	75.20	76.45	77.70	78.96	80.22	81.50	82.78	84.06	85.36	86.66	87.97	89.28	90.60	91.93	93.26	95.94
16.00	74.19	75.42	76.65	77.89	79.14	80.40	81.66	82.93	84.21	85.49	86.78	88.08	89.38	90.69	92.00	94.65
16.25	73.20	74.41	75.63	76.86	78.09	79.33	80.57	81.83	83.09	84.35	85.63	86.91	88.19	89.48	90.78	93.39
16.50	72.24	73.43	74.63	75.84	77.06	78.28	79.51	80.75	81.99	83.24	84.50	85.76	87.03	88.30	89.58	92.15
16.75	71.29	72.47	73.66	74.85	76.05	77.26	78.47	79.69	80.92	82.15	83.39	84.64	85.89	87.15	88.41	90.95
17.00	70.37	71.53	72.70	73.88	75.07	76.26	77.46	78.66	79.87	81.09	82.31	83.54	84.78	86.02	87.26	89.77
17.25	69.47	70.62	71.77	72.94	74.11	75.28	76.46	77.65	78.85	80.05	81.26	82.47	83.69	84.92	86.15	88.62
17.50	68.59	69.72	70.86	72.01	73.16	74.33	75.49	76.67	77.85	79.03	80.23	81.43	82.63	83.84	85.05	87.50
17.75	67.72	68.84	69.97	71.10	72.25	73.39	74.55	75.70	76.87	78.04	79.22	80.40	81.59	82.78	83.98	86.40
18.00	66.88	67.99	69.10	70.22	71.35	72.48	73.62	74.76	75.91	77.07	78.23	79.40	80.57	81.75	82.94	85.32
18.25	66.06	67.15	68.25	69.35	70.47	71.58	72.71	73.84	74.98	76.12	77.27	78.42	79.58	80.75	81.92	84.27
18.50	65.25	66.33	67.41	68.51	69.61	70.71	71.82	72.94	74.06	75.19	76.32	77.46	78.61	79.76	80.92	83.24
18.75	64.46	65.53	66.60	67.68	68.76	69.86	70.95	72.06	73.17	74.28	75.40	76.53	77.66	78.80	79.94	82.23
19.00	63.69	64.74	65.80	66.87	67.94	69.02	70.10	71.19	72.29	73.39	74.50	75.61	76.73	77.85	78.98	81.25
20.00	60.76	61.76	62.77	63.79	64.81	65.84	66.88	67.92	68.96	70.01	71.07	72.13	73.20	74.27	75.35	77.51
25.00	49.19	50.01	50.83	51.65	52.48	53.31	54.15	54.99	55.84	56.69	57.54	58.40	59.27	60.13	61.00	62.76
30.00	41.18	41.86	42.54	43.23	43.93	44.62	45.32	46.03	46.74	47.45	48.17	48.89	49.61	50.33	51.06	52.53

Description: This table shows the yield to maturity of a mortgage purchased at the price shown in the index.

Example: The yield to maturity of a 15.00 %, 20 year mortgage at a price of 125.00 is 11.31 %.

INTEREST RATE, %

PRICE	11.00%	11.25%	11.50%	11.75%	12.00%	12.25%	12.50%	12.75%	13.00%	13.25%	13.50%	13.75%	14.00%	14.25%	14.50%	15.00%
250	–	.07	.23	.39	.55	.71	.87	1.03	1.19	1.35	1.50	1.66	1.82	1.97	2.12	2.43
240	–	.48	.64	.81	.97	1.13	1.29	1.46	1.62	1.78	1.94	2.09	2.25	2.41	2.57	2.88
230	.74	.91	1.08	1.25	1.41	1.58	1.74	1.91	2.07	2.23	2.39	2.55	2.71	2.87	3.03	3.35
220	1.20	1.37	1.54	1.71	1.88	2.05	2.22	2.38	2.55	2.71	2.88	3.04	3.21	3.37	3.53	3.85
210	1.69	1.86	2.04	2.21	2.38	2.55	2.72	2.89	3.06	3.23	3.40	3.56	3.73	3.90	4.06	4.39
200	2.21	2.39	2.56	2.74	2.91	3.09	3.26	3.44	3.61	3.78	3.95	4.12	4.29	4.46	4.63	4.97
195	2.48	2.66	2.84	3.02	3.19	3.37	3.55	3.72	3.90	4.07	4.24	4.42	4.59	4.76	4.93	5.27
190	2.77	2.95	3.13	3.31	3.49	3.66	3.84	4.02	4.20	4.37	4.55	4.72	4.90	5.07	5.24	5.59
185	3.06	3.24	3.43	3.61	3.79	3.97	4.15	4.33	4.51	4.68	4.86	5.04	5.22	5.39	5.57	5.91
180	3.37	3.55	3.74	3.92	4.10	4.29	4.47	4.65	4.83	5.01	5.19	5.37	5.55	5.73	5.90	6.26
175	3.69	3.87	4.06	4.25	4.43	4.62	4.80	4.98	5.17	5.35	5.53	5.71	5.89	6.07	6.25	6.61
170	4.02	4.21	4.40	4.58	4.77	4.96	5.15	5.33	5.52	5.70	5.89	6.07	6.25	6.44	6.62	6.98
165	4.36	4.56	4.75	4.94	5.13	5.32	5.51	5.70	5.88	6.07	6.26	6.45	6.63	6.82	7.00	7.37
160	4.72	4.92	5.11	5.31	5.50	5.69	5.88	6.08	6.27	6.46	6.65	6.84	7.03	7.22	7.40	7.78
155	5.10	5.30	5.50	5.69	5.89	6.09	6.28	6.47	6.67	6.86	7.06	7.25	7.44	7.63	7.82	8.20
150	5.50	5.70	5.90	6.10	6.30	6.50	6.70	6.89	7.09	7.29	7.48	7.68	7.88	8.07	8.27	8.65
145	5.92	6.12	6.32	6.53	6.73	6.93	7.13	7.33	7.53	7.73	7.93	8.13	8.33	8.53	8.73	9.13
140	6.35	6.56	6.77	6.97	7.18	7.39	7.59	7.80	8.00	8.21	8.41	8.61	8.82	9.02	9.22	9.62
135	6.82	7.03	7.24	7.45	7.66	7.87	8.08	8.29	8.50	8.70	8.91	9.12	9.33	9.53	9.74	10.15
130	7.30	7.52	7.73	7.95	8.16	8.38	8.59	8.81	9.02	9.23	9.44	9.66	9.87	10.08	10.29	10.71
125	7.82	8.04	8.26	8.48	8.70	8.92	9.14	9.36	9.57	9.79	10.01	10.23	10.44	10.66	10.87	11.31
120	8.37	8.60	8.82	9.05	9.27	9.50	9.72	9.94	10.17	10.39	10.61	10.83	11.05	11.28	11.50	11.94
115	8.96	9.19	9.42	9.65	9.88	10.11	10.34	10.57	10.80	11.03	11.25	11.48	11.71	11.94	12.17	12.62
113	9.21	9.44	9.67	9.90	10.14	10.37	10.60	10.83	11.06	11.29	11.52	11.76	11.99	12.22	12.45	12.91
112	9.33	9.57	9.80	10.03	10.27	10.50	10.73	10.97	11.20	11.43	11.66	11.89	12.13	12.36	12.59	13.05
111	9.46	9.70	9.93	10.17	10.40	10.63	10.87	11.10	11.34	11.57	11.80	12.04	12.27	12.50	12.74	13.20
110	9.59	9.83	10.06	10.30	10.53	10.77	11.00	11.24	11.48	11.71	11.95	12.18	12.41	12.65	12.88	13.35
109	9.72	9.96	10.20	10.43	10.67	10.91	11.14	11.38	11.62	11.85	12.09	12.33	12.56	12.95	13.03	13.50
108	9.85	10.09	10.33	10.57	10.81	11.05	11.28	11.52	11.76	12.00	12.24	12.47	12.71	12.95	13.19	13.66
107	9.99	10.23	10.47	10.71	10.95	11.19	11.43	11.67	11.91	12.15	12.38	12.62	12.86	13.10	13.34	13.82
106	10.13	10.37	10.61	10.85	11.09	11.33	11.57	11.81	12.05	12.30	12.54	12.78	13.02	13.26	13.50	13.98
105	10.27	10.51	10.75	10.99	11.24	11.48	11.72	11.96	12.21	12.45	12.69	12.93	13.17	13.42	13.66	14.14
104	10.41	10.65	10.90	11.14	11.38	11.63	11.87	12.11	12.36	12.60	12.85	13.09	13.33	13.58	13.82	14.31
103	10.55	10.80	11.04	11.29	11.53	11.78	12.02	12.27	12.51	12.76	13.00	13.25	13.49	13.74	13.98	14.47
102	10.70	10.94	11.19	11.44	11.68	11.93	12.18	12.42	12.67	12.92	13.16	13.41	13.66	13.90	14.15	14.64
101	10.84	11.09	11.34	11.59	11.84	12.09	12.34	12.58	12.83	13.08	13.33	13.58	13.83	14.07	14.32	14.82
100	11.00	11.25	11.50	11.75	12.00	12.25	12.50	12.75	13.00	13.25	13.50	13.75	14.00	14.25	14.50	15.00
99	11.15	11.40	11.65	11.90	12.15	12.41	12.66	12.91	13.16	13.41	13.66	13.92	14.17	14.42	14.67	15.17
98	11.30	11.56	11.81	12.06	12.32	12.57	12.82	13.08	13.33	13.58	13.84	14.09	14.34	14.60	14.85	15.36
97	11.46	11.72	11.97	12.23	12.48	12.74	12.99	13.25	13.50	13.76	14.01	14.27	14.52	14.78	15.03	15.54
96	11.62	11.88	12.14	12.39	12.65	12.91	13.16	13.42	13.68	13.93	14.19	14.45	14.70	14.96	15.22	15.73
95	11.79	12.04	12.30	12.56	12.82	13.08	13.34	13.59	13.85	14.11	14.37	14.63	14.89	15.15	15.41	15.93
94	11.95	12.21	12.47	12.73	12.99	13.25	13.51	13.77	14.03	14.29	14.56	14.82	15.08	15.34	15.60	16.12
93	12.12	12.38	12.64	12.91	13.17	13.43	13.69	13.96	14.22	14.48	14.74	15.01	15.27	15.53	15.80	16.32
92	12.29	12.56	12.82	13.08	13.35	13.61	13.88	14.14	14.41	14.67	14.94	15.20	15.47	15.73	16.00	16.53
91	12.47	12.73	13.00	13.27	13.53	13.80	14.06	14.33	14.60	14.86	15.13	15.40	15.66	15.93	16.20	16.73
90	12.65	12.91	13.18	13.45	13.72	13.99	14.25	14.52	14.79	15.06	15.33	15.60	15.87	16.14	16.41	16.95
89	12.83	13.10	13.37	13.64	13.91	14.18	14.45	14.72	14.99	15.26	15.53	15.80	16.07	16.35	16.62	17.16
88	13.01	13.29	13.56	13.83	14.10	14.37	14.65	14.92	15.19	15.46	15.74	16.01	16.29	16.56	16.83	17.38
87	13.20	13.48	13.75	14.02	14.30	14.57	14.85	15.12	15.40	15.67	15.95	16.22	16.50	16.78	17.05	17.61
86	13.40	13.67	13.95	14.22	14.50	14.78	15.05	15.33	15.61	15.89	16.16	16.44	16.72	17.00	17.28	17.84
85	13.59	13.87	14.15	14.43	14.70	14.98	15.26	15.54	15.82	16.10	16.38	16.66	16.94	17.23	17.51	18.07
84	13.79	14.07	14.35	14.63	14.91	15.20	15.48	15.76	16.04	16.32	16.61	16.89	17.17	17.46	17.74	18.31
83	14.00	14.28	14.56	14.84	15.13	15.41	15.70	15.98	16.26	16.55	16.84	17.12	17.41	17.69	17.98	18.55
82	14.20	14.49	14.77	15.06	15.35	15.63	15.92	16.21	16.49	16.78	17.07	17.36	17.65	17.93	18.22	18.80
81	14.42	14.70	14.99	15.28	15.57	15.86	16.15	16.44	16.73	17.02	17.31	17.60	17.89	18.18	18.47	19.06
80	14.63	14.92	15.21	15.51	15.80	16.09	16.38	16.67	16.96	17.26	17.55	17.84	18.14	18.43	18.73	19.32
79	14.86	15.15	15.44	15.73	16.03	16.32	16.62	16.91	17.21	17.50	17.80	18.10	18.39	18.69	18.99	19.59
78	15.08	15.38	15.67	15.97	16.27	16.56	16.86	17.16	17.46	17.76	18.05	18.35	18.65	18.96	19.26	19.86
77	15.32	15.61	15.91	16.21	16.51	16.81	17.11	17.41	17.71	18.01	18.32	18.62	18.92	19.23	19.53	20.14
76	15.55	15.85	16.15	16.46	16.76	17.06	17.36	17.67	17.97	18.28	18.58	18.89	19.19	19.50	19.81	20.42
75	15.79	16.10	16.40	16.71	17.01	17.32	17.62	17.93	18.24	18.55	18.86	19.16	19.47	19.78	20.09	20.72
74	16.04	16.35	16.66	16.96	17.27	17.58	17.89	18.20	18.51	18.82	19.14	19.45	19.76	20.07	20.39	21.02
73	16.30	16.61	16.92	17.23	17.54	17.85	18.16	18.48	18.79	19.11	19.42	19.74	20.05	20.37	20.69	21.33
70	17.10	17.42	17.74	18.06	18.38	18.70	19.03	19.35	19.67	20.00	20.33	20.65	20.98	21.31	21.64	22.30
65	18.57	18.91	19.25	19.59	19.93	20.28	20.62	20.96	21.31	21.65	22.00	22.35	22.70	23.05	23.40	24.10
60	20.27	20.63	20.99	21.36	21.72	22.09	22.45	22.82	23.19	23.56	23.93	24.30	24.68	25.05	25.43	26.18
55	22.24	22.63	23.02	23.41	23.80	24.20	24.59	24.99	25.39	25.79	26.19	26.59	27.00	27.40	27.81	28.62

Description: This table shows the price to pay for a monthly payment mortgage loan at the yield rate.

Example: The price of a 6.75 %, 21 year mortgage loan to yield 8.00 % to maturity is $ 90.60.

INTEREST RATE, %

YIELD	0.00%	1.00%	2.00%	3.00%	4.00%	4.25%	4.50%	4.75%	5.00%	5.25%	5.50%	5.75%	6.00%	6.25%	6.50%	6.75%
0.00	100.00	110.91	122.55	134.91	147.97	151.34	154.76	158.21	161.71	165.25	168.83	172.45	176.11	179.81	183.55	187.32
1.00	90.16	100.00	110.49	121.64	133.42	136.46	139.54	142.65	145.81	149.00	152.23	155.49	158.79	162.12	165.49	168.90
2.00	81.60	90.50	100.00	110.08	120.74	123.50	126.28	129.10	131.96	134.85	137.77	140.72	143.71	146.73	149.78	152.86
3.00	74.13	82.21	90.84	100.00	109.68	112.18	114.71	117.28	119.87	122.49	125.15	127.83	130.54	133.29	136.06	138.85
4.00	67.58	74.95	82.82	91.17	100.00	102.28	104.59	106.92	109.29	111.68	114.10	116.55	119.02	121.52	124.04	126.60
4.25	66.08	73.28	80.97	89.14	97.77	100.00	102.26	104.54	106.85	109.19	111.56	113.95	116.37	118.81	121.28	123.77
4.50	64.62	71.67	79.19	87.17	95.61	97.79	100.00	102.23	104.49	106.78	109.09	111.43	113.80	116.19	118.60	121.04
4.75	63.21	70.10	77.46	85.27	93.52	95.66	97.81	100.00	102.21	104.45	106.71	109.00	111.31	113.65	116.01	118.40
5.00	61.84	68.58	75.78	83.42	91.50	93.59	95.70	97.84	100.00	102.19	104.40	106.64	108.90	111.19	113.50	115.84
5.25	60.51	67.11	74.16	81.64	89.54	91.58	93.65	95.74	97.86	100.00	102.17	104.36	106.57	108.81	111.07	113.36
5.50	59.23	65.69	72.59	79.91	87.64	89.64	91.66	93.71	95.78	97.88	100.00	102.14	104.31	106.50	108.72	110.95
5.75	57.99	64.31	71.06	78.23	85.80	87.76	89.74	91.74	93.77	95.82	97.90	100.00	102.12	104.27	106.43	108.62
6.00	56.78	62.98	69.59	76.60	84.02	85.94	87.87	89.84	91.82	93.83	95.87	97.92	100.00	102.10	104.22	106.37
6.25	55.61	61.68	68.15	75.03	82.29	84.17	86.07	87.99	89.94	91.90	93.89	95.91	97.94	100.00	102.08	104.18
6.50	54.48	60.43	66.77	73.50	80.62	82.45	84.31	86.20	88.10	90.03	91.98	93.96	95.95	97.96	100.00	102.06
6.75	53.38	59.21	65.42	72.02	78.99	80.79	82.62	84.46	86.33	88.22	90.13	92.06	94.02	95.99	97.98	100.00
7.00	52.32	58.03	64.12	70.58	77.42	79.18	80.97	82.78	84.61	86.46	88.33	90.23	92.14	94.08	96.03	98.01
7.25	51.29	56.88	62.85	69.19	75.89	77.62	79.37	81.14	82.94	84.75	86.59	88.44	90.32	92.22	94.13	96.07
7.50	50.28	55.77	61.62	67.84	74.41	76.10	77.82	79.56	81.32	83.10	84.90	86.72	88.56	90.42	92.30	94.19
7.75	49.31	54.69	60.43	66.52	72.97	74.63	76.31	78.02	79.74	81.49	83.25	85.04	86.84	88.67	90.51	92.37
8.00	48.37	53.64	59.27	65.25	71.57	73.20	74.85	76.53	78.22	79.93	81.66	83.41	85.18	86.97	88.78	90.60
8.25	47.45	52.63	58.15	64.02	70.21	71.81	73.44	75.08	76.74	78.42	80.11	81.83	83.57	85.32	87.10	88.89
8.50	46.56	51.64	57.06	62.82	68.90	70.47	72.06	73.67	75.30	76.95	78.61	80.30	82.00	83.72	85.46	87.22
8.75	45.70	50.68	56.00	61.65	67.62	69.16	70.72	72.30	73.90	75.52	77.15	78.81	80.48	82.17	83.88	85.60
9.00	44.86	49.75	54.98	60.52	66.38	67.89	69.42	70.98	72.54	74.13	75.74	77.36	79.00	80.66	82.34	84.03
9.25	44.05	48.85	53.98	59.42	65.17	66.66	68.16	69.69	71.23	72.79	74.36	75.96	77.57	79.20	80.84	82.51
9.50	43.25	47.97	53.01	58.35	64.00	65.46	66.94	68.43	69.95	71.48	73.03	74.59	76.18	77.77	79.39	81.02
9.75	42.48	47.12	52.06	57.31	62.86	64.30	65.75	67.22	68.70	70.21	71.73	73.27	74.82	76.39	77.98	79.58
10.00	41.74	46.29	51.15	56.31	61.76	63.17	64.59	66.03	67.49	68.97	70.47	71.98	73.50	75.05	76.61	78.18
10.25	41.01	45.48	50.26	55.33	60.68	62.07	63.47	64.88	66.32	67.77	69.24	70.72	72.22	73.74	75.27	76.82
10.50	40.30	44.70	49.39	54.37	59.64	61.00	62.37	63.77	65.18	66.60	68.05	69.50	70.98	72.47	73.98	75.50
10.75	39.62	43.94	48.55	53.44	58.62	59.96	61.31	62.68	64.06	65.47	66.88	68.32	69.77	71.23	72.71	74.21
11.00	38.95	43.20	47.73	52.54	57.63	58.94	60.27	61.62	62.98	64.36	65.76	67.17	68.59	70.03	71.49	72.96
11.25	38.30	42.48	46.93	51.67	56.67	57.96	59.27	60.59	61.93	63.29	64.66	66.04	67.45	68.86	70.29	71.74
11.50	37.66	41.77	46.16	50.81	55.73	57.00	58.29	59.59	60.91	62.24	63.59	64.95	66.33	67.72	69.13	70.55
11.75	37.05	41.09	45.40	49.98	54.82	56.07	57.34	58.62	59.91	61.22	62.55	63.89	65.25	66.62	68.00	69.40
12.00	36.45	40.43	44.67	49.17	53.93	55.16	56.41	57.67	58.94	60.23	61.54	62.86	64.19	65.54	66.90	68.28
12.25	35.87	39.78	43.95	48.39	53.07	54.28	55.51	56.75	58.00	59.27	60.55	61.85	63.16	64.49	65.83	67.19
12.50	35.30	39.15	43.26	47.62	52.23	53.42	54.63	55.85	57.08	58.33	59.59	60.87	62.16	63.47	64.79	66.12
12.75	34.74	38.53	42.58	46.87	51.41	52.58	53.77	54.97	56.19	57.42	58.66	59.92	61.19	62.47	63.77	65.08
13.00	34.21	37.94	41.92	46.15	50.61	51.77	52.94	54.12	55.32	56.53	57.75	58.99	60.24	61.51	62.78	64.07
13.25	33.68	37.35	41.27	45.44	49.84	50.97	52.12	53.29	54.47	55.66	56.86	58.08	59.32	60.56	61.82	63.09
13.50	33.17	36.79	40.65	44.75	49.08	50.20	51.33	52.48	53.64	54.81	56.00	57.20	58.41	59.64	60.88	62.13
13.75	32.67	36.23	40.04	44.07	48.34	49.44	50.56	51.69	52.83	53.99	55.16	56.34	57.54	58.75	59.97	61.20
14.00	32.18	35.70	39.44	43.42	47.62	48.71	49.81	50.92	52.05	53.19	54.34	55.50	56.68	57.87	59.07	60.29
14.25	31.71	35.17	38.86	42.78	46.92	47.99	49.07	50.17	51.28	52.40	53.54	54.69	55.85	57.02	58.20	59.40
14.50	31.25	34.66	38.29	42.16	46.24	47.29	48.36	49.44	50.53	51.64	52.76	53.89	55.03	56.19	57.36	58.54
14.75	30.80	34.16	37.74	41.55	45.57	46.61	47.66	48.73	49.80	50.89	52.00	53.11	54.24	55.38	56.53	57.69
15.00	30.36	33.67	37.20	40.96	44.92	45.95	46.98	48.03	49.09	50.17	51.26	52.35	53.47	54.59	55.72	56.87
15.25	29.93	33.20	36.68	40.38	44.29	45.30	46.32	47.35	48.40	49.46	50.53	51.62	52.71	53.82	54.94	56.07
15.50	29.51	32.73	36.17	39.81	43.67	44.66	45.67	46.69	47.72	48.77	49.83	50.89	51.97	53.07	54.17	55.28
15.75	29.10	32.28	35.67	39.26	43.06	44.05	45.04	46.05	47.06	48.09	49.14	50.19	51.25	52.33	53.42	54.52
16.00	28.70	31.84	35.18	38.72	42.47	43.44	44.42	45.42	46.42	47.44	48.46	49.50	50.55	51.61	52.69	53.77
16.25	28.32	31.40	34.70	38.20	41.90	42.85	43.82	44.80	45.79	46.79	47.81	48.83	49.87	50.91	51.97	53.04
16.50	27.94	30.98	34.23	37.69	41.34	42.28	43.23	44.20	45.18	46.16	47.16	48.18	49.20	50.23	51.28	52.33
16.75	27.56	30.57	33.78	37.19	40.79	41.72	42.66	43.61	44.58	45.55	46.54	47.54	48.55	49.56	50.59	51.64
17.00	27.20	30.17	33.34	36.70	40.25	41.17	42.10	43.04	43.99	44.95	45.93	46.91	47.91	48.91	49.93	50.96
17.25	26.85	29.78	32.90	36.22	39.73	40.63	41.55	42.48	43.42	44.37	45.33	46.30	47.28	48.28	49.28	50.29
17.50	26.50	29.39	32.48	35.75	39.22	40.11	41.01	41.93	42.86	43.80	44.74	45.70	46.67	47.65	48.64	49.65
17.75	26.16	29.02	32.06	35.30	38.72	39.60	40.49	41.40	42.31	43.24	44.17	45.12	46.08	47.05	48.02	49.01
18.00	25.83	28.65	31.66	34.85	38.23	39.10	39.98	40.87	41.78	42.69	43.62	44.55	45.50	46.45	47.42	48.39
18.25	25.51	28.29	31.26	34.42	37.75	38.61	39.48	40.36	41.25	42.16	43.07	43.99	44.93	45.87	46.82	47.79
18.50	25.20	27.94	30.88	33.99	37.28	38.13	38.99	39.86	40.74	41.64	42.54	43.45	44.37	45.30	46.25	47.20
18.75	24.89	27.60	30.50	33.57	36.82	37.66	38.51	39.37	40.24	41.13	42.02	42.92	43.83	44.75	45.68	46.62
19.00	24.58	27.27	30.13	33.17	36.38	37.21	38.05	38.90	39.76	40.63	41.51	42.40	43.30	44.21	45.12	46.05
20.00	23.44	26.00	28.73	31.62	34.68	35.47	36.28	37.09	37.91	38.74	39.57	40.42	41.28	42.15	43.02	43.91
25.00	18.94	21.01	23.21	25.55	28.03	28.67	29.31	29.97	30.63	31.30	31.98	32.67	33.36	34.06	34.77	35.48
30.00	15.84	17.57	19.41	21.37	23.44	23.97	24.52	25.06	25.62	26.18	26.75	27.32	27.90	28.48	29.08	29.67

Description: This table shows the yield to maturity of a mortgage purchased at the price shown in the index.

Example: The yield to maturity of a 6.75 %, 21 year mortgage at a price of 80.00 is 9.67 %.

INTEREST RATE, %

PRICE	0.00%	1.00%	2.00%	3.00%	4.00%	4.25%	4.50%	4.75%	5.00%	5.25%	5.50%	5.75%	6.00%	6.25%	6.50%	6.75%
100	0.00	1.00	2.00	3.00	4.00	4.25	4.50	4.75	5.00	5.25	5.50	5.75	6.00	6.25	6.50	6.75
99	.09	1.09	2.10	3.10	4.11	4.36	4.61	4.86	5.11	5.36	5.61	5.86	6.12	6.37	6.62	6.87
98	.19	1.19	2.20	3.21	4.22	4.47	4.72	4.98	5.23	5.48	5.73	5.99	6.24	6.49	6.74	7.00
97	.29	1.30	2.31	3.32	4.33	4.59	4.84	5.09	5.35	5.60	5.85	6.11	6.36	6.62	6.87	7.12
96	.38	1.40	2.42	3.43	4.45	4.70	4.96	5.21	5.47	5.72	5.98	6.23	6.49	6.74	7.00	7.25
95	.49	1.50	2.52	3.55	4.57	4.82	5.08	5.34	5.59	5.85	6.10	6.36	6.62	6.87	7.13	7.39
94	.59	1.61	2.63	3.66	4.69	4.94	5.20	5.46	5.72	5.97	6.23	6.49	6.75	7.00	7.26	7.52
93	.69	1.72	2.75	3.78	4.81	5.07	5.33	5.58	5.84	6.10	6.36	6.62	6.88	7.14	7.40	7.66
92	.80	1.83	2.86	3.90	4.93	5.19	5.45	5.71	5.97	6.23	6.49	6.75	7.01	7.27	7.54	7.80
91	.90	1.94	2.98	4.02	5.06	5.32	5.58	5.84	6.10	6.36	6.63	6.89	7.15	7.41	7.68	7.94
90	1.01	2.05	3.09	4.14	5.19	5.45	5.71	5.97	6.24	6.50	6.76	7.03	7.29	7.55	7.82	8.08
89	1.12	2.17	3.21	4.26	5.32	5.58	5.84	6.11	6.37	6.64	6.90	7.17	7.43	7.70	7.96	8.23
88	1.24	2.28	3.33	4.39	5.45	5.71	5.98	6.24	6.51	6.78	7.04	7.31	7.58	7.84	8.11	8.38
87	1.35	2.40	3.46	4.52	5.58	5.85	6.11	6.38	6.65	6.92	7.19	7.45	7.72	7.99	8.26	8.53
86	1.46	2.52	3.58	4.65	5.72	5.99	6.25	6.52	6.79	7.06	7.33	7.60	7.87	8.14	8.41	8.68
85	1.58	2.64	3.71	4.78	5.86	6.13	6.40	6.67	6.94	7.21	7.48	7.75	8.02	8.30	8.57	8.84
84	1.70	2.77	3.84	4.92	6.00	6.27	6.54	6.81	7.08	7.36	7.63	7.90	8.18	8.45	8.73	9.00
83	1.82	2.89	3.97	5.05	6.14	6.41	6.69	6.96	7.24	7.51	7.78	8.06	8.33	8.61	8.89	9.16
82	1.95	3.02	4.11	5.19	6.29	6.56	6.84	7.11	7.39	7.66	7.94	8.22	8.50	8.77	9.05	9.33
81	2.07	3.15	4.24	5.34	6.44	6.71	6.99	7.27	7.54	7.82	8.10	8.38	8.66	8.94	9.22	9.50
80	2.20	3.29	4.38	5.48	6.59	6.87	7.15	7.42	7.70	7.98	8.26	8.54	8.83	9.11	9.39	9.67
79	2.33	3.42	4.52	5.63	6.74	7.02	7.30	7.58	7.87	8.15	8.43	8.71	9.00	9.28	9.56	9.85
78	2.46	3.56	4.67	5.78	6.90	7.18	7.47	7.75	8.03	8.31	8.60	8.88	9.17	9.46	9.74	10.03
77	2.59	3.70	4.81	5.93	7.06	7.35	7.63	7.91	8.20	8.49	8.77	9.06	9.35	9.63	9.92	10.21
76	2.73	3.84	4.96	6.09	7.23	7.51	7.80	8.08	8.37	8.66	8.95	9.24	9.53	9.82	10.11	10.40
75	2.87	3.99	5.11	6.25	7.39	7.68	7.97	8.26	8.55	8.84	9.13	9.42	9.71	10.00	10.30	10.59
74	3.01	4.14	5.27	6.41	7.56	7.85	8.14	8.44	8.73	9.02	9.31	9.61	9.90	10.19	10.49	10.79
73	3.16	4.29	5.43	6.58	7.74	8.03	8.32	8.62	8.91	9.20	9.50	9.80	10.09	10.39	10.69	10.99
72	3.31	4.44	5.59	6.75	7.92	8.21	8.51	8.80	9.10	9.39	9.69	9.99	10.29	10.59	10.89	11.19
71	3.46	4.60	5.76	6.92	8.10	8.40	8.69	8.99	9.29	9.59	9.89	10.19	10.49	10.79	11.10	11.40
70	3.61	4.76	5.92	7.10	8.29	8.58	8.88	9.18	9.48	9.79	10.09	10.39	10.70	11.00	11.31	11.61
69	3.77	4.93	6.10	7.28	8.48	8.78	9.08	9.38	9.68	9.99	10.29	10.60	10.91	11.22	11.52	11.83
68	3.93	5.09	6.27	7.46	8.67	8.97	9.28	9.58	9.89	10.20	10.50	10.81	11.12	11.43	11.75	12.06
67	4.09	5.26	6.45	7.65	8.87	9.18	9.48	9.79	10.10	10.41	10.72	11.03	11.34	11.66	11.97	12.29
66	4.26	5.44	6.64	7.85	9.07	9.38	9.69	10.00	10.31	10.63	10.94	11.26	11.57	11.89	12.21	12.52
65	4.43	5.62	6.82	8.05	9.28	9.59	9.91	10.22	10.53	10.85	11.17	11.48	11.80	12.12	12.44	12.77
64	4.60	5.80	7.02	8.25	9.50	9.81	10.13	10.44	10.76	11.08	11.40	11.72	12.04	12.36	12.69	13.01
63	4.78	5.99	7.22	8.46	9.71	10.03	10.35	10.67	10.99	11.31	11.64	11.96	12.29	12.61	12.94	13.27
62	4.96	6.18	7.42	8.67	9.94	10.26	10.58	10.90	11.23	11.55	11.88	12.21	12.54	12.87	13.20	13.53
61	5.15	6.38	7.62	8.89	10.17	10.49	10.82	11.15	11.47	11.80	12.13	12.46	12.79	13.13	13.46	13.80
60	5.34	6.58	7.84	9.11	10.41	10.73	11.06	11.39	11.72	12.06	12.39	12.72	13.06	13.40	13.74	14.08
59	5.54	6.79	8.06	9.34	10.65	10.98	11.31	11.65	11.98	12.32	12.65	12.99	13.33	13.67	14.02	14.36
58	5.74	7.00	8.28	9.58	10.90	11.23	11.57	11.91	12.25	12.58	12.93	13.27	13.61	13.96	14.30	14.65
57	5.95	7.22	8.51	9.82	11.16	11.50	11.83	12.18	12.52	12.86	13.21	13.55	13.90	14.25	14.60	14.95
56	6.16	7.44	8.75	10.07	11.42	11.76	12.11	12.45	12.80	13.15	13.50	13.85	14.20	14.55	14.91	15.27
55	6.38	7.67	8.99	10.33	11.70	12.04	12.39	12.74	13.09	13.44	13.79	14.15	14.51	14.86	15.22	15.59
54	6.60	7.91	9.24	10.59	11.98	12.33	12.68	13.03	13.39	13.74	14.10	14.46	14.82	15.19	15.55	15.92
53	6.83	8.15	9.50	10.87	12.27	12.62	12.98	13.33	13.69	14.05	14.42	14.78	15.15	15.52	15.89	16.26
52	7.07	8.40	9.76	11.15	12.56	12.92	13.28	13.65	14.01	14.38	14.74	15.11	15.49	15.86	16.24	16.61
51	7.32	8.66	10.04	11.44	12.87	13.24	13.60	13.97	14.34	14.71	15.08	15.46	15.84	16.21	16.60	16.98
50	7.57	8.93	10.32	11.74	13.19	13.56	13.93	14.30	14.68	15.05	15.43	15.81	16.20	16.58	16.97	17.36
49	7.83	9.20	10.61	12.05	13.52	13.90	14.27	14.65	15.03	15.41	15.80	16.18	16.57	16.96	17.35	17.75
48	8.09	9.49	10.91	12.37	13.86	14.24	14.62	15.01	15.39	15.78	16.17	16.56	16.96	17.36	17.75	18.16
47	8.37	9.78	11.22	12.70	14.22	14.60	14.99	15.38	15.77	16.16	16.56	16.96	17.36	17.76	18.17	18.58
46	8.66	10.08	11.55	13.05	14.58	14.97	15.37	15.76	16.16	16.56	16.96	17.37	17.78	18.19	18.60	19.02
45	8.95	10.40	11.88	13.40	14.96	15.36	15.76	16.16	16.57	16.98	17.39	17.80	18.21	18.63	19.05	19.47
44	9.26	10.72	12.23	13.77	15.36	15.76	16.17	16.58	16.99	17.41	17.82	18.24	18.67	19.09	19.52	19.95
43	9.58	11.06	12.59	14.16	15.77	16.18	16.60	17.01	17.43	17.85	18.28	18.71	19.14	19.57	20.01	20.45
42	9.91	11.41	12.96	14.56	16.20	16.62	17.04	17.46	17.89	18.32	18.75	19.19	19.63	20.07	20.52	20.96
41	10.25	11.78	13.35	14.98	16.65	17.07	17.50	17.93	18.37	18.81	19.25	19.69	20.14	20.59	21.05	21.50
40	10.60	12.16	13.76	15.41	17.11	17.55	17.99	18.43	18.87	19.32	19.77	20.22	20.68	21.14	21.60	22.07
39	10.98	12.55	14.18	15.87	17.60	18.04	18.49	18.94	19.39	19.85	20.31	20.77	21.24	21.71	22.18	22.66
35	12.63	14.33	16.09	17.91	19.80	20.28	20.77	21.26	21.76	22.26	22.76	23.27	23.79	24.30	24.82	25.35
30	15.20	17.10	19.08	21.15	23.30	23.85	24.41	24.97	25.54	26.11	26.69	27.27	27.86	28.46	29.06	29.67
25	18.65	20.85	23.15	25.57	28.10	28.75	29.41	30.07	30.75	31.43	32.11	32.81	33.51	34.22	34.93	35.65
20	23.63	26.29	29.10	32.07	35.20	36.01	36.82	37.65	38.48	39.33	40.18	41.05	41.92	42.80	43.69	44.59
15	31.70	35.18	38.89	42.82	46.97	48.04	49.12	50.22	51.33	52.46	53.59	54.74	55.90	57.08	58.26	59.46
10	47.61	52.81	58.35	64.24	70.46	72.06	73.69	75.34	77.00	78.69	80.39	82.12	83.86	85.62	87.40	89.20

Description: This table shows the price to pay for a monthly payment mortgage loan at the yield rate.

Example: The price of a 10.75 %, 21 year mortgage loan to yield 8.00 % to maturity is $ 122.09.

INTEREST RATE, %

YIELD	7.00%	7.25%	7.50%	7.75%	8.00%	8.25%	8.50%	8.75%	9.00%	9.25%	9.50%	9.75%	10.00%	10.25%	10.50%	10.75%
0.00	191.13	194.98	198.87	202.79	206.75	210.74	214.76	218.82	222.91	227.04	231.19	235.38	239.60	243.84	248.12	252.42
1.00	172.34	175.81	179.31	182.85	186.41	190.01	193.64	197.30	200.99	204.71	208.45	212.23	216.03	219.86	223.71	227.60
2.00	155.97	159.11	162.28	165.48	168.71	171.96	175.25	178.56	181.90	185.26	188.66	192.07	195.51	198.98	202.47	205.98
3.00	141.68	144.53	147.41	150.32	153.25	156.21	159.19	162.20	165.24	168.29	171.37	174.48	177.60	180.75	183.92	187.11
4.00	129.17	131.77	134.40	137.05	139.72	142.42	145.14	147.88	150.65	153.44	156.24	159.07	161.92	164.79	167.68	170.59
4.25	126.29	128.84	131.40	134.00	136.61	139.25	141.91	144.59	147.29	150.02	152.76	155.53	158.31	161.12	163.95	166.79
4.50	123.51	125.99	128.50	131.04	133.59	136.17	138.77	141.40	144.04	146.71	149.39	152.10	154.82	157.56	160.33	163.11
4.75	120.81	123.24	125.70	128.17	130.68	133.20	135.74	138.31	140.89	143.50	146.13	148.77	151.44	154.12	156.82	159.54
5.00	118.19	120.57	122.98	125.40	127.85	130.32	132.81	135.32	137.85	140.40	142.97	145.55	148.16	150.79	153.43	156.09
5.25	115.66	117.99	120.34	122.72	125.11	127.53	129.96	132.42	134.89	137.39	139.90	142.44	144.99	147.56	150.15	152.75
5.50	113.21	115.49	117.79	120.11	122.46	124.82	127.21	129.61	132.03	134.48	136.94	139.42	141.91	144.43	146.96	149.51
5.75	110.83	113.07	115.32	117.59	119.89	122.20	124.54	126.89	129.26	131.65	134.06	136.49	138.93	141.40	143.88	146.37
6.00	108.53	110.72	112.92	115.15	117.40	119.66	121.95	124.25	126.58	128.92	131.28	133.65	136.05	138.46	140.89	143.33
6.25	106.30	108.44	110.60	112.78	114.98	117.20	119.44	121.70	123.97	126.27	128.58	130.90	133.25	135.61	137.99	140.38
6.50	104.13	106.23	108.35	110.48	112.64	114.81	117.01	119.22	121.45	123.69	125.96	128.24	130.54	132.85	135.18	137.52
6.75	102.04	104.09	106.16	108.26	110.37	112.50	114.65	116.82	119.00	121.20	123.42	125.65	127.91	130.17	132.46	134.75
7.00	100.00	102.01	104.05	106.10	108.17	110.26	112.36	114.49	116.63	118.78	120.96	123.15	125.35	127.58	129.81	132.07
7.25	98.03	100.00	101.99	104.00	106.03	108.08	110.14	112.23	114.32	116.44	118.57	120.72	122.88	125.06	127.25	129.46
7.50	96.11	98.05	100.00	101.97	103.96	105.97	107.99	110.03	112.09	114.16	116.25	118.36	120.48	122.61	124.76	126.93
7.75	94.25	96.15	98.07	100.00	101.95	103.92	105.90	107.91	109.92	111.96	114.01	116.07	118.15	120.24	122.35	124.47
8.00	92.45	94.31	96.19	98.09	100.00	101.93	103.88	105.84	107.82	109.81	111.82	113.85	115.89	117.94	120.01	122.09
8.25	90.70	92.52	94.37	96.23	98.11	100.00	101.91	103.84	105.78	107.73	109.71	111.69	113.69	115.71	117.74	119.78
8.50	89.00	90.79	92.60	94.43	96.27	98.13	100.00	101.89	103.79	105.72	107.65	109.60	111.56	113.54	115.53	117.53
8.75	87.35	89.11	90.88	92.67	94.48	96.31	98.15	100.00	101.87	103.75	105.65	107.57	109.49	111.43	113.39	115.35
9.00	85.74	87.47	89.21	90.97	92.75	94.54	96.34	98.16	100.00	101.85	103.71	105.59	107.48	109.39	111.31	113.24
9.25	84.19	85.88	87.59	89.32	91.06	92.82	94.59	96.38	98.18	100.00	101.83	103.67	105.53	107.40	109.29	111.18
9.50	82.67	84.34	86.02	87.71	89.43	91.15	92.89	94.65	96.42	98.20	100.00	101.81	103.63	105.47	107.32	109.18
9.75	81.20	82.84	84.49	86.15	87.84	89.53	91.24	92.97	94.70	96.46	98.22	100.00	101.79	103.60	105.41	107.24
10.00	79.77	81.38	83.00	84.64	86.29	87.96	89.64	91.33	93.04	94.76	96.49	98.24	100.00	101.77	103.56	105.35
10.25	78.38	79.96	81.56	83.16	84.79	86.42	88.07	89.74	91.42	93.11	94.81	96.53	98.26	100.00	101.75	103.52
10.50	77.03	78.58	80.15	81.73	83.33	84.93	86.56	88.19	89.84	91.50	93.18	94.87	96.57	98.28	100.00	101.73
10.75	75.72	77.24	78.78	80.34	81.91	83.49	85.08	86.69	88.31	89.94	91.59	93.25	94.92	96.60	98.29	100.00
11.00	74.44	75.94	77.45	78.98	80.52	82.08	83.65	85.23	86.82	88.43	90.04	91.67	93.32	94.97	96.64	98.31
11.25	73.20	74.67	76.16	77.66	79.18	80.71	82.25	83.80	85.37	86.95	88.54	90.14	91.76	93.39	95.02	96.67
11.50	71.99	73.44	74.90	76.38	77.87	79.37	80.89	82.42	83.96	85.51	87.08	88.65	90.24	91.84	93.45	95.07
11.75	70.81	72.24	73.68	75.13	76.60	78.08	79.57	81.07	82.59	84.11	85.65	87.21	88.77	90.34	91.93	93.52
12.00	69.67	71.07	72.49	73.92	75.36	76.81	78.28	79.76	81.25	82.75	84.27	85.79	87.33	88.88	90.44	92.01
12.25	68.55	69.93	71.33	72.73	74.15	75.58	77.03	78.48	79.95	81.43	82.92	84.42	85.93	87.46	88.99	90.53
12.50	67.47	68.83	70.20	71.58	72.98	74.39	75.81	77.24	78.68	80.14	81.61	83.08	84.57	86.07	87.58	89.10
12.75	66.41	67.75	69.10	70.46	71.83	73.22	74.62	76.03	77.45	78.88	80.33	81.78	83.25	84.72	86.21	87.70
13.00	65.38	66.70	68.02	69.37	70.72	72.08	73.46	74.85	76.25	77.66	79.08	80.51	81.96	83.41	84.87	86.34
13.25	64.38	65.67	66.98	68.30	69.63	70.98	72.33	73.70	75.08	76.47	77.87	79.28	80.70	82.13	83.57	85.02
13.50	63.40	64.67	65.96	67.26	68.58	69.90	71.24	72.58	73.94	75.31	76.68	78.07	79.47	80.88	82.30	83.73
13.75	62.44	63.70	64.97	66.25	67.55	68.85	70.16	71.49	72.83	74.17	75.53	76.90	78.28	79.66	81.06	82.47
14.00	61.52	62.75	64.01	65.27	66.54	67.83	69.12	70.43	71.74	73.07	74.41	75.76	77.11	78.48	79.86	81.24
14.25	60.61	61.83	63.06	64.31	65.56	66.83	68.10	69.39	70.69	72.00	73.31	74.64	75.98	77.32	78.68	80.05
14.50	59.73	60.93	62.14	63.37	64.61	65.85	67.11	68.38	69.66	70.95	72.25	73.55	74.87	76.20	77.53	78.88
14.75	58.87	60.05	61.25	62.46	63.67	64.90	66.14	67.39	68.65	69.92	71.20	72.49	73.79	75.10	76.42	77.74
15.00	58.03	59.19	60.37	61.57	62.77	63.98	65.20	66.43	67.67	68.93	70.19	71.46	72.74	74.03	75.33	76.63
15.25	57.21	58.36	59.52	60.70	61.88	63.07	64.28	65.49	66.72	67.95	69.20	70.45	71.71	72.98	74.26	75.55
15.50	56.41	57.54	58.69	59.85	61.01	62.19	63.38	64.58	65.79	67.00	68.23	69.46	70.71	71.96	73.22	74.49
15.75	55.63	56.75	57.88	59.02	60.17	61.33	62.50	63.68	64.88	66.08	67.29	68.50	69.73	70.97	72.21	73.46
16.00	54.87	55.97	57.09	58.21	59.35	60.49	61.65	62.81	63.99	65.17	66.36	67.57	68.78	69.99	71.22	72.46
16.25	54.12	55.21	56.31	57.42	58.54	59.67	60.81	61.96	63.12	64.29	65.46	66.65	67.84	69.05	70.26	71.48
16.50	53.40	54.47	55.56	56.65	57.76	58.87	60.00	61.13	62.27	63.43	64.59	65.76	66.93	68.12	69.31	70.52
16.75	52.69	53.75	54.82	55.90	56.99	58.09	59.20	60.32	61.45	62.58	63.73	64.88	66.04	67.22	68.39	69.58
17.00	51.99	53.04	54.10	55.16	56.24	57.33	58.42	59.53	60.64	61.76	62.89	64.03	65.18	66.33	67.49	68.67
17.25	51.32	52.35	53.39	54.45	55.51	56.58	57.66	58.75	59.85	60.96	62.07	63.20	64.33	65.47	66.62	67.77
17.50	50.66	51.68	52.71	53.74	54.79	55.85	56.92	57.99	59.08	60.17	61.27	62.38	63.50	64.62	65.76	66.90
17.75	50.01	51.02	52.03	53.06	54.09	55.14	56.19	57.25	58.32	59.40	60.49	61.59	62.69	63.80	64.92	66.05
18.00	49.38	50.37	51.38	52.39	53.41	54.44	55.48	56.53	57.59	58.65	59.73	60.81	61.90	62.99	64.10	65.21
18.25	48.76	49.74	50.73	51.73	52.74	53.76	54.79	55.82	56.87	57.92	58.98	60.05	61.12	62.21	63.30	64.40
18.50	48.16	49.13	50.11	51.09	52.09	53.10	54.11	55.13	56.16	57.20	58.25	59.30	60.37	61.44	62.51	63.60
18.75	47.57	48.52	49.49	50.47	51.45	52.45	53.45	54.46	55.48	56.50	57.54	58.58	59.63	60.68	61.75	62.82
19.00	46.99	47.94	48.89	49.85	50.83	51.81	52.80	53.80	54.80	55.82	56.84	57.87	58.90	59.95	61.00	62.06
20.00	44.80	45.70	46.61	47.53	48.46	49.40	50.34	51.29	52.25	53.22	54.19	55.17	56.16	57.16	58.16	59.17
25.00	36.21	36.93	37.67	38.41	39.16	39.92	40.68	41.45	42.22	43.01	43.79	44.59	45.38	46.19	47.00	47.81
30.00	30.28	30.89	31.50	32.13	32.75	33.38	34.02	34.66	35.31	35.97	36.62	37.29	37.96	38.63	39.31	39.99

Description: This table shows the yield to maturity of a mortgage purchased at the price shown in the index.

Example: The yield to maturity of a 10.75 %, 21 year mortgage at a price of 111.00 is 9.27 %.

INTEREST RATE, %

PRICE	7.00%	7.25%	7.50%	7.75%	8.00%	8.25%	8.50%	8.75%	9.00%	9.25%	9.50%	9.75%	10.00%	10.25%	10.50%	10.75%
165	1.43	1.63	1.83	2.02	2.22	2.42	2.62	2.81	3.01	3.21	3.40	3.59	3.79	3.98	4.17	4.37
160	1.74	1.94	2.14	2.34	2.54	2.74	2.94	3.14	3.34	3.54	3.73	3.93	4.13	4.32	4.52	4.71
155	2.06	2.26	2.47	2.67	2.87	3.08	3.28	3.48	3.68	3.88	4.08	4.28	4.48	4.68	4.88	5.08
150	2.40	2.60	2.81	3.02	3.22	3.43	3.63	3.84	4.04	4.25	4.45	4.65	4.85	5.06	5.26	5.46
145	2.75	2.96	3.17	3.38	3.59	3.80	4.01	4.21	4.42	4.63	4.83	5.04	5.24	5.45	5.65	5.86
140	3.12	3.34	3.55	3.76	3.97	4.18	4.40	4.61	4.82	5.03	5.24	5.45	5.65	5.86	6.07	6.28
135	3.51	3.73	3.95	4.16	4.38	4.59	4.81	5.02	5.24	5.45	5.66	5.88	6.09	6.30	6.51	6.72
130	3.92	4.15	4.37	4.58	4.80	5.02	5.24	5.46	5.68	5.90	6.11	6.33	6.55	6.76	6.98	7.19
125	4.36	4.58	4.81	5.03	5.26	5.48	5.70	5.92	6.15	6.37	6.59	6.81	7.03	7.25	7.47	7.69
122	4.63	4.86	5.09	5.31	5.54	5.76	5.99	6.21	6.44	6.66	6.89	7.11	7.34	7.56	7.78	8.00
121	4.73	4.95	5.18	5.41	5.64	5.86	6.09	6.31	6.54	6.77	6.99	7.22	7.44	7.66	7.89	8.11
120	4.82	5.05	5.28	5.51	5.73	5.96	6.19	6.42	6.64	6.87	7.09	7.32	7.55	7.77	8.00	8.22
119	4.92	5.15	5.38	5.60	5.83	6.06	6.29	6.52	6.75	6.97	7.20	7.43	7.65	7.88	8.11	8.33
118	5.01	5.24	5.47	5.70	5.93	6.16	6.39	6.62	6.85	7.08	7.31	7.53	7.76	7.99	8.22	8.44
117	5.11	5.34	5.57	5.80	6.04	6.27	6.50	6.73	6.96	7.18	7.41	7.64	7.87	8.10	8.33	8.56
116	5.21	5.44	5.68	5.91	6.14	6.37	6.60	6.83	7.06	7.29	7.52	7.75	7.98	8.21	8.44	8.67
115	5.31	5.54	5.78	6.01	6.24	6.48	6.71	6.94	7.17	7.40	7.63	7.86	8.10	8.33	8.56	8.79
114	5.41	5.65	5.88	6.12	6.35	6.58	6.82	7.05	7.28	7.51	7.75	7.98	8.21	8.44	8.67	8.90
113	5.52	5.75	5.99	6.22	6.46	6.69	6.92	7.16	7.39	7.63	7.86	8.09	8.33	8.56	8.79	9.02
112	5.62	5.86	6.09	6.33	6.56	6.80	7.04	7.27	7.51	7.74	7.97	8.21	8.44	8.68	8.91	9.14
111	5.73	5.96	6.20	6.44	6.67	6.91	7.15	7.38	7.62	7.86	8.09	8.33	8.56	8.80	9.03	9.27
110	5.83	6.07	6.31	6.55	6.79	7.02	7.26	7.50	7.74	7.97	8.21	8.45	8.68	8.92	9.16	9.39
109	5.94	6.18	6.42	6.66	6.90	7.14	7.38	7.62	7.85	8.09	8.33	8.57	8.81	9.04	9.28	9.52
108	6.05	6.29	6.53	6.77	7.01	7.25	7.49	7.73	7.97	8.21	8.45	8.69	8.93	9.17	9.41	9.65
107	6.17	6.41	6.65	6.89	7.13	7.37	7.61	7.85	8.09	8.34	8.58	8.82	9.06	9.30	9.54	9.78
106	6.28	6.52	6.76	7.01	7.25	7.49	7.73	7.98	8.22	8.46	8.70	8.94	9.18	9.43	9.67	9.91
105	6.39	6.64	6.88	7.13	7.37	7.61	7.86	8.10	8.34	8.59	8.83	9.07	9.31	9.56	9.80	10.04
104	6.51	6.76	7.00	7.25	7.49	7.74	7.98	8.22	8.47	8.71	8.96	9.20	9.45	9.69	9.93	10.18
103	6.63	6.88	7.12	7.37	7.61	7.86	8.11	8.35	8.60	8.84	9.09	9.33	9.58	9.83	10.07	10.32
102	6.75	7.00	7.24	7.49	7.74	7.99	8.23	8.48	8.73	8.98	9.22	9.47	9.72	9.96	10.21	10.46
101	6.87	7.12	7.37	7.62	7.87	8.11	8.36	8.61	8.86	9.11	9.36	9.61	9.85	10.10	10.35	10.60
100	7.00	7.25	7.50	7.75	8.00	8.25	8.50	8.75	9.00	9.25	9.50	9.75	10.00	10.25	10.50	10.75
99	7.12	7.37	7.62	7.87	8.13	8.38	8.63	8.88	9.13	9.38	9.63	9.89	10.14	10.39	10.64	10.89
98	7.25	7.50	7.75	8.01	8.26	8.51	8.76	9.02	9.27	9.52	9.78	10.03	10.28	10.54	10.79	11.04
97	7.38	7.63	7.89	8.14	8.39	8.65	8.90	9.16	9.41	9.67	9.92	10.18	10.43	10.68	10.94	11.19
96	7.51	7.77	8.02	8.28	8.53	8.79	9.04	9.30	9.56	9.81	10.07	10.32	10.58	10.84	11.09	11.35
95	7.64	7.90	8.16	8.41	8.67	8.93	9.19	9.44	9.70	9.96	10.22	10.47	10.73	10.99	11.25	11.51
94	7.78	8.04	8.30	8.56	8.81	9.07	9.33	9.59	9.85	10.11	10.37	10.63	10.89	11.15	11.41	11.67
93	7.92	8.18	8.44	8.70	8.96	9.22	9.48	9.74	10.00	10.26	10.52	10.78	11.05	11.31	11.57	11.83
92	8.06	8.32	8.58	8.84	9.11	9.37	9.63	9.89	10.15	10.42	10.68	10.94	11.21	11.47	11.73	12.00
91	8.20	8.46	8.73	8.99	9.25	9.52	9.78	10.05	10.31	10.57	10.84	11.10	11.37	11.63	11.90	12.17
90	8.35	8.61	8.88	9.14	9.41	9.67	9.94	10.20	10.47	10.74	11.00	11.27	11.54	11.80	12.07	12.34
89	8.49	8.76	9.03	9.29	9.56	9.83	10.10	10.36	10.63	10.90	11.17	11.44	11.71	11.97	12.24	12.51
88	8.65	8.91	9.18	9.45	9.72	9.99	10.26	10.53	10.80	11.07	11.34	11.61	11.88	12.15	12.42	12.69
87	8.80	9.07	9.34	9.61	9.88	10.15	10.42	10.69	10.96	11.24	11.51	11.78	12.05	12.33	12.60	12.87
86	8.95	9.23	9.50	9.77	10.04	10.32	10.59	10.86	11.14	11.41	11.68	11.96	12.23	12.51	12.78	13.06
85	9.11	9.39	9.66	9.93	10.21	10.48	10.76	11.03	11.31	11.59	11.86	12.14	12.42	12.69	12.97	13.25
84	9.28	9.55	9.83	10.10	10.38	10.66	10.93	11.21	11.49	11.77	12.04	12.32	12.60	12.88	13.16	13.44
83	9.44	9.72	10.00	10.27	10.55	10.83	11.11	11.39	11.67	11.95	12.23	12.51	12.79	13.07	13.36	13.64
82	9.61	9.89	10.17	10.45	10.73	11.01	11.29	11.57	11.85	12.14	12.42	12.70	12.99	13.27	13.55	13.84
81	9.78	10.06	10.34	10.63	10.91	11.19	11.47	11.76	12.04	12.33	12.61	12.90	13.18	13.47	13.76	14.04
80	9.95	10.24	10.52	10.81	11.09	11.38	11.66	11.95	12.24	12.52	12.81	13.10	13.39	13.68	13.96	14.25
79	10.13	10.42	10.71	10.99	11.28	11.57	11.85	12.14	12.43	12.72	13.01	13.30	13.59	13.88	14.18	14.47
78	10.32	10.60	10.89	11.18	11.47	11.76	12.05	12.34	12.63	12.92	13.22	13.51	13.80	14.10	14.39	14.69
77	10.50	10.79	11.08	11.37	11.67	11.96	12.25	12.54	12.84	13.13	13.43	13.72	14.02	14.32	14.61	14.91
76	10.69	10.98	11.28	11.57	11.86	12.16	12.46	12.75	13.05	13.34	13.64	13.94	14.24	14.54	14.84	15.14
75	10.89	11.18	11.48	11.77	12.07	12.37	12.66	12.96	13.26	13.56	13.86	14.16	14.47	14.77	15.07	15.37
74	11.08	11.38	11.68	11.98	12.28	12.58	12.88	13.18	13.48	13.78	14.09	14.39	14.70	15.00	15.31	15.61
73	11.29	11.59	11.89	12.19	12.49	12.79	13.10	13.40	13.71	14.01	14.32	14.62	14.93	15.24	15.55	15.86
70	11.92	12.23	12.54	12.85	13.16	13.47	13.78	14.10	14.41	14.73	15.04	15.36	15.68	15.99	16.31	16.63
65	13.09	13.41	13.74	14.06	14.39	14.72	15.05	15.38	15.71	16.04	16.38	16.71	17.05	17.38	17.72	18.06
60	14.42	14.76	15.10	15.45	15.80	16.14	16.49	16.84	17.20	17.55	17.90	18.26	18.62	18.98	19.34	19.70
55	15.95	16.32	16.68	17.05	17.42	17.79	18.17	18.54	18.92	19.30	19.68	20.06	20.45	20.83	21.22	21.61
50	17.75	18.14	18.54	18.94	19.33	19.74	20.14	20.55	20.95	21.36	21.78	22.19	22.61	23.03	23.45	23.87
45	19.90	20.33	20.76	21.19	21.63	22.07	22.51	22.96	23.40	23.85	24.30	24.76	25.21	25.67	26.14	26.60
40	22.54	23.01	23.49	23.97	24.46	24.94	25.43	25.93	26.42	26.92	27.43	27.93	28.44	28.95	29.47	29.99
35	25.88	26.41	26.95	27.49	28.04	28.59	29.15	29.70	30.27	30.83	31.40	31.98	32.55	33.14	33.72	34.31
30	30.28	30.89	31.52	32.14	32.78	33.41	34.06	34.70	35.35	36.01	36.67	37.34	38.01	38.69	39.37	40.05

MORTGAGE PRICE

21 YEARS

Description: This table shows the price to pay for a monthly payment mortgage loan at the yield rate.

Example: The price of a 15.00 %, 21 year mortgage loan to yield 8.00 % to maturity is $ 159.32.

INTEREST RATE, %

YIELD	11.00%	11.25%	11.50%	11.75%	12.00%	12.25%	12.50%	12.75%	13.00%	13.25%	13.50%	13.75%	14.00%	14.25%	14.50%	15.00%
0.00	256.76	261.12	265.50	269.91	274.35	278.82	283.30	287.81	292.35	296.91	301.49	306.09	310.71	315.35	320.01	329.39
1.00	231.50	235.43	239.39	243.37	247.37	251.39	255.44	259.51	263.59	267.70	271.83	275.98	280.15	284.33	288.54	297.00
2.00	209.51	213.07	216.65	220.25	223.87	227.52	231.18	234.86	238.56	242.28	246.01	249.77	253.54	257.33	261.13	268.79
3.00	190.32	193.55	196.80	200.07	203.36	206.67	210.00	213.34	216.70	220.08	223.48	226.89	230.31	233.75	237.21	244.16
4.00	173.52	176.47	179.43	182.4i	185.41	188.43	191.46	194.51	197.57	200.65	203.75	206.86	209.98	213.12	216.27	222.61
4.25	169.65	172.53	175.43	178.35	181.28	184.23	187.19	190.17	193.17	196.18	199.21	202.25	205.30	208.37	211.45	217.65
4.50	165.91	168.73	171.56	174.41	177.28	180.16	183.06	185.98	188.91	191.85	194.81	197.78	200.77	203.77	206.78	212.84
4.75	162.28	165.04	167.81	170.60	173.41	176.23	179.06	181.91	184.78	187.66	190.55	193.46	196.38	199.32	202.26	208.19
5.00	158.77	161.47	164.18	166.91	169.65	172.41	175.19	177.98	180.78	183.60	186.43	189.28	192.14	195.01	197.89	203.69
5.25	155.37	158.01	160.66	163.33	166.02	168.72	171.44	174.17	176.91	179.67	182.44	185.22	188.02	190.83	193.65	199.33
5.50	152.08	154.66	157.26	159.87	162.50	165.14	167.80	170.47	173.16	175.86	178.57	181.30	184.03	186.78	189.54	195.10
5.75	148.88	151.41	153.96	156.52	159.09	161.68	164.28	166.89	169.52	172.17	174.82	177.49	180.17	182.86	185.57	191.01
6.00	145.79	148.27	150.76	153.26	155.78	158.32	160.87	163.43	166.00	168.59	171.19	173.80	176.43	179.06	181.71	187.04
6.25	142.79	145.22	147.66	150.11	152.58	155.06	157.56	160.07	162.59	165.12	167.67	170.23	172.80	175.38	177.97	183.19
6.50	139.89	142.26	144.65	147.05	149.47	151.90	154.35	156.81	159.28	161.76	164.25	166.76	169.28	171.81	174.35	179.46
6.75	137.07	139.39	141.74	144.09	146.46	148.84	151.24	153.65	156.07	158.50	160.94	163.40	165.87	168.35	170.83	175.84
7.00	134.33	136.61	138.91	141.22	143.54	145.87	148.22	150.58	152.95	155.34	157.73	160.14	162.56	164.99	167.43	172.34
7.25	131.68	133.92	136.17	138.43	140.70	142.99	145.30	147.61	149.93	152.27	154.62	156.98	159.35	161.73	164.12	168.93
7.50	129.11	131.30	133.51	135.72	137.96	140.20	142.46	144.72	147.01	149.30	151.60	153.91	156.24	158.57	160.92	165.63
7.75	126.61	128.76	130.92	133.10	135.29	137.49	139.70	141.93	144.16	146.41	148.67	150.94	153.22	155.50	157.80	162.43
8.00	124.19	126.30	128.42	130.55	132.70	134.86	137.03	139.21	141.40	143.61	145.82	148.05	150.28	152.53	154.78	159.32
8.25	121.84	123.90	125.99	128.08	130.19	132.30	134.43	136.57	138.73	140.89	143.06	145.24	147.44	149.64	151.85	156.30
8.50	119.55	121.58	123.62	125.68	127.75	129.82	131.91	134.01	136.13	138.25	140.38	142.52	144.67	146.84	149.01	153.37
8.75	117.33	119.33	121.33	123.35	125.38	127.42	129.47	131.53	133.60	135.68	137.78	139.88	141.99	144.11	146.24	150.53
9.00	115.18	117.14	119.10	121.08	123.08	125.08	127.09	129.11	131.15	133.19	135.25	137.31	139.38	141.47	143.56	147.77
9.25	113.09	115.01	116.94	118.88	120.84	122.81	124.78	126.77	128.77	130.77	132.79	134.82	136.85	138.90	140.95	145.08
9.50	111.06	112.94	114.84	116.75	118.67	120.60	122.54	124.49	126.45	128.42	130.40	132.39	134.39	136.40	138.42	142.48
9.75	109.08	110.93	112.80	114.67	116.56	118.45	120.36	122.28	124.20	126.14	128.08	130.04	132.00	133.97	135.96	139.94
10.00	107.16	108.98	110.81	112.65	114.51	116.37	118.24	120.12	122.02	123.92	125.83	127.75	129.68	131.62	133.56	137.48
10.25	105.30	107.08	108.88	110.69	112.51	114.34	116.18	118.03	119.89	121.76	123.64	125.53	127.42	129.32	131.24	135.08
10.50	103.48	105.24	107.01	108.78	110.57	112.37	114.18	116.00	117.83	119.66	121.51	123.36	125.23	127.10	128.98	132.76
10.75	101.72	103.44	105.18	106.93	108.69	110.46	112.23	114.02	115.82	117.62	119.44	121.26	123.09	124.93	126.78	130.49
11.00	100.00	101.70	103.41	105.12	106.85	108.59	110.34	112.10	113.86	115.64	117.42	119.21	121.01	122.82	124.64	128.29
11.25	98.33	100.00	101.68	103.37	105.07	106.78	108.50	110.23	111.96	113.71	115.46	117.22	118.99	120.77	122.56	126.15
11.50	96.71	98.35	100.00	101.66	103.33	105.01	106.70	108.40	110.11	111.83	113.55	115.29	117.03	118.78	120.53	124.06
11.75	95.12	96.74	98.37	100.00	101.64	103.30	104.96	106.63	108.31	110.00	111.70	113.40	115.11	116.83	118.56	122.04
12.00	93.59	95.18	96.77	98.38	100.00	101.63	103.26	104.91	106.56	108.22	109.89	111.57	113.25	114.94	116.64	120.06
12.25	92.09	93.65	95.22	96.81	98.40	100.00	101.61	103.23	104.85	106.49	108.13	109.78	111.44	113.10	114.78	118.14
12.50	90.63	92.17	93.72	95.27	96.84	98.42	100.00	101.59	103.19	104.80	106.42	108.04	109.67	111.31	112.96	116.27
12.75	89.21	90.72	92.25	93.78	95.32	96.87	98.43	100.00	101.58	103.16	104.75	106.35	107.95	109.57	111.19	114.45
13.00	87.83	89.32	90.82	92.33	93.84	95.37	96.91	98.45	100.00	101.56	103.13	104.70	106.28	107.87	109.46	112.67
13.25	86.48	87.95	89.42	90.91	92.40	93.91	95.42	96.94	98.47	100.00	101.54	103.09	104.65	106.21	107.78	110.94
13.50	85.16	86.61	88.06	89.53	91.00	92.48	93.97	95.47	96.97	98.48	100.00	101.53	103.06	104.60	106.15	109.26
13.75	83.88	85.31	86.74	88.18	89.63	91.09	92.56	94.03	95.51	97.00	98.50	100.00	101.51	103.03	104.55	107.61
14.00	82.64	84.04	85.45	86.87	88.30	89.74	91.18	92.63	94.09	95.56	97.03	98.51	100.00	101.49	102.99	106.01
14.25	81.42	82.80	84.19	85.59	87.00	88.41	89.84	91.27	92.71	94.15	95.60	97.06	98.53	100.00	101.48	104.45
14.50	80.23	81.60	82.97	84.35	85.73	87.13	88.53	89.94	91.36	92.78	94.21	95.65	97.09	98.54	100.00	102.93
14.75	79.08	80.42	81.77	83.13	84.50	85.87	87.25	88.64	90.04	91.44	92.85	94.27	95.69	97.12	98.56	101.45
15.00	77.95	79.27	80.60	81.94	83.29	84.65	86.01	87.38	88.75	90.14	91.53	92.92	94.33	95.74	97.15	100.00
15.25	76.85	78.15	79.46	80.79	82.11	83.45	84.79	86.14	87.50	88.86	90.23	91.61	93.00	94.38	95.78	98.59
15.50	75.77	77.06	78.35	79.66	80.97	82.28	83.61	84.94	86.28	87.62	88.97	90.33	91.70	93.07	94.44	97.21
15.75	74.72	75.99	77.27	78.55	79.85	81.14	82.45	83.76	85.08	86.41	87.74	89.08	90.43	91.78	93.13	95.86
16.00	73.70	74.95	76.21	77.48	78.75	80.03	81.32	82.62	83.92	85.23	86.54	87.86	89.19	90.52	91.86	94.55
16.25	72.70	73.94	75.18	76.43	77.69	78.95	80.22	81.50	82.78	84.07	85.37	86.67	87.98	89.29	90.61	93.27
16.50	71.73	72.94	74.17	75.40	76.64	77.89	79.14	80.40	81.67	82.94	84.22	85.51	86.80	88.10	89.40	92.02
16.75	70.77	71.98	73.19	74.40	75.62	76.86	78.09	79.34	80.59	81.84	83.10	84.37	85.65	86.93	88.21	90.80
17.00	69.84	71.03	72.22	73.42	74.63	75.84	77.07	78.29	79.53	80.77	82.01	83.26	84.52	85.78	87.05	89.60
17.25	68.93	70.11	71.28	72.47	73.66	74.86	76.06	77.27	78.49	79.71	80.94	82.18	83.42	84.67	85.92	88.44
17.50	68.05	69.20	70.36	71.53	72.71	73.89	75.08	76.28	77.48	78.69	79.90	81.12	82.35	83.58	84.81	87.30
17.75	67.18	68.32	69.47	70.62	71.78	72.95	74.12	75.31	76.49	77.68	78.88	80.09	81.30	82.51	83.73	86.18
18.00	66.33	67.46	68.59	69.73	70.88	72.03	73.19	74.35	75.53	76.70	77.89	79.07	80.27	81.47	82.67	85.10
18.25	65.50	66.61	67.73	68.86	69.99	71.13	72.27	73.42	74.58	75.74	76.91	78.09	79.26	80.45	81.64	84.03
18.50	64.69	65.79	66.89	68.01	69.12	70.25	71.38	72.52	73.66	74.81	75.96	77.12	78.28	79.45	80.63	82.99
18.75	63.90	64.98	66.07	67.17	68.28	69.39	70.50	71.63	72.75	73.89	75.03	76.17	77.32	78.48	79.64	81.97
19.00	63.12	64.19	65.27	66.36	67.45	68.54	69.65	70.76	71.87	72.99	74.12	75.25	76.39	77.53	78.67	80.98
20.00	60.18	61.21	62.23	63.27	64.31	65.35	66.41	67.46	68.53	69.59	70.67	71.75	72.83	73.92	75.01	77.21
25.00	48.63	49.46	50.29	51.13	51.97	52.81	53.66	54.52	55.38	56.24	57.11	57.98	58.85	59.73	60.62	62.39
30.00	40.67	41.36	42.06	42.76	43.46	44.17	44.88	45.59	46.31	47.03	47.76	48.49	49.22	49.96	50.69	52.18

Description: This table shows the yield to maturity of a mortgage purchased at the price shown in the index.

Example: The yield to maturity of a 15.00 %, 21 year mortgage at a price of 125.00 is 11.38 %.

INTEREST RATE, %

PRICE	11.00%	11.25%	11.50%	11.75%	12.00%	12.25%	12.50%	12.75%	13.00%	13.25%	13.50%	13.75%	14.00%	14.25%	14.50%	15.00%
250	.25	.41	.57	.73	.89	1.05	1.21	1.36	1.52	1.68	1.83	1.99	2.14	2.29	2.44	2.75
240	.64	.81	.97	1.13	1.29	1.46	1.62	1.77	1.93	2.09	2.25	2.41	2.56	2.72	2.87	3.18
230	1.06	1.23	1.39	1.56	1.72	1.88	2.05	2.21	2.37	2.53	2.69	2.85	3.01	3.17	3.32	3.64
220	1.50	1.67	1.84	2.01	2.17	2.34	2.51	2.67	2.84	3.00	3.16	3.32	3.49	3.65	3.81	4.13
210	1.97	2.14	2.32	2.49	2.66	2.83	2.99	3.16	3.33	3.50	3.66	3.83	3.99	4.16	4.32	4.65
200	2.47	2.65	2.82	3.00	3.17	3.35	3.52	3.69	3.86	4.03	4.20	4.37	4.54	4.71	4.87	5.21
195	2.74	2.92	3.09	3.27	3.44	3.62	3.79	3.97	4.14	4.31	4.48	4.66	4.83	5.00	5.16	5.50
190	3.01	3.19	3.37	3.55	3.73	3.90	4.08	4.26	4.43	4.60	4.78	4.95	5.12	5.30	5.47	5.81
185	3.30	3.48	3.66	3.84	4.02	4.20	4.38	4.55	4.73	4.91	5.08	5.26	5.43	5.61	5.78	6.13
180	3.59	3.78	3.96	4.14	4.32	4.51	4.69	4.87	5.04	5.22	5.40	5.58	5.76	5.93	6.11	6.46
175	3.90	4.09	4.27	4.46	4.64	4.82	5.01	5.19	5.37	5.55	5.73	5.91	6.09	6.27	6.45	6.80
170	4.22	4.41	4.60	4.79	4.97	5.16	5.34	5.53	5.71	5.90	6.08	6.26	6.44	6.62	6.81	7.17
165	4.56	4.75	4.94	5.13	5.32	5.51	5.69	5.88	6.07	6.25	6.44	6.63	6.81	6.99	7.18	7.54
160	4.91	5.10	5.29	5.49	5.68	5.87	6.06	6.25	6.44	6.63	6.82	7.01	7.19	7.38	7.57	7.94
155	5.27	5.47	5.67	5.86	6.06	6.25	6.44	6.64	6.83	7.02	7.21	7.41	7.60	7.79	7.98	8.36
150	5.66	5.86	6.06	6.25	6.45	6.65	6.85	7.04	7.24	7.44	7.63	7.83	8.02	8.21	8.41	8.79
145	6.06	6.26	6.47	6.67	6.87	7.07	7.27	7.47	7.67	7.87	8.07	8.27	8.47	8.66	8.86	9.25
140	6.48	6.69	6.90	7.10	7.31	7.51	7.72	7.92	8.13	8.33	8.53	8.73	8.94	9.14	9.34	9.74
135	6.93	7.14	7.35	7.56	7.77	7.98	8.19	8.40	8.61	8.81	9.02	9.23	9.43	9.64	9.84	10.25
130	7.41	7.62	7.84	8.05	8.26	8.48	8.69	8.90	9.11	9.33	9.54	9.75	9.96	10.17	10.38	10.80
125	7.91	8.13	8.35	8.57	8.79	9.00	9.22	9.44	9.66	9.87	10.09	10.31	10.52	10.74	10.96	11.38
120	8.45	8.67	8.89	9.12	9.34	9.56	9.79	10.01	10.23	10.45	10.68	10.90	11.12	11.34	11.56	12.00
115	9.02	9.25	9.48	9.71	9.93	10.16	10.39	10.62	10.85	11.08	11.30	11.53	11.76	11.99	12.21	12.67
113	9.26	9.49	9.72	9.95	10.18	10.41	10.65	10.88	11.11	11.34	11.57	11.80	12.03	12.26	12.49	12.95
112	9.38	9.61	9.84	10.08	10.31	10.54	10.78	11.01	11.24	11.47	11.70	11.94	12.17	12.40	12.63	13.09
111	9.50	9.74	9.97	10.21	10.44	10.67	10.91	11.14	11.37	11.61	11.84	12.07	12.31	12.54	12.77	13.24
110	9.63	9.86	10.10	10.33	10.57	10.81	11.04	11.28	11.51	11.75	11.98	12.21	12.45	12.68	12.92	13.38
109	9.76	9.99	10.23	10.47	10.70	10.94	11.18	11.41	11.65	11.88	12.12	12.36	12.59	12.83	13.06	13.53
108	9.88	10.12	10.36	10.60	10.84	11.08	11.31	11.55	11.79	12.03	12.26	12.50	12.74	12.98	13.21	13.69
107	10.02	10.26	10.50	10.74	10.97	11.21	11.45	11.69	11.93	12.17	12.41	12.65	12.89	13.13	13.36	13.84
106	10.15	10.39	10.63	10.87	11.11	11.35	11.60	11.84	12.08	12.32	12.56	12.80	13.04	13.28	13.52	14.00
105	10.29	10.53	10.77	11.01	11.25	11.50	11.74	11.98	12.22	12.47	12.71	12.95	13.19	13.43	13.67	14.16
104	10.42	10.67	10.91	11.15	11.40	11.64	11.89	12.13	12.37	12.62	12.86	13.10	13.35	13.59	13.83	14.32
103	10.56	10.81	11.05	11.30	11.54	11.79	12.03	12.28	12.52	12.77	13.01	13.26	13.50	13.75	13.99	14.48
102	10.70	10.95	11.20	11.44	11.69	11.94	12.19	12.43	12.68	12.93	13.17	13.42	13.67	13.91	14.16	14.65
101	10.85	11.10	11.35	11.59	11.84	12.09	12.34	12.59	12.84	13.08	13.33	13.58	13.83	14.08	14.33	14.82
100	11.00	11.25	11.50	11.75	12.00	12.25	12.50	12.75	13.00	13.25	13.50	13.75	14.00	14.25	14.50	15.00
99	11.14	11.40	11.65	11.90	12.15	12.40	12.65	12.91	13.16	13.41	13.66	13.91	14.16	14.42	14.67	15.17
98	11.30	11.55	11.80	12.06	12.31	12.56	12.82	13.07	13.32	13.58	13.83	14.08	14.34	14.59	14.84	15.35
97	11.45	11.70	11.96	12.21	12.47	12.72	12.98	13.23	13.49	13.75	14.00	14.26	14.51	14.77	15.02	15.53
96	11.61	11.86	12.12	12.38	12.63	12.89	13.15	13.40	13.66	13.92	14.17	14.43	14.69	14.95	15.20	15.72
95	11.77	12.02	12.28	12.54	12.80	13.06	13.32	13.58	13.83	14.09	14.35	14.61	14.87	15.13	15.39	15.91
94	11.93	12.19	12.45	12.71	12.97	13.23	13.49	13.75	14.01	14.27	14.53	14.79	15.06	15.32	15.58	16.10
93	12.09	12.35	12.62	12.88	13.14	13.40	13.67	13.93	14.19	14.45	14.72	14.98	15.24	15.51	15.77	16.30
92	12.26	12.52	12.79	13.05	13.32	13.58	13.85	14.11	14.37	14.64	14.91	15.17	15.44	15.70	15.97	16.50
91	12.43	12.70	12.96	13.23	13.50	13.76	14.03	14.29	14.56	14.83	15.10	15.36	15.63	15.90	16.17	16.70
90	12.60	12.87	13.14	13.41	13.68	13.95	14.21	14.48	14.75	15.02	15.29	15.56	15.83	16.10	16.37	16.91
89	12.78	13.05	13.32	13.59	13.86	14.13	14.40	14.68	14.95	15.22	15.49	15.76	16.03	16.31	16.58	17.12
88	12.96	13.23	13.51	13.78	14.05	14.32	14.60	14.87	15.14	15.42	15.69	15.97	16.24	16.52	16.79	17.34
87	13.15	13.42	13.70	13.97	14.24	14.52	14.80	15.07	15.35	15.62	15.90	16.18	16.45	16.73	17.01	17.56
86	13.34	13.61	13.89	14.16	14.44	14.72	15.00	15.27	15.55	15.83	16.11	16.39	16.67	16.95	17.23	17.79
85	13.53	13.81	14.08	14.36	14.64	14.92	15.20	15.48	15.76	16.04	16.32	16.61	16.89	17.17	17.45	18.02
84	13.72	14.00	14.28	14.57	14.85	15.13	15.41	15.69	15.98	16.26	16.54	16.83	17.11	17.40	17.68	18.25
83	13.92	14.20	14.49	14.77	15.06	15.34	15.63	15.91	16.20	16.48	16.77	17.06	17.34	17.63	17.92	18.49
82	14.12	14.41	14.70	14.98	15.27	15.56	15.84	16.13	16.42	16.71	17.00	17.29	17.58	17.87	18.16	18.74
81	14.33	14.62	14.91	15.20	15.49	15.78	16.07	16.36	16.65	16.94	17.23	17.52	17.82	18.11	18.40	18.99
80	14.54	14.84	15.13	15.42	15.71	16.00	16.30	16.59	16.88	17.18	17.47	17.77	18.06	18.36	18.65	19.25
79	14.76	15.06	15.35	15.64	15.94	16.23	16.53	16.82	17.12	17.42	17.72	18.01	18.31	18.61	18.91	19.51
78	14.98	15.28	15.58	15.87	16.17	16.47	16.77	17.07	17.37	17.67	17.97	18.27	18.57	18.87	19.17	19.78
77	15.21	15.51	15.81	16.11	16.41	16.71	17.01	17.31	17.62	17.92	18.22	18.53	18.83	19.14	19.44	20.05
76	15.44	15.74	16.05	16.35	16.65	16.96	17.26	17.57	17.87	18.18	18.48	18.79	19.10	19.41	19.72	20.34
75	15.68	15.98	16.29	16.59	16.90	17.21	17.52	17.82	18.13	18.44	18.75	19.06	19.37	19.69	20.00	20.62
74	15.92	16.23	16.54	16.85	17.16	17.47	17.78	18.09	18.40	18.71	19.03	19.34	19.66	19.97	20.29	20.92
73	16.17	16.48	16.79	17.11	17.42	17.73	18.05	18.36	18.68	18.99	19.31	19.63	19.95	20.26	20.58	21.22
70	16.95	17.27	17.60	17.92	18.24	18.57	18.89	19.22	19.54	19.87	20.20	20.53	20.86	21.19	21.52	22.18
65	18.40	18.74	19.08	19.42	19.77	20.11	20.46	20.80	21.15	21.50	21.85	22.20	22.55	22.90	23.25	23.96
60	20.06	20.42	20.79	21.16	21.52	21.89	22.26	22.63	23.00	23.38	23.75	24.13	24.50	24.88	25.26	26.02
55	22.00	22.39	22.78	23.18	23.57	23.97	24.37	24.77	25.17	25.57	25.98	26.39	26.79	27.20	27.61	28.44

Description: This table shows the price to pay for a monthly payment mortgage loan at the yield rate.

Example: The price of a 6.75 %, 22 year mortgage loan to yield 8.00 % to maturity is $ 90.32.

INTEREST RATE, %

YIELD	0.00%	1.00%	2.00%	3.00%	4.00%	4.25%	4.50%	4.75%	5.00%	5.25%	5.50%	5.75%	6.00%	6.25%	6.50%	6.75%
0.00	100.00	111.44	123.69	136.72	150.53	154.10	157.71	161.37	165.07	168.82	172.62	176.45	180.33	184.25	188.22	192.22
1.00	89.73	100.00	110.99	122.68	135.07	138.27	141.51	144.80	148.12	151.49	154.89	158.33	161.81	165.33	168.89	172.48
2.00	80.85	90.10	100.00	110.54	121.70	124.58	127.50	130.46	133.46	136.49	139.56	142.66	145.79	148.96	152.17	155.40
3.00	73.14	81.51	90.47	100.00	110.10	112.71	115.35	118.03	120.73	123.48	126.25	129.06	131.89	134.76	137.66	140.59
4.00	66.43	74.04	82.17	90.83	100.00	102.37	104.77	107.20	109.66	112.15	114.67	117.22	119.80	122.40	125.04	127.70
4.25	64.89	72.32	80.27	88.73	97.68	100.00	102.35	104.72	107.12	109.56	112.02	114.51	117.03	119.57	122.14	124.74
4.50	63.41	70.66	78.43	86.69	95.45	97.71	100.00	102.32	104.67	107.05	109.45	111.88	114.34	116.83	119.34	121.88
4.75	61.97	69.06	76.65	84.73	93.28	95.49	97.73	100.00	102.30	104.62	106.97	109.35	111.75	114.18	116.64	119.12
5.00	60.58	67.51	74.93	82.83	91.19	93.35	95.54	97.76	100.00	102.27	104.57	106.89	109.24	111.62	114.02	116.44
5.25	59.23	66.01	73.27	80.99	89.16	91.28	93.42	95.58	97.78	100.00	102.25	104.52	106.82	109.14	111.49	113.86
5.50	57.93	64.56	71.66	79.21	87.20	89.27	91.36	93.48	95.63	97.80	100.00	102.22	104.47	106.74	109.04	111.36
5.75	56.67	63.16	70.10	77.49	85.31	87.33	89.38	91.45	93.55	95.68	97.83	100.00	102.20	104.42	106.67	108.94
6.00	55.45	61.80	68.59	75.82	83.47	85.45	87.46	89.48	91.54	93.62	95.72	97.85	100.00	102.17	104.37	106.59
6.25	54.27	60.48	67.13	74.20	81.70	83.63	85.59	87.58	89.59	91.63	93.68	95.77	97.87	100.00	102.15	104.32
6.50	53.13	59.21	65.72	72.64	79.98	81.87	83.79	85.74	87.70	89.70	91.71	93.75	95.81	97.89	100.00	102.13
6.75	52.02	57.98	64.35	71.13	78.31	80.17	82.05	83.95	85.88	87.83	89.80	91.80	93.82	95.86	97.92	100.00
7.00	50.95	56.78	63.02	69.66	76.70	78.51	80.36	82.22	84.11	86.02	87.95	89.91	91.88	93.88	95.90	97.94
7.25	49.91	55.63	61.74	68.24	75.13	76.91	78.72	80.54	82.39	84.27	86.16	88.07	90.01	91.97	93.94	95.94
7.50	48.91	54.50	60.49	66.87	73.62	75.36	77.13	78.92	80.73	82.57	84.42	86.30	88.19	90.11	92.05	94.01
7.75	47.93	53.42	59.29	65.53	72.15	73.86	75.59	77.35	79.12	80.92	82.74	84.58	86.44	88.31	90.21	92.13
8.00	46.99	52.36	58.12	64.24	70.73	72.40	74.10	75.82	77.56	79.32	81.10	82.91	84.73	86.57	88.43	90.32
8.25	46.07	51.34	56.98	62.99	69.35	70.99	72.65	74.34	76.05	77.77	79.52	81.29	83.08	84.88	86.71	88.55
8.50	45.18	50.35	55.88	61.77	68.01	69.62	71.25	72.91	74.58	76.27	77.99	79.72	81.47	83.24	85.04	86.84
8.75	44.32	49.39	54.82	60.59	66.71	68.29	69.89	71.51	73.16	74.82	76.50	78.20	79.92	81.66	83.41	85.19
9.00	43.48	48.46	53.78	59.45	65.45	67.00	68.57	70.16	71.77	73.40	75.05	76.72	78.41	80.11	81.84	83.58
9.25	42.67	47.55	52.78	58.34	64.23	65.75	67.29	68.85	70.43	72.03	73.65	75.29	76.94	78.62	80.31	82.02
9.50	41.88	46.67	51.80	57.26	63.04	64.54	66.05	67.58	69.13	70.70	72.29	73.90	75.52	77.17	78.82	80.50
9.75	41.11	45.82	50.85	56.21	61.89	63.36	64.84	66.35	67.87	69.41	70.97	72.55	74.14	75.76	77.38	79.03
10.00	40.37	44.99	49.94	55.20	60.77	62.21	63.67	65.15	66.64	68.16	69.69	71.24	72.80	74.39	75.99	77.60
10.25	39.65	44.19	49.04	54.21	59.68	61.10	62.53	63.98	65.45	66.94	68.44	69.96	71.50	73.06	74.63	76.22
10.50	38.95	43.41	48.18	53.25	58.63	60.02	61.43	62.85	64.30	65.76	67.23	68.73	70.24	71.77	73.31	74.87
10.75	38.27	42.65	47.33	52.32	57.61	58.97	60.35	61.75	63.17	64.61	66.06	67.53	69.01	70.51	72.03	73.56
11.00	37.61	41.91	46.52	51.42	56.61	57.95	59.31	60.69	62.08	63.49	64.92	66.36	67.82	69.29	70.78	72.29
11.25	36.96	41.19	45.72	50.54	55.64	56.96	58.30	59.65	61.02	62.40	63.81	65.22	66.66	68.11	69.57	71.05
11.50	36.34	40.50	44.95	49.68	54.70	56.00	57.31	58.64	59.99	61.35	62.73	64.12	65.53	66.96	68.40	69.85
11.75	35.73	39.82	44.20	48.85	53.79	55.06	56.35	57.66	58.98	60.32	61.68	63.05	64.43	65.84	67.25	68.68
12.00	35.14	39.16	43.46	48.05	52.90	54.15	55.42	56.71	58.01	59.32	60.66	62.01	63.37	64.75	66.14	67.55
12.25	34.57	38.52	42.75	47.26	52.03	53.26	54.51	55.78	57.06	58.35	59.66	60.99	62.33	63.69	65.06	66.44
12.50	34.01	37.90	42.06	46.49	51.19	52.40	53.63	54.87	56.13	57.41	58.70	60.00	61.32	62.66	64.00	65.37
12.75	33.46	37.29	41.39	45.75	50.37	51.56	52.77	54.00	55.24	56.49	57.76	59.04	60.34	61.65	62.98	64.32
13.00	32.93	36.70	40.73	45.03	49.57	50.75	51.94	53.14	54.36	55.60	56.85	58.11	59.39	60.68	61.98	63.30
13.25	32.42	36.13	40.10	44.32	48.79	49.95	51.12	52.31	53.51	54.73	55.96	57.20	58.46	59.73	61.01	62.31
13.50	31.91	35.57	39.47	43.63	48.04	49.18	50.33	51.50	52.68	53.88	55.09	56.31	57.55	58.80	60.07	61.34
13.75	31.42	35.02	38.87	42.97	47.30	48.42	49.56	50.71	51.87	53.05	54.24	55.45	56.67	57.90	59.15	60.40
14.00	30.95	34.49	38.28	42.31	46.59	47.69	48.81	49.94	51.09	52.25	53.42	54.61	55.81	57.02	58.25	59.49
14.25	30.48	33.97	37.71	41.68	45.89	46.98	48.08	49.19	50.32	51.46	52.62	53.79	54.97	56.17	57.38	58.60
14.50	30.03	33.47	37.15	41.06	45.21	46.28	47.36	48.46	49.58	50.70	51.84	52.99	54.16	55.34	56.53	57.73
14.75	29.59	32.98	36.60	40.46	44.54	45.60	46.67	47.75	48.85	49.96	51.08	52.22	53.36	54.52	55.70	56.88
15.00	29.16	32.50	36.07	39.87	43.90	44.94	45.99	47.06	48.14	49.23	50.34	51.46	52.59	53.73	54.89	56.06
15.25	28.74	32.03	35.55	39.30	43.27	44.29	45.33	46.38	47.45	48.53	49.62	50.72	51.83	52.96	54.10	55.25
15.50	28.34	31.58	35.05	38.74	42.65	43.66	44.69	45.72	46.77	47.84	48.91	50.00	51.10	52.21	53.33	54.47
15.75	27.94	31.13	34.56	38.20	42.05	43.05	44.06	45.08	46.12	47.16	48.22	49.30	50.38	51.47	52.58	53.70
16.00	27.55	30.70	34.07	37.67	41.47	42.45	43.45	44.45	45.48	46.51	47.55	48.61	49.68	50.76	51.85	52.95
16.25	27.17	30.28	33.61	37.15	40.90	41.87	42.85	43.84	44.85	45.87	46.90	47.94	48.99	50.06	51.14	52.22
16.50	26.80	29.87	33.15	36.64	40.34	41.30	42.27	43.25	44.24	45.24	46.26	47.29	48.33	49.38	50.44	51.51
16.75	26.44	29.46	32.70	36.15	39.80	40.74	41.70	42.66	43.64	44.63	45.64	46.65	47.68	48.71	49.76	50.82
17.00	26.09	29.07	32.27	35.67	39.27	40.20	41.14	42.09	43.06	44.04	45.03	46.03	47.04	48.06	49.10	50.14
17.25	25.74	28.69	31.84	35.20	38.75	39.67	40.60	41.54	42.49	43.46	44.43	45.42	46.42	47.43	48.45	49.48
17.50	25.41	28.31	31.42	34.74	38.24	39.15	40.07	41.00	41.94	42.89	43.85	44.83	45.81	46.81	47.82	48.83
17.75	25.08	27.95	31.02	34.29	37.75	38.64	39.55	40.47	41.40	42.34	43.29	44.25	45.22	46.21	47.20	48.20
18.00	24.76	27.59	30.62	33.85	37.27	38.15	39.04	39.95	40.87	41.80	42.73	43.68	44.64	45.62	46.60	47.59
18.25	24.44	27.24	30.23	33.42	36.79	37.67	38.55	39.44	40.35	41.27	42.19	43.13	44.08	45.04	46.01	46.99
18.50	24.14	26.90	29.86	33.00	36.33	37.19	38.07	38.95	39.84	40.75	41.66	42.59	43.53	44.47	45.43	46.40
18.75	23.84	26.57	29.49	32.59	35.88	36.73	37.59	38.47	39.35	40.24	41.15	42.06	42.99	43.92	44.87	45.82
19.00	23.55	26.24	29.12	32.19	35.44	36.28	37.13	37.99	38.87	39.75	40.64	41.55	42.46	43.38	44.32	45.26
20.00	22.44	25.01	27.75	30.68	33.78	34.58	35.39	36.21	37.04	37.88	38.73	39.59	40.46	41.34	42.23	43.13
25.00	18.10	20.18	22.39	24.75	27.25	27.90	28.55	29.21	29.88	30.56	31.25	31.94	32.65	33.36	34.07	34.80
30.00	15.13	16.86	18.71	20.69	22.77	23.31	23.86	24.41	24.97	25.54	26.12	26.70	27.28	27.88	28.48	29.08

Description: This table shows the yield to maturity of a mortgage purchased at the price shown in the index.

Example: The yield to maturity of a 6.75 %, 22 year mortgage at a price of 80.00 is 9.58 %.

INTEREST RATE, %

PRICE	0.00%	1.00%	2.00%	3.00%	4.00%	4.25%	4.50%	4.75%	5.00%	5.25%	5.50%	5.75%	6.00%	6.25%	6.50%	6.75%
100	0.00	1.00	2.00	3.00	4.00	4.25	4.50	4.75	5.00	5.25	5.50	5.75	6.00	6.25	6.50	6.75
99	.09	1.09	2.09	3.10	4.10	4.35	4.60	4.86	5.11	5.36	5.61	5.86	6.11	6.36	6.61	6.87
98	.18	1.19	2.19	3.20	4.21	4.46	4.72	4.97	5.22	5.47	5.72	5.98	6.23	6.48	6.73	6.99
97	.27	1.28	2.29	3.31	4.32	4.57	4.83	5.08	5.33	5.59	5.84	6.10	6.35	6.60	6.86	7.11
96	.37	1.38	2.40	3.41	4.43	4.69	4.94	5.20	5.45	5.71	5.96	6.22	6.47	6.73	6.98	7.24
95	.46	1.48	2.50	3.52	4.55	4.80	5.06	5.31	5.57	5.83	6.08	6.34	6.60	6.85	7.11	7.37
94	.56	1.58	2.61	3.63	4.66	4.92	5.18	5.43	5.69	5.95	6.21	6.46	6.72	6.98	7.24	7.50
93	.66	1.69	2.72	3.75	4.78	5.04	5.30	5.55	5.81	6.07	6.33	6.59	6.85	7.11	7.37	7.63
92	.76	1.79	2.82	3.86	4.90	5.16	5.42	5.68	5.94	6.20	6.46	6.72	6.98	7.24	7.50	7.76
91	.86	1.90	2.94	3.98	5.02	5.28	5.54	5.80	6.06	6.33	6.59	6.85	7.11	7.37	7.64	7.90
90	.97	2.01	3.05	4.09	5.14	5.40	5.67	5.93	6.19	6.46	6.72	6.98	7.25	7.51	7.77	8.04
89	1.07	2.12	3.16	4.21	5.27	5.53	5.79	6.06	6.32	6.59	6.85	7.12	7.38	7.65	7.91	8.18
88	1.18	2.23	3.28	4.33	5.39	5.66	5.92	6.19	6.46	6.72	6.99	7.26	7.52	7.79	8.06	8.33
87	1.29	2.34	3.40	4.46	5.52	5.79	6.06	6.32	6.59	6.86	7.13	7.40	7.66	7.93	8.20	8.47
86	1.40	2.45	3.52	4.58	5.65	5.92	6.19	6.46	6.73	7.00	7.27	7.54	7.81	8.08	8.35	8.62
85	1.51	2.57	3.64	4.71	5.79	6.06	6.33	6.60	6.87	7.14	7.41	7.68	7.95	8.23	8.50	8.77
84	1.62	2.69	3.76	4.84	5.92	6.19	6.47	6.74	7.01	7.28	7.56	7.83	8.10	8.38	8.65	8.93
83	1.74	2.81	3.89	4.97	6.06	6.33	6.61	6.88	7.16	7.43	7.71	7.98	8.26	8.53	8.81	9.09
82	1.86	2.93	4.02	5.11	6.20	6.48	6.75	7.03	7.30	7.58	7.86	8.13	8.41	8.69	8.97	9.25
81	1.98	3.06	4.15	5.24	6.35	6.62	6.90	7.18	7.45	7.73	8.01	8.29	8.57	8.85	9.13	9.41
80	2.10	3.19	4.28	5.38	6.49	6.77	7.05	7.33	7.61	7.89	8.17	8.45	8.73	9.01	9.30	9.58
79	2.22	3.32	4.42	5.52	6.64	6.92	7.20	7.48	7.76	8.05	8.33	8.61	8.90	9.18	9.47	9.75
78	2.35	3.45	4.55	5.67	6.79	7.07	7.36	7.64	7.92	8.21	8.49	8.78	9.06	9.35	9.64	9.92
77	2.48	3.58	4.70	5.82	6.95	7.23	7.52	7.80	8.09	8.37	8.66	8.95	9.24.	9.52	9.81	10.10
76	2.61	3.72	4.84	5.97	7.11	7.39	7.68	7.97	8.25	8.54	8.83	9.12	9.41	9.70	9.99	10.28
75	2.74	3.86	4.98	6.12	7.27	7.55	7.84	8.13	8.42	8.71	9.00	9.30	9.59	9.88	10.18	10.47
74	2.88	4.00	5.13	6.28	7.43	7.72	8.01	8.30	8.60	8.89	9.18	9.48	9.77	10.07	10.36	10.66
73	3.01	4.15	5.29	6.44	7.60	7.89	8.18	8.48	8.77	9.07	9.36	9.66	9.96	10.26	10.55	10.85
72	3.16	4.29	5.44	6.60	7.77	8.07	8.36	8.66	8.95	9.25	9.55	9.85	10.15	10.45	10.75	11.05
71	3.30	4.44	5.60	6.77	7.95	8.24	8.54	8.84	9.14	9.44	9.74	10.04	10.34	10.65	10.95	11.26
70	3.45	4.60	5.76	6.94	8.13	8.42	8.72	9.03	9.33	9.63	9.93	10.24	10.54	10.85	11.16	11.46
69	3.60	4.75	5.93	7.11	8.31	8.61	8.91	9.22	9.52	9.83	10.13	10.44	10.75	11.06	11.37	11.68
68	3.75	4.92	6.10	7.29	8.50	8.80	9.11	9.41	9.72	10.03	10.34	10.65	10.96	11.27	11.58	11.89
67	3.90	5.08	6.27	7.47	8.69	9.00	9.30	9.61	9.92	10.23	10.54	10.86	11.17	11.49	11.80	12.12
66	4.06	5.25	6.44	7.66	8.88	9.19	9.50	9.82	10.13	10.44	10.76	11.07	11.39	11.71	12.03	12.35
65	4.23	5.42	6.62	7.85	9.09	9.40	9.71	10.03	10.34	10.66	10.98	11.30	11.62	11.94	12.26	12.58
64	4.39	5.59	6.81	8.04	9.29	9.61	9.92	10.24	10.56	10.88	11.20	11.52	11.85	12.17	12.50	12.82
63	4.57	5.77	7.00	8.24	9.50	9.82	10.14	10.46	10.78	11.11	11.43	11.76	12.08	12.41	12.74	13.07
62	4.74	5.96	7.19	8.45	9.72	10.04	10.36	10.69	11.01	11.34	11.67	12.00	12.33	12.66	12.99	13.32
61	4.92	6.15	7.39	8.66	9.94	10.27	10.59	10.92	11.25	11.58	11.91	12.24	12.58	12.91	13.25	13.59
60	5.10	6.34	7.60	8.87	10.17	10.50	10.83	11.16	11.49	11.83	12.16	12.50	12.83	13.17	13.51	13.85
59	5.29	6.54	7.81	9.09	10.41	10.74	11.07	11.40	11.74	12.08	12.42	12.76	13.10	13.44	13.79	14.13
58	5.48	6.74	8.02	9.32	10.65	10.98	11.32	11.66	12.00	12.34	12.68	13.02	13.37	13.72	14.07	14.42
57	5.68	6.95	8.24	9.56	10.90	11.23	11.58	11.92	12.26	12.61	12.95	13.30	13.65	14.00	14.35	14.71
56	5.88	7.16	8.47	9.80	11.15	11.49	11.84	12.18	12.53	12.88	13.23	13.58	13.94	14.30	14.65	15.01
55	6.09	7.38	8.70	10.04	11.41	11.76	12.11	12.46	12.81	13.17	13.52	13.88	14.24	14.60	14.96	15.32
54	6.30	7.61	8.94	10.30	11.69	12.04	12.39	12.74	13.10	13.46	13.82	14.18	14.54	14.91	15.28	15.65
53	6.52	7.84	9.19	10.56	11.97	12.32	12.68	13.04	13.40	13.76	14.13	14.49	14.86	15.23	15.60	15.98
52	6.75	8.08	9.44	10.83	12.25	12.61	12.98	13.34	13.71	14.07	14.44	14.82	15.19	15.57	15.94	16.32
51	6.98	8.33	9.71	11.11	12.55	12.92	13.28	13.65	14.02	14.40	14.77	15.15	15.53	15.91	16.29	16.68
50	7.22	8.59	9.98	11.40	12.86	13.23	13.60	13.98	14.35	14.73	15.11	15.49	15.88	16.27	16.66	17.05
49	7.47	8.85	10.26	11.70	13.18	13.55	13.93	14.31	14.69	15.08	15.46	15.85	16.24	16.64	17.03	17.43
48	7.73	9.12	10.55	12.01	13.51	13.89	14.27	14.66	15.04	15.44	15.83	16.22	16.62	17.02	17.42	17.83
47	7.99	9.40	10.85	12.33	13.85	14.24	14.63	15.02	15.41	15.81	16.21	16.61	17.01	17.42	17.83	18.24
46	8.26	9.69	11.16	12.66	14.20	14.60	14.99	15.39	15.79	16.19	16.60	17.01	17.42	17.83	18.25	18.67
45	8.55	9.99	11.48	13.00	14.57	14.97	15.37	15.78	16.18	16.59	17.01	17.42	17.84	18.26	18.69	19.11
44	8.84	10.30	11.81	13.36	14.95	15.36	15.77	16.18	16.59	17.01	17.43	17.85	18.28	18.71	19.14	19.58
43	9.14	10.63	12.16	13.73	15.35	15.77	16.18	16.60	17.02	17.45	17.87	18.31	18.74	19.18	19.62	20.06
42	9.46	10.96	12.52	14.12	15.77	16.19	16.61	17.04	17.47	17.90	18.34	18.78	19.22	19.66	20.11	20.56
41	9.78	11.31	12.89	14.52	16.20	16.63	17.06	17.49	17.93	18.37	18.82	19.27	19.72	20.17	20.63	21.09
40	10.12	11.68	13.28	14.94	16.65	17.09	17.53	17.97	18.42	18.87	19.32	19.78	20.24	20.70	21.17	21.64
39	10.48	12.06	13.69	15.38	17.12	17.57	18.02	18.47	18.93	19.39	19.85	20.32	20.79	21.26	21.74	22.22
35	12.06	13.75	15.52	17.35	19.25	19.74	20.23	20.72	21.22	21.73	22.24	22.75	23.27	23.79	24.32	24.85
30	14.51	16.41	18.40	20.47	22.64	23.19	23.76	24.32	24.90	25.47	26.06	26.65	27.25	27.85	28.45	29.07
25	17.80	20.00	22.31	24.74	27.29	27.95	28.61	29.28	29.96	30.65	31.35	32.05	32.76	33.47	34.20	34.93
20	22.56	25.22	28.04	31.03	34.19	35.00	35.82	36.66	37.50	38.35	39.22	40.09	40.97	41.87	42.77	43.68
15	30.26	33.74	37.47	41.42	45.61	46.69	47.78	48.89	50.02	51.15	52.30	53.47	54.64	55.83	57.03	58.24
10	45.45	50.65	56.22	62.14	68.42	70.04	71.68	73.35	75.03	76.73	78.46	80.20	81.96	83.75	85.55	87.37

Description: This table shows the price to pay for a monthly payment mortgage loan at the yield rate.

Example: The price of a 10.75 %, 22 year mortgage loan to yield 8.00 % to maturity is $ 122.78.

INTEREST RATE, %

YIELD	7.00%	7.25%	7.50%	7.75%	8.00%	8.25%	8.50%	8.75%	9.00%	9.25%	9.50%	9.75%	10.00%	10.25%	10.50%	10.75%
0.00	196.26	200.35	204.47	208.63	212.83	217.07	221.34	225.65	229.99	234.37	238.78	243.22	247.70	252.20	256.74	261.31
1.00	176.11	179.77	183.47	187.21	190.97	194.78	198.61	202.47	206.37	210.30	214.26	218.24	222.26	226.30	230.38	234.48
2.00	158.67	161.98	165.31	168.67	172.07	175.49	178.95	182.43	185.94	189.48	193.05	196.64	200.26	203.90	207.57	211.26
3.00	143.55	146.53	149.55	152.59	155.66	158.76	161.89	165.04	168.21	171.42	174.64	177.89	181.17	184.46	187.78	191.12
4.00	130.38	133.10	135.84	138.60	141.39	144.20	147.04	149.90	152.79	155.70	158.63	161.58	164.55	167.55	170.56	173.60
4.25	127.36	130.02	132.69	135.39	138.12	140.86	143.64	146.43	149.25	152.09	154.95	157.84	160.74	163.67	166.61	169.58
4.50	124.45	127.04	129.65	132.29	134.95	137.64	140.35	143.08	145.83	148.61	151.40	154.22	157.06	159.92	162.79	165.69
4.75	121.62	124.15	126.71	129.29	131.89	134.52	137.16	139.83	142.52	145.24	147.97	150.72	153.50	156.29	159.10	161.93
5.00	118.89	121.37	123.87	126.39	128.93	131.50	134.08	136.69	139.33	141.98	144.65	147.34	150.05	152.78	155.53	158.30
5.25	116.25	118.67	121.12	123.58	126.07	128.58	131.11	133.66	136.23	138.82	141.44	144.07	146.72	149.39	152.08	154.78
5.50	113.70	116.07	118.45	120.86	123.30	125.75	128.23	130.72	133.24	135.77	138.33	140.90	143.50	146.11	148.74	151.38
5.75	111.23	113.54	115.88	118.24	120.62	123.02	125.44	127.88	130.34	132.82	135.32	137.84	140.38	142.93	145.50	148.09
6.00	108.84	111.10	113.39	115.69	118.02	120.37	122.74	125.13	127.54	129.96	132.41	134.87	137.36	139.86	142.37	144.91
6.25	106.52	108.74	110.97	113.23	115.51	117.81	120.13	122.47	124.82	127.20	129.59	132.00	134.43	136.88	139.34	141.82
6.50	104.28	106.45	108.64	110.85	113.08	115.33	117.60	119.89	122.19	124.52	126.86	129.22	131.60	134.00	136.41	138.84
6.75	102.10	104.23	106.37	108.54	110.72	112.93	115.15	117.39	119.65	121.93	124.22	126.53	128.86	131.21	133.57	135.94
7.00	100.00	102.08	104.18	106.30	108.44	110.60	112.78	114.97	117.18	119.41	121.66	123.93	126.21	128.50	130.81	133.14
7.25	97.96	100.00	102.06	104.13	106.23	108.35	110.48	112.63	114.80	116.98	119.18	121.40	123.63	125.88	128.15	130.43
7.50	95.99	97.98	100.00	102.04	104.09	106.16	108.25	110.36	112.48	114.62	116.78	118.95	121.14	123.34	125.56	127.80
7.75	94.07	96.03	98.01	100.00	102.01	104.04	106.09	108.16	110.24	112.34	114.45	116.58	118.72	120.88	123.06	125.25
8.00	92.22	94.13	96.07	98.03	100.00	101.99	104.00	106.02	108.06	110.12	112.19	114.28	116.38	118.50	120.63	122.78
8.25	90.42	92.30	94.20	96.11	98.05	100.00	101.97	103.95	105.95	107.97	110.00	112.05	114.11	116.19	118.28	120.38
8.50	88.67	90.52	92.38	94.26	96.16	98.07	100.00	101.95	103.91	105.89	107.88	109.89	111.91	113.94	115.99	118.06
8.75	86.98	88.79	90.62	92.46	94.32	96.20	98.09	100.00	101.92	103.86	105.82	107.79	109.77	111.77	113.78	115.80
9.00	85.34	87.11	88.90	90.71	92.54	94.38	96.24	98.11	100.00	101.90	103.82	105.75	107.70	109.66	111.63	113.62
9.25	83.74	85.48	87.24	89.02	90.81	92.62	94.44	96.28	98.13	100.00	101.88	103.78	105.69	107.61	109.55	111.50
9.50	82.20	83.91	85.63	87.37	89.13	90.91	92.70	94.50	96.32	98.15	100.00	101.86	103.74	105.62	107.52	109.44
9.75	80.69	82.37	84.07	85.78	87.51	89.25	91.00	92.77	94.56	96.36	98.17	100.00	101.84	103.69	105.56	107.44
10.00	79.24	80.88	82.55	84.23	85.92	87.63	89.36	91.10	92.85	94.62	96.40	98.19	100.00	101.82	103.65	105.50
10.25	77.82	79.44	81.07	82.72	84.39	86.07	87.76	89.47	91.19	92.93	94.68	96.44	98.21	100.00	101.80	103.61
10.50	76.44	78.03	79.64	81.26	82.90	84.55	86.21	87.89	89.58	91.29	93.00	94.73	96.48	98.23	100.00	101.78
10.75	75.11	76.67	78.25	79.84	81.45	83.07	84.70	86.35	88.01	89.69	91.38	93.08	94.79	96.52	98.25	100.00
11.00	73.81	75.35	76.90	78.46	80.04	81.63	83.24	84.86	86.49	88.14	89.80	91.47	93.15	94.85	96.55	98.27
11.25	72.55	74.06	75.58	77.12	78.67	80.24	81.82	83.41	85.01	86.63	88.26	89.90	91.56	93.22	94.90	96.59
11.50	71.32	72.80	74.30	75.81	77.34	78.88	80.43	82.00	83.58	85.17	86.77	88.38	90.01	91.65	93.30	94.96
11.75	70.13	71.59	73.06	74.55	76.05	77.56	79.09	80.63	82.18	83.74	85.32	86.91	88.50	90.12	91.74	93.37
12.00	68.97	70.40	71.85	73.31	74.79	76.28	77.78	79.29	80.82	82.36	83.91	85.47	87.04	88.62	90.22	91.82
12.25	67.84	69.25	70.68	72.11	73.57	75.03	76.51	78.00	79.50	81.01	82.53	84.07	85.62	87.17	88.74	90.32
12.50	66.74	68.13	69.53	70.95	72.37	73.82	75.27	76.73	78.21	79.70	81.20	82.71	84.23	85.76	87.31	88.86
12.75	65.67	67.04	68.42	69.81	71.22	72.63	74.06	75.50	76.96	78.42	79.90	81.39	82.88	84.39	85.91	87.44
13.00	64.63	65.98	67.34	68.71	70.09	71.48	72.89	74.31	75.74	77.18	78.63	80.10	81.57	83.05	84.55	86.05
13.25	63.62	64.94	66.28	67.63	68.99	70.36	71.75	73.15	74.55	75.97	77.40	78.84	80.29	81.75	83.23	84.71
13.50	62.64	63.94	65.25	66.58	67.92	69.27	70.64	72.01	73.40	74.80	76.20	77.62	79.05	80.49	81.94	83.39
13.75	61.68	62.96	64.25	65.56	66.88	68.21	69.56	70.91	72.27	73.65	75.04	76.43	77.84	79.25	80.68	82.12
14.00	60.74	62.00	63.28	64.57	65.87	67.18	68.50	69.83	71.18	72.53	73.90	75.27	76.66	78.05	79.46	80.87
14.25	59.83	61.08	62.33	63.60	64.88	66.17	67.47	68.79	70.11	71.45	72.79	74.14	75.51	76.88	78.27	79.66
14.50	58.94	60.17	61.41	62.66	63.92	65.19	66.47	67.77	69.07	70.39	71.71	73.05	74.39	75.74	77.11	78.48
14.75	58.08	59.29	60.51	61.74	62.98	64.23	65.50	66.77	68.06	69.35	70.66	71.97	73.30	74.63	75.97	77.33
15.00	57.24	58.43	59.63	60.84	62.07	63.30	64.55	65.80	67.07	68.35	69.63	70.93	72.23	73.55	74.87	76.20
15.25	56.41	57.59	58.77	59.97	61.18	62.39	63.62	64.86	66.11	67.37	68.63	69.91	71.20	72.49	73.80	75.11
15.50	55.61	56.77	57.94	59.12	60.31	61.51	62.72	63.94	65.17	66.41	67.66	68.92	70.19	71.46	72.75	74.04
15.75	54.83	55.97	57.12	58.29	59.46	60.64	61.84	63.04	64.25	65.47	66.71	67.95	69.20	70.46	71.73	73.00
16.00	54.07	55.19	56.33	57.47	58.63	59.80	60.98	62.16	63.36	64.56	65.78	67.00	68.24	69.48	70.73	71.99
16.25	53.32	54.43	55.55	56.68	57.82	58.98	60.14	61.31	62.49	63.68	64.87	66.08	67.30	68.52	69.76	71.00
16.50	52.60	53.69	54.80	55.91	57.04	58.17	59.32	60.47	61.64	62.81	63.99	65.18	66.38	67.59	68.81	70.03
16.75	51.89	52.97	54.06	55.16	56.27	57.39	58.52	59.66	60.81	61.96	63.13	64.30	65.49	66.68	67.88	69.09
17.00	51.20	52.26	53.34	54.42	55.52	56.62	57.74	58.86	60.00	61.14	62.29	63.45	64.61	65.79	66.97	68.17
17.25	50.52	51.57	52.63	53.71	54.79	55.88	56.98	58.09	59.20	60.33	61.47	62.61	63.76	64.92	66.09	67.27
17.50	49.86	50.90	51.95	53.00	54.07	55.15	56.23	57.33	58.43	59.54	60.66	61.79	62.93	64.07	65.23	66.39
17.75	49.22	50.24	51.28	52.32	53.37	54.43	55.51	56.59	57.68	58.77	59.88	60.99	62.12	63.25	64.38	65.53
18.00	48.59	49.60	50.62	51.65	52.69	53.74	54.80	55.86	56.94	58.02	59.11	60.21	61.32	62.44	63.56	64.69
18.25	47.97	48.97	49.98	51.00	52.02	53.06	54.10	55.16	56.22	57.29	58.37	59.45	60.55	61.65	62.76	63.87
18.50	47.37	48.36	49.35	50.36	51.37	52.39	53.43	54.46	55.51	56.57	57.63	58.71	59.79	60.87	61.97	63.07
18.75	46.79	47.76	48.74	49.73	50.73	51.74	52.76	53.79	54.82	55.87	56.92	57.98	59.05	60.12	61.20	62.29
19.00	46.21	47.17	48.14	49.12	50.11	51.11	52.11	53.13	54.15	55.18	56.22	57.27	58.32	59.38	60.45	61.53
20.00	44.04	44.95	45.88	46.81	47.75	48.71	49.66	50.63	51.61	52.59	53.58	54.57	55.58	56.59	57.61	58.63
25.00	35.53	36.27	37.02	37.77	38.53	39.30	40.07	40.85	41.64	42.43	43.23	44.03	44.84	45.66	46.48	47.31
30.00	29.69	30.31	30.93	31.56	32.20	32.84	33.49	34.14	34.80	35.46	36.13	36.80	37.47	38.16	38.84	39.53

Description: This table shows the yield to maturity of a mortgage purchased at the price shown in the index.

Example: The yield to maturity of a 10.75 %, 22 year mortgage at a price of 111.00 is 9.30 %.

INTEREST RATE, %

PRICE	7.00%	7.25%	7.50%	7.75%	8.00%	8.25%	8.50%	8.75%	9.00%	9.25%	9.50%	9.75%	10.00%	10.25%	10.50%	10.75%
165	1.62	1.81	2.01	2.21	2.41	2.61	2.80	3.00	3.19	3.39	3.58	3.77	3.97	4.16	4.35	4.54
160	1.91	2.12	2.32	2.52	2.72	2.92	3.11	3.31	3.51	3.71	3.90	4.10	4.29	4.49	4.68	4.88
155	2.23	2.43	2.63	2.84	3.04	3.24	3.44	3.64	3.84	4.04	4.24	4.44	4.64	4.84	5.03	5.23
150	2.55	2.76	2.96	3.17	3.38	3.58	3.78	3.99	4.19	4.39	4.60	4.80	5.00	5.20	5.40	5.60
145	2.89	3.10	3.31	3.52	3.73	3.94	4.14	4.35	4.56	4.76	4.97	5.17	5.38	5.58	5.78	5.99
140	3.25	3.46	3.68	3.89	4.10	4.31	4.52	4.73	4.94	5.15	5.36	5.57	5.78	5.98	6.19	6.40
135	3.63	3.84	4.06	4.28	4.49	4.71	4.92	5.13	5.35	5.56	5.77	5.98	6.20	6.41	6.62	6.83
130	4.03	4.25	4.47	4.68	4.90	5.12	5.34	5.56	5.77	5.99	6.21	6.42	6.64	6.86	7.07	7.29
125	4.45	4.67	4.89	5.12	5.34	5.56	5.79	6.01	6.23	6.45	6.67	6.89	7.11	7.33	7.55	7.77
122	4.71	4.94	5.16	5.39	5.61	5.84	6.07	6.29	6.51	6.74	6.96	7.18	7.41	7.63	7.85	8.08
121	4.80	5.03	5.26	5.48	5.71	5.93	6.16	6.39	6.61	6.84	7.06	7.29	7.51	7.73	7.96	8.18
120	4.89	5.12	5.35	5.58	5.80	6.03	6.26	6.48	6.71	6.94	7.16	7.39	7.61	7.84	8.06	8.29
119	4.99	5.21	5.44	5.67	5.90	6.13	6.36	6.58	6.81	7.04	7.26	7.49	7.72	7.94	8.17	8.39
118	5.08	5.31	5.54	5.77	6.00	6.23	6.45	6.68	6.91	7.14	7.37	7.59	7.82	8.05	8.28	8.50
117	5.17	5.40	5.64	5.87	6.10	6.33	6.56	6.78	7.01	7.24	7.47	7.70	7.93	8.16	8.38	8.61
116	5.27	5.50	5.73	5.96	6.20	6.43	6.66	6.89	7.12	7.35	7.58	7.81	8.04	8.27	8.49	8.72
115	5.37	5.60	5.83	6.06	6.30	6.53	6.76	6.99	7.22	7.45	7.69	7.92	8.15	8.38	8.61	8.84
114	5.47	5.70	5.93	6.17	6.40	6.63	6.87	7.10	7.33	7.56	7.79	8.03	8.26	8.49	8.72	8.95
113	5.56	5.80	6.03	6.27	6.50	6.74	6.97	7.20	7.44	7.67	7.90	8.14	8.37	8.60	8.83	9.07
112	5.67	5.90	6.14	6.37	6.61	6.84	7.08	7.31	7.55	7.78	8.02	8.25	8.48	8.72	8.95	9.18
111	5.77	6.01	6.24	6.48	6.72	6.95	7.19	7.42	7.66	7.89	8.13	8.37	8.60	8.84	9.07	9.30
110	5.87	6.11	6.35	6.59	6.82	7.06	7.30	7.53	7.77	8.01	8.25	8.48	8.72	8.95	9.19	9.43
109	5.98	6.22	6.46	6.69	6.93	7.17	7.41	7.65	7.89	8.12	8.36	8.60	8.84	9.07	9.31	9.55
108	6.08	6.32	6.56	6.80	7.04	7.28	7.52	7.76	8.00	8.24	8.48	8.72	8.96	9.20	9.44	9.67
107	6.19	6.43	6.67	6.92	7.16	7.40	7.64	7.88	8.12	8.36	8.60	8.84	9.08	9.32	9.56	9.80
106	6.30	6.54	6.79	7.03	7.27	7.51	7.76	8.00	8.24	8.48	8.72	8.96	9.21	9.45	9.69	9.93
105	6.41	6.66	6.90	7.14	7.39	7.63	7.87	8.12	8.36	8.60	8.85	9.09	9.33	9.57	9.82	10.06
104	6.53	6.77	7.02	7.26	7.51	7.75	7.99	8.24	8.48	8.73	8.97	9.22	9.46	9.70	9.95	10.19
103	6.64	6.89	7.13	7.38	7.63	7.87	8.12	8.36	8.61	8.85	9.10	9.35	9.59	9.84	10.08	10.33
102	6.76	7.00	7.25	7.50	7.75	7.99	8.24	8.49	8.74	8.98	9.23	9.48	9.72	9.97	10.22	10.46
101	6.88	7.12	7.37	7.62	7.87	8.12	8.37	8.62	8.86	9.11	9.36	9.61	9.86	10.11	10.36	10.60
100	7.00	7.25	7.50	7.75	8.00	8.25	8.50	8.75	9.00	9.25	9.50	9.75	10.00	10.25	10.50	10.75
99	7.12	7.37	7.62	7.87	8.12	8.37	8.63	8.88	9.13	9.38	9.63	9.88	10.13	10.39	10.64	10.89
98	7.24	7.49	7.75	8.00	8.25	8.50	8.76	9.01	9.26	9.52	9.77	10.02	10.28	10.53	10.78	11.03
97	7.37	7.62	7.87	8.13	8.38	8.64	8.89	9.15	9.40	9.65	9.91	10.16	10.42	10.67	10.93	11.18
96	7.49	7.75	8.00	8.26	8.52	8.77	9.03	9.28	9.54	9.80	10.05	10.31	10.57	10.82	11.08	11.33
95	7.62	7.88	8.14	8.39	8.65	8.91	9.17	9.42	9.68	9.94	10.20	10.46	10.71	10.97	11.23	11.49
94	7.75	8.01	8.27	8.53	8.79	9.05	9.31	9.57	9.83	10.09	10.35	10.60	10.86	11.12	11.38	11.64
93	7.89	8.15	8.41	8.67	8.93	9.19	9.45	9.71	9.97	10.23	10.50	10.76	11.02	11.28	11.54	11.80
92	8.02	8.29	8.55	8.81	9.07	9.33	9.60	9.86	10.12	10.39	10.65	10.91	11.18	11.44	11.70	11.97
91	8.16	8.43	8.69	8.95	9.22	9.48	9.75	10.01	10.27	10.54	10.80	11.07	11.33	11.60	11.87	12.13
90	8.30	8.57	8.83	9.10	9.36	9.63	9.90	10.16	10.43	10.70	10.96	11.23	11.50	11.76	12.03	12.30
89	8.45	8.71	8.98	9.25	9.52	9.78	10.05	10.32	10.59	10.86	11.12	11.39	11.66	11.93	12.20	12.47
88	8.59	8.86	9.13	9.40	9.67	9.94	10.21	10.48	10.75	11.02	11.29	11.56	11.83	12.10	12.37	12.65
87	8.74	9.01	9.28	9.55	9.82	10.10	10.37	10.64	10.91	11.18	11.46	11.73	12.00	12.28	12.55	12.82
86	8.89	9.17	9.44	9.71	9.98	10.26	10.53	10.80	11.08	11.35	11.63	11.90	12.18	12.45	12.73	13.00
85	9.05	9.32	9.60	9.87	10.14	10.42	10.70	10.97	11.25	11.52	11.80	12.08	12.35	12.63	12.91	13.19
84	9.20	9.48	9.76	10.03	10.31	10.59	10.86	11.14	11.42	11.70	11.98	12.26	12.54	12.82	13.10	13.38
83	9.36	9.64	9.92	10.20	10.48	10.76	11.04	11.32	11.60	11.88	12.16	12.44	12.72	13.01	13.29	13.57
82	9.53	9.81	10.09	10.37	10.65	10.93	11.21	11.49	11.78	12.06	12.34	12.63	12.91	13.20	13.48	13.77
81	9.69	9.98	10.26	10.54	10.82	11.11	11.39	11.68	11.96	12.25	12.53	12.82	13.11	13.39	13.68	13.97
80	9.86	10.15	10.43	10.72	11.00	11.29	11.57	11.86	12.15	12.44	12.73	13.01	13.30	13.59	13.88	14.17
79	10.04	10.32	10.61	10.90	11.18	11.47	11.76	12.05	12.34	12.63	12.92	13.21	13.51	13.80	14.09	14.38
78	10.21	10.50	10.79	11.08	11.37	11.66	11.95	12.24	12.54	12.83	13.12	13.42	13.71	14.01	14.30	14.60
77	10.39	10.68	10.98	11.27	11.56	11.85	12.15	12.44	12.74	13.03	13.33	13.62	13.92	14.22	14.52	14.82
76	10.58	10.87	11.16	11.46	11.75	12.05	12.35	12.64	12.94	13.24	13.54	13.84	14.14	14.44	14.74	15.04
75	10.77	11.06	11.36	11.65	11.95	12.25	12.55	12.85	13.15	13.45	13.75	14.05	14.36	14.66	14.97	15.27
74	10.96	11.26	11.56	11.85	12.16	12.46	12.76	13.06	13.36	13.67	13.97	14.28	14.58	14.89	15.20	15.51
73	11.15	11.46	11.76	12.06	12.36	12.67	12.97	13.28	13.58	13.89	14.20	14.51	14.81	15.12	15.43	15.75
70	11.77	12.08	12.39	12.70	13.01	13.33	13.64	13.96	14.27	14.59	14.90	15.22	15.54	15.86	16.18	16.50
65	12.91	13.23	13.56	13.89	14.21	14.54	14.88	15.21	15.54	15.87	16.21	16.55	16.88	17.22	17.56	17.90
60	14.20	14.54	14.89	15.24	15.58	15.93	16.29	16.64	16.99	17.35	17.71	18.06	18.42	18.79	19.15	19.51
55	15.69	16.06	16.43	16.80	17.17	17.55	17.92	18.30	18.68	19.06	19.45	19.83	20.22	20.61	21.00	21.39
50	17.44	17.84	18.24	18.64	19.04	19.45	19.85	20.26	20.67	21.09	21.50	21.92	22.34	22.76	23.19	23.61
45	19.54	19.97	20.41	20.85	21.29	21.73	22.17	22.62	23.07	23.53	23.98	24.44	24.90	25.37	25.83	26.30
40	22.12	22.60	23.08	23.56	24.05	24.54	25.04	25.54	26.04	26.55	27.05	27.57	28.08	28.60	29.12	29.64
35	25.38	25.92	26.47	27.01	27.57	28.12	28.68	29.25	29.82	30.39	30.97	31.55	32.13	32.72	33.31	33.91
30	29.69	30.31	30.94	31.57	32.21	32.86	33.51	34.16	34.82	35.49	36.16	36.83	37.51	38.20	38.89	39.58

Description: This table shows the price to pay for a monthly payment mortgage loan at the yield rate.

Example: The price of a 15.00 %, 22 year mortgage loan to yield 8.00 % to maturity is $ 161.12.

INTEREST RATE, %

YIELD	11.00%	11.25%	11.50%	11.75%	12.00%	12.25%	12.50%	12.75%	13.00%	13.25%	13.50%	13.75%	14.00%	14.25%	14.50%	15.00%
0.00	265.91	270.53	275.19	279.87	284.58	289.31	294.07	298.85	303.66	308.49	313.34	318.22	323.12	328.04	332.97	342.91
1.00	238.60	242.75	246.93	251.13	255.35	259.60	263.87	268.16	272.48	276.81	281.17	285.54	289.94	294.35	298.78	307.69
2.00	214.98	218.72	222.48	226.27	230.07	233.90	237.75	241.61	245.50	249.41	253.33	257.27	261.23	265.21	269.20	277.23
3.00	194.48	197.87	201.27	204.69	208.14	211.60	215.08	218.58	222.10	225.63	229.18	232.75	236.33	239.92	243.54	250.80
4.00	176.65	179.72	182.81	185.92	189.05	192.20	195.36	198.54	201.73	204.94	208.16	211.40	214.66	217.92	221.20	227.80
4.25	172.56	175.56	178.58	181.62	184.67	187.75	190.83	193.94	197.06	200.19	203.34	206.51	209.69	212.88	216.08	222.53
4.50	168.61	171.54	174.49	177.46	180.44	183.44	186.46	189.49	192.54	195.61	198.68	201.78	204.88	208.00	211.13	217.43
4.75	164.78	167.65	170.53	173.43	176.35	179.28	182.23	185.20	188.18	191.17	194.18	197.20	200.23	203.28	206.34	212.50
5.00	161.08	163.89	166.70	169.54	172.39	175.26	178.14	181.04	183.95	186.88	189.82	192.77	195.74	198.72	201.71	207.73
5.25	157.51	160.25	163.00	165.78	168.56	171.37	174.19	177.02	179.87	182.73	185.61	188.49	191.39	194.31	197.23	203.12
5.50	154.05	156.73	159.42	162.13	164.86	167.60	170.36	173.13	175.92	178.71	181.53	184.35	187.19	190.04	192.90	198.65
5.75	150.70	153.32	155.96	158.61	161.28	163.96	166.66	169.37	172.09	174.83	177.58	180.34	183.12	185.91	188.70	194.33
6.00	147.45	150.02	152.60	155.20	157.81	160.43	163.07	165.72	168.39	171.07	173.76	176.46	179.18	181.91	184.65	190.15
6.25	144.32	146.83	149.35	151.89	154.45	157.02	159.60	162.20	164.81	167.43	170.06	172.71	175.37	178.04	180.72	186.11
6.50	141.28	143.74	146.21	148.70	151.20	153.71	156.24	158.78	161.34	163.90	166.48	169.07	171.67	174.29	176.91	182.19
6.75	138.33	140.74	143.16	145.60	148.05	150.51	152.99	155.47	157.98	160.49	163.01	165.55	168.10	170.66	173.23	178.39
7.00	135.48	137.84	140.21	142.60	145.00	147.41	149.83	152.27	154.72	157.18	159.65	162.14	164.63	167.14	169.66	174.72
7.25	132.72	135.03	137.35	139.69	142.04	144.40	146.78	149.17	151.57	153.98	156.40	158.83	161.28	163.73	166.20	171.16
7.50	130.05	132.31	134.58	136.87	139.18	141.49	143.82	146.16	148.51	150.87	153.25	155.63	158.03	160.43	162.85	167.71
7.75	127.45	129.67	131.90	134.14	136.40	138.67	140.95	143.24	145.55	147.86	150.19	152.53	154.87	157.23	159.60	164.36
8.00	124.94	127.11	129.30	131.50	133.71	135.93	138.17	140.42	142.68	144.95	147.23	149.52	151.82	154.13	156.45	161.12
8.25	122.50	124.63	126.78	128.93	131.10	133.28	135.47	137.68	139.89	142.12	144.35	146.60	148.86	151.12	153.40	157.97
8.50	120.14	122.23	124.33	126.44	128.57	130.71	132.86	135.02	137.19	139.37	141.57	143.77	145.98	148.20	150.44	154.92
8.75	117.84	119.89	121.95	124.03	126.12	128.21	130.32	132.44	134.57	136.71	138.86	141.03	143.20	145.38	147.56	151.97
9.00	115.62	117.63	119.65	121.69	123.73	125.79	127.86	129.94	132.03	134.13	136.24	138.36	140.49	142.63	144.78	149.10
9.25	113.46	115.43	117.42	119.41	121.42	123.44	125.47	127.51	129.57	131.63	133.70	135.78	137.87	139.97	142.07	146.31
9.50	111.36	113.30	115.25	117.21	119.18	121.16	123.16	125.16	127.17	129.20	131.23	133.27	135.32	137.38	139.45	143.61
9.75	109.33	111.23	113.14	115.07	117.00	118.95	120.91	122.87	124.85	126.84	128.83	130.84	132.85	134.87	136.90	140.99
10.00	107.35	109.22	111.10	112.99	114.89	116.80	118.72	120.65	122.59	124.54	126.50	128.47	130.45	132.43	134.43	138.44
10.25	105.43	107.27	109.11	110.97	112.84	114.71	116.60	118.50	120.40	122.32	124.24	126.18	128.12	130.07	132.03	135.96
10.50	103.57	105.37	107.18	109.01	110.84	112.68	114.54	116.40	118.27	120.16	122.05	123.95	125.85	127.77	129.69	133.56
10.75	101.76	103.53	105.31	107.10	108.90	110.72	112.54	114.37	116.21	118.06	119.91	121.78	123.65	125.54	127.42	131.23
11.00	100.00	101.74	103.49	105.25	107.02	108.80	110.59	112.39	114.20	116.01	117.84	119.67	121.52	123.36	125.22	128.96
11.25	98.29	100.00	101.72	103.45	105.19	106.94	108.70	110.47	112.25	114.03	115.82	117.63	119.44	121.26	123.08	126.75
11.50	96.63	98.31	100.00	101.70	103.41	105.13	106.86	108.60	110.35	112.10	113.87	115.64	117.42	119.20	121.00	124.61
11.75	95.01	96.66	98.33	100.00	101.68	103.37	105.07	106.78	108.50	110.23	111.96	113.70	115.45	117.21	118.98	122.53
12.00	93.44	95.07	96.70	98.35	100.00	101.66	103.34	105.02	106.71	108.40	110.11	111.82	113.54	115.27	117.01	120.50
12.25	91.91	93.51	95.12	96.74	98.36	100.00	101.64	103.30	104.96	106.63	108.31	109.99	111.69	113.39	115.09	118.53
12.50	90.42	92.00	93.58	95.17	96.77	98.38	100.00	101.63	103.26	104.90	106.55	108.21	109.88	111.55	113.23	116.61
12.75	88.98	90.52	92.08	93.65	95.22	96.81	98.40	100.00	101.61	103.23	104.85	106.48	108.12	109.77	111.42	114.74
13.00	87.57	89.09	90.62	92.16	93.72	95.27	96.84	98.42	100.00	101.59	103.19	104.79	106.41	108.03	109.65	112.93
13.25	86.20	87.70	89.20	90.72	92.25	93.78	95.32	96.88	98.43	100.00	101.57	103.15	104.74	106.34	107.94	111.16
13.50	84.86	86.34	87.82	89.32	90.82	92.33	93.85	95.37	96.91	98.45	100.00	101.56	103.12	104.69	106.26	109.44
13.75	83.56	85.01	86.48	87.95	89.43	90.91	92.41	93.91	95.42	96.94	98.47	100.00	101.54	103.08	104.64	107.76
14.00	82.29	83.73	85.17	86.61	88.07	89.54	91.01	92.49	93.98	95.47	96.98	98.48	100.00	101.52	103.05	106.13
14.25	81.06	82.47	83.89	85.32	86.75	88.19	89.65	91.10	92.57	94.04	95.52	97.01	98.50	100.00	101.51	104.53
14.50	79.86	81.25	82.65	84.05	85.46	86.89	88.32	89.75	91.20	92.65	94.10	95.57	97.04	98.52	100.00	102.98
14.75	78.69	80.06	81.43	82.82	84.21	85.61	87.02	88.44	89.86	91.29	92.72	94.17	95.62	97.07	98.53	101.47
15.00	77.54	78.89	80.25	81.62	82.99	84.37	85.76	87.15	88.55	89.96	91.38	92.80	94.23	95.66	97.10	100.00
15.25	76.43	77.76	79.10	80.44	81.80	83.16	84.53	85.90	87.28	88.67	90.07	91.47	92.88	94.29	95.71	98.56
15.50	75.35	76.66	77.97	79.30	80.64	81.98	83.32	84.68	86.04	87.41	88.79	90.17	91.56	92.95	94.35	97.16
15.75	74.29	75.58	76.88	78.19	79.50	80.82	82.15	83.49	84.83	86.18	87.54	88.90	90.27	91.64	93.02	95.80
16.00	73.25	74.53	75.81	77.10	78.40	79.70	81.01	82.33	83.65	84.98	86.32	87.66	89.01	90.37	91.73	94.47
16.25	72.25	73.50	74.77	76.04	77.32	78.60	79.90	81.20	82.50	83.81	85.13	86.46	87.79	89.13	90.47	93.17
16.50	71.26	72.50	73.75	75.00	76.26	77.53	78.81	80.09	81.38	82.67	83.97	85.28	86.59	87.91	89.24	91.90
16.75	70.30	71.52	72.75	73.99	75.24	76.49	77.75	79.01	80.28	81.56	82.84	84.13	85.43	86.73	88.03	90.66
17.00	69.36	70.57	71.79	73.01	74.23	75.47	76.71	77.96	79.21	80.47	81.74	83.01	84.29	85.57	86.86	89.45
17.25	68.45	69.64	70.84	72.04	73.25	74.47	75.70	76.93	78.17	79.41	80.66	81.92	83.18	84.44	85.71	88.27
17.50	67.56	68.73	69.91	71.10	72.30	73.50	74.71	75.93	77.15	78.37	79.61	80.85	82.09	83.34	84.59	87.12
17.75	66.68	67.84	69.01	70.18	71.36	72.55	73.74	74.94	76.15	77.36	78.58	79.80	81.03	82.26	83.50	85.99
18.00	65.83	66.98	68.13	69.29	70.45	71.62	72.80	73.99	75.18	76.37	77.57	78.78	79.99	81.21	82.43	84.89
18.25	65.00	66.13	67.27	68.41	69.56	70.72	71.88	73.05	74.22	75.41	76.59	77.78	78.98	80.18	81.39	83.82
18.50	64.18	65.30	66.42	67.55	68.69	69.83	70.98	72.13	73.29	74.46	75.63	76.81	77.99	79.18	80.37	82.77
18.75	63.39	64.49	65.60	66.71	67.84	68.97	70.10	71.24	72.39	73.54	74.69	75.86	77.02	78.20	79.37	81.74
19.00	62.61	63.70	64.79	65.90	67.00	68.12	69.24	70.37	71.50	72.63	73.78	74.93	76.08	77.24	78.40	80.74
20.00	59.66	60.70	61.75	62.80	63.85	64.92	65.98	67.06	68.13	69.22	70.31	71.40	72.50	73.60	74.71	76.94
25.00	48.14	48.98	49.82	50.67	51.52	52.37	53.24	54.10	54.97	55.85	56.73	57.61	58.49	59.38	60.28	62.08
30.00	40.23	40.93	41.63	42.34	43.05	43.77	44.49	45.21	45.94	46.67	47.41	48.14	48.88	49.63	50.38	51.88

Description: This table shows the yield to maturity of a mortgage purchased at the price shown in the index.

Example: The yield to maturity of a 15.00 %, 22 year mortgage at a price of 125.00 is 11.45 %.

INTEREST RATE, %

PRICE	11.00%	11.25%	11.50%	11.75%	12.00%	12.25%	12.50%	12.75%	13.00%	13.25%	13.50%	13.75%	14.00%	14.25%	14.50%	15.00%
250	.56	.72	.88	1.04	1.20	1.35	1.51	1.66	1.82	1.97	2.12	2.28	2.43	2.58	2.73	3.03
240	.94	1.10	1.26	1.42	1.59	1.74	1.90	2.06	2.22	2.37	2.53	2.68	2.84	2.99	3.14	3.45
230	1.34	1.51	1.67	1.84	2.00	2.16	2.32	2.48	2.64	2.80	2.96	3.12	3.27	3.43	3.58	3.89
220	1.77	1.94	2.10	2.27	2.44	2.60	2.77	2.93	3.09	3.25	3.41	3.58	3.74	3.89	4.05	4.37
210	2.23	2.40	2.57	2.74	2.90	3.07	3.24	3.41	3.57	3.74	3.90	4.07	4.23	4.39	4.55	4.87
200	2.71	2.89	3.06	3.23	3.40	3.58	3.75	3.92	4.09	4.26	4.42	4.59	4.76	4.92	5.09	5.42
195	2.97	3.14	3.32	3.49	3.67	3.84	4.01	4.19	4.36	4.53	4.70	4.87	5.04	5.21	5.37	5.71
190	3.23	3.41	3.59	3.77	3.94	4.12	4.29	4.47	4.64	4.81	4.98	5.16	5.33	5.50	5.67	6.00
185	3.51	3.69	3.87	4.05	4.23	4.40	4.58	4.76	4.93	5.11	5.28	5.46	5.63	5.80	5.97	6.31
180	3.80	3.98	4.16	4.34	4.52	4.70	4.88	5.06	5.24	5.41	5.59	5.77	5.94	6.12	6.29	6.64
175	4.09	4.28	4.46	4.65	4.83	5.01	5.19	5.37	5.55	5.73	5.91	6.09	6.27	6.45	6.62	6.98
170	4.41	4.59	4.78	4.97	5.15	5.33	5.52	5.70	5.89	6.07	6.25	6.43	6.61	6.79	6.97	7.33
165	4.73	4.92	5.11	5.30	5.49	5.67	5.86	6.05	6.23	6.42	6.60	6.78	6.97	7.15	7.33	7.70
160	5.07	5.26	5.45	5.65	5.84	6.03	6.22	6.40	6.59	6.78	6.97	7.16	7.34	7.53	7.71	8.08
155	5.43	5.62	5.82	6.01	6.20	6.40	6.59	6.78	6.97	7.16	7.36	7.55	7.73	7.92	8.11	8.49
150	5.80	6.00	6.19	6.39	6.59	6.79	6.98	7.18	7.37	7.57	7.76	7.95	8.15	8.34	8.53	8.92
145	6.19	6.39	6.59	6.79	6.99	7.19	7.39	7.59	7.79	7.99	8.19	8.39	8.58	8.78	8.97	9.37
140	6.60	6.81	7.01	7.22	7.42	7.63	7.83	8.03	8.24	8.44	8.64	8.84	9.04	9.24	9.44	9.84
135	7.04	7.25	7.46	7.67	7.87	8.08	8.29	8.50	8.70	8.91	9.12	9.32	9.53	9.73	9.94	10.34
130	7.50	7.71	7.93	8.14	8.35	8.57	8.78	8.99	9.20	9.41	9.62	9.83	10.04	10.25	10.46	10.88
125	7.99	8.21	8.43	8.64	8.86	9.08	9.30	9.51	9.73	9.94	10.16	10.38	10.59	10.81	11.02	11.45
120	8.51	8.73	8.96	9.18	9.40	9.63	9.85	10.07	10.29	10.51	10.73	10.96	11.18	11.40	11.62	12.06
115	9.07	9.29	9.52	9.75	9.98	10.21	10.44	10.67	10.89	11.12	11.35	11.58	11.80	12.03	12.26	12.71
113	9.30	9.53	9.76	9.99	10.22	10.46	10.69	10.92	11.15	11.38	11.61	11.84	12.07	12.30	12.53	12.98
112	9.42	9.65	9.88	10.12	10.35	10.58	10.81	11.05	11.28	11.51	11.74	11.97	12.20	12.43	12.66	13.12
111	9.54	9.77	10.01	10.24	10.47	10.71	10.94	11.18	11.41	11.64	11.87	12.11	12.34	12.57	12.80	13.27
110	9.66	9.90	10.13	10.37	10.60	10.84	11.07	11.31	11.54	11.78	12.01	12.24	12.48	12.71	12.95	13.41
109	9.79	10.02	10.26	10.50	10.73	10.97	11.20	11.44	11.68	11.91	12.15	12.38	12.62	12.85	13.09	13.56
108	9.91	10.15	10.39	10.63	10.86	11.10	11.34	11.58	11.81	12.05	12.29	12.53	12.76	13.00	13.24	13.71
107	10.04	10.28	10.52	10.76	11.00	11.24	11.48	11.71	11.95	12.19	12.43	12.67	12.91	13.15	13.38	13.86
106	10.17	10.41	10.65	10.89	11.13	11.37	11.61	11.86	12.10	12.34	12.58	12.82	13.06	13.30	13.54	14.01
105	10.30	10.54	10.79	11.03	11.27	11.51	11.76	12.00	12.24	12.48	12.72	12.96	13.21	13.45	13.69	14.17
104	10.44	10.68	10.92	11.17	11.41	11.66	11.90	12.14	12.39	12.63	12.87	13.12	13.36	13.60	13.84	14.33
103	10.57	10.82	11.06	11.31	11.55	11.80	12.04	12.29	12.53	12.78	13.02	13.27	13.51	13.76	14.00	14.49
102	10.71	10.96	11.21	11.45	11.70	11.95	12.19	12.44	12.69	12.93	13.18	13.42	13.67	13.92	14.16	14.66
101	10.85	11.10	11.35	11.60	11.85	12.09	12.34	12.59	12.84	13.09	13.34	13.58	13.83	14.08	14.33	14.82
100	11.00	11.25	11.50	11.75	12.00	12.25	12.50	12.75	13.00	13.25	13.50	13.75	14.00	14.25	14.50	15.00
99	11.14	11.39	11.64	11.90	12.15	12.40	12.65	12.90	13.15	13.41	13.66	13.91	14.16	14.41	14.66	15.17
98	11.29	11.54	11.79	12.05	12.30	12.55	12.81	13.06	13.32	13.57	13.82	14.08	14.33	14.58	14.84	15.34
97	11.44	11.69	11.95	12.20	12.46	12.71	12.97	13.22	13.48	13.74	13.99	14.25	14.50	14.76	15.01	15.52
96	11.59	11.85	12.10	12.36	12.62	12.88	13.13	13.39	13.65	13.90	14.16	14.42	14.68	14.93	15.19	15.71
95	11.75	12.01	12.26	12.52	12.78	13.04	13.30	13.56	13.82	14.08	14.34	14.60	14.86	15.11	15.37	15.89
94	11.91	12.17	12.43	12.69	12.95	13.21	13.47	13.73	13.99	14.25	14.51	14.78	15.04	15.30	15.56	16.08
93	12.07	12.33	12.59	12.85	13.12	13.38	13.64	13.90	14.17	14.43	14.69	14.96	15.22	15.49	15.75	16.28
92	12.23	12.49	12.76	13.02	13.29	13.55	13.82	14.08	14.35	14.61	14.88	15.14	15.41	15.68	15.94	16.47
91	12.40	12.66	12.93	13.20	13.46	13.73	14.00	14.26	14.53	14.80	15.07	15.33	15.60	15.87	16.14	16.68
90	12.57	12.84	13.10	13.37	13.64	13.91	14.18	14.45	14.72	14.99	15.26	15.53	15.80	16.07	16.34	16.88
89	12.74	13.01	13.28	13.55	13.82	14.09	14.37	14.64	14.91	15.18	15.45	15.73	16.00	16.27	16.54	17.09
88	12.92	13.19	13.46	13.74	14.01	14.28	14.56	14.83	15.10	15.38	15.65	15.93	16.20	16.48	16.75	17.30
87	13.10	13.37	13.65	13.92	14.20	14.47	14.75	15.03	15.30	15.58	15.85	16.13	16.41	16.69	16.96	17.52
86	13.28	13.56	13.84	14.11	14.39	14.67	14.95	15.22	15.50	15.78	16.06	16.34	16.62	16.90	17.18	17.74
85	13.47	13.75	14.03	14.31	14.59	14.87	15.15	15.43	15.71	15.99	16.27	16.56	16.84	17.12	17.40	17.97
84	13.66	13.94	14.22	14.51	14.79	15.07	15.35	15.64	15.92	16.21	16.49	16.77	17.06	17.34	17.63	18.20
83	13.85	14.14	14.42	14.71	14.99	15.28	15.56	15.85	16.14	16.42	16.71	17.00	17.29	17.57	17.86	18.44
82	14.05	14.34	14.63	14.91	15.20	15.49	15.78	16.07	16.36	16.65	16.94	17.23	17.52	17.81	18.10	18.68
81	14.26	14.55	14.84	15.13	15.42	15.71	16.00	16.29	16.58	16.87	17.17	17.46	17.75	18.05	18.34	18.93
80	14.47	14.76	15.05	15.34	15.63	15.93	16.22	16.52	16.81	17.11	17.40	17.70	17.99	18.29	18.59	19.18
79	14.68	14.97	15.27	15.56	15.86	16.15	16.45	16.75	17.05	17.34	17.64	17.94	18.24	18.54	18.84	19.44
78	14.89	15.19	15.49	15.79	16.09	16.39	16.68	16.99	17.29	17.59	17.89	18.19	18.49	18.80	19.10	19.71
77	15.12	15.42	15.72	16.02	16.32	16.62	16.92	17.23	17.53	17.84	18.14	18.45	18.75	19.06	19.36	19.98
76	15.34	15.65	15.95	16.25	16.56	16.86	17.17	17.48	17.78	18.09	18.40	18.71	19.02	19.33	19.64	20.26
75	15.58	15.88	16.19	16.50	16.80	17.11	17.42	17.73	18.04	18.35	18.66	18.97	19.29	19.60	19.91	20.54
74	15.81	16.12	16.43	16.74	17.05	17.37	17.68	17.99	18.30	18.62	18.93	19.25	19.57	19.88	20.20	20.83
73	16.06	16.37	16.68	17.00	17.31	17.63	17.94	18.26	18.58	18.89	19.21	19.53	19.85	20.17	20.49	21.13
70	16.82	17.15	17.47	17.80	18.12	18.45	18.77	19.10	19.43	19.76	20.09	20.42	20.75	21.08	21.41	22.08
65	18.24	18.59	18.93	19.28	19.62	19.97	20.31	20.66	21.01	21.36	21.71	22.07	22.42	22.77	23.13	23.84
60	19.88	20.24	20.61	20.98	21.35	21.72	22.09	22.47	22.84	23.22	23.59	23.97	24.35	24.73	25.11	25.88
55	21.78	22.18	22.57	22.97	23.37	23.77	24.17	24.58	24.98	25.39	25.80	26.21	26.62	27.03	27.44	28.27

Description: This table shows the price to pay for a monthly payment mortgage loan at the yield rate.

Example: The price of a 6.75 %, 23 year mortgage loan to yield 8.00 % to maturity is $ 90.04.

YIELD	0.00%	1.00%	2.00%	3.00%	4.00%	4.25%	4.50%	4.75%	5.00%	5.25%	5.50%	5.75%	6.00%	6.25%	6.50%	6.75%
0.00	100.00	111.98	124.84	138.56	153.11	156.88	160.69	164.56	168.47	172.43	176.44	180.50	184.60	188.75	192.94	197.18
1.00	89.30	100.00	111.48	123.73	136.73	140.09	143.50	146.95	150.45	153.98	157.56	161.19	164.85	168.55	172.30	176.08
2.00	80.10	89.70	100.00	110.99	122.65	125.66	128.72	131.82	134.95	138.13	141.34	144.59	147.87	151.19	154.55	157.95
3.00	72.17	80.82	90.10	100.00	110.50	113.22	115.98	118.77	121.59	124.45	127.34	130.27	133.23	136.23	139.25	142.31
4.00	65.31	73.14	81.53	90.49	100.00	102.46	104.95	107.48	110.03	112.62	115.24	117.89	120.57	123.28	126.01	128.78
4.25	63.74	71.38	79.58	88.32	97.60	100.00	102.43	104.90	107.39	109.92	112.47	115.06	117.67	120.32	122.99	125.69
4.50	62.23	69.69	77.69	86.22	95.28	97.63	100.00	102.41	104.84	107.31	109.80	112.33	114.88	117.46	120.07	122.70
4.75	60.77	68.05	75.86	84.20	93.04	95.33	97.65	100.00	102.38	104.79	107.22	109.69	112.18	114.70	117.25	119.82
5.00	59.36	66.47	74.10	82.24	90.88	93.12	95.38	97.68	100.00	102.35	104.73	107.14	109.57	112.04	114.52	117.04
5.25	57.99	64.94	72.40	80.35	88.79	90.98	93.19	95.43	97.70	100.00	102.33	104.68	107.06	109.46	111.89	114.35
5.50	56.68	63.47	70.75	78.53	86.78	88.91	91.07	93.26	95.48	97.73	100.00	102.30	104.62	106.97	109.35	111.75
5.75	55.40	62.04	69.16	76.76	84.83	86.91	89.03	91.17	93.34	95.53	97.75	100.00	102.27	104.57	106.89	109.24
6.00	54.17	60.66	67.63	75.06	82.94	84.98	87.05	89.14	91.26	93.41	95.58	97.78	100.00	102.25	104.52	106.81
6.25	52.98	59.33	66.14	73.41	81.12	83.11	85.14	87.18	89.26	91.36	93.48	95.63	97.80	100.00	102.22	104.47
6.50	51.83	58.04	64.70	71.81	79.36	81.31	83.29	85.29	87.32	89.37	91.45	93.55	95.68	97.83	100.00	102.20
6.75	50.72	56.79	63.31	70.27	77.65	79.56	81.50	83.46	85.44	87.45	89.48	91.54	93.62	95.73	97.85	100.00
7.00	49.64	55.59	61.97	68.78	76.00	77.87	79.77	81.68	83.63	85.59	87.58	89.60	91.63	93.69	95.77	97.88
7.25	48.60	54.42	60.67	67.33	74.41	76.24	78.09	79.97	81.87	83.80	85.74	87.71	89.71	91.72	93.76	95.82
7.50	47.59	53.29	59.41	65.93	72.86	74.65	76.47	78.31	80.17	82.06	83.96	85.89	87.85	89.82	91.81	93.83
7.75	46.61	52.19	58.19	64.58	71.36	73.12	74.90	76.70	78.52	80.37	82.24	84.13	86.04	87.98	89.93	91.90
8.00	45.66	51.13	57.01	63.27	69.92	71.64	73.38	75.14	76.93	78.74	80.57	82.42	84.30	86.19	88.10	90.04
8.25	44.75	50.11	55.86	62.00	68.51	70.20	71.91	73.64	75.39	77.16	78.95	80.77	82.60	84.46	86.34	88.23
8.50	43.86	49.11	54.75	60.77	67.15	68.81	70.48	72.17	73.89	75.63	77.39	79.17	80.97	82.78	84.62	86.48
8.75	43.00	48.15	53.68	59.58	65.84	67.46	69.10	70.76	72.44	74.15	75.87	77.61	79.38	81.16	82.96	84.79
9.00	42.17	47.22	52.64	58.42	64.56	66.15	67.76	69.39	71.04	72.71	74.40	76.11	77.84	79.59	81.36	83.14
9.25	41.36	46.31	51.63	57.30	63.32	64.88	66.46	68.06	69.68	71.32	72.97	74.65	76.35	78.06	79.80	81.55
9.50	40.57	45.44	50.65	56.22	62.12	63.65	65.20	66.77	68.36	69.96	71.59	73.24	74.90	76.58	78.28	80.00
9.75	39.81	44.59	49.70	55.17	60.96	62.46	63.98	65.52	67.08	68.65	70.25	71.87	73.50	75.15	76.82	78.51
10.00	39.08	43.76	48.78	54.14	59.83	61.30	62.79	64.31	65.83	67.38	68.95	70.53	72.14	73.76	75.40	77.05
10.25	38.36	42.96	47.89	53.15	58.74	60.18	61.65	63.13	64.63	66.15	67.69	69.24	70.82	72.41	74.02	75.64
10.50	37.67	42.18	47.02	52.19	57.67	59.09	60.53	61.99	63.46	64.95	66.46	67.99	69.54	71.10	72.68	74.27
10.75	36.99	41.43	46.18	51.26	56.64	58.04	59.45	60.88	62.33	63.79	65.27	66.78	68.29	69.83	71.38	72.95
11.00	36.34	40.69	45.37	50.35	55.64	57.01	58.40	59.80	61.22	62.66	64.12	65.59	67.09	68.59	70.12	71.66
11.25	35.71	39.98	44.57	49.47	54.67	56.01	57.38	58.76	60.15	61.57	63.00	64.45	65.91	67.39	68.89	70.40
11.50	35.09	39.29	43.80	48.62	53.72	55.05	56.39	57.74	59.11	60.50	61.91	63.33	64.77	66.23	67.70	69.19
11.75	34.49	38.62	43.06	47.79	52.81	54.11	55.42	56.76	58.10	59.47	60.85	62.25	63.67	65.10	66.54	68.01
12.00	33.91	37.97	42.33	46.98	51.92	53.19	54.49	55.80	57.12	58.47	59.83	61.20	62.59	64.00	65.42	66.86
12.25	33.34	37.34	41.62	46.20	51.05	52.30	53.58	54.87	56.17	57.49	58.83	60.18	61.55	62.93	64.33	65.74
12.50	32.79	36.72	40.94	45.43	50.21	51.44	52.69	53.96	55.24	56.54	57.86	59.19	60.53	61.89	63.27	64.66
12.75	32.26	36.12	40.27	44.69	49.39	50.60	51.83	53.08	54.34	55.62	56.91	58.22	59.55	60.88	62.24	63.60
13.00	31.74	35.54	39.62	43.97	48.59	49.79	51.00	52.22	53.47	54.72	56.00	57.28	58.58	59.90	61.23	62.58
13.25	31.23	34.97	38.99	43.27	47.82	48.99	50.18	51.39	52.61	53.85	55.10	56.37	57.65	58.95	60.26	61.58
13.50	30.74	34.42	38.37	42.59	47.06	48.22	49.39	50.58	51.78	53.00	54.23	55.48	56.74	58.02	59.31	60.61
13.75	30.26	33.88	37.77	41.92	46.33	47.47	48.62	49.79	50.98	52.18	53.39	54.62	55.86	57.11	58.38	59.66
14.00	29.79	33.36	37.19	41.28	45.61	46.74	47.87	49.02	50.19	51.37	52.57	53.77	55.00	56.23	57.48	58.74
14.25	29.34	32.85	36.62	40.65	44.92	46.02	47.14	48.28	49.43	50.59	51.76	52.95	54.16	55.37	56.60	57.85
14.50	28.90	32.36	36.07	40.04	44.24	45.33	46.43	47.55	48.68	49.83	50.98	52.16	53.34	54.54	55.75	56.98
14.75	28.46	31.88	35.54	39.44	43.58	44.65	45.74	46.84	47.96	49.08	50.22	51.38	52.55	53.73	54.92	56.13
15.00	28.05	31.41	35.01	38.86	42.94	44.00	45.07	46.15	47.25	48.36	49.48	50.62	51.77	52.94	54.11	55.30
15.25	27.64	30.95	34.50	38.29	42.31	43.36	44.41	45.48	46.56	47.66	48.76	49.88	51.02	52.16	53.32	54.49
15.50	27.24	30.50	34.00	37.74	41.71	42.73	43.77	44.82	45.89	46.97	48.06	49.17	50.28	51.41	52.55	53.71
15.75	26.85	30.07	33.52	37.20	41.11	42.12	43.15	44.18	45.24	46.30	47.38	48.46	49.57	50.68	51.81	52.94
16.00	26.47	29.64	33.05	36.68	40.53	41.53	42.54	43.56	44.60	45.65	46.71	47.78	48.87	49.97	51.07	52.20
16.25	26.10	29.23	32.59	36.17	39.97	40.95	41.94	42.95	43.98	45.01	46.06	47.11	48.19	49.27	50.36	51.47
16.50	25.74	28.83	32.14	35.67	39.41	40.38	41.37	42.36	43.37	44.39	45.42	46.47	47.52	48.59	49.67	50.76
16.75	25.39	28.43	31.70	35.18	38.88	39.83	40.80	41.78	42.78	43.78	44.80	45.83	46.87	47.93	48.99	50.07
17.00	25.05	28.05	31.27	34.71	38.35	39.30	40.25	41.22	42.20	43.19	44.20	45.21	46.24	47.28	48.33	49.39
17.25	24.71	27.68	30.85	34.24	37.84	38.77	39.71	40.67	41.64	42.62	43.61	44.61	45.62	46.65	47.68	48.73
17.50	24.39	27.31	30.45	33.79	37.34	38.26	39.19	40.13	41.09	42.05	43.03	44.02	45.02	46.03	47.05	48.09
17.75	24.07	26.95	30.05	33.35	36.85	37.76	38.68	39.61	40.55	41.50	42.47	43.44	44.43	45.43	46.44	47.46
18.00	23.76	26.60	29.66	32.92	36.38	37.27	38.18	39.10	40.03	40.97	41.92	42.88	43.86	44.84	45.84	46.85
18.25	23.45	26.26	29.28	32.50	35.91	36.79	37.69	38.60	39.51	40.44	41.38	42.33	43.30	44.27	45.25	46.25
18.50	23.16	25.93	28.91	32.09	35.46	36.33	37.21	38.11	39.01	39.93	40.86	41.80	42.75	43.71	44.68	45.66
18.75	22.87	25.61	28.55	31.68	35.01	35.87	36.75	37.63	38.52	39.43	40.35	41.28	42.21	43.16	44.12	45.09
19.00	22.58	25.29	28.19	31.29	34.58	35.43	36.29	37.16	38.05	38.94	39.85	40.76	41.69	42.63	43.57	44.53
20.00	21.51	24.09	26.86	29.81	32.94	33.75	34.57	35.40	36.24	37.09	37.96	38.83	39.71	40.60	41.51	42.42
25.00	17.33	19.41	21.64	24.02	26.54	27.19	27.85	28.52	29.20	29.89	30.58	31.29	32.00	32.72	33.44	34.18
30.00	14.48	16.21	18.07	20.06	22.17	22.71	23.26	23.82	24.39	24.96	25.54	26.13	26.72	27.32	27.93	28.55

Description: This table shows the yield to maturity of a mortgage purchased at the price shown in the index.

Example: The yield to maturity of a 6.75 %, 23 year mortgage at a price of 80.00 is 9.50 %.

INTEREST RATE, %

PRICE	0.00%	1.00%	2.00%	3.00%	4.00%	4.25%	4.50%	4.75%	5.00%	5.25%	5.50%	5.75%	6.00%	6.25%	6.50%	6.75%
100	0.00	1.00	2.00	3.00	4.00	4.25	4.50	4.75	5.00	5.25	5.50	5.75	6.00	6.25	6.50	6.75
99	.08	1.09	2.09	3.09	4.10	4.35	4.60	4.85	5.10	5.35	5.61	5.86	6.11	6.36	6.61	6.86
98	.17	1.18	2.19	3.19	4.20	4.45	4.71	4.96	5.21	5.46	5.72	5.97	6.22	6.47	6.73	6.98
97	.26	1.27	2.28	3.30	4.31	4.56	4.82	5.07	5.32	5.58	5.83	6.08	6.34	6.59	6.85	7.10
96	.35	1.37	2.38	3.40	4.42	4.67	4.93	5.18	5.44	5.69	5.95	6.20	6.46	6.71	6.97	7.22
95	.44	1.46	2.48	3.50	4.53	4.78	5.04	5.29	5.55	5.81	6.06	6.32	6.58	6.83	7.09	7.35
94	.54	1.56	2.58	3.61	4.64	4.89	5.15	5.41	5.67	5.92	6.18	6.44	6.70	6.96	7.21	7.47
93	.63	1.66	2.69	3.72	4.75	5.01	5.27	5.53	5.79	6.04	6.30	6.56	6.82	7.08	7.34	7.60
92	.73	1.76	2.79	3.83	4.86	5.12	5.38	5.64	5.91	6.17	6.43	6.69	6.95	7.21	7.47	7.73
91	.83	1.86	2.90	3.94	4.98	5.24	5.50	5.77	6.03	6.29	6.55	6.81	7.08	7.34	7.60	7.87
90	.92	1.96	3.01	4.05	5.10	5.36	5.63	5.89	6.15	6.41	6.68	6.94	7.21	7.47	7.74	8.00
89	1.03	2.07	3.12	4.17	5.22	5.48	5.75	6.01	6.28	6.54	6.81	7.07	7.34	7.61	7.87	8.14
88	1.13	2.18	3.23	4.28	5.34	5.61	5.87	6.14	6.41	6.67	6.94	7.21	7.47	7.74	8.01	8.28
87	1.23	2.28	3.34	4.40	5.47	5.73	6.00	6.27	6.54	6.80	7.07	7.34	7.61	7.88	8.15	8.42
86	1.34	2.39	3.46	4.52	5.59	5.86	6.13	6.40	6.67	6.94	7.21	7.48	7.75	8.02	8.29	8.57
85	1.44	2.51	3.57	4.65	5.72	5.99	6.26	6.53	6.81	7.08	7.35	7.62	7.89	8.17	8.44	8.71
84	1.55	2.62	3.69	4.77	5.85	6.13	6.40	6.67	6.94	7.22	7.49	7.76	8.04	8.31	8.59	8.86
83	1.66	2.74	3.81	4.90	5.99	6.26	6.53	6.81	7.08	7.36	7.63	7.91	8.19	8.46	8.74	9.02
82	1.78	2.85	3.94	5.03	6.12	6.40	6.67	6.95	7.23	7.50	7.78	8.06	8.34	8.61	8.89	9.17
81	1.89	2.97	4.06	5.16	6.26	6.54	6.82	7.09	7.37	7.65	7.93	8.21	8.49	8.77	9.05	9.33
80	2.01	3.10	4.19	5.29	6.40	6.68	6.96	7.24	7.52	7.80	8.08	8.36	8.65	8.93	9.21	9.50
79	2.13	3.22	4.32	5.43	6.55	6.83	7.11	7.39	7.67	7.95	8.24	8.52	8.81	9.09	9.38	9.66
78	2.25	3.35	4.45	5.57	6.69	6.98	7.26	7.54	7.83	8.11	8.40	8.68	8.97	9.26	9.54	9.83
77	2.37	3.47	4.59	5.71	6.84	7.13	7.41	7.70	7.98	8.27	8.56	8.85	9.13	9.42	9.71	10.00
76	2.49	3.61	4.73	5.86	7.00	7.28	7.57	7.86	8.14	8.43	8.72	9.01	9.30	9.60	9.89	10.18
75	2.62	3.74	4.87	6.00	7.15	7.44	7.73	8.02	8.31	8.60	8.89	9.18	9.48	9.77	10.07	10.36
74	2.75	3.88	5.01	6.15	7.31	7.60	7.89	8.18	8.48	8.77	9.06	9.36	9.65	9.95	10.25	10.55
73	2.88	4.01	5.16	6.31	7.47	7.76	8.06	8.35	8.65	8.94	9.24	9.54	9.84	10.13	10.43	10.73
72	3.02	4.16	5.30	6.47	7.64	7.93	8.23	8.53	8.82	9.12	9.42	9.72	10.02	10.32	10.62	10.93
71	3.16	4.30	5.46	6.63	7.81	8.10	8.40	8.70	9.00	9.30	9.60	9.91	10.21	10.51	10.82	11.13
70	3.30	4.45	5.61	6.79	7.98	8.28	8.58	8.88	9.18	9.49	9.79	10.10	10.40	10.71	11.02	11.33
69	3.44	4.60	5.77	6.96	8.16	8.46	8.76	9.07	9.37	9.68	9.99	10.29	10.60	10.91	11.22	11.53
68	3.59	4.75	5.93	7.13	8.34	8.64	8.95	9.26	9.56	9.87	10.18	10.49	10.80	11.12	11.43	11.75
67	3.74	4.91	6.10	7.30	8.52	8.83	9.14	9.45	9.76	10.07	10.38	10.70	11.01	11.33	11.65	11.96
66	3.89	5.07	6.27	7.48	8.71	9.02	9.34	9.65	9.96	10.28	10.59	10.91	11.23	11.55	11.87	12.19
65	4.04	5.24	6.44	7.67	8.91	9.22	9.54	9.85	10.17	10.49	10.80	11.12	11.44	11.77	12.09	12.42
64	4.20	5.40	6.62	7.85	9.11	9.42	9.74	10.06	10.38	10.70	11.02	11.34	11.67	11.99	12.32	12.65
63	4.37	5.58	6.80	8.05	9.31	9.63	9.95	10.27	10.60	10.92	11.25	11.57	11.90	12.23	12.56	12.89
62	4.53	5.75	6.99	8.25	9.52	9.84	10.17	10.49	10.82	11.15	11.47	11.80	12.14	12.47	12.80	13.14
61	4.70	5.93	7.18	8.45	9.74	10.06	10.39	10.72	11.05	11.38	11.71	12.04	12.38	12.72	13.05	13.39
60	4.88	6.12	7.38	8.66	9.96	10.29	10.62	10.95	11.28	11.62	11.95	12.29	12.63	12.97	13.31	13.65
59	5.06	6.31	7.58	8.87	10.18	10.52	10.85	11.19	11.52	11.86	12.20	12.54	12.89	13.23	13.58	13.92
58	5.24	6.50	7.78	9.09	10.42	10.75	11.09	11.43	11.77	12.11	12.46	12.80	13.15	13.50	13.85	14.20
57	5.43	6.70	8.00	9.31	10.66	11.00	11.34	11.68	12.03	12.37	12.72	13.07	13.42	13.78	14.13	14.49
56	5.63	6.91	8.21	9.55	10.90	11.25	11.59	11.94	12.29	12.64	12.99	13.35	13.70	14.06	14.42	14.78
55	5.83	7.12	8.44	9.79	11.16	11.51	11.86	12.21	12.56	12.92	13.27	13.63	13.99	14.36	14.72	15.09
54	6.03	7.34	8.67	10.03	11.42	11.77	12.13	12.48	12.84	13.20	13.56	13.93	14.29	14.66	15.03	15.40
53	6.24	7.56	8.91	10.28	11.69	12.05	12.41	12.77	13.13	13.50	13.86	14.23	14.60	14.97	15.35	15.73
52	6.46	7.79	9.15	10.55	11.97	12.33	12.70	13.06	13.43	13.80	14.17	14.54	14.92	15.30	15.68	16.06
51	6.68	8.03	9.41	10.82	12.26	12.63	12.99	13.36	13.74	14.11	14.49	14.87	15.25	15.63	16.02	16.41
50	6.91	8.27	9.67	11.09	12.56	12.93	13.30	13.68	14.06	14.44	14.82	15.21	15.59	15.98	16.37	16.77
49	7.15	8.52	9.94	11.38	12.87	13.24	13.62	14.00	14.39	14.77	15.16	15.55	15.95	16.34	16.74	17.14
48	7.39	8.79	10.21	11.68	13.19	13.57	13.95	14.34	14.73	15.12	15.52	15.91	16.31	16.72	17.12	17.53
47	7.64	9.05	10.50	11.99	13.52	13.90	14.30	14.69	15.08	15.48	15.88	16.29	16.70	17.10	17.52	17.93
46	7.91	9.33	10.80	12.31	13.86	14.25	14.65	15.05	15.45	15.86	16.27	16.68	17.09	17.51	17.93	18.35
45	8.18	9.62	11.11	12.64	14.22	14.62	15.02	15.43	15.84	16.25	16.66	17.08	17.50	17.93	18.35	18.78
44	8.45	9.92	11.43	12.99	14.59	14.99	15.40	15.82	16.24	16.65	17.08	17.50	17.93	18.36	18.80	19.24
43	8.74	10.23	11.76	13.34	14.97	15.39	15.80	16.23	16.65	17.08	17.51	17.94	18.38	18.82	19.26	19.71
42	9.05	10.55	12.11	13.72	15.37	15.80	16.22	16.65	17.08	17.52	17.96	18.40	18.85	19.30	19.75	20.20
41	9.36	10.89	12.47	14.10	15.79	16.22	16.66	17.09	17.53	17.98	18.43	18.88	19.33	19.79	20.25	20.72
40	9.68	11.24	12.85	14.51	16.23	16.67	17.11	17.56	18.01	18.46	18.92	19.38	19.84	20.31	20.78	21.26
39	10.02	11.60	13.24	14.93	16.69	17.14	17.59	18.04	18.50	18.97	19.43	19.90	20.38	20.86	21.34	21.83
35	11.53	13.23	15.00	16.84	18.75	19.24	19.74	20.23	20.74	21.25	21.76	22.28	22.80	23.33	23.86	24.39
30	13.88	15.78	17.78	19.86	22.04	22.60	23.17	23.74	24.32	24.90	25.49	26.09	26.69	27.30	27.91	28.53
25	17.03	19.23	21.55	23.99	26.56	27.22	27.89	28.57	29.26	29.95	30.65	31.36	32.08	32.80	33.53	34.27
20	21.58	24.24	27.08	30.08	33.26	34.08	34.92	35.76	36.61	37.47	38.35	39.23	40.12	41.02	41.94	42.86
15	28.94	32.43	36.17	40.15	44.37	45.47	46.57	47.69	48.83	49.98	51.14	52.31	53.50	54.71	55.92	57.15
10	43.47	48.68	54.27	60.24	66.57	68.20	69.86	71.54	73.24	74.97	76.71	78.47	80.26	82.06	83.88	85.73

Description: This table shows the price to pay for a monthly payment mortgage loan at the yield rate.

Example: The price of a 10.75 %, 23 year mortgage loan to yield 8.00 % to maturity is $ 123.43.

INTEREST RATE, %

YIELD	7.00%	7.25%	7.50%	7.75%	8.00%	8.25%	8.50%	8.75%	9.00%	9.25%	9.50%	9.75%	10.00%	10.25%	10.50%	10.75%
0.00	201.46	205.78	210.14	214.55	218.99	223.48	228.00	232.56	237.16	241.79	246.46	251.16	255.90	260.67	265.48	270.31
1.00	179.90	183.76	187.66	191.59	195.56	199.57	203.60	207.68	211.78	215.92	220.09	224.29	228.52	232.78	237.07	241.39
2.00	161.37	164.84	168.33	171.86	175.42	179.01	182.64	186.29	189.97	193.68	197.42	201.19	204.99	208.81	212.65	216.53
3.00	145.40	148.52	151.67	154.85	158.05	161.29	164.55	167.85	171.16	174.51	177.88	181.27	184.69	188.13	191.60	195.09
4.00	131.58	134.40	137.25	140.13	143.03	145.96	148.91	151.89	154.89	157.92	160.97	164.04	167.13	170.25	173.39	176.54
4.25	128.42	131.17	133.95	136.76	139.60	142.45	145.34	148.24	151.17	154.13	157.10	160.10	163.12	166.16	169.23	172.31
4.50	125.37	128.06	130.77	133.51	136.28	139.07	141.89	144.72	147.58	150.47	153.37	156.30	159.25	162.22	165.21	168.21
4.75	122.42	125.05	127.70	130.38	133.08	135.80	138.55	141.32	144.12	146.93	149.77	152.63	155.51	158.41	161.33	164.26
5.00	119.58	122.14	124.73	127.35	129.99	132.65	135.33	138.04	140.77	143.52	146.29	149.08	151.90	154.73	157.58	160.45
5.25	116.83	119.34	121.87	124.42	127.00	129.60	132.22	134.87	137.54	140.22	142.93	145.66	148.41	151.17	153.96	156.76
5.50	114.18	116.63	119.10	121.60	124.12	126.66	129.22	131.80	134.41	137.04	139.68	142.35	145.03	147.74	150.46	153.20
5.75	111.61	114.01	116.42	118.86	121.33	123.81	126.32	128.84	131.39	133.96	136.54	139.15	141.77	144.42	147.08	149.76
6.00	109.13	111.47	113.84	116.22	118.63	121.06	123.51	125.98	128.47	130.98	133.51	136.06	138.62	141.21	143.81	146.43
6.25	106.73	109.02	111.33	113.67	116.02	118.40	120.79	123.21	125.65	128.10	130.58	133.07	135.58	138.11	140.65	143.21
6.50	104.41	106.65	108.92	111.20	113.50	115.83	118.17	120.53	122.92	125.32	127.74	130.18	132.63	135.10	137.59	140.10
6.75	102.17	104.36	106.58	108.81	111.06	113.34	115.63	117.94	120.28	122.63	124.99	127.38	129.78	132.20	134.64	137.09
7.00	100.00	102.15	104.31	106.50	108.70	110.93	113.18	115.44	117.72	120.02	122.34	124.67	127.03	129.39	131.78	134.18
7.25	97.90	100.00	102.12	104.26	106.42	108.60	110.80	113.01	115.25	117.50	119.77	122.06	124.36	126.68	129.01	131.36
7.50	95.87	97.92	100.00	102.10	104.21	106.35	108.50	110.67	112.86	115.06	117.28	119.52	121.77	124.05	126.33	128.63
7.75	93.90	95.91	97.95	100.00	102.07	104.16	106.27	108.40	110.54	112.70	114.87	117.07	119.27	121.50	123.74	125.99
8.00	91.99	93.97	95.96	97.97	100.00	102.05	104.11	106.20	108.29	110.41	112.54	114.69	116.85	119.03	121.23	123.43
8.25	90.15	92.08	94.03	96.00	97.99	100.00	102.02	104.06	106.12	108.20	110.28	112.39	114.51	116.64	118.79	120.96
8.50	88.36	90.25	92.17	94.10	96.05	98.02	100.00	102.00	104.02	106.05	108.10	110.16	112.24	114.33	116.44	118.56
8.75	86.63	88.48	90.36	92.25	94.17	96.09	98.04	100.00	101.98	103.97	105.98	108.00	110.04	112.09	114.15	116.23
9.00	84.95	86.77	88.61	90.47	92.34	94.23	96.14	98.06	100.00	101.95	103.92	105.91	107.90	109.92	111.94	113.98
9.25	83.32	85.11	86.91	88.73	90.57	92.43	94.30	96.18	98.08	100.00	101.93	103.88	105.84	107.81	109.80	111.79
9.50	81.74	83.49	85.26	87.05	88.86	90.67	92.51	94.36	96.23	98.11	100.00	101.91	103.83	105.77	107.72	109.68
9.75	80.21	81.93	83.67	85.42	87.19	88.98	90.78	92.59	94.42	96.27	98.13	100.00	101.89	103.79	105.70	107.62
10.00	78.72	80.41	82.12	83.84	85.58	87.33	89.10	90.88	92.68	94.49	96.31	98.15	100.00	101.86	103.74	105.63
10.25	77.28	78.94	80.62	82.31	84.01	85.73	87.47	89.22	90.98	92.76	94.55	96.35	98.17	100.00	101.84	103.70
10.50	75.89	77.51	79.16	80.82	82.49	84.18	85.88	87.60	89.33	91.08	92.84	94.61	96.39	98.19	100.00	101.82
10.75	74.53	76.13	77.74	79.37	81.02	82.67	84.35	86.03	87.74	89.45	91.18	92.92	94.67	96.43	98.21	100.00
11.00	73.21	74.78	76.37	77.97	79.58	81.21	82.86	84.51	86.18	87.87	89.57	91.27	93.00	94.73	96.48	98.23
11.25	71.93	73.47	75.03	76.61	78.19	79.79	81.41	83.04	84.68	86.33	88.00	89.68	91.37	93.07	94.79	96.52
11.50	70.69	72.21	73.74	75.28	76.84	78.42	80.00	81.60	83.22	84.84	86.48	88.13	89.79	91.47	93.15	94.85
11.75	69.48	70.97	72.48	74.00	75.53	77.08	78.64	80.21	81.79	83.39	85.00	86.63	88.26	89.90	91.56	93.23
12.00	68.31	69.77	71.25	72.75	74.25	75.77	77.31	78.85	80.41	81.98	83.57	85.16	86.77	88.39	90.01	91.65
12.25	67.17	68.61	70.06	71.53	73.01	74.51	76.02	77.54	79.07	80.62	82.17	83.74	85.32	86.91	88.51	90.12
12.50	66.06	67.48	68.91	70.35	71.81	73.28	74.76	76.26	77.77	79.29	80.82	82.36	83.91	85.48	87.05	88.64
12.75	64.98	66.38	67.78	69.20	70.64	72.08	73.54	75.01	76.50	77.99	79.50	81.02	82.54	84.08	85.63	87.19
13.00	63.93	65.31	66.69	68.09	69.50	70.92	72.36	73.80	75.26	76.73	78.22	79.71	81.21	82.73	84.25	85.78
13.25	62.91	64.26	65.63	67.00	68.39	69.79	71.20	72.63	74.06	75.51	76.97	78.44	79.92	81.41	82.91	84.42
13.50	61.92	63.25	64.59	65.95	67.31	68.69	70.08	71.48	72.90	74.32	75.76	77.20	78.66	80.12	81.60	83.09
13.75	60.96	62.27	63.59	64.92	66.26	67.62	68.99	70.37	71.76	73.16	74.57	76.00	77.43	78.87	80.33	81.79
14.00	60.02	61.31	62.61	63.92	65.24	66.58	67.93	69.28	70.65	72.03	73.42	74.83	76.24	77.66	79.09	80.53
14.25	59.10	60.37	61.65	62.94	64.25	65.56	66.89	68.23	69.58	70.94	72.31	73.69	75.08	76.48	77.88	79.30
14.50	58.21	59.46	60.72	61.99	63.28	64.57	65.88	67.20	68.53	69.87	71.22	72.58	73.94	75.32	76.71	78.11
14.75	57.34	58.58	59.82	61.07	62.34	63.61	64.90	66.20	67.51	68.83	70.15	71.49	72.84	74.20	75.57	76.94
15.00	56.50	57.71	58.94	60.17	61.42	62.68	63.94	65.22	66.51	67.81	69.12	70.44	71.77	73.11	74.45	75.81
15.25	55.68	56.87	58.08	59.29	60.52	61.76	63.01	64.27	65.54	66.82	68.11	69.41	70.72	72.04	73.37	74.70
15.50	54.87	56.05	57.24	58.44	59.65	60.87	62.10	63.35	64.60	65.86	67.13	68.41	69.70	71.00	72.31	73.63
15.75	54.09	55.25	56.42	57.61	58.80	60.00	61.22	62.44	63.68	64.92	66.18	67.44	68.71	69.99	71.28	72.58
16.00	53.33	54.47	55.63	56.79	57.97	59.16	60.36	61.56	62.78	64.01	65.24	66.49	67.74	69.00	70.28	71.56
16.25	52.59	53.71	54.85	56.00	57.16	58.33	59.51	60.70	61.90	63.11	64.33	65.56	66.80	68.04	69.30	70.56
16.50	51.86	52.97	54.10	55.23	56.37	57.53	58.69	59.87	61.05	62.24	63.45	64.66	65.88	67.10	68.34	69.58
16.75	51.15	52.25	53.36	54.48	55.61	56.74	57.89	59.05	60.22	61.39	62.58	63.77	64.98	66.19	67.41	68.64
17.00	50.46	51.55	52.64	53.74	54.85	55.98	57.11	58.25	59.40	60.57	61.74	62.91	64.10	65.29	66.50	67.71
17.25	49.79	50.86	51.94	53.02	54.12	55.23	56.35	57.48	58.61	59.76	60.91	62.07	63.24	64.42	65.61	66.80
17.50	49.13	50.19	51.25	52.32	53.41	54.50	55.60	56.72	57.84	58.97	60.11	61.25	62.41	63.57	64.74	65.92
17.75	48.49	49.53	50.58	51.64	52.71	53.79	54.88	55.98	57.08	58.20	59.32	60.45	61.59	62.74	63.90	65.06
18.00	47.86	48.89	49.93	50.97	52.03	53.09	54.17	55.25	56.34	57.44	58.55	59.67	60.80	61.93	63.07	64.22
18.25	47.25	48.26	49.29	50.32	51.36	52.41	53.48	54.54	55.62	56.71	57.81	58.91	60.02	61.14	62.26	63.40
18.50	46.65	47.65	48.66	49.68	50.71	51.75	52.80	53.85	54.92	55.99	57.07	58.16	59.26	60.36	61.48	62.60
18.75	46.07	47.06	48.05	49.06	50.08	51.10	52.14	53.18	54.23	55.29	56.36	57.43	58.52	59.61	60.71	61.81
19.00	45.50	46.47	47.46	48.45	49.46	50.47	51.49	52.52	53.56	54.61	55.66	56.72	57.79	58.87	59.95	61.05
20.00	43.34	44.27	45.21	46.15	47.11	48.07	49.05	50.03	51.02	52.01	53.02	54.03	55.05	56.08	57.11	58.15
25.00	34.92	35.67	36.42	37.19	37.96	38.73	39.52	40.31	41.11	41.91	42.72	43.53	44.35	45.18	46.01	46.85
30.00	29.16	29.79	30.42	31.06	31.70	32.35	33.01	33.67	34.33	35.00	35.68	36.36	37.05	37.74	38.43	39.13

MORTGAGE YIELD

Description: This table shows the yield to maturity of a mortgage purchased at the price shown in the index.

Example: The yield to maturity of a 10.75 %, 23 year mortgage at a price of 111.00 is 9.34 %.

INTEREST RATE, %

PRICE	7.00%	7.25%	7.50%	7.75%	8.00%	8.25%	8.50%	8.75%	9.00%	9.25%	9.50%	9.75%	10.00%	10.25%	10.50%	10.75%
165	1.79	1.99	2.18	2.38	2.58	2.77	2.97	3.16	3.36	3.55	3.74	3.94	4.13	4.32	4.51	4.70
160	2.08	2.28	2.48	2.68	2.88	3.07	3.27	3.47	3.67	3.86	4.06	4.25	4.45	4.64	4.83	5.02
155	2.38	2.58	2.78	2.99	3.19	3.39	3.59	3.79	3.99	4.19	4.38	4.58	4.78	4.98	5.17	5.37
150	2.69	2.90	3.10	3.31	3.51	3.72	3.92	4.12	4.33	4.53	4.73	4.93	5.13	5.33	5.53	5.73
145	3.02	3.23	3.44	3.65	3.86	4.06	4.27	4.48	4.68	4.89	5.09	5.29	5.50	5.70	5.90	6.10
140	3.37	3.58	3.79	4.00	4.22	4.43	4.64	4.84	5.05	5.26	5.47	5.68	5.88	6.09	6.30	6.50
135	3.73	3.95	4.16	4.38	4.59	4.81	5.02	5.23	5.45	5.66	5.87	6.08	6.29	6.50	6.71	6.92
130	4.12	4.34	4.56	4.78	4.99	5.21	5.43	5.65	5.86	6.08	6.30	6.51	6.73	6.94	7.15	7.37
125	4.53	4.75	4.97	5.20	5.42	5.64	5.86	6.08	6.30	6.52	6.74	6.96	7.18	7.40	7.62	7.84
122	4.78	5.01	5.23	5.46	5.68	5.91	6.13	6.36	6.58	6.80	7.03	7.25	7.47	7.70	7.92	8.14
121	4.87	5.10	5.32	5.55	5.77	6.00	6.23	6.45	6.68	6.90	7.12	7.35	7.57	7.79	8.02	8.24
120	4.96	5.19	5.41	5.64	5.87	6.09	6.32	6.55	6.77	7.00	7.22	7.45	7.67	7.90	8.12	8.34
119	5.05	5.28	5.50	5.73	5.96	6.19	6.42	6.64	6.87	7.10	7.32	7.55	7.77	8.00	8.22	8.45
118	5.14	5.37	5.60	5.83	6.05	6.28	6.51	6.74	6.97	7.19	7.42	7.65	7.88	8.10	8.33	8.55
117	5.23	5.46	5.69	5.92	6.15	6.38	6.61	6.84	7.07	7.30	7.52	7.75	7.98	8.21	8.43	8.66
116	5.32	5.55	5.79	6.02	6.25	6.48	6.71	6.94	7.17	7.40	7.63	7.86	8.09	8.31	8.54	8.77
115	5.42	5.65	5.88	6.11	6.35	6.58	6.81	7.04	7.27	7.50	7.73	7.96	8.19	8.42	8.65	8.88
114	5.51	5.75	5.98	6.21	6.44	6.68	6.91	7.14	7.37	7.61	7.84	8.07	8.30	8.53	8.76	8.99
113	5.61	5.84	6.08	6.31	6.55	6.78	7.01	7.25	7.48	7.71	7.95	8.18	8.41	8.64	8.87	9.11
112	5.71	5.94	6.18	6.41	6.65	6.88	7.12	7.35	7.59	7.82	8.05	8.29	8.52	8.75	8.99	9.22
111	5.81	6.04	6.28	6.52	6.75	6.99	7.22	7.46	7.69	7.93	8.16	8.40	8.63	8.87	9.10	9.34
110	5.91	6.14	6.38	6.62	6.86	7.09	7.33	7.57	7.80	8.04	8.28	8.51	8.75	8.99	9.22	9.46
109	6.01	6.25	6.49	6.72	6.96	7.20	7.44	7.68	7.92	8.15	8.39	8.63	8.87	9.10	9.34	9.58
108	6.11	6.35	6.59	6.83	7.07	7.31	7.55	7.79	8.03	8.27	8.51	8.74	8.98	9.22	9.46	9.70
107	6.22	6.46	6.70	6.94	7.18	7.42	7.66	7.90	8.14	8.38	8.62	8.86	9.10	9.34	9.58	9.82
106	6.32	6.57	6.81	7.05	7.29	7.53	7.78	8.02	8.26	8.50	8.74	8.98	9.22	9.47	9.71	9.95
105	6.43	6.67	6.92	7.16	7.40	7.65	7.89	8.13	8.38	8.62	8.86	9.11	9.35	9.59	9.83	10.08
104	6.54	6.79	7.03	7.27	7.52	7.76	8.01	8.25	8.50	8.74	8.99	9.23	9.47	9.72	9.96	10.21
103	6.65	6.90	7.14	7.39	7.64	7.88	8.13	8.37	8.62	8.86	9.11	9.36	9.60	9.85	10.09	10.34
102	6.76	7.01	7.26	7.51	7.75	8.00	8.25	8.50	8.74	8.99	9.24	9.48	9.73	9.98	10.22	10.47
101	6.88	7.13	7.38	7.62	7.87	8.12	8.37	8.62	8.87	9.12	9.36	9.61	9.86	10.11	10.36	10.61
100	7.00	7.25	7.50	7.75	8.00	8.25	8.50	8.75	9.00	9.25	9.50	9.75	10.00	10.25	10.50	10.75
99	7.11	7.36	7.62	7.87	8.12	8.37	8.62	8.87	9.12	9.38	9.63	9.88	10.13	10.38	10.63	10.89
98	7.23	7.49	7.74	7.99	8.24	8.50	8.75	9.00	9.26	9.51	9.76	10.02	10.27	10.52	10.78	11.03
97	7.35	7.61	7.86	8.12	8.37	8.63	8.88	9.14	9.39	9.64	9.90	10.15	10.41	10.66	10.92	11.17
96	7.48	7.73	7.99	8.25	8.50	8.76	9.01	9.27	9.53	9.78	10.04	10.29	10.55	10.81	11.06	11.32
95	7.60	7.86	8.12	8.38	8.63	8.89	9.15	9.41	9.66	9.92	10.18	10.44	10.70	10.95	11.21	11.47
94	7.73	7.99	8.25	8.51	8.77	9.03	9.29	9.55	9.80	10.06	10.32	10.58	10.84	11.10	11.36	11.62
93	7.86	8.12	8.38	8.64	8.90	9.16	9.43	9.69	9.95	10.21	10.47	10.73	10.99	11.26	11.52	11.78
92	7.99	8.26	8.52	8.78	9.04	9.31	9.57	9.83	10.09	10.36	10.62	10.88	11.15	11.41	11.68	11.94
91	8.13	8.39	8.66	8.92	9.18	9.45	9.71	9.98	10.24	10.51	10.77	11.04	11.30	11.57	11.83	12.10
90	8.27	8.53	8.80	9.06	9.33	9.59	9.86	10.13	10.39	10.66	10.93	11.19	11.46	11.73	12.00	12.27
89	8.40	8.67	8.94	9.21	9.47	9.74	10.01	10.28	10.55	10.82	11.08	11.35	11.62	11.89	12.16	12.43
88	8.55	8.81	9.08	9.35	9.62	9.89	10.16	10.43	10.70	10.97	11.25	11.52	11.79	12.06	12.33	12.60
87	8.69	8.96	9.23	9.50	9.77	10.05	10.32	10.59	10.86	11.14	11.41	11.68	11.96	12.23	12.50	12.78
86	8.84	9.11	9.38	9.66	9.93	10.20	10.48	10.75	11.03	11.30	11.58	11.85	12.13	12.40	12.68	12.96
85	8.99	9.26	9.54	9.81	10.09	10.36	10.64	10.91	11.19	11.47	11.75	12.02	12.30	12.58	12.86	13.14
84	9.14	9.42	9.69	9.97	10.25	10.52	10.80	11.08	11.36	11.64	11.92	12.20	12.48	12.76	13.04	13.32
83	9.29	9.57	9.85	10.13	10.41	10.69	10.97	11.25	11.53	11.81	12.10	12.38	12.66	12.94	13.23	13.51
82	9.45	9.73	10.01	10.30	10.58	10.86	11.14	11.42	11.71	11.99	12.28	12.56	12.85	13.13	13.42	13.70
81	9.61	9.90	10.18	10.46	10.75	11.03	11.32	11.60	11.89	12.17	12.46	12.75	13.04	13.32	13.61	13.90
80	9.78	10.06	10.35	10.64	10.92	11.21	11.50	11.78	12.07	12.36	12.65	12.94	13.23	13.52	13.81	14.10
79	9.95	10.23	10.52	10.81	11.10	11.39	11.68	11.97	12.26	12.55	12.84	13.13	13.43	13.72	14.01	14.31
78	10.12	10.41	10.70	10.99	11.28	11.57	11.86	12.16	12.45	12.74	13.04	13.33	13.63	13.92	14.22	14.52
77	10.30	10.59	10.88	11.17	11.47	11.76	12.05	12.35	12.65	12.94	13.24	13.54	13.83	14.13	14.43	14.73
76	10.47	10.77	11.06	11.36	11.65	11.95	12.25	12.55	12.85	13.14	13.44	13.74	14.05	14.35	14.65	14.95
75	10.66	10.95	11.25	11.55	11.85	12.15	12.45	12.75	13.05	13.35	13.65	13.96	14.26	14.57	14.87	15.18
74	10.84	11.14	11.44	11.74	12.05	12.35	12.65	12.95	13.26	13.56	13.87	14.18	14.48	14.79	15.10	15.41
73	11.04	11.34	11.64	11.94	12.25	12.55	12.86	13.17	13.47	13.78	14.09	14.40	14.71	15.02	15.33	15.64
70	11.64	11.95	12.26	12.57	12.88	13.20	13.51	13.83	14.15	14.46	14.78	15.10	15.42	15.74	16.06	16.39
65	12.74	13.07	13.40	13.72	14.06	14.39	14.72	15.05	15.39	15.72	16.06	16.40	16.74	17.08	17.42	17.76
60	14.00	14.35	14.69	15.04	15.39	15.75	16.10	16.45	16.81	17.17	17.53	17.89	18.25	18.61	18.98	19.35
55	15.46	15.83	16.20	16.57	16.95	17.32	17.70	18.08	18.47	18.85	19.24	19.62	20.01	20.41	20.80	21.19
50	17.17	17.57	17.97	18.37	18.78	19.18	19.59	20.01	20.42	20.84	21.26	21.68	22.10	22.53	22.96	23.39
45	19.22	19.65	20.09	20.53	20.98	21.42	21.87	22.33	22.78	23.24	23.70	24.16	24.63	25.10	25.57	26.04
40	21.74	22.22	22.71	23.20	23.69	24.19	24.69	25.19	25.70	26.21	26.72	27.24	27.76	28.28	28.81	29.34
35	24.94	25.48	26.03	26.58	27.14	27.71	28.27	28.84	29.42	30.00	30.58	31.17	31.76	32.36	32.95	33.56
30	29.15	29.78	30.42	31.06	31.71	32.36	33.02	33.68	34.35	35.02	35.70	36.39	37.07	37.77	38.46	39.16

Description: This table shows the price to pay for a monthly payment mortgage loan at the yield rate.

Example: The price of a 15.00 %, 23 year mortgage loan to yield 8.00 % to maturity is $ 162.82.

INTEREST RATE, %

YIELD	11.00%	11.25%	11.50%	11.75%	12.00%	12.25%	12.50%	12.75%	13.00%	13.25%	13.50%	13.75%	14.00%	14.25%	14.50%	15.00%
0.00	275.17	280.07	284.99	289.94	294.92	299.93	304.96	310.02	315.10	320.21	325.34	330.49	335.66	340.86	346.07	356.56
1.00	245.73	250.10	254.50	258.92	263.37	267.84	272.33	276.85	281.39	285.95	290.53	295.13	299.75	304.39	309.04	318.41
2.00	220.42	224.34	228.29	232.25	236.24	240.25	244.28	248.34	252.41	256.50	260.61	264.73	268.88	273.04	277.22	285.62
3.00	198.60	202.13	205.69	209.26	212.85	216.47	220.10	223.75	227.42	231.10	234.81	238.52	242.26	246.01	249.77	257.34
4.00	179.72	182.92	186.13	189.37	192.62	195.89	199.18	202.48	205.80	209.13	212.48	215.85	219.23	222.62	226.03	232.88
4.25	175.41	178.53	181.67	184.82	188.00	191.19	194.40	197.62	200.86	204.11	207.38	210.67	213.97	217.28	220.60	227.29
4.50	171.24	174.29	177.35	180.43	183.53	186.65	189.78	192.93	196.09	199.27	202.46	205.67	208.89	212.12	215.36	221.89
4.75	167.22	170.19	173.19	176.20	179.22	182.26	185.32	188.40	191.48	194.59	197.70	200.83	203.98	207.14	210.31	216.68
5.00	163.34	166.24	169.16	172.10	175.06	178.03	181.02	184.02	187.04	190.07	193.11	196.17	199.24	202.32	205.42	211.65
5.25	159.58	162.42	165.28	168.15	171.04	173.94	176.86	179.79	182.74	185.70	188.67	191.66	194.66	197.67	200.70	206.78
5.50	155.96	158.73	161.52	164.33	167.15	169.99	172.84	175.71	178.59	181.48	184.39	187.31	190.24	193.18	196.14	202.08
5.75	152.45	155.16	157.89	160.63	163.39	166.17	168.95	171.76	174.57	177.40	180.24	183.10	185.96	188.84	191.73	197.54
6.00	149.06	151.72	154.38	157.06	159.76	162.47	165.20	167.94	170.69	173.46	176.24	179.03	181.83	184.65	187.47	193.15
6.25	145.79	148.38	150.99	153.61	156.25	158.90	161.57	164.25	166.94	169.65	172.37	175.09	177.84	180.59	183.35	188.91
6.50	142.62	145.16	147.71	150.28	152.86	155.45	158.06	160.68	163.31	165.96	168.62	171.29	173.97	176.66	179.37	184.80
6.75	139.56	142.04	144.54	147.05	149.57	152.11	154.66	157.23	159.81	162.40	165.00	167.61	170.23	172.87	175.51	180.83
7.00	136.59	139.02	141.47	143.92	146.39	148.88	151.38	153.89	156.41	158.95	161.49	164.05	166.62	169.20	171.79	176.99
7.25	133.72	136.10	138.49	140.90	143.32	145.75	148.20	150.66	153.13	155.61	158.10	160.60	163.12	165.64	168.18	173.27
7.50	130.95	133.28	135.62	137.97	140.34	142.73	145.12	147.53	149.95	152.38	154.82	157.27	159.73	162.20	164.68	169.68
7.75	128.26	130.54	132.83	135.14	137.46	139.80	142.14	144.50	146.87	149.25	151.64	154.04	156.45	158.87	161.30	166.19
8.00	125.65	127.89	130.14	132.40	134.67	136.96	139.26	141.57	143.89	146.22	148.56	150.91	153.28	155.65	158.03	162.82
8.25	123.13	125.32	127.53	129.74	131.97	134.21	136.46	138.73	141.00	143.28	145.58	147.89	150.20	152.53	154.86	159.55
8.50	120.69	122.84	125.00	127.17	129.35	131.55	133.76	135.97	138.20	140.44	142.69	144.95	147.22	149.50	151.79	156.39
8.75	118.32	120.43	122.55	124.67	126.82	128.97	131.13	133.31	135.49	137.69	139.89	142.11	144.33	146.57	148.81	153.32
9.00	116.03	118.09	120.17	122.26	124.36	126.47	128.59	130.72	132.87	135.02	137.18	139.35	141.54	143.73	145.93	150.35
9.25	113.81	115.83	117.87	119.91	121.97	124.04	126.13	128.22	130.32	132.43	134.55	136.68	138.82	140.97	143.13	147.47
9.50	111.65	113.64	115.63	117.64	119.66	121.69	123.74	125.79	127.85	129.92	132.00	134.09	136.19	138.30	140.42	144.67
9.75	109.56	111.51	113.47	115.44	117.42	119.42	121.42	123.43	125.46	127.49	129.53	131.58	133.64	135.71	137.79	141.96
10.00	107.53	109.44	111.37	113.30	115.25	117.21	119.17	121.15	123.13	125.13	127.13	129.15	131.17	133.20	135.24	139.34
10.25	105.56	107.44	109.33	111.23	113.14	115.06	116.99	118.93	120.88	122.84	124.81	126.78	128.77	130.76	132.76	136.79
10.50	103.65	105.50	107.35	109.22	111.09	112.98	114.87	116.78	118.69	120.62	122.55	124.49	126.44	128.40	130.36	134.31
10.75	101.80	103.61	105.43	107.26	109.11	110.96	112.82	114.69	116.57	118.46	120.36	122.26	124.18	126.10	128.03	131.91
11.00	100.00	101.78	103.57	105.37	107.18	109.00	110.83	112.66	114.51	116.37	118.23	120.10	121.98	123.87	125.77	129.58
11.25	98.25	100.00	101.76	103.53	105.30	107.09	108.89	110.69	112.51	114.33	116.16	118.00	119.85	121.71	123.57	127.31
11.50	96.55	98.27	100.00	101.74	103.48	105.24	107.01	108.78	110.57	112.36	114.16	115.96	117.78	119.60	121.43	125.11
11.75	94.91	96.59	98.29	100.00	101.72	103.44	105.18	106.92	108.68	110.44	112.21	113.98	115.77	117.56	119.36	122.98
12.00	93.30	94.96	96.63	98.31	100.00	101.70	103.40	105.12	106.84	108.57	110.31	112.06	113.81	115.58	117.34	120.90
12.25	91.75	93.38	95.02	96.67	98.33	100.00	101.68	103.36	105.06	106.76	108.47	110.19	111.91	113.65	115.38	118.88
12.50	90.23	91.84	93.45	95.08	96.71	98.35	100.00	101.66	103.32	105.00	106.68	108.37	110.07	111.77	113.48	116.92
12.75	88.76	90.34	91.93	93.52	95.13	96.75	98.37	100.00	101.64	103.29	104.94	106.60	108.27	109.95	111.63	115.01
13.00	87.33	88.88	90.44	92.02	93.60	95.18	96.78	98.39	100.00	101.62	103.25	104.88	106.53	108.17	109.83	113.16
13.25	85.94	87.46	89.00	90.55	92.10	93.67	95.24	96.82	98.41	100.00	101.60	103.21	104.83	106.45	108.08	111.35
13.50	84.58	86.09	87.60	89.12	90.65	92.19	93.74	95.29	96.85	98.42	100.00	101.58	103.17	104.77	106.37	109.60
13.75	83.26	84.74	86.23	87.73	89.24	90.75	92.28	93.81	95.34	96.89	98.44	100.00	101.57	103.14	104.72	107.89
14.00	81.98	83.44	84.90	86.38	87.86	89.35	90.85	92.36	93.87	95.40	96.92	98.46	100.00	101.55	103.10	106.23
14.25	80.73	82.17	83.61	85.06	86.52	87.99	89.47	90.95	92.44	93.94	95.45	96.96	98.48	100.00	101.53	104.61
14.50	79.51	80.93	82.35	83.78	85.22	86.67	88.12	89.58	91.05	92.53	94.01	95.50	96.99	98.49	100.00	103.03
14.75	78.33	79.72	81.12	82.53	83.95	85.37	86.81	88.25	89.69	91.15	92.61	94.07	95.55	97.03	98.51	101.50
15.00	77.17	78.55	79.93	81.32	82.71	84.12	85.53	86.95	88.37	89.80	91.24	92.69	94.14	95.60	97.06	100.00
15.25	76.05	77.40	78.76	80.13	81.51	82.89	84.28	85.68	87.08	88.50	89.91	91.34	92.77	94.20	95.64	98.54
15.50	74.95	76.29	77.63	78.98	80.33	81.70	83.07	84.44	85.83	87.22	88.62	90.02	91.43	92.84	94.27	97.12
15.75	73.88	75.20	76.52	77.85	79.19	80.53	81.88	83.24	84.61	85.98	87.35	88.74	90.13	91.52	92.92	95.74
16.00	72.84	74.14	75.44	76.75	78.07	79.40	80.73	82.07	83.41	84.76	86.12	87.49	88.86	90.23	91.61	94.39
16.25	71.83	73.11	74.39	75.68	76.98	78.29	79.60	80.92	82.25	83.58	84.92	86.27	87.62	88.97	90.33	93.07
16.50	70.84	72.10	73.36	74.64	75.92	77.21	78.51	79.81	81.12	82.43	83.75	85.08	86.41	87.75	89.09	91.79
16.75	69.87	71.11	72.36	73.62	74.89	76.16	77.43	78.72	80.01	81.31	82.61	83.92	85.23	86.55	87.87	90.54
17.00	68.93	70.15	71.39	72.63	73.87	75.13	76.39	77.66	78.93	80.21	81.49	82.78	84.08	85.38	86.69	89.31
17.25	68.01	69.22	70.43	71.66	72.89	74.13	75.37	76.62	77.88	79.14	80.40	81.68	82.96	84.24	85.53	88.12
17.50	67.11	68.30	69.50	70.71	71.93	73.15	74.37	75.61	76.85	78.09	79.34	80.60	81.86	83.13	84.40	86.96
17.75	66.23	67.41	68.60	69.79	70.99	72.19	73.40	74.62	75.84	77.07	78.31	79.55	80.79	82.04	83.30	85.82
18.00	65.38	66.54	67.71	68.88	70.07	71.26	72.45	73.65	74.86	76.08	77.29	78.52	79.75	80.98	82.22	84.71
18.25	64.54	65.69	66.84	68.00	69.17	70.35	71.53	72.71	73.90	75.10	76.31	77.51	78.73	79.95	81.17	83.63
18.50	63.72	64.86	66.00	67.14	68.30	69.46	70.62	71.79	72.97	74.15	75.34	76.53	77.73	78.93	80.14	82.57
18.75	62.92	64.04	65.17	66.30	67.44	68.59	69.74	70.89	72.05	73.22	74.40	75.57	76.76	77.94	79.14	81.54
19.00	62.14	63.25	64.36	65.48	66.60	67.74	68.87	70.01	71.16	72.32	73.47	74.64	75.81	76.98	78.16	80.53
20.00	59.20	60.25	61.31	62.37	63.44	64.52	65.60	66.69	67.79	68.88	69.99	71.10	72.21	73.33	74.45	76.70
25.00	47.69	48.54	49.40	50.25	51.12	51.99	52.86	53.73	54.62	55.50	56.39	57.28	58.18	59.08	59.98	61.80
30.00	39.84	40.55	41.26	41.97	42.70	43.42	44.15	44.88	45.62	46.36	47.10	47.84	48.59	49.35	50.10	51.62

Description: This table shows the yield to maturity of a mortgage purchased at the price shown in the index.

Example: The yield to maturity of a 15.00 %, 23 year mortgage at a price of 125.00 is 11.51 %.

INTEREST RATE, %

PRICE	11.00%	11.25%	11.50%	11.75%	12.00%	12.25%	12.50%	12.75%	13.00%	13.25%	13.50%	13.75%	14.00%	14.25%	14.50%	15.00%
250	.84	1.00	1.16	1.31	1.47	1.62	1.78	1.93	2.09	2.24	2.39	2.54	2.69	2.84	2.99	3.28
240	1.21	1.37	1.53	1.69	1.85	2.00	2.16	2.32	2.47	2.63	2.78	2.93	3.09	3.24	3.39	3.69
230	1.60	1.76	1.92	2.09	2.25	2.41	2.57	2.73	2.88	3.04	3.20	3.35	3.51	3.66	3.82	4.12
220	2.01	2.18	2.34	2.51	2.67	2.84	3.00	3.16	3.32	3.48	3.64	3.80	3.96	4.12	4.27	4.58
210	2.45	2.62	2.79	2.96	3.13	3.29	3.46	3.62	3.79	3.95	4.12	4.28	4.44	4.60	4.76	5.08
200	2.93	3.10	3.27	3.44	3.61	3.78	3.95	4.12	4.29	4.46	4.62	4.79	4.95	5.12	5.28	5.61
195	3.17	3.35	3.52	3.70	3.87	4.04	4.21	4.38	4.55	4.72	4.89	5.06	5.23	5.39	5.56	5.89
190	3.43	3.61	3.79	3.96	4.14	4.31	4.48	4.66	4.83	5.00	5.17	5.34	5.51	5.68	5.85	6.18
185	3.70	3.88	4.06	4.24	4.41	4.59	4.76	4.94	5.11	5.29	5.46	5.63	5.80	5.97	6.14	6.48
180	3.98	4.16	4.34	4.52	4.70	4.88	5.06	5.23	5.41	5.58	5.76	5.93	6.11	6.28	6.45	6.80
175	4.27	4.45	4.64	4.82	5.00	5.18	5.36	5.54	5.72	5.90	6.07	6.25	6.43	6.60	6.78	7.13
170	4.57	4.76	4.94	5.13	5.31	5.49	5.68	5.86	6.04	6.22	6.40	6.58	6.76	6.94	7.12	7.47
165	4.89	5.08	5.26	5.45	5.64	5.82	6.01	6.19	6.38	6.56	6.74	6.93	7.11	7.29	7.47	7.83
160	5.22	5.41	5.60	5.79	5.98	6.17	6.36	6.54	6.73	6.92	7.10	7.29	7.47	7.66	7.84	8.21
155	5.56	5.76	5.95	6.14	6.34	6.53	6.72	6.91	7.10	7.29	7.48	7.67	7.86	8.05	8.23	8.61
150	5.93	6.12	6.32	6.52	6.71	6.91	7.10	7.30	7.49	7.68	7.88	8.07	8.26	8.45	8.64	9.02
145	6.31	6.51	6.71	6.91	7.11	7.31	7.51	7.70	7.90	8.10	8.29	8.49	8.69	8.88	9.08	9.47
140	6.71	6.91	7.12	7.32	7.52	7.73	7.93	8.13	8.33	8.53	8.74	8.94	9.14	9.34	9.53	9.93
135	7.13	7.34	7.55	7.76	7.97	8.17	8.38	8.59	8.79	9.00	9.20	9.41	9.61	9.82	10.02	10.42
130	7.58	7.80	8.01	8.22	8.43	8.64	8.86	9.07	9.28	9.49	9.70	9.91	10.12	10.32	10.53	10.95
125	8.06	8.28	8.49	8.71	8.93	9.15	9.36	9.58	9.79	10.01	10.22	10.44	10.65	10.87	11.08	11.51
120	8.57	8.79	9.01	9.24	9.46	9.68	9.90	10.12	10.34	10.57	10.79	11.01	11.23	11.45	11.67	12.11
115	9.11	9.34	9.57	9.80	10.02	10.25	10.48	10.71	10.93	11.16	11.39	11.62	11.84	12.07	12.29	12.75
113	9.34	9.57	9.80	10.03	10.26	10.49	10.72	10.95	11.18	11.41	11.64	11.87	12.10	12.33	12.56	13.02
112	9.45	9.69	9.92	10.15	10.38	10.62	10.85	11.08	11.31	11.54	11.77	12.00	12.23	12.46	12.69	13.15
111	9.57	9.81	10.04	10.27	10.51	10.74	10.97	11.21	11.44	11.67	11.90	12.14	12.37	12.60	12.83	13.29
110	9.69	9.93	10.16	10.40	10.63	10.87	11.10	11.33	11.57	11.80	12.04	12.27	12.50	12.74	12.97	13.44
109	9.81	10.05	10.29	10.52	10.76	10.99	11.23	11.47	11.70	11.94	12.17	12.41	12.64	12.88	13.11	13.58
108	9.94	10.17	10.41	10.65	10.89	11.12	11.36	11.60	11.84	12.07	12.31	12.55	12.78	13.02	13.26	13.73
107	10.06	10.30	10.54	10.78	11.02	11.26	11.50	11.73	11.97	12.21	12.45	12.69	12.93	13.16	13.40	13.88
106	10.19	10.43	10.67	10.91	11.15	11.39	11.63	11.87	12.11	12.35	12.59	12.83	13.07	13.31	13.55	14.03
105	10.32	10.56	10.80	11.04	11.29	11.53	11.77	12.01	12.25	12.49	12.74	12.98	13.22	13.46	13.70	14.18
104	10.45	10.69	10.94	11.18	11.42	11.67	11.91	12.15	12.40	12.64	12.88	13.13	13.37	13.61	13.86	14.34
103	10.58	10.83	11.07	11.32	11.56	11.81	12.05	12.30	12.54	12.79	13.03	13.28	13.52	13.77	14.01	14.50
102	10.72	10.96	11.21	11.46	11.70	11.95	12.20	12.44	12.69	12.94	13.18	13.43	13.68	13.92	14.17	14.66
101	10.86	11.10	11.35	11.60	11.85	12.10	12.35	12.59	12.84	13.09	13.34	13.59	13.83	14.08	14.33	14.83
100	11.00	11.25	11.50	11.75	12.00	12.25	12.50	12.75	13.00	13.25	13.50	13.75	14.00	14.25	14.50	15.00
99	11.14	11.39	11.64	11.89	12.14	12.40	12.65	12.90	13.15	13.40	13.65	13.91	14.16	14.41	14.66	15.17
98	11.28	11.54	11.79	12.04	12.30	12.55	12.80	13.06	13.31	13.56	13.82	14.07	14.32	14.58	14.83	15.34
97	11.43	11.68	11.94	12.19	12.45	12.70	12.96	13.22	13.47	13.73	13.98	14.24	14.49	14.75	15.01	15.52
96	11.58	11.84	12.09	12.35	12.61	12.86	13.12	13.38	13.64	13.89	14.15	14.41	14.67	14.92	15.18	15.70
95	11.73	11.99	12.25	12.51	12.77	13.03	13.28	13.54	13.80	14.06	14.32	14.58	14.84	15.10	15.36	15.88
94	11.89	12.15	12.41	12.67	12.93	13.19	13.45	13.71	13.97	14.23	14.50	14.76	15.02	15.28	15.54	16.07
93	12.04	12.31	12.57	12.83	13.09	13.36	13.62	13.88	14.15	14.41	14.67	14.94	15.20	15.47	15.73	16.26
92	12.20	12.47	12.73	13.00	13.26	13.53	13.79	14.06	14.32	14.59	14.86	15.12	15.39	15.65	15.92	16.45
91	12.37	12.63	12.90	13.17	13.43	13.70	13.97	14.24	14.50	14.77	15.04	15.31	15.58	15.85	16.11	16.65
90	12.53	12.80	13.07	13.34	13.61	13.88	14.15	14.42	14.69	14.96	15.23	15.50	15.77	16.04	16.31	16.85
89	12.70	12.97	13.25	13.52	13.79	14.06	14.33	14.60	14.88	15.15	15.42	15.69	15.97	16.24	16.51	17.06
88	12.88	13.15	13.42	13.70	13.97	14.24	14.52	14.79	15.07	15.34	15.62	15.89	16.17	16.44	16.72	17.27
87	13.05	13.33	13.60	13.88	14.16	14.43	14.71	14.98	15.26	15.54	15.82	16.09	16.37	16.65	16.93	17.49
86	13.23	13.51	13.79	14.07	14.34	14.62	14.90	15.18	15.46	15.74	16.02	16.30	16.58	16.86	17.14	17.71
85	13.42	13.70	13.98	14.26	14.54	14.82	15.10	15.38	15.66	15.95	16.23	16.51	16.79	17.08	17.36	17.93
84	13.60	13.89	14.17	14.45	14.74	15.02	15.30	15.59	15.87	16.16	16.44	16.73	17.01	17.30	17.58	18.16
83	13.80	14.08	14.37	14.65	14.94	15.22	15.51	15.80	16.08	16.37	16.66	16.95	17.24	17.52	17.81	18.39
82	13.99	14.28	14.57	14.85	15.14	15.43	15.72	16.01	16.30	16.59	16.88	17.17	17.46	17.75	18.05	18.63
81	14.19	14.48	14.77	15.06	15.35	15.64	15.94	16.23	16.52	16.81	17.11	17.40	17.70	17.99	18.29	18.88
80	14.39	14.69	14.98	15.27	15.57	15.86	16.16	16.45	16.75	17.04	17.34	17.64	17.93	18.23	18.53	19.13
79	14.60	14.90	15.19	15.49	15.79	16.08	16.38	16.68	16.98	17.28	17.58	17.88	18.18	18.48	18.78	19.38
78	14.82	15.11	15.41	15.71	16.01	16.31	16.61	16.91	17.22	17.52	17.82	18.12	18.43	18.73	19.04	19.65
77	15.03	15.33	15.64	15.94	16.24	16.54	16.85	17.15	17.46	17.76	18.07	18.38	18.68	18.99	19.30	19.91
76	15.26	15.56	15.86	16.17	16.48	16.78	17.09	17.40	17.71	18.01	18.32	18.63	18.94	19.25	19.57	20.19
75	15.48	15.79	16.10	16.41	16.72	17.03	17.34	17.65	17.96	18.27	18.58	18.90	19.21	19.53	19.84	20.47
74	15.72	16.03	16.34	16.65	16.96	17.28	17.59	17.90	18.22	18.54	18.85	19.17	19.49	19.80	20.12	20.76
73	15.96	16.27	16.59	16.90	17.22	17.53	17.85	18.17	18.49	18.81	19.13	19.45	19.77	20.09	20.41	21.06
70	16.71	17.04	17.36	17.69	18.01	18.34	18.67	19.00	19.33	19.66	19.99	20.32	20.66	20.99	21.32	21.99
65	18.11	18.45	18.80	19.14	19.49	19.84	20.19	20.54	20.89	21.25	21.60	21.95	22.31	22.66	23.02	23.74
60	19.71	20.08	20.45	20.82	21.20	21.57	21.95	22.32	22.70	23.08	23.46	23.84	24.22	24.60	24.99	25.76
55	21.59	21.99	22.39	22.79	23.19	23.60	24.00	24.41	24.82	25.23	25.64	26.05	26.47	26.88	27.30	28.13

MORTGAGE PRICE

24 YEARS

Description: This table shows the price to pay for a monthly payment mortgage loan at the yield rate.

Example: The price of a 6.75 %, 24 year mortgage loan to yield 8.00 % to maturity is $ 89.77.

INTEREST RATE, %

YIELD	0.00%	1.00%	2.00%	3.00%	4.00%	4.25%	4.50%	4.75%	5.00%	5.25%	5.50%	5.75%	6.00%	6.25%	6.50%	6.75%
0.00	100.00	112.52	125.99	140.40	155.72	159.69	163.71	167.78	171.91	176.08	180.31	184.59	188.92	193.30	197.72	202.20
1.00	88.87	100.00	111.97	124.78	138.39	141.92	145.49	149.11	152.78	156.49	160.25	164.05	167.90	171.79	175.72	179.70
2.00	79.37	89.31	100.00	111.44	123.59	126.74	129.93	133.16	136.44	139.76	143.11	146.51	149.94	153.42	156.93	160.48
3.00	71.22	80.14	89.74	100.00	110.91	113.73	116.60	119.50	122.44	125.41	128.43	131.47	134.56	137.67	140.83	144.01
4.00	64.22	72.26	80.91	90.16	100.00	102.55	105.13	107.75	110.40	113.08	115.79	118.54	121.32	124.13	126.98	129.85
4.25	62.62	70.46	78.90	87.92	97.52	100.00	102.52	105.07	107.65	110.27	112.92	115.60	118.31	121.05	123.82	126.62
4.50	61.08	68.73	76.96	85.77	95.12	97.54	100.00	102.49	105.01	107.56	110.14	112.76	115.40	118.08	120.78	123.51
4.75	59.60	67.06	75.09	83.68	92.81	95.18	97.57	100.00	102.46	104.95	107.47	110.02	112.60	115.21	117.85	120.51
5.00	58.17	65.45	73.29	81.67	90.58	92.89	95.23	97.60	100.00	102.43	104.89	107.38	109.90	112.44	115.02	117.62
5.25	56.79	63.90	71.55	79.74	88.43	90.69	92.97	95.28	97.63	100.00	102.40	104.83	107.29	109.78	112.29	114.83
5.50	55.46	62.40	69.88	77.87	86.36	88.56	90.79	93.05	95.34	97.65	100.00	102.37	104.77	107.20	109.66	112.14
5.75	54.17	60.96	68.26	76.06	84.36	86.51	88.69	90.89	93.13	95.39	97.68	100.00	102.35	104.72	107.11	109.54
6.00	52.93	59.56	66.69	74.32	82.43	84.52	86.65	88.81	90.99	93.21	95.44	97.71	100.00	102.32	104.66	107.03
6.25	51.73	58.21	65.18	72.64	80.56	82.61	84.69	86.80	88.93	91.09	93.28	95.50	97.74	100.00	102.29	104.60
6.50	50.58	56.91	63.72	71.01	78.76	80.76	82.80	84.86	86.94	89.06	91.19	93.36	95.55	97.76	100.00	102.26
6.75	49.46	55.65	62.31	69.44	77.01	78.98	80.96	82.98	85.02	87.09	89.18	91.29	93.43	95.60	97.79	100.00
7.00	48.38	54.43	60.95	67.92	75.33	77.25	79.19	81.17	83.16	85.18	87.23	89.30	91.39	93.51	95.65	97.81
7.25	47.33	53.26	59.63	66.45	73.70	75.58	77.48	79.41	81.36	83.34	85.34	87.37	89.42	91.49	93.58	95.70
7.50	46.32	52.12	58.36	65.04	72.13	73.97	75.83	77.72	79.63	81.56	83.52	85.50	87.51	89.54	91.59	93.66
7.75	45.34	51.02	57.13	63.66	70.61	72.41	74.23	76.08	77.95	79.84	81.76	83.70	85.66	87.65	89.66	91.68
8.00	44.40	49.96	55.94	62.34	69.14	70.90	72.68	74.49	76.32	78.18	80.06	81.96	83.88	85.82	87.79	89.77
8.25	43.48	48.93	54.79	61.05	67.71	69.44	71.19	72.96	74.75	76.57	78.41	80.27	82.15	84.06	85.98	87.92
8.50	42.60	47.93	53.67	59.81	66.34	68.03	69.74	71.47	73.23	75.01	76.81	78.64	80.48	82.34	84.23	86.13
8.75	41.74	46.97	52.59	58.61	65.00	66.66	68.34	70.04	71.76	73.50	75.27	77.05	78.86	80.69	82.54	84.40
9.00	40.91	46.04	51.55	57.44	63.71	65.33	66.98	68.65	70.33	72.04	73.77	75.52	77.30	79.09	80.90	82.73
9.25	40.11	45.13	50.54	56.32	62.46	64.05	65.66	67.30	68.95	70.63	72.33	74.04	75.78	77.53	79.31	81.10
9.50	39.33	44.26	49.56	55.22	61.25	62.81	64.39	65.99	67.62	69.26	70.92	72.61	74.31	76.03	77.77	79.53
9.75	38.58	43.41	48.61	54.17	60.08	61.61	63.16	64.73	66.32	67.93	69.56	71.21	72.88	74.57	76.28	78.01
10.00	37.85	42.59	47.69	53.14	58.94	60.44	61.96	63.50	65.06	66.65	68.25	69.87	71.50	73.16	74.84	76.53
10.25	37.14	41.79	46.80	52.15	57.84	59.31	60.80	62.32	63.85	65.40	66.97	68.56	70.17	71.79	73.44	75.10
10.50	36.45	41.02	45.93	51.18	56.77	58.21	59.68	61.16	62.67	64.19	65.73	67.29	68.87	70.47	72.08	73.71
10.75	35.79	40.27	45.09	50.25	55.73	57.15	58.59	60.05	61.52	63.02	64.53	66.06	67.61	69.18	70.76	72.36
11.00	35.14	39.54	44.28	49.34	54.72	56.12	57.53	58.96	60.41	61.88	63.37	64.87	66.39	67.93	69.49	71.06
11.25	34.52	38.84	43.49	48.46	53.75	55.12	56.51	57.91	59.34	60.78	62.24	63.71	65.21	66.72	68.25	69.79
11.50	33.91	38.15	42.72	47.61	52.80	54.15	55.51	56.89	58.29	59.71	61.14	62.59	64.06	65.54	67.05	68.56
11.75	33.32	37.49	41.98	46.78	51.88	53.20	54.54	55.90	57.28	58.67	60.08	61.50	62.95	64.40	65.88	67.37
12.00	32.75	36.85	41.26	45.97	50.99	52.29	53.61	54.94	56.29	57.66	59.04	60.44	61.86	63.30	64.74	66.21
12.25	32.19	36.22	40.56	45.19	50.12	51.40	52.69	54.01	55.33	56.68	58.04	59.42	60.81	62.22	63.64	65.08
12.50	31.65	35.61	39.87	44.43	49.28	50.54	51.81	53.10	54.40	55.73	57.07	58.42	59.79	61.17	62.58	63.99
12.75	31.12	35.02	39.21	43.70	48.46	49.70	50.95	52.22	53.50	54.80	56.12	57.45	58.80	60.16	61.54	62.93
13.00	30.61	34.44	38.57	42.98	47.67	48.88	50.11	51.36	52.62	53.90	55.20	56.51	57.83	59.17	60.53	61.90
13.25	30.12	33.89	37.94	42.28	46.90	48.09	49.30	50.53	51.77	53.03	54.30	55.59	56.90	58.21	59.55	60.89
13.50	29.63	33.34	37.34	41.61	46.14	47.32	48.51	49.72	50.94	52.18	53.43	54.70	55.98	57.28	58.59	59.92
13.75	29.16	32.82	36.75	40.95	45.41	46.57	47.74	48.93	50.14	51.35	52.59	53.84	55.10	56.37	57.66	58.97
14.00	28.71	32.30	36.17	40.31	44.70	45.84	47.00	48.17	49.35	50.55	51.76	52.99	54.24	55.49	56.76	58.05
14.25	28.26	31.80	35.61	39.68	44.01	45.13	46.27	47.42	48.59	49.77	50.96	52.17	53.40	54.63	55.88	57.15
14.50	27.83	31.32	35.07	39.08	43.34	44.44	45.56	46.70	47.84	49.01	50.18	51.38	52.58	53.80	55.03	56.27
14.75	27.41	30.84	34.54	38.49	42.68	43.77	44.87	45.99	47.12	48.27	49.43	50.60	51.79	52.99	54.20	55.42
15.00	27.00	30.38	34.02	37.91	42.05	43.12	44.20	45.30	46.42	47.55	48.69	49.84	51.01	52.19	53.39	54.60
15.25	26.60	29.93	33.52	37.35	41.43	42.48	43.55	44.63	45.73	46.84	47.97	49.11	50.26	51.42	52.60	53.79
15.50	26.21	29.50	33.03	36.81	40.82	41.86	42.91	43.98	45.06	46.16	47.27	48.39	49.52	50.67	51.83	53.00
15.75	25.84	29.07	32.55	36.27	40.23	41.26	42.30	43.35	44.41	45.49	46.59	47.69	48.81	49.94	51.08	52.24
16.00	25.47	28.66	32.09	35.76	39.66	40.67	41.69	42.73	43.78	44.84	45.92	47.01	48.11	49.23	50.36	51.49
16.25	25.11	28.25	31.63	35.25	39.10	40.09	41.10	42.13	43.16	44.21	45.27	46.35	47.43	48.53	49.65	50.77
16.50	24.76	27.86	31.19	34.76	38.55	39.53	40.53	41.54	42.56	43.59	44.64	45.70	46.77	47.86	48.95	50.06
16.75	24.42	27.47	30.76	34.28	38.02	38.99	39.97	40.97	41.97	42.99	44.03	45.07	46.13	47.20	48.28	49.37
17.00	24.08	27.10	30.34	33.81	37.50	38.46	39.43	40.41	41.40	42.41	43.43	44.46	45.50	46.55	47.62	48.70
17.25	23.76	26.73	29.93	33.36	37.00	37.94	38.89	39.86	40.84	41.84	42.84	43.86	44.88	45.92	46.98	48.04
17.50	23.44	26.38	29.53	32.91	36.50	37.43	38.38	39.33	40.30	41.28	42.27	43.27	44.29	45.31	46.35	47.40
17.75	23.13	26.03	29.15	32.48	36.02	36.94	37.87	38.81	39.77	40.73	41.71	42.70	43.70	44.71	45.74	46.77
18.00	22.83	25.69	28.76	32.05	35.55	36.46	37.37	38.30	39.25	40.20	41.17	42.14	43.13	44.13	45.14	46.16
18.25	22.54	25.36	28.39	31.64	35.09	35.99	36.89	37.81	38.74	39.68	40.63	41.60	42.57	43.56	44.56	45.57
18.50	22.25	25.03	28.03	31.24	34.64	35.53	36.42	37.33	38.25	39.17	40.12	41.07	42.03	43.00	43.99	44.98
18.75	21.97	24.72	27.68	30.84	34.21	35.08	35.96	36.86	37.76	38.68	39.61	40.55	41.50	42.46	43.43	44.42
19.00	21.69	24.41	27.33	30.46	33.78	34.64	35.51	36.39	37.29	38.20	39.11	40.04	40.98	41.93	42.89	43.86
20.00	20.65	23.24	26.02	29.00	32.16	32.98	33.81	34.65	35.51	36.37	37.24	38.13	39.02	39.93	40.84	41.76
25.00	16.62	18.70	20.94	23.34	25.88	26.54	27.21	27.89	28.58	29.27	29.97	30.68	31.40	32.13	32.87	33.61
30.00	13.88	15.62	17.48	19.48	21.61	22.16	22.72	23.28	23.86	24.44	25.02	25.62	26.22	26.83	27.44	28.06

Description: This table shows the yield to maturity of a mortgage purchased at the price shown in the index.

Example: The yield to maturity of a 6.75 %, 24 year mortgage at a price of 80.00 is 9.42 %.

							INTEREST RATE, %										
PRICE	0.00%	1.00%	2.00%	3.00%	4.00%	4.25%	4.50%	4.75%	5.00%	5.25%	5.50%	5.75%	6.00%	6.25%	6.50%	6.75%
100	0.00	1.00	2.00	3.00	4.00	4.25	4.50	4.75	5.00	5.25	5.50	5.75	6.00	6.25	6.50	6.75
99	.08	1.08	2.09	3.09	4.09	4.35	4.60	4.85	5.10	5.35	5.60	5.85	6.10	6.36	6.61	6.86
98	.16	1.17	2.18	3.19	4.20	4.45	4.70	4.95	5.21	5.46	5.71	5.96	6.22	6.47	6.72	6.97
97	.25	1.26	2.27	3.28	4.30	4.55	4.81	5.06	5.31	5.57	5.82	6.07	6.33	6.58	6.84	7.09
96	.34	1.35	2.37	3.38	4.40	4.66	4.91	5.17	5.42	5.68	5.93	6.19	6.44	6.70	6.95	7.21
95	.42	1.44	2.46	3.48	4.51	4.76	5.02	5.28	5.53	5.79	6.05	6.30	6.56	6.82	7.07	7.33
94	.51	1.54	2.56	3.59	4.62	4.87	5.13	5.39	5.65	5.90	6.16	6.42	6.68	6.94	7.19	7.45
93	.61	1.63	2.66	3.69	4.72	4.98	5.24	5.50	5.76	6.02	6.28	6.54	6.80	7.06	7.32	7.58
92	.70	1.73	2.76	3.80	4.84	5.10	5.36	5.62	5.88	6.14	6.40	6.66	6.92	7.18	7.44	7.70
91	.79	1.83	2.86	3.90	4.95	5.21	5.47	5.73	5.99	6.26	6.52	6.78	7.04	7.31	7.57	7.83
90	.89	1.93	2.97	4.01	5.06	5.32	5.59	5.85	6.11	6.38	6.64	6.91	7.17	7.44	7.70	7.96
89	.98	2.03	3.07	4.12	5.18	5.44	5.71	5.97	6.24	6.50	6.77	7.03	7.30	7.57	7.83	8.10
88	1.08	2.13	3.18	4.24	5.30	5.56	5.83	6.09	6.36	6.63	6.90	7.16	7.43	7.70	7.97	8.23
87	1.18	2.23	3.29	4.35	5.42	5.68	5.95	6.22	6.49	6.76	7.02	7.29	7.56	7.83	8.10	8.37
86	1.28	2.34	3.40	4.47	5.54	5.81	6.08	6.35	6.62	6.89	7.16	7.43	7.70	7.97	8.24	8.51
85	1.38	2.45	3.51	4.59	5.66	5.93	6.21	6.48	6.75	7.02	7.29	7.56	7.84	8.11	8.38	8.66
84	1.49	2.56	3.63	4.71	5.79	6.06	6.34	6.61	6.88	7.15	7.43	7.70	7.98	8.25	8.53	8.80
83	1.59	2.67	3.74	4.83	5.92	6.19	6.47	6.74	7.02	7.29	7.57	7.84	8.12	8.40	8.68	8.95
82	1.70	2.78	3.86	4.95	6.05	6.33	6.60	6.88	7.16	7.43	7.71	7.99	8.27	8.55	8.83	9.11
81	1.81	2.89	3.98	5.08	6.19	6.46	6.74	7.02	7.30	7.58	7.86	8.14	8.42	8.70	8.98	9.26
80	1.92	3.01	4.11	5.21	6.32	6.60	6.88	7.16	7.44	7.72	8.00	8.29	8.57	8.85	9.14	9.42
79	2.04	3.13	4.23	5.34	6.46	6.74	7.02	7.31	7.59	7.87	8.15	8.44	8.72	9.01	9.29	9.58
78	2.15	3.25	4.36	5.48	6.60	6.89	7.17	7.45	7.74	8.02	8.31	8.59	8.88	9.17	9.46	9.75
77	2.27	3.38	4.49	5.61	6.75	7.03	7.32	7.60	7.89	8.18	8.47	8.75	9.04	9.33	9.62	9.91
76	2.39	3.50	4.62	5.75	6.89	7.18	7.47	7.76	8.05	8.34	8.63	8.92	9.21	9.50	9.79	10.09
75	2.51	3.63	4.76	5.90	7.05	7.33	7.62	7.91	8.21	8.50	8.79	9.08	9.38	9.67	9.97	10.26
74	2.64	3.76	4.90	6.04	7.20	7.49	7.78	8.07	8.37	8.66	8.96	9.25	9.55	9.85	10.14	10.44
73	2.76	3.89	5.04	6.19	7.36	7.65	7.94	8.24	8.53	8.83	9.13	9.43	9.72	10.02	10.32	10.63
72	2.89	4.03	5.18	6.34	7.52	7.81	8.11	8.41	8.70	9.00	9.30	9.60	9.90	10.21	10.51	10.81
71	3.02	4.17	5.33	6.50	7.68	7.98	8.28	8.58	8.88	9.18	9.48	9.78	10.09	10.39	10.70	11.01
70	3.16	4.31	5.48	6.65	7.85	8.15	8.45	8.75	9.05	9.36	9.66	9.97	10.28	10.58	10.89	11.20
69	3.30	4.46	5.63	6.82	8.02	8.32	8.63	8.93	9.24	9.54	9.85	10.16	10.47	10.78	11.09	11.41
68	3.44	4.60	5.79	6.98	8.19	8.50	8.81	9.11	9.42	9.73	10.04	10.35	10.67	10.98	11.30	11.61
67	3.58	4.75	5.94	7.15	8.37	8.68	8.99	9.30	9.61	9.93	10.24	10.55	10.87	11.19	11.50	11.82
66	3.73	4.91	6.11	7.32	8.56	8.87	9.18	9.49	9.81	10.12	10.44	10.76	11.08	11.40	11.72	12.04
65	3.88	5.07	6.28	7.50	8.75	9.06	9.37	9.69	10.01	10.33	10.65	10.97	11.29	11.61	11.94	12.26
64	4.03	5.23	6.45	7.68	8.94	9.26	9.57	9.89	10.21	10.54	10.86	11.18	11.51	11.84	12.16	12.49
63	4.19	5.39	6.62	7.87	9.14	9.46	9.78	10.10	10.42	10.75	11.08	11.40	11.73	12.06	12.39	12.73
62	4.35	5.56	6.80	8.06	9.34	9.66	9.99	10.31	10.64	10.97	11.30	11.63	11.96	12.30	12.63	12.97
61	4.51	5.74	6.99	8.26	9.55	9.87	10.20	10.53	10.86	11.19	11.53	11.86	12.20	12.54	12.88	13.22
60	4.68	5.92	7.17	8.46	9.76	10.09	10.42	10.76	11.09	11.43	11.76	12.10	12.44	12.78	13.13	13.47
59	4.85	6.10	7.37	8.66	9.98	10.31	10.65	10.99	11.32	11.66	12.01	12.35	12.69	13.04	13.39	13.74
58	5.03	6.28	7.57	8.87	10.21	10.54	10.88	11.22	11.57	11.91	12.26	12.60	12.95	13.30	13.65	14.01
57	5.21	6.48	7.77	9.09	10.44	10.78	11.12	11.47	11.81	12.16	12.51	12.86	13.22	13.57	13.93	14.29
56	5.39	6.67	7.98	9.32	10.68	11.02	11.37	11.72	12.07	12.42	12.78	13.13	13.49	13.85	14.21	14.58
55	5.58	6.88	8.20	9.55	10.93	11.27	11.63	11.98	12.33	12.69	13.05	13.41	13.77	14.14	14.50	14.87
54	5.78	7.09	8.42	9.79	11.18	11.53	11.89	12.25	12.61	12.97	13.33	13.70	14.06	14.43	14.81	15.18
53	5.98	7.30	8.65	10.03	11.44	11.80	12.16	12.52	12.89	13.25	13.62	13.99	14.37	14.74	15.12	15.50
52	6.19	7.52	8.89	10.28	11.71	12.08	12.44	12.81	13.18	13.55	13.92	14.30	14.68	15.06	15.44	15.82
51	6.40	7.75	9.13	10.54	11.99	12.36	12.73	13.10	13.48	13.85	14.23	14.62	15.00	15.39	15.77	16.16
50	6.62	7.98	9.38	10.81	12.28	12.65	13.03	13.41	13.79	14.17	14.56	14.94	15.33	15.72	16.12	16.52
49	6.85	8.23	9.64	11.09	12.58	12.96	13.34	13.72	14.11	14.50	14.89	15.28	15.68	16.08	16.48	16.88
48	7.08	8.48	9.91	11.38	12.89	13.27	13.66	14.05	14.44	14.84	15.23	15.63	16.04	16.44	16.85	17.26
47	7.33	8.74	10.19	11.68	13.21	13.60	13.99	14.39	14.79	15.19	15.59	16.00	16.41	16.82	17.24	17.65
46	7.58	9.01	10.47	11.99	13.54	13.94	14.34	14.74	15.15	15.55	15.97	16.38	16.80	17.21	17.64	18.06
45	7.84	9.28	10.77	12.31	13.89	14.29	14.70	15.11	15.52	15.93	16.35	16.77	17.20	17.62	18.05	18.49
44	8.10	9.57	11.08	12.64	14.25	14.66	15.07	15.49	15.91	16.33	16.76	17.18	17.62	18.05	18.49	18.93
43	8.38	9.87	11.40	12.99	14.62	15.04	15.46	15.88	16.31	16.74	17.18	17.61	18.05	18.50	18.94	19.39
42	8.67	10.18	11.74	13.35	15.01	15.44	15.87	16.30	16.73	17.17	17.61	18.06	18.51	18.96	19.42	19.88
41	8.97	10.50	12.09	13.72	15.42	15.85	16.29	16.73	17.17	17.62	18.07	18.53	18.99	19.45	19.91	20.38
40	9.28	10.84	12.45	14.12	15.85	16.29	16.73	17.18	17.63	18.09	18.55	19.02	19.48	19.96	20.43	20.91
39	9.60	11.19	12.83	14.53	16.29	16.74	17.19	17.65	18.12	18.58	19.05	19.53	20.01	20.49	20.98	21.47
35	11.05	12.75	14.53	16.37	18.30	18.79	19.29	19.79	20.30	20.81	21.33	21.85	22.38	22.91	23.44	23.99
30	13.30	15.21	17.20	19.30	21.49	22.06	22.63	23.20	23.79	24.38	24.97	25.57	26.18	26.80	27.42	28.04
25	16.32	18.52	20.85	23.30	25.89	26.56	27.24	27.92	28.61	29.31	30.02	30.74	31.46	32.20	32.94	33.68
20	20.68	23.35	26.19	29.22	32.42	33.25	34.09	34.94	35.80	36.67	37.56	38.45	39.35	40.26	41.19	42.12
15	27.73	31.23	34.98	38.99	43.25	44.35	45.47	46.60	47.75	48.91	50.08	51.27	52.47	53.69	54.92	56.16
10	41.66	46.88	52.49	58.50	64.88	66.53	68.21	69.90	71.62	73.36	75.13	76.91	78.71	80.54	82.38	84.24

Description: This table shows the price to pay for a monthly payment mortgage loan at the yield rate.

Example: The price of a 10.75 %, 24 year mortgage loan to yield 8.00 % to maturity is $ 124.06.

INTEREST RATE, %

YIELD	7.00%	7.25%	7.50%	7.75%	8.00%	8.25%	8.50%	8.75%	9.00%	9.25%	9.50%	9.75%	10.00%	10.25%	10.50%	10.75%
0.00	206.71	211.28	215.89	220.54	225.23	229.97	234.74	239.56	244.42	249.31	254.24	259.21	264.21	269.24	274.31	279.42
1.00	183.71	187.77	191.86	196.00	200.17	204.38	208.62	212.90	217.22	221.57	225.95	230.36	234.81	239.28	243.79	248.32
2.00	164.07	167.69	171.35	175.04	178.76	182.52	186.31	190.14	193.99	197.87	201.79	205.73	209.70	213.70	217.72	221.77
3.00	147.23	150.48	153.76	157.07	160.42	163.79	167.19	170.62	174.08	177.57	181.08	184.62	188.18	191.77	195.38	199.01
4.00	132.75	135.68	138.64	141.63	144.64	147.68	150.75	153.84	156.96	160.10	163.27	166.46	169.67	172.90	176.16	179.44
4.25	129.45	132.31	135.19	138.11	141.05	144.01	147.00	150.02	153.06	156.12	159.21	162.32	165.45	168.61	171.78	174.98
4.50	126.27	129.06	131.87	134.72	137.58	140.48	143.39	146.34	149.30	152.29	155.30	158.34	161.39	164.47	167.56	170.68
4.75	123.21	125.93	128.67	131.44	134.24	137.06	139.91	142.78	145.68	148.59	151.53	154.49	157.47	160.47	163.50	166.54
5.00	120.25	122.90	125.58	128.29	131.02	133.77	136.55	139.35	142.18	145.03	147.89	150.78	153.69	156.62	159.57	162.54
5.25	117.40	119.99	122.60	125.25	127.91	130.60	133.31	136.05	138.81	141.58	144.38	147.21	150.05	152.91	155.79	158.68
5.50	114.64	117.17	119.73	122.31	124.91	127.54	130.19	132.86	135.55	138.26	141.00	143.75	146.53	149.32	152.13	154.96
5.75	111.98	114.46	116.95	119.47	122.02	124.58	127.17	129.78	132.41	135.06	137.73	140.42	143.13	145.86	148.61	151.37
6.00	109.42	111.83	114.27	116.73	119.22	121.73	124.25	126.80	129.37	131.96	134.57	137.20	139.85	142.52	145.20	147.90
6.25	106.94	109.30	111.69	114.09	116.52	118.97	121.44	123.93	126.44	128.98	131.53	134.10	136.68	139.29	141.91	144.55
6.50	104.55	106.86	109.19	111.54	113.91	116.31	118.72	121.16	123.61	126.09	128.58	131.09	133.62	136.17	138.74	141.32
6.75	102.23	104.49	106.77	109.07	111.39	113.73	116.10	118.48	120.88	123.30	125.74	128.20	130.67	133.16	135.67	138.19
7.00	100.00	102.21	104.44	106.69	108.96	111.25	113.56	115.89	118.24	120.61	122.99	125.39	127.81	130.25	132.70	135.17
7.25	97.84	100.00	102.18	104.38	106.60	108.85	111.11	113.39	115.68	118.00	120.33	122.68	125.05	127.44	129.84	132.25
7.50	95.75	97.87	100.00	102.15	104.33	106.52	108.73	110.97	113.21	115.48	117.77	120.07	122.38	124.72	127.06	129.43
7.75	93.73	95.80	97.89	100.00	102.13	104.28	106.44	108.63	110.83	113.05	115.28	117.53	119.80	122.09	124.38	126.70
8.00	91.78	93.80	95.85	97.92	100.00	102.10	104.22	106.36	108.52	110.69	112.88	115.08	117.31	119.54	121.79	124.06
8.25	89.89	91.87	93.88	95.90	97.94	100.00	102.08	104.17	106.28	108.41	110.55	112.71	114.89	117.08	119.28	121.50
8.50	88.06	90.00	91.97	93.95	95.95	97.97	100.00	102.05	104.12	106.20	108.30	110.42	112.55	114.70	116.86	119.03
8.75	86.29	88.19	90.12	92.06	94.02	96.00	97.99	100.00	102.03	104.07	106.13	108.20	110.29	112.39	114.51	116.64
9.00	84.58	86.44	88.33	90.23	92.15	94.09	96.04	98.01	100.00	102.00	104.02	106.05	108.10	110.16	112.23	114.32
9.25	82.92	84.75	86.59	88.46	90.34	92.24	94.16	96.09	98.04	100.00	101.98	103.97	105.98	108.00	110.03	112.08
9.50	81.31	83.10	84.91	86.74	88.59	90.45	92.33	94.23	96.14	98.06	100.00	101.95	103.92	105.90	107.90	109.90
9.75	79.75	81.51	83.29	85.08	86.89	88.72	90.56	92.42	94.29	96.18	98.08	100.00	101.93	103.87	105.83	107.80
10.00	78.24	79.97	81.71	83.47	85.25	87.04	88.85	90.67	92.51	94.36	96.23	98.11	100.00	101.91	103.83	105.76
10.25	76.78	78.47	80.18	81.91	83.65	85.41	87.19	88.97	90.78	92.60	94.43	96.27	98.13	100.00	101.88	103.78
10.50	75.36	77.02	78.70	80.40	82.11	83.83	85.57	87.33	89.10	90.88	92.68	94.49	96.32	98.15	100.00	101.86
10.75	73.98	75.61	77.26	78.93	80.61	82.30	84.01	85.74	87.47	89.22	90.99	92.77	94.56	96.36	98.17	100.00
11.00	72.65	74.25	75.87	77.50	79.15	80.82	82.50	84.19	85.89	87.61	89.35	91.09	92.85	94.62	96.40	98.20
11.25	71.35	72.93	74.52	76.12	77.74	79.38	81.03	82.69	84.36	86.05	87.75	89.47	91.20	92.93	94.68	96.44
11.50	70.09	71.64	73.20	74.78	76.37	77.98	79.60	81.23	82.88	84.54	86.21	87.89	89.59	91.30	93.02	94.75
11.75	68.87	70.39	71.93	73.48	75.04	76.62	78.21	79.82	81.43	83.06	84.71	86.36	88.03	89.71	91.40	93.10
12.00	67.69	69.18	70.69	72.22	73.75	75.30	76.87	78.44	80.03	81.64	83.25	84.88	86.51	88.16	89.82	91.50
12.25	66.54	68.01	69.49	70.99	72.50	74.02	75.56	77.11	78.67	80.25	81.84	83.43	85.04	86.67	88.30	89.94
12.50	65.42	66.86	68.32	69.80	71.28	72.78	74.29	75.82	77.35	78.90	80.46	82.03	83.62	85.21	86.81	88.43
12.75	64.33	65.76	67.19	68.64	70.10	71.57	73.06	74.56	76.07	77.59	79.13	80.67	82.23	83.80	85.37	86.96
13.00	63.28	64.68	66.09	67.51	68.95	70.40	71.86	73.33	74.82	76.32	77.83	79.35	80.88	82.42	83.97	85.54
13.25	62.25	63.63	65.02	66.42	67.83	69.26	70.70	72.15	73.61	75.08	76.57	78.06	79.57	81.09	82.61	84.15
13.50	61.26	62.61	63.97	65.35	66.74	68.15	69.56	70.99	72.43	73.88	75.34	76.81	78.29	79.79	81.29	82.80
13.75	60.29	61.62	62.96	64.32	65.69	67.07	68.46	69.87	71.28	72.71	74.15	75.60	77.05	78.52	80.00	81.49
14.00	59.34	60.65	61.98	63.31	64.66	66.02	67.39	68.77	70.17	71.57	72.99	74.41	75.85	77.29	78.75	80.21
14.25	58.43	59.72	61.02	62.33	63.66	65.00	66.35	67.71	69.08	70.46	71.86	73.26	74.68	76.10	77.53	78.97
14.50	57.53	58.80	60.08	61.38	62.69	64.00	65.33	66.67	68.02	69.39	70.76	72.14	73.53	74.94	76.35	77.77
14.75	56.66	57.91	59.18	60.45	61.74	63.04	64.35	65.67	67.00	68.34	69.69	71.05	72.42	73.80	75.19	76.59
15.00	55.82	57.05	58.29	59.55	60.82	62.09	63.38	64.69	66.00	67.32	68.65	69.99	71.34	72.70	74.07	75.45
15.25	54.99	56.21	57.43	58.67	59.92	61.18	62.45	63.73	65.02	66.32	67.64	68.96	70.29	71.63	72.98	74.33
15.50	54.19	55.39	56.59	57.81	59.04	60.28	61.54	62.80	64.07	65.36	66.65	67.95	69.26	70.58	71.91	73.25
15.75	53.41	54.59	55.78	56.98	58.19	59.41	60.65	61.89	63.15	64.41	65.69	66.97	68.26	69.56	70.87	72.19
16.00	52.65	53.81	54.98	56.17	57.36	58.57	59.78	61.01	62.25	63.49	64.75	66.01	67.29	68.57	69.86	71.16
16.25	51.90	53.05	54.21	55.37	56.55	57.74	58.94	60.15	61.37	62.60	63.83	65.08	66.34	67.60	68.88	70.16
16.50	51.18	52.31	53.45	54.60	55.76	56.94	58.12	59.31	60.51	61.72	62.94	64.17	65.41	66.66	67.91	69.18
16.75	50.47	51.59	52.71	53.85	54.99	56.15	57.32	58.49	59.68	60.87	62.08	63.29	64.51	65.74	66.98	68.22
17.00	49.78	50.88	51.99	53.11	54.24	55.38	56.53	57.69	58.86	60.04	61.23	62.43	63.63	64.84	66.06	67.29
17.25	49.11	50.20	51.29	52.40	53.51	54.64	55.77	56.92	58.07	59.23	60.40	61.58	62.77	63.97	65.17	66.39
17.50	48.46	49.53	50.61	51.70	52.80	53.91	55.03	56.16	57.29	58.44	59.60	60.76	61.93	63.11	64.30	65.50
17.75	47.82	48.87	49.94	51.02	52.10	53.20	54.30	55.42	56.54	57.67	58.81	59.96	61.12	62.28	63.45	64.64
18.00	47.19	48.24	49.29	50.35	51.42	52.50	53.59	54.69	55.80	56.92	58.04	59.18	60.32	61.47	62.63	63.79
18.25	46.58	47.61	48.65	49.70	50.76	51.82	52.90	53.99	55.08	56.18	57.29	58.41	59.54	60.68	61.82	62.97
18.50	45.99	47.00	48.03	49.06	50.11	51.16	52.23	53.30	54.38	55.47	56.56	57.67	58.78	59.90	61.03	62.16
18.75	45.41	46.41	47.42	48.44	49.48	50.52	51.57	52.62	53.69	54.76	55.85	56.94	58.04	59.14	60.26	61.38
19.00	44.84	45.83	46.83	47.84	48.86	49.88	50.92	51.97	53.02	54.08	55.15	56.23	57.31	58.40	59.50	60.61
20.00	42.70	43.64	44.59	45.55	46.52	47.50	48.49	49.48	50.48	51.49	52.51	53.54	54.57	55.61	56.66	57.71
25.00	34.36	35.12	35.89	36.66	37.44	38.23	39.02	39.82	40.63	41.44	42.26	43.09	43.92	44.76	45.60	46.45
30.00	28.69	29.32	29.96	30.61	31.26	31.91	32.58	33.25	33.92	34.60	35.28	35.97	36.67	37.36	38.07	38.78

Description: This table shows the yield to maturity of a mortgage purchased at the price shown in the index.

Example: The yield to maturity of a 10.75 %, 24 year mortgage at a price of 111.00 is 9.37 %.

INTEREST RATE, %

PRICE	7.00%	7.25%	7.50%	7.75%	8.00%	8.25%	8.50%	8.75%	9.00%	9.25%	9.50%	9.75%	10.00%	10.25%	10.50%	10.75%
165	1.94	2.14	2.34	2.53	2.73	2.93	3.12	3.31	3.51	3.70	3.89	4.08	4.27	4.46	4.65	4.84
160	2.22	2.42	2.62	2.82	3.02	3.22	3.41	3.61	3.81	4.00	4.20	4.39	4.58	4.78	4.97	5.16
155	2.51	2.72	2.92	3.12	3.32	3.52	3.72	3.92	4.12	4.32	4.51	4.71	4.91	5.10	5.30	5.49
150	2.82	3.03	3.23	3.43	3.64	3.84	4.04	4.25	4.45	4.65	4.85	5.05	5.25	5.45	5.65	5.84
145	3.14	3.35	3.56	3.76	3.97	4.18	4.38	4.59	4.79	5.00	5.20	5.40	5.61	5.81	6.01	6.21
140	3.48	3.69	3.90	4.11	4.32	4.53	4.74	4.95	5.16	5.36	5.57	5.78	5.98	6.19	6.39	6.60
135	3.83	4.04	4.26	4.47	4.69	4.90	5.11	5.33	5.54	5.75	5.96	6.17	6.38	6.59	6.80	7.01
130	4.20	4.42	4.64	4.86	5.08	5.29	5.51	5.73	5.94	6.16	6.37	6.59	6.80	7.02	7.23	7.44
125	4.60	4.82	5.04	5.27	5.49	5.71	5.93	6.15	6.37	6.59	6.81	7.03	7.25	7.47	7.69	7.90
122	4.85	5.07	5.30	5.52	5.75	5.97	6.19	6.42	6.64	6.86	7.09	7.31	7.53	7.75	7.97	8.20
121	4.93	5.16	5.38	5.61	5.83	6.06	6.28	6.51	6.73	6.96	7.18	7.40	7.63	7.85	8.07	8.30
120	5.02	5.24	5.47	5.70	5.92	6.15	6.38	6.60	6.83	7.05	7.28	7.50	7.73	7.95	8.17	8.40
119	5.10	5.33	5.56	5.79	6.02	6.24	6.47	6.70	6.92	7.15	7.37	7.60	7.82	8.05	8.27	8.50
118	5.19	5.42	5.65	5.88	6.11	6.34	6.56	6.79	7.02	7.25	7.47	7.70	7.92	8.15	8.38	8.60
117	5.28	5.51	5.74	5.97	6.20	6.43	6.66	6.89	7.12	7.34	7.57	7.80	8.03	8.25	8.48	8.71
116	5.37	5.60	5.83	6.06	6.29	6.52	6.75	6.98	7.21	7.44	7.67	7.90	8.13	8.36	8.59	8.81
115	5.46	5.69	5.93	6.16	6.39	6.62	6.85	7.08	7.31	7.54	7.77	8.00	8.23	8.46	8.69	8.92
114	5.55	5.79	6.02	6.25	6.49	6.72	6.95	7.18	7.41	7.65	7.88	8.11	8.34	8.57	8.80	9.03
113	5.65	5.88	6.12	6.35	6.58	6.82	7.05	7.28	7.52	7.75	7.98	8.21	8.45	8.68	8.91	9.14
112	5.74	5.98	6.21	6.45	6.68	6.92	7.15	7.39	7.62	7.85	8.09	8.32	8.56	8.79	9.02	9.25
111	5.84	6.08	6.31	6.55	6.78	7.02	7.26	7.49	7.73	7.96	8.20	8.43	8.67	8.90	9.13	9.37
110	5.94	6.18	6.41	6.65	6.89	7.12	7.36	7.60	7.83	8.07	8.31	8.54	8.78	9.01	9.25	9.48
109	6.04	6.28	6.51	6.75	6.99	7.23	7.47	7.70	7.94	8.18	8.42	8.65	8.89	9.13	9.36	9.60
108	6.14	6.38	6.62	6.86	7.10	7.34	7.57	7.81	8.05	8.29	8.53	8.77	9.01	9.24	9.48	9.72
107	6.24	6.48	6.72	6.96	7.20	7.44	7.68	7.92	8.16	8.40	8.64	8.88	9.12	9.36	9.60	9.84
106	6.34	6.58	6.83	7.07	7.31	7.55	7.79	8.04	8.28	8.52	8.76	9.00	9.24	9.48	9.72	9.96
105	6.45	6.69	6.93	7.18	7.42	7.66	7.91	8.15	8.39	8.64	8.88	9.12	9.36	9.61	9.85	10.09
104	6.55	6.80	7.04	7.29	7.53	7.78	8.02	8.26	8.51	8.75	9.00	9.24	9.49	9.73	9.97	10.22
103	6.66	6.91	7.15	7.40	7.64	7.89	8.14	8.38	8.63	8.87	9.12	9.36	9.61	9.86	10.10	10.35
102	6.77	7.02	7.27	7.51	7.76	8.01	8.25	8.50	8.75	9.00	9.24	9.49	9.74	9.98	10.23	10.48
101	6.88	7.13	7.38	7.63	7.88	8.13	8.37	8.62	8.87	9.12	9.37	9.62	9.86	10.11	10.36	10.61
100	7.00	7.25	7.50	7.75	8.00	8.25	8.50	8.75	9.00	9.25	9.50	9.75	10.00	10.25	10.50	10.75
99	7.11	7.36	7.61	7.86	8.12	8.37	8.62	8.87	9.12	9.37	9.62	9.88	10.13	10.38	10.63	10.88
98	7.23	7.48	7.73	7.98	8.24	8.49	8.74	9.00	9.25	9.50	9.76	10.01	10.26	10.52	10.77	11.02
97	7.34	7.60	7.85	8.11	8.36	8.62	8.87	9.13	9.38	9.64	9.89	10.14	10.40	10.65	10.91	11.16
96	7.46	7.72	7.98	8.23	8.49	8.74	9.00	9.26	9.51	9.77	10.03	10.28	10.54	10.80	11.05	11.31
95	7.59	7.84	8.10	8.36	8.62	8.87	9.13	9.39	9.65	9.91	10.16	10.42	10.68	10.94	11.20	11.46
94	7.71	7.97	8.23	8.49	8.75	9.01	9.27	9.53	9.79	10.05	10.31	10.57	10.83	11.09	11.35	11.61
93	7.84	8.10	8.36	8.62	8.88	9.14	9.40	9.66	9.93	10.19	10.45	10.71	10.97	11.24	11.50	11.76
92	7.97	8.23	8.49	8.75	9.02	9.28	9.54	9.80	10.07	10.33	10.59	10.86	11.12	11.39	11.65	11.92
91	8.10	8.36	8.62	8.89	9.15	9.42	9.68	9.95	10.21	10.48	10.74	11.01	11.27	11.54	11.81	12.07
90	8.23	8.50	8.76	9.03	9.29	9.56	9.83	10.09	10.36	10.63	10.89	11.16	11.43	11.70	11.97	12.24
89	8.37	8.63	8.90	9.17	9.44	9.70	9.97	10.24	10.51	10.78	11.05	11.32	11.59	11.86	12.13	12.40
88	8.50	8.77	9.04	9.31	9.58	9.85	10.12	10.39	10.66	10.93	11.21	11.48	11.75	12.02	12.29	12.57
87	8.64	8.91	9.19	9.46	9.73	10.00	10.27	10.55	10.82	11.09	11.37	11.64	11.91	12.19	12.46	12.74
86	8.79	9.06	9.33	9.61	9.88	10.15	10.43	10.70	10.98	11.25	11.53	11.81	12.08	12.36	12.64	12.91
85	8.93	9.21	9.48	9.76	10.03	10.31	10.59	10.86	11.14	11.42	11.70	11.97	12.25	12.53	12.81	13.09
84	9.08	9.36	9.63	9.91	10.19	10.47	10.75	11.03	11.31	11.59	11.87	12.15	12.43	12.71	12.99	13.27
83	9.23	9.51	9.79	10.07	10.35	10.63	10.91	11.19	11.47	11.76	12.04	12.32	12.61	12.89	13.17	13.46
82	9.39	9.67	9.95	10.23	10.51	10.80	11.08	11.36	11.65	11.93	12.22	12.50	12.79	13.07	13.36	13.65
81	9.54	9.83	10.11	10.39	10.68	10.96	11.25	11.54	11.82	12.11	12.40	12.68	12.97	13.26	13.55	13.84
80	9.70	9.99	10.28	10.56	10.85	11.14	11.42	11.71	12.00	12.29	12.58	12.87	13.16	13.45	13.75	14.04
79	9.87	10.16	10.44	10.73	11.02	11.31	11.60	11.89	12.18	12.48	12.77	13.06	13.36	13.65	13.94	14.24
78	10.04	10.33	10.62	10.91	11.20	11.49	11.78	12.08	12.37	12.67	12.96	13.26	13.55	13.85	14.15	14.45
77	10.21	10.50	10.79	11.09	11.38	11.67	11.97	12.27	12.56	12.86	13.16	13.46	13.76	14.06	14.36	14.66
76	10.38	10.68	10.97	11.27	11.56	11.86	12.16	12.46	12.76	13.06	13.36	13.66	13.96	14.27	14.57	14.87
75	10.56	10.86	11.15	11.45	11.75	12.05	12.35	12.66	12.96	13.26	13.57	13.87	14.18	14.48	14.79	15.09
74	10.74	11.04	11.34	11.64	11.95	12.25	12.55	12.86	13.16	13.47	13.78	14.08	14.39	14.70	15.01	15.32
73	10.93	11.23	11.53	11.84	12.14	12.45	12.76	13.06	13.37	13.68	13.99	14.30	14.61	14.93	15.24	15.55
70	11.51	11.83	12.14	12.45	12.77	13.08	13.40	13.71	14.03	14.35	14.67	14.99	15.31	15.64	15.96	16.28
65	12.59	12.92	13.25	13.58	13.91	14.24	14.58	14.91	15.25	15.59	15.93	16.27	16.61	16.95	17.29	17.64
60	13.82	14.17	14.52	14.87	15.22	15.58	15.93	16.29	16.65	17.01	17.37	17.73	18.09	18.46	18.83	19.20
55	15.24	15.61	15.99	16.36	16.74	17.12	17.50	17.89	18.27	18.66	19.05	19.44	19.83	20.23	20.62	21.02
50	16.92	17.32	17.72	18.13	18.54	18.95	19.36	19.78	20.20	20.62	21.04	21.46	21.89	22.32	22.75	23.19
45	18.92	19.36	19.81	20.25	20.70	21.15	21.60	22.06	22.52	22.98	23.45	23.91	24.38	24.86	25.33	25.81
40	21.40	21.88	22.37	22.87	23.37	23.87	24.37	24.88	25.39	25.91	26.43	26.95	27.48	28.00	28.54	29.07
35	24.53	25.08	25.64	26.20	26.76	27.33	27.90	28.48	29.06	29.65	30.24	30.83	31.43	32.03	32.64	33.25
30	28.67	29.31	29.95	30.60	31.26	31.92	32.58	33.25	33.93	34.61	35.30	35.99	36.68	37.38	38.09	38.80

Description: This table shows the price to pay for a monthly payment mortgage loan at the yield rate.

Example: The price of a 15.00 %, 24 year mortgage loan to yield 8.00 % to maturity is $ 164.43.

INTEREST RATE, %

YIELD	11.00%	11.25%	11.50%	11.75%	12.00%	12.25%	12.50%	12.75%	13.00%	13.25%	13.50%	13.75%	14.00%	14.25%	14.50%	15.00%
0.00	284.55	289.72	294.91	300.14	305.39	310.67	315.98	321.31	326.67	332.05	337.46	342.89	348.34	353.81	359.30	370.35
1.00	252.89	257.48	262.10	266.74	271.41	276.10	280.82	285.56	290.32	295.10	299.91	304.73	309.58	314.44	319.32	329.14
2.00	225.84	229.94	234.07	238.21	242.38	246.57	250.79	255.02	259.27	263.54	267.84	272.14	276.47	280.81	285.17	293.94
3.00	202.67	206.35	210.05	213.77	217.51	221.27	225.05	228.85	232.67	236.50	240.35	244.22	248.10	252.00	255.91	263.78
4.00	182.73	186.05	189.39	192.74	196.12	199.51	202.92	206.34	209.78	213.24	216.71	220.20	223.70	227.21	230.74	237.83
4.25	178.19	181.43	184.68	187.95	191.24	194.55	197.87	201.21	204.57	207.94	211.33	214.73	218.14	221.57	225.01	231.92
4.50	173.82	176.97	180.15	183.34	186.55	189.77	193.01	196.27	199.55	202.83	206.14	209.45	212.78	216.12	219.48	226.23
4.75	169.60	172.68	175.77	178.89	182.02	185.17	188.33	191.51	194.70	197.91	201.13	204.37	207.62	210.88	214.15	220.73
5.00	165.53	168.53	171.55	174.59	177.65	180.72	183.81	186.91	190.03	193.16	196.30	199.46	202.63	205.82	209.01	215.44
5.25	161.60	164.53	167.48	170.45	173.43	176.43	179.45	182.48	185.52	188.57	191.65	194.73	197.82	200.93	204.05	210.32
5.50	157.81	160.67	163.56	166.45	169.37	172.29	175.24	178.20	181.17	184.15	187.15	190.16	193.18	196.22	199.27	205.39
5.75	154.15	156.95	159.76	162.59	165.44	168.30	171.18	174.06	176.97	179.88	182.81	185.75	188.71	191.67	194.65	200.63
6.00	150.62	153.35	156.10	158.87	161.65	164.44	167.25	170.08	172.91	175.76	178.62	181.50	184.38	187.28	190.19	196.03
6.25	147.21	149.88	152.57	155.27	157.99	160.72	163.47	166.22	169.00	171.78	174.58	177.39	180.21	183.04	185.88	191.59
6.50	143.91	146.53	149.15	151.80	154.45	157.12	159.81	162.50	165.21	167.94	170.67	173.42	176.17	178.94	181.72	187.31
6.75	140.73	143.28	145.85	148.44	151.04	153.65	156.27	158.91	161.56	164.22	166.90	169.58	172.28	174.98	177.70	183.16
7.00	137.65	140.15	142.67	145.19	147.73	150.29	152.86	155.44	158.03	160.63	163.25	165.87	168.51	171.16	173.82	179.16
7.25	134.68	137.13	139.58	142.06	144.54	147.04	149.56	152.08	154.62	157.16	159.72	162.29	164.87	167.46	170.06	175.29
7.50	131.81	134.20	136.61	139.03	141.46	143.90	146.36	148.83	151.32	153.81	156.31	158.83	161.35	163.89	166.43	171.55
7.75	129.03	131.37	133.72	136.09	138.48	140.87	143.28	145.69	148.12	150.56	153.02	155.48	157.95	160.43	162.92	167.93
8.00	126.34	128.63	130.94	133.26	135.59	137.93	140.29	142.66	145.04	147.43	149.83	152.24	154.66	157.09	159.53	164.43
8.25	123.74	125.98	128.24	130.51	132.80	135.09	137.40	139.72	142.05	144.39	146.74	149.10	151.47	153.85	156.24	161.04
8.50	121.22	123.42	125.63	127.86	130.10	132.34	134.61	136.88	139.16	141.45	143.76	146.07	148.39	150.72	153.06	157.77
8.75	118.78	120.94	123.11	125.29	127.48	129.68	131.90	134.13	136.36	138.61	140.87	143.13	145.41	147.69	149.98	154.59
9.00	116.42	118.53	120.66	122.80	124.95	127.11	129.28	131.46	133.65	135.86	138.07	140.29	142.52	144.76	147.00	151.52
9.25	114.14	116.21	118.29	120.39	122.49	124.61	126.74	128.88	131.03	133.19	135.36	137.53	139.72	141.92	144.12	148.55
9.50	111.92	113.95	116.00	118.05	120.12	122.20	124.28	126.38	128.49	130.61	132.73	134.87	137.01	139.16	141.32	145.67
9.75	109.78	111.77	113.78	115.79	117.82	119.85	121.90	123.96	126.03	128.10	130.19	132.28	134.39	136.50	138.62	142.88
10.00	107.70	109.65	111.62	113.60	115.59	117.59	119.59	121.61	123.64	125.68	127.72	129.78	131.84	133.91	135.99	140.17
10.25	105.69	107.60	109.53	111.47	113.42	115.39	117.36	119.34	121.33	123.33	125.33	127.35	129.38	131.41	133.45	137.55
10.50	103.73	105.61	107.51	109.41	111.33	113.25	115.19	117.13	119.09	121.05	123.02	125.00	126.98	128.98	130.98	135.01
10.75	101.84	103.69	105.55	107.42	109.30	111.19	113.08	114.99	116.91	118.84	120.77	122.71	124.67	126.62	128.59	132.54
11.00	100.00	101.82	103.64	105.48	107.32	109.18	111.04	112.92	114.80	116.69	118.59	120.50	122.42	124.34	126.27	130.15
11.25	98.22	100.00	101.79	103.60	105.41	107.23	109.06	110.91	112.75	114.61	116.48	118.35	120.23	122.12	124.02	127.83
11.50	96.49	98.24	100.00	101.77	103.55	105.34	107.14	108.95	110.77	112.59	114.43	116.27	118.12	119.97	121.83	125.58
11.75	94.81	96.53	98.26	100.00	101.75	103.51	105.28	107.05	108.84	110.63	112.43	114.24	116.06	117.88	119.71	123.39
12.00	93.18	94.87	96.57	98.28	100.00	101.73	103.47	105.21	106.97	108.73	110.50	112.28	114.06	115.85	117.65	121.27
12.25	91.59	93.26	94.93	96.61	98.30	100.00	101.71	103.42	105.15	106.88	108.62	110.37	112.12	113.89	115.65	119.21
12.50	90.05	91.69	93.33	94.99	96.65	98.32	100.00	101.69	103.38	105.09	106.80	108.52	110.24	111.97	113.71	117.21
12.75	88.56	90.17	91.78	93.41	95.05	96.69	98.34	100.00	101.67	103.34	105.03	106.71	108.41	110.11	111.82	115.26
13.00	87.11	88.69	90.28	91.88	93.49	95.10	96.73	98.36	100.00	101.65	103.30	104.96	106.63	108.31	109.99	113.37
13.25	85.70	87.25	88.82	90.39	91.97	93.56	95.16	96.77	98.38	100.00	101.63	103.26	104.90	106.55	108.21	111.53
13.50	84.32	85.85	87.39	88.94	90.50	92.06	93.63	95.22	96.80	98.40	100.00	101.61	103.22	104.85	106.47	109.75
13.75	82.99	84.49	86.01	87.53	89.06	90.60	92.15	93.71	95.27	96.84	98.42	100.00	101.59	103.19	104.79	108.01
14.00	81.69	83.17	84.66	86.16	87.67	89.19	90.71	92.24	93.78	95.32	96.88	98.44	100.00	101.57	103.15	106.32
14.25	80.43	81.89	83.35	84.83	86.31	87.81	89.31	90.81	92.33	93.85	95.38	96.91	98.45	100.00	101.55	104.67
14.50	79.20	80.63	82.08	83.53	85.00	86.46	87.94	89.43	90.92	92.42	93.92	95.43	96.95	98.47	100.00	103.07
14.75	78.00	79.41	80.84	82.27	83.71	85.16	86.61	88.07	89.54	91.02	92.50	93.99	95.48	96.98	98.49	101.52
15.00	76.83	78.23	79.63	81.04	82.46	83.89	85.32	86.76	88.21	89.66	91.12	92.58	94.06	95.53	97.02	100.00
15.25	75.70	77.07	78.46	79.85	81.24	82.65	84.06	85.48	86.90	88.34	89.77	91.22	92.67	94.12	95.58	98.52
15.50	74.59	75.95	77.31	78.68	80.06	81.44	82.83	84.23	85.63	87.05	88.46	89.89	91.32	92.75	94.19	97.09
15.75	73.52	74.85	76.19	77.54	78.90	80.27	81.64	83.01	84.40	85.79	87.19	88.59	90.00	91.41	92.83	95.68
16.00	72.47	73.78	75.11	76.44	77.78	79.12	80.47	81.83	83.19	84.57	85.94	87.32	88.71	90.11	91.51	94.32
16.25	71.45	72.74	74.05	75.36	76.68	78.00	79.34	80.68	82.02	83.37	84.73	86.09	87.46	88.84	90.21	92.99
16.50	70.45	71.73	73.01	74.31	75.61	76.92	78.23	79.55	80.88	82.21	83.55	84.89	86.24	87.60	88.96	91.69
16.75	69.48	70.74	72.01	73.28	74.57	75.85	77.15	78.45	79.76	81.08	82.40	83.72	85.05	86.39	87.73	90.43
17.00	68.53	69.77	71.02	72.28	73.55	74.82	76.10	77.38	78.67	79.97	81.27	82.58	83.89	85.21	86.53	89.19
17.25	67.61	68.83	70.07	71.31	72.56	73.81	75.07	76.34	77.61	78.89	80.17	81.46	82.76	84.06	85.36	87.99
17.50	66.70	67.91	69.13	70.36	71.59	72.83	74.07	75.32	76.58	77.84	79.11	80.38	81.66	82.94	84.23	86.82
17.75	65.82	67.02	68.22	69.43	70.64	71.86	73.09	74.33	75.57	76.81	78.06	79.32	80.58	81.84	83.11	85.67
18.00	64.96	66.14	67.33	68.52	69.72	70.93	72.14	73.36	74.58	75.81	77.04	78.28	79.53	80.78	82.03	84.55
18.25	64.13	65.29	66.46	67.64	68.82	70.01	71.21	72.41	73.62	74.83	76.05	77.27	78.50	79.73	80.97	83.46
18.50	63.31	64.46	65.61	66.77	67.94	69.12	70.30	71.48	72.68	73.87	75.08	76.28	77.50	78.71	79.94	82.39
18.75	62.51	63.64	64.78	65.93	67.08	68.24	69.41	70.58	71.76	72.94	74.13	75.32	76.52	77.72	78.93	81.35
19.00	61.73	62.85	63.97	65.11	66.25	67.39	68.54	69.70	70.86	72.03	73.20	74.38	75.56	76.75	77.94	80.34
20.00	58.77	59.84	60.91	61.99	63.08	64.17	65.27	66.37	67.47	68.59	69.70	70.82	71.95	73.08	74.21	76.50
25.00	47.30	48.16	49.02	49.89	50.76	51.64	52.52	53.41	54.30	55.20	56.09	57.00	57.90	58.81	59.73	61.56
30.00	39.49	40.21	40.93	41.65	42.38	43.11	43.85	44.59	45.33	46.08	46.83	47.58	48.34	49.10	49.86	51.40

Description: This table shows the yield to maturity of a mortgage purchased at the price shown in the index.

Example: The yield to maturity of a 15.00 %, 24 year mortgage at a price of 125.00 is 11.56 %.

INTEREST RATE, %

PRICE	11.00%	11.25%	11.50%	11.75%	12.00%	12.25%	12.50%	12.75%	13.00%	13.25%	13.50%	13.75%	14.00%	14.25%	14.50%	15.00%
250	1.09	1.25	1.41	1.56	1.72	1.87	2.02	2.18	2.33	2.48	2.63	2.78	2.92	3.07	3.22	3.51
240	1.45	1.61	1.77	1.93	2.08	2.24	2.40	2.55	2.70	2.86	3.01	3.16	3.31	3.46	3.61	3.91
230	1.83	1.99	2.15	2.31	2.47	2.63	2.79	2.95	3.10	3.26	3.41	3.57	3.72	3.87	4.03	4.33
220	2.23	2.40	2.56	2.73	2.89	3.05	3.21	3.37	3.53	3.69	3.85	4.00	4.16	4.32	4.47	4.78
210	2.66	2.83	3.00	3.16	3.33	3.49	3.66	3.82	3.98	4.15	4.31	4.47	4.63	4.79	4.95	5.26
200	3.12	3.29	3.46	3.63	3.80	3.97	4.14	4.31	4.47	4.64	4.80	4.97	5.13	5.29	5.46	5.78
195	3.36	3.54	3.71	3.88	4.05	4.22	4.39	4.56	4.73	4.90	5.06	5.23	5.40	5.56	5.73	6.05
190	3.61	3.79	3.96	4.14	4.31	4.48	4.65	4.83	5.00	5.17	5.34	5.50	5.67	5.84	6.01	6.34
185	3.87	4.05	4.23	4.40	4.58	4.75	4.93	5.10	5.27	5.45	5.62	5.79	5.96	6.13	6.30	6.63
180	4.14	4.32	4.50	4.68	4.86	5.04	5.21	5.39	5.56	5.74	5.91	6.09	6.26	6.43	6.60	6.94
175	4.43	4.61	4.79	4.97	5.15	5.33	5.51	5.69	5.87	6.04	6.22	6.39	6.57	6.74	6.92	7.26
170	4.72	4.91	5.09	5.27	5.46	5.64	5.82	6.00	6.18	6.36	6.54	6.72	6.90	7.07	7.25	7.60
165	5.03	5.22	5.40	5.59	5.77	5.96	6.14	6.33	6.51	6.69	6.87	7.06	7.24	7.42	7.60	7.95
160	5.35	5.54	5.73	5.92	6.11	6.29	6.48	6.67	6.85	7.04	7.22	7.41	7.59	7.78	7.96	8.32
155	5.69	5.88	6.07	6.26	6.46	6.65	6.84	7.03	7.22	7.41	7.59	7.78	7.97	8.16	8.34	8.71
150	6.04	6.24	6.43	6.63	6.82	7.02	7.21	7.40	7.60	7.79	7.98	8.17	8.36	8.55	8.74	9.12
145	6.41	6.61	6.81	7.01	7.21	7.41	7.60	7.80	8.00	8.19	8.39	8.59	8.78	8.97	9.17	9.55
140	6.80	7.01	7.21	7.41	7.62	7.82	8.02	8.22	8.42	8.62	8.82	9.02	9.22	9.42	9.62	10.01
135	7.22	7.43	7.63	7.84	8.05	8.25	8.46	8.66	8.87	9.07	9.28	9.48	9.69	9.89	10.09	10.50
130	7.66	7.87	8.08	8.29	8.50	8.71	8.93	9.14	9.35	9.55	9.76	9.97	10.18	10.39	10.60	11.01
125	8.12	8.34	8.56	8.77	8.99	9.21	9.42	9.64	9.85	10.07	10.28	10.49	10.71	10.92	11.14	11.56
120	8.62	8.84	9.06	9.29	9.51	9.73	9.95	10.17	10.39	10.61	10.83	11.05	11.27	11.49	11.71	12.15
115	9.15	9.38	9.61	9.83	10.06	10.29	10.52	10.74	10.97	11.20	11.42	11.65	11.88	12.10	12.33	12.78
113	9.37	9.60	9.83	10.06	10.30	10.53	10.76	10.99	11.21	11.44	11.67	11.90	12.13	12.36	12.59	13.04
112	9.49	9.72	9.95	10.18	10.41	10.65	10.88	11.11	11.34	11.57	11.80	12.03	12.26	12.49	12.72	13.18
111	9.60	9.84	10.07	10.30	10.53	10.77	11.00	11.23	11.47	11.70	11.93	12.16	12.39	12.62	12.86	13.32
110	9.72	9.95	10.19	10.42	10.66	10.89	11.13	11.36	11.59	11.83	12.06	12.29	12.53	12.76	12.99	13.46
109	9.84	10.07	10.31	10.55	10.78	11.02	11.25	11.49	11.72	11.96	12.19	12.43	12.66	12.90	13.13	13.60
108	9.96	10.20	10.43	10.67	10.91	11.15	11.38	11.62	11.86	12.09	12.33	12.57	12.80	13.04	13.27	13.75
107	10.08	10.32	10.56	10.80	11.04	11.28	11.51	11.75	11.99	12.23	12.47	12.70	12.94	13.18	13.42	13.89
106	10.21	10.45	10.69	10.93	11.17	11.41	11.65	11.89	12.13	12.37	12.61	12.85	13.09	13.33	13.56	14.04
105	10.33	10.57	10.82	11.06	11.30	11.54	11.78	12.02	12.27	12.51	12.75	12.99	13.23	13.47	13.71	14.19
104	10.46	10.70	10.95	11.19	11.43	11.68	11.92	12.16	12.41	12.65	12.89	13.14	13.38	13.62	13.86	14.35
103	10.59	10.84	11.08	11.33	11.57	11.82	12.06	12.31	12.55	12.79	13.04	13.28	13.53	13.77	14.02	14.51
102	10.72	10.97	11.22	11.46	11.71	11.96	12.20	12.45	12.70	12.94	13.19	13.44	13.68	13.93	14.17	14.67
101	10.86	11.11	11.35	11.60	11.85	12.10	12.35	12.60	12.84	13.09	13.34	13.59	13.84	14.09	14.33	14.83
100	11.00	11.25	11.50	11.75	12.00	12.25	12.50	12.75	13.00	13.25	13.50	13.75	14.00	14.25	14.50	15.00
99	11.13	11.39	11.64	11.89	12.14	12.39	12.64	12.90	13.15	13.40	13.65	13.90	14.16	14.41	14.66	15.16
98	11.28	11.53	11.78	12.04	12.29	12.54	12.80	13.05	13.30	13.56	13.81	14.07	14.32	14.57	14.83	15.34
97	11.42	11.68	11.93	12.19	12.44	12.70	12.95	13.21	13.46	13.72	13.97	14.23	14.49	14.74	15.00	15.51
96	11.57	11.82	12.08	12.34	12.60	12.85	13.11	13.37	13.63	13.88	14.14	14.40	14.66	14.91	15.17	15.69
95	11.72	11.97	12.23	12.49	12.75	13.01	13.27	13.53	13.79	14.05	14.31	14.57	14.83	15.09	15.35	15.87
94	11.87	12.13	12.39	12.65	12.91	13.17	13.43	13.70	13.96	14.22	14.48	14.74	15.01	15.27	15.53	16.05
93	12.02	12.29	12.55	12.81	13.07	13.34	13.60	13.86	14.13	14.39	14.66	14.92	15.18	15.45	15.71	16.24
92	12.18	12.44	12.71	12.97	13.24	13.51	13.77	14.04	14.30	14.57	14.83	15.10	15.37	15.63	15.90	16.43
91	12.34	12.61	12.87	13.14	13.41	13.68	13.94	14.21	14.48	14.75	15.02	15.29	15.55	15.82	16.09	16.63
90	12.50	12.77	13.04	13.31	13.58	13.85	14.12	14.39	14.66	14.93	15.20	15.47	15.74	16.02	16.29	16.83
89	12.67	12.94	13.21	13.48	13.76	14.03	14.30	14.57	14.85	15.12	15.39	15.67	15.94	16.21	16.49	17.03
88	12.84	13.11	13.39	13.66	13.94	14.21	14.48	14.76	15.03	15.31	15.58	15.86	16.14	16.41	16.69	17.24
87	13.01	13.29	13.57	13.84	14.12	14.39	14.67	14.95	15.23	15.50	15.78	16.06	16.34	16.62	16.90	17.46
86	13.19	13.47	13.75	14.03	14.30	14.58	14.86	15.14	15.42	15.70	15.98	16.26	16.55	16.83	17.11	17.67
85	13.37	13.65	13.93	14.21	14.49	14.78	15.06	15.34	15.62	15.91	16.19	16.47	16.76	17.04	17.32	17.89
84	13.55	13.84	14.12	14.40	14.69	14.97	15.26	15.54	15.83	16.11	16.40	16.68	16.97	17.26	17.55	18.12
83	13.74	14.03	14.31	14.60	14.89	15.17	15.46	15.75	16.04	16.32	16.61	16.90	17.19	17.48	17.77	18.35
82	13.93	14.22	14.51	14.80	15.09	15.38	15.67	15.96	16.25	16.54	16.83	17.12	17.42	17.71	18.00	18.59
81	14.13	14.42	14.71	15.00	15.30	15.59	15.88	16.17	16.47	16.76	17.06	17.35	17.65	17.94	18.24	18.83
80	14.33	14.62	14.92	15.21	15.51	15.80	16.10	16.39	16.69	16.99	17.29	17.58	17.88	18.18	18.48	19.08
79	14.54	14.83	15.13	15.43	15.72	16.02	16.32	16.62	16.92	17.22	17.52	17.82	18.12	18.42	18.73	19.33
78	14.74	15.04	15.34	15.64	15.94	16.25	16.55	16.85	17.15	17.46	17.76	18.06	18.37	18.67	18.98	19.59
77	14.96	15.26	15.56	15.87	16.17	16.48	16.78	17.09	17.39	17.70	18.01	18.31	18.62	18.93	19.24	19.86
76	15.18	15.48	15.79	16.10	16.40	16.71	17.02	17.33	17.64	17.95	18.26	18.57	18.88	19.19	19.50	20.13
75	15.40	15.71	16.02	16.33	16.64	16.95	17.26	17.57	17.89	18.20	18.51	18.83	19.14	19.46	19.78	20.41
74	15.63	15.94	16.26	16.57	16.88	17.20	17.51	17.83	18.14	18.46	18.78	19.10	19.42	19.74	20.06	20.70
73	15.87	16.18	16.50	16.82	17.13	17.45	17.77	18.09	18.41	18.73	19.05	19.37	19.69	20.02	20.34	20.99
70	16.61	16.94	17.26	17.59	17.92	18.25	18.58	18.91	19.24	19.57	19.91	20.24	20.57	20.91	21.25	21.92
65	17.98	18.33	18.68	19.03	19.38	19.73	20.08	20.43	20.79	21.14	21.50	21.85	22.21	22.57	22.93	23.65
60	19.57	19.94	20.31	20.69	21.06	21.44	21.82	22.19	22.57	22.96	23.34	23.72	24.11	24.49	24.88	25.66
55	21.42	21.82	22.22	22.63	23.03	23.44	23.85	24.26	24.67	25.09	25.50	25.92	26.33	26.75	27.17	28.02

Description: This table shows the price to pay for a monthly payment mortgage loan at the yield rate.

Example: The price of a 6.75 %, 25 year mortgage loan to yield 8.00 % to maturity is $ 89.52.

INTEREST RATE, %

YIELD	0.00%	1.00%	2.00%	3.00%	4.00%	4.25%	4.50%	4.75%	5.00%	5.25%	5.50%	5.75%	6.00%	6.25%	6.50%	6.75%
0.00	100.00	113.06	127.16	142.26	158.35	162.52	166.75	171.04	175.38	179.77	184.23	188.73	193.29	197.90	202.56	207.27
1.00	88.45	100.00	112.47	125.83	140.06	143.75	147.49	151.28	155.12	159.01	162.94	166.93	170.96	175.04	179.16	183.33
2.00	78.64	88.92	100.00	111.88	124.53	127.81	131.14	134.51	137.92	141.38	144.88	148.43	152.01	155.64	159.30	163.01
3.00	70.29	79.47	89.38	100.00	111.31	114.24	117.21	120.22	123.28	126.37	129.50	132.66	135.87	139.11	142.39	145.70
4.00	63.15	71.40	80.30	89.84	100.00	102.63	105.30	108.01	110.75	113.53	116.34	119.19	122.06	124.98	127.92	130.89
4.25	61.53	69.57	78.24	87.54	97.43	100.00	102.60	105.24	107.91	110.62	113.36	116.13	118.93	121.77	124.64	127.54
4.50	59.97	67.80	76.26	85.32	94.96	97.46	100.00	102.57	105.17	107.81	110.48	113.18	115.92	118.68	121.48	124.30
4.75	58.47	66.10	74.35	83.18	92.58	95.02	97.49	100.00	102.54	105.11	107.71	110.35	113.01	115.71	118.43	121.19
5.00	57.02	64.47	72.50	81.12	90.29	92.67	95.08	97.52	100.00	102.51	105.05	107.61	110.21	112.84	115.50	118.19
5.25	55.63	62.89	70.73	79.13	88.08	90.40	92.76	95.14	97.55	100.00	102.48	104.98	107.52	110.08	112.68	115.30
5.50	54.28	61.37	69.02	77.22	85.95	88.22	90.51	92.84	95.20	97.58	100.00	102.45	104.92	107.42	109.95	112.51
5.75	52.99	59.91	67.37	75.38	83.90	86.11	88.35	90.62	92.92	95.25	97.61	100.00	102.42	104.86	107.33	109.82
6.00	51.74	58.49	65.79	73.60	81.92	84.08	86.27	88.49	90.73	93.01	95.31	97.64	100.00	102.39	104.80	107.23
6.25	50.53	57.13	64.25	71.89	80.02	82.12	84.26	86.42	88.62	90.84	93.09	95.37	97.67	100.00	102.36	104.74
6.50	49.37	55.82	62.77	70.23	78.17	80.23	82.32	84.44	86.58	88.75	90.95	93.17	95.42	97.70	100.00	102.33
6.75	48.25	54.55	61.35	68.64	76.40	78.41	80.45	82.52	84.61	86.73	88.88	91.05	93.25	95.48	97.73	100.00
7.00	47.16	53.32	59.97	67.09	74.68	76.65	78.64	80.66	82.71	84.79	86.89	89.01	91.16	93.33	95.53	97.75
7.25	46.12	52.14	58.64	65.61	73.03	74.95	76.90	78.88	80.88	82.91	84.96	87.04	89.14	91.26	93.41	95.59
7.50	45.11	51.00	57.36	64.17	71.43	73.31	75.22	77.15	79.11	81.09	83.10	85.13	87.19	89.27	91.37	93.49
7.75	44.13	49.90	56.12	62.78	69.88	71.72	73.59	75.48	77.40	79.34	81.30	83.29	85.30	87.34	89.39	91.47
8.00	43.19	48.83	54.92	61.44	68.39	70.19	72.02	73.87	75.74	77.64	79.56	81.51	83.48	85.47	87.48	89.52
8.25	42.28	47.80	53.76	60.14	66.95	68.71	70.50	72.31	74.14	76.00	77.89	79.79	81.72	83.67	85.64	87.63
8.50	41.40	46.80	52.64	58.89	65.55	67.28	69.03	70.80	72.60	74.42	76.26	78.13	80.01	81.92	83.85	85.80
8.75	40.54	45.84	51.55	57.68	64.20	65.89	67.61	69.35	71.11	72.89	74.69	76.52	78.37	80.24	82.13	84.04
9.00	39.72	44.91	50.51	56.51	62.90	64.55	66.23	67.94	69.66	71.41	73.18	74.97	76.78	78.61	80.46	82.33
9.25	38.92	44.01	49.49	55.37	61.64	63.26	64.90	66.57	68.26	69.97	71.71	73.46	75.24	77.03	78.84	80.68
9.50	38.15	43.14	48.51	54.28	60.41	62.01	63.62	65.25	66.91	68.59	70.29	72.01	73.74	75.50	77.28	79.08
9.75	37.41	42.29	47.56	53.21	59.23	60.79	62.37	63.98	65.60	67.25	68.91	70.60	72.30	74.03	75.77	77.53
10.00	36.68	41.47	46.64	52.19	58.09	59.62	61.17	62.74	64.33	65.95	67.58	69.23	70.90	72.59	74.30	76.03
10.25	35.98	40.68	45.75	51.19	56.98	58.48	60.00	61.54	63.10	64.69	66.29	67.91	69.55	71.21	72.89	74.58
10.50	35.30	39.92	44.89	50.22	55.90	57.38	58.87	60.38	61.91	63.47	65.04	66.63	68.24	69.87	71.51	73.18
10.75	34.65	39.17	44.06	49.29	54.86	56.31	57.77	59.26	60.76	62.29	63.83	65.39	66.97	68.57	70.18	71.81
11.00	34.01	38.45	43.25	48.38	53.85	55.27	56.71	58.17	59.65	61.14	62.65	64.19	65.74	67.31	68.89	70.49
11.25	33.39	37.75	42.46	47.50	52.88	54.27	55.68	57.11	58.56	60.03	61.52	63.02	64.54	66.08	67.64	69.21
11.50	32.79	37.08	41.70	46.65	51.93	53.30	54.68	56.09	57.51	58.95	60.41	61.89	63.39	64.90	66.43	67.97
11.75	32.21	36.42	40.96	45.83	51.01	52.35	53.71	55.09	56.49	57.91	59.34	60.80	62.26	63.75	65.25	66.77
12.00	31.65	35.78	40.24	45.02	50.12	51.44	52.77	54.13	55.50	56.90	58.31	59.73	61.17	62.63	64.11	65.60
12.25	31.10	35.16	39.55	44.25	49.25	50.55	51.86	53.20	54.55	55.91	57.30	58.70	60.12	61.55	63.00	64.47
12.50	30.57	34.56	38.87	43.49	48.41	49.68	50.98	52.29	53.61	54.96	56.32	57.70	59.09	60.50	61.93	63.37
12.75	30.06	33.98	38.22	42.76	47.59	48.85	50.12	51.41	52.71	54.03	55.37	56.72	58.09	59.48	60.88	62.30
13.00	29.56	33.42	37.58	42.05	46.80	48.03	49.28	50.55	51.83	53.13	54.45	55.78	57.13	58.49	59.87	61.26
13.25	29.07	32.87	36.96	41.35	46.03	47.24	48.47	49.72	50.98	52.26	53.55	54.86	56.19	57.53	58.88	60.25
13.50	28.60	32.33	36.36	40.68	45.28	46.48	47.68	48.91	50.15	51.41	52.68	53.97	55.27	56.59	57.93	59.27
13.75	28.14	31.81	35.78	40.03	44.56	45.73	46.92	48.12	49.35	50.58	51.84	53.10	54.39	55.68	57.00	58.32
14.00	27.69	31.31	35.21	39.39	43.85	45.00	46.17	47.36	48.56	49.78	51.01	52.26	53.52	54.80	56.09	57.40
14.25	27.26	30.82	34.66	38.78	43.16	44.30	45.45	46.62	47.80	49.00	50.21	51.44	52.69	53.94	55.21	56.50
14.50	26.83	30.34	34.12	38.18	42.49	43.61	44.75	45.90	47.06	48.24	49.44	50.65	51.87	53.11	54.36	55.62
14.75	26.42	29.88	33.60	37.59	41.84	42.95	44.06	45.19	46.34	47.50	48.68	49.87	51.08	52.29	53.53	54.77
15.00	26.02	29.42	33.09	37.02	41.21	42.30	43.40	44.51	45.64	46.79	47.94	49.12	50.30	51.50	52.72	53.94
15.25	25.64	28.98	32.60	36.47	40.59	41.66	42.75	43.85	44.96	46.09	47.23	48.38	49.55	50.73	51.93	53.14
15.50	25.26	28.56	32.12	35.93	40.00	41.05	42.12	43.20	44.30	45.41	46.53	47.67	48.82	49.98	51.16	52.35
15.75	24.89	28.14	31.65	35.41	39.41	40.45	41.50	42.57	43.65	44.74	45.85	46.97	48.11	49.26	50.42	51.59
16.00	24.53	27.73	31.19	34.90	38.84	39.87	40.90	41.95	43.02	44.10	45.19	46.30	47.41	48.54	49.69	50.84
16.25	24.18	27.34	30.75	34.40	38.29	39.30	40.32	41.36	42.41	43.47	44.55	45.64	46.74	47.85	48.98	50.12
16.50	23.84	26.95	30.31	33.91	37.75	38.74	39.75	40.77	41.81	42.86	43.92	44.99	46.08	47.18	48.29	49.41
16.75	23.51	26.58	29.89	33.44	37.22	38.20	39.20	40.21	41.23	42.26	43.31	44.37	45.44	46.52	47.62	48.72
17.00	23.18	26.21	29.48	32.98	36.71	37.68	38.66	39.65	40.66	41.68	42.71	43.75	44.81	45.88	46.96	48.05
17.25	22.87	25.85	29.08	32.53	36.21	37.17	38.13	39.11	40.11	41.11	42.13	43.16	44.20	45.26	46.32	47.40
17.50	22.56	25.51	28.69	32.09	35.72	36.67	37.62	38.59	39.57	40.56	41.56	42.58	43.61	44.65	45.70	46.76
17.75	22.26	25.17	28.30	31.67	35.25	36.18	37.12	38.07	39.04	40.02	41.01	42.01	43.03	44.05	45.09	46.14
18.00	21.97	24.84	27.93	31.25	34.78	35.70	36.63	37.57	38.53	39.49	40.47	41.46	42.46	43.47	44.50	45.53
18.25	21.68	24.51	27.57	30.84	34.33	35.24	36.15	37.08	38.02	38.98	39.94	40.92	41.91	42.91	43.92	44.94
18.50	21.40	24.20	27.21	30.45	33.89	34.78	35.69	36.61	37.53	38.48	39.43	40.39	41.37	42.35	43.35	44.36
18.75	21.13	23.89	26.87	30.06	33.46	34.34	35.23	36.14	37.06	37.99	38.93	39.88	40.84	41.82	42.80	43.80
19.00	20.86	23.59	26.53	29.68	33.04	33.91	34.79	35.68	36.59	37.51	38.44	39.38	40.33	41.29	42.26	43.24
20.00	19.86	22.45	25.25	28.25	31.45	32.28	33.12	33.97	34.83	35.70	36.59	37.48	38.39	39.30	40.23	41.16
25.00	15.97	18.05	20.30	22.72	25.28	25.95	26.63	27.31	28.00	28.70	29.42	30.13	30.86	31.60	32.34	33.10
30.00	13.33	15.07	16.94	18.96	21.10	21.66	22.22	22.79	23.37	23.96	24.55	25.15	25.76	26.37	26.99	27.62

MORTGAGE YIELD

25 YEARS

Description: This table shows the yield to maturity of a mortgage purchased at the price shown in the index.

Example: The yield to maturity of a 6.75 %, 25 year mortgage at a price of 80.00 is 9.35 %.

INTEREST RATE, %

PRICE	0.00%	1.00%	2.00%	3.00%	4.00%	4.25%	4.50%	4.75%	5.00%	5.25%	5.50%	5.75%	6.00%	6.25%	6.50%	6.75%
100	0.00	1.00	2.00	3.00	4.00	4.25	4.50	4.75	5.00	5.25	5.50	5.75	6.00	6.25	6.50	6.75
99	.08	1.08	2.08	3.09	4.09	4.34	4.59	4.84	5.10	5.35	5.60	5.85	6.10	6.35	6.60	6.86
98	.16	1.16	2.17	3.18	4.19	4.44	4.69	4.95	5.20	5.45	5.70	5.96	6.21	6.46	6.71	6.97
97	.24	1.25	2.26	3.27	4.29	4.54	4.80	5.05	5.30	5.56	5.81	6.06	6.32	6.57	6.83	7.08
96	.32	1.34	2.35	3.37	4.39	4.64	4.90	5.15	5.41	5.66	5.92	6.17	6.43	6.69	6.94	7.20
95	.41	1.43	2.45	3.47	4.49	4.75	5.00	5.26	5.52	5.77	6.03	6.29	6.54	6.80	7.06	7.31
94	.49	1.52	2.54	3.57	4.60	4.85	5.11	5.37	5.63	5.88	6.14	6.40	6.66	6.92	7.18	7.43
93	.58	1.61	2.64	3.67	4.70	4.96	5.22	5.48	5.74	6.00	6.26	6.52	6.77	7.03	7.29	7.56
92	.67	1.70	2.73	3.77	4.81	5.07	5.33	5.59	5.85	6.11	6.37	6.63	6.89	7.16	7.42	7.68
91	.76	1.79	2.83	3.87	4.92	5.18	5.44	5.70	5.96	6.23	6.49	6.75	7.01	7.28	7.54	7.80
90	.85	1.89	2.93	3.98	5.03	5.29	5.55	5.82	6.08	6.34	6.61	6.87	7.14	7.40	7.67	7.93
89	.94	1.99	3.03	4.09	5.14	5.40	5.67	5.93	6.20	6.46	6.73	7.00	7.26	7.53	7.80	8.06
88	1.04	2.09	3.14	4.19	5.25	5.52	5.79	6.05	6.32	6.59	6.85	7.12	7.39	7.66	7.93	8.20
87	1.13	2.19	3.24	4.30	5.37	5.64	5.91	6.17	6.44	6.71	6.98	7.25	7.52	7.79	8.06	8.33
86	1.23	2.29	3.35	4.42	5.49	5.76	6.03	6.30	6.57	6.84	7.11	7.38	7.65	7.92	8.20	8.47
85	1.33	2.39	3.46	4.53	5.61	5.88	6.15	6.42	6.69	6.97	7.24	7.51	7.79	8.06	8.33	8.61
84	1.43	2.50	3.57	4.65	5.73	6.01	6.28	6.55	6.82	7.10	7.37	7.65	7.92	8.20	8.47	8.75
83	1.53	2.60	3.68	4.77	5.86	6.13	6.41	6.68	6.96	7.23	7.51	7.79	8.06	8.34	8.62	8.90
82	1.63	2.71	3.80	4.89	5.99	6.26	6.54	6.81	7.09	7.37	7.65	7.93	8.20	8.48	8.76	9.04
81	1.74	2.82	3.91	5.01	6.11	6.39	6.67	6.95	7.23	7.51	7.79	8.07	8.35	8.63	8.91	9.20
80	1.85	2.93	4.03	5.13	6.25	6.53	6.81	7.09	7.37	7.65	7.93	8.21	8.50	8.78	9.07	9.35
79	1.96	3.05	4.15	5.26	6.38	6.66	6.94	7.23	7.51	7.79	8.08	8.36	8.65	8.93	9.22	9.51
78	2.07	3.17	4.27	5.39	6.52	6.80	7.09	7.37	7.66	7.94	8.23	8.51	8.80	9.09	9.38	9.67
77	2.18	3.29	4.40	5.52	6.66	6.94	7.23	7.52	7.80	8.09	8.38	8.67	8.96	9.25	9.54	9.83
76	2.29	3.41	4.53	5.66	6.80	7.09	7.38	7.67	7.96	8.25	8.54	8.83	9.12	9.41	9.71	10.00
75	2.41	3.53	4.66	5.80	6.95	7.24	7.53	7.82	8.11	8.40	8.70	8.99	9.28	9.58	9.88	10.17
74	2.53	3.66	4.79	5.94	7.10	7.39	7.68	7.97	8.27	8.56	8.86	9.15	9.45	9.75	10.05	10.35
73	2.65	3.78	4.93	6.08	7.25	7.54	7.84	8.13	8.43	8.73	9.02	9.32	9.62	9.92	10.22	10.53
72	2.78	3.92	5.07	6.23	7.40	7.70	8.00	8.30	8.59	8.89	9.19	9.50	9.80	10.10	10.41	10.71
71	2.90	4.05	5.21	6.38	7.56	7.86	8.16	8.46	8.76	9.07	9.37	9.67	9.98	10.28	10.59	10.90
70	3.03	4.19	5.35	6.53	7.73	8.03	8.33	8.63	8.94	9.24	9.55	9.85	10.16	10.47	10.78	11.09
69	3.16	4.32	5.50	6.69	7.89	8.20	8.50	8.81	9.11	9.42	9.73	10.04	10.35	10.66	10.97	11.29
68	3.30	4.47	5.65	6.85	8.06	8.37	8.68	8.98	9.29	9.60	9.92	10.23	10.54	10.86	11.17	11.49
67	3.44	4.61	5.80	7.01	8.24	8.54	8.85	9.17	9.48	9.79	10.11	10.42	10.74	11.06	11.38	11.70
66	3.58	4.76	5.96	7.18	8.41	8.73	9.04	9.35	9.67	9.98	10.30	10.62	10.94	11.26	11.58	11.91
65	3.72	4.91	6.12	7.35	8.60	8.91	9.23	9.54	9.86	10.18	10.50	10.83	11.15	11.47	11.80	12.13
64	3.87	5.07	6.29	7.53	8.78	9.10	9.42	9.74	10.06	10.38	10.71	11.03	11.36	11.69	12.02	12.35
63	4.02	5.23	6.46	7.71	8.98	9.30	9.62	9.94	10.27	10.59	10.92	11.25	11.58	11.91	12.25	12.58
62	4.17	5.39	6.63	7.89	9.17	9.50	9.82	10.15	10.48	10.81	11.14	11.47	11.80	12.14	12.48	12.82
61	4.33	5.56	6.81	8.08	9.37	9.70	10.03	10.36	10.69	11.03	11.36	11.70	12.04	12.38	12.72	13.06
60	4.49	5.73	6.99	8.27	9.58	9.91	10.25	10.58	10.91	11.25	11.59	11.93	12.27	12.62	12.96	13.31
59	4.66	5.90	7.18	8.47	9.79	10.13	10.47	10.80	11.14	11.48	11.83	12.17	12.52	12.87	13.21	13.57
58	4.82	6.08	7.37	8.68	10.01	10.35	10.69	11.03	11.38	11.72	12.07	12.42	12.77	13.12	13.48	13.83
57	5.00	6.27	7.57	8.89	10.24	10.58	10.93	11.27	11.62	11.97	12.32	12.67	13.03	13.39	13.74	14.10
56	5.18	6.46	7.77	9.11	10.47	10.82	11.17	11.52	11.87	12.22	12.58	12.94	13.30	13.66	14.02	14.39
55	5.36	6.65	7.98	9.33	10.71	11.06	11.41	11.77	12.13	12.48	12.84	13.21	13.57	13.94	14.31	14.68
54	5.55	6.86	8.19	9.56	10.96	11.31	11.67	12.03	12.39	12.75	13.12	13.49	13.86	14.23	14.60	14.98
53	5.74	7.06	8.41	9.80	11.21	11.57	11.93	12.30	12.66	13.03	13.40	13.78	14.15	14.53	14.91	15.29
52	5.94	7.28	8.64	10.04	11.48	11.84	12.21	12.58	12.95	13.32	13.70	14.07	14.45	14.84	15.22	15.61
51	6.15	7.49	8.88	10.29	11.75	12.12	12.49	12.86	13.24	13.62	14.00	14.38	14.77	15.16	15.55	15.94
50	6.36	7.72	9.12	10.55	12.03	12.40	12.78	13.16	13.54	13.93	14.31	14.70	15.10	15.49	15.89	16.29
49	6.58	7.95	9.37	10.82	12.32	12.70	13.08	13.47	13.85	14.25	14.64	15.03	15.43	15.83	16.24	16.64
48	6.80	8.20	9.63	11.10	12.62	13.01	13.39	13.79	14.18	14.58	14.98	15.38	15.78	16.19	16.60	17.02
47	7.03	8.44	9.90	11.39	12.93	13.32	13.72	14.12	14.52	14.92	15.33	15.74	16.15	16.56	16.98	17.40
46	7.27	8.70	10.18	11.69	13.26	13.65	14.05	14.46	14.87	15.28	15.69	16.11	16.53	16.95	17.37	17.80
45	7.52	8.97	10.46	12.00	13.59	14.00	14.40	14.82	15.23	15.65	16.07	16.49	16.92	17.35	17.78	18.22
44	7.78	9.25	10.76	12.33	13.94	14.35	14.77	15.19	15.61	16.03	16.46	16.89	17.33	17.77	18.21	18.65
43	8.05	9.53	11.07	12.66	14.30	14.72	15.15	15.57	16.00	16.44	16.87	17.31	17.76	18.20	18.65	19.11
42	8.32	9.83	11.40	13.01	14.68	15.11	15.54	15.98	16.41	16.86	17.30	17.75	18.20	18.66	19.12	19.58
41	8.61	10.14	11.73	13.38	15.08	15.52	15.95	16.40	16.84	17.29	17.75	18.21	18.67	19.13	19.60	20.08
40	8.91	10.47	12.08	13.76	15.49	15.94	16.39	16.84	17.29	17.75	18.22	18.69	19.16	19.63	20.11	20.60
39	9.22	10.80	12.45	14.15	15.93	16.38	16.84	17.30	17.76	18.23	18.71	19.19	19.67	20.16	20.65	21.14
35	10.61	12.31	14.09	15.94	17.88	18.37	18.88	19.38	19.89	20.41	20.93	21.46	21.99	22.53	23.07	23.62
30	12.77	14.68	16.68	18.78	20.99	21.56	22.14	22.72	23.31	23.90	24.50	25.11	25.72	26.34	26.97	27.60
25	15.67	17.87	20.20	22.67	25.28	25.96	26.64	27.33	28.03	28.74	29.45	30.17	30.91	31.65	32.39	33.15
20	19.85	22.52	25.38	28.42	31.65	32.49	33.34	34.19	35.06	35.94	36.84	37.74	38.65	39.57	40.51	41.45
15	26.63	30.13	33.90	37.93	42.22	43.33	44.46	45.60	46.76	47.93	49.12	50.32	51.54	52.77	54.01	55.27
10	39.99	45.22	50.86	56.90	63.34	65.00	66.70	68.41	70.15	71.91	73.69	75.49	77.31	79.16	81.02	82.91

Description: This table shows the price to pay for a monthly payment mortgage loan at the yield rate.

Example: The price of a 10.75 %, 25 year mortgage loan to yield 8.00 % to maturity is $ 124.65.

INTEREST RATE, %

YIELD	7.00%	7.25%	7.50%	7.75%	8.00%	8.25%	8.50%	8.75%	9.00%	9.25%	9.50%	9.75%	10.00%	10.25%	10.50%	10.75%
0.00	212.03	216.84	221.70	226.60	231.54	236.54	241.57	246.64	251.76	256.91	262.11	267.34	272.61	277.91	283.25	288.63
1.00	187.54	191.79	196.09	200.42	204.80	209.21	213.66	218.15	222.67	227.23	231.83	236.46	241.12	245.81	250.53	255.28
2.00	166.75	170.53	174.35	178.20	182.09	186.02	189.98	193.97	197.99	202.05	206.13	210.25	214.39	218.56	222.76	226.99
3.00	149.04	152.42	155.84	159.28	162.76	166.27	169.80	173.37	176.97	180.59	184.24	187.92	191.62	195.35	199.11	202.88
4.00	133.90	136.94	140.00	143.10	146.22	149.37	152.55	155.76	158.99	162.24	165.52	168.83	172.16	175.51	178.88	182.27
4.25	130.47	133.42	136.41	139.43	142.47	145.54	148.64	151.76	154.91	158.08	161.28	164.50	167.74	171.00	174.29	177.59
4.50	127.16	130.04	132.95	135.89	138.86	141.85	144.87	147.91	150.98	154.07	157.19	160.32	163.48	166.67	169.87	173.09
4.75	123.97	126.78	129.62	132.49	135.38	138.30	141.24	144.21	147.20	150.21	153.25	156.31	159.39	162.49	165.61	168.75
5.00	120.90	123.64	126.41	129.21	132.03	134.87	137.74	140.64	143.55	146.49	149.45	152.44	155.44	158.47	161.51	164.58
5.25	117.94	120.62	123.32	126.05	128.80	131.57	134.37	137.20	140.04	142.91	145.80	148.71	151.64	154.59	157.56	160.55
5.50	115.09	117.70	120.34	123.00	125.69	128.39	131.13	133.88	136.66	139.46	142.28	145.12	147.98	150.86	153.75	156.67
5.75	112.35	114.89	117.47	120.06	122.68	125.33	128.00	130.68	133.39	136.13	138.88	141.65	144.44	147.25	150.08	152.93
6.00	109.70	112.18	114.70	117.23	119.79	122.37	124.98	127.60	130.25	132.92	135.60	138.31	141.04	143.78	146.54	149.32
6.25	107.14	109.57	112.02	114.50	117.00	119.52	122.07	124.63	127.21	129.82	132.44	135.09	137.75	140.43	143.13	145.84
6.50	104.68	107.05	109.45	111.87	114.31	116.77	119.26	121.76	124.29	126.83	129.40	131.98	134.58	137.20	139.84	142.49
6.75	102.30	104.62	106.96	109.32	111.71	114.12	116.55	118.99	121.46	123.95	126.46	128.98	131.52	134.08	136.66	139.25
7.00	100.00	102.27	104.56	106.87	109.20	111.56	113.93	116.32	118.74	121.17	123.62	126.08	128.57	131.07	133.59	136.12
7.25	97.78	100.00	102.24	104.50	106.78	109.08	111.40	113.74	116.10	118.48	120.88	123.29	125.72	128.16	130.63	133.11
7.50	95.64	97.81	100.00	102.21	104.44	106.69	108.96	111.25	113.56	115.89	118.23	120.59	122.97	125.36	127.77	130.19
7.75	93.57	95.69	97.84	100.00	102.18	104.39	106.61	108.85	111.10	113.38	115.67	117.98	120.31	122.65	125.00	127.37
8.00	91.57	93.65	95.75	97.86	100.00	102.16	104.33	106.52	108.73	110.96	113.20	115.46	117.74	120.03	122.33	124.65
8.25	89.64	91.67	93.73	95.80	97.89	100.00	102.13	104.27	106.44	108.62	110.81	113.02	115.25	117.49	119.75	122.02
8.50	87.77	89.76	91.77	93.80	95.85	97.92	100.00	102.10	104.22	106.35	108.50	110.67	112.85	115.05	117.26	119.48
8.75	85.97	87.92	89.89	91.87	93.88	95.90	97.94	100.00	102.07	104.16	106.27	108.39	110.53	112.68	114.84	117.02
9.00	84.22	86.13	88.06	90.01	91.97	93.95	95.95	97.97	100.00	102.05	104.11	106.19	108.28	110.39	112.51	114.64
9.25	82.53	84.40	86.29	88.20	90.13	92.07	94.03	96.00	97.99	100.00	102.02	104.06	106.11	108.17	110.25	112.34
9.50	80.90	82.73	84.58	86.45	88.34	90.24	92.16	94.10	96.05	98.02	100.00	102.00	104.01	106.03	108.07	110.12
9.75	79.31	81.11	82.93	84.76	86.61	88.48	90.36	92.26	94.17	96.10	98.04	100.00	101.97	103.96	105.95	107.96
10.00	77.78	79.54	81.32	83.12	84.94	86.77	88.61	90.47	92.35	94.24	96.15	98.07	100.00	101.95	103.90	105.88
10.25	76.29	78.02	79.77	81.54	83.31	85.11	86.92	88.75	90.59	92.44	94.31	96.20	98.09	100.00	101.92	103.85
10.50	74.86	76.55	78.27	80.00	81.74	83.51	85.28	87.07	88.88	90.70	92.53	94.38	96.24	98.11	100.00	101.90
10.75	73.46	75.13	76.81	78.51	80.22	81.95	83.70	85.45	87.23	89.01	90.81	92.62	94.45	96.29	98.14	100.00
11.00	72.11	73.75	75.40	77.07	78.75	80.44	82.16	83.88	85.62	87.38	89.14	90.92	92.71	94.52	96.33	98.16
11.25	70.80	72.41	74.03	75.67	77.32	78.98	80.66	82.36	84.07	85.79	87.52	89.27	91.03	92.80	94.58	96.38
11.50	69.53	71.11	72.70	74.31	75.93	77.57	79.22	80.88	82.56	84.25	85.95	87.67	89.40	91.14	92.89	94.65
11.75	68.30	69.85	71.41	72.99	74.59	76.19	77.81	79.45	81.10	82.76	84.43	86.12	87.81	89.52	91.24	92.97
12.00	67.11	68.63	70.16	71.72	73.28	74.86	76.45	78.06	79.68	81.31	82.95	84.61	86.28	87.96	89.65	91.35
12.25	65.95	67.44	68.95	70.48	72.01	73.57	75.13	76.71	78.30	79.91	81.52	83.15	84.79	86.44	88.10	89.77
12.50	64.82	66.29	67.78	69.27	70.79	72.31	73.85	75.40	76.97	78.54	80.13	81.73	83.34	84.96	86.59	88.24
12.75	63.73	65.17	66.63	68.11	69.59	71.09	72.60	74.13	75.67	77.22	78.78	80.35	81.93	83.53	85.13	86.75
13.00	62.67	64.09	65.52	66.97	68.43	69.91	71.40	72.90	74.41	75.93	77.47	79.01	80.57	82.14	83.72	85.30
13.25	61.64	63.03	64.45	65.87	67.31	68.76	70.22	71.70	73.18	74.68	76.19	77.71	79.24	80.79	82.34	83.90
13.50	60.63	62.01	63.40	64.80	66.21	67.64	69.08	70.53	71.99	73.47	74.95	76.45	77.96	79.47	81.00	82.54
13.75	59.66	61.01	62.38	63.76	65.15	66.55	67.97	69.40	70.84	72.29	73.75	75.22	76.71	78.20	79.70	81.21
14.00	58.71	60.05	61.39	62.75	64.12	65.50	66.89	68.30	69.71	71.14	72.58	74.03	75.49	76.96	78.44	79.92
14.25	57.79	59.10	60.43	61.76	63.11	64.47	65.84	67.23	68.62	70.03	71.44	72.87	74.31	75.75	77.21	78.67
14.50	56.90	58.19	59.49	60.81	62.13	63.47	64.82	66.19	67.56	68.94	70.34	71.74	73.15	74.58	76.01	77.45
14.75	56.03	57.30	58.58	59.88	61.18	62.50	63.83	65.17	66.53	67.89	69.26	70.64	72.04	73.44	74.85	76.27
15.00	55.18	56.43	57.70	58.97	60.26	61.56	62.87	64.19	65.52	66.86	68.21	69.57	70.95	72.33	73.72	75.11
15.25	54.36	55.59	56.83	58.09	59.36	60.64	61.93	63.23	64.54	65.86	67.19	68.54	69.89	71.25	72.61	73.99
15.50	53.55	54.77	55.99	57.23	58.48	59.74	61.01	62.30	63.59	64.89	66.20	67.52	68.85	70.19	71.54	72.90
15.75	52.77	53.97	55.18	56.40	57.63	58.87	60.12	61.39	62.66	63.94	65.24	66.54	67.85	69.17	70.50	71.84
16.00	52.01	53.19	54.38	55.58	56.80	58.02	59.26	60.50	61.76	63.02	64.29	65.58	66.87	68.17	69.48	70.80
16.25	51.27	52.43	53.61	54.79	55.99	57.19	58.41	59.64	60.88	62.12	63.38	64.64	65.92	67.20	68.49	69.79
16.50	50.55	51.69	52.85	54.02	55.20	56.39	57.59	58.80	60.02	61.25	62.49	63.73	64.99	66.25	67.53	68.81
16.75	49.84	50.97	52.12	53.27	54.43	55.60	56.79	57.98	59.18	60.39	61.61	62.84	64.08	65.33	66.59	67.85
17.00	49.16	50.27	51.40	52.53	53.68	54.84	56.00	57.18	58.37	59.56	60.77	61.98	63.20	64.43	65.67	66.91
17.25	48.49	49.59	50.70	51.82	52.95	54.09	55.24	56.40	57.57	58.75	59.94	61.14	62.34	63.55	64.77	66.00
17.50	47.84	48.92	50.02	51.12	52.24	53.36	54.50	55.64	56.80	57.96	59.13	60.31	61.50	62.70	63.90	65.11
17.75	47.20	48.27	49.35	50.44	51.54	52.65	53.77	54.90	56.04	57.19	58.35	59.51	60.68	61.86	63.05	64.25
18.00	46.58	47.63	48.70	49.78	50.86	51.96	53.07	54.18	55.30	56.44	57.58	58.73	59.88	61.05	62.22	63.40
18.25	45.97	47.01	48.07	49.13	50.20	51.28	52.37	53.47	54.58	55.70	56.83	57.96	59.10	60.25	61.41	62.58
18.50	45.38	46.41	47.45	48.50	49.56	50.62	51.70	52.79	53.88	54.98	56.10	57.22	58.34	59.48	60.62	61.77
18.75	44.80	45.82	46.84	47.88	48.92	49.98	51.04	52.11	53.20	54.29	55.38	56.49	57.60	58.72	59.85	60.99
19.00	44.24	45.24	46.25	47.28	48.31	49.35	50.40	51.46	52.53	53.60	54.69	55.78	56.88	57.98	59.10	60.22
20.00	42.11	43.06	44.03	45.00	45.98	46.97	47.97	48.98	50.00	51.02	52.05	53.09	54.14	55.19	56.25	57.32
25.00	33.86	34.62	35.40	36.18	36.97	37.77	38.57	39.38	40.20	41.02	41.85	42.69	43.53	44.37	45.23	46.09
30.00	28.25	28.89	29.54	30.19	30.85	31.52	32.19	32.87	33.55	34.23	34.93	35.62	36.33	37.03	37.74	38.46

Description: This table shows the yield to maturity of a mortgage purchased at the price shown in the index.

Example: The yield to maturity of a 10.75 %, 25 year mortgage at a price of 111.00 is 9.39 %.

INTEREST RATE, %

PRICE	7.00%	7.25%	7.50%	7.75%	8.00%	8.25%	8.50%	8.75%	9.00%	9.25%	9.50%	9.75%	10.00%	10.25%	10.50%	10.75%
165	2.09	2.28	2.48	2.68	2.87	3.06	3.26	3.45	3.64	3.83	4.03	4.22	4.40	4.59	4.78	4.97
160	2.36	2.56	2.76	2.95	3.15	3.35	3.54	3.74	3.93	4.13	4.32	4.51	4.71	4.90	5.09	5.28
155	2.64	2.84	3.04	3.24	3.45	3.64	3.84	4.04	4.24	4.44	4.63	4.83	5.02	5.22	5.41	5.61
150	2.94	3.14	3.35	3.55	3.75	3.96	4.16	4.36	4.56	4.76	4.96	5.16	5.36	5.55	5.75	5.95
145	3.25	3.46	3.66	3.87	4.08	4.28	4.49	4.69	4.89	5.10	5.30	5.50	5.70	5.91	6.11	6.31
140	3.57	3.78	4.00	4.21	4.41	4.62	4.83	5.04	5.25	5.46	5.66	5.87	6.07	6.28	6.48	6.69
135	3.92	4.13	4.35	4.56	4.77	4.99	5.20	5.41	5.62	5.83	6.04	6.25	6.46	6.67	6.88	7.09
130	4.28	4.50	4.72	4.93	5.15	5.37	5.58	5.80	6.02	6.23	6.44	6.66	6.87	7.09	7.30	7.51
125	4.66	4.89	5.11	5.33	5.55	5.77	5.99	6.21	6.43	6.65	6.87	7.09	7.31	7.53	7.75	7.96
122	4.90	5.13	5.35	5.58	5.80	6.03	6.25	6.47	6.70	6.92	7.14	7.36	7.58	7.81	8.03	8.25
121	4.99	5.21	5.44	5.66	5.89	6.11	6.34	6.56	6.79	7.01	7.23	7.46	7.68	7.90	8.12	8.34
120	5.07	5.30	5.52	5.75	5.98	6.20	6.43	6.65	6.88	7.10	7.33	7.55	7.77	8.00	8.22	8.44
119	5.15	5.38	5.61	5.84	6.06	6.29	6.52	6.74	6.97	7.20	7.42	7.65	7.87	8.10	8.32	8.54
118	5.24	5.47	5.70	5.93	6.15	6.38	6.61	6.84	7.06	7.29	7.52	7.74	7.97	8.19	8.42	8.64
117	5.33	5.56	5.79	6.02	6.25	6.47	6.70	6.93	7.16	7.39	7.61	7.84	8.07	8.29	8.52	8.75
116	5.41	5.65	5.88	6.11	6.34	6.57	6.80	7.03	7.25	7.48	7.71	7.94	8.17	8.40	8.62	8.85
115	5.50	5.74	5.97	6.20	6.43	6.66	6.89	7.12	7.35	7.58	7.81	8.04	8.27	8.50	8.73	8.96
114	5.59	5.83	6.06	6.29	6.52	6.76	6.99	7.22	7.45	7.68	7.91	8.14	8.37	8.60	8.83	9.06
113	5.68	5.92	6.15	6.39	6.62	6.85	7.09	7.32	7.55	7.78	8.02	8.25	8.48	8.71	8.94	9.17
112	5.78	6.01	6.25	6.48	6.72	6.95	7.19	7.42	7.65	7.89	8.12	8.35	8.59	8.82	9.05	9.28
111	5.87	6.11	6.34	6.58	6.81	7.05	7.29	7.52	7.76	7.99	8.23	8.46	8.69	8.93	9.16	9.39
110	5.97	6.20	6.44	6.68	6.91	7.15	7.39	7.62	7.86	8.10	8.33	8.57	8.80	9.04	9.27	9.51
109	6.06	6.30	6.54	6.78	7.02	7.25	7.49	7.73	7.97	8.20	8.44	8.68	8.91	9.15	9.39	9.62
108	6.16	6.40	6.64	6.88	7.12	7.36	7.60	7.83	8.07	8.31	8.55	8.79	9.03	9.27	9.50	9.74
107	6.26	6.50	6.74	6.98	7.22	7.46	7.70	7.94	8.18	8.42	8.66	8.90	9.14	9.38	9.62	9.86
106	6.36	6.60	6.84	7.09	7.33	7.57	7.81	8.05	8.29	8.53	8.78	9.02	9.26	9.50	9.74	9.98
105	6.46	6.71	6.95	7.19	7.43	7.68	7.92	8.16	8.41	8.65	8.89	9.13	9.38	9.62	9.86	10.10
104	6.57	6.81	7.05	7.30	7.54	7.79	8.03	8.28	8.52	8.76	9.01	9.25	9.50	9.74	9.98	10.23
103	6.67	6.92	7.16	7.41	7.65	7.90	8.14	8.39	8.64	8.88	9.13	9.37	9.62	9.86	10.11	10.35
102	6.78	7.02	7.27	7.52	7.77	8.01	8.26	8.51	8.75	9.00	9.25	9.49	9.74	9.99	10.23	10.48
101	6.89	7.13	7.38	7.63	7.88	8.13	8.38	8.62	8.87	9.12	9.37	9.62	9.87	10.12	10.36	10.61
100	7.00	7.25	7.50	7.75	8.00	8.25	8.50	8.75	9.00	9.25	9.50	9.75	10.00	10.25	10.50	10.75
99	7.11	7.36	7.61	7.86	8.11	8.36	8.62	8.87	9.12	9.37	9.62	9.87	10.12	10.38	10.63	10.88
98	7.22	7.47	7.73	7.98	8.23	8.48	8.74	8.99	9.24	9.50	9.75	10.00	10.26	10.51	10.76	11.02
97	7.34	7.59	7.84	8.10	8.35	8.61	8.86	9.12	9.37	9.63	9.88	10.14	10.39	10.65	10.90	11.16
96	7.45	7.71	7.96	8.22	8.48	8.73	8.99	9.25	9.50	9.76	10.01	10.27	10.53	10.79	11.04	11.30
95	7.57	7.83	8.09	8.34	8.60	8.86	9.12	9.38	9.63	9.89	10.15	10.41	10.67	10.93	11.18	11.44
94	7.69	7.95	8.21	8.47	8.73	8.99	9.25	9.51	9.77	10.03	10.29	10.55	10.81	11.07	11.33	11.59
93	7.82	8.08	8.34	8.60	8.86	9.12	9.38	9.64	9.90	10.17	10.43	10.69	10.95	11.22	11.48	11.74
92	7.94	8.20	8.47	8.73	8.99	9.25	9.52	9.78	10.04	10.31	10.57	10.84	11.10	11.36	11.63	11.89
91	8.07	8.33	8.60	8.86	9.13	9.39	9.66	9.92	10.19	10.45	10.72	10.98	11.25	11.52	11.78	12.05
90	8.20	8.46	8.73	9.00	9.26	9.53	9.80	10.06	10.33	10.60	10.87	11.13	11.40	11.67	11.94	12.21
89	8.33	8.60	8.87	9.13	9.40	9.67	9.94	10.21	10.48	10.75	11.02	11.29	11.56	11.83	12.10	12.37
88	8.46	8.73	9.00	9.27	9.54	9.81	10.08	10.36	10.63	10.90	11.17	11.44	11.72	11.99	12.26	12.53
87	8.60	8.87	9.14	9.42	9.69	9.96	10.23	10.51	10.78	11.05	11.33	11.60	11.88	12.15	12.43	12.70
86	8.74	9.01	9.29	9.56	9.84	10.11	10.38	10.66	10.94	11.21	11.49	11.76	12.04	12.32	12.60	12.87
85	8.88	9.16	9.43	9.71	9.99	10.26	10.54	10.82	11.09	11.37	11.65	11.93	12.21	12.49	12.77	13.05
84	9.03	9.30	9.58	9.86	10.14	10.42	10.70	10.98	11.26	11.54	11.82	12.10	12.38	12.66	12.94	13.23
83	9.17	9.45	9.73	10.01	10.29	10.58	10.86	11.14	11.42	11.70	11.99	12.27	12.55	12.84	13.12	13.41
82	9.33	9.61	9.89	10.17	10.45	10.74	11.02	11.31	11.59	11.88	12.16	12.45	12.73	13.02	13.31	13.60
81	9.48	9.76	10.05	10.33	10.62	10.90	11.19	11.47	11.76	12.05	12.34	12.63	12.92	13.21	13.50	13.79
80	9.64	9.92	10.21	10.49	10.78	11.07	11.36	11.65	11.94	12.23	12.52	12.81	13.10	13.39	13.69	13.98
79	9.80	10.08	10.37	10.66	10.95	11.24	11.53	11.83	12.12	12.41	12.70	13.00	13.29	13.59	13.88	14.18
78	9.96	10.25	10.54	10.83	11.12	11.42	11.71	12.01	12.30	12.60	12.89	13.19	13.49	13.78	14.08	14.38
77	10.13	10.42	10.71	11.01	11.30	11.60	11.89	12.19	12.49	12.79	13.09	13.39	13.69	13.99	14.29	14.59
76	10.30	10.59	10.89	11.18	11.48	11.78	12.08	12.38	12.68	12.98	13.28	13.59	13.89	14.19	14.50	14.80
75	10.47	10.77	11.07	11.37	11.67	11.97	12.27	12.57	12.88	13.18	13.49	13.79	14.10	14.40	14.71	15.02
74	10.65	10.95	11.25	11.55	11.86	12.16	12.47	12.77	13.08	13.38	13.69	14.00	14.31	14.62	14.93	15.24
73	10.83	11.13	11.44	11.74	12.05	12.36	12.66	12.97	13.28	13.59	13.90	14.22	14.53	14.84	15.16	15.47
70	11.40	11.71	12.03	12.34	12.66	12.98	13.29	13.61	13.93	14.25	14.57	14.89	15.22	15.54	15.87	16.19
65	12.45	12.78	13.12	13.45	13.78	14.12	14.45	14.79	15.13	15.47	15.81	16.15	16.49	16.84	17.18	17.53
60	13.66	14.01	14.36	14.71	15.07	15.42	15.78	16.14	16.50	16.86	17.23	17.59	17.96	18.33	18.70	19.07
55	15.05	15.42	15.80	16.18	16.56	16.94	17.33	17.71	18.10	18.49	18.88	19.28	19.67	20.07	20.47	20.87
50	16.69	17.09	17.50	17.91	18.32	18.74	19.15	19.57	19.99	20.42	20.84	21.27	21.70	22.14	22.57	23.01
45	18.66	19.10	19.55	20.00	20.45	20.90	21.36	21.82	22.28	22.75	23.22	23.69	24.17	24.64	25.12	25.61
40	21.08	21.58	22.07	22.57	23.07	23.58	24.09	24.60	25.12	25.64	26.17	26.69	27.22	27.76	28.29	28.83
35	24.17	24.72	25.28	25.85	26.42	26.99	27.57	28.16	28.74	29.34	29.93	30.53	31.14	31.74	32.36	32.97
30	28.24	28.88	29.53	30.19	30.85	31.52	32.19	32.87	33.55	34.24	34.94	35.64	36.34	37.05	37.76	38.48

Description: This table shows the price to pay for a monthly payment mortgage loan at the yield rate.

Example: The price of a 15.00 %, 25 year mortgage loan to yield 8.00 % to maturity is $ 165.95.

INTEREST RATE, %

YIELD	11.00%	11.25%	11.50%	11.75%	12.00%	12.25%	12.50%	12.75%	13.00%	13.25%	13.50%	13.75%	14.00%	14.25%	14.50%	15.00%
0.00	294.03	299.47	304.94	310.44	315.97	321.52	327.11	332.72	338.35	344.01	349.69	355.40	361.13	366.88	372.65	384.25
1.00	260.06	264.87	269.71	274.58	279.46	284.38	289.32	294.28	299.26	304.27	309.29	314.34	319.41	324.49	329.60	339.86
2.00	231.24	235.51	239.82	244.14	248.49	252.86	257.25	261.66	266.09	270.54	275.01	279.50	284.00	288.53	293.06	302.19
3.00	206.68	210.51	214.35	218.21	222.10	226.01	229.93	233.87	237.83	241.81	245.81	249.82	253.84	257.89	261.94	270.10
4.00	185.68	189.12	192.57	196.05	199.54	203.04	206.57	210.11	213.67	217.25	220.83	224.44	228.06	231.69	235.33	242.66
4.25	180.92	184.27	187.63	191.01	194.42	197.83	201.27	204.72	208.19	211.67	215.17	218.68	222.20	225.74	229.29	236.43
4.50	176.33	179.59	182.87	186.17	189.49	192.82	196.17	199.53	202.91	206.30	209.71	213.13	216.57	220.02	223.48	230.43
4.75	171.91	175.09	178.29	181.51	184.74	187.99	191.25	194.53	197.83	201.13	204.46	207.79	211.14	214.50	217.88	224.66
5.00	167.66	170.76	173.88	177.01	180.16	183.33	186.52	189.71	192.93	196.15	199.40	202.65	205.92	209.19	212.48	219.10
5.25	163.56	166.58	169.62	172.68	175.76	178.85	181.95	185.07	188.21	191.36	194.52	197.69	200.88	204.08	207.29	213.74
5.50	159.60	162.56	165.53	168.51	171.51	174.53	177.56	180.60	183.66	186.73	189.82	192.91	196.02	199.15	202.28	208.57
5.75	155.79	158.68	161.57	164.49	167.42	170.36	173.32	176.29	179.28	182.27	185.29	188.31	191.34	194.39	197.45	203.60
6.00	152.12	154.93	157.76	160.61	163.47	166.34	169.23	172.13	175.05	177.98	180.92	183.87	186.83	189.81	192.79	198.79
6.25	148.58	151.32	154.09	156.87	159.66	162.47	165.29	168.12	170.97	173.83	176.70	179.58	182.48	185.38	188.30	194.16
6.50	145.16	147.84	150.54	153.26	155.99	158.73	161.48	164.25	167.04	169.83	172.64	175.45	178.28	181.12	183.97	189.69
6.75	141.86	144.48	147.12	149.77	152.44	155.12	157.81	160.52	163.24	165.97	168.71	171.46	174.23	177.00	179.79	185.38
7.00	138.67	141.24	143.82	146.41	149.02	151.64	154.27	156.92	159.57	162.24	164.92	167.61	170.32	173.03	175.75	181.22
7.25	135.60	138.11	140.63	143.16	145.71	148.28	150.85	153.44	156.04	158.65	161.27	163.90	166.54	169.19	171.85	177.20
7.50	132.63	135.08	137.55	140.03	142.52	145.03	147.55	150.08	152.62	155.17	157.73	160.31	162.89	165.49	168.09	173.32
7.75	129.76	132.16	134.57	137.00	139.44	141.89	144.35	146.83	149.32	151.81	154.32	156.84	159.37	161.91	164.45	169.57
8.00	126.99	129.34	131.70	134.07	136.46	138.86	141.27	143.69	146.13	148.57	151.03	153.49	155.96	158.45	160.94	165.95
8.25	124.31	126.61	128.92	131.24	133.58	135.93	138.29	140.66	143.04	145.44	147.84	150.25	152.67	155.11	157.54	162.45
8.50	121.72	123.97	126.23	128.51	130.80	133.10	135.41	137.73	140.06	142.41	144.76	147.12	149.49	151.87	154.26	159.06
8.75	119.21	121.42	123.64	125.87	128.11	130.36	132.62	134.90	137.18	139.48	141.78	144.09	146.42	148.75	151.09	155.79
9.00	116.79	118.95	121.12	123.31	125.50	127.71	129.93	132.16	134.39	136.64	138.90	141.17	143.44	145.73	148.02	152.63
9.25	114.45	116.56	118.69	120.83	122.99	125.15	127.32	129.50	131.70	133.90	136.11	138.33	140.56	142.80	145.05	149.56
9.50	112.18	114.25	116.34	118.44	120.55	122.67	124.80	126.94	129.09	131.25	133.42	135.59	137.78	139.97	142.17	146.60
9.75	109.98	112.02	114.06	116.12	118.19	120.27	122.36	124.45	126.56	128.68	130.80	132.94	135.08	137.23	139.39	143.73
10.00	107.86	109.85	111.86	113.88	115.90	117.94	119.99	122.05	124.12	126.19	128.28	130.37	132.47	134.58	136.70	140.95
10.25	105.80	107.76	109.72	111.70	113.69	115.69	117.70	119.72	121.75	123.78	125.83	127.88	129.94	132.01	134.09	138.26
10.50	103.81	105.73	107.66	109.60	111.55	113.51	115.48	117.46	119.45	121.45	123.46	125.47	127.49	129.52	131.56	135.66
10.75	101.87	103.76	105.65	107.56	109.47	111.40	113.33	115.27	117.23	119.19	121.16	123.13	125.12	127.11	129.11	133.13
11.00	100.00	101.85	103.71	105.58	107.46	109.35	111.25	113.16	115.07	117.00	118.93	120.87	122.82	124.77	126.74	130.68
11.25	98.18	100.00	101.83	103.66	105.51	107.36	109.23	111.10	112.98	114.87	116.77	118.68	120.59	122.51	124.44	128.31
11.50	96.42	98.21	100.00	101.80	103.62	105.44	107.27	109.11	110.96	112.81	114.68	116.55	118.43	120.31	122.20	126.01
11.75	94.72	96.47	98.23	100.00	101.78	103.57	105.37	107.18	108.99	110.81	112.64	114.48	116.33	118.18	120.04	123.78
12.00	93.06	94.78	96.51	98.25	100.00	101.76	103.53	105.30	107.08	108.88	110.67	112.48	114.29	116.11	117.94	121.61
12.25	91.45	93.14	94.84	96.55	98.27	100.00	101.74	103.48	105.23	106.99	108.76	110.54	112.32	114.11	115.90	119.51
12.50	89.89	91.55	93.22	94.90	96.59	98.29	100.00	101.71	103.44	105.17	106.91	108.65	110.40	112.16	113.92	117.47
12.75	88.37	90.01	91.65	93.30	94.97	96.64	98.31	100.00	101.69	103.39	105.10	106.82	108.54	110.27	112.00	115.49
13.00	86.90	88.51	90.13	91.75	93.38	95.03	96.68	98.33	100.00	101.67	103.35	105.04	106.73	108.43	110.14	113.57
13.25	85.47	87.05	88.64	90.24	91.85	93.46	95.09	96.72	98.35	100.00	101.65	103.31	104.98	106.65	108.32	111.70
13.50	84.08	85.64	87.20	88.77	90.36	91.94	93.54	95.14	96.76	98.37	100.00	101.63	103.27	104.91	106.56	109.88
13.75	82.73	84.26	85.80	87.35	88.90	90.47	92.04	93.62	95.20	96.80	98.39	100.00	101.61	103.23	104.85	108.12
14.00	81.42	82.93	84.44	85.96	87.49	89.03	90.58	92.13	93.69	95.26	96.83	98.41	100.00	101.59	103.19	106.40
14.25	80.14	81.63	83.12	84.62	86.12	87.64	89.16	90.69	92.22	93.77	95.32	96.87	98.43	100.00	101.57	104.73
14.50	78.90	80.36	81.83	83.31	84.79	86.28	87.78	89.28	90.80	92.31	93.84	95.37	96.91	98.45	100.00	103.11
14.75	77.70	79.13	80.58	82.03	83.49	84.96	86.44	87.92	89.41	90.90	92.40	93.91	95.43	96.95	98.47	101.54
15.00	76.52	77.94	79.36	80.79	82.23	83.68	85.13	86.59	88.05	89.53	91.01	92.49	93.98	95.48	96.98	100.00
15.25	75.38	76.77	78.17	79.58	81.00	82.43	83.86	85.29	86.74	88.19	89.65	91.11	92.58	94.05	95.53	98.51
15.50	74.27	75.64	77.02	78.41	79.81	81.21	82.62	84.04	85.46	86.89	88.32	89.76	91.21	92.66	94.12	97.05
15.75	73.18	74.54	75.90	77.26	78.64	80.02	81.41	82.81	84.21	85.62	87.03	88.45	89.88	91.31	92.75	95.64
16.00	72.13	73.46	74.80	76.15	77.51	78.87	80.24	81.61	83.00	84.39	85.78	87.18	88.58	89.99	91.41	94.26
16.25	71.10	72.41	73.74	75.06	76.40	77.74	79.09	80.45	81.81	83.18	84.56	85.94	87.32	88.71	90.11	92.91
16.50	70.10	71.39	72.70	74.01	75.32	76.65	77.98	79.32	80.66	82.01	83.36	84.73	86.09	87.46	88.84	91.60
16.75	69.12	70.40	71.68	72.98	74.28	75.58	76.89	78.21	79.54	80.87	82.20	83.55	84.89	86.24	87.60	90.33
17.00	68.17	69.43	70.70	71.97	73.25	74.54	75.84	77.14	78.44	79.75	81.07	82.39	83.72	85.06	86.39	89.08
17.25	67.24	68.48	69.73	70.99	72.26	73.53	74.80	76.09	77.37	78.67	79.97	81.27	82.58	83.90	85.22	87.87
17.50	66.33	67.56	68.80	70.04	71.28	72.54	73.80	75.06	76.33	77.61	78.89	80.18	81.47	82.77	84.07	86.69
17.75	65.45	66.66	67.88	69.10	70.33	71.57	72.81	74.06	75.32	76.58	77.84	79.11	80.39	81.67	82.95	85.53
18.00	64.59	65.78	66.99	68.19	69.41	70.63	71.86	73.09	74.33	75.57	76.82	78.07	79.33	80.59	81.86	84.41
18.25	63.75	64.93	66.11	67.31	68.51	69.71	70.92	72.14	73.36	74.59	75.82	77.05	78.30	79.54	80.79	83.31
18.50	62.93	64.09	65.26	66.44	67.62	68.81	70.01	71.21	72.41	73.63	74.84	76.06	77.29	78.52	79.75	82.24
18.75	62.13	63.28	64.43	65.59	66.76	67.94	69.12	70.30	71.49	72.69	73.89	75.09	76.30	77.52	78.74	81.19
19.00	61.35	62.48	63.62	64.77	65.92	67.08	68.25	69.42	70.59	71.77	72.96	74.15	75.34	76.54	77.75	80.17
20.00	58.39	59.47	60.56	61.65	62.75	63.85	64.96	66.08	67.19	68.32	69.45	70.58	71.72	72.86	74.01	76.31
25.00	46.95	47.82	48.69	49.57	50.45	51.34	52.23	53.12	54.02	54.93	55.84	56.75	57.66	58.58	59.50	61.35
30.00	39.18	39.91	40.63	41.37	42.10	42.84	43.59	44.34	45.09	45.84	46.60	47.36	48.12	48.89	49.66	51.20

Description: This table shows the yield to maturity of a mortgage purchased at the price shown in the index.

Example: The yield to maturity of a 15.00 %, 25 year mortgage at a price of 125.00 is 11.61 %.

INTEREST RATE, %

PRICE	11.00%	11.25%	11.50%	11.75%	12.00%	12.25%	12.50%	12.75%	13.00%	13.25%	13.50%	13.75%	14.00%	14.25%	14.50%	15.00%
250	1.33	1.48	1.64	1.79	1.94	2.09	2.25	2.40	2.54	2.69	2.84	2.99	3.13	3.28	3.42	3.71
240	1.67	1.83	1.99	2.14	2.30	2.45	2.61	2.76	2.91	3.06	3.21	3.36	3.51	3.66	3.81	4.10
230	2.04	2.20	2.36	2.52	2.68	2.84	2.99	3.15	3.30	3.46	3.61	3.76	3.91	4.06	4.22	4.51
220	2.43	2.60	2.76	2.92	3.08	3.24	3.40	3.56	3.72	3.87	4.03	4.19	4.34	4.50	4.65	4.95
210	2.85	3.02	3.18	3.35	3.51	3.68	3.84	4.00	4.16	4.32	4.48	4.64	4.80	4.96	5.11	5.43
200	3.30	3.47	3.64	3.80	3.97	4.14	4.31	4.47	4.64	4.80	4.96	5.13	5.29	5.45	5.61	5.93
195	3.53	3.70	3.88	4.05	4.22	4.39	4.55	4.72	4.89	5.05	5.22	5.38	5.55	5.71	5.88	6.20
190	3.78	3.95	4.12	4.30	4.47	4.64	4.81	4.98	5.15	5.32	5.49	5.65	5.82	5.98	6.15	6.48
185	4.03	4.21	4.38	4.56	4.73	4.90	5.08	5.25	5.42	5.59	5.76	5.93	6.10	6.27	6.43	6.77
180	4.29	4.47	4.65	4.83	5.00	5.18	5.35	5.53	5.70	5.88	6.05	6.22	6.39	6.56	6.73	7.07
175	4.57	4.75	4.93	5.11	5.29	5.47	5.64	5.82	6.00	6.17	6.35	6.52	6.70	6.87	7.04	7.39
170	4.86	5.04	5.22	5.40	5.59	5.77	5.95	6.13	6.31	6.48	6.66	6.84	7.02	7.19	7.37	7.72
165	5.16	5.34	5.53	5.71	5.90	6.08	6.26	6.45	6.63	6.81	6.99	7.17	7.35	7.53	7.71	8.06
160	5.47	5.66	5.85	6.04	6.22	6.41	6.60	6.78	6.97	7.15	7.33	7.52	7.70	7.88	8.06	8.43
155	5.80	5.99	6.18	6.37	6.56	6.75	6.94	7.13	7.32	7.51	7.69	7.88	8.07	8.25	8.44	8.81
150	6.14	6.34	6.53	6.73	6.92	7.12	7.31	7.50	7.69	7.88	8.07	8.26	8.45	8.64	8.83	9.21
145	6.51	6.71	6.90	7.10	7.30	7.50	7.69	7.89	8.09	8.28	8.48	8.67	8.86	9.06	9.25	9.63
140	6.89	7.09	7.30	7.50	7.70	7.90	8.10	8.30	8.50	8.70	8.90	9.10	9.29	9.49	9.69	10.08
135	7.29	7.50	7.71	7.91	8.12	8.33	8.53	8.74	8.94	9.14	9.35	9.55	9.75	9.95	10.16	10.56
130	7.72	7.94	8.15	8.36	8.57	8.78	8.99	9.20	9.41	9.62	9.82	10.03	10.24	10.45	10.65	11.07
125	8.18	8.40	8.61	8.83	9.04	9.26	9.47	9.69	9.90	10.12	10.33	10.54	10.76	10.97	11.18	11.61
120	8.67	8.89	9.11	9.33	9.55	9.77	9.99	10.21	10.43	10.65	10.87	11.09	11.31	11.53	11.75	12.19
115	9.19	9.41	9.64	9.87	10.10	10.32	10.55	10.78	11.00	11.23	11.46	11.68	11.91	12.13	12.36	12.81
113	9.40	9.63	9.86	10.09	10.32	10.55	10.78	11.01	11.24	11.47	11.70	11.93	12.16	12.39	12.61	13.07
112	9.52	9.75	9.98	10.21	10.44	10.67	10.90	11.13	11.37	11.60	11.83	12.06	12.29	12.52	12.75	13.20
111	9.63	9.86	10.09	10.33	10.56	10.79	11.03	11.26	11.49	11.72	11.95	12.18	12.42	12.65	12.88	13.34
110	9.74	9.98	10.21	10.45	10.68	10.91	11.15	11.38	11.62	11.85	12.08	12.32	12.55	12.78	13.01	13.48
109	9.86	10.10	10.33	10.57	10.80	11.04	11.27	11.51	11.74	11.98	12.21	12.45	12.68	12.92	13.15	13.62
108	9.98	10.22	10.45	10.69	10.93	11.16	11.40	11.64	11.87	12.11	12.35	12.58	12.82	13.05	13.29	13.76
107	10.10	10.34	10.58	10.81	11.05	11.29	11.53	11.77	12.01	12.24	12.48	12.72	12.96	13.20	13.43	13.91
106	10.22	10.46	10.70	10.94	11.18	11.42	11.66	11.90	12.14	12.38	12.62	12.86	13.10	13.34	13.58	14.05
105	10.34	10.59	10.83	11.07	11.31	11.55	11.79	12.04	12.28	12.52	12.76	13.00	13.24	13.48	13.72	14.20
104	10.47	10.71	10.96	11.20	11.44	11.69	11.93	12.17	12.42	12.66	12.90	13.14	13.39	13.63	13.87	14.36
103	10.60	10.84	11.09	11.33	11.58	11.82	12.07	12.31	12.56	12.80	13.05	13.29	13.54	13.78	14.02	14.51
102	10.73	10.97	11.22	11.47	11.71	11.96	12.21	12.45	12.70	12.95	13.19	13.44	13.69	13.93	14.18	14.67
101	10.86	11.11	11.36	11.61	11.85	12.10	12.35	12.60	12.85	13.09	13.34	13.59	13.84	14.09	14.34	14.83
100	11.00	11.25	11.50	11.75	12.00	12.25	12.50	12.75	13.00	13.25	13.50	13.75	14.00	14.25	14.50	15.00
99	11.13	11.38	11.64	11.89	12.14	12.39	12.64	12.89	13.15	13.40	13.65	13.90	14.15	14.41	14.66	15.16
98	11.27	11.52	11.78	12.03	12.29	12.54	12.79	13.05	13.30	13.55	13.81	14.06	14.32	14.57	14.82	15.33
97	11.41	11.67	11.92	12.18	12.43	12.69	12.95	13.20	13.46	13.71	13.97	14.22	14.48	14.74	14.99	15.50
96	11.56	11.81	12.07	12.33	12.59	12.84	13.10	13.36	13.62	13.87	14.13	14.39	14.65	14.91	15.16	15.68
95	11.70	11.96	12.22	12.48	12.74	13.00	13.26	13.52	13.78	14.04	14.30	14.56	14.82	15.08	15.34	15.86
94	11.85	12.11	12.37	12.64	12.90	13.16	13.42	13.68	13.94	14.21	14.47	14.73	14.99	15.25	15.52	16.04
93	12.00	12.27	12.53	12.79	13.06	13.32	13.58	13.85	14.11	14.38	14.64	14.90	15.17	15.43	15.70	16.23
92	12.16	12.42	12.69	12.95	13.22	13.49	13.75	14.02	14.28	14.55	14.82	15.08	15.35	15.62	15.88	16.42
91	12.32	12.58	12.85	13.12	13.39	13.65	13.92	14.19	14.46	14.73	15.00	15.27	15.53	15.80	16.07	16.61
90	12.48	12.75	13.02	13.29	13.56	13.83	14.10	14.37	14.64	14.91	15.18	15.45	15.72	15.99	16.27	16.81
89	12.64	12.91	13.18	13.46	13.73	14.00	14.27	14.55	14.82	15.09	15.37	15.64	15.91	16.19	16.46	17.01
88	12.81	13.08	13.36	13.63	13.90	14.18	14.45	14.73	15.01	15.28	15.56	15.83	16.11	16.39	16.66	17.22
87	12.98	13.25	13.53	13.81	14.08	14.36	14.64	14.92	15.19	15.47	15.75	16.03	16.31	16.59	16.87	17.43
86	13.15	13.43	13.71	13.99	14.27	14.55	14.83	15.11	15.39	15.67	15.95	16.23	16.51	16.80	17.08	17.64
85	13.33	13.61	13.89	14.17	14.46	14.74	15.02	15.30	15.59	15.87	16.15	16.44	16.72	17.01	17.29	17.86
84	13.51	13.79	14.08	14.36	14.65	14.93	15.22	15.50	15.79	16.07	16.36	16.65	16.94	17.22	17.51	18.09
83	13.70	13.98	14.27	14.55	14.84	15.13	15.42	15.71	15.99	16.28	16.57	16.86	17.15	17.44	17.73	18.32
82	13.88	14.17	14.46	14.75	15.04	15.33	15.62	15.91	16.21	16.50	16.79	17.08	17.38	17.67	17.96	18.56
81	14.08	14.37	14.66	14.95	15.25	15.54	15.83	16.13	16.42	16.72	17.01	17.31	17.60	17.90	18.20	18.79
80	14.27	14.57	14.86	15.16	15.45	15.75	16.05	16.34	16.64	16.94	17.24	17.54	17.84	18.14	18.44	19.04
79	14.48	14.77	15.07	15.37	15.67	15.97	16.27	16.57	16.87	17.17	17.47	17.77	18.07	18.38	18.68	19.29
78	14.68	14.98	15.28	15.58	15.89	16.19	16.49	16.79	17.10	17.40	17.71	18.01	18.32	18.62	18.93	19.55
77	14.89	15.20	15.50	15.80	16.11	16.41	16.72	17.03	17.33	17.64	17.95	18.26	18.57	18.88	19.19	19.81
76	15.11	15.41	15.72	16.03	16.34	16.65	16.96	17.27	17.58	17.89	18.20	18.51	18.82	19.14	19.45	20.08
75	15.33	15.64	15.95	16.26	16.57	16.88	17.20	17.51	17.82	18.14	18.45	18.77	19.09	19.40	19.72	20.36
74	15.56	15.87	16.18	16.50	16.81	17.13	17.44	17.76	18.08	18.40	18.72	19.04	19.36	19.68	20.00	20.64
73	15.79	16.10	16.42	16.74	17.06	17.38	17.70	18.02	18.34	18.66	18.98	19.31	19.63	19.96	20.28	20.93
70	16.52	16.85	17.18	17.50	17.83	18.17	18.50	18.83	19.16	19.50	19.83	20.17	20.50	20.84	21.18	21.85
65	17.88	18.22	18.57	18.92	19.28	19.63	19.98	20.34	20.69	21.05	21.41	21.77	22.13	22.49	22.85	23.57
60	19.44	19.81	20.19	20.56	20.94	21.32	21.70	22.08	22.47	22.85	23.23	23.62	24.01	24.40	24.78	25.57
55	21.27	21.67	22.08	22.49	22.90	23.31	23.72	24.13	24.55	24.96	25.38	25.80	26.22	26.64	27.06	27.91

MORTGAGE PRICE

Description: This table shows the price to pay for a monthly payment mortgage loan at the yield rate.

Example: The price of a 6.75 %, 26 year mortgage loan to yield 8.00 % to maturity is $ 89.27.

INTEREST RATE, %

YIELD	0.00%	1.00%	2.00%	3.00%	4.00%	4.25%	4.50%	4.75%	5.00%	5.25%	5.50%	5.75%	6.00%	6.25%	6.50%	6.75%
0.00	100.00	113.60	128.32	144.14	161.01	165.38	169.82	174.32	178.88	183.50	188.18	192.92	197.71	202.55	207.45	212.41
1.00	88.02	100.00	112.96	126.88	141.73	145.58	149.49	153.45	157.46	161.53	165.65	169.81	174.03	178.30	182.61	186.97
2.00	77.93	88.53	100.00	112.32	125.47	128.88	132.34	135.85	139.40	143.00	146.64	150.33	154.07	157.84	161.66	165.52
3.00	69.38	78.82	89.03	100.00	111.70	114.74	117.82	120.94	124.11	127.31	130.56	133.84	137.17	140.53	143.93	147.36
4.00	62.11	70.56	79.70	89.52	100.00	102.72	105.48	108.27	111.10	113.97	116.88	119.82	122.79	125.80	128.85	131.92
4.25	60.47	68.69	77.59	87.15	97.35	100.00	102.68	105.40	108.16	110.96	113.78	116.65	119.54	122.47	125.44	128.43
4.50	58.88	66.90	75.56	84.88	94.81	97.39	100.00	102.65	105.34	108.06	110.81	113.60	116.42	119.27	122.16	125.08
4.75	57.36	65.17	73.61	82.68	92.36	94.87	97.42	100.00	102.62	105.27	107.95	110.67	113.41	116.19	119.01	121.85
5.00	55.90	63.51	71.74	80.58	90.01	92.45	94.94	97.45	100.00	102.58	105.20	107.84	110.52	113.23	115.97	118.74
5.25	54.50	61.91	69.93	78.55	87.74	90.13	92.55	95.00	97.48	100.00	102.55	105.13	107.74	110.38	113.05	115.75
5.50	53.14	60.37	68.19	76.60	85.56	87.89	90.24	92.64	95.06	97.51	100.00	102.52	105.06	107.64	110.24	112.87
5.75	51.84	58.89	66.52	74.72	83.46	85.73	88.03	90.36	92.73	95.12	97.55	100.00	102.48	105.00	107.54	110.10
6.00	50.58	57.46	64.91	72.90	81.44	83.65	85.90	88.17	90.48	92.82	95.18	97.58	100.00	102.45	104.93	107.44
6.25	49.37	56.09	63.35	71.16	79.49	81.65	83.84	86.06	88.31	90.59	92.90	95.24	97.61	100.00	102.42	104.86
6.50	48.20	54.76	61.86	69.48	77.61	79.72	81.86	84.03	86.23	88.45	90.71	92.99	95.30	97.64	100.00	102.39
6.75	47.08	53.48	60.41	67.86	75.80	77.86	79.95	82.07	84.22	86.39	88.59	90.82	93.08	95.36	97.67	100.00
7.00	46.00	52.25	59.02	66.30	74.06	76.07	78.11	80.18	82.28	84.40	86.55	88.73	90.94	93.17	95.42	97.70
7.25	44.95	51.07	57.68	64.79	72.37	74.34	76.34	78.36	80.41	82.48	84.59	86.72	88.87	91.05	93.25	95.48
7.50	43.94	49.92	56.39	63.34	70.75	72.67	74.62	76.60	78.60	80.63	82.69	84.77	86.88	89.01	91.16	93.34
7.75	42.97	48.81	55.14	61.93	69.18	71.06	72.97	74.90	76.86	78.85	80.86	82.89	84.95	87.03	89.14	91.27
8.00	42.03	47.75	53.93	60.58	67.67	69.51	71.37	73.27	75.18	77.12	79.09	81.08	83.09	85.13	87.19	89.27
8.25	41.12	46.72	52.77	59.27	66.21	68.01	69.83	71.69	73.56	75.46	77.38	79.33	81.30	83.29	85.31	87.35
8.50	40.25	45.72	51.65	58.01	64.80	66.56	68.35	70.16	71.99	73.85	75.74	77.64	79.57	81.52	83.49	85.49
8.75	39.40	44.76	50.56	56.79	63.44	65.16	66.91	68.68	70.48	72.30	74.14	76.01	77.90	79.81	81.74	83.69
9.00	38.58	43.83	49.51	55.61	62.12	63.81	65.52	67.26	69.02	70.80	72.60	74.43	76.28	78.15	80.04	81.95
9.25	37.79	42.93	48.50	54.47	60.85	62.50	64.18	65.88	67.60	69.35	71.12	72.91	74.72	76.55	78.40	80.27
9.50	37.03	42.07	47.52	53.37	59.62	61.24	62.88	64.55	66.24	67.95	69.68	71.43	73.21	75.00	76.82	78.65
9.75	36.29	41.23	46.57	52.31	58.43	60.02	61.63	63.26	64.91	66.59	68.29	70.01	71.75	73.50	75.28	77.08
10.00	35.57	40.41	45.65	51.28	57.28	58.83	60.41	62.01	63.64	65.28	66.94	68.63	70.33	72.06	73.80	75.56
10.25	34.88	39.63	44.76	50.28	56.16	57.69	59.24	60.81	62.40	64.01	65.64	67.29	68.96	70.66	72.36	74.09
10.50	34.21	38.87	43.90	49.31	55.08	56.58	58.10	59.64	61.20	62.78	64.38	66.00	67.64	69.30	70.98	72.67
10.75	33.56	38.13	43.07	48.38	54.04	55.51	57.00	58.51	60.04	61.59	63.16	64.75	66.36	67.99	69.63	71.29
11.00	32.94	37.42	42.27	47.47	53.03	54.47	55.93	57.42	58.92	60.44	61.98	63.54	65.12	66.71	68.33	69.96
11.25	32.33	36.73	41.49	46.60	52.05	53.47	54.90	56.36	57.83	59.32	60.84	62.37	63.92	65.48	67.07	68.67
11.50	31.74	36.06	40.73	45.75	51.10	52.49	53.90	55.33	56.78	58.24	59.73	61.23	62.75	64.29	65.84	67.42
11.75	31.17	35.41	40.00	44.92	50.18	51.55	52.93	54.33	55.75	57.19	58.65	60.13	61.62	63.13	64.66	66.20
12.00	30.61	34.78	39.29	44.13	49.29	50.63	51.99	53.37	54.76	56.18	57.61	59.06	60.53	62.01	63.51	65.03
12.25	30.08	34.17	38.60	43.35	48.43	49.74	51.08	52.43	53.80	55.19	56.60	58.02	59.46	60.92	62.40	63.89
12.50	29.56	33.58	37.93	42.60	47.59	48.88	50.19	51.52	52.87	54.24	55.62	57.02	58.43	59.87	61.32	62.78
12.75	29.05	33.00	37.28	41.87	46.77	48.04	49.33	50.64	51.97	53.31	54.67	56.04	57.43	58.84	60.27	61.71
13.00	28.56	32.45	36.65	41.17	45.98	47.23	48.50	49.79	51.09	52.41	53.74	55.10	56.47	57.85	59.25	60.66
13.25	28.08	31.90	36.04	40.48	45.22	46.45	47.69	48.96	50.24	51.53	52.85	54.18	55.52	56.88	58.26	59.65
13.50	27.62	31.38	35.45	39.81	44.47	45.68	46.91	48.15	49.41	50.69	51.98	53.29	54.61	55.95	57.30	58.67
13.75	27.17	30.87	34.87	39.17	43.75	44.94	46.14	47.37	48.61	49.86	51.13	52.42	53.72	55.04	56.37	57.72
14.00	26.74	30.37	34.31	38.54	43.05	44.22	45.40	46.61	47.83	49.06	50.31	51.58	52.86	54.15	55.46	56.79
14.25	26.31	29.89	33.76	37.93	42.36	43.52	44.68	45.87	47.07	48.28	49.51	50.76	52.02	53.30	54.59	55.89
14.50	25.90	29.42	33.24	37.33	41.70	42.83	43.98	45.15	46.33	47.53	48.74	49.96	51.21	52.46	53.73	55.01
14.75	25.50	28.97	32.72	36.75	41.06	42.17	43.30	44.45	45.61	46.79	47.98	49.19	50.41	51.65	52.90	54.16
15.00	25.11	28.53	32.22	36.19	40.43	41.53	42.64	43.77	44.92	46.08	47.25	48.44	49.64	50.86	52.09	53.33
15.25	24.73	28.09	31.73	35.65	39.82	40.90	42.00	43.11	44.24	45.38	46.54	47.71	48.89	50.09	51.30	52.53
15.50	24.36	27.68	31.26	35.11	39.22	40.29	41.37	42.47	43.58	44.70	45.84	47.00	48.16	49.34	50.54	51.75
15.75	24.00	27.27	30.80	34.60	38.65	39.70	40.76	41.84	42.94	44.04	45.17	46.30	47.45	48.62	49.79	50.98
16.00	23.65	26.87	30.35	34.09	38.08	39.12	40.17	41.23	42.31	43.40	44.51	45.63	46.76	47.91	49.07	50.24
16.25	23.31	26.48	29.92	33.60	37.53	38.56	39.59	40.64	41.70	42.78	43.87	44.97	46.09	47.22	48.36	49.52
16.50	22.98	26.11	29.49	33.12	37.00	38.01	39.03	40.06	41.11	42.17	43.25	44.33	45.44	46.55	47.68	48.81
16.75	22.66	25.74	29.08	32.66	36.48	37.47	38.48	39.50	40.53	41.58	42.64	43.71	44.80	45.90	47.01	48.13
17.00	22.34	25.38	28.67	32.21	35.97	36.95	37.94	38.95	39.97	41.00	42.05	43.10	44.17	45.26	46.35	47.46
17.25	22.04	25.03	28.28	31.76	35.48	36.45	37.42	38.42	39.42	40.44	41.47	42.51	43.57	44.64	45.72	46.81
17.50	21.74	24.70	27.90	31.33	35.00	35.95	36.92	37.89	38.89	39.89	40.91	41.94	42.98	44.03	45.10	46.17
17.75	21.45	24.36	27.52	30.91	34.53	35.47	36.42	37.39	38.36	39.35	40.36	41.37	42.40	43.44	44.49	45.55
18.00	21.16	24.04	27.16	30.50	34.07	35.00	35.94	36.89	37.86	38.83	39.82	40.83	41.84	42.86	43.90	44.95
18.25	20.88	23.73	26.80	30.10	33.63	34.54	35.47	36.41	37.36	38.32	39.30	40.29	41.29	42.30	43.33	44.36
18.50	20.61	23.42	26.45	29.71	33.19	34.09	35.01	35.94	36.88	37.83	38.79	39.77	40.76	41.76	42.77	43.79
18.75	20.35	23.12	26.11	29.33	32.77	33.66	34.56	35.48	36.40	37.34	38.30	39.26	40.23	41.22	42.22	43.23
19.00	20.09	22.83	25.78	28.96	32.35	33.23	34.12	35.03	35.94	36.87	37.81	38.76	39.72	40.70	41.68	42.68
20.00	19.12	21.72	24.54	27.56	30.78	31.62	32.47	33.33	34.20	35.09	35.98	36.89	37.80	38.73	39.67	40.61
25.00	15.36	17.45	19.71	22.14	24.73	25.40	26.08	26.78	27.48	28.19	28.90	29.63	30.37	31.11	31.86	32.63
30.00	12.81	14.56	16.44	18.47	20.63	21.19	21.76	22.34	22.92	23.52	24.11	24.72	25.34	25.96	26.58	27.22

Description: This table shows the yield to maturity of a mortgage purchased at the price shown in the index.

Example: The yield to maturity of a 6.75 %, 26 year mortgage at a price of 80.00 is 9.29 %.

INTEREST RATE, %

PRICE	0.00%	1.00%	2.00%	3.00%	4.00%	4.25%	4.50%	4.75%	5.00%	5.25%	5.50%	5.75%	6.00%	6.25%	6.50%	6.75%
100	0.00	1.00	2.00	3.00	4.00	4.25	4.50	4.75	5.00	5.25	5.50	5.75	6.00	6.25	6.50	6.75
99	.07	1.08	2.08	3.08	4.09	4.34	4.59	4.84	5.09	5.34	5.60	5.85	6.10	6.35	6.60	6.85
98	.15	1.16	2.17	3.17	4.18	4.44	4.69	4.94	5.19	5.45	5.70	5.95	6.20	6.46	6.71	6.96
97	.23	1.24	2.25	3.27	4.28	4.53	4.79	5.04	5.29	5.55	5.80	6.06	6.31	6.56	6.82	7.07
96	.31	1.32	2.34	3.36	4.38	4.63	4.89	5.14	5.40	5.65	5.91	6.16	6.42	6.67	6.93	7.19
95	.39	1.41	2.43	3.45	4.48	4.73	4.99	5.24	5.50	5.76	6.01	6.27	6.53	6.79	7.04	7.30
94	.47	1.50	2.52	3.55	4.58	4.83	5.09	5.35	5.61	5.87	6.12	6.38	6.64	6.90	7.16	7.42
93	.56	1.58	2.61	3.65	4.68	4.94	5.20	5.46	5.72	5.97	6.23	6.49	6.75	7.01	7.27	7.53
92	.64	1.67	2.71	3.74	4.78	5.04	5.30	5.56	5.82	6.09	6.35	6.61	6.87	7.13	7.39	7.66
91	.73	1.76	2.80	3.84	4.89	5.15	5.41	5.67	5.94	6.20	6.46	6.72	6.99	7.25	7.51	7.78
90	.82	1.86	2.90	3.95	5.00	5.26	5.52	5.79	6.05	6.31	6.58	6.84	7.11	7.37	7.64	7.90
89	.91	1.95	3.00	4.05	5.10	5.37	5.63	5.90	6.16	6.43	6.70	6.96	7.23	7.50	7.76	8.03
88	1.00	2.05	3.10	4.15	5.22	5.48	5.75	6.02	6.28	6.55	6.82	7.08	7.35	7.62	7.89	8.16
87	1.09	2.14	3.20	4.26	5.33	5.60	5.86	6.13	6.40	6.67	6.94	7.21	7.48	7.75	8.02	8.29
86	1.18	2.24	3.30	4.37	5.44	5.71	5.98	6.25	6.52	6.79	7.06	7.34	7.61	7.88	8.15	8.43
85	1.28	2.34	3.41	4.48	5.56	5.83	6.10	6.37	6.65	6.92	7.19	7.47	7.74	8.01	8.29	8.56
84	1.37	2.44	3.51	4.59	5.68	5.95	6.23	6.50	6.77	7.05	7.32	7.60	7.87	8.15	8.42	8.70
83	1.47	2.54	3.62	4.71	5.80	6.08	6.35	6.63	6.90	7.18	7.45	7.73	8.01	8.29	8.56	8.84
82	1.57	2.65	3.73	4.83	5.92	6.20	6.48	6.75	7.03	7.31	7.59	7.87	8.15	8.43	8.71	8.99
81	1.67	2.76	3.85	4.94	6.05	6.33	6.61	6.89	7.16	7.44	7.73	8.01	8.29	8.57	8.85	9.14
80	1.78	2.86	3.96	5.07	6.18	6.46	6.74	7.02	7.30	7.58	7.87	8.15	8.43	8.72	9.00	9.29
79	1.88	2.97	4.08	5.19	6.31	6.59	6.87	7.16	7.44	7.72	8.01	8.29	8.58	8.87	9.15	9.44
78	1.99	3.09	4.20	5.31	6.44	6.73	7.01	7.30	7.58	7.87	8.15	8.44	8.73	9.02	9.31	9.60
77	2.10	3.20	4.32	5.44	6.58	6.86	7.15	7.44	7.73	8.01	8.30	8.59	8.88	9.17	9.47	9.76
76	2.21	3.32	4.44	5.57	6.72	7.00	7.29	7.58	7.87	8.16	8.45	8.75	9.04	9.33	9.63	9.92
75	2.32	3.44	4.57	5.71	6.86	7.15	7.44	7.73	8.02	8.32	8.61	8.90	9.20	9.50	9.79	10.09
74	2.43	3.56	4.69	5.84	7.00	7.30	7.59	7.88	8.18	8.47	8.77	9.06	9.36	9.66	9.96	10.26
73	2.55	3.68	4.83	5.98	7.15	7.45	7.74	8.04	8.33	8.63	8.93	9.23	9.53	9.83	10.13	10.44
72	2.67	3.81	4.96	6.12	7.30	7.60	7.90	8.19	8.49	8.79	9.10	9.40	9.70	10.00	10.31	10.62
71	2.79	3.94	5.10	6.27	7.46	7.75	8.06	8.36	8.66	8.96	9.27	9.57	9.88	10.18	10.49	10.80
70	2.92	4.07	5.24	6.42	7.61	7.92	8.22	8.52	8.83	9.13	9.44	9.75	10.05	10.36	10.68	10.99
69	3.04	4.20	5.38	6.57	7.77	8.08	8.38	8.69	9.00	9.31	9.62	9.93	10.24	10.55	10.87	11.18
68	3.17	4.34	5.52	6.72	7.94	8.25	8.55	8.86	9.17	9.49	9.80	10.11	10.43	10.74	11.06	11.38
67	3.30	4.48	5.67	6.88	8.11	8.42	8.73	9.04	9.35	9.67	9.98	10.30	10.62	10.94	11.26	11.58
66	3.44	4.62	5.82	7.04	8.28	8.59	8.91	9.22	9.54	9.86	10.18	10.50	10.82	11.14	11.46	11.79
65	3.58	4.77	5.98	7.21	8.46	8.77	9.09	9.41	9.73	10.05	10.37	10.69	11.02	11.35	11.67	12.00
64	3.72	4.92	6.14	7.38	8.64	8.96	9.28	9.60	9.92	10.25	10.57	10.90	11.23	11.56	11.89	12.22
63	3.86	5.07	6.30	7.55	8.83	9.15	9.47	9.80	10.12	10.45	10.78	11.11	11.44	11.77	12.11	12.44
62	4.01	5.23	6.47	7.73	9.02	9.34	9.67	10.00	10.33	10.66	10.99	11.32	11.66	12.00	12.34	12.68
61	4.16	5.39	6.64	7.92	9.21	9.54	9.87	10.20	10.54	10.87	11.21	11.55	11.89	12.23	12.57	12.91
60	4.32	5.56	6.82	8.10	9.42	9.75	10.08	10.42	10.75	11.09	11.43	11.77	12.12	12.46	12.81	13.16
59	4.48	5.73	7.00	8.30	9.62	9.96	10.30	10.64	10.98	11.32	11.66	12.01	12.36	12.71	13.06	13.41
58	4.64	5.90	7.18	8.50	9.84	10.18	10.52	10.86	11.21	11.55	11.90	12.25	12.60	12.96	13.31	13.67
57	4.81	6.08	7.38	8.70	10.06	10.40	10.74	11.09	11.44	11.79	12.14	12.50	12.86	13.21	13.58	13.94
56	4.98	6.26	7.57	8.91	10.28	10.63	10.98	11.33	11.68	12.04	12.40	12.76	13.12	13.48	13.85	14.21
55	5.15	6.45	7.77	9.13	10.51	10.87	11.22	11.58	11.93	12.29	12.66	13.02	13.39	13.76	14.13	14.50
54	5.34	6.64	7.98	9.35	10.75	11.11	11.47	11.83	12.19	12.56	12.93	13.29	13.67	14.04	14.42	14.79
53	5.52	6.84	8.19	9.58	11.00	11.36	11.73	12.09	12.46	12.83	13.20	13.58	13.95	14.33	14.71	15.10
52	5.71	7.05	8.42	9.82	11.26	11.62	11.99	12.36	12.74	13.11	13.49	13.87	14.25	14.64	15.02	15.41
51	5.91	7.26	8.64	10.06	11.52	11.89	12.27	12.64	13.02	13.40	13.79	14.17	14.56	14.95	15.34	15.74
50	6.11	7.48	8.88	10.32	11.80	12.17	12.55	12.93	13.32	13.70	14.09	14.48	14.88	15.28	15.68	16.08
49	6.32	7.70	9.12	10.58	12.08	12.46	12.84	13.23	13.62	14.01	14.41	14.81	15.21	15.61	16.02	16.43
48	6.54	7.93	9.37	10.85	12.37	12.76	13.15	13.54	13.94	14.34	14.74	15.14	15.55	15.96	16.38	16.79
47	6.76	8.18	9.63	11.13	12.67	13.07	13.47	13.86	14.27	14.67	15.08	15.49	15.91	16.33	16.75	17.17
46	6.99	8.42	9.90	11.42	12.99	13.39	13.79	14.20	14.61	15.02	15.44	15.86	16.28	16.70	17.13	17.56
45	7.23	8.68	10.18	11.72	13.32	13.72	14.13	14.55	14.96	15.38	15.81	16.23	16.66	17.10	17.53	17.97
44	7.48	8.95	10.47	12.04	13.66	14.07	14.49	14.91	15.33	15.76	16.19	16.63	17.07	17.51	17.95	18.40
43	7.74	9.23	10.77	12.36	14.01	14.43	14.86	15.29	15.72	16.16	16.60	17.04	17.49	17.94	18.39	18.85
42	8.00	9.51	11.08	12.70	14.38	14.81	15.24	15.68	16.12	16.57	17.01	17.47	17.92	18.38	18.85	19.31
41	8.28	9.81	11.40	13.05	14.77	15.20	15.65	16.09	16.54	17.00	17.45	17.91	18.38	18.85	19.32	19.80
40	8.57	10.13	11.74	13.42	15.17	15.62	16.07	16.52	16.98	17.44	17.91	18.38	18.86	19.34	19.82	20.31
39	8.87	10.45	12.10	13.81	15.59	16.05	16.51	16.97	17.44	17.91	18.39	18.87	19.36	19.85	20.35	20.85
35	10.20	11.91	13.69	15.55	17.49	17.99	18.50	19.01	19.52	20.05	20.57	21.10	21.64	22.18	22.73	23.28
30	12.28	14.19	16.20	18.31	20.53	21.11	21.69	22.27	22.87	23.47	24.07	24.68	25.30	25.93	26.56	27.20
25	15.07	17.27	19.61	22.10	24.72	25.40	26.09	26.79	27.49	28.21	28.93	29.66	30.40	31.15	31.90	32.67
20	19.09	21.76	24.63	27.69	30.95	31.79	32.65	33.51	34.39	35.28	36.18	37.09	38.01	38.95	39.89	40.84
15	25.60	29.11	32.89	36.95	41.28	42.40	43.54	44.69	45.86	47.05	48.25	49.46	50.69	51.93	53.19	54.46
10	38.45	43.69	49.35	55.43	61.92	63.60	65.31	67.04	68.80	70.57	72.37	74.19	76.04	77.90	79.79	81.69

Description: This table shows the price to pay for a monthly payment mortgage loan at the yield rate.

Example: The price of a 10.75 %, 26 year mortgage loan to yield 8.00 % to maturity is $ 125.22.

INTEREST RATE, %

YIELD	7.00%	7.25%	7.50%	7.75%	8.00%	8.25%	8.50%	8.75%	9.00%	9.25%	9.50%	9.75%	10.00%	10.25%	10.50%	10.75%
0.00	217.41	222.47	227.58	232.73	237.93	243.18	248.47	253.81	259.19	264.61	270.07	275.57	281.10	286.68	292.29	297.94
1.00	191.38	195.83	200.32	204.86	209.44	214.06	218.72	223.41	228.15	232.92	237.73	242.57	247.44	252.35	257.29	262.26
2.00	169.42	173.36	177.34	181.36	185.41	189.50	193.63	197.78	201.98	206.20	210.46	214.74	219.06	223.40	227.77	232.17
3.00	150.84	154.34	157.89	161.46	165.07	168.71	172.38	176.09	179.82	183.58	187.37	191.18	195.02	198.89	202.79	206.70
4.00	135.03	138.17	141.34	144.55	147.78	151.04	154.32	157.64	160.98	164.34	167.74	171.15	174.59	178.05	181.54	185.05
4.25	131.46	134.52	137.60	140.72	143.87	147.04	150.24	153.47	156.72	159.99	163.30	166.62	169.97	173.34	176.73	180.15
4.50	128.02	131.00	134.01	137.04	140.11	143.20	146.31	149.45	152.62	155.81	159.03	162.27	165.53	168.81	172.12	175.44
4.75	124.72	127.62	130.55	133.50	136.49	139.50	142.53	145.60	148.68	151.79	154.92	158.08	161.26	164.45	167.67	170.91
5.00	121.54	124.37	127.22	130.10	133.01	135.94	138.90	141.88	144.89	147.92	150.97	154.05	157.14	160.26	163.40	166.55
5.25	118.48	121.23	124.02	126.83	129.66	132.52	135.40	138.31	141.24	144.20	147.17	150.17	153.19	156.23	159.28	162.36
5.50	115.53	118.22	120.93	123.67	126.44	129.23	132.04	134.87	137.73	140.61	143.51	146.44	149.38	152.34	155.32	158.32
5.75	112.70	115.32	117.97	120.64	123.33	126.05	128.80	131.56	134.35	137.16	139.99	142.84	145.71	148.60	151.51	154.44
6.00	109.97	112.52	115.11	117.71	120.34	123.00	125.68	128.38	131.10	133.84	136.60	139.38	142.18	145.00	147.84	150.70
6.25	107.34	109.83	112.35	114.90	117.47	120.06	122.67	125.30	127.96	130.63	133.33	136.05	138.78	141.53	144.30	147.09
6.50	104.80	107.24	109.70	112.18	114.69	117.22	119.77	122.34	124.94	127.55	130.18	132.83	135.50	138.19	140.89	143.62
6.75	102.36	104.74	107.14	109.57	112.02	114.49	116.98	119.49	122.02	124.57	127.15	129.73	132.34	134.97	137.61	140.27
7.00	100.00	102.33	104.67	107.04	109.44	111.85	114.28	116.74	119.21	121.71	124.22	126.75	129.30	131.86	134.44	137.04
7.25	97.73	100.00	102.30	104.61	106.95	109.31	111.69	114.09	116.50	118.94	121.40	123.87	126.36	128.86	131.38	133.92
7.50	95.53	97.76	100.00	102.26	104.55	106.86	109.18	111.53	113.89	116.27	118.67	121.09	123.52	125.97	128.44	130.92
7.75	93.42	95.59	97.79	100.00	102.23	104.49	106.76	109.06	111.37	113.70	116.04	118.41	120.79	123.18	125.59	128.02
8.00	91.38	93.50	95.65	97.81	100.00	102.21	104.43	106.67	108.93	111.21	113.51	115.82	118.15	120.49	122.85	125.22
8.25	89.40	91.48	93.58	95.70	97.84	100.00	102.18	104.37	106.58	108.81	111.06	113.32	115.60	117.89	120.20	122.52
8.50	87.50	89.54	91.59	93.66	95.76	97.87	100.00	102.15	104.31	106.49	108.69	110.91	113.13	115.38	117.64	119.91
8.75	85.66	87.65	89.66	91.70	93.74	95.81	97.90	100.00	102.12	104.25	106.41	108.57	110.76	112.95	115.16	117.39
9.00	83.88	85.83	87.80	89.79	91.80	93.82	95.87	97.92	100.00	102.09	104.20	106.32	108.46	110.61	112.77	114.95
9.25	82.16	84.08	86.01	87.95	89.92	91.90	93.90	95.92	97.95	100.00	102.06	104.14	106.24	108.34	110.46	112.60
9.50	80.50	82.38	84.27	86.17	88.10	90.04	92.00	93.98	95.97	97.98	100.00	102.04	104.09	106.15	108.23	110.32
9.75	78.90	80.73	82.58	84.45	86.34	88.25	90.17	92.10	94.06	96.02	98.00	100.00	102.01	104.03	106.07	108.12
10.00	77.34	79.14	80.96	82.79	84.64	86.51	88.39	90.29	92.20	94.13	96.07	98.03	100.00	101.98	103.98	105.99
10.25	75.84	77.60	79.38	81.18	83.00	84.83	86.67	88.53	90.41	92.30	94.21	96.12	98.06	100.00	101.96	103.93
10.50	74.38	76.11	77.86	79.62	81.40	83.20	85.01	86.83	88.67	90.53	92.40	94.28	96.17	98.08	100.00	101.93
10.75	72.97	74.67	76.38	78.11	79.86	81.62	83.40	85.19	86.99	88.81	90.65	92.49	94.35	96.22	98.11	100.00
11.00	71.61	73.27	74.95	76.65	78.37	80.09	81.84	83.59	85.37	87.15	88.95	90.76	92.59	94.42	96.27	98.13
11.25	70.29	71.92	73.57	75.24	76.92	78.62	80.33	82.05	83.79	85.54	87.31	89.09	90.88	92.68	94.49	96.32
11.50	69.00	70.61	72.23	73.87	75.52	77.18	78.86	80.56	82.26	83.98	85.72	87.46	89.22	90.99	92.77	94.56
11.75	67.76	69.34	70.93	72.54	74.16	75.79	77.44	79.11	80.78	82.47	84.17	85.89	87.61	89.35	91.10	92.86
12.00	66.56	68.11	69.67	71.25	72.84	74.45	76.07	77.70	79.35	81.01	82.68	84.36	86.06	87.76	89.48	91.21
12.25	65.39	66.91	68.45	70.00	71.56	73.14	74.73	76.34	77.95	79.59	81.23	82.88	84.55	86.22	87.91	89.61
12.50	64.26	65.75	67.26	68.79	70.32	71.87	73.44	75.02	76.60	78.21	79.82	81.45	83.08	84.73	86.39	88.06
12.75	63.16	64.63	66.11	67.61	69.12	70.64	72.18	73.73	75.29	76.87	78.46	80.05	81.66	83.28	84.91	86.55
13.00	62.09	63.54	65.00	66.47	67.95	69.45	70.96	72.49	74.02	75.57	77.13	78.70	80.28	81.88	83.48	85.09
13.25	61.06	62.48	63.91	65.36	66.82	68.29	69.78	71.28	72.79	74.31	75.85	77.39	78.94	80.51	82.09	83.67
13.50	60.05	61.45	62.86	64.28	65.72	67.17	68.63	70.11	71.59	73.09	74.60	76.12	77.65	79.19	80.73	82.29
13.75	59.08	60.45	61.84	63.24	64.65	66.08	67.52	68.97	70.43	71.90	73.38	74.88	76.38	77.90	79.42	80.96
14.00	58.13	59.48	60.84	62.22	63.61	65.02	66.43	67.86	69.30	70.74	72.20	73.68	75.16	76.65	78.15	79.66
14.25	57.21	58.54	59.88	61.24	62.60	63.98	65.38	66.78	68.20	69.62	71.06	72.51	73.96	75.43	76.91	78.39
14.50	56.31	57.62	58.94	60.28	61.62	62.98	64.35	65.74	67.13	68.53	69.95	71.37	72.81	74.25	75.70	77.16
14.75	55.44	56.73	58.03	59.34	60.67	62.01	63.36	64.72	66.09	67.47	68.86	70.27	71.68	73.10	74.53	75.97
15.00	54.59	55.86	57.14	58.44	59.74	61.06	62.39	63.73	65.08	66.44	67.81	69.19	70.58	71.98	73.39	74.81
15.25	53.77	55.02	56.28	57.55	58.84	60.14	61.45	62.77	64.10	65.44	66.79	68.15	69.52	70.90	72.28	73.68
15.50	52.96	54.20	55.44	56.70	57.96	59.24	60.53	61.83	63.14	64.46	65.79	67.13	68.48	69.84	71.21	72.58
15.75	52.18	53.40	54.62	55.86	57.11	58.37	59.64	60.92	62.21	63.51	64.82	66.14	67.47	68.81	70.16	71.51
16.00	51.42	52.62	53.83	55.05	56.28	57.52	58.77	60.03	61.30	62.59	63.88	65.18	66.49	67.81	69.14	70.47
16.25	50.68	51.86	53.05	54.26	55.47	56.69	57.92	59.17	60.42	61.69	62.96	64.24	65.53	66.83	68.14	69.46
16.50	49.96	51.13	52.30	53.48	54.68	55.88	57.10	58.33	59.56	60.81	62.06	63.33	64.60	65.88	67.17	68.47
16.75	49.26	50.41	51.56	52.73	53.91	55.10	56.30	57.51	58.73	59.95	61.19	62.44	63.69	64.96	66.23	67.51
17.00	48.58	49.71	50.85	52.00	53.16	54.33	55.52	56.71	57.91	59.12	60.34	61.57	62.81	64.05	65.31	66.57
17.25	47.91	49.03	50.15	51.29	52.43	53.59	54.76	55.93	57.12	58.31	59.51	60.73	61.95	63.18	64.41	65.66
17.50	47.26	48.36	49.47	50.59	51.72	52.86	54.01	55.17	56.34	57.52	58.71	59.90	61.11	62.32	63.54	64.77
17.75	46.63	47.71	48.81	49.91	51.03	52.15	53.29	54.43	55.59	56.75	57.92	59.10	60.29	61.48	62.69	63.90
18.00	46.01	47.08	48.16	49.25	50.35	51.46	52.58	53.71	54.85	56.00	57.15	58.32	59.49	60.67	61.86	63.05
18.25	45.41	46.46	47.53	48.61	49.69	50.79	51.89	53.01	54.13	55.26	56.40	57.55	58.71	59.87	61.04	62.22
18.50	44.82	45.86	46.91	47.98	49.05	50.13	51.22	52.32	53.43	54.55	55.67	56.81	57.95	59.10	60.25	61.42
18.75	44.24	45.27	46.31	47.36	48.42	49.49	50.56	51.65	52.74	53.85	54.96	56.08	57.21	58.34	59.48	60.63
19.00	43.68	44.70	45.73	46.76	47.81	48.86	49.92	51.00	52.08	53.17	54.26	55.37	56.48	57.60	58.73	59.86
20.00	41.57	42.54	43.51	44.50	45.49	46.50	47.51	48.53	49.56	50.59	51.64	52.69	53.75	54.81	55.89	56.97
25.00	33.39	34.17	34.96	35.75	36.55	37.35	38.16	38.98	39.81	40.64	41.48	42.33	43.18	44.03	44.90	45.76
30.00	27.86	28.51	29.16	29.82	30.49	31.16	31.84	32.52	33.21	33.91	34.61	35.31	36.02	36.74	37.46	38.18

Description: This table shows the yield to maturity of a mortgage purchased at the price shown in the index.

Example: The yield to maturity of a 10.75 %, 26 year mortgage at a price of 111.00 is 9.42 %.

INTEREST RATE, %

PRICE	7.00%	7.25%	7.50%	7.75%	8.00%	8.25%	8.50%	8.75%	9.00%	9.25%	9.50%	9.75%	10.00%	10.25%	10.50%	10.75%
175	1.72	1.92	2.11	2.30	2.49	2.67	2.86	3.05	3.24	3.42	3.61	3.79	3.97	4.16	4.34	4.52
170	1.97	2.16	2.35	2.55	2.74	2.93	3.12	3.31	3.50	3.68	3.87	4.06	4.24	4.43	4.61	4.80
165	2.22	2.41	2.61	2.80	3.00	3.19	3.38	3.58	3.77	3.96	4.15	4.34	4.53	4.71	4.90	5.09
160	2.48	2.68	2.88	3.08	3.27	3.47	3.66	3.86	4.05	4.24	4.44	4.63	4.82	5.01	5.20	5.39
155	2.76	2.96	3.16	3.36	3.56	3.76	3.95	4.15	4.35	4.54	4.74	4.94	5.13	5.32	5.52	5.71
150	3.04	3.25	3.45	3.65	3.86	4.06	4.26	4.46	4.66	4.86	5.06	5.26	5.45	5.65	5.85	6.04
145	3.35	3.55	3.76	3.97	4.17	4.38	4.58	4.78	4.99	5.19	5.39	5.59	5.79	6.00	6.19	6.39
140	3.66	3.87	4.08	4.29	4.50	4.71	4.92	5.13	5.33	5.54	5.74	5.95	6.15	6.36	6.56	6.77
135	4.00	4.21	4.43	4.64	4.85	5.06	5.27	5.49	5.70	5.91	6.12	6.33	6.53	6.74	6.95	7.16
130	4.35	4.57	4.79	5.00	5.22	5.44	5.65	5.87	6.08	6.30	6.51	6.72	6.94	7.15	7.36	7.57
125	4.72	4.95	5.17	5.39	5.61	5.83	6.05	6.27	6.49	6.71	6.93	7.15	7.36	7.58	7.80	8.02
120	5.12	5.35	5.57	5.80	6.02	6.25	6.47	6.70	6.92	7.15	7.37	7.60	7.82	8.04	8.26	8.49
119	5.20	5.43	5.66	5.88	6.11	6.34	6.56	6.79	7.01	7.24	7.46	7.69	7.91	8.14	8.36	8.58
118	5.29	5.51	5.74	5.97	6.20	6.43	6.65	6.88	7.11	7.33	7.56	7.78	8.01	8.23	8.46	8.68
117	5.37	5.60	5.83	6.06	6.29	6.51	6.74	6.97	7.20	7.43	7.65	7.88	8.11	8.33	8.56	8.78
116	5.45	5.69	5.92	6.15	6.38	6.61	6.83	7.06	7.29	7.52	7.75	7.98	8.20	8.43	8.66	8.89
115	5.54	5.77	6.00	6.24	6.47	6.70	6.93	7.16	7.39	7.62	7.85	8.08	8.30	8.53	8.76	8.99
114	5.63	5.86	6.09	6.33	6.56	6.79	7.02	7.25	7.48	7.72	7.95	8.18	8.41	8.64	8.87	9.09
113	5.72	5.95	6.19	6.42	6.65	6.88	7.12	7.35	7.58	7.81	8.05	8.28	8.51	8.74	8.97	9.20
112	5.81	6.04	6.28	6.51	6.75	6.98	7.21	7.45	7.68	7.91	8.15	8.38	8.61	8.85	9.08	9.31
111	5.90	6.14	6.37	6.61	6.84	7.08	7.31	7.55	7.78	8.02	8.25	8.49	8.72	8.95	9.19	9.42
110	5.99	6.23	6.47	6.70	6.94	7.18	7.41	7.65	7.88	8.12	8.36	8.59	8.83	9.06	9.30	9.53
109	6.09	6.32	6.56	6.80	7.04	7.28	7.51	7.75	7.99	8.23	8.46	8.70	8.94	9.17	9.41	9.64
108	6.18	6.42	6.66	6.90	7.14	7.38	7.62	7.85	8.09	8.33	8.57	8.81	9.05	9.28	9.52	9.76
107	6.28	6.52	6.76	7.00	7.24	7.48	7.72	7.96	8.20	8.44	8.68	8.92	9.16	9.40	9.64	9.88
106	6.38	6.62	6.86	7.10	7.34	7.58	7.83	8.07	8.31	8.55	8.79	9.03	9.27	9.51	9.75	9.99
105	6.48	6.72	6.96	7.20	7.45	7.69	7.93	8.18	8.42	8.66	8.90	9.15	9.39	9.63	9.87	10.11
104	6.58	6.82	7.06	7.31	7.55	7.80	8.04	8.29	8.53	8.77	9.02	9.26	9.51	9.75	9.99	10.24
103	6.68	6.92	7.17	7.42	7.66	7.91	8.15	8.40	8.64	8.89	9.13	9.38	9.62	9.87	10.12	10.36
102	6.78	7.03	7.28	7.52	7.77	8.02	8.26	8.51	8.76	9.01	9.25	9.50	9.75	9.99	10.24	10.49
101	6.89	7.14	7.38	7.63	7.88	8.13	8.38	8.63	8.88	9.12	9.37	9.62	9.87	10.12	10.37	10.61
100	7.00	7.25	7.50	7.75	8.00	8.25	8.50	8.75	9.00	9.25	9.50	9.75	10.00	10.25	10.50	10.75
99	7.10	7.36	7.61	7.86	8.11	8.36	8.61	8.86	9.12	9.37	9.62	9.87	10.12	10.37	10.63	10.88
98	7.21	7.47	7.72	7.97	8.23	8.48	8.73	8.99	9.24	9.49	9.75	10.00	10.25	10.51	10.76	11.01
97	7.33	7.58	7.84	8.09	8.34	8.60	8.85	9.11	9.36	9.62	9.87	10.13	10.38	10.64	10.89	11.15
96	7.44	7.70	7.95	8.21	8.47	8.72	8.98	9.23	9.49	9.75	10.00	10.26	10.52	10.78	11.03	11.29
95	7.56	7.81	8.07	8.33	8.59	8.85	9.10	9.36	9.62	9.88	10.14	10.40	10.66	10.91	11.17	11.43
94	7.68	7.93	8.19	8.45	8.71	8.97	9.23	9.49	9.75	10.01	10.27	10.53	10.79	11.05	11.32	11.58
93	7.80	8.06	8.32	8.58	8.84	9.10	9.36	9.62	9.89	10.15	10.41	10.67	10.94	11.20	11.46	11.72
92	7.92	8.18	8.44	8.71	8.97	9.23	9.50	9.76	10.02	10.29	10.55	10.82	11.08	11.34	11.61	11.87
91	8.04	8.31	8.57	8.84	9.10	9.37	9.63	9.90	10.16	10.43	10.69	10.96	11.23	11.49	11.76	12.03
90	8.17	8.43	8.70	8.97	9.23	9.50	9.77	10.04	10.30	10.57	10.84	11.11	11.38	11.65	11.91	12.18
89	8.30	8.57	8.83	9.10	9.37	9.64	9.91	10.18	10.45	10.72	10.99	11.26	11.53	11.80	12.07	12.34
88	8.43	8.70	8.97	9.24	9.51	9.78	10.05	10.32	10.59	10.87	11.14	11.41	11.68	11.96	12.23	12.50
87	8.56	8.83	9.11	9.38	9.65	9.92	10.20	10.47	10.74	11.02	11.29	11.57	11.84	12.12	12.39	12.67
86	8.70	8.97	9.25	9.52	9.79	10.07	10.34	10.62	10.90	11.17	11.45	11.73	12.00	12.28	12.56	12.84
85	8.84	9.11	9.39	9.66	9.94	10.22	10.50	10.77	11.05	11.33	11.61	11.89	12.17	12.45	12.73	13.01
84	8.98	9.26	9.53	9.81	10.09	10.37	10.65	10.93	11.21	11.49	11.77	12.06	12.34	12.62	12.90	13.19
83	9.12	9.40	9.68	9.96	10.24	10.53	10.81	11.09	11.37	11.66	11.94	12.22	12.51	12.79	13.08	13.37
82	9.27	9.55	9.83	10.12	10.40	10.68	10.97	11.25	11.54	11.82	12.11	12.40	12.68	12.97	13.26	13.55
81	9.42	9.70	9.99	10.27	10.56	10.85	11.13	11.42	11.71	12.00	12.28	12.57	12.86	13.15	13.45	13.74
80	9.57	9.86	10.15	10.43	10.72	11.01	11.30	11.59	11.88	12.17	12.46	12.75	13.05	13.34	13.63	13.93
79	9.73	10.02	10.31	10.60	10.89	11.18	11.47	11.76	12.06	12.35	12.64	12.94	13.23	13.53	13.83	14.12
78	9.89	10.18	10.47	10.76	11.06	11.35	11.65	11.94	12.24	12.53	12.83	13.13	13.43	13.72	14.02	14.32
77	10.05	10.35	10.64	10.93	11.23	11.53	11.82	12.12	12.42	12.72	13.02	13.32	13.62	13.92	14.23	14.53
76	10.22	10.51	10.81	11.11	11.41	11.71	12.01	12.31	12.61	12.91	13.21	13.52	13.82	14.13	14.43	14.74
75	10.39	10.69	10.99	11.29	11.59	11.89	12.19	12.50	12.80	13.11	13.41	13.72	14.03	14.34	14.64	14.95
74	10.56	10.86	11.17	11.47	11.77	12.08	12.39	12.69	13.00	13.31	13.62	13.93	14.24	14.55	14.86	15.17
73	10.74	11.04	11.35	11.66	11.96	12.27	12.58	12.89	13.20	13.51	13.83	14.14	14.45	14.77	15.08	15.40
70	11.30	11.61	11.93	12.24	12.56	12.88	13.20	13.52	13.84	14.16	14.48	14.81	15.13	15.46	15.78	16.11
65	12.33	12.66	12.99	13.33	13.66	14.00	14.34	14.68	15.02	15.36	15.70	16.04	16.39	16.73	17.08	17.43
60	13.51	13.86	14.21	14.57	14.92	15.28	15.64	16.00	16.37	16.73	17.10	17.47	17.83	18.20	18.58	18.95
55	14.87	15.25	15.63	16.01	16.39	16.78	17.16	17.55	17.94	18.34	18.73	19.13	19.53	19.93	20.33	20.73
50	16.48	16.89	17.30	17.71	18.13	18.54	18.96	19.39	19.81	20.24	20.67	21.10	21.53	21.97	22.41	22.85
45	18.42	18.86	19.31	19.76	20.22	20.68	21.14	21.61	22.07	22.54	23.02	23.49	23.97	24.45	24.94	25.42
40	20.80	21.30	21.80	22.30	22.81	23.32	23.83	24.35	24.88	25.40	25.93	26.46	27.00	27.54	28.08	28.62
35	23.84	24.40	24.96	25.53	26.11	26.69	27.27	27.86	28.46	29.06	29.66	30.26	30.87	31.49	32.11	32.73
30	27.85	28.50	29.16	29.82	30.49	31.16	31.84	32.53	33.22	33.91	34.61	35.32	36.03	36.75	37.47	38.19

MORTGAGE PRICE

Description: This table shows the price to pay for a monthly payment mortgage loan at the yield rate.

Example: The price of a 15.00 %, 26 year mortgage loan to yield 8.00 % to maturity is $ 167.38.

INTEREST RATE, %

YIELD	11.00%	11.25%	11.50%	11.75%	12.00%	12.25%	12.50%	12.75%	13.00%	13.25%	13.50%	13.75%	14.00%	14.25%	14.50%	15.00%
0.00	303.62	309.33	315.07	320.85	326.65	332.48	338.34	344.23	350.14	356.08	362.04	368.02	374.03	380.06	386.10	398.26
1.00	267.26	272.29	277.34	282.42	287.53	292.67	297.82	303.01	308.21	313.44	318.68	323.95	329.24	334.54	339.87	350.57
2.00	236.60	241.05	245.53	250.03	254.55	259.09	263.66	268.25	272.85	277.48	282.13	286.79	291.47	296.17	300.88	310.35
3.00	210.64	214.61	218.59	222.60	226.62	230.67	234.73	238.82	242.92	247.04	251.17	255.33	259.49	263.67	267.87	276.30
4.00	188.57	192.12	195.69	199.27	202.88	206.50	210.14	213.80	217.47	221.16	224.86	228.57	232.31	236.05	239.81	247.35
4.25	183.58	187.04	190.51	194.00	197.51	201.04	204.58	208.14	211.71	215.30	218.91	222.53	226.16	229.80	233.46	240.81
4.50	178.78	182.15	185.53	188.93	192.35	195.78	199.23	202.70	206.18	209.68	213.19	216.71	220.25	223.80	227.36	234.51
4.75	174.17	177.45	180.74	184.05	187.38	190.73	194.09	197.47	200.86	204.26	207.68	211.12	214.56	218.02	221.49	228.46
5.00	169.73	172.92	176.13	179.36	182.60	185.87	189.14	192.43	195.74	199.06	202.39	205.73	209.09	212.46	215.84	222.64
5.25	165.46	168.57	171.70	174.84	178.01	181.19	184.38	187.59	190.81	194.04	197.29	200.55	203.83	207.11	210.41	217.03
5.50	161.34	164.38	167.43	170.50	173.58	176.68	179.80	182.92	186.07	189.22	192.39	195.57	198.76	201.96	205.18	211.64
5.75	157.38	160.34	163.32	166.31	169.32	172.35	175.38	178.43	181.50	184.58	187.67	190.77	193.88	197.01	200.14	206.44
6.00	153.57	156.46	159.36	162.28	165.22	168.17	171.13	174.11	177.10	180.10	183.12	186.14	189.18	192.23	195.29	201.44
6.25	149.89	152.71	155.55	158.40	161.27	164.14	167.04	169.94	172.86	175.79	178.74	181.69	184.66	187.63	190.62	196.62
6.50	146.35	149.11	151.87	154.66	157.46	160.27	163.09	165.93	168.78	171.64	174.51	177.40	180.29	183.20	186.12	191.97
6.75	142.94	145.63	148.33	151.05	153.78	156.53	159.29	162.06	164.84	167.64	170.44	173.26	176.09	178.93	181.77	187.50
7.00	139.65	142.28	144.92	147.57	150.24	152.93	155.62	158.33	161.05	163.78	166.52	169.27	172.04	174.81	177.59	183.18
7.25	136.48	139.04	141.62	144.22	146.83	149.45	152.08	154.73	157.39	160.06	162.74	165.43	168.13	170.84	173.55	179.02
7.50	133.41	135.92	138.45	140.98	143.53	146.10	148.67	151.26	153.86	156.47	159.09	161.71	164.35	167.00	169.66	175.00
7.75	130.46	132.91	135.38	137.86	140.36	142.86	145.38	147.91	150.45	153.00	155.56	158.13	160.71	163.30	165.90	171.13
8.00	127.61	130.01	132.42	134.85	137.29	139.74	142.20	144.68	147.16	149.66	152.16	154.68	157.20	159.73	162.28	167.38
8.25	124.85	127.20	129.56	131.94	134.33	136.72	139.13	141.55	143.99	146.43	148.88	151.34	153.81	156.29	158.77	163.77
8.50	122.19	124.49	126.80	129.13	131.46	133.81	136.17	138.54	140.92	143.31	145.71	148.11	150.53	152.96	155.39	160.28
8.75	119.62	121.88	124.14	126.41	128.70	131.00	133.31	135.63	137.96	140.29	142.64	145.00	147.37	149.74	152.13	156.91
9.00	117.14	119.35	121.56	123.79	126.03	128.28	130.54	132.81	135.09	137.38	139.68	141.99	144.31	146.63	148.97	153.66
9.25	114.74	116.90	119.07	121.25	123.45	125.65	127.87	130.09	132.33	134.57	136.82	139.08	141.35	143.63	145.92	150.51
9.50	112.42	114.54	116.66	118.80	120.95	123.11	125.28	127.46	129.65	131.85	134.05	136.27	138.49	140.73	142.97	147.47
9.75	110.18	112.25	114.34	116.43	118.54	120.65	122.78	124.92	127.06	129.22	131.38	133.55	135.73	137.92	140.11	144.52
10.00	108.01	110.04	112.08	114.14	116.20	118.28	120.36	122.46	124.56	126.67	128.79	130.92	133.06	135.20	137.35	141.68
10.25	105.91	107.90	109.90	111.92	113.94	115.98	118.02	120.07	122.14	124.21	126.29	128.37	130.47	132.57	134.68	138.92
10.50	103.87	105.83	107.79	109.77	111.75	113.75	115.76	117.77	119.79	121.82	123.86	125.91	127.96	130.03	132.10	136.25
10.75	101.91	103.82	105.75	107.69	109.64	111.59	113.56	115.54	117.52	119.51	121.52	123.52	125.54	127.56	129.59	133.67
11.00	100.00	101.88	103.77	105.67	107.59	109.51	111.44	113.38	115.32	117.28	119.24	121.21	123.19	125.18	127.17	131.17
11.25	98.15	100.00	101.86	103.72	105.60	107.49	109.38	111.28	113.19	115.11	117.04	118.97	120.92	122.87	124.82	128.75
11.50	96.36	98.18	100.00	101.83	103.67	105.53	107.39	109.25	111.13	113.01	114.91	116.81	118.71	120.63	122.54	126.40
11.75	94.63	96.41	98.20	100.00	101.81	103.63	105.45	107.29	109.13	110.98	112.84	114.70	116.58	118.45	120.34	124.13
12.00	92.95	94.70	96.46	98.22	100.00	101.79	103.58	105.38	107.19	109.01	110.83	112.67	114.50	116.35	118.20	121.92
12.25	91.32	93.04	94.76	96.50	98.25	100.00	101.76	103.53	105.31	107.10	108.89	110.69	112.50	114.31	116.13	119.78
12.50	89.74	91.42	93.12	94.83	96.54	98.27	100.00	101.74	103.49	105.24	107.00	108.77	110.55	112.33	114.12	117.71
12.75	88.20	89.86	91.53	93.21	94.89	96.59	98.29	100.00	101.72	103.44	105.17	106.91	108.66	110.41	112.17	115.70
13.00	86.71	88.34	89.98	91.63	93.29	94.96	96.63	98.31	100.00	101.70	103.40	105.11	106.82	108.54	110.27	113.74
13.25	85.27	86.87	88.48	90.11	91.74	93.37	95.02	96.67	98.33	100.00	101.67	103.35	105.04	106.73	108.43	111.85
13.50	83.86	85.44	87.03	88.62	90.23	91.84	93.45	95.08	96.71	98.35	100.00	101.65	103.31	104.98	106.65	110.00
13.75	82.50	84.05	85.61	87.18	88.76	90.34	91.94	93.53	95.14	96.75	98.37	100.00	101.63	103.27	104.91	108.22
14.00	81.17	82.70	84.24	85.78	87.33	88.89	90.46	92.03	93.61	95.20	96.79	98.39	100.00	101.61	103.23	106.48
14.25	79.89	81.39	82.90	84.42	85.95	87.48	89.02	90.57	92.13	93.69	95.26	96.83	98.41	100.00	101.59	104.79
14.50	78.64	80.12	81.60	83.10	84.60	86.11	87.63	89.15	90.69	92.22	93.77	95.32	96.87	98.43	100.00	103.15
14.75	77.42	78.88	80.34	81.81	83.29	84.78	86.27	87.77	89.28	90.80	92.32	93.84	95.37	96.91	98.45	101.55
15.00	76.24	77.67	79.11	80.56	82.02	83.48	84.96	86.43	87.92	89.41	90.91	92.41	93.92	95.43	96.95	100.00
15.25	75.08	76.50	77.92	79.35	80.78	82.22	83.67	85.13	86.59	88.06	89.53	91.01	92.50	93.99	95.48	98.49
15.50	73.96	75.36	76.76	78.16	79.58	81.00	82.42	83.86	85.30	86.75	88.20	89.66	91.12	92.59	94.06	97.02
15.75	72.87	74.25	75.62	77.01	78.40	79.80	81.21	82.62	84.04	85.47	86.90	88.33	89.78	91.22	92.67	95.59
16.00	71.81	73.16	74.52	75.89	77.26	78.64	80.03	81.42	82.82	84.22	85.63	87.05	88.47	89.89	91.32	94.20
16.25	70.78	72.11	73.45	74.80	76.15	77.51	78.88	80.25	81.63	83.01	84.40	85.80	87.20	88.60	90.01	92.84
16.50	69.77	71.09	72.41	73.73	75.07	76.41	77.75	79.11	80.47	81.83	83.20	84.58	85.96	87.34	88.73	91.52
16.75	68.79	70.09	71.39	72.70	74.01	75.33	76.66	78.00	79.34	80.68	82.03	83.39	84.75	86.11	87.48	90.24
17.00	67.84	69.11	70.40	71.69	72.99	74.29	75.60	76.91	78.23	79.56	80.89	82.23	83.57	84.92	86.27	88.99
17.25	66.91	68.17	69.43	70.70	71.98	73.27	74.56	75.86	77.16	78.47	79.78	81.10	82.42	83.75	85.09	87.76
17.50	66.00	67.24	68.49	69.75	71.01	72.27	73.55	74.83	76.11	77.40	78.70	80.00	81.31	82.62	83.93	86.57
17.75	65.12	66.34	67.57	68.81	70.05	71.31	72.56	73.82	75.09	76.37	77.64	78.93	80.22	81.51	82.81	85.41
18.00	64.25	65.46	66.68	67.90	69.13	70.36	71.60	72.85	74.10	75.35	76.62	77.88	79.15	80.43	81.71	84.28
18.25	63.41	64.60	65.80	67.01	68.22	69.44	70.66	71.89	73.13	74.37	75.61	76.86	78.12	79.37	80.64	83.18
18.50	62.59	63.77	64.95	66.14	67.34	68.54	69.75	70.96	72.18	73.40	74.63	75.87	77.10	78.35	79.59	82.10
18.75	61.79	62.95	64.12	65.29	66.47	67.66	68.85	70.05	71.25	72.46	73.68	74.89	76.12	77.34	78.57	81.05
19.00	61.00	62.15	63.31	64.47	65.63	66.80	67.98	69.16	70.35	71.54	72.74	73.94	75.15	76.36	77.58	80.02
20.00	58.05	59.14	60.24	61.35	62.46	63.57	64.69	65.82	66.95	68.08	69.22	70.37	71.51	72.67	73.82	76.15
25.00	46.64	47.51	48.39	49.28	50.17	51.07	51.97	52.87	53.78	54.69	55.61	56.53	57.45	58.38	59.31	61.17
30.00	38.91	39.64	40.38	41.12	41.86	42.61	43.36	44.11	44.87	45.63	46.39	47.16	47.93	48.70	49.48	51.04

Description: This table shows the yield to maturity of a mortgage purchased at the price shown in the index.

Example: The yield to maturity of a 15.00 %, 26 year mortgage at a price of 125.00 is 11.65 %.

INTEREST RATE, %

PRICE	11.00%	11.25%	11.50%	11.75%	12.00%	12.25%	12.50%	12.75%	13.00%	13.25%	13.50%	13.75%	14.00%	14.25%	14.50%	15.00%
250	1.54	1.69	1.84	2.00	2.15	2.30	2.45	2.60	2.74	2.89	3.04	3.18	3.33	3.47	3.61	3.90
240	1.88	2.03	2.19	2.34	2.50	2.65	2.80	2.95	3.10	3.25	3.40	3.55	3.70	3.84	3.99	4.28
230	2.23	2.39	2.55	2.71	2.86	3.02	3.18	3.33	3.48	3.64	3.79	3.94	4.09	4.24	4.39	4.68
220	2.62	2.78	2.94	3.10	3.26	3.42	3.57	3.73	3.89	4.04	4.20	4.35	4.51	4.66	4.81	5.11
210	3.02	3.19	3.35	3.52	3.68	3.84	4.00	4.16	4.32	4.48	4.64	4.80	4.95	5.11	5.26	5.57
200	3.46	3.63	3.79	3.96	4.13	4.29	4.46	4.62	4.79	4.95	5.11	5.27	5.43	5.59	5.75	6.07
195	3.69	3.86	4.03	4.20	4.37	4.53	4.70	4.87	5.03	5.20	5.36	5.52	5.69	5.85	6.01	6.33
190	3.93	4.10	4.27	4.44	4.61	4.78	4.95	5.12	5.29	5.45	5.62	5.79	5.95	6.12	6.28	6.60
185	4.17	4.35	4.52	4.70	4.87	5.04	5.21	5.38	5.55	5.72	5.89	6.06	6.23	6.39	6.56	6.89
180	4.43	4.61	4.78	4.96	5.14	5.31	5.48	5.66	5.83	6.00	6.17	6.34	6.51	6.68	6.85	7.19
175	4.70	4.88	5.06	5.24	5.41	5.59	5.77	5.94	6.12	6.29	6.47	6.64	6.81	6.98	7.15	7.50
170	4.98	5.16	5.34	5.52	5.70	5.88	6.06	6.24	6.42	6.60	6.77	6.95	7.12	7.30	7.47	7.82
165	5.27	5.46	5.64	5.83	6.01	6.19	6.37	6.55	6.73	6.91	7.09	7.27	7.45	7.63	7.81	8.16
160	5.58	5.77	5.95	6.14	6.33	6.51	6.70	6.88	7.07	7.25	7.43	7.61	7.80	7.98	8.16	8.52
155	5.90	6.09	6.28	6.47	6.66	6.85	7.04	7.23	7.41	7.60	7.79	7.97	8.16	8.34	8.52	8.89
150	6.24	6.43	6.63	6.82	7.01	7.20	7.40	7.59	7.78	7.97	8.16	8.35	8.54	8.72	8.91	9.29
145	6.59	6.79	6.99	7.19	7.38	7.58	7.77	7.97	8.16	8.36	8.55	8.75	8.94	9.13	9.32	9.70
140	6.97	7.17	7.37	7.57	7.77	7.97	8.17	8.37	8.57	8.77	8.97	9.17	9.36	9.56	9.76	10.15
135	7.36	7.57	7.78	7.98	8.19	8.39	8.60	8.80	9.00	9.21	9.41	9.61	9.81	10.01	10.21	10.62
130	7.78	8.00	8.21	8.42	8.63	8.84	9.04	9.25	9.46	9.67	9.88	10.08	10.29	10.50	10.70	11.11
125	8.23	8.45	8.66	8.88	9.09	9.31	9.52	9.74	9.95	10.16	10.38	10.59	10.80	11.01	11.23	11.65
120	8.71	8.93	9.15	9.37	9.59	9.81	10.03	10.25	10.47	10.69	10.91	11.13	11.35	11.57	11.78	12.22
115	9.22	9.45	9.67	9.90	10.13	10.35	10.58	10.81	11.03	11.26	11.48	11.71	11.93	12.16	12.38	12.83
113	9.43	9.66	9.89	10.12	10.35	10.58	10.81	11.04	11.27	11.50	11.73	11.95	12.18	12.41	12.64	13.09
112	9.54	9.77	10.00	10.24	10.47	10.70	10.93	11.16	11.39	11.62	11.85	12.08	12.31	12.54	12.77	13.22
111	9.65	9.89	10.12	10.35	10.58	10.82	11.05	11.28	11.51	11.74	11.97	12.21	12.44	12.67	12.90	13.36
110	9.77	10.00	10.23	10.47	10.70	10.94	11.17	11.40	11.64	11.87	12.10	12.33	12.57	12.80	13.03	13.50
109	9.88	10.12	10.35	10.59	10.82	11.06	11.29	11.53	11.76	12.00	12.23	12.46	12.70	12.93	13.17	13.63
108	10.00	10.23	10.47	10.71	10.94	11.18	11.42	11.65	11.89	12.13	12.36	12.60	12.83	13.07	13.30	13.78
107	10.11	10.35	10.59	10.83	11.07	11.31	11.54	11.78	12.02	12.26	12.50	12.73	12.97	13.21	13.45	13.92
106	10.23	10.47	10.71	10.95	11.19	11.43	11.67	11.91	12.15	12.39	12.63	12.87	13.11	13.35	13.59	14.07
105	10.36	10.60	10.84	11.08	11.32	11.56	11.80	12.05	12.29	12.53	12.77	13.01	13.25	13.49	13.73	14.21
104	10.48	10.72	10.97	11.21	11.45	11.70	11.94	12.18	12.42	12.67	12.91	13.15	13.39	13.64	13.88	14.36
103	10.61	10.85	11.09	11.34	11.58	11.83	12.07	12.32	12.56	12.81	13.05	13.30	13.54	13.79	14.03	14.52
102	10.73	10.98	11.23	11.47	11.72	11.97	12.21	12.46	12.70	12.95	13.20	13.44	13.69	13.94	14.18	14.67
101	10.86	11.11	11.36	11.61	11.86	12.10	12.35	12.60	12.85	13.10	13.34	13.59	13.84	14.09	14.34	14.83
100	11.00	11.25	11.50	11.75	12.00	12.25	12.50	12.75	13.00	13.25	13.50	13.75	14.00	14.25	14.50	15.00
99	11.13	11.38	11.63	11.88	12.14	12.39	12.64	12.89	13.14	13.40	13.65	13.90	14.15	14.40	14.66	15.16
98	11.27	11.52	11.77	12.03	12.28	12.53	12.79	13.04	13.30	13.55	13.80	14.06	14.31	14.57	14.82	15.33
97	11.41	11.66	11.92	12.17	12.43	12.68	12.94	13.19	13.45	13.71	13.96	14.22	14.47	14.73	14.99	15.50
96	11.55	11.80	12.06	12.32	12.58	12.83	13.09	13.35	13.61	13.87	14.12	14.38	14.64	14.90	15.16	15.67
95	11.69	11.95	12.21	12.47	12.73	12.99	13.25	13.51	13.77	14.03	14.29	14.55	14.81	15.07	15.33	15.85
94	11.84	12.10	12.36	12.62	12.88	13.15	13.41	13.67	13.93	14.19	14.46	14.72	14.98	15.24	15.51	16.03
93	11.99	12.25	12.51	12.78	13.04	13.31	13.57	13.83	14.10	14.36	14.63	14.89	15.16	15.42	15.69	16.22
92	12.14	12.40	12.67	12.94	13.20	13.47	13.73	14.00	14.27	14.53	14.80	15.07	15.33	15.60	15.87	16.40
91	12.29	12.56	12.83	13.10	13.37	13.63	13.90	14.17	14.44	14.71	14.98	15.25	15.52	15.79	16.06	16.60
90	12.45	12.72	12.99	13.26	13.53	13.80	14.07	14.35	14.62	14.89	15.16	15.43	15.70	15.97	16.25	16.79
89	12.61	12.89	13.16	13.43	13.70	13.98	14.25	14.52	14.80	15.07	15.34	15.62	15.89	16.17	16.44	16.99
88	12.78	13.05	13.33	13.60	13.88	14.15	14.43	14.70	14.98	15.26	15.53	15.81	16.09	16.36	16.64	17.20
87	12.95	13.22	13.50	13.78	14.05	14.33	14.61	14.89	15.17	15.45	15.73	16.00	16.28	16.56	16.84	17.40
86	13.12	13.40	13.68	13.96	14.24	14.52	14.80	15.08	15.36	15.64	15.92	16.20	16.49	16.77	17.05	17.62
85	13.29	13.57	13.86	14.14	14.42	14.70	14.99	15.27	15.55	15.84	16.12	16.41	16.69	16.98	17.26	17.84
84	13.47	13.75	14.04	14.32	14.61	14.89	15.18	15.47	15.75	16.04	16.33	16.62	16.90	17.19	17.48	18.06
83	13.65	13.94	14.23	14.51	14.80	15.09	15.38	15.67	15.96	16.25	16.54	16.83	17.12	17.41	17.70	18.29
82	13.84	14.13	14.42	14.71	15.00	15.29	15.58	15.87	16.17	16.46	16.75	17.05	17.34	17.63	17.93	18.52
81	14.03	14.32	14.61	14.91	15.20	15.49	15.79	16.08	16.38	16.67	16.97	17.27	17.56	17.86	18.16	18.76
80	14.22	14.52	14.81	15.11	15.41	15.70	16.00	16.30	16.60	16.90	17.20	17.50	17.80	18.10	18.40	19.00
79	14.42	14.72	15.02	15.32	15.62	15.92	16.22	16.52	16.82	17.12	17.43	17.73	18.03	18.34	18.64	19.25
78	14.62	14.93	15.23	15.53	15.83	16.14	16.44	16.74	17.05	17.35	17.66	17.97	18.27	18.58	18.89	19.50
77	14.83	15.14	15.44	15.75	16.05	16.36	16.67	16.97	17.28	17.59	17.90	18.21	18.52	18.83	19.14	19.77
76	15.05	15.35	15.66	15.97	16.28	16.59	16.90	17.21	17.52	17.83	18.15	18.46	18.77	19.09	19.40	20.03
75	15.26	15.57	15.89	16.20	16.51	16.82	17.14	17.45	17.77	18.08	18.40	18.72	19.03	19.35	19.67	20.31
74	15.49	15.80	16.12	16.43	16.75	17.07	17.38	17.70	18.02	18.34	18.66	18.98	19.30	19.62	19.95	20.59
73	15.72	16.03	16.35	16.67	16.99	17.31	17.63	17.96	18.28	18.60	18.93	19.25	19.58	19.90	20.23	20.88
70	16.44	16.77	17.10	17.43	17.76	18.09	18.43	18.76	19.09	19.43	19.77	20.10	20.44	20.78	21.12	21.80
65	17.78	18.13	18.48	18.83	19.19	19.54	19.90	20.25	20.61	20.97	21.33	21.69	22.05	22.41	22.78	23.51
60	19.32	19.70	20.08	20.46	20.84	21.22	21.60	21.98	22.37	22.76	23.14	23.53	23.92	24.31	24.70	25.49
55	21.14	21.54	21.95	22.36	22.77	23.19	23.60	24.02	24.43	24.85	25.27	25.70	26.12	26.54	26.97	27.82

MORTGAGE PRICE

27 YEARS

Description: This table shows the price to pay for a monthly payment mortgage loan at the yield rate.

Example: The price of a 6.75 %, 27 year mortgage loan to yield 8.00 % to maturity is $ 89.04.

INTEREST RATE, %

YIELD	0.00%	1.00%	2.00%	3.00%	4.00%	4.25%	4.50%	4.75%	5.00%	5.25%	5.50%	5.75%	6.00%	6.25%	6.50%	6.75%
0.00	100.00	114.15	129.50	146.03	163.69	168.27	172.93	177.64	182.42	187.27	192.18	197.14	202.17	207.26	212.40	217.60
1.00	87.61	100.00	113.45	127.93	143.40	147.42	151.49	155.62	159.81	164.06	168.36	172.71	177.11	181.57	186.07	190.63
2.00	77.22	88.15	100.00	112.76	126.40	129.94	133.53	137.18	140.87	144.61	148.40	152.24	156.12	160.04	164.02	168.03
3.00	68.48	78.17	88.68	100.00	112.09	115.23	118.42	121.65	124.93	128.24	131.60	135.01	138.45	141.93	145.45	149.01
4.00	61.09	69.74	79.11	89.21	100.00	102.80	105.64	108.53	111.45	114.41	117.40	120.44	123.51	126.62	129.76	132.94
4.25	59.43	67.83	76.96	86.78	97.27	100.00	102.76	105.57	108.41	111.29	114.20	117.16	120.14	123.17	126.22	129.31
4.50	57.83	66.01	74.89	84.45	94.66	97.31	100.00	102.73	105.49	108.29	111.13	114.01	116.91	119.85	122.83	125.83
4.75	56.29	64.26	72.90	82.20	92.14	94.73	97.34	100.00	102.69	105.42	108.18	110.98	113.81	116.67	119.57	122.49
5.00	54.82	62.57	70.99	80.05	89.73	92.24	94.79	97.38	100.00	102.66	105.35	108.07	110.82	113.61	116.43	119.28
5.25	53.40	60.95	69.15	77.98	87.41	89.86	92.34	94.86	97.41	100.00	102.62	105.27	107.96	110.67	113.42	116.20
5.50	52.04	59.40	67.39	75.99	85.18	87.56	89.98	92.44	94.93	97.45	100.00	102.58	105.20	107.85	110.52	113.23
5.75	50.72	57.90	65.69	74.07	83.03	85.36	87.72	90.11	92.53	94.99	97.48	100.00	102.55	105.13	107.74	110.38
6.00	49.46	56.46	64.05	72.23	80.96	83.23	85.53	87.87	90.23	92.63	95.06	97.51	100.00	102.52	105.06	107.63
6.25	48.25	55.08	62.48	70.46	78.98	81.19	83.44	85.71	88.02	90.36	92.72	95.12	97.55	100.00	102.48	104.99
6.50	47.08	53.74	60.97	68.75	77.07	79.22	81.42	83.64	85.89	88.17	90.48	92.82	95.18	97.58	100.00	102.45
6.75	45.96	52.46	59.51	67.11	75.22	77.33	79.47	81.64	83.84	86.06	88.32	90.60	92.91	95.25	97.61	100.00
7.00	44.87	51.22	58.11	65.53	73.45	75.51	77.60	79.71	81.86	84.03	86.23	88.46	90.72	93.00	95.31	97.64
7.25	43.83	50.03	56.76	64.00	71.74	73.75	75.79	77.86	79.96	82.08	84.23	86.41	88.61	90.84	93.09	95.37
7.50	42.82	48.88	55.46	62.53	70.10	72.06	74.05	76.07	78.12	80.19	82.30	84.42	86.58	88.75	90.96	93.18
7.75	41.85	47.78	54.20	61.12	68.51	70.43	72.38	74.35	76.35	78.38	80.43	82.51	84.62	86.74	88.90	91.07
8.00	40.92	46.71	52.99	59.75	66.98	68.86	70.76	72.69	74.65	76.63	78.64	80.67	82.73	84.81	86.91	89.04
8.25	40.02	45.68	51.82	58.44	65.50	67.34	69.20	71.09	73.00	74.94	76.90	78.89	80.90	82.94	85.00	87.08
8.50	39.15	44.69	50.70	57.16	64.08	65.87	67.69	69.54	71.41	73.31	75.23	77.18	79.14	81.13	83.15	85.18
8.75	38.31	43.73	49.61	55.94	62.70	64.46	66.24	68.05	69.88	71.74	73.62	75.52	77.45	79.39	81.36	83.36
9.00	37.50	42.80	48.56	54.75	61.38	63.10	64.84	66.61	68.40	70.22	72.06	73.92	75.81	77.71	79.64	81.59
9.25	36.71	41.91	47.54	53.61	60.10	61.78	63.49	65.22	66.97	68.75	70.55	72.38	74.22	76.09	77.98	79.89
9.50	35.96	41.04	46.56	52.51	58.86	60.51	62.18	63.88	65.59	67.34	69.10	70.89	72.69	74.52	76.37	78.24
9.75	35.23	40.21	45.62	51.44	57.66	59.28	60.92	62.58	64.26	65.97	67.70	69.45	71.22	73.01	74.82	76.65
10.00	34.52	39.40	44.70	50.41	56.50	58.09	59.69	61.32	62.97	64.65	66.34	68.05	69.79	71.54	73.32	75.11
10.25	33.84	38.62	43.82	49.41	55.39	56.94	58.51	60.11	61.73	63.37	65.03	66.71	68.41	70.13	71.87	73.63
10.50	33.18	37.87	42.96	48.45	54.31	55.83	57.37	58.94	60.52	62.13	63.76	65.41	67.07	68.76	70.47	72.19
10.75	32.54	37.14	42.14	47.51	53.26	54.75	56.27	57.80	59.36	60.93	62.53	64.15	65.78	67.44	69.11	70.80
11.00	31.92	36.44	41.34	46.61	52.25	53.71	55.20	56.70	58.23	59.77	61.34	62.93	64.53	66.15	67.80	69.46
11.25	31.32	35.75	40.56	45.74	51.27	52.70	54.16	55.64	57.14	58.65	60.19	61.75	63.32	64.91	66.52	68.15
11.50	30.74	35.09	39.81	44.89	50.32	51.73	53.16	54.61	56.08	57.57	59.08	60.60	62.15	63.71	65.29	66.89
11.75	30.18	34.45	39.08	44.07	49.40	50.78	52.19	53.61	55.06	56.52	58.00	59.50	61.01	62.55	64.10	65.67
12.00	29.64	33.83	38.38	43.28	48.51	49.87	51.25	52.65	54.06	55.50	56.95	58.43	59.92	61.42	62.95	64.49
12.25	29.11	33.23	37.70	42.51	47.65	48.98	50.34	51.71	53.10	54.51	55.94	57.39	58.85	60.33	61.83	63.34
12.50	28.60	32.64	37.03	41.76	46.81	48.12	49.45	50.80	52.17	53.56	54.96	56.38	57.82	59.27	60.74	62.23
12.75	28.10	32.08	36.39	41.04	46.00	47.29	48.60	49.92	51.27	52.63	54.01	55.40	56.82	58.24	59.69	61.15
13.00	27.62	31.53	35.77	40.34	45.21	46.48	47.77	49.07	50.39	51.73	53.08	54.46	55.84	57.25	58.67	60.11
13.25	27.16	31.00	35.17	39.65	44.45	45.70	46.96	48.24	49.54	50.85	52.19	53.54	54.90	56.28	57.68	59.09
13.50	26.70	30.48	34.58	38.99	43.71	44.93	46.18	47.44	48.71	50.01	51.32	52.64	53.99	55.34	56.72	58.11
13.75	26.26	29.98	34.01	38.35	42.99	44.20	45.42	46.66	47.91	49.19	50.47	51.78	53.10	54.43	55.79	57.15
14.00	25.84	29.49	33.46	37.73	42.29	43.48	44.68	45.90	47.13	48.39	49.65	50.94	52.24	53.55	54.88	56.22
14.25	25.42	29.02	32.92	37.13	41.62	42.78	43.96	45.16	46.38	47.61	48.86	50.12	51.40	52.69	54.00	55.32
14.50	25.02	28.56	32.40	36.54	40.96	42.10	43.27	44.45	45.65	46.86	48.09	49.33	50.59	51.86	53.15	54.45
14.75	24.63	28.12	31.90	35.97	40.32	41.45	42.59	43.75	44.93	46.13	47.33	48.56	49.80	51.05	52.31	53.60
15.00	24.25	27.68	31.40	35.41	39.69	40.81	41.93	43.08	44.24	45.41	46.60	47.81	49.03	50.26	51.51	52.77
15.25	23.88	27.26	30.93	34.87	39.09	40.18	41.30	42.42	43.56	44.72	45.89	47.08	48.28	49.49	50.72	51.96
15.50	23.52	26.85	30.46	34.35	38.50	39.58	40.67	41.78	42.91	44.05	45.20	46.37	47.55	48.75	49.96	51.18
15.75	23.17	26.45	30.01	33.84	37.93	38.99	40.07	41.16	42.27	43.39	44.53	45.68	46.85	48.02	49.22	50.42
16.00	22.83	26.06	29.57	33.34	37.37	38.42	39.48	40.56	41.65	42.76	43.88	45.01	46.16	47.32	48.49	49.68
16.25	22.50	25.68	29.14	32.86	36.83	37.86	38.91	39.97	41.05	42.14	43.24	44.36	45.49	46.63	47.79	48.96
16.50	22.18	25.32	28.72	32.39	36.30	37.32	38.35	39.40	40.46	41.53	42.62	43.72	44.84	45.97	47.11	48.26
16.75	21.86	24.96	28.31	31.93	35.79	36.79	37.81	38.84	39.89	40.94	42.02	43.10	44.20	45.31	46.44	47.58
17.00	21.56	24.61	27.92	31.48	35.29	36.28	37.28	38.30	39.33	40.37	41.43	42.50	43.58	44.68	45.79	46.91
17.25	21.26	24.27	27.53	31.05	34.80	35.78	36.76	37.77	38.78	39.81	40.86	41.91	42.98	44.06	45.16	46.26
17.50	20.97	23.94	27.16	30.62	34.32	35.29	36.26	37.25	38.25	39.27	40.30	41.34	42.39	43.46	44.54	45.63
17.75	20.69	23.61	26.79	30.21	33.86	34.81	35.77	36.75	37.74	38.74	39.76	40.78	41.82	42.87	43.94	45.01
18.00	20.41	23.30	26.43	29.81	33.41	34.35	35.30	36.26	37.23	38.22	39.22	40.24	41.26	42.30	43.35	44.41
18.25	20.14	22.99	26.08	29.41	32.97	33.89	34.83	35.78	36.74	37.72	38.71	39.71	40.72	41.75	42.78	43.83
18.50	19.88	22.69	25.74	29.03	32.54	33.45	34.38	35.31	36.26	37.23	38.20	39.19	40.19	41.20	42.22	43.26
18.75	19.62	22.40	25.41	28.65	32.12	33.02	33.93	34.86	35.80	36.75	37.71	38.69	39.67	40.67	41.68	42.70
19.00	19.37	22.11	25.09	28.29	31.71	32.60	33.50	34.41	35.34	36.28	37.23	38.19	39.17	40.15	41.15	42.16
20.00	18.43	21.04	23.87	26.91	30.17	31.01	31.87	32.74	33.62	34.52	35.42	36.34	37.26	38.20	39.15	40.11
25.00	14.80	16.89	19.16	21.61	24.22	24.90	25.59	26.28	26.99	27.71	28.43	29.17	29.91	30.67	31.43	32.20
30.00	12.34	14.09	15.98	18.02	20.20	20.77	21.34	21.92	22.51	23.11	23.72	24.33	24.95	25.58	26.21	26.86

Description: This table shows the yield to maturity of a mortgage purchased at the price shown in the index.

Example: The yield to maturity of a 6.75 %, 27 year mortgage at a price of 80.00 is 9.23 %.

INTEREST RATE, %

PRICE	0.00%	1.00%	2.00%	3.00%	4.00%	4.25%	4.50%	4.75%	5.00%	5.25%	5.50%	5.75%	6.00%	6.25%	6.50%	6.75%
100	0.00	1.00	2.00	3.00	4.00	4.25	4.50	4.75	5.00	5.25	5.50	5.75	6.00	6.25	6.50	6.75
99	.07	1.07	2.08	3.08	4.09	4.34	4.59	4.84	5.09	5.34	5.59	5.84	6.10	6.35	6.60	6.85
98	.14	1.15	2.16	3.17	4.18	4.43	4.68	4.93	5.19	5.44	5.69	5.95	6.20	6.45	6.70	6.96
97	.22	1.23	2.24	3.26	4.27	4.52	4.78	5.03	5.29	5.54	5.79	6.05	6.30	6.56	6.81	7.06
96	.30	1.31	2.33	3.35	4.37	4.62	4.88	5.13	5.39	5.64	5.90	6.15	6.41	6.66	6.92	7.17
95	.38	1.40	2.42	3.44	4.46	4.72	4.97	5.23	5.49	5.74	6.00	6.26	6.51	6.77	7.03	7.29
94	.46	1.48	2.50	3.53	4.56	4.82	5.07	5.33	5.59	5.85	6.11	6.37	6.62	6.88	7.14	7.40
93	.54	1.56	2.59	3.62	4.66	4.92	5.18	5.44	5.70	5.96	6.21	6.47	6.73	7.00	7.26	7.52
92	.62	1.65	2.68	3.72	4.76	5.02	5.28	5.54	5.80	6.06	6.32	6.59	6.85	7.11	7.37	7.63
91	.70	1.74	2.78	3.82	4.86	5.12	5.39	5.65	5.91	6.17	6.44	6.70	6.96	7.23	7.49	7.75
90	.79	1.83	2.87	3.92	4.97	5.23	5.49	5.76	6.02	6.29	6.55	6.81	7.08	7.34	7.61	7.88
89	.87	1.92	2.96	4.02	5.07	5.34	5.60	5.87	6.13	6.40	6.66	6.93	7.20	7.47	7.73	8.00
88	.96	2.01	3.06	4.12	5.18	5.45	5.71	5.98	6.25	6.51	6.78	7.05	7.32	7.59	7.86	8.13
87	1.05	2.10	3.16	4.22	5.29	5.56	5.83	6.09	6.36	6.63	6.90	7.17	7.44	7.71	7.98	8.25
86	1.14	2.20	3.26	4.33	5.40	5.67	5.94	6.21	6.48	6.75	7.02	7.30	7.57	7.84	8.11	8.39
85	1.23	2.29	3.36	4.43	5.52	5.79	6.06	6.33	6.60	6.87	7.15	7.42	7.70	7.97	8.24	8.52
84	1.32	2.39	3.46	4.54	5.63	5.90	6.18	6.45	6.72	7.00	7.27	7.55	7.83	8.10	8.38	8.66
83	1.42	2.49	3.57	4.65	5.75	6.02	6.30	6.57	6.85	7.13	7.40	7.68	7.96	8.24	8.52	8.79
82	1.51	2.59	3.68	4.77	5.87	6.14	6.42	6.70	6.98	7.26	7.53	7.81	8.09	8.37	8.65	8.94
81	1.61	2.69	3.78	4.88	5.99	6.27	6.55	6.83	7.11	7.39	7.67	7.95	8.23	8.51	8.80	9.08
80	1.71	2.80	3.90	5.00	6.12	6.40	6.68	6.96	7.24	7.52	7.80	8.09	8.37	8.66	8.94	9.23
79	1.81	2.90	4.01	5.12	6.24	6.52	6.81	7.09	7.37	7.66	7.94	8.23	8.52	8.80	9.09	9.38
78	1.91	3.01	4.12	5.24	6.37	6.66	6.94	7.23	7.51	7.80	8.09	8.37	8.66	8.95	9.24	9.53
77	2.02	3.12	4.24	5.37	6.50	6.79	7.08	7.36	7.65	7.94	8.23	8.52	8.81	9.10	9.40	9.69
76	2.12	3.24	4.36	5.49	6.64	6.93	7.22	7.51	7.80	8.09	8.38	8.67	8.97	9.26	9.55	9.85
75	2.23	3.35	4.48	5.62	6.78	7.07	7.36	7.65	7.94	8.24	8.53	8.83	9.12	9.42	9.72	10.01
74	2.34	3.47	4.61	5.75	6.92	7.21	7.50	7.80	8.09	8.39	8.68	8.98	9.28	9.58	9.88	10.18
73	2.46	3.59	4.73	5.89	7.06	7.36	7.65	7.95	8.25	8.54	8.84	9.14	9.44	9.75	10.05	10.35
72	2.57	3.71	4.86	6.03	7.21	7.50	7.80	8.10	8.40	8.70	9.00	9.31	9.61	9.92	10.22	10.53
71	2.69	3.83	4.99	6.17	7.36	7.66	7.96	8.26	8.56	8.87	9.17	9.48	9.78	10.09	10.40	10.71
70	2.81	3.96	5.13	6.31	7.51	7.81	8.12	8.42	8.73	9.03	9.34	9.65	9.96	10.27	10.58	10.89
69	2.93	4.09	5.27	6.46	7.67	7.97	8.28	8.58	8.89	9.20	9.51	9.82	10.14	10.45	10.77	11.08
68	3.06	4.22	5.41	6.61	7.83	8.13	8.44	8.75	9.06	9.38	9.69	10.00	10.32	10.64	10.96	11.27
67	3.18	4.36	5.55	6.76	7.99	8.30	8.61	8.93	9.24	9.56	9.87	10.19	10.51	10.83	11.15	11.47
66	3.31	4.50	5.70	6.92	8.16	8.47	8.79	9.10	9.42	9.74	10.06	10.38	10.70	11.03	11.35	11.68
65	3.45	4.64	5.85	7.08	8.33	8.65	8.97	9.29	9.61	9.93	10.25	10.57	10.90	11.23	11.56	11.89
64	3.58	4.78	6.00	7.25	8.51	8.83	9.15	9.47	9.80	10.12	10.45	10.77	11.10	11.43	11.77	12.10
63	3.72	4.93	6.16	7.41	8.69	9.01	9.34	9.66	9.99	10.32	10.65	10.98	11.31	11.65	11.98	12.32
62	3.86	5.08	6.32	7.59	8.88	9.20	9.53	9.86	10.19	10.52	10.86	11.19	11.53	11.87	12.21	12.55
61	4.01	5.24	6.49	7.77	9.07	9.40	9.73	10.06	10.39	10.73	11.07	11.41	11.75	12.09	12.43	12.78
60	4.16	5.40	6.66	7.95	9.26	9.60	9.93	10.27	10.61	10.95	11.29	11.63	11.98	12.32	12.67	13.02
59	4.31	5.56	6.84	8.14	9.47	9.80	10.14	10.48	10.82	11.17	11.51	11.86	12.21	12.56	12.91	13.27
58	4.47	5.73	7.02	8.33	9.67	10.01	10.36	10.70	11.05	11.39	11.74	12.10	12.45	12.81	13.16	13.52
57	4.63	5.90	7.20	8.53	9.89	10.23	10.58	10.93	11.28	11.63	11.98	12.34	12.70	13.06	13.42	13.79
56	4.79	6.08	7.39	8.73	10.11	10.46	10.81	11.16	11.51	11.87	12.23	12.59	12.95	13.32	13.69	14.06
55	4.96	6.26	7.58	8.94	10.33	10.69	11.04	11.40	11.76	12.12	12.48	12.85	13.22	13.59	13.96	14.34
54	5.14	6.45	7.79	9.16	10.57	10.92	11.28	11.65	12.01	12.38	12.75	13.12	13.49	13.87	14.25	14.63
53	5.32	6.64	7.99	9.38	10.81	11.17	11.54	11.90	12.27	12.64	13.02	13.39	13.77	14.15	14.54	14.92
52	5.50	6.84	8.21	9.61	11.06	11.42	11.79	12.17	12.54	12.92	13.30	13.68	14.06	14.45	14.84	15.23
51	5.69	7.04	8.43	9.85	11.31	11.69	12.06	12.44	12.82	13.20	13.59	13.98	14.37	14.76	15.16	15.55
50	5.89	7.25	8.65	10.10	11.58	11.96	12.34	12.72	13.11	13.50	13.89	14.28	14.68	15.08	15.48	15.89
49	6.09	7.47	8.89	10.35	11.86	12.24	12.63	13.02	13.41	13.80	14.20	14.60	15.00	15.41	15.82	16.23
48	6.30	7.69	9.13	10.61	12.14	12.53	12.92	13.32	13.72	14.12	14.52	14.93	15.34	15.75	16.17	16.59
47	6.51	7.93	9.38	10.89	12.44	12.83	13.23	13.63	14.04	14.45	14.86	15.27	15.69	16.11	16.53	16.96
46	6.74	8.17	9.64	11.17	12.75	13.15	13.55	13.96	14.37	14.79	15.21	15.63	16.05	16.48	16.91	17.35
45	6.97	8.41	9.91	11.46	13.06	13.47	13.89	14.30	14.72	15.14	15.57	16.00	16.43	16.87	17.31	17.75
44	7.20	8.67	10.19	11.77	13.40	13.81	14.23	14.66	15.08	15.51	15.95	16.38	16.83	17.27	17.72	18.17
43	7.45	8.94	10.48	12.08	13.74	14.17	14.59	15.02	15.46	15.90	16.34	16.79	17.24	17.69	18.15	18.61
42	7.71	9.22	10.79	12.41	14.10	14.53	14.97	15.41	15.85	16.30	16.75	17.21	17.67	18.13	18.60	19.07
41	7.97	9.51	11.10	12.76	14.48	14.92	15.36	15.81	16.26	16.72	17.18	17.65	18.12	18.59	19.07	19.55
40	8.25	9.81	11.43	13.12	14.87	15.32	15.77	16.23	16.69	17.16	17.63	18.11	18.59	19.07	19.56	20.05
39	8.54	10.12	11.77	13.49	15.28	15.74	16.20	16.67	17.14	17.62	18.10	18.59	19.08	19.57	20.07	20.58
35	9.82	11.53	13.32	15.19	17.14	17.64	18.15	18.67	19.19	19.71	20.24	20.78	21.32	21.86	22.42	22.97
30	11.83	13.74	15.75	17.87	20.11	20.69	21.27	21.86	22.46	23.07	23.68	24.30	24.92	25.55	26.19	26.84
25	14.51	16.71	19.06	21.56	24.21	24.89	25.59	26.29	27.00	27.72	28.45	29.19	29.94	30.69	31.45	32.23
20	18.38	21.06	23.94	27.02	30.30	31.15	32.01	32.89	33.77	34.67	35.58	36.50	37.43	38.37	39.33	40.29
15	24.65	28.16	31.96	36.05	40.41	41.54	42.69	43.86	45.04	46.23	47.45	48.67	49.91	51.17	52.44	53.72
10	37.03	42.27	47.96	54.08	60.62	62.32	64.04	65.79	67.56	69.35	71.17	73.01	74.87	76.76	78.66	80.59

MORTGAGE PRICE

27 YEARS

Description: This table shows the price to pay for a monthly payment mortgage loan at the yield rate.

Example: The price of a 10.75 %, 27 year mortgage loan to yield 8.00 % to maturity is $ 125.76.

INTEREST RATE, %

YIELD	7.00%	7.25%	7.50%	7.75%	8.00%	8.25%	8.50%	8.75%	9.00%	9.25%	9.50%	9.75%	10.00%	10.25%	10.50%	10.75%
0.00	222.85	228.16	233.52	238.93	244.39	249.89	255.45	261.05	266.69	272.38	278.11	283.88	289.69	295.53	301.42	307.34
1.00	195.23	199.88	204.57	209.31	214.10	218.92	223.79	228.69	233.64	238.62	243.64	248.69	253.78	258.90	264.06	269.24
2.00	172.09	176.19	180.32	184.50	188.72	192.97	197.26	201.58	205.94	210.33	214.76	219.21	223.70	228.21	232.76	237.33
3.00	152.61	156.24	159.91	163.62	167.36	171.13	174.93	178.77	182.63	186.53	190.45	194.40	198.38	202.38	206.41	210.47
4.00	136.14	139.39	142.66	145.97	149.30	152.67	156.06	159.48	162.93	166.40	169.90	173.43	176.98	180.55	184.14	187.76
4.25	132.43	135.59	138.77	141.99	145.23	148.50	151.81	155.13	158.49	161.87	165.27	168.70	172.15	175.63	179.12	182.64
4.50	128.87	131.94	135.04	138.17	141.32	144.51	147.72	150.96	154.22	157.51	160.83	164.16	167.52	170.90	174.31	177.73
4.75	125.45	128.44	131.45	134.50	137.57	140.67	143.80	146.95	150.13	153.33	156.56	159.80	163.07	166.36	169.68	173.01
5.00	122.16	125.07	128.01	130.97	133.97	136.98	140.03	143.10	146.19	149.31	152.45	155.61	158.80	162.00	165.23	168.47
5.25	119.00	121.83	124.70	127.58	130.50	133.44	136.41	139.40	142.41	145.45	148.51	151.59	154.69	157.81	160.95	164.12
5.50	115.96	118.72	121.51	124.33	127.17	130.03	132.92	135.84	138.77	141.73	144.72	147.72	150.74	153.78	156.84	159.92
5.75	113.04	115.73	118.45	121.19	123.96	126.76	129.57	132.42	135.28	138.16	141.07	144.00	146.94	149.91	152.89	155.90
6.00	110.23	112.85	115.50	118.18	120.88	123.61	126.35	129.12	131.91	134.73	137.56	140.41	143.29	146.18	149.09	152.02
6.25	107.52	110.09	112.67	115.28	117.91	120.57	123.25	125.95	128.68	131.42	134.19	136.97	139.77	142.59	145.43	148.29
6.50	104.92	107.42	109.94	112.49	115.06	117.65	120.27	122.90	125.56	128.24	130.94	133.65	136.39	139.14	141.91	144.70
6.75	102.41	104.85	107.32	109.80	112.31	114.84	117.39	119.97	122.56	125.18	127.81	130.46	133.13	135.82	138.52	141.24
7.00	100.00	102.38	104.79	107.21	109.66	112.13	114.63	117.14	119.67	122.22	124.80	127.38	129.99	132.61	135.25	137.91
7.25	97.67	100.00	102.35	104.72	107.11	109.53	111.96	114.42	116.89	119.38	121.89	124.42	126.97	129.53	132.11	134.70
7.50	95.43	97.71	100.00	102.32	104.65	107.01	109.39	111.79	114.21	116.64	119.10	121.57	124.05	126.56	129.08	131.61
7.75	93.27	95.49	97.74	100.00	102.28	104.59	106.91	109.26	111.62	114.00	116.40	118.81	121.25	123.69	126.15	128.63
8.00	91.19	93.36	95.55	97.77	100.00	102.25	104.53	106.82	109.13	111.45	113.80	116.16	118.54	120.93	123.34	125.76
8.25	89.18	91.30	93.45	95.61	97.80	100.00	102.22	104.46	106.72	109.00	111.29	113.60	115.92	118.26	120.62	122.99
8.50	87.24	89.32	91.41	93.53	95.67	97.83	100.00	102.19	104.40	106.63	108.87	111.13	113.40	115.69	118.00	120.31
8.75	85.37	87.40	89.45	91.53	93.62	95.73	97.85	100.00	102.16	104.34	106.54	108.75	110.97	113.21	115.46	117.73
9.00	83.56	85.55	87.56	89.59	91.64	93.70	95.78	97.88	100.00	102.13	104.28	106.44	108.62	110.81	113.02	115.24
9.25	81.82	83.76	85.73	87.72	89.72	91.74	93.78	95.84	97.91	100.00	102.10	104.22	106.35	108.50	110.66	112.83
9.50	80.13	82.04	83.97	85.91	87.87	89.85	91.85	93.87	95.89	97.94	100.00	102.07	104.16	106.27	108.38	110.51
9.75	78.50	80.37	82.26	84.17	86.09	88.03	89.99	91.96	93.95	95.95	97.97	100.00	102.05	104.11	106.18	108.26
10.00	76.93	78.76	80.61	82.48	84.36	86.26	88.18	90.11	92.06	94.03	96.00	97.99	100.00	102.02	104.05	106.09
10.25	75.41	77.20	79.02	80.85	82.69	84.56	86.44	88.33	90.24	92.17	94.10	96.06	98.02	100.00	101.99	103.99
10.50	73.93	75.70	77.47	79.27	81.08	82.91	84.75	86.61	88.48	90.37	92.27	94.18	96.11	98.05	100.00	101.96
10.75	72.51	74.24	75.98	77.74	79.52	81.31	83.12	84.94	86.78	88.63	90.49	92.37	94.26	96.16	98.07	100.00
11.00	71.13	72.83	74.54	76.26	78.01	79.76	81.54	83.32	85.13	86.94	88.77	90.61	92.47	94.33	96.21	98.10
11.25	69.80	71.46	73.14	74.83	76.54	78.27	80.01	81.76	83.53	85.31	87.11	88.91	90.73	92.56	94.41	96.26
11.50	68.51	70.14	71.79	73.45	75.13	76.82	78.53	80.25	81.98	83.73	85.49	87.27	89.05	90.85	92.66	94.48
11.75	67.26	68.86	70.47	72.11	73.76	75.42	77.09	78.78	80.49	82.20	83.93	85.67	87.43	89.19	90.97	92.75
12.00	66.04	67.62	69.20	70.81	72.43	74.06	75.70	77.36	79.04	80.72	82.42	84.13	85.85	87.58	89.33	91.08
12.25	64.87	66.41	67.97	69.55	71.14	72.74	74.36	75.99	77.63	79.29	80.95	82.63	84.32	86.03	87.74	89.46
12.50	63.73	65.25	66.78	68.33	69.89	71.46	73.05	74.65	76.27	77.89	79.53	81.18	82.84	84.52	86.20	87.89
12.75	62.63	64.12	65.62	67.14	68.68	70.23	71.79	73.36	74.95	76.55	78.16	79.78	81.41	83.05	84.71	86.37
13.00	61.56	63.02	64.50	66.00	67.50	69.03	70.56	72.11	73.67	75.24	76.82	78.41	80.02	81.63	83.26	84.89
13.25	60.52	61.96	63.41	64.88	66.37	67.86	69.37	70.89	72.42	73.97	75.52	77.09	78.67	80.25	81.85	83.46
13.50	59.51	60.93	62.36	63.80	65.26	66.73	68.21	69.71	71.22	72.73	74.26	75.81	77.36	78.92	80.49	82.07
13.75	58.53	59.92	61.33	62.75	64.19	65.63	67.09	68.56	70.04	71.54	73.04	74.56	76.08	77.62	79.17	80.72
14.00	57.58	58.95	60.34	61.73	63.14	64.57	66.00	67.45	68.91	70.38	71.86	73.35	74.85	76.36	77.88	79.41
14.25	56.66	58.01	59.37	60.74	62.13	63.53	64.94	66.37	67.80	69.25	70.71	72.17	73.65	75.14	76.63	78.14
14.50	55.76	57.09	58.43	59.78	61.15	62.53	63.92	65.32	66.73	68.15	69.59	71.03	72.48	73.95	75.42	76.90
14.75	54.89	56.20	57.52	58.85	60.19	61.55	62.92	64.30	65.69	67.09	68.50	69.92	71.35	72.79	74.24	75.70
15.00	54.04	55.33	56.63	57.94	59.26	60.60	61.95	63.30	64.67	66.05	67.44	68.84	70.25	71.67	73.09	74.53
15.25	53.22	54.49	55.77	57.06	58.36	59.68	61.00	62.34	63.69	65.05	66.41	67.79	69.18	70.58	71.98	73.39
15.50	52.42	53.67	54.93	56.20	57.48	58.78	60.08	61.40	62.73	64.07	65.41	66.77	68.14	69.51	70.90	72.29
15.75	51.64	52.87	54.11	55.36	56.63	57.90	59.19	60.49	61.80	63.11	64.44	65.78	67.13	68.48	69.84	71.22
16.00	50.88	52.09	53.32	54.55	55.80	57.05	58.32	59.60	60.89	62.19	63.50	64.81	66.14	67.47	68.82	70.17
16.25	50.14	51.34	52.54	53.76	54.99	56.23	57.48	58.74	60.01	61.29	62.58	63.87	65.18	66.50	67.82	69.15
16.50	49.42	50.60	51.79	52.99	54.20	55.42	56.65	57.89	59.15	60.41	61.68	62.96	64.25	65.54	66.85	68.16
16.75	48.72	49.88	51.06	52.24	53.43	54.64	55.85	57.08	58.31	59.55	60.81	62.07	63.34	64.62	65.90	67.20
17.00	48.04	49.19	50.34	51.51	52.69	53.87	55.07	56.28	57.49	58.72	59.95	61.20	62.45	63.71	64.98	66.26
17.25	47.38	48.51	49.65	50.80	51.96	53.13	54.31	55.50	56.70	57.91	59.13	60.35	61.59	62.83	64.08	65.34
17.50	46.73	47.84	48.97	50.10	51.25	52.40	53.57	54.74	55.92	57.12	58.32	59.53	60.75	61.97	63.21	64.45
17.75	46.10	47.20	48.31	49.43	50.56	51.69	52.84	54.00	55.17	56.35	57.53	58.73	59.93	61.14	62.35	63.58
18.00	45.49	46.57	47.66	48.77	49.88	51.01	52.14	53.28	54.43	55.59	56.76	57.94	59.13	60.32	61.52	62.73
18.25	44.89	45.96	47.03	48.12	49.22	50.33	51.45	52.58	53.72	54.86	56.02	57.18	58.35	59.53	60.71	61.90
18.50	44.30	45.36	46.42	47.50	48.58	49.68	50.78	51.89	53.02	54.15	55.29	56.43	57.59	58.75	59.92	61.10
18.75	43.73	44.77	45.82	46.88	47.96	49.04	50.13	51.23	52.33	53.45	54.57	55.71	56.85	57.99	59.15	60.31
19.00	43.17	44.20	45.24	46.29	47.35	48.41	49.49	50.57	51.67	52.77	53.88	55.00	56.12	57.25	58.39	59.54
20.00	41.07	42.05	43.04	44.04	45.04	46.06	47.08	48.11	49.15	50.20	51.26	52.32	53.39	54.47	55.55	56.65
25.00	32.97	33.76	34.55	35.35	36.16	36.97	37.80	38.63	39.46	40.30	41.15	42.00	42.86	43.73	44.60	45.47
30.00	27.50	28.16	28.82	29.49	30.16	30.84	31.53	32.22	32.91	33.62	34.32	35.04	35.75	36.47	37.20	37.93

Description: This table shows the yield to maturity of a mortgage purchased at the price shown in the index.

Example: The yield to maturity of a 10.75 %, 27 year mortgage at a price of 111.00 is 9.44 %.

INTEREST RATE, %

PRICE	7.00%	7.25%	7.50%	7.75%	8.00%	8.25%	8.50%	8.75%	9.00%	9.25%	9.50%	9.75%	10.00%	10.25%	10.50%	10.75%
175	1.86	2.05	2.24	2.43	2.62	2.80	2.99	3.18	3.36	3.55	3.73	3.91	4.10	4.28	4.46	4.64
170	2.09	2.29	2.48	2.67	2.86	3.05	3.24	3.43	3.62	3.80	3.99	4.18	4.36	4.54	4.73	4.91
165	2.34	2.53	2.73	2.92	3.12	3.31	3.50	3.69	3.88	4.07	4.26	4.45	4.64	4.82	5.01	5.19
160	2.60	2.79	2.99	3.19	3.38	3.58	3.77	3.97	4.16	4.35	4.54	4.73	4.92	5.11	5.30	5.49
155	2.86	3.06	3.26	3.46	3.66	3.86	4.06	4.25	4.45	4.64	4.84	5.03	5.23	5.42	5.61	5.80
150	3.14	3.35	3.55	3.75	3.95	4.15	4.35	4.55	4.75	4.95	5.15	5.35	5.54	5.74	5.93	6.13
145	3.44	3.64	3.85	4.05	4.26	4.46	4.67	4.87	5.07	5.27	5.48	5.68	5.88	6.08	6.28	6.47
140	3.75	3.96	4.16	4.37	4.58	4.79	5.00	5.20	5.41	5.62	5.82	6.02	6.23	6.43	6.63	6.84
135	4.07	4.28	4.50	4.71	4.92	5.13	5.34	5.56	5.77	5.97	6.18	6.39	6.60	6.81	7.01	7.22
130	4.41	4.63	4.85	5.07	5.28	5.50	5.71	5.93	6.14	6.36	6.57	6.78	6.99	7.21	7.42	7.63
125	4.78	5.00	5.22	5.44	5.66	5.88	6.10	6.32	6.54	6.76	6.98	7.20	7.41	7.63	7.85	8.06
120	5.16	5.39	5.62	5.84	6.07	6.29	6.52	6.74	6.97	7.19	7.41	7.64	7.86	8.08	8.30	8.52
119	5.25	5.47	5.70	5.93	6.15	6.38	6.60	6.83	7.05	7.28	7.50	7.73	7.95	8.18	8.40	8.62
118	5.33	5.55	5.78	6.01	6.24	6.46	6.69	6.92	7.14	7.37	7.60	7.82	8.05	8.27	8.49	8.72
117	5.41	5.64	5.87	6.10	6.32	6.55	6.78	7.01	7.23	7.46	7.69	7.91	8.14	8.37	8.59	8.82
116	5.49	5.72	5.95	6.18	6.41	6.64	6.87	7.10	7.33	7.55	7.78	8.01	8.24	8.46	8.69	8.92
115	5.58	5.81	6.04	6.27	6.50	6.73	6.96	7.19	7.42	7.65	7.88	8.11	8.34	8.56	8.79	9.02
114	5.66	5.89	6.13	6.36	6.59	6.82	7.05	7.28	7.51	7.75	7.98	8.21	8.44	8.66	8.89	9.12
113	5.75	5.98	6.22	6.45	6.68	6.91	7.15	7.38	7.61	7.84	8.07	8.30	8.54	8.77	9.00	9.23
112	5.84	6.07	6.31	6.54	6.77	7.01	7.24	7.47	7.71	7.94	8.17	8.41	8.64	8.87	9.10	9.33
111	5.93	6.16	6.40	6.63	6.87	7.10	7.34	7.57	7.81	8.04	8.27	8.51	8.74	8.98	9.21	9.44
110	6.02	6.25	6.49	6.73	6.96	7.20	7.43	7.67	7.91	8.14	8.38	8.61	8.85	9.08	9.32	9.55
109	6.11	6.35	6.58	6.82	7.06	7.30	7.53	7.77	8.01	8.24	8.48	8.72	8.95	9.19	9.43	9.66
108	6.20	6.44	6.68	6.92	7.16	7.40	7.63	7.87	8.11	8.35	8.59	8.83	9.06	9.30	9.54	9.77
107	6.29	6.54	6.78	7.02	7.26	7.50	7.74	7.98	8.22	8.46	8.69	8.93	9.17	9.41	9.65	9.89
106	6.39	6.63	6.87	7.12	7.36	7.60	7.84	8.08	8.32	8.56	8.80	9.04	9.28	9.53	9.77	10.01
105	6.49	6.73	6.97	7.22	7.46	7.70	7.94	8.19	8.43	8.67	8.91	9.16	9.40	9.64	9.88	10.12
104	6.59	6.83	7.07	7.32	7.56	7.81	8.05	8.30	8.54	8.78	9.03	9.27	9.51	9.76	10.00	10.24
103	6.69	6.93	7.18	7.42	7.67	7.91	8.16	8.41	8.65	8.90	9.14	9.39	9.63	9.88	10.12	10.37
102	6.79	7.03	7.28	7.53	7.78	8.02	8.27	8.52	8.76	9.01	9.26	9.50	9.75	10.00	10.24	10.49
101	6.89	7.14	7.39	7.64	7.88	8.13	8.38	8.63	8.88	9.13	9.38	9.62	9.87	10.12	10.37	10.62
100	7.00	7.25	7.50	7.75	8.00	8.25	8.50	8.75	9.00	9.25	9.50	9.75	10.00	10.25	10.50	10.75
99	7.10	7.35	7.60	7.86	8.11	8.36	8.61	8.86	9.11	9.37	9.62	9.87	10.12	10.37	10.62	10.88
98	7.21	7.46	7.72	7.97	8.22	8.47	8.73	8.98	9.23	9.49	9.74	9.99	10.25	10.50	10.75	11.01
97	7.32	7.57	7.83	8.08	8.34	8.59	8.85	9.10	9.36	9.61	9.87	10.12	10.38	10.63	10.89	11.14
96	7.43	7.69	7.94	8.20	8.46	8.71	8.97	9.23	9.48	9.74	10.00	10.25	10.51	10.77	11.02	11.28
95	7.54	7.80	8.06	8.32	8.58	8.83	9.09	9.35	9.61	9.87	10.13	10.38	10.64	10.90	11.16	11.42
94	7.66	7.92	8.18	8.44	8.70	8.96	9.22	9.48	9.74	10.00	10.26	10.52	10.78	11.04	11.30	11.56
93	7.78	8.04	8.30	8.56	8.82	9.08	9.35	9.61	9.87	10.13	10.39	10.66	10.92	11.18	11.45	11.71
92	7.90	8.16	8.42	8.69	8.95	9.21	9.48	9.74	10.00	10.27	10.53	10.80	11.06	11.33	11.59	11.86
91	8.02	8.28	8.55	8.81	9.08	9.34	9.61	9.87	10.14	10.41	10.67	10.94	11.21	11.47	11.74	12.01
90	8.14	8.41	8.67	8.94	9.21	9.48	9.74	10.01	10.28	10.55	10.82	11.08	11.35	11.62	11.89	12.16
89	8.27	8.54	8.80	9.07	9.34	9.61	9.88	10.15	10.42	10.69	10.96	11.23	11.50	11.77	12.05	12.32
88	8.40	8.67	8.94	9.21	9.48	9.75	10.02	10.29	10.56	10.84	11.11	11.38	11.66	11.93	12.20	12.48
87	8.53	8.80	9.07	9.34	9.62	9.89	10.16	10.44	10.71	10.99	11.26	11.54	11.81	12.09	12.36	12.64
86	8.66	8.93	9.21	9.48	9.76	10.03	10.31	10.58	10.86	11.14	11.42	11.69	11.97	12.25	12.53	12.81
85	8.80	9.07	9.35	9.62	9.90	10.18	10.46	10.74	11.01	11.29	11.57	11.85	12.13	12.41	12.70	12.98
84	8.93	9.21	9.49	9.77	10.05	10.33	10.61	10.89	11.17	11.45	11.73	12.02	12.30	12.58	12.87	13.15
83	9.07	9.35	9.64	9.92	10.20	10.48	10.76	11.05	11.33	11.61	11.90	12.18	12.47	12.75	13.04	13.33
82	9.22	9.50	9.78	10.07	10.35	10.64	10.92	11.21	11.49	11.78	12.07	12.35	12.64	12.93	13.22	13.51
81	9.37	9.65	9.94	10.22	10.51	10.79	11.08	11.37	11.66	11.95	12.24	12.53	12.82	13.11	13.40	13.69
80	9.51	9.80	10.09	10.38	10.67	10.96	11.25	11.54	11.83	12.12	12.41	12.70	13.00	13.29	13.59	13.88
79	9.67	9.96	10.25	10.54	10.83	11.12	11.41	11.71	12.00	12.30	12.59	12.89	13.18	13.48	13.78	14.07
78	9.82	10.12	10.41	10.70	11.00	11.29	11.59	11.88	12.18	12.48	12.77	13.07	13.37	13.67	13.97	14.27
77	9.98	10.28	10.57	10.87	11.17	11.46	11.76	12.06	12.36	12.66	12.96	13.26	13.56	13.87	14.17	14.47
76	10.15	10.44	10.74	11.04	11.34	11.64	11.94	12.24	12.55	12.85	13.15	13.46	13.76	14.07	14.37	14.68
75	10.31	10.61	10.91	11.22	11.52	11.82	12.12	12.43	12.73	13.04	13.35	13.66	13.96	14.27	14.58	14.89
74	10.48	10.79	11.09	11.39	11.70	12.01	12.31	12.62	12.93	13.24	13.55	13.86	14.17	14.48	14.80	15.11
73	10.66	10.96	11.27	11.58	11.89	12.20	12.51	12.82	13.13	13.44	13.75	14.07	14.38	14.70	15.02	15.33
70	11.21	11.52	11.84	12.15	12.47	12.79	13.11	13.43	13.75	14.08	14.40	14.73	15.05	15.38	15.71	16.04
65	12.22	12.55	12.88	13.22	13.55	13.89	14.23	14.57	14.91	15.26	15.60	15.95	16.29	16.64	16.99	17.34
60	13.37	13.73	14.08	14.44	14.80	15.16	15.52	15.88	16.25	16.61	16.98	17.35	17.72	18.10	18.47	18.84
55	14.71	15.09	15.47	15.86	16.24	16.63	17.02	17.41	17.80	18.20	18.59	18.99	19.39	19.80	20.20	20.61
50	16.29	16.70	17.12	17.53	17.95	18.37	18.79	19.22	19.65	20.08	20.51	20.95	21.38	21.82	22.26	22.71
45	18.20	18.65	19.10	19.56	20.01	20.48	20.94	21.41	21.88	22.36	22.83	23.31	23.80	24.28	24.77	25.26
40	20.55	21.05	21.55	22.06	22.57	23.09	23.60	24.13	24.65	25.19	25.72	26.26	26.80	27.34	27.89	28.44
35	23.53	24.10	24.67	25.25	25.83	26.42	27.01	27.60	28.20	28.81	29.41	30.03	30.64	31.26	31.88	32.51
30	27.49	28.15	28.81	29.48	30.16	30.84	31.52	32.22	32.92	33.62	34.33	35.04	35.76	36.48	37.21	37.94

Description: This table shows the price to pay for a monthly payment mortgage loan at the yield rate.

Example: The price of a 15.00 %, 27 year mortgage loan to yield 8.00 % to maturity is $ 168.74.

INTEREST RATE, %

YIELD	11.00%	11.25%	11.50%	11.75%	12.00%	12.25%	12.50%	12.75%	13.00%	13.25%	13.50%	13.75%	14.00%	14.25%	14.50%	15.00%
0.00	313.29	319.28	325.30	331.35	337.43	343.54	349.68	355.84	362.03	368.24	374.48	380.74	387.03	393.33	399.66	412.37
1.00	274.46	279.71	284.98	290.28	295.61	300.96	306.34	311.74	317.16	322.60	328.07	333.55	339.06	344.58	350.12	361.26
2.00	241.92	246.55	251.20	255.87	260.56	265.28	270.02	274.78	279.56	284.36	289.18	294.01	298.86	303.73	308.62	318.43
3.00	214.54	218.64	222.77	226.91	231.07	235.26	239.46	243.68	247.92	252.18	256.45	260.74	265.04	269.36	273.69	282.39
4.00	191.40	195.05	198.73	202.43	206.14	209.87	213.62	217.39	221.17	224.97	228.78	232.60	236.44	240.30	244.16	251.92
4.25	186.18	189.74	193.32	196.91	200.52	204.16	207.80	211.47	215.14	218.84	222.54	226.27	230.00	233.75	237.51	245.06
4.50	181.17	184.63	188.11	191.61	195.13	198.66	202.21	205.78	209.36	212.95	216.56	220.18	223.81	227.46	231.12	238.47
4.75	176.36	179.73	183.12	186.53	189.95	193.39	196.84	200.31	203.80	207.29	210.81	214.33	217.87	221.42	224.98	232.13
5.00	171.74	175.02	178.32	181.64	184.97	188.32	191.68	195.06	198.45	201.86	205.28	208.71	212.16	215.61	219.08	226.05
5.25	167.29	170.49	173.71	176.94	180.18	183.45	186.72	190.01	193.32	196.64	199.97	203.31	206.67	210.04	213.41	220.20
5.50	163.02	166.14	169.27	172.42	175.58	178.76	181.96	185.16	188.38	191.62	194.86	198.12	201.39	204.67	207.96	214.58
5.75	158.92	161.95	165.01	168.07	171.16	174.26	177.37	180.50	183.64	186.79	189.95	193.13	196.32	199.52	202.72	209.17
6.00	154.96	157.93	160.90	163.90	166.90	169.92	172.96	176.01	179.07	182.14	185.23	188.33	191.44	194.55	197.68	203.97
6.25	151.16	154.05	156.95	159.87	162.81	165.76	168.72	171.69	174.68	177.68	180.69	183.71	186.74	189.78	192.83	198.96
6.50	147.50	150.32	153.15	156.00	158.87	161.74	164.63	167.53	170.45	173.37	176.31	179.26	182.22	185.19	188.16	194.15
6.75	143.98	146.73	149.49	152.28	155.07	157.88	160.70	163.53	166.38	169.23	172.10	174.98	177.86	180.76	183.67	189.51
7.00	140.58	143.27	145.97	148.69	151.41	154.16	156.91	159.68	162.45	165.24	168.04	170.85	173.67	176.50	179.34	185.04
7.25	137.31	139.94	142.58	145.23	147.89	150.57	153.26	155.96	158.67	161.40	164.13	166.88	169.63	172.39	175.17	180.74
7.50	134.16	136.73	139.30	141.89	144.50	147.11	149.74	152.38	155.03	157.69	160.37	163.05	165.74	168.44	171.15	176.59
7.75	131.12	133.63	136.15	138.68	141.23	143.78	146.35	148.93	151.52	154.12	156.74	159.36	161.99	164.62	167.27	172.59
8.00	128.20	130.65	133.11	135.58	138.07	140.57	143.08	145.61	148.14	150.68	153.23	155.80	158.37	160.95	163.54	168.74
8.25	125.37	127.77	130.17	132.60	135.03	137.47	139.93	142.40	144.87	147.36	149.86	152.36	154.88	157.40	159.93	165.02
8.50	122.64	124.99	127.34	129.71	132.09	134.48	136.89	139.30	141.72	144.16	146.60	149.05	151.51	153.98	156.45	161.43
8.75	120.01	122.31	124.61	126.93	129.26	131.60	133.95	136.31	138.68	141.06	143.45	145.85	148.26	150.67	153.10	157.97
9.00	117.47	119.72	121.98	124.24	126.52	128.81	131.12	133.43	135.75	138.08	140.42	142.77	145.12	147.49	149.86	154.62
9.25	115.02	117.22	119.43	121.65	123.88	126.12	128.38	130.64	132.91	135.20	137.49	139.78	142.09	144.41	146.73	151.39
9.50	112.65	114.80	116.97	119.14	121.33	123.53	125.73	127.95	130.18	132.41	134.65	136.90	139.16	141.43	143.71	148.28
9.75	110.36	112.47	114.59	116.72	118.86	121.02	123.18	125.35	127.53	129.72	131.92	134.12	136.34	138.56	140.78	145.26
10.00	108.15	110.21	112.29	114.38	116.48	118.59	120.71	122.84	124.97	127.12	129.27	131.43	133.60	135.78	137.96	142.35
10.25	106.01	108.03	110.07	112.12	114.18	116.24	118.32	120.41	122.50	124.60	126.71	128.83	130.96	133.09	135.23	139.53
10.50	103.94	105.93	107.92	109.93	111.95	113.97	116.01	118.06	120.11	122.17	124.24	126.32	128.40	130.49	132.59	136.81
10.75	101.94	103.89	105.84	107.81	109.79	111.78	113.78	115.78	117.80	119.82	121.85	123.88	125.93	127.98	130.04	134.17
11.00	100.00	101.91	103.83	105.76	107.70	109.65	111.61	113.58	115.56	117.54	119.53	121.53	123.54	125.55	127.57	131.62
11.25	98.12	100.00	101.89	103.78	105.68	107.60	109.52	111.45	113.39	115.34	117.29	119.25	121.22	123.19	125.18	129.16
11.50	96.31	98.15	100.00	101.86	103.73	105.61	107.49	109.39	111.29	113.20	115.12	117.04	118.98	120.91	122.86	126.77
11.75	94.55	96.36	98.17	100.00	101.84	103.68	105.53	107.39	109.26	111.13	113.02	114.91	116.80	118.71	120.62	124.45
12.00	92.85	94.62	96.40	98.20	100.00	101.81	103.63	105.46	107.29	109.13	110.98	112.84	114.70	116.57	118.44	122.21
12.25	91.20	92.94	94.69	96.45	98.22	100.00	101.79	103.58	105.38	107.19	109.01	110.83	112.66	114.49	116.34	120.04
12.50	89.59	91.31	93.03	94.76	96.50	98.24	100.00	101.76	103.53	105.31	107.09	108.89	110.68	112.49	114.29	117.93
12.75	88.04	89.73	91.42	93.12	94.83	96.54	98.27	100.00	101.74	103.49	105.24	107.00	108.76	110.54	112.31	115.89
13.00	86.54	88.19	89.85	91.53	93.20	94.89	96.59	98.29	100.00	101.72	103.44	105.17	106.91	108.65	110.39	113.90
13.25	85.08	86.70	88.34	89.98	91.63	93.29	94.96	96.63	98.31	100.00	101.69	103.39	105.10	106.81	108.53	111.98
13.50	83.66	85.26	86.87	88.48	90.11	91.74	93.38	95.02	96.67	98.33	100.00	101.67	103.35	105.03	106.72	110.12
13.75	82.28	83.86	85.44	87.03	88.62	90.23	91.84	93.46	95.08	96.72	98.36	100.00	101.65	103.31	104.97	108.31
14.00	80.95	82.49	84.05	85.61	87.18	88.76	90.35	91.94	93.54	95.15	96.76	98.38	100.00	101.63	103.26	106.55
14.25	79.65	81.17	82.70	84.24	85.79	87.34	88.90	90.47	92.04	93.62	95.21	96.80	98.40	100.00	101.61	104.84
14.50	78.39	79.89	81.39	82.91	84.43	85.96	87.49	89.04	90.58	92.14	93.70	95.27	96.84	98.42	100.00	103.18
14.75	77.16	78.64	80.12	81.61	83.11	84.61	86.13	87.64	89.17	90.70	92.24	93.78	95.33	96.88	98.44	101.57
15.00	75.97	77.43	78.89	80.35	81.83	83.31	84.80	86.29	87.79	89.30	90.81	92.33	93.85	95.38	96.92	100.00
15.25	74.82	76.25	77.68	79.13	80.58	82.04	83.50	84.98	86.46	87.94	89.43	90.92	92.43	93.93	95.44	98.48
15.50	73.69	75.10	76.51	77.94	79.37	80.80	82.25	83.70	85.15	86.62	88.08	89.56	91.03	92.52	94.00	96.99
15.75	72.59	73.98	75.38	76.78	78.19	79.60	81.03	82.45	83.89	85.33	86.77	88.22	89.68	91.14	92.61	95.55
16.00	71.53	72.90	74.27	75.65	77.04	78.43	79.84	81.24	82.66	84.08	85.50	86.93	88.36	89.80	91.25	94.15
16.25	70.49	71.84	73.19	74.55	75.92	77.30	78.68	80.06	81.46	82.86	84.26	85.67	87.08	88.50	89.92	92.78
16.50	69.48	70.81	72.14	73.49	74.83	76.19	77.55	78.92	80.29	81.67	83.05	84.44	85.83	87.23	88.64	91.45
16.75	68.50	69.81	71.12	72.45	73.78	75.11	76.45	77.80	79.15	80.51	81.88	83.25	84.62	86.00	87.38	90.16
17.00	67.54	68.83	70.13	71.43	72.74	74.06	75.38	76.71	78.05	79.39	80.73	82.08	83.44	84.80	86.16	88.90
17.25	66.61	67.88	69.16	70.45	71.74	73.04	74.34	75.65	76.97	78.29	79.62	80.95	82.28	83.62	84.97	87.67
17.50	65.70	66.95	68.21	69.48	70.76	72.04	73.33	74.62	75.92	77.22	78.53	79.84	81.16	82.48	83.81	86.47
17.75	64.81	66.05	67.29	68.55	69.80	71.07	72.34	73.61	74.89	76.18	77.47	78.76	80.06	81.37	82.68	85.31
18.00	63.95	65.17	66.40	67.63	68.87	70.12	71.37	72.63	73.89	75.16	76.43	77.71	79.00	80.28	81.57	84.17
18.25	63.10	64.31	65.52	66.74	67.96	69.19	70.43	71.67	72.92	74.17	75.43	76.69	77.95	79.22	80.50	83.06
18.50	62.28	63.47	64.67	65.87	67.08	68.29	69.51	70.74	71.97	73.20	74.44	75.69	76.94	78.19	79.45	81.98
18.75	61.48	62.65	63.83	65.02	66.21	67.41	68.62	69.83	71.04	72.26	73.49	74.71	75.95	77.18	78.43	80.92
19.00	60.69	61.85	63.02	64.19	65.37	66.55	67.74	68.94	70.14	71.34	72.55	73.76	74.98	76.20	77.43	79.89
20.00	57.74	58.85	59.96	61.07	62.19	63.32	64.45	65.59	66.73	67.87	69.02	70.18	71.33	72.50	73.66	76.00
25.00	46.36	47.24	48.13	49.03	49.93	50.83	51.74	52.65	53.57	54.49	55.41	56.34	57.27	58.20	59.13	61.01
30.00	38.67	39.40	40.15	40.89	41.64	42.40	43.16	43.92	44.68	45.45	46.22	46.99	47.77	48.54	49.32	50.89

MORTGAGE YIELD

Description: This table shows the yield to maturity of a mortgage purchased at the price shown in the index.

Example: The yield to maturity of a 15.00 %, 27 year mortgage at a price of 125.00 is 11.68 %.

INTEREST RATE, %

PRICE	11.00%	11.25%	11.50%	11.75%	12.00%	12.25%	12.50%	12.75%	13.00%	13.25%	13.50%	13.75%	14.00%	14.25%	14.50%	15.00%
250	1.73	1.88	2.03	2.18	2.33	2.48	2.63	2.78	2.92	3.07	3.21	3.36	3.50	3.64	3.78	4.06
240	2.06	2.21	2.37	2.52	2.67	2.83	2.98	3.13	3.27	3.42	3.57	3.72	3.86	4.01	4.15	4.44
230	2.41	2.57	2.72	2.88	3.03	3.19	3.34	3.49	3.65	3.80	3.95	4.10	4.25	4.39	4.54	4.83
220	2.78	2.94	3.10	3.26	3.42	3.58	3.73	3.89	4.04	4.20	4.35	4.50	4.65	4.81	4.96	5.25
210	3.18	3.34	3.51	3.67	3.83	3.99	4.15	4.31	4.47	4.62	4.78	4.94	5.09	5.25	5.40	5.71
200	3.60	3.77	3.94	4.10	4.27	4.43	4.60	4.76	4.92	5.08	5.24	5.40	5.56	5.72	5.88	6.19
195	3.83	4.00	4.17	4.33	4.50	4.67	4.83	5.00	5.16	5.33	5.49	5.65	5.81	5.97	6.13	6.45
190	4.06	4.23	4.40	4.57	4.74	4.91	5.08	5.25	5.41	5.58	5.74	5.91	6.07	6.23	6.40	6.72
185	4.30	4.48	4.65	4.82	4.99	5.16	5.33	5.50	5.67	5.84	6.01	6.17	6.34	6.51	6.67	7.00
180	4.55	4.73	4.91	5.08	5.25	5.43	5.60	5.77	5.94	6.11	6.28	6.45	6.62	6.79	6.96	7.29
175	4.82	5.00	5.17	5.35	5.53	5.70	5.88	6.05	6.23	6.40	6.57	6.74	6.91	7.09	7.26	7.59
170	5.09	5.27	5.45	5.63	5.81	5.99	6.17	6.35	6.52	6.70	6.87	7.05	7.22	7.40	7.57	7.91
165	5.38	5.56	5.75	5.93	6.11	6.29	6.47	6.65	6.83	7.01	7.19	7.37	7.54	7.72	7.90	8.25
160	5.68	5.86	6.05	6.24	6.42	6.61	6.79	6.97	7.16	7.34	7.52	7.70	7.88	8.06	8.24	8.60
155	5.99	6.18	6.37	6.56	6.75	6.94	7.12	7.31	7.50	7.68	7.87	8.05	8.24	8.42	8.60	8.97
150	6.32	6.52	6.71	6.90	7.09	7.29	7.48	7.67	7.86	8.05	8.23	8.42	8.61	8.80	8.98	9.36
145	6.67	6.87	7.07	7.26	7.46	7.65	7.85	8.04	8.24	8.43	8.62	8.81	9.00	9.20	9.39	9.77
140	7.04	7.24	7.44	7.64	7.84	8.04	8.24	8.44	8.64	8.83	9.03	9.23	9.42	9.62	9.81	10.20
135	7.43	7.63	7.84	8.04	8.25	8.45	8.65	8.86	9.06	9.26	9.46	9.67	9.87	10.07	10.27	10.67
130	7.84	8.05	8.26	8.47	8.68	8.89	9.10	9.30	9.51	9.72	9.93	10.13	10.34	10.54	10.75	11.16
125	8.28	8.49	8.71	8.92	9.14	9.35	9.57	9.78	9.99	10.20	10.42	10.63	10.84	11.05	11.26	11.68
120	8.75	8.97	9.19	9.41	9.63	9.85	10.07	10.29	10.51	10.73	10.94	11.16	11.38	11.60	11.82	12.25
115	9.25	9.47	9.70	9.93	10.15	10.38	10.61	10.83	11.06	11.28	11.51	11.73	11.96	12.18	12.41	12.86
113	9.46	9.69	9.92	10.15	10.38	10.60	10.83	11.06	11.29	11.52	11.75	11.98	12.20	12.43	12.66	13.11
112	9.57	9.80	10.03	10.26	10.49	10.72	10.95	11.18	11.41	11.64	11.87	12.10	12.33	12.56	12.79	13.24
111	9.67	9.91	10.14	10.37	10.60	10.84	11.07	11.30	11.53	11.76	11.99	12.22	12.45	12.68	12.92	13.38
110	9.79	10.02	10.25	10.49	10.72	10.95	11.19	11.42	11.65	11.89	12.12	12.35	12.58	12.82	13.05	13.51
109	9.90	10.13	10.37	10.60	10.84	11.07	11.31	11.54	11.78	12.01	12.25	12.48	12.71	12.95	13.18	13.65
108	10.01	10.25	10.49	10.72	10.96	11.20	11.43	11.67	11.90	12.14	12.38	12.61	12.85	13.08	13.32	13.79
107	10.13	10.37	10.60	10.84	11.08	11.32	11.56	11.79	12.03	12.27	12.51	12.74	12.98	13.22	13.46	13.93
106	10.25	10.49	10.73	10.97	11.21	11.45	11.68	11.92	12.16	12.40	12.64	12.88	13.12	13.36	13.60	14.07
105	10.37	10.61	10.85	11.09	11.33	11.57	11.81	12.06	12.30	12.54	12.78	13.02	13.26	13.50	13.74	14.22
104	10.49	10.73	10.97	11.22	11.46	11.70	11.95	12.19	12.43	12.67	12.92	13.16	13.40	13.64	13.89	14.37
103	10.61	10.86	11.10	11.35	11.59	11.83	12.08	12.32	12.57	12.81	13.06	13.30	13.55	13.79	14.03	14.52
102	10.74	10.98	11.23	11.48	11.72	11.97	12.22	12.46	12.71	12.95	13.20	13.45	13.69	13.94	14.19	14.68
101	10.86	11.11	11.36	11.61	11.86	12.11	12.35	12.60	12.85	13.10	13.35	13.59	13.84	14.09	14.34	14.83
100	11.00	11.25	11.50	11.75	12.00	12.25	12.50	12.75	13.00	13.25	13.50	13.75	14.00	14.25	14.50	15.00
99	11.13	11.38	11.63	11.88	12.13	12.39	12.64	12.89	13.14	13.39	13.65	13.90	14.15	14.40	14.65	15.16
98	11.26	11.52	11.77	12.02	12.28	12.53	12.78	13.04	13.29	13.55	13.80	14.05	14.31	14.56	14.82	15.32
97	11.40	11.65	11.91	12.17	12.42	12.68	12.93	13.19	13.44	13.70	13.96	14.21	14.47	14.73	14.98	15.49
96	11.54	11.80	12.05	12.31	12.57	12.83	13.08	13.34	13.60	13.86	14.12	14.37	14.63	14.89	15.15	15.67
95	11.68	11.94	12.20	12.46	12.72	12.98	13.24	13.50	13.76	14.02	14.28	14.54	14.80	15.06	15.32	15.84
94	11.82	12.09	12.35	12.61	12.87	13.13	13.40	13.66	13.92	14.18	14.44	14.71	14.97	15.23	15.50	16.02
93	11.97	12.24	12.50	12.76	13.03	13.29	13.56	13.82	14.08	14.35	14.61	14.88	15.14	15.41	15.67	16.20
92	12.12	12.39	12.65	12.92	13.19	13.45	13.72	13.99	14.25	14.52	14.79	15.05	15.32	15.59	15.86	16.39
91	12.28	12.54	12.81	13.08	13.35	13.62	13.88	14.15	14.42	14.69	14.96	15.23	15.50	15.77	16.04	16.58
90	12.43	12.70	12.97	13.24	13.51	13.78	14.05	14.33	14.60	14.87	15.14	15.41	15.69	15.96	16.23	16.78
89	12.59	12.86	13.13	13.41	13.68	13.95	14.23	14.50	14.78	15.05	15.32	15.60	15.87	16.15	16.42	16.97
88	12.75	13.03	13.30	13.58	13.85	14.13	14.40	14.68	14.96	15.23	15.51	15.79	16.07	16.34	16.62	17.18
87	12.92	13.19	13.47	13.75	14.03	14.31	14.58	14.86	15.14	15.42	15.70	15.98	16.26	16.54	16.82	17.38
86	13.09	13.37	13.65	13.93	14.21	14.49	14.77	15.05	15.33	15.61	15.90	16.18	16.46	16.74	17.03	17.60
85	13.26	13.54	13.82	14.11	14.39	14.67	14.96	15.24	15.53	15.81	16.09	16.38	16.67	16.95	17.24	17.81
84	13.43	13.72	14.00	14.29	14.58	14.86	15.15	15.44	15.72	16.01	16.30	16.59	16.88	17.16	17.45	18.03
83	13.61	13.90	14.19	14.48	14.77	15.06	15.34	15.63	15.92	16.22	16.51	16.80	17.09	17.38	17.67	18.26
82	13.80	14.09	14.38	14.67	14.96	15.25	15.55	15.84	16.13	16.42	16.72	17.01	17.31	17.60	17.90	18.49
81	13.99	14.28	14.57	14.87	15.16	15.45	15.75	16.05	16.34	16.64	16.94	17.23	17.53	17.83	18.13	18.73
80	14.18	14.47	14.77	15.07	15.36	15.66	15.96	16.26	16.56	16.86	17.16	17.46	17.76	18.06	18.36	18.97
79	14.37	14.67	14.97	15.27	15.57	15.87	16.17	16.48	16.78	17.08	17.39	17.69	17.99	18.30	18.60	19.22
78	14.57	14.88	15.18	15.48	15.79	16.09	16.39	16.70	17.01	17.31	17.62	17.93	18.23	18.54	18.85	19.47
77	14.78	15.08	15.39	15.70	16.00	16.31	16.62	16.93	17.24	17.55	17.86	18.17	18.48	18.79	19.10	19.73
76	14.99	15.30	15.61	15.92	16.23	16.54	16.85	17.16	17.48	17.79	18.10	18.42	18.73	19.05	19.36	20.00
75	15.20	15.52	15.83	16.14	16.46	16.77	17.09	17.40	17.72	18.04	18.35	18.67	18.99	19.31	19.63	20.27
74	15.43	15.74	16.06	16.38	16.69	17.01	17.33	17.65	17.97	18.29	18.61	18.93	19.25	19.58	19.90	20.55
73	15.65	15.97	16.29	16.61	16.93	17.25	17.58	17.90	18.22	18.55	18.87	19.20	19.53	19.85	20.18	20.84
70	16.37	16.70	17.03	17.36	17.69	18.03	18.36	18.70	19.03	19.37	19.71	20.05	20.39	20.73	21.07	21.75
65	17.69	18.04	18.40	18.75	19.11	19.46	19.82	20.18	20.54	20.90	21.26	21.62	21.99	22.35	22.72	23.45
60	19.22	19.60	19.98	20.36	20.74	21.13	21.51	21.90	22.29	22.67	23.06	23.45	23.85	24.24	24.63	25.42
55	21.02	21.43	21.84	22.25	22.66	23.08	23.50	23.92	24.34	24.76	25.18	25.61	26.03	26.46	26.89	27.75

Description: This table shows the price to pay for a monthly payment mortgage loan at the yield rate.

Example: The price of a 6.75 %, 28 year mortgage loan to yield 8.00 % to maturity is $ 88.81.

INTEREST RATE, %

YIELD	0.00%	1.00%	2.00%	3.00%	4.00%	4.25%	4.50%	4.75%	5.00%	5.25%	5.50%	5.75%	6.00%	6.25%	6.50%	6.75%
0.00	100.00	114.69	130.68	147.93	166.39	171.19	176.06	180.99	186.00	191.07	196.21	201.42	206.68	212.01	217.40	222.84
1.00	87.19	100.00	113.94	128.98	145.07	149.26	153.50	157.81	162.17	166.59	171.07	175.61	180.20	184.85	189.55	194.29
2.00	76.52	87.77	100.00	113.20	127.33	131.00	134.72	138.50	142.33	146.21	150.15	154.13	158.16	162.23	166.36	170.53
3.00	67.60	77.53	88.34	100.00	112.48	115.72	119.01	122.35	125.74	129.17	132.64	136.16	139.72	143.32	146.96	150.64
4.00	60.10	68.93	78.54	88.90	100.00	102.88	105.81	108.78	111.79	114.83	117.92	121.05	124.21	127.42	130.65	133.93
4.25	58.41	67.00	76.34	86.41	97.20	100.00	102.84	105.73	108.65	111.62	114.62	117.66	120.73	123.85	126.99	130.17
4.50	56.80	65.15	74.23	84.02	94.51	97.23	100.00	102.80	105.65	108.53	111.45	114.40	117.39	120.42	123.48	126.57
4.75	55.25	63.37	72.20	81.73	91.93	94.58	97.27	100.00	102.77	105.57	108.41	111.28	114.19	117.14	120.11	123.12
5.00	53.76	61.66	70.26	79.53	89.46	92.04	94.65	97.31	100.00	102.73	105.49	108.29	111.12	113.98	116.88	119.81
5.25	52.34	60.03	68.39	77.42	87.08	89.59	92.14	94.73	97.35	100.00	102.69	105.41	108.17	110.96	113.78	116.63
5.50	50.97	58.45	66.60	75.39	84.80	87.25	89.73	92.24	94.80	97.38	100.00	102.65	105.34	108.05	110.80	113.57
5.75	49.65	56.94	64.88	73.45	82.61	84.99	87.41	89.86	92.35	94.87	97.42	100.00	102.61	105.26	107.93	110.64
6.00	48.38	55.49	63.23	71.57	80.51	82.83	85.18	87.57	89.99	92.45	94.93	97.45	100.00	102.58	105.18	107.82
6.25	47.17	54.10	61.64	69.78	78.48	80.75	83.04	85.37	87.73	90.13	92.55	95.00	97.49	100.00	102.54	105.11
6.50	46.00	52.76	60.11	68.05	76.54	78.74	80.98	83.26	85.56	87.89	90.26	92.65	95.07	97.52	100.00	102.51
6.75	44.87	51.47	58.64	66.38	74.67	76.82	79.00	81.22	83.47	85.74	88.05	90.38	92.75	95.14	97.56	100.00
7.00	43.79	50.23	57.23	64.78	72.87	74.97	77.10	79.26	81.45	83.68	85.93	88.21	90.51	92.84	95.20	97.59
7.25	42.75	49.03	55.87	63.24	71.14	73.19	75.27	77.38	79.52	81.69	83.88	86.11	88.36	90.64	92.94	95.27
7.50	41.75	47.88	54.56	61.76	69.47	71.47	73.50	75.56	77.65	79.77	81.92	84.09	86.29	88.51	90.76	93.04
7.75	40.78	46.78	53.30	60.33	67.86	69.82	71.80	73.82	75.86	77.93	80.02	82.15	84.29	86.47	88.66	90.89
8.00	39.85	45.71	52.08	58.96	66.31	68.23	70.17	72.14	74.13	76.15	78.20	80.27	82.37	84.50	86.64	88.81
8.25	38.96	44.68	50.91	57.63	64.82	66.69	68.59	70.51	72.46	74.44	76.44	78.47	80.52	82.60	84.70	86.82
8.50	38.10	43.69	49.78	56.35	63.39	65.22	67.07	68.95	70.86	72.79	74.75	76.73	78.74	80.77	82.82	84.89
8.75	37.26	42.74	48.70	55.12	62.00	63.79	65.60	67.44	69.31	71.20	73.11	75.05	77.02	79.00	81.01	83.04
9.00	36.46	41.82	47.65	53.93	60.67	62.41	64.19	65.99	67.82	69.66	71.54	73.44	75.36	77.30	79.26	81.25
9.25	35.68	40.93	46.63	52.79	59.38	61.09	62.83	64.59	66.37	68.18	70.02	71.87	73.75	75.65	77.58	79.52
9.50	34.94	40.07	45.66	51.68	58.13	59.81	61.51	63.23	64.98	66.75	68.55	70.37	72.21	74.07	75.95	77.85
9.75	34.21	39.24	44.71	50.61	56.93	58.57	60.24	61.93	63.64	65.38	67.13	68.91	70.72	72.54	74.38	76.25
10.00	33.52	38.44	43.80	49.58	55.77	57.38	59.01	60.66	62.34	64.04	65.76	67.51	69.27	71.06	72.87	74.69
10.25	32.84	37.67	42.92	48.59	54.65	56.22	57.82	59.44	61.09	62.76	64.44	66.15	67.88	69.63	71.40	73.19
10.50	32.19	36.92	42.07	47.62	53.57	55.11	56.68	58.27	59.88	61.51	63.17	64.84	66.54	68.25	69.99	71.74
10.75	31.56	36.20	41.25	46.69	52.52	54.03	55.57	57.13	58.71	60.31	61.93	63.57	65.23	66.92	68.62	70.34
11.00	30.95	35.50	40.45	45.79	51.51	52.99	54.50	56.03	57.58	59.15	60.74	62.35	63.98	65.63	67.29	68.98
11.25	30.37	34.83	39.68	44.92	50.53	51.98	53.46	54.96	56.48	58.02	59.58	61.16	62.76	64.38	66.01	67.67
11.50	29.80	34.17	38.94	44.08	49.58	51.01	52.46	53.93	55.42	56.93	58.46	60.01	61.58	63.17	64.78	66.40
11.75	29.24	33.54	38.22	43.26	48.66	50.06	51.49	52.93	54.40	55.88	57.38	58.90	60.44	62.00	63.58	65.17
12.00	28.71	32.93	37.52	42.47	47.77	49.15	50.55	51.96	53.40	54.86	56.33	57.83	59.34	60.87	62.42	63.98
12.25	28.19	32.34	36.84	41.71	46.91	48.26	49.64	51.03	52.44	53.87	55.32	56.79	58.27	59.77	61.29	62.83
12.50	27.69	31.76	36.19	40.97	46.08	47.41	48.76	50.12	51.51	52.91	54.34	55.78	57.24	58.71	60.20	61.71
12.75	27.21	31.21	35.56	40.25	45.27	46.58	47.90	49.24	50.61	51.99	53.38	54.80	56.23	57.68	59.15	60.63
13.00	26.74	30.67	34.94	39.55	44.49	45.77	47.07	48.39	49.73	51.09	52.46	53.85	55.26	56.69	58.13	59.58
13.25	26.28	30.14	34.34	38.88	43.73	44.99	46.27	47.57	48.88	50.22	51.57	52.93	54.32	55.72	57.13	58.57
13.50	25.84	29.64	33.77	38.22	42.99	44.23	45.49	46.77	48.06	49.37	50.70	52.04	53.40	54.78	56.17	57.58
13.75	25.41	29.14	33.20	37.59	42.28	43.50	44.73	45.99	47.26	48.55	49.86	51.18	52.52	53.87	55.24	56.62
14.00	24.99	28.66	32.66	36.97	41.59	42.78	44.00	45.24	46.49	47.75	49.04	50.34	51.65	52.99	54.33	55.69
14.25	24.59	28.20	32.13	36.37	40.91	42.09	43.29	44.50	45.73	46.98	48.24	49.52	50.82	52.13	53.45	54.79
14.50	24.20	27.75	31.62	35.79	40.26	41.42	42.60	43.79	45.00	46.23	47.47	48.73	50.01	51.30	52.60	53.92
14.75	23.81	27.31	31.12	35.23	39.62	40.77	41.93	43.10	44.29	45.50	46.73	47.96	49.22	50.49	51.77	53.07
15.00	23.44	26.89	30.64	34.68	39.01	40.13	41.27	42.43	43.60	44.79	46.00	47.22	48.45	49.70	50.96	52.24
15.25	23.08	26.47	30.16	34.15	38.41	39.52	40.64	41.78	42.93	44.11	45.29	46.49	47.71	48.94	50.18	51.44
15.50	22.73	26.07	29.71	33.63	37.83	38.92	40.02	41.14	42.28	43.44	44.60	45.79	46.98	48.20	49.42	50.66
15.75	22.39	25.68	29.26	33.12	37.26	38.33	39.42	40.53	41.65	42.79	43.94	45.10	46.28	47.47	48.68	49.90
16.00	22.06	25.30	28.83	32.63	36.71	37.77	38.84	39.93	41.03	42.15	43.29	44.43	45.60	46.77	47.96	49.16
16.25	21.74	24.93	28.41	32.16	36.17	37.21	38.27	39.35	40.43	41.54	42.65	43.78	44.93	46.09	47.26	48.44
16.50	21.42	24.57	28.00	31.69	35.65	36.68	37.72	38.78	39.85	40.94	42.04	43.15	44.28	45.42	46.58	47.74
16.75	21.12	24.22	27.60	31.24	35.14	36.15	37.18	38.23	39.28	40.35	41.44	42.54	43.65	44.78	45.91	47.06
17.00	20.82	23.88	27.21	30.80	34.65	35.65	36.66	37.69	38.73	39.79	40.86	41.94	43.04	44.15	45.27	46.40
17.25	20.53	23.55	26.83	30.37	34.16	35.15	36.15	37.16	38.19	39.23	40.29	41.36	42.44	43.53	44.64	45.76
17.50	20.25	23.23	26.46	29.96	33.70	34.67	35.65	36.65	37.67	38.69	39.73	40.79	41.85	42.93	44.02	45.13
17.75	19.98	22.91	26.10	29.55	33.24	34.20	35.17	36.16	37.16	38.17	39.20	40.23	41.29	42.35	43.43	44.52
18.00	19.71	22.60	25.75	29.15	32.79	33.74	34.70	35.67	36.66	37.66	38.67	39.69	40.73	41.78	42.84	43.92
18.25	19.45	22.30	25.41	28.77	32.36	33.29	34.24	35.20	36.17	37.16	38.16	39.17	40.19	41.23	42.28	43.34
18.50	19.19	22.01	25.08	28.39	31.93	32.85	33.79	34.74	35.70	36.67	37.66	38.66	39.67	40.69	41.72	42.77
18.75	18.94	21.73	24.76	28.02	31.52	32.43	33.35	34.29	35.24	36.20	37.17	38.16	39.15	40.16	41.18	42.21
19.00	18.70	21.45	24.44	27.66	31.12	32.01	32.92	33.85	34.78	35.73	36.69	37.67	38.65	39.65	40.66	41.67
20.00	17.79	20.40	23.25	26.31	29.60	30.45	31.32	32.20	33.09	33.99	34.90	35.83	36.76	37.71	38.67	39.64
25.00	14.27	16.37	18.65	21.11	23.75	24.43	25.13	25.83	26.55	27.27	28.00	28.75	29.50	30.26	31.03	31.80
30.00	11.90	13.65	15.55	17.61	19.80	20.37	20.95	21.54	22.14	22.74	23.35	23.97	24.60	25.23	25.87	26.52

Description: This table shows the yield to maturity of a mortgage purchased at the price shown in the index.

Example: The yield to maturity of a 6.75 %, 28 year mortgage at a price of 80.00 is 9.17 %.

INTEREST RATE, %

PRICE	0.00%	1.00%	2.00%	3.00%	4.00%	4.25%	4.50%	4.75%	5.00%	5.25%	5.50%	5.75%	6.00%	6.25%	6.50%	6.75%
100	0.00	1.00	2.00	3.00	4.00	4.25	4.50	4.75	5.00	5.25	5.50	5.75	6.00	6.25	6.50	6.75
99	.07	1.07	2.07	3.08	4.08	4.33	4.59	4.84	5.09	5.34	5.59	5.84	6.09	6.34	6.60	6.85
98	.14	1.15	2.15	3.16	4.17	4.42	4.68	4.93	5.18	5.44	5.69	5.94	6.19	6.45	6.70	6.95
97	.21	1.22	2.24	3.25	4.26	4.52	4.77	5.02	5.28	5.53	5.79	6.04	6.29	6.55	6.80	7.06
96	.29	1.30	2.32	3.34	4.36	4.61	4.87	5.12	5.38	5.63	5.89	6.14	6.40	6.65	6.91	7.17
95	.36	1.38	2.40	3.42	4.45	4.70	4.96	5.22	5.47	5.73	5.99	6.25	6.50	6.76	7.02	7.27
94	.44	1.46	2.49	3.51	4.54	4.80	5.06	5.32	5.58	5.83	6.09	6.35	6.61	6.87	7.13	7.39
93	.52	1.54	2.57	3.61	4.64	4.90	5.16	5.42	5.68	5.94	6.20	6.46	6.72	6.98	7.24	7.50
92	.60	1.63	2.66	3.70	4.74	5.00	5.26	5.52	5.78	6.04	6.30	6.57	6.83	7.09	7.35	7.61
91	.68	1.71	2.75	3.79	4.84	5.10	5.36	5.62	5.89	6.15	6.41	6.68	6.94	7.20	7.47	7.73
90	.76	1.80	2.84	3.89	4.94	5.20	5.47	5.73	5.99	6.26	6.52	6.79	7.05	7.32	7.58	7.85
89	.84	1.89	2.93	3.99	5.04	5.31	5.57	5.84	6.10	6.37	6.64	6.90	7.17	7.44	7.70	7.97
88	.93	1.97	3.03	4.08	5.15	5.41	5.68	5.95	6.21	6.48	6.75	7.02	7.29	7.56	7.83	8.10
87	1.01	2.06	3.12	4.19	5.25	5.52	5.79	6.06	6.33	6.60	6.87	7.14	7.41	7.68	7.95	8.22
86	1.10	2.16	3.22	4.29	5.36	5.63	5.90	6.17	6.44	6.71	6.99	7.26	7.53	7.80	8.08	8.35
85	1.19	2.25	3.32	4.39	5.47	5.74	6.02	6.29	6.56	6.83	7.11	7.38	7.66	7.93	8.21	8.48
84	1.28	2.34	3.42	4.50	5.59	5.86	6.13	6.41	6.68	6.96	7.23	7.51	7.78	8.06	8.34	8.61
83	1.37	2.44	3.52	4.61	5.70	5.97	6.25	6.53	6.80	7.08	7.36	7.63	7.91	8.19	8.47	8.75
82	1.46	2.54	3.62	4.72	5.82	6.09	6.37	6.65	6.93	7.21	7.48	7.76	8.04	8.33	8.61	8.89
81	1.55	2.64	3.73	4.83	5.94	6.21	6.49	6.77	7.05	7.33	7.62	7.90	8.18	8.46	8.75	9.03
80	1.65	2.74	3.83	4.94	6.06	6.34	6.62	6.90	7.18	7.46	7.75	8.03	8.32	8.60	8.89	9.17
79	1.75	2.84	3.94	5.06	6.18	6.46	6.75	7.03	7.31	7.60	7.88	8.17	8.46	8.75	9.03	9.32
78	1.85	2.95	4.06	5.18	6.31	6.59	6.88	7.16	7.45	7.74	8.02	8.31	8.60	8.89	9.18	9.47
77	1.95	3.05	4.17	5.30	6.43	6.72	7.01	7.30	7.59	7.87	8.16	8.46	8.75	9.04	9.33	9.63
76	2.05	3.16	4.28	5.42	6.57	6.85	7.14	7.43	7.73	8.02	8.31	8.60	8.90	9.19	9.49	9.78
75	2.15	3.27	4.40	5.54	6.70	6.99	7.28	7.57	7.87	8.16	8.46	8.75	9.05	9.35	9.65	9.94
74	2.26	3.39	4.52	5.67	6.84	7.13	7.42	7.72	8.01	8.31	8.61	8.91	9.21	9.51	9.81	10.11
73	2.37	3.50	4.65	5.80	6.98	7.27	7.57	7.87	8.16	8.46	8.76	9.06	9.37	9.67	9.97	10.28
72	2.48	3.62	4.77	5.94	7.12	7.42	7.72	8.02	8.32	8.62	8.92	9.22	9.53	9.83	10.14	10.45
71	2.59	3.74	4.90	6.07	7.26	7.57	7.87	8.17	8.47	8.78	9.08	9.39	9.70	10.01	10.31	10.63
70	2.71	3.86	5.03	6.21	7.41	7.72	8.02	8.33	8.63	8.94	9.25	9.56	9.87	10.18	10.49	10.81
69	2.83	3.99	5.16	6.36	7.57	7.87	8.18	8.49	8.80	9.11	9.42	9.73	10.04	10.36	10.67	10.99
68	2.95	4.11	5.30	6.50	7.72	8.03	8.34	8.65	8.96	9.28	9.59	9.91	10.22	10.54	10.86	11.18
67	3.07	4.24	5.44	6.65	7.88	8.19	8.51	8.82	9.14	9.45	9.77	10.09	10.41	10.73	11.05	11.38
66	3.19	4.38	5.58	6.80	8.05	8.36	8.68	8.99	9.31	9.63	9.95	10.27	10.60	10.92	11.25	11.58
65	3.32	4.52	5.73	6.96	8.22	8.53	8.85	9.17	9.49	9.81	10.14	10.46	10.79	11.12	11.45	11.78
64	3.45	4.66	5.88	7.12	8.39	8.71	9.03	9.35	9.68	10.00	10.33	10.66	10.99	11.32	11.66	11.99
63	3.59	4.80	6.03	7.29	8.56	8.89	9.21	9.54	9.87	10.20	10.53	10.86	11.20	11.53	11.87	12.21
62	3.72	4.94	6.19	7.45	8.75	9.07	9.40	9.73	10.06	10.40	10.73	11.07	11.41	11.75	12.09	12.43
61	3.87	5.10	6.35	7.63	8.93	9.26	9.59	9.93	10.26	10.60	10.94	11.28	11.62	11.97	12.31	12.66
60	4.01	5.25	6.51	7.80	9.12	9.46	9.79	10.13	10.47	10.81	11.15	11.50	11.84	12.19	12.54	12.89
59	4.16	5.41	6.68	7.99	9.32	9.66	10.00	10.34	10.68	11.03	11.37	11.72	12.07	12.43	12.78	13.14
58	4.31	5.57	6.86	8.17	9.52	9.86	10.21	10.55	10.90	11.25	11.60	11.95	12.31	12.67	13.03	13.39
57	4.46	5.74	7.04	8.37	9.73	10.08	10.42	10.77	11.13	11.48	11.84	12.19	12.55	12.92	13.28	13.65
56	4.62	5.91	7.22	8.57	9.94	10.29	10.65	11.00	11.36	11.72	12.08	12.44	12.80	13.17	13.54	13.91
55	4.79	6.08	7.41	8.77	10.17	10.52	10.88	11.24	11.60	11.96	12.33	12.69	13.06	13.44	13.81	14.19
54	4.95	6.26	7.60	8.98	10.39	10.75	11.11	11.48	11.84	12.21	12.58	12.96	13.33	13.71	14.09	14.47
53	5.13	6.45	7.81	9.20	10.63	10.99	11.36	11.73	12.10	12.47	12.85	13.23	13.61	13.99	14.38	14.77
52	5.31	6.64	8.01	9.42	10.87	11.24	11.61	11.99	12.36	12.74	13.12	13.51	13.89	14.28	14.68	15.07
51	5.49	6.84	8.23	9.65	11.12	11.50	11.87	12.25	12.64	13.02	13.41	13.80	14.19	14.59	14.98	15.38
50	5.68	7.04	8.45	9.89	11.38	11.76	12.14	12.53	12.92	13.31	13.70	14.10	14.50	14.90	15.30	15.71
49	5.87	7.25	8.67	10.14	11.65	12.04	12.42	12.82	13.21	13.61	14.01	14.41	14.82	15.22	15.64	16.05
48	6.07	7.47	8.91	10.40	11.93	12.32	12.72	13.11	13.51	13.92	14.32	14.73	15.15	15.56	15.98	16.40
47	6.28	7.69	9.15	10.66	12.22	12.62	13.02	13.42	13.83	14.24	14.65	15.07	15.49	15.91	16.34	16.77
46	6.49	7.93	9.41	10.94	12.52	12.92	13.33	13.74	14.16	14.57	14.99	15.42	15.85	16.28	16.71	17.15
45	6.72	8.17	9.67	11.22	12.83	13.24	13.66	14.07	14.50	14.92	15.35	15.78	16.22	16.66	17.10	17.55
44	6.95	8.42	9.94	11.52	13.15	13.57	14.00	14.42	14.85	15.28	15.72	16.16	16.61	17.05	17.51	17.96
43	7.18	8.68	10.22	11.83	13.49	13.92	14.35	14.78	15.22	15.66	16.11	16.56	17.01	17.47	17.93	18.39
42	7.43	8.94	10.52	12.15	13.84	14.28	14.72	15.16	15.61	16.06	16.51	16.97	17.43	17.90	18.37	18.84
41	7.69	9.22	10.82	12.48	14.21	14.65	15.10	15.55	16.01	16.47	16.93	17.40	17.87	18.35	18.83	19.32
40	7.96	9.52	11.14	12.83	14.60	15.05	15.50	15.97	16.43	16.90	17.37	17.85	18.34	18.82	19.31	19.81
39	8.23	9.82	11.47	13.20	15.00	15.46	15.93	16.40	16.87	17.35	17.84	18.33	18.82	19.32	19.82	20.33
35	9.47	11.18	12.97	14.85	16.82	17.32	17.83	18.35	18.87	19.40	19.94	20.48	21.02	21.57	22.13	22.69
30	11.40	13.31	15.33	17.47	19.72	20.30	20.89	21.49	22.09	22.70	23.32	23.94	24.57	25.21	25.86	26.51
25	13.99	16.20	18.56	21.07	23.73	24.42	25.12	25.83	26.55	27.28	28.01	28.76	29.51	30.28	31.05	31.83
20	17.72	20.41	23.29	26.39	29.70	30.56	31.43	32.31	33.21	34.11	35.03	35.96	36.90	37.85	38.82	39.79
15	23.77	27.29	31.10	35.21	39.61	40.75	41.91	43.09	44.28	45.49	46.71	47.95	49.21	50.47	51.76	53.05
10	35.71	40.96	46.67	52.83	59.42	61.13	62.87	64.64	66.42	68.24	70.07	71.93	73.81	75.71	77.64	79.58

Description: This table shows the price to pay for a monthly payment mortgage loan at the yield rate.

Example: The price of a 10.75 %, 28 year mortgage loan to yield 8.00 % to maturity is $ 126.27.

INTEREST RATE, %

YIELD	7.00%	7.25%	7.50%	7.75%	8.00%	8.25%	8.50%	8.75%	9.00%	9.25%	9.50%	9.75%	10.00%	10.25%	10.50%	10.75%
0.00	228.35	233.91	239.52	245.19	250.91	256.68	262.50	268.36	274.28	280.23	286.23	292.27	298.35	304.48	310.63	316.83
1.00	199.09	203.94	208.84	213.78	218.77	223.80	228.87	233.98	239.14	244.33	249.56	254.83	260.13	265.47	270.84	276.24
2.00	174.74	178.99	183.29	187.63	192.00	196.42	200.87	205.36	209.88	214.44	219.03	223.65	228.31	232.99	237.70	242.44
3.00	154.36	158.12	161.92	165.75	169.61	173.52	177.45	181.41	185.41	189.44	193.49	197.58	201.69	205.82	209.99	214.17
4.00	137.24	140.58	143.95	147.36	150.80	154.26	157.76	161.29	164.84	168.42	172.02	175.65	179.31	182.99	186.69	190.41
4.25	133.39	136.64	139.92	143.23	146.57	149.94	153.34	156.77	160.22	163.70	167.20	170.73	174.28	177.86	181.46	185.07
4.50	129.70	132.86	136.05	139.27	142.52	145.79	149.10	152.43	155.79	159.17	162.58	166.01	169.46	172.94	176.44	179.96
4.75	126.16	129.24	132.34	135.47	138.63	141.82	145.03	148.27	151.54	154.83	158.14	161.48	164.84	168.22	171.63	175.05
5.00	122.77	125.76	128.78	131.82	134.90	138.00	141.13	144.28	147.46	150.66	153.89	157.14	160.41	163.70	167.01	170.34
5.25	119.51	122.42	125.36	128.32	131.32	134.34	137.38	140.45	143.54	146.66	149.80	152.96	156.15	159.35	162.57	165.81
5.50	116.38	119.21	122.07	124.96	127.88	130.82	133.78	136.77	139.79	142.82	145.88	148.96	152.06	155.18	158.31	161.47
5.75	113.37	116.13	118.92	121.73	124.57	127.44	130.33	133.24	136.17	139.13	142.11	145.11	148.13	151.17	154.23	157.30
6.00	110.48	113.17	115.89	118.63	121.40	124.19	127.01	129.84	132.70	135.59	138.49	141.41	144.35	147.32	150.30	153.29
6.25	107.71	110.33	112.98	115.65	118.35	121.07	123.81	126.58	129.37	132.18	135.01	137.86	140.73	143.61	146.52	149.44
6.50	105.04	107.59	110.18	112.78	115.42	118.07	120.75	123.46	126.18	128.90	131.66	134.44	137.24	140.05	142.89	145.74
6.75	102.47	104.97	107.48	110.03	112.59	115.18	117.79	120.43	123.08	125.75	128.44	131.16	133.88	136.63	139.39	142.17
7.00	100.00	102.43	104.89	107.38	109.88	112.41	114.96	117.52	120.11	122.72	125.35	127.99	130.66	133.34	136.03	138.75
7.25	97.62	100.00	102.40	104.82	107.27	109.74	112.22	114.73	117.26	119.80	122.37	124.95	127.55	130.17	132.80	135.45
7.50	95.33	97.66	100.00	102.37	104.75	107.16	109.59	112.04	114.51	117.00	119.50	122.02	124.56	127.12	129.69	132.27
7.75	93.13	95.40	97.69	100.00	102.33	104.69	107.06	109.45	111.86	114.29	116.74	119.20	121.68	124.18	126.69	129.22
8.00	91.01	93.22	95.46	97.72	100.00	102.30	104.62	106.96	109.31	111.69	114.08	116.48	118.91	121.35	123.80	126.27
8.25	88.96	91.13	93.32	95.52	97.75	100.00	102.27	104.55	106.86	109.18	111.51	113.87	116.24	118.62	121.02	123.43
8.50	86.99	89.11	91.25	93.41	95.59	97.78	100.00	102.23	104.49	106.76	109.04	111.34	113.66	115.99	118.34	120.70
8.75	85.09	87.16	89.25	91.36	93.50	95.65	97.81	100.00	102.20	104.42	106.66	108.91	111.17	113.46	115.75	118.06
9.00	83.25	85.28	87.33	89.40	91.48	93.58	95.71	97.84	100.00	102.17	104.36	106.56	108.78	111.01	113.26	115.51
9.25	81.49	83.47	85.47	87.50	89.54	91.60	93.67	95.76	97.87	100.00	102.14	104.30	106.47	108.65	110.85	113.06
9.50	79.78	81.72	83.68	85.66	87.66	89.68	91.71	93.76	95.82	97.90	100.00	102.11	104.24	106.37	108.52	110.69
9.75	78.13	80.03	81.95	83.89	85.85	87.82	89.81	91.82	93.84	95.88	97.93	100.00	102.08	104.17	106.28	108.40
10.00	76.54	78.40	80.28	82.18	84.10	86.03	87.98	89.95	91.93	93.93	95.94	97.96	100.00	102.05	104.12	106.19
10.25	75.00	76.82	78.67	80.53	82.41	84.30	86.21	88.14	90.08	92.04	94.01	95.99	97.99	100.00	102.02	104.06
10.50	73.51	75.30	77.11	78.93	80.77	82.63	84.50	86.39	88.30	90.21	92.14	94.09	96.05	98.02	100.00	101.99
10.75	72.07	73.83	75.60	77.39	79.19	81.02	82.85	84.70	86.57	88.45	90.34	92.25	94.17	96.10	98.04	100.00
11.00	70.68	72.40	74.14	75.90	77.67	79.45	81.25	83.07	84.90	86.74	88.60	90.47	92.35	94.25	96.15	98.07
11.25	69.34	71.03	72.73	74.45	76.19	77.94	79.71	81.49	83.29	85.09	86.92	88.75	90.60	92.46	94.33	96.21
11.50	68.04	69.70	71.37	73.06	74.76	76.48	78.21	79.96	81.72	83.50	85.29	87.09	88.90	90.72	92.56	94.40
11.75	66.78	68.41	70.05	71.71	73.38	75.07	76.77	78.48	80.21	81.95	83.71	85.47	87.25	89.04	90.84	92.65
12.00	65.56	67.16	68.77	70.40	72.04	73.69	75.37	77.05	78.75	80.46	82.18	83.91	85.66	87.42	89.19	90.96
12.25	64.38	65.95	67.53	69.13	70.74	72.37	74.01	75.66	77.33	79.01	80.70	82.40	84.12	85.84	87.58	89.33
12.50	63.24	64.78	66.33	67.90	69.48	71.08	72.69	74.32	75.96	77.60	79.27	80.94	82.62	84.32	86.02	87.74
12.75	62.13	63.64	65.17	66.71	68.27	69.84	71.42	73.02	74.62	76.24	77.88	79.52	81.17	82.84	84.52	86.20
13.00	61.05	62.54	64.04	65.56	67.09	68.63	70.18	71.75	73.33	74.93	76.53	78.15	79.77	81.41	83.05	84.71
13.25	60.01	61.47	62.95	64.44	65.94	67.46	68.99	70.53	72.08	73.65	75.22	76.81	78.41	80.02	81.64	83.27
13.50	59.00	60.44	61.89	63.35	64.83	66.32	67.83	69.34	70.87	72.41	73.96	75.52	77.09	78.67	80.26	81.86
13.75	58.02	59.43	60.86	62.30	63.75	65.22	66.70	68.19	69.69	71.20	72.73	74.26	75.81	77.36	78.93	80.50
14.00	57.07	58.46	59.86	61.28	62.71	64.15	65.60	67.07	68.55	70.04	71.54	73.05	74.57	76.10	77.63	79.18
14.25	56.15	57.51	58.89	60.29	61.69	63.11	64.54	65.99	67.44	68.90	70.38	71.86	73.36	74.86	76.38	77.90
14.50	55.25	56.59	57.95	59.32	60.71	62.10	63.51	64.93	66.36	67.80	69.25	70.72	72.19	73.67	75.16	76.66
14.75	54.38	55.70	57.04	58.39	59.75	61.13	62.51	63.91	65.32	66.73	68.16	69.60	71.05	72.51	73.97	75.45
15.00	53.53	54.84	56.15	57.48	58.82	60.17	61.54	62.91	64.30	65.70	67.10	68.52	69.94	71.38	72.82	74.27
15.25	52.71	53.99	55.29	56.60	57.92	59.25	60.59	61.95	63.31	64.69	66.07	67.46	68.87	70.28	71.70	73.13
15.50	51.91	53.17	54.45	55.74	57.04	58.35	59.67	61.01	62.35	63.70	65.07	66.44	67.82	69.22	70.62	72.02
15.75	51.13	52.38	53.63	54.90	56.18	57.48	58.78	60.09	61.42	62.75	64.09	65.45	66.81	68.18	69.56	70.94
16.00	50.38	51.60	52.84	54.09	55.35	56.63	57.91	59.20	60.51	61.82	63.15	64.48	65.82	67.17	68.53	69.89
16.25	49.64	50.85	52.07	53.30	54.54	55.80	57.06	58.34	59.62	60.92	62.22	63.54	64.86	66.19	67.53	68.87
16.50	48.92	50.11	51.32	52.53	53.76	54.99	56.24	57.50	58.76	60.04	61.33	62.62	63.92	65.23	66.55	67.88
16.75	48.23	49.40	50.59	51.78	52.99	54.21	55.44	56.68	57.93	59.18	60.45	61.73	63.01	64.30	65.60	66.91
17.00	47.55	48.71	49.87	51.05	52.25	53.45	54.66	55.88	57.11	58.35	59.60	60.86	62.12	63.40	64.68	65.97
17.25	46.89	48.03	49.18	50.34	51.52	52.70	53.90	55.10	56.32	57.54	58.77	60.01	61.26	62.52	63.78	65.05
17.50	46.24	47.37	48.51	49.65	50.81	51.98	53.16	54.35	55.54	56.75	57.96	59.19	60.42	61.66	62.91	64.16
17.75	45.61	46.73	47.85	48.98	50.12	51.27	52.44	53.61	54.79	55.98	57.18	58.38	59.60	60.82	62.05	63.29
18.00	45.00	46.10	47.21	48.32	49.45	50.59	51.73	52.89	54.05	55.23	56.41	57.60	58.80	60.01	61.22	62.44
18.25	44.41	45.49	46.58	47.68	48.79	49.92	51.05	52.19	53.34	54.50	55.66	56.84	58.02	59.21	60.41	61.61
18.50	43.82	44.89	45.97	47.06	48.15	49.26	50.38	51.50	52.64	53.78	54.93	56.09	57.26	58.43	59.62	60.81
18.75	43.26	44.31	45.37	46.45	47.53	48.62	49.73	50.84	51.96	53.09	54.22	55.37	56.52	57.68	58.84	60.02
19.00	42.70	43.74	44.79	45.85	46.92	48.00	49.09	50.19	51.29	52.41	53.53	54.66	55.80	56.94	58.09	59.25
20.00	40.62	41.61	42.61	43.61	44.63	45.66	46.69	47.74	48.79	49.85	50.91	51.99	53.07	54.16	55.26	56.36
25.00	32.59	33.38	34.18	34.99	35.81	36.63	37.46	38.30	39.14	39.99	40.85	41.71	42.58	43.45	44.33	45.22
30.00	27.18	27.84	28.51	29.18	29.86	30.55	31.24	31.94	32.64	33.35	34.07	34.79	35.51	36.24	36.97	37.71

Description: This table shows the yield to maturity of a mortgage purchased at the price shown in the index.

Example: The yield to maturity of a 10.75 %, 28 year mortgage at a price of 111.00 is 9.46 %.

INTEREST RATE, %

PRICE	7.00%	7.25%	7.50%	7.75%	8.00%	8.25%	8.50%	8.75%	9.00%	9.25%	9.50%	9.75%	10.00%	10.25%	10.50%	10.75%
175	1.98	2.17	2.36	2.55	2.74	2.92	3.11	3.30	3.48	3.66	3.85	4.03	4.21	4.39	4.57	4.75
170	2.21	2.40	2.60	2.79	2.98	3.17	3.35	3.54	3.73	3.91	4.10	4.28	4.47	4.65	4.83	5.01
165	2.45	2.65	2.84	3.03	3.22	3.42	3.61	3.80	3.99	4.17	4.36	4.55	4.74	4.92	5.11	5.29
160	2.70	2.90	3.09	3.29	3.48	3.68	3.87	4.07	4.26	4.45	4.64	4.83	5.02	5.21	5.39	5.58
155	2.96	3.16	3.36	3.56	3.76	3.95	4.15	4.35	4.54	4.73	4.93	5.12	5.31	5.51	5.70	5.89
150	3.23	3.44	3.64	3.84	4.04	4.24	4.44	4.64	4.84	5.04	5.23	5.43	5.62	5.82	6.01	6.21
145	3.52	3.73	3.93	4.14	4.34	4.54	4.75	4.95	5.15	5.35	5.55	5.75	5.95	6.15	6.35	6.55
140	3.82	4.03	4.24	4.45	4.66	4.86	5.07	5.28	5.48	5.69	5.89	6.09	6.30	6.50	6.70	6.90
135	4.14	4.35	4.56	4.78	4.99	5.20	5.41	5.62	5.83	6.04	6.25	6.45	6.66	6.87	7.07	7.28
130	4.47	4.69	4.91	5.12	5.34	5.55	5.77	5.98	6.20	6.41	6.62	6.84	7.05	7.26	7.47	7.68
125	4.83	5.05	5.27	5.49	5.71	5.93	6.15	6.37	6.59	6.81	7.02	7.24	7.46	7.67	7.89	8.11
120	5.21	5.43	5.66	5.88	6.11	6.33	6.56	6.78	7.00	7.23	7.45	7.67	7.90	8.12	8.34	8.56
119	5.28	5.51	5.74	5.96	6.19	6.42	6.64	6.87	7.09	7.32	7.54	7.76	7.99	8.21	8.43	8.65
118	5.36	5.59	5.82	6.05	6.27	6.50	6.73	6.95	7.18	7.40	7.63	7.85	8.08	8.30	8.53	8.75
117	5.44	5.67	5.90	6.13	6.36	6.59	6.81	7.04	7.27	7.49	7.72	7.95	8.17	8.40	8.62	8.85
116	5.53	5.76	5.99	6.22	6.44	6.67	6.90	7.13	7.36	7.59	7.81	8.04	8.27	8.49	8.72	8.95
115	5.61	5.84	6.07	6.30	6.53	6.76	6.99	7.22	7.45	7.68	7.91	8.14	8.36	8.59	8.82	9.05
114	5.69	5.92	6.16	6.39	6.62	6.85	7.08	7.31	7.54	7.77	8.00	8.23	8.46	8.69	8.92	9.15
113	5.78	6.01	6.24	6.48	6.71	6.94	7.17	7.40	7.64	7.87	8.10	8.33	8.56	8.79	9.02	9.25
112	5.86	6.10	6.33	6.57	6.80	7.03	7.27	7.50	7.73	7.96	8.20	8.43	8.66	8.89	9.12	9.36
111	5.95	6.19	6.42	6.66	6.89	7.13	7.36	7.59	7.83	8.06	8.30	8.53	8.76	9.00	9.23	9.46
110	6.04	6.27	6.51	6.75	6.98	7.22	7.46	7.69	7.93	8.16	8.40	8.63	8.87	9.10	9.34	9.57
109	6.13	6.37	6.60	6.84	7.08	7.32	7.55	7.79	8.03	8.26	8.50	8.74	8.97	9.21	9.44	9.68
108	6.22	6.46	6.70	6.94	7.17	7.41	7.65	7.89	8.13	8.37	8.60	8.84	9.08	9.32	9.55	9.79
107	6.31	6.55	6.79	7.03	7.27	7.51	7.75	7.99	8.23	8.47	8.71	8.95	9.19	9.43	9.66	9.90
106	6.40	6.65	6.89	7.13	7.37	7.61	7.85	8.09	8.33	8.57	8.82	9.06	9.30	9.54	9.78	10.02
105	6.50	6.74	6.98	7.23	7.47	7.71	7.96	8.20	8.44	8.68	8.92	9.17	9.41	9.65	9.89	10.13
104	6.59	6.84	7.08	7.33	7.57	7.82	8.06	8.30	8.55	8.79	9.03	9.28	9.52	9.77	10.01	10.25
103	6.69	6.94	7.18	7.43	7.68	7.92	8.17	8.41	8.66	8.90	9.15	9.39	9.64	9.88	10.13	10.37
102	6.79	7.04	7.29	7.53	7.78	8.03	8.27	8.52	8.77	9.01	9.26	9.51	9.75	10.00	10.25	10.49
101	6.89	7.14	7.39	7.64	7.89	8.14	8.38	8.63	8.88	9.13	9.38	9.63	9.87	10.12	10.37	10.62
100	7.00	7.25	7.50	7.75	8.00	8.25	8.50	8.75	9.00	9.25	9.50	9.75	10.00	10.25	10.50	10.75
99	7.10	7.35	7.60	7.85	8.11	8.36	8.61	8.86	9.11	9.36	9.61	9.87	10.12	10.37	10.62	10.87
98	7.20	7.46	7.71	7.96	8.22	8.47	8.72	8.98	9.23	9.48	9.74	9.99	10.24	10.50	10.75	11.00
97	7.31	7.57	7.82	8.08	8.33	8.59	8.84	9.10	9.35	9.61	9.86	10.12	10.37	10.63	10.88	11.14
96	7.42	7.68	7.93	8.19	8.45	8.70	8.96	9.22	9.47	9.73	9.99	10.24	10.50	10.76	11.02	11.27
95	7.53	7.79	8.05	8.31	8.56	8.82	9.08	9.34	9.60	9.86	10.12	10.37	10.63	10.89	11.15	11.41
94	7.65	7.90	8.16	8.42	8.68	8.94	9.20	9.46	9.72	9.99	10.25	10.51	10.77	11.03	11.29	11.55
93	7.76	8.02	8.28	8.54	8.81	9.07	9.33	9.59	9.85	10.12	10.38	10.64	10.91	11.17	11.43	11.69
92	7.88	8.14	8.40	8.67	8.93	9.19	9.46	9.72	9.99	10.25	10.51	10.78	11.04	11.31	11.58	11.84
91	8.00	8.26	8.53	8.79	9.06	9.32	9.59	9.85	10.12	10.39	10.65	10.92	11.19	11.45	11.72	11.99
90	8.12	8.38	8.65	8.92	9.18	9.45	9.72	9.99	10.26	10.52	10.79	11.06	11.33	11.60	11.87	12.14
89	8.24	8.51	8.78	9.05	9.32	9.59	9.85	10.13	10.40	10.67	10.94	11.21	11.48	11.75	12.02	12.30
88	8.37	8.64	8.91	9.18	9.45	9.72	9.99	10.26	10.54	10.81	11.08	11.36	11.63	11.90	12.18	12.45
87	8.49	8.77	9.04	9.31	9.59	9.86	10.13	10.41	10.68	10.96	11.23	11.51	11.78	12.06	12.34	12.61
86	8.62	8.90	9.17	9.45	9.72	10.00	10.28	10.55	10.83	11.11	11.38	11.66	11.94	12.22	12.50	12.78
85	8.76	9.03	9.31	9.59	9.87	10.14	10.42	10.70	10.98	11.26	11.54	11.82	12.10	12.38	12.66	12.95
84	8.89	9.17	9.45	9.73	10.01	10.29	10.57	10.85	11.13	11.42	11.70	11.98	12.26	12.55	12.83	13.12
83	9.03	9.31	9.59	9.87	10.16	10.44	10.72	11.01	11.29	11.57	11.86	12.15	12.43	12.72	13.00	13.29
82	9.17	9.45	9.74	10.02	10.31	10.59	10.88	11.16	11.45	11.74	12.02	12.31	12.60	12.89	13.18	13.47
81	9.32	9.60	9.89	10.17	10.46	10.75	11.04	11.32	11.61	11.90	12.19	12.48	12.78	13.07	13.36	13.65
80	9.46	9.75	10.04	10.33	10.62	10.91	11.20	11.49	11.78	12.07	12.37	12.66	12.95	13.25	13.54	13.84
79	9.61	9.90	10.19	10.48	10.78	11.07	11.36	11.66	11.95	12.25	12.54	12.84	13.14	13.43	13.73	14.03
78	9.76	10.06	10.35	10.65	10.94	11.24	11.53	11.83	12.13	12.42	12.72	13.02	13.32	13.62	13.92	14.23
77	9.92	10.22	10.51	10.81	11.11	11.41	11.70	12.00	12.30	12.61	12.91	13.21	13.51	13.82	14.12	14.43
76	10.08	10.38	10.68	10.98	11.28	11.58	11.88	12.18	12.49	12.79	13.10	13.40	13.71	14.01	14.32	14.63
75	10.24	10.55	10.85	11.15	11.45	11.76	12.06	12.37	12.67	12.98	13.29	13.60	13.91	14.22	14.53	14.84
74	10.41	10.72	11.02	11.33	11.63	11.94	12.25	12.56	12.86	13.18	13.49	13.80	14.11	14.42	14.74	15.05
73	10.58	10.89	11.20	11.51	11.81	12.12	12.44	12.75	13.06	13.37	13.69	14.00	14.32	14.64	14.96	15.27
70	11.12	11.44	11.75	12.07	12.39	12.71	13.03	13.36	13.68	14.00	14.33	14.65	14.98	15.31	15.64	15.97
65	12.11	12.45	12.78	13.12	13.46	13.80	14.14	14.48	14.82	15.17	15.51	15.86	16.21	16.56	16.91	17.26
60	13.25	13.60	13.96	14.32	14.68	15.04	15.41	15.77	16.14	16.51	16.88	17.25	17.62	18.00	18.37	18.75
55	14.57	14.95	15.33	15.72	16.10	16.49	16.88	17.28	17.67	18.07	18.47	18.87	19.28	19.68	20.09	20.50
50	16.12	16.53	16.95	17.37	17.79	18.21	18.64	19.07	19.50	19.93	20.37	20.81	21.25	21.69	22.14	22.58
45	18.00	18.45	18.91	19.37	19.83	20.29	20.76	21.24	21.71	22.19	22.67	23.15	23.64	24.13	24.62	25.12
40	20.31	20.82	21.32	21.84	22.35	22.87	23.40	23.92	24.46	24.99	25.53	26.07	26.62	27.17	27.72	28.27
35	23.26	23.83	24.41	24.99	25.58	26.17	26.76	27.37	27.97	28.58	29.19	29.81	30.43	31.06	31.69	32.32
30	27.16	27.83	28.50	29.18	29.86	30.55	31.24	31.94	32.64	33.35	34.07	34.79	35.51	36.24	36.97	37.71

Description: This table shows the price to pay for a monthly payment mortgage loan at the yield rate.

Example: The price of a 15.00 %, 28 year mortgage loan to yield 8.00 % to maturity is $ 170.01.

INTEREST RATE, %

YIELD	11.00%	11.25%	11.50%	11.75%	12.00%	12.25%	12.50%	12.75%	13.00%	13.25%	13.50%	13.75%	14.00%	14.25%	14.50%	15.00%
0.00	323.06	329.32	335.62	341.94	348.30	354.69	361.10	367.55	374.01	380.51	387.02	393.56	400.12	406.70	413.30	426.57
1.00	281.67	287.13	292.62	298.14	303.68	309.25	314.84	320.46	326.10	331.76	337.44	343.14	348.86	354.60	360.35	371.92
2.00	247.21	252.00	256.82	261.66	266.53	271.42	276.32	281.25	286.20	291.17	296.16	301.16	306.18	311.22	316.27	326.42
3.00	218.39	222.62	226.88	231.15	235.45	239.77	244.10	248.46	252.83	257.22	261.62	266.05	270.48	274.93	279.39	288.36
4.00	194.16	197.92	201.70	205.51	209.33	213.17	217.02	220.89	224.78	228.68	232.60	236.53	240.47	244.43	248.39	256.36
4.25	188.71	192.37	196.05	199.75	203.46	207.19	210.94	214.70	218.48	222.27	226.08	229.90	233.73	237.58	241.43	249.18
4.50	183.50	187.05	190.63	194.22	197.83	201.46	205.11	208.76	212.44	216.13	219.83	223.54	227.27	231.01	234.76	242.29
4.75	178.49	181.95	185.43	188.92	192.44	195.97	199.51	203.07	206.64	210.23	213.83	217.44	221.07	224.70	228.35	235.68
5.00	173.69	177.05	180.44	183.84	187.26	190.69	194.14	197.60	201.08	204.57	208.07	211.59	215.12	218.66	222.21	229.34
5.25	169.07	172.35	175.65	178.96	182.29	185.63	188.99	192.36	195.74	199.14	202.55	205.97	209.41	212.85	216.31	223.25
5.50	164.65	167.84	171.05	174.27	177.51	180.77	184.04	187.32	190.62	193.93	197.25	200.58	203.92	207.28	210.64	217.40
5.75	160.39	163.50	166.63	169.77	172.93	176.10	179.28	182.48	185.69	188.92	192.15	195.40	198.65	201.92	205.20	211.78
6.00	156.31	159.34	162.38	165.44	168.52	171.61	174.71	177.83	180.96	184.10	187.25	190.42	193.59	196.78	199.97	206.39
6.25	152.38	155.33	158.30	161.29	164.29	167.30	170.32	173.36	176.41	179.48	182.55	185.63	188.73	191.83	194.95	201.20
6.50	148.60	151.48	154.38	157.29	160.21	163.15	166.10	169.07	172.04	175.03	178.02	181.03	184.05	187.08	190.11	196.21
6.75	144.97	147.78	150.61	153.45	156.30	159.16	162.04	164.93	167.84	170.75	173.67	176.61	179.55	182.51	185.47	191.42
7.00	141.48	144.22	146.98	149.75	152.53	155.33	158.14	160.96	163.79	166.63	169.49	172.35	175.22	178.11	181.00	186.80
7.25	138.11	140.79	143.48	146.19	148.91	151.64	154.38	157.13	159.90	162.67	165.46	168.25	171.06	173.87	176.69	182.36
7.50	134.87	137.49	140.12	142.76	145.41	148.08	150.76	153.45	156.15	158.86	161.58	164.31	167.05	169.80	172.55	178.09
7.75	131.76	134.31	136.88	139.46	142.05	144.66	147.27	149.90	152.54	155.19	157.84	160.51	163.19	165.87	168.56	173.97
8.00	128.75	131.25	133.76	136.28	138.81	141.36	143.92	146.48	149.06	151.65	154.25	156.85	159.47	162.09	164.72	170.01
8.25	125.86	128.30	130.75	133.22	135.69	138.18	140.68	143.19	145.71	148.24	150.78	153.33	155.88	158.45	161.02	166.19
8.50	123.07	125.46	127.85	130.26	132.69	135.12	137.56	140.02	142.48	144.95	147.44	149.93	152.43	154.93	157.45	162.50
8.75	120.38	122.71	125.06	127.42	129.79	132.17	134.56	136.96	139.37	141.79	144.21	146.65	149.10	151.55	154.01	158.95
9.00	117.79	120.07	122.36	124.67	126.99	129.32	131.66	134.01	136.36	138.73	141.11	143.49	145.88	148.28	150.69	155.52
9.25	115.28	117.52	119.76	122.02	124.29	126.57	128.86	131.16	133.46	135.78	138.11	140.44	142.78	145.13	147.49	152.22
9.50	112.87	115.05	117.25	119.46	121.69	123.92	126.16	128.41	130.67	132.94	135.21	137.50	139.79	142.09	144.39	149.03
9.75	110.53	112.68	114.83	116.99	119.17	121.36	123.55	125.75	127.97	130.19	132.42	134.65	136.90	139.15	141.41	145.95
10.00	108.28	110.38	112.49	114.61	116.74	118.88	121.03	123.19	125.36	127.53	129.72	131.91	134.11	136.32	138.53	142.97
10.25	106.10	108.16	110.23	112.31	114.39	116.49	118.60	120.71	122.84	124.97	127.11	129.26	131.41	133.58	135.74	140.10
10.50	104.00	106.02	108.04	110.08	112.13	114.18	116.25	118.32	120.40	122.49	124.59	126.70	128.81	130.93	133.05	137.32
10.75	101.97	103.94	105.93	107.93	109.93	111.95	113.97	116.01	118.05	120.10	122.16	124.22	126.29	128.37	130.45	134.64
11.00	100.00	101.94	103.89	105.85	107.81	109.79	111.78	113.77	115.77	117.78	119.80	121.82	123.85	125.89	127.94	132.04
11.25	98.10	100.00	101.91	103.83	105.76	107.70	109.65	111.61	113.57	115.54	117.52	119.51	121.50	123.50	125.50	129.53
11.50	96.26	98.12	100.00	101.89	103.78	105.68	107.59	109.51	111.44	113.37	115.32	117.26	119.22	121.18	123.15	127.10
11.75	94.48	96.31	98.15	100.00	101.86	103.73	105.60	107.49	109.38	111.28	113.18	115.09	117.01	118.94	120.87	124.75
12.00	92.75	94.55	96.36	98.17	100.00	101.83	103.68	105.52	107.38	109.25	111.12	112.99	114.88	116.77	118.66	122.47
12.25	91.08	92.85	94.62	96.41	98.20	100.00	101.81	103.62	105.45	107.28	109.12	110.96	112.81	114.66	116.53	120.26
12.50	89.46	91.20	92.94	94.69	96.45	98.22	100.00	101.78	103.57	105.37	107.18	108.99	110.81	112.63	114.46	118.13
12.75	87.90	89.60	91.31	93.03	94.76	96.50	98.25	100.00	101.76	103.53	105.30	107.08	108.86	110.65	112.45	116.06
13.00	86.38	88.05	89.73	91.43	93.13	94.83	96.55	98.27	100.00	101.74	103.48	105.23	106.98	108.74	110.51	114.05
13.25	84.90	86.55	88.20	89.87	91.54	93.22	94.90	96.59	98.29	100.00	101.71	103.43	105.16	106.88	108.62	112.11
13.50	83.47	85.09	86.72	88.35	90.00	91.65	93.30	94.97	96.64	98.32	100.00	101.69	103.38	105.09	106.79	110.22
13.75	82.09	83.68	85.28	86.88	88.50	90.12	91.75	93.39	95.03	96.68	98.34	100.00	101.67	103.34	105.02	108.39
14.00	80.74	82.31	83.88	85.46	87.05	88.65	90.25	91.86	93.47	95.10	96.73	98.36	100.00	101.64	103.29	106.61
14.25	79.43	80.97	82.52	84.08	85.64	87.21	88.79	90.37	91.96	93.56	95.16	96.77	98.38	100.00	101.62	104.88
14.50	78.16	79.68	81.20	82.73	84.27	85.82	87.37	88.93	90.49	92.06	93.64	95.22	96.81	98.40	100.00	103.21
14.75	76.93	78.42	79.92	81.43	82.94	84.46	85.99	87.53	89.07	90.61	92.16	93.72	95.28	96.85	98.42	101.58
15.00	75.73	77.20	78.68	80.16	81.65	83.15	84.65	86.16	87.68	89.20	90.73	92.26	93.80	95.34	96.89	100.00
15.25	74.57	76.02	77.47	78.93	80.40	81.87	83.35	84.84	86.33	87.83	89.34	90.84	92.36	93.88	95.40	98.46
15.50	73.44	74.86	76.29	77.73	79.18	80.63	82.09	83.55	85.02	86.50	87.98	89.47	90.96	92.45	93.96	96.97
15.75	72.34	73.74	75.15	76.57	77.99	79.42	80.86	82.30	83.75	85.20	86.66	88.13	89.60	91.07	92.55	95.52
16.00	71.27	72.65	74.04	75.44	76.84	78.25	79.66	81.08	82.51	83.94	85.38	86.82	88.27	89.72	91.18	94.10
16.25	70.23	71.59	72.96	74.33	75.72	77.10	78.50	79.90	81.31	82.72	84.13	85.55	86.98	88.41	89.85	92.73
16.50	69.21	70.56	71.91	73.26	74.62	75.99	77.37	78.75	80.13	81.52	82.92	84.32	85.73	87.14	88.55	91.39
16.75	68.23	69.55	70.88	72.22	73.56	74.91	76.26	77.62	78.99	80.36	81.74	83.12	84.50	85.89	87.29	90.09
17.00	67.27	68.57	69.88	71.20	72.52	73.85	75.19	76.53	77.88	79.23	80.59	81.95	83.31	84.69	86.06	88.82
17.25	66.33	67.62	68.91	70.21	71.52	72.83	74.14	75.47	76.80	78.13	79.47	80.81	82.16	83.51	84.86	87.59
17.50	65.42	66.69	67.96	69.25	70.53	71.83	73.13	74.43	75.74	77.06	78.37	79.70	81.03	82.36	83.70	86.38
17.75	64.53	65.78	67.04	68.31	69.58	70.85	72.13	73.42	74.71	76.01	77.31	78.62	79.93	81.24	82.56	85.21
18.00	63.67	64.90	66.14	67.39	68.64	69.90	71.17	72.44	73.71	74.99	76.27	77.56	78.86	80.15	81.45	84.07
18.25	62.82	64.04	65.27	66.50	67.73	68.98	70.22	71.48	72.73	74.00	75.26	76.53	77.81	79.09	80.37	82.95
18.50	62.00	63.20	64.41	65.63	66.85	68.07	69.30	70.54	71.78	73.03	74.28	75.53	76.79	78.05	79.32	81.87
18.75	61.20	62.38	63.58	64.78	65.98	67.19	68.41	69.63	70.85	72.08	73.32	74.55	75.80	77.04	78.29	80.81
19.00	60.42	61.59	62.76	63.95	65.14	66.33	67.53	68.74	69.94	71.16	72.38	73.60	74.83	76.06	77.29	79.77
20.00	57.47	58.58	59.70	60.83	61.96	63.09	64.23	65.38	66.53	67.68	68.84	70.01	71.17	72.34	73.52	75.88
25.00	46.11	47.00	47.90	48.80	49.71	50.62	51.54	52.46	53.38	54.30	55.23	56.17	57.10	58.04	58.99	60.88
30.00	38.45	39.20	39.94	40.70	41.45	42.21	42.98	43.74	44.51	45.29	46.06	46.84	47.62	48.40	49.19	50.77

Description: This table shows the yield to maturity of a mortgage purchased at the price shown in the index.

Example: The yield to maturity of a 15.00 %, 28 year mortgage at a price of 125.00 is 11.72 %.

INTEREST RATE, %

PRICE	11.00%	11.25%	11.50%	11.75%	12.00%	12.25%	12.50%	12.75%	13.00%	13.25%	13.50%	13.75%	14.00%	14.25%	14.50%	15.00%
250	1.91	2.06	2.21	2.36	2.50	2.65	2.80	2.94	3.09	3.23	3.38	3.52	3.66	3.80	3.94	4.22
240	2.23	2.38	2.53	2.69	2.84	2.99	3.14	3.28	3.43	3.58	3.72	3.87	4.01	4.16	4.30	4.58
230	2.57	2.73	2.88	3.04	3.19	3.34	3.49	3.65	3.80	3.94	4.09	4.24	4.39	4.53	4.68	4.97
220	2.93	3.09	3.25	3.41	3.57	3.72	3.88	4.03	4.18	4.34	4.49	4.64	4.79	4.94	5.09	5.38
210	3.32	3.48	3.65	3.81	3.97	4.13	4.28	4.44	4.60	4.75	4.91	5.06	5.22	5.37	5.52	5.83
200	3.74	3.90	4.07	4.23	4.40	4.56	4.72	4.88	5.04	5.20	5.36	5.52	5.68	5.84	5.99	6.30
195	3.96	4.13	4.29	4.46	4.63	4.79	4.95	5.12	5.28	5.44	5.60	5.76	5.92	6.08	6.24	6.56
190	4.18	4.36	4.52	4.69	4.86	5.03	5.20	5.36	5.53	5.69	5.85	6.02	6.18	6.34	6.50	6.82
185	4.42	4.59	4.77	4.94	5.11	5.28	5.45	5.61	5.78	5.95	6.11	6.28	6.44	6.61	6.77	7.10
180	4.67	4.84	5.02	5.19	5.36	5.54	5.71	5.88	6.05	6.22	6.38	6.55	6.72	6.89	7.05	7.38
175	4.93	5.10	5.28	5.46	5.63	5.81	5.98	6.15	6.32	6.50	6.67	6.84	7.01	7.18	7.35	7.68
170	5.19	5.37	5.55	5.73	5.91	6.09	6.26	6.44	6.62	6.79	6.96	7.14	7.31	7.48	7.65	8.00
165	5.47	5.66	5.84	6.02	6.20	6.38	6.56	6.74	6.92	7.10	7.27	7.45	7.63	7.80	7.98	8.32
160	5.77	5.95	6.14	6.32	6.51	6.69	6.87	7.06	7.24	7.42	7.60	7.78	7.96	8.14	8.32	8.67
155	6.08	6.27	6.45	6.64	6.83	7.02	7.20	7.39	7.57	7.76	7.94	8.13	8.31	8.49	8.67	9.03
150	6.40	6.59	6.79	6.98	7.17	7.36	7.55	7.74	7.93	8.11	8.30	8.49	8.68	8.86	9.05	9.42
145	6.74	6.94	7.14	7.33	7.53	7.72	7.91	8.11	8.30	8.49	8.68	8.87	9.07	9.26	9.45	9.82
140	7.10	7.30	7.50	7.70	7.90	8.10	8.30	8.50	8.69	8.89	9.09	9.28	9.48	9.67	9.87	10.25
135	7.49	7.69	7.89	8.10	8.30	8.50	8.71	8.91	9.11	9.31	9.51	9.71	9.91	10.11	10.31	10.71
130	7.89	8.10	8.31	8.52	8.73	8.93	9.14	9.35	9.56	9.76	9.97	10.17	10.38	10.58	10.79	11.20
125	8.32	8.54	8.75	8.96	9.18	9.39	9.60	9.82	10.03	10.24	10.45	10.67	10.88	11.09	11.30	11.72
120	8.78	9.00	9.22	9.44	9.66	9.88	10.10	10.32	10.54	10.76	10.97	11.19	11.41	11.63	11.84	12.28
115	9.27	9.50	9.73	9.95	10.18	10.41	10.63	10.86	11.08	11.31	11.53	11.76	11.98	12.20	12.43	12.88
113	9.48	9.71	9.94	10.17	10.40	10.63	10.85	11.08	11.31	11.54	11.77	11.99	12.22	12.45	12.68	13.13
112	9.59	9.82	10.05	10.28	10.51	10.74	10.97	11.20	11.43	11.66	11.89	12.12	12.34	12.57	12.80	13.26
111	9.69	9.93	10.16	10.39	10.62	10.85	11.09	11.32	11.55	11.78	12.01	12.24	12.47	12.70	12.93	13.39
110	9.80	10.04	10.27	10.50	10.74	10.97	11.20	11.44	11.67	11.90	12.13	12.37	12.60	12.83	13.06	13.52
109	9.91	10.15	10.38	10.62	10.85	11.09	11.32	11.56	11.79	12.03	12.26	12.49	12.73	12.96	13.19	13.66
108	10.03	10.26	10.50	10.74	10.97	11.21	11.45	11.68	11.92	12.15	12.39	12.62	12.86	13.09	13.33	13.80
107	10.14	10.38	10.62	10.86	11.09	11.33	11.57	11.81	12.04	12.28	12.52	12.76	12.99	13.23	13.47	13.94
106	10.26	10.50	10.74	10.98	11.22	11.46	11.69	11.93	12.17	12.41	12.65	12.89	13.13	13.37	13.61	14.08
105	10.38	10.62	10.86	11.10	11.34	11.58	11.82	12.06	12.30	12.54	12.79	13.03	13.27	13.51	13.75	14.23
104	10.49	10.74	10.98	11.22	11.47	11.71	11.95	12.20	12.44	12.68	12.92	13.16	13.41	13.65	13.89	14.38
103	10.62	10.86	11.11	11.35	11.60	11.84	12.08	12.33	12.57	12.82	13.06	13.31	13.55	13.79	14.04	14.53
102	10.74	10.99	11.23	11.48	11.73	11.97	12.22	12.47	12.71	12.96	13.20	13.45	13.70	13.94	14.19	14.68
101	10.87	11.12	11.36	11.61	11.86	12.11	12.36	12.60	12.85	13.10	13.35	13.60	13.84	14.09	14.34	14.84
100	11.00	11.25	11.50	11.75	12.00	12.25	12.50	12.75	13.00	13.25	13.50	13.75	14.00	14.25	14.50	15.00
99	11.13	11.38	11.63	11.88	12.13	12.38	12.64	12.89	13.14	13.39	13.64	13.90	14.15	14.40	14.65	15.16
98	11.26	11.51	11.77	12.02	12.27	12.53	12.78	13.03	13.29	13.54	13.80	14.05	14.31	14.56	14.81	15.32
97	11.39	11.65	11.90	12.16	12.42	12.67	12.93	13.18	13.44	13.70	13.95	14.21	14.46	14.72	14.98	15.49
96	11.53	11.79	12.05	12.30	12.56	12.82	13.08	13.34	13.59	13.85	14.11	14.37	14.63	14.89	15.14	15.66
95	11.67	11.93	12.19	12.45	12.71	12.97	13.23	13.49	13.75	14.01	14.27	14.53	14.79	15.05	15.31	15.84
94	11.81	12.07	12.34	12.60	12.86	13.12	13.39	13.65	13.91	14.17	14.44	14.70	14.96	15.22	15.49	16.01
93	11.96	12.22	12.49	12.75	13.01	13.28	13.54	13.81	14.07	14.34	14.60	14.87	15.13	15.40	15.66	16.20
92	12.11	12.37	12.64	12.90	13.17	13.44	13.70	13.97	14.24	14.51	14.77	15.04	15.31	15.58	15.84	16.38
91	12.26	12.53	12.79	13.06	13.33	13.60	13.87	14.14	14.41	14.68	14.95	15.22	15.49	15.76	16.03	16.57
90	12.41	12.68	12.95	13.22	13.49	13.77	14.04	14.31	14.58	14.85	15.12	15.40	15.67	15.94	16.22	16.76
89	12.57	12.84	13.11	13.39	13.66	13.93	14.21	14.48	14.76	15.03	15.31	15.58	15.86	16.13	16.41	16.96
88	12.73	13.00	13.28	13.55	13.83	14.11	14.38	14.66	14.94	15.21	15.49	15.77	16.05	16.32	16.60	17.16
87	12.89	13.17	13.45	13.73	14.00	14.28	14.56	14.84	15.12	15.40	15.68	15.96	16.24	16.52	16.80	17.37
86	13.06	13.34	13.62	13.90	14.18	14.46	14.74	15.03	15.31	15.59	15.87	16.16	16.44	16.72	17.01	17.58
85	13.23	13.51	13.79	14.08	14.36	14.65	14.93	15.21	15.50	15.78	16.07	16.36	16.64	16.93	17.22	17.79
84	13.40	13.69	13.97	14.26	14.55	14.83	15.12	15.41	15.70	15.98	16.27	16.56	16.85	17.14	17.43	18.01
83	13.58	13.87	14.16	14.44	14.73	15.02	15.31	15.60	15.90	16.19	16.48	16.77	17.06	17.35	17.65	18.23
82	13.76	14.05	14.34	14.63	14.93	15.22	15.51	15.81	16.10	16.39	16.69	16.98	17.28	17.57	17.87	18.46
81	13.95	14.24	14.53	14.83	15.12	15.42	15.72	16.01	16.31	16.61	16.90	17.20	17.50	17.80	18.10	18.70
80	14.14	14.43	14.73	15.03	15.33	15.62	15.92	16.22	16.52	16.82	17.13	17.43	17.73	18.03	18.33	18.94
79	14.33	14.63	14.93	15.23	15.53	15.83	16.14	16.44	16.74	17.05	17.35	17.66	17.96	18.27	18.57	19.19
78	14.53	14.83	15.13	15.44	15.74	16.05	16.35	16.66	16.97	17.27	17.58	17.89	18.20	18.51	18.82	19.44
77	14.73	15.04	15.34	15.65	15.96	16.27	16.58	16.89	17.20	17.51	17.82	18.13	18.44	18.76	19.07	19.70
76	14.94	15.25	15.56	15.87	16.18	16.49	16.81	17.12	17.43	17.75	18.06	18.38	18.69	19.01	19.33	19.96
75	15.15	15.47	15.78	16.09	16.41	16.72	17.04	17.36	17.67	17.99	18.31	18.63	18.95	19.27	19.59	20.23
74	15.37	15.69	16.00	16.32	16.64	16.96	17.28	17.60	17.92	18.24	18.57	18.89	19.21	19.54	19.86	20.51
73	15.59	15.91	16.24	16.56	16.88	17.20	17.53	17.85	18.18	18.50	18.83	19.16	19.48	19.81	20.14	20.80
70	16.30	16.63	16.97	17.30	17.63	17.97	18.31	18.64	18.98	19.32	19.66	20.00	20.34	20.68	21.02	21.71
65	17.61	17.97	18.32	18.68	19.04	19.39	19.75	20.11	20.48	20.84	21.20	21.56	21.93	22.30	22.66	23.40
60	19.13	19.51	19.89	20.28	20.66	21.05	21.43	21.82	22.21	22.60	22.99	23.39	23.78	24.17	24.57	25.36
55	20.91	21.32	21.74	22.15	22.57	22.99	23.41	23.83	24.25	24.68	25.10	25.53	25.96	26.39	26.82	27.68

Description: This table shows the price to pay for a monthly payment mortgage loan at the yield rate.

Example: The price of a 6.75 %, 29 year mortgage loan to yield 8.00 % to maturity is $ 88.60.

INTEREST RATE, %

YIELD	0.00%	1.00%	2.00%	3.00%	4.00%	4.25%	4.50%	4.75%	5.00%	5.25%	5.50%	5.75%	6.00%	6.25%	6.50%	6.75%
0.00	100.00	115.24	131.87	149.85	169.12	174.13	179.22	184.38	189.61	194.92	200.29	205.73	211.24	216.81	222.45	228.14
1.00	86.77	100.00	114.43	130.03	146.75	151.10	155.52	159.99	164.53	169.14	173.80	178.52	183.30	188.14	193.03	197.97
2.00	75.83	87.39	100.00	113.63	128.25	132.05	135.91	139.82	143.79	147.81	151.88	156.01	160.19	164.41	168.69	173.01
3.00	66.73	76.91	88.00	100.00	112.86	116.21	119.60	123.04	126.54	130.08	133.66	137.29	140.97	144.69	148.45	152.25
4.00	59.13	68.14	77.97	88.60	100.00	102.96	105.97	109.02	112.12	115.25	118.43	121.65	124.90	128.20	131.53	134.90
4.25	57.43	66.18	75.73	86.05	97.12	100.00	102.92	105.89	108.89	111.94	115.02	118.15	121.31	124.51	127.75	131.02
4.50	55.80	64.30	73.58	83.61	94.37	97.16	100.00	102.88	105.80	108.76	111.76	114.79	117.87	120.98	124.12	127.30
4.75	54.24	62.50	71.52	81.27	91.72	94.44	97.20	100.00	102.84	105.71	108.63	111.58	114.57	117.59	120.65	123.74
5.00	52.74	60.78	69.55	79.03	89.19	91.84	94.52	97.24	100.00	102.80	105.63	108.50	111.41	114.34	117.32	120.32
5.25	51.30	59.12	67.65	76.88	86.77	89.34	91.95	94.59	97.28	100.00	102.76	105.55	108.37	111.23	114.12	117.05
5.50	49.93	57.54	65.84	74.82	84.44	86.94	89.48	92.06	94.67	97.32	100.00	102.72	105.47	108.25	111.06	113.91
5.75	48.61	56.02	64.10	72.84	82.20	84.64	87.11	89.62	92.17	94.74	97.36	100.00	102.68	105.39	108.13	110.89
6.00	47.34	54.56	62.43	70.94	80.06	82.43	84.84	87.28	89.76	92.27	94.82	97.39	100.00	102.64	105.31	108.00
6.25	46.12	53.15	60.82	69.11	78.00	80.31	82.66	85.04	87.46	89.90	92.38	94.89	97.43	100.00	102.60	105.23
6.50	44.95	51.81	59.28	67.36	76.03	78.28	80.57	82.89	85.24	87.62	90.04	92.49	94.96	97.47	100.00	102.56
6.75	43.83	50.51	57.80	65.68	74.13	76.33	78.55	80.82	83.11	85.44	87.79	90.18	92.59	95.03	97.50	100.00
7.00	42.75	49.27	56.38	64.06	72.30	74.45	76.62	78.83	81.06	83.33	85.63	87.96	90.31	92.69	95.10	97.54
7.25	41.72	48.07	55.01	62.51	70.55	72.64	74.76	76.91	79.10	81.31	83.55	85.82	88.12	90.44	92.80	95.17
7.50	40.72	46.92	53.69	61.01	68.86	70.90	72.97	75.08	77.21	79.37	81.55	83.77	86.01	88.28	90.58	92.90
7.75	39.76	45.82	52.43	59.58	67.24	69.23	71.25	73.31	75.39	77.50	79.63	81.79	83.98	86.20	88.44	90.71
8.00	38.83	44.75	51.21	58.19	65.68	67.62	69.60	71.60	73.64	75.69	77.78	79.89	82.03	84.20	86.39	88.60
8.25	37.95	43.73	50.04	56.86	64.17	66.07	68.01	69.96	71.95	73.96	76.00	78.07	80.16	82.27	84.41	86.57
8.50	37.09	42.74	48.91	55.58	62.72	64.58	66.47	68.38	70.33	72.29	74.29	76.30	78.35	80.41	82.50	84.62
8.75	36.26	41.79	47.82	54.34	61.33	63.15	64.99	66.86	68.76	70.68	72.63	74.61	76.60	78.62	80.67	82.73
9.00	35.47	40.88	46.77	53.15	59.99	61.76	63.57	65.40	67.25	69.13	71.04	72.97	74.92	76.90	78.90	80.92
9.25	34.70	39.99	45.76	52.00	58.69	60.43	62.19	63.98	65.80	67.64	69.51	71.39	73.31	75.24	77.19	79.17
9.50	33.96	39.14	44.79	50.89	57.44	59.14	60.87	62.62	64.40	66.20	68.03	69.87	71.74	73.64	75.55	77.49
9.75	33.25	38.32	43.85	49.82	56.23	57.90	59.59	61.31	63.05	64.81	66.60	68.41	70.24	72.09	73.96	75.86
10.00	32.56	37.53	42.94	48.79	55.07	56.70	58.36	60.04	61.74	63.47	65.22	66.99	68.78	70.60	72.43	74.29
10.25	31.90	36.76	42.06	47.80	53.95	55.54	57.17	58.81	60.48	62.17	63.89	65.62	67.38	69.16	70.96	72.77
10.50	31.26	36.02	41.22	46.84	52.86	54.43	56.02	57.63	59.27	60.92	62.60	64.30	66.03	67.77	69.53	71.31
10.75	30.64	35.31	40.40	45.91	51.81	53.35	54.91	56.49	58.09	59.72	61.36	63.03	64.72	66.42	68.15	69.90
11.00	30.04	34.62	39.61	45.01	50.80	52.31	53.83	55.38	56.96	58.55	60.16	61.80	63.45	65.13	66.82	68.53
11.25	29.46	33.95	38.85	44.14	49.82	51.30	52.80	54.32	55.86	57.42	59.00	60.61	62.23	63.87	65.53	67.21
11.50	28.90	33.30	38.11	43.31	48.88	50.32	51.79	53.29	54.80	56.33	57.88	59.46	61.05	62.66	64.29	65.93
11.75	28.36	32.68	37.40	42.49	47.96	49.38	50.82	52.29	53.77	55.28	56.80	58.34	59.90	61.48	63.08	64.70
12.00	27.83	32.08	36.71	41.71	47.07	48.47	49.89	51.32	52.78	54.25	55.75	57.26	58.80	60.35	61.92	63.50
12.25	27.33	31.49	36.04	40.95	46.22	47.59	48.98	50.39	51.82	53.27	54.73	56.22	57.73	59.25	60.79	62.35
12.50	26.84	30.93	35.39	40.21	45.39	46.73	48.10	49.48	50.89	52.31	53.75	55.21	56.69	58.19	59.70	61.23
12.75	26.36	30.38	34.76	39.50	44.58	45.90	47.24	48.61	49.98	51.38	52.80	54.23	55.69	57.15	58.64	60.14
13.00	25.90	29.85	34.16	38.81	43.80	45.10	46.42	47.76	49.11	50.49	51.88	53.29	54.71	56.16	57.62	59.09
13.25	25.45	29.33	33.57	38.14	43.05	44.32	45.62	46.93	48.27	49.62	50.98	52.37	53.77	55.19	56.62	58.07
13.50	25.02	28.84	33.00	37.49	42.32	43.57	44.84	46.14	47.44	48.77	50.12	51.48	52.86	54.25	55.66	57.09
13.75	24.60	28.35	32.44	36.87	41.61	42.84	44.09	45.36	46.65	47.95	49.28	50.61	51.97	53.34	54.73	56.13
14.00	24.20	27.88	31.91	36.26	40.92	42.13	43.36	44.61	45.88	47.16	48.46	49.78	51.11	52.46	53.82	55.20
14.25	23.80	27.43	31.39	35.66	40.25	41.44	42.65	43.88	45.13	46.39	47.67	48.97	50.28	51.60	52.94	54.30
14.50	23.42	26.99	30.88	35.09	39.60	40.78	41.97	43.18	44.40	45.64	46.90	48.18	49.47	50.77	52.09	53.43
14.75	23.05	26.56	30.39	34.53	38.97	40.13	41.30	42.49	43.70	44.92	46.16	47.41	48.68	49.96	51.26	52.58
15.00	22.68	26.14	29.91	33.99	38.36	39.50	40.65	41.82	43.01	44.21	45.43	46.67	47.92	49.18	50.46	51.75
15.25	22.33	25.74	29.45	33.46	37.77	38.89	40.02	41.18	42.35	43.53	44.73	45.94	47.17	48.42	49.68	50.95
15.50	21.99	25.34	29.00	32.95	37.19	38.29	39.41	40.55	41.70	42.86	44.05	45.24	46.45	47.68	48.92	50.17
15.75	21.66	24.96	28.56	32.46	36.63	37.72	38.82	39.94	41.07	42.22	43.38	44.56	45.75	46.96	48.18	49.42
16.00	21.34	24.59	28.14	31.97	36.09	37.15	38.24	39.34	40.46	41.59	42.74	43.90	45.07	46.26	47.46	48.68
16.25	21.02	24.23	27.72	31.50	35.55	36.61	37.68	38.76	39.86	40.98	42.11	43.25	44.41	45.58	46.77	47.96
16.50	20.72	23.88	27.32	31.05	35.04	36.08	37.13	38.20	39.28	40.38	41.50	42.62	43.76	44.92	46.09	47.27
16.75	20.42	23.53	26.93	30.60	34.54	35.56	36.60	37.65	38.72	39.80	40.90	42.01	43.14	44.28	45.43	46.59
17.00	20.13	23.20	26.55	30.17	34.05	35.06	36.08	37.12	38.17	39.24	40.32	41.42	42.53	43.65	44.78	45.93
17.25	19.85	22.88	26.18	29.75	33.57	34.57	35.58	36.60	37.64	38.69	39.76	40.84	41.93	43.04	44.16	45.29
17.50	19.58	22.56	25.82	29.33	33.11	34.09	35.08	36.10	37.12	38.16	39.21	40.28	41.35	42.44	43.55	44.66
17.75	19.31	22.25	25.46	28.93	32.66	33.62	34.61	35.60	36.61	37.64	38.67	39.73	40.79	41.87	42.95	44.05
18.00	19.05	21.95	25.12	28.54	32.22	33.17	34.14	35.12	36.12	37.13	38.15	39.19	40.24	41.30	42.37	43.46
18.25	18.80	21.66	24.79	28.16	31.79	32.73	33.69	34.66	35.64	36.64	37.65	38.67	39.70	40.75	41.81	42.88
18.50	18.55	21.38	24.46	27.79	31.37	32.30	33.24	34.20	35.17	36.15	37.15	38.16	39.18	40.22	41.26	42.32
18.75	18.31	21.10	24.14	27.43	30.96	31.88	32.81	33.75	34.71	35.68	36.67	37.66	38.67	39.69	40.72	41.77
19.00	18.07	20.83	23.83	27.08	30.56	31.47	32.39	33.32	34.27	35.23	36.20	37.18	38.18	39.18	40.20	41.23
20.00	17.19	19.81	22.66	25.75	29.07	29.93	30.80	31.69	32.59	33.50	34.42	35.36	36.30	37.26	38.23	39.21
25.00	13.78	15.88	18.17	20.65	23.31	24.00	24.70	25.41	26.13	26.86	27.60	28.35	29.11	29.88	30.66	31.44
30.00	11.49	13.24	15.15	17.22	19.44	20.01	20.60	21.19	21.79	22.40	23.02	23.64	24.28	24.92	25.56	26.22

Description: This table shows the yield to maturity of a mortgage purchased at the price shown in the index.

Example: The yield to maturity of a 6.75 %, 29 year mortgage at a price of 80.00 is 9.13 %.

INTEREST RATE, %

PRICE	0.00%	1.00%	2.00%	3.00%	4.00%	4.25%	4.50%	4.75%	5.00%	5.25%	5.50%	5.75%	6.00%	6.25%	6.50%	6.75%
100	0.00	1.00	2.00	3.00	4.00	4.25	4.50	4.75	5.00	5.25	5.50	5.75	6.00	6.25	6.50	6.75
99	.06	1.07	2.07	3.08	4.08	4.33	4.58	4.83	5.09	5.34	5.59	5.84	6.09	6.34	6.59	6.85
98	.13	1.14	2.15	3.16	4.17	4.42	4.67	4.93	5.18	5.43	5.68	5.94	6.19	6.44	6.69	6.95
97	.21	1.22	2.23	3.24	4.26	4.51	4.76	5.02	5.27	5.53	5.78	6.03	6.29	6.54	6.80	7.05
96	.28	1.29	2.31	3.33	4.35	4.60	4.86	5.11	5.37	5.62	5.88	6.13	6.39	6.64	6.90	7.16
95	.35	1.37	2.39	3.41	4.44	4.69	4.95	5.21	5.46	5.72	5.98	6.23	6.49	6.75	7.01	7.26
94	.43	1.45	2.47	3.50	4.53	4.79	5.04	5.30	5.56	5.82	6.08	6.34	6.60	6.85	7.11	7.37
93	.50	1.53	2.56	3.59	4.62	4.88	5.14	5.40	5.66	5.92	6.18	6.44	6.70	6.96	7.22	7.48
92	.58	1.61	2.64	3.68	4.72	4.98	5.24	5.50	5.76	6.02	6.28	6.55	6.81	7.07	7.33	7.60
91	.65	1.69	2.73	3.77	4.82	5.08	5.34	5.60	5.86	6.13	6.39	6.65	6.92	7.18	7.45	7.71
90	.73	1.77	2.82	3.86	4.91	5.18	5.44	5.71	5.97	6.23	6.50	6.76	7.03	7.30	7.56	7.83
89	.81	1.86	2.90	3.96	5.01	5.28	5.54	5.81	6.08	6.34	6.61	6.88	7.14	7.41	7.68	7.95
88	.89	1.94	3.00	4.05	5.12	5.38	5.65	5.92	6.19	6.45	6.72	6.99	7.26	7.53	7.80	8.07
87	.98	2.03	3.09	4.15	5.22	5.49	5.76	6.03	6.30	6.57	6.84	7.11	7.38	7.65	7.92	8.19
86	1.06	2.12	3.18	4.25	5.33	5.60	5.87	6.14	6.41	6.68	6.95	7.22	7.50	7.77	8.04	8.32
85	1.14	2.21	3.28	4.35	5.43	5.71	5.98	6.25	6.52	6.80	7.07	7.34	7.62	7.89	8.17	8.45
84	1.23	2.30	3.37	4.45	5.54	5.82	6.09	6.36	6.64	6.91	7.19	7.47	7.74	8.02	8.30	8.58
83	1.32	2.39	3.47	4.56	5.65	5.93	6.21	6.48	6.76	7.04	7.31	7.59	7.87	8.15	8.43	8.71
82	1.41	2.49	3.57	4.67	5.77	6.05	6.32	6.60	6.88	7.16	7.44	7.72	8.00	8.28	8.56	8.85
81	1.50	2.58	3.67	4.77	5.88	6.16	6.44	6.72	7.00	7.28	7.57	7.85	8.13	8.41	8.70	8.98
80	1.59	2.68	3.78	4.89	6.00	6.28	6.56	6.85	7.13	7.41	7.70	7.98	8.27	8.55	8.84	9.13
79	1.69	2.78	3.88	5.00	6.12	6.41	6.69	6.97	7.26	7.54	7.83	8.12	8.40	8.69	8.98	9.27
78	1.78	2.88	3.99	5.11	6.25	6.53	6.82	7.10	7.39	7.68	7.97	8.25	8.54	8.83	9.13	9.42
77	1.88	2.99	4.10	5.23	6.37	6.66	6.95	7.23	7.52	7.81	8.10	8.40	8.69	8.98	9.27	9.57
76	1.98	3.09	4.21	5.35	6.50	6.79	7.08	7.37	7.66	7.95	8.25	8.54	8.83	9.13	9.43	9.72
75	2.08	3.20	4.33	5.47	6.63	6.92	7.21	7.51	7.80	8.09	8.39	8.69	8.98	9.28	9.58	9.88
74	2.18	3.31	4.45	5.60	6.76	7.06	7.35	7.65	7.94	8.24	8.54	8.84	9.14	9.44	9.74	10.04
73	2.29	3.42	4.56	5.72	6.90	7.19	7.49	7.79	8.09	8.39	8.69	8.99	9.29	9.60	9.90	10.21
72	2.39	3.53	4.69	5.85	7.04	7.34	7.64	7.94	8.24	8.54	8.84	9.15	9.45	9.76	10.07	10.38
71	2.50	3.65	4.81	5.99	7.18	7.48	7.78	8.09	8.39	8.70	9.00	9.31	9.62	9.93	10.24	10.55
70	2.61	3.77	4.94	6.12	7.33	7.63	7.93	8.24	8.55	8.85	9.16	9.47	9.79	10.10	10.41	10.73
69	2.73	3.89	5.07	6.26	7.47	7.78	8.09	8.40	8.71	9.02	9.33	9.64	9.96	10.27	10.59	10.91
68	2.84	4.01	5.20	6.40	7.63	7.94	8.25	8.56	8.87	9.18	9.50	9.82	10.13	10.45	10.77	11.09
67	2.96	4.14	5.33	6.55	7.78	8.09	8.41	8.72	9.04	9.36	9.67	9.99	10.31	10.64	10.96	11.29
66	3.08	4.27	5.47	6.70	7.94	8.26	8.57	8.89	9.21	9.53	9.85	10.18	10.50	10.83	11.15	11.48
65	3.21	4.40	5.61	6.85	8.11	8.42	8.74	9.06	9.39	9.71	10.04	10.36	10.69	11.02	11.35	11.68
64	3.33	4.54	5.76	7.01	8.27	8.60	8.92	9.24	9.57	9.90	10.22	10.55	10.89	11.22	11.55	11.89
63	3.46	4.67	5.91	7.17	8.45	8.77	9.10	9.42	9.75	10.08	10.42	10.75	11.09	11.42	11.76	12.10
62	3.60	4.82	6.06	7.33	8.62	8.95	9.28	9.61	9.94	10.28	10.62	10.95	11.29	11.63	11.98	12.32
61	3.73	4.96	6.22	7.50	8.81	9.14	9.47	9.80	10.14	10.48	10.82	11.16	11.51	11.85	12.20	12.55
60	3.87	5.11	6.38	7.67	8.99	9.33	9.66	10.00	10.34	10.69	11.03	11.38	11.72	12.07	12.43	12.78
59	4.01	5.26	6.54	7.85	9.18	9.52	9.86	10.21	10.55	10.90	11.25	11.60	11.95	12.30	12.66	13.02
58	4.16	5.42	6.71	8.03	9.38	9.72	10.07	10.42	10.76	11.12	11.47	11.82	12.18	12.54	12.90	13.26
57	4.31	5.58	6.88	8.22	9.58	9.93	10.28	10.63	10.99	11.34	11.70	12.06	12.42	12.78	13.15	13.52
56	4.46	5.75	7.06	8.41	9.79	10.15	10.50	10.85	11.21	11.57	11.93	12.30	12.67	13.03	13.41	13.78
55	4.62	5.92	7.25	8.61	10.01	10.37	10.72	11.08	11.45	11.81	12.18	12.55	12.92	13.29	13.67	14.05
54	4.78	6.09	7.44	8.82	10.23	10.59	10.96	11.32	11.69	12.06	12.43	12.81	13.18	13.56	13.95	14.33
53	4.95	6.27	7.63	9.03	10.46	10.83	11.20	11.57	11.94	12.31	12.69	13.07	13.46	13.84	14.23	14.62
52	5.12	6.46	7.83	9.25	10.70	11.07	11.44	11.82	12.20	12.58	12.96	13.35	13.74	14.13	14.52	14.92
51	5.30	6.65	8.04	9.47	10.95	11.32	11.70	12.08	12.46	12.85	13.24	13.63	14.03	14.43	14.83	15.23
50	5.48	6.85	8.25	9.70	11.20	11.58	11.96	12.35	12.74	13.13	13.53	13.93	14.33	14.73	15.14	15.55
49	5.67	7.05	8.47	9.94	11.46	11.85	12.24	12.63	13.03	13.43	13.83	14.23	14.64	15.05	15.47	15.89
48	5.86	7.26	8.70	10.19	11.73	12.13	12.52	12.92	13.33	13.73	14.14	14.55	14.97	15.39	15.81	16.23
47	6.06	7.48	8.94	10.45	12.02	12.42	12.82	13.22	13.63	14.05	14.46	14.88	15.30	15.73	16.16	16.59
46	6.27	7.70	9.19	10.72	12.31	12.72	13.13	13.54	13.95	14.37	14.80	15.23	15.66	16.09	16.53	16.97
45	6.49	7.94	9.44	11.00	12.61	13.03	13.44	13.86	14.29	14.72	15.15	15.58	16.02	16.46	16.91	17.36
44	6.71	8.18	9.70	11.29	12.93	13.35	13.78	14.20	14.64	15.07	15.51	15.96	16.40	16.85	17.31	17.77
43	6.94	8.43	9.98	11.59	13.26	13.69	14.12	14.56	15.00	15.44	15.89	16.34	16.80	17.26	17.73	18.19
42	7.18	8.69	10.26	11.90	13.61	14.04	14.48	14.93	15.38	15.83	16.29	16.75	17.22	17.69	18.16	18.64
41	7.42	8.96	10.56	12.23	13.97	14.41	14.86	15.31	15.77	16.24	16.70	17.17	17.65	18.13	18.62	19.10
40	7.68	9.24	10.87	12.57	14.34	14.80	15.25	15.72	16.19	16.66	17.14	17.62	18.11	18.60	19.09	19.59
39	7.95	9.54	11.19	12.93	14.73	15.20	15.67	16.14	16.62	17.10	17.59	18.09	18.58	19.09	19.59	20.10
35	9.15	10.86	12.65	14.53	16.51	17.02	17.54	18.06	18.59	19.12	19.66	20.20	20.75	21.31	21.87	22.44
30	11.01	12.92	14.95	17.09	19.36	19.95	20.54	21.14	21.75	22.36	22.99	23.62	24.25	24.90	25.55	26.20
25	13.51	15.72	18.08	20.61	23.29	23.99	24.69	25.41	26.13	26.87	27.61	28.36	29.12	29.89	30.67	31.46
20	17.11	19.80	22.70	25.82	29.15	30.01	30.89	31.78	32.68	33.60	34.53	35.46	36.41	37.38	38.35	39.33
15	22.95	26.47	30.30	34.44	38.87	40.02	41.19	42.38	43.58	44.80	46.04	47.29	48.56	49.84	51.13	52.44
10	34.48	39.73	45.47	51.67	58.31	60.04	61.79	63.57	65.38	67.21	69.06	70.94	72.84	74.76	76.70	78.67

Description: This table shows the price to pay for a monthly payment mortgage loan at the yield rate.

Example: The price of a 10.75 %, 29 year mortgage loan to yield 8.00 % to maturity is $ 126.76.

INTEREST RATE, %

YIELD	7.00%	7.25%	7.50%	7.75%	8.00%	8.25%	8.50%	8.75%	9.00%	9.25%	9.50%	9.75%	10.00%	10.25%	10.50%	10.75%
0.00	233.90	239.72	245.59	251.52	257.50	263.54	269.62	275.75	281.93	288.16	294.43	300.75	307.10	313.50	319.93	326.40
1.00	202.97	208.01	213.11	218.25	223.45	228.68	233.96	239.28	244.65	250.05	255.49	260.97	266.49	272.04	277.62	283.23
2.00	177.37	181.78	186.24	190.73	195.27	199.85	204.46	209.11	213.80	218.52	223.28	228.07	232.88	237.73	242.61	247.52
3.00	156.09	159.98	163.89	167.85	171.84	175.87	179.93	184.02	188.15	192.30	196.49	200.70	204.94	209.21	213.51	217.82
4.00	138.31	141.75	145.22	148.72	152.26	155.83	159.43	163.05	166.71	170.39	174.10	177.83	181.59	185.37	189.18	193.00
4.25	134.33	137.67	141.04	144.44	147.88	151.34	154.84	158.36	161.91	165.49	169.09	172.71	176.36	180.04	183.73	187.45
4.50	130.51	133.76	137.03	140.34	143.68	147.05	150.44	153.87	157.31	160.79	164.29	167.81	171.36	174.93	178.52	182.13
4.75	126.86	130.01	133.20	136.41	139.66	142.93	146.23	149.56	152.91	156.29	159.69	163.11	166.56	170.03	173.52	177.03
5.00	123.36	126.43	129.52	132.65	135.80	138.99	142.20	145.43	148.69	151.97	155.28	158.61	161.96	165.34	168.73	172.14
5.25	120.00	122.99	126.00	129.04	132.11	135.21	138.33	141.47	144.64	147.84	151.06	154.30	157.56	160.84	164.14	167.46
5.50	116.78	119.69	122.62	125.58	128.57	131.58	134.62	137.68	140.76	143.87	147.00	150.16	153.33	156.52	159.73	162.97
5.75	113.69	116.52	119.38	122.26	125.16	128.10	131.06	134.04	137.04	140.07	143.12	146.19	149.27	152.38	155.51	158.66
6.00	110.73	113.48	116.26	119.07	121.90	124.76	127.64	130.54	133.47	136.42	139.38	142.37	145.38	148.41	151.46	154.52
6.25	107.88	110.57	113.27	116.01	118.77	121.55	124.36	127.19	130.04	132.91	135.80	138.71	141.65	144.60	147.56	150.55
6.50	105.15	107.76	110.40	113.07	115.76	118.47	121.21	123.96	126.74	129.54	132.36	135.20	138.06	140.93	143.82	146.73
6.75	102.52	105.07	107.65	110.25	112.87	115.51	118.18	120.87	123.58	126.31	129.06	131.82	134.61	137.41	140.23	143.07
7.00	100.00	102.49	105.00	107.53	110.09	112.67	115.27	117.89	120.54	123.20	125.88	128.58	131.30	134.03	136.78	139.55
7.25	97.57	100.00	102.45	104.92	107.42	109.94	112.47	115.03	117.61	120.21	122.82	125.46	128.11	130.78	133.46	136.16
7.50	95.24	97.61	100.00	102.41	104.85	107.31	109.78	112.28	114.80	117.33	119.89	122.46	125.05	127.65	130.27	132.90
7.75	93.00	95.31	97.64	100.00	102.38	104.78	107.20	109.64	112.09	114.57	117.06	119.57	122.10	124.64	127.20	129.77
8.00	90.84	93.09	95.37	97.68	100.00	102.34	104.71	107.09	109.49	111.91	114.34	116.79	119.26	121.75	124.24	126.76
8.25	88.76	90.96	93.19	95.44	97.71	100.00	102.31	104.64	106.98	109.34	111.72	114.12	116.53	118.96	121.40	123.85
8.50	86.75	88.91	91.09	93.29	95.51	97.74	100.00	102.27	104.57	106.88	109.20	111.54	113.90	116.27	118.66	121.06
8.75	84.82	86.93	89.06	91.21	93.38	95.57	97.78	100.00	102.24	104.50	106.77	109.06	111.37	113.69	116.02	118.37
9.00	82.96	85.03	87.11	89.21	91.33	93.47	95.63	97.81	100.00	102.21	104.43	106.67	108.93	111.19	113.48	115.77
9.25	81.17	83.19	85.23	87.28	89.36	91.45	93.57	95.69	97.84	100.00	102.18	104.37	106.57	108.79	111.02	113.27
9.50	79.44	81.42	83.41	85.42	87.46	89.51	91.57	93.66	95.76	97.87	100.00	102.14	104.30	106.47	108.66	110.86
9.75	77.77	79.71	81.66	83.63	85.62	87.63	89.65	91.69	93.74	95.82	97.90	100.00	102.11	104.24	106.38	108.53
10.00	76.16	78.06	79.97	81.90	83.85	85.81	87.79	89.79	91.80	93.83	95.87	97.93	100.00	102.08	104.18	106.28
10.25	74.61	76.47	78.34	80.23	82.14	84.06	86.00	87.96	89.93	91.92	93.92	95.93	97.96	100.00	102.05	104.12
10.50	73.11	74.93	76.76	78.62	80.49	82.37	84.27	86.19	88.12	90.07	92.03	94.00	95.99	97.99	100.00	102.02
10.75	71.66	73.44	75.24	77.06	78.89	80.74	82.60	84.48	86.38	88.28	90.21	92.14	94.09	96.05	98.02	100.00
11.00	70.26	72.01	73.77	75.55	77.35	79.16	80.99	82.83	84.69	86.56	88.44	90.34	92.25	94.17	96.10	98.05
11.25	68.91	70.62	72.35	74.10	75.86	77.64	79.43	81.24	83.06	84.89	86.74	88.60	90.47	92.36	94.25	96.16
11.50	67.60	69.28	70.98	72.69	74.42	76.16	77.92	79.69	81.48	83.28	85.09	86.92	88.75	90.60	92.46	94.33
11.75	66.33	67.98	69.65	71.33	73.02	74.74	76.46	78.20	79.95	81.72	83.50	85.29	87.09	88.90	90.73	92.56
12.00	65.11	66.73	68.36	70.01	71.68	73.35	75.05	76.76	78.48	80.21	81.96	83.71	85.48	87.26	89.05	90.85
12.25	63.92	65.51	67.11	68.74	70.37	72.02	73.68	75.36	77.05	78.75	80.46	82.19	83.92	85.67	87.43	89.20
12.50	62.77	64.33	65.91	67.50	69.11	70.73	72.36	74.00	75.66	77.33	79.02	80.71	82.42	84.13	85.86	87.60
12.75	61.66	63.19	64.74	66.30	67.88	69.47	71.08	72.69	74.32	75.96	77.62	79.28	80.96	82.64	84.34	86.05
13.00	60.58	62.09	63.61	65.15	66.70	68.26	69.83	71.42	73.02	74.64	76.26	77.90	79.54	81.20	82.87	84.54
13.25	59.54	61.02	62.51	64.02	65.55	67.08	68.63	70.19	71.77	73.35	74.95	76.55	78.17	79.80	81.44	83.08
13.50	58.53	59.98	61.45	62.94	64.43	65.94	67.46	69.00	70.55	72.10	73.67	75.25	76.84	78.44	80.05	81.67
13.75	57.55	58.98	60.42	61.88	63.35	64.84	66.33	67.84	69.36	70.90	72.44	73.99	75.56	77.13	78.71	80.30
14.00	56.59	58.00	59.42	60.86	62.30	63.76	65.24	66.72	68.22	69.72	71.24	72.77	74.31	75.85	77.41	78.97
14.25	55.67	57.05	58.45	59.86	61.29	62.72	64.17	65.63	67.10	68.58	70.08	71.58	73.09	74.61	76.15	77.69
14.50	54.77	56.14	57.51	58.90	60.30	61.71	63.14	64.57	66.02	67.48	68.95	70.43	71.92	73.41	74.92	76.43
14.75	53.90	55.24	56.60	57.96	59.34	60.73	62.13	63.55	64.97	66.41	67.85	69.31	70.77	72.25	73.73	75.22
15.00	53.06	54.38	55.71	57.05	58.41	59.78	61.16	62.55	63.95	65.37	66.79	68.22	69.66	71.11	72.57	74.04
15.25	52.24	53.54	54.85	56.17	57.51	58.85	60.21	61.58	62.96	64.35	65.75	67.16	68.58	70.01	71.45	72.89
15.50	51.44	52.72	54.01	55.31	56.63	57.95	59.29	60.64	62.00	63.37	64.75	66.14	67.54	68.94	70.36	71.78
15.75	50.66	51.92	53.19	54.48	55.77	57.08	58.40	59.73	61.07	62.41	63.77	65.14	66.52	67.90	69.30	70.70
16.00	49.91	51.15	52.40	53.67	54.94	56.23	57.53	58.84	60.16	61.49	62.82	64.17	65.53	66.89	68.26	69.64
16.25	49.17	50.40	51.63	52.88	54.14	55.40	56.68	57.97	59.27	60.58	61.90	63.23	64.56	65.91	67.26	68.62
16.50	48.46	49.67	50.88	52.11	53.35	54.60	55.86	57.13	58.41	59.70	61.00	62.31	63.63	64.95	66.28	67.62
16.75	47.77	48.95	50.15	51.36	52.59	53.82	55.06	56.31	57.57	58.85	60.13	61.42	62.71	64.02	65.33	66.66
17.00	47.09	48.26	49.44	50.64	51.84	53.06	54.28	55.52	56.76	58.01	59.28	60.55	61.83	63.11	64.41	65.71
17.25	46.43	47.59	48.75	49.93	51.12	52.31	53.52	54.74	55.97	57.20	58.45	59.70	60.96	62.23	63.51	64.79
17.50	45.79	46.93	48.08	49.24	50.41	51.59	52.78	53.98	55.19	56.41	57.64	58.88	60.12	61.37	62.63	63.90
17.75	45.17	46.29	47.42	48.57	49.72	50.89	52.06	53.25	54.44	55.64	56.85	58.07	59.30	60.54	61.78	63.03
18.00	44.56	45.66	46.78	47.91	49.05	50.20	51.36	52.53	53.71	54.89	56.09	57.29	58.50	59.72	60.94	62.18
18.25	43.96	45.06	46.16	47.27	48.40	49.53	50.68	51.83	52.99	54.16	55.34	56.53	57.72	58.92	60.13	61.35
18.50	43.39	44.46	45.55	46.65	47.76	48.88	50.01	51.15	52.29	53.45	54.61	55.78	56.96	58.15	59.34	60.54
18.75	42.82	43.89	44.96	46.05	47.14	48.25	49.36	50.48	51.61	52.75	53.90	55.06	56.22	57.39	58.57	59.76
19.00	42.27	43.32	44.38	45.45	46.54	47.63	48.73	49.83	50.95	52.08	53.21	54.35	55.50	56.66	57.82	58.99
20.00	40.20	41.20	42.21	43.23	44.26	45.29	46.34	47.39	48.46	49.53	50.60	51.69	52.78	53.88	54.99	56.10
25.00	32.24	33.04	33.85	34.67	35.49	36.32	37.16	38.01	38.86	39.72	40.58	41.45	42.33	43.21	44.09	44.99
30.00	26.88	27.55	28.22	28.90	29.59	30.29	30.99	31.69	32.40	33.12	33.84	34.56	35.29	36.03	36.77	37.51

Description: This table shows the yield to maturity of a mortgage purchased at the price shown in the index.

Example: The yield to maturity of a 10.75 %, 29 year mortgage at a price of 111.00 is 9.48 %.

INTEREST RATE, %

PRICE	7.00%	7.25%	7.50%	7.75%	8.00%	8.25%	8.50%	8.75%	9.00%	9.25%	9.50%	9.75%	10.00%	10.25%	10.50%	10.75%
175	2.10	2.29	2.48	2.66	2.85	3.03	3.22	3.40	3.59	3.77	3.95	4.13	4.31	4.49	4.67	4.85
170	2.32	2.51	2.70	2.89	3.08	3.27	3.46	3.64	3.83	4.01	4.20	4.38	4.56	4.75	4.93	5.11
165	2.55	2.75	2.94	3.13	3.32	3.52	3.71	3.89	4.08	4.27	4.46	4.64	4.83	5.01	5.20	5.38
160	2.80	2.99	3.19	3.38	3.58	3.77	3.96	4.16	4.35	4.54	4.73	4.92	5.11	5.29	5.48	5.67
155	3.05	3.25	3.45	3.65	3.84	4.04	4.24	4.43	4.63	4.82	5.01	5.20	5.39	5.59	5.78	5.97
150	3.32	3.52	3.72	3.92	4.12	4.32	4.52	4.72	4.92	5.11	5.31	5.50	5.70	5.89	6.09	6.28
145	3.60	3.80	4.01	4.21	4.42	4.62	4.82	5.02	5.22	5.42	5.62	5.82	6.02	6.22	6.42	6.61
140	3.89	4.10	4.31	4.52	4.72	4.93	5.14	5.34	5.55	5.75	5.95	6.16	6.36	6.56	6.76	6.96
135	4.20	4.41	4.63	4.84	5.05	5.26	5.47	5.68	5.89	6.09	6.30	6.51	6.72	6.92	7.13	7.33
130	4.53	4.75	4.96	5.18	5.39	5.61	5.82	6.03	6.25	6.46	6.67	6.88	7.10	7.31	7.52	7.73
125	4.88	5.10	5.32	5.54	5.76	5.98	6.20	6.41	6.63	6.85	7.07	7.28	7.50	7.71	7.93	8.15
120	5.25	5.47	5.70	5.92	6.15	6.37	6.59	6.82	7.04	7.26	7.49	7.71	7.93	8.15	8.37	8.59
119	5.32	5.55	5.77	6.00	6.23	6.45	6.68	6.90	7.13	7.35	7.57	7.80	8.02	8.24	8.46	8.69
118	5.40	5.63	5.85	6.08	6.31	6.53	6.76	6.99	7.21	7.44	7.66	7.89	8.11	8.33	8.56	8.78
117	5.48	5.71	5.93	6.16	6.39	6.62	6.85	7.07	7.30	7.52	7.75	7.98	8.20	8.43	8.65	8.88
116	5.56	5.79	6.02	6.25	6.47	6.70	6.93	7.16	7.39	7.61	7.84	8.07	8.29	8.52	8.75	8.97
115	5.64	5.87	6.10	6.33	6.56	6.79	7.02	7.25	7.48	7.71	7.93	8.16	8.39	8.62	8.84	9.07
114	5.72	5.95	6.18	6.41	6.65	6.88	7.11	7.34	7.57	7.80	8.03	8.26	8.49	8.71	8.94	9.17
113	5.80	6.04	6.27	6.50	6.73	6.97	7.20	7.43	7.66	7.89	8.12	8.35	8.58	8.81	9.04	9.27
112	5.89	6.12	6.35	6.59	6.82	7.06	7.29	7.52	7.75	7.99	8.22	8.45	8.68	8.91	9.14	9.38
111	5.97	6.21	6.44	6.68	6.91	7.15	7.38	7.61	7.85	8.08	8.32	8.55	8.78	9.01	9.25	9.48
110	6.06	6.29	6.53	6.77	7.00	7.24	7.47	7.71	7.95	8.18	8.41	8.65	8.88	9.12	9.35	9.59
109	6.15	6.38	6.62	6.86	7.10	7.33	7.57	7.81	8.04	8.28	8.52	8.75	8.99	9.22	9.46	9.69
108	6.23	6.47	6.71	6.95	7.19	7.43	7.67	7.90	8.14	8.38	8.62	8.86	9.09	9.33	9.57	9.80
107	6.32	6.57	6.81	7.05	7.29	7.52	7.76	8.00	8.24	8.48	8.72	8.96	9.20	9.44	9.68	9.91
106	6.42	6.66	6.90	7.14	7.38	7.62	7.86	8.10	8.35	8.59	8.83	9.07	9.31	9.55	9.79	10.03
105	6.51	6.75	6.99	7.24	7.48	7.72	7.97	8.21	8.45	8.69	8.93	9.18	9.42	9.66	9.90	10.14
104	6.60	6.85	7.09	7.34	7.58	7.82	8.07	8.31	8.56	8.80	9.04	9.29	9.53	9.77	10.02	10.26
103	6.70	6.94	7.19	7.44	7.68	7.93	8.17	8.42	8.66	8.91	9.15	9.40	9.64	9.89	10.13	10.38
102	6.80	7.04	7.29	7.54	7.78	8.03	8.28	8.52	8.77	9.02	9.26	9.51	9.76	10.00	10.25	10.50
101	6.89	7.14	7.39	7.64	7.89	8.14	8.39	8.63	8.88	9.13	9.38	9.63	9.88	10.12	10.37	10.62
100	7.00	7.25	7.50	7.75	8.00	8.25	8.50	8.75	9.00	9.25	9.50	9.75	10.00	10.25	10.50	10.75
99	7.10	7.35	7.60	7.85	8.10	8.35	8.61	8.86	9.11	9.36	9.61	9.86	10.12	10.37	10.62	10.87
98	7.20	7.45	7.71	7.96	8.21	8.47	8.72	8.97	9.23	9.48	9.73	9.99	10.24	10.49	10.75	11.00
97	7.31	7.56	7.81	8.07	8.32	8.58	8.83	9.09	9.34	9.60	9.86	10.11	10.37	10.62	10.88	11.13
96	7.41	7.67	7.93	8.18	8.44	8.69	8.95	9.21	9.47	9.72	9.98	10.24	10.49	10.75	11.01	11.27
95	7.52	7.78	8.04	8.30	8.55	8.81	9.07	9.33	9.59	9.85	10.11	10.36	10.62	10.88	11.14	11.40
94	7.63	7.89	8.15	8.41	8.67	8.93	9.19	9.45	9.71	9.97	10.23	10.50	10.76	11.02	11.28	11.54
93	7.74	8.01	8.27	8.53	8.79	9.05	9.32	9.58	9.84	10.10	10.37	10.63	10.89	11.16	11.42	11.68
92	7.86	8.12	8.39	8.65	8.91	9.18	9.44	9.70	9.97	10.23	10.50	10.76	11.03	11.29	11.56	11.83
91	7.98	8.24	8.51	8.77	9.04	9.30	9.57	9.83	10.10	10.37	10.64	10.90	11.17	11.44	11.71	11.97
90	8.09	8.36	8.63	8.90	9.16	9.43	9.70	9.97	10.24	10.50	10.77	11.04	11.31	11.58	11.85	12.12
89	8.22	8.48	8.75	9.02	9.29	9.56	9.83	10.10	10.37	10.64	10.92	11.19	11.46	11.73	12.00	12.28
88	8.34	8.61	8.88	9.15	9.42	9.69	9.97	10.24	10.51	10.79	11.06	11.33	11.61	11.88	12.16	12.43
87	8.46	8.74	9.01	9.28	9.56	9.83	10.10	10.38	10.65	10.93	11.21	11.48	11.76	12.04	12.31	12.59
86	8.59	8.87	9.14	9.42	9.69	9.97	10.25	10.52	10.80	11.08	11.36	11.63	11.91	12.19	12.47	12.75
85	8.72	9.00	9.28	9.55	9.83	10.11	10.39	10.67	10.95	11.23	11.51	11.79	12.07	12.35	12.64	12.92
84	8.85	9.13	9.41	9.69	9.97	10.25	10.54	10.82	11.10	11.38	11.67	11.95	12.23	12.52	12.80	13.09
83	8.99	9.27	9.55	9.84	10.12	10.40	10.68	10.97	11.25	11.54	11.82	12.11	12.40	12.68	12.97	13.26
82	9.13	9.41	9.70	9.98	10.27	10.55	10.84	11.12	11.41	11.70	11.99	12.28	12.57	12.86	13.15	13.44
81	9.27	9.56	9.84	10.13	10.42	10.70	10.99	11.28	11.57	11.86	12.15	12.45	12.74	13.03	13.32	13.62
80	9.41	9.70	9.99	10.28	10.57	10.86	11.15	11.44	11.74	12.03	12.32	12.62	12.91	13.21	13.50	13.80
79	9.56	9.85	10.14	10.43	10.73	11.02	11.32	11.61	11.91	12.20	12.50	12.80	13.09	13.39	13.69	13.99
78	9.71	10.00	10.30	10.59	10.89	11.18	11.48	11.78	12.08	12.38	12.68	12.98	13.28	13.58	13.88	14.18
77	9.86	10.16	10.46	10.75	11.05	11.35	11.65	11.95	12.25	12.56	12.86	13.16	13.47	13.77	14.08	14.38
76	10.02	10.32	10.62	10.92	11.22	11.52	11.83	12.13	12.43	12.74	13.04	13.35	13.66	13.97	14.27	14.58
75	10.18	10.48	10.79	11.09	11.39	11.70	12.00	12.31	12.62	12.93	13.23	13.54	13.86	14.17	14.48	14.79
74	10.35	10.65	10.96	11.26	11.57	11.88	12.19	12.50	12.81	13.12	13.43	13.74	14.06	14.37	14.69	15.00
73	10.51	10.82	11.13	11.44	11.75	12.06	12.37	12.69	13.00	13.31	13.63	13.95	14.26	14.58	14.90	15.22
70	11.04	11.36	11.68	12.00	12.32	12.64	12.96	13.28	13.61	13.94	14.26	14.59	14.92	15.25	15.58	15.91
65	12.02	12.35	12.69	13.03	13.37	13.71	14.05	14.39	14.74	15.08	15.43	15.78	16.13	16.48	16.83	17.19
60	13.13	13.49	13.85	14.21	14.57	14.94	15.30	15.67	16.04	16.41	16.78	17.16	17.53	17.91	18.29	18.67
55	14.43	14.81	15.20	15.59	15.98	16.37	16.76	17.16	17.56	17.96	18.36	18.77	19.17	19.58	19.99	20.40
50	15.96	16.38	16.80	17.22	17.64	18.07	18.50	18.93	19.36	19.80	20.24	20.68	21.13	21.57	22.02	22.47
45	17.81	18.27	18.73	19.19	19.66	20.13	20.60	21.08	21.56	22.04	22.52	23.01	23.50	23.99	24.49	24.99
40	20.10	20.61	21.12	21.63	22.16	22.68	23.21	23.74	24.28	24.82	25.36	25.91	26.46	27.01	27.57	28.12
35	23.01	23.59	24.17	24.75	25.35	25.94	26.55	27.15	27.76	28.38	29.00	29.62	30.25	30.88	31.51	32.15
30	26.87	27.54	28.22	28.90	29.59	30.28	30.98	31.69	32.40	33.11	33.84	34.56	35.29	36.03	36.77	37.51

Description: This table shows the price to pay for a monthly payment mortgage loan at the yield rate.

Example: The price of a 15.00 %, 29 year mortgage loan to yield 8.00 % to maturity is $ 171.20.

INTEREST RATE, %

YIELD	11.00%	11.25%	11.50%	11.75%	12.00%	12.25%	12.50%	12.75%	13.00%	13.25%	13.50%	13.75%	14.00%	14.25%	14.50%	15.00%
0.00	332.91	339.45	346.02	352.63	359.26	365.93	372.62	379.34	386.08	392.85	399.65	406.46	413.30	420.16	427.03	440.85
1.00	288.88	294.55	300.26	305.99	311.75	317.53	323.34	329.17	335.02	340.90	346.79	352.70	358.64	364.59	370.56	382.54
2.00	252.45	257.41	262.40	267.41	272.44	277.49	282.57	287.66	292.78	297.91	303.06	308.23	313.42	318.62	323.83	334.31
3.00	222.17	226.53	230.92	235.32	239.75	244.20	248.67	253.15	257.65	262.17	266.70	271.25	275.81	280.39	284.98	294.20
4.00	196.85	200.72	204.60	208.51	212.43	216.37	220.33	224.30	228.29	232.29	236.31	240.34	244.38	248.44	252.51	260.67
4.25	191.18	194.94	198.71	202.51	206.32	210.14	213.99	217.85	221.72	225.61	229.51	233.42	237.35	241.29	245.24	253.17
4.50	185.76	189.41	193.07	196.76	200.46	204.18	207.91	211.66	215.43	219.20	222.99	226.80	230.61	234.44	238.28	245.98
4.75	180.56	184.10	187.67	191.25	194.85	198.46	202.09	205.74	209.40	213.07	216.75	220.45	224.16	227.88	231.61	239.10
5.00	175.57	179.02	182.49	185.97	189.47	192.99	196.52	200.06	203.62	207.19	210.77	214.37	217.97	221.59	225.22	232.50
5.25	170.80	174.15	177.52	180.91	184.32	187.74	191.17	194.62	198.08	201.55	205.04	208.53	212.04	215.56	219.09	226.17
5.50	166.21	169.48	172.76	176.06	179.37	182.70	186.04	189.40	192.76	196.14	199.53	202.94	206.35	209.78	213.21	220.11
5.75	161.82	165.00	168.19	171.40	174.63	177.87	181.12	184.39	187.66	190.96	194.26	197.57	200.89	204.23	207.57	214.28
6.00	157.60	160.69	163.81	166.93	170.07	173.23	176.40	179.58	182.77	185.98	189.19	192.42	195.66	198.90	202.16	208.70
6.25	153.55	156.56	159.60	162.64	165.70	168.78	171.86	174.96	178.07	181.20	184.33	187.47	190.63	193.79	196.96	203.33
6.50	149.66	152.60	155.55	158.52	161.50	164.50	167.51	170.53	173.56	176.61	179.66	182.72	185.80	188.88	191.97	198.18
6.75	145.92	148.79	151.67	154.56	157.47	160.39	163.33	166.27	169.23	172.20	175.17	178.16	181.16	184.16	187.18	193.23
7.00	142.33	145.12	147.93	150.76	153.60	156.44	159.31	162.18	165.06	167.96	170.86	173.77	176.70	179.63	182.57	188.48
7.25	138.87	141.60	144.35	147.10	149.87	152.65	155.44	158.24	161.06	163.88	166.72	169.56	172.41	175.27	178.14	183.90
7.50	135.55	138.22	140.89	143.58	146.28	149.00	151.72	154.46	157.21	159.96	162.73	165.50	168.29	171.08	173.88	179.50
7.75	132.36	134.96	137.57	140.20	142.84	145.49	148.15	150.82	153.50	156.19	158.89	161.60	164.32	167.05	169.78	175.27
8.00	129.28	131.82	134.38	136.94	139.52	142.11	144.71	147.31	149.93	152.56	155.20	157.85	160.50	163.17	165.84	171.20
8.25	126.32	128.81	131.30	133.81	136.32	138.85	141.39	143.94	146.50	149.07	151.65	154.23	156.83	159.43	162.04	167.28
8.50	123.47	125.90	128.34	130.79	133.25	135.72	138.20	140.69	143.19	145.71	148.23	150.75	153.29	155.83	158.38	163.51
8.75	120.73	123.10	125.48	127.88	130.28	132.70	135.13	137.56	140.01	142.46	144.93	147.40	149.88	152.37	154.86	159.87
9.00	118.08	120.40	122.73	125.07	127.43	129.79	132.16	134.55	136.94	139.34	141.75	144.17	146.59	149.03	151.47	156.36
9.25	115.53	117.80	120.08	122.37	124.67	126.99	129.31	131.64	133.98	136.33	138.69	141.05	143.43	145.81	148.19	152.99
9.50	113.07	115.29	117.52	119.76	122.02	124.28	126.55	128.84	131.13	133.43	135.73	138.05	140.37	142.70	145.04	149.73
9.75	110.69	112.87	115.05	117.25	119.46	121.67	123.90	126.13	128.37	130.63	132.88	135.15	137.42	139.70	141.99	146.58
10.00	108.40	110.53	112.67	114.82	116.98	119.15	121.33	123.52	125.72	127.92	130.13	132.35	134.58	136.81	139.05	143.55
10.25	106.19	108.28	110.37	112.48	114.60	116.72	118.86	121.00	123.15	125.31	127.48	129.65	131.83	134.02	136.22	140.62
10.50	104.06	106.10	108.15	110.22	112.29	114.38	116.47	118.57	120.68	122.79	124.92	127.05	129.18	131.33	133.48	137.79
10.75	101.99	104.00	106.01	108.03	110.07	112.11	114.16	116.22	118.28	120.36	122.44	124.53	126.62	128.72	130.83	135.06
11.00	100.00	101.96	103.94	105.92	107.92	109.92	111.93	113.95	115.97	118.01	120.05	122.09	124.15	126.21	128.27	132.42
11.25	98.07	100.00	101.94	103.88	105.84	107.80	109.77	111.75	113.74	115.73	117.73	119.74	121.76	123.78	125.80	129.87
11.50	96.21	98.10	100.00	101.91	103.83	105.75	107.69	109.63	111.58	113.53	115.50	117.47	119.44	121.43	123.41	127.40
11.75	94.41	96.26	98.13	100.00	101.88	103.77	105.67	107.58	109.49	111.41	113.33	115.27	117.21	119.15	121.10	125.02
12.00	92.66	94.48	96.31	98.15	100.00	101.86	103.72	105.59	107.47	109.35	111.24	113.14	115.04	116.95	118.86	122.71
12.25	90.98	92.76	94.56	96.37	98.18	100.00	101.83	103.67	105.51	107.36	109.21	111.08	112.95	114.82	116.70	120.47
12.50	89.34	91.10	92.86	94.63	96.42	98.20	100.00	101.80	103.61	105.43	107.25	109.08	110.92	112.76	114.60	118.31
12.75	87.76	89.48	91.22	92.96	94.71	96.46	98.23	100.00	101.78	103.56	105.35	107.15	108.95	110.76	112.57	116.21
13.00	86.23	87.92	89.62	91.33	93.05	94.78	96.51	98.25	100.00	101.75	103.51	105.28	107.05	108.83	110.61	114.18
13.25	84.74	86.41	88.08	89.76	91.45	93.15	94.85	96.56	98.28	100.00	101.73	103.46	105.20	106.95	108.70	112.22
13.50	83.30	84.94	86.58	88.23	89.89	91.56	93.24	94.92	96.61	98.30	100.00	101.71	103.42	105.13	106.85	110.31
13.75	81.90	83.51	85.13	86.76	88.39	90.03	91.67	93.33	94.99	96.65	98.32	100.00	101.68	103.37	105.06	108.46
14.00	80.55	82.13	83.72	85.32	86.93	88.54	90.16	91.78	93.41	95.05	96.70	98.35	100.00	101.66	103.32	106.67
14.25	79.23	80.79	82.36	83.93	85.51	87.09	88.69	90.28	91.89	93.50	95.12	96.74	98.37	100.00	101.64	104.92
14.50	77.96	79.49	81.03	82.58	84.13	85.69	87.26	88.83	90.41	92.00	93.59	95.18	96.78	98.39	100.00	103.23
14.75	76.72	78.23	79.74	81.26	82.79	84.33	85.87	87.42	88.97	90.53	92.10	93.67	95.25	96.83	98.41	101.59
15.00	75.52	77.00	78.49	79.99	81.49	83.01	84.52	86.05	87.58	89.11	90.65	92.20	93.75	95.31	96.87	100.00
15.25	74.35	75.81	77.28	78.75	80.23	81.72	83.22	84.72	86.22	87.73	89.25	90.77	92.30	93.83	95.37	98.45
15.50	73.21	74.65	76.09	77.55	79.01	80.47	81.94	83.42	84.90	86.39	87.89	89.39	90.89	92.40	93.91	96.95
15.75	72.11	73.52	74.95	76.38	77.81	79.26	80.71	82.16	83.62	85.09	86.56	88.04	89.52	91.00	92.49	95.49
16.00	71.03	72.43	73.83	75.24	76.66	78.08	79.51	80.94	82.38	83.82	85.27	86.73	88.19	89.65	91.12	94.06
16.25	69.99	71.36	72.75	74.13	75.53	76.93	78.34	79.75	81.17	82.59	84.02	85.45	86.89	88.33	89.78	92.68
16.50	68.97	70.33	71.69	73.06	74.43	75.81	77.20	78.59	79.99	81.39	82.80	84.21	85.63	87.05	88.47	91.34
16.75	67.98	69.32	70.66	72.01	73.37	74.73	76.09	77.47	78.84	80.23	81.61	83.00	84.40	85.80	87.21	90.03
17.00	67.02	68.34	69.66	70.99	72.33	73.67	75.02	76.37	77.73	79.09	80.46	81.83	83.21	84.59	85.97	88.75
17.25	66.08	67.38	68.69	70.00	71.32	72.64	73.97	75.30	76.64	77.98	79.33	80.69	82.04	83.40	84.77	87.51
17.50	65.17	66.45	67.74	69.03	70.33	71.64	72.95	74.26	75.58	76.91	78.24	79.57	80.91	82.25	83.60	86.30
17.75	64.28	65.55	66.82	68.09	69.37	70.66	71.95	73.25	74.55	75.86	77.17	78.49	79.81	81.13	82.46	85.13
18.00	63.42	64.66	65.91	67.17	68.44	69.71	70.98	72.26	73.55	74.84	76.13	77.43	78.73	80.04	81.35	83.98
18.25	62.57	63.80	65.04	66.28	67.53	68.78	70.04	71.30	72.57	73.84	75.12	76.40	77.68	78.97	80.26	82.86
18.50	61.75	62.96	64.18	65.41	66.64	67.87	69.12	70.36	71.61	72.87	74.13	75.39	76.66	77.93	79.21	81.77
18.75	60.95	62.14	63.35	64.56	65.77	66.99	68.22	69.45	70.68	71.92	73.16	74.41	75.66	76.92	78.18	80.71
19.00	60.16	61.35	62.53	63.73	64.93	66.13	67.34	68.55	69.77	71.00	72.22	73.46	74.69	75.93	77.17	79.67
20.00	57.22	58.34	59.47	60.60	61.74	62.89	64.04	65.20	66.35	67.52	68.69	69.86	71.03	72.21	73.39	75.77
25.00	45.88	46.78	47.69	48.60	49.52	50.43	51.36	52.28	53.21	54.15	55.08	56.02	56.96	57.91	58.86	60.76
30.00	38.26	39.01	39.77	40.52	41.29	42.05	42.82	43.59	44.37	45.15	45.93	46.71	47.50	48.28	49.08	50.66

Description: This table shows the yield to maturity of a mortgage purchased at the price shown in the index.

Example: The yield to maturity of a 15.00 %, 29 year mortgage at a price of 125.00 is 11.75 %.

INTEREST RATE, %

PRICE	11.00%	11.25%	11.50%	11.75%	12.00%	12.25%	12.50%	12.75%	13.00%	13.25%	13.50%	13.75%	14.00%	14.25%	14.50%	15.00%
250	2.07	2.22	2.37	2.51	2.66	2.81	2.95	3.10	3.24	3.38	3.52	3.66	3.80	3.94	4.08	4.35
240	2.38	2.54	2.69	2.84	2.99	3.14	3.28	3.43	3.57	3.72	3.86	4.01	4.15	4.29	4.43	4.71
230	2.72	2.87	3.03	3.18	3.33	3.48	3.63	3.78	3.93	4.08	4.23	4.37	4.52	4.66	4.81	5.09
220	3.07	3.23	3.39	3.54	3.70	3.85	4.01	4.16	4.31	4.46	4.61	4.76	4.91	5.06	5.21	5.50
210	3.45	3.61	3.78	3.93	4.09	4.25	4.41	4.56	4.72	4.87	5.03	5.18	5.33	5.49	5.64	5.94
200	3.86	4.03	4.19	4.35	4.52	4.68	4.84	5.00	5.16	5.32	5.47	5.63	5.79	5.94	6.10	6.41
195	4.08	4.24	4.41	4.57	4.74	4.90	5.06	5.23	5.39	5.55	5.71	5.87	6.03	6.18	6.34	6.65
190	4.30	4.47	4.64	4.80	4.97	5.14	5.30	5.47	5.63	5.79	5.95	6.12	6.28	6.44	6.60	6.91
185	4.53	4.70	4.87	5.04	5.21	5.38	5.55	5.71	5.88	6.05	6.21	6.37	6.54	6.70	6.86	7.18
180	4.77	4.95	5.12	5.29	5.46	5.63	5.80	5.97	6.14	6.31	6.48	6.64	6.81	6.97	7.14	7.47
175	5.02	5.20	5.38	5.55	5.72	5.90	6.07	6.24	6.41	6.58	6.75	6.92	7.09	7.26	7.43	7.76
170	5.29	5.47	5.64	5.82	6.00	6.18	6.35	6.53	6.70	6.87	7.05	7.22	7.39	7.56	7.73	8.07
165	5.56	5.74	5.93	6.11	6.29	6.47	6.64	6.82	7.00	7.18	7.35	7.53	7.70	7.88	8.05	8.39
160	5.85	6.04	6.22	6.40	6.59	6.77	6.95	7.13	7.31	7.49	7.67	7.85	8.03	8.21	8.38	8.74
155	6.15	6.34	6.53	6.72	6.90	7.09	7.27	7.46	7.64	7.83	8.01	8.19	8.37	8.55	8.73	9.09
150	6.47	6.66	6.86	7.05	7.24	7.43	7.61	7.80	7.99	8.18	8.36	8.55	8.74	8.92	9.11	9.47
145	6.81	7.00	7.20	7.39	7.59	7.78	7.97	8.17	8.36	8.55	8.74	8.93	9.12	9.31	9.50	9.87
140	7.16	7.36	7.56	7.76	7.96	8.16	8.35	8.55	8.75	8.94	9.14	9.33	9.53	9.72	9.91	10.30
135	7.54	7.74	7.95	8.15	8.35	8.55	8.76	8.96	9.16	9.36	9.56	9.76	9.96	10.16	10.35	10.75
130	7.94	8.14	8.35	8.56	8.77	8.98	9.18	9.39	9.60	9.80	10.01	10.21	10.42	10.62	10.83	11.23
125	8.36	8.57	8.79	9.00	9.21	9.43	9.64	9.85	10.06	10.28	10.49	10.70	10.91	11.12	11.33	11.75
120	8.81	9.03	9.25	9.47	9.69	9.91	10.13	10.35	10.56	10.78	11.00	11.22	11.43	11.65	11.87	12.30
115	9.30	9.52	9.75	9.98	10.20	10.43	10.65	10.88	11.10	11.33	11.55	11.78	12.00	12.22	12.45	12.89
113	9.50	9.73	9.96	10.19	10.42	10.65	10.87	11.10	11.33	11.56	11.78	12.01	12.24	12.47	12.69	13.14
112	9.61	9.84	10.07	10.30	10.53	10.76	10.99	11.22	11.45	11.67	11.90	12.13	12.36	12.59	12.82	13.27
111	9.71	9.94	10.18	10.41	10.64	10.87	11.10	11.33	11.56	11.79	12.02	12.25	12.48	12.71	12.94	13.40
110	9.82	10.05	10.29	10.52	10.75	10.99	11.22	11.45	11.68	11.92	12.15	12.38	12.61	12.84	13.07	13.54
109	9.93	10.16	10.40	10.63	10.87	11.10	11.34	11.57	11.80	12.04	12.27	12.51	12.74	12.97	13.21	13.67
108	10.04	10.28	10.51	10.75	10.99	11.22	11.46	11.69	11.93	12.16	12.40	12.63	12.87	13.10	13.34	13.81
107	10.15	10.39	10.63	10.87	11.10	11.34	11.58	11.82	12.05	12.29	12.53	12.76	13.00	13.24	13.47	13.95
106	10.27	10.51	10.75	10.99	11.23	11.46	11.70	11.94	12.18	12.42	12.66	12.90	13.14	13.37	13.61	14.09
105	10.38	10.62	10.87	11.11	11.35	11.59	11.83	12.07	12.31	12.55	12.79	13.03	13.27	13.51	13.75	14.23
104	10.50	10.74	10.99	11.23	11.47	11.72	11.96	12.20	12.44	12.69	12.93	13.17	13.41	13.65	13.90	14.38
103	10.62	10.87	11.11	11.36	11.60	11.84	12.09	12.33	12.58	12.82	13.07	13.31	13.55	13.80	14.04	14.53
102	10.74	10.99	11.24	11.48	11.73	11.98	12.22	12.47	12.71	12.96	13.21	13.45	13.70	13.94	14.19	14.68
101	10.87	11.12	11.36	11.61	11.86	12.11	12.36	12.61	12.85	13.10	13.35	13.60	13.85	14.09	14.34	14.84
100	11.00	11.25	11.50	11.75	12.00	12.25	12.50	12.75	13.00	13.25	13.50	13.75	14.00	14.25	14.50	15.00
99	11.12	11.38	11.63	11.88	12.13	12.38	12.64	12.89	13.14	13.39	13.64	13.90	14.15	14.40	14.65	15.16
98	11.25	11.51	11.76	12.02	12.27	12.52	12.78	13.03	13.29	13.54	13.79	14.05	14.30	14.56	14.81	15.32
97	11.39	11.64	11.90	12.16	12.41	12.67	12.92	13.18	13.44	13.69	13.95	14.20	14.46	14.72	14.97	15.49
96	11.52	11.78	12.04	12.30	12.56	12.81	13.07	13.33	13.59	13.85	14.10	14.36	14.62	14.88	15.14	15.66
95	11.66	11.92	12.18	12.44	12.70	12.96	13.22	13.48	13.74	14.00	14.26	14.52	14.79	15.05	15.31	15.83
94	11.80	12.06	12.33	12.59	12.85	13.11	13.38	13.64	13.90	14.16	14.43	14.69	14.95	15.22	15.48	16.01
93	11.95	12.21	12.47	12.74	13.00	13.27	13.53	13.80	14.06	14.33	14.59	14.86	15.12	15.39	15.65	16.19
92	12.09	12.36	12.63	12.89	13.16	13.43	13.69	13.96	14.23	14.49	14.76	15.03	15.30	15.57	15.83	16.37
91	12.24	12.51	12.78	13.05	13.32	13.59	13.86	14.12	14.39	14.66	14.93	15.20	15.48	15.75	16.02	16.56
90	12.39	12.66	12.94	13.21	13.48	13.75	14.02	14.29	14.57	14.84	15.11	15.38	15.66	15.93	16.20	16.75
89	12.55	12.82	13.10	13.37	13.64	13.92	14.19	14.47	14.74	15.02	15.29	15.57	15.84	16.12	16.39	16.95
88	12.71	12.98	13.26	13.53	13.81	14.09	14.36	14.64	14.92	15.20	15.47	15.75	16.03	16.31	16.59	17.15
87	12.87	13.15	13.42	13.70	13.98	14.26	14.54	14.82	15.10	15.38	15.66	15.94	16.22	16.50	16.79	17.35
86	13.03	13.31	13.59	13.88	14.16	14.44	14.72	15.00	15.29	15.57	15.85	16.14	16.42	16.70	16.99	17.56
85	13.20	13.48	13.77	14.05	14.34	14.62	14.91	15.19	15.48	15.76	16.05	16.34	16.62	16.91	17.20	17.77
84	13.37	13.66	13.95	14.23	14.52	14.81	15.09	15.38	15.67	15.96	16.25	16.54	16.83	17.12	17.41	17.99
83	13.55	13.84	14.13	14.42	14.71	15.00	15.29	15.58	15.87	16.16	16.45	16.75	17.04	17.33	17.63	18.21
82	13.73	14.02	14.31	14.60	14.90	15.19	15.48	15.78	16.07	16.37	16.66	16.96	17.25	17.55	17.85	18.44
81	13.91	14.21	14.50	14.80	15.09	15.39	15.69	15.98	16.28	16.58	16.88	17.18	17.47	17.77	18.07	18.68
80	14.10	14.40	14.69	14.99	15.29	15.59	15.89	16.19	16.49	16.79	17.10	17.40	17.70	18.00	18.31	18.91
79	14.29	14.59	14.89	15.19	15.50	15.80	16.10	16.41	16.71	17.02	17.32	17.63	17.93	18.24	18.55	19.16
78	14.49	14.79	15.10	15.40	15.71	16.01	16.32	16.63	16.93	17.24	17.55	17.86	18.17	18.48	18.79	19.41
77	14.69	14.99	15.30	15.61	15.92	16.23	16.54	16.85	17.16	17.47	17.79	18.10	18.41	18.72	19.04	19.67
76	14.89	15.20	15.52	15.83	16.14	16.45	16.77	17.08	17.40	17.71	18.03	18.34	18.66	18.98	19.30	19.93
75	15.10	15.42	15.73	16.05	16.36	16.68	17.00	17.32	17.64	17.95	18.27	18.59	18.92	19.24	19.56	20.20
74	15.32	15.64	15.96	16.28	16.60	16.92	17.24	17.56	17.88	18.20	18.53	18.85	19.18	19.50	19.83	20.48
73	15.54	15.86	16.19	16.51	16.83	17.16	17.48	17.81	18.13	18.46	18.79	19.12	19.45	19.77	20.10	20.77
70	16.24	16.58	16.91	17.24	17.58	17.92	18.25	18.59	18.93	19.27	19.61	19.95	20.30	20.64	20.98	21.67
65	17.54	17.90	18.26	18.61	18.97	19.33	19.69	20.06	20.42	20.78	21.15	21.51	21.88	22.25	22.62	23.35
60	19.05	19.43	19.81	20.20	20.59	20.97	21.36	21.75	22.15	22.54	22.93	23.33	23.72	24.12	24.52	25.31
55	20.81	21.23	21.65	22.06	22.48	22.91	23.33	23.75	24.18	24.60	25.03	25.46	25.89	26.32	26.76	27.62

MORTGAGE PRICE

Description: This table shows the price to pay for a monthly payment mortgage loan at the yield rate.

Example: The price of a 6.75 %, 30 year mortgage loan to yield 8.00 % to maturity is $ 88.39.

INTEREST RATE, %

YIELD	0.00%	1.00%	2.00%	3.00%	4.00%	4.25%	4.50%	4.75%	5.00%	5.25%	5.50%	5.75%	6.00%	6.25%	6.50%	6.75%
0.00	100.00	115.79	133.06	151.78	171.87	177.10	182.41	187.79	193.26	198.79	204.40	210.09	215.84	221.66	227.54	233.50
1.00	86.36	100.00	114.92	131.08	148.43	152.95	157.53	162.18	166.90	171.68	176.53	181.44	186.40	191.43	196.51	201.65
2.00	75.15	87.02	100.00	114.06	129.16	133.09	137.08	141.13	145.24	149.40	153.61	157.88	162.21	166.58	171.01	175.48
3.00	65.89	76.29	87.67	100.00	113.24	116.68	120.18	123.73	127.33	130.98	134.67	138.42	142.21	146.04	149.92	153.84
4.00	58.18	67.37	77.42	88.31	100.00	103.04	106.13	109.26	112.44	115.67	118.93	122.24	125.58	128.97	132.39	135.86
4.25	56.47	65.38	75.14	85.70	97.05	100.00	103.00	106.04	109.12	112.25	115.42	118.63	121.87	125.16	128.48	131.84
4.50	54.82	63.48	72.95	83.21	94.22	97.09	100.00	102.95	105.95	108.98	112.06	115.17	118.33	121.52	124.75	128.01
4.75	53.25	61.66	70.86	80.82	91.52	94.31	97.13	100.00	102.91	105.86	108.85	111.87	114.93	118.03	121.17	124.34
5.00	51.74	59.92	68.85	78.54	88.93	91.64	94.39	97.17	100.00	102.87	105.77	108.71	111.69	114.70	117.74	120.82
5.25	50.30	58.25	66.94	76.35	86.46	89.09	91.76	94.47	97.21	100.00	102.82	105.68	108.57	111.50	114.46	117.46
5.50	48.92	56.65	65.10	74.25	84.08	86.64	89.24	91.87	94.55	97.26	100.00	102.78	105.59	108.44	111.32	114.23
5.75	47.60	55.12	63.34	72.25	81.81	84.30	86.82	89.39	91.99	94.62	97.30	100.00	102.74	105.51	108.31	111.14
6.00	46.33	53.65	61.65	70.32	79.63	82.05	84.51	87.01	89.54	92.10	94.70	97.34	100.00	102.70	105.42	108.18
6.25	45.11	52.24	60.03	68.47	77.54	79.90	82.29	84.72	87.19	89.68	92.22	94.78	97.37	100.00	102.66	105.34
6.50	43.95	50.89	58.48	66.70	75.53	77.83	80.16	82.53	84.93	87.36	89.83	92.33	94.86	97.41	100.00	102.62
6.75	42.83	49.59	56.99	65.00	73.61	75.85	78.12	80.43	82.77	85.14	87.54	89.97	92.44	94.93	97.45	100.00
7.00	41.75	48.34	55.56	63.37	71.76	73.94	76.16	78.41	80.69	83.00	85.34	87.72	90.12	92.55	95.00	97.49
7.25	40.72	47.15	54.18	61.80	69.98	72.11	74.27	76.47	78.69	80.95	83.23	85.55	87.89	90.26	92.65	95.08
7.50	39.73	46.00	52.86	60.30	68.28	70.36	72.46	74.60	76.77	78.97	81.20	83.46	85.75	88.06	90.40	92.76
7.75	38.77	44.90	51.59	58.85	66.64	68.67	70.73	72.81	74.93	77.08	79.25	81.46	83.69	85.94	88.23	90.53
8.00	37.86	43.83	50.37	57.46	65.06	67.04	69.05	71.09	73.16	75.26	77.38	79.53	81.71	83.91	86.14	88.39
8.25	36.97	42.81	49.20	56.12	63.55	65.48	67.44	69.44	71.46	73.50	75.58	77.68	79.81	81.96	84.13	86.33
8.50	36.13	41.83	48.07	54.83	62.09	63.98	65.90	67.84	69.82	71.82	73.84	75.90	77.97	80.08	82.20	84.35
8.75	35.31	40.88	46.98	53.59	60.69	62.53	64.41	66.31	68.24	70.19	72.17	74.18	76.21	78.27	80.34	82.45
9.00	34.52	39.97	45.94	52.40	59.33	61.14	62.97	64.83	66.72	68.63	70.57	72.53	74.51	76.52	78.55	80.61
9.25	33.77	39.10	44.93	51.25	58.03	59.80	61.59	63.41	65.25	67.12	69.02	70.94	72.88	74.84	76.83	78.84
9.50	33.04	38.25	43.96	50.14	56.78	58.50	60.26	62.04	63.84	65.67	67.53	69.40	71.30	73.23	75.17	77.14
9.75	32.33	37.44	43.02	49.07	55.57	57.26	58.97	60.72	62.48	64.27	66.09	67.92	69.78	71.67	73.57	75.49
10.00	31.65	36.65	42.12	48.04	54.40	56.06	57.74	59.44	61.17	62.92	64.70	66.50	68.32	70.16	72.02	73.91
10.25	31.00	35.89	41.25	47.05	53.28	54.90	56.54	58.21	59.91	61.62	63.36	65.12	66.91	68.71	70.54	72.38
10.50	30.37	35.16	40.41	46.09	52.19	53.78	55.39	57.03	58.69	60.37	62.07	63.80	65.54	67.31	69.10	70.91
10.75	29.76	34.46	39.60	45.16	51.14	52.70	54.28	55.88	57.51	59.16	60.82	62.52	64.23	65.96	67.71	69.48
11.00	29.17	33.77	38.81	44.27	50.13	51.66	53.21	54.78	56.37	57.98	59.62	61.28	62.96	64.65	66.37	68.11
11.25	28.60	33.12	38.06	43.41	49.15	50.65	52.17	53.71	55.27	56.85	58.46	60.08	61.73	63.39	65.08	66.78
11.50	28.05	32.48	37.32	42.57	48.21	49.68	51.17	52.68	54.21	55.76	57.34	58.93	60.54	62.18	63.83	65.50
11.75	27.52	31.86	36.62	41.77	47.30	48.74	50.20	51.68	53.18	54.71	56.25	57.81	59.40	61.00	62.62	64.26
12.00	27.01	31.27	35.93	40.99	46.41	47.83	49.26	50.71	52.19	53.68	55.20	56.73	58.29	59.86	61.45	63.06
12.25	26.51	30.69	35.27	40.23	45.56	46.95	48.35	49.78	51.23	52.70	54.18	55.69	57.21	58.76	60.32	61.90
12.50	26.03	30.14	34.63	39.50	44.73	46.09	47.48	48.88	50.30	51.74	53.20	54.68	56.18	57.69	59.22	60.77
12.75	25.56	29.60	34.01	38.80	43.93	45.27	46.63	48.00	49.40	50.82	52.25	53.70	55.17	56.66	58.16	59.69
13.00	25.11	29.08	33.41	38.11	43.16	44.47	45.80	47.16	48.53	49.92	51.33	52.75	54.20	55.66	57.14	58.63
13.25	24.67	28.57	32.83	37.45	42.41	43.70	45.01	46.34	47.68	49.05	50.44	51.84	53.26	54.69	56.15	57.61
13.50	24.25	28.08	32.27	36.81	41.68	42.95	44.24	45.54	46.87	48.21	49.57	50.95	52.34	53.76	55.18	56.63
13.75	23.84	27.61	31.72	36.19	40.98	42.22	43.49	44.77	46.07	47.39	48.73	50.09	51.46	52.85	54.25	55.67
14.00	23.44	27.15	31.19	35.58	40.29	41.52	42.76	44.03	45.31	46.60	47.92	49.25	50.60	51.96	53.34	54.74
14.25	23.06	26.70	30.68	35.00	39.63	40.84	42.06	43.30	44.56	45.84	47.13	48.44	49.77	51.11	52.47	53.84
14.50	22.68	26.27	30.18	34.43	38.99	40.17	41.38	42.60	43.84	45.09	46.37	47.66	48.96	50.28	51.62	52.97
14.75	22.32	25.85	29.70	33.88	38.36	39.53	40.71	41.92	43.14	44.37	45.62	46.89	48.18	49.48	50.79	52.12
15.00	21.97	25.44	29.23	33.34	37.76	38.91	40.07	41.26	42.46	43.67	44.90	46.15	47.42	48.69	49.99	51.30
15.25	21.63	25.04	28.78	32.82	37.17	38.30	39.45	40.61	41.79	42.99	44.20	45.43	46.68	47.94	49.21	50.50
15.50	21.29	24.66	28.33	32.32	36.60	37.71	38.84	39.99	41.15	42.33	43.52	44.73	45.96	47.20	48.45	49.72
15.75	20.97	24.28	27.90	31.83	36.04	37.14	38.25	39.38	40.53	41.69	42.86	44.06	45.26	46.48	47.72	48.96
16.00	20.66	23.92	27.49	31.35	35.50	36.58	37.68	38.79	39.92	41.06	42.22	43.40	44.58	45.79	47.00	48.23
16.25	20.35	23.56	27.08	30.89	34.98	36.04	37.12	38.22	39.33	40.46	41.60	42.75	43.93	45.11	46.31	47.52
16.50	20.05	23.22	26.68	30.44	34.47	35.52	36.58	37.66	38.76	39.87	40.99	42.13	43.28	44.45	45.63	46.83
16.75	19.77	22.89	26.30	30.00	33.97	35.00	36.05	37.12	38.20	39.29	40.40	41.52	42.66	43.81	44.97	46.15
17.00	19.48	22.56	25.93	29.57	33.49	34.51	35.54	36.59	37.65	38.73	39.83	40.93	42.05	43.19	44.33	45.49
17.25	19.21	22.24	25.56	29.16	33.02	34.02	35.04	36.08	37.12	38.19	39.27	40.36	41.46	42.58	43.71	44.86
17.50	18.94	21.94	25.21	28.75	32.56	33.55	34.55	35.58	36.61	37.66	38.72	39.80	40.89	41.99	43.11	44.23
17.75	18.68	21.63	24.86	28.36	32.11	33.09	34.08	35.09	36.11	37.14	38.19	39.25	40.33	41.42	42.52	43.63
18.00	18.43	21.34	24.53	27.97	31.68	32.64	33.62	34.61	35.62	36.64	37.67	38.72	39.78	40.85	41.94	43.04
18.25	18.19	21.06	24.20	27.60	31.25	32.21	33.17	34.15	35.14	36.15	37.17	38.20	39.25	40.31	41.38	42.46
18.50	17.94	20.78	23.88	27.24	30.84	31.78	32.73	33.70	34.68	35.67	36.68	37.70	38.73	39.78	40.83	41.90
18.75	17.71	20.51	23.57	26.88	30.44	31.37	32.31	33.26	34.23	35.21	36.20	37.21	38.23	39.26	40.30	41.35
19.00	17.48	20.24	23.26	26.53	30.05	30.96	31.89	32.83	33.79	34.75	35.73	36.73	37.73	38.75	39.78	40.82
20.00	16.62	19.25	22.12	25.23	28.57	29.44	30.32	31.22	32.13	33.05	33.98	34.92	35.88	36.85	37.83	38.81
25.00	13.33	15.43	17.73	20.22	22.90	23.60	24.31	25.02	25.75	26.49	27.24	27.99	28.76	29.54	30.32	31.11
30.00	11.11	12.86	14.78	16.86	19.09	19.67	20.26	20.86	21.47	22.09	22.71	23.34	23.98	24.63	25.28	25.94

Description: This table shows the yield to maturity of a mortgage purchased at the price shown in the index.

Example: The yield to maturity of a 6.75 %, 30 year mortgage at a price of 80.00 is 9.08 %.

INTEREST RATE, %

PRICE	0.00%	1.00%	2.00%	3.00%	4.00%	4.25%	4.50%	4.75%	5.00%	5.25%	5.50%	5.75%	6.00%	6.25%	6.50%	6.75%
100	0.00	1.00	2.00	3.00	4.00	4.25	4.50	4.75	5.00	5.25	5.50	5.75	6.00	6.25	6.50	6.75
99	.06	1.07	2.07	3.07	4.08	4.33	4.58	4.83	5.08	5.33	5.59	5.84	6.09	6.34	6.59	6.84
98	.13	1.14	2.14	3.15	4.16	4.42	4.67	4.92	5.17	5.43	5.68	5.93	6.18	6.44	6.69	6.94
97	.20	1.21	2.22	3.23	4.25	4.50	4.76	5.01	5.26	5.52	5.77	6.03	6.28	6.54	6.79	7.04
96	.27	1.28	2.30	3.32	4.34	4.59	4.85	5.10	5.36	5.61	5.87	6.12	6.38	6.64	6.89	7.15
95	.34	1.36	2.38	3.40	4.43	4.68	4.94	5.19	5.45	5.71	5.97	6.22	6.48	6.74	7.00	7.25
94	.41	1.43	2.46	3.49	4.52	4.77	5.03	5.29	5.55	5.81	6.06	6.32	6.58	6.84	7.10	7.36
93	.48	1.51	2.54	3.57	4.61	4.87	5.13	5.39	5.64	5.90	6.17	6.43	6.69	6.95	7.21	7.47
92	.56	1.59	2.62	3.66	4.70	4.96	5.22	5.48	5.74	6.01	6.27	6.53	6.79	7.05	7.32	7.58
91	.63	1.67	2.71	3.75	4.79	5.06	5.32	5.58	5.84	6.11	6.37	6.63	6.90	7.16	7.43	7.69
90	.71	1.75	2.79	3.84	4.89	5.15	5.42	5.68	5.95	6.21	6.48	6.74	7.01	7.27	7.54	7.81
89	.79	1.83	2.88	3.93	4.99	5.25	5.52	5.79	6.05	6.32	6.58	6.85	7.12	7.39	7.65	7.92
88	.86	1.91	2.97	4.02	5.09	5.35	5.62	5.89	6.16	6.43	6.69	6.96	7.23	7.50	7.77	8.04
87	.94	2.00	3.06	4.12	5.19	5.46	5.73	6.00	6.27	6.54	6.81	7.08	7.35	7.62	7.89	8.16
86	1.02	2.08	3.15	4.22	5.29	5.56	5.83	6.10	6.38	6.65	6.92	7.19	7.46	7.74	8.01	8.29
85	1.11	2.17	3.24	4.31	5.40	5.67	5.94	6.21	6.49	6.76	7.03	7.31	7.58	7.86	8.14	8.41
84	1.19	2.26	3.33	4.41	5.50	5.78	6.05	6.33	6.60	6.88	7.15	7.43	7.71	7.98	8.26	8.54
83	1.28	2.35	3.43	4.52	5.61	5.89	6.16	6.44	6.72	7.00	7.27	7.55	7.83	8.11	8.39	8.67
82	1.36	2.44	3.53	4.62	5.72	6.00	6.28	6.56	6.84	7.12	7.40	7.68	7.96	8.24	8.52	8.80
81	1.45	2.53	3.62	4.73	5.84	6.12	6.40	6.68	6.96	7.24	7.52	7.80	8.09	8.37	8.66	8.94
80	1.54	2.63	3.73	4.83	5.95	6.23	6.51	6.80	7.08	7.36	7.65	7.93	8.22	8.51	8.79	9.08
79	1.63	2.72	3.83	4.94	6.07	6.35	6.64	6.92	7.21	7.49	7.78	8.07	8.35	8.64	8.93	9.22
78	1.72	2.82	3.93	5.06	6.19	6.47	6.76	7.05	7.33	7.62	7.91	8.20	8.49	8.78	9.07	9.37
77	1.82	2.92	4.04	5.17	6.31	6.60	6.89	7.18	7.47	7.76	8.05	8.34	8.63	8.93	9.22	9.52
76	1.91	3.02	4.15	5.29	6.44	6.73	7.02	7.31	7.60	7.89	8.19	8.48	8.78	9.07	9.37	9.67
75	2.01	3.13	4.26	5.40	6.56	6.85	7.15	7.44	7.74	8.03	8.33	8.62	8.92	9.22	9.52	9.82
74	2.11	3.23	4.37	5.53	6.69	6.99	7.28	7.58	7.88	8.17	8.47	8.77	9.07	9.37	9.68	9.98
73	2.21	3.34	4.49	5.65	6.83	7.12	7.42	7.72	8.02	8.32	8.62	8.92	9.23	9.53	9.84	10.14
72	2.31	3.45	4.61	5.78	6.96	7.26	7.56	7.86	8.16	8.47	8.77	9.08	9.38	9.69	10.00	10.31
71	2.42	3.57	4.73	5.91	7.10	7.40	7.70	8.01	8.31	8.62	8.93	9.23	9.54	9.85	10.17	10.48
70	2.53	3.68	4.85	6.04	7.24	7.55	7.85	8.16	8.47	8.78	9.09	9.40	9.71	10.02	10.34	10.65
69	2.64	3.80	4.98	6.17	7.39	7.69	8.00	8.31	8.62	8.93	9.25	9.56	9.88	10.19	10.51	10.83
68	2.75	3.92	5.10	6.31	7.54	7.85	8.16	8.47	8.78	9.10	9.41	9.73	10.05	10.37	10.69	11.01
67	2.86	4.04	5.24	6.45	7.69	8.00	8.32	8.63	8.95	9.27	9.59	9.91	10.23	10.55	10.88	11.20
66	2.98	4.17	5.37	6.60	7.85	8.16	8.48	8.80	9.12	9.44	9.76	10.08	10.41	10.74	11.07	11.40
65	3.10	4.29	5.51	6.75	8.01	8.32	8.64	8.97	9.29	9.61	9.94	10.27	10.60	10.93	11.26	11.59
64	3.22	4.43	5.65	6.90	8.17	8.49	8.81	9.14	9.47	9.79	10.12	10.46	10.79	11.12	11.46	11.80
63	3.35	4.56	5.79	7.05	8.34	8.66	8.99	9.32	9.65	9.98	10.31	10.65	10.99	11.32	11.67	12.01
62	3.48	4.70	5.94	7.21	8.51	8.84	9.17	9.50	9.84	10.17	10.51	10.85	11.19	11.53	11.88	12.22
61	3.61	4.84	6.09	7.38	8.69	9.02	9.35	9.69	10.03	10.37	10.71	11.05	11.40	11.74	12.09	12.44
60	3.74	4.98	6.25	7.55	8.87	9.21	9.54	9.88	10.23	10.57	10.92	11.26	11.61	11.96	12.32	12.67
59	3.88	5.13	6.41	7.72	9.06	9.40	9.74	10.08	10.43	10.78	11.13	11.48	11.83	12.19	12.55	12.91
58	4.02	5.28	6.57	7.90	9.25	9.60	9.94	10.29	10.64	10.99	11.35	11.70	12.06	12.42	12.78	13.15
57	4.17	5.44	6.74	8.08	9.45	9.80	10.15	10.50	10.86	11.21	11.57	11.93	12.30	12.66	13.03	13.40
56	4.31	5.60	6.92	8.27	9.65	10.01	10.36	10.72	11.08	11.44	11.80	12.17	12.54	12.91	13.28	13.66
55	4.47	5.76	7.10	8.46	9.87	10.22	10.58	10.94	11.31	11.67	12.04	12.41	12.79	13.16	13.54	13.92
54	4.62	5.93	7.28	8.66	10.08	10.44	10.81	11.18	11.55	11.92	12.29	12.67	13.05	13.43	13.81	14.20
53	4.79	6.11	7.47	8.87	10.31	10.67	11.04	11.42	11.79	12.17	12.55	12.93	13.31	13.70	14.09	14.49
52	4.95	6.29	7.66	9.08	10.54	10.91	11.29	11.66	12.04	12.43	12.81	13.20	13.59	13.98	14.38	14.78
51	5.12	6.47	7.87	9.30	10.78	11.16	11.54	11.92	12.31	12.69	13.09	13.48	13.88	14.28	14.68	15.09
50	5.30	6.66	8.07	9.53	11.03	11.41	11.80	12.19	12.58	12.97	13.37	13.77	14.17	14.58	14.99	15.40
49	5.48	6.86	8.29	9.76	11.29	11.67	12.07	12.46	12.86	13.26	13.66	14.07	14.48	14.90	15.31	15.73
48	5.67	7.07	8.51	10.01	11.55	11.95	12.34	12.75	13.15	13.56	13.97	14.38	14.80	15.22	15.65	16.08
47	5.86	7.28	8.74	10.26	11.83	12.23	12.63	13.04	13.45	13.87	14.29	14.71	15.13	15.56	16.00	16.43
46	6.06	7.50	8.98	10.52	12.12	12.52	12.93	13.35	13.77	14.19	14.62	15.05	15.48	15.92	16.36	16.80
45	6.27	7.72	9.23	10.79	12.41	12.83	13.25	13.67	14.10	14.53	14.96	15.40	15.84	16.29	16.74	17.19
44	6.48	7.96	9.48	11.07	12.72	13.15	13.57	14.00	14.44	14.88	15.32	15.77	16.22	16.67	17.13	17.59
43	6.71	8.20	9.75	11.37	13.05	13.48	13.91	14.35	14.79	15.24	15.69	16.15	16.61	17.07	17.54	18.01
42	6.94	8.45	10.03	11.67	13.38	13.82	14.27	14.71	15.17	15.62	16.08	16.55	17.02	17.49	17.97	18.45
41	7.18	8.71	10.32	11.99	13.74	14.18	14.64	15.09	15.55	16.02	16.49	16.97	17.45	17.93	18.42	18.91
40	7.43	8.99	10.62	12.32	14.10	14.56	15.02	15.49	15.96	16.44	16.92	17.40	17.89	18.39	18.89	19.39
39	7.68	9.27	10.93	12.67	14.49	14.96	15.43	15.91	16.39	16.87	17.37	17.86	18.37	18.87	19.38	19.90
35	8.84	10.55	12.35	14.24	16.23	16.75	17.27	17.79	18.32	18.86	19.40	19.95	20.51	21.07	21.63	22.20
30	10.64	12.56	14.59	16.74	19.03	19.62	20.21	20.82	21.43	22.05	22.68	23.32	23.96	24.61	25.26	25.93
25	13.06	15.27	17.64	20.18	22.89	23.59	24.30	25.02	25.75	26.49	27.24	28.00	28.77	29.54	30.33	31.12
20	16.54	19.23	22.14	25.28	28.63	29.51	30.39	31.29	32.20	33.13	34.06	35.01	35.97	36.94	37.92	38.91
15	22.19	25.71	29.56	33.72	38.19	39.35	40.53	41.73	42.94	44.17	45.42	46.68	47.96	49.25	50.56	51.88
10	33.33	38.59	44.35	50.59	57.29	59.03	60.80	62.59	64.41	66.26	68.13	70.02	71.94	73.88	75.84	77.83

Description: This table shows the price to pay for a monthly payment mortgage loan at the yield rate.

Example: The price of a 10.75 %, 30 year mortgage loan to yield 8.00 % to maturity is $ 127.22.

INTEREST RATE, %

YIELD	7.00%	7.25%	7.50%	7.75%	8.00%	8.25%	8.50%	8.75%	9.00%	9.25%	9.50%	9.75%	10.00%	10.25%	10.50%	10.75%
0.00	239.51	245.58	251.72	257.91	264.16	270.46	276.81	283.21	289.66	296.16	302.71	309.30	315.93	322.60	329.31	336.05
1.00	206.85	212.09	217.39	222.74	228.13	233.57	239.06	244.59	250.16	255.78	261.43	267.12	272.84	278.60	284.40	290.23
2.00	180.00	184.56	189.17	193.82	198.52	203.25	208.03	212.84	217.69	222.57	227.49	232.44	237.43	242.44	247.48	252.55
3.00	157.80	161.80	165.85	169.93	174.04	178.19	182.38	186.60	190.85	195.13	199.44	203.78	208.15	212.55	216.97	221.41
4.00	139.36	142.89	146.46	150.06	153.70	157.36	161.06	164.78	168.54	172.32	176.13	179.96	183.82	187.70	191.60	195.53
4.25	135.24	138.67	142.13	145.63	149.16	152.72	156.30	159.92	163.56	167.23	170.93	174.65	178.39	182.16	185.95	189.76
4.50	131.30	134.64	138.00	141.39	144.82	148.27	151.75	155.26	158.80	162.36	165.95	169.56	173.20	176.86	180.53	184.23
4.75	127.54	130.77	134.04	137.34	140.66	144.02	147.40	150.81	154.25	157.71	161.19	164.70	168.23	171.78	175.36	178.95
5.00	123.93	127.08	130.25	133.45	136.69	139.95	143.23	146.55	149.89	153.25	156.64	160.04	163.48	166.93	170.40	173.89
5.25	120.48	123.54	126.62	129.74	132.88	136.05	139.24	142.47	145.71	148.98	152.27	155.59	158.92	162.28	165.65	169.05
5.50	117.17	120.15	123.15	126.18	129.23	132.31	135.42	138.56	141.71	144.89	148.09	151.32	154.56	157.82	161.11	164.41
5.75	114.01	116.90	119.82	122.76	125.74	128.74	131.76	134.81	137.88	140.97	144.09	147.22	150.38	153.55	156.75	159.96
6.00	110.97	113.78	116.62	119.49	122.39	125.30	128.25	131.22	134.20	137.22	140.25	143.30	146.37	149.46	152.57	155.70
6.25	108.05	110.79	113.56	116.35	119.17	122.01	124.88	127.77	130.68	133.61	136.57	139.54	142.53	145.54	148.56	151.61
6.50	105.26	107.93	110.62	113.34	116.09	118.86	121.65	124.46	127.30	130.16	133.03	135.93	138.84	141.77	144.72	147.69
6.75	102.58	105.18	107.80	110.46	113.13	115.83	118.55	121.29	124.06	126.84	129.64	132.46	135.30	138.16	141.03	143.92
7.00	100.00	102.54	105.10	107.68	110.29	112.92	115.57	118.25	120.94	123.65	126.39	129.14	131.91	134.69	137.49	140.31
7.25	97.53	100.00	102.50	105.02	107.56	110.13	112.71	115.32	117.95	120.60	123.26	125.94	128.64	131.36	134.09	136.84
7.50	95.15	97.56	100.00	102.46	104.94	107.44	109.97	112.51	115.08	117.66	120.26	122.87	125.51	128.16	130.82	133.50
7.75	92.87	95.22	97.60	100.00	102.42	104.87	107.33	109.81	112.31	114.83	117.37	119.92	122.50	125.08	127.68	130.30
8.00	90.67	92.97	95.29	97.64	100.00	102.39	104.79	107.21	109.66	112.12	114.59	117.09	119.60	122.12	124.66	127.22
8.25	88.56	90.80	93.07	95.36	97.67	100.00	102.35	104.72	107.10	109.51	111.92	114.36	116.81	119.28	121.76	124.25
8.50	86.53	88.72	90.94	93.17	95.43	97.70	100.00	102.31	104.64	106.99	109.36	111.74	114.13	116.54	118.97	121.40
8.75	84.57	86.71	88.88	91.07	93.27	95.50	97.74	100.00	102.28	104.57	106.88	109.21	111.55	113.91	116.28	118.66
9.00	82.69	84.78	86.90	89.04	91.19	93.37	95.56	97.77	100.00	102.24	104.50	106.78	109.07	111.37	113.69	116.01
9.25	80.87	82.92	84.99	87.08	89.19	91.32	93.46	95.63	97.81	100.00	102.21	104.43	106.67	108.93	111.19	113.47
9.50	79.12	81.13	83.16	85.20	87.26	89.35	91.44	93.56	95.69	97.84	100.00	102.18	104.37	106.57	108.79	111.02
9.75	77.44	79.40	81.38	83.39	85.41	87.44	89.50	91.57	93.65	95.75	97.87	100.00	102.14	104.30	106.47	108.65
10.00	75.81	77.73	79.68	81.64	83.61	85.61	87.62	89.65	91.69	93.74	95.82	97.90	100.00	102.11	104.24	106.37
10.25	74.24	76.13	78.03	79.95	81.88	83.84	85.81	87.79	89.79	91.81	93.83	95.88	97.93	100.00	102.08	104.17
10.50	72.73	74.58	76.44	78.32	80.22	82.13	84.06	86.00	87.96	89.94	91.92	93.92	95.94	97.96	100.00	102.05
10.75	71.27	73.08	74.90	76.75	78.61	80.48	82.37	84.28	86.20	88.13	90.08	92.04	94.01	96.00	97.99	100.00
11.00	69.86	71.63	73.42	75.23	77.05	78.89	80.74	82.61	84.49	86.39	88.30	90.22	92.15	94.10	96.05	98.02
11.25	68.50	70.24	71.99	73.76	75.55	77.35	79.17	81.00	82.84	84.70	86.57	88.46	90.35	92.26	94.18	96.11
11.50	67.18	68.89	70.61	72.34	74.10	75.86	77.65	79.44	81.25	83.07	84.91	86.76	88.62	90.49	92.37	94.26
11.75	65.91	67.58	69.27	70.97	72.69	74.43	76.17	77.94	79.71	81.50	83.30	85.11	86.94	88.77	90.62	92.48
12.00	64.68	66.32	67.98	69.65	71.34	73.04	74.75	76.48	78.22	79.98	81.75	83.53	85.32	87.12	88.93	90.75
12.25	63.49	65.10	66.73	68.37	70.02	71.69	73.38	75.07	76.78	78.51	80.24	81.99	83.75	85.51	87.29	89.08
12.50	62.34	63.92	65.52	67.13	68.75	70.39	72.05	73.71	75.39	77.08	78.79	80.50	82.23	83.96	85.71	87.47
12.75	61.22	62.78	64.34	65.93	67.52	69.13	70.76	72.39	74.04	75.70	77.38	79.06	80.76	82.46	84.18	85.90
13.00	60.14	61.67	63.21	64.76	66.33	67.91	69.51	71.12	72.74	74.37	76.01	77.67	79.33	81.01	82.69	84.39
13.25	59.10	60.60	62.11	63.64	65.18	66.73	68.30	69.88	71.47	73.08	74.69	76.32	77.95	79.60	81.25	82.92
13.50	58.08	59.56	61.04	62.55	64.06	65.59	67.13	68.68	70.25	71.82	73.41	75.01	76.62	78.23	79.86	81.50
13.75	57.10	58.55	60.01	61.49	62.98	64.48	65.99	67.52	69.06	70.61	72.17	73.74	75.32	76.91	78.51	80.12
14.00	56.15	57.57	59.01	60.46	61.93	63.40	64.89	66.40	67.91	69.43	70.97	72.51	74.06	75.63	77.20	78.78
14.25	55.23	56.63	58.04	59.47	60.91	62.36	63.83	65.30	66.79	68.29	69.80	71.32	72.85	74.38	75.93	77.49
14.50	54.33	55.71	57.10	58.50	59.92	61.35	62.79	64.24	65.71	67.18	68.67	70.16	71.66	73.18	74.70	76.23
14.75	53.46	54.82	56.19	57.57	58.96	60.37	61.79	63.22	64.66	66.11	67.57	69.04	70.52	72.01	73.50	75.01
15.00	52.62	53.95	55.30	56.66	58.03	59.41	60.81	62.22	63.63	65.06	66.50	67.95	69.40	70.87	72.34	73.83
15.25	51.80	53.11	54.44	55.78	57.13	58.49	59.86	61.25	62.64	64.05	65.46	66.89	68.32	69.76	71.22	72.68
15.50	51.00	52.29	53.60	54.92	56.25	57.59	58.94	60.31	61.68	63.06	64.46	65.86	67.27	68.69	70.12	71.56
15.75	50.23	51.50	52.79	54.08	55.39	56.72	58.05	59.39	60.74	62.11	63.48	64.86	66.25	67.65	69.06	70.47
16.00	49.47	50.73	52.00	53.27	54.56	55.87	57.18	58.50	59.83	61.18	62.53	63.89	65.26	66.64	68.02	69.42
16.25	48.74	49.98	51.23	52.49	53.76	55.04	56.33	57.64	58.95	60.27	61.60	62.94	64.29	65.65	67.02	68.39
16.50	48.03	49.25	50.48	51.72	52.97	54.24	55.51	56.80	58.09	59.39	60.71	62.03	63.36	64.69	66.04	67.39
16.75	47.34	48.54	49.75	50.98	52.21	53.46	54.71	55.98	57.25	58.54	59.83	61.13	62.44	63.76	65.09	66.42
17.00	46.67	47.85	49.04	50.25	51.47	52.70	53.93	55.18	56.44	57.70	58.98	60.26	61.55	62.85	64.16	65.48
17.25	46.01	47.18	48.36	49.54	50.74	51.96	53.18	54.41	55.65	56.89	58.15	59.42	60.69	61.97	63.26	64.56
17.50	45.37	46.52	47.68	48.86	50.04	51.23	52.44	53.65	54.87	56.10	57.34	58.59	59.85	61.11	62.38	63.66
17.75	44.75	45.89	47.03	48.19	49.36	50.53	51.72	52.92	54.12	55.34	56.56	57.79	59.03	60.27	61.53	62.79
18.00	44.14	45.26	46.40	47.54	48.69	49.85	51.02	52.20	53.39	54.59	55.79	57.01	58.23	59.46	60.70	61.94
18.25	43.55	44.66	45.77	46.90	48.04	49.18	50.34	51.50	52.68	53.86	55.05	56.25	57.45	58.66	59.88	61.11
18.50	42.98	44.07	45.17	46.28	47.40	48.53	49.67	50.82	51.98	53.15	54.32	55.50	56.69	57.89	59.09	60.30
18.75	42.42	43.49	44.58	45.68	46.78	47.90	49.03	50.16	51.30	52.45	53.61	54.78	55.95	57.13	58.32	59.52
19.00	41.87	42.93	44.01	45.09	46.18	47.28	48.39	49.51	50.64	51.78	52.92	54.07	55.23	56.40	57.57	58.75
20.00	39.81	40.82	41.84	42.87	43.91	44.96	46.01	47.08	48.15	49.23	50.32	51.42	52.52	53.63	54.74	55.86
25.00	31.92	32.72	33.54	34.37	35.20	36.04	36.89	37.74	38.60	39.46	40.34	41.21	42.10	42.99	43.88	44.78
30.00	26.61	27.28	27.96	28.65	29.35	30.05	30.75	31.46	32.18	32.90	33.63	34.36	35.10	35.84	36.58	37.33

MORTGAGE YIELD

Description: This table shows the yield to maturity of a mortgage purchased at the price shown in the index.

Example: The yield to maturity of a 10.75 %, 30 year mortgage at a price of 111.00 is 9.50 %.

PRICE	7.00%	7.25%	7.50%	7.75%	8.00%	8.25%	8.50%	8.75%	9.00%	9.25%	9.50%	9.75%	10.00%	10.25%	10.50%	10.75%
175	2.20	2.39	2.58	2.77	2.95	3.14	3.32	3.50	3.69	3.87	4.05	4.23	4.41	4.59	4.76	4.94
170	2.42	2.61	2.80	2.99	3.18	3.37	3.55	3.74	3.92	4.11	4.29	4.47	4.65	4.84	5.02	5.19
165	2.65	2.84	3.04	3.23	3.42	3.61	3.80	3.98	4.17	4.36	4.54	4.73	4.91	5.10	5.28	5.46
160	2.89	3.08	3.28	3.47	3.67	3.86	4.05	4.24	4.43	4.62	4.81	5.00	5.18	5.37	5.56	5.74
155	3.14	3.33	3.53	3.73	3.93	4.12	4.32	4.51	4.70	4.90	5.09	5.28	5.47	5.66	5.85	6.04
150	3.40	3.60	3.80	4.00	4.20	4.40	4.59	4.79	4.99	5.18	5.38	5.57	5.77	5.96	6.15	6.35
145	3.67	3.87	4.08	4.28	4.48	4.69	4.89	5.09	5.29	5.49	5.69	5.89	6.08	6.28	6.48	6.67
140	3.96	4.17	4.37	4.58	4.79	4.99	5.20	5.40	5.61	5.81	6.01	6.21	6.42	6.62	6.82	7.02
135	4.26	4.47	4.68	4.89	5.10	5.31	5.52	5.73	5.94	6.15	6.35	6.56	6.77	6.97	7.18	7.38
130	4.58	4.80	5.01	5.23	5.44	5.66	5.87	6.08	6.29	6.51	6.72	6.93	7.14	7.35	7.56	7.77
125	4.92	5.14	5.36	5.58	5.80	6.02	6.24	6.45	6.67	6.89	7.10	7.32	7.54	7.75	7.97	8.18
120	5.28	5.51	5.73	5.96	6.18	6.40	6.63	6.85	7.07	7.29	7.52	7.74	7.96	8.18	8.40	8.62
119	5.36	5.58	5.81	6.03	6.26	6.48	6.71	6.93	7.16	7.38	7.60	7.83	8.05	8.27	8.49	8.71
118	5.43	5.66	5.89	6.11	6.34	6.56	6.79	7.02	7.24	7.47	7.69	7.91	8.14	8.36	8.58	8.81
117	5.51	5.74	5.96	6.19	6.42	6.65	6.87	7.10	7.33	7.55	7.78	8.00	8.23	8.45	8.68	8.90
116	5.59	5.82	6.05	6.27	6.50	6.73	6.96	7.19	7.41	7.64	7.87	8.09	8.32	8.55	8.77	9.00
115	5.67	5.90	6.13	6.36	6.59	6.82	7.04	7.27	7.50	7.73	7.96	8.19	8.41	8.64	8.87	9.09
114	5.75	5.98	6.21	6.44	6.67	6.90	7.13	7.36	7.59	7.82	8.05	8.28	8.51	8.74	8.96	9.19
113	5.83	6.06	6.29	6.52	6.76	6.99	7.22	7.45	7.68	7.91	8.14	8.37	8.60	8.83	9.06	9.29
112	5.91	6.14	6.38	6.61	6.84	7.08	7.31	7.54	7.77	8.01	8.24	8.47	8.70	8.93	9.16	9.39
111	5.99	6.23	6.46	6.70	6.93	7.17	7.40	7.63	7.87	8.10	8.33	8.57	8.80	9.03	9.26	9.50
110	6.08	6.31	6.55	6.79	7.02	7.26	7.49	7.73	7.96	8.20	8.43	8.67	8.90	9.13	9.37	9.60
109	6.16	6.40	6.64	6.87	7.11	7.35	7.59	7.82	8.06	8.29	8.53	8.77	9.00	9.24	9.47	9.71
108	6.25	6.49	6.73	6.97	7.20	7.44	7.68	7.92	8.16	8.39	8.63	8.87	9.11	9.34	9.58	9.82
107	6.34	6.58	6.82	7.06	7.30	7.54	7.78	8.02	8.26	8.49	8.73	8.97	9.21	9.45	9.69	9.93
106	6.43	6.67	6.91	7.15	7.39	7.63	7.87	8.12	8.36	8.60	8.84	9.08	9.32	9.56	9.80	10.04
105	6.52	6.76	7.00	7.25	7.49	7.73	7.97	8.22	8.46	8.70	8.94	9.18	9.43	9.67	9.91	10.15
104	6.61	6.86	7.10	7.34	7.59	7.83	8.07	8.32	8.56	8.81	9.05	9.29	9.54	9.78	10.02	10.26
103	6.70	6.95	7.20	7.44	7.69	7.93	8.18	8.42	8.67	8.91	9.16	9.40	9.65	9.89	10.14	10.38
102	6.80	7.05	7.29	7.54	7.79	8.03	8.28	8.53	8.78	9.02	9.27	9.51	9.76	10.01	10.25	10.50
101	6.90	7.15	7.39	7.64	7.89	8.14	8.39	8.64	8.88	9.13	9.38	9.63	9.88	10.13	10.37	10.62
100	7.00	7.25	7.50	7.75	8.00	8.25	8.50	8.75	9.00	9.25	9.50	9.75	10.00	10.25	10.50	10.75
99	7.09	7.35	7.60	7.85	8.10	8.35	8.60	8.86	9.11	9.36	9.61	9.86	10.11	10.37	10.62	10.87
98	7.20	7.45	7.70	7.96	8.21	8.46	8.72	8.97	9.22	9.48	9.73	9.98	10.24	10.49	10.74	11.00
97	7.30	7.55	7.81	8.06	8.32	8.57	8.83	9.08	9.34	9.59	9.85	10.11	10.36	10.62	10.87	11.13
96	7.40	7.66	7.92	8.17	8.43	8.69	8.94	9.20	9.46	9.72	9.97	10.23	10.49	10.74	11.00	11.26
95	7.51	7.77	8.03	8.29	8.54	8.80	9.06	9.32	9.58	9.84	10.10	10.36	10.62	10.87	11.13	11.39
94	7.62	7.88	8.14	8.40	8.66	8.92	9.18	9.44	9.70	9.96	10.22	10.49	10.75	11.01	11.27	11.53
93	7.73	7.99	8.25	8.52	8.78	9.04	9.30	9.56	9.83	10.09	10.35	10.62	10.88	11.14	11.41	11.67
92	7.84	8.11	8.37	8.63	8.90	9.16	9.43	9.69	9.95	10.22	10.48	10.75	11.02	11.28	11.55	11.81
91	7.96	8.22	8.49	8.75	9.02	9.28	9.55	9.82	10.08	10.35	10.62	10.89	11.15	11.42	11.69	11.96
90	8.07	8.34	8.61	8.88	9.14	9.41	9.68	9.95	10.22	10.49	10.76	11.03	11.30	11.57	11.84	12.11
89	8.19	8.46	8.73	9.00	9.27	9.54	9.81	10.08	10.35	10.62	10.90	11.17	11.44	11.71	11.98	12.26
88	8.31	8.58	8.85	9.13	9.40	9.67	9.94	10.22	10.49	10.76	11.04	11.31	11.59	11.86	12.14	12.41
87	8.44	8.71	8.98	9.26	9.53	9.80	10.08	10.35	10.63	10.91	11.18	11.46	11.74	12.01	12.29	12.57
86	8.56	8.84	9.11	9.39	9.66	9.94	10.22	10.50	10.77	11.05	11.33	11.61	11.89	12.17	12.45	12.73
85	8.69	8.97	9.24	9.52	9.80	10.08	10.36	10.64	10.92	11.20	11.48	11.76	12.04	12.33	12.61	12.89
84	8.82	9.10	9.38	9.66	9.94	10.22	10.50	10.79	11.07	11.35	11.64	11.92	12.20	12.49	12.77	13.06
83	8.95	9.23	9.52	9.80	10.08	10.37	10.65	10.94	11.22	11.51	11.79	12.08	12.37	12.65	12.94	13.23
82	9.09	9.37	9.66	9.94	10.23	10.51	10.80	11.09	11.38	11.66	11.95	12.24	12.53	12.82	13.11	13.41
81	9.23	9.51	9.80	10.09	10.38	10.67	10.95	11.24	11.54	11.83	12.12	12.41	12.70	13.00	13.29	13.58
80	9.37	9.66	9.95	10.24	10.53	10.82	11.11	11.40	11.70	11.99	12.29	12.58	12.88	13.17	13.47	13.77
79	9.51	9.80	10.10	10.39	10.68	10.98	11.27	11.57	11.86	12.16	12.46	12.76	13.05	13.35	13.65	13.95
78	9.66	9.95	10.25	10.54	10.84	11.14	11.44	11.73	12.03	12.33	12.63	12.93	13.24	13.54	13.84	14.15
77	9.81	10.11	10.41	10.70	11.00	11.30	11.60	11.91	12.21	12.51	12.81	13.12	13.42	13.73	14.03	14.34
76	9.97	10.27	10.57	10.87	11.17	11.47	11.78	12.08	12.38	12.69	13.00	13.30	13.61	13.92	14.23	14.54
75	10.12	10.43	10.73	11.03	11.34	11.64	11.95	12.26	12.57	12.88	13.19	13.50	13.81	14.12	14.43	14.75
74	10.28	10.59	10.90	11.20	11.51	11.82	12.13	12.44	12.75	13.07	13.38	13.69	14.01	14.32	14.64	14.96
73	10.45	10.76	11.07	11.38	11.69	12.00	12.31	12.63	12.94	13.26	13.58	13.89	14.21	14.53	14.85	15.17
70	10.97	11.29	11.61	11.93	12.25	12.57	12.90	13.22	13.55	13.87	14.20	14.53	14.86	15.19	15.52	15.86
65	11.93	12.27	12.60	12.94	13.28	13.63	13.97	14.32	14.66	15.01	15.36	15.71	16.06	16.41	16.77	17.12
60	13.03	13.39	13.75	14.11	14.47	14.84	15.21	15.58	15.95	16.32	16.70	17.07	17.45	17.83	18.21	18.59
55	14.31	14.69	15.08	15.47	15.86	16.26	16.65	17.05	17.45	17.86	18.26	18.67	19.08	19.49	19.90	20.31
50	15.82	16.24	16.66	17.08	17.51	17.94	18.37	18.81	19.24	19.68	20.12	20.57	21.02	21.47	21.92	22.37
45	17.64	18.10	18.57	19.03	19.50	19.98	20.45	20.93	21.41	21.90	22.39	22.88	23.37	23.87	24.37	24.87
40	19.90	20.41	20.93	21.45	21.98	22.51	23.04	23.57	24.12	24.66	25.21	25.76	26.31	26.87	27.43	27.99
35	22.78	23.36	23.95	24.54	25.14	25.74	26.35	26.96	27.57	28.19	28.82	29.45	30.08	30.72	31.35	32.00
30	26.60	27.27	27.96	28.65	29.34	30.04	30.75	31.46	32.18	32.90	33.63	34.36	35.10	35.84	36.58	37.33

MORTGAGE PRICE

Description: This table shows the price to pay for a monthly payment mortgage loan at the yield rate.

Example: The price of a 15.00 %, 30 year mortgage loan to yield 8.00 % to maturity is $ 172.32.

INTEREST RATE, %

YIELD	11.00%	11.25%	11.50%	11.75%	12.00%	12.25%	12.50%	12.75%	13.00%	13.25%	13.50%	13.75%	14.00%	14.25%	14.50%	15.00%
0.00	342.84	349.65	356.50	363.39	370.30	377.24	384.21	391.21	398.23	405.28	412.35	419.44	426.55	433.69	440.84	455.20
1.00	296.08	301.97	307.89	313.83	319.80	325.80	331.82	337.86	343.93	350.01	356.12	362.24	368.39	374.55	380.72	393.12
2.00	257.65	262.77	267.92	273.09	278.29	283.51	288.75	294.00	299.28	304.58	309.89	315.22	320.57	325.93	331.30	342.09
3.00	225.88	230.37	234.89	239.42	243.98	248.55	253.14	257.75	262.38	267.02	271.68	276.35	281.04	285.74	290.45	299.91
4.00	199.47	203.44	207.43	211.43	215.45	219.49	223.55	227.62	231.71	235.81	239.92	244.05	248.18	252.34	256.50	264.85
4.25	193.59	197.43	201.30	205.19	209.09	213.01	216.95	220.90	224.86	228.84	232.84	236.84	240.86	244.89	248.92	257.03
4.50	187.95	191.69	195.45	199.22	203.01	206.81	210.64	214.47	218.32	222.18	226.06	229.95	233.85	237.76	241.68	249.55
4.75	182.56	186.19	189.84	193.50	197.19	200.88	204.59	208.32	212.06	215.81	219.58	223.35	227.14	230.94	234.75	242.39
5.00	177.40	180.93	184.47	188.03	191.61	195.20	198.81	202.43	206.06	209.71	213.37	217.04	220.72	224.41	228.11	235.54
5.25	172.46	175.89	179.33	182.80	186.27	189.77	193.27	196.79	200.32	203.87	207.43	210.99	214.57	218.16	221.76	228.98
5.50	167.72	171.06	174.41	177.78	181.16	184.56	187.97	191.39	194.83	198.27	201.73	205.20	208.68	212.17	215.67	222.70
5.75	163.19	166.43	169.69	172.97	176.26	179.57	182.88	186.21	189.56	192.91	196.28	199.65	203.04	206.43	209.84	216.67
6.00	158.84	162.00	165.17	168.36	171.56	174.78	178.01	181.25	184.50	187.77	191.05	194.33	197.63	200.93	204.25	210.90
6.25	154.67	157.74	160.84	163.94	167.06	170.19	173.34	176.49	179.66	182.84	186.03	189.23	192.44	195.66	198.88	205.36
6.50	150.67	153.66	156.67	159.70	162.74	165.79	168.85	171.93	175.01	178.11	181.22	184.33	187.46	190.59	193.74	200.05
6.75	146.83	149.75	152.68	155.63	158.59	161.56	164.55	167.54	170.55	173.57	176.60	179.64	182.68	185.74	188.80	194.95
7.00	143.14	145.99	148.85	151.72	154.61	157.51	160.42	163.34	166.27	169.21	172.16	175.13	178.10	181.07	184.06	190.06
7.25	139.60	142.38	145.17	147.97	150.78	153.61	156.45	159.30	162.16	165.03	167.91	170.79	173.69	176.59	179.51	185.35
7.50	136.20	138.91	141.63	144.36	147.11	149.87	152.64	155.42	158.21	161.01	163.81	166.63	169.46	172.29	175.13	180.84
7.75	132.93	135.57	138.23	140.90	143.58	146.27	148.97	151.69	154.41	157.14	159.88	162.63	165.39	168.16	170.93	176.50
8.00	129.79	132.37	134.96	137.57	140.18	142.81	145.45	148.10	150.76	153.42	156.10	158.79	161.48	164.18	166.89	172.32
8.25	126.76	129.28	131.82	134.36	136.92	139.48	142.06	144.65	147.24	149.85	152.46	155.09	157.72	160.35	163.00	168.31
8.50	123.85	126.32	128.79	131.28	133.77	136.28	138.80	141.33	143.87	146.41	148.97	151.53	154.10	156.67	159.26	164.45
8.75	121.05	123.46	125.88	128.31	130.75	133.20	135.66	138.13	140.61	143.10	145.60	148.10	150.61	153.13	155.66	160.73
9.00	118.36	120.71	123.08	125.45	127.84	130.23	132.64	135.06	137.48	139.91	142.35	144.80	147.26	149.72	152.19	157.15
9.25	115.76	118.06	120.37	122.70	125.03	127.38	129.73	132.09	134.46	136.84	139.23	141.62	144.03	146.44	148.85	153.70
9.50	113.26	115.51	117.77	120.05	122.33	124.62	126.93	129.24	131.56	133.88	136.22	138.56	140.91	143.27	145.63	150.38
9.75	110.84	113.05	115.26	117.49	119.72	121.97	124.22	126.48	128.75	131.03	133.32	135.61	137.91	140.22	142.53	147.17
10.00	108.52	110.68	112.84	115.02	117.21	119.41	121.61	123.83	126.05	128.28	130.52	132.77	135.02	137.28	139.54	144.08
10.25	106.27	108.39	110.51	112.64	114.79	116.94	119.10	121.27	123.45	125.63	127.82	130.02	132.23	134.44	136.65	141.11
10.50	104.11	106.18	108.26	110.35	112.45	114.56	116.67	118.80	120.93	123.07	125.22	127.37	129.53	131.70	133.87	138.23
10.75	102.02	104.05	106.09	108.13	110.19	112.26	114.33	116.41	118.50	120.60	122.70	124.81	126.93	129.05	131.18	135.45
11.00	100.00	101.99	103.99	105.99	108.01	110.04	112.07	114.11	116.16	118.21	120.28	122.34	124.42	126.50	128.59	132.77
11.25	98.05	100.00	101.96	103.93	105.90	107.89	109.88	111.88	113.89	115.91	117.93	119.96	121.99	124.03	126.08	130.19
11.50	96.17	98.08	100.00	101.93	103.87	105.82	107.77	109.73	111.70	113.68	115.66	117.65	119.65	121.65	123.66	127.68
11.75	94.34	96.22	98.11	100.00	101.90	103.81	105.73	107.66	109.59	111.53	113.47	115.43	117.38	119.35	121.31	125.27
12.00	92.58	94.42	96.27	98.13	100.00	101.87	103.76	105.65	107.54	109.45	111.36	113.27	115.19	117.12	119.05	122.93
12.25	90.88	92.69	94.50	96.33	98.16	100.00	101.85	103.70	105.56	107.43	109.31	111.19	113.07	114.96	116.86	120.66
12.50	89.23	91.01	92.79	94.58	96.38	98.19	100.00	101.82	103.65	105.48	107.32	109.17	111.02	112.88	114.74	118.48
12.75	87.63	89.38	91.13	92.89	94.66	96.43	98.21	100.00	101.80	103.60	105.40	107.22	109.03	110.86	112.69	116.36
13.00	86.09	87.80	89.52	91.25	92.99	94.73	96.48	98.24	100.00	101.77	103.54	105.33	107.11	108.90	110.70	114.31
13.25	84.59	86.28	87.97	89.66	91.37	93.08	94.80	96.53	98.26	100.00	101.74	103.49	105.25	107.01	108.77	112.32
13.50	83.14	84.80	86.46	88.13	89.80	91.49	93.18	94.87	96.58	98.29	100.00	101.72	103.45	105.17	106.91	110.39
13.75	81.74	83.36	85.00	86.64	88.28	89.94	91.60	93.27	94.94	96.62	98.31	100.00	101.70	103.40	105.10	108.53
14.00	80.37	81.97	83.58	85.19	86.81	88.44	90.07	91.71	93.36	95.01	96.67	98.33	100.00	101.67	103.35	106.72
14.25	79.05	80.62	82.20	83.79	85.38	86.98	88.59	90.21	91.82	93.45	95.08	96.71	98.36	100.00	101.65	104.96
14.50	77.77	79.32	80.87	82.43	84.00	85.57	87.15	88.74	90.33	91.93	93.54	95.15	96.76	98.38	100.00	103.26
14.75	76.52	78.05	79.57	81.11	82.65	84.20	85.76	87.32	88.89	90.46	92.04	93.62	95.21	96.80	98.40	101.60
15.00	75.32	76.81	78.32	79.83	81.35	82.87	84.41	85.94	87.49	89.03	90.59	92.14	93.71	95.27	96.85	100.00
15.25	74.14	75.62	77.10	78.59	80.08	81.58	83.09	84.60	86.12	87.65	89.17	90.71	92.25	93.79	95.34	98.44
15.50	73.00	74.45	75.91	77.38	78.85	80.33	81.81	83.30	84.80	86.30	87.80	89.31	90.83	92.35	93.87	96.93
15.75	71.89	73.32	74.76	76.20	77.65	79.11	80.57	82.04	83.51	84.99	86.47	87.96	89.45	90.95	92.45	95.46
16.00	70.82	72.23	73.64	75.06	76.49	77.92	79.36	80.81	82.26	83.72	85.18	86.64	88.11	89.58	91.06	94.03
16.25	69.77	71.16	72.55	73.95	75.36	76.77	78.19	79.62	81.04	82.48	83.92	85.36	86.81	88.26	89.72	92.64
16.50	68.75	70.12	71.49	72.87	74.26	75.65	77.05	78.45	79.86	81.27	82.69	84.11	85.54	86.97	88.41	91.29
16.75	67.76	69.11	70.46	71.82	73.19	74.56	75.94	77.32	78.71	80.10	81.50	82.90	84.31	85.72	87.13	89.97
17.00	66.80	68.13	69.46	70.80	72.15	73.50	74.86	76.22	77.59	78.96	80.34	81.72	83.11	84.50	85.89	88.69
17.25	65.86	67.17	68.49	69.81	71.14	72.47	73.81	75.15	76.50	77.86	79.21	80.58	81.94	83.31	84.69	87.45
17.50	64.95	66.24	67.54	68.84	70.15	71.46	72.78	74.11	75.44	76.78	78.11	79.46	80.81	82.16	83.51	86.23
17.75	64.06	65.33	66.61	67.90	69.19	70.49	71.79	73.09	74.41	75.72	77.04	78.37	79.70	81.03	82.37	85.05
18.00	63.19	64.45	65.71	66.98	68.25	69.53	70.82	72.11	73.40	74.70	76.00	77.31	78.62	79.93	81.25	83.90
18.25	62.35	63.58	64.83	66.08	67.34	68.60	69.87	71.14	72.42	73.70	74.99	76.28	77.57	78.87	80.17	82.78
18.50	61.52	62.75	63.97	65.21	66.45	67.70	68.95	70.20	71.46	72.73	74.00	75.27	76.54	77.82	79.11	81.69
18.75	60.72	61.93	63.14	64.36	65.58	66.81	68.05	69.29	70.53	71.78	73.03	74.29	75.55	76.81	78.08	80.62
19.00	59.94	61.13	62.33	63.53	64.74	65.95	67.17	68.39	69.62	70.85	72.09	73.33	74.57	75.82	77.07	79.58
20.00	56.99	58.12	59.26	60.41	61.56	62.71	63.87	65.03	66.20	67.37	68.55	69.72	70.91	72.09	73.28	75.67
25.00	45.68	46.59	47.51	48.42	49.34	50.27	51.20	52.13	53.07	54.00	54.95	55.89	56.84	57.79	58.74	60.66
30.00	38.09	38.85	39.61	40.37	41.14	41.91	42.68	43.46	44.24	45.02	45.81	46.60	47.39	48.18	48.98	50.57

Description: This table shows the yield to maturity of a mortgage purchased at the price shown in the index.

Example: The yield to maturity of a 15.00 %, 30 year mortgage at a price of 125.00 is 11.77 %.

INTEREST RATE, %

PRICE	11.00%	11.25%	11.50%	11.75%	12.00%	12.25%	12.50%	12.75%	13.00%	13.25%	13.50%	13.75%	14.00%	14.25%	14.50%	15.00%
250	2.22	2.37	2.51	2.66	2.81	2.95	3.09	3.24	3.38	3.52	3.66	3.80	3.93	4.07	4.21	4.48
240	2.53	2.68	2.83	2.98	3.12	3.27	3.42	3.56	3.71	3.85	3.99	4.13	4.27	4.42	4.55	4.83
230	2.85	3.01	3.16	3.31	3.46	3.61	3.76	3.91	4.06	4.20	4.35	4.49	4.64	4.78	4.92	5.21
220	3.20	3.36	3.51	3.67	3.82	3.98	4.13	4.28	4.43	4.58	4.73	4.88	5.02	5.17	5.32	5.61
210	3.57	3.73	3.89	4.05	4.21	4.37	4.52	4.68	4.83	4.98	5.14	5.29	5.44	5.59	5.74	6.03
200	3.97	4.14	4.30	4.46	4.62	4.78	4.94	5.10	5.26	5.42	5.57	5.73	5.88	6.04	6.19	6.50
195	4.18	4.35	4.51	4.68	4.84	5.00	5.17	5.33	5.49	5.65	5.81	5.96	6.12	6.28	6.43	6.74
190	4.40	4.57	4.74	4.90	5.07	5.23	5.40	5.56	5.72	5.89	6.05	6.21	6.37	6.53	6.68	7.00
185	4.63	4.80	4.97	5.14	5.31	5.47	5.64	5.81	5.97	6.13	6.30	6.46	6.62	6.78	6.94	7.26
180	4.87	5.04	5.21	5.38	5.55	5.72	5.89	6.06	6.23	6.39	6.56	6.73	6.89	7.05	7.22	7.54
175	5.12	5.29	5.46	5.64	5.81	5.98	6.15	6.33	6.50	6.67	6.83	7.00	7.17	7.34	7.50	7.83
170	5.37	5.55	5.73	5.90	6.08	6.26	6.43	6.60	6.78	6.95	7.12	7.29	7.46	7.63	7.80	8.14
165	5.64	5.82	6.00	6.18	6.36	6.54	6.72	6.90	7.07	7.25	7.42	7.60	7.77	7.94	8.12	8.46
160	5.93	6.11	6.29	6.48	6.66	6.84	7.02	7.20	7.38	7.56	7.74	7.92	8.09	8.27	8.44	8.80
155	6.22	6.41	6.60	6.78	6.97	7.15	7.34	7.52	7.71	7.89	8.07	8.25	8.43	8.61	8.79	9.15
150	6.54	6.73	6.92	7.11	7.30	7.49	7.67	7.86	8.05	8.23	8.42	8.61	8.79	8.97	9.16	9.52
145	6.87	7.06	7.26	7.45	7.64	7.84	8.03	8.22	8.41	8.60	8.79	8.98	9.17	9.36	9.55	9.92
140	7.22	7.42	7.61	7.81	8.01	8.21	8.40	8.60	8.79	8.99	9.18	9.38	9.57	9.76	9.96	10.34
135	7.59	7.79	7.99	8.19	8.40	8.60	8.80	9.00	9.20	9.40	9.60	9.80	10.00	10.19	10.39	10.79
130	7.98	8.19	8.39	8.60	8.81	9.02	9.22	9.43	9.63	9.84	10.04	10.25	10.45	10.65	10.86	11.26
125	8.40	8.61	8.82	9.04	9.25	9.46	9.67	9.88	10.09	10.31	10.52	10.73	10.94	11.15	11.36	11.77
120	8.84	9.06	9.28	9.50	9.72	9.94	10.15	10.37	10.59	10.81	11.02	11.24	11.46	11.67	11.89	12.32
115	9.32	9.55	9.77	10.00	10.22	10.45	10.67	10.90	11.12	11.35	11.57	11.79	12.02	12.24	12.46	12.91
113	9.52	9.75	9.98	10.21	10.44	10.66	10.89	11.12	11.35	11.57	11.80	12.03	12.25	12.48	12.71	13.16
112	9.62	9.85	10.08	10.31	10.54	10.77	11.00	11.23	11.46	11.69	11.92	12.15	12.37	12.60	12.83	13.29
111	9.73	9.96	10.19	10.42	10.65	10.89	11.12	11.35	11.58	11.81	12.04	12.27	12.50	12.73	12.96	13.42
110	9.83	10.07	10.30	10.53	10.77	11.00	11.23	11.46	11.70	11.93	12.16	12.39	12.62	12.85	13.08	13.55
109	9.94	10.18	10.41	10.65	10.88	11.11	11.35	11.58	11.82	12.05	12.28	12.52	12.75	12.98	13.22	13.68
108	10.05	10.29	10.52	10.76	11.00	11.23	11.47	11.70	11.94	12.17	12.41	12.64	12.88	13.11	13.35	13.82
107	10.16	10.40	10.64	10.88	11.11	11.35	11.59	11.83	12.06	12.30	12.54	12.77	13.01	13.25	13.48	13.96
106	10.28	10.52	10.76	10.99	11.23	11.47	11.71	11.95	12.19	12.43	12.67	12.90	13.14	13.38	13.62	14.10
105	10.39	10.63	10.87	11.11	11.36	11.60	11.84	12.08	12.32	12.56	12.80	13.04	13.28	13.52	13.76	14.24
104	10.51	10.75	10.99	11.24	11.48	11.72	11.96	12.21	12.45	12.69	12.93	13.18	13.42	13.66	13.90	14.39
103	10.63	10.87	11.12	11.36	11.60	11.85	12.09	12.34	12.58	12.83	13.07	13.31	13.56	13.80	14.05	14.53
102	10.75	10.99	11.24	11.49	11.73	11.98	12.22	12.47	12.72	12.96	13.21	13.46	13.70	13.95	14.19	14.68
101	10.87	11.12	11.37	11.61	11.86	12.11	12.36	12.61	12.85	13.10	13.35	13.60	13.85	14.09	14.34	14.84
100	11.00	11.25	11.50	11.75	12.00	12.25	12.50	12.75	13.00	13.25	13.50	13.75	14.00	14.25	14.50	15.00
99	11.12	11.37	11.63	11.88	12.13	12.38	12.63	12.89	13.14	13.39	13.64	13.89	14.15	14.40	14.65	15.15
98	11.25	11.51	11.76	12.01	12.27	12.52	12.78	13.03	13.28	13.54	13.79	14.05	14.30	14.55	14.81	15.32
97	11.38	11.64	11.89	12.15	12.41	12.66	12.92	13.18	13.43	13.69	13.94	14.20	14.46	14.71	14.97	15.48
96	11.52	11.78	12.03	12.29	12.55	12.81	13.07	13.32	13.58	13.84	14.10	14.36	14.62	14.88	15.13	15.65
95	11.65	11.91	12.17	12.43	12.69	12.95	13.22	13.48	13.74	14.00	14.26	14.52	14.78	15.04	15.30	15.82
94	11.79	12.06	12.32	12.58	12.84	13.10	13.37	13.63	13.89	14.16	14.42	14.68	14.95	15.21	15.47	16.00
93	11.94	12.20	12.46	12.73	12.99	13.26	13.52	13.79	14.05	14.32	14.58	14.85	15.12	15.38	15.65	16.18
92	12.08	12.35	12.61	12.88	13.15	13.41	13.68	13.95	14.22	14.48	14.75	15.02	15.29	15.56	15.82	16.36
91	12.23	12.50	12.76	13.03	13.30	13.57	13.84	14.11	14.38	14.65	14.92	15.19	15.46	15.74	16.01	16.55
90	12.38	12.65	12.92	13.19	13.46	13.74	14.01	14.28	14.55	14.83	15.10	15.37	15.64	15.92	16.19	16.74
89	12.53	12.80	13.08	13.35	13.63	13.90	14.18	14.45	14.73	15.00	15.28	15.55	15.83	16.10	16.38	16.93
88	12.69	12.96	13.24	13.52	13.79	14.07	14.35	14.62	14.90	15.18	15.46	15.74	16.02	16.29	16.57	17.13
87	12.85	13.13	13.40	13.68	13.96	14.24	14.52	14.80	15.08	15.36	15.64	15.92	16.21	16.49	16.77	17.34
86	13.01	13.29	13.57	13.85	14.14	14.42	14.70	14.98	15.27	15.55	15.84	16.12	16.40	16.69	16.97	17.54
85	13.18	13.46	13.74	14.03	14.31	14.60	14.88	15.17	15.46	15.74	16.03	16.32	16.60	16.89	17.18	17.76
84	13.35	13.63	13.92	14.21	14.49	14.78	15.07	15.36	15.65	15.94	16.23	16.52	16.81	17.10	17.39	17.97
83	13.52	13.81	14.10	14.39	14.68	14.97	15.26	15.55	15.85	16.14	16.43	16.72	17.02	17.31	17.61	18.20
82	13.70	13.99	14.28	14.58	14.87	15.16	15.46	15.75	16.05	16.34	16.64	16.94	17.23	17.53	17.83	18.42
81	13.88	14.17	14.47	14.77	15.06	15.36	15.66	15.96	16.25	16.55	16.85	17.15	17.45	17.75	18.05	18.66
80	14.06	14.36	14.66	14.96	15.26	15.56	15.86	16.16	16.47	16.77	17.07	17.37	17.68	17.98	18.28	18.89
79	14.25	14.56	14.86	15.16	15.46	15.77	16.07	16.38	16.68	16.99	17.29	17.60	17.91	18.21	18.52	19.14
78	14.45	14.75	15.06	15.37	15.67	15.98	16.29	16.59	16.90	17.21	17.52	17.83	18.14	18.45	18.76	19.39
77	14.65	14.96	15.27	15.57	15.88	16.20	16.51	16.82	17.13	17.44	17.76	18.07	18.38	18.70	19.01	19.64
76	14.85	15.16	15.48	15.79	16.10	16.42	16.73	17.05	17.36	17.68	18.00	18.31	18.63	18.95	19.27	19.91
75	15.06	15.38	15.69	16.01	16.33	16.64	16.96	17.28	17.60	17.92	18.24	18.56	18.88	19.21	19.53	20.18
74	15.28	15.59	15.91	16.23	16.56	16.88	17.20	17.52	17.85	18.17	18.49	18.82	19.14	19.47	19.80	20.45
73	15.50	15.82	16.14	16.47	16.79	17.12	17.44	17.77	18.10	18.42	18.75	19.08	19.41	19.74	20.07	20.74
70	16.19	16.52	16.86	17.20	17.53	17.87	18.21	18.55	18.89	19.23	19.57	19.92	20.26	20.60	20.95	21.64
65	17.48	17.84	18.20	18.56	18.92	19.28	19.64	20.00	20.37	20.74	21.10	21.47	21.84	22.21	22.57	23.32
60	18.97	19.36	19.75	20.13	20.52	20.91	21.30	21.69	22.09	22.48	22.88	23.27	23.67	24.07	24.47	25.27
55	20.73	21.15	21.57	21.99	22.41	22.83	23.26	23.68	24.11	24.54	24.97	25.40	25.83	26.27	26.70	27.58

TABLE **26**

Prepayment Mortgage Price and Yield

Interest Rates:	6 to 15% by .25%.
Terms:	30 years.
Payment:	Monthly.
Prepayment Terms:	1 to 12 years, each year; 15, 20, 25, 30 years.

This table shows the price of a mortgage at a yield rate and the yield of a mortgage at a price, when the term and the interest rate are the same for both. In each case, the yield is to prepayment.

Example: An 8%, 30 year mortgage is for sale. It is estimated that the mortgage will prepay in 12 years. To yield 9% to prepayment in 12 years, the price is $93.07.

To yield 7% to prepayment in 12 years, the price is $107.64.

If the 8% mortgage is sold at a price of 93, the yield is 9.01% to prepayment in 12 years.

The prices and yields in the example are shown in the table beginning on page 26-18.

Prepayment. A 30 year residential mortgage may be prepaid in full prior to maturity. Prepayment may be the result of selling the residence or of refinancing the mortgage. Whatever the reason for prepayment, if the mortgage was purchased as an investment with the expectation that the mortgage would run to maturity, the yield to the investor is different than expected. If the original purchase price was a premium price, the yield to prepayment is less; if the price was a discount price, the yield is more.

Prepayment Price. The mortgage price is a function of yield. The yield creates the price. The price is the present value of all future payments at the yield rate. The future payments of a mortgage that is prepaid include the balance of the loan as of the date of prepayment. The price is computed directly from this formula:

$$\text{Price} = \text{Payment} \times A_{\overline{n}|} + \text{Balance} \times V^n$$

where:

$A_{\overline{n}|}$ = Present Worth of 1 Per Period at the yield rate

V^n = Present Worth of 1 at the yield rate

Example: The monthly payment per 100 for an 8%, 30 year mortgage is .73376457. The balance at the end of 12 years is 83.8624%.

At 8% for 12 years, the Present Worth of 1 Per Period is 92.3828 and the the Present Worth of 1 is .384115. Multiply the 2 factors and add the products for the price:

$$\text{Price} = .733765 \times 92.3828 + 83.8624 \times .384115$$
$$= 100$$

The price of an 8% mortgage to yield 8% is par.

At 9%, the Present Worth of 1 Per Period is 87.871092 and the Present Worth of 1 is .340967. Multiply the 2 factors and add the products:

$$\text{Price} = .733765 \times 87.8710 + 83.8624 \times .340967$$
$$= 93.07$$

To yield 9%, the price is below par.

At 7%, the Present Worth of 1 Per Period is 97.240216 and the Present Worth of 1 is .432765. Multiply the 2 factors and add the products:

$$\text{Price} = .733765 \times 97.2402 + 83.8624 \times .432765$$
$$= 107.64$$

To yield 7%, the price is above par.

Mortgage Yield. There is no direct way to compute a yield for a given price. In practice, the process is one of trial and error, that is, a price is computed at a trial rate. If the computed price is too high, a greater rate is used. The process is continued until the yield is found that computes the price exactly. The process is called iteration. A program for computing a yield is described in the Appendix.

Premium and Discount. A premium price is higher than par and the yield is less than the interest rate on the mortgage. The $107.64 in the example is a premium price and the yield is 7% on the 8% mortgage.

PREPAYMENT MORTGAGE PRICE AND YIELD

A discount price is less than par and the yield is greater than the interest rate. The $93.07 in the example is a discount price and the yield is 9%.

For all fixed-rate securities, price up, yield down and yield up, price down. "Yield" is that rate at which the investment is amortized over the term.

Example: The underlying security of a mortgage is the loan. The first few lines and the final lines of the borrower's schedule look like this:

Loan:	100.0000	Term:	30 years
Rate:	8%	Payment:	.7338

Payment	Interest	Principal	Balance
1	.6667	.0671	99.9329
2	.6662	.0676	99.8653
3	.6658	.0680	99.7973
⋮	⋮	⋮	⋮
143	—	—	84.0358
144	.5602	.1735	83.8623

If the investor buys at a premium price to yield 7% and the mortgage is prepaid in 12 years, the first few lines and the final lines of the investor's schedule look like this:

Loan:	107.6400	Prepayment term:	12 years
Rate:	7%	Payment:	.7338

Payment	Interest	Principal	Balance
1	.6279	.1059	107.5341
2	.6273	.1065	107.4276
3	.6267	.1071	107.3205
⋮	⋮	⋮	⋮
143	—	—	84.0874
144	.4905	.2433	83.8441

If the investor buys at a discount price to yield 9%, and the mortgage is prepaid in 12 years, the first few lines and the final lines of the investor's schedule look like this:

Loan:	93.0700	Prepayment term:	12 years
Rate:	9%	Payment:	.7338

Payment	Interest	Principal	Balance
1	.6980	.0358	93.0342
2	.6978	.0360	92.9982
3	.6975	.0363	92.9619
⋮	⋮	⋮	⋮
143	—	—	83.9543
144	.6297	.1041	83.8502

Each schedule has the same payment and term. The lender creates the stream of payments by making the original loan. The investor buys the stream of payments at a yield rate and allocates the payment to amortize the investment over the term to prepayment. The schedules are also a proof of the yield calculation. If the balance at line 144 on the investor's schedule is the same as that on the borrower's, since that is what is being prepaid, then the price-yield calculation is correct.

PREPAYMENT MORTGAGE PRICE AND YIELD

PREPAYMENT MORTGAGE PRICE

6.00 %

Description: This table shows the price to pay for a monthly payment loan, at a yield rate and assuming prepayment.

Example: The price of a 6.00 %, 30 year mortgage to yield 8.00 %, if prepaid in 6 years, is $ 90.84.

30 YEAR MORTGAGE PREPAID IN

YIELD	1 yr	2 yr	3 yr	4 yr	5 yr	6 yr	7 yr	8 yr	9 yr	10 yr	11 yr	12 yr	15 yr	20 yr	25 yr	30 yr
0.00	105.97	111.86	117.67	123.39	129.03	134.57	140.00	145.33	150.54	155.63	160.59	165.41	178.97	197.90	210.88	215.84
1.00	104.95	109.78	114.50	119.11	123.59	127.96	132.20	136.32	140.31	144.16	147.88	151.47	161.33	174.59	183.24	186.40
2.00	103.94	107.74	111.43	114.98	118.41	121.72	124.90	127.95	130.88	133.69	136.37	138.92	145.82	154.73	160.27	162.21
3.00	102.94	105.75	108.44	111.02	113.47	115.82	118.05	120.18	122.20	124.11	125.92	127.62	132.15	137.77	141.09	142.21
4.00	101.95	103.79	105.54	107.20	108.77	110.25	111.64	112.96	114.19	115.35	116.44	117.45	120.09	123.24	125.01	125.58
4.25	101.70	103.31	104.83	106.27	107.62	108.90	110.10	111.23	112.29	113.28	114.21	115.07	117.30	119.94	121.41	121.87
4.50	101.46	102.83	104.13	105.35	106.50	107.58	108.59	109.54	110.43	111.26	112.03	112.75	114.59	116.76	117.95	118.33
4.75	101.21	102.35	103.43	104.43	105.38	106.27	107.10	107.88	108.60	109.27	109.90	110.48	111.97	113.70	114.64	114.93
5.00	100.97	101.88	102.73	103.53	104.28	104.98	105.63	106.24	106.81	107.34	107.83	108.28	109.43	110.76	111.47	111.69
5.25	100.73	101.40	102.04	102.63	103.19	103.71	104.19	104.64	105.06	105.44	105.80	106.13	106.96	107.92	108.42	108.57
5.50	100.48	100.93	101.36	101.75	102.11	102.45	102.77	103.06	103.34	103.59	103.82	104.03	104.57	105.18	105.50	105.59
5.75	100.24	100.47	100.68	100.87	101.05	101.22	101.37	101.52	101.65	101.77	101.89	101.99	102.25	102.54	102.69	102.74
6.00	100.00	100.00	100.00	100.00	100.00	100.00	100.00	100.00	100.00	100.00	100.00	100.00	100.00	100.00	100.00	100.00
6.25	99.76	99.54	99.33	99.14	98.96	98.80	98.65	98.51	98.38	98.26	98.16	98.06	97.82	97.55	97.41	97.37
6.50	99.52	99.08	98.66	98.29	97.94	97.61	97.32	97.04	96.79	96.57	96.36	96.17	95.70	95.18	94.93	94.86
6.75	99.28	98.62	98.00	97.44	96.92	96.44	96.01	95.61	95.24	94.90	94.60	94.32	93.64	92.90	92.54	92.44
7.00	99.04	98.16	97.35	96.60	95.92	95.29	94.72	94.19	93.71	93.28	92.88	92.52	91.64	90.70	90.25	90.12
7.25	98.80	97.71	96.70	95.77	94.93	94.16	93.45	92.81	92.22	91.69	91.21	90.77	89.70	88.58	88.04	87.89
7.50	98.57	97.25	96.05	94.95	93.95	93.04	92.20	91.44	90.76	90.13	89.57	89.06	87.82	86.53	85.91	85.75
7.75	98.33	96.80	95.41	94.14	92.98	91.93	90.97	90.11	89.32	88.61	87.97	87.39	86.00	84.55	83.87	83.69
8.00	98.09	96.36	94.78	93.34	92.03	90.84	89.76	88.79	87.91	87.12	86.40	85.76	84.22	82.64	81.91	81.71
8.25	97.86	95.91	94.14	92.54	91.08	89.77	88.58	87.50	86.53	85.66	84.88	84.18	82.50	80.79	80.01	79.81
8.50	97.62	95.47	93.52	91.75	90.15	88.71	87.40	86.23	85.18	84.23	83.39	82.63	80.83	79.01	78.19	77.97
8.75	97.39	95.03	92.89	90.97	89.23	87.66	86.25	84.99	83.85	82.84	81.93	81.12	79.20	77.29	76.43	76.21
9.00	97.16	94.59	92.28	90.19	88.32	86.63	85.12	83.76	82.55	81.47	80.50	79.65	77.62	75.62	74.74	74.51
9.25	96.92	94.15	91.66	89.42	87.42	85.61	84.00	82.56	81.27	80.13	79.11	78.21	76.09	74.01	73.11	72.88
9.50	96.69	93.72	91.05	88.66	86.52	84.61	82.90	81.38	80.02	78.82	77.75	76.81	74.60	72.46	71.53	71.30
9.75	96.46	93.29	90.45	87.91	85.65	83.62	81.82	80.22	78.80	77.54	76.42	75.44	73.15	70.95	70.02	69.78
10.00	96.23	92.86	89.85	87.17	84.78	82.65	80.76	79.08	77.60	76.28	75.12	74.11	71.74	69.50	68.55	68.32
10.25	96.00	92.43	89.25	86.43	83.92	81.69	79.71	77.96	76.42	75.05	73.86	72.80	70.38	68.09	67.14	66.91
10.50	95.77	92.01	88.66	85.70	83.07	80.74	78.68	76.86	75.26	73.85	72.61	71.53	69.05	66.73	65.77	65.54
10.75	95.54	91.58	88.08	84.97	82.23	79.80	77.66	75.78	74.13	72.67	71.40	70.29	67.75	65.41	64.45	64.23
11.00	95.31	91.16	87.49	84.25	81.40	78.88	76.67	74.72	73.01	71.52	70.22	69.08	66.50	64.13	63.18	62.96
11.25	95.08	90.74	86.92	83.54	80.58	77.97	75.68	73.68	71.92	70.39	69.06	67.90	65.28	62.89	61.95	61.73
11.50	94.86	90.33	86.34	82.84	79.77	77.07	74.71	72.65	70.85	69.29	67.93	66.74	64.09	61.69	60.76	60.54
11.75	94.63	89.91	85.77	82.14	78.97	76.19	73.76	71.65	69.80	68.20	66.82	65.62	62.93	60.53	59.61	59.40
12.00	94.40	89.50	85.21	81.45	78.17	75.31	72.82	70.66	68.78	67.15	65.74	64.52	61.81	59.41	58.49	58.29
12.25	94.18	89.09	84.65	80.77	77.39	74.45	71.90	69.69	67.77	66.11	64.68	63.44	60.71	58.32	57.41	57.21
12.50	93.95	88.68	84.09	80.09	76.62	73.60	70.99	68.73	66.78	65.09	63.64	62.40	59.65	57.26	56.37	56.18
12.75	93.73	88.27	83.53	79.42	75.85	72.77	70.10	67.79	65.81	64.10	62.63	61.37	58.61	56.24	55.36	55.17
13.00	93.50	87.87	82.98	78.76	75.10	71.94	69.22	66.87	64.85	63.12	61.64	60.37	57.60	55.24	54.38	54.20
13.25	93.28	87.47	82.44	78.10	74.35	71.13	68.35	65.96	63.92	62.17	60.67	59.40	56.62	54.28	53.44	53.26
13.50	93.06	87.07	81.90	77.45	73.61	70.32	67.50	65.07	63.00	61.23	59.72	58.44	55.66	53.34	52.52	52.34
13.75	92.84	86.67	81.36	76.80	72.88	69.53	66.65	64.20	62.10	60.32	58.80	57.51	54.73	52.43	51.63	51.46
14.00	92.62	86.27	80.83	76.16	72.16	68.75	65.83	63.34	61.22	59.42	57.89	56.60	53.83	51.55	50.76	50.60
14.25	92.39	85.88	80.30	75.53	71.45	67.97	65.01	62.49	60.35	58.54	57.01	55.71	52.94	50.70	49.92	49.77
14.50	92.17	85.48	79.77	74.90	70.75	67.21	64.21	61.66	59.50	57.68	56.14	54.84	52.08	49.86	49.11	48.96
14.75	91.95	85.09	79.25	74.28	70.05	66.46	63.42	60.85	58.67	56.84	55.29	53.99	51.25	49.06	48.32	48.18
15.00	91.74	84.71	78.73	73.66	69.36	65.72	62.64	60.04	57.85	56.01	54.46	53.17	50.43	48.27	47.56	47.42
15.25	91.52	84.32	78.22	73.05	68.68	64.99	61.88	59.25	57.05	55.20	53.65	52.35	49.64	47.51	46.81	46.68
15.50	91.30	83.93	77.71	72.45	68.01	64.27	61.12	58.48	56.26	54.41	52.86	51.56	48.86	46.77	46.09	45.96
15.75	91.08	83.55	77.20	71.85	67.35	63.56	60.38	57.72	55.49	53.63	52.08	50.79	48.11	46.04	45.39	45.26
16.00	90.86	83.17	76.70	71.26	66.69	62.86	59.65	56.97	54.73	52.87	51.32	50.03	47.37	45.34	44.70	44.58
16.25	90.65	82.79	76.20	70.67	66.04	62.17	58.93	56.23	53.99	52.12	50.57	49.29	46.65	44.66	44.04	43.93
16.50	90.43	82.42	75.70	70.09	65.40	61.48	58.22	55.51	53.26	51.39	49.84	48.57	45.95	44.00	43.39	43.28
16.75	90.22	82.04	75.21	69.51	64.76	60.81	57.52	54.80	52.54	50.67	49.13	47.86	45.27	43.35	42.77	42.66
17.00	90.00	81.67	74.72	68.94	64.14	60.15	56.84	54.10	51.84	49.97	48.43	47.17	44.60	42.72	42.16	42.05
17.25	89.79	81.30	74.24	68.38	63.51	59.49	56.16	53.41	51.14	49.28	47.75	46.49	43.96	42.11	41.56	41.46
17.50	89.58	80.93	73.75	67.82	62.90	58.84	55.49	52.74	50.47	48.60	47.08	45.83	43.32	41.51	40.98	40.89
17.75	89.36	80.56	73.28	67.26	62.30	58.20	54.84	52.07	49.80	47.94	46.42	45.19	42.70	40.93	40.42	40.33
18.00	89.15	80.19	72.80	66.71	61.70	57.58	54.19	51.42	49.15	47.29	45.78	44.55	42.10	40.36	39.87	39.78
18.25	88.94	79.83	72.33	66.17	61.11	56.95	53.55	50.78	48.51	46.66	45.15	43.93	41.51	39.81	39.33	39.25
18.50	88.73	79.47	71.86	65.63	60.52	56.34	52.93	50.14	47.88	46.03	44.54	43.33	40.94	39.27	38.81	38.73
18.75	88.52	79.11	71.40	65.09	59.94	55.74	52.31	49.52	47.26	45.42	43.94	42.74	40.38	38.75	38.30	38.23
19.00	88.31	78.75	70.94	64.56	59.37	55.14	51.70	48.91	46.65	44.82	43.35	42.16	39.83	38.24	37.80	37.73
20.00	87.47	77.33	69.13	62.50	57.15	52.83	49.36	46.57	44.33	42.54	41.10	39.96	37.76	36.31	35.94	35.88
25.00	83.43	70.66	60.82	53.25	47.43	42.97	39.55	36.93	34.93	33.40	32.24	31.36	29.81	28.96	28.78	28.76
30.00	79.59	64.61	53.62	45.57	39.68	35.38	32.23	29.94	28.28	27.07	26.19	25.56	24.53	24.06	23.99	23.98

Description: This table shows the yield to prepayment of a monthly payment mortgage purchased at a price in the index.

Example: The yield to prepayment in 10 years of a 6.00 %, 30 year mortgage at a price of 104.00 is 5.44 %.

30 YEAR MORTGAGE PREPAID IN

PRICE	1 yr	2 yr	3 yr	4 yr	5 yr	6 yr	7 yr	8 yr	9 yr	10 yr	11 yr	12 yr	15 yr	20 yr	25 yr	30 yr
140	–	–	–	–	–	–	–	–	1.03	1.38	1.67	1.90	2.41	2.85	3.06	3.12
135	–	–	–	–	–	–	–	1.15	1.55	1.86	2.12	2.33	2.78	3.17	3.35	3.41
130	–	–	–	–	–	–	1.29	1.74	2.09	2.37	2.59	2.78	3.16	3.51	3.67	3.71
125	–	–	–	–	–	1.46	1.98	2.37	2.66	2.90	3.09	3.24	3.57	3.87	4.00	4.03
120	–	–	–	–	1.68	2.28	2.70	3.02	3.26	3.45	3.61	3.73	4.00	4.24	4.35	4.38
119	–	–	–	1.02	1.88	2.45	2.85	3.15	3.38	3.57	3.72	3.84	4.09	4.32	4.42	4.45
118	–	–	–	1.26	2.08	2.62	3.00	3.29	3.51	3.68	3.82	3.94	4.18	4.40	4.49	4.52
117	–	–	–	1.50	2.28	2.79	3.16	3.43	3.63	3.80	3.93	4.04	4.27	4.48	4.57	4.59
116	–	–	–	1.74	2.48	2.96	3.31	3.56	3.76	3.92	4.04	4.15	4.36	4.56	4.64	4.67
115	–	–	–	1.99	2.68	3.14	3.46	3.70	3.89	4.04	4.16	4.25	4.46	4.64	4.72	4.74
114	–	–	1.16	2.24	2.89	3.32	3.62	3.85	4.02	4.16	4.27	4.36	4.55	4.72	4.79	4.82
113	–	–	1.48	2.49	3.09	3.49	3.78	3.99	4.15	4.28	4.38	4.47	4.65	4.80	4.87	4.89
112	–	–	1.81	2.74	3.30	3.67	3.94	4.13	4.28	4.40	4.50	4.58	4.74	4.89	4.95	4.97
111	–	–	2.14	3.00	3.51	3.86	4.10	4.28	4.42	4.53	4.62	4.69	4.84	4.97	5.03	5.05
110	–	–	2.47	3.26	3.73	4.04	4.26	4.43	4.55	4.65	4.73	4.80	4.94	5.06	5.11	5.13
109	–	1.38	2.81	3.52	3.94	4.23	4.43	4.58	4.69	4.78	4.85	4.91	5.04	5.15	5.20	5.21
108	–	1.87	3.15	3.78	4.16	4.41	4.59	4.73	4.83	4.91	4.97	5.03	5.14	5.24	5.28	5.29
107	–	2.37	3.49	4.05	4.38	4.60	4.76	4.88	4.97	5.04	5.10	5.14	5.24	5.33	5.37	5.38
106	–	2.87	3.84	4.32	4.61	4.80	4.93	5.03	5.11	5.17	5.22	5.26	5.34	5.42	5.45	5.46
105	–	3.38	4.19	4.59	4.83	4.99	5.10	5.19	5.25	5.30	5.35	5.38	5.45	5.51	5.54	5.55
104	1.93	3.89	4.54	4.86	5.06	5.19	5.28	5.35	5.40	5.44	5.47	5.50	5.56	5.61	5.63	5.63
103.75	2.18	4.02	4.63	4.93	5.12	5.24	5.32	5.39	5.43	5.47	5.50	5.53	5.58	5.63	5.65	5.66
103.50	2.43	4.15	4.72	5.00	5.17	5.29	5.37	5.43	5.47	5.51	5.54	5.56	5.61	5.65	5.67	5.68
103.25	2.68	4.28	4.81	5.07	5.23	5.34	5.41	5.47	5.51	5.54	5.57	5.59	5.64	5.68	5.69	5.70
103.00	2.93	4.41	4.90	5.14	5.29	5.39	5.45	5.51	5.54	5.58	5.60	5.62	5.66	5.70	5.72	5.72
102.75	3.18	4.54	4.99	5.21	5.35	5.44	5.50	5.55	5.58	5.61	5.63	5.65	5.69	5.72	5.74	5.74
102.50	3.43	4.67	5.08	5.28	5.41	5.49	5.54	5.59	5.62	5.64	5.67	5.68	5.72	5.75	5.76	5.77
102.25	3.69	4.80	5.17	5.35	5.46	5.54	5.59	5.63	5.66	5.68	5.70	5.71	5.75	5.77	5.79	5.79
102.00	3.94	4.93	5.26	5.42	5.52	5.59	5.63	5.67	5.69	5.71	5.73	5.74	5.77	5.80	5.81	5.81
101.75	4.20	5.06	5.35	5.49	5.58	5.64	5.68	5.71	5.73	5.75	5.76	5.77	5.80	5.82	5.83	5.83
101.50	4.45	5.19	5.44	5.57	5.64	5.69	5.72	5.75	5.77	5.78	5.80	5.81	5.83	5.85	5.85	5.86
101.25	4.71	5.33	5.53	5.64	5.70	5.74	5.77	5.79	5.81	5.82	5.83	5.84	5.86	5.87	5.88	5.88
101.00	4.96	5.46	5.63	5.71	5.76	5.79	5.81	5.83	5.84	5.85	5.86	5.87	5.88	5.90	5.90	5.90
100.75	5.22	5.59	5.72	5.78	5.82	5.84	5.86	5.87	5.88	5.89	5.89	5.90	5.91	5.92	5.92	5.93
100.50	5.48	5.73	5.81	5.85	5.88	5.89	5.90	5.91	5.92	5.92	5.93	5.93	5.94	5.95	5.95	5.95
100.25	5.74	5.86	5.90	5.92	5.94	5.94	5.95	5.95	5.96	5.96	5.96	5.96	5.97	5.97	5.97	5.97
100.00	6.00	6.00	6.00	6.00	6.00	6.00	6.00	6.00	6.00	6.00	6.00	6.00	6.02	6.02	6.02	6.02
99.75	6.26	6.13	6.09	6.07	6.05	6.05	6.04	6.04	6.03	6.03	6.03	6.03	6.02	6.02	6.02	6.02
99.50	6.52	6.26	6.18	6.14	6.12	6.10	6.09	6.08	6.07	6.07	6.06	6.06	6.05	6.05	6.04	6.04
99.25	6.78	6.40	6.27	6.21	6.18	6.15	6.13	6.12	6.11	6.10	6.10	6.09	6.08	6.07	6.07	6.07
99.00	7.04	6.54	6.37	6.29	6.24	6.20	6.18	6.16	6.15	6.14	6.13	6.12	6.11	6.10	6.09	6.09
98.75	7.30	6.67	6.46	6.36	6.30	6.26	6.23	6.20	6.19	6.17	6.16	6.16	6.14	6.12	6.11	6.11
98.50	7.57	6.81	6.56	6.43	6.36	6.31	6.27	6.25	6.23	6.21	6.20	6.19	6.17	6.15	6.14	6.14
98.25	7.83	6.95	6.65	6.51	6.42	6.36	6.32	6.29	6.27	6.25	6.23	6.22	6.19	6.17	6.16	6.16
98.00	8.10	7.08	6.75	6.58	6.48	6.41	6.37	6.33	6.30	6.28	6.27	6.25	6.22	6.20	6.19	6.18
97.75	8.36	7.22	6.84	6.65	6.54	6.47	6.41	6.37	6.34	6.32	6.30	6.29	6.25	6.22	6.21	6.21
97.50	8.63	7.36	6.94	6.73	6.60	6.52	6.46	6.42	6.38	6.36	6.34	6.32	6.28	6.25	6.24	6.23
97.25	8.90	7.50	7.03	6.80	6.66	6.57	6.51	6.46	6.42	6.39	6.37	6.35	6.31	6.28	6.26	6.26
97	9.16	7.64	7.13	6.88	6.73	6.63	6.56	6.50	6.46	6.43	6.41	6.38	6.34	6.30	6.29	6.28
96	10.24	8.20	7.52	7.18	6.97	6.84	6.75	6.68	6.62	6.58	6.55	6.52	6.46	6.41	6.39	6.38
95	11.34	8.76	7.91	7.48	7.23	7.06	6.94	6.85	6.78	6.73	6.69	6.65	6.58	6.51	6.49	6.48
94	12.44	9.33	8.30	7.79	7.48	7.28	7.14	7.03	6.95	6.88	6.83	6.79	6.70	6.62	6.59	6.58
93	13.56	9.91	8.70	8.10	7.74	7.50	7.33	7.21	7.11	7.04	6.98	6.93	6.82	6.73	6.70	6.69
92	14.69	10.50	9.11	8.42	8.00	7.73	7.54	7.39	7.28	7.20	7.13	7.07	6.95	6.85	6.80	6.79
91	15.84	11.09	9.52	8.73	8.27	7.96	7.74	7.58	7.45	7.35	7.28	7.21	7.08	6.96	6.91	6.90
90	17.00	11.69	9.93	9.06	8.54	8.19	7.95	7.76	7.63	7.52	7.43	7.36	7.21	7.08	7.02	7.01
89	18.17	12.30	10.35	9.38	8.81	8.43	8.16	7.95	7.80	7.68	7.58	7.50	7.34	7.19	7.13	7.12
88	19.36	12.91	10.78	9.72	9.08	8.66	8.37	8.15	7.98	7.85	7.74	7.65	7.47	7.31	7.25	7.23
87	20.57	13.54	11.21	10.05	9.36	8.91	8.58	8.34	8.16	8.02	7.90	7.80	7.61	7.44	7.37	7.35
86	21.79	14.17	11.64	10.39	9.64	9.15	8.80	8.54	8.34	8.19	8.06	7.96	7.74	7.56	7.48	7.46
85	23.02	14.81	12.09	10.74	9.93	9.40	9.02	8.74	8.53	8.36	8.22	8.11	7.88	7.69	7.61	7.58
80	29.45	18.13	14.39	12.53	11.42	10.69	10.18	9.79	9.50	9.27	9.08	8.93	8.62	8.36	8.25	8.22
75	36.34	21.68	16.85	14.45	13.03	12.09	11.42	10.93	10.55	10.26	10.02	9.83	9.43	9.09	8.96	8.92
70	43.77	25.51	19.51	16.53	14.76	13.60	12.77	12.16	11.70	11.33	11.04	10.80	10.32	9.91	9.75	9.71
65	51.81	29.66	22.39	18.79	16.65	15.24	14.25	13.52	12.96	12.52	12.17	11.88	11.30	10.82	10.64	10.60
60	60.57	34.17	25.53	21.26	18.72	17.05	15.88	15.01	14.35	13.83	13.42	13.09	12.41	11.86	11.66	11.61
55	70.19	39.12	28.98	23.97	21.01	19.05	17.68	16.67	15.91	15.31	14.83	14.45	13.67	13.06	12.84	12.79
50	80.84	44.61	32.81	27.00	23.56	21.30	19.72	18.55	17.67	16.98	16.44	16.01	15.13	14.45	14.22	14.17

PREPAYMENT MORTGAGE PRICE

6.25 %

Description: This table shows the price to pay for a monthly payment loan, at a yield rate and assuming prepayment.

Example: The price of a 6.25 %, 30 year mortgage to yield 8.00 %, if prepaid in 6 years, is $ 91.97.

30 YEAR MORTGAGE PREPAID IN

YIELD	1 yr	2 yr	3 yr	4 yr	5 yr	6 yr	7 yr	8 yr	9 yr	10 yr	11 yr	12 yr	15 yr	20 yr	25 yr	30 yr
0.00	106.22	112.36	118.42	124.40	130.28	136.07	141.75	147.33	152.79	158.12	163.33	168.39	182.64	202.61	216.37	221.66
1.00	105.19	110.27	115.24	120.08	124.81	129.41	133.88	138.22	142.43	146.51	150.44	154.23	164.69	178.78	188.03	191.43
2.00	104.18	108.23	112.15	115.94	119.59	123.11	126.51	129.77	132.90	135.90	138.76	141.50	148.89	158.48	164.48	166.58
3.00	103.18	106.23	109.15	111.95	114.62	117.17	119.60	121.91	124.11	126.19	128.17	130.03	134.97	141.14	144.81	146.04
4.00	102.19	104.27	106.24	108.11	109.88	111.55	113.12	114.61	116.01	117.32	118.55	119.70	122.69	126.28	128.31	128.97
4.25	101.94	103.79	105.53	107.17	108.73	110.19	111.57	112.86	114.08	115.22	116.28	117.28	119.85	122.91	124.62	125.16
4.50	101.70	103.30	104.82	106.25	107.59	108.85	110.04	111.15	112.19	113.17	114.08	114.92	117.10	119.66	121.07	121.52
4.75	101.45	102.82	104.11	105.33	106.47	107.53	108.54	109.47	110.35	111.16	111.92	112.62	114.42	116.53	117.68	118.03
5.00	101.21	102.35	103.42	104.42	105.36	106.23	107.05	107.82	108.53	109.20	109.81	110.38	111.83	113.51	114.42	114.70
5.25	100.97	101.87	102.72	103.52	104.26	104.95	105.60	106.20	106.76	107.28	107.75	108.20	109.32	110.61	111.29	111.50
5.50	100.72	101.40	102.03	102.62	103.18	103.69	104.16	104.61	105.02	105.40	105.75	106.07	106.88	107.81	108.29	108.44
5.75	100.48	100.93	101.35	101.74	102.10	102.44	102.75	103.04	103.31	103.56	103.79	103.99	104.52	105.11	105.42	105.51
6.00	100.24	100.46	100.67	100.87	101.05	101.21	101.37	101.51	101.64	101.76	101.87	101.97	102.23	102.51	102.65	102.70
6.25	100.00	100.00	100.00	100.00	100.00	100.00	100.00	100.00	100.00	100.00	100.00	100.00	100.00	100.00	100.00	100.00
6.50	99.76	99.54	99.33	99.14	98.97	98.80	98.66	98.52	98.39	98.28	98.17	98.08	97.84	97.58	97.45	97.41
6.75	99.52	99.08	98.67	98.29	97.94	97.63	97.33	97.06	96.82	96.59	96.39	96.20	95.74	95.25	95.00	94.93
7.00	99.28	98.62	98.01	97.45	96.94	96.46	96.03	95.64	95.27	94.95	94.65	94.38	93.71	92.99	92.65	92.55
7.25	99.04	98.16	97.36	96.62	95.94	95.32	94.75	94.23	93.76	93.33	92.94	92.59	91.73	90.82	90.38	90.26
7.50	98.81	97.71	96.71	95.79	94.95	94.19	93.49	92.85	92.28	91.75	91.28	90.85	89.81	88.72	88.20	88.06
7.75	98.57	97.26	96.06	94.97	93.98	93.07	92.25	91.50	90.82	90.21	89.66	89.16	87.95	86.70	86.11	85.94
8.00	98.33	96.81	95.42	94.16	93.02	91.97	91.03	90.17	89.40	88.70	88.07	87.51	86.14	84.74	84.09	83.91
8.25	98.10	96.36	94.79	93.36	92.06	90.89	89.83	88.87	88.00	87.22	86.52	85.89	84.39	82.85	82.15	81.96
8.50	97.86	95.92	94.16	92.57	91.12	89.82	88.64	87.58	86.63	85.77	85.01	84.32	82.68	81.03	80.27	80.08
8.75	97.63	95.48	93.54	91.78	90.19	88.77	87.48	86.32	85.29	84.36	83.53	82.78	81.03	79.26	78.47	78.27
9.00	97.39	95.04	92.91	91.00	89.28	87.73	86.33	85.09	83.97	82.97	82.08	81.29	79.42	77.56	76.73	76.52
9.25	97.16	94.60	92.30	90.23	88.37	86.70	85.21	83.87	82.68	81.61	80.67	79.83	77.85	75.91	75.06	74.84
9.50	96.93	94.17	91.69	89.46	87.47	85.69	84.10	82.67	81.41	80.28	79.29	78.40	76.33	74.32	73.44	73.23
9.75	96.70	93.73	91.08	88.71	86.58	84.69	83.00	81.50	80.17	78.98	77.94	77.01	74.86	72.78	71.89	71.67
10.00	96.46	93.30	90.48	87.96	85.71	83.71	81.93	80.35	78.95	77.71	76.62	75.65	73.42	71.29	70.38	70.16
10.25	96.23	92.87	89.88	87.21	84.84	82.74	80.87	79.22	77.75	76.46	75.33	74.33	72.02	69.84	68.93	68.71
10.50	96.00	92.45	89.28	86.48	83.99	81.78	79.83	78.10	76.58	75.24	74.07	73.04	70.67	68.45	67.53	67.31
10.75	95.77	92.02	88.70	85.75	83.14	80.84	78.80	77.01	75.43	74.05	72.84	71.78	69.35	67.10	66.18	65.96
11.00	95.54	91.60	88.11	85.03	82.30	79.91	77.79	75.94	74.31	72.88	71.63	70.54	68.07	65.79	64.87	64.65
11.25	95.32	91.18	87.53	84.31	81.48	78.99	76.80	74.88	73.20	71.73	70.45	69.34	66.82	64.52	63.61	63.39
11.50	95.09	90.76	86.95	83.60	80.66	78.08	75.82	73.84	72.12	70.61	69.30	68.17	65.61	63.29	62.38	62.18
11.75	94.86	90.35	86.38	82.90	79.85	77.19	74.86	72.83	71.05	69.51	68.18	67.02	64.43	62.11	61.20	61.00
12.00	94.63	89.93	85.81	82.21	79.06	76.31	73.91	71.82	70.01	68.44	67.08	65.90	63.28	60.95	60.06	59.86
12.25	94.41	89.52	85.25	81.52	78.27	75.44	72.98	70.84	68.99	67.39	66.00	64.81	62.16	59.84	58.95	58.76
12.50	94.18	89.11	84.69	80.84	77.49	74.58	72.06	69.87	67.99	66.36	64.95	63.74	61.08	58.75	57.88	57.69
12.75	93.96	88.70	84.13	80.16	76.72	73.74	71.15	68.92	67.00	65.35	63.92	62.70	60.02	57.70	56.85	56.66
13.00	93.73	88.30	83.58	79.49	75.96	72.90	70.26	67.99	66.04	64.36	62.92	61.69	58.99	56.68	55.84	55.66
13.25	93.51	87.89	83.03	78.83	75.21	72.08	69.39	67.07	65.09	63.39	61.93	60.69	57.99	55.70	54.87	54.69
13.50	93.29	87.49	82.49	78.18	74.46	71.27	68.52	66.17	64.16	62.44	60.97	59.72	57.01	54.74	53.93	53.76
13.75	93.07	87.09	81.95	77.53	73.73	70.47	67.68	65.29	63.25	61.51	60.03	58.77	56.06	53.81	53.01	52.85
14.00	92.84	86.69	81.41	76.88	73.00	69.68	66.84	64.42	62.35	60.60	59.11	57.85	55.14	52.90	52.12	51.96
14.25	92.62	86.30	80.88	76.24	72.28	68.90	66.02	63.56	61.47	59.71	58.21	56.94	54.23	52.03	51.26	51.11
14.50	92.40	85.90	80.35	75.61	71.57	68.13	65.20	62.72	60.61	58.83	57.33	56.06	53.36	51.17	50.43	50.28
14.75	92.18	85.51	79.83	74.99	70.87	67.37	64.41	61.89	59.77	57.97	56.46	55.19	52.50	50.35	49.62	49.48
15.00	91.96	85.12	79.31	74.37	70.18	66.62	63.62	61.08	58.94	57.14	55.62	54.35	51.67	49.54	48.83	48.69
15.25	91.74	84.74	78.79	73.75	69.49	65.89	62.85	60.28	58.12	56.31	54.79	53.53	50.86	48.76	48.07	47.94
15.50	91.53	84.35	78.28	73.15	68.81	65.16	62.08	59.50	57.33	55.51	53.99	52.72	50.06	48.00	47.33	47.20
15.75	91.31	83.97	77.77	72.54	68.14	64.44	61.33	58.73	56.54	54.72	53.20	51.93	49.29	47.26	46.61	46.48
16.00	91.09	83.58	77.26	71.95	67.48	63.73	60.59	57.97	55.77	53.94	52.42	51.16	48.54	46.54	45.91	45.79
16.25	90.87	83.20	76.76	71.36	66.83	63.04	59.87	57.22	55.02	53.19	51.67	50.41	47.81	45.84	45.22	45.11
16.50	90.66	82.83	76.26	70.77	66.18	62.35	59.15	56.49	54.28	52.44	50.92	49.67	47.09	45.16	44.56	44.45
16.75	90.44	82.45	75.77	70.19	65.54	61.67	58.44	55.77	53.55	51.71	50.20	48.95	46.40	44.50	43.92	43.81
17.00	90.23	82.07	75.28	69.62	64.91	60.99	57.75	55.06	52.84	51.00	49.49	48.25	45.72	43.85	43.29	43.19
17.25	90.01	81.70	74.79	69.05	64.28	60.33	57.06	54.36	52.14	50.30	48.79	47.56	45.05	43.22	42.68	42.58
17.50	89.80	81.33	74.31	68.48	63.66	59.68	56.39	53.68	51.45	49.61	48.11	46.88	44.41	42.61	42.08	41.99
17.75	89.59	80.96	73.83	67.93	63.05	59.04	55.73	53.01	50.77	48.94	47.45	46.22	43.77	42.02	41.50	41.42
18.00	89.37	80.60	73.35	67.37	62.45	58.40	55.07	52.34	50.11	48.28	46.79	45.58	43.16	41.43	40.94	40.85
18.25	89.16	80.23	72.87	66.82	61.85	57.77	54.43	51.69	49.46	47.64	46.15	44.95	42.56	40.87	40.39	40.31
18.50	88.95	79.87	72.40	66.28	61.26	57.15	53.80	51.05	48.82	47.00	45.53	44.33	41.97	40.32	39.85	39.78
18.75	88.74	79.51	71.94	65.74	60.68	56.54	53.17	50.43	48.19	46.38	44.91	43.73	41.39	39.78	39.33	39.26
19.00	88.53	79.15	71.47	65.21	60.10	55.94	52.56	49.81	47.58	45.77	44.31	43.14	40.83	39.26	38.82	38.75
20.00	87.69	77.72	69.65	63.13	57.86	53.61	50.19	47.43	45.22	43.45	42.03	40.90	38.72	37.28	36.91	36.85
25.00	83.64	71.03	61.30	53.82	48.06	43.64	40.25	37.66	35.67	34.16	33.01	32.13	30.59	29.73	29.56	29.54
30.00	79.80	64.96	54.07	46.09	40.25	35.97	32.85	30.57	28.91	27.71	26.83	26.20	25.18	24.71	24.63	24.63

Description: This table shows the yield to prepayment of a monthly payment mortgage purchased at a price in the index.

Example: The yield to prepayment in 10 years of a 6.25 %, 30 year mortgage at a price of 104.00 is 5.68 %.

30 YEAR MORTGAGE PREPAID IN

PRICE	1 yr	2 yr	3 yr	4 yr	5 yr	6 yr	7 yr	8 yr	9 yr	10 yr	11 yr	12 yr	15 yr	20 yr	25 yr	30 yr
140	–	–	–	–	–	–	–	–	1.24	1.60	1.88	2.12	2.62	3.07	3.27	3.33
135	–	–	–	–	–	–	–	1.37	1.77	2.08	2.34	2.55	2.99	3.39	3.57	3.62
130	–	–	–	–	–	–	1.51	1.97	2.32	2.59	2.81	3.00	3.39	3.73	3.88	3.93
125	–	–	–	–	–	1.69	2.21	2.59	2.89	3.12	3.31	3.47	3.80	4.09	4.22	4.26
120	–	–	–	1.01	1.91	2.51	2.93	3.25	3.49	3.68	3.84	3.96	4.23	4.47	4.57	4.60
119	–	–	–	1.25	2.11	2.68	3.08	3.38	3.62	3.80	3.95	4.07	4.32	4.55	4.65	4.67
118	–	–	–	1.49	2.31	2.85	3.24	3.52	3.74	3.91	4.05	4.17	4.41	4.63	4.72	4.75
117	–	–	–	1.73	2.51	3.02	3.39	3.66	3.87	4.03	4.17	4.27	4.50	4.71	4.80	4.82
116	–	–	–	1.98	2.71	3.20	3.54	3.80	4.00	4.15	4.28	4.38	4.60	4.79	4.87	4.90
115	–	–	1.07	2.23	2.92	3.37	3.70	3.94	4.13	4.27	4.39	4.49	4.69	4.87	4.95	4.97
114	–	–	1.39	2.48	3.12	3.55	3.86	4.08	4.26	4.39	4.50	4.59	4.79	4.95	5.03	5.05
113	–	–	1.72	2.73	3.33	3.73	4.01	4.23	4.39	4.52	4.62	4.70	4.88	5.04	5.11	5.13
112	–	–	2.04	2.98	3.54	3.91	4.18	4.37	4.52	4.64	4.74	4.81	4.98	5.12	5.19	5.21
111	–	–	2.37	3.24	3.75	4.10	4.34	4.52	4.66	4.77	4.85	4.93	5.08	5.21	5.27	5.29
110	–	1.13	2.71	3.50	3.97	4.28	4.50	4.67	4.79	4.89	4.97	5.04	5.18	5.30	5.35	5.37
109	–	1.62	3.05	3.76	4.19	4.47	4.67	4.82	4.93	5.02	5.09	5.15	5.28	5.39	5.44	5.45
108	–	2.11	3.39	4.02	4.40	4.66	4.83	4.97	5.07	5.15	5.21	5.27	5.38	5.48	5.52	5.53
107	–	2.61	3.73	4.29	4.63	4.85	5.00	5.12	5.21	5.28	5.34	5.38	5.48	5.57	5.61	5.62
106	–	3.11	4.08	4.56	4.85	5.04	5.18	5.28	5.35	5.41	5.46	5.50	5.59	5.66	5.69	5.70
105	1.19	3.62	4.43	4.83	5.08	5.24	5.35	5.43	5.50	5.55	5.59	5.62	5.69	5.76	5.78	5.79
104	2.18	4.13	4.79	5.11	5.30	5.43	5.52	5.59	5.64	5.68	5.72	5.74	5.80	5.85	5.87	5.88
103.75	2.43	4.26	4.88	5.18	5.36	5.48	5.57	5.63	5.68	5.72	5.75	5.77	5.83	5.87	5.89	5.90
103.50	2.68	4.39	4.96	5.25	5.42	5.53	5.61	5.67	5.72	5.75	5.78	5.81	5.86	5.90	5.92	5.92
103.25	2.93	4.52	5.05	5.32	5.48	5.58	5.66	5.71	5.75	5.79	5.81	5.84	5.88	5.92	5.94	5.94
103.00	3.18	4.65	5.14	5.39	5.54	5.63	5.70	5.75	5.79	5.82	5.85	5.87	5.91	5.95	5.96	5.97
102.75	3.43	4.78	5.24	5.46	5.59	5.68	5.75	5.79	5.83	5.86	5.88	5.90	5.94	5.97	5.99	5.99
102.50	3.68	4.92	5.33	5.53	5.65	5.73	5.79	5.83	5.87	5.89	5.91	5.93	5.96	6.00	6.01	6.01
102.25	3.93	5.05	5.42	5.60	5.71	5.78	5.84	5.87	5.90	5.93	5.94	5.96	5.99	6.02	6.03	6.04
102.00	4.19	5.18	5.51	5.67	5.77	5.83	5.88	5.91	5.94	5.96	5.98	6.00	6.02	6.04	6.06	6.06
101.75	4.44	5.31	5.60	5.74	5.83	5.89	5.93	5.96	5.98	6.00	6.01	6.02	6.05	6.07	6.08	6.08
101.50	4.70	5.44	5.69	5.81	5.89	5.94	5.97	6.00	6.02	6.03	6.04	6.05	6.08	6.09	6.10	6.10
101.25	4.95	5.58	5.78	5.89	5.95	5.99	6.02	6.04	6.05	6.07	6.08	6.09	6.10	6.12	6.13	6.13
101.00	5.21	5.71	5.87	5.96	6.01	6.04	6.06	6.08	6.09	6.10	6.11	6.12	6.13	6.14	6.15	6.15
100.75	5.47	5.84	5.97	6.03	6.07	6.09	6.11	6.12	6.13	6.14	6.14	6.15	6.16	6.17	6.17	6.17
100.50	5.73	5.98	6.06	6.10	6.13	6.14	6.15	6.16	6.17	6.17	6.18	6.18	6.19	6.19	6.20	6.20
100.25	5.99	6.11	6.15	6.17	6.18	6.19	6.20	6.20	6.21	6.21	6.21	6.21	6.22	6.22	6.22	6.22
100.00	6.25	6.25	6.25	6.25	6.25	6.25	6.25	6.25	6.25	6.25	6.25	6.25	6.27	6.27	6.27	6.27
99.75	6.51	6.38	6.34	6.32	6.31	6.30	6.29	6.29	6.28	6.28	6.28	6.28	6.27	6.27	6.27	6.27
99.50	6.77	6.52	6.43	6.39	6.37	6.35	6.34	6.33	6.32	6.32	6.31	6.31	6.30	6.30	6.29	6.29
99.25	7.03	6.65	6.53	6.46	6.43	6.40	6.38	6.37	6.36	6.35	6.35	6.34	6.33	6.32	6.32	6.32
99.00	7.29	6.79	6.62	6.54	6.49	6.45	6.43	6.41	6.40	6.39	6.38	6.37	6.36	6.35	6.34	6.34
98.75	7.55	6.92	6.71	6.61	6.55	6.51	6.48	6.46	6.44	6.43	6.42	6.41	6.39	6.37	6.37	6.36
98.50	7.82	7.06	6.81	6.68	6.61	6.56	6.52	6.50	6.48	6.46	6.45	6.44	6.42	6.40	6.39	6.39
98.25	8.08	7.20	6.90	6.76	6.67	6.61	6.57	6.54	6.52	6.50	6.48	6.47	6.45	6.42	6.42	6.41
98.00	8.35	7.34	7.00	6.83	6.73	6.67	6.62	6.58	6.56	6.54	6.52	6.51	6.48	6.45	6.44	6.44
97.75	8.61	7.47	7.09	6.91	6.79	6.72	6.67	6.63	6.60	6.57	6.55	6.54	6.51	6.48	6.47	6.46
97.50	8.88	7.61	7.19	6.98	6.85	6.77	6.71	6.67	6.64	6.61	6.59	6.57	6.54	6.50	6.49	6.49
97.25	9.15	7.75	7.29	7.05	6.92	6.83	6.76	6.71	6.68	6.65	6.62	6.60	6.56	6.53	6.52	6.51
97	9.42	7.89	7.38	7.13	6.98	6.88	6.81	6.76	6.72	6.68	6.66	6.64	6.59	6.56	6.54	6.54
96	10.50	8.45	7.77	7.43	7.23	7.10	7.00	6.93	6.88	6.83	6.80	6.77	6.71	6.66	6.64	6.64
95	11.59	9.02	8.16	7.74	7.48	7.31	7.20	7.11	7.04	6.99	6.94	6.91	6.84	6.77	6.75	6.74
94	12.70	9.59	8.56	8.05	7.74	7.54	7.39	7.29	7.21	7.14	7.09	7.05	6.96	6.88	6.85	6.84
93	13.82	10.17	8.96	8.36	8.00	7.76	7.59	7.47	7.37	7.30	7.24	7.19	7.08	6.99	6.96	6.95
92	14.95	10.76	9.37	8.67	8.26	7.99	7.80	7.65	7.54	7.46	7.39	7.33	7.21	7.11	7.07	7.05
91	16.10	11.35	9.78	8.99	8.53	8.22	8.00	7.84	7.71	7.62	7.54	7.47	7.34	7.22	7.18	7.16
90	17.26	11.95	10.19	9.32	8.80	8.45	8.21	8.03	7.89	7.78	7.69	7.62	7.47	7.34	7.29	7.27
89	18.44	12.56	10.62	9.65	9.07	8.69	8.42	8.22	8.07	7.94	7.85	7.77	7.60	7.46	7.40	7.39
88	19.63	13.18	11.04	9.98	9.35	8.93	8.63	8.41	8.24	8.11	8.01	7.92	7.74	7.58	7.52	7.50
87	20.83	13.80	11.47	10.32	9.63	9.17	8.85	8.61	8.43	8.28	8.17	8.07	7.88	7.71	7.64	7.62
86	22.05	14.43	11.91	10.66	9.91	9.42	9.07	8.81	8.61	8.46	8.33	8.23	8.02	7.83	7.76	7.74
85	23.29	15.07	12.36	11.00	10.20	9.67	9.29	9.01	8.80	8.63	8.50	8.39	8.16	7.96	7.88	7.86
80	29.73	18.40	14.66	12.81	11.70	10.97	10.45	10.07	9.78	9.55	9.36	9.22	8.90	8.64	8.53	8.51
75	36.63	21.97	17.14	14.74	13.31	12.37	11.71	11.22	10.84	10.55	10.31	10.12	9.72	9.39	9.25	9.22
70	44.06	25.81	19.80	16.83	15.06	13.89	13.07	12.46	12.00	11.63	11.34	11.11	10.62	10.22	10.06	10.02
65	52.11	29.96	22.69	19.09	16.96	15.55	14.56	13.83	13.27	12.83	12.48	12.20	11.62	11.15	10.97	10.93
60	60.89	34.49	25.85	21.57	19.04	17.37	16.20	15.33	14.68	14.16	13.75	13.42	12.75	12.21	12.01	11.96
55	70.52	39.45	29.31	24.31	21.34	19.39	18.02	17.02	16.25	15.66	15.18	14.80	14.03	13.43	13.21	13.16
50	81.19	44.95	33.16	27.35	23.91	21.66	20.08	18.92	18.04	17.35	16.81	16.38	15.52	14.85	14.63	14.58

Description: This table shows the price to pay for a monthly payment loan, at a yield rate and assuming prepayment.

Example: The price of a 6.50 %, 30 year mortgage to yield 8.00 %, if prepaid in 6 years, is $ 93.11.

30 YEAR MORTGAGE PREPAID IN

YIELD	1 yr	2 yr	3 yr	4 yr	5 yr	6 yr	7 yr	8 yr	9 yr	10 yr	11 yr	12 yr	15 yr	20 yr	25 yr	30 yr
0.00	106.47	112.86	119.17	125.40	131.54	137.57	143.51	149.34	155.04	160.62	166.07	171.38	186.33	207.36	221.92	227.54
1.00	105.44	110.77	115.98	121.06	126.02	130.86	135.56	140.13	144.57	148.86	153.01	157.01	168.07	183.02	192.88	196.51
2.00	104.43	108.72	112.87	116.89	120.77	124.51	128.12	131.59	134.92	138.11	141.17	144.08	151.99	162.27	168.73	171.01
3.00	103.43	106.71	109.86	112.88	115.76	118.52	121.14	123.65	126.03	128.29	130.42	132.45	137.82	144.54	148.56	149.92
4.00	102.43	104.75	106.94	109.02	110.99	112.85	114.61	116.27	117.83	119.29	120.67	121.96	125.31	129.35	131.65	132.39
4.25	102.19	104.26	106.22	108.08	109.83	111.48	113.04	114.50	115.88	117.17	118.37	119.50	122.42	125.90	127.86	128.48
4.50	101.94	103.78	105.51	107.15	108.69	110.13	111.50	112.77	113.97	115.09	116.13	117.11	119.61	122.58	124.23	124.75
4.75	101.70	103.30	104.80	106.22	107.55	108.80	109.98	111.07	112.10	113.05	113.94	114.77	116.89	119.38	120.74	121.17
5.00	101.45	102.82	104.10	105.31	106.44	107.49	108.48	109.40	110.26	111.06	111.81	112.50	114.26	116.30	117.40	117.74
5.25	101.21	102.34	103.41	104.40	105.33	106.20	107.01	107.77	108.47	109.12	109.72	110.28	111.70	113.32	114.20	114.46
5.50	100.97	101.87	102.71	103.50	104.24	104.93	105.56	106.16	106.71	107.21	107.68	108.12	109.21	110.46	111.12	111.32
5.75	100.72	101.40	102.03	102.61	103.16	103.67	104.14	104.57	104.98	105.35	105.69	106.01	106.81	107.70	108.17	108.31
6.00	100.48	100.93	101.35	101.73	102.09	102.43	102.74	103.02	103.29	103.53	103.75	103.96	104.47	105.04	105.34	105.42
6.25	100.24	100.46	100.67	100.86	101.04	101.21	101.36	101.50	101.63	101.74	101.85	101.95	102.20	102.47	102.61	102.66
6.50	100.00	100.00	100.00	100.00	100.00	100.00	100.00	100.00	100.00	100.00	100.00	100.00	100.00	100.00	100.00	100.00
6.75	99.76	99.54	99.33	99.15	98.97	98.81	98.66	98.53	98.41	98.29	98.19	98.10	97.86	97.61	97.49	97.45
7.00	99.52	99.08	98.67	98.30	97.95	97.64	97.35	97.08	96.84	96.62	96.42	96.24	95.79	95.31	95.07	95.00
7.25	99.28	98.62	98.02	97.46	96.95	96.48	96.06	95.67	95.31	94.99	94.69	94.43	93.78	93.09	92.75	92.65
7.50	99.04	98.17	97.36	96.63	95.96	95.34	94.78	94.27	93.81	93.39	93.01	92.66	91.82	90.94	90.51	90.40
7.75	98.81	97.72	96.72	95.81	94.98	94.22	93.53	92.90	92.34	91.82	91.36	90.94	89.92	88.87	88.36	88.23
8.00	98.57	97.27	96.08	94.99	94.01	93.11	92.30	91.56	90.89	90.29	89.75	89.26	88.08	86.86	86.29	86.14
8.25	98.33	96.82	95.44	94.18	93.05	92.02	91.08	90.24	89.48	88.79	88.17	87.62	86.29	84.93	84.30	84.13
8.50	98.10	96.37	94.81	93.39	92.10	90.94	89.89	88.94	88.09	87.32	86.64	86.02	84.55	83.06	82.38	82.20
8.75	97.86	95.93	94.18	92.59	91.16	89.87	88.71	87.67	86.73	85.89	85.13	84.46	82.86	81.26	80.53	80.34
9.00	97.63	95.49	93.55	91.81	90.24	88.82	87.55	86.41	85.39	84.48	83.67	82.94	81.22	79.51	78.75	78.55
9.25	97.40	95.05	92.93	91.03	89.32	87.79	86.41	85.18	84.08	83.10	82.23	81.46	79.63	77.83	77.03	76.83
9.50	97.16	94.61	92.32	90.26	88.42	86.77	85.29	83.98	82.80	81.76	80.83	80.01	78.08	76.20	75.38	75.17
9.75	96.93	94.18	91.71	89.50	87.53	85.76	84.19	82.79	81.54	80.44	79.46	78.59	76.57	74.62	73.78	73.57
10.00	96.70	93.75	91.11	88.75	86.64	84.77	83.10	81.62	80.31	79.15	78.12	77.21	75.11	73.09	72.24	72.02
10.25	96.47	93.32	90.50	88.00	85.77	83.79	82.03	80.48	79.10	77.88	76.81	75.87	73.69	71.62	70.75	70.54
10.50	96.24	92.89	89.91	87.26	84.91	82.83	80.98	79.35	77.91	76.64	75.53	74.55	72.30	70.19	69.31	69.10
10.75	96.01	92.46	89.32	86.53	84.06	81.87	79.95	78.25	76.75	75.43	74.28	73.27	70.96	68.81	67.92	67.71
11.00	95.78	92.04	88.73	85.80	83.22	80.93	78.93	77.16	75.61	74.25	73.06	72.02	69.65	67.47	66.58	66.37
11.25	95.55	91.62	88.14	85.08	82.38	80.01	77.92	76.09	74.49	73.08	71.86	70.80	68.38	66.17	65.28	65.08
11.50	95.32	91.20	87.56	84.37	81.56	79.09	76.93	75.04	73.39	71.95	70.69	69.60	67.14	64.91	64.03	63.83
11.75	95.09	90.78	86.99	83.66	80.75	78.19	75.96	74.01	72.31	70.83	69.55	68.44	65.94	63.69	62.82	62.62
12.00	94.87	90.36	86.42	82.96	79.94	77.30	75.00	73.00	71.25	69.74	68.43	67.30	64.77	62.51	61.65	61.45
12.25	94.64	89.95	85.85	82.27	79.15	76.43	74.06	72.00	70.22	68.67	67.34	66.19	63.63	61.37	60.51	60.32
12.50	94.42	89.54	85.29	81.59	78.36	75.56	73.13	71.02	69.20	67.63	66.27	65.10	62.52	60.26	59.41	59.22
12.75	94.19	89.13	84.73	80.91	77.59	74.71	72.22	70.06	68.20	66.60	65.23	64.04	61.44	59.19	58.35	58.16
13.00	93.97	88.72	84.18	80.23	76.82	73.87	71.32	69.12	67.23	65.60	64.20	63.01	60.39	58.14	57.32	57.14
13.25	93.74	88.32	83.63	79.57	76.06	73.04	70.43	68.19	66.27	64.62	63.20	62.00	59.37	57.13	56.32	56.15
13.50	93.52	87.92	83.08	78.91	75.31	72.22	69.56	67.28	65.32	63.65	62.23	61.01	58.37	56.15	55.35	55.18
13.75	93.30	87.52	82.54	78.25	74.57	71.41	68.70	66.38	64.40	62.71	61.27	60.05	57.40	55.19	54.41	54.25
14.00	93.07	87.12	82.00	77.61	73.84	70.61	67.86	65.50	63.49	61.78	60.33	59.10	56.46	54.27	53.50	53.34
14.25	92.85	86.72	81.46	76.96	73.12	69.83	67.02	64.63	62.60	60.88	59.42	58.18	55.54	53.37	52.62	52.47
14.50	92.63	86.32	80.93	76.33	72.40	69.05	66.20	63.78	61.73	59.99	58.52	57.28	54.64	52.50	51.76	51.62
14.75	92.41	85.93	80.41	75.70	71.69	68.29	65.40	62.95	60.87	59.12	57.65	56.40	53.77	51.65	50.93	50.79
15.00	92.19	85.54	79.88	75.08	70.99	67.53	64.60	62.12	60.03	58.27	56.79	55.55	52.92	50.82	50.13	49.99
15.25	91.97	85.15	79.36	74.46	70.30	66.79	63.82	61.32	59.21	57.44	55.95	54.71	52.09	50.02	49.34	49.21
15.50	91.75	84.76	78.85	73.85	69.62	66.05	63.05	60.52	58.40	56.62	55.13	53.88	51.28	49.24	48.58	48.45
15.75	91.53	84.38	78.34	73.24	68.94	65.33	62.29	59.74	57.60	55.82	54.32	53.08	50.49	48.49	47.84	47.72
16.00	91.32	84.00	77.83	72.64	68.28	64.61	61.54	58.97	56.82	55.03	53.54	52.30	49.72	47.75	47.12	47.00
16.25	91.10	83.62	77.33	72.04	67.62	63.91	60.81	58.22	56.06	54.26	52.77	51.53	48.97	47.03	46.42	46.31
16.50	90.88	83.24	76.82	71.46	66.96	63.21	60.08	57.48	55.31	53.51	52.01	50.78	48.24	46.33	45.74	45.63
16.75	90.67	82.86	76.33	70.87	66.32	62.53	59.37	56.75	54.57	52.77	51.28	50.05	47.53	45.66	45.08	44.97
17.00	90.45	82.48	75.83	70.29	65.68	61.85	58.67	56.03	53.84	52.04	50.55	49.33	46.84	44.99	44.44	44.33
17.25	90.24	82.11	75.34	69.72	65.05	61.18	57.97	55.32	53.13	51.33	49.85	48.63	46.16	44.35	43.81	43.71
17.50	90.02	81.74	74.86	69.15	64.43	60.52	57.29	54.63	52.44	50.63	49.15	47.94	45.50	43.72	43.20	43.11
17.75	89.81	81.37	74.38	68.59	63.81	59.87	56.62	53.95	51.75	49.95	48.48	47.27	44.85	43.11	42.60	42.52
18.00	89.60	81.00	73.90	68.04	63.21	59.23	55.96	53.28	51.08	49.28	47.81	46.62	44.22	42.52	42.02	41.94
18.25	89.39	80.63	73.42	67.48	62.60	58.60	55.31	52.62	50.42	48.62	47.16	45.97	43.61	41.94	41.46	41.38
18.50	89.17	80.27	72.95	66.94	62.01	57.97	54.67	51.97	49.77	47.98	46.53	45.35	43.01	41.37	40.91	40.83
18.75	88.96	79.91	72.48	66.40	61.42	57.36	54.04	51.33	49.13	47.35	45.90	44.73	42.42	40.82	40.37	40.30
19.00	88.75	79.54	72.01	65.86	60.84	56.75	53.42	50.71	48.51	46.73	45.29	44.13	41.85	40.28	39.85	39.78
20.00	87.91	78.12	70.18	63.77	58.58	54.39	51.02	48.30	46.12	44.37	42.97	41.85	39.69	38.26	37.88	37.83
25.00	83.86	71.40	61.79	54.39	48.70	44.33	40.97	38.40	36.43	34.92	33.78	32.91	31.37	30.52	30.34	30.32
30.00	80.01	65.31	54.53	46.61	40.81	36.57	33.47	31.20	29.56	28.36	27.49	26.86	25.84	25.36	25.29	25.28

Description: This table shows the yield to prepayment of a monthly payment mortgage purchased at a price in the index.

Example: The yield to prepayment in 10 years of a 6.50 %, 30 year mortgage at a price of 104.00 is 5.93 %.

30 YEAR MORTGAGE PREPAID IN

PRICE	1 yr	2 yr	3 yr	4 yr	5 yr	6 yr	7 yr	8 yr	9 yr	10 yr	11 yr	12 yr	15 yr	20 yr	25 yr	30 yr
140	–	–	–	–	–	–	–	1.01	1.46	1.81	2.10	2.33	2.83	3.28	3.48	3.54
135	–	–	–	–	–	–	1.07	1.59	1.99	2.30	2.56	2.77	3.21	3.61	3.78	3.83
130	–	–	–	–	–	1.13	1.74	2.19	2.54	2.81	3.04	3.22	3.61	3.95	4.10	4.15
125	–	–	–	–	1.19	1.92	2.43	2.82	3.12	3.35	3.54	3.69	4.02	4.31	4.44	4.48
120	–	–	–	1.25	2.15	2.74	3.17	3.48	3.72	3.91	4.07	4.19	4.46	4.70	4.80	4.83
119	–	–	–	1.48	2.34	2.91	3.32	3.62	3.85	4.03	4.18	4.30	4.55	4.78	4.87	4.90
118	–	–	–	1.73	2.54	3.08	3.47	3.75	3.97	4.15	4.29	4.40	4.64	4.86	4.95	4.98
117	–	–	–	1.97	2.74	3.26	3.62	3.89	4.10	4.27	4.40	4.51	4.74	4.94	5.03	5.05
116	–	–	–	2.21	2.95	3.43	3.78	4.03	4.23	4.38	4.51	4.61	4.83	5.02	5.10	5.13
115	–	–	1.31	2.46	3.15	3.61	3.93	4.17	4.36	4.51	4.62	4.72	4.92	5.10	5.18	5.20
114	–	–	1.63	2.71	3.36	3.79	4.09	4.32	4.49	4.63	4.74	4.83	5.02	5.19	5.26	5.28
113	–	–	1.95	2.96	3.57	3.97	4.25	4.46	4.62	4.75	4.85	4.94	5.12	5.27	5.34	5.36
112	–	–	2.28	3.22	3.78	4.15	4.41	4.61	4.76	4.88	4.97	5.05	5.22	5.36	5.42	5.44
111	–	–	2.61	3.48	3.99	4.33	4.58	4.76	4.89	5.00	5.09	5.16	5.31	5.45	5.51	5.52
110	–	1.37	2.95	3.74	4.21	4.52	4.74	4.91	5.03	5.13	5.21	5.28	5.42	5.54	5.59	5.60
109	–	1.86	3.29	4.00	4.43	4.71	4.91	5.06	5.17	5.26	5.33	5.39	5.52	5.63	5.67	5.69
108	–	2.35	3.63	4.27	4.65	4.90	5.08	5.21	5.31	5.39	5.46	5.51	5.62	5.72	5.76	5.77
107	–	2.85	3.97	4.53	4.87	5.09	5.25	5.36	5.45	5.52	5.58	5.63	5.72	5.81	5.85	5.86
106	–	3.36	4.32	4.81	5.09	5.28	5.42	5.52	5.60	5.66	5.71	5.75	5.83	5.90	5.94	5.94
105	1.43	3.86	4.68	5.08	5.32	5.48	5.59	5.68	5.74	5.79	5.83	5.87	5.94	6.00	6.03	6.03
104	2.42	4.38	5.03	5.36	5.55	5.68	5.77	5.84	5.89	5.93	5.96	5.99	6.05	6.10	6.12	6.12
103.75	2.67	4.51	5.12	5.43	5.61	5.73	5.81	5.88	5.93	5.96	6.00	6.02	6.07	6.12	6.14	6.14
103.50	2.92	4.64	5.21	5.50	5.67	5.78	5.86	5.92	5.96	6.00	6.03	6.05	6.10	6.14	6.16	6.17
103.25	3.17	4.77	5.30	5.57	5.72	5.83	5.90	5.96	6.00	6.03	6.06	6.08	6.13	6.17	6.19	6.19
103.00	3.42	4.90	5.39	5.64	5.78	5.88	5.95	6.00	6.04	6.07	6.09	6.11	6.16	6.19	6.21	6.21
102.75	3.68	5.03	5.48	5.71	5.84	5.93	5.99	6.04	6.08	6.10	6.13	6.14	6.18	6.22	6.23	6.24
102.50	3.93	5.16	5.57	5.78	5.90	5.98	6.04	6.08	6.11	6.14	6.16	6.18	6.21	6.24	6.26	6.26
102.25	4.18	5.29	5.66	5.85	5.96	6.03	6.08	6.12	6.15	6.17	6.19	6.21	6.24	6.27	6.28	6.28
102.00	4.44	5.43	5.76	5.92	6.02	6.08	6.13	6.16	6.19	6.21	6.23	6.24	6.27	6.29	6.30	6.31
101.75	4.69	5.56	5.85	5.99	6.08	6.13	6.17	6.20	6.23	6.24	6.26	6.27	6.30	6.32	6.33	6.33
101.50	4.95	5.69	5.94	6.06	6.14	6.18	6.22	6.24	6.26	6.28	6.29	6.30	6.32	6.34	6.35	6.35
101.25	5.20	5.82	6.03	6.13	6.20	6.24	6.26	6.29	6.30	6.32	6.33	6.33	6.35	6.37	6.37	6.38
101.00	5.46	5.96	6.12	6.21	6.25	6.29	6.31	6.33	6.34	6.35	6.36	6.37	6.38	6.39	6.40	6.40
100.75	5.72	6.09	6.22	6.28	6.31	6.34	6.36	6.37	6.38	6.39	6.39	6.40	6.41	6.42	6.42	6.42
100.50	5.98	6.23	6.31	6.35	6.37	6.39	6.40	6.41	6.42	6.42	6.43	6.43	6.44	6.44	6.45	6.45
100.25	6.24	6.36	6.40	6.42	6.43	6.44	6.45	6.45	6.46	6.46	6.46	6.46	6.47	6.47	6.47	6.47
100.00	6.50	6.50	6.50	6.50	6.50	6.50	6.50	6.50	6.50	6.50	6.50	6.50	6.50	6.50	6.50	6.50
99.75	6.76	6.63	6.59	6.57	6.56	6.55	6.54	6.54	6.53	6.53	6.53	6.53	6.52	6.52	6.52	6.52
99.50	7.02	6.77	6.68	6.64	6.62	6.60	6.59	6.58	6.57	6.57	6.56	6.56	6.55	6.55	6.54	6.54
99.25	7.28	6.90	6.78	6.71	6.68	6.65	6.63	6.62	6.61	6.60	6.60	6.59	6.58	6.57	6.57	6.57
99.00	7.54	7.04	6.87	6.79	6.74	6.71	6.68	6.66	6.65	6.64	6.63	6.63	6.61	6.60	6.59	6.59
98.75	7.81	7.18	6.97	6.86	6.80	6.76	6.73	6.71	6.69	6.68	6.67	6.66	6.64	6.62	6.62	6.62
98.50	8.07	7.31	7.06	6.94	6.86	6.81	6.78	6.75	6.73	6.71	6.70	6.69	6.67	6.65	6.64	6.64
98.25	8.33	7.45	7.16	7.01	6.92	6.86	6.82	6.79	6.77	6.75	6.74	6.72	6.70	6.68	6.67	6.67
98.00	8.60	7.59	7.25	7.08	6.98	6.92	6.87	6.84	6.81	6.79	6.77	6.76	6.73	6.70	6.69	6.69
97.75	8.87	7.73	7.35	7.16	7.05	6.97	6.92	6.88	6.85	6.83	6.81	6.79	6.76	6.73	6.72	6.72
97.50	9.13	7.86	7.44	7.23	7.11	7.02	6.97	6.92	6.89	6.86	6.84	6.82	6.79	6.76	6.74	6.74
97.25	9.40	8.00	7.54	7.31	7.17	7.08	7.01	6.97	6.93	6.90	6.88	6.86	6.82	6.78	6.77	6.77
97	9.67	8.14	7.64	7.38	7.23	7.13	7.06	7.01	6.97	6.94	6.91	6.89	6.85	6.81	6.79	6.79
96	10.75	8.70	8.02	7.69	7.48	7.35	7.26	7.19	7.13	7.09	7.06	7.03	6.97	6.92	6.90	6.89
95	11.85	9.27	8.42	7.99	7.74	7.57	7.45	7.36	7.30	7.24	7.20	7.17	7.09	7.03	7.00	7.00
94	12.96	9.85	8.82	8.30	8.00	7.79	7.65	7.54	7.46	7.40	7.35	7.31	7.22	7.14	7.11	7.10
93	14.08	10.43	9.22	8.62	8.26	8.02	7.85	7.73	7.63	7.56	7.50	7.45	7.34	7.25	7.22	7.21
92	15.21	11.02	9.63	8.93	8.52	8.25	8.06	7.91	7.80	7.72	7.65	7.59	7.47	7.37	7.33	7.32
91	16.36	11.61	10.04	9.26	8.79	8.48	8.26	8.10	7.98	7.88	7.80	7.74	7.60	7.49	7.44	7.43
90	17.52	12.22	10.46	9.58	9.06	8.72	8.47	8.29	8.15	8.04	7.96	7.88	7.73	7.61	7.55	7.54
89	18.70	12.83	10.88	9.91	9.33	8.95	8.68	8.48	8.33	8.21	8.11	8.03	7.87	7.73	7.67	7.65
88	19.89	13.44	11.31	10.25	9.61	9.19	8.90	8.68	8.51	8.38	8.27	8.19	8.01	7.85	7.79	7.77
87	21.10	14.07	11.74	10.58	9.89	9.44	9.12	8.88	8.69	8.55	8.44	8.34	8.15	7.98	7.91	7.89
86	22.32	14.70	12.18	10.93	10.18	9.69	9.34	9.08	8.88	8.72	8.60	8.50	8.29	8.11	8.03	8.01
85	23.56	15.34	12.62	11.27	10.47	9.94	9.56	9.28	9.07	8.90	8.77	8.66	8.43	8.24	8.16	8.14
80	30.01	18.68	14.94	13.08	11.98	11.25	10.73	10.35	10.06	9.83	9.65	9.50	9.19	8.92	8.82	8.79
75	36.92	22.25	17.42	15.03	13.60	12.66	12.00	11.51	11.13	10.84	10.60	10.41	10.01	9.68	9.55	9.52
70	44.36	26.10	20.10	17.12	15.36	14.19	13.37	12.76	12.30	11.94	11.65	11.41	10.93	10.53	10.37	10.34
65	52.42	30.27	23.00	19.40	17.27	15.86	14.87	14.14	13.58	13.15	12.80	12.52	11.94	11.48	11.30	11.26
60	61.21	34.81	26.16	21.89	19.36	17.70	16.52	15.66	15.00	14.49	14.09	13.76	13.09	12.56	12.36	12.32
55	70.86	39.79	29.65	24.64	21.68	19.73	18.37	17.36	16.60	16.00	15.53	15.16	14.39	13.80	13.59	13.54
50	81.54	45.30	33.51	27.70	24.27	22.02	20.44	19.28	18.41	17.73	17.19	16.76	15.90	15.25	15.03	14.99

Description: This table shows the price to pay for a monthly payment loan, at a yield rate and assuming prepayment.

Example: The price of a 6.75 %, 30 year mortgage to yield 8.00 %, if prepaid in 6 years, is $ 94.25.

30 YEAR MORTGAGE PREPAID IN

YIELD	1 yr	2 yr	3 yr	4 yr	5 yr	6 yr	7 yr	8 yr	9 yr	10 yr	11 yr	12 yr	15 yr	20 yr	25 yr	30 yr
0.00	106.72	113.36	119.92	126.40	132.79	139.08	145.27	151.35	157.30	163.13	168.83	174.38	190.04	212.15	227.53	233.50
1.00	105.69	111.26	116.72	122.04	127.24	132.31	137.25	142.05	146.71	151.22	155.59	159.80	171.46	187.28	197.77	201.65
2.00	104.68	109.21	113.60	117.85	121.95	125.92	129.74	133.41	136.95	140.34	143.59	146.69	155.10	166.09	173.02	175.48
3.00	103.67	107.20	110.58	113.81	116.91	119.87	122.70	125.39	127.95	130.39	132.69	134.87	140.68	147.97	152.35	153.84
4.00	102.68	105.22	107.64	109.93	112.10	114.16	116.10	117.93	119.66	121.28	122.80	124.23	127.95	132.45	135.02	135.86
4.25	102.43	104.74	106.92	108.98	110.94	112.78	114.51	116.15	117.68	119.13	120.47	121.73	125.01	128.92	131.13	131.84
4.50	102.19	104.25	106.20	108.05	109.78	111.42	112.96	114.40	115.75	117.02	118.20	119.30	122.15	125.53	127.41	128.01
4.75	101.94	103.77	105.49	107.12	108.64	110.08	111.42	112.68	113.86	114.96	115.98	116.93	119.38	122.25	123.84	124.34
5.00	101.70	103.29	104.79	106.20	107.52	108.76	109.91	110.99	112.00	112.94	113.81	114.62	116.69	119.10	120.41	120.82
5.25	101.45	102.81	104.09	105.29	106.41	107.45	108.43	109.34	110.18	110.97	111.70	112.37	114.09	116.07	117.13	117.46
5.50	101.21	102.34	103.40	104.38	105.31	106.17	106.97	107.71	108.40	109.04	109.63	110.18	111.56	113.14	113.98	114.23
5.75	100.96	101.87	102.71	103.49	104.22	104.90	105.53	106.11	106.65	107.15	107.61	108.04	109.11	110.32	110.95	111.14
6.00	100.72	101.40	102.02	102.60	103.15	103.65	104.11	104.54	104.94	105.31	105.64	105.95	106.73	107.60	108.05	108.18
6.25	100.48	100.93	101.34	101.73	102.08	102.41	102.72	103.00	103.26	103.50	103.72	103.92	104.42	104.97	105.26	105.34
6.50	100.24	100.46	100.67	100.86	101.04	101.20	101.35	101.49	101.61	101.73	101.84	101.93	102.18	102.44	102.58	102.62
6.75	100.00	100.00	100.00	100.00	100.00	100.00	100.00	100.00	100.00	100.00	100.00	100.00	100.00	100.00	100.00	100.00
7.00	99.76	99.54	99.34	99.15	98.98	98.82	98.67	98.54	98.42	98.31	98.21	98.11	97.89	97.64	97.52	97.49
7.25	99.52	99.08	98.68	98.30	97.96	97.65	97.37	97.10	96.87	96.65	96.45	96.27	95.84	95.37	95.14	95.08
7.50	99.28	98.63	98.02	97.47	96.96	96.50	96.08	95.70	95.35	95.03	94.74	94.48	93.85	93.17	92.85	92.76
7.75	99.05	98.17	97.37	96.64	95.98	95.37	94.81	94.31	93.86	93.44	93.07	92.73	91.91	91.05	90.65	90.53
8.00	98.81	97.72	96.73	95.82	95.00	94.25	93.57	92.95	92.39	91.89	91.43	91.02	90.03	89.01	88.52	88.39
8.25	98.57	97.27	96.09	95.01	94.03	93.15	92.34	91.62	90.96	90.37	89.84	89.36	88.21	87.03	86.48	86.33
8.50	98.34	96.82	95.45	94.21	93.08	92.06	91.14	90.30	89.55	88.88	88.28	87.73	86.44	85.12	84.51	84.35
8.75	98.10	96.38	94.82	93.41	92.14	90.99	89.95	89.02	88.18	87.42	86.75	86.15	84.72	83.27	82.62	82.45
9.00	97.87	95.94	94.19	92.62	91.20	89.93	88.78	87.75	86.83	86.00	85.26	84.60	83.04	81.49	80.79	80.61
9.25	97.63	95.50	93.57	91.84	90.28	88.88	87.63	86.51	85.50	84.60	83.80	83.09	81.42	79.76	79.03	78.84
9.50	97.40	95.06	92.96	91.07	89.37	87.85	86.50	85.28	84.20	83.24	82.38	81.62	79.84	78.09	77.33	77.14
9.75	97.17	94.62	92.34	90.30	88.47	86.84	85.38	84.08	82.93	81.90	80.99	80.19	78.31	76.48	75.69	75.49
10.00	96.93	94.19	91.73	89.54	87.58	85.84	84.28	82.90	81.68	80.59	79.63	78.78	76.81	74.92	74.11	73.91
10.25	96.70	93.76	91.13	88.79	86.70	84.85	83.20	81.74	80.45	79.31	78.30	77.42	75.36	73.41	72.58	72.38
10.50	96.47	93.33	90.53	88.04	85.84	83.88	82.14	80.61	79.25	78.05	77.00	76.08	73.95	71.95	71.11	70.91
10.75	96.24	92.90	89.94	87.31	84.98	82.92	81.09	79.49	78.07	76.83	75.73	74.78	72.58	70.53	69.68	69.48
11.00	96.01	92.48	89.35	86.58	84.13	81.97	80.06	78.39	76.91	75.62	74.49	73.50	71.25	69.16	68.31	68.11
11.25	95.78	92.05	88.76	85.85	83.29	81.03	79.05	77.31	75.78	74.44	73.28	72.26	69.95	67.83	66.98	66.78
11.50	95.55	91.63	88.18	85.14	82.46	80.11	78.05	76.25	74.67	73.29	72.09	71.05	68.69	66.55	65.69	65.50
11.75	95.33	91.21	87.60	84.43	81.64	79.20	77.07	75.20	73.58	72.16	70.93	69.86	67.46	65.30	64.45	64.26
12.00	95.10	90.80	87.03	83.72	80.83	78.31	76.10	74.18	72.51	71.05	69.79	68.71	66.27	64.09	63.25	63.06
12.25	94.87	90.38	86.46	83.03	80.03	77.42	75.15	73.17	71.46	69.97	68.68	67.58	65.10	62.92	62.08	61.90
12.50	94.65	89.97	85.89	82.34	79.24	76.55	74.21	72.18	70.43	68.91	67.60	66.47	63.97	61.78	60.96	60.77
12.75	94.42	89.56	85.33	81.65	78.46	75.69	73.29	71.21	69.41	67.87	66.54	65.40	62.87	60.68	59.87	59.69
13.00	94.20	89.15	84.77	80.98	77.68	74.84	72.38	70.25	68.42	66.85	65.50	64.34	61.80	59.62	58.81	58.63
13.25	93.97	88.75	84.22	80.31	76.92	74.00	71.48	69.31	67.45	65.85	64.48	63.32	60.76	58.58	57.78	57.61
13.50	93.75	88.34	83.67	79.64	76.17	73.17	70.60	68.39	66.50	64.87	63.49	62.31	59.74	57.57	56.79	56.63
13.75	93.53	87.94	83.13	78.98	75.42	72.36	69.73	67.48	65.56	63.92	62.52	61.33	58.75	56.60	55.83	55.67
14.00	93.30	87.54	82.59	78.33	74.68	71.55	68.88	66.59	64.64	62.98	61.57	60.37	57.79	55.65	54.90	54.74
14.25	93.08	87.14	82.05	77.69	73.95	70.76	68.04	65.71	63.74	62.06	60.64	59.43	56.85	54.73	53.99	53.84
14.50	92.86	86.75	81.52	77.05	73.23	69.98	67.21	64.85	62.85	61.16	59.73	58.52	55.94	53.83	53.11	52.97
14.75	92.64	86.35	80.99	76.41	72.52	69.21	66.39	64.01	61.99	60.28	58.84	57.62	55.04	52.97	52.26	52.12
15.00	92.42	85.96	80.46	75.79	71.81	68.44	65.59	63.17	61.13	59.41	57.97	56.75	54.18	52.12	51.43	51.30
15.25	92.20	85.57	79.94	75.16	71.12	67.69	64.80	62.36	60.30	58.57	57.11	55.90	53.33	51.30	50.63	50.50
15.50	91.98	85.18	79.42	74.55	70.43	66.95	64.02	61.55	59.48	57.74	56.28	55.06	52.50	50.50	49.85	49.72
15.75	91.76	84.79	78.91	73.94	69.75	66.22	63.25	60.76	58.67	56.92	55.46	54.24	51.70	49.73	49.09	48.96
16.00	91.54	84.41	78.40	73.33	69.08	65.50	62.50	59.98	57.88	56.12	54.66	53.45	50.92	48.97	48.35	48.23
16.25	91.33	84.03	77.89	72.74	68.41	64.79	61.75	59.22	57.10	55.34	53.88	52.66	50.15	48.24	47.63	47.52
16.50	91.11	83.65	77.39	72.14	67.75	64.08	61.02	58.47	56.34	54.58	53.11	51.90	49.41	47.52	46.93	46.83
16.75	90.89	83.27	76.89	71.56	67.10	63.39	60.30	57.73	55.59	53.83	52.36	51.16	48.68	46.83	46.26	46.15
17.00	90.68	82.89	76.39	70.97	66.46	62.71	59.59	57.00	54.86	53.09	51.63	50.43	47.97	46.15	45.59	45.49
17.25	90.46	82.52	75.90	70.40	65.83	62.03	58.89	56.29	54.14	52.37	50.91	49.71	47.28	45.49	44.95	44.86
17.50	90.25	82.14	75.41	69.83	65.20	61.37	58.20	55.59	53.43	51.66	50.21	49.01	46.60	44.85	44.33	44.23
17.75	90.04	81.77	74.93	69.26	64.58	60.71	57.52	54.90	52.74	50.97	49.52	48.33	45.94	44.22	43.72	43.63
18.00	89.82	81.40	74.45	68.70	63.96	60.06	56.85	54.22	52.06	50.29	48.84	47.66	45.30	43.61	43.12	43.04
18.25	89.61	81.04	73.97	68.15	63.36	59.42	56.20	53.55	51.39	49.62	48.18	47.01	44.67	43.02	42.54	42.46
18.50	89.40	80.67	73.49	67.60	62.76	58.79	55.55	52.89	50.73	48.97	47.53	46.37	44.06	42.44	41.98	41.90
18.75	89.19	80.31	73.02	67.05	62.17	58.17	54.91	52.25	50.08	48.32	46.90	45.74	43.46	41.87	41.43	41.35
19.00	88.97	79.94	72.55	66.51	61.58	57.56	54.28	51.61	49.45	47.69	46.28	45.13	42.88	41.32	40.89	40.82
20.00	88.14	78.51	70.72	64.41	59.30	55.18	51.86	49.18	47.03	45.30	43.91	42.81	40.67	39.25	38.87	38.81
25.00	84.07	71.77	62.28	54.97	49.34	45.01	41.69	39.14	37.19	35.69	34.56	33.69	32.16	31.31	31.14	31.11
30.00	80.22	65.67	54.98	47.14	41.38	37.17	34.09	31.84	30.20	29.01	28.14	27.52	26.50	26.03	25.95	25.94

Description: This table shows the yield to prepayment of a monthly payment mortgage purchased at a price in the index.

Example: The yield to prepayment in 10 years of a 6.75 %, 30 year mortgage at a price of 104.00 is 6.18 %.

30 YEAR MORTGAGE PREPAID IN

PRICE	1 yr	2 yr	3 yr	4 yr	5 yr	6 yr	7 yr	8 yr	9 yr	10 yr	11 yr	12 yr	15 yr	20 yr	25 yr	30 yr
140	–	–	–	–	–	–	–	1.23	1.67	2.03	2.31	2.55	3.05	3.49	3.69	3.75
135	–	–	–	–	–	–	1.29	1.81	2.20	2.52	2.77	2.98	3.43	3.82	4.00	4.05
130	–	–	–	–	–	1.35	1.96	2.41	2.76	3.04	3.26	3.44	3.83	4.17	4.32	4.36
125	–	–	–	–	1.41	2.14	2.66	3.05	3.34	3.58	3.76	3.92	4.25	4.53	4.66	4.70
120	–	–	–	1.48	2.38	2.97	3.40	3.71	3.95	4.14	4.30	4.42	4.69	4.92	5.03	5.06
119	–	–	–	1.72	2.57	3.14	3.55	3.85	4.08	4.26	4.41	4.53	4.78	5.00	5.10	5.13
118	–	–	–	1.96	2.77	3.32	3.70	3.99	4.20	4.38	4.52	4.63	4.87	5.08	5.18	5.20
117	–	–	–	2.20	2.98	3.49	3.85	4.13	4.33	4.50	4.63	4.74	4.97	5.17	5.26	5.28
116	–	–	1.22	2.45	3.18	3.67	4.01	4.27	4.46	4.62	4.74	4.85	5.06	5.25	5.33	5.36
115	–	–	1.54	2.70	3.39	3.84	4.17	4.41	4.59	4.74	4.86	4.95	5.16	5.33	5.41	5.43
114	–	–	1.86	2.95	3.59	4.02	4.33	4.55	4.73	4.86	4.97	5.06	5.25	5.42	5.49	5.51
113	–	–	2.19	3.20	3.80	4.20	4.49	4.70	4.86	4.99	5.09	5.17	5.35	5.51	5.57	5.59
112	–	–	2.52	3.46	4.02	4.39	4.65	4.85	5.00	5.11	5.21	5.29	5.45	5.59	5.66	5.67
111	–	1.12	2.85	3.72	4.23	4.57	4.81	4.99	5.13	5.24	5.33	5.40	5.55	5.68	5.74	5.76
110	–	1.61	3.19	3.98	4.45	4.76	4.98	5.14	5.27	5.37	5.45	5.52	5.65	5.77	5.83	5.84
109	–	2.10	3.53	4.24	4.67	4.95	5.15	5.30	5.41	5.50	5.57	5.63	5.76	5.86	5.91	5.92
108	–	2.59	3.87	4.51	4.89	5.14	5.32	5.45	5.55	5.63	5.70	5.75	5.86	5.96	6.00	6.01
107	–	3.09	4.22	4.78	5.11	5.33	5.49	5.61	5.69	5.77	5.82	5.87	5.97	6.05	6.09	6.10
106	–	3.60	4.57	5.05	5.34	5.53	5.66	5.76	5.84	5.90	5.95	5.99	6.07	6.15	6.18	6.19
105	1.68	4.11	4.92	5.32	5.57	5.72	5.84	5.92	5.99	6.04	6.08	6.11	6.18	6.24	6.27	6.28
104	2.67	4.63	5.28	5.60	5.80	5.92	6.02	6.08	6.13	6.18	6.21	6.23	6.29	6.34	6.36	6.37
103.75	2.92	4.76	5.37	5.67	5.85	5.97	6.06	6.12	6.17	6.21	6.24	6.27	6.32	6.36	6.38	6.39
103.50	3.17	4.89	5.46	5.74	5.91	6.02	6.10	6.16	6.21	6.24	6.27	6.30	6.35	6.39	6.41	6.41
103.25	3.42	5.02	5.55	5.81	5.97	6.08	6.15	6.20	6.25	6.28	6.31	6.33	6.37	6.41	6.43	6.44
103.00	3.67	5.15	5.64	5.88	6.03	6.13	6.19	6.25	6.28	6.31	6.34	6.36	6.40	6.44	6.45	6.46
102.75	3.92	5.28	5.73	5.95	6.09	6.18	6.24	6.29	6.32	6.35	6.37	6.39	6.43	6.46	6.48	6.48
102.50	4.18	5.41	5.82	6.02	6.15	6.23	6.28	6.33	6.36	6.39	6.41	6.42	6.46	6.49	6.50	6.51
102.25	4.43	5.54	5.91	6.10	6.21	6.28	6.33	6.37	6.40	6.42	6.44	6.45	6.49	6.51	6.53	6.53
102.00	4.68	5.67	6.00	6.17	6.27	6.33	6.38	6.41	6.44	6.46	6.47	6.49	6.51	6.54	6.55	6.55
101.75	4.94	5.81	6.10	6.24	6.32	6.38	6.42	6.45	6.47	6.49	6.51	6.52	6.54	6.56	6.57	6.58
101.50	5.20	5.94	6.19	6.31	6.38	6.43	6.47	6.49	6.51	6.53	6.54	6.55	6.57	6.59	6.60	6.60
101.25	5.45	6.07	6.28	6.38	6.44	6.48	6.51	6.53	6.55	6.56	6.57	6.58	6.60	6.62	6.62	6.62
101.00	5.71	6.21	6.37	6.45	6.50	6.54	6.56	6.58	6.59	6.60	6.61	6.61	6.63	6.64	6.65	6.65
100.75	5.97	6.34	6.46	6.53	6.56	6.59	6.61	6.62	6.63	6.64	6.64	6.65	6.66	6.67	6.67	6.67
100.50	6.23	6.48	6.56	6.60	6.62	6.64	6.65	6.66	6.67	6.67	6.68	6.68	6.69	6.69	6.70	6.70
100.25	6.48	6.61	6.65	6.67	6.68	6.69	6.70	6.70	6.71	6.71	6.71	6.71	6.72	6.72	6.72	6.72
100.00	6.75	6.75	6.75	6.75	6.75	6.75	6.75	6.75	6.75	6.75	6.75	6.75	6.75	6.75	6.75	6.75
99.75	7.01	6.88	6.84	6.82	6.81	6.80	6.79	6.79	6.78	6.78	6.78	6.78	6.77	6.77	6.77	6.77
99.50	7.27	7.02	6.93	6.89	6.87	6.85	6.84	6.83	6.82	6.82	6.81	6.81	6.80	6.80	6.79	6.79
99.25	7.53	7.15	7.03	6.97	6.93	6.90	6.89	6.87	6.86	6.86	6.85	6.84	6.83	6.82	6.82	6.82
99.00	7.79	7.29	7.12	7.04	6.99	6.96	6.93	6.92	6.90	6.89	6.88	6.88	6.86	6.85	6.84	6.84
98.75	8.06	7.43	7.22	7.11	7.05	7.01	6.98	6.96	6.94	6.93	6.92	6.91	6.89	6.88	6.87	6.87
98.50	8.32	7.56	7.31	7.19	7.11	7.06	7.03	7.00	6.98	6.97	6.95	6.94	6.92	6.90	6.90	6.89
98.25	8.59	7.70	7.41	7.26	7.17	7.12	7.08	7.05	7.02	7.00	6.99	6.98	6.95	6.93	6.92	6.92
98.00	8.85	7.84	7.50	7.34	7.24	7.17	7.12	7.09	7.06	7.04	7.02	7.01	6.98	6.96	6.95	6.94
97.75	9.12	7.98	7.60	7.41	7.30	7.22	7.17	7.13	7.10	7.08	7.06	7.04	7.01	6.98	6.97	6.97
97.50	9.39	8.12	7.70	7.49	7.36	7.28	7.22	7.18	7.14	7.12	7.09	7.08	7.04	7.01	7.00	6.99
97.25	9.65	8.26	7.79	7.56	7.42	7.33	7.27	7.22	7.18	7.15	7.13	7.11	7.07	7.04	7.02	7.02
97	9.92	8.40	7.89	7.64	7.49	7.39	7.32	7.26	7.22	7.19	7.17	7.15	7.10	7.06	7.05	7.04
96	11.01	8.96	8.28	7.94	7.74	7.61	7.51	7.44	7.39	7.34	7.31	7.28	7.22	7.17	7.15	7.15
95	12.10	9.53	8.67	8.25	7.99	7.83	7.71	7.62	7.55	7.50	7.46	7.42	7.35	7.29	7.26	7.25
94	13.21	10.10	9.07	8.56	8.25	8.05	7.91	7.80	7.72	7.66	7.60	7.56	7.48	7.40	7.37	7.36
93	14.34	10.69	9.48	8.87	8.52	8.28	8.11	7.99	7.89	7.82	7.76	7.71	7.60	7.52	7.48	7.47
92	15.47	11.28	9.89	9.19	8.78	8.51	8.32	8.17	8.06	7.98	7.91	7.85	7.73	7.63	7.59	7.58
91	16.62	11.87	10.30	9.52	9.05	8.74	8.52	8.36	8.24	8.14	8.06	8.00	7.87	7.75	7.70	7.69
90	17.79	12.48	10.72	9.84	9.32	8.98	8.73	8.55	8.42	8.31	8.22	8.15	8.00	7.87	7.82	7.81
89	18.96	13.09	11.14	10.17	9.60	9.22	8.95	8.75	8.60	8.47	8.38	8.30	8.14	8.00	7.94	7.92
88	20.16	13.71	11.57	10.51	9.88	9.46	9.16	8.95	8.78	8.65	8.54	8.45	8.27	8.12	8.06	8.04
87	21.37	14.33	12.01	10.85	10.16	9.71	9.38	9.15	8.96	8.82	8.70	8.61	8.41	8.25	8.18	8.16
86	22.59	14.97	12.45	11.19	10.45	9.95	9.61	9.35	9.15	8.99	8.87	8.77	8.56	8.38	8.31	8.29
85	23.83	15.61	12.89	11.54	10.74	10.21	9.83	9.55	9.34	9.17	9.04	8.93	8.70	8.51	8.43	8.41
80	30.28	18.96	15.22	13.36	12.25	11.53	11.01	10.63	10.34	10.11	9.93	9.78	9.47	9.21	9.11	9.08
75	37.20	22.54	17.71	15.31	13.89	12.95	12.28	11.79	11.42	11.13	10.89	10.70	10.31	9.98	9.85	9.82
70	44.66	26.40	20.39	17.42	15.65	14.49	13.67	13.06	12.60	12.24	11.95	11.72	11.24	10.84	10.69	10.65
65	52.73	30.57	23.30	19.71	17.57	16.17	15.18	14.45	13.90	13.46	13.12	12.84	12.27	11.81	11.63	11.59
60	61.53	35.12	26.48	22.21	19.68	18.02	16.85	15.99	15.33	14.82	14.42	14.09	13.43	12.90	12.71	12.67
55	71.19	40.12	29.98	24.98	22.02	20.07	18.71	17.71	16.95	16.36	15.89	15.51	14.76	14.17	13.97	13.92
50	81.89	45.65	33.86	28.06	24.63	22.38	20.80	19.65	18.78	18.10	17.57	17.14	16.30	15.66	15.45	15.40

Description: This table shows the price to pay for a monthly payment loan, at a yield rate and assuming prepayment.

Example: The price of a 7.00 %, 30 year mortgage to yield 8.00 %, if prepaid in 6 years, is $ 95.39.

30 YEAR MORTGAGE PREPAID IN

YIELD	1 yr	2 yr	3 yr	4 yr	5 yr	6 yr	7 yr	8 yr	9 yr	10 yr	11 yr	12 yr	15 yr	20 yr	25 yr	30 yr
0.00	106.97	113.86	120.68	127.41	134.05	140.59	147.03	153.36	159.57	165.65	171.59	177.39	193.77	216.97	233.19	239.51
1.00	105.94	111.76	117.45	123.02	128.46	133.77	138.94	143.97	148.86	153.59	158.18	162.60	174.88	191.58	202.70	206.85
2.00	104.92	109.70	114.33	118.81	123.14	127.32	131.36	135.25	138.98	142.57	146.01	149.30	158.23	169.94	177.35	180.00
3.00	103.92	107.68	111.29	114.75	118.06	121.23	124.25	127.14	129.88	132.50	134.97	137.31	143.56	151.43	156.18	157.80
4.00	102.92	105.70	108.34	110.85	113.22	115.47	117.59	119.60	121.49	123.27	124.94	126.51	130.61	135.57	138.42	139.36
4.25	102.68	105.21	107.62	109.89	112.04	114.08	115.99	117.80	119.50	121.09	122.58	123.98	127.61	131.97	134.44	135.24
4.50	102.43	104.73	106.90	108.95	110.88	112.71	114.42	116.03	117.54	118.96	120.28	121.51	124.70	128.50	130.63	131.30
4.75	102.18	104.24	106.19	108.02	109.74	111.35	112.87	114.30	115.63	116.87	118.03	119.11	121.88	125.15	126.97	127.54
5.00	101.94	103.76	105.48	107.09	108.60	110.02	111.35	112.59	113.75	114.83	115.83	116.76	119.15	121.93	123.46	123.93
5.25	101.69	103.28	104.78	106.17	107.48	108.71	109.85	110.92	111.91	112.83	113.69	114.48	116.50	118.83	120.09	120.48
5.50	101.45	102.81	104.08	105.27	106.38	107.41	108.37	109.27	110.10	110.88	111.59	112.25	113.92	115.84	116.86	117.17
5.75	101.21	102.33	103.39	104.37	105.28	106.13	106.92	107.66	108.33	108.96	109.54	110.08	111.43	112.95	113.76	114.01
6.00	100.96	101.86	102.70	103.48	104.20	104.87	105.49	106.07	106.60	107.09	107.54	107.96	109.00	110.17	110.78	110.97
6.25	100.72	101.39	102.02	102.59	103.13	103.63	104.09	104.51	104.90	105.26	105.59	105.89	106.65	107.49	107.93	108.05
6.50	100.48	100.93	101.34	101.72	102.08	102.40	102.70	102.98	103.23	103.47	103.68	103.88	104.37	104.90	105.18	105.26
6.75	100.24	100.46	100.67	100.86	101.03	101.19	101.34	101.48	101.60	101.72	101.82	101.92	102.15	102.41	102.54	102.58
7.00	100.00	100.00	100.00	100.00	100.00	100.00	100.00	100.00	100.00	100.00	100.00	100.00	100.00	100.00	100.00	100.00
7.25	99.76	99.54	99.34	99.15	98.98	98.82	98.68	98.55	98.43	98.32	98.22	98.13	97.91	97.68	97.56	97.53
7.50	99.52	99.08	98.68	98.31	97.97	97.66	97.38	97.12	96.89	96.68	96.48	96.31	95.88	95.43	95.21	95.15
7.75	99.28	98.63	98.03	97.48	96.98	96.52	96.10	95.73	95.38	95.07	94.79	94.53	93.91	93.26	92.95	92.87
8.00	99.05	98.18	97.38	96.65	95.99	95.39	94.85	94.35	93.90	93.50	93.13	92.80	92.00	91.17	90.78	90.67
8.25	98.81	97.72	96.74	95.84	95.02	94.28	93.61	93.00	92.45	91.96	91.51	91.11	90.14	89.15	88.68	88.56
8.50	98.57	97.28	96.10	95.03	94.06	93.18	92.39	91.67	91.03	90.45	89.93	89.46	88.34	87.19	86.67	86.53
8.75	98.34	96.83	95.46	94.23	93.11	92.10	91.19	90.37	89.63	88.97	88.38	87.85	86.58	85.31	84.72	84.57
9.00	98.10	96.39	94.84	93.43	92.17	91.03	90.01	89.09	88.26	87.53	86.87	86.28	84.88	83.48	82.85	82.69
9.25	97.87	95.95	94.21	92.65	91.24	89.98	88.85	87.83	86.92	86.11	85.39	84.74	83.22	81.72	81.04	80.87
9.50	97.63	95.51	93.59	91.87	90.33	88.94	87.70	86.60	85.61	84.73	83.94	83.25	81.61	80.01	79.30	79.12
9.75	97.40	95.07	92.98	91.10	89.42	87.92	86.58	85.38	84.32	83.37	82.53	81.79	80.05	78.36	77.62	77.44
10.00	97.17	94.63	92.36	90.34	88.52	86.91	85.47	84.19	83.05	82.04	81.15	80.36	78.53	76.76	76.00	75.81
10.25	96.94	94.20	91.76	89.58	87.64	85.91	84.38	83.02	81.81	80.74	79.80	78.97	77.05	75.22	74.44	74.24
10.50	96.71	93.77	91.16	88.83	86.76	84.93	83.30	81.87	80.59	79.47	78.48	77.62	75.61	73.72	72.93	72.73
10.75	96.48	93.34	90.56	88.09	85.90	83.96	82.25	80.73	79.40	78.23	77.19	76.29	74.22	72.27	71.47	71.27
11.00	96.25	92.92	89.97	87.35	85.04	83.01	81.21	79.62	78.23	77.01	75.93	75.00	72.86	70.87	70.06	69.86
11.25	96.02	92.49	89.38	86.63	84.20	82.06	80.18	78.53	77.08	75.81	74.70	73.74	71.53	69.51	68.69	68.50
11.50	95.79	92.07	88.79	85.90	83.36	81.13	79.17	77.46	75.95	74.64	73.50	72.50	70.25	68.19	67.37	67.18
11.75	95.56	91.65	88.21	85.19	82.54	80.21	78.18	76.40	74.85	73.49	72.32	71.30	69.00	66.92	66.10	65.91
12.00	95.33	91.23	87.64	84.48	81.72	79.31	77.20	75.36	73.76	72.37	71.17	70.12	67.78	65.68	64.87	64.68
12.25	95.10	90.82	87.06	83.78	80.92	78.42	76.24	74.35	72.70	71.27	70.04	68.97	66.59	64.48	63.67	63.49
12.50	94.88	90.40	86.50	83.09	80.12	77.54	75.29	73.34	71.66	70.20	68.94	67.85	65.44	63.32	62.52	62.34
12.75	94.65	89.99	85.93	82.40	79.33	76.67	74.36	72.36	70.63	69.14	67.86	66.76	64.32	62.20	61.40	61.22
13.00	94.43	89.58	85.37	81.72	78.55	75.81	73.44	71.39	69.63	68.11	66.80	65.69	63.22	61.10	60.32	60.14
13.25	94.20	89.17	84.82	81.05	77.78	74.97	72.54	70.44	68.64	67.10	65.77	64.64	62.16	60.04	59.27	59.10
13.50	93.98	88.77	84.27	80.38	77.02	74.13	71.65	69.51	67.68	66.11	64.76	63.62	61.12	59.01	58.25	58.08
13.75	93.76	88.37	83.72	79.72	76.27	73.31	70.77	68.59	66.73	65.13	63.78	62.62	60.12	58.01	57.26	57.10
14.00	93.53	87.96	83.17	79.06	75.53	72.50	69.90	67.69	65.80	64.18	62.81	61.65	59.13	57.04	56.30	56.15
14.25	93.31	87.56	82.64	78.41	74.79	71.70	69.05	66.80	64.88	63.25	61.87	60.69	58.17	56.10	55.38	55.23
14.50	93.09	87.17	82.10	77.77	74.07	70.91	68.22	65.93	63.98	62.34	60.94	59.76	57.24	55.18	54.48	54.33
14.75	92.87	86.77	81.57	77.13	73.35	70.13	67.39	65.07	63.10	61.44	60.04	58.85	56.33	54.30	53.60	53.46
15.00	92.65	86.38	81.04	76.50	72.64	69.36	66.58	64.23	62.24	60.56	59.15	57.96	55.45	53.43	52.75	52.62
15.25	92.43	85.99	80.52	75.87	71.94	68.60	65.78	63.40	61.39	59.70	58.28	57.09	54.58	52.59	51.93	51.80
15.50	92.21	85.60	80.00	75.25	71.24	67.85	65.00	62.59	60.56	58.86	57.44	56.25	53.74	51.77	51.13	51.00
15.75	91.99	85.21	79.48	74.64	70.56	67.12	64.22	61.79	59.75	58.04	56.61	55.41	52.92	50.98	50.35	50.23
16.00	91.77	84.82	78.97	74.03	69.88	66.39	63.46	61.00	58.94	57.23	55.79	54.60	52.12	50.21	49.59	49.47
16.25	91.55	84.44	78.46	73.43	69.21	65.67	62.70	60.23	58.16	56.43	55.00	53.81	51.34	49.45	48.86	48.74
16.50	91.34	84.06	77.95	72.83	68.55	64.96	61.96	59.47	57.38	55.65	54.22	53.03	50.58	48.72	48.14	48.03
16.75	91.12	83.68	77.45	72.24	67.89	64.26	61.24	58.72	56.63	54.89	53.46	52.27	49.84	48.01	47.44	47.34
17.00	90.90	83.30	76.95	71.66	67.24	63.57	60.52	57.98	55.88	54.14	52.71	51.53	49.11	47.32	46.77	46.67
17.25	90.69	82.93	76.46	71.08	66.60	62.89	59.81	57.26	55.15	53.41	51.98	50.80	48.41	46.64	46.11	46.01
17.50	90.47	82.55	75.97	70.50	65.97	62.22	59.11	56.55	54.43	52.69	51.26	50.09	47.72	45.98	45.46	45.37
17.75	90.26	82.18	75.48	69.93	65.35	61.56	58.43	55.85	53.73	51.99	50.56	49.40	47.04	45.34	44.84	44.75
18.00	90.05	81.81	75.00	69.37	64.73	60.90	57.75	55.16	53.04	51.30	49.88	48.72	46.39	44.72	44.23	44.14
18.25	89.83	81.44	74.52	68.81	64.12	60.26	57.09	54.49	52.36	50.62	49.20	48.05	45.75	44.11	43.64	43.55
18.50	89.62	81.07	74.04	68.26	63.51	59.62	56.43	53.82	51.69	49.96	48.55	47.40	45.12	43.51	43.06	42.98
18.75	89.41	80.71	73.57	67.71	62.91	58.99	55.78	53.17	51.04	49.31	47.90	46.76	44.51	42.94	42.49	42.42
19.00	89.20	80.34	73.10	67.17	62.32	58.37	55.15	52.53	50.40	48.67	47.27	46.14	43.91	42.37	41.94	41.87
20.00	88.36	78.91	71.25	65.05	60.03	55.97	52.70	50.06	47.94	46.23	44.87	43.77	41.66	40.25	39.87	39.81
25.00	84.29	72.15	62.78	55.55	49.98	45.70	42.41	39.89	37.95	36.47	35.34	34.48	32.96	32.11	31.94	31.92
30.00	80.42	66.02	55.44	47.66	41.96	37.78	34.72	32.49	30.86	29.67	28.81	28.18	27.17	26.69	26.62	26.61

PREPAYMENT MORTGAGE YIELD, 30 YEAR TERM   7.00 %

Description: This table shows the yield to prepayment of a monthly payment mortgage purchased at a price in the index.

Example: The yield to prepayment in 10 years of a 7.00 %, 30 year mortgage at a price of 104.00 is 6.42 %.

30 YEAR MORTGAGE PREPAID IN

PRICE	1 yr	2 yr	3 yr	4 yr	5 yr	6 yr	7 yr	8 yr	9 yr	10 yr	11 yr	12 yr	15 yr	20 yr	25 yr	30 yr
140	–	–	–	–	–	–	–	1.44	1.89	2.24	2.53	2.76	3.26	3.70	3.90	3.96
135	–	–	–	–	–	–	1.51	2.02	2.42	2.74	2.99	3.20	3.64	4.03	4.21	4.26
130	–	–	–	–	–	1.57	2.18	2.63	2.98	3.26	3.48	3.66	4.04	4.39	4.54	4.58
125	–	–	–	–	1.64	2.37	2.89	3.27	3.57	3.80	3.99	4.14	4.47	4.76	4.88	4.92
120	–	–	–	1.71	2.61	3.20	3.63	3.94	4.18	4.37	4.53	4.65	4.92	5.15	5.25	5.28
119	–	–	–	1.95	2.81	3.38	3.78	4.08	4.31	4.49	4.64	4.76	5.01	5.23	5.33	5.36
118	–	–	–	2.19	3.01	3.55	3.93	4.22	4.44	4.61	4.75	4.86	5.10	5.31	5.41	5.43
117	–	–	1.14	2.44	3.21	3.72	4.09	4.36	4.57	4.73	4.86	4.97	5.20	5.40	5.48	5.51
116	–	–	1.46	2.68	3.41	3.90	4.24	4.50	4.70	4.85	4.98	5.08	5.29	5.48	5.56	5.59
115	–	–	1.78	2.93	3.62	4.08	4.40	4.64	4.83	4.97	5.09	5.19	5.39	5.57	5.64	5.67
114	–	–	2.10	3.18	3.83	4.26	4.56	4.79	4.96	5.10	5.21	5.30	5.49	5.65	5.73	5.75
113	–	–	2.43	3.44	4.04	4.44	4.72	4.93	5.10	5.22	5.33	5.41	5.59	5.74	5.81	5.83
112	–	–	2.76	3.70	4.25	4.63	4.89	5.08	5.23	5.35	5.45	5.52	5.69	5.83	5.89	5.91
111	–	1.36	3.09	3.95	4.47	4.81	5.05	5.23	5.37	5.48	5.57	5.64	5.79	5.92	5.98	5.99
110	–	1.85	3.43	4.22	4.69	5.00	5.22	5.38	5.51	5.61	5.69	5.75	5.89	6.01	6.06	6.08
109	–	2.34	3.77	4.48	4.91	5.19	5.39	5.54	5.65	5.74	5.81	5.87	6.00	6.10	6.15	6.16
108	–	2.84	4.11	4.75	5.13	5.38	5.56	5.69	5.79	5.87	5.94	5.99	6.10	6.20	6.24	6.25
107	–	3.34	4.46	5.02	5.35	5.57	5.73	5.85	5.94	6.01	6.06	6.11	6.21	6.29	6.33	6.34
106	–	3.84	4.81	5.29	5.58	5.77	5.91	6.01	6.08	6.14	6.19	6.23	6.32	6.39	6.42	6.43
105	1.92	4.35	5.16	5.57	5.81	5.97	6.08	6.17	6.23	6.28	6.32	6.36	6.42	6.49	6.51	6.52
104	2.91	4.87	5.52	5.85	6.04	6.17	6.26	6.33	6.38	6.42	6.45	6.48	6.54	6.58	6.61	6.61
103.75	3.16	5.00	5.61	5.92	6.10	6.22	6.31	6.37	6.42	6.46	6.49	6.51	6.56	6.61	6.63	6.63
103.50	3.41	5.13	5.70	5.99	6.16	6.27	6.35	6.41	6.45	6.49	6.52	6.54	6.59	6.63	6.65	6.66
103.25	3.66	5.26	5.79	6.06	6.22	6.32	6.40	6.45	6.49	6.53	6.55	6.57	6.62	6.66	6.68	6.68
103.00	3.92	5.39	5.89	6.13	6.28	6.37	6.44	6.49	6.53	6.56	6.59	6.61	6.65	6.68	6.70	6.70
102.75	4.17	5.53	5.98	6.20	6.33	6.42	6.49	6.53	6.57	6.60	6.62	6.64	6.68	6.71	6.72	6.73
102.50	4.42	5.66	6.07	6.27	6.39	6.47	6.53	6.57	6.61	6.63	6.65	6.67	6.71	6.74	6.75	6.75
102.25	4.68	5.79	6.16	6.34	6.45	6.53	6.58	6.62	6.65	6.67	6.69	6.70	6.73	6.76	6.77	6.78
102.00	4.93	5.92	6.25	6.42	6.51	6.58	6.62	6.66	6.68	6.70	6.72	6.73	6.76	6.79	6.80	6.80
101.75	5.19	6.05	6.34	6.49	6.57	6.63	6.67	6.70	6.72	6.74	6.75	6.77	6.79	6.81	6.82	6.82
101.50	5.44	6.19	6.44	6.56	6.63	6.68	6.72	6.74	6.76	6.78	6.79	6.80	6.82	6.84	6.85	6.85
101.25	5.70	6.32	6.53	6.63	6.69	6.73	6.76	6.78	6.80	6.81	6.82	6.83	6.85	6.86	6.87	6.87
101.00	5.96	6.46	6.62	6.70	6.75	6.79	6.81	6.83	6.84	6.85	6.86	6.86	6.88	6.89	6.90	6.90
100.75	6.22	6.59	6.71	6.78	6.81	6.84	6.85	6.87	6.88	6.89	6.89	6.90	6.91	6.92	6.92	6.92
100.50	6.48	6.72	6.81	6.85	6.87	6.89	6.90	6.91	6.92	6.92	6.93	6.93	6.94	6.94	6.94	6.95
100.25	6.73	6.86	6.90	6.92	6.93	6.94	6.95	6.95	6.96	6.96	6.96	6.96	6.97	6.97	6.97	6.97
100.00	7.00	7.00	7.00	7.00	7.00	7.00	7.00	7.00	7.00	7.00	7.00	7.00	7.00	7.00	7.00	7.00
99.75	7.26	7.13	7.09	7.07	7.06	7.05	7.04	7.04	7.03	7.03	7.03	7.03	7.02	7.02	7.02	7.02
99.50	7.52	7.27	7.18	7.14	7.12	7.10	7.09	7.08	7.07	7.07	7.06	7.06	7.05	7.05	7.05	7.04
99.25	7.78	7.40	7.28	7.22	7.18	7.15	7.14	7.12	7.11	7.11	7.10	7.09	7.08	7.07	7.07	7.07
99.00	8.04	7.54	7.37	7.29	7.24	7.21	7.18	7.17	7.15	7.14	7.13	7.13	7.11	7.10	7.10	7.09
98.75	8.31	7.68	7.47	7.36	7.30	7.26	7.23	7.21	7.19	7.18	7.17	7.16	7.14	7.13	7.12	7.12
98.50	8.57	7.82	7.56	7.44	7.36	7.31	7.28	7.25	7.23	7.22	7.21	7.20	7.17	7.16	7.15	7.15
98.25	8.84	7.95	7.66	7.51	7.43	7.37	7.33	7.30	7.27	7.26	7.24	7.23	7.20	7.18	7.17	7.17
98.00	9.10	8.09	7.76	7.59	7.49	7.42	7.38	7.34	7.31	7.29	7.28	7.26	7.23	7.21	7.20	7.20
97.75	9.37	8.23	7.85	7.66	7.55	7.48	7.42	7.38	7.35	7.33	7.31	7.30	7.26	7.24	7.23	7.22
97.50	9.64	8.37	7.95	7.74	7.61	7.53	7.47	7.43	7.40	7.37	7.35	7.33	7.30	7.26	7.25	7.25
97.25	9.91	8.51	8.05	7.81	7.68	7.59	7.52	7.47	7.44	7.41	7.38	7.37	7.33	7.29	7.28	7.27
97	10.18	8.65	8.14	7.89	7.74	7.64	7.57	7.52	7.48	7.45	7.42	7.40	7.36	7.32	7.30	7.30
96	11.26	9.21	8.53	8.20	7.99	7.86	7.77	7.70	7.64	7.60	7.57	7.54	7.48	7.43	7.41	7.40
95	12.36	9.78	8.93	8.50	8.25	8.08	7.96	7.88	7.81	7.76	7.71	7.68	7.61	7.54	7.52	7.51
94	13.47	10.36	9.33	8.82	8.51	8.31	8.17	8.06	7.98	7.91	7.86	7.82	7.73	7.66	7.63	7.62
93	14.59	10.95	9.74	9.13	8.77	8.54	8.37	8.25	8.15	8.07	8.01	7.97	7.86	7.78	7.74	7.73
92	15.73	11.54	10.15	9.45	9.04	8.77	8.58	8.43	8.32	8.24	8.17	8.11	8.00	7.89	7.85	7.84
91	16.88	12.13	10.56	9.78	9.31	9.00	8.79	8.62	8.50	8.40	8.32	8.26	8.13	8.02	7.97	7.96
90	18.05	12.74	10.98	10.11	9.58	9.24	9.00	8.82	8.68	8.57	8.48	8.41	8.26	8.14	8.09	8.07
89	19.23	13.35	11.41	10.44	9.86	9.48	9.21	9.01	8.86	8.74	8.64	8.57	8.40	8.26	8.21	8.19
88	20.42	13.97	11.84	10.78	10.14	9.73	9.43	9.21	9.04	8.91	8.81	8.72	8.54	8.39	8.33	8.31
87	21.63	14.60	12.27	11.12	10.43	9.97	9.65	9.41	9.23	9.09	8.97	8.88	8.69	8.52	8.45	8.44
86	22.86	15.24	12.71	11.46	10.72	10.22	9.87	9.62	9.42	9.26	9.14	9.04	8.83	8.65	8.58	8.56
85	24.10	15.88	13.16	11.81	11.01	10.48	10.10	9.82	9.61	9.45	9.31	9.20	8.98	8.79	8.71	8.69
80	30.56	19.23	15.49	13.64	12.53	11.80	11.29	10.91	10.62	10.39	10.21	10.06	9.75	9.50	9.39	9.37
75	37.49	22.83	17.99	15.60	14.17	13.23	12.57	12.08	11.71	11.42	11.18	10.99	10.60	10.28	10.15	10.12
70	44.95	26.69	20.69	17.72	15.95	14.79	13.97	13.36	12.91	12.54	12.25	12.02	11.54	11.15	11.00	10.97
65	53.04	30.88	23.61	20.02	17.88	16.48	15.49	14.77	14.21	13.78	13.44	13.16	12.59	12.14	11.97	11.93
60	61.85	35.44	26.80	22.54	20.01	18.35	17.18	16.32	15.67	15.16	14.76	14.43	13.77	13.26	13.07	13.03
55	71.53	40.45	30.32	25.32	22.36	20.42	19.05	18.05	17.30	16.71	16.24	15.87	15.12	14.55	14.35	14.31
50	82.25	46.01	34.22	28.41	24.99	22.74	21.17	20.02	19.15	18.48	17.95	17.53	16.69	16.06	15.86	15.82

Description: This table shows the price to pay for a monthly payment loan, at a yield rate and assuming prepayment.

Example: The price of a 7.25 %, 30 year mortgage to yield 8.00 %, if prepaid in 6 years, is $ 96.54.

30 YEAR MORTGAGE PREPAID IN

YIELD	1 yr	2 yr	3 yr	4 yr	5 yr	6 yr	7 yr	8 yr	9 yr	10 yr	11 yr	12 yr	15 yr	20 yr	25 yr	30 yr
0.00	107.22	114.36	121.43	128.42	135.31	142.11	148.80	155.38	161.84	168.17	174.36	180.41	197.52	221.83	238.90	245.58
1.00	106.19	112.26	118.20	124.01	129.69	135.23	140.63	145.90	151.01	155.97	160.77	165.42	178.31	195.91	207.68	212.09
2.00	105.17	110.19	115.05	119.77	124.32	128.73	132.98	137.08	141.03	144.82	148.45	151.92	161.38	173.81	181.73	184.56
3.00	104.16	108.16	112.00	115.69	119.21	122.59	125.81	128.89	131.82	134.61	137.26	139.77	146.46	154.92	160.05	161.80
4.00	103.17	106.18	109.04	111.76	114.34	116.78	119.09	121.27	123.33	125.27	127.10	128.80	133.28	138.72	141.86	142.89
4.25	102.92	105.69	108.32	110.80	113.16	115.38	117.48	119.45	121.32	123.06	124.70	126.23	130.23	135.04	137.78	138.67
4.50	102.67	105.20	107.59	109.85	111.99	114.00	115.89	117.67	119.34	120.90	122.37	123.73	127.27	131.49	133.87	134.64
4.75	102.43	104.72	106.88	108.91	110.83	112.63	114.33	115.91	117.40	118.79	120.08	121.29	124.40	128.08	130.12	130.77
5.00	102.18	104.23	106.17	107.98	109.69	111.29	112.79	114.19	115.50	116.72	117.86	118.91	121.62	124.79	126.53	127.08
5.25	101.94	103.75	105.46	107.06	108.56	109.96	111.27	112.50	113.64	114.70	115.68	116.59	118.92	121.62	123.08	123.54
5.50	101.69	103.28	104.76	106.15	107.45	108.66	109.79	110.84	111.81	112.72	113.56	114.33	116.30	118.56	119.77	120.15
5.75	101.45	102.80	104.07	105.25	106.34	107.37	108.32	109.20	110.02	110.78	111.48	112.13	113.76	115.61	116.60	116.90
6.00	101.21	102.33	103.38	104.35	105.26	106.10	106.88	107.60	108.27	108.88	109.45	109.98	111.29	112.77	113.55	113.78
6.25	100.96	101.86	102.69	103.46	104.18	104.84	105.46	106.03	106.55	107.03	107.47	107.88	108.90	110.03	110.62	110.79
6.50	100.72	101.39	102.01	102.58	103.12	103.61	104.06	104.48	104.86	105.22	105.54	105.83	106.57	107.39	107.81	107.93
6.75	100.48	100.92	101.34	101.71	102.07	102.39	102.69	102.96	103.21	103.44	103.65	103.84	104.32	104.84	105.10	105.18
7.00	100.24	100.46	100.67	100.85	101.03	101.19	101.33	101.47	101.59	101.70	101.80	101.90	102.13	102.38	102.50	102.54
7.25	100.00	100.00	100.00	100.00	100.00	100.00	100.00	100.00	100.00	100.00	100.00	100.00	100.00	100.00	100.00	100.00
7.50	99.76	99.54	99.34	99.15	98.99	98.83	98.69	98.56	98.44	98.34	98.24	98.15	97.93	97.71	97.59	97.56
7.75	99.52	99.08	98.68	98.32	97.98	97.68	97.40	97.15	96.91	96.71	96.52	96.35	95.93	95.49	95.28	95.22
8.00	99.28	98.63	98.03	97.49	96.99	96.54	96.13	95.76	95.42	95.11	94.83	94.59	93.98	93.35	93.05	92.97
8.25	99.05	98.18	97.39	96.67	96.01	95.42	94.88	94.39	93.95	93.55	93.19	92.87	92.09	91.28	90.91	90.80
8.50	98.81	97.73	96.75	95.85	95.04	94.31	93.65	93.05	92.51	92.02	91.58	91.19	90.25	89.29	88.84	88.72
8.75	98.57	97.28	96.11	95.05	94.09	93.22	92.44	91.73	91.10	90.53	90.01	89.56	88.46	87.36	86.85	86.71
9.00	98.34	96.84	95.48	94.25	93.14	92.14	91.24	90.44	89.71	89.06	88.48	87.96	86.73	85.49	84.93	84.78
9.25	98.10	96.39	94.85	93.46	92.21	91.08	90.07	89.16	88.35	87.63	86.98	86.40	85.04	83.69	83.08	82.92
9.50	97.87	95.95	94.23	92.68	91.28	90.04	88.92	87.92	87.02	86.22	85.52	84.89	83.40	81.94	81.29	81.13
9.75	97.64	95.51	93.61	91.90	90.37	89.00	87.78	86.69	85.71	84.85	84.08	83.40	81.81	80.25	79.57	79.40
10.00	97.40	95.08	93.00	91.13	89.47	87.98	86.66	85.48	84.43	83.50	82.68	81.96	80.26	78.62	77.91	77.73
10.25	97.17	94.64	92.39	90.37	88.58	86.98	85.56	84.30	83.18	82.19	81.31	80.54	78.75	77.04	76.31	76.13
10.50	96.94	94.21	91.78	89.62	87.70	85.99	84.47	83.13	81.94	80.90	79.97	79.16	77.29	75.51	74.76	74.58
10.75	96.71	93.78	91.18	88.87	86.82	85.01	83.41	81.99	80.74	79.63	78.67	77.82	75.86	74.03	73.26	73.08
11.00	96.48	93.36	90.59	88.13	85.96	84.05	82.35	80.86	79.55	78.40	77.39	76.50	74.48	72.59	71.82	71.63
11.25	96.25	92.93	89.99	87.40	85.11	83.10	81.32	79.76	78.39	77.19	76.14	75.22	73.13	71.20	70.42	70.24
11.50	96.02	92.51	89.41	86.68	84.27	82.16	80.30	78.67	77.25	76.00	74.91	73.97	71.82	69.86	69.07	68.89
11.75	95.79	92.09	88.82	85.96	83.44	81.23	79.30	77.60	76.13	74.84	73.72	72.74	70.54	68.55	67.76	67.58
12.00	95.56	91.67	88.25	85.25	82.62	80.32	78.31	76.56	75.03	73.70	72.55	71.55	69.30	67.29	66.50	66.32
12.25	95.34	91.25	87.67	84.54	81.81	79.42	77.34	75.53	73.95	72.58	71.40	70.38	68.10	66.06	65.28	65.10
12.50	95.11	90.83	87.10	83.84	81.00	78.53	76.38	74.51	72.89	71.49	70.28	69.24	66.92	64.88	64.09	63.92
12.75	94.88	90.42	86.53	83.15	80.21	77.65	75.44	73.52	71.86	70.42	69.19	68.13	65.78	63.72	62.95	62.78
13.00	94.66	90.01	85.97	82.47	79.42	76.79	74.51	72.54	70.84	69.38	68.12	67.04	64.66	62.60	61.84	61.67
13.25	94.43	89.60	85.41	81.79	78.65	75.94	73.60	71.58	69.84	68.35	67.07	65.98	63.58	61.52	60.76	60.60
13.50	94.21	89.20	84.86	81.12	77.88	75.10	72.70	70.63	68.86	67.34	66.05	64.94	62.52	60.47	59.72	59.56
13.75	93.99	88.79	84.31	80.45	77.12	74.27	71.81	69.70	67.90	66.36	65.04	63.92	61.49	59.44	58.71	58.55
14.00	93.76	88.39	83.76	79.79	76.38	73.45	70.94	68.79	66.96	65.39	64.06	62.93	60.49	58.45	57.73	57.57
14.25	93.54	87.99	83.22	79.14	75.63	72.64	70.08	67.89	66.03	64.45	63.10	61.96	59.51	57.49	56.77	56.63
14.50	93.32	87.59	82.69	78.49	74.90	71.84	69.23	67.01	65.12	63.52	62.16	61.02	58.56	56.55	55.85	55.71
14.75	93.10	87.19	82.15	77.85	74.18	71.06	68.40	66.14	64.23	62.61	61.24	60.09	57.63	55.64	54.95	54.82
15.00	92.88	86.80	81.62	77.21	73.46	70.28	67.58	65.29	63.36	61.72	60.34	59.19	56.73	54.75	54.08	53.95
15.25	92.65	86.41	81.09	76.58	72.76	69.51	66.77	64.45	62.50	60.85	59.46	58.30	55.85	53.89	53.24	53.11
15.50	92.44	86.02	80.57	75.96	72.06	68.76	65.98	63.63	61.65	59.99	58.60	57.44	54.99	53.06	52.42	52.29
15.75	92.22	85.63	80.05	75.34	71.37	68.02	65.19	62.82	60.83	59.16	57.76	56.59	54.15	52.24	51.62	51.50
16.00	92.00	85.24	79.54	74.73	70.68	67.28	64.42	62.02	60.01	58.33	56.93	55.77	53.34	51.45	50.85	50.73
16.25	91.78	84.85	79.03	74.13	70.01	66.56	63.66	61.24	59.22	57.53	56.13	54.96	52.54	50.68	50.09	49.98
16.50	91.56	84.47	78.52	73.53	69.34	65.84	62.91	60.47	58.43	56.74	55.33	54.17	51.76	49.93	49.36	49.25
16.75	91.35	84.09	78.01	72.93	68.68	65.13	62.18	59.71	57.67	55.97	54.56	53.40	51.01	49.20	48.64	48.54
17.00	91.13	83.71	77.51	72.34	68.03	64.44	61.45	58.97	56.91	55.21	53.80	52.64	50.27	48.49	47.95	47.85
17.25	90.91	83.33	77.02	71.76	67.38	63.75	60.74	58.24	56.17	54.46	53.06	51.90	49.55	47.80	47.27	47.18
17.50	90.70	82.96	76.52	71.18	66.75	63.07	60.03	57.52	55.44	53.73	52.33	51.18	48.84	47.13	46.61	46.52
17.75	90.48	82.59	76.04	70.61	66.12	62.40	59.34	56.81	54.73	53.02	51.62	50.47	48.15	46.47	45.97	45.89
18.00	90.27	82.21	75.55	70.04	65.49	61.74	58.65	56.11	54.03	52.32	50.92	49.78	47.48	45.83	45.35	45.26
18.25	90.06	81.84	75.07	69.48	64.88	61.09	57.98	55.43	53.34	51.63	50.24	49.10	46.83	45.21	44.74	44.66
18.50	89.84	81.48	74.59	68.92	64.27	60.45	57.32	54.76	52.66	50.96	49.57	48.44	46.19	44.60	44.15	44.07
18.75	89.63	81.11	74.11	68.37	63.67	59.81	56.67	54.10	52.00	50.30	48.91	47.79	45.57	44.01	43.57	43.49
19.00	89.42	80.75	73.64	67.82	63.07	59.19	56.02	53.44	51.35	49.65	48.27	47.15	44.96	43.43	43.01	42.93
20.00	88.58	79.31	71.78	65.69	60.76	56.77	53.54	50.95	48.86	47.17	45.83	44.75	42.66	41.26	40.88	40.82
25.00	84.50	72.52	63.27	56.13	50.63	46.40	43.14	40.64	38.72	37.26	36.14	35.28	33.77	32.92	32.75	32.72
30.00	80.63	66.38	55.89	48.19	42.54	38.39	35.36	33.14	31.52	30.34	29.48	28.85	27.84	27.37	27.29	27.28

Description: This table shows the yield to prepayment of a monthly payment mortgage purchased at a price in the index.

Example: The yield to prepayment in 10 years of a 7.25 %, 30 year mortgage at a price of 104.00 is 6.67 %.

30 YEAR MORTGAGE PREPAID IN

PRICE	1 yr	2 yr	3 yr	4 yr	5 yr	6 yr	7 yr	8 yr	9 yr	10 yr	11 yr	12 yr	15 yr	20 yr	25 yr	30 yr
140	–	–	–	–	–	–	1.08	1.66	2.10	2.46	2.74	2.97	3.47	3.91	4.11	4.17
135	–	–	–	–	–	1.03	1.73	2.24	2.64	2.96	3.21	3.42	3.86	4.25	4.42	4.47
130	–	–	–	–	–	1.80	2.40	2.86	3.20	3.48	3.70	3.88	4.26	4.60	4.75	4.80
125	–	–	–	–	1.87	2.60	3.11	3.50	3.79	4.03	4.21	4.37	4.69	4.98	5.10	5.14
120	–	–	–	1.94	2.84	3.43	3.86	4.17	4.41	4.60	4.75	4.88	5.14	5.38	5.48	5.51
119	–	–	–	2.18	3.04	3.61	4.01	4.31	4.54	4.72	4.87	4.99	5.24	5.46	5.56	5.58
118	–	–	1.06	2.42	3.24	3.78	4.16	4.45	4.67	4.84	4.98	5.09	5.33	5.54	5.63	5.66
117	–	–	1.37	2.67	3.44	3.96	4.32	4.59	4.80	4.96	5.09	5.20	5.43	5.63	5.71	5.74
116	–	–	1.69	2.92	3.65	4.13	4.48	4.73	4.93	5.08	5.21	5.31	5.52	5.71	5.79	5.82
115	–	–	2.01	3.17	3.86	4.31	4.64	4.88	5.06	5.21	5.32	5.42	5.62	5.80	5.87	5.90
114	–	–	2.34	3.42	4.07	4.49	4.80	5.02	5.20	5.33	5.44	5.53	5.72	5.89	5.96	5.98
113	–	–	2.66	3.67	4.28	4.68	4.96	5.17	5.33	5.46	5.56	5.65	5.82	5.97	6.04	6.06
112	–	1.12	3.00	3.93	4.49	4.86	5.12	5.32	5.47	5.59	5.68	5.76	5.92	6.06	6.13	6.14
111	–	1.60	3.33	4.19	4.71	5.05	5.29	5.47	5.61	5.72	5.80	5.88	6.03	6.16	6.21	6.23
110	–	2.09	3.67	4.46	4.93	5.24	5.46	5.62	5.75	5.85	5.93	5.99	6.13	6.25	6.30	6.31
109	–	2.58	4.01	4.72	5.15	5.43	5.63	5.78	5.89	5.98	6.05	6.11	6.23	6.34	6.39	6.40
108	–	3.08	4.35	4.99	5.37	5.62	5.80	5.93	6.03	6.11	6.18	6.23	6.34	6.44	6.48	6.49
107	–	3.58	4.70	5.26	5.60	5.82	5.97	6.09	6.18	6.25	6.31	6.35	6.45	6.53	6.57	6.58
106	1.18	4.09	5.05	5.54	5.82	6.01	6.15	6.25	6.33	6.39	6.43	6.47	6.56	6.63	6.66	6.67
105	2.16	4.60	5.41	5.81	6.05	6.21	6.33	6.41	6.47	6.53	6.57	6.60	6.67	6.73	6.75	6.76
104	3.16	5.12	5.77	6.09	6.29	6.42	6.51	6.57	6.62	6.67	6.70	6.72	6.78	6.83	6.85	6.86
103.75	3.41	5.25	5.86	6.16	6.35	6.47	6.55	6.61	6.66	6.70	6.73	6.76	6.81	6.85	6.87	6.88
103.50	3.66	5.38	5.95	6.23	6.40	6.52	6.60	6.66	6.70	6.74	6.77	6.79	6.84	6.88	6.90	6.90
103.25	3.91	5.51	6.04	6.31	6.46	6.57	6.64	6.70	6.74	6.77	6.80	6.82	6.87	6.91	6.92	6.93
103.00	4.16	5.64	6.13	6.38	6.52	6.62	6.69	6.74	6.78	6.81	6.83	6.85	6.89	6.93	6.95	6.95
102.75	4.42	5.77	6.22	6.45	6.58	6.67	6.73	6.78	6.82	6.84	6.87	6.88	6.92	6.96	6.97	6.97
102.50	4.67	5.90	6.31	6.52	6.64	6.72	6.78	6.82	6.85	6.88	6.90	6.92	6.95	6.98	7.00	7.00
102.25	4.92	6.04	6.41	6.59	6.70	6.77	6.83	6.86	6.89	6.92	6.93	6.95	6.98	7.01	7.02	7.02
102.00	5.18	6.17	6.50	6.66	6.76	6.83	6.87	6.91	6.93	6.95	6.97	6.98	7.01	7.03	7.04	7.05
101.75	5.44	6.30	6.59	6.73	6.82	6.88	6.92	6.95	6.97	6.99	7.00	7.01	7.04	7.06	7.07	7.07
101.50	5.69	6.44	6.68	6.81	6.88	6.93	6.96	6.99	7.01	7.02	7.04	7.05	7.07	7.09	7.09	7.10
101.25	5.95	6.57	6.78	6.88	6.94	6.98	7.01	7.03	7.05	7.06	7.07	7.08	7.10	7.11	7.12	7.12
101.00	6.21	6.70	6.87	6.95	7.00	7.03	7.06	7.07	7.09	7.10	7.11	7.11	7.13	7.14	7.14	7.15
100.75	6.47	6.84	6.96	7.03	7.06	7.09	7.10	7.12	7.13	7.13	7.14	7.15	7.16	7.17	7.17	7.17
100.50	6.72	6.97	7.06	7.10	7.12	7.14	7.15	7.16	7.17	7.17	7.18	7.18	7.19	7.19	7.19	7.19
100.25	6.98	7.11	7.15	7.17	7.18	7.19	7.20	7.20	7.21	7.21	7.21	7.21	7.22	7.22	7.22	7.22
100.00	7.25	7.25	7.25	7.25	7.25	7.25	7.25	7.25	7.25	7.25	7.25	7.25	7.25	7.25	7.25	7.25
99.75	7.51	7.38	7.34	7.32	7.31	7.30	7.29	7.29	7.28	7.28	7.28	7.28	7.27	7.27	7.27	7.27
99.50	7.77	7.52	7.43	7.39	7.37	7.35	7.34	7.33	7.33	7.32	7.32	7.31	7.30	7.30	7.30	7.30
99.25	8.03	7.65	7.53	7.47	7.43	7.40	7.39	7.37	7.36	7.36	7.35	7.35	7.33	7.33	7.32	7.32
99.00	8.30	7.79	7.62	7.54	7.49	7.46	7.44	7.42	7.40	7.39	7.39	7.38	7.37	7.35	7.35	7.35
98.75	8.56	7.93	7.72	7.62	7.55	7.51	7.48	7.46	7.45	7.43	7.42	7.41	7.40	7.38	7.37	7.37
98.50	8.82	8.07	7.82	7.69	7.62	7.57	7.53	7.51	7.49	7.47	7.46	7.45	7.43	7.41	7.40	7.40
98.25	9.09	8.21	7.91	7.77	7.68	7.62	7.58	7.55	7.53	7.51	7.49	7.48	7.46	7.43	7.43	7.42
98.00	9.36	8.34	8.01	7.84	7.74	7.67	7.63	7.59	7.57	7.55	7.53	7.52	7.49	7.46	7.45	7.45
97.75	9.62	8.48	8.10	7.92	7.80	7.73	7.68	7.64	7.61	7.58	7.57	7.55	7.52	7.49	7.48	7.48
97.50	9.89	8.62	8.20	7.99	7.87	7.78	7.73	7.68	7.65	7.62	7.60	7.58	7.55	7.52	7.51	7.50
97.25	10.16	8.76	8.30	8.07	7.93	7.84	7.77	7.73	7.69	7.66	7.64	7.62	7.58	7.55	7.53	7.53
97	10.43	8.90	8.40	8.14	7.99	7.89	7.82	7.77	7.73	7.70	7.67	7.65	7.61	7.57	7.56	7.55
96	11.52	9.47	8.79	8.45	8.25	8.11	8.02	7.95	7.90	7.85	7.82	7.79	7.74	7.69	7.67	7.66
95	12.62	10.04	9.19	8.76	8.51	8.34	8.22	8.13	8.07	8.01	7.97	7.94	7.86	7.80	7.78	7.77
94	13.73	10.62	9.59	9.07	8.77	8.57	8.42	8.32	8.24	8.17	8.12	8.08	7.99	7.92	7.89	7.88
93	14.85	11.20	9.99	9.39	9.03	8.80	8.63	8.50	8.41	8.33	8.27	8.23	8.12	8.04	8.00	7.99
92	15.99	11.80	10.40	9.71	9.30	9.03	8.84	8.69	8.58	8.50	8.43	8.37	8.26	8.16	8.12	8.11
91	17.14	12.40	10.82	10.04	9.57	9.26	9.05	8.89	8.76	8.67	8.59	8.52	8.39	8.28	8.23	8.22
90	18.31	13.00	11.24	10.37	9.85	9.50	9.26	9.08	8.94	8.83	8.75	8.68	8.53	8.40	8.35	8.34
89	19.49	13.62	11.67	10.70	10.13	9.75	9.48	9.28	9.13	9.01	8.91	8.83	8.67	8.53	8.48	8.46
88	20.69	14.24	12.10	11.04	10.41	9.99	9.70	9.48	9.31	9.18	9.07	8.99	8.81	8.66	8.60	8.58
87	21.90	14.87	12.54	11.38	10.69	10.24	9.92	9.68	9.50	9.36	9.24	9.15	8.96	8.79	8.73	8.71
86	23.13	15.50	12.98	11.73	10.98	10.49	10.14	9.89	9.69	9.54	9.41	9.31	9.10	8.93	8.85	8.84
85	24.37	16.15	13.43	12.08	11.28	10.75	10.37	10.10	9.88	9.72	9.58	9.48	9.25	9.06	8.99	8.97
80	30.84	19.51	15.77	13.92	12.81	12.08	11.57	11.19	10.90	10.67	10.49	10.34	10.04	9.78	9.68	9.66
75	37.78	23.11	18.28	15.88	14.46	13.52	12.86	12.37	12.00	11.71	11.48	11.29	10.90	10.58	10.46	10.43
70	45.25	26.99	20.99	18.01	16.25	15.09	14.27	13.66	13.20	12.85	12.56	12.33	11.85	11.47	11.32	11.29
65	53.35	31.19	23.92	20.33	18.19	16.79	15.81	15.08	14.53	14.10	13.76	13.48	12.92	12.47	12.30	12.27
60	62.17	35.76	27.12	22.86	20.33	18.67	17.51	16.65	16.00	15.49	15.09	14.77	14.12	13.61	13.43	13.39
55	71.86	40.79	30.65	25.65	22.70	20.76	19.40	18.40	17.65	17.06	16.60	16.23	15.49	14.92	14.73	14.69
50	82.60	46.36	34.57	28.77	25.35	23.11	21.54	20.39	19.53	18.86	18.33	17.91	17.09	16.47	16.28	16.24

Description: This table shows the price to pay for a monthly payment loan, at a yield rate and assuming prepayment.

Example: The price of a 7.50 %, 30 year mortgage to yield 8.00 %, if prepaid in 6 years, is $ 97.69.

30 YEAR MORTGAGE PREPAID IN

YIELD	1 yr	2 yr	3 yr	4 yr	5 yr	6 yr	7 yr	8 yr	9 yr	10 yr	11 yr	12 yr	15 yr	20 yr	25 yr	30 yr
0.00	107.47	114.87	122.19	129.42	136.57	143.62	150.57	157.40	164.12	170.70	177.14	183.44	201.29	226.72	244.66	251.72
1.00	106.44	112.75	118.94	124.99	130.91	136.69	142.33	147.82	153.17	158.35	163.38	168.24	181.75	200.27	212.71	217.39
2.00	105.42	110.68	115.78	120.73	125.51	130.14	134.61	138.92	143.07	147.06	150.89	154.56	164.55	177.72	186.14	189.17
3.00	104.41	108.65	112.72	116.62	120.37	123.95	127.38	130.65	133.77	136.74	139.55	142.23	149.37	158.43	163.95	165.85
4.00	103.41	106.66	109.74	112.68	115.46	118.10	120.59	122.95	125.18	127.28	129.25	131.11	135.96	141.89	145.33	146.46
4.25	103.16	106.17	109.01	111.71	114.27	116.68	118.96	121.12	123.14	125.04	126.83	128.50	132.86	138.13	141.15	142.13
4.50	102.92	105.68	108.29	110.76	113.09	115.29	117.36	119.31	121.14	122.86	124.46	125.96	129.85	134.51	137.15	138.00
4.75	102.67	105.19	107.57	109.81	111.93	113.92	115.78	117.54	119.18	120.72	122.15	123.48	126.94	131.02	133.31	134.04
5.00	102.42	104.71	106.86	108.88	110.78	112.56	114.23	115.80	117.26	118.62	119.89	121.07	124.10	127.66	129.63	130.25
5.25	102.18	104.23	106.15	107.95	109.64	111.22	112.70	114.09	115.37	116.57	117.69	118.72	121.36	124.43	126.10	126.62
5.50	101.93	103.75	105.44	107.03	108.52	109.91	111.20	112.41	113.53	114.57	115.53	116.42	118.69	121.30	122.71	123.15
5.75	101.69	103.27	104.75	106.12	107.41	108.61	109.72	110.76	111.72	112.61	113.43	114.18	116.10	118.29	119.46	119.82
6.00	101.45	102.80	104.05	105.22	106.31	107.33	108.27	109.14	109.94	110.69	111.37	112.00	113.59	115.39	116.34	116.62
6.25	101.20	102.32	103.37	104.33	105.23	106.06	106.83	107.54	108.20	108.81	109.36	109.88	111.16	112.59	113.34	113.56
6.50	100.96	101.85	102.68	103.45	104.16	104.82	105.42	105.98	106.50	106.97	107.40	107.80	108.79	109.89	110.46	110.62
6.75	100.72	101.39	102.00	102.57	103.10	103.59	104.03	104.45	104.82	105.17	105.49	105.78	106.50	107.29	107.69	107.80
7.00	100.48	100.92	101.33	101.71	102.06	102.37	102.67	102.94	103.18	103.41	103.62	103.80	104.27	104.77	105.02	105.10
7.25	100.24	100.46	100.66	100.85	101.02	101.18	101.32	101.46	101.58	101.69	101.79	101.88	102.10	102.34	102.46	102.50
7.50	100.00	100.00	100.00	100.00	100.00	100.00	100.00	100.00	100.00	100.00	100.00	100.00	100.00	100.00	100.00	100.00
7.75	99.76	99.54	99.34	99.16	98.99	98.84	98.70	98.57	98.45	98.35	98.25	98.17	97.96	97.74	97.63	97.60
8.00	99.52	99.09	98.69	98.32	97.99	97.69	97.42	97.17	96.94	96.73	96.55	96.38	95.97	95.55	95.35	95.29
8.25	99.29	98.63	98.04	97.50	97.01	96.56	96.15	95.79	95.45	95.15	94.88	94.64	94.05	93.44	93.15	93.07
8.50	99.05	98.18	97.40	96.68	96.03	95.44	94.91	94.43	93.99	93.60	93.25	92.94	92.18	91.40	91.03	90.94
8.75	98.81	97.73	96.76	95.87	95.07	94.34	93.69	93.10	92.57	92.09	91.66	91.28	90.36	89.42	88.99	88.88
9.00	98.58	97.29	96.12	95.07	94.12	93.26	92.48	91.79	91.16	90.60	90.10	89.66	88.59	87.52	87.03	86.90
9.25	98.34	96.84	95.49	94.27	93.17	92.19	91.30	90.50	89.79	89.15	88.58	88.07	86.87	85.67	85.13	84.99
9.50	98.11	96.40	94.87	93.49	92.24	91.13	90.13	89.24	88.44	87.73	87.10	86.53	85.20	83.89	83.31	83.16
9.75	97.87	95.96	94.25	92.71	91.32	90.09	88.98	88.00	87.12	86.34	85.64	85.03	83.58	82.16	81.54	81.38
10.00	97.64	95.52	93.63	91.93	90.42	89.06	87.85	86.78	85.82	84.97	84.22	83.56	82.00	80.49	79.84	79.68
10.25	97.41	95.09	93.02	91.17	89.52	88.05	86.74	85.58	84.55	83.64	82.83	82.12	80.47	78.88	78.20	78.03
10.50	97.18	94.66	92.41	90.41	88.63	87.05	85.65	84.40	83.30	82.33	81.47	80.72	78.98	77.31	76.61	76.44
10.75	96.94	94.22	91.81	89.66	87.75	86.06	84.57	83.25	82.08	81.05	80.15	79.35	77.52	75.80	75.08	74.90
11.00	96.71	93.80	91.21	88.92	86.89	85.09	83.51	82.11	80.88	79.80	78.85	78.02	76.11	74.33	73.60	73.42
11.25	96.48	93.37	90.61	88.18	86.03	84.13	82.46	80.99	79.70	78.57	77.58	76.71	74.74	72.91	72.17	71.99
11.50	96.25	92.94	90.02	87.45	85.18	83.19	81.43	79.89	78.54	77.37	76.34	75.44	73.40	71.54	70.78	70.61
11.75	96.02	92.52	89.44	86.73	84.34	82.25	80.42	78.81	77.41	76.19	75.12	74.20	72.10	70.20	69.45	69.27
12.00	95.80	92.10	88.86	86.01	83.52	81.33	79.42	77.75	76.30	75.03	73.94	72.98	70.84	68.91	68.15	67.98
12.25	95.57	91.68	88.28	85.30	82.70	80.42	78.44	76.71	75.21	73.90	72.77	71.80	69.61	67.66	66.90	66.73
12.50	95.34	91.27	87.71	84.60	81.89	79.53	77.47	75.69	74.14	72.80	71.64	70.64	68.41	66.44	65.69	65.52
12.75	95.12	90.85	87.14	83.90	81.09	78.64	76.52	74.68	73.09	71.71	70.53	69.51	67.24	65.26	64.51	64.34
13.00	94.89	90.44	86.57	83.21	80.30	77.77	75.58	73.69	72.06	70.65	69.44	68.40	66.11	64.12	63.37	63.21
13.25	94.66	90.03	86.01	82.53	79.52	76.91	74.66	72.72	71.05	69.61	68.38	67.32	65.00	63.01	62.27	62.11
13.50	94.44	89.62	85.46	81.86	78.74	76.06	73.75	71.76	70.05	68.59	67.34	66.27	63.92	61.93	61.20	61.04
13.75	94.22	89.22	84.90	81.19	77.98	75.22	72.86	70.82	69.08	67.59	66.32	65.23	62.88	60.88	60.17	60.01
14.00	93.99	88.81	84.36	80.52	77.23	74.40	71.97	69.90	68.12	66.61	65.32	64.23	61.85	59.87	59.16	59.01
14.25	93.77	88.41	83.81	79.86	76.48	73.58	71.11	68.99	67.19	65.65	64.35	63.24	60.86	58.88	58.19	58.04
14.50	93.55	88.01	83.27	79.21	75.74	72.78	70.25	68.10	66.27	64.71	63.39	62.28	59.89	57.92	57.24	57.10
14.75	93.32	87.61	82.73	78.57	75.01	71.99	69.41	67.22	65.36	63.79	62.46	61.34	58.94	56.99	56.32	56.19
15.00	93.10	87.22	82.20	77.93	74.29	71.20	68.58	66.36	64.48	62.89	61.55	60.42	58.02	56.09	55.43	55.30
15.25	92.88	86.83	81.67	77.30	73.58	70.43	67.76	65.51	63.61	62.00	60.65	59.52	57.12	55.21	54.56	54.44
15.50	92.66	86.43	81.15	76.67	72.88	69.67	66.96	64.68	62.75	61.13	59.78	58.64	56.25	54.35	53.72	53.60
15.75	92.44	86.04	80.63	76.05	72.18	68.92	66.17	63.86	61.91	60.28	58.92	57.78	55.39	53.52	52.91	52.79
16.00	92.22	85.66	80.11	75.43	71.49	68.18	65.39	63.05	61.09	59.45	58.08	56.94	54.56	52.71	52.11	52.00
16.25	92.01	85.27	79.60	74.82	70.81	67.44	64.62	62.26	60.28	58.63	57.26	56.12	53.75	51.92	51.34	51.23
16.50	91.79	84.89	79.09	74.22	70.14	66.72	63.87	61.48	59.49	57.83	56.46	55.32	52.96	51.16	50.59	50.48
16.75	91.57	84.50	78.58	73.62	69.47	66.01	63.12	60.71	58.71	57.05	55.67	54.53	52.18	50.41	49.86	49.75
17.00	91.35	84.12	78.08	73.03	68.82	65.31	62.39	59.96	57.95	56.28	54.90	53.76	51.43	49.68	49.14	49.04
17.25	91.14	83.74	77.58	72.44	68.17	64.61	61.66	59.22	57.20	55.52	54.14	53.01	50.69	48.97	48.45	48.36
17.50	90.92	83.37	77.08	71.86	67.52	63.93	60.95	58.49	56.46	54.78	53.40	52.27	49.97	48.29	47.78	47.68
17.75	90.71	82.99	76.59	71.28	66.89	63.25	60.25	57.78	55.73	54.06	52.68	51.55	49.27	47.61	47.12	47.03
18.00	90.49	82.62	76.10	70.71	66.26	62.59	59.56	57.07	55.02	53.35	51.97	50.85	48.59	46.96	46.48	46.40
18.25	90.28	82.25	75.62	70.15	65.64	61.93	58.88	56.38	54.33	52.65	51.28	50.16	47.92	46.32	45.86	45.77
18.50	90.07	81.88	75.14	69.59	65.03	61.28	58.21	55.70	53.64	51.96	50.60	49.49	47.27	45.70	45.25	45.17
18.75	89.85	81.51	74.66	69.03	64.42	60.64	57.55	55.03	52.97	51.29	49.93	48.83	46.63	45.09	44.66	44.58
19.00	89.64	81.15	74.18	68.48	63.82	60.01	56.90	54.37	52.31	50.63	49.28	48.18	46.01	44.50	44.08	44.01
20.00	88.80	79.70	72.32	66.34	61.49	57.57	54.40	51.84	49.78	48.12	46.79	45.73	43.66	42.27	41.90	41.84
25.00	84.72	72.90	63.77	56.72	51.28	47.09	43.87	41.40	39.50	38.05	36.93	36.09	34.59	33.74	33.57	33.54
30.00	80.84	66.73	56.35	48.72	43.12	39.01	35.99	33.79	32.18	31.01	30.15	29.53	28.53	28.05	27.97	27.96

Description: This table shows the yield to prepayment of a monthly payment mortgage purchased at a price in the index.

Example: The yield to prepayment in 10 years of a 7.50 %, 30 year mortgage at a price of 104.00 is 6.91 %.

30 YEAR MORTGAGE PREPAID IN

PRICE	1 yr	2 yr	3 yr	4 yr	5 yr	6 yr	7 yr	8 yr	9 yr	10 yr	11 yr	12 yr	15 yr	20 yr	25 yr	30 yr
140	–	–	–	–	–	–	1.29	1.87	2.32	2.67	2.95	3.19	3.68	4.12	4.32	4.37
135	–	–	–	–	–	1.25	1.94	2.46	2.86	3.17	3.43	3.63	4.07	4.46	4.63	4.68
130	–	–	–	–	1.16	2.02	2.62	3.08	3.42	3.70	3.92	4.10	4.48	4.82	4.97	5.01
125	–	–	–	–	2.09	2.82	3.34	3.72	4.02	4.25	4.44	4.59	4.92	5.20	5.33	5.36
120	–	–	–	2.17	3.07	3.66	4.09	4.40	4.64	4.83	4.98	5.11	5.37	5.60	5.70	5.73
119	–	–	–	2.41	3.27	3.84	4.24	4.54	4.77	4.95	5.10	5.21	5.47	5.69	5.78	5.81
118	–	–	1.29	2.66	3.47	4.01	4.39	4.68	4.90	5.07	5.21	5.32	5.56	5.77	5.86	5.89
117	–	–	1.61	2.90	3.68	4.19	4.55	4.82	5.03	5.19	5.32	5.43	5.66	5.86	5.94	5.96
116	–	–	1.92	3.15	3.88	4.37	4.71	4.97	5.16	5.32	5.44	5.54	5.76	5.94	6.02	6.05
115	–	–	2.25	3.40	4.09	4.55	4.87	5.11	5.30	5.44	5.56	5.65	5.85	6.03	6.11	6.13
114	–	–	2.57	3.66	4.30	4.73	5.03	5.26	5.43	5.57	5.68	5.77	5.95	6.12	6.19	6.21
113	–	–	2.90	3.91	4.51	4.91	5.20	5.41	5.57	5.69	5.80	5.88	6.06	6.21	6.27	6.29
112	–	1.36	3.23	4.17	4.73	5.10	5.36	5.56	5.71	5.82	5.92	6.00	6.16	6.30	6.36	6.38
111	–	1.84	3.57	4.43	4.95	5.29	5.53	5.71	5.85	5.95	6.04	6.11	6.26	6.39	6.45	6.46
110	–	2.33	3.91	4.70	5.17	5.48	5.70	5.86	5.99	6.09	6.17	6.23	6.37	6.48	6.54	6.55
109	–	2.82	4.25	4.96	5.39	5.67	5.87	6.02	6.13	6.22	6.29	6.35	6.47	6.58	6.63	6.64
108	–	3.32	4.60	5.23	5.61	5.86	6.04	6.17	6.27	6.35	6.42	6.47	6.58	6.68	6.72	6.73
107	–	3.82	4.94	5.50	5.84	6.06	6.22	6.33	6.42	6.49	6.55	6.59	6.69	6.77	6.81	6.82
106	1.42	4.33	5.30	5.78	6.07	6.26	6.39	6.49	6.57	6.63	6.68	6.72	6.80	6.87	6.90	6.91
105	2.41	4.84	5.65	6.06	6.30	6.46	6.57	6.65	6.72	6.77	6.81	6.84	6.91	6.97	7.00	7.00
104	3.40	5.36	6.01	6.34	6.53	6.66	6.75	6.82	6.87	6.91	6.94	6.97	7.03	7.07	7.09	7.10
103.75	3.65	5.49	6.11	6.41	6.59	6.71	6.80	6.86	6.91	6.95	6.98	7.00	7.05	7.10	7.12	7.12
103.50	3.91	5.62	6.20	6.48	6.65	6.76	6.84	6.90	6.95	6.98	7.01	7.03	7.08	7.12	7.14	7.15
103.25	4.16	5.76	6.29	6.55	6.71	6.81	6.89	6.94	6.98	7.02	7.04	7.07	7.11	7.15	7.17	7.17
103.00	4.41	5.89	6.38	6.62	6.77	6.87	6.93	6.98	7.02	7.05	7.08	7.10	7.14	7.18	7.19	7.20
102.75	4.66	6.02	6.47	6.69	6.83	6.92	6.98	7.03	7.06	7.09	7.11	7.13	7.17	7.20	7.22	7.22
102.50	4.92	6.15	6.56	6.77	6.89	6.97	7.03	7.07	7.10	7.13	7.15	7.16	7.20	7.23	7.24	7.24
102.25	5.17	6.28	6.65	6.84	6.95	7.02	7.07	7.11	7.14	7.16	7.18	7.20	7.23	7.25	7.27	7.27
102.00	5.43	6.42	6.75	6.91	7.01	7.07	7.12	7.15	7.18	7.20	7.22	7.23	7.26	7.28	7.29	7.29
101.75	5.68	6.55	6.84	6.98	7.07	7.13	7.17	7.19	7.22	7.24	7.25	7.26	7.29	7.31	7.32	7.32
101.50	5.94	6.68	6.93	7.06	7.13	7.18	7.21	7.24	7.26	7.27	7.28	7.29	7.32	7.33	7.34	7.34
101.25	6.20	6.82	7.03	7.13	7.19	7.23	7.26	7.28	7.30	7.31	7.32	7.33	7.35	7.36	7.37	7.37
101.00	6.46	6.95	7.12	7.20	7.25	7.28	7.31	7.32	7.34	7.35	7.35	7.36	7.38	7.39	7.39	7.39
100.75	6.71	7.09	7.21	7.27	7.31	7.34	7.35	7.37	7.38	7.38	7.39	7.39	7.40	7.41	7.42	7.42
100.50	6.97	7.22	7.31	7.35	7.37	7.39	7.40	7.41	7.42	7.42	7.42	7.43	7.43	7.44	7.44	7.44
100.25	7.23	7.36	7.40	7.42	7.43	7.44	7.45	7.45	7.46	7.46	7.46	7.46	7.46	7.47	7.47	7.47
100.00	7.50	7.50	7.50	7.50	7.50	7.50	7.50	7.50	7.50	7.50	7.50	7.50	7.50	7.50	7.50	7.50
99.75	7.76	7.63	7.59	7.57	7.56	7.55	7.54	7.54	7.54	7.53	7.53	7.53	7.53	7.52	7.52	7.52
99.50	8.02	7.77	7.68	7.64	7.62	7.60	7.59	7.58	7.58	7.57	7.57	7.56	7.56	7.55	7.55	7.55
99.25	8.28	7.91	7.78	7.72	7.68	7.66	7.64	7.63	7.62	7.61	7.60	7.60	7.59	7.58	7.57	7.57
99.00	8.55	8.04	7.88	7.79	7.74	7.71	7.69	7.67	7.66	7.65	7.64	7.63	7.62	7.60	7.60	7.60
98.75	8.81	8.18	7.97	7.87	7.80	7.76	7.73	7.71	7.70	7.68	7.67	7.66	7.65	7.63	7.63	7.62
98.50	9.08	8.32	8.07	7.94	7.87	7.82	7.78	7.76	7.74	7.72	7.71	7.70	7.68	7.66	7.65	7.65
98.25	9.34	8.46	8.16	8.02	7.93	7.87	7.83	7.80	7.78	7.76	7.75	7.73	7.71	7.69	7.68	7.68
98.00	9.61	8.60	8.26	8.09	7.99	7.93	7.88	7.85	7.82	7.80	7.78	7.77	7.74	7.72	7.71	7.70
97.75	9.88	8.74	8.36	8.17	8.06	7.98	7.93	7.89	7.86	7.84	7.82	7.80	7.77	7.74	7.73	7.73
97.50	10.15	8.88	8.45	8.24	8.12	8.04	7.98	7.94	7.90	7.88	7.85	7.84	7.80	7.77	7.76	7.76
97.25	10.41	9.02	8.55	8.32	8.18	8.09	8.03	7.98	7.94	7.91	7.89	7.87	7.83	7.80	7.79	7.78
97	10.68	9.16	8.65	8.40	8.25	8.15	8.08	8.02	7.98	7.95	7.93	7.91	7.86	7.83	7.81	7.81
96	11.77	9.72	9.04	8.70	8.50	8.37	8.28	8.21	8.15	8.11	8.08	8.05	7.99	7.94	7.92	7.92
95	12.87	10.30	9.44	9.02	8.76	8.60	8.48	8.39	8.32	8.27	8.23	8.19	8.12	8.06	8.03	8.03
94	13.99	10.88	9.84	9.33	9.03	8.82	8.68	8.58	8.49	8.43	8.38	8.34	8.25	8.18	8.15	8.14
93	15.11	11.46	10.25	9.65	9.29	9.05	8.89	8.76	8.67	8.59	8.53	8.49	8.38	8.30	8.26	8.25
92	16.25	12.06	10.66	9.97	9.56	9.29	9.10	8.95	8.85	8.76	8.69	8.64	8.52	8.42	8.38	8.37
91	17.41	12.66	11.08	10.30	9.83	9.53	9.31	9.15	9.02	8.93	8.85	8.79	8.66	8.54	8.50	8.49
90	18.57	13.26	11.51	10.63	10.11	9.77	9.52	9.34	9.21	9.10	9.01	8.94	8.80	8.67	8.62	8.61
89	19.76	13.88	11.93	10.97	10.39	10.01	9.74	9.54	9.39	9.27	9.18	9.10	8.94	8.80	8.74	8.73
88	20.95	14.50	12.37	11.31	10.67	10.26	9.96	9.74	9.58	9.45	9.34	9.26	9.08	8.93	8.87	8.85
87	22.17	15.13	12.81	11.65	10.96	10.51	10.19	9.95	9.77	9.63	9.51	9.42	9.23	9.06	9.00	8.98
86	23.40	15.77	13.25	12.00	11.25	10.76	10.41	10.16	9.96	9.81	9.68	9.58	9.37	9.20	9.13	9.11
85	24.64	16.42	13.70	12.35	11.55	11.02	10.64	10.37	10.16	9.99	9.86	9.75	9.53	9.34	9.26	9.24
80	31.12	19.79	16.05	14.19	13.09	12.36	11.85	11.47	11.18	10.95	10.77	10.63	10.32	10.07	9.97	9.95
75	38.06	23.40	18.57	16.17	14.75	13.81	13.15	12.67	12.29	12.00	11.77	11.58	11.20	10.88	10.76	10.73
70	45.55	27.28	21.28	18.31	16.55	15.39	14.57	13.97	13.51	13.15	12.87	12.64	12.16	11.78	11.64	11.61
65	53.65	31.49	24.23	20.64	18.51	17.11	16.12	15.40	14.85	14.42	14.08	13.80	13.25	12.80	12.64	12.60
60	62.49	36.08	27.45	23.18	20.66	19.00	17.84	16.98	16.33	15.83	15.43	15.11	14.47	13.96	13.79	13.75
55	72.20	41.12	30.99	25.99	23.04	21.10	19.75	18.76	18.00	17.42	16.96	16.59	15.86	15.31	15.12	15.08
50	82.96	46.71	34.93	29.13	25.71	23.47	21.91	20.77	19.90	19.24	18.72	18.30	17.49	16.89	16.70	16.66

Description: This table shows the price to pay for a monthly payment loan, at a yield rate and assuming prepayment.

Example: The price of a 7.75 %, 30 year mortgage to yield 8.00 %, if prepaid in 6 years, is $ 98.84.

30 YEAR MORTGAGE PREPAID IN

YIELD	1 yr	2 yr	3 yr	4 yr	5 yr	6 yr	7 yr	8 yr	9 yr	10 yr	11 yr	12 yr	15 yr	20 yr	25 yr	30 yr
0.00	107.72	115.37	122.94	130.43	137.83	145.14	152.34	159.43	166.40	173.24	179.93	186.48	205.06	231.63	250.47	257.91
1.00	106.69	113.25	119.68	125.97	132.13	138.15	144.03	149.76	155.33	160.74	165.99	171.07	185.22	204.66	217.78	222.74
2.00	105.67	111.17	116.51	121.69	126.70	131.55	136.24	140.77	145.13	149.32	153.34	157.20	167.73	181.64	190.59	193.82
3.00	104.66	109.13	113.43	117.56	121.52	125.31	128.94	132.41	135.72	138.87	141.86	144.70	152.30	161.96	167.88	169.93
4.00	103.66	107.14	110.45	113.59	116.58	119.41	122.10	124.64	127.03	129.30	131.42	133.42	138.67	145.08	148.82	150.06
4.25	103.41	106.64	109.71	112.63	115.38	117.99	120.45	122.78	124.97	127.03	128.97	130.78	135.51	141.25	144.55	145.63
4.50	103.16	106.15	108.99	111.67	114.20	116.59	118.84	120.96	122.95	124.82	126.57	128.20	132.45	137.55	140.45	141.39
4.75	102.91	105.67	108.26	110.72	113.03	115.20	117.25	119.17	120.97	122.65	124.22	125.69	129.48	133.99	136.53	137.34
5.00	102.67	105.18	107.55	109.77	111.87	113.84	115.68	117.41	119.02	120.53	121.93	123.24	126.60	130.56	132.76	133.45
5.25	102.42	104.70	106.84	108.84	110.73	112.49	114.14	115.68	117.12	118.45	119.70	120.85	123.81	127.25	129.15	129.74
5.50	102.18	104.22	106.13	107.92	109.60	111.16	112.62	113.98	115.25	116.42	117.51	118.52	121.10	124.07	125.68	126.18
5.75	101.93	103.74	105.43	107.01	108.48	109.85	111.13	112.31	113.42	114.44	115.38	116.25	118.47	120.99	122.35	122.76
6.00	101.69	103.26	104.73	106.10	107.37	108.56	109.66	110.68	111.62	112.49	113.30	114.04	115.91	118.03	119.15	119.49
6.25	101.44	102.79	104.04	105.20	106.28	107.28	108.21	109.07	109.86	110.59	111.26	111.88	113.43	115.17	116.08	116.35
6.50	101.20	102.32	103.36	104.32	105.21	106.03	106.79	107.49	108.14	108.73	109.28	109.78	111.03	112.41	113.13	113.34
6.75	100.96	101.85	102.67	103.44	104.14	104.79	105.39	105.94	106.44	106.91	107.33	107.72	108.69	109.75	110.30	110.46
7.00	100.72	101.38	102.00	102.56	103.09	103.57	104.01	104.41	104.79	105.13	105.44	105.72	106.42	107.19	107.57	107.68
7.25	100.48	100.92	101.33	101.70	102.05	102.36	102.65	102.92	103.16	103.38	103.58	103.77	104.22	104.71	104.95	105.02
7.50	100.24	100.46	100.66	100.85	101.02	101.17	101.31	101.45	101.56	101.67	101.77	101.86	102.08	102.31	102.43	102.46
7.75	100.00	100.00	100.00	100.00	100.00	100.00	100.00	100.00	100.00	100.00	100.00	100.00	100.00	100.00	100.00	100.00
8.00	99.76	99.54	99.34	99.16	99.00	98.84	98.71	98.58	98.47	98.36	98.27	98.19	97.98	97.77	97.66	97.64
8.25	99.52	99.09	98.69	98.33	98.00	97.70	97.43	97.19	96.96	96.76	96.58	96.42	96.02	95.61	95.41	95.36
8.50	99.29	98.64	98.05	97.51	97.02	96.58	96.18	95.82	95.49	95.19	94.93	94.69	94.11	93.52	93.25	93.17
8.75	99.05	98.19	97.40	96.69	96.05	95.47	94.94	94.47	94.04	93.66	93.31	93.00	92.26	91.51	91.16	91.07
9.00	98.81	97.74	96.77	95.89	95.09	94.37	93.73	93.15	92.62	92.15	91.73	91.36	90.46	89.56	89.15	89.04
9.25	98.58	97.29	96.13	95.09	94.14	93.29	92.53	91.85	91.23	90.68	90.19	89.75	88.72	87.68	87.21	87.08
9.50	98.34	96.85	95.50	94.29	93.21	92.23	91.35	90.57	89.87	89.24	88.68	88.19	87.02	85.85	85.33	85.20
9.75	98.11	96.41	94.88	93.51	92.28	91.18	90.19	89.31	88.53	87.83	87.21	86.66	85.36	84.09	83.53	83.39
10.00	97.88	95.97	94.26	92.73	91.37	90.14	89.05	88.08	87.22	86.45	85.77	85.17	83.76	82.38	81.79	81.64
10.25	97.64	95.53	93.65	91.96	90.46	89.12	87.93	86.87	85.93	85.10	84.36	83.71	82.19	80.73	80.10	79.95
10.50	97.41	95.10	93.04	91.20	89.57	88.11	86.82	85.68	84.67	83.77	82.98	82.29	80.67	79.13	78.48	78.32
10.75	97.18	94.67	92.43	90.45	88.68	87.12	85.73	84.51	83.43	82.47	81.63	80.90	79.20	77.59	76.91	76.75
11.00	96.95	94.24	91.83	89.70	87.81	86.14	84.66	83.36	82.21	81.20	80.32	79.54	77.76	76.09	75.40	75.23
11.25	96.72	93.81	91.23	88.96	86.95	85.17	83.61	82.23	81.02	79.96	79.03	78.22	76.36	74.64	73.93	73.76
11.50	96.49	93.38	90.64	88.22	86.09	84.22	82.57	81.12	79.85	78.74	77.77	76.92	75.00	73.23	72.51	72.34
11.75	96.26	92.96	90.05	87.50	85.25	83.28	81.54	80.03	78.70	77.55	76.54	75.66	73.68	71.87	71.14	70.97
12.00	96.03	92.54	89.47	86.78	84.42	82.35	80.54	78.96	77.58	76.38	75.33	74.43	72.39	70.54	69.82	69.65
12.25	95.80	92.12	88.89	86.06	83.59	81.43	79.54	77.90	76.47	75.23	74.15	73.22	71.13	69.26	68.53	68.37
12.50	95.57	91.70	88.31	85.36	82.78	80.53	78.57	76.87	75.39	74.11	73.00	72.04	69.91	68.02	67.29	67.13
12.75	95.35	91.29	87.74	84.66	81.97	79.64	77.61	75.85	74.32	73.01	71.87	70.89	68.72	66.82	66.09	65.93
13.00	95.12	90.87	87.18	83.96	81.17	78.76	76.66	74.85	73.28	71.93	70.77	69.77	67.57	65.65	64.92	64.76
13.25	94.90	90.46	86.61	83.28	80.39	77.89	75.73	73.86	72.26	70.88	69.69	68.67	66.44	64.51	63.79	63.64
13.50	94.67	90.05	86.05	82.60	79.61	77.03	74.81	72.90	71.25	69.84	68.63	67.60	65.34	63.41	62.70	62.55
13.75	94.45	89.65	85.50	81.92	78.84	76.19	73.91	71.95	70.27	68.83	67.60	66.55	64.27	62.34	61.64	61.49
14.00	94.22	89.24	84.95	81.26	78.08	75.35	73.01	71.01	69.30	67.84	66.59	65.53	63.23	61.30	60.61	60.46
14.25	94.00	88.84	84.40	80.59	77.33	74.53	72.14	70.09	68.35	66.86	65.60	64.52	62.21	60.29	59.61	59.47
14.50	93.78	88.44	83.86	79.94	76.59	73.72	71.27	69.19	67.42	65.91	64.63	63.55	61.23	59.31	58.64	58.50
14.75	93.55	88.04	83.32	79.29	75.85	72.92	70.42	68.30	66.50	64.97	63.68	62.59	60.26	58.36	57.70	57.57
15.00	93.33	87.64	82.79	78.65	75.13	72.13	69.59	67.43	65.60	64.06	62.76	61.66	59.32	57.43	56.79	56.66
15.25	93.11	87.24	82.25	78.01	74.41	71.35	68.76	66.57	64.72	63.16	61.85	60.75	58.41	56.53	55.90	55.78
15.50	92.89	86.85	81.73	77.38	73.70	70.58	67.95	65.73	63.86	62.28	60.96	59.85	57.51	55.66	55.04	54.92
15.75	92.67	86.46	81.20	76.76	73.00	69.83	67.15	64.90	63.01	61.42	60.09	58.98	56.64	54.81	54.20	54.08
16.00	92.45	86.07	80.68	76.14	72.30	69.08	66.36	64.08	62.17	60.57	59.24	58.12	55.79	53.98	53.39	53.27
16.25	92.23	85.68	80.17	75.52	71.62	68.34	65.59	63.28	61.35	59.74	58.40	57.29	54.97	53.17	52.60	52.49
16.50	92.02	85.30	79.65	74.92	70.94	67.61	64.82	62.49	60.55	58.93	57.59	56.47	54.16	52.39	51.83	51.72
16.75	91.80	84.92	79.15	74.31	70.27	66.89	64.07	61.72	59.76	58.14	56.79	55.67	53.37	51.63	51.08	50.98
17.00	91.58	84.53	78.64	73.72	69.61	66.18	63.33	60.96	58.99	57.35	56.00	54.89	52.60	50.88	50.35	50.25
17.25	91.36	84.15	78.14	73.13	68.95	65.48	62.60	60.21	58.23	56.59	55.24	54.12	51.85	50.16	49.64	49.54
17.50	91.15	83.78	77.64	72.54	68.31	64.79	61.88	59.47	57.48	55.84	54.49	53.38	51.12	49.45	48.95	48.86
17.75	90.93	83.40	77.15	71.96	67.67	64.11	61.17	58.75	56.75	55.10	53.75	52.64	50.40	48.77	48.28	48.19
18.00	90.72	83.03	76.66	71.39	67.03	63.44	60.47	58.03	56.03	54.38	53.03	51.93	49.70	48.10	47.62	47.54
18.25	90.50	82.66	76.17	70.82	66.41	62.77	59.79	57.33	55.32	53.67	52.32	51.23	49.02	47.44	46.98	46.90
18.50	90.29	82.28	75.69	70.26	65.79	62.12	59.11	56.64	54.62	52.98	51.63	50.54	48.36	46.81	46.36	46.28
18.75	90.08	81.92	75.21	69.70	65.18	61.47	58.44	55.96	53.94	52.29	50.95	49.87	47.71	46.19	45.75	45.68
19.00	89.87	81.55	74.73	69.14	64.57	60.84	57.78	55.30	53.27	51.63	50.29	49.21	47.07	45.58	45.16	45.09
20.00	89.02	80.10	72.86	66.98	62.22	58.37	55.25	52.74	50.71	49.08	47.77	46.72	44.68	43.30	42.93	42.87
25.00	84.93	73.28	64.26	57.30	51.93	47.80	44.61	42.16	40.28	38.84	37.74	36.90	35.41	34.57	34.39	34.37
30.00	81.05	67.09	56.81	49.25	43.70	39.62	36.64	34.45	32.85	31.68	30.83	30.22	29.21	28.74	28.66	28.65

Description: This table shows the yield to prepayment of a monthly payment mortgage purchased at a price in the index.

Example: The yield to prepayment in 10 years of a 7.75 %, 30 year mortgage at a price of 104.00 is 7.16 %.

30 YEAR MORTGAGE PREPAID IN

PRICE	1 yr	2 yr	3 yr	4 yr	5 yr	6 yr	7 yr	8 yr	9 yr	10 yr	11 yr	12 yr	15 yr	20 yr	25 yr	30 yr
140	–	–	–	–	–	–	1.50	2.08	2.53	2.88	3.17	3.40	3.89	4.33	4.52	4.58
135	–	–	–	–	–	1.47	2.16	2.68	3.07	3.39	3.64	3.85	4.29	4.67	4.85	4.89
130	–	–	–	–	1.38	2.24	2.85	3.30	3.64	3.92	4.14	4.32	4.70	5.04	5.18	5.23
125	–	–	–	1.22	2.32	3.05	3.56	3.95	4.24	4.47	4.66	4.81	5.14	5.42	5.55	5.58
120	–	–	–	2.40	3.30	3.89	4.31	4.63	4.87	5.06	5.21	5.34	5.60	5.83	5.93	5.96
119	–	–	1.21	2.64	3.50	4.07	4.47	4.77	5.00	5.18	5.32	5.44	5.69	5.91	6.01	6.03
118	–	–	1.52	2.89	3.70	4.24	4.63	4.91	5.13	5.30	5.44	5.55	5.79	6.00	6.09	6.11
117	–	–	1.84	3.13	3.91	4.42	4.78	5.05	5.26	5.42	5.55	5.66	5.89	6.08	6.17	6.19
116	–	–	2.16	3.38	4.12	4.60	4.94	5.20	5.39	5.55	5.67	5.77	5.99	6.17	6.25	6.27
115	–	–	2.48	3.64	4.33	4.78	5.10	5.34	5.53	5.67	5.79	5.89	6.09	6.26	6.34	6.36
114	–	–	2.81	3.89	4.54	4.96	5.27	5.49	5.66	5.80	5.91	6.00	6.19	6.35	6.42	6.44
113	–	1.11	3.14	4.15	4.75	5.15	5.43	5.64	5.80	5.93	6.03	6.11	6.29	6.44	6.51	6.52
112	–	1.59	3.47	4.41	4.97	5.34	5.60	5.79	5.94	6.06	6.15	6.23	6.39	6.53	6.59	6.61
111	–	2.08	3.81	4.67	5.18	5.53	5.77	5.95	6.08	6.19	6.28	6.35	6.50	6.63	6.68	6.70
110	–	2.57	4.15	4.94	5.41	5.72	5.94	6.10	6.23	6.32	6.40	6.47	6.60	6.72	6.77	6.79
109	–	3.06	4.49	5.20	5.63	5.91	6.11	6.26	6.37	6.46	6.53	6.59	6.71	6.82	6.86	6.87
108	–	3.56	4.84	5.47	5.85	6.10	6.28	6.41	6.51	6.59	6.66	6.71	6.82	6.91	6.95	6.97
107	–	4.06	5.19	5.75	6.08	6.30	6.46	6.57	6.66	6.73	6.79	6.83	6.93	7.01	7.05	7.06
106	1.67	4.57	5.54	6.02	6.31	6.50	6.64	6.73	6.81	6.87	6.92	6.96	7.04	7.11	7.14	7.15
105	2.65	5.09	5.90	6.30	6.54	6.70	6.81	6.90	6.96	7.01	7.05	7.09	7.16	7.21	7.24	7.25
104	3.65	5.61	6.26	6.58	6.78	6.91	7.00	7.06	7.12	7.16	7.19	7.21	7.27	7.32	7.34	7.34
103.75	3.90	5.74	6.35	6.66	6.84	6.96	7.04	7.11	7.15	7.19	7.22	7.25	7.30	7.34	7.36	7.37
103.50	4.15	5.87	6.44	6.73	6.90	7.01	7.09	7.15	7.19	7.23	7.26	7.28	7.33	7.37	7.39	7.39
103.25	4.40	6.00	6.53	6.80	6.96	7.06	7.13	7.19	7.23	7.26	7.29	7.31	7.36	7.40	7.41	7.42
103.00	4.66	6.13	6.63	6.87	7.02	7.11	7.18	7.23	7.27	7.30	7.32	7.34	7.39	7.42	7.44	7.44
102.75	4.91	6.27	6.72	6.94	7.08	7.16	7.23	7.27	7.31	7.34	7.36	7.38	7.42	7.45	7.46	7.47
102.50	5.16	6.40	6.81	7.01	7.14	7.22	7.27	7.32	7.35	7.37	7.39	7.41	7.45	7.48	7.49	7.49
102.25	5.42	6.53	6.90	7.09	7.20	7.27	7.32	7.36	7.39	7.41	7.43	7.44	7.47	7.50	7.51	7.52
102.00	5.67	6.67	6.99	7.16	7.26	7.32	7.37	7.40	7.43	7.45	7.46	7.48	7.50	7.53	7.54	7.54
101.75	5.93	6.80	7.09	7.23	7.32	7.37	7.41	7.44	7.47	7.48	7.50	7.51	7.53	7.55	7.56	7.57
101.50	6.19	6.93	7.18	7.30	7.38	7.43	7.46	7.49	7.51	7.52	7.53	7.54	7.56	7.58	7.59	7.59
101.25	6.45	7.07	7.27	7.38	7.44	7.48	7.51	7.53	7.54	7.56	7.57	7.58	7.59	7.61	7.62	7.62
101.00	6.70	7.20	7.37	7.45	7.50	7.53	7.55	7.57	7.58	7.59	7.60	7.61	7.62	7.64	7.64	7.64
100.75	6.96	7.34	7.46	7.52	7.56	7.58	7.60	7.61	7.62	7.63	7.64	7.64	7.65	7.66	7.67	7.67
100.50	7.22	7.47	7.56	7.60	7.62	7.64	7.65	7.66	7.66	7.67	7.67	7.68	7.68	7.69	7.69	7.69
100.25	7.48	7.61	7.65	7.67	7.68	7.69	7.70	7.70	7.70	7.71	7.71	7.71	7.71	7.72	7.72	7.72
100.00	7.75	7.75	7.75	7.75	7.75	7.75	7.75	7.75	7.75	7.75	7.75	7.75	7.75	7.75	7.75	7.75
99.75	8.01	7.88	7.84	7.82	7.81	7.80	7.79	7.79	7.79	7.78	7.78	7.78	7.78	7.77	7.77	7.77
99.50	8.27	8.02	7.94	7.89	7.87	7.85	7.84	7.83	7.83	7.82	7.82	7.81	7.81	7.80	7.80	7.80
99.25	8.53	8.16	8.03	7.97	7.93	7.91	7.89	7.88	7.87	7.86	7.85	7.85	7.84	7.83	7.82	7.82
99.00	8.80	8.29	8.13	8.04	7.99	7.96	7.94	7.92	7.91	7.90	7.89	7.88	7.87	7.86	7.85	7.85
98.75	9.06	8.43	8.22	8.12	8.06	8.02	7.99	7.96	7.95	7.94	7.93	7.92	7.90	7.88	7.88	7.88
98.50	9.33	8.57	8.32	8.19	8.12	8.07	8.04	8.01	7.99	7.97	7.96	7.95	7.93	7.91	7.90	7.90
98.25	9.59	8.71	8.42	8.27	8.18	8.12	8.08	8.05	8.03	8.01	8.00	7.99	7.96	7.94	7.93	7.93
98.00	9.86	8.85	8.51	8.35	8.25	8.18	8.13	8.10	8.07	8.05	8.03	8.02	7.99	7.97	7.96	7.96
97.75	10.13	8.99	8.61	8.42	8.31	8.23	8.18	8.14	8.11	8.09	8.07	8.06	8.02	8.00	7.99	7.98
97.50	10.40	9.13	8.71	8.50	8.37	8.29	8.23	8.19	8.16	8.13	8.11	8.09	8.06	8.03	8.01	8.01
97.25	10.67	9.27	8.80	8.57	8.44	8.35	8.28	8.23	8.20	8.17	8.15	8.13	8.09	8.05	8.04	8.04
97	10.94	9.41	8.90	8.65	8.50	8.40	8.33	8.28	8.24	8.21	8.18	8.16	8.12	8.08	8.07	8.06
96	12.03	9.98	9.30	8.96	8.76	8.62	8.53	8.46	8.41	8.37	8.33	8.30	8.25	8.20	8.18	8.17
95	13.13	10.55	9.70	9.27	9.02	8.85	8.73	8.65	8.58	8.53	8.48	8.45	8.38	8.32	8.29	8.29
94	14.24	11.13	10.10	9.59	9.28	9.08	8.94	8.83	8.75	8.69	8.64	8.60	8.51	8.44	8.41	8.40
93	15.37	11.72	10.51	9.91	9.55	9.31	9.15	9.02	8.93	8.85	8.79	8.75	8.64	8.56	8.52	8.52
92	16.51	12.32	10.92	10.23	9.82	9.55	9.36	9.22	9.11	9.02	8.95	8.90	8.78	8.68	8.64	8.63
91	17.67	12.92	11.34	10.56	10.10	9.79	9.57	9.41	9.29	9.19	9.11	9.05	8.92	8.81	8.76	8.75
90	18.84	13.53	11.77	10.89	10.37	10.03	9.79	9.61	9.47	9.36	9.28	9.21	9.06	8.94	8.89	8.88
89	20.02	14.14	12.20	11.23	10.66	10.28	10.01	9.81	9.66	9.54	9.44	9.36	9.20	9.07	9.01	9.00
88	21.22	14.77	12.63	11.57	10.94	10.52	10.23	10.01	9.85	9.71	9.61	9.53	9.35	9.20	9.14	9.13
87	22.43	15.40	13.07	11.92	11.23	10.78	10.45	10.22	10.04	9.89	9.78	9.69	9.50	9.34	9.27	9.26
86	23.66	16.04	13.52	12.27	11.52	11.03	10.68	10.43	10.23	10.08	9.95	9.85	9.65	9.47	9.41	9.39
85	24.91	16.69	13.97	12.62	11.82	11.29	10.92	10.64	10.43	10.26	10.13	10.02	9.80	9.61	9.54	9.52
80	31.40	20.07	16.33	14.47	13.37	12.64	12.13	11.75	11.46	11.24	11.06	10.91	10.61	10.36	10.26	10.24
75	38.35	23.68	18.85	16.46	15.04	14.10	13.44	12.96	12.59	12.30	12.06	11.88	11.49	11.18	11.06	11.03
70	45.84	27.58	21.58	18.61	16.85	15.69	14.87	14.27	13.81	13.46	13.17	12.94	12.48	12.10	11.96	11.93
65	53.96	31.80	24.54	20.95	18.82	17.42	16.44	15.71	15.17	14.74	14.40	14.13	13.57	13.14	12.98	12.94
60	62.82	36.41	27.77	23.51	20.98	19.33	18.17	17.31	16.67	16.17	15.77	15.45	14.81	14.32	14.15	14.11
55	72.54	41.46	31.33	26.33	23.38	21.45	20.10	19.11	18.36	17.78	17.32	16.96	16.23	15.69	15.51	15.47
50	83.31	47.07	35.29	29.49	26.07	23.84	22.28	21.14	20.28	19.62	19.11	18.70	17.89	17.30	17.12	17.08

Description: This table shows the price to pay for a monthly payment loan, at a yield rate and assuming prepayment.

Example: The price of a 8.00 %, 30 year mortgage to yield 8.00 %, if prepaid in 6 years, is $ 100.00.

30 YEAR MORTGAGE PREPAID IN

YIELD	1 yr	2 yr	3 yr	4 yr	5 yr	6 yr	7 yr	8 yr	9 yr	10 yr	11 yr	12 yr	15 yr	20 yr	25 yr	30 yr
0.00	107.97	115.87	123.70	131.44	139.10	146.66	154.11	161.46	168.68	175.78	182.73	189.52	208.86	236.58	256.32	264.16
1.00	106.94	113.74	120.42	126.96	133.36	139.62	145.73	151.69	157.50	163.14	168.61	173.91	188.69	209.07	222.88	228.13
2.00	105.91	111.66	117.24	122.65	127.89	132.97	137.88	142.62	147.18	151.58	155.80	159.85	170.92	185.60	195.08	198.52
3.00	104.90	109.62	114.15	118.50	122.68	126.68	130.51	134.18	137.67	141.00	144.17	147.18	155.24	165.52	171.84	174.04
4.00	103.90	107.61	111.15	114.51	117.71	120.74	123.61	126.33	128.89	131.32	133.60	135.74	141.38	148.30	152.35	153.70
4.25	103.65	107.12	110.41	113.54	116.50	119.30	121.95	124.45	126.81	129.03	131.11	133.06	138.17	144.38	147.98	149.'6
4.50	103.40	106.63	109.68	112.57	115.31	117.88	120.32	122.61	124.76	126.78	128.68	130.45	135.06	140.61	143.79	144.8
4.75	103.16	106.14	108.96	111.62	114.13	116.49	118.71	120.80	122.76	124.59	126.30	127.90	132.04	136.98	139.77	140.66
5.00	102.91	105.65	108.24	110.67	112.96	115.11	117.13	119.02	120.79	122.44	123.98	125.42	129.11	133.48	135.91	136.69
5.25	102.66	105.17	107.52	109.74	111.81	113.75	115.57	117.28	118.86	120.34	121.72	123.00	126.27	130.10	132.22	132.88
5.50	102.42	104.69	106.81	108.81	110.67	112.42	114.04	115.56	116.97	118.29	119.51	120.63	123.51	126.85	128.67	129.23
5.75	102.17	104.21	106.11	107.89	109.55	111.10	112.54	113.88	115.12	116.28	117.35	118.33	120.84	123.71	125.26	125.74
6.00	101.93	103.73	105.41	106.98	108.44	109.79	111.05	112.22	113.31	114.31	115.23	116.09	118.24	120.69	121.99	122.39
6.25	101.69	103.26	104.72	106.08	107.34	108.51	109.59	110.60	111.53	112.38	113.17	113.90	115.72	117.77	118.85	119.17
6.50	101.44	102.78	104.03	105.18	106.25	107.24	108.16	109.00	109.78	110.50	111.16	111.76	113.27	114.96	115.83	116.09
6.75	101.20	102.31	103.34	104.30	105.18	105.99	106.74	107.43	108.07	108.65	109.19	109.68	110.89	112.24	112.93	113.13
7.00	100.96	101.85	102.67	103.42	104.12	104.76	105.35	105.89	106.39	106.85	107.26	107.64	108.59	109.62	110.14	110.29
7.25	100.72	101.38	101.99	102.55	103.07	103.55	103.98	104.38	104.75	105.08	105.38	105.66	106.35	107.09	107.46	107.56
7.50	100.48	100.92	101.32	101.69	102.04	102.35	102.63	102.90	103.13	103.35	103.55	103.73	104.17	104.64	104.87	104.94
7.75	100.24	100.46	100.66	100.84	101.01	101.17	101.31	101.43	101.55	101.66	101.75	101.84	102.05	102.28	102.39	102.42
8.00	100.00	100.00	100.00	100.00	100.00	100.00	100.00	100.00	100.00	100.00	100.00	100.00	100.00	100.00	100.00	100.00
8.25	99.76	99.54	99.35	99.16	99.00	98.85	98.71	98.59	98.48	98.38	98.29	98.20	98.00	97.80	97.70	97.67
8.50	99.52	99.09	98.70	98.34	98.01	97.72	97.45	97.21	96.99	96.79	96.61	96.45	96.07	95.67	95.48	95.43
8.75	99.29	98.64	98.05	97.52	97.03	96.60	96.20	95.84	95.52	95.23	94.97	94.74	94.18	93.61	93.34	93.27
9.00	99.05	98.19	97.41	96.71	96.07	95.49	94.98	94.51	94.09	93.71	93.37	93.07	92.35	91.62	91.28	91.19
9.25	98.81	97.74	96.78	95.90	95.11	94.41	93.77	93.19	92.68	92.22	91.81	91.44	90.57	89.69	89.30	89.19
9.50	98.58	97.30	96.14	95.11	94.17	93.33	92.58	91.90	91.30	90.76	90.28	89.85	88.84	87.83	87.38	87.26
9.75	98.35	96.86	95.52	94.32	93.24	92.27	91.41	90.64	89.95	89.33	88.78	88.30	87.16	86.03	85.53	85.41
10.00	98.11	96.42	94.90	93.54	92.32	91.23	90.26	89.39	88.62	87.93	87.32	86.78	85.52	84.29	83.75	83.61
10.25	97.88	95.98	94.28	92.76	91.41	90.20	89.12	88.16	87.31	86.56	85.89	85.30	83.93	82.60	82.03	81.88
10.50	97.65	95.54	93.67	91.99	90.51	89.18	88.00	86.96	86.04	85.22	84.50	83.86	82.38	80.97	80.37	80.22
10.75	97.41	95.11	93.06	91.24	89.62	88.18	86.91	85.78	84.78	83.90	83.13	82.45	80.88	79.39	78.76	78.61
11.00	97.18	94.68	92.45	90.48	88.74	87.19	85.82	84.62	83.55	82.62	81.79	81.07	79.42	77.86	77.21	77.05
11.25	96.95	94.25	91.86	89.74	87.87	86.21	84.76	83.47	82.35	81.35	80.49	79.73	77.99	76.37	75.71	75.55
11.50	96.72	93.82	91.26	89.00	87.01	85.25	83.71	82.35	81.16	80.12	79.21	78.41	76.61	74.94	74.26	74.10
11.75	96.49	93.40	90.67	88.27	86.16	84.30	82.67	81.25	80.00	78.91	77.96	77.13	75.26	73.54	72.85	72.69
12.00	96.26	92.97	90.08	87.54	85.32	83.37	81.66	80.16	78.86	77.72	76.74	75.88	73.94	72.19	71.50	71.34
12.25	96.03	92.55	89.50	86.83	84.49	82.44	80.66	79.10	77.74	76.56	75.54	74.65	72.67	70.88	70.18	70.02
12.50	95.81	92.13	88.92	86.12	83.67	81.53	79.67	78.05	76.64	75.43	74.37	73.46	71.42	69.61	68.91	68.75
12.75	95.58	91.72	88.35	85.41	82.86	80.63	78.70	77.02	75.57	74.31	73.23	72.29	70.21	68.38	67.68	67.52
13.00	95.35	91.30	87.78	84.72	82.05	79.74	77.74	76.01	74.51	73.22	72.11	71.15	69.03	67.19	66.49	66.33
13.25	95.13	90.89	87.21	84.02	81.26	78.87	76.80	75.01	73.47	72.15	71.01	70.04	67.88	66.03	65.33	65.18
13.50	94.90	90.48	86.65	83.34	80.48	78.00	75.87	74.04	72.46	71.10	69.94	68.95	66.77	64.90	64.21	64.06
13.75	94.68	90.07	86.10	82.66	79.70	77.15	74.96	73.07	71.46	70.07	68.89	67.88	65.68	63.81	63.12	62.98
14.00	94.45	89.67	85.54	81.99	78.94	76.31	74.06	72.13	70.48	69.07	67.86	66.84	64.62	62.74	62.07	61.93
14.25	94.23	89.26	84.99	81.33	78.18	75.48	73.17	71.20	69.52	68.08	66.86	65.82	63.58	61.71	61.05	60.91
14.50	94.01	88.86	84.45	80.67	77.43	74.67	72.30	70.29	68.57	67.11	65.88	64.83	62.57	60.71	60.06	59.92
14.75	93.78	88.46	83.91	80.01	76.69	73.86	71.44	69.39	67.65	66.17	64.91	63.86	61.59	59.74	59.09	58.96
15.00	93.56	88.06	83.37	79.37	75.96	73.06	70.60	68.51	66.74	65.24	63.97	62.91	60.63	58.79	58.16	58.03
15.25	93.34	87.67	82.84	78.73	75.24	72.28	69.76	67.64	65.84	64.33	63.05	61.98	59.70	57.87	57.25	57.13
15.50	93.12	87.27	82.31	78.09	74.52	71.50	68.94	66.79	64.97	63.44	62.15	61.07	58.79	56.98	56.37	56.25
15.75	92.90	86.88	81.78	77.46	73.82	70.74	68.14	65.95	64.11	62.56	61.26	60.18	57.90	56.11	55.51	55.39
16.00	92.68	86.49	81.26	76.84	73.12	69.98	67.34	65.12	63.26	61.70	60.40	59.31	57.04	55.26	54.68	54.56
16.25	92.46	86.10	80.74	76.22	72.43	69.24	66.56	64.31	62.43	60.86	59.55	58.46	56.19	54.44	53.87	53.76
16.50	92.24	85.71	80.22	75.61	71.74	68.50	65.78	63.51	61.62	60.04	58.72	57.63	55.37	53.63	53.08	52.97
16.75	92.02	85.33	79.71	75.01	71.07	67.78	65.02	62.73	60.82	59.23	57.91	56.82	54.57	52.85	52.31	52.21
17.00	91.81	84.95	79.21	74.41	70.40	67.06	64.28	61.96	60.03	58.44	57.12	56.02	53.78	52.09	51.57	51.47
17.25	91.59	84.57	78.70	73.81	69.74	66.35	63.54	61.20	59.26	57.66	56.34	55.25	53.02	51.35	50.84	50.74
17.50	91.37	84.19	78.20	73.23	69.09	65.66	62.81	60.45	58.51	56.90	55.57	54.49	52.27	50.63	50.13	50.04
17.75	91.16	83.81	77.71	72.64	68.45	64.97	62.09	59.72	57.76	56.15	54.83	53.74	51.54	49.93	49.44	49.36
18.00	90.94	83.43	77.21	72.07	67.81	64.29	61.39	59.00	57.03	55.42	54.10	53.01	50.83	49.24	48.77	48.69
18.25	90.73	83.06	76.72	71.49	67.18	63.62	60.70	58.29	56.32	54.70	53.38	52.30	50.13	48.57	48.12	48.04
18.50	90.52	82.69	76.24	70.93	66.55	62.96	60.01	57.59	55.61	54.00	52.68	51.60	49.45	47.92	47.48	47.40
18.75	90.30	82.32	75.76	70.36	65.94	62.31	59.34	56.91	54.92	53.30	51.99	50.92	48.79	47.29	46.86	46.78
19.00	90.09	81.95	75.28	69.81	65.33	61.66	58.67	56.23	54.24	52.63	51.31	50.25	48.14	46.67	46.25	46.18
20.00	89.24	80.50	73.40	67.63	62.96	59.17	56.11	53.64	51.64	50.04	48.75	47.71	45.70	44.34	43.97	43.91
25.00	85.15	73.65	64.76	57.89	52.59	48.50	45.35	42.93	41.07	39.64	38.55	37.72	36.24	35.40	35.22	35.20
30.00	81.26	67.45	57.28	49.79	44.29	40.25	37.28	35.11	33.53	32.37	31.52	30.91	29.91	29.43	29.35	29.35

PREPAYMENT MORTGAGE YIELD, 30 YEAR TERM

8.00 %

Description: This table shows the yield to prepayment of a monthly payment mortgage purchased at a price in the index.

Example: The yield to prepayment in 10 years of a 8.00 %, 30 year mortgage at a price of 104.00 is 7.40 %.

30 YEAR MORTGAGE PREPAID IN

PRICE	1 yr	2 yr	3 yr	4 yr	5 yr	6 yr	7 yr	8 yr	9 yr	10 yr	11 yr	12 yr	15 yr	20 yr	25 yr	30 yr
140	–	–	–	–	–	–	1.72	2.30	2.74	3.09	3.38	3.61	4.10	4.54	4.73	4.79
135	–	–	–	–	–	1.68	2.38	2.89	3.29	3.60	3.86	4.06	4.50	4.89	5.06	5.10
130	–	–	–	–	1.60	2.46	3.07	3.52	3.86	4.14	4.36	4.54	4.92	5.25	5.40	5.44
125	–	–	–	1.44	2.54	3.27	3.79	4.17	4.47	4.70	4.88	5.04	5.36	5.64	5.76	5.80
120	–	–	1.13	2.63	3.53	4.12	4.54	4.86	5.10	5.29	5.44	5.56	5.82	6.05	6.15	6.18
119	–	–	1.44	2.87	3.73	4.30	4.70	5.00	5.23	5.41	5.55	5.67	5.92	6.14	6.23	6.26
118	–	–	1.75	3.12	3.93	4.47	4.86	5.14	5.36	5.53	5.67	5.78	6.02	6.23	6.31	6.34
117	–	–	2.07	3.37	4.14	4.65	5.02	5.28	5.49	5.65	5.79	5.89	6.12	6.31	6.40	6.42
116	–	–	2.39	3.62	4.35	4.83	5.18	5.43	5.63	5.78	5.90	6.00	6.22	6.40	6.48	6.50
115	–	–	2.72	3.87	4.56	5.02	5.34	5.58	5.76	5.91	6.02	6.12	6.32	6.49	6.57	6.59
114	–	–	3.04	4.13	4.77	5.20	5.50	5.73	5.90	6.03	6.14	6.23	6.42	6.58	6.65	6.67
113	–	1.35	3.37	4.38	4.99	5.39	5.67	5.88	6.04	6.16	6.27	6.35	6.52	6.67	6.74	6.76
112	–	1.83	3.71	4.64	5.20	5.57	5.84	6.03	6.18	6.30	6.39	6.47	6.63	6.77	6.83	6.84
111	–	2.32	4.05	4.91	5.42	5.76	6.00	6.18	6.32	6.43	6.51	6.59	6.73	6.86	6.92	6.93
110	–	2.81	4.39	5.17	5.64	5.96	6.18	6.34	6.46	6.56	6.64	6.71	6.84	6.96	7.01	7.02
109	–	3.30	4.73	5.44	5.87	6.15	6.35	6.50	6.61	6.70	6.77	6.83	6.95	7.06	7.10	7.11
108	–	3.80	5.08	5.71	6.09	6.35	6.52	6.65	6.76	6.83	6.90	6.95	7.06	7.15	7.19	7.20
107	–	4.31	5.43	5.99	6.32	6.54	6.70	6.82	6.90	6.97	7.03	7.08	7.17	7.25	7.29	7.30
106	1.91	4.82	5.78	6.27	6.55	6.74	6.88	6.98	7.05	7.11	7.16	7.20	7.28	7.35	7.38	7.39
105	2.90	5.33	6.14	6.55	6.79	6.95	7.06	7.14	7.21	7.26	7.30	7.33	7.40	7.46	7.48	7.49
104	3.89	5.85	6.51	6.83	7.02	7.15	7.24	7.31	7.36	7.40	7.43	7.46	7.51	7.56	7.58	7.59
103.75	4.15	5.98	6.60	6.90	7.08	7.20	7.29	7.35	7.40	7.44	7.47	7.49	7.54	7.59	7.61	7.61
103.50	4.40	6.12	6.69	6.97	7.14	7.25	7.33	7.39	7.44	7.47	7.50	7.52	7.57	7.61	7.63	7.64
103.25	4.65	6.25	6.78	7.04	7.20	7.31	7.38	7.43	7.48	7.51	7.54	7.56	7.60	7.64	7.66	7.66
103.00	4.90	6.38	6.87	7.12	7.26	7.36	7.43	7.48	7.52	7.55	7.57	7.59	7.63	7.67	7.68	7.69
102.75	5.16	6.51	6.96	7.19	7.32	7.41	7.47	7.52	7.56	7.58	7.61	7.62	7.66	7.69	7.71	7.71
102.50	5.41	6.65	7.06	7.26	7.38	7.46	7.52	7.56	7.59	7.62	7.64	7.66	7.69	7.72	7.73	7.74
102.25	5.67	6.78	7.15	7.33	7.44	7.52	7.57	7.60	7.63	7.66	7.68	7.69	7.72	7.75	7.76	7.76
102.00	5.92	6.91	7.24	7.41	7.50	7.57	7.61	7.65	7.67	7.69	7.71	7.72	7.75	7.78	7.79	7.79
101.75	6.18	7.05	7.34	7.48	7.56	7.62	7.66	7.69	7.71	7.73	7.75	7.76	7.78	7.80	7.81	7.81
101.50	6.44	7.18	7.43	7.55	7.63	7.67	7.71	7.73	7.75	7.77	7.78	7.79	7.81	7.83	7.84	7.84
101.25	6.69	7.32	7.52	7.63	7.69	7.73	7.76	7.78	7.79	7.81	7.82	7.82	7.84	7.86	7.86	7.86
101.00	6.95	7.45	7.62	7.70	7.75	7.78	7.80	7.82	7.83	7.84	7.85	7.86	7.87	7.88	7.89	7.89
100.75	7.21	7.59	7.71	7.77	7.81	7.83	7.85	7.86	7.87	7.88	7.89	7.89	7.90	7.91	7.92	7.92
100.50	7.47	7.72	7.81	7.85	7.87	7.89	7.90	7.91	7.91	7.92	7.92	7.93	7.93	7.94	7.94	7.94
100.25	7.73	7.86	7.90	7.92	7.93	7.94	7.95	7.95	7.95	7.96	7.96	7.96	7.96	7.97	7.97	7.97
100.00	8.00	8.00	8.00	8.00	8.00	8.00	8.00	8.00	8.00	8.00	8.00	8.00	8.00	8.00	8.00	8.00
99.75	8.26	8.13	8.09	8.07	8.06	8.05	8.04	8.04	8.04	8.03	8.03	8.03	8.03	8.02	8.02	8.02
99.50	8.52	8.27	8.19	8.14	8.12	8.10	8.09	8.08	8.08	8.07	8.07	8.06	8.06	8.05	8.05	8.05
99.25	8.78	8.41	8.28	8.22	8.18	8.16	8.14	8.13	8.12	8.11	8.10	8.10	8.09	8.08	8.08	8.07
99.00	9.05	8.55	8.38	8.29	8.25	8.21	8.19	8.17	8.16	8.15	8.14	8.13	8.12	8.11	8.10	8.10
98.75	9.31	8.68	8.47	8.37	8.31	8.27	8.24	8.22	8.20	8.19	8.18	8.17	8.15	8.14	8.13	8.13
98.50	9.58	8.82	8.57	8.45	8.37	8.32	8.29	8.26	8.24	8.23	8.21	8.20	8.18	8.16	8.16	8.15
98.25	9.85	8.96	8.67	8.52	8.43	8.38	8.34	8.31	8.28	8.26	8.25	8.24	8.21	8.19	8.18	8.18
98.00	10.11	9.10	8.76	8.60	8.50	8.43	8.39	8.35	8.32	8.30	8.29	8.27	8.25	8.22	8.21	8.21
97.75	10.38	9.24	8.86	8.67	8.56	8.49	8.44	8.40	8.37	8.34	8.32	8.31	8.28	8.25	8.24	8.24
97.50	10.65	9.38	8.96	8.75	8.63	8.54	8.48	8.44	8.41	8.38	8.36	8.34	8.31	8.28	8.27	8.26
97.25	10.92	9.52	9.06	8.83	8.69	8.60	8.53	8.49	8.45	8.42	8.40	8.38	8.34	8.31	8.29	8.29
97	11.19	9.66	9.16	8.90	8.75	8.65	8.58	8.53	8.49	8.46	8.44	8.42	8.37	8.34	8.32	8.32
96	12.28	10.23	9.55	9.21	9.01	8.88	8.79	8.72	8.66	8.62	8.59	8.56	8.50	8.46	8.44	8.43
95	13.38	10.81	9.95	9.53	9.28	9.11	8.99	8.90	8.84	8.78	8.74	8.71	8.64	8.58	8.55	8.54
94	14.50	11.39	10.36	9.85	9.54	9.34	9.20	9.09	9.01	8.95	8.90	8.86	8.77	8.70	8.67	8.66
93	15.63	11.98	10.77	10.17	9.81	9.57	9.41	9.28	9.19	9.11	9.05	9.01	8.91	8.82	8.79	8.78
92	16.77	12.58	11.18	10.49	10.08	9.81	9.62	9.48	9.37	9.28	9.21	9.16	9.04	8.95	8.91	8.90
91	17.93	13.18	11.61	10.82	10.36	10.05	9.83	9.67	9.55	9.45	9.38	9.31	9.18	9.07	9.03	9.02
90	19.10	13.79	12.03	11.16	10.64	10.29	10.05	9.87	9.73	9.63	9.54	9.47	9.33	9.20	9.16	9.14
89	20.29	14.41	12.46	11.50	10.92	10.54	10.27	10.07	9.92	9.80	9.71	9.63	9.47	9.34	9.28	9.27
88	21.49	15.03	12.90	11.84	11.21	10.79	10.50	10.28	10.11	9.98	9.88	9.79	9.62	9.47	9.41	9.40
87	22.70	15.67	13.34	12.18	11.50	11.04	10.72	10.49	10.31	10.16	10.05	9.96	9.77	9.61	9.55	9.53
86	23.93	16.31	13.79	12.54	11.79	11.30	10.95	10.70	10.50	10.35	10.23	10.13	9.92	9.75	9.68	9.66
85	25.18	16.96	14.24	12.89	12.09	11.56	11.19	10.91	10.70	10.54	10.40	10.30	10.08	9.89	9.82	9.80
80	31.68	20.34	16.60	14.75	13.65	12.92	12.41	12.03	11.74	11.52	11.34	11.19	10.89	10.65	10.55	10.53
75	38.64	23.97	19.14	16.75	15.33	14.39	13.73	13.25	12.88	12.59	12.36	12.17	11.79	11.48	11.37	11.34
70	46.14	27.88	21.88	18.91	17.15	15.99	15.17	14.57	14.12	13.76	13.48	13.25	12.79	12.42	12.28	12.25
65	54.27	32.11	24.85	21.26	19.13	17.73	16.75	16.03	15.49	15.06	14.72	14.45	13.90	13.47	13.32	13.28
60	63.14	36.73	28.09	23.83	21.31	19.66	18.50	17.65	17.01	16.51	16.11	15.80	15.16	14.68	14.51	14.47
55	72.88	41.80	31.67	26.68	23.73	21.80	20.45	19.46	18.72	18.14	17.69	17.33	16.61	16.07	15.90	15.86
50	83.67	47.42	35.64	29.85	26.44	24.21	22.65	21.52	20.67	20.01	19.50	19.09	18.29	17.72	17.54	17.51

Description: This table shows the price to pay for a monthly payment loan, at a yield rate and assuming prepayment.

Example: The price of a 8.25 %, 30 year mortgage to yield 8.00 %, if prepaid in 6 years, is $ 101.16.

30 YEAR MORTGAGE PREPAID IN

YIELD	1 yr	2 yr	3 yr	4 yr	5 yr	6 yr	7 yr	8 yr	9 yr	10 yr	11 yr	12 yr	15 yr	20 yr	25 yr	30 yr
0.00	108.22	116.37	124.45	132.45	140.36	148.18	155.89	163.49	170.97	178.32	185.53	192.58	212.67	241.56	262.21	270.46
1.00	107.19	114.24	121.16	127.95	134.59	141.09	147.44	153.63	159.67	165.54	171.24	176.76	192.18	213.51	228.03	233.57
2.00	106.16	112.15	117.97	123.61	129.09	134.39	139.51	144.47	149.25	153.85	158.27	162.51	174.13	189.58	199.60	203.25
3.00	105.15	110.10	114.87	119.44	123.84	128.05	132.09	135.94	139.63	143.14	146.49	149.66	158.19	169.10	175.84	178.19
4.00	104.14	108.09	111.85	115.43	118.83	122.06	125.12	128.02	130.76	133.34	135.78	138.07	144.11	151.53	155.90	157.36
4.25	103.90	107.60	111.12	114.45	117.62	120.61	123.45	126.12	128.65	131.03	133.26	135.36	140.85	147.54	151.43	152.72
4.50	103.65	107.11	110.38	113.48	116.42	119.19	121.80	124.26	126.58	128.76	130.80	132.71	137.68	143.69	147.14	148.27
4.75	103.40	106.61	109.65	112.52	115.23	117.78	120.18	122.44	124.55	126.54	128.39	130.12	134.62	139.99	143.03	144.02
5.00	103.15	106.13	108.93	111.57	114.06	116.39	118.58	120.64	122.56	124.36	126.04	127.60	131.64	136.42	139.09	139.95
5.25	102.91	105.64	108.21	110.63	112.90	115.02	117.01	118.88	120.62	122.24	123.75	125.15	128.75	132.97	135.31	136.05
5.50	102.66	105.16	107.50	109.70	111.75	113.67	115.47	117.15	118.71	120.16	121.51	122.75	125.95	129.65	131.68	132.31
5.75	102.42	104.68	106.79	108.77	110.62	112.34	113.95	115.44	116.83	118.12	119.32	120.42	123.22	126.45	128.20	128.74
6.00	102.17	104.20	106.09	107.86	109.50	111.03	112.45	113.77	115.00	116.13	117.18	118.14	120.58	123.37	124.85	125.30
6.25	101.93	103.72	105.39	106.95	108.39	109.74	110.98	112.13	113.20	114.18	115.09	115.92	118.02	120.39	121.64	122.01
6.50	101.68	103.25	104.70	106.05	107.30	108.46	109.53	110.52	111.43	112.27	113.04	113.75	115.53	117.52	118.55	118.86
6.75	101.44	102.78	104.02	105.16	106.22	107.20	108.10	108.94	109.70	110.40	111.05	111.64	113.11	114.74	115.58	115.83
7.00	101.20	102.31	103.33	104.28	105.15	105.96	106.70	107.38	108.00	108.58	109.10	109.58	110.76	112.07	112.73	112.92
7.25	100.96	101.84	102.66	103.41	104.10	104.73	105.32	105.85	106.34	106.79	107.20	107.57	108.48	109.48	109.98	110.13
7.50	100.72	101.38	101.99	102.54	103.06	103.53	103.96	104.35	104.71	105.04	105.33	105.60	106.27	106.99	107.34	107.44
7.75	100.48	100.92	101.32	101.69	102.03	102.33	102.62	102.87	103.11	103.32	103.52	103.69	104.12	104.58	104.80	104.87
8.00	100.24	100.46	100.66	100.84	101.01	101.16	101.30	101.42	101.54	101.64	101.74	101.82	102.03	102.25	102.36	102.39
8.25	100.00	100.00	100.00	100.00	100.00	100.00	100.00	100.00	100.00	100.00	100.00	100.00	100.00	100.00	100.00	100.00
8.50	99.76	99.55	99.35	99.17	99.00	98.86	98.72	98.60	98.49	98.39	98.30	98.22	98.03	97.83	97.73	97.70
8.75	99.52	99.09	98.70	98.34	98.02	97.73	97.46	97.23	97.01	96.82	96.64	96.49	96.11	95.72	95.54	95.50
9.00	99.29	98.64	98.06	97.53	97.05	96.62	96.23	95.87	95.56	95.27	95.02	94.79	94.25	93.69	93.44	93.37
9.25	99.05	98.19	97.42	96.72	96.09	95.52	95.01	94.55	94.13	93.76	93.43	93.14	92.44	91.73	91.41	91.32
9.50	98.82	97.75	96.79	95.92	95.14	94.44	93.81	93.24	92.74	92.29	91.88	91.52	90.67	89.83	89.45	89.35
9.75	98.58	97.30	96.16	95.13	94.20	93.37	92.63	91.96	91.37	90.84	90.37	89.95	88.96	87.99	87.55	87.44
10.00	98.35	96.86	95.53	94.34	93.27	92.32	91.46	90.70	90.02	89.42	88.88	88.41	87.30	86.21	85.73	85.61
10.25	98.11	96.42	94.91	93.56	92.35	91.28	90.32	89.46	88.70	88.03	87.44	86.91	85.68	84.49	83.97	83.84
10.50	97.88	95.99	94.30	92.79	91.45	90.25	89.19	88.25	87.41	86.67	86.02	85.44	84.10	82.82	82.27	82.13
10.75	97.65	95.55	93.69	92.03	90.55	89.24	88.08	87.05	86.14	85.34	84.63	84.01	82.57	81.20	80.62	80.48
11.00	97.42	95.12	93.08	91.27	89.67	88.24	86.99	85.88	84.90	84.04	83.28	82.61	81.08	79.64	79.04	78.89
11.25	97.19	94.69	92.48	90.52	88.79	87.26	85.91	84.72	83.68	82.76	81.95	81.25	79.63	78.12	77.50	77.35
11.50	96.95	94.26	91.88	89.78	87.92	86.29	84.85	83.59	82.48	81.51	80.66	79.91	78.22	76.66	76.02	75.86
11.75	96.72	93.83	91.29	89.04	87.07	85.33	83.81	82.47	81.30	80.28	79.39	78.61	76.85	75.23	74.58	74.43
12.00	96.50	93.41	90.70	88.31	86.22	84.39	82.78	81.38	80.15	79.08	78.15	77.34	75.51	73.85	73.19	73.04
12.25	96.27	92.99	90.11	87.59	85.39	83.46	81.77	80.30	79.02	77.90	76.93	76.10	74.21	72.52	71.85	71.69
12.50	96.04	92.57	89.53	86.88	84.56	82.54	80.77	79.24	77.91	76.75	75.75	74.88	72.94	71.22	70.55	70.39
12.75	95.81	92.15	88.96	86.17	83.74	81.63	79.79	78.20	76.82	75.62	74.59	73.70	71.71	69.96	69.29	69.13
13.00	95.58	91.74	88.38	85.47	82.94	80.74	78.83	77.18	75.75	74.51	73.45	72.54	70.51	68.74	68.06	67.91
13.25	95.36	91.32	87.82	84.77	82.14	79.85	77.88	76.17	74.70	73.43	72.34	71.40	69.34	67.55	66.88	66.73
13.50	95.13	90.91	87.25	84.09	81.35	78.98	76.94	75.18	73.67	72.37	71.25	70.30	68.20	66.40	65.74	65.59
13.75	94.91	90.50	86.69	83.40	80.57	78.12	76.02	74.21	72.66	71.33	70.19	69.22	67.09	65.28	64.62	64.48
14.00	94.68	90.09	86.14	82.73	79.80	77.27	75.11	73.25	71.66	70.31	69.15	68.16	66.01	64.20	63.54	63.40
14.25	94.46	89.69	85.59	82.06	79.03	76.44	74.22	72.31	70.69	69.31	68.13	67.13	64.96	63.15	62.50	62.36
14.50	94.23	89.28	85.04	81.40	78.28	75.61	73.33	71.39	69.73	68.32	67.13	66.12	63.93	62.12	61.48	61.35
14.75	94.01	88.88	84.49	80.74	77.53	74.80	72.47	70.48	68.80	67.36	66.15	65.13	62.93	61.13	60.50	60.37
15.00	93.79	88.48	83.95	80.09	76.80	74.00	71.61	69.59	67.87	66.42	65.20	64.16	61.95	60.16	59.54	59.41
15.25	93.57	88.09	83.42	79.45	76.07	73.20	70.77	68.71	66.97	65.50	64.26	63.22	61.00	59.22	58.61	58.49
15.50	93.35	87.69	82.89	78.81	75.35	72.42	69.94	67.85	66.08	64.60	63.34	62.30	60.08	58.30	57.71	57.59
15.75	93.13	87.30	82.36	78.18	74.64	71.65	69.13	67.00	65.21	63.71	62.45	61.39	59.17	57.41	56.83	56.72
16.00	92.91	86.91	81.83	77.55	73.93	70.89	68.32	66.17	64.36	62.84	61.57	60.51	58.29	56.55	55.98	55.87
16.25	92.69	86.52	81.31	76.93	73.24	70.14	67.53	65.35	63.52	61.99	60.71	59.65	57.43	55.71	55.15	55.04
16.50	92.47	86.13	80.80	76.31	72.55	69.39	66.75	64.54	62.69	61.15	59.87	58.80	56.59	54.89	54.34	54.24
16.75	92.25	85.74	80.28	75.70	71.87	68.66	65.98	63.75	61.88	60.33	59.04	57.98	55.77	54.09	53.56	53.46
17.00	92.03	85.36	79.77	75.10	71.20	67.94	65.23	62.97	61.09	59.53	58.24	57.17	54.97	53.31	52.79	52.70
17.25	91.82	84.98	79.27	74.50	70.53	67.23	64.48	62.20	60.31	58.74	57.44	56.38	54.19	52.55	52.05	51.96
17.50	91.60	84.60	78.77	73.91	69.88	66.53	63.75	61.44	59.54	57.97	56.67	55.60	53.43	51.82	51.32	51.23
17.75	91.38	84.22	78.27	73.32	69.23	65.83	63.02	60.70	58.79	57.21	55.91	54.85	52.69	51.10	50.62	50.53
18.00	91.17	83.84	77.77	72.74	68.58	65.15	62.31	59.97	58.05	56.46	55.17	54.11	51.96	50.40	49.93	49.85
18.25	90.95	83.47	77.28	72.17	67.95	64.47	61.61	59.25	57.32	55.74	54.44	53.38	51.25	49.72	49.26	49.18
18.50	90.74	83.10	76.79	71.60	67.32	63.80	60.92	58.55	56.61	55.02	53.73	52.67	50.56	49.05	48.61	48.53
18.75	90.53	82.73	76.31	71.03	66.70	63.15	60.24	57.85	55.91	54.32	53.03	51.98	49.88	48.40	47.97	47.90
19.00	90.31	82.36	75.83	70.47	66.09	62.50	59.56	57.17	55.22	53.63	52.34	51.30	49.22	47.77	47.35	47.28
20.00	89.47	80.90	73.94	68.28	63.70	59.98	56.98	54.55	52.59	51.01	49.73	48.71	46.73	45.38	45.02	44.96
25.00	85.36	74.03	65.26	58.48	53.25	49.21	46.10	43.70	41.86	40.45	39.37	38.54	37.07	36.24	36.06	36.04
30.00	81.47	67.81	57.74	50.33	44.88	40.87	37.93	35.78	34.20	33.05	32.21	31.60	30.61	30.13	30.05	30.05

Description: This table shows the yield to prepayment of a monthly payment mortgage purchased at a price in the index.

Example: The yield to prepayment in 10 years of a 8.25 %, 30 year mortgage at a price of 104.00 is 7.65 %.

30 YEAR MORTGAGE PREPAID IN

PRICE	1 yr	2 yr	3 yr	4 yr	5 yr	6 yr	7 yr	8 yr	9 yr	10 yr	11 yr	12 yr	15 yr	20 yr	25 yr	30 yr
140	–	–	–	–	–	1.15	1.93	2.51	2.96	3.31	3.59	3.82	4.31	4.74	4.94	4.99
135	–	–	–	–	–	1.90	2.59	3.11	3.51	3.82	4.07	4.28	4.71	5.10	5.27	5.31
130	–	–	–	–	1.83	2.68	3.29	3.74	4.08	4.36	4.58	4.76	5.14	5.47	5.61	5.66
125	–	–	–	1.67	2.77	3.50	4.01	4.40	4.69	4.92	5.11	5.26	5.58	5.86	5.98	6.02
120	–	–	1.36	2.86	3.76	4.35	4.77	5.09	5.33	5.51	5.67	5.79	6.05	6.28	6.38	6.40
119	–	–	1.67	3.10	3.96	4.53	4.93	5.23	5.46	5.64	5.78	5.90	6.15	6.36	6.46	6.48
118	–	–	1.98	3.35	4.17	4.71	5.09	5.37	5.59	5.76	5.90	6.01	6.25	6.45	6.54	6.56
117	–	–	2.30	3.60	4.37	4.88	5.25	5.52	5.72	5.89	6.02	6.12	6.35	6.54	6.62	6.65
116	–	–	2.63	3.85	4.58	5.07	5.41	5.66	5.86	6.01	6.14	6.24	6.45	6.63	6.71	6.73
115	–	–	2.95	4.10	4.79	5.25	5.57	5.81	5.99	6.14	6.26	6.35	6.55	6.72	6.80	6.82
114	–	1.11	3.28	4.36	5.01	5.43	5.74	5.96	6.13	6.27	6.38	6.47	6.65	6.81	6.88	6.90
113	–	1.59	3.61	4.62	5.22	5.62	5.90	6.11	6.27	6.40	6.50	6.58	6.76	6.91	6.97	6.99
112	–	2.07	3.95	4.88	5.44	5.81	6.07	6.27	6.41	6.53	6.63	6.70	6.86	7.00	7.06	7.08
111	–	2.55	4.28	5.15	5.66	6.00	6.24	6.42	6.56	6.66	6.75	6.82	6.97	7.10	7.15	7.17
110	–	3.04	4.63	5.41	5.88	6.19	6.41	6.58	6.70	6.80	6.88	6.94	7.08	7.19	7.24	7.26
109	–	3.54	4.97	5.68	6.11	6.39	6.59	6.73	6.85	6.94	7.01	7.07	7.19	7.29	7.34	7.35
108	–	4.04	5.32	5.96	6.33	6.59	6.76	6.89	7.00	7.08	7.14	7.19	7.30	7.39	7.43	7.44
107	1.17	4.55	5.67	6.23	6.56	6.79	6.94	7.06	7.15	7.22	7.27	7.32	7.41	7.49	7.53	7.54
106	2.15	5.06	6.03	6.51	6.80	6.99	7.12	7.22	7.30	7.36	7.40	7.44	7.53	7.60	7.63	7.63
105	3.14	5.58	6.39	6.79	7.03	7.19	7.30	7.39	7.45	7.50	7.54	7.57	7.64	7.70	7.73	7.73
104	4.14	6.10	6.75	7.08	7.27	7.40	7.49	7.55	7.61	7.65	7.68	7.70	7.76	7.81	7.83	7.83
103.75	4.39	6.23	6.84	7.15	7.33	7.45	7.53	7.60	7.64	7.68	7.71	7.74	7.79	7.83	7.85	7.86
103.50	4.64	6.36	6.93	7.22	7.39	7.50	7.58	7.64	7.68	7.72	7.75	7.77	7.82	7.86	7.88	7.88
103.25	4.90	6.49	7.03	7.29	7.45	7.55	7.63	7.68	7.72	7.76	7.78	7.80	7.85	7.89	7.90	7.91
103.00	5.15	6.63	7.12	7.36	7.51	7.60	7.67	7.72	7.76	7.79	7.82	7.84	7.88	7.91	7.93	7.93
102.75	5.40	6.76	7.21	7.44	7.57	7.66	7.72	7.77	7.80	7.83	7.85	7.87	7.91	7.94	7.95	7.96
102.50	5.66	6.89	7.30	7.51	7.63	7.71	7.77	7.81	7.84	7.87	7.89	7.90	7.94	7.97	7.98	7.98
102.25	5.91	7.03	7.40	7.58	7.69	7.76	7.81	7.85	7.88	7.90	7.92	7.94	7.97	7.99	8.01	8.01
102.00	6.17	7.16	7.49	7.65	7.75	7.82	7.86	7.90	7.92	7.94	7.96	7.97	8.00	8.02	8.03	8.03
101.75	6.43	7.29	7.58	7.73	7.81	7.87	7.91	7.94	7.96	7.98	7.99	8.00	8.03	8.05	8.06	8.06
101.50	6.68	7.43	7.68	7.80	7.87	7.92	7.96	7.98	8.00	8.02	8.03	8.04	8.06	8.08	8.08	8.09
101.25	6.94	7.56	7.77	7.87	7.94	7.98	8.00	8.03	8.04	8.05	8.06	8.07	8.09	8.11	8.11	8.11
101.00	7.20	7.70	7.87	7.95	8.00	8.03	8.05	8.07	8.08	8.09	8.10	8.11	8.12	8.13	8.14	8.14
100.75	7.46	7.84	7.96	8.02	8.06	8.08	8.10	8.11	8.12	8.13	8.14	8.14	8.15	8.16	8.16	8.17
100.50	7.72	7.97	8.05	8.10	8.12	8.14	8.15	8.16	8.16	8.17	8.17	8.18	8.18	8.19	8.19	8.19
100.25	7.98	8.11	8.15	8.17	8.18	8.19	8.20	8.20	8.20	8.21	8.21	8.21	8.21	8.22	8.22	8.22
100.00	8.25	8.25	8.25	8.25	8.25	8.25	8.25	8.25	8.25	8.25	8.25	8.25	8.25	8.25	8.25	8.25
99.75	8.51	8.38	8.34	8.32	8.31	8.30	8.29	8.29	8.29	8.28	8.28	8.28	8.28	8.27	8.27	8.27
99.50	8.77	8.52	8.44	8.39	8.37	8.35	8.34	8.33	8.33	8.32	8.32	8.31	8.31	8.30	8.30	8.30
99.25	9.04	8.66	8.53	8.47	8.43	8.41	8.39	8.38	8.37	8.36	8.35	8.35	8.34	8.33	8.33	8.33
99.00	9.30	8.80	8.63	8.55	8.50	8.46	8.44	8.42	8.41	8.40	8.39	8.38	8.37	8.36	8.35	8.35
98.75	9.57	8.94	8.73	8.62	8.56	8.52	8.49	8.47	8.45	8.44	8.43	8.42	8.40	8.39	8.38	8.38
98.50	9.83	9.07	8.82	8.70	8.62	8.57	8.54	8.51	8.49	8.48	8.47	8.46	8.43	8.42	8.41	8.41
98.25	10.10	9.21	8.92	8.77	8.69	8.63	8.59	8.56	8.54	8.52	8.50	8.49	8.47	8.45	8.44	8.43
98.00	10.37	9.35	9.02	8.85	8.75	8.68	8.64	8.60	8.58	8.56	8.54	8.53	8.50	8.47	8.46	8.46
97.75	10.64	9.49	9.12	8.93	8.81	8.74	8.69	8.65	8.62	8.60	8.58	8.56	8.53	8.50	8.49	8.49
97.50	10.90	9.63	9.21	9.00	8.88	8.80	8.74	8.69	8.66	8.64	8.62	8.60	8.56	8.53	8.52	8.52
97.25	11.17	9.78	9.31	9.08	8.94	8.85	8.79	8.74	8.70	8.68	8.65	8.63	8.60	8.56	8.55	8.55
97	11.45	9.92	9.41	9.16	9.01	8.91	8.84	8.79	8.75	8.72	8.69	8.67	8.63	8.59	8.58	8.57
96	12.54	10.49	9.81	9.47	9.27	9.14	9.04	8.97	8.92	8.88	8.84	8.82	8.76	8.71	8.69	8.69
95	13.64	11.06	10.21	9.78	9.53	9.36	9.25	9.16	9.09	9.04	9.00	8.96	8.89	8.83	8.81	8.80
94	14.76	11.65	10.62	10.10	9.80	9.60	9.45	9.35	9.27	9.21	9.16	9.11	9.03	8.96	8.93	8.92
93	15.89	12.24	11.03	10.43	10.07	9.83	9.67	9.54	9.45	9.37	9.31	9.27	9.17	9.08	9.05	9.04
92	17.03	12.84	11.44	10.75	10.34	10.07	9.88	9.74	9.63	9.54	9.48	9.42	9.31	9.21	9.17	9.16
91	18.19	13.44	11.87	11.08	10.62	10.31	10.10	9.94	9.81	9.72	9.64	9.58	9.45	9.34	9.30	9.28
90	19.36	14.05	12.29	11.42	10.90	10.56	10.32	10.14	10.00	9.89	9.81	9.74	9.59	9.47	9.42	9.41
89	20.55	14.67	12.73	11.76	11.18	10.81	10.54	10.34	10.19	10.07	9.98	9.90	9.74	9.61	9.55	9.54
88	21.75	15.30	13.16	12.10	11.47	11.06	10.76	10.55	10.38	10.25	10.15	10.06	9.89	9.74	9.69	9.67
87	22.97	15.93	13.61	12.45	11.77	11.31	10.99	10.76	10.58	10.43	10.32	10.23	10.04	9.88	9.82	9.80
86	24.20	16.58	14.06	12.81	12.06	11.57	11.22	10.97	10.77	10.62	10.50	10.40	10.19	10.02	9.96	9.94
85	25.45	17.23	14.51	13.16	12.36	11.83	11.46	11.18	10.97	10.81	10.68	10.57	10.35	10.17	10.10	10.08
80	31.95	20.62	16.88	15.03	13.93	13.20	12.69	12.32	12.03	11.81	11.62	11.48	11.18	10.94	10.84	10.82
75	38.93	24.26	19.43	17.04	15.62	14.68	14.03	13.54	13.17	12.88	12.66	12.47	12.09	11.79	11.67	11.64
70	46.44	28.18	22.18	19.21	17.45	16.29	15.48	14.88	14.42	14.07	13.79	13.56	13.10	12.74	12.60	12.57
65	54.58	32.42	25.16	21.57	19.44	18.05	17.07	16.35	15.81	15.38	15.05	14.78	14.23	13.81	13.66	13.63
60	63.46	37.05	28.42	24.16	21.64	19.99	18.83	17.99	17.34	16.85	16.46	16.14	15.52	15.04	14.87	14.84
55	73.22	42.14	32.01	27.02	24.07	22.15	20.80	19.82	19.08	18.50	18.05	17.69	16.99	16.46	16.29	16.26
50	84.03	47.78	36.00	30.22	26.81	24.58	23.03	21.90	21.05	20.40	19.89	19.49	18.70	18.14	17.97	17.94

PREPAYMENT MORTGAGE PRICE

8.50 %

Description: This table shows the price to pay for a monthly payment loan, at a yield rate and assuming prepayment.

Example: The price of a 8.50 %, 30 year mortgage to yield 8.00 %, if prepaid in 6 years, is $ 102.32.

30 YEAR MORTGAGE PREPAID IN

YIELD	1 yr	2 yr	3 yr	4 yr	5 yr	6 yr	7 yr	8 yr	9 yr	10 yr	11 yr	12 yr	15 yr	20 yr	25 yr	30 yr
0.00	108.47	116.88	125.21	133.46	141.63	149.70	157.67	165.53	173.27	180.87	188.34	195.64	216.49	246.56	268.15	276.81
1.00	107.43	114.74	121.90	128.93	135.82	142.56	149.14	155.57	161.84	167.95	173.87	179.62	195.69	217.97	233.22	239.06
2.00	106.41	112.64	118.70	124.58	130.28	135.80	141.15	146.32	151.31	156.12	160.74	165.18	177.35	193.58	204.15	208.03
3.00	105.39	110.59	115.58	120.38	125.00	129.42	133.66	137.72	141.59	145.29	148.81	152.16	161.16	172.70	179.87	182.38
4.00	104.39	108.57	112.56	116.35	119.96	123.38	126.63	129.71	132.63	135.38	137.97	140.41	146.85	154.79	159.48	161.06
4.25	104.14	108.08	111.82	115.37	118.74	121.93	124.95	127.80	130.49	133.03	135.42	137.66	143.55	150.72	154.91	156.30
4.50	103.89	107.58	111.08	114.39	117.53	120.49	123.28	125.92	128.40	130.73	132.92	134.97	140.32	146.80	150.53	151.75
4.75	103.64	107.09	110.35	113.43	116.33	119.07	121.65	124.08	126.35	128.49	130.49	132.35	137.20	143.01	146.33	147.40
5.00	103.40	106.60	109.62	112.47	115.15	117.67	120.04	122.26	124.34	126.29	128.11	129.80	134.17	139.37	142.30	143.23
5.25	103.15	106.11	108.90	111.52	113.99	116.29	118.46	120.48	122.37	124.14	125.78	127.31	131.24	135.86	138.43	139.24
5.50	102.90	105.63	108.19	110.59	112.83	114.93	116.90	118.73	120.44	122.03	123.51	124.88	128.39	132.47	134.72	135.42
5.75	102.66	105.15	107.48	109.66	111.69	113.59	115.37	117.02	118.55	119.97	121.29	122.51	125.62	129.21	131.16	131.76
6.00	102.41	104.67	106.77	108.74	110.57	112.27	113.86	115.33	116.69	117.96	119.13	120.20	122.94	126.06	127.73	128.25
6.25	102.17	104.19	106.07	107.82	109.45	110.97	112.37	113.67	114.87	115.98	117.01	117.95	120.33	123.02	124.45	124.88
6.50	101.92	103.71	105.38	106.92	108.35	109.68	110.91	112.04	113.09	114.05	114.94	115.75	117.80	120.09	121.29	121.65
6.75	101.68	103.24	104.69	106.03	107.27	108.41	109.47	110.44	111.34	112.16	112.92	113.61	115.34	117.26	118.26	118.55
7.00	101.44	102.77	104.00	105.14	106.19	107.16	108.05	108.87	109.62	110.31	110.94	111.52	112.95	114.53	115.34	115.57
7.25	101.20	102.30	103.32	104.26	105.13	105.92	106.66	107.33	107.94	108.50	109.01	109.48	110.64	111.90	112.53	112.71
7.50	100.96	101.84	102.65	103.39	104.08	104.71	105.28	105.81	106.29	106.73	107.13	107.49	108.38	109.35	109.83	109.97
7.75	100.72	101.38	101.98	102.53	103.04	103.51	103.93	104.32	104.67	104.99	105.28	105.55	106.20	106.89	107.23	107.33
8.00	100.48	100.91	101.32	101.68	102.02	102.32	102.60	102.85	103.08	103.29	103.48	103.65	104.07	104.51	104.73	104.79
8.25	100.24	100.46	100.66	100.84	101.00	101.15	101.29	101.41	101.53	101.63	101.72	101.80	102.01	102.22	102.32	102.35
8.50	100.00	100.00	100.00	100.00	100.00	100.00	100.00	100.00	100.00	100.00	100.00	100.00	100.00	100.00	100.00	100.00
8.75	99.76	99.55	99.35	99.17	99.01	98.86	98.73	98.61	98.50	98.41	98.32	98.24	98.05	97.86	97.76	97.74
9.00	99.53	99.09	98.70	98.35	98.03	97.74	97.48	97.25	97.03	96.84	96.67	96.52	96.15	95.78	95.61	95.56
9.25	99.29	98.65	98.06	97.54	97.06	96.64	96.25	95.90	95.59	95.31	95.07	94.84	94.31	93.78	93.53	93.46
9.50	99.05	98.20	97.43	96.73	96.11	95.54	95.04	94.59	94.18	93.82	93.49	93.20	92.52	91.84	91.53	91.44
9.75	98.82	97.75	96.80	95.93	95.16	94.47	93.85	93.29	92.79	92.35	91.96	91.61	90.78	89.96	89.59	89.50
10.00	98.58	97.31	96.17	95.14	94.23	93.41	92.67	92.02	91.43	90.91	90.45	90.04	89.08	88.14	87.73	87.62
10.25	98.35	96.87	95.55	94.36	93.30	92.36	91.52	90.77	90.10	89.51	88.98	88.52	87.44	86.38	85.92	85.81
10.50	98.12	96.43	94.93	93.59	92.39	91.33	90.38	89.54	88.79	88.13	87.55	87.03	85.83	84.68	84.18	84.06
10.75	97.88	96.00	94.31	92.82	91.49	90.31	89.26	88.33	87.51	86.78	86.14	85.58	84.28	83.03	82.50	82.37
11.00	97.65	95.56	93.71	92.06	90.60	89.30	88.16	87.14	86.25	85.46	84.77	84.16	82.76	81.43	80.88	80.74
11.25	97.42	95.13	93.10	91.30	89.71	88.31	87.07	85.98	85.01	84.17	83.42	82.77	81.28	79.89	79.31	79.17
11.50	97.19	94.70	92.50	90.56	88.84	87.33	86.00	84.83	83.80	82.90	82.11	81.42	79.85	78.39	77.79	77.65
11.75	96.96	94.27	91.90	89.82	87.98	86.37	84.95	83.70	82.61	81.66	80.82	80.10	78.45	76.93	76.32	76.17
12.00	96.73	93.85	91.31	89.09	87.13	85.41	83.91	82.59	81.44	80.44	79.57	78.81	77.09	75.53	74.90	74.75
12.25	96.50	93.42	90.73	88.36	86.29	84.47	82.89	81.50	80.30	79.25	78.34	77.55	75.77	74.16	73.52	73.38
12.50	96.27	93.00	90.14	87.64	85.45	83.55	81.88	80.43	79.17	78.08	77.13	76.31	74.48	72.83	72.19	72.05
12.75	96.04	92.58	89.56	86.93	84.63	82.63	80.89	79.38	78.07	76.94	75.95	75.11	73.22	71.55	70.90	70.76
13.00	95.82	92.17	88.99	86.22	83.82	81.73	79.92	78.35	76.99	75.81	74.80	73.93	72.00	70.30	69.65	69.51
13.25	95.59	91.75	88.42	85.53	83.01	80.84	78.96	77.33	75.93	74.72	73.67	72.78	70.81	69.09	68.44	68.30
13.50	95.36	91.34	87.85	84.83	82.22	79.96	78.01	76.33	74.88	73.64	72.57	71.66	69.65	67.92	67.27	67.13
13.75	95.14	90.93	87.29	84.15	81.43	79.09	77.08	75.35	73.86	72.58	71.49	70.56	68.52	66.77	66.13	65.99
14.00	94.91	90.52	86.73	83.47	80.66	78.24	76.16	74.38	72.85	71.55	70.43	69.49	67.42	65.67	65.03	64.89
14.25	94.69	90.11	86.18	82.80	79.89	77.40	75.26	73.43	71.87	70.54	69.40	68.44	66.34	64.59	63.96	63.83
14.50	94.46	89.71	85.63	82.13	79.13	76.56	74.37	72.50	70.90	69.54	68.39	67.41	65.30	63.54	62.92	62.79
14.75	94.24	89.31	85.08	81.47	78.38	75.74	73.49	71.58	69.95	68.57	67.40	66.41	64.28	62.53	61.91	61.79
15.00	94.02	88.91	84.54	80.81	77.64	74.93	72.63	70.68	69.02	67.61	66.43	65.43	63.28	61.54	60.93	60.81
15.25	93.80	88.51	84.00	80.17	76.90	74.13	71.78	69.79	68.10	66.68	65.48	64.47	62.32	60.58	59.98	59.86
15.50	93.58	88.11	83.47	79.52	76.18	73.34	70.94	68.92	67.20	65.76	64.55	63.53	61.37	59.64	59.06	58.94
15.75	93.35	87.72	82.94	78.89	75.46	72.57	70.12	68.06	66.32	64.86	63.64	62.61	60.45	58.73	58.16	58.05
16.00	93.13	87.32	82.41	78.26	74.75	71.80	69.31	67.21	65.46	63.98	62.75	61.71	59.55	57.85	57.29	57.18
16.25	92.91	86.93	81.89	77.63	74.05	71.04	68.51	66.38	64.60	63.12	61.87	60.84	58.67	56.99	56.44	56.33
16.50	92.70	86.54	81.37	77.02	73.36	70.29	67.72	65.57	63.77	62.27	61.02	59.98	57.82	56.15	55.61	55.51
16.75	92.48	86.16	80.85	76.40	72.67	69.55	66.94	64.77	62.95	61.44	60.18	59.14	56.98	55.34	54.81	54.71
17.00	92.26	85.77	80.34	75.80	72.00	68.83	66.18	63.98	62.14	60.62	59.36	58.32	56.17	54.54	54.03	53.93
17.25	92.04	85.39	79.83	75.19	71.33	68.11	65.43	63.20	61.35	59.82	58.56	57.51	55.37	53.77	53.27	53.18
17.50	91.83	85.01	79.33	74.60	70.67	67.40	64.68	62.44	60.58	59.04	57.77	56.73	54.60	53.01	52.53	52.44
17.75	91.61	84.63	78.83	74.01	70.01	66.70	63.95	61.69	59.81	58.27	57.00	55.96	53.84	52.28	51.81	51.72
18.00	91.39	84.25	78.33	73.42	69.36	66.01	63.23	60.95	59.06	57.52	56.25	55.21	53.10	51.56	51.10	51.02
18.25	91.18	83.88	77.84	72.84	68.72	65.33	62.53	60.22	58.33	56.78	55.51	54.47	52.38	50.86	50.42	50.34
18.50	90.96	83.50	77.35	72.27	68.09	64.65	61.83	59.51	57.61	56.05	54.78	53.75	51.67	50.18	49.75	49.67
18.75	90.75	83.13	76.86	71.70	67.47	63.99	61.14	58.80	56.90	55.34	54.07	53.04	50.98	49.52	49.10	49.03
19.00	90.54	82.76	76.38	71.14	66.85	63.33	60.46	58.11	56.20	54.64	53.38	52.35	50.31	48.87	48.46	48.39
20.00	89.69	81.30	74.48	68.94	64.44	60.80	57.85	55.46	53.53	51.98	50.73	49.72	47.77	46.44	46.07	46.01
25.00	85.58	74.41	65.76	59.08	53.91	49.92	46.85	44.48	42.66	41.26	40.19	39.37	37.91	37.09	36.91	36.89
30.00	81.68	68.17	58.20	50.87	45.47	41.50	38.59	36.45	34.89	33.74	32.91	32.30	31.31	30.84	30.76	30.75

PREPAYMENT MORTGAGE YIELD, 30 YEAR TERM 8.50 %

Description: This table shows the yield to prepayment of a monthly payment mortgage purchased at a price in the index.

Example: The yield to prepayment in 10 years of a 8.50 %, 30 year mortgage at a price of 104.00 is 7.89 %.

30 YEAR MORTGAGE PREPAID IN

PRICE	1 yr	2 yr	3 yr	4 yr	5 yr	6 yr	7 yr	8 yr	9 yr	10 yr	11 yr	12 yr	15 yr	20 yr	25 yr	30 yr
140	–	–	–	–	–	1.37	2.14	2.72	3.17	3.52	3.80	4.03	4.52	4.95	5.14	5.20
135	–	–	–	–	1.14	2.12	2.81	3.33	3.72	4.03	4.29	4.49	4.93	5.31	5.48	5.52
130	–	–	–	–	2.05	2.90	3.51	3.96	4.30	4.58	4.80	4.98	5.35	5.68	5.83	5.87
125	–	–	–	1.90	2.99	3.72	4.24	4.62	4.91	5.14	5.33	5.48	5.80	6.08	6.20	6.24
120	–	–	1.58	3.09	3.99	4.58	5.00	5.31	5.55	5.74	5.89	6.02	6.28	6.50	6.60	6.63
119	–	–	1.90	3.33	4.19	4.76	5.16	5.46	5.69	5.87	6.01	6.13	6.38	6.59	6.68	6.71
118	–	–	2.22	3.58	4.40	4.94	5.32	5.60	5.82	5.99	6.13	6.24	6.47	6.68	6.77	6.79
117	–	–	2.54	3.83	4.60	5.12	5.48	5.75	5.95	6.12	6.25	6.35	6.58	6.77	6.85	6.87
116	–	–	2.86	4.08	4.82	5.30	5.64	5.89	6.09	6.24	6.37	6.47	6.68	6.86	6.94	6.96
115	–	–	3.19	4.34	5.03	5.48	5.81	6.04	6.23	6.37	6.49	6.58	6.78	6.95	7.02	7.04
114	–	1.34	3.51	4.60	5.24	5.67	5.97	6.19	6.37	6.50	6.61	6.70	6.88	7.04	7.11	7.13
113	–	1.82	3.85	4.86	5.46	5.86	6.14	6.35	6.51	6.63	6.73	6.82	6.99	7.14	7.20	7.22
112	–	2.30	4.18	5.12	5.68	6.05	6.31	6.50	6.65	6.77	6.86	6.94	7.10	7.23	7.29	7.31
111	–	2.79	4.52	5.38	5.90	6.24	6.48	6.66	6.79	6.90	6.99	7.06	7.21	7.33	7.39	7.40
110	–	3.28	4.86	5.65	6.12	6.43	6.65	6.81	6.94	7.04	7.12	7.18	7.31	7.43	7.48	7.49
109	–	3.78	5.21	5.92	6.35	6.63	6.83	6.97	7.09	7.18	7.25	7.30	7.43	7.53	7.57	7.59
108	–	4.28	5.56	6.20	6.58	6.83	7.00	7.14	7.24	7.32	7.38	7.43	7.54	7.63	7.67	7.68
107	1.42	4.79	5.91	6.47	6.81	7.03	7.18	7.30	7.39	7.46	7.51	7.56	7.65	7.73	7.77	7.78
106	2.40	5.30	6.27	6.75	7.04	7.23	7.36	7.46	7.54	7.60	7.65	7.69	7.77	7.84	7.87	7.87
105	3.39	5.82	6.63	7.04	7.28	7.43	7.55	7.63	7.69	7.74	7.78	7.82	7.88	7.94	7.97	7.97
104	4.39	6.34	7.00	7.32	7.51	7.64	7.73	7.80	7.85	7.89	7.92	7.95	8.00	8.05	8.07	8.07
103.75	4.64	6.48	7.09	7.39	7.57	7.69	7.78	7.84	7.89	7.93	7.96	7.98	8.03	8.08	8.10	8.10
103.50	4.89	6.61	7.18	7.46	7.63	7.75	7.83	7.88	7.93	7.96	7.99	8.02	8.06	8.10	8.12	8.13
103.25	5.14	6.74	7.27	7.54	7.69	7.80	7.87	7.93	7.97	8.00	8.03	8.05	8.09	8.13	8.15	8.15
103.00	5.40	6.87	7.36	7.61	7.76	7.85	7.92	7.97	8.01	8.04	8.06	8.08	8.12	8.16	8.17	8.18
102.75	5.65	7.01	7.46	7.68	7.82	7.90	7.97	8.01	8.05	8.08	8.10	8.12	8.15	8.19	8.20	8.20
102.50	5.91	7.14	7.55	7.75	7.88	7.96	8.01	8.06	8.09	8.11	8.13	8.15	8.18	8.21	8.23	8.23
102.25	6.16	7.27	7.64	7.83	7.94	8.01	8.06	8.10	8.13	8.15	8.17	8.18	8.22	8.24	8.25	8.26
102.00	6.42	7.41	7.74	7.90	8.00	8.06	8.11	8.14	8.17	8.19	8.21	8.22	8.25	8.27	8.28	8.28
101.75	6.68	7.54	7.83	7.97	8.06	8.12	8.16	8.19	8.21	8.23	8.24	8.25	8.28	8.30	8.31	8.31
101.50	6.93	7.68	7.93	8.05	8.12	8.17	8.20	8.23	8.25	8.26	8.28	8.29	8.31	8.33	8.33	8.33
101.25	7.19	7.81	8.02	8.12	8.18	8.22	8.25	8.27	8.29	8.30	8.31	8.32	8.34	8.35	8.36	8.36
101.00	7.45	7.95	8.11	8.20	8.25	8.28	8.30	8.32	8.33	8.34	8.35	8.36	8.37	8.38	8.39	8.39
100.75	7.71	8.08	8.21	8.27	8.31	8.33	8.35	8.36	8.37	8.38	8.39	8.39	8.40	8.41	8.41	8.41
100.50	7.97	8.22	8.30	8.35	8.37	8.39	8.40	8.41	8.41	8.42	8.42	8.43	8.43	8.44	8.44	8.44
100.25	8.23	8.36	8.40	8.42	8.43	8.44	8.45	8.45	8.45	8.46	8.46	8.46	8.46	8.47	8.47	8.47
100.00	8.50	8.50	8.50	8.50	8.50	8.50	8.50	8.50	8.50	8.50	8.50	8.50	8.50	8.50	8.50	8.50
99.75	8.76	8.63	8.59	8.57	8.56	8.55	8.54	8.54	8.54	8.53	8.53	8.53	8.53	8.52	8.52	8.52
99.50	9.02	8.77	8.69	8.65	8.62	8.60	8.59	8.58	8.58	8.57	8.57	8.57	8.56	8.55	8.55	8.55
99.25	9.29	8.91	8.78	8.72	8.68	8.66	8.64	8.63	8.62	8.61	8.61	8.60	8.59	8.58	8.58	8.58
99.00	9.55	9.05	8.88	8.80	8.75	8.71	8.69	8.67	8.66	8.65	8.64	8.64	8.62	8.61	8.61	8.60
98.75	9.82	9.19	8.98	8.87	8.81	8.77	8.74	8.72	8.70	8.69	8.68	8.67	8.65	8.64	8.63	8.63
98.50	10.08	9.33	9.07	8.95	8.87	8.83	8.79	8.77	8.75	8.73	8.72	8.71	8.69	8.67	8.66	8.66
98.25	10.35	9.47	9.17	9.03	8.94	8.88	8.84	8.81	8.79	8.77	8.76	8.74	8.72	8.70	8.69	8.69
98.00	10.62	9.61	9.27	9.10	9.00	8.94	8.89	8.86	8.83	8.81	8.79	8.78	8.75	8.73	8.72	8.72
97.75	10.89	9.75	9.37	9.18	9.07	8.99	8.94	8.90	8.87	8.85	8.83	8.82	8.78	8.76	8.75	8.74
97.50	11.16	9.89	9.47	9.26	9.13	9.05	8.99	8.95	8.92	8.89	8.87	8.85	8.82	8.79	8.78	8.77
97.25	11.43	10.03	9.56	9.33	9.20	9.11	9.04	8.99	8.96	8.93	8.91	8.89	8.85	8.82	8.80	8.80
97	11.70	10.17	9.66	9.41	9.26	9.16	9.09	9.04	9.00	8.97	8.94	8.92	8.88	8.85	8.83	8.83
96	12.79	10.74	10.06	9.72	9.52	9.39	9.30	9.23	9.17	9.13	9.10	9.07	9.02	8.97	8.95	8.94
95	13.90	11.32	10.46	10.04	9.79	9.62	9.50	9.42	9.35	9.30	9.26	9.22	9.15	9.09	9.07	9.06
94	15.02	11.91	10.87	10.36	10.06	9.85	9.71	9.61	9.53	9.46	9.41	9.37	9.29	9.22	9.19	9.18
93	16.15	12.50	11.29	10.69	10.33	10.09	9.92	9.80	9.71	9.63	9.57	9.53	9.43	9.34	9.31	9.30
92	17.29	13.10	11.70	11.01	10.60	10.33	10.14	10.00	9.89	9.81	9.74	9.68	9.57	9.47	9.44	9.43
91	18.45	13.70	12.13	11.35	10.88	10.57	10.36	10.20	10.08	9.98	9.90	9.84	9.71	9.61	9.56	9.55
90	19.63	14.32	12.56	11.68	11.16	10.82	10.58	10.40	10.26	10.16	10.07	10.00	9.86	9.74	9.69	9.68
89	20.82	14.94	12.99	12.02	11.45	11.07	10.80	10.61	10.45	10.34	10.24	10.17	10.01	9.88	9.82	9.81
88	22.02	15.57	13.43	12.37	11.74	11.32	11.03	10.81	10.65	10.52	10.42	10.33	10.16	10.01	9.96	9.94
87	23.24	16.20	13.88	12.72	12.03	11.58	11.26	11.03	10.85	10.70	10.59	10.50	10.31	10.16	10.09	10.08
86	24.47	16.85	14.33	13.07	12.33	11.84	11.49	11.24	11.04	10.89	10.77	10.67	10.47	10.30	10.23	10.22
85	25.72	17.50	14.78	13.43	12.63	12.10	11.73	11.46	11.25	11.08	10.95	10.85	10.63	10.45	10.38	10.36
80	32.23	20.90	17.16	15.31	14.21	13.48	12.97	12.60	12.31	12.09	11.91	11.76	11.47	11.23	11.13	11.11
75	39.22	24.55	19.72	17.33	15.91	14.97	14.32	13.83	13.47	13.18	12.95	12.77	12.39	12.09	11.98	11.95
70	46.74	28.48	22.48	19.51	17.75	16.59	15.78	15.19	14.73	14.38	14.10	13.87	13.42	13.06	12.93	12.90
65	54.90	32.73	25.47	21.88	19.76	18.37	17.39	16.67	16.13	15.71	15.37	15.11	14.57	14.15	14.00	13.97
60	63.79	37.37	28.74	24.49	21.97	20.32	19.17	18.32	17.68	17.19	16.80	16.49	15.87	15.40	15.24	15.21
55	73.56	42.48	32.35	27.36	24.42	22.50	21.16	20.17	19.44	18.87	18.42	18.06	17.36	16.85	16.69	16.65
50	84.39	48.14	36.36	30.58	27.18	24.95	23.41	22.28	21.44	20.79	20.28	19.89	19.11	18.56	18.40	18.37

PREPAYMENT MORTGAGE PRICE

8.75 %

Description: This table shows the price to pay for a monthly payment loan, at a yield rate and assuming prepayment.

Example: The price of a 8.75 %, 30 year mortgage to yield 8.00 %, if prepaid in 6 years, is $ 103.49.

30 YEAR MORTGAGE PREPAID IN

YIELD	1 yr	2 yr	3 yr	4 yr	5 yr	6 yr	7 yr	8 yr	9 yr	10 yr	11 yr	12 yr	15 yr	20 yr	25 yr	30 yr
0.00	108.72	117.38	125.96	134.47	142.89	151.22	159.45	167.56	175.56	183.43	191.15	198.71	220.32	251.58	274.13	283.21
1.00	107.68	115.23	122.65	129.92	137.05	144.03	150.85	157.52	164.02	170.36	176.51	182.48	199.20	222.46	238.44	244.59
2.00	106.66	113.13	119.43	125.54	131.47	137.23	142.79	148.18	153.38	158.40	163.22	167.86	180.58	197.60	208.74	212.84
3.00	105.64	111.07	116.30	121.33	126.16	130.79	135.24	139.49	143.56	147.45	151.15	154.66	164.14	176.33	183.92	186.60
4.00	104.63	109.05	113.26	117.27	121.09	124.71	128.15	131.41	134.50	137.42	140.17	142.76	149.60	158.07	163.09	164.78
4.25	104.38	108.55	112.52	116.28	119.86	123.24	126.45	129.48	132.34	135.04	137.58	139.97	146.23	153.91	158.42	159.92
4.50	104.13	108.06	111.78	115.30	118.64	121.79	124.77	127.58	130.23	132.72	135.06	137.24	142.97	149.91	153.94	155.26
4.75	103.89	107.57	111.04	114.33	117.44	120.37	123.12	125.72	128.16	130.45	132.59	134.59	139.80	146.06	149.64	150.81
5.00	103.64	107.07	110.32	113.37	116.25	118.96	121.50	123.89	126.13	128.22	130.18	132.00	136.72	142.35	145.52	146.55
5.25	103.39	106.59	109.59	112.42	115.07	117.57	119.90	122.09	124.14	126.05	127.82	129.48	133.74	138.76	141.57	142.47
5.50	103.15	106.10	108.87	111.48	113.91	116.20	118.33	120.33	122.18	123.92	125.52	127.02	130.84	135.31	137.78	138.56
5.75	102.90	105.62	108.16	110.54	112.77	114.85	116.78	118.59	120.27	121.83	123.28	124.62	128.03	131.98	134.14	134.81
6.00	102.65	105.14	107.45	109.62	111.63	113.51	115.26	116.89	118.39	119.79	121.08	122.27	125.30	128.77	130.64	131.22
6.25	102.41	104.66	106.75	108.70	110.51	112.20	113.76	115.21	116.55	117.79	118.94	119.99	122.65	125.67	127.28	127.77
6.50	102.17	104.18	106.05	107.79	109.41	110.90	112.29	113.57	114.75	115.84	116.84	117.76	120.08	122.68	124.05	124.46
6.75	101.92	103.71	105.36	106.89	108.31	109.62	110.83	111.95	112.98	113.93	114.79	115.59	117.58	119.80	120.95	121.29
7.00	101.68	103.24	104.67	106.00	107.23	108.36	109.40	110.36	111.24	112.05	112.79	113.47	115.15	117.01	117.97	118.25
7.25	101.44	102.77	103.99	105.12	106.16	107.12	108.00	108.80	109.54	110.22	110.84	111.40	112.80	114.32	115.10	115.32
7.50	101.20	102.30	103.31	104.25	105.10	105.89	106.61	107.27	107.87	108.42	108.93	109.38	110.51	111.73	112.34	112.51
7.75	100.96	101.83	102.64	103.38	104.06	104.68	105.25	105.76	106.24	106.67	107.06	107.41	108.28	109.22	109.68	109.81
8.00	100.72	101.37	101.97	102.52	103.03	103.49	103.90	104.29	104.63	104.95	105.23	105.49	106.12	106.79	107.12	107.21
8.25	100.48	100.91	101.31	101.67	102.01	102.31	102.58	102.83	103.06	103.26	103.45	103.62	104.02	104.45	104.66	104.72
8.50	100.24	100.46	100.65	100.83	101.00	101.15	101.28	101.40	101.51	101.61	101.70	101.79	101.98	102.19	102.29	102.31
8.75	100.00	100.00	100.00	100.00	100.00	100.00	100.00	100.00	100.00	100.00	100.00	100.00	100.00	100.00	100.00	100.00
9.00	99.76	99.55	99.35	99.17	99.01	98.87	98.74	98.62	98.51	98.42	98.33	98.26	98.07	97.88	97.80	97.77
9.25	99.53	99.10	98.71	98.36	98.04	97.75	97.50	97.27	97.06	96.87	96.70	96.55	96.20	95.84	95.67	95.63
9.50	99.29	98.65	98.07	97.55	97.08	96.65	96.27	95.93	95.63	95.35	95.11	94.89	94.38	93.86	93.62	93.56
9.75	99.05	98.20	97.43	96.75	96.13	95.57	95.07	94.63	94.23	93.87	93.55	93.27	92.60	91.94	91.64	91.57
10.00	98.82	97.76	96.81	95.95	95.18	94.50	93.89	93.34	92.85	92.42	92.03	91.69	90.88	90.09	89.74	89.65
10.25	98.58	97.32	96.18	95.16	94.26	93.44	92.72	92.07	91.50	90.99	90.54	90.14	89.21	88.29	87.89	87.79
10.50	98.35	96.88	95.56	94.38	93.34	92.40	91.57	90.83	90.18	89.60	89.08	88.63	87.58	86.56	86.11	86.00
10.75	98.12	96.44	94.94	93.61	92.43	91.37	90.44	89.61	88.88	88.23	87.66	87.16	85.99	84.87	84.40	84.28
11.00	97.89	96.00	94.33	92.85	91.53	90.36	89.33	88.41	87.60	86.89	86.27	85.72	84.45	83.24	82.73	82.61
11.25	97.65	95.57	93.72	92.09	90.64	89.36	88.23	87.23	86.35	85.58	84.90	84.31	82.94	81.66	81.13	81.00
11.50	97.42	95.14	93.12	91.34	89.76	88.37	87.15	86.07	85.13	84.30	83.57	82.94	81.48	80.13	79.58	79.44
11.75	97.19	94.71	92.52	90.59	88.90	87.40	86.09	84.93	83.92	83.04	82.27	81.59	80.06	78.65	78.07	77.94
12.00	96.96	94.29	91.93	89.86	88.04	86.44	85.04	83.81	82.74	81.81	80.99	80.28	78.68	77.21	76.62	76.48
12.25	96.73	93.86	91.34	89.13	87.19	85.49	84.01	82.71	81.58	80.60	79.74	79.00	77.33	75.82	75.21	75.07
12.50	96.50	93.44	90.75	88.41	86.35	84.56	82.99	81.63	80.45	79.42	78.52	77.75	76.02	74.46	73.85	73.71
12.75	96.27	93.02	90.17	87.69	85.52	83.64	81.99	80.57	79.33	78.26	77.33	76.53	74.74	73.15	72.53	72.39
13.00	96.05	92.60	89.60	86.98	84.70	82.73	81.01	79.52	78.23	77.12	76.16	75.33	73.49	71.88	71.26	71.12
13.25	95.82	92.18	89.02	86.28	83.89	81.83	80.04	78.49	77.16	76.01	75.02	74.17	72.28	70.64	70.02	69.88
13.50	95.59	91.77	88.45	85.58	83.09	80.94	79.09	77.48	76.10	74.92	73.90	73.02	71.10	69.44	68.82	68.68
13.75	95.37	91.36	87.89	84.89	82.30	80.07	78.15	76.49	75.07	73.85	72.80	71.91	69.95	68.28	67.66	67.52
14.00	95.14	90.95	87.33	84.21	81.52	79.21	77.22	75.51	74.05	72.80	71.73	70.82	68.83	67.14	66.53	66.40
14.25	94.92	90.54	86.77	83.53	80.75	78.36	76.31	74.55	73.05	71.77	70.68	69.75	67.74	66.04	65.43	65.30
14.50	94.69	90.13	86.22	82.86	79.98	77.52	75.41	73.61	72.07	70.77	69.65	68.71	66.67	64.98	64.37	64.24
14.75	94.47	89.73	85.67	82.20	79.23	76.69	74.53	72.68	71.11	69.78	68.65	67.69	65.63	63.94	63.34	63.22
15.00	94.25	89.33	85.13	81.54	78.48	75.87	73.65	71.77	70.17	68.81	67.66	66.70	64.62	62.93	62.34	62.22
15.25	94.03	88.93	84.59	80.89	77.74	75.07	72.80	70.87	69.24	67.86	66.70	65.72	63.64	61.95	61.37	61.25
15.50	93.80	88.53	84.05	80.24	77.01	74.27	71.95	69.99	68.33	66.93	65.76	64.77	62.67	60.99	60.42	60.31
15.75	93.58	88.14	83.52	79.60	76.29	73.49	71.12	69.12	67.44	66.02	64.83	63.84	61.73	60.06	59.50	59.39
16.00	93.36	87.74	82.99	78.97	75.57	72.71	70.30	68.27	66.56	65.13	63.93	62.93	60.82	59.16	58.61	58.50
16.25	93.14	87.35	82.46	78.34	74.87	71.95	69.49	67.43	65.70	64.25	63.04	62.03	59.93	58.28	57.74	57.64
16.50	92.92	86.96	81.94	77.72	74.17	71.19	68.69	66.60	64.85	63.39	62.18	61.16	59.05	57.42	56.90	56.80
16.75	92.70	86.57	81.42	77.10	73.48	70.45	67.91	65.79	64.02	62.55	61.33	60.31	58.20	56.59	56.08	55.98
17.00	92.49	86.19	80.91	76.49	72.80	69.71	67.14	64.99	63.21	61.72	60.49	59.48	57.37	55.78	55.28	55.18
17.25	92.27	85.80	80.40	75.89	72.12	68.99	66.38	64.21	62.41	60.91	59.68	58.66	56.56	54.99	54.50	54.41
17.50	92.05	85.42	79.89	75.29	71.46	68.27	65.63	63.44	61.62	60.12	58.88	57.86	55.77	54.22	53.74	53.65
17.75	91.83	85.04	79.39	74.69	70.80	67.57	64.89	62.68	60.85	59.34	58.10	57.08	55.00	53.47	53.00	52.92
18.00	91.62	84.66	78.89	74.11	70.15	66.87	64.16	61.93	60.09	58.57	57.33	56.31	54.25	52.74	52.28	52.20
18.25	91.40	84.28	78.39	73.52	69.50	66.18	63.45	61.19	59.34	57.82	56.58	55.56	53.51	52.02	51.58	51.50
18.50	91.19	83.91	77.90	72.95	68.86	65.50	62.74	60.47	58.61	57.09	55.84	54.83	52.79	51.33	50.90	50.82
18.75	90.97	83.54	77.41	72.37	68.23	64.83	62.04	59.76	57.89	56.37	55.12	54.11	52.09	50.65	50.23	50.16
19.00	90.76	83.17	76.93	71.81	67.61	64.17	61.36	59.06	57.19	55.66	54.42	53.41	51.40	49.99	49.58	49.51
20.00	89.91	81.70	75.02	69.59	65.19	61.61	58.72	56.38	54.48	52.96	51.73	50.74	48.81	47.50	47.14	47.08
25.00	85.80	74.79	66.27	59.67	54.57	50.64	47.60	45.26	43.46	42.08	41.02	40.21	38.76	37.94	37.76	37.74
30.00	81.89	68.53	58.67	51.41	46.06	42.13	39.25	37.13	35.58	34.44	33.61	33.01	32.02	31.55	31.47	31.46

Description: This table shows the yield to prepayment of a monthly payment mortgage purchased at a price in the index.

Example: The yield to prepayment in 10 years of a 8.75 %, 30 year mortgage at a price of 104.00 is 8.14 %.

30 YEAR MORTGAGE PREPAID IN

PRICE	1 yr	2 yr	3 yr	4 yr	5 yr	6 yr	7 yr	8 yr	9 yr	10 yr	11 yr	12 yr	15 yr	20 yr	25 yr	30 yr
140	–	–	–	–	–	1.58	2.36	2.93	3.38	3.73	4.01	4.24	4.73	5.16	5.35	5.40
135	–	–	–	–	1.36	2.33	3.03	3.54	3.94	4.25	4.50	4.71	5.14	5.52	5.68	5.73
130	–	–	–	–	2.27	3.12	3.73	4.18	4.52	4.79	5.01	5.19	5.57	5.90	6.04	6.08
125	–	–	–	2.12	3.22	3.95	4.46	4.84	5.14	5.37	5.55	5.70	6.02	6.30	6.42	6.45
120	–	–	1.81	3.32	4.22	4.81	5.23	5.54	5.78	5.97	6.12	6.24	6.50	6.73	6.82	6.85
119	–	–	2.13	3.56	4.42	4.99	5.39	5.69	5.91	6.09	6.24	6.36	6.60	6.82	6.91	6.93
118	–	–	2.45	3.81	4.63	5.17	5.55	5.83	6.05	6.22	6.36	6.47	6.70	6.91	6.99	7.02
117	–	–	2.77	4.06	4.84	5.35	5.71	5.98	6.18	6.35	6.48	6.58	6.80	7.00	7.08	7.10
116	–	–	3.09	4.32	5.05	5.53	5.87	6.13	6.32	6.47	6.60	6.70	6.91	7.09	7.17	7.19
115	–	1.10	3.42	4.57	5.26	5.72	6.04	6.28	6.46	6.60	6.72	6.81	7.01	7.18	7.25	7.27
114	–	1.58	3.75	4.83	5.48	5.90	6.21	6.43	6.60	6.74	6.84	6.93	7.12	7.28	7.34	7.36
113	–	2.06	4.08	5.09	5.69	6.09	6.37	6.58	6.74	6.87	6.97	7.05	7.22	7.37	7.43	7.45
112	–	2.54	4.42	5.36	5.91	6.28	6.54	6.74	6.89	7.00	7.10	7.17	7.33	7.47	7.53	7.54
111	–	3.03	4.76	5.62	6.14	6.48	6.72	6.89	7.03	7.14	7.22	7.29	7.44	7.57	7.62	7.63
110	–	3.52	5.10	5.89	6.36	6.67	6.89	7.05	7.18	7.28	7.35	7.42	7.55	7.67	7.71	7.73
109	–	4.02	5.45	6.16	6.59	6.87	7.07	7.21	7.33	7.41	7.49	7.54	7.66	7.77	7.81	7.82
108	–	4.52	5.80	6.44	6.82	7.07	7.24	7.38	7.48	7.55	7.62	7.67	7.78	7.87	7.91	7.92
107	1.66	5.03	6.16	6.72	7.05	7.27	7.42	7.54	7.63	7.70	7.75	7.80	7.89	7.97	8.01	8.02
106	2.64	5.55	6.51	7.00	7.28	7.47	7.61	7.71	7.78	7.84	7.89	7.93	8.01	8.08	8.11	8.12
105	3.63	6.07	6.88	7.28	7.52	7.68	7.79	7.87	7.94	7.99	8.03	8.06	8.13	8.19	8.21	8.22
104	4.63	6.59	7.24	7.57	7.76	7.89	7.98	8.04	8.09	8.14	8.17	8.19	8.25	8.29	8.31	8.32
103.75	4.88	6.72	7.33	7.64	7.82	7.94	8.02	8.09	8.13	8.17	8.20	8.23	8.28	8.32	8.34	8.34
103.50	5.14	6.85	7.43	7.71	7.88	7.99	8.07	8.13	8.17	8.21	8.24	8.26	8.31	8.35	8.37	8.37
103.25	5.39	6.99	7.52	7.78	7.94	8.04	8.12	8.17	8.21	8.25	8.27	8.29	8.34	8.38	8.39	8.40
103.00	5.64	7.12	7.61	7.86	8.00	8.10	8.17	8.22	8.25	8.28	8.31	8.33	8.37	8.40	8.42	8.42
102.75	5.90	7.25	7.70	7.93	8.06	8.15	8.21	8.26	8.29	8.32	8.34	8.36	8.40	8.43	8.45	8.45
102.50	6.15	7.39	7.80	8.00	8.12	8.20	8.26	8.30	8.33	8.36	8.38	8.40	8.43	8.46	8.47	8.48
102.25	6.41	7.52	7.89	8.08	8.18	8.26	8.31	8.35	8.38	8.40	8.42	8.43	8.46	8.49	8.50	8.50
102.00	6.67	7.66	7.99	8.15	8.25	8.31	8.36	8.39	8.42	8.44	8.45	8.47	8.49	8.52	8.53	8.53
101.75	6.92	7.79	8.08	8.22	8.31	8.36	8.40	8.43	8.46	8.47	8.49	8.50	8.52	8.54	8.55	8.56
101.50	7.18	7.93	8.17	8.30	8.37	8.42	8.45	8.48	8.50	8.51	8.52	8.53	8.56	8.57	8.58	8.58
101.25	7.44	8.06	8.27	8.37	8.43	8.47	8.50	8.52	8.54	8.55	8.56	8.57	8.59	8.60	8.61	8.61
101.00	7.70	8.20	8.36	8.45	8.49	8.53	8.55	8.57	8.58	8.59	8.60	8.60	8.62	8.63	8.63	8.64
100.75	7.96	8.33	8.46	8.52	8.56	8.58	8.60	8.61	8.62	8.63	8.63	8.64	8.65	8.66	8.66	8.66
100.50	8.22	8.47	8.55	8.59	8.62	8.64	8.65	8.66	8.66	8.67	8.67	8.67	8.68	8.69	8.69	8.69
100.25	8.48	8.61	8.65	8.67	8.68	8.69	8.70	8.70	8.70	8.71	8.71	8.71	8.71	8.72	8.72	8.72
100.00	8.75	8.75	8.75	8.75	8.75	8.75	8.75	8.75	8.75	8.75	8.75	8.75	8.75	8.75	8.75	8.75
99.75	9.01	8.88	8.84	8.82	8.81	8.80	8.80	8.79	8.79	8.78	8.78	8.78	8.78	8.77	8.77	8.77
99.50	9.27	9.02	8.94	8.90	8.87	8.86	8.84	8.84	8.83	8.82	8.82	8.82	8.81	8.80	8.80	8.80
99.25	9.54	9.16	9.03	8.97	8.94	8.91	8.89	8.88	8.87	8.86	8.86	8.85	8.84	8.83	8.83	8.83
99.00	9.80	9.30	9.13	9.05	9.00	8.97	8.94	8.93	8.91	8.90	8.89	8.89	8.87	8.86	8.86	8.86
98.75	10.07	9.44	9.23	9.12	9.06	9.02	8.99	8.97	8.96	8.94	8.93	8.92	8.91	8.89	8.89	8.88
98.50	10.34	9.58	9.33	9.20	9.13	9.08	9.04	9.02	9.00	8.98	8.97	8.96	8.94	8.92	8.91	8.91
98.25	10.60	9.72	9.42	9.28	9.19	9.13	9.09	9.06	9.04	9.02	9.01	9.00	8.97	8.95	8.94	8.94
98.00	10.87	9.86	9.52	9.36	9.26	9.19	9.14	9.11	9.08	9.06	9.05	9.03	9.00	8.98	8.97	8.97
97.75	11.14	10.00	9.62	9.43	9.32	9.25	9.19	9.16	9.13	9.10	9.08	9.07	9.04	9.01	9.00	9.00
97.50	11.41	10.14	9.72	9.51	9.38	9.30	9.24	9.20	9.17	9.14	9.12	9.11	9.07	9.04	9.03	9.03
97.25	11.68	10.28	9.82	9.59	9.45	9.36	9.30	9.25	9.21	9.18	9.16	9.14	9.10	9.07	9.06	9.06
97	11.95	10.42	9.92	9.67	9.52	9.42	9.35	9.29	9.25	9.22	9.20	9.18	9.14	9.10	9.09	9.08
96	13.05	11.00	10.32	9.98	9.78	9.65	9.55	9.48	9.43	9.39	9.35	9.33	9.27	9.22	9.21	9.20
95	14.15	11.58	10.72	10.30	10.04	9.88	9.76	9.67	9.61	9.55	9.51	9.48	9.41	9.35	9.33	9.32
94	15.27	12.16	11.13	10.62	10.31	10.11	9.97	9.87	9.79	9.72	9.67	9.63	9.55	9.48	9.45	9.44
93	16.41	12.76	11.55	10.94	10.59	10.35	10.18	10.06	9.97	9.89	9.84	9.79	9.69	9.61	9.57	9.56
92	17.55	13.36	11.97	11.27	10.86	10.59	10.40	10.26	10.15	10.07	10.00	9.95	9.83	9.74	9.70	9.69
91	18.71	13.96	12.39	11.61	11.14	10.84	10.62	10.46	10.34	10.24	10.17	10.11	9.98	9.87	9.83	9.82
90	19.89	14.58	12.82	11.95	11.43	11.08	10.84	10.67	10.53	10.42	10.34	10.27	10.13	10.01	9.96	9.95
89	21.08	15.20	13.26	12.29	11.71	11.34	11.07	10.87	10.72	10.60	10.51	10.43	10.28	10.15	10.09	10.08
88	22.28	15.83	13.70	12.64	12.01	11.59	11.30	11.08	10.92	10.79	10.68	10.60	10.43	10.29	10.23	10.22
87	23.51	16.47	14.14	12.99	12.30	11.85	11.53	11.29	11.12	10.97	10.86	10.77	10.58	10.43	10.37	10.35
86	24.74	17.12	14.60	13.34	12.60	12.11	11.77	11.51	11.32	11.16	11.04	10.95	10.74	10.58	10.51	10.50
85	25.99	17.77	15.05	13.71	12.90	12.38	12.00	11.73	11.52	11.36	11.23	11.12	10.90	10.73	10.66	10.64
80	32.51	21.18	17.44	15.59	14.49	13.77	13.26	12.88	12.59	12.37	12.19	12.05	11.76	11.52	11.43	11.40
75	39.51	24.84	20.01	17.62	16.20	15.27	14.61	14.13	13.76	13.48	13.25	13.07	12.69	12.39	12.28	12.26
70	47.04	28.77	22.77	19.81	18.05	16.90	16.09	15.49	15.04	14.69	14.41	14.19	13.73	13.38	13.25	13.22
65	55.21	33.04	25.78	22.20	20.07	18.68	17.71	16.99	16.45	16.03	15.70	15.43	14.90	14.49	14.35	14.32
60	64.11	37.70	29.07	24.81	22.30	20.65	19.50	18.66	18.02	17.53	17.15	16.84	16.22	15.76	15.61	15.58
55	73.90	42.82	32.69	27.71	24.77	22.85	21.51	20.53	19.80	19.23	18.79	18.44	17.75	17.24	17.08	17.05
50	84.75	48.50	36.73	30.95	27.55	25.33	23.79	22.67	21.83	21.18	20.68	20.29	19.52	18.99	18.83	18.81

Description: This table shows the price to pay for a monthly payment loan, at a yield rate and assuming prepayment.

Example: The price of a 9.00 %, 30 year mortgage to yield 8.00 %, if prepaid in 6 years, is $ 104.65.

30 YEAR MORTGAGE PREPAID IN

YIELD	1 yr	2 yr	3 yr	4 yr	5 yr	6 yr	7 yr	8 yr	9 yr	10 yr	11 yr	12 yr	15 yr	20 yr	25 yr	30 yr
0.00	108.97	117.88	126.72	135.48	144.16	152.74	161.23	169.60	177.86	185.98	193.97	201.79	224.16	256.63	280.15	289.66
1.00	107.93	115.73	123.39	130.91	138.28	145.50	152.56	159.47	166.21	172.77	179.15	185.35	202.73	226.97	243.69	250.16
2.00	106.90	113.62	120.16	126.50	132.67	138.65	144.44	150.04	155.46	160.68	165.71	170.54	183.82	201.64	213.35	217.69
3.00	105.89	111.56	117.02	122.27	127.32	132.17	136.82	141.27	145.53	149.60	153.48	157.18	167.13	179.97	188.00	190.85
4.00	104.88	109.53	113.97	118.19	122.22	126.04	129.67	133.11	136.38	139.46	142.37	145.11	152.36	161.36	166.72	168.54
4.25	104.63	109.03	113.22	117.20	120.98	124.56	127.95	131.16	134.20	137.06	139.75	142.28	148.94	157.13	161.95	163.56
4.50	104.38	108.54	112.48	116.21	119.75	123.10	126.26	129.25	132.06	134.71	137.19	139.52	145.62	153.05	157.37	158.80
4.75	104.13	108.04	111.74	115.24	118.54	121.66	124.60	127.37	129.97	132.41	134.70	136.83	142.40	149.12	152.98	154.25
5.00	103.88	107.55	111.01	114.27	117.35	120.24	122.96	125.52	127.92	130.16	132.26	134.21	139.28	145.34	148.77	149.89
5.25	103.63	107.06	110.28	113.32	116.17	118.84	121.35	123.70	125.90	127.96	129.87	131.65	136.25	141.69	144.73	145.71
5.50	103.39	106.57	109.56	112.37	115.00	117.46	119.77	121.92	123.93	125.80	127.54	129.16	133.31	138.17	140.86	141.71
5.75	103.14	106.09	108.85	111.43	113.84	116.10	118.21	120.17	122.00	123.69	125.27	126.73	130.45	134.77	137.14	137.88
6.00	102.90	105.60	108.13	110.50	112.70	114.76	116.67	118.45	120.10	121.63	123.04	124.35	127.68	131.50	133.56	134.20
6.25	102.65	105.12	107.43	109.58	111.57	113.43	115.16	116.76	118.24	119.61	120.87	122.04	124.98	128.34	130.13	130.68
6.50	102.41	104.65	106.73	108.66	110.46	112.13	113.67	115.10	116.41	117.63	118.75	119.78	122.37	125.29	126.83	127.30
6.75	102.16	104.17	106.03	107.76	109.36	110.84	112.20	113.46	114.63	115.69	116.68	117.58	119.83	122.35	123.66	124.06
7.00	101.92	103.70	105.34	106.86	108.27	109.57	110.76	111.86	112.87	113.80	114.65	115.43	117.36	119.51	120.61	120.94
7.25	101.68	103.23	104.66	105.98	107.19	108.31	109.34	110.28	111.15	111.94	112.67	113.33	114.97	116.77	117.68	117.95
7.50	101.44	102.76	103.98	105.10	106.13	107.08	107.94	108.74	109.46	110.13	110.73	111.28	112.64	114.12	114.86	115.08
7.75	101.20	102.29	103.30	104.23	105.08	105.86	106.57	107.22	107.81	108.35	108.84	109.29	110.38	111.56	112.15	112.31
8.00	100.96	101.83	102.63	103.37	104.04	104.65	105.21	105.72	106.19	106.61	106.99	107.34	108.19	109.09	109.53	109.66
8.25	100.72	101.37	101.97	102.51	103.01	103.47	103.88	104.25	104.59	104.90	105.18	105.44	106.05	106.70	107.01	107.10
8.50	100.48	100.91	101.31	101.67	102.00	102.29	102.57	102.81	103.03	103.23	103.42	103.58	103.98	104.39	104.59	104.64
8.75	100.24	100.45	100.65	100.83	100.99	101.14	101.27	101.39	101.50	101.60	101.69	101.77	101.96	102.16	102.25	102.28
9.00	100.00	100.00	100.00	100.00	100.00	100.00	100.00	100.00	100.00	100.00	100.00	100.00	100.00	100.00	100.00	100.00
9.25	99.76	99.55	99.35	99.18	99.02	98.88	98.75	98.63	98.53	98.43	98.35	98.27	98.09	97.91	97.83	97.81
9.50	99.53	99.10	98.71	98.36	98.05	97.77	97.51	97.29	97.08	96.90	96.73	96.59	96.24	95.89	95.73	95.69
9.75	99.29	98.65	98.08	97.56	97.09	96.67	96.30	95.96	95.66	95.39	95.16	94.94	94.44	93.94	93.71	93.65
10.00	99.05	98.21	97.44	96.76	96.14	95.60	95.10	94.66	94.27	93.92	93.61	93.34	92.69	92.05	91.76	91.69
10.25	98.82	97.76	96.82	95.97	95.21	94.53	93.93	93.39	92.91	92.48	92.10	91.77	90.98	90.22	89.88	89.79
10.50	98.59	97.32	96.19	95.18	94.28	93.48	92.77	92.13	91.57	91.07	90.63	90.24	89.33	88.44	88.06	87.96
10.75	98.35	96.88	95.57	94.41	93.37	92.45	91.63	90.90	90.25	89.69	89.18	88.74	87.71	86.73	86.30	86.20
11.00	98.12	96.45	94.96	93.64	92.46	91.42	90.50	89.69	88.97	88.33	87.77	87.28	86.14	85.06	84.60	84.49
11.25	97.89	96.01	94.35	92.88	91.57	90.42	89.39	88.49	87.70	87.00	86.39	85.85	84.62	83.45	82.96	82.84
11.50	97.66	95.58	93.74	92.12	90.69	89.42	88.30	87.32	86.46	85.70	85.04	84.46	83.13	81.89	81.38	81.25
11.75	97.43	95.15	93.14	91.37	89.81	88.44	87.23	86.17	85.24	84.43	83.72	83.10	81.68	80.37	79.84	79.71
12.00	97.19	94.72	92.55	90.63	88.95	87.47	86.18	85.04	84.05	83.18	82.42	81.77	80.27	78.91	78.35	78.22
12.25	96.96	94.30	91.95	89.90	88.10	86.52	85.13	83.93	82.87	81.96	81.16	80.47	78.90	77.48	76.92	76.78
12.50	96.74	93.87	91.37	89.17	87.25	85.57	84.11	82.83	81.72	80.76	79.92	79.20	77.57	76.10	75.53	75.39
12.75	96.51	93.45	90.78	88.45	86.42	84.64	83.10	81.76	80.59	79.58	78.71	77.95	76.27	74.76	74.18	74.04
13.00	96.28	93.03	90.20	87.74	85.59	83.73	82.11	80.70	79.48	78.43	77.52	76.74	75.00	73.46	72.87	72.74
13.25	96.05	92.62	89.63	87.03	84.78	82.82	81.13	79.66	78.40	77.30	76.36	75.56	73.77	72.20	71.61	71.47
13.50	95.83	92.20	89.06	86.33	83.97	81.93	80.16	78.64	77.33	76.20	75.23	74.40	72.56	70.98	70.38	70.25
13.75	95.60	91.79	88.49	85.64	83.17	81.05	79.22	77.64	76.28	75.12	74.12	73.27	71.39	69.79	69.19	69.06
14.00	95.37	91.38	87.93	84.95	82.39	80.18	78.28	76.65	75.25	74.05	73.03	72.16	70.25	68.63	68.04	67.91
14.25	95.15	90.97	87.37	84.27	81.61	79.32	77.36	75.68	74.24	73.01	71.97	71.08	69.14	67.51	66.92	66.79
14.50	94.92	90.56	86.81	83.60	80.84	78.47	76.45	74.72	73.25	71.99	70.93	70.02	68.06	66.42	65.83	65.71
14.75	94.70	90.16	86.26	82.93	80.08	77.64	75.56	73.79	72.28	70.99	69.91	68.98	67.00	65.36	64.78	64.66
15.00	94.48	89.75	85.71	82.27	79.32	76.82	74.68	72.86	71.32	70.01	68.91	67.97	65.97	64.33	63.75	63.63
15.25	94.25	89.35	85.17	81.61	78.58	76.00	73.81	71.96	70.38	69.05	67.93	66.98	64.96	63.32	62.76	62.64
15.50	94.03	88.95	84.63	80.96	77.84	75.20	72.96	71.06	69.46	68.11	66.97	66.02	63.98	62.35	61.79	61.68
15.75	93.81	88.56	84.10	80.32	77.12	74.41	72.12	70.19	68.56	67.19	66.04	65.07	63.03	61.40	60.85	60.74
16.00	93.59	88.16	83.57	79.68	76.40	73.63	71.29	69.32	67.67	66.28	65.12	64.14	62.10	60.48	59.94	59.83
16.25	93.37	87.77	83.04	79.05	75.69	72.86	70.47	68.47	66.80	65.39	64.22	63.24	61.19	59.58	59.05	58.95
16.50	93.15	87.38	82.51	78.42	74.98	72.09	69.67	67.64	65.94	64.52	63.34	62.35	60.30	58.71	58.19	58.09
16.75	92.93	86.99	81.99	77.80	74.29	71.34	68.88	66.82	65.10	63.67	62.48	61.49	59.43	57.86	57.35	57.25
17.00	92.71	86.60	81.48	77.19	73.60	70.60	68.10	66.01	64.27	62.83	61.63	60.64	58.59	57.03	56.53	56.44
17.25	92.49	86.22	80.97	76.58	72.92	69.87	67.33	65.22	63.46	62.01	60.80	59.81	57.76	56.22	55.74	55.65
17.50	92.28	85.83	80.46	75.98	72.25	69.15	66.57	64.44	62.67	61.20	59.99	59.00	56.96	55.43	54.96	54.87
17.75	92.06	85.45	79.95	75.38	71.59	68.44	65.83	63.67	61.88	60.41	59.20	58.20	56.17	54.67	54.21	54.12
18.00	91.84	85.07	79.45	74.79	70.93	67.73	65.09	62.91	61.12	59.64	58.42	57.42	55.40	53.92	53.47	53.39
18.25	91.63	84.69	78.95	74.20	70.28	67.04	64.37	62.17	60.36	58.88	57.66	56.66	54.65	53.19	52.75	52.68
18.50	91.41	84.32	78.46	73.62	69.64	66.36	63.66	61.44	59.62	58.13	56.91	55.92	53.92	52.48	52.06	51.98
18.75	91.20	83.94	77.97	73.05	69.00	65.68	62.95	60.72	58.89	57.40	56.18	55.19	53.20	51.79	51.37	51.30
19.00	90.98	83.57	77.48	72.48	68.38	65.01	62.26	60.01	58.18	56.68	55.46	54.47	52.50	51.11	50.71	50.64
20.00	90.13	82.10	75.56	70.25	65.93	62.43	59.59	57.30	55.44	53.94	52.73	51.76	49.86	48.57	48.21	48.15
25.00	86.01	75.17	66.77	60.27	55.24	51.35	48.36	46.05	44.27	42.90	41.85	41.05	39.62	38.80	38.62	38.60
30.00	82.10	68.89	59.14	51.95	46.66	42.77	39.91	37.81	36.27	35.14	34.32	33.72	32.74	32.27	32.19	32.18

Description: This table shows the yield to prepayment of a monthly payment mortgage purchased at a price in the index.

Example: The yield to prepayment in 10 years of a 9.00 %, 30 year mortgage at a price of 104.00 is 8.38 %.

30 YEAR MORTGAGE PREPAID IN

PRICE	1 yr	2 yr	3 yr	4 yr	5 yr	6 yr	7 yr	8 yr	9 yr	10 yr	11 yr	12 yr	15 yr	20 yr	25 yr	30 yr
140	–	–	–	–	–	1.79	2.57	3.15	3.59	3.94	4.22	4.45	4.94	5.36	5.55	5.61
135	–	–	–	–	1.57	2.55	3.24	3.76	4.15	4.46	4.71	4.92	5.35	5.73	5.89	5.94
130	–	–	–	1.20	2.49	3.34	3.95	4.40	4.74	5.01	5.23	5.41	5.79	6.11	6.25	6.29
125	–	–	–	2.35	3.44	4.17	4.68	5.07	5.36	5.59	5.77	5.93	6.24	6.52	6.64	6.67
120	–	–	2.04	3.55	4.44	5.04	5.46	5.77	6.01	6.20	6.35	6.47	6.73	6.95	7.05	7.07
119	–	–	2.36	3.79	4.65	5.22	5.62	5.91	6.14	6.32	6.47	6.58	6.83	7.04	7.13	7.16
118	–	–	2.68	4.04	4.86	5.40	5.78	6.06	6.28	6.45	6.58	6.70	6.93	7.13	7.22	7.24
117	–	–	3.00	4.30	5.07	5.58	5.94	6.21	6.41	6.58	6.71	6.81	7.03	7.22	7.30	7.33
116	–	–	3.33	4.55	5.28	5.76	6.11	6.36	6.55	6.71	6.83	6.93	7.14	7.32	7.39	7.41
115	–	1.34	3.65	4.81	5.49	5.95	6.27	6.51	6.69	6.84	6.95	7.05	7.24	7.41	7.48	7.50
114	–	1.81	3.98	5.07	5.71	6.14	6.44	6.66	6.83	6.97	7.08	7.16	7.35	7.51	7.57	7.59
113	–	2.29	4.32	5.33	5.93	6.33	6.61	6.82	6.98	7.10	7.20	7.28	7.46	7.60	7.67	7.68
112	–	2.78	4.66	5.59	6.15	6.52	6.78	6.97	7.12	7.24	7.33	7.41	7.57	7.70	7.76	7.77
111	–	3.27	5.00	5.86	6.37	6.71	6.95	7.13	7.27	7.37	7.46	7.53	7.68	7.80	7.85	7.87
110	–	3.76	5.34	6.13	6.60	6.91	7.13	7.29	7.42	7.51	7.59	7.65	7.79	7.90	7.95	7.96
109	–	4.26	5.69	6.40	6.83	7.11	7.31	7.45	7.56	7.65	7.72	7.78	7.90	8.00	8.05	8.06
108	–	4.77	6.04	6.68	7.06	7.31	7.48	7.62	7.72	7.79	7.86	7.91	8.02	8.11	8.15	8.16
107	1.90	5.28	6.40	6.96	7.29	7.51	7.67	7.78	7.87	7.94	7.99	8.04	8.13	8.21	8.25	8.26
106	2.88	5.79	6.76	7.24	7.53	7.72	7.85	7.95	8.02	8.08	8.13	8.17	8.25	8.32	8.35	8.36
105	3.87	6.31	7.12	7.52	7.76	7.92	8.03	8.12	8.18	8.23	8.27	8.30	8.37	8.43	8.45	8.46
104	4.88	6.84	7.49	7.81	8.00	8.13	8.22	8.29	8.34	8.38	8.41	8.44	8.49	8.54	8.56	8.56
103.75	5.13	6.97	7.58	7.88	8.06	8.18	8.27	8.33	8.38	8.42	8.45	8.47	8.52	8.57	8.58	8.59
103.50	5.38	7.10	7.67	7.96	8.13	8.24	8.32	8.38	8.42	8.45	8.48	8.51	8.55	8.59	8.61	8.61
103.25	5.63	7.23	7.76	8.03	8.19	8.29	8.36	8.42	8.46	8.49	8.52	8.54	8.58	8.62	8.64	8.64
103.00	5.89	7.37	7.86	8.10	8.25	8.34	8.41	8.46	8.50	8.53	8.55	8.57	8.62	8.65	8.66	8.67
102.75	6.14	7.50	7.95	8.18	8.31	8.40	8.46	8.51	8.54	8.57	8.59	8.61	8.65	8.68	8.69	8.69
102.50	6.40	7.63	8.04	8.25	8.37	8.45	8.51	8.55	8.58	8.61	8.63	8.64	8.68	8.71	8.72	8.72
102.25	6.66	7.77	8.14	8.32	8.43	8.50	8.56	8.59	8.62	8.65	8.66	8.68	8.71	8.73	8.75	8.75
102.00	6.91	7.90	8.23	8.40	8.49	8.56	8.60	8.64	8.66	8.68	8.70	8.71	8.74	8.76	8.77	8.78
101.75	7.17	8.04	8.33	8.47	8.56	8.61	8.65	8.68	8.70	8.72	8.74	8.75	8.77	8.79	8.80	8.80
101.50	7.43	8.17	8.42	8.54	8.62	8.67	8.70	8.73	8.75	8.76	8.77	8.78	8.80	8.82	8.83	8.83
101.25	7.69	8.31	8.52	8.62	8.68	8.72	8.75	8.77	8.79	8.80	8.81	8.82	8.83	8.85	8.86	8.86
101.00	7.95	8.45	8.61	8.69	8.74	8.78	8.80	8.82	8.83	8.84	8.85	8.85	8.87	8.88	8.88	8.88
100.75	8.21	8.58	8.71	8.77	8.81	8.83	8.85	8.86	8.87	8.88	8.88	8.89	8.90	8.91	8.91	8.91
100.50	8.47	8.72	8.80	8.84	8.87	8.88	8.90	8.90	8.91	8.92	8.92	8.92	8.93	8.94	8.94	8.94
100.25	8.73	8.86	8.90	8.92	8.93	8.94	8.95	8.95	8.95	8.96	8.96	8.96	8.96	8.97	8.97	8.97
100.00	9.00	9.00	9.00	9.00	9.00	9.00	9.00	9.00	9.00	9.00	9.00	9.00	9.00	9.00	9.00	9.00
99.75	9.26	9.13	9.09	9.07	9.06	9.05	9.04	9.04	9.04	9.03	9.03	9.03	9.03	9.02	9.02	9.02
99.50	9.52	9.27	9.19	9.15	9.12	9.11	9.09	9.09	9.08	9.07	9.07	9.07	9.06	9.05	9.05	9.05
99.25	9.79	9.41	9.29	9.22	9.19	9.16	9.14	9.13	9.12	9.11	9.11	9.10	9.09	9.08	9.08	9.08
99.00	10.05	9.55	9.38	9.30	9.25	9.22	9.19	9.18	9.16	9.15	9.15	9.14	9.13	9.11	9.11	9.11
98.75	10.32	9.69	9.48	9.38	9.31	9.27	9.24	9.22	9.21	9.19	9.18	9.18	9.16	9.14	9.14	9.14
98.50	10.59	9.83	9.58	9.45	9.38	9.33	9.29	9.27	9.25	9.23	9.22	9.21	9.19	9.17	9.17	9.16
98.25	10.86	9.97	9.68	9.53	9.44	9.39	9.35	9.32	9.29	9.27	9.26	9.25	9.22	9.20	9.20	9.19
98.00	11.12	10.11	9.77	9.61	9.51	9.44	9.40	9.36	9.34	9.31	9.30	9.29	9.26	9.23	9.22	9.22
97.75	11.39	10.25	9.87	9.69	9.57	9.50	9.45	9.41	9.38	9.36	9.34	9.32	9.29	9.26	9.25	9.25
97.50	11.66	10.39	9.97	9.76	9.64	9.56	9.50	9.45	9.42	9.40	9.38	9.36	9.32	9.30	9.28	9.28
97.25	11.94	10.54	10.07	9.84	9.70	9.61	9.55	9.50	9.47	9.44	9.41	9.40	9.36	9.33	9.31	9.31
97	12.21	10.68	10.17	9.92	9.77	9.67	9.60	9.55	9.51	9.48	9.45	9.43	9.39	9.36	9.34	9.34
96	13.30	11.25	10.57	10.23	10.03	9.90	9.81	9.74	9.69	9.64	9.61	9.58	9.53	9.48	9.46	9.46
95	14.41	11.83	10.98	10.55	10.30	10.13	10.02	9.93	9.86	9.81	9.77	9.74	9.67	9.61	9.58	9.58
94	15.53	12.42	11.39	10.88	10.57	10.37	10.23	10.12	10.04	9.98	9.93	9.89	9.81	9.74	9.71	9.70
93	16.67	13.01	11.80	11.20	10.85	10.61	10.44	10.32	10.23	10.15	10.10	10.05	9.95	9.87	9.84	9.83
92	17.81	13.62	12.23	11.54	11.12	10.85	10.66	10.52	10.41	10.33	10.26	10.21	10.10	10.00	9.96	9.95
91	18.98	14.23	12.65	11.87	11.41	11.10	10.88	10.72	10.60	10.51	10.43	10.37	10.24	10.14	10.10	10.08
90	20.15	14.84	13.08	12.21	11.69	11.35	11.11	10.93	10.79	10.69	10.60	10.53	10.39	10.27	10.23	10.22
89	21.34	15.47	13.52	12.55	11.98	11.60	11.34	11.14	10.99	10.87	10.78	10.70	10.54	10.42	10.36	10.35
88	22.55	16.10	13.96	12.90	12.27	11.86	11.57	11.35	11.19	11.06	10.95	10.87	10.70	10.56	10.50	10.49
87	23.77	16.74	14.41	13.26	12.57	12.12	11.80	11.56	11.39	11.25	11.13	11.04	10.86	10.70	10.64	10.63
86	25.01	17.39	14.86	13.61	12.87	12.38	12.04	11.78	11.59	11.44	11.32	11.22	11.02	10.85	10.79	10.77
85	26.26	18.04	15.32	13.98	13.18	12.65	12.28	12.00	11.80	11.63	11.50	11.40	11.18	11.00	10.94	10.92
80	32.79	21.46	17.72	15.87	14.77	14.05	13.54	13.16	12.88	12.66	12.48	12.34	12.04	11.81	11.72	11.70
75	39.79	25.12	20.30	17.91	16.49	15.56	14.90	14.42	14.06	13.77	13.55	13.36	13.00	12.70	12.59	12.57
70	47.34	29.07	23.07	20.11	18.35	17.20	16.39	15.80	15.35	15.00	14.72	14.50	14.05	13.70	13.57	13.55
65	55.52	33.35	26.09	22.51	20.39	19.00	18.03	17.31	16.78	16.36	16.03	15.76	15.24	14.83	14.69	14.66
60	64.44	38.02	29.39	25.14	22.63	20.99	19.84	19.00	18.37	17.88	17.49	17.19	16.58	16.13	15.98	15.95
55	74.24	43.16	33.03	28.06	25.12	23.20	21.87	20.89	20.16	19.60	19.16	18.81	18.13	17.64	17.48	17.45
50	85.11	48.86	37.09	31.31	27.92	25.70	24.17	23.05	22.22	21.58	21.08	20.69	19.94	19.42	19.27	19.24

PREPAYMENT MORTGAGE PRICE

Description: This table shows the price to pay for a monthly payment loan, at a yield rate and assuming prepayment.

Example: The price of a 9.25 %, 30 year mortgage to yield 8.00 %, if prepaid in 6 years, is $ 105.82.

30 YEAR MORTGAGE PREPAID IN

YIELD	1 yr	2 yr	3 yr	4 yr	5 yr	6 yr	7 yr	8 yr	9 yr	10 yr	11 yr	12 yr	15 yr	20 yr	25 yr	30 yr
0.00	109.22	118.38	127.47	136.49	145.42	154.27	163.01	171.65	180.16	188.55	196.79	204.87	228.02	261.70	286.20	296.16
1.00	108.18	116.23	124.13	131.89	139.51	146.97	154.28	161.42	168.39	175.19	181.80	188.23	206.26	231.50	248.98	255.78
2.00	107.15	114.11	120.89	127.47	133.87	140.07	146.08	151.90	157.53	162.96	168.20	173.23	187.07	205.71	218.00	222.57
3.00	106.13	112.04	117.73	123.21	128.48	133.54	138.40	143.05	147.51	151.77	155.83	159.69	170.12	183.63	192.11	195.13
4.00	105.12	110.01	114.67	119.12	123.35	127.37	131.19	134.82	138.26	141.51	144.58	147.47	155.13	164.67	170.38	172.32
4.25	104.87	109.51	113.92	118.12	122.10	125.88	129.46	132.85	136.06	139.08	141.93	144.61	151.66	160.36	165.50	167.23
4.50	104.62	109.01	113.18	117.13	120.87	124.41	127.76	130.92	133.90	136.70	139.34	141.81	148.28	156.20	160.83	162.36
4.75	104.37	108.52	112.44	116.15	119.65	122.96	126.08	129.02	131.78	134.38	136.81	139.09	145.02	152.20	156.34	157.71
5.00	104.13	108.02	111.70	115.18	118.45	121.53	124.43	127.15	129.71	132.10	134.34	136.43	141.85	148.34	152.04	153.25
5.25	103.88	107.53	110.97	114.21	117.26	120.12	122.80	125.32	127.67	129.87	131.93	133.84	138.77	144.62	147.92	148.98
5.50	103.63	107.04	110.25	113.26	116.08	118.73	121.20	123.52	125.68	127.69	129.57	131.31	135.78	141.04	143.96	144.89
5.75	103.38	106.56	109.53	112.32	114.92	117.36	119.63	121.75	123.72	125.56	127.26	128.84	132.88	137.58	140.16	140.97
6.00	103.14	106.07	108.82	111.38	113.77	116.00	118.08	120.01	121.81	123.47	125.01	126.44	130.06	134.24	136.51	137.22
6.25	102.89	105.59	108.11	110.45	112.64	114.67	116.55	118.31	119.93	121.43	122.81	124.09	127.33	131.02	133.00	133.61
6.50	102.65	105.11	107.41	109.54	111.52	113.35	115.05	116.63	118.08	119.43	120.66	121.80	124.67	127.91	129.63	130.16
6.75	102.40	104.64	106.71	108.63	110.41	112.05	113.57	114.98	116.28	117.47	118.56	119.57	122.09	124.92	126.39	126.84
7.00	102.16	104.16	106.01	107.73	109.31	110.77	112.12	113.36	114.50	115.55	116.51	117.39	119.58	122.02	123.28	123.65
7.25	101.92	103.69	105.33	106.84	108.23	109.51	110.69	111.77	112.76	113.67	114.51	115.26	117.15	119.22	120.28	120.60
7.50	101.68	103.22	104.64	105.95	107.16	108.26	109.28	110.21	111.06	111.84	112.54	113.19	114.79	116.52	117.40	117.66
7.75	101.43	102.75	103.97	105.08	106.10	107.03	107.89	108.67	109.39	110.04	110.63	111.17	112.49	113.92	114.63	114.83
8.00	101.19	102.29	103.29	104.21	105.05	105.82	106.52	107.16	107.74	108.27	108.75	109.19	110.26	111.40	111.96	112.12
8.25	100.95	101.83	102.62	103.35	104.02	104.62	105.18	105.68	106.14	106.55	106.92	107.26	108.09	108.96	109.39	109.51
8.50	100.71	101.37	101.96	102.50	103.00	103.44	103.85	104.22	104.56	104.86	105.13	105.38	105.98	106.61	106.91	106.99
8.75	100.48	100.91	101.30	101.66	101.99	102.28	102.55	102.79	103.01	103.21	103.38	103.54	103.93	104.33	104.52	104.57
9.00	100.24	100.45	100.65	100.83	100.99	101.13	101.26	101.38	101.49	101.59	101.67	101.75	101.94	102.13	102.22	102.24
9.25	100.00	100.00	100.00	100.00	100.00	100.00	100.00	100.00	100.00	100.00	100.00	100.00	100.00	100.00	100.00	100.00
9.50	99.76	99.55	99.36	99.18	99.02	98.88	98.76	98.64	98.54	98.45	98.36	98.29	98.12	97.94	97.86	97.84
9.75	99.53	99.10	98.72	98.37	98.06	97.78	97.53	97.31	97.10	96.92	96.76	96.62	96.28	95.95	95.79	95.75
10.00	99.29	98.65	98.08	97.57	97.11	96.69	96.32	95.99	95.70	95.43	95.20	94.99	94.50	94.02	93.80	93.74
10.25	99.06	98.21	97.45	96.77	96.16	95.62	95.14	94.70	94.32	93.98	93.67	93.40	92.77	92.15	91.88	91.81
10.50	98.82	97.77	96.83	95.98	95.23	94.56	93.97	93.43	92.96	92.55	92.18	91.85	91.08	90.34	90.02	89.94
10.75	98.59	97.33	96.20	95.20	94.31	93.52	92.81	92.19	91.63	91.14	90.71	90.33	89.44	88.59	88.22	88.13
11.00	98.35	96.89	95.59	94.43	93.40	92.49	91.68	90.96	90.33	89.77	89.28	88.85	87.85	86.89	86.49	86.39
11.25	98.12	96.45	94.97	93.66	92.50	91.47	90.56	89.76	89.05	88.43	87.88	87.40	86.29	85.25	84.81	84.70
11.50	97.89	96.02	94.37	92.90	91.61	90.47	89.46	88.58	87.80	87.11	86.51	85.99	84.78	83.66	83.19	83.07
11.75	97.66	95.59	93.76	92.15	90.73	89.48	88.38	87.41	86.56	85.82	85.17	84.60	83.31	82.11	81.62	81.50
12.00	97.43	95.16	93.16	91.41	89.86	88.50	87.31	86.27	85.36	84.56	83.86	83.25	81.88	80.61	80.10	79.98
12.25	97.20	94.73	92.57	90.67	89.00	87.54	86.26	85.15	84.17	83.32	82.58	81.94	80.48	79.16	78.63	78.51
12.50	96.97	94.31	91.98	89.94	88.15	86.59	85.23	84.04	83.01	82.10	81.32	80.65	79.13	77.75	77.21	77.08
12.75	96.74	93.89	91.39	89.21	87.31	85.65	84.21	82.95	81.86	80.92	80.10	79.39	77.80	76.39	75.83	75.70
13.00	96.51	93.47	90.81	88.50	86.48	84.73	83.21	81.89	80.74	79.75	78.89	78.16	76.51	75.06	74.50	74.37
13.25	96.28	93.05	90.23	87.79	85.66	83.82	82.22	80.84	79.64	78.61	77.72	76.95	75.26	73.77	73.20	73.08
13.50	96.06	92.63	89.66	87.08	84.85	82.92	81.25	79.80	78.56	77.49	76.57	75.78	74.04	72.52	71.95	71.82
13.75	95.83	92.22	89.09	86.38	84.05	82.03	80.29	78.79	77.50	76.39	75.44	74.63	72.84	71.31	70.74	70.61
14.00	95.60	91.81	88.52	85.69	83.25	81.15	79.34	77.79	76.46	75.32	74.34	73.51	71.68	70.13	69.56	69.43
14.25	95.38	91.39	87.96	85.01	82.47	80.29	78.41	76.81	75.44	74.26	73.26	72.41	70.55	68.98	68.41	68.29
14.50	95.15	90.99	87.41	84.33	81.69	79.43	77.50	75.84	74.43	73.23	72.20	71.33	69.45	67.87	67.30	67.18
14.75	94.93	90.58	86.85	83.66	80.93	78.59	76.60	74.90	73.45	72.21	71.17	70.28	68.37	66.79	66.22	66.11
15.00	94.71	90.18	86.30	82.99	80.17	77.76	75.71	73.96	72.48	71.22	70.16	69.26	67.32	65.73	65.18	65.06
15.25	94.48	89.77	85.76	82.34	79.42	76.94	74.83	73.05	71.53	70.25	69.16	68.25	66.30	64.71	64.16	64.05
15.50	94.26	89.37	85.22	81.68	78.68	76.13	73.97	72.14	70.60	69.29	68.19	67.27	65.30	63.72	63.17	63.06
15.75	94.04	88.98	84.68	81.04	77.95	75.33	73.12	71.26	69.68	68.36	67.24	66.31	64.33	62.75	62.21	62.11
16.00	93.82	88.58	84.15	80.39	77.22	74.55	72.29	70.38	68.78	67.44	66.31	65.37	63.38	61.81	61.28	61.18
16.25	93.60	88.19	83.62	79.76	76.51	73.77	71.46	69.53	67.90	66.54	65.40	64.45	62.46	60.89	60.37	60.27
16.50	93.38	87.79	83.09	79.13	75.80	73.00	70.65	68.68	67.03	65.66	64.51	63.55	61.55	60.00	59.49	59.39
16.75	93.16	87.40	82.57	78.51	75.10	72.24	69.85	67.85	66.18	64.79	63.63	62.67	60.67	59.13	58.63	58.54
17.00	92.94	87.02	82.05	77.89	74.41	71.50	69.06	67.04	65.35	63.94	62.78	61.81	59.81	58.28	57.80	57.70
17.25	92.72	86.63	81.53	77.28	73.72	70.76	68.29	66.23	64.53	63.11	61.94	60.97	58.97	57.46	56.98	56.89
17.50	92.50	86.24	81.02	76.67	73.05	70.03	67.52	65.44	63.72	62.29	61.11	60.14	58.15	56.65	56.19	56.10
17.75	92.29	85.86	80.52	76.07	72.38	69.31	66.77	64.67	62.93	61.49	60.31	59.33	57.35	55.87	55.42	55.34
18.00	92.07	85.48	80.01	75.48	71.72	68.60	66.03	63.90	62.15	60.70	59.52	58.54	56.57	55.11	54.67	54.59
18.25	91.85	85.10	79.51	74.89	71.06	67.90	65.30	63.15	61.38	59.93	58.74	57.77	55.80	54.37	53.94	53.86
18.50	91.64	84.73	79.01	74.30	70.42	67.21	64.58	62.41	60.63	59.18	57.99	57.01	55.05	53.64	53.22	53.15
18.75	91.42	84.35	78.52	73.72	69.78	66.53	63.87	61.68	59.90	58.44	57.24	56.27	54.33	52.93	52.52	52.45
19.00	91.21	83.98	78.03	73.15	69.14	65.86	63.17	60.97	59.17	57.71	56.51	55.55	53.61	52.24	51.85	51.78
20.00	90.36	82.50	76.11	70.91	66.68	63.25	60.47	58.22	56.40	54.93	53.74	52.79	50.92	49.64	49.29	49.23
25.00	86.23	75.55	67.27	60.87	55.91	52.08	49.12	46.84	45.08	43.73	42.69	41.90	40.48	39.66	39.49	39.46
30.00	82.31	69.25	59.61	52.50	47.26	43.41	40.57	38.49	36.96	35.85	35.03	34.43	33.46	32.99	32.91	32.90

Description: This table shows the yield to prepayment of a monthly payment mortgage purchased at a price in the index.

Example: The yield to prepayment in 10 years of a 9.25 %, 30 year mortgage at a price of 104.00 is 8.62 %.

30 YEAR MORTGAGE PREPAID IN

PRICE	1 yr	2 yr	3 yr	4 yr	5 yr	6 yr	7 yr	8 yr	9 yr	10 yr	11 yr	12 yr	15 yr	20 yr	25 yr	30 yr
140	–	–	–	–	–	2.01	2.78	3.36	3.80	4.15	4.43	4.66	5.14	5.57	5.76	5.81
135	–	–	–	–	1.79	2.77	3.46	3.97	4.37	4.68	4.93	5.13	5.56	5.94	6.10	6.15
130	–	–	–	1.42	2.71	3.56	4.17	4.62	4.96	5.23	5.45	5.63	6.00	6.33	6.47	6.51
125	–	–	–	2.57	3.67	4.39	4.91	5.29	5.58	5.81	6.00	6.15	6.46	6.74	6.86	6.89
120	–	–	2.27	3.78	4.67	5.27	5.69	6.00	6.24	6.42	6.57	6.70	6.95	7.17	7.27	7.29
119	–	–	2.59	4.02	4.88	5.45	5.85	6.14	6.37	6.55	6.69	6.81	7.05	7.27	7.36	7.38
118	–	–	2.91	4.27	5.09	5.63	6.01	6.29	6.51	6.68	6.81	6.92	7.16	7.36	7.44	7.47
117	–	–	3.23	4.53	5.30	5.81	6.17	6.44	6.64	6.81	6.93	7.04	7.26	7.45	7.53	7.55
116	–	1.10	3.56	4.78	5.51	6.00	6.34	6.59	6.78	6.94	7.06	7.16	7.37	7.54	7.62	7.64
115	–	1.57	3.89	5.04	5.73	6.18	6.50	6.74	6.92	7.07	7.18	7.28	7.47	7.64	7.71	7.73
114	–	2.05	4.22	5.30	5.95	6.37	6.67	6.90	7.07	7.20	7.31	7.40	7.58	7.74	7.80	7.82
113	–	2.53	4.55	5.56	6.16	6.56	6.84	7.05	7.21	7.34	7.44	7.52	7.69	7.83	7.90	7.91
112	–	3.02	4.89	5.83	6.39	6.76	7.02	7.21	7.36	7.47	7.57	7.64	7.80	7.93	7.99	8.01
111	–	3.51	5.24	6.10	6.61	6.95	7.19	7.37	7.50	7.61	7.70	7.77	7.91	8.04	8.09	8.10
110	–	4.00	5.58	6.37	6.84	7.15	7.37	7.53	7.65	7.75	7.83	7.89	8.02	8.14	8.18	8.20
109	–	4.50	5.93	6.64	7.07	7.35	7.54	7.69	7.80	7.89	7.96	8.02	8.14	8.24	8.28	8.29
108	1.17	5.01	6.28	6.92	7.30	7.55	7.72	7.86	7.96	8.03	8.10	8.15	8.26	8.35	8.38	8.39
107	2.14	5.52	6.64	7.20	7.53	7.75	7.91	8.02	8.11	8.18	8.23	8.28	8.37	8.45	8.49	8.49
106	3.13	6.03	7.00	7.48	7.77	7.96	8.09	8.19	8.27	8.33	8.37	8.41	8.49	8.56	8.59	8.60
105	4.12	6.55	7.36	7.77	8.01	8.17	8.28	8.36	8.42	8.47	8.51	8.55	8.61	8.67	8.69	8.70
104	5.12	7.08	7.73	8.06	8.25	8.38	8.47	8.53	8.58	8.62	8.66	8.68	8.74	8.78	8.80	8.81
103.75	5.37	7.21	7.82	8.13	8.31	8.43	8.51	8.58	8.62	8.66	8.69	8.72	8.77	8.81	8.83	8.83
103.50	5.63	7.35	7.92	8.20	8.37	8.48	8.56	8.62	8.67	8.70	8.73	8.75	8.80	8.84	8.85	8.86
103.25	5.88	7.48	8.01	8.28	8.43	8.54	8.61	8.66	8.71	8.74	8.76	8.79	8.83	8.87	8.88	8.89
103.00	6.14	7.61	8.10	8.35	8.49	8.59	8.66	8.71	8.75	8.78	8.80	8.82	8.86	8.90	8.91	8.91
102.75	6.39	7.75	8.20	8.42	8.56	8.64	8.71	8.75	8.79	8.81	8.84	8.85	8.89	8.92	8.94	8.94
102.50	6.65	7.88	8.29	8.50	8.62	8.70	8.75	8.80	8.83	8.85	8.87	8.89	8.92	8.95	8.96	8.97
102.25	6.90	8.02	8.39	8.57	8.68	8.75	8.80	8.84	8.87	8.89	8.91	8.92	8.96	8.98	8.99	8.99
102.00	7.16	8.15	8.48	8.64	8.74	8.81	8.85	8.88	8.91	8.93	8.95	8.96	8.99	9.01	9.02	9.02
101.75	7.42	8.29	8.58	8.72	8.80	8.86	8.90	8.93	8.95	8.97	8.98	9.00	9.02	9.04	9.05	9.05
101.50	7.68	8.42	8.67	8.79	8.87	8.91	8.95	8.97	8.99	9.01	9.02	9.03	9.05	9.07	9.08	9.08
101.25	7.94	8.56	8.77	8.87	8.93	8.97	9.00	9.02	9.03	9.05	9.06	9.07	9.08	9.10	9.10	9.10
101.00	8.20	8.70	8.86	8.94	8.99	9.02	9.05	9.06	9.08	9.09	9.09	9.10	9.12	9.13	9.13	9.13
100.75	8.46	8.83	8.96	9.02	9.05	9.08	9.10	9.11	9.12	9.13	9.13	9.14	9.15	9.16	9.16	9.16
100.50	8.72	8.97	9.05	9.09	9.12	9.13	9.15	9.15	9.16	9.16	9.17	9.17	9.18	9.19	9.19	9.19
100.25	8.98	9.11	9.15	9.17	9.18	9.19	9.20	9.20	9.20	9.21	9.21	9.21	9.21	9.22	9.22	9.22
100.00	9.25	9.25	9.25	9.25	9.25	9.25	9.25	9.25	9.25	9.25	9.25	9.25	9.25	9.25	9.25	9.25
99.75	9.51	9.38	9.34	9.32	9.31	9.30	9.29	9.29	9.29	9.28	9.28	9.28	9.28	9.27	9.27	9.27
99.50	9.77	9.52	9.44	9.40	9.37	9.36	9.34	9.34	9.33	9.32	9.32	9.32	9.31	9.30	9.30	9.30
99.25	10.04	9.66	9.54	9.47	9.44	9.41	9.40	9.38	9.37	9.37	9.36	9.35	9.34	9.34	9.33	9.33
99.00	10.30	9.80	9.63	9.55	9.50	9.47	9.45	9.43	9.42	9.41	9.40	9.39	9.38	9.37	9.36	9.36
98.75	10.57	9.94	9.73	9.63	9.57	9.52	9.50	9.47	9.46	9.45	9.44	9.43	9.41	9.40	9.39	9.39
98.50	10.84	10.08	9.83	9.70	9.63	9.58	9.55	9.52	9.50	9.49	9.47	9.47	9.44	9.43	9.42	9.42
98.25	11.11	10.22	9.93	9.78	9.70	9.64	9.60	9.57	9.54	9.53	9.51	9.50	9.48	9.46	9.45	9.45
98.00	11.38	10.36	10.03	9.86	9.76	9.69	9.65	9.61	9.59	9.57	9.55	9.54	9.51	9.49	9.48	9.48
97.75	11.65	10.50	10.13	9.94	9.83	9.75	9.70	9.66	9.63	9.61	9.59	9.58	9.54	9.52	9.51	9.51
97.50	11.92	10.65	10.23	10.02	9.89	9.81	9.75	9.71	9.68	9.65	9.63	9.61	9.58	9.55	9.54	9.53
97.25	12.19	10.79	10.33	10.09	9.96	9.87	9.80	9.76	9.72	9.69	9.67	9.65	9.61	9.58	9.57	9.56
97	12.46	10.93	10.42	10.17	10.02	9.92	9.85	9.80	9.76	9.73	9.71	9.69	9.65	9.61	9.60	9.59
96	13.56	11.51	10.83	10.49	10.29	10.16	10.06	9.99	9.94	9.90	9.87	9.84	9.78	9.74	9.72	9.72
95	14.67	12.09	11.23	10.81	10.56	10.39	10.27	10.19	10.12	10.07	10.03	9.99	9.92	9.87	9.84	9.84
94	15.79	12.68	11.65	11.13	10.83	10.63	10.49	10.38	10.30	10.24	10.19	10.15	10.07	10.00	9.97	9.96
93	16.93	13.27	12.06	11.46	11.11	10.87	10.70	10.58	10.49	10.41	10.36	10.31	10.21	10.13	10.10	10.09
92	18.08	13.88	12.49	11.80	11.39	11.11	10.92	10.78	10.68	10.59	10.52	10.47	10.36	10.27	10.23	10.22
91	19.24	14.49	12.91	12.13	11.67	11.36	11.15	10.99	10.87	10.77	10.70	10.63	10.51	10.40	10.36	10.35
90	20.42	15.10	13.35	12.47	11.96	11.61	11.37	11.19	11.06	10.95	10.87	10.80	10.66	10.54	10.50	10.49
89	21.61	15.73	13.78	12.82	12.25	11.87	11.60	11.40	11.26	11.14	11.04	10.97	10.81	10.69	10.64	10.62
88	22.82	16.36	14.23	13.17	12.54	12.13	11.83	11.62	11.45	11.33	11.22	11.14	10.97	10.83	10.78	10.76
87	24.04	17.00	14.68	13.52	12.84	12.39	12.07	11.83	11.66	11.52	11.41	11.32	11.13	10.98	10.92	10.91
86	25.28	17.65	15.13	13.88	13.14	12.65	12.31	12.05	11.86	11.71	11.59	11.49	11.29	11.13	11.07	11.05
85	26.54	18.31	15.60	14.25	13.45	12.92	12.55	12.28	12.07	11.91	11.78	11.67	11.46	11.28	11.22	11.20
80	33.07	21.74	18.00	16.15	15.05	14.33	13.82	13.45	13.16	12.94	12.76	12.62	12.33	12.10	12.01	11.99
75	40.08	25.41	20.58	18.20	16.78	15.85	15.20	14.72	14.35	14.07	13.84	13.66	13.30	13.01	12.90	12.88
70	47.64	29.37	23.37	20.41	18.66	17.51	16.70	16.11	15.66	15.31	15.03	14.81	14.37	14.02	13.90	13.87
65	55.83	33.67	26.41	22.82	20.71	19.32	18.35	17.64	17.10	16.68	16.36	16.09	15.57	15.17	15.04	15.01
60	64.77	38.35	29.72	25.47	22.96	21.32	20.18	19.34	18.71	18.22	17.84	17.54	16.94	16.49	16.35	16.32
55	74.59	43.50	33.38	28.40	25.47	23.56	22.23	21.26	20.53	19.97	19.53	19.19	18.51	18.03	17.88	17.86
50	85.47	49.22	37.45	31.68	28.29	26.08	24.55	23.44	22.61	21.98	21.48	21.10	20.36	19.85	19.71	19.68

PREPAYMENT MORTGAGE PRICE

9.50 %

Description: This table shows the price to pay for a monthly payment loan, at a yield rate and assuming prepayment.

Example: The price of a 9.50 %, 30 year mortgage to yield 8.00 %, if prepaid in 6 years, is $ 106.99.

30 YEAR MORTGAGE PREPAID IN

YIELD	1 yr	2 yr	3 yr	4 yr	5 yr	6 yr	7 yr	8 yr	9 yr	10 yr	11 yr	12 yr	15 yr	20 yr	25 yr	30 yr
0.00	109.47	118.89	128.23	137.50	146.69	155.79	164.80	173.69	182.47	191.11	199.61	207.96	231.88	266.79	292.29	302.71
1.00	108.43	116.72	124.88	132.88	140.74	148.44	155.99	163.37	170.58	177.61	184.46	191.11	209.81	236.04	254.30	261.43
2.00	107.40	114.60	121.62	128.44	135.06	141.49	147.73	153.77	159.61	165.25	170.69	175.92	190.34	209.79	222.68	227.49
3.00	106.38	112.53	118.45	124.16	129.65	134.92	139.98	144.84	149.49	153.93	158.17	162.22	173.13	187.30	196.25	199.44
4.00	105.37	110.49	115.38	120.04	124.48	128.70	132.72	136.53	140.14	143.56	146.79	149.84	157.91	168.00	174.06	176.13
4.25	105.12	109.99	114.63	119.04	123.22	127.20	130.97	134.54	137.92	141.10	144.11	146.93	154.39	163.61	169.08	170.93
4.50	104.87	109.49	113.88	118.04	121.99	125.72	129.25	132.59	135.74	138.70	141.49	144.10	150.97	159.37	164.30	165.95
4.75	104.62	108.99	113.13	117.05	120.76	124.26	127.56	130.67	133.60	136.35	138.93	141.34	147.65	155.30	159.73	161.19
5.00	104.37	108.50	112.40	116.08	119.55	122.82	125.90	128.79	131.50	134.05	136.43	138.65	144.43	151.37	155.34	156.64
5.25	104.12	108.00	111.66	115.11	118.35	121.40	124.26	126.94	129.45	131.79	133.98	136.02	141.30	147.58	151.13	152.27
5.50	103.87	107.51	110.94	114.15	117.17	120.00	122.64	125.12	127.43	129.59	131.60	133.46	138.26	143.92	147.08	148.09
5.75	103.63	107.03	110.22	113.20	116.00	118.61	121.06	123.33	125.46	127.43	129.27	130.96	135.32	140.40	143.20	144.09
6.00	103.38	106.54	109.50	112.26	114.84	117.25	119.49	121.58	123.52	125.32	126.99	128.53	132.46	137.00	139.47	140.25
6.25	103.13	106.06	108.79	111.33	113.70	115.91	117.95	119.86	121.62	123.25	124.76	126.15	129.68	133.72	135.89	136.57
6.50	102.89	105.58	108.08	110.41	112.57	114.58	116.44	118.16	119.76	121.23	122.58	123.83	126.98	130.55	132.45	133.03
6.75	102.64	105.10	107.38	109.50	111.46	113.27	114.95	116.50	117.93	119.25	120.46	121.57	124.36	127.50	129.14	129.64
7.00	102.40	104.63	106.69	108.59	110.35	111.98	113.48	114.86	116.14	117.31	118.38	119.36	121.81	124.55	125.96	126.39
7.25	102.16	104.15	106.00	107.70	109.26	110.71	112.04	113.26	114.38	115.41	116.35	117.21	119.34	121.70	122.90	123.26
7.50	101.92	103.68	105.31	106.81	108.19	109.45	110.61	111.68	112.66	113.55	114.36	115.10	116.94	118.94	119.96	120.26
7.75	101.67	103.21	104.63	105.93	107.12	108.21	109.21	110.13	110.97	111.73	112.42	113.05	114.61	116.29	117.13	117.37
8.00	101.43	102.75	103.95	105.06	106.07	106.99	107.84	108.61	109.31	109.95	110.52	111.05	112.34	113.72	114.40	114.59
8.25	101.19	102.28	103.28	104.19	105.03	105.79	106.48	107.11	107.68	108.20	108.67	109.10	110.13	111.23	111.77	111.92
8.50	100.95	101.82	102.62	103.34	104.00	104.60	105.14	105.64	106.08	106.49	106.86	107.19	107.99	108.83	109.24	109.36
8.75	100.71	101.36	101.95	102.49	102.98	103.42	103.83	104.19	104.52	104.82	105.08	105.33	105.91	106.51	106.80	106.88
9.00	100.48	100.91	101.30	101.65	101.98	102.27	102.53	102.77	102.98	103.18	103.35	103.51	103.88	104.27	104.45	104.50
9.25	100.24	100.45	100.65	100.82	100.98	101.13	101.26	101.37	101.48	101.57	101.66	101.73	101.91	102.10	102.19	102.21
9.50	100.00	100.00	100.00	100.00	100.00	100.00	100.00	100.00	100.00	100.00	100.00	100.00	100.00	100.00	100.00	100.00
9.75	99.76	99.55	99.36	99.18	99.03	98.89	98.76	98.65	98.55	98.46	98.38	98.31	98.14	97.97	97.89	97.87
10.00	99.53	99.10	98.72	98.38	98.07	97.79	97.55	97.33	97.13	96.95	96.80	96.66	96.33	96.00	95.85	95.82
10.25	99.29	98.66	98.09	97.58	97.12	96.71	96.35	96.02	95.73	95.47	95.25	95.04	94.57	94.10	93.89	93.83
10.50	99.06	98.21	97.46	96.78	96.18	95.65	95.17	94.74	94.36	94.03	93.73	93.47	92.85	92.25	91.99	91.92
10.75	98.82	97.77	96.84	96.00	95.26	94.59	94.00	93.48	93.02	92.61	92.25	91.93	91.18	90.47	90.16	90.08
11.00	98.59	97.33	96.22	95.22	94.34	93.56	92.86	92.25	91.70	91.22	90.80	90.42	89.56	88.74	88.38	88.30
11.25	98.36	96.90	95.60	94.45	93.43	92.53	91.73	91.03	90.41	89.86	89.38	88.96	87.98	87.06	86.67	86.57
11.50	98.12	96.46	94.99	93.69	92.54	91.52	90.62	89.83	89.14	88.53	87.99	87.52	86.44	85.43	85.01	84.91
11.75	97.89	96.03	94.38	92.93	91.65	90.52	89.53	88.66	87.89	87.22	86.63	86.12	84.95	83.86	83.41	83.30
12.00	97.66	95.60	93.78	92.18	90.78	89.54	88.45	87.50	86.67	85.94	85.30	84.75	83.49	82.33	81.86	81.75
12.25	97.43	95.17	93.19	91.44	89.91	88.57	87.39	86.37	85.47	84.69	84.00	83.41	82.07	80.85	80.36	80.24
12.50	97.20	94.75	92.59	90.71	89.06	87.61	86.35	85.25	84.29	83.46	82.73	82.11	80.69	79.41	78.91	78.79
12.75	96.97	94.32	92.00	89.98	88.21	86.67	85.32	84.15	83.14	82.25	81.49	80.83	79.35	78.02	77.50	77.38
13.00	96.74	93.90	91.42	89.26	87.37	85.73	84.31	83.07	82.00	81.07	80.27	79.58	78.04	76.67	76.13	76.01
13.25	96.52	93.48	90.84	88.54	86.55	84.81	83.31	82.01	80.89	79.92	79.08	78.36	76.76	75.35	74.81	74.69
13.50	96.29	93.06	90.26	87.83	85.73	83.91	82.33	80.97	79.79	78.78	77.91	77.17	75.51	74.08	73.53	73.41
13.75	96.06	92.65	89.69	87.13	84.92	83.01	81.36	79.94	78.72	77.67	76.77	76.00	74.30	72.84	72.29	72.17
14.00	95.83	92.23	89.12	86.44	84.12	82.13	80.41	78.93	77.67	76.58	75.65	74.86	73.12	71.63	71.09	70.97
14.25	95.61	91.82	88.56	85.75	83.33	81.26	79.47	77.94	76.63	75.51	74.56	73.74	71.97	70.47	69.92	69.80
14.50	95.38	91.41	88.00	85.07	82.55	80.40	78.55	76.97	75.62	74.47	73.49	72.65	70.85	69.33	68.78	68.67
14.75	95.16	91.01	87.44	84.39	81.78	79.55	77.64	76.01	74.62	73.44	72.44	71.59	69.75	68.23	67.68	67.57
15.00	94.94	90.60	86.89	83.72	81.02	78.71	76.74	75.07	73.64	72.43	71.41	70.55	68.69	67.15	66.61	66.50
15.25	94.71	90.20	86.35	83.06	80.26	77.88	75.86	74.14	72.68	71.45	70.41	69.53	67.64	66.11	65.57	65.46
15.50	94.49	89.80	85.80	82.40	79.52	77.07	74.99	73.23	71.74	70.48	69.42	68.53	66.63	65.09	64.57	64.46
15.75	94.27	89.40	85.26	81.75	78.78	76.26	74.13	72.33	70.81	69.53	68.46	67.55	65.64	64.11	63.58	63.48
16.00	94.05	89.00	84.73	81.11	78.05	75.47	73.29	71.45	69.90	68.60	67.51	66.60	64.67	63.14	62.63	62.53
16.25	93.83	88.60	84.19	80.47	77.33	74.68	72.45	70.58	69.01	67.69	66.59	65.67	63.73	62.21	61.70	61.60
16.50	93.60	88.21	83.67	79.84	76.62	73.91	71.64	69.73	68.13	66.80	65.68	64.75	62.81	61.30	60.80	60.71
16.75	93.38	87.82	83.14	79.21	75.91	73.15	70.83	68.89	67.27	65.92	64.79	63.86	61.91	60.41	59.92	59.83
17.00	93.17	87.43	82.62	78.59	75.21	72.39	70.03	68.06	66.42	65.06	63.92	62.98	61.04	59.55	59.07	58.98
17.25	92.95	87.04	82.10	77.97	74.53	71.65	69.25	67.25	65.59	64.21	63.07	62.13	60.18	58.71	58.24	58.15
17.50	92.73	86.66	81.59	77.36	73.84	70.91	68.48	66.45	64.78	63.39	62.24	61.29	59.35	57.89	57.43	57.34
17.75	92.51	86.27	81.08	76.76	73.17	70.19	67.72	65.67	63.97	62.57	61.42	60.47	58.53	57.09	56.64	56.56
18.00	92.29	85.89	80.57	76.16	72.50	69.47	66.97	64.90	63.19	61.78	60.62	59.67	57.73	56.31	55.87	55.79
18.25	92.08	85.51	80.07	75.57	71.85	68.77	66.23	64.14	62.41	61.00	59.83	58.88	56.96	55.55	55.12	55.05
18.50	91.86	85.13	79.57	74.98	71.19	68.07	65.50	63.39	61.65	60.23	59.06	58.11	56.20	54.81	54.39	54.32
18.75	91.65	84.76	79.08	74.40	70.55	67.38	64.79	62.65	60.91	59.48	58.31	57.36	55.45	54.09	53.68	53.61
19.00	91.43	84.38	78.59	73.82	69.91	66.71	64.08	61.93	60.17	58.74	57.57	56.62	54.73	53.38	52.99	52.92
20.00	90.58	82.90	76.65	71.57	67.44	64.08	61.36	59.15	57.36	55.92	54.76	53.82	51.99	50.73	50.38	50.32
25.00	86.45	75.93	67.78	61.47	56.58	52.80	49.88	47.63	45.89	44.56	43.53	42.75	41.34	40.54	40.36	40.34
30.00	82.52	69.61	60.08	53.05	47.86	44.05	41.24	39.18	37.66	36.56	35.75	35.15	34.18	33.72	33.64	33.63

PREPAYMENT MORTGAGE YIELD, 30 YEAR TERM — 9.50 %

Description: This table shows the yield to prepayment of a monthly payment mortgage purchased at a price in the index.

Example: The yield to prepayment in 10 years of a 9.50 %, 30 year mortgage at a price of 104.00 is 8.87 %.

30 YEAR MORTGAGE PREPAID IN

PRICE	1 yr	2 yr	3 yr	4 yr	5 yr	6 yr	7 yr	8 yr	9 yr	10 yr	11 yr	12 yr	15 yr	20 yr	25 yr	30 yr
140	–	–	–	–	1.12	2.22	2.99	3.57	4.01	4.36	4.64	4.87	5.35	5.77	5.96	6.01
135	–	–	–	–	2.01	2.98	3.67	4.19	4.58	4.89	5.14	5.34	5.77	6.15	6.31	6.35
130	–	–	–	1.64	2.93	3.78	4.39	4.83	5.18	5.45	5.67	5.84	6.22	6.54	6.68	6.72
125	–	–	–	2.80	3.89	4.62	5.13	5.51	5.80	6.03	6.22	6.37	6.68	6.96	7.07	7.10
120	–	–	2.50	4.01	4.90	5.49	5.91	6.22	6.46	6.65	6.80	6.92	7.18	7.40	7.49	7.52
119	–	–	2.82	4.25	5.11	5.67	6.07	6.37	6.60	6.78	6.92	7.04	7.28	7.49	7.58	7.60
118	–	–	3.14	4.51	5.32	5.86	6.24	6.52	6.74	6.91	7.04	7.15	7.38	7.58	7.67	7.69
117	–	–	3.46	4.76	5.53	6.04	6.40	6.67	6.87	7.04	7.16	7.27	7.49	7.68	7.76	7.78
116	–	1.33	3.79	5.02	5.74	6.23	6.57	6.82	7.01	7.17	7.29	7.39	7.59	7.77	7.85	7.87
115	–	1.81	4.12	5.27	5.96	6.42	6.74	6.97	7.16	7.30	7.41	7.51	7.70	7.87	7.94	7.96
114	–	2.28	4.45	5.54	6.18	6.61	6.91	7.13	7.30	7.44	7.54	7.63	7.81	7.97	8.03	8.05
113	–	2.77	4.79	5.80	6.40	6.80	7.08	7.29	7.44	7.57	7.67	7.75	7.92	8.07	8.13	8.14
112	–	3.25	5.13	6.07	6.62	6.99	7.25	7.44	7.59	7.71	7.80	7.88	8.03	8.17	8.22	8.24
111	–	3.74	5.47	6.33	6.85	7.19	7.43	7.60	7.74	7.85	7.93	8.00	8.15	8.27	8.32	8.33
110	–	4.24	5.82	6.61	7.08	7.39	7.60	7.77	7.89	7.99	8.07	8.13	8.26	8.37	8.42	8.43
109	–	4.74	6.17	6.88	7.31	7.59	7.78	7.93	8.04	8.13	8.20	8.26	8.38	8.48	8.52	8.53
108	1.41	5.25	6.52	7.16	7.54	7.79	7.96	8.10	8.20	8.27	8.34	8.39	8.49	8.58	8.62	8.63
107	2.38	5.76	6.88	7.44	7.77	7.99	8.15	8.26	8.35	8.42	8.48	8.52	8.61	8.69	8.72	8.73
106	3.37	6.28	7.24	7.72	8.01	8.20	8.33	8.43	8.51	8.57	8.62	8.65	8.73	8.80	8.83	8.84
105	4.36	6.80	7.61	8.01	8.25	8.41	8.52	8.60	8.67	8.72	8.76	8.79	8.86	8.91	8.94	8.94
104	5.37	7.33	7.98	8.30	8.49	8.62	8.71	8.78	8.83	8.87	8.90	8.93	8.98	9.03	9.04	9.05
103.75	5.62	7.46	8.07	8.37	8.56	8.68	8.76	8.82	8.87	8.91	8.94	8.96	9.01	9.05	9.07	9.08
103.50	5.87	7.59	8.16	8.45	8.62	8.73	8.81	8.87	8.91	8.95	8.97	9.00	9.04	9.08	9.10	9.10
103.25	6.13	7.73	8.26	8.52	8.68	8.78	8.86	8.91	8.95	8.98	9.01	9.03	9.07	9.11	9.13	9.13
103.00	6.38	7.86	8.35	8.59	8.74	8.84	8.90	8.95	8.99	9.02	9.05	9.07	9.11	9.14	9.15	9.16
102.75	6.64	7.99	8.44	8.67	8.80	8.89	8.95	9.00	9.03	9.06	9.08	9.10	9.14	9.17	9.18	9.19
102.50	6.89	8.13	8.54	8.74	8.86	8.94	9.00	9.04	9.07	9.10	9.12	9.14	9.17	9.20	9.21	9.21
102.25	7.15	8.26	8.63	8.82	8.93	9.00	9.05	9.09	9.12	9.14	9.16	9.17	9.20	9.23	9.24	9.24
102.00	7.41	8.40	8.73	8.89	8.99	9.05	9.10	9.13	9.16	9.18	9.19	9.21	9.23	9.26	9.27	9.27
101.75	7.67	8.53	8.82	8.97	9.05	9.11	9.15	9.18	9.20	9.22	9.23	9.24	9.27	9.29	9.29	9.30
101.50	7.93	8.67	8.92	9.04	9.11	9.16	9.20	9.22	9.24	9.26	9.27	9.28	9.30	9.32	9.32	9.32
101.25	8.19	8.81	9.01	9.12	9.18	9.22	9.25	9.27	9.28	9.30	9.31	9.31	9.33	9.35	9.35	9.35
101.00	8.45	8.94	9.11	9.19	9.24	9.27	9.30	9.31	9.33	9.34	9.34	9.35	9.36	9.37	9.38	9.38
100.75	8.71	9.08	9.21	9.27	9.30	9.33	9.35	9.36	9.37	9.38	9.38	9.39	9.40	9.40	9.41	9.41
100.50	8.97	9.22	9.30	9.34	9.37	9.38	9.40	9.40	9.41	9.41	9.42	9.42	9.43	9.43	9.44	9.44
100.25	9.23	9.36	9.40	9.42	9.43	9.44	9.44	9.45	9.45	9.45	9.46	9.46	9.46	9.46	9.47	9.47
100.00	9.50	9.50	9.50	9.50	9.50	9.50	9.50	9.50	9.50	9.50	9.50	9.50	9.50	9.50	9.50	9.50
99.75	9.76	9.63	9.59	9.57	9.56	9.55	9.55	9.54	9.54	9.54	9.53	9.53	9.53	9.53	9.52	9.52
99.50	10.02	9.77	9.69	9.65	9.62	9.61	9.60	9.59	9.58	9.58	9.57	9.57	9.56	9.56	9.55	9.55
99.25	10.29	9.91	9.79	9.72	9.69	9.66	9.65	9.63	9.62	9.62	9.61	9.61	9.59	9.59	9.58	9.58
99.00	10.56	10.05	9.89	9.80	9.75	9.72	9.70	9.68	9.67	9.66	9.65	9.64	9.63	9.62	9.61	9.61
98.75	10.82	10.19	9.98	9.88	9.82	9.78	9.75	9.73	9.71	9.70	9.69	9.68	9.66	9.65	9.64	9.64
98.50	11.09	10.33	10.08	9.96	9.88	9.83	9.80	9.77	9.75	9.74	9.73	9.72	9.70	9.68	9.67	9.67
98.25	11.36	10.47	10.18	10.03	9.95	9.89	9.85	9.82	9.80	9.78	9.77	9.75	9.73	9.71	9.70	9.70
98.00	11.63	10.62	10.28	10.11	10.01	9.95	9.90	9.87	9.84	9.82	9.80	9.79	9.76	9.74	9.73	9.73
97.75	11.90	10.76	10.38	10.19	10.08	10.00	9.95	9.91	9.89	9.86	9.84	9.83	9.80	9.77	9.76	9.76
97.50	12.17	10.90	10.48	10.27	10.14	10.06	10.00	9.96	9.93	9.90	9.88	9.87	9.83	9.80	9.79	9.79
97.25	12.44	11.04	10.58	10.35	10.21	10.12	10.06	10.01	9.97	9.95	9.92	9.90	9.87	9.84	9.82	9.82
97	12.71	11.19	10.68	10.43	10.28	10.18	10.11	10.06	10.02	9.99	9.96	9.94	9.90	9.87	9.85	9.85
96	13.81	11.76	11.08	10.74	10.54	10.41	10.32	10.25	10.20	10.16	10.12	10.10	10.04	10.00	9.98	9.97
95	14.92	12.35	11.49	11.07	10.81	10.65	10.53	10.44	10.38	10.33	10.29	10.25	10.18	10.13	10.10	10.10
94	16.05	12.94	11.90	11.39	11.09	10.89	10.75	10.64	10.56	10.50	10.45	10.41	10.33	10.26	10.23	10.22
93	17.18	13.53	12.32	11.72	11.37	11.13	10.96	10.84	10.75	10.68	10.62	10.57	10.47	10.39	10.36	10.35
92	18.34	14.14	12.75	12.06	11.65	11.38	11.19	11.05	10.94	10.85	10.79	10.73	10.62	10.53	10.49	10.48
91	19.50	14.75	13.18	12.39	11.93	11.63	11.41	11.25	11.13	11.04	10.96	10.90	10.77	10.67	10.63	10.62
90	20.68	15.37	13.61	12.74	12.22	11.88	11.64	11.46	11.32	11.22	11.13	11.07	10.93	10.81	10.77	10.76
89	21.87	15.99	14.05	13.08	12.51	12.13	11.87	11.67	11.52	11.41	11.31	11.24	11.08	10.96	10.91	10.90
88	23.08	16.63	14.50	13.44	12.81	12.39	12.10	11.89	11.72	11.60	11.49	11.41	11.24	11.10	11.05	11.04
87	24.31	17.27	14.95	13.79	13.11	12.66	12.34	12.11	11.93	11.79	11.68	11.59	11.40	11.25	11.20	11.18
86	25.55	17.92	15.40	14.15	13.41	12.92	12.58	12.33	12.13	11.98	11.86	11.77	11.57	11.41	11.35	11.33
85	26.81	18.58	15.87	14.52	13.72	13.19	12.82	12.55	12.34	12.18	12.05	11.95	11.74	11.56	11.50	11.48
80	33.35	22.02	18.28	16.43	15.33	14.61	14.10	13.73	13.45	13.23	13.05	12.91	12.62	12.39	12.31	12.29
75	40.37	25.70	20.87	18.49	17.07	16.14	15.49	15.01	14.65	14.37	14.14	13.96	13.60	13.31	13.21	13.19
70	47.94	29.67	23.68	20.71	18.96	17.81	17.01	16.42	15.97	15.62	15.35	15.13	14.69	14.35	14.23	14.20
65	56.14	33.98	26.72	23.14	21.02	19.64	18.67	17.96	17.43	17.01	16.69	16.43	15.91	15.52	15.39	15.36
60	65.09	38.68	30.05	25.80	23.30	21.66	20.52	19.68	19.05	18.57	18.19	17.89	17.30	16.86	16.72	16.70
55	74.93	43.84	33.72	28.75	25.82	23.91	22.58	21.62	20.89	20.34	19.91	19.56	18.90	18.43	18.29	18.26
50	85.84	49.58	37.82	32.05	28.66	26.46	24.93	23.83	23.00	22.37	21.89	21.51	20.78	20.29	20.15	20.12

Description: This table shows the price to pay for a monthly payment loan, at a yield rate and assuming prepayment.

Example: The price of a 9.75 %, 30 year mortgage to yield 8.00 %, if prepaid in 6 years, is $ 108.16.

30 YEAR MORTGAGE PREPAID IN

YIELD	1 yr	2 yr	3 yr	4 yr	5 yr	6 yr	7 yr	8 yr	9 yr	10 yr	11 yr	12 yr	15 yr	20 yr	25 yr	30 yr
0.00	109.72	119.39	128.99	138.51	147.96	157.32	166.58	175.73	184.77	193.68	202.44	211.05	235.75	271.90	298.42	309.30
1.00	108.68	117.22	125.62	133.87	141.97	149.92	157.70	165.32	172.77	180.03	187.11	193.99	213.36	240.61	259.65	267.12
2.00	107.65	115.10	122.35	129.40	136.26	142.92	149.38	155.64	161.69	167.54	173.19	178.62	193.61	213.89	227.38	232.44
3.00	106.62	113.01	119.17	125.10	130.81	136.30	141.57	146.63	151.47	156.10	160.53	164.74	176.15	191.00	200.41	203.78
4.00	105.61	110.97	116.09	120.96	125.61	130.04	134.24	138.24	142.03	145.62	149.01	152.21	160.70	171.34	177.76	179.96
4.25	105.36	110.47	115.33	119.95	124.35	128.52	132.48	136.23	139.78	143.13	146.29	149.27	157.13	166.87	172.67	174.65
4.50	105.11	109.97	114.58	118.95	123.10	127.03	130.75	134.26	137.58	140.70	143.64	146.40	153.65	162.56	167.80	169.56
4.75	104.86	109.47	113.83	117.96	121.87	125.56	129.04	132.33	135.42	138.33	141.05	143.61	150.28	158.41	163.13	164.70
5.00	104.61	108.97	113.09	116.98	120.65	124.11	127.37	130.43	133.30	136.00	138.52	140.88	147.01	154.40	158.65	160.04
5.25	104.36	108.48	112.36	116.01	119.45	122.68	125.71	128.56	131.23	133.72	136.05	138.22	143.84	150.54	154.35	155.59
5.50	104.12	107.99	111.63	115.05	118.26	121.27	124.09	126.72	129.19	131.49	133.63	135.62	140.76	146.82	150.22	151.32
5.75	103.87	107.50	110.90	114.09	117.08	119.87	122.49	124.92	127.19	129.31	131.27	133.09	137.77	143.23	146.26	147.22
6.00	103.62	107.01	110.18	113.15	115.92	118.50	120.91	123.15	125.24	127.17	128.97	130.63	134.86	139.77	142.46	143.30
6.25	103.38	106.53	109.47	112.21	114.77	117.15	119.36	121.41	123.32	125.08	126.71	128.22	132.04	136.43	138.80	139.54
6.50	103.13	106.05	108.76	111.28	113.63	115.81	117.83	119.70	121.43	123.03	124.51	125.87	129.30	133.20	135.29	135.93
6.75	102.89	105.57	108.06	110.37	112.51	114.49	116.33	118.02	119.59	121.03	122.36	123.57	126.64	130.09	131.91	132.46
7.00	102.64	105.09	107.36	109.46	111.40	113.19	114.85	116.37	117.78	119.07	120.25	121.34	124.05	127.08	128.66	129.14
7.25	102.40	104.62	106.66	108.56	110.30	111.91	113.39	114.75	116.00	117.15	118.20	119.15	121.54	124.18	125.54	125.94
7.50	102.16	104.14	105.98	107.66	109.22	110.64	111.95	113.16	114.26	115.27	116.19	117.02	119.10	121.38	122.53	122.87
7.75	101.91	103.67	105.29	106.78	108.14	109.40	110.54	111.59	112.55	113.42	114.22	114.94	116.73	118.67	119.64	119.92
8.00	101.67	103.21	104.61	105.90	107.08	108.16	109.15	110.05	110.87	111.62	112.30	112.92	114.43	116.05	116.86	117.09
8.25	101.43	102.74	103.94	105.04	106.04	106.95	107.78	108.54	109.23	109.85	110.42	110.93	112.19	113.52	114.17	114.36
8.50	101.19	102.28	103.27	104.18	105.00	105.75	106.43	107.05	107.62	108.13	108.59	109.00	110.01	111.08	111.59	111.74
8.75	100.95	101.82	102.61	103.33	103.98	104.57	105.11	105.59	106.03	106.43	106.79	107.11	107.90	108.71	109.10	109.21
9.00	100.71	101.36	101.95	102.48	102.97	103.40	103.80	104.16	104.48	104.77	105.04	105.27	105.84	106.42	106.70	106.78
9.25	100.47	100.90	101.29	101.65	101.97	102.25	102.51	102.75	102.96	103.15	103.32	103.47	103.84	104.21	104.39	104.43
9.50	100.24	100.45	100.64	100.82	100.98	101.12	101.25	101.36	101.47	101.56	101.64	101.72	101.89	102.07	102.15	102.18
9.75	100.00	100.00	100.00	100.00	100.00	100.00	100.00	100.00	100.00	100.00	100.00	100.00	100.00	100.00	100.00	100.00
10.00	99.76	99.55	99.36	99.19	99.03	98.90	98.77	98.66	98.56	98.47	98.39	98.32	98.16	98.00	97.92	97.90
10.25	99.53	99.10	98.72	98.38	98.08	97.81	97.56	97.34	97.15	96.98	96.83	96.69	96.37	96.05	95.91	95.88
10.50	99.29	98.66	98.09	97.59	97.13	96.73	96.37	96.05	95.77	95.51	95.29	95.09	94.63	94.17	93.97	93.92
10.75	99.06	98.22	97.47	96.80	96.20	95.67	95.20	94.78	94.41	94.08	93.79	93.53	92.93	92.35	92.10	92.04
11.00	98.82	97.78	96.85	96.02	95.28	94.62	94.04	93.53	93.07	92.67	92.32	92.01	91.28	90.59	90.29	90.22
11.25	98.59	97.34	96.23	95.24	94.37	93.59	92.91	92.30	91.77	91.30	90.88	90.52	89.68	88.88	88.54	88.46
11.50	98.36	96.90	95.61	94.47	93.47	92.57	91.79	91.09	90.48	89.95	89.48	89.06	88.11	87.22	86.85	86.76
11.75	98.13	96.47	95.01	93.71	92.57	91.57	90.68	89.91	89.22	88.62	88.10	87.64	86.59	85.62	85.21	85.11
12.00	97.90	96.04	94.40	92.96	91.69	90.58	89.60	88.74	87.99	87.33	86.75	86.25	85.11	84.06	83.63	83.53
12.25	97.66	95.61	93.80	92.22	90.82	89.60	88.53	87.59	86.77	86.06	85.44	84.90	83.67	82.55	82.10	81.99
12.50	97.43	95.18	93.21	91.48	89.96	88.63	87.48	86.46	85.58	84.81	84.15	83.57	82.27	81.08	80.61	80.50
12.75	97.20	94.76	92.62	90.74	89.11	87.68	86.44	85.35	84.41	83.60	82.89	82.27	80.90	79.66	79.17	79.06
13.00	96.98	94.33	92.03	90.02	88.27	86.74	85.42	84.26	83.27	82.40	81.65	81.01	79.56	78.28	77.78	77.67
13.25	96.75	93.91	91.45	89.30	87.43	85.82	84.41	83.19	82.14	81.23	80.44	79.77	78.27	76.94	76.43	76.32
13.50	96.52	93.49	90.87	88.59	86.61	84.90	83.42	82.14	81.03	80.08	79.26	78.56	77.00	75.64	75.12	75.01
13.75	96.29	93.08	90.29	87.88	85.80	84.00	82.44	81.10	79.95	78.96	78.10	77.37	75.77	74.38	73.86	73.74
14.00	96.07	92.66	89.72	87.18	84.99	83.11	81.48	80.08	78.88	77.85	76.97	76.22	74.57	73.15	72.63	72.51
14.25	95.84	92.25	89.16	86.49	84.20	82.23	80.53	79.08	77.84	76.77	75.86	75.09	73.40	71.96	71.43	71.32
14.50	95.61	91.84	88.60	85.81	83.41	81.36	79.60	78.10	76.81	75.71	74.78	73.98	72.25	70.80	70.27	70.16
14.75	95.39	91.43	88.04	85.13	82.64	80.50	78.68	77.13	75.80	74.67	73.71	72.90	71.14	69.67	69.15	69.04
15.00	95.17	91.03	87.48	84.45	81.87	79.66	77.78	76.17	74.81	73.65	72.67	71.84	70.05	68.58	68.06	67.95
15.25	94.94	90.62	86.93	83.79	81.11	78.83	76.89	75.24	73.84	72.65	71.65	70.81	69.00	67.51	67.00	66.89
15.50	94.72	90.22	86.39	83.13	80.36	78.00	76.01	74.32	72.88	71.67	70.65	69.79	67.96	66.48	65.97	65.86
15.75	94.50	89.82	85.85	82.47	79.61	77.19	75.14	73.41	71.95	70.71	69.68	68.80	66.96	65.47	64.96	64.86
16.00	94.27	89.42	85.31	81.83	78.88	76.39	74.29	72.52	71.03	69.77	68.72	67.84	65.97	64.49	63.99	63.89
16.25	94.05	89.02	84.77	81.18	78.15	75.60	73.45	71.64	70.12	68.85	67.78	66.89	65.01	63.53	63.04	62.94
16.50	93.83	88.63	84.24	80.55	77.44	74.82	72.62	70.78	69.23	67.94	66.86	65.96	64.08	62.61	62.12	62.03
16.75	93.61	88.24	83.72	79.92	76.73	74.05	71.81	69.93	68.36	67.05	65.96	65.05	63.16	61.70	61.23	61.13
17.00	93.39	87.85	83.19	79.29	76.02	73.29	71.00	69.10	67.50	66.18	65.08	64.17	62.27	60.82	60.35	60.26
17.25	93.17	87.46	82.67	78.67	75.33	72.54	70.21	68.28	66.66	65.32	64.22	63.30	61.40	59.96	59.50	59.42
17.50	92.96	87.07	82.16	78.06	74.64	71.80	69.43	67.47	65.84	64.49	63.37	62.45	60.55	59.12	58.68	58.59
17.75	92.74	86.69	81.65	77.45	73.97	71.07	68.67	66.67	65.03	63.66	62.54	61.61	59.72	58.31	57.87	57.79
18.00	92.52	86.30	81.14	76.85	73.29	70.35	67.91	65.89	64.23	62.86	61.73	60.80	58.91	57.51	57.09	57.01
18.25	92.30	85.92	80.63	76.25	72.63	69.64	67.16	65.12	63.44	62.06	60.93	60.00	58.12	56.74	56.32	56.25
18.50	92.09	85.54	80.13	75.66	71.97	68.93	66.43	64.37	62.68	61.29	60.15	59.22	57.34	55.98	55.58	55.50
18.75	91.87	85.17	79.63	75.08	71.33	68.24	65.71	63.62	61.92	60.52	59.38	58.45	56.59	55.25	54.85	54.78
19.00	91.66	84.79	79.14	74.50	70.68	67.56	64.99	62.89	61.18	59.78	58.63	57.71	55.85	54.53	54.14	54.07
20.00	90.80	83.31	77.20	72.23	68.19	64.91	62.24	60.08	58.33	56.92	55.78	54.86	53.06	51.82	51.47	51.42
25.00	86.66	76.31	68.29	62.07	57.25	53.53	50.65	48.43	46.71	45.39	44.38	43.61	42.21	41.41	41.24	41.21
30.00	82.73	69.97	60.55	53.60	48.47	44.69	41.91	39.87	38.37	37.27	36.47	35.88	34.91	34.45	34.37	34.36

Description: This table shows the yield to prepayment of a monthly payment mortgage purchased at a price in the index.

Example: The yield to prepayment in 10 years of a 9.75 %, 30 year mortgage at a price of 104.00 is 9.11 %.

30 YEAR MORTGAGE PREPAID IN

PRICE	1 yr	2 yr	3 yr	4 yr	5 yr	6 yr	7 yr	8 yr	9 yr	10 yr	11 yr	12 yr	15 yr	20 yr	25 yr	30 yr
140	–	–	–	–	1.33	2.43	3.20	3.78	4.22	4.57	4.85	5.08	5.56	5.98	6.16	6.21
135	–	–	–	–	2.22	3.20	3.89	4.40	4.79	5.10	5.35	5.56	5.98	6.35	6.52	6.56
130	–	–	–	1.86	3.15	4.00	4.60	5.05	5.39	5.67	5.88	6.06	6.43	6.75	6.89	6.93
125	–	–	1.18	3.02	4.12	4.84	5.35	5.73	6.03	6.25	6.44	6.59	6.90	7.17	7.29	7.32
120	–	–	2.73	4.23	5.13	5.72	6.14	6.45	6.69	6.88	7.03	7.15	7.40	7.62	7.71	7.74
119	–	–	3.05	4.48	5.34	5.90	6.30	6.60	6.83	7.00	7.15	7.26	7.51	7.71	7.80	7.83
118	–	–	3.37	4.74	5.55	6.09	6.47	6.75	6.96	7.13	7.27	7.38	7.61	7.81	7.89	7.91
117	–	1.10	3.70	4.99	5.76	6.27	6.63	6.90	7.10	7.26	7.39	7.50	7.72	7.90	7.98	8.00
116	–	1.57	4.02	5.25	5.98	6.46	6.80	7.05	7.25	7.40	7.52	7.62	7.82	8.00	8.07	8.09
115	–	2.04	4.35	5.51	6.19	6.65	6.97	7.21	7.39	7.53	7.65	7.74	7.93	8.10	8.17	8.19
114	–	2.52	4.69	5.77	6.41	6.84	7.14	7.36	7.53	7.67	7.77	7.86	8.04	8.20	8.26	8.28
113	–	3.00	5.03	6.03	6.64	7.03	7.31	7.52	7.68	7.80	7.90	7.98	8.15	8.30	8.36	8.37
112	–	3.49	5.37	6.30	6.86	7.23	7.49	7.68	7.83	7.94	8.03	8.11	8.27	8.40	8.45	8.47
111	–	3.98	5.71	6.57	7.09	7.42	7.66	7.84	7.98	8.08	8.17	8.24	8.38	8.50	8.55	8.57
110	–	4.48	6.06	6.85	7.31	7.62	7.84	8.00	8.13	8.22	8.30	8.37	8.50	8.61	8.65	8.67
109	–	4.98	6.41	7.12	7.55	7.82	8.02	8.17	8.28	8.37	8.44	8.50	8.61	8.71	8.76	8.77
108	1.65	5.49	6.77	7.40	7.78	8.03	8.21	8.34	8.44	8.51	8.58	8.63	8.73	8.82	8.86	8.87
107	2.63	6.00	7.12	7.68	8.02	8.23	8.39	8.50	8.59	8.66	8.72	8.76	8.85	8.93	8.96	8.97
106	3.61	6.52	7.49	7.97	8.25	8.44	8.58	8.68	8.75	8.81	8.86	8.90	8.98	9.04	9.07	9.08
105	4.61	7.04	7.85	8.26	8.50	8.65	8.77	8.85	8.91	8.96	9.00	9.03	9.10	9.15	9.18	9.18
104	5.61	7.57	8.22	8.55	8.74	8.87	8.96	9.02	9.07	9.11	9.15	9.17	9.22	9.27	9.29	9.29
103.75	5.86	7.70	8.32	8.62	8.80	8.92	9.00	9.07	9.11	9.15	9.18	9.21	9.26	9.30	9.32	9.32
103.50	6.12	7.84	8.41	8.69	8.86	8.97	9.05	9.11	9.16	9.19	9.22	9.24	9.29	9.33	9.34	9.35
103.25	6.37	7.97	8.50	8.77	8.92	9.03	9.10	9.16	9.20	9.23	9.26	9.28	9.32	9.36	9.37	9.37
103.00	6.63	8.11	8.60	8.84	8.99	9.08	9.15	9.20	9.24	9.27	9.29	9.31	9.35	9.39	9.40	9.40
102.75	6.88	8.24	8.69	8.92	9.05	9.14	9.20	9.24	9.28	9.31	9.33	9.35	9.38	9.41	9.43	9.43
102.50	7.14	8.38	8.79	8.99	9.11	9.19	9.25	9.29	9.32	9.35	9.37	9.38	9.42	9.44	9.46	9.46
102.25	7.40	8.51	8.88	9.06	9.17	9.25	9.30	9.33	9.36	9.39	9.40	9.42	9.45	9.47	9.48	9.49
102.00	7.66	8.65	8.98	9.14	9.24	9.30	9.35	9.38	9.41	9.43	9.44	9.45	9.48	9.50	9.51	9.51
101.75	7.91	8.78	9.07	9.21	9.30	9.36	9.40	9.42	9.45	9.46	9.48	9.49	9.51	9.53	9.54	9.54
101.50	8.17	8.92	9.17	9.29	9.36	9.41	9.44	9.47	9.49	9.50	9.52	9.53	9.55	9.56	9.57	9.57
101.25	8.43	9.06	9.26	9.36	9.43	9.47	9.49	9.52	9.53	9.54	9.55	9.56	9.58	9.59	9.60	9.60
101.00	8.69	9.19	9.36	9.44	9.49	9.52	9.54	9.56	9.57	9.58	9.59	9.60	9.61	9.62	9.63	9.63
100.75	8.96	9.33	9.45	9.52	9.55	9.58	9.59	9.61	9.62	9.62	9.63	9.63	9.65	9.65	9.66	9.66
100.50	9.22	9.47	9.55	9.59	9.62	9.63	9.64	9.65	9.66	9.66	9.67	9.67	9.68	9.68	9.69	9.69
100.25	9.48	9.61	9.65	9.67	9.68	9.69	9.69	9.70	9.70	9.70	9.71	9.71	9.71	9.71	9.72	9.72
100.00	9.75	9.75	9.75	9.75	9.75	9.75	9.75	9.75	9.75	9.75	9.75	9.75	9.75	9.75	9.75	9.75
99.75	10.01	9.88	9.84	9.82	9.81	9.80	9.80	9.79	9.79	9.79	9.78	9.78	9.78	9.78	9.77	9.77
99.50	10.27	10.02	9.94	9.90	9.87	9.86	9.85	9.84	9.83	9.83	9.82	9.82	9.81	9.81	9.80	9.80
99.25	10.54	10.16	10.04	9.98	9.94	9.91	9.90	9.88	9.87	9.87	9.86	9.86	9.85	9.84	9.83	9.83
99.00	10.81	10.30	10.14	10.05	10.00	9.97	9.95	9.93	9.92	9.91	9.90	9.89	9.88	9.87	9.86	9.86
98.75	11.07	10.44	10.23	10.13	10.07	10.03	10.00	9.98	9.96	9.95	9.94	9.93	9.91	9.90	9.89	9.89
98.50	11.34	10.59	10.33	10.21	10.13	10.09	10.05	10.03	10.01	9.99	9.98	9.97	9.95	9.93	9.92	9.92
98.25	11.61	10.73	10.43	10.29	10.20	10.14	10.10	10.07	10.05	10.03	10.02	10.01	9.98	9.96	9.95	9.95
98.00	11.88	10.87	10.53	10.37	10.27	10.20	10.15	10.12	10.09	10.07	10.06	10.04	10.02	9.99	9.99	9.98
97.75	12.15	11.01	10.63	10.44	10.33	10.26	10.21	10.17	10.14	10.12	10.10	10.08	10.05	10.03	10.02	10.01
97.50	12.42	11.15	10.73	10.52	10.40	10.32	10.26	10.22	10.18	10.16	10.14	10.12	10.09	10.06	10.05	10.04
97.25	12.70	11.30	10.83	10.60	10.46	10.37	10.31	10.26	10.23	10.20	10.18	10.16	10.12	10.09	10.08	10.07
97	12.97	11.44	10.93	10.68	10.53	10.43	10.36	10.31	10.27	10.24	10.22	10.20	10.16	10.12	10.11	10.11
96	14.07	12.02	11.34	11.00	10.80	10.67	10.57	10.51	10.45	10.41	10.38	10.35	10.30	10.25	10.23	10.23
95	15.18	12.60	11.75	11.32	11.07	10.90	10.79	10.70	10.64	10.58	10.54	10.51	10.44	10.38	10.36	10.36
94	16.31	13.19	12.16	11.65	11.35	11.15	11.00	10.90	10.82	10.76	10.71	10.67	10.59	10.52	10.49	10.49
93	17.44	13.79	12.58	11.98	11.63	11.39	11.22	11.10	11.01	10.94	10.88	10.83	10.73	10.66	10.62	10.62
92	18.60	14.40	13.01	12.32	11.91	11.64	11.45	11.31	11.20	11.12	11.05	11.00	10.89	10.79	10.76	10.75
91	19.76	15.01	13.44	12.66	12.19	11.89	11.67	11.51	11.39	11.30	11.22	11.16	11.04	10.94	10.90	10.89
90	20.94	15.63	13.87	13.00	12.48	12.14	11.90	11.73	11.59	11.48	11.40	11.33	11.19	11.08	11.04	11.03
89	22.14	16.26	14.31	13.35	12.78	12.40	12.13	11.94	11.79	11.67	11.58	11.51	11.35	11.23	11.18	11.17
88	23.35	16.90	14.76	13.70	13.07	12.66	12.37	12.16	11.99	11.86	11.76	11.68	11.51	11.38	11.32	11.31
87	24.58	17.54	15.21	14.06	13.38	12.93	12.61	12.38	12.20	12.06	11.95	11.86	11.68	11.53	11.47	11.46
86	25.82	18.19	15.67	14.42	13.68	13.19	12.85	12.60	12.41	12.26	12.14	12.04	11.84	11.68	11.62	11.61
85	27.08	18.85	16.14	14.79	13.99	13.47	13.10	12.83	12.62	12.46	12.33	12.23	12.01	11.84	11.78	11.76
80	33.63	22.30	18.56	16.71	15.61	14.89	14.39	14.02	13.73	13.51	13.34	13.20	12.91	12.68	12.60	12.58
75	40.66	25.99	21.16	18.78	17.36	16.44	15.79	15.31	14.95	14.67	14.44	14.26	13.90	13.62	13.52	13.50
70	48.24	29.97	23.98	21.02	19.27	18.12	17.31	16.72	16.28	15.93	15.66	15.44	15.01	14.67	14.56	14.53
65	56.46	34.29	27.03	23.46	21.34	19.96	18.99	18.29	17.75	17.34	17.02	16.76	16.25	15.86	15.74	15.71
60	65.42	39.00	30.38	26.13	23.63	22.00	20.86	20.02	19.40	18.92	18.54	18.25	17.66	17.23	17.10	17.07
55	75.27	44.19	34.07	29.10	26.18	24.27	22.95	21.98	21.26	20.71	20.28	19.94	19.29	18.83	18.69	18.67
50	86.20	49.94	38.19	32.42	29.04	26.84	25.32	24.22	23.40	22.78	22.29	21.92	21.20	20.72	20.59	20.57

PREPAYMENT MORTGAGE PRICE

10.00 %

Description: This table shows the price to pay for a monthly payment loan, at a yield rate and assuming prepayment.

Example: The price of a 10.00 %, 30 year mortgage to yield 8.00 %, if prepaid in 6 years, is $ 109.34.

30 YEAR MORTGAGE PREPAID IN

YIELD	1 yr	2 yr	3 yr	4 yr	5 yr	6 yr	7 yr	8 yr	9 yr	10 yr	11 yr	12 yr	15 yr	20 yr	25 yr	30 yr
0.00	109.97	119.89	129.74	139.53	149.23	158.84	168.37	177.78	187.08	196.25	205.27	214.14	239.63	277.02	304.57	315.93
1.00	108.93	117.72	126.36	134.86	143.20	151.39	159.42	167.28	174.96	182.46	189.77	196.89	216.92	245.19	265.03	272.84
2.00	107.89	115.59	123.08	130.37	137.46	144.35	151.03	157.51	163.78	169.84	175.69	181.32	196.89	218.00	232.11	237.43
3.00	106.87	113.50	119.89	126.05	131.98	137.68	143.16	148.41	153.45	158.28	162.88	167.28	179.18	194.71	204.59	208.15
4.00	105.86	111.45	116.79	121.89	126.75	131.37	135.77	139.95	143.92	147.68	151.23	154.59	163.50	174.70	181.48	183.82
4.25	105.61	110.95	116.03	120.87	125.48	129.85	134.00	137.93	141.65	145.17	148.49	151.61	159.87	170.14	176.29	178.39
4.50	105.35	110.44	115.28	119.87	124.22	128.35	132.25	135.94	139.42	142.71	145.80	148.71	156.35	165.76	171.32	173.20
4.75	105.10	109.94	114.53	118.87	122.98	126.86	130.53	133.99	137.24	140.31	143.18	145.88	152.93	161.53	166.55	168.23
5.00	104.86	109.45	113.79	117.89	121.75	125.40	128.84	132.07	135.10	137.95	140.62	143.11	149.61	157.45	161.98	163.48
5.25	104.61	108.95	113.05	116.91	120.54	123.96	127.17	130.18	133.01	135.65	138.12	140.42	146.39	153.53	157.59	158.92
5.50	104.36	108.46	112.32	115.94	119.34	122.54	125.53	128.33	130.95	133.40	135.67	137.79	143.26	149.74	153.38	154.56
5.75	104.11	107.97	111.59	114.98	118.16	121.14	123.92	126.51	128.93	131.19	133.28	135.23	140.22	146.08	149.34	150.38
6.00	103.86	107.48	110.87	114.03	116.99	119.75	122.33	124.73	126.96	129.03	130.95	132.73	137.27	142.55	145.46	146.37
6.25	103.62	107.00	110.15	113.09	115.83	118.39	120.76	122.97	125.02	126.91	128.67	130.29	134.41	139.15	141.72	142.53
6.50	103.37	106.51	109.44	112.16	114.69	117.04	119.22	121.24	123.11	124.84	126.44	127.91	131.63	135.87	138.14	138.84
6.75	103.13	106.03	108.73	111.24	113.56	115.71	117.71	119.55	121.25	122.82	124.26	125.59	128.92	132.70	134.69	135.30
7.00	102.88	105.55	108.03	110.32	112.44	114.40	116.21	117.88	119.42	120.83	122.13	123.32	126.30	129.63	131.38	131.91
7.25	102.64	105.08	107.33	109.42	111.34	113.11	114.74	116.24	117.62	118.89	120.05	121.11	123.75	126.68	128.19	128.64
7.50	102.40	104.61	106.64	108.52	110.25	111.84	113.30	114.64	115.86	116.99	118.01	118.95	121.27	123.82	125.12	125.51
7.75	102.15	104.13	105.96	107.63	109.17	110.58	111.87	113.06	114.14	115.12	116.02	116.84	118.86	121.06	122.17	122.50
8.00	101.91	103.67	105.28	106.75	108.10	109.34	110.47	111.50	112.44	113.30	114.08	114.79	116.52	118.40	119.33	119.60
8.25	101.67	103.20	104.60	105.88	107.05	108.12	109.09	109.98	110.78	111.51	112.18	112.78	114.25	115.82	116.59	116.81
8.50	101.43	102.74	103.93	105.01	106.01	106.91	107.73	108.48	109.15	109.76	110.32	110.82	112.04	113.33	113.95	114.13
8.75	101.19	102.27	103.26	104.16	104.98	105.72	106.39	107.00	107.55	108.05	108.50	108.91	109.89	110.92	111.41	111.55
9.00	100.95	101.81	102.60	103.31	103.96	104.54	105.07	105.55	105.98	106.37	106.72	107.04	107.80	108.59	108.96	109.07
9.25	100.71	101.36	101.94	102.47	102.95	103.38	103.77	104.13	104.45	104.73	104.99	105.22	105.77	106.33	106.60	106.67
9.50	100.47	100.90	101.29	101.64	101.96	102.24	102.50	102.73	102.94	103.12	103.29	103.44	103.79	104.15	104.32	104.37
9.75	100.24	100.45	100.64	100.82	100.97	101.11	101.24	101.35	101.45	101.54	101.63	101.70	101.87	102.04	102.12	102.14
10.00	100.00	100.00	100.00	100.00	100.00	100.00	100.00	100.00	100.00	100.00	100.00	100.00	100.00	100.00	100.00	100.00
10.25	99.76	99.55	99.36	99.19	99.04	98.90	98.78	98.67	98.57	98.49	98.41	98.34	98.18	98.02	97.95	97.93
10.50	99.53	99.11	98.73	98.39	98.09	97.82	97.58	97.36	97.17	97.00	96.85	96.72	96.41	96.11	95.97	95.94
10.75	99.29	98.66	98.10	97.60	97.15	96.75	96.40	96.08	95.80	95.55	95.33	95.14	94.69	94.25	94.06	94.01
11.00	99.06	98.22	97.48	96.81	96.22	95.70	95.23	94.82	94.45	94.13	93.85	93.59	93.01	92.45	92.21	92.15
11.25	98.83	97.78	96.86	96.03	95.30	94.66	94.08	93.58	93.13	92.74	92.39	92.08	91.38	90.71	90.43	90.35
11.50	98.59	97.35	96.24	95.26	94.39	93.63	92.95	92.36	91.83	91.37	90.97	90.61	89.79	89.02	88.70	88.62
11.75	98.36	96.91	95.63	94.50	93.50	92.62	91.84	91.16	90.56	90.03	89.57	89.17	88.25	87.38	87.03	86.94
12.00	98.13	96.48	95.02	93.74	92.61	91.62	90.75	89.98	89.31	88.72	88.21	87.76	86.74	85.80	85.41	85.32
12.25	97.90	96.05	94.42	92.99	91.73	90.63	89.67	88.82	88.08	87.44	86.87	86.38	85.27	84.26	83.84	83.75
12.50	97.67	95.62	93.82	92.25	90.87	89.66	88.60	87.68	86.88	86.18	85.57	85.04	83.85	82.76	82.33	82.23
12.75	97.44	95.19	93.23	91.51	90.01	88.70	87.56	86.56	85.69	84.94	84.29	83.72	82.46	81.31	80.86	80.76
13.00	97.21	94.77	92.64	90.78	89.16	87.75	86.53	85.46	84.53	83.73	83.04	82.44	81.10	79.91	79.44	79.33
13.25	96.98	94.35	92.05	90.06	88.32	86.82	85.51	84.38	83.39	82.55	81.81	81.18	79.78	78.54	78.06	77.95
13.50	96.75	93.93	91.47	89.34	87.50	85.90	84.51	83.31	82.28	81.38	80.62	79.96	78.49	77.21	76.73	76.62
13.75	96.52	93.51	90.90	88.63	86.68	84.99	83.52	82.26	81.18	80.24	79.44	78.76	77.24	75.93	75.43	75.32
14.00	96.30	93.09	90.32	87.93	85.87	84.09	82.55	81.23	80.10	79.13	78.29	77.58	76.02	74.68	74.18	74.06
14.25	96.07	92.68	89.76	87.24	85.07	83.20	81.60	80.22	79.04	78.03	77.17	76.43	74.83	73.46	72.96	72.85
14.50	95.84	92.27	89.19	86.55	84.28	82.33	80.66	79.23	78.00	76.96	76.07	75.31	73.67	72.28	71.77	71.66
14.75	95.62	91.86	88.63	85.86	83.49	81.46	79.73	78.25	76.98	75.91	74.99	74.22	72.53	71.13	70.63	70.52
15.00	95.39	91.45	88.07	85.19	82.72	80.61	78.82	77.28	75.98	74.87	73.94	73.14	71.43	70.01	69.51	69.40
15.25	95.17	91.05	87.52	84.52	81.95	79.77	77.92	76.34	75.00	73.86	72.90	72.09	70.35	68.93	68.43	68.32
15.50	94.95	90.64	86.97	83.85	81.20	78.94	77.03	75.41	74.03	72.87	71.89	71.06	69.30	67.87	67.37	67.27
15.75	94.72	90.24	86.43	83.19	80.45	78.12	76.16	74.49	73.08	71.90	70.90	70.06	68.28	66.84	66.35	66.25
16.00	94.50	89.84	85.89	82.54	79.71	77.32	75.29	73.59	72.15	70.94	69.93	69.08	67.28	65.84	65.36	65.26
16.25	94.28	89.44	85.35	81.90	78.98	76.52	74.45	72.70	71.24	70.01	68.98	68.12	66.30	64.87	64.39	64.29
16.50	94.06	89.05	84.82	81.26	78.26	75.73	73.61	71.83	70.34	69.09	68.05	67.17	65.35	63.92	63.45	63.36
16.75	93.84	88.65	84.29	80.62	77.54	74.96	72.79	70.97	69.46	68.19	67.13	66.25	64.42	63.00	62.53	62.44
17.00	93.62	88.26	83.77	79.99	76.84	74.19	71.98	70.13	68.59	67.31	66.24	65.35	63.51	62.10	61.64	61.55
17.25	93.40	87.87	83.24	79.37	76.14	73.43	71.18	69.30	67.74	66.44	65.36	64.47	62.63	61.22	60.78	60.69
17.50	93.18	87.48	82.73	78.76	75.45	72.69	70.39	68.49	66.90	65.59	64.50	63.61	61.76	60.37	59.93	59.85
17.75	92.96	87.10	82.21	78.14	74.76	71.95	69.62	67.68	66.08	64.76	63.66	62.76	60.92	59.54	59.11	59.03
18.00	92.75	86.71	81.70	77.54	74.09	71.22	68.85	66.89	65.27	63.94	62.84	61.93	60.09	58.73	58.31	58.23
18.25	92.53	86.33	81.20	76.94	73.42	70.51	68.10	66.12	64.48	63.14	62.03	61.12	59.29	57.94	57.53	57.45
18.50	92.31	85.95	80.69	76.35	72.76	69.80	67.36	65.35	63.70	62.35	61.24	60.33	58.50	57.16	56.76	56.69
18.75	92.10	85.57	80.19	75.76	72.10	69.10	66.63	64.60	62.94	61.58	60.46	59.55	57.73	56.41	56.02	55.95
19.00	91.88	85.20	79.70	75.17	71.46	68.41	65.91	63.86	62.18	60.82	59.70	58.79	56.98	55.68	55.30	55.23
20.00	91.03	83.71	77.75	72.89	68.95	65.74	63.13	61.02	59.31	57.92	56.80	55.90	54.13	52.91	52.57	52.52
25.00	86.88	76.69	68.79	62.67	57.93	54.25	51.42	49.23	47.54	46.23	45.23	44.47	43.09	42.30	42.12	42.10
30.00	82.94	70.34	61.02	54.15	49.07	45.34	42.59	40.56	39.08	37.99	37.19	36.61	35.65	35.19	35.11	35.10

PREPAYMENT MORTGAGE YIELD, 30 YEAR TERM

10.00 %

Description: This table shows the yield to prepayment of a monthly payment mortgage purchased at a price in the index.

Example: The yield to prepayment in 10 years of a 10.00 %, 30 year mortgage at a price of 104.00 is 9.36 %.

30 YEAR MORTGAGE PREPAID IN

PRICE	1 yr	2 yr	3 yr	4 yr	5 yr	6 yr	7 yr	8 yr	9 yr	10 yr	11 yr	12 yr	15 yr	20 yr	25 yr	30 yr
140	–	–	–	–	1.55	2.64	3.41	3.99	4.43	4.78	5.06	5.28	5.76	6.18	6.36	6.42
135	–	–	–	–	2.44	3.41	4.10	4.61	5.01	5.32	5.56	5.77	6.19	6.56	6.72	6.77
130	–	–	–	2.08	3.37	4.22	4.82	5.27	5.61	5.88	6.10	6.28	6.64	6.96	7.10	7.14
125	–	–	1.41	3.24	4.34	5.06	5.58	5.96	6.25	6.48	6.66	6.81	7.12	7.39	7.51	7.54
120	–	–	2.96	4.46	5.36	5.95	6.37	6.68	6.92	7.10	7.25	7.37	7.63	7.84	7.94	7.96
119	–	–	3.28	4.71	5.57	6.13	6.53	6.83	7.05	7.23	7.37	7.49	7.73	7.94	8.02	8.05
118	–	–	3.60	4.97	5.78	6.32	6.70	6.98	7.19	7.36	7.50	7.61	7.84	8.03	8.12	8.14
117	–	1.33	3.93	5.22	5.99	6.50	6.86	7.13	7.33	7.49	7.62	7.73	7.94	8.13	8.21	8.23
116	–	1.80	4.26	5.48	6.21	6.69	7.03	7.28	7.48	7.63	7.75	7.85	8.05	8.23	8.30	8.32
115	–	2.27	4.59	5.74	6.43	6.88	7.20	7.44	7.62	7.76	7.88	7.97	8.16	8.33	8.39	8.41
114	–	2.75	4.92	6.00	6.65	7.07	7.37	7.60	7.77	7.90	8.01	8.09	8.27	8.43	8.49	8.51
113	–	3.24	5.26	6.27	6.87	7.27	7.55	7.75	7.91	8.04	8.14	8.22	8.39	8.53	8.59	8.60
112	–	3.73	5.60	6.54	7.10	7.46	7.72	7.91	8.06	8.18	8.27	8.34	8.50	8.63	8.69	8.70
111	–	4.22	5.95	6.81	7.32	7.66	7.90	8.08	8.21	8.32	8.40	8.47	8.62	8.74	8.79	8.80
110	–	4.72	6.30	7.08	7.55	7.86	8.08	8.24	8.36	8.46	8.54	8.60	8.73	8.84	8.89	8.90
109	–	5.22	6.65	7.36	7.78	8.06	8.26	8.41	8.52	8.61	8.68	8.73	8.85	8.95	8.99	9.00
108	1.89	5.73	7.01	7.64	8.02	8.27	8.44	8.58	8.67	8.75	8.82	8.87	8.97	9.06	9.10	9.11
107	2.87	6.24	7.37	7.92	8.26	8.48	8.63	8.75	8.83	8.90	8.96	9.00	9.09	9.17	9.20	9.21
106	3.85	6.76	7.73	8.21	8.50	8.69	8.82	8.92	8.99	9.05	9.10	9.14	9.22	9.28	9.31	9.32
105	4.85	7.29	8.10	8.50	8.74	8.90	9.01	9.09	9.15	9.20	9.24	9.28	9.34	9.40	9.42	9.43
104	5.86	7.82	8.47	8.79	8.98	9.11	9.20	9.27	9.32	9.36	9.39	9.42	9.47	9.51	9.53	9.54
103.75	6.11	7.95	8.56	8.87	9.05	9.17	9.25	9.31	9.36	9.40	9.43	9.45	9.50	9.54	9.56	9.56
103.50	6.36	8.08	8.66	8.94	9.11	9.22	9.30	9.36	9.40	9.44	9.46	9.49	9.53	9.57	9.59	9.59
103.25	6.62	8.22	8.75	9.01	9.17	9.27	9.35	9.40	9.44	9.47	9.50	9.52	9.56	9.60	9.62	9.62
103.00	6.87	8.35	8.84	9.09	9.23	9.33	9.40	9.45	9.48	9.51	9.54	9.56	9.60	9.63	9.64	9.65
102.75	7.13	8.49	8.94	9.16	9.30	9.38	9.45	9.49	9.53	9.55	9.58	9.59	9.63	9.66	9.67	9.68
102.50	7.39	8.62	9.03	9.24	9.36	9.44	9.49	9.54	9.57	9.59	9.61	9.63	9.66	9.69	9.70	9.70
102.25	7.64	8.76	9.13	9.31	9.42	9.49	9.54	9.58	9.61	9.63	9.65	9.66	9.70	9.72	9.73	9.73
102.00	7.90	8.89	9.22	9.39	9.48	9.55	9.59	9.63	9.65	9.67	9.69	9.70	9.73	9.75	9.76	9.76
101.75	8.16	9.03	9.32	9.46	9.55	9.60	9.64	9.67	9.69	9.71	9.73	9.74	9.76	9.78	9.79	9.79
101.50	8.42	9.17	9.41	9.54	9.61	9.66	9.69	9.72	9.74	9.75	9.76	9.77	9.79	9.81	9.82	9.82
101.25	8.68	9.30	9.51	9.61	9.67	9.71	9.74	9.76	9.78	9.79	9.80	9.81	9.83	9.84	9.85	9.85
101.00	8.94	9.44	9.61	9.69	9.74	9.77	9.79	9.81	9.82	9.83	9.84	9.85	9.86	9.87	9.88	9.88
100.75	9.21	9.58	9.70	9.77	9.80	9.83	9.84	9.86	9.87	9.87	9.88	9.88	9.89	9.90	9.91	9.91
100.50	9.47	9.72	9.80	9.84	9.87	9.88	9.89	9.90	9.91	9.91	9.92	9.92	9.93	9.93	9.94	9.94
100.25	9.73	9.86	9.90	9.92	9.93	9.94	9.94	9.95	9.95	9.95	9.96	9.96	9.96	9.96	9.97	9.97
100.00	10.00	10.00	10.00	10.00	10.00	10.00	10.00	10.00	10.00	10.00	10.00	10.00	10.00	10.00	10.00	10.00
99.75	10.26	10.13	10.09	10.07	10.06	10.05	10.05	10.04	10.04	10.04	10.03	10.03	10.03	10.03	10.03	10.02
99.50	10.53	10.27	10.19	10.15	10.12	10.11	10.10	10.09	10.08	10.08	10.07	10.07	10.06	10.06	10.06	10.05
99.25	10.79	10.41	10.29	10.23	10.19	10.17	10.15	10.14	10.13	10.12	10.11	10.11	10.10	10.10	10.09	10.08
99.00	11.06	10.55	10.39	10.30	10.26	10.22	10.20	10.18	10.17	10.16	10.15	10.15	10.13	10.12	10.12	10.11
98.75	11.33	10.70	10.49	10.38	10.32	10.28	10.25	10.23	10.21	10.20	10.19	10.18	10.17	10.15	10.15	10.15
98.50	11.59	10.84	10.59	10.46	10.39	10.34	10.30	10.28	10.26	10.24	10.23	10.22	10.20	10.18	10.18	10.18
98.25	11.86	10.98	10.69	10.54	10.45	10.40	10.35	10.33	10.30	10.28	10.27	10.26	10.24	10.22	10.21	10.21
98.00	12.13	11.12	10.78	10.62	10.52	10.45	10.41	10.37	10.35	10.33	10.31	10.30	10.27	10.25	10.24	10.24
97.75	12.41	11.26	10.88	10.70	10.58	10.51	10.46	10.42	10.39	10.37	10.35	10.34	10.31	10.28	10.27	10.27
97.50	12.68	11.41	10.99	10.78	10.65	10.57	10.51	10.47	10.44	10.41	10.39	10.37	10.34	10.31	10.30	10.30
97.25	12.95	11.55	11.09	10.86	10.72	10.63	10.56	10.52	10.48	10.45	10.43	10.41	10.38	10.34	10.33	10.33
97	13.22	11.69	11.19	10.93	10.78	10.69	10.62	10.57	10.53	10.50	10.47	10.45	10.41	10.38	10.36	10.36
96	14.32	12.27	11.59	11.26	11.05	10.92	10.83	10.76	10.71	10.67	10.63	10.61	10.55	10.51	10.49	10.49
95	15.44	12.86	12.00	11.58	11.33	11.16	11.04	10.96	10.89	10.84	10.80	10.77	10.70	10.64	10.62	10.62
94	16.56	13.45	12.42	11.91	11.60	11.40	11.26	11.16	11.08	11.02	10.97	10.93	10.85	10.78	10.75	10.75
93	17.70	14.05	12.84	12.24	11.88	11.65	11.48	11.36	11.27	11.20	11.14	11.09	11.00	10.92	10.89	10.88
92	18.86	14.66	13.27	12.58	12.17	11.90	11.71	11.57	11.46	11.38	11.31	11.26	11.15	11.06	11.02	11.02
91	20.03	15.27	13.70	12.92	12.46	12.15	11.94	11.78	11.66	11.56	11.49	11.43	11.30	11.20	11.16	11.15
90	21.21	15.90	14.14	13.27	12.75	12.41	12.17	11.99	11.86	11.75	11.67	11.60	11.46	11.35	11.31	11.30
89	22.41	16.52	14.58	13.62	13.04	12.67	12.40	12.21	12.06	11.94	11.85	11.77	11.62	11.50	11.45	11.44
88	23.62	17.16	15.03	13.97	13.34	12.93	12.64	12.42	12.26	12.13	12.03	11.95	11.79	11.65	11.60	11.59
87	24.85	17.81	15.48	14.33	13.65	13.20	12.88	12.65	12.47	12.33	12.22	12.13	11.95	11.80	11.75	11.74
86	26.09	18.46	15.94	14.69	13.95	13.47	13.12	12.87	12.68	12.53	12.41	12.32	12.12	11.96	11.90	11.89
85	27.35	19.13	16.41	15.06	14.27	13.74	13.37	13.10	12.89	12.73	12.61	12.50	12.29	12.12	12.06	12.04
80	33.91	22.58	18.84	16.99	15.90	15.18	14.67	14.30	14.02	13.80	13.63	13.49	13.20	12.98	12.90	12.88
75	40.95	26.28	21.46	19.07	17.66	16.73	16.08	15.61	15.24	14.96	14.74	14.57	14.21	13.93	13.83	13.81
70	48.54	30.27	24.28	21.32	19.57	18.42	17.62	17.03	16.59	16.25	15.98	15.76	15.33	15.00	14.88	14.86
65	56.77	34.60	27.35	23.77	21.66	20.28	19.32	18.61	18.08	17.67	17.35	17.09	16.59	16.21	16.09	16.06
60	65.75	39.33	30.71	26.47	23.97	22.33	21.20	20.37	19.75	19.27	18.90	18.60	18.02	17.61	17.47	17.45
55	75.62	44.53	34.42	29.45	26.53	24.63	23.31	22.35	21.63	21.09	20.66	20.33	19.68	19.23	19.10	19.08
50	86.56	50.31	38.55	32.80	29.42	27.23	25.71	24.61	23.80	23.18	22.70	22.33	21.63	21.16	21.04	21.02

26 - 35

PREPAYMENT MORTGAGE PRICE

10.25 %

Description: This table shows the price to pay for a monthly payment loan, at a yield rate and assuming prepayment.

Example: The price of a 10.25 %, 30 year mortgage to yield 8.00 %, if prepaid in 6 years, is $ 110.52.

30 YEAR MORTGAGE PREPAID IN

YIELD	1 yr	2 yr	3 yr	4 yr	5 yr	6 yr	7 yr	8 yr	9 yr	10 yr	11 yr	12 yr	15 yr	20 yr	25 yr	30 yr
0.00	110.23	120.39	130.50	140.54	150.50	160.37	170.15	179.83	189.39	198.82	208.11	217.24	243.51	282.17	310.76	322.60
1.00	109.18	118.21	127.11	135.85	144.44	152.87	161.14	169.23	177.16	184.89	192.44	199.78	220.49	249.79	270.43	278.60
2.00	108.14	116.08	123.81	131.34	138.66	145.77	152.68	159.38	165.87	172.14	178.20	184.03	200.17	222.13	236.86	242.44
3.00	107.12	113.99	120.61	126.99	133.14	139.06	144.75	150.21	155.44	160.45	165.24	169.82	182.21	198.43	208.79	212.55
4.00	106.10	111.93	117.50	122.81	127.88	132.71	137.30	141.67	145.81	149.74	153.46	156.97	166.31	178.07	185.22	187.70
4.25	105.85	111.43	116.74	121.79	126.60	131.17	135.51	139.62	143.52	147.20	150.68	153.96	162.63	173.44	179.93	182.16
4.50	105.60	110.92	115.98	120.78	125.34	129.66	133.75	137.62	141.27	144.72	147.97	151.02	159.05	168.97	174.86	176.86
4.75	105.35	110.42	115.23	119.78	124.09	128.17	132.02	135.65	139.07	142.29	145.31	148.15	155.58	164.67	170.00	171.78
5.00	105.10	109.92	114.48	118.79	122.86	126.69	130.31	133.71	136.91	139.91	142.72	145.35	152.21	160.52	165.33	166.93
5.25	104.85	109.43	113.74	117.81	121.64	125.24	128.63	131.81	134.79	137.58	140.19	142.63	148.94	156.52	160.86	162.28
5.50	104.60	108.93	113.01	116.84	120.43	123.81	126.98	129.94	132.71	135.30	137.72	139.96	145.77	152.66	156.56	157.82
5.75	104.35	108.44	112.28	115.87	119.24	122.40	125.35	128.11	130.68	133.07	135.30	137.37	142.69	148.94	152.43	153.55
6.00	104.11	107.95	111.55	114.92	118.07	121.00	123.75	126.30	128.68	130.89	132.94	134.84	139.69	145.35	148.47	149.46
6.25	103.86	107.46	110.83	113.97	116.90	119.63	122.17	124.53	126.72	128.75	130.63	132.37	136.79	141.89	144.67	145.54
6.50	103.61	106.98	110.12	113.04	115.75	118.27	120.62	122.79	124.80	126.66	128.37	129.96	133.96	138.54	141.01	141.77
6.75	103.37	106.50	109.41	112.11	114.61	116.94	119.09	121.08	122.91	124.61	126.17	127.60	131.22	135.31	137.49	138.16
7.00	103.12	106.02	108.70	111.19	113.49	115.62	117.58	119.39	121.06	122.60	124.01	125.31	128.55	132.20	134.11	134.69
7.25	102.88	105.54	108.00	110.28	112.38	114.32	116.10	117.74	119.25	120.64	121.91	123.07	125.97	129.19	130.86	131.36
7.50	102.64	105.07	107.31	109.38	111.28	113.03	114.64	116.12	117.47	118.71	119.85	120.88	123.45	126.28	127.73	128.16
7.75	102.39	104.59	106.62	108.48	110.19	111.76	113.20	114.52	115.73	116.83	117.83	118.75	121.01	123.47	124.72	125.08
8.00	102.15	104.13	105.94	107.60	109.12	110.52	111.79	112.95	114.02	114.98	115.86	116.66	118.63	120.75	121.82	122.12
8.25	101.91	103.66	105.26	106.72	108.06	109.28	110.40	111.41	112.34	113.18	113.94	114.63	116.32	118.13	119.02	119.28
8.50	101.67	103.19	104.58	105.85	107.01	108.07	109.03	109.90	110.69	111.41	112.06	112.65	114.08	115.59	116.33	116.54
8.75	101.43	102.73	103.91	104.99	105.98	106.87	107.68	108.41	109.07	109.68	110.22	110.71	111.89	113.14	113.74	113.91
9.00	101.19	102.27	103.25	104.14	104.95	105.68	106.35	106.95	107.49	107.98	108.42	108.81	109.77	110.76	111.24	111.37
9.25	100.95	101.81	102.59	103.30	103.94	104.52	105.04	105.51	105.93	106.32	106.66	106.97	107.71	108.47	108.83	108.93
9.50	100.71	101.35	101.94	102.46	102.94	103.36	103.75	104.10	104.41	104.69	104.94	105.16	105.70	106.25	106.50	106.57
9.75	100.47	100.90	101.29	101.63	101.95	102.23	102.48	102.71	102.91	103.09	103.26	103.40	103.75	104.10	104.26	104.30
10.00	100.24	100.45	100.64	100.81	100.97	101.11	101.23	101.34	101.44	101.53	101.61	101.68	101.85	102.02	102.09	102.11
10.25	100.00	100.00	100.00	100.00	100.00	100.00	100.00	100.00	100.00	100.00	100.00	100.00	100.00	100.00	100.00	100.00
10.50	99.76	99.55	99.36	99.19	99.04	98.91	98.79	98.68	98.59	98.50	98.43	98.36	98.20	98.05	97.98	97.96
10.75	99.53	99.11	98.73	98.40	98.10	97.83	97.59	97.38	97.20	97.03	96.88	96.75	96.45	96.16	96.03	96.00
11.00	99.29	98.67	98.11	97.61	97.16	96.77	96.42	96.11	95.83	95.59	95.38	95.19	94.75	94.33	94.14	94.10
11.25	99.06	98.23	97.48	96.82	96.24	95.72	95.26	94.86	94.50	94.18	93.90	93.66	93.09	92.55	92.32	92.26
11.50	98.83	97.79	96.87	96.05	95.33	94.69	94.12	93.62	93.19	92.80	92.46	92.16	91.48	90.83	90.56	90.49
11.75	98.59	97.35	96.25	95.28	94.42	93.67	93.00	92.41	91.90	91.45	91.05	90.70	89.91	89.16	88.85	88.77
12.00	98.36	96.92	95.64	94.52	93.53	92.66	91.89	91.22	90.63	90.12	89.67	89.27	88.38	87.54	87.20	87.12
12.25	98.13	96.49	95.04	93.77	92.65	91.67	90.81	90.05	89.39	88.82	88.32	87.88	86.89	85.97	85.60	85.51
12.50	97.90	96.06	94.44	93.02	91.77	90.69	89.73	88.90	88.18	87.54	86.99	86.51	85.44	84.45	84.06	83.96
12.75	97.67	95.63	93.84	92.28	90.91	89.72	88.68	87.77	86.98	86.29	85.70	85.18	84.02	82.97	82.56	82.46
13.00	97.44	95.20	93.25	91.55	90.06	88.76	87.64	86.66	85.81	85.07	84.43	83.88	82.64	81.54	81.11	81.01
13.25	97.21	94.78	92.66	90.82	89.22	87.82	86.61	85.56	84.65	83.87	83.19	82.61	81.30	80.15	79.70	79.60
13.50	96.98	94.36	92.08	90.10	88.38	86.89	85.60	84.49	83.52	82.69	81.98	81.36	80.00	78.80	78.34	78.23
13.75	96.75	93.94	91.50	89.39	87.56	85.98	84.61	83.43	82.41	81.54	80.79	80.14	78.72	77.48	77.02	76.91
14.00	96.53	93.52	90.93	88.68	86.74	85.07	83.63	82.39	81.32	80.41	79.62	78.95	77.48	76.21	75.73	75.63
14.25	96.30	93.11	90.35	87.98	85.94	84.18	82.66	81.37	80.25	79.30	78.48	77.79	76.27	74.97	74.49	74.38
14.50	96.07	92.70	89.79	87.29	85.14	83.30	81.71	80.36	79.20	78.21	77.37	76.65	75.09	73.77	73.28	73.18
14.75	95.85	92.28	89.23	86.60	84.35	82.43	80.78	79.37	78.17	77.15	76.28	75.54	73.94	72.59	72.11	72.01
15.00	95.62	91.88	88.67	85.92	83.57	81.57	79.86	78.40	77.16	76.10	75.21	74.45	72.81	71.46	70.97	70.87
15.25	95.40	91.47	88.11	85.25	82.80	80.72	78.95	77.44	76.16	75.08	74.16	73.38	71.72	70.35	69.87	69.76
15.50	95.18	91.06	87.56	84.58	82.04	79.88	78.05	76.50	75.18	74.07	73.13	72.34	70.65	69.27	68.79	68.69
15.75	94.95	90.66	87.01	83.92	81.29	79.06	77.17	75.57	74.23	73.09	72.13	71.32	69.61	68.22	67.75	67.65
16.00	94.73	90.26	86.47	83.26	80.54	78.25	76.30	74.66	73.28	72.12	71.14	70.32	68.59	67.20	66.73	66.64
16.25	94.51	89.86	85.93	82.61	79.81	77.44	75.45	73.77	72.36	71.17	70.18	69.35	67.60	66.21	65.75	65.65
16.50	94.29	89.47	85.40	81.97	79.08	76.65	74.60	72.89	71.45	70.24	69.24	68.39	66.63	65.24	64.78	64.69
16.75	94.07	89.07	84.87	81.33	78.36	75.87	73.77	72.02	70.56	69.33	68.31	67.46	65.68	64.30	63.85	63.76
17.00	93.85	88.68	84.34	80.70	77.65	75.09	72.96	71.17	69.68	68.44	67.40	66.54	64.76	63.39	62.94	62.85
17.25	93.63	88.29	83.82	80.07	76.94	74.33	72.15	70.33	68.82	67.56	66.51	65.65	63.86	62.49	62.06	61.97
17.50	93.41	87.90	83.30	79.45	76.25	73.58	71.36	69.51	67.97	66.70	65.64	64.77	62.98	61.62	61.19	61.11
17.75	93.19	87.51	82.78	78.84	75.56	72.84	70.57	68.70	67.14	65.85	64.79	63.92	62.12	60.77	60.35	60.27
18.00	92.97	87.13	82.27	78.23	74.88	72.10	69.80	67.90	66.32	65.02	63.95	63.08	61.28	59.95	59.54	59.46
18.25	92.75	86.74	81.76	77.63	74.21	71.38	69.04	67.11	65.52	64.21	63.14	62.25	60.46	59.14	58.74	58.66
18.50	92.54	86.36	81.25	77.03	73.54	70.66	68.29	66.34	64.73	63.41	62.33	61.45	59.66	58.35	57.96	57.89
18.75	92.32	85.98	80.75	76.44	72.88	69.96	67.55	65.58	63.96	62.63	61.55	60.66	58.88	57.59	57.20	57.13
19.00	92.11	85.60	80.25	75.85	72.23	69.26	66.83	64.83	63.20	61.86	60.77	59.89	58.11	56.84	56.46	56.40
20.00	91.25	84.11	78.30	73.56	69.70	66.57	64.02	61.96	60.28	58.93	57.83	56.95	55.22	54.02	53.68	53.63
25.00	87.10	77.08	69.30	63.27	58.60	54.99	52.19	50.03	48.36	47.08	46.09	45.33	43.97	43.18	43.01	42.99
30.00	83.16	70.70	61.50	54.70	49.68	45.99	43.26	41.26	39.79	38.71	37.92	37.34	36.39	35.93	35.85	35.84

Description: This table shows the yield to prepayment of a monthly payment mortgage purchased at a price in the index.

Example: The yield to prepayment in 10 years of a 10.25 %, 30 year mortgage at a price of 104.00 is 9.60 %.

30 YEAR MORTGAGE PREPAID IN

PRICE	1 yr	2 yr	3 yr	4 yr	5 yr	6 yr	7 yr	8 yr	9 yr	10 yr	11 yr	12 yr	15 yr	20 yr	25 yr	30 yr
140	–	–	–	–	1.76	2.85	3.63	4.20	4.64	4.99	5.26	5.49	5.97	6.38	6.57	6.62
135	–	–	–	1.18	2.65	3.63	4.32	4.83	5.22	5.53	5.78	5.98	6.40	6.77	6.93	6.97
130	–	–	–	2.30	3.59	4.44	5.04	5.49	5.83	6.10	6.31	6.49	6.86	7.18	7.31	7.35
125	–	–	1.63	3.47	4.56	5.29	5.80	6.18	6.47	6.70	6.88	7.03	7.34	7.61	7.72	7.75
120	–	–	3.19	4.69	5.59	6.18	6.60	6.90	7.14	7.33	7.48	7.60	7.85	8.07	8.16	8.18
119	–	–	3.51	4.94	5.80	6.36	6.76	7.05	7.28	7.46	7.60	7.72	7.96	8.16	8.25	8.27
118	–	1.09	3.83	5.20	6.01	6.55	6.93	7.21	7.42	7.59	7.72	7.83	8.06	8.26	8.34	8.36
117	–	1.56	4.16	5.45	6.22	6.73	7.09	7.36	7.56	7.72	7.85	7.95	8.17	8.36	8.43	8.45
116	–	2.03	4.49	5.71	6.44	6.92	7.26	7.51	7.71	7.86	7.98	8.08	8.28	8.45	8.53	8.55
115	–	2.51	4.82	5.97	6.66	7.11	7.43	7.67	7.85	7.99	8.11	8.20	8.39	8.55	8.62	8.64
114	–	2.99	5.16	6.24	6.88	7.31	7.61	7.83	8.00	8.13	8.24	8.32	8.50	8.66	8.72	8.74
113	–	3.47	5.50	6.50	7.10	7.50	7.78	7.99	8.15	8.27	8.37	8.45	8.62	8.76	8.82	8.83
112	–	3.96	5.84	6.77	7.33	7.70	7.96	8.15	8.30	8.41	8.50	8.58	8.73	8.86	8.92	8.93
111	–	4.46	6.19	7.05	7.56	7.90	8.14	8.31	8.45	8.55	8.64	8.71	8.85	8.97	9.02	9.03
110	–	4.96	6.54	7.32	7.79	8.10	8.32	8.48	8.60	8.70	8.78	8.84	8.97	9.08	9.12	9.13
109	1.17	5.46	6.89	7.60	8.02	8.30	8.50	8.65	8.76	8.84	8.91	8.97	9.09	9.19	9.23	9.24
108	2.13	5.97	7.25	7.88	8.26	8.51	8.68	8.81	8.91	8.99	9.05	9.10	9.21	9.30	9.33	9.34
107	3.11	6.48	7.61	8.17	8.50	8.72	8.87	8.99	9.07	9.14	9.20	9.24	9.33	9.41	9.44	9.45
106	4.10	7.00	7.97	8.45	8.74	8.93	9.06	9.16	9.23	9.29	9.34	9.38	9.46	9.52	9.55	9.56
105	5.09	7.53	8.34	8.74	8.98	9.14	9.25	9.33	9.40	9.45	9.49	9.52	9.58	9.64	9.66	9.67
104	6.10	8.06	8.71	9.04	9.23	9.36	9.45	9.51	9.56	9.60	9.63	9.66	9.71	9.76	9.77	9.78
103.75	6.36	8.20	8.81	9.11	9.29	9.41	9.49	9.56	9.60	9.64	9.67	9.70	9.74	9.79	9.80	9.81
103.50	6.61	8.33	8.90	9.18	9.35	9.47	9.54	9.60	9.65	9.68	9.71	9.73	9.78	9.82	9.83	9.84
103.25	6.86	8.46	9.00	9.26	9.42	9.52	9.59	9.65	9.69	9.72	9.75	9.77	9.81	9.85	9.86	9.86
103.00	7.12	8.60	9.09	9.33	9.48	9.57	9.64	9.69	9.73	9.76	9.78	9.80	9.84	9.88	9.89	9.89
102.75	7.38	8.73	9.18	9.41	9.54	9.63	9.69	9.74	9.77	9.80	9.82	9.84	9.88	9.91	9.92	9.92
102.50	7.63	8.87	9.28	9.48	9.60	9.68	9.74	9.78	9.81	9.84	9.86	9.88	9.91	9.94	9.95	9.95
102.25	7.89	9.01	9.37	9.56	9.67	9.74	9.79	9.83	9.86	9.88	9.90	9.91	9.94	9.97	9.98	9.98
102.00	8.15	9.14	9.47	9.63	9.73	9.80	9.84	9.87	9.90	9.92	9.94	9.95	9.97	10.00	10.01	10.01
101.75	8.41	9.28	9.57	9.71	9.79	9.85	9.89	9.92	9.94	9.96	9.97	9.98	10.01	10.03	10.04	10.04
101.50	8.67	9.42	9.66	9.79	9.86	9.91	9.94	9.97	9.98	10.00	10.01	10.02	10.04	10.06	10.06	10.07
101.25	8.93	9.55	9.76	9.86	9.92	9.96	9.99	10.01	10.03	10.04	10.05	10.06	10.08	10.09	10.09	10.10
101.00	9.19	9.69	9.86	9.94	9.99	10.02	10.04	10.06	10.07	10.08	10.09	10.10	10.11	10.12	10.12	10.13
100.75	9.45	9.83	9.95	10.01	10.05	10.08	10.09	10.10	10.11	10.12	10.13	10.13	10.14	10.15	10.15	10.16
100.50	9.72	9.97	10.05	10.09	10.12	10.13	10.14	10.15	10.16	10.16	10.17	10.17	10.18	10.18	10.18	10.18
100.25	9.98	10.11	10.15	10.17	10.18	10.19	10.19	10.20	10.20	10.20	10.21	10.21	10.21	10.21	10.21	10.21
100.00	10.25	10.25	10.25	10.25	10.25	10.25	10.25	10.25	10.25	10.25	10.25	10.25	10.25	10.25	10.25	10.25
99.75	10.51	10.38	10.34	10.32	10.31	10.30	10.30	10.29	10.29	10.29	10.28	10.28	10.28	10.28	10.28	10.28
99.50	10.78	10.52	10.44	10.40	10.38	10.36	10.35	10.34	10.33	10.33	10.32	10.32	10.31	10.31	10.31	10.31
99.25	11.04	10.67	10.54	10.48	10.44	10.42	10.40	10.39	10.38	10.37	10.36	10.36	10.35	10.34	10.34	10.34
99.00	11.31	10.81	10.64	10.56	10.51	10.47	10.45	10.43	10.42	10.41	10.40	10.40	10.38	10.37	10.37	10.37
98.75	11.58	10.95	10.74	10.63	10.57	10.53	10.50	10.48	10.47	10.45	10.44	10.43	10.42	10.40	10.40	10.40
98.50	11.85	11.09	10.84	10.71	10.64	10.59	10.56	10.53	10.51	10.50	10.48	10.47	10.45	10.44	10.43	10.43
98.25	12.12	11.23	10.94	10.79	10.70	10.65	10.61	10.58	10.55	10.54	10.52	10.51	10.49	10.47	10.46	10.46
98.00	12.39	11.37	11.04	10.87	10.77	10.71	10.66	10.63	10.60	10.58	10.56	10.55	10.52	10.50	10.49	10.49
97.75	12.66	11.52	11.14	10.95	10.84	10.76	10.71	10.67	10.64	10.62	10.60	10.59	10.56	10.53	10.52	10.52
97.50	12.93	11.66	11.24	11.03	10.90	10.82	10.77	10.72	10.69	10.66	10.64	10.63	10.59	10.57	10.56	10.55
97.25	13.20	11.80	11.34	11.11	10.97	10.88	10.82	10.77	10.74	10.71	10.69	10.67	10.63	10.60	10.59	10.58
97	13.48	11.95	11.44	11.19	11.04	10.94	10.87	10.82	10.78	10.75	10.73	10.71	10.67	10.63	10.62	10.62
96	14.58	12.53	11.85	11.51	11.31	11.18	11.09	11.02	10.96	10.92	10.89	10.86	10.81	10.77	10.75	10.74
95	15.69	13.12	12.26	11.84	11.58	11.42	11.30	11.22	11.15	11.10	11.06	11.03	10.96	10.90	10.88	10.87
94	16.82	13.71	12.68	12.17	11.86	11.66	11.52	11.42	11.34	11.28	11.23	11.19	11.11	11.04	11.01	11.01
93	17.96	14.31	13.10	12.50	12.14	11.91	11.74	11.62	11.53	11.46	11.40	11.35	11.26	11.18	11.15	11.14
92	19.12	14.92	13.53	12.84	12.43	12.16	11.97	11.83	11.72	11.64	11.58	11.52	11.41	11.32	11.29	11.28
91	20.29	15.54	13.96	13.18	12.72	12.41	12.20	12.04	11.92	11.83	11.75	11.69	11.57	11.47	11.43	11.42
90	21.47	16.16	14.40	13.53	13.01	12.67	12.43	12.26	12.12	12.02	11.93	11.87	11.73	11.62	11.58	11.57
89	22.67	16.79	14.85	13.88	13.31	12.93	12.67	12.47	12.33	12.21	12.12	12.04	11.89	11.77	11.72	11.71
88	23.89	17.43	15.30	14.24	13.61	13.20	12.91	12.69	12.53	12.40	12.30	12.22	12.06	11.92	11.87	11.86
87	25.11	18.08	15.75	14.60	13.92	13.47	13.15	12.92	12.74	12.60	12.49	12.41	12.23	12.08	12.03	12.01
86	26.36	18.73	16.21	14.97	14.23	13.74	13.40	13.14	12.95	12.80	12.69	12.59	12.41	12.24	12.18	12.17
85	27.62	19.40	16.68	15.34	14.54	14.01	13.65	13.38	13.17	13.01	12.88	12.78	12.57	12.40	12.34	12.33
80	34.19	22.86	19.12	17.27	16.18	15.46	14.96	14.59	14.30	14.09	13.91	13.77	13.49	13.27	13.19	13.17
75	41.24	26.57	21.75	19.36	17.95	17.03	16.38	15.90	15.54	15.26	15.04	14.87	14.51	14.24	14.14	14.12
70	48.85	30.57	24.58	21.62	19.88	18.73	17.93	17.34	16.90	16.56	16.29	16.08	15.65	15.33	15.21	15.19
65	57.09	34.92	27.66	24.09	21.98	20.60	19.64	18.94	18.41	18.00	17.68	17.43	16.93	16.56	16.44	16.41
60	66.08	39.66	31.04	26.80	24.30	22.67	21.54	20.71	20.10	19.62	19.25	18.96	18.39	17.98	17.85	17.83
55	75.96	44.88	34.77	29.80	26.89	24.99	23.67	22.72	22.01	21.46	21.04	20.71	20.07	19.64	19.51	19.49
50	86.93	50.67	38.92	33.17	29.80	27.61	26.10	25.01	24.20	23.59	23.11	22.75	22.06	21.60	21.48	21.47

PREPAYMENT MORTGAGE PRICE

10.50 %

Description: This table shows the price to pay for a monthly payment loan, at a yield rate and assuming prepayment.

Example: The price of a 10.50 %, 30 year mortgage to yield 8.00 %, if prepaid in 6 years, is $ 111.69.

30 YEAR MORTGAGE PREPAID IN

YIELD	1 yr	2 yr	3 yr	4 yr	5 yr	6 yr	7 yr	8 yr	9 yr	10 yr	11 yr	12 yr	15 yr	20 yr	25 yr	30 yr
0.00	110.48	120.90	131.26	141.55	151.77	161.90	171.94	181.87	191.70	201.39	210.94	220.34	247.41	287.33	316.98	329.31
1.00	109.43	118.71	127.85	136.84	145.67	154.35	162.85	171.19	179.35	187.32	195.10	202.68	224.07	254.41	275.87	284.40
2.00	108.39	116.57	124.54	132.30	139.86	147.20	154.33	161.25	167.95	174.44	180.70	186.74	203.47	226.28	241.64	247.48
3.00	107.36	114.47	121.33	127.94	134.31	140.44	146.34	152.00	157.43	162.63	167.61	172.36	185.25	202.17	213.02	216.97
4.00	106.35	112.41	118.21	123.74	129.02	134.04	138.83	143.38	147.71	151.81	155.69	159.36	169.13	181.45	188.98	191.60
4.25	106.09	111.91	117.44	122.71	127.73	132.50	137.03	141.32	145.39	149.24	152.88	156.31	165.39	176.74	183.59	185.95
4.50	105.84	111.40	116.68	121.70	126.46	130.98	135.25	139.30	143.12	146.73	150.13	153.33	161.76	172.20	178.42	180.53
4.75	105.59	110.90	115.93	120.69	125.20	129.47	133.50	137.31	140.90	144.28	147.45	150.43	158.24	167.82	173.46	175.36
5.00	105.34	110.40	115.18	119.70	123.96	127.99	131.78	135.36	138.72	141.87	144.83	147.60	154.82	163.60	168.70	170.40
5.25	105.09	109.90	114.43	118.71	122.74	126.53	130.09	133.44	136.58	139.52	142.27	144.84	151.51	159.53	164.14	165.65
5.50	104.84	109.40	113.70	117.73	121.52	125.08	128.42	131.55	134.48	137.22	139.77	142.14	148.28	155.60	159.75	161.11
5.75	104.60	108.91	112.96	116.76	120.33	123.66	126.78	129.70	132.42	134.96	137.32	139.51	145.16	151.81	155.55	156.75
6.00	104.35	108.42	112.23	115.80	119.14	122.26	125.17	127.88	130.40	132.75	134.93	136.95	142.12	148.16	151.51	152.57
6.25	104.10	107.93	111.51	114.85	117.97	120.87	123.58	126.09	128.43	130.59	132.60	134.45	139.17	144.63	147.62	148.56
6.50	103.85	107.45	110.80	113.91	116.81	119.51	122.01	124.33	126.48	128.47	130.31	132.01	136.30	141.23	143.89	144.72
6.75	103.61	106.96	110.08	112.98	115.67	118.16	120.47	122.61	124.58	126.40	128.08	129.62	133.52	137.94	140.31	141.03
7.00	103.36	106.48	109.38	112.06	114.54	116.83	118.95	120.91	122.71	124.37	125.90	127.30	130.82	134.77	136.86	137.49
7.25	103.12	106.01	108.67	111.14	113.42	115.52	117.46	119.24	120.88	122.39	123.77	125.03	128.19	131.71	133.54	134.09
7.50	102.88	105.53	107.98	110.23	112.31	114.23	115.99	117.60	119.08	120.44	121.68	122.82	125.64	128.75	130.35	130.82
7.75	102.63	105.06	107.29	109.34	111.22	112.95	114.54	115.99	117.32	118.54	119.65	120.66	123.15	125.89	127.27	127.68
8.00	102.39	104.58	106.60	108.45	110.14	111.69	113.11	114.41	115.59	116.67	117.65	118.55	120.74	123.12	124.32	124.66
8.25	102.15	104.12	105.92	107.57	109.07	110.45	111.71	112.85	113.90	114.85	115.71	116.49	118.40	120.45	121.47	121.76
8.50	101.91	103.65	105.24	106.69	108.02	109.23	110.33	111.33	112.23	113.06	113.80	114.48	116.12	117.86	118.72	118.97
8.75	101.67	103.19	104.57	105.83	106.98	108.02	108.96	109.82	110.60	111.30	111.94	112.51	113.90	115.37	116.08	116.28
9.00	101.43	102.72	103.90	104.97	105.94	106.83	107.62	108.35	109.00	109.59	110.12	110.59	111.75	112.95	113.53	113.69
9.25	101.19	102.26	103.24	104.12	104.92	105.65	106.30	106.89	107.43	107.91	108.34	108.72	109.65	110.61	111.07	111.19
9.50	100.95	101.81	102.58	103.28	103.92	104.49	105.00	105.47	105.88	106.26	106.59	106.90	107.61	108.35	108.69	108.79
9.75	100.71	101.35	101.93	102.45	102.92	103.34	103.72	104.07	104.37	104.65	104.89	105.11	105.63	106.16	106.40	106.47
10.00	100.47	100.90	101.28	101.63	101.94	102.21	102.46	102.69	102.89	103.07	103.22	103.37	103.70	104.04	104.19	104.24
10.25	100.24	100.45	100.64	100.81	100.96	101.10	101.22	101.33	101.43	101.52	101.59	101.66	101.83	101.99	102.06	102.08
10.50	100.00	100.00	100.00	100.00	100.00	100.00	100.00	100.00	100.00	100.00	100.00	100.00	100.00	100.00	100.00	100.00
10.75	99.76	99.55	99.37	99.20	99.05	98.92	98.80	98.69	98.60	98.51	98.44	98.37	98.22	98.07	98.01	97.99
11.00	99.53	99.11	98.74	98.40	98.11	97.84	97.61	97.40	97.22	97.06	96.91	96.79	96.49	96.21	96.08	96.05
11.25	99.30	98.67	98.11	97.62	97.18	96.79	96.44	96.14	95.87	95.63	95.42	95.24	94.81	94.40	94.22	94.18
11.50	99.06	98.23	97.49	96.84	96.26	95.75	95.29	94.89	94.54	94.23	93.96	93.72	93.17	92.65	92.43	92.37
11.75	98.83	97.79	96.88	96.06	95.35	94.72	94.16	93.67	93.24	92.86	92.53	92.24	91.57	90.95	90.69	90.62
12.00	98.60	97.36	96.26	95.30	94.45	93.70	93.05	92.47	91.96	91.52	91.13	90.79	90.02	89.30	89.00	88.93
12.25	98.36	96.92	95.66	94.54	93.56	92.70	91.95	91.29	90.71	90.20	89.76	89.38	88.51	87.70	87.37	87.29
12.50	98.13	96.49	95.05	93.79	92.68	91.71	90.87	90.12	89.48	88.91	88.42	88.00	87.03	86.15	85.79	85.71
12.75	97.90	96.06	94.46	93.05	91.82	90.74	89.80	88.98	88.27	87.65	87.11	86.64	85.59	84.64	84.27	84.18
13.00	97.67	95.64	93.86	92.31	90.96	89.78	88.75	87.86	87.08	86.41	85.83	85.32	84.20	83.18	82.79	82.69
13.25	97.44	95.21	93.27	91.58	90.11	88.83	87.72	86.75	85.92	85.19	84.57	84.03	82.83	81.77	81.35	81.25
13.50	97.21	94.79	92.69	90.86	89.27	87.89	86.70	85.67	84.77	84.00	83.34	82.77	81.50	80.39	79.96	79.86
13.75	96.99	94.37	92.10	90.14	88.44	86.97	85.70	84.60	83.65	82.84	82.14	81.54	80.21	79.05	78.61	78.51
14.00	96.76	93.95	91.53	89.43	87.62	86.05	84.71	83.55	82.55	81.69	80.96	80.33	78.94	77.75	77.30	77.20
14.25	96.53	93.54	90.95	88.73	86.81	85.15	83.73	82.51	81.47	80.57	79.80	79.15	77.71	76.49	76.03	75.93
14.50	96.31	93.12	90.38	88.03	86.00	84.27	82.78	81.50	80.40	79.47	78.67	77.99	76.51	75.26	74.80	74.70
14.75	96.08	92.71	89.82	87.34	85.21	83.39	81.83	80.50	79.36	78.39	77.57	76.86	75.34	74.07	73.60	73.50
15.00	95.85	92.30	89.26	86.65	84.43	82.52	80.90	79.52	78.34	77.33	76.48	75.76	74.20	72.91	72.44	72.34
15.25	95.63	91.89	88.70	85.98	83.65	81.67	79.98	78.55	77.33	76.30	75.42	74.68	73.09	71.78	71.31	71.22
15.50	95.41	91.49	88.15	85.31	82.89	80.83	79.08	77.60	76.34	75.28	74.38	73.62	72.00	70.68	70.22	70.12
15.75	95.18	91.08	87.60	84.64	82.13	80.00	78.19	76.66	75.37	74.28	73.36	72.59	70.94	69.61	69.15	69.06
16.00	94.96	90.68	87.06	83.98	81.38	79.18	77.31	75.74	74.42	73.30	72.36	71.58	69.91	68.57	68.12	68.02
16.25	94.74	90.28	86.51	83.33	80.64	78.37	76.45	74.84	73.48	72.34	71.39	70.59	68.90	67.56	67.11	67.02
16.50	94.52	89.88	85.98	82.68	79.90	77.57	75.60	73.95	72.56	71.40	70.43	69.62	67.92	66.57	66.13	66.04
16.75	94.29	89.49	85.44	82.04	79.18	76.78	74.76	73.07	71.66	70.48	69.49	68.67	66.95	65.61	65.17	65.09
17.00	94.07	89.09	84.91	81.40	78.46	76.00	73.94	72.21	70.77	69.57	68.57	67.74	66.02	64.68	64.25	64.16
17.25	93.85	88.70	84.39	80.78	77.75	75.23	73.12	71.36	69.90	68.68	67.67	66.83	65.10	63.77	63.34	63.26
17.50	93.63	88.31	83.87	80.15	77.05	74.47	72.32	70.53	69.04	67.81	66.79	65.94	64.20	62.88	62.46	62.38
17.75	93.42	87.92	83.35	79.53	76.36	73.72	71.53	69.71	68.20	66.95	65.92	65.07	63.33	62.02	61.61	61.53
18.00	93.20	87.54	82.83	78.92	75.68	72.98	70.75	68.90	67.38	66.12	65.08	64.22	62.48	61.17	60.77	60.70
18.25	92.98	87.15	82.32	78.32	75.00	72.25	69.98	68.11	66.56	65.29	64.25	63.39	61.64	60.35	59.96	59.88
18.50	92.76	86.77	81.81	77.72	74.33	71.53	69.23	67.33	65.77	64.48	63.43	62.57	60.83	59.55	59.16	59.09
18.75	92.55	86.39	81.31	77.12	73.67	70.82	68.48	66.56	64.98	63.69	62.63	61.77	60.03	58.77	58.39	58.32
19.00	92.33	86.01	80.81	76.53	73.01	70.12	67.75	65.80	64.21	62.91	61.85	60.98	59.25	58.00	57.64	57.57
20.00	91.47	84.52	78.84	74.22	70.46	67.40	64.92	62.90	61.26	59.94	58.87	58.01	56.31	55.13	54.80	54.74
25.00	87.31	77.46	69.81	63.88	59.28	55.72	52.96	50.84	49.19	47.93	46.95	46.20	44.86	44.08	43.90	43.88
30.00	83.37	71.06	61.97	55.25	50.29	46.64	43.94	41.96	40.50	39.43	38.65	38.08	37.13	36.67	36.59	36.58

Description: This table shows the yield to prepayment of a monthly payment mortgage purchased at a price in the index.

Example: The yield to prepayment in 10 years of a 10.50 %, 30 year mortgage at a price of 104.00 is 9.85 %.

30 YEAR MORTGAGE PREPAID IN

PRICE	1 yr	2 yr	3 yr	4 yr	5 yr	6 yr	7 yr	8 yr	9 yr	10 yr	11 yr	12 yr	15 yr	20 yr	25 yr	30 yr
140	–	–	–	–	1.97	3.06	3.83	4.41	4.85	5.19	5.47	5.70	6.17	6.59	6.77	6.82
135	–	–	–	1.40	2.87	3.84	4.53	5.04	5.43	5.74	5.99	6.19	6.61	6.98	7.13	7.18
130	–	–	–	2.52	3.81	4.66	5.26	5.70	6.05	6.31	6.53	6.71	7.07	7.39	7.52	7.56
125	–	–	1.85	3.69	4.79	5.51	6.02	6.40	6.69	6.92	7.10	7.25	7.56	7.82	7.94	7.97
120	–	–	3.42	4.92	5.81	6.40	6.82	7.13	7.37	7.55	7.70	7.82	8.07	8.29	8.38	8.40
119	–	–	3.74	5.17	6.02	6.59	6.99	7.28	7.51	7.68	7.83	7.94	8.18	8.38	8.47	8.49
118	–	1.33	4.06	5.43	6.24	6.78	7.15	7.43	7.65	7.82	7.95	8.06	8.29	8.48	8.56	8.58
117	–	1.79	4.39	5.68	6.45	6.96	7.32	7.59	7.79	7.95	8.08	8.18	8.40	8.58	8.66	8.68
116	–	2.26	4.72	5.94	6.67	7.15	7.49	7.74	7.94	8.09	8.21	8.30	8.51	8.68	8.75	8.77
115	–	2.74	5.05	6.21	6.89	7.35	7.66	7.90	8.08	8.22	8.34	8.43	8.62	8.78	8.85	8.87
114	–	3.22	5.39	6.47	7.11	7.54	7.84	8.06	8.23	8.36	8.47	8.55	8.73	8.89	8.95	8.96
113	–	3.71	5.73	6.74	7.34	7.74	8.01	8.22	8.38	8.50	8.60	8.68	8.85	8.99	9.05	9.06
112	–	4.20	6.08	7.01	7.57	7.93	8.19	8.38	8.53	8.65	8.74	8.81	8.97	9.10	9.15	9.16
111	–	4.69	6.42	7.28	7.80	8.13	8.37	8.55	8.68	8.79	8.87	8.94	9.08	9.20	9.25	9.26
110	–	5.19	6.77	7.56	8.03	8.34	8.55	8.72	8.84	8.93	9.01	9.07	9.20	9.31	9.36	9.37
109	1.41	5.70	7.13	7.84	8.26	8.54	8.74	8.88	8.99	9.08	9.15	9.21	9.32	9.42	9.46	9.47
108	2.37	6.21	7.49	8.12	8.50	8.75	8.92	9.05	9.15	9.23	9.29	9.34	9.45	9.53	9.57	9.58
107	3.35	6.73	7.85	8.41	8.74	8.96	9.11	9.23	9.31	9.38	9.44	9.48	9.57	9.65	9.68	9.69
106	4.34	7.25	8.21	8.70	8.98	9.17	9.30	9.40	9.48	9.53	9.58	9.62	9.70	9.76	9.79	9.80
105	5.34	7.77	8.58	8.99	9.23	9.38	9.50	9.58	9.64	9.69	9.73	9.76	9.83	9.88	9.90	9.91
104	6.35	8.31	8.96	9.28	9.47	9.60	9.69	9.76	9.81	9.85	9.88	9.90	9.96	10.00	10.02	10.02
103.75	6.60	8.44	9.05	9.36	9.54	9.66	9.74	9.80	9.85	9.89	9.92	9.94	9.99	10.03	10.05	10.05
103.50	6.86	8.58	9.15	9.43	9.60	9.71	9.79	9.85	9.89	9.93	9.95	9.98	10.02	10.06	10.08	10.08
103.25	7.11	8.71	9.24	9.51	9.66	9.77	9.84	9.89	9.93	9.97	9.99	10.01	10.05	10.09	10.10	10.11
103.00	7.37	8.85	9.34	9.58	9.73	9.82	9.89	9.94	9.98	10.01	10.03	10.05	10.09	10.12	10.13	10.14
102.75	7.62	8.98	9.43	9.66	9.79	9.88	9.94	9.98	10.02	10.05	10.07	10.08	10.12	10.15	10.16	10.17
102.50	7.88	9.12	9.53	9.73	9.85	9.93	9.99	10.03	10.06	10.09	10.11	10.12	10.15	10.18	10.19	10.20
102.25	8.14	9.25	9.62	9.81	9.92	9.99	10.04	10.08	10.10	10.13	10.14	10.16	10.19	10.21	10.22	10.22
102.00	8.40	9.39	9.72	9.88	9.98	10.04	10.09	10.12	10.15	10.17	10.18	10.20	10.22	10.24	10.25	10.25
101.75	8.66	9.53	9.81	9.96	10.04	10.10	10.14	10.17	10.19	10.21	10.22	10.23	10.26	10.27	10.28	10.28
101.50	8.92	9.66	9.91	10.03	10.11	10.15	10.19	10.21	10.23	10.25	10.26	10.27	10.29	10.31	10.31	10.31
101.25	9.18	9.80	10.01	10.11	10.17	10.21	10.24	10.26	10.28	10.29	10.30	10.31	10.32	10.34	10.34	10.34
101.00	9.44	9.94	10.10	10.19	10.24	10.27	10.29	10.31	10.32	10.33	10.34	10.34	10.36	10.37	10.37	10.37
100.75	9.70	10.08	10.20	10.26	10.30	10.32	10.34	10.35	10.36	10.37	10.38	10.38	10.39	10.40	10.40	10.40
100.50	9.97	10.22	10.30	10.34	10.36	10.38	10.39	10.40	10.41	10.41	10.42	10.42	10.43	10.43	10.43	10.43
100.25	10.23	10.36	10.40	10.42	10.43	10.44	10.44	10.45	10.45	10.45	10.46	10.46	10.46	10.46	10.46	10.46
100.00	10.50	10.50	10.50	10.50	10.50	10.50	10.50	10.50	10.50	10.50	10.50	10.50	10.50	10.50	10.50	10.50
99.75	10.76	10.64	10.59	10.57	10.56	10.55	10.55	10.54	10.54	10.54	10.53	10.53	10.53	10.53	10.53	10.53
99.50	11.03	10.78	10.69	10.65	10.63	10.61	10.60	10.59	10.58	10.58	10.57	10.57	10.56	10.56	10.56	10.56
99.25	11.29	10.92	10.79	10.73	10.69	10.67	10.65	10.64	10.63	10.62	10.61	10.61	10.60	10.59	10.59	10.59
99.00	11.56	11.06	10.89	10.81	10.76	10.73	10.70	10.69	10.67	10.66	10.65	10.65	10.63	10.62	10.62	10.62
98.75	11.83	11.20	10.99	10.89	10.82	10.78	10.75	10.73	10.72	10.70	10.69	10.69	10.67	10.66	10.65	10.65
98.50	12.10	11.34	11.09	10.96	10.89	10.84	10.81	10.78	10.76	10.75	10.74	10.73	10.71	10.69	10.68	10.68
98.25	12.37	11.48	11.19	11.04	10.96	10.90	10.86	10.83	10.81	10.79	10.78	10.76	10.74	10.72	10.71	10.71
98.00	12.64	11.63	11.29	11.12	11.02	10.96	10.91	10.88	10.85	10.83	10.82	10.80	10.78	10.75	10.75	10.74
97.75	12.91	11.77	11.39	11.20	11.09	11.02	10.97	10.93	10.90	10.88	10.86	10.84	10.81	10.79	10.78	10.78
97.50	13.18	11.91	11.49	11.28	11.16	11.08	11.02	10.98	10.94	10.92	10.90	10.88	10.85	10.82	10.81	10.81
97.25	13.46	12.06	11.59	11.36	11.23	11.14	11.07	11.03	10.99	10.96	10.94	10.92	10.88	10.85	10.84	10.84
97	13.73	12.20	11.69	11.44	11.29	11.19	11.13	11.07	11.04	11.00	10.98	10.96	10.92	10.89	10.88	10.87
96	14.83	12.78	12.10	11.77	11.57	11.43	11.34	11.27	11.22	11.18	11.15	11.12	11.07	11.02	11.01	11.00
95	15.95	13.37	12.52	12.09	11.84	11.68	11.56	11.47	11.41	11.36	11.32	11.28	11.22	11.16	11.14	11.13
94	17.08	13.97	12.94	12.43	12.12	11.92	11.78	11.68	11.60	11.54	11.49	11.45	11.37	11.30	11.28	11.27
93	18.22	14.57	13.36	12.76	12.40	12.17	12.01	11.88	11.79	11.72	11.66	11.62	11.52	11.44	11.41	11.41
92	19.38	15.18	13.79	13.10	12.69	12.42	12.23	12.09	11.99	11.90	11.84	11.79	11.68	11.59	11.56	11.55
91	20.55	15.80	14.22	13.45	12.98	12.68	12.46	12.31	12.19	12.09	12.02	11.96	11.84	11.74	11.70	11.69
90	21.74	16.42	14.67	13.79	13.28	12.94	12.70	12.52	12.39	12.28	12.20	12.13	12.00	11.89	11.85	11.84
89	22.94	17.06	15.11	14.15	13.58	13.20	12.94	12.74	12.59	12.48	12.39	12.31	12.16	12.04	12.00	11.98
88	24.15	17.70	15.56	14.51	13.88	13.47	13.18	12.96	12.80	12.68	12.57	12.49	12.33	12.20	12.15	12.14
87	25.38	18.35	16.02	14.87	14.19	13.74	13.42	13.19	13.01	12.88	12.77	12.68	12.50	12.36	12.30	12.29
86	26.63	19.00	16.48	15.24	14.50	14.01	13.67	13.42	13.23	13.08	12.96	12.87	12.67	12.52	12.46	12.45
85	27.89	19.67	16.95	15.61	14.81	14.29	13.92	13.65	13.45	13.29	13.16	13.06	12.85	12.69	12.62	12.61
80	34.47	23.14	19.40	17.56	16.46	15.74	15.24	14.87	14.59	14.37	14.20	14.06	13.79	13.57	13.49	13.47
75	41.53	26.86	22.04	19.65	18.24	17.32	16.67	16.20	15.84	15.56	15.35	15.17	14.82	14.55	14.45	14.43
70	49.15	30.88	24.88	21.93	20.18	19.04	18.24	17.66	17.22	16.88	16.61	16.40	15.97	15.65	15.55	15.52
65	57.40	35.23	27.98	24.41	22.30	20.92	19.96	19.27	18.74	18.33	18.02	17.77	17.27	16.91	16.79	16.77
60	66.41	39.99	31.37	27.13	24.64	23.01	21.88	21.06	20.45	19.97	19.61	19.32	18.75	18.35	18.21	18.21
55	76.31	45.22	35.11	30.16	27.24	25.35	24.04	23.09	22.38	21.84	21.42	21.09	20.47	20.04	19.92	19.90
50	87.29	51.04	39.29	33.54	30.18	28.00	26.49	25.41	24.60	23.99	23.53	23.17	22.49	22.05	21.93	21.92

Description: This table shows the price to pay for a monthly payment loan, at a yield rate and assuming prepayment.

Example: The price of a 10.75 %, 30 year mortgage to yield 8.00 %, if prepaid in 6 years, is $ 112.87.

30 YEAR MORTGAGE PREPAID IN

YIELD	1 yr	2 yr	3 yr	4 yr	5 yr	6 yr	7 yr	8 yr	9 yr	10 yr	11 yr	12 yr	15 yr	20 yr	25 yr	30 yr
0.00	110.73	121.40	132.01	142.56	153.04	163.43	173.73	183.92	194.01	203.97	213.78	223.44	251.30	292.50	323.23	336.05
1.00	109.68	119.21	128.59	137.83	146.91	155.82	164.57	173.15	181.55	189.76	197.77	205.58	227.65	259.04	281.32	290.23
2.00	108.64	117.06	125.27	133.27	141.06	148.63	155.99	163.12	170.05	176.74	183.22	189.46	206.77	230.44	246.44	252.55
3.00	107.61	114.96	122.05	128.89	135.48	141.82	147.93	153.79	159.42	164.82	169.98	174.91	188.30	205.92	217.27	221.41
4.00	106.59	112.89	118.92	124.67	130.15	135.38	140.36	145.10	149.60	153.88	157.92	161.75	171.95	184.85	192.76	195.53
4.25	106.34	112.39	118.15	123.64	128.86	133.83	138.54	143.02	147.27	151.28	155.08	158.66	168.16	180.06	187.26	189.76
4.50	106.09	111.88	117.38	122.61	127.58	132.29	136.76	140.98	144.98	148.75	152.30	155.65	164.48	175.43	181.99	184.23
4.75	105.84	111.37	116.63	121.60	126.32	130.78	134.99	138.98	142.73	146.27	149.59	152.71	160.91	170.98	176.94	178.95
5.00	105.59	110.87	115.87	120.60	125.07	129.29	133.26	137.01	140.53	143.84	146.94	149.85	157.44	166.69	172.09	173.89
5.25	105.34	110.37	115.13	119.61	123.83	127.81	131.55	135.07	138.37	141.46	144.35	147.05	154.08	162.55	167.43	169.05
5.50	105.09	109.88	114.39	118.63	122.62	126.36	129.87	133.17	136.25	139.13	141.82	144.32	150.81	158.55	162.96	164.41
5.75	104.84	109.38	113.65	117.65	121.41	124.93	128.22	131.30	134.17	136.85	139.35	141.66	147.64	154.70	158.67	159.96
6.00	104.59	108.89	112.92	116.69	120.22	123.51	126.59	129.46	132.13	134.62	136.93	139.07	144.55	150.98	154.55	155.70
6.25	104.34	108.40	112.19	115.74	119.04	122.12	124.99	127.66	130.13	132.43	134.57	136.54	141.56	147.39	150.60	151.61
6.50	104.10	107.91	111.47	114.79	117.87	120.74	123.41	125.88	128.17	130.30	132.26	134.06	138.65	143.93	146.79	147.69
6.75	103.85	107.43	110.76	113.85	116.72	119.39	121.85	124.14	126.25	128.20	130.00	131.65	135.83	140.58	143.13	143.92
7.00	103.60	106.95	110.05	112.92	115.59	118.05	120.32	122.43	124.37	126.15	127.79	129.30	133.09	137.36	139.62	140.31
7.25	103.36	106.47	109.35	112.00	114.46	116.73	118.82	120.74	122.51	124.14	125.63	127.00	130.42	134.24	136.23	136.84
7.50	103.12	105.99	108.65	111.09	113.35	115.43	117.33	119.09	120.70	122.18	123.53	124.76	127.83	131.22	132.98	133.50
7.75	102.87	105.52	107.95	110.19	112.25	114.14	115.87	117.46	118.92	120.25	121.46	122.57	125.31	128.31	129.85	130.30
8.00	102.63	105.04	107.26	109.30	111.16	112.87	114.44	115.87	117.17	118.36	119.45	120.43	122.86	125.50	126.83	127.22
8.25	102.39	104.57	106.58	108.41	110.09	111.62	113.02	114.30	115.46	116.52	117.48	118.35	120.48	122.78	123.92	124.25
8.50	102.15	104.11	105.90	107.53	109.03	110.39	111.63	112.75	113.78	114.71	115.55	116.31	118.17	120.15	121.12	121.40
8.75	101.90	103.64	105.22	106.67	107.98	109.17	110.25	111.24	112.13	112.94	113.66	114.32	115.92	117.61	118.43	118.66
9.00	101.66	103.18	104.55	105.80	106.94	107.97	108.90	109.75	110.51	111.20	111.82	112.38	113.73	115.15	115.82	116.01
9.25	101.42	102.72	103.89	104.95	105.91	106.78	107.57	108.28	108.92	109.50	110.02	110.48	111.61	112.77	113.32	113.47
9.50	101.19	102.26	103.23	104.11	104.90	105.62	106.26	106.84	107.36	107.83	108.26	108.63	109.54	110.46	110.90	111.02
9.75	100.95	101.80	102.57	103.27	103.90	104.46	104.97	105.43	105.84	106.20	106.53	106.82	107.52	108.23	108.56	108.65
10.00	100.71	101.35	101.92	102.44	102.91	103.32	103.70	104.03	104.34	104.60	104.84	105.06	105.56	106.07	106.31	106.37
10.25	100.47	100.90	101.28	101.62	101.93	102.20	102.45	102.67	102.86	103.04	103.19	103.33	103.66	103.99	104.13	104.17
10.50	100.24	100.45	100.64	100.81	100.96	101.09	101.21	101.32	101.42	101.50	101.58	101.65	101.80	101.96	102.03	102.05
10.75	100.00	100.00	100.00	100.00	100.00	100.00	100.00	100.00	100.00	100.00	100.00	100.00	100.00	100.00	100.00	100.00
11.00	99.76	99.55	99.37	99.20	99.05	98.92	98.80	98.70	98.61	98.53	98.45	98.39	98.24	98.10	98.04	98.02
11.25	99.53	99.11	98.74	98.41	98.12	97.86	97.63	97.42	97.24	97.08	96.94	96.82	96.53	96.26	96.14	96.11
11.50	99.30	98.67	98.12	97.63	97.19	96.81	96.47	96.17	95.90	95.67	95.46	95.28	94.87	94.47	94.31	94.26
11.75	99.06	98.23	97.50	96.85	96.28	95.77	95.33	94.93	94.59	94.28	94.02	93.78	93.25	92.74	92.53	92.48
12.00	98.83	97.80	96.89	96.08	95.37	94.75	94.20	93.72	93.29	92.92	92.60	92.32	91.67	91.06	90.81	90.75
12.25	98.60	97.36	96.28	95.32	94.48	93.74	93.09	92.52	92.03	91.59	91.21	90.88	90.13	89.44	89.15	89.08
12.50	98.37	96.93	95.67	94.56	93.59	92.74	92.00	91.35	90.78	90.28	89.86	89.48	88.63	87.86	87.54	87.47
12.75	98.14	96.50	95.07	93.82	92.72	91.76	90.93	90.20	89.56	89.01	88.53	88.11	87.17	86.32	85.98	85.90
13.00	97.91	96.07	94.47	93.08	91.86	90.79	89.87	89.06	88.36	87.75	87.23	86.77	85.75	84.83	84.47	84.39
13.25	97.68	95.65	93.88	92.34	91.00	89.84	88.82	87.95	87.18	86.52	85.95	85.46	84.37	83.39	83.01	82.92
13.50	97.45	95.22	93.29	91.61	90.16	88.89	87.80	86.85	86.03	85.32	84.71	84.18	83.02	81.99	81.59	81.50
13.75	97.22	94.80	92.71	90.89	89.32	87.96	86.78	85.77	84.89	84.14	83.49	82.93	81.70	80.62	80.21	80.12
14.00	96.99	94.38	92.13	90.18	88.50	87.04	85.79	84.71	83.78	82.98	82.29	81.71	80.42	79.30	78.88	78.78
14.25	96.76	93.97	91.55	89.47	87.68	86.13	84.81	83.66	82.68	81.84	81.13	80.51	79.17	78.01	77.58	77.49
14.50	96.54	93.55	90.98	88.77	86.87	85.24	83.84	82.64	81.61	80.73	79.98	79.34	77.95	76.76	76.33	76.23
14.75	96.31	93.14	90.42	88.08	86.07	84.36	82.89	81.63	80.55	79.64	78.86	78.20	76.76	75.55	75.11	75.01
15.00	96.08	92.73	89.85	87.39	85.28	83.48	81.95	80.64	79.52	78.57	77.76	77.08	75.60	74.36	73.92	73.83
15.25	95.86	92.32	89.29	86.71	84.50	82.62	81.02	79.66	78.50	77.52	76.68	75.98	74.47	73.21	72.77	72.68
15.50	95.63	91.91	88.74	86.03	83.73	81.77	80.11	78.70	77.50	76.49	75.63	74.91	73.36	72.09	71.65	71.56
15.75	95.41	91.51	88.19	85.36	82.97	80.94	79.21	77.75	76.52	75.48	74.60	73.86	72.28	71.01	70.56	70.47
16.00	95.19	91.10	87.64	84.70	82.21	80.11	78.33	76.82	75.56	74.49	73.59	72.83	71.23	69.95	69.51	69.42
16.25	94.97	90.70	87.10	84.05	81.47	79.29	77.46	75.91	74.61	73.52	72.60	71.83	70.21	68.92	68.48	68.39
16.50	94.74	90.30	86.56	83.39	80.73	78.49	76.60	75.01	73.68	72.56	71.63	70.85	69.21	67.91	67.48	67.39
16.75	94.52	89.91	86.02	82.75	80.00	77.69	75.75	74.13	72.77	71.63	70.69	69.89	68.23	66.93	66.51	66.42
17.00	94.30	89.51	85.49	82.11	79.28	76.91	74.92	73.26	71.87	70.71	69.75	68.94	67.27	65.98	65.56	65.48
17.25	94.08	89.12	84.96	81.48	78.57	76.13	74.10	72.40	70.99	69.81	68.83	68.02	66.34	65.05	64.64	64.56
17.50	93.86	88.73	84.44	80.85	77.86	75.37	73.29	71.56	70.12	68.93	67.94	67.12	65.43	64.15	63.74	63.66
17.75	93.64	88.34	83.92	80.23	77.16	74.61	72.49	70.73	69.27	68.06	67.06	66.24	64.54	63.27	62.87	62.79
18.00	93.42	87.95	83.40	79.62	76.47	73.87	71.70	69.91	68.43	67.21	66.20	65.37	63.68	62.41	62.01	61.94
18.25	93.21	87.57	82.89	79.01	75.79	73.13	70.93	69.11	67.61	66.38	65.36	64.52	62.83	61.57	61.18	61.11
18.50	92.99	87.18	82.38	78.40	75.12	72.40	70.17	68.32	66.80	65.56	64.53	63.70	62.00	60.75	60.37	60.30
18.75	92.77	86.80	81.87	77.80	74.45	71.69	69.41	67.55	66.01	64.75	63.72	62.88	61.19	59.95	59.58	59.52
19.00	92.56	86.42	81.37	77.21	73.79	70.98	68.67	66.78	65.23	63.97	62.93	62.09	60.40	59.18	58.82	58.75
20.00	91.70	84.92	79.39	74.89	71.22	68.24	65.81	63.84	62.25	60.95	59.91	59.06	57.40	56.24	55.92	55.86
25.00	87.53	77.84	70.32	64.49	59.96	56.46	53.74	51.65	50.03	48.78	47.82	47.08	45.75	44.97	44.80	44.78
30.00	83.58	71.43	62.44	55.81	50.91	47.29	44.62	42.66	41.22	40.16	39.38	38.82	37.88	37.42	37.34	37.33

PREPAYMENT MORTGAGE YIELD, 30 YEAR TERM   10.75 %

Description: This table shows the yield to prepayment of a monthly payment mortgage purchased at a price in the index.

Example: The yield to prepayment in 10 years of a 10.75 %, 30 year mortgage at a price of 104.00 is 10.09 %.

30 YEAR MORTGAGE PREPAID IN

PRICE	1 yr	2 yr	3 yr	4 yr	5 yr	6 yr	7 yr	8 yr	9 yr	10 yr	11 yr	12 yr	15 yr	20 yr	25 yr	30 yr
140	–	–	–	–	2.18	3.27	4.04	4.62	5.06	5.40	5.68	5.90	6.38	6.79	6.97	7.02
135	–	–	–	1.61	3.08	4.06	4.74	5.25	5.64	5.95	6.20	6.40	6.82	7.18	7.34	7.38
130	–	–	–	2.74	4.02	4.87	5.48	5.92	6.26	6.53	6.74	6.92	7.29	7.60	7.73	7.77
125	–	–	2.08	3.91	5.01	5.73	6.24	6.62	6.91	7.14	7.32	7.47	7.78	8.04	8.15	8.18
120	–	–	3.65	5.15	6.04	6.63	7.05	7.36	7.59	7.78	7.93	8.05	8.30	8.51	8.60	8.62
119	–	1.09	3.97	5.40	6.25	6.82	7.21	7.51	7.73	7.91	8.05	8.17	8.40	8.61	8.69	8.71
118	–	1.56	4.29	5.66	6.47	7.00	7.38	7.66	7.88	8.04	8.18	8.29	8.51	8.71	8.79	8.81
117	–	2.02	4.62	5.91	6.68	7.19	7.55	7.82	8.02	8.18	8.31	8.41	8.62	8.81	8.88	8.90
116	–	2.50	4.95	6.18	6.90	7.38	7.72	7.97	8.17	8.32	8.44	8.53	8.74	8.91	8.98	9.00
115	–	2.97	5.29	6.44	7.12	7.58	7.90	8.13	8.31	8.45	8.57	8.66	8.85	9.01	9.08	9.09
114	–	3.46	5.63	6.71	7.35	7.77	8.07	8.29	8.46	8.59	8.70	8.79	8.96	9.11	9.18	9.19
113	–	3.94	5.97	6.97	7.57	7.97	8.25	8.45	8.61	8.74	8.83	8.91	9.08	9.22	9.28	9.29
112	–	4.43	6.31	7.25	7.80	8.17	8.43	8.62	8.76	8.88	8.97	9.04	9.20	9.33	9.38	9.39
111	–	4.93	6.66	7.52	8.03	8.37	8.61	8.78	8.92	9.02	9.11	9.18	9.32	9.44	9.48	9.50
110	–	5.43	7.01	7.80	8.27	8.57	8.79	8.95	9.07	9.17	9.25	9.31	9.44	9.55	9.59	9.60
109	1.65	5.94	7.37	8.08	8.50	8.78	8.98	9.12	9.23	9.32	9.39	9.44	9.56	9.66	9.70	9.71
108	2.61	6.45	7.73	8.36	8.74	8.99	9.16	9.29	9.39	9.47	9.53	9.58	9.69	9.77	9.81	9.82
107	3.59	6.97	8.09	8.65	8.98	9.20	9.35	9.47	9.55	9.62	9.68	9.72	9.81	9.89	9.92	9.93
106	4.58	7.49	8.46	8.94	9.22	9.41	9.55	9.64	9.72	9.78	9.82	9.86	9.94	10.00	10.03	10.04
105	5.58	8.02	8.83	9.23	9.47	9.63	9.74	9.82	9.88	9.93	9.97	10.00	10.07	10.12	10.14	10.15
104	6.59	8.55	9.20	9.53	9.72	9.85	9.94	10.00	10.05	10.09	10.12	10.15	10.20	10.24	10.26	10.26
103.75	6.85	8.69	9.30	9.60	9.78	9.90	9.98	10.05	10.09	10.13	10.16	10.18	10.23	10.27	10.29	10.29
103.50	7.10	8.82	9.39	9.68	9.84	9.96	10.03	10.09	10.14	10.17	10.20	10.22	10.27	10.30	10.32	10.32
103.25	7.36	8.96	9.49	9.75	9.91	10.01	10.08	10.14	10.18	10.21	10.24	10.26	10.30	10.33	10.35	10.35
103.00	7.61	9.09	9.58	9.83	9.97	10.07	10.13	10.18	10.22	10.25	10.27	10.29	10.33	10.37	10.38	10.38
102.75	7.87	9.23	9.68	9.90	10.03	10.12	10.18	10.23	10.26	10.29	10.31	10.33	10.37	10.40	10.41	10.41
102.50	8.13	9.36	9.77	9.98	10.10	10.18	10.23	10.28	10.31	10.33	10.35	10.37	10.40	10.43	10.44	10.44
102.25	8.39	9.50	9.87	10.06	10.16	10.23	10.28	10.32	10.35	10.37	10.39	10.40	10.43	10.46	10.47	10.47
102.00	8.65	9.64	9.97	10.13	10.23	10.29	10.34	10.37	10.39	10.41	10.43	10.44	10.47	10.49	10.50	10.50
101.75	8.91	9.77	10.06	10.21	10.29	10.35	10.39	10.41	10.44	10.45	10.47	10.48	10.50	10.52	10.53	10.53
101.50	9.17	9.91	10.16	10.28	10.35	10.40	10.44	10.46	10.48	10.50	10.51	10.52	10.54	10.55	10.56	10.56
101.25	9.43	10.05	10.26	10.36	10.42	10.46	10.49	10.51	10.52	10.54	10.55	10.55	10.57	10.58	10.59	10.59
101.00	9.69	10.19	10.35	10.44	10.48	10.52	10.54	10.56	10.57	10.58	10.59	10.59	10.61	10.62	10.62	10.62
100.75	9.95	10.33	10.45	10.51	10.55	10.57	10.59	10.60	10.61	10.62	10.63	10.63	10.64	10.65	10.65	10.65
100.50	10.22	10.47	10.55	10.59	10.61	10.63	10.64	10.65	10.66	10.66	10.67	10.67	10.68	10.68	10.68	10.68
100.25	10.48	10.61	10.65	10.67	10.68	10.69	10.69	10.70	10.70	10.70	10.71	10.71	10.71	10.71	10.71	10.71
100.00	10.75	10.75	10.75	10.75	10.75	10.75	10.75	10.75	10.75	10.75	10.75	10.75	10.75	10.75	10.75	10.75
99.75	11.01	10.89	10.84	10.82	10.81	10.80	10.80	10.79	10.79	10.79	10.79	10.79	10.78	10.78	10.78	10.78
99.50	11.28	11.03	10.94	10.90	10.88	10.86	10.85	10.84	10.83	10.83	10.83	10.82	10.82	10.81	10.81	10.81
99.25	11.54	11.17	11.04	10.98	10.94	10.92	10.90	10.89	10.88	10.87	10.87	10.86	10.85	10.84	10.84	10.84
99.00	11.81	11.31	11.14	11.06	11.01	10.98	10.95	10.94	10.92	10.91	10.91	10.90	10.89	10.88	10.87	10.87
98.75	12.08	11.45	11.24	11.14	11.08	11.04	11.01	10.99	10.97	10.96	10.95	10.94	10.92	10.91	10.90	10.90
98.50	12.35	11.59	11.34	11.22	11.14	11.09	11.06	11.03	11.01	11.00	10.99	10.98	10.96	10.94	10.94	10.93
98.25	12.62	11.74	11.44	11.30	11.21	11.15	11.11	11.08	11.06	11.04	11.03	11.02	10.99	10.97	10.97	10.97
98.00	12.89	11.88	11.54	11.38	11.28	11.21	11.17	11.13	11.11	11.09	11.07	11.06	11.03	11.01	11.00	11.00
97.75	13.16	12.02	11.64	11.46	11.34	11.27	11.22	11.18	11.15	11.13	11.11	11.10	11.07	11.04	11.03	11.03
97.50	13.44	12.17	11.74	11.54	11.41	11.33	11.27	11.23	11.20	11.17	11.15	11.14	11.10	11.08	11.06	11.06
97.25	13.71	12.31	11.85	11.62	11.48	11.39	11.33	11.28	11.24	11.22	11.19	11.18	11.14	11.11	11.10	11.09
97	13.98	12.46	11.95	11.70	11.55	11.45	11.38	11.33	11.29	11.26	11.24	11.22	11.18	11.14	11.13	11.13
96	15.09	13.04	12.36	12.02	11.82	11.69	11.60	11.53	11.48	11.44	11.40	11.38	11.32	11.28	11.26	11.26
95	16.21	13.63	12.77	12.35	12.10	11.93	11.82	11.73	11.67	11.61	11.57	11.54	11.47	11.42	11.40	11.39
94	17.34	14.23	13.19	12.68	12.38	12.18	12.04	11.94	11.86	11.80	11.75	11.71	11.63	11.56	11.54	11.53
93	18.48	14.83	13.62	13.02	12.66	12.43	12.27	12.14	12.05	11.98	11.92	11.88	11.78	11.71	11.68	11.67
92	19.64	15.44	14.05	13.36	12.95	12.68	12.50	12.36	12.25	12.17	12.10	12.05	11.94	11.85	11.82	11.81
91	20.81	16.06	14.49	13.71	13.25	12.94	12.73	12.57	12.45	12.36	12.28	12.22	12.10	12.00	11.97	11.96
90	22.00	16.69	14.93	14.06	13.54	13.20	12.96	12.79	12.65	12.55	12.47	12.40	12.27	12.16	12.12	12.11
89	23.20	17.32	15.38	14.41	13.84	13.47	13.20	13.01	12.86	12.75	12.66	12.58	12.43	12.31	12.27	12.26
88	24.42	17.96	15.83	14.77	14.15	13.73	13.45	13.23	13.07	12.95	12.85	12.77	12.60	12.47	12.42	12.41
87	25.65	18.61	16.29	15.14	14.46	14.01	13.69	13.46	13.28	13.15	13.04	12.95	12.78	12.63	12.58	12.57
86	26.90	19.27	16.75	15.51	14.77	14.28	13.94	13.69	13.50	13.35	13.24	13.14	12.95	12.80	12.74	12.73
85	28.17	19.94	17.23	15.88	15.09	14.56	14.20	13.93	13.72	13.56	13.44	13.33	13.13	12.97	12.91	12.89
80	34.76	23.42	19.68	17.84	16.75	16.03	15.53	15.16	14.88	14.66	14.49	14.35	14.08	13.86	13.78	13.77
75	41.83	27.15	22.33	19.95	18.54	17.62	16.97	16.50	16.14	15.86	15.65	15.47	15.13	14.86	14.75	14.75
70	49.45	31.18	25.19	22.23	20.49	19.35	18.55	17.97	17.53	17.19	16.93	16.71	16.30	15.98	15.88	15.86
65	57.72	35.55	28.30	24.73	22.62	21.25	20.29	19.59	19.07	18.67	18.35	18.10	17.62	17.26	17.15	17.12
60	66.74	40.32	31.70	27.47	24.98	23.35	22.23	21.41	20.80	20.33	19.96	19.68	19.12	18.73	18.61	18.59
55	76.65	45.57	35.46	30.51	27.60	25.71	24.40	23.46	22.75	22.22	21.80	21.48	20.87	20.45	20.33	20.31
50	87.66	51.41	39.66	33.92	30.56	28.38	26.88	25.81	25.01	24.41	23.94	23.59	22.92	22.50	22.39	22.37

Description: This table shows the price to pay for a monthly payment loan, at a yield rate and assuming prepayment.

Example: The price of a 11.00 %, 30 year mortgage to yield 8.00 %, if prepaid in 6 years, is $ 114.05.

30 YEAR MORTGAGE PREPAID IN

YIELD	1 yr	2 yr	3 yr	4 yr	5 yr	6 yr	7 yr	8 yr	9 yr	10 yr	11 yr	12 yr	15 yr	20 yr	25 yr	30 yr
0.00	110.98	121.90	132.77	143.57	154.30	164.95	175.51	185.97	196.32	206.54	216.62	226.55	255.21	297.69	329.50	342.84
1.00	109.93	119.71	129.34	138.82	148.14	157.30	166.29	175.11	183.75	192.19	200.44	208.48	231.24	263.68	286.81	296.08
2.00	108.89	117.55	126.01	134.24	142.26	150.06	157.64	165.00	172.14	179.05	185.73	192.18	210.08	234.61	251.26	257.65
3.00	107.86	115.44	122.77	129.83	136.65	143.21	149.52	155.59	161.41	167.00	172.35	177.46	191.36	209.68	221.53	225.88
4.00	106.84	113.38	119.62	125.59	131.29	136.72	141.90	146.82	151.50	155.95	160.16	164.14	174.78	188.26	196.56	199.47
4.25	106.58	112.86	118.85	124.56	129.99	135.15	140.06	144.73	149.15	153.33	157.29	161.02	170.93	183.38	190.96	193.59
4.50	106.33	112.36	118.09	123.53	128.70	133.61	138.26	142.67	146.83	150.77	154.48	157.97	167.20	178.68	185.58	187.95
4.75	106.08	111.85	117.33	122.52	127.43	132.09	136.49	140.64	144.56	148.26	151.74	155.00	163.58	174.15	180.43	182.56
5.00	105.83	111.35	116.57	121.51	126.18	130.58	134.74	138.65	142.34	145.80	149.06	152.10	160.07	169.79	175.49	177.40
5.25	105.58	110.85	115.82	120.51	124.93	129.10	133.02	136.70	140.16	143.40	146.44	149.27	156.65	165.58	170.74	172.46
5.50	105.33	110.35	115.08	119.52	123.71	127.64	131.32	134.78	138.02	141.05	143.88	146.51	153.34	161.51	166.19	167.72
5.75	105.08	109.85	114.34	118.55	122.49	126.19	129.66	132.90	135.92	138.74	141.37	143.82	150.12	157.59	161.82	163.19
6.00	104.83	109.36	113.60	117.58	121.29	124.77	128.02	131.04	133.86	136.49	138.93	141.19	147.00	153.81	157.62	158.84
6.25	104.58	108.87	112.88	116.62	120.11	123.37	126.40	129.22	131.85	134.28	136.54	138.63	143.96	150.16	153.58	154.67
6.50	104.34	108.38	112.15	115.67	118.94	121.98	124.81	127.43	129.87	132.12	134.20	136.12	141.01	146.64	149.70	150.67
6.75	104.09	107.90	111.44	114.73	117.78	120.61	123.24	125.67	127.92	130.00	131.92	133.68	138.15	143.24	145.98	146.83
7.00	103.84	107.41	110.72	113.79	116.63	119.27	121.70	123.95	126.02	127.93	129.69	131.30	135.36	139.95	142.39	143.14
7.25	103.60	106.93	110.02	112.87	115.50	117.94	120.18	122.25	124.15	125.90	127.50	128.97	132.66	136.78	138.94	139.60
7.50	103.36	106.45	109.31	111.95	114.38	116.62	118.68	120.58	122.32	123.91	125.37	126.70	130.03	133.71	135.62	136.20
7.75	103.11	105.98	108.62	111.05	113.28	115.33	117.21	118.94	120.52	121.97	123.28	124.49	127.47	130.75	132.43	132.93
8.00	102.87	105.50	107.92	110.15	112.19	114.05	115.76	117.33	118.76	120.06	121.25	122.32	124.99	127.89	129.35	129.79
8.25	102.63	105.03	107.24	109.26	111.10	112.79	114.34	115.74	117.02	118.19	119.25	120.21	122.57	125.12	126.39	126.76
8.50	102.38	104.56	106.56	108.38	110.04	111.55	112.93	114.19	115.33	116.36	117.30	118.15	120.23	122.44	123.54	123.85
8.75	102.14	104.10	105.88	107.50	108.98	110.32	111.55	112.65	113.66	114.57	115.39	116.14	117.94	119.85	120.79	121.05
9.00	101.90	103.63	105.21	106.64	107.94	109.11	110.18	111.15	112.03	112.82	113.53	114.17	115.72	117.35	118.14	118.36
9.25	101.66	103.17	104.54	105.78	106.90	107.92	108.84	109.67	110.42	111.10	111.70	112.25	113.56	114.93	115.58	115.76
9.50	101.42	102.71	103.88	104.93	105.88	106.74	107.52	108.22	108.85	109.41	109.92	110.37	111.46	112.58	113.11	113.26
9.75	101.18	102.25	103.22	104.09	104.87	105.58	106.22	106.79	107.30	107.76	108.17	108.54	109.42	110.32	110.73	110.84
10.00	100.95	101.80	102.57	103.26	103.88	104.43	104.94	105.38	105.79	106.15	106.47	106.75	107.43	108.12	108.43	108.52
10.25	100.71	101.35	101.92	102.43	102.89	103.30	103.67	104.00	104.30	104.56	104.80	105.01	105.50	105.99	106.21	106.27
10.50	100.47	100.89	101.27	101.61	101.92	102.19	102.43	102.65	102.84	103.01	103.16	103.30	103.62	103.93	104.07	104.11
10.75	100.24	100.45	100.63	100.80	100.95	101.09	101.21	101.31	101.41	101.49	101.56	101.63	101.78	101.93	102.00	102.02
11.00	100.00	100.00	100.00	100.00	100.00	100.00	100.00	100.00	100.00	100.00	100.00	100.00	100.00	100.00	100.00	100.00
11.25	99.77	99.56	99.37	99.20	99.06	98.93	98.81	98.71	98.62	98.54	98.47	98.41	98.26	98.13	98.07	98.05
11.50	99.53	99.11	98.74	98.42	98.13	97.87	97.64	97.44	97.27	97.11	96.97	96.85	96.57	96.31	96.19	96.17
11.75	99.30	98.67	98.12	97.64	97.21	96.83	96.49	96.20	95.94	95.71	95.51	95.33	94.93	94.55	94.38	94.34
12.00	99.06	98.24	97.51	96.86	96.30	95.80	95.36	94.97	94.63	94.33	94.07	93.84	93.32	92.84	92.63	92.58
12.25	98.83	97.80	96.90	96.10	95.40	94.78	94.24	93.76	93.35	92.99	92.67	92.39	91.76	91.18	90.94	90.88
12.50	98.60	97.37	96.29	95.34	94.51	93.78	93.14	92.58	92.09	91.67	91.29	90.97	90.24	89.57	89.30	89.23
12.75	98.37	96.94	95.68	94.59	93.63	92.79	92.05	91.41	90.86	90.37	89.95	89.58	88.76	88.01	87.71	87.63
13.00	98.14	96.51	95.09	93.84	92.76	91.81	90.99	90.27	89.64	89.10	88.63	88.23	87.31	86.49	86.17	86.09
13.25	97.91	96.08	94.49	93.10	91.90	90.85	89.93	89.14	88.45	87.86	87.34	86.90	85.91	85.02	84.67	84.59
13.50	97.68	95.66	93.90	92.37	91.05	89.90	88.90	88.03	87.29	86.64	86.08	85.60	84.54	83.59	83.23	83.14
13.75	97.45	95.24	93.31	91.65	90.21	88.96	87.88	86.94	86.14	85.44	84.85	84.33	83.20	82.20	81.82	81.74
14.00	97.22	94.81	92.73	90.93	89.37	88.03	86.87	85.87	85.01	84.27	83.64	83.09	81.90	80.86	80.46	80.37
14.25	96.99	94.40	92.15	90.22	88.55	87.12	85.88	84.82	83.90	83.12	82.45	81.88	80.62	79.54	79.14	79.05
14.50	96.77	93.98	91.58	89.52	87.74	86.21	84.90	83.78	82.82	82.00	81.29	80.69	79.39	78.27	77.86	77.77
14.75	96.54	93.57	91.01	88.82	86.94	85.32	83.94	82.76	81.75	80.89	80.16	79.53	78.18	77.03	76.61	76.52
15.00	96.31	93.15	90.45	88.13	86.14	84.44	83.00	81.76	80.70	79.81	79.04	78.40	77.00	75.83	75.41	75.32
15.25	96.09	92.74	89.88	87.44	85.36	83.58	82.06	80.77	79.67	78.74	77.95	77.29	75.85	74.66	74.23	74.14
15.50	95.86	92.34	89.33	86.76	84.58	82.72	81.14	79.80	78.66	77.70	76.89	76.20	74.73	73.52	73.09	73.00
15.75	95.64	91.93	88.77	86.09	83.81	81.88	80.24	78.85	77.67	76.68	75.84	75.14	73.63	72.41	71.98	71.89
16.00	95.42	91.53	88.22	85.42	83.05	81.04	79.34	77.91	76.70	75.68	74.82	74.10	72.56	71.33	70.90	70.82
16.25	95.19	91.12	87.68	84.76	82.30	80.22	78.46	76.99	75.74	74.69	73.81	73.08	71.52	70.28	69.86	69.77
16.50	94.97	90.72	87.14	84.11	81.56	79.41	77.60	76.08	74.80	73.73	72.83	72.08	70.50	69.26	68.84	68.75
16.75	94.75	90.33	86.60	83.46	80.82	78.61	76.74	75.18	73.87	72.78	71.87	71.11	69.51	68.26	67.84	67.76
17.00	94.53	89.93	86.06	82.82	80.10	77.81	75.90	74.30	72.97	71.85	70.92	70.15	68.54	67.29	66.88	66.80
17.25	94.31	89.53	85.53	82.18	79.38	77.03	75.07	73.44	72.08	70.94	70.00	69.22	67.59	66.34	65.94	65.86
17.50	94.09	89.14	85.01	81.55	78.67	76.26	74.26	72.59	71.20	70.05	69.09	68.30	66.67	65.42	65.02	64.95
17.75	93.87	88.75	84.48	80.93	77.97	75.50	73.45	71.75	70.34	69.17	68.20	67.40	65.76	64.52	64.13	64.06
18.00	93.65	88.36	83.97	80.31	77.27	74.75	72.66	70.93	69.49	68.31	67.33	66.53	64.88	63.65	63.26	63.19
18.25	93.43	87.98	83.45	79.70	76.59	74.01	71.88	70.12	68.66	67.46	66.48	65.67	64.02	62.79	62.42	62.35
18.50	93.21	87.59	82.94	79.09	75.91	73.28	71.11	69.32	67.85	66.63	65.64	64.83	63.17	61.96	61.59	61.52
18.75	93.00	87.21	82.43	78.49	75.23	72.55	70.35	68.53	67.04	65.82	64.82	64.00	62.35	61.15	60.78	60.72
19.00	92.78	86.83	81.93	77.89	74.57	71.84	69.60	67.76	66.25	65.02	64.02	63.19	61.55	60.35	60.00	59.94
20.00	91.92	85.32	79.94	75.56	71.99	69.08	66.71	64.79	63.23	61.97	60.95	60.13	58.50	57.37	57.05	56.99
25.00	87.75	78.23	70.83	65.09	60.64	57.19	54.52	52.46	50.86	49.63	48.68	47.96	46.64	45.88	45.71	45.68
30.00	83.79	71.79	62.92	56.36	51.52	47.94	45.31	43.37	41.94	40.89	40.12	39.56	38.63	38.18	38.10	38.09

PREPAYMENT MORTGAGE YIELD, 30 YEAR TERM

11.00 %

Description: This table shows the yield to prepayment of a monthly payment mortgage purchased at a price in the index.

Example: The yield to prepayment in 10 years of a 11.00 %, 30 year mortgage at a price of 104.00 is 10.33 %.

30 YEAR MORTGAGE PREPAID IN

PRICE	1 yr	2 yr	3 yr	4 yr	5 yr	6 yr	7 yr	8 yr	9 yr	10 yr	11 yr	12 yr	15 yr	20 yr	25 yr	30 yr
140	–	–	–	–	2.39	3.48	4.25	4.83	5.26	5.61	5.88	6.11	6.58	6.99	7.17	7.22
135	–	–	–	1.83	3.30	4.27	4.96	5.47	5.86	6.16	6.41	6.61	7.03	7.39	7.54	7.59
130	–	–	–	2.96	4.24	5.09	5.69	6.14	6.48	6.75	6.96	7.13	7.50	7.81	7.94	7.98
125	–	–	2.30	4.14	5.23	5.95	6.46	6.84	7.13	7.36	7.54	7.69	7.99	8.26	8.37	8.40
120	–	–	3.87	5.37	6.27	6.86	7.27	7.58	7.82	8.00	8.15	8.27	8.52	8.73	8.82	8.84
119	–	1.32	4.20	5.63	6.48	7.04	7.44	7.74	7.96	8.14	8.28	8.39	8.63	8.83	8.91	8.93
118	–	1.79	4.52	5.89	6.70	7.23	7.61	7.89	8.10	8.27	8.40	8.51	8.74	8.93	9.01	9.03
117	–	2.26	4.85	6.15	6.91	7.42	7.78	8.05	8.25	8.41	8.53	8.64	8.85	9.03	9.10	9.12
116	–	2.73	5.19	6.41	7.13	7.62	7.95	8.20	8.40	8.55	8.66	8.76	8.96	9.13	9.20	9.22
115	–	3.21	5.52	6.67	7.36	7.81	8.13	8.36	8.54	8.68	8.80	8.89	9.08	9.24	9.30	9.32
114	–	3.69	5.86	6.94	7.58	8.01	8.30	8.53	8.69	8.83	8.93	9.02	9.19	9.34	9.40	9.42
113	–	4.18	6.20	7.21	7.81	8.20	8.48	8.69	8.85	8.97	9.07	9.15	9.31	9.45	9.51	9.52
112	–	4.67	6.55	7.48	8.04	8.40	8.66	8.85	9.00	9.11	9.20	9.28	9.43	9.56	9.61	9.62
111	–	5.17	6.90	7.76	8.27	8.61	8.84	9.02	9.15	9.26	9.34	9.41	9.55	9.67	9.72	9.73
110	–	5.67	7.25	8.04	8.50	8.81	9.03	9.19	9.31	9.41	9.48	9.55	9.67	9.78	9.82	9.83
109	1.88	6.18	7.61	8.32	8.74	9.02	9.22	9.36	9.47	9.56	9.63	9.68	9.80	9.89	9.93	9.94
108	2.85	6.69	7.97	8.60	8.98	9.23	9.40	9.53	9.63	9.71	9.77	9.82	9.92	10.01	10.04	10.05
107	3.83	7.21	8.33	8.89	9.22	9.44	9.59	9.71	9.79	9.86	9.92	9.96	10.05	10.13	10.16	10.16
106	4.82	7.73	8.70	9.18	9.47	9.65	9.79	9.88	9.96	10.02	10.06	10.10	10.18	10.24	10.27	10.28
105	5.83	8.26	9.07	9.47	9.71	9.87	9.98	10.06	10.13	10.18	10.21	10.25	10.31	10.36	10.39	10.39
104	6.84	8.80	9.45	9.77	9.96	10.09	10.18	10.25	10.30	10.33	10.37	10.39	10.44	10.49	10.50	10.51
103.75	7.09	8.93	9.54	9.85	10.03	10.15	10.23	10.29	10.34	10.38	10.40	10.43	10.48	10.52	10.53	10.54
103.50	7.35	9.07	9.64	9.92	10.09	10.20	10.28	10.34	10.38	10.42	10.44	10.47	10.51	10.55	10.56	10.57
103.25	7.60	9.20	9.73	10.00	10.15	10.26	10.33	10.38	10.42	10.46	10.48	10.50	10.54	10.58	10.59	10.60
103.00	7.86	9.34	9.83	10.07	10.22	10.31	10.38	10.43	10.47	10.50	10.52	10.54	10.58	10.61	10.62	10.63
102.75	8.12	9.47	9.92	10.15	10.28	10.37	10.43	10.48	10.51	10.54	10.56	10.58	10.61	10.64	10.65	10.66
102.50	8.37	9.61	10.02	10.22	10.34	10.42	10.48	10.52	10.55	10.58	10.60	10.61	10.65	10.67	10.68	10.69
102.25	8.63	9.75	10.12	10.30	10.41	10.48	10.53	10.57	10.60	10.62	10.64	10.65	10.68	10.70	10.71	10.72
102.00	8.89	9.88	10.21	10.38	10.47	10.54	10.58	10.62	10.64	10.66	10.68	10.69	10.72	10.74	10.75	10.75
101.75	9.15	10.02	10.31	10.45	10.54	10.59	10.63	10.66	10.68	10.70	10.72	10.73	10.75	10.77	10.78	10.78
101.50	9.41	10.16	10.41	10.53	10.60	10.65	10.68	10.71	10.73	10.74	10.76	10.76	10.78	10.80	10.81	10.81
101.25	9.68	10.30	10.50	10.61	10.67	10.71	10.74	10.76	10.77	10.78	10.79	10.80	10.82	10.83	10.84	10.84
101.00	9.94	10.44	10.60	10.68	10.73	10.76	10.79	10.80	10.82	10.83	10.83	10.84	10.85	10.86	10.87	10.87
100.75	10.20	10.58	10.70	10.76	10.80	10.82	10.84	10.85	10.86	10.87	10.87	10.88	10.89	10.90	10.90	10.90
100.50	10.47	10.72	10.80	10.84	10.86	10.88	10.89	10.90	10.91	10.91	10.91	10.92	10.92	10.93	10.93	10.93
100.25	10.73	10.85	10.90	10.92	10.93	10.94	10.94	10.95	10.95	10.95	10.95	10.96	10.96	10.96	10.96	10.96
100.00	11.00	11.00	11.00	11.00	11.00	11.00	11.00	11.00	11.00	11.00	11.00	11.00	11.00	11.00	11.00	11.00
99.75	11.26	11.14	11.09	11.07	11.06	11.05	11.05	11.04	11.04	11.04	11.04	11.03	11.03	11.03	11.03	11.03
99.50	11.53	11.28	11.19	11.15	11.13	11.11	11.10	11.09	11.09	11.08	11.08	11.07	11.07	11.06	11.06	11.06
99.25	11.80	11.42	11.29	11.23	11.19	11.17	11.15	11.14	11.13	11.12	11.12	11.11	11.10	11.09	11.09	11.09
99.00	12.06	11.56	11.39	11.31	11.26	11.23	11.21	11.19	11.18	11.17	11.16	11.15	11.14	11.13	11.12	11.12
98.75	12.33	11.70	11.49	11.39	11.33	11.29	11.26	11.24	11.22	11.21	11.20	11.19	11.17	11.16	11.16	11.15
98.50	12.60	11.84	11.59	11.47	11.39	11.35	11.31	11.29	11.27	11.25	11.24	11.23	11.21	11.19	11.19	11.19
98.25	12.87	11.99	11.69	11.55	11.46	11.40	11.36	11.34	11.31	11.30	11.28	11.27	11.25	11.23	11.22	11.22
98.00	13.14	12.13	11.80	11.63	11.53	11.46	11.42	11.38	11.36	11.34	11.32	11.31	11.28	11.26	11.25	11.25
97.75	13.42	12.27	11.90	11.71	11.60	11.52	11.47	11.43	11.41	11.38	11.36	11.35	11.32	11.30	11.29	11.28
97.50	13.69	12.42	12.00	11.79	11.66	11.58	11.53	11.48	11.45	11.43	11.41	11.39	11.36	11.33	11.32	11.32
97.25	13.96	12.56	12.10	11.87	11.73	11.64	11.58	11.53	11.50	11.47	11.45	11.43	11.39	11.36	11.35	11.35
97	14.24	12.71	12.20	11.95	11.80	11.70	11.63	11.58	11.54	11.51	11.49	11.47	11.43	11.40	11.39	11.38
96	15.34	13.29	12.61	12.28	12.08	11.95	11.85	11.78	11.73	11.69	11.66	11.63	11.58	11.54	11.52	11.52
95	16.46	13.88	13.03	12.61	12.36	12.19	12.07	11.99	11.92	11.87	11.83	11.80	11.73	11.68	11.66	11.65
94	17.60	14.48	13.45	12.94	12.64	12.44	12.30	12.20	12.12	12.06	12.01	11.97	11.89	11.82	11.80	11.79
93	18.74	15.09	13.88	13.28	12.92	12.69	12.53	12.41	12.31	12.24	12.19	12.14	12.05	11.97	11.94	11.94
92	19.90	15.70	14.31	13.62	13.21	12.95	12.76	12.62	12.51	12.43	12.37	12.31	12.21	12.12	12.09	12.08
91	21.08	16.32	14.75	13.97	13.51	13.20	12.99	12.83	12.72	12.62	12.55	12.49	12.37	12.27	12.24	12.23
90	22.26	16.95	15.19	14.32	13.81	13.47	13.23	13.05	12.92	12.82	12.74	12.67	12.54	12.43	12.39	12.38
89	23.47	17.59	15.64	14.68	14.11	13.73	13.47	13.28	13.13	13.02	12.92	12.85	12.70	12.59	12.54	12.53
88	24.69	18.23	16.10	15.04	14.41	14.00	13.71	13.50	13.34	13.22	13.12	13.04	12.88	12.75	12.70	12.69
87	25.92	18.88	16.56	15.41	14.73	14.28	13.96	13.73	13.56	13.42	13.31	13.23	13.05	12.91	12.86	12.85
86	27.17	19.54	17.03	15.78	15.04	14.55	14.21	13.96	13.78	13.63	13.51	13.42	13.23	13.08	13.02	13.01
85	28.44	20.21	17.50	16.16	15.36	14.84	14.47	14.20	14.00	13.84	13.71	13.61	13.41	13.25	13.19	13.18
80	35.04	23.70	19.97	18.12	17.03	16.31	15.81	15.44	15.17	14.95	14.78	14.64	14.37	14.16	14.08	14.06
75	42.12	27.44	22.62	20.24	18.83	17.91	17.27	16.80	16.44	16.17	15.95	15.78	15.43	15.17	15.08	15.06
70	49.75	31.48	25.49	22.54	20.79	19.66	18.86	18.28	17.84	17.51	17.24	17.03	16.62	16.31	16.21	16.19
65	58.03	35.86	28.61	25.04	22.94	21.57	20.62	19.92	19.40	19.00	18.69	18.44	17.96	17.61	17.50	17.48
60	67.07	40.65	32.03	27.80	25.31	23.70	22.57	21.76	21.15	20.68	20.32	20.04	19.49	19.11	19.00	18.97
55	77.00	45.92	35.81	30.86	27.96	26.07	24.77	23.83	23.13	22.60	22.19	21.87	21.26	20.86	20.75	20.73
50	88.03	51.77	40.03	34.30	30.94	28.77	27.28	26.21	25.41	24.82	24.36	24.01	23.36	22.94	22.84	22.82

Description: This table shows the price to pay for a monthly payment loan, at a yield rate and assuming prepayment.

Example: The price of a 11.25 %, 30 year mortgage to yield 8.00 %, if prepaid in 6 years, is $ 115.23.

30 YEAR MORTGAGE PREPAID IN

YIELD	1 yr	2 yr	3 yr	4 yr	5 yr	6 yr	7 yr	8 yr	9 yr	10 yr	11 yr	12 yr	15 yr	20 yr	25 yr	30 yr
0.00	111.23	122.41	133.53	144.59	155.57	166.48	177.30	188.02	198.63	209.12	219.47	229.66	259.11	302.89	335.79	349.65
1.00	110.18	120.20	130.08	139.81	149.37	158.78	168.01	177.07	185.95	194.63	203.12	211.39	234.83	268.34	292.31	301.97
2.00	109.13	118.05	126.74	135.21	143.46	151.49	159.29	166.88	174.23	181.36	188.25	194.90	213.39	238.79	256.10	262.77
3.00	108.10	115.93	123.49	130.78	137.81	144.59	151.11	157.38	163.41	169.19	174.72	180.01	194.42	213.46	225.82	230.37
4.00	107.08	113.86	120.33	126.52	132.43	138.06	143.43	148.54	153.41	158.02	162.40	166.54	177.61	191.68	200.37	203.44
4.25	106.83	113.34	119.56	125.48	131.12	136.48	141.58	146.43	151.02	155.38	159.50	163.38	173.71	186.72	194.66	197.43
4.50	106.58	112.83	118.79	124.45	129.82	134.93	139.77	144.35	148.69	152.79	156.66	160.30	169.93	181.95	189.19	191.69
4.75	106.32	112.33	118.02	123.43	128.55	133.39	137.98	142.31	146.40	150.26	153.88	157.29	166.26	177.34	183.94	186.19
5.00	106.07	111.82	117.27	122.42	127.28	131.88	136.22	140.31	144.16	147.77	151.17	154.36	162.70	172.90	178.90	180.93
5.25	105.82	111.32	116.51	121.41	126.03	130.39	134.48	138.34	141.95	145.35	148.52	151.49	159.24	168.62	174.07	175.89
5.50	105.57	110.82	115.77	120.42	124.80	128.91	132.78	136.40	139.79	142.97	145.94	148.70	155.88	164.48	169.43	171.06
5.75	105.32	110.33	115.03	119.44	123.58	127.46	131.10	134.50	137.68	140.64	143.41	145.98	152.61	160.50	164.97	166.43
6.00	105.07	109.83	114.29	118.46	122.37	126.03	129.44	132.63	135.60	138.36	140.93	143.32	149.44	156.65	160.69	162.00
6.25	104.83	109.34	113.56	117.50	121.18	124.61	127.81	130.79	133.56	136.13	138.52	140.72	146.36	152.94	156.58	157.74
6.50	104.58	108.85	112.83	116.54	120.00	123.22	126.21	128.98	131.56	133.95	136.15	138.19	143.37	149.36	152.63	153.66
6.75	104.33	108.36	112.11	115.60	118.84	121.84	124.63	127.21	129.60	131.81	133.84	135.72	140.47	145.90	148.83	149.75
7.00	104.09	107.88	111.40	114.66	117.68	120.48	123.07	125.47	127.68	129.71	131.59	133.31	137.64	142.56	145.18	145.99
7.25	103.84	107.40	110.69	113.73	116.55	119.15	121.54	123.75	125.79	127.66	129.38	130.95	134.90	139.33	141.66	142.38
7.50	103.60	106.92	109.98	112.81	115.42	117.82	120.04	122.07	123.94	125.65	127.22	128.65	132.23	136.21	138.28	138.91
7.75	103.35	106.44	109.28	111.90	114.31	116.52	118.55	120.42	122.12	123.68	125.11	126.41	129.64	133.20	135.03	135.57
8.00	103.11	105.96	108.59	111.00	113.21	115.23	117.09	118.79	120.34	121.76	123.05	124.22	127.12	130.28	131.89	132.37
8.25	102.86	105.49	107.90	110.10	112.12	113.97	115.65	117.19	118.59	119.87	121.03	122.08	124.67	127.47	128.87	129.28
8.50	102.62	105.02	107.21	109.22	111.05	112.71	114.23	115.62	116.88	118.02	119.06	119.99	122.29	124.75	125.96	126.32
8.75	102.38	104.55	106.53	108.34	109.98	111.48	112.84	114.07	115.19	116.21	117.13	117.95	119.97	122.11	123.16	123.46
9.00	102.14	104.09	105.86	107.47	108.93	110.26	111.46	112.56	113.54	114.43	115.24	115.96	117.72	119.56	120.46	120.71
9.25	101.90	103.62	105.19	106.61	107.89	109.06	110.11	111.06	111.92	112.70	113.39	114.02	115.53	117.10	117.85	118.06
9.50	101.66	103.16	104.52	105.75	106.87	107.87	108.78	109.60	110.33	110.99	111.59	112.12	113.40	114.71	115.34	115.51
9.75	101.42	102.70	103.86	104.91	105.85	106.70	107.47	108.15	108.77	109.33	109.82	110.26	111.32	112.41	112.91	113.05
10.00	101.18	102.25	103.21	104.07	104.85	105.55	106.17	106.74	107.24	107.69	108.09	108.45	109.31	110.17	110.57	110.68
10.25	100.94	101.79	102.56	103.24	103.86	104.41	104.90	105.34	105.74	106.09	106.40	106.68	107.34	108.01	108.31	108.39
10.50	100.71	101.34	101.91	102.42	102.88	103.28	103.65	103.97	104.26	104.52	104.75	104.95	105.43	105.91	106.12	106.18
10.75	100.47	100.89	101.27	101.61	101.91	102.17	102.41	102.63	102.82	102.98	103.13	103.26	103.57	103.88	104.01	104.05
11.00	100.24	100.45	100.63	100.80	100.95	101.08	101.20	101.30	101.39	101.48	101.55	101.61	101.76	101.91	101.97	101.99
11.25	100.00	100.00	100.00	100.00	100.00	100.00	100.00	100.00	100.00	100.00	100.00	100.00	100.00	100.00	100.00	100.00
11.50	99.77	99.56	99.37	99.21	99.06	98.93	98.82	98.72	98.63	98.55	98.48	98.42	98.28	98.15	98.09	98.08
11.75	99.53	99.12	98.75	98.42	98.14	97.88	97.66	97.46	97.29	97.13	97.00	96.88	96.61	96.36	96.25	96.22
12.00	99.30	98.68	98.13	97.65	97.22	96.84	96.51	96.22	95.97	95.74	95.55	95.38	94.98	94.62	94.46	94.42
12.25	99.07	98.24	97.52	96.88	96.31	95.82	95.39	95.01	94.67	94.38	94.13	93.91	93.40	92.93	92.73	92.69
12.50	98.83	97.81	96.91	96.11	95.42	94.81	94.28	93.81	93.40	93.05	92.74	92.47	91.85	91.29	91.06	91.01
12.75	98.60	97.37	96.30	95.36	94.53	93.81	93.18	92.63	92.15	91.74	91.37	91.06	90.35	89.70	89.44	89.38
13.00	98.37	96.94	95.70	94.61	93.66	92.83	92.11	91.48	90.93	90.45	90.04	89.68	88.88	88.16	87.87	87.80
13.25	98.14	96.52	95.10	93.87	92.79	91.86	91.05	90.34	89.73	89.20	88.74	88.34	87.45	86.66	86.35	86.28
13.50	97.91	96.09	94.51	93.13	91.94	90.90	90.00	89.22	88.55	87.96	87.46	87.03	86.06	85.21	84.87	84.80
13.75	97.68	95.67	93.92	92.40	91.09	89.95	88.97	88.12	87.39	86.75	86.21	85.74	84.70	83.79	83.44	83.36
14.00	97.45	95.25	93.34	91.68	90.25	89.02	87.96	87.04	86.25	85.57	84.98	84.48	83.38	82.42	82.05	81.97
14.25	97.22	94.83	92.76	90.97	89.43	88.10	86.96	85.97	85.13	84.40	83.78	83.25	82.09	81.08	80.71	80.62
14.50	97.00	94.41	92.18	90.26	88.61	87.19	85.97	84.93	84.03	83.26	82.61	82.05	80.83	79.79	79.40	79.32
14.75	96.77	93.99	91.61	89.56	87.80	86.29	85.00	83.90	82.95	82.15	81.46	80.87	79.60	78.53	78.13	78.05
15.00	96.54	93.58	91.04	88.86	87.00	85.41	84.05	82.88	81.89	81.05	80.33	79.72	78.40	77.30	76.90	76.81
15.25	96.32	93.17	90.48	88.17	86.21	84.53	83.10	81.89	80.85	79.97	79.23	78.60	77.24	76.11	75.70	75.62
15.50	96.09	92.76	89.92	87.49	85.43	83.67	82.18	80.91	79.83	78.92	78.15	77.49	76.10	74.95	74.54	74.45
15.75	95.87	92.35	89.36	86.82	84.65	82.82	81.26	79.94	78.83	77.88	77.09	76.42	74.98	73.82	73.41	73.32
16.00	95.65	91.95	88.81	86.15	83.89	81.98	80.36	79.00	77.84	76.87	76.05	75.36	73.90	72.72	72.31	72.23
16.25	95.42	91.54	88.26	85.48	83.13	81.15	79.47	78.06	76.87	75.87	75.03	74.33	72.84	71.65	71.24	71.16
16.50	95.20	91.14	87.72	84.83	82.39	80.33	78.60	77.15	75.92	74.90	74.04	73.32	71.81	70.61	70.20	70.12
16.75	94.98	90.74	87.18	84.17	81.65	79.52	77.74	76.24	74.99	73.94	73.06	72.33	70.80	69.59	69.19	69.11
17.00	94.76	90.35	86.64	83.53	80.92	78.73	76.89	75.35	74.07	73.00	72.10	71.36	69.81	68.60	68.20	68.13
17.25	94.54	89.95	86.11	82.89	80.19	77.94	76.05	74.48	73.17	72.08	71.17	70.41	68.85	67.64	67.25	67.17
17.50	94.31	89.56	85.58	82.25	79.48	77.16	75.23	73.62	72.28	71.17	70.25	69.48	67.91	66.70	66.31	66.24
17.75	94.10	89.17	85.05	81.63	78.77	76.39	74.42	72.77	71.41	70.28	69.35	68.58	66.99	65.78	65.40	65.33
18.00	93.88	88.78	84.53	81.00	78.07	75.64	73.62	71.94	70.56	69.41	68.46	67.69	66.09	64.89	64.52	64.45
18.25	93.66	88.39	84.02	80.39	77.38	74.89	72.83	71.12	69.72	68.56	67.60	66.81	65.21	64.02	63.65	63.58
18.50	93.44	88.00	83.50	79.78	76.70	74.15	72.05	70.32	68.89	67.72	66.75	65.96	64.36	63.17	62.81	62.75
18.75	93.22	87.62	82.99	79.17	76.02	73.42	71.28	69.52	68.08	66.89	65.92	65.12	63.52	62.35	61.99	61.93
19.00	93.00	87.24	82.49	78.57	75.35	72.70	70.53	68.74	67.28	66.08	65.10	64.31	62.70	61.54	61.19	61.13
20.00	92.14	85.73	80.50	76.23	72.75	69.92	67.62	65.74	64.22	62.99	62.00	61.19	59.60	58.49	58.18	58.12
25.00	87.97	78.61	71.35	65.70	61.33	57.93	55.31	53.27	51.70	50.49	49.56	48.84	47.54	46.78	46.62	46.59
30.00	84.00	72.16	63.40	56.92	52.13	48.60	46.00	44.08	42.66	41.63	40.86	40.31	39.38	38.93	38.85	38.85

Description: This table shows the yield to prepayment of a monthly payment mortgage purchased at a price in the index.

Example: The yield to prepayment in 10 years of a 11.25 %, 30 year mortgage at a price of 104.00 is 10.58 %.

30 YEAR MORTGAGE PREPAID IN

PRICE	1 yr	2 yr	3 yr	4 yr	5 yr	6 yr	7 yr	8 yr	9 yr	10 yr	11 yr	12 yr	15 yr	20 yr	25 yr	30 yr
140	–	–	–	–	2.60	3.69	4.46	5.03	5.47	5.81	6.09	6.32	6.79	7.19	7.37	7.42
135	–	–	–	2.04	3.51	4.48	5.17	5.68	6.07	6.37	6.62	6.82	7.24	7.59	7.75	7.79
130	–	–	1.02	3.18	4.46	5.31	5.91	6.35	6.69	6.96	7.17	7.35	7.71	8.02	8.15	8.19
125	–	–	2.53	4.36	5.45	6.18	6.69	7.06	7.35	7.58	7.76	7.91	8.21	8.47	8.58	8.61
120	–	1.09	4.10	5.60	6.50	7.09	7.50	7.81	8.04	8.23	8.37	8.49	8.74	8.95	9.04	9.06
119	–	1.55	4.43	5.86	6.71	7.27	7.67	7.96	8.19	8.36	8.50	8.62	8.85	9.05	9.13	9.16
118	–	2.02	4.75	6.12	6.93	7.46	7.84	8.12	8.33	8.50	8.63	8.74	8.96	9.15	9.23	9.25
117	–	2.49	5.08	6.38	7.15	7.65	8.01	8.27	8.48	8.64	8.76	8.86	9.08	9.26	9.33	9.35
116	–	2.96	5.42	6.64	7.37	7.85	8.18	8.43	8.62	8.77	8.89	8.99	9.19	9.36	9.43	9.45
115	–	3.44	5.75	6.90	7.59	8.04	8.36	8.59	8.77	8.91	9.03	9.12	9.31	9.46	9.53	9.55
114	–	3.92	6.09	7.17	7.81	8.24	8.54	8.76	8.93	9.06	9.16	9.25	9.42	9.57	9.63	9.65
113	–	4.41	6.44	7.44	8.04	8.44	8.72	8.92	9.08	9.20	9.30	9.38	9.54	9.68	9.74	9.75
112	–	4.91	6.78	7.72	8.27	8.64	8.90	9.09	9.23	9.35	9.44	9.51	9.66	9.79	9.84	9.85
111	–	5.41	7.13	7.99	8.51	8.84	9.08	9.26	9.39	9.49	9.58	9.65	9.78	9.90	9.95	9.96
110	1.16	5.91	7.49	8.27	8.74	9.05	9.27	9.43	9.55	9.64	9.72	9.78	9.91	10.01	10.06	10.07
109	2.12	6.42	7.85	8.56	8.98	9.26	9.45	9.60	9.71	9.79	9.86	9.92	10.03	10.13	10.17	10.18
108	3.09	6.93	8.21	8.84	9.22	9.47	9.64	9.77	9.87	9.95	10.01	10.06	10.16	10.25	10.28	10.29
107	4.08	7.45	8.57	9.13	9.46	9.68	9.83	9.95	10.03	10.10	10.16	10.20	10.29	10.36	10.39	10.40
106	5.07	7.98	8.94	9.42	9.71	9.90	10.03	10.13	10.20	10.26	10.31	10.34	10.42	10.48	10.51	10.52
105	6.07	8.51	9.32	9.72	9.96	10.11	10.23	10.31	10.37	10.42	10.46	10.49	10.55	10.61	10.63	10.63
104	7.08	9.04	9.69	10.02	10.21	10.34	10.42	10.49	10.54	10.58	10.61	10.64	10.69	10.73	10.75	10.75
103.75	7.34	9.18	9.79	10.09	10.27	10.39	10.47	10.54	10.58	10.62	10.65	10.67	10.72	10.76	10.78	10.78
103.50	7.59	9.31	9.88	10.17	10.34	10.45	10.52	10.58	10.63	10.66	10.69	10.71	10.75	10.79	10.81	10.81
103.25	7.85	9.45	9.98	10.24	10.40	10.50	10.58	10.63	10.67	10.70	10.73	10.75	10.79	10.82	10.84	10.84
103.00	8.11	9.58	10.07	10.32	10.46	10.56	10.63	10.68	10.71	10.74	10.77	10.78	10.82	10.86	10.87	10.87
102.75	8.36	9.72	10.17	10.39	10.53	10.61	10.68	10.72	10.76	10.78	10.80	10.82	10.86	10.89	10.90	10.90
102.50	8.62	9.86	10.27	10.47	10.59	10.67	10.73	10.77	10.80	10.82	10.84	10.86	10.89	10.92	10.93	10.93
102.25	8.88	9.99	10.36	10.55	10.66	10.73	10.78	10.82	10.84	10.87	10.88	10.90	10.93	10.95	10.96	10.96
102.00	9.14	10.13	10.46	10.62	10.72	10.78	10.83	10.86	10.89	10.91	10.92	10.94	10.96	10.98	10.99	10.99
101.75	9.40	10.27	10.56	10.70	10.79	10.84	10.88	10.91	10.93	10.95	10.96	10.97	11.00	11.02	11.02	11.02
101.50	9.66	10.41	10.65	10.78	10.85	10.90	10.93	10.96	10.98	10.99	11.00	11.01	11.03	11.05	11.05	11.06
101.25	9.92	10.55	10.75	10.86	10.92	10.96	10.98	11.00	11.02	11.03	11.04	11.05	11.07	11.08	11.09	11.09
101.00	10.19	10.69	10.85	10.93	10.98	11.01	11.04	11.05	11.07	11.08	11.08	11.09	11.10	11.11	11.12	11.12
100.75	10.45	10.82	10.95	11.01	11.05	11.07	11.09	11.10	11.11	11.12	11.12	11.13	11.14	11.15	11.15	11.15
100.50	10.71	10.96	11.05	11.09	11.11	11.13	11.14	11.15	11.15	11.16	11.16	11.17	11.17	11.18	11.18	11.18
100.25	10.98	11.10	11.15	11.17	11.18	11.19	11.19	11.20	11.20	11.20	11.20	11.21	11.21	11.21	11.21	11.21
100.00	11.25	11.25	11.25	11.25	11.25	11.25	11.25	11.25	11.25	11.25	11.25	11.25	11.25	11.25	11.25	11.25
99.75	11.51	11.39	11.34	11.32	11.31	11.30	11.30	11.29	11.29	11.29	11.29	11.28	11.28	11.28	11.28	11.28
99.50	11.78	11.53	11.44	11.40	11.38	11.36	11.35	11.34	11.34	11.33	11.33	11.32	11.32	11.31	11.31	11.31
99.25	12.05	11.67	11.54	11.48	11.44	11.42	11.40	11.39	11.38	11.37	11.37	11.36	11.35	11.35	11.34	11.34
99.00	12.32	11.81	11.64	11.56	11.51	11.48	11.46	11.44	11.43	11.42	11.41	11.40	11.39	11.38	11.38	11.37
98.75	12.58	11.95	11.74	11.64	11.58	11.54	11.51	11.49	11.47	11.46	11.45	11.44	11.43	11.41	11.41	11.41
98.50	12.85	12.10	11.85	11.72	11.65	11.60	11.56	11.54	11.52	11.50	11.49	11.48	11.46	11.45	11.44	11.44
98.25	13.13	12.24	11.95	11.80	11.71	11.66	11.62	11.59	11.57	11.55	11.53	11.52	11.50	11.48	11.47	11.47
98.00	13.40	12.38	12.05	11.88	11.78	11.72	11.67	11.64	11.61	11.59	11.58	11.56	11.54	11.52	11.51	11.51
97.75	13.67	12.53	12.15	11.96	11.85	11.78	11.73	11.69	11.66	11.64	11.62	11.60	11.57	11.55	11.54	11.54
97.50	13.94	12.67	12.25	12.04	11.92	11.84	11.78	11.74	11.71	11.68	11.66	11.64	11.61	11.58	11.57	11.57
97.25	14.22	12.82	12.35	12.12	11.99	11.90	11.83	11.79	11.75	11.72	11.70	11.68	11.65	11.62	11.61	11.61
97	14.49	12.96	12.46	12.20	12.06	11.96	11.89	11.84	11.80	11.77	11.75	11.73	11.69	11.65	11.64	11.64
96	15.60	13.55	12.87	12.53	12.33	12.20	12.11	12.04	11.99	11.95	11.92	11.89	11.84	11.80	11.78	11.78
95	16.72	14.14	13.29	12.86	12.61	12.45	12.33	12.25	12.18	12.13	12.09	12.06	11.99	11.94	11.92	11.91
94	17.85	14.74	13.71	13.20	12.90	12.70	12.56	12.46	12.38	12.32	12.27	12.23	12.15	12.09	12.06	12.06
93	19.00	15.35	14.14	13.54	13.19	12.95	12.79	12.67	12.58	12.50	12.45	12.40	12.31	12.23	12.21	12.20
92	20.16	15.96	14.57	13.88	13.48	13.21	13.02	12.88	12.78	12.69	12.63	12.58	12.47	12.39	12.35	12.35
91	21.34	16.58	15.01	14.23	13.77	13.47	13.26	13.10	12.98	12.89	12.81	12.76	12.64	12.54	12.50	12.50
90	22.53	17.21	15.46	14.59	14.07	13.73	13.49	13.32	13.19	13.08	13.00	12.94	12.80	12.70	12.66	12.65
89	23.73	17.85	15.91	14.95	14.38	14.00	13.74	13.54	13.40	13.28	13.19	13.12	12.97	12.86	12.81	12.80
88	24.95	18.50	16.36	15.31	14.68	14.27	13.98	13.77	13.61	13.49	13.39	13.31	13.15	13.02	12.97	12.96
87	26.19	19.15	16.83	15.68	15.00	14.55	14.23	14.00	13.83	13.69	13.59	13.50	13.33	13.19	13.14	13.13
86	27.44	19.81	17.30	16.05	15.31	14.83	14.49	14.24	14.05	13.90	13.79	13.69	13.51	13.36	13.30	13.29
85	28.71	20.49	17.77	16.43	15.63	15.11	14.75	14.48	14.27	14.12	13.99	13.89	13.69	13.53	13.47	13.46
80	35.32	23.98	20.25	18.40	17.31	16.60	16.10	15.73	15.45	15.24	15.07	14.93	14.66	14.45	14.38	14.36
75	42.41	27.73	22.91	20.53	19.13	18.21	17.57	17.10	16.74	16.47	16.25	16.08	15.74	15.48	15.40	15.38
70	50.05	31.78	25.79	22.84	21.10	19.97	19.17	18.59	18.16	17.83	17.56	17.36	16.95	16.64	16.54	16.52
65	58.35	36.18	28.93	25.36	23.27	21.90	20.94	20.25	19.73	19.34	19.03	18.78	18.31	17.96	17.86	17.84
60	67.40	40.98	32.37	28.14	25.65	24.04	22.92	22.11	21.50	21.04	20.68	20.40	19.86	19.49	19.38	19.36
55	77.35	46.26	36.16	31.22	28.32	26.44	25.14	24.20	23.51	22.98	22.58	22.26	21.67	21.27	21.16	21.15
50	88.39	52.14	40.41	34.68	31.33	29.16	27.68	26.61	25.82	25.23	24.78	24.43	23.80	23.40	23.30	23.28

Description: This table shows the price to pay for a monthly payment loan, at a yield rate and assuming prepayment.

Example: The price of a 11.50 %, 30 year mortgage to yield 8.00 %, if prepaid in 6 years, is $ 116.42.

30 YEAR MORTGAGE PREPAID IN

YIELD	1 yr	2 yr	3 yr	4 yr	5 yr	6 yr	7 yr	8 yr	9 yr	10 yr	11 yr	12 yr	15 yr	20 yr	25 yr	30 yr
0.00	111.48	122.91	134.28	145.60	156.84	168.01	179.09	190.07	200.94	211.70	222.31	232.77	263.02	308.11	342.12	356.50
1.00	110.42	120.70	130.83	140.80	150.61	160.25	169.73	179.03	188.15	197.07	205.79	214.30	238.43	273.00	297.84	307.89
2.00	109.38	118.54	127.47	136.18	144.66	152.92	160.95	168.75	176.33	183.67	190.77	197.63	216.71	242.98	260.96	267.92
3.00	108.35	116.42	124.21	131.73	138.98	145.97	152.71	159.18	165.40	171.37	177.10	182.57	197.48	217.25	230.12	234.89
4.00	107.33	114.34	121.04	127.45	133.56	139.40	144.97	150.27	155.31	160.10	164.64	168.95	180.45	195.11	204.21	207.43
4.25	107.07	113.82	120.26	126.40	132.25	137.81	143.11	148.13	152.91	157.43	161.71	165.75	176.50	190.07	198.39	201.30
4.50	106.82	113.31	119.49	125.36	130.95	136.25	141.27	146.04	150.55	154.81	158.84	162.63	172.67	185.22	192.81	195.45
4.75	106.57	112.80	118.72	124.34	129.66	134.70	139.47	143.98	148.24	152.25	156.03	159.59	168.95	180.53	187.46	189.84
5.00	106.32	112.30	117.96	123.32	128.39	133.18	137.70	141.96	145.97	149.75	153.29	156.62	165.33	176.02	182.33	184.47
5.25	106.06	111.80	117.21	122.32	127.13	131.67	135.95	139.97	143.75	147.29	150.62	153.72	161.83	171.67	177.41	179.33
5.50	105.81	111.30	116.46	121.32	125.89	130.19	134.23	138.02	141.57	144.89	148.00	150.90	158.42	167.47	172.68	174.41
5.75	105.56	110.80	115.71	120.33	124.66	128.73	132.54	136.10	139.43	142.54	145.44	148.14	155.11	163.41	168.14	169.69
6.00	105.32	110.30	114.97	119.35	123.45	127.29	130.87	134.21	137.33	140.24	142.94	145.45	151.90	159.50	163.78	165.17
6.25	105.07	109.81	114.24	118.38	122.25	125.86	129.23	132.36	135.28	137.98	140.50	142.82	148.77	155.73	159.60	160.84
6.50	104.82	109.32	113.51	117.42	121.07	124.46	127.61	130.54	133.26	135.78	138.11	140.26	145.74	152.09	155.57	156.67
6.75	104.57	108.83	112.79	116.47	119.89	123.07	126.02	128.75	131.28	133.61	135.77	137.76	142.79	148.57	151.70	152.68
7.00	104.33	108.34	112.07	115.53	118.74	121.70	124.45	126.99	129.34	131.50	133.49	135.32	139.93	145.17	147.98	148.85
7.25	104.08	107.86	111.36	114.60	117.59	120.36	122.91	125.26	127.43	129.42	131.26	132.93	137.15	141.89	144.40	145.17
7.50	103.84	107.38	110.65	113.67	116.46	119.03	121.39	123.56	125.56	127.39	129.07	130.61	134.44	138.72	140.95	141.63
7.75	103.59	106.90	109.95	112.76	115.34	117.71	119.89	121.89	123.73	125.40	126.94	128.34	131.81	135.65	137.63	138.23
8.00	103.35	106.42	109.25	111.85	114.23	116.42	118.42	120.25	121.93	123.46	124.85	126.12	129.26	132.69	134.44	134.96
8.25	103.10	105.95	108.56	110.95	113.14	115.14	116.97	118.64	120.16	121.55	122.81	123.96	126.77	129.83	131.37	131.82
8.50	102.86	105.48	107.87	110.06	112.06	113.88	115.54	117.05	118.43	119.68	120.81	121.84	124.36	127.06	128.40	128.79
8.75	102.62	105.01	107.19	109.18	110.99	112.64	114.13	115.50	116.73	117.85	118.86	119.78	122.01	124.38	125.54	125.88
9.00	102.38	104.54	106.51	108.30	109.93	111.41	112.75	113.96	115.06	116.06	116.95	117.76	119.72	121.79	122.79	123.08
9.25	102.14	104.08	105.84	107.44	108.89	110.20	111.38	112.46	113.43	114.30	115.09	115.79	117.50	119.28	120.13	120.37
9.50	101.90	103.62	105.17	106.58	107.85	109.00	110.04	110.98	111.82	112.58	113.26	113.87	115.34	116.85	117.57	117.77
9.75	101.66	103.16	104.51	105.73	106.83	107.82	108.72	109.52	110.24	110.89	111.47	111.99	113.23	114.50	115.10	115.26
10.00	101.42	102.70	103.85	104.89	105.82	106.66	107.41	108.09	108.70	109.24	109.72	110.16	111.19	112.23	112.71	112.84
10.25	101.18	102.24	103.20	104.05	104.82	105.51	106.13	106.68	107.18	107.62	108.01	108.36	109.19	110.03	110.41	110.51
10.50	100.94	101.79	102.55	103.23	103.84	104.38	104.87	105.30	105.69	106.03	106.34	106.61	107.26	107.89	108.18	108.26
10.75	100.71	101.34	101.90	102.41	102.86	103.26	103.62	103.94	104.23	104.48	104.70	104.90	105.37	105.83	106.03	106.09
11.00	100.47	100.89	101.27	101.60	101.90	102.16	102.40	102.61	102.79	102.96	103.10	103.23	103.53	103.82	103.95	103.99
11.25	100.23	100.44	100.63	100.80	100.94	101.07	101.19	101.29	101.38	101.46	101.53	101.60	101.74	101.88	101.94	101.96
11.50	100.00	100.00	100.00	100.00	100.00	100.00	100.00	100.00	100.00	100.00	100.00	100.00	100.00	100.00	100.00	100.00
11.75	99.77	99.56	99.37	99.21	99.07	98.94	98.83	98.73	98.64	98.57	98.50	98.44	98.30	98.17	98.12	98.11
12.00	99.53	99.12	98.75	98.43	98.15	97.90	97.67	97.48	97.31	97.16	97.03	96.91	96.65	96.40	96.30	96.27
12.25	99.30	98.68	98.14	97.66	97.23	96.86	96.54	96.25	96.00	95.78	95.59	95.42	95.04	94.69	94.54	94.50
12.50	99.07	98.25	97.52	96.89	96.33	95.85	95.42	95.04	94.72	94.43	94.18	93.97	93.47	93.02	92.83	92.79
12.75	98.83	97.81	96.92	96.13	95.44	94.84	94.32	93.86	93.46	93.11	92.80	92.54	91.95	91.40	91.18	91.13
13.00	98.60	97.38	96.31	95.38	94.56	93.85	93.23	92.69	92.22	91.81	91.45	91.15	90.46	89.83	89.58	89.52
13.25	98.37	96.95	95.71	94.63	93.69	92.87	92.16	91.54	91.00	90.54	90.13	89.79	89.01	88.31	88.03	87.97
13.50	98.14	96.52	95.12	93.89	92.83	91.91	91.10	90.41	89.81	89.29	88.84	88.45	87.59	86.83	86.53	86.46
13.75	97.91	96.10	94.53	93.16	91.98	90.95	90.07	89.30	88.64	88.07	87.57	87.15	86.21	85.39	85.07	85.00
14.00	97.68	95.68	93.94	92.44	91.14	90.01	89.04	88.21	87.49	86.87	86.33	85.88	84.87	83.99	83.65	83.58
14.25	97.46	95.26	93.36	91.72	90.30	89.08	88.03	87.13	86.36	85.69	85.12	84.63	83.56	82.63	82.28	82.20
14.50	97.23	94.84	92.78	91.01	89.48	88.17	87.04	86.07	85.25	84.54	83.93	83.41	82.28	81.31	80.95	80.87
14.75	97.00	94.42	92.20	90.30	88.67	87.26	86.06	85.03	84.16	83.40	82.76	82.22	81.03	80.03	79.66	79.57
15.00	96.77	94.01	91.63	89.60	87.86	86.37	85.10	84.01	83.08	82.29	81.62	81.05	79.82	78.78	78.40	78.32
15.25	96.55	93.59	91.07	88.91	87.07	85.49	84.15	83.01	82.03	81.21	80.51	79.91	78.63	77.57	77.18	77.10
15.50	96.32	93.18	90.51	88.22	86.28	84.62	83.21	82.02	81.00	80.14	79.41	78.79	77.47	76.38	75.99	75.91
15.75	96.10	92.78	89.95	87.54	85.50	83.76	82.29	81.04	79.99	79.09	78.34	77.70	76.34	75.23	74.84	74.76
16.00	95.87	92.37	89.39	86.87	84.73	82.92	81.38	80.08	78.99	78.06	77.29	76.63	75.24	74.11	73.72	73.64
16.25	95.65	91.97	88.84	86.20	83.97	82.08	80.49	79.14	78.01	77.06	76.26	75.59	74.16	73.02	72.63	72.55
16.50	95.43	91.56	88.30	85.54	83.22	81.26	79.61	78.22	77.05	76.07	75.25	74.56	73.11	71.96	71.57	71.49
16.75	95.21	91.16	87.76	84.89	82.47	80.44	78.74	77.30	76.10	75.10	74.26	73.56	72.09	70.93	70.54	70.46
17.00	94.98	90.76	87.22	84.24	81.74	79.64	77.88	76.41	75.18	74.15	73.29	72.58	71.08	69.92	69.54	69.46
17.25	94.76	90.37	86.68	83.59	81.01	78.84	77.04	75.52	74.26	73.21	72.34	71.61	70.11	68.94	68.56	68.49
17.50	94.54	89.97	86.15	82.96	80.29	78.06	76.20	74.66	73.37	72.30	71.41	70.67	69.15	67.98	67.61	67.54
17.75	94.32	89.58	85.63	82.33	79.58	77.29	75.38	73.80	72.49	71.40	70.50	69.75	68.22	67.05	66.68	66.61
18.00	94.10	89.19	85.10	81.70	78.87	76.53	74.58	72.96	71.62	70.52	69.60	68.85	67.31	66.14	65.78	65.71
18.25	93.88	88.80	84.58	81.08	78.18	75.77	73.78	72.13	70.77	69.65	68.73	67.97	66.41	65.26	64.90	64.83
18.50	93.66	88.41	84.07	80.47	77.49	75.03	73.00	71.32	69.94	68.80	67.87	67.10	65.54	64.39	64.04	63.97
18.75	93.45	88.03	83.55	79.86	76.81	74.29	72.22	70.52	69.12	67.97	67.02	66.25	64.69	63.55	63.20	63.14
19.00	93.23	87.65	83.05	79.26	76.13	73.57	71.46	69.73	68.31	67.15	66.20	65.42	63.86	62.73	62.39	62.33
20.00	92.37	86.13	81.05	76.90	73.52	70.76	68.52	66.70	65.22	64.02	63.05	62.26	60.71	59.63	59.32	59.26
25.00	88.18	79.00	71.86	66.31	62.01	58.68	56.09	54.09	52.55	51.35	50.43	49.72	48.44	47.70	47.53	47.51
30.00	84.21	72.52	63.88	57.48	52.75	49.26	46.69	44.79	43.39	42.36	41.61	41.06	40.14	39.69	39.61	39.61

Description: This table shows the yield to prepayment of a monthly payment mortgage purchased at a price in the index.

Example: The yield to prepayment in 10 years of a 11.50 %, 30 year mortgage at a price of 104.00 is 10.82 %.

30 YEAR MORTGAGE PREPAID IN

PRICE	1 yr	2 yr	3 yr	4 yr	5 yr	6 yr	7 yr	8 yr	9 yr	10 yr	11 yr	12 yr	15 yr	20 yr	25 yr	30 yr
140	–	–	–	1.16	2.81	3.90	4.67	5.24	5.68	6.02	6.30	6.52	6.99	7.39	7.57	7.61
135	–	–	–	2.26	3.73	4.70	5.38	5.89	6.28	6.58	6.83	7.03	7.44	7.80	7.95	7.99
130	–	–	1.24	3.39	4.68	5.53	6.13	6.57	6.91	7.18	7.39	7.56	7.92	8.23	8.36	8.39
125	–	–	2.75	4.58	5.68	6.40	6.91	7.28	7.57	7.80	7.98	8.12	8.43	8.69	8.79	8.82
120	–	1.32	4.33	5.83	6.72	7.31	7.73	8.03	8.27	8.45	8.60	8.72	8.96	9.17	9.26	9.28
119	–	1.78	4.65	6.09	6.94	7.50	7.90	8.19	8.41	8.59	8.73	8.84	9.08	9.27	9.35	9.38
118	–	2.25	4.98	6.34	7.16	7.69	8.07	8.35	8.56	8.72	8.86	8.97	9.19	9.38	9.45	9.47
117	–	2.72	5.31	6.61	7.37	7.88	8.24	8.50	8.71	8.86	8.99	9.09	9.30	9.48	9.55	9.57
116	–	3.19	5.65	6.87	7.60	8.08	8.41	8.66	8.85	9.00	9.12	9.22	9.42	9.58	9.65	9.67
115	–	3.67	5.99	7.14	7.82	8.27	8.59	8.83	9.00	9.14	9.26	9.35	9.53	9.69	9.76	9.77
114	–	4.16	6.33	7.41	8.05	8.47	8.77	8.99	9.16	9.29	9.39	9.48	9.65	9.80	9.86	9.87
113	–	4.65	6.67	7.68	8.28	8.67	8.95	9.15	9.31	9.43	9.53	9.61	9.77	9.91	9.96	9.98
112	–	5.14	7.02	7.95	8.51	8.87	9.13	9.32	9.47	9.58	9.67	9.74	9.89	10.02	10.07	10.08
111	–	5.64	7.37	8.23	8.74	9.08	9.32	9.49	9.62	9.73	9.81	9.88	10.02	10.13	10.18	10.19
110	1.40	6.15	7.73	8.51	8.98	9.29	9.50	9.66	9.78	9.88	9.96	10.02	10.14	10.25	10.29	10.30
109	2.36	6.66	8.09	8.80	9.22	9.50	9.69	9.84	9.95	10.03	10.10	10.16	10.27	10.36	10.40	10.41
108	3.33	7.17	8.45	9.08	9.46	9.71	9.88	10.01	10.11	10.19	10.25	10.30	10.40	10.48	10.52	10.52
107	4.32	7.69	8.81	9.37	9.70	9.92	10.08	10.19	10.27	10.34	10.40	10.44	10.53	10.60	10.63	10.64
106	5.31	8.22	9.19	9.67	9.95	10.14	10.27	10.37	10.44	10.50	10.55	10.58	10.66	10.72	10.75	10.76
105	6.31	8.75	9.56	9.96	10.20	10.36	10.47	10.55	10.61	10.66	10.70	10.73	10.79	10.85	10.87	10.87
104	7.33	9.29	9.94	10.26	10.45	10.58	10.67	10.73	10.78	10.82	10.85	10.88	10.93	10.97	10.99	10.99
103.75	7.58	9.42	10.03	10.34	10.52	10.64	10.72	10.78	10.83	10.86	10.89	10.92	10.96	11.00	11.02	11.02
103.50	7.84	9.56	10.13	10.41	10.58	10.69	10.77	10.83	10.87	10.91	10.93	10.95	11.00	11.04	11.05	11.05
103.25	8.09	9.69	10.22	10.49	10.65	10.75	10.82	10.87	10.91	10.95	10.97	10.99	11.03	11.07	11.08	11.08
103.00	8.35	9.83	10.32	10.56	10.71	10.80	10.87	10.92	10.96	10.99	11.01	11.03	11.07	11.10	11.11	11.12
102.75	8.61	9.97	10.42	10.64	10.77	10.86	10.92	10.97	11.00	11.03	11.05	11.07	11.10	11.13	11.14	11.15
102.50	8.87	10.10	10.51	10.72	10.84	10.92	10.97	11.02	11.05	11.07	11.09	11.11	11.14	11.16	11.17	11.18
102.25	9.13	10.24	10.61	10.79	10.90	10.97	11.03	11.06	11.09	11.11	11.13	11.14	11.17	11.20	11.21	11.21
102.00	9.39	10.38	10.71	10.87	10.97	11.03	11.08	11.11	11.13	11.15	11.17	11.18	11.21	11.23	11.24	11.24
101.75	9.65	10.52	10.81	10.95	11.03	11.09	11.13	11.16	11.18	11.20	11.21	11.22	11.24	11.26	11.27	11.27
101.50	9.91	10.66	10.90	11.03	11.10	11.15	11.18	11.21	11.22	11.24	11.25	11.26	11.28	11.30	11.30	11.30
101.25	10.17	10.79	11.00	11.10	11.16	11.20	11.23	11.25	11.27	11.28	11.29	11.30	11.31	11.33	11.33	11.33
101.00	10.44	10.93	11.10	11.18	11.23	11.26	11.28	11.30	11.31	11.32	11.33	11.34	11.35	11.36	11.37	11.37
100.75	10.70	11.07	11.20	11.26	11.30	11.32	11.34	11.35	11.36	11.37	11.37	11.38	11.39	11.39	11.40	11.40
100.50	10.96	11.21	11.30	11.34	11.36	11.38	11.39	11.40	11.40	11.41	11.41	11.42	11.42	11.43	11.43	11.43
100.25	11.23	11.35	11.40	11.42	11.43	11.44	11.44	11.45	11.45	11.45	11.45	11.46	11.46	11.46	11.46	11.46
100.00	11.50	11.50	11.50	11.50	11.50	11.50	11.50	11.50	11.50	11.50	11.50	11.50	11.50	11.50	11.50	11.50
99.75	11.76	11.64	11.59	11.57	11.56	11.55	11.55	11.54	11.54	11.54	11.54	11.53	11.53	11.53	11.53	11.53
99.50	12.03	11.78	11.69	11.65	11.63	11.61	11.60	11.59	11.59	11.58	11.58	11.57	11.57	11.56	11.56	11.56
99.25	12.30	11.92	11.79	11.73	11.70	11.67	11.65	11.64	11.63	11.63	11.62	11.61	11.60	11.60	11.59	11.59
99.00	12.57	12.06	11.90	11.81	11.76	11.73	11.71	11.69	11.68	11.67	11.66	11.65	11.64	11.63	11.63	11.63
98.75	12.84	12.21	12.00	11.89	11.83	11.79	11.76	11.74	11.73	11.71	11.70	11.69	11.68	11.67	11.66	11.66
98.50	13.11	12.35	12.10	11.97	11.90	11.85	11.82	11.79	11.77	11.76	11.74	11.74	11.72	11.70	11.69	11.69
98.25	13.38	12.49	12.20	12.05	11.97	11.91	11.87	11.84	11.82	11.80	11.79	11.78	11.75	11.73	11.73	11.73
98.00	13.65	12.64	12.30	12.13	12.03	11.97	11.92	11.89	11.86	11.85	11.83	11.82	11.79	11.77	11.76	11.76
97.75	13.92	12.78	12.40	12.21	12.10	12.03	11.98	11.94	11.91	11.89	11.87	11.86	11.83	11.80	11.80	11.79
97.50	14.20	12.93	12.50	12.30	12.17	12.09	12.03	11.99	11.96	11.93	11.91	11.90	11.87	11.84	11.83	11.83
97.25	14.47	13.07	12.61	12.38	12.24	12.15	12.09	12.04	12.01	11.98	11.96	11.94	11.90	11.87	11.86	11.86
97	14.75	13.22	12.71	12.46	12.31	12.21	12.14	12.09	12.05	12.02	12.00	11.98	11.94	11.91	11.90	11.89
96	15.85	13.80	13.12	12.79	12.59	12.46	12.36	12.30	12.25	12.21	12.17	12.15	12.10	12.05	12.04	12.03
95	16.98	14.40	13.54	13.12	12.87	12.71	12.59	12.50	12.44	12.39	12.35	12.32	12.25	12.20	12.18	12.17
94	18.11	15.00	13.97	13.46	13.16	12.96	12.82	12.71	12.64	12.58	12.53	12.49	12.41	12.35	12.32	12.32
93	19.26	15.61	14.40	13.80	13.45	13.21	13.05	12.93	12.84	12.77	12.71	12.66	12.57	12.50	12.47	12.46
92	20.42	16.22	14.83	14.15	13.74	13.47	13.28	13.14	13.04	12.96	12.89	12.84	12.74	12.65	12.62	12.61
91	21.60	16.85	15.28	14.50	14.04	13.73	13.52	13.36	13.25	13.15	13.08	13.02	12.90	12.81	12.77	12.76
90	22.79	17.48	15.72	14.85	14.34	14.00	13.76	13.59	13.45	13.35	13.27	13.21	13.07	12.97	12.93	12.92
89	24.00	18.12	16.17	15.21	14.64	14.27	14.01	13.81	13.67	13.55	13.46	13.39	13.25	13.13	13.09	13.08
88	25.22	18.76	16.63	15.58	14.95	14.54	14.25	14.04	13.88	13.76	13.66	13.58	13.42	13.30	13.25	13.24
87	26.46	19.42	17.10	15.95	15.27	14.82	14.51	14.28	14.10	13.97	13.86	13.77	13.60	13.47	13.42	13.40
86	27.71	20.08	17.57	16.32	15.58	15.10	14.76	14.51	14.32	14.18	14.06	13.97	13.78	13.64	13.58	13.57
85	28.98	20.76	18.04	16.70	15.91	15.39	15.02	14.75	14.55	14.39	14.27	14.17	13.97	13.81	13.76	13.74
80	35.60	24.26	20.53	18.69	17.60	16.88	16.38	16.02	15.74	15.53	15.36	15.23	14.96	14.75	14.68	14.66
75	42.70	28.02	23.21	20.83	19.42	18.50	17.86	17.40	17.04	16.77	16.56	16.39	16.05	15.80	15.71	15.69
70	50.36	32.09	26.10	23.15	21.41	20.28	19.48	18.91	18.48	18.14	17.88	17.68	17.27	16.98	16.88	16.86
65	58.66	36.49	29.25	25.68	23.59	22.22	21.27	20.58	20.07	19.67	19.37	19.12	18.65	18.32	18.22	18.20
60	67.73	41.31	32.70	28.47	25.99	24.38	23.27	22.46	21.86	21.40	21.04	20.76	20.23	19.87	19.76	19.75
55	77.70	46.61	36.52	31.57	28.68	26.80	25.51	24.58	23.89	23.37	22.96	22.65	22.07	21.69	21.58	21.57
50	88.76	52.51	40.78	35.06	31.71	29.56	28.07	27.01	26.23	25.65	25.20	24.86	24.24	23.85	23.76	23.74

PREPAYMENT MORTGAGE PRICE

11.75 %

Description: This table shows the price to pay for a monthly payment loan, at a yield rate and assuming prepayment.

Example: The price of a 11.75 %, 30 year mortgage to yield 8.00 %, if prepaid in 6 years, is $ 117.60.

30 YEAR MORTGAGE PREPAID IN

YIELD	1 yr	2 yr	3 yr	4 yr	5 yr	6 yr	7 yr	8 yr	9 yr	10 yr	11 yr	12 yr	15 yr	20 yr	25 yr	30 yr
0.00	111.73	123.41	135.04	146.61	158.11	169.54	180.88	192.12	203.26	214.27	225.15	235.88	266.94	313.33	348.46	363.39
1.00	110.67	121.20	131.57	141.79	151.84	161.73	171.45	180.99	190.35	199.51	208.47	217.21	242.03	277.68	303.38	313.83
2.00	109.63	119.03	128.20	137.14	145.86	154.35	162.60	170.63	178.42	185.98	193.29	200.36	220.03	247.19	265.84	273.09
3.00	108.59	116.90	124.93	132.68	140.15	147.36	154.30	160.98	167.40	173.56	179.47	185.13	200.55	221.04	234.44	239.42
4.00	107.57	114.82	121.75	128.37	134.70	140.74	146.50	151.99	157.21	162.18	166.89	171.35	183.29	198.55	208.05	211.43
4.25	107.32	114.30	120.97	127.32	133.38	139.14	144.63	149.84	154.79	159.48	163.92	168.12	179.29	193.43	202.13	205.19
4.50	107.06	113.79	120.19	126.28	132.07	137.57	142.78	147.73	152.41	156.84	161.02	164.96	175.41	188.50	196.45	199.22
4.75	106.81	113.28	119.42	125.25	130.78	136.01	140.97	145.65	150.08	154.25	158.19	161.88	171.64	183.74	191.00	193.50
5.00	106.56	112.77	118.66	124.23	129.50	134.48	139.18	143.61	147.79	151.72	155.42	158.88	167.97	179.15	185.78	188.03
5.25	106.31	112.27	117.90	123.22	128.23	132.96	137.42	141.61	145.55	149.24	152.71	155.95	164.42	174.73	180.76	182.80
5.50	106.06	111.77	117.15	122.22	126.99	131.47	135.68	139.64	143.35	146.82	150.06	153.09	160.97	170.46	175.95	177.78
5.75	105.81	111.27	116.40	121.22	125.75	130.00	133.98	137.70	141.19	144.44	147.48	150.30	157.61	166.34	171.33	172.97
6.00	105.56	110.77	115.66	120.24	124.53	128.54	132.30	135.80	139.07	142.12	144.95	147.58	154.35	162.36	166.89	168.36
6.25	105.31	110.28	114.92	119.27	123.32	127.11	130.64	133.93	136.99	139.84	142.48	144.92	151.19	158.53	162.62	163.94
6.50	105.06	109.79	114.19	118.30	122.13	125.70	129.01	132.10	134.96	137.61	140.06	142.33	148.11	154.82	158.52	159.70
6.75	104.81	109.30	113.47	117.35	120.95	124.30	127.41	130.29	132.96	135.42	137.70	139.80	145.13	151.25	154.58	155.63
7.00	104.57	108.81	112.75	116.40	119.79	122.93	125.83	128.52	131.00	133.28	135.39	137.33	142.22	147.79	150.79	151.72
7.25	104.32	108.32	112.03	115.46	118.63	121.57	124.27	126.77	129.07	131.19	133.14	134.92	139.40	144.46	147.14	147.97
7.50	104.08	107.84	111.32	114.53	117.50	120.23	122.74	125.06	127.19	129.14	130.93	132.57	136.66	141.23	143.63	144.36
7.75	103.83	107.36	110.62	113.61	116.37	118.91	121.24	123.37	125.33	127.13	128.77	130.27	133.99	138.12	140.25	140.90
8.00	103.59	106.88	109.92	112.70	115.26	117.60	119.75	121.72	123.52	125.16	126.66	128.02	131.40	135.10	137.00	137.57
8.25	103.34	106.41	109.22	111.80	114.16	116.31	118.29	120.09	121.73	123.23	124.60	125.83	128.88	132.19	133.87	134.36
8.50	103.10	105.94	108.53	110.90	113.07	115.05	116.85	118.49	119.99	121.34	122.58	123.69	126.43	129.38	130.85	131.28
8.75	102.86	105.47	107.85	110.02	111.99	113.79	115.43	116.92	118.27	119.49	120.60	121.60	124.05	126.65	127.94	128.31
9.00	102.62	105.00	107.17	109.14	110.93	112.56	114.03	115.37	116.59	117.68	118.67	119.56	121.73	124.02	125.13	125.45
9.25	102.38	104.53	106.49	108.27	109.88	111.34	112.66	113.85	114.93	115.91	116.78	117.57	119.48	121.47	122.43	122.70
9.50	102.13	104.07	105.82	107.41	108.84	110.13	111.30	112.36	113.31	114.17	114.93	115.62	117.28	119.00	119.82	120.05
9.75	101.90	103.61	105.15	106.55	107.81	108.95	109.97	110.89	111.72	112.46	113.13	113.72	115.15	116.61	117.30	117.49
10.00	101.66	103.15	104.49	105.71	106.80	107.78	108.66	109.45	110.16	110.79	111.36	111.87	113.07	114.30	114.87	115.02
10.25	101.42	102.69	103.84	104.87	105.79	106.62	107.36	108.03	108.62	109.15	109.63	110.05	111.05	112.06	112.52	112.64
10.50	101.18	102.24	103.19	104.04	104.80	105.48	106.09	106.63	107.12	107.55	107.94	108.28	109.08	109.89	110.25	110.35
10.75	100.94	101.79	102.54	103.21	103.82	104.35	104.83	105.26	105.64	105.98	106.28	106.54	107.17	107.79	108.06	108.13
11.00	100.71	101.34	101.90	102.40	102.85	103.24	103.60	103.91	104.19	104.44	104.66	104.85	105.30	105.75	105.94	105.99
11.25	100.47	100.89	101.26	101.59	101.89	102.15	102.38	102.59	102.77	102.93	103.07	103.20	103.49	103.77	103.90	103.93
11.50	100.23	100.44	100.63	100.79	100.94	101.07	101.18	101.28	101.37	101.45	101.52	101.58	101.72	101.86	101.92	101.93
11.75	100.00	100.00	100.00	100.00	100.00	100.00	100.00	100.00	100.00	100.00	100.00	100.00	100.00	100.00	100.00	100.00
12.00	99.77	99.56	99.38	99.21	99.07	98.95	98.84	98.74	98.65	98.58	98.51	98.46	98.32	98.20	98.15	98.13
12.25	99.53	99.12	98.76	98.44	98.16	97.91	97.69	97.50	97.33	97.19	97.06	96.95	96.69	96.45	96.35	96.33
12.50	99.30	98.68	98.14	97.67	97.25	96.88	96.56	96.28	96.03	95.82	95.63	95.47	95.10	94.76	94.61	94.58
12.75	99.07	98.25	97.53	96.90	96.35	95.87	95.45	95.08	94.76	94.48	94.24	94.03	93.55	93.11	92.93	92.89
13.00	98.84	97.82	96.93	96.15	95.47	94.87	94.35	93.90	93.51	93.17	92.87	92.61	92.04	91.51	91.30	91.25
13.25	98.60	97.39	96.32	95.40	94.59	93.89	93.27	92.74	92.28	91.88	91.53	91.23	90.56	89.96	89.72	89.66
13.50	98.37	96.96	95.73	94.65	93.72	92.91	92.21	91.60	91.07	90.62	90.22	89.88	89.13	88.45	88.19	88.13
13.75	98.14	96.53	95.13	93.92	92.87	91.95	91.16	90.48	89.89	89.38	88.94	88.57	87.73	86.99	86.70	86.64
14.00	97.92	96.11	94.54	93.19	92.02	91.01	90.13	89.38	88.73	88.17	87.69	87.27	86.36	85.57	85.26	85.19
14.25	97.69	95.69	93.96	92.47	91.18	90.07	89.11	88.29	87.58	86.98	86.46	86.01	85.03	84.18	83.86	83.79
14.50	97.46	95.27	93.38	91.75	90.35	89.15	88.11	87.22	86.46	85.81	85.25	84.78	83.73	82.84	82.51	82.43
14.75	97.23	94.85	92.80	91.04	89.53	88.24	87.13	86.17	85.36	84.67	84.07	83.57	82.47	81.53	81.19	81.11
15.00	97.00	94.43	92.23	90.34	88.72	87.34	86.15	85.14	84.28	83.54	82.92	82.39	81.23	80.26	79.91	79.83
15.25	96.78	94.02	91.66	89.64	87.92	86.45	85.20	84.13	83.22	82.44	81.79	81.23	80.03	79.03	78.66	78.59
15.50	96.55	93.61	91.10	88.96	87.13	85.57	84.25	83.13	82.17	81.36	80.68	80.10	78.85	77.82	77.46	77.38
15.75	96.33	93.20	90.54	88.27	86.35	84.71	83.32	82.14	81.15	80.30	79.59	78.99	77.70	76.65	76.28	76.20
16.00	96.10	92.79	89.98	87.59	85.57	83.86	82.40	81.18	80.14	79.26	78.53	77.91	76.58	75.51	75.14	75.06
16.25	95.88	92.39	89.43	86.92	84.81	83.01	81.50	80.23	79.15	78.24	77.48	76.84	75.49	74.40	74.03	73.95
16.50	95.66	91.98	88.88	86.26	84.05	82.18	80.61	79.29	78.18	77.24	76.46	75.81	74.42	73.32	72.95	72.87
16.75	95.43	91.58	88.34	85.60	83.30	81.36	79.73	78.37	77.22	76.26	75.46	74.79	73.38	72.27	71.90	71.82
17.00	95.21	91.18	87.80	84.95	82.56	80.55	78.87	77.46	76.28	75.30	74.48	73.79	72.36	71.25	70.88	70.80
17.25	94.99	90.78	87.26	84.30	81.83	79.75	78.02	76.57	75.36	74.35	73.52	72.82	71.37	70.25	69.88	69.81
17.50	94.77	90.39	86.73	83.66	81.10	78.96	77.18	75.69	74.46	73.43	72.57	71.87	70.40	69.27	68.91	68.84
17.75	94.55	90.00	86.20	83.03	80.38	78.18	76.35	74.83	73.57	72.52	71.65	70.93	69.45	68.33	67.97	67.90
18.00	94.33	89.60	85.67	82.40	79.68	77.42	75.54	73.98	72.69	71.62	70.74	70.02	68.52	67.40	67.05	66.98
18.25	94.11	89.21	85.15	81.77	78.98	76.66	74.73	73.15	71.83	70.75	69.85	69.12	67.62	66.50	66.15	66.08
18.50	93.89	88.83	84.63	81.16	78.28	75.91	73.94	72.32	70.99	69.89	68.98	68.24	66.73	65.62	65.27	65.21
18.75	93.67	88.44	84.12	80.55	77.60	75.17	73.16	71.51	70.16	69.04	68.13	67.38	65.87	64.76	64.42	64.36
19.00	93.46	88.06	83.61	79.94	76.92	74.44	72.39	70.72	69.34	68.21	67.29	66.54	65.02	63.92	63.59	63.53
20.00	92.59	86.54	81.60	77.57	74.28	71.60	69.43	67.65	66.21	65.05	64.10	63.34	61.82	60.76	60.46	60.41
25.00	88.40	79.38	72.37	66.93	62.70	59.42	56.88	54.91	53.39	52.22	51.31	50.61	49.35	48.61	48.45	48.42
30.00	84.43	72.89	64.35	58.04	53.37	49.92	47.38	45.50	44.12	43.10	42.36	41.81	40.90	40.46	40.38	40.37

PREPAYMENT MORTGAGE YIELD, 30 YEAR TERM   11.75 %

Description: This table shows the yield to prepayment of a monthly payment mortgage purchased at a price in the index.

Example: The yield to prepayment in 10 years of a 11.75 %, 30 year mortgage at a price of 104.00 is 11.07 %.

30 YEAR MORTGAGE PREPAID IN

PRICE	1 yr	2 yr	3 yr	4 yr	5 yr	6 yr	7 yr	8 yr	9 yr	10 yr	11 yr	12 yr	15 yr	20 yr	25 yr	30 yr
140	–	–	–	1.38	3.02	4.11	4.88	5.45	5.88	6.23	6.50	6.73	7.19	7.59	7.76	7.81
135	–	–	–	2.47	3.94	4.91	5.59	6.10	6.49	6.79	7.04	7.24	7.65	8.00	8.15	8.19
130	–	–	1.46	3.61	4.90	5.74	6.34	6.79	7.12	7.39	7.60	7.77	8.13	8.44	8.57	8.60
125	–	–	2.97	4.81	5.90	6.62	7.13	7.50	7.79	8.02	8.20	8.34	8.64	8.90	9.01	9.04
120	–	1.54	4.56	6.06	6.95	7.54	7.95	8.26	8.49	8.68	8.82	8.94	9.19	9.39	9.48	9.50
119	–	2.01	4.88	6.31	7.17	7.73	8.12	8.41	8.64	8.81	8.95	9.07	9.30	9.50	9.58	9.60
118	–	2.48	5.21	6.57	7.38	7.92	8.29	8.57	8.78	8.95	9.08	9.19	9.41	9.60	9.67	9.69
117	–	2.95	5.54	6.84	7.60	8.11	8.47	8.73	8.93	9.09	9.22	9.32	9.53	9.70	9.78	9.79
116	–	3.43	5.88	7.10	7.83	8.31	8.64	8.89	9.08	9.23	9.35	9.45	9.64	9.81	9.88	9.89
115	–	3.91	6.22	7.37	8.05	8.50	8.82	9.06	9.23	9.37	9.49	9.58	9.76	9.92	9.98	10.00
114	–	4.39	6.56	7.64	8.28	8.70	9.00	9.22	9.39	9.52	9.62	9.71	9.88	10.03	10.09	10.10
113	–	4.88	6.91	7.91	8.51	8.91	9.18	9.39	9.54	9.67	9.76	9.84	10.00	10.14	10.19	10.21
112	–	5.38	7.26	8.19	8.74	9.11	9.37	9.56	9.70	9.81	9.90	9.98	10.13	10.25	10.30	10.31
111	–	5.88	7.61	8.47	8.98	9.31	9.55	9.73	9.86	9.96	10.05	10.11	10.25	10.37	10.41	10.42
110	1.64	6.39	7.96	8.75	9.22	9.52	9.74	9.90	10.02	10.12	10.19	10.25	10.38	10.48	10.52	10.53
109	2.60	6.90	8.32	9.03	9.46	9.73	9.93	10.07	10.18	10.27	10.34	10.39	10.51	10.60	10.64	10.65
108	3.58	7.41	8.69	9.32	9.70	9.95	10.12	10.25	10.35	10.42	10.49	10.53	10.64	10.72	10.75	10.76
107	4.56	7.93	9.06	9.61	9.94	10.16	10.32	10.43	10.51	10.58	10.64	10.68	10.77	10.84	10.87	10.88
106	5.55	8.46	9.43	9.91	10.19	10.38	10.51	10.61	10.68	10.74	10.79	10.82	10.90	10.96	10.99	10.99
105	6.56	8.99	9.80	10.21	10.44	10.60	10.71	10.79	10.86	10.90	10.94	10.97	11.04	11.09	11.11	11.11
104	7.57	9.53	10.18	10.51	10.70	10.82	10.91	10.98	11.03	11.07	11.10	11.12	11.17	11.22	11.23	11.24
103.75	7.83	9.67	10.28	10.58	10.76	10.88	10.96	11.03	11.07	11.11	11.14	11.16	11.21	11.25	11.26	11.27
103.50	8.08	9.80	10.37	10.66	10.83	10.94	11.02	11.07	11.12	11.15	11.18	11.20	11.24	11.28	11.29	11.30
103.25	8.34	9.94	10.47	10.73	10.89	10.99	11.07	11.12	11.16	11.19	11.22	11.24	11.28	11.31	11.33	11.33
103.00	8.60	10.08	10.57	10.81	10.96	11.05	11.12	11.17	11.20	11.23	11.26	11.28	11.31	11.34	11.36	11.36
102.75	8.86	10.21	10.66	10.89	11.02	11.11	11.17	11.21	11.25	11.28	11.30	11.31	11.35	11.38	11.39	11.39
102.50	9.12	10.35	10.76	10.96	11.08	11.16	11.22	11.26	11.29	11.32	11.34	11.35	11.38	11.41	11.42	11.42
102.25	9.38	10.49	10.86	11.04	11.15	11.22	11.27	11.31	11.34	11.36	11.38	11.39	11.42	11.44	11.45	11.45
102.00	9.64	10.63	10.96	11.12	11.22	11.28	11.32	11.36	11.38	11.40	11.42	11.43	11.46	11.48	11.48	11.49
101.75	9.90	10.77	11.05	11.20	11.28	11.34	11.38	11.40	11.43	11.44	11.46	11.47	11.49	11.51	11.52	11.52
101.50	10.16	10.90	11.15	11.27	11.35	11.39	11.43	11.45	11.47	11.49	11.50	11.51	11.53	11.54	11.55	11.55
101.25	10.42	11.04	11.25	11.35	11.41	11.45	11.48	11.50	11.52	11.53	11.54	11.55	11.56	11.58	11.58	11.58
101.00	10.68	11.18	11.35	11.43	11.48	11.51	11.53	11.55	11.56	11.57	11.58	11.59	11.60	11.61	11.61	11.61
100.75	10.95	11.32	11.45	11.51	11.54	11.57	11.59	11.60	11.61	11.62	11.62	11.63	11.64	11.64	11.65	11.65
100.50	11.21	11.46	11.55	11.59	11.61	11.63	11.64	11.65	11.65	11.66	11.66	11.67	11.67	11.68	11.68	11.68
100.25	11.48	11.60	11.65	11.67	11.68	11.69	11.69	11.70	11.70	11.70	11.70	11.71	11.71	11.71	11.71	11.71
100.00	11.75	11.75	11.75	11.75	11.75	11.75	11.75	11.75	11.75	11.75	11.75	11.75	11.75	11.75	11.75	11.75
99.75	12.01	11.89	11.85	11.82	11.81	11.80	11.80	11.79	11.79	11.79	11.79	11.79	11.78	11.78	11.78	11.78
99.50	12.28	12.03	11.95	11.90	11.88	11.86	11.85	11.84	11.84	11.83	11.83	11.83	11.82	11.81	11.81	11.81
99.25	12.55	12.17	12.05	11.98	11.95	11.92	11.91	11.89	11.88	11.88	11.87	11.87	11.86	11.85	11.85	11.84
99.00	12.82	12.31	12.15	12.06	12.01	11.98	11.96	11.94	11.93	11.92	11.91	11.91	11.89	11.88	11.88	11.88
98.75	13.09	12.46	12.25	12.14	12.08	12.04	12.01	11.99	11.98	11.96	11.95	11.95	11.93	11.92	11.91	11.91
98.50	13.36	12.60	12.35	12.22	12.15	12.10	12.07	12.04	12.02	12.01	12.00	11.99	11.97	11.95	11.95	11.95
98.25	13.63	12.74	12.45	12.31	12.22	12.16	12.12	12.09	12.07	12.05	12.04	12.03	12.01	11.99	11.98	11.98
98.00	13.90	12.89	12.55	12.39	12.29	12.22	12.18	12.14	12.12	12.10	12.08	12.07	12.04	12.02	12.02	12.01
97.75	14.18	13.03	12.66	12.47	12.36	12.28	12.23	12.19	12.17	12.14	12.13	12.11	12.08	12.06	12.05	12.05
97.50	14.45	13.18	12.76	12.55	12.43	12.34	12.29	12.24	12.21	12.19	12.17	12.15	12.12	12.09	12.08	12.08
97.25	14.72	13.32	12.86	12.63	12.49	12.41	12.34	12.30	12.26	12.23	12.21	12.19	12.16	12.13	12.12	12.12
97	15.00	13.47	12.96	12.71	12.56	12.47	12.40	12.35	12.31	12.28	12.25	12.24	12.20	12.17	12.15	12.15
96	16.11	14.06	13.38	13.04	12.84	12.71	12.62	12.55	12.50	12.46	12.43	12.40	12.35	12.31	12.29	12.29
95	17.23	14.65	13.80	13.38	13.13	12.96	12.85	12.76	12.70	12.65	12.61	12.58	12.51	12.46	12.44	12.43
94	18.37	15.26	14.23	13.72	13.41	13.22	13.08	12.97	12.90	12.84	12.79	12.75	12.67	12.61	12.59	12.58
93	19.52	15.87	14.66	14.06	13.71	13.47	13.31	13.19	13.10	13.03	12.97	12.93	12.83	12.76	12.73	12.73
92	20.68	16.48	15.10	14.41	14.00	13.73	13.55	13.41	13.30	13.22	13.16	13.11	13.00	12.92	12.89	12.88
91	21.86	17.11	15.54	14.76	14.30	14.00	13.78	13.63	13.51	13.42	13.35	13.29	13.17	13.08	13.04	13.03
90	23.06	17.74	15.99	15.12	14.60	14.26	14.03	13.85	13.72	13.62	13.54	13.47	13.34	13.24	13.20	13.19
89	24.26	18.38	16.44	15.48	14.91	14.54	14.27	14.08	13.94	13.82	13.73	13.66	13.52	13.40	13.35	13.35
88	25.49	19.03	16.90	15.85	15.22	14.81	14.52	14.31	14.15	14.03	13.93	13.85	13.70	13.57	13.53	13.52
87	26.73	19.69	17.37	16.22	15.54	15.09	14.78	14.55	14.37	14.24	14.13	14.05	13.88	13.74	13.69	13.68
86	27.98	20.36	17.84	16.59	15.86	15.37	15.03	14.79	14.60	14.45	14.34	14.25	14.06	13.92	13.87	13.85
85	29.26	21.03	18.32	16.98	16.18	15.66	15.30	15.03	14.83	14.67	14.55	14.45	14.25	14.10	14.04	14.03
80	35.88	24.54	20.81	18.97	17.88	17.17	16.67	16.30	16.03	15.82	15.65	15.52	15.25	15.05	14.98	14.96
75	42.99	28.32	23.50	21.12	19.72	18.80	18.16	17.70	17.34	17.07	16.86	16.69	16.36	16.11	16.03	16.01
70	50.66	32.39	26.40	23.46	21.72	20.59	19.80	19.22	18.79	18.46	18.20	18.00	17.60	17.31	17.21	17.20
65	58.98	36.81	29.57	26.01	23.91	22.55	21.60	20.92	20.40	20.01	19.71	19.47	19.00	18.67	18.57	18.56
60	68.06	41.64	33.03	28.81	26.33	24.73	23.61	22.81	22.21	21.76	21.40	21.13	20.61	20.25	20.15	20.13
55	78.05	46.96	36.87	31.93	29.04	27.17	25.88	24.95	24.27	23.75	23.35	23.05	22.47	22.10	22.00	21.99
50	89.13	52.88	41.16	35.44	32.10	29.95	28.47	27.42	26.65	26.07	25.63	25.29	24.68	24.30	24.22	24.20

PREPAYMENT MORTGAGE PRICE

12.00 %

Description: This table shows the price to pay for a monthly payment loan, at a yield rate and assuming prepayment.

Example: The price of a 12.00 %, 30 year mortgage to yield 8.00 %, if prepaid in 6 years, is $ 118.79.

30 YEAR MORTGAGE PREPAID IN

YIELD	1 yr	2 yr	3 yr	4 yr	5 yr	6 yr	7 yr	8 yr	9 yr	10 yr	11 yr	12 yr	15 yr	20 yr	25 yr	30 yr
0.00	111.98	123.91	135.80	147.62	159.38	171.06	182.66	194.17	205.57	216.85	228.00	238.99	270.86	318.56	354.83	370.30
1.00	110.92	121.70	132.31	142.78	153.08	163.21	173.17	182.95	192.55	201.95	211.14	220.12	245.64	282.37	308.95	319.80
2.00	109.88	119.52	128.93	138.11	147.06	155.78	164.26	172.51	180.52	188.29	195.81	203.09	223.35	251.40	270.74	278.29
3.00	108.84	117.39	125.65	133.62	141.32	148.74	155.89	162.78	169.40	175.76	181.85	187.69	203.63	224.85	238.77	243.98
4.00	107.82	115.30	122.46	129.30	135.84	142.08	148.04	153.72	159.12	164.26	169.14	173.76	186.14	202.00	211.91	215.45
4.25	107.56	114.78	121.67	128.24	134.51	140.47	146.15	151.55	156.67	161.53	166.14	170.49	182.09	196.80	205.88	209.09
4.50	107.31	114.27	120.90	127.20	133.19	138.89	144.29	149.42	154.27	158.87	163.21	167.30	178.15	191.79	200.10	203.01
4.75	107.06	113.76	120.12	126.16	131.89	137.32	142.46	147.32	151.92	156.26	160.34	164.18	174.33	186.95	194.56	197.19
5.00	106.80	113.25	119.36	125.14	130.61	135.78	140.66	145.27	149.61	153.70	157.54	161.15	170.62	182.29	189.24	191.61
5.25	106.55	112.74	118.60	124.12	129.34	134.25	138.89	143.25	147.35	151.20	154.81	158.18	167.02	177.79	184.13	186.27
5.50	106.30	112.24	117.84	123.11	128.08	132.75	137.14	141.26	145.13	148.75	152.13	155.29	163.52	173.46	179.23	181.16
5.75	106.05	111.74	117.09	122.12	126.84	131.27	135.42	139.31	142.95	146.35	149.52	152.47	160.12	169.27	174.52	176.26
6.00	105.80	111.24	116.35	121.13	125.61	129.80	133.73	137.39	140.81	144.00	146.96	149.72	156.82	165.23	170.00	171.56
6.25	105.55	110.75	115.61	120.15	124.40	128.36	132.06	135.50	138.71	141.70	144.46	147.03	153.61	161.33	165.66	167.06
6.50	105.30	110.25	114.87	119.18	123.20	126.94	130.42	133.65	136.66	139.44	142.02	144.41	150.49	157.57	161.49	162.74
6.75	105.05	109.76	114.14	118.22	122.01	125.53	128.80	131.83	134.64	137.24	139.64	141.85	147.47	153.94	157.47	158.59
7.00	104.81	109.27	113.42	117.27	120.84	124.15	127.21	130.04	132.66	135.08	137.30	139.35	144.52	150.42	153.61	154.61
7.25	104.56	108.79	112.70	116.33	119.68	122.78	125.64	128.28	130.72	132.96	135.02	136.91	141.66	147.03	149.90	150.78
7.50	104.32	108.30	111.99	115.39	118.53	121.43	124.10	126.55	128.81	130.89	132.79	134.53	138.88	143.76	146.32	147.11
7.75	104.07	107.82	111.28	114.47	117.40	120.10	122.58	124.86	126.94	128.86	130.60	132.20	136.18	140.59	142.88	143.58
8.00	103.83	107.34	110.58	113.55	116.28	118.79	121.08	123.19	125.11	126.87	128.47	129.93	133.55	137.53	139.57	140.18
8.25	103.58	106.87	109.88	112.64	115.18	117.49	119.61	121.54	123.31	124.92	126.38	127.71	131.00	134.57	136.38	136.92
8.50	103.34	106.39	109.19	111.75	114.08	116.21	118.16	119.93	121.54	123.01	124.34	125.55	128.51	131.70	133.31	133.77
8.75	103.10	105.92	108.50	110.85	113.00	114.95	116.73	118.34	119.81	121.14	122.35	123.43	126.10	128.94	130.34	130.75
9.00	102.85	105.45	107.82	109.97	111.93	113.71	115.32	116.78	118.11	119.31	120.39	121.37	123.74	126.26	127.49	127.84
9.25	102.61	104.99	107.14	109.10	110.87	112.48	113.93	115.25	116.44	117.51	118.48	119.35	121.46	123.66	124.73	125.03
9.50	102.37	104.52	106.47	108.23	109.83	111.27	112.57	113.74	114.80	115.76	116.61	117.38	119.23	121.15	122.07	122.33
9.75	102.13	104.06	105.80	107.37	108.79	110.07	111.23	112.26	113.20	114.03	114.78	115.46	117.07	118.73	119.51	119.72
10.00	101.89	103.60	105.14	106.52	107.77	108.89	109.90	110.81	111.62	112.35	113.00	113.58	114.96	116.37	117.03	117.21
10.25	101.65	103.14	104.48	105.68	106.76	107.73	108.60	109.37	110.07	110.69	111.25	111.74	112.91	114.10	114.64	114.79
10.50	101.42	102.69	103.83	104.85	105.76	106.58	107.31	107.97	108.55	109.07	109.53	109.94	110.92	111.89	112.33	112.45
10.75	101.18	102.23	103.18	104.02	104.77	105.45	106.05	106.58	107.06	107.48	107.86	108.19	108.97	109.75	110.10	110.19
11.00	100.94	101.78	102.53	103.20	103.80	104.33	104.80	105.22	105.59	105.92	106.22	106.48	107.08	107.68	107.94	108.01
11.25	100.71	101.33	101.89	102.39	102.83	103.22	103.57	103.88	104.16	104.40	104.61	104.80	105.24	105.67	105.86	105.90
11.50	100.47	100.89	101.26	101.59	101.88	102.14	102.36	102.57	102.75	102.90	103.04	103.16	103.45	103.72	103.84	103.87
11.75	100.23	100.44	100.63	100.79	100.93	101.06	101.17	101.27	101.36	101.44	101.50	101.56	101.70	101.83	101.89	101.90
12.00	100.00	100.00	100.00	100.00	100.00	100.00	100.00	100.00	100.00	100.00	100.00	100.00	100.00	100.00	100.00	100.00
12.25	99.77	99.56	99.38	99.22	99.08	98.95	98.84	98.75	98.66	98.59	98.53	98.47	98.34	98.22	98.17	98.16
12.50	99.53	99.12	98.76	98.44	98.16	97.92	97.71	97.52	97.35	97.21	97.08	96.98	96.73	96.50	96.40	96.38
12.75	99.30	98.69	98.15	97.68	97.26	96.90	96.58	96.31	96.07	95.86	95.67	95.51	95.15	94.82	94.69	94.66
13.00	99.07	98.25	97.54	96.92	96.37	95.89	95.48	95.12	94.80	94.53	94.29	94.08	93.62	93.20	93.03	92.99
13.25	98.84	97.82	96.94	96.16	95.49	94.90	94.39	93.95	93.56	93.23	92.94	92.69	92.13	91.62	91.42	91.37
13.50	98.61	97.39	96.34	95.42	94.62	93.92	93.32	92.80	92.34	91.95	91.61	91.32	90.67	90.09	89.86	89.80
13.75	98.38	96.97	95.74	94.68	93.75	92.95	92.26	91.66	91.15	90.70	90.31	89.98	89.25	88.60	88.34	88.28
14.00	98.15	96.54	95.15	93.94	92.90	92.00	91.22	90.55	89.97	89.47	89.04	88.68	87.86	87.15	86.87	86.81
14.25	97.92	96.12	94.56	93.22	92.06	91.06	90.20	89.45	88.82	88.27	87.80	87.40	86.51	85.74	85.45	85.38
14.50	97.69	95.70	93.98	92.50	91.22	90.13	89.19	88.38	87.68	87.09	86.58	86.15	85.19	84.37	84.07	84.00
14.75	97.46	95.28	93.40	91.79	90.40	89.21	88.19	87.32	86.57	85.93	85.39	84.92	83.91	83.04	82.73	82.65
15.00	97.23	94.86	92.83	91.08	89.59	88.31	87.21	86.27	85.48	84.80	84.22	83.72	82.65	81.75	81.42	81.35
15.25	97.01	94.45	92.25	90.38	88.78	87.41	86.24	85.25	84.40	83.68	83.07	82.55	81.43	80.49	80.15	80.08
15.50	96.78	94.03	91.69	89.69	87.98	86.53	85.29	84.24	83.35	82.59	81.95	81.40	80.24	79.27	78.92	78.85
15.75	96.56	93.62	91.13	89.00	87.19	85.66	84.35	83.25	82.31	81.52	80.85	80.28	79.07	78.08	77.73	77.65
16.00	96.33	93.21	90.57	88.32	86.41	84.80	83.43	82.27	81.29	80.47	79.77	79.18	77.93	76.92	76.56	76.49
16.25	96.11	92.81	90.01	87.65	85.64	83.95	82.52	81.31	80.29	79.43	78.71	78.11	76.82	75.79	75.43	75.36
16.50	95.88	92.40	89.46	86.98	84.88	83.11	81.62	80.37	79.31	78.42	77.68	77.06	75.74	74.69	74.33	74.26
16.75	95.66	92.00	88.92	86.32	84.13	82.28	80.74	79.44	78.34	77.43	76.66	76.03	74.68	73.62	73.26	73.19
17.00	95.44	91.60	88.37	85.66	83.38	81.47	79.86	78.52	77.40	76.46	75.67	75.02	73.65	72.58	72.22	72.15
17.25	95.22	91.20	87.83	85.01	82.64	80.66	79.00	77.62	76.46	75.50	74.70	74.03	72.64	71.56	71.21	71.14
17.50	95.00	90.81	87.30	84.37	81.91	79.87	78.16	76.73	75.55	74.56	73.74	73.06	71.65	70.57	70.22	70.15
17.75	94.77	90.41	86.77	83.73	81.19	79.08	77.32	75.86	74.65	73.64	72.81	72.11	70.69	69.60	69.26	69.19
18.00	94.55	90.02	86.24	83.10	80.48	78.31	76.50	75.00	73.76	72.74	71.89	71.19	69.75	68.66	68.32	68.25
18.25	94.34	89.63	85.72	82.47	79.77	77.54	75.69	74.16	72.89	71.85	70.99	70.28	68.83	67.74	67.40	67.34
18.50	94.12	89.24	85.20	81.85	79.08	76.79	74.89	73.33	72.04	70.98	70.11	69.39	67.93	66.85	66.51	66.45
18.75	93.90	88.85	84.68	81.23	78.39	76.04	74.10	72.51	71.20	70.12	69.24	68.52	67.05	65.97	65.64	65.58
19.00	93.68	88.47	84.17	80.62	77.71	75.30	73.33	71.71	70.38	69.28	68.39	67.66	66.19	65.12	64.80	64.74
20.00	92.81	86.94	82.15	78.24	75.05	72.45	70.33	68.61	67.21	66.08	65.16	64.41	62.94	61.91	61.61	61.56
25.00	88.62	79.77	72.89	67.54	63.39	60.17	57.67	55.74	54.24	53.08	52.19	51.50	50.26	49.53	49.37	49.34
30.00	84.64	73.26	64.83	58.60	53.99	50.58	48.07	46.22	44.85	43.84	43.11	42.56	41.67	41.23	41.15	41.14

Description: This table shows the yield to prepayment of a monthly payment mortgage purchased at a price in the index.

Example: The yield to prepayment in 10 years of a 12.00 %, 30 year mortgage at a price of 104.00 is 11.31 %.

30 YEAR MORTGAGE PREPAID IN

PRICE	1 yr	2 yr	3 yr	4 yr	5 yr	6 yr	7 yr	8 yr	9 yr	10 yr	11 yr	12 yr	15 yr	20 yr	25 yr	30 yr
140	–	–	–	1.59	3.23	4.32	5.09	5.66	6.09	6.43	6.71	6.93	7.39	7.79	7.96	8.01
135	–	–	–	2.68	4.15	5.12	5.81	6.31	6.70	7.00	7.25	7.44	7.86	8.21	8.36	8.40
130	–	–	1.68	3.83	5.11	5.96	6.56	7.00	7.34	7.60	7.82	7.99	8.34	8.65	8.77	8.81
125	–	–	3.20	5.03	6.12	6.84	7.35	7.72	8.01	8.23	8.41	8.56	8.86	9.12	9.22	9.25
120	–	1.77	4.79	6.28	7.18	7.76	8.18	8.48	8.72	8.90	9.05	9.16	9.41	9.61	9.70	9.72
119	–	2.24	5.11	6.54	7.39	7.95	8.35	8.64	8.86	9.04	9.18	9.29	9.52	9.72	9.80	9.82
118	–	2.71	5.44	6.80	7.61	8.15	8.52	8.80	9.01	9.18	9.31	9.42	9.64	9.82	9.90	9.92
117	–	3.18	5.78	7.07	7.83	8.34	8.70	8.96	9.16	9.32	9.44	9.54	9.75	9.93	10.00	10.02
116	–	3.66	6.11	7.33	8.06	8.54	8.87	9.12	9.31	9.46	9.58	9.67	9.87	10.04	10.10	10.12
115	–	4.14	6.45	7.60	8.28	8.74	9.05	9.29	9.46	9.60	9.72	9.81	9.99	10.14	10.21	10.22
114	–	4.63	6.79	7.87	8.51	8.94	9.23	9.45	9.62	9.75	9.85	9.94	10.11	10.26	10.31	10.33
113	–	5.12	7.14	8.15	8.74	9.14	9.42	9.62	9.78	9.90	9.99	10.07	10.23	10.37	10.42	10.44
112	–	5.62	7.49	8.42	8.98	9.34	9.60	9.79	9.93	10.05	10.14	10.21	10.36	10.48	10.53	10.54
111	–	6.12	7.85	8.70	9.21	9.55	9.79	9.96	10.09	10.20	10.28	10.35	10.48	10.60	10.64	10.65
110	1.88	6.62	8.20	8.99	9.45	9.76	9.98	10.14	10.26	10.35	10.43	10.49	10.61	10.72	10.76	10.77
109	2.84	7.14	8.56	9.27	9.69	9.97	10.17	10.31	10.42	10.51	10.57	10.63	10.74	10.83	10.87	10.88
108	3.82	7.65	8.93	9.56	9.94	10.19	10.36	10.49	10.59	10.66	10.72	10.77	10.87	10.96	10.99	11.00
107	4.80	8.18	9.30	9.85	10.19	10.40	10.56	10.67	10.75	10.82	10.88	10.92	11.01	11.08	11.11	11.11
106	5.79	8.70	9.67	10.15	10.44	10.62	10.75	10.85	10.93	10.98	11.03	11.07	11.14	11.20	11.23	11.23
105	6.80	9.24	10.05	10.45	10.69	10.84	10.95	11.04	11.10	11.15	11.18	11.22	11.28	11.33	11.35	11.36
104	7.82	9.78	10.43	10.75	10.94	11.07	11.16	11.22	11.27	11.31	11.34	11.37	11.42	11.46	11.47	11.48
103.75	8.07	9.91	10.52	10.83	11.01	11.13	11.21	11.27	11.32	11.35	11.38	11.40	11.45	11.49	11.51	11.51
103.50	8.33	10.05	10.62	10.90	11.07	11.18	11.26	11.32	11.36	11.39	11.42	11.44	11.49	11.52	11.54	11.54
103.25	8.59	10.19	10.72	10.98	11.14	11.24	11.31	11.36	11.41	11.44	11.46	11.48	11.52	11.56	11.57	11.57
103.00	8.84	10.32	10.81	11.06	11.20	11.30	11.36	11.41	11.45	11.48	11.50	11.52	11.56	11.59	11.60	11.60
102.75	9.10	10.46	10.91	11.13	11.27	11.35	11.41	11.46	11.49	11.52	11.54	11.56	11.59	11.62	11.63	11.64
102.50	9.36	10.60	11.01	11.21	11.33	11.41	11.47	11.51	11.54	11.56	11.58	11.60	11.63	11.66	11.67	11.67
102.25	9.62	10.74	11.10	11.29	11.40	11.47	11.52	11.56	11.58	11.61	11.62	11.64	11.67	11.69	11.70	11.70
102.00	9.88	10.87	11.20	11.37	11.46	11.53	11.57	11.60	11.63	11.65	11.66	11.68	11.70	11.72	11.73	11.73
101.75	10.14	11.01	11.30	11.44	11.53	11.58	11.62	11.65	11.67	11.69	11.70	11.72	11.74	11.76	11.76	11.76
101.50	10.41	11.15	11.40	11.52	11.59	11.64	11.68	11.70	11.72	11.73	11.75	11.76	11.77	11.79	11.80	11.80
101.25	10.67	11.29	11.50	11.60	11.66	11.70	11.73	11.75	11.77	11.78	11.79	11.79	11.81	11.82	11.83	11.83
101.00	10.93	11.43	11.60	11.68	11.73	11.76	11.78	11.80	11.81	11.82	11.83	11.83	11.85	11.86	11.86	11.86
100.75	11.20	11.57	11.70	11.76	11.79	11.82	11.83	11.85	11.86	11.86	11.87	11.87	11.88	11.89	11.89	11.90
100.50	11.46	11.71	11.80	11.84	11.86	11.88	11.89	11.90	11.90	11.91	11.91	11.91	11.92	11.93	11.93	11.93
100.25	11.73	11.85	11.90	11.92	11.93	11.94	11.94	11.95	11.95	11.95	11.95	11.95	11.96	11.96	11.96	11.96
100.00	12.00	12.00	12.00	12.00	12.00	12.00	12.00	12.00	12.00	12.00	12.00	12.00	12.00	12.00	12.00	12.00
99.75	12.26	12.14	12.10	12.07	12.06	12.05	12.05	12.04	12.04	12.04	12.04	12.04	12.03	12.03	12.03	12.03
99.50	12.53	12.28	12.20	12.15	12.13	12.11	12.10	12.09	12.09	12.08	12.08	12.08	12.07	12.06	12.06	12.06
99.25	12.80	12.42	12.30	12.23	12.20	12.17	12.16	12.14	12.13	12.13	12.12	12.12	12.11	12.10	12.10	12.10
99.00	13.07	12.57	12.40	12.32	12.27	12.23	12.21	12.19	12.18	12.17	12.16	12.16	12.15	12.13	12.13	12.13
98.75	13.34	12.71	12.50	12.40	12.33	12.29	12.27	12.24	12.23	12.22	12.21	12.20	12.18	12.17	12.17	12.16
98.50	13.61	12.85	12.60	12.48	12.40	12.35	12.32	12.30	12.28	12.26	12.25	12.24	12.22	12.21	12.20	12.20
98.25	13.88	13.00	12.70	12.56	12.47	12.41	12.38	12.35	12.32	12.31	12.29	12.28	12.26	12.24	12.23	12.23
98.00	14.16	13.14	12.81	12.64	12.54	12.48	12.43	12.40	12.37	12.35	12.34	12.32	12.30	12.28	12.27	12.27
97.75	14.43	13.29	12.91	12.72	12.61	12.54	12.49	12.45	12.42	12.40	12.38	12.36	12.34	12.31	12.30	12.30
97.50	14.70	13.43	13.01	12.80	12.68	12.60	12.54	12.50	12.47	12.44	12.42	12.41	12.37	12.35	12.34	12.34
97.25	14.98	13.58	13.11	12.88	12.75	12.66	12.60	12.55	12.52	12.49	12.47	12.45	12.41	12.39	12.37	12.37
97	15.25	13.72	13.22	12.97	12.82	12.72	12.65	12.60	12.56	12.53	12.51	12.49	12.45	12.42	12.41	12.41
96	16.37	14.31	13.64	13.30	13.10	12.97	12.88	12.81	12.76	12.72	12.69	12.66	12.61	12.57	12.55	12.55
95	17.49	14.91	14.06	13.64	13.38	13.22	13.10	13.02	12.96	12.91	12.87	12.83	12.77	12.72	12.70	12.69
94	18.63	15.52	14.49	13.98	13.67	13.48	13.34	13.23	13.16	13.10	13.05	13.01	12.93	12.87	12.85	12.84
93	19.78	16.13	14.92	14.32	13.97	13.73	13.57	13.45	13.36	13.29	13.23	13.19	13.10	13.03	13.00	12.99
92	20.95	16.75	15.36	14.67	14.26	14.00	13.81	13.67	13.57	13.49	13.42	13.37	13.27	13.18	13.15	13.15
91	22.13	17.37	15.80	15.02	14.56	14.26	14.05	13.89	13.78	13.68	13.61	13.55	13.44	13.35	13.31	13.30
90	23.32	18.01	16.25	15.38	14.87	14.53	14.29	14.12	13.99	13.89	13.81	13.74	13.61	13.51	13.47	13.46
89	24.53	18.65	16.71	15.75	15.18	14.80	14.54	14.35	14.21	14.09	14.00	13.93	13.79	13.68	13.64	13.63
88	25.76	19.30	17.17	16.11	15.49	15.08	14.79	14.58	14.42	14.30	14.20	14.13	13.97	13.85	13.80	13.79
87	27.00	19.96	17.64	16.49	15.81	15.36	15.05	14.82	14.65	14.51	14.41	14.32	14.15	14.02	13.97	13.96
86	28.25	20.63	18.11	16.87	16.13	15.65	15.31	15.06	14.87	14.73	14.62	14.52	14.34	14.20	14.15	14.14
85	29.53	21.30	18.59	17.25	16.46	15.94	15.57	15.31	15.11	14.95	14.83	14.73	14.53	14.38	14.33	14.31
80	36.16	24.83	21.09	19.25	18.16	17.45	16.96	16.59	16.32	16.11	15.94	15.81	15.55	15.35	15.28	15.26
75	43.28	28.61	23.79	21.42	20.01	19.10	18.46	18.00	17.65	17.38	17.17	17.00	16.67	16.42	16.34	16.33
70	50.96	32.69	26.71	23.76	22.03	20.90	20.11	19.54	19.11	18.78	18.53	18.32	17.93	17.64	17.55	17.53
65	59.29	37.12	29.88	26.33	24.24	22.88	21.93	21.25	20.74	20.35	20.05	19.81	19.35	19.03	18.93	18.92
60	68.39	41.97	33.37	29.15	26.68	25.07	23.96	23.16	22.57	22.12	21.77	21.50	20.98	20.64	20.54	20.52
55	78.39	47.31	37.22	32.29	29.40	27.54	26.25	25.33	24.65	24.14	23.75	23.44	22.88	22.52	22.42	22.41
50	89.50	53.25	41.53	35.82	32.49	30.34	28.88	27.83	27.06	26.49	26.05	25.72	25.12	24.76	24.68	24.67

Description: This table shows the price to pay for a monthly payment loan, at a yield rate and assuming prepayment.

Example: The price of a 12.25 %, 30 year mortgage to yield 8.00 %, if prepaid in 6 years, is $ 119.97.

30 YEAR MORTGAGE PREPAID IN

YIELD	1 yr	2 yr	3 yr	4 yr	5 yr	6 yr	7 yr	8 yr	9 yr	10 yr	11 yr	12 yr	15 yr	20 yr	25 yr	30 yr
0.00	112.23	124.42	136.55	148.63	160.65	172.59	184.45	196.22	207.88	219.43	230.84	242.10	274.78	323.80	361.21	377.24
1.00	111.17	122.19	133.06	143.77	154.31	164.69	174.89	184.91	194.75	204.39	213.82	223.04	249.25	287.06	314.53	325.80
2.00	110.12	120.01	129.66	139.08	148.26	157.21	165.92	174.39	182.61	190.60	198.33	205.82	226.68	255.63	275.65	283.51
3.00	109.09	117.87	126.37	134.57	142.49	150.13	157.49	164.58	171.40	177.95	184.23	190.25	206.71	228.66	243.12	248.55
4.00	108.06	115.78	123.16	130.23	136.98	143.42	149.58	155.44	161.03	166.34	171.39	176.17	189.00	205.46	215.79	219.49
4.25	107.81	115.26	122.38	129.17	135.64	141.81	147.67	153.26	158.56	163.59	168.35	172.86	184.89	200.18	209.65	213.01
4.50	107.55	114.75	121.60	128.12	134.32	140.21	145.80	151.11	156.14	160.90	165.39	169.64	180.90	195.08	203.77	206.81
4.75	107.30	114.24	120.82	127.08	133.01	138.63	143.96	149.00	153.76	158.26	162.50	166.49	177.03	190.17	198.12	200.88
5.00	107.05	113.73	120.05	126.05	131.72	137.08	142.14	146.92	151.43	155.68	159.67	163.42	173.27	185.44	192.71	195.20
5.25	106.79	113.22	119.29	125.02	130.44	135.54	140.35	144.89	149.15	153.15	156.90	160.42	169.62	180.87	187.51	189.77
5.50	106.54	112.71	118.53	124.01	129.17	134.03	138.60	142.88	146.91	150.67	154.20	157.50	166.08	176.47	182.52	184.56
5.75	106.29	112.21	117.78	123.01	127.93	132.54	136.86	140.91	144.71	148.25	151.56	154.64	162.63	172.21	177.73	179.57
6.00	106.04	111.71	117.03	122.02	126.69	131.06	135.16	138.98	142.55	145.88	148.98	151.86	159.29	168.11	173.13	174.78
6.25	105.79	111.22	116.29	121.04	125.47	129.61	133.48	137.08	140.43	143.55	146.45	149.14	156.04	164.15	168.71	170.19
6.50	105.54	110.72	115.55	120.06	124.26	128.18	131.82	135.21	138.36	141.28	143.98	146.49	152.88	160.32	164.46	165.79
6.75	105.30	110.23	114.82	119.10	123.07	126.76	130.19	133.37	136.32	139.05	141.57	143.90	149.81	156.63	160.37	161.56
7.00	105.05	109.74	114.10	118.14	121.89	125.37	128.59	131.57	134.32	136.87	139.21	141.37	146.83	153.06	156.44	157.51
7.25	104.80	109.25	113.38	117.19	120.73	123.99	127.01	129.80	132.36	134.73	136.90	138.90	143.93	149.62	152.66	153.61
7.50	104.56	108.77	112.66	116.26	119.57	122.63	125.46	128.05	130.44	132.64	134.65	136.49	141.11	146.29	149.03	149.87
7.75	104.31	108.29	111.95	115.33	118.43	121.29	123.92	126.34	128.55	130.58	132.44	134.14	138.37	143.07	145.52	146.27
8.00	104.07	107.81	111.24	114.41	117.31	119.97	122.42	124.65	126.70	128.58	130.28	131.84	135.71	139.96	142.15	142.81
8.25	103.82	107.33	110.54	113.49	116.19	118.67	120.93	123.00	124.89	126.61	128.17	129.60	133.12	136.95	138.90	139.48
8.50	103.58	106.85	109.85	112.59	115.09	117.38	119.47	121.37	123.10	124.68	126.11	127.41	130.60	134.04	135.77	136.28
8.75	103.33	106.38	109.16	111.69	114.01	116.11	118.03	119.77	121.35	122.79	124.09	125.27	128.15	131.22	132.76	133.20
9.00	103.09	105.91	108.47	110.81	112.93	114.86	116.61	118.20	119.64	120.94	122.12	123.18	125.76	128.50	129.85	130.23
9.25	102.85	105.44	107.79	109.93	111.87	113.62	115.21	116.65	117.95	119.13	120.18	121.14	123.44	125.87	127.04	127.38
9.50	102.61	104.97	107.12	109.06	110.81	112.40	113.84	115.13	116.30	117.35	118.29	119.14	121.19	123.32	124.34	124.62
9.75	102.37	104.51	106.45	108.20	109.77	111.20	112.48	113.64	114.68	115.61	116.45	117.20	118.99	120.85	121.72	121.97
10.00	102.13	104.05	105.78	107.34	108.75	110.01	111.15	112.17	113.08	113.90	114.64	115.29	116.86	118.46	119.20	119.41
10.25	101.89	103.59	105.12	106.50	107.73	108.84	109.83	110.72	111.52	112.23	112.87	113.43	114.78	116.14	116.77	116.94
10.50	101.65	103.13	104.46	105.66	106.72	107.68	108.54	109.30	109.98	110.59	111.13	111.62	112.76	113.90	114.42	114.56
10.75	101.41	102.68	103.81	104.83	105.73	106.54	107.26	107.90	108.48	108.99	109.44	109.84	110.79	111.72	112.14	112.26
11.00	101.18	102.23	103.17	104.00	104.75	105.41	106.00	106.53	107.00	107.41	107.78	108.11	108.87	109.61	109.95	110.04
11.25	100.94	101.78	102.52	103.19	103.78	104.30	104.77	105.18	105.55	105.87	106.16	106.41	107.00	107.57	107.82	107.89
11.50	100.70	101.33	101.89	102.38	102.82	103.20	103.55	103.85	104.12	104.36	104.57	104.75	105.18	105.59	105.77	105.82
11.75	100.47	100.88	101.25	101.58	101.87	102.12	102.35	102.55	102.72	102.88	103.01	103.13	103.41	103.67	103.78	103.81
12.00	100.23	100.44	100.62	100.79	100.93	101.05	101.17	101.26	101.35	101.42	101.49	101.55	101.68	101.81	101.86	101.87
12.25	100.00	100.00	100.00	100.00	100.00	100.00	100.00	100.00	100.00	100.00	100.00	100.00	100.00	100.00	100.00	100.00
12.50	99.77	99.56	99.38	99.22	99.08	98.96	98.85	98.76	98.68	98.60	98.54	98.49	98.36	98.25	98.20	98.19
12.75	99.53	99.12	98.77	98.45	98.17	97.93	97.72	97.54	97.38	97.23	97.11	97.01	96.76	96.54	96.45	96.43
13.00	99.30	98.69	98.15	97.69	97.28	96.92	96.61	96.34	96.10	95.89	95.71	95.56	95.21	94.89	94.76	94.73
13.25	99.07	98.26	97.55	96.93	96.39	95.92	95.51	95.15	94.85	94.58	94.34	94.14	93.69	93.28	93.12	93.08
13.50	98.84	97.83	96.95	96.18	95.51	94.93	94.43	93.99	93.61	93.29	93.00	92.76	92.21	91.72	91.53	91.49
13.75	98.61	97.40	96.35	95.44	94.64	93.96	93.36	92.85	92.40	92.02	91.69	91.41	90.77	90.21	89.99	89.94
14.00	98.38	96.97	95.75	94.70	93.79	93.00	92.31	91.73	91.22	90.78	90.40	90.08	89.37	88.74	88.50	88.44
14.25	98.15	96.55	95.16	93.97	92.94	92.05	91.28	90.62	90.05	89.56	89.14	88.79	87.99	87.31	87.04	86.98
14.50	97.92	96.13	94.58	93.25	92.10	91.11	90.26	89.53	88.91	88.37	87.91	87.52	86.66	85.92	85.64	85.57
14.75	97.69	95.71	94.00	92.53	91.27	90.19	89.26	88.46	87.78	87.20	86.70	86.28	85.35	84.56	84.27	84.20
15.00	97.46	95.29	93.42	91.82	90.45	89.27	88.27	87.41	86.68	86.05	85.52	85.06	84.08	83.25	82.94	82.87
15.25	97.24	94.87	92.85	91.12	89.64	88.37	87.29	86.37	85.59	84.92	84.36	83.88	82.84	81.97	81.65	81.58
15.50	97.01	94.46	92.28	90.42	88.84	87.48	86.33	85.36	84.52	83.82	83.22	82.72	81.63	80.72	80.40	80.33
15.75	96.79	94.05	91.72	89.73	88.04	86.61	85.39	84.35	83.48	82.73	82.11	81.58	80.44	79.51	79.18	79.11
16.00	96.56	93.64	91.15	89.05	87.26	85.74	84.46	83.37	82.45	81.67	81.02	80.47	79.29	78.33	78.00	77.92
16.25	96.34	93.23	90.60	88.37	86.48	84.89	83.54	82.40	81.44	80.63	79.95	79.38	78.16	77.18	76.84	76.77
16.50	96.11	92.82	90.05	87.70	85.71	84.04	82.63	81.44	80.44	79.60	78.90	78.31	77.06	76.06	75.72	75.65
16.75	95.89	92.42	89.50	87.03	84.96	83.21	81.74	80.50	79.47	78.60	77.87	77.27	75.99	74.97	74.63	74.56
17.00	95.67	92.02	88.95	86.37	84.20	82.39	80.86	79.58	78.51	77.61	76.87	76.24	74.94	73.91	73.57	73.50
17.25	95.44	91.62	88.41	85.72	83.46	81.57	79.99	78.67	77.57	76.65	75.88	75.24	73.91	72.88	72.54	72.47
17.50	95.22	91.22	87.87	85.07	82.73	80.77	79.14	77.78	76.64	75.70	74.91	74.26	72.91	71.87	71.53	71.46
17.75	95.00	90.83	87.34	84.43	82.00	79.98	78.30	76.90	75.73	74.77	73.96	73.30	71.93	70.89	70.55	70.49
18.00	94.78	90.43	86.81	83.79	81.29	79.20	77.47	76.03	74.84	73.85	73.03	72.36	70.98	69.93	69.60	69.53
18.25	94.56	90.04	86.28	83.16	80.58	78.43	76.65	75.18	73.96	72.95	72.12	71.44	70.04	68.99	68.66	68.60
18.50	94.34	89.65	85.76	82.54	79.87	77.67	75.84	74.34	73.10	72.07	71.23	70.54	69.13	68.08	67.76	67.70
18.75	94.12	89.26	85.24	81.92	79.18	76.92	75.05	73.51	72.25	71.21	70.35	69.65	68.24	67.19	66.87	66.81
19.00	93.91	88.88	84.73	81.31	78.49	76.17	74.27	72.70	71.41	70.36	69.49	68.79	67.36	66.32	66.01	65.95
20.00	93.04	87.35	82.70	78.91	75.82	73.30	71.24	69.57	68.22	67.11	66.22	65.50	64.06	63.05	62.76	62.71
25.00	88.84	80.15	73.40	68.15	64.08	60.91	58.46	56.56	55.09	53.95	53.08	52.40	51.18	50.46	50.29	50.27
30.00	84.85	73.62	65.31	59.16	54.61	51.25	48.77	46.93	45.58	44.59	43.86	43.32	42.44	42.00	41.92	41.91

Description: This table shows the yield to prepayment of a monthly payment mortgage purchased at a price in the index.

Example: The yield to prepayment in 10 years of a 12.25 %, 30 year mortgage at a price of 104.00 is 11.56 %.

30 YEAR MORTGAGE PREPAID IN

PRICE	1 yr	2 yr	3 yr	4 yr	5 yr	6 yr	7 yr	8 yr	9 yr	10 yr	11 yr	12 yr	15 yr	20 yr	25 yr	30 yr
140	–	–	–	1.80	3.44	4.53	5.30	5.86	6.30	6.64	6.91	7.13	7.60	7.99	8.16	8.21
135	–	–	–	2.90	4.37	5.33	6.02	6.52	6.91	7.21	7.46	7.65	8.06	8.41	8.56	8.60
130	–	–	1.89	4.05	5.33	6.18	6.77	7.22	7.55	7.82	8.03	8.20	8.56	8.86	8.98	9.02
125	–	–	3.42	5.25	6.34	7.06	7.57	7.94	8.23	8.45	8.63	8.78	9.08	9.33	9.43	9.46
120	–	2.00	5.01	6.51	7.40	7.99	8.40	8.71	8.94	9.12	9.27	9.39	9.63	9.83	9.92	9.94
119	–	2.47	5.34	6.77	7.62	8.18	8.58	8.87	9.09	9.26	9.40	9.51	9.74	9.94	10.02	10.04
118	–	2.94	5.67	7.03	7.84	8.37	8.75	9.03	9.24	9.40	9.53	9.64	9.86	10.04	10.12	10.14
117	–	3.41	6.01	7.30	8.06	8.57	8.93	9.19	9.39	9.54	9.67	9.77	9.98	10.15	10.22	10.24
116	–	3.89	6.34	7.56	8.29	8.77	9.10	9.35	9.54	9.69	9.81	9.90	10.10	10.26	10.33	10.34
115	–	4.37	6.68	7.83	8.52	8.97	9.28	9.52	9.69	9.83	9.94	10.03	10.22	10.37	10.43	10.45
114	–	4.86	7.03	8.11	8.75	9.17	9.47	9.68	9.85	9.98	10.08	10.17	10.34	10.48	10.54	10.55
113	–	5.35	7.38	8.38	8.98	9.37	9.65	9.85	10.01	10.13	10.23	10.30	10.46	10.60	10.65	10.66
112	–	5.85	7.73	8.66	9.21	9.58	9.83	10.02	10.17	10.28	10.37	10.44	10.59	10.71	10.76	10.77
111	1.16	6.35	8.08	8.94	9.45	9.79	10.02	10.20	10.33	10.43	10.51	10.58	10.72	10.83	10.87	10.89
110	2.11	6.86	8.44	9.22	9.69	10.00	10.21	10.37	10.49	10.59	10.66	10.72	10.85	10.95	10.99	11.00
109	3.08	7.38	8.80	9.51	9.93	10.21	10.41	10.55	10.66	10.74	10.81	10.87	10.98	11.07	11.11	11.11
108	4.06	7.89	9.17	9.80	10.18	10.43	10.60	10.73	10.83	10.90	10.96	11.01	11.11	11.19	11.22	11.23
107	5.04	8.42	9.54	10.10	10.43	10.64	10.80	10.91	10.99	11.06	11.11	11.16	11.24	11.32	11.34	11.35
106	6.04	8.95	9.91	10.39	10.68	10.86	11.00	11.09	11.17	11.22	11.27	11.31	11.38	11.44	11.47	11.47
105	7.04	9.48	10.29	10.69	10.93	11.09	11.20	11.28	11.34	11.39	11.43	11.46	11.52	11.57	11.59	11.60
104	8.06	10.02	10.67	11.00	11.19	11.31	11.40	11.47	11.52	11.56	11.59	11.61	11.66	11.70	11.72	11.72
103.75	8.32	10.16	10.77	11.07	11.25	11.37	11.45	11.51	11.56	11.60	11.63	11.65	11.70	11.73	11.75	11.75
103.50	8.57	10.29	10.87	11.15	11.32	11.43	11.51	11.56	11.61	11.64	11.67	11.69	11.73	11.77	11.78	11.78
103.25	8.83	10.43	10.96	11.23	11.38	11.48	11.56	11.61	11.65	11.68	11.71	11.73	11.77	11.80	11.81	11.82
103.00	9.09	10.57	11.06	11.30	11.45	11.54	11.61	11.66	11.70	11.72	11.75	11.77	11.80	11.83	11.85	11.85
102.75	9.35	10.71	11.16	11.38	11.51	11.60	11.66	11.71	11.74	11.77	11.79	11.80	11.84	11.87	11.88	11.88
102.50	9.61	10.84	11.25	11.46	11.58	11.66	11.71	11.75	11.79	11.81	11.83	11.84	11.88	11.90	11.91	11.91
102.25	9.87	10.98	11.35	11.54	11.64	11.72	11.77	11.80	11.83	11.85	11.87	11.88	11.91	11.93	11.94	11.95
102.00	10.13	11.12	11.45	11.61	11.71	11.77	11.82	11.85	11.88	11.90	11.91	11.92	11.95	11.97	11.98	11.98
101.75	10.39	11.26	11.55	11.69	11.78	11.83	11.87	11.90	11.92	11.94	11.95	11.96	11.98	12.00	12.01	12.01
101.50	10.65	11.40	11.65	11.77	11.84	11.89	11.92	11.95	11.97	11.98	11.99	12.00	12.02	12.04	12.04	12.04
101.25	10.92	11.54	11.75	11.85	11.91	11.95	11.98	12.00	12.01	12.03	12.03	12.04	12.06	12.07	12.08	12.08
101.00	11.18	11.68	11.85	11.93	11.98	12.01	12.03	12.05	12.06	12.07	12.08	12.08	12.10	12.11	12.11	12.11
100.75	11.45	11.82	11.94	12.01	12.04	12.07	12.08	12.10	12.11	12.11	12.12	12.12	12.13	12.14	12.14	12.14
100.50	11.71	11.96	12.04	12.09	12.11	12.13	12.14	12.15	12.15	12.16	12.16	12.16	12.17	12.18	12.18	12.18
100.25	11.98	12.10	12.14	12.17	12.18	12.19	12.19	12.20	12.20	12.20	12.20	12.20	12.21	12.21	12.21	12.21
100.00	12.25	12.25	12.25	12.25	12.25	12.25	12.25	12.25	12.25	12.25	12.25	12.25	12.25	12.25	12.25	12.25
99.75	12.51	12.39	12.35	12.33	12.31	12.30	12.30	12.30	12.29	12.29	12.29	12.29	12.28	12.28	12.28	12.28
99.50	12.78	12.53	12.45	12.41	12.38	12.36	12.35	12.35	12.34	12.33	12.33	12.33	12.32	12.32	12.31	12.31
99.25	13.05	12.67	12.55	12.49	12.45	12.42	12.41	12.40	12.39	12.38	12.37	12.37	12.36	12.35	12.35	12.35
99.00	13.32	12.82	12.65	12.57	12.52	12.49	12.46	12.45	12.43	12.42	12.42	12.41	12.40	12.39	12.38	12.38
98.75	13.59	12.96	12.75	12.65	12.59	12.55	12.52	12.50	12.48	12.47	12.46	12.45	12.44	12.42	12.42	12.42
98.50	13.86	13.10	12.85	12.73	12.66	12.61	12.57	12.55	12.53	12.51	12.50	12.49	12.47	12.46	12.45	12.45
98.25	14.13	13.25	12.96	12.81	12.72	12.67	12.63	12.60	12.58	12.56	12.55	12.53	12.51	12.49	12.49	12.49
98.00	14.41	13.39	13.06	12.89	12.79	12.73	12.68	12.65	12.62	12.60	12.59	12.58	12.55	12.53	12.52	12.52
97.75	14.68	13.54	13.16	12.97	12.86	12.79	12.74	12.70	12.67	12.65	12.63	12.62	12.59	12.57	12.56	12.56
97.50	14.96	13.69	13.26	13.06	12.93	12.85	12.79	12.75	12.72	12.70	12.68	12.66	12.63	12.60	12.59	12.59
97.25	15.23	13.83	13.37	13.14	13.00	12.91	12.85	12.80	12.77	12.74	12.72	12.70	12.67	12.64	12.63	12.63
97	15.51	13.98	13.47	13.22	13.07	12.98	12.91	12.86	12.82	12.79	12.76	12.75	12.71	12.68	12.67	12.66
96	16.62	14.57	13.89	13.55	13.36	13.22	13.13	13.07	13.01	12.97	12.94	12.92	12.87	12.83	12.81	12.81
95	17.75	15.17	14.32	13.89	13.64	13.48	13.36	13.28	13.21	13.16	13.12	13.09	13.03	12.98	12.96	12.95
94	18.89	15.77	14.74	14.23	13.93	13.73	13.60	13.49	13.42	13.36	13.31	13.27	13.19	13.13	13.11	13.10
93	20.04	16.39	15.18	14.58	14.23	13.99	13.83	13.71	13.62	13.55	13.50	13.45	13.36	13.29	13.26	13.26
92	21.21	17.01	15.62	14.93	14.52	14.26	14.07	13.93	13.83	13.75	13.69	13.63	13.53	13.45	13.42	13.41
91	22.39	17.64	16.06	15.29	14.83	14.52	14.31	14.16	14.04	13.95	13.88	13.82	13.70	13.61	13.58	13.57
90	23.59	18.27	16.52	15.65	15.13	14.80	14.56	14.39	14.26	14.15	14.07	14.01	13.88	13.78	13.74	13.74
89	24.80	18.91	16.97	16.01	15.44	15.07	14.81	14.62	14.47	14.36	14.27	14.20	14.06	13.95	13.91	13.90
88	26.02	19.57	17.44	16.38	15.76	15.35	15.06	14.85	14.70	14.57	14.48	14.40	14.24	14.12	14.08	14.07
87	27.27	20.23	17.91	16.76	16.08	15.63	15.32	15.09	14.92	14.79	14.68	14.60	14.43	14.30	14.25	14.24
86	28.53	20.90	18.38	17.14	16.40	15.92	15.58	15.34	15.15	15.01	14.89	14.80	14.62	14.48	14.43	14.42
85	29.80	21.57	18.86	17.52	16.73	16.21	15.85	15.58	15.38	15.23	15.11	15.01	14.81	14.66	14.61	14.60
80	36.44	25.11	21.38	19.54	18.45	17.74	17.24	16.88	16.61	16.41	16.23	16.10	15.84	15.64	15.58	15.56
75	43.58	28.90	24.08	21.71	20.31	19.40	18.76	18.30	17.95	17.68	17.47	17.31	16.98	16.74	16.66	16.64
70	51.27	33.00	27.01	24.07	22.34	21.21	20.42	19.85	19.43	19.10	18.85	18.65	18.26	17.98	17.89	17.87
65	59.61	37.44	30.20	26.65	24.56	23.20	22.26	21.58	21.07	20.69	20.39	20.15	19.70	19.39	19.30	19.28
60	68.72	42.30	33.70	29.49	27.02	25.42	24.31	23.52	22.93	22.48	22.13	21.86	21.36	21.02	20.93	20.91
55	78.74	47.66	37.58	32.65	29.77	27.91	26.63	25.71	25.04	24.53	24.14	23.84	23.29	22.94	22.85	22.83
50	89.87	53.62	41.91	36.20	32.88	30.74	29.28	28.24	27.48	26.91	26.48	26.16	25.57	25.22	25.14	25.13

PREPAYMENT MORTGAGE PRICE

12.50 %

Description: This table shows the price to pay for a monthly payment loan, at a yield rate and assuming prepayment.

Example: The price of a 12.50 %, 30 year mortgage to yield 8.00 %, if prepaid in 6 years, is $ 121.16.

30 YEAR MORTGAGE PREPAID IN

YIELD	1 yr	2 yr	3 yr	4 yr	5 yr	6 yr	7 yr	8 yr	9 yr	10 yr	11 yr	12 yr	15 yr	20 yr	25 yr	30 yr
0.00	112.48	124.92	137.31	149.65	161.92	174.12	186.24	198.27	210.20	222.01	233.69	245.22	278.70	329.05	367.62	384.21
1.00	111.42	122.69	133.80	144.76	155.55	166.17	176.61	186.88	196.95	206.83	216.50	225.95	252.86	291.77	320.14	331.82
2.00	110.37	120.50	130.40	140.05	149.46	158.64	167.57	176.27	184.71	192.91	200.86	208.55	230.01	259.86	280.58	288.75
3.00	109.33	118.36	127.09	135.52	143.66	151.51	159.09	166.38	173.40	180.14	186.62	192.82	209.79	232.48	247.49	253.14
4.00	108.31	116.26	123.87	131.16	138.12	144.77	151.11	157.17	162.94	168.42	173.64	178.58	191.85	208.93	219.68	223.55
4.25	108.05	115.74	123.08	130.09	136.77	143.14	149.20	154.97	160.44	165.65	170.57	175.24	187.69	203.56	213.43	216.95
4.50	107.80	115.23	122.30	129.03	135.44	141.53	147.31	152.80	158.00	162.93	167.58	171.98	183.66	198.39	207.44	210.64
4.75	107.54	114.71	121.52	127.99	134.12	139.94	145.45	150.67	155.61	160.26	164.66	168.79	179.73	193.40	201.70	204.59
5.00	107.29	114.20	120.75	126.95	132.82	138.38	143.63	148.58	153.25	157.66	161.80	165.69	175.93	188.60	196.19	198.81
5.25	107.04	113.69	119.98	125.93	131.54	136.83	141.83	146.53	150.95	155.11	159.01	162.66	172.23	183.96	190.90	193.27
5.50	106.79	113.19	119.22	124.91	130.27	135.31	140.05	144.51	148.69	152.61	156.27	159.70	168.64	179.48	185.83	187.97
5.75	106.53	112.68	118.47	123.91	129.01	133.81	138.31	142.52	146.47	150.16	153.60	156.82	165.15	175.16	180.95	182.88
6.00	106.28	112.18	117.72	122.91	127.77	132.33	136.59	140.57	144.29	147.76	150.99	154.00	161.76	171.00	176.27	178.01
6.25	106.03	111.69	116.97	121.92	126.54	130.86	134.90	138.65	142.16	145.42	148.44	151.25	158.47	166.97	171.77	173.34
6.50	105.79	111.19	116.23	120.94	125.33	129.42	133.23	136.77	140.06	143.12	145.95	148.57	155.27	163.09	167.45	168.85
6.75	105.54	110.70	115.50	119.97	124.13	128.00	131.59	134.92	138.01	140.87	143.51	145.95	152.16	159.33	163.29	164.55
7.00	105.29	110.21	114.77	119.01	122.94	126.59	129.97	133.10	135.99	138.66	141.12	143.39	149.13	155.71	159.29	160.42
7.25	105.04	109.72	114.05	118.06	121.77	125.21	128.38	131.31	134.01	136.50	138.79	140.90	146.20	152.21	155.44	156.45
7.50	104.80	109.23	113.33	117.12	120.61	123.84	126.81	129.55	132.07	134.39	136.51	138.46	143.34	148.83	151.74	152.64
7.75	104.55	108.75	112.62	116.18	119.47	122.49	125.27	127.82	130.17	132.32	134.28	136.08	140.56	145.56	148.17	148.97
8.00	104.30	108.27	111.91	115.26	118.33	121.16	123.75	126.12	128.30	130.29	132.10	133.75	137.86	142.39	144.74	145.45
8.25	104.06	107.79	111.21	114.34	117.21	119.85	122.25	124.45	126.46	128.30	129.97	131.49	135.24	139.34	141.44	142.06
8.50	103.82	107.31	110.51	113.43	116.11	118.55	120.78	122.81	124.66	126.35	127.88	129.27	132.69	136.38	138.25	138.80
8.75	103.57	106.84	109.82	112.53	115.01	117.27	119.33	121.20	122.90	124.44	125.84	127.10	130.20	133.52	135.18	135.66
9.00	103.33	106.36	109.13	111.64	113.93	116.01	117.90	119.61	121.17	122.57	123.84	124.99	127.79	130.75	132.22	132.64
9.25	103.09	105.90	108.45	110.76	112.86	114.76	116.49	118.05	119.46	120.74	121.89	122.93	125.44	128.08	129.36	129.73
9.50	102.85	105.43	107.77	109.89	111.80	113.54	115.10	116.52	117.79	118.94	119.98	120.91	123.15	125.48	126.61	126.93
9.75	102.61	104.96	107.09	109.02	110.76	112.32	113.74	115.01	116.16	117.19	118.11	118.94	120.92	122.97	123.95	124.22
10.00	102.37	104.50	106.43	108.16	109.72	111.13	112.39	113.53	114.55	115.46	116.28	117.01	118.76	120.54	121.38	121.61
10.25	102.13	104.04	105.76	107.31	108.70	109.95	111.07	112.07	112.97	113.77	114.49	115.13	116.65	118.19	118.90	119.10
10.50	101.89	103.58	105.10	106.47	107.69	108.78	109.76	110.64	111.42	112.12	112.74	113.29	114.60	115.91	116.51	116.67
10.75	101.65	103.13	104.45	105.63	106.69	107.63	108.48	109.23	109.90	110.49	111.02	111.49	112.60	113.70	114.20	114.33
11.00	101.41	102.67	103.80	104.80	105.70	106.50	107.21	107.84	108.41	108.90	109.35	109.74	110.65	111.56	111.96	112.07
11.25	101.18	102.22	103.16	103.99	104.72	105.38	105.96	106.48	106.94	107.35	107.70	108.02	108.76	109.48	109.80	109.88
11.50	100.94	101.77	102.52	103.17	103.76	104.28	104.73	105.14	105.50	105.82	106.10	106.34	106.92	107.47	107.71	107.77
11.75	100.70	101.33	101.88	102.37	102.80	103.19	103.52	103.82	104.09	104.32	104.52	104.70	105.12	105.52	105.69	105.73
12.00	100.47	100.88	101.25	101.57	101.86	102.11	102.33	102.53	102.70	102.85	102.98	103.10	103.37	103.62	103.73	103.76
12.25	100.23	100.44	100.62	100.78	100.92	101.05	101.16	101.25	101.34	101.41	101.48	101.53	101.66	101.78	101.83	101.85
12.50	100.00	100.00	100.00	100.00	100.00	100.00	100.00	100.00	100.00	100.00	100.00	100.00	100.00	100.00	100.00	100.00
12.75	99.77	99.56	99.38	99.22	99.09	98.97	98.86	98.77	98.69	98.62	98.55	98.50	98.38	98.27	98.22	98.21
13.00	99.53	99.13	98.77	98.46	98.18	97.95	97.74	97.56	97.40	97.26	97.14	97.04	96.80	96.59	96.50	96.48
13.25	99.30	98.69	98.16	97.70	97.29	96.94	96.63	96.36	96.13	95.93	95.75	95.60	95.26	94.96	94.83	94.80
13.50	99.07	98.26	97.56	96.94	96.41	95.94	95.54	95.19	94.89	94.62	94.40	94.20	93.76	93.37	93.21	93.18
13.75	98.84	97.83	96.96	96.19	95.53	94.96	94.47	94.04	93.67	93.34	93.07	92.83	92.30	91.83	91.64	91.60
14.00	98.61	97.40	96.36	95.45	94.67	93.99	93.41	92.90	92.47	92.09	91.77	91.49	90.87	90.33	90.12	90.07
14.25	98.38	96.98	95.77	94.72	93.82	93.04	92.37	91.79	91.29	90.86	90.49	90.18	89.48	88.88	88.64	88.59
14.50	98.15	96.56	95.18	93.99	92.97	92.09	91.34	90.69	90.13	89.65	89.24	88.89	88.13	87.46	87.21	87.15
14.75	97.92	96.14	94.60	93.27	92.14	91.16	90.33	89.61	88.99	88.47	88.02	87.64	86.80	86.09	85.82	85.76
15.00	97.70	95.72	94.02	92.56	91.31	90.24	89.33	88.55	87.88	87.31	86.82	86.41	85.51	84.75	84.47	84.41
15.25	97.47	95.30	93.44	91.85	90.50	89.34	88.35	87.50	86.78	86.17	85.65	85.21	84.25	83.45	83.15	83.09
15.50	97.24	94.88	92.87	91.15	89.69	88.44	87.38	86.47	85.70	85.05	84.50	84.03	83.02	82.18	81.88	81.81
15.75	97.02	94.47	92.31	90.46	88.89	87.56	86.42	85.46	84.65	83.95	83.37	82.88	81.82	80.95	80.64	80.57
16.00	96.79	94.06	91.74	89.77	88.10	86.68	85.48	84.47	83.61	82.88	82.27	81.75	80.65	79.75	79.43	79.36
16.25	96.57	93.65	91.18	89.09	87.32	85.82	84.56	83.49	82.58	81.82	81.18	80.65	79.50	78.58	78.26	78.19
16.50	96.34	93.25	90.63	88.42	86.55	84.97	83.64	82.52	81.58	80.79	80.12	79.57	78.39	77.44	77.12	77.05
16.75	96.12	92.84	90.08	87.75	85.79	84.13	82.74	81.57	80.59	79.77	79.08	78.51	77.30	76.33	76.01	75.94
17.00	95.89	92.44	89.53	87.08	85.03	83.30	81.86	80.64	79.63	78.77	78.06	77.47	76.23	75.25	74.93	74.86
17.25	95.67	92.04	88.99	86.43	84.28	82.49	80.98	79.72	78.67	77.80	77.07	76.46	75.19	74.20	73.87	73.81
17.50	95.45	91.64	88.45	85.78	83.54	81.68	80.12	78.82	77.74	76.84	76.09	75.46	74.17	73.17	72.85	72.78
17.75	95.23	91.24	87.91	85.13	82.81	80.88	79.27	77.93	76.82	75.89	75.13	74.49	73.18	72.18	71.85	71.79
18.00	95.01	90.85	87.38	84.49	82.09	80.09	78.43	77.06	75.91	74.97	74.19	73.54	72.21	71.20	70.88	70.82
18.25	94.79	90.45	86.85	83.86	81.38	79.32	77.61	76.20	75.03	74.06	73.26	72.61	71.26	70.25	69.93	69.87
18.50	94.57	90.06	86.33	83.23	80.67	78.55	76.80	75.35	74.15	73.17	72.36	71.69	70.33	69.32	69.01	68.95
18.75	94.35	89.67	85.81	82.61	79.97	77.79	76.00	74.51	73.30	72.29	71.47	70.80	69.43	68.42	68.11	68.05
19.00	94.13	89.29	85.29	82.00	79.28	77.04	75.21	73.69	72.45	71.43	70.60	69.92	68.54	67.53	67.23	67.17
20.00	93.26	87.76	83.26	79.59	76.59	74.15	72.16	70.54	69.22	68.15	67.28	66.58	65.19	64.20	63.92	63.87
25.00	89.06	80.54	73.92	68.77	64.77	61.66	59.25	57.39	55.94	54.83	53.96	53.30	52.09	51.38	51.22	51.20
30.00	85.06	73.99	65.79	59.72	55.23	51.92	49.46	47.65	46.32	45.34	44.62	44.09	43.21	42.77	42.69	42.68

Description: This table shows the yield to prepayment of a monthly payment mortgage purchased at a price in the index.

Example: The yield to prepayment in 10 years of a 12.50 %, 30 year mortgage at a price of 104.00 is 11.80 %.

30 YEAR MORTGAGE PREPAID IN

PRICE	1 yr	2 yr	3 yr	4 yr	5 yr	6 yr	7 yr	8 yr	9 yr	10 yr	11 yr	12 yr	15 yr	20 yr	25 yr	30 yr
140	–	–	–	2.01	3.65	4.74	5.50	6.07	6.50	6.84	7.11	7.34	7.80	8.19	8.36	8.40
135	–	–	–	3.11	4.58	5.55	6.23	6.73	7.12	7.42	7.66	7.86	8.27	8.61	8.76	8.80
130	–	–	2.11	4.27	5.55	6.39	6.99	7.43	7.77	8.03	8.24	8.41	8.77	9.06	9.19	9.22
125	–	–	3.64	5.47	6.56	7.28	7.79	8.16	8.45	8.67	8.85	8.99	9.29	9.54	9.65	9.67
120	–	2.23	5.24	6.74	7.63	8.22	8.63	8.93	9.17	9.35	9.49	9.61	9.85	10.05	10.13	10.15
119	–	2.69	5.57	7.00	7.85	8.41	8.80	9.09	9.31	9.49	9.63	9.74	9.97	10.16	10.24	10.26
118	–	3.17	5.90	7.26	8.07	8.60	8.98	9.25	9.46	9.63	9.76	9.87	10.08	10.27	10.34	10.36
117	–	3.64	6.24	7.53	8.29	8.80	9.15	9.42	9.62	9.77	9.90	10.00	10.20	10.37	10.44	10.46
116	–	4.12	6.57	7.79	8.52	9.00	9.33	9.58	9.77	9.92	10.03	10.13	10.32	10.48	10.55	10.57
115	–	4.60	6.92	8.07	8.75	9.20	9.51	9.75	9.92	10.06	10.17	10.26	10.45	10.60	10.66	10.67
114	–	5.09	7.26	8.34	8.98	9.40	9.70	9.92	10.08	10.21	10.31	10.40	10.57	10.71	10.77	10.78
113	–	5.59	7.61	8.62	9.21	9.61	9.88	10.09	10.24	10.36	10.46	10.54	10.69	10.83	10.88	10.89
112	–	6.09	7.96	8.89	9.45	9.81	10.07	10.26	10.40	10.51	10.60	10.67	10.82	10.94	10.99	11.00
111	1.40	6.59	8.32	9.18	9.69	10.02	10.26	10.43	10.56	10.67	10.75	10.81	10.95	11.06	11.11	11.12
110	2.35	7.10	8.68	9.46	9.93	10.23	10.45	10.61	10.73	10.82	10.90	10.96	11.08	11.18	11.22	11.23
109	3.32	7.61	9.04	9.75	10.17	10.45	10.64	10.79	10.89	10.98	11.05	11.10	11.21	11.30	11.34	11.35
108	4.30	8.13	9.41	10.04	10.42	10.66	10.84	10.97	11.06	11.14	11.20	11.25	11.35	11.43	11.46	11.47
107	5.28	8.66	9.78	10.34	10.67	10.88	11.04	11.15	11.23	11.30	11.35	11.40	11.48	11.55	11.58	11.59
106	6.28	9.19	10.16	10.63	10.92	11.11	11.24	11.33	11.41	11.46	11.51	11.55	11.62	11.68	11.71	11.71
105	7.29	9.73	10.53	10.94	11.17	11.33	11.44	11.52	11.58	11.63	11.67	11.70	11.76	11.81	11.83	11.84
104	8.31	10.27	10.92	11.24	11.43	11.56	11.65	11.71	11.76	11.80	11.83	11.85	11.90	11.94	11.96	11.96
103.75	8.56	10.40	11.01	11.32	11.50	11.62	11.70	11.76	11.81	11.84	11.87	11.89	11.94	11.98	11.99	12.00
103.50	8.82	10.54	11.11	11.39	11.56	11.67	11.75	11.81	11.85	11.88	11.91	11.93	11.98	12.01	12.02	12.03
103.25	9.08	10.68	11.21	11.47	11.63	11.73	11.80	11.86	11.90	11.93	11.95	11.97	12.01	12.04	12.06	12.06
103.00	9.34	10.82	11.31	11.55	11.69	11.79	11.85	11.90	11.94	11.97	11.99	12.01	12.05	12.08	12.09	12.09
102.75	9.60	10.95	11.40	11.63	11.76	11.85	11.91	11.95	11.99	12.01	12.03	12.05	12.08	12.11	12.12	12.13
102.50	9.86	11.09	11.50	11.70	11.82	11.90	11.96	12.00	12.03	12.06	12.07	12.09	12.12	12.15	12.16	12.16
102.25	10.12	11.23	11.60	11.78	11.89	11.96	12.01	12.05	12.08	12.10	12.12	12.13	12.16	12.18	12.19	12.19
102.00	10.38	11.37	11.70	11.86	11.96	12.02	12.07	12.10	12.12	12.14	12.16	12.17	12.19	12.22	12.22	12.22
101.75	10.64	11.51	11.80	11.94	12.02	12.08	12.12	12.15	12.17	12.19	12.20	12.21	12.23	12.25	12.26	12.26
101.50	10.90	11.65	11.90	12.02	12.09	12.14	12.17	12.20	12.21	12.23	12.24	12.25	12.27	12.28	12.29	12.29
101.25	11.17	11.79	11.99	12.10	12.16	12.20	12.23	12.25	12.26	12.27	12.28	12.29	12.31	12.32	12.32	12.32
101.00	11.43	11.93	12.09	12.18	12.22	12.26	12.28	12.30	12.31	12.32	12.33	12.33	12.34	12.35	12.36	12.36
100.75	11.70	12.07	12.19	12.26	12.29	12.32	12.33	12.34	12.35	12.36	12.37	12.37	12.38	12.39	12.39	12.39
100.50	11.96	12.21	12.29	12.33	12.36	12.38	12.39	12.39	12.40	12.41	12.41	12.41	12.42	12.42	12.43	12.43
100.25	12.23	12.35	12.39	12.41	12.43	12.44	12.44	12.44	12.45	12.45	12.45	12.45	12.46	12.46	12.46	12.46
100.00	12.50	12.50	12.50	12.50	12.50	12.50	12.50	12.50	12.50	12.50	12.50	12.50	12.50	12.50	12.50	12.50
99.75	12.76	12.64	12.60	12.58	12.56	12.56	12.55	12.55	12.54	12.54	12.54	12.54	12.53	12.53	12.53	12.53
99.50	13.03	12.78	12.70	12.66	12.63	12.62	12.60	12.60	12.59	12.58	12.58	12.58	12.57	12.57	12.56	12.56
99.25	13.30	12.92	12.80	12.74	12.70	12.68	12.66	12.65	12.64	12.63	12.62	12.62	12.61	12.60	12.60	12.60
99.00	13.57	13.07	12.90	12.82	12.77	12.74	12.71	12.70	12.68	12.68	12.67	12.66	12.65	12.64	12.63	12.63
98.75	13.84	13.21	13.00	12.90	12.84	12.80	12.77	12.75	12.73	12.72	12.71	12.70	12.69	12.67	12.67	12.67
98.50	14.11	13.36	13.11	12.98	12.91	12.86	12.82	12.80	12.78	12.77	12.75	12.75	12.73	12.71	12.71	12.70
98.25	14.39	13.50	13.21	13.06	12.98	12.92	12.88	12.85	12.83	12.81	12.80	12.79	12.77	12.75	12.74	12.74
98.00	14.66	13.65	13.31	13.14	13.05	12.98	12.94	12.90	12.88	12.86	12.84	12.83	12.80	12.78	12.78	12.78
97.75	14.93	13.79	13.41	13.23	13.12	13.04	12.99	12.95	12.93	12.90	12.89	12.87	12.84	12.82	12.81	12.81
97.50	15.21	13.94	13.52	13.31	13.19	13.11	13.05	13.01	12.97	12.95	12.93	12.92	12.88	12.86	12.85	12.85
97.25	15.49	14.09	13.62	13.39	13.26	13.17	13.10	13.06	13.02	13.00	12.98	12.96	12.92	12.90	12.89	12.88
97	15.76	14.23	13.73	13.48	13.33	13.23	13.16	13.11	13.07	13.04	13.02	13.00	12.96	12.93	12.92	12.92
96	16.88	14.83	14.15	13.81	13.61	13.48	13.39	13.32	13.27	13.23	13.20	13.18	13.12	13.08	13.07	13.07
95	18.00	15.43	14.57	14.15	13.90	13.74	13.62	13.54	13.47	13.42	13.38	13.35	13.29	13.24	13.22	13.22
94	19.14	16.03	15.00	14.49	14.19	13.99	13.85	13.75	13.68	13.62	13.57	13.53	13.46	13.39	13.37	13.37
93	20.30	16.65	15.44	14.84	14.49	14.26	14.09	13.97	13.88	13.81	13.76	13.71	13.62	13.55	13.53	13.52
92	21.47	17.27	15.88	15.19	14.79	14.52	14.33	14.20	14.09	14.01	13.95	13.90	13.80	13.72	13.69	13.68
91	22.65	17.90	16.33	15.55	15.09	14.79	14.58	14.42	14.31	14.22	14.14	14.09	13.97	13.88	13.85	13.84
90	23.85	18.54	16.78	15.91	15.40	15.06	14.83	14.65	14.52	14.42	14.34	14.28	14.15	14.05	14.02	14.01
89	25.06	19.18	17.24	16.28	15.71	15.34	15.08	14.89	14.74	14.63	14.54	14.47	14.33	14.22	14.18	14.18
88	26.29	19.83	17.70	16.65	16.03	15.62	15.33	15.13	14.97	14.85	14.75	14.67	14.52	14.40	14.36	14.35
87	27.54	20.50	18.17	17.03	16.35	15.90	15.59	15.37	15.19	15.06	14.96	14.87	14.71	14.58	14.53	14.52
86	28.80	21.17	18.65	17.41	16.67	16.19	15.86	15.61	15.43	15.29	15.17	15.08	14.90	14.76	14.71	14.70
85	30.07	21.85	19.14	17.80	17.01	16.49	16.12	15.86	15.66	15.51	15.39	15.29	15.10	14.95	14.90	14.88
80	36.73	25.39	21.66	19.82	18.73	18.03	17.53	17.17	16.90	16.69	16.52	16.39	16.14	15.94	15.88	15.86
75	43.87	29.19	24.38	22.01	20.61	19.70	19.06	18.60	18.25	17.99	17.78	17.61	17.29	17.05	16.98	16.96
70	51.57	33.30	27.32	24.38	22.65	21.52	20.74	20.17	19.75	19.42	19.17	18.97	18.59	18.31	18.23	18.21
65	59.93	37.76	30.52	26.97	24.89	23.53	22.59	21.92	21.41	21.03	20.73	20.50	20.05	19.75	19.66	19.64
60	69.05	42.64	34.04	29.83	27.36	25.77	24.66	23.87	23.28	22.84	22.50	22.23	21.74	21.41	21.32	21.30
55	79.09	48.01	37.93	33.01	30.13	28.28	27.00	26.09	25.42	24.92	24.53	24.24	23.70	23.36	23.27	23.26
50	90.24	53.99	42.29	36.59	33.27	31.14	29.68	28.65	27.90	27.33	26.91	26.59	26.02	25.68	25.61	25.60

Description: This table shows the price to pay for a monthly payment loan, at a yield rate and assuming prepayment.

Example: The price of a 12.75 %, 30 year mortgage to yield 8.00 %, if prepaid in 6 years, is $ 122.35.

30 YEAR MORTGAGE PREPAID IN

YIELD	1 yr	2 yr	3 yr	4 yr	5 yr	6 yr	7 yr	8 yr	9 yr	10 yr	11 yr	12 yr	15 yr	20 yr	25 yr	30 yr
0.00	112.73	125.42	138.07	150.66	163.19	175.65	188.03	200.32	212.51	224.59	236.53	248.33	282.62	334.31	374.04	391.21
1.00	111.67	123.19	134.55	145.75	156.78	167.64	178.33	188.84	199.15	209.27	219.18	228.87	256.47	296.48	325.75	337.86
2.00	110.62	121.00	131.13	141.02	150.67	160.07	169.23	178.14	186.81	195.22	203.38	211.28	233.35	264.10	285.53	294.00
3.00	109.58	118.85	127.81	136.47	144.83	152.90	160.68	168.18	175.40	182.34	189.00	195.38	212.87	236.31	251.87	257.75
4.00	108.55	116.74	124.58	132.08	139.26	146.11	152.65	158.90	164.85	170.51	175.89	181.00	194.72	212.40	223.58	227.62
4.25	108.30	116.22	123.79	131.01	137.90	144.47	150.72	156.67	162.33	167.70	172.80	177.62	190.50	206.95	217.22	220.90
4.50	108.04	115.70	123.00	129.95	136.56	142.85	148.82	154.49	159.87	164.96	169.77	174.32	186.41	201.70	211.13	214.47
4.75	107.79	115.19	122.22	128.90	135.24	141.25	146.95	152.35	157.45	162.27	166.82	171.10	182.44	196.64	205.29	208.32
5.00	107.53	114.68	121.45	127.86	133.93	139.68	145.11	150.24	155.08	159.64	163.93	167.96	178.59	191.76	199.69	202.43
5.25	107.28	114.17	120.68	126.83	132.64	138.13	143.30	148.17	152.75	157.06	161.11	164.90	174.84	187.05	194.31	196.79
5.50	107.03	113.66	119.92	125.81	131.36	136.59	141.51	146.13	150.47	154.54	158.35	161.91	171.20	182.50	189.14	191.39
5.75	106.78	113.16	119.16	124.80	130.10	135.08	139.75	144.13	148.23	152.07	155.65	158.99	167.67	178.12	184.18	186.21
6.00	106.53	112.65	118.40	123.80	128.85	133.59	138.02	142.16	146.04	149.65	153.01	156.15	164.23	173.89	179.42	181.25
6.25	106.28	112.15	117.66	122.80	127.62	132.12	136.31	140.23	143.88	147.28	150.44	153.37	160.90	169.80	174.84	176.49
6.50	106.03	111.66	116.91	121.82	126.40	130.66	134.64	138.33	141.77	144.96	147.91	150.65	157.66	165.86	170.44	171.93
6.75	105.78	111.16	116.18	120.85	125.19	129.23	132.98	136.46	139.69	142.68	145.45	148.00	154.51	162.05	166.21	167.54
7.00	105.53	110.67	115.45	119.88	124.00	127.82	131.35	134.63	137.66	140.46	143.04	145.42	151.44	158.36	162.14	163.34
7.25	105.28	110.18	114.72	118.93	122.82	126.42	129.75	132.83	135.66	138.28	140.68	142.89	148.47	154.81	158.23	159.30
7.50	105.04	109.69	114.00	117.98	121.65	125.04	128.17	131.05	133.70	136.14	138.38	140.43	145.57	151.37	154.46	155.42
7.75	104.79	109.21	113.28	117.04	120.50	123.69	126.62	129.31	131.78	134.05	136.12	138.02	142.76	148.05	150.83	151.69
8.00	104.54	108.73	112.57	116.11	119.36	122.35	125.09	127.60	129.90	132.00	133.92	135.67	140.03	144.84	147.34	148.10
8.25	104.30	108.25	111.87	115.19	118.24	121.02	123.58	125.91	128.04	129.99	131.76	133.38	137.37	141.73	143.98	144.65
8.50	104.06	107.77	111.17	114.28	117.12	119.72	122.09	124.26	126.23	128.02	129.65	131.13	134.78	138.73	140.73	141.33
8.75	103.81	107.29	110.47	113.37	116.02	118.43	120.63	122.63	124.45	126.09	127.59	128.94	132.26	135.82	137.61	138.13
9.00	103.57	106.82	109.78	112.48	114.93	117.16	119.19	121.03	122.70	124.21	125.57	126.81	129.81	133.01	134.60	135.06
9.25	103.33	106.35	109.10	111.59	113.86	115.91	117.77	119.45	120.98	122.36	123.60	124.72	127.43	130.29	131.69	132.09
9.50	103.08	105.88	108.42	110.71	112.79	114.67	116.37	117.91	119.29	120.54	121.67	122.67	125.11	127.66	128.89	129.24
9.75	102.84	105.42	107.74	109.84	111.74	113.45	115.00	116.39	117.64	118.76	119.78	120.68	122.86	125.11	126.18	126.48
10.00	102.60	104.95	107.07	108.98	110.70	112.25	113.64	114.89	116.02	117.02	117.93	118.73	120.66	122.64	123.57	123.83
10.25	102.36	104.49	106.40	108.12	109.67	111.06	112.30	113.42	114.42	115.32	116.12	116.83	118.52	120.25	121.05	121.27
10.50	102.12	104.03	105.74	107.28	108.65	109.89	110.99	111.98	112.86	113.64	114.34	114.97	116.44	117.93	118.61	118.80
10.75	101.89	103.57	105.09	106.44	107.65	108.73	109.69	110.55	111.32	112.00	112.61	113.15	114.42	115.68	116.26	116.41
11.00	101.65	103.12	104.43	105.61	106.65	107.59	108.42	109.16	109.81	110.40	110.91	111.37	112.45	113.51	113.98	114.11
11.25	101.41	102.67	103.79	104.78	105.67	106.46	107.16	107.78	108.33	108.82	109.25	109.64	110.53	111.40	111.78	111.88
11.50	101.17	102.22	103.14	103.97	104.70	105.35	105.92	106.43	106.88	107.28	107.63	107.94	108.66	109.35	109.66	109.73
11.75	100.94	101.77	102.51	103.16	103.74	104.25	104.70	105.10	105.45	105.76	106.04	106.28	106.83	107.37	107.60	107.66
12.00	100.70	101.32	101.87	102.36	102.79	103.17	103.50	103.79	104.05	104.28	104.48	104.65	105.06	105.44	105.60	105.65
12.25	100.47	100.88	101.24	101.57	101.85	102.10	102.32	102.51	102.68	102.83	102.95	103.07	103.33	103.57	103.68	103.70
12.50	100.23	100.44	100.62	100.78	100.92	101.04	101.15	101.24	101.33	101.40	101.46	101.52	101.64	101.76	101.81	101.82
12.75	100.00	100.00	100.00	100.00	100.00	100.00	100.00	100.00	100.00	100.00	100.00	100.00	100.00	100.00	100.00	100.00
13.00	99.77	99.56	99.38	99.23	99.09	98.97	98.87	98.78	98.70	98.63	98.57	98.52	98.40	98.29	98.25	98.24
13.25	99.53	99.13	98.77	98.46	98.19	97.96	97.75	97.57	97.42	97.28	97.17	97.07	96.84	96.63	96.55	96.53
13.50	99.30	98.70	98.17	97.71	97.30	96.96	96.65	96.39	96.16	95.96	95.79	95.65	95.32	95.02	94.90	94.87
13.75	99.07	98.27	97.56	96.95	96.43	95.97	95.57	95.23	94.93	94.67	94.45	94.26	93.83	93.45	93.30	93.27
14.00	98.84	97.84	96.97	96.21	95.56	94.99	94.50	94.08	93.72	93.40	93.13	92.90	92.39	91.93	91.75	91.71
14.25	98.61	97.41	96.37	95.47	94.70	94.03	93.45	92.96	92.53	92.16	91.84	91.57	90.97	90.45	90.25	90.21
14.50	98.38	96.99	95.78	94.74	93.85	93.08	92.42	91.85	91.36	90.94	90.58	90.27	89.60	89.01	88.79	88.74
14.75	98.15	96.56	95.20	94.02	93.01	92.14	91.40	90.76	90.21	89.74	89.34	89.00	88.25	87.61	87.38	87.32
15.00	97.93	96.14	94.61	93.30	92.18	91.22	90.39	89.68	89.08	88.57	88.13	87.76	86.94	86.25	86.00	85.94
15.25	97.70	95.73	94.04	92.59	91.36	90.30	89.40	88.63	87.97	87.42	86.94	86.54	85.67	84.93	84.66	84.60
15.50	97.47	95.31	93.46	91.89	90.54	89.40	88.42	87.59	86.89	86.29	85.78	85.35	84.42	83.64	83.36	83.30
15.75	97.24	94.90	92.90	91.19	89.74	88.51	87.46	86.57	85.82	85.18	84.64	84.18	83.20	82.39	82.10	82.04
16.00	97.02	94.48	92.33	90.50	88.95	87.63	86.51	85.57	84.77	84.09	83.52	83.04	82.01	81.17	80.87	80.81
16.25	96.79	94.07	91.77	89.82	88.16	86.76	85.58	84.58	83.73	83.02	82.42	81.92	80.85	79.98	79.68	79.62
16.50	96.57	93.67	91.21	89.14	87.38	85.90	84.66	83.60	82.72	81.97	81.35	80.83	79.72	78.82	78.52	78.45
16.75	96.35	93.26	90.66	88.46	86.62	85.06	83.75	82.65	81.72	80.95	80.30	79.75	78.61	77.70	77.39	77.32
17.00	96.12	92.86	90.11	87.80	85.86	84.22	82.85	81.71	80.74	79.94	79.27	78.70	77.53	76.60	76.29	76.22
17.25	95.90	92.46	89.56	87.14	85.10	83.40	81.97	80.78	79.78	78.95	78.25	77.68	76.47	75.53	75.22	75.15
17.50	95.68	92.06	89.02	86.48	84.36	82.59	81.10	79.87	78.84	77.98	77.26	76.67	75.44	74.48	74.17	74.11
17.75	95.46	91.66	88.48	85.84	83.63	81.78	80.25	78.97	77.91	77.02	76.29	75.69	74.43	73.47	73.16	73.09
18.00	95.23	91.26	87.95	85.19	82.90	80.99	79.40	78.09	76.99	76.09	75.34	74.72	73.45	72.48	72.17	72.11
18.25	95.01	90.87	87.42	84.56	82.18	80.21	78.57	77.22	76.10	75.17	74.40	73.77	72.48	71.51	71.20	71.14
18.50	94.79	90.48	86.89	83.93	81.47	79.43	77.75	76.36	75.21	74.27	73.49	72.85	71.54	70.56	70.26	70.20
18.75	94.57	90.09	86.37	83.30	80.76	78.67	76.94	75.52	74.35	73.38	72.59	71.94	70.62	69.64	69.34	69.29
19.00	94.36	89.70	85.85	82.68	80.07	77.92	76.15	74.69	73.49	72.51	71.71	71.05	69.72	68.75	68.45	68.39
20.00	93.49	88.16	83.81	80.26	77.36	75.00	73.07	71.50	70.23	69.19	68.35	67.67	66.31	65.36	65.08	65.03
25.00	89.27	80.93	74.43	69.38	65.46	62.41	60.05	58.22	56.80	55.70	54.85	54.20	53.01	52.31	52.15	52.13
30.00	85.27	74.36	66.27	60.29	55.86	52.58	50.16	48.38	47.06	46.09	45.37	44.85	43.98	43.55	43.47	43.46

Description: This table shows the yield to prepayment of a monthly payment mortgage purchased at a price in the index.

Example: The yield to prepayment in 10 years of a 12.75 %, 30 year mortgage at a price of 104.00 is 12.04 %.

30 YEAR MORTGAGE PREPAID IN

PRICE	1 yr	2 yr	3 yr	4 yr	5 yr	6 yr	7 yr	8 yr	9 yr	10 yr	11 yr	12 yr	15 yr	20 yr	25 yr	30 yr
140	–	–	–	2.22	3.86	4.94	5.71	6.28	6.71	7.05	7.32	7.54	8.00	8.39	8.55	8.60
135	–	–	–	3.33	4.79	5.76	6.44	6.94	7.33	7.63	7.87	8.07	8.47	8.82	8.96	9.00
130	–	–	2.33	4.48	5.77	6.61	7.21	7.65	7.98	8.24	8.45	8.62	8.98	9.27	9.39	9.43
125	–	–	3.86	5.70	6.78	7.50	8.01	8.38	8.67	8.89	9.07	9.21	9.51	9.76	9.86	9.88
120	–	2.46	5.47	6.96	7.85	8.44	8.85	9.16	9.39	9.57	9.71	9.83	10.07	10.27	10.35	10.37
119	–	2.92	5.80	7.23	8.08	8.63	9.03	9.32	9.54	9.71	9.85	9.96	10.19	10.38	10.45	10.47
118	–	3.40	6.13	7.49	8.30	8.83	9.20	9.48	9.69	9.85	9.98	10.09	10.31	10.49	10.56	10.58
117	–	3.87	6.47	7.76	8.52	9.03	9.38	9.64	9.84	10.00	10.12	10.22	10.43	10.60	10.67	10.68
116	–	4.35	6.81	8.03	8.75	9.23	9.56	9.81	10.00	10.14	10.26	10.36	10.55	10.71	10.77	10.79
115	–	4.84	7.15	8.30	8.98	9.43	9.74	9.98	10.15	10.29	10.40	10.49	10.67	10.82	10.88	10.90
114	–	5.33	7.50	8.57	9.21	9.63	9.93	10.15	10.31	10.44	10.54	10.63	10.80	10.94	10.99	11.01
113	–	5.82	7.84	8.85	9.45	9.84	10.11	10.32	10.47	10.59	10.69	10.77	10.92	11.05	11.11	11.12
112	–	6.32	8.20	9.13	9.68	10.05	10.30	10.49	10.63	10.75	10.83	10.91	11.05	11.17	11.22	11.23
111	1.63	6.83	8.56	9.41	9.92	10.26	10.49	10.67	10.80	10.90	10.98	11.05	11.18	11.29	11.34	11.35
110	2.59	7.34	8.92	9.70	10.16	10.47	10.69	10.84	10.96	11.06	11.13	11.19	11.31	11.41	11.45	11.46
109	3.56	7.85	9.28	9.99	10.41	10.69	10.88	11.02	11.13	11.22	11.28	11.34	11.45	11.54	11.57	11.58
108	4.54	8.37	9.65	10.28	10.66	10.90	11.08	11.21	11.30	11.38	11.44	11.49	11.58	11.66	11.70	11.70
107	5.52	8.90	10.02	10.58	10.91	11.12	11.28	11.39	11.47	11.54	11.59	11.64	11.72	11.79	11.82	11.83
106	6.52	9.43	10.40	10.88	11.16	11.35	11.48	11.58	11.65	11.71	11.75	11.79	11.86	11.92	11.94	11.95
105	7.53	9.97	10.78	11.18	11.42	11.57	11.68	11.76	11.83	11.87	11.91	11.94	12.00	12.05	12.07	12.08
104	8.55	10.51	11.16	11.49	11.68	11.80	11.89	11.96	12.00	12.04	12.07	12.10	12.15	12.19	12.20	12.21
103.75	8.81	10.65	11.26	11.56	11.74	11.86	11.94	12.00	12.05	12.09	12.11	12.14	12.18	12.22	12.24	12.24
103.50	9.07	10.79	11.36	11.64	11.81	11.92	11.99	12.05	12.09	12.13	12.16	12.18	12.22	12.25	12.27	12.27
103.25	9.32	10.92	11.45	11.72	11.87	11.98	12.05	12.10	12.14	12.17	12.20	12.22	12.26	12.29	12.30	12.30
103.00	9.58	11.06	11.55	11.79	11.94	12.03	12.10	12.15	12.19	12.21	12.24	12.26	12.29	12.32	12.33	12.34
102.75	9.84	11.20	11.65	11.87	12.00	12.09	12.15	12.20	12.23	12.26	12.28	12.30	12.33	12.36	12.37	12.37
102.50	10.10	11.34	11.75	11.95	12.07	12.15	12.21	12.25	12.28	12.30	12.32	12.34	12.37	12.39	12.40	12.40
102.25	10.36	11.48	11.85	12.03	12.14	12.21	12.26	12.30	12.32	12.35	12.36	12.38	12.40	12.43	12.44	12.44
102.00	10.63	11.62	11.94	12.11	12.20	12.27	12.31	12.34	12.37	12.39	12.40	12.42	12.44	12.46	12.47	12.47
101.75	10.89	11.76	12.04	12.19	12.27	12.33	12.37	12.39	12.42	12.43	12.45	12.46	12.48	12.50	12.50	12.50
101.50	11.15	11.90	12.14	12.27	12.34	12.39	12.42	12.44	12.46	12.48	12.49	12.50	12.52	12.53	12.54	12.54
101.25	11.41	12.04	12.24	12.34	12.41	12.45	12.47	12.49	12.51	12.52	12.53	12.54	12.55	12.57	12.57	12.57
101.00	11.68	12.18	12.34	12.42	12.47	12.50	12.53	12.54	12.56	12.57	12.57	12.58	12.59	12.60	12.61	12.61
100.75	11.94	12.32	12.44	12.50	12.54	12.56	12.58	12.59	12.60	12.61	12.62	12.62	12.63	12.64	12.64	12.64
100.50	12.21	12.46	12.54	12.58	12.61	12.62	12.64	12.64	12.65	12.66	12.66	12.66	12.67	12.67	12.68	12.68
100.25	12.48	12.60	12.64	12.66	12.68	12.68	12.69	12.69	12.70	12.70	12.70	12.70	12.71	12.71	12.71	12.71
100.00	12.75	12.75	12.75	12.75	12.75	12.75	12.75	12.75	12.75	12.75	12.75	12.75	12.75	12.75	12.75	12.75
99.75	13.01	12.89	12.85	12.83	12.81	12.81	12.80	12.80	12.79	12.79	12.79	12.79	12.78	12.78	12.78	12.78
99.50	13.28	13.03	12.95	12.91	12.88	12.87	12.85	12.85	12.84	12.84	12.83	12.83	12.82	12.82	12.82	12.82
99.25	13.55	13.17	13.05	12.99	12.95	12.93	12.91	12.90	12.89	12.88	12.88	12.87	12.86	12.85	12.85	12.85
99.00	13.82	13.32	13.15	13.07	13.02	12.99	12.97	12.95	12.94	12.93	12.92	12.91	12.90	12.89	12.89	12.89
98.75	14.09	13.46	13.25	13.15	13.09	13.05	13.02	13.00	12.98	12.97	12.96	12.96	12.94	12.93	12.92	12.92
98.50	14.37	13.61	13.36	13.23	13.16	13.11	13.08	13.05	13.03	13.02	13.01	13.00	12.98	12.96	12.96	12.96
98.25	14.64	13.75	13.46	13.32	13.23	13.17	13.13	13.10	13.08	13.06	13.05	13.04	13.02	13.00	12.99	12.99
98.00	14.91	13.90	13.56	13.40	13.30	13.23	13.19	13.16	13.13	13.11	13.10	13.08	13.06	13.04	13.03	13.03
97.75	15.19	14.05	13.67	13.48	13.37	13.30	13.25	13.21	13.18	13.16	13.14	13.13	13.10	13.08	13.07	13.07
97.50	15.46	14.19	13.77	13.56	13.44	13.36	13.30	13.26	13.23	13.20	13.19	13.17	13.14	13.11	13.10	13.10
97.25	15.74	14.34	13.88	13.65	13.51	13.42	13.36	13.31	13.28	13.25	13.23	13.21	13.18	13.15	13.14	13.14
97	16.02	14.49	13.98	13.73	13.58	13.48	13.42	13.37	13.33	13.30	13.28	13.26	13.22	13.19	13.18	13.18
96	17.13	15.08	14.40	14.07	13.87	13.74	13.65	13.58	13.53	13.49	13.46	13.43	13.38	13.34	13.33	13.32
95	18.26	15.68	14.83	14.41	14.16	13.99	13.88	13.79	13.73	13.68	13.64	13.61	13.55	13.50	13.48	13.48
94	19.40	16.29	15.26	14.75	14.45	14.25	14.11	14.01	13.94	13.88	13.83	13.79	13.72	13.66	13.64	13.63
93	20.56	16.91	15.70	15.10	14.75	14.52	14.35	14.23	14.15	14.08	14.02	13.98	13.89	13.82	13.79	13.79
92	21.73	17.53	16.14	15.46	15.05	14.78	14.60	14.46	14.36	14.28	14.21	14.16	14.06	13.98	13.95	13.95
91	22.91	18.16	16.59	15.81	15.35	15.05	14.84	14.69	14.57	14.48	14.41	14.35	14.24	14.15	14.12	14.11
90	24.11	18.80	17.05	16.18	15.66	15.33	15.09	14.92	14.79	14.69	14.61	14.55	14.42	14.32	14.29	14.28
89	25.33	19.45	17.51	16.55	15.98	15.61	15.35	15.16	15.01	14.90	14.81	14.75	14.61	14.50	14.46	14.45
88	26.56	20.10	17.97	16.92	16.30	15.89	15.60	15.40	15.24	15.12	15.02	14.95	14.79	14.68	14.63	14.62
87	27.81	20.77	18.44	17.30	16.62	16.18	15.87	15.64	15.47	15.34	15.23	15.15	14.98	14.86	14.81	14.80
86	29.07	21.44	18.92	17.68	16.95	16.47	16.13	15.89	15.70	15.56	15.45	15.36	15.18	15.04	14.99	14.98
85	30.35	22.12	19.41	18.07	17.28	16.76	16.40	16.14	15.94	15.79	15.66	15.57	15.38	15.23	15.18	15.17
80	37.01	25.67	21.94	20.10	19.02	18.31	17.82	17.46	17.19	16.98	16.82	16.69	16.43	16.24	16.18	16.16
75	44.16	29.49	24.67	22.30	20.90	19.99	19.36	18.90	18.56	18.29	18.09	17.92	17.60	17.37	17.30	17.28
70	51.88	33.60	27.62	24.69	22.96	21.83	21.05	20.49	20.07	19.74	19.49	19.30	18.92	18.65	18.57	18.55
65	60.25	38.08	30.84	27.29	25.21	23.86	22.93	22.25	21.75	21.37	21.07	20.84	20.41	20.11	20.02	20.00
60	69.39	42.97	34.38	30.17	27.71	26.11	25.02	24.23	23.65	23.20	22.87	22.60	22.12	21.79	21.71	21.69
55	79.44	48.36	38.29	33.37	30.50	28.65	27.38	26.47	25.81	25.31	24.93	24.64	24.11	23.78	23.70	23.68
50	90.61	54.37	42.67	36.97	33.66	31.54	30.09	29.06	28.32	27.76	27.34	27.03	26.47	26.15	26.07	26.06

Description: This table shows the price to pay for a monthly payment loan, at a yield rate and assuming prepayment.

Example: The price of a 13.00 %, 30 year mortgage to yield 8.00 %, if prepaid in 6 years, is $ 123.53.

30 YEAR MORTGAGE PREPAID IN

YIELD	1 yr	2 yr	3 yr	4 yr	5 yr	6 yr	7 yr	8 yr	9 yr	10 yr	11 yr	12 yr	15 yr	20 yr	25 yr	30 yr
0.00	112.98	125.93	138.82	151.67	164.45	177.17	189.81	202.37	214.82	227.16	239.38	251.44	286.55	339.57	380.48	398.23
1.00	111.92	123.68	135.29	146.74	158.01	169.12	180.05	190.80	201.35	211.71	221.86	231.78	260.09	301.20	331.39	343.93
2.00	110.87	121.49	131.86	141.99	151.87	161.50	170.89	180.02	188.91	197.54	205.91	214.02	236.69	268.35	290.49	299.28
3.00	109.83	119.33	128.53	137.41	146.00	154.29	162.28	169.98	177.40	184.53	191.38	197.95	215.96	240.15	256.26	262.38
4.00	108.80	117.22	125.29	133.01	140.39	147.45	154.19	160.62	166.76	172.59	178.14	183.41	197.58	215.88	227.49	231.71
4.25	108.54	116.70	124.50	131.94	139.03	145.80	152.25	158.39	164.22	169.76	175.02	180.00	193.32	210.35	221.03	224.86
4.50	108.29	116.18	123.71	130.87	137.69	144.17	150.33	156.19	161.73	166.99	171.97	176.66	189.17	205.02	214.83	218.32
4.75	108.03	115.67	122.92	129.82	136.36	142.57	148.45	154.02	159.30	164.28	168.98	173.41	185.15	199.89	208.89	212.06
5.00	107.78	115.15	122.15	128.77	135.04	140.98	146.59	151.90	156.90	161.62	166.06	170.24	181.25	194.93	203.19	206.06
5.25	107.52	114.64	121.37	127.74	133.74	139.42	144.77	149.81	154.56	159.02	163.21	167.14	177.46	190.15	197.72	200.32
5.50	107.27	114.13	120.61	126.71	132.46	137.87	142.97	147.76	152.25	156.47	160.42	164.12	173.77	185.53	192.47	194.83
5.75	107.02	113.63	119.85	125.69	131.19	136.35	141.20	145.74	150.00	153.98	157.70	161.17	170.19	181.08	187.42	189.56
6.00	106.77	113.12	119.09	124.69	129.93	134.85	139.45	143.76	147.78	151.54	155.04	158.29	166.71	176.79	182.58	184.50
6.25	106.52	112.62	118.34	123.69	128.69	133.37	137.73	141.81	145.61	149.14	152.43	155.48	163.34	172.64	177.92	179.66
6.50	106.27	112.13	117.60	122.70	127.47	131.91	136.04	139.89	143.47	146.80	149.88	152.74	160.05	168.63	173.45	175.01
6.75	106.02	111.63	116.86	121.72	126.25	130.46	134.38	138.01	141.38	144.50	147.39	150.06	156.86	164.76	169.14	170.55
7.00	105.77	111.14	116.12	120.75	125.05	129.04	132.74	136.16	139.33	142.26	144.96	147.45	153.76	161.02	165.00	166.27
7.25	105.52	110.65	115.39	119.79	123.87	127.64	131.12	134.34	137.31	140.05	142.58	144.89	150.74	157.41	161.02	162.16
7.50	105.28	110.16	114.67	118.84	122.69	126.25	129.53	132.55	135.34	137.90	140.25	142.40	147.81	153.92	157.19	158.21
7.75	105.03	109.67	113.95	117.90	121.54	124.88	127.96	130.80	133.40	135.78	137.97	139.97	144.96	150.55	153.50	154.41
8.00	104.78	109.19	113.24	116.96	120.39	123.53	126.42	129.07	131.49	133.71	135.74	137.59	142.19	147.29	149.95	150.76
8.25	104.54	108.71	112.53	116.04	119.26	122.20	124.90	127.37	129.63	131.68	133.56	135.27	139.50	144.13	146.53	147.24
8.50	104.29	108.23	111.83	115.12	118.14	120.89	123.41	125.70	127.79	129.70	131.43	133.00	136.87	141.08	143.23	143.87
8.75	104.05	107.75	111.13	114.21	117.03	119.59	121.93	124.06	125.99	127.75	129.34	130.79	134.32	138.13	140.05	140.61
9.00	103.81	107.28	110.44	113.32	115.93	118.32	120.48	122.45	124.23	125.84	127.30	128.62	131.84	135.28	136.98	137.48
9.25	103.56	106.80	109.75	112.42	114.85	117.05	119.05	120.86	122.49	123.97	125.31	126.51	129.43	132.51	134.03	134.46
9.50	103.32	106.33	109.07	111.54	113.78	115.81	117.64	119.30	120.79	122.14	123.35	124.44	127.08	129.84	131.18	131.56
9.75	103.08	105.87	108.39	110.67	112.72	114.58	116.26	117.76	119.12	120.35	121.44	122.43	124.79	127.25	128.42	128.75
10.00	102.84	105.40	107.71	109.80	111.68	113.37	114.89	116.26	117.48	118.59	119.57	120.46	122.57	124.74	125.77	126.05
10.25	102.60	104.94	107.05	108.94	110.64	112.17	113.54	114.77	115.88	116.86	117.74	118.53	120.40	122.31	123.20	123.45
10.50	102.36	104.48	106.38	108.09	109.62	110.99	112.22	113.32	114.30	115.17	115.95	116.65	118.30	119.96	120.72	120.93
10.75	102.12	104.02	105.72	107.25	108.61	109.82	110.91	111.88	112.75	113.52	114.20	114.81	116.24	117.67	118.33	118.50
11.00	101.88	103.57	105.07	106.41	107.61	108.67	109.63	110.47	111.22	111.89	112.49	113.01	114.24	115.46	116.01	116.16
11.25	101.65	103.11	104.42	105.58	106.62	107.54	108.36	109.09	109.73	110.30	110.81	111.25	112.30	113.32	113.77	113.89
11.50	101.41	102.66	103.77	104.76	105.64	106.42	107.11	107.72	108.26	108.74	109.16	109.53	110.40	111.24	111.61	111.70
11.75	101.17	102.21	103.13	103.95	104.67	105.31	105.88	106.38	106.82	107.21	107.55	107.85	108.55	109.22	109.51	109.59
12.00	100.94	101.77	102.50	103.15	103.72	104.22	104.67	105.06	105.41	105.71	105.98	106.21	106.75	107.27	107.49	107.54
12.25	100.70	101.32	101.87	102.35	102.77	103.15	103.48	103.76	104.02	104.24	104.44	104.61	105.00	105.37	105.52	105.56
12.50	100.47	100.88	101.24	101.56	101.84	102.08	102.30	102.49	102.65	102.80	102.93	103.04	103.29	103.53	103.62	103.65
12.75	100.23	100.44	100.62	100.78	100.91	101.04	101.14	101.23	101.32	101.39	101.45	101.50	101.62	101.74	101.78	101.80
13.00	100.00	100.00	100.00	100.00	100.00	100.00	100.00	100.00	100.00	100.00	100.00	100.00	100.00	100.00	100.00	100.00
13.25	99.77	99.56	99.39	99.23	99.10	98.98	98.88	98.79	98.71	98.64	98.58	98.53	98.42	98.31	98.27	98.26
13.50	99.54	99.13	98.78	98.47	98.20	97.97	97.77	97.59	97.44	97.31	97.19	97.09	96.87	96.67	96.60	96.58
13.75	99.30	98.70	98.17	97.72	97.32	96.97	96.68	96.42	96.19	96.00	95.83	95.69	95.37	95.08	94.97	94.94
14.00	99.07	98.27	97.57	96.97	96.44	95.99	95.60	95.26	94.97	94.72	94.50	94.32	93.90	93.54	93.39	93.36
14.25	98.84	97.84	96.98	96.23	95.58	95.02	94.54	94.13	93.77	93.46	93.20	92.97	92.47	92.03	91.86	91.82
14.50	98.61	97.42	96.38	95.49	94.73	94.07	93.50	93.01	92.59	92.23	91.92	91.65	91.07	90.57	90.38	90.33
14.75	98.38	96.99	95.80	94.77	93.88	93.12	92.47	91.91	91.43	91.02	90.67	90.37	89.71	89.15	88.94	88.89
15.00	98.16	96.57	95.21	94.05	93.05	92.19	91.45	90.83	90.29	89.83	89.44	89.11	88.38	87.77	87.54	87.49
15.25	97.93	96.15	94.63	93.33	92.22	91.27	90.45	89.76	89.17	88.67	88.24	87.87	87.08	86.42	86.18	86.12
15.50	97.70	95.74	94.06	92.62	91.40	90.36	89.47	88.71	88.07	87.52	87.06	86.67	85.82	85.11	84.85	84.80
15.75	97.47	95.32	93.49	91.92	90.59	89.46	88.50	87.68	86.99	86.40	85.91	85.49	84.58	83.84	83.57	83.51
16.00	97.25	94.91	92.92	91.23	89.79	88.58	87.54	86.67	85.93	85.30	84.77	84.33	83.38	82.60	82.32	82.26
16.25	97.02	94.50	92.36	90.54	89.00	87.70	86.60	85.67	84.89	84.22	83.67	83.20	82.20	81.39	81.10	81.04
16.50	96.80	94.09	91.80	89.86	88.22	86.84	85.67	84.69	83.86	83.16	82.58	82.09	81.05	80.21	79.92	79.86
16.75	96.57	93.68	91.24	89.18	87.45	85.99	84.76	83.72	82.85	82.12	81.51	81.00	79.92	79.06	78.77	78.71
17.00	96.35	93.28	90.69	88.51	86.68	85.15	83.85	82.77	81.86	81.10	80.47	79.94	78.83	77.95	77.65	77.59
17.25	96.13	92.87	90.14	87.85	85.93	84.31	82.97	81.84	80.89	80.10	79.45	78.90	77.76	76.86	76.56	76.50
17.50	95.90	92.47	89.60	87.19	85.18	83.50	82.09	80.92	79.94	79.12	78.44	77.88	76.71	75.80	75.50	75.44
17.75	95.68	92.07	89.06	86.54	84.44	82.69	81.23	80.01	79.00	78.16	77.46	76.88	75.68	74.76	74.47	74.41
18.00	95.46	91.68	88.52	85.89	83.71	81.89	80.37	79.12	78.07	77.21	76.49	75.90	74.68	73.76	73.46	73.40
18.25	95.24	91.28	87.99	85.25	82.98	81.10	79.53	78.24	77.17	76.28	75.55	74.95	73.71	72.77	72.48	72.42
18.50	95.02	90.89	87.46	84.62	82.27	80.32	78.71	77.38	76.28	75.37	74.62	74.01	72.75	71.81	71.52	71.46
18.75	94.80	90.50	86.94	83.99	81.56	79.55	77.89	76.52	75.40	74.47	73.71	73.09	71.82	70.88	70.58	70.53
19.00	94.58	90.11	86.42	83.37	80.86	78.79	77.09	75.69	74.54	73.59	72.82	72.19	70.90	69.96	69.67	69.62
20.00	93.71	88.57	84.37	80.94	78.13	75.85	73.99	72.47	71.23	70.23	69.42	68.76	67.45	66.52	66.25	66.20
25.00	89.49	81.31	74.95	70.00	66.15	63.16	60.85	59.05	57.66	56.58	55.75	55.10	53.94	53.25	53.09	53.07
30.00	85.49	74.73	66.76	60.85	56.48	53.25	50.86	49.10	47.80	46.84	46.13	45.62	44.75	44.33	44.25	44.24

Description: This table shows the yield to prepayment of a monthly payment mortgage purchased at a price in the index.

Example: The yield to prepayment in 10 years of a 13.00 %, 30 year mortgage at a price of 104.00 is 12.29 %.

30 YEAR MORTGAGE PREPAID IN

PRICE	1 yr	2 yr	3 yr	4 yr	5 yr	6 yr	7 yr	8 yr	9 yr	10 yr	11 yr	12 yr	15 yr	20 yr	25 yr	30 yr
140	–	–	–	2.42	4.07	5.15	5.92	6.48	6.91	7.25	7.52	7.74	8.20	8.59	8.75	8.79
135	–	–	1.08	3.54	5.00	5.97	6.65	7.15	7.54	7.84	8.08	8.27	8.68	9.02	9.16	9.20
130	–	–	2.55	4.70	5.98	6.83	7.42	7.86	8.19	8.46	8.67	8.84	9.19	9.48	9.60	9.63
125	–	–	4.09	5.92	7.01	7.72	8.23	8.60	8.89	9.11	9.28	9.43	9.72	9.97	10.07	10.09
120	–	2.68	5.69	7.19	8.08	8.67	9.08	9.38	9.61	9.79	9.94	10.05	10.29	10.49	10.57	10.59
119	–	3.15	6.03	7.45	8.30	8.86	9.25	9.54	9.76	9.94	10.07	10.18	10.41	10.60	10.67	10.69
118	–	3.62	6.36	7.72	8.53	9.06	9.43	9.71	9.92	10.08	10.21	10.31	10.53	10.71	10.78	10.80
117	–	4.10	6.70	7.99	8.75	9.26	9.61	9.87	10.07	10.22	10.35	10.45	10.65	10.82	10.89	10.90
116	–	4.58	7.04	8.26	8.98	9.46	9.79	10.04	10.23	10.37	10.49	10.58	10.77	10.93	11.00	11.01
115	–	5.07	7.38	8.53	9.21	9.66	9.97	10.21	10.38	10.52	10.63	10.72	10.90	11.05	11.11	11.12
114	–	5.56	7.73	8.80	9.44	9.86	10.16	10.38	10.54	10.67	10.77	10.86	11.03	11.16	11.22	11.23
113	–	6.06	8.08	9.08	9.68	10.07	10.35	10.55	10.70	10.82	10.92	11.00	11.15	11.28	11.33	11.35
112	–	6.56	8.43	9.36	9.92	10.28	10.54	10.72	10.87	10.98	11.07	11.14	11.28	11.40	11.45	11.46
111	1.87	7.06	8.79	9.65	10.16	10.49	10.73	10.90	11.03	11.13	11.22	11.28	11.42	11.52	11.57	11.58
110	2.83	7.58	9.15	9.94	10.40	10.71	10.92	11.08	11.20	11.29	11.37	11.43	11.55	11.65	11.69	11.70
109	3.80	8.09	9.52	10.23	10.65	10.92	11.12	11.26	11.37	11.45	11.52	11.57	11.68	11.77	11.81	11.82
108	4.78	8.61	9.89	10.52	10.90	11.14	11.32	11.44	11.54	11.62	11.68	11.72	11.82	11.90	11.93	11.94
107	5.77	9.14	10.26	10.82	11.15	11.37	11.52	11.63	11.71	11.78	11.83	11.87	11.96	12.03	12.06	12.06
106	6.76	9.67	10.64	11.12	11.40	11.59	11.72	11.82	11.89	11.95	11.99	12.03	12.10	12.16	12.18	12.19
105	7.78	10.21	11.02	11.42	11.66	11.82	11.93	12.01	12.07	12.12	12.15	12.18	12.24	12.29	12.31	12.32
104	8.80	10.76	11.41	11.73	11.92	12.05	12.13	12.20	12.25	12.29	12.32	12.34	12.39	12.43	12.44	12.45
103.75	9.05	10.89	11.50	11.81	11.99	12.10	12.19	12.25	12.29	12.33	12.36	12.38	12.43	12.46	12.48	12.48
103.50	9.31	11.03	11.60	11.88	12.05	12.16	12.24	12.30	12.34	12.37	12.40	12.42	12.46	12.50	12.51	12.51
103.25	9.57	11.17	11.70	11.96	12.12	12.22	12.29	12.35	12.39	12.42	12.44	12.46	12.50	12.53	12.55	12.55
103.00	9.83	11.31	11.80	12.04	12.18	12.28	12.35	12.39	12.43	12.46	12.48	12.50	12.54	12.57	12.58	12.58
102.75	10.09	11.45	11.90	12.12	12.25	12.34	12.40	12.44	12.48	12.50	12.52	12.54	12.58	12.60	12.61	12.62
102.50	10.35	11.58	11.99	12.20	12.32	12.40	12.45	12.49	12.52	12.55	12.57	12.58	12.61	12.64	12.65	12.65
102.25	10.61	11.72	12.09	12.28	12.38	12.46	12.51	12.54	12.57	12.59	12.61	12.62	12.65	12.67	12.68	12.68
102.00	10.87	11.86	12.19	12.36	12.45	12.51	12.56	12.59	12.62	12.64	12.65	12.66	12.69	12.71	12.72	12.72
101.75	11.14	12.00	12.29	12.43	12.52	12.57	12.61	12.64	12.66	12.68	12.69	12.70	12.73	12.74	12.75	12.75
101.50	11.40	12.14	12.39	12.51	12.59	12.63	12.67	12.69	12.71	12.72	12.74	12.75	12.76	12.78	12.78	12.79
101.25	11.66	12.28	12.49	12.59	12.65	12.69	12.72	12.74	12.76	12.77	12.78	12.79	12.80	12.81	12.82	12.82
101.00	11.93	12.43	12.59	12.67	12.72	12.75	12.78	12.79	12.80	12.81	12.82	12.83	12.84	12.85	12.85	12.85
100.75	12.19	12.57	12.69	12.75	12.79	12.81	12.83	12.84	12.85	12.86	12.86	12.87	12.88	12.89	12.89	12.89
100.50	12.46	12.71	12.79	12.83	12.86	12.87	12.89	12.89	12.90	12.90	12.91	12.91	12.92	12.92	12.92	12.92
100.25	12.73	12.85	12.89	12.91	12.93	12.93	12.94	12.94	12.95	12.95	12.95	12.95	12.96	12.96	12.96	12.96
100.00	13.00	13.00	13.00	13.00	13.00	13.00	13.00	13.00	13.00	13.00	13.00	13.00	13.00	13.00	13.00	13.00
99.75	13.26	13.14	13.10	13.08	13.06	13.06	13.05	13.05	13.04	13.04	13.04	13.04	13.03	13.03	13.03	13.03
99.50	13.53	13.28	13.20	13.16	13.13	13.12	13.11	13.10	13.09	13.09	13.08	13.08	13.07	13.07	13.07	13.07
99.25	13.80	13.43	13.30	13.24	13.20	13.18	13.16	13.15	13.14	13.13	13.13	13.12	13.11	13.11	13.10	13.10
99.00	14.07	13.57	13.40	13.32	13.27	13.24	13.22	13.20	13.19	13.18	13.17	13.16	13.15	13.14	13.14	13.14
98.75	14.35	13.72	13.51	13.40	13.34	13.30	13.27	13.25	13.24	13.22	13.22	13.21	13.19	13.18	13.18	13.17
98.50	14.62	13.86	13.61	13.49	13.41	13.36	13.33	13.30	13.29	13.27	13.26	13.25	13.23	13.22	13.21	13.21
98.25	14.89	14.01	13.71	13.57	13.48	13.43	13.39	13.36	13.33	13.32	13.30	13.29	13.27	13.25	13.25	13.25
98.00	15.17	14.15	13.82	13.65	13.55	13.49	13.44	13.41	13.38	13.36	13.35	13.34	13.31	13.29	13.28	13.28
97.75	15.44	14.30	13.92	13.73	13.62	13.55	13.50	13.46	13.43	13.41	13.39	13.38	13.35	13.33	13.32	13.32
97.50	15.72	14.45	14.03	13.82	13.69	13.61	13.56	13.51	13.48	13.46	13.44	13.42	13.39	13.37	13.36	13.36
97.25	15.99	14.59	14.13	13.90	13.76	13.68	13.61	13.57	13.53	13.51	13.48	13.47	13.43	13.41	13.40	13.39
97	16.27	14.74	14.23	13.98	13.84	13.74	13.67	13.62	13.58	13.55	13.53	13.51	13.47	13.44	13.43	13.43
96	17.39	15.34	14.66	14.32	14.12	13.99	13.90	13.83	13.78	13.75	13.71	13.69	13.64	13.60	13.59	13.58
95	18.52	15.94	15.09	14.66	14.41	14.25	14.14	14.05	13.99	13.94	13.90	13.87	13.81	13.76	13.74	13.74
94	19.66	16.55	15.52	15.01	14.71	14.51	14.37	14.27	14.20	14.14	14.09	14.05	13.98	13.92	13.90	13.89
93	20.82	17.17	15.96	15.36	15.01	14.78	14.62	14.50	14.41	14.34	14.28	14.24	14.15	14.08	14.06	14.05
92	21.99	17.79	16.40	15.72	15.31	15.05	14.86	14.72	14.62	14.54	14.48	14.43	14.33	14.25	14.22	14.22
91	23.18	18.42	16.85	16.08	15.62	15.32	15.11	14.95	14.84	14.75	14.68	14.62	14.51	14.42	14.39	14.38
90	24.38	19.06	17.31	16.44	15.93	15.59	15.36	15.19	15.06	14.96	14.88	14.82	14.69	14.59	14.56	14.55
89	25.60	19.71	17.77	16.81	16.25	15.87	15.62	15.43	15.28	15.17	15.09	15.02	14.88	14.77	14.73	14.73
88	26.83	20.37	18.24	17.19	16.57	16.16	15.88	15.67	15.51	15.39	15.29	15.22	15.07	14.95	14.91	14.90
87	28.07	21.04	18.71	17.57	16.89	16.45	16.14	15.91	15.74	15.61	15.51	15.43	15.26	15.14	15.09	15.08
86	29.34	21.71	19.20	17.95	17.22	16.74	16.41	16.16	15.98	15.84	15.72	15.64	15.46	15.32	15.28	15.27
85	30.62	22.39	19.68	18.35	17.56	17.04	16.68	16.42	16.22	16.06	15.94	15.85	15.66	15.52	15.47	15.46
80	37.29	25.95	22.23	20.39	19.31	18.60	18.11	17.75	17.48	17.27	17.11	16.98	16.73	16.54	16.48	16.47
75	44.45	29.78	24.97	22.60	21.20	20.29	19.66	19.20	18.86	18.60	18.39	18.23	17.92	17.69	17.62	17.60
70	52.18	33.91	27.93	24.99	23.27	22.15	21.37	20.81	20.39	20.07	19.82	19.62	19.25	18.98	18.90	18.89
65	60.56	38.39	31.16	27.62	25.54	24.19	23.26	22.59	22.09	21.71	21.42	21.19	20.76	20.47	20.38	20.37
60	69.72	43.30	34.71	30.51	28.05	26.46	25.37	24.59	24.01	23.57	23.23	22.98	22.50	22.18	22.10	22.09
55	79.79	48.71	38.64	33.73	30.86	29.02	27.76	26.86	26.20	25.70	25.33	25.04	24.52	24.20	24.12	24.11
50	90.98	54.74	43.04	37.36	34.05	31.94	30.50	29.48	28.74	28.19	27.78	27.47	26.92	26.61	26.54	26.53

Description: This table shows the price to pay for a monthly payment loan, at a yield rate and assuming prepayment.

Example: The price of a 13.25 %, 30 year mortgage to yield 8.00 %, if prepaid in 6 years, is $ 124.72.

30 YEAR MORTGAGE PREPAID IN

YIELD	1 yr	2 yr	3 yr	4 yr	5 yr	6 yr	7 yr	8 yr	9 yr	10 yr	11 yr	12 yr	15 yr	20 yr	25 yr	30 yr
0.00	113.23	126.43	139.58	152.68	165.72	178.70	191.60	204.42	217.13	229.74	242.22	254.56	290.47	344.84	386.93	405.28
1.00	112.17	124.18	136.03	147.72	159.25	170.60	181.77	192.76	203.56	214.15	224.54	234.70	263.70	305.92	337.04	350.01
2.00	111.12	121.98	132.59	142.95	153.07	162.93	172.54	181.90	191.01	199.85	208.44	216.75	240.03	272.60	295.46	304.58
3.00	110.07	119.82	129.25	138.36	147.17	155.67	163.88	171.78	179.40	186.73	193.77	200.52	219.05	243.99	260.66	267.02
4.00	109.04	117.70	126.00	133.94	141.53	148.80	155.73	162.35	168.67	174.68	180.40	185.83	200.45	219.37	231.41	235.81
4.25	108.79	117.18	125.20	132.86	140.17	147.13	153.77	160.10	166.11	171.82	177.24	182.38	196.13	213.76	224.84	228.84
4.50	108.53	116.66	124.41	131.79	138.81	145.50	151.85	157.88	163.60	169.03	174.16	179.01	191.94	208.35	218.55	222.18
4.75	108.28	116.14	123.62	130.73	137.48	143.88	149.95	155.70	161.14	166.29	171.15	175.72	187.87	203.14	212.50	215.81
5.00	108.02	115.63	122.84	129.68	136.15	142.28	148.08	153.56	158.73	163.61	168.20	172.52	183.91	198.11	206.71	209.71
5.25	107.77	115.12	122.07	128.64	134.85	140.71	146.24	151.45	156.36	160.98	165.32	169.39	180.07	193.25	201.14	203.87
5.50	107.51	114.61	121.30	127.61	133.56	139.16	144.43	149.38	154.04	158.41	162.50	166.33	176.34	188.57	195.80	198.27
5.75	107.26	114.10	120.54	126.59	132.28	137.62	142.64	147.35	151.76	155.89	159.75	163.35	172.72	184.05	190.67	192.91
6.00	107.01	113.60	119.78	125.58	131.02	136.11	140.89	145.35	149.53	153.42	157.06	160.44	169.20	179.69	185.75	187.77
6.25	106.76	113.09	119.02	124.57	129.77	134.62	139.16	143.39	147.33	151.01	154.43	157.60	165.78	175.48	181.01	182.84
6.50	106.51	112.59	118.28	123.58	128.53	133.15	137.45	141.46	145.18	148.64	151.85	154.83	162.45	171.41	176.46	178.11
6.75	106.26	112.10	117.53	122.60	127.31	131.70	135.77	139.56	143.07	146.33	149.34	152.12	159.22	167.49	172.08	173.57
7.00	106.01	111.60	116.80	121.63	126.11	130.27	134.12	137.69	141.00	144.06	146.88	149.48	156.08	163.69	167.88	169.21
7.25	105.76	111.11	116.07	120.66	124.91	128.85	132.49	135.86	138.97	141.83	144.47	146.90	153.02	160.02	163.83	165.03
7.50	105.52	110.62	115.34	119.70	123.74	127.46	130.89	134.06	136.97	139.65	142.12	144.38	150.06	156.48	159.93	161.01
7.75	105.27	110.13	114.62	118.76	122.57	126.08	129.31	132.29	135.01	137.52	139.81	141.91	147.17	153.06	156.18	157.14
8.00	105.02	109.65	113.90	117.82	121.42	124.72	127.76	130.54	133.09	135.43	137.56	139.51	144.36	149.74	152.56	153.42
8.25	104.78	109.17	113.19	116.89	120.28	123.38	126.23	128.83	131.21	133.38	135.36	137.16	141.63	146.54	149.08	149.85
8.50	104.53	108.69	112.49	115.97	119.15	122.06	124.72	127.15	129.36	131.37	133.21	134.87	138.98	143.44	145.73	146.41
8.75	104.29	108.21	111.79	115.06	118.04	120.76	123.24	125.49	127.54	129.41	131.10	132.63	136.39	140.45	142.50	143.10
9.00	104.04	107.73	111.09	114.15	116.94	119.47	121.77	123.86	125.76	127.48	129.04	130.44	133.88	137.55	139.38	139.91
9.25	103.80	107.26	110.40	113.26	115.85	118.20	120.33	122.26	124.01	125.59	127.02	128.31	131.43	134.74	136.37	136.84
9.50	103.56	106.79	109.72	112.37	114.77	116.95	118.91	120.69	122.30	123.74	125.05	126.22	129.05	132.02	133.47	133.88
9.75	103.32	106.32	109.04	111.49	113.71	115.71	117.52	119.14	120.61	121.93	123.11	124.18	126.74	129.39	130.67	131.03
10.00	103.08	105.85	108.36	110.62	112.65	114.49	116.14	117.62	118.96	120.15	121.22	122.18	124.48	126.85	127.97	128.28
10.25	102.84	105.39	107.69	109.76	111.61	113.28	114.78	116.13	117.33	118.41	119.37	120.23	122.29	124.38	125.36	125.63
10.50	102.60	104.93	107.02	108.90	110.59	112.09	113.45	114.66	115.74	116.70	117.56	118.33	120.15	121.99	122.84	123.07
10.75	102.36	104.47	106.36	108.05	109.57	110.92	112.13	113.21	114.17	115.03	115.79	116.47	118.07	119.67	120.40	120.60
11.00	102.12	104.01	105.70	107.21	108.56	109.76	110.83	111.79	112.64	113.39	114.06	114.65	116.04	117.42	118.05	118.21
11.25	101.88	103.56	105.05	106.38	107.57	108.62	109.56	110.39	111.13	111.78	112.36	112.87	114.07	115.24	115.77	115.91
11.50	101.64	103.11	104.40	105.56	106.58	107.49	108.30	109.01	109.65	110.21	110.70	111.13	112.15	113.13	113.57	113.68
11.75	101.41	102.66	103.76	104.74	105.61	106.38	107.06	107.66	108.19	108.66	109.07	109.43	110.27	111.08	111.44	111.53
12.00	101.17	102.21	103.12	103.93	104.65	105.28	105.84	106.33	106.76	107.14	107.48	107.77	108.45	109.10	109.37	109.45
12.25	100.94	101.76	102.49	103.13	103.70	104.20	104.64	105.02	105.36	105.66	105.92	106.15	106.67	107.17	107.38	107.43
12.50	100.70	101.32	101.86	102.34	102.76	103.13	103.45	103.74	103.98	104.20	104.39	104.56	104.94	105.30	105.45	105.48
12.75	100.47	100.88	101.24	101.55	101.83	102.07	102.28	102.47	102.63	102.77	102.90	103.01	103.25	103.48	103.57	103.60
13.00	100.23	100.44	100.62	100.77	100.91	101.03	101.13	101.22	101.30	101.37	101.43	101.49	101.60	101.71	101.76	101.77
13.25	100.00	100.00	100.00	100.00	100.00	100.00	100.00	100.00	100.00	100.00	100.00	100.00	100.00	100.00	100.00	100.00
13.50	99.77	99.57	99.39	99.23	99.10	98.98	98.88	98.80	98.72	98.65	98.60	98.55	98.44	98.34	98.30	98.29
13.75	99.54	99.13	98.78	98.48	98.21	97.98	97.78	97.61	97.46	97.33	97.22	97.12	96.91	96.72	96.64	96.62
14.00	99.30	98.70	98.18	97.73	97.33	96.99	96.70	96.44	96.23	96.04	95.87	95.73	95.42	95.15	95.04	95.01
14.25	99.07	98.27	97.58	96.98	96.46	96.02	95.63	95.30	95.01	94.76	94.55	94.37	93.97	93.62	93.48	93.45
14.50	98.84	97.85	96.99	96.24	95.60	95.05	94.58	94.17	93.82	93.52	93.26	93.04	92.55	92.13	91.97	91.93
14.75	98.61	97.42	96.40	95.51	94.75	94.10	93.54	93.06	92.65	92.29	91.99	91.74	91.17	90.69	90.50	90.46
15.00	98.39	97.00	95.81	94.79	93.91	93.16	92.52	91.97	91.50	91.09	90.75	90.46	89.82	89.28	89.08	89.03
15.25	98.16	96.58	95.23	94.07	93.08	92.23	91.51	90.89	90.37	89.92	89.54	89.21	88.51	87.91	87.69	87.65
15.50	97.93	96.16	94.65	93.36	92.26	91.32	90.52	89.84	89.26	88.76	88.34	87.99	87.22	86.58	86.35	86.30
15.75	97.70	95.75	94.08	92.66	91.44	90.41	89.54	88.80	88.16	87.63	87.18	86.79	85.97	85.29	85.04	84.99
16.00	97.48	95.33	93.51	91.96	90.64	89.52	88.58	87.77	87.09	86.52	86.03	85.62	84.75	84.03	83.77	83.72
16.25	97.25	94.92	92.94	91.27	89.84	88.64	87.63	86.76	86.04	85.43	84.91	84.48	83.55	82.80	82.53	82.48
16.50	97.03	94.51	92.38	90.58	89.06	87.77	86.69	85.77	85.00	84.36	83.81	83.35	82.38	81.60	81.33	81.27
16.75	96.80	94.10	91.82	89.90	88.28	86.91	85.77	84.80	83.99	83.30	82.73	82.25	81.24	80.44	80.16	80.10
17.00	96.58	93.70	91.27	89.23	87.51	86.07	84.86	83.84	82.99	82.27	81.68	81.18	80.13	79.30	79.02	78.96
17.25	96.35	93.29	90.72	88.56	86.75	85.23	83.96	82.89	82.00	81.26	80.64	80.12	79.04	78.20	77.91	77.86
17.50	96.13	92.89	90.17	87.90	86.00	84.41	83.08	81.97	81.04	80.27	79.63	79.09	77.98	77.12	76.83	76.78
17.75	95.91	92.49	89.63	87.24	85.25	83.59	82.20	81.05	80.09	79.29	78.63	78.08	76.94	76.07	75.78	75.72
18.00	95.69	92.09	89.09	86.60	84.52	82.79	81.35	80.15	79.16	78.33	77.65	77.09	75.93	75.04	74.75	74.70
18.25	95.47	91.70	88.56	85.95	83.79	81.99	80.50	79.26	78.24	77.39	76.70	76.12	74.94	74.04	73.76	73.70
18.50	95.25	91.30	88.03	85.32	83.07	81.21	79.67	78.39	77.34	76.47	75.76	75.17	73.97	73.07	72.78	72.73
18.75	95.03	90.91	87.50	84.68	82.35	80.43	78.84	77.53	76.45	75.57	74.84	74.24	73.02	72.11	71.83	71.78
19.00	94.81	90.52	86.98	84.06	81.65	79.67	78.03	76.69	75.58	74.68	73.93	73.32	72.09	71.18	70.90	70.85
20.00	93.93	88.98	84.92	81.61	78.91	76.70	74.90	73.44	72.24	71.28	70.49	69.85	68.58	67.68	67.42	67.37
25.00	89.71	81.70	75.46	70.62	66.85	63.92	61.64	59.88	58.51	57.46	56.64	56.01	54.86	54.18	54.03	54.00
30.00	85.70	75.10	67.24	61.42	57.11	53.92	51.57	49.83	48.54	47.59	46.90	46.39	45.53	45.11	45.03	45.02

Description: This table shows the yield to prepayment of a monthly payment mortgage purchased at a price in the index.

Example: The yield to prepayment in 10 years of a 13.25 %, 30 year mortgage at a price of 104.00 is 12.53 %.

30 YEAR MORTGAGE PREPAID IN

PRICE	1 yr	2 yr	3 yr	4 yr	5 yr	6 yr	7 yr	8 yr	9 yr	10 yr	11 yr	12 yr	15 yr	20 yr	25 yr	30 yr
140	–	–	–	2.63	4.28	5.36	6.12	6.69	7.12	7.45	7.72	7.94	8.40	8.78	8.94	8.99
135	–	–	1.29	3.75	5.22	6.18	6.86	7.36	7.75	8.05	8.29	8.48	8.88	9.22	9.36	9.40
130	–	–	2.77	4.92	6.20	7.04	7.64	8.07	8.41	8.67	8.88	9.05	9.39	9.69	9.81	9.84
125	–	–	4.31	6.14	7.23	7.94	8.45	8.82	9.10	9.32	9.50	9.64	9.94	10.18	10.28	10.31
120	–	2.91	5.92	7.42	8.31	8.89	9.30	9.61	9.84	10.02	10.16	10.28	10.51	10.71	10.79	10.81
119	–	3.38	6.25	7.68	8.53	9.09	9.48	9.77	9.99	10.16	10.30	10.41	10.63	10.82	10.89	10.91
118	–	3.85	6.59	7.95	8.75	9.28	9.66	9.93	10.14	10.30	10.43	10.54	10.75	10.93	11.00	11.02
117	–	4.33	6.93	8.22	8.98	9.48	9.84	10.10	10.30	10.45	10.57	10.67	10.88	11.04	11.11	11.13
116	–	4.81	7.27	8.49	9.21	9.69	10.02	10.27	10.45	10.60	10.72	10.81	11.00	11.16	11.22	11.23
115	–	5.30	7.61	8.76	9.44	9.89	10.20	10.44	10.61	10.75	10.86	10.95	11.13	11.27	11.33	11.35
114	–	5.79	7.96	9.04	9.68	10.10	10.39	10.61	10.77	10.90	11.00	11.09	11.25	11.39	11.45	11.46
113	–	6.29	8.31	9.32	9.91	10.30	10.58	10.78	10.94	11.06	11.15	11.23	11.38	11.51	11.56	11.57
112	1.15	6.79	8.67	9.60	10.15	10.52	10.77	10.96	11.10	11.21	11.30	11.37	11.51	11.63	11.68	11.69
111	2.11	7.30	9.03	9.89	10.39	10.73	10.96	11.14	11.27	11.37	11.45	11.51	11.65	11.76	11.80	11.81
110	3.07	7.81	9.39	10.17	10.64	10.94	11.16	11.32	11.43	11.53	11.60	11.66	11.78	11.88	11.92	11.93
109	4.04	8.33	9.76	10.47	10.89	11.16	11.36	11.50	11.61	11.69	11.76	11.81	11.92	12.01	12.04	12.05
108	5.02	8.85	10.13	10.76	11.14	11.38	11.56	11.68	11.78	11.85	11.91	11.96	12.06	12.14	12.17	12.17
107	6.01	9.38	10.50	11.06	11.39	11.61	11.76	11.87	11.95	12.02	12.07	12.11	12.20	12.27	12.29	12.30
106	7.01	9.92	10.88	11.36	11.64	11.83	11.96	12.06	12.13	12.19	12.23	12.27	12.34	12.40	12.42	12.43
105	8.02	10.46	11.27	11.67	11.90	12.06	12.17	12.25	12.31	12.36	12.40	12.43	12.49	12.54	12.55	12.56
104	9.04	11.00	11.65	11.97	12.17	12.29	12.38	12.44	12.49	12.53	12.56	12.58	12.63	12.67	12.69	12.69
103.75	9.30	11.14	11.75	12.05	12.23	12.35	12.43	12.49	12.54	12.57	12.60	12.62	12.67	12.71	12.72	12.72
103.50	9.56	11.28	11.85	12.13	12.30	12.41	12.48	12.54	12.58	12.62	12.64	12.66	12.71	12.74	12.75	12.76
103.25	9.82	11.42	11.95	12.21	12.36	12.47	12.54	12.59	12.63	12.66	12.69	12.71	12.75	12.78	12.79	12.79
103.00	10.07	11.55	12.04	12.29	12.43	12.53	12.59	12.64	12.68	12.71	12.73	12.75	12.78	12.81	12.82	12.83
102.75	10.34	11.69	12.14	12.37	12.50	12.58	12.64	12.69	12.72	12.75	12.77	12.79	12.82	12.85	12.86	12.86
102.50	10.60	11.83	12.24	12.44	12.56	12.64	12.70	12.74	12.77	12.79	12.81	12.83	12.86	12.88	12.89	12.89
102.25	10.86	11.97	12.34	12.52	12.63	12.70	12.75	12.79	12.82	12.84	12.86	12.87	12.90	12.92	12.93	12.93
102.00	11.12	12.11	12.44	12.60	12.70	12.76	12.81	12.84	12.86	12.88	12.90	12.91	12.93	12.95	12.96	12.96
101.75	11.38	12.25	12.54	12.68	12.77	12.82	12.86	12.89	12.91	12.93	12.94	12.95	12.97	12.99	13.00	13.00
101.50	11.65	12.39	12.64	12.76	12.83	12.88	12.91	12.94	12.96	12.97	12.98	12.99	13.01	13.03	13.03	13.03
101.25	11.91	12.53	12.74	12.84	12.90	12.94	12.97	12.99	13.01	13.02	13.03	13.03	13.05	13.06	13.07	13.07
101.00	12.18	12.67	12.84	12.92	12.97	13.00	13.02	13.04	13.05	13.06	13.07	13.08	13.09	13.10	13.10	13.10
100.75	12.44	12.82	12.94	13.00	13.04	13.06	13.08	13.09	13.10	13.11	13.11	13.12	13.13	13.13	13.14	13.14
100.50	12.71	12.96	13.04	13.08	13.11	13.12	13.13	13.14	13.15	13.15	13.16	13.16	13.17	13.17	13.17	13.17
100.25	12.98	13.10	13.14	13.16	13.18	13.18	13.19	13.19	13.20	13.20	13.20	13.20	13.21	13.21	13.21	13.21
100.00	13.25	13.25	13.25	13.25	13.25	13.25	13.25	13.25	13.25	13.25	13.25	13.25	13.25	13.25	13.25	13.25
99.75	13.51	13.39	13.35	13.33	13.31	13.31	13.30	13.30	13.29	13.29	13.29	13.29	13.28	13.28	13.28	13.28
99.50	13.78	13.53	13.45	13.41	13.38	13.37	13.36	13.35	13.34	13.34	13.33	13.33	13.32	13.32	13.32	13.32
99.25	14.05	13.68	13.55	13.49	13.45	13.43	13.41	13.40	13.39	13.38	13.38	13.37	13.36	13.36	13.35	13.35
99.00	14.33	13.82	13.65	13.57	13.52	13.49	13.47	13.45	13.44	13.43	13.42	13.42	13.40	13.39	13.39	13.39
98.75	14.60	13.97	13.76	13.65	13.59	13.55	13.53	13.50	13.49	13.48	13.47	13.46	13.44	13.43	13.43	13.43
98.50	14.87	14.11	13.86	13.74	13.66	13.62	13.58	13.56	13.54	13.52	13.51	13.50	13.48	13.47	13.46	13.46
98.25	15.14	14.26	13.97	13.82	13.73	13.68	13.64	13.61	13.59	13.57	13.56	13.55	13.53	13.51	13.50	13.50
98.00	15.42	14.40	14.07	13.90	13.81	13.74	13.70	13.66	13.64	13.62	13.60	13.59	13.57	13.55	13.54	13.54
97.75	15.69	14.55	14.17	13.99	13.88	13.80	13.75	13.72	13.69	13.67	13.65	13.63	13.61	13.58	13.58	13.57
97.50	15.97	14.70	14.28	14.07	13.95	13.87	13.81	13.77	13.74	13.71	13.69	13.68	13.65	13.62	13.61	13.61
97.25	16.25	14.85	14.38	14.15	14.02	13.93	13.87	13.82	13.79	13.76	13.74	13.72	13.69	13.66	13.65	13.65
97	16.52	15.00	14.49	14.24	14.09	13.99	13.93	13.88	13.84	13.81	13.79	13.77	13.73	13.70	13.69	13.69
96	17.64	15.59	14.91	14.58	14.38	14.25	14.16	14.09	14.04	14.00	13.97	13.95	13.90	13.86	13.84	13.84
95	18.77	16.20	15.34	14.92	14.67	14.51	14.39	14.31	14.25	14.20	14.16	14.13	14.07	14.02	14.00	14.00
94	19.92	16.81	15.78	15.27	14.97	14.77	14.63	14.53	14.46	14.40	14.35	14.31	14.24	14.18	14.16	14.16
93	21.08	17.43	16.22	15.62	15.27	15.04	14.88	14.76	14.67	14.60	14.55	14.50	14.42	14.35	14.32	14.32
92	22.25	18.05	16.67	15.98	15.57	15.31	15.12	14.99	14.89	14.81	14.74	14.69	14.59	14.52	14.49	14.48
91	23.44	18.69	17.12	16.34	15.88	15.58	15.37	15.22	15.10	15.01	14.94	14.89	14.78	14.69	14.66	14.65
90	24.64	19.33	17.57	16.71	16.20	15.86	15.63	15.46	15.33	15.23	15.15	15.09	14.96	14.87	14.83	14.83
89	25.86	19.98	18.04	17.08	16.51	16.14	15.88	15.70	15.55	15.44	15.36	15.29	15.15	15.05	15.01	15.00
88	27.09	20.64	18.51	17.46	16.84	16.43	16.15	15.94	15.78	15.66	15.57	15.49	15.34	15.23	15.19	15.18
87	28.34	21.31	18.98	17.84	17.16	16.72	16.41	16.19	16.02	15.89	15.78	15.70	15.54	15.42	15.37	15.36
86	29.61	21.98	19.47	18.23	17.49	17.02	16.68	16.44	16.25	16.11	16.00	15.91	15.74	15.61	15.56	15.55
85	30.89	22.67	19.96	18.62	17.83	17.31	16.96	16.69	16.50	16.34	16.22	16.13	15.94	15.80	15.75	15.74
80	37.57	26.24	22.51	20.67	19.59	18.89	18.39	18.04	17.77	17.56	17.40	17.27	17.02	16.84	16.78	16.76
75	44.75	30.07	25.26	22.89	21.50	20.59	19.96	19.51	19.16	18.90	18.70	18.54	18.23	18.01	17.93	17.92
70	52.49	34.21	28.24	25.30	23.58	22.46	21.69	21.13	20.71	20.39	20.14	19.95	19.58	19.32	19.25	19.23
65	60.88	38.71	31.48	27.94	25.87	24.52	23.59	22.92	22.43	22.05	21.76	21.54	21.11	20.83	20.75	20.74
60	70.05	43.64	35.05	30.85	28.40	26.81	25.72	24.94	24.37	23.94	23.60	23.35	22.88	22.57	22.50	22.48
55	80.15	49.07	39.00	34.09	31.23	29.39	28.14	27.24	26.59	26.10	25.73	25.44	24.93	24.63	24.55	24.54
50	91.36	55.12	43.42	37.74	34.45	32.34	30.91	29.89	29.16	28.62	28.21	27.91	27.38	27.08	27.01	27.00

Description: This table shows the price to pay for a monthly payment loan, at a yield rate and assuming prepayment.

Example: The price of a 13.50 %, 30 year mortgage to yield 8.00 %, if prepaid in 6 years, is $ 125.91.

30 YEAR MORTGAGE PREPAID IN

YIELD	1 yr	2 yr	3 yr	4 yr	5 yr	6 yr	7 yr	8 yr	9 yr	10 yr	11 yr	12 yr	15 yr	20 yr	25 yr	30 yr
0.00	113.48	126.93	140.34	153.69	166.99	180.22	193.39	206.46	219.45	232.32	245.06	257.67	294.40	350.12	393.40	412.35
1.00	112.42	124.68	136.78	148.71	160.48	172.08	183.49	194.72	205.76	216.59	227.21	237.61	267.32	310.65	342.70	356.12
2.00	111.36	122.47	133.32	143.92	154.27	164.36	174.20	183.78	193.11	202.17	210.96	219.49	243.37	276.86	300.44	309.89
3.00	110.32	120.31	129.97	139.31	148.34	157.06	165.47	173.59	181.40	188.93	196.16	203.09	222.15	247.84	265.08	271.68
4.00	109.29	118.18	126.71	134.87	142.67	150.14	157.27	164.08	170.58	176.77	182.66	188.25	203.32	222.86	235.34	239.92
4.25	109.03	117.66	125.91	133.78	141.30	148.47	155.30	161.81	168.00	173.88	179.47	184.76	198.95	217.17	228.67	232.84
4.50	108.77	117.14	125.11	132.71	139.94	146.82	153.36	159.57	165.47	171.06	176.35	181.36	194.70	211.68	222.27	226.06
4.75	108.52	116.62	124.32	131.64	138.59	145.19	151.45	157.38	162.99	168.30	173.31	178.04	190.58	206.39	216.13	219.58
5.00	108.26	116.11	123.54	130.59	137.26	143.59	149.56	155.22	160.56	165.59	170.33	174.80	186.58	201.29	210.23	213.37
5.25	108.01	115.59	122.76	129.54	135.95	142.00	147.71	153.10	158.17	162.94	167.43	171.63	182.69	196.36	204.58	207.43
5.50	107.76	115.08	121.99	128.51	134.65	140.44	145.89	151.01	155.83	160.35	164.58	168.55	178.92	191.61	199.15	201.73
5.75	107.51	114.57	121.22	127.48	133.37	138.90	144.09	148.96	153.53	157.80	161.80	165.53	175.25	187.03	193.93	196.28
6.00	107.25	114.07	120.46	126.47	132.10	137.38	142.32	146.95	151.27	155.31	159.08	162.59	171.68	182.60	188.92	191.05
6.25	107.00	113.56	119.71	125.46	130.84	135.87	140.58	144.97	149.06	152.88	156.42	159.72	168.22	178.33	184.11	186.03
6.50	106.75	113.06	118.96	124.46	129.60	134.39	138.86	143.02	146.89	150.49	153.83	156.92	164.85	174.20	179.48	181.22
6.75	106.50	112.56	118.21	123.48	128.37	132.93	137.17	141.11	144.76	148.15	151.28	154.18	161.58	170.21	175.03	176.60
7.00	106.25	112.07	117.47	122.50	127.16	131.49	135.51	139.23	142.67	145.86	148.80	151.51	158.40	166.36	170.76	172.16
7.25	106.00	111.57	116.74	121.53	125.96	130.07	133.87	137.38	140.62	143.61	146.37	148.90	155.31	162.64	166.64	167.91
7.50	105.76	111.08	116.01	120.57	124.78	128.66	132.25	135.56	138.61	141.41	143.99	146.35	152.30	159.04	162.68	163.81
7.75	105.51	110.60	115.29	119.62	123.60	127.28	130.66	133.77	136.63	139.26	141.66	143.86	149.38	155.57	158.86	159.88
8.00	105.26	110.11	114.57	118.67	122.45	125.91	129.10	132.02	134.70	137.15	139.39	141.43	146.53	152.21	155.19	156.10
8.25	105.02	109.63	113.86	117.74	121.30	124.56	127.55	130.29	132.79	135.08	137.16	139.06	143.77	148.96	151.65	152.46
8.50	104.77	109.14	113.15	116.81	120.17	123.23	126.04	128.59	130.93	133.05	134.99	136.74	141.08	145.81	148.24	148.97
8.75	104.53	108.66	112.44	115.90	119.05	121.92	124.54	126.92	129.09	131.07	132.86	134.48	138.46	142.77	144.95	145.60
9.00	104.28	108.19	111.75	114.99	117.94	120.62	123.07	125.28	127.30	129.12	130.77	132.27	135.92	139.82	141.78	142.35
9.25	104.04	107.71	111.05	114.09	116.84	119.35	121.61	123.67	125.53	127.21	128.73	130.10	133.44	136.97	138.72	139.23
9.50	103.80	107.24	110.37	113.20	115.76	118.08	120.18	122.08	123.80	125.35	126.74	127.99	131.03	134.22	135.77	136.22
9.75	103.56	106.77	109.68	112.31	114.69	116.84	118.78	120.52	122.10	123.51	124.79	125.93	128.68	131.54	132.93	133.32
10.00	103.31	106.31	109.00	111.44	113.63	115.61	117.39	118.99	120.43	121.72	122.88	123.91	126.40	128.96	130.18	130.52
10.25	103.07	105.84	108.33	110.57	112.59	114.40	116.02	117.48	118.79	119.96	121.01	121.94	124.17	126.45	127.52	127.82
10.50	102.83	105.38	107.66	109.71	111.55	113.20	114.68	116.00	117.18	118.24	119.18	120.02	122.01	124.02	124.96	125.22
10.75	102.59	104.92	107.00	108.86	110.53	112.02	113.35	114.54	115.60	116.55	117.39	118.13	119.90	121.67	122.48	122.70
11.00	102.35	104.46	106.34	108.02	109.52	110.85	112.04	113.11	114.05	114.89	115.63	116.29	117.85	119.39	120.09	120.28
11.25	102.12	104.00	105.68	107.18	108.52	109.70	110.76	111.70	112.53	113.26	113.92	114.49	115.85	117.18	117.77	117.93
11.50	101.88	103.55	105.03	106.35	107.53	108.57	109.49	110.31	111.03	111.67	112.24	112.74	113.90	115.03	115.53	115.66
11.75	101.64	103.10	104.39	105.53	106.55	107.45	108.24	108.94	109.56	110.11	110.59	111.02	112.00	112.95	113.37	113.47
12.00	101.41	102.65	103.75	104.72	105.58	106.34	107.01	107.60	108.12	108.58	108.98	109.34	110.15	110.93	111.27	111.36
12.25	101.17	102.20	103.11	103.92	104.63	105.25	105.80	106.28	106.71	107.08	107.41	107.69	108.35	108.97	109.24	109.31
12.50	100.93	101.76	102.48	103.12	103.68	104.17	104.60	104.98	105.32	105.61	105.86	106.08	106.59	107.07	107.27	107.32
12.75	100.70	101.31	101.85	102.33	102.74	103.11	103.43	103.71	103.95	104.16	104.35	104.51	104.88	105.22	105.37	105.40
13.00	100.47	100.87	101.23	101.55	101.82	102.06	102.27	102.45	102.61	102.75	102.87	102.98	103.21	103.43	103.52	103.54
13.25	100.23	100.44	100.61	100.77	100.90	101.02	101.13	101.22	101.29	101.36	101.42	101.47	101.59	101.69	101.73	101.74
13.50	100.00	100.00	100.00	100.00	100.00	100.00	100.00	100.00	100.00	100.00	100.00	100.00	100.00	100.00	100.00	100.00
13.75	99.77	99.57	99.39	99.24	99.11	98.99	98.89	98.80	98.73	98.66	98.61	98.56	98.45	98.36	98.32	98.31
14.00	99.54	99.13	98.79	98.48	98.22	97.99	97.80	97.63	97.48	97.36	97.25	97.15	96.94	96.76	96.69	96.67
14.25	99.31	98.70	98.18	97.74	97.35	97.01	96.72	96.47	96.26	96.07	95.91	95.77	95.47	95.21	95.10	95.08
14.50	99.08	98.28	97.59	96.99	96.48	96.04	95.66	95.33	95.05	94.81	94.60	94.43	94.04	93.70	93.57	93.54
14.75	98.85	97.85	97.00	96.26	95.63	95.08	94.61	94.21	93.87	93.57	93.32	93.11	92.64	92.23	92.07	92.04
15.00	98.62	97.43	96.41	95.53	94.78	94.14	93.58	93.11	92.71	92.36	92.07	91.82	91.27	90.80	90.63	90.59
15.25	98.39	97.01	95.82	94.81	93.94	93.20	92.57	92.03	91.57	91.17	90.84	90.55	89.93	89.41	89.22	89.17
15.50	98.16	96.59	95.24	94.10	93.12	92.28	91.57	90.96	90.44	90.00	89.63	89.32	88.63	88.06	87.85	87.80
15.75	97.93	96.17	94.67	93.39	92.30	91.37	90.58	89.91	89.34	88.86	88.45	88.10	87.36	86.74	86.52	86.47
16.00	97.71	95.76	94.10	92.69	91.49	90.47	89.61	88.88	88.26	87.73	87.29	86.92	86.12	85.46	85.23	85.18
16.25	97.48	95.34	93.53	91.99	90.69	89.58	88.65	87.86	87.19	86.63	86.16	85.76	84.91	84.21	83.97	83.92
16.50	97.25	94.93	92.96	91.30	89.90	88.71	87.71	86.86	86.15	85.55	85.04	84.62	83.72	83.00	82.75	82.69
16.75	97.03	94.52	92.41	90.62	89.11	87.84	86.78	85.88	85.12	84.49	83.95	83.51	82.57	81.81	81.55	81.50
17.00	96.81	94.12	91.85	89.94	88.34	86.99	85.86	84.91	84.11	83.44	82.89	82.42	81.44	80.66	80.40	80.34
17.25	96.58	93.71	91.30	89.27	87.57	86.15	84.95	83.95	83.12	82.42	81.84	81.35	80.34	79.54	79.27	79.21
17.50	96.36	93.31	90.75	88.61	86.82	85.32	84.06	83.02	82.14	81.42	80.81	80.31	79.26	78.44	78.17	78.11
17.75	96.14	92.91	90.21	87.95	86.07	84.50	83.18	82.09	81.18	80.43	79.80	79.28	78.20	77.37	77.10	77.04
18.00	95.91	92.51	89.67	87.30	85.33	83.68	82.32	81.18	80.24	79.46	78.81	78.28	77.17	76.33	76.06	76.00
18.25	95.69	92.11	89.13	86.65	84.59	82.88	81.47	80.29	79.32	78.51	77.85	77.30	76.17	75.31	75.04	74.99
18.50	95.47	91.71	88.60	86.01	83.87	82.09	80.62	79.41	78.41	77.58	76.89	76.33	75.18	74.32	74.05	74.00
18.75	95.25	91.32	88.07	85.38	83.15	81.31	79.79	78.54	77.51	76.66	75.96	75.39	74.22	73.35	73.08	73.03
19.00	95.03	90.93	87.54	84.75	82.44	80.54	78.98	77.69	76.63	75.76	75.05	74.46	73.28	72.41	72.14	72.09
20.00	94.16	89.38	85.48	82.29	79.68	77.56	75.82	74.41	73.26	72.32	71.56	70.95	69.72	68.85	68.59	68.55
25.00	89.93	82.09	75.98	71.23	67.54	64.67	62.44	60.72	59.38	58.34	57.54	56.92	55.79	55.12	54.97	54.95
30.00	85.91	75.46	67.72	61.98	57.74	54.59	52.27	50.55	49.28	48.35	47.66	47.16	46.31	45.89	45.82	45.81

PREPAYMENT MORTGAGE YIELD, 30 YEAR TERM

13.50 %

Description: This table shows the yield to prepayment of a monthly payment mortgage purchased at a price in the index.

Example: The yield to prepayment in 10 years of a 13.50 %, 30 year mortgage at a price of 104.00 is 12.77 %.

30 YEAR MORTGAGE PREPAID IN

PRICE	1 yr	2 yr	3 yr	4 yr	5 yr	6 yr	7 yr	8 yr	9 yr	10 yr	11 yr	12 yr	15 yr	20 yr	25 yr	30 yr
140	–	–	–	2.84	4.48	5.57	6.33	6.89	7.32	7.66	7.93	8.15	8.60	8.98	9.14	9.18
135	–	–	1.51	3.96	5.43	6.39	7.07	7.57	7.96	8.25	8.49	8.69	9.09	9.42	9.56	9.60
130	–	–	2.99	5.14	6.41	7.26	7.85	8.29	8.62	8.88	9.09	9.26	9.60	9.89	10.01	10.04
125	–	–	4.53	6.36	7.45	8.16	8.67	9.04	9.32	9.54	9.72	9.86	10.15	10.39	10.49	10.52
120	–	3.14	6.15	7.64	8.53	9.12	9.53	9.83	10.06	10.24	10.38	10.50	10.73	10.93	11.00	11.02
119	–	3.61	6.48	7.91	8.76	9.31	9.71	9.99	10.21	10.38	10.52	10.63	10.85	11.04	11.11	11.13
118	–	4.08	6.82	8.17	8.98	9.51	9.88	10.16	10.37	10.53	10.66	10.76	10.98	11.15	11.22	11.24
117	–	4.56	7.16	8.44	9.21	9.71	10.07	10.33	10.52	10.68	10.80	10.90	11.10	11.27	11.33	11.35
116	–	5.05	7.50	8.72	9.44	9.92	10.25	10.49	10.68	10.83	10.94	11.04	11.23	11.38	11.44	11.46
115	–	5.53	7.84	8.99	9.67	10.12	10.43	10.67	10.84	10.98	11.09	11.17	11.35	11.50	11.56	11.57
114	–	6.03	8.19	9.27	9.91	10.33	10.62	10.84	11.00	11.13	11.23	11.31	11.48	11.62	11.67	11.68
113	–	6.53	8.55	9.55	10.15	10.54	10.81	11.01	11.17	11.29	11.38	11.46	11.61	11.74	11.79	11.80
112	1.39	7.03	8.90	9.83	10.39	10.75	11.00	11.19	11.33	11.44	11.53	11.60	11.75	11.86	11.91	11.92
111	2.34	7.54	9.26	10.12	10.63	10.96	11.20	11.37	11.50	11.60	11.68	11.75	11.88	11.99	12.03	12.04
110	3.30	8.05	9.63	10.41	10.88	11.18	11.39	11.55	11.67	11.76	11.84	11.90	12.02	12.11	12.15	12.16
109	4.27	8.57	10.00	10.70	11.12	11.40	11.59	11.73	11.84	11.93	11.99	12.05	12.15	12.24	12.27	12.28
108	5.26	9.09	10.37	11.00	11.38	11.62	11.79	11.92	12.02	12.09	12.15	12.20	12.29	12.37	12.40	12.41
107	6.25	9.62	10.74	11.30	11.63	11.85	12.00	12.11	12.19	12.26	12.31	12.35	12.44	12.50	12.53	12.54
106	7.25	10.16	11.12	11.60	11.89	12.07	12.20	12.30	12.37	12.43	12.47	12.51	12.58	12.64	12.66	12.67
105	8.26	10.70	11.51	11.91	12.15	12.30	12.41	12.49	12.55	12.60	12.64	12.67	12.73	12.78	12.79	12.80
104	9.29	11.25	11.90	12.22	12.41	12.54	12.62	12.69	12.74	12.77	12.80	12.83	12.88	12.92	12.93	12.93
103.75	9.54	11.38	11.99	12.30	12.48	12.59	12.68	12.74	12.78	12.82	12.85	12.87	12.91	12.95	12.96	12.97
103.50	9.80	11.52	12.09	12.38	12.54	12.65	12.73	12.79	12.83	12.86	12.89	12.91	12.95	12.99	13.00	13.00
103.25	10.06	11.66	12.19	12.45	12.61	12.71	12.78	12.84	12.88	12.91	12.93	12.95	12.99	13.02	13.03	13.04
103.00	10.32	11.80	12.29	12.53	12.68	12.77	12.84	12.89	12.92	12.95	12.97	12.99	13.03	13.06	13.07	13.07
102.75	10.58	11.94	12.39	12.61	12.74	12.83	12.89	12.94	12.97	12.99	13.02	13.03	13.07	13.09	13.10	13.10
102.50	10.84	12.08	12.49	12.69	12.81	12.89	12.94	12.99	13.02	13.04	13.06	13.07	13.10	13.13	13.14	13.14
102.25	11.10	12.22	12.59	12.77	12.88	12.95	13.00	13.04	13.06	13.08	13.10	13.11	13.14	13.16	13.17	13.17
102.00	11.37	12.36	12.69	12.85	12.95	13.01	13.05	13.09	13.11	13.13	13.14	13.16	13.18	13.20	13.21	13.21
101.75	11.63	12.50	12.79	12.93	13.01	13.07	13.11	13.14	13.16	13.17	13.19	13.20	13.22	13.24	13.24	13.24
101.50	11.89	12.64	12.89	13.01	13.08	13.13	13.16	13.19	13.21	13.22	13.23	13.24	13.26	13.27	13.28	13.28
101.25	12.16	12.78	12.99	13.09	13.15	13.19	13.22	13.24	13.25	13.27	13.27	13.28	13.30	13.31	13.31	13.32
101.00	12.43	12.92	13.09	13.17	13.22	13.25	13.27	13.29	13.30	13.31	13.32	13.32	13.34	13.35	13.35	13.35
100.75	12.69	13.07	13.19	13.25	13.29	13.31	13.33	13.34	13.35	13.36	13.36	13.37	13.38	13.38	13.39	13.39
100.50	12.96	13.21	13.29	13.33	13.36	13.37	13.38	13.39	13.40	13.40	13.41	13.41	13.42	13.42	13.42	13.42
100.25	13.23	13.35	13.39	13.41	13.43	13.43	13.44	13.44	13.45	13.45	13.45	13.45	13.46	13.46	13.46	13.46
100.00	13.50	13.50	13.50	13.50	13.50	13.50	13.50	13.50	13.50	13.50	13.50	13.50	13.50	13.50	13.50	13.50
99.75	13.76	13.64	13.60	13.58	13.56	13.56	13.55	13.55	13.55	13.54	13.54	13.54	13.54	13.53	13.53	13.53
99.50	14.03	13.78	13.70	13.66	13.63	13.62	13.61	13.60	13.59	13.59	13.58	13.58	13.58	13.57	13.57	13.57
99.25	14.31	13.93	13.80	13.74	13.70	13.68	13.66	13.65	13.64	13.63	13.63	13.62	13.62	13.61	13.61	13.60
99.00	14.58	14.07	13.91	13.82	13.77	13.74	13.72	13.70	13.69	13.68	13.67	13.67	13.66	13.65	13.64	13.64
98.75	14.85	14.22	14.01	13.91	13.85	13.81	13.78	13.76	13.74	13.73	13.72	13.71	13.70	13.68	13.68	13.68
98.50	15.12	14.36	14.11	13.99	13.92	13.87	13.83	13.81	13.79	13.78	13.76	13.76	13.74	13.72	13.72	13.72
98.25	15.40	14.51	14.22	14.07	13.99	13.93	13.89	13.86	13.84	13.82	13.81	13.80	13.78	13.76	13.76	13.75
98.00	15.67	14.66	14.32	14.16	14.06	13.99	13.95	13.92	13.89	13.87	13.86	13.84	13.82	13.80	13.79	13.79
97.75	15.95	14.80	14.43	14.24	14.13	14.06	14.01	13.97	13.94	13.92	13.90	13.89	13.86	13.84	13.83	13.83
97.50	16.22	14.95	14.53	14.32	14.20	14.12	14.06	14.02	13.99	13.97	13.95	13.93	13.90	13.88	13.87	13.87
97.25	16.50	15.10	14.64	14.41	14.27	14.18	14.12	14.08	14.04	14.02	13.99	13.98	13.94	13.92	13.91	13.91
97	16.78	15.25	14.74	14.49	14.34	14.25	14.18	14.13	14.09	14.06	14.04	14.02	13.99	13.96	13.95	13.94
96	17.90	15.85	15.17	14.83	14.64	14.51	14.41	14.35	14.30	14.26	14.23	14.20	14.15	14.12	14.10	14.10
95	19.03	16.45	15.60	15.18	14.93	14.77	14.65	14.57	14.51	14.46	14.42	14.39	14.33	14.28	14.26	14.26
94	20.18	17.07	16.04	15.53	15.23	15.03	14.89	14.79	14.72	14.66	14.61	14.58	14.50	14.44	14.42	14.42
93	21.34	17.69	16.48	15.88	15.53	15.30	15.14	15.02	14.93	14.86	14.81	14.77	14.68	14.61	14.59	14.58
92	22.51	18.31	16.93	16.24	15.84	15.57	15.39	15.25	15.15	15.07	15.01	14.96	14.86	14.78	14.76	14.75
91	23.70	18.95	17.38	16.61	16.15	15.85	15.64	15.49	15.37	15.28	15.21	15.16	15.04	14.96	14.93	14.92
90	24.91	19.59	17.84	16.97	16.46	16.13	15.89	15.72	15.60	15.50	15.42	15.36	15.23	15.14	15.11	15.10
89	26.13	20.25	18.31	17.35	16.78	16.41	16.15	15.97	15.82	15.71	15.63	15.56	15.42	15.32	15.28	15.28
88	27.36	20.91	18.78	17.73	17.11	16.70	16.42	16.21	16.06	15.94	15.84	15.77	15.62	15.51	15.47	15.46
87	28.61	21.57	19.25	18.11	17.43	16.99	16.68	16.46	16.29	16.16	16.06	15.98	15.82	15.70	15.65	15.64
86	29.88	22.25	19.74	18.50	17.77	17.29	16.96	16.71	16.53	16.39	16.28	16.19	16.02	15.89	15.84	15.84
85	31.17	22.94	20.23	18.89	18.11	17.59	17.23	16.97	16.77	16.62	16.51	16.41	16.23	16.09	16.04	16.03
80	37.86	26.52	22.79	20.96	19.88	19.17	18.68	18.33	18.06	17.86	17.70	17.57	17.32	17.14	17.08	17.07
75	45.04	30.36	25.55	23.19	21.80	20.89	20.26	19.81	19.47	19.21	19.01	18.85	18.54	18.32	18.25	18.24
70	52.79	34.52	28.55	25.61	23.89	22.77	22.00	21.44	21.03	20.71	20.47	20.28	19.91	19.66	19.59	19.57
65	61.20	39.03	31.81	28.27	26.19	24.85	23.93	23.26	22.77	22.40	22.11	21.89	21.47	21.19	21.11	21.10
60	70.39	43.97	35.39	31.19	28.74	27.16	26.08	25.30	24.73	24.30	23.98	23.72	23.26	22.97	22.89	22.88
55	80.50	49.42	39.36	34.45	31.60	29.77	28.52	27.63	26.98	26.49	26.13	25.85	25.35	25.05	24.98	24.97
50	91.73	55.49	43.81	38.13	34.84	32.74	31.32	30.31	29.59	29.05	28.65	28.35	27.83	27.55	27.48	27.48

Description: This table shows the price to pay for a monthly payment loan, at a yield rate and assuming prepayment.

Example: The price of a 13.75 %, 30 year mortgage to yield 8.00 %, if prepaid in 6 years, is $ 127.10.

30 YEAR MORTGAGE PREPAID IN

YIELD	1 yr	2 yr	3 yr	4 yr	5 yr	6 yr	7 yr	8 yr	9 yr	10 yr	11 yr	12 yr	15 yr	20 yr	25 yr	30 yr
0.00	113.73	127.43	141.09	154.70	168.26	181.75	195.17	208.51	221.76	234.89	247.91	260.78	298.32	355.40	399.89	419.44
1.00	112.67	125.18	137.52	149.70	161.72	173.55	185.21	196.68	207.96	219.03	229.89	240.53	270.94	315.39	348.37	362.24
2.00	111.61	122.96	134.06	144.89	155.47	165.79	175.86	185.66	195.20	204.48	213.49	222.23	246.71	281.12	305.44	315.22
3.00	110.57	120.79	130.69	140.26	149.51	158.44	167.07	175.39	183.41	191.12	198.54	205.67	225.24	251.70	269.50	276.35
4.00	109.53	118.67	127.42	135.79	143.81	151.48	158.81	165.81	172.49	178.85	184.91	190.67	206.19	226.36	239.29	244.05
4.25	109.27	118.14	126.61	134.71	142.43	149.80	156.83	163.52	169.89	175.95	181.70	187.15	201.77	220.59	232.50	236.84
4.50	109.02	117.62	125.82	133.63	141.06	148.14	154.87	161.27	167.34	173.10	178.55	183.71	197.45	215.02	226.00	229.95
4.75	108.76	117.10	125.02	132.56	139.71	146.50	152.95	159.05	164.84	170.31	175.48	180.35	193.30	209.65	219.76	223.35
5.00	108.51	116.58	124.24	131.50	138.37	144.89	151.05	156.88	162.38	167.58	172.47	177.08	189.25	204.48	213.77	217.04
5.25	108.25	116.07	123.46	130.45	137.05	143.29	149.18	154.74	159.97	164.90	169.53	173.88	185.32	199.48	208.02	210.99
5.50	108.00	115.55	122.68	129.41	135.75	141.72	147.35	152.64	157.61	162.28	166.66	170.76	181.50	194.66	202.50	205.20
5.75	107.75	115.04	121.91	128.38	134.46	140.17	145.54	150.57	155.29	159.72	163.85	167.72	177.78	190.01	197.20	199.65
6.00	107.50	114.54	121.15	127.36	133.18	138.64	143.75	148.54	153.02	157.20	161.11	164.75	174.17	185.52	192.11	194.33
6.25	107.24	114.03	120.39	126.35	131.92	137.13	142.00	146.55	150.79	154.74	158.42	161.84	170.67	181.18	187.22	189.23
6.50	106.99	113.53	119.64	125.34	130.67	135.64	140.27	144.58	148.60	152.33	155.80	159.01	167.26	176.99	182.51	184.33
6.75	106.74	113.03	118.89	124.35	129.44	134.17	138.57	142.66	146.45	149.97	153.23	156.25	163.95	172.95	177.99	179.64
7.00	106.49	112.53	118.15	123.37	128.22	132.72	136.89	140.76	144.34	147.66	150.72	153.54	160.73	169.04	173.64	175.13
7.25	106.24	112.04	117.41	122.39	127.01	131.29	135.24	138.90	142.28	145.39	148.26	150.91	157.59	165.26	169.46	170.79
7.50	106.00	111.55	116.68	121.43	125.82	129.87	133.61	137.07	140.25	143.17	145.86	148.33	154.55	161.61	165.43	166.63
7.75	105.75	111.06	115.96	120.47	124.64	128.48	132.01	135.26	138.25	141.00	143.51	145.82	151.59	158.09	161.55	162.63
8.00	105.50	110.57	115.23	119.53	123.47	127.10	130.44	133.49	136.30	138.87	141.21	143.36	148.71	154.67	157.82	158.79
8.25	105.26	110.08	114.52	118.59	122.32	125.75	128.88	131.75	134.38	136.78	138.97	140.96	145.91	151.37	154.22	155.09
8.50	105.01	109.60	113.81	117.66	121.18	124.41	127.35	130.04	132.50	134.73	136.77	138.62	143.19	148.18	150.75	151.53
8.75	104.77	109.12	113.10	116.74	120.06	123.08	125.84	128.36	130.65	132.73	134.62	136.33	140.54	145.09	147.41	148.10
9.00	104.52	108.64	112.40	115.83	118.94	121.78	124.36	126.70	128.83	130.76	132.51	134.09	137.96	142.11	144.19	144.80
9.25	104.28	108.17	111.71	114.92	117.84	120.49	122.90	125.08	127.05	128.84	130.45	131.91	135.45	139.21	141.08	141.62
9.50	104.03	107.70	111.02	114.03	116.75	119.22	121.46	123.48	125.30	126.95	128.43	129.77	133.01	136.41	138.08	138.56
9.75	103.79	107.22	110.33	113.14	115.68	117.97	120.04	121.91	123.59	125.10	126.46	127.68	130.63	133.70	135.19	135.61
10.00	103.55	106.76	109.65	112.26	114.61	116.73	118.64	120.36	121.90	123.29	124.53	125.64	128.32	131.07	132.39	132.77
10.25	103.31	106.29	108.97	111.39	113.56	115.51	117.26	118.84	120.25	121.51	122.64	123.65	126.06	128.53	129.70	130.02
10.50	103.07	105.83	108.30	110.52	112.52	114.31	115.91	117.34	118.62	119.77	120.79	121.70	123.87	126.06	127.09	127.37
10.75	102.83	105.36	107.64	109.67	111.49	113.12	114.57	115.87	117.03	118.06	118.98	119.80	121.73	123.67	124.57	124.81
11.00	102.59	104.91	106.97	108.82	110.47	111.94	113.26	114.42	115.47	116.39	117.21	117.94	119.65	121.36	122.13	122.34
11.25	102.35	104.45	106.32	107.98	109.47	110.79	111.96	113.00	113.93	114.75	115.48	116.12	117.63	119.11	119.78	119.96
11.50	102.11	103.99	105.67	107.15	108.47	109.64	110.68	111.60	112.42	113.14	113.78	114.34	115.65	116.93	117.50	117.65
11.75	101.88	103.54	105.02	106.33	107.49	108.51	109.42	110.23	110.94	111.56	112.12	112.60	113.73	114.82	115.30	115.43
12.00	101.64	103.09	104.37	105.51	106.51	107.40	108.18	108.87	109.48	110.02	110.49	110.90	111.86	112.77	113.17	113.27
12.25	101.40	102.64	103.74	104.70	105.55	106.30	106.96	107.54	108.05	108.50	108.89	109.24	110.03	110.78	111.10	111.19
12.50	101.17	102.20	103.10	103.90	104.60	105.22	105.76	106.23	106.65	107.01	107.33	107.61	108.25	108.85	109.10	109.17
12.75	100.93	101.75	102.47	103.11	103.66	104.15	104.57	104.95	105.27	105.56	105.81	106.02	106.52	106.98	107.17	107.22
13.00	100.70	101.31	101.85	102.32	102.73	103.09	103.40	103.68	103.92	104.13	104.31	104.47	104.82	105.16	105.29	105.33
13.25	100.47	100.87	101.23	101.54	101.81	102.05	102.25	102.43	102.59	102.72	102.84	102.94	103.18	103.39	103.47	103.49
13.50	100.23	100.44	100.61	100.77	100.90	101.02	101.12	101.21	101.28	101.35	101.41	101.46	101.57	101.67	101.71	101.72
13.75	100.00	100.00	100.00	100.00	100.00	100.00	100.00	100.00	100.00	100.00	100.00	100.00	100.00	100.00	100.00	100.00
14.00	99.77	99.57	99.39	99.24	99.11	99.00	98.90	98.81	98.74	98.68	98.62	98.58	98.47	98.38	98.34	98.33
14.25	99.54	99.14	98.79	98.49	98.23	98.01	97.81	97.65	97.50	97.38	97.27	97.18	96.98	96.80	96.73	96.71
14.50	99.31	98.71	98.19	97.74	97.36	97.03	96.74	96.50	96.29	96.11	95.95	95.82	95.52	95.27	95.17	95.15
14.75	99.08	98.28	97.60	97.01	96.50	96.06	95.69	95.37	95.09	94.86	94.65	94.48	94.10	93.78	93.65	93.62
15.00	98.85	97.86	97.01	96.28	95.65	95.11	94.65	94.26	93.92	93.63	93.38	93.17	92.72	92.32	92.18	92.14
15.25	98.62	97.43	96.42	95.55	94.81	94.17	93.63	93.16	92.77	92.43	92.14	91.90	91.36	90.91	90.75	90.71
15.50	98.39	97.01	95.84	94.83	93.97	93.24	92.62	92.09	91.63	91.25	90.92	90.64	90.04	89.54	89.35	89.31
15.75	98.16	96.60	95.26	94.12	93.15	92.33	91.62	91.03	90.52	90.09	89.73	89.42	88.75	88.20	88.00	87.96
16.00	97.94	96.18	94.69	93.42	92.34	91.42	90.64	89.98	89.43	88.95	88.55	88.22	87.50	86.90	86.69	86.64
16.25	97.71	95.77	94.12	92.72	91.53	90.53	89.68	88.96	88.35	87.84	87.41	87.04	86.27	85.63	85.41	85.36
16.50	97.48	95.35	93.55	92.02	90.74	89.65	88.73	87.95	87.30	86.74	86.28	85.89	85.07	84.40	84.16	84.11
16.75	97.26	94.94	92.99	91.34	89.95	88.78	87.79	86.96	86.26	85.67	85.18	84.77	83.89	83.19	82.95	82.90
17.00	97.03	94.53	92.43	90.66	89.17	87.92	86.86	85.98	85.24	84.62	84.10	83.66	82.75	82.02	81.77	81.72
17.25	96.81	94.13	91.88	89.99	88.40	87.07	85.95	85.02	84.24	83.58	83.04	82.58	81.63	80.88	80.63	80.58
17.50	96.59	93.72	91.33	89.32	87.64	86.23	85.05	84.07	83.25	82.57	82.00	81.52	80.54	79.77	79.51	79.46
17.75	96.36	93.32	90.78	88.66	86.88	85.40	84.17	83.14	82.28	81.57	80.98	80.49	79.47	78.68	78.42	78.37
18.00	96.14	92.92	90.24	88.00	86.14	84.58	83.29	82.22	81.33	80.59	79.98	79.47	78.42	77.62	77.36	77.31
18.25	95.92	92.52	89.70	87.35	85.40	83.78	82.43	81.32	80.39	79.63	79.00	78.48	77.40	76.59	76.33	76.28
18.50	95.70	92.13	89.16	86.71	84.67	82.98	81.58	80.43	79.47	78.69	78.04	77.50	76.40	75.58	75.32	75.27
18.75	95.48	91.73	88.63	86.07	83.95	82.20	80.75	79.55	78.57	77.76	77.09	76.54	75.43	74.60	74.34	74.29
19.00	95.26	91.34	88.11	85.44	83.23	81.42	79.92	78.69	77.68	76.85	76.17	75.61	74.47	73.64	73.38	73.33
20.00	94.38	89.79	86.03	82.96	80.46	78.41	76.74	75.38	74.27	73.37	72.64	72.04	70.86	70.02	69.77	69.72
25.00	90.15	82.47	76.50	71.85	68.24	65.43	63.25	61.55	60.24	59.22	58.44	57.83	56.72	56.07	55.91	55.89
30.00	86.12	75.83	68.20	62.55	58.37	55.27	52.98	51.28	50.03	49.11	48.43	47.93	47.10	46.68	46.61	46.60

PREPAYMENT MORTGAGE YIELD, 30 YEAR TERM

13.75 %

Description: This table shows the yield to prepayment of a monthly payment mortgage purchased at a price in the index.

Example: The yield to prepayment in 10 years of a 13.75 %, 30 year mortgage at a price of 104.00 is 13.02 %.

30 YEAR MORTGAGE PREPAID IN

PRICE	1 yr	2 yr	3 yr	4 yr	5 yr	6 yr	7 yr	8 yr	9 yr	10 yr	11 yr	12 yr	15 yr	20 yr	25 yr	30 yr
140	–	–	–	3.05	4.69	5.77	6.53	7.10	7.53	7.86	8.13	8.35	8.80	9.18	9.33	9.38
135	–	–	1.72	4.18	5.64	6.60	7.28	7.78	8.16	8.46	8.70	8.89	9.29	9.62	9.76	9.80
130	–	–	3.20	5.35	6.63	7.47	8.06	8.50	8.83	9.09	9.30	9.47	9.81	10.10	10.22	10.25
125	–	1.07	4.75	6.58	7.67	8.38	8.89	9.26	9.54	9.76	9.93	10.08	10.37	10.61	10.70	10.73
120	–	3.37	6.37	7.87	8.76	9.34	9.75	10.05	10.28	10.46	10.60	10.72	10.95	11.15	11.22	11.24
119	–	3.84	6.71	8.14	8.98	9.54	9.93	10.22	10.44	10.61	10.74	10.85	11.07	11.26	11.33	11.35
118	–	4.31	7.05	8.40	9.21	9.74	10.11	10.38	10.59	10.75	10.88	10.99	11.20	11.37	11.44	11.46
117	–	4.79	7.39	8.67	9.44	9.94	10.29	10.55	10.75	10.90	11.03	11.12	11.32	11.49	11.55	11.57
116	–	5.28	7.73	8.95	9.67	10.14	10.48	10.72	10.91	11.05	11.17	11.26	11.45	11.60	11.66	11.68
115	–	5.77	8.08	9.22	9.90	10.35	10.66	10.90	11.07	11.21	11.31	11.40	11.58	11.72	11.78	11.79
114	–	6.26	8.43	9.50	10.14	10.56	10.85	11.07	11.23	11.36	11.46	11.54	11.71	11.84	11.90	11.91
113	–	6.76	8.78	9.78	10.38	10.77	11.04	11.25	11.40	11.52	11.61	11.69	11.84	11.97	12.02	12.03
112	1.63	7.26	9.14	10.07	10.62	10.98	11.24	11.42	11.57	11.68	11.76	11.83	11.98	12.09	12.14	12.15
111	2.58	7.77	9.50	10.36	10.86	11.20	11.43	11.60	11.73	11.84	11.92	11.98	12.11	12.22	12.26	12.27
110	3.54	8.29	9.87	10.65	11.11	11.42	11.63	11.79	11.91	12.00	12.07	12.13	12.25	12.35	12.38	12.39
109	4.51	8.81	10.24	10.94	11.36	11.64	11.83	11.97	12.08	12.16	12.23	12.28	12.39	12.48	12.51	12.52
108	5.50	9.33	10.61	11.24	11.61	11.86	12.03	12.16	12.25	12.33	12.39	12.43	12.53	12.61	12.64	12.64
107	6.49	9.86	10.99	11.54	11.87	12.09	12.24	12.35	12.43	12.50	12.55	12.59	12.67	12.74	12.77	12.77
106	7.49	10.40	11.37	11.84	12.13	12.31	12.44	12.54	12.61	12.67	12.71	12.75	12.82	12.88	12.90	12.90
105	8.51	10.94	11.75	12.15	12.39	12.55	12.65	12.73	12.79	12.84	12.88	12.91	12.97	13.02	13.03	13.04
104	9.53	11.49	12.14	12.46	12.65	12.78	12.87	12.93	12.98	13.02	13.05	13.07	13.12	13.16	13.17	13.18
103.75	9.79	11.63	12.24	12.54	12.72	12.84	12.92	12.98	13.03	13.06	13.09	13.11	13.16	13.19	13.21	13.21
103.50	10.05	11.77	12.34	12.62	12.79	12.90	12.97	13.03	13.07	13.11	13.13	13.15	13.20	13.23	13.24	13.24
103.25	10.31	11.91	12.44	12.70	12.85	12.96	13.03	13.08	13.12	13.15	13.18	13.19	13.23	13.26	13.28	13.28
103.00	10.57	12.05	12.54	12.78	12.92	13.02	13.08	13.13	13.17	13.20	13.22	13.24	13.27	13.30	13.31	13.31
102.75	10.83	12.19	12.63	12.86	12.99	13.08	13.14	13.18	13.21	13.24	13.26	13.28	13.31	13.34	13.35	13.35
102.50	11.09	12.32	12.73	12.94	13.06	13.14	13.19	13.23	13.26	13.29	13.30	13.32	13.35	13.37	13.38	13.38
102.25	11.35	12.47	12.83	13.02	13.12	13.20	13.25	13.28	13.31	13.33	13.35	13.36	13.39	13.41	13.42	13.42
102.00	11.61	12.61	12.93	13.10	13.19	13.26	13.30	13.33	13.36	13.38	13.39	13.40	13.43	13.45	13.45	13.46
101.75	11.88	12.75	13.03	13.18	13.26	13.32	13.36	13.38	13.41	13.42	13.43	13.45	13.47	13.48	13.49	13.49
101.50	12.14	12.89	13.14	13.26	13.33	13.38	13.41	13.43	13.45	13.47	13.48	13.49	13.51	13.52	13.53	13.53
101.25	12.41	13.03	13.24	13.34	13.40	13.44	13.47	13.49	13.50	13.51	13.52	13.53	13.55	13.56	13.56	13.56
101.00	12.67	13.17	13.34	13.42	13.47	13.50	13.52	13.54	13.55	13.56	13.57	13.57	13.58	13.59	13.60	13.60
100.75	12.94	13.31	13.44	13.50	13.54	13.56	13.58	13.59	13.60	13.61	13.61	13.62	13.62	13.63	13.63	13.64
100.50	13.21	13.46	13.54	13.58	13.61	13.62	13.63	13.64	13.65	13.65	13.66	13.66	13.66	13.67	13.67	13.67
100.25	13.48	13.60	13.64	13.66	13.68	13.68	13.69	13.69	13.70	13.70	13.70	13.70	13.70	13.71	13.71	13.71
100.00	13.75	13.75	13.75	13.75	13.75	13.75	13.75	13.75	13.75	13.75	13.75	13.75	13.75	13.75	13.75	13.75
99.75	14.01	13.89	13.85	13.83	13.81	13.81	13.80	13.80	13.79	13.79	13.79	13.79	13.79	13.78	13.78	13.78
99.50	14.29	14.03	13.95	13.91	13.89	13.87	13.86	13.85	13.84	13.84	13.84	13.83	13.83	13.82	13.82	13.82
99.25	14.56	14.18	14.05	13.99	13.96	13.93	13.91	13.90	13.89	13.89	13.88	13.88	13.87	13.86	13.86	13.86
99.00	14.83	14.32	14.16	14.08	14.03	13.99	13.97	13.96	13.94	13.93	13.93	13.92	13.91	13.90	13.89	13.89
98.75	15.10	14.47	14.26	14.16	14.10	14.06	14.03	14.01	13.99	13.98	13.97	13.96	13.95	13.94	13.93	13.93
98.50	15.37	14.62	14.37	14.24	14.17	14.12	14.09	14.06	14.04	14.03	14.02	14.01	13.99	13.98	13.97	13.97
98.25	15.65	14.76	14.47	14.33	14.24	14.18	14.14	14.12	14.09	14.08	14.06	14.05	14.03	14.01	14.01	14.01
98.00	15.92	14.91	14.58	14.41	14.31	14.25	14.20	14.17	14.14	14.12	14.11	14.10	14.07	14.05	14.05	14.05
97.75	16.20	15.06	14.68	14.49	14.38	14.31	14.26	14.22	14.19	14.17	14.16	14.14	14.11	14.09	14.09	14.08
97.50	16.48	15.21	14.79	14.58	14.45	14.37	14.32	14.28	14.25	14.22	14.20	14.19	14.16	14.13	14.12	14.12
97.25	16.75	15.35	14.89	14.66	14.53	14.44	14.38	14.33	14.30	14.27	14.25	14.23	14.20	14.17	14.16	14.16
97	17.03	15.50	15.00	14.75	14.60	14.50	14.43	14.39	14.35	14.32	14.30	14.28	14.24	14.21	14.20	14.20
96	18.15	16.10	15.43	15.09	14.89	14.76	14.67	14.60	14.55	14.52	14.49	14.46	14.41	14.37	14.36	14.36
95	19.29	16.71	15.86	15.44	15.19	15.02	14.91	14.83	14.76	14.72	14.68	14.65	14.59	14.54	14.52	14.52
94	20.44	17.32	16.30	15.79	15.49	15.29	15.15	15.05	14.98	14.92	14.87	14.84	14.76	14.71	14.69	14.68
93	21.60	17.95	16.74	16.14	15.79	15.56	15.40	15.28	15.19	15.13	15.07	15.03	14.94	14.88	14.85	14.85
92	22.78	18.58	17.19	16.50	16.10	15.83	15.65	15.52	15.41	15.34	15.27	15.22	15.13	15.05	15.03	15.02
91	23.97	19.21	17.64	16.87	16.41	16.11	15.90	15.75	15.64	15.55	15.48	15.42	15.31	15.23	15.20	15.19
90	25.17	19.86	18.11	17.24	16.73	16.39	16.16	15.99	15.86	15.76	15.69	15.63	15.50	15.41	15.38	15.37
89	26.39	20.51	18.57	17.61	17.05	16.68	16.42	16.23	16.09	15.98	15.90	15.83	15.70	15.60	15.56	15.55
88	27.63	21.17	19.05	18.00	17.38	16.97	16.69	16.48	16.33	16.21	16.12	16.04	15.89	15.78	15.75	15.74
87	28.88	21.84	19.53	18.38	17.71	17.26	16.96	16.73	16.57	16.44	16.33	16.25	16.10	15.98	15.93	15.93
86	30.15	22.52	20.01	18.77	18.04	17.56	17.23	16.99	16.81	16.67	16.56	16.47	16.30	16.17	16.13	16.12
85	31.44	23.21	20.50	19.17	18.38	17.87	17.51	17.25	17.05	16.90	16.79	16.69	16.51	16.37	16.33	16.32
80	38.14	26.80	23.08	21.24	20.16	19.46	18.97	18.62	18.35	18.15	17.99	17.86	17.62	17.44	17.38	17.37
75	45.33	30.66	25.85	23.49	22.10	21.19	20.57	20.11	19.78	19.52	19.32	19.16	18.86	18.64	18.58	18.56
70	53.09	34.82	28.85	25.92	24.20	23.09	22.32	21.76	21.35	21.04	20.80	20.61	20.25	20.00	19.93	19.92
65	61.52	39.35	32.13	28.59	26.52	25.18	24.26	23.60	23.11	22.74	22.46	22.24	21.83	21.56	21.48	21.47
60	70.72	44.31	35.73	31.54	29.09	27.52	26.44	25.66	25.10	24.67	24.35	24.10	23.64	23.36	23.29	23.27
55	80.85	49.77	39.72	34.82	31.97	30.14	28.90	28.01	27.37	26.89	26.53	26.26	25.77	25.48	25.41	25.40
50	92.10	55.87	44.19	38.52	35.24	33.15	31.73	30.73	30.01	29.48	29.09	28.80	28.29	28.01	27.96	27.95

PREPAYMENT MORTGAGE PRICE

14.00 %

Description: This table shows the price to pay for a monthly payment loan, at a yield rate and assuming prepayment.

Example: The price of a 14.00 %, 30 year mortgage to yield 8.00 %, if prepaid in 6 years, is $ 128.29.

30 YEAR MORTGAGE PREPAID IN

YIELD	1 yr	2 yr	3 yr	4 yr	5 yr	6 yr	7 yr	8 yr	9 yr	10 yr	11 yr	12 yr	15 yr	20 yr	25 yr	30 yr
0.00	113.99	127.94	141.85	155.71	169.52	183.27	196.96	210.56	224.07	237.47	250.75	263.89	302.25	360.68	406.38	426.55
1.00	112.92	125.67	138.27	150.69	162.95	175.03	186.93	198.64	210.16	221.47	232.57	243.44	274.56	320.12	354.06	368.39
2.00	111.86	123.45	134.79	145.86	156.67	167.22	177.51	187.54	197.30	206.80	216.02	224.96	250.06	285.39	310.45	320.57
3.00	110.81	121.28	131.41	141.21	150.68	159.83	168.67	177.19	185.41	193.32	200.93	208.24	228.34	255.56	273.94	281.04
4.00	109.78	119.15	128.12	136.72	144.95	152.83	160.35	167.54	174.40	180.94	187.17	193.09	209.06	229.86	243.24	248.18
4.25	109.52	118.62	127.32	135.63	143.56	151.13	158.35	165.23	171.78	178.01	183.92	189.53	204.59	224.01	236.35	240.86
4.50	109.26	118.10	126.52	134.54	142.19	149.46	156.38	162.96	169.21	175.13	180.75	186.06	200.24	218.37	229.74	233.85
4.75	109.01	117.58	125.72	133.47	140.83	147.82	154.45	160.73	166.69	172.32	177.64	182.67	196.02	212.92	223.40	227.14
5.00	108.75	117.06	124.94	132.41	139.49	146.19	152.54	158.54	164.21	169.56	174.61	179.36	191.93	207.67	217.31	220.72
5.25	108.50	116.54	124.15	131.35	138.16	144.59	150.66	156.38	161.78	166.86	171.64	176.13	187.94	202.60	211.47	214.57
5.50	108.24	116.03	123.37	130.31	136.84	143.00	148.81	154.27	159.40	164.22	168.74	172.98	184.08	197.71	205.86	208.68
5.75	107.99	115.52	122.60	129.27	135.55	141.44	146.98	152.18	157.06	161.63	165.91	169.90	180.32	192.99	200.48	203.04
6.00	107.74	115.01	121.84	128.25	134.26	139.90	145.19	150.14	154.77	159.10	163.14	166.90	176.67	188.44	195.31	197.63
6.25	107.49	114.50	121.08	127.23	132.99	138.38	143.42	148.13	152.52	156.61	160.42	163.97	173.12	184.04	190.33	192.44
6.50	107.24	114.00	120.32	126.23	131.74	136.88	141.68	146.15	150.31	154.18	157.77	161.11	169.67	179.79	185.55	187.46
6.75	106.98	113.50	119.57	125.23	130.50	135.40	139.97	144.21	148.14	151.80	155.18	158.31	166.31	175.69	180.96	182.68
7.00	106.73	113.00	118.83	124.24	129.27	133.94	138.28	142.30	146.02	149.46	152.64	155.58	163.05	171.72	176.54	178.10
7.25	106.49	112.50	118.09	123.26	128.06	132.50	136.61	140.42	143.93	147.17	150.16	152.92	159.88	167.89	172.28	173.69
7.50	106.24	112.01	117.35	122.29	126.86	131.08	134.98	138.57	141.88	144.93	147.74	150.31	156.80	164.19	168.19	169.46
7.75	105.99	111.52	116.62	121.33	125.68	129.68	133.36	136.76	139.87	142.74	145.36	147.77	153.81	160.61	164.25	165.39
8.00	105.74	111.03	115.90	120.38	124.50	128.29	131.77	134.97	137.90	140.59	143.04	145.29	150.89	157.15	160.45	161.48
8.25	105.50	110.54	115.18	119.44	123.35	126.93	130.21	133.22	135.97	138.48	140.77	142.86	148.06	153.80	156.80	157.72
8.50	105.25	110.06	114.47	118.51	122.20	125.58	128.67	131.49	134.07	136.41	138.55	140.49	145.30	150.56	153.28	154.10
8.75	105.00	109.58	113.76	117.58	121.07	124.25	127.15	129.79	132.20	134.39	136.38	138.18	142.61	147.42	149.88	150.61
9.00	104.76	109.10	113.06	116.66	119.95	122.94	125.66	128.13	130.37	132.41	134.25	135.92	140.00	144.39	146.60	147.26
9.25	104.52	108.62	112.36	115.75	118.84	121.64	124.18	126.49	128.57	130.46	132.17	133.71	137.46	141.46	143.44	144.03
9.50	104.27	108.15	111.67	114.85	117.74	120.36	122.73	124.87	126.81	128.56	130.13	131.55	134.99	138.61	140.40	140.91
9.75	104.03	107.68	110.98	113.96	116.66	119.10	121.30	123.29	125.08	126.69	128.14	129.44	132.58	135.86	137.46	137.91
10.00	103.79	107.21	110.29	113.08	115.59	117.86	119.89	121.73	123.38	124.86	126.19	127.38	130.24	133.20	134.62	135.02
10.25	103.55	106.74	109.62	112.20	114.53	116.63	118.51	120.19	121.71	123.07	124.28	125.36	127.96	130.61	131.87	132.23
10.50	103.31	106.28	108.94	111.34	113.49	115.41	117.14	118.69	120.07	121.31	122.41	123.39	125.73	128.11	129.22	129.53
10.75	103.07	105.81	108.27	110.48	112.45	114.22	115.79	117.20	118.46	119.58	120.58	121.47	123.57	125.68	126.66	126.93
11.00	102.83	105.35	107.61	109.63	111.43	113.04	114.47	115.75	116.88	117.89	118.79	119.59	121.46	123.33	124.19	124.42
11.25	102.59	104.89	106.95	108.78	110.42	111.87	113.16	114.31	115.33	116.24	117.04	117.75	119.41	121.05	121.79	121.99
11.50	102.35	104.44	106.30	107.95	109.42	110.72	111.87	112.90	113.81	114.61	115.32	115.95	117.41	118.84	119.48	119.65
11.75	102.11	103.98	105.65	107.12	108.43	109.58	110.61	111.51	112.31	113.02	113.64	114.19	115.46	116.70	117.24	117.38
12.00	101.87	103.53	105.00	106.30	107.45	108.46	109.36	110.15	110.84	111.46	112.00	112.47	113.56	114.62	115.07	115.19
12.25	101.64	103.08	104.36	105.49	106.48	107.35	108.13	108.80	109.40	109.93	110.38	110.79	111.71	112.60	112.97	113.07
12.50	101.40	102.64	103.72	104.68	105.52	106.26	106.91	107.48	107.98	108.42	108.81	109.14	109.91	110.63	110.94	111.02
12.75	101.17	102.19	103.09	103.88	104.58	105.18	105.72	106.18	106.59	106.95	107.26	107.53	108.15	108.73	108.97	109.03
13.00	100.93	101.75	102.46	103.09	103.64	104.12	104.54	104.91	105.23	105.51	105.75	105.96	106.44	106.88	107.07	107.11
13.25	100.70	101.31	101.84	102.31	102.72	103.07	103.38	103.65	103.89	104.09	104.27	104.42	104.77	105.09	105.22	105.25
13.50	100.46	100.87	101.22	101.53	101.80	102.03	102.24	102.41	102.57	102.70	102.82	102.91	103.14	103.34	103.43	103.45
13.75	100.23	100.43	100.61	100.76	100.90	101.01	101.11	101.20	101.27	101.34	101.39	101.44	101.55	101.65	101.69	101.70
14.00	100.00	100.00	100.00	100.00	100.00	100.00	100.00	100.00	100.00	100.00	100.00	100.00	100.00	100.00	100.00	100.00
14.25	99.77	99.57	99.39	99.24	99.11	99.00	98.91	98.82	98.75	98.68	98.64	98.59	98.49	98.40	98.36	98.36
14.50	99.54	99.14	98.79	98.50	98.24	98.02	97.83	97.66	97.52	97.40	97.30	97.21	97.01	96.84	96.77	96.76
14.75	99.31	98.71	98.20	97.75	97.37	97.05	96.77	96.52	96.32	96.14	95.99	95.86	95.57	95.33	95.23	95.21
15.00	99.08	98.29	97.60	97.02	96.52	96.09	95.72	95.40	95.13	94.90	94.70	94.54	94.17	93.85	93.73	93.71
15.25	98.85	97.86	97.02	96.29	95.67	95.14	94.69	94.30	93.97	93.69	93.45	93.24	92.80	92.42	92.28	92.25
15.50	98.62	97.44	96.43	95.57	94.83	94.21	93.67	93.21	92.82	92.49	92.21	91.97	91.46	91.02	90.86	90.83
15.75	98.39	97.02	95.85	94.85	94.01	93.28	92.67	92.14	91.70	91.32	91.00	90.73	90.15	89.67	89.49	89.45
16.00	98.16	96.60	95.28	94.15	93.19	92.37	91.68	91.09	90.60	90.17	89.82	89.52	88.88	88.34	88.15	88.11
16.25	97.94	96.19	94.70	93.44	92.38	91.47	90.71	90.06	89.51	89.05	88.66	88.33	87.63	87.05	86.85	86.81
16.50	97.71	95.77	94.14	92.75	91.57	90.58	89.75	89.04	88.44	87.94	87.52	87.17	86.41	85.80	85.59	85.54
16.75	97.49	95.36	93.57	92.06	90.78	89.71	88.80	88.04	87.40	86.86	86.40	86.03	85.22	84.58	84.36	84.31
17.00	97.26	94.95	93.01	91.38	90.00	88.84	87.87	87.05	86.37	85.79	85.31	84.91	84.06	83.39	83.16	83.11
17.25	97.04	94.55	92.46	90.70	89.22	87.99	86.95	86.08	85.35	84.75	84.24	83.81	82.93	82.23	81.99	81.94
17.50	96.81	94.14	91.90	90.03	88.46	87.14	86.04	85.12	84.36	83.72	83.19	82.74	81.82	81.10	80.85	80.81
17.75	96.59	93.74	91.35	89.36	87.70	86.31	85.15	84.18	83.38	82.71	82.15	81.69	80.73	79.99	79.75	79.70
18.00	96.37	93.34	90.81	88.70	86.95	85.49	84.27	83.26	82.42	81.72	81.14	80.66	79.68	78.92	78.67	78.62
18.25	96.15	92.94	90.27	88.05	86.21	84.67	83.40	82.35	81.47	80.75	80.15	79.66	78.64	77.87	77.62	77.57
18.50	95.92	92.54	89.73	87.40	85.47	83.87	82.55	81.45	80.54	79.80	79.18	78.67	77.63	76.84	76.59	76.54
18.75	95.70	92.15	89.20	86.76	84.75	83.08	81.70	80.57	79.63	78.86	78.22	77.70	76.64	75.84	75.59	75.55
19.00	95.48	91.75	88.67	86.13	84.03	82.30	80.87	79.70	78.73	77.94	77.29	76.75	75.67	74.87	74.62	74.57
20.00	94.61	90.20	86.59	83.64	81.23	79.27	77.66	76.35	75.29	74.42	73.72	73.14	72.00	71.19	70.95	70.91
25.00	90.36	82.86	77.02	72.47	68.93	66.18	64.05	62.39	61.10	60.11	59.34	58.74	57.66	57.01	56.86	56.84
30.00	86.34	76.20	68.69	63.12	58.99	55.94	53.68	52.01	50.78	49.87	49.20	48.71	47.88	47.47	47.40	47.39

PREPAYMENT MORTGAGE YIELD, 30 YEAR TERM   14.00 %

Description: This table shows the yield to prepayment of a monthly payment mortgage purchased at a price in the index.

Example: The yield to prepayment in 10 years of a 14.00 %, 30 year mortgage at a price of 104.00 is 13.26 %.

30 YEAR MORTGAGE PREPAID IN

PRICE	1 yr	2 yr	3 yr	4 yr	5 yr	6 yr	7 yr	8 yr	9 yr	10 yr	11 yr	12 yr	15 yr	20 yr	25 yr	30 yr
140	–	–	–	3.26	4.90	5.98	6.74	7.30	7.73	8.06	8.33	8.55	9.00	9.37	9.53	9.57
135	–	–	1.93	4.39	5.85	6.81	7.49	7.99	8.37	8.67	8.91	9.10	9.49	9.82	9.96	10.00
130	–	–	3.42	5.57	6.85	7.69	8.28	8.71	9.05	9.31	9.51	9.68	10.02	10.31	10.42	10.45
125	–	1.30	4.97	6.80	7.89	8.60	9.11	9.48	9.76	9.98	10.15	10.29	10.58	10.82	10.91	10.94
120	–	3.59	6.60	8.10	8.98	9.57	9.98	10.28	10.51	10.68	10.83	10.94	11.17	11.36	11.44	11.46
119	–	4.06	6.94	8.36	9.21	9.77	10.16	10.44	10.66	10.83	10.97	11.07	11.30	11.48	11.55	11.57
118	–	4.54	7.27	8.63	9.44	9.97	10.34	10.61	10.82	10.98	11.11	11.21	11.42	11.59	11.66	11.68
117	–	5.02	7.62	8.90	9.67	10.17	10.52	10.78	10.98	11.13	11.25	11.35	11.55	11.71	11.77	11.79
116	–	5.51	7.96	9.18	9.90	10.37	10.71	10.95	11.14	11.28	11.40	11.49	11.68	11.83	11.89	11.90
115	–	6.00	8.31	9.45	10.13	10.58	10.89	11.12	11.30	11.43	11.54	11.63	11.81	11.95	12.00	12.02
114	–	6.49	8.66	9.73	10.37	10.79	11.08	11.30	11.46	11.59	11.69	11.77	11.94	12.07	12.12	12.13
113	–	6.99	9.02	10.02	10.61	11.00	11.28	11.48	11.63	11.75	11.84	11.92	12.07	12.19	12.24	12.25
112	1.86	7.50	9.37	10.30	10.85	11.22	11.47	11.66	11.80	11.91	11.99	12.06	12.21	12.32	12.36	12.37
111	2.81	8.01	9.74	10.59	11.10	11.43	11.67	11.84	11.97	12.07	12.15	12.21	12.34	12.45	12.49	12.50
110	3.78	8.53	10.10	10.89	11.35	11.65	11.87	12.02	12.14	12.23	12.31	12.36	12.48	12.58	12.61	12.62
109	4.75	9.05	10.47	11.18	11.60	11.87	12.07	12.21	12.32	12.40	12.46	12.52	12.62	12.71	12.74	12.75
108	5.74	9.57	10.85	11.48	11.85	12.10	12.27	12.40	12.49	12.57	12.62	12.67	12.77	12.84	12.87	12.88
107	6.73	10.11	11.23	11.78	12.11	12.33	12.48	12.59	12.67	12.74	12.79	12.83	12.91	12.98	13.00	13.01
106	7.73	10.64	11.61	12.09	12.37	12.56	12.69	12.78	12.85	12.91	12.95	12.99	13.06	13.12	13.14	13.14
105	8.75	11.19	12.00	12.40	12.63	12.79	12.90	12.98	13.04	13.08	13.12	13.15	13.21	13.26	13.27	13.28
104	9.78	11.74	12.39	12.71	12.90	13.02	13.11	13.18	13.22	13.26	13.29	13.31	13.36	13.40	13.41	13.42
103.75	10.03	11.87	12.48	12.79	12.97	13.08	13.16	13.22	13.27	13.31	13.33	13.36	13.40	13.44	13.45	13.45
103.50	10.29	12.01	12.58	12.87	13.03	13.14	13.22	13.28	13.32	13.35	13.38	13.40	13.44	13.47	13.48	13.49
103.25	10.55	12.15	12.68	12.94	13.10	13.20	13.27	13.33	13.36	13.40	13.42	13.44	13.48	13.51	13.52	13.52
103.00	10.81	12.29	12.78	13.02	13.17	13.26	13.33	13.38	13.41	13.44	13.46	13.48	13.52	13.54	13.56	13.56
102.75	11.07	12.43	12.88	13.10	13.24	13.32	13.38	13.43	13.46	13.49	13.51	13.52	13.56	13.58	13.59	13.59
102.50	11.34	12.57	12.98	13.18	13.30	13.38	13.44	13.48	13.51	13.53	13.55	13.56	13.59	13.62	13.63	13.63
102.25	11.60	12.71	13.08	13.26	13.37	13.44	13.49	13.53	13.56	13.58	13.59	13.61	13.63	13.66	13.66	13.66
102.00	11.86	12.85	13.18	13.34	13.44	13.50	13.55	13.58	13.60	13.62	13.64	13.65	13.67	13.69	13.70	13.70
101.75	12.13	12.99	13.28	13.42	13.51	13.56	13.60	13.63	13.65	13.67	13.68	13.69	13.71	13.73	13.74	13.74
101.50	12.39	13.14	13.38	13.51	13.58	13.62	13.66	13.68	13.70	13.71	13.73	13.74	13.75	13.77	13.77	13.77
101.25	12.66	13.28	13.48	13.59	13.65	13.69	13.71	13.73	13.75	13.76	13.77	13.78	13.79	13.80	13.81	13.81
101.00	12.92	13.42	13.59	13.67	13.72	13.75	13.77	13.79	13.80	13.81	13.82	13.82	13.83	13.84	13.85	13.85
100.75	13.19	13.56	13.69	13.75	13.79	13.81	13.83	13.84	13.85	13.85	13.86	13.86	13.87	13.88	13.88	13.88
100.50	13.46	13.71	13.79	13.83	13.86	13.87	13.88	13.89	13.90	13.90	13.90	13.91	13.91	13.92	13.92	13.92
100.25	13.73	13.85	13.89	13.91	13.92	13.93	13.94	13.94	13.95	13.95	13.95	13.95	13.95	13.96	13.96	13.96
100.00	14.00	14.00	14.00	14.00	14.00	14.00	14.00	14.00	14.00	14.00	14.00	14.00	14.00	14.00	14.00	14.00
99.75	14.27	14.14	14.10	14.08	14.07	14.06	14.05	14.05	14.04	14.04	14.04	14.04	14.04	14.03	14.03	14.03
99.50	14.54	14.28	14.20	14.16	14.14	14.12	14.11	14.10	14.09	14.09	14.09	14.08	14.08	14.07	14.07	14.07
99.25	14.81	14.43	14.31	14.24	14.21	14.18	14.17	14.15	14.14	14.14	14.13	14.13	14.12	14.11	14.11	14.11
99.00	15.08	14.58	14.41	14.33	14.28	14.25	14.22	14.21	14.19	14.19	14.18	14.17	14.16	14.15	14.15	14.15
98.75	15.35	14.72	14.51	14.41	14.35	14.31	14.28	14.26	14.25	14.23	14.22	14.22	14.20	14.19	14.19	14.18
98.50	15.63	14.87	14.62	14.49	14.42	14.37	14.34	14.31	14.30	14.28	14.27	14.26	14.24	14.23	14.22	14.22
98.25	15.90	15.02	14.72	14.58	14.49	14.44	14.40	14.37	14.35	14.33	14.32	14.31	14.28	14.27	14.26	14.26
98.00	16.18	15.16	14.83	14.66	14.56	14.50	14.45	14.42	14.40	14.38	14.36	14.35	14.33	14.31	14.30	14.30
97.75	16.45	15.31	14.93	14.75	14.64	14.56	14.51	14.48	14.45	14.43	14.41	14.40	14.37	14.35	14.34	14.34
97.50	16.73	15.46	15.04	14.83	14.71	14.63	14.57	14.53	14.50	14.48	14.46	14.44	14.41	14.39	14.38	14.38
97.25	17.01	15.61	15.15	14.92	14.78	14.69	14.63	14.59	14.55	14.52	14.50	14.49	14.45	14.43	14.42	14.42
97	17.29	15.76	15.25	15.00	14.85	14.76	14.69	14.64	14.60	14.57	14.55	14.53	14.50	14.47	14.46	14.46
96	18.41	16.36	15.68	15.35	15.15	15.02	14.93	14.86	14.81	14.77	14.74	14.72	14.67	14.63	14.62	14.62
95	19.55	16.97	16.12	15.69	15.45	15.28	15.17	15.09	15.02	14.97	14.94	14.91	14.85	14.80	14.78	14.78
94	20.70	17.58	16.55	16.05	15.75	15.55	15.41	15.31	15.24	15.18	15.13	15.10	15.03	14.97	14.95	14.95
93	21.86	18.21	17.00	16.40	16.05	15.82	15.66	15.54	15.46	15.39	15.33	15.29	15.21	15.14	15.12	15.12
92	23.04	18.84	17.45	16.77	16.36	16.10	15.91	15.78	15.68	15.60	15.54	15.49	15.39	15.32	15.29	15.29
91	24.23	19.48	17.91	17.13	16.68	16.38	16.17	16.02	15.90	15.81	15.75	15.69	15.58	15.50	15.47	15.46
90	25.44	20.12	18.37	17.51	16.99	16.66	16.43	16.26	16.13	16.03	15.96	15.90	15.77	15.68	15.65	15.64
89	26.66	20.78	18.84	17.88	17.32	16.95	16.69	16.50	16.36	16.26	16.17	16.10	15.97	15.87	15.84	15.83
88	27.90	21.44	19.31	18.26	17.65	17.24	16.96	16.75	16.60	16.48	16.39	16.32	16.17	16.06	16.02	16.02
87	29.15	22.11	19.80	18.65	17.98	17.54	17.23	17.01	16.84	16.71	16.61	16.53	16.37	16.26	16.22	16.21
86	30.42	22.80	20.28	19.05	18.31	17.84	17.51	17.27	17.08	16.95	16.84	16.75	16.58	16.45	16.41	16.40
85	31.71	23.49	20.78	19.44	18.66	18.14	17.79	17.53	17.33	17.18	17.07	16.97	16.79	16.66	16.61	16.60
80	38.42	27.08	23.36	21.53	20.45	19.75	19.26	18.91	18.64	18.44	18.28	18.16	17.92	17.74	17.69	17.68
75	45.63	30.95	26.14	23.78	22.39	21.49	20.87	20.42	20.08	19.83	19.63	19.47	19.17	18.96	18.90	18.88
70	53.40	35.13	29.16	26.23	24.52	23.40	22.64	22.08	21.67	21.36	21.12	20.94	20.58	20.34	20.27	20.26
65	61.84	39.67	32.45	28.92	26.85	25.52	24.60	23.94	23.45	23.09	22.81	22.59	22.18	21.92	21.85	21.84
60	71.05	44.64	36.07	31.88	29.44	27.87	26.79	26.02	25.46	25.04	24.72	24.48	24.03	23.75	23.68	23.67
55	81.20	50.13	40.08	35.18	32.34	30.52	29.28	28.40	27.76	27.29	26.93	26.66	26.19	25.91	25.84	25.83
50	92.47	56.24	44.57	38.91	35.64	33.55	32.14	31.15	30.44	29.92	29.53	29.25	28.75	28.49	28.43	28.43

Description: This table shows the price to pay for a monthly payment loan, at a yield rate and assuming prepayment.

Example: The price of a 14.25 %, 30 year mortgage to yield 8.00 %, if prepaid in 6 years, is $ 129.48.

30 YEAR MORTGAGE PREPAID IN

YIELD	1 yr	2 yr	3 yr	4 yr	5 yr	6 yr	7 yr	8 yr	9 yr	10 yr	11 yr	12 yr	15 yr	20 yr	25 yr	30 yr
0.00	114.24	128.44	142.60	156.72	170.79	184.80	198.74	212.60	226.37	240.04	253.59	267.00	306.17	365.97	412.89	433.69
1.00	113.17	126.17	139.01	151.68	164.18	176.51	188.65	200.60	212.36	223.91	235.25	246.36	278.18	324.87	359.76	374.55
2.00	112.11	123.95	135.52	146.83	157.87	168.65	179.17	189.42	199.40	209.11	218.55	227.70	253.40	289.66	315.46	325.93
3.00	111.06	121.77	132.13	142.15	151.85	161.21	170.26	178.99	187.41	195.52	203.32	210.81	231.44	259.42	278.38	285.74
4.00	110.02	119.63	128.83	137.65	146.09	154.17	161.89	169.27	176.31	183.03	189.43	195.51	211.94	233.37	247.20	252.34
4.25	109.76	119.10	128.02	136.55	144.69	152.47	159.88	166.94	173.67	180.07	186.15	191.92	207.41	227.44	240.20	244.89
4.50	109.51	118.58	127.22	135.46	143.31	150.79	157.90	164.66	171.08	177.17	182.95	188.41	203.02	221.71	233.49	237.76
4.75	109.25	118.05	126.42	134.38	141.95	149.13	155.95	162.41	168.53	174.33	179.81	184.99	198.75	216.19	227.04	230.94
5.00	109.00	117.53	125.63	133.31	140.60	147.49	154.02	160.20	166.04	171.55	176.75	181.64	194.60	210.87	220.86	224.41
5.25	108.74	117.02	124.85	132.26	139.26	145.88	152.13	158.03	163.59	168.83	173.75	178.38	190.57	205.73	214.93	218.16
5.50	108.49	116.50	124.07	131.21	137.94	144.29	150.27	155.90	161.19	166.16	170.83	175.20	186.66	200.77	209.23	212.17
5.75	108.23	115.99	123.29	130.17	136.63	142.72	148.43	153.80	158.83	163.55	167.96	172.09	182.86	195.99	203.76	206.43
6.00	107.98	115.48	122.52	129.14	135.34	141.17	146.62	151.74	156.52	160.99	165.16	169.06	179.16	191.37	198.51	200.93
6.25	107.73	114.97	121.76	128.12	134.07	139.64	144.84	149.71	154.25	158.48	162.43	166.09	175.57	186.90	193.46	195.66
6.50	107.48	114.47	121.00	127.11	132.81	138.13	143.09	147.72	152.02	156.03	159.75	163.20	172.08	182.59	188.60	190.59
6.75	107.23	113.97	120.25	126.11	131.56	136.64	141.36	145.76	149.84	153.62	157.13	160.38	168.68	178.43	183.93	185.74
7.00	106.98	113.47	119.50	125.11	130.33	135.17	139.66	143.83	147.69	151.27	154.57	157.62	165.38	174.41	179.44	181.07
7.25	106.73	112.97	118.76	124.13	129.11	133.72	137.99	141.94	145.59	148.96	152.06	154.93	162.18	170.52	175.12	176.59
7.50	106.48	112.47	118.02	123.16	127.90	132.29	136.34	140.08	143.52	146.70	149.61	152.30	159.06	166.77	170.96	172.29
7.75	106.23	111.98	117.29	122.19	126.71	130.88	134.71	138.25	141.50	144.48	147.22	149.73	156.02	163.13	166.96	168.16
8.00	105.98	111.49	116.57	121.24	125.53	129.48	133.11	136.45	139.51	142.31	144.87	147.22	153.07	159.62	163.10	164.18
8.25	105.73	111.00	115.84	120.29	124.37	128.11	131.54	134.68	137.55	140.18	142.58	144.77	150.20	156.23	159.38	160.35
8.50	105.49	110.52	115.13	119.35	123.22	126.75	129.99	132.94	135.64	138.10	140.33	142.37	147.41	152.94	155.80	156.67
8.75	105.24	110.04	114.42	118.42	122.08	125.41	128.46	131.23	133.76	136.05	138.14	140.03	144.69	149.76	152.35	153.13
9.00	105.00	109.56	113.71	117.50	120.95	124.09	126.95	129.55	131.91	134.05	135.99	137.75	142.05	146.68	149.02	149.72
9.25	104.75	109.08	113.01	116.59	119.84	122.79	125.47	127.90	130.10	132.09	133.89	135.51	139.48	143.70	145.81	146.44
9.50	104.51	108.60	112.32	115.68	118.74	121.50	124.01	126.27	128.32	130.16	131.83	133.33	136.97	140.82	142.72	143.27
9.75	104.27	108.13	111.63	114.79	117.65	120.23	122.57	124.67	126.57	128.28	129.82	131.20	134.53	138.03	139.73	140.22
10.00	104.02	107.66	110.94	113.90	116.57	118.98	121.15	123.10	124.85	126.43	127.85	129.11	132.16	135.32	136.84	137.28
10.25	103.78	107.19	110.26	113.02	115.51	117.74	119.75	121.55	123.17	124.62	125.92	127.08	129.85	132.70	134.06	134.44
10.50	103.54	106.72	109.58	112.15	114.45	116.52	118.37	120.03	121.52	122.84	124.03	125.09	127.60	130.16	131.36	131.70
10.75	103.30	106.26	108.91	111.29	113.41	115.32	117.02	118.54	119.89	121.10	122.18	123.14	125.41	127.70	128.76	129.05
11.00	103.06	105.80	108.25	110.43	112.38	114.13	115.68	117.07	118.30	119.40	120.37	121.24	123.28	125.31	126.25	126.50
11.25	102.82	105.34	107.58	109.58	111.37	112.95	114.36	115.62	116.73	117.72	118.60	119.38	121.20	123.00	123.81	124.03
11.50	102.58	104.88	106.93	108.74	110.36	111.79	113.07	114.20	115.20	116.08	116.87	117.56	119.17	120.75	121.46	121.65
11.75	102.35	104.43	106.27	107.91	109.36	110.65	111.79	112.80	113.69	114.47	115.17	115.78	117.20	118.58	119.19	119.35
12.00	102.11	103.97	105.63	107.09	108.38	109.52	110.53	111.42	112.21	112.90	113.51	114.04	115.28	116.46	116.98	117.12
12.25	101.87	103.52	104.98	106.27	107.41	108.41	109.29	110.07	110.75	111.35	111.88	112.34	113.40	114.41	114.85	114.96
12.50	101.64	103.08	104.35	105.46	106.45	107.31	108.07	108.74	109.32	109.83	110.28	110.67	111.57	112.42	112.78	112.88
12.75	101.40	102.63	103.71	104.66	105.49	106.22	106.86	107.43	107.92	108.35	108.72	109.05	109.79	110.49	110.78	110.86
13.00	101.17	102.19	103.08	103.87	104.55	105.15	105.68	106.14	106.54	106.89	107.19	107.46	108.06	108.61	108.85	108.90
13.25	100.93	101.74	102.46	103.08	103.62	104.10	104.51	104.87	105.18	105.46	105.69	105.90	106.36	106.79	106.97	107.01
13.50	100.70	101.31	101.84	102.30	102.70	103.05	103.36	103.62	103.85	104.05	104.23	104.38	104.71	105.02	105.14	105.17
13.75	100.46	100.87	101.22	101.53	101.79	102.02	102.22	102.39	102.55	102.68	102.79	102.89	103.10	103.30	103.38	103.40
14.00	100.23	100.43	100.61	100.76	100.89	101.00	101.10	101.19	101.26	101.32	101.38	101.43	101.53	101.63	101.66	101.67
14.25	100.00	100.00	100.00	100.00	100.00	100.00	100.00	100.00	100.00	100.00	100.00	100.00	100.00	100.00	100.00	100.00
14.50	99.77	99.57	99.40	99.25	99.12	99.01	98.91	98.83	98.76	98.70	98.65	98.60	98.50	98.42	98.39	98.38
14.75	99.54	99.14	98.80	98.50	98.25	98.03	97.84	97.68	97.54	97.42	97.32	97.24	97.05	96.88	96.82	96.80
15.00	99.31	98.71	98.20	97.76	97.39	97.06	96.79	96.55	96.35	96.17	96.03	95.90	95.62	95.38	95.29	95.27
15.25	99.08	98.29	97.61	97.03	96.54	96.11	95.75	95.44	95.17	94.95	94.75	94.59	94.23	93.93	93.81	93.79
15.50	98.85	97.87	97.03	96.31	95.69	95.17	94.72	94.34	94.02	93.74	93.51	93.31	92.88	92.51	92.38	92.35
15.75	98.62	97.45	96.44	95.59	94.86	94.24	93.71	93.26	92.88	92.56	92.28	92.05	91.55	91.13	90.98	90.95
16.00	98.39	97.03	95.87	94.88	94.04	93.32	92.72	92.20	91.77	91.40	91.09	90.82	90.26	89.79	89.62	89.58
16.25	98.17	96.61	95.29	94.17	93.22	92.42	91.73	91.16	90.67	90.26	89.91	89.62	88.99	88.48	88.30	88.26
16.50	97.94	96.20	94.72	93.47	92.42	91.52	90.77	90.13	89.59	89.14	88.76	88.44	87.76	87.21	87.01	86.97
16.75	97.71	95.78	94.15	92.78	91.62	90.64	89.81	89.12	88.54	88.04	87.63	87.29	86.56	85.97	85.76	85.72
17.00	97.49	95.37	93.59	92.09	90.83	89.77	88.87	88.12	87.49	86.97	86.53	86.16	85.38	84.76	84.54	84.50
17.25	97.27	94.97	93.03	91.41	90.05	88.91	87.95	87.14	86.47	85.91	85.44	85.05	84.23	83.58	83.36	83.31
17.50	97.04	94.56	92.48	90.74	89.28	88.06	87.03	86.18	85.47	84.87	84.38	83.96	83.10	82.43	82.20	82.16
17.75	96.82	94.16	91.93	90.07	88.51	87.22	86.13	85.23	84.48	83.85	83.33	82.90	82.00	81.31	81.08	81.03
18.00	96.59	93.75	91.38	89.41	87.76	86.39	85.25	84.30	83.51	82.85	82.31	81.86	80.93	80.22	79.98	79.93
18.25	96.37	93.35	90.84	88.75	87.01	85.57	84.37	83.38	82.55	81.87	81.31	80.84	79.88	79.15	78.91	78.87
18.50	96.15	92.95	90.30	88.10	86.28	84.76	83.51	82.47	81.62	80.91	80.32	79.84	78.85	78.11	77.87	77.82
18.75	95.93	92.56	89.77	87.46	85.54	83.96	82.66	81.58	80.69	79.96	79.36	78.86	77.85	77.09	76.86	76.81
19.00	95.71	92.16	89.23	86.82	84.82	83.18	81.82	80.70	79.79	79.03	78.41	77.90	76.87	76.10	75.86	75.82
20.00	94.83	90.60	87.15	84.32	82.01	80.12	78.58	77.33	76.31	75.47	74.80	74.25	73.15	72.37	72.14	72.09
25.00	90.58	83.25	77.54	73.09	69.63	66.94	64.85	63.23	61.97	61.00	60.24	59.66	58.60	57.96	57.81	57.79
30.00	86.55	76.57	69.17	63.69	59.62	56.62	54.39	52.74	51.53	50.63	49.97	49.48	48.67	48.26	48.19	48.18

Description: This table shows the yield to prepayment of a monthly payment mortgage purchased at a price in the index.

Example: The yield to prepayment in 10 years of a 14.25 %, 30 year mortgage at a price of 104.00 is 13.50 %.

30 YEAR MORTGAGE PREPAID IN

PRICE	1 yr	2 yr	3 yr	4 yr	5 yr	6 yr	7 yr	8 yr	9 yr	10 yr	11 yr	12 yr	15 yr	20 yr	25 yr	30 yr
140	–	–	–	3.47	5.11	6.19	6.95	7.51	7.93	8.27	8.53	8.75	9.19	9.57	9.72	9.76
135	–	–	2.15	4.60	6.06	7.02	7.70	8.20	8.58	8.88	9.11	9.30	9.70	10.03	10.16	10.19
130	–	–	3.64	5.79	7.06	7.90	8.49	8.93	9.26	9.52	9.72	9.89	10.23	10.51	10.62	10.65
125	–	1.52	5.20	7.02	8.11	8.82	9.32	9.69	9.97	10.19	10.37	10.51	10.79	11.03	11.12	11.15
120	–	3.82	6.83	8.32	9.21	9.79	10.20	10.50	10.73	10.91	11.05	11.16	11.39	11.58	11.65	11.67
119	–	4.29	7.16	8.59	9.43	9.99	10.38	10.67	10.88	11.05	11.19	11.30	11.52	11.70	11.77	11.78
118	–	4.77	7.50	8.86	9.66	10.19	10.56	10.84	11.04	11.20	11.33	11.43	11.64	11.81	11.88	11.90
117	–	5.25	7.85	9.13	9.90	10.40	10.75	11.01	11.20	11.35	11.48	11.57	11.77	11.93	11.99	12.01
116	–	5.74	8.19	9.41	10.13	10.60	10.93	11.18	11.36	11.51	11.62	11.71	11.90	12.05	12.11	12.12
115	–	6.23	8.54	9.69	10.37	10.81	11.12	11.35	11.53	11.66	11.77	11.86	12.03	12.17	12.23	12.24
114	–	6.73	8.89	9.97	10.60	11.02	11.31	11.53	11.69	11.82	11.92	12.00	12.16	12.30	12.35	12.36
113	1.15	7.23	9.25	10.25	10.85	11.23	11.51	11.71	11.86	11.98	12.07	12.15	12.30	12.42	12.47	12.48
112	2.10	7.74	9.61	10.54	11.09	11.45	11.70	11.89	12.03	12.14	12.23	12.30	12.44	12.55	12.59	12.60
111	3.05	8.25	9.97	10.83	11.34	11.67	11.90	12.07	12.20	12.30	12.38	12.45	12.57	12.68	12.72	12.73
110	4.02	8.76	10.34	11.12	11.59	11.89	12.10	12.26	12.38	12.47	12.54	12.60	12.72	12.81	12.85	12.85
109	4.99	9.29	10.71	11.42	11.84	12.11	12.30	12.45	12.55	12.63	12.70	12.75	12.86	12.94	12.97	12.98
108	5.98	9.81	11.09	11.72	12.09	12.34	12.51	12.63	12.73	12.80	12.86	12.91	13.00	13.08	13.11	13.11
107	6.97	10.35	11.47	12.02	12.35	12.57	12.72	12.83	12.91	12.98	13.03	13.07	13.15	13.22	13.24	13.25
106	7.98	10.89	11.85	12.33	12.61	12.80	12.93	13.02	13.09	13.15	13.19	13.23	13.30	13.36	13.38	13.38
105	8.99	11.43	12.24	12.64	12.88	13.03	13.14	13.22	13.28	13.33	13.36	13.39	13.45	13.50	13.52	13.52
104	10.02	11.98	12.63	12.95	13.14	13.27	13.35	13.42	13.47	13.50	13.53	13.56	13.60	13.64	13.66	13.66
103.75	10.28	12.12	12.73	13.03	13.21	13.33	13.41	13.47	13.51	13.55	13.58	13.60	13.64	13.68	13.69	13.69
103.50	10.54	12.26	12.83	13.11	13.28	13.39	13.46	13.52	13.56	13.59	13.62	13.64	13.68	13.72	13.73	13.73
103.25	10.80	12.40	12.93	13.19	13.35	13.45	13.52	13.57	13.61	13.64	13.66	13.68	13.72	13.75	13.76	13.77
103.00	11.06	12.54	13.03	13.27	13.41	13.51	13.57	13.62	13.66	13.69	13.71	13.73	13.76	13.79	13.80	13.80
102.75	11.32	12.68	13.13	13.35	13.48	13.57	13.63	13.67	13.71	13.73	13.75	13.77	13.80	13.83	13.84	13.84
102.50	11.58	12.82	13.23	13.43	13.55	13.63	13.68	13.72	13.75	13.78	13.80	13.81	13.84	13.86	13.87	13.87
102.25	11.85	12.96	13.33	13.51	13.62	13.69	13.74	13.77	13.80	13.82	13.84	13.85	13.88	13.90	13.91	13.91
102.00	12.11	13.10	13.43	13.59	13.69	13.75	13.79	13.83	13.85	13.87	13.88	13.90	13.92	13.94	13.95	13.95
101.75	12.37	13.24	13.53	13.67	13.76	13.81	13.85	13.88	13.90	13.92	13.93	13.94	13.96	13.98	13.98	13.98
101.50	12.64	13.38	13.63	13.75	13.83	13.87	13.91	13.93	13.95	13.96	13.97	13.98	14.00	14.01	14.02	14.02
101.25	12.90	13.53	13.73	13.83	13.89	13.93	13.96	13.98	14.00	14.01	14.02	14.03	14.04	14.05	14.06	14.06
101.00	13.17	13.67	13.83	13.92	13.96	14.00	14.02	14.03	14.05	14.06	14.06	14.07	14.08	14.09	14.09	14.09
100.75	13.44	13.81	13.94	14.00	14.03	14.06	14.07	14.09	14.10	14.10	14.11	14.11	14.12	14.13	14.13	14.13
100.50	13.71	13.96	14.04	14.08	14.10	14.12	14.13	14.14	14.15	14.15	14.15	14.16	14.16	14.17	14.17	14.17
100.25	13.98	14.10	14.14	14.16	14.17	14.18	14.19	14.19	14.20	14.20	14.20	14.20	14.20	14.21	14.21	14.21
100.00	14.25	14.25	14.25	14.25	14.25	14.25	14.25	14.25	14.25	14.25	14.25	14.29	14.25	14.25	14.25	14.25
99.75	14.52	14.39	14.35	14.33	14.32	14.31	14.30	14.30	14.30	14.30	14.29	14.29	14.29	14.28	14.28	14.28
99.50	14.79	14.54	14.45	14.41	14.39	14.37	14.36	14.35	14.35	14.34	14.34	14.33	14.33	14.32	14.32	14.32
99.25	15.06	14.68	14.56	14.49	14.46	14.43	14.42	14.40	14.40	14.39	14.38	14.38	14.37	14.36	14.36	14.36
99.00	15.33	14.83	14.66	14.58	14.53	14.50	14.47	14.46	14.45	14.44	14.43	14.42	14.41	14.40	14.40	14.40
98.75	15.60	14.97	14.76	14.66	14.60	14.56	14.53	14.51	14.50	14.49	14.48	14.47	14.45	14.44	14.44	14.44
98.50	15.88	15.12	14.87	14.75	14.67	14.62	14.59	14.57	14.55	14.53	14.52	14.51	14.50	14.48	14.48	14.48
98.25	16.15	15.27	14.98	14.83	14.74	14.69	14.65	14.62	14.60	14.58	14.57	14.56	14.54	14.52	14.52	14.51
98.00	16.43	15.42	15.08	14.91	14.82	14.75	14.71	14.68	14.65	14.63	14.62	14.60	14.58	14.56	14.56	14.55
97.75	16.71	15.56	15.19	15.00	14.89	14.82	14.77	14.73	14.70	14.68	14.66	14.65	14.62	14.60	14.60	14.59
97.50	16.98	15.71	15.29	15.08	14.96	14.88	14.83	14.78	14.75	14.73	14.71	14.70	14.67	14.64	14.64	14.63
97.25	17.26	15.86	15.40	15.17	15.04	14.95	14.88	14.84	14.81	14.78	14.76	14.74	14.71	14.68	14.68	14.67
97	17.54	16.01	15.51	15.26	15.11	15.01	14.94	14.90	14.86	14.83	14.81	14.79	14.75	14.73	14.72	14.71
96	18.67	16.61	15.94	15.60	15.40	15.27	15.18	15.12	15.07	15.03	15.00	14.98	14.93	14.89	14.88	14.88
95	19.80	17.22	16.37	15.95	15.70	15.54	15.43	15.34	15.28	15.23	15.20	15.17	15.11	15.06	15.04	15.04
94	20.95	17.84	16.81	16.31	16.01	15.81	15.67	15.57	15.50	15.44	15.40	15.36	15.29	15.23	15.21	15.21
93	22.12	18.47	17.26	16.66	16.31	16.08	15.92	15.81	15.72	15.65	15.60	15.56	15.47	15.41	15.39	15.38
92	23.30	19.10	17.71	17.03	16.62	16.36	16.18	16.04	15.94	15.86	15.80	15.76	15.66	15.59	15.56	15.56
91	24.49	19.74	18.17	17.40	16.94	16.64	16.43	16.28	16.17	16.08	16.01	15.96	15.85	15.77	15.74	15.74
90	25.70	20.39	18.64	17.77	17.26	16.93	16.70	16.53	16.40	16.30	16.23	16.17	16.05	15.96	15.92	15.92
89	26.93	21.04	19.11	18.15	17.59	17.22	16.96	16.77	16.63	16.53	16.44	16.38	16.24	16.15	16.11	16.10
88	28.17	21.71	19.58	18.53	17.92	17.51	17.23	17.03	16.87	16.76	16.66	16.59	16.45	16.34	16.30	16.29
87	29.42	22.38	20.07	18.92	18.25	17.81	17.50	17.28	17.12	16.99	16.89	16.81	16.65	16.54	16.50	16.49
86	30.70	23.07	20.56	19.32	18.59	18.11	17.78	17.54	17.36	17.22	17.12	17.03	16.86	16.74	16.70	16.69
85	31.99	23.76	21.05	19.72	18.93	18.42	18.07	17.81	17.61	17.46	17.35	17.26	17.08	16.94	16.90	16.89
80	38.70	27.37	23.65	21.81	20.74	20.04	19.55	19.20	18.94	18.73	18.58	18.45	18.22	18.04	17.99	17.98
75	45.92	31.25	26.44	24.08	22.69	21.79	21.17	20.72	20.39	20.13	19.94	19.78	19.49	19.28	19.22	19.21
70	53.71	35.44	29.47	26.54	24.83	23.72	22.96	22.40	22.00	21.69	21.45	21.27	20.92	20.68	20.61	20.60
65	62.16	39.99	32.77	29.24	27.18	25.85	24.93	24.28	23.80	23.43	23.15	22.94	22.54	22.29	22.22	22.21
60	71.39	44.98	36.40	32.22	29.79	28.22	27.15	26.39	25.83	25.41	25.10	24.85	24.42	24.15	24.08	24.07
55	81.55	50.48	40.43	35.55	32.71	30.90	29.66	28.79	28.16	27.69	27.34	27.07	26.61	26.34	26.28	26.27
50	92.85	56.62	44.95	39.30	36.04	33.96	32.56	31.58	30.87	30.36	29.98	29.70	29.21	28.96	28.91	28.90

PREPAYMENT MORTGAGE PRICE

14.50 %

Description: This table shows the price to pay for a monthly payment loan, at a yield rate and assuming prepayment.

Example: The price of a 14.50 %, 30 year mortgage to yield 8.00 %, if prepaid in 6 years, is $ 130.68.

30 YEAR MORTGAGE PREPAID IN

YIELD	1 yr	2 yr	3 yr	4 yr	5 yr	6 yr	7 yr	8 yr	9 yr	10 yr	11 yr	12 yr	15 yr	20 yr	25 yr	30 yr
0.00	114.49	128.94	143.36	157.73	172.06	186.32	200.52	214.65	228.68	242.62	256.43	270.11	310.10	371.26	419.41	440.84
1.00	113.41	126.67	139.75	152.67	165.41	177.98	190.37	202.56	214.56	226.35	237.93	249.27	281.80	329.61	365.46	380.72
2.00	112.35	124.44	136.25	147.80	159.07	170.08	180.82	191.30	201.50	211.42	221.07	230.44	256.75	293.94	320.49	331.30
3.00	111.30	122.25	132.85	143.10	153.02	162.60	171.86	180.80	189.41	197.72	205.71	213.38	234.54	263.29	282.84	290.45
4.00	110.27	120.11	129.54	138.58	147.23	155.51	163.45	171.00	178.23	185.12	191.69	197.94	214.82	236.89	251.17	256.50
4.25	110.01	119.58	128.73	137.47	145.83	153.80	161.41	168.66	175.56	182.13	188.38	194.31	210.24	230.87	244.06	248.92
4.50	109.75	119.05	127.92	136.38	144.44	152.11	159.41	166.35	172.95	179.21	185.14	190.76	205.79	225.07	237.24	241.68
4.75	109.49	118.53	127.12	135.30	143.06	150.44	157.44	164.09	170.38	176.34	181.98	187.30	201.47	219.47	230.70	234.75
5.00	109.24	118.01	126.33	134.22	141.71	148.80	155.51	161.86	167.87	173.54	178.89	183.93	197.28	214.07	224.42	228.11
5.25	108.98	117.49	125.54	133.16	140.36	147.17	153.60	159.67	165.40	170.79	175.87	180.63	193.20	208.86	218.40	221.76
5.50	108.73	116.97	124.76	132.11	139.04	145.57	151.73	157.52	162.98	168.10	172.91	177.42	189.24	203.83	212.61	215.67
5.75	108.48	116.46	123.98	131.06	137.72	143.99	149.88	155.41	160.60	165.46	170.02	174.28	185.40	198.98	207.05	209.84
6.00	108.22	115.95	123.21	130.03	136.43	142.43	148.06	153.33	158.27	162.88	167.19	171.21	181.66	194.30	201.72	204.25
6.25	107.97	115.44	122.44	129.00	135.14	140.89	146.27	151.29	155.98	160.35	164.43	168.22	178.02	189.77	196.59	198.88
6.50	107.72	114.94	121.68	127.99	133.88	139.37	144.50	149.28	153.73	157.88	161.73	165.30	174.49	185.40	191.65	193.74
6.75	107.47	114.43	120.93	126.98	132.62	137.88	142.76	147.31	151.53	155.45	159.08	162.44	171.06	181.18	186.91	188.80
7.00	107.22	113.93	120.18	125.99	131.38	136.40	141.05	145.37	149.37	153.07	156.50	159.66	167.72	177.10	182.35	184.06
7.25	106.97	113.43	119.43	125.00	130.16	134.94	139.36	143.46	147.24	150.74	153.97	156.94	164.47	173.16	177.96	179.51
7.50	106.72	112.94	118.69	124.02	128.95	133.50	137.70	141.58	145.16	148.46	151.49	154.28	161.31	169.35	173.73	175.13
7.75	106.47	112.44	117.96	123.05	127.75	132.08	136.07	139.74	143.12	146.22	149.07	151.68	158.24	165.67	169.67	170.93
8.00	106.22	111.95	117.23	122.09	126.56	130.68	134.45	137.93	141.11	144.03	146.70	149.15	155.26	162.10	165.75	166.89
8.25	105.97	111.46	116.51	121.14	125.39	129.29	132.87	136.14	139.14	141.88	144.39	146.67	152.35	158.66	161.98	163.00
8.50	105.73	110.98	115.79	120.20	124.23	127.93	131.30	134.39	137.21	139.78	142.12	144.25	149.53	155.32	158.34	159.26
8.75	105.48	110.49	115.08	119.26	123.09	126.58	129.76	132.67	135.31	137.72	139.90	141.89	146.77	152.10	154.83	155.66
9.00	105.24	110.01	114.37	118.34	121.96	125.25	128.25	130.97	133.45	135.70	137.73	139.58	144.10	148.98	151.45	152.19
9.25	104.99	109.53	113.67	117.42	120.84	123.94	126.75	129.31	131.62	133.71	135.61	137.32	141.49	145.96	148.19	148.85
9.50	104.75	109.06	112.97	116.51	119.73	122.64	125.28	127.67	129.82	131.77	133.53	135.11	138.96	143.03	145.04	145.63
9.75	104.50	108.58	112.27	115.61	118.63	121.36	123.83	126.05	128.06	129.87	131.50	132.96	136.49	140.20	142.01	142.53
10.00	104.26	108.11	111.59	114.72	117.55	120.10	122.40	124.47	126.33	128.00	129.51	130.85	134.09	137.45	139.08	139.54
10.25	104.02	107.64	110.90	113.84	116.48	118.86	120.99	122.91	124.63	126.18	127.56	128.79	131.75	134.79	136.24	136.65
10.50	103.78	107.17	110.22	112.96	115.42	117.63	119.61	121.38	122.96	124.38	125.65	126.78	129.47	132.21	133.51	133.87
10.75	103.54	106.71	109.55	112.10	114.38	116.42	118.24	119.87	121.33	122.63	123.78	124.81	127.25	129.72	130.86	131.18
11.00	103.30	106.25	108.88	111.24	113.34	115.22	116.89	118.39	119.72	120.90	121.95	122.89	125.09	127.30	128.31	128.59
11.25	103.06	105.79	108.22	110.39	112.32	114.04	115.57	116.93	118.14	119.21	120.16	121.01	122.99	124.95	125.84	126.08
11.50	102.82	105.33	107.56	109.54	111.31	112.87	114.26	115.50	116.59	117.56	118.41	119.17	120.94	122.67	123.45	123.66
11.75	102.58	104.87	106.90	108.71	110.30	111.72	112.97	114.08	115.07	115.93	116.70	117.37	118.94	120.46	121.14	121.31
12.00	102.34	104.42	106.25	107.88	109.31	110.58	111.71	112.70	113.57	114.34	115.02	115.61	116.99	118.32	118.90	119.05
12.25	102.11	103.97	105.61	107.06	108.34	109.46	110.46	111.33	112.10	112.78	113.37	113.89	115.09	116.24	116.73	116.86
12.50	101.87	103.52	104.97	106.24	107.37	108.36	109.23	109.99	110.66	111.25	111.76	112.21	113.24	114.22	114.63	114.74
12.75	101.63	103.07	104.33	105.44	106.41	107.26	108.01	108.67	109.24	109.74	110.18	110.56	111.44	112.25	112.60	112.69
13.00	101.40	102.62	103.70	104.64	105.46	106.19	106.82	107.37	107.85	108.27	108.64	108.95	109.68	110.35	110.63	110.70
13.25	101.16	102.18	103.07	103.85	104.53	105.12	105.64	106.09	106.48	106.82	107.12	107.38	107.96	108.50	108.72	108.77
13.50	100.93	101.74	102.45	103.06	103.60	104.07	104.48	104.83	105.14	105.41	105.64	105.84	106.29	106.70	106.87	106.91
13.75	100.70	101.30	101.83	102.29	102.69	103.03	103.33	103.59	103.82	104.02	104.19	104.33	104.66	104.95	105.07	105.10
14.00	100.46	100.87	101.22	101.52	101.78	102.01	102.21	102.38	102.52	102.65	102.76	102.86	103.07	103.26	103.33	103.35
14.25	100.23	100.43	100.61	100.76	100.89	101.00	101.09	101.18	101.25	101.31	101.37	101.41	101.51	101.61	101.64	101.65
14.50	100.00	100.00	100.00	100.00	100.00	100.00	100.00	100.00	100.00	100.00	100.00	100.00	100.00	100.00	100.00	100.00
14.75	99.77	99.57	99.40	99.25	99.12	99.01	98.92	98.84	98.77	98.71	98.66	98.62	98.52	98.44	98.41	98.40
15.00	99.54	99.14	98.80	98.51	98.26	98.04	97.86	97.70	97.56	97.45	97.35	97.26	97.08	96.92	96.86	96.85
15.25	99.31	98.72	98.21	97.77	97.40	97.08	96.81	96.58	96.38	96.21	96.06	95.94	95.67	95.44	95.36	95.34
15.50	99.08	98.29	97.62	97.04	96.55	96.13	95.78	95.47	95.21	94.99	94.80	94.64	94.30	94.00	93.89	93.87
15.75	98.85	97.87	97.04	96.32	95.72	95.20	94.76	94.38	94.07	93.79	93.57	93.37	92.95	92.60	92.47	92.45
16.00	98.62	97.45	96.46	95.61	94.89	94.27	93.75	93.31	92.94	92.62	92.35	92.13	91.64	91.24	91.09	91.06
16.25	98.40	97.03	95.88	94.90	94.07	93.36	92.77	92.26	91.83	91.47	91.17	90.91	90.36	89.91	89.75	89.72
16.50	98.17	96.62	95.31	94.20	93.26	92.46	91.79	91.22	90.75	90.34	90.00	89.72	89.11	88.62	88.44	88.41
16.75	97.94	96.21	94.74	93.50	92.45	91.57	90.83	90.20	89.68	89.23	88.86	88.55	87.89	87.36	87.17	87.13
17.00	97.72	95.79	94.17	92.81	91.66	90.69	89.88	89.20	88.63	88.15	87.74	87.41	86.70	86.13	85.93	85.89
17.25	97.49	95.39	93.61	92.13	90.88	89.83	88.95	88.21	87.59	87.08	86.65	86.29	85.53	84.93	84.73	84.69
17.50	97.27	94.98	93.06	91.45	90.10	88.97	88.03	87.24	86.58	86.03	85.57	85.19	84.39	83.76	83.55	83.51
17.75	97.04	94.57	92.50	90.78	89.33	88.13	87.12	86.28	85.58	85.00	84.51	84.11	83.28	82.63	82.41	82.37
18.00	96.82	94.17	91.96	90.11	88.57	87.29	86.22	85.34	84.60	83.99	83.48	83.06	82.19	81.52	81.30	81.25
18.25	96.60	93.77	91.41	89.45	87.82	86.47	85.34	84.41	83.64	82.99	82.46	82.03	81.12	80.43	80.21	80.17
18.50	96.38	93.37	90.87	88.80	87.08	85.65	84.47	83.50	82.69	82.02	81.47	81.01	80.08	79.38	79.15	79.11
18.75	96.16	92.97	90.33	88.15	86.34	84.85	83.62	82.60	81.76	81.06	80.49	80.02	79.07	78.35	78.12	78.08
19.00	95.93	92.57	89.80	87.51	85.62	84.06	82.77	81.71	80.84	80.12	79.53	79.05	78.07	77.34	77.11	77.07
20.00	95.06	91.01	87.70	85.00	82.79	80.98	79.51	78.30	77.32	76.53	75.88	75.35	74.30	73.55	73.32	73.28
25.00	90.80	83.64	78.06	73.71	70.33	67.70	65.66	64.07	62.84	61.89	61.15	60.58	59.53	58.91	58.76	58.74
30.00	86.76	76.94	69.66	64.26	60.26	57.29	55.10	53.48	52.28	51.39	50.74	50.26	49.46	49.06	48.98	48.98

Description: This table shows the yield to prepayment of a monthly payment mortgage purchased at a price in the index.

Example: The yield to prepayment in 10 years of a 14.50 %, 30 year mortgage at a price of 104.00 is 13.75 %.

30 YEAR MORTGAGE PREPAID IN

PRICE	1 yr	2 yr	3 yr	4 yr	5 yr	6 yr	7 yr	8 yr	9 yr	10 yr	11 yr	12 yr	15 yr	20 yr	25 yr	30 yr
140	–	–	–	3.68	5.31	6.39	7.15	7.71	8.14	8.47	8.73	8.95	9.39	9.76	9.92	9.96
135	–	–	2.36	4.81	6.27	7.23	7.91	8.41	8.79	9.08	9.32	9.51	9.90	10.23	10.36	10.39
130	–	–	3.85	6.00	7.28	8.12	8.71	9.14	9.47	9.73	9.93	10.10	10.44	10.72	10.83	10.86
125	–	1.74	5.42	7.24	8.33	9.04	9.54	9.91	10.19	10.41	10.58	10.72	11.01	11.24	11.33	11.36
120	–	4.05	7.05	8.55	9.43	10.02	10.42	10.72	10.95	11.13	11.27	11.38	11.61	11.80	11.87	11.89
119	–	4.52	7.39	8.82	9.66	10.22	10.61	10.89	11.11	11.28	11.41	11.52	11.74	11.91	11.98	12.00
118	–	5.00	7.73	9.09	9.89	10.42	10.79	11.06	11.27	11.43	11.55	11.66	11.86	12.03	12.10	12.11
117	–	5.48	8.07	9.36	10.12	10.62	10.98	11.23	11.43	11.58	11.70	11.80	11.99	12.15	12.21	12.23
116	–	5.97	8.42	9.64	10.36	10.83	11.16	11.41	11.59	11.73	11.85	11.94	12.12	12.27	12.33	12.35
115	–	6.46	8.77	9.92	10.60	11.04	11.35	11.58	11.76	11.89	12.00	12.08	12.26	12.40	12.45	12.46
114	–	6.96	9.13	10.20	10.84	11.25	11.55	11.76	11.92	12.05	12.15	12.23	12.39	12.52	12.57	12.58
113	1.38	7.46	9.48	10.48	11.08	11.47	11.74	11.94	12.09	12.21	12.30	12.38	12.53	12.65	12.70	12.71
112	2.33	7.97	9.84	10.77	11.32	11.68	11.94	12.12	12.26	12.37	12.46	12.53	12.67	12.78	12.82	12.83
111	3.29	8.48	10.21	11.06	11.57	11.90	12.14	12.31	12.44	12.54	12.61	12.68	12.81	12.91	12.95	12.96
110	4.25	9.00	10.58	11.36	11.82	12.12	12.34	12.49	12.61	12.70	12.77	12.83	12.95	13.04	13.08	13.08
109	5.23	9.52	10.95	11.66	12.08	12.35	12.54	12.68	12.79	12.87	12.94	12.99	13.09	13.18	13.21	13.22
108	6.22	10.05	11.33	11.96	12.33	12.58	12.75	12.87	12.97	13.04	13.10	13.15	13.24	13.31	13.34	13.35
107	7.21	10.59	11.71	12.26	12.59	12.81	12.96	13.07	13.15	13.21	13.27	13.31	13.39	13.45	13.48	13.48
106	8.22	11.13	12.09	12.57	12.85	13.04	13.17	13.26	13.33	13.39	13.43	13.47	13.54	13.59	13.62	13.62
105	9.24	11.67	12.48	12.88	13.12	13.27	13.38	13.46	13.52	13.57	13.60	13.63	13.69	13.74	13.76	13.76
104	10.27	12.23	12.88	13.20	13.39	13.51	13.60	13.66	13.71	13.75	13.78	13.80	13.85	13.88	13.90	13.90
103.75	10.52	12.36	12.97	13.28	13.45	13.57	13.65	13.71	13.76	13.79	13.82	13.84	13.89	13.92	13.93	13.94
103.50	10.78	12.50	13.07	13.36	13.52	13.63	13.71	13.76	13.81	13.84	13.86	13.89	13.93	13.96	13.97	13.97
103.25	11.04	12.64	13.17	13.44	13.59	13.69	13.76	13.82	13.85	13.88	13.91	13.93	13.97	14.00	14.01	14.01
103.00	11.31	12.78	13.27	13.52	13.66	13.75	13.82	13.87	13.90	13.93	13.95	13.97	14.01	14.03	14.04	14.05
102.75	11.57	12.92	13.37	13.60	13.73	13.81	13.87	13.92	13.95	13.98	14.00	14.01	14.05	14.07	14.08	14.08
102.50	11.83	13.07	13.47	13.68	13.80	13.87	13.93	13.97	14.00	14.02	14.04	14.06	14.09	14.11	14.12	14.12
102.25	12.09	13.21	13.57	13.76	13.87	13.94	13.99	14.02	14.05	14.07	14.09	14.10	14.13	14.15	14.15	14.16
102.00	12.36	13.35	13.68	13.84	13.93	14.00	14.04	14.07	14.10	14.12	14.13	14.14	14.17	14.18	14.19	14.19
101.75	12.62	13.49	13.78	13.92	14.00	14.06	14.10	14.13	14.15	14.16	14.18	14.19	14.21	14.22	14.23	14.23
101.50	12.89	13.63	13.88	14.00	14.07	14.12	14.15	14.18	14.20	14.21	14.22	14.23	14.25	14.26	14.27	14.27
101.25	13.15	13.78	13.98	14.08	14.14	14.18	14.21	14.23	14.25	14.26	14.27	14.27	14.29	14.30	14.30	14.30
101.00	13.42	13.92	14.08	14.16	14.21	14.24	14.27	14.28	14.29	14.30	14.31	14.32	14.33	14.34	14.34	14.34
100.75	13.69	14.06	14.19	14.25	14.28	14.31	14.32	14.34	14.34	14.35	14.36	14.36	14.37	14.38	14.38	14.38
100.50	13.96	14.21	14.29	14.33	14.35	14.37	14.38	14.39	14.39	14.40	14.40	14.41	14.41	14.42	14.42	14.42
100.25	14.23	14.35	14.39	14.41	14.42	14.43	14.44	14.44	14.44	14.45	14.45	14.45	14.45	14.46	14.46	14.46
100.00	14.50	14.50	14.50	14.50	14.50	14.50	14.50	14.50	14.50	14.50	14.50	14.50	14.50	14.50	14.50	14.50
99.75	14.77	14.64	14.60	14.58	14.57	14.56	14.55	14.55	14.55	14.54	14.54	14.54	14.54	14.53	14.53	14.53
99.50	15.04	14.79	14.70	14.66	14.64	14.62	14.61	14.60	14.60	14.60	14.59	14.59	14.58	14.57	14.57	14.57
99.25	15.31	14.93	14.81	14.75	14.71	14.69	14.67	14.66	14.65	14.64	14.63	14.63	14.62	14.61	14.61	14.61
99.00	15.58	15.08	14.91	14.83	14.78	14.75	14.73	14.71	14.70	14.69	14.68	14.68	14.66	14.65	14.65	14.65
98.75	15.86	15.23	15.02	14.91	14.85	14.81	14.78	14.76	14.75	14.74	14.73	14.72	14.71	14.69	14.69	14.69
98.50	16.13	15.37	15.12	15.00	14.92	14.88	14.84	14.82	14.80	14.79	14.78	14.77	14.75	14.74	14.73	14.73
98.25	16.41	15.52	15.23	15.08	15.00	14.94	14.90	14.87	14.85	14.84	14.82	14.81	14.79	14.78	14.77	14.77
98.00	16.68	15.67	15.33	15.17	15.07	15.01	14.96	14.93	14.90	14.89	14.87	14.86	14.83	14.82	14.81	14.81
97.75	16.96	15.82	15.44	15.25	15.14	15.07	15.02	14.98	14.96	14.93	14.92	14.90	14.88	14.86	14.85	14.85
97.50	17.24	15.97	15.55	15.34	15.22	15.14	15.08	15.04	15.01	14.98	14.97	14.95	14.92	14.90	14.89	14.89
97.25	17.52	16.12	15.65	15.42	15.29	15.20	15.14	15.09	15.06	15.03	15.01	15.00	14.97	14.94	14.93	14.93
97	17.80	16.27	15.76	15.51	15.36	15.27	15.20	15.15	15.11	15.08	15.06	15.04	15.01	14.98	14.97	14.97
96	18.92	16.87	16.19	15.86	15.66	15.53	15.44	15.37	15.33	15.29	15.26	15.23	15.19	15.15	15.14	15.13
95	20.06	17.48	16.63	16.21	15.96	15.80	15.69	15.60	15.54	15.49	15.46	15.43	15.37	15.32	15.31	15.30
94	21.21	18.10	17.07	16.57	16.27	16.07	15.93	15.83	15.76	15.70	15.66	15.62	15.55	15.50	15.48	15.47
93	22.38	18.73	17.52	16.93	16.57	16.35	16.19	16.07	15.98	15.91	15.86	15.82	15.74	15.67	15.65	15.65
92	23.56	19.36	17.97	17.29	16.89	16.62	16.44	16.31	16.21	16.13	16.07	16.02	15.93	15.85	15.83	15.82
91	24.76	20.00	18.43	17.66	17.21	16.91	16.70	16.55	16.44	16.35	16.28	16.23	16.12	16.04	16.01	16.01
90	25.97	20.65	18.90	18.04	17.53	17.19	16.96	16.80	16.67	16.57	16.50	16.44	16.32	16.23	16.20	16.19
89	27.19	21.31	19.37	18.42	17.85	17.49	17.23	17.05	16.91	16.80	16.71	16.65	16.52	16.42	16.39	16.38
88	28.44	21.98	19.85	18.80	18.19	17.78	17.50	17.30	17.15	17.03	16.94	16.86	16.72	16.62	16.58	16.57
87	29.69	22.65	20.34	19.19	18.52	18.08	17.78	17.56	17.39	17.26	17.16	17.09	16.93	16.82	16.78	16.77
86	30.97	23.34	20.83	19.59	18.86	18.39	18.06	17.82	17.64	17.50	17.39	17.31	17.14	17.02	16.98	16.97
85	32.26	24.03	21.33	19.99	19.21	18.70	18.34	18.09	17.89	17.74	17.63	17.54	17.36	17.23	17.19	17.18
80	38.99	27.65	23.93	22.10	21.02	20.32	19.84	19.49	19.23	19.03	18.87	18.75	18.52	18.35	18.29	18.28
75	46.21	31.54	26.74	24.38	22.99	22.10	21.48	21.03	20.70	20.44	20.25	20.09	19.80	19.60	19.54	19.53
70	54.01	35.74	29.78	26.85	25.14	24.04	23.27	22.73	22.32	22.01	21.78	21.60	21.25	21.02	20.96	20.95
65	62.48	40.31	33.10	29.57	27.51	26.18	25.27	24.62	24.14	23.78	23.50	23.29	22.90	22.65	22.59	22.57
60	71.72	45.31	36.75	32.57	30.14	28.57	27.51	26.75	26.20	25.78	25.47	25.23	24.80	24.54	24.48	24.47
55	81.91	50.84	40.79	35.91	33.09	31.28	30.05	29.18	28.55	28.09	27.75	27.49	27.03	26.77	26.71	26.70
50	93.22	57.00	45.34	39.70	36.44	34.37	32.98	32.00	31.30	30.80	30.42	30.15	29.68	29.43	29.39	29.38

Description: This table shows the price to pay for a monthly payment loan, at a yield rate and assuming prepayment.

Example: The price of a 14.75 %, 30 year mortgage to yield 8.00 %, if prepaid in 6 years, is $ 131.87.

30 YEAR MORTGAGE PREPAID IN

YIELD	1 yr	2 yr	3 yr	4 yr	5 yr	6 yr	7 yr	8 yr	9 yr	10 yr	11 yr	12 yr	15 yr	20 yr	25 yr	30 yr
0.00	114.74	129.44	144.11	158.74	173.32	187.85	202.31	216.69	230.99	245.19	259.27	273.22	314.02	376.55	425.94	448.01
1.00	113.66	127.16	140.50	153.66	166.65	179.46	192.08	204.52	216.76	228.79	240.60	252.19	285.42	334.36	371.18	386.92
2.00	112.60	124.93	136.98	148.76	160.27	171.51	182.48	193.17	203.60	213.74	223.60	233.17	260.09	298.22	325.53	336.69
3.00	111.55	122.74	133.57	144.05	154.19	163.99	173.46	182.60	191.42	199.91	208.09	215.96	237.64	267.16	287.30	295.18
4.00	110.51	120.59	130.25	139.51	148.37	156.86	164.97	172.73	180.14	187.21	193.95	200.36	217.69	240.40	255.15	260.67
4.25	110.25	120.06	129.44	138.40	146.95	155.13	162.93	170.37	177.45	184.20	190.61	196.69	213.06	234.30	247.93	252.97
4.50	110.00	119.53	128.63	137.30	145.56	153.43	160.92	168.05	174.82	181.25	187.34	193.11	208.57	228.42	241.01	245.61
4.75	109.74	119.01	127.83	136.21	144.18	151.75	158.94	165.77	172.23	178.36	184.15	189.62	204.20	222.75	234.36	238.57
5.00	109.48	118.48	127.03	135.13	142.82	150.10	157.00	163.52	169.70	175.53	181.03	186.21	199.96	217.28	227.99	231.82
5.25	109.23	117.97	126.24	134.06	141.47	148.47	155.08	161.32	167.21	172.76	177.98	182.89	195.84	212.00	221.87	225.37
5.50	108.97	117.45	125.45	133.01	140.13	146.85	153.19	159.15	164.77	170.04	174.99	179.64	191.83	206.90	216.00	219.18
5.75	108.72	116.93	124.67	131.96	138.81	145.26	151.33	157.02	162.37	167.38	172.08	176.47	187.94	201.98	210.35	213.25
6.00	108.46	116.42	123.90	130.92	137.51	143.70	149.49	154.93	160.02	164.78	169.22	173.37	184.15	197.23	204.93	207.57
6.25	108.21	115.91	123.13	129.89	136.22	142.15	147.69	152.87	157.71	162.22	166.43	170.35	180.48	192.64	199.72	202.12
6.50	107.96	115.40	122.36	128.87	134.95	140.62	145.91	150.85	155.45	159.73	163.70	167.40	176.90	188.21	194.71	196.89
6.75	107.71	114.90	121.61	127.86	133.69	139.11	144.16	148.86	153.22	157.28	161.03	164.51	173.43	183.93	189.90	191.87
7.00	107.46	114.40	120.85	126.86	132.44	137.62	142.44	146.90	151.04	154.88	158.42	161.70	170.05	179.80	185.26	187.05
7.25	107.21	113.90	120.11	125.87	131.21	136.16	140.74	144.98	148.90	152.53	155.87	158.95	166.77	175.80	180.81	182.43
7.50	106.96	113.40	119.37	124.88	129.99	134.71	139.07	143.09	146.80	150.22	153.37	156.26	163.57	171.94	176.52	177.98
7.75	106.71	112.91	118.63	123.91	128.78	133.28	137.42	141.23	144.74	147.97	150.93	153.64	160.47	168.20	172.38	173.71
8.00	106.46	112.41	117.90	122.95	127.59	131.87	135.80	139.40	142.72	145.75	148.54	151.08	157.44	164.59	168.41	169.60
8.25	106.21	111.92	117.17	121.99	126.41	130.47	134.20	137.61	140.73	143.59	146.20	148.58	154.50	161.09	164.57	165.65
8.50	105.97	111.44	116.45	121.04	125.25	129.10	132.62	135.84	138.78	141.46	143.91	146.13	151.64	157.71	160.88	161.85
8.75	105.72	110.95	115.73	120.11	124.10	127.74	131.07	134.10	136.87	139.38	141.67	143.74	148.86	154.44	157.32	158.19
9.00	105.47	110.47	115.02	119.18	122.96	126.41	129.54	132.40	134.99	137.34	139.48	141.41	146.15	151.28	153.88	154.67
9.25	105.23	109.99	114.32	118.26	121.83	125.09	128.04	130.72	133.14	135.34	137.33	139.13	143.51	148.21	150.57	151.27
9.50	104.99	109.51	113.62	117.34	120.72	123.78	126.56	129.06	131.33	133.38	135.23	136.90	140.95	145.24	147.38	148.00
9.75	104.74	109.04	112.92	116.44	119.62	122.50	125.09	127.44	129.56	131.46	133.18	134.72	138.45	142.37	144.29	144.85
10.00	104.50	108.56	112.23	115.54	118.53	121.23	123.66	125.84	127.81	129.58	131.17	132.59	136.02	139.59	141.31	141.81
10.25	104.26	108.09	111.55	114.66	117.46	119.97	122.24	124.27	126.10	127.73	129.20	130.51	133.65	136.89	138.44	138.88
10.50	104.01	107.62	110.86	113.78	116.39	118.74	120.84	122.73	124.41	125.92	127.27	128.47	131.34	134.27	135.66	136.05
10.75	103.77	107.16	110.19	112.91	115.34	117.52	119.46	121.21	122.76	124.15	125.39	126.49	129.10	131.74	132.97	133.32
11.00	103.53	106.69	109.52	112.04	114.30	116.31	118.11	119.71	121.14	122.41	123.54	124.54	126.91	129.28	130.38	130.68
11.25	103.29	106.23	108.85	111.19	113.27	115.12	116.77	118.24	119.55	120.70	121.73	122.64	124.78	126.90	127.87	128.13
11.50	103.05	105.77	108.19	110.34	112.25	113.95	115.46	116.79	117.98	119.03	119.96	120.78	122.70	124.59	125.44	125.67
11.75	102.82	105.31	107.53	109.50	111.24	112.79	114.16	115.37	116.44	117.39	118.23	118.96	120.68	122.35	123.09	123.29
12.00	102.58	104.86	106.88	108.67	110.25	111.65	112.88	113.97	114.93	115.78	116.53	117.18	118.70	120.17	120.82	120.99
12.25	102.34	104.41	106.23	107.84	109.26	110.52	111.62	112.60	113.45	114.21	114.87	115.45	116.78	118.06	118.62	118.76
12.50	102.10	103.96	105.59	107.03	108.29	109.40	110.38	111.24	112.00	112.66	113.24	113.75	114.91	116.01	116.48	116.60
12.75	101.87	103.51	104.95	106.22	107.33	108.30	109.16	109.91	110.57	111.14	111.64	112.08	113.08	114.02	114.42	114.52
13.00	101.63	103.06	104.32	105.41	106.38	107.22	107.96	108.60	109.16	109.65	110.08	110.45	111.30	112.09	112.42	112.50
13.25	101.40	102.62	103.69	104.62	105.44	106.15	106.77	107.31	107.78	108.19	108.55	108.86	109.56	110.21	110.48	110.54
13.50	101.16	102.18	103.06	103.83	104.50	105.09	105.60	106.04	106.43	106.76	107.05	107.30	107.87	108.39	108.60	108.65
13.75	100.93	101.74	102.44	103.05	103.58	104.05	104.45	104.79	105.10	105.36	105.58	105.78	106.22	106.61	106.77	106.81
14.00	100.70	101.30	101.82	102.28	102.67	103.01	103.31	103.57	103.79	103.98	104.14	104.29	104.61	104.89	105.00	105.03
14.25	100.46	100.86	101.21	101.51	101.77	102.00	102.19	102.36	102.50	102.63	102.74	102.83	103.03	103.21	103.29	103.30
14.50	100.23	100.43	100.60	100.75	100.88	100.99	101.09	101.17	101.24	101.30	101.35	101.40	101.50	101.58	101.62	101.63
14.75	100.00	100.00	100.00	100.00	100.00	100.00	100.00	100.00	100.00	100.00	100.00	100.00	100.00	100.00	100.00	100.00
15.00	99.77	99.57	99.40	99.25	99.13	99.02	98.93	98.85	98.78	98.72	98.67	98.63	98.54	98.46	98.43	98.42
15.25	99.54	99.14	98.81	98.52	98.27	98.05	97.87	97.72	97.58	97.47	97.37	97.29	97.11	96.96	96.90	96.89
15.50	99.31	98.72	98.21	97.78	97.41	97.10	96.83	96.60	96.41	96.24	96.10	95.98	95.72	95.50	95.42	95.40
15.75	99.08	98.30	97.63	97.06	96.57	96.16	95.80	95.50	95.25	95.03	94.85	94.69	94.36	94.08	93.97	93.95
16.00	98.85	97.88	97.05	96.34	95.74	95.23	94.79	94.43	94.11	93.85	93.63	93.44	93.03	92.69	92.57	92.54
16.25	98.63	97.46	96.47	95.63	94.91	94.31	93.80	93.36	93.00	92.69	92.42	92.20	91.73	91.34	91.20	91.17
16.50	98.40	97.04	95.89	94.92	94.10	93.40	92.81	92.32	91.90	91.55	91.25	91.00	90.47	90.03	89.88	89.84
16.75	98.17	96.63	95.32	94.22	93.29	92.51	91.84	91.29	90.82	90.42	90.09	89.82	89.23	88.75	88.59	88.55
17.00	97.95	96.21	94.76	93.53	92.49	91.62	90.89	90.27	89.76	89.33	88.96	88.66	88.02	87.50	87.33	87.29
17.25	97.72	95.80	94.19	92.84	91.70	90.75	89.95	89.28	88.72	88.25	87.85	87.52	86.84	86.29	86.10	86.06
17.50	97.50	95.40	93.63	92.16	90.92	89.89	89.02	88.30	87.69	87.19	86.76	86.41	85.68	85.10	84.91	84.87
17.75	97.27	94.99	93.08	91.48	90.15	89.04	88.11	87.33	86.68	86.15	85.70	85.33	84.55	83.95	83.75	83.71
18.00	97.05	94.58	92.53	90.82	89.39	88.20	87.20	86.38	85.69	85.12	84.65	84.26	83.45	82.82	82.62	82.57
18.25	96.83	94.18	91.98	90.15	88.63	87.37	86.31	85.44	84.72	84.12	83.62	83.21	82.37	81.72	81.51	81.47
18.50	96.60	93.78	91.44	89.50	87.88	86.55	85.44	84.52	83.76	83.14	82.62	82.19	81.31	80.65	80.44	80.40
18.75	96.38	93.38	90.90	88.84	87.14	85.74	84.57	83.61	82.82	82.17	81.63	81.19	80.28	79.60	79.39	79.35
19.00	96.16	92.99	90.36	88.20	86.41	84.94	83.72	82.72	81.90	81.22	80.66	80.20	79.27	78.58	78.37	78.32
20.00	95.28	91.42	88.26	85.68	83.57	81.84	80.43	79.28	78.35	77.58	76.96	76.46	75.45	74.73	74.51	74.47
25.00	91.02	84.02	78.57	74.33	71.03	68.46	66.46	64.91	63.71	62.78	62.05	61.49	60.47	59.86	59.72	59.70
30.00	86.97	77.31	70.14	64.83	60.89	57.97	55.81	54.21	53.03	52.16	51.52	51.04	50.25	49.85	49.78	49.77

PREPAYMENT MORTGAGE YIELD, 30 YEAR TERM

14.75 %

Description: This table shows the yield to prepayment of a monthly payment mortgage purchased at a price in the index.

Example: The yield to prepayment in 10 years of a 14.75 %, 30 year mortgage at a price of 104.00 is 13.99 %.

30 YEAR MORTGAGE PREPAID IN

PRICE	1 yr	2 yr	3 yr	4 yr	5 yr	6 yr	7 yr	8 yr	9 yr	10 yr	11 yr	12 yr	15 yr	20 yr	25 yr	30 yr
140	–	–	1.13	3.88	5.52	6.60	7.36	7.91	8.34	8.67	8.93	9.15	9.59	9.96	10.11	10.15
135	–	–	2.57	5.03	6.48	7.44	8.12	8.62	8.99	9.29	9.52	9.71	10.10	10.42	10.56	10.59
130	–	–	4.07	6.22	7.49	8.33	8.92	9.35	9.68	9.94	10.14	10.31	10.64	10.92	11.03	11.06
125	–	1.96	5.64	7.47	8.55	9.26	9.76	10.13	10.41	10.62	10.80	10.94	11.22	11.45	11.54	11.56
120	–	4.27	7.28	8.77	9.66	10.24	10.65	10.95	11.17	11.35	11.49	11.60	11.83	12.02	12.09	12.10
119	–	4.75	7.62	9.04	9.89	10.44	10.83	11.12	11.33	11.50	11.63	11.74	11.96	12.13	12.20	12.22
118	–	5.23	7.96	9.31	10.12	10.65	11.02	11.29	11.49	11.65	11.78	11.88	12.09	12.25	12.32	12.33
117	–	5.71	8.30	9.59	10.35	10.85	11.20	11.46	11.65	11.81	11.93	12.02	12.22	12.37	12.43	12.45
116	–	6.20	8.65	9.87	10.59	11.06	11.39	11.63	11.82	11.96	12.07	12.16	12.35	12.50	12.55	12.57
115	–	6.70	9.00	10.15	10.83	11.27	11.58	11.81	11.98	12.12	12.22	12.31	12.48	12.62	12.67	12.69
114	–	7.19	9.36	10.43	11.07	11.48	11.78	11.99	12.15	12.28	12.38	12.46	12.62	12.75	12.80	12.81
113	1.62	7.70	9.72	10.72	11.31	11.70	11.97	12.17	12.32	12.44	12.53	12.61	12.76	12.88	12.92	12.93
112	2.57	8.21	10.08	11.01	11.56	11.92	12.17	12.35	12.49	12.60	12.69	12.76	12.90	13.01	13.05	13.06
111	3.52	8.72	10.45	11.30	11.81	12.14	12.37	12.54	12.67	12.77	12.85	12.91	13.04	13.14	13.18	13.19
110	4.49	9.24	10.82	11.60	12.06	12.36	12.57	12.73	12.85	12.94	13.01	13.07	13.18	13.27	13.31	13.32
109	5.47	9.76	11.19	11.89	12.31	12.59	12.78	12.92	13.02	13.11	13.17	13.22	13.33	13.41	13.44	13.45
108	6.46	10.29	11.57	12.20	12.57	12.81	12.99	13.11	13.21	13.28	13.34	13.38	13.48	13.55	13.58	13.58
107	7.45	10.83	11.95	12.50	12.83	13.05	13.20	13.31	13.39	13.45	13.50	13.54	13.63	13.69	13.71	13.72
106	8.46	11.37	12.33	12.81	13.09	13.28	13.41	13.50	13.57	13.63	13.67	13.71	13.78	13.83	13.85	13.86
105	9.48	11.92	12.73	13.13	13.36	13.52	13.62	13.70	13.76	13.81	13.85	13.87	13.93	13.98	14.00	14.00
104	10.51	12.47	13.12	13.44	13.63	13.76	13.84	13.91	13.95	13.99	14.02	14.04	14.09	14.13	14.14	14.14
103.75	10.77	12.61	13.22	13.52	13.70	13.82	13.90	13.96	14.00	14.04	14.06	14.09	14.13	14.16	14.18	14.18
103.50	11.03	12.75	13.32	13.60	13.77	13.88	13.95	14.01	14.05	14.08	14.11	14.13	14.17	14.20	14.21	14.22
103.25	11.29	12.89	13.42	13.68	13.84	13.94	14.01	14.06	14.10	14.13	14.15	14.17	14.21	14.24	14.25	14.25
103.00	11.55	13.03	13.52	13.76	13.90	14.00	14.06	14.11	14.15	14.18	14.20	14.22	14.25	14.28	14.29	14.29
102.75	11.81	13.17	13.62	13.84	13.97	14.06	14.12	14.16	14.20	14.22	14.24	14.26	14.29	14.32	14.32	14.33
102.50	12.08	13.31	13.72	13.92	14.04	14.12	14.18	14.22	14.25	14.27	14.29	14.30	14.33	14.35	14.36	14.36
102.25	12.34	13.45	13.82	14.00	14.11	14.18	14.23	14.27	14.29	14.32	14.33	14.35	14.37	14.39	14.40	14.40
102.00	12.60	13.60	13.92	14.09	14.18	14.24	14.29	14.32	14.34	14.36	14.38	14.39	14.41	14.43	14.44	14.44
101.75	12.87	13.74	14.02	14.17	14.25	14.31	14.34	14.37	14.39	14.41	14.42	14.43	14.45	14.47	14.48	14.48
101.50	13.13	13.88	14.13	14.25	14.32	14.37	14.40	14.43	14.44	14.46	14.47	14.48	14.49	14.51	14.51	14.51
101.25	13.40	14.02	14.23	14.33	14.39	14.43	14.46	14.48	14.49	14.50	14.51	14.52	14.54	14.55	14.55	14.55
101.00	13.67	14.17	14.33	14.41	14.46	14.49	14.51	14.53	14.54	14.55	14.56	14.57	14.58	14.59	14.59	14.59
100.75	13.94	14.31	14.43	14.50	14.53	14.56	14.57	14.58	14.59	14.60	14.61	14.61	14.62	14.63	14.63	14.63
100.50	14.21	14.46	14.54	14.58	14.60	14.62	14.63	14.63	14.64	14.64	14.65	14.66	14.66	14.67	14.67	14.67
100.25	14.47	14.60	14.64	14.66	14.67	14.68	14.68	14.69	14.69	14.69	14.70	14.70	14.70	14.71	14.71	14.71
100.00	14.75	14.75	14.75	14.75	14.75	14.75	14.75	14.75	14.75	14.75	14.75	14.75	14.75	14.75	14.75	14.75
99.75	15.02	14.89	14.85	14.83	14.82	14.81	14.80	14.80	14.80	14.79	14.79	14.79	14.79	14.79	14.78	14.78
99.50	15.29	15.04	14.95	14.91	14.89	14.87	14.86	14.85	14.85	14.84	14.84	14.84	14.83	14.83	14.82	14.82
99.25	15.56	15.18	15.06	15.00	14.96	14.94	14.92	14.91	14.90	14.89	14.89	14.88	14.87	14.87	14.86	14.86
99.00	15.83	15.33	15.16	15.08	15.03	15.00	14.98	14.96	14.95	14.94	14.93	14.93	14.92	14.91	14.90	14.90
98.75	16.11	15.48	15.27	15.17	15.10	15.06	15.04	15.02	15.00	14.99	14.98	14.97	14.96	14.95	14.94	14.94
98.50	16.38	15.62	15.37	15.25	15.18	15.13	15.10	15.07	15.05	15.04	15.03	15.02	15.00	14.99	14.98	14.98
98.25	16.66	15.77	15.48	15.34	15.25	15.19	15.16	15.13	15.11	15.09	15.08	15.07	15.05	15.03	15.02	15.02
98.00	16.94	15.92	15.59	15.42	15.32	15.26	15.21	15.18	15.16	15.14	15.12	15.11	15.09	15.07	15.06	15.06
97.75	17.21	16.07	15.69	15.51	15.40	15.32	15.27	15.24	15.21	15.19	15.17	15.16	15.13	15.11	15.11	15.10
97.50	17.49	16.22	15.80	15.59	15.47	15.39	15.33	15.29	15.26	15.24	15.22	15.21	15.18	15.15	15.15	15.14
97.25	17.77	16.37	15.91	15.68	15.54	15.46	15.39	15.35	15.32	15.29	15.27	15.25	15.22	15.20	15.19	15.19
97	18.05	16.52	16.01	15.77	15.62	15.52	15.45	15.41	15.37	15.34	15.32	15.30	15.26	15.24	15.23	15.23
96	19.18	17.13	16.45	16.11	15.92	15.79	15.70	15.63	15.58	15.54	15.51	15.49	15.44	15.41	15.40	15.39
95	20.32	17.74	16.89	16.47	16.22	16.06	15.94	15.86	15.80	15.75	15.71	15.68	15.63	15.58	15.57	15.56
94	21.47	18.36	17.33	16.82	16.53	16.33	16.19	16.09	16.02	15.96	15.92	15.88	15.81	15.76	15.74	15.74
93	22.64	18.99	17.78	17.19	16.84	16.61	16.45	16.33	16.24	16.18	16.12	16.08	16.00	15.94	15.92	15.91
92	23.82	19.62	18.24	17.55	17.15	16.89	16.70	16.57	16.47	16.39	16.33	16.29	16.19	16.12	16.10	16.09
91	25.02	20.27	18.70	17.93	17.47	17.17	16.97	16.82	16.70	16.62	16.55	16.49	16.39	16.31	16.28	16.28
90	26.23	20.92	19.17	18.30	17.79	17.46	17.23	17.06	16.94	16.84	16.77	16.71	16.59	16.50	16.47	16.47
89	27.46	21.58	19.64	18.69	18.12	17.76	17.50	17.32	17.18	17.07	16.99	16.92	16.79	16.70	16.66	16.66
88	28.70	22.25	20.12	19.07	18.46	18.05	17.77	17.57	17.42	17.30	17.21	17.14	17.00	16.89	16.86	16.85
87	29.96	22.92	20.61	19.47	18.79	18.36	18.05	17.83	17.67	17.54	17.44	17.36	17.21	17.10	17.06	17.05
86	31.24	23.61	21.10	19.86	19.14	18.66	18.33	18.10	17.92	17.78	17.67	17.59	17.43	17.31	17.27	17.26
85	32.53	24.31	21.60	20.27	19.49	18.98	18.62	18.36	18.17	18.03	17.91	17.82	17.65	17.52	17.48	17.47
80	39.27	27.93	24.21	22.39	21.31	20.61	20.13	19.78	19.52	19.32	19.17	19.05	18.81	18.65	18.60	18.59
75	46.51	31.83	27.03	24.67	23.29	22.40	21.78	21.33	21.00	20.75	20.56	20.41	20.12	19.92	19.86	19.85
70	54.32	36.05	30.09	27.17	25.46	24.35	23.59	23.05	22.65	22.34	22.11	21.93	21.59	21.36	21.30	21.29
65	62.79	40.63	33.42	29.90	27.84	26.52	25.61	24.96	24.48	24.13	23.85	23.65	23.26	23.02	22.96	22.94
60	72.06	45.65	37.09	32.91	30.49	28.93	27.87	27.11	26.56	26.16	25.85	25.61	25.19	24.94	24.88	24.87
55	82.26	51.19	41.16	36.28	33.46	31.66	30.43	29.57	28.95	28.49	28.15	27.90	27.45	27.20	27.15	27.14
50	93.60	57.37	45.72	40.09	36.84	34.78	33.39	32.43	31.74	31.24	30.87	30.60	30.14	29.91	29.86	29.86

Description: This table shows the price to pay for a monthly payment loan, at a yield rate and assuming prepayment.

Example: The price of a 15.00 %, 30 year mortgage to yield 8.00 %, if prepaid in 6 years, is $ 133.06.

30 YEAR MORTGAGE PREPAID IN

YIELD	1 yr	2 yr	3 yr	4 yr	5 yr	6 yr	7 yr	8 yr	9 yr	10 yr	11 yr	12 yr	15 yr	20 yr	25 yr	30 yr
0.00	114.99	129.95	144.87	159.75	174.59	189.37	204.09	218.73	233.30	247.76	262.11	276.32	317.94	381.84	432.48	455.20
1.00	113.91	127.66	141.24	154.65	167.88	180.93	193.80	206.48	218.96	231.23	243.28	255.10	289.04	339.11	376.91	393.12
2.00	112.85	125.42	137.71	149.73	161.47	172.94	184.13	195.05	205.69	216.05	226.12	235.91	263.44	302.50	330.57	342.09
3.00	111.80	123.22	134.29	145.00	155.35	165.37	175.05	184.40	193.42	202.11	210.48	218.53	240.74	271.04	291.77	299.91
4.00	110.76	121.07	130.96	140.43	149.51	158.20	166.51	174.46	182.05	189.30	196.21	202.78	220.57	243.92	259.14	264.85
4.25	110.50	120.54	130.14	139.32	148.09	156.47	164.46	172.08	179.35	186.26	192.84	199.08	215.89	237.74	251.81	257.03
4.50	110.24	120.01	129.33	138.22	146.69	154.76	162.44	169.74	176.69	183.28	189.54	195.47	211.35	231.78	244.78	249.55
4.75	109.98	119.48	128.53	137.12	145.30	153.07	160.44	167.45	174.08	180.37	186.32	191.94	206.93	226.03	238.03	242.39
5.00	109.73	118.96	127.73	136.04	143.93	151.40	158.48	165.19	171.53	177.52	183.17	188.50	202.64	220.49	231.56	235.54
5.25	109.47	118.44	126.93	134.97	142.57	149.76	156.55	162.97	169.02	174.72	180.09	185.14	198.47	215.14	225.35	228.98
5.50	109.22	117.92	126.14	133.91	141.23	148.14	154.65	160.78	166.55	171.98	177.08	181.86	194.42	209.97	219.39	222.70
5.75	108.96	117.41	125.36	132.85	139.90	146.54	152.78	158.64	164.14	169.30	174.13	178.66	190.48	204.98	213.66	216.67
6.00	108.71	116.89	124.58	131.81	138.59	144.96	150.93	156.53	161.77	166.67	171.25	175.53	186.65	200.17	208.15	210.90
6.25	108.45	116.38	123.81	130.77	137.30	143.40	149.11	154.45	159.44	164.10	168.44	172.48	182.94	195.52	202.86	205.36
6.50	108.20	115.87	123.05	129.75	136.02	141.86	147.32	152.41	157.16	161.58	165.68	169.49	179.32	191.03	197.78	200.05
6.75	107.95	115.37	122.29	128.74	134.75	140.35	145.56	150.41	154.92	159.10	162.99	166.58	175.81	186.69	192.89	194.95
7.00	107.70	114.86	121.53	127.73	133.49	138.85	143.82	148.44	152.72	156.68	160.35	163.74	172.39	182.50	188.19	190.06
7.25	107.45	114.36	120.78	126.73	132.26	137.37	142.11	146.50	150.56	154.31	157.77	160.96	169.07	178.44	183.66	185.35
7.50	107.20	113.86	120.04	125.75	131.03	135.92	140.43	144.60	148.44	151.99	155.25	158.25	165.83	174.53	179.30	180.84
7.75	106.95	113.37	119.30	124.77	129.82	134.48	138.77	142.73	146.36	149.71	152.78	155.60	162.69	170.74	175.11	176.50
8.00	106.70	112.87	118.56	123.80	128.62	133.06	137.14	140.88	144.32	147.48	150.37	153.01	159.63	167.08	171.07	172.32
8.25	106.45	112.38	117.83	122.84	127.44	131.66	135.53	139.07	142.32	145.29	148.01	150.48	156.66	163.53	167.18	168.31
8.50	106.21	111.90	117.11	121.89	126.27	130.28	133.94	137.29	140.35	143.15	145.70	148.01	153.76	160.11	163.43	164.45
8.75	105.96	111.41	116.39	120.95	125.11	128.91	132.38	135.54	138.42	141.05	143.43	145.60	150.95	156.79	159.81	160.73
9.00	105.71	110.93	115.68	120.01	123.97	127.56	130.84	133.82	136.53	138.99	141.22	143.24	148.20	153.58	156.32	157.15
9.25	105.47	110.44	114.97	119.09	122.83	126.24	129.32	132.13	134.67	136.97	139.05	140.94	145.54	150.47	152.96	153.70
9.50	105.22	109.96	114.27	118.17	121.71	124.92	127.83	130.46	132.84	134.99	136.93	138.68	142.94	147.46	149.71	150.38
9.75	104.98	109.49	113.57	117.27	120.61	123.63	126.36	128.83	131.05	133.05	134.86	136.48	140.41	144.55	146.58	147.17
10.00	104.74	109.01	112.88	116.37	119.51	122.35	124.91	127.22	129.29	131.15	132.83	134.33	137.95	141.72	143.56	144.08
10.25	104.49	108.54	112.19	115.47	118.43	121.09	123.48	125.63	127.56	129.29	130.84	132.23	135.55	138.99	140.64	141.11
10.50	104.25	108.07	111.51	114.59	117.36	119.85	122.08	124.07	125.86	127.46	128.89	130.17	133.22	136.34	137.81	138.23
10.75	104.01	107.60	110.83	113.72	116.30	118.62	120.69	122.54	124.20	125.67	126.99	128.16	130.94	133.76	135.09	135.45
11.00	103.77	107.14	110.15	112.85	115.26	117.41	119.32	121.03	122.56	123.92	125.12	126.20	128.73	131.27	132.45	132.77
11.25	103.53	106.68	109.48	111.99	114.22	116.21	117.98	119.55	120.95	122.20	123.30	124.27	126.57	128.86	129.90	130.19
11.50	103.29	106.22	108.82	111.14	113.20	115.03	116.65	118.09	119.37	120.51	121.51	122.40	124.47	126.51	127.44	127.68
11.75	103.05	105.76	108.16	110.29	112.18	113.86	115.35	116.66	117.82	118.85	119.76	120.56	122.42	124.24	125.05	125.27
12.00	102.81	105.30	107.51	109.46	111.18	112.71	114.06	115.25	116.30	117.23	118.04	118.76	120.42	122.03	122.74	122.93
12.25	102.57	104.85	106.86	108.63	110.19	111.57	112.79	113.86	114.81	115.63	116.36	117.00	118.48	119.89	120.50	120.66
12.50	102.34	104.40	106.21	107.81	109.22	110.45	111.54	112.50	113.34	114.07	114.72	115.28	116.58	117.81	118.34	118.48
12.75	102.10	103.95	105.57	107.00	108.25	109.35	110.31	111.15	111.89	112.54	113.11	113.60	114.73	115.79	116.24	116.36
13.00	101.86	103.50	104.93	106.19	107.29	108.25	109.10	109.83	110.48	111.04	111.53	111.96	112.93	113.83	114.21	114.31
13.25	101.63	103.05	104.30	105.39	106.34	107.17	107.90	108.53	109.08	109.56	109.98	110.35	111.17	111.92	112.24	112.32
13.50	101.39	102.61	103.67	104.60	105.41	106.11	106.72	107.25	107.72	108.12	108.47	108.77	109.45	110.07	110.33	110.39
13.75	101.16	102.17	103.05	103.82	104.48	105.06	105.56	106.00	106.37	106.70	106.98	107.23	107.78	108.28	108.48	108.53
14.00	100.93	101.73	102.43	103.04	103.56	104.02	104.42	104.76	105.05	105.31	105.53	105.72	106.15	106.53	106.68	106.72
14.25	100.69	101.30	101.82	102.27	102.66	103.00	103.29	103.54	103.76	103.94	104.11	104.24	104.55	104.83	104.93	104.96
14.50	100.46	100.86	101.21	101.51	101.76	101.98	102.18	102.34	102.48	102.60	102.71	102.80	103.00	103.17	103.24	103.26
14.75	100.23	100.43	100.60	100.75	100.88	100.99	101.08	101.16	101.23	101.29	101.34	101.38	101.48	101.56	101.60	101.60
15.00	100.00	100.00	100.00	100.00	100.00	100.00	100.00	100.00	100.00	100.00	100.00	100.00	100.00	100.00	100.00	100.00
15.25	99.77	99.57	99.40	99.26	99.13	99.03	98.94	98.86	98.79	98.73	98.69	98.64	98.55	98.48	98.45	98.44
15.50	99.54	99.15	98.81	98.52	98.28	98.07	97.89	97.73	97.60	97.49	97.40	97.32	97.14	97.00	96.94	96.93
15.75	99.31	98.72	98.22	97.79	97.43	97.12	96.85	96.63	96.44	96.27	96.13	96.02	95.77	95.55	95.47	95.46
16.00	99.08	98.30	97.64	97.07	96.59	96.18	95.83	95.54	95.29	95.08	94.90	94.75	94.42	94.15	94.05	94.03
16.25	98.85	97.88	97.06	96.35	95.76	95.26	94.83	94.47	94.16	93.90	93.68	93.50	93.11	92.78	92.66	92.64
16.50	98.63	97.46	96.48	95.64	94.94	94.34	93.84	93.41	93.05	92.75	92.49	92.28	91.82	91.45	91.31	91.29
16.75	98.40	97.05	95.91	94.94	94.13	93.44	92.86	92.37	91.96	91.62	91.33	91.08	90.57	90.15	90.00	89.97
17.00	98.17	96.63	95.34	94.24	93.32	92.55	91.90	91.35	90.89	90.51	90.18	89.91	89.34	88.88	88.72	88.69
17.25	97.95	96.22	94.77	93.55	92.53	91.67	90.95	90.35	89.84	89.42	89.06	88.77	88.14	87.65	87.48	87.45
17.50	97.72	95.81	94.21	92.87	91.75	90.80	90.02	89.36	88.80	88.34	87.96	87.64	86.97	86.45	86.27	86.23
17.75	97.50	95.41	93.66	92.19	90.97	89.95	89.09	88.38	87.79	87.29	86.88	86.54	85.83	85.27	85.09	85.05
18.00	97.28	95.00	93.10	91.52	90.20	89.10	88.18	87.42	86.79	86.26	85.82	85.46	84.71	84.13	83.94	83.90
18.25	97.05	94.60	92.55	90.85	89.44	88.26	87.29	86.48	85.80	85.25	84.79	84.40	83.62	83.01	82.82	82.78
18.50	96.83	94.20	92.01	90.19	88.69	87.44	86.40	85.55	84.84	84.25	83.77	83.37	82.55	81.93	81.72	81.69
18.75	96.61	93.80	91.47	89.54	87.94	86.62	85.53	84.63	83.89	83.27	82.77	82.35	81.50	80.86	80.66	80.62
19.00	96.39	93.40	90.93	88.89	87.21	85.82	84.67	83.73	82.95	82.31	81.79	81.36	80.48	79.83	79.62	79.58
20.00	95.51	91.83	88.82	86.36	84.34	82.70	81.36	80.26	79.37	78.64	78.05	77.57	76.61	75.91	75.71	75.67
25.00	91.24	84.41	79.09	74.95	71.73	69.22	67.27	65.76	64.58	63.67	62.96	62.42	61.42	60.82	60.68	60.66
30.00	87.19	77.68	70.63	65.40	61.52	58.65	56.52	54.95	53.78	52.93	52.29	51.82	51.04	50.65	50.58	50.57

Description: This table shows the yield to prepayment of a monthly payment mortgage purchased at a price in the index.

Example: The yield to prepayment in 10 years of a 15.00 %, 30 year mortgage at a price of 104.00 is 14.23 %.

30 YEAR MORTGAGE PREPAID IN

PRICE	1 yr	2 yr	3 yr	4 yr	5 yr	6 yr	7 yr	8 yr	9 yr	10 yr	11 yr	12 yr	15 yr	20 yr	25 yr	30 yr
140	–	–	1.34	4.09	5.73	6.80	7.56	8.12	8.54	8.87	9.14	9.35	9.79	10.15	10.30	10.34
135	–	–	2.78	5.24	6.70	7.65	8.33	8.82	9.20	9.49	9.73	9.92	10.30	10.62	10.75	10.79
130	–	–	4.29	6.43	7.71	8.55	9.13	9.57	9.89	10.15	10.35	10.52	10.85	11.13	11.24	11.26
125	–	2.18	5.86	7.69	8.77	9.48	9.98	10.35	10.62	10.84	11.01	11.15	11.43	11.66	11.75	11.77
120	–	4.50	7.51	9.00	9.88	10.46	10.87	11.17	11.40	11.57	11.71	11.82	12.05	12.23	12.30	12.32
119	–	4.98	7.85	9.27	10.11	10.67	11.05	11.34	11.55	11.72	11.85	11.96	12.18	12.35	12.42	12.43
118	–	5.46	8.19	9.54	10.35	10.87	11.24	11.51	11.72	11.88	12.00	12.10	12.31	12.47	12.53	12.55
117	–	5.94	8.53	9.82	10.58	11.08	11.43	11.69	11.88	12.03	12.15	12.25	12.44	12.59	12.65	12.67
116	–	6.43	8.88	10.10	10.82	11.29	11.62	11.86	12.04	12.19	12.30	12.39	12.57	12.72	12.77	12.79
115	–	6.93	9.23	10.38	11.06	11.50	11.81	12.04	12.21	12.35	12.45	12.54	12.71	12.84	12.90	12.91
114	–	7.43	9.59	10.66	11.30	11.72	12.01	12.22	12.38	12.51	12.61	12.69	12.85	12.97	13.02	13.03
113	1.85	7.93	9.95	10.95	11.54	11.93	12.20	12.40	12.55	12.67	12.76	12.84	12.98	13.10	13.15	13.16
112	2.80	8.44	10.31	11.24	11.79	12.15	12.40	12.59	12.73	12.83	12.92	12.99	13.13	13.24	13.28	13.29
111	3.76	8.96	10.68	11.54	12.04	12.37	12.60	12.77	12.90	13.00	13.08	13.14	13.27	13.37	13.41	13.42
110	4.73	9.48	11.05	11.83	12.29	12.60	12.81	12.96	13.08	13.17	13.24	13.30	13.41	13.51	13.54	13.55
109	5.71	10.00	11.43	12.13	12.55	12.82	13.01	13.15	13.26	13.34	13.41	13.46	13.56	13.64	13.67	13.68
108	6.70	10.53	11.81	12.44	12.81	13.05	13.22	13.35	13.44	13.52	13.57	13.62	13.71	13.78	13.81	13.82
107	7.69	11.07	12.19	12.74	13.07	13.29	13.44	13.55	13.63	13.69	13.74	13.78	13.86	13.93	13.95	13.96
106	8.70	11.61	12.58	13.05	13.34	13.52	13.65	13.74	13.82	13.87	13.91	13.95	14.02	14.07	14.09	14.10
105	9.72	12.16	12.97	13.37	13.60	13.76	13.87	13.95	14.01	14.05	14.09	14.12	14.17	14.22	14.24	14.24
104	10.75	12.72	13.36	13.69	13.88	14.00	14.09	14.15	14.20	14.23	14.26	14.29	14.33	14.37	14.38	14.39
103.75	11.01	12.85	13.46	13.77	13.94	14.06	14.14	14.20	14.25	14.28	14.31	14.33	14.37	14.41	14.42	14.42
103.50	11.27	12.99	13.56	13.85	14.01	14.12	14.20	14.25	14.29	14.33	14.35	14.37	14.41	14.44	14.46	14.46
103.25	11.54	13.14	13.66	13.93	14.08	14.18	14.25	14.30	14.34	14.37	14.40	14.42	14.45	14.48	14.49	14.50
103.00	11.80	13.28	13.77	14.01	14.15	14.24	14.31	14.36	14.39	14.42	14.44	14.46	14.49	14.52	14.53	14.53
102.75	12.06	13.42	13.87	14.09	14.22	14.31	14.37	14.41	14.44	14.47	14.49	14.50	14.54	14.56	14.57	14.57
102.50	12.32	13.56	13.97	14.17	14.29	14.37	14.42	14.46	14.49	14.51	14.53	14.55	14.58	14.60	14.61	14.61
102.25	12.59	13.70	14.07	14.25	14.36	14.43	14.48	14.51	14.54	14.56	14.58	14.59	14.62	14.64	14.64	14.65
102.00	12.85	13.84	14.17	14.33	14.43	14.49	14.53	14.57	14.59	14.61	14.62	14.64	14.66	14.68	14.68	14.68
101.75	13.12	13.99	14.27	14.41	14.50	14.55	14.59	14.62	14.64	14.66	14.67	14.68	14.70	14.72	14.72	14.72
101.50	13.38	14.13	14.37	14.50	14.57	14.62	14.65	14.67	14.69	14.70	14.72	14.72	14.74	14.76	14.76	14.76
101.25	13.65	14.27	14.48	14.58	14.64	14.68	14.71	14.73	14.74	14.75	14.76	14.77	14.78	14.79	14.80	14.80
101.00	13.92	14.42	14.58	14.66	14.71	14.74	14.76	14.78	14.79	14.80	14.81	14.81	14.83	14.83	14.84	14.84
100.75	14.19	14.56	14.68	14.74	14.78	14.80	14.82	14.83	14.84	14.85	14.85	14.86	14.87	14.87	14.88	14.88
100.50	14.45	14.70	14.79	14.83	14.85	14.87	14.88	14.89	14.89	14.90	14.90	14.90	14.91	14.91	14.92	14.92
100.25	14.72	14.85	14.89	14.91	14.92	14.93	14.94	14.94	14.94	14.95	14.95	14.95	14.95	14.95	14.96	14.96
100.00	15.00	15.00	15.00	15.00	15.00	15.00	15.00	15.00	15.00	15.00	15.00	15.00	15.00	15.00	15.00	15.00
99.75	15.27	15.14	15.10	15.08	15.07	15.06	15.05	15.05	15.05	15.04	15.04	15.04	15.04	15.04	15.03	15.03
99.50	15.54	15.29	15.20	15.16	15.14	15.12	15.11	15.10	15.10	15.09	15.09	15.09	15.08	15.08	15.07	15.07
99.25	15.81	15.43	15.31	15.25	15.21	15.19	15.17	15.16	15.15	15.14	15.14	15.13	15.12	15.12	15.11	15.11
99.00	16.09	15.58	15.41	15.33	15.28	15.25	15.23	15.21	15.20	15.19	15.18	15.18	15.17	15.16	15.16	15.15
98.75	16.36	15.73	15.52	15.42	15.36	15.32	15.29	15.27	15.25	15.24	15.23	15.23	15.21	15.20	15.20	15.19
98.50	16.64	15.88	15.63	15.50	15.43	15.38	15.35	15.32	15.31	15.29	15.28	15.27	15.25	15.24	15.24	15.24
98.25	16.91	16.03	15.73	15.59	15.50	15.45	15.41	15.38	15.36	15.34	15.33	15.32	15.30	15.28	15.28	15.28
98.00	17.19	16.17	15.84	15.67	15.58	15.51	15.47	15.44	15.41	15.39	15.38	15.37	15.34	15.32	15.32	15.32
97.75	17.47	16.32	15.95	15.76	15.65	15.58	15.53	15.49	15.46	15.44	15.43	15.41	15.39	15.37	15.36	15.36
97.50	17.74	16.47	16.05	15.85	15.72	15.64	15.59	15.55	15.52	15.49	15.47	15.46	15.43	15.41	15.40	15.40
97.25	18.02	16.62	16.16	15.93	15.80	15.71	15.65	15.60	15.57	15.54	15.52	15.51	15.48	15.45	15.44	15.44
97	18.30	16.77	16.27	16.02	15.87	15.78	15.71	15.66	15.62	15.60	15.57	15.56	15.52	15.49	15.49	15.48
96	19.43	17.38	16.70	16.37	16.17	16.04	15.95	15.89	15.84	15.80	15.77	15.75	15.70	15.67	15.65	15.65
95	20.57	18.00	17.14	16.72	16.48	16.31	16.20	16.12	16.06	16.01	15.97	15.94	15.89	15.84	15.83	15.82
94	21.73	18.62	17.59	17.08	16.78	16.59	16.45	16.36	16.28	16.22	16.18	16.14	16.07	16.02	16.00	16.00
93	22.90	19.25	18.04	17.45	17.10	16.87	16.71	16.59	16.51	16.44	16.39	16.35	16.27	16.20	16.18	16.18
92	24.08	19.88	18.50	17.82	17.41	17.15	16.97	16.84	16.74	16.66	16.60	16.55	16.46	16.39	16.37	16.36
91	25.28	20.53	18.96	18.19	17.73	17.44	17.23	17.08	16.97	16.88	16.82	16.76	16.66	16.58	16.55	16.55
90	26.50	21.18	19.43	18.57	18.06	17.73	17.50	17.33	17.21	17.11	17.04	16.98	16.86	16.77	16.75	16.74
89	27.73	21.84	19.91	18.95	18.39	18.02	17.77	17.59	17.45	17.34	17.26	17.19	17.07	16.97	16.94	16.93
88	28.97	22.52	20.39	19.34	18.73	18.32	18.05	17.84	17.69	17.58	17.49	17.41	17.28	17.17	17.14	17.13
87	30.23	23.19	20.88	19.74	19.07	18.63	18.33	18.11	17.94	17.82	17.72	17.64	17.49	17.38	17.34	17.34
86	31.51	23.88	21.37	20.14	19.41	18.94	18.61	18.37	18.19	18.06	17.95	17.87	17.71	17.59	17.55	17.54
85	32.81	24.58	21.88	20.54	19.76	19.25	18.90	18.64	18.45	18.31	18.19	18.10	17.93	17.80	17.76	17.76
80	39.55	28.22	24.50	22.67	21.60	20.90	20.42	20.07	19.81	19.62	19.46	19.34	18.95	18.90	18.89	18.89
75	46.80	32.13	27.33	24.97	23.59	22.70	22.08	21.64	21.31	21.06	20.87	20.72	20.44	20.24	20.19	20.18
70	54.62	36.35	30.39	27.48	25.77	24.67	23.91	23.37	22.97	22.67	22.44	22.26	21.93	21.71	21.65	21.64
65	63.11	40.95	33.74	30.22	28.17	26.85	25.95	25.30	24.83	24.47	24.21	24.00	23.62	23.39	23.33	23.32
60	72.39	45.99	37.43	33.26	30.84	29.29	28.23	27.48	26.93	26.53	26.22	25.99	25.58	25.34	25.28	25.27
55	82.61	51.55	41.52	36.65	33.83	32.04	30.82	29.97	29.35	28.90	28.56	28.31	27.87	27.63	27.58	27.58
50	93.97	57.75	46.11	40.48	37.24	35.19	33.81	32.86	32.17	31.68	31.32	31.05	30.61	30.38	30.34	30.34

TABLE *27*

Bond Price and Yield

Coupon Rates: 0, 1, 2, 3%;
4 to 15% by .25%.

Terms: 1 to 30 years, each year.

Payment: Semiannual coupons.

This table shows the price of a bond at a yield rate and the yield of a bond at a price, when the yield is to maturity.

Example: An 8%, 30 year bond is for sale. To yield 9% to maturity, the price is $89.68. This means that for every $100 of face amount the purchaser will pay $89.68. A $100,000 bond will sell for $89,680.

To yield 7% to maturity, the price is $112.47.

If the 8% bond is sold at a price of $89, the yield is 9.07% to maturity.

An 8%, 30 year bond is held for 5 years before it is sold. It is now a 25 year bond.

The prices and yields in the example are shown in the table on page 27-178.

Bond. A bond is evidence of a loan that has been made to a borrower who has agreed to make regular periodic payments of interest for a specified time and, at the maturity date, to repay the principal amount. The bond document states, among other things, the face amount, the coupon rate, and the term.

The face amount of a bond is usually $1,000. Bonds are bought and sold based on a price per 100. An 8% bond issued on June 1, 1987 and due in 10 years has attached to it 20 semi-annual coupons, each for $40, each uniquely dated June 1 and December 1 for each year through 1996. When a coupon comes due, it is clipped and presented to a bank for payment. At maturity, the bond certificate is presented for redemption of the face amount.

Once a bond is issued, it is a document that represents a specific stream of payments in the future: the series of semiannual interest payments plus the repayment of the principal amount at maturity. The value is determined by the market and prevailing interest rate.

This table shows the price-yield relationship of a bond purchased for investment. The yield is the return on the investment.

Bond Price. A bond price is a function of yield. The yield creates the price. The price is the present value of all future payments at the yield rate. The price is computed directly from this formula:

$$\text{Price} = \frac{\text{Coupon rate}}{2} \times A_{\overline{n}|} + \text{Principal} \times V^n$$

where:

$A_{\overline{n}|}$ = Present Worth of 1 Per Period at the yield rate

V^n = Present Worth of 1 at the yield rate

Example: The annual coupon per 100 for an 8%, 30 year bond is $8. A 30 year semiannual-coupon bond has 60 periods.

At 8%, the Present Worth of 1 Per Period is 22.623490 and the Present Worth of 1 is .095060. Multiply the factors and add the 2 products for the price.

$$\text{Price} = \frac{8.00}{2} \times 22.6234 + 100 \times .095060$$
$$= 90.494 + 9.508$$
$$= 100.00$$

The price of an 8% bond to yield 8% is par.

At 9%, the Present Worth of 1 Per Period is 20.638022 and the Present Worth of 1 is .071289. Multiply the factors and add the 2 products:

$$\text{Price} = \frac{8.00}{2} \times 20.6380 + 100 \times .071289$$
$$= 89.68$$

To yield 9%, the price is below par.

At 7%, the Present Worth of 1 Per Period is 24.944734 and the Present Worth of 1 is .126934. Multiply the factors and add the 2 products:

$$\text{Price} = \frac{8.00}{2} \times 24.944734 + 100 \times .126934$$
$$= 112.47$$

To yield 7%, the price is above par.

BOND PRICE AND YIELD

Bond Yield. There is no direct way to compute a yield for a given price. In practice, the process is by trial and error, that is, a price is computed at a trial rate. If the price is too high, the rate is increased and a new price is computed. The process is continued until the yield is found that computes the price exactly. The process is called iteration. The description of a program to calculate a yield is found in the Appendix.

Premium and Discount. A premium price is higher than par and the yield is less than the coupon rate on the bond. The $112.47 in the example is a premium price and the yield is 7% on the 8% bond.

A discount price is less than par and the yield is greater than the interest rate. The $89.68 in the example is a discount price and the yield is 9%.

For all fixed-rate securities, price up, yield down and yield up, price down. The yield is that rate at which the investment is amortized over the term.

Example: The underlying security of a bond is the loan. The first few lines and the final lines of the borrower's schedule look like this:

Loan: 100.00		Term: 30 years	
Rate: 8%		Payment: 4.00 semiannual	
Payment	*Interest*	*Principal*	*Balance*
1	4.00	.00	100.00
2	4.00	.00	100.00
3	4.00	.00	100.00
⋮	⋮	⋮	⋮
59	—	—	100.00
60	4.00	.00	100.00

As shown in the final balance, at maturity the bond is redeemed at par.

If the investor buys at a premium price to yield 7%, the first few lines and the final lines of the investor's schedule look like this:

Loan: 112.47		Term: 30 years	
Rate: 7%		Payment: 4.00 semiannual	
Payment	*Interest*	*Principal*	*Balance*
1	3.94	.06	112.41
2	3.93	.07	112.34
3	3.93	.07	112.27
⋮	⋮	⋮	⋮
59	—	—	100.42
60	3.58	.42	100.00

As shown in the final balance, at maturity the bond is redeemed at par.

With a premium bond, the coupon pays the interest and, in addition, a small amount of principal each period. At maturity, the face amount of the bond is paid.

If the investor buys at a discount price to yield 9%, the first few lines and the final lines of the investor's schedule look like this:

Loan: 89.68		Term: 30 years	
Rate: 9%		Payment: 4.00 semiannual	
Payment	*Interest*	*Principal*	*Balance*
1	4.04	.04	89.72
2	4.04	.04	89.76
3	4.04	.04	89.80
⋮	⋮	⋮	⋮
59	—	—	99.57
60	4.43	.43	100.00

As shown in the final balance, at maturity the bond is redeemed at par.

With a discount bond, the coupon does not pay all the interest. This deficiency is added to the balance and is paid when the bond matures.

Each schedule has the same payment and term. The lender creates the stream of payments by making the original loan. The investor buys the stream of payments at a yield rate and allocates the payment to amortize the investment over the term of the original loan.

Current Yield. The "current yield" is the cash return on the investment. It is the coupon income divided by the price. The formula is:

$$\text{Current yield} = \frac{\text{Coupon}}{\text{Price}}$$

The current yield, shown on page 27-182, overstates the return on premium bonds and understates the return on discount bonds.

Callable Bond. A "callable" bond is a bond called by the issuer prior to maturity. The issuer usually pays a premium for the privilege of calling the bond.

Example: A 4% bond due in 10 years is subject to call in 2 years at a price of 102. What is the price to yield 10% where the issuer pays $1,020 for each $1,000 unit?

The 0% bond value is used to get the present worth of the call premium. The price of a callable bond at a yield is computed in 2 steps.

1. Find the bond price. On page 27-8, the price of a 4%, 2 year bond to yield 10% is $89.36.

2. Add the present worth of the call premium at the yield rate. The price of a 0%, 2 year bond to yield 10% is $82.27. The value of a 2% call premium is 1.6445.

The price of the bond to call date:

$$= \$89.36 + \$1.64$$
$$= \$91.00$$

A schedule shows the verification of the price to call date:

Loan: 91.00 Term: 2 years
Rate: 10% Payment: 2.00 semiannual

Payment	Interest	Principal	Balance
	—	—	91.00
1	4.55	2.55	93.55
2	4.68	2.68	96.23
3	4.81	2.81	99.04
4	4.96	2.96	102.00

The final balance shows the face amount of the bond plus the call premium.

Description: This table shows the price to pay for a bond at the yield rate. The yield is to maturity.

Example: The price of a 6.75 %, 1 year bond to yield 8 % to maturity is $ 98.82.

COUPON RATE, %

YIELD	0.00%	1.00%	2.00%	3.00%	4.00%	4.25%	4.50%	4.75%	5.00%	5.25%	5.50%	5.75%	6.00%	6.25%	6.50%	6.75%
0.00	100.00	101.00	102.00	103.00	104.00	104.25	104.50	104.75	105.00	105.25	105.50	105.75	106.00	106.25	106.50	106.75
1.00	99.01	100.00	100.99	101.99	102.98	103.23	103.47	103.72	103.97	104.22	104.47	104.71	104.96	105.21	105.46	105.71
2.00	98.03	99.01	100.00	100.99	101.97	102.22	102.46	102.71	102.96	103.20	103.45	103.69	103.94	104.19	104.43	104.68
3.00	97.07	98.04	99.02	100.00	100.98	101.22	101.47	101.71	101.96	102.20	102.44	102.69	102.93	103.18	103.42	103.67
4.00	96.12	97.09	98.06	99.03	100.00	100.24	100.49	100.73	100.97	101.21	101.46	101.70	101.94	102.18	102.43	102.67
4.25	95.88	96.85	97.82	98.79	99.76	100.00	100.24	100.48	100.73	100.97	101.21	101.45	101.70	101.94	102.18	102.42
4.50	95.65	96.61	97.58	98.55	99.52	99.76	100.00	100.24	100.48	100.73	100.97	101.21	101.45	101.69	101.93	102.18
4.75	95.41	96.38	97.34	98.31	99.28	99.52	99.76	100.00	100.24	100.48	100.72	100.97	101.21	101.45	101.69	101.93
5.00	95.18	96.15	97.11	98.07	99.04	99.28	99.52	99.76	100.00	100.24	100.48	100.72	100.96	101.20	101.45	101.69
5.25	94.95	95.91	96.87	97.84	98.80	99.04	99.28	99.52	99.76	100.00	100.24	100.48	100.72	100.96	101.20	101.44
5.50	94.72	95.68	96.64	97.60	98.56	98.80	99.04	99.28	99.52	99.76	100.00	100.24	100.48	100.72	100.96	101.20
5.75	94.49	95.45	96.41	97.36	98.32	98.56	98.80	99.04	99.28	99.52	99.76	100.00	100.24	100.48	100.72	100.96
6.00	94.26	95.22	96.17	97.13	98.09	98.33	98.56	98.80	99.04	99.28	99.52	99.76	100.00	100.24	100.48	100.72
6.25	94.03	94.99	95.94	96.90	97.85	98.09	98.33	98.57	98.81	99.04	99.28	99.52	99.76	100.00	100.24	100.48
6.50	93.80	94.76	95.71	96.66	97.62	97.86	98.09	98.33	98.57	98.81	99.05	99.29	99.52	99.76	100.00	100.24
6.75	93.58	94.53	95.48	96.43	97.38	97.62	97.86	98.10	98.33	98.57	98.81	99.05	99.29	99.52	99.76	100.00
7.00	93.35	94.30	95.25	96.20	97.15	97.39	97.63	97.86	98.10	98.34	98.58	98.81	99.05	99.29	99.53	99.76
7.25	93.13	94.07	95.02	95.97	96.92	97.16	97.39	97.63	97.87	98.10	98.34	98.58	98.81	99.05	99.29	99.53
7.50	92.90	93.85	94.79	95.74	96.69	96.92	97.16	97.40	97.63	97.87	98.11	98.34	98.58	98.82	99.05	99.29
7.75	92.68	93.62	94.57	95.51	96.46	96.69	96.93	97.17	97.40	97.64	97.87	98.11	98.35	98.58	98.82	99.06
8.00	92.46	93.40	94.34	95.28	96.23	96.46	96.70	96.94	97.17	97.41	97.64	97.88	98.11	98.35	98.59	98.82
8.25	92.23	93.18	94.12	95.06	96.00	96.23	96.47	96.71	96.94	97.18	97.41	97.65	97.88	98.12	98.35	98.59
8.50	92.01	92.95	93.89	94.83	95.77	96.01	96.24	96.48	96.71	96.95	97.18	97.42	97.65	97.89	98.12	98.36
8.75	91.79	92.73	93.67	94.61	95.54	95.78	96.01	96.25	96.48	96.72	96.95	97.19	97.42	97.65	97.89	98.12
9.00	91.57	92.51	93.45	94.38	95.32	95.55	95.79	96.02	96.25	96.49	96.72	96.96	97.19	97.43	97.66	97.89
9.25	91.35	92.29	93.22	94.16	95.09	95.33	95.56	95.79	96.03	96.26	96.49	96.73	96.96	97.20	97.43	97.66
9.50	91.14	92.07	93.00	93.94	94.87	95.10	95.33	95.57	95.80	96.03	96.27	96.50	96.73	96.97	97.20	97.43
9.75	90.92	91.85	92.78	93.71	94.64	94.88	95.11	95.34	95.58	95.81	96.04	96.27	96.51	96.74	96.97	97.21
10.00	90.70	91.63	92.56	93.49	94.42	94.65	94.89	95.12	95.35	95.58	95.82	96.05	96.28	96.51	96.75	96.98
10.25	90.49	91.42	92.34	93.27	94.20	94.43	94.66	94.90	95.13	95.36	95.59	95.82	96.06	96.29	96.52	96.75
10.50	90.27	91.20	92.13	93.05	93.98	94.21	94.44	94.67	94.90	95.14	95.37	95.60	95.83	96.06	96.29	96.53
10.75	90.06	90.98	91.91	92.83	93.76	93.99	94.22	94.45	94.68	94.91	95.14	95.38	95.61	95.84	96.07	96.30
11.00	89.85	90.77	91.69	92.61	93.54	93.77	94.00	94.23	94.46	94.69	94.92	95.15	95.38	95.61	95.85	96.08
11.25	89.63	90.55	91.48	92.40	93.32	93.55	93.78	94.01	94.24	94.47	94.70	94.93	95.16	95.39	95.62	95.85
11.50	89.42	90.34	91.26	92.18	93.10	93.33	93.56	93.79	94.02	94.25	94.48	94.71	94.94	95.17	95.40	95.63
11.75	89.21	90.13	91.05	91.96	92.88	93.11	93.34	93.57	93.80	94.03	94.26	94.49	94.72	94.95	95.18	95.41
12.00	89.00	89.92	90.83	91.75	92.67	92.90	93.12	93.35	93.58	93.81	94.04	94.27	94.50	94.73	94.96	95.19
12.25	88.79	89.71	90.62	91.54	92.45	92.68	92.91	93.14	93.37	93.59	93.82	94.05	94.28	94.51	94.74	94.97
12.50	88.58	89.49	90.41	91.32	92.24	92.46	92.69	92.92	93.15	93.38	93.61	93.83	94.06	94.29	94.52	94.75
12.75	88.37	89.29	90.20	91.11	92.02	92.25	92.48	92.70	92.93	93.16	93.39	93.62	93.84	94.07	94.30	94.53
13.00	88.17	89.08	89.99	90.90	91.81	92.03	92.26	92.49	92.72	92.95	93.17	93.40	93.63	93.86	94.08	94.31
13.25	87.96	88.87	89.78	90.69	91.59	91.82	92.05	92.28	92.50	92.73	92.96	93.18	93.41	93.64	93.87	94.09
13.50	87.75	88.66	89.57	90.47	91.38	91.61	91.84	92.06	92.29	92.52	92.74	92.97	93.20	93.42	93.65	93.88
13.75	87.55	88.45	89.36	90.27	91.17	91.40	91.62	91.85	92.08	92.30	92.53	92.76	92.98	93.21	93.43	93.66
14.00	87.34	88.25	89.15	90.06	90.96	91.19	91.41	91.64	91.86	92.09	92.32	92.54	92.77	92.99	93.22	93.45
14.25	87.14	88.04	88.95	89.85	90.75	90.98	91.20	91.43	91.65	91.88	92.10	92.33	92.55	92.78	93.01	93.23
14.50	86.94	87.84	88.74	89.64	90.54	90.77	90.99	91.22	91.44	91.67	91.89	92.12	92.34	92.57	92.79	93.02
14.75	86.73	87.63	88.53	89.43	90.33	90.56	90.78	91.01	91.23	91.46	91.68	91.91	92.13	92.36	92.58	92.81
15.00	86.53	87.43	88.33	89.23	90.12	90.35	90.57	90.80	91.02	91.25	91.47	91.70	91.92	92.14	92.37	92.59
15.25	86.33	87.23	88.12	89.02	89.92	90.14	90.37	90.59	90.81	91.04	91.26	91.49	91.71	91.93	92.16	92.38
15.50	86.13	87.03	87.92	88.82	89.71	89.93	90.16	90.38	90.61	90.83	91.05	91.28	91.50	91.72	91.95	92.17
15.75	85.93	86.83	87.72	88.61	89.51	89.73	89.95	90.18	90.40	90.62	90.85	91.07	91.29	91.51	91.74	91.96
16.00	85.73	86.63	87.52	88.41	89.30	89.52	89.75	89.97	90.19	90.41	90.64	90.86	91.08	91.31	91.53	91.75
16.25	85.54	86.43	87.32	88.21	89.10	89.32	89.54	89.76	89.99	90.21	90.43	90.65	90.88	91.10	91.32	91.54
16.50	85.34	86.23	87.12	88.00	88.89	89.11	89.34	89.56	89.78	90.00	90.23	90.45	90.67	90.89	91.11	91.34
16.75	85.14	86.03	86.92	87.80	88.69	88.91	89.13	89.36	89.58	89.80	90.02	90.24	90.46	90.69	90.91	91.13
17.00	84.95	85.83	86.72	87.60	88.49	88.71	88.93	89.15	89.37	89.59	89.82	90.04	90.26	90.48	90.70	90.92
17.25	84.75	85.63	86.52	87.40	88.29	88.51	88.73	88.95	89.17	89.39	89.61	89.83	90.05	90.28	90.50	90.72
17.50	84.56	85.44	86.32	87.20	88.09	88.31	88.53	88.75	88.97	89.19	89.41	89.63	89.85	90.07	90.29	90.51
17.75	84.36	85.24	86.12	87.00	87.89	88.11	88.33	88.55	88.77	88.99	89.21	89.43	89.65	89.87	90.09	90.31
18.00	84.17	85.05	85.93	86.81	87.69	87.91	88.13	88.35	88.57	88.79	89.01	89.23	89.45	89.67	89.89	90.10
18.25	83.98	84.85	85.73	86.61	87.49	87.71	87.93	88.15	88.37	88.59	88.80	89.02	89.24	89.46	89.68	89.90
18.50	83.78	84.66	85.54	86.41	87.29	87.51	87.73	87.95	88.17	88.39	88.60	88.82	89.04	89.26	89.48	89.70
18.75	83.59	84.47	85.34	86.22	87.09	87.31	87.53	87.75	87.97	88.19	88.40	88.62	88.84	89.06	89.28	89.50
19.00	83.40	84.27	85.15	86.02	86.90	87.11	87.33	87.55	87.77	87.99	88.21	88.42	88.64	88.86	89.08	89.30
20.00	82.64	83.51	84.38	85.25	86.12	86.33	86.55	86.77	86.98	87.20	87.42	87.63	87.85	88.07	88.29	88.50
25.00	79.01	79.85	80.69	81.53	82.37	82.58	82.79	83.00	83.21	83.42	83.63	83.84	84.05	84.26	84.47	84.68
30.00	75.61	76.43	77.24	78.05	78.87	79.07	79.27	79.48	79.68	79.88	80.09	80.29	80.49	80.69	80.90	81.10

Description: This table shows the yield to maturity of a bond purchased at the price shown in the index.

Example: The yield to maturity of a 6.75 %, 1 year bond at a price of 95.00 is 12.21 %.

PRICE	0.00%	1.00%	2.00%	3.00%	4.00%	4.25%	4.50%	4.75%	5.00%	5.25%	5.50%	5.75%	6.00%	6.25%	6.50%	6.75%
100	0.00	1.00	2.00	3.00	4.00	4.25	4.50	4.75	5.00	5.25	5.50	5.75	6.00	6.25	6.50	6.75
99.75	.25	1.25	2.25	3.25	4.25	4.50	4.75	5.00	5.26	5.51	5.76	6.01	6.26	6.51	6.76	7.01
99.50	.50	1.50	2.50	3.51	4.51	4.76	5.01	5.26	5.52	5.77	6.02	6.27	6.52	6.77	7.02	7.27
99.25	.75	1.76	2.76	3.77	4.77	5.02	5.27	5.53	5.78	6.03	6.28	6.53	6.78	7.03	7.29	7.54
99.00	1.00	2.01	3.02	4.03	5.03	5.28	5.54	5.79	6.04	6.29	6.54	6.80	7.05	7.30	7.55	7.80
98.75	1.26	2.27	3.28	4.29	5.30	5.55	5.80	6.05	6.30	6.56	6.81	7.06	7.31	7.57	7.82	8.07
98.50	1.51	2.52	3.54	4.55	5.56	5.81	6.06	6.32	6.57	6.82	7.08	7.33	7.58	7.83	8.09	8.34
98.25	1.77	2.78	3.80	4.81	5.82	6.08	6.33	6.58	6.84	7.09	7.34	7.60	7.85	8.10	8.36	8.61
98.00	2.03	3.04	4.06	5.07	6.09	6.34	6.59	6.85	7.10	7.36	7.61	7.86	8.12	8.37	8.63	8.88
97.75	2.28	3.30	4.32	5.34	6.35	6.61	6.86	7.12	7.37	7.62	7.88	8.13	8.39	8.64	8.90	9.15
97.50	2.54	3.56	4.58	5.60	6.62	6.87	7.13	7.38	7.64	7.89	8.15	8.40	8.66	8.91	9.17	9.42
97.25	2.80	3.82	4.85	5.87	6.89	7.14	7.40	7.65	7.91	8.16	8.42	8.68	8.93	9.19	9.44	9.70
97.00	3.06	4.09	5.11	6.13	7.16	7.41	7.67	7.92	8.18	8.44	8.69	8.95	9.20	9.46	9.72	9.97
96.75	3.33	4.35	5.38	6.40	7.43	7.68	7.94	8.20	8.45	8.71	8.97	9.22	9.48	9.73	9.99	10.25
96.50	3.59	4.62	5.64	6.67	7.70	7.96	8.21	8.47	8.73	8.98	9.24	9.50	9.75	10.01	10.27	10.52
96.25	3.85	4.88	5.91	6.94	7.97	8.23	8.49	8.74	9.00	9.26	9.51	9.77	10.03	10.29	10.54	10.80
96.00	4.12	5.15	6.18	7.21	8.24	8.50	8.76	9.02	9.28	9.53	9.79	10.05	10.31	10.56	10.82	11.08
95.75	4.39	5.42	6.45	7.49	8.52	8.78	9.04	9.29	9.55	9.81	10.07	10.33	10.59	10.84	11.10	11.36
95.50	4.65	5.69	6.72	7.76	8.79	9.05	9.31	9.57	9.83	10.09	10.35	10.61	10.87	11.12	11.38	11.64
95.25	4.92	5.96	7.00	8.03	9.07	9.33	9.59	9.85	10.11	10.37	10.63	10.89	11.15	11.41	11.66	11.92
95.00	5.19	6.23	7.27	8.31	9.35	9.61	9.87	10.13	10.39	10.65	10.91	11.17	11.43	11.69	11.95	12.21
94.75	5.46	6.50	7.54	8.59	9.63	9.89	10.15	10.41	10.67	10.93	11.19	11.45	11.71	11.97	12.23	12.49
94.50	5.73	6.78	7.82	8.86	9.91	10.17	10.43	10.69	10.95	11.21	11.47	11.73	11.99	12.26	12.52	12.78
94.25	6.01	7.05	8.10	9.14	10.19	10.45	10.71	10.97	11.23	11.50	11.76	12.02	12.28	12.54	12.80	13.06
94.00	6.28	7.33	8.37	9.42	10.47	10.73	10.99	11.26	11.52	11.78	12.04	12.30	12.57	12.83	13.09	13.35
93.75	6.55	7.60	8.65	9.70	10.75	11.02	11.28	11.54	11.80	12.07	12.33	12.59	12.85	13.12	13.38	13.64
93.50	6.83	7.88	8.93	9.99	11.04	11.30	11.56	11.83	12.09	12.35	12.62	12.88	13.14	13.41	13.67	13.93
93.25	7.11	8.16	9.22	10.27	11.32	11.59	11.85	12.11	12.38	12.64	12.91	13.17	13.43	13.70	13.96	14.22
93.00	7.39	8.44	9.50	10.55	11.61	11.87	12.14	12.40	12.67	12.93	13.20	13.46	13.72	13.99	14.25	14.52
92.75	7.66	8.72	9.78	10.84	11.90	12.16	12.43	12.69	12.96	13.22	13.49	13.75	14.02	14.28	14.55	14.81
92.50	7.95	9.01	10.07	11.13	12.19	12.45	12.72	12.98	13.25	13.51	13.78	14.04	14.31	14.57	14.84	15.11
92.25	8.23	9.29	10.35	11.42	12.48	12.74	13.01	13.28	13.54	13.81	14.07	14.34	14.60	14.87	15.14	15.40
92.00	8.51	9.57	10.64	11.70	12.77	13.04	13.30	13.57	13.83	14.10	14.37	14.63	14.90	15.17	15.43	15.70
91.75	8.79	9.86	10.93	11.99	13.06	13.33	13.60	13.86	14.13	14.40	14.66	14.93	15.20	15.46	15.73	16.00
91	9.65	10.73	11.80	12.87	13.95	14.22	14.48	14.75	15.02	15.29	15.56	15.83	16.10	16.36	16.63	16.90
90	10.81	11.90	12.98	14.06	15.15	15.42	15.69	15.96	16.23	16.50	16.77	17.04	17.31	17.58	17.85	18.12
89	11.99	13.09	14.18	15.27	16.36	16.64	16.91	17.18	17.46	17.73	18.00	18.28	18.55	18.82	19.09	19.37
88	13.20	14.30	15.40	16.50	17.60	17.88	18.15	18.43	18.70	18.98	19.26	19.53	19.81	20.08	20.36	20.63
87	14.42	15.53	16.64	17.75	18.86	19.14	19.42	19.70	19.97	20.25	20.53	20.81	21.09	21.36	21.64	21.92
86	15.66	16.78	17.90	19.02	20.14	20.43	20.71	20.99	21.27	21.55	21.83	22.11	22.39	22.67	22.95	23.23
85	16.93	18.06	19.19	20.32	21.45	21.73	22.02	22.30	22.58	22.86	23.15	23.43	23.71	24.00	24.28	24.56
84	18.21	19.35	20.50	21.64	22.78	23.06	23.35	23.63	23.92	24.21	24.49	24.78	25.06	25.35	25.63	25.92
83	19.52	20.68	21.83	22.98	24.13	24.42	24.71	25.00	25.28	25.57	25.86	26.15	26.44	26.72	27.01	27.30
82	20.86	22.02	23.18	24.35	25.51	25.80	26.09	26.38	26.67	26.96	27.25	27.54	27.84	28.13	28.42	28.71
81	22.22	23.39	24.56	25.74	26.91	27.20	27.50	27.79	28.09	28.38	28.67	28.97	29.26	29.55	29.85	30.14
80	23.60	24.79	25.97	27.16	28.34	28.64	28.93	29.23	29.53	29.82	30.12	30.42	30.71	31.01	31.31	31.60
79	25.01	26.21	27.40	28.60	29.80	30.10	30.40	30.70	30.99	31.29	31.59	31.89	32.19	32.49	32.79	33.09
78	26.45	27.66	28.87	30.07	31.28	31.58	31.89	32.19	32.49	32.79	33.10	33.40	33.70	34.00	34.31	34.61
77	27.92	29.14	30.36	31.58	32.80	33.10	33.41	33.71	34.02	34.32	34.63	34.93	35.24	35.54	35.85	36.16
76	29.41	30.64	31.87	33.11	34.34	34.65	34.96	35.27	35.57	35.88	36.19	36.50	36.81	37.12	37.42	37.73
75	30.94	32.18	33.42	34.67	35.92	36.23	36.54	36.85	37.16	37.47	37.78	38.10	38.41	38.72	39.03	39.34
74	32.49	33.75	35.01	36.26	37.52	37.84	38.15	38.47	38.78	39.10	39.41	39.73	40.04	40.36	40.67	40.99
73	34.08	35.35	36.62	37.89	39.16	39.48	39.80	40.12	40.43	40.75	41.07	41.39	41.71	42.03	42.34	42.66
72	35.70	36.98	38.27	39.55	40.84	41.16	41.48	41.80	42.12	42.44	42.77	43.09	43.41	43.73	44.05	44.38
71	37.35	38.65	39.95	41.25	42.55	42.87	43.20	43.52	43.85	44.17	44.50	44.82	45.15	45.47	45.80	46.12
70	39.04	40.35	41.67	42.98	44.29	44.62	44.95	45.28	45.61	45.94	46.27	46.59	46.92	47.25	47.58	47.91
69	40.77	42.09	43.42	44.75	46.08	46.41	46.74	47.08	47.41	47.74	48.07	48.41	48.74	49.07	49.40	49.74
68	42.53	43.87	45.22	46.56	47.90	48.24	48.58	48.91	49.25	49.58	49.92	50.26	50.59	50.93	51.27	51.60
67	44.33	45.69	47.05	48.41	49.77	50.11	50.45	50.79	51.13	51.47	51.81	52.15	52.49	52.83	53.17	53.51
66	46.18	47.55	48.93	50.30	51.68	52.02	52.36	52.71	53.05	53.40	53.74	54.09	54.43	54.77	55.12	55.46
65	48.06	49.45	50.85	52.24	53.63	53.98	54.33	54.67	55.02	55.37	55.72	56.07	56.42	56.76	57.11	57.46
64	50.00	51.40	52.81	54.22	55.63	55.98	56.33	56.68	57.04	57.39	57.74	58.10	58.45	58.80	59.15	59.51
63	51.97	53.40	54.82	56.25	57.67	58.03	58.39	58.74	59.10	59.46	59.82	60.17	60.53	60.89	61.24	61.60
62	54.00	55.44	56.88	58.32	59.77	60.13	60.49	60.85	61.21	61.58	61.94	62.30	62.66	63.02	63.39	63.75
61	56.07	57.53	58.99	60.45	61.92	62.28	62.65	63.01	63.38	63.75	64.11	64.48	64.85	65.21	65.58	65.95
60	58.19	59.67	61.15	62.64	64.12	64.49	64.86	65.23	65.60	65.97	66.34	66.71	67.09	67.46	67.83	68.20
59	60.37	61.87	63.37	64.87	66.38	66.75	67.13	67.50	67.88	68.26	68.63	69.01	69.38	69.76	70.14	70.51
58	62.61	64.13	65.65	67.17	68.69	69.07	69.45	69.83	70.22	70.60	70.98	71.36	71.74	72.12	72.50	72.89

Description: This table shows the price to pay for a bond at the yield rate. The yield is to maturity.

Example: The price of a 10.75 %, 1 year bond to yield 8 % to maturity is $ 102.59.

COUPON RATE, %

YIELD	7.00%	7.25%	7.50%	7.75%	8.00%	8.25%	8.50%	8.75%	9.00%	9.25%	9.50%	9.75%	10.00%	10.25%	10.50%	10.75%
0.00	107.00	107.25	107.50	107.75	108.00	108.25	108.50	108.75	109.00	109.25	109.50	109.75	110.00	110.25	110.50	110.75
1.00	105.96	106.20	106.45	106.70	106.95	107.20	107.44	107.69	107.94	108.19	108.44	108.68	108.93	109.18	109.43	109.68
2.00	104.93	105.17	105.42	105.66	105.91	106.16	106.40	106.65	106.90	107.14	107.39	107.64	107.88	108.13	108.37	108.62
3.00	103.91	104.16	104.40	104.65	104.89	105.13	105.38	105.62	105.87	106.11	106.36	106.60	106.85	107.09	107.33	107.58
4.00	102.91	103.16	103.40	103.64	103.88	104.13	104.37	104.61	104.85	105.10	105.34	105.58	105.82	106.07	106.31	106.55
4.25	102.66	102.91	103.15	103.39	103.63	103.88	104.12	104.36	104.60	104.85	105.09	105.33	105.57	105.81	106.06	106.30
4.50	102.42	102.66	102.90	103.14	103.39	103.63	103.87	104.11	104.35	104.59	104.84	105.08	105.32	105.56	105.80	106.05
4.75	102.17	102.41	102.66	102.90	103.14	103.38	103.62	103.86	104.10	104.34	104.59	104.83	105.07	105.31	105.55	105.79
5.00	101.93	102.17	102.41	102.65	102.89	103.13	103.37	103.61	103.85	104.10	104.34	104.58	104.82	105.06	105.30	105.54
5.25	101.68	101.92	102.16	102.40	102.65	102.89	103.13	103.37	103.61	103.85	104.09	104.33	104.57	104.81	105.05	105.29
5.50	101.44	101.68	101.92	102.16	102.40	102.64	102.88	103.12	103.36	103.60	103.84	104.08	104.32	104.56	104.80	105.04
5.75	101.20	101.44	101.68	101.92	102.16	102.40	102.64	102.88	103.12	103.35	103.59	103.83	104.07	104.31	104.55	104.79
6.00	100.96	101.20	101.44	101.67	101.91	102.15	102.39	102.63	102.87	103.11	103.35	103.59	103.83	104.07	104.31	104.54
6.25	100.72	100.96	101.19	101.43	101.67	101.91	102.15	102.39	102.63	102.87	103.10	103.34	103.58	103.82	104.06	104.30
6.50	100.48	100.71	100.95	101.19	101.43	101.67	101.91	102.14	102.38	102.62	102.86	103.10	103.34	103.57	103.81	104.05
6.75	100.24	100.48	100.71	100.95	101.19	101.43	101.67	101.90	102.14	102.38	102.62	102.85	103.09	103.33	103.57	103.81
7.00	100.00	100.24	100.47	100.71	100.95	101.19	101.42	101.66	101.90	102.14	102.37	102.61	102.85	103.09	103.32	103.56
7.25	99.76	100.00	100.24	100.47	100.71	100.95	101.19	101.42	101.66	101.90	102.13	102.37	102.61	102.84	103.08	103.32
7.50	99.53	99.76	100.00	100.24	100.47	100.71	100.95	101.18	101.42	101.66	101.89	102.13	102.37	102.60	102.84	103.08
7.75	99.29	99.53	99.76	100.00	100.24	100.47	100.71	100.94	101.18	101.42	101.65	101.89	102.13	102.36	102.60	102.83
8.00	99.06	99.29	99.53	99.76	100.00	100.24	100.47	100.71	100.94	101.18	101.41	101.65	101.89	102.12	102.36	102.59
8.25	98.82	99.06	99.29	99.53	99.76	100.00	100.24	100.47	100.71	100.94	101.18	101.41	101.65	101.88	102.12	102.35
8.50	98.59	98.83	99.06	99.30	99.53	99.77	100.00	100.23	100.47	100.70	100.94	101.17	101.41	101.64	101.88	102.11
8.75	98.36	98.59	98.83	99.06	99.30	99.53	99.77	100.00	100.23	100.47	100.70	100.94	101.17	101.41	101.64	101.88
9.00	98.13	98.36	98.60	98.83	99.06	99.30	99.53	99.77	100.00	100.23	100.47	100.70	100.94	101.17	101.40	101.64
9.25	97.90	98.13	98.36	98.60	98.83	99.07	99.30	99.53	99.77	100.00	100.23	100.47	100.70	100.93	101.17	101.40
9.50	97.67	97.90	98.13	98.37	98.60	98.83	99.07	99.30	99.53	99.77	100.00	100.23	100.47	100.70	100.93	101.17
9.75	97.44	97.67	97.90	98.14	98.37	98.60	98.84	99.07	99.30	99.53	99.77	100.00	100.23	100.47	100.70	100.93
10.00	97.21	97.44	97.68	97.91	98.14	98.37	98.61	98.84	99.07	99.30	99.54	99.77	100.00	100.23	100.46	100.70
10.25	96.98	97.22	97.45	97.68	97.91	98.14	98.38	98.61	98.84	99.07	99.30	99.54	99.77	100.00	100.23	100.46
10.50	96.76	96.99	97.22	97.45	97.68	97.92	98.15	98.38	98.61	98.84	99.07	99.31	99.54	99.77	100.00	100.23
10.75	96.53	96.76	96.99	97.23	97.46	97.69	97.92	98.15	98.38	98.61	98.84	99.08	99.31	99.54	99.77	100.00
11.00	96.31	96.54	96.77	97.00	97.23	97.46	97.69	97.92	98.15	98.38	98.62	98.85	99.08	99.31	99.54	99.77
11.25	96.08	96.31	96.54	96.77	97.01	97.24	97.47	97.70	97.93	98.16	98.39	98.62	98.85	99.08	99.31	99.54
11.50	95.86	96.09	96.32	96.55	96.78	97.01	97.24	97.47	97.70	97.93	98.16	98.39	98.62	98.85	99.08	99.31
11.75	95.64	95.87	96.10	96.33	96.56	96.79	97.02	97.25	97.47	97.70	97.93	98.16	98.39	98.62	98.85	99.08
12.00	95.42	95.65	95.87	96.10	96.33	96.56	96.79	97.02	97.25	97.48	97.71	97.94	98.17	98.40	98.62	98.85
12.25	95.20	95.42	95.65	95.88	96.11	96.34	96.57	96.80	97.03	97.25	97.48	97.71	97.94	98.17	98.40	98.63
12.50	94.98	95.20	95.43	95.66	95.89	96.12	96.35	96.57	96.80	97.03	97.26	97.49	97.72	97.94	98.17	98.40
12.75	94.76	94.98	95.21	95.44	95.67	95.90	96.12	96.35	96.58	96.81	97.04	97.26	97.49	97.72	97.95	98.18
13.00	94.54	94.77	94.99	95.22	95.45	95.68	95.90	96.13	96.36	96.59	96.81	97.04	97.27	97.50	97.72	97.95
13.25	94.32	94.55	94.77	95.00	95.23	95.46	95.68	95.91	96.14	96.37	96.59	96.82	97.05	97.27	97.50	97.73
13.50	94.10	94.33	94.56	94.78	95.01	95.24	95.46	95.69	95.92	96.14	96.37	96.60	96.82	97.05	97.28	97.51
13.75	93.89	94.11	94.34	94.57	94.79	95.02	95.25	95.47	95.70	95.92	96.15	96.38	96.60	96.83	97.06	97.28
14.00	93.67	93.90	94.12	94.35	94.58	94.80	95.03	95.25	95.48	95.71	95.93	96.16	96.38	96.61	96.84	97.06
14.25	93.46	93.68	93.91	94.13	94.36	94.59	94.81	95.04	95.26	95.49	95.71	95.94	96.16	96.39	96.62	96.84
14.50	93.24	93.47	93.69	93.92	94.14	94.37	94.59	94.82	95.05	95.27	95.50	95.72	95.95	96.17	96.40	96.62
14.75	93.03	93.26	93.48	93.70	93.93	94.15	94.38	94.60	94.83	95.05	95.28	95.50	95.73	95.95	96.18	96.40
15.00	92.82	93.04	93.27	93.49	93.72	93.94	94.16	94.39	94.61	94.84	95.06	95.29	95.51	95.74	95.96	96.18
15.25	92.61	92.83	93.05	93.28	93.50	93.73	93.95	94.17	94.40	94.62	94.85	95.07	95.29	95.52	95.74	95.97
15.50	92.40	92.62	92.84	93.07	93.29	93.51	93.74	93.96	94.18	94.41	94.63	94.86	95.08	95.30	95.53	95.75
15.75	92.18	92.41	92.63	92.85	93.08	93.30	93.52	93.75	93.97	94.19	94.42	94.64	94.86	95.09	95.31	95.53
16.00	91.98	92.20	92.42	92.64	92.87	93.09	93.31	93.54	93.76	93.98	94.20	94.43	94.65	94.87	95.10	95.32
16.25	91.77	91.99	92.21	92.43	92.66	92.88	93.10	93.32	93.55	93.77	93.99	94.21	94.44	94.66	94.88	95.10
16.50	91.56	91.78	92.00	92.22	92.45	92.67	92.89	93.11	93.34	93.56	93.78	94.00	94.22	94.45	94.67	94.89
16.75	91.35	91.57	91.79	92.02	92.24	92.46	92.68	92.90	93.13	93.35	93.57	93.79	94.01	94.23	94.46	94.68
17.00	91.14	91.37	91.59	91.81	92.03	92.25	92.47	92.69	92.92	93.14	93.36	93.58	93.80	94.02	94.24	94.47
17.25	90.94	91.16	91.38	91.60	91.82	92.04	92.26	92.49	92.71	92.93	93.15	93.37	93.59	93.81	94.03	94.25
17.50	90.73	90.95	91.17	91.40	91.62	91.84	92.06	92.28	92.50	92.72	92.94	93.16	93.38	93.60	93.82	94.04
17.75	90.53	90.75	90.97	91.19	91.41	91.63	91.85	92.07	92.29	92.51	92.73	92.95	93.17	93.39	93.61	93.83
18.00	90.32	90.54	90.76	90.98	91.20	91.42	91.64	91.86	92.08	92.30	92.52	92.74	92.96	93.18	93.40	93.62
18.25	90.12	90.34	90.56	90.78	91.00	91.22	91.44	91.66	91.88	92.10	92.32	92.54	92.76	92.98	93.19	93.41
18.50	89.92	90.14	90.36	90.58	90.80	91.02	91.23	91.45	91.67	91.89	92.11	92.33	92.55	92.77	92.99	93.21
18.75	89.72	89.94	90.16	90.37	90.59	90.81	91.03	91.25	91.47	91.69	91.91	92.12	92.34	92.56	92.78	93.00
19.00	89.52	89.73	89.95	90.17	90.39	90.61	90.83	91.05	91.26	91.48	91.70	91.92	92.14	92.36	92.57	92.79
20.00	88.72	88.94	89.15	89.37	89.59	89.80	90.02	90.24	90.45	90.67	90.89	91.11	91.32	91.54	91.76	91.97
25.00	84.89	85.10	85.31	85.52	85.73	85.94	86.15	86.36	86.57	86.78	86.99	87.20	87.41	87.62	87.83	88.04
30.00	81.30	81.51	81.71	81.91	82.12	82.32	82.52	82.73	82.93	83.13	83.34	83.54	83.74	83.95	84.15	84.35

Description: This table shows the yield to maturity of a bond purchased at the price shown in the index.

Example: The yield to maturity of a 10.75 %, 1 year bond at a price of 100.00 is 10.75 %.

COUPON RATE, %

PRICE	7.00%	7.25%	7.50%	7.75%	8.00%	8.25%	8.50%	8.75%	9.00%	9.25%	9.50%	9.75%	10.00%	10.25%	10.50%	10.75%
105	1.92	2.16	2.40	2.65	2.89	3.13	3.37	3.61	3.85	4.09	4.33	4.57	4.81	5.05	5.30	5.54
104.75	2.17	2.41	2.65	2.89	3.13	3.37	3.62	3.86	4.10	4.34	4.58	4.82	5.06	5.31	5.55	5.79
104.50	2.41	2.66	2.90	3.14	3.38	3.62	3.86	4.11	4.35	4.59	4.83	5.07	5.31	5.56	5.80	6.04
104.25	2.66	2.90	3.14	3.39	3.63	3.87	4.11	4.36	4.60	4.84	5.08	5.32	5.57	5.81	6.05	6.29
104.00	2.91	3.15	3.39	3.64	3.88	4.12	4.36	4.61	4.85	5.09	5.33	5.58	5.82	6.06	6.30	6.55
103.75	3.16	3.40	3.64	3.89	4.13	4.37	4.61	4.86	5.10	5.34	5.59	5.83	6.07	6.32	6.56	6.80
103.50	3.41	3.65	3.89	4.14	4.38	4.62	4.87	5.11	5.35	5.60	5.84	6.08	6.33	6.57	6.82	7.06
103.25	3.66	3.90	4.14	4.39	4.63	4.88	5.12	5.36	5.61	5.85	6.10	6.34	6.58	6.83	7.07	7.32
103.00	3.91	4.15	4.40	4.64	4.88	5.13	5.37	5.62	5.86	6.11	6.35	6.60	6.84	7.08	7.33	7.57
102.75	4.16	4.40	4.65	4.89	5.14	5.38	5.63	5.87	6.12	6.36	6.61	6.85	7.10	7.34	7.59	7.83
102.50	4.41	4.66	4.90	5.15	5.39	5.64	5.88	6.13	6.37	6.62	6.87	7.11	7.36	7.60	7.85	8.09
102.25	4.67	4.91	5.16	5.40	5.65	5.90	6.14	6.39	6.63	6.88	7.12	7.37	7.62	7.86	8.11	8.35
102.00	4.92	5.17	5.41	5.66	5.91	6.15	6.40	6.64	6.89	7.14	7.38	7.63	7.88	8.12	8.37	8.61
101.75	5.18	5.42	5.67	5.92	6.16	6.41	6.66	6.90	7.15	7.40	7.64	7.89	8.14	8.38	8.63	8.88
101.50	5.43	5.68	5.93	6.18	6.42	6.67	6.92	7.16	7.41	7.66	7.91	8.15	8.40	8.65	8.89	9.14
101.25	5.69	5.94	6.19	6.43	6.68	6.93	7.18	7.43	7.67	7.92	8.17	8.42	8.66	8.91	9.16	9.41
101.00	5.95	6.20	6.45	6.69	6.94	7.19	7.44	7.69	7.94	8.18	8.43	8.68	8.93	9.18	9.42	9.67
100.75	6.21	6.46	6.71	6.96	7.20	7.45	7.70	7.95	8.20	8.45	8.70	8.94	9.19	9.44	9.69	9.94
100.50	6.47	6.72	6.97	7.22	7.47	7.72	7.97	8.21	8.46	8.71	8.96	9.21	9.46	9.71	9.96	10.21
100.25	6.73	6.98	7.23	7.48	7.73	7.98	8.23	8.48	8.73	8.98	9.23	9.48	9.73	9.98	10.23	10.48
100.00	7.00	7.25	7.50	7.75	8.00	8.25	8.50	8.75	9.00	9.25	9.50	9.75	10.00	10.25	10.50	10.75
99.75	7.26	7.51	7.76	8.01	8.26	8.51	8.76	9.01	9.26	9.51	9.76	10.01	10.26	10.52	10.77	11.02
99.50	7.52	7.77	8.03	8.28	8.53	8.78	9.03	9.28	9.53	9.78	10.03	10.28	10.53	10.79	11.04	11.29
99.25	7.79	8.04	8.29	8.54	8.79	9.05	9.30	9.55	9.80	10.05	10.30	10.56	10.81	11.06	11.31	11.56
99.00	8.06	8.31	8.56	8.81	9.06	9.32	9.57	9.82	10.07	10.32	10.58	10.83	11.08	11.33	11.58	11.83
98.75	8.32	8.58	8.83	9.08	9.33	9.59	9.84	10.09	10.34	10.60	10.85	11.10	11.35	11.60	11.86	12.11
98.50	8.59	8.85	9.10	9.35	9.60	9.86	10.11	10.36	10.62	10.87	11.12	11.37	11.63	11.88	12.13	12.39
98.25	8.86	9.12	9.37	9.62	9.88	10.13	10.38	10.64	10.89	11.14	11.40	11.65	11.90	12.16	12.41	12.66
98.00	9.13	9.39	9.64	9.89	10.15	10.40	10.66	10.91	11.16	11.42	11.67	11.93	12.18	12.43	12.69	12.94
97.75	9.41	9.66	9.91	10.17	10.42	10.68	10.93	11.19	11.44	11.69	11.95	12.20	12.46	12.71	12.97	13.22
97.50	9.68	9.93	10.19	10.44	10.70	10.95	11.21	11.46	11.72	11.97	12.23	12.48	12.74	12.99	13.25	13.50
97.25	9.95	10.21	10.46	10.72	10.97	11.23	11.48	11.74	12.00	12.25	12.51	12.76	13.02	13.27	13.53	13.78
97.00	10.23	10.48	10.74	10.99	11.25	11.51	11.76	12.02	12.27	12.53	12.79	13.04	13.30	13.55	13.81	14.07
96.75	10.50	10.76	11.02	11.27	11.53	11.79	12.04	12.30	12.55	12.81	13.07	13.32	13.58	13.84	14.09	14.35
96.50	10.78	11.04	11.29	11.55	11.81	12.07	12.32	12.58	12.84	13.09	13.35	13.61	13.86	14.12	14.38	14.63
96.25	11.06	11.32	11.57	11.83	12.09	12.35	12.60	12.86	13.12	13.38	13.63	13.89	14.15	14.41	14.66	14.92
96.00	11.34	11.60	11.85	12.11	12.37	12.63	12.89	13.14	13.40	13.66	13.92	14.18	14.43	14.69	14.95	15.21
95.75	11.62	11.88	12.14	12.39	12.65	12.91	13.17	13.43	13.69	13.94	14.20	14.46	14.72	14.98	15.24	15.50
95.50	11.90	12.16	12.42	12.68	12.94	13.20	13.45	13.71	13.97	14.23	14.49	14.75	15.01	15.27	15.53	15.78
95.25	12.18	12.44	12.70	12.96	13.22	13.48	13.74	14.00	14.26	14.52	14.78	15.04	15.30	15.56	15.82	16.08
95.00	12.47	12.73	12.99	13.25	13.51	13.77	14.03	14.29	14.55	14.81	15.07	15.33	15.59	15.85	16.11	16.37
94.75	12.75	13.01	13.27	13.53	13.79	14.05	14.32	14.58	14.84	15.10	15.36	15.62	15.88	16.14	16.40	16.66
94	13.61	13.88	14.14	14.40	14.66	14.93	15.19	15.45	15.71	15.97	16.24	16.50	16.76	17.02	17.28	17.55
93	14.78	15.04	15.31	15.57	15.84	16.10	16.37	16.63	16.89	17.16	17.42	17.69	17.95	18.22	18.48	18.74
92	15.97	16.23	16.50	16.76	17.03	17.30	17.56	17.83	18.10	18.36	18.63	18.90	19.16	19.43	19.70	19.96
91	17.17	17.44	17.71	17.98	18.24	18.51	18.78	19.05	19.32	19.59	19.86	20.13	20.39	20.66	20.93	21.20
90	18.40	18.67	18.94	19.21	19.48	19.75	20.02	20.29	20.56	20.83	21.10	21.38	21.65	21.92	22.19	22.46
89	19.64	19.91	20.19	20.46	20.73	21.01	21.28	21.55	21.83	22.10	22.37	22.65	22.92	23.19	23.47	23.74
88	20.91	21.18	21.46	21.74	22.01	22.29	22.56	22.84	23.11	23.39	23.67	23.94	24.22	24.49	24.77	25.04
87	22.20	22.48	22.75	23.03	23.31	23.59	23.87	24.14	24.42	24.70	24.98	25.26	25.54	25.81	26.09	26.37
86	23.51	23.79	24.07	24.35	24.63	24.91	25.19	25.47	25.75	26.04	26.32	26.60	26.88	27.16	27.44	27.72
85	24.85	25.13	25.41	25.69	25.98	26.26	26.54	26.83	27.11	27.39	27.68	27.96	28.24	28.53	28.81	29.09
84	26.20	26.49	26.78	27.06	27.35	27.63	27.92	28.20	28.49	28.78	29.06	29.35	29.63	29.92	30.21	30.49
83	27.59	27.88	28.17	28.45	28.74	29.03	29.32	29.61	29.90	30.18	30.47	30.76	31.05	31.34	31.63	31.92
82	29.00	29.29	29.58	29.87	30.16	30.45	30.75	31.04	31.33	31.62	31.91	32.20	32.49	32.78	33.07	33.37
81	30.44	30.73	31.02	31.32	31.61	31.90	32.20	32.49	32.79	33.08	33.37	33.67	33.96	34.26	34.55	34.84
80	31.90	32.20	32.49	32.79	33.09	33.38	33.68	33.98	34.27	34.57	34.87	35.16	35.46	35.76	36.05	36.35
79	33.39	33.69	33.99	34.29	34.59	34.89	35.19	35.49	35.79	36.09	36.39	36.69	36.99	37.29	37.59	37.88
78	34.91	35.21	35.52	35.82	36.12	36.42	36.73	37.03	37.33	37.63	37.94	38.24	38.54	38.84	39.15	39.45
77	36.46	36.77	37.07	37.38	37.68	37.99	38.29	38.60	38.91	39.21	39.52	39.82	40.13	40.43	40.74	41.05
76	38.04	38.35	38.66	38.97	39.28	39.59	39.89	40.20	40.51	40.82	41.13	41.44	41.75	42.06	42.37	42.67
75	39.65	39.97	40.28	40.59	40.90	41.21	41.53	41.84	42.15	42.46	42.77	43.09	43.40	43.71	44.02	44.34
74	41.30	41.62	41.93	42.25	42.56	42.88	43.19	43.51	43.82	44.14	44.45	44.77	45.08	45.40	45.72	46.03
73	42.98	43.30	43.62	43.94	44.26	44.57	44.89	45.21	45.53	45.85	46.17	46.49	46.81	47.12	47.44	47.76
72	44.70	45.02	45.34	45.66	45.99	46.31	46.63	46.95	47.27	47.60	47.92	48.24	48.56	48.88	49.21	49.53
71	46.45	46.77	47.10	47.43	47.75	48.08	48.40	48.73	49.05	49.38	49.71	50.03	50.36	50.68	51.01	51.33
70	48.24	48.57	48.90	49.23	49.56	49.89	50.21	50.54	50.87	51.20	51.53	51.86	52.19	52.52	52.85	53.18
69	50.07	50.40	50.73	51.07	51.40	51.73	52.07	52.40	52.73	53.07	53.40	53.73	54.07	54.40	54.73	55.07

Description: This table shows the price to pay for a bond at the yield rate. The yield is to maturity.

Example: The price of a 15.00 %, 1 year bond to yield 8 % to maturity is $ 106.60.

COUPON RATE, %

YIELD	11.00%	11.25%	11.50%	11.75%	12.00%	12.25%	12.50%	12.75%	13.00%	13.25%	13.50%	13.75%	14.00%	14.25%	14.50%	15.00%
0.00	111.00	111.25	111.50	111.75	112.00	112.25	112.50	112.75	113.00	113.25	113.50	113.75	114.00	114.25	114.50	115.00
1.00	109.93	110.17	110.42	110.67	110.92	111.17	111.41	111.66	111.91	112.16	112.41	112.66	112.90	113.15	113.40	113.90
2.00	108.87	109.11	109.36	109.61	109.85	110.10	110.34	110.59	110.84	111.08	111.33	111.58	111.82	112.07	112.31	112.81
3.00	107.82	108.07	108.31	108.56	108.80	109.05	109.29	109.53	109.78	110.02	110.27	110.51	110.76	111.00	111.25	111.74
4.00	106.80	107.04	107.28	107.52	107.77	108.01	108.25	108.49	108.74	108.98	109.22	109.47	109.71	109.95	110.19	110.68
4.25	106.54	106.78	107.03	107.27	107.51	107.75	107.99	108.24	108.48	108.72	108.96	109.21	109.45	109.69	109.93	110.42
4.50	106.29	106.53	106.77	107.01	107.25	107.50	107.74	107.98	108.22	108.46	108.71	108.95	109.19	109.43	109.67	110.16
4.75	106.03	106.28	106.52	106.76	107.00	107.24	107.48	107.72	107.97	108.21	108.45	108.69	108.93	109.17	109.41	109.90
5.00	105.78	106.02	106.26	106.51	106.75	106.99	107.23	107.47	107.71	107.95	108.19	108.43	108.67	108.91	109.16	109.64
5.25	105.53	105.77	106.01	106.25	106.49	106.73	106.97	107.21	107.46	107.70	107.94	108.18	108.42	108.66	108.90	109.38
5.50	105.28	105.52	105.76	106.00	106.24	106.48	106.72	106.96	107.20	107.44	107.68	107.92	108.16	108.40	108.64	109.12
5.75	105.03	105.27	105.51	105.75	105.99	106.23	106.47	106.71	106.95	107.19	107.43	107.67	107.91	108.15	108.39	108.87
6.00	104.78	105.02	105.26	105.50	105.74	105.98	106.22	106.46	106.70	106.94	107.18	107.41	107.65	107.89	108.13	108.61
6.25	104.54	104.78	105.01	105.25	105.49	105.73	105.97	106.21	106.45	106.69	106.92	107.16	107.40	107.64	107.88	108.36
6.50	104.29	104.53	104.77	105.00	105.24	105.48	105.72	105.96	106.20	106.43	106.67	106.91	107.15	107.39	107.63	108.10
6.75	104.04	104.28	104.52	104.76	105.00	105.23	105.47	105.71	105.95	106.19	106.42	106.66	106.90	107.14	107.37	107.85
7.00	103.80	104.04	104.27	104.51	104.75	104.99	105.22	105.46	105.70	105.94	106.17	106.41	106.65	106.89	107.12	107.60
7.25	103.56	103.79	104.03	104.27	104.50	104.74	104.98	105.21	105.45	105.69	105.93	106.16	106.40	106.64	106.87	107.35
7.50	103.31	103.55	103.79	104.02	104.26	104.50	104.73	104.97	105.21	105.44	105.68	105.92	106.15	106.39	106.63	107.10
7.75	103.07	103.31	103.54	103.78	104.02	104.25	104.49	104.72	104.96	105.20	105.43	105.67	105.90	106.14	106.38	106.85
8.00	102.83	103.06	103.30	103.54	103.77	104.01	104.24	104.48	104.72	104.95	105.19	105.42	105.66	105.89	106.13	106.60
8.25	102.59	102.82	103.06	103.29	103.53	103.77	104.00	104.24	104.47	104.71	104.94	105.18	105.41	105.65	105.88	106.35
8.50	102.35	102.58	102.82	103.05	103.29	103.52	103.76	103.99	104.23	104.46	104.70	104.93	105.17	105.40	105.64	106.11
8.75	102.11	102.35	102.58	102.81	103.05	103.28	103.52	103.75	103.99	104.22	104.46	104.69	104.92	105.16	105.39	105.86
9.00	101.87	102.11	102.34	102.57	102.81	103.04	103.28	103.51	103.75	103.98	104.21	104.45	104.68	104.92	105.15	105.62
9.25	101.64	101.87	102.10	102.34	102.57	102.80	103.04	103.27	103.51	103.74	103.97	104.21	104.44	104.67	104.91	105.37
9.50	101.40	101.63	101.87	102.10	102.33	102.57	102.80	103.03	103.27	103.50	103.73	103.97	104.20	104.43	104.67	105.13
9.75	101.16	101.40	101.63	101.86	102.10	102.33	102.56	102.79	103.03	103.26	103.49	103.73	103.96	104.19	104.42	104.89
10.00	100.93	101.16	101.39	101.63	101.86	102.09	102.32	102.56	102.79	103.02	103.25	103.49	103.72	103.95	104.18	104.65
10.25	100.70	100.93	101.16	101.39	101.62	101.86	102.09	102.32	102.55	102.78	103.02	103.25	103.48	103.71	103.94	104.41
10.50	100.46	100.69	100.93	101.16	101.39	101.62	101.85	102.08	102.32	102.55	102.78	103.01	103.24	103.47	103.71	104.17
10.75	100.23	100.46	100.69	100.92	101.16	101.39	101.62	101.85	102.08	102.31	102.54	102.77	103.01	103.24	103.47	103.93
11.00	100.00	100.23	100.46	100.69	100.92	101.15	101.38	101.62	101.85	102.08	102.31	102.54	102.77	103.00	103.23	103.69
11.25	99.77	100.00	100.23	100.46	100.69	100.92	101.15	101.38	101.61	101.84	102.07	102.30	102.53	102.76	102.99	103.46
11.50	99.54	99.77	100.00	100.23	100.46	100.69	100.92	101.15	101.38	101.61	101.84	102.07	102.30	102.53	102.76	103.22
11.75	99.31	99.54	99.77	100.00	100.23	100.46	100.69	100.92	101.15	101.38	101.61	101.84	102.07	102.30	102.53	102.98
12.00	99.08	99.31	99.54	99.77	100.00	100.23	100.46	100.69	100.92	101.15	101.38	101.60	101.83	102.06	102.29	102.75
12.25	98.86	99.08	99.31	99.54	99.77	100.00	100.23	100.46	100.69	100.92	101.14	101.37	101.60	101.83	102.06	102.52
12.50	98.63	98.86	99.09	99.31	99.54	99.77	100.00	100.23	100.46	100.69	100.91	101.14	101.37	101.60	101.83	102.28
12.75	98.40	98.63	98.86	99.09	99.32	99.54	99.77	100.00	100.23	100.46	100.68	100.91	101.14	101.37	101.60	102.05
13.00	98.18	98.41	98.63	98.86	99.09	99.32	99.54	99.77	100.00	100.23	100.46	100.68	100.91	101.14	101.37	101.82
13.25	97.96	98.18	98.41	98.64	98.86	99.09	99.32	99.55	99.77	100.00	100.23	100.45	100.68	100.91	101.14	101.59
13.50	97.73	97.96	98.19	98.41	98.64	98.87	99.09	99.32	99.55	99.77	100.00	100.23	100.45	100.68	100.91	101.36
13.75	97.51	97.74	97.96	98.19	98.42	98.64	98.87	99.09	99.32	99.55	99.77	100.00	100.23	100.45	100.68	101.13
14.00	97.29	97.51	97.74	97.97	98.19	98.42	98.64	98.87	99.10	99.32	99.55	99.77	100.00	100.23	100.45	100.90
14.25	97.07	97.29	97.52	97.74	97.97	98.20	98.42	98.65	98.87	99.10	99.32	99.55	99.77	100.00	100.23	100.68
14.50	96.85	97.07	97.30	97.52	97.75	97.97	98.20	98.42	98.65	98.87	99.10	99.32	99.55	99.77	100.00	100.45
14.75	96.63	96.85	97.08	97.30	97.53	97.75	97.98	98.20	98.43	98.65	98.88	99.10	99.33	99.55	99.78	100.22
15.00	96.41	96.63	96.86	97.08	97.31	97.53	97.76	97.98	98.20	98.43	98.65	98.88	99.10	99.33	99.55	100.00
15.25	96.19	96.42	96.64	96.86	97.09	97.31	97.54	97.76	97.98	98.21	98.43	98.66	98.88	99.10	99.33	99.78
15.50	95.97	96.20	96.42	96.64	96.87	97.09	97.32	97.54	97.76	97.99	98.21	98.43	98.66	98.88	99.11	99.55
15.75	95.76	95.98	96.20	96.43	96.65	96.87	97.10	97.32	97.54	97.77	97.99	98.21	98.44	98.66	98.88	99.33
16.00	95.54	95.76	95.99	96.21	96.43	96.66	96.88	97.10	97.33	97.55	97.77	97.99	98.22	98.44	98.66	99.11
16.25	95.33	95.55	95.77	95.99	96.22	96.44	96.66	96.88	97.11	97.33	97.55	97.77	98.00	98.22	98.44	98.89
16.50	95.11	95.33	95.56	95.78	96.00	96.22	96.45	96.67	96.89	97.11	97.33	97.56	97.78	98.00	98.22	98.67
16.75	94.90	95.12	95.34	95.56	95.79	96.01	96.23	96.45	96.67	96.90	97.12	97.34	97.56	97.78	98.00	98.45
17.00	94.69	94.91	95.13	95.35	95.57	95.79	96.01	96.24	96.46	96.68	96.90	97.12	97.34	97.56	97.79	98.23
17.25	94.47	94.70	94.92	95.14	95.36	95.58	95.80	96.02	96.24	96.46	96.68	96.91	97.13	97.35	97.57	98.01
17.50	94.26	94.48	94.70	94.93	95.15	95.37	95.59	95.81	96.03	96.25	96.47	96.69	96.91	97.13	97.35	97.79
17.75	94.05	94.27	94.49	94.71	94.93	95.15	95.37	95.59	95.82	96.04	96.26	96.48	96.70	96.92	97.14	97.58
18.00	93.84	94.06	94.28	94.50	94.72	94.94	95.16	95.38	95.60	95.82	96.04	96.26	96.48	96.70	96.92	97.36
18.25	93.63	93.85	94.07	94.29	94.51	94.73	94.95	95.17	95.39	95.61	95.83	96.05	96.27	96.49	96.71	97.15
18.50	93.43	93.64	93.86	94.08	94.30	94.52	94.74	94.96	95.18	95.40	95.62	95.84	96.06	96.27	96.49	96.93
18.75	93.22	93.44	93.66	93.87	94.09	94.31	94.53	94.75	94.97	95.19	95.41	95.62	95.84	96.06	96.28	96.72
19.00	93.01	93.23	93.45	93.67	93.88	94.10	94.32	94.54	94.76	94.98	95.20	95.41	95.63	95.85	96.07	96.51
20.00	92.19	92.41	92.62	92.84	93.06	93.27	93.49	93.71	93.93	94.14	94.36	94.58	94.79	95.01	95.23	95.66
25.00	88.25	88.46	88.67	88.88	89.09	89.30	89.51	89.72	89.93	90.14	90.35	90.56	90.77	90.98	91.19	91.60
30.00	84.56	84.76	84.96	85.17	85.37	85.57	85.78	85.98	86.18	86.38	86.59	86.79	86.99	87.20	87.40	87.81

Description: This table shows the yield to maturity of a bond purchased at the price shown in the index.

Example: The yield to maturity of a 15.00 %, 1 year bond at a price of 102.00 is 12.80 %.

							COUPON RATE, %									
PRICE	11.00%	11.25%	11.50%	11.75%	12.00%	12.25%	12.50%	12.75%	13.00%	13.25%	13.50%	13.75%	14.00%	14.25%	14.50%	15.00%
110	.93	1.16	1.39	1.62	1.86	2.09	2.32	2.55	2.79	3.02	3.25	3.48	3.72	3.95	4.18	4.65
109	1.87	2.10	2.34	2.57	2.80	3.04	3.27	3.51	3.74	3.98	4.21	4.44	4.68	4.91	5.15	5.61
108	2.82	3.06	3.30	3.53	3.77	4.00	4.24	4.48	4.71	4.95	5.18	5.42	5.65	5.89	6.13	6.60
107	3.79	4.03	4.27	4.51	4.74	4.98	5.22	5.46	5.69	5.93	6.17	6.41	6.64	6.88	7.12	7.59
106	4.78	5.02	5.26	5.50	5.74	5.97	6.21	6.45	6.69	6.93	7.17	7.41	7.65	7.89	8.13	8.60
105.75	5.03	5.27	5.51	5.75	5.99	6.23	6.46	6.70	6.94	7.18	7.42	7.66	7.90	8.14	8.38	8.86
105.50	5.28	5.52	5.76	6.00	6.24	6.48	6.72	6.96	7.20	7.44	7.68	7.92	8.16	8.40	8.64	9.12
105.25	5.53	5.77	6.01	6.25	6.49	6.73	6.97	7.21	7.45	7.69	7.93	8.17	8.41	8.65	8.89	9.37
105.00	5.78	6.02	6.26	6.50	6.74	6.98	7.22	7.46	7.70	7.95	8.19	8.43	8.67	8.91	9.15	9.63
104.75	6.03	6.27	6.51	6.75	6.99	7.24	7.48	7.72	7.96	8.20	8.44	8.68	8.92	9.17	9.41	9.89
104.50	6.28	6.52	6.77	7.01	7.25	7.49	7.73	7.97	8.22	8.46	8.70	8.94	9.18	9.42	9.67	10.15
104.25	6.54	6.78	7.02	7.26	7.50	7.75	7.99	8.23	8.47	8.72	8.96	9.20	9.44	9.68	9.93	10.41
104.00	6.79	7.03	7.28	7.52	7.76	8.00	8.25	8.49	8.73	8.97	9.22	9.46	9.70	9.94	10.19	10.67
103.75	7.05	7.29	7.53	7.77	8.02	8.26	8.50	8.75	8.99	9.23	9.48	9.72	9.96	10.21	10.45	10.93
103.50	7.30	7.55	7.79	8.03	8.28	8.52	8.76	9.01	9.25	9.49	9.74	9.98	10.22	10.47	10.71	11.20
103.25	7.56	7.80	8.05	8.29	8.54	8.78	9.02	9.27	9.51	9.76	10.00	10.24	10.49	10.73	10.98	11.46
103.00	7.82	8.06	8.31	8.55	8.80	9.04	9.28	9.53	9.77	10.02	10.26	10.51	10.75	11.00	11.24	11.73
102.75	8.08	8.32	8.57	8.81	9.06	9.30	9.55	9.79	10.04	10.28	10.53	10.77	11.02	11.26	11.51	12.00
102.50	8.34	8.58	8.83	9.07	9.32	9.56	9.81	10.05	10.30	10.55	10.79	11.04	11.28	11.53	11.77	12.26
102.25	8.60	8.84	9.09	9.34	9.58	9.83	10.07	10.32	10.57	10.81	11.06	11.30	11.55	11.79	12.04	12.53
102.00	8.86	9.11	9.35	9.60	9.85	10.09	10.34	10.58	10.83	11.08	11.32	11.57	11.82	12.06	12.31	12.80
101.75	9.12	9.37	9.62	9.86	10.11	10.36	10.60	10.85	11.10	11.34	11.59	11.84	12.08	12.33	12.58	13.07
101.50	9.39	9.64	9.88	10.13	10.38	10.62	10.87	11.12	11.37	11.61	11.86	12.11	12.35	12.60	12.85	13.34
101.25	9.65	9.90	10.15	10.40	10.64	10.89	11.14	11.39	11.63	11.88	12.13	12.38	12.63	12.87	13.12	13.62
101.00	9.92	10.17	10.42	10.66	10.91	11.16	11.41	11.66	11.90	12.15	12.40	12.65	12.90	13.15	13.39	13.89
100.75	10.19	10.44	10.68	10.93	11.18	11.43	11.68	11.93	12.18	12.42	12.67	12.92	13.17	13.42	13.67	14.16
100.50	10.46	10.70	10.95	11.20	11.45	11.70	11.95	12.20	12.45	12.70	12.95	13.20	13.44	13.69	13.94	14.44
100.25	10.72	10.97	11.22	11.47	11.72	11.97	12.22	12.47	12.72	12.97	13.22	13.47	13.72	13.97	14.22	14.72
100.00	11.00	11.25	11.50	11.75	12.00	12.25	12.50	12.75	13.00	13.25	13.50	13.75	14.00	14.25	14.50	15.00
99.75	11.27	11.52	11.77	12.02	12.27	12.52	12.77	13.02	13.27	13.52	13.77	14.02	14.27	14.52	14.77	15.27
99.50	11.54	11.79	12.04	12.29	12.54	12.79	13.04	13.30	13.55	13.80	14.05	14.30	14.55	14.80	15.05	15.55
99.25	11.81	12.06	12.32	12.57	12.82	13.07	13.32	13.57	13.82	14.08	14.33	14.58	14.83	15.08	15.33	15.84
99.00	12.09	12.34	12.59	12.84	13.09	13.35	13.60	13.85	14.10	14.35	14.61	14.86	15.11	15.36	15.61	16.12
98.75	12.36	12.61	12.87	13.12	13.37	13.62	13.88	14.13	14.38	14.63	14.89	15.14	15.39	15.64	15.90	16.40
98.50	12.64	12.89	13.14	13.40	13.65	13.90	14.16	14.41	14.66	14.91	15.17	15.42	15.67	15.93	16.18	16.69
98.25	12.92	13.17	13.42	13.68	13.93	14.18	14.44	14.69	14.94	15.20	15.45	15.70	15.96	16.21	16.46	16.97
98.00	13.20	13.45	13.70	13.96	14.21	14.46	14.72	14.97	15.23	15.48	15.73	15.99	16.24	16.50	16.75	17.26
97.75	13.48	13.73	13.98	14.24	14.49	14.75	15.00	15.26	15.51	15.76	16.02	16.27	16.53	16.78	17.04	17.55
97.50	13.76	14.01	14.27	14.52	14.78	15.03	15.29	15.54	15.80	16.05	16.30	16.56	16.81	17.07	17.32	17.83
97.25	14.04	14.29	14.55	14.80	15.06	15.31	15.57	15.83	16.08	16.34	16.59	16.85	17.10	17.36	17.61	18.12
97.00	14.32	14.58	14.83	15.09	15.34	15.60	15.86	16.11	16.37	16.62	16.88	17.14	17.39	17.65	17.90	18.42
96.75	14.61	14.86	15.12	15.37	15.63	15.89	16.14	16.40	16.66	16.91	17.17	17.43	17.68	17.94	18.20	18.71
96.50	14.89	15.15	15.40	15.66	15.92	16.18	16.43	16.69	16.95	17.20	17.46	17.72	17.97	18.23	18.49	19.00
96.25	15.18	15.43	15.69	15.95	16.21	16.46	16.72	16.98	17.24	17.49	17.75	18.01	18.27	18.52	18.78	19.30
96.00	15.46	15.72	15.98	16.24	16.50	16.75	17.01	17.27	17.53	17.79	18.04	18.30	18.56	18.82	19.08	19.59
95.75	15.75	16.01	16.27	16.53	16.79	17.05	17.30	17.56	17.82	18.08	18.34	18.60	18.86	19.11	19.37	19.89
95.50	16.04	16.30	16.56	16.82	17.08	17.34	17.60	17.86	18.12	18.37	18.63	18.89	19.15	19.41	19.67	20.19
95.25	16.33	16.59	16.85	17.11	17.37	17.63	17.89	18.15	18.41	18.67	18.93	19.19	19.45	19.71	19.97	20.49
95.00	16.63	16.89	17.15	17.41	17.67	17.93	18.19	18.45	18.71	18.97	19.23	19.49	19.75	20.01	20.27	20.79
94.75	16.92	17.18	17.44	17.70	17.96	18.22	18.48	18.74	19.00	19.27	19.53	19.79	20.05	20.31	20.57	21.09
94.50	17.22	17.48	17.74	18.00	18.26	18.52	18.78	19.04	19.30	19.56	19.83	20.09	20.35	20.61	20.87	21.39
94.25	17.51	17.77	18.03	18.30	18.56	18.82	19.08	19.34	19.60	19.87	20.13	20.39	20.65	20.91	21.17	21.70
94.00	17.81	18.07	18.33	18.59	18.86	19.12	19.38	19.64	19.91	20.17	20.43	20.69	20.95	21.22	21.48	22.00
93.75	18.11	18.37	18.63	18.89	19.16	19.42	19.68	19.95	20.21	20.47	20.73	21.00	21.26	21.52	21.78	22.31
93	19.01	19.27	19.54	19.80	20.07	20.33	20.59	20.86	21.12	21.39	21.65	21.92	22.18	22.44	22.71	23.24
92	20.23	20.50	20.76	21.03	21.29	21.56	21.83	22.09	22.36	22.63	22.89	23.16	23.43	23.69	23.96	24.49
91	21.47	21.74	22.01	22.28	22.54	22.81	23.08	23.35	23.62	23.89	24.16	24.43	24.69	24.96	25.23	25.77
90	22.73	23.00	23.27	23.54	23.82	24.09	24.36	24.63	24.90	25.17	25.44	25.71	25.98	26.26	26.53	27.07
89	24.01	24.29	24.56	24.83	25.11	25.38	25.65	25.93	26.20	26.47	26.75	27.02	27.30	27.57	27.84	28.39
88	25.32	25.60	25.87	26.15	26.42	26.70	26.97	27.25	27.53	27.80	28.08	28.35	28.63	28.91	29.18	29.73
87	26.65	26.93	27.20	27.48	27.76	28.04	28.32	28.60	28.87	29.15	29.43	29.71	29.99	30.27	30.54	31.10
86	28.00	28.28	28.56	28.84	29.12	29.40	29.68	29.97	30.25	30.53	30.81	31.09	31.37	31.65	31.93	32.49
85	29.38	29.66	29.94	30.23	30.51	30.79	31.08	31.36	31.64	31.93	32.21	32.49	32.78	33.06	33.34	33.91
84	30.78	31.06	31.35	31.63	31.92	32.21	32.49	32.78	33.06	33.35	33.64	33.92	34.21	34.49	34.78	35.35
83	32.20	32.49	32.78	33.07	33.36	33.65	33.94	34.22	34.51	34.80	35.09	35.38	35.67	35.96	36.25	36.82
82	33.66	33.95	34.24	34.53	34.82	35.11	35.41	35.70	35.99	36.28	36.57	36.86	37.15	37.45	37.74	38.32
81	35.14	35.43	35.73	36.02	36.31	36.61	36.90	37.20	37.49	37.79	38.08	38.37	38.67	38.96	39.26	39.85
80	36.65	36.94	37.24	37.54	37.83	38.13	38.43	38.73	39.02	39.32	39.62	39.91	40.21	40.51	40.81	41.40

Description: This table shows the price to pay for a bond at the yield rate. The yield is to maturity.

Example: The price of a 6.75 %, 2 year bond to yield 8 % to maturity is $ 97.73.

COUPON RATE, %

YIELD	0.00%	1.00%	2.00%	3.00%	4.00%	4.25%	4.50%	4.75%	5.00%	5.25%	5.50%	5.75%	6.00%	6.25%	6.50%	6.75%
0.00	100.00	102.00	104.00	106.00	108.00	108.50	109.00	109.50	110.00	110.50	111.00	111.50	112.00	112.50	113.00	113.50
1.00	98.02	100.00	101.98	103.95	105.93	106.42	106.91	107.41	107.90	108.39	108.89	109.38	109.88	110.37	110.86	111.36
2.00	96.10	98.05	100.00	101.95	103.90	104.39	104.88	105.37	105.85	106.34	106.83	107.32	107.80	108.29	108.78	109.27
3.00	94.22	96.15	98.07	100.00	101.93	102.41	102.89	103.37	103.85	104.34	104.82	105.30	105.78	106.26	106.75	107.23
4.00	92.38	94.29	96.19	98.10	100.00	100.48	100.95	101.43	101.90	102.38	102.86	103.33	103.81	104.28	104.76	105.24
4.25	91.93	93.83	95.73	97.63	99.53	100.00	100.47	100.95	101.42	101.90	102.37	102.85	103.32	103.80	104.27	104.75
4.50	91.48	93.38	95.27	97.16	99.05	99.53	100.00	100.47	100.95	101.42	101.89	102.37	102.84	103.31	103.78	104.26
4.75	91.04	92.93	94.81	96.70	98.59	99.06	99.53	100.00	100.47	100.94	101.41	101.89	102.36	102.83	103.30	103.77
5.00	90.60	92.48	94.36	96.24	98.12	98.59	99.06	99.53	100.00	100.47	100.94	101.41	101.88	102.35	102.82	103.29
5.25	90.15	92.03	93.91	95.78	97.66	98.12	98.59	99.06	99.53	100.00	100.47	100.94	101.41	101.88	102.34	102.81
5.50	89.72	91.59	93.46	95.33	97.20	97.66	98.13	98.60	99.07	99.53	100.00	100.47	100.93	101.40	101.87	102.34
5.75	89.28	91.15	93.01	94.87	96.74	97.20	97.67	98.14	98.60	99.07	99.53	100.00	100.47	100.93	101.40	101.86
6.00	88.85	90.71	92.57	94.42	96.28	96.75	97.21	97.68	98.14	98.61	99.07	99.54	100.00	100.46	100.93	101.39
6.25	88.42	90.27	92.12	93.98	95.83	96.29	96.76	97.22	97.68	98.15	98.61	99.07	99.54	100.00	100.46	100.93
6.50	87.99	89.84	91.69	93.53	95.38	95.84	96.31	96.77	97.23	97.69	98.15	98.61	99.08	99.54	100.00	100.46
6.75	87.57	89.41	91.25	93.09	94.93	95.39	95.86	96.32	96.78	97.24	97.70	98.16	98.62	99.08	99.54	100.00
7.00	87.14	88.98	90.82	92.65	94.49	94.95	95.41	95.87	96.33	96.79	97.25	97.70	98.16	98.62	99.08	99.54
7.25	86.72	88.56	90.39	92.22	94.05	94.51	94.96	95.42	95.88	96.34	96.80	97.25	97.71	98.17	98.63	99.08
7.50	86.31	88.13	89.96	91.78	93.61	94.07	94.52	94.98	95.44	95.89	96.35	96.81	97.26	97.72	98.17	98.63
7.75	85.89	87.71	89.53	91.35	93.17	93.63	94.08	94.54	94.99	95.45	95.90	96.36	96.81	97.27	97.72	98.18
8.00	85.48	87.30	89.11	90.93	92.74	93.19	93.65	94.10	94.56	95.01	95.46	95.92	96.37	96.82	97.28	97.73
8.25	85.07	86.88	88.69	90.50	92.31	92.76	93.21	93.67	94.12	94.57	95.02	95.48	95.93	96.38	96.83	97.29
8.50	84.66	86.47	88.27	90.08	91.88	92.33	92.78	93.23	93.68	94.14	94.59	95.04	95.49	95.94	96.39	96.84
8.75	84.26	86.06	87.86	89.66	91.45	91.90	92.35	92.80	93.25	93.70	94.15	94.60	95.05	95.50	95.95	96.40
9.00	83.86	85.65	87.44	89.24	91.03	91.48	91.93	92.38	92.82	93.27	93.72	94.17	94.62	95.07	95.52	95.96
9.25	83.46	85.24	87.03	88.82	90.61	91.06	91.50	91.95	92.40	92.85	93.29	93.74	94.19	94.63	95.08	95.53
9.50	83.06	84.84	86.63	88.41	90.19	90.64	91.08	91.53	91.98	92.42	92.87	93.31	93.76	94.20	94.65	95.10
9.75	82.66	84.44	86.22	88.00	89.78	90.22	90.66	91.11	91.55	92.00	92.44	92.89	93.33	93.78	94.22	94.67
10.00	82.27	84.04	85.82	87.59	89.36	89.81	90.25	90.69	91.14	91.58	92.02	92.46	92.91	93.35	93.79	94.24
10.25	81.88	83.65	85.42	87.18	88.95	89.39	89.83	90.28	90.72	91.16	91.60	92.04	92.49	92.93	93.37	93.81
10.50	81.49	83.25	85.02	86.78	88.54	88.98	89.42	89.86	90.30	90.75	91.19	91.63	92.07	92.51	92.95	93.39
10.75	81.11	82.86	84.62	86.38	88.14	88.58	89.01	89.45	89.89	90.33	90.77	91.21	91.65	92.09	92.53	92.97
11.00	80.72	82.47	84.23	85.98	87.73	88.17	88.61	89.05	89.48	89.92	90.36	90.80	91.24	91.68	92.11	92.55
11.25	80.34	82.09	83.84	85.58	87.33	87.77	88.20	88.64	89.08	89.51	89.95	90.39	90.83	91.26	91.70	92.14
11.50	79.96	81.70	83.45	85.19	86.93	87.37	87.80	88.24	88.67	89.11	89.54	89.98	90.42	90.85	91.29	91.72
11.75	79.58	81.32	83.06	84.80	86.53	86.97	87.40	87.84	88.27	88.71	89.14	89.57	90.01	90.44	90.88	91.31
12.00	79.21	80.94	82.67	84.41	86.14	86.57	87.01	87.44	87.87	88.31	88.74	89.17	89.60	90.04	90.47	90.90
12.25	78.84	80.56	82.29	84.02	85.75	86.18	86.61	87.04	87.47	87.91	88.34	88.77	89.20	89.63	90.07	90.50
12.50	78.47	80.19	81.91	83.63	85.36	85.79	86.22	86.65	87.08	87.51	87.94	88.37	88.80	89.23	89.66	90.09
12.75	78.10	79.82	81.53	83.25	84.97	85.40	85.83	86.26	86.69	87.12	87.55	87.98	88.40	88.83	89.26	89.69
13.00	77.73	79.45	81.16	82.87	84.58	85.01	85.44	85.87	86.30	86.73	87.15	87.58	88.01	88.44	88.87	89.29
13.25	77.37	79.08	80.78	82.49	84.20	84.63	85.05	85.48	85.91	86.34	86.76	87.19	87.62	88.04	88.47	88.90
13.50	77.01	78.71	80.41	82.12	83.82	84.25	84.67	85.10	85.52	85.95	86.37	86.80	87.23	87.65	88.08	88.50
13.75	76.65	78.35	80.04	81.74	83.44	83.87	84.29	84.71	85.14	85.56	85.99	86.41	86.84	87.26	87.69	88.11
14.00	76.29	77.98	79.68	81.37	83.06	83.49	83.91	84.33	84.76	85.18	85.60	86.03	86.45	86.87	87.30	87.72
14.25	75.93	77.62	79.31	81.00	82.69	83.11	83.53	83.96	84.38	84.80	85.22	85.64	86.07	86.49	86.91	87.33
14.50	75.58	77.26	78.95	80.63	82.32	82.74	83.16	83.58	84.00	84.42	84.84	85.26	85.69	86.11	86.53	86.95
14.75	75.23	76.91	78.59	80.27	81.95	82.37	82.79	83.21	83.63	84.05	84.47	84.89	85.31	85.73	86.15	86.57
15.00	74.88	76.55	78.23	79.90	81.58	82.00	82.42	82.83	83.25	83.67	84.09	84.51	84.93	85.35	85.77	86.18
15.25	74.53	76.20	77.87	79.54	81.21	81.63	82.05	82.47	82.88	83.30	83.72	84.14	84.55	84.97	85.39	85.81
15.50	74.19	75.85	77.52	79.18	80.85	81.27	81.68	82.10	82.51	82.93	83.35	83.76	84.18	84.60	85.01	85.43
15.75	73.84	75.50	77.17	78.83	80.49	80.90	81.32	81.73	82.15	82.56	82.98	83.39	83.81	84.22	84.64	85.05
16.00	73.50	75.16	76.82	78.47	80.13	80.54	80.96	81.37	81.78	82.20	82.61	83.03	83.44	83.85	84.27	84.68
16.25	73.16	74.82	76.47	78.12	79.77	80.18	80.60	81.01	81.42	81.83	82.25	82.66	83.07	83.49	83.90	84.31
16.50	72.83	74.47	76.12	77.77	79.41	79.83	80.24	80.65	81.06	81.47	81.88	82.30	82.71	83.12	83.53	83.94
16.75	72.49	74.13	75.78	77.42	79.06	79.47	79.88	80.29	80.70	81.11	81.52	81.93	82.34	82.76	83.17	83.58
17.00	72.16	73.80	75.43	77.07	78.71	79.12	79.53	79.94	80.35	80.76	81.17	81.57	81.98	82.39	82.80	83.21
17.25	71.83	73.46	75.09	76.73	78.36	78.77	79.18	79.58	79.99	80.40	80.81	81.22	81.63	82.03	82.44	82.85
17.50	71.50	73.12	74.75	76.38	78.01	78.42	78.83	79.23	79.64	80.05	80.45	80.86	81.27	81.68	82.08	82.49
17.75	71.17	72.79	74.42	76.04	77.67	78.07	78.48	78.88	79.29	79.70	80.10	80.51	80.91	81.32	81.73	82.13
18.00	70.84	72.46	74.08	75.70	77.32	77.73	78.13	78.54	78.94	79.35	79.75	80.16	80.56	80.97	81.37	81.78
18.25	70.52	72.13	73.75	75.36	76.98	77.38	77.79	78.19	78.60	79.00	79.40	79.81	80.21	80.61	81.02	81.42
18.50	70.20	71.81	73.42	75.03	76.64	77.04	77.45	77.85	78.25	78.65	79.06	79.46	79.86	80.27	80.67	81.07
18.75	69.88	71.48	73.09	74.70	76.30	76.70	77.11	77.51	77.91	78.31	78.71	79.11	79.52	79.92	80.32	80.72
19.00	69.56	71.16	72.76	74.36	75.97	76.37	76.77	77.17	77.57	77.97	78.37	78.77	79.17	79.57	79.97	80.37
20.00	68.30	69.89	71.47	73.06	74.64	75.04	75.43	75.83	76.23	76.62	77.02	77.41	77.81	78.21	78.60	79.00
25.00	62.43	63.93	65.44	66.94	68.44	68.82	69.19	69.57	69.94	70.32	70.70	71.07	71.45	71.82	72.20	72.57
30.00	57.18	58.60	60.03	61.46	62.89	63.24	63.60	63.96	64.31	64.67	65.03	65.38	65.74	66.10	66.45	66.81

Description: This table shows the yield to maturity of a bond purchased at the price shown in the index.

Example: The yield to maturity of a 6.75 %, 2 year bond at a price of 95.00 is 9.55 %.

PRICE	0.00%	1.00%	2.00%	3.00%	4.00%	4.25%	COUPON RATE, % 4.50%	4.75%	5.00%	5.25%	5.50%	5.75%	6.00%	6.25%	6.50%	6.75%
100	0.00	1.00	2.00	3.00	4.00	4.25	4.50	4.75	5.00	5.25	5.50	5.75	6.00	6.25	6.50	6.75
99.75	.12	1.12	2.12	3.12	4.13	4.38	4.63	4.88	5.13	5.38	5.63	5.88	6.13	6.38	6.63	6.88
99.50	.25	1.25	2.25	3.26	4.26	4.51	4.76	5.01	5.26	5.51	5.76	6.01	6.26	6.52	6.77	7.02
99.25	.37	1.38	2.38	3.39	4.39	4.64	4.89	5.14	5.40	5.65	5.90	6.15	6.40	6.65	6.90	7.15
99.00	.50	1.50	2.51	3.52	4.52	4.78	5.03	5.28	5.53	5.78	6.03	6.28	6.54	6.79	7.04	7.29
98.75	.62	1.63	2.64	3.65	4.66	4.91	5.16	5.41	5.66	5.92	6.17	6.42	6.67	6.93	7.18	7.43
98.50	.75	1.76	2.77	3.78	4.79	5.04	5.30	5.55	5.80	6.05	6.31	6.56	6.81	7.06	7.31	7.57
98.25	.88	1.89	2.90	3.91	4.92	5.18	5.43	5.68	5.94	6.19	6.44	6.69	6.95	7.20	7.45	7.71
98.00	1.01	2.02	3.03	4.05	5.06	5.31	5.57	5.82	6.07	6.33	6.58	6.83	7.09	7.34	7.59	7.85
97.75	1.14	2.15	3.16	4.18	5.19	5.45	5.70	5.96	6.21	6.46	6.72	6.97	7.22	7.48	7.73	7.98
97.50	1.26	2.28	3.30	4.31	5.33	5.58	5.84	6.09	6.35	6.60	6.85	7.11	7.36	7.62	7.87	8.12
97.25	1.39	2.41	3.43	4.45	5.47	5.72	5.97	6.23	6.48	6.74	6.99	7.25	7.50	7.76	8.01	8.27
97.00	1.52	2.54	3.56	4.58	5.60	5.86	6.11	6.37	6.62	6.88	7.13	7.39	7.64	7.90	8.15	8.41
96.75	1.65	2.67	3.70	4.72	5.74	5.99	6.25	6.50	6.76	7.02	7.27	7.53	7.78	8.04	8.29	8.55
96.50	1.78	2.81	3.83	4.85	5.88	6.13	6.39	6.64	6.90	7.15	7.41	7.67	7.92	8.18	8.43	8.69
96.25	1.92	2.94	3.96	4.99	6.01	6.27	6.53	6.78	7.04	7.29	7.55	7.81	8.06	8.32	8.58	8.83
96.00	2.05	3.07	4.10	5.12	6.15	6.41	6.66	6.92	7.18	7.43	7.69	7.95	8.20	8.46	8.72	8.97
95.75	2.18	3.21	4.23	5.26	6.29	6.55	6.80	7.06	7.32	7.58	7.83	8.09	8.35	8.60	8.86	9.12
95.50	2.31	3.34	4.37	5.40	6.43	6.69	6.94	7.20	7.46	7.72	7.97	8.23	8.49	8.75	9.00	9.26
95.25	2.44	3.47	4.51	5.54	6.57	6.83	7.08	7.34	7.60	7.86	8.12	8.37	8.63	8.89	9.15	9.41
95.00	2.58	3.61	4.64	5.68	6.71	6.97	7.23	7.48	7.74	8.00	8.26	8.52	8.78	9.03	9.29	9.55
94.75	2.71	3.74	4.78	5.81	6.85	7.11	7.37	7.63	7.88	8.14	8.40	8.66	8.92	9.18	9.44	9.70
94.50	2.84	3.88	4.92	5.95	6.99	7.25	7.51	7.77	8.03	8.29	8.55	8.80	9.06	9.32	9.58	9.84
94.25	2.98	4.02	5.05	6.09	7.13	7.39	7.65	7.91	8.17	8.43	8.69	8.95	9.21	9.47	9.73	9.99
94.00	3.11	4.15	5.19	6.23	7.27	7.53	7.79	8.05	8.31	8.57	8.83	9.09	9.35	9.61	9.87	10.13
93.75	3.25	4.29	5.33	6.37	7.42	7.68	7.94	8.20	8.46	8.72	8.98	9.24	9.50	9.76	10.02	10.28
93.50	3.38	4.43	5.47	6.51	7.56	7.82	8.08	8.34	8.60	8.86	9.12	9.39	9.65	9.91	10.17	10.43
93.25	3.52	4.57	5.61	6.66	7.70	7.96	8.22	8.49	8.75	9.01	9.27	9.53	9.79	10.05	10.32	10.58
93.00	3.66	4.70	5.75	6.80	7.85	8.11	8.37	8.63	8.89	9.15	9.42	9.68	9.94	10.20	10.46	10.73
92.75	3.79	4.84	5.89	6.94	7.99	8.25	8.51	8.78	9.04	9.30	9.56	9.83	10.09	10.35	10.61	10.88
92.50	3.93	4.98	6.03	7.08	8.13	8.40	8.66	8.92	9.19	9.45	9.71	9.97	10.24	10.50	10.76	11.03
92.25	4.07	5.12	6.17	7.23	8.28	8.54	8.81	9.07	9.33	9.60	9.86	10.12	10.39	10.65	10.91	11.18
92.00	4.21	5.26	6.32	7.37	8.43	8.69	8.95	9.22	9.48	9.74	10.01	10.27	10.54	10.80	11.06	11.33
91.75	4.35	5.40	6.46	7.51	8.57	8.84	9.10	9.36	9.63	9.89	10.16	10.42	10.69	10.95	11.21	11.48
91	4.77	5.83	6.89	7.95	9.01	9.28	9.54	9.81	10.08	10.34	10.61	10.87	11.14	11.40	11.67	11.94
90	5.33	6.40	7.47	8.54	9.61	9.88	10.15	10.41	10.68	10.95	11.22	11.48	11.75	12.02	12.29	12.55
89	5.91	6.98	8.06	9.14	10.22	10.48	10.75	11.02	11.29	11.56	11.83	12.10	12.37	12.64	12.91	13.18
88	6.49	7.57	8.66	9.74	10.83	11.10	11.37	11.64	11.91	12.19	12.46	12.73	13.00	13.27	13.54	13.82
87	7.08	8.17	9.27	10.36	11.45	11.73	12.00	12.27	12.55	12.82	13.09	13.37	13.64	13.91	14.19	14.46
86	7.68	8.78	9.88	10.98	12.08	12.36	12.63	12.91	13.19	13.46	13.74	14.01	14.29	14.56	14.84	15.12
85	8.29	9.40	10.51	11.62	12.73	13.00	13.28	13.56	13.84	14.11	14.39	14.67	14.95	15.23	15.50	15.78
84	8.91	10.02	11.14	12.26	13.38	13.66	13.94	14.22	14.50	14.78	15.06	15.34	15.62	15.90	16.18	16.46
83	9.53	10.66	11.78	12.91	14.04	14.32	14.60	14.88	15.17	15.45	15.73	16.01	16.29	16.58	16.86	17.14
82	10.17	11.30	12.44	13.57	14.71	14.99	15.28	15.56	15.85	16.13	16.42	16.70	16.98	17.27	17.55	17.84
81	10.81	11.96	13.10	14.25	15.39	15.68	15.96	16.25	16.54	16.82	17.11	17.40	17.68	17.97	18.26	18.55
80	11.47	12.62	13.77	14.93	16.08	16.37	16.66	16.95	17.24	17.53	17.82	18.11	18.40	18.69	18.97	19.26
79	12.14	13.30	14.46	15.62	16.79	17.08	17.37	17.66	17.95	18.24	18.54	18.83	19.12	19.41	19.70	19.99
78	12.81	13.98	15.16	16.33	17.50	17.80	18.09	18.38	18.68	18.97	19.27	19.56	19.85	20.15	20.44	20.74
77	13.50	14.68	15.86	17.05	18.23	18.53	18.82	19.12	19.42	19.71	20.01	20.31	20.60	20.90	21.20	21.49
76	14.20	15.39	16.58	17.78	18.97	19.27	19.57	19.87	20.17	20.46	20.76	21.06	21.36	21.66	21.96	22.26
75	14.91	16.11	17.31	18.52	19.72	20.02	20.32	20.63	20.93	21.23	21.53	21.83	22.14	22.44	22.74	23.04
74	15.63	16.84	18.06	19.27	20.49	20.79	21.10	21.40	21.70	22.01	22.31	22.62	22.92	23.23	23.53	23.84
73	16.37	17.59	18.81	20.04	21.27	21.57	21.88	22.19	22.49	22.80	23.11	23.42	23.72	24.03	24.34	24.65
72	17.11	18.35	19.58	20.82	22.06	22.37	22.68	22.99	23.30	23.61	23.92	24.23	24.54	24.85	25.16	25.47
71	17.87	19.12	20.37	21.61	22.86	23.18	23.49	23.80	24.11	24.43	24.74	25.05	25.37	25.68	25.99	26.31
70	18.65	19.90	21.16	22.42	23.68	24.00	24.32	24.63	24.95	25.26	25.58	25.90	26.21	26.53	26.85	27.16
69	19.44	20.70	21.98	23.25	24.52	24.84	25.16	25.48	25.80	26.12	26.43	26.75	27.07	27.39	27.71	28.03
68	20.24	21.52	22.80	24.09	25.37	25.69	26.02	26.34	26.66	26.98	27.31	27.63	27.95	28.27	28.60	28.92
67	21.06	22.35	23.64	24.94	26.24	26.57	26.89	27.22	27.54	27.87	28.19	28.52	28.84	29.17	29.50	29.82
66	21.89	23.19	24.50	25.81	27.13	27.45	27.78	28.11	28.44	28.77	29.10	29.43	29.76	30.08	30.41	30.74
65	22.74	24.06	25.38	26.70	28.03	28.36	28.69	29.02	29.36	29.69	30.02	30.35	30.68	31.02	31.35	31.68
64	23.60	24.94	26.27	27.61	28.95	29.28	29.62	29.95	30.29	30.63	30.96	31.30	31.63	31.97	32.31	32.64
63	24.48	25.83	27.18	28.53	29.89	30.23	30.56	30.90	31.24	31.58	31.92	32.26	32.60	32.94	33.28	33.62
62	25.38	26.75	28.11	29.48	30.84	31.19	31.53	31.87	32.22	32.56	32.90	33.25	33.59	33.93	34.28	34.62
61	26.30	27.68	29.06	30.44	31.82	32.17	32.52	32.86	33.21	33.56	33.90	34.25	34.60	34.95	35.29	35.64
60	27.24	28.63	30.02	31.42	32.82	33.17	33.52	33.87	34.22	34.57	34.93	35.28	35.63	35.98	36.33	36.68
59	28.20	29.60	31.01	32.43	33.84	34.20	34.55	34.91	35.26	35.62	35.97	36.33	36.68	37.04	37.39	37.75
58	29.17	30.60	32.02	33.45	34.88	35.24	35.60	35.96	36.32	36.68	37.04	37.40	37.76	38.12	38.48	38.84

Description: This table shows the price to pay for a bond at the yield rate. The yield is to maturity.

Example: The price of a 10.75 %, 2 year bond to yield 8 % to maturity is $ 104.99.

COUPON RATE, %

YIELD	7.00%	7.25%	7.50%	7.75%	8.00%	8.25%	8.50%	8.75%	9.00%	9.25%	9.50%	9.75%	10.00%	10.25%	10.50%	10.75%
0.00	114.00	114.50	115.00	115.50	116.00	116.50	117.00	117.50	118.00	118.50	119.00	119.50	120.00	120.50	121.00	121.50
1.00	111.85	112.35	112.84	113.33	113.83	114.32	114.81	115.31	115.80	116.30	116.79	117.28	117.78	118.27	118.76	119.26
2.00	109.75	110.24	110.73	111.22	111.71	112.19	112.68	113.17	113.66	114.14	114.63	115.12	115.61	116.10	116.58	117.07
3.00	107.71	108.19	108.67	109.15	109.64	110.12	110.60	111.08	111.56	112.04	112.53	113.01	113.49	113.97	114.45	114.94
4.00	105.71	106.19	106.66	107.14	107.62	108.09	108.57	109.04	109.52	110.00	110.47	110.95	111.42	111.90	112.38	112.85
4.25	105.22	105.69	106.17	106.64	107.12	107.59	108.07	108.54	109.02	109.49	109.97	110.44	110.91	111.39	111.86	112.34
4.50	104.73	105.20	105.68	106.15	106.62	107.10	107.57	108.04	108.52	108.99	109.46	109.93	110.41	110.88	111.35	111.83
4.75	104.24	104.72	105.19	105.66	106.13	106.60	107.07	107.55	108.02	108.49	108.96	109.43	109.90	110.38	110.85	111.32
5.00	103.76	104.23	104.70	105.17	105.64	106.11	106.58	107.05	107.52	107.99	108.46	108.93	109.40	109.88	110.35	110.82
5.25	103.28	103.75	104.22	104.69	105.16	105.63	106.09	106.56	107.03	107.50	107.97	108.44	108.91	109.38	109.85	110.31
5.50	102.80	103.27	103.74	104.21	104.67	105.14	105.61	106.08	106.54	107.01	107.48	107.95	108.41	108.88	109.35	109.82
5.75	102.33	102.80	103.26	103.73	104.19	104.66	105.13	105.59	106.06	106.52	106.99	107.46	107.92	108.39	108.85	109.32
6.00	101.86	102.32	102.79	103.25	103.72	104.18	104.65	105.11	105.58	106.04	106.50	106.97	107.43	107.90	108.36	108.83
6.25	101.39	101.85	102.32	102.78	103.24	103.71	104.17	104.63	105.10	105.56	106.02	106.49	106.95	107.41	107.88	108.34
6.50	100.92	101.39	101.85	102.31	102.77	103.23	103.69	104.16	104.62	105.08	105.54	106.00	106.47	106.93	107.39	107.85
6.75	100.46	100.92	101.38	101.84	102.30	102.76	103.22	103.68	104.14	104.61	105.07	105.53	105.99	106.45	106.91	107.37
7.00	100.00	100.46	100.92	101.38	101.84	102.30	102.75	103.21	103.67	104.13	104.59	105.05	105.51	105.97	106.43	106.89
7.25	99.54	100.00	100.46	100.92	101.37	101.83	102.29	102.75	103.20	103.66	104.12	104.58	105.04	105.49	105.95	106.41
7.50	99.09	99.54	100.00	100.46	100.91	101.37	101.83	102.28	102.74	103.19	103.65	104.11	104.56	105.02	105.48	105.93
7.75	98.63	99.09	99.54	100.00	100.46	100.91	101.37	101.82	102.28	102.73	103.19	103.64	104.10	104.55	105.01	105.46
8.00	98.19	98.64	99.09	99.55	100.00	100.45	100.91	101.36	101.81	102.27	102.72	103.18	103.63	104.08	104.54	104.99
8.25	97.74	98.19	98.64	99.10	99.55	100.00	100.45	100.90	101.36	101.81	102.26	102.71	103.17	103.62	104.07	104.52
8.50	97.29	97.74	98.20	98.65	99.10	99.55	100.00	100.45	100.90	101.35	101.80	102.26	102.71	103.16	103.61	104.06
8.75	96.85	97.30	97.75	98.20	98.65	99.10	99.55	100.00	100.45	100.90	101.35	101.80	102.25	102.70	103.15	103.60
9.00	96.41	96.86	97.31	97.76	98.21	98.65	99.10	99.55	100.00	100.45	100.90	101.35	101.79	102.24	102.69	103.14
9.25	95.98	96.42	96.87	97.32	97.76	98.21	98.66	99.11	99.55	100.00	100.45	100.89	101.34	101.79	102.24	102.68
9.50	95.54	95.99	96.43	96.88	97.33	97.77	98.22	98.66	99.11	99.55	100.00	100.45	100.89	101.34	101.78	102.23
9.75	95.11	95.55	96.00	96.44	96.89	97.33	97.78	98.22	98.67	99.11	99.56	100.00	100.44	100.89	101.33	101.78
10.00	94.68	95.12	95.57	96.01	96.45	96.90	97.34	97.78	98.23	98.67	99.11	99.56	100.00	100.44	100.89	101.33
10.25	94.25	94.70	95.14	95.58	96.02	96.46	96.91	97.35	97.79	98.23	98.67	99.12	99.56	100.00	100.44	100.88
10.50	93.83	94.27	94.71	95.15	95.59	96.03	96.47	96.92	97.36	97.80	98.24	98.68	99.12	99.56	100.00	100.44
10.75	93.41	93.85	94.29	94.73	95.17	95.61	96.05	96.48	96.92	97.36	97.80	98.24	98.68	99.12	99.56	100.00
11.00	92.99	93.43	93.87	94.30	94.74	95.18	95.62	96.06	96.49	96.93	97.37	97.81	98.25	98.69	99.12	99.56
11.25	92.57	93.01	93.45	93.88	94.32	94.76	95.19	95.63	96.07	96.50	96.94	97.38	97.82	98.25	98.69	99.13
11.50	92.16	92.59	93.03	93.47	93.90	94.34	94.77	95.21	95.64	96.08	96.51	96.95	97.39	97.82	98.26	98.69
11.75	91.75	92.18	92.62	93.05	93.48	93.92	94.35	94.79	95.22	95.66	96.09	96.52	96.96	97.39	97.83	98.26
12.00	91.34	91.77	92.20	92.64	93.07	93.50	93.94	94.37	94.80	95.24	95.67	96.10	96.53	96.97	97.40	97.83
12.25	90.93	91.36	91.79	92.23	92.66	93.09	93.52	93.95	94.39	94.82	95.25	95.68	96.11	96.54	96.98	97.41
12.50	90.53	90.96	91.39	91.82	92.25	92.68	93.11	93.54	93.97	94.40	94.83	95.26	95.69	96.12	96.55	96.99
12.75	90.12	90.55	90.98	91.41	91.84	92.27	92.70	93.13	93.56	93.99	94.42	94.85	95.28	95.71	96.13	96.56
13.00	89.72	90.15	90.58	91.01	91.44	91.86	92.29	92.72	93.15	93.58	94.00	94.43	94.86	95.29	95.72	96.15
13.25	89.32	89.75	90.18	90.61	91.03	91.46	91.89	92.31	92.74	93.17	93.59	94.02	94.45	94.88	95.30	95.73
13.50	88.93	89.35	89.78	90.21	90.63	91.06	91.48	91.91	92.34	92.76	93.19	93.61	94.04	94.46	94.89	95.32
13.75	88.54	88.96	89.39	89.81	90.23	90.66	91.08	91.51	91.93	92.36	92.78	93.21	93.63	94.06	94.48	94.90
14.00	88.14	88.57	88.99	89.41	89.84	90.26	90.69	91.11	91.53	91.96	92.38	92.80	93.23	93.65	94.07	94.50
14.25	87.76	88.18	88.60	89.02	89.44	89.87	90.29	90.71	91.13	91.56	91.98	92.40	92.82	93.24	93.67	94.09
14.50	87.37	87.79	88.21	88.63	89.05	89.47	89.90	90.32	90.74	91.16	91.58	92.00	92.42	92.84	93.26	93.68
14.75	86.98	87.40	87.82	88.24	88.66	89.08	89.50	89.92	90.34	90.76	91.18	91.60	92.02	92.44	92.86	93.28
15.00	86.60	87.02	87.44	87.86	88.28	88.70	89.11	89.53	89.95	90.37	90.79	91.21	91.63	92.05	92.46	92.88
15.25	86.22	86.64	87.06	87.48	87.89	88.31	88.73	89.15	89.56	89.98	90.40	90.82	91.23	91.65	92.07	92.49
15.50	85.84	86.26	86.68	87.09	87.51	87.93	88.34	88.76	89.18	89.59	90.01	90.42	90.84	91.26	91.67	92.09
15.75	85.47	85.88	86.30	86.71	87.13	87.54	87.96	88.38	88.79	89.21	89.62	90.04	90.45	90.87	91.28	91.70
16.00	85.10	85.51	85.92	86.34	86.75	87.17	87.58	87.99	88.41	88.82	89.24	89.65	90.06	90.48	90.89	91.31
16.25	84.72	85.14	85.55	85.96	86.38	86.79	87.20	87.61	88.03	88.44	88.85	89.27	89.68	90.09	90.50	90.92
16.50	84.35	84.77	85.18	85.59	86.00	86.41	86.82	87.24	87.65	88.06	88.47	88.88	89.30	89.71	90.12	90.53
16.75	83.99	84.40	84.81	85.22	85.63	86.04	86.45	86.86	87.27	87.68	88.09	88.50	88.91	89.32	89.74	90.15
17.00	83.62	84.03	84.44	84.85	85.26	85.67	86.08	86.49	86.90	87.31	87.72	88.13	88.54	88.94	89.35	89.76
17.25	83.26	83.67	84.08	84.48	84.89	85.30	85.71	86.12	86.53	86.93	87.34	87.75	88.16	88.57	88.98	89.38
17.50	82.90	83.30	83.71	84.12	84.53	84.93	85.34	85.75	86.16	86.56	86.97	87.38	87.78	88.19	88.60	89.01
17.75	82.54	82.94	83.35	83.76	84.16	84.57	84.98	85.38	85.79	86.19	86.60	87.01	87.41	87.82	88.22	88.63
18.00	82.18	82.59	82.99	83.40	83.80	84.21	84.61	85.02	85.42	85.83	86.23	86.64	87.04	87.45	87.85	88.26
18.25	81.83	82.23	82.63	83.04	83.44	83.85	84.25	84.65	85.06	85.46	85.87	86.27	86.67	87.08	87.48	87.88
18.50	81.47	81.88	82.28	82.68	83.08	83.49	83.89	84.29	84.70	85.10	85.50	85.90	86.31	86.71	87.11	87.51
18.75	81.12	81.52	81.93	82.33	82.73	83.13	83.53	83.93	84.34	84.74	85.14	85.54	85.94	86.34	86.75	87.15
19.00	80.77	81.17	81.57	81.97	82.38	82.78	83.18	83.58	83.98	84.38	84.78	85.18	85.58	85.98	86.38	86.78
20.00	79.40	79.79	80.19	80.58	80.98	81.38	81.77	82.17	82.57	82.96	83.36	83.75	84.15	84.55	84.94	85.34
25.00	72.95	73.32	73.70	74.08	74.45	74.83	75.20	75.58	75.95	76.33	76.71	77.08	77.46	77.83	78.21	78.58
30.00	67.17	67.52	67.88	68.24	68.60	68.95	69.31	69.67	70.02	70.38	70.74	71.09	71.45	71.81	72.16	72.52

Description: This table shows the yield to maturity of a bond purchased at the price shown in the index.

Example: The yield to maturity of a 10.75 %, 2 year bond at a price of 100.00 is 10.75 %.

COUPON RATE, %

PRICE	7.00%	7.25%	7.50%	7.75%	8.00%	8.25%	8.50%	8.75%	9.00%	9.25%	9.50%	9.75%	10.00%	10.25%	10.50%	10.75%
105	4.36	4.60	4.84	5.08	5.33	5.57	5.81	6.05	6.30	6.54	6.78	7.02	7.26	7.51	7.75	7.99
104.75	4.49	4.73	4.97	5.21	5.46	5.70	5.94	6.18	6.43	6.67	6.91	7.15	7.40	7.64	7.88	8.12
104.50	4.61	4.86	5.10	5.34	5.59	5.83	6.07	6.31	6.56	6.80	7.04	7.29	7.53	7.77	8.02	8.26
104.25	4.74	4.99	5.23	5.47	5.72	5.96	6.20	6.45	6.69	6.93	7.18	7.42	7.66	7.91	8.15	8.39
104.00	4.87	5.12	5.36	5.60	5.85	6.09	6.33	6.58	6.82	7.07	7.31	7.55	7.80	8.04	8.28	8.53
103.75	5.00	5.25	5.49	5.73	5.98	6.22	6.47	6.71	6.95	7.20	7.44	7.69	7.93	8.17	8.42	8.66
103.50	5.13	5.38	5.62	5.86	6.11	6.35	6.60	6.84	7.09	7.33	7.58	7.82	8.07	8.31	8.55	8.80
103.25	5.26	5.51	5.75	6.00	6.24	6.49	6.73	6.98	7.22	7.47	7.71	7.96	8.20	8.44	8.69	8.93
103.00	5.39	5.64	5.88	6.13	6.37	6.62	6.86	7.11	7.35	7.60	7.85	8.09	8.34	8.58	8.83	9.07
102.75	5.52	5.77	6.02	6.26	6.51	6.75	7.00	7.24	7.49	7.73	7.98	8.23	8.47	8.72	8.96	9.21
102.50	5.66	5.90	6.15	6.39	6.64	6.89	7.13	7.38	7.62	7.87	8.12	8.36	8.61	8.85	9.10	9.35
102.25	5.79	6.03	6.28	6.53	6.77	7.02	7.27	7.51	7.76	8.01	8.25	8.50	8.74	8.99	9.24	9.48
102.00	5.92	6.17	6.41	6.66	6.91	7.15	7.40	7.65	7.89	8.14	8.39	8.63	8.88	9.13	9.38	9.62
101.75	6.05	6.30	6.55	6.79	7.04	7.29	7.54	7.78	8.03	8.28	8.52	8.77	9.02	9.27	9.51	9.76
101.50	6.19	6.43	6.68	6.93	7.18	7.42	7.67	7.92	8.17	8.41	8.66	8.91	9.16	9.40	9.65	9.90
101.25	6.32	6.57	6.82	7.06	7.31	7.56	7.81	8.06	8.30	8.55	8.80	9.05	9.30	9.54	9.79	10.04
101.00	6.45	6.70	6.95	7.20	7.45	7.70	7.94	8.19	8.44	8.69	8.94	9.19	9.43	9.68	9.93	10.18
100.75	6.59	6.84	7.09	7.34	7.58	7.83	8.08	8.33	8.58	8.83	9.08	9.33	9.57	9.82	10.07	10.32
100.50	6.72	6.97	7.22	7.47	7.72	7.97	8.22	8.47	8.72	8.97	9.22	9.46	9.71	9.96	10.21	10.46
100.25	6.86	7.11	7.36	7.61	7.86	8.11	8.36	8.61	8.86	9.11	9.36	9.60	9.85	10.10	10.35	10.60
100.00	7.00	7.25	7.50	7.75	8.00	8.25	8.50	8.75	9.00	9.25	9.50	9.75	10.00	10.25	10.50	10.75
99.75	7.13	7.38	7.63	7.88	8.13	8.38	8.63	8.88	9.13	9.39	9.64	9.89	10.14	10.39	10.64	10.89
99.50	7.27	7.52	7.77	8.02	8.27	8.52	8.77	9.02	9.27	9.53	9.78	10.03	10.28	10.53	10.78	11.03
99.25	7.41	7.66	7.91	8.16	8.41	8.66	8.91	9.16	9.42	9.67	9.92	10.17	10.42	10.67	10.92	11.17
99.00	7.54	7.79	8.05	8.30	8.55	8.80	9.05	9.30	9.56	9.81	10.06	10.31	10.56	10.81	11.07	11.32
98.75	7.68	7.93	8.19	8.44	8.69	8.94	9.19	9.45	9.70	9.95	10.20	10.45	10.71	10.96	11.21	11.46
98.50	7.82	8.07	8.32	8.58	8.83	9.08	9.33	9.59	9.84	10.09	10.34	10.60	10.85	11.10	11.35	11.61
98.25	7.96	8.21	8.46	8.72	8.97	9.22	9.48	9.73	9.98	10.23	10.49	10.74	10.99	11.25	11.50	11.75
98.00	8.10	8.35	8.60	8.86	9.11	9.36	9.62	9.87	10.12	10.38	10.63	10.88	11.14	11.39	11.64	11.90
97.75	8.24	8.49	8.75	9.00	9.25	9.51	9.76	10.01	10.27	10.52	10.78	11.03	11.28	11.54	11.79	12.04
97.50	8.38	8.63	8.89	9.14	9.40	9.65	9.90	10.16	10.41	10.67	10.92	11.17	11.43	11.68	11.94	12.19
97.25	8.52	8.77	9.03	9.28	9.54	9.79	10.05	10.30	10.56	10.81	11.07	11.32	11.57	11.83	12.08	12.34
97.00	8.66	8.92	9.17	9.43	9.68	9.94	10.19	10.45	10.70	10.96	11.21	11.47	11.72	11.98	12.23	12.49
96.75	8.80	9.06	9.31	9.57	9.82	10.08	10.34	10.59	10.85	11.10	11.36	11.61	11.87	12.12	12.38	12.63
96.50	8.95	9.20	9.46	9.71	9.97	10.22	10.48	10.74	10.99	11.25	11.50	11.76	12.02	12.27	12.53	12.78
96.25	9.09	9.34	9.60	9.86	10.11	10.37	10.63	10.88	11.14	11.39	11.65	11.91	12.16	12.42	12.68	12.93
96.00	9.23	9.49	9.74	10.00	10.26	10.51	10.77	11.03	11.29	11.54	11.80	12.06	12.31	12.57	12.83	13.08
95.75	9.37	9.63	9.89	10.15	10.40	10.66	10.92	11.18	11.43	11.69	11.95	12.20	12.46	12.72	12.98	13.23
95.50	9.52	9.78	10.03	10.29	10.55	10.81	11.06	11.32	11.58	11.84	12.10	12.35	12.61	12.87	13.13	13.38
95.25	9.66	9.92	10.18	10.44	10.70	10.95	11.21	11.47	11.73	11.99	12.24	12.50	12.76	13.02	13.28	13.54
95.00	9.81	10.07	10.33	10.58	10.84	11.10	11.36	11.62	11.88	12.14	12.39	12.65	12.91	13.17	13.43	13.69
94.75	9.95	10.21	10.47	10.73	10.99	11.25	11.51	11.77	12.03	12.29	12.54	12.80	13.06	13.32	13.58	13.84
94	10.39	10.66	10.92	11.18	11.44	11.70	11.96	12.22	12.48	12.74	13.00	13.26	13.52	13.78	14.04	14.30
93	10.99	11.25	11.51	11.78	12.04	12.30	12.56	12.82	13.09	13.35	13.61	13.87	14.13	14.40	14.66	14.92
92	11.59	11.86	12.12	12.38	12.65	12.91	13.18	13.44	13.70	13.97	14.23	14.50	14.76	15.02	15.29	15.55
91	12.20	12.47	12.73	13.00	13.27	13.53	13.80	14.06	14.33	14.60	14.86	15.13	15.39	15.66	15.93	16.19
90	12.82	13.09	13.36	13.62	13.89	14.16	14.43	14.70	14.96	15.23	15.50	15.77	16.04	16.30	16.57	16.84
89	13.45	13.72	13.99	14.26	14.53	14.80	15.07	15.34	15.61	15.88	16.15	16.42	16.69	16.96	17.23	17.50
88	14.09	14.36	14.63	14.90	15.18	15.45	15.72	15.99	16.26	16.53	16.81	17.08	17.35	17.62	17.89	18.17
87	14.74	15.01	15.28	15.56	15.83	16.10	16.38	16.65	16.93	17.20	17.47	17.75	18.02	18.30	18.57	18.85
86	15.39	15.67	15.94	16.22	16.50	16.77	17.05	17.32	17.60	17.88	18.15	18.43	18.71	18.98	19.26	19.53
85	16.06	16.34	16.62	16.89	17.17	17.45	17.73	18.01	18.28	18.56	18.84	19.12	19.40	19.68	19.96	20.23
84	16.74	17.02	17.30	17.58	17.86	18.14	18.42	18.70	18.98	19.26	19.54	19.82	20.10	20.38	20.66	20.94
83	17.42	17.71	17.99	18.27	18.55	18.84	19.12	19.40	19.69	19.97	20.25	20.53	20.82	21.10	21.38	21.67
82	18.12	18.41	18.69	18.98	19.26	19.55	19.83	20.12	20.40	20.69	20.97	21.26	21.54	21.83	22.11	22.40
81	18.83	19.12	19.41	19.69	19.98	20.27	20.56	20.84	21.13	21.42	21.71	21.99	22.28	22.57	22.86	23.14
80	19.55	19.84	20.13	20.42	20.71	21.00	21.29	21.58	21.87	22.16	22.45	22.74	23.03	23.32	23.61	23.90
79	20.29	20.58	20.87	21.16	21.45	21.75	22.04	22.33	22.62	22.92	23.21	23.50	23.79	24.09	24.38	24.67
78	21.03	21.33	21.62	21.92	22.21	22.50	22.80	23.09	23.39	23.68	23.98	24.27	24.57	24.86	25.16	25.45
77	21.79	22.09	22.38	22.68	22.98	23.28	23.57	23.87	24.17	24.46	24.76	25.06	25.36	25.66	25.95	26.25
76	22.56	22.86	23.16	23.46	23.76	24.06	24.36	24.66	24.96	25.26	25.56	25.86	26.16	26.46	26.76	27.06
75	23.34	23.65	23.95	24.25	24.55	24.86	25.16	25.46	25.76	26.07	26.37	26.67	26.98	27.28	27.58	27.89
74	24.14	24.45	24.75	25.06	25.36	25.67	25.97	26.28	26.58	26.89	27.20	27.50	27.81	28.11	28.42	28.73
73	24.95	25.26	25.57	25.88	26.19	26.49	26.80	27.11	27.42	27.73	28.04	28.34	28.65	28.96	29.27	29.58
72	25.78	26.09	26.40	26.71	27.02	27.33	27.65	27.96	28.27	28.58	28.89	29.20	29.51	29.83	30.14	30.45
71	26.62	26.94	27.25	27.56	27.88	28.19	28.51	28.82	29.13	29.45	29.76	30.08	30.39	30.71	31.02	31.34
70	27.48	27.80	28.11	28.43	28.75	29.06	29.38	29.70	30.02	30.33	30.65	30.97	31.29	31.60	31.92	32.24
69	28.35	28.67	28.99	29.31	29.63	29.95	30.27	30.59	30.91	31.23	31.56	31.88	32.20	32.52	32.84	33.16

Description: This table shows the price to pay for a bond at the yield rate. The yield is to maturity.

Example: The price of a 15.00 %, 2 year bond to yield 8 % to maturity is $ 112.70.

COUPON RATE, %

YIELD	11.00%	11.25%	11.50%	11.75%	12.00%	12.25%	12.50%	12.75%	13.00%	13.25%	13.50%	13.75%	14.00%	14.25%	14.50%	15.00%
0.00	122.00	122.50	123.00	123.50	124.00	124.50	125.00	125.50	126.00	126.50	127.00	127.50	128.00	128.50	129.00	130.00
1.00	119.75	120.25	120.74	121.23	121.73	122.22	122.72	123.21	123.70	124.20	124.69	125.18	125.68	126.17	126.67	127.65
2.00	117.56	118.05	118.53	119.02	119.51	120.00	120.49	120.97	121.46	121.95	122.44	122.92	123.41	123.90	124.39	125.36
3.00	115.42	115.90	116.38	116.86	117.34	117.83	118.31	118.79	119.27	119.75	120.24	120.72	121.20	121.68	122.16	123.13
4.00	113.33	113.80	114.28	114.75	115.23	115.71	116.18	116.66	117.13	117.61	118.09	118.56	119.04	119.51	119.99	120.94
4.25	112.81	113.29	113.76	114.24	114.71	115.18	115.66	116.13	116.61	117.08	117.56	118.03	118.51	118.98	119.46	120.40
4.50	112.30	112.77	113.25	113.72	114.19	114.67	115.14	115.61	116.09	116.56	117.03	117.50	117.98	118.45	118.92	119.87
4.75	111.79	112.26	112.73	113.21	113.68	114.15	114.62	115.09	115.56	116.04	116.51	116.98	117.45	117.92	118.39	119.34
5.00	111.29	111.76	112.23	112.70	113.17	113.64	114.11	114.58	115.05	115.52	115.99	116.46	116.93	117.40	117.87	118.81
5.25	110.78	111.25	111.72	112.19	112.66	113.13	113.60	114.07	114.53	115.00	115.47	115.94	116.41	116.88	117.35	118.28
5.50	110.28	110.75	111.22	111.69	112.15	112.62	113.09	113.56	114.02	114.49	114.96	115.43	115.89	116.36	116.83	117.76
5.75	109.79	110.25	110.72	111.18	111.65	112.12	112.58	113.05	113.51	113.98	114.45	114.91	115.38	115.85	116.31	117.24
6.00	109.29	109.76	110.22	110.69	111.15	111.62	112.08	112.55	113.01	113.47	113.94	114.40	114.87	115.33	115.80	116.73
6.25	108.80	109.27	109.73	110.19	110.65	111.12	111.58	112.04	112.51	112.97	113.43	113.90	114.36	114.82	115.29	116.21
6.50	108.31	108.78	109.24	109.70	110.16	110.62	111.08	111.55	112.01	112.47	112.93	113.39	113.86	114.32	114.78	115.70
6.75	107.83	108.29	108.75	109.21	109.67	110.13	110.59	111.05	111.51	111.97	112.43	112.89	113.35	113.82	114.28	115.20
7.00	107.35	107.81	108.26	108.72	109.18	109.64	110.10	110.56	111.02	111.48	111.94	112.40	112.86	113.31	113.77	114.69
7.25	106.87	107.32	107.78	108.24	108.70	109.16	109.61	110.07	110.53	110.99	111.44	111.90	112.36	112.82	113.28	114.19
7.50	106.39	106.85	107.30	107.76	108.22	108.67	109.13	109.58	110.04	110.50	110.95	111.41	111.87	112.32	112.78	113.69
7.75	105.92	106.37	106.83	107.28	107.74	108.19	108.65	109.10	109.56	110.01	110.47	110.92	111.38	111.83	112.29	113.20
8.00	105.44	105.90	106.35	106.81	107.26	107.71	108.17	108.62	109.07	109.53	109.98	110.44	110.89	111.34	111.80	112.70
8.25	104.98	105.43	105.88	106.33	106.79	107.24	107.69	108.14	108.60	109.05	109.50	109.95	110.41	110.86	111.31	112.21
8.50	104.51	104.96	105.41	105.86	106.32	106.77	107.22	107.67	108.12	108.57	109.02	109.47	109.92	110.37	110.83	111.73
8.75	104.05	104.50	104.95	105.40	105.85	106.30	106.75	107.20	107.65	108.10	108.55	109.00	109.44	109.89	110.34	111.24
9.00	103.59	104.04	104.48	104.93	105.38	105.83	106.28	106.73	107.18	107.62	108.07	108.52	108.97	109.42	109.87	110.76
9.25	103.13	103.58	104.02	104.47	104.92	105.37	105.81	106.26	106.71	107.15	107.60	108.05	108.50	108.94	109.39	110.28
9.50	102.67	103.12	103.57	104.01	104.46	104.90	105.35	105.80	106.24	106.69	107.13	107.58	108.02	108.47	108.92	109.81
9.75	102.22	102.67	103.11	103.56	104.00	104.45	104.89	105.33	105.78	106.22	106.67	107.11	107.56	108.00	108.45	109.34
10.00	101.77	102.22	102.66	103.10	103.55	103.99	104.43	104.88	105.32	105.76	106.21	106.65	107.09	107.54	107.98	108.86
10.25	101.33	101.77	102.21	102.65	103.09	103.54	103.98	104.42	104.86	105.30	105.75	106.19	106.63	107.07	107.51	108.40
10.50	100.88	101.32	101.76	102.20	102.64	103.08	103.53	103.97	104.41	104.85	105.29	105.73	106.17	106.61	107.05	107.93
10.75	100.44	100.88	101.32	101.76	102.20	102.64	103.08	103.52	103.95	104.39	104.83	105.27	105.71	106.15	106.59	107.47
11.00	100.00	100.44	100.88	101.31	101.75	102.19	102.63	103.07	103.51	103.94	104.38	104.82	105.26	105.70	106.13	107.01
11.25	99.56	100.00	100.44	100.87	101.31	101.75	102.18	102.62	103.06	103.50	103.93	104.37	104.81	105.24	105.68	106.55
11.50	99.13	99.56	100.00	100.44	100.87	101.31	101.74	102.18	102.61	103.05	103.49	103.92	104.36	104.79	105.23	106.10
11.75	98.70	99.13	99.57	100.00	100.43	100.87	101.30	101.74	102.17	102.61	103.04	103.48	103.91	104.34	104.78	105.65
12.00	98.27	98.70	99.13	99.57	100.00	100.43	100.87	101.30	101.73	102.17	102.60	103.03	103.47	103.90	104.33	105.20
12.25	97.84	98.27	98.70	99.14	99.57	100.00	100.43	100.86	101.30	101.73	102.16	102.59	103.02	103.46	103.89	104.75
12.50	97.42	97.85	98.28	98.71	99.14	99.57	100.00	100.43	100.86	101.29	101.72	102.15	102.58	103.01	103.45	104.31
12.75	96.99	97.42	97.85	98.28	98.71	99.14	99.57	100.00	100.43	100.86	101.29	101.72	102.15	102.58	103.01	103.87
13.00	96.57	97.00	97.43	97.86	98.29	98.72	99.14	99.57	100.00	100.43	100.86	101.28	101.71	102.14	102.57	103.43
13.25	96.16	96.58	97.01	97.44	97.86	98.29	98.72	99.15	99.57	100.00	100.43	100.85	101.28	101.71	102.14	102.99
13.50	95.74	96.17	96.59	97.02	97.45	97.87	98.30	98.72	99.15	99.57	100.00	100.43	100.85	101.28	101.70	102.55
13.75	95.33	95.75	96.18	96.60	97.03	97.45	97.88	98.30	98.73	99.15	99.58	100.00	100.42	100.85	101.27	102.12
14.00	94.92	95.34	95.77	96.19	96.61	97.04	97.46	97.88	98.31	98.73	99.15	99.58	100.00	100.42	100.85	101.69
14.25	94.51	94.93	95.36	95.78	96.20	96.62	97.04	97.47	97.89	98.31	98.73	99.16	99.58	100.00	100.42	101.27
14.50	94.11	94.53	94.95	95.37	95.79	96.21	96.63	97.05	97.47	97.89	98.32	98.74	99.16	99.58	100.00	100.84
14.75	93.70	94.12	94.54	94.96	95.38	95.80	96.22	96.64	97.06	97.48	97.90	98.32	98.74	99.16	99.58	100.42
15.00	93.30	93.72	94.14	94.56	94.98	95.39	95.81	96.23	96.65	97.07	97.49	97.91	98.33	98.74	99.16	100.00
15.25	92.90	93.32	93.74	94.16	94.57	94.99	95.41	95.83	96.24	96.66	97.08	97.50	97.91	98.33	98.75	99.58
15.50	92.51	92.92	93.34	93.76	94.17	94.59	95.00	95.42	95.84	96.25	96.67	97.09	97.50	97.92	98.33	99.17
15.75	92.11	92.53	92.94	93.36	93.77	94.19	94.60	95.02	95.43	95.85	96.26	96.68	97.09	97.51	97.92	98.75
16.00	91.72	92.13	92.55	92.96	93.38	93.79	94.20	94.62	95.03	95.45	95.86	96.27	96.69	97.10	97.52	98.34
16.25	91.33	91.74	92.16	92.57	92.98	93.39	93.81	94.22	94.63	95.05	95.46	95.87	96.28	96.70	97.11	97.94
16.50	90.94	91.35	91.77	92.18	92.59	93.00	93.41	93.82	94.24	94.65	95.06	95.47	95.88	96.29	96.71	97.53
16.75	90.56	90.97	91.38	91.79	92.20	92.61	93.02	93.43	93.84	94.25	94.66	95.07	95.48	95.89	96.30	97.13
17.00	90.17	90.58	90.99	91.40	91.81	92.22	92.63	93.04	93.45	93.86	94.27	94.68	95.09	95.50	95.91	96.72
17.25	89.79	90.20	90.61	91.02	91.43	91.83	92.24	92.65	93.06	93.47	93.88	94.28	94.69	95.10	95.51	96.33
17.50	89.41	89.82	90.23	90.63	91.04	91.45	91.86	92.26	92.67	93.08	93.48	93.89	94.30	94.71	95.11	95.93
17.75	89.04	89.44	89.85	90.25	90.66	91.07	91.47	91.88	92.28	92.69	93.10	93.50	93.91	94.31	94.72	95.53
18.00	88.66	89.07	89.47	89.88	90.28	90.69	91.09	91.50	91.90	92.31	92.71	93.12	93.52	93.93	94.33	95.14
18.25	88.29	88.69	89.10	89.50	89.90	90.31	90.71	91.12	91.52	91.92	92.33	92.73	93.13	93.54	93.94	94.75
18.50	87.92	88.32	88.72	89.13	89.53	89.93	90.33	90.74	91.14	91.54	91.94	92.35	92.75	93.15	93.56	94.36
18.75	87.55	87.95	88.35	88.75	89.16	89.56	89.96	90.36	90.76	91.16	91.57	91.97	92.37	92.77	93.17	93.98
19.00	87.18	87.58	87.98	88.38	88.78	89.18	89.59	89.99	90.39	90.79	91.19	91.59	91.99	92.39	92.79	93.59
20.00	85.74	86.13	86.53	86.92	87.32	87.72	88.11	88.51	88.91	89.30	89.70	90.09	90.49	90.89	91.28	92.08
25.00	78.96	79.34	79.71	80.09	80.46	80.84	81.21	81.59	81.97	82.34	82.72	83.09	83.47	83.84	84.22	84.97
30.00	72.88	73.23	73.59	73.95	74.31	74.66	75.02	75.38	75.73	76.09	76.45	76.80	77.16	77.52	77.87	78.59

Description: This table shows the yield to maturity of a bond purchased at the price shown in the index.

Example: The yield to maturity of a 15.00 %, 2 year bond at a price of 102.00 is 13.82 %.

COUPON RATE, %

PRICE	11.00%	11.25%	11.50%	11.75%	12.00%	12.25%	12.50%	12.75%	13.00%	13.25%	13.50%	13.75%	14.00%	14.25%	14.50%	15.00%
110	5.64	5.87	6.11	6.34	6.58	6.81	7.05	7.28	7.52	7.75	7.99	8.22	8.46	8.69	8.92	9.39
109	6.14	6.38	6.62	6.85	7.09	7.33	7.56	7.80	8.03	8.27	8.51	8.74	8.98	9.21	9.45	9.92
108	6.66	6.89	7.13	7.37	7.61	7.85	8.08	8.32	8.56	8.80	9.03	9.27	9.51	9.75	9.98	10.46
107	7.18	7.41	7.65	7.89	8.13	8.37	8.61	8.85	9.09	9.33	9.57	9.81	10.04	10.28	10.52	11.00
106	7.70	7.94	8.18	8.42	8.66	8.90	9.14	9.38	9.63	9.87	10.11	10.35	10.59	10.83	11.07	11.55
105.75	7.83	8.07	8.31	8.56	8.80	9.04	9.28	9.52	9.76	10.00	10.24	10.48	10.72	10.97	11.21	11.69
105.50	7.97	8.21	8.45	8.69	8.93	9.17	9.41	9.66	9.90	10.14	10.38	10.62	10.86	11.10	11.34	11.83
105.25	8.10	8.34	8.58	8.82	9.07	9.31	9.55	9.79	10.03	10.27	10.52	10.76	11.00	11.24	11.48	11.97
105.00	8.23	8.47	8.72	8.96	9.20	9.44	9.69	9.93	10.17	10.41	10.65	10.90	11.14	11.38	11.62	12.11
104.75	8.37	8.61	8.85	9.09	9.34	9.58	9.82	10.06	10.31	10.55	10.79	11.03	11.28	11.52	11.76	12.25
104.50	8.50	8.74	8.99	9.23	9.47	9.72	9.96	10.20	10.44	10.69	10.93	11.17	11.41	11.66	11.90	12.39
104.25	8.64	8.88	9.12	9.37	9.61	9.85	10.10	10.34	10.58	10.82	11.07	11.31	11.55	11.80	12.04	12.53
104.00	8.77	9.01	9.26	9.50	9.75	9.99	10.23	10.48	10.72	10.96	11.21	11.45	11.69	11.94	12.18	12.67
103.75	8.91	9.15	9.39	9.64	9.88	10.13	10.37	10.61	10.86	11.10	11.35	11.59	11.83	12.08	12.32	12.81
103.50	9.04	9.29	9.53	9.78	10.02	10.26	10.51	10.75	11.00	11.24	11.49	11.73	11.98	12.22	12.46	12.95
103.25	9.18	9.42	9.67	9.91	10.16	10.40	10.65	10.89	11.14	11.38	11.63	11.87	12.12	12.36	12.61	13.10
103.00	9.32	9.56	9.81	10.05	10.30	10.54	10.79	11.03	11.28	11.52	11.77	12.01	12.26	12.50	12.75	13.24
102.75	9.45	9.70	9.94	10.19	10.44	10.68	10.93	11.17	11.42	11.66	11.91	12.15	12.40	12.65	12.89	13.38
102.50	9.59	9.84	10.08	10.33	10.58	10.82	11.07	11.31	11.56	11.81	12.05	12.30	12.54	12.79	13.03	13.53
102.25	9.73	9.98	10.22	10.47	10.72	10.96	11.21	11.45	11.70	11.95	12.19	12.44	12.69	12.93	13.18	13.67
102.00	9.87	10.12	10.36	10.61	10.86	11.10	11.35	11.60	11.84	12.09	12.34	12.58	12.83	13.08	13.32	13.82
101.75	10.01	10.26	10.50	10.75	11.00	11.24	11.49	11.74	11.99	12.23	12.48	12.73	12.97	13.22	13.47	13.96
101.50	10.15	10.40	10.64	10.89	11.14	11.39	11.63	11.88	12.13	12.38	12.62	12.87	13.12	13.37	13.61	14.11
101.25	10.29	10.54	10.78	11.03	11.28	11.53	11.78	12.02	12.27	12.52	12.77	13.02	13.26	13.51	13.76	14.25
101.00	10.43	10.68	10.92	11.17	11.42	11.67	11.92	12.17	12.42	12.66	12.91	13.16	13.41	13.66	13.91	14.40
100.75	10.57	10.82	11.07	11.32	11.56	11.81	12.06	12.31	12.56	12.81	13.06	13.31	13.55	13.80	14.05	14.55
100.50	10.71	10.96	11.21	11.46	11.71	11.96	12.21	12.45	12.70	12.95	13.20	13.45	13.70	13.95	14.20	14.70
100.25	10.85	11.10	11.35	11.60	11.85	12.10	12.35	12.60	12.85	13.10	13.35	13.60	13.85	14.10	14.35	14.85
100.00	11.00	11.25	11.50	11.75	12.00	12.25	12.50	12.75	13.00	13.25	13.50	13.75	14.00	14.25	14.50	15.00
99.75	11.14	11.39	11.64	11.89	12.14	12.39	12.64	12.89	13.14	13.39	13.64	13.89	14.14	14.39	14.64	15.14
99.50	11.28	11.53	11.78	12.03	12.28	12.54	12.79	13.04	13.29	13.54	13.79	14.04	14.29	14.54	14.79	15.29
99.25	11.43	11.68	11.93	12.18	12.43	12.68	12.93	13.18	13.44	13.69	13.94	14.19	14.44	14.69	14.94	15.45
99.00	11.57	11.82	12.07	12.32	12.58	12.83	13.08	13.33	13.58	13.83	14.09	14.34	14.59	14.84	15.09	15.60
98.75	11.71	11.97	12.22	12.47	12.72	12.97	13.23	13.48	13.73	13.98	14.24	14.49	14.74	14.99	15.24	15.75
98.50	11.86	12.11	12.36	12.62	12.87	13.12	13.37	13.63	13.88	14.13	14.38	14.53	14.79	15.04	15.29	15.55
98.25	12.01	12.26	12.51	12.76	13.02	13.27	13.52	13.78	14.03	14.28	14.53	14.79	15.04	15.29	15.55	16.05
98.00	12.15	12.40	12.66	12.91	13.16	13.42	13.67	13.93	14.18	14.43	14.69	14.94	15.19	15.45	15.70	16.21
97.75	12.30	12.55	12.81	13.06	13.31	13.57	13.82	14.07	14.33	14.58	14.84	15.09	15.34	15.60	15.85	16.36
97.50	12.45	12.70	12.95	13.21	13.46	13.72	13.97	14.23	14.48	14.73	14.99	15.24	15.50	15.75	16.00	16.51
97.25	12.59	12.85	13.10	13.36	13.61	13.87	14.12	14.38	14.63	14.89	15.14	15.39	15.65	15.90	16.16	16.67
97.00	12.74	13.00	13.25	13.51	13.76	14.02	14.27	14.53	14.78	15.04	15.29	15.55	15.80	16.06	16.31	16.82
96.75	12.89	13.15	13.40	13.66	13.91	14.17	14.42	14.68	14.93	15.19	15.45	15.70	15.96	16.21	16.47	16.98
96.50	13.04	13.30	13.55	13.81	14.06	14.32	14.58	14.83	15.09	15.34	15.60	15.86	16.11	16.37	16.62	17.14
96.25	13.19	13.45	13.70	13.96	14.21	14.47	14.73	14.98	15.24	15.50	15.75	16.01	16.27	16.52	16.78	17.29
96.00	13.34	13.60	13.85	14.11	14.37	14.62	14.88	15.14	15.39	15.65	15.91	16.16	16.42	16.68	16.94	17.45
95.75	13.49	13.75	14.00	14.26	14.52	14.78	15.03	15.29	15.55	15.81	16.06	16.32	16.58	16.84	17.09	17.61
95.50	13.64	13.90	14.16	14.41	14.67	14.93	15.19	15.45	15.70	15.96	16.22	16.48	16.73	16.99	17.25	17.77
95.25	13.79	14.05	14.31	14.57	14.83	15.08	15.34	15.60	15.86	16.12	16.38	16.63	16.89	17.15	17.41	17.93
95.00	13.95	14.20	14.46	14.72	14.98	15.24	15.50	15.76	16.01	16.27	16.53	16.79	17.05	17.31	17.57	18.08
94.75	14.10	14.36	14.62	14.88	15.13	15.39	15.65	15.91	16.17	16.43	16.69	16.95	17.21	17.47	17.73	18.24
94.50	14.25	14.51	14.77	15.03	15.29	15.55	15.81	16.07	16.33	16.59	16.85	17.11	17.37	17.63	17.89	18.41
94.25	14.41	14.67	14.93	15.19	15.45	15.71	15.97	16.23	16.49	16.75	17.01	17.27	17.53	17.79	18.05	18.57
94.00	14.56	14.82	15.08	15.34	15.60	15.86	16.12	16.38	16.64	16.90	17.17	17.43	17.69	17.95	18.21	18.73
93.75	14.72	14.98	15.24	15.50	15.76	16.02	16.28	16.54	16.80	17.06	17.33	17.59	17.85	18.11	18.37	18.89
93	15.18	15.45	15.71	15.97	16.23	16.50	16.76	17.02	17.28	17.55	17.81	18.07	18.33	18.59	18.86	19.38
92	15.82	16.08	16.34	16.61	16.87	17.14	17.40	17.67	17.93	18.19	18.46	18.72	18.99	19.25	19.52	20.05
91	16.46	16.72	16.99	17.26	17.52	17.79	18.05	18.32	18.59	18.85	19.12	19.39	19.65	19.92	20.19	20.72
90	17.11	17.38	17.64	17.91	18.18	18.45	18.72	18.99	19.25	19.52	19.79	20.06	20.33	20.60	20.86	21.40
89	17.77	18.04	18.31	18.58	18.85	19.12	19.39	19.66	19.93	20.20	20.47	20.74	21.01	21.28	21.55	22.09
88	18.44	18.71	18.98	19.26	19.53	19.80	20.07	20.35	20.62	20.89	21.16	21.43	21.71	21.98	22.25	22.80
87	19.12	19.39	19.67	19.94	20.22	20.49	20.77	21.04	21.31	21.59	21.86	22.14	22.41	22.69	22.96	23.51
86	19.81	20.09	20.36	20.64	20.92	21.19	21.47	21.75	22.02	22.30	22.58	22.85	23.13	23.41	23.68	24.24
85	20.51	20.79	21.07	21.35	21.63	21.91	22.18	22.46	22.74	23.02	23.30	23.58	23.86	24.14	24.42	24.97
84	21.22	21.51	21.79	22.07	22.35	22.63	22.91	23.19	23.47	23.75	24.04	24.32	24.60	24.88	25.16	25.72
83	21.95	22.23	22.52	22.80	23.08	23.36	23.65	23.93	24.21	24.50	24.78	25.07	25.35	25.63	25.92	26.48
82	22.68	22.97	23.26	23.54	23.83	24.11	24.40	24.68	24.97	25.26	25.54	25.83	26.11	26.40	26.68	27.26
81	23.43	23.72	24.01	24.30	24.58	24.87	25.16	25.45	25.74	26.02	26.31	26.60	26.89	27.18	27.47	28.04
80	24.19	24.48	24.77	25.06	25.35	25.64	25.93	26.22	26.52	26.81	27.10	27.39	27.68	27.97	28.26	28.84

Description: This table shows the price to pay for a bond at the yield rate. The yield is to maturity.

Example: The price of a 6.75 %, 3 year bond to yield 8 % to maturity is $ 96.72.

							COUPON RATE, %									
YIELD	0.00%	1.00%	2.00%	3.00%	4.00%	4.25%	4.50%	4.75%	5.00%	5.25%	5.50%	5.75%	6.00%	6.25%	6.50%	6.75%
0.00	100.00	103.00	106.00	109.00	112.00	112.75	113.50	114.25	115.00	115.75	116.50	117.25	118.00	118.75	119.50	120.25
1.00	97.05	100.00	102.95	105.90	108.84	109.58	110.32	111.06	111.79	112.53	113.27	114.00	114.74	115.48	116.22	116.95
2.00	94.20	97.10	100.00	102.90	105.80	106.52	107.24	107.97	108.69	109.42	110.14	110.87	111.59	112.32	113.04	113.76
3.00	91.45	94.30	97.15	100.00	102.85	103.56	104.27	104.99	105.70	106.41	107.12	107.83	108.55	109.26	109.97	110.68
4.00	88.80	91.60	94.40	97.20	100.00	100.70	101.40	102.10	102.80	103.50	104.20	104.90	105.60	106.30	107.00	107.70
4.25	88.15	90.94	93.72	96.51	99.30	100.00	100.70	101.39	102.09	102.79	103.49	104.18	104.88	105.58	106.28	106.97
4.50	87.50	90.28	93.06	95.83	98.61	99.31	100.00	100.69	101.39	102.08	102.78	103.47	104.17	104.86	105.55	106.25
4.75	86.86	89.63	92.39	95.16	97.93	98.62	99.31	100.00	100.69	101.38	102.07	102.77	103.46	104.15	104.84	105.53
5.00	86.23	88.98	91.74	94.49	97.25	97.93	98.62	99.31	100.00	100.69	101.38	102.07	102.75	103.44	104.13	104.82
5.25	85.60	88.34	91.09	93.83	96.57	97.26	97.94	98.63	99.31	100.00	100.69	101.37	102.06	102.74	103.43	104.11
5.50	84.98	87.71	90.44	93.17	95.90	96.59	97.27	97.95	98.63	99.32	100.00	100.68	101.37	102.05	102.73	103.41
5.75	84.36	87.08	89.80	92.52	95.24	95.92	96.60	97.28	97.96	98.64	99.32	100.00	100.68	101.36	102.04	102.72
6.00	83.75	86.46	89.17	91.87	94.58	95.26	95.94	96.61	97.29	97.97	98.65	99.32	100.00	100.68	101.36	102.03
6.25	83.14	85.84	88.54	91.23	93.93	94.61	95.28	95.95	96.63	97.30	97.98	98.65	99.33	100.00	100.67	101.35
6.50	82.54	85.23	87.91	90.60	93.28	93.96	94.63	95.30	95.97	96.64	97.31	97.99	98.66	99.33	100.00	100.67
6.75	81.94	84.62	87.29	89.97	92.64	93.31	93.98	94.65	95.32	95.99	96.66	97.32	97.99	98.66	99.33	100.00
7.00	81.35	84.01	86.68	89.34	92.01	92.67	93.34	94.01	94.67	95.34	96.00	96.67	97.34	98.00	98.67	99.33
7.25	80.76	83.42	86.07	88.72	91.38	92.04	92.70	93.37	94.03	94.69	95.36	96.02	96.68	97.35	98.01	98.67
7.50	80.18	82.82	85.47	88.11	90.75	91.41	92.07	92.73	93.39	94.05	94.71	95.38	96.04	96.70	97.36	98.02
7.75	79.60	82.24	84.87	87.50	90.13	90.79	91.45	92.10	92.76	93.42	94.08	94.74	95.39	96.05	96.71	97.37
8.00	79.03	81.65	84.27	86.89	89.52	90.17	90.83	91.48	92.14	92.79	93.45	94.10	94.76	95.41	96.07	96.72
8.25	78.46	81.07	83.68	86.30	88.91	89.56	90.21	90.86	91.52	92.17	92.82	93.47	94.13	94.78	95.43	96.08
8.50	77.90	80.50	83.10	85.70	88.30	88.95	89.60	90.25	90.90	91.55	92.20	92.85	93.50	94.15	94.80	95.45
8.75	77.34	79.93	82.52	85.11	87.70	88.35	89.00	89.64	90.29	90.94	91.58	92.23	92.88	93.53	94.17	94.82
9.00	76.79	79.37	81.95	84.53	87.11	87.75	88.39	89.04	89.68	90.33	90.97	91.62	92.26	92.91	93.55	94.20
9.25	76.24	78.81	81.38	83.95	86.52	87.16	87.80	88.44	89.08	89.73	90.37	91.01	91.65	92.29	92.94	93.58
9.50	75.70	78.25	80.81	83.37	85.93	86.57	87.21	87.85	88.49	89.13	89.77	90.41	91.05	91.69	92.33	92.96
9.75	75.16	77.70	80.25	82.80	85.35	85.99	86.62	87.26	87.90	88.53	89.17	89.81	90.44	91.08	91.72	92.36
10.00	74.62	77.16	79.70	82.24	84.77	85.41	86.04	86.68	87.31	87.95	88.58	89.21	89.85	90.48	91.12	91.75
10.25	74.09	76.62	79.15	81.67	84.20	84.83	85.47	86.10	86.73	87.36	87.99	88.63	89.26	89.89	90.52	91.15
10.50	73.56	76.08	78.60	81.12	83.64	84.26	84.89	85.52	86.15	86.78	87.41	88.04	88.67	89.30	89.93	90.56
10.75	73.04	75.55	78.06	80.57	83.07	83.70	84.33	84.95	85.58	86.21	86.83	87.46	88.09	88.72	89.34	89.97
11.00	72.52	75.02	77.52	80.02	82.52	83.14	83.76	84.39	85.01	85.64	86.26	86.89	87.51	88.14	88.76	89.38
11.25	72.01	74.50	76.99	79.47	81.96	82.58	83.21	83.83	84.45	85.07	85.69	86.32	86.94	87.56	88.18	88.80
11.50	71.50	73.98	76.46	78.94	81.41	82.03	82.65	83.27	83.89	84.51	85.13	85.75	86.37	86.99	87.61	88.23
11.75	71.00	73.47	75.93	78.40	80.87	81.49	82.10	82.72	83.34	83.96	84.57	85.19	85.81	86.42	87.04	87.66
12.00	70.50	72.95	75.41	77.87	80.33	80.95	81.56	82.17	82.79	83.40	84.02	84.63	85.25	85.86	86.48	87.09
12.25	70.00	72.45	74.90	77.35	79.80	80.41	81.02	81.63	82.24	82.86	83.47	84.08	84.69	85.31	85.92	86.53
12.50	69.51	71.95	74.39	76.83	79.26	79.87	80.48	81.09	81.70	82.31	82.92	83.53	84.14	84.75	85.36	85.97
12.75	69.02	71.45	73.88	76.31	78.74	79.35	79.95	80.56	81.17	81.78	82.38	82.99	83.60	84.21	84.81	85.42
13.00	68.53	70.95	73.37	75.79	78.22	78.82	79.43	80.03	80.64	81.24	81.85	82.45	83.06	83.66	84.27	84.87
13.25	68.05	70.46	72.87	75.29	77.70	78.30	78.90	79.51	80.11	80.71	81.31	81.92	82.52	83.12	83.72	84.33
13.50	67.58	69.98	72.38	74.78	77.18	77.78	78.38	78.98	79.58	80.19	80.79	81.39	81.99	82.59	83.19	83.79
13.75	67.10	69.50	71.89	74.28	76.67	77.27	77.87	78.47	79.07	79.66	80.26	80.86	81.46	82.06	82.65	83.25
14.00	66.63	69.02	71.40	73.78	76.17	76.76	77.36	77.95	78.55	79.15	79.74	80.34	80.93	81.53	82.13	82.72
14.25	66.17	68.54	70.92	73.29	75.67	76.26	76.85	77.45	78.04	78.63	79.23	79.82	80.41	81.01	81.60	82.19
14.50	65.71	68.07	70.44	72.80	75.17	75.76	76.35	76.94	77.53	78.12	78.72	79.31	79.90	80.49	81.08	81.67
14.75	65.25	67.61	69.96	72.32	74.67	75.26	75.85	76.44	77.03	77.62	78.21	78.80	79.39	79.97	80.56	81.15
15.00	64.80	67.14	69.49	71.84	74.18	74.77	75.36	75.94	76.53	77.12	77.70	78.29	78.88	79.46	80.05	80.64
15.25	64.35	66.68	69.02	71.36	73.70	74.28	74.87	75.45	76.04	76.62	77.20	77.79	78.37	78.96	79.54	80.13
15.50	63.90	66.23	68.56	70.89	73.22	73.80	74.38	74.96	75.54	76.13	76.71	77.29	77.87	78.46	79.04	79.62
15.75	63.46	65.78	68.10	70.42	72.74	73.32	73.90	74.48	75.06	75.64	76.22	76.80	77.38	77.96	78.54	79.12
16.00	63.02	65.33	67.64	69.95	72.26	72.84	73.42	74.00	74.57	75.15	75.73	76.31	76.89	77.46	78.04	78.62
16.25	62.58	64.88	67.19	69.49	71.79	72.37	72.94	73.52	74.09	74.67	75.25	75.82	76.40	76.97	77.55	78.12
16.50	62.15	64.44	66.74	69.03	71.32	71.90	72.47	73.05	73.62	74.19	74.77	75.34	75.91	76.49	77.06	77.63
16.75	61.72	64.01	66.29	68.58	70.86	71.43	72.00	72.58	73.15	73.72	74.29	74.86	75.43	76.00	76.57	77.15
17.00	61.29	63.57	65.85	68.12	70.40	70.97	71.54	72.11	72.68	73.25	73.82	74.39	74.96	75.52	76.09	76.66
17.25	60.87	63.14	65.41	67.68	69.95	70.51	71.08	71.65	72.21	72.78	73.35	73.92	74.48	75.05	75.62	76.18
17.50	60.45	62.71	64.97	67.23	69.49	70.06	70.62	71.19	71.75	72.32	72.88	73.45	74.01	74.58	75.14	75.71
17.75	60.04	62.29	64.54	66.79	69.04	69.61	70.17	70.73	71.30	71.86	72.42	72.98	73.55	74.11	74.67	75.24
18.00	59.63	61.87	64.11	66.36	68.60	69.16	69.72	70.28	70.84	71.40	71.96	72.52	73.08	73.65	74.21	74.77
18.25	59.22	61.45	63.69	65.92	68.16	68.72	69.27	69.83	70.39	70.95	71.51	72.07	72.63	73.18	73.74	74.30
18.50	58.81	61.04	63.27	65.49	67.72	68.27	68.83	69.39	69.94	70.50	71.06	71.61	72.17	72.73	73.28	73.84
18.75	58.41	60.63	62.85	65.06	67.28	67.84	68.39	68.95	69.50	70.06	70.61	71.16	71.72	72.27	72.83	73.38
19.00	58.01	60.22	62.43	64.64	66.85	67.40	67.96	68.51	69.06	69.61	70.17	70.72	71.27	71.82	72.38	72.93
20.00	56.45	58.63	60.80	62.98	65.16	65.70	66.25	66.79	67.34	67.88	68.42	68.97	69.51	70.06	70.60	71.15
25.00	49.33	51.35	53.38	55.41	57.43	57.94	58.45	58.95	59.46	59.97	60.48	60.98	61.49	62.00	62.50	63.01
30.00	43.23	45.13	47.02	48.91	50.80	51.27	51.75	52.22	52.69	53.17	53.64	54.11	54.59	55.06	55.53	56.01

Description: This table shows the yield to maturity of a bond purchased at the price shown in the index.

Example: The yield to maturity of a 6.75 %, 3 year bond at a price of 95.00 is 8.67 %.

PRICE	0.00%	1.00%	2.00%	3.00%	4.00%	4.25%	4.50%	4.75%	5.00%	5.25%	5.50%	5.75%	6.00%	6.25%	6.50%	6.75%
100	0.00	1.00	2.00	3.00	4.00	4.25	4.50	4.75	5.00	5.25	5.50	5.75	6.00	6.25	6.50	6.75
99.75	.08	1.08	2.08	3.08	4.08	4.33	4.59	4.84	5.09	5.34	5.59	5.84	6.09	6.34	6.59	6.84
99.50	.16	1.17	2.17	3.17	4.17	4.42	4.68	4.93	5.18	5.43	5.68	5.93	6.18	6.43	6.68	6.93
99.25	.25	1.25	2.26	3.26	4.26	4.52	4.77	5.02	5.27	5.52	5.77	6.02	6.27	6.52	6.78	7.03
99.00	.33	1.34	2.34	3.35	4.35	4.61	4.86	5.11	5.36	5.61	5.86	6.11	6.37	6.62	6.87	7.12
98.75	.41	1.42	2.43	3.44	4.44	4.70	4.95	5.20	5.45	5.70	5.96	6.21	6.46	6.71	6.96	7.22
98.50	.50	1.51	2.52	3.53	4.54	4.79	5.04	5.29	5.54	5.80	6.05	6.30	6.55	6.81	7.06	7.31
98.25	.58	1.59	2.61	3.62	4.63	4.88	5.13	5.38	5.64	5.89	6.14	6.40	6.65	6.90	7.15	7.41
98.00	.67	1.68	2.69	3.71	4.72	4.97	5.22	5.48	5.73	5.98	6.24	6.49	6.74	7.00	7.25	7.50
97.75	.76	1.77	2.78	3.80	4.81	5.06	5.32	5.57	5.82	6.08	6.33	6.58	6.84	7.09	7.34	7.60
97.50	.84	1.86	2.87	3.89	4.90	5.16	5.41	5.66	5.92	6.17	6.42	6.68	6.93	7.19	7.44	7.69
97.25	.93	1.94	2.96	3.98	4.99	5.25	5.50	5.76	6.01	6.26	6.52	6.77	7.03	7.28	7.54	7.79
97.00	1.01	2.03	3.05	4.07	5.09	5.34	5.60	5.85	6.10	6.36	6.61	6.87	7.12	7.38	7.63	7.89
96.75	1.10	2.12	3.14	4.16	5.18	5.43	5.69	5.94	6.20	6.45	6.71	6.96	7.22	7.47	7.73	7.98
96.50	1.19	2.21	3.23	4.25	5.27	5.53	5.78	6.04	6.29	6.55	6.80	7.06	7.32	7.57	7.83	8.08
96.25	1.27	2.30	3.32	4.34	5.37	5.62	5.88	6.13	6.39	6.64	6.90	7.16	7.41	7.67	7.92	8.18
96.00	1.36	2.38	3.41	4.43	5.46	5.71	5.97	6.23	6.48	6.74	7.00	7.25	7.51	7.77	8.02	8.28
95.75	1.45	2.47	3.50	4.53	5.55	5.81	6.07	6.32	6.58	6.84	7.09	7.35	7.61	7.86	8.12	8.38
95.50	1.54	2.56	3.59	4.62	5.65	5.90	6.16	6.42	6.68	6.93	7.19	7.45	7.70	7.96	8.22	8.48
95.25	1.62	2.65	3.68	4.71	5.74	6.00	6.26	6.51	6.77	7.03	7.29	7.54	7.80	8.06	8.32	8.57
95.00	1.71	2.74	3.77	4.80	5.84	6.09	6.35	6.61	6.87	7.13	7.38	7.64	7.90	8.16	8.42	8.67
94.75	1.80	2.83	3.87	4.90	5.93	6.19	6.45	6.71	6.96	7.22	7.48	7.74	8.00	8.26	8.52	8.77
94.50	1.89	2.92	3.96	4.99	6.03	6.29	6.54	6.80	7.06	7.32	7.58	7.84	8.10	8.36	8.61	8.87
94.25	1.98	3.01	4.05	5.09	6.12	6.38	6.64	6.90	7.16	7.42	7.68	7.94	8.20	8.46	8.71	8.97
94.00	2.07	3.11	4.14	5.18	6.22	6.48	6.74	7.00	7.26	7.52	7.78	8.04	8.30	8.56	8.81	9.07
93.75	2.16	3.20	4.24	5.28	6.31	6.57	6.83	7.09	7.35	7.61	7.87	8.13	8.40	8.66	8.92	9.18
93.50	2.25	3.29	4.33	5.37	6.41	6.67	6.93	7.19	7.45	7.71	7.97	8.23	8.50	8.76	9.02	9.28
93.25	2.34	3.38	4.42	5.47	6.51	6.77	7.03	7.29	7.55	7.81	8.07	8.33	8.60	8.86	9.12	9.38
93.00	2.43	3.47	4.52	5.56	6.61	6.87	7.13	7.39	7.65	7.91	8.17	8.43	8.70	8.96	9.22	9.48
92.75	2.52	3.56	4.61	5.66	6.70	6.96	7.23	7.49	7.75	8.01	8.27	8.54	8.80	9.06	9.32	9.58
92.50	2.61	3.66	4.71	5.75	6.80	7.06	7.33	7.59	7.85	8.11	8.37	8.64	8.90	9.16	9.42	9.69
92.25	2.70	3.75	4.80	5.85	6.90	7.16	7.42	7.69	7.95	8.21	8.47	8.74	9.00	9.26	9.53	9.79
92.00	2.79	3.84	4.89	5.95	7.00	7.26	7.52	7.79	8.05	8.31	8.58	8.84	9.10	9.37	9.63	9.89
91.75	2.89	3.94	4.99	6.04	7.10	7.36	7.62	7.89	8.15	8.41	8.68	8.94	9.20	9.47	9.73	10.00
91	3.16	4.22	5.28	6.34	7.40	7.66	7.92	8.19	8.45	8.72	8.98	9.25	9.51	9.78	10.04	10.31
90	3.54	4.60	5.67	6.73	7.80	8.06	8.33	8.60	8.86	9.13	9.40	9.66	9.93	10.20	10.47	10.73
89	3.92	4.99	6.06	7.13	8.21	8.47	8.74	9.01	9.28	9.55	9.82	10.09	10.35	10.62	10.89	11.16
88	4.30	5.38	6.46	7.54	8.62	8.89	9.16	9.43	9.70	9.97	10.24	10.51	10.78	11.05	11.32	11.60
87	4.69	5.78	6.86	7.95	9.04	9.31	9.58	9.86	10.13	10.40	10.67	10.95	11.22	11.49	11.76	12.04
86	5.09	6.18	7.27	8.37	9.46	9.74	10.01	10.29	10.56	10.84	11.11	11.38	11.66	11.93	12.21	12.48
85	5.49	6.59	7.69	8.79	9.90	10.17	10.45	10.72	11.00	11.28	11.55	11.83	12.11	12.38	12.66	12.94
84	5.89	7.00	8.11	9.22	10.33	10.61	10.89	11.17	11.45	11.73	12.00	12.28	12.56	12.84	13.12	13.40
83	6.30	7.42	8.54	9.66	10.78	11.06	11.34	11.62	11.90	12.18	12.46	12.74	13.02	13.30	13.58	13.86
82	6.72	7.85	8.97	10.10	11.23	11.51	11.79	12.08	12.36	12.64	12.92	13.21	13.49	13.77	14.05	14.34
81	7.14	8.28	9.41	10.55	11.69	11.97	12.25	12.54	12.82	13.11	13.39	13.68	13.96	14.25	14.53	14.82
80	7.57	8.72	9.86	11.00	12.15	12.44	12.72	13.01	13.30	13.58	13.87	14.16	14.45	14.73	15.02	15.31
79	8.01	9.16	10.31	11.47	12.62	12.91	13.20	13.49	13.78	14.07	14.36	14.65	14.93	15.22	15.51	15.80
78	8.45	9.61	10.77	11.93	13.10	13.39	13.68	13.97	14.26	14.56	14.85	15.14	15.43	15.72	16.02	16.31
77	8.90	10.07	11.24	12.41	13.58	13.88	14.17	14.47	14.76	15.05	15.35	15.64	15.94	16.23	16.53	16.82
76	9.36	10.53	11.71	12.89	14.08	14.37	14.67	14.97	15.26	15.56	15.86	16.15	16.45	16.75	17.04	17.34
75	9.82	11.01	12.20	13.39	14.58	14.88	15.18	15.48	15.77	16.07	16.37	16.67	16.97	17.27	17.57	17.87
74	10.29	11.49	12.68	13.89	15.09	15.39	15.69	15.99	16.29	16.60	16.90	17.20	17.50	17.80	18.11	18.41
73	10.77	11.97	13.18	14.39	15.61	15.91	16.22	16.52	16.82	17.13	17.43	17.74	18.04	18.35	18.65	18.96
72	11.25	12.47	13.69	14.91	16.13	16.44	16.75	17.05	17.36	17.67	17.97	18.28	18.59	18.90	19.20	19.51
71	11.74	12.97	14.20	15.43	16.67	16.98	17.29	17.60	17.91	18.22	18.53	18.84	19.15	19.46	19.77	20.08
70	12.24	13.48	14.72	15.97	17.22	17.53	17.84	18.15	18.46	18.78	19.09	19.40	19.72	20.03	20.34	20.65
69	12.75	14.00	15.26	16.51	17.77	18.08	18.40	18.71	19.03	19.35	19.66	19.98	20.29	20.61	20.93	21.24
68	13.27	14.53	15.80	17.06	18.33	18.65	18.97	19.29	19.61	19.92	20.24	20.56	20.88	21.20	21.52	21.84
67	13.80	15.07	16.35	17.63	18.91	19.23	19.55	19.87	20.19	20.51	20.84	21.16	21.48	21.80	22.13	22.45
66	14.34	15.62	16.91	18.20	19.49	19.82	20.14	20.47	20.79	21.12	21.44	21.77	22.09	22.42	22.74	23.07
65	14.88	16.18	17.48	18.78	20.09	20.42	20.74	21.07	21.40	21.73	22.06	22.38	22.71	23.04	23.37	23.70
64	15.44	16.75	18.06	19.38	20.70	21.03	21.36	21.69	22.02	22.35	22.68	23.01	23.35	23.68	24.01	24.34
63	16.00	17.33	18.65	19.98	21.32	21.65	21.98	22.32	22.65	22.99	23.32	23.66	23.99	24.33	24.66	25.00
62	16.58	17.92	19.26	20.60	21.95	22.28	22.62	22.96	23.30	23.64	23.97	24.31	24.65	24.99	25.33	25.67
61	17.17	18.52	19.87	21.23	22.59	22.93	23.27	23.61	23.96	24.30	24.64	24.98	25.33	25.67	26.01	26.35
60	17.77	19.13	20.50	21.87	23.25	23.59	23.94	24.28	24.63	24.97	25.32	25.67	26.01	26.36	26.71	27.05
59	18.38	19.76	21.14	22.53	23.92	24.27	24.61	24.96	25.31	25.66	26.01	26.36	26.71	27.06	27.41	27.77
58	19.00	20.40	21.79	23.20	24.60	24.95	25.31	25.66	26.01	26.37	26.72	27.07	27.43	27.78	28.14	28.49

Description: This table shows the price to pay for a bond at the yield rate. The yield is to maturity.

Example: The price of a 10.75 %, 3 year bond to yield 8 % to maturity is $ 107.21.

								COUPON RATE, %								
YIELD	7.00%	7.25%	7.50%	7.75%	8.00%	8.25%	8.50%	8.75%	9.00%	9.25%	9.50%	9.75%	10.00%	10.25%	10.50%	10.75%
0.00	121.00	121.75	122.50	123.25	124.00	124.75	125.50	126.25	127.00	127.75	128.50	129.25	130.00	130.75	131.50	132.25
1.00	117.69	118.43	119.16	119.90	120.64	121.37	122.11	122.85	123.59	124.32	125.06	125.80	126.53	127.27	128.01	128.74
2.00	114.49	115.21	115.94	116.66	117.39	118.11	118.84	119.56	120.28	121.01	121.73	122.46	123.18	123.91	124.63	125.36
3.00	111.39	112.11	112.82	113.53	114.24	114.96	115.67	116.38	117.09	117.80	118.52	119.23	119.94	120.65	121.36	122.08
4.00	108.40	109.10	109.80	110.50	111.20	111.90	112.60	113.30	114.00	114.70	115.40	116.10	116.80	117.50	118.20	118.90
4.25	107.67	108.37	109.06	109.76	110.46	111.16	111.85	112.55	113.25	113.94	114.64	115.34	116.04	116.73	117.43	118.13
4.50	106.94	107.64	108.33	109.03	109.72	110.41	111.11	111.80	112.50	113.19	113.89	114.58	115.27	115.97	116.66	117.36
4.75	106.22	106.91	107.61	108.30	108.99	109.68	110.37	111.06	111.75	112.45	113.14	113.83	114.52	115.21	115.90	116.59
5.00	105.51	106.20	106.89	107.57	108.26	108.95	109.64	110.33	111.02	111.70	112.39	113.08	113.77	114.46	115.15	115.84
5.25	104.80	105.49	106.17	106.86	107.54	108.23	108.91	109.60	110.28	110.97	111.66	112.34	113.03	113.71	114.40	115.08
5.50	104.10	104.78	105.46	106.15	106.83	107.51	108.19	108.88	109.56	110.24	110.92	111.61	112.29	112.97	113.66	114.34
5.75	103.40	104.08	104.76	105.44	106.12	106.80	107.48	108.16	108.84	109.52	110.20	110.88	111.56	112.24	112.92	113.60
6.00	102.71	103.39	104.06	104.74	105.42	106.09	106.77	107.45	108.13	108.80	109.48	110.16	110.83	111.51	112.19	112.87
6.25	102.02	102.70	103.37	104.05	104.72	105.39	106.07	106.74	107.42	108.09	108.77	109.44	110.12	110.79	111.46	112.14
6.50	101.34	102.01	102.69	103.36	104.03	104.70	105.37	106.04	106.72	107.39	108.06	108.73	109.40	110.07	110.75	111.42
6.75	100.67	101.34	102.01	102.68	103.34	104.01	104.68	105.35	106.02	106.69	107.36	108.03	108.69	109.36	110.03	110.70
7.00	100.00	100.67	101.33	102.00	102.66	103.33	104.00	104.66	105.33	105.99	106.66	107.33	107.99	108.66	109.32	109.99
7.25	99.34	100.00	100.66	101.33	101.99	102.65	103.32	103.98	104.64	105.31	105.97	106.63	107.30	107.96	108.62	109.29
7.50	98.68	99.34	100.00	100.66	101.32	101.98	102.64	103.30	103.96	104.62	105.29	105.95	106.61	107.27	107.93	108.59
7.75	98.03	98.68	99.34	100.00	100.66	101.32	101.97	102.63	103.29	103.95	104.61	105.26	105.92	106.58	107.24	107.90
8.00	97.38	98.03	98.69	99.34	100.00	100.66	101.31	101.97	102.62	103.28	103.93	104.59	105.24	105.90	106.55	107.21
8.25	96.74	97.39	98.04	98.69	99.35	100.00	100.65	101.31	101.96	102.61	103.26	103.92	104.57	105.22	105.87	106.53
8.50	96.10	96.75	97.40	98.05	98.70	99.35	100.00	100.65	101.30	101.95	102.60	103.25	103.90	104.55	105.20	105.85
8.75	95.47	96.12	96.76	97.41	98.06	98.71	99.35	100.00	100.65	101.29	101.94	102.59	103.24	103.88	104.53	105.18
9.00	94.84	95.49	96.13	96.78	97.42	98.07	98.71	99.36	100.00	100.64	101.29	101.93	102.58	103.22	103.87	104.51
9.25	94.22	94.86	95.51	96.15	96.79	97.43	98.07	98.72	99.36	100.00	100.64	101.28	101.93	102.57	103.21	103.85
9.50	93.60	94.24	94.88	95.52	96.16	96.80	97.44	98.08	98.72	99.36	100.00	100.64	101.28	101.92	102.56	103.20
9.75	92.99	93.63	94.27	94.90	95.54	96.18	96.81	97.45	98.09	98.73	99.36	100.00	100.64	101.28	101.92	102.55
10.00	92.39	93.02	93.66	94.29	94.92	95.56	96.19	96.83	97.46	98.10	98.73	99.37	100.00	100.63	101.27	101.90
10.25	91.78	92.42	93.05	93.68	94.31	94.94	95.58	96.21	96.84	97.47	98.10	98.73	99.37	100.00	100.63	101.26
10.50	91.19	91.82	92.45	93.08	93.71	94.34	94.96	95.59	96.22	96.85	97.48	98.11	98.74	99.37	100.00	100.63
10.75	90.60	91.22	91.85	92.48	93.10	93.73	94.36	94.98	95.61	96.24	96.87	97.49	98.12	98.75	99.37	100.00
11.00	90.01	90.63	91.26	91.88	92.51	93.13	93.76	94.38	95.00	95.63	96.25	96.88	97.50	98.13	98.75	99.38
11.25	89.43	90.05	90.67	91.29	91.91	92.54	93.16	93.78	94.40	95.02	95.65	96.27	96.89	97.51	98.13	98.76
11.50	88.85	89.47	90.09	90.71	91.33	91.95	92.57	93.19	93.80	94.42	95.04	95.66	96.28	96.90	97.52	98.14
11.75	88.28	88.89	89.51	90.13	90.74	91.36	91.98	92.59	93.21	93.83	94.45	95.06	95.68	96.30	96.91	97.53
12.00	87.71	88.32	88.94	89.55	90.17	90.78	91.39	92.01	92.62	93.24	93.85	94.47	95.08	95.70	96.31	96.93
12.25	87.14	87.75	88.37	88.98	89.59	90.20	90.82	91.43	92.04	92.65	93.27	93.88	94.49	95.10	95.71	96.33
12.50	86.58	87.19	87.80	88.41	89.02	89.63	90.24	90.85	91.46	92.07	92.68	93.29	93.90	94.51	95.12	95.73
12.75	86.03	86.64	87.24	87.85	88.46	89.07	89.67	90.28	90.89	91.50	92.10	92.71	93.32	93.93	94.53	95.14
13.00	85.48	86.08	86.69	87.29	87.90	88.50	89.11	89.71	90.32	90.92	91.53	92.13	92.74	93.34	93.95	94.55
13.25	84.93	85.53	86.14	86.74	87.34	87.94	88.55	89.15	89.75	90.36	90.96	91.56	92.16	92.77	93.37	93.97
13.50	84.39	84.99	85.59	86.19	86.79	87.39	87.99	88.59	89.19	89.79	90.39	90.99	91.59	92.19	92.79	93.40
13.75	83.85	84.45	85.05	85.65	86.24	86.84	87.44	88.04	88.64	89.23	89.83	90.43	91.03	91.63	92.22	92.82
14.00	83.32	83.91	84.51	85.10	85.70	86.30	86.89	87.49	88.08	88.68	89.28	89.87	90.47	91.06	91.66	92.25
14.25	82.79	83.38	83.97	84.57	85.16	85.76	86.35	86.94	87.54	88.13	88.72	89.32	89.91	90.50	91.10	91.69
14.50	82.26	82.85	83.45	84.04	84.63	85.22	85.81	86.40	86.99	87.58	88.18	88.77	89.36	89.95	90.54	91.13
14.75	81.74	82.33	82.92	83.51	84.10	84.69	85.28	85.86	86.45	87.04	87.63	88.22	88.81	89.40	89.99	90.58
15.00	81.22	81.81	82.40	82.98	83.57	84.16	84.74	85.33	85.92	86.51	87.09	87.68	88.27	88.85	89.44	90.03
15.25	80.71	81.30	81.88	82.47	83.05	83.63	84.22	84.80	85.39	85.97	86.56	87.14	87.73	88.31	88.89	89.48
15.50	80.20	80.79	81.37	81.95	82.53	83.11	83.70	84.28	84.86	85.44	86.03	86.61	87.19	87.77	88.35	88.94
15.75	79.70	80.28	80.86	81.44	82.02	82.60	83.18	83.76	84.34	84.92	85.50	86.08	86.66	87.24	87.82	88.40
16.00	79.20	79.77	80.35	80.93	81.51	82.09	82.66	83.24	83.82	84.40	84.98	85.55	86.13	86.71	87.29	87.86
16.25	78.70	79.28	79.85	80.43	81.00	81.58	82.15	82.73	83.31	83.88	84.46	85.03	85.61	86.18	86.76	87.34
16.50	78.21	78.78	79.35	79.93	80.50	81.07	81.65	82.22	82.79	83.37	83.94	84.52	85.09	85.66	86.24	86.81
16.75	77.72	78.29	78.86	79.43	80.00	80.57	81.15	81.72	82.29	82.86	83.43	84.00	84.57	85.15	85.72	86.29
17.00	77.23	77.80	78.37	78.94	79.51	80.08	80.65	81.22	81.79	82.35	82.92	83.49	84.06	84.63	85.20	85.77
17.25	76.75	77.32	77.88	78.45	79.02	79.59	80.15	80.72	81.29	81.85	82.42	82.99	83.56	84.12	84.69	85.26
17.50	76.27	76.84	77.40	77.97	78.53	79.10	79.66	80.23	80.79	81.36	81.92	82.49	83.05	83.62	84.18	84.75
17.75	75.80	76.36	76.92	77.49	78.05	78.61	79.18	79.74	80.30	80.86	81.43	81.99	82.55	83.11	83.68	84.24
18.00	75.33	75.89	76.45	77.01	77.57	78.13	78.69	79.25	79.81	80.37	80.93	81.50	82.06	82.62	83.18	83.74
18.25	74.86	75.42	75.98	76.54	77.10	77.65	78.21	78.77	79.33	79.89	80.45	81.01	81.56	82.12	82.68	83.24
18.50	74.40	74.95	75.51	76.07	76.62	77.18	77.74	78.29	78.85	79.41	79.96	80.52	81.08	81.63	82.19	82.75
18.75	73.94	74.49	75.05	75.60	76.16	76.71	77.26	77.82	78.37	78.93	79.48	80.04	80.59	81.15	81.70	82.26
19.00	73.48	74.03	74.59	75.14	75.69	76.24	76.80	77.35	77.90	78.45	79.01	79.56	80.11	80.66	81.22	81.77
20.00	71.69	72.24	72.78	73.32	73.87	74.41	74.96	75.50	76.05	76.59	77.13	77.68	78.22	78.77	79.31	79.86
25.00	63.52	64.02	64.53	65.04	65.54	66.05	66.56	67.06	67.57	68.08	68.58	69.09	69.60	70.10	70.61	71.12
30.00	56.48	56.95	57.42	57.90	58.37	58.84	59.32	59.79	60.26	60.74	61.21	61.68	62.16	62.63	63.10	63.57

Description: This table shows the yield to maturity of a bond purchased at the price shown in the index.

Example: The yield to maturity of a 10.75 %, 3 year bond at a price of 100.00 is 10.75 %.

COUPON RATE, %

PRICE	7.00%	7.25%	7.50%	7.75%	8.00%	8.25%	8.50%	8.75%	9.00%	9.25%	9.50%	9.75%	10.00%	10.25%	10.50%	10.75%
105	5.17	5.42	5.66	5.90	6.14	6.39	6.63	6.87	7.11	7.36	7.60	7.84	8.08	8.33	8.57	8.81
104.75	5.26	5.51	5.75	5.99	6.23	6.48	6.72	6.96	7.21	7.45	7.69	7.93	8.18	8.42	8.66	8.91
104.50	5.35	5.59	5.84	6.08	6.32	6.57	6.81	7.05	7.30	7.54	7.78	8.03	8.27	8.51	8.76	9.00
104.25	5.44	5.68	5.93	6.17	6.42	6.66	6.90	7.15	7.39	7.63	7.88	8.12	8.36	8.61	8.85	9.09
104.00	5.53	5.77	6.02	6.26	6.51	6.75	6.99	7.24	7.48	7.73	7.97	8.21	8.46	8.70	8.95	9.19
103.75	5.62	5.86	6.11	6.35	6.60	6.84	7.09	7.33	7.57	7.82	8.06	8.31	8.55	8.80	9.04	9.28
103.50	5.71	5.95	6.20	6.44	6.69	6.93	7.18	7.42	7.67	7.91	8.16	8.40	8.65	8.89	9.13	9.38
103.25	5.80	6.04	6.29	6.53	6.78	7.02	7.27	7.51	7.76	8.00	8.25	8.49	8.74	8.99	9.23	9.48
103.00	5.89	6.13	6.38	6.63	6.87	7.12	7.36	7.61	7.85	8.10	8.34	8.59	8.83	9.08	9.33	9.57
102.75	5.98	6.23	6.47	6.72	6.96	7.21	7.46	7.70	7.95	8.19	8.44	8.68	8.93	9.18	9.42	9.67
102.50	6.07	6.32	6.56	6.81	7.06	7.30	7.55	7.79	8.04	8.29	8.53	8.78	9.03	9.27	9.52	9.76
102.25	6.16	6.41	6.66	6.90	7.15	7.39	7.64	7.89	8.13	8.38	8.63	8.87	9.12	9.37	9.61	9.86
102.00	6.25	6.50	6.75	6.99	7.24	7.49	7.74	7.98	8.23	8.48	8.72	8.97	9.22	9.46	9.71	9.96
101.75	6.35	6.59	6.84	7.09	7.33	7.58	7.83	8.08	8.32	8.57	8.82	9.07	9.31	9.56	9.81	10.05
101.50	6.44	6.68	6.93	7.18	7.43	7.68	7.92	8.17	8.42	8.67	8.91	9.16	9.41	9.66	9.90	10.15
101.25	6.53	6.78	7.03	7.27	7.52	7.77	8.02	8.27	8.51	8.76	9.01	9.26	9.51	9.75	10.00	10.25
101.00	6.62	6.87	7.12	7.37	7.62	7.86	8.11	8.36	8.61	8.86	9.11	9.36	9.60	9.85	10.10	10.35
100.75	6.71	6.96	7.21	7.46	7.71	7.96	8.21	8.46	8.71	8.95	9.20	9.45	9.70	9.95	10.20	10.45
100.50	6.81	7.06	7.31	7.56	7.80	8.05	8.30	8.55	8.80	9.05	9.30	9.55	9.80	10.05	10.30	10.55
100.25	6.90	7.15	7.40	7.65	7.90	8.15	8.40	8.65	8.90	9.15	9.40	9.65	9.90	10.15	10.40	10.65
100.00	7.00	7.25	7.50	7.75	8.00	8.25	8.50	8.75	9.00	9.25	9.50	9.75	10.00	10.25	10.50	10.75
99.75	7.09	7.34	7.59	7.84	8.09	8.34	8.59	8.84	9.09	9.34	9.59	9.84	10.09	10.34	10.59	10.84
99.50	7.18	7.43	7.68	7.94	8.19	8.44	8.69	8.94	9.19	9.44	9.69	9.94	10.19	10.44	10.69	10.95
99.25	7.28	7.53	7.78	8.03	8.28	8.53	8.78	9.04	9.29	9.54	9.79	10.04	10.29	10.54	10.79	11.05
99.00	7.37	7.62	7.88	8.13	8.38	8.63	8.88	9.13	9.39	9.64	9.89	10.14	10.39	10.64	10.89	11.15
98.75	7.47	7.72	7.97	8.22	8.48	8.73	8.98	9.23	9.48	9.74	9.99	10.24	10.49	10.74	11.00	11.25
98.50	7.56	7.82	8.07	8.32	8.57	8.83	9.08	9.33	9.58	9.83	10.09	10.34	10.59	10.84	11.10	11.35
98.25	7.66	7.91	8.16	8.42	8.67	8.92	9.18	9.43	9.68	9.93	10.19	10.44	10.69	10.95	11.20	11.45
98.00	7.76	8.01	8.26	8.51	8.77	9.02	9.27	9.53	9.78	10.03	10.29	10.54	10.79	11.05	11.30	11.55
97.75	7.85	8.11	8.36	8.61	8.87	9.12	9.37	9.63	9.88	10.13	10.39	10.64	10.89	11.15	11.40	11.66
97.50	7.95	8.20	8.46	8.71	8.96	9.22	9.47	9.73	9.98	10.23	10.49	10.74	11.00	11.25	11.50	11.76
97.25	8.05	8.30	8.55	8.81	9.06	9.32	9.57	9.83	10.08	10.33	10.59	10.84	11.10	11.35	11.61	11.86
97.00	8.14	8.40	8.65	8.91	9.16	9.42	9.67	9.93	10.18	10.44	10.69	10.95	11.20	11.45	11.71	11.96
96.75	8.24	8.50	8.75	9.01	9.26	9.52	9.77	10.03	10.28	10.54	10.79	11.05	11.30	11.56	11.81	12.07
96.50	8.34	8.59	8.85	9.10	9.36	9.62	9.87	10.13	10.38	10.64	10.89	11.15	11.41	11.66	11.92	12.17
96.25	8.44	8.69	8.95	9.20	9.46	9.72	9.97	10.23	10.48	10.74	11.00	11.25	11.51	11.76	12.02	12.28
96.00	8.53	8.79	9.05	9.30	9.56	9.82	10.07	10.33	10.59	10.84	11.10	11.36	11.61	11.87	12.13	12.38
95.75	8.63	8.89	9.15	9.40	9.66	9.92	10.17	10.43	10.69	10.95	11.20	11.46	11.72	11.97	12.23	12.49
95.50	8.73	8.99	9.25	9.50	9.76	10.02	10.28	10.53	10.79	11.05	11.31	11.56	11.82	12.08	12.34	12.59
95.25	8.83	9.09	9.35	9.61	9.86	10.12	10.38	10.64	10.89	11.15	11.41	11.67	11.92	12.18	12.44	12.70
95.00	8.93	9.19	9.45	9.71	9.96	10.22	10.48	10.74	11.00	11.26	11.51	11.77	12.03	12.29	12.55	12.80
94.75	9.03	9.29	9.55	9.81	10.07	10.32	10.58	10.84	11.10	11.36	11.62	11.88	12.14	12.39	12.65	12.91
94	9.33	9.59	9.85	10.11	10.37	10.63	10.89	11.15	11.41	11.67	11.93	12.19	12.45	12.71	12.97	13.23
93	9.74	10.00	10.27	10.53	10.79	11.05	11.31	11.57	11.83	12.10	12.36	12.62	12.88	13.14	13.41	13.67
92	10.16	10.42	10.68	10.95	11.21	11.47	11.74	12.00	12.26	12.53	12.79	13.05	13.32	13.58	13.84	14.11
91	10.57	10.84	11.10	11.37	11.63	11.90	12.17	12.43	12.70	12.96	13.23	13.49	13.76	14.02	14.29	14.55
90	11.00	11.27	11.53	11.80	12.07	12.33	12.60	12.87	13.14	13.40	13.67	13.94	14.20	14.47	14.74	15.01
89	11.43	11.70	11.97	12.24	12.50	12.77	13.04	13.31	13.58	13.85	14.12	14.39	14.66	14.93	15.20	15.47
88	11.87	12.14	12.41	12.68	12.95	13.22	13.49	13.76	14.03	14.30	14.58	14.85	15.12	15.39	15.66	15.93
87	12.31	12.58	12.85	13.13	13.40	13.67	13.95	14.22	14.49	14.76	15.04	15.31	15.58	15.86	16.13	16.40
86	12.76	13.03	13.31	13.58	13.86	14.13	14.41	14.68	14.96	15.23	15.51	15.78	16.06	16.33	16.61	16.88
85	13.21	13.49	13.77	14.04	14.32	14.60	14.87	15.15	15.43	15.71	15.98	16.26	16.54	16.82	17.09	17.37
84	13.68	13.95	14.23	14.51	14.79	15.07	15.35	15.63	15.91	16.19	16.47	16.75	17.03	17.31	17.58	17.86
83	14.14	14.43	14.71	14.99	15.27	15.55	15.83	16.11	16.39	16.68	16.96	17.24	17.52	17.80	18.08	18.37
82	14.62	14.90	15.19	15.47	15.75	16.04	16.32	16.60	16.89	17.17	17.46	17.74	18.02	18.31	18.59	18.88
81	15.10	15.39	15.68	15.96	16.25	16.53	16.82	17.10	17.39	17.68	17.96	18.25	18.53	18.82	19.11	19.39
80	15.60	15.88	16.17	16.46	16.75	17.03	17.32	17.61	17.90	18.19	18.48	18.76	19.05	19.34	19.63	19.92
79	16.09	16.38	16.67	16.96	17.25	17.54	17.84	18.13	18.42	18.71	19.00	19.29	19.58	19.87	20.16	20.45
78	16.60	16.89	17.19	17.48	17.77	18.06	18.36	18.65	18.94	19.24	19.53	19.82	20.12	20.41	20.70	21.00
77	17.12	17.41	17.71	18.00	18.30	18.59	18.89	19.18	19.48	19.77	20.07	20.36	20.66	20.96	21.25	21.55
76	17.64	17.94	18.23	18.53	18.83	19.13	19.42	19.72	20.02	20.32	20.62	20.92	21.21	21.51	21.81	22.11
75	18.17	18.47	18.77	19.07	19.37	19.67	19.97	20.27	20.57	20.87	21.17	21.48	21.78	22.08	22.38	22.68
74	18.71	19.01	19.32	19.62	19.92	20.22	20.53	20.83	21.13	21.44	21.74	22.05	22.35	22.65	22.96	23.26
73	19.26	19.57	19.87	20.18	20.48	20.79	21.09	21.40	21.71	22.01	22.32	22.63	22.93	23.24	23.55	23.85
72	19.82	20.13	20.44	20.74	21.05	21.36	21.67	21.98	22.29	22.60	22.91	23.22	23.53	23.83	24.14	24.45
71	20.39	20.70	21.01	21.32	21.63	21.95	22.26	22.57	22.88	23.19	23.50	23.82	24.13	24.44	24.75	25.07
70	20.97	21.28	21.60	21.91	22.22	22.54	22.85	23.17	23.48	23.80	24.11	24.43	24.74	25.06	25.37	25.69
69	21.56	21.88	22.19	22.51	22.83	23.14	23.46	23.78	24.10	24.41	24.73	25.05	25.37	25.69	26.01	26.33

Description: This table shows the price to pay for a bond at the yield rate. The yield is to maturity.

Example: The price of a 15.00 %, 3 year bond to yield 8 % to maturity is $ 118.35.

COUPON RATE, %

YIELD	11.00%	11.25%	11.50%	11.75%	12.00%	12.25%	12.50%	12.75%	13.00%	13.25%	13.50%	13.75%	14.00%	14.25%	14.50%	15.00%
0.00	133.00	133.75	134.50	135.25	136.00	136.75	137.50	138.25	139.00	139.75	140.50	141.25	142.00	142.75	143.50	145.00
1.00	129.48	130.22	130.96	131.69	132.43	133.17	133.90	134.64	135.38	136.12	136.85	137.59	138.33	139.06	139.80	141.27
2.00	126.08	126.80	127.53	128.25	128.98	129.70	130.43	131.15	131.88	132.60	133.32	134.05	134.77	135.50	136.22	137.67
3.00	122.79	123.50	124.21	124.93	125.64	126.35	127.06	127.77	128.49	129.20	129.91	130.62	131.33	132.05	132.76	134.18
4.00	119.61	120.31	121.01	121.71	122.41	123.11	123.81	124.51	125.21	125.91	126.61	127.31	128.01	128.71	129.41	130.81
4.25	118.83	119.52	120.22	120.92	121.61	122.31	123.01	123.71	124.40	125.10	125.80	126.49	127.19	127.89	128.59	129.98
4.50	118.05	118.75	119.44	120.13	120.83	121.52	122.22	122.91	123.61	124.30	125.00	125.69	126.38	127.08	127.77	129.16
4.75	117.29	117.98	118.67	119.36	120.05	120.74	121.43	122.12	122.82	123.51	124.20	124.89	125.58	126.27	126.96	128.35
5.00	116.52	117.21	117.90	118.59	119.28	119.97	120.66	121.34	122.03	122.72	123.41	124.10	124.79	125.48	126.16	127.54
5.25	115.77	116.46	117.14	117.83	118.51	119.20	119.88	120.57	121.26	121.94	122.63	123.31	124.00	124.68	125.37	126.74
5.50	115.02	115.70	116.39	117.07	117.75	118.44	119.12	119.80	120.48	121.17	121.85	122.53	123.22	123.90	124.58	125.95
5.75	114.28	114.96	115.64	116.32	117.00	117.68	118.36	119.04	119.72	120.40	121.08	121.76	122.44	123.12	123.80	125.16
6.00	113.54	114.22	114.90	115.57	116.25	116.93	117.61	118.28	118.96	119.64	120.31	120.99	121.67	122.35	123.02	124.38
6.25	112.81	113.49	114.16	114.84	115.51	116.18	116.86	117.53	118.21	118.88	119.56	120.23	120.90	121.58	122.25	123.60
6.50	112.09	112.76	113.43	114.10	114.77	115.45	116.12	116.79	117.46	118.13	118.80	119.48	120.15	120.82	121.49	122.83
6.75	111.37	112.04	112.71	113.38	114.05	114.71	115.38	116.05	116.72	117.39	118.06	118.73	119.40	120.06	120.73	122.07
7.00	110.66	111.32	111.99	112.66	113.32	113.99	114.65	115.32	115.99	116.65	117.32	117.98	118.65	119.32	119.98	121.31
7.25	109.95	110.61	111.28	111.94	112.60	113.27	113.93	114.59	115.26	115.92	116.58	117.25	117.91	118.57	119.24	120.56
7.50	109.25	109.91	110.57	111.23	111.89	112.55	113.21	113.87	114.53	115.19	115.86	116.52	117.18	117.84	118.50	119.82
7.75	108.55	109.21	109.87	110.53	111.19	111.84	112.50	113.16	113.82	114.47	115.13	115.79	116.45	117.11	117.76	119.08
8.00	107.86	108.52	109.17	109.83	110.48	111.14	111.79	112.45	113.11	113.76	114.42	115.07	115.73	116.38	117.04	118.35
8.25	107.18	107.83	108.48	109.14	109.79	110.44	111.09	111.75	112.40	113.05	113.70	114.36	115.01	115.66	116.32	117.62
8.50	106.50	107.15	107.80	108.45	109.10	109.75	110.40	111.05	111.70	112.35	113.00	113.65	114.30	114.95	115.60	116.90
8.75	105.83	106.47	107.12	107.77	108.42	109.06	109.71	110.36	111.00	111.65	112.30	112.95	113.59	114.24	114.89	116.18
9.00	105.16	105.80	106.45	107.09	107.74	108.38	109.03	109.67	110.32	110.96	111.61	112.25	112.89	113.54	114.18	115.47
9.25	104.49	105.14	105.78	106.42	107.06	107.71	108.35	108.99	109.63	110.27	110.92	111.56	112.20	112.84	113.48	114.77
9.50	103.84	104.48	105.12	105.76	106.40	107.04	107.67	108.31	108.95	109.59	110.23	110.87	111.51	112.15	112.79	114.07
9.75	103.19	103.82	104.46	105.10	105.73	106.37	107.01	107.64	108.28	108.92	109.56	110.19	110.83	111.47	112.10	113.38
10.00	102.54	103.17	103.81	104.44	105.08	105.71	106.34	106.98	107.61	108.25	108.88	109.52	110.15	110.79	111.42	112.69
10.25	101.90	102.53	103.16	103.79	104.42	105.06	105.69	106.32	106.95	107.58	108.22	108.85	109.48	110.11	110.74	112.01
10.50	101.26	101.89	102.52	103.15	103.78	104.41	105.04	105.66	106.29	106.92	107.55	108.18	108.81	109.44	110.07	111.33
10.75	100.63	101.25	101.88	102.51	103.13	103.76	104.39	105.02	105.64	106.27	106.90	107.52	108.15	108.78	109.40	110.66
11.00	100.00	100.62	101.25	101.87	102.50	103.12	103.75	104.37	105.00	105.62	106.24	106.87	107.49	108.12	108.74	109.99
11.25	99.38	100.00	100.62	101.24	101.87	102.49	103.11	103.73	104.35	104.98	105.60	106.22	106.84	107.46	108.09	109.33
11.50	98.76	99.38	100.00	100.62	101.24	101.86	102.48	103.10	103.72	104.34	104.96	105.58	106.20	106.81	107.43	108.67
11.75	98.15	98.77	99.38	100.00	100.62	101.23	101.85	102.47	103.09	103.70	104.32	104.94	105.55	106.17	106.79	108.02
12.00	97.54	98.16	98.77	99.39	100.00	100.61	101.23	101.84	102.46	103.07	103.69	104.30	104.92	105.53	106.15	107.38
12.25	96.94	97.55	98.16	98.78	99.39	100.00	100.61	101.22	101.84	102.45	103.06	103.67	104.29	104.90	105.51	106.73
12.50	96.34	96.95	97.56	98.17	98.78	99.39	100.00	100.61	101.22	101.83	102.44	103.05	103.66	104.27	104.88	106.10
12.75	95.75	96.36	96.96	97.57	98.18	98.79	99.39	100.00	100.61	101.21	101.82	102.43	103.04	103.64	104.25	105.47
13.00	95.16	95.76	96.37	96.97	97.58	98.18	98.79	99.39	100.00	100.61	101.21	101.82	102.42	103.03	103.63	104.84
13.25	94.57	95.18	95.78	96.38	96.99	97.59	98.19	98.79	99.40	100.00	100.60	101.21	101.81	102.41	103.01	104.22
13.50	94.00	94.60	95.20	95.80	96.40	97.00	97.60	98.20	98.80	99.40	100.00	100.60	101.20	101.80	102.40	103.60
13.75	93.42	94.02	94.62	95.22	95.81	96.41	97.01	97.61	98.21	98.80	99.40	100.00	100.60	101.20	101.79	102.99
14.00	92.85	93.45	94.04	94.64	95.23	95.83	96.43	97.02	97.62	98.21	98.81	99.40	100.00	100.60	101.19	102.38
14.25	92.28	92.88	93.47	94.06	94.66	95.25	95.85	96.44	97.03	97.63	98.22	98.81	99.41	100.00	100.59	101.78
14.50	91.72	92.31	92.91	93.50	94.09	94.68	95.27	95.86	96.45	97.04	97.64	98.23	98.82	99.41	100.00	101.18
14.75	91.17	91.75	92.34	92.93	93.52	94.11	94.70	95.29	95.88	96.47	97.06	97.64	98.23	98.82	99.41	100.59
15.00	90.61	91.20	91.79	92.37	92.96	93.55	94.13	94.72	95.31	95.89	96.48	97.07	97.65	98.24	98.83	100.00
15.25	90.06	90.65	91.23	91.82	92.40	92.99	93.57	94.16	94.74	95.32	95.91	96.49	97.08	97.66	98.25	99.42
15.50	89.52	90.10	90.68	91.27	91.85	92.43	93.01	93.60	94.18	94.76	95.34	95.92	96.51	97.09	97.67	98.84
15.75	88.98	89.56	90.14	90.72	91.30	91.88	92.46	93.04	93.62	94.20	94.78	95.36	95.94	96.52	97.10	98.26
16.00	88.44	89.02	89.60	90.18	90.75	91.33	91.91	92.49	93.07	93.64	94.22	94.80	95.38	95.95	96.53	97.69
16.25	87.91	88.49	89.06	89.64	90.21	90.79	91.36	91.94	92.52	93.09	93.67	94.24	94.82	95.39	95.97	97.12
16.50	87.38	87.96	88.53	89.10	89.68	90.25	90.82	91.40	91.97	92.54	93.12	93.69	94.26	94.84	95.41	96.56
16.75	86.86	87.43	88.00	88.57	89.14	89.72	90.29	90.86	91.43	92.00	92.57	93.14	93.72	94.29	94.86	96.00
17.00	86.34	86.91	87.48	88.05	88.62	89.19	89.75	90.32	90.89	91.46	92.03	92.60	93.17	93.74	94.31	95.45
17.25	85.82	86.39	86.96	87.52	88.09	88.66	89.23	89.79	90.36	90.93	91.49	92.06	92.63	93.20	93.76	94.90
17.50	85.31	85.88	86.44	87.01	87.57	88.14	88.70	89.27	89.83	90.40	90.96	91.53	92.09	92.66	93.22	94.35
17.75	84.80	85.37	85.93	86.49	87.05	87.62	88.18	88.74	89.31	89.87	90.43	90.99	91.56	92.12	92.68	93.81
18.00	84.30	84.86	85.42	85.98	86.54	87.10	87.66	88.22	88.79	89.35	89.91	90.47	91.03	91.59	92.15	93.27
18.25	83.80	84.36	84.92	85.47	86.03	86.59	87.15	87.71	88.27	88.83	89.39	89.94	90.50	91.06	91.62	92.74
18.50	83.30	83.86	84.42	84.97	85.53	86.09	86.64	87.20	87.76	88.31	88.87	89.42	89.98	90.54	91.09	92.21
18.75	82.81	83.36	83.92	84.47	85.03	85.58	86.14	86.69	87.25	87.80	88.35	88.91	89.46	90.02	90.57	91.68
19.00	82.32	82.87	83.43	83.98	84.53	85.08	85.64	86.19	86.74	87.29	87.85	88.40	88.95	89.50	90.06	91.16
20.00	80.40	80.95	81.49	82.03	82.58	83.12	83.67	84.21	84.76	85.30	85.85	86.39	86.93	87.48	88.02	89.11
25.00	71.62	72.13	72.64	73.14	73.65	74.16	74.66	75.17	75.68	76.18	76.69	77.20	77.70	78.21	78.72	79.73
30.00	64.05	64.52	64.99	65.47	65.94	66.41	66.89	67.36	67.83	68.30	68.78	69.25	69.72	70.20	70.67	71.62

BOND YIELD

Description: This table shows the yield to maturity of a bond purchased at the price shown in the index.

Example: The yield to maturity of a 15.00 %, 3 year bond at a price of 102.00 is 14.15 %.

COUPON RATE, %

PRICE	11.00%	11.25%	11.50%	11.75%	12.00%	12.25%	12.50%	12.75%	13.00%	13.25%	13.50%	13.75%	14.00%	14.25%	14.50%	15.00%
110	7.23	7.46	7.70	7.93	8.17	8.40	8.64	8.87	9.11	9.35	9.58	9.82	10.05	10.29	10.52	10.99
109	7.58	7.82	8.06	8.29	8.53	8.77	9.00	9.24	9.48	9.71	9.95	10.19	10.42	10.66	10.90	11.37
108	7.95	8.18	8.42	8.66	8.90	9.14	9.37	9.61	9.85	10.09	10.33	10.56	10.80	11.04	11.28	11.75
107	8.31	8.55	8.79	9.03	9.27	9.51	9.75	9.99	10.23	10.47	10.71	10.94	11.18	11.42	11.66	12.14
106	8.68	8.92	9.16	9.40	9.64	9.88	10.13	10.37	10.61	10.85	11.09	11.33	11.57	11.81	12.05	12.53
105.75	8.77	9.01	9.26	9.50	9.74	9.98	10.22	10.46	10.70	10.94	11.19	11.43	11.67	11.91	12.15	12.63
105.50	8.87	9.11	9.35	9.59	9.83	10.08	10.32	10.56	10.80	11.04	11.28	11.52	11.77	12.01	12.25	12.73
105.25	8.96	9.20	9.44	9.69	9.93	10.17	10.41	10.65	10.90	11.14	11.38	11.62	11.86	12.11	12.35	12.83
105.00	9.05	9.30	9.54	9.78	10.02	10.27	10.51	10.75	10.99	11.24	11.48	11.72	11.96	12.20	12.45	12.93
104.75	9.15	9.39	9.63	9.88	10.12	10.36	10.61	10.85	11.09	11.33	11.58	11.82	12.06	12.30	12.55	13.03
104.50	9.24	9.49	9.73	9.97	10.22	10.46	10.70	10.94	11.19	11.43	11.67	11.92	12.16	12.40	12.65	13.13
104.25	9.34	9.58	9.82	10.07	10.31	10.56	10.80	11.04	11.29	11.53	11.77	12.02	12.26	12.50	12.75	13.23
104.00	9.43	9.68	9.92	10.16	10.41	10.65	10.90	11.14	11.38	11.63	11.87	12.12	12.36	12.60	12.85	13.33
103.75	9.53	9.77	10.02	10.26	10.51	10.75	10.99	11.24	11.48	11.73	11.97	12.21	12.46	12.70	12.95	13.44
103.50	9.62	9.87	10.11	10.36	10.60	10.85	11.09	11.34	11.58	11.83	12.07	12.31	12.56	12.80	13.05	13.54
103.25	9.72	9.97	10.21	10.45	10.70	10.94	11.19	11.43	11.68	11.92	12.17	12.41	12.66	12.90	13.15	13.64
103.00	9.82	10.06	10.31	10.55	10.80	11.04	11.29	11.53	11.78	12.02	12.27	12.51	12.76	13.01	13.25	13.74
102.75	9.91	10.16	10.40	10.65	10.90	11.14	11.39	11.63	11.88	12.12	12.37	12.62	12.86	13.11	13.35	13.84
102.50	10.01	10.26	10.50	10.75	10.99	11.24	11.49	11.73	11.98	12.22	12.47	12.72	12.96	13.21	13.56	14.05
102.25	10.11	10.35	10.60	10.85	11.09	11.34	11.59	11.83	12.08	12.33	12.57	12.82	13.06	13.31	13.56	14.05
102.00	10.20	10.45	10.70	10.94	11.19	11.44	11.69	11.93	12.18	12.43	12.67	12.92	13.17	13.41	13.66	14.15
101.75	10.30	10.55	10.80	11.04	11.29	11.54	11.79	12.03	12.28	12.53	12.77	13.02	13.27	13.52	13.76	14.26
101.50	10.40	10.65	10.90	11.14	11.39	11.64	11.89	12.13	12.38	12.63	12.88	13.12	13.37	13.62	13.87	14.36
101.25	10.50	10.75	10.99	11.24	11.49	11.74	11.99	12.23	12.48	12.73	12.98	13.23	13.47	13.72	13.97	14.47
101.00	10.60	10.85	11.09	11.34	11.59	11.84	12.09	12.34	12.58	12.83	13.08	13.33	13.58	13.83	14.07	14.57
100.75	10.70	10.95	11.19	11.44	11.69	11.94	12.19	12.44	12.69	12.94	13.18	13.43	13.68	13.93	14.18	14.68
100.50	10.80	11.04	11.29	11.54	11.79	12.04	12.29	12.54	12.79	13.04	13.29	13.54	13.79	14.04	14.28	14.78
100.25	10.90	11.14	11.39	11.64	11.89	12.14	12.39	12.64	12.89	13.14	13.39	13.64	13.89	14.14	14.39	14.89
100.00	11.00	11.25	11.50	11.75	12.00	12.25	12.50	12.75	13.00	13.25	13.50	13.75	14.00	14.25	14.50	15.00
99.75	11.10	11.35	11.60	11.85	12.10	12.35	12.60	12.85	13.10	13.35	13.60	13.85	14.10	14.35	14.60	15.10
99.50	11.20	11.45	11.70	11.95	12.20	12.45	12.70	12.95	13.20	13.45	13.70	13.95	14.21	14.46	14.71	15.21
99.25	11.30	11.55	11.80	12.05	12.30	12.55	12.80	13.06	13.31	13.56	13.81	14.06	14.31	14.56	14.81	15.32
99.00	11.40	11.65	11.90	12.15	12.40	12.66	12.91	13.16	13.41	13.66	13.91	14.17	14.42	14.67	14.92	15.42
98.75	11.50	11.75	12.00	12.26	12.51	12.76	13.01	13.26	13.52	13.77	14.02	14.27	14.52	14.78	15.03	15.53
98.50	11.60	11.85	12.11	12.36	12.61	12.86	13.12	13.37	13.62	13.87	14.13	14.38	14.63	14.88	15.14	15.64
98.25	11.70	11.96	12.21	12.46	12.71	12.97	13.22	13.47	13.73	13.98	14.23	14.48	14.74	14.99	15.24	15.75
98.00	11.81	12.06	12.31	12.57	12.82	13.07	13.33	13.58	13.83	14.09	14.34	14.59	14.85	15.10	15.35	15.86
97.75	11.91	12.16	12.42	12.67	12.92	13.18	13.43	13.68	13.94	14.19	14.45	14.70	14.95	15.21	15.46	15.97
97.50	12.01	12.27	12.52	12.77	13.03	13.28	13.54	13.79	14.04	14.30	14.55	14.81	15.06	15.32	15.57	16.08
97.25	12.12	12.37	12.62	12.88	13.13	13.39	13.64	13.90	14.15	14.41	14.66	14.92	15.17	15.42	15.68	16.19
97.00	12.22	12.47	12.73	12.98	13.24	13.49	13.75	14.00	14.26	14.51	14.77	15.02	15.28	15.53	15.79	16.30
96.75	12.32	12.58	12.83	13.09	13.35	13.60	13.86	14.11	14.37	14.62	14.88	15.13	15.39	15.64	15.90	16.41
96.50	12.43	12.68	12.94	13.20	13.45	13.71	13.96	14.22	14.47	14.73	14.99	15.24	15.50	15.75	16.01	16.52
96.25	12.53	12.79	13.05	13.30	13.56	13.81	14.07	14.33	14.58	14.84	15.10	15.35	15.61	15.86	16.12	16.63
96.00	12.64	12.90	13.15	13.41	13.66	13.92	14.18	14.43	14.69	14.95	15.20	15.46	15.72	15.98	16.23	16.75
95.75	12.74	13.00	13.26	13.52	13.77	14.03	14.29	14.54	14.80	15.06	15.31	15.57	15.83	16.09	16.34	16.86
95.50	12.85	13.11	13.36	13.62	13.88	14.14	14.39	14.65	14.91	15.17	15.43	15.68	15.94	16.20	16.46	16.97
95.25	12.96	13.21	13.47	13.73	13.99	14.25	14.50	14.76	15.02	15.28	15.54	15.79	16.05	16.31	16.57	17.08
95.00	13.06	13.32	13.58	13.84	14.10	14.35	14.61	14.87	15.13	15.39	15.65	15.91	16.16	16.42	16.68	17.20
94.75	13.17	13.43	13.69	13.95	14.21	14.46	14.72	14.98	15.24	15.50	15.76	16.02	16.28	16.53	16.79	17.31
94.50	13.28	13.54	13.80	14.05	14.31	14.57	14.83	15.09	15.35	15.61	15.87	16.13	16.39	16.65	16.91	17.43
94.25	13.39	13.64	13.90	14.16	14.42	14.68	14.94	15.20	15.46	15.72	15.98	16.24	16.50	16.76	17.02	17.54
94.00	13.49	13.75	14.01	14.27	14.53	14.79	15.05	15.31	15.57	15.83	16.09	16.36	16.62	16.88	17.14	17.66
93.75	13.60	13.86	14.12	14.38	14.64	14.90	15.17	15.43	15.69	15.95	16.21	16.47	16.73	16.99	17.25	17.77
93	13.93	14.19	14.45	14.71	14.98	15.24	15.50	15.76	16.02	16.29	16.55	16.81	17.07	17.34	17.60	18.12
92	14.37	14.64	14.90	15.16	15.43	15.69	15.95	16.22	16.48	16.75	17.01	17.27	17.54	17.80	18.07	18.59
91	14.82	15.09	15.35	15.62	15.88	16.15	16.41	16.68	16.94	17.21	17.48	17.74	18.01	18.27	18.54	19.07
90	15.27	15.54	15.81	16.08	16.34	16.61	16.88	17.15	17.41	17.68	17.95	18.22	18.49	18.75	19.02	19.56
89	15.74	16.00	16.27	16.54	16.81	17.08	17.35	17.62	17.89	18.16	18.43	18.70	18.97	19.24	19.51	20.05
88	16.20	16.47	16.75	17.02	17.29	17.56	17.83	18.10	18.38	18.65	18.92	19.19	19.46	19.73	20.01	20.55
87	16.68	16.95	17.22	17.50	17.77	18.05	18.32	18.59	18.87	19.14	19.41	19.69	19.96	20.24	20.51	21.06
86	17.16	17.43	17.71	17.99	18.26	18.54	18.81	19.09	19.36	19.64	19.92	20.19	20.47	20.74	21.02	21.57
85	17.65	17.93	18.20	18.48	18.76	19.04	19.31	19.59	19.87	20.15	20.43	20.71	20.98	21.26	21.54	22.10
84	18.14	18.42	18.70	18.98	19.26	19.54	19.82	20.10	20.38	20.66	20.95	21.23	21.51	21.79	22.07	22.63
83	18.65	18.93	19.21	19.49	19.78	20.06	20.34	20.62	20.91	21.19	21.47	21.75	22.04	22.32	22.60	23.17
82	19.16	19.44	19.73	20.01	20.30	20.58	20.87	21.15	21.44	21.72	22.01	22.29	22.58	22.86	23.15	23.72
81	19.68	19.97	20.25	20.54	20.83	21.11	21.40	21.69	21.97	22.26	22.55	22.84	23.12	23.41	23.70	24.27
80	20.21	20.50	20.79	21.08	21.36	21.65	21.94	22.23	22.52	22.81	23.10	23.39	23.68	23.97	24.26	24.84

Description: This table shows the price to pay for a bond at the yield rate. The yield is to maturity.

Example: The price of a 6.75 %, 4 year bond to yield 8 % to maturity is $ 95.79.

YIELD	0.00%	1.00%	2.00%	3.00%	4.00%	4.25%	COUPON RATE, % 4.50%	4.75%	5.00%	5.25%	5.50%	5.75%	6.00%	6.25%	6.50%	6.75%
0.00	100.00	104.00	108.00	112.00	116.00	117.00	118.00	119.00	120.00	121.00	122.00	123.00	124.00	125.00	126.00	127.00
1.00	96.09	100.00	103.91	107.82	111.73	112.71	113.69	114.67	115.65	116.62	117.60	118.58	119.56	120.54	121.51	122.49
2.00	92.35	96.17	100.00	103.83	107.65	108.61	109.56	110.52	111.48	112.43	113.39	114.35	115.30	116.26	117.22	118.17
3.00	88.77	92.51	96.26	100.00	103.74	104.68	105.61	106.55	107.49	108.42	109.36	110.29	111.23	112.16	113.10	114.04
4.00	85.35	89.01	92.67	96.34	100.00	100.92	101.83	102.75	103.66	104.58	105.49	106.41	107.33	108.24	109.16	110.07
4.25	84.52	88.16	91.80	95.45	99.09	100.00	100.91	101.82	102.73	103.64	104.55	105.46	106.38	107.29	108.20	109.11
4.50	83.69	87.32	90.94	94.56	98.19	99.09	100.00	100.91	101.81	102.72	103.62	104.53	105.44	106.34	107.25	108.15
4.75	82.88	86.48	90.09	93.69	97.30	98.20	99.10	100.00	100.90	101.80	102.70	103.60	104.51	105.41	106.31	107.21
5.00	82.07	85.66	89.24	92.83	96.41	97.31	98.21	99.10	100.00	100.90	101.79	102.69	103.59	104.48	105.38	106.27
5.25	81.28	84.84	88.41	91.98	95.54	96.43	97.33	98.22	99.11	100.00	100.89	101.78	102.67	103.57	104.46	105.35
5.50	80.49	84.04	87.58	91.13	94.68	95.57	96.45	97.34	98.23	99.11	100.00	100.89	101.77	102.66	103.55	104.43
5.75	79.71	83.24	86.77	90.30	93.83	94.71	95.59	96.47	97.35	98.24	99.12	100.00	100.88	101.76	102.65	103.53
6.00	78.94	82.45	85.96	89.47	92.98	93.86	94.74	95.61	96.49	97.37	98.25	99.12	100.00	100.88	101.75	102.63
6.25	78.18	81.67	85.16	88.65	92.14	93.02	93.89	94.76	95.64	96.51	97.38	98.25	99.13	100.00	100.88	101.75
6.50	77.42	80.90	84.37	87.84	91.32	92.19	93.05	93.92	94.79	95.66	96.53	97.40	98.26	99.13	100.00	100.87
6.75	76.68	80.13	83.59	87.04	90.50	91.36	92.23	93.09	93.95	94.82	95.68	96.55	97.41	98.27	99.14	100.00
7.00	75.94	79.38	82.82	86.25	89.69	90.55	91.41	92.27	93.13	93.99	94.84	95.70	96.56	97.42	98.28	99.14
7.25	75.21	78.63	82.05	85.47	88.89	89.74	90.60	91.45	92.31	93.16	94.02	94.87	95.73	96.58	97.44	98.29
7.50	74.49	77.89	81.29	84.69	88.10	88.95	89.80	90.65	91.50	92.35	93.20	94.05	94.90	95.75	96.60	97.45
7.75	73.78	77.16	80.54	83.93	87.31	88.15	89.00	89.85	90.69	91.54	92.39	93.23	94.08	94.92	95.77	96.62
8.00	73.07	76.44	79.80	83.17	86.53	87.38	88.22	89.06	89.90	90.74	91.58	92.43	93.27	94.11	94.95	95.79
8.25	72.37	75.72	79.07	82.42	85.77	86.60	87.44	88.28	89.12	89.95	90.79	91.63	92.46	93.30	94.14	94.98
8.50	71.68	75.01	78.34	81.67	85.01	85.84	86.67	87.51	88.34	89.17	90.00	90.84	91.67	92.50	93.34	94.17
8.75	71.00	74.31	77.62	80.94	84.25	85.08	85.91	86.74	87.57	88.40	89.23	90.06	90.88	91.71	92.54	93.37
9.00	70.32	73.62	76.91	80.21	83.51	84.33	85.16	85.98	86.81	87.63	88.46	89.28	90.11	90.93	91.76	92.58
9.25	69.65	72.93	76.21	79.49	82.77	83.59	84.41	85.23	86.06	86.88	87.70	88.52	89.34	90.16	90.98	91.80
9.50	68.99	72.25	75.52	78.78	82.05	82.86	83.68	84.49	85.31	86.13	86.94	87.76	88.57	89.39	90.21	91.02
9.75	68.33	71.58	74.83	78.08	81.32	82.14	82.95	83.76	84.57	85.38	86.20	87.01	87.82	88.63	89.44	90.26
10.00	67.68	70.92	74.15	77.38	80.61	81.42	82.23	83.03	83.84	84.65	85.46	86.27	87.07	87.88	88.69	89.50
10.25	67.04	70.26	73.47	76.69	79.90	80.71	81.51	82.32	83.12	83.92	84.73	85.53	86.33	87.14	87.94	88.75
10.50	66.41	69.61	72.81	76.01	79.21	80.01	80.80	81.60	82.40	83.20	84.00	84.80	85.60	86.40	87.20	88.00
10.75	65.78	68.96	72.15	75.33	78.51	79.31	80.11	80.90	81.70	82.49	83.29	84.08	84.88	85.68	86.47	87.27
11.00	65.16	68.33	71.49	74.66	77.83	78.62	79.41	80.20	81.00	81.79	82.58	83.37	84.16	84.96	85.75	86.54
11.25	64.55	67.70	70.85	74.00	77.15	77.94	78.73	79.52	80.30	81.09	81.88	82.67	83.45	84.24	85.03	85.82
11.50	63.94	67.07	70.21	73.35	76.48	77.27	78.05	78.83	79.62	80.40	81.18	81.97	82.75	83.54	84.32	85.10
11.75	63.34	66.46	69.58	72.70	75.82	76.60	77.38	78.16	78.94	79.72	80.50	81.28	82.06	82.84	83.62	84.40
12.00	62.74	65.85	68.95	72.06	75.16	75.94	76.71	77.49	78.27	79.04	79.82	80.59	81.37	82.15	82.92	83.70
12.25	62.15	65.24	68.33	71.42	74.51	75.28	76.06	76.83	77.60	78.37	79.15	79.92	80.69	81.46	82.23	83.01
12.50	61.57	64.64	67.72	70.79	73.87	74.64	75.40	76.17	76.94	77.71	78.48	79.25	80.02	80.78	81.55	82.32
12.75	60.99	64.05	67.11	70.17	73.23	74.00	74.76	75.53	76.29	77.05	77.82	78.58	79.35	80.11	80.88	81.64
13.00	60.42	63.47	66.51	69.56	72.60	73.36	74.12	74.88	75.64	76.41	77.17	77.93	78.69	79.45	80.21	80.97
13.25	59.86	62.89	65.92	68.95	71.98	72.73	73.49	74.25	75.01	75.76	76.52	77.28	78.04	78.79	79.55	80.31
13.50	59.30	62.32	65.33	68.34	71.36	72.11	72.87	73.62	74.37	75.13	75.88	76.64	77.39	78.14	78.90	79.65
13.75	58.75	61.75	64.75	67.75	70.75	71.50	72.25	73.00	73.75	74.50	75.25	76.00	76.75	77.50	78.25	79.00
14.00	58.20	61.19	64.17	67.16	70.14	70.89	71.64	72.38	73.13	73.88	74.62	75.37	76.11	76.86	77.61	78.35
14.25	57.66	60.63	63.60	66.57	69.54	70.29	71.03	71.77	72.52	73.26	74.00	74.74	75.49	76.23	76.97	77.72
14.50	57.12	60.08	63.04	66.00	68.95	69.69	70.43	71.17	71.91	72.65	73.39	74.13	74.87	75.61	76.34	77.08
14.75	56.59	59.54	62.48	65.42	68.37	69.10	69.84	70.57	71.31	72.04	72.78	73.52	74.25	74.99	75.72	76.46
15.00	56.07	59.00	61.93	64.86	67.78	68.52	69.25	69.98	70.71	71.45	72.18	72.91	73.64	74.37	75.11	75.84
15.25	55.55	58.47	61.38	64.30	67.21	67.94	68.67	69.40	70.12	70.85	71.58	72.31	73.04	73.77	74.50	75.23
15.50	55.04	57.94	60.84	63.74	66.64	67.37	68.09	68.82	69.54	70.27	70.99	71.72	72.44	73.17	73.89	74.62
15.75	54.53	57.42	60.30	63.19	66.08	66.80	67.52	68.24	68.96	69.69	70.41	71.13	71.85	72.57	73.30	74.02
16.00	54.03	56.90	59.77	62.65	65.52	66.24	66.96	67.68	68.39	69.11	69.83	70.55	71.27	71.99	72.70	73.42
16.25	53.53	56.39	59.25	62.11	64.97	65.68	66.40	67.11	67.83	68.54	69.26	69.97	70.69	71.40	72.12	72.83
16.50	53.04	55.88	58.73	61.58	64.42	65.13	65.84	66.56	67.27	67.98	68.69	69.40	70.11	70.83	71.54	72.25
16.75	52.55	55.38	58.22	61.05	63.88	64.59	65.30	66.01	66.71	67.42	68.13	68.84	69.55	70.25	70.96	71.67
17.00	52.07	54.89	57.71	60.53	63.35	64.05	64.76	65.46	66.16	66.87	67.57	68.28	68.98	69.69	70.39	71.10
17.25	51.59	54.40	57.20	60.01	62.82	63.52	64.22	64.92	65.62	66.32	67.02	67.73	68.43	69.13	69.83	70.53
17.50	51.12	53.91	56.70	59.50	62.29	62.99	63.69	64.39	65.08	65.78	66.48	67.18	67.88	68.58	69.27	69.97
17.75	50.65	53.43	56.21	58.99	61.77	62.47	63.16	63.86	64.55	65.25	65.94	66.64	67.33	68.03	68.72	69.42
18.00	50.19	52.95	55.72	58.49	61.26	61.95	62.64	63.33	64.02	64.72	65.41	66.10	66.79	67.48	68.17	68.87
18.25	49.73	52.48	55.24	57.99	60.75	61.44	62.12	62.81	63.50	64.19	64.88	65.57	66.26	66.94	67.63	68.32
18.50	49.28	52.02	54.76	57.50	60.24	60.93	61.61	62.30	62.98	63.67	64.36	65.04	65.73	66.41	67.10	67.78
18.75	48.83	51.56	54.28	57.01	59.74	60.43	61.11	61.79	62.47	63.16	63.84	64.52	65.20	65.88	66.57	67.25
19.00	48.38	51.10	53.82	56.53	59.25	59.93	60.61	61.29	61.97	62.65	63.32	64.00	64.68	65.36	66.04	66.72
20.00	46.65	49.32	51.99	54.65	57.32	57.99	58.65	59.32	59.99	60.65	61.32	61.99	62.66	63.32	63.99	64.66
25.00	38.97	41.42	43.86	46.30	48.74	49.35	49.96	50.57	51.18	51.79	52.40	53.01	53.62	54.23	54.84	55.45
30.00	32.69	34.93	37.18	39.42	41.66	42.23	42.79	43.35	43.91	44.47	45.03	45.59	46.15	46.71	47.27	47.83

Description: This table shows the yield to maturity of a bond purchased at the price shown in the index.

Example: The yield to maturity of a 6.75 %, 4 year bond at a price of 95.00 is 8.24 %.

PRICE	0.00%	1.00%	2.00%	3.00%	4.00%	4.25%	4.50%	4.75%	5.00%	5.25%	5.50%	5.75%	6.00%	6.25%	6.50%	6.75%
100	0.00	1.00	2.00	3.00	4.00	4.25	4.50	4.75	5.00	5.25	5.50	5.75	6.00	6.25	6.50	6.75
99.75	.06	1.06	2.06	3.06	4.06	4.31	4.56	4.81	5.06	5.32	5.57	5.82	6.07	6.32	6.57	6.82
99.50	.12	1.12	2.13	3.13	4.13	4.38	4.63	4.88	5.13	5.39	5.64	5.89	6.14	6.39	6.64	6.89
99.25	.18	1.19	2.19	3.20	4.20	4.45	4.70	4.95	5.21	5.46	5.71	5.96	6.21	6.46	6.71	6.96
99.00	.25	1.25	2.26	3.26	4.27	4.52	4.77	5.02	5.28	5.53	5.78	6.03	6.28	6.53	6.78	7.04
98.75	.31	1.32	2.32	3.33	4.34	4.59	4.84	5.09	5.35	5.60	5.85	6.10	6.35	6.61	6.86	7.11
98.50	.37	1.38	2.39	3.40	4.41	4.66	4.91	5.16	5.42	5.67	5.92	6.17	6.43	6.68	6.93	7.18
98.25	.44	1.45	2.46	3.47	4.48	4.73	4.98	5.24	5.49	5.74	5.99	6.25	6.50	6.75	7.00	7.26
98.00	.50	1.51	2.52	3.54	4.55	4.80	5.05	5.31	5.56	5.81	6.07	6.32	6.57	6.82	7.08	7.33
97.75	.56	1.58	2.59	3.60	4.62	4.87	5.12	5.38	5.63	5.88	6.14	6.39	6.64	6.90	7.15	7.41
97.50	.63	1.64	2.66	3.67	4.69	4.94	5.20	5.45	5.70	5.96	6.21	6.46	6.72	6.97	7.23	7.48
97.25	.69	1.71	2.73	3.74	4.76	5.01	5.27	5.52	5.77	6.03	6.28	6.54	6.79	7.05	7.30	7.55
97.00	.76	1.78	2.79	3.81	4.83	5.08	5.34	5.59	5.85	6.10	6.36	6.61	6.87	7.12	7.37	7.63
96.75	.82	1.84	2.86	3.88	4.90	5.15	5.41	5.66	5.92	6.17	6.43	6.68	6.94	7.19	7.45	7.70
96.50	.89	1.91	2.93	3.95	4.97	5.23	5.48	5.74	5.99	6.25	6.50	6.76	7.01	7.27	7.52	7.78
96.25	.95	1.97	3.00	4.02	5.04	5.30	5.55	5.81	6.07	6.32	6.58	6.83	7.09	7.34	7.60	7.86
96.00	1.02	2.04	3.07	4.09	5.11	5.37	5.63	5.88	6.14	6.39	6.65	6.91	7.16	7.42	7.68	7.93
95.75	1.08	2.11	3.13	4.16	5.19	5.44	5.70	5.95	6.21	6.47	6.72	6.98	7.24	7.49	7.75	8.01
95.50	1.15	2.18	3.20	4.23	5.26	5.51	5.77	6.03	6.28	6.54	6.80	7.06	7.31	7.57	7.83	8.08
95.25	1.22	2.24	3.27	4.30	5.33	5.59	5.84	6.10	6.36	6.62	6.87	7.13	7.39	7.65	7.90	8.16
95.00	1.28	2.31	3.34	4.37	5.40	5.66	5.92	6.18	6.43	6.69	6.95	7.21	7.46	7.72	7.98	8.24
94.75	1.35	2.38	3.41	4.44	5.47	5.73	5.99	6.25	6.51	6.77	7.02	7.28	7.54	7.80	8.06	8.31
94.50	1.41	2.45	3.48	4.51	5.55	5.81	6.06	6.32	6.58	6.84	7.10	7.36	7.62	7.87	8.13	8.39
94.25	1.48	2.52	3.55	4.58	5.62	5.88	6.14	6.40	6.66	6.92	7.17	7.43	7.69	7.95	8.21	8.47
94.00	1.55	2.58	3.62	4.66	5.69	5.95	6.21	6.47	6.73	6.99	7.25	7.51	7.77	8.03	8.29	8.55
93.75	1.62	2.65	3.69	4.73	5.77	6.03	6.29	6.55	6.81	7.07	7.33	7.59	7.85	8.11	8.37	8.63
93.50	1.68	2.72	3.76	4.80	5.84	6.10	6.36	6.62	6.88	7.14	7.40	7.66	7.92	8.18	8.44	8.70
93.25	1.75	2.79	3.83	4.87	5.91	6.18	6.44	6.70	6.96	7.22	7.48	7.74	8.00	8.26	8.52	8.78
93.00	1.82	2.86	3.90	4.95	5.99	6.25	6.51	6.77	7.03	7.29	7.56	7.82	8.08	8.34	8.60	8.86
92.75	1.89	2.93	3.97	5.02	6.06	6.33	6.59	6.85	7.11	7.37	7.63	7.89	8.16	8.42	8.68	8.94
92.50	1.95	3.00	4.04	5.09	6.14	6.40	6.66	6.92	7.19	7.45	7.71	7.97	8.23	8.50	8.76	9.02
92.25	2.02	3.07	4.12	5.16	6.21	6.48	6.74	7.00	7.26	7.52	7.79	8.05	8.31	8.57	8.84	9.10
92.00	2.09	3.14	4.19	5.24	6.29	6.55	6.81	7.08	7.34	7.60	7.87	8.13	8.39	8.65	8.92	9.18
91.75	2.16	3.21	4.26	5.31	6.36	6.63	6.89	7.15	7.42	7.68	7.94	8.21	8.47	8.73	9.00	9.26
91	2.37	3.42	4.48	5.53	6.59	6.86	7.12	7.38	7.65	7.91	8.18	8.44	8.71	8.97	9.24	9.50
90	2.65	3.71	4.77	5.83	6.90	7.16	7.43	7.70	7.96	8.23	8.50	8.76	9.03	9.30	9.56	9.83
89	2.93	4.00	5.07	6.14	7.21	7.48	7.75	8.01	8.28	8.55	8.82	9.09	9.36	9.62	9.89	10.16
88	3.22	4.29	5.37	6.45	7.53	7.79	8.06	8.33	8.60	8.87	9.14	9.41	9.69	9.96	10.23	10.50
87	3.51	4.59	5.67	6.76	7.84	8.12	8.39	8.66	8.93	9.20	9.48	9.75	10.02	10.29	10.56	10.84
86	3.80	4.89	5.98	7.08	8.17	8.44	8.72	8.99	9.26	9.54	9.81	10.09	10.36	10.63	10.91	11.18
85	4.10	5.20	6.30	7.40	8.50	8.77	9.05	9.32	9.60	9.88	10.15	10.43	10.70	10.98	11.26	11.53
84	4.40	5.51	6.61	7.72	8.83	9.11	9.39	9.66	9.94	10.22	10.50	10.77	11.05	11.33	11.61	11.89
83	4.71	5.82	6.94	8.05	9.17	9.45	9.73	10.01	10.29	10.57	10.85	11.13	11.41	11.69	11.97	12.25
82	5.02	6.14	7.26	8.39	9.51	9.79	10.07	10.36	10.64	10.92	11.20	11.48	11.77	12.05	12.33	12.61
81	5.33	6.46	7.59	8.72	9.86	10.14	10.43	10.71	10.99	11.28	11.56	11.85	12.13	12.42	12.70	12.98
80	5.65	6.79	7.93	9.07	10.21	10.50	10.78	11.07	11.36	11.64	11.93	12.21	12.50	12.79	13.07	13.36
79	5.98	7.12	8.27	9.42	10.57	10.86	11.15	11.43	11.72	12.01	12.30	12.59	12.88	13.17	13.46	13.74
78	6.30	7.46	8.61	9.77	10.93	11.22	11.51	11.80	12.09	12.39	12.68	12.97	13.26	13.55	13.84	14.13
77	6.64	7.80	8.96	10.13	11.30	11.59	11.89	12.18	12.47	12.77	13.06	13.35	13.65	13.94	14.23	14.53
76	6.97	8.15	9.32	10.50	11.68	11.97	12.27	12.56	12.86	13.15	13.45	13.74	14.04	14.34	14.63	14.93
75	7.32	8.50	9.68	10.87	12.06	12.35	12.65	12.95	13.25	13.55	13.84	14.14	14.44	14.74	15.04	15.34
74	7.67	8.86	10.05	11.25	12.44	12.74	13.04	13.34	13.64	13.94	14.25	14.55	14.85	15.15	15.45	15.75
73	8.02	9.22	10.42	11.63	12.84	13.14	13.44	13.74	14.05	14.35	14.65	14.96	15.26	15.57	15.87	16.17
72	8.38	9.59	10.80	12.02	13.24	13.54	13.85	14.15	14.46	14.76	15.07	15.38	15.68	15.99	16.30	16.60
71	8.74	9.96	11.19	12.41	13.64	13.95	14.26	14.57	14.87	15.18	15.49	15.80	16.11	16.42	16.73	17.04
70	9.11	10.34	11.58	12.81	14.05	14.37	14.68	14.99	15.30	15.61	15.92	16.23	16.55	16.86	17.17	17.48
69	9.49	10.73	11.98	13.22	14.47	14.79	15.10	15.42	15.73	16.04	16.36	16.67	16.99	17.30	17.62	17.93
68	9.87	11.12	12.38	13.64	14.90	15.22	15.53	15.85	16.17	16.49	16.80	17.12	17.44	17.76	18.08	18.39
67	10.26	11.52	12.79	14.06	15.34	15.66	15.98	16.30	16.62	16.94	17.26	17.58	17.90	18.22	18.54	18.86
66	10.66	11.93	13.21	14.49	15.78	16.10	16.42	16.75	17.07	17.39	17.72	18.04	18.37	18.69	19.01	19.34
65	11.06	12.35	13.64	14.93	16.23	16.56	16.88	17.21	17.53	17.86	18.19	18.51	18.84	19.17	19.50	19.83
64	11.47	12.77	14.07	15.38	16.69	17.02	17.35	17.68	18.01	18.34	18.67	19.00	19.33	19.66	19.99	20.32
63	11.89	13.20	14.51	15.83	17.16	17.49	17.82	18.15	18.49	18.82	19.15	19.49	19.82	20.16	20.49	20.83
62	12.31	13.63	14.96	16.30	17.63	17.97	18.31	18.64	18.98	19.31	19.65	19.99	20.33	20.66	21.00	21.34
61	12.74	14.08	15.42	16.77	18.12	18.46	18.80	19.14	19.48	19.82	20.16	20.50	20.84	21.18	21.53	21.87
60	13.18	14.53	15.89	17.25	18.62	18.96	19.30	19.65	19.99	20.33	20.68	21.02	21.37	21.71	22.06	22.40
59	13.63	14.99	16.36	17.74	19.12	19.47	19.82	20.16	20.51	20.86	21.21	21.55	21.90	22.25	22.60	22.95
58	14.09	15.47	16.85	18.24	19.64	19.99	20.34	20.69	21.04	21.39	21.75	22.10	22.45	22.80	23.16	23.51

BOND PRICE

Description: This table shows the price to pay for a bond at the yield rate. The yield is to maturity.

Example: The price of a 10.75 %, 4 year bond to yield 8 % to maturity is $ 109.26.

COUPON RATE, %

YIELD	7.00%	7.25%	7.50%	7.75%	8.00%	8.25%	8.50%	8.75%	9.00%	9.25%	9.50%	9.75%	10.00%	10.25%	10.50%	10.75%
0.00	128.00	129.00	130.00	131.00	132.00	133.00	134.00	135.00	136.00	137.00	138.00	139.00	140.00	141.00	142.00	143.00
1.00	123.47	124.45	125.42	126.40	127.38	128.36	129.34	130.31	131.29	132.27	133.25	134.23	135.20	136.18	137.16	138.14
2.00	119.13	120.09	121.04	122.00	122.96	123.91	124.87	125.82	126.78	127.74	128.69	129.65	130.61	131.56	132.52	133.48
3.00	114.97	115.91	116.84	117.78	118.71	119.65	120.59	121.52	122.46	123.39	124.33	125.26	126.20	127.14	128.07	129.01
4.00	110.99	111.90	112.82	113.74	114.65	115.57	116.48	117.40	118.31	119.23	120.15	121.06	121.98	122.89	123.81	124.72
4.25	110.02	110.93	111.84	112.75	113.66	114.57	115.48	116.39	117.30	118.22	119.13	120.04	120.95	121.86	122.77	123.68
4.50	109.06	109.96	110.87	111.78	112.68	113.59	114.49	115.40	116.31	117.21	118.12	119.02	119.93	120.84	121.74	122.65
4.75	108.11	109.01	109.91	110.81	111.71	112.61	113.52	114.42	115.32	116.22	117.12	118.02	118.92	119.82	120.72	121.63
5.00	107.17	108.07	108.96	109.86	110.76	111.65	112.55	113.44	114.34	115.24	116.13	117.03	117.93	118.82	119.72	120.61
5.25	106.24	107.13	108.02	108.92	109.81	110.70	111.59	112.48	113.37	114.26	115.16	116.05	116.94	117.83	118.72	119.61
5.50	105.32	106.21	107.09	107.98	108.87	109.75	110.64	111.53	112.42	113.30	114.19	115.08	115.96	116.85	117.74	118.62
5.75	104.41	105.29	106.17	107.06	107.94	108.82	109.70	110.59	111.47	112.35	113.23	114.11	115.00	115.88	116.76	117.64
6.00	103.51	104.39	105.26	106.14	107.02	107.90	108.77	109.65	110.53	111.41	112.28	113.16	114.04	114.92	115.79	116.67
6.25	102.62	103.49	104.36	105.24	106.11	106.98	107.86	108.73	109.60	110.47	111.35	112.22	113.09	113.97	114.84	115.71
6.50	101.74	102.60	103.47	104.34	105.21	106.08	106.95	107.81	108.68	109.55	110.42	111.29	112.16	113.02	113.89	114.76
6.75	100.86	101.73	102.59	103.45	104.32	105.18	106.05	106.91	107.77	108.64	109.50	110.36	111.23	112.09	112.96	113.82
7.00	100.00	100.86	101.72	102.58	103.44	104.30	105.16	106.01	106.87	107.73	108.59	109.45	110.31	111.17	112.03	112.89
7.25	99.15	100.00	100.85	101.71	102.56	103.42	104.27	105.13	105.98	106.84	107.69	108.55	109.40	110.26	111.11	111.97
7.50	98.30	99.15	100.00	100.85	101.70	102.55	103.40	104.25	105.10	105.95	106.80	107.65	108.50	109.35	110.20	111.05
7.75	97.46	98.31	99.15	100.00	100.85	101.69	102.54	103.38	104.23	105.08	105.92	106.77	107.61	108.46	109.31	110.15
8.00	96.63	97.48	98.32	99.16	100.00	100.84	101.68	102.52	103.37	104.21	105.05	105.89	106.73	107.57	108.42	109.26
8.25	95.81	96.65	97.49	98.33	99.16	100.00	100.84	101.67	102.51	103.35	104.19	105.02	105.86	106.70	107.54	108.37
8.50	95.00	95.84	96.67	97.50	98.33	99.17	100.00	100.83	101.67	102.50	103.33	104.16	105.00	105.83	106.66	107.50
8.75	94.20	95.03	95.86	96.69	97.51	98.34	99.17	100.00	100.83	101.66	102.49	103.31	104.14	104.97	105.80	106.63
9.00	93.40	94.23	95.05	95.88	96.70	97.53	98.35	99.18	100.00	100.82	101.65	102.47	103.30	104.12	104.95	105.77
9.25	92.62	93.44	94.26	95.08	95.90	96.72	97.54	98.36	99.18	100.00	100.82	101.64	102.46	103.28	104.10	104.92
9.50	91.84	92.65	93.47	94.29	95.10	95.92	96.74	97.55	98.37	99.18	100.00	100.82	101.63	102.45	103.26	104.08
9.75	91.07	91.88	92.69	93.50	94.32	95.13	95.94	96.75	97.56	98.38	99.18	100.00	100.81	101.63	102.45	103.25
10.00	90.31	91.11	91.92	92.73	93.54	94.34	95.15	95.96	96.77	97.58	98.38	99.19	100.00	100.81	101.62	102.44
10.25	89.55	90.35	91.16	91.96	92.77	93.57	94.37	95.18	95.98	96.78	97.59	98.39	99.20	100.00	100.81	101.62
10.50	88.80	89.60	90.40	91.20	92.00	92.80	93.60	94.40	95.20	96.00	96.80	97.60	98.40	99.20	100.00	100.80
10.75	88.06	88.86	89.65	90.45	91.25	92.04	92.84	93.63	94.43	95.23	96.02	96.82	97.61	98.41	99.20	100.00
11.00	87.33	88.12	88.91	89.71	90.50	91.29	92.08	92.87	93.67	94.46	95.25	96.04	96.83	97.62	98.42	99.21
11.25	86.61	87.39	88.18	88.97	89.76	90.55	91.33	92.12	92.91	93.70	94.48	95.27	96.06	96.85	97.64	98.42
11.50	85.89	86.67	87.46	88.24	89.02	89.81	90.59	91.38	92.16	92.94	93.73	94.51	95.30	96.08	96.86	97.65
11.75	85.18	85.96	86.74	87.52	88.30	89.08	89.86	90.64	91.42	92.20	92.98	93.76	94.54	95.32	96.10	96.88
12.00	84.48	85.25	86.03	86.80	87.58	88.36	89.13	89.91	90.69	91.46	92.24	93.01	93.79	94.57	95.34	96.12
12.25	83.78	84.55	85.32	86.10	86.87	87.64	88.41	89.19	89.96	90.73	91.50	92.28	93.05	93.82	94.59	95.37
12.50	83.09	83.86	84.63	85.40	86.17	86.93	87.70	88.47	89.24	90.01	90.78	91.55	92.31	93.08	93.85	94.62
12.75	82.41	83.17	83.94	84.70	85.47	86.23	87.00	87.76	88.53	89.29	90.06	90.82	91.59	92.35	93.12	93.88
13.00	81.73	82.49	83.26	84.02	84.78	85.54	86.30	87.06	87.82	88.58	89.34	90.11	90.87	91.63	92.39	93.15
13.25	81.07	81.82	82.58	83.34	84.09	84.85	85.61	86.37	87.12	87.88	88.64	89.40	90.15	90.91	91.67	92.43
13.50	80.40	81.16	81.91	82.66	83.42	84.17	84.93	85.68	86.43	87.19	87.94	88.69	89.45	90.20	90.96	91.71
13.75	79.75	80.50	81.25	82.00	82.75	83.50	84.25	85.00	85.75	86.50	87.25	88.00	88.75	89.50	90.25	91.00
14.00	79.10	79.85	80.59	81.34	82.09	82.83	83.58	84.33	85.07	85.82	86.56	87.31	88.06	88.80	89.55	90.30
14.25	78.46	79.20	79.94	80.69	81.43	82.17	82.92	83.66	84.40	85.14	85.89	86.63	87.37	88.12	88.86	89.60
14.50	77.82	78.56	79.30	80.04	80.78	81.52	82.26	83.00	83.74	84.48	85.22	85.95	86.69	87.43	88.17	88.91
14.75	77.19	77.93	78.67	79.40	80.14	80.87	81.61	82.34	83.08	83.81	84.55	85.29	86.02	86.76	87.49	88.23
15.00	76.57	77.30	78.04	78.77	79.50	80.23	80.96	81.70	82.43	83.16	83.89	84.62	85.36	86.09	86.82	87.55
15.25	75.95	76.68	77.41	78.14	78.87	79.60	80.33	81.05	81.78	82.51	83.24	83.97	84.70	85.43	86.16	86.88
15.50	75.34	76.07	76.79	77.52	78.24	78.97	79.69	80.42	81.14	81.87	82.60	83.32	84.05	84.77	85.50	86.22
15.75	74.74	75.46	76.18	76.90	77.63	78.35	79.07	79.79	80.51	81.23	81.96	82.68	83.40	84.12	84.84	85.57
16.00	74.14	74.86	75.58	76.30	77.01	77.73	78.45	79.17	79.89	80.61	81.32	82.04	82.76	83.48	84.20	84.92
16.25	73.55	74.26	74.98	75.69	76.41	77.12	77.84	78.55	79.27	79.98	80.70	81.41	82.13	82.84	83.56	84.27
16.50	72.96	73.67	74.38	75.10	75.81	76.52	77.23	77.94	78.65	79.36	80.08	80.79	81.50	82.21	82.92	83.63
16.75	72.38	73.09	73.80	74.50	75.21	75.92	76.63	77.34	78.05	78.75	79.46	80.17	80.88	81.59	82.29	83.00
17.00	71.80	72.51	73.21	73.92	74.62	75.33	76.03	76.74	77.44	78.15	78.85	79.56	80.26	80.97	81.67	82.38
17.25	71.23	71.94	72.64	73.34	74.04	74.74	75.44	76.15	76.85	77.55	78.25	78.95	79.65	80.36	81.06	81.76
17.50	70.67	71.37	72.07	72.77	73.46	74.16	74.86	75.56	76.26	76.96	77.65	78.35	79.05	79.75	80.45	81.15
17.75	70.11	70.81	71.50	72.20	72.89	73.59	74.28	74.98	75.67	76.37	77.06	77.76	78.45	79.15	79.84	80.54
18.00	69.56	70.25	70.94	71.63	72.33	73.02	73.71	74.40	75.09	75.79	76.48	77.17	77.86	78.55	79.24	79.94
18.25	69.01	69.70	70.39	71.08	71.77	72.45	73.14	73.83	74.52	75.21	75.90	76.59	77.27	77.96	78.65	79.34
18.50	68.47	69.15	69.84	70.52	71.21	71.90	72.58	73.27	73.95	74.64	75.32	76.01	76.69	77.38	78.06	78.75
18.75	67.93	68.61	69.30	69.98	70.66	71.34	72.03	72.71	73.39	74.07	74.75	75.44	76.12	76.80	77.48	78.17
19.00	67.40	68.08	68.76	69.44	70.12	70.80	71.47	72.15	72.83	73.51	74.19	74.87	75.55	76.23	76.91	77.59
20.00	65.32	65.99	66.66	67.32	67.99	68.66	69.32	69.99	70.66	71.32	71.99	72.66	73.33	73.99	74.66	75.33
25.00	56.06	56.67	57.28	57.89	58.50	59.11	59.72	60.33	60.94	61.55	62.16	62.77	63.38	63.99	64.61	65.22
30.00	48.40	48.96	49.52	50.08	50.64	51.20	51.76	52.32	52.88	53.44	54.00	54.57	55.13	55.69	56.25	56.81

Description: This table shows the yield to maturity of a bond purchased at the price shown in the index.

Example: The yield to maturity of a 10.75 %, 4 year bond at a price of 100.00 is 10.75 %.

COUPON RATE, %

PRICE	7.00%	7.25%	7.50%	7.75%	8.00%	8.25%	8.50%	8.75%	9.00%	9.25%	9.50%	9.75%	10.00%	10.25%	10.50%	10.75%
105	5.58	5.83	6.07	6.31	6.55	6.80	7.04	7.28	7.52	7.77	8.01	8.25	8.49	8.74	8.98	9.22
104.75	5.65	5.89	6.14	6.38	6.62	6.87	7.11	7.35	7.60	7.84	8.08	8.32	8.57	8.81	9.05	9.30
104.50	5.72	5.96	6.21	6.45	6.69	6.94	7.18	7.42	7.67	7.91	8.15	8.40	8.64	8.88	9.13	9.37
104.25	5.79	6.03	6.28	6.52	6.76	7.01	7.25	7.50	7.74	7.98	8.23	8.47	8.71	8.96	9.20	9.44
104.00	5.86	6.10	6.35	6.59	6.84	7.08	7.32	7.57	7.81	8.06	8.30	8.54	8.79	9.03	9.28	9.52
103.75	5.93	6.17	6.42	6.66	6.91	7.15	7.39	7.64	7.88	8.13	8.37	8.62	8.86	9.11	9.35	9.59
103.50	6.00	6.24	6.49	6.73	6.98	7.22	7.47	7.71	7.96	8.20	8.45	8.69	8.94	9.18	9.42	9.67
103.25	6.07	6.31	6.56	6.80	7.05	7.29	7.54	7.78	8.03	8.27	8.52	8.76	9.01	9.25	9.50	9.74
103.00	6.14	6.38	6.63	6.87	7.12	7.37	7.61	7.86	8.10	8.35	8.59	8.84	9.08	9.33	9.57	9.82
102.75	6.21	6.45	6.70	6.95	7.19	7.44	7.68	7.93	8.18	8.42	8.67	8.91	9.16	9.40	9.65	9.90
102.50	6.28	6.52	6.77	7.02	7.26	7.51	7.76	8.00	8.25	8.49	8.74	8.99	9.23	9.48	9.73	9.97
102.25	6.35	6.60	6.84	7.09	7.34	7.58	7.83	8.08	8.32	8.57	8.82	9.06	9.31	9.55	9.80	10.05
102.00	6.42	6.67	6.91	7.16	7.41	7.66	7.90	8.15	8.40	8.64	8.89	9.14	9.38	9.63	9.88	10.12
101.75	6.49	6.74	6.99	7.23	7.48	7.73	7.98	8.22	8.47	8.72	8.96	9.21	9.46	9.71	9.95	10.20
101.50	6.56	6.81	7.06	7.31	7.55	7.80	8.05	8.30	8.54	8.79	9.04	9.29	9.54	9.78	10.03	10.28
101.25	6.63	6.88	7.13	7.38	7.63	7.87	8.12	8.37	8.62	8.87	9.12	9.36	9.61	9.86	10.11	10.36
101.00	6.71	6.95	7.20	7.45	7.70	7.95	8.20	8.45	8.69	8.94	9.19	9.44	9.69	9.94	10.18	10.43
100.75	6.78	7.03	7.28	7.52	7.77	8.02	8.27	8.52	8.77	9.02	9.27	9.52	9.76	10.01	10.26	10.51
100.50	6.85	7.10	7.35	7.60	7.85	8.10	8.35	8.59	8.84	9.09	9.34	9.59	9.84	10.09	10.34	10.59
100.25	6.92	7.17	7.42	7.67	7.92	8.17	8.42	8.67	8.92	9.17	9.42	9.67	9.92	10.17	10.42	10.67
100.00	7.00	7.25	7.50	7.75	8.00	8.25	8.50	8.75	9.00	9.25	9.50	9.75	10.00	10.25	10.50	10.75
99.75	7.07	7.32	7.57	7.82	8.07	8.32	8.57	8.82	9.07	9.32	9.57	9.82	10.07	10.32	10.57	10.82
99.50	7.14	7.39	7.64	7.89	8.14	8.39	8.65	8.90	9.15	9.40	9.65	9.90	10.15	10.40	10.65	10.90
99.25	7.21	7.47	7.72	7.97	8.22	8.47	8.72	8.97	9.22	9.47	9.73	9.98	10.23	10.48	10.73	10.98
99.00	7.29	7.54	7.79	8.04	8.29	8.55	8.80	9.05	9.30	9.55	9.80	10.05	10.31	10.56	10.81	11.06
98.75	7.36	7.61	7.87	8.12	8.37	8.62	8.87	9.13	9.38	9.63	9.88	10.13	10.38	10.64	10.89	11.14
98.50	7.44	7.69	7.94	8.19	8.44	8.70	8.95	9.20	9.45	9.71	9.96	10.21	10.46	10.72	10.97	11.22
98.25	7.51	7.76	8.02	8.27	8.52	8.77	9.03	9.28	9.53	9.78	10.04	10.29	10.54	10.80	11.05	11.30
98.00	7.58	7.84	8.09	8.34	8.60	8.85	9.10	9.36	9.61	9.86	10.12	10.37	10.62	10.87	11.13	11.38
97.75	7.66	7.91	8.17	8.42	8.67	8.93	9.18	9.43	9.69	9.94	10.19	10.45	10.70	10.95	11.21	11.46
97.50	7.73	7.99	8.24	8.50	8.75	9.00	9.26	9.51	9.77	10.02	10.27	10.53	10.78	11.03	11.29	11.54
97.25	7.81	8.06	8.32	8.57	8.83	9.08	9.33	9.59	9.84	10.10	10.35	10.61	10.86	11.12	11.37	11.62
97.00	7.88	8.14	8.39	8.65	8.90	9.16	9.41	9.67	9.92	10.18	10.43	10.69	10.94	11.20	11.45	11.71
96.75	7.96	8.21	8.47	8.73	8.98	9.24	9.49	9.75	10.00	10.26	10.51	10.77	11.02	11.28	11.53	11.79
96.50	8.04	8.29	8.55	8.80	9.06	9.31	9.57	9.82	10.08	10.34	10.59	10.85	11.10	11.36	11.61	11.87
96.25	8.11	8.37	8.62	8.88	9.14	9.39	9.65	9.90	10.16	10.42	10.67	10.93	11.18	11.44	11.70	11.95
96.00	8.19	8.44	8.70	8.96	9.21	9.47	9.73	9.98	10.24	10.50	10.75	11.01	11.26	11.52	11.78	12.03
95.75	8.26	8.52	8.78	9.03	9.29	9.55	9.81	10.06	10.32	10.58	10.83	11.09	11.35	11.60	11.86	12.12
95.50	8.34	8.60	8.86	9.11	9.37	9.63	9.88	10.14	10.40	10.66	10.91	11.17	11.43	11.69	11.94	12.20
95.25	8.42	8.68	8.93	9.19	9.45	9.71	9.96	10.22	10.48	10.74	10.99	11.25	11.51	11.77	12.03	12.28
95.00	8.50	8.75	9.01	9.27	9.53	9.79	10.04	10.30	10.56	10.82	11.08	11.33	11.59	11.85	12.11	12.37
94.75	8.57	8.83	9.09	9.35	9.61	9.87	10.12	10.38	10.64	10.90	11.16	11.42	11.68	11.93	12.19	12.45
94	8.81	9.07	9.33	9.59	9.85	10.11	10.37	10.63	10.89	11.15	11.40	11.66	11.92	12.18	12.44	12.70
93	9.12	9.38	9.65	9.91	10.17	10.43	10.69	10.95	11.21	11.48	11.74	12.00	12.26	12.52	12.78	13.05
92	9.44	9.71	9.97	10.23	10.50	10.76	11.02	11.29	11.55	11.81	12.08	12.34	12.60	12.87	13.13	13.39
91	9.77	10.03	10.30	10.56	10.83	11.09	11.36	11.62	11.89	12.15	12.42	12.68	12.95	13.21	13.48	13.74
90	10.10	10.36	10.63	10.90	11.16	11.43	11.70	11.96	12.23	12.50	12.77	13.03	13.30	13.57	13.83	14.10
89	10.43	10.70	10.97	11.23	11.50	11.77	12.04	12.31	12.58	12.85	13.12	13.39	13.66	13.92	14.19	14.46
88	10.77	11.04	11.31	11.58	11.85	12.12	12.39	12.66	12.93	13.20	13.47	13.74	14.02	14.29	14.56	14.83
87	11.11	11.38	11.65	11.93	12.20	12.47	12.74	13.02	13.29	13.56	13.84	14.11	14.38	14.66	14.93	15.20
86	11.46	11.73	12.00	12.28	12.55	12.83	13.10	13.38	13.65	13.93	14.20	14.48	14.75	15.03	15.30	15.58
85	11.81	12.08	12.36	12.64	12.91	13.19	13.47	13.74	14.02	14.30	14.58	14.85	15.13	15.41	15.68	15.96
84	12.17	12.44	12.72	13.00	13.28	13.56	13.84	14.12	14.40	14.67	14.95	15.23	15.51	15.79	16.07	16.35
83	12.53	12.81	13.09	13.37	13.65	13.93	14.21	14.49	14.78	15.06	15.34	15.62	15.90	16.18	16.46	16.75
82	12.90	13.18	13.46	13.74	14.03	14.31	14.59	14.88	15.16	15.44	15.73	16.01	16.30	16.58	16.86	17.15
81	13.27	13.55	13.84	14.12	14.41	14.70	14.98	15.27	15.55	15.84	16.12	16.41	16.70	16.98	17.27	17.55
80	13.65	13.94	14.22	14.51	14.80	15.09	15.37	15.66	15.95	16.24	16.53	16.81	17.10	17.39	17.68	17.97
79	14.03	14.32	14.61	14.90	15.19	15.48	15.77	16.06	16.35	16.64	16.93	17.23	17.52	17.81	18.10	18.39
78	14.43	14.72	15.01	15.30	15.59	15.89	16.18	16.47	16.76	17.06	17.35	17.64	17.94	18.23	18.52	18.82
77	14.82	15.12	15.41	15.71	16.00	16.30	16.59	16.89	17.18	17.48	17.77	18.07	18.36	18.66	18.95	19.25
76	15.23	15.52	15.82	16.12	16.41	16.71	17.01	17.31	17.60	17.90	18.20	18.50	18.80	19.10	19.39	19.69
75	15.64	15.94	16.24	16.54	16.83	17.13	17.43	17.74	18.04	18.34	18.64	18.94	19.24	19.54	19.84	20.14
74	16.05	16.36	16.66	16.96	17.26	17.57	17.87	18.17	18.47	18.78	19.08	19.38	19.69	19.99	20.30	20.60
73	16.48	16.78	17.09	17.39	17.70	18.00	18.31	18.61	18.92	19.23	19.53	19.84	20.14	20.45	20.76	21.06
72	16.91	17.22	17.52	17.83	18.14	18.45	18.76	19.06	19.37	19.68	19.99	20.30	20.61	20.92	21.23	21.54
71	17.35	17.66	17.97	18.28	18.59	18.90	19.21	19.52	19.84	20.15	20.46	20.77	21.08	21.40	21.71	22.02
70	17.80	18.11	18.42	18.74	19.05	19.36	19.68	19.99	20.31	20.62	20.93	21.25	21.57	21.88	22.20	22.51
69	18.25	18.57	18.88	19.20	19.52	19.83	20.15	20.47	20.78	21.10	21.42	21.74	22.06	22.37	22.69	23.01

Description: This table shows the price to pay for a bond at the yield rate. The yield is to maturity.

Example: The price of a 15.00 %, 4 year bond to yield 8 % to maturity is $ 123.56.

COUPON RATE, %

YIELD	11.00%	11.25%	11.50%	11.75%	12.00%	12.25%	12.50%	12.75%	13.00%	13.25%	13.50%	13.75%	14.00%	14.25%	14.50%	15.00%
0.00	144.00	145.00	146.00	147.00	148.00	149.00	150.00	151.00	152.00	153.00	154.00	155.00	156.00	157.00	158.00	160.00
1.00	139.11	140.09	141.07	142.05	143.03	144.00	144.98	145.96	146.94	147.92	148.89	149.87	150.85	151.83	152.80	154.76
2.00	134.43	135.39	136.35	137.30	138.26	139.21	140.17	141.13	142.08	143.04	144.00	144.95	145.91	146.87	147.82	149.74
3.00	129.94	130.88	131.82	132.75	133.69	134.62	135.56	136.49	137.43	138.37	139.30	140.24	141.17	142.11	143.04	144.92
4.00	125.64	126.55	127.47	128.39	129.30	130.22	131.13	132.05	132.96	133.88	134.80	135.71	136.63	137.54	138.46	140.29
4.25	124.59	125.50	126.41	127.32	128.23	129.14	130.06	130.97	131.88	132.79	133.70	134.61	135.52	136.43	137.34	139.16
4.50	123.55	124.46	125.37	126.27	127.18	128.08	128.99	129.89	130.80	131.71	132.61	133.52	134.42	135.33	136.24	138.05
4.75	122.53	123.43	124.33	125.23	126.13	127.03	127.93	128.83	129.74	130.64	131.54	132.44	133.34	134.24	135.14	136.94
5.00	121.51	122.41	123.30	124.20	125.10	125.99	126.89	127.78	128.68	129.58	130.47	131.37	132.27	133.16	134.06	135.85
5.25	120.50	121.40	122.29	123.18	124.07	124.96	125.85	126.75	127.64	128.53	129.42	130.31	131.20	132.09	132.99	134.77
5.50	119.51	120.40	121.28	122.17	123.06	123.94	124.83	125.72	126.60	127.49	128.38	129.26	130.15	131.04	131.92	133.70
5.75	118.52	119.41	120.29	121.17	122.05	122.93	123.82	124.70	125.58	126.46	127.35	128.23	129.11	129.99	130.87	132.64
6.00	117.55	118.43	119.30	120.18	121.06	121.94	122.81	123.69	124.57	125.45	126.32	127.20	128.08	128.96	129.83	131.59
6.25	116.58	117.46	118.33	119.20	120.08	120.95	121.82	122.69	123.57	124.44	125.31	126.19	127.06	127.93	128.80	130.55
6.50	115.63	116.50	117.37	118.23	119.10	119.97	120.84	121.71	122.58	123.44	124.31	125.18	126.05	126.92	127.78	129.52
6.75	114.68	115.55	116.41	117.27	118.14	119.00	119.87	120.73	121.59	122.46	123.32	124.18	125.05	125.91	126.78	128.50
7.00	113.75	114.61	115.47	116.33	117.18	118.04	118.90	119.76	120.62	121.48	122.34	123.20	124.06	124.92	125.78	127.50
7.25	112.82	113.68	114.53	115.39	116.24	117.10	117.95	118.81	119.66	120.51	121.37	122.22	123.08	123.93	124.79	126.50
7.50	111.90	112.76	113.61	114.46	115.31	116.16	117.01	117.86	118.71	119.56	120.41	121.26	122.11	122.96	123.81	125.51
7.75	111.00	111.84	112.69	113.54	114.38	115.23	116.07	116.92	117.77	118.61	119.46	120.30	121.15	121.99	122.84	124.53
8.00	110.10	110.94	111.78	112.62	113.47	114.31	115.15	115.99	116.83	117.67	118.52	119.36	120.20	121.04	121.88	123.56
8.25	109.21	110.05	110.88	111.72	112.56	113.40	114.23	115.07	115.91	116.75	117.58	118.42	119.26	120.09	120.93	122.61
8.50	108.33	109.16	110.00	110.83	111.66	112.49	113.33	114.16	114.99	115.83	116.66	117.49	118.33	119.16	119.99	121.66
8.75	107.46	108.29	109.12	109.94	110.77	111.60	112.43	113.26	114.09	114.92	115.75	116.57	117.40	118.23	119.06	120.72
9.00	106.60	107.42	108.24	109.07	109.89	110.72	111.54	112.37	113.19	114.02	114.84	115.67	116.49	117.31	118.14	119.79
9.25	105.74	106.56	107.38	108.20	109.02	109.84	110.66	111.48	112.30	113.12	113.94	114.77	115.59	116.41	117.23	118.87
9.50	104.90	105.71	106.53	107.35	108.16	108.98	109.79	110.61	111.43	112.24	113.06	113.87	114.69	115.51	116.32	117.95
9.75	104.06	104.87	105.68	106.50	107.31	108.12	108.93	109.74	110.56	111.37	112.18	112.99	113.80	114.62	115.43	117.05
10.00	103.23	104.04	104.85	105.66	106.46	107.27	108.08	108.89	109.69	110.50	111.31	112.12	112.93	113.73	114.54	116.16
10.25	102.41	103.22	104.02	104.82	105.63	106.43	107.23	108.04	108.84	109.65	110.45	111.25	112.06	112.86	113.67	115.27
10.50	101.60	102.40	103.20	104.00	104.80	105.60	106.40	107.20	108.00	108.80	109.60	110.40	111.20	112.00	112.80	114.40
10.75	100.80	101.59	102.39	103.18	103.98	104.77	105.57	106.37	107.16	107.96	108.75	109.55	110.35	111.14	111.94	113.53
11.00	100.00	100.79	101.58	102.38	103.17	103.96	104.75	105.54	106.33	107.13	107.92	108.71	109.50	110.29	111.09	112.67
11.25	99.21	100.00	100.79	101.58	102.36	103.15	103.94	104.73	105.52	106.30	107.09	107.88	108.67	109.45	110.24	111.82
11.50	98.43	99.22	100.00	100.78	101.57	102.35	103.14	103.92	104.70	105.49	106.27	107.06	107.84	108.62	109.41	110.98
11.75	97.66	98.44	99.22	100.00	100.78	101.56	102.34	103.12	103.90	104.68	105.46	106.24	107.02	107.80	108.58	110.14
12.00	96.90	97.67	98.45	99.22	100.00	100.78	101.55	102.33	103.10	103.88	104.66	105.43	106.21	106.99	107.76	109.31
12.25	96.14	96.91	97.68	98.46	99.23	100.00	100.77	101.54	102.32	103.09	103.86	104.63	105.41	106.18	106.95	108.50
12.50	95.39	96.16	96.93	97.69	98.46	99.23	100.00	100.77	101.54	102.31	103.07	103.84	104.61	105.38	106.15	107.69
12.75	94.65	95.41	96.18	96.94	97.71	98.47	99.24	100.00	100.76	101.53	102.29	103.06	103.82	104.59	105.35	106.88
13.00	93.91	94.67	95.43	96.19	96.96	97.72	98.48	99.24	100.00	100.76	101.52	102.28	103.04	103.81	104.57	106.09
13.25	93.18	93.94	94.70	95.46	96.21	96.97	97.73	98.49	99.24	100.00	100.76	101.51	102.27	103.03	103.79	105.30
13.50	92.46	93.22	93.97	94.72	95.48	96.23	96.99	97.74	98.49	99.25	100.00	100.75	101.51	102.26	103.01	104.52
13.75	91.75	92.50	93.25	94.00	94.75	95.50	96.25	97.00	97.75	98.50	99.25	100.00	100.75	101.50	102.25	103.75
14.00	91.04	91.79	92.54	93.28	94.03	94.78	95.52	96.27	97.01	97.76	98.51	99.25	100.00	100.75	101.49	102.99
14.25	90.34	91.09	91.83	92.57	93.31	94.06	94.80	95.54	96.29	97.03	97.77	98.51	99.26	100.00	100.74	102.23
14.50	89.65	90.39	91.13	91.87	92.61	93.35	94.09	94.83	95.56	96.30	97.04	97.78	98.52	99.26	100.00	101.48
14.75	88.96	89.70	90.44	91.17	91.91	92.64	93.38	94.11	94.85	95.59	96.32	97.06	97.79	98.53	99.26	100.74
15.00	88.29	89.02	89.75	90.48	91.21	91.95	92.68	93.41	94.14	94.87	95.61	96.34	97.07	97.80	98.54	100.00
15.25	87.61	88.34	89.07	89.80	90.53	91.26	91.98	92.71	93.44	94.17	94.90	95.63	96.36	97.09	97.81	99.27
15.50	86.95	87.67	88.40	89.12	89.85	90.57	91.30	92.02	92.75	93.47	94.20	94.92	95.65	96.37	97.10	98.55
15.75	86.29	87.01	87.73	88.45	89.17	89.90	90.62	91.34	92.06	92.78	93.50	94.23	94.95	95.67	96.39	97.83
16.00	85.63	86.35	87.07	87.79	88.51	89.23	89.94	90.66	91.38	92.10	92.82	93.54	94.25	94.97	95.69	97.13
16.25	84.99	85.70	86.42	87.13	87.85	88.56	89.28	89.99	90.71	91.42	92.14	92.85	93.57	94.28	95.00	96.43
16.50	84.35	85.06	85.77	86.48	87.19	87.90	88.61	89.33	90.04	90.75	91.46	92.17	92.88	93.60	94.31	95.73
16.75	83.71	84.42	85.13	85.84	86.54	87.25	87.96	88.67	89.38	90.08	90.79	91.50	92.21	92.92	93.63	95.04
17.00	83.08	83.79	84.49	85.20	85.90	86.61	87.31	88.02	88.72	89.43	90.13	90.84	91.54	92.25	92.95	94.36
17.25	82.46	83.16	83.86	84.56	85.27	85.97	86.67	87.37	88.07	88.77	89.48	90.18	90.88	91.58	92.28	93.69
17.50	81.84	82.54	83.24	83.94	84.64	85.34	86.03	86.73	87.43	88.13	88.83	89.53	90.22	90.92	91.62	93.02
17.75	81.23	81.93	82.62	83.32	84.01	84.71	85.40	86.10	86.79	87.49	88.18	88.88	89.57	90.27	90.96	92.35
18.00	80.63	81.32	82.01	82.70	83.40	84.09	84.78	85.47	86.16	86.85	87.55	88.24	88.93	89.62	90.31	91.70
18.25	80.03	80.72	81.41	82.10	82.78	83.47	84.16	84.85	85.54	86.23	86.92	87.60	88.29	88.98	89.67	91.05
18.50	79.44	80.12	80.81	81.49	82.18	82.86	83.55	84.23	84.92	85.61	86.29	86.98	87.66	88.35	89.03	90.40
18.75	78.85	79.53	80.21	80.90	81.58	82.26	82.94	83.62	84.31	84.99	85.67	86.35	87.04	87.72	88.40	89.77
19.00	78.27	78.95	79.62	80.30	80.98	81.66	82.34	83.02	83.70	84.38	85.06	85.74	86.42	87.10	87.77	89.13
20.00	75.99	76.66	77.33	77.99	78.66	79.33	79.99	80.66	81.33	81.99	82.66	83.33	84.00	84.66	85.33	86.66
25.00	65.83	66.44	67.05	67.66	68.27	68.88	69.49	70.10	70.71	71.32	71.93	72.54	73.15	73.76	74.37	75.59
30.00	57.37	57.93	58.49	59.05	59.61	60.18	60.74	61.30	61.86	62.42	62.98	63.54	64.10	64.66	65.22	66.35

Description: This table shows the yield to maturity of a bond purchased at the price shown in the index.

Example: The yield to maturity of a 15.00 %, 4 year bond at a price of 102.00 is 14.32 %.

PRICE	11.00%	11.25%	11.50%	11.75%	12.00%	12.25%	12.50%	12.75%	13.00%	13.25%	13.50%	13.75%	14.00%	14.25%	14.50%	15.00%
110	8.02	8.26	8.49	8.73	8.96	9.20	9.44	9.67	9.91	10.14	10.38	10.61	10.85	11.08	11.32	11.79
109	8.30	8.54	8.78	9.01	9.25	9.49	9.73	9.96	10.20	10.44	10.67	10.91	11.14	11.38	11.62	12.09
108	8.59	8.83	9.07	9.30	9.54	9.78	10.02	10.26	10.49	10.73	10.97	11.21	11.45	11.68	11.92	12.40
107	8.88	9.12	9.36	9.60	9.84	10.08	10.31	10.55	10.79	11.03	11.27	11.51	11.75	11.99	12.23	12.71
106	9.17	9.41	9.65	9.89	10.13	10.37	10.62	10.86	11.10	11.34	11.58	11.82	12.06	12.30	12.54	13.02
105.75	9.24	9.48	9.73	9.97	10.21	10.45	10.69	10.93	11.17	11.41	11.66	11.90	12.14	12.38	12.62	13.10
105.50	9.32	9.56	9.80	10.04	10.28	10.52	10.77	11.01	11.25	11.49	11.73	11.97	12.22	12.46	12.70	13.18
105.25	9.39	9.63	9.87	10.12	10.36	10.60	10.84	11.08	11.33	11.57	11.81	12.05	12.29	12.54	12.78	13.26
105.00	9.46	9.71	9.95	10.19	10.43	10.68	10.92	11.16	11.40	11.65	11.89	12.13	12.37	12.61	12.86	13.34
104.75	9.54	9.78	10.02	10.27	10.51	10.75	11.00	11.24	11.48	11.72	11.97	12.21	12.45	12.69	12.94	13.42
104.50	9.61	9.86	10.10	10.34	10.59	10.83	11.07	11.32	11.56	11.80	12.04	12.29	12.53	12.77	13.02	13.50
104.25	9.69	9.93	10.18	10.42	10.66	10.91	11.15	11.39	11.64	11.88	12.12	12.37	12.61	12.85	13.10	13.58
104.00	9.76	10.01	10.25	10.49	10.74	10.98	11.23	11.47	11.71	11.96	12.20	12.45	12.69	12.93	13.18	13.66
103.75	9.84	10.08	10.33	10.57	10.82	11.06	11.30	11.55	11.79	12.04	12.28	12.52	12.77	13.01	13.26	13.75
103.50	9.91	10.16	10.40	10.65	10.89	11.14	11.38	11.63	11.87	12.12	12.36	12.60	12.85	13.09	13.34	13.83
103.25	9.99	10.23	10.48	10.72	10.97	11.21	11.46	11.70	11.95	12.19	12.44	12.68	12.93	13.17	13.42	13.91
103.00	10.07	10.31	10.56	10.80	11.05	11.29	11.54	11.78	12.03	12.27	12.52	12.76	13.01	13.25	13.50	13.99
102.75	10.14	10.39	10.63	10.88	11.12	11.37	11.62	11.86	12.11	12.35	12.60	12.84	13.09	13.34	13.58	14.07
102.50	10.22	10.46	10.71	10.96	11.20	11.45	11.69	11.94	12.19	12.43	12.68	12.92	13.17	13.42	13.66	14.16
102.25	10.29	10.54	10.79	11.03	11.28	11.53	11.77	12.02	12.27	12.51	12.76	13.01	13.25	13.50	13.75	14.24
102.00	10.37	10.62	10.87	11.11	11.36	11.61	11.85	12.10	12.35	12.59	12.84	13.09	13.33	13.58	13.83	14.32
101.75	10.45	10.70	10.94	11.19	11.44	11.68	11.93	12.18	12.43	12.67	12.92	13.17	13.42	13.66	13.91	14.40
101.50	10.53	10.77	11.02	11.27	11.52	11.76	12.01	12.26	12.51	12.75	13.00	13.25	13.50	13.75	13.99	14.49
101.25	10.60	10.85	11.10	11.35	11.60	11.84	12.09	12.34	12.59	12.84	13.08	13.33	13.58	13.83	14.08	14.57
101.00	10.68	10.93	11.18	11.43	11.67	11.92	12.17	12.42	12.67	12.92	13.17	13.41	13.66	13.91	14.16	14.66
100.75	10.76	11.01	11.26	11.51	11.75	12.00	12.25	12.50	12.75	13.00	13.25	13.50	13.75	13.99	14.24	14.74
100.50	10.84	11.09	11.34	11.59	11.83	12.08	12.33	12.58	12.83	13.08	13.33	13.58	13.83	14.08	14.33	14.82
100.25	10.92	11.17	11.42	11.67	11.91	12.16	12.41	12.66	12.91	13.16	13.41	13.66	13.91	14.16	14.41	14.91
100.00	11.00	11.25	11.50	11.75	12.00	12.25	12.50	12.75	13.00	13.25	13.50	13.75	14.00	14.25	14.50	15.00
99.75	11.07	11.32	11.57	11.83	12.08	12.33	12.58	12.83	13.08	13.33	13.58	13.83	14.08	14.33	14.58	15.08
99.50	11.15	11.40	11.65	11.91	12.16	12.41	12.66	12.91	13.16	13.41	13.66	13.91	14.16	14.41	14.66	15.17
99.25	11.23	11.48	11.74	11.99	12.24	12.49	12.74	12.99	13.24	13.49	13.75	14.00	14.25	14.50	14.75	15.25
99.00	11.31	11.56	11.82	12.07	12.32	12.57	12.82	13.07	13.33	13.58	13.83	14.08	14.33	14.58	14.84	15.34
98.75	11.39	11.64	11.90	12.15	12.40	12.65	12.90	13.16	13.41	13.66	13.91	14.17	14.42	14.67	14.92	15.43
98.50	11.47	11.73	11.98	12.23	12.48	12.74	12.99	13.24	13.49	13.75	14.00	14.25	14.50	14.75	15.01	15.51
98.25	11.55	11.81	12.06	12.31	12.57	12.82	13.07	13.32	13.58	13.83	14.08	14.34	14.59	14.84	15.09	15.60
98.00	11.63	11.89	12.14	12.39	12.65	12.90	13.15	13.41	13.66	13.91	14.17	14.42	14.67	14.93	15.18	15.69
97.75	11.72	11.97	12.22	12.48	12.73	12.98	13.24	13.49	13.74	14.00	14.25	14.51	14.76	15.01	15.27	15.77
97.50	11.80	12.05	12.31	12.56	12.81	13.07	13.32	13.58	13.83	14.08	14.34	14.59	14.85	15.10	15.35	15.86
97.25	11.88	12.13	12.39	12.64	12.90	13.15	13.41	13.66	13.91	14.17	14.42	14.68	14.93	15.19	15.44	15.95
97.00	11.96	12.22	12.47	12.73	12.98	13.24	13.49	13.74	14.00	14.25	14.51	14.76	15.02	15.27	15.53	16.04
96.75	12.04	12.30	12.55	12.81	13.06	13.32	13.57	13.83	14.09	14.34	14.60	14.85	15.11	15.36	15.62	16.13
96.50	12.13	12.38	12.64	12.89	13.15	13.40	13.66	13.92	14.17	14.43	14.68	14.94	15.19	15.45	15.71	16.22
96.25	12.21	12.46	12.72	12.98	13.23	13.49	13.74	14.00	14.26	14.51	14.77	15.03	15.28	15.54	15.80	16.31
96.00	12.29	12.55	12.80	13.06	13.32	13.57	13.83	14.09	14.34	14.60	14.86	15.11	15.37	15.63	15.88	16.40
95.75	12.37	12.63	12.89	13.15	13.40	13.66	13.92	14.17	14.43	14.69	14.94	15.20	15.46	15.72	15.97	16.49
95.50	12.46	12.72	12.97	13.23	13.49	13.74	14.00	14.26	14.52	14.78	15.03	15.29	15.55	15.81	16.06	16.58
95.25	12.54	12.80	13.06	13.32	13.57	13.83	14.09	14.35	14.60	14.86	15.12	15.38	15.64	15.90	16.15	16.67
95.00	12.63	12.88	13.14	13.40	13.66	13.92	14.18	14.43	14.69	14.95	15.21	15.47	15.73	15.98	16.24	16.76
94.75	12.71	12.97	13.23	13.49	13.74	14.00	14.26	14.52	14.78	15.04	15.30	15.56	15.82	16.07	16.33	16.85
94.50	12.79	13.05	13.31	13.57	13.83	14.09	14.35	14.61	14.87	15.13	15.39	15.65	15.91	16.17	16.42	16.94
94.25	12.88	13.14	13.40	13.66	13.92	14.18	14.44	14.70	14.96	15.22	15.48	15.74	16.00	16.26	16.52	17.04
94.00	12.96	13.22	13.48	13.74	14.01	14.27	14.53	14.79	15.05	15.31	15.57	15.83	16.09	16.35	16.61	17.13
93.75	13.05	13.31	13.57	13.83	14.09	14.35	14.61	14.87	15.13	15.40	15.66	15.92	16.18	16.44	16.70	17.22
93	13.31	13.57	13.83	14.09	14.36	14.62	14.88	15.14	15.40	15.67	15.93	16.19	16.45	16.71	16.98	17.50
92	13.66	13.92	14.18	14.45	14.71	14.98	15.24	15.50	15.77	16.03	16.30	16.56	16.82	17.09	17.35	17.88
91	14.01	14.28	14.54	14.81	15.07	15.34	15.60	15.87	16.14	16.40	16.67	16.93	17.20	17.47	17.73	18.26
90	14.37	14.64	14.90	15.17	15.44	15.71	15.97	16.24	16.51	16.78	17.04	17.31	17.58	17.85	18.12	18.65
89	14.73	15.00	15.27	15.54	15.81	16.08	16.35	16.62	16.89	17.16	17.43	17.70	17.97	18.24	18.51	19.05
88	15.10	15.37	15.64	15.92	16.19	16.46	16.73	17.00	17.27	17.55	17.82	18.09	18.36	18.63	18.90	19.45
87	15.47	15.75	16.02	16.30	16.57	16.84	17.12	17.39	17.66	17.94	18.21	18.49	18.76	19.03	19.31	19.86
86	15.85	16.13	16.41	16.68	16.96	17.23	17.51	17.78	18.06	18.34	18.61	18.89	19.16	19.44	19.72	20.27
85	16.24	16.52	16.79	17.07	17.35	17.63	17.91	18.18	18.46	18.74	19.02	19.30	19.58	19.85	20.13	20.69
84	16.63	16.91	17.19	17.47	17.75	18.03	18.31	18.59	18.87	19.15	19.43	19.71	19.99	20.27	20.55	21.12
83	17.03	17.31	17.59	17.87	18.16	18.44	18.72	19.00	19.29	19.57	19.85	20.13	20.42	20.70	20.98	21.55
82	17.43	17.72	18.00	18.28	18.57	18.85	19.14	19.42	19.71	19.99	20.28	20.56	20.85	21.13	21.42	21.99
81	17.84	18.13	18.41	18.70	18.99	19.27	19.56	19.85	20.14	20.42	20.71	21.00	21.29	21.57	21.86	22.44
80	18.26	18.55	18.84	19.12	19.41	19.70	19.99	20.28	20.57	20.86	21.15	21.44	21.73	22.02	22.31	22.89

Description: This table shows the price to pay for a bond at the yield rate. The yield is to maturity.

Example: The price of a 6.75 %, 5 year bond to yield 8 % to maturity is $ 94.93.

COUPON RATE, %

YIELD	0.00%	1.00%	2.00%	3.00%	4.00%	4.25%	4.50%	4.75%	5.00%	5.25%	5.50%	5.75%	6.00%	6.25%	6.50%	6.75%
0.00	100.00	105.00	110.00	115.00	120.00	121.25	122.50	123.75	125.00	126.25	127.50	128.75	130.00	131.25	132.50	133.75
1.00	95.13	100.00	104.87	109.73	114.60	115.81	117.03	118.24	119.46	120.68	121.89	123.11	124.33	125.54	126.76	127.97
2.00	90.53	95.26	100.00	104.74	109.47	110.66	111.84	113.02	114.21	115.39	116.57	117.76	118.94	120.13	121.31	122.49
3.00	86.17	90.78	95.39	100.00	104.61	105.76	106.92	108.07	109.22	110.37	111.53	112.68	113.83	114.99	116.14	117.29
4.00	82.03	86.53	91.02	95.51	100.00	101.12	102.25	103.37	104.49	105.61	106.74	107.86	108.98	110.11	111.23	112.35
4.25	81.04	85.50	89.96	94.42	98.88	100.00	101.12	102.23	103.35	104.46	105.58	106.69	107.81	108.92	110.04	111.16
4.50	80.05	84.48	88.92	93.35	97.78	98.89	100.00	101.11	102.22	103.32	104.43	105.54	106.65	107.76	108.87	109.97
4.75	79.08	83.48	87.89	92.29	96.70	97.80	98.90	100.00	101.10	102.20	103.30	104.40	105.51	106.61	107.71	108.81
5.00	78.12	82.50	86.87	91.25	95.62	96.72	97.81	98.91	100.00	101.09	102.19	103.28	104.38	105.47	106.56	107.66
5.25	77.17	81.52	85.87	90.22	94.57	95.65	96.74	97.83	98.91	100.00	101.09	102.17	103.26	104.35	105.43	106.52
5.50	76.24	80.56	84.88	89.20	93.52	94.60	95.68	96.76	97.84	98.92	100.00	101.08	102.16	103.24	104.32	105.40
5.75	75.32	79.61	83.90	88.20	92.49	93.56	94.63	95.71	96.78	97.85	98.93	100.00	101.07	102.15	103.22	104.29
6.00	74.41	78.67	82.94	87.20	91.47	92.54	93.60	94.67	95.73	96.80	97.87	98.93	100.00	101.07	102.13	103.20
6.25	73.51	77.75	81.99	86.23	90.46	91.52	92.58	93.64	94.70	95.76	96.82	97.88	98.94	100.00	101.06	102.12
6.50	72.63	76.84	81.05	85.26	89.47	90.52	91.58	92.63	93.68	94.74	95.79	96.84	97.89	98.95	100.00	101.05
6.75	71.75	75.94	80.12	84.31	88.49	89.54	90.58	91.63	92.68	93.72	94.77	95.82	96.86	97.91	98.95	100.00
7.00	70.89	75.05	79.21	83.37	87.53	88.56	89.60	90.64	91.68	92.72	93.76	94.80	95.84	96.88	97.92	98.96
7.25	70.04	74.17	78.31	82.44	86.57	87.60	88.64	89.67	90.70	91.74	92.77	93.80	94.83	95.87	96.90	97.93
7.50	69.20	73.31	77.41	81.52	85.63	86.65	87.68	88.71	89.73	90.76	91.79	92.81	93.84	94.87	95.89	96.92
7.75	68.37	72.45	76.54	80.62	84.70	85.72	86.74	87.76	88.78	89.80	90.82	91.84	92.86	93.88	94.90	95.92
8.00	67.56	71.61	75.67	79.72	83.78	84.79	85.81	86.82	87.83	88.85	89.86	90.88	91.89	92.90	93.92	94.93
8.25	66.75	70.78	74.81	78.84	82.87	83.88	84.89	85.89	86.90	87.91	88.92	89.92	90.93	91.94	92.95	93.95
8.50	65.95	69.96	73.96	77.97	81.98	82.98	83.98	84.98	85.98	86.98	87.98	88.99	89.99	90.99	91.99	92.99
8.75	65.17	69.15	73.13	77.11	81.09	82.09	83.08	84.08	85.07	86.07	87.06	88.06	89.05	90.05	91.04	92.04
9.00	64.39	68.35	72.31	76.26	80.22	81.21	82.20	83.19	84.17	85.16	86.15	87.14	88.13	89.12	90.11	91.10
9.25	63.63	67.56	71.49	75.42	79.36	80.34	81.32	82.31	83.29	84.27	85.25	86.24	87.22	88.20	89.19	90.17
9.50	62.87	66.78	70.69	74.60	78.51	79.48	80.46	81.44	82.41	83.39	84.37	85.34	86.32	87.30	88.28	89.25
9.75	62.13	66.01	69.90	73.78	77.66	78.64	79.61	80.58	81.55	82.52	83.49	84.46	85.43	86.40	87.38	88.35
10.00	61.39	65.25	69.11	72.97	76.83	77.80	78.77	79.73	80.70	81.66	82.63	83.59	84.56	85.52	86.49	87.45
10.25	60.67	64.50	68.34	72.18	76.02	76.97	77.93	78.89	79.85	80.81	81.77	82.73	83.69	84.65	85.61	86.57
10.50	59.95	63.76	67.58	71.39	75.21	76.16	77.11	78.07	79.02	79.97	80.93	81.88	82.84	83.79	84.74	85.70
10.75	59.24	63.03	66.82	70.62	74.41	75.36	76.30	77.25	78.20	79.15	80.09	81.04	81.99	82.94	83.89	84.83
11.00	58.54	62.31	66.08	69.85	73.62	74.56	75.50	76.44	77.39	78.33	79.27	80.21	81.16	82.10	83.04	83.98
11.25	57.85	61.60	65.35	69.09	72.84	73.78	74.71	75.65	76.59	77.52	78.46	79.40	80.33	81.27	82.20	83.14
11.50	57.17	60.90	64.62	68.35	72.07	73.00	73.93	74.86	75.79	76.72	77.66	78.59	79.52	80.45	81.38	82.31
11.75	56.50	60.20	63.91	67.61	71.31	72.24	73.16	74.09	75.01	75.94	76.86	77.79	78.71	79.64	80.56	81.49
12.00	55.84	59.52	63.20	66.88	70.56	71.48	72.40	73.32	74.24	75.16	76.08	77.00	77.92	78.84	79.76	80.68
12.25	55.19	58.84	62.50	66.16	69.82	70.73	71.65	72.56	73.48	74.39	75.31	76.22	77.14	78.05	78.96	79.88
12.50	54.54	58.18	61.81	65.45	69.09	70.00	70.91	71.81	72.72	73.63	74.54	75.45	76.36	77.27	78.18	79.09
12.75	53.90	57.52	61.13	64.75	68.36	69.27	70.17	71.08	71.98	72.88	73.79	74.69	75.60	76.50	77.40	78.31
13.00	53.27	56.87	60.46	64.06	67.65	68.55	69.45	70.35	71.24	72.14	73.04	73.94	74.84	75.74	76.64	77.53
13.25	52.65	56.22	59.80	63.37	66.95	67.84	68.73	69.63	70.52	71.41	72.31	73.20	74.09	74.99	75.88	76.77
13.50	52.04	55.59	59.14	62.70	66.25	67.14	68.03	68.91	69.80	70.69	71.58	72.47	73.35	74.24	75.13	76.02
13.75	51.43	54.96	58.50	62.03	65.56	66.44	67.33	68.21	69.09	69.98	70.86	71.74	72.63	73.51	74.39	75.27
14.00	50.83	54.35	57.86	61.37	64.88	65.76	66.64	67.52	68.39	69.27	70.15	71.03	71.91	72.78	73.66	74.54
14.25	50.24	53.74	57.23	60.72	64.21	65.08	65.96	66.83	67.70	68.58	69.45	70.32	71.19	72.07	72.94	73.81
14.50	49.66	53.13	56.61	60.08	63.55	64.42	65.28	66.15	67.02	67.89	68.76	69.62	70.49	71.36	72.23	73.10
14.75	49.09	52.54	55.99	59.44	62.89	63.76	64.62	65.48	66.35	67.21	68.07	68.93	69.80	70.66	71.52	72.39
15.00	48.52	51.95	55.38	58.82	62.25	63.11	63.96	64.82	65.68	66.54	67.40	68.25	69.11	69.97	70.83	71.69
15.25	47.96	51.37	54.78	58.20	61.61	62.46	63.32	64.17	65.02	65.87	66.73	67.58	68.43	69.29	70.14	70.99
15.50	47.41	50.80	54.19	57.58	60.98	61.83	62.67	63.52	64.37	65.22	66.07	66.92	67.76	68.61	69.46	70.31
15.75	46.86	50.23	53.61	56.98	60.36	61.20	62.04	62.89	63.73	64.57	65.42	66.26	67.10	67.95	68.79	69.63
16.00	46.32	49.67	53.03	56.38	59.74	60.58	61.42	62.26	63.09	63.93	64.77	65.61	66.45	67.29	68.13	68.97
16.25	45.79	49.12	52.46	55.80	59.13	59.97	60.80	61.63	62.47	63.30	64.14	64.97	65.80	66.64	67.47	68.31
16.50	45.26	48.58	51.90	55.21	58.53	59.36	60.19	61.02	61.85	62.68	63.51	64.34	65.17	66.00	66.82	67.65
16.75	44.74	48.04	51.34	54.64	57.94	58.76	59.59	60.41	61.24	62.06	62.89	63.71	64.54	65.36	66.18	67.01
17.00	44.23	47.51	50.79	54.07	57.35	58.17	58.99	59.81	60.63	61.45	62.27	63.09	63.91	64.73	65.55	66.37
17.25	43.72	46.98	50.25	53.51	56.77	57.59	58.40	59.22	60.03	60.85	61.67	62.48	63.30	64.11	64.93	65.74
17.50	43.22	46.47	49.71	52.96	56.20	57.01	57.82	58.63	59.44	60.26	61.07	61.88	62.69	63.50	64.31	65.12
17.75	42.73	45.96	49.18	52.41	55.63	56.44	57.25	58.05	58.86	59.67	60.47	61.28	62.09	62.89	63.70	64.51
18.00	42.24	45.45	48.66	51.87	55.08	55.88	56.68	57.48	58.29	59.09	59.89	60.69	61.49	62.30	63.10	63.90
18.25	41.76	44.95	48.14	51.33	54.52	55.32	56.12	56.92	57.72	58.51	59.31	60.11	60.91	61.71	62.50	63.30
18.50	41.28	44.46	47.63	50.81	53.98	54.77	55.57	56.36	57.15	57.95	58.74	59.53	60.33	61.12	61.91	62.71
18.75	40.81	43.97	47.13	50.28	53.44	54.23	55.02	55.81	56.60	57.39	58.18	58.97	59.75	60.54	61.33	62.12
19.00	40.35	43.49	46.63	49.77	52.91	53.69	54.48	55.26	56.05	56.83	57.62	58.40	59.19	59.97	60.76	61.54
20.00	38.55	41.63	44.70	47.77	50.84	51.61	52.38	53.15	53.92	54.68	55.45	56.22	56.99	57.76	58.52	59.29
25.00	30.79	33.56	36.33	39.10	41.87	42.56	43.25	43.94	44.64	45.33	46.02	46.71	47.40	48.10	48.79	49.48
30.00	24.72	27.23	29.74	32.25	34.76	35.38	36.01	36.64	37.27	37.89	38.52	39.15	39.77	40.40	41.03	41.66

Description: This table shows the yield to maturity of a bond purchased at the price shown in the index.

Example: The yield to maturity of a 6.75 %, 5 year bond at a price of 95.00 is 7.98 %.

COUPON RATE, %

PRICE	0.00%	1.00%	2.00%	3.00%	4.00%	4.25%	4.50%	4.75%	5.00%	5.25%	5.50%	5.75%	6.00%	6.25%	6.50%	6.75%
100	0.00	1.00	2.00	3.00	4.00	4.25	4.50	4.75	5.00	5.25	5.50	5.75	6.00	6.25	6.50	6.75
99.75	.05	1.05	2.05	3.05	4.05	4.30	4.55	4.80	5.05	5.30	5.55	5.80	6.05	6.30	6.55	6.80
99.50	.10	1.10	2.10	3.10	4.11	4.36	4.61	4.86	5.11	5.36	5.61	5.86	6.11	6.36	6.61	6.86
99.25	.15	1.15	2.15	3.16	4.16	4.41	4.66	4.92	5.17	5.42	5.67	5.92	6.17	6.42	6.67	6.93
99.00	.20	1.20	2.21	3.21	4.22	4.47	4.72	4.97	5.22	5.48	5.73	5.98	6.23	6.48	6.73	6.99
98.75	.25	1.25	2.26	3.27	4.28	4.53	4.78	5.03	5.28	5.53	5.79	6.04	6.29	6.54	6.79	7.05
98.50	.30	1.31	2.31	3.32	4.33	4.58	4.84	5.09	5.34	5.59	5.85	6.10	6.35	6.60	6.85	7.11
98.25	.35	1.36	2.37	3.38	4.39	4.64	4.89	5.15	5.40	5.65	5.90	6.16	6.41	6.66	6.92	7.17
98.00	.40	1.41	2.42	3.43	4.45	4.70	4.95	5.20	5.46	5.71	5.96	6.22	6.47	6.72	6.98	7.23
97.75	.45	1.46	2.48	3.49	4.50	4.76	5.01	5.26	5.52	5.77	6.02	6.28	6.53	6.78	7.04	7.29
97.50	.50	1.52	2.53	3.55	4.56	4.81	5.07	5.32	5.57	5.83	6.08	6.34	6.59	6.84	7.10	7.35
97.25	.55	1.57	2.58	3.60	4.62	4.87	5.13	5.38	5.63	5.89	6.14	6.40	6.65	6.90	7.16	7.41
97.00	.61	1.62	2.64	3.66	4.67	4.93	5.18	5.44	5.69	5.95	6.20	6.46	6.71	6.97	7.22	7.48
96.75	.66	1.68	2.69	3.71	4.73	4.99	5.24	5.50	5.75	6.01	6.26	6.52	6.77	7.03	7.28	7.54
96.50	.71	1.73	2.75	3.77	4.79	5.05	5.30	5.56	5.81	6.07	6.32	6.58	6.83	7.09	7.34	7.60
96.25	.76	1.78	2.80	3.83	4.85	5.10	5.36	5.62	5.87	6.13	6.38	6.64	6.89	7.15	7.41	7.66
96.00	.81	1.84	2.86	3.88	4.91	5.16	5.42	5.68	5.93	6.19	6.44	6.70	6.96	7.21	7.47	7.72
95.75	.87	1.89	2.91	3.94	4.97	5.22	5.48	5.73	5.99	6.25	6.50	6.76	7.02	7.27	7.53	7.79
95.50	.92	1.94	2.97	4.00	5.02	5.28	5.54	5.79	6.05	6.31	6.57	6.82	7.08	7.34	7.59	7.85
95.25	.97	2.00	3.03	4.05	5.08	5.34	5.60	5.85	6.11	6.37	6.63	6.88	7.14	7.40	7.66	7.91
95.00	1.02	2.05	3.08	4.11	5.14	5.40	5.66	5.91	6.17	6.43	6.69	6.95	7.20	7.46	7.72	7.98
94.75	1.08	2.11	3.14	4.17	5.20	5.46	5.72	5.98	6.23	6.49	6.75	7.01	7.27	7.52	7.78	8.04
94.50	1.13	2.16	3.19	4.23	5.26	5.52	5.78	6.04	6.29	6.55	6.81	7.07	7.33	7.59	7.85	8.10
94.25	1.18	2.22	3.25	4.29	5.32	5.58	5.84	6.10	6.36	6.61	6.87	7.13	7.39	7.65	7.91	8.17
94.00	1.24	2.27	3.31	4.34	5.38	5.64	5.90	6.16	6.42	6.68	6.94	7.20	7.45	7.71	7.97	8.23
93.75	1.29	2.33	3.36	4.40	5.44	5.70	5.96	6.22	6.48	6.74	7.00	7.26	7.52	7.78	8.04	8.30
93.50	1.34	2.38	3.42	4.46	5.50	5.76	6.02	6.28	6.54	6.80	7.06	7.32	7.58	7.84	8.10	8.36
93.25	1.40	2.44	3.48	4.52	5.56	5.82	6.08	6.34	6.60	6.86	7.12	7.38	7.64	7.91	8.17	8.43
93.00	1.45	2.49	3.53	4.58	5.62	5.88	6.14	6.40	6.66	6.93	7.19	7.45	7.71	7.97	8.23	8.49
92.75	1.51	2.55	3.59	4.64	5.68	5.94	6.20	6.47	6.73	6.99	7.25	7.51	7.77	8.03	8.30	8.56
92.50	1.56	2.60	3.65	4.70	5.74	6.00	6.27	6.53	6.79	7.05	7.31	7.58	7.84	8.10	8.36	8.62
92.25	1.61	2.66	3.71	4.76	5.80	6.07	6.33	6.59	6.85	7.11	7.38	7.64	7.90	8.16	8.43	8.69
92.00	1.67	2.72	3.77	4.81	5.86	6.13	6.39	6.65	6.92	7.18	7.44	7.70	7.97	8.23	8.49	8.76
91.75	1.72	2.77	3.82	4.87	5.93	6.19	6.45	6.72	6.98	7.24	7.50	7.77	8.03	8.29	8.56	8.82
91	1.89	2.94	4.00	5.05	6.11	6.38	6.64	6.90	7.17	7.43	7.70	7.96	8.23	8.49	8.76	9.02
90	2.11	3.17	4.24	5.30	6.36	6.63	6.89	7.16	7.43	7.69	7.96	8.22	8.49	8.76	9.02	9.29
89	2.34	3.41	4.48	5.54	6.62	6.88	7.15	7.42	7.69	7.95	8.22	8.49	8.76	9.03	9.30	9.56
88	2.57	3.64	4.72	5.79	6.87	7.14	7.41	7.68	7.95	8.22	8.49	8.76	9.03	9.30	9.57	9.84
87	2.80	3.88	4.96	6.05	7.13	7.40	7.68	7.95	8.22	8.49	8.76	9.03	9.31	9.58	9.85	10.12
86	3.03	4.12	5.21	6.30	7.40	7.67	7.94	8.22	8.49	8.76	9.04	9.31	9.59	9.86	10.13	10.41
85	3.27	4.37	5.46	6.56	7.66	7.94	8.21	8.49	8.76	9.04	9.32	9.59	9.87	10.14	10.42	10.70
84	3.51	4.62	5.72	6.83	7.93	8.21	8.49	8.77	9.04	9.32	9.60	9.88	10.16	10.43	10.71	10.99
83	3.76	4.87	5.98	7.09	8.21	8.49	8.77	9.05	9.33	9.61	9.89	10.17	10.45	10.73	11.01	11.29
82	4.00	5.12	6.24	7.36	8.49	8.77	9.05	9.33	9.61	9.90	10.18	10.46	10.74	11.02	11.31	11.59
81	4.25	5.38	6.51	7.64	8.77	9.05	9.34	9.62	9.91	10.19	10.47	10.76	11.04	11.33	11.61	11.90
80	4.51	5.64	6.78	7.92	9.06	9.34	9.63	9.92	10.20	10.49	10.77	11.06	11.35	11.63	11.92	12.21
79	4.77	5.91	7.05	8.20	9.35	9.64	9.92	10.21	10.50	10.79	11.08	11.37	11.66	11.94	12.23	12.52
78	5.03	6.18	7.33	8.49	9.64	9.93	10.23	10.52	10.81	11.10	11.39	11.68	11.97	12.26	12.55	12.84
77	5.29	6.45	7.61	8.78	9.95	10.24	10.53	10.82	11.12	11.41	11.70	11.99	12.29	12.58	12.88	13.17
76	5.56	6.73	7.90	9.07	10.25	10.54	10.84	11.13	11.43	11.73	12.02	12.32	12.61	12.91	13.20	13.50
75	5.83	7.01	8.19	9.37	10.56	10.86	11.15	11.45	11.75	12.05	12.34	12.64	12.94	13.24	13.54	13.84
74	6.11	7.29	8.48	9.68	10.87	11.17	11.47	11.77	12.07	12.37	12.67	12.98	13.28	13.58	13.88	14.18
73	6.39	7.58	8.78	9.99	11.19	11.50	11.80	12.10	12.40	12.71	13.01	13.31	13.62	13.92	14.22	14.53
72	6.67	7.88	9.09	10.30	11.52	11.82	12.13	12.43	12.74	13.04	13.35	13.66	13.96	14.27	14.58	14.88
71	6.96	8.18	9.40	10.62	11.85	12.16	12.46	12.77	13.08	13.39	13.70	14.00	14.31	14.62	14.93	15.24
70	7.26	8.48	9.71	10.95	12.18	12.49	12.80	13.11	13.43	13.74	14.05	14.36	14.67	14.98	15.30	15.61
69	7.56	8.79	10.03	11.28	12.52	12.84	13.15	13.46	13.78	14.09	14.41	14.72	15.04	15.35	15.67	15.98
68	7.86	9.11	10.36	11.61	12.87	13.19	13.50	13.82	14.14	14.45	14.77	15.09	15.41	15.72	16.04	16.36
67	8.17	9.42	10.69	11.95	13.23	13.54	13.86	14.18	14.50	14.82	15.14	15.46	15.78	16.11	16.43	16.75
66	8.48	9.75	11.02	12.30	13.59	13.91	14.23	14.55	14.87	15.20	15.52	15.84	16.17	16.49	16.82	17.14
65	8.80	10.08	11.36	12.66	13.95	14.28	14.60	14.93	15.25	15.58	15.91	16.23	16.56	16.89	17.22	17.54
64	9.12	10.41	11.71	13.02	14.32	14.65	14.98	15.31	15.64	15.97	16.30	16.63	16.96	17.29	17.62	17.95
63	9.45	10.76	12.07	13.38	14.70	15.04	15.37	15.70	16.03	16.37	16.70	17.03	17.37	17.70	18.04	18.37
62	9.79	11.10	12.43	13.76	15.09	15.43	15.76	16.10	16.43	16.77	17.11	17.44	17.78	18.12	18.46	18.80
61	10.13	11.46	12.79	14.14	15.49	15.82	16.16	16.50	16.84	17.18	17.52	17.86	18.21	18.55	18.89	19.23
60	10.48	11.82	13.17	14.53	15.89	16.23	16.57	16.92	17.26	17.60	17.95	18.29	18.64	18.98	19.33	19.68
59	10.83	12.19	13.55	14.92	16.30	16.65	16.99	17.34	17.69	18.03	18.38	18.73	19.08	19.43	19.78	20.13
58	11.19	12.56	13.94	15.33	16.72	17.07	17.42	17.77	18.12	18.47	18.82	19.18	19.53	19.88	20.24	20.59

Description: This table shows the price to pay for a bond at the yield rate. The yield is to maturity.

Example: The price of a 10.75 %, 5 year bond to yield 8 % to maturity is $ 111.15.

YIELD	7.00%	7.25%	7.50%	7.75%	8.00%	8.25%	COUPON RATE, % 8.50%	8.75%	9.00%	9.25%	9.50%	9.75%	10.00%	10.25%	10.50%	10.75%
0.00	135.00	136.25	137.50	138.75	140.00	141.25	142.50	143.75	145.00	146.25	147.50	148.75	150.00	151.25	152.50	153.75
1.00	129.19	130.41	131.62	132.84	134.06	135.27	136.49	137.71	138.92	140.14	141.35	142.57	143.79	145.00	146.22	147.44
2.00	123.68	124.86	126.05	127.23	128.41	129.60	130.78	131.97	133.15	134.33	135.52	136.70	137.89	139.07	140.25	141.44
3.00	118.44	119.60	120.75	121.90	123.06	124.21	125.36	126.51	127.67	128.82	129.97	131.12	132.28	133.43	134.58	135.74
4.00	113.47	114.60	115.72	116.84	117.97	119.09	120.21	121.33	122.46	123.58	124.70	125.82	126.95	128.07	129.19	130.32
4.25	112.27	113.39	114.50	115.62	116.73	117.85	118.96	120.08	121.19	122.31	123.43	124.54	125.66	126.77	127.89	129.00
4.50	111.08	112.19	113.30	114.41	115.52	116.62	117.73	118.84	119.95	121.06	122.17	123.27	124.38	125.49	126.60	127.71
4.75	109.91	111.01	112.11	113.21	114.31	115.42	116.52	117.62	118.72	119.82	120.92	122.02	123.12	124.22	125.33	126.43
5.00	108.75	109.85	110.94	112.03	113.13	114.22	115.32	116.41	117.50	118.60	119.69	120.79	121.88	122.97	124.07	125.16
5.25	107.61	108.70	109.78	110.87	111.96	113.04	114.13	115.22	116.30	117.39	118.48	119.57	120.65	121.74	122.83	123.91
5.50	106.48	107.56	108.64	109.72	110.80	111.88	112.96	114.04	115.12	116.20	117.28	118.36	119.44	120.52	121.60	122.68
5.75	105.37	106.44	107.51	108.58	109.66	110.73	111.80	112.88	113.95	115.02	116.10	117.17	118.24	119.32	120.39	121.46
6.00	104.27	105.33	106.40	107.46	108.53	109.60	110.66	111.73	112.80	113.86	114.93	115.99	117.06	118.13	119.19	120.26
6.25	103.18	104.24	105.30	106.36	107.42	108.48	109.54	110.60	111.65	112.71	113.77	114.83	115.89	116.95	118.01	119.07
6.50	102.11	103.16	104.21	105.26	106.32	107.37	108.42	109.48	110.53	111.58	112.63	113.69	114.74	115.79	116.84	117.90
6.75	101.05	102.09	103.14	104.18	105.23	106.28	107.32	108.37	109.42	110.46	111.51	112.55	113.60	114.65	115.69	116.74
7.00	100.00	101.04	102.08	103.12	104.16	105.20	106.24	107.28	108.32	109.36	110.40	111.44	112.47	113.51	114.55	115.59
7.25	98.97	100.00	101.03	102.07	103.10	104.13	105.17	106.20	107.23	108.26	109.30	110.33	111.36	112.40	113.43	114.46
7.50	97.95	98.97	100.00	101.03	102.05	103.08	104.11	105.13	106.16	107.19	108.21	109.24	110.27	111.29	112.32	113.35
7.75	96.94	97.96	98.98	100.00	101.02	102.04	103.06	104.08	105.10	106.12	107.14	108.16	109.18	110.20	111.22	112.24
8.00	95.94	96.96	97.97	98.99	100.00	101.01	102.03	103.04	104.06	105.07	106.08	107.10	108.11	109.12	110.14	111.15
8.25	94.96	95.97	96.98	97.98	98.99	100.00	101.01	102.02	103.02	104.03	105.04	106.05	107.05	108.06	109.07	110.08
8.50	93.99	94.99	95.99	97.00	98.00	99.00	100.00	101.00	102.00	103.00	104.01	105.01	106.01	107.01	108.01	109.01
8.75	93.03	94.03	95.02	96.02	97.01	98.01	99.00	100.00	101.00	101.99	102.99	103.98	104.98	105.97	106.97	107.96
9.00	92.09	93.08	94.07	95.05	96.04	97.03	98.02	99.01	100.00	100.99	101.98	102.97	103.96	104.95	105.93	106.92
9.25	91.15	92.14	93.12	94.10	95.08	96.07	97.05	98.03	99.02	100.00	100.98	101.97	102.95	103.93	104.92	105.90
9.50	90.23	91.21	92.18	93.16	94.14	95.11	96.09	97.07	98.05	99.02	100.00	100.98	101.95	102.93	103.91	104.89
9.75	89.32	90.29	91.26	92.23	93.20	94.17	95.14	96.12	97.09	98.06	99.03	100.00	100.97	101.94	102.91	103.88
10.00	88.42	89.38	90.35	91.31	92.28	93.24	94.21	95.17	96.14	97.10	98.07	99.03	100.00	100.97	101.93	102.90
10.25	87.53	88.49	89.45	90.41	91.37	92.32	93.28	94.24	95.20	96.16	97.12	98.08	99.04	100.00	100.96	101.92
10.50	86.65	87.60	88.56	89.51	90.46	91.42	92.37	93.32	94.28	95.23	96.19	97.14	98.09	99.05	100.00	100.95
10.75	85.78	86.73	87.68	88.63	89.57	90.52	91.47	92.42	93.36	94.31	95.26	96.21	97.16	98.10	99.05	100.00
11.00	84.92	85.87	86.81	87.75	88.69	89.64	90.58	91.52	92.46	93.40	94.35	95.29	96.23	97.17	98.12	99.06
11.25	84.08	85.01	85.95	86.89	87.82	88.76	89.70	90.63	91.57	92.51	93.44	94.38	95.32	96.25	97.19	98.13
11.50	83.24	84.17	85.10	86.03	86.97	87.90	88.83	89.76	90.69	91.62	92.55	93.48	94.41	95.34	96.28	97.21
11.75	82.42	83.34	84.27	85.19	86.12	87.04	87.97	88.89	89.82	90.75	91.67	92.60	93.52	94.45	95.37	96.30
12.00	81.60	82.52	83.44	84.36	85.28	86.20	87.12	88.04	88.96	89.88	90.80	91.72	92.64	93.56	94.48	95.40
12.25	80.79	81.71	82.62	83.54	84.45	85.37	86.28	87.20	88.11	89.02	89.94	90.85	91.77	92.68	93.60	94.51
12.50	80.00	80.91	81.82	82.72	83.63	84.54	85.45	86.36	87.27	88.18	89.09	90.00	90.91	91.82	92.73	93.64
12.75	79.21	80.11	81.02	81.92	82.83	83.73	84.63	85.54	86.44	87.35	88.25	89.15	90.06	90.96	91.87	92.77
13.00	78.43	79.33	80.23	81.13	82.03	82.93	83.83	84.72	85.62	86.52	87.42	88.32	89.22	90.12	91.01	91.91
13.25	77.67	78.56	79.45	80.35	81.24	82.13	83.03	83.92	84.81	85.71	86.60	87.49	88.39	89.28	90.17	91.07
13.50	76.91	77.80	78.68	79.57	80.46	81.35	82.24	83.12	84.01	84.90	85.79	86.68	87.57	88.45	89.34	90.23
13.75	76.16	77.04	77.92	78.81	79.69	80.57	81.46	82.34	83.22	84.11	84.99	85.87	86.75	87.64	88.52	89.40
14.00	75.42	76.30	77.17	78.05	78.93	79.81	80.69	81.56	82.44	83.32	84.20	85.07	85.95	86.83	87.71	88.59
14.25	74.69	75.56	76.43	77.30	78.18	79.05	79.92	80.80	81.67	82.54	83.41	84.29	85.16	86.03	86.91	87.78
14.50	73.96	74.83	75.70	76.57	77.43	78.30	79.17	80.04	80.91	81.77	82.64	83.51	84.38	85.25	86.11	86.98
14.75	73.25	74.11	74.98	75.84	76.70	77.56	78.43	79.29	80.15	81.02	81.88	82.74	83.60	84.47	85.33	86.19
15.00	72.54	73.40	74.26	75.12	75.98	76.83	77.69	78.55	79.41	80.27	81.12	81.98	82.84	83.70	84.56	85.41
15.25	71.85	72.70	73.55	74.41	75.26	76.11	76.97	77.82	78.67	79.52	80.38	81.23	82.08	82.94	83.79	84.64
15.50	71.16	72.01	72.85	73.70	74.55	75.40	76.25	77.10	77.94	78.79	79.64	80.49	81.34	82.19	83.03	83.88
15.75	70.48	71.32	72.16	73.01	73.85	74.69	75.54	76.38	77.23	78.07	78.91	79.76	80.60	81.44	82.29	83.13
16.00	69.80	70.64	71.48	72.32	73.16	74.00	74.84	75.68	76.51	77.35	78.19	79.03	79.87	80.71	81.55	82.39
16.25	69.14	69.97	70.81	71.64	72.48	73.31	74.14	74.98	75.81	76.65	77.48	78.31	79.15	79.98	80.82	81.65
16.50	68.48	69.31	70.14	70.97	71.80	72.63	73.46	74.29	75.12	75.95	76.78	77.61	78.44	79.27	80.09	80.92
16.75	67.83	68.66	69.48	70.31	71.13	71.96	72.78	73.61	74.43	75.26	76.08	76.91	77.73	78.56	79.38	80.21
17.00	67.19	68.01	68.83	69.65	70.47	71.29	72.11	72.93	73.75	74.57	75.39	76.22	77.04	77.86	78.68	79.50
17.25	66.56	67.38	68.19	69.01	69.82	70.64	71.45	72.27	73.08	73.90	74.72	75.53	76.35	77.16	77.98	78.79
17.50	65.93	66.74	67.56	68.37	69.18	69.99	70.80	71.61	72.42	73.23	74.04	74.86	75.67	76.48	77.29	78.10
17.75	65.31	66.12	66.93	67.73	68.54	69.35	70.15	70.96	71.77	72.57	73.38	74.19	74.99	75.80	76.61	77.41
18.00	64.70	65.51	66.31	67.11	67.91	68.71	69.52	70.32	71.12	71.92	72.72	73.53	74.33	75.13	75.93	76.74
18.25	64.10	64.90	65.69	66.49	67.29	68.09	68.89	69.68	70.48	71.28	72.08	72.87	73.67	74.47	75.27	76.07
18.50	63.50	64.29	65.09	65.88	66.67	67.47	68.26	69.06	69.85	70.64	71.44	72.23	73.02	73.82	74.61	75.40
18.75	62.91	63.70	64.49	65.28	66.07	66.86	67.65	68.43	69.22	70.01	70.80	71.59	72.38	73.17	73.96	74.75
19.00	62.33	63.11	63.90	64.68	65.47	66.25	67.04	67.82	68.61	69.39	70.18	70.96	71.75	72.53	73.32	74.10
20.00	60.06	60.83	61.60	62.36	63.13	63.90	64.67	65.44	66.20	66.97	67.74	68.51	69.28	70.05	70.81	71.58
25.00	50.17	50.86	51.56	52.25	52.94	53.63	54.32	55.02	55.71	56.40	57.09	57.78	58.48	59.17	59.86	60.55
30.00	42.28	42.91	43.54	44.17	44.79	45.42	46.05	46.68	47.30	47.93	48.56	49.18	49.81	50.44	51.07	51.69

Description: This table shows the yield to maturity of a bond purchased at the price shown in the index.

Example: The yield to maturity of a 10.75 %, 5 year bond at a price of 100.00 is 10.75 %.

PRICE	7.00%	7.25%	7.50%	7.75%	8.00%	8.25%	8.50%	8.75%	9.00%	9.25%	9.50%	9.75%	10.00%	10.25%	10.50%	10.75%
105	5.83	6.07	6.31	6.56	6.80	7.04	7.28	7.53	7.77	8.01	8.25	8.50	8.74	8.98	9.22	9.47
104.75	5.88	6.13	6.37	6.61	6.86	7.10	7.34	7.59	7.83	8.07	8.31	8.56	8.80	9.04	9.29	9.53
104.50	5.94	6.18	6.43	6.67	6.92	7.16	7.40	7.65	7.89	8.13	8.37	8.62	8.86	9.10	9.35	9.59
104.25	6.00	6.24	6.49	6.73	6.97	7.22	7.46	7.70	7.95	8.19	8.44	8.68	8.92	9.17	9.41	9.65
104.00	6.06	6.30	6.54	6.79	7.03	7.28	7.52	7.76	8.01	8.25	8.50	8.74	8.98	9.23	9.47	9.72
103.75	6.11	6.36	6.60	6.85	7.09	7.34	7.58	7.82	8.07	8.31	8.56	8.80	9.05	9.29	9.53	9.78
103.50	6.17	6.42	6.66	6.91	7.15	7.39	7.64	7.88	8.13	8.37	8.62	8.86	9.11	9.35	9.60	9.84
103.25	6.23	6.47	6.72	6.96	7.21	7.45	7.70	7.94	8.19	8.43	8.68	8.92	9.17	9.42	9.66	9.91
103.00	6.29	6.53	6.78	7.02	7.27	7.51	7.76	8.01	8.25	8.50	8.74	8.99	9.23	9.48	9.72	9.97
102.75	6.34	6.59	6.84	7.08	7.33	7.57	7.82	8.07	8.31	8.56	8.80	9.05	9.29	9.54	9.79	10.03
102.50	6.40	6.65	6.90	7.14	7.39	7.63	7.88	8.13	8.37	8.62	8.87	9.11	9.36	9.60	9.85	10.10
102.25	6.46	6.71	6.95	7.20	7.45	7.69	7.94	8.19	8.43	8.68	8.93	9.17	9.42	9.67	9.91	10.16
102.00	6.52	6.77	7.01	7.26	7.51	7.75	8.00	8.25	8.50	8.74	8.99	9.24	9.48	9.73	9.98	10.22
101.75	6.58	6.83	7.07	7.32	7.57	7.82	8.06	8.31	8.56	8.80	9.05	9.30	9.55	9.79	10.04	10.29
101.50	6.64	6.89	7.13	7.38	7.63	7.88	8.12	8.37	8.62	8.87	9.11	9.36	9.61	9.86	10.11	10.35
101.25	6.70	6.94	7.19	7.44	7.69	7.94	8.19	8.43	8.68	8.93	9.18	9.43	9.67	9.92	10.17	10.42
101.00	6.76	7.00	7.25	7.50	7.75	8.00	8.25	8.50	8.74	8.99	9.24	9.49	9.74	9.99	10.23	10.48
100.75	6.82	7.06	7.31	7.56	7.81	8.06	8.31	8.56	8.81	9.06	9.30	9.55	9.80	10.05	10.30	10.55
100.50	6.88	7.12	7.37	7.62	7.87	8.12	8.37	8.62	8.87	9.12	9.37	9.62	9.87	10.12	10.36	10.61
100.25	6.93	7.18	7.43	7.68	7.93	8.18	8.43	8.68	8.93	9.18	9.43	9.68	9.93	10.18	10.43	10.68
100.00	7.00	7.25	7.50	7.75	8.00	8.25	8.50	8.75	9.00	9.25	9.50	9.75	10.00	10.25	10.50	10.75
99.75	7.06	7.31	7.56	7.81	8.06	8.31	8.56	8.81	9.06	9.31	9.56	9.81	10.06	10.31	10.56	10.81
99.50	7.12	7.37	7.62	7.87	8.12	8.37	8.62	8.87	9.12	9.37	9.62	9.87	10.12	10.38	10.63	10.88
99.25	7.18	7.43	7.68	7.93	8.18	8.43	8.68	8.93	9.19	9.44	9.69	9.94	10.19	10.44	10.69	10.94
99.00	7.24	7.49	7.74	7.99	8.24	8.49	8.75	9.00	9.25	9.50	9.75	10.00	10.26	10.51	10.76	11.01
98.75	7.30	7.55	7.80	8.05	8.31	8.56	8.81	9.06	9.31	9.57	9.82	10.07	10.32	10.57	10.83	11.08
98.50	7.36	7.61	7.86	8.12	8.37	8.62	8.87	9.13	9.38	9.63	9.88	10.13	10.39	10.64	10.89	11.14
98.25	7.42	7.67	7.93	8.18	8.43	8.68	8.94	9.19	9.44	9.69	9.95	10.20	10.45	10.71	10.96	11.21
98.00	7.48	7.74	7.99	8.24	8.49	8.75	9.00	9.25	9.51	9.76	10.01	10.27	10.52	10.77	11.03	11.28
97.75	7.54	7.80	8.05	8.30	8.56	8.81	9.06	9.32	9.57	9.83	10.08	10.33	10.59	10.84	11.09	11.35
97.50	7.61	7.86	8.11	8.37	8.62	8.88	9.13	9.38	9.64	9.89	10.14	10.40	10.65	10.91	11.16	11.42
97.25	7.67	7.92	8.18	8.43	8.68	8.94	9.19	9.45	9.70	9.96	10.21	10.47	10.72	10.97	11.23	11.48
97.00	7.73	7.98	8.24	8.49	8.75	9.00	9.26	9.51	9.77	10.02	10.28	10.53	10.79	11.04	11.30	11.55
96.75	7.79	8.05	8.30	8.56	8.81	9.07	9.32	9.58	9.83	10.09	10.34	10.60	10.85	11.11	11.37	11.62
96.50	7.86	8.11	8.37	8.62	8.88	9.13	9.39	9.64	9.90	10.16	10.41	10.67	10.92	11.18	11.43	11.69
96.25	7.92	8.17	8.43	8.69	8.94	9.20	9.45	9.71	9.97	10.22	10.48	10.73	10.99	11.25	11.50	11.76
96.00	7.98	8.24	8.49	8.75	9.01	9.26	9.52	9.78	10.03	10.29	10.54	10.80	11.06	11.31	11.57	11.83
95.75	8.04	8.30	8.56	8.81	9.07	9.33	9.58	9.84	10.10	10.36	10.61	10.87	11.13	11.38	11.64	11.90
95.50	8.11	8.36	8.62	8.88	9.14	9.39	9.65	9.91	10.17	10.42	10.68	10.94	11.19	11.45	11.71	11.97
95.25	8.17	8.43	8.69	8.94	9.20	9.46	9.72	9.97	10.23	10.49	10.75	11.01	11.26	11.52	11.78	12.04
95.00	8.24	8.49	8.75	9.01	9.27	9.53	9.78	10.04	10.30	10.56	10.82	11.07	11.33	11.59	11.85	12.11
94.75	8.30	8.56	8.82	9.07	9.33	9.59	9.85	10.11	10.37	10.63	10.88	11.14	11.40	11.66	11.92	12.18
94	8.49	8.75	9.01	9.27	9.53	9.79	10.05	10.31	10.57	10.83	11.09	11.35	11.61	11.87	12.13	12.39
93	8.75	9.02	9.28	9.54	9.80	10.06	10.32	10.58	10.85	11.11	11.37	11.63	11.89	12.15	12.42	12.68
92	9.02	9.28	9.54	9.81	10.07	10.33	10.60	10.86	11.12	11.39	11.65	11.91	12.18	12.44	12.71	12.97
91	9.29	9.55	9.82	10.08	10.35	10.61	10.88	11.14	11.41	11.67	11.94	12.20	12.47	12.73	13.00	13.26
90	9.56	9.82	10.09	10.36	10.62	10.89	11.16	11.43	11.69	11.96	12.23	12.49	12.76	13.03	13.30	13.56
89	9.83	10.10	10.37	10.64	10.91	11.18	11.45	11.71	11.98	12.25	12.52	12.79	13.06	13.33	13.60	13.87
88	10.11	10.38	10.65	10.92	11.19	11.47	11.74	12.01	12.28	12.55	12.82	13.09	13.36	13.63	13.90	14.18
87	10.39	10.67	10.94	11.21	11.49	11.76	12.03	12.30	12.58	12.85	13.12	13.40	13.67	13.94	14.22	14.49
86	10.68	10.96	11.23	11.51	11.78	12.05	12.33	12.60	12.88	13.15	13.43	13.70	13.98	14.26	14.53	14.81
85	10.97	11.25	11.53	11.80	12.08	12.36	12.63	12.91	13.19	13.46	13.74	14.02	14.30	14.57	14.85	15.13
84	11.27	11.55	11.83	12.10	12.38	12.66	12.94	13.22	13.50	13.78	14.06	14.34	14.62	14.90	15.18	15.46
83	11.57	11.85	12.13	12.41	12.69	12.97	13.25	13.53	13.82	14.10	14.38	14.66	14.94	15.22	15.51	15.79
82	11.87	12.15	12.44	12.72	13.00	13.29	13.57	13.85	14.14	14.42	14.71	14.99	15.27	15.56	15.84	16.13
81	12.18	12.47	12.75	13.04	13.32	13.61	13.89	14.18	14.46	14.75	15.04	15.32	15.61	15.90	16.18	16.47
80	12.49	12.78	13.07	13.36	13.64	13.93	14.22	14.51	14.80	15.08	15.37	15.66	15.95	16.24	16.53	16.82
79	12.81	13.10	13.39	13.68	13.97	14.26	14.55	14.84	15.13	15.42	15.71	16.01	16.30	16.59	16.88	17.17
78	13.14	13.43	13.72	14.01	14.30	14.60	14.89	15.18	15.48	15.77	16.06	16.36	16.65	16.94	17.24	17.53
77	13.46	13.76	14.05	14.35	14.64	14.94	15.23	15.53	15.82	16.12	16.42	16.71	17.01	17.30	17.60	17.90
76	13.80	14.09	14.39	14.69	14.99	15.28	15.58	15.88	16.18	16.48	16.77	17.07	17.37	17.67	17.97	18.27
75	14.14	14.44	14.74	15.04	15.34	15.64	15.94	16.24	16.54	16.84	17.14	17.44	17.74	18.04	18.35	18.65
74	14.48	14.78	15.09	15.39	15.69	15.99	16.30	16.60	16.90	17.21	17.51	17.82	18.12	18.42	18.73	19.03
73	14.83	15.14	15.44	15.75	16.05	16.36	16.66	16.97	17.28	17.58	17.89	18.20	18.50	18.81	19.12	19.43
72	15.19	15.50	15.80	16.11	16.42	16.73	17.04	17.35	17.66	17.97	18.27	18.58	18.89	19.20	19.52	19.83
71	15.55	15.86	16.17	16.48	16.80	17.11	17.42	17.73	18.04	18.35	18.67	18.98	19.29	19.61	19.92	20.23
70	15.92	16.24	16.55	16.86	17.18	17.49	17.81	18.12	18.43	18.75	19.07	19.38	19.70	20.01	20.33	20.65
69	16.30	16.61	16.93	17.25	17.56	17.88	18.20	18.52	18.84	19.15	19.47	19.79	20.11	20.43	20.75	21.07

Description: This table shows the price to pay for a bond at the yield rate. The yield is to maturity.

Example: The price of a 15.00 %, 5 year bond to yield 8 % to maturity is $ 128.39.

COUPON RATE, %

YIELD	11.00%	11.25%	11.50%	11.75%	12.00%	12.25%	12.50%	12.75%	13.00%	13.25%	13.50%	13.75%	14.00%	14.25%	14.50%	15.00%
0.00	155.00	156.25	157.50	158.75	160.00	161.25	162.50	163.75	165.00	166.25	167.50	168.75	170.00	171.25	172.50	175.00
1.00	148.65	149.87	151.08	152.30	153.52	154.73	155.95	157.17	158.38	159.60	160.82	162.03	163.25	164.46	165.68	168.11
2.00	142.62	143.80	144.99	146.17	147.36	148.54	149.72	150.91	152.09	153.28	154.46	155.64	156.83	158.01	159.20	161.56
3.00	136.89	138.04	139.19	140.35	141.50	142.65	143.81	144.96	146.11	147.26	148.42	149.57	150.72	151.87	153.03	155.33
4.00	131.44	132.56	133.68	134.81	135.93	137.05	138.18	139.30	140.42	141.54	142.67	143.79	144.91	146.04	147.16	149.40
4.25	130.12	131.23	132.35	133.47	134.58	135.70	136.81	137.93	139.04	140.16	141.27	142.39	143.51	144.62	145.74	147.97
4.50	128.82	129.92	131.03	132.14	133.25	134.36	135.46	136.57	137.68	138.79	139.90	141.01	142.11	143.22	144.33	146.55
4.75	127.53	128.63	129.73	130.83	131.93	133.03	134.13	135.24	136.34	137.44	138.54	139.64	140.74	141.84	142.94	145.15
5.00	126.26	127.35	128.44	129.54	130.63	131.73	132.82	133.91	135.01	136.10	137.20	138.29	139.38	140.48	141.57	143.76
5.25	125.00	126.09	127.17	128.26	129.35	130.44	131.52	132.61	133.70	134.78	135.87	136.96	138.04	139.13	140.22	142.39
5.50	123.76	124.84	125.92	127.00	128.08	129.16	130.24	131.32	132.40	133.48	134.56	135.64	136.72	137.80	138.88	141.04
5.75	122.54	123.61	124.68	125.75	126.83	127.90	128.97	130.05	131.12	132.19	133.27	134.34	135.41	136.49	137.56	139.71
6.00	121.33	122.39	123.46	124.52	125.59	126.66	127.72	128.79	129.86	130.92	131.99	133.05	134.12	135.19	136.25	138.39
6.25	120.13	121.19	122.25	123.31	124.37	125.43	126.49	127.55	128.61	129.67	130.73	131.79	132.84	133.90	134.96	137.08
6.50	118.95	120.00	121.06	122.11	123.16	124.21	125.27	126.32	127.37	128.43	129.48	130.53	131.58	132.64	133.69	135.80
6.75	117.78	118.83	119.88	120.92	121.97	123.02	124.06	125.11	126.15	127.20	128.25	129.29	130.34	131.38	132.43	134.52
7.00	116.63	117.67	118.71	119.75	120.79	121.83	122.87	123.91	124.95	125.99	127.03	128.07	129.11	130.15	131.19	133.27
7.25	115.50	116.53	117.56	118.60	119.63	120.66	121.69	122.73	123.76	124.79	125.83	126.86	127.89	128.93	129.96	132.02
7.50	114.37	115.40	116.43	117.45	118.48	119.51	120.53	121.56	122.59	123.61	124.64	125.66	126.69	127.72	128.74	130.80
7.75	113.26	114.28	115.30	116.32	117.34	118.36	119.38	120.40	121.42	122.44	123.46	124.48	125.51	126.53	127.55	129.59
8.00	112.17	113.18	114.19	115.21	116.22	117.24	118.25	119.26	120.28	121.29	122.30	123.32	124.33	125.35	126.36	128.39
8.25	111.08	112.09	113.10	114.11	115.11	116.12	117.13	118.14	119.14	120.15	121.16	122.17	123.17	124.18	125.19	127.20
8.50	110.01	111.01	112.02	113.02	114.02	115.02	116.02	117.02	118.02	119.03	120.03	121.03	122.03	123.03	124.03	126.04
8.75	108.96	109.95	110.95	111.94	112.94	113.93	114.93	115.92	116.92	117.91	118.91	119.90	120.90	121.89	122.89	124.88
9.00	107.91	108.90	109.89	110.88	111.87	112.86	113.85	114.84	115.83	116.81	117.80	118.79	119.78	120.77	121.76	123.74
9.25	106.88	107.86	108.85	109.83	110.81	111.80	112.78	113.76	114.75	115.73	116.71	117.69	118.68	119.66	120.64	122.61
9.50	105.86	106.84	107.82	108.79	109.77	110.75	111.72	112.70	113.68	114.66	115.63	116.61	117.59	118.56	119.54	121.49
9.75	104.86	105.83	106.80	107.77	108.74	109.71	110.68	111.65	112.62	113.60	114.57	115.54	116.51	117.48	118.45	120.39
10.00	103.86	104.83	105.79	106.76	107.72	108.69	109.65	110.62	111.58	112.55	113.51	114.48	115.44	116.41	117.37	119.30
10.25	102.88	103.84	104.80	105.76	106.72	107.68	108.63	109.59	110.55	111.51	112.47	113.43	114.39	115.35	116.31	118.23
10.50	101.91	102.86	103.81	104.77	105.72	106.68	107.63	108.58	109.54	110.49	111.44	112.40	113.35	114.30	115.26	117.16
10.75	100.95	101.90	102.84	103.79	104.74	105.69	106.64	107.58	108.53	109.48	110.43	111.37	112.32	113.27	114.22	116.11
11.00	100.00	100.94	101.88	102.83	103.77	104.71	105.65	106.60	107.54	108.48	109.42	110.36	111.31	112.25	113.19	115.08
11.25	99.06	100.00	100.94	101.87	102.81	103.75	104.68	105.62	106.56	107.49	108.43	109.37	110.30	111.24	112.18	114.05
11.50	98.14	99.07	100.00	100.93	101.86	102.79	103.72	104.66	105.59	106.52	107.45	108.38	109.31	110.24	111.17	113.03
11.75	97.22	98.15	99.07	100.00	100.93	101.85	102.78	103.70	104.63	105.55	106.48	107.40	108.33	109.25	110.18	112.03
12.00	96.32	97.24	98.16	99.08	100.00	100.92	101.84	102.76	103.68	104.60	105.52	106.44	107.36	108.28	109.20	111.04
12.25	95.43	96.34	97.26	98.17	99.09	100.00	100.91	101.83	102.74	103.66	104.57	105.49	106.40	107.32	108.23	110.06
12.50	94.54	95.45	96.36	97.27	98.18	99.09	100.00	100.91	101.82	102.73	103.64	104.55	105.46	106.36	107.27	109.09
12.75	93.67	94.58	95.48	96.38	97.29	98.19	99.10	100.00	100.90	101.81	102.71	103.62	104.52	105.42	106.33	108.13
13.00	92.81	93.71	94.61	95.51	96.41	97.30	98.20	99.10	100.00	100.90	101.80	102.70	103.59	104.49	105.39	107.19
13.25	91.96	92.85	93.75	94.64	95.53	96.43	97.32	98.21	99.11	100.00	100.89	101.79	102.68	103.57	104.47	106.25
13.50	91.12	92.01	92.89	93.78	94.67	95.56	96.45	97.34	98.22	99.11	100.00	100.89	101.78	102.66	103.55	105.33
13.75	90.29	91.17	92.05	92.94	93.82	94.70	95.58	96.47	97.35	98.23	99.12	100.00	100.88	101.77	102.65	104.42
14.00	89.46	90.34	91.22	92.10	92.98	93.85	94.73	95.61	96.49	97.37	98.24	99.12	100.00	100.88	101.76	103.51
14.25	88.65	89.53	90.40	91.27	92.14	93.02	93.89	94.76	95.64	96.51	97.38	98.25	99.13	100.00	100.87	102.62
14.50	87.85	88.72	89.59	90.45	91.32	92.19	93.06	93.92	94.79	95.66	96.53	97.40	98.26	99.13	100.00	101.74
14.75	87.06	87.92	88.78	89.64	90.51	91.37	92.23	93.10	93.96	94.82	95.69	96.55	97.41	98.27	99.14	100.86
15.00	86.27	87.13	87.99	88.85	89.70	90.56	91.42	92.28	93.14	93.99	94.85	95.71	96.57	97.43	98.28	100.00
15.25	85.50	86.35	87.20	88.06	88.91	89.76	90.62	91.47	92.32	93.17	94.03	94.88	95.73	96.59	97.44	99.15
15.50	84.73	85.58	86.43	87.28	88.12	88.97	89.82	90.67	91.52	92.37	93.21	94.06	94.91	95.76	96.61	98.30
15.75	83.97	84.82	85.66	86.50	87.35	88.19	89.03	89.88	90.72	91.56	92.41	93.25	94.10	94.94	95.78	97.47
16.00	83.22	84.06	84.90	85.74	86.58	87.42	88.26	89.10	89.93	90.77	91.61	92.45	93.29	94.13	94.97	96.64
16.25	82.48	83.32	84.15	84.99	85.82	86.66	87.49	88.32	89.16	89.99	90.83	91.66	92.49	93.33	94.16	95.83
16.50	81.75	82.58	83.41	84.24	85.07	85.90	86.73	87.56	88.39	89.22	90.05	90.88	91.71	92.54	93.36	95.02
16.75	81.03	81.86	82.68	83.50	84.33	85.15	85.98	86.80	87.63	88.45	89.28	90.10	90.93	91.75	92.58	94.23
17.00	80.32	81.14	81.96	82.78	83.60	84.42	85.24	86.06	86.88	87.70	88.52	89.34	90.16	90.98	91.80	93.44
17.25	79.61	80.43	81.24	82.06	82.87	83.69	84.50	85.32	86.13	86.95	87.77	88.58	89.40	90.21	91.03	92.66
17.50	78.91	79.72	80.53	81.34	82.16	82.97	83.78	84.59	85.40	86.21	87.02	87.83	88.64	89.46	90.27	91.89
17.75	78.22	79.03	79.83	80.64	81.45	82.25	83.06	83.87	84.67	85.48	86.29	87.09	87.90	88.71	89.51	91.13
18.00	77.54	78.34	79.14	79.94	80.75	81.55	82.35	83.15	83.96	84.76	85.56	86.36	87.16	87.97	88.77	90.37
18.25	76.86	77.66	78.46	79.26	80.05	80.85	81.65	82.45	83.25	84.04	84.84	85.64	86.44	87.24	88.03	89.63
18.50	76.20	76.99	77.78	78.58	79.37	80.16	80.96	81.75	82.54	83.34	84.13	84.92	85.72	86.51	87.30	88.89
18.75	75.54	76.33	77.12	77.90	78.69	79.48	80.27	81.06	81.85	82.64	83.43	84.22	85.01	85.80	86.58	88.16
19.00	74.88	75.67	76.45	77.24	78.02	78.81	79.59	80.38	81.16	81.95	82.73	83.52	84.30	85.09	85.87	87.44
20.00	72.35	73.12	73.89	74.65	75.42	76.19	76.96	77.73	78.49	79.26	80.03	80.80	81.57	82.33	83.10	84.64
25.00	61.24	61.94	62.63	63.32	64.01	64.71	65.40	66.09	66.78	67.47	68.17	68.86	69.55	70.24	70.93	72.32
30.00	52.32	52.95	53.58	54.20	54.83	55.46	56.09	56.71	57.34	57.97	58.60	59.22	59.85	60.48	61.10	62.36

BOND YIELD

Description: This table shows the yield to maturity of a bond purchased at the price shown in the index.

Example: The yield to maturity of a 15.00 %, 5 year bond at a price of 102.00 is 14.42 %.

COUPON RATE, %

PRICE	11.00%	11.25%	11.50%	11.75%	12.00%	12.25%	12.50%	12.75%	13.00%	13.25%	13.50%	13.75%	14.00%	14.25%	14.50%	15.00%
110	8.50	8.73	8.97	9.20	9.44	9.68	9.91	10.15	10.38	10.62	10.85	11.09	11.32	11.56	11.79	12.26
109	8.73	8.97	9.21	9.44	9.68	9.92	10.15	10.39	10.63	10.86	11.10	11.34	11.57	11.81	12.05	12.52
108	8.97	9.21	9.45	9.69	9.93	10.16	10.40	10.64	10.88	11.12	11.35	11.59	11.83	12.07	12.31	12.78
107	9.22	9.46	9.70	9.93	10.17	10.41	10.65	10.89	11.13	11.37	11.61	11.85	12.09	12.33	12.57	13.05
106	9.46	9.70	9.94	10.18	10.42	10.67	10.91	11.15	11.39	11.63	11.87	12.11	12.35	12.59	12.83	13.31
105.75	9.52	9.76	10.01	10.25	10.49	10.73	10.97	11.21	11.45	11.69	11.93	12.18	12.42	12.66	12.90	13.38
105.50	9.58	9.83	10.07	10.31	10.55	10.79	11.03	11.28	11.52	11.76	12.00	12.24	12.48	12.72	12.97	13.45
105.25	9.65	9.89	10.13	10.37	10.61	10.86	11.10	11.34	11.58	11.82	12.07	12.31	12.55	12.79	13.03	13.52
105.00	9.71	9.95	10.19	10.44	10.68	10.92	11.16	11.41	11.65	11.89	12.13	12.37	12.62	12.86	13.10	13.58
104.75	9.77	10.01	10.26	10.50	10.74	10.98	11.23	11.47	11.71	11.96	12.20	12.44	12.68	12.93	13.17	13.65
104.50	9.83	10.08	10.32	10.56	10.81	11.05	11.29	11.54	11.78	12.02	12.26	12.51	12.75	12.99	13.24	13.72
104.25	9.90	10.14	10.38	10.63	10.87	11.11	11.36	11.60	11.84	12.09	12.33	12.57	12.82	13.06	13.30	13.79
104.00	9.96	10.20	10.45	10.69	10.94	11.18	11.42	11.67	11.91	12.15	12.40	12.64	12.89	13.13	13.37	13.86
103.75	10.02	10.27	10.51	10.76	11.00	11.24	11.49	11.73	11.98	12.22	12.46	12.71	12.95	13.20	13.44	13.93
103.50	10.09	10.33	10.58	10.82	11.06	11.31	11.55	11.80	12.04	12.29	12.53	12.78	13.02	13.27	13.51	14.00
103.25	10.15	10.40	10.64	10.88	11.13	11.37	11.62	11.86	12.11	12.35	12.60	12.84	13.09	13.33	13.58	14.07
103.00	10.21	10.46	10.70	10.95	11.20	11.44	11.69	11.93	12.18	12.42	12.67	12.91	13.16	13.40	13.65	14.14
102.75	10.28	10.52	10.77	11.02	11.26	11.51	11.75	12.00	12.24	12.49	12.73	12.98	13.23	13.47	13.72	14.21
102.50	10.34	10.59	10.83	11.08	11.33	11.57	11.82	12.06	12.31	12.56	12.80	13.05	13.29	13.54	13.79	14.28
102.25	10.41	10.65	10.90	11.15	11.39	11.64	11.89	12.13	12.38	12.62	12.87	13.12	13.36	13.61	13.86	14.35
102.00	10.47	10.72	10.96	11.21	11.46	11.71	11.95	12.20	12.45	12.69	12.94	13.19	13.43	13.68	13.93	14.42
101.75	10.54	10.78	11.03	11.28	11.52	11.77	12.02	12.27	12.51	12.76	13.01	13.26	13.50	13.75	14.00	14.49
101.50	10.60	10.85	11.10	11.34	11.59	11.84	12.09	12.33	12.58	12.83	13.08	13.32	13.57	13.82	14.07	14.56
101.25	10.67	10.91	11.16	11.41	11.66	11.91	12.15	12.40	12.65	12.90	13.15	13.39	13.64	13.89	14.14	14.63
101.00	10.73	10.98	11.23	11.48	11.73	11.97	12.22	12.47	12.72	12.97	13.22	13.46	13.71	13.96	14.21	14.71
100.75	10.80	11.05	11.29	11.54	11.79	12.04	12.29	12.54	12.79	13.04	13.28	13.53	13.78	14.03	14.28	14.78
100.50	10.86	11.11	11.36	11.61	11.86	12.11	12.36	12.61	12.86	13.11	13.35	13.60	13.85	14.10	14.35	14.85
100.25	10.93	11.18	11.43	11.68	11.93	12.18	12.43	12.68	12.93	13.18	13.42	13.67	13.92	14.17	14.42	14.92
100.00	11.00	11.25	11.50	11.75	12.00	12.25	12.50	12.75	13.00	13.25	13.50	13.75	14.00	14.25	14.50	15.00
99.75	11.06	11.31	11.56	11.81	12.06	12.31	12.56	12.81	13.06	13.32	13.57	13.82	14.07	14.32	14.57	15.07
99.50	11.13	11.38	11.63	11.88	12.13	12.38	12.63	12.88	13.13	13.39	13.64	13.89	14.14	14.39	14.64	15.14
99.25	11.19	11.45	11.70	11.95	12.20	12.45	12.70	12.95	13.20	13.46	13.71	13.96	14.21	14.46	14.71	15.21
99.00	11.26	11.51	11.77	12.02	12.27	12.52	12.77	13.02	13.28	13.53	13.78	14.03	14.28	14.53	14.79	15.29
98.75	11.33	11.58	11.83	12.09	12.34	12.59	12.84	13.09	13.35	13.60	13.85	14.10	14.35	14.61	14.86	15.36
98.50	11.40	11.65	11.90	12.15	12.41	12.66	12.91	13.16	13.42	13.67	13.92	14.17	14.43	14.68	14.93	15.44
98.25	11.46	11.72	11.97	12.22	12.48	12.73	12.98	13.23	13.49	13.74	13.99	14.25	14.50	14.75	15.01	15.51
98.00	11.53	11.79	12.04	12.29	12.55	12.80	13.05	13.31	13.56	13.81	14.07	14.32	14.57	14.83	15.08	15.59
97.75	11.60	11.85	12.11	12.36	12.62	12.87	13.12	13.38	13.63	13.88	14.14	14.39	14.65	14.90	15.15	15.66
97.50	11.67	11.92	12.18	12.43	12.69	12.94	13.19	13.45	13.70	13.96	14.21	14.46	14.72	14.97	15.23	15.74
97.25	11.74	11.99	12.25	12.50	12.76	13.01	13.26	13.52	13.77	14.03	14.28	14.54	14.79	15.05	15.30	15.81
97.00	11.81	12.06	12.32	12.57	12.83	13.08	13.34	13.59	13.85	14.10	14.36	14.61	14.87	15.12	15.38	15.89
96.75	11.88	12.13	12.39	12.64	12.90	13.15	13.41	13.66	13.92	14.17	14.43	14.69	14.94	15.20	15.45	15.96
96.50	11.94	12.20	12.46	12.71	12.97	13.22	13.48	13.74	13.99	14.25	14.50	14.76	15.02	15.27	15.53	16.04
96.25	12.01	12.27	12.53	12.78	13.04	13.30	13.55	13.81	14.06	14.32	14.58	14.83	15.09	15.35	15.60	16.12
96.00	12.08	12.34	12.60	12.85	13.11	13.37	13.62	13.88	14.14	14.39	14.65	14.91	15.17	15.42	15.68	16.19
95.75	12.15	12.41	12.67	12.93	13.18	13.44	13.70	13.95	14.21	14.47	14.73	14.98	15.24	15.50	15.75	16.27
95.50	12.22	12.48	12.74	13.00	13.25	13.51	13.77	14.03	14.29	14.54	14.80	15.06	15.32	15.57	15.83	16.35
95.25	12.29	12.55	12.81	13.07	13.33	13.58	13.84	14.10	14.36	14.62	14.88	15.13	15.39	15.65	15.91	16.42
95.00	12.37	12.62	12.88	13.14	13.40	13.66	13.92	14.17	14.43	14.69	14.95	15.21	15.47	15.73	15.98	16.50
94.75	12.44	12.70	12.95	13.21	13.47	13.73	13.99	14.25	14.51	14.77	15.03	15.28	15.54	15.80	16.06	16.58
94.50	12.51	12.77	13.03	13.29	13.54	13.80	14.06	14.32	14.58	14.84	15.10	15.36	15.62	15.88	16.14	16.66
94.25	12.58	12.84	13.10	13.36	13.62	13.88	14.14	14.40	14.66	14.92	15.18	15.44	15.70	15.96	16.22	16.74
94.00	12.65	12.91	13.17	13.43	13.69	13.95	14.21	14.47	14.73	14.99	15.25	15.51	15.77	16.03	16.30	16.82
93.75	12.72	12.98	13.24	13.50	13.77	14.03	14.29	14.55	14.81	15.07	15.33	15.59	15.85	16.11	16.37	16.90
93	12.94	13.20	13.46	13.73	13.99	14.25	14.51	14.77	15.04	15.30	15.56	15.82	16.09	16.35	16.61	17.14
92	13.23	13.50	13.76	14.02	14.29	14.55	14.82	15.08	15.34	15.61	15.87	16.14	16.40	16.67	16.93	17.46
91	13.53	13.80	14.06	14.33	14.59	14.86	15.13	15.39	15.66	15.92	16.19	16.46	16.72	16.99	17.25	17.79
90	13.83	14.10	14.37	14.63	14.90	15.17	15.44	15.71	15.97	16.24	16.51	16.78	17.05	17.31	17.58	18.12
89	14.14	14.41	14.68	14.95	15.22	15.49	15.76	16.03	16.30	16.57	16.84	17.11	17.38	17.65	17.92	18.46
88	14.45	14.72	14.99	15.26	15.53	15.81	16.08	16.35	16.62	16.89	17.17	17.44	17.71	17.98	18.26	18.80
87	14.76	15.04	15.31	15.58	15.86	16.13	16.41	16.68	16.95	17.23	17.50	17.78	18.05	18.33	18.60	19.15
86	15.08	15.36	15.63	15.91	16.19	16.46	16.74	17.01	17.29	17.57	17.84	18.12	18.40	18.67	18.95	19.50
85	15.41	15.68	15.96	16.24	16.52	16.80	17.08	17.35	17.63	17.91	18.19	18.47	18.75	19.03	19.31	19.86
84	15.74	16.02	16.30	16.58	16.86	17.14	17.42	17.70	17.98	18.26	18.54	18.82	19.10	19.38	19.67	20.23
83	16.07	16.35	16.64	16.92	17.20	17.48	17.77	18.05	18.33	18.62	18.90	19.18	19.47	19.75	20.03	20.60
82	16.41	16.70	16.98	17.26	17.55	17.83	18.12	18.41	18.69	18.98	19.26	19.55	19.83	20.12	20.41	20.98
81	16.76	17.04	17.33	17.62	17.90	18.19	18.48	18.77	19.06	19.34	19.63	19.92	20.21	20.50	20.78	21.36
80	17.11	17.40	17.69	17.98	18.26	18.55	18.84	19.14	19.43	19.72	20.01	20.30	20.59	20.88	21.17	21.75

Description: This table shows the price to pay for a bond at the yield rate. The yield is to maturity.

Example: The price of a 6.75 %, 6 year bond to yield 8 % to maturity is $ 94.13.

COUPON RATE, %

YIELD	0.00%	1.00%	2.00%	3.00%	4.00%	4.25%	4.50%	4.75%	5.00%	5.25%	5.50%	5.75%	6.00%	6.25%	6.50%	6.75%
0.00	100.00	106.00	112.00	118.00	124.00	125.50	127.00	128.50	130.00	131.50	133.00	134.50	136.00	137.50	139.00	140.50
1.00	94.19	100.00	105.81	111.62	117.43	118.88	120.33	121.79	123.24	124.69	126.14	127.59	129.05	130.50	131.95	133.40
2.00	88.74	94.37	100.00	105.63	111.26	112.66	114.07	115.48	116.88	118.29	119.70	121.10	122.51	123.92	125.32	126.73
3.00	83.64	89.09	94.55	100.00	105.45	106.82	108.18	109.54	110.91	112.27	113.63	115.00	116.36	117.72	119.09	120.45
4.00	78.85	84.14	89.42	94.71	100.00	101.32	102.64	103.97	105.29	106.61	107.93	109.25	110.58	111.90	113.22	114.54
4.25	77.70	82.95	88.19	93.44	98.69	100.00	101.31	102.62	103.94	105.25	106.56	107.87	109.18	110.49	111.81	113.12
4.50	76.57	81.77	86.98	92.19	97.40	98.70	100.00	101.30	102.60	103.91	105.21	106.51	107.81	109.11	111.81	111.72
4.75	75.45	80.62	85.79	90.96	96.12	97.42	98.71	100.00	101.29	102.58	103.88	105.17	106.46	107.75	109.04	110.34
5.00	74.36	79.48	84.61	89.74	94.87	96.15	97.44	98.72	100.00	101.28	102.56	103.85	105.13	106.41	107.69	108.98
5.25	73.28	78.37	83.46	88.55	93.64	94.91	96.18	97.45	98.73	100.00	101.27	102.55	103.82	105.09	106.36	107.64
5.50	72.21	77.27	82.32	87.37	92.42	93.68	94.95	96.21	97.47	98.74	100.00	101.26	102.53	103.79	105.05	106.32
5.75	71.17	76.18	81.20	86.21	91.22	92.48	93.73	94.99	96.24	97.49	98.75	100.00	101.25	102.51	103.76	105.01
6.00	70.14	75.11	80.09	85.07	90.05	91.29	92.53	93.78	95.02	96.27	97.51	98.76	100.00	101.24	102.49	103.73
6.25	69.12	74.06	79.00	83.94	88.88	90.12	91.35	92.59	93.82	95.06	96.29	97.53	98.76	100.00	101.24	102.47
6.50	68.13	73.03	77.93	82.84	87.74	88.97	90.19	91.42	92.64	93.87	95.10	96.32	97.55	98.77	100.00	101.23
6.75	67.15	72.01	76.88	81.75	86.61	87.83	89.05	90.27	91.48	92.70	93.92	95.13	96.35	97.57	98.78	100.00
7.00	66.18	71.01	75.84	80.67	85.50	86.71	87.92	89.13	90.34	91.54	92.75	93.96	95.17	96.38	97.58	98.79
7.25	65.23	70.02	74.82	79.62	84.41	85.61	86.81	88.01	89.21	90.41	91.61	92.81	94.00	95.20	96.40	97.60
7.50	64.29	69.05	73.81	78.57	83.34	84.53	85.72	86.91	88.10	89.29	90.48	91.67	92.86	94.05	95.24	96.43
7.75	63.37	68.09	72.82	77.55	82.27	83.46	84.64	85.82	87.00	88.18	89.36	90.55	91.73	92.91	94.09	95.27
8.00	62.46	67.15	71.84	76.54	81.23	82.40	83.58	84.75	85.92	87.10	88.27	89.44	90.61	91.79	92.96	94.13
8.25	61.57	66.22	70.88	75.54	80.20	81.37	82.53	83.69	84.86	86.02	87.19	88.35	89.52	90.68	91.85	93.01
8.50	60.69	65.31	69.94	74.56	79.19	80.34	81.50	82.66	83.81	84.97	86.12	87.28	88.44	89.59	90.75	91.91
8.75	59.82	64.41	69.00	73.60	78.19	79.34	80.48	81.63	82.78	83.93	85.08	86.22	87.37	88.52	89.67	90.82
9.00	58.97	63.53	68.08	72.64	77.20	78.34	79.48	80.62	81.76	82.90	84.04	85.18	86.32	87.46	88.60	89.74
9.25	58.13	62.65	67.18	71.71	76.23	77.37	78.50	79.63	80.76	81.89	83.02	84.16	85.29	86.42	87.55	88.68
9.50	57.30	61.79	66.29	70.78	75.28	76.40	77.53	78.65	79.77	80.90	82.02	83.14	84.27	85.39	86.52	87.64
9.75	56.49	60.95	65.41	69.87	74.34	75.45	76.57	77.68	78.80	79.92	81.03	82.15	83.26	84.38	85.50	86.61
10.00	55.68	60.12	64.55	68.98	73.41	74.52	75.63	76.73	77.84	78.95	80.06	81.17	82.27	83.38	84.49	85.60
10.25	54.89	59.29	63.70	68.10	72.50	73.60	74.70	75.80	76.90	78.00	79.10	80.20	81.30	82.40	83.50	84.60
10.50	54.12	58.49	62.86	67.23	71.60	72.69	73.78	74.87	75.97	77.06	78.15	79.24	80.34	81.43	82.52	83.61
10.75	53.35	57.69	62.03	66.37	70.71	71.79	72.88	73.96	75.05	76.13	77.22	78.30	79.39	80.47	81.56	82.64
11.00	52.60	56.91	61.22	65.53	69.84	70.91	71.99	73.07	74.14	75.22	76.30	77.38	78.45	79.53	80.61	81.69
11.25	51.86	56.14	60.41	64.69	68.97	70.04	71.11	72.18	73.25	74.32	75.39	76.46	77.53	78.60	79.67	80.74
11.50	51.13	55.38	59.63	63.88	68.13	69.19	70.25	71.31	72.38	73.44	74.50	75.56	76.63	77.69	78.75	79.81
11.75	50.41	54.63	58.85	63.07	67.29	68.34	69.40	70.45	71.51	72.56	73.62	74.68	75.73	76.79	77.84	78.90
12.00	49.70	53.89	58.08	62.27	66.46	67.51	68.56	69.61	70.66	71.70	72.75	73.80	74.85	75.90	76.94	77.99
12.25	49.00	53.16	57.33	61.49	65.65	66.69	67.73	68.77	69.82	70.86	71.90	72.94	73.98	75.02	76.06	77.10
12.50	48.31	52.45	56.58	60.72	64.85	65.89	66.92	67.95	68.99	70.02	71.05	72.09	73.12	74.16	75.19	76.22
12.75	47.63	51.74	55.85	59.96	64.06	65.09	66.12	67.14	68.17	69.20	70.22	71.25	72.28	73.30	74.33	75.36
13.00	46.97	51.05	55.13	59.21	63.29	64.31	65.33	66.35	67.37	68.38	69.40	70.42	71.44	72.46	73.48	74.50
13.25	46.31	50.36	54.42	58.47	62.52	63.53	64.55	65.56	66.57	67.58	68.60	69.61	70.62	71.64	72.65	73.66
13.50	45.67	49.69	53.71	57.74	61.76	62.77	63.78	64.78	65.79	66.80	67.80	68.81	69.81	70.82	71.83	72.83
13.75	45.03	49.03	53.02	57.02	61.02	62.02	63.02	64.02	65.02	66.02	67.02	68.02	69.02	70.02	71.01	72.01
14.00	44.40	48.37	52.34	56.32	60.29	61.28	62.27	63.27	64.26	65.25	66.24	67.24	68.23	69.22	70.21	71.21
14.25	43.78	47.73	51.67	55.62	59.56	60.55	61.54	62.52	63.51	64.49	65.48	66.47	67.45	68.44	69.43	70.41
14.50	43.18	47.09	51.01	54.93	58.85	59.83	60.81	61.79	62.77	63.75	64.73	65.71	66.69	67.67	68.65	69.63
14.75	42.58	46.47	50.36	54.26	58.15	59.12	60.09	61.07	62.04	63.01	63.99	64.96	65.93	66.91	67.88	68.85
15.00	41.99	45.85	49.72	53.59	57.46	58.42	59.39	60.36	61.32	62.29	63.26	64.22	65.19	66.16	67.13	68.09
15.25	41.40	45.25	49.09	52.93	56.77	57.73	58.69	59.66	60.62	61.58	62.54	63.50	64.46	65.42	66.38	67.34
15.50	40.83	44.65	48.47	52.28	56.10	57.05	58.01	58.96	59.92	60.87	61.83	62.78	63.74	64.69	65.64	66.60
15.75	40.27	44.06	47.85	51.64	55.44	56.39	57.33	58.28	59.23	60.18	61.13	62.07	63.02	63.97	64.92	65.87
16.00	39.71	43.48	47.25	51.02	54.78	55.73	56.67	57.61	58.55	59.49	60.44	61.38	62.32	63.26	64.20	65.15
16.25	39.16	42.91	46.65	50.40	54.14	55.07	56.01	56.95	57.88	58.82	59.75	60.69	61.63	62.56	63.50	64.43
16.50	38.62	42.34	46.06	49.78	53.50	54.43	55.36	56.29	57.22	58.15	59.08	60.01	60.94	61.87	62.80	63.73
16.75	38.09	41.79	45.49	49.18	52.88	53.80	54.73	55.65	56.57	57.50	58.42	59.34	60.27	61.19	62.12	63.04
17.00	37.57	41.24	44.91	48.59	52.26	53.18	54.10	55.01	55.93	56.85	57.77	58.69	59.60	60.52	61.44	62.36
17.25	37.05	40.70	44.35	48.00	51.65	52.56	53.48	54.39	55.30	56.21	57.12	58.04	58.95	59.86	60.77	61.69
17.50	36.55	40.17	43.80	47.42	51.05	51.96	52.86	53.77	54.68	55.58	56.49	57.40	58.30	59.21	60.12	61.02
17.75	36.05	39.65	43.25	46.86	50.46	51.36	52.26	53.16	54.06	54.96	55.86	56.76	57.66	58.57	59.47	60.37
18.00	35.55	39.13	42.71	46.29	49.87	50.77	51.67	52.56	53.46	54.35	55.25	56.14	57.04	57.93	58.83	59.72
18.25	35.07	38.63	42.18	45.74	49.30	50.19	51.08	51.97	52.86	53.75	54.64	55.53	56.42	57.30	58.19	59.08
18.50	34.59	38.13	41.66	45.20	48.73	49.62	50.50	51.38	52.27	53.15	54.04	54.92	55.80	56.69	57.57	58.46
18.75	34.12	37.63	41.15	44.66	48.17	49.05	49.93	50.81	51.69	52.56	53.44	54.32	55.20	56.08	56.96	57.84
19.00	33.65	37.15	40.64	44.13	47.62	48.49	49.37	50.24	51.11	51.99	52.86	53.73	54.61	55.48	56.35	57.22
20.00	31.86	35.27	38.68	42.08	45.49	46.34	47.19	48.05	48.90	49.75	50.60	51.45	52.30	53.16	54.01	54.86
25.00	24.33	27.36	30.39	33.41	36.44	37.20	37.95	38.71	39.47	40.22	40.98	41.74	42.49	43.25	44.01	44.76
30.00	18.69	21.40	24.11	26.82	29.53	30.21	30.89	31.56	32.24	32.92	33.60	34.27	34.95	35.63	36.31	36.99

Description: This table shows the yield to maturity of a bond purchased at the price shown in the index.

Example: The yield to maturity of a 6.75 %, 6 year bond at a price of 80.00 is 11.44 %.

COUPON RATE, %

PRICE	0.00%	1.00%	2.00%	3.00%	4.00%	4.25%	4.50%	4.75%	5.00%	5.25%	5.50%	5.75%	6.00%	6.25%	6.50%	6.75%
100	0.00	1.00	2.00	3.00	4.00	4.25	4.50	4.75	5.00	5.25	5.50	5.75	6.00	6.25	6.50	6.75
99	.16	1.17	2.17	3.18	4.19	4.44	4.69	4.94	5.19	5.44	5.69	5.95	6.20	6.45	6.70	6.95
98	.33	1.34	2.35	3.37	4.38	4.63	4.88	5.14	5.39	5.64	5.90	6.15	6.40	6.65	6.91	7.16
97	.50	1.52	2.54	3.55	4.57	4.83	5.08	5.34	5.59	5.85	6.10	6.35	6.61	6.86	7.12	7.37
96	.68	1.70	2.72	3.75	4.77	5.03	5.28	5.54	5.79	6.05	6.31	6.56	6.82	7.07	7.33	7.59
95	.85	1.88	2.91	3.94	4.97	5.23	5.48	5.74	6.00	6.26	6.52	6.77	7.03	7.29	7.55	7.80
94	1.03	2.06	3.10	4.13	5.17	5.43	5.69	5.95	6.21	6.47	6.73	6.99	7.25	7.51	7.77	8.02
93	1.21	2.25	3.29	4.33	5.38	5.64	5.90	6.16	6.42	6.68	6.94	7.20	7.46	7.73	7.99	8.25
92	1.39	2.44	3.48	4.53	5.58	5.85	6.11	6.37	6.63	6.90	7.16	7.42	7.68	7.95	8.21	8.47
91	1.57	2.63	3.68	4.74	5.79	6.06	6.32	6.59	6.85	7.11	7.38	7.64	7.91	8.17	8.44	8.70
90	1.76	2.82	3.88	4.94	6.00	6.27	6.54	6.80	7.07	7.34	7.60	7.87	8.13	8.40	8.67	8.93
89	1.95	3.01	4.08	5.15	6.22	6.49	6.76	7.02	7.29	7.56	7.83	8.10	8.36	8.63	8.90	9.17
88	2.14	3.21	4.28	5.36	6.44	6.71	6.98	7.25	7.52	7.79	8.06	8.33	8.60	8.87	9.14	9.41
87	2.33	3.41	4.49	5.57	6.66	6.93	7.20	7.47	7.75	8.02	8.29	8.56	8.83	9.11	9.38	9.65
86	2.52	3.61	4.70	5.79	6.88	7.16	7.43	7.70	7.98	8.25	8.52	8.80	9.07	9.35	9.62	9.90
85	2.72	3.82	4.91	6.01	7.11	7.39	7.66	7.94	8.21	8.49	8.76	9.04	9.32	9.59	9.87	10.14
84	2.92	4.02	5.13	6.23	7.34	7.62	7.89	8.17	8.45	8.73	9.01	9.28	9.56	9.84	10.12	10.40
83	3.12	4.23	5.34	6.46	7.57	7.85	8.13	8.41	8.69	8.97	9.25	9.53	9.81	10.09	10.37	10.65
82	3.33	4.45	5.57	6.69	7.81	8.09	8.37	8.65	8.94	9.22	9.50	9.78	10.06	10.35	10.63	10.91
81	3.54	4.66	5.79	6.92	8.05	8.33	8.62	8.90	9.19	9.47	9.75	10.04	10.32	10.61	10.89	11.18
80	3.75	4.88	6.02	7.15	8.29	8.58	8.87	9.15	9.44	9.72	10.01	10.30	10.58	10.87	11.16	11.44
79	3.96	5.10	6.25	7.39	8.54	8.83	9.12	9.41	9.69	9.98	10.27	10.56	10.85	11.14	11.43	11.72
78	4.18	5.33	6.48	7.63	8.79	9.08	9.37	9.66	9.95	10.24	10.54	10.83	11.12	11.41	11.70	11.99
77	4.40	5.56	6.72	7.88	9.05	9.34	9.63	9.92	10.22	10.51	10.80	11.10	11.39	11.69	11.98	12.27
76	4.62	5.79	6.96	8.13	9.31	9.60	9.90	10.19	10.49	10.78	11.08	11.37	11.67	11.97	12.26	12.56
75	4.85	6.02	7.20	8.38	9.57	9.87	10.16	10.46	10.76	11.06	11.35	11.65	11.95	12.25	12.55	12.85
74	5.08	6.26	7.45	8.64	9.84	10.14	10.43	10.74	11.04	11.34	11.64	11.94	12.24	12.54	12.84	13.14
73	5.31	6.50	7.70	8.90	10.11	10.41	10.71	11.01	11.32	11.62	11.92	12.23	12.53	12.84	13.14	13.44
72	5.55	6.75	7.96	9.17	10.38	10.69	10.99	11.30	11.60	11.91	12.21	12.52	12.83	13.13	13.44	13.75
71	5.79	7.00	8.21	9.44	10.66	10.97	11.28	11.59	11.89	12.20	12.51	12.82	13.13	13.44	13.75	14.06
70	6.03	7.25	8.48	9.71	10.95	11.26	11.57	11.88	12.19	12.50	12.81	13.12	13.44	13.75	14.06	14.38
69	6.28	7.51	8.75	9.99	11.24	11.55	11.86	12.18	12.49	12.81	13.12	13.43	13.75	14.07	14.38	14.70
68	6.53	7.77	9.02	10.27	11.53	11.85	12.16	12.48	12.80	13.11	13.43	13.75	14.07	14.39	14.71	15.03
67	6.78	8.04	9.30	10.56	11.83	12.15	12.47	12.79	13.11	13.43	13.75	14.07	14.39	14.71	15.04	15.36
66	7.04	8.31	9.58	10.85	12.14	12.46	12.78	13.10	13.43	13.75	14.07	14.40	14.72	15.05	15.37	15.70
65	7.31	8.58	9.86	11.15	12.45	12.77	13.10	13.42	13.75	14.08	14.40	14.73	15.06	15.39	15.72	16.05
64	7.57	8.86	10.16	11.46	12.77	13.09	13.42	13.75	14.08	14.41	14.74	15.07	15.40	15.73	16.07	16.40
63	7.85	9.15	10.45	11.77	13.09	13.42	13.75	14.08	14.42	14.75	15.08	15.42	15.75	16.09	16.42	16.76
62	8.12	9.43	10.75	12.08	13.42	13.75	14.09	14.42	14.76	15.10	15.43	15.77	16.11	16.45	16.79	17.13
61	8.41	9.73	11.06	12.40	13.75	14.09	14.43	14.77	15.11	15.45	15.79	16.13	16.47	16.82	17.16	17.50
60	8.69	10.03	11.38	12.73	14.09	14.44	14.78	15.12	15.47	15.81	16.15	16.50	16.85	17.19	17.54	17.89
59	8.99	10.34	11.70	13.06	14.44	14.79	15.13	15.48	15.83	16.18	16.53	16.88	17.23	17.58	17.93	18.28
58	9.28	10.65	12.02	13.41	14.80	15.15	15.50	15.85	16.20	16.55	16.91	17.26	17.61	17.97	18.32	18.68
57	9.59	10.97	12.35	13.75	15.16	15.52	15.87	16.22	16.58	16.94	17.29	17.65	18.01	18.37	18.73	19.09
56	9.90	11.29	12.69	14.11	15.53	15.89	16.25	16.61	16.97	17.33	17.69	18.05	18.41	18.78	19.14	19.51
55	10.21	11.62	13.04	14.47	15.91	16.27	16.64	17.00	17.36	17.73	18.10	18.46	18.83	19.20	19.56	19.93
54	10.53	11.96	13.39	14.84	16.30	16.67	17.03	17.40	17.77	18.14	18.51	18.88	19.25	19.63	20.00	20.37
53	10.86	12.30	13.75	15.22	16.70	17.07	17.44	17.81	18.19	18.56	18.93	19.31	19.69	20.06	20.44	20.82
52	11.20	12.65	14.12	15.61	17.10	17.48	17.85	18.23	18.61	18.99	19.37	19.75	20.13	20.51	20.90	21.28
51	11.54	13.01	14.50	16.00	17.52	17.90	18.28	18.66	19.04	19.43	19.81	20.20	20.59	20.97	21.36	21.75
50	11.89	13.38	14.89	16.41	17.94	18.33	18.71	19.10	19.49	19.88	20.27	20.66	21.05	21.45	21.84	22.24
49	12.24	13.76	15.28	16.82	18.38	18.77	19.16	19.55	19.95	20.34	20.74	21.14	21.53	21.93	22.33	22.73
48	12.61	14.14	15.68	17.25	18.82	19.22	19.62	20.02	20.42	20.82	21.22	21.62	22.03	22.43	22.84	23.24
47	12.98	14.53	16.10	17.68	19.28	19.68	20.09	20.49	20.90	21.30	21.71	22.12	22.53	22.94	23.35	23.77
46	13.37	14.94	16.52	18.13	19.75	20.16	20.57	20.98	21.39	21.80	22.22	22.63	23.05	23.47	23.89	24.31
45	13.76	15.35	16.96	18.59	20.23	20.65	21.06	21.48	21.90	22.32	22.74	23.16	23.58	24.01	24.43	24.86
44	14.16	15.77	17.40	19.06	20.73	21.15	21.57	22.00	22.42	22.85	23.28	23.70	24.13	24.57	25.00	25.43
43	14.57	16.20	17.86	19.54	21.24	21.67	22.10	22.53	22.96	23.39	23.83	24.26	24.70	25.14	25.58	26.02
42	14.99	16.65	18.33	20.04	21.76	22.20	22.64	23.07	23.51	23.95	24.40	24.84	25.28	25.73	26.18	26.63
41	15.42	17.11	18.82	20.55	22.30	22.75	23.19	23.64	24.08	24.53	24.98	25.43	25.89	26.34	26.80	27.25
40	15.86	17.58	19.31	21.08	22.86	23.31	23.76	24.22	24.67	25.13	25.59	26.05	26.51	26.97	27.44	27.90
39	16.32	18.06	19.83	21.62	23.44	23.89	24.35	24.82	25.28	25.75	26.21	26.68	27.15	27.62	28.10	28.57
38	16.79	18.56	20.35	22.18	24.03	24.50	24.97	25.44	25.91	26.38	26.86	27.34	27.82	28.30	28.78	29.27
37	17.27	19.07	20.90	22.76	24.64	25.12	25.60	26.08	26.56	27.04	27.53	28.02	28.50	29.00	29.49	29.98
36	17.77	19.60	21.46	23.35	25.28	25.76	26.25	26.74	27.23	27.72	28.22	28.72	29.22	29.72	30.22	30.73
35	18.28	20.14	22.04	23.97	25.93	26.43	26.93	27.43	27.93	28.43	28.94	29.45	29.96	30.47	30.99	31.50
30	21.10	23.16	25.27	27.41	29.61	30.17	30.73	31.29	31.85	32.42	32.99	33.57	34.15	34.73	35.31	35.90
25	24.49	26.81	29.20	31.65	34.17	34.81	35.46	36.11	36.76	37.42	38.09	38.75	39.43	40.10	40.78	41.47

BOND PRICE

6 YEARS

Description: This table shows the price to pay for a bond at the yield rate. The yield is to maturity.

Example: The price of a 10.75 %, 6 year bond to yield 8 % to maturity is $ 112.90.

YIELD	7.00%	7.25%	7.50%	7.75%	8.00%	8.25%	8.50%	8.75%	9.00%	9.25%	9.50%	9.75%	10.00%	10.25%	10.50%	10.75%
0.00	142.00	143.50	145.00	146.50	148.00	149.50	151.00	152.50	154.00	155.50	157.00	158.50	160.00	161.50	163.00	164.50
1.00	134.86	136.31	137.76	139.21	140.67	142.12	143.57	145.02	146.48	147.93	149.38	150.83	152.29	153.74	155.19	156.64
2.00	128.14	129.54	130.95	132.36	133.77	135.17	136.58	137.99	139.39	140.80	142.21	143.61	145.02	146.43	147.83	149.24
3.00	121.82	123.18	124.54	125.91	127.27	128.63	130.00	131.36	132.72	134.09	135.45	136.81	138.18	139.54	140.90	142.27
4.00	115.86	117.18	118.51	119.83	121.15	122.47	123.79	125.12	126.44	127.76	129.08	130.40	131.73	133.05	134.37	135.69
4.25	114.43	115.74	117.05	118.37	119.68	120.99	122.30	123.61	124.92	126.24	127.55	128.86	130.17	131.48	132.80	134.11
4.50	113.02	114.32	115.62	116.92	118.23	119.53	120.83	122.13	123.43	124.74	126.04	127.34	128.64	129.94	131.24	132.55
4.75	111.63	112.92	114.21	115.50	116.80	118.09	119.38	120.67	121.96	123.26	124.55	125.84	127.13	128.42	129.72	131.01
5.00	110.26	111.54	112.82	114.10	115.39	116.67	117.95	119.23	120.52	121.80	123.08	124.36	125.64	126.93	128.21	129.49
5.25	108.91	110.18	111.45	112.73	114.00	115.27	116.54	117.82	119.09	120.36	121.63	122.91	124.18	125.45	126.72	128.00
5.50	107.58	108.84	110.10	111.37	112.63	113.89	115.16	116.42	117.68	118.95	120.21	121.47	122.73	124.00	125.26	126.52
5.75	106.27	107.52	108.78	110.03	111.28	112.54	113.79	115.04	116.30	117.55	118.80	120.06	121.31	122.56	123.82	125.07
6.00	104.98	106.22	107.47	108.71	109.95	111.20	112.44	113.69	114.93	116.18	117.42	118.66	119.91	121.15	122.40	123.64
6.25	103.71	104.94	106.18	107.41	108.65	109.88	111.12	112.35	113.59	114.82	116.06	117.29	118.53	119.76	121.00	122.23
6.50	102.45	103.68	104.90	106.13	107.36	108.58	109.81	111.03	112.26	113.48	114.71	115.94	117.16	118.39	119.61	120.84
6.75	101.22	102.43	103.65	104.87	106.08	107.30	108.52	109.73	110.95	112.17	113.39	114.60	115.82	117.04	118.25	119.47
7.00	100.00	101.21	102.42	103.62	104.83	106.04	107.25	108.46	109.66	110.87	112.08	113.29	114.50	115.70	116.91	118.12
7.25	98.80	100.00	101.20	102.40	103.60	104.80	106.00	107.19	108.39	109.59	110.79	111.99	113.19	114.39	115.59	116.79
7.50	97.62	98.81	100.00	101.19	102.38	103.57	104.76	105.95	107.14	108.33	109.52	110.71	111.90	113.09	114.28	115.47
7.75	96.45	97.64	98.82	100.00	101.18	102.36	103.55	104.73	105.91	107.09	108.27	109.45	110.64	111.82	113.00	114.18
8.00	95.31	96.48	97.65	98.83	100.00	101.17	102.35	103.52	104.69	105.87	107.04	108.21	109.39	110.56	111.73	112.90
8.25	94.18	95.34	96.51	97.67	98.84	100.00	101.16	102.33	103.49	104.66	105.82	106.99	108.15	109.32	110.48	111.65
8.50	93.06	94.22	95.37	96.53	97.69	98.84	100.00	101.16	102.31	103.47	104.63	105.78	106.94	108.09	109.25	110.41
8.75	91.96	93.11	94.26	95.41	96.56	97.70	98.85	100.00	101.15	102.30	103.44	104.59	105.74	106.89	108.04	109.18
9.00	90.88	92.02	93.16	94.30	95.44	96.58	97.72	98.86	100.00	101.14	102.28	103.42	104.56	105.70	106.84	107.98
9.25	89.81	90.95	92.08	93.21	94.34	95.47	96.60	97.74	98.87	100.00	101.13	102.26	103.40	104.53	105.66	106.79
9.50	88.76	89.89	91.01	92.13	93.26	94.38	95.51	96.63	97.75	98.88	100.00	101.12	102.25	103.37	104.49	105.62
9.75	87.73	88.84	89.96	91.07	92.19	93.31	94.42	95.54	96.65	97.77	98.88	100.00	101.12	102.23	103.35	104.46
10.00	86.71	87.81	88.92	90.03	91.14	92.24	93.35	94.46	95.57	96.68	97.78	98.89	100.00	101.11	102.22	103.32
10.25	85.70	86.80	87.90	89.00	90.10	91.20	92.30	93.40	94.50	95.60	96.70	97.80	98.90	100.00	101.10	102.20
10.50	84.71	85.80	86.89	87.98	89.08	90.17	91.26	92.35	93.45	94.54	95.63	96.72	97.82	98.91	100.00	101.09
10.75	83.73	84.81	85.90	86.98	88.07	89.15	90.24	91.32	92.41	93.49	94.58	95.66	96.75	97.83	98.92	100.00
11.00	82.76	83.84	84.92	85.99	87.07	88.15	89.23	90.30	91.38	92.46	93.54	94.61	95.69	96.77	97.85	98.92
11.25	81.81	82.88	83.95	85.02	86.09	87.16	88.23	89.30	90.37	91.44	92.51	93.58	94.65	95.72	96.79	97.86
11.50	80.88	81.94	83.00	84.06	85.13	86.19	87.25	88.31	89.38	90.44	91.50	92.56	93.63	94.69	95.75	96.81
11.75	79.95	81.01	82.06	83.12	84.17	85.23	86.28	87.34	88.39	89.45	90.50	91.56	92.61	93.67	94.72	95.78
12.00	79.04	80.09	81.14	82.18	83.23	84.28	85.33	86.38	87.42	88.47	89.52	90.57	91.62	92.66	93.71	94.76
12.25	78.14	79.18	80.22	81.26	82.31	83.35	84.39	85.43	86.47	87.51	88.55	89.59	90.63	91.67	92.71	93.75
12.50	77.26	78.29	79.32	80.36	81.39	82.43	83.46	84.49	85.53	86.56	87.59	88.63	89.66	90.70	91.73	92.76
12.75	76.38	77.41	78.44	79.46	80.49	81.52	82.54	83.57	84.60	85.63	86.65	87.68	88.71	89.73	90.76	91.79
13.00	75.52	76.54	77.56	78.58	79.60	80.62	81.64	82.66	83.68	84.70	85.72	86.74	87.76	88.78	89.80	90.82
13.25	74.68	75.69	76.70	77.71	78.73	79.74	80.75	81.77	82.78	83.79	84.81	85.82	86.83	87.84	88.86	89.87
13.50	73.84	74.85	75.85	76.86	77.86	78.87	79.88	80.88	81.89	82.89	83.90	84.91	85.91	86.92	87.93	88.93
13.75	73.01	74.01	75.01	76.01	77.01	78.01	79.01	80.01	81.01	82.01	83.01	84.01	85.01	86.01	87.01	88.01
14.00	72.20	73.19	74.19	75.18	76.17	77.16	78.16	79.15	80.14	81.14	82.13	83.12	84.11	85.11	86.10	87.09
14.25	71.40	72.38	73.37	74.36	75.34	76.33	77.32	78.30	79.29	80.27	81.26	82.25	83.23	84.22	85.21	86.19
14.50	70.61	71.59	72.57	73.55	74.53	75.51	76.49	77.47	78.45	79.43	80.41	81.38	82.36	83.34	84.32	85.30
14.75	69.83	70.80	71.77	72.75	73.72	74.69	75.67	76.64	77.61	78.59	79.56	80.53	81.51	82.48	83.45	84.43
15.00	69.06	70.03	70.99	71.96	72.93	73.89	74.86	75.83	76.79	77.76	78.73	79.69	80.66	81.63	82.60	83.56
15.25	68.30	69.26	70.22	71.18	72.14	73.10	74.06	75.02	75.99	76.95	77.91	78.87	79.83	80.79	81.75	82.71
15.50	67.55	68.51	69.46	70.42	71.37	72.32	73.28	74.23	75.19	76.14	77.10	78.05	79.00	79.96	80.91	81.87
15.75	66.82	67.76	68.71	69.66	70.61	71.56	72.50	73.45	74.40	75.35	76.30	77.24	78.19	79.14	80.09	81.04
16.00	66.09	67.03	67.97	68.91	69.86	70.80	71.74	72.68	73.62	74.57	75.51	76.45	77.39	78.33	79.28	80.22
16.25	65.37	66.31	67.24	68.18	69.11	70.05	70.99	71.92	72.86	73.79	74.73	75.67	76.60	77.54	78.47	79.41
16.50	64.66	65.59	66.52	67.45	68.38	69.31	70.24	71.17	72.10	73.03	73.96	74.89	75.82	76.75	77.68	78.61
16.75	63.96	64.89	65.81	66.74	67.66	68.58	69.51	70.43	71.36	72.28	73.20	74.13	75.05	75.98	76.90	77.82
17.00	63.28	64.19	65.11	66.03	66.95	67.87	68.79	69.70	70.62	71.54	72.46	73.38	74.29	75.21	76.13	77.05
17.25	62.60	63.51	64.42	65.33	66.25	67.16	68.07	68.98	69.90	70.81	71.72	72.63	73.54	74.46	75.37	76.28
17.50	61.93	62.83	63.74	64.65	65.55	66.46	67.37	68.27	69.18	70.09	70.99	71.90	72.81	73.71	74.62	75.53
17.75	61.27	62.17	63.07	63.97	64.87	65.77	66.67	67.57	68.47	69.37	70.28	71.18	72.08	72.98	73.88	74.78
18.00	60.62	61.51	62.41	63.30	64.20	65.09	65.99	66.88	67.78	68.67	69.57	70.46	71.36	72.25	73.15	74.04
18.25	59.97	60.86	61.75	62.64	63.53	64.42	65.31	66.20	67.09	67.98	68.87	69.76	70.65	71.54	72.43	73.32
18.50	59.34	60.22	61.11	61.99	62.88	63.76	64.64	65.53	66.41	67.29	68.18	69.06	69.95	70.83	71.71	72.60
18.75	58.71	59.59	60.47	61.35	62.23	63.11	63.98	64.86	65.74	66.62	67.50	68.38	69.26	70.13	71.01	71.89
19.00	58.10	58.97	59.84	60.72	61.59	62.46	63.33	64.21	65.08	65.95	66.83	67.70	68.57	69.45	70.32	71.19
20.00	55.71	56.56	57.41	58.27	59.12	59.97	60.82	61.67	62.52	63.38	64.23	65.08	65.93	66.78	67.63	68.49
25.00	45.52	46.28	47.03	47.79	48.55	49.30	50.06	50.82	51.57	52.33	53.09	53.84	54.60	55.36	56.11	56.87
30.00	37.66	38.34	39.02	39.70	40.37	41.05	41.73	42.41	43.08	43.76	44.44	45.12	45.79	46.47	47.15	47.83

Description: This table shows the yield to maturity of a bond purchased at the price shown in the index.

Example: The yield to maturity of a 10.75 %, 6 year bond at a price of 105.00 is 9.63 %.

PRICE	7.00%	7.25%	7.50%	7.75%	8.00%	8.25%	8.50%	8.75%	9.00%	9.25%	9.50%	9.75%	10.00%	10.25%	10.50%	10.75%
125	2.48	2.70	2.92	3.14	3.36	3.58	3.80	4.01	4.23	4.45	4.67	4.89	5.10	5.32	5.54	5.76
124	2.64	2.86	3.08	3.30	3.52	3.74	3.96	4.18	4.40	4.62	4.84	5.06	5.28	5.49	5.71	5.93
123	2.80	3.02	3.24	3.47	3.69	3.91	4.13	4.35	4.57	4.79	5.01	5.23	5.45	5.67	5.89	6.11
122	2.96	3.19	3.41	3.63	3.85	4.07	4.30	4.52	4.74	4.96	5.18	5.40	5.62	5.84	6.07	6.29
121	3.13	3.35	3.57	3.80	4.02	4.24	4.47	4.69	4.91	5.13	5.36	5.58	5.80	6.02	6.24	6.47
120	3.29	3.52	3.74	3.97	4.19	4.41	4.64	4.86	5.08	5.31	5.53	5.76	5.98	6.20	6.42	6.65
119	3.46	3.69	3.91	4.14	4.36	4.59	4.81	5.04	5.26	5.49	5.71	5.93	6.16	6.38	6.61	6.83
118	3.63	3.86	4.08	4.31	4.53	4.76	4.99	5.21	5.44	5.66	5.89	6.12	6.34	6.57	6.79	7.02
117	3.80	4.03	4.25	4.48	4.71	4.94	5.16	5.39	5.62	5.84	6.07	6.30	6.53	6.75	6.98	7.20
116	3.97	4.20	4.43	4.66	4.89	5.11	5.34	5.57	5.80	6.03	6.26	6.48	6.71	6.94	7.17	7.39
115	4.15	4.38	4.60	4.83	5.06	5.29	5.52	5.75	5.98	6.21	6.44	6.67	6.90	7.13	7.36	7.59
114	4.32	4.55	4.78	5.01	5.24	5.48	5.71	5.94	6.17	6.40	6.63	6.86	7.09	7.32	7.55	7.78
113	4.50	4.73	4.96	5.19	5.43	5.66	5.89	6.12	6.35	6.59	6.82	7.05	7.28	7.51	7.74	7.98
112	4.68	4.91	5.14	5.38	5.61	5.84	6.08	6.31	6.54	6.78	7.01	7.24	7.48	7.71	7.94	8.17
111	4.86	5.09	5.33	5.56	5.80	6.03	6.27	6.50	6.74	6.97	7.20	7.44	7.67	7.91	8.14	8.37
110	5.04	5.28	5.51	5.75	5.99	6.22	6.46	6.69	6.93	7.16	7.40	7.64	7.87	8.11	8.34	8.58
109	5.23	5.47	5.70	5.94	6.18	6.41	6.65	6.89	7.13	7.36	7.60	7.84	8.07	8.31	8.55	8.78
108	5.42	5.65	5.89	6.13	6.37	6.61	6.85	7.08	7.32	7.56	7.80	8.04	8.28	8.51	8.75	8.99
107	5.60	5.84	6.08	6.32	6.56	6.80	7.04	7.28	7.52	7.76	8.00	8.24	8.48	8.72	8.96	9.20
106	5.80	6.04	6.28	6.52	6.76	7.00	7.24	7.49	7.73	7.97	8.21	8.45	8.69	8.93	9.17	9.41
105	5.99	6.23	6.48	6.72	6.96	7.20	7.45	7.69	7.93	8.17	8.42	8.66	8.90	9.14	9.39	9.63
104	6.19	6.43	6.67	6.92	7.16	7.41	7.65	7.90	8.14	8.38	8.63	8.87	9.11	9.36	9.60	9.85
103	6.39	6.63	6.88	7.12	7.37	7.61	7.86	8.10	8.35	8.59	8.84	9.09	9.33	9.58	9.82	10.07
102	6.59	6.83	7.08	7.33	7.57	7.82	8.07	8.31	8.56	8.81	9.06	9.30	9.55	9.80	10.04	10.29
101	6.79	7.04	7.29	7.53	7.78	8.03	8.28	8.53	8.78	9.03	9.27	9.52	9.77	10.02	10.27	10.52
100	7.00	7.25	7.50	7.75	8.00	8.25	8.50	8.75	9.00	9.25	9.50	9.75	10.00	10.25	10.50	10.75
99	7.20	7.45	7.71	7.96	8.21	8.46	8.71	8.96	9.22	9.47	9.72	9.97	10.22	10.47	10.73	10.98
98	7.41	7.67	7.92	8.17	8.43	8.68	8.93	9.19	9.44	9.69	9.95	10.20	10.45	10.71	10.96	11.21
97	7.63	7.88	8.14	8.39	8.65	8.90	9.16	9.41	9.67	9.92	10.18	10.43	10.69	10.94	11.20	11.45
96	7.84	8.10	8.36	8.61	8.87	9.13	9.38	9.64	9.90	10.15	10.41	10.66	10.92	11.18	11.43	11.69
95	8.06	8.32	8.58	8.84	9.09	9.35	9.61	9.87	10.13	10.39	10.64	10.90	11.16	11.42	11.68	11.94
94	8.28	8.54	8.80	9.06	9.32	9.58	9.84	10.10	10.36	10.62	10.88	11.14	11.40	11.66	11.92	12.18
93	8.51	8.77	9.03	9.29	9.56	9.82	10.08	10.34	10.60	10.86	11.13	11.39	11.65	11.91	12.17	12.44
92	8.74	9.00	9.26	9.53	9.79	10.05	10.32	10.58	10.84	11.11	11.37	11.63	11.90	12.16	12.43	12.69
91	8.97	9.23	9.50	9.76	10.03	10.29	10.56	10.82	11.09	11.35	11.62	11.89	12.15	12.42	12.68	12.95
90	9.20	9.47	9.74	10.00	10.27	10.54	10.80	11.07	11.34	11.61	11.87	12.14	12.41	12.68	12.94	13.21
89	9.44	9.71	9.98	10.24	10.51	10.78	11.05	11.32	11.59	11.86	12.13	12.40	12.67	12.94	13.21	13.48
88	9.68	9.95	10.22	10.49	10.76	11.03	11.30	11.57	11.85	12.12	12.39	12.66	12.93	13.20	13.47	13.75
87	9.92	10.20	10.47	10.74	11.01	11.29	11.56	11.83	12.11	12.38	12.65	12.93	13.20	13.47	13.75	14.02
86	10.17	10.44	10.72	10.99	11.27	11.54	11.82	12.09	12.37	12.64	12.92	13.20	13.47	13.75	14.02	14.30
85	10.42	10.70	10.97	11.25	11.53	11.80	12.08	12.36	12.64	12.91	13.19	13.47	13.75	14.03	14.30	14.58
84	10.67	10.95	11.23	11.51	11.79	12.07	12.35	12.63	12.91	13.19	13.47	13.75	14.03	14.31	14.59	14.87
83	10.93	11.21	11.50	11.78	12.06	12.34	12.62	12.90	13.18	13.47	13.75	14.03	14.31	14.59	14.88	15.16
82	11.20	11.48	11.76	12.04	12.33	12.61	12.90	13.18	13.46	13.75	14.03	14.32	14.60	14.89	15.17	15.46
81	11.46	11.75	12.03	12.32	12.60	12.89	13.18	13.46	13.75	14.03	14.32	14.61	14.89	15.18	15.47	15.76
80	11.73	12.02	12.31	12.59	12.88	13.17	13.46	13.75	14.04	14.33	14.61	14.90	15.19	15.48	15.77	16.06
79	12.01	12.30	12.59	12.88	13.17	13.46	13.75	14.04	14.33	14.62	14.91	15.20	15.50	15.79	16.08	16.37
78	12.29	12.58	12.87	13.16	13.46	13.75	14.04	14.34	14.63	14.92	15.22	15.51	15.80	16.10	16.39	16.69
77	12.57	12.86	13.16	13.45	13.75	14.04	14.34	14.64	14.93	15.23	15.52	15.82	16.12	16.42	16.71	17.01
76	12.86	13.15	13.45	13.75	14.05	14.34	14.64	14.94	15.24	15.54	15.84	16.14	16.44	16.74	17.04	17.34
75	13.15	13.45	13.75	14.05	14.35	14.65	14.95	15.25	15.55	15.86	16.16	16.46	16.76	17.06	17.37	17.67
74	13.45	13.75	14.05	14.35	14.66	14.96	15.27	15.57	15.87	16.18	16.48	16.79	17.09	17.40	17.70	18.01
73	13.75	14.05	14.36	14.67	14.97	15.28	15.58	15.89	16.20	16.51	16.81	17.12	17.43	17.74	18.05	18.35
72	14.06	14.37	14.67	14.98	15.29	15.60	15.91	16.22	16.53	16.84	17.15	17.46	17.77	18.08	18.39	18.71
71	14.37	14.68	14.99	15.30	15.62	15.93	16.24	16.55	16.87	17.18	17.49	17.81	18.12	18.43	18.75	19.06
70	14.69	15.00	15.32	15.63	15.95	16.26	16.58	16.89	17.21	17.53	17.84	18.16	18.48	18.79	19.11	19.43
69	15.01	15.33	15.65	15.97	16.28	16.60	16.92	17.24	17.56	17.88	18.20	18.52	18.84	19.16	19.48	19.80
68	15.35	15.67	15.99	16.31	16.63	16.95	17.27	17.59	17.91	18.24	18.56	18.88	19.21	19.53	19.86	20.18
67	15.68	16.01	16.33	16.65	16.98	17.30	17.63	17.95	18.28	18.60	18.93	19.26	19.58	19.91	20.24	20.57
66	16.03	16.35	16.68	17.01	17.33	17.66	17.99	18.32	18.65	18.98	19.31	19.64	19.97	20.30	20.63	20.96
65	16.38	16.71	17.04	17.37	17.70	18.03	18.36	18.69	19.03	19.36	19.69	20.03	20.36	20.70	21.03	21.37
64	16.73	17.07	17.40	17.73	18.07	18.40	18.74	19.08	19.41	19.75	20.09	20.42	20.76	21.10	21.44	21.78
63	17.10	17.43	17.77	18.11	18.45	18.79	19.13	19.46	19.81	20.15	20.49	20.83	21.17	21.51	21.86	22.20
62	17.47	17.81	18.15	18.49	18.83	19.18	19.52	19.86	20.21	20.55	20.90	21.24	21.59	21.93	22.28	22.63
60	18.23	18.58	18.93	19.28	19.63	19.98	20.33	20.69	21.04	21.39	21.74	22.10	22.45	22.81	23.16	23.52
55	20.30	20.67	21.05	21.42	21.79	22.16	22.54	22.91	23.29	23.66	24.04	24.42	24.79	25.17	25.55	25.93
50	22.63	23.03	23.43	23.83	24.22	24.63	25.03	25.43	25.83	26.24	26.64	27.05	27.45	27.86	28.27	28.68
45	25.29	25.72	26.15	26.58	27.01	27.44	27.88	28.32	28.75	29.19	29.63	30.07	30.51	30.96	31.40	31.84

BOND PRICE

Description: This table shows the price to pay for a bond at the yield rate. The yield is to maturity.

Example: The price of a 15.00 %, 6 year bond to yield 8 % to maturity is $ 132.85.

COUPON RATE, %

YIELD	11.00%	11.25%	11.50%	11.75%	12.00%	12.25%	12.50%	12.75%	13.00%	13.25%	13.50%	13.75%	14.00%	14.25%	14.50%	15.00%
0.00	166.00	167.50	169.00	170.50	172.00	173.50	175.00	176.50	178.00	179.50	181.00	182.50	184.00	185.50	187.00	190.00
1.00	158.09	159.55	161.00	162.45	163.90	165.36	166.81	168.26	169.71	171.17	172.62	174.07	175.52	176.98	178.43	181.33
2.00	150.65	152.05	153.46	154.87	156.28	157.68	159.09	160.50	161.90	163.31	164.72	166.12	167.53	168.94	170.34	173.16
3.00	143.63	144.99	146.36	147.72	149.08	150.45	151.81	153.17	154.54	155.90	157.26	158.63	159.99	161.35	162.72	165.45
4.00	137.01	138.34	139.66	140.98	142.30	143.62	144.95	146.27	147.59	148.91	150.23	151.55	152.88	154.20	155.52	158.16
4.25	135.42	136.73	138.04	139.35	140.67	141.98	143.29	144.60	145.91	147.23	148.54	149.85	151.16	152.47	153.78	156.41
4.50	133.85	135.15	136.45	137.75	139.06	140.36	141.66	142.96	144.26	145.56	146.87	148.17	149.47	150.77	152.07	154.68
4.75	132.30	133.59	134.88	136.18	137.47	138.76	140.05	141.34	142.64	143.93	145.22	146.51	147.80	149.10	150.39	152.97
5.00	130.77	132.06	133.34	134.62	135.90	137.18	138.47	139.75	141.03	142.31	143.60	144.88	146.16	147.44	148.72	151.29
5.25	129.27	130.54	131.81	133.09	134.36	135.63	136.90	138.18	139.45	140.72	141.99	143.27	144.54	145.81	147.09	149.63
5.50	127.79	129.05	130.31	131.58	132.84	134.10	135.36	136.63	137.89	139.15	140.42	141.68	142.94	144.21	145.47	147.99
5.75	126.33	127.58	128.83	130.09	131.34	132.59	133.85	135.10	136.35	137.61	138.86	140.11	141.37	142.62	143.88	146.38
6.00	124.89	126.13	127.37	128.62	129.86	131.11	132.35	133.59	134.84	136.08	137.33	138.57	139.82	141.06	142.30	144.79
6.25	123.47	124.70	125.94	127.17	128.41	129.64	130.88	132.11	133.35	134.58	135.82	137.05	138.29	139.52	140.76	143.23
6.50	122.07	123.29	124.52	125.74	126.97	128.20	129.42	130.65	131.87	133.10	134.32	135.55	136.78	138.00	139.23	141.68
6.75	120.69	121.90	123.12	124.34	125.55	126.77	127.99	129.20	130.42	131.64	132.85	134.07	135.29	136.51	137.72	140.16
7.00	119.33	120.53	121.74	122.95	124.16	125.37	126.57	127.78	128.99	130.20	131.41	132.61	133.82	135.03	136.24	138.65
7.25	117.99	119.19	120.38	121.58	122.78	123.98	125.18	126.38	127.58	128.78	129.98	131.18	132.38	133.57	134.77	137.17
7.50	116.66	117.86	119.05	120.24	121.43	122.62	123.81	125.00	126.19	127.38	128.57	129.76	130.95	132.14	133.33	135.71
7.75	115.36	116.54	117.73	118.91	120.09	121.27	122.45	123.63	124.82	126.00	127.18	128.36	129.54	130.72	131.91	134.27
8.00	114.08	115.25	116.42	117.60	118.77	119.94	121.12	122.29	123.46	124.64	125.81	126.98	128.16	129.33	130.50	132.85
8.25	112.81	113.98	115.14	116.31	117.47	118.63	119.80	120.96	122.13	123.29	124.46	125.62	126.79	127.95	129.12	131.45
8.50	111.56	112.72	113.88	115.03	116.19	117.34	118.50	119.66	120.81	121.97	123.13	124.28	125.44	126.59	127.75	130.06
8.75	110.33	111.48	112.63	113.78	114.92	116.07	117.22	118.37	119.52	120.66	121.81	122.96	124.11	125.26	126.40	128.70
9.00	109.12	110.26	111.40	112.54	113.68	114.82	115.96	117.10	118.24	119.38	120.52	121.66	122.80	123.94	125.08	127.36
9.25	107.92	109.05	110.19	111.32	112.45	113.58	114.71	115.84	116.98	118.11	119.24	120.37	121.50	122.63	123.77	126.03
9.50	106.74	107.87	108.99	110.11	111.24	112.36	113.48	114.61	115.73	116.86	117.98	119.10	120.23	121.35	122.47	124.72
9.75	105.58	106.69	107.81	108.93	110.04	111.16	112.27	113.39	114.50	115.62	116.74	117.85	118.97	120.08	121.20	123.43
10.00	104.43	105.54	106.65	107.76	108.86	109.97	111.08	112.19	113.29	114.40	115.51	116.62	117.73	118.83	119.94	122.16
10.25	103.30	104.40	105.50	106.60	107.70	108.80	109.90	111.00	112.10	113.20	114.30	115.40	116.50	117.60	118.70	120.90
10.50	102.18	103.28	104.37	105.46	106.55	107.65	108.74	109.83	110.92	112.02	113.11	114.20	115.29	116.39	117.48	119.66
10.75	101.08	102.17	103.25	104.34	105.42	106.51	107.59	108.68	109.76	110.85	111.93	113.02	114.10	115.19	116.27	118.44
11.00	100.00	101.08	102.15	103.23	104.31	105.39	106.46	107.54	108.62	109.70	110.77	111.85	112.93	114.01	115.08	117.24
11.25	98.93	100.00	101.07	102.14	103.21	104.28	105.35	106.42	107.49	108.56	109.63	110.70	111.77	112.84	113.91	116.05
11.50	97.88	98.94	100.00	101.06	102.12	103.19	104.25	105.31	106.37	107.44	108.50	109.56	110.62	111.69	112.75	114.87
11.75	96.83	97.89	98.94	100.00	101.06	102.11	103.17	104.22	105.28	106.33	107.39	108.44	109.50	110.55	111.61	113.72
12.00	95.81	96.86	97.90	98.95	100.00	101.05	102.10	103.14	104.19	105.24	106.29	107.34	108.38	109.43	110.48	112.58
12.25	94.80	95.84	96.88	97.92	98.96	100.00	101.04	102.08	103.12	104.16	105.20	106.25	107.29	108.33	109.37	111.45
12.50	93.80	94.83	95.86	96.90	97.93	98.97	100.00	101.03	102.07	103.10	104.14	105.17	106.20	107.24	108.27	110.34
12.75	92.81	93.84	94.87	95.89	96.92	97.95	98.97	100.00	101.03	102.05	103.08	104.11	105.13	106.16	107.19	109.24
13.00	91.84	92.86	93.88	94.90	95.92	96.94	97.96	98.98	100.00	101.02	102.04	103.06	104.08	105.10	106.12	108.16
13.25	90.88	91.90	92.91	93.92	94.94	95.95	96.96	97.97	98.99	100.00	101.01	102.03	103.04	104.05	105.06	107.09
13.50	89.94	90.94	91.95	92.96	93.96	94.97	95.98	96.98	97.99	98.99	100.00	101.01	102.01	103.02	104.02	106.04
13.75	89.01	90.01	91.00	92.00	93.00	94.00	95.00	96.00	97.00	98.00	99.00	100.00	101.00	102.00	103.00	105.00
14.00	88.09	89.08	90.07	91.06	92.06	93.05	94.04	95.04	96.03	97.02	98.01	99.01	100.00	100.99	101.99	103.97
14.25	87.18	88.16	89.15	90.14	91.12	92.11	93.10	94.08	95.07	96.05	97.04	98.03	99.01	100.00	100.99	102.96
14.50	86.28	87.26	88.24	89.22	90.20	91.18	92.16	93.14	94.12	95.10	96.08	97.06	98.04	99.02	100.00	101.96
14.75	85.40	86.37	87.35	88.32	89.29	90.27	91.24	92.21	93.19	94.16	95.13	96.11	97.08	98.05	99.03	100.97
15.00	84.53	85.50	86.46	87.43	88.40	89.36	90.33	91.30	92.26	93.23	94.20	95.17	96.13	97.10	98.07	100.00
15.25	83.67	84.63	85.59	86.55	87.51	88.47	89.43	90.39	91.35	92.32	93.28	94.24	95.20	96.16	97.12	99.04
15.50	82.82	83.78	84.73	85.68	86.64	87.59	88.55	89.50	90.46	91.41	92.37	93.32	94.27	95.23	96.18	98.09
15.75	81.99	82.93	83.88	84.83	85.78	86.73	87.67	88.62	89.57	90.52	91.47	92.41	93.36	94.31	95.26	97.16
16.00	81.16	82.10	83.04	83.99	84.93	85.87	86.81	87.75	88.70	89.64	90.58	91.52	92.46	93.41	94.35	96.23
16.25	80.35	81.28	82.22	83.15	84.09	85.02	85.96	86.90	87.83	88.77	89.70	90.64	91.58	92.51	93.45	95.32
16.50	79.54	80.47	81.40	82.33	83.26	84.19	85.12	86.05	86.98	87.91	88.84	89.77	90.70	91.63	92.56	94.42
16.75	78.75	79.67	80.60	81.52	82.44	83.37	84.29	85.22	86.14	87.06	87.99	88.91	89.84	90.76	91.68	93.53
17.00	77.97	78.88	79.80	80.72	81.64	82.56	83.47	84.39	85.31	86.23	87.15	88.06	88.98	89.90	90.82	92.66
17.25	77.19	78.11	79.02	79.93	80.84	81.75	82.67	83.58	84.49	85.40	86.32	87.23	88.14	89.05	89.97	91.79
17.50	76.43	77.34	78.24	79.15	80.06	80.96	81.87	82.78	83.68	84.59	85.50	86.40	87.31	88.22	89.12	90.94
17.75	75.68	76.58	77.48	78.38	79.28	80.18	81.08	81.98	82.89	83.79	84.69	85.59	86.49	87.39	88.29	90.09
18.00	74.94	75.83	76.73	77.62	78.52	79.41	80.31	81.20	82.10	82.99	83.89	84.78	85.68	86.57	87.47	89.26
18.25	74.21	75.09	75.98	76.87	77.76	78.65	79.54	80.43	81.32	82.21	83.10	83.99	84.88	85.77	86.66	88.44
18.50	73.48	74.37	75.25	76.13	77.02	77.90	78.79	79.67	80.55	81.44	82.32	83.21	84.09	84.97	85.86	87.63
18.75	72.77	73.65	74.53	75.40	76.28	77.16	78.04	78.92	79.80	80.67	81.55	82.43	83.31	84.19	85.07	86.82
19.00	72.06	72.94	73.81	74.68	75.56	76.43	77.30	78.18	79.05	79.92	80.79	81.67	82.54	83.41	84.29	86.03
20.00	69.34	70.19	71.04	71.89	72.75	73.60	74.45	75.30	76.15	77.00	77.86	78.71	79.56	80.41	81.26	82.97
25.00	57.63	58.38	59.14	59.90	60.65	61.41	62.17	62.92	63.68	64.44	65.19	65.95	66.71	67.46	68.22	69.73
30.00	48.50	49.18	49.86	50.54	51.21	51.89	52.57	53.25	53.92	54.60	55.28	55.96	56.64	57.31	57.99	59.35

Description: This table shows the yield to maturity of a bond purchased at the price shown in the index.

Example: The yield to maturity of a 15.00 %, 6 year bond at a price of 116.00 is 11.26 %.

COUPON RATE, %

PRICE	11.00%	11.25%	11.50%	11.75%	12.00%	12.25%	12.50%	12.75%	13.00%	13.25%	13.50%	13.75%	14.00%	14.25%	14.50%	15.00%
160	.75	.94	1.12	1.31	1.50	1.69	1.87	2.06	2.25	2.43	2.62	2.81	2.99	3.18	3.37	3.74
155	1.40	1.59	1.79	1.98	2.17	2.36	2.55	2.74	2.93	3.12	3.31	3.50	3.69	3.88	4.07	4.45
150	2.08	2.28	2.47	2.67	2.86	3.06	3.25	3.45	3.64	3.84	4.03	4.22	4.42	4.61	4.80	5.19
145	2.80	2.99	3.19	3.39	3.59	3.79	3.99	4.18	4.38	4.58	4.78	4.98	5.17	5.37	5.57	5.96
140	3.54	3.74	3.94	4.15	4.35	4.55	4.75	4.96	5.16	5.36	5.56	5.76	5.97	6.17	6.37	6.77
135	4.31	4.52	4.73	4.93	5.14	5.35	5.55	5.76	5.97	6.17	6.38	6.59	6.79	7.00	7.21	7.62
130	5.12	5.34	5.55	5.76	5.97	6.18	6.40	6.61	6.82	7.03	7.24	7.45	7.66	7.87	8.09	8.51
129	5.29	5.50	5.72	5.93	6.14	6.36	6.57	6.78	6.99	7.21	7.42	7.63	7.84	8.05	8.27	8.69
128	5.46	5.67	5.89	6.10	6.32	6.53	6.74	6.96	7.17	7.38	7.60	7.81	8.02	8.24	8.45	8.87
127	5.63	5.84	6.06	6.27	6.49	6.70	6.92	7.13	7.35	7.56	7.78	7.99	8.21	8.42	8.63	9.06
126	5.80	6.02	6.23	6.45	6.67	6.88	7.10	7.31	7.53	7.74	7.96	8.18	8.39	8.61	8.82	9.25
125	5.97	6.19	6.41	6.63	6.84	7.06	7.28	7.49	7.71	7.93	8.14	8.36	8.58	8.79	9.01	9.44
124	6.15	6.37	6.59	6.81	7.02	7.24	7.46	7.68	7.90	8.11	8.33	8.55	8.77	8.98	9.20	9.63
123	6.33	6.55	6.77	6.99	7.21	7.42	7.64	7.86	8.08	8.30	8.52	8.74	8.96	9.17	9.39	9.83
122	6.51	6.73	6.95	7.17	7.39	7.61	7.83	8.05	8.27	8.49	8.71	8.93	9.15	9.37	9.59	10.03
121	6.69	6.91	7.13	7.35	7.57	7.80	8.02	8.24	8.46	8.68	8.90	9.12	9.34	9.56	9.78	10.23
120	6.87	7.09	7.32	7.54	7.76	7.98	8.21	8.43	8.65	8.87	9.10	9.32	9.54	9.76	9.98	10.43
119	7.06	7.28	7.50	7.73	7.95	8.17	8.40	8.62	8.85	9.07	9.29	9.52	9.74	9.96	10.18	10.63
118	7.24	7.47	7.69	7.92	8.14	8.37	8.59	8.82	9.04	9.27	9.49	9.72	9.94	10.16	10.39	10.84
117	7.43	7.66	7.88	8.11	8.34	8.56	8.79	9.01	9.24	9.47	9.69	9.92	10.14	10.37	10.59	11.04
116	7.62	7.85	8.08	8.30	8.53	8.76	8.99	9.21	9.44	9.67	9.89	10.12	10.35	10.58	10.80	11.26
115	7.82	8.04	8.27	8.50	8.73	8.96	9.19	9.42	9.64	9.87	10.10	10.33	10.56	10.78	11.01	11.47
114	8.01	8.24	8.47	8.70	8.93	9.16	9.39	9.62	9.85	10.08	10.31	10.54	10.77	11.00	11.23	11.68
113	8.21	8.44	8.67	8.90	9.13	9.36	9.59	9.83	10.06	10.29	10.52	10.75	10.98	11.21	11.44	11.90
112	8.41	8.64	8.87	9.10	9.34	9.57	9.80	10.03	10.27	10.50	10.73	10.96	11.19	11.43	11.66	12.12
111	8.61	8.84	9.08	9.31	9.54	9.78	10.01	10.25	10.48	10.71	10.95	11.18	11.41	11.65	11.88	12.35
110	8.81	9.05	9.28	9.52	9.75	9.99	10.22	10.46	10.69	10.93	11.16	11.40	11.63	11.87	12.10	12.57
109	9.02	9.26	9.49	9.73	9.97	10.20	10.44	10.68	10.91	11.15	11.38	11.62	11.86	12.09	12.33	12.80
108	9.23	9.47	9.70	9.94	10.18	10.42	10.66	10.89	11.13	11.37	11.61	11.84	12.08	12.32	12.56	13.03
107	9.44	9.68	9.92	10.16	10.40	10.64	10.88	11.12	11.35	11.59	11.83	12.07	12.31	12.55	12.79	13.27
106	9.65	9.89	10.14	10.38	10.62	10.86	11.10	11.34	11.58	11.82	12.06	12.30	12.54	12.78	13.02	13.50
105	9.87	10.11	10.36	10.60	10.84	11.08	11.32	11.57	11.81	12.05	12.29	12.53	12.78	13.02	13.26	13.74
104	10.09	10.33	10.58	10.82	11.06	11.31	11.55	11.80	12.04	12.28	12.53	12.77	13.01	13.26	13.50	13.99
103	10.31	10.56	10.80	11.05	11.29	11.54	11.78	12.03	12.27	12.52	12.76	13.01	13.25	13.50	13.74	14.23
102	10.54	10.78	11.03	11.28	11.52	11.77	12.02	12.26	12.51	12.76	13.00	13.25	13.50	13.74	13.99	14.48
101	10.76	11.01	11.26	11.51	11.76	12.01	12.25	12.50	12.75	13.00	13.25	13.50	13.74	13.99	14.24	14.74
100	11.00	11.25	11.50	11.75	12.00	12.25	12.50	12.75	13.00	13.25	13.50	13.75	14.00	14.25	14.50	15.00
99	11.23	11.48	11.73	11.98	12.24	12.49	12.74	12.99	13.24	13.49	13.75	14.00	14.25	14.50	14.75	15.26
98	11.47	11.72	11.97	12.23	12.48	12.73	12.99	13.24	13.49	13.75	14.00	14.25	14.51	14.76	15.01	15.52
97	11.71	11.96	12.22	12.47	12.73	12.98	13.24	13.49	13.75	14.00	14.26	14.51	14.77	15.02	15.28	15.79
96	11.95	12.20	12.46	12.72	12.98	13.23	13.49	13.75	14.00	14.26	14.52	14.77	15.03	15.29	15.54	16.06
95	12.19	12.45	12.71	12.97	13.23	13.49	13.75	14.00	14.26	14.52	14.78	15.04	15.30	15.56	15.82	16.33
94	12.44	12.70	12.96	13.22	13.49	13.75	14.01	14.27	14.53	14.79	15.05	15.31	15.57	15.83	16.09	16.61
93	12.70	12.96	13.22	13.48	13.75	14.01	14.27	14.53	14.80	15.06	15.32	15.58	15.84	16.11	16.37	16.90
92	12.95	13.22	13.48	13.75	14.01	14.27	14.54	14.80	15.07	15.33	15.60	15.86	16.13	16.39	16.65	17.18
91	13.21	13.48	13.75	14.01	14.28	14.54	14.81	15.08	15.34	15.61	15.88	16.14	16.41	16.68	16.94	17.48
90	13.48	13.75	14.01	14.28	14.55	14.82	15.09	15.36	15.62	15.89	16.16	16.43	16.70	16.97	17.23	17.77
89	13.75	14.02	14.29	14.56	14.83	15.10	15.37	15.64	15.91	16.18	16.45	16.72	16.99	17.26	17.53	18.07
88	14.02	14.29	14.56	14.83	15.11	15.38	15.65	15.92	16.20	16.47	16.74	17.01	17.29	17.56	17.83	18.38
87	14.29	14.57	14.84	15.12	15.39	15.67	15.94	16.21	16.49	16.76	17.04	17.31	17.59	17.86	18.14	18.69
86	14.57	14.85	15.13	15.40	15.68	15.96	16.23	16.51	16.79	17.06	17.34	17.62	17.90	18.17	18.45	19.01
85	14.86	15.14	15.42	15.69	15.97	16.25	16.53	16.81	17.09	17.37	17.65	17.93	18.21	18.49	18.77	19.33
84	15.15	15.43	15.71	15.99	16.27	16.55	16.83	17.12	17.40	17.68	17.96	18.24	18.52	18.81	19.09	19.65
83	15.44	15.73	16.01	16.29	16.57	16.86	17.14	17.43	17.71	17.99	18.28	18.56	18.85	19.13	19.41	19.98
82	15.74	16.03	16.31	16.60	16.88	17.17	17.45	17.74	18.03	18.31	18.60	18.89	19.17	19.46	19.75	20.32
81	16.04	16.33	16.62	16.91	17.20	17.48	17.77	18.06	18.35	18.64	18.93	19.22	19.51	19.79	20.08	20.66
80	16.35	16.64	16.93	17.22	17.51	17.80	18.10	18.39	18.68	18.97	19.26	19.55	19.84	20.14	20.43	21.01
79	16.67	16.96	17.25	17.54	17.84	18.13	18.42	18.72	19.01	19.31	19.60	19.89	20.19	20.48	20.78	21.37
78	16.98	17.28	17.57	17.87	18.17	18.46	18.76	19.05	19.35	19.65	19.94	20.24	20.54	20.84	21.13	21.73
77	17.31	17.61	17.90	18.20	18.50	18.80	19.10	19.40	19.70	20.00	20.30	20.60	20.90	21.20	21.50	22.10
76	17.64	17.94	18.24	18.54	18.84	19.14	19.45	19.75	20.05	20.35	20.65	20.96	21.26	21.56	21.87	22.47
75	17.97	18.28	18.58	18.88	19.19	19.49	19.80	20.10	20.41	20.71	21.02	21.32	21.63	21.94	22.24	22.85
74	18.32	18.62	18.93	19.24	19.54	19.85	20.16	20.46	20.77	21.08	21.39	21.70	22.01	22.32	22.63	23.24
73	18.66	18.97	19.28	19.59	19.90	20.21	20.52	20.83	21.14	21.46	21.77	22.08	22.39	22.70	23.02	23.64
72	19.02	19.33	19.64	19.96	20.27	20.58	20.90	21.21	21.52	21.84	22.15	22.47	22.78	23.10	23.41	24.05
71	19.38	19.69	20.01	20.33	20.64	20.96	21.28	21.59	21.91	22.23	22.55	22.86	23.18	23.50	23.82	24.46
70	19.75	20.07	20.39	20.70	21.02	21.34	21.66	21.98	22.31	22.63	22.95	23.27	23.59	23.91	24.24	24.88
65	21.70	22.04	22.37	22.71	23.05	23.39	23.73	24.06	24.40	24.74	25.08	25.42	25.76	26.10	26.44	27.13

Description: This table shows the price to pay for a bond at the yield rate. The yield is to maturity.

Example: The price of a 6.75 %, 7 year bond to yield 8 % to maturity is $ 93.40.

COUPON RATE, %

YIELD	0.00%	1.00%	2.00%	3.00%	4.00%	4.25%	4.50%	4.75%	5.00%	5.25%	5.50%	5.75%	6.00%	6.25%	6.50%	6.75%
0.00	100.00	107.00	114.00	121.00	128.00	129.75	131.50	133.25	135.00	136.75	138.50	140.25	142.00	143.75	145.50	147.25
1.00	93.26	100.00	106.74	113.49	120.23	121.92	123.61	125.29	126.98	128.66	130.35	132.04	133.72	135.41	137.09	138.78
2.00	87.00	93.50	100.00	106.50	113.00	114.63	116.25	117.88	119.51	121.13	122.76	124.38	126.01	127.63	129.26	130.88
3.00	81.18	87.46	93.73	100.00	106.27	107.84	109.41	110.98	112.54	114.11	115.68	117.25	118.82	120.38	121.95	123.52
4.00	75.79	81.84	87.89	93.95	100.00	101.51	103.03	104.54	106.05	107.57	109.08	110.59	112.11	113.62	115.13	116.65
4.25	74.50	80.50	86.50	92.50	98.50	100.00	101.50	103.00	104.50	106.00	107.50	109.00	110.50	112.00	113.50	115.00
4.50	73.23	79.18	85.13	91.08	97.03	98.51	100.00	101.49	102.97	104.46	105.95	107.43	108.92	110.41	111.90	113.38
4.75	71.99	77.89	83.78	89.68	95.58	97.05	98.53	100.00	101.47	102.95	104.42	105.90	107.37	108.84	110.32	111.79
5.00	70.77	76.62	82.46	88.31	94.15	95.62	97.08	98.54	100.00	101.46	102.92	104.38	105.85	107.31	108.77	110.23
5.25	69.58	75.37	81.17	86.96	92.76	94.20	95.65	97.10	98.55	100.00	101.45	102.90	104.35	105.80	107.24	108.69
5.50	68.42	74.15	79.89	85.64	91.38	92.82	94.25	95.69	97.13	98.56	100.00	101.44	102.87	104.31	105.75	107.18
5.75	67.25	72.94	78.64	84.33	90.03	91.46	92.88	94.30	95.73	97.15	98.58	100.00	101.42	102.85	104.27	105.70
6.00	66.11	71.76	77.41	83.06	88.70	90.12	91.53	92.94	94.35	95.76	97.18	98.59	100.00	101.41	102.82	104.24
6.25	65.00	70.60	76.20	81.80	87.40	88.80	90.20	91.60	93.00	94.40	95.80	97.20	98.60	100.00	101.40	102.80
6.50	63.91	69.46	75.01	80.56	86.12	87.51	88.89	90.28	91.67	93.06	94.45	95.84	97.22	98.61	100.00	101.39
6.75	62.83	68.34	73.84	79.35	84.86	86.23	87.61	88.99	90.36	91.74	93.12	94.49	95.87	97.25	98.62	100.00
7.00	61.78	67.24	72.70	78.16	83.62	84.98	86.35	87.71	89.08	90.44	91.81	93.17	94.54	95.90	97.27	98.63
7.25	60.74	66.16	71.57	76.99	82.40	83.76	85.11	86.46	87.82	89.17	90.52	91.88	93.23	94.59	95.94	97.29
7.50	59.73	65.10	70.47	75.84	81.21	82.55	83.89	85.23	86.58	87.92	89.26	90.60	91.95	93.29	94.63	95.97
7.75	58.73	64.05	69.38	74.70	80.03	81.36	82.69	84.02	85.36	86.69	88.02	89.35	90.68	92.01	93.34	94.67
8.00	57.75	63.03	68.31	73.59	78.87	80.19	81.51	82.83	84.16	85.48	86.80	88.12	89.44	90.76	92.08	93.40
8.25	56.78	62.02	67.26	72.50	77.74	79.05	80.36	81.67	82.98	84.29	85.59	86.90	88.21	89.52	90.83	92.14
8.50	55.84	61.03	66.23	71.43	76.62	77.92	79.22	80.52	81.82	83.11	84.41	85.71	87.01	88.31	89.61	90.91
8.75	54.91	60.06	65.22	70.37	75.52	76.81	78.10	79.39	80.68	81.96	83.25	84.54	85.83	87.12	88.41	89.69
9.00	54.00	59.11	64.22	69.33	74.44	75.72	77.00	78.28	79.55	80.83	82.11	83.39	84.67	85.94	87.22	88.50
9.25	53.10	58.17	63.24	68.31	73.38	74.65	75.92	77.18	78.45	79.72	80.99	82.25	83.52	84.79	86.06	87.32
9.50	52.22	57.25	62.28	67.31	72.34	73.60	74.85	76.11	77.37	78.63	79.88	81.14	82.40	83.65	84.91	86.17
9.75	51.36	56.35	61.33	66.32	71.31	72.56	73.81	75.05	76.30	77.55	78.80	80.04	81.29	82.54	83.79	85.03
10.00	50.51	55.46	60.41	65.35	70.30	71.54	72.78	74.02	75.25	76.49	77.73	78.97	80.20	81.44	82.68	83.91
10.25	49.67	54.58	59.49	64.40	69.31	70.54	71.77	72.99	74.22	75.45	76.68	77.90	79.13	80.36	81.59	82.81
10.50	48.85	53.72	58.60	63.47	68.34	69.56	70.77	71.99	73.21	74.43	75.64	76.86	78.08	79.30	80.52	81.73
10.75	48.05	52.88	57.71	62.55	67.38	68.59	69.80	71.00	72.21	73.42	74.63	75.84	77.04	78.25	79.46	80.67
11.00	47.26	52.05	56.85	61.64	66.44	67.63	68.83	70.03	71.23	72.43	73.63	74.83	76.03	77.22	78.42	79.62
11.25	46.48	51.24	55.99	60.75	65.51	66.70	67.89	69.08	70.27	71.46	72.65	73.83	75.02	76.21	77.40	78.59
11.50	45.72	50.44	55.16	59.88	64.60	65.78	66.96	68.14	69.32	70.50	71.68	72.86	74.04	75.22	76.40	77.58
11.75	44.97	49.65	54.33	59.02	63.70	64.87	66.04	67.21	68.39	69.56	70.73	71.90	73.07	74.24	75.41	76.58
12.00	44.23	48.88	53.53	58.17	62.82	63.98	65.14	66.31	67.47	68.63	69.79	70.95	72.12	73.28	74.44	75.60
12.25	43.51	48.12	52.73	57.34	61.95	63.11	64.26	65.41	66.56	67.72	68.87	70.02	71.18	72.33	73.48	74.64
12.50	42.80	47.37	51.95	56.52	61.10	62.24	63.39	64.53	65.68	66.82	67.97	69.11	70.25	71.40	72.54	73.69
12.75	42.10	46.64	51.18	55.72	60.26	61.40	62.53	63.67	64.80	65.94	67.07	68.21	69.35	70.48	71.62	72.75
13.00	41.41	45.92	50.42	54.93	59.44	60.56	61.69	62.82	63.94	65.07	66.20	67.32	68.45	69.58	70.71	71.83
13.25	40.74	45.21	49.68	54.15	58.63	59.74	60.86	61.98	63.10	64.22	65.34	66.45	67.57	68.69	69.81	70.93
13.50	40.07	44.51	48.95	53.39	57.83	58.94	60.05	61.16	62.27	63.38	64.49	65.60	66.71	67.82	68.93	70.04
13.75	39.42	43.83	48.23	52.64	57.04	58.15	59.25	60.35	61.45	62.55	63.65	64.75	65.86	66.96	68.06	69.16
14.00	38.78	43.15	47.53	51.90	56.27	57.37	58.46	59.55	60.65	61.74	62.83	63.92	65.02	66.11	67.20	68.30
14.25	38.15	42.49	46.83	51.17	55.51	56.60	57.68	58.77	59.85	60.94	62.02	63.11	64.19	65.28	66.36	67.45
14.50	37.54	41.84	46.15	50.46	54.77	55.84	56.92	58.00	59.07	60.15	61.23	62.31	63.38	64.46	65.54	66.61
14.75	36.93	41.20	45.48	49.76	54.03	55.10	56.17	57.24	58.31	59.38	60.45	61.52	62.58	63.65	64.72	65.79
15.00	36.33	40.58	44.82	49.07	53.31	54.37	55.43	56.49	57.55	58.62	59.68	60.74	61.80	62.86	63.92	64.98
15.25	35.75	39.96	44.17	48.39	52.60	53.65	54.71	55.76	56.81	57.87	58.92	59.97	61.03	62.08	63.13	64.19
15.50	35.17	39.35	43.53	47.72	51.90	52.95	53.99	55.04	56.08	57.13	58.17	59.22	60.26	61.31	62.36	63.40
15.75	34.60	38.75	42.91	47.06	51.21	52.25	53.29	54.33	55.36	56.40	57.44	58.48	59.52	60.55	61.59	62.63
16.00	34.05	38.17	42.29	46.41	50.53	51.57	52.60	53.63	54.66	55.69	56.72	57.75	58.78	59.81	60.84	61.87
16.25	33.50	37.59	41.68	45.78	49.87	50.89	51.91	52.94	53.96	54.98	56.01	57.03	58.05	59.08	60.10	61.12
16.50	32.96	37.02	41.09	45.15	49.21	50.23	51.24	52.26	53.28	54.29	55.31	56.32	57.34	58.35	59.37	60.39
16.75	32.43	36.47	40.50	44.53	48.57	49.58	50.59	51.59	52.60	53.61	54.62	55.63	56.64	57.64	58.65	59.66
17.00	31.91	35.92	39.92	43.93	47.93	48.94	49.94	50.94	51.94	52.94	53.94	54.94	55.94	56.95	57.95	58.95
17.25	31.40	35.38	39.36	43.33	47.31	48.30	49.30	50.29	51.29	52.28	53.28	54.27	55.26	56.26	57.25	58.25
17.50	30.90	34.85	38.80	42.75	46.70	47.68	48.67	49.66	50.64	51.63	52.62	53.61	54.59	55.58	56.57	57.55
17.75	30.41	34.33	38.25	42.17	46.09	47.07	48.05	49.03	50.01	50.99	51.97	52.95	53.93	54.91	55.89	56.87
18.00	29.92	33.82	37.71	41.60	45.50	46.47	47.44	48.42	49.39	50.36	51.34	52.31	53.28	54.26	55.23	56.20
18.25	29.45	33.31	37.18	41.05	44.91	45.88	46.84	47.81	48.78	49.74	50.71	51.68	52.64	53.61	54.58	55.54
18.50	28.98	32.82	36.66	40.50	44.34	45.30	46.26	47.21	48.17	49.13	50.09	51.05	52.01	52.97	53.93	54.89
18.75	28.52	32.33	36.14	39.96	43.77	44.72	45.68	46.63	47.58	48.53	49.49	50.44	51.39	52.35	53.30	54.25
19.00	28.07	31.85	35.64	39.43	43.21	44.16	45.10	46.05	47.00	47.94	48.89	49.84	50.78	51.73	52.68	53.62
20.00	26.33	30.02	33.70	37.38	41.07	41.99	42.91	43.83	44.75	45.67	46.59	47.51	48.43	49.35	50.27	51.20
25.00	19.22	22.46	25.69	28.92	32.15	32.96	33.76	34.57	35.38	36.19	37.00	37.80	38.61	39.42	40.23	41.03
30.00	14.13	17.00	19.86	22.72	25.58	26.30	27.01	27.73	28.44	29.16	29.88	30.59	31.31	32.02	32.74	33.45

Description: This table shows the yield to maturity of a bond purchased at the price shown in the index.

Example: The yield to maturity of a 6.75 %, 7 year bond at a price of 80.00 is 10.90 %.

COUPON RATE, %

PRICE	0.00%	1.00%	2.00%	3.00%	4.00%	4.25%	4.50%	4.75%	5.00%	5.25%	5.50%	5.75%	6.00%	6.25%	6.50%	6.75%
100	0.00	1.00	2.00	3.00	4.00	4.25	4.50	4.75	5.00	5.25	5.50	5.75	6.00	6.25	6.50	6.75
99	.14	1.14	2.15	3.16	4.16	4.41	4.66	4.92	5.17	5.42	5.67	5.92	6.17	6.42	6.68	6.93
98	.28	1.29	2.31	3.32	4.33	4.58	4.84	5.09	5.34	5.59	5.85	6.10	6.35	6.61	6.86	7.11
97	.43	1.45	2.46	3.48	4.50	4.75	5.01	5.26	5.52	5.77	6.03	6.28	6.54	6.79	7.05	7.30
96	.58	1.60	2.62	3.65	4.67	4.93	5.18	5.44	5.70	5.95	6.21	6.46	6.72	6.98	7.23	7.49
95	.73	1.76	2.79	3.82	4.85	5.10	5.36	5.62	5.88	6.13	6.39	6.65	6.91	7.17	7.42	7.68
94	.88	1.92	2.95	3.99	5.02	5.28	5.54	5.80	6.06	6.32	6.58	6.84	7.10	7.36	7.62	7.88
93	1.03	2.07	3.12	4.16	5.20	5.46	5.72	5.98	6.24	6.51	6.77	7.03	7.29	7.55	7.81	8.07
92	1.19	2.24	3.28	4.33	5.38	5.64	5.91	6.17	6.43	6.70	6.96	7.22	7.48	7.75	8.01	8.27
91	1.35	2.40	3.45	4.51	5.57	5.83	6.09	6.36	6.62	6.89	7.15	7.42	7.68	7.95	8.21	8.48
90	1.51	2.57	3.63	4.69	5.75	6.02	6.28	6.55	6.82	7.08	7.35	7.61	7.88	8.15	8.41	8.68
89	1.67	2.73	3.80	4.87	5.94	6.21	6.47	6.74	7.01	7.28	7.55	7.82	8.08	8.35	8.62	8.89
88	1.83	2.90	3.98	5.05	6.13	6.40	6.67	6.94	7.21	7.48	7.75	8.02	8.29	8.56	8.83	9.10
87	1.99	3.07	4.15	5.24	6.32	6.59	6.87	7.14	7.41	7.68	7.95	8.23	8.50	8.77	9.04	9.31
86	2.16	3.25	4.34	5.43	6.52	6.79	7.07	7.34	7.61	7.89	8.16	8.43	8.71	8.98	9.26	9.53
85	2.33	3.42	4.52	5.62	6.72	6.99	7.27	7.54	7.82	8.09	8.37	8.65	8.92	9.20	9.48	9.75
84	2.50	3.60	4.70	5.81	6.92	7.19	7.47	7.75	8.03	8.31	8.58	8.86	9.14	9.42	9.70	9.98
83	2.67	3.78	4.89	6.01	7.12	7.40	7.68	7.96	8.24	8.52	8.80	9.08	9.36	9.64	9.92	10.20
82	2.85	3.97	5.08	6.20	7.33	7.61	7.89	8.17	8.46	8.74	9.02	9.30	9.58	9.87	10.15	10.43
81	3.03	4.15	5.28	6.41	7.54	7.82	8.11	8.39	8.67	8.96	9.24	9.53	9.81	10.10	10.38	10.67
80	3.21	4.34	5.47	6.61	7.75	8.04	8.32	8.61	8.90	9.18	9.47	9.76	10.04	10.33	10.62	10.90
79	3.39	4.53	5.67	6.82	7.97	8.26	8.54	8.83	9.12	9.41	9.70	9.99	10.28	10.57	10.86	11.15
78	3.58	4.72	5.87	7.03	8.19	8.48	8.77	9.06	9.35	9.64	9.93	10.22	10.51	10.81	11.10	11.39
77	3.76	4.92	6.08	7.24	8.41	8.70	8.99	9.29	9.58	9.87	10.17	10.46	10.76	11.05	11.34	11.64
76	3.95	5.12	6.29	7.46	8.64	8.93	9.23	9.52	9.82	10.11	10.41	10.70	11.00	11.30	11.60	11.89
75	4.15	5.32	6.50	7.68	8.87	9.16	9.46	9.76	10.06	10.35	10.65	10.95	11.25	11.55	11.85	12.15
74	4.34	5.52	6.71	7.90	9.10	9.40	9.70	10.00	10.30	10.60	10.90	11.20	11.50	11.81	12.11	12.41
73	4.54	5.73	6.93	8.13	9.34	9.64	9.94	10.24	10.55	10.85	11.15	11.46	11.76	12.07	12.37	12.68
72	4.74	5.94	7.15	8.36	9.58	9.88	10.19	10.49	10.80	11.10	11.41	11.72	12.03	12.33	12.64	12.95
71	4.95	6.16	7.37	8.60	9.82	10.13	10.44	10.75	11.05	11.36	11.67	11.98	12.29	12.60	12.91	13.22
70	5.16	6.38	7.60	8.83	10.07	10.38	10.69	11.00	11.31	11.63	11.94	12.25	12.56	12.88	13.19	13.51
69	5.37	6.60	7.83	9.08	10.32	10.64	10.95	11.27	11.58	11.89	12.21	12.53	12.84	13.16	13.47	13.79
68	5.58	6.82	8.07	9.32	10.58	10.90	11.22	11.53	11.85	12.17	12.49	12.80	13.12	13.44	13.76	14.08
67	5.80	7.05	8.31	9.57	10.85	11.16	11.48	11.80	12.12	12.44	12.77	13.09	13.41	13.73	14.06	14.38
66	6.02	7.28	8.55	9.83	11.11	11.43	11.76	12.08	12.40	12.73	13.05	13.38	13.70	14.03	14.35	14.68
65	6.24	7.52	8.80	10.09	11.38	11.71	12.04	12.36	12.69	13.02	13.34	13.67	14.00	14.33	14.66	14.99
64	6.47	7.76	9.05	10.35	11.66	11.99	12.32	12.65	12.98	13.31	13.64	13.97	14.30	14.64	14.97	15.30
63	6.71	8.00	9.31	10.62	11.94	12.28	12.61	12.94	13.27	13.61	13.94	14.28	14.61	14.95	15.29	15.62
62	6.94	8.25	9.57	10.90	12.23	12.57	12.90	13.24	13.58	13.91	14.25	14.59	14.93	15.27	15.61	15.95
61	7.18	8.50	9.83	11.17	12.52	12.86	13.20	13.54	13.88	14.23	14.57	14.91	15.25	15.60	15.94	16.29
60	7.43	8.76	10.11	11.46	12.82	13.17	13.51	13.85	14.20	14.54	14.89	15.24	15.58	15.93	16.28	16.63
59	7.68	9.02	10.38	11.75	13.13	13.48	13.82	14.17	14.52	14.87	15.22	15.57	15.92	16.27	16.62	16.98
58	7.93	9.29	10.66	12.05	13.44	13.79	14.14	14.49	14.85	15.20	15.55	15.91	16.26	16.62	16.98	17.33
57	8.19	9.56	10.95	12.35	13.76	14.11	14.47	14.82	15.18	15.54	15.90	16.26	16.62	16.98	17.34	17.70
56	8.45	9.84	11.24	12.66	14.08	14.44	14.80	15.16	15.52	15.89	16.25	16.61	16.97	17.34	17.71	18.07
55	8.72	10.13	11.54	12.97	14.42	14.78	15.14	15.51	15.87	16.24	16.61	16.97	17.34	17.71	18.08	18.45
54	8.99	10.41	11.85	13.30	14.76	15.12	15.49	15.86	16.23	16.60	16.97	17.35	17.72	18.09	18.47	18.84
53	9.27	10.71	12.16	13.62	15.10	15.48	15.85	16.22	16.60	16.97	17.35	17.73	18.11	18.48	18.86	19.25
52	9.56	11.01	12.48	13.96	15.46	15.84	16.21	16.59	16.97	17.35	17.73	18.12	18.50	18.88	19.27	19.66
51	9.85	11.32	12.80	14.31	15.82	16.20	16.59	16.97	17.36	17.74	18.13	18.52	18.91	19.30	19.69	20.08
50	10.15	11.63	13.14	14.66	16.20	16.58	16.97	17.36	17.75	18.14	18.53	18.93	19.32	19.72	20.11	20.51
49	10.45	11.96	13.48	15.02	16.58	16.97	17.36	17.76	18.15	18.55	18.95	19.35	19.75	20.15	20.55	20.96
48	10.76	12.28	13.83	15.39	16.97	17.37	17.77	18.17	18.57	18.97	19.37	19.78	20.19	20.59	21.00	21.41
47	11.08	12.62	14.18	15.77	17.37	17.77	18.18	18.59	18.99	19.40	19.81	20.22	20.64	21.05	21.47	21.88
46	11.40	12.97	14.55	16.16	17.78	18.19	18.60	19.02	19.43	19.85	20.26	20.68	21.10	21.52	21.94	22.37
45	11.73	13.32	14.93	16.56	18.21	18.62	19.04	19.46	19.88	20.30	20.73	21.15	21.58	22.00	22.43	22.86
44	12.07	13.68	15.31	16.97	18.64	19.07	19.49	19.92	20.34	20.77	21.20	21.63	22.07	22.50	22.94	23.38
43	12.42	14.05	15.71	17.39	19.09	19.52	19.95	20.38	20.82	21.26	21.69	22.13	22.57	23.02	23.46	23.90
42	12.78	14.43	16.11	17.82	19.55	19.99	20.43	20.87	21.31	21.75	22.20	22.65	23.09	23.55	24.00	24.45
41	13.15	14.83	16.53	18.27	20.03	20.47	20.92	21.37	21.82	22.27	22.72	23.18	23.63	24.09	24.55	25.01
40	13.52	15.23	16.96	18.72	20.52	20.97	21.42	21.88	22.34	22.80	23.26	23.72	24.19	24.66	25.13	25.60
39	13.91	15.64	17.40	19.20	21.02	21.48	21.95	22.41	22.88	23.35	23.82	24.29	24.77	25.24	25.72	26.20
38	14.31	16.07	17.86	19.69	21.54	22.01	22.49	22.96	23.44	23.91	24.39	24.88	25.36	25.85	26.34	26.83
37	14.72	16.51	18.33	20.19	22.08	22.56	23.04	23.53	24.01	24.50	24.99	25.48	25.98	26.48	26.98	27.48
36	15.14	16.96	18.82	20.71	22.64	23.13	23.62	24.12	24.61	25.11	25.61	26.11	26.62	27.13	27.64	28.15
35	15.57	17.42	19.32	21.25	23.22	23.72	24.22	24.73	25.23	25.74	26.25	26.77	27.29	27.81	28.33	28.85
30	17.96	20.00	22.11	24.26	26.47	27.03	27.60	28.17	28.74	29.31	29.89	30.48	31.06	31.65	32.25	32.84
25	20.81	23.12	25.51	27.97	30.52	31.17	31.82	32.48	33.15	33.82	34.49	35.18	35.86	36.55	37.25	37.95

Description: This table shows the price to pay for a bond at the yield rate. The yield is to maturity.

Example: The price of a 10.75 %, 7 year bond to yield 8 % to maturity is $ 114.52.

COUPON RATE, %

YIELD	7.00%	7.25%	7.50%	7.75%	8.00%	8.25%	8.50%	8.75%	9.00%	9.25%	9.50%	9.75%	10.00%	10.25%	10.50%	10.75%
0.00	149.00	150.75	152.50	154.25	156.00	157.75	159.50	161.25	163.00	164.75	166.50	168.25	170.00	171.75	173.50	175.25
1.00	140.47	142.15	143.84	145.52	147.21	148.90	150.58	152.27	153.95	155.64	157.33	159.01	160.70	162.39	164.07	165.76
2.00	132.51	134.13	135.76	137.39	139.01	140.64	142.26	143.89	145.51	147.14	148.76	150.39	152.01	153.64	155.27	156.89
3.00	125.09	126.65	128.22	129.79	131.36	132.93	134.49	136.06	137.63	139.20	140.77	142.33	143.90	145.47	147.04	148.61
4.00	118.16	119.67	121.19	122.70	124.21	125.73	127.24	128.75	130.27	131.78	133.29	134.81	136.32	137.83	139.35	140.86
4.25	116.50	118.00	119.50	121.00	122.50	124.00	125.50	127.00	128.50	130.00	131.50	133.00	134.50	136.00	137.50	139.00
4.50	114.87	116.36	117.84	119.33	120.82	122.30	123.79	125.28	126.77	128.25	129.74	131.23	132.71	134.20	135.69	137.17
4.75	113.27	114.74	116.22	117.69	119.16	120.64	122.11	123.59	125.06	126.53	128.01	129.48	130.96	132.43	133.90	135.38
5.00	111.69	113.15	114.61	116.08	117.54	119.00	120.46	121.92	123.38	124.84	126.30	127.77	129.23	130.69	132.15	133.61
5.25	110.14	111.59	113.04	114.49	115.94	117.39	118.83	120.28	121.73	123.18	124.63	126.08	127.53	128.98	130.42	131.87
5.50	108.62	110.05	111.49	112.93	114.36	115.80	117.24	118.67	120.11	121.55	122.98	124.42	125.85	127.29	128.73	130.16
5.75	107.12	108.54	109.97	111.39	112.82	114.24	115.67	117.09	118.51	119.94	121.36	122.79	124.21	125.63	127.06	128.48
6.00	105.65	107.06	108.47	109.88	111.30	112.71	114.12	115.53	116.94	118.36	119.77	121.18	122.59	124.00	125.42	126.83
6.25	104.20	105.60	107.00	108.40	109.80	111.20	112.60	114.00	115.40	116.80	118.20	119.60	121.00	122.40	123.80	125.20
6.50	102.78	104.16	105.55	106.94	108.33	109.72	111.11	112.49	113.88	115.27	116.66	118.05	119.44	120.82	122.21	123.60
6.75	101.38	102.75	104.13	105.51	106.88	108.26	109.64	111.01	112.39	113.77	115.14	116.52	117.90	119.27	120.65	122.03
7.00	100.00	101.37	102.73	104.10	105.46	106.83	108.19	109.56	110.92	112.29	113.65	115.02	116.38	117.75	119.11	120.48
7.25	98.65	100.00	101.35	102.71	104.06	105.41	106.77	108.12	109.48	110.83	112.18	113.54	114.89	116.24	117.60	118.95
7.50	97.32	98.66	100.00	101.34	102.68	104.03	105.37	106.71	108.05	109.40	110.74	112.08	113.42	114.77	116.11	117.45
7.75	96.01	97.34	98.67	100.00	101.33	102.66	103.99	105.33	106.66	107.99	109.32	110.65	111.98	113.31	114.64	115.98
8.00	94.72	96.04	97.36	98.68	100.00	101.32	102.64	103.96	105.28	106.60	107.92	109.24	110.56	111.88	113.20	114.52
8.25	93.45	94.76	96.07	97.38	98.69	100.00	101.31	102.62	103.93	105.24	106.55	107.86	109.17	110.48	111.79	113.10
8.50	92.21	93.51	94.80	96.10	97.40	98.70	100.00	101.30	102.60	103.90	105.20	106.49	107.79	109.09	110.39	111.69
8.75	90.98	92.27	93.56	94.85	96.14	97.42	98.71	100.00	101.29	102.58	103.86	105.15	106.44	107.73	109.02	110.31
9.00	89.78	91.06	92.33	93.61	94.89	96.17	97.44	98.72	100.00	101.28	102.56	103.83	105.11	106.39	107.67	108.94
9.25	88.59	89.86	91.13	92.39	93.66	94.93	96.20	97.46	98.73	100.00	101.27	102.54	103.80	105.07	106.34	107.61
9.50	87.43	88.68	89.94	91.20	92.46	93.71	94.97	96.23	97.49	98.74	100.00	101.26	102.51	103.77	105.03	106.29
9.75	86.28	87.53	88.77	90.02	91.27	92.52	93.76	95.01	96.26	97.51	98.75	100.00	101.25	102.49	103.74	104.99
10.00	85.15	86.39	87.63	88.86	90.10	91.34	92.58	93.81	95.05	96.29	97.53	98.76	100.00	101.24	102.47	103.71
10.25	84.04	85.27	86.50	87.72	88.95	90.18	91.41	92.63	93.86	95.09	96.32	97.54	98.77	100.00	101.23	102.46
10.50	82.95	84.17	85.39	86.60	87.82	89.04	90.26	91.48	92.69	93.91	95.13	96.35	97.56	98.78	100.00	101.22
10.75	81.88	83.09	84.29	85.50	86.71	87.92	89.13	90.33	91.54	92.75	93.96	95.17	96.38	97.58	98.79	100.00
11.00	80.82	82.02	83.22	84.42	85.62	86.81	88.01	89.21	90.41	91.61	92.81	94.01	95.21	96.40	97.60	98.80
11.25	79.78	80.97	82.16	83.35	84.54	85.73	86.92	88.11	89.30	90.49	91.67	92.86	94.05	95.24	96.43	97.62
11.50	78.76	79.94	81.12	82.30	83.48	84.66	85.84	87.02	88.20	89.38	90.56	91.74	92.92	94.10	95.28	96.46
11.75	77.75	78.92	80.09	81.27	82.44	83.61	84.78	85.95	87.12	88.29	89.46	90.63	91.80	92.97	94.15	95.32
12.00	76.76	77.92	79.09	80.25	81.41	82.57	83.73	84.90	86.06	87.22	88.38	89.54	90.71	91.87	93.03	94.19
12.25	75.79	76.94	78.09	79.25	80.40	81.55	82.71	83.86	85.01	86.16	87.32	88.47	89.62	90.78	91.93	93.08
12.50	74.83	75.97	77.12	78.26	79.41	80.55	81.69	82.84	83.98	85.13	86.27	87.41	88.56	89.70	90.85	91.99
12.75	73.89	75.02	76.16	77.29	78.43	79.56	80.70	81.83	82.97	84.10	85.24	86.38	87.51	88.65	89.78	90.92
13.00	72.96	74.09	75.21	76.34	77.47	78.59	79.72	80.85	81.97	83.10	84.23	85.35	86.48	87.61	88.73	89.86
13.25	72.05	73.16	74.28	75.40	76.52	77.64	78.75	79.87	80.99	82.11	83.23	84.35	85.46	86.58	87.70	88.82
13.50	71.15	72.26	73.37	74.48	75.59	76.69	77.80	78.91	80.02	81.13	82.24	83.35	84.46	85.57	86.68	87.79
13.75	70.26	71.36	72.46	73.57	74.67	75.77	76.87	77.97	79.07	80.17	81.28	82.38	83.48	84.58	85.68	86.78
14.00	69.39	70.48	71.58	72.67	73.76	74.86	75.95	77.04	78.14	79.23	80.32	81.42	82.51	83.60	84.70	85.79
14.25	68.53	69.62	70.70	71.79	72.87	73.96	75.04	76.13	77.21	78.30	79.38	80.47	81.55	82.64	83.72	84.81
14.50	67.69	68.77	69.84	70.92	72.00	73.08	74.15	75.23	76.31	77.38	78.46	79.54	80.61	81.69	82.77	83.85
14.75	66.86	67.93	69.00	70.07	71.14	72.21	73.27	74.34	75.41	76.48	77.55	78.62	79.69	80.76	81.83	82.90
15.00	66.04	67.10	68.17	69.23	70.29	71.35	72.41	73.47	74.53	75.59	76.65	77.72	78.78	79.84	80.90	81.96
15.25	65.24	66.29	67.35	68.40	69.45	70.51	71.56	72.61	73.67	74.72	75.77	76.83	77.88	78.93	79.99	81.04
15.50	64.45	65.49	66.54	67.58	68.63	69.68	70.72	71.77	72.81	73.86	74.90	75.95	77.00	78.04	79.09	80.13
15.75	63.67	64.71	65.74	66.78	67.82	68.86	69.90	70.93	71.97	73.01	74.05	75.09	76.12	77.16	78.20	79.24
16.00	62.90	63.93	64.96	65.99	67.02	68.05	69.08	70.11	71.15	72.18	73.21	74.24	75.27	76.30	77.33	78.36
16.25	62.15	63.17	64.19	65.21	66.24	67.26	68.28	69.31	70.33	71.35	72.38	73.40	74.42	75.45	76.47	77.49
16.50	61.40	62.42	63.43	64.45	65.47	66.48	67.50	68.51	69.53	70.54	71.56	72.58	73.59	74.61	75.62	76.64
16.75	60.67	61.68	62.69	63.70	64.70	65.71	66.72	67.73	68.74	69.75	70.75	71.76	72.77	73.78	74.79	75.80
17.00	59.95	60.95	61.95	62.95	63.95	64.96	65.96	66.96	67.96	68.96	69.96	70.96	71.96	72.97	73.97	74.97
17.25	59.24	60.23	61.23	62.22	63.22	64.21	65.20	66.20	67.19	68.19	69.18	70.18	71.17	72.16	73.16	74.15
17.50	58.54	59.53	60.52	61.50	62.49	63.48	64.46	65.45	66.44	67.43	68.41	69.40	70.39	71.37	72.36	73.35
17.75	57.85	58.83	59.81	60.79	61.77	62.75	63.73	64.71	65.69	66.67	67.66	68.64	69.62	70.60	71.58	72.56
18.00	57.18	58.15	59.12	60.10	61.07	62.04	63.02	63.99	64.96	65.94	66.91	67.88	68.86	69.83	70.80	71.78
18.25	56.51	57.48	58.44	59.41	60.38	61.34	62.31	63.27	64.24	65.21	66.17	67.14	68.11	69.07	70.04	71.01
18.50	55.85	56.81	57.77	58.73	59.69	60.65	61.61	62.57	63.53	64.49	65.45	66.41	67.37	68.33	69.29	70.25
18.75	55.21	56.16	57.11	58.06	59.02	59.97	60.92	61.88	62.83	63.78	64.74	65.69	66.64	67.60	68.55	69.50
19.00	54.57	55.52	56.46	57.41	58.35	59.30	60.25	61.19	62.14	63.09	64.03	64.98	65.93	66.87	67.82	68.77
20.00	52.12	53.04	53.96	54.88	55.80	56.72	57.64	58.56	59.48	60.40	61.32	62.25	63.17	64.09	65.01	65.93
25.00	41.84	42.65	43.46	44.27	45.07	45.88	46.69	47.50	48.30	49.11	49.92	50.73	51.53	52.34	53.15	53.96
30.00	34.17	34.88	35.60	36.32	37.03	37.75	38.46	39.18	39.89	40.61	41.32	42.04	42.76	43.47	44.19	44.90

Description: This table shows the yield to maturity of a bond purchased at the price shown in the index.

Example: The yield to maturity of a 10.75 %, 7 year bond at a price of 105.00 is 9.74 %.

PRICE	7.00%	7.25%	7.50%	7.75%	8.00%	8.25%	8.50%	8.75%	9.00%	9.25%	9.50%	9.75%	10.00%	10.25%	10.50%	10.75%
125	3.01	3.23	3.44	3.66	3.88	4.10	4.32	4.54	4.75	4.97	5.19	5.41	5.62	5.84	6.06	6.28
124	3.15	3.37	3.59	3.81	4.03	4.25	4.46	4.68	4.90	5.12	5.34	5.56	5.78	6.00	6.21	6.43
123	3.29	3.51	3.73	3.95	4.17	4.39	4.61	4.83	5.05	5.27	5.49	5.71	5.93	6.15	6.37	6.59
122	3.43	3.65	3.88	4.10	4.32	4.54	4.76	4.98	5.20	5.43	5.65	5.87	6.09	6.31	6.53	6.75
121	3.58	3.80	4.02	4.25	4.47	4.69	4.91	5.14	5.36	5.58	5.80	6.02	6.25	6.47	6.69	6.91
120	3.72	3.95	4.17	4.39	4.62	4.84	5.07	5.29	5.51	5.74	5.96	6.18	6.40	6.63	6.85	7.07
119	3.87	4.10	4.32	4.55	4.77	4.99	5.22	5.44	5.67	5.89	6.12	6.34	6.57	6.79	7.01	7.24
118	4.02	4.25	4.47	4.70	4.92	5.15	5.38	5.60	5.83	6.05	6.28	6.50	6.73	6.95	7.18	7.40
117	4.17	4.40	4.62	4.85	5.08	5.31	5.53	5.76	5.99	6.21	6.44	6.67	6.89	7.12	7.34	7.57
116	4.32	4.55	4.78	5.01	5.24	5.46	5.69	5.92	6.15	6.38	6.60	6.83	7.06	7.29	7.51	7.74
115	4.47	4.70	4.93	5.16	5.39	5.62	5.85	6.08	6.31	6.54	6.77	7.00	7.23	7.46	7.68	7.91
114	4.63	4.86	5.09	5.32	5.55	5.78	6.01	6.25	6.48	6.71	6.94	7.17	7.40	7.63	7.86	8.09
113	4.79	5.02	5.25	5.48	5.72	5.95	6.18	6.41	6.64	6.87	7.11	7.34	7.57	7.80	8.03	8.26
112	4.95	5.18	5.41	5.65	5.88	6.11	6.34	6.58	6.81	7.04	7.28	7.51	7.74	7.97	8.21	8.44
111	5.11	5.34	5.58	5.81	6.04	6.28	6.51	6.75	6.98	7.22	7.45	7.68	7.92	8.15	8.39	8.62
110	5.27	5.50	5.74	5.98	6.21	6.45	6.68	6.92	7.15	7.39	7.62	7.86	8.10	8.33	8.57	8.80
109	5.43	5.67	5.91	6.14	6.38	6.62	6.85	7.09	7.33	7.57	7.80	8.04	8.28	8.51	8.75	8.98
108	5.60	5.84	6.07	6.31	6.55	6.79	7.03	7.27	7.50	7.74	7.98	8.22	8.46	8.70	8.93	9.17
107	5.77	6.01	6.25	6.48	6.72	6.96	7.20	7.44	7.68	7.92	8.16	8.40	8.64	8.88	9.12	9.36
106	5.93	6.18	6.42	6.66	6.90	7.14	7.38	7.62	7.86	8.10	8.35	8.59	8.83	9.07	9.31	9.55
105	6.11	6.35	6.59	6.83	7.08	7.32	7.56	7.80	8.05	8.29	8.53	8.77	9.02	9.26	9.50	9.74
104	6.28	6.52	6.77	7.01	7.26	7.50	7.74	7.99	8.23	8.48	8.72	8.96	9.21	9.45	9.69	9.94
103	6.46	6.70	6.95	7.19	7.44	7.68	7.93	8.17	8.42	8.66	8.91	9.16	9.40	9.65	9.89	10.14
102	6.63	6.88	7.13	7.37	7.62	7.87	8.11	8.36	8.61	8.86	9.10	9.35	9.60	9.84	10.09	10.34
101	6.81	7.06	7.31	7.56	7.81	8.06	8.30	8.55	8.80	9.05	9.30	9.55	9.79	10.04	10.29	10.54
100	7.00	7.25	7.50	7.75	8.00	8.25	8.50	8.75	9.00	9.25	9.50	9.75	10.00	10.25	10.50	10.75
99	7.18	7.43	7.68	7.93	8.19	8.44	8.69	8.94	9.19	9.44	9.70	9.95	10.20	10.45	10.70	10.95
98	7.37	7.62	7.87	8.13	8.38	8.63	8.88	9.14	9.39	9.64	9.90	10.15	10.40	10.66	10.91	11.16
97	7.55	7.81	8.06	8.32	8.57	8.83	9.08	9.34	9.59	9.85	10.10	10.36	10.61	10.87	11.12	11.38
96	7.75	8.00	8.26	8.52	8.77	9.03	9.28	9.54	9.80	10.05	10.31	10.57	10.82	11.08	11.34	11.60
95	7.94	8.20	8.46	8.71	8.97	9.23	9.49	9.75	10.01	10.26	10.52	10.78	11.04	11.30	11.56	11.81
94	8.14	8.40	8.66	8.92	9.18	9.44	9.70	9.96	10.22	10.48	10.74	11.00	11.26	11.52	11.78	12.04
93	8.34	8.60	8.86	9.12	9.38	9.64	9.91	10.17	10.43	10.69	10.95	11.22	11.48	11.74	12.00	12.26
92	8.54	8.80	9.06	9.33	9.59	9.85	10.12	10.38	10.65	10.91	11.17	11.44	11.70	11.96	12.23	12.49
91	8.74	9.01	9.27	9.54	9.80	10.07	10.33	10.60	10.86	11.13	11.40	11.66	11.93	12.19	12.46	12.73
90	8.95	9.22	9.48	9.75	10.02	10.28	10.55	10.82	11.09	11.35	11.62	11.89	12.16	12.43	12.69	12.96
89	9.16	9.43	9.70	9.97	10.23	10.50	10.77	11.04	11.31	11.58	11.85	12.12	12.39	12.66	12.93	13.20
88	9.37	9.64	9.91	10.18	10.46	10.73	11.00	11.27	11.54	11.81	12.08	12.36	12.63	12.90	13.17	13.44
87	9.59	9.86	10.13	10.41	10.68	10.95	11.23	11.50	11.77	12.05	12.32	12.59	12.87	13.14	13.42	13.69
86	9.81	10.08	10.36	10.63	10.91	11.18	11.46	11.73	12.01	12.28	12.56	12.84	13.11	13.39	13.67	13.94
85	10.03	10.31	10.58	10.86	11.14	11.41	11.69	11.97	12.25	12.53	12.80	13.08	13.36	13.64	13.92	14.20
84	10.25	10.53	10.81	11.09	11.37	11.65	11.93	12.21	12.49	12.77	13.05	13.33	13.61	13.89	14.17	14.45
83	10.48	10.76	11.05	11.33	11.61	11.89	12.17	12.46	12.74	13.02	13.30	13.59	13.87	14.15	14.43	14.72
82	10.72	11.00	11.28	11.57	11.85	12.13	12.42	12.70	12.99	13.27	13.56	13.84	14.13	14.41	14.70	14.98
81	10.95	11.24	11.52	11.81	12.10	12.38	12.67	12.96	13.24	13.53	13.82	14.10	14.39	14.68	14.97	15.26
80	11.19	11.48	11.77	12.06	12.35	12.63	12.92	13.21	13.50	13.79	14.08	14.37	14.66	14.95	15.24	15.53
79	11.44	11.73	12.02	12.31	12.60	12.89	13.18	13.47	13.76	14.06	14.35	14.64	14.93	15.23	15.52	15.81
78	11.68	11.98	12.27	12.56	12.86	13.15	13.44	13.74	14.03	14.33	14.62	14.92	15.21	15.51	15.80	16.10
77	11.93	12.23	12.53	12.82	13.12	13.41	13.71	14.01	14.30	14.60	14.90	15.20	15.49	15.79	16.09	16.39
76	12.19	12.49	12.79	13.08	13.38	13.68	13.98	14.28	14.58	14.88	15.18	15.48	15.78	16.08	16.38	16.68
75	12.45	12.75	13.05	13.35	13.65	13.96	14.26	14.56	14.86	15.16	15.47	15.77	16.07	16.38	16.68	16.99
74	12.71	13.02	13.32	13.63	13.93	14.23	14.54	14.84	15.15	15.45	15.76	16.07	16.37	16.68	16.98	17.29
73	12.98	13.29	13.60	13.90	14.21	14.52	14.82	15.13	15.44	15.75	16.06	16.37	16.67	16.98	17.29	17.60
72	13.26	13.57	13.88	14.18	14.49	14.80	15.12	15.43	15.74	16.05	16.36	16.67	16.98	17.30	17.61	17.92
71	13.54	13.85	14.16	14.47	14.78	15.10	15.41	15.73	16.04	16.35	16.67	16.98	17.30	17.61	17.93	18.25
70	13.82	14.13	14.45	14.76	15.08	15.40	15.71	16.03	16.35	16.67	16.98	17.30	17.62	17.94	18.26	18.58
69	14.11	14.43	14.74	15.06	15.38	15.70	16.02	16.34	16.66	16.98	17.30	17.63	17.95	18.27	18.59	18.92
68	14.40	14.72	15.05	15.37	15.69	16.01	16.33	16.66	16.98	17.31	17.63	17.96	18.28	18.61	18.93	19.26
67	14.70	15.03	15.35	15.68	16.00	16.33	16.65	16.98	17.31	17.64	17.96	18.29	18.62	18.95	19.28	19.61
66	15.01	15.34	15.66	15.99	16.32	16.65	16.98	17.31	17.64	17.97	18.30	18.64	18.97	19.30	19.64	19.97
65	15.32	15.65	15.98	16.31	16.65	16.98	17.31	17.65	17.98	18.32	18.65	18.99	19.32	19.66	20.00	20.34
64	15.64	15.97	16.31	16.64	16.98	17.32	17.65	17.99	18.33	18.67	19.01	19.35	19.69	20.03	20.37	20.71
63	15.96	16.30	16.64	16.98	17.32	17.66	18.00	18.34	18.68	19.03	19.37	19.71	20.06	20.40	20.75	21.09
62	16.29	16.64	16.98	17.32	17.67	18.01	18.36	18.70	19.05	19.39	19.74	20.09	20.44	20.78	21.13	21.48
60	16.98	17.33	17.68	18.03	18.38	18.73	19.09	19.44	19.80	20.15	20.51	20.86	21.22	21.58	21.94	22.29
55	18.83	19.20	19.57	19.95	20.32	20.70	21.07	21.45	21.83	22.21	22.59	22.97	23.35	23.73	24.12	24.50
50	20.91	21.31	21.71	22.11	22.52	22.92	23.32	23.73	24.14	24.55	24.95	25.36	25.78	26.19	26.60	27.02
45	23.29	23.73	24.16	24.60	25.03	25.47	25.91	26.35	26.80	27.24	27.69	28.13	28.58	29.03	29.48	29.93

Description: This table shows the price to pay for a bond at the yield rate. The yield is to maturity.

Example: The price of a 15.00 %, 7 year bond to yield 8 % to maturity is $ 136.97.

YIELD	11.00%	11.25%	11.50%	11.75%	12.00%	12.25%	12.50%	12.75%	13.00%	13.25%	13.50%	13.75%	14.00%	14.25%	14.50%	15.00%
0.00	177.00	178.75	180.50	182.25	184.00	185.75	187.50	189.25	191.00	192.75	194.50	196.25	198.00	199.75	201.50	205.00
1.00	167.44	169.13	170.82	172.50	174.19	175.87	177.56	179.25	180.93	182.62	184.30	185.99	187.68	189.36	191.05	194.42
2.00	158.52	160.14	161.77	163.39	165.02	166.64	168.27	169.89	171.52	173.15	174.77	176.40	178.02	179.65	181.27	184.52
3.00	150.17	151.74	153.31	154.88	156.45	158.01	159.58	161.15	162.72	164.28	165.85	167.42	168.99	170.56	172.12	175.26
4.00	142.37	143.89	145.40	146.91	148.42	149.94	151.45	152.96	154.48	155.99	157.50	159.02	160.53	162.04	163.56	166.58
4.25	140.50	142.00	143.50	145.00	146.50	148.00	149.50	151.00	152.50	154.00	155.50	157.00	158.50	160.00	161.50	164.50
4.50	138.66	140.15	141.64	143.12	144.61	146.10	147.58	149.07	150.56	152.04	153.53	155.02	156.51	157.99	159.48	162.45
4.75	136.85	138.33	139.80	141.27	142.75	144.22	145.70	147.17	148.65	150.12	151.59	153.07	154.54	156.02	157.49	160.44
5.00	135.07	136.53	138.00	139.46	140.92	142.38	143.84	145.30	146.76	148.23	149.69	151.15	152.61	154.07	155.53	158.45
5.25	133.32	134.77	136.22	137.67	139.12	140.57	142.01	143.46	144.91	146.36	147.81	149.26	150.71	152.16	153.61	156.50
5.50	131.60	133.04	134.47	135.91	137.35	138.78	140.22	141.65	143.09	144.53	145.96	147.40	148.84	150.27	151.71	154.58
5.75	129.91	131.33	132.75	134.18	135.60	137.03	138.45	139.88	141.30	142.72	144.15	145.57	147.00	148.42	149.84	152.69
6.00	128.24	129.65	131.06	132.48	133.89	135.30	136.71	138.12	139.54	140.95	142.36	143.77	145.18	146.60	148.01	150.83
6.25	126.60	128.00	129.40	130.80	132.20	133.60	135.00	136.40	137.80	139.20	140.60	142.00	143.40	144.80	146.20	149.00
6.50	124.99	126.38	127.76	129.15	130.54	131.93	133.32	134.71	136.09	137.48	138.87	140.26	141.65	143.04	144.42	147.20
6.75	123.40	124.78	126.16	127.53	128.91	130.28	131.66	133.04	134.41	135.79	137.17	138.54	139.92	141.30	142.67	145.43
7.00	121.84	123.21	124.57	125.94	127.30	128.67	130.03	131.40	132.76	134.13	135.49	136.86	138.22	139.59	140.95	143.68
7.25	120.31	121.66	123.01	124.37	125.72	127.07	128.43	129.78	131.13	132.49	133.84	135.20	136.55	137.90	139.26	141.96
7.50	118.79	120.14	121.48	122.82	124.16	125.51	126.85	128.19	129.53	130.88	132.22	133.56	134.90	136.25	137.59	140.27
7.75	117.31	118.64	119.97	121.30	122.63	123.96	125.30	126.63	127.96	129.29	130.62	131.95	133.28	134.62	135.95	138.61
8.00	115.84	117.17	118.49	119.81	121.13	122.45	123.77	125.09	126.41	127.73	129.05	130.37	131.69	133.01	134.33	136.97
8.25	114.41	115.71	117.02	118.33	119.64	120.95	122.26	123.57	124.88	126.19	127.50	128.81	130.12	131.43	132.74	135.36
8.50	112.99	114.29	115.59	116.89	118.18	119.48	120.78	122.08	123.38	124.68	125.98	127.28	128.57	129.87	131.17	133.77
8.75	111.59	112.88	114.17	115.46	116.75	118.04	119.32	120.61	121.90	123.19	124.48	125.77	127.05	128.34	129.63	132.21
9.00	110.22	111.50	112.78	114.06	115.33	116.61	117.89	119.17	120.45	121.72	123.00	124.28	125.56	126.83	128.11	130.67
9.25	108.87	110.14	111.41	112.68	113.94	115.21	116.48	117.75	119.01	120.28	121.55	122.82	124.08	125.35	126.62	129.15
9.50	107.54	108.80	110.06	111.32	112.57	113.83	115.09	116.35	117.60	118.86	120.12	121.37	122.63	123.89	125.15	127.66
9.75	106.24	107.48	108.73	109.98	111.23	112.47	113.72	114.97	116.21	117.46	118.71	119.96	121.20	122.45	123.70	126.19
10.00	104.95	106.19	107.42	108.66	109.90	111.14	112.37	113.61	114.85	116.09	117.32	118.56	119.80	121.03	122.27	124.75
10.25	103.68	104.91	106.14	107.37	108.59	109.82	111.05	112.28	113.50	114.73	115.96	117.19	118.41	119.64	120.87	123.32
10.50	102.44	103.65	104.87	106.09	107.31	108.52	109.74	110.96	112.18	113.40	114.61	115.83	117.05	118.27	119.48	121.92
10.75	101.21	102.42	103.62	104.83	106.04	107.25	108.46	109.67	110.87	112.08	113.29	114.50	115.71	116.91	118.12	120.54
11.00	100.00	101.20	102.40	103.60	104.79	105.99	107.19	108.39	109.59	110.79	111.99	113.19	114.38	115.58	116.78	119.18
11.25	98.81	100.00	101.19	102.38	103.57	104.76	105.95	107.14	108.33	109.51	110.70	111.89	113.08	114.27	115.46	117.84
11.50	97.64	98.82	100.00	101.18	102.36	103.54	104.72	105.90	107.08	108.26	109.44	110.62	111.80	112.98	114.16	116.52
11.75	96.49	97.66	98.83	100.00	101.17	102.34	103.51	104.68	105.85	107.03	108.20	109.37	110.54	111.71	112.88	115.22
12.00	95.35	96.51	97.68	98.84	100.00	101.16	102.32	103.49	104.65	105.81	106.97	108.13	109.29	110.46	111.62	113.94
12.25	94.24	95.39	96.54	97.69	98.85	100.00	101.15	102.31	103.46	104.61	105.76	106.92	108.07	109.22	110.38	112.68
12.50	93.14	94.28	95.42	96.57	97.71	98.86	100.00	101.14	102.29	103.43	104.58	105.72	106.86	108.01	109.15	111.44
12.75	92.05	93.19	94.32	95.46	96.59	97.73	98.86	100.00	101.14	102.27	103.41	104.54	105.68	106.81	107.95	110.22
13.00	90.99	92.11	93.24	94.37	95.49	96.62	97.75	98.87	100.00	101.13	102.25	103.38	104.51	105.63	106.76	109.01
13.25	89.94	91.05	92.17	93.29	94.41	95.53	96.65	97.76	98.88	100.00	101.12	102.24	103.35	104.47	105.59	107.83
13.50	88.90	90.01	91.12	92.23	93.34	94.45	95.56	96.67	97.78	98.89	100.00	101.11	102.22	103.33	104.44	106.66
13.75	87.88	88.99	90.09	91.19	92.29	93.39	94.49	95.59	96.70	97.80	98.90	100.00	101.10	102.20	103.30	105.51
14.00	86.88	87.97	89.07	90.16	91.25	92.35	93.44	94.53	95.63	96.72	97.81	98.91	100.00	101.09	102.19	104.37
14.25	85.89	86.98	88.06	89.15	90.23	91.32	92.40	93.49	94.57	95.66	96.74	97.83	98.91	100.00	101.09	103.26
14.50	84.92	86.00	87.08	88.15	89.23	90.31	91.38	92.46	93.54	94.62	95.69	96.77	97.85	98.92	100.00	102.15
14.75	83.96	85.03	86.10	87.17	88.24	89.31	90.38	91.45	92.52	93.59	94.65	95.72	96.79	97.86	98.93	101.07
15.00	83.02	84.08	85.14	86.21	87.27	88.33	89.39	90.45	91.51	92.57	93.63	94.69	95.76	96.82	97.88	100.00
15.25	82.09	83.15	84.20	85.25	86.31	87.36	88.41	89.47	90.52	91.57	92.63	93.68	94.73	95.79	96.84	98.95
15.50	81.18	82.22	83.27	84.32	85.36	86.41	87.45	88.50	89.54	90.59	91.63	92.68	93.73	94.77	95.82	97.91
15.75	80.28	81.32	82.35	83.39	84.43	85.47	86.51	87.54	88.58	89.62	90.66	91.70	92.73	93.77	94.81	96.89
16.00	79.39	80.42	81.45	82.48	83.51	84.54	85.57	86.60	87.63	88.66	89.69	90.73	91.76	92.79	93.82	95.88
16.25	78.52	79.54	80.56	81.58	82.61	83.63	84.65	85.68	86.70	87.72	88.75	89.77	90.79	91.82	92.84	94.88
16.50	77.65	78.67	79.69	80.70	81.72	82.73	83.75	84.76	85.78	86.80	87.81	88.83	89.84	90.86	91.87	93.91
16.75	76.81	77.81	78.82	79.83	80.84	81.85	82.86	83.86	84.87	85.88	86.89	87.90	88.91	89.92	90.92	92.94
17.00	75.97	76.97	77.97	78.97	79.97	80.98	81.98	82.98	83.98	84.98	85.98	86.98	87.98	88.99	89.99	91.99
17.25	75.15	76.14	77.13	78.13	79.12	80.12	81.11	82.11	83.10	84.09	85.09	86.08	87.08	88.07	89.06	91.05
17.50	74.34	75.32	76.31	77.30	78.28	79.27	80.26	81.24	82.23	83.22	84.21	85.19	86.18	87.17	88.15	90.13
17.75	73.54	74.52	75.50	76.48	77.46	78.44	79.42	80.40	81.38	82.36	83.34	84.32	85.30	86.28	87.26	89.22
18.00	72.75	73.72	74.70	75.67	76.64	77.61	78.59	79.56	80.53	81.51	82.48	83.45	84.43	85.40	86.37	88.32
18.25	71.97	72.94	73.91	74.87	75.84	76.80	77.77	78.74	79.70	80.67	81.64	82.60	83.57	84.54	85.50	87.44
18.50	71.21	72.17	73.13	74.09	75.05	76.01	76.97	77.93	78.89	79.85	80.81	81.77	82.72	83.68	84.64	86.56
18.75	70.45	71.41	72.36	73.31	74.27	75.22	76.17	77.13	78.08	79.03	79.99	80.94	81.89	82.84	83.80	85.70
19.00	69.71	70.66	71.61	72.55	73.50	74.45	75.39	76.34	77.28	78.23	79.18	80.12	81.07	82.02	82.96	84.86
20.00	66.85	67.77	68.69	69.61	70.53	71.45	72.37	73.30	74.22	75.14	76.06	76.98	77.90	78.82	79.74	81.58
25.00	54.77	55.57	56.38	57.19	58.00	58.80	59.61	60.42	61.23	62.04	62.84	63.65	64.46	65.27	66.07	67.69
30.00	45.62	46.33	47.05	47.76	48.48	49.20	49.91	50.63	51.34	52.06	52.77	53.49	54.20	54.92	55.64	57.07

Description: This table shows the yield to maturity of a bond purchased at the price shown in the index.

Example: The yield to maturity of a 15.00 %, 7 year bond at a price of 116.00 is 11.59 %.

PRICE	11.00%	11.25%	11.50%	11.75%	12.00%	12.25%	12.50%	12.75%	13.00%	13.25%	13.50%	13.75%	14.00%	14.25%	14.50%	15.00%
160	1.82	2.01	2.20	2.39	2.57	2.76	2.95	3.13	3.32	3.50	3.69	3.87	4.06	4.25	4.43	4.80
155	2.41	2.60	2.79	2.98	3.17	3.36	3.55	3.74	3.93	4.12	4.31	4.50	4.69	4.88	5.06	5.44
150	3.02	3.21	3.41	3.60	3.79	3.99	4.18	4.37	4.57	4.76	4.95	5.15	5.34	5.53	5.72	6.11
145	3.65	3.85	4.05	4.25	4.44	4.64	4.84	5.04	5.23	5.43	5.63	5.82	6.02	6.22	6.41	6.81
140	4.31	4.52	4.72	4.92	5.12	5.32	5.53	5.73	5.93	6.13	6.33	6.53	6.73	6.93	7.13	7.54
135	5.01	5.21	5.42	5.63	5.83	6.04	6.25	6.45	6.66	6.86	7.07	7.27	7.48	7.69	7.89	8.30
130	5.73	5.94	6.15	6.37	6.58	6.79	7.00	7.21	7.42	7.63	7.84	8.05	8.26	8.47	8.68	9.10
129	5.88	6.09	6.31	6.52	6.73	6.94	7.16	7.37	7.58	7.79	8.00	8.21	8.43	8.64	8.85	9.27
128	6.03	6.25	6.46	6.67	6.89	7.10	7.31	7.53	7.74	7.95	8.16	8.38	8.59	8.80	9.01	9.44
127	6.18	6.40	6.61	6.83	7.04	7.26	7.47	7.69	7.90	8.11	8.33	8.54	8.75	8.97	9.18	9.61
126	6.34	6.55	6.77	6.98	7.20	7.42	7.63	7.85	8.06	8.28	8.49	8.71	8.92	9.14	9.35	9.78
125	6.49	6.71	6.93	7.14	7.36	7.58	7.79	8.01	8.23	8.44	8.66	8.87	9.09	9.30	9.52	9.95
124	6.65	6.87	7.09	7.30	7.52	7.74	7.96	8.17	8.39	8.61	8.83	9.04	9.26	9.48	9.69	10.13
123	6.81	7.03	7.25	7.47	7.68	7.90	8.12	8.34	8.56	8.78	9.00	9.21	9.43	9.65	9.87	10.30
122	6.97	7.19	7.41	7.63	7.85	8.07	8.29	8.51	8.73	8.95	9.17	9.39	9.61	9.82	10.04	10.48
121	7.13	7.35	7.57	7.80	8.02	8.24	8.46	8.68	8.90	9.12	9.34	9.56	9.78	10.00	10.22	10.66
120	7.30	7.52	7.74	7.96	8.18	8.41	8.63	8.85	9.07	9.29	9.52	9.74	9.96	10.18	10.40	10.84
119	7.46	7.68	7.91	8.13	8.35	8.58	8.80	9.02	9.25	9.47	9.69	9.92	10.14	10.36	10.58	11.03
118	7.63	7.85	8.08	8.30	8.53	8.75	8.98	9.20	9.42	9.65	9.87	10.10	10.32	10.54	10.77	11.21
117	7.80	8.02	8.25	8.48	8.70	8.93	9.15	9.38	9.60	9.83	10.05	10.28	10.50	10.73	10.95	11.40
116	7.97	8.20	8.42	8.65	8.88	9.10	9.33	9.56	9.78	10.01	10.24	10.46	10.69	10.92	11.14	11.59
115	8.14	8.37	8.60	8.83	9.05	9.28	9.51	9.74	9.97	10.19	10.42	10.65	10.88	11.11	11.33	11.79
114	8.32	8.55	8.78	9.01	9.23	9.46	9.69	9.92	10.15	10.38	10.61	10.84	11.07	11.30	11.53	11.98
113	8.49	8.72	8.95	9.19	9.42	9.65	9.88	10.11	10.34	10.57	10.80	11.03	11.26	11.49	11.72	12.18
112	8.67	8.90	9.14	9.37	9.60	9.83	10.07	10.30	10.53	10.76	10.99	11.22	11.46	11.69	11.92	12.38
111	8.85	9.09	9.32	9.55	9.79	10.02	10.25	10.49	10.72	10.95	11.19	11.42	11.65	11.89	12.12	12.58
110	9.04	9.27	9.51	9.74	9.98	10.21	10.45	10.68	10.91	11.15	11.38	11.62	11.85	12.09	12.32	12.79
109	9.22	9.46	9.69	9.93	10.17	10.40	10.64	10.88	11.11	11.35	11.58	11.82	12.05	12.29	12.53	13.00
108	9.41	9.65	9.88	10.12	10.36	10.60	10.83	11.07	11.31	11.55	11.78	12.02	12.26	12.50	12.73	13.21
107	9.60	9.84	10.08	10.32	10.56	10.79	11.03	11.27	11.51	11.75	11.99	12.23	12.47	12.71	12.94	13.42
106	9.79	10.03	10.27	10.51	10.75	10.99	11.23	11.47	11.72	11.96	12.20	12.44	12.68	12.92	13.16	13.64
105	9.99	10.23	10.47	10.71	10.95	11.20	11.44	11.68	11.92	12.16	12.41	12.65	12.89	13.13	13.37	13.86
104	10.18	10.43	10.67	10.91	11.16	11.40	11.64	11.89	12.13	12.37	12.62	12.86	13.10	13.35	13.59	14.08
103	10.38	10.63	10.87	11.12	11.36	11.61	11.85	12.10	12.34	12.59	12.83	13.08	13.32	13.57	13.81	14.30
102	10.58	10.83	11.08	11.32	11.57	11.82	12.06	12.31	12.56	12.80	13.05	13.30	13.54	13.79	14.04	14.53
101	10.79	11.04	11.28	11.53	11.78	12.03	12.28	12.53	12.77	13.02	13.27	13.52	13.77	14.02	14.26	14.76
100	11.00	11.25	11.50	11.75	12.00	12.25	12.50	12.75	13.00	13.25	13.50	13.75	14.00	14.25	14.50	15.00
99	11.20	11.46	11.71	11.96	12.21	12.46	12.72	12.97	13.22	13.47	13.72	13.97	14.23	14.48	14.73	15.23
98	11.42	11.67	11.92	12.18	12.43	12.68	12.94	13.19	13.44	13.70	13.95	14.21	14.46	14.71	14.97	15.47
97	11.63	11.89	12.14	12.40	12.65	12.91	13.16	13.42	13.67	13.93	14.19	14.44	14.70	14.95	15.21	15.72
96	11.85	12.11	12.37	12.62	12.88	13.14	13.39	13.65	13.91	14.16	14.42	14.68	14.94	15.19	15.45	15.96
95	12.07	12.33	12.59	12.85	13.11	13.37	13.63	13.88	14.14	14.40	14.66	14.92	15.18	15.44	15.70	16.22
94	12.30	12.56	12.82	13.08	13.34	13.60	13.86	14.12	14.38	14.64	14.90	15.17	15.43	15.69	15.95	16.47
93	12.53	12.79	13.05	13.31	13.58	13.84	14.10	14.36	14.63	14.89	15.15	15.41	15.68	15.94	16.20	16.73
92	12.76	13.02	13.29	13.55	13.81	14.08	14.34	14.61	14.87	15.14	15.40	15.67	15.93	16.20	16.46	16.99
91	12.99	13.26	13.52	13.79	14.06	14.32	14.59	14.86	15.12	15.39	15.66	15.92	16.19	16.46	16.72	17.26
90	13.23	13.50	13.77	14.03	14.30	14.57	14.84	15.11	15.38	15.65	15.92	16.18	16.45	16.72	16.99	17.53
89	13.47	13.74	14.01	14.28	14.55	14.82	15.09	15.36	15.64	15.91	16.18	16.45	16.72	16.99	17.26	17.81
88	13.72	13.99	14.26	14.53	14.81	15.08	15.35	15.62	15.90	16.17	16.44	16.72	16.99	17.26	17.54	18.09
87	13.97	14.24	14.51	14.79	15.06	15.34	15.61	15.89	16.16	16.44	16.71	16.99	17.27	17.54	17.82	18.37
86	14.22	14.49	14.77	15.05	15.33	15.60	15.88	16.16	16.43	16.71	16.99	17.27	17.55	17.82	18.10	18.66
85	14.47	14.75	15.03	15.31	15.59	15.87	16.15	16.43	16.71	16.99	17.27	17.55	17.83	18.11	18.39	18.95
84	14.74	15.02	15.30	15.58	15.86	16.14	16.43	16.71	16.99	17.27	17.55	17.84	18.12	18.40	18.68	19.25
83	15.00	15.28	15.57	15.85	16.14	16.42	16.70	16.99	17.27	17.56	17.84	18.13	18.41	18.70	18.98	19.56
82	15.27	15.56	15.84	16.13	16.42	16.70	16.99	17.28	17.56	17.85	18.14	18.42	18.71	19.00	19.29	19.86
81	15.54	15.83	16.12	16.41	16.70	16.99	17.28	17.57	17.86	18.15	18.44	18.73	19.02	19.31	19.60	20.18
80	15.82	16.11	16.40	16.70	16.99	17.28	17.57	17.86	18.16	18.45	18.74	19.03	19.33	19.62	19.91	20.50
79	16.11	16.40	16.69	16.99	17.28	17.58	17.87	18.17	18.46	18.76	19.05	19.35	19.64	19.94	20.23	20.83
78	16.39	16.69	16.99	17.28	17.58	17.88	18.17	18.47	18.77	19.07	19.37	19.66	19.96	20.26	20.56	21.16
77	16.69	16.99	17.29	17.58	17.88	18.18	18.48	18.78	19.09	19.39	19.69	19.99	20.29	20.59	20.89	21.50
76	16.99	17.29	17.59	17.89	18.19	18.50	18.80	19.10	19.41	19.71	20.01	20.32	20.62	20.93	21.23	21.84
75	17.29	17.59	17.90	18.20	18.51	18.82	19.12	19.43	19.73	20.04	20.35	20.65	20.96	21.27	21.58	22.19
74	17.60	17.91	18.21	18.52	18.83	19.14	19.45	19.76	20.07	20.38	20.69	21.00	21.31	21.62	21.93	22.55
73	17.91	18.23	18.54	18.85	19.16	19.47	19.78	20.10	20.41	20.72	21.03	21.35	21.66	21.98	22.29	22.92
72	18.24	18.55	18.86	19.18	19.49	19.81	20.12	20.44	20.75	21.07	21.39	21.70	22.02	22.34	22.66	23.29
71	18.56	18.88	19.20	19.52	19.83	20.15	20.47	20.79	21.11	21.43	21.75	22.07	22.39	22.71	23.03	23.67
70	18.90	19.22	19.54	19.86	20.18	20.50	20.82	21.15	21.47	21.79	22.12	22.44	22.76	23.09	23.41	24.06
65	20.67	21.01	21.35	21.69	22.03	22.37	22.71	23.05	23.39	23.74	24.08	24.42	24.76	25.11	25.45	26.14

Description: This table shows the price to pay for a bond at the yield rate. The yield is to maturity.

Example: The price of a 6.75 %, 8 year bond to yield 8 % to maturity is $ 92.72.

YIELD	0.00%	1.00%	2.00%	3.00%	4.00%	4.25%	4.50%	4.75%	5.00%	5.25%	5.50%	5.75%	6.00%	6.25%	6.50%	6.75%
0.00	100.00	108.00	116.00	124.00	132.00	134.00	136.00	138.00	140.00	142.00	144.00	146.00	148.00	150.00	152.00	154.00
1.00	92.33	100.00	107.67	115.34	123.01	124.93	126.84	128.76	130.68	132.60	134.51	136.43	138.35	140.27	142.18	144.10
2.00	85.28	92.64	100.00	107.36	114.72	116.56	118.40	120.24	122.08	123.92	125.76	127.60	129.44	131.28	133.12	134.95
3.00	78.80	85.87	92.93	100.00	107.07	108.83	110.60	112.36	114.13	115.90	117.66	119.43	121.20	122.96	124.73	126.50
4.00	72.84	79.63	86.42	93.21	100.00	101.70	103.39	105.09	106.79	108.49	110.18	111.88	113.58	115.27	116.97	118.67
4.25	71.43	78.15	84.88	91.60	98.32	100.00	101.68	103.36	105.04	106.72	108.40	110.08	111.76	113.44	115.12	116.81
4.50	70.05	76.70	83.36	90.02	96.67	98.34	100.00	101.66	103.33	104.99	106.66	108.32	109.98	111.65	113.31	114.98
4.75	68.69	75.28	81.87	88.46	95.06	96.70	98.35	100.00	101.65	103.30	104.94	106.59	108.24	109.89	111.54	113.18
5.00	67.36	73.89	80.42	86.94	93.47	95.10	96.74	98.37	100.00	101.63	103.26	104.90	106.53	108.16	109.79	111.42
5.25	66.06	72.53	78.99	85.45	91.92	93.54	95.15	96.77	98.38	100.00	101.62	103.23	104.85	106.46	108.08	109.70
5.50	64.79	71.19	77.59	83.99	90.40	92.00	93.60	95.20	96.80	98.40	100.00	101.60	103.20	104.80	106.40	108.00
5.75	63.54	69.88	76.22	82.56	88.90	90.49	92.07	93.66	95.24	96.83	98.41	100.00	101.59	103.17	104.76	106.34
6.00	62.32	68.60	74.88	81.16	87.44	89.01	90.58	92.15	93.72	95.29	96.86	98.43	100.00	101.57	103.14	104.71
6.25	61.12	67.34	73.56	79.78	86.00	87.56	89.11	90.67	92.22	93.78	95.33	96.89	98.44	100.00	101.56	103.11
6.50	59.95	66.11	72.27	78.43	84.59	86.14	87.68	89.22	90.76	92.30	93.84	95.38	96.92	98.46	100.00	101.54
6.75	58.80	64.90	71.00	77.11	83.21	84.74	86.27	87.79	89.32	90.84	92.37	93.90	95.42	96.95	98.47	100.00
7.00	57.67	63.72	69.76	75.81	81.86	83.37	84.88	86.39	87.91	89.42	90.93	92.44	93.95	95.46	96.98	98.49
7.25	56.57	62.56	68.55	74.54	80.53	82.03	83.53	85.02	86.52	88.02	89.52	91.01	92.51	94.01	95.51	97.00
7.50	55.49	61.42	67.36	73.29	79.23	80.71	82.19	83.68	85.16	86.65	88.13	89.61	91.10	92.58	94.06	95.55
7.75	54.43	60.31	66.19	72.07	77.95	79.42	80.89	82.36	83.83	85.30	86.77	88.24	89.71	91.18	92.65	94.12
8.00	53.39	59.22	65.04	70.87	76.70	78.15	79.61	81.07	82.52	83.98	85.43	86.89	88.35	89.80	91.26	92.72
8.25	52.37	58.15	63.92	69.69	75.47	76.91	78.35	79.80	81.24	82.68	84.12	85.57	87.01	88.45	89.90	91.34
8.50	51.38	57.10	62.82	68.54	74.26	75.69	77.12	78.55	79.98	81.41	82.84	84.27	85.70	87.13	88.56	89.99
8.75	50.40	56.07	61.74	67.41	73.08	74.49	75.91	77.33	78.74	80.16	81.58	83.00	84.41	85.83	87.25	88.66
9.00	49.45	55.06	60.68	66.30	71.91	73.32	74.72	76.13	77.53	78.94	80.34	81.74	83.15	84.55	85.96	87.36
9.25	48.51	54.08	59.64	65.21	70.78	72.17	73.56	74.95	76.34	77.73	79.13	80.52	81.91	83.30	84.69	86.08
9.50	47.59	53.11	58.63	64.14	69.66	71.04	72.42	73.80	75.18	76.55	77.93	79.31	80.69	82.07	83.45	84.83
9.75	46.69	52.16	57.63	63.09	68.56	69.93	71.30	72.66	74.03	75.40	76.76	78.13	79.50	80.86	82.23	83.60
10.00	45.81	51.23	56.65	62.07	67.49	68.84	70.20	71.55	72.91	74.26	75.62	76.97	78.32	79.68	81.03	82.39
10.25	44.95	50.32	55.69	61.06	66.43	67.77	69.12	70.46	71.80	73.15	74.49	75.83	77.17	78.52	79.86	81.20
10.50	44.10	49.42	54.75	60.07	65.40	66.73	68.06	69.39	70.72	72.05	73.38	74.71	76.04	77.37	78.71	80.04
10.75	43.27	48.55	53.83	59.10	64.38	65.70	67.02	68.34	69.66	70.98	72.30	73.61	74.93	76.25	77.57	78.89
11.00	42.46	47.69	52.92	58.15	63.38	64.69	66.00	67.31	68.61	69.92	71.23	72.54	73.84	75.15	76.46	77.77
11.25	41.66	46.85	52.03	57.22	62.40	63.70	65.00	66.29	67.59	68.89	70.18	71.48	72.78	74.07	75.37	76.66
11.50	40.88	46.02	51.16	56.30	61.44	62.73	64.01	65.30	66.58	67.87	69.15	70.44	71.73	73.01	74.30	75.58
11.75	40.11	45.21	50.31	55.40	60.50	61.78	63.05	64.32	65.60	66.87	68.15	69.42	70.69	71.97	73.24	74.52
12.00	39.36	44.42	49.47	54.52	59.58	60.84	62.10	63.37	64.63	65.89	67.16	68.42	69.68	70.95	72.21	73.47
12.25	38.63	43.64	48.65	53.66	58.67	59.92	61.17	62.43	63.68	64.93	66.18	67.44	68.69	69.94	71.19	72.45
12.50	37.91	42.88	47.84	52.81	57.78	59.02	60.26	61.50	62.75	63.99	65.23	66.47	67.71	68.95	70.20	71.44
12.75	37.20	42.13	47.05	51.98	56.90	58.13	59.37	60.60	61.83	63.06	64.29	65.52	66.75	67.99	69.22	70.45
13.00	36.51	41.39	46.28	51.16	56.05	57.27	58.49	59.71	60.93	62.15	63.37	64.59	65.81	67.03	68.25	69.48
13.25	35.83	40.67	45.52	50.36	55.20	56.41	57.62	58.83	60.05	61.26	62.47	63.68	64.89	66.10	67.31	68.52
13.50	35.17	39.97	44.77	49.57	54.38	55.58	56.78	57.98	59.18	60.38	61.58	62.78	63.98	65.18	66.38	67.58
13.75	34.51	39.28	44.04	48.80	53.56	54.75	55.95	57.14	58.33	59.52	60.71	61.90	63.09	64.28	65.47	66.66
14.00	33.87	38.60	43.32	48.04	52.77	53.95	55.13	56.31	57.49	58.67	59.85	61.03	62.21	63.39	64.58	65.76
14.25	33.25	37.93	42.62	47.30	51.98	53.16	54.33	55.50	56.67	57.84	59.01	60.18	61.35	62.52	63.70	64.87
14.50	32.63	37.28	41.92	46.57	51.22	52.38	53.54	54.70	55.86	57.02	58.19	59.35	60.51	61.67	62.83	63.99
14.75	32.03	36.64	41.25	45.85	50.46	51.61	52.77	53.92	55.07	56.22	57.37	58.53	59.68	60.83	61.98	63.13
15.00	31.44	36.01	40.58	45.15	49.72	50.86	52.01	53.15	54.29	55.44	56.58	57.72	58.86	60.01	61.15	62.29
15.25	30.86	35.39	39.93	44.46	48.99	50.13	51.26	52.40	53.53	54.66	55.80	56.93	58.06	59.20	60.33	61.46
15.50	30.29	34.79	39.29	43.78	48.28	49.41	50.53	51.65	52.78	53.90	55.03	56.15	57.28	58.40	59.52	60.65
15.75	29.73	34.20	38.66	43.12	47.58	48.70	49.81	50.93	52.04	53.16	54.27	55.39	56.50	57.62	58.73	59.85
16.00	29.19	33.61	38.04	42.47	46.89	48.00	49.10	50.21	51.32	52.42	53.53	54.64	55.74	56.85	57.96	59.06
16.25	28.65	33.04	37.43	41.83	46.22	47.31	48.41	49.51	50.61	51.70	52.80	53.90	55.00	56.09	57.19	58.29
16.50	28.13	32.48	36.84	41.20	45.55	46.64	47.73	48.82	49.91	51.00	52.09	53.17	54.26	55.35	56.44	57.53
16.75	27.61	31.94	36.26	40.58	44.90	45.98	47.06	48.14	49.22	50.30	51.38	52.46	53.54	54.62	55.70	56.78
17.00	27.11	31.40	35.69	39.97	44.26	45.33	46.40	47.48	48.55	49.62	50.69	51.76	52.84	53.91	54.98	56.05
17.25	26.61	30.87	35.12	39.38	43.63	44.70	45.76	46.82	47.89	48.95	50.01	51.08	52.14	53.20	54.27	55.33
17.50	26.13	30.35	34.57	38.79	43.01	44.07	45.12	46.18	47.24	48.29	49.35	50.40	51.46	52.51	53.57	54.62
17.75	25.65	29.84	34.03	38.22	42.41	43.45	44.50	45.55	46.60	47.64	48.69	49.74	50.78	51.83	52.88	53.93
18.00	25.19	29.34	33.50	37.66	41.81	42.85	43.89	44.93	45.97	47.01	48.05	49.09	50.12	51.16	52.20	53.24
18.25	24.73	28.85	32.98	37.10	41.23	42.26	43.29	44.32	45.35	46.38	47.41	48.44	49.48	50.51	51.54	52.57
18.50	24.28	28.37	32.47	36.56	40.65	41.68	42.70	43.72	44.75	45.77	46.79	47.81	48.84	49.86	50.88	51.91
18.75	23.84	27.90	31.96	36.03	40.09	41.10	42.12	43.13	44.15	45.16	46.18	47.20	48.21	49.23	50.24	51.26
19.00	23.41	27.44	31.47	35.50	39.53	40.54	41.55	42.56	43.56	44.57	45.58	46.59	47.60	48.60	49.61	50.62
20.00	21.76	25.67	29.59	33.50	37.41	38.39	39.37	40.34	41.32	42.30	43.28	44.26	45.23	46.21	47.19	48.17
25.00	15.19	18.58	21.97	25.37	28.76	29.61	30.46	31.30	32.15	33.00	33.85	34.70	35.54	36.39	37.24	38.09
30.00	10.69	13.66	16.64	19.62	22.59	23.34	24.08	24.83	25.57	26.32	27.06	27.80	28.55	29.29	30.04	30.78

Description: This table shows the yield to maturity of a bond purchased at the price shown in the index.

Example: The yield to maturity of a 6.75 %, 8 year bond at a price of 80.00 is 10.50 %.

	COUPON RATE, %															
PRICE	0.00%	1.00%	2.00%	3.00%	4.00%	4.25%	4.50%	4.75%	5.00%	5.25%	5.50%	5.75%	6.00%	6.25%	6.50%	6.75%
100	0.00	1.00	2.00	3.00	4.00	4.25	4.50	4.75	5.00	5.25	5.50	5.75	6.00	6.25	6.50	6.75
99	.12	1.13	2.13	3.14	4.14	4.39	4.65	4.90	5.15	5.40	5.65	5.90	6.16	6.41	6.66	6.91
98	.25	1.26	2.27	3.28	4.29	4.55	4.80	5.05	5.31	5.56	5.81	6.06	6.32	6.57	6.82	7.08
97	.38	1.39	2.41	3.43	4.44	4.70	4.95	5.21	5.46	5.72	5.97	6.23	6.48	6.74	6.99	7.25
96	.51	1.53	2.55	3.57	4.60	4.85	5.11	5.37	5.62	5.88	6.14	6.39	6.65	6.90	7.16	7.42
95	.64	1.67	2.69	3.72	4.75	5.01	5.27	5.53	5.78	6.04	6.30	6.56	6.82	7.07	7.33	7.59
94	.77	1.80	2.84	3.87	4.91	5.17	5.43	5.69	5.95	6.21	6.47	6.73	6.99	7.25	7.51	7.77
93	.90	1.94	2.99	4.03	5.07	5.33	5.59	5.85	6.11	6.38	6.64	6.90	7.16	7.42	7.68	7.94
92	1.04	2.09	3.13	4.18	5.23	5.49	5.76	6.02	6.28	6.55	6.81	7.07	7.33	7.60	7.86	8.12
91	1.18	2.23	3.28	4.34	5.40	5.66	5.92	6.19	6.45	6.72	6.98	7.25	7.51	7.78	8.04	8.31
90	1.32	2.38	3.44	4.50	5.56	5.83	6.09	6.36	6.63	6.89	7.16	7.43	7.69	7.96	8.23	8.49
89	1.46	2.52	3.59	4.66	5.73	6.00	6.26	6.53	6.80	7.07	7.34	7.61	7.87	8.14	8.41	8.68
88	1.60	2.67	3.75	4.82	5.90	6.17	6.44	6.71	6.98	7.25	7.52	7.79	8.06	8.33	8.60	8.87
87	1.74	2.82	3.90	4.99	6.07	6.34	6.61	6.89	7.16	7.43	7.70	7.97	8.25	8.52	8.79	9.07
86	1.89	2.97	4.06	5.15	6.25	6.52	6.79	7.07	7.34	7.61	7.89	8.16	8.44	8.71	8.99	9.26
85	2.04	3.13	4.22	5.32	6.42	6.70	6.97	7.25	7.53	7.80	8.08	8.35	8.63	8.91	9.18	9.46
84	2.19	3.29	4.39	5.49	6.60	6.88	7.16	7.43	7.71	7.99	8.27	8.55	8.83	9.10	9.38	9.66
83	2.34	3.44	4.56	5.67	6.78	7.06	7.34	7.62	7.90	8.18	8.46	8.74	9.02	9.31	9.59	9.87
82	2.49	3.61	4.72	5.84	6.97	7.25	7.53	7.81	8.10	8.38	8.66	8.94	9.23	9.51	9.79	10.08
81	2.65	3.77	4.89	6.02	7.16	7.44	7.72	8.01	8.29	8.58	8.86	9.15	9.43	9.72	10.00	10.29
80	2.80	3.93	5.07	6.21	7.35	7.63	7.92	8.20	8.49	8.78	9.06	9.35	9.64	9.93	10.21	10.50
79	2.96	4.10	5.24	6.39	7.54	7.83	8.12	8.40	8.69	8.98	9.27	9.56	9.85	10.14	10.43	10.72
78	3.13	4.27	5.42	6.58	7.73	8.03	8.32	8.61	8.90	9.19	9.48	9.77	10.07	10.36	10.65	10.94
77	3.29	4.44	5.60	6.77	7.93	8.23	8.52	8.81	9.11	9.40	9.69	9.99	10.28	10.58	10.87	11.17
76	3.46	4.62	5.79	6.96	8.14	8.43	8.73	9.02	9.32	9.61	9.91	10.21	10.50	10.80	11.10	11.40
75	3.62	4.80	5.97	7.15	8.34	8.64	8.94	9.23	9.53	9.83	10.13	10.43	10.73	11.03	11.33	11.63
74	3.79	4.98	6.16	7.35	8.55	8.85	9.15	9.45	9.75	10.05	10.35	10.66	10.96	11.26	11.56	11.87
73	3.97	5.16	6.35	7.55	8.76	9.06	9.37	9.67	9.97	10.28	10.58	10.89	11.19	11.50	11.80	12.11
72	4.14	5.34	6.55	7.76	8.98	9.28	9.59	9.89	10.20	10.51	10.81	11.12	11.43	11.74	12.05	12.36
71	4.32	5.53	6.75	7.97	9.20	9.50	9.81	10.12	10.43	10.74	11.05	11.36	11.67	11.98	12.29	12.61
70	4.50	5.72	6.95	8.18	9.42	9.73	10.04	10.35	10.66	10.98	11.29	11.60	11.92	12.23	12.54	12.86
69	4.69	5.92	7.15	8.39	9.64	9.96	10.27	10.59	10.90	11.22	11.53	11.85	12.17	12.48	12.80	13.12
68	4.87	6.11	7.36	8.61	9.88	10.19	10.51	10.83	11.14	11.46	11.78	12.10	12.42	12.74	13.06	13.38
67	5.06	6.31	7.57	8.84	10.11	10.43	10.75	11.07	11.39	11.71	12.03	12.36	12.68	13.00	13.33	13.65
66	5.26	6.52	7.79	9.06	10.35	10.67	10.99	11.32	11.64	11.97	12.29	12.62	12.94	13.27	13.60	13.93
65	5.45	6.72	8.00	9.29	10.59	10.92	11.24	11.57	11.90	12.23	12.56	12.88	13.21	13.54	13.88	14.21
64	5.65	6.93	8.23	9.53	10.84	11.17	11.50	11.83	12.16	12.49	12.82	13.16	13.49	13.82	14.16	14.49
63	5.85	7.15	8.45	9.77	11.09	11.42	11.76	12.09	12.43	12.76	13.10	13.43	13.77	14.11	14.45	14.78
62	6.06	7.37	8.68	10.01	11.35	11.69	12.02	12.36	12.70	13.04	13.38	13.72	14.06	14.40	14.74	15.08
61	6.27	7.59	8.92	10.26	11.61	11.95	12.29	12.63	12.98	13.32	13.66	14.00	14.35	14.69	15.04	15.39
60	6.48	7.82	9.16	10.51	11.88	12.22	12.57	12.91	13.26	13.60	13.95	14.30	14.65	15.00	15.35	15.70
59	6.70	8.05	9.40	10.77	12.15	12.50	12.85	13.20	13.55	13.90	14.25	14.60	14.95	15.31	15.66	16.02
58	6.92	8.28	9.65	11.04	12.43	12.78	13.14	13.49	13.84	14.20	14.55	14.91	15.26	15.62	15.98	16.34
57	7.15	8.52	9.90	11.30	12.72	13.07	13.43	13.79	14.14	14.50	14.86	15.22	15.58	15.95	16.31	16.67
56	7.38	8.76	10.16	11.58	13.01	13.37	13.73	14.09	14.45	14.82	15.18	15.54	15.91	16.28	16.64	17.01
55	7.61	9.01	10.43	11.86	13.31	13.67	14.03	14.40	14.77	15.14	15.50	15.87	16.24	16.62	16.99	17.36
54	7.85	9.26	10.70	12.15	13.61	13.98	14.35	14.72	15.09	15.46	15.84	16.21	16.59	16.96	17.34	17.72
53	8.09	9.52	10.97	12.44	13.92	14.29	14.67	15.04	15.42	15.80	16.18	16.56	16.94	17.32	17.70	18.08
52	8.34	9.79	11.25	12.74	14.24	14.62	15.00	15.38	15.76	16.14	16.53	16.91	17.30	17.68	18.07	18.46
51	8.59	10.06	11.54	13.04	14.57	14.95	15.33	15.72	16.11	16.49	16.88	17.27	17.66	18.06	18.45	18.85
50	8.85	10.33	11.84	13.36	14.90	15.29	15.68	16.07	16.46	16.86	17.25	17.65	18.04	18.44	18.84	19.24
49	9.11	10.62	12.14	13.68	15.24	15.64	16.03	16.43	16.83	17.23	17.63	18.03	18.43	18.84	19.24	19.65
48	9.38	10.90	12.45	14.01	15.59	15.99	16.40	16.80	17.20	17.61	18.01	18.42	18.83	19.24	19.65	20.07
47	9.66	11.20	12.76	14.35	15.96	16.36	16.77	17.18	17.59	18.00	18.41	18.83	19.24	19.66	20.08	20.50
46	9.94	11.50	13.09	14.69	16.33	16.74	17.15	17.57	17.98	18.40	18.82	19.24	19.66	20.09	20.51	20.94
45	10.23	11.81	13.42	15.05	16.71	17.12	17.54	17.97	18.39	18.81	19.24	19.67	20.10	20.53	20.96	21.40
44	10.53	12.13	13.76	15.41	17.10	17.52	17.95	18.38	18.81	19.24	19.67	20.11	20.55	20.98	21.43	21.87
43	10.83	12.45	14.11	15.79	17.50	17.93	18.37	18.80	19.24	19.68	20.12	20.56	21.01	21.45	21.90	22.35
42	11.14	12.79	14.47	16.18	17.92	18.36	18.80	19.24	19.69	20.13	20.58	21.03	21.49	21.94	22.40	22.86
41	11.46	13.13	14.84	16.57	18.34	18.79	19.24	19.69	20.14	20.60	21.06	21.52	21.98	22.44	22.91	23.37
40	11.78	13.48	15.22	16.98	18.78	19.24	19.70	20.16	20.62	21.08	21.55	22.02	22.49	22.96	23.44	23.91
39	12.12	13.85	15.61	17.41	19.24	19.70	20.17	20.64	21.11	21.58	22.06	22.54	23.02	23.50	23.98	24.47
38	12.46	14.22	16.01	17.84	19.71	20.18	20.66	21.14	21.62	22.10	22.58	23.07	23.56	24.05	24.55	25.05
37	12.82	14.60	16.43	18.29	20.20	20.68	21.16	21.65	22.14	22.64	23.13	23.63	24.13	24.63	25.14	25.65
36	13.18	15.00	16.86	18.76	20.70	21.19	21.69	22.19	22.69	23.19	23.70	24.21	24.72	25.23	25.75	26.27
35	13.56	15.41	17.30	19.24	21.22	21.73	22.23	22.74	23.25	23.77	24.29	24.81	25.33	25.86	26.39	26.92
30	15.63	17.67	19.77	21.93	24.16	24.73	25.30	25.88	26.46	27.04	27.63	28.22	28.82	29.42	30.03	30.64
25	18.10	20.40	22.79	25.27	27.84	28.50	29.17	29.84	30.52	31.20	31.89	32.59	33.29	34.00	34.71	35.43

Description: This table shows the price to pay for a bond at the yield rate. The yield is to maturity.

Example: The price of a 10.75 %, 8 year bond to yield 8 % to maturity is $ 116.02.

YIELD	7.00%	7.25%	7.50%	7.75%	8.00%	8.25%	COUPON RATE, % 8.50%	8.75%	9.00%	9.25%	9.50%	9.75%	10.00%	10.25%	10.50%	10.75%
0.00	156.00	158.00	160.00	162.00	164.00	166.00	168.00	170.00	172.00	174.00	176.00	178.00	180.00	182.00	184.00	186.00
1.00	146.02	147.94	149.85	151.77	153.69	155.61	157.52	159.44	161.36	163.28	165.19	167.11	169.03	170.95	172.86	174.78
2.00	136.79	138.63	140.47	142.31	144.15	145.99	147.83	149.67	151.51	153.35	155.19	157.03	158.87	160.71	162.55	164.39
3.00	128.26	130.03	131.80	133.56	135.33	137.09	138.86	140.63	142.39	144.16	145.93	147.69	149.46	151.23	152.99	154.76
4.00	120.37	122.06	123.76	125.46	127.16	128.85	130.55	132.25	133.94	135.64	137.34	139.04	140.73	142.43	144.13	145.82
4.25	118.49	120.17	121.85	123.53	125.21	126.89	128.57	130.25	131.93	133.61	135.29	136.97	138.65	140.33	142.01	143.69
4.50	116.64	118.30	119.97	121.63	123.30	124.96	126.63	128.29	129.95	131.62	133.28	134.95	136.61	138.27	139.94	141.60
4.75	114.83	116.48	118.13	119.77	121.42	123.07	124.72	126.37	128.01	129.66	131.31	132.96	134.61	136.25	137.90	139.55
5.00	113.06	114.69	116.32	117.95	119.58	121.21	122.85	124.48	126.11	127.74	129.37	131.01	132.64	134.27	135.90	137.53
5.25	111.31	112.93	114.55	116.16	117.78	119.39	121.01	122.63	124.24	125.86	127.47	129.09	130.71	132.32	133.94	135.55
5.50	109.60	111.20	112.80	114.41	116.01	117.61	119.21	120.81	122.41	124.01	125.61	127.21	128.81	130.41	132.01	133.61
5.75	107.93	109.51	111.10	112.68	114.27	115.85	117.44	119.02	120.61	122.19	123.78	125.36	126.95	128.53	130.12	131.70
6.00	106.28	107.85	109.42	110.99	112.56	114.13	115.70	117.27	118.84	120.41	121.98	123.55	125.12	126.69	128.26	129.83
6.25	104.67	106.22	107.78	109.33	110.89	112.44	114.00	115.55	117.11	118.66	120.22	121.77	123.33	124.88	126.44	127.99
6.50	103.08	104.62	106.16	107.70	109.24	110.78	112.32	113.86	115.41	116.95	118.49	120.03	121.57	123.11	124.65	126.19
6.75	101.53	103.05	104.58	106.10	107.63	109.16	110.68	112.21	113.73	115.26	116.79	118.31	119.84	121.36	122.89	124.42
7.00	100.00	101.51	103.02	104.54	106.05	107.56	109.07	110.58	112.09	113.61	115.12	116.63	118.14	119.65	121.16	122.68
7.25	98.50	100.00	101.50	103.00	104.49	105.99	107.49	108.99	110.48	111.98	113.48	114.98	116.47	117.97	119.47	120.97
7.50	97.03	98.52	100.00	101.48	102.97	104.45	105.94	107.42	108.90	110.39	111.87	113.35	114.84	116.32	117.81	119.29
7.75	95.59	97.06	98.53	100.00	101.47	102.94	104.41	105.88	107.35	108.82	110.29	111.76	113.23	114.70	116.17	117.64
8.00	94.17	95.63	97.09	98.54	100.00	101.46	102.91	104.37	105.83	107.28	108.74	110.20	111.65	113.11	114.57	116.02
8.25	92.78	94.23	95.67	97.11	98.56	100.00	101.44	102.89	104.33	105.77	107.22	108.66	110.10	111.55	112.99	114.43
8.50	91.42	92.85	94.28	95.71	97.14	98.57	100.00	101.43	102.86	104.29	105.72	107.15	108.58	110.01	111.44	112.87
8.75	90.08	91.50	92.91	94.33	95.75	97.17	98.58	100.00	101.42	102.83	104.25	105.67	107.09	108.50	109.92	111.34
9.00	88.77	90.17	91.57	92.98	94.38	95.79	97.19	98.60	100.00	101.40	102.81	104.21	105.62	107.02	108.43	109.83
9.25	87.48	88.87	90.26	91.65	93.04	94.43	95.83	97.22	98.61	100.00	101.39	102.78	104.17	105.57	106.96	108.35
9.50	86.21	87.59	88.97	90.35	91.73	93.10	94.48	95.86	97.24	98.62	100.00	101.38	102.76	104.14	105.52	106.90
9.75	84.96	86.33	87.70	89.07	90.43	91.80	93.17	94.53	95.90	97.27	98.63	100.00	101.37	102.73	104.10	105.47
10.00	83.74	85.10	86.45	87.81	89.16	90.52	91.87	93.23	94.58	95.94	97.29	98.65	100.00	101.35	102.71	104.06
10.25	82.54	83.89	85.23	86.57	87.92	89.26	90.60	91.94	93.29	94.63	95.97	97.31	98.66	100.00	101.34	102.69
10.50	81.37	82.70	84.03	85.36	86.69	88.02	89.35	90.68	92.01	93.35	94.68	96.01	97.34	98.67	100.00	101.33
10.75	80.21	81.53	82.85	84.17	85.49	86.81	88.13	89.45	90.77	92.08	93.40	94.72	96.04	97.36	98.68	100.00
11.00	79.08	80.38	81.69	83.00	84.31	85.61	86.92	88.23	89.54	90.85	92.15	93.46	94.77	96.08	97.38	98.69
11.25	77.96	79.26	80.55	81.85	83.15	84.44	85.74	87.04	88.33	89.63	90.93	92.22	93.52	94.81	96.11	97.41
11.50	76.87	78.15	79.44	80.72	82.01	83.29	84.58	85.86	87.15	88.43	89.72	91.00	92.29	93.57	94.86	96.14
11.75	75.79	77.07	78.34	79.61	80.89	82.16	83.44	84.71	85.98	87.26	88.53	89.81	91.08	92.36	93.63	94.90
12.00	74.74	76.00	77.26	78.52	79.79	81.05	82.31	83.58	84.84	86.10	87.37	88.63	89.89	91.16	92.42	93.68
12.25	73.70	74.95	76.20	77.46	78.71	79.96	81.21	82.47	83.72	84.97	86.22	87.48	88.73	89.98	91.23	92.49
12.50	72.68	73.92	75.16	76.41	77.65	78.89	80.13	81.37	82.61	83.86	85.10	86.34	87.58	88.82	90.07	91.31
12.75	71.68	72.91	74.14	75.37	76.60	77.84	79.07	80.30	81.53	82.76	83.99	85.22	86.46	87.69	88.92	90.15
13.00	70.70	71.92	73.14	74.36	75.58	76.80	78.02	79.24	80.46	81.69	82.91	84.13	85.35	86.57	87.79	89.01
13.25	69.73	70.94	72.15	73.36	74.57	75.79	77.00	78.21	79.42	80.63	81.84	83.05	84.26	85.47	86.68	87.89
13.50	68.78	69.98	71.18	72.39	73.59	74.79	75.99	77.19	78.39	79.59	80.79	81.99	83.19	84.39	85.59	86.79
13.75	67.85	69.04	70.23	71.42	72.61	73.81	75.00	76.19	77.38	78.57	79.76	80.95	82.14	83.33	84.52	85.71
14.00	66.94	68.12	69.30	70.48	71.66	72.84	74.02	75.20	76.38	77.56	78.75	79.93	81.11	82.29	83.47	84.65
14.25	66.04	67.21	68.38	69.55	70.72	71.89	73.06	74.24	75.41	76.58	77.75	78.92	80.09	81.26	82.43	83.60
14.50	65.15	66.32	67.48	68.64	69.80	70.96	72.12	73.29	74.45	75.61	76.77	77.93	79.09	80.25	81.42	82.58
14.75	64.29	65.44	66.59	67.74	68.89	70.05	71.20	72.35	73.50	74.66	75.81	76.96	78.11	79.26	80.42	81.57
15.00	63.43	64.58	65.72	66.86	68.00	69.15	70.29	71.43	72.58	73.72	74.86	76.00	77.15	78.29	79.43	80.57
15.25	62.60	63.73	64.86	66.00	67.13	68.26	69.40	70.53	71.66	72.80	73.93	75.06	76.20	77.33	78.46	79.60
15.50	61.77	62.90	64.02	65.15	66.27	67.39	68.52	69.64	70.77	71.89	73.02	74.14	75.26	76.39	77.51	78.64
15.75	60.96	62.08	63.19	64.31	65.43	66.54	67.66	68.77	69.89	71.00	72.12	73.23	74.35	75.46	76.58	77.69
16.00	60.17	61.28	62.38	63.49	64.59	65.70	66.81	67.91	69.02	70.13	71.23	72.34	73.45	74.55	75.66	76.77
16.25	59.39	60.49	61.58	62.68	63.78	64.88	65.97	67.07	68.17	69.27	70.36	71.46	72.56	73.66	74.75	75.85
16.50	58.62	59.71	60.80	61.89	62.98	64.06	65.15	66.24	67.33	68.42	69.51	70.60	71.69	72.78	73.87	74.95
16.75	57.87	58.95	60.03	61.11	62.19	63.27	64.35	65.43	66.51	67.59	68.67	69.75	70.83	71.91	72.99	74.07
17.00	57.12	58.20	59.27	60.34	61.41	62.48	63.55	64.63	65.70	66.77	67.84	68.91	69.99	71.06	72.13	73.20
17.25	56.39	57.46	58.52	59.58	60.65	61.71	62.78	63.84	64.90	65.97	67.03	68.09	69.16	70.22	71.28	72.35
17.50	55.68	56.73	57.79	58.84	59.90	60.95	62.01	63.06	64.12	65.18	66.23	67.29	68.34	69.40	70.45	71.51
17.75	54.97	56.02	57.07	58.11	59.16	60.21	61.26	62.30	63.35	64.40	65.44	66.49	67.54	68.59	69.63	70.68
18.00	54.28	55.32	56.36	57.40	58.44	59.48	60.52	61.55	62.59	63.63	64.67	65.71	66.75	67.79	68.83	69.87
18.25	53.60	54.63	55.66	56.69	57.72	58.76	59.79	60.82	61.85	62.88	63.91	64.94	65.97	67.00	68.04	69.07
18.50	52.93	53.95	54.98	56.00	57.02	58.05	59.07	60.09	61.12	62.14	63.16	64.19	65.21	66.23	67.26	68.28
18.75	52.27	53.29	54.30	55.32	56.34	57.35	58.37	59.38	60.40	61.41	62.43	63.44	64.46	65.47	66.49	67.51
19.00	51.63	52.63	53.64	54.65	55.66	56.67	57.67	58.68	59.69	60.70	61.70	62.71	63.72	64.73	65.74	66.74
20.00	49.15	50.12	51.10	52.08	53.06	54.04	55.01	55.99	56.97	57.95	58.93	59.90	60.88	61.86	62.84	63.82
25.00	38.94	39.78	40.63	41.48	42.33	43.18	44.03	44.87	45.72	46.57	47.42	48.27	49.11	49.96	50.81	51.66
30.00	31.53	32.27	33.01	33.76	34.50	35.25	35.99	36.74	37.48	38.22	38.97	39.71	40.46	41.20	41.95	42.69

Description: This table shows the yield to maturity of a bond purchased at the price shown in the index.

Example: The yield to maturity of a 10.75 %, 8 year bond at a price of 105.00 is 9.83 %.

PRICE	7.00%	7.25%	7.50%	7.75%	8.00%	8.25%	8.50%	8.75%	9.00%	9.25%	9.50%	9.75%	10.00%	10.25%	10.50%	10.75%
125	3.40	3.62	3.84	4.05	4.27	4.49	4.71	4.93	5.14	5.36	5.58	5.79	6.01	6.23	6.45	6.66
124	3.53	3.74	3.96	4.18	4.40	4.62	4.84	5.06	5.28	5.50	5.71	5.93	6.15	6.37	6.59	6.80
123	3.65	3.87	4.09	4.31	4.53	4.75	4.97	5.19	5.41	5.63	5.85	6.07	6.29	6.51	6.73	6.95
122	3.78	4.00	4.22	4.45	4.67	4.89	5.11	5.33	5.55	5.77	5.99	6.21	6.43	6.65	6.87	7.09
121	3.91	4.13	4.36	4.58	4.80	5.02	5.25	5.47	5.69	5.91	6.13	6.36	6.58	6.80	7.02	7.24
120	4.04	4.27	4.49	4.71	4.94	5.16	5.38	5.61	5.83	6.05	6.28	6.50	6.72	6.94	7.17	7.39
119	4.18	4.40	4.63	4.85	5.08	5.30	5.52	5.75	5.97	6.20	6.42	6.64	6.87	7.09	7.32	7.54
118	4.31	4.54	4.76	4.99	5.21	5.44	5.67	5.89	6.12	6.34	6.57	6.79	7.02	7.24	7.47	7.69
117	4.45	4.67	4.90	5.13	5.35	5.58	5.81	6.03	6.26	6.49	6.71	6.94	7.17	7.39	7.62	7.84
116	4.58	4.81	5.04	5.27	5.50	5.72	5.95	6.18	6.41	6.63	6.86	7.09	7.32	7.54	7.77	8.00
115	4.72	4.95	5.18	5.41	5.64	5.87	6.10	6.33	6.56	6.78	7.01	7.24	7.47	7.70	7.93	8.16
114	4.86	5.09	5.32	5.55	5.78	6.01	6.24	6.47	6.70	6.94	7.17	7.39	7.62	7.85	8.08	8.31
113	5.00	5.23	5.47	5.70	5.93	6.16	6.39	6.62	6.86	7.09	7.32	7.55	7.78	8.01	8.24	8.47
112	5.15	5.38	5.61	5.85	6.08	6.31	6.54	6.78	7.01	7.24	7.47	7.71	7.94	8.17	8.40	8.64
111	5.29	5.52	5.76	5.99	6.23	6.46	6.70	6.93	7.16	7.40	7.63	7.87	8.10	8.33	8.57	8.80
110	5.44	5.67	5.91	6.14	6.38	6.61	6.85	7.09	7.32	7.56	7.79	8.03	8.26	8.50	8.73	8.97
109	5.58	5.82	6.06	6.30	6.53	6.77	7.01	7.24	7.48	7.72	7.95	8.19	8.43	8.66	8.90	9.13
108	5.73	5.97	6.21	6.45	6.69	6.93	7.16	7.40	7.64	7.88	8.12	8.35	8.59	8.83	9.07	9.30
107	5.89	6.12	6.36	6.60	6.84	7.08	7.32	7.56	7.80	8.04	8.28	8.52	8.76	9.00	9.24	9.48
106	6.04	6.28	6.52	6.76	7.00	7.24	7.48	7.73	7.97	8.21	8.45	8.69	8.93	9.17	9.41	9.65
105	6.19	6.44	6.68	6.92	7.16	7.41	7.65	7.89	8.13	8.37	8.62	8.86	9.10	9.34	9.59	9.83
104	6.35	6.59	6.84	7.08	7.33	7.57	7.81	8.06	8.30	8.54	8.79	9.03	9.28	9.52	9.76	10.01
103	6.51	6.75	7.00	7.24	7.49	7.74	7.98	8.23	8.47	8.72	8.96	9.21	9.45	9.70	9.94	10.19
102	6.67	6.92	7.16	7.41	7.66	7.90	8.15	8.40	8.64	8.89	9.14	9.38	9.63	9.88	10.12	10.37
101	6.83	7.08	7.33	7.58	7.82	8.07	8.32	8.57	8.82	9.07	9.31	9.56	9.81	10.06	10.31	10.56
100	7.00	7.25	7.50	7.75	8.00	8.25	8.50	8.75	9.00	9.25	9.50	9.75	10.00	10.25	10.50	10.75
99	7.16	7.41	7.66	7.92	8.17	8.42	8.67	8.92	9.17	9.43	9.68	9.93	10.18	10.43	10.68	10.94
98	7.33	7.58	7.84	8.09	8.34	8.60	8.85	9.10	9.36	9.61	9.86	10.12	10.37	10.62	10.88	11.13
97	7.50	7.76	8.01	8.27	8.52	8.77	9.03	9.28	9.54	9.79	10.05	10.30	10.56	10.81	11.07	11.33
96	7.67	7.93	8.19	8.44	8.70	8.96	9.21	9.47	9.73	9.98	10.24	10.50	10.75	11.01	11.27	11.52
95	7.85	8.11	8.36	8.62	8.88	9.14	9.40	9.66	9.92	10.17	10.43	10.69	10.95	11.21	11.47	11.73
94	8.03	8.29	8.55	8.81	9.07	9.33	9.59	9.85	10.11	10.37	10.63	10.89	11.15	11.41	11.67	11.93
93	8.21	8.47	8.73	8.99	9.25	9.51	9.78	10.04	10.30	10.56	10.83	11.09	11.35	11.61	11.87	12.14
92	8.39	8.65	8.92	9.18	9.44	9.71	9.97	10.23	10.50	10.76	11.03	11.29	11.55	11.82	12.08	12.35
91	8.57	8.84	9.10	9.37	9.63	9.90	10.17	10.43	10.70	10.96	11.23	11.50	11.76	12.03	12.29	12.56
90	8.76	9.03	9.29	9.56	9.83	10.10	10.36	10.63	10.90	11.17	11.44	11.70	11.97	12.24	12.51	12.78
89	8.95	9.22	9.49	9.76	10.03	10.30	10.57	10.84	11.11	11.38	11.65	11.92	12.19	12.46	12.73	13.00
88	9.14	9.41	9.69	9.96	10.23	10.50	10.77	11.04	11.31	11.59	11.86	12.13	12.40	12.68	12.95	13.22
87	9.34	9.61	9.88	10.16	10.43	10.71	10.98	11.25	11.53	11.80	12.07	12.35	12.62	12.90	13.17	13.45
86	9.54	9.81	10.09	10.36	10.64	10.91	11.19	11.47	11.74	12.02	12.29	12.57	12.85	13.12	13.40	13.68
85	9.74	10.02	10.29	10.57	10.85	11.13	11.40	11.68	11.96	12.24	12.52	12.80	13.07	13.35	13.63	13.91
84	9.94	10.22	10.50	10.78	11.06	11.34	11.62	11.90	12.18	12.46	12.74	13.02	13.31	13.59	13.87	14.15
83	10.15	10.43	10.71	10.99	11.28	11.56	11.84	12.12	12.41	12.69	12.97	13.26	13.54	13.82	14.11	14.39
82	10.36	10.64	10.93	11.21	11.50	11.78	12.07	12.35	12.64	12.92	13.21	13.49	13.78	14.06	14.35	14.64
81	10.57	10.86	11.15	11.43	11.72	12.01	12.29	12.58	12.87	13.16	13.44	13.73	14.02	14.31	14.60	14.89
80	10.79	11.08	11.37	11.66	11.95	12.24	12.53	12.82	13.11	13.40	13.69	13.98	14.27	14.56	14.85	15.14
79	11.01	11.30	11.59	11.89	12.18	12.47	12.76	13.05	13.35	13.64	13.93	14.22	14.52	14.81	15.11	15.40
78	11.24	11.53	11.82	12.12	12.41	12.71	13.00	13.30	13.59	13.89	14.18	14.48	14.77	15.07	15.37	15.66
77	11.46	11.76	12.06	12.35	12.65	12.95	13.24	13.54	13.84	14.14	14.44	14.73	15.03	15.33	15.63	15.93
76	11.70	11.99	12.29	12.59	12.89	13.19	13.49	13.79	14.09	14.39	14.69	15.00	15.30	15.60	15.90	16.20
75	11.93	12.23	12.53	12.84	13.14	13.44	13.74	14.05	14.35	14.65	14.96	15.26	15.57	15.87	16.18	16.48
74	12.17	12.48	12.78	13.08	13.39	13.70	14.00	14.31	14.61	14.92	15.23	15.53	15.84	16.15	16.46	16.77
73	12.42	12.72	13.03	13.34	13.65	13.95	14.26	14.57	14.88	15.19	15.50	15.81	16.12	16.43	16.74	17.05
72	12.66	12.97	13.28	13.59	13.91	14.22	14.53	14.84	15.15	15.46	15.78	16.09	16.40	16.72	17.03	17.35
71	12.92	13.23	13.54	13.86	14.17	14.48	14.80	15.11	15.43	15.75	16.06	16.38	16.70	17.01	17.33	17.65
70	13.18	13.49	13.81	14.12	14.44	14.76	15.08	15.39	15.71	16.03	16.35	16.67	16.99	17.31	17.63	17.95
69	13.44	13.76	14.08	14.40	14.72	15.04	15.36	15.68	16.00	16.32	16.65	16.97	17.29	17.62	17.94	18.27
68	13.70	14.03	14.35	14.67	15.00	15.32	15.64	15.97	16.30	16.62	16.95	17.27	17.60	17.93	18.26	18.58
67	13.98	14.30	14.63	14.96	15.28	15.61	15.94	16.27	16.60	16.92	17.25	17.58	17.92	18.25	18.58	18.91
66	14.26	14.58	14.91	15.24	15.57	15.91	16.24	16.57	16.90	17.23	17.57	17.90	18.24	18.57	18.91	19.24
65	14.54	14.87	15.20	15.54	15.87	16.21	16.54	16.88	17.21	17.55	17.89	18.23	18.56	18.90	19.24	19.58
64	14.83	15.16	15.50	15.84	16.18	16.52	16.85	17.19	17.53	17.87	18.22	18.56	18.90	19.24	19.59	19.93
63	15.12	15.46	15.80	16.15	16.49	16.83	17.17	17.52	17.86	18.20	18.55	18.90	19.24	19.59	19.94	20.29
62	15.43	15.77	16.11	16.46	16.80	17.15	17.50	17.85	18.19	18.54	18.89	19.24	19.59	19.94	20.30	20.65
60	16.05	16.40	16.75	17.11	17.46	17.82	18.17	18.53	18.88	19.24	19.60	19.96	20.32	20.68	21.04	21.40
55	17.74	18.11	18.49	18.86	19.24	19.62	20.00	20.38	20.76	21.15	21.53	21.91	22.30	22.68	23.07	23.46
50	19.64	20.05	20.45	20.86	21.26	21.67	22.08	22.49	22.90	23.31	23.73	24.14	24.56	24.98	25.39	25.81
45	21.83	22.27	22.71	23.15	23.59	24.04	24.48	24.93	25.38	25.83	26.28	26.73	27.19	27.64	28.10	28.56

BOND PRICE

Description: This table shows the price to pay for a bond at the yield rate. The yield is to maturity.

Example: The price of a 15.00 %, 8 year bond to yield 8 % to maturity is $ 140.78.

COUPON RATE, %

YIELD	11.00%	11.25%	11.50%	11.75%	12.00%	12.25%	12.50%	12.75%	13.00%	13.25%	13.50%	13.75%	14.00%	14.25%	14.50%	15.00%
0.00	188.00	190.00	192.00	194.00	196.00	198.00	200.00	202.00	204.00	206.00	208.00	210.00	212.00	214.00	216.00	220.00
1.00	176.70	178.62	180.53	182.45	184.37	186.29	188.20	190.12	192.04	193.96	195.87	197.79	199.71	201.63	203.54	207.38
2.00	166.23	168.07	169.91	171.75	173.59	175.43	177.27	179.11	180.95	182.79	184.63	186.47	188.31	190.15	191.99	195.67
3.00	156.53	158.29	160.06	161.82	163.59	165.36	167.12	168.89	170.66	172.42	174.19	175.96	177.72	179.49	181.25	184.79
4.00	147.52	149.22	150.92	152.61	154.31	156.01	157.71	159.40	161.10	162.80	164.49	166.19	167.89	169.59	171.28	174.68
4.25	145.37	147.05	148.74	150.42	152.10	153.78	155.46	157.14	158.82	160.50	162.18	163.86	165.54	167.22	168.90	172.26
4.50	143.27	144.93	146.59	148.26	149.92	151.59	153.25	154.91	156.58	158.24	159.91	161.57	163.23	164.90	166.56	169.89
4.75	141.20	142.84	144.49	146.14	147.79	149.44	151.08	152.73	154.38	156.03	157.68	159.32	160.97	162.62	164.27	167.56
5.00	139.17	140.80	142.43	144.06	145.69	147.32	148.96	150.59	152.22	153.85	155.48	157.12	158.75	160.38	162.01	165.28
5.25	137.17	138.79	140.40	142.02	143.64	145.25	146.87	148.48	150.10	151.72	153.33	154.95	156.56	158.18	159.80	163.03
5.50	135.21	136.81	138.41	140.01	141.61	143.22	144.82	146.42	148.02	149.62	151.22	152.82	154.42	156.02	157.62	160.82
5.75	133.29	134.88	136.46	138.05	139.63	141.22	142.80	144.39	145.97	147.56	149.14	150.73	152.31	153.90	155.48	158.65
6.00	131.40	132.97	134.54	136.11	137.68	139.25	140.82	142.39	143.96	145.53	147.10	148.67	150.24	151.81	153.38	156.52
6.25	129.55	131.10	132.66	134.22	135.77	137.33	138.88	140.44	141.99	143.55	145.10	146.66	148.21	149.77	151.32	154.43
6.50	127.73	129.27	130.81	132.35	133.89	135.43	136.97	138.51	140.05	141.59	143.14	144.68	146.22	147.76	149.30	152.38
6.75	125.94	127.47	129.00	130.52	132.05	133.57	135.10	136.63	138.15	139.68	141.20	142.73	144.26	145.78	147.31	150.36
7.00	124.19	125.70	127.21	128.72	130.24	131.75	133.26	134.77	136.28	137.79	139.31	140.82	142.33	143.84	145.35	148.38
7.25	122.47	123.96	125.46	126.96	128.46	129.95	131.45	132.95	134.45	135.94	137.44	138.94	140.44	141.93	143.43	146.43
7.50	120.77	122.26	123.74	125.22	126.71	128.19	129.68	131.16	132.64	134.13	135.61	137.09	138.58	140.06	141.55	144.51
7.75	119.11	120.58	122.05	123.52	124.99	126.46	127.93	129.40	130.87	132.34	133.81	135.28	136.75	138.22	139.69	142.63
8.00	117.48	118.93	120.39	121.85	123.30	124.76	126.22	127.67	129.13	130.59	132.04	133.50	134.96	136.41	137.87	140.78
8.25	115.88	117.32	118.76	120.20	121.65	123.09	124.53	125.98	127.42	128.86	130.31	131.75	133.19	134.64	136.08	138.97
8.50	114.30	115.73	117.16	118.59	120.02	121.45	122.88	124.31	125.74	127.17	128.60	130.03	131.46	132.89	134.32	137.18
8.75	112.75	114.17	115.59	117.00	118.42	119.84	121.26	122.67	124.09	125.51	126.92	128.34	129.76	131.18	132.59	135.43
9.00	111.23	112.64	114.04	115.45	116.85	118.26	119.66	121.06	122.47	123.87	125.28	126.68	128.09	129.49	130.89	133.70
9.25	109.74	111.13	112.52	113.92	115.31	116.70	118.09	119.48	120.87	122.27	123.66	125.05	126.44	127.83	129.22	132.01
9.50	108.27	109.65	111.03	112.41	113.79	115.17	116.55	117.93	119.31	120.69	122.07	123.45	124.82	126.20	127.58	130.34
9.75	106.83	108.20	109.57	110.93	112.30	113.67	115.04	116.40	117.77	119.14	120.50	121.87	123.24	124.60	125.97	128.70
10.00	105.42	106.77	108.13	109.48	110.84	112.19	113.55	114.90	116.26	117.61	118.97	120.32	121.68	123.03	124.38	127.09
10.25	104.03	105.37	106.71	108.06	109.40	110.74	112.08	113.43	114.77	116.11	117.46	118.80	120.14	121.48	122.83	125.51
10.50	102.66	103.99	105.32	106.65	107.99	109.32	110.65	111.98	113.31	114.64	115.97	117.30	118.63	119.96	121.29	123.96
10.75	101.32	102.64	103.96	105.28	106.60	107.92	109.23	110.55	111.87	113.19	114.51	115.83	117.15	118.47	119.79	122.43
11.00	100.00	101.31	102.62	103.92	105.23	106.54	107.85	109.15	110.46	111.77	113.08	114.39	115.69	117.00	118.31	120.92
11.25	98.70	100.00	101.30	102.59	103.89	105.19	106.48	107.78	109.07	110.37	111.67	112.96	114.26	115.56	116.85	119.45
11.50	97.43	98.71	100.00	101.29	102.57	103.86	105.14	106.43	107.71	109.00	110.28	111.57	112.85	114.14	115.42	117.99
11.75	96.18	97.45	98.73	100.00	101.27	102.55	103.82	105.10	106.37	107.64	108.92	110.19	111.47	112.74	114.02	116.56
12.00	94.95	96.21	97.47	98.74	100.00	101.26	102.53	103.79	105.05	106.32	107.58	108.84	110.11	111.37	112.63	115.16
12.25	93.74	94.99	96.24	97.50	98.75	100.00	101.25	102.50	105.01	106.26	107.51	108.77	110.02	111.27	113.78
12.50	92.55	93.79	95.03	96.27	97.52	98.76	100.00	101.24	102.48	103.73	104.97	106.21	107.45	108.69	109.93	112.42
12.75	91.38	92.61	93.84	95.07	96.31	97.54	98.77	100.00	101.23	102.46	103.69	104.93	106.16	107.39	108.62	111.08
13.00	90.23	91.45	92.67	93.90	95.12	96.34	97.56	98.78	100.00	101.22	102.44	103.66	104.88	106.10	107.33	109.77
13.25	89.10	90.31	91.52	92.74	93.95	95.16	96.37	97.58	98.79	100.00	101.21	102.42	103.63	104.84	106.05	108.48
13.50	87.99	89.19	90.39	91.60	92.80	94.00	95.20	96.40	97.60	98.80	100.00	101.20	102.40	103.60	104.80	107.20
13.75	86.90	88.09	89.28	90.47	91.67	92.86	94.05	95.24	96.43	97.62	98.81	100.00	101.19	102.38	103.57	105.95
14.00	85.83	87.01	88.19	89.37	90.55	91.73	92.92	94.10	95.28	96.46	97.64	98.82	100.00	101.18	102.36	104.72
14.25	84.78	85.95	87.12	88.29	89.46	90.63	91.80	92.97	94.14	95.32	96.49	97.66	98.83	100.00	101.17	103.51
14.50	83.74	84.90	86.06	87.22	88.38	89.55	90.71	91.87	93.03	94.19	95.35	96.52	97.68	98.84	100.00	102.32
14.75	82.72	83.87	85.02	86.18	87.33	88.48	89.63	90.78	91.94	93.09	94.24	95.39	96.54	97.70	98.85	101.15
15.00	81.72	82.86	84.00	85.15	86.29	87.43	88.57	89.72	90.86	92.00	93.14	94.29	95.43	96.57	97.71	100.00
15.25	80.73	81.86	83.00	84.13	85.27	86.40	87.53	88.67	89.80	90.93	92.07	93.20	94.33	95.47	96.60	98.87
15.50	79.76	80.89	82.01	83.14	84.26	85.38	86.51	87.63	88.76	89.88	91.01	92.13	93.25	94.38	95.50	97.75
15.75	78.81	79.92	81.04	82.15	83.27	84.39	85.50	86.62	87.73	88.85	89.96	91.08	92.19	93.31	94.42	96.65
16.00	77.87	78.98	80.08	81.19	82.30	83.40	84.51	85.62	86.72	87.83	88.94	90.04	91.15	92.26	93.36	95.57
16.25	76.95	78.05	79.14	80.24	81.34	82.44	83.54	84.63	85.73	86.83	87.93	89.02	90.12	91.22	92.32	94.51
16.50	76.04	77.13	78.22	79.31	80.40	81.49	82.58	83.67	84.75	85.84	86.93	88.02	89.11	90.20	91.29	93.47
16.75	75.15	76.23	77.31	78.39	79.47	80.55	81.63	82.71	83.79	84.87	85.96	87.04	88.12	89.20	90.28	92.44
17.00	74.27	75.35	76.42	77.49	78.56	79.63	80.71	81.78	82.85	83.92	84.99	86.07	87.14	88.21	89.28	91.42
17.25	73.41	74.47	75.54	76.60	77.67	78.73	79.79	80.86	81.92	82.98	84.05	85.11	86.17	87.24	88.30	90.43
17.50	72.56	73.62	74.67	75.73	76.78	77.84	78.89	79.95	81.00	82.06	83.12	84.17	85.23	86.28	87.34	89.45
17.75	71.73	72.77	73.82	74.87	75.92	76.96	78.01	79.06	80.10	81.15	82.20	83.25	84.29	85.34	86.39	88.48
18.00	70.91	71.95	72.98	74.02	75.06	76.10	77.14	78.18	79.22	80.26	81.30	82.34	83.37	84.41	85.45	87.53
18.25	70.10	71.13	72.16	73.19	74.22	75.25	76.28	77.32	78.35	79.38	80.41	81.44	82.47	83.50	84.53	86.60
18.50	69.30	70.33	71.35	72.37	73.40	74.42	75.44	76.47	77.49	78.51	79.54	80.56	81.58	82.60	83.63	85.67
18.75	68.52	69.54	70.55	71.57	72.58	73.60	74.61	75.63	76.64	77.66	78.68	79.69	80.71	81.72	82.74	84.77
19.00	67.75	68.76	69.77	70.77	71.78	72.79	73.80	74.81	75.81	76.82	77.83	78.84	79.84	80.85	81.86	83.88
20.00	64.79	65.77	66.75	67.73	68.71	69.68	70.66	71.64	72.62	73.59	74.57	75.55	76.53	77.51	78.48	80.44
25.00	52.51	53.35	54.20	55.05	55.90	56.75	57.60	58.44	59.29	60.14	60.99	61.84	62.68	63.53	64.38	66.08
30.00	43.43	44.18	44.92	45.67	46.41	47.16	47.90	48.64	49.39	50.13	50.88	51.62	52.37	53.11	53.85	55.34

Description: This table shows the yield to maturity of a bond purchased at the price shown in the index.

Example: The yield to maturity of a 15.00 %, 8 year bond at a price of 116.00 is 11.84 %.

COUPON RATE, %

PRICE	11.00%	11.25%	11.50%	11.75%	12.00%	12.25%	12.50%	12.75%	13.00%	13.25%	13.50%	13.75%	14.00%	14.25%	14.50%	15.00%
160	2.63	2.81	3.00	3.19	3.37	3.56	3.74	3.93	4.11	4.30	4.48	4.67	4.85	5.04	5.22	5.59
155	3.16	3.35	3.54	3.73	3.92	4.11	4.30	4.49	4.67	4.86	5.05	5.24	5.43	5.61	5.80	6.18
150	3.71	3.91	4.10	4.29	4.49	4.68	4.87	5.06	5.26	5.45	5.64	5.83	6.02	6.22	6.41	6.79
145	4.29	4.49	4.68	4.88	5.08	5.28	5.47	5.67	5.87	6.06	6.26	6.45	6.65	6.85	7.04	7.43
140	4.89	5.09	5.30	5.50	5.70	5.90	6.10	6.30	6.50	6.70	6.90	7.10	7.30	7.50	7.70	8.10
135	5.52	5.73	5.94	6.14	6.35	6.55	6.76	6.96	7.17	7.37	7.58	7.78	7.99	8.19	8.40	8.81
130	6.18	6.40	6.61	6.82	7.03	7.24	7.45	7.66	7.87	8.08	8.29	8.50	8.71	8.92	9.13	9.55
129	6.32	6.53	6.74	6.96	7.17	7.38	7.59	7.80	8.01	8.23	8.44	8.65	8.86	9.07	9.28	9.70
128	6.46	6.67	6.88	7.10	7.31	7.52	7.74	7.95	8.16	8.37	8.58	8.80	9.01	9.22	9.43	9.85
127	6.60	6.81	7.03	7.24	7.45	7.67	7.88	8.09	8.31	8.52	8.73	8.95	9.16	9.37	9.58	10.01
126	6.74	6.95	7.17	7.38	7.60	7.81	8.03	8.24	8.46	8.67	8.88	9.10	9.31	9.53	9.74	10.17
125	6.88	7.10	7.31	7.53	7.74	7.96	8.18	8.39	8.61	8.82	9.04	9.25	9.47	9.68	9.90	10.33
124	7.02	7.24	7.46	7.67	7.89	8.11	8.33	8.54	8.76	8.98	9.19	9.41	9.62	9.84	10.06	10.49
123	7.17	7.39	7.60	7.82	8.04	8.26	8.48	8.69	8.91	9.13	9.35	9.57	9.78	10.00	10.22	10.65
122	7.31	7.53	7.75	7.97	8.19	8.41	8.63	8.85	9.07	9.29	9.51	9.72	9.94	10.16	10.38	10.82
121	7.46	7.68	7.90	8.12	8.34	8.56	8.78	9.01	9.23	9.45	9.67	9.88	10.10	10.32	10.54	10.98
120	7.61	7.83	8.05	8.28	8.50	8.72	8.94	9.16	9.38	9.61	9.83	10.05	10.27	10.49	10.71	11.15
119	7.76	7.99	8.21	8.43	8.65	8.88	9.10	9.32	9.54	9.77	9.99	10.21	10.43	10.66	10.88	11.32
118	7.91	8.14	8.36	8.59	8.81	9.04	9.26	9.48	9.71	9.93	10.15	10.38	10.60	10.82	11.05	11.49
117	8.07	8.29	8.52	8.75	8.97	9.20	9.42	9.65	9.87	10.10	10.32	10.55	10.77	11.00	11.22	11.67
116	8.23	8.45	8.68	8.91	9.13	9.36	9.59	9.81	10.04	10.26	10.49	10.72	10.94	11.17	11.39	11.84
115	8.38	8.61	8.84	9.07	9.30	9.52	9.75	9.98	10.21	10.43	10.66	10.89	11.12	11.34	11.57	12.02
114	8.54	8.77	9.00	9.23	9.46	9.69	9.92	10.15	10.38	10.61	10.83	11.06	11.29	11.52	11.75	12.20
113	8.70	8.94	9.17	9.40	9.63	9.86	10.09	10.32	10.55	10.78	11.01	11.24	11.47	11.70	11.93	12.39
112	8.87	9.10	9.33	9.56	9.80	10.03	10.26	10.49	10.72	10.95	11.19	11.42	11.65	11.88	12.11	12.57
111	9.03	9.27	9.50	9.73	9.97	10.20	10.43	10.67	10.90	11.13	11.36	11.60	11.83	12.06	12.30	12.76
110	9.20	9.44	9.67	9.91	10.14	10.37	10.61	10.84	11.08	11.31	11.55	11.78	12.01	12.25	12.48	12.95
109	9.37	9.61	9.84	10.08	10.32	10.55	10.79	11.02	11.26	11.49	11.73	11.97	12.20	12.44	12.67	13.14
108	9.54	9.78	10.02	10.26	10.49	10.73	10.97	11.20	11.44	11.68	11.92	12.15	12.39	12.63	12.86	13.34
107	9.72	9.96	10.19	10.43	10.67	10.91	11.15	11.39	11.63	11.87	12.10	12.34	12.58	12.82	13.06	13.54
106	9.89	10.13	10.37	10.61	10.85	11.09	11.33	11.57	11.81	12.06	12.30	12.54	12.78	13.02	13.26	13.74
105	10.07	10.31	10.55	10.80	11.04	11.28	11.52	11.76	12.01	12.25	12.49	12.73	12.97	13.21	13.46	13.94
104	10.25	10.49	10.74	10.98	11.22	11.47	11.71	11.95	12.20	12.44	12.68	12.93	13.17	13.41	13.66	14.14
103	10.43	10.68	10.92	11.17	11.41	11.66	11.90	12.15	12.39	12.64	12.88	13.13	13.37	13.62	13.86	14.35
102	10.62	10.86	11.11	11.36	11.60	11.85	12.10	12.34	12.59	12.84	13.08	13.33	13.58	13.82	14.07	14.56
101	10.81	11.05	11.30	11.55	11.80	12.05	12.30	12.54	12.79	13.04	13.29	13.54	13.78	14.03	14.28	14.78
100	11.00	11.25	11.50	11.75	12.00	12.25	12.50	12.75	13.00	13.25	13.50	13.75	14.00	14.25	14.50	15.00
99	11.19	11.44	11.69	11.94	12.19	12.45	12.70	12.95	13.20	13.45	13.70	13.96	14.21	14.46	14.71	15.22
98	11.38	11.64	11.89	12.14	12.40	12.65	12.90	13.16	13.41	13.66	13.92	14.17	14.42	14.68	14.93	15.44
97	11.58	11.84	12.09	12.35	12.60	12.86	13.11	13.37	13.62	13.88	14.13	14.39	14.64	14.90	15.15	15.67
96	11.78	12.04	12.29	12.55	12.81	13.07	13.32	13.58	13.84	14.09	14.35	14.61	14.87	15.12	15.38	15.90
95	11.98	12.24	12.50	12.76	13.02	13.28	13.54	13.80	14.06	14.31	14.57	14.83	15.09	15.35	15.61	16.13
94	12.19	12.45	12.71	12.97	13.23	13.49	13.76	14.02	14.28	14.54	14.80	15.06	15.32	15.58	15.84	16.37
93	12.40	12.66	12.92	13.19	13.45	13.71	13.98	14.24	14.50	14.77	15.03	15.29	15.55	15.82	16.08	16.61
92	12.61	12.88	13.14	13.41	13.67	13.94	14.20	14.47	14.73	15.00	15.26	15.53	15.79	16.06	16.32	16.85
91	12.83	13.09	13.36	13.63	13.89	14.16	14.43	14.69	14.96	15.23	15.50	15.76	16.03	16.30	16.57	17.10
90	13.05	13.31	13.58	13.85	14.12	14.39	14.66	14.93	15.20	15.47	15.74	16.01	16.27	16.54	16.81	17.35
89	13.27	13.54	13.81	14.08	14.35	14.62	14.89	15.16	15.44	15.71	15.98	16.25	16.52	16.79	17.07	17.61
88	13.49	13.77	14.04	14.31	14.59	14.86	15.13	15.41	15.68	15.95	16.23	16.50	16.77	17.05	17.32	17.87
87	13.72	14.00	14.27	14.55	14.82	15.10	15.37	15.65	15.93	16.20	16.48	16.75	17.03	17.31	17.58	18.14
86	13.96	14.23	14.51	14.79	15.06	15.34	15.62	15.90	16.18	16.46	16.73	17.01	17.29	17.57	17.85	18.41
85	14.19	14.47	14.75	15.03	15.31	15.59	15.87	16.15	16.43	16.71	16.99	17.27	17.56	17.84	18.12	18.68
84	14.43	14.71	15.00	15.28	15.56	15.84	16.13	16.41	16.69	16.97	17.26	17.54	17.82	18.11	18.39	18.96
83	14.68	14.96	15.24	15.53	15.81	16.10	16.38	16.67	16.95	17.24	17.53	17.81	18.10	18.38	18.67	19.24
82	14.92	15.21	15.50	15.78	16.07	16.36	16.65	16.94	17.22	17.51	17.80	18.09	18.38	18.67	18.95	19.53
81	15.18	15.47	15.76	16.05	16.33	16.62	16.92	17.21	17.50	17.79	18.08	18.37	18.66	18.95	19.24	19.83
80	15.43	15.73	16.02	16.31	16.60	16.89	17.19	17.48	17.77	18.07	18.36	18.66	18.95	19.24	19.54	20.13
79	15.69	15.99	16.28	16.58	16.87	17.17	17.47	17.76	18.06	18.35	18.65	18.95	19.24	19.54	19.84	20.43
78	15.96	16.26	16.56	16.85	17.15	17.45	17.75	18.05	18.35	18.64	18.94	19.24	19.54	19.84	20.14	20.75
77	16.23	16.53	16.83	17.13	17.43	17.73	18.04	18.34	18.64	18.94	19.24	19.55	19.85	20.15	20.46	21.06
76	16.51	16.81	17.11	17.42	17.72	18.02	18.33	18.63	18.94	19.24	19.55	19.85	20.16	20.47	20.77	21.39
75	16.79	17.09	17.40	17.71	18.01	18.32	18.63	18.94	19.24	19.55	19.86	20.17	20.48	20.79	21.10	21.72
74	17.07	17.38	17.69	18.00	18.31	18.62	18.93	19.24	19.55	19.87	20.18	20.49	20.80	21.11	21.43	22.05
73	17.37	17.68	17.99	18.30	18.62	18.93	19.24	19.56	19.87	20.19	20.50	20.82	21.13	21.45	21.76	22.40
72	17.66	17.98	18.29	18.61	18.93	19.24	19.56	19.88	20.20	20.51	20.83	21.15	21.47	21.79	22.11	22.75
71	17.97	18.28	18.60	18.92	19.24	19.56	19.88	20.20	20.53	20.85	21.17	21.49	21.81	22.14	22.46	23.11
70	18.28	18.60	18.92	19.24	19.57	19.89	20.21	20.54	20.86	21.19	21.51	21.84	22.17	22.49	22.82	23.47
65	19.92	20.26	20.61	20.95	21.29	21.63	21.98	22.32	22.66	23.01	23.35	23.70	24.05	24.39	24.74	25.44

Description: This table shows the price to pay for a bond at the yield rate. The yield is to maturity.

Example: The price of a 6.75 %, 9 year bond to yield 8 % to maturity is $ 92.09.

COUPON RATE, %

YIELD	0.00%	1.00%	2.00%	3.00%	4.00%	4.25%	4.50%	4.75%	5.00%	5.25%	5.50%	5.75%	6.00%	6.25%	6.50%	6.75%
0.00	100.00	109.00	118.00	127.00	136.00	138.25	140.50	142.75	145.00	147.25	149.50	151.75	154.00	156.25	158.50	160.75
1.00	91.41	100.00	108.59	117.17	125.76	127.91	130.05	132.20	134.35	136.49	138.64	140.79	142.93	145.08	147.23	149.37
2.00	83.60	91.80	100.00	108.20	116.40	118.45	120.50	122.55	124.60	126.65	128.70	130.75	132.80	134.85	136.90	138.95
3.00	76.49	84.33	92.16	100.00	107.84	109.80	111.75	113.71	115.67	117.63	119.59	121.55	123.51	125.47	127.43	129.39
4.00	70.02	77.51	85.01	92.50	100.00	101.87	103.75	105.62	107.50	109.37	111.24	113.12	114.99	116.87	118.74	120.61
4.25	68.49	75.90	83.32	90.73	98.15	100.00	101.85	103.71	105.56	107.41	109.27	111.12	112.97	114.83	116.68	118.54
4.50	67.00	74.33	81.67	89.00	96.33	98.17	100.00	101.83	103.67	105.50	107.33	109.17	111.00	112.83	114.67	116.50
4.75	65.54	72.80	80.05	87.30	94.56	96.37	98.19	100.00	101.81	103.63	105.44	107.25	109.07	110.88	112.70	114.51
5.00	64.12	71.29	78.47	85.65	92.82	94.62	96.41	98.21	100.00	101.79	103.59	105.38	107.18	108.97	110.77	112.56
5.25	62.73	69.83	76.93	84.03	91.13	92.90	94.68	96.45	98.23	100.00	101.77	103.55	105.32	107.10	108.87	110.65
5.50	61.37	68.39	75.41	82.44	89.46	91.22	92.98	94.73	96.49	98.24	100.00	101.76	103.51	105.27	107.02	108.78
5.75	60.04	66.99	73.94	80.89	87.84	89.58	91.31	93.05	94.79	96.53	98.26	100.00	101.74	103.47	105.21	106.95
6.00	58.74	65.62	72.49	79.37	86.25	87.97	89.68	91.40	93.12	94.84	96.56	98.28	100.00	101.72	103.44	105.16
6.25	57.47	64.28	71.08	77.88	84.69	86.39	88.09	89.79	91.49	93.20	94.90	96.60	98.30	100.00	101.70	103.40
6.50	56.23	62.97	69.70	76.43	83.17	84.85	86.53	88.22	89.90	91.58	93.27	94.95	96.63	98.32	100.00	101.68
6.75	55.02	61.68	68.35	75.01	81.67	83.34	85.01	86.67	88.34	90.00	91.67	93.34	95.00	96.67	98.33	100.00
7.00	53.84	60.43	67.03	73.62	80.22	81.86	83.51	85.16	86.81	88.46	90.11	91.76	93.41	95.05	96.70	98.35
7.25	52.68	59.21	65.73	72.26	78.79	80.42	82.05	83.68	85.31	86.95	88.58	90.21	91.84	93.47	95.10	96.74
7.50	51.55	58.01	64.47	70.93	77.39	79.00	80.62	82.23	83.85	85.46	87.08	88.69	90.31	91.92	93.54	95.15
7.75	50.44	56.84	63.23	69.63	76.02	77.62	79.22	80.82	82.42	84.01	85.61	87.21	88.81	90.41	92.01	93.61
8.00	49.36	55.69	62.02	68.35	74.68	76.26	77.85	79.43	81.01	82.59	84.18	85.76	87.34	88.92	90.51	92.09
8.25	48.31	54.57	60.84	67.10	73.37	74.94	76.50	78.07	79.64	81.20	82.77	84.34	85.90	87.47	89.03	90.60
8.50	47.27	53.48	59.68	65.88	72.09	73.64	75.19	76.74	78.29	79.84	81.39	82.94	84.49	86.04	87.59	89.14
8.75	46.27	52.41	58.55	64.69	70.83	72.37	73.90	75.44	76.97	78.51	80.04	81.58	83.11	84.65	86.18	87.72
9.00	45.28	51.36	57.44	63.52	69.60	71.12	72.64	74.16	75.68	77.20	78.72	80.24	81.76	83.28	84.80	86.32
9.25	44.32	50.34	56.36	62.38	68.40	69.90	71.41	72.91	74.42	75.92	77.43	78.93	80.44	81.94	83.45	84.95
9.50	43.37	49.33	55.30	61.26	67.22	68.71	70.20	71.69	73.18	74.67	76.16	77.65	79.14	80.63	82.12	83.61
9.75	42.45	48.35	54.26	60.16	66.06	67.54	69.01	70.49	71.96	73.44	74.92	76.39	77.87	79.34	80.82	82.29
10.00	41.55	47.40	53.24	59.09	64.93	66.39	67.85	69.31	70.78	72.24	73.70	75.16	76.62	78.08	79.54	81.00
10.25	40.67	46.46	52.25	58.04	63.82	65.27	66.72	68.17	69.61	71.06	72.51	73.95	75.40	76.85	78.29	79.74
10.50	39.81	45.54	51.28	57.01	62.74	64.17	65.61	67.04	68.47	69.91	71.34	72.77	74.20	75.64	77.07	78.50
10.75	38.97	44.65	50.32	56.00	61.68	63.10	64.52	65.94	67.36	68.78	70.19	71.61	73.03	74.45	75.87	77.29
11.00	38.15	43.77	49.39	55.02	60.64	62.04	63.45	64.86	66.26	67.67	69.07	70.48	71.88	73.29	74.70	76.10
11.25	37.34	42.91	48.48	54.05	59.62	61.01	62.41	63.80	65.19	66.58	67.97	69.37	70.76	72.15	73.54	74.94
11.50	36.56	42.07	47.59	53.11	58.62	60.00	61.38	62.76	64.14	65.52	66.90	68.28	69.66	71.04	72.42	73.79
11.75	35.79	41.25	46.72	52.18	57.65	59.01	60.38	61.75	63.11	64.48	65.84	67.21	68.58	69.94	71.31	72.68
12.00	35.03	40.45	45.86	51.28	56.69	58.04	59.40	60.75	62.10	63.46	64.81	66.16	67.52	68.87	70.22	71.58
12.25	34.30	39.66	45.03	50.39	55.75	57.09	58.43	59.77	61.12	62.46	63.80	65.14	66.48	67.82	69.16	70.50
12.50	33.58	38.89	44.21	49.52	54.83	56.16	57.49	58.82	60.15	61.48	62.80	64.13	65.46	66.79	68.12	69.45
12.75	32.88	38.14	43.41	48.67	53.93	55.25	56.57	57.88	59.20	60.52	61.83	63.15	64.46	65.78	67.10	68.41
13.00	32.19	37.41	42.62	47.84	53.05	54.36	55.66	56.97	58.27	59.57	60.88	62.18	63.49	64.79	66.09	67.40
13.25	31.52	36.69	41.85	47.02	52.19	53.48	54.78	56.07	57.36	58.65	59.94	61.24	62.53	63.82	65.11	66.40
13.50	30.86	35.98	41.10	46.22	51.35	52.63	53.91	55.19	56.47	57.75	59.03	60.31	61.59	62.87	64.15	65.43
13.75	30.22	35.29	40.37	45.44	50.52	51.79	53.05	54.32	55.59	56.86	58.13	59.40	60.67	61.94	63.20	64.47
14.00	29.59	34.62	39.65	44.68	49.70	50.96	52.22	53.48	54.73	55.99	57.25	58.51	59.76	61.02	62.28	63.54
14.25	28.97	33.96	38.94	43.92	48.91	50.16	51.40	52.65	53.89	55.14	56.39	57.63	58.88	60.12	61.37	62.62
14.50	28.37	33.31	38.25	43.19	48.13	49.36	50.60	51.83	53.07	54.30	55.54	56.77	58.01	59.24	60.48	61.71
14.75	27.78	32.68	37.57	42.47	47.37	48.59	49.81	51.04	52.26	53.49	54.71	55.93	57.16	58.38	59.61	60.83
15.00	27.20	32.06	36.91	41.76	46.62	47.83	49.04	50.26	51.47	52.68	53.90	55.11	56.32	57.54	58.75	59.96
15.25	26.64	31.45	36.26	41.07	45.88	47.09	48.29	49.49	50.69	51.90	53.10	54.30	55.50	56.71	57.91	59.11
15.50	26.09	30.86	35.63	40.40	45.16	46.36	47.55	48.74	49.93	51.12	52.32	53.51	54.70	55.89	57.09	58.28
15.75	25.55	30.28	35.01	39.73	44.46	45.64	46.82	48.00	49.19	50.37	51.55	52.73	53.91	55.09	56.28	57.46
16.00	25.02	29.71	34.40	39.08	43.77	44.94	46.11	47.28	48.45	49.63	50.80	51.97	53.14	54.31	55.48	56.66
16.25	24.51	29.15	33.80	38.45	43.09	44.25	45.41	46.58	47.74	48.90	50.06	51.22	52.38	53.54	54.71	55.87
16.50	24.00	28.61	33.22	37.82	42.43	43.58	44.73	45.88	47.03	48.19	49.34	50.49	51.64	52.79	53.94	55.09
16.75	23.51	28.08	32.64	37.21	41.78	42.92	44.06	45.20	46.34	47.49	48.63	49.77	50.91	52.05	53.19	54.34
17.00	23.03	27.56	32.08	36.61	41.14	42.27	43.40	44.54	45.67	46.80	47.93	49.06	50.19	51.33	52.46	53.59
17.25	22.56	27.05	31.54	36.02	40.51	41.64	42.76	43.88	45.00	46.13	47.25	48.37	49.49	50.62	51.74	52.86
17.50	22.09	26.55	31.00	35.45	39.90	41.01	42.13	43.24	44.35	45.47	46.58	47.69	48.80	49.92	51.03	52.14
17.75	21.64	26.06	30.47	34.89	39.30	40.40	41.51	42.61	43.71	44.82	45.92	47.03	48.13	49.23	50.34	51.44
18.00	21.20	25.58	29.95	34.33	38.71	39.81	40.90	41.99	43.09	44.18	45.28	46.37	47.47	48.56	49.66	50.75
18.25	20.77	25.11	29.45	33.79	38.13	39.22	40.30	41.39	42.47	43.56	44.65	45.73	46.82	47.90	48.99	50.07
18.50	20.34	24.65	28.95	33.26	37.57	38.64	39.72	40.80	41.87	42.95	44.02	45.10	46.18	47.25	48.33	49.41
18.75	19.93	24.20	28.47	32.74	37.01	38.08	39.15	40.21	41.28	42.35	43.42	44.48	45.55	46.62	47.69	48.75
19.00	19.52	23.76	27.99	32.23	36.47	37.52	38.58	39.64	40.70	41.76	42.82	43.88	44.94	46.00	47.05	48.11
20.00	17.99	22.09	26.19	30.29	34.39	35.41	36.44	37.46	38.49	39.51	40.54	41.56	42.59	43.62	44.64	45.67
25.00	12.00	15.52	19.04	22.56	26.08	26.96	27.84	28.72	29.60	30.48	31.36	32.24	33.12	34.00	34.88	35.76
30.00	8.08	11.14	14.21	17.27	20.34	21.10	21.87	22.63	23.40	24.17	24.93	25.70	26.46	27.23	28.00	28.76

Description: This table shows the yield to maturity of a bond purchased at the price shown in the index.

Example: The yield to maturity of a 6.75 %, 9 year bond at a price of 80.00 is 10.19 %.

COUPON RATE, %

PRICE	0.00%	1.00%	2.00%	3.00%	4.00%	4.25%	4.50%	4.75%	5.00%	5.25%	5.50%	5.75%	6.00%	6.25%	6.50%	6.75%
100	0.00	1.00	2.00	3.00	4.00	4.25	4.50	4.75	5.00	5.25	5.50	5.75	6.00	6.25	6.50	6.75
99	.11	1.11	2.12	3.12	4.13	4.38	4.63	4.88	5.14	5.39	5.64	5.89	6.14	6.39	6.64	6.90
98	.22	1.23	2.24	3.25	4.26	4.52	4.77	5.02	5.28	5.53	5.78	6.04	6.29	6.54	6.80	7.05
97	.33	1.35	2.37	3.38	4.40	4.66	4.91	5.17	5.42	5.68	5.93	6.18	6.44	6.69	6.95	7.20
96	.45	1.47	2.49	3.52	4.54	4.80	5.05	5.31	5.57	5.82	6.08	6.34	6.59	6.85	7.10	7.36
95	.57	1.59	2.62	3.65	4.68	4.94	5.20	5.46	5.71	5.97	6.23	6.49	6.75	7.00	7.26	7.52
94	.68	1.72	2.75	3.79	4.82	5.08	5.34	5.60	5.86	6.12	6.38	6.64	6.90	7.16	7.42	7.68
93	.80	1.84	2.88	3.93	4.97	5.23	5.49	5.75	6.01	6.28	6.54	6.80	7.06	7.32	7.58	7.84
92	.92	1.97	3.02	4.07	5.12	5.38	5.64	5.90	6.17	6.43	6.69	6.96	7.22	7.48	7.75	8.01
91	1.05	2.10	3.15	4.21	5.26	5.53	5.79	6.06	6.32	6.59	6.85	7.12	7.38	7.65	7.91	8.18
90	1.17	2.23	3.29	4.35	5.41	5.68	5.95	6.21	6.48	6.75	7.01	7.28	7.55	7.81	8.08	8.35
89	1.29	2.36	3.43	4.49	5.57	5.83	6.10	6.37	6.64	6.91	7.18	7.44	7.71	7.98	8.25	8.52
88	1.42	2.49	3.57	4.64	5.72	5.99	6.26	6.53	6.80	7.07	7.34	7.61	7.88	8.15	8.42	8.70
87	1.55	2.63	3.71	4.79	5.88	6.15	6.42	6.69	6.96	7.24	7.51	7.78	8.05	8.33	8.60	8.87
86	1.68	2.76	3.85	4.94	6.03	6.31	6.58	6.86	7.13	7.40	7.68	7.95	8.23	8.50	8.78	9.05
85	1.81	2.90	4.00	5.09	6.19	6.47	6.75	7.02	7.30	7.57	7.85	8.13	8.40	8.68	8.96	9.24
84	1.94	3.04	4.14	5.25	6.36	6.64	6.91	7.19	7.47	7.75	8.03	8.30	8.58	8.86	9.14	9.42
83	2.08	3.18	4.29	5.41	6.52	6.80	7.08	7.36	7.64	7.92	8.20	8.48	8.77	9.05	9.33	9.61
82	2.21	3.33	4.44	5.57	6.69	6.97	7.25	7.54	7.82	8.10	8.38	8.67	8.95	9.23	9.52	9.80
81	2.35	3.47	4.60	5.73	6.86	7.14	7.43	7.71	8.00	8.28	8.57	8.85	9.14	9.42	9.71	10.00
80	2.49	3.62	4.75	5.89	7.03	7.32	7.60	7.89	8.18	8.47	8.75	9.04	9.33	9.62	9.90	10.19
79	2.63	3.77	4.91	6.06	7.21	7.50	7.78	8.07	8.36	8.65	8.94	9.23	9.52	9.81	10.10	10.39
78	2.77	3.92	5.07	6.23	7.39	7.68	7.97	8.26	8.55	8.84	9.13	9.43	9.72	10.01	10.30	10.60
77	2.92	4.07	5.23	6.40	7.57	7.86	8.15	8.45	8.74	9.03	9.33	9.62	9.92	10.21	10.51	10.81
76	3.07	4.23	5.40	6.57	7.75	8.04	8.34	8.64	8.93	9.23	9.53	9.82	10.12	10.42	10.72	11.02
75	3.22	4.39	5.56	6.75	7.94	8.23	8.53	8.83	9.13	9.43	9.73	10.03	10.33	10.63	10.93	11.23
74	3.37	4.55	5.73	6.93	8.12	8.42	8.73	9.03	9.33	9.63	9.93	10.24	10.54	10.84	11.15	11.45
73	3.52	4.71	5.91	7.11	8.32	8.62	8.92	9.23	9.53	9.84	10.14	10.45	10.75	11.06	11.36	11.67
72	3.68	4.88	6.08	7.29	8.51	8.82	9.12	9.43	9.74	10.04	10.35	10.66	10.97	11.28	11.59	11.90
71	3.84	5.04	6.26	7.48	8.71	9.02	9.33	9.64	9.95	10.26	10.57	10.88	11.19	11.50	11.82	12.13
70	4.00	5.21	6.44	7.67	8.91	9.22	9.54	9.85	10.16	10.47	10.79	11.10	11.42	11.73	12.05	12.36
69	4.16	5.39	6.62	7.87	9.12	9.43	9.75	10.06	10.38	10.69	11.01	11.33	11.65	11.96	12.28	12.60
68	4.33	5.56	6.81	8.06	9.33	9.65	9.96	10.28	10.60	10.92	11.24	11.56	11.88	12.20	12.52	12.85
67	4.49	5.74	7.00	8.27	9.54	9.86	10.18	10.50	10.83	11.15	11.47	11.79	12.12	12.44	12.77	13.09
66	4.67	5.92	7.19	8.47	9.76	10.08	10.41	10.73	11.06	11.38	11.71	12.03	12.36	12.69	13.02	13.35
65	4.84	6.11	7.39	8.68	9.98	10.31	10.63	10.96	11.29	11.62	11.95	12.28	12.61	12.94	13.27	13.61
64	5.02	6.30	7.59	8.89	10.20	10.53	10.87	11.20	11.53	11.86	12.19	12.53	12.86	13.20	13.53	13.87
63	5.20	6.49	7.79	9.11	10.43	10.77	11.10	11.44	11.77	12.11	12.45	12.78	13.12	13.46	13.80	14.14
62	5.38	6.68	8.00	9.33	10.67	11.01	11.34	11.68	12.02	12.36	12.70	13.04	13.38	13.73	14.07	14.42
61	5.56	6.88	8.21	9.55	10.91	11.25	11.59	11.93	12.27	12.62	12.96	13.31	13.65	14.00	14.35	14.70
60	5.75	7.08	8.43	9.78	11.15	11.50	11.84	12.19	12.53	12.88	13.23	13.58	13.93	14.28	14.63	14.98
59	5.94	7.29	8.64	10.02	11.40	11.75	12.10	12.45	12.80	13.15	13.50	13.86	14.21	14.57	14.92	15.28
58	6.14	7.50	8.87	10.25	11.65	12.01	12.36	12.71	13.07	13.42	13.78	14.14	14.50	14.86	15.22	15.58
57	6.34	7.71	9.10	10.50	11.91	12.27	12.63	12.99	13.35	13.71	14.07	14.43	14.79	15.16	15.52	15.89
56	6.54	7.93	9.33	10.75	12.18	12.54	12.90	13.26	13.63	13.99	14.36	14.73	15.09	15.46	15.83	16.20
55	6.75	8.15	9.57	11.00	12.45	12.81	13.18	13.55	13.92	14.29	14.66	15.03	15.40	15.78	16.15	16.53
54	6.96	8.38	9.81	11.26	12.73	13.10	13.47	13.84	14.21	14.59	14.96	15.34	15.72	16.10	16.48	16.86
53	7.18	8.61	10.06	11.52	13.01	13.39	13.76	14.14	14.52	14.90	15.28	15.66	16.04	16.43	16.81	17.20
52	7.39	8.84	10.31	11.79	13.30	13.68	14.06	14.44	14.83	15.21	15.60	15.98	16.37	16.76	17.15	17.55
51	7.62	9.08	10.57	12.07	13.60	13.98	14.37	14.76	15.15	15.54	15.93	16.32	16.71	17.11	17.51	17.90
50	7.85	9.33	10.83	12.36	13.90	14.29	14.69	15.08	15.47	15.87	16.27	16.66	17.06	17.47	17.87	18.27
49	8.08	9.58	11.10	12.65	14.22	14.61	15.01	15.41	15.81	16.21	16.61	17.02	17.42	17.83	18.24	18.65
48	8.32	9.84	11.38	12.95	14.54	14.94	15.34	15.75	16.15	16.56	16.97	17.38	17.79	18.21	18.62	19.04
47	8.56	10.10	11.66	13.25	14.87	15.27	15.68	16.09	16.51	16.92	17.34	17.75	18.17	18.59	19.02	19.44
46	8.81	10.37	11.95	13.57	15.20	15.62	16.03	16.45	16.87	17.29	17.72	18.14	18.57	18.99	19.42	19.85
45	9.07	10.65	12.25	13.89	15.55	15.97	16.40	16.82	17.25	17.67	18.10	18.54	18.97	19.40	19.84	20.28
44	9.33	10.93	12.56	14.22	15.91	16.34	16.77	17.20	17.63	18.07	18.51	18.94	19.39	19.83	20.27	20.72
43	9.60	11.22	12.87	14.56	16.28	16.71	17.15	17.59	18.03	18.47	18.92	19.37	19.81	20.27	20.72	21.17
42	9.87	11.52	13.20	14.91	16.66	17.10	17.55	17.99	18.44	18.89	19.35	19.80	20.26	20.72	21.18	21.64
41	10.15	11.82	13.53	15.27	17.05	17.50	17.95	18.41	18.87	19.33	19.79	20.25	20.72	21.19	21.66	22.13
40	10.44	12.14	13.87	15.64	17.45	17.91	18.37	18.84	19.30	19.77	20.24	20.72	21.19	21.67	22.15	22.63
39	10.74	12.46	14.22	16.03	17.87	18.34	18.81	19.28	19.76	20.24	20.72	21.20	21.68	22.17	22.66	23.16
38	11.04	12.79	14.59	16.42	18.30	18.78	19.26	19.74	20.23	20.71	21.21	21.70	22.19	22.69	23.20	23.70
37	11.35	13.14	14.96	16.83	18.75	19.24	19.73	20.22	20.71	21.21	21.71	22.22	22.72	23.23	23.75	24.26
36	11.68	13.49	15.35	17.26	19.21	19.71	20.21	20.71	21.22	21.73	22.24	22.76	23.28	23.80	24.32	24.85
35	12.01	13.85	15.75	17.69	19.69	20.20	20.71	21.23	21.74	22.27	22.79	23.32	23.85	24.38	24.92	25.46
30	13.83	15.87	17.97	20.15	22.40	22.98	23.55	24.14	24.73	25.32	25.92	26.52	27.13	27.74	28.36	28.98
25	16.01	18.30	20.70	23.20	25.81	26.48	27.15	27.84	28.53	29.23	29.93	30.64	31.36	32.09	32.82	33.56

Description: This table shows the price to pay for a bond at the yield rate. The yield is to maturity.

Example: The price of a 10.75 %, 9 year bond to yield 8 % to maturity is $ 117.41.

COUPON RATE, %

YIELD	7.00%	7.25%	7.50%	7.75%	8.00%	8.25%	8.50%	8.75%	9.00%	9.25%	9.50%	9.75%	10.00%	10.25%	10.50%	10.75%
0.00	163.00	165.25	167.50	169.75	172.00	174.25	176.50	178.75	181.00	183.25	185.50	187.75	190.00	192.25	194.50	196.75
1.00	151.52	153.66	155.81	157.96	160.10	162.25	164.40	166.54	168.69	170.84	172.98	175.13	177.28	179.42	181.57	183.72
2.00	141.00	143.05	145.10	147.15	149.19	151.24	153.29	155.34	157.39	159.44	161.49	163.54	165.59	167.64	169.69	171.74
3.00	131.35	133.30	135.26	137.22	139.18	141.14	143.10	145.06	147.02	148.98	150.94	152.89	154.85	156.81	158.77	160.73
4.00	122.49	124.36	126.24	128.11	129.98	131.86	133.73	135.61	137.48	139.35	141.23	143.10	144.98	146.85	148.72	150.60
4.25	120.39	122.24	124.10	125.95	127.80	129.66	131.51	133.36	135.22	137.07	138.92	140.78	142.63	144.49	146.34	148.19
4.50	118.33	120.17	122.00	123.83	125.67	127.50	129.34	131.17	133.00	134.84	136.67	138.50	140.34	142.17	144.00	145.84
4.75	116.32	118.14	119.95	121.76	123.58	125.39	127.20	129.02	130.83	132.65	134.46	136.27	138.09	139.90	141.71	143.53
5.00	114.35	116.15	117.94	119.74	121.53	123.32	125.12	126.91	128.71	130.50	132.30	134.09	135.88	137.68	139.47	141.27
5.25	112.42	114.20	115.97	117.75	119.52	121.30	123.07	124.85	126.62	128.40	130.17	131.95	133.72	135.50	137.27	139.05
5.50	110.54	112.29	114.05	115.80	117.56	119.32	121.07	122.83	124.59	126.34	128.10	129.85	131.61	133.37	135.12	136.88
5.75	108.69	110.42	112.16	113.90	115.64	117.37	119.11	120.85	122.59	124.32	126.06	127.80	129.54	131.27	133.01	134.75
6.00	106.88	108.60	110.32	112.03	113.75	115.47	117.19	118.91	120.63	122.35	124.07	125.79	127.51	129.23	130.95	132.66
6.25	105.10	106.80	108.51	110.21	111.91	113.61	115.31	117.01	118.71	120.41	122.12	123.82	125.52	127.22	128.92	130.62
6.50	103.37	105.05	106.73	108.42	110.10	111.78	113.47	115.15	116.83	118.52	120.20	121.88	123.57	125.25	126.93	128.62
6.75	101.67	103.33	105.00	106.66	108.33	110.00	111.66	113.33	114.99	116.66	118.33	119.99	121.66	123.32	124.99	126.65
7.00	100.00	101.65	103.30	104.95	106.59	108.24	109.89	111.54	113.19	114.84	116.49	118.14	119.78	121.43	123.08	124.73
7.25	98.37	100.00	101.63	103.26	104.90	106.53	108.16	109.79	111.42	113.05	114.69	116.32	117.95	119.58	121.21	122.84
7.50	96.77	98.38	100.00	101.62	103.23	104.85	106.46	108.08	109.69	111.31	112.92	114.54	116.15	117.77	119.38	121.00
7.75	95.20	96.80	98.40	100.00	101.60	103.20	104.80	106.39	107.99	109.59	111.19	112.79	114.39	115.99	117.58	119.18
8.00	93.67	95.25	96.84	98.42	100.00	101.58	103.16	104.75	106.33	107.91	109.49	111.08	112.66	114.24	115.82	117.41
8.25	92.17	93.73	95.30	96.87	98.43	100.00	101.57	103.13	104.70	106.27	107.83	109.40	110.97	112.53	114.10	115.66
8.50	90.70	92.25	93.80	95.35	96.90	98.45	100.00	101.55	103.10	104.65	106.20	107.75	109.30	110.86	112.41	113.96
8.75	89.25	90.79	92.32	93.86	95.39	96.93	98.46	100.00	101.54	103.07	104.61	106.14	107.68	109.21	110.75	112.28
9.00	87.84	89.36	90.88	92.40	93.92	95.44	96.96	98.48	100.00	101.52	103.04	104.56	106.08	107.60	109.12	110.64
9.25	86.46	87.96	89.47	90.97	92.48	93.98	95.49	96.99	98.50	100.00	101.50	103.01	104.51	106.02	107.52	109.03
9.50	85.10	86.59	88.08	89.57	91.06	92.55	94.04	95.53	97.02	98.51	100.00	101.49	102.98	104.47	105.96	107.45
9.75	83.77	85.24	86.72	88.20	89.67	91.15	92.62	94.10	95.57	97.05	98.52	100.00	101.48	102.95	104.43	105.90
10.00	82.47	83.93	85.39	86.85	88.31	89.77	91.23	92.69	94.16	95.62	97.08	98.54	100.00	101.46	102.92	104.38
10.25	81.19	82.64	84.08	85.53	86.98	88.42	89.87	91.32	92.76	94.21	95.66	97.11	98.55	100.00	101.45	102.89
10.50	79.94	81.37	82.80	84.24	85.67	87.10	88.54	89.97	91.40	92.83	94.27	95.70	97.13	98.57	100.00	101.43
10.75	78.71	80.13	81.55	82.97	84.39	85.81	87.23	88.65	90.06	91.48	92.90	94.32	95.74	97.16	98.58	100.00
11.00	77.51	78.91	80.32	81.73	83.13	84.54	85.94	87.35	88.75	90.16	91.57	92.97	94.38	95.78	97.19	98.59
11.25	76.33	77.72	79.11	80.51	81.90	83.29	84.68	86.08	87.47	88.86	90.25	91.65	93.04	94.43	95.82	97.22
11.50	75.17	76.55	77.93	79.31	80.69	82.07	83.45	84.83	86.21	87.59	88.97	90.35	91.72	93.10	94.48	95.86
11.75	74.04	75.41	76.77	78.14	79.51	80.87	82.24	83.61	84.97	86.34	87.70	89.07	90.44	91.80	93.17	94.54
12.00	72.93	74.28	75.64	76.99	78.34	79.70	81.05	82.41	83.76	85.11	86.47	87.82	89.17	90.53	91.88	93.23
12.25	71.84	73.18	74.52	75.86	77.21	78.55	79.89	81.23	82.57	83.91	85.25	86.59	87.93	89.27	90.61	91.95
12.50	70.78	72.10	73.43	74.76	76.09	77.42	78.75	80.07	81.40	82.73	84.06	85.39	86.72	88.04	89.37	90.70
12.75	69.73	71.04	72.36	73.68	74.99	76.31	77.63	78.94	80.26	81.57	82.89	84.21	85.52	86.84	88.15	89.47
13.00	68.70	70.01	71.31	72.61	73.92	75.22	76.53	77.83	79.14	80.44	81.74	83.05	84.35	85.66	86.96	88.26
13.25	67.70	68.99	70.28	71.57	72.87	74.16	75.45	76.74	78.03	79.33	80.62	81.91	83.20	84.49	85.79	87.08
13.50	66.71	67.99	69.27	70.55	71.83	73.11	74.39	75.67	76.95	78.23	79.51	80.79	82.07	83.35	84.64	85.92
13.75	65.74	67.01	68.28	69.55	70.82	72.09	73.36	74.62	75.89	77.16	78.43	79.70	80.97	82.24	83.51	84.77
14.00	64.79	66.05	67.31	68.57	69.82	71.08	72.34	73.59	74.85	76.11	77.37	78.62	79.88	81.14	82.40	83.65
14.25	63.86	65.11	66.35	67.60	68.85	70.09	71.34	72.59	73.83	75.08	76.32	77.57	78.82	80.06	81.31	82.55
14.50	62.95	64.18	65.42	66.65	67.89	69.12	70.36	71.59	72.83	74.06	75.30	76.53	77.77	79.00	80.24	81.47
14.75	62.05	63.28	64.50	65.73	66.95	68.17	69.40	70.62	71.85	73.07	74.29	75.52	76.74	77.97	79.19	80.42
15.00	61.18	62.39	63.60	64.82	66.03	67.24	68.46	69.67	70.88	72.10	73.31	74.52	75.73	76.95	78.16	79.37
15.25	60.31	61.52	62.72	63.92	65.12	66.33	67.53	68.73	69.94	71.14	72.34	73.54	74.75	75.95	77.15	78.35
15.50	59.47	60.66	61.85	63.05	64.24	65.43	66.62	67.81	69.01	70.20	71.39	72.58	73.77	74.97	76.16	77.35
15.75	58.64	59.82	61.00	62.19	63.37	64.55	65.73	66.91	68.09	69.28	70.46	71.64	72.82	74.00	75.18	76.37
16.00	57.83	59.00	60.17	61.34	62.51	63.68	64.86	66.03	67.20	68.37	69.54	70.71	71.88	73.06	74.23	75.40
16.25	57.03	58.19	59.35	60.51	61.67	62.84	64.00	65.16	66.32	67.48	68.64	69.80	70.97	72.13	73.29	74.45
16.50	56.25	57.40	58.55	59.70	60.85	62.00	63.15	64.31	65.46	66.61	67.76	68.91	70.06	71.21	72.37	73.52
16.75	55.48	56.62	57.76	58.90	60.04	61.18	62.33	63.47	64.61	65.75	66.89	68.03	69.18	70.32	71.46	72.60
17.00	54.72	55.85	56.99	58.12	59.25	60.38	61.51	62.65	63.78	64.91	66.04	67.17	68.31	69.44	70.57	71.70
17.25	53.98	55.10	56.23	57.35	58.47	59.59	60.72	61.84	62.96	64.08	65.21	66.33	67.45	68.57	69.70	70.82
17.50	53.26	54.37	55.48	56.60	57.71	58.82	59.93	61.05	62.16	63.27	64.39	65.50	66.61	67.72	68.84	69.95
17.75	52.54	53.65	54.75	55.85	56.96	58.06	59.17	60.27	61.37	62.48	63.58	64.68	65.79	66.89	67.99	69.10
18.00	51.84	52.94	54.03	55.13	56.22	57.32	58.41	59.51	60.60	61.69	62.79	63.88	64.98	66.07	67.17	68.26
18.25	51.16	52.24	53.33	54.41	55.50	56.58	57.67	58.76	59.84	60.93	62.01	63.10	64.18	65.27	66.35	67.44
18.50	50.48	51.56	52.64	53.71	54.79	55.87	56.94	58.02	59.10	60.17	61.25	62.32	63.40	64.48	65.55	66.63
18.75	49.82	50.89	51.96	53.02	54.09	55.16	56.23	57.30	58.36	59.43	60.50	61.57	62.63	63.70	64.77	65.84
19.00	49.17	50.23	51.29	52.35	53.41	54.47	55.53	56.58	57.64	58.70	59.76	60.82	61.88	62.94	64.00	65.06
20.00	46.69	47.72	48.74	49.77	50.79	51.82	52.84	53.87	54.89	55.92	56.94	57.97	58.99	60.02	61.04	62.07
25.00	36.64	37.52	38.40	39.28	40.16	41.04	41.92	42.80	43.68	44.56	45.44	46.32	47.20	48.08	48.96	49.84
30.00	29.53	30.29	31.06	31.83	32.59	33.36	34.12	34.89	35.66	36.42	37.19	37.95	38.72	39.49	40.25	41.02

Description: This table shows the yield to maturity of a bond purchased at the price shown in the index.

Example: The yield to maturity of a 10.75 %, 9 year bond at a price of 105.00 is 9.89 %.

COUPON RATE, %

PRICE	7.00%	7.25%	7.50%	7.75%	8.00%	8.25%	8.50%	8.75%	9.00%	9.25%	9.50%	9.75%	10.00%	10.25%	10.50%	10.75%
125	3.70	3.92	4.14	4.36	4.57	4.79	5.01	5.23	5.44	5.66	5.88	6.09	6.31	6.53	6.74	6.96
124	3.82	4.04	4.26	4.48	4.69	4.91	5.13	5.35	5.57	5.79	6.00	6.22	6.44	6.66	6.87	7.09
123	3.93	4.16	4.38	4.60	4.82	5.03	5.25	5.47	5.69	5.91	6.13	6.35	6.57	6.79	7.01	7.22
122	4.05	4.27	4.50	4.72	4.94	5.16	5.38	5.60	5.82	6.04	6.26	6.48	6.70	6.92	7.14	7.36
121	4.17	4.39	4.62	4.84	5.06	5.28	5.50	5.73	5.95	6.17	6.39	6.61	6.83	7.05	7.27	7.49
120	4.29	4.52	4.74	4.96	5.19	5.41	5.63	5.85	6.08	6.30	6.52	6.74	6.97	7.19	7.41	7.63
119	4.41	4.64	4.86	5.09	5.31	5.54	5.76	5.98	6.21	6.43	6.65	6.88	7.10	7.32	7.55	7.77
118	4.54	4.76	4.99	5.21	5.44	5.66	5.89	6.11	6.34	6.56	6.79	7.01	7.24	7.46	7.69	7.91
117	4.66	4.89	5.11	5.34	5.57	5.79	6.02	6.25	6.47	6.70	6.92	7.15	7.38	7.60	7.83	8.05
116	4.79	5.01	5.24	5.47	5.70	5.93	6.15	6.38	6.61	6.83	7.06	7.29	7.52	7.74	7.97	8.20
115	4.91	5.14	5.37	5.60	5.83	6.06	6.29	6.52	6.74	6.97	7.20	7.43	7.66	7.89	8.11	8.34
114	5.04	5.27	5.50	5.73	5.96	6.19	6.42	6.65	6.88	7.11	7.34	7.57	7.80	8.03	8.26	8.49
113	5.17	5.40	5.63	5.86	6.10	6.33	6.56	6.79	7.02	7.25	7.48	7.71	7.95	8.18	8.41	8.64
112	5.30	5.53	5.77	6.00	6.23	6.47	6.70	6.93	7.16	7.40	7.63	7.86	8.09	8.32	8.56	8.79
111	5.43	5.67	5.90	6.14	6.37	6.60	6.84	7.07	7.31	7.54	7.77	8.01	8.24	8.47	8.71	8.94
110	5.57	5.80	6.04	6.27	6.51	6.74	6.98	7.21	7.45	7.68	7.92	8.15	8.39	8.62	8.86	9.09
109	5.70	5.94	6.18	6.41	6.65	6.89	7.12	7.36	7.60	7.83	8.07	8.31	8.54	8.78	9.01	9.25
108	5.84	6.08	6.32	6.55	6.79	7.03	7.27	7.51	7.74	7.98	8.22	8.46	8.69	8.93	9.17	9.41
107	5.98	6.22	6.46	6.70	6.94	7.18	7.42	7.65	7.89	8.13	8.37	8.61	8.85	9.09	9.33	9.57
106	6.12	6.36	6.60	6.84	7.08	7.32	7.56	7.80	8.05	8.29	8.53	8.77	9.01	9.25	9.49	9.73
105	6.26	6.50	6.74	6.99	7.23	7.47	7.71	7.96	8.20	8.44	8.68	8.92	9.17	9.41	9.65	9.89
104	6.40	6.65	6.89	7.13	7.38	7.62	7.87	8.11	8.35	8.60	8.84	9.08	9.33	9.57	9.82	10.06
103	6.55	6.79	7.04	7.28	7.53	7.78	8.02	8.27	8.51	8.76	9.00	9.25	9.49	9.74	9.98	10.23
102	6.70	6.94	7.19	7.44	7.68	7.93	8.18	8.42	8.67	8.92	9.16	9.41	9.66	9.90	10.15	10.40
101	6.84	7.09	7.34	7.59	7.84	8.09	8.33	8.58	8.83	9.08	9.33	9.58	9.83	10.07	10.32	10.57
100	7.00	7.25	7.50	7.75	8.00	8.25	8.50	8.75	9.00	9.25	9.50	9.75	10.00	10.25	10.50	10.75
99	7.15	7.40	7.65	7.90	8.15	8.41	8.66	8.91	9.16	9.41	9.66	9.92	10.17	10.42	10.67	10.92
98	7.30	7.56	7.81	8.06	8.32	8.57	8.82	9.08	9.33	9.58	9.84	10.09	10.34	10.60	10.85	11.10
97	7.46	7.71	7.97	8.22	8.48	8.73	8.99	9.24	9.50	9.75	10.01	10.26	10.52	10.77	11.03	11.28
96	7.62	7.87	8.13	8.39	8.64	8.90	9.16	9.41	9.67	9.93	10.18	10.44	10.70	10.96	11.21	11.47
95	7.78	8.04	8.29	8.55	8.81	9.07	9.33	9.59	9.85	10.10	10.36	10.62	10.88	11.14	11.40	11.66
94	7.94	8.20	8.46	8.72	8.98	9.24	9.50	9.76	10.02	10.28	10.54	10.80	11.06	11.33	11.59	11.85
93	8.11	8.37	8.63	8.89	9.15	9.42	9.68	9.94	10.20	10.46	10.73	10.99	11.25	11.51	11.78	12.04
92	8.27	8.54	8.80	9.06	9.33	9.59	9.86	10.12	10.38	10.65	10.91	11.18	11.44	11.71	11.97	12.24
91	8.44	8.71	8.97	9.24	9.51	9.77	10.04	10.30	10.57	10.84	11.10	11.37	11.64	11.90	12.17	12.44
90	8.61	8.88	9.15	9.42	9.69	9.95	10.22	10.49	10.76	11.03	11.29	11.56	11.83	12.10	12.37	12.64
89	8.79	9.06	9.33	9.60	9.87	10.14	10.41	10.68	10.95	11.22	11.49	11.76	12.03	12.30	12.57	12.84
88	8.97	9.24	9.51	9.78	10.05	10.32	10.60	10.87	11.14	11.41	11.69	11.96	12.23	12.50	12.78	13.05
87	9.15	9.42	9.69	9.97	10.24	10.51	10.79	11.06	11.34	11.61	11.89	12.16	12.44	12.71	12.99	13.26
86	9.33	9.60	9.88	10.16	10.43	10.71	10.98	11.26	11.54	11.81	12.09	12.37	12.64	12.92	13.20	13.48
85	9.51	9.79	10.07	10.35	10.62	10.90	11.18	11.46	11.74	12.02	12.30	12.58	12.86	13.14	13.42	13.70
84	9.70	9.98	10.26	10.54	10.82	11.10	11.38	11.66	11.94	12.23	12.51	12.79	13.07	13.35	13.64	13.92
83	9.89	10.17	10.46	10.74	11.02	11.30	11.59	11.87	12.15	12.44	12.72	13.01	13.29	13.57	13.86	14.14
82	10.09	10.37	10.65	10.94	11.22	11.51	11.79	12.08	12.37	12.65	12.94	13.23	13.51	13.80	14.09	14.37
81	10.28	10.57	10.86	11.14	11.43	11.72	12.01	12.29	12.58	12.87	13.16	13.45	13.74	14.03	14.32	14.61
80	10.48	10.77	11.06	11.35	11.64	11.93	12.22	12.51	12.80	13.09	13.38	13.68	13.97	14.26	14.55	14.84
79	10.69	10.98	11.27	11.56	11.85	12.15	12.44	12.73	13.03	13.32	13.61	13.91	14.20	14.50	14.79	15.09
78	10.89	11.19	11.48	11.78	12.07	12.37	12.66	12.96	13.25	13.55	13.85	14.14	14.44	14.74	15.03	15.33
77	11.10	11.40	11.70	11.99	12.29	12.59	12.89	13.19	13.48	13.78	14.08	14.38	14.68	14.98	15.28	15.58
76	11.32	11.62	11.91	12.21	12.52	12.82	13.12	13.42	13.72	14.02	14.32	14.63	14.93	15.23	15.54	15.84
75	11.53	11.84	12.14	12.44	12.74	13.05	13.35	13.65	13.96	14.26	14.57	14.87	15.18	15.49	15.79	16.10
74	11.75	12.06	12.36	12.67	12.98	13.28	13.59	13.90	14.20	14.51	14.82	15.13	15.44	15.75	16.06	16.36
73	11.98	12.29	12.60	12.90	13.21	13.52	13.83	14.14	14.45	14.76	15.07	15.39	15.70	16.01	16.32	16.64
72	12.21	12.52	12.83	13.14	13.45	13.77	14.08	14.39	14.71	15.02	15.33	15.65	15.96	16.28	16.60	16.91
71	12.44	12.76	13.07	13.38	13.70	14.02	14.33	14.65	14.96	15.28	15.60	15.92	16.24	16.55	16.87	17.19
70	12.68	13.00	13.31	13.63	13.95	14.27	14.59	14.91	15.23	15.55	15.87	16.19	16.51	16.83	17.16	17.48
69	12.92	13.24	13.56	13.88	14.21	14.53	14.85	15.17	15.50	15.82	16.15	16.47	16.80	17.12	17.45	17.77
68	13.17	13.49	13.82	14.14	14.47	14.79	15.12	15.44	15.77	16.10	16.43	16.75	17.08	17.41	17.74	18.07
67	13.42	13.75	14.08	14.40	14.73	15.06	15.39	15.72	16.05	16.38	16.71	17.05	17.38	17.71	18.05	18.38
66	13.68	14.01	14.34	14.67	15.00	15.34	15.67	16.00	16.34	16.67	17.01	17.34	17.68	18.02	18.35	18.69
65	13.94	14.27	14.61	14.94	15.28	15.62	15.95	16.29	16.63	16.97	17.31	17.65	17.99	18.33	18.67	19.01
64	14.21	14.55	14.88	15.22	15.56	15.90	16.24	16.59	16.93	17.27	17.61	17.93	18.28	18.63	18.99	19.68
63	14.48	14.82	15.17	15.51	15.85	16.20	16.54	16.89	17.23	17.58	17.93	18.28	18.63	18.97	19.32	19.68
62	14.76	15.11	15.45	15.80	16.15	16.50	16.84	17.19	17.55	17.90	18.25	18.60	18.95	19.31	19.66	20.02
60	15.34	15.69	16.05	16.40	16.76	17.12	17.47	17.83	18.19	18.55	18.91	19.28	19.64	20.00	20.37	20.73
55	16.90	17.28	17.66	18.04	18.42	18.80	19.19	19.57	19.95	20.34	20.73	21.12	21.50	21.89	22.29	22.68
50	18.68	19.08	19.49	19.90	20.31	20.72	21.14	21.55	21.97	22.39	22.81	23.23	23.65	24.07	24.49	24.92
45	20.72	21.16	21.61	22.05	22.50	22.95	23.40	23.86	24.31	24.77	25.23	25.69	26.15	26.61	27.08	27.54

BOND PRICE

Description: This table shows the price to pay for a bond at the yield rate. The yield is to maturity.

Example: The price of a 15.00 %, 9 year bond to yield 8 % to maturity is $ 144.31.

COUPON RATE, %

YIELD	11.00%	11.25%	11.50%	11.75%	12.00%	12.25%	12.50%	12.75%	13.00%	13.25%	13.50%	13.75%	14.00%	14.25%	14.50%	15.00%
0.00	199.00	201.25	203.50	205.75	208.00	210.25	212.50	214.75	217.00	219.25	221.50	223.75	226.00	228.25	230.50	235.00
1.00	185.86	188.01	190.16	192.30	194.45	196.60	198.74	200.89	203.04	205.18	207.33	209.48	211.62	213.77	215.92	220.21
2.00	173.79	175.84	177.89	179.94	181.99	184.04	186.09	188.14	190.19	192.24	194.29	196.34	198.39	200.44	202.49	206.59
3.00	162.69	164.65	166.61	168.57	170.53	172.49	174.44	176.40	178.36	180.32	182.28	184.24	186.20	188.16	190.12	194.04
4.00	152.47	154.35	156.22	158.09	159.97	161.84	163.72	165.59	167.46	169.34	171.21	173.09	174.96	176.83	178.71	182.46
4.25	150.05	151.90	153.75	155.61	157.46	159.31	161.17	163.02	164.87	166.73	168.58	170.44	172.29	174.14	176.00	179.70
4.50	147.67	149.50	151.34	153.17	155.00	156.84	158.67	160.50	162.34	164.17	166.00	167.84	169.67	171.50	173.34	177.01
4.75	145.34	147.16	148.97	150.78	152.60	154.41	156.22	158.04	159.85	161.66	163.48	165.29	167.11	168.92	170.73	174.36
5.00	143.06	144.85	146.65	148.44	150.24	152.03	153.83	155.62	157.41	159.21	161.00	162.80	164.59	166.38	168.18	171.77
5.25	140.82	142.60	144.37	146.15	147.92	149.70	151.47	153.25	155.02	156.80	158.57	160.35	162.12	163.90	165.67	169.22
5.50	138.63	140.39	142.15	143.90	145.66	147.41	149.17	150.93	152.68	154.44	156.20	157.95	159.71	161.46	163.22	166.73
5.75	136.49	138.22	139.96	141.70	143.44	145.17	146.91	148.65	150.39	152.12	153.86	155.60	157.34	159.07	160.81	164.29
6.00	134.38	136.10	137.82	139.54	141.26	142.98	144.70	146.42	148.14	149.86	151.58	153.29	155.01	156.73	158.45	161.89
6.25	132.32	134.02	135.72	137.43	139.13	140.83	142.53	144.23	145.93	147.63	149.33	151.03	152.74	154.44	156.14	159.54
6.50	130.30	131.98	133.67	135.35	137.03	138.72	140.40	142.09	143.77	145.45	147.14	148.82	150.50	152.19	153.87	157.24
6.75	128.32	129.99	131.65	133.32	134.98	136.65	138.32	139.98	141.65	143.31	144.98	146.65	148.31	149.98	151.64	154.98
7.00	126.38	128.03	129.68	131.33	132.97	134.62	136.27	137.92	139.57	141.22	142.87	144.52	146.16	147.81	149.46	152.76
7.25	124.48	126.11	127.74	129.37	131.00	132.64	134.27	135.90	137.53	139.16	140.79	142.43	144.06	145.69	147.32	150.58
7.50	122.61	124.23	125.84	127.46	129.07	130.69	132.30	133.92	135.53	137.15	138.76	140.38	141.99	143.61	145.22	148.45
7.75	120.78	122.38	123.98	125.58	127.18	128.78	130.37	131.97	133.57	135.17	136.77	138.37	139.97	141.56	143.16	146.36
8.00	118.99	120.57	122.15	123.74	125.32	126.90	128.48	130.07	131.65	133.23	134.81	136.40	137.98	139.56	141.14	144.31
8.25	117.23	118.80	120.36	121.93	123.50	125.06	126.63	128.20	129.76	131.33	132.90	134.46	136.03	137.59	139.16	142.29
8.50	115.51	117.06	118.61	120.16	121.71	123.26	124.81	126.36	127.91	129.46	131.01	132.57	134.12	135.67	137.22	140.32
8.75	113.82	115.35	116.89	118.42	119.96	121.49	123.03	124.56	126.10	127.63	129.17	130.71	132.24	133.78	135.31	138.38
9.00	112.16	113.68	115.20	116.72	118.24	119.76	121.28	122.80	124.32	125.84	127.36	128.88	130.40	131.92	133.44	136.48
9.25	110.53	112.04	113.54	115.05	116.55	118.06	119.56	121.07	122.57	124.08	125.58	127.09	128.59	130.10	131.60	134.61
9.50	108.94	110.43	111.92	113.41	114.90	116.39	117.88	119.37	120.86	122.35	123.84	125.33	126.82	128.31	129.80	132.78
9.75	107.38	108.85	110.33	111.80	113.28	114.76	116.23	117.71	119.18	120.66	122.13	123.61	125.08	126.56	128.04	130.99
10.00	105.84	107.31	108.77	110.23	111.69	113.15	114.61	116.07	117.53	119.00	120.46	121.92	123.38	124.84	126.30	129.22
10.25	104.34	105.79	107.24	108.68	110.13	111.58	113.02	114.47	115.92	117.36	118.81	120.26	121.71	123.15	124.60	127.49
10.50	102.87	104.30	105.73	107.17	108.60	110.03	111.46	112.90	114.33	115.76	117.20	118.63	120.06	121.50	122.93	125.80
10.75	101.42	102.84	104.26	105.68	107.10	108.52	109.94	111.35	112.77	114.19	115.61	117.03	118.45	119.87	121.29	124.13
11.00	100.00	101.41	102.81	104.22	105.62	107.03	108.43	109.84	111.25	112.65	114.06	115.46	116.87	118.27	119.68	122.49
11.25	98.61	100.00	101.39	102.78	104.18	105.57	106.96	108.35	109.75	111.14	112.53	113.92	115.32	116.71	118.10	120.89
11.50	97.24	98.62	100.00	101.38	102.76	104.14	105.52	106.90	108.28	109.65	111.03	112.41	113.79	115.17	116.55	119.31
11.75	95.90	97.27	98.63	100.00	101.37	102.73	104.10	105.46	106.83	108.20	109.56	110.93	112.30	113.66	115.03	117.76
12.00	94.59	95.94	97.29	98.65	100.00	101.35	102.71	104.06	105.41	106.77	108.12	109.47	110.83	112.18	113.53	116.24
12.25	93.30	94.64	95.98	97.32	98.66	100.00	101.34	102.68	104.02	105.36	106.70	108.05	109.39	110.73	112.07	114.75
12.50	92.03	93.36	94.69	96.01	97.34	98.67	100.00	101.33	102.66	103.99	105.31	106.64	107.97	109.30	110.63	113.28
12.75	90.79	92.10	93.42	94.74	96.05	97.37	98.68	100.00	101.32	102.63	103.95	105.26	106.58	107.90	109.21	111.85
13.00	89.57	90.87	92.18	93.48	94.78	96.09	97.39	98.70	100.00	101.30	102.61	103.91	105.22	106.52	107.82	110.43
13.25	88.37	89.66	90.96	92.25	93.54	94.83	96.12	97.42	98.71	100.00	101.29	102.58	103.88	105.17	106.46	109.04
13.50	87.20	88.48	89.76	91.04	92.32	93.60	94.88	96.16	97.44	98.72	100.00	101.28	102.56	103.84	105.12	107.68
13.75	86.04	87.31	88.58	89.85	91.12	92.39	93.66	94.92	96.19	97.46	98.73	100.00	101.27	102.54	103.81	106.34
14.00	84.91	86.17	87.43	88.68	89.94	91.20	92.46	93.71	94.97	96.23	97.49	98.74	100.00	101.26	102.51	105.03
14.25	83.80	85.05	86.29	87.54	88.78	90.03	91.28	92.52	93.77	95.02	96.26	97.51	98.75	100.00	101.25	103.74
14.50	82.71	83.94	85.18	86.41	87.65	88.88	90.12	91.35	92.59	93.82	95.06	96.29	97.53	98.76	100.00	102.47
14.75	81.64	82.86	84.09	85.31	86.54	87.76	88.98	90.21	91.43	92.66	93.88	95.10	96.33	97.55	98.78	101.22
15.00	80.59	81.80	83.01	84.23	85.44	86.65	87.87	89.08	90.29	91.51	92.72	93.93	95.15	96.36	97.57	100.00
15.25	79.56	80.76	81.96	83.16	84.37	85.57	86.77	87.97	89.18	90.38	91.58	92.78	93.99	95.19	96.39	98.80
15.50	78.54	79.73	80.93	82.12	83.31	84.50	85.70	86.89	88.08	89.27	90.46	91.66	92.85	94.04	95.23	97.62
15.75	77.55	78.73	79.91	81.09	82.27	83.46	84.64	85.82	87.00	88.18	89.36	90.55	91.73	92.91	94.09	96.45
16.00	76.57	77.74	78.91	80.08	81.26	82.43	83.60	84.77	85.94	87.11	88.29	89.46	90.63	91.80	92.97	95.31
16.25	75.61	76.77	77.93	79.09	80.26	81.42	82.58	83.74	84.90	86.06	87.22	88.39	89.55	90.71	91.87	94.19
16.50	74.67	75.82	76.97	78.12	79.27	80.43	81.58	82.73	83.88	85.03	86.18	87.33	88.49	89.64	90.79	93.09
16.75	73.74	74.88	76.03	77.17	78.31	79.45	80.59	81.73	82.88	84.02	85.16	86.30	87.44	88.58	89.73	92.01
17.00	72.83	73.97	75.10	76.23	77.36	78.49	79.63	80.76	81.89	83.02	84.15	85.28	86.42	87.55	88.68	90.94
17.25	71.94	73.06	74.19	75.31	76.43	77.55	78.67	79.80	80.92	82.04	83.16	84.29	85.41	86.53	87.65	89.90
17.50	71.06	72.18	73.29	74.40	75.52	76.63	77.74	78.85	79.97	81.08	82.19	83.31	84.42	85.53	86.64	88.87
17.75	70.20	71.31	72.41	73.51	74.62	75.72	76.82	77.93	79.03	80.13	81.24	82.34	83.45	84.55	85.65	87.86
18.00	69.36	70.45	71.54	72.64	73.73	74.83	75.92	77.02	78.11	79.21	80.30	81.39	82.49	83.58	84.68	86.87
18.25	68.52	69.61	70.69	71.78	72.87	73.95	75.04	76.12	77.21	78.29	79.38	80.46	81.55	82.63	83.72	85.89
18.50	67.71	68.78	69.86	70.94	72.01	73.09	74.17	75.24	76.32	77.39	78.47	79.55	80.62	81.70	82.78	84.93
18.75	66.90	67.97	69.04	70.11	71.17	72.24	73.31	74.38	75.44	76.51	77.58	78.65	79.72	80.78	81.85	83.99
19.00	66.11	67.17	68.23	69.29	70.35	71.41	72.47	73.53	74.59	75.65	76.70	77.76	78.82	79.88	80.94	83.06
20.00	63.09	64.12	65.14	66.17	67.19	68.22	69.24	70.27	71.30	72.32	73.35	74.37	75.40	76.42	77.45	79.50
25.00	50.72	51.60	52.48	53.36	54.24	55.12	56.00	56.88	57.76	58.64	59.52	60.40	61.28	62.16	63.04	64.80
30.00	41.78	42.55	43.32	44.08	44.85	45.61	46.38	47.15	47.91	48.68	49.44	50.21	50.98	51.74	52.51	54.04

Description: This table shows the yield to maturity of a bond purchased at the price shown in the index.

Example: The yield to maturity of a 15.00 %, 9 year bond at a price of 116.00 is 12.04 %.

COUPON RATE, %

PRICE	11.00%	11.25%	11.50%	11.75%	12.00%	12.25%	12.50%	12.75%	13.00%	13.25%	13.50%	13.75%	14.00%	14.25%	14.50%	15.00%
160	3.25	3.44	3.62	3.81	3.99	4.18	4.36	4.55	4.73	4.91	5.10	5.28	5.46	5.65	5.83	6.20
155	3.74	3.93	4.12	4.31	4.50	4.68	4.87	5.06	5.25	5.44	5.62	5.81	6.00	6.18	6.37	6.74
150	4.25	4.44	4.64	4.83	5.02	5.21	5.40	5.60	5.79	5.98	6.17	6.36	6.55	6.74	6.93	7.31
145	4.78	4.98	5.18	5.37	5.57	5.76	5.96	6.16	6.35	6.55	6.74	6.94	7.13	7.33	7.52	7.91
140	5.34	5.54	5.74	5.94	6.14	6.34	6.54	6.74	6.94	7.14	7.34	7.54	7.74	7.94	8.14	8.54
135	5.92	6.13	6.33	6.54	6.74	6.95	7.15	7.36	7.56	7.77	7.97	8.17	8.38	8.58	8.79	9.19
130	6.53	6.74	6.95	7.16	7.37	7.58	7.79	8.00	8.21	8.42	8.63	8.84	9.05	9.26	9.47	9.88
129	6.66	6.87	7.08	7.29	7.50	7.72	7.93	8.14	8.35	8.56	8.77	8.98	9.19	9.40	9.61	10.03
128	6.79	7.00	7.21	7.42	7.64	7.85	8.06	8.27	8.48	8.69	8.91	9.12	9.33	9.54	9.75	10.17
127	6.91	7.13	7.34	7.56	7.77	7.98	8.19	8.41	8.62	8.83	9.05	9.26	9.47	9.68	9.89	10.32
126	7.04	7.26	7.47	7.69	7.90	8.12	8.33	8.55	8.76	8.97	9.19	9.40	9.61	9.83	10.04	10.46
125	7.18	7.39	7.61	7.82	8.04	8.25	8.47	8.68	8.90	9.11	9.33	9.54	9.76	9.97	10.19	10.61
124	7.31	7.53	7.74	7.96	8.18	8.39	8.61	8.82	9.04	9.26	9.47	9.69	9.90	10.12	10.33	10.76
123	7.44	7.66	7.88	8.10	8.31	8.53	8.75	8.97	9.18	9.40	9.62	9.83	10.05	10.27	10.48	10.92
122	7.58	7.80	8.02	8.24	8.45	8.67	8.89	9.11	9.33	9.55	9.76	9.98	10.20	10.42	10.64	11.07
121	7.71	7.94	8.16	8.38	8.60	8.82	9.04	9.26	9.47	9.69	9.91	10.13	10.35	10.57	10.79	11.23
120	7.85	8.08	8.30	8.52	8.74	8.96	9.18	9.40	9.62	9.84	10.06	10.28	10.50	10.72	10.95	11.38
119	7.99	8.22	8.44	8.66	8.88	9.11	9.33	9.55	9.77	9.99	10.22	10.44	10.66	10.88	11.10	11.54
118	8.14	8.36	8.58	8.81	9.03	9.25	9.48	9.70	9.92	10.15	10.37	10.59	10.82	11.04	11.26	11.71
117	8.28	8.50	8.73	8.95	9.18	9.40	9.63	9.85	10.08	10.30	10.53	10.75	10.97	11.20	11.42	11.87
116	8.42	8.65	8.88	9.10	9.33	9.55	9.78	10.01	10.23	10.46	10.68	10.91	11.13	11.36	11.58	12.04
115	8.57	8.80	9.02	9.25	9.48	9.71	9.93	10.16	10.39	10.62	10.84	11.07	11.30	11.52	11.75	12.20
114	8.72	8.95	9.18	9.40	9.63	9.86	10.09	10.32	10.55	10.78	11.00	11.23	11.46	11.69	11.92	12.37
113	8.87	9.10	9.33	9.56	9.79	10.02	10.25	10.48	10.71	10.94	11.17	11.40	11.63	11.86	12.09	12.54
112	9.02	9.25	9.48	9.71	9.95	10.18	10.41	10.64	10.87	11.10	11.33	11.56	11.80	12.03	12.26	12.72
111	9.17	9.41	9.64	9.87	10.10	10.34	10.57	10.80	11.04	11.27	11.50	11.73	11.97	12.20	12.43	12.89
110	9.33	9.56	9.80	10.03	10.27	10.50	10.73	10.97	11.20	11.44	11.67	11.90	12.14	12.37	12.61	13.07
109	9.49	9.72	9.96	10.19	10.43	10.66	10.90	11.14	11.37	11.61	11.84	12.08	12.31	12.55	12.78	13.25
108	9.64	9.88	10.12	10.36	10.59	10.83	11.07	11.31	11.54	11.78	12.02	12.25	12.49	12.73	12.96	13.44
107	9.81	10.05	10.28	10.52	10.76	11.00	11.24	11.48	11.72	11.95	12.19	12.43	12.67	12.91	13.15	13.62
106	9.97	10.21	10.45	10.69	10.93	11.17	11.41	11.65	11.89	12.13	12.37	12.61	12.85	13.09	13.33	13.81
105	10.13	10.38	10.62	10.86	11.10	11.34	11.59	11.83	12.07	12.31	12.55	12.79	13.04	13.28	13.52	14.00
104	10.30	10.55	10.79	11.03	11.28	11.52	11.76	12.01	12.25	12.49	12.74	12.98	13.22	13.46	13.71	14.19
103	10.47	10.72	10.96	11.21	11.45	11.70	11.94	12.19	12.43	12.68	12.92	13.17	13.41	13.66	13.90	14.39
102	10.64	10.89	11.14	11.38	11.63	11.88	12.12	12.37	12.62	12.86	13.11	13.36	13.60	13.85	14.10	14.59
101	10.82	11.07	11.31	11.56	11.81	12.06	12.31	12.56	12.80	13.05	13.30	13.55	13.80	14.05	14.29	14.79
100	11.00	11.25	11.50	11.75	12.00	12.25	12.50	12.75	13.00	13.25	13.50	13.75	14.00	14.25	14.50	15.00
99	11.17	11.43	11.68	11.93	12.18	12.43	12.68	12.94	13.19	13.44	13.69	13.94	14.20	14.45	14.70	15.20
98	11.36	11.61	11.86	12.12	12.37	12.62	12.88	13.13	13.38	13.64	13.89	14.14	14.40	14.65	14.91	15.41
97	11.54	11.80	12.05	12.31	12.56	12.82	13.07	13.33	13.58	13.84	14.09	14.35	14.60	14.86	15.12	15.63
96	11.73	11.98	12.24	12.50	12.76	13.01	13.27	13.53	13.78	14.04	14.30	14.56	14.81	15.07	15.33	15.84
95	11.92	12.17	12.43	12.69	12.95	13.21	13.47	13.73	13.99	14.25	14.51	14.77	15.03	15.29	15.55	16.06
94	12.11	12.37	12.63	12.89	13.15	13.41	13.67	13.94	14.20	14.46	14.72	14.98	15.24	15.50	15.77	16.29
93	12.30	12.57	12.83	13.09	13.35	13.62	13.88	14.14	14.41	14.67	14.93	15.20	15.46	15.72	15.99	16.52
92	12.50	12.77	13.03	13.30	13.56	13.83	14.09	14.36	14.62	14.89	15.15	15.42	15.68	15.95	16.22	16.75
91	12.70	12.97	13.24	13.50	13.77	14.04	14.30	14.57	14.84	15.11	15.37	15.64	15.91	16.18	16.45	16.98
90	12.91	13.17	13.44	13.71	13.98	14.25	14.52	14.79	15.06	15.33	15.60	15.87	16.14	16.41	16.68	17.22
89	13.11	13.38	13.66	13.93	14.20	14.47	14.74	15.01	15.28	15.56	15.83	16.10	16.37	16.65	16.92	17.46
88	13.32	13.60	13.87	14.14	14.42	14.69	14.97	15.24	15.51	15.79	16.06	16.34	16.61	16.89	17.16	17.71
87	13.54	13.81	14.09	14.36	14.64	14.92	15.19	15.47	15.75	16.02	16.30	16.58	16.85	17.13	17.41	17.96
86	13.75	14.03	14.31	14.59	14.87	15.15	15.42	15.70	15.98	16.26	16.54	16.82	17.10	17.38	17.66	18.22
85	13.98	14.26	14.54	14.82	15.10	15.38	15.66	15.94	16.22	16.50	16.78	17.07	17.35	17.63	17.91	18.48
84	14.20	14.48	14.77	15.05	15.33	15.61	15.90	16.18	16.47	16.75	17.03	17.32	17.60	17.89	18.17	18.74
83	14.43	14.71	15.00	15.28	15.57	15.86	16.14	16.43	16.71	17.00	17.29	17.57	17.86	18.15	18.44	19.01
82	14.66	14.95	15.24	15.52	15.81	16.10	16.39	16.68	16.97	17.26	17.55	17.83	18.12	18.41	18.70	19.29
81	14.90	15.19	15.48	15.77	16.06	16.35	16.64	16.93	17.22	17.52	17.81	18.10	18.39	18.69	18.98	19.56
80	15.14	15.43	15.72	16.02	16.31	16.60	16.90	17.19	17.49	17.78	18.08	18.37	18.67	18.96	19.26	19.85
79	15.38	15.68	15.97	16.27	16.57	16.86	17.16	17.46	17.75	18.05	18.35	18.65	18.94	19.24	19.54	20.14
78	15.63	15.93	16.23	16.53	16.83	17.13	17.43	17.73	18.03	18.33	18.63	18.93	19.23	19.53	19.83	20.44
77	15.88	16.19	16.49	16.79	17.09	17.39	17.70	18.00	18.30	18.61	18.91	19.21	19.52	19.82	20.13	20.74
76	16.14	16.45	16.75	17.06	17.36	17.67	17.97	18.28	18.59	18.89	19.20	19.51	19.81	20.12	20.43	21.05
75	16.41	16.71	17.02	17.33	17.64	17.95	18.26	18.56	18.87	19.18	19.49	19.80	20.12	20.43	20.74	21.36
74	16.68	16.99	17.30	17.61	17.92	18.23	18.54	18.86	19.17	19.48	19.79	20.11	20.42	20.74	21.05	21.68
73	16.95	17.26	17.58	17.89	18.21	18.52	18.84	19.15	19.47	19.78	20.10	20.42	20.74	21.05	21.37	22.01
72	17.23	17.55	17.86	18.18	18.50	18.82	19.14	19.46	19.78	20.10	20.42	20.74	21.06	21.38	21.70	22.34
71	17.51	17.83	18.15	18.48	18.80	19.12	19.44	19.76	20.09	20.41	20.74	21.06	21.38	21.71	22.04	22.69
70	17.80	18.13	18.45	18.78	19.10	19.43	19.75	20.08	20.41	20.74	21.06	21.39	21.72	22.05	22.38	23.04
65	19.36	19.70	20.04	20.39	20.73	21.08	21.42	21.77	22.12	22.47	22.81	23.16	23.51	23.86	24.21	24.92

Description: This table shows the price to pay for a bond at the yield rate. The yield is to maturity.

Example: The price of a 6.75 %, 10 year bond to yield 8 % to maturity is $ 91.51.

COUPON RATE, %

YIELD	0.00%	1.00%	2.00%	3.00%	4.00%	4.25%	4.50%	4.75%	5.00%	5.25%	5.50%	5.75%	6.00%	6.25%	6.50%	6.75%
0.00	100.00	110.00	120.00	130.00	140.00	142.50	145.00	147.50	150.00	152.50	155.00	157.50	160.00	162.50	165.00	167.50
1.00	90.51	100.00	109.49	118.99	128.48	130.85	133.23	135.60	137.97	140.35	142.72	145.10	147.47	149.84	152.22	154.59
2.00	81.95	90.98	100.00	109.02	118.05	120.30	122.56	124.81	127.07	129.32	131.58	133.84	136.09	138.35	140.60	142.86
3.00	74.25	82.83	91.42	100.00	108.58	110.73	112.88	115.02	117.17	119.31	121.46	123.61	125.75	127.90	130.05	132.19
4.00	67.30	75.47	83.65	91.82	100.00	102.04	104.09	106.13	108.18	110.22	112.26	114.31	116.35	118.40	120.44	122.48
4.25	65.67	73.75	81.82	89.90	97.98	100.00	102.02	104.04	106.06	108.08	110.10	112.12	114.14	116.16	118.18	120.19
4.50	64.08	72.06	80.05	88.03	96.01	98.00	100.00	102.00	103.99	105.99	107.98	109.98	111.97	113.97	115.96	117.96
4.75	62.53	70.42	78.31	86.20	94.08	96.06	98.03	100.00	101.97	103.94	105.92	107.89	109.86	111.83	113.80	115.77
5.00	61.03	68.82	76.62	84.41	92.21	94.15	96.10	98.05	100.00	101.95	103.90	105.85	107.79	109.74	111.69	113.64
5.25	59.56	67.26	74.96	82.67	90.37	92.30	94.22	96.15	98.07	100.00	101.93	103.85	105.78	107.70	109.63	111.55
5.50	58.13	65.74	73.35	80.97	88.58	90.48	92.39	94.29	96.19	98.10	100.00	101.90	103.81	105.71	107.61	109.52
5.75	56.73	64.25	71.78	79.31	86.83	88.71	90.59	92.47	94.36	96.24	98.12	100.00	101.88	103.76	105.64	107.53
6.00	55.37	62.81	70.25	77.68	85.12	86.99	88.84	90.70	92.56	94.42	96.28	98.14	100.00	101.86	103.72	105.58
6.25	54.04	61.39	68.75	76.10	83.45	85.29	87.13	88.97	90.81	92.65	94.48	96.32	98.16	100.00	101.84	103.68
6.50	52.75	60.02	67.29	74.56	81.83	83.64	85.46	87.28	89.10	90.91	92.73	94.55	96.37	98.18	100.00	101.82
6.75	51.49	58.67	65.86	73.05	80.24	82.03	83.83	85.63	87.42	89.22	91.02	92.81	94.61	96.41	98.20	100.00
7.00	50.26	57.36	64.47	71.58	78.68	80.46	82.23	84.01	85.79	87.56	89.34	91.12	92.89	94.67	96.45	98.22
7.25	49.06	56.08	63.11	70.14	77.16	78.92	80.68	82.43	84.19	85.95	87.70	89.46	91.22	92.97	94.73	96.49
7.50	47.89	54.84	61.79	68.73	75.68	77.42	79.16	80.89	82.63	84.37	86.10	87.84	89.58	91.31	93.05	94.79
7.75	46.75	53.62	60.49	67.36	74.23	75.95	77.67	79.39	81.10	82.82	84.54	86.26	87.98	89.69	91.41	93.13
8.00	45.64	52.43	59.23	66.02	72.82	74.52	76.22	77.92	79.61	81.31	83.01	84.71	86.41	88.11	89.81	91.51
8.25	44.56	51.28	58.00	64.72	71.44	73.12	74.80	76.48	78.16	79.84	81.52	83.20	84.88	86.56	88.24	89.92
8.50	43.50	50.15	56.79	63.44	70.09	71.75	73.41	75.07	76.73	78.40	80.06	81.72	83.38	85.04	86.71	88.37
8.75	42.47	49.04	55.62	62.19	68.77	70.41	72.06	73.70	75.34	76.99	78.63	80.28	81.92	83.56	85.21	86.85
9.00	41.46	47.97	54.47	60.98	67.48	69.11	70.73	72.36	73.98	75.61	77.24	78.86	80.49	82.11	83.74	85.37
9.25	40.48	46.92	53.35	59.79	66.22	67.83	69.44	71.05	72.66	74.26	75.87	77.48	79.09	80.70	82.31	83.91
9.50	39.53	45.89	52.26	58.63	64.99	66.58	68.17	69.76	71.36	72.95	74.54	76.13	77.72	79.31	80.90	82.50
9.75	38.60	44.90	51.19	57.49	63.79	65.36	66.94	68.51	70.09	71.66	73.23	74.81	76.38	77.96	79.53	81.11
10.00	37.69	43.92	50.15	56.38	62.61	64.17	65.73	67.29	68.84	70.40	71.96	73.52	75.08	76.63	78.19	79.75
10.25	36.80	42.97	49.13	55.30	61.47	63.01	64.55	66.09	67.63	69.17	70.71	72.25	73.80	75.34	76.88	78.42
10.50	35.94	42.04	48.14	54.24	60.34	61.87	63.39	64.92	66.44	67.97	69.49	71.02	72.54	74.07	75.60	77.12
10.75	35.10	41.13	47.17	53.21	59.25	60.76	62.26	63.77	65.28	66.79	68.30	69.81	71.32	72.83	74.34	75.85
11.00	34.27	40.25	46.22	52.20	58.17	59.67	61.16	62.66	64.15	65.64	67.14	68.63	70.12	71.62	73.11	74.61
11.25	33.47	39.38	45.30	51.21	57.13	58.60	60.08	61.56	63.04	64.52	66.00	67.47	68.95	70.43	71.91	73.39
11.50	32.69	38.54	44.39	50.25	56.10	57.56	59.03	60.49	61.95	63.42	64.88	66.34	67.81	69.27	70.73	72.20
11.75	31.93	37.72	43.51	49.31	55.10	56.55	58.00	59.44	60.89	62.34	63.79	65.24	66.69	68.14	69.58	71.03
12.00	31.18	36.92	42.65	48.39	54.12	55.55	56.99	58.42	59.86	61.29	62.72	64.16	65.59	67.02	68.46	69.89
12.25	30.45	36.13	41.81	47.49	53.16	54.58	56.00	57.42	58.84	60.26	61.68	63.10	64.52	65.94	67.36	68.78
12.50	29.75	35.37	40.99	46.61	52.23	53.63	55.04	56.44	57.85	59.25	60.66	62.06	63.47	64.87	66.28	67.68
12.75	29.05	34.62	40.18	45.75	51.31	52.70	54.09	55.48	56.88	58.27	59.66	61.05	62.44	63.83	65.22	66.61
13.00	28.38	33.89	39.40	44.91	50.42	51.79	53.17	54.55	55.93	57.30	58.68	60.06	61.44	62.81	64.19	65.57
13.25	27.72	33.18	38.63	44.09	49.54	50.91	52.27	53.63	55.00	56.36	57.72	59.09	60.45	61.82	63.18	64.54
13.50	27.08	32.48	37.88	43.28	48.69	50.04	51.39	52.74	54.09	55.44	56.79	58.14	59.49	60.84	62.19	63.54
13.75	26.45	31.80	37.15	42.50	47.85	49.19	50.52	51.86	53.20	54.53	55.87	57.21	58.55	59.88	61.22	62.56
14.00	25.84	31.14	36.44	41.73	47.03	48.35	49.68	51.00	52.33	53.65	54.98	56.30	57.62	58.95	60.27	61.60
14.25	25.25	30.49	35.74	40.98	46.23	47.54	48.85	50.16	51.47	52.79	54.10	55.41	56.72	58.03	59.34	60.66
14.50	24.66	29.86	35.05	40.25	45.45	46.74	48.04	49.34	50.64	51.94	53.24	54.54	55.84	57.14	58.44	59.73
14.75	24.10	29.24	34.39	39.53	44.68	45.97	47.25	48.54	49.83	51.11	52.40	53.69	54.97	56.26	57.54	58.83
15.00	23.54	28.64	33.74	38.83	43.93	45.20	46.48	47.75	49.03	50.30	51.58	52.85	54.12	55.40	56.67	57.95
15.25	23.00	28.05	33.10	38.15	43.20	44.46	45.72	46.98	48.25	49.51	50.77	52.03	53.30	54.56	55.82	57.08
15.50	22.47	27.47	32.48	37.48	42.48	43.73	44.98	46.23	47.48	48.73	49.98	51.23	52.48	53.73	54.98	56.23
15.75	21.96	26.91	31.87	36.82	41.78	43.02	44.26	45.49	46.73	47.97	49.21	50.45	51.69	52.93	54.17	55.40
16.00	21.45	26.36	31.27	36.18	41.09	42.32	43.55	44.77	46.00	47.23	48.45	49.68	50.91	52.14	53.36	54.59
16.25	20.96	25.83	30.69	35.56	40.42	41.64	42.85	44.07	45.28	46.50	47.71	48.93	50.15	51.36	52.58	53.79
16.50	20.49	25.30	30.12	34.94	39.76	40.97	42.17	43.38	44.58	45.79	46.99	48.19	49.40	50.60	51.81	53.01
16.75	20.02	24.79	29.57	34.34	39.12	40.31	41.51	42.70	43.89	45.09	46.28	47.47	48.67	49.86	51.06	52.25
17.00	19.56	24.29	29.02	33.76	38.49	39.67	40.85	42.04	43.22	44.40	45.59	46.77	47.95	49.13	50.32	51.50
17.25	19.12	23.81	28.49	33.18	37.87	39.04	40.22	41.39	42.56	43.73	44.91	46.08	47.25	48.42	49.59	50.77
17.50	18.68	23.33	27.98	32.62	37.27	38.43	39.59	40.75	41.92	43.08	44.24	45.40	46.56	47.72	48.89	50.05
17.75	18.26	22.86	27.47	32.07	36.68	37.83	38.98	40.13	41.28	42.43	43.59	44.74	45.89	47.04	48.19	49.34
18.00	17.84	22.41	26.97	31.54	36.10	37.24	38.38	39.52	40.66	41.81	42.95	44.09	45.23	46.37	47.51	48.65
18.25	17.44	21.96	26.49	31.01	35.53	36.67	37.80	38.93	40.06	41.19	42.32	43.45	44.58	45.71	46.84	47.98
18.50	17.04	21.53	26.01	30.50	34.98	36.10	37.22	38.34	39.46	40.59	41.71	42.83	43.95	45.07	46.19	47.31
18.75	16.66	21.10	25.55	29.99	34.44	35.55	36.66	37.77	38.88	39.99	41.11	42.22	43.33	44.44	45.55	46.66
19.00	16.28	20.69	25.09	29.50	33.91	35.01	36.11	37.21	38.31	39.41	40.52	41.62	42.72	43.82	44.92	46.02
20.00	14.86	19.12	23.38	27.63	31.89	32.96	34.02	35.08	36.15	37.21	38.28	39.34	40.41	41.47	42.53	43.60
25.00	9.48	13.10	16.72	20.35	23.97	24.87	25.78	26.68	27.59	28.49	29.40	30.30	31.21	32.11	33.02	33.92
30.00	6.11	9.24	12.37	15.50	18.63	19.41	20.19	20.98	21.76	22.54	23.32	24.11	24.89	25.67	26.45	27.24

Description: This table shows the yield to maturity of a bond purchased at the price shown in the index.

Example: The yield to maturity of a 6.75 %, 10 year bond at a price of 80.00 is 9.95 %.

PRICE	0.00%	1.00%	2.00%	3.00%	4.00%	4.25%	4.50%	4.75%	5.00%	5.25%	5.50%	5.75%	6.00%	6.25%	6.50%	6.75%
100	0.00	1.00	2.00	3.00	4.00	4.25	4.50	4.75	5.00	5.25	5.50	5.75	6.00	6.25	6.50	6.75
99	.10	1.10	2.11	3.11	4.12	4.37	4.62	4.87	5.12	5.38	5.63	5.88	6.13	6.38	6.63	6.89
98	.20	1.21	2.22	3.23	4.24	4.50	4.75	5.00	5.25	5.51	5.76	6.01	6.27	6.52	6.77	7.03
97	.30	1.32	2.33	3.35	4.37	4.62	4.88	5.13	5.39	5.64	5.90	6.15	6.41	6.66	6.92	7.17
96	.40	1.43	2.45	3.47	4.50	4.75	5.01	5.26	5.52	5.78	6.03	6.29	6.55	6.80	7.06	7.32
95	.51	1.54	2.57	3.59	4.63	4.88	5.14	5.40	5.66	5.91	6.17	6.43	6.69	6.95	7.21	7.46
94	.61	1.65	2.68	3.72	4.76	5.02	5.27	5.53	5.79	6.05	6.31	6.57	6.83	7.09	7.35	7.61
93	.72	1.76	2.80	3.85	4.89	5.15	5.41	5.67	5.93	6.19	6.46	6.72	6.98	7.24	7.50	7.76
92	.83	1.88	2.92	3.97	5.02	5.29	5.55	5.81	6.07	6.34	6.60	6.86	7.13	7.39	7.65	7.92
91	.94	1.99	3.05	4.10	5.16	5.42	5.69	5.95	6.22	6.48	6.75	7.01	7.28	7.54	7.81	8.07
90	1.05	2.11	3.17	4.23	5.30	5.56	5.83	6.10	6.36	6.63	6.90	7.16	7.43	7.70	7.96	8.23
89	1.16	2.23	3.30	4.36	5.44	5.70	5.97	6.24	6.51	6.78	7.05	7.32	7.58	7.85	8.12	8.39
88	1.28	2.35	3.42	4.50	5.58	5.85	6.12	6.39	6.66	6.93	7.20	7.47	7.74	8.01	8.28	8.56
87	1.39	2.47	3.55	4.63	5.72	5.99	6.26	6.54	6.81	7.08	7.35	7.63	7.90	8.17	8.45	8.72
86	1.51	2.59	3.68	4.77	5.87	6.14	6.41	6.69	6.96	7.24	7.51	7.79	8.06	8.34	8.61	8.89
85	1.63	2.72	3.81	4.91	6.01	6.29	6.56	6.84	7.12	7.39	7.67	7.95	8.23	8.50	8.78	9.06
84	1.75	2.85	3.95	5.05	6.16	6.44	6.72	7.00	7.28	7.55	7.83	8.11	8.39	8.67	8.95	9.23
83	1.87	2.97	4.08	5.20	6.31	6.59	6.87	7.15	7.44	7.72	8.00	8.28	8.56	8.84	9.12	9.41
82	1.99	3.10	4.22	5.34	6.47	6.75	7.03	7.31	7.60	7.88	8.16	8.45	8.73	9.01	9.30	9.58
81	2.11	3.23	4.36	5.49	6.62	6.91	7.19	7.48	7.76	8.05	8.33	8.62	8.90	9.19	9.48	9.76
80	2.24	3.37	4.50	5.64	6.78	7.07	7.36	7.64	7.93	8.22	8.51	8.79	9.08	9.37	9.66	9.95
79	2.37	3.50	4.64	5.79	6.94	7.23	7.52	7.81	8.10	8.39	8.68	8.97	9.26	9.55	9.84	10.14
78	2.50	3.64	4.79	5.95	7.11	7.40	7.69	7.98	8.27	8.56	8.86	9.15	9.44	9.74	10.03	10.33
77	2.63	3.78	4.94	6.10	7.27	7.57	7.86	8.15	8.45	8.74	9.04	9.33	9.63	9.93	10.22	10.52
76	2.76	3.92	5.09	6.26	7.44	7.74	8.03	8.33	8.63	8.92	9.22	9.52	9.82	10.12	10.42	10.72
75	2.89	4.06	5.24	6.42	7.61	7.91	8.21	8.51	8.81	9.11	9.41	9.71	10.01	10.31	10.61	10.92
74	3.03	4.21	5.39	6.59	7.79	8.09	8.39	8.69	8.99	9.29	9.60	9.90	10.20	10.51	10.81	11.12
73	3.17	4.36	5.55	6.75	7.96	8.27	8.57	8.87	9.18	9.48	9.79	10.10	10.40	10.71	11.02	11.33
72	3.31	4.50	5.71	6.92	8.14	8.45	8.76	9.06	9.37	9.68	9.99	10.30	10.61	10.92	11.23	11.54
71	3.45	4.66	5.87	7.09	8.33	8.63	8.94	9.25	9.56	9.88	10.19	10.50	10.81	11.12	11.44	11.75
70	3.59	4.81	6.04	7.27	8.51	8.82	9.14	9.45	9.76	10.08	10.39	10.71	11.02	11.34	11.65	11.97
69	3.74	4.97	6.20	7.45	8.70	9.02	9.33	9.65	9.96	10.28	10.60	10.92	11.23	11.55	11.87	12.19
68	3.89	5.13	6.37	7.63	8.89	9.21	9.53	9.85	10.17	10.49	10.81	11.13	11.45	11.78	12.10	12.42
67	4.04	5.29	6.54	7.81	9.09	9.41	9.73	10.05	10.38	10.70	11.02	11.35	11.67	12.00	12.33	12.65
66	4.19	5.45	6.72	8.00	9.29	9.61	9.94	10.26	10.59	10.92	11.24	11.57	11.90	12.23	12.56	12.89
65	4.35	5.62	6.90	8.19	9.49	9.82	10.15	10.48	10.81	11.14	11.47	11.80	12.13	12.46	12.80	13.13
64	4.51	5.79	7.08	8.38	9.70	10.03	10.36	10.70	11.03	11.36	11.70	12.03	12.37	12.70	13.04	13.38
63	4.67	5.96	7.27	8.58	9.91	10.25	10.58	10.92	11.25	11.59	11.93	12.27	12.61	12.95	13.29	13.63
62	4.83	6.14	7.45	8.78	10.13	10.47	10.80	11.14	11.48	11.83	12.17	12.51	12.85	13.20	13.54	13.89
61	5.00	6.32	7.65	8.99	10.35	10.69	11.03	11.38	11.72	12.06	12.41	12.76	13.10	13.45	13.80	14.15
60	5.17	6.50	7.84	9.20	10.57	10.92	11.26	11.61	11.96	12.31	12.66	13.01	13.36	13.71	14.07	14.42
59	5.34	6.68	8.04	9.41	10.80	11.15	11.50	11.85	12.21	12.56	12.91	13.27	13.62	13.98	14.34	14.70
58	5.52	6.87	8.24	9.63	11.04	11.39	11.74	12.10	12.46	12.81	13.17	13.53	13.89	14.25	14.62	14.98
57	5.70	7.07	8.45	9.85	11.28	11.63	11.99	12.35	12.71	13.07	13.44	13.80	14.17	14.53	14.90	15.27
56	5.88	7.26	8.66	10.08	11.52	11.88	12.25	12.61	12.98	13.34	13.71	14.08	14.45	14.82	15.19	15.57
55	6.06	7.46	8.88	10.32	11.77	12.14	12.50	12.87	13.24	13.62	13.99	14.36	14.74	15.11	15.49	15.87
54	6.25	7.67	9.10	10.55	12.03	12.40	12.77	13.14	13.52	13.90	14.27	14.65	15.03	15.41	15.80	16.18
53	6.45	7.88	9.33	10.80	12.29	12.66	13.04	13.42	13.80	14.18	14.57	14.95	15.34	15.72	16.11	16.50
52	6.64	8.09	9.56	11.04	12.56	12.94	13.32	13.70	14.09	14.48	14.87	15.26	15.65	16.04	16.43	16.83
51	6.84	8.31	9.79	11.30	12.83	13.22	13.61	14.00	14.39	14.78	15.17	15.57	15.97	16.36	16.76	17.16
50	7.05	8.53	10.03	11.56	13.11	13.51	13.90	14.29	14.69	15.09	15.49	15.89	16.29	16.70	17.10	17.51
49	7.26	8.76	10.28	11.83	13.40	13.80	14.20	14.60	15.00	15.41	15.81	16.22	16.63	17.04	17.45	17.87
48	7.47	8.99	10.53	12.10	13.70	14.10	14.51	14.92	15.32	15.74	16.15	16.56	16.98	17.40	17.81	18.24
47	7.69	9.23	10.79	12.38	14.00	14.41	14.83	15.24	15.66	16.07	16.49	16.91	17.34	17.76	18.19	18.61
46	7.91	9.47	11.05	12.67	14.32	14.73	15.15	15.57	16.00	16.42	16.85	17.27	17.70	18.14	18.57	19.00
45	8.14	9.72	11.33	12.97	14.64	15.06	15.49	15.92	16.35	16.78	17.21	17.65	18.08	18.52	18.96	19.41
44	8.38	9.97	11.61	13.27	14.97	15.40	15.83	16.27	16.71	17.14	17.59	18.03	18.47	18.92	19.37	19.82
43	8.62	10.24	11.89	13.58	15.31	15.75	16.19	16.63	17.08	17.52	17.97	18.43	18.88	19.34	19.79	20.25
42	8.86	10.51	12.19	13.91	15.67	16.11	16.56	17.01	17.46	17.92	18.37	18.83	19.30	19.76	20.23	20.70
41	9.11	10.78	12.49	14.24	16.03	16.48	16.94	17.40	17.86	18.32	18.79	19.26	19.73	20.20	20.68	21.16
40	9.37	11.07	12.80	14.58	16.40	16.87	17.33	17.80	18.27	18.74	19.22	19.70	20.18	20.66	21.15	21.64
39	9.64	11.36	13.12	14.93	16.79	17.26	17.74	18.21	18.69	19.18	19.66	20.15	20.64	21.14	21.64	22.14
38	9.91	11.66	13.46	15.30	17.19	17.67	18.16	18.64	19.13	19.63	20.12	20.62	21.13	21.63	22.14	22.65
37	10.19	11.97	13.80	15.68	17.61	18.10	18.59	19.09	19.59	20.10	20.60	21.11	21.63	22.15	22.67	23.19
36	10.48	12.29	14.15	16.07	18.04	18.54	19.05	19.55	20.07	20.58	21.10	21.62	22.15	22.68	23.21	23.75
35	10.77	12.62	14.52	16.47	18.49	19.00	19.52	20.04	20.56	21.09	21.62	22.16	22.69	23.24	23.78	24.34
30	12.40	14.44	16.55	18.74	21.02	21.60	22.18	22.78	23.38	23.98	24.59	25.20	25.82	26.44	27.07	27.71
25	14.35	16.64	19.05	21.57	24.22	24.90	25.59	26.28	26.99	27.70	28.42	29.15	29.89	30.63	31.39	32.15

Description: This table shows the price to pay for a bond at the yield rate. The yield is to maturity.

Example: The price of a 10.75 %, 10 year bond to yield 8 % to maturity is $ 118.69.

COUPON RATE, %

YIELD	7.00%	7.25%	7.50%	7.75%	8.00%	8.25%	8.50%	8.75%	9.00%	9.25%	9.50%	9.75%	10.00%	10.25%	10.50%	10.75%
0.00	170.00	172.50	175.00	177.50	180.00	182.50	185.00	187.50	190.00	192.50	195.00	197.50	200.00	202.50	205.00	207.50
1.00	156.96	159.34	161.71	164.08	166.46	168.83	171.20	173.58	175.95	178.32	180.70	183.07	185.44	187.82	190.19	192.56
2.00	145.11	147.37	149.63	151.88	154.14	156.39	158.65	160.90	163.16	165.42	167.67	169.93	172.18	174.44	176.69	178.95
3.00	134.34	136.48	138.63	140.78	142.92	145.07	147.21	149.36	151.51	153.65	155.80	157.94	160.09	162.24	164.38	166.53
4.00	124.53	126.57	128.62	130.66	132.70	134.75	136.79	138.83	140.88	142.92	144.97	147.01	149.05	151.10	153.14	155.19
4.25	122.21	124.23	126.25	128.27	130.29	132.31	134.33	136.35	138.37	140.39	142.41	144.43	146.45	148.47	150.49	152.51
4.50	119.95	121.95	123.95	125.94	127.94	129.93	131.93	133.92	135.92	137.91	139.91	141.90	143.90	145.90	147.89	149.89
4.75	117.75	119.72	121.69	123.66	125.63	127.61	129.58	131.55	133.52	135.49	137.47	139.44	141.41	143.38	145.35	147.32
5.00	115.59	117.54	119.49	121.44	123.38	125.33	127.28	129.23	131.18	133.13	135.08	137.02	138.97	140.92	142.87	144.82
5.25	113.48	115.41	117.33	119.26	121.18	123.11	125.04	126.96	128.89	130.81	132.74	134.66	136.59	138.52	140.44	142.37
5.50	111.42	113.32	115.23	117.13	119.03	120.94	122.84	124.74	126.65	128.55	130.45	132.36	134.26	136.16	138.07	139.97
5.75	109.41	111.29	113.17	115.05	116.93	118.81	120.69	122.58	124.46	126.34	128.22	130.10	131.98	133.86	135.75	137.63
6.00	107.44	109.30	111.16	113.02	114.88	116.74	118.60	120.46	122.32	124.18	126.04	127.90	129.75	131.61	133.47	135.33
6.25	105.52	107.35	109.19	111.03	112.87	114.71	116.55	118.38	120.22	122.06	123.90	125.74	127.58	129.41	131.25	133.09
6.50	103.63	105.45	107.27	109.09	110.90	112.72	114.54	116.36	118.17	119.99	121.81	123.63	125.44	127.26	129.08	130.90
6.75	101.80	103.59	105.39	107.19	108.98	110.78	112.58	114.37	116.17	117.97	119.76	121.56	123.36	125.16	126.95	128.75
7.00	100.00	101.78	103.55	105.33	107.11	108.88	110.66	112.44	114.21	115.99	117.77	119.54	121.32	123.10	124.87	126.65
7.25	98.24	100.00	101.76	103.51	105.27	107.03	108.78	110.54	112.30	114.05	115.81	117.57	119.32	121.08	122.84	124.59
7.50	96.53	98.26	100.00	101.74	103.47	105.21	106.95	108.69	110.42	112.16	113.90	115.63	117.37	119.11	120.84	122.58
7.75	94.85	96.56	98.28	100.00	101.72	103.44	105.15	106.87	108.59	110.31	112.02	113.74	115.46	117.18	118.90	120.61
8.00	93.20	94.90	96.60	98.30	100.00	101.70	103.40	105.10	106.80	108.49	110.19	111.89	113.59	115.29	116.99	118.69
8.25	91.60	93.28	94.96	96.64	98.32	100.00	101.68	103.36	105.04	106.72	108.40	110.08	111.76	113.44	115.12	116.80
8.50	90.03	91.69	93.35	95.01	96.68	98.34	100.00	101.66	103.32	104.99	106.65	108.31	109.97	111.63	113.29	114.96
8.75	88.49	90.14	91.78	93.43	95.07	96.71	98.36	100.00	101.64	103.29	104.93	106.57	108.22	109.86	111.51	113.15
9.00	86.99	88.62	90.24	91.87	93.50	95.12	96.75	98.37	100.00	101.63	103.25	104.88	106.50	108.13	109.76	111.38
9.25	85.52	87.13	88.74	90.35	91.96	93.57	95.17	96.78	98.39	100.00	101.61	103.22	104.83	106.43	108.04	109.65
9.50	84.09	85.68	87.27	88.86	90.45	92.04	93.63	95.23	96.82	98.41	100.00	101.59	103.18	104.77	106.37	107.96
9.75	82.68	84.26	85.83	87.40	88.98	90.55	92.13	93.70	95.28	96.85	98.43	100.00	101.57	103.15	104.72	106.30
10.00	81.31	82.86	84.42	85.98	87.54	89.10	90.65	92.21	93.77	95.33	96.88	98.44	100.00	101.56	103.12	104.67
10.25	79.96	81.50	83.04	84.59	86.13	87.67	89.21	90.75	92.29	93.83	95.38	96.92	98.46	100.00	101.54	103.08
10.50	78.65	80.17	81.70	83.22	84.75	86.27	87.80	89.32	90.85	92.37	93.90	95.42	96.95	98.47	100.00	101.53
10.75	77.36	78.87	80.38	81.89	83.40	84.91	86.42	87.92	89.43	90.94	92.45	93.96	95.47	96.98	98.49	100.00
11.00	76.10	77.59	79.09	80.58	82.07	83.57	85.06	86.56	88.05	89.54	91.04	92.53	94.02	95.52	97.01	98.51
11.25	74.87	76.35	77.82	79.30	80.78	82.26	83.74	85.22	86.69	88.17	89.65	91.13	92.61	94.09	95.56	97.04
11.50	73.66	75.12	76.59	78.05	79.51	80.98	82.44	83.90	85.37	86.83	88.29	89.76	91.22	92.68	94.15	95.61
11.75	72.48	73.93	75.38	76.83	78.27	79.72	81.17	82.62	84.07	85.52	86.96	88.41	89.86	91.31	92.76	94.21
12.00	71.33	72.76	74.19	75.63	77.06	78.49	79.93	81.36	82.80	84.23	85.66	87.10	88.53	89.96	91.40	92.83
12.25	70.19	71.61	73.03	74.45	75.87	77.29	78.71	80.13	81.55	82.97	84.39	85.81	87.23	88.65	90.06	91.48
12.50	69.09	70.49	71.90	73.30	74.71	76.11	77.52	78.92	80.33	81.73	83.14	84.54	85.95	87.35	88.76	90.16
12.75	68.00	69.40	70.79	72.18	73.57	74.96	76.35	77.74	79.13	80.52	81.92	83.31	84.70	86.09	87.48	88.87
13.00	66.94	68.32	69.70	71.08	72.45	73.83	75.21	76.59	77.96	79.34	80.72	82.09	83.47	84.85	86.23	87.60
13.25	65.91	67.27	68.63	70.00	71.36	72.73	74.09	75.45	76.82	78.18	79.54	80.91	82.27	83.64	85.00	86.36
13.50	64.89	66.24	67.59	68.94	70.29	71.64	72.99	74.34	75.69	77.04	78.39	79.74	81.09	82.45	83.80	85.15
13.75	63.90	65.23	66.57	67.91	69.24	70.58	71.92	73.26	74.59	75.93	77.27	78.60	79.94	81.28	82.62	83.95
14.00	62.92	64.25	65.57	66.89	68.22	69.54	70.87	72.19	73.51	74.84	76.16	77.49	78.81	80.14	81.46	82.78
14.25	61.97	63.28	64.59	65.90	67.21	68.52	69.84	71.15	72.46	73.77	75.08	76.39	77.70	79.02	80.33	81.64
14.50	61.03	62.33	63.63	64.93	66.23	67.53	68.83	70.13	71.42	72.72	74.02	75.32	76.62	77.92	79.22	80.52
14.75	60.12	61.40	62.69	63.98	65.26	66.55	67.84	69.12	70.41	71.70	72.98	74.27	75.56	76.84	78.13	79.42
15.00	59.22	60.50	61.77	63.04	64.32	65.59	66.87	68.14	69.42	70.69	71.97	73.24	74.51	75.79	77.06	78.34
15.25	58.34	59.61	60.87	62.13	63.39	64.66	65.92	67.18	68.44	69.71	70.97	72.23	73.49	74.75	76.02	77.28
15.50	57.49	58.74	59.99	61.24	62.49	63.74	64.99	66.24	67.49	68.74	69.99	71.24	72.49	73.74	74.99	76.24
15.75	56.64	57.88	59.12	60.36	61.60	62.84	64.08	65.31	66.55	67.79	69.03	70.27	71.51	72.75	73.99	75.22
16.00	55.82	57.05	58.27	59.50	60.73	61.95	63.18	64.41	65.64	66.86	68.09	69.32	70.55	71.77	73.00	74.23
16.25	55.01	56.23	57.44	58.66	59.87	61.09	62.31	63.52	64.74	65.95	67.17	68.39	69.60	70.82	72.03	73.25
16.50	54.22	55.42	56.63	57.83	59.04	60.24	61.45	62.65	63.86	65.06	66.27	67.47	68.68	69.88	71.09	72.29
16.75	53.44	54.64	55.83	57.02	58.22	59.41	60.61	61.80	62.99	64.19	65.38	66.57	67.77	68.96	70.16	71.35
17.00	52.68	53.87	55.05	56.23	57.41	58.60	59.78	60.96	62.15	63.33	64.51	65.70	66.88	68.06	69.24	70.43
17.25	51.94	53.11	54.28	55.46	56.63	57.80	58.97	60.14	61.32	62.49	63.66	64.83	66.01	67.18	68.35	69.52
17.50	51.21	52.37	53.53	54.69	55.86	57.02	58.18	59.34	60.50	61.66	62.83	63.99	65.15	66.31	67.47	68.63
17.75	50.49	51.65	52.80	53.95	55.10	56.25	57.40	58.55	59.70	60.86	62.01	63.16	64.31	65.46	66.61	67.76
18.00	49.79	50.93	52.08	53.22	54.36	55.50	56.64	57.78	58.92	60.06	61.20	62.34	63.49	64.63	65.77	66.91
18.25	49.11	50.24	51.37	52.50	53.63	54.76	55.89	57.02	58.15	59.28	60.42	61.55	62.68	63.81	64.94	66.07
18.50	48.43	49.55	50.67	51.80	52.92	54.04	55.16	56.28	57.40	58.52	59.64	60.76	61.89	63.01	64.13	65.25
18.75	47.77	48.88	50.00	51.11	52.22	53.33	54.44	55.55	56.66	57.77	58.88	60.00	61.11	62.22	63.33	64.44
19.00	47.13	48.23	49.33	50.43	51.53	52.63	53.73	54.84	55.94	57.04	58.14	59.24	60.34	61.45	62.55	63.65
20.00	44.66	45.73	46.79	47.85	48.92	49.98	51.05	52.11	53.18	54.24	55.30	56.37	57.43	58.50	59.56	60.62
25.00	34.83	35.73	36.64	37.54	38.45	39.35	40.26	41.16	42.07	42.97	43.88	44.78	45.69	46.60	47.50	48.41
30.00	28.02	28.80	29.58	30.36	31.15	31.93	32.71	33.49	34.28	35.06	35.84	36.62	37.41	38.19	38.97	39.75

Description: This table shows the yield to maturity of a bond purchased at the price shown in the index.

Example: The yield to maturity of a 10.75 %, 10 year bond at a price of 105.00 is 9.94 %.

						COUPON RATE, %										
PRICE	7.00%	7.25%	7.50%	7.75%	8.00%	8.25%	8.50%	8.75%	9.00%	9.25%	9.50%	9.75%	10.00%	10.25%	10.50%	10.75%
125	3.94	4.16	4.38	4.60	4.81	5.03	5.25	5.47	5.68	5.90	6.12	6.33	6.55	6.76	6.98	7.20
124	4.05	4.27	4.49	4.71	4.93	5.14	5.36	5.58	5.80	6.02	6.23	6.45	6.67	6.88	7.10	7.32
123	4.16	4.38	4.60	4.82	5.04	5.26	5.48	5.70	5.91	6.13	6.35	6.57	6.79	7.01	7.22	7.44
122	4.27	4.49	4.71	4.93	5.15	5.37	5.59	5.81	6.03	6.25	6.47	6.69	6.91	7.13	7.35	7.57
121	4.38	4.60	4.82	5.04	5.27	5.49	5.71	5.93	6.15	6.37	6.59	6.81	7.03	7.25	7.48	7.70
120	4.49	4.71	4.94	5.16	5.38	5.60	5.83	6.05	6.27	6.49	6.72	6.94	7.16	7.38	7.60	7.82
119	4.60	4.83	5.05	5.28	5.50	5.72	5.95	6.17	6.39	6.62	6.84	7.06	7.29	7.51	7.73	7.95
118	4.72	4.94	5.17	5.39	5.62	5.84	6.07	6.29	6.52	6.74	6.97	7.19	7.41	7.64	7.86	8.09
117	4.83	5.06	5.28	5.51	5.74	5.96	6.19	6.42	6.64	6.87	7.09	7.32	7.54	7.77	7.99	8.22
116	4.95	5.17	5.40	5.63	5.86	6.09	6.31	6.54	6.77	6.99	7.22	7.45	7.67	7.90	8.13	8.35
115	5.06	5.29	5.52	5.75	5.98	6.21	6.44	6.67	6.89	7.12	7.35	7.58	7.81	8.03	8.26	8.49
114	5.18	5.41	5.64	5.87	6.10	6.33	6.56	6.79	7.02	7.25	7.48	7.71	7.94	8.17	8.40	8.63
113	5.30	5.53	5.77	6.00	6.23	6.46	6.69	6.92	7.15	7.38	7.61	7.84	8.08	8.31	8.54	8.77
112	5.42	5.66	5.89	6.12	6.35	6.59	6.82	7.05	7.28	7.52	7.75	7.98	8.21	8.44	8.68	8.91
111	5.55	5.78	6.01	6.25	6.48	6.72	6.95	7.18	7.42	7.65	7.88	8.12	8.35	8.58	8.82	9.05
110	5.67	5.91	6.14	6.38	6.61	6.85	7.08	7.32	7.55	7.79	8.02	8.26	8.49	8.73	8.96	9.19
109	5.80	6.03	6.27	6.51	6.74	6.98	7.22	7.45	7.69	7.92	8.16	8.40	8.63	8.87	9.10	9.34
108	5.92	6.16	6.40	6.64	6.88	7.11	7.35	7.59	7.83	8.06	8.30	8.54	8.78	9.01	9.25	9.49
107	6.05	6.29	6.53	6.77	7.01	7.25	7.49	7.73	7.97	8.21	8.44	8.68	8.92	9.16	9.40	9.64
106	6.18	6.42	6.66	6.90	7.14	7.39	7.63	7.87	8.11	8.35	8.59	8.83	9.07	9.31	9.55	9.79
105	6.31	6.56	6.80	7.04	7.28	7.52	7.77	8.01	8.25	8.49	8.73	8.98	9.22	9.46	9.70	9.94
104	6.45	6.69	6.93	7.18	7.42	7.66	7.91	8.15	8.40	8.64	8.88	9.13	9.37	9.61	9.86	10.10
103	6.58	6.83	7.07	7.32	7.56	7.81	8.05	8.30	8.54	8.79	9.03	9.28	9.52	9.77	10.01	10.26
102	6.72	6.96	7.21	7.46	7.70	7.95	8.20	8.44	8.69	8.94	9.18	9.43	9.68	9.92	10.17	10.42
101	6.86	7.10	7.35	7.60	7.85	8.10	8.35	8.59	8.84	9.09	9.34	9.59	9.84	10.08	10.33	10.58
100	7.00	7.25	7.50	7.75	8.00	8.25	8.50	8.75	9.00	9.25	9.50	9.75	10.00	10.25	10.50	10.75
99	7.14	7.39	7.64	7.89	8.14	8.39	8.65	8.90	9.15	9.40	9.65	9.90	10.16	10.41	10.66	10.91
98	7.28	7.53	7.79	8.04	8.29	8.55	8.80	9.05	9.31	9.56	9.81	10.07	10.32	10.57	10.83	11.08
97	7.43	7.68	7.94	8.19	8.45	8.70	8.96	9.21	9.47	9.72	9.98	10.23	10.49	10.74	11.00	11.25
96	7.57	7.83	8.09	8.34	8.60	8.86	9.11	9.37	9.63	9.88	10.14	10.40	10.66	10.91	11.17	11.43
95	7.72	7.98	8.24	8.50	8.76	9.01	9.27	9.53	9.79	10.05	10.31	10.57	10.83	11.08	11.34	11.60
94	7.87	8.13	8.39	8.65	8.91	9.17	9.44	9.70	9.96	10.22	10.48	10.74	11.00	11.26	11.52	11.78
93	8.03	8.29	8.55	8.81	9.08	9.34	9.60	9.86	10.12	10.39	10.65	10.91	11.18	11.44	11.70	11.96
92	8.18	8.45	8.71	8.97	9.24	9.50	9.77	10.03	10.30	10.56	10.82	11.09	11.35	11.62	11.88	12.15
91	8.34	8.61	8.87	9.14	9.40	9.67	9.94	10.20	10.47	10.74	11.00	11.27	11.54	11.80	12.07	12.34
90	8.50	8.77	9.04	9.30	9.57	9.84	10.11	10.38	10.64	10.91	11.18	11.45	11.72	11.99	12.26	12.53
89	8.66	8.93	9.20	9.47	9.74	10.01	10.28	10.55	10.82	11.09	11.36	11.64	11.91	12.18	12.45	12.72
88	8.83	9.10	9.37	9.64	9.91	10.19	10.46	10.73	11.00	11.28	11.55	11.82	12.10	12.37	12.64	12.92
87	8.99	9.27	9.54	9.82	10.09	10.36	10.64	10.91	11.19	11.46	11.74	12.01	12.29	12.56	12.84	13.12
86	9.16	9.44	9.72	9.99	10.27	10.54	10.82	11.10	11.38	11.65	11.93	12.21	12.48	12.76	13.04	13.32
85	9.34	9.61	9.89	10.17	10.45	10.73	11.01	11.29	11.57	11.84	12.12	12.40	12.68	12.96	13.24	13.53
84	9.51	9.79	10.07	10.35	10.63	10.91	11.20	11.48	11.76	12.04	12.32	12.60	12.89	13.17	13.45	13.74
83	9.69	9.97	10.25	10.54	10.82	11.10	11.39	11.67	11.95	12.24	12.52	12.81	13.09	13.38	13.66	13.95
82	9.87	10.15	10.44	10.72	11.01	11.30	11.58	11.87	12.15	12.44	12.73	13.01	13.30	13.59	13.88	14.17
81	10.05	10.34	10.63	10.91	11.20	11.49	11.78	12.07	12.36	12.65	12.94	13.23	13.52	13.81	14.10	14.39
80	10.24	10.53	10.82	11.11	11.40	11.69	11.98	12.27	12.56	12.86	13.15	13.44	13.73	14.03	14.32	14.61
79	10.43	10.72	11.01	11.30	11.60	11.89	12.19	12.48	12.77	13.07	13.36	13.66	13.95	14.25	14.54	14.84
78	10.62	10.91	11.21	11.51	11.80	12.10	12.39	12.69	12.99	13.28	13.58	13.88	14.18	14.48	14.78	15.07
77	10.82	11.11	11.41	11.71	12.01	12.31	12.61	12.90	13.20	13.50	13.81	14.11	14.41	14.71	15.01	15.31
76	11.01	11.32	11.62	11.92	12.22	12.52	12.82	13.12	13.43	13.73	14.03	14.34	14.64	14.94	15.25	15.55
75	11.22	11.52	11.82	12.13	12.43	12.74	13.04	13.35	13.65	13.96	14.26	14.57	14.88	15.19	15.49	15.80
74	11.42	11.73	12.04	12.34	12.65	12.96	13.27	13.57	13.88	14.19	14.50	14.81	15.12	15.43	15.74	16.05
73	11.63	11.94	12.25	12.56	12.87	13.18	13.49	13.80	14.12	14.43	14.74	15.05	15.37	15.68	16.00	16.31
72	11.85	12.16	12.47	12.79	13.10	13.41	13.73	14.04	14.36	14.67	14.99	15.30	15.62	15.94	16.25	16.57
71	12.07	12.38	12.70	13.01	13.33	13.65	13.96	14.28	14.60	14.92	15.24	15.56	15.88	16.20	16.52	16.84
70	12.29	12.61	12.93	13.24	13.56	13.88	14.20	14.53	14.85	15.17	15.49	15.82	16.14	16.46	16.79	17.11
69	12.52	12.84	13.16	13.48	13.80	14.13	14.45	14.78	15.10	15.43	15.75	16.08	16.41	16.73	17.06	17.39
68	12.75	13.07	13.40	13.72	14.05	14.38	14.70	15.03	15.36	15.69	16.02	16.35	16.68	17.01	17.34	17.68
67	12.98	13.31	13.64	13.97	14.30	14.63	14.96	15.29	15.62	15.96	16.29	16.63	16.96	17.30	17.63	17.97
66	13.22	13.55	13.89	14.22	14.55	14.89	15.22	15.56	15.90	16.23	16.57	16.91	17.25	17.59	17.93	18.27
65	13.47	13.80	14.14	14.48	14.81	15.15	15.49	15.83	16.17	16.51	16.85	17.20	17.54	17.88	18.23	18.57
64	13.72	14.06	14.40	14.74	15.08	15.42	15.77	16.11	16.45	16.80	17.14	17.49	17.84	18.19	18.53	18.88
63	13.97	14.32	14.66	15.01	15.35	15.70	16.05	16.39	16.74	17.09	17.44	17.79	18.14	18.50	18.85	19.20
62	14.24	14.58	14.93	15.28	15.63	15.98	16.33	16.69	17.04	17.39	17.75	18.10	18.46	18.82	19.17	19.53
60	14.78	15.13	15.49	15.85	16.21	16.57	16.93	17.29	17.65	18.01	18.38	18.74	19.11	19.48	19.84	20.21
55	16.25	16.63	17.01	17.39	17.78	18.16	18.55	18.94	19.33	19.72	20.11	20.50	20.89	21.29	21.68	22.08
50	17.92	18.33	18.74	19.16	19.57	19.99	20.41	20.83	21.25	21.67	22.09	22.52	22.94	23.37	23.80	24.23
45	19.85	20.30	20.75	21.20	21.66	22.11	22.57	23.03	23.49	23.95	24.42	24.88	25.35	25.82	26.30	26.77

Description: This table shows the price to pay for a bond at the yield rate. The yield is to maturity.

Example: The price of a 15.00 %, 10 year bond to yield 8 % to maturity is $ 147.57.

COUPON RATE, %

YIELD	11.00%	11.25%	11.50%	11.75%	12.00%	12.25%	12.50%	12.75%	13.00%	13.25%	13.50%	13.75%	14.00%	14.25%	14.50%	15.00%
0.00	210.00	212.50	215.00	217.50	220.00	222.50	225.00	227.50	230.00	232.50	235.00	237.50	240.00	242.50	245.00	250.00
1.00	194.94	197.31	199.68	202.06	204.43	206.80	209.18	211.55	213.92	216.30	218.67	221.04	223.42	225.79	228.17	232.91
2.00	181.20	183.46	185.72	187.97	190.23	192.48	194.74	196.99	199.25	201.51	203.76	206.02	208.27	210.53	212.78	217.30
3.00	168.67	170.82	172.97	175.11	177.26	179.40	181.55	183.70	185.84	187.99	190.14	192.28	194.43	196.57	198.72	203.01
4.00	157.23	159.27	161.32	163.36	165.41	167.45	169.49	171.54	173.58	175.63	177.67	179.71	181.76	183.80	185.85	189.93
4.25	154.53	156.55	158.57	160.58	162.60	164.62	166.64	168.66	170.68	172.70	174.72	176.74	178.76	180.78	182.80	186.84
4.50	151.88	153.88	155.87	157.87	159.86	161.86	163.85	165.85	167.85	169.84	171.84	173.83	175.83	177.82	179.82	183.81
4.75	149.30	151.27	153.24	155.21	157.18	159.16	161.13	163.10	165.07	167.04	169.01	170.99	172.96	174.93	176.90	180.85
5.00	146.77	148.72	150.66	152.61	154.56	156.51	158.46	160.41	162.36	164.31	166.25	168.20	170.15	172.10	174.05	177.95
5.25	144.29	146.22	148.15	150.07	152.00	153.92	155.85	157.77	159.70	161.63	163.55	165.48	167.40	169.33	171.26	175.11
5.50	141.87	143.78	145.68	147.59	149.49	151.39	153.30	155.20	157.10	159.01	160.91	162.81	164.72	166.62	168.52	172.33
5.75	139.51	141.39	143.27	145.15	147.03	148.92	150.80	152.68	154.56	156.44	158.32	160.20	162.08	163.97	165.85	169.61
6.00	137.19	139.05	140.91	142.77	144.63	146.49	148.35	150.21	152.07	153.93	155.79	157.65	159.51	161.37	163.23	166.95
6.25	134.93	136.77	138.61	140.44	142.28	144.12	145.96	147.80	149.64	151.47	153.31	155.15	156.99	158.83	160.67	164.34
6.50	132.71	134.53	136.35	138.17	139.98	141.80	143.62	145.44	147.25	149.07	150.89	152.71	154.52	156.34	158.16	161.79
6.75	130.55	132.34	134.14	135.94	137.73	139.53	141.33	143.12	144.92	146.72	148.51	150.31	152.11	153.90	155.70	159.29
7.00	128.42	130.20	131.98	133.75	135.53	137.31	139.08	140.86	142.64	144.41	146.19	147.97	149.74	151.52	153.30	156.85
7.25	126.35	128.11	129.86	131.62	133.38	135.13	136.89	138.65	140.40	142.16	143.92	145.67	147.43	149.19	150.94	154.46
7.50	124.32	126.06	127.79	129.53	131.27	133.00	134.74	136.48	138.21	139.95	141.69	143.43	145.16	146.90	148.64	152.11
7.75	122.33	124.05	125.77	127.48	129.20	130.92	132.64	134.36	136.07	137.79	139.51	141.23	142.94	144.66	146.38	149.81
8.00	120.39	122.08	123.78	125.48	127.18	128.88	130.58	132.28	133.98	135.67	137.37	139.07	140.77	142.47	144.17	147.57
8.25	118.48	120.16	121.84	123.52	125.20	126.88	128.56	130.24	131.92	133.60	135.28	136.96	138.64	140.32	142.00	145.36
8.50	116.62	118.28	119.94	121.60	123.27	124.93	126.59	128.25	129.91	131.57	133.24	134.90	136.56	138.22	139.88	143.21
8.75	114.79	116.44	118.08	119.72	121.37	123.01	124.66	126.30	127.94	129.59	131.23	132.87	134.52	136.16	137.81	141.09
9.00	113.01	114.63	116.26	117.89	119.51	121.14	122.76	124.39	126.02	127.64	129.27	130.89	132.52	134.15	135.77	139.02
9.25	111.26	112.87	114.48	116.09	117.69	119.30	120.91	122.52	124.13	125.74	127.34	128.95	130.56	132.17	133.78	137.00
9.50	109.55	111.14	112.73	114.32	115.91	117.50	119.10	120.69	122.28	123.87	125.46	127.05	128.64	130.24	131.83	135.01
9.75	107.87	109.45	111.02	112.60	114.17	115.74	117.32	118.89	120.47	122.04	123.62	125.19	126.77	128.34	129.91	133.06
10.00	106.23	107.79	109.35	110.90	112.46	114.02	115.58	117.14	118.69	120.25	121.81	123.37	124.92	126.48	128.04	131.16
10.25	104.62	106.17	107.71	109.25	110.79	112.33	113.87	115.41	116.96	118.50	120.04	121.58	123.12	124.66	126.20	129.29
10.50	103.05	104.58	106.10	107.63	109.15	110.68	112.20	113.73	115.25	116.78	118.30	119.83	121.35	122.88	124.40	127.46
10.75	101.51	103.02	104.53	106.04	107.55	109.06	110.57	112.08	113.58	115.09	116.60	118.11	119.62	121.13	122.64	125.66
11.00	100.00	101.49	102.99	104.48	105.98	107.47	108.96	110.46	111.95	113.44	114.94	116.43	117.93	119.42	120.91	123.90
11.25	98.52	100.00	101.48	102.96	104.44	105.91	107.39	108.87	110.35	111.83	113.31	114.78	116.26	117.74	119.22	122.18
11.50	97.07	98.54	100.00	101.46	102.93	104.39	105.85	107.32	108.78	110.24	111.71	113.17	114.63	116.10	117.56	120.49
11.75	95.65	97.10	98.55	100.00	101.45	102.90	104.35	105.79	107.24	108.69	110.14	111.59	113.04	114.48	115.93	118.83
12.00	94.27	95.70	97.13	98.57	100.00	101.43	102.87	104.30	105.73	107.17	108.60	110.04	111.47	112.90	114.34	117.20
12.25	92.90	94.32	95.74	97.16	98.58	100.00	101.42	102.84	104.26	105.68	107.10	108.52	109.94	111.35	112.77	115.61
12.50	91.57	92.97	94.38	95.78	97.19	98.59	100.00	101.41	102.81	104.22	105.62	107.03	108.43	109.84	111.24	114.05
12.75	90.26	91.65	93.04	94.44	95.83	97.22	98.61	100.00	101.39	102.78	104.17	105.56	106.96	108.35	109.74	112.52
13.00	88.98	90.36	91.74	93.11	94.49	95.87	97.25	98.62	100.00	101.38	102.75	104.13	105.51	106.89	108.26	111.02
13.25	87.73	89.09	90.45	91.82	93.18	94.55	95.91	97.27	98.64	100.00	101.36	102.73	104.09	105.45	106.82	109.55
13.50	86.50	87.85	89.20	90.55	91.90	93.25	94.60	95.95	97.30	98.65	100.00	101.35	102.70	104.05	105.40	108.10
13.75	85.29	86.63	87.97	89.30	90.64	91.98	93.31	94.65	95.99	97.33	98.66	100.00	101.34	102.67	104.01	106.69
14.00	84.11	85.43	86.76	88.08	89.41	90.73	92.05	93.38	94.70	96.03	97.35	98.68	100.00	101.32	102.65	105.30
14.25	82.95	84.26	85.57	86.89	88.20	89.51	90.82	92.13	93.44	94.75	96.07	97.38	98.69	100.00	101.31	103.93
14.50	81.82	83.11	84.41	85.71	87.01	88.31	89.61	90.91	92.21	93.51	94.80	96.10	97.40	98.70	100.00	102.60
14.75	80.70	81.99	83.28	84.56	85.85	87.13	88.42	89.71	90.99	92.28	93.57	94.85	96.14	97.43	98.71	101.29
15.00	79.61	80.89	82.16	83.43	84.71	85.98	87.26	88.53	89.81	91.08	92.35	93.63	94.90	96.18	97.45	100.00
15.25	78.54	79.80	81.07	82.33	83.59	84.85	86.11	87.38	88.64	89.90	91.16	92.43	93.69	94.95	96.21	98.74
15.50	77.49	78.74	79.99	81.24	82.49	83.74	84.99	86.25	87.50	88.75	90.00	91.25	92.50	93.75	95.00	97.50
15.75	76.46	77.70	78.94	80.18	81.42	82.66	83.90	85.13	86.37	87.61	88.85	90.09	91.33	92.57	93.81	96.28
16.00	75.45	76.68	77.91	79.14	80.36	81.59	82.82	84.05	85.27	86.50	87.73	88.95	90.18	91.41	92.64	95.09
16.25	74.47	75.68	76.90	78.11	79.33	80.55	81.76	82.98	84.19	85.41	86.62	87.84	89.06	90.27	91.49	93.92
16.50	73.50	74.70	75.90	77.11	78.31	79.52	80.72	81.93	83.13	84.34	85.54	86.75	87.95	89.16	90.36	92.77
16.75	72.54	73.74	74.93	76.12	77.32	78.51	79.71	80.90	82.09	83.29	84.48	85.67	86.87	88.06	89.26	91.64
17.00	71.61	72.79	73.98	75.16	76.34	77.52	78.71	79.89	81.07	82.26	83.44	84.62	85.80	86.99	88.17	90.54
17.25	70.69	71.87	73.04	74.21	75.38	76.56	77.73	78.90	80.07	81.24	82.42	83.59	84.76	85.93	87.11	89.45
17.50	69.80	70.96	72.12	73.28	74.44	75.60	76.77	77.93	79.09	80.25	81.41	82.57	83.74	84.90	86.06	88.38
17.75	68.91	70.07	71.22	72.37	73.52	74.67	75.82	76.97	78.13	79.28	80.43	81.58	82.73	83.88	85.03	87.34
18.00	68.05	69.19	70.33	71.47	72.61	73.76	74.90	76.04	77.18	78.32	79.46	80.60	81.74	82.88	84.03	86.31
18.25	67.20	68.33	69.46	70.59	71.73	72.86	73.99	75.12	76.25	77.38	78.51	79.64	80.77	81.90	83.04	85.30
18.50	66.37	67.49	68.61	69.73	70.85	71.97	73.10	74.22	75.34	76.46	77.58	78.70	79.82	80.94	82.06	84.31
18.75	65.55	66.66	67.77	68.89	70.00	71.11	72.22	73.33	74.44	75.55	76.66	77.78	78.89	80.00	81.11	83.33
19.00	64.75	65.85	66.95	68.06	69.16	70.26	71.36	72.46	73.56	74.66	75.77	76.87	77.97	79.07	80.17	82.38
20.00	61.69	62.75	63.82	64.88	65.95	67.01	68.07	69.14	70.20	71.27	72.33	73.40	74.46	75.52	76.59	78.72
25.00	49.31	50.22	51.12	52.03	52.93	53.84	54.74	55.65	56.55	57.46	58.36	59.27	60.17	61.08	61.98	63.79
30.00	40.54	41.32	42.10	42.88	43.67	44.45	45.23	46.01	46.80	47.58	48.36	49.14	49.93	50.71	51.49	53.06

Description: This table shows the yield to maturity of a bond purchased at the price shown in the index.

Example: The yield to maturity of a 15.00 %, 10 year bond at a price of 116.00 is 12.18 %.

COUPON RATE, %

PRICE	11.00%	11.25%	11.50%	11.75%	12.00%	12.25%	12.50%	12.75%	13.00%	13.25%	13.50%	13.75%	14.00%	14.25%	14.50%	15.00%
160	3.74	3.93	4.11	4.30	4.48	4.67	4.85	5.03	5.22	5.40	5.58	5.76	5.95	6.13	6.31	6.67
155	4.20	4.39	4.58	4.77	4.95	5.14	5.33	5.51	5.70	5.89	6.07	6.26	6.45	6.63	6.82	7.19
150	4.68	4.87	5.06	5.25	5.44	5.63	5.83	6.02	6.21	6.40	6.59	6.78	6.97	7.16	7.35	7.72
145	5.17	5.37	5.57	5.76	5.96	6.15	6.35	6.54	6.74	6.93	7.13	7.32	7.51	7.71	7.90	8.29
140	5.69	5.89	6.09	6.29	6.49	6.69	6.89	7.09	7.29	7.49	7.69	7.89	8.08	8.28	8.48	8.88
135	6.24	6.44	6.65	6.85	7.06	7.26	7.46	7.67	7.87	8.08	8.28	8.48	8.69	8.89	9.09	9.50
130	6.81	7.02	7.23	7.44	7.65	7.86	8.07	8.28	8.48	8.69	8.90	9.11	9.32	9.53	9.73	10.15
129	6.93	7.14	7.35	7.56	7.77	7.98	8.19	8.40	8.61	8.82	9.03	9.24	9.45	9.66	9.87	10.28
128	7.05	7.26	7.47	7.68	7.89	8.10	8.32	8.53	8.74	8.95	9.16	9.37	9.58	9.79	10.00	10.42
127	7.17	7.38	7.59	7.80	8.02	8.23	8.44	8.65	8.87	9.08	9.29	9.50	9.71	9.92	10.14	10.56
126	7.29	7.50	7.72	7.93	8.14	8.36	8.57	8.78	9.00	9.21	9.42	9.64	9.85	10.06	10.27	10.70
125	7.41	7.63	7.84	8.06	8.27	8.49	8.70	8.91	9.13	9.34	9.56	9.77	9.98	10.20	10.41	10.84
124	7.53	7.75	7.97	8.18	8.40	8.62	8.83	9.05	9.26	9.48	9.69	9.91	10.12	10.34	10.55	10.98
123	7.66	7.88	8.10	8.31	8.53	8.75	8.96	9.18	9.40	9.61	9.83	10.05	10.26	10.48	10.69	11.12
122	7.79	8.01	8.22	8.44	8.66	8.88	9.10	9.32	9.53	9.75	9.97	10.19	10.40	10.62	10.84	11.27
121	7.92	8.14	8.36	8.57	8.79	9.01	9.23	9.45	9.67	9.89	10.11	10.33	10.55	10.76	10.98	11.42
120	8.05	8.27	8.49	8.71	8.93	9.15	9.37	9.59	9.81	10.03	10.25	10.47	10.69	10.91	11.13	11.57
119	8.18	8.40	8.62	8.84	9.06	9.29	9.51	9.73	9.95	10.17	10.39	10.62	10.84	11.06	11.28	11.72
118	8.31	8.53	8.76	8.98	9.20	9.43	9.65	9.87	10.09	10.32	10.54	10.76	10.98	11.21	11.43	11.87
117	8.44	8.67	8.89	9.12	9.34	9.57	9.79	10.01	10.24	10.46	10.69	10.91	11.13	11.36	11.58	12.03
116	8.58	8.81	9.03	9.26	9.48	9.71	9.93	10.16	10.38	10.61	10.84	11.06	11.28	11.51	11.73	12.18
115	8.72	8.94	9.17	9.40	9.63	9.85	10.08	10.31	10.53	10.76	10.99	11.21	11.44	11.66	11.89	12.34
114	8.86	9.08	9.31	9.54	9.77	10.00	10.23	10.45	10.68	10.91	11.14	11.37	11.59	11.82	12.05	12.50
113	9.00	9.23	9.46	9.69	9.92	10.15	10.37	10.60	10.83	11.06	11.29	11.52	11.75	11.98	12.21	12.67
112	9.14	9.37	9.60	9.83	10.06	10.29	10.53	10.76	10.99	11.22	11.45	11.68	11.91	12.14	12.37	12.83
111	9.28	9.52	9.75	9.98	10.21	10.45	10.68	10.91	11.14	11.37	11.61	11.84	12.07	12.30	12.53	13.00
110	9.43	9.66	9.90	10.13	10.36	10.60	10.83	11.07	11.30	11.53	11.77	12.00	12.23	12.47	12.70	13.17
109	9.58	9.81	10.05	10.28	10.52	10.75	10.99	11.22	11.46	11.69	11.93	12.16	12.40	12.63	12.87	13.34
108	9.73	9.96	10.20	10.44	10.67	10.91	11.15	11.38	11.62	11.86	12.09	12.33	12.57	12.80	13.04	13.51
107	9.88	10.12	10.35	10.59	10.83	11.07	11.31	11.55	11.78	12.02	12.26	12.50	12.74	12.98	13.21	13.69
106	10.03	10.27	10.51	10.75	10.99	11.23	11.47	11.71	11.95	12.19	12.43	12.67	12.91	13.15	13.39	13.87
105	10.19	10.43	10.67	10.91	11.15	11.39	11.64	11.88	12.12	12.36	12.60	12.84	13.08	13.33	13.57	14.05
104	10.34	10.59	10.83	11.07	11.32	11.56	11.80	12.05	12.29	12.53	12.78	13.02	13.26	13.50	13.75	14.23
103	10.50	10.75	10.99	11.24	11.48	11.73	11.97	12.22	12.46	12.71	12.95	13.20	13.44	13.69	13.93	14.42
102	10.66	10.91	11.16	11.40	11.65	11.90	12.14	12.39	12.64	12.88	13.13	13.38	13.62	13.87	14.12	14.61
101	10.83	11.08	11.33	11.57	11.82	12.07	12.32	12.57	12.81	13.06	13.31	13.56	13.81	14.06	14.30	14.80
100	11.00	11.25	11.50	11.75	12.00	12.25	12.50	12.75	13.00	13.25	13.50	13.75	14.00	14.25	14.50	15.00
99	11.16	11.42	11.67	11.92	12.17	12.42	12.67	12.93	13.18	13.43	13.68	13.93	14.19	14.44	14.69	15.19
98	11.33	11.59	11.84	12.10	12.35	12.60	12.86	13.11	13.36	13.62	13.87	14.12	14.38	14.63	14.89	15.39
97	11.51	11.76	12.02	12.27	12.53	12.79	13.04	13.30	13.55	13.81	14.06	14.32	14.57	14.83	15.09	15.60
96	11.68	11.94	12.20	12.46	12.71	12.97	13.23	13.49	13.74	14.00	14.26	14.52	14.77	15.03	15.29	15.80
95	11.86	12.12	12.38	12.64	12.90	13.16	13.42	13.68	13.94	14.20	14.46	14.72	14.98	15.23	15.49	16.01
94	12.04	12.30	12.57	12.83	13.09	13.35	13.61	13.87	14.13	14.40	14.66	14.92	15.18	15.44	15.70	16.23
93	12.23	12.49	12.75	13.02	13.28	13.54	13.81	14.07	14.33	14.60	14.86	15.13	15.39	15.65	15.92	16.44
92	12.41	12.68	12.94	13.21	13.47	13.74	14.01	14.27	14.54	14.80	15.07	15.33	15.60	15.87	16.13	16.67
91	12.60	12.87	13.14	13.41	13.67	13.94	14.21	14.48	14.74	15.01	15.28	15.55	15.82	16.08	16.35	16.89
90	12.80	13.07	13.33	13.60	13.87	14.14	14.41	14.68	14.95	15.22	15.49	15.76	16.04	16.31	16.58	17.12
89	12.99	13.26	13.53	13.81	14.08	14.35	14.62	14.89	15.17	15.44	15.71	15.98	16.26	16.53	16.80	17.35
88	13.19	13.46	13.74	14.01	14.29	14.56	14.83	15.11	15.38	15.66	15.93	16.21	16.48	16.76	17.03	17.59
87	13.39	13.67	13.94	14.22	14.50	14.77	15.05	15.33	15.60	15.88	16.16	16.44	16.71	16.99	17.27	17.83
86	13.60	13.88	14.15	14.43	14.71	14.99	15.27	15.55	15.83	16.11	16.39	16.67	16.95	17.23	17.51	18.07
85	13.81	14.09	14.37	14.65	14.93	15.21	15.49	15.78	16.06	16.34	16.62	16.90	17.19	17.47	17.75	18.32
84	14.02	14.30	14.59	14.87	15.15	15.44	15.72	16.01	16.29	16.57	16.86	17.14	17.43	17.72	18.00	18.57
83	14.23	14.52	14.81	15.09	15.38	15.67	15.95	16.24	16.53	16.81	17.10	17.39	17.68	17.97	18.25	18.83
82	14.45	14.74	15.03	15.32	15.61	15.90	16.19	16.48	16.77	17.06	17.35	17.64	17.93	18.22	18.51	19.09
81	14.68	14.97	15.26	15.55	15.84	16.14	16.43	16.72	17.01	17.31	17.60	17.89	18.19	18.48	18.77	19.36
80	14.91	15.20	15.49	15.79	16.08	16.38	16.67	16.97	17.26	17.56	17.86	18.15	18.45	18.74	19.04	19.64
79	15.14	15.43	15.73	16.03	16.33	16.62	16.92	17.22	17.52	17.82	18.12	18.42	18.71	19.01	19.31	19.91
78	15.37	15.67	15.97	16.27	16.57	16.87	17.18	17.48	17.78	18.08	18.38	18.68	18.99	19.29	19.59	20.20
77	15.61	15.92	16.22	16.52	16.83	17.13	17.43	17.74	18.04	18.35	18.65	18.96	19.26	19.57	19.88	20.49
76	15.86	16.16	16.47	16.78	17.08	17.39	17.70	18.01	18.31	18.62	18.93	19.24	19.55	19.86	20.17	20.79
75	16.11	16.42	16.73	17.04	17.35	17.66	17.97	18.28	18.59	18.90	19.21	19.52	19.84	20.15	20.46	21.09
74	16.36	16.68	16.99	17.30	17.61	17.93	18.24	18.56	18.87	19.18	19.50	19.82	20.13	20.45	20.76	21.40
73	16.62	16.94	17.26	17.57	17.89	18.20	18.52	18.84	19.16	19.48	19.79	20.11	20.43	20.75	21.07	21.71
72	16.89	17.21	17.53	17.85	18.17	18.49	18.81	19.13	19.45	19.77	20.10	20.42	20.74	21.06	21.39	22.04
71	17.16	17.48	17.81	18.13	18.45	18.78	19.10	19.43	19.75	20.08	20.40	20.73	21.06	21.38	21.71	22.37
70	17.44	17.76	18.09	18.42	18.74	19.07	19.40	19.73	20.06	20.39	20.72	21.05	21.38	21.71	22.04	22.71
65	18.92	19.26	19.61	19.96	20.30	20.65	21.00	21.35	21.70	22.05	22.40	22.75	23.11	23.46	23.81	24.52

Description: This table shows the price to pay for a bond at the yield rate. The yield is to maturity.

Example: The price of a 6.75 %, 11 year bond to yield 8 % to maturity is $ 90.97.

COUPON RATE, %

YIELD	0.00%	1.00%	2.00%	3.00%	4.00%	4.25%	4.50%	4.75%	5.00%	5.25%	5.50%	5.75%	6.00%	6.25%	6.50%	6.75%
0.00	100.00	111.00	122.00	133.00	144.00	146.75	149.50	152.25	155.00	157.75	160.50	163.25	166.00	168.75	171.50	174.25
1.00	89.61	100.00	110.39	120.78	131.18	133.77	136.37	138.97	141.57	144.17	146.76	149.36	151.96	154.56	157.16	159.75
2.00	80.34	90.17	100.00	109.83	119.66	122.12	124.58	127.03	129.49	131.95	134.41	136.86	139.32	141.78	144.24	146.69
3.00	72.07	81.38	90.69	100.00	109.31	111.64	113.97	116.29	118.62	120.95	123.28	125.60	127.93	130.26	132.59	134.91
4.00	64.68	73.51	82.34	91.17	100.00	102.21	104.41	106.62	108.83	111.04	113.24	115.45	117.66	119.87	122.07	124.28
4.25	62.96	71.68	80.39	89.11	97.82	100.00	102.18	104.36	106.54	108.71	110.89	113.07	115.25	117.43	119.61	121.79
4.50	61.29	69.89	78.50	87.10	95.70	97.85	100.00	102.15	104.30	106.45	108.60	110.75	112.90	115.05	117.20	119.35
4.75	59.67	68.16	76.65	85.14	93.63	95.75	97.88	100.00	102.12	104.25	106.37	108.49	110.61	112.74	114.86	116.98
5.00	58.09	66.47	74.85	83.23	91.62	93.71	95.81	97.90	100.00	102.10	104.19	106.29	108.38	110.48	112.57	114.67
5.25	56.55	64.83	73.10	81.38	89.65	91.72	93.79	95.86	97.93	100.00	102.07	104.14	106.21	108.28	110.35	112.41
5.50	55.06	63.23	71.40	79.57	87.74	89.79	91.83	93.87	95.91	97.96	100.00	102.04	104.09	106.13	108.17	110.21
5.75	53.60	61.67	69.74	77.81	85.88	87.90	89.91	91.93	93.95	95.97	97.98	100.00	102.02	104.03	106.05	108.07
6.00	52.19	60.16	68.13	76.09	84.06	86.06	88.05	90.04	92.03	94.02	96.02	98.01	100.00	101.99	103.98	105.98
6.25	50.82	58.68	66.55	74.42	82.29	84.26	86.23	88.20	90.16	92.13	94.10	96.07	98.03	100.00	101.97	103.93
6.50	49.48	57.25	65.02	72.80	80.57	82.51	84.45	86.40	88.34	90.28	92.23	94.17	96.11	98.06	100.00	101.94
6.75	48.18	55.86	63.53	71.21	78.89	80.81	82.73	84.65	86.56	88.48	90.40	92.32	94.24	96.16	98.08	100.00
7.00	46.92	54.50	62.08	69.67	77.25	79.15	81.04	82.94	84.83	86.73	88.62	90.52	92.42	94.31	96.21	98.10
7.25	45.69	53.18	60.67	68.16	75.65	77.53	79.40	81.27	83.14	85.02	86.89	88.76	90.64	92.51	94.38	96.25
7.50	44.49	51.89	59.29	66.69	74.10	75.95	77.80	79.65	81.50	83.35	85.20	87.05	88.90	90.75	92.60	94.45
7.75	43.33	50.64	57.95	65.26	72.58	74.41	76.23	78.06	79.89	81.72	83.55	85.37	87.20	89.03	90.86	92.69
8.00	42.20	49.42	56.65	63.87	71.10	72.90	74.71	76.52	78.32	80.13	81.94	83.74	85.55	87.36	89.16	90.97
8.25	41.10	48.24	55.38	62.52	69.66	71.44	73.23	75.01	76.80	78.58	80.37	82.15	83.94	85.72	87.51	89.29
8.50	40.02	47.08	54.14	61.19	68.25	70.01	71.78	73.54	75.30	77.07	78.83	80.60	82.36	84.12	85.89	87.65
8.75	38.98	45.96	52.93	59.90	66.88	68.62	70.36	72.11	73.85	75.59	77.34	79.08	80.82	82.57	84.31	86.05
9.00	37.97	44.86	51.75	58.65	65.54	67.26	68.99	70.71	72.43	74.15	75.88	77.60	79.32	81.05	82.77	84.49
9.25	36.98	43.80	50.61	57.42	64.23	65.94	67.64	69.34	71.05	72.75	74.45	76.16	77.86	79.56	81.27	82.97
9.50	36.03	42.76	49.49	56.23	62.96	64.65	66.33	68.01	69.70	71.38	73.06	74.75	76.43	78.11	79.80	81.48
9.75	35.09	41.75	48.41	55.06	61.72	63.39	65.05	66.71	68.38	70.04	71.71	73.37	75.04	76.70	78.36	80.03
10.00	34.18	40.77	47.35	53.93	60.51	62.16	63.80	65.45	67.09	68.74	70.38	72.03	73.67	75.32	76.96	78.61
10.25	33.30	39.81	46.32	52.82	59.33	60.96	62.58	64.21	65.84	67.46	69.09	70.72	72.34	73.97	75.60	77.23
10.50	32.44	38.88	45.31	51.74	58.18	59.79	61.40	63.00	64.61	66.22	67.83	69.44	71.05	72.66	74.26	75.87
10.75	31.61	37.97	44.33	50.69	57.06	58.65	60.24	61.83	63.42	65.01	66.60	68.19	69.78	71.37	72.96	74.55
11.00	30.79	37.08	43.38	49.67	55.96	57.53	59.10	60.68	62.25	63.82	65.40	66.97	68.54	70.11	71.69	73.26
11.25	30.00	36.22	42.45	48.67	54.89	56.44	58.00	59.56	61.11	62.67	64.22	65.78	67.33	68.89	70.44	72.00
11.50	29.23	35.38	41.54	47.69	53.85	55.38	56.92	58.46	60.00	61.54	63.08	64.62	66.15	67.69	69.23	70.77
11.75	28.48	34.57	40.65	46.74	52.83	54.35	55.87	57.39	58.91	60.44	61.96	63.48	65.00	66.52	68.04	69.57
12.00	27.75	33.77	39.79	45.81	51.83	53.34	54.84	56.35	57.85	59.36	60.86	62.37	63.88	65.38	66.89	68.39
12.25	27.04	33.00	38.95	44.91	50.86	52.35	53.84	55.33	56.82	58.31	59.80	61.29	62.78	64.26	65.75	67.24
12.50	26.35	32.24	38.13	44.03	49.92	51.39	52.86	54.34	55.81	57.28	58.76	60.23	61.70	63.17	64.65	66.12
12.75	25.68	31.51	37.33	43.16	48.99	50.45	51.91	53.37	54.82	56.28	57.74	59.19	60.65	62.11	63.57	65.02
13.00	25.02	30.79	36.56	42.32	48.09	49.53	50.98	52.42	53.86	55.30	56.74	58.18	59.63	61.07	62.51	63.95
13.25	24.38	30.09	35.80	41.50	47.21	48.64	50.06	51.49	52.92	54.34	55.77	57.20	58.63	60.05	61.48	62.91
13.50	23.76	29.41	35.06	40.70	46.35	47.76	49.18	50.59	52.00	53.41	54.82	56.23	57.65	59.06	60.47	61.88
13.75	23.16	28.75	34.34	39.92	45.51	46.91	48.31	49.70	51.10	52.50	53.90	55.29	56.69	58.09	59.48	60.88
14.00	22.57	28.10	33.63	39.16	44.69	46.08	47.46	48.84	50.22	51.61	52.99	54.37	55.76	57.14	58.52	59.90
14.25	22.00	27.47	32.95	38.42	43.89	45.26	46.63	48.00	49.37	50.74	52.10	53.47	54.84	56.21	57.58	58.95
14.50	21.44	26.86	32.28	37.70	43.11	44.47	45.82	47.18	48.53	49.89	51.24	52.59	53.95	55.30	56.66	58.01
14.75	20.90	26.26	31.62	36.99	42.35	43.69	45.03	46.37	47.71	49.05	50.39	51.74	53.08	54.42	55.76	57.10
15.00	20.37	25.68	30.99	36.30	41.61	42.93	44.26	45.59	46.91	48.24	49.57	50.90	52.22	53.55	54.88	56.20
15.25	19.86	25.11	30.37	35.62	40.88	42.19	43.51	44.82	46.13	47.45	48.76	50.07	51.39	52.70	54.02	55.33
15.50	19.36	24.56	29.76	34.96	40.17	41.47	42.77	44.07	45.37	46.67	47.97	49.27	50.57	51.87	53.17	54.48
15.75	18.87	24.02	29.17	34.32	39.47	40.76	42.05	43.34	44.62	45.91	47.20	48.49	49.78	51.06	52.35	53.64
16.00	18.39	23.49	28.59	33.70	38.80	40.07	41.35	42.62	43.90	45.17	46.45	47.72	49.00	50.27	51.55	52.82
16.25	17.93	22.98	28.03	33.08	38.13	39.40	40.66	41.92	43.18	44.45	45.71	46.97	48.23	49.50	50.76	52.02
16.50	17.48	22.48	27.48	32.49	37.49	38.74	39.99	41.24	42.49	43.74	44.99	46.24	47.49	48.74	49.99	51.24
16.75	17.04	22.00	26.95	31.90	36.85	38.09	39.33	40.57	41.81	43.04	44.28	45.52	46.76	48.00	49.24	50.47
17.00	16.62	21.52	26.43	31.33	36.24	37.46	38.69	39.92	41.14	42.37	43.59	44.82	46.05	47.27	48.50	49.72
17.25	16.20	21.06	25.92	30.77	35.63	36.85	38.06	39.28	40.49	41.71	42.92	44.13	45.35	46.56	47.78	48.99
17.50	15.80	20.61	25.42	30.23	35.04	36.25	37.45	38.65	39.85	41.06	42.26	43.46	44.67	45.87	47.07	48.27
17.75	15.40	20.17	24.93	29.70	34.47	35.66	36.85	38.04	39.23	40.42	41.62	42.81	44.00	45.19	46.38	47.57
18.00	15.02	19.74	24.46	29.18	33.90	35.08	36.26	37.44	38.62	39.80	40.98	42.17	43.35	44.53	45.71	46.89
18.25	14.64	19.32	24.00	28.68	33.35	34.52	35.69	36.86	38.03	39.20	40.37	41.54	42.71	43.88	45.04	46.21
18.50	14.28	18.91	23.55	28.18	32.81	33.97	35.13	36.29	37.45	38.61	39.76	40.92	42.08	43.24	44.40	45.56
18.75	13.93	18.52	23.11	27.70	32.29	33.44	34.58	35.73	36.88	38.03	39.17	40.32	41.47	42.62	43.76	44.91
19.00	13.58	18.13	22.68	27.22	31.77	32.91	34.05	35.18	36.32	37.46	38.60	39.73	40.87	42.01	43.14	44.28
20.00	12.28	16.67	21.06	25.44	29.83	30.92	32.02	33.12	34.21	35.31	36.41	37.50	38.60	39.70	40.79	41.89
25.00	7.49	11.19	14.89	18.59	22.29	23.22	24.14	25.07	25.99	26.92	27.84	28.77	29.69	30.62	31.54	32.47
30.00	4.62	7.80	10.98	14.16	17.34	18.13	18.93	19.72	20.52	21.31	22.11	22.90	23.70	24.49	25.29	26.08

Description: This table shows the yield to maturity of a bond purchased at the price shown in the index.

Example: The yield to maturity of a 6.75 %, 11 year bond at a price of 80.00 is 9.75 %.

PRICE	0.00%	1.00%	2.00%	3.00%	4.00%	4.25%	4.50%	4.75%	5.00%	5.25%	5.50%	5.75%	6.00%	6.25%	6.50%	6.75%
100	0.00	1.00	2.00	3.00	4.00	4.25	4.50	4.75	5.00	5.25	5.50	5.75	6.00	6.25	6.50	6.75
99	.09	1.09	2.10	3.10	4.11	4.36	4.61	4.86	5.12	5.37	5.62	5.87	6.12	6.37	6.62	6.88
98	.18	1.19	2.20	3.21	4.22	4.48	4.73	4.98	5.24	5.49	5.74	6.00	6.25	6.50	6.76	7.01
97	.27	1.29	2.31	3.32	4.34	4.60	4.85	5.10	5.36	5.61	5.87	6.12	6.38	6.63	6.89	7.14
96	.37	1.39	2.41	3.43	4.46	4.72	4.97	5.23	5.48	5.74	6.00	6.25	6.51	6.77	7.02	7.28
95	.46	1.49	2.52	3.55	4.58	4.84	5.09	5.35	5.61	5.87	6.13	6.38	6.64	6.90	7.16	7.42
94	.56	1.59	2.63	3.66	4.70	4.96	5.22	5.48	5.74	6.00	6.26	6.52	6.78	7.04	7.30	7.56
93	.66	1.70	2.74	3.78	4.82	5.08	5.35	5.61	5.87	6.13	6.39	6.65	6.91	7.18	7.44	7.70
92	.75	1.80	2.85	3.90	4.95	5.21	5.47	5.74	6.00	6.26	6.53	6.79	7.05	7.32	7.58	7.84
91	.85	1.91	2.96	4.02	5.07	5.34	5.60	5.87	6.13	6.40	6.66	6.93	7.19	7.46	7.72	7.99
90	.96	2.01	3.07	4.14	5.20	5.47	5.73	6.00	6.27	6.53	6.80	7.07	7.34	7.60	7.87	8.14
89	1.06	2.12	3.19	4.26	5.33	5.60	5.87	6.14	6.40	6.67	6.94	7.21	7.48	7.75	8.02	8.29
88	1.16	2.23	3.31	4.38	5.46	5.73	6.00	6.27	6.54	6.81	7.08	7.36	7.63	7.90	8.17	8.44
87	1.27	2.34	3.42	4.51	5.59	5.87	6.14	6.41	6.68	6.96	7.23	7.50	7.78	8.05	8.32	8.60
86	1.37	2.46	3.54	4.63	5.73	6.00	6.28	6.55	6.83	7.10	7.38	7.65	7.93	8.20	8.48	8.75
85	1.48	2.57	3.66	4.76	5.87	6.14	6.42	6.69	6.97	7.25	7.52	7.80	8.08	8.36	8.63	8.91
84	1.59	2.69	3.79	4.89	6.00	6.28	6.56	6.84	7.12	7.40	7.68	7.96	8.23	8.51	8.79	9.08
83	1.70	2.80	3.91	5.03	6.14	6.42	6.71	6.99	7.27	7.55	7.83	8.11	8.39	8.67	8.96	9.24
82	1.81	2.92	4.04	5.16	6.29	6.57	6.85	7.13	7.42	7.70	7.98	8.27	8.55	8.84	9.12	9.41
81	1.92	3.04	4.17	5.30	6.43	6.72	7.00	7.29	7.57	7.86	8.14	8.43	8.72	9.00	9.29	9.58
80	2.03	3.16	4.30	5.44	6.58	6.87	7.15	7.44	7.73	8.02	8.30	8.59	8.88	9.17	9.46	9.75
79	2.15	3.29	4.43	5.58	6.73	7.02	7.31	7.60	7.89	8.18	8.47	8.76	9.05	9.34	9.63	9.93
78	2.27	3.41	4.56	5.72	6.88	7.17	7.46	7.75	8.05	8.34	8.63	8.93	9.22	9.51	9.81	10.10
77	2.39	3.54	4.70	5.86	7.03	7.33	7.62	7.92	8.21	8.51	8.80	9.10	9.39	9.69	9.99	10.29
76	2.51	3.67	4.83	6.01	7.19	7.49	7.78	8.08	8.38	8.68	8.97	9.27	9.57	9.87	10.17	10.47
75	2.63	3.80	4.97	6.16	7.35	7.65	7.95	8.25	8.55	8.85	9.15	9.45	9.75	10.05	10.36	10.66
74	2.75	3.93	5.12	6.31	7.51	7.81	8.11	8.42	8.72	9.02	9.33	9.63	9.93	10.24	10.55	10.85
73	2.88	4.06	5.26	6.46	7.67	7.98	8.28	8.59	8.89	9.20	9.51	9.81	10.12	10.43	10.74	11.05
72	3.00	4.20	5.41	6.62	7.84	8.15	8.46	8.76	9.07	9.38	9.69	10.00	10.31	10.62	10.93	11.25
71	3.13	4.34	5.55	6.78	8.01	8.32	8.63	8.94	9.25	9.57	9.88	10.19	10.50	10.82	11.13	11.45
70	3.26	4.48	5.71	6.94	8.18	8.50	8.81	9.12	9.44	9.75	10.07	10.38	10.70	11.02	11.34	11.65
69	3.40	4.62	5.86	7.10	8.36	8.68	8.99	9.31	9.63	9.94	10.26	10.58	10.90	11.22	11.54	11.86
68	3.53	4.77	6.01	7.27	8.54	8.86	9.18	9.50	9.82	10.14	10.46	10.78	11.11	11.43	11.75	12.08
67	3.67	4.92	6.17	7.44	8.72	9.04	9.37	9.69	10.01	10.34	10.66	10.99	11.32	11.64	11.97	12.30
66	3.81	5.07	6.33	7.62	8.91	9.23	9.56	9.89	10.21	10.54	10.87	11.20	11.53	11.86	12.19	12.52
65	3.95	5.22	6.50	7.79	9.10	9.43	9.75	10.08	10.42	10.75	11.08	11.41	11.75	12.08	12.41	12.75
64	4.09	5.37	6.67	7.97	9.29	9.62	9.95	10.29	10.62	10.96	11.29	11.63	11.97	12.31	12.64	12.98
63	4.24	5.53	6.84	8.15	9.49	9.82	10.16	10.50	10.83	11.17	11.51	11.85	12.19	12.54	12.88	13.22
62	4.39	5.69	7.01	8.34	9.69	10.03	10.37	10.71	11.05	11.39	11.74	12.08	12.42	12.77	13.12	13.47
61	4.54	5.86	7.19	8.53	9.89	10.24	10.58	10.92	11.27	11.62	11.96	12.31	12.66	13.01	13.36	13.72
60	4.69	6.02	7.37	8.73	10.10	10.45	10.80	11.15	11.49	11.85	12.20	12.55	12.90	13.26	13.61	13.97
59	4.85	6.19	7.55	8.92	10.32	10.67	11.02	11.37	11.73	12.08	12.44	12.79	13.15	13.51	13.87	14.23
58	5.01	6.36	7.74	9.13	10.53	10.89	11.25	11.60	11.96	12.32	12.68	13.04	13.40	13.77	14.13	14.50
57	5.17	6.54	7.93	9.33	10.76	11.12	11.48	11.84	12.20	12.56	12.93	13.30	13.66	14.03	14.40	14.77
56	5.34	6.72	8.12	9.54	10.99	11.35	11.71	12.08	12.45	12.82	13.19	13.56	13.93	14.30	14.68	15.05
55	5.50	6.90	8.32	9.76	11.22	11.59	11.96	12.33	12.70	13.07	13.45	13.82	14.20	14.58	14.96	15.34
54	5.68	7.09	8.52	9.98	11.46	11.83	12.21	12.58	12.96	13.34	13.72	14.10	14.48	14.86	15.25	15.64
53	5.85	7.28	8.73	10.20	11.70	12.08	12.46	12.84	13.22	13.61	13.99	14.38	14.77	15.16	15.55	15.94
52	6.03	7.47	8.94	10.44	11.95	12.34	12.72	13.11	13.49	13.88	14.27	14.67	15.06	15.46	15.85	16.25
51	6.21	7.67	9.16	10.67	12.21	12.60	12.99	13.38	13.77	14.17	14.57	14.96	15.36	15.76	16.17	16.57
50	6.40	7.88	9.38	10.91	12.47	12.87	13.26	13.66	14.06	14.46	14.86	15.27	15.67	16.08	16.49	16.90
49	6.59	8.08	9.61	11.16	12.74	13.14	13.55	13.95	14.35	14.76	15.17	15.58	15.99	16.41	16.82	17.24
48	6.78	8.30	9.84	11.42	13.02	13.43	13.83	14.24	14.66	15.07	15.49	15.90	16.32	16.74	17.17	17.59
47	6.98	8.51	10.08	11.68	13.31	13.72	14.13	14.55	14.97	15.39	15.81	16.24	16.66	17.09	17.52	17.95
46	7.18	8.74	10.32	11.94	13.60	14.02	14.44	14.86	15.29	15.72	16.15	16.58	17.01	17.45	17.89	18.33
45	7.39	8.96	10.57	12.22	13.90	14.33	14.76	15.19	15.62	16.05	16.49	16.93	17.37	17.82	18.26	18.71
44	7.60	9.20	10.83	12.50	14.21	14.64	15.08	15.52	15.96	16.40	16.85	17.29	17.74	18.20	18.65	19.11
43	7.82	9.44	11.10	12.79	14.53	14.97	15.42	15.86	16.31	16.76	17.21	17.67	18.13	18.59	19.05	19.52
42	8.04	9.68	11.37	13.09	14.86	15.31	15.76	16.22	16.67	17.13	17.60	18.06	18.53	19.00	19.47	19.95
41	8.27	9.94	11.65	13.40	15.20	15.66	16.12	16.58	17.05	17.52	17.99	18.46	18.94	19.42	19.90	20.39
40	8.50	10.19	11.93	13.72	15.55	16.02	16.49	16.96	17.44	17.92	18.40	18.88	19.37	19.86	20.35	20.85
39	8.74	10.46	12.23	14.05	15.92	16.39	16.87	17.35	17.84	18.33	18.82	19.31	19.81	20.31	20.82	21.32
35	9.77	11.61	13.51	15.48	17.51	18.03	18.55	19.08	19.61	20.15	20.69	21.23	21.78	22.33	22.88	23.44
30	11.25	13.28	15.40	17.60	19.90	20.49	21.09	21.69	22.30	22.91	23.53	24.15	24.79	25.42	26.07	26.71
25	13.00	15.30	17.71	20.26	22.94	23.64	24.34	25.05	25.77	26.50	27.23	27.98	28.74	29.50	30.27	31.06
20	15.17	17.84	20.70	23.77	27.06	27.92	28.79	29.68	30.58	31.50	32.43	33.38	34.33	35.31	36.29	37.29
15	18.01	21.28	24.89	28.87	33.27	34.43	35.63	36.85	38.09	39.36	40.66	41.98	43.32	44.69	46.08	47.50
10	22.06	26.50	31.68	37.74	44.78	46.69	48.66	50.69	52.76	54.89	57.06	59.27	61.52	63.80	66.11	68.45

Description: This table shows the price to pay for a bond at the yield rate. The yield is to maturity.

Example: The price of a 10.75 %, 11 year bond to yield 8 % to maturity is $ 119.87.

COUPON RATE, %

YIELD	7.00%	7.25%	7.50%	7.75%	8.00%	8.25%	8.50%	8.75%	9.00%	9.25%	9.50%	9.75%	10.00%	10.25%	10.50%	10.75%
0.00	177.00	179.75	182.50	185.25	188.00	190.75	193.50	196.25	199.00	201.75	204.50	207.25	210.00	212.75	215.50	218.25
1.00	162.35	164.95	167.55	170.15	172.74	175.34	177.94	180.54	183.14	185.73	188.33	190.93	193.53	196.13	198.72	201.32
2.00	149.15	151.61	154.07	156.52	158.98	161.44	163.90	166.35	168.81	171.27	173.73	176.18	178.64	181.10	183.56	186.01
3.00	137.24	139.57	141.90	144.22	146.55	148.88	151.21	153.53	155.86	158.19	160.52	162.85	165.17	167.50	169.83	172.16
4.00	126.49	128.69	130.90	133.11	135.32	137.52	139.73	141.94	144.15	146.35	148.56	150.77	152.97	155.18	157.39	159.60
4.25	123.96	126.14	128.32	130.50	132.68	134.86	137.04	139.21	141.39	143.57	145.75	147.93	150.11	152.29	154.46	156.64
4.50	121.50	123.65	125.81	127.96	130.11	132.26	134.41	136.56	138.71	140.86	143.01	145.16	147.31	149.46	151.61	153.76
4.75	119.11	121.23	123.35	125.47	127.60	129.72	131.84	133.96	136.09	138.21	140.33	142.46	144.58	146.70	148.82	150.95
5.00	116.77	118.86	120.96	123.05	125.15	127.24	129.34	131.44	133.53	135.63	137.72	139.82	141.91	144.01	146.10	148.20
5.25	114.48	116.55	118.62	120.69	122.76	124.83	126.90	128.97	131.04	133.10	135.17	137.24	139.31	141.38	143.45	145.52
5.50	112.26	114.30	116.34	118.39	120.43	122.47	124.52	126.56	128.60	130.64	132.69	134.73	136.77	138.82	140.86	142.90
5.75	110.09	112.10	114.12	116.14	118.16	120.17	122.19	124.21	126.22	128.24	130.26	132.28	134.29	136.31	138.33	140.35
6.00	107.97	109.96	111.95	113.94	115.94	117.93	119.92	121.91	123.91	125.90	127.89	129.88	131.87	133.87	135.86	137.85
6.25	105.90	107.87	109.84	111.80	113.77	115.74	117.71	119.67	121.64	123.61	125.58	127.54	129.51	131.48	133.45	135.41
6.50	103.89	105.83	107.77	109.72	111.66	113.60	115.55	117.49	119.43	121.37	123.32	125.26	127.20	129.15	131.09	133.03
6.75	101.92	103.84	105.76	107.68	109.60	111.52	113.44	115.35	117.27	119.19	121.11	123.03	124.95	126.87	128.79	130.71
7.00	100.00	101.90	103.79	105.69	107.58	109.48	111.38	113.27	115.17	117.06	118.96	120.85	122.75	124.65	126.54	128.44
7.25	98.13	100.00	101.87	103.75	105.62	107.49	109.36	111.24	113.11	114.98	116.86	118.73	120.60	122.47	124.35	126.22
7.50	96.30	98.15	100.00	101.85	103.70	105.55	107.40	109.25	111.10	112.95	114.80	116.65	118.50	120.35	122.20	124.05
7.75	94.52	96.34	98.17	100.00	101.83	103.66	105.48	107.31	109.14	110.97	112.80	114.63	116.45	118.28	120.11	121.94
8.00	92.77	94.58	96.39	98.19	100.00	101.81	103.61	105.42	107.23	109.03	110.84	112.64	114.45	116.26	118.06	119.87
8.25	91.08	92.86	94.65	96.43	98.22	100.00	101.78	103.57	105.35	107.14	108.92	110.71	112.49	114.28	116.06	117.85
8.50	89.42	91.18	92.94	94.71	96.47	98.24	100.00	101.76	103.53	105.29	107.06	108.82	110.58	112.35	114.11	115.88
8.75	87.80	89.54	91.28	93.03	94.77	96.51	98.26	100.00	101.74	103.49	105.23	106.97	108.72	110.46	112.20	113.95
9.00	86.22	87.94	89.66	91.38	93.11	94.83	96.55	98.28	100.00	101.72	103.45	105.17	106.89	108.62	110.34	112.06
9.25	84.67	86.38	88.08	89.78	91.48	93.19	94.89	96.59	98.30	100.00	101.70	103.41	105.11	106.81	108.52	110.22
9.50	83.16	84.85	86.53	88.22	89.90	91.58	93.27	94.95	96.63	98.32	100.00	101.68	103.37	105.05	106.73	108.42
9.75	81.69	83.36	85.02	86.69	88.35	90.01	91.68	93.34	95.01	96.67	98.34	100.00	101.66	103.33	104.99	106.66
10.00	80.26	81.90	83.55	85.19	86.84	88.48	90.13	91.77	93.42	95.06	96.71	98.35	100.00	101.65	103.29	104.94
10.25	78.85	80.48	82.11	83.73	85.36	86.99	88.61	90.24	91.87	93.49	95.12	96.75	98.37	100.00	101.63	103.25
10.50	77.48	79.09	80.70	82.31	83.91	85.52	87.13	88.74	90.35	91.96	93.57	95.17	96.78	98.39	100.00	101.61
10.75	76.14	77.73	79.32	80.91	82.50	84.09	85.69	87.28	88.87	90.46	92.05	93.64	95.23	96.82	98.41	100.00
11.00	74.83	76.41	77.98	79.55	81.13	82.70	84.27	85.84	87.42	88.99	90.56	92.14	93.71	95.28	96.85	98.43
11.25	73.56	75.11	76.67	78.22	79.78	81.33	82.89	84.44	86.00	87.56	89.11	90.67	92.22	93.78	95.33	96.89
11.50	72.31	73.85	75.38	76.92	78.46	80.00	81.54	83.08	84.62	86.15	87.69	89.23	90.77	92.31	93.85	95.38
11.75	71.09	72.61	74.13	75.65	77.17	78.70	80.22	81.74	83.26	84.78	86.30	87.83	89.35	90.87	92.39	93.91
12.00	69.90	71.40	72.91	74.41	75.92	77.42	78.93	80.43	81.94	83.44	84.95	86.45	87.96	89.46	90.97	92.47
12.25	68.73	70.22	71.71	73.20	74.69	76.18	77.67	79.15	80.64	82.13	83.62	85.11	86.60	88.09	89.58	91.07
12.50	67.59	69.07	70.54	72.01	73.49	74.96	76.43	77.90	79.38	80.85	82.32	83.80	85.27	86.74	88.22	89.69
12.75	66.48	67.94	69.40	70.85	72.31	73.77	75.23	76.68	78.14	79.60	81.05	82.51	83.97	85.43	86.88	88.34
13.00	65.39	66.84	68.28	69.72	71.16	72.60	74.05	75.49	76.93	78.37	79.81	81.26	82.70	84.14	85.58	87.02
13.25	64.33	65.76	67.19	68.61	70.04	71.47	72.89	74.32	75.75	77.17	78.60	80.03	81.45	82.88	84.31	85.73
13.50	63.29	64.71	66.12	67.53	68.94	70.35	71.76	73.18	74.59	76.00	77.41	78.82	80.23	81.65	83.06	84.47
13.75	62.28	63.68	65.07	66.47	67.87	69.26	70.66	72.06	73.46	74.85	76.25	77.65	79.04	80.44	81.84	83.23
14.00	61.29	62.67	64.05	65.43	66.82	68.20	69.58	70.96	72.35	73.73	75.11	76.49	77.88	79.26	80.64	82.03
14.25	60.32	61.68	63.05	64.42	65.79	67.16	68.53	69.89	71.26	72.63	74.00	75.37	76.74	78.10	79.47	80.84
14.50	59.37	60.72	62.08	63.43	64.78	66.14	67.49	68.85	70.20	71.56	72.91	74.27	75.62	76.97	78.33	79.68
14.75	58.44	59.78	61.12	62.46	63.80	65.14	66.48	67.82	69.16	70.50	71.85	73.19	74.53	75.87	77.21	78.55
15.00	57.53	58.86	60.19	61.51	62.84	64.17	65.49	66.82	68.15	69.48	70.80	72.13	73.46	74.78	76.11	77.44
15.25	56.64	57.96	59.27	60.59	61.90	63.21	64.53	65.84	67.15	68.47	69.78	71.10	72.41	73.72	75.04	76.35
15.50	55.78	57.08	58.38	59.68	60.98	62.28	63.58	64.88	66.18	67.48	68.78	70.08	71.38	72.69	73.99	75.29
15.75	54.93	56.21	57.50	58.79	60.08	61.37	62.65	63.94	65.23	66.52	67.81	69.09	70.38	71.67	72.96	74.24
16.00	54.10	55.37	56.65	57.92	59.20	60.47	61.75	63.02	64.30	65.57	66.85	68.12	69.40	70.67	71.95	73.22
16.25	53.28	54.55	55.81	57.07	58.33	59.60	60.86	62.12	63.38	64.65	65.91	67.17	68.44	69.70	70.96	72.22
16.50	52.49	53.74	54.99	56.24	57.49	58.74	59.99	61.24	62.49	63.74	64.99	66.24	67.49	68.74	69.99	71.24
16.75	51.71	52.95	54.19	55.43	56.66	57.90	59.14	60.38	61.62	62.86	64.09	65.33	66.57	67.81	69.05	70.28
17.00	50.95	52.18	53.40	54.63	55.86	57.08	58.31	59.53	60.76	61.99	63.21	64.44	65.67	66.89	68.12	69.34
17.25	50.21	51.42	52.64	53.85	55.06	56.28	57.49	58.71	59.92	61.14	62.35	63.57	64.78	65.99	67.21	68.42
17.50	49.48	50.68	51.88	53.09	54.29	55.49	56.70	57.90	59.10	60.30	61.51	62.71	63.91	65.12	66.32	67.52
17.75	48.76	49.96	51.15	52.34	53.53	54.72	55.91	57.11	58.30	59.49	60.68	61.87	63.06	64.25	65.45	66.64
18.00	48.07	49.25	50.43	51.61	52.79	53.97	55.15	56.33	57.51	58.69	59.87	61.05	62.23	63.41	64.59	65.77
18.25	47.38	48.55	49.72	50.89	52.06	53.23	54.40	55.57	56.74	57.91	59.08	60.25	61.41	62.58	63.75	64.92
18.50	46.71	47.87	49.03	50.19	51.35	52.51	53.66	54.82	55.98	57.14	58.30	59.46	60.62	61.77	62.93	64.09
18.75	46.06	47.21	48.36	49.50	50.65	51.80	52.95	54.09	55.24	56.39	57.54	58.68	59.83	60.98	62.13	63.27
19.00	45.42	46.56	47.69	48.83	49.97	51.10	52.24	53.38	54.52	55.65	56.79	57.93	59.06	60.20	61.34	62.48
20.00	42.98	44.08	45.18	46.27	47.37	48.47	49.56	50.66	51.76	52.85	53.95	55.05	56.14	57.24	58.34	59.43
25.00	33.39	34.32	35.24	36.17	37.10	38.02	38.95	39.87	40.80	41.72	42.65	43.57	44.50	45.42	46.35	47.27
30.00	26.88	27.67	28.47	29.26	30.05	30.85	31.64	32.44	33.23	34.03	34.82	35.62	36.41	37.21	38.00	38.80

Description: This table shows the yield to maturity of a bond purchased at the price shown in the index.

Example: The yield to maturity of a 10.75 %, 11 year bond at a price of 113.00 is 8.87 %.

PRICE	7.00%	7.25%	7.50%	7.75%	8.00%	8.25%	8.50%	8.75%	9.00%	9.25%	9.50%	9.75%	10.00%	10.25%	10.50%	10.75%
145	2.33	2.53	2.73	2.93	3.13	3.33	3.52	3.72	3.92	4.12	4.31	4.51	4.71	4.90	5.10	5.29
140	2.75	2.96	3.16	3.36	3.57	3.77	3.97	4.17	4.37	4.58	4.78	4.98	5.18	5.38	5.58	5.78
135	3.20	3.40	3.61	3.82	4.02	4.23	4.44	4.64	4.85	5.06	5.26	5.47	5.67	5.88	6.08	6.29
130	3.66	3.87	4.08	4.29	4.51	4.72	4.93	5.14	5.35	5.56	5.77	5.98	6.19	6.40	6.61	6.82
129	3.75	3.97	4.18	4.39	4.60	4.82	5.03	5.24	5.45	5.67	5.88	6.09	6.30	6.51	6.72	6.93
128	3.85	4.06	4.28	4.49	4.70	4.92	5.13	5.34	5.56	5.77	5.98	6.20	6.41	6.62	6.83	7.04
127	3.94	4.16	4.38	4.59	4.81	5.02	5.23	5.45	5.66	5.88	6.09	6.30	6.52	6.73	6.94	7.16
126	4.04	4.26	4.48	4.69	4.91	5.12	5.34	5.55	5.77	5.98	6.20	6.41	6.63	6.84	7.06	7.27
125	4.14	4.36	4.58	4.79	5.01	5.23	5.44	5.66	5.88	6.09	6.31	6.52	6.74	6.95	7.17	7.39
124	4.24	4.46	4.68	4.90	5.11	5.33	5.55	5.77	5.98	6.20	6.42	6.64	6.85	7.07	7.29	7.50
123	4.34	4.56	4.78	5.00	5.22	5.44	5.66	5.88	6.09	6.31	6.53	6.75	6.97	7.18	7.40	7.62
122	4.44	4.66	4.89	5.11	5.33	5.55	5.77	5.99	6.21	6.42	6.64	6.86	7.08	7.30	7.52	7.74
121	4.55	4.77	4.99	5.21	5.43	5.65	5.88	6.10	6.32	6.54	6.76	6.98	7.20	7.42	7.64	7.86
120	4.65	4.87	5.10	5.32	5.54	5.76	5.99	6.21	6.43	6.65	6.87	7.09	7.32	7.54	7.76	7.98
119	4.76	4.98	5.20	5.43	5.65	5.87	6.10	6.32	6.54	6.77	6.99	7.21	7.44	7.66	7.88	8.10
118	4.86	5.09	5.31	5.54	5.76	5.99	6.21	6.44	6.66	6.88	7.11	7.33	7.56	7.78	8.00	8.23
117	4.97	5.20	5.42	5.65	5.87	6.10	6.33	6.55	6.78	7.00	7.23	7.45	7.68	7.90	8.13	8.35
116	5.08	5.31	5.53	5.76	5.99	6.21	6.44	6.67	6.90	7.12	7.35	7.57	7.80	8.03	8.25	8.48
115	5.19	5.42	5.65	5.87	6.10	6.33	6.56	6.79	7.02	7.24	7.47	7.70	7.93	8.15	8.38	8.61
114	5.30	5.53	5.76	5.99	6.22	6.45	6.68	6.91	7.14	7.37	7.59	7.82	8.05	8.28	8.51	8.74
113	5.41	5.64	5.87	6.10	6.34	6.57	6.80	7.03	7.26	7.49	7.72	7.95	8.18	8.41	8.64	8.87
112	5.52	5.76	5.99	6.22	6.45	6.69	6.92	7.15	7.38	7.61	7.85	8.08	8.31	8.54	8.77	9.00
111	5.64	5.87	6.11	6.34	6.57	6.81	7.04	7.27	7.51	7.74	7.97	8.21	8.44	8.67	8.91	9.14
110	5.76	5.99	6.23	6.46	6.70	6.93	7.17	7.40	7.63	7.87	8.10	8.34	8.57	8.81	9.04	9.28
109	5.87	6.11	6.35	6.58	6.82	7.05	7.29	7.53	7.76	8.00	8.24	8.47	8.71	8.94	9.18	9.41
108	5.99	6.23	6.47	6.71	6.94	7.18	7.42	7.66	7.89	8.13	8.37	8.61	8.84	9.08	9.32	9.55
107	6.11	6.35	6.59	6.83	7.07	7.31	7.55	7.79	8.02	8.26	8.50	8.74	8.98	9.22	9.46	9.70
106	6.23	6.47	6.71	6.96	7.20	7.44	7.68	7.92	8.16	8.40	8.64	8.88	9.12	9.36	9.60	9.84
105	6.36	6.60	6.84	7.08	7.33	7.57	7.81	8.05	8.29	8.54	8.78	9.02	9.26	9.50	9.74	9.99
104	6.48	6.72	6.97	7.21	7.46	7.70	7.94	8.19	8.43	8.67	8.92	9.16	9.40	9.65	9.89	10.13
103	6.61	6.85	7.10	7.34	7.59	7.83	8.08	8.32	8.57	8.81	9.06	9.30	9.55	9.79	10.04	10.28
102	6.73	6.98	7.23	7.48	7.72	7.97	8.22	8.46	8.71	8.96	9.20	9.45	9.70	9.94	10.19	10.44
101	6.86	7.11	7.36	7.61	7.86	8.11	8.35	8.60	8.85	9.10	9.35	9.60	9.84	10.09	10.34	10.59
100	7.00	7.25	7.50	7.75	8.00	8.25	8.50	8.75	9.00	9.25	9.50	9.75	10.00	10.25	10.50	10.75
99	7.13	7.38	7.63	7.88	8.13	8.39	8.64	8.89	9.14	9.39	9.64	9.90	10.15	10.40	10.65	10.90
98	7.26	7.52	7.77	8.02	8.28	8.53	8.78	9.04	9.29	9.54	9.80	10.05	10.30	10.56	10.81	11.06
97	7.40	7.65	7.91	8.16	8.42	8.67	8.93	9.18	9.44	9.69	9.95	10.21	10.46	10.72	10.97	11.23
96	7.54	7.79	8.05	8.31	8.56	8.82	9.08	9.33	9.59	9.85	10.11	10.36	10.62	10.88	11.13	11.39
95	7.68	7.94	8.19	8.45	8.71	8.97	9.23	9.49	9.75	10.01	10.26	10.52	10.78	11.04	11.30	11.56
94	7.82	8.08	8.34	8.60	8.86	9.12	9.38	9.64	9.90	10.16	10.42	10.69	10.95	11.21	11.47	11.73
93	7.96	8.22	8.49	8.75	9.01	9.27	9.54	9.80	10.06	10.32	10.59	10.85	11.11	11.38	11.64	11.90
92	8.11	8.37	8.64	8.90	9.16	9.43	9.69	9.96	10.22	10.49	10.75	11.02	11.28	11.55	11.81	12.08
91	8.26	8.52	8.79	9.05	9.32	9.59	9.85	10.12	10.39	10.65	10.92	11.19	11.45	11.72	11.99	12.26
90	8.41	8.67	8.94	9.21	9.48	9.75	10.02	10.28	10.55	10.82	11.09	11.36	11.63	11.90	12.17	12.44
89	8.56	8.83	9.10	9.37	9.64	9.91	10.18	10.45	10.72	10.99	11.26	11.54	11.81	12.08	12.35	12.62
88	8.71	8.99	9.26	9.53	9.80	10.07	10.35	10.62	10.89	11.17	11.44	11.71	11.99	12.26	12.54	12.81
87	8.87	9.14	9.42	9.69	9.97	10.24	10.52	10.79	11.07	11.34	11.62	11.89	12.17	12.45	12.72	13.00
86	9.03	9.31	9.58	9.86	10.14	10.41	10.69	10.97	11.25	11.52	11.80	12.08	12.36	12.64	12.91	13.19
85	9.19	9.47	9.75	10.03	10.31	10.59	10.87	11.15	11.42	11.71	11.99	12.27	12.55	12.83	13.11	13.39
84	9.36	9.64	9.92	10.20	10.48	10.76	11.04	11.33	11.61	11.89	12.17	12.46	12.74	13.02	13.31	13.59
83	9.52	9.81	10.09	10.37	10.66	10.94	11.22	11.51	11.79	12.08	12.36	12.65	12.94	13.22	13.51	13.79
82	9.69	9.98	10.26	10.55	10.84	11.12	11.41	11.70	11.98	12.27	12.56	12.85	13.13	13.42	13.71	14.00
81	9.86	10.15	10.44	10.73	11.02	11.31	11.60	11.89	12.18	12.47	12.76	13.05	13.34	13.63	13.92	14.21
80	10.04	10.33	10.62	10.91	11.20	11.49	11.79	12.08	12.37	12.66	12.96	13.25	13.54	13.84	14.13	14.43
79	10.22	10.51	10.80	11.10	11.39	11.69	11.98	12.28	12.57	12.87	13.16	13.46	13.75	14.05	14.35	14.64
78	10.40	10.70	10.99	11.29	11.58	11.88	12.18	12.48	12.77	13.07	13.37	13.67	13.97	14.27	14.57	14.87
77	10.58	10.88	11.18	11.48	11.78	12.08	12.38	12.68	12.98	13.28	13.58	13.88	14.19	14.49	14.79	15.10
76	10.77	11.07	11.37	11.68	11.98	12.28	12.58	12.89	13.19	13.49	13.80	14.10	14.41	14.71	15.02	15.33
75	10.96	11.27	11.57	11.88	12.18	12.49	12.79	13.10	13.41	13.71	14.02	14.33	14.64	14.94	15.25	15.56
74	11.16	11.46	11.77	12.08	12.39	12.70	13.00	13.31	13.62	13.93	14.24	14.56	14.87	15.18	15.49	15.80
70	11.97	12.29	12.61	12.93	13.25	13.58	13.90	14.22	14.54	14.87	15.19	15.52	15.84	16.17	16.49	16.82
65	13.09	13.42	13.76	14.10	14.44	14.78	15.12	15.46	15.81	16.15	16.49	16.84	17.18	17.53	17.87	18.22
60	14.33	14.69	15.05	15.41	15.77	16.13	16.49	16.86	17.22	17.59	17.95	18.32	18.69	19.06	19.43	19.80
55	15.72	16.11	16.49	16.88	17.27	17.65	18.04	18.44	18.83	19.22	19.62	20.01	20.41	20.81	21.21	21.61
50	17.32	17.73	18.15	18.56	18.98	19.40	19.83	20.25	20.68	21.10	21.53	21.96	22.39	22.83	23.26	23.70
45	19.16	19.61	20.07	20.53	20.99	21.45	21.91	22.38	22.84	23.31	23.79	24.26	24.73	25.21	25.69	26.17
40	21.35	21.85	22.35	22.86	23.37	23.89	24.40	24.92	25.44	25.97	26.50	27.03	27.56	28.09	28.63	29.17
35	24.01	24.58	25.15	25.72	26.30	26.89	27.47	28.06	28.66	29.26	29.86	30.47	31.08	31.69	32.31	32.93

Description: This table shows the price to pay for a bond at the yield rate. The yield is to maturity.

Example: The price of a 15.00 %, 11 year bond to yield 8 % to maturity is $ 150.58.

YIELD	11.00%	11.25%	11.50%	11.75%	12.00%	12.25%	12.50%	12.75%	13.00%	13.25%	13.50%	13.75%	14.00%	14.25%	14.50%	15.00%
0.00	221.00	223.75	226.50	229.25	232.00	234.75	237.50	240.25	243.00	245.75	248.50	251.25	254.00	256.75	259.50	265.00
1.00	203.92	206.52	209.12	211.71	214.31	216.91	219.51	222.11	224.70	227.30	229.90	232.50	235.10	237.69	240.29	245.49
2.00	188.47	190.93	193.39	195.84	198.30	200.76	203.22	205.67	208.13	210.59	213.05	215.50	217.96	220.42	222.88	227.79
3.00	174.48	176.81	179.14	181.47	183.79	186.12	188.45	190.78	193.10	195.43	197.76	200.09	202.41	204.74	207.07	211.72
4.00	161.80	164.01	166.22	168.42	170.63	172.84	175.05	177.25	179.46	181.67	183.88	186.08	188.29	190.50	192.70	197.12
4.25	158.82	161.00	163.18	165.36	167.54	169.71	171.89	174.07	176.25	178.43	180.61	182.79	184.96	187.14	189.32	193.68
4.50	155.91	158.06	160.21	162.36	164.51	166.66	168.81	170.96	173.11	175.26	177.42	179.57	181.72	183.87	186.02	190.32
4.75	153.07	155.19	157.32	159.44	161.56	163.68	165.81	167.93	170.05	172.17	174.30	176.42	178.54	180.67	182.79	187.03
5.00	150.30	152.39	154.49	156.58	158.68	160.77	162.87	164.97	167.06	169.16	171.25	173.35	175.44	177.54	179.64	183.83
5.25	147.59	149.66	151.73	153.80	155.86	157.93	160.00	162.07	164.14	166.21	168.28	170.35	172.42	174.49	176.56	180.69
5.50	144.94	146.99	149.03	151.07	153.12	155.16	157.20	159.25	161.29	163.33	165.37	167.42	169.46	171.50	173.55	177.63
5.75	142.36	144.38	146.40	148.42	150.43	152.45	154.47	156.48	158.50	160.52	162.54	164.55	166.57	168.59	170.61	174.64
6.00	139.84	141.83	143.83	145.82	147.81	149.80	151.79	153.79	155.78	157.77	159.76	161.76	163.75	165.74	167.73	171.72
6.25	137.38	139.35	141.32	143.28	145.25	147.22	149.18	151.15	153.12	155.09	157.05	159.02	160.99	162.96	164.92	168.86
6.50	134.98	136.92	138.86	140.81	142.75	144.69	146.64	148.58	150.52	152.46	154.41	156.35	158.29	160.24	162.18	166.07
6.75	132.63	134.55	136.47	138.39	140.31	142.22	144.14	146.06	147.98	149.90	151.82	153.74	155.66	157.58	159.50	163.34
7.00	130.33	132.23	134.13	136.02	137.92	139.81	141.71	143.61	145.50	147.40	149.29	151.19	153.08	154.98	156.88	160.67
7.25	128.09	129.97	131.84	133.71	135.59	137.46	139.33	141.20	143.08	144.95	146.82	148.70	150.57	152.44	154.31	158.06
7.50	125.90	127.76	129.61	131.46	133.31	135.16	137.01	138.86	140.71	142.56	144.41	146.26	148.11	149.96	151.81	155.51
7.75	123.77	125.59	127.42	129.25	131.08	132.91	134.74	136.56	138.39	140.22	142.05	143.88	145.70	147.53	149.36	153.02
8.00	121.68	123.48	125.29	127.10	128.90	130.71	132.52	134.32	136.13	137.93	139.74	141.55	143.35	145.16	146.97	150.58
8.25	119.63	121.42	123.20	124.99	126.77	128.56	130.34	132.13	133.91	135.70	137.48	139.27	141.05	142.84	144.62	148.19
8.50	117.64	119.40	121.17	122.93	124.70	126.46	128.22	129.99	131.75	133.52	135.28	137.04	138.81	140.57	142.34	145.86
8.75	115.69	117.43	119.18	120.92	122.66	124.41	126.15	127.89	129.64	131.38	133.12	134.87	136.61	138.35	140.10	143.58
9.00	113.78	115.51	117.23	118.95	120.68	122.40	124.12	125.85	127.57	129.29	131.01	132.74	134.46	136.18	137.91	141.35
9.25	111.92	113.62	115.33	117.03	118.73	120.44	122.14	123.84	125.55	127.25	128.95	130.66	132.36	134.06	135.77	139.17
9.50	110.10	111.78	113.47	115.15	116.84	118.52	120.20	121.89	123.57	125.25	126.94	128.62	130.30	131.99	133.67	137.04
9.75	108.32	109.99	111.65	113.31	114.98	116.64	118.31	119.97	121.64	123.30	124.96	126.63	128.29	129.96	131.62	134.95
10.00	106.58	108.23	109.87	111.52	113.16	114.81	116.45	118.10	119.74	121.39	123.04	124.68	126.33	127.97	129.62	132.91
10.25	104.88	106.51	108.13	109.76	111.39	113.01	114.64	116.27	117.89	119.52	121.15	122.77	124.40	126.03	127.66	130.91
10.50	103.22	104.83	106.43	108.04	109.65	111.26	112.87	114.48	116.09	117.69	119.30	120.91	122.52	124.13	125.74	128.95
10.75	101.59	103.18	104.77	106.36	107.95	109.54	111.13	112.72	114.31	115.91	117.50	119.09	120.68	122.27	123.86	127.04
11.00	100.00	101.57	103.15	104.72	106.29	107.86	109.44	111.01	112.58	114.16	115.73	117.30	118.87	120.45	122.02	125.17
11.25	98.44	100.00	101.56	103.11	104.67	106.22	107.78	109.33	110.89	112.44	114.00	115.56	117.11	118.67	120.22	123.33
11.50	96.92	98.46	100.00	101.54	103.08	104.62	106.15	107.69	109.23	110.77	112.31	113.85	115.38	116.92	118.46	121.54
11.75	95.43	96.96	98.48	100.00	101.52	103.04	104.57	106.09	107.61	109.13	110.65	112.17	113.70	115.22	116.74	119.78
12.00	93.98	95.48	96.99	98.49	100.00	101.51	103.01	104.52	106.02	107.53	109.03	110.54	112.04	113.55	115.05	118.06
12.25	92.56	94.04	95.53	97.02	98.51	100.00	101.49	102.98	104.47	105.96	107.44	108.93	110.42	111.91	113.40	116.38
12.50	91.16	92.63	94.11	95.58	97.05	98.53	100.00	101.47	102.95	104.42	105.89	107.37	108.84	110.31	111.78	114.73
12.75	89.80	91.26	92.71	94.17	95.63	97.09	98.54	100.00	101.46	102.91	104.37	105.83	107.29	108.74	110.20	113.12
13.00	88.46	89.91	91.35	92.79	94.23	95.67	97.12	98.56	100.00	101.44	102.88	104.33	105.77	107.21	108.65	111.54
13.25	87.16	88.59	90.01	91.44	92.87	94.29	95.72	97.15	98.57	100.00	101.43	102.85	104.28	105.71	107.13	109.99
13.50	85.88	87.29	88.71	90.12	91.53	92.94	94.35	95.76	97.18	98.59	100.00	101.41	102.82	104.24	105.65	108.47
13.75	84.63	86.03	87.43	88.82	90.22	91.62	93.01	94.41	95.81	97.21	98.60	100.00	101.40	102.79	104.19	106.99
14.00	83.41	84.79	86.17	87.56	88.94	90.32	91.70	93.09	94.47	95.85	97.23	98.62	100.00	101.38	102.77	105.53
14.25	82.21	83.58	84.95	86.32	87.68	89.05	90.42	91.79	93.16	94.53	95.89	97.26	98.63	100.00	101.37	104.11
14.50	81.04	82.39	83.75	85.10	86.46	87.81	89.16	90.52	91.87	93.23	94.58	95.94	97.29	98.65	100.00	102.71
14.75	79.89	81.23	82.57	83.91	85.25	86.59	87.93	89.27	90.62	91.96	93.30	94.64	95.98	97.32	98.66	101.34
15.00	78.77	80.09	81.42	82.75	84.07	85.40	86.73	88.06	89.38	90.71	92.04	93.36	94.69	96.02	97.35	100.00
15.25	77.67	78.98	80.29	81.61	82.92	84.23	85.55	86.86	88.18	89.49	90.80	92.12	93.43	94.74	96.06	98.69
15.50	76.59	77.89	79.19	80.49	81.79	83.09	84.39	85.69	86.99	88.29	89.59	90.90	92.20	93.50	94.80	97.40
15.75	75.53	76.82	78.11	79.40	80.68	81.97	83.26	84.55	85.83	87.12	88.41	89.70	90.99	92.27	93.56	96.14
16.00	74.50	75.77	77.05	78.32	79.60	80.87	82.15	83.42	84.70	85.97	87.25	88.52	89.80	91.07	92.35	94.90
16.25	73.49	74.75	76.01	77.27	78.54	79.80	81.06	82.32	83.59	84.85	86.11	87.37	88.64	89.90	91.16	93.69
16.50	72.49	73.74	74.99	76.24	77.50	78.75	80.00	81.25	82.50	83.75	85.00	86.25	87.50	88.75	90.00	92.50
16.75	71.52	72.76	74.00	75.24	76.48	77.71	78.95	80.19	81.43	82.67	83.90	85.14	86.38	87.62	88.86	91.33
17.00	70.57	71.80	73.02	74.25	75.48	76.70	77.93	79.15	80.38	81.61	82.83	84.06	85.29	86.51	87.74	90.19
17.25	69.64	70.85	72.07	73.28	74.50	75.71	76.92	78.14	79.35	80.57	81.78	83.00	84.21	85.43	86.64	89.07
17.50	68.72	69.93	71.13	72.33	73.54	74.74	75.94	77.14	78.35	79.55	80.75	81.96	83.16	84.36	85.57	87.97
17.75	67.83	69.02	70.21	71.40	72.60	73.79	74.98	76.17	77.36	78.55	79.74	80.94	82.13	83.32	84.51	86.89
18.00	66.95	68.13	69.31	70.49	71.67	72.85	74.03	75.21	76.39	77.57	78.75	79.93	81.12	82.30	83.48	85.84
18.25	66.09	67.26	68.43	69.60	70.77	71.94	73.11	74.28	75.45	76.61	77.78	78.95	80.12	81.29	82.46	84.80
18.50	65.25	66.41	67.57	68.72	69.88	71.04	72.20	73.36	74.52	75.67	76.83	77.99	79.15	80.31	81.47	83.78
18.75	64.42	65.57	66.72	67.87	69.01	70.16	71.31	72.46	73.60	74.75	75.90	77.05	78.19	79.34	80.49	82.79
19.00	63.61	64.75	65.89	67.02	68.16	69.30	70.44	71.57	72.71	73.85	74.98	76.12	77.26	78.39	79.53	81.81
20.00	60.53	61.62	62.72	63.82	64.91	66.01	67.11	68.20	69.30	70.40	71.49	72.59	73.69	74.78	75.88	78.07
25.00	48.20	49.12	50.05	50.97	51.90	52.82	53.75	54.67	55.60	56.52	57.45	58.37	59.30	60.22	61.15	63.00
30.00	39.59	40.39	41.18	41.98	42.77	43.57	44.36	45.16	45.95	46.75	47.54	48.34	49.13	49.93	50.72	52.31

Description: This table shows the yield to maturity of a bond purchased at the price shown in the index.

Example: The yield to maturity of a 15.00 %, 11 year bond at a price of 117.00 is 12.15 %.

COUPON RATE, %

PRICE	11.00%	11.25%	11.50%	11.75%	12.00%	12.25%	12.50%	12.75%	13.00%	13.25%	13.50%	13.75%	14.00%	14.25%	14.50%	15.00%
190	1.89	2.06	2.22	2.39	2.56	2.72	2.89	3.05	3.21	3.38	3.54	3.71	3.87	4.03	4.19	4.52
185	2.23	2.40	2.57	2.74	2.91	3.08	3.24	3.41	3.58	3.74	3.91	4.08	4.24	4.41	4.57	4.90
180	2.59	2.76	2.93	3.10	3.27	3.44	3.61	3.78	3.95	4.12	4.29	4.46	4.63	4.80	4.97	5.30
175	2.96	3.13	3.30	3.48	3.65	3.83	4.00	4.17	4.34	4.52	4.69	4.86	5.03	5.20	5.37	5.71
170	3.34	3.51	3.69	3.87	4.05	4.22	4.40	4.57	4.75	4.92	5.10	5.27	5.45	5.62	5.80	6.14
165	3.73	3.91	4.09	4.27	4.45	4.63	4.81	4.99	5.17	5.35	5.53	5.71	5.88	6.06	6.24	6.59
160	4.15	4.33	4.51	4.70	4.88	5.06	5.25	5.43	5.61	5.79	5.97	6.15	6.34	6.52	6.70	7.06
155	4.57	4.76	4.95	5.14	5.32	5.51	5.70	5.88	6.07	6.25	6.44	6.62	6.81	6.99	7.18	7.55
150	5.02	5.21	5.40	5.60	5.79	5.98	6.17	6.36	6.55	6.74	6.92	7.11	7.30	7.49	7.68	8.06
145	5.49	5.69	5.88	6.08	6.27	6.46	6.66	6.85	7.05	7.24	7.43	7.63	7.82	8.01	8.20	8.59
140	5.98	6.18	6.38	6.58	6.78	6.98	7.17	7.37	7.57	7.77	7.97	8.16	8.36	8.56	8.76	9.15
135	6.49	6.70	6.90	7.10	7.31	7.51	7.72	7.92	8.12	8.32	8.53	8.73	8.93	9.13	9.34	9.74
130	7.03	7.24	7.45	7.66	7.87	8.08	8.29	8.49	8.70	8.91	9.12	9.32	9.53	9.74	9.95	10.36
125	7.60	7.81	8.03	8.24	8.46	8.67	8.89	9.10	9.31	9.53	9.74	9.95	10.17	10.38	10.59	11.02
123	7.84	8.05	8.27	8.49	8.70	8.92	9.14	9.35	9.57	9.78	10.00	10.22	10.43	10.65	10.86	11.29
122	7.96	8.17	8.39	8.61	8.83	9.05	9.26	9.48	9.70	9.91	10.13	10.35	10.56	10.78	11.00	11.43
121	8.08	8.30	8.52	8.73	8.95	9.17	9.39	9.61	9.83	10.05	10.26	10.48	10.70	10.92	11.14	11.57
120	8.20	8.42	8.64	8.86	9.08	9.30	9.52	9.74	9.96	10.18	10.40	10.62	10.84	11.06	11.28	11.71
119	8.32	8.55	8.77	8.99	9.21	9.43	9.65	9.87	10.09	10.32	10.54	10.76	10.98	11.20	11.42	11.86
118	8.45	8.67	8.90	9.12	9.34	9.56	9.79	10.01	10.23	10.45	10.67	10.90	11.12	11.34	11.56	12.00
117	8.58	8.80	9.03	9.25	9.47	9.70	9.92	10.14	10.37	10.59	10.81	11.04	11.26	11.48	11.71	12.15
116	8.70	8.93	9.16	9.38	9.61	9.83	10.06	10.28	10.51	10.73	10.96	11.18	11.41	11.63	11.85	12.30
115	8.83	9.06	9.29	9.52	9.74	9.97	10.20	10.42	10.65	10.87	11.10	11.33	11.55	11.78	12.00	12.45
114	8.97	9.19	9.42	9.65	9.88	10.11	10.33	10.56	10.79	11.02	11.24	11.47	11.70	11.93	12.15	12.61
113	9.10	9.33	9.56	9.79	10.02	10.25	10.48	10.71	10.93	11.16	11.39	11.62	11.85	12.08	12.31	12.76
112	9.23	9.47	9.70	9.93	10.16	10.39	10.62	10.85	11.08	11.31	11.54	11.77	12.00	12.23	12.46	12.92
111	9.37	9.60	9.84	10.07	10.30	10.53	10.76	11.00	11.23	11.46	11.69	11.92	12.16	12.39	12.62	13.08
110	9.51	9.74	9.98	10.21	10.44	10.68	10.91	11.14	11.38	11.61	11.84	12.08	12.31	12.54	12.78	13.24
109	9.65	9.88	10.12	10.36	10.59	10.83	11.06	11.30	11.53	11.77	12.00	12.23	12.47	12.70	12.94	13.41
108	9.79	10.03	10.26	10.50	10.74	10.97	11.21	11.45	11.68	11.92	12.16	12.39	12.63	12.87	13.10	13.57
107	9.93	10.17	10.41	10.65	10.89	11.13	11.36	11.60	11.84	12.08	12.32	12.55	12.79	13.03	13.27	13.74
106	10.08	10.32	10.56	10.80	11.04	11.28	11.52	11.76	12.00	12.24	12.48	12.72	12.96	13.20	13.44	13.91
105	10.23	10.47	10.71	10.95	11.19	11.43	11.68	11.92	12.16	12.40	12.64	12.88	13.12	13.36	13.61	14.09
104	10.38	10.62	10.86	11.11	11.35	11.59	11.84	12.08	12.32	12.56	12.81	13.05	13.29	13.54	13.78	14.26
103	10.53	10.77	11.02	11.26	11.51	11.75	12.00	12.24	12.49	12.73	12.98	13.22	13.46	13.71	13.95	14.44
102	10.68	10.93	11.17	11.42	11.67	11.91	12.16	12.41	12.65	12.90	13.15	13.39	13.64	13.89	14.13	14.62
101	10.84	11.09	11.33	11.58	11.83	12.08	12.33	12.57	12.82	13.07	13.32	13.57	13.82	14.06	14.31	14.81
100	11.00	11.25	11.50	11.75	12.00	12.25	12.50	12.75	13.00	13.25	13.50	13.75	14.00	14.25	14.50	15.00
99	11.16	11.41	11.66	11.91	12.16	12.41	12.67	12.92	13.17	13.42	13.67	13.93	14.18	14.43	14.68	15.18
98	11.32	11.57	11.82	12.08	12.33	12.59	12.84	13.09	13.35	13.60	13.85	14.11	14.36	14.62	14.87	15.38
97	11.48	11.74	11.99	12.25	12.50	12.76	13.02	13.27	13.53	13.78	14.04	14.29	14.55	14.81	15.06	15.57
96	11.65	11.91	12.16	12.42	12.68	12.94	13.19	13.45	13.71	13.97	14.23	14.48	14.74	15.00	15.26	15.77
95	11.82	12.08	12.34	12.60	12.86	13.12	13.38	13.64	13.90	14.16	14.41	14.67	14.93	15.19	15.45	15.97
94	11.99	12.25	12.51	12.78	13.04	13.30	13.56	13.82	14.08	14.35	14.61	14.87	15.13	15.39	15.66	16.18
93	12.17	12.43	12.69	12.96	13.22	13.48	13.75	14.01	14.28	14.54	14.80	15.07	15.33	15.60	15.86	16.39
92	12.34	12.61	12.88	13.14	13.41	13.67	13.94	14.20	14.47	14.74	15.00	15.27	15.54	15.80	16.07	16.60
91	12.52	12.79	13.06	13.33	13.60	13.86	14.13	14.40	14.67	14.94	15.20	15.47	15.74	16.01	16.28	16.82
90	12.71	12.98	13.25	13.52	13.79	14.06	14.33	14.60	14.87	15.14	15.41	15.68	15.95	16.22	16.49	17.04
89	12.89	13.17	13.44	13.71	13.98	14.26	14.53	14.80	15.07	15.35	15.62	15.89	16.17	16.44	16.71	17.26
88	13.08	13.36	13.63	13.91	14.18	14.46	14.73	15.01	15.28	15.56	15.83	16.11	16.38	16.66	16.94	17.49
87	13.28	13.55	13.83	14.11	14.38	14.66	14.94	15.22	15.49	15.77	16.05	16.33	16.61	16.88	17.16	17.72
86	13.47	13.75	14.03	14.31	14.59	14.87	15.15	15.43	15.71	15.99	16.27	16.55	16.83	17.11	17.39	17.96
85	13.67	13.95	14.23	14.52	14.80	15.08	15.36	15.65	15.93	16.21	16.49	16.78	17.06	17.34	17.63	18.20
84	13.87	14.16	14.44	14.73	15.01	15.30	15.58	15.87	16.15	16.44	16.72	17.01	17.29	17.58	17.87	18.44
83	14.08	14.37	14.65	14.94	15.23	15.52	15.80	16.09	16.38	16.67	16.96	17.24	17.53	17.82	18.11	18.69
82	14.29	14.58	14.87	15.16	15.45	15.74	16.03	16.32	16.61	16.90	17.19	17.48	17.78	18.07	18.36	18.95
81	14.50	14.80	15.09	15.38	15.67	15.97	16.26	16.55	16.85	17.14	17.43	17.73	18.02	18.32	18.61	19.20
80	14.72	15.02	15.31	15.61	15.90	16.20	16.49	16.79	17.09	17.38	17.68	17.98	18.28	18.57	18.87	19.47
79	14.94	15.24	15.54	15.84	16.14	16.43	16.73	17.03	17.33	17.63	17.93	18.23	18.53	18.83	19.14	19.74
78	15.17	15.47	15.77	16.07	16.37	16.68	16.98	17.28	17.58	17.89	18.19	18.49	18.80	19.10	19.41	20.01
77	15.40	15.70	16.01	16.31	16.62	16.92	17.23	17.53	17.84	18.14	18.45	18.76	19.06	19.37	19.68	20.30
76	15.63	15.94	16.25	16.56	16.86	17.17	17.48	17.79	18.10	18.41	18.72	19.03	19.34	19.65	19.96	20.58
75	15.87	16.18	16.49	16.80	17.12	17.43	17.74	18.05	18.36	18.68	18.99	19.30	19.62	19.93	20.25	20.88
74	16.12	16.43	16.74	17.06	17.37	17.69	18.00	18.32	18.64	18.95	19.27	19.59	19.90	20.22	20.54	21.18
73	16.37	16.68	17.00	17.32	17.64	17.96	18.27	18.59	18.91	19.23	19.55	19.87	20.20	20.52	20.84	21.48
70	17.15	17.48	17.80	18.13	18.46	18.79	19.12	19.45	19.78	20.11	20.45	20.78	21.11	21.45	21.78	22.45
65	18.57	18.92	19.27	19.62	19.97	20.32	20.67	21.02	21.38	21.73	22.08	22.44	22.79	23.15	23.50	24.22
60	20.17	20.55	20.92	21.30	21.67	22.05	22.42	22.80	23.18	23.56	23.94	24.32	24.70	25.09	25.47	26.24

Description: This table shows the price to pay for a bond at the yield rate. The yield is to maturity.

Example: The price of a 6.75 %, 12 year bond to yield 8 % to maturity is $ 90.47.

YIELD	0.00%	1.00%	2.00%	3.00%	4.00%	4.25%	4.50%	4.75%	5.00%	5.25%	5.50%	5.75%	6.00%	6.25%	6.50%	6.75%
0.00	100.00	112.00	124.00	136.00	148.00	151.00	154.00	157.00	160.00	163.00	166.00	169.00	172.00	175.00	178.00	181.00
1.00	88.72	100.00	111.28	122.56	133.84	136.66	139.49	142.31	145.13	147.95	150.77	153.59	156.41	159.23	162.05	164.87
2.00	78.76	89.38	100.00	110.62	121.24	123.90	126.55	129.21	131.87	134.52	137.18	139.83	142.49	145.14	147.80	150.45
3.00	69.95	79.97	89.98	100.00	110.02	112.52	115.02	117.53	120.03	122.53	125.04	127.54	130.05	132.55	135.05	137.56
4.00	62.17	71.63	81.09	90.54	100.00	102.36	104.73	107.09	109.46	111.82	114.19	116.55	118.91	121.28	123.64	126.01
4.25	60.37	69.70	79.02	88.34	97.67	100.00	102.33	104.66	106.99	109.32	111.66	113.99	116.32	118.65	120.98	123.31
4.50	58.62	67.82	77.01	86.21	95.40	97.70	100.00	102.30	104.60	106.90	109.19	111.49	113.79	116.09	118.39	120.69
4.75	56.93	66.00	75.07	84.13	93.20	95.47	97.73	100.00	102.27	104.53	106.80	109.07	111.33	113.60	115.87	118.13
5.00	55.29	64.23	73.17	82.12	91.06	93.29	95.53	97.76	100.00	102.24	104.47	106.71	108.94	111.18	113.41	115.65
5.25	53.69	62.51	71.33	80.15	88.97	91.18	93.38	95.59	97.79	100.00	102.21	104.41	106.62	108.82	111.03	113.23
5.50	52.15	60.85	69.55	78.25	86.95	89.12	91.30	93.47	95.65	97.82	100.00	102.18	104.35	106.53	108.70	110.88
5.75	50.65	59.23	67.81	76.40	84.98	87.13	89.27	91.42	93.56	95.71	97.85	100.00	102.15	104.29	106.44	108.58
6.00	49.19	57.66	66.13	74.60	83.06	85.18	87.30	89.42	91.53	93.65	95.77	97.88	100.00	102.12	104.23	106.35
6.25	47.78	56.14	64.49	72.85	81.20	83.29	85.38	87.47	89.56	91.65	93.73	95.82	97.91	100.00	102.09	104.18
6.50	46.41	54.66	62.90	71.15	79.39	81.45	83.51	85.57	87.63	89.69	91.76	93.82	95.88	97.94	100.00	102.06
6.75	45.08	53.22	61.36	69.49	77.63	79.66	81.69	83.73	85.76	87.80	89.83	91.86	93.90	95.93	97.97	100.00
7.00	43.80	51.82	59.85	67.88	75.91	77.92	79.93	81.93	83.94	85.95	87.96	89.96	91.97	93.98	95.99	97.99
7.25	42.55	50.47	58.39	66.32	74.24	76.23	78.21	80.19	82.17	84.15	86.13	88.11	90.09	92.08	94.06	96.04
7.50	41.33	49.15	56.98	64.80	72.62	74.58	76.53	78.49	80.44	82.40	84.36	86.31	88.27	90.22	92.18	94.13
7.75	40.15	47.88	55.60	63.32	71.04	72.97	74.90	76.83	78.76	80.70	82.63	84.56	86.49	88.42	90.35	92.28
8.00	39.01	46.64	54.26	61.88	69.51	71.41	73.32	75.22	77.13	79.04	80.94	82.85	84.75	86.66	88.56	90.47
8.25	37.90	45.43	52.96	60.48	68.01	69.89	71.77	73.66	75.54	77.42	79.30	81.18	83.06	84.95	86.83	88.71
8.50	36.83	44.26	51.69	59.12	66.54	68.41	70.27	72.13	73.99	75.85	77.70	79.56	81.42	83.28	85.14	86.99
8.75	35.78	43.12	50.46	57.80	65.14	66.97	68.81	70.64	72.48	74.31	76.15	77.98	79.82	81.65	83.49	85.32
9.00	34.77	42.02	49.27	56.51	63.76	65.57	67.39	69.20	71.01	72.82	74.63	76.44	78.26	80.07	81.88	83.69
9.25	33.79	40.95	48.10	55.26	62.42	64.21	66.00	67.79	69.58	71.37	73.16	74.95	76.74	78.53	80.32	82.10
9.50	32.83	39.90	46.97	54.04	61.11	62.88	64.65	66.42	68.18	69.95	71.72	73.49	75.25	77.02	78.79	80.56
9.75	31.91	38.89	45.87	52.86	59.84	61.59	63.33	65.08	66.83	68.57	70.32	72.06	73.81	75.56	77.30	79.05
10.00	31.01	37.91	44.81	51.70	58.60	60.33	62.05	63.78	65.50	67.23	68.95	70.68	72.40	74.13	75.85	77.58
10.25	30.13	36.95	43.77	50.58	57.40	59.10	60.81	62.51	64.21	65.92	67.62	69.33	71.03	72.74	74.44	76.14
10.50	29.29	36.02	42.76	49.49	56.23	57.91	59.59	61.28	62.96	64.64	66.33	68.01	69.69	71.38	73.06	74.75
10.75	28.46	35.12	41.77	48.43	55.08	56.75	58.41	60.07	61.74	63.40	65.06	66.73	68.39	70.05	71.72	73.38
11.00	27.67	34.24	40.82	47.39	53.97	55.61	57.26	58.90	60.54	62.19	63.83	65.48	67.12	68.76	70.41	72.05
11.25	26.89	33.39	39.89	46.39	52.88	54.51	56.13	57.76	59.38	61.01	62.63	64.26	65.88	67.51	69.13	70.76
11.50	26.14	32.56	38.98	45.41	51.83	53.43	55.04	56.65	58.25	59.86	61.46	63.07	64.67	66.28	67.89	69.49
11.75	25.41	31.76	38.10	44.45	50.80	52.39	53.97	55.56	57.15	58.74	60.32	61.91	63.50	65.08	66.67	68.26
12.00	24.70	30.97	37.25	43.52	49.80	51.37	52.94	54.50	56.07	57.64	59.21	60.78	62.35	63.92	65.49	67.06
12.25	24.01	30.21	36.42	42.62	48.82	50.37	51.92	53.47	55.03	56.58	58.13	59.68	61.23	62.78	64.33	65.88
12.50	23.34	29.47	35.61	41.74	47.87	49.40	50.94	52.47	54.00	55.54	57.07	58.60	60.14	61.67	63.20	64.74
12.75	22.69	28.75	34.82	40.88	46.94	48.46	49.98	51.49	53.01	54.52	56.04	57.56	59.07	60.59	62.10	63.62
13.00	22.06	28.06	34.05	40.05	46.04	47.54	49.04	50.54	52.04	53.54	55.03	56.53	58.03	59.53	61.03	62.53
13.25	21.45	27.38	33.30	39.23	45.16	46.64	48.13	49.61	51.09	52.57	54.05	55.54	57.02	58.50	59.98	61.46
13.50	20.85	26.72	32.58	38.44	44.30	45.77	47.24	48.70	50.17	51.63	53.10	54.56	56.03	57.50	58.96	60.43
13.75	20.28	26.07	31.87	37.67	43.47	44.92	46.37	47.82	49.27	50.72	52.17	53.61	55.06	56.51	57.96	59.41
14.00	19.71	25.45	31.18	36.92	42.65	44.09	45.52	46.95	48.39	49.82	51.26	52.69	54.12	55.56	56.99	58.42
14.25	19.17	24.84	30.51	36.19	41.86	43.28	44.70	46.11	47.53	48.95	50.37	51.79	53.20	54.62	56.04	57.46
14.50	18.64	24.25	29.86	35.47	41.08	42.49	43.89	45.29	46.70	48.10	49.50	50.90	52.31	53.71	55.11	56.51
14.75	18.13	23.68	29.23	34.78	40.33	41.72	43.11	44.49	45.88	47.27	48.66	50.04	51.43	52.82	54.21	55.59
15.00	17.63	23.12	28.61	34.10	39.59	40.97	42.34	43.71	45.09	46.46	47.83	49.20	50.58	51.95	53.32	54.70
15.25	17.14	22.58	28.01	33.44	38.88	40.23	41.59	42.95	44.31	45.67	47.03	48.38	49.74	51.10	52.46	53.82
15.50	16.67	22.05	27.42	32.80	38.18	39.52	40.86	42.21	43.55	44.90	46.24	47.58	48.93	50.27	51.62	52.96
15.75	16.21	21.53	26.85	32.17	37.49	38.82	40.15	41.48	42.81	44.14	45.47	46.80	48.13	49.46	50.79	52.12
16.00	15.77	21.03	26.30	31.56	36.83	38.14	39.46	40.78	42.09	43.41	44.72	46.04	47.36	48.67	49.99	51.30
16.25	15.34	20.55	25.76	30.97	36.18	37.48	38.78	40.09	41.39	42.69	43.99	45.30	46.60	47.90	49.20	50.51
16.50	14.92	20.08	25.23	30.39	35.54	36.83	38.12	39.41	40.70	41.99	43.28	44.57	45.86	47.15	48.44	49.72
16.75	14.51	19.61	24.72	29.82	34.93	36.20	37.48	38.75	40.03	41.31	42.58	43.86	45.13	46.41	47.69	48.96
17.00	14.12	19.17	24.22	29.27	34.32	35.59	36.85	38.11	39.38	40.64	41.90	43.16	44.43	45.69	46.95	48.22
17.25	13.73	18.73	23.73	28.73	33.73	34.99	36.24	37.49	38.74	39.99	41.24	42.49	43.74	44.99	46.24	47.49
17.50	13.36	18.31	23.26	28.21	33.16	34.40	35.64	36.87	38.11	39.35	40.59	41.83	43.06	44.30	45.54	46.78
17.75	12.99	17.90	22.80	27.70	32.60	33.83	35.05	36.28	37.50	38.73	39.95	41.18	42.40	43.63	44.85	46.08
18.00	12.64	17.49	22.35	27.20	32.05	33.27	34.48	35.69	36.91	38.12	39.33	40.55	41.76	42.97	44.19	45.40
18.25	12.30	17.10	21.91	26.71	31.52	32.72	33.92	35.12	36.33	37.53	38.73	39.93	41.13	42.33	43.53	44.74
18.50	11.96	16.72	21.48	26.24	31.00	32.19	33.38	34.57	35.76	36.95	38.14	39.33	40.52	41.71	42.90	44.09
18.75	11.64	16.35	21.07	25.78	30.49	31.67	32.85	34.02	35.20	36.38	37.56	38.74	39.92	41.09	42.27	43.45
19.00	11.33	15.99	20.66	25.33	29.99	31.16	32.33	33.49	34.66	35.83	36.99	38.16	39.33	40.49	41.66	42.83
20.00	10.15	14.64	19.14	23.63	28.12	29.25	30.37	31.49	32.61	33.74	34.86	35.98	37.11	38.23	39.35	40.48
25.00	5.92	9.68	13.45	17.21	20.97	21.91	22.85	23.80	24.74	25.68	26.62	27.56	28.50	29.44	30.38	31.32
30.00	3.49	6.71	9.93	13.14	16.36	17.17	17.97	18.77	19.58	20.38	21.19	21.99	22.79	23.60	24.40	25.21

Description: This table shows the yield to maturity of a bond purchased at the price shown in the index.

Example: The yield to maturity of a 6.75 %, 12 year bond at a price of 80.00 is 9.59 %.

PRICE	0.00%	1.00%	2.00%	3.00%	4.00%	4.25%	4.50%	4.75%	5.00%	5.25%	5.50%	5.75%	6.00%	6.25%	6.50%	6.75%
100	0.00	1.00	2.00	3.00	4.00	4.25	4.50	4.75	5.00	5.25	5.50	5.75	6.00	6.25	6.50	6.75
99	.08	1.08	2.09	3.10	4.10	4.35	4.60	4.86	5.11	5.36	5.61	5.86	6.11	6.37	6.62	6.87
98	.16	1.17	2.19	3.20	4.21	4.46	4.72	4.97	5.22	5.47	5.73	5.98	6.23	6.49	6.74	6.99
97	.25	1.27	2.28	3.30	4.32	4.57	4.83	5.08	5.34	5.59	5.85	6.10	6.36	6.61	6.87	7.12
96	.34	1.36	2.38	3.40	4.43	4.68	4.94	5.20	5.45	5.71	5.97	6.22	6.48	6.74	6.99	7.25
95	.42	1.45	2.48	3.51	4.54	4.80	5.06	5.31	5.57	5.83	6.09	6.35	6.61	6.86	7.12	7.38
94	.51	1.54	2.58	3.62	4.65	4.91	5.17	5.43	5.69	5.95	6.21	6.47	6.73	6.99	7.25	7.51
93	.60	1.64	2.68	3.72	4.77	5.03	5.29	5.55	5.81	6.08	6.34	6.60	6.86	7.12	7.38	7.65
92	.69	1.74	2.78	3.83	4.88	5.15	5.41	5.67	5.94	6.20	6.46	6.73	6.99	7.26	7.52	7.78
91	.78	1.83	2.89	3.94	5.00	5.27	5.53	5.80	6.06	6.33	6.59	6.86	7.12	7.39	7.66	7.92
90	.87	1.93	2.99	4.06	5.12	5.39	5.65	5.92	6.19	6.46	6.72	6.99	7.26	7.53	7.79	8.06
89	.97	2.03	3.10	4.17	5.24	5.51	5.78	6.05	6.32	6.59	6.85	7.12	7.39	7.66	7.93	8.20
88	1.06	2.13	3.21	4.28	5.36	5.63	5.91	6.18	6.45	6.72	6.99	7.26	7.53	7.80	8.08	8.35
87	1.16	2.24	3.32	4.40	5.49	5.76	6.03	6.31	6.58	6.85	7.13	7.40	7.67	7.95	8.22	8.49
86	1.26	2.34	3.43	4.52	5.61	5.89	6.16	6.44	6.71	6.99	7.26	7.54	7.81	8.09	8.37	8.64
85	1.35	2.45	3.54	4.64	5.74	6.02	6.30	6.57	6.85	7.13	7.40	7.68	7.96	8.24	8.52	8.79
84	1.45	2.55	3.65	4.76	5.87	6.15	6.43	6.71	6.99	7.27	7.55	7.83	8.11	8.39	8.67	8.95
83	1.55	2.66	3.77	4.88	6.00	6.28	6.56	6.85	7.13	7.41	7.69	7.97	8.25	8.54	8.82	9.10
82	1.66	2.77	3.89	5.01	6.14	6.42	6.70	6.99	7.27	7.55	7.84	8.12	8.41	8.69	8.98	9.26
81	1.76	2.88	4.01	5.14	6.27	6.56	6.84	7.13	7.41	7.70	7.99	8.27	8.56	8.85	9.13	9.42
80	1.86	2.99	4.13	5.27	6.41	6.70	6.98	7.27	7.56	7.85	8.14	8.43	8.72	9.01	9.30	9.59
79	1.97	3.11	4.25	5.40	6.55	6.84	7.13	7.42	7.71	8.00	8.29	8.58	8.88	9.17	9.46	9.75
78	2.08	3.22	4.37	5.53	6.69	6.98	7.28	7.57	7.86	8.15	8.45	8.74	9.04	9.33	9.63	9.92
77	2.18	3.34	4.50	5.66	6.84	7.13	7.42	7.72	8.02	8.31	8.61	8.90	9.20	9.50	9.80	10.09
76	2.30	3.46	4.62	5.80	6.98	7.28	7.58	7.87	8.17	8.47	8.77	9.07	9.37	9.67	9.97	10.27
75	2.41	3.58	4.75	5.94	7.13	7.43	7.73	8.03	8.33	8.63	8.93	9.24	9.54	9.84	10.15	10.45
74	2.52	3.70	4.88	6.08	7.28	7.58	7.89	8.19	8.49	8.80	9.10	9.41	9.71	10.02	10.32	10.63
73	2.63	3.82	5.02	6.22	7.44	7.74	8.05	8.35	8.66	8.96	9.27	9.58	9.89	10.20	10.51	10.82
72	2.75	3.95	5.15	6.37	7.59	7.90	8.21	8.52	8.83	9.14	9.45	9.76	10.07	10.38	10.69	11.01
71	2.87	4.08	5.29	6.52	7.75	8.06	8.37	8.68	9.00	9.31	9.62	9.94	10.25	10.57	10.88	11.20
70	2.99	4.21	5.43	6.67	7.91	8.23	8.54	8.86	9.17	9.49	9.80	10.12	10.44	10.76	11.07	11.39
69	3.11	4.34	5.57	6.82	8.08	8.40	8.71	9.03	9.35	9.67	9.99	10.31	10.63	10.95	11.27	11.59
68	3.23	4.47	5.72	6.98	8.25	8.57	8.89	9.21	9.53	9.85	10.17	10.50	10.82	11.15	11.47	11.80
67	3.36	4.61	5.86	7.14	8.42	8.74	9.06	9.39	9.71	10.04	10.36	10.69	11.02	11.35	11.68	12.01
66	3.49	4.74	6.01	7.30	8.59	8.92	9.24	9.57	9.90	10.23	10.56	10.89	11.22	11.55	11.89	12.22
65	3.62	4.89	6.17	7.46	8.77	9.10	9.43	9.76	10.09	10.42	10.76	11.09	11.43	11.76	12.10	12.44
64	3.75	5.03	6.32	7.63	8.95	9.28	9.62	9.95	10.29	10.62	10.96	11.30	11.64	11.98	12.32	12.66
63	3.88	5.17	6.48	7.80	9.14	9.47	9.81	10.15	10.49	10.83	11.17	11.51	11.85	12.20	12.54	12.89
62	4.02	5.32	6.64	7.97	9.32	9.66	10.01	10.35	10.69	11.03	11.38	11.73	12.07	12.42	12.77	13.12
61	4.16	5.47	6.80	8.15	9.52	9.86	10.21	10.55	10.90	11.25	11.60	11.95	12.30	12.65	13.00	13.36
60	4.30	5.63	6.97	8.33	9.71	10.06	10.41	10.76	11.11	11.46	11.82	12.17	12.53	12.88	13.24	13.60
59	4.44	5.78	7.14	8.52	9.91	10.27	10.62	10.97	11.33	11.69	12.04	12.40	12.76	13.12	13.49	13.85
58	4.59	5.94	7.31	8.71	10.12	10.48	10.83	11.19	11.55	11.91	12.27	12.64	13.00	13.37	13.74	14.10
57	4.73	6.10	7.49	8.90	10.33	10.69	11.05	11.41	11.78	12.14	12.51	12.88	13.25	13.62	13.99	14.37
56	4.89	6.27	7.67	9.10	10.54	10.91	11.28	11.64	12.01	12.38	12.75	13.13	13.50	13.88	14.26	14.63
55	5.04	6.44	7.86	9.30	10.76	11.13	11.50	11.87	12.25	12.63	13.00	13.38	13.76	14.14	14.53	14.91
54	5.20	6.61	8.04	9.50	10.99	11.36	11.74	12.12	12.50	12.88	13.26	13.64	14.03	14.41	14.80	15.19
53	5.36	6.78	8.24	9.71	11.22	11.60	11.98	12.36	12.75	13.13	13.52	13.91	14.30	14.69	15.09	15.48
52	5.52	6.96	8.43	9.93	11.45	11.84	12.23	12.61	13.00	13.40	13.79	14.19	14.58	14.98	15.38	15.78
51	5.69	7.15	8.63	10.15	11.70	12.09	12.48	12.87	13.27	13.67	14.07	14.47	14.87	15.28	15.68	16.09
50	5.86	7.33	8.84	10.38	11.94	12.34	12.74	13.14	13.54	13.94	14.35	14.76	15.17	15.58	15.99	16.41
49	6.03	7.52	9.05	10.61	12.20	12.60	13.01	13.41	13.82	14.23	14.64	15.06	15.47	15.89	16.31	16.73
48	6.21	7.72	9.27	10.85	12.46	12.87	13.28	13.69	14.11	14.52	14.94	15.36	15.79	16.21	16.64	17.07
47	6.39	7.92	9.49	11.09	12.73	13.14	13.56	13.98	14.40	14.83	15.25	15.68	16.11	16.54	16.98	17.42
46	6.57	8.13	9.72	11.34	13.01	13.43	13.85	14.28	14.71	15.14	15.57	16.01	16.45	16.89	17.33	17.77
45	6.76	8.34	9.95	11.60	13.29	13.72	14.15	14.59	15.02	15.46	15.90	16.35	16.79	17.24	17.69	18.14
44	6.95	8.55	10.19	11.87	13.59	14.02	14.46	14.90	15.35	15.79	16.24	16.69	17.15	17.61	18.07	18.53
43	7.15	8.77	10.43	12.14	13.89	14.33	14.78	15.23	15.68	16.14	16.59	17.06	17.52	17.98	18.45	18.93
42	7.36	9.00	10.69	12.42	14.20	14.65	15.11	15.57	16.03	16.49	16.96	17.43	17.90	18.38	18.86	19.34
41	7.56	9.23	10.95	12.71	14.52	14.98	15.45	15.92	16.39	16.86	17.34	17.82	18.30	18.78	19.27	19.76
40	7.78	9.47	11.21	13.01	14.86	15.33	15.80	16.28	16.76	17.24	17.73	18.22	18.71	19.21	19.71	20.21
39	8.00	9.72	11.49	13.32	15.20	15.68	16.16	16.65	17.14	17.63	18.13	18.63	19.14	19.64	20.16	20.67
35	8.94	10.78	12.69	14.66	16.71	17.24	17.77	18.30	18.84	19.38	19.93	20.48	21.03	21.59	22.16	22.73
30	10.28	12.32	14.44	16.67	18.99	19.59	20.19	20.80	21.42	22.05	22.68	23.31	23.96	24.61	25.26	25.92
25	11.89	14.18	16.61	19.18	21.91	22.61	23.33	24.05	24.79	25.53	26.29	27.05	27.82	28.61	29.40	30.20
20	13.87	16.54	19.42	22.53	25.89	26.77	27.66	28.57	29.50	30.45	31.40	32.38	33.37	34.37	35.39	36.42
15	16.45	19.72	23.37	27.44	31.97	33.17	34.41	35.67	36.97	38.28	39.63	41.00	42.40	43.82	45.26	46.72
10	20.13	24.59	29.86	36.14	43.50	45.51	47.57	49.68	51.85	54.06	56.31	58.60	60.92	63.27	65.65	68.04

Description: This table shows the price to pay for a bond at the yield rate. The yield is to maturity.

Example: The price of a 10.75 %, 12 year bond to yield 8 % to maturity is $ 120.96.

YIELD	7.00%	7.25%	7.50%	7.75%	8.00%	8.25%	8.50%	8.75%	9.00%	9.25%	9.50%	9.75%	10.00%	10.25%	10.50%	10.75%
0.00	184.00	187.00	190.00	193.00	196.00	199.00	202.00	205.00	208.00	211.00	214.00	217.00	220.00	223.00	226.00	229.00
1.00	167.69	170.51	173.33	176.15	178.97	181.79	184.61	187.43	190.25	193.07	195.89	198.71	201.53	204.35	207.17	209.99
2.00	153.11	155.76	158.42	161.07	163.73	166.39	169.04	171.70	174.35	177.01	179.66	182.32	184.97	187.63	190.28	192.94
3.00	140.06	142.56	145.07	147.57	150.08	152.58	155.08	157.59	160.09	162.60	165.10	167.60	170.11	172.61	175.11	177.62
4.00	128.37	130.74	133.10	135.46	137.83	140.19	142.56	144.92	147.28	149.65	152.01	154.38	156.74	159.11	161.47	163.83
4.25	125.64	127.97	130.30	132.64	134.97	137.30	139.63	141.96	144.29	146.62	148.95	151.28	153.62	155.95	158.28	160.61
4.50	122.99	125.28	127.58	129.88	132.18	134.48	136.78	139.08	141.38	143.67	145.97	148.27	150.57	152.87	155.17	157.47
4.75	120.40	122.67	124.93	127.20	129.47	131.74	134.00	136.27	138.54	140.80	143.07	145.34	147.60	149.87	152.14	154.40
5.00	117.88	120.12	122.36	124.59	126.83	129.06	131.30	133.53	135.77	138.01	140.24	142.48	144.71	146.95	149.18	151.42
5.25	115.44	117.64	119.85	122.05	124.26	126.46	128.67	130.87	133.08	135.28	137.49	139.69	141.90	144.10	146.31	148.51
5.50	113.05	115.23	117.40	119.58	121.75	123.93	126.10	128.28	130.45	132.63	134.80	136.98	139.15	141.33	143.50	145.68
5.75	110.73	112.87	115.02	117.17	119.31	121.46	123.60	125.75	127.89	130.04	132.19	134.33	136.48	138.62	140.77	142.91
6.00	108.47	110.58	112.70	114.82	116.94	119.05	121.17	123.29	125.40	127.52	129.64	131.75	133.87	135.99	138.10	140.22
6.25	106.27	108.35	110.44	112.53	114.62	116.71	118.80	120.89	122.98	125.06	127.15	129.24	131.33	133.42	135.51	137.60
6.50	104.12	106.18	108.24	110.31	112.37	114.43	116.49	118.55	120.61	122.67	124.73	126.79	128.85	130.92	132.98	135.04
6.75	102.03	104.07	106.10	108.14	110.17	112.20	114.24	116.27	118.31	120.34	122.37	124.41	126.44	128.47	130.51	132.54
7.00	100.00	102.01	104.01	106.02	108.03	110.04	112.04	114.05	116.06	118.07	120.07	122.08	124.09	126.09	128.10	130.11
7.25	98.02	100.00	101.98	103.96	105.94	107.92	109.91	111.89	113.87	115.85	117.83	119.81	121.79	123.77	125.76	127.74
7.50	96.09	98.04	100.00	101.96	103.91	105.87	107.82	109.78	111.73	113.69	115.64	117.60	119.56	121.51	123.47	125.42
7.75	94.21	96.14	98.07	100.00	101.93	103.86	105.79	107.72	109.65	111.58	113.51	115.44	117.37	119.30	121.24	123.17
8.00	92.38	94.28	96.19	98.09	100.00	101.91	103.81	105.72	107.62	109.53	111.44	113.34	115.25	117.15	119.06	120.96
8.25	90.59	92.47	94.35	96.24	98.12	100.00	101.88	103.76	105.65	107.53	109.41	111.29	113.17	115.05	116.94	118.82
8.50	88.85	90.71	92.57	94.43	96.28	98.14	100.00	101.86	103.72	105.57	107.43	109.29	111.15	113.01	114.86	116.72
8.75	87.16	88.99	90.83	92.66	94.50	96.33	98.17	100.00	101.83	103.67	105.50	107.34	109.17	111.01	112.84	114.68
9.00	85.50	87.32	89.13	90.94	92.75	94.56	96.38	98.19	100.00	101.81	103.62	105.44	107.25	109.06	110.87	112.68
9.25	83.89	85.68	87.47	89.26	91.05	92.84	94.63	96.42	98.21	100.00	101.79	103.58	105.37	107.16	108.95	110.74
9.50	82.32	84.09	85.86	87.63	89.39	91.16	92.93	94.70	96.46	98.23	100.00	101.77	103.54	105.30	107.07	108.84
9.75	80.79	82.54	84.29	86.03	87.78	89.52	91.27	93.02	94.76	96.51	98.25	100.00	101.75	103.49	105.24	106.98
10.00	79.30	81.03	82.75	84.48	86.20	87.93	89.65	91.38	93.10	94.83	96.55	98.28	100.00	101.72	103.45	105.17
10.25	77.85	79.55	81.26	82.96	84.66	86.37	88.07	89.78	91.48	93.18	94.89	96.59	98.30	100.00	101.70	103.41
10.50	76.43	78.11	79.80	81.48	83.16	84.85	86.53	88.21	89.90	91.58	93.27	94.95	96.63	98.32	100.00	101.68
10.75	75.05	76.71	78.37	80.04	81.70	83.36	85.03	86.69	88.35	90.02	91.68	93.35	95.01	96.67	98.34	100.00
11.00	73.70	75.34	76.98	78.63	80.27	81.92	83.56	85.20	86.85	88.49	90.14	91.78	93.42	95.07	96.71	98.36
11.25	72.38	74.01	75.63	77.25	78.88	80.50	82.13	83.75	85.38	87.00	88.63	90.25	91.88	93.50	95.13	96.75
11.50	71.10	72.70	74.31	75.91	77.52	79.13	80.73	82.34	83.94	85.55	87.15	88.76	90.37	91.97	93.58	95.18
11.75	69.85	71.43	73.02	74.61	76.19	77.78	79.37	80.96	82.54	84.13	85.72	87.30	88.89	90.48	92.06	93.65
12.00	68.62	70.19	71.76	73.33	74.90	76.47	78.04	79.61	81.17	82.74	84.31	85.88	87.45	89.02	90.59	92.16
12.25	67.43	68.98	70.53	72.08	73.64	75.19	76.74	78.29	79.84	81.39	82.94	84.49	86.04	87.59	89.14	90.69
12.50	66.27	67.80	69.34	70.87	72.40	73.94	75.47	77.00	78.54	80.07	81.60	83.13	84.67	86.20	87.73	89.27
12.75	65.14	66.65	68.17	69.68	71.20	72.71	74.23	75.75	77.26	78.78	80.29	81.81	83.33	84.84	86.36	87.87
13.00	64.03	65.53	67.03	68.52	70.02	71.52	73.02	74.52	76.02	77.52	79.02	80.52	82.01	83.51	85.01	86.51
13.25	62.95	64.43	65.91	67.39	68.88	70.36	71.84	73.32	74.80	76.29	77.77	79.25	80.73	82.21	83.70	85.18
13.50	61.89	63.36	64.82	66.29	67.75	69.22	70.69	72.15	73.62	75.08	76.55	78.01	79.48	80.95	82.41	83.88
13.75	60.86	62.31	63.76	65.21	66.66	68.11	69.56	71.01	72.46	73.91	75.36	76.81	78.26	79.71	81.16	82.61
14.00	59.86	61.29	62.72	64.16	65.59	67.03	68.46	69.89	71.33	72.76	74.19	75.63	77.06	78.49	79.93	81.36
14.25	58.88	60.29	61.71	63.13	64.55	65.97	67.38	68.80	70.22	71.64	73.06	74.47	75.89	77.31	78.73	80.15
14.50	57.92	59.32	60.72	62.13	63.53	64.93	66.33	67.74	69.14	70.54	71.95	73.35	74.75	76.15	77.56	78.96
14.75	56.98	58.37	59.76	61.14	62.53	63.92	65.31	66.70	68.08	69.47	70.86	72.25	73.63	75.02	76.41	77.80
15.00	56.07	57.44	58.81	60.19	61.56	62.93	64.31	65.68	67.05	68.42	69.80	71.17	72.54	73.92	75.29	76.66
15.25	55.18	56.53	57.89	59.25	60.61	61.97	63.33	64.68	66.04	67.40	68.76	70.12	71.48	72.83	74.19	75.55
15.50	54.30	55.65	56.99	58.34	59.68	61.02	62.37	63.71	65.06	66.40	67.74	69.09	70.43	71.78	73.12	74.46
15.75	53.45	54.78	56.11	57.44	58.77	60.10	61.43	62.76	64.09	65.42	66.75	68.08	69.41	70.74	72.07	73.40
16.00	52.62	53.94	55.25	56.57	57.88	59.20	60.52	61.83	63.15	64.47	65.78	67.10	68.41	69.73	71.05	72.36
16.25	51.81	53.11	54.41	55.72	57.02	58.32	59.62	60.93	62.23	63.53	64.83	66.14	67.44	68.74	70.04	71.35
16.50	51.01	52.30	53.59	54.88	56.17	57.46	58.75	60.04	61.33	62.62	63.90	65.19	66.48	67.77	69.06	70.35
16.75	50.24	51.51	52.79	54.07	55.34	56.62	57.89	59.17	60.45	61.72	63.00	64.27	65.55	66.83	68.10	69.38
17.00	49.48	50.74	52.01	53.27	54.53	55.79	57.06	58.32	59.58	60.85	62.11	63.37	64.64	65.90	67.16	68.42
17.25	48.74	49.99	51.24	52.49	53.74	54.99	56.24	57.49	58.74	59.99	61.24	62.49	63.74	64.99	66.24	67.49
17.50	48.01	49.25	50.49	51.73	52.97	54.20	55.44	56.68	57.92	59.15	60.39	61.63	62.87	64.10	65.34	66.58
17.75	47.31	48.53	49.76	50.98	52.21	53.43	54.66	55.88	57.11	58.33	59.56	60.79	62.01	63.24	64.46	65.69
18.00	46.61	47.83	49.04	50.25	51.47	52.68	53.89	55.11	56.32	57.53	58.75	59.96	61.17	62.39	63.60	64.81
18.25	45.94	47.14	48.34	49.54	50.74	51.94	53.15	54.35	55.55	56.75	57.95	59.15	60.35	61.56	62.76	63.96
18.50	45.28	46.46	47.65	48.84	50.03	51.22	52.41	53.60	54.79	55.98	57.17	58.36	59.55	60.74	61.93	63.12
18.75	44.63	45.81	46.98	48.16	49.34	50.52	51.70	52.87	54.05	55.23	56.41	57.59	58.77	59.94	61.12	62.30
19.00	44.00	45.16	46.33	47.50	48.66	49.83	51.00	52.16	53.33	54.50	55.66	56.83	58.00	59.16	60.33	61.50
20.00	41.60	42.72	43.85	44.97	46.09	47.21	48.34	49.46	50.58	51.71	52.83	53.95	55.08	56.20	57.32	58.45
25.00	32.26	33.20	34.14	35.08	36.03	36.97	37.91	38.85	39.79	40.73	41.67	42.61	43.55	44.49	45.43	46.37
30.00	26.01	26.82	27.62	28.42	29.23	30.03	30.84	31.64	32.45	33.25	34.05	34.86	35.66	36.47	37.27	38.07

Description: This table shows the yield to maturity of a bond purchased at the price shown in the index.

Example: The yield to maturity of a 10.75 %, 12 year bond at a price of 113.00 is 8.95 %.

PRICE	7.00%	7.25%	7.50%	7.75%	8.00%	8.25%	COUPON RATE, % 8.50%	8.75%	9.00%	9.25%	9.50%	9.75%	10.00%	10.25%	10.50%	10.75%
145	2.60	2.80	3.00	3.20	3.40	3.59	3.79	3.99	4.19	4.38	4.58	4.77	4.97	5.17	5.36	5.56
140	3.00	3.20	3.41	3.61	3.81	4.01	4.21	4.41	4.62	4.82	5.02	5.22	5.42	5.62	5.82	6.02
135	3.41	3.62	3.83	4.04	4.24	4.45	4.65	4.86	5.07	5.27	5.48	5.68	5.89	6.09	6.29	6.50
130	3.85	4.06	4.27	4.48	4.70	4.91	5.12	5.33	5.54	5.75	5.96	6.17	6.38	6.59	6.80	7.01
129	3.94	4.15	4.36	4.58	4.79	5.00	5.21	5.42	5.64	5.85	6.06	6.27	6.48	6.69	6.90	7.11
128	4.03	4.24	4.46	4.67	4.88	5.10	5.31	5.52	5.73	5.95	6.16	6.37	6.58	6.79	7.01	7.22
127	4.12	4.33	4.55	4.76	4.98	5.19	5.41	5.62	5.83	6.05	6.26	6.47	6.69	6.90	7.11	7.32
126	4.21	4.43	4.64	4.86	5.07	5.29	5.51	5.72	5.93	6.15	6.36	6.58	6.79	7.01	7.22	7.43
125	4.30	4.52	4.74	4.96	5.17	5.39	5.60	5.82	6.04	6.25	6.47	6.68	6.90	7.11	7.33	7.54
124	4.40	4.62	4.83	5.05	5.27	5.49	5.70	5.92	6.14	6.36	6.57	6.79	7.00	7.22	7.44	7.65
123	4.49	4.71	4.93	5.15	5.37	5.59	5.81	6.02	6.24	6.46	6.68	6.90	7.11	7.33	7.55	7.76
122	4.59	4.81	5.03	5.25	5.47	5.69	5.91	6.13	6.35	6.57	6.79	7.00	7.22	7.44	7.66	7.88
121	4.69	4.91	5.13	5.35	5.57	5.79	6.01	6.23	6.45	6.67	6.89	7.11	7.33	7.55	7.77	7.99
120	4.78	5.01	5.23	5.45	5.67	5.90	6.12	6.34	6.56	6.78	7.00	7.22	7.44	7.67	7.89	8.11
119	4.88	5.11	5.33	5.55	5.78	6.00	6.22	6.45	6.67	6.89	7.11	7.34	7.56	7.78	8.00	8.22
118	4.98	5.21	5.43	5.66	5.88	6.11	6.33	6.55	6.78	7.00	7.23	7.45	7.67	7.90	8.12	8.34
117	5.08	5.31	5.54	5.76	5.99	6.21	6.44	6.66	6.89	7.11	7.34	7.56	7.79	8.01	8.24	8.46
116	5.19	5.41	5.64	5.87	6.10	6.32	6.55	6.78	7.00	7.23	7.45	7.68	7.91	8.13	8.36	8.58
115	5.29	5.52	5.75	5.98	6.20	6.43	6.66	6.89	7.12	7.34	7.57	7.80	8.02	8.25	8.48	8.71
114	5.39	5.62	5.85	6.08	6.31	6.54	6.77	7.00	7.23	7.46	7.69	7.92	8.14	8.37	8.60	8.83
113	5.50	5.73	5.96	6.19	6.42	6.65	6.89	7.12	7.35	7.58	7.81	8.04	8.27	8.50	8.73	8.95
112	5.61	5.84	6.07	6.30	6.54	6.77	7.00	7.23	7.46	7.70	7.93	8.16	8.39	8.62	8.85	9.08
111	5.72	5.95	6.18	6.42	6.65	6.88	7.12	7.35	7.58	7.82	8.05	8.28	8.51	8.75	8.98	9.21
110	5.82	6.06	6.29	6.53	6.76	7.00	7.23	7.47	7.70	7.94	8.17	8.41	8.64	8.87	9.11	9.34
109	5.94	6.17	6.41	6.64	6.88	7.12	7.35	7.59	7.82	8.06	8.30	8.53	8.77	9.00	9.24	9.47
108	6.05	6.29	6.52	6.76	7.00	7.24	7.47	7.71	7.95	8.19	8.42	8.66	8.90	9.13	9.37	9.61
107	6.16	6.40	6.64	6.88	7.12	7.36	7.60	7.83	8.07	8.31	8.55	8.79	9.03	9.27	9.50	9.74
106	6.28	6.52	6.76	7.00	7.24	7.48	7.72	7.96	8.20	8.44	8.68	8.92	9.16	9.40	9.64	9.88
105	6.39	6.63	6.88	7.12	7.36	7.60	7.84	8.09	8.33	8.57	8.81	9.05	9.29	9.54	9.78	10.02
104	6.51	6.75	7.00	7.24	7.48	7.73	7.97	8.21	8.46	8.70	8.94	9.19	9.43	9.67	9.92	10.16
103	6.63	6.87	7.12	7.36	7.61	7.85	8.10	8.34	8.59	8.83	9.08	9.32	9.57	9.81	10.06	10.30
102	6.75	7.00	7.24	7.49	7.74	7.98	8.23	8.48	8.72	8.97	9.22	9.46	9.71	9.96	10.20	10.45
101	6.87	7.12	7.37	7.62	7.86	8.11	8.36	8.61	8.86	9.11	9.35	9.60	9.85	10.10	10.35	10.60
100	7.00	7.25	7.50	7.75	8.00	8.25	8.50	8.75	9.00	9.25	9.50	9.75	10.00	10.25	10.50	10.75
99	7.12	7.37	7.62	7.88	8.13	8.38	8.63	8.88	9.13	9.39	9.64	9.89	10.14	10.39	10.64	10.90
98	7.25	7.50	7.75	8.01	8.26	8.51	8.77	9.02	9.27	9.53	9.78	10.04	10.29	10.54	10.80	11.05
97	7.38	7.63	7.89	8.14	8.40	8.65	8.91	9.16	9.42	9.67	9.93	10.18	10.44	10.69	10.95	11.21
96	7.51	7.76	8.02	8.28	8.53	8.79	9.05	9.31	9.56	9.82	10.08	10.33	10.59	10.85	11.11	11.36
95	7.64	7.90	8.16	8.42	8.67	8.93	9.19	9.45	9.71	9.97	10.23	10.49	10.75	11.01	11.27	11.52
94	7.77	8.03	8.29	8.55	8.82	9.08	9.34	9.60	9.86	10.12	10.38	10.64	10.90	11.16	11.43	11.69
93	7.91	8.17	8.43	8.70	8.96	9.22	9.48	9.75	10.01	10.27	10.54	10.80	11.06	11.33	11.59	11.85
92	8.05	8.31	8.58	8.84	9.10	9.37	9.63	9.90	10.16	10.43	10.69	10.96	11.22	11.49	11.76	12.02
91	8.19	8.45	8.72	8.99	9.25	9.52	9.79	10.05	10.32	10.59	10.85	11.12	11.39	11.66	11.92	12.19
90	8.33	8.60	8.87	9.13	9.40	9.67	9.94	10.21	10.48	10.75	11.02	11.29	11.56	11.83	12.10	12.37
89	8.47	8.74	9.01	9.28	9.56	9.83	10.10	10.37	10.64	10.91	11.18	11.45	11.73	12.00	12.27	12.54
88	8.62	8.89	9.16	9.44	9.71	9.98	10.26	10.53	10.80	11.08	11.35	11.62	11.90	12.17	12.45	12.72
87	8.77	9.04	9.32	9.59	9.87	10.14	10.42	10.69	10.97	11.25	11.52	11.80	12.07	12.35	12.63	12.90
86	8.92	9.20	9.47	9.75	10.03	10.30	10.58	10.86	11.14	11.42	11.70	11.97	12.25	12.53	12.81	13.09
85	9.07	9.35	9.63	9.91	10.19	10.47	10.75	11.03	11.31	11.59	11.87	12.15	12.43	12.72	13.00	13.28
84	9.23	9.51	9.79	10.07	10.35	10.64	10.92	11.20	11.48	11.77	12.05	12.33	12.62	12.90	13.19	13.47
83	9.39	9.67	9.95	10.24	10.52	10.81	11.09	11.38	11.66	11.95	12.23	12.52	12.81	13.09	13.38	13.67
82	9.55	9.83	10.12	10.41	10.69	10.98	11.27	11.56	11.84	12.13	12.42	12.71	13.00	13.29	13.58	13.87
81	9.71	10.00	10.29	10.58	10.87	11.16	11.45	11.74	12.03	12.32	12.61	12.90	13.19	13.48	13.78	14.07
80	9.88	10.17	10.46	10.75	11.04	11.34	11.63	11.92	12.21	12.51	12.80	13.10	13.39	13.69	13.98	14.28
79	10.05	10.34	10.63	10.93	11.22	11.52	11.81	12.11	12.41	12.70	13.00	13.30	13.59	13.89	14.19	14.49
78	10.22	10.51	10.81	11.11	11.41	11.70	12.00	12.30	12.60	12.90	13.20	13.50	13.80	14.10	14.40	14.70
77	10.39	10.69	10.99	11.29	11.59	11.89	12.19	12.50	12.80	13.10	13.40	13.70	14.01	14.31	14.62	14.92
76	10.57	10.87	11.18	11.48	11.78	12.09	12.39	12.69	13.00	13.30	13.61	13.92	14.22	14.53	14.84	15.14
75	10.75	11.06	11.36	11.67	11.98	12.28	12.59	12.90	13.20	13.51	13.82	14.13	14.44	14.75	15.06	15.37
74	10.94	11.25	11.55	11.86	12.17	12.48	12.79	13.10	13.41	13.73	14.04	14.35	14.66	14.98	15.29	15.60
70	11.71	12.03	12.36	12.68	13.00	13.32	13.65	13.97	14.30	14.62	14.95	15.27	15.60	15.93	16.26	16.58
65	12.78	13.11	13.45	13.79	14.14	14.48	14.82	15.16	15.51	15.85	16.20	16.55	16.89	17.24	17.59	17.94
60	13.96	14.32	14.68	15.04	15.41	15.77	16.14	16.51	16.87	17.24	17.61	17.98	18.35	18.73	19.10	19.48
55	15.29	15.68	16.07	16.46	16.85	17.24	17.64	18.03	18.43	18.82	19.22	19.62	20.02	20.42	20.83	21.23
50	16.82	17.24	17.66	18.08	18.51	18.93	19.36	19.79	20.22	20.65	21.09	21.52	21.96	22.40	22.84	23.28
45	18.60	19.06	19.52	19.98	20.45	20.91	21.38	21.86	22.33	22.81	23.28	23.77	24.25	24.73	25.22	25.71
40	20.71	21.22	21.74	22.25	22.77	23.29	23.82	24.34	24.88	25.41	25.95	26.48	27.03	27.57	28.12	28.67
35	23.30	23.88	24.46	25.05	25.64	26.23	26.83	27.44	28.04	28.65	29.27	29.89	30.51	31.13	31.76	32.39

Description: This table shows the price to pay for a bond at the yield rate. The yield is to maturity.

Example: The price of a 15.00 %, 12 year bond to yield 8 % to maturity is $ 153.36.

COUPON RATE, %

YIELD	11.00%	11.25%	11.50%	11.75%	12.00%	12.25%	12.50%	12.75%	13.00%	13.25%	13.50%	13.75%	14.00%	14.25%	14.50%	15.00%
0.00	232.00	235.00	238.00	241.00	244.00	247.00	250.00	253.00	256.00	259.00	262.00	265.00	268.00	271.00	274.00	280.00
1.00	212.81	215.63	218.46	221.28	224.10	226.92	229.74	232.56	235.38	238.20	241.02	243.84	246.66	249.48	252.30	257.94
2.00	195.60	198.25	200.91	203.56	206.22	208.87	211.53	214.18	216.84	219.49	222.15	224.80	227.46	230.12	232.77	238.08
3.00	180.12	182.63	185.13	187.63	190.14	192.64	195.14	197.65	200.15	202.66	205.16	207.66	210.17	212.67	215.17	220.18
4.00	166.20	168.56	170.93	173.29	175.66	178.02	180.38	182.75	185.11	187.48	189.84	192.21	194.57	196.93	199.30	204.03
4.25	162.94	165.27	167.60	169.93	172.26	174.60	176.93	179.26	181.59	183.92	186.25	188.58	190.91	193.24	195.58	200.24
4.50	159.76	162.06	164.36	166.66	168.96	171.26	173.56	175.85	178.15	180.45	182.75	185.05	187.35	189.65	191.95	196.54
4.75	156.67	158.94	161.20	163.47	165.74	168.00	170.27	172.54	174.80	177.07	179.34	181.61	183.87	186.14	188.41	192.94
5.00	153.65	155.89	158.13	160.36	162.60	164.83	167.07	169.30	171.54	173.78	176.01	178.25	180.48	182.72	184.95	189.42
5.25	150.72	152.92	155.13	157.33	159.54	161.74	163.95	166.15	168.36	170.56	172.77	174.97	177.18	179.38	181.59	186.00
5.50	147.85	150.03	152.20	154.38	156.55	158.73	160.90	163.08	165.25	167.43	169.60	171.78	173.95	176.13	178.30	182.65
5.75	145.06	147.21	149.35	151.50	153.64	155.79	157.93	160.08	162.23	164.37	166.52	168.66	170.81	172.95	175.10	179.39
6.00	142.34	144.46	146.57	148.69	150.81	152.92	155.04	157.16	159.27	161.39	163.51	165.63	167.74	169.86	171.98	176.21
6.25	139.69	141.77	143.86	145.95	148.04	150.13	152.22	154.31	156.40	158.48	160.57	162.66	164.75	166.84	168.93	173.11
6.50	137.10	139.16	141.22	143.28	145.34	147.40	149.47	151.53	153.59	155.65	157.71	159.77	161.83	163.89	165.95	170.08
6.75	134.58	136.61	138.64	140.68	142.71	144.75	146.78	148.81	150.85	152.88	154.92	156.95	158.98	161.02	163.05	167.12
7.00	132.12	134.12	136.13	138.14	140.15	142.15	144.16	146.17	148.18	150.18	152.19	154.20	156.20	158.21	160.22	164.23
7.25	129.72	131.70	133.68	135.66	137.64	139.62	141.61	143.59	145.57	147.55	149.53	151.51	153.49	155.47	157.45	161.42
7.50	127.38	129.33	131.29	133.25	135.20	137.16	139.11	141.07	143.02	144.98	146.93	148.89	150.85	152.80	154.76	158.67
7.75	125.10	127.03	128.96	130.89	132.82	134.75	136.68	138.61	140.54	142.47	144.40	146.33	148.26	150.19	152.12	155.98
8.00	122.87	124.78	126.68	128.59	130.49	132.40	134.31	136.21	138.12	140.02	141.93	143.84	145.74	147.65	149.55	153.36
8.25	120.70	122.58	124.46	126.34	128.23	130.11	131.99	133.87	135.75	137.63	139.52	141.40	143.28	145.16	147.04	150.81
8.50	118.58	120.44	122.30	124.15	126.01	127.87	129.73	131.59	133.44	135.30	137.16	139.02	140.88	142.73	144.59	148.31
8.75	116.51	118.35	120.18	122.02	123.85	125.69	127.52	129.36	131.19	133.03	134.86	136.70	138.53	140.36	142.20	145.87
9.00	114.50	116.31	118.12	119.93	121.74	123.56	125.37	127.18	128.99	130.80	132.61	134.43	136.24	138.05	139.86	143.49
9.25	112.53	114.32	116.11	117.90	119.68	121.47	123.26	125.05	126.84	128.63	130.42	132.21	134.00	135.79	137.58	141.16
9.50	110.61	112.37	114.14	115.91	117.68	119.44	121.21	122.98	124.75	126.51	128.28	130.05	131.82	133.58	135.35	138.89
9.75	108.73	110.48	112.22	113.97	115.71	117.46	119.21	120.95	122.70	124.44	126.19	127.94	129.68	131.43	133.17	136.67
10.00	106.90	108.62	110.35	112.07	113.80	115.52	117.25	118.97	120.70	122.42	124.15	125.87	127.60	129.32	131.05	134.50
10.25	105.11	106.82	108.52	110.22	111.93	113.63	115.34	117.04	118.74	120.45	122.15	123.86	125.56	127.26	128.97	132.38
10.50	103.37	105.05	106.73	108.42	110.10	111.79	113.47	115.15	116.84	118.52	120.20	121.89	123.57	125.25	126.94	130.31
10.75	101.66	103.33	104.99	106.65	108.32	109.98	111.65	113.31	114.97	116.64	118.30	119.96	121.63	123.29	124.95	128.28
11.00	100.00	101.64	103.29	104.93	106.58	108.22	109.86	111.51	113.15	114.80	116.44	118.08	119.73	121.37	123.02	126.30
11.25	98.38	100.00	101.62	103.25	104.87	106.50	108.12	109.75	111.37	113.00	114.62	116.25	117.87	119.50	121.12	124.37
11.50	96.79	98.39	100.00	101.61	103.21	104.82	106.42	108.03	109.63	111.24	112.85	114.45	116.06	117.66	119.27	122.48
11.75	95.24	96.83	98.41	100.00	101.59	103.17	104.76	106.35	107.94	109.52	111.11	112.70	114.28	115.87	117.46	120.63
12.00	93.72	95.29	96.86	98.43	100.00	101.57	103.14	104.71	106.28	107.84	109.41	110.98	112.55	114.12	115.69	118.83
12.25	92.25	93.80	95.35	96.90	98.45	100.00	101.55	103.10	104.65	106.20	107.75	109.31	110.86	112.41	113.96	117.06
12.50	90.80	92.33	93.87	95.40	96.93	98.47	100.00	101.53	103.07	104.60	106.13	107.67	109.20	110.73	112.27	115.33
12.75	89.39	90.90	92.42	93.94	95.45	96.97	98.48	100.00	101.52	103.03	104.55	106.06	107.58	109.10	110.61	113.64
13.00	88.01	89.51	91.01	92.51	94.00	95.50	97.00	98.50	100.00	101.50	103.00	104.50	106.00	107.49	108.99	111.99
13.25	86.66	88.14	89.63	91.11	92.59	94.07	95.55	97.04	98.52	100.00	101.48	102.96	104.45	105.93	107.41	110.37
13.50	85.34	86.81	88.27	89.74	91.21	92.67	94.14	95.60	97.07	98.53	100.00	101.47	102.93	104.40	105.86	108.79
13.75	84.06	85.50	86.95	88.40	89.85	91.30	92.75	94.20	95.65	97.10	98.55	100.00	101.45	102.90	104.35	107.25
14.00	82.80	84.23	85.66	87.10	88.53	89.96	91.40	92.83	94.27	95.70	97.13	98.57	100.00	101.43	102.87	105.73
14.25	81.57	82.98	84.40	85.82	87.24	88.66	90.07	91.49	92.91	94.33	95.75	97.16	98.58	100.00	101.42	104.25
14.50	80.36	81.76	83.17	84.57	85.97	87.38	88.78	90.18	91.58	92.99	94.39	95.79	97.19	98.60	100.00	102.81
14.75	79.18	80.57	81.96	83.35	84.74	86.12	87.51	88.90	90.29	91.67	93.06	94.45	95.84	97.22	98.61	101.39
15.00	78.03	79.41	80.78	82.15	83.53	84.90	86.27	87.64	89.02	90.39	91.76	93.14	94.51	95.88	97.25	100.00
15.25	76.91	78.27	79.63	80.98	82.34	83.70	85.06	86.42	87.78	89.13	90.49	91.85	93.21	94.57	95.93	98.64
15.50	75.81	77.15	78.50	79.84	81.18	82.53	83.87	85.22	86.56	87.90	89.25	90.59	91.94	93.28	94.62	97.31
15.75	74.73	76.06	77.39	78.72	80.05	81.38	82.71	84.04	85.37	86.70	88.03	89.36	90.69	92.02	93.35	96.01
16.00	73.68	74.99	76.31	77.63	78.94	80.26	81.57	82.89	84.21	85.52	86.84	88.16	89.47	90.79	92.10	94.74
16.25	72.65	73.95	75.25	76.56	77.86	79.16	80.46	81.77	83.07	84.37	85.67	86.98	88.28	89.58	90.88	93.49
16.50	71.64	72.93	74.22	75.51	76.80	78.09	79.37	80.66	81.95	83.24	84.53	85.82	87.11	88.40	89.69	92.27
16.75	70.65	71.93	73.20	74.48	75.76	77.03	78.31	79.58	80.86	82.14	83.41	84.69	85.96	87.24	88.52	91.07
17.00	69.69	70.95	72.21	73.48	74.74	76.00	77.27	78.53	79.79	81.05	82.32	83.58	84.84	86.11	87.37	89.90
17.25	68.74	69.99	71.24	72.49	73.74	74.99	76.24	77.49	78.75	80.00	81.25	82.50	83.75	85.00	86.25	88.75
17.50	67.82	69.06	70.29	71.53	72.77	74.01	75.24	76.48	77.72	78.96	80.20	81.43	82.67	83.91	85.15	87.62
17.75	66.91	68.14	69.36	70.59	71.81	73.04	74.27	75.49	76.72	77.94	79.17	80.39	81.62	82.84	84.07	86.52
18.00	66.03	67.24	68.45	69.67	70.88	72.09	73.31	74.52	75.73	76.95	78.16	79.37	80.59	81.80	83.01	85.44
18.25	65.16	66.36	67.56	68.76	69.96	71.17	72.37	73.57	74.77	75.97	77.17	78.37	79.58	80.78	81.98	84.38
18.50	64.31	65.50	66.69	67.88	69.07	70.26	71.45	72.64	73.83	75.02	76.21	77.40	78.59	79.78	80.97	83.34
18.75	63.48	64.66	65.83	67.01	68.19	69.37	70.55	71.72	72.90	74.08	75.26	76.44	77.62	78.79	79.97	82.33
19.00	62.66	63.83	65.00	66.16	67.33	68.50	69.66	70.83	72.00	73.16	74.33	75.50	76.66	77.83	79.00	81.33
20.00	59.57	60.69	61.81	62.94	64.06	65.18	66.31	67.43	68.55	69.68	70.80	71.92	73.05	74.17	75.29	77.54
25.00	47.32	48.26	49.20	50.14	51.08	52.02	52.96	53.90	54.84	55.78	56.72	57.66	58.60	59.55	60.49	62.37
30.00	38.88	39.68	40.49	41.29	42.10	42.90	43.70	44.51	45.31	46.12	46.92	47.73	48.53	49.33	50.14	51.75

Description: This table shows the yield to maturity of a bond purchased at the price shown in the index.

Example: The yield to maturity of a 15.00 %, 12 year bond at a price of 117.00 is 12.25 %.

COUPON RATE, %

PRICE	11.00%	11.25%	11.50%	11.75%	12.00%	12.25%	12.50%	12.75%	13.00%	13.25%	13.50%	13.75%	14.00%	14.25%	14.50%	15.00%
190	2.34	2.51	2.67	2.84	3.00	3.17	3.33	3.50	3.66	3.82	3.98	4.15	4.31	4.47	4.63	4.95
185	2.67	2.84	3.00	3.17	3.34	3.50	3.67	3.84	4.00	4.17	4.33	4.50	4.66	4.83	4.99	5.32
180	3.00	3.17	3.34	3.51	3.68	3.85	4.02	4.19	4.36	4.53	4.70	4.86	5.03	5.20	5.37	5.70
175	3.35	3.52	3.70	3.87	4.04	4.22	4.39	4.56	4.73	4.90	5.07	5.24	5.41	5.58	5.75	6.09
170	3.71	3.89	4.06	4.24	4.42	4.59	4.77	4.94	5.12	5.29	5.46	5.64	5.81	5.98	6.16	6.50
165	4.09	4.27	4.45	4.62	4.80	4.98	5.16	5.34	5.52	5.69	5.87	6.05	6.22	6.40	6.58	6.93
160	4.48	4.66	4.84	5.02	5.21	5.39	5.57	5.75	5.93	6.11	6.29	6.47	6.66	6.83	7.01	7.37
155	4.88	5.07	5.26	5.44	5.63	5.81	6.00	6.18	6.37	6.55	6.74	6.92	7.11	7.29	7.47	7.84
150	5.31	5.50	5.69	5.88	6.07	6.26	6.45	6.63	6.82	7.01	7.20	7.39	7.58	7.76	7.95	8.33
145	5.75	5.95	6.14	6.33	6.53	6.72	6.91	7.11	7.30	7.49	7.69	7.88	8.07	8.26	8.45	8.84
140	6.22	6.41	6.61	6.81	7.01	7.21	7.41	7.60	7.80	8.00	8.19	8.39	8.59	8.78	8.98	9.37
135	6.70	6.91	7.11	7.31	7.52	7.72	7.92	8.12	8.33	8.53	8.73	8.93	9.13	9.33	9.53	9.94
130	7.22	7.42	7.63	7.84	8.05	8.26	8.46	8.67	8.88	9.09	9.29	9.50	9.71	9.91	10.12	10.53
125	7.76	7.97	8.18	8.40	8.61	8.82	9.04	9.25	9.46	9.68	9.89	10.10	10.31	10.53	10.74	11.16
123	7.98	8.20	8.41	8.63	8.85	9.06	9.28	9.49	9.71	9.92	10.14	10.35	10.57	10.78	11.00	11.43
122	8.09	8.31	8.53	8.75	8.96	9.18	9.40	9.61	9.83	10.05	10.26	10.48	10.70	10.91	11.13	11.56
121	8.21	8.43	8.65	8.87	9.08	9.30	9.52	9.74	9.96	10.17	10.39	10.61	10.83	11.04	11.26	11.69
120	8.33	8.55	8.77	8.99	9.21	9.43	9.65	9.86	10.08	10.30	10.52	10.74	10.96	11.18	11.40	11.83
119	8.44	8.67	8.89	9.11	9.33	9.55	9.77	9.99	10.21	10.43	10.65	10.87	11.09	11.31	11.53	11.97
118	8.56	8.79	9.01	9.23	9.45	9.68	9.90	10.12	10.34	10.56	10.78	11.01	11.23	11.45	11.67	12.11
117	8.69	8.91	9.13	9.36	9.58	9.80	10.03	10.25	10.47	10.70	10.92	11.14	11.36	11.59	11.81	12.25
116	8.81	9.03	9.26	9.48	9.71	9.93	10.16	10.38	10.61	10.83	11.05	11.28	11.50	11.73	11.95	12.40
115	8.93	9.16	9.38	9.61	9.84	10.06	10.29	10.52	10.74	10.97	11.19	11.42	11.64	11.87	12.09	12.54
114	9.06	9.29	9.51	9.74	9.97	10.20	10.42	10.65	10.88	11.10	11.33	11.56	11.79	12.01	12.24	12.69
113	9.18	9.41	9.64	9.87	10.10	10.33	10.56	10.79	11.02	11.24	11.47	11.70	11.93	12.16	12.39	12.84
112	9.31	9.54	9.77	10.00	10.24	10.47	10.70	10.93	11.16	11.39	11.62	11.85	12.08	12.31	12.53	12.99
111	9.44	9.68	9.91	10.14	10.37	10.60	10.83	11.07	11.30	11.53	11.76	11.99	12.22	12.45	12.69	13.15
110	9.58	9.81	10.04	10.28	10.51	10.74	10.98	11.21	11.44	11.67	11.91	12.14	12.37	12.61	12.84	13.30
109	9.71	9.94	10.18	10.41	10.65	10.88	11.12	11.35	11.59	11.82	12.06	12.29	12.53	12.76	12.99	13.46
108	9.84	10.08	10.32	10.55	10.79	11.03	11.26	11.50	11.74	11.97	12.21	12.44	12.68	12.92	13.15	13.62
107	9.98	10.22	10.46	10.70	10.93	11.17	11.41	11.65	11.89	12.12	12.36	12.60	12.84	13.07	13.31	13.79
106	10.12	10.36	10.60	10.84	11.08	11.32	11.56	11.80	12.04	12.28	12.52	12.76	12.99	13.23	13.47	13.95
105	10.26	10.50	10.74	10.99	11.23	11.47	11.71	11.95	12.19	12.43	12.67	12.91	13.16	13.40	13.64	14.12
104	10.40	10.65	10.89	11.13	11.38	11.62	11.86	12.10	12.35	12.59	12.83	13.08	13.32	13.56	13.80	14.29
103	10.55	10.79	11.04	11.28	11.53	11.77	12.02	12.26	12.51	12.75	12.99	13.24	13.48	13.73	13.97	14.46
102	10.70	10.94	11.19	11.43	11.68	11.93	12.17	12.42	12.67	12.91	13.16	13.41	13.65	13.90	14.14	14.64
101	10.84	11.09	11.34	11.59	11.84	12.08	12.33	12.58	12.83	13.08	13.33	13.57	13.82	14.07	14.32	14.81
100	11.00	11.25	11.50	11.75	12.00	12.25	12.50	12.75	13.00	13.25	13.50	13.75	14.00	14.25	14.50	15.00
99	11.15	11.40	11.65	11.90	12.16	12.41	12.66	12.91	13.16	13.41	13.67	13.92	14.17	14.42	14.67	15.18
98	11.30	11.56	11.81	12.06	12.32	12.57	12.83	13.08	13.33	13.59	13.84	14.10	14.35	14.60	14.86	15.37
97	11.46	11.72	11.97	12.23	12.48	12.74	13.00	13.25	13.51	13.76	14.02	14.27	14.53	14.79	15.04	15.55
96	11.62	11.88	12.14	12.39	12.65	12.91	13.17	13.43	13.68	13.94	14.20	14.46	14.71	14.97	15.23	15.75
95	11.78	12.04	12.30	12.56	12.82	13.08	13.34	13.60	13.86	14.12	14.38	14.64	14.90	15.16	15.42	15.94
94	11.95	12.21	12.47	12.73	13.00	13.26	13.52	13.78	14.04	14.31	14.57	14.83	15.09	15.35	15.62	16.14
93	12.12	12.38	12.64	12.91	13.17	13.44	13.70	13.96	14.23	14.49	14.68	14.95	15.22	15.48	15.75	16.34
92	12.29	12.55	12.82	13.08	13.35	13.62	13.88	14.15	14.42	14.68	14.95	15.14	15.41	15.68	15.95	16.55
91	12.46	12.73	13.00	13.26	13.53	13.80	14.07	14.34	14.61	14.88	15.14	15.41	15.68	15.95	16.22	16.76
90	12.64	12.91	13.18	13.45	13.72	13.99	14.26	14.53	14.80	15.07	15.34	15.61	15.89	16.16	16.43	16.97
89	12.81	13.09	13.36	13.63	13.91	14.18	14.45	14.73	15.00	15.27	15.55	15.82	16.09	16.37	16.64	17.19
88	13.00	13.27	13.55	13.82	14.10	14.37	14.65	14.92	15.20	15.48	15.75	16.03	16.30	16.58	16.86	17.41
87	13.18	13.46	13.74	14.01	14.29	14.57	14.85	15.13	15.40	15.68	15.96	16.24	16.52	16.80	17.08	17.64
86	13.37	13.65	13.93	14.21	14.49	14.77	15.05	15.33	15.61	15.89	16.17	16.46	16.74	17.02	17.30	17.86
85	13.56	13.84	14.13	14.41	14.69	14.97	15.26	15.54	15.82	16.11	16.39	16.68	16.96	17.24	17.53	18.10
84	13.76	14.04	14.33	14.61	14.90	15.18	15.47	15.75	16.04	16.33	16.61	16.90	17.19	17.47	17.76	18.34
83	13.95	14.24	14.53	14.82	15.11	15.39	15.68	15.97	16.26	16.55	16.84	17.13	17.42	17.71	18.00	18.58
82	14.16	14.45	14.74	15.03	15.32	15.61	15.90	16.19	16.48	16.78	17.07	17.36	17.65	17.95	18.24	18.83
81	14.36	14.65	14.95	15.24	15.54	15.83	16.12	16.42	16.71	17.01	17.30	17.60	17.89	18.19	18.49	19.08
80	14.57	14.87	15.16	15.46	15.76	16.05	16.35	16.65	16.95	17.24	17.54	17.84	18.14	18.44	18.74	19.34
79	14.78	15.08	15.38	15.68	15.98	16.28	16.58	16.88	17.18	17.48	17.79	18.09	18.39	18.69	18.99	19.60
78	15.00	15.30	15.61	15.91	16.21	16.52	16.82	17.12	17.43	17.73	18.04	18.34	18.65	18.95	19.26	19.87
77	15.22	15.53	15.83	16.14	16.45	16.75	17.06	17.37	17.67	17.98	18.29	18.60	18.86	19.17	19.52	20.14
76	15.45	15.76	16.07	16.38	16.69	17.00	17.31	17.62	17.93	18.24	18.55	18.81	19.13	19.45	19.76	20.42
75	15.68	15.99	16.31	16.62	16.93	17.24	17.56	17.87	18.18	18.50	18.81	19.13	19.45	19.76	20.08	20.71
74	15.92	16.23	16.55	16.86	17.18	17.50	17.81	18.13	18.45	18.77	19.09	19.40	19.72	20.04	20.36	21.00
73	16.16	16.48	16.80	17.12	17.44	17.76	18.08	18.40	18.72	19.04	19.36	19.69	20.01	20.33	20.66	21.30
70	16.91	17.24	17.57	17.90	18.24	18.57	18.90	19.23	19.57	19.90	20.23	20.57	20.90	21.24	21.57	22.25
65	18.29	18.64	18.99	19.35	19.70	20.05	20.41	20.76	21.12	21.47	21.83	22.19	22.55	22.90	23.26	23.98
60	19.85	20.23	20.60	20.98	21.36	21.74	22.12	22.50	22.89	23.27	23.65	24.04	24.42	24.81	25.20	25.97

Description: This table shows the price to pay for a bond at the yield rate. The yield is to maturity.

Example: The price of a 6.75 %, 13 year bond to yield 8 % to maturity is $ 90.01.

COUPON RATE, %

YIELD	0.00%	1.00%	2.00%	3.00%	4.00%	4.25%	4.50%	4.75%	5.00%	5.25%	5.50%	5.75%	6.00%	6.25%	6.50%	6.75%
0.00	100.00	113.00	126.00	139.00	152.00	155.25	158.50	161.75	165.00	168.25	171.50	174.75	178.00	181.25	184.50	187.75
1.00	87.84	100.00	112.16	124.32	136.49	139.53	142.57	145.61	148.65	151.69	154.73	157.77	160.81	163.85	166.89	169.93
2.00	77.20	88.60	100.00	111.40	122.80	125.64	128.49	131.34	134.19	137.04	139.89	142.74	145.59	148.44	151.29	154.14
3.00	67.90	78.60	89.30	100.00	110.70	113.37	116.05	118.72	121.40	124.07	126.75	129.42	132.10	134.77	137.45	140.12
4.00	59.76	69.82	79.88	89.94	100.00	102.52	105.03	107.55	110.06	112.58	115.09	117.61	120.12	122.64	125.15	127.67
4.25	57.89	67.79	77.70	87.61	97.52	100.00	102.48	104.95	107.43	109.91	112.39	114.86	117.34	119.82	122.30	124.77
4.50	56.07	65.83	75.60	85.36	95.12	97.56	100.00	102.44	104.88	107.32	109.76	112.20	114.64	117.08	119.52	121.96
4.75	54.32	63.94	73.55	83.17	92.79	95.19	97.60	100.00	102.40	104.81	107.21	109.62	112.02	114.43	116.83	119.23
5.00	52.62	62.10	71.57	81.05	90.52	92.89	95.26	97.63	100.00	102.37	104.74	107.11	109.48	111.84	114.21	116.58
5.25	50.98	60.32	69.66	78.99	88.33	90.66	93.00	95.33	97.67	100.00	102.33	104.67	107.00	109.34	111.67	114.01
5.50	49.39	58.59	67.80	77.00	86.20	88.50	90.80	93.10	95.40	97.70	100.00	102.30	104.60	106.90	109.20	111.50
5.75	47.86	56.93	65.99	75.06	84.13	86.40	88.66	90.93	93.20	95.47	97.73	100.00	102.27	104.53	106.80	109.07
6.00	46.37	55.31	64.25	73.18	82.12	84.36	86.59	88.83	91.06	93.30	95.53	97.77	100.00	102.23	104.47	106.70
6.25	44.93	53.74	62.55	71.36	80.17	82.38	84.58	86.78	88.99	91.19	93.39	95.59	97.80	100.00	102.20	104.41
6.50	43.54	52.22	60.91	69.60	78.28	80.46	82.63	84.80	86.97	89.14	91.31	93.49	95.66	97.83	100.00	102.17
6.75	42.19	50.75	59.32	67.88	76.45	78.59	80.73	82.87	85.01	87.15	89.29	91.44	93.58	95.72	97.86	100.00
7.00	40.88	49.33	57.77	66.22	74.66	76.78	78.89	81.00	83.11	85.22	87.33	89.44	91.55	93.67	95.78	97.89
7.25	39.62	47.95	56.28	64.61	72.93	75.02	77.10	79.18	81.26	83.34	85.43	87.51	89.59	91.67	93.75	95.84
7.50	38.40	46.61	54.83	63.04	71.25	73.31	75.36	77.41	79.47	81.52	83.57	85.63	87.68	89.73	91.79	93.84
7.75	37.21	45.32	53.42	61.52	69.62	71.65	73.67	75.70	77.72	79.75	81.77	83.80	85.82	87.85	89.87	91.90
8.00	36.07	44.06	52.05	60.04	68.03	70.03	72.03	74.03	76.03	78.02	80.02	82.02	84.02	86.02	88.01	90.01
8.25	34.96	42.84	50.73	58.61	66.49	68.47	70.44	72.41	74.38	76.35	78.32	80.29	82.26	84.23	86.20	88.17
8.50	33.89	41.66	49.44	57.22	65.00	66.94	68.89	70.83	72.78	74.72	76.67	78.61	80.55	82.50	84.44	86.39
8.75	32.85	40.52	48.20	55.87	63.55	65.46	67.38	69.30	71.22	73.14	75.06	76.98	78.89	80.81	82.73	84.65
9.00	31.84	39.41	46.99	54.56	62.13	64.03	65.92	67.81	69.71	71.60	73.49	75.39	77.28	79.17	81.07	82.96
9.25	30.87	38.34	45.81	53.29	60.76	62.63	64.50	66.37	68.24	70.10	71.97	73.84	75.71	77.58	79.45	81.32
9.50	29.92	37.30	44.68	52.05	59.43	61.27	63.12	64.96	66.81	68.65	70.49	72.34	74.18	76.03	77.87	79.71
9.75	29.01	36.29	43.57	50.85	58.13	59.95	61.77	63.59	65.41	67.23	69.06	70.88	72.70	74.52	76.34	78.16
10.00	28.12	35.31	42.50	49.69	56.87	58.67	60.47	62.27	64.06	65.86	67.66	69.45	71.25	73.05	74.84	76.64
10.25	27.27	34.36	41.46	48.55	55.65	57.42	59.20	60.97	62.75	64.52	66.29	68.07	69.84	71.62	73.39	75.16
10.50	26.44	33.44	40.45	47.46	54.46	56.21	57.96	59.72	61.47	63.22	64.97	66.72	68.47	70.22	71.98	73.73
10.75	25.63	32.55	39.47	46.39	53.31	55.03	56.76	58.49	60.22	61.95	63.68	65.41	67.14	68.87	70.60	72.33
11.00	24.86	31.69	38.52	45.35	52.18	53.89	55.60	57.30	59.01	60.72	62.43	64.14	65.84	67.55	69.26	70.97
11.25	24.10	30.85	37.60	44.34	51.09	52.77	54.46	56.15	57.83	59.52	61.21	62.89	64.58	66.27	67.95	69.64
11.50	23.37	30.04	36.70	43.36	50.03	51.69	53.36	55.02	56.69	58.35	60.02	61.69	63.35	65.02	66.68	68.35
11.75	22.67	29.25	35.83	42.41	48.99	50.64	52.28	53.93	55.57	57.22	58.86	60.51	62.16	63.80	65.45	67.09
12.00	21.98	28.48	34.98	41.49	47.99	49.61	51.24	52.86	54.49	56.11	57.74	59.37	60.99	62.62	64.24	65.87
12.25	21.32	27.74	34.16	40.59	47.01	48.62	50.22	51.83	53.43	55.04	56.64	58.25	59.86	61.46	63.07	64.67
12.50	20.68	27.02	33.37	39.71	46.06	47.65	49.23	50.82	52.41	53.99	55.58	57.16	58.75	60.34	61.92	63.51
12.75	20.05	26.32	32.59	38.86	45.13	46.70	48.27	49.84	51.40	52.97	54.54	56.11	57.67	59.24	60.81	62.38
13.00	19.45	25.65	31.84	38.04	44.23	45.78	47.33	48.88	50.43	51.98	53.53	55.08	56.63	58.18	59.72	61.27
13.25	18.87	24.99	31.11	37.24	43.36	44.89	46.42	47.95	49.48	51.01	52.54	54.07	55.61	57.14	58.67	60.20
13.50	18.30	24.35	30.40	36.46	42.51	44.02	45.53	47.05	48.56	50.07	51.58	53.10	54.61	56.12	57.64	59.15
13.75	17.75	23.73	29.71	35.70	41.68	43.17	44.67	46.16	47.66	49.16	50.65	52.15	53.64	55.14	56.63	58.13
14.00	17.22	23.13	29.05	34.96	40.87	42.35	43.83	45.31	46.78	48.26	49.74	51.22	52.70	54.18	55.65	57.13
14.25	16.70	22.55	28.40	34.24	40.09	41.55	43.01	44.47	45.93	47.39	48.85	50.32	51.78	53.24	54.70	56.16
14.50	16.21	21.98	27.76	33.54	39.32	40.77	42.21	43.66	45.10	46.55	47.99	49.43	50.88	52.32	53.77	55.21
14.75	15.72	21.44	27.15	32.86	38.58	40.01	41.43	42.86	44.29	45.72	47.15	48.58	50.00	51.43	52.86	54.29
15.00	15.25	20.90	26.55	32.20	37.85	39.27	40.68	42.09	43.50	44.92	46.33	47.74	49.15	50.56	51.98	53.39
15.25	14.80	20.39	25.97	31.56	37.15	38.54	39.94	41.34	42.73	44.13	45.53	46.92	48.32	49.72	51.11	52.51
15.50	14.36	19.89	25.41	30.94	36.46	37.84	39.22	40.60	41.99	43.37	44.75	46.13	47.51	48.89	50.27	51.65
15.75	13.93	19.40	24.86	30.33	35.79	37.16	38.52	39.89	41.26	42.62	43.99	45.35	46.72	48.09	49.45	50.82
16.00	13.52	18.93	24.33	29.74	35.14	36.49	37.84	39.19	40.55	41.90	43.25	44.60	45.95	47.30	48.65	50.00
16.25	13.12	18.47	23.81	29.16	34.51	35.84	37.18	38.52	39.85	41.19	42.53	43.86	45.20	46.54	47.87	49.21
16.50	12.73	18.02	23.31	28.60	33.89	35.21	36.53	37.85	39.18	40.50	41.82	43.14	44.47	45.79	47.11	48.43
16.75	12.36	17.59	22.82	28.05	33.29	34.59	35.90	37.21	38.52	39.83	41.13	42.44	43.75	45.06	46.37	47.67
17.00	11.99	17.17	22.34	27.52	32.70	33.99	35.29	36.58	37.88	39.17	40.46	41.76	43.05	44.35	45.64	46.94
17.25	11.64	16.76	21.88	27.00	32.13	33.41	34.69	35.97	37.25	38.53	39.81	41.09	42.37	43.65	44.93	46.21
17.50	11.29	16.36	21.43	26.50	31.57	32.84	34.10	35.37	36.64	37.91	39.17	40.44	41.71	42.97	44.24	45.51
17.75	10.96	15.98	20.99	26.01	31.03	32.28	33.53	34.79	36.04	37.30	38.55	39.80	41.06	42.31	43.57	44.82
18.00	10.64	15.60	20.57	25.53	30.50	31.74	32.98	34.22	35.46	36.70	37.94	39.19	40.43	41.67	42.91	44.15
18.25	10.33	15.24	20.15	25.07	29.98	31.21	32.44	33.67	34.89	36.12	37.35	38.58	39.81	41.04	42.27	43.49
18.50	10.02	14.89	19.75	24.61	29.48	30.69	31.91	33.13	34.34	35.56	36.77	37.99	39.21	40.42	41.64	42.85
18.75	9.73	14.54	19.36	24.17	28.99	30.19	31.40	32.60	33.80	35.01	36.21	37.41	38.62	39.82	41.02	42.23
19.00	9.45	14.21	18.98	23.74	28.51	29.70	30.89	32.08	33.28	34.47	35.66	36.85	38.04	39.23	40.42	41.62
20.00	8.39	12.97	17.55	22.13	26.71	27.86	29.00	30.15	31.29	32.44	33.58	34.73	35.87	37.02	38.16	39.31
25.00	4.68	8.49	12.30	16.12	19.93	20.88	21.84	22.79	23.74	24.70	25.65	26.60	27.56	28.51	29.46	30.41
30.00	2.64	5.89	9.13	12.38	15.62	16.43	17.25	18.06	18.87	19.68	20.49	21.30	22.11	22.92	23.74	24.55

Description: This table shows the yield to maturity of a bond purchased at the price shown in the index.

Example: The yield to maturity of a 6.75 %, 13 year bond at a price of 80.00 is 9.45 %.

COUPON RATE, %

PRICE	0.00%	1.00%	2.00%	3.00%	4.00%	4.25%	4.50%	4.75%	5.00%	5.25%	5.50%	5.75%	6.00%	6.25%	6.50%	6.75%
100	0.00	1.00	2.00	3.00	4.00	4.25	4.50	4.75	5.00	5.25	5.50	5.75	6.00	6.25	6.50	6.75
99	.07	1.08	2.08	3.09	4.10	4.35	4.60	4.85	5.10	5.35	5.60	5.86	6.11	6.36	6.61	6.86
98	.15	1.16	2.17	3.18	4.20	4.45	4.70	4.96	5.21	5.46	5.72	5.97	6.22	6.47	6.73	6.98
97	.23	1.25	2.26	3.28	4.30	4.55	4.81	5.06	5.32	5.57	5.83	6.08	6.34	6.59	6.85	7.10
96	.31	1.33	2.35	3.38	4.40	4.66	4.92	5.17	5.43	5.68	5.94	6.20	6.45	6.71	6.97	7.22
95	.39	1.42	2.45	3.48	4.51	4.77	5.02	5.28	5.54	5.80	6.06	6.31	6.57	6.83	7.09	7.35
94	.47	1.51	2.54	3.58	4.61	4.87	5.13	5.39	5.65	5.91	6.17	6.43	6.69	6.95	7.21	7.47
93	.55	1.59	2.63	3.68	4.72	4.98	5.24	5.51	5.77	6.03	6.29	6.55	6.82	7.08	7.34	7.60
92	.64	1.68	2.73	3.78	4.83	5.09	5.36	5.62	5.88	6.15	6.41	6.68	6.94	7.20	7.47	7.73
91	.72	1.77	2.83	3.88	4.94	5.21	5.47	5.74	6.00	6.27	6.53	6.80	7.06	7.33	7.60	7.86
90	.81	1.87	2.93	3.99	5.05	5.32	5.59	5.85	6.12	6.39	6.66	6.92	7.19	7.46	7.73	8.00
89	.89	1.96	3.03	4.10	5.17	5.44	5.71	5.97	6.24	6.51	6.78	7.05	7.32	7.59	7.86	8.13
88	.98	2.05	3.13	4.20	5.28	5.55	5.82	6.10	6.37	6.64	6.91	7.18	7.45	7.72	8.00	8.27
87	1.07	2.15	3.23	4.31	5.40	5.67	5.95	6.22	6.49	6.76	7.04	7.31	7.59	7.86	8.13	8.41
86	1.16	2.24	3.33	4.42	5.52	5.79	6.07	6.34	6.62	6.89	7.17	7.44	7.72	8.00	8.27	8.55
85	1.25	2.34	3.44	4.54	5.64	5.92	6.19	6.47	6.75	7.02	7.30	7.58	7.86	8.14	8.42	8.69
84	1.34	2.44	3.54	4.65	5.76	6.04	6.32	6.60	6.88	7.16	7.44	7.72	8.00	8.28	8.56	8.84
83	1.43	2.54	3.65	4.76	5.88	6.17	6.45	6.73	7.01	7.29	7.57	7.86	8.14	8.42	8.71	8.99
82	1.53	2.64	3.76	4.88	6.01	6.29	6.58	6.86	7.14	7.43	7.71	8.00	8.28	8.57	8.85	9.14
81	1.62	2.74	3.87	5.00	6.14	6.42	6.71	6.99	7.28	7.57	7.85	8.14	8.43	8.72	9.01	9.29
80	1.72	2.85	3.98	5.12	6.27	6.56	6.84	7.13	7.42	7.71	8.00	8.29	8.58	8.87	9.16	9.45
79	1.82	2.95	4.10	5.24	6.40	6.69	6.98	7.27	7.56	7.85	8.14	8.44	8.73	9.02	9.32	9.61
78	1.92	3.06	4.21	5.37	6.53	6.83	7.12	7.41	7.70	8.00	8.29	8.59	8.88	9.18	9.47	9.77
77	2.02	3.17	4.33	5.49	6.67	6.96	7.26	7.55	7.85	8.15	8.44	8.74	9.04	9.34	9.64	9.94
76	2.12	3.28	4.45	5.62	6.81	7.10	7.40	7.70	8.00	8.30	8.60	8.90	9.20	9.50	9.80	10.10
75	2.22	3.39	4.57	5.75	6.95	7.25	7.55	7.85	8.15	8.45	8.75	9.06	9.36	9.66	9.97	10.27
74	2.32	3.50	4.69	5.89	7.09	7.39	7.70	8.00	8.30	8.61	8.91	9.22	9.53	9.83	10.14	10.45
73	2.43	3.62	4.81	6.02	7.24	7.54	7.85	8.15	8.46	8.77	9.08	9.38	9.69	10.00	10.31	10.62
72	2.54	3.73	4.94	6.16	7.38	7.69	8.00	8.31	8.62	8.93	9.24	9.55	9.86	10.18	10.49	10.80
71	2.65	3.85	5.07	6.30	7.53	7.84	8.16	8.47	8.78	9.09	9.41	9.72	10.04	10.35	10.67	10.99
70	2.76	3.97	5.20	6.44	7.69	8.00	8.31	8.63	8.95	9.26	9.58	9.90	10.22	10.54	10.86	11.18
69	2.87	4.10	5.33	6.58	7.84	8.16	8.48	8.80	9.11	9.43	9.75	10.08	10.40	10.72	11.04	11.37
68	2.98	4.22	5.47	6.73	8.00	8.32	8.64	8.96	9.29	9.61	9.93	10.26	10.58	10.91	11.24	11.56
67	3.10	4.35	5.60	6.88	8.16	8.49	8.81	9.13	9.46	9.79	10.11	10.44	10.77	11.10	11.43	11.76
66	3.22	4.47	5.74	7.03	8.33	8.65	8.98	9.31	9.64	9.97	10.30	10.63	10.96	11.30	11.63	11.97
65	3.34	4.60	5.89	7.18	8.49	8.82	9.16	9.49	9.82	10.15	10.49	10.82	11.16	11.50	11.84	12.18
64	3.46	4.74	6.03	7.34	8.67	9.00	9.33	9.67	10.01	10.34	10.68	11.02	11.36	11.70	12.05	12.39
63	3.58	4.87	6.18	7.50	8.84	9.18	9.52	9.86	10.20	10.54	10.88	11.22	11.57	11.91	12.26	12.61
62	3.71	5.01	6.33	7.67	9.02	9.36	9.70	10.05	10.39	10.74	11.08	11.43	11.78	12.13	12.48	12.83
61	3.83	5.15	6.48	7.83	9.20	9.55	9.89	10.24	10.59	10.94	11.29	11.64	11.99	12.35	12.70	13.06
60	3.96	5.29	6.64	8.00	9.39	9.74	10.09	10.44	10.79	11.14	11.50	11.86	12.21	12.57	12.93	13.29
59	4.10	5.44	6.80	8.18	9.58	9.93	10.28	10.64	11.00	11.36	11.72	12.08	12.44	12.80	13.17	13.53
58	4.23	5.58	6.96	8.35	9.77	10.13	10.49	10.85	11.21	11.57	11.94	12.30	12.67	13.04	13.41	13.78
57	4.37	5.73	7.12	8.54	9.97	10.33	10.70	11.06	11.43	11.79	12.16	12.53	12.91	13.28	13.65	14.03
56	4.51	5.89	7.29	8.72	10.17	10.54	10.91	11.28	11.65	12.02	12.40	12.77	13.15	13.53	13.91	14.29
55	4.65	6.04	7.46	8.91	10.38	10.75	11.13	11.50	11.88	12.25	12.63	13.01	13.40	13.78	14.17	14.55
54	4.79	6.20	7.64	9.10	10.59	10.97	11.35	11.73	12.11	12.49	12.88	13.26	13.65	14.04	14.43	14.82
53	4.94	6.37	7.82	9.30	10.81	11.19	11.58	11.96	12.35	12.74	13.13	13.52	13.91	14.31	14.71	15.11
52	5.09	6.53	8.00	9.51	11.04	11.42	11.81	12.20	12.60	12.99	13.39	13.78	14.18	14.59	14.99	15.39
51	5.24	6.70	8.19	9.71	11.27	11.66	12.05	12.45	12.85	13.25	13.65	14.05	14.46	14.87	15.28	15.69
50	5.40	6.88	8.39	9.93	11.50	11.90	12.30	12.70	13.11	13.51	13.92	14.33	14.75	15.16	15.58	16.00
49	5.56	7.05	8.58	10.15	11.74	12.15	12.55	12.96	13.37	13.79	14.20	14.62	15.04	15.46	15.89	16.31
48	5.72	7.24	8.79	10.37	11.99	12.40	12.82	13.23	13.65	14.07	14.49	14.92	15.34	15.77	16.20	16.64
47	5.89	7.42	8.99	10.60	12.25	12.67	13.09	13.51	13.93	14.36	14.79	15.22	15.66	16.09	16.53	16.97
46	6.06	7.61	9.20	10.84	12.51	12.94	13.36	13.79	14.22	14.66	15.10	15.54	15.98	16.42	16.87	17.32
45	6.23	7.81	9.42	11.08	12.78	13.21	13.65	14.09	14.53	14.97	15.41	15.86	16.31	16.77	17.22	17.68
44	6.41	8.01	9.65	11.33	13.06	13.50	13.94	14.39	14.84	15.29	15.74	16.20	16.66	17.12	17.58	18.05
43	6.59	8.21	9.88	11.59	13.35	13.80	14.25	14.70	15.16	15.62	16.08	16.55	17.01	17.49	17.96	18.44
42	6.78	8.42	10.11	11.86	13.65	14.10	14.56	15.02	15.49	15.96	16.43	16.91	17.38	17.87	18.35	18.84
41	6.97	8.64	10.36	12.13	13.95	14.42	14.89	15.36	15.83	16.31	16.79	17.28	17.77	18.26	18.75	19.25
40	7.17	8.86	10.61	12.41	14.27	14.75	15.22	15.71	16.19	16.68	17.17	17.67	18.17	18.67	19.18	19.69
39	7.37	9.09	10.87	12.70	14.60	15.09	15.57	16.07	16.56	17.06	17.56	18.07	18.58	19.10	19.61	20.14
35	8.24	10.08	11.99	13.98	16.05	16.58	17.11	17.65	18.20	18.75	19.30	19.86	20.43	20.99	21.57	22.15
30	9.47	11.51	13.64	15.88	18.24	18.84	19.46	20.08	20.70	21.34	21.98	22.63	23.28	23.95	24.61	25.29
25	10.95	13.24	15.68	18.28	21.05	21.77	22.50	23.24	23.99	24.75	25.52	26.30	27.10	27.90	28.71	29.53
20	12.77	15.44	18.34	21.50	24.93	25.83	26.75	27.68	28.64	29.61	30.59	31.60	32.61	33.65	34.70	35.76
15	15.13	18.41	22.11	26.26	30.93	32.18	33.45	34.76	36.10	37.47	38.86	40.28	41.72	43.19	44.67	46.18
10	18.52	22.98	28.37	34.87	42.55	44.64	46.78	48.98	51.23	53.51	55.83	58.18	60.56	62.96	65.37	67.80

Description: This table shows the price to pay for a bond at the yield rate. The yield is to maturity.

Example: The price of a 10.75 %, 13 year bond to yield 8 % to maturity is $ 121.98.

YIELD	7.00%	7.25%	7.50%	7.75%	8.00%	8.25%	8.50%	8.75%	9.00%	9.25%	9.50%	9.75%	10.00%	10.25%	10.50%	10.75%
0.00	191.00	194.25	197.50	200.75	204.00	207.25	210.50	213.75	217.00	220.25	223.50	226.75	230.00	233.25	236.50	239.75
1.00	172.97	176.01	179.05	182.09	185.13	188.17	191.22	194.26	197.30	200.34	203.38	206.42	209.46	212.50	215.54	218.58
2.00	156.99	159.84	162.69	165.54	168.39	171.24	174.08	176.93	179.78	182.63	185.48	188.33	191.18	194.03	196.88	199.73
3.00	142.80	145.47	148.15	150.82	153.50	156.17	158.85	161.52	164.20	166.87	169.55	172.22	174.90	177.57	180.24	182.92
4.00	130.18	132.70	135.21	137.73	140.24	142.76	145.27	147.79	150.30	152.82	155.33	157.85	160.36	162.88	165.39	167.91
4.25	127.25	129.73	132.21	134.68	137.16	139.64	142.11	144.59	147.07	149.55	152.02	154.50	156.98	159.46	161.93	164.41
4.50	124.40	126.84	129.28	131.73	134.17	136.61	139.05	141.49	143.93	146.37	148.81	151.25	153.69	156.13	158.57	161.01
4.75	121.64	124.04	126.45	128.85	131.25	133.66	136.06	138.47	140.87	143.28	145.68	148.08	150.49	152.89	155.30	157.70
5.00	118.95	121.32	123.69	126.06	128.43	130.79	133.16	135.53	137.90	140.27	142.64	145.01	147.38	149.75	152.11	154.48
5.25	116.34	118.67	121.01	123.34	125.68	128.01	130.34	132.68	135.01	137.35	139.68	142.02	144.35	146.68	149.02	151.35
5.50	113.80	116.10	118.40	120.70	123.00	125.30	127.60	129.90	132.20	134.50	136.80	139.10	141.41	143.71	146.01	148.31
5.75	111.34	113.60	115.87	118.14	120.40	122.67	124.94	127.21	129.47	131.74	134.01	136.27	138.54	140.81	143.07	145.34
6.00	108.94	111.17	113.41	115.64	117.88	120.11	122.35	124.58	126.82	129.05	131.28	133.52	135.75	137.99	140.22	142.46
6.25	106.61	108.81	111.01	113.22	115.42	117.62	119.83	122.03	124.23	126.43	128.64	130.84	133.04	135.24	137.45	139.65
6.50	104.34	106.51	108.69	110.86	113.03	115.20	117.37	119.54	121.72	123.89	126.06	128.23	130.40	132.57	134.75	136.92
6.75	102.14	104.28	106.42	108.56	110.71	112.85	114.99	117.13	119.27	121.41	123.55	125.69	127.84	129.98	132.12	134.26
7.00	100.00	102.11	104.22	106.33	108.45	110.56	112.67	114.78	116.89	119.00	121.11	123.22	125.34	127.45	129.56	131.67
7.25	97.92	100.00	102.08	104.16	106.25	108.33	110.41	112.49	114.57	116.66	118.74	120.82	122.90	124.98	127.07	129.15
7.50	95.89	97.95	100.00	102.05	104.11	106.16	108.21	110.27	112.32	114.37	116.43	118.48	120.53	122.59	124.64	126.69
7.75	93.92	95.95	97.97	100.00	102.03	104.05	106.08	108.10	110.13	112.15	114.18	116.20	118.23	120.25	122.28	124.30
8.00	92.01	94.01	96.00	98.00	100.00	102.00	104.00	105.99	107.99	109.99	111.99	113.98	115.98	117.98	119.98	121.98
8.25	90.15	92.12	94.09	96.06	98.03	100.00	101.97	103.94	105.91	107.88	109.85	111.83	113.80	115.77	117.74	119.71
8.50	88.33	90.28	92.22	94.17	96.11	98.06	100.00	101.94	103.89	105.83	107.78	109.72	111.67	113.61	115.56	117.50
8.75	86.57	88.49	90.41	92.33	94.24	96.16	98.08	100.00	101.92	103.84	105.76	107.67	109.59	111.51	113.43	115.35
9.00	84.85	86.75	88.64	90.53	92.43	94.32	96.21	98.11	100.00	101.89	103.79	105.68	107.57	109.47	111.36	113.25
9.25	83.18	85.05	86.92	88.79	90.66	92.53	94.39	96.26	98.13	100.00	101.87	103.74	105.61	107.47	109.34	111.21
9.50	81.56	83.40	85.25	87.09	88.94	90.78	92.62	94.47	96.31	98.16	100.00	101.84	103.69	105.53	107.38	109.22
9.75	79.98	81.80	83.62	85.44	87.26	89.08	90.90	92.72	94.54	96.36	98.18	100.00	101.82	103.64	105.46	107.28
10.00	78.44	80.23	82.03	83.83	85.62	87.42	89.22	91.02	92.81	94.61	96.41	98.20	100.00	101.80	103.59	105.39
10.25	76.94	78.71	80.49	82.26	84.03	85.81	87.58	89.36	91.13	92.90	94.68	96.45	98.23	100.00	101.77	103.55
10.50	75.48	77.23	78.98	80.73	82.49	84.24	85.99	87.74	89.49	91.24	92.99	94.75	96.50	98.25	100.00	101.75
10.75	74.06	75.79	77.52	79.25	80.98	82.71	84.44	86.16	87.89	89.62	91.35	93.08	94.81	96.54	98.27	100.00
11.00	72.68	74.38	76.09	77.80	79.51	81.21	82.92	84.63	86.34	88.05	89.75	91.46	93.17	94.88	96.58	98.29
11.25	71.33	73.01	74.70	76.39	78.07	79.76	81.45	83.13	84.82	86.51	88.19	89.88	91.57	93.25	94.94	96.63
11.50	70.02	71.68	73.35	75.01	76.68	78.34	80.01	81.68	83.34	85.01	86.67	88.34	90.01	91.67	93.34	95.00
11.75	68.74	70.38	72.03	73.67	75.32	76.96	78.61	80.26	81.90	83.55	85.19	86.84	88.48	90.13	91.77	93.42
12.00	67.49	69.12	70.74	72.37	73.99	75.62	77.24	78.87	80.50	82.12	83.75	85.37	87.00	88.62	90.25	91.87
12.25	66.28	67.88	69.49	71.10	72.70	74.31	75.91	77.52	79.13	80.73	82.34	83.94	85.55	87.15	88.76	90.37
12.50	65.10	66.68	68.27	69.86	71.44	73.03	74.62	76.20	77.79	79.38	80.96	82.55	84.14	85.72	87.31	88.89
12.75	63.95	65.51	67.08	68.65	70.22	71.78	73.35	74.92	76.49	78.05	79.62	81.19	82.76	84.32	85.89	87.46
13.00	62.82	64.37	65.92	67.47	69.02	70.57	72.12	73.67	75.22	76.76	78.31	79.86	81.41	82.96	84.51	86.06
13.25	61.73	63.26	64.79	66.32	67.85	69.38	70.91	72.44	73.98	75.51	77.04	78.57	80.10	81.63	83.16	84.69
13.50	60.66	62.18	63.69	65.20	66.71	68.23	69.74	71.25	72.77	74.28	75.79	77.31	78.82	80.33	81.84	83.36
13.75	59.62	61.12	62.61	64.11	65.60	67.10	68.60	70.09	71.59	73.08	74.58	76.07	77.57	79.06	80.56	82.05
14.00	58.61	60.09	61.57	63.04	64.52	66.00	67.48	68.96	70.44	71.91	73.39	74.87	76.35	77.83	79.30	80.78
14.25	57.62	59.08	60.54	62.01	63.47	64.93	66.39	67.85	69.31	70.77	72.23	73.70	75.16	76.62	78.08	79.54
14.50	56.66	58.10	59.55	60.99	62.44	63.88	65.33	66.77	68.22	69.66	71.11	72.55	73.99	75.44	76.88	78.33
14.75	55.72	57.15	58.58	60.00	61.43	62.86	64.29	65.72	67.15	68.57	70.00	71.43	72.86	74.29	75.72	77.15
15.00	54.80	56.21	57.63	59.04	60.45	61.86	63.28	64.69	66.10	67.51	68.93	70.34	71.75	73.16	74.58	75.99
15.25	53.91	55.30	56.70	58.10	59.50	60.89	62.29	63.69	65.08	66.48	67.88	69.27	70.67	72.07	73.46	74.86
15.50	53.04	54.42	55.80	57.18	58.56	59.94	61.32	62.71	64.09	65.47	66.85	68.23	69.61	70.99	72.37	73.76
15.75	52.19	53.55	54.92	56.28	57.65	59.02	60.38	61.75	63.11	64.48	65.85	67.21	68.58	69.95	71.31	72.68
16.00	51.36	52.71	54.06	55.41	56.76	58.11	59.46	60.81	62.17	63.52	64.87	66.22	67.57	68.92	70.27	71.62
16.25	50.55	51.88	53.22	54.55	55.89	57.23	58.56	59.90	61.24	62.57	63.91	65.25	66.58	67.92	69.26	70.59
16.50	49.75	51.08	52.40	53.72	55.04	56.37	57.69	59.01	60.33	61.65	62.98	64.30	65.62	66.94	68.27	69.59
16.75	48.98	50.29	51.60	52.91	54.22	55.52	56.83	58.14	59.45	60.76	62.06	63.37	64.68	65.99	67.30	68.60
17.00	48.23	49.52	50.82	52.11	53.41	54.70	56.00	57.29	58.58	59.88	61.17	62.47	63.76	65.05	66.35	67.64
17.25	47.49	48.77	50.06	51.34	52.62	53.90	55.18	56.46	57.74	59.02	60.30	61.58	62.86	64.14	65.42	66.70
17.50	46.78	48.04	49.31	50.58	51.85	53.11	54.38	55.65	56.91	58.18	59.45	60.72	61.98	63.25	64.52	65.78
17.75	46.08	47.33	48.58	49.84	51.09	52.35	53.60	54.85	56.11	57.36	58.62	59.87	61.12	62.38	63.63	64.89
18.00	45.39	46.63	47.87	49.11	50.36	51.60	52.84	54.08	55.32	56.56	57.80	59.04	60.28	61.53	62.77	64.01
18.25	44.72	45.95	47.18	48.41	49.64	50.86	52.09	53.32	54.55	55.78	57.01	58.23	59.46	60.69	61.92	63.15
18.50	44.07	45.28	46.50	47.72	48.93	50.15	51.36	52.58	53.80	55.01	56.23	57.44	58.66	59.88	61.09	62.31
18.75	43.43	44.63	45.84	47.04	48.25	49.45	50.65	51.86	53.06	54.26	55.47	56.67	57.87	59.08	60.28	61.48
19.00	42.81	44.00	45.19	46.38	47.57	48.77	49.96	51.15	52.34	53.53	54.72	55.91	57.11	58.30	59.49	60.68
20.00	40.45	41.60	42.74	43.89	45.03	46.18	47.32	48.47	49.61	50.76	51.91	53.05	54.20	55.34	56.49	57.63
25.00	31.37	32.32	33.27	34.23	35.18	36.13	37.09	38.04	38.99	39.95	40.90	41.85	42.81	43.76	44.71	45.67
30.00	25.36	26.17	26.98	27.79	28.60	29.42	30.23	31.04	31.85	32.66	33.47	34.28	35.09	35.91	36.72	37.53

Description: This table shows the yield to maturity of a bond purchased at the price shown in the index.

Example: The yield to maturity of a 10.75 %, 13 year bond at a price of 113.00 is 9.03 %.

COUPON RATE, %

PRICE	7.00%	7.25%	7.50%	7.75%	8.00%	8.25%	8.50%	8.75%	9.00%	9.25%	9.50%	9.75%	10.00%	10.25%	10.50%	10.75%
145	2.83	3.03	3.23	3.43	3.62	3.82	4.02	4.21	4.41	4.60	4.80	5.00	5.19	5.39	5.58	5.77
140	3.21	3.41	3.61	3.81	4.01	4.22	4.42	4.62	4.82	5.02	5.22	5.42	5.62	5.82	6.01	6.21
135	3.60	3.81	4.01	4.22	4.42	4.63	4.84	5.04	5.25	5.45	5.66	5.86	6.06	6.27	6.47	6.67
130	4.01	4.22	4.43	4.64	4.86	5.07	5.28	5.49	5.70	5.91	6.12	6.32	6.53	6.74	6.95	7.16
129	4.09	4.31	4.52	4.73	4.94	5.16	5.37	5.58	5.79	6.00	6.21	6.42	6.63	6.84	7.05	7.26
128	4.18	4.39	4.61	4.82	5.03	5.25	5.46	5.67	5.88	6.09	6.31	6.52	6.73	6.94	7.15	7.36
127	4.27	4.48	4.70	4.91	5.12	5.34	5.55	5.76	5.98	6.19	6.40	6.62	6.83	7.04	7.25	7.46
126	4.35	4.57	4.78	5.00	5.22	5.43	5.64	5.86	6.07	6.29	6.50	6.71	6.93	7.14	7.35	7.57
125	4.44	4.66	4.88	5.09	5.31	5.52	5.74	5.95	6.17	6.38	6.60	6.81	7.03	7.24	7.46	7.67
124	4.53	4.75	4.97	5.18	5.40	5.62	5.83	6.05	6.27	6.48	6.70	6.92	7.13	7.35	7.56	7.78
123	4.62	4.84	5.06	5.28	5.50	5.71	5.93	6.15	6.37	6.58	6.80	7.02	7.23	7.45	7.67	7.88
122	4.71	4.93	5.15	5.37	5.59	5.81	6.03	6.25	6.47	6.68	6.90	7.12	7.34	7.56	7.77	7.99
121	4.80	5.02	5.25	5.47	5.69	5.91	6.13	6.35	6.57	6.79	7.01	7.23	7.45	7.66	7.88	8.10
120	4.90	5.12	5.34	5.56	5.78	6.01	6.23	6.45	6.67	6.89	7.11	7.33	7.55	7.77	7.99	8.21
119	4.99	5.21	5.44	5.66	5.88	6.11	6.33	6.55	6.77	7.00	7.22	7.44	7.66	7.88	8.10	8.32
118	5.09	5.31	5.53	5.76	5.98	6.21	6.43	6.65	6.88	7.10	7.32	7.55	7.77	7.99	8.22	8.44
117	5.18	5.41	5.63	5.86	6.08	6.31	6.53	6.76	6.98	7.21	7.43	7.66	7.88	8.10	8.33	8.55
116	5.28	5.51	5.73	5.96	6.19	6.41	6.64	6.86	7.09	7.32	7.54	7.77	7.99	8.22	8.44	8.67
115	5.38	5.60	5.83	6.06	6.29	6.52	6.74	6.97	7.20	7.43	7.65	7.88	8.11	8.33	8.56	8.79
114	5.48	5.70	5.93	6.16	6.39	6.62	6.85	7.08	7.31	7.54	7.77	7.99	8.22	8.45	8.68	8.91
113	5.58	5.81	6.04	6.27	6.50	6.73	6.96	7.19	7.42	7.65	7.88	8.11	8.34	8.57	8.80	9.03
112	5.68	5.91	6.14	6.37	6.60	6.84	7.07	7.30	7.53	7.76	7.99	8.22	8.46	8.69	8.92	9.15
111	5.78	6.01	6.25	6.48	6.71	6.95	7.18	7.41	7.64	7.88	8.11	8.34	8.57	8.81	9.04	9.27
110	5.88	6.12	6.35	6.59	6.82	7.06	7.29	7.53	7.76	7.99	8.23	8.46	8.70	8.93	9.16	9.40
109	5.99	6.22	6.46	6.70	6.93	7.17	7.40	7.64	7.88	8.11	8.35	8.58	8.82	9.05	9.29	9.52
108	6.09	6.33	6.57	6.81	7.05	7.28	7.52	7.76	7.99	8.23	8.47	8.70	8.94	9.18	9.42	9.65
107	6.20	6.44	6.68	6.92	7.16	7.40	7.64	7.87	8.11	8.35	8.59	8.83	9.07	9.31	9.54	9.78
106	6.31	6.55	6.79	7.03	7.27	7.51	7.75	7.99	8.23	8.47	8.71	8.95	9.19	9.43	9.67	9.91
105	6.42	6.66	6.91	7.15	7.39	7.63	7.87	8.12	8.36	8.60	8.84	9.08	9.32	9.56	9.81	10.05
104	6.53	6.78	7.02	7.26	7.51	7.75	7.99	8.24	8.48	8.72	8.97	9.21	9.45	9.70	9.94	10.18
103	6.65	6.89	7.14	7.38	7.63	7.87	8.12	8.36	8.61	8.85	9.10	9.34	9.59	9.83	10.08	10.32
102	6.76	7.01	7.25	7.50	7.75	7.99	8.24	8.49	8.73	8.98	9.23	9.47	9.72	9.97	10.21	10.46
101	6.88	7.13	7.37	7.62	7.87	8.12	8.37	8.62	8.86	9.11	9.36	9.61	9.86	10.11	10.35	10.60
100	7.00	7.25	7.50	7.75	8.00	8.25	8.50	8.75	9.00	9.25	9.50	9.75	10.00	10.25	10.50	10.75
99	7.11	7.37	7.62	7.87	8.12	8.37	8.62	8.88	9.13	9.38	9.63	9.88	10.14	10.39	10.64	10.89
98	7.24	7.49	7.74	8.00	8.25	8.50	8.76	9.01	9.26	9.52	9.77	10.02	10.28	10.53	10.78	11.04
97	7.36	7.61	7.87	8.12	8.38	8.63	8.89	9.14	9.40	9.66	9.91	10.17	10.42	10.68	10.93	11.19
96	7.48	7.74	8.00	8.25	8.51	8.77	9.02	9.28	9.54	9.80	10.05	10.31	10.57	10.83	11.08	11.34
95	7.61	7.87	8.13	8.38	8.64	8.90	9.16	9.42	9.68	9.94	10.20	10.46	10.72	10.98	11.24	11.50
94	7.74	8.00	8.26	8.52	8.78	9.04	9.30	9.56	9.82	10.08	10.34	10.61	10.87	11.13	11.39	11.65
93	7.86	8.13	8.39	8.65	8.92	9.18	9.44	9.70	9.97	10.23	10.49	10.76	11.02	11.28	11.55	11.81
92	8.00	8.26	8.53	8.79	9.05	9.32	9.58	9.85	10.11	10.38	10.65	10.91	11.18	11.44	11.71	11.97
91	8.13	8.40	8.66	8.93	9.20	9.46	9.73	10.00	10.26	10.53	10.80	11.07	11.34	11.60	11.87	12.14
90	8.26	8.53	8.80	9.07	9.34	9.61	9.88	10.15	10.42	10.69	10.96	11.23	11.50	11.77	12.04	12.31
89	8.40	8.67	8.94	9.21	9.49	9.76	10.03	10.30	10.57	10.84	11.11	11.39	11.66	11.93	12.20	12.48
88	8.54	8.81	9.09	9.36	9.63	9.91	10.18	10.45	10.73	11.00	11.28	11.55	11.83	12.10	12.38	12.65
87	8.68	8.96	9.23	9.51	9.78	10.06	10.34	10.61	10.89	11.16	11.44	11.72	11.99	12.27	12.55	12.83
86	8.83	9.10	9.38	9.66	9.94	10.21	10.49	10.77	11.05	11.33	11.61	11.89	12.17	12.45	12.73	13.01
85	8.97	9.25	9.53	9.81	10.09	10.37	10.65	10.93	11.22	11.50	11.78	12.06	12.34	12.62	12.91	13.19
84	9.12	9.40	9.69	9.97	10.25	10.53	10.82	11.10	11.38	11.67	11.95	12.23	12.52	12.80	13.09	13.37
83	9.27	9.56	9.84	10.13	10.41	10.70	10.98	11.27	11.55	11.84	12.13	12.41	12.70	12.99	13.28	13.56
82	9.43	9.71	10.00	10.29	10.57	10.86	11.15	11.44	11.73	12.02	12.31	12.60	12.88	13.17	13.47	13.76
81	9.58	9.87	10.16	10.45	10.74	11.03	11.32	11.61	11.90	12.20	12.49	12.78	13.07	13.37	13.66	13.95
80	9.74	10.03	10.33	10.62	10.91	11.20	11.50	11.79	12.08	12.38	12.67	12.97	13.26	13.56	13.86	14.15
79	9.90	10.20	10.49	10.79	11.08	11.38	11.67	11.97	12.27	12.57	12.86	13.16	13.46	13.76	14.06	14.36
78	10.07	10.36	10.66	10.96	11.26	11.56	11.86	12.16	12.46	12.76	13.06	13.36	13.66	13.96	14.26	14.56
77	10.23	10.53	10.83	11.14	11.44	11.74	12.04	12.34	12.65	12.95	13.25	13.56	13.86	14.17	14.47	14.78
76	10.41	10.71	11.01	11.31	11.62	11.92	12.23	12.53	12.84	13.15	13.45	13.76	14.07	14.38	14.68	14.99
75	10.58	10.88	11.19	11.50	11.80	12.11	12.42	12.73	13.04	13.35	13.66	13.97	14.28	14.59	14.90	15.21
74	10.76	11.06	11.37	11.68	11.99	12.30	12.62	12.93	13.24	13.55	13.87	14.18	14.49	14.81	15.12	15.44
70	11.50	11.82	12.14	12.47	12.79	13.11	13.44	13.76	14.09	14.42	14.75	15.07	15.40	15.73	16.06	16.39
65	12.52	12.86	13.20	13.54	13.88	14.23	14.57	14.92	15.27	15.61	15.96	16.31	16.66	17.01	17.36	17.71
60	13.65	14.02	14.38	14.75	15.11	15.48	15.85	16.22	16.59	16.96	17.33	17.71	18.08	18.46	18.83	19.21
55	14.94	15.33	15.72	16.11	16.51	16.90	17.30	17.70	18.10	18.50	18.90	19.30	19.71	20.12	20.52	20.93
50	16.42	16.84	17.26	17.69	18.12	18.55	18.98	19.41	19.85	20.29	20.72	21.16	21.61	22.05	22.50	22.94
45	18.14	18.60	19.07	19.54	20.01	20.48	20.96	21.44	21.92	22.40	22.88	23.37	23.86	24.35	24.85	25.34
40	20.20	20.72	21.24	21.76	22.29	22.81	23.35	23.88	24.42	24.96	25.51	26.06	26.61	27.16	27.72	28.28
35	22.73	23.32	23.91	24.51	25.11	25.72	26.33	26.94	27.56	28.18	28.81	29.44	30.07	30.71	31.35	31.99

Description: This table shows the price to pay for a bond at the yield rate. The yield is to maturity.

Example: The price of a 15.00 %, 13 year bond to yield 8 % to maturity is $ 155.94.

COUPON RATE, %

YIELD	11.00%	11.25%	11.50%	11.75%	12.00%	12.25%	12.50%	12.75%	13.00%	13.25%	13.50%	13.75%	14.00%	14.25%	14.50%	15.00%
0.00	243.00	246.25	249.50	252.75	256.00	259.25	262.50	265.75	269.00	272.25	275.50	278.75	282.00	285.25	288.50	295.00
1.00	221.62	224.66	227.70	230.74	233.78	236.82	239.86	242.90	245.94	248.98	252.03	255.07	258.11	261.15	264.19	270.27
2.00	202.58	205.43	208.28	211.13	213.98	216.83	219.67	222.52	225.37	228.22	231.07	233.92	236.77	239.62	242.47	248.17
3.00	185.59	188.27	190.94	193.62	196.29	198.97	201.64	204.32	206.99	209.67	212.34	215.02	217.69	220.37	223.04	228.39
4.00	170.42	172.94	175.45	177.97	180.48	183.00	185.51	188.03	190.54	193.06	195.57	198.09	200.61	203.12	205.64	210.67
4.25	166.89	169.37	171.84	174.32	176.80	179.28	181.75	184.23	186.71	189.18	191.66	194.14	196.62	199.09	201.57	206.53
4.50	163.45	165.89	168.33	170.77	173.21	175.65	178.09	180.53	182.97	185.41	187.85	190.29	192.73	195.18	197.62	202.50
4.75	160.11	162.51	164.91	167.32	169.72	172.13	174.53	176.94	179.34	181.74	184.15	186.55	188.96	191.36	193.76	198.57
5.00	156.85	159.22	161.59	163.96	166.33	168.70	171.06	173.43	175.80	178.17	180.54	182.91	185.28	187.65	190.02	194.75
5.25	153.69	156.02	158.35	160.69	163.02	165.36	167.69	170.03	172.36	174.69	177.03	179.36	181.70	184.03	186.36	191.03
5.50	150.61	152.91	155.21	157.51	159.81	162.11	164.41	166.71	169.01	171.31	173.61	175.91	178.21	180.51	182.81	187.41
5.75	147.61	149.88	152.14	154.41	156.68	158.94	161.21	163.48	165.75	168.01	170.28	172.55	174.81	177.08	179.35	183.88
6.00	144.69	146.93	149.16	151.40	153.63	155.87	158.10	160.33	162.57	164.80	167.04	169.27	171.51	173.74	175.98	180.45
6.25	141.85	144.06	146.26	148.46	150.66	152.87	155.07	157.27	159.48	161.68	163.88	166.08	168.29	170.49	172.69	177.10
6.50	139.09	141.26	143.43	145.60	147.78	149.95	152.12	154.29	156.46	158.63	160.81	162.98	165.15	167.32	169.49	173.84
6.75	136.40	138.54	140.68	142.82	144.96	147.11	149.25	151.39	153.53	155.67	157.81	159.95	162.09	164.23	166.38	170.66
7.00	133.78	135.89	138.00	140.11	142.23	144.34	146.45	148.56	150.67	152.78	154.89	157.00	159.12	161.23	163.34	167.56
7.25	131.23	133.31	135.39	137.48	139.56	141.64	143.72	145.81	147.89	149.97	152.05	154.13	156.22	158.30	160.38	164.54
7.50	128.75	130.80	132.85	134.91	136.96	139.01	141.07	143.12	145.17	147.23	149.28	151.33	153.39	155.44	157.50	161.60
7.75	126.33	128.35	130.38	132.41	134.43	136.46	138.48	140.51	142.53	144.56	146.58	148.61	150.63	152.66	154.68	158.73
8.00	123.97	125.97	127.97	129.97	131.97	133.96	135.96	137.96	139.96	141.95	143.95	145.95	147.95	149.95	151.94	155.94
8.25	121.68	123.65	125.62	127.59	129.56	131.53	133.51	135.48	137.45	139.42	141.39	143.36	145.33	147.30	149.27	153.21
8.50	119.45	121.39	123.33	125.28	127.22	129.17	131.11	133.06	135.00	136.95	138.89	140.84	142.78	144.72	146.67	150.56
8.75	117.27	119.19	121.11	123.02	124.94	126.86	128.78	130.70	132.62	134.54	136.45	138.37	140.29	142.21	144.13	147.97
9.00	115.15	117.04	118.93	120.83	122.72	124.61	126.51	128.40	130.29	132.19	134.08	135.97	137.87	139.76	141.65	145.44
9.25	113.08	114.95	116.82	118.68	120.55	122.42	124.29	126.16	128.03	129.90	131.76	133.63	135.50	137.37	139.24	142.98
9.50	111.06	112.91	114.75	116.60	118.44	120.29	122.13	123.97	125.82	127.66	129.51	131.35	133.19	135.04	136.88	140.57
9.75	109.10	110.92	112.74	114.56	116.38	118.20	120.02	121.84	123.66	125.48	127.30	129.12	130.94	132.77	134.59	138.23
10.00	107.19	108.98	110.78	112.58	114.38	116.17	117.97	119.77	121.56	123.36	125.16	126.95	128.75	130.55	132.34	135.94
10.25	105.32	107.10	108.87	110.64	112.42	114.19	115.97	117.74	119.51	121.29	123.06	124.84	126.61	128.38	130.16	133.71
10.50	103.50	105.25	107.01	108.76	110.51	112.26	114.01	115.76	117.51	119.27	121.02	122.77	124.52	126.27	128.02	131.53
10.75	101.73	103.46	105.19	106.92	108.65	110.38	112.11	113.84	115.56	117.29	119.02	120.75	122.48	124.21	125.94	129.40
11.00	100.00	101.71	103.42	105.12	106.83	108.54	110.25	111.95	113.66	115.37	117.08	118.79	120.49	122.20	123.91	127.32
11.25	98.31	100.00	101.69	103.37	105.06	106.75	108.43	110.12	111.81	113.49	115.18	116.87	118.55	120.24	121.93	125.30
11.50	96.67	98.33	100.00	101.67	103.33	105.00	106.66	108.33	109.99	111.66	113.33	114.99	116.66	118.32	119.99	123.32
11.75	95.06	96.71	98.35	100.00	101.65	103.29	104.94	106.58	108.23	109.87	111.52	113.16	114.81	116.45	118.10	121.39
12.00	93.50	95.12	96.75	98.37	100.00	101.63	103.25	104.88	106.50	108.13	109.75	111.38	113.00	114.63	116.25	119.50
12.25	91.97	93.58	95.18	96.79	98.39	100.00	101.61	103.21	104.82	106.42	108.03	109.63	111.24	112.85	114.45	117.66
12.50	90.48	92.07	93.65	95.24	96.83	98.41	100.00	101.59	103.17	104.76	106.35	107.93	109.52	111.11	112.69	115.86
12.75	89.03	90.59	92.16	93.73	95.30	96.86	98.43	100.00	101.57	103.14	104.70	106.27	107.84	109.41	110.97	114.11
13.00	87.61	89.16	90.71	92.25	93.80	95.35	96.90	98.45	100.00	101.55	103.10	104.65	106.20	107.75	109.29	112.39
13.25	86.22	87.75	89.28	90.81	92.35	93.88	95.41	96.94	98.47	100.00	101.53	103.06	104.59	106.12	107.65	110.72
13.50	84.87	86.38	87.90	89.41	90.92	92.44	93.95	95.46	96.97	98.49	100.00	101.51	103.03	104.54	106.05	109.08
13.75	83.55	85.05	86.54	88.04	89.53	91.03	92.52	94.02	95.51	97.01	98.50	100.00	101.50	102.99	104.49	107.48
14.00	82.26	83.74	85.22	86.70	88.17	89.65	91.13	92.61	94.09	95.57	97.04	98.52	100.00	101.48	102.96	105.91
14.25	81.00	82.46	83.93	85.39	86.85	88.31	89.77	91.23	92.69	94.15	95.62	97.08	98.54	100.00	101.46	104.38
14.50	79.77	81.22	82.66	84.11	85.55	87.00	88.44	89.89	91.33	92.78	94.22	95.67	97.11	98.56	100.00	102.89
14.75	78.57	80.00	81.43	82.86	84.29	85.72	87.14	88.57	90.00	91.43	92.86	94.29	95.71	97.14	98.57	101.43
15.00	77.40	78.81	80.23	81.64	83.05	84.46	85.88	87.29	88.70	90.11	91.53	92.94	94.35	95.76	97.18	100.00
15.25	76.26	77.65	79.05	80.45	81.84	83.24	84.64	86.03	87.43	88.83	90.22	91.62	93.02	94.41	95.81	98.60
15.50	75.14	76.52	77.90	79.28	80.66	82.04	83.42	84.81	86.19	87.57	88.95	90.33	91.71	93.09	94.47	97.24
15.75	74.04	75.41	76.78	78.14	79.51	80.87	82.24	83.61	84.97	86.34	87.70	89.07	90.44	91.80	93.17	95.90
16.00	72.98	74.33	75.68	77.03	78.38	79.73	81.08	82.43	83.79	85.14	86.49	87.84	89.19	90.54	91.89	94.60
16.25	71.93	73.27	74.60	75.94	77.28	78.61	79.95	81.29	82.62	83.96	85.30	86.63	87.97	89.31	90.64	93.32
16.50	70.91	72.23	73.55	74.88	76.20	77.52	78.84	80.17	81.49	82.81	84.13	85.46	86.78	88.10	89.42	92.07
16.75	69.91	71.22	72.53	73.84	75.15	76.45	77.76	79.07	80.38	81.69	82.99	84.30	85.61	86.92	88.23	90.84
17.00	68.94	70.23	71.53	72.82	74.11	75.41	76.70	78.00	79.29	80.59	81.88	83.17	84.47	85.76	87.06	89.65
17.25	67.98	69.26	70.55	71.83	73.11	74.39	75.67	76.95	78.23	79.51	80.79	82.07	83.35	84.63	85.91	88.47
17.50	67.05	68.32	69.59	70.85	72.12	73.39	74.66	75.92	77.19	78.46	79.72	80.99	82.26	83.53	84.79	87.33
17.75	66.14	67.39	68.65	69.90	71.16	72.41	73.66	74.92	76.17	77.43	78.68	79.93	81.19	82.44	83.70	86.21
18.00	65.25	66.49	67.73	68.97	70.21	71.45	72.70	73.94	75.18	76.42	77.66	78.90	80.14	81.38	82.62	85.11
18.25	64.38	65.60	66.83	68.06	69.29	70.52	71.75	72.98	74.20	75.43	76.66	77.89	79.12	80.35	81.57	84.03
18.50	63.52	64.74	65.96	67.17	68.39	69.60	70.82	72.03	73.25	74.47	75.68	76.90	78.11	79.33	80.55	82.98
18.75	62.69	63.89	65.10	66.30	67.50	68.71	69.91	71.11	72.32	73.52	74.72	75.93	77.13	78.34	79.54	81.95
19.00	61.87	63.06	64.25	65.45	66.64	67.83	69.02	70.21	71.40	72.60	73.79	74.98	76.17	77.36	78.55	80.94
20.00	58.78	59.92	61.07	62.21	63.36	64.50	65.65	66.79	67.94	69.08	70.23	71.37	72.52	73.66	74.81	77.10
25.00	46.62	47.57	48.53	49.48	50.43	51.39	52.34	53.29	54.25	55.20	56.15	57.10	58.06	59.01	59.96	61.87
30.00	38.34	39.15	39.96	40.77	41.58	42.40	43.21	44.02	44.83	45.64	46.45	47.26	48.08	48.89	49.70	51.32

Description: This table shows the yield to maturity of a bond purchased at the price shown in the index.

Example: The yield to maturity of a 15.00 %, 13 year bond at a price of 117.00 is 12.34 %.

COUPON RATE, %

PRICE	11.00%	11.25%	11.50%	11.75%	12.00%	12.25%	12.50%	12.75%	13.00%	13.25%	13.50%	13.75%	14.00%	14.25%	14.50%	15.00%
190	2.72	2.89	3.05	3.22	3.38	3.54	3.71	3.87	4.03	4.19	4.35	4.51	4.68	4.84	5.00	5.32
185	3.03	3.20	3.37	3.53	3.70	3.86	4.03	4.19	4.36	4.52	4.69	4.85	5.01	5.18	5.34	5.67
180	3.35	3.52	3.69	3.86	4.03	4.20	4.36	4.53	4.70	4.87	5.03	5.20	5.37	5.53	5.70	6.03
175	3.68	3.85	4.03	4.20	4.37	4.54	4.71	4.88	5.05	5.22	5.39	5.56	5.73	5.90	6.07	6.41
170	4.02	4.20	4.38	4.55	4.72	4.90	5.07	5.25	5.42	5.59	5.77	5.94	6.11	6.28	6.45	6.80
165	4.38	4.56	4.74	4.92	5.09	5.27	5.45	5.63	5.80	5.98	6.16	6.33	6.51	6.68	6.86	7.21
160	4.75	4.94	5.12	5.30	5.48	5.66	5.84	6.02	6.20	6.38	6.56	6.74	6.92	7.10	7.28	7.63
155	5.14	5.33	5.51	5.70	5.88	6.07	6.25	6.43	6.62	6.80	6.99	7.17	7.35	7.53	7.72	8.08
150	5.55	5.73	5.92	6.11	6.30	6.49	6.68	6.87	7.05	7.24	7.43	7.62	7.80	7.99	8.18	8.55
145	5.97	6.16	6.36	6.55	6.74	6.93	7.13	7.32	7.51	7.70	7.89	8.09	8.28	8.47	8.66	9.04
140	6.41	6.61	6.81	7.01	7.20	7.40	7.60	7.79	7.99	8.19	8.38	8.58	8.77	8.97	9.17	9.56
135	6.88	7.08	7.28	7.49	7.69	7.89	8.09	8.29	8.50	8.70	8.90	9.10	9.30	9.50	9.70	10.10
130	7.37	7.58	7.78	7.99	8.20	8.41	8.61	8.82	9.03	9.23	9.44	9.65	9.85	10.06	10.26	10.67
125	7.89	8.10	8.31	8.53	8.74	8.95	9.16	9.38	9.59	9.80	10.01	10.23	10.44	10.65	10.86	11.28
123	8.10	8.32	8.53	8.75	8.96	9.18	9.39	9.61	9.82	10.04	10.25	10.47	10.68	10.89	11.11	11.54
122	8.21	8.43	8.64	8.86	9.08	9.29	9.51	9.73	9.94	10.16	10.37	10.59	10.81	11.02	11.24	11.67
121	8.32	8.54	8.76	8.98	9.19	9.41	9.63	9.85	10.06	10.28	10.50	10.71	10.93	11.15	11.36	11.80
120	8.43	8.65	8.87	9.09	9.31	9.53	9.75	9.97	10.19	10.40	10.62	10.84	11.06	11.28	11.49	11.93
119	8.55	8.77	8.99	9.21	9.43	9.65	9.87	10.09	10.31	10.53	10.75	10.97	11.19	11.41	11.63	12.06
118	8.66	8.88	9.10	9.33	9.55	9.77	9.99	10.21	10.43	10.65	10.88	11.10	11.32	11.54	11.76	12.20
117	8.78	9.00	9.22	9.45	9.67	9.89	10.12	10.34	10.56	10.78	11.01	11.23	11.45	11.67	11.89	12.34
116	8.89	9.12	9.34	9.57	9.79	10.02	10.24	10.46	10.69	10.91	11.14	11.36	11.58	11.81	12.03	12.48
115	9.01	9.24	9.46	9.69	9.92	10.14	10.37	10.59	10.82	11.04	11.27	11.49	11.72	11.94	12.17	12.62
114	9.13	9.36	9.59	9.82	10.04	10.27	10.50	10.72	10.95	11.18	11.40	11.63	11.86	12.08	12.31	12.76
113	9.25	9.48	9.71	9.94	10.17	10.40	10.63	10.86	11.08	11.31	11.54	11.77	12.00	12.22	12.45	12.91
112	9.38	9.61	9.84	10.07	10.30	10.53	10.76	10.99	11.22	11.45	11.68	11.91	12.14	12.37	12.59	13.05
111	9.50	9.74	9.97	10.20	10.43	10.66	10.89	11.12	11.36	11.59	11.82	12.05	12.28	12.51	12.74	13.20
110	9.63	9.86	10.10	10.33	10.56	10.80	11.03	11.26	11.49	11.73	11.96	12.19	12.42	12.66	12.89	13.35
109	9.76	9.99	10.23	10.46	10.70	10.93	11.17	11.40	11.63	11.87	12.10	12.34	12.57	12.81	13.04	13.51
108	9.89	10.12	10.36	10.60	10.83	11.07	11.31	11.54	11.78	12.01	12.25	12.48	12.72	12.96	13.19	13.66
107	10.02	10.26	10.50	10.73	10.97	11.21	11.45	11.68	11.92	12.16	12.40	12.63	12.87	13.11	13.35	13.82
106	10.15	10.39	10.63	10.87	11.11	11.35	11.59	11.83	12.07	12.31	12.55	12.79	13.03	13.26	13.50	13.98
105	10.29	10.53	10.77	11.01	11.25	11.49	11.74	11.98	12.22	12.46	12.70	12.94	13.18	13.42	13.66	14.14
104	10.43	10.67	10.91	11.15	11.40	11.64	11.88	12.13	12.37	12.61	12.85	13.10	13.34	13.58	13.82	14.31
103	10.57	10.81	11.05	11.30	11.54	11.79	12.03	12.28	12.52	12.77	13.01	13.25	13.50	13.74	13.99	14.48
102	10.71	10.95	11.20	11.45	11.69	11.94	12.18	12.43	12.68	12.92	13.17	13.42	13.66	13.91	14.15	14.65
101	10.85	11.10	11.35	11.59	11.84	12.09	12.34	12.59	12.83	13.08	13.33	13.58	13.83	14.08	14.32	14.82
100	11.00	11.25	11.50	11.75	12.00	12.25	12.50	12.75	13.00	13.25	13.50	13.75	14.00	14.25	14.50	15.00
99	11.14	11.39	11.65	11.90	12.15	12.40	12.65	12.91	13.16	13.41	13.66	13.91	14.17	14.42	14.67	15.17
98	11.29	11.55	11.80	12.05	12.31	12.56	12.82	13.07	13.32	13.58	13.83	14.08	14.34	14.59	14.85	15.35
97	11.44	11.70	11.96	12.21	12.47	12.72	12.98	13.23	13.49	13.75	14.00	14.26	14.51	14.77	15.03	15.54
96	11.60	11.86	12.11	12.37	12.63	12.89	13.15	13.40	13.66	13.92	14.18	14.44	14.69	14.95	15.21	15.73
95	11.76	12.01	12.27	12.53	12.79	13.05	13.31	13.57	13.83	14.09	14.35	14.61	14.88	15.14	15.40	15.92
94	11.91	12.18	12.44	12.70	12.96	13.22	13.49	13.75	14.01	14.27	14.54	14.80	15.06	15.32	15.59	16.11
93	12.08	12.34	12.60	12.87	13.13	13.40	13.66	13.93	14.19	14.45	14.72	14.98	15.25	15.51	15.78	16.31
92	12.24	12.51	12.77	13.04	13.31	13.57	13.84	14.10	14.37	14.64	14.91	15.17	15.44	15.71	15.97	16.51
91	12.41	12.68	12.94	13.21	13.48	13.75	14.02	14.29	14.56	14.83	15.10	15.36	15.63	15.90	16.17	16.71
90	12.58	12.85	13.12	13.39	13.66	13.93	14.20	14.47	14.75	15.02	15.29	15.56	15.83	16.10	16.38	16.92
89	12.75	13.02	13.30	13.57	13.84	14.12	14.39	14.66	14.94	15.21	15.49	15.76	16.03	16.31	16.58	17.13
88	12.93	13.20	13.48	13.75	14.03	14.30	14.58	14.86	15.13	15.41	15.69	15.96	16.24	16.52	16.79	17.35
87	13.10	13.38	13.66	13.94	14.22	14.49	14.77	15.05	15.33	15.61	15.89	16.17	16.45	16.73	17.01	17.57
86	13.29	13.57	13.85	14.13	14.41	14.69	14.97	15.25	15.53	15.81	16.10	16.38	16.66	16.94	17.23	17.79
85	13.47	13.75	14.04	14.32	14.60	14.89	15.17	15.46	15.74	16.02	16.31	16.59	16.88	17.16	17.45	18.02
84	13.66	13.94	14.23	14.52	14.80	15.09	15.38	15.66	15.95	16.24	16.52	16.81	17.10	17.39	17.68	18.25
83	13.85	14.14	14.43	14.72	15.01	15.29	15.58	15.87	16.16	16.45	16.74	17.03	17.32	17.62	17.91	18.49
82	14.05	14.34	14.63	14.92	15.21	15.50	15.80	16.09	16.38	16.67	16.97	17.26	17.56	17.85	18.14	18.73
81	14.25	14.54	14.83	15.13	15.42	15.72	16.01	16.31	16.60	16.90	17.20	17.49	17.79	18.09	18.38	18.98
80	14.45	14.75	15.04	15.34	15.64	15.94	16.23	16.53	16.83	17.13	17.43	17.73	18.03	18.33	18.63	19.23
79	14.66	14.96	15.26	15.56	15.86	16.16	16.46	16.76	17.06	17.37	17.67	17.97	18.27	18.58	18.88	19.49
78	14.87	15.17	15.47	15.78	16.08	16.38	16.69	16.99	17.30	17.61	17.91	18.22	18.52	18.83	19.14	19.75
77	15.08	15.39	15.69	16.00	16.31	16.62	16.92	17.23	17.54	17.85	18.16	18.47	18.78	19.09	19.40	20.02
76	15.30	15.61	15.92	16.23	16.54	16.85	17.16	17.48	17.79	18.10	18.41	18.73	19.04	19.35	19.67	20.30
75	15.53	15.84	16.15	16.47	16.78	17.09	17.41	17.72	18.04	18.36	18.67	18.99	19.31	19.62	19.94	20.58
74	15.76	16.07	16.39	16.71	17.02	17.34	17.66	17.98	18.30	18.62	18.94	19.26	19.58	19.90	20.22	20.87
73	15.99	16.31	16.63	16.95	17.27	17.59	17.92	18.24	18.56	18.89	19.21	19.53	19.86	20.18	20.51	21.16
70	16.72	17.05	17.39	17.72	18.05	18.39	18.72	19.05	19.39	19.73	20.06	20.40	20.74	21.07	21.41	22.09
65	18.07	18.42	18.77	19.13	19.48	19.84	20.20	20.55	20.91	21.27	21.63	21.99	22.35	22.71	23.07	23.80
60	19.59	19.97	20.35	20.73	21.11	21.50	21.88	22.26	22.65	23.04	23.42	23.81	24.20	24.59	24.98	25.76

Description: This table shows the price to pay for a bond at the yield rate. The yield is to maturity.

Example: The price of a 6.75 %, 14 year bond to yield 8 % to maturity is $ 89.59.

COUPON RATE, %

YIELD	0.00%	1.00%	2.00%	3.00%	4.00%	4.25%	4.50%	4.75%	5.00%	5.25%	5.50%	5.75%	6.00%	6.25%	6.50%	6.75%
0.00	100.00	114.00	128.00	142.00	156.00	159.50	163.00	166.50	170.00	173.50	177.00	180.50	184.00	187.50	191.00	194.50
1.00	86.97	100.00	113.03	126.07	139.10	142.36	145.62	148.88	152.14	155.39	158.65	161.91	165.17	168.43	171.69	174.94
2.00	75.68	87.84	100.00	112.16	124.32	127.36	130.40	133.44	136.47	139.51	142.55	145.59	148.63	151.67	154.71	157.75
3.00	65.91	77.27	88.64	100.00	111.36	114.20	117.05	119.89	122.73	125.57	128.41	131.25	134.09	136.93	139.77	142.61
4.00	57.44	68.08	78.72	89.36	100.00	102.66	105.32	107.98	110.64	113.30	115.96	118.62	121.28	123.94	126.60	129.26
4.25	55.50	65.97	76.44	86.91	97.38	100.00	102.62	105.24	107.85	110.47	113.09	115.71	118.32	120.94	123.56	126.18
4.50	53.63	63.94	74.24	84.54	94.85	97.42	100.00	102.58	105.15	107.73	110.30	112.88	115.46	118.03	120.61	123.18
4.75	51.83	61.97	72.11	82.25	92.39	94.93	97.46	100.00	102.54	105.07	107.61	110.14	112.68	115.21	117.75	120.28
5.00	50.09	60.07	70.05	80.04	90.02	92.51	95.01	97.50	100.00	102.50	104.99	107.49	109.98	112.48	114.97	117.47
5.25	48.41	58.23	68.06	77.89	87.72	90.17	92.63	95.09	97.54	100.00	102.46	104.91	107.37	109.83	112.28	114.74
5.50	46.79	56.46	66.14	75.81	85.49	87.91	90.32	92.74	95.16	97.58	100.00	102.42	104.84	107.26	109.68	112.09
5.75	45.22	54.75	64.27	73.80	83.33	85.71	88.09	90.47	92.85	95.24	97.62	100.00	102.38	104.76	107.15	109.53
6.00	43.71	53.09	62.47	71.85	81.24	83.58	85.93	88.27	90.62	92.96	95.31	97.65	100.00	102.35	104.69	107.04
6.25	42.25	51.49	60.73	69.97	79.21	81.52	83.83	86.14	88.45	90.76	93.07	95.38	97.69	100.00	102.31	104.62
6.50	40.84	49.94	59.04	68.14	77.25	79.52	81.80	84.07	86.35	88.62	90.90	93.17	95.45	97.72	100.00	102.28
6.75	39.48	48.45	57.41	66.38	75.34	77.58	79.83	82.07	84.31	86.55	88.79	91.03	93.28	95.52	97.76	100.00
7.00	38.17	47.00	55.83	64.67	73.50	75.71	77.92	80.12	82.33	84.54	86.75	88.96	91.17	93.37	95.58	97.79
7.25	36.90	45.60	54.30	63.01	71.71	73.89	76.06	78.24	80.42	82.59	84.77	86.94	89.12	91.30	93.47	95.65
7.50	35.67	44.25	52.83	61.40	69.98	72.12	74.27	76.41	78.56	80.70	82.85	84.99	87.13	89.28	91.42	93.57
7.75	34.49	42.94	51.40	59.85	68.30	70.41	72.53	74.64	76.75	78.87	80.98	83.09	85.21	87.32	89.43	91.55
8.00	33.35	41.68	50.01	58.34	66.67	68.76	70.84	72.92	75.01	77.09	79.17	81.25	83.34	85.42	87.50	89.59
8.25	32.24	40.46	48.67	56.88	65.10	67.15	69.20	71.26	73.31	75.36	77.41	79.47	81.52	83.57	85.63	87.68
8.50	31.18	39.28	47.37	55.47	63.57	65.59	67.61	69.64	71.66	73.69	75.71	77.73	79.76	81.78	83.81	85.83
8.75	30.15	38.13	46.12	54.10	62.08	64.08	66.07	68.07	70.06	72.06	74.06	76.05	78.05	80.04	82.04	84.03
9.00	29.16	37.03	44.90	52.77	60.64	62.61	64.58	66.55	68.51	70.48	72.45	74.42	76.39	78.35	80.32	82.29
9.25	28.20	35.96	43.72	51.48	59.25	61.19	63.13	65.07	67.01	68.95	70.89	72.83	74.77	76.71	78.65	80.59
9.50	27.27	34.93	42.58	50.24	57.89	59.81	61.72	63.64	65.55	67.46	69.38	71.29	73.20	75.12	77.03	78.95
9.75	26.37	33.93	41.48	49.03	56.58	58.47	60.36	62.24	64.13	66.02	67.91	69.79	71.68	73.57	75.46	77.35
10.00	25.51	32.96	40.41	47.86	55.31	57.17	59.03	60.89	62.75	64.62	66.48	68.34	70.20	72.07	73.93	75.79
10.25	24.67	32.02	39.37	46.72	54.07	55.91	57.74	59.58	61.42	63.26	65.09	66.93	68.77	70.60	72.44	74.28
10.50	23.87	31.12	38.37	45.62	52.87	54.68	56.49	58.31	60.12	61.93	63.75	65.56	67.37	69.18	71.00	72.81
10.75	23.09	30.24	37.40	44.55	51.71	53.49	55.28	57.07	58.86	60.65	62.44	64.23	66.01	67.80	69.59	71.38
11.00	22.33	29.39	36.45	43.51	50.58	52.34	54.11	55.87	57.64	59.40	61.17	62.93	64.70	66.46	68.23	69.99
11.25	21.60	28.57	35.54	42.51	49.48	51.22	52.96	54.70	56.45	58.19	59.93	61.67	63.42	65.16	66.90	68.64
11.50	20.90	27.78	34.66	41.53	48.41	50.13	51.85	53.57	55.29	57.01	58.73	60.45	62.17	63.89	65.61	67.33
11.75	20.22	27.01	33.80	40.59	47.38	49.08	50.77	52.47	54.17	55.87	57.56	59.26	60.96	62.66	64.35	66.05
12.00	19.56	26.27	32.97	39.67	46.38	48.05	49.73	51.40	53.08	54.75	56.43	58.11	59.78	61.46	63.13	64.81
12.25	18.93	25.55	32.16	38.78	45.40	47.06	48.71	50.36	52.02	53.67	55.33	56.98	58.64	60.29	61.95	63.60
12.50	18.31	24.85	31.38	37.92	44.45	46.09	47.72	49.35	50.99	52.62	54.26	55.89	57.52	59.16	60.79	62.42
12.75	17.72	24.17	30.63	37.08	43.53	45.15	46.76	48.37	49.99	51.60	53.21	54.83	56.44	58.05	59.67	61.28
13.00	17.15	23.52	29.89	36.27	42.64	44.23	45.83	47.42	49.01	50.61	52.20	53.79	55.39	56.98	58.57	60.17
13.25	16.59	22.89	29.18	35.48	41.77	43.35	44.92	46.49	48.07	49.64	51.22	52.79	54.36	55.94	57.51	59.08
13.50	16.06	22.28	28.49	34.71	40.93	42.48	44.04	45.59	47.15	48.70	50.26	51.81	53.37	54.92	56.47	58.03
13.75	15.54	21.68	27.83	33.97	40.11	41.65	43.18	44.72	46.25	47.79	49.32	50.86	52.40	53.93	55.47	57.00
14.00	15.04	21.11	27.18	33.25	39.31	40.83	42.35	43.87	45.38	46.90	48.42	49.93	51.45	52.97	54.49	56.00
14.25	14.56	20.55	26.55	32.54	38.54	40.04	41.54	43.04	44.54	46.04	47.53	49.03	50.53	52.03	53.53	55.03
14.50	14.09	20.01	25.94	31.86	37.79	39.27	40.75	42.23	43.71	45.19	46.68	48.16	49.64	51.12	52.60	54.08
14.75	13.64	19.49	25.35	31.20	37.06	38.52	39.98	41.45	42.91	44.38	45.84	47.30	48.77	50.23	51.70	53.16
15.00	13.20	18.99	24.77	30.56	36.35	37.79	39.24	40.69	42.13	43.58	45.03	46.47	47.92	49.37	50.81	52.26
15.25	12.78	18.50	24.22	29.94	35.66	37.09	38.51	39.94	41.37	42.80	44.23	45.66	47.09	48.52	49.95	51.38
15.50	12.37	18.02	23.68	29.33	34.98	36.40	37.81	39.22	40.64	42.05	43.46	44.88	46.29	47.70	49.12	50.53
15.75	11.97	17.56	23.15	28.74	34.33	35.73	37.12	38.52	39.92	41.32	42.71	44.11	45.51	46.90	48.30	49.70
16.00	11.59	17.12	22.64	28.17	33.69	35.07	36.46	37.84	39.22	40.60	41.98	43.36	44.74	46.13	47.51	48.89
16.25	11.22	16.69	22.15	27.61	33.08	34.44	35.81	37.17	38.54	39.90	41.27	42.64	44.00	45.37	46.73	48.10
16.50	10.86	16.27	21.67	27.07	32.47	33.82	35.17	36.52	37.88	39.23	40.58	41.93	43.28	44.63	45.98	47.33
16.75	10.52	15.86	21.20	26.55	31.89	33.22	34.56	35.89	37.23	38.57	39.90	41.24	42.57	43.91	45.24	46.58
17.00	10.19	15.47	20.75	26.03	31.32	32.64	33.96	35.28	36.60	37.92	39.24	40.56	41.88	43.21	44.53	45.85
17.25	9.86	15.09	20.31	25.54	30.76	32.07	33.38	34.68	35.99	37.30	38.60	39.91	41.21	42.52	43.83	45.13
17.50	9.55	14.72	19.89	25.06	30.22	31.52	32.81	34.10	35.39	36.68	37.98	39.27	40.56	41.85	43.15	44.44
17.75	9.25	14.36	19.47	24.59	29.70	30.98	32.25	33.53	34.81	36.09	37.37	38.65	39.92	41.20	42.48	43.76
18.00	8.95	14.01	19.07	24.13	29.19	30.45	31.72	32.98	34.25	35.51	36.77	38.04	39.30	40.57	41.83	43.10
18.25	8.67	13.68	18.68	23.68	28.69	29.94	31.19	32.44	33.69	34.94	36.20	37.45	38.70	39.95	41.20	42.45
18.50	8.40	13.35	18.30	23.25	28.20	29.44	30.68	31.92	33.16	34.39	35.63	36.87	38.11	39.34	40.58	41.82
18.75	8.13	13.03	17.93	22.83	27.73	28.96	30.18	31.41	32.63	33.86	35.08	36.31	37.53	38.76	39.98	41.21
19.00	7.88	12.73	17.57	22.42	27.27	28.48	29.70	30.91	32.12	33.33	34.54	35.76	36.97	38.18	39.39	40.61
20.00	6.93	11.59	16.24	20.89	25.55	26.71	27.87	29.04	30.20	31.36	32.53	33.69	34.85	36.02	37.18	38.34
25.00	3.70	7.55	11.40	15.25	19.10	20.07	21.03	21.99	22.96	23.92	24.88	25.85	26.81	27.77	28.74	29.70
30.00	2.00	5.26	8.53	11.80	15.06	15.88	16.70	17.51	18.33	19.15	19.96	20.78	21.60	22.41	23.23	24.05

Description: This table shows the yield to maturity of a bond purchased at the price shown in the index.

Example: The yield to maturity of a 6.75 %, 14 year bond at a price of 80.00 is 9.33 %.

COUPON RATE, %

PRICE	0.00%	1.00%	2.00%	3.00%	4.00%	4.25%	4.50%	4.75%	5.00%	5.25%	5.50%	5.75%	6.00%	6.25%	6.50%	6.75%
100	0.00	1.00	2.00	3.00	4.00	4.25	4.50	4.75	5.00	5.25	5.50	5.75	6.00	6.25	6.50	6.75
99	.07	1.07	2.08	3.08	4.09	4.34	4.59	4.84	5.10	5.35	5.60	5.85	6.10	6.35	6.61	6.86
98	.14	1.15	2.16	3.17	4.19	4.44	4.69	4.94	5.20	5.45	5.70	5.96	6.21	6.46	6.72	6.97
97	.21	1.23	2.25	3.26	4.28	4.54	4.79	5.05	5.30	5.56	5.81	6.07	6.32	6.58	6.83	7.09
96	.29	1.31	2.33	3.36	4.38	4.64	4.89	5.15	5.41	5.66	5.92	6.18	6.43	6.69	6.95	7.20
95	.36	1.39	2.42	3.45	4.48	4.74	5.00	5.25	5.51	5.77	6.03	6.29	6.55	6.80	7.06	7.32
94	.44	1.47	2.51	3.54	4.58	4.84	5.10	5.36	5.62	5.88	6.14	6.40	6.66	6.92	7.18	7.44
93	.51	1.55	2.59	3.64	4.68	4.94	5.21	5.47	5.73	5.99	6.25	6.52	6.78	7.04	7.30	7.56
92	.59	1.64	2.68	3.73	4.79	5.05	5.31	5.58	5.84	6.10	6.37	6.63	6.90	7.16	7.42	7.69
91	.67	1.72	2.78	3.83	4.89	5.16	5.42	5.69	5.95	6.22	6.48	6.75	7.02	7.28	7.55	7.81
90	.75	1.81	2.87	3.93	5.00	5.26	5.53	5.80	6.07	6.33	6.60	6.87	7.14	7.40	7.67	7.94
89	.83	1.89	2.96	4.03	5.10	5.37	5.64	5.91	6.18	6.45	6.72	6.99	7.26	7.53	7.80	8.07
88	.91	1.98	3.06	4.13	5.21	5.48	5.76	6.03	6.30	6.57	6.84	7.11	7.39	7.66	7.93	8.20
87	.99	2.07	3.15	4.24	5.32	5.60	5.87	6.14	6.42	6.69	6.96	7.24	7.51	7.79	8.06	8.34
86	1.08	2.16	3.25	4.34	5.44	5.71	5.99	6.26	6.54	6.81	7.09	7.36	7.64	7.92	8.19	8.47
85	1.16	2.25	3.35	4.45	5.55	5.83	6.10	6.38	6.66	6.94	7.22	7.49	7.77	8.05	8.33	8.61
84	1.24	2.34	3.45	4.55	5.67	5.95	6.22	6.50	6.78	7.06	7.34	7.62	7.91	8.19	8.47	8.75
83	1.33	2.44	3.55	4.66	5.78	6.06	6.35	6.63	6.91	7.19	7.47	7.76	8.04	8.32	8.61	8.89
82	1.42	2.53	3.65	4.77	5.90	6.19	6.47	6.75	7.04	7.32	7.61	7.89	8.18	8.46	8.75	9.04
81	1.51	2.63	3.75	4.89	6.02	6.31	6.60	6.88	7.17	7.46	7.74	8.03	8.32	8.61	8.90	9.18
80	1.60	2.72	3.86	5.00	6.15	6.43	6.72	7.01	7.30	7.59	7.88	8.17	8.46	8.75	9.04	9.33
79	1.69	2.82	3.96	5.11	6.27	6.56	6.85	7.14	7.43	7.73	8.02	8.31	8.60	8.90	9.19	9.49
78	1.78	2.92	4.07	5.23	6.40	6.69	6.98	7.28	7.57	7.87	8.16	8.46	8.75	9.05	9.34	9.64
77	1.87	3.02	4.18	5.35	6.53	6.82	7.12	7.41	7.71	8.01	8.31	8.60	8.90	9.20	9.50	9.80
76	1.96	3.13	4.29	5.47	6.66	6.96	7.25	7.55	7.85	8.15	8.45	8.75	9.05	9.36	9.66	9.96
75	2.06	3.23	4.41	5.59	6.79	7.09	7.39	7.69	8.00	8.30	8.60	8.91	9.21	9.51	9.82	10.12
74	2.16	3.34	4.52	5.72	6.93	7.23	7.53	7.84	8.14	8.45	8.75	9.06	9.37	9.67	9.98	10.29
73	2.26	3.44	4.64	5.85	7.06	7.37	7.68	7.98	8.29	8.60	8.91	9.22	9.53	9.84	10.15	10.46
72	2.36	3.55	4.76	5.98	7.20	7.51	7.82	8.13	8.44	8.75	9.07	9.38	9.69	10.01	10.32	10.64
71	2.46	3.66	4.88	6.11	7.35	7.66	7.97	8.28	8.60	8.91	9.23	9.54	9.86	10.18	10.49	10.81
70	2.56	3.77	5.00	6.24	7.49	7.81	8.12	8.44	8.76	9.07	9.39	9.71	10.03	10.35	10.67	10.99
69	2.66	3.89	5.13	6.38	7.64	7.96	8.28	8.60	8.92	9.24	9.56	9.88	10.20	10.53	10.85	11.18
68	2.77	4.00	5.25	6.52	7.79	8.11	8.43	8.76	9.08	9.40	9.73	10.05	10.38	10.71	11.04	11.37
67	2.88	4.12	5.38	6.66	7.94	8.27	8.59	8.92	9.25	9.57	9.90	10.23	10.56	10.89	11.23	11.56
66	2.99	4.24	5.51	6.80	8.10	8.43	8.76	9.09	9.42	9.75	10.08	10.41	10.75	11.08	11.42	11.76
65	3.10	4.36	5.65	6.95	8.26	8.59	8.92	9.26	9.59	9.93	10.26	10.60	10.94	11.28	11.62	11.96
64	3.21	4.49	5.78	7.09	8.42	8.76	9.09	9.43	9.77	10.11	10.45	10.79	11.13	11.47	11.82	12.16
63	3.32	4.61	5.92	7.25	8.59	8.93	9.27	9.61	9.95	10.29	10.64	10.98	11.33	11.67	12.02	12.37
62	3.44	4.74	6.06	7.40	8.76	9.10	9.44	9.79	10.14	10.48	10.83	11.18	11.53	11.88	12.23	12.59
61	3.56	4.87	6.21	7.56	8.93	9.28	9.63	9.97	10.32	10.68	11.03	11.38	11.74	12.09	12.45	12.81
60	3.68	5.00	6.35	7.72	9.11	9.46	9.81	10.16	10.52	10.87	11.23	11.59	11.95	12.31	12.67	13.03
59	3.80	5.14	6.50	7.88	9.29	9.64	10.00	10.36	10.72	11.08	11.44	11.80	12.16	12.53	12.90	13.26
58	3.92	5.28	6.65	8.05	9.48	9.83	10.19	10.56	10.92	11.28	11.65	12.02	12.39	12.76	13.13	13.50
57	4.05	5.42	6.81	8.22	9.66	10.03	10.39	10.76	11.13	11.50	11.87	12.24	12.62	12.99	13.37	13.75
56	4.18	5.56	6.97	8.40	9.86	10.23	10.60	10.97	11.34	11.72	12.09	12.47	12.85	13.23	13.61	14.00
55	4.31	5.71	7.13	8.58	10.06	10.43	10.80	11.18	11.56	11.94	12.32	12.70	13.09	13.48	13.86	14.25
54	4.45	5.86	7.30	8.76	10.26	10.64	11.02	11.40	11.78	12.17	12.56	12.94	13.34	13.73	14.12	14.52
53	4.58	6.01	7.47	8.95	10.47	10.85	11.24	11.62	12.01	12.40	12.80	13.19	13.59	13.99	14.39	14.79
52	4.72	6.16	7.64	9.14	10.68	11.07	11.46	11.85	12.25	12.65	13.05	13.45	13.85	14.25	14.66	15.07
51	4.86	6.32	7.82	9.34	10.90	11.30	11.69	12.09	12.49	12.90	13.30	13.71	14.12	14.53	14.94	15.36
50	5.01	6.49	8.00	9.54	11.13	11.53	11.93	12.33	12.74	13.15	13.56	13.98	14.39	14.81	15.23	15.65
49	5.16	6.65	8.18	9.75	11.36	11.76	12.17	12.58	13.00	13.42	13.83	14.25	14.68	15.10	15.53	15.96
48	5.31	6.82	8.37	9.96	11.59	12.01	12.42	12.84	13.26	13.69	14.11	14.54	14.97	15.40	15.84	16.28
47	5.46	6.99	8.57	10.18	11.84	12.26	12.68	13.11	13.54	13.97	14.40	14.84	15.27	15.71	16.16	16.60
46	5.62	7.17	8.77	10.41	12.09	12.52	12.95	13.38	13.82	14.26	14.70	15.14	15.59	16.04	16.49	16.94
45	5.78	7.36	8.97	10.64	12.35	12.78	13.22	13.66	14.11	14.55	15.00	15.46	15.91	16.37	16.83	17.29
44	5.95	7.54	9.19	10.88	12.62	13.06	13.51	13.96	14.41	14.86	15.32	15.78	16.25	16.71	17.18	17.66
43	6.12	7.73	9.40	11.12	12.89	13.34	13.80	14.26	14.72	15.18	15.65	16.12	16.59	17.07	17.55	18.03
42	6.29	7.93	9.63	11.37	13.18	13.64	14.10	14.57	15.04	15.51	15.99	16.47	16.95	17.44	17.93	18.42
41	6.47	8.13	9.86	11.64	13.47	13.94	14.42	14.89	15.37	15.85	16.34	16.83	17.33	17.82	18.33	18.83
40	6.65	8.34	10.09	11.90	13.78	14.26	14.74	15.23	15.72	16.21	16.71	17.21	17.71	18.22	18.74	19.25
39	6.84	8.55	10.34	12.18	14.10	14.58	15.08	15.57	16.07	16.58	17.09	17.60	18.12	18.64	19.17	19.69
35	7.64	9.48	11.40	13.40	15.49	16.02	16.57	17.11	17.66	18.22	18.78	19.35	19.92	20.50	21.08	21.67
30	8.78	10.82	12.96	15.22	17.60	18.22	18.84	19.47	20.11	20.75	21.40	22.06	22.73	23.41	24.09	24.78
25	10.15	12.44	14.90	17.52	20.34	21.07	21.81	22.57	23.33	24.11	24.90	25.70	26.51	27.33	28.16	29.00
20	11.83	14.50	17.43	20.63	24.14	25.06	26.00	26.96	27.94	28.94	29.95	30.98	32.03	33.09	34.17	35.26
15	14.02	17.30	21.04	25.29	30.10	31.38	32.70	34.05	35.43	36.85	38.28	39.74	41.23	42.74	44.26	45.80
10	17.14	21.63	27.13	33.86	41.85	44.01	46.23	48.50	50.80	53.15	55.52	57.92	60.33	62.77	65.21	67.67

Description: This table shows the price to pay for a bond at the yield rate. The yield is to maturity.

Example: The price of a 10.75 %, 14 year bond to yield 8 % to maturity is $ 122.91.

COUPON RATE, %

YIELD	7.00%	7.25%	7.50%	7.75%	8.00%	8.25%	8.50%	8.75%	9.00%	9.25%	9.50%	9.75%	10.00%	10.25%	10.50%	10.75%
0.00	198.00	201.50	205.00	208.50	212.00	215.50	219.00	222.50	226.00	229.50	233.00	236.50	240.00	243.50	247.00	250.50
1.00	178.20	181.46	184.72	187.98	191.24	194.50	197.75	201.01	204.27	207.53	210.79	214.05	217.30	220.56	223.82	227.08
2.00	160.79	163.83	166.87	169.91	172.95	175.99	179.03	182.07	185.11	188.15	191.19	194.23	197.27	200.31	203.34	206.38
3.00	145.45	148.29	151.14	153.98	156.82	159.66	162.50	165.34	168.18	171.02	173.86	176.70	179.54	182.38	185.23	188.07
4.00	131.92	134.58	137.24	139.90	142.56	145.22	147.88	150.54	153.20	155.86	158.52	161.18	163.84	166.50	169.16	171.82
4.25	128.79	131.41	134.03	136.65	139.26	141.88	144.50	147.12	149.73	152.35	154.97	157.59	160.20	162.82	165.44	168.06
4.50	125.76	128.34	130.91	133.49	136.06	138.64	141.22	143.79	146.37	148.94	151.52	154.10	156.67	159.25	161.82	164.40
4.75	122.82	125.35	127.89	130.42	132.96	135.49	138.03	140.57	143.10	145.64	148.17	150.71	153.24	155.78	158.31	160.85
5.00	119.96	122.46	124.96	127.45	129.95	132.44	134.94	137.43	139.93	142.43	144.92	147.42	149.91	152.41	154.90	157.40
5.25	117.20	119.65	122.11	124.57	127.02	129.48	131.94	134.40	136.85	139.31	141.77	144.22	146.68	149.14	151.59	154.05
5.50	114.51	116.93	119.35	121.77	124.19	126.61	129.03	131.45	133.86	136.28	138.70	141.12	143.54	145.96	148.38	150.80
5.75	111.91	114.29	116.67	119.05	121.44	123.82	126.20	128.58	130.96	133.34	135.73	138.11	140.49	142.87	145.25	147.64
6.00	109.38	111.73	114.07	116.42	118.76	121.11	123.46	125.80	128.15	130.49	132.84	135.18	137.53	139.87	142.22	144.56
6.25	106.93	109.24	111.55	113.86	116.17	118.48	120.79	123.10	125.41	127.72	130.03	132.34	134.65	136.96	139.27	141.58
6.50	104.55	106.83	109.10	111.38	113.65	115.93	118.20	120.48	122.75	125.03	127.30	129.58	131.86	134.13	136.41	138.68
6.75	102.24	104.48	106.72	108.97	111.21	113.45	115.69	117.93	120.17	122.42	124.66	126.90	129.14	131.38	133.62	135.86
7.00	100.00	102.21	104.42	106.63	108.83	111.04	113.25	115.46	117.67	119.88	122.08	124.29	126.50	128.71	130.92	133.13
7.25	97.82	100.00	102.18	104.35	106.53	108.70	110.88	113.06	115.23	117.41	119.58	121.76	123.94	126.11	128.29	130.46
7.50	95.71	97.86	100.00	102.14	104.29	106.43	108.58	110.72	112.87	115.01	117.15	119.30	121.44	123.59	125.73	127.88
7.75	93.66	95.77	97.89	100.00	102.11	104.23	106.34	108.45	110.57	112.68	114.79	116.91	119.02	121.13	123.25	125.36
8.00	91.67	93.75	95.83	97.92	100.00	102.08	104.17	106.25	108.33	110.41	112.50	114.58	116.66	118.75	120.83	122.91
8.25	89.73	91.79	93.84	95.89	97.95	100.00	102.05	104.11	106.16	108.21	110.27	112.32	114.37	116.43	118.48	120.53
8.50	87.86	89.88	91.90	93.93	95.95	97.98	100.00	102.02	104.05	106.07	108.10	110.12	112.14	114.17	116.19	118.22
8.75	86.03	88.03	90.02	92.02	94.01	96.01	98.00	100.00	102.00	103.99	105.99	107.98	109.98	111.97	113.97	115.97
9.00	84.26	86.22	88.19	90.16	92.13	94.10	96.06	98.03	100.00	101.97	103.94	105.90	107.87	109.84	111.81	113.78
9.25	82.53	84.48	86.42	88.36	90.30	92.24	94.18	96.12	98.06	100.00	101.94	103.88	105.82	107.76	109.70	111.64
9.50	80.86	82.77	84.69	86.60	88.52	90.43	92.34	94.26	96.17	98.09	100.00	101.91	103.83	105.74	107.66	109.57
9.75	79.23	81.12	83.01	84.90	86.79	88.67	90.56	92.45	94.34	96.22	98.11	100.00	101.89	103.78	105.66	107.55
10.00	77.65	79.52	81.38	83.24	85.10	86.96	88.83	90.69	92.55	94.41	96.28	98.14	100.00	101.86	103.72	105.59
10.25	76.12	77.95	79.79	81.63	83.46	85.30	87.14	88.98	90.81	92.65	94.49	96.33	98.16	100.00	101.84	103.67
10.50	74.62	76.43	78.25	80.06	81.87	83.69	85.50	87.31	89.12	90.94	92.75	94.56	96.37	98.19	100.00	101.81
10.75	73.17	74.96	76.75	78.54	80.32	82.11	83.90	85.69	87.48	89.27	91.06	92.85	94.63	96.42	98.21	100.00
11.00	71.76	73.52	75.29	77.05	78.82	80.58	82.35	84.11	85.88	87.64	89.41	91.17	92.94	94.70	96.47	98.23
11.25	70.38	72.13	73.87	75.61	77.35	79.09	80.84	82.58	84.32	86.06	87.81	89.55	91.29	93.03	94.77	96.52
11.50	69.05	70.77	72.49	74.21	75.93	77.65	79.37	81.08	82.80	84.52	86.24	87.96	89.68	91.40	93.12	94.84
11.75	67.75	69.45	71.14	72.84	74.54	76.24	77.93	79.63	81.33	83.03	84.72	86.42	88.12	89.82	91.51	93.21
12.00	66.48	68.16	69.84	71.51	73.19	74.86	76.54	78.21	79.89	81.57	83.24	84.92	86.59	88.27	89.95	91.62
12.25	65.25	66.91	68.56	70.22	71.87	73.53	75.18	76.84	78.49	80.15	81.80	83.45	85.11	86.76	88.42	90.07
12.50	64.06	65.69	67.33	68.96	70.59	72.23	73.86	75.49	77.13	78.76	80.40	82.03	83.66	85.30	86.93	88.56
12.75	62.89	64.51	66.12	67.73	69.35	70.96	72.57	74.19	75.80	77.41	79.03	80.64	82.25	83.87	85.48	87.09
13.00	61.76	63.35	64.95	66.54	68.13	69.73	71.32	72.91	74.51	76.10	77.69	79.29	80.88	82.47	84.07	85.66
13.25	60.66	62.23	63.80	65.38	66.95	68.53	70.10	71.67	73.25	74.82	76.39	77.97	79.54	81.12	82.69	84.26
13.50	59.58	61.14	62.69	64.25	65.80	67.36	68.91	70.46	72.02	73.57	75.13	76.68	78.24	79.79	81.35	82.90
13.75	58.54	60.07	61.61	63.14	64.68	66.22	67.75	69.29	70.82	72.36	73.89	75.43	76.97	78.50	80.04	81.57
14.00	57.52	59.04	60.55	62.07	63.59	65.11	66.62	68.14	69.66	71.17	72.69	74.21	75.73	77.24	78.76	80.28
14.25	56.53	58.03	59.53	61.03	62.52	64.02	65.52	67.02	68.52	70.02	71.52	73.02	74.52	76.02	77.51	79.01
14.50	55.56	57.04	58.53	60.01	61.49	62.97	64.45	65.93	67.41	68.89	70.38	71.86	73.34	74.82	76.30	77.78
14.75	54.62	56.09	57.55	59.01	60.48	61.94	63.41	64.87	66.33	67.80	69.26	70.72	72.19	73.65	75.12	76.58
15.00	53.71	55.15	56.60	58.05	59.49	60.94	62.39	63.83	65.28	66.73	68.17	69.62	71.07	72.51	73.96	75.41
15.25	52.81	54.24	55.67	57.10	58.53	59.96	61.39	62.82	64.25	65.68	67.11	68.54	69.97	71.40	72.83	74.26
15.50	51.94	53.36	54.77	56.18	57.60	59.01	60.42	61.84	63.25	64.66	66.08	67.49	68.90	70.32	71.73	73.15
15.75	51.10	52.49	53.89	55.29	56.69	58.08	59.48	60.88	62.27	63.67	65.07	66.47	67.86	69.26	70.66	72.06
16.00	50.27	51.65	53.03	54.41	55.80	57.18	58.56	59.94	61.32	62.70	64.08	65.47	66.85	68.23	69.61	70.99
16.25	49.46	50.83	52.20	53.56	54.93	56.29	57.66	59.03	60.39	61.76	63.12	64.49	65.85	67.22	68.59	69.95
16.50	48.68	50.03	51.38	52.73	54.08	55.43	56.78	58.13	59.48	60.83	62.19	63.54	64.89	66.24	67.59	68.94
16.75	47.91	49.25	50.59	51.92	53.26	54.59	55.93	57.26	58.60	59.93	61.27	62.61	63.94	65.28	66.61	67.95
17.00	47.17	48.49	49.81	51.13	52.45	53.77	55.09	56.41	57.73	59.05	60.38	61.70	63.02	64.34	65.66	66.98
17.25	46.44	47.75	49.05	50.36	51.67	52.97	54.28	55.58	56.89	58.20	59.50	60.81	62.12	63.42	64.73	66.03
17.50	45.73	47.02	48.31	49.61	50.90	52.19	53.48	54.77	56.07	57.36	58.65	59.94	61.24	62.53	63.82	65.11
17.75	45.04	46.32	47.59	48.87	50.15	51.43	52.71	53.98	55.26	56.54	57.82	59.10	60.38	61.65	62.93	64.21
18.00	44.36	45.63	46.89	48.15	49.42	50.68	51.95	53.21	54.48	55.74	57.01	58.27	59.54	60.80	62.06	63.33
18.25	43.70	44.95	46.20	47.46	48.71	49.96	51.21	52.46	53.71	54.96	56.21	57.46	58.71	59.97	61.22	62.47
18.50	43.06	44.30	45.53	46.77	48.01	49.25	50.49	51.72	52.96	54.20	55.44	56.67	57.91	59.15	60.39	61.63
18.75	42.43	43.66	44.88	46.11	47.33	48.55	49.78	51.00	52.23	53.45	54.68	55.90	57.13	58.35	59.58	60.80
19.00	41.82	43.03	44.24	45.45	46.67	47.88	49.09	50.30	51.51	52.73	53.94	55.15	56.36	57.58	58.79	60.00
20.00	39.51	40.67	41.83	43.00	44.16	45.32	46.49	47.65	48.81	49.98	51.14	52.30	53.47	54.63	55.79	56.96
25.00	30.66	31.62	32.59	33.55	34.51	35.48	36.44	37.40	38.37	39.33	40.29	41.25	42.22	43.18	44.14	45.11
30.00	24.86	25.68	26.50	27.31	28.13	28.95	29.76	30.58	31.40	32.21	33.03	33.85	34.66	35.48	36.30	37.11

Description: This table shows the yield to maturity of a bond purchased at the price shown in the index.

Example: The yield to maturity of a 10.75 %, 14 year bond at a price of 113.00 is 9.09 %.

PRICE	7.00%	7.25%	7.50%	7.75%	8.00%	8.25%	8.50%	8.75%	9.00%	9.25%	9.50%	9.75%	10.00%	10.25%	10.50%	10.75%
145	3.03	3.22	3.42	3.62	3.82	4.01	4.21	4.40	4.60	4.79	4.99	5.18	5.38	5.57	5.77	5.96
140	3.38	3.58	3.79	3.99	4.19	4.39	4.59	4.79	4.99	5.19	5.39	5.59	5.79	5.98	6.18	6.38
135	3.76	3.96	4.17	4.37	4.58	4.79	4.99	5.19	5.40	5.60	5.81	6.01	6.21	6.42	6.62	6.82
130	4.15	4.36	4.57	4.78	4.99	5.20	5.41	5.62	5.83	6.04	6.25	6.46	6.67	6.87	7.08	7.29
129	4.23	4.44	4.65	4.86	5.08	5.29	5.50	5.71	5.92	6.13	6.34	6.55	6.76	6.97	7.18	7.39
128	4.31	4.52	4.74	4.95	5.16	5.37	5.58	5.80	6.01	6.22	6.43	6.64	6.85	7.06	7.27	7.48
127	4.39	4.61	4.82	5.03	5.25	5.46	5.67	5.89	6.10	6.31	6.52	6.74	6.95	7.16	7.37	7.58
126	4.47	4.69	4.91	5.12	5.33	5.55	5.76	5.98	6.19	6.40	6.62	6.83	7.04	7.26	7.47	7.68
125	4.56	4.78	4.99	5.21	5.42	5.64	5.85	6.07	6.28	6.50	6.71	6.93	7.14	7.35	7.57	7.78
124	4.64	4.86	5.08	5.30	5.51	5.73	5.94	6.16	6.38	6.59	6.81	7.02	7.24	7.45	7.67	7.88
123	4.73	4.95	5.17	5.38	5.60	5.82	6.04	6.25	6.47	6.69	6.91	7.12	7.34	7.55	7.77	7.99
122	4.82	5.04	5.25	5.47	5.69	5.91	6.13	6.35	6.57	6.79	7.00	7.22	7.44	7.66	7.87	8.09
121	4.90	5.12	5.34	5.57	5.79	6.01	6.23	6.44	6.66	6.88	7.10	7.32	7.54	7.76	7.98	8.20
120	4.99	5.21	5.44	5.66	5.88	6.10	6.32	6.54	6.76	6.98	7.20	7.42	7.64	7.86	8.08	8.30
119	5.08	5.30	5.53	5.75	5.97	6.20	6.42	6.64	6.86	7.08	7.30	7.53	7.75	7.97	8.19	8.41
118	5.17	5.40	5.62	5.84	6.07	6.29	6.51	6.74	6.96	7.18	7.41	7.63	7.85	8.07	8.30	8.52
117	5.26	5.49	5.71	5.94	6.16	6.39	6.61	6.84	7.06	7.29	7.51	7.74	7.96	8.18	8.41	8.63
116	5.36	5.58	5.81	6.04	6.26	6.49	6.71	6.94	7.17	7.39	7.62	7.84	8.07	8.29	8.52	8.74
115	5.45	5.68	5.90	6.13	6.36	6.59	6.82	7.04	7.27	7.50	7.72	7.95	8.18	8.40	8.63	8.85
114	5.54	5.77	6.00	6.23	6.46	6.69	6.92	7.15	7.37	7.60	7.83	8.06	8.29	8.51	8.74	8.97
113	5.64	5.87	6.10	6.33	6.56	6.79	7.02	7.25	7.48	7.71	7.94	8.17	8.40	8.63	8.86	9.09
112	5.74	5.97	6.20	6.43	6.66	6.89	7.13	7.36	7.59	7.82	8.05	8.28	8.51	8.74	8.97	9.20
111	5.83	6.07	6.30	6.53	6.77	7.00	7.23	7.46	7.70	7.93	8.16	8.39	8.63	8.86	9.09	9.32
110	5.93	6.17	6.40	6.64	6.87	7.11	7.34	7.57	7.81	8.04	8.28	8.51	8.74	8.98	9.21	9.44
109	6.03	6.27	6.51	6.74	6.98	7.21	7.45	7.68	7.92	8.15	8.39	8.63	8.86	9.10	9.33	9.56
108	6.14	6.37	6.61	6.85	7.08	7.32	7.56	7.80	8.03	8.27	8.51	8.74	8.98	9.22	9.45	9.69
107	6.24	6.48	6.72	6.95	7.19	7.43	7.67	7.91	8.15	8.39	8.62	8.86	9.10	9.34	9.58	9.81
106	6.34	6.58	6.82	7.06	7.30	7.54	7.78	8.02	8.26	8.50	8.74	8.98	9.22	9.46	9.70	9.94
105	6.45	6.69	6.93	7.17	7.41	7.66	7.90	8.14	8.38	8.62	8.86	9.11	9.35	9.59	9.83	10.07
104	6.55	6.80	7.04	7.28	7.53	7.77	8.01	8.26	8.50	8.74	8.99	9.23	9.47	9.72	9.96	10.20
103	6.66	6.91	7.15	7.40	7.64	7.89	8.13	8.38	8.62	8.87	9.11	9.36	9.60	9.85	10.09	10.33
102	6.77	7.02	7.26	7.51	7.76	8.00	8.25	8.50	8.74	8.99	9.24	9.48	9.73	9.98	10.22	10.47
101	6.88	7.13	7.38	7.63	7.88	8.12	8.37	8.62	8.87	9.12	9.37	9.61	9.86	10.11	10.36	10.61
100	7.00	7.25	7.50	7.75	8.00	8.25	8.50	8.75	9.00	9.25	9.50	9.75	10.00	10.25	10.50	10.75
99	7.11	7.36	7.61	7.86	8.12	8.37	8.62	8.87	9.12	9.37	9.63	9.88	10.13	10.38	10.63	10.89
98	7.22	7.48	7.73	7.98	8.24	8.49	8.75	9.00	9.25	9.51	9.76	10.01	10.27	10.52	10.77	11.03
97	7.34	7.60	7.85	8.11	8.36	8.62	8.87	9.13	9.38	9.64	9.90	10.15	10.41	10.66	10.92	11.17
96	7.46	7.72	7.97	8.23	8.49	8.75	9.00	9.26	9.52	9.78	10.03	10.29	10.55	10.81	11.06	11.32
95	7.58	7.84	8.10	8.36	8.62	8.88	9.14	9.39	9.65	9.91	10.17	10.43	10.69	10.95	11.21	11.47
94	7.70	7.96	8.22	8.49	8.75	9.01	9.27	9.53	9.79	10.05	10.31	10.58	10.84	11.10	11.36	11.62
93	7.83	8.09	8.35	8.62	8.88	9.14	9.40	9.67	9.93	10.19	10.46	10.72	10.99	11.25	11.51	11.78
92	7.95	8.22	8.48	8.75	9.01	9.28	9.54	9.81	10.07	10.34	10.60	10.87	11.14	11.40	11.67	11.93
91	8.08	8.35	8.61	8.88	9.15	9.42	9.68	9.95	10.22	10.49	10.75	11.02	11.29	11.56	11.83	12.09
90	8.21	8.48	8.75	9.02	9.29	9.56	9.83	10.09	10.36	10.63	10.90	11.17	11.45	11.72	11.99	12.26
89	8.34	8.61	8.88	9.16	9.43	9.70	9.97	10.24	10.51	10.79	11.06	11.33	11.60	11.88	12.15	12.42
88	8.48	8.75	9.02	9.30	9.57	9.84	10.12	10.39	10.67	10.94	11.21	11.49	11.76	12.04	12.31	12.59
87	8.61	8.89	9.16	9.44	9.71	9.99	10.27	10.54	10.82	11.10	11.37	11.65	11.93	12.21	12.48	12.76
86	8.75	9.03	9.30	9.58	9.86	10.14	10.42	10.70	10.98	11.26	11.53	11.81	12.09	12.37	12.65	12.94
85	8.89	9.17	9.45	9.73	10.01	10.29	10.57	10.85	11.14	11.42	11.70	11.98	12.26	12.55	12.83	13.11
84	9.03	9.31	9.60	9.88	10.16	10.45	10.73	11.01	11.30	11.58	11.87	12.15	12.44	12.72	13.01	13.29
83	9.18	9.46	9.75	10.03	10.32	10.60	10.89	11.18	11.46	11.75	12.04	12.32	12.61	12.90	13.19	13.48
82	9.32	9.61	9.90	10.19	10.47	10.76	11.05	11.34	11.63	11.92	12.21	12.50	12.79	13.08	13.37	13.66
81	9.47	9.76	10.05	10.34	10.64	10.93	11.22	11.51	11.80	12.09	12.39	12.68	12.97	13.27	13.56	13.85
80	9.63	9.92	10.21	10.50	10.80	11.09	11.39	11.68	11.98	12.27	12.57	12.86	13.16	13.46	13.75	14.05
79	9.78	10.08	10.37	10.67	10.96	11.26	11.56	11.86	12.15	12.45	12.75	13.05	13.35	13.65	13.95	14.25
78	9.94	10.24	10.54	10.83	11.13	11.43	11.73	12.03	12.33	12.64	12.94	13.24	13.54	13.84	14.15	14.45
77	10.10	10.40	10.70	11.00	11.31	11.61	11.91	12.22	12.52	12.82	13.13	13.43	13.74	14.04	14.35	14.66
76	10.26	10.57	10.87	11.18	11.48	11.79	12.09	12.40	12.71	13.01	13.32	13.63	13.94	14.25	14.56	14.87
75	10.43	10.74	11.05	11.35	11.66	11.97	12.28	12.59	12.90	13.21	13.52	13.83	14.14	14.46	14.77	15.08
74	10.60	10.91	11.22	11.53	11.84	12.16	12.47	12.78	13.09	13.41	13.72	14.04	14.35	14.67	14.99	15.30
70	11.32	11.64	11.96	12.29	12.61	12.94	13.27	13.59	13.92	14.25	14.58	14.91	15.24	15.57	15.90	16.23
65	12.30	12.64	12.98	13.33	13.67	14.02	14.37	14.71	15.06	15.41	15.76	16.11	16.47	16.82	17.17	17.53
60	13.40	13.76	14.13	14.50	14.87	15.24	15.61	15.98	16.35	16.73	17.10	17.48	17.86	18.23	18.61	18.99
55	14.64	15.04	15.43	15.83	16.22	16.62	17.02	17.42	17.83	18.23	18.64	19.05	19.45	19.86	20.28	20.69
50	16.08	16.50	16.93	17.36	17.80	18.23	18.67	19.10	19.54	19.99	20.43	20.88	21.32	21.77	22.22	22.67
45	17.76	18.23	18.70	19.17	19.65	20.13	20.61	21.09	21.58	22.07	22.56	23.05	23.55	24.05	24.55	25.05
40	19.77	20.30	20.82	21.36	21.89	22.43	22.97	23.51	24.06	24.61	25.16	25.72	26.28	26.84	27.40	27.97
35	22.26	22.86	23.47	24.07	24.68	25.30	25.92	26.55	27.17	27.81	28.44	29.09	29.73	30.38	31.03	31.68

Description: This table shows the price to pay for a bond at the yield rate. The yield is to maturity.

Example: The price of a 15.00 %, 14 year bond to yield 8 % to maturity is $ 158.32.

COUPON RATE, %

YIELD	11.00%	11.25%	11.50%	11.75%	12.00%	12.25%	12.50%	12.75%	13.00%	13.25%	13.50%	13.75%	14.00%	14.25%	14.50%	15.00%
0.00	254.00	257.50	261.00	264.50	268.00	271.50	275.00	278.50	282.00	285.50	289.00	292.50	296.00	299.50	303.00	310.00
1.00	230.34	233.60	236.86	240.11	243.37	246.63	249.89	253.15	256.41	259.66	262.92	266.18	269.44	272.70	275.96	282.47
2.00	209.42	212.46	215.50	218.54	221.58	224.62	227.66	230.70	233.74	236.78	239.82	242.86	245.90	248.94	251.98	258.06
3.00	190.91	193.75	196.59	199.43	202.27	205.11	207.95	210.79	213.63	216.47	219.32	222.16	225.00	227.84	230.68	236.36
4.00	174.48	177.14	179.80	182.46	185.13	187.79	190.45	193.11	195.77	198.43	201.09	203.75	206.41	209.07	211.73	217.05
4.25	170.67	173.29	175.91	178.53	181.14	183.76	186.38	189.00	191.62	194.23	196.85	199.47	202.09	204.70	207.32	212.56
4.50	166.98	169.55	172.13	174.70	177.28	179.86	182.43	185.01	187.58	190.16	192.74	195.31	197.89	200.46	203.04	208.19
4.75	163.38	165.92	168.45	170.99	173.52	176.06	178.60	181.13	183.67	186.20	188.74	191.27	193.81	196.34	198.88	203.95
5.00	159.89	162.39	164.89	167.38	169.88	172.37	174.87	177.36	179.86	182.36	184.85	187.35	189.84	192.34	194.83	199.82
5.25	156.51	158.96	161.42	163.88	166.33	168.79	171.25	173.70	176.16	178.62	181.07	183.53	185.99	188.44	190.90	195.81
5.50	153.21	155.63	158.05	160.47	162.89	165.31	167.73	170.15	172.57	174.98	177.40	179.82	182.24	184.66	187.08	191.92
5.75	150.02	152.40	154.78	157.16	159.54	161.93	164.31	166.69	169.07	171.45	173.83	176.22	178.60	180.98	183.36	188.13
6.00	146.91	149.26	151.60	153.95	156.29	158.64	160.98	163.33	165.67	168.02	170.37	172.71	175.06	177.40	179.75	184.44
6.25	143.89	146.20	148.51	150.82	153.13	155.44	157.75	160.06	162.37	164.68	166.99	169.30	171.61	173.92	176.23	180.85
6.50	140.96	143.23	145.51	147.78	150.06	152.33	154.61	156.89	159.16	161.44	163.71	165.99	168.26	170.54	172.81	177.36
6.75	138.11	140.35	142.59	144.83	147.07	149.31	151.55	153.80	156.04	158.28	160.52	162.76	165.00	167.25	169.49	173.97
7.00	135.33	137.54	139.75	141.96	144.17	146.38	148.58	150.79	153.00	155.21	157.42	159.63	161.83	164.04	166.25	170.67
7.25	132.64	134.82	136.99	139.17	141.34	143.52	145.70	147.87	150.05	152.22	154.40	156.57	158.75	160.93	163.10	167.45
7.50	130.02	132.16	134.31	136.45	138.60	140.74	142.89	145.03	147.17	149.32	151.46	153.61	155.75	157.89	160.04	164.33
7.75	127.47	129.59	131.70	133.81	135.92	138.04	140.15	142.26	144.38	146.49	148.60	150.72	152.83	154.94	157.06	161.28
8.00	124.99	127.08	129.16	131.24	133.33	135.41	137.49	139.57	141.66	143.74	145.82	147.91	149.99	152.07	154.15	158.32
8.25	122.59	124.64	126.69	128.74	130.80	132.85	134.90	136.96	139.01	141.06	143.12	145.17	147.22	149.28	151.33	155.44
8.50	120.24	122.27	124.29	126.31	128.34	130.36	132.39	134.41	136.43	138.46	140.48	142.51	144.53	146.55	148.58	152.63
8.75	117.96	119.96	121.95	123.95	125.94	127.94	129.94	131.93	133.93	135.92	137.92	139.91	141.91	143.91	145.90	149.89
9.00	115.74	117.71	119.68	121.65	123.61	125.58	127.55	129.52	131.49	133.45	135.42	137.39	139.36	141.33	143.29	147.23
9.25	113.58	115.52	117.47	119.41	121.35	123.29	125.23	127.17	129.11	131.05	132.99	134.93	136.87	138.81	140.75	144.63
9.50	111.48	113.40	115.31	117.23	119.14	121.05	122.97	124.88	126.80	128.71	130.62	132.54	134.45	136.36	138.28	142.11
9.75	109.44	111.33	113.21	115.10	116.99	118.88	120.77	122.65	124.54	126.43	128.32	130.21	132.09	133.98	135.87	139.64
10.00	107.45	109.31	111.17	113.04	114.90	116.76	118.62	120.48	122.35	124.21	126.07	127.93	129.80	131.66	133.52	137.25
10.25	105.51	107.35	109.19	111.02	112.86	114.70	116.54	118.37	120.21	122.05	123.88	125.72	127.56	129.40	131.23	134.91
10.50	103.63	105.44	107.25	109.06	110.88	112.69	114.50	116.31	118.13	119.94	121.75	123.57	125.38	127.19	129.00	132.63
10.75	101.79	103.58	105.37	107.15	108.94	110.73	112.52	114.31	116.10	117.89	119.68	121.46	123.25	125.04	126.83	130.41
11.00	100.00	101.77	103.53	105.30	107.06	108.83	110.59	112.36	114.12	115.89	117.65	119.42	121.18	122.95	124.71	128.24
11.25	98.26	100.00	101.74	103.48	105.23	106.97	108.71	110.45	112.19	113.94	115.68	117.42	119.16	120.91	122.65	126.13
11.50	96.56	98.28	100.00	101.72	103.44	105.16	106.88	108.60	110.32	112.04	113.76	115.48	117.20	118.92	120.63	124.07
11.75	94.91	96.61	98.30	100.00	101.70	103.39	105.09	106.79	108.49	110.18	111.88	113.58	115.28	116.97	118.67	122.07
12.00	93.30	94.97	96.65	98.32	100.00	101.68	103.35	105.03	106.70	108.38	110.05	111.73	113.41	115.08	116.76	120.11
12.25	91.73	93.38	95.04	96.69	98.35	100.00	101.65	103.31	104.96	106.62	108.27	109.93	111.58	113.24	114.89	118.20
12.50	90.20	91.83	93.47	95.10	96.73	98.37	100.00	101.63	103.27	104.90	106.53	108.17	109.80	111.44	113.07	116.34
12.75	88.71	90.32	91.93	93.55	95.16	96.77	98.39	100.00	101.61	103.23	104.84	106.45	108.07	109.68	111.29	114.52
13.00	87.25	88.85	90.44	92.03	93.63	95.22	96.81	98.41	100.00	101.59	103.19	104.78	106.37	107.97	109.56	112.75
13.25	85.84	87.41	88.98	90.56	92.13	93.71	95.28	96.85	98.43	100.00	101.57	103.15	104.72	106.29	107.87	111.02
13.50	84.46	86.01	87.56	89.12	90.67	92.23	93.78	95.34	96.89	98.45	100.00	101.55	103.11	104.66	106.22	109.33
13.75	83.11	84.64	86.18	87.71	89.25	90.79	92.32	93.86	95.39	96.93	98.46	100.00	101.54	103.07	104.61	107.68
14.00	81.79	83.31	84.83	86.35	87.86	89.38	90.90	92.41	93.93	95.45	96.97	98.48	100.00	101.52	103.03	106.07
14.25	80.51	82.01	83.51	85.01	86.51	88.01	89.51	91.01	92.50	94.00	95.50	97.00	98.50	100.00	101.50	104.50
14.50	79.26	80.74	82.23	83.71	85.19	86.67	88.15	89.63	91.11	92.59	94.08	95.56	97.04	98.52	100.00	102.96
14.75	78.04	79.51	80.97	82.43	83.90	85.36	86.83	88.29	89.75	91.22	92.68	94.14	95.61	97.07	98.54	101.46
15.00	76.85	78.30	79.75	81.19	82.64	84.09	85.53	86.98	88.43	89.87	91.32	92.77	94.21	95.66	97.11	100.00
15.25	75.69	77.12	78.55	79.98	81.41	82.84	84.27	85.70	87.13	88.56	89.99	91.42	92.85	94.28	95.71	98.57
15.50	74.56	75.97	77.39	78.80	80.21	81.63	83.04	84.45	85.87	87.28	88.69	90.11	91.52	92.93	94.35	97.17
15.75	73.45	74.85	76.25	77.64	79.04	80.44	81.84	83.23	84.63	86.03	87.42	88.82	90.22	91.62	93.01	95.81
16.00	72.37	73.75	75.14	76.52	77.90	79.28	80.66	82.04	83.42	84.80	86.19	87.57	88.95	90.33	91.71	94.47
16.25	71.32	72.68	74.05	75.42	76.78	78.15	79.51	80.88	82.24	83.61	84.98	86.34	87.71	89.07	90.44	93.17
16.50	70.29	71.64	72.99	74.34	75.69	77.04	78.39	79.74	81.09	82.44	83.79	85.14	86.49	87.85	89.20	91.90
16.75	69.28	70.62	71.95	73.29	74.62	75.96	77.30	78.63	79.97	81.30	82.64	83.97	85.31	86.64	87.98	90.65
17.00	68.30	69.62	70.94	72.26	73.58	74.90	76.23	77.55	78.87	80.19	81.51	82.83	84.15	85.47	86.79	89.43
17.25	67.34	68.65	69.95	71.26	72.57	73.87	75.18	76.49	77.79	79.10	80.40	81.71	83.02	84.32	85.63	88.24
17.50	66.40	67.70	68.99	70.28	71.57	72.86	74.16	75.45	76.74	78.03	79.33	80.62	81.91	83.20	84.49	87.08
17.75	65.49	66.77	68.04	69.32	70.60	71.88	73.16	74.44	75.71	76.99	78.27	79.55	80.83	82.11	83.38	85.94
18.00	64.59	65.86	67.12	68.39	69.65	70.92	72.18	73.45	74.71	75.97	77.24	78.50	79.77	81.03	82.30	84.83
18.25	63.72	64.97	66.22	67.47	68.72	69.97	71.23	72.48	73.73	74.98	76.23	77.48	78.73	79.98	81.23	83.74
18.50	62.86	64.10	65.34	66.58	67.82	69.05	70.29	71.53	72.77	74.00	75.24	76.48	77.72	78.96	80.19	82.67
18.75	62.03	63.25	64.48	65.70	66.93	68.15	69.38	70.60	71.83	73.05	74.28	75.50	76.73	77.95	79.18	81.63
19.00	61.21	62.42	63.64	64.85	66.06	67.27	68.48	69.70	70.91	72.12	73.33	74.55	75.76	76.97	78.18	80.61
20.00	58.12	59.28	60.45	61.61	62.77	63.94	65.10	66.26	67.43	68.59	69.75	70.92	72.08	73.24	74.41	76.73
25.00	46.07	47.03	48.00	48.96	49.92	50.88	51.85	52.81	53.77	54.74	55.70	56.66	57.63	58.59	59.55	61.48
30.00	37.93	38.75	39.57	40.38	41.20	42.02	42.83	43.65	44.47	45.28	46.10	46.92	47.73	48.55	49.37	51.00

Description: This table shows the yield to maturity of a bond purchased at the price shown in the index.

Example: The yield to maturity of a 15.00 %, 14 year bond at a price of 117.00 is 12.41 %.

					COUPON RATE, %											
PRICE	11.00%	11.25%	11.50%	11.75%	12.00%	12.25%	12.50%	12.75%	13.00%	13.25%	13.50%	13.75%	14.00%	14.25%	14.50%	15.00%
190	3.05	3.21	3.37	3.54	3.70	3.86	4.02	4.18	4.34	4.50	4.67	4.83	4.98	5.14	5.30	5.62
185	3.34	3.51	3.67	3.84	4.00	4.17	4.33	4.50	4.66	4.82	4.99	5.15	5.31	5.47	5.63	5.96
180	3.65	3.81	3.98	4.15	4.32	4.49	4.65	4.82	4.99	5.15	5.32	5.48	5.65	5.81	5.98	6.31
175	3.96	4.13	4.30	4.48	4.65	4.82	4.99	5.16	5.32	5.49	5.66	5.83	6.00	6.17	6.33	6.67
170	4.29	4.46	4.64	4.81	4.99	5.16	5.33	5.51	5.68	5.85	6.02	6.19	6.36	6.54	6.71	7.05
165	4.63	4.81	4.99	5.16	5.34	5.52	5.69	5.87	6.05	6.22	6.40	6.57	6.75	6.92	7.09	7.44
160	4.99	5.17	5.35	5.53	5.71	5.89	6.07	6.25	6.43	6.61	6.79	6.96	7.14	7.32	7.50	7.85
155	5.36	5.54	5.73	5.91	6.10	6.28	6.46	6.65	6.83	7.01	7.19	7.38	7.56	7.74	7.92	8.28
150	5.75	5.94	6.12	6.31	6.50	6.69	6.87	7.06	7.25	7.44	7.62	7.81	7.99	8.18	8.37	8.74
145	6.15	6.35	6.54	6.73	6.92	7.11	7.31	7.50	7.69	7.88	8.07	8.26	8.45	8.64	8.83	9.21
140	6.58	6.78	6.97	7.17	7.37	7.56	7.76	7.96	8.15	8.35	8.54	8.74	8.93	9.13	9.32	9.71
135	7.03	7.23	7.43	7.63	7.83	8.03	8.24	8.44	8.64	8.84	9.04	9.24	9.44	9.64	9.84	10.23
130	7.50	7.70	7.91	8.12	8.33	8.53	8.74	8.94	9.15	9.36	9.56	9.77	9.97	10.18	10.38	10.79
125	7.99	8.21	8.42	8.63	8.85	9.06	9.27	9.48	9.69	9.91	10.12	10.33	10.54	10.75	10.96	11.38
123	8.20	8.42	8.63	8.85	9.06	9.28	9.49	9.71	9.92	10.13	10.35	10.56	10.78	10.99	11.20	11.63
122	8.31	8.52	8.74	8.96	9.17	9.39	9.60	9.82	10.04	10.25	10.47	10.68	10.90	11.11	11.32	11.75
121	8.41	8.63	8.85	9.07	9.28	9.50	9.72	9.94	10.15	10.37	10.58	10.80	11.02	11.23	11.45	11.88
120	8.52	8.74	8.96	9.18	9.40	9.62	9.83	10.05	10.27	10.49	10.71	10.92	11.14	11.36	11.58	12.01
119	8.63	8.85	9.07	9.29	9.51	9.73	9.95	10.17	10.39	10.61	10.83	11.05	11.27	11.48	11.70	12.14
118	8.74	8.96	9.18	9.41	9.63	9.85	10.07	10.29	10.51	10.73	10.95	11.17	11.39	11.61	11.83	12.27
117	8.85	9.08	9.30	9.52	9.74	9.97	10.19	10.41	10.63	10.86	11.08	11.30	11.52	11.74	11.96	12.41
116	8.97	9.19	9.41	9.64	9.86	10.09	10.31	10.53	10.76	10.98	11.20	11.43	11.65	11.87	12.10	12.54
115	9.08	9.31	9.53	9.76	9.98	10.21	10.43	10.66	10.88	11.11	11.33	11.56	11.78	12.01	12.23	12.68
114	9.20	9.42	9.65	9.88	10.10	10.33	10.56	10.78	11.01	11.24	11.46	11.69	11.91	12.14	12.37	12.82
113	9.31	9.54	9.77	10.00	10.23	10.46	10.68	10.91	11.14	11.37	11.60	11.82	12.05	12.28	12.50	12.96
112	9.43	9.66	9.89	10.12	10.35	10.58	10.81	11.04	11.27	11.50	11.73	11.96	12.19	12.42	12.64	13.10
111	9.55	9.79	10.02	10.25	10.48	10.71	10.94	11.17	11.40	11.63	11.86	12.10	12.33	12.56	12.79	13.25
110	9.68	9.91	10.14	10.37	10.61	10.84	11.07	11.31	11.54	11.77	12.00	12.23	12.47	12.70	12.93	13.39
109	9.80	10.03	10.27	10.50	10.74	10.97	11.21	11.44	11.67	11.91	12.14	12.38	12.61	12.84	13.08	13.54
108	9.93	10.16	10.40	10.63	10.87	11.11	11.34	11.58	11.81	12.05	12.28	12.52	12.75	12.99	13.23	13.70
107	10.05	10.29	10.53	10.77	11.00	11.24	11.48	11.72	11.95	12.19	12.43	12.66	12.90	13.14	13.38	13.85
106	10.18	10.42	10.66	10.90	11.14	11.38	11.62	11.86	12.10	12.33	12.57	12.81	13.05	13.29	13.53	14.01
105	10.31	10.55	10.79	11.04	11.28	11.52	11.76	12.00	12.24	12.48	12.72	12.96	13.20	13.44	13.68	14.16
104	10.44	10.69	10.93	11.17	11.42	11.66	11.90	12.14	12.39	12.63	12.87	13.11	13.36	13.60	13.84	14.33
103	10.58	10.82	11.07	11.31	11.56	11.80	12.05	12.29	12.54	12.78	13.02	13.27	13.51	13.76	14.00	14.49
102	10.72	10.96	11.21	11.45	11.70	11.95	12.19	12.44	12.69	12.93	13.18	13.42	13.67	13.92	14.16	14.65
101	10.85	11.10	11.35	11.60	11.85	12.10	12.34	12.59	12.84	13.09	13.34	13.58	13.83	14.08	14.33	14.82
100	11.00	11.25	11.50	11.75	12.00	12.25	12.50	12.75	13.00	13.25	13.50	13.75	14.00	14.25	14.50	15.00
99	11.14	11.39	11.64	11.89	12.15	12.40	12.65	12.90	13.15	13.41	13.66	13.91	14.16	14.41	14.67	15.17
98	11.28	11.54	11.79	12.04	12.30	12.55	12.81	13.06	13.31	13.57	13.82	14.08	14.33	14.58	14.84	15.35
97	11.43	11.69	11.94	12.20	12.45	12.71	12.97	13.22	13.48	13.73	13.99	14.25	14.50	14.76	15.01	15.53
96	11.58	11.84	12.09	12.35	12.61	12.87	13.13	13.38	13.64	13.90	14.16	14.42	14.68	14.93	15.19	15.71
95	11.73	11.99	12.25	12.51	12.77	13.03	13.29	13.55	13.81	14.07	14.33	14.59	14.85	15.11	15.37	15.90
94	11.89	12.15	12.41	12.67	12.93	13.20	13.46	13.72	13.98	14.25	14.51	14.77	15.03	15.30	15.56	16.09
93	12.04	12.31	12.57	12.83	13.10	13.36	13.63	13.89	14.16	14.42	14.69	14.95	15.22	15.48	15.75	16.28
92	12.20	12.47	12.73	13.00	13.27	13.53	13.80	14.07	14.33	14.60	14.87	15.14	15.40	15.67	15.94	16.47
91	12.36	12.63	12.90	13.17	13.44	13.71	13.98	14.25	14.52	14.79	15.05	15.32	15.59	15.86	16.13	16.67
90	12.53	12.80	13.07	13.34	13.61	13.88	14.16	14.43	14.70	14.97	15.24	15.52	15.79	16.06	16.33	16.88
89	12.70	12.97	13.24	13.52	13.79	14.06	14.34	14.61	14.89	15.16	15.44	15.71	15.98	16.26	16.53	17.09
88	12.87	13.14	13.42	13.69	13.97	14.25	14.52	14.80	15.08	15.35	15.63	15.91	16.19	16.46	16.74	17.30
87	13.04	13.32	13.60	13.87	14.15	14.43	14.71	14.99	15.27	15.55	15.83	16.11	16.39	16.67	16.95	17.51
86	13.22	13.50	13.78	14.06	14.34	14.62	14.90	15.19	15.47	15.75	16.03	16.32	16.60	16.88	17.16	17.73
85	13.40	13.68	13.96	14.25	14.53	14.82	15.10	15.38	15.67	15.95	16.24	16.53	16.81	17.10	17.38	17.96
84	13.58	13.87	14.15	14.44	14.73	15.01	15.30	15.59	15.87	16.16	16.45	16.74	17.03	17.32	17.61	18.18
83	13.77	14.05	14.34	14.63	14.92	15.21	15.50	15.79	16.08	16.38	16.67	16.96	17.25	17.54	17.83	18.42
82	13.96	14.25	14.54	14.83	15.12	15.42	15.71	16.00	16.30	16.59	16.89	17.18	17.47	17.77	18.06	18.65
81	14.15	14.44	14.74	15.03	15.33	15.63	15.92	16.22	16.52	16.81	17.11	17.41	17.70	18.00	18.30	18.90
80	14.35	14.64	14.94	15.24	15.54	15.84	16.14	16.44	16.74	17.04	17.34	17.64	17.94	18.24	18.54	19.15
79	14.55	14.85	15.15	15.45	15.75	16.06	16.36	16.66	16.96	17.27	17.57	17.88	18.18	18.48	18.79	19.40
78	14.75	15.06	15.36	15.67	15.97	16.28	16.58	16.89	17.20	17.50	17.81	18.12	18.43	18.73	19.04	19.66
77	14.96	15.27	15.58	15.89	16.20	16.50	16.81	17.12	17.43	17.74	18.05	18.36	18.68	18.99	19.30	19.92
76	15.18	15.49	15.80	16.11	16.42	16.74	17.05	17.36	17.67	17.99	18.30	18.62	18.93	19.25	19.56	20.19
75	15.40	15.71	16.03	16.34	16.66	16.97	17.29	17.61	17.92	18.24	18.56	18.88	19.19	19.51	19.83	20.47
74	15.62	15.94	16.26	16.58	16.89	17.21	17.53	17.85	18.18	18.50	18.82	19.14	19.46	19.78	20.11	20.76
73	15.85	16.17	16.49	16.81	17.14	17.46	17.78	18.11	18.43	18.76	19.08	19.41	19.74	20.06	20.39	21.05
70	16.57	16.90	17.23	17.57	17.90	18.24	18.57	18.91	19.25	19.59	19.92	20.26	20.60	20.94	21.28	21.96
65	17.88	18.24	18.59	18.95	19.31	19.67	20.03	20.39	20.75	21.11	21.47	21.83	22.20	22.56	22.92	23.65
60	19.38	19.76	20.14	20.53	20.91	21.30	21.69	22.07	22.46	22.85	23.24	23.63	24.03	24.42	24.81	25.60

Description: This table shows the price to pay for a bond at the yield rate. The yield is to maturity.

Example: The price of a 6.75 %, 15 year bond to yield 8 % to maturity is $ 89.19.

YIELD	0.00%	1.00%	2.00%	3.00%	4.00%	4.25%	4.50%	4.75%	5.00%	5.25%	5.50%	5.75%	6.00%	6.25%	6.50%	6.75%
0.00	100.00	115.00	130.00	145.00	160.00	163.75	167.50	171.25	175.00	178.75	182.50	186.25	190.00	193.75	197.50	201.25
1.00	86.10	100.00	113.90	127.79	141.69	145.17	148.64	152.11	155.59	159.06	162.54	166.01	169.49	172.96	176.43	179.91
2.00	74.19	87.10	100.00	112.90	125.81	129.03	132.26	135.49	138.71	141.94	145.16	148.39	151.62	154.84	158.07	161.29
3.00	63.98	75.98	87.99	100.00	112.01	115.01	118.01	121.01	124.02	127.02	130.02	133.02	136.02	139.03	142.03	145.03
4.00	55.21	66.41	77.60	88.80	100.00	102.80	105.60	108.40	111.20	114.00	116.80	119.60	122.40	125.20	128.00	130.80
4.25	53.22	64.22	75.23	86.24	97.25	100.00	102.75	105.50	108.26	111.01	113.76	116.51	119.26	122.02	124.77	127.52
4.50	51.30	62.12	72.94	83.77	94.59	97.29	100.00	102.71	105.41	108.12	110.82	113.53	116.23	118.94	121.65	124.35
4.75	49.45	60.09	70.74	81.38	92.02	94.68	97.34	100.00	102.66	105.32	107.98	110.64	113.30	115.96	118.62	121.28
5.00	47.67	58.14	68.60	79.07	89.53	92.15	94.77	97.38	100.00	102.62	105.23	107.85	110.47	113.08	115.70	118.31
5.25	45.96	56.26	66.55	76.84	87.13	89.71	92.28	94.85	97.43	100.00	102.57	105.15	107.72	110.29	112.87	115.44
5.50	44.31	54.44	64.56	74.69	84.81	87.34	89.88	92.41	94.94	97.47	100.00	102.53	105.06	107.59	110.12	112.66
5.75	42.73	52.69	62.65	72.61	82.57	85.06	87.55	90.04	92.53	95.02	97.51	100.00	102.49	104.98	107.47	109.96
6.00	41.20	51.00	60.80	70.60	80.40	82.85	85.30	87.75	90.20	92.65	95.10	97.55	100.00	102.45	104.90	107.35
6.25	39.73	49.37	59.01	68.66	78.30	80.71	83.12	85.53	87.95	90.36	92.77	95.18	97.59	100.00	102.41	104.82
6.50	38.31	47.80	57.29	66.78	76.27	78.65	81.02	83.39	85.76	88.14	90.51	92.88	95.25	97.63	100.00	102.37
6.75	36.94	46.28	55.63	64.97	74.31	76.65	78.98	81.32	83.65	85.99	88.32	90.66	92.99	95.33	97.66	100.00
7.00	35.63	44.82	54.02	63.22	72.41	74.71	77.01	79.31	81.61	83.91	86.21	88.50	90.80	93.10	95.40	97.70
7.25	34.36	43.41	52.47	61.52	70.58	72.84	75.10	77.37	79.63	81.89	84.16	86.42	88.68	90.95	93.21	95.47
7.50	33.14	42.05	50.97	59.88	68.80	71.03	73.26	75.48	77.71	79.94	82.17	84.40	86.63	88.86	91.09	93.31
7.75	31.96	40.74	49.52	58.30	67.08	69.27	71.47	73.66	75.86	78.05	80.25	82.44	84.64	86.83	89.03	91.22
8.00	30.83	39.48	48.12	56.77	65.42	67.58	69.74	71.90	74.06	76.22	78.38	80.55	82.71	84.87	87.03	89.19
8.25	29.74	38.26	46.77	55.29	63.81	65.93	68.06	70.19	72.32	74.45	76.58	78.71	80.84	82.97	85.10	87.23
8.50	28.69	37.08	45.47	53.86	62.25	64.34	66.44	68.54	70.64	72.73	74.83	76.93	79.03	81.12	83.22	85.32
8.75	27.68	35.94	44.21	52.47	60.74	62.80	64.87	66.94	69.00	71.07	73.14	75.20	77.27	79.34	81.40	83.47
9.00	26.70	34.84	42.99	51.13	59.28	61.31	63.35	65.39	67.42	69.46	71.49	73.53	75.57	77.60	79.64	81.68
9.25	25.76	33.79	41.81	49.84	57.86	59.87	61.88	63.88	65.89	67.90	69.90	71.91	73.92	75.92	77.93	79.93
9.50	24.85	32.76	40.67	48.58	56.49	58.47	60.45	62.43	64.40	66.38	68.36	70.34	72.31	74.29	76.27	78.25
9.75	23.98	31.78	39.57	47.37	55.17	57.12	59.07	61.02	62.96	64.91	66.86	68.81	70.76	72.71	74.66	76.61
10.00	23.14	30.82	38.51	46.20	53.88	55.80	57.73	59.65	61.57	63.49	65.41	67.33	69.26	71.18	73.10	75.02
10.25	22.33	29.90	37.48	45.06	52.64	54.53	56.43	58.32	60.22	62.11	64.00	65.90	67.79	69.69	71.58	73.48
10.50	21.54	29.02	36.49	43.96	51.43	53.30	55.17	57.04	58.90	60.77	62.64	64.51	66.38	68.24	70.11	71.98
10.75	20.79	28.16	35.53	42.90	50.26	52.11	53.95	55.79	57.63	59.47	61.32	63.16	65.00	66.84	68.68	70.53
11.00	20.06	27.33	34.60	41.87	49.13	50.95	52.77	54.58	56.40	58.22	60.03	61.85	63.67	65.48	67.30	69.12
11.25	19.36	26.53	33.70	40.87	48.03	49.83	51.62	53.41	55.20	56.99	58.79	60.58	62.37	64.16	65.95	67.75
11.50	18.69	25.76	32.83	39.90	46.97	48.74	50.51	52.27	54.04	55.81	57.58	59.34	61.11	62.88	64.65	66.42
11.75	18.04	25.01	31.99	38.96	45.94	47.68	49.43	51.17	52.92	54.66	56.40	58.15	59.89	61.63	63.38	65.12
12.00	17.41	24.29	31.18	38.06	44.94	46.66	48.38	50.10	51.82	53.54	55.26	56.98	58.71	60.43	62.15	63.87
12.25	16.81	23.60	30.39	37.18	43.97	45.67	47.37	49.07	50.76	52.46	54.16	55.86	57.55	59.25	60.95	62.65
12.50	16.22	22.93	29.63	36.33	43.03	44.71	46.38	48.06	49.73	51.41	53.08	54.76	56.44	58.11	59.79	61.46
12.75	15.66	22.28	28.89	35.51	42.12	43.77	45.43	47.08	48.73	50.39	52.04	53.70	55.35	57.00	58.66	60.31
13.00	15.12	21.65	28.18	34.71	41.24	42.87	44.50	46.13	47.77	49.40	51.03	52.66	54.29	55.93	57.56	59.19
13.25	14.60	21.04	27.49	33.93	40.38	41.99	43.60	45.21	46.82	48.44	50.05	51.66	53.27	54.88	56.49	58.10
13.50	14.09	20.46	26.82	33.18	39.55	41.14	42.73	44.32	45.91	47.50	49.09	50.68	52.27	53.86	55.45	57.05
13.75	13.61	19.89	26.17	32.46	38.74	40.31	41.88	43.45	45.02	46.59	48.16	49.73	51.30	52.88	54.45	56.02
14.00	13.14	19.34	25.55	31.75	37.95	39.51	41.06	42.61	44.16	45.71	47.26	48.81	50.36	51.91	53.47	55.02
14.25	12.68	18.81	24.94	31.07	37.19	38.73	40.26	41.79	43.32	44.85	46.39	47.92	49.45	50.98	52.51	54.04
14.50	12.25	18.30	24.35	30.40	36.46	37.97	39.48	40.99	42.51	44.02	45.53	47.05	48.56	50.07	51.59	53.10
14.75	11.83	17.81	23.78	29.76	35.74	37.23	38.73	40.22	41.72	43.21	44.71	46.20	47.69	49.19	50.68	52.18
15.00	11.42	17.33	23.23	29.14	35.04	36.52	38.00	39.47	40.95	42.42	43.90	45.38	46.85	48.33	49.81	51.28
15.25	11.03	16.86	22.70	28.53	34.37	35.83	37.28	38.74	40.20	41.66	43.12	44.58	46.04	47.49	48.95	50.41
15.50	10.65	16.42	22.18	27.95	33.71	35.15	36.59	38.03	39.47	40.92	42.36	43.80	45.24	46.68	48.12	49.56
15.75	10.29	15.98	21.68	27.38	33.07	34.50	35.92	37.34	38.77	40.19	41.62	43.04	44.46	45.89	47.31	48.74
16.00	9.94	15.57	21.20	26.82	32.45	33.86	35.27	36.67	38.08	39.49	40.90	42.30	43.71	45.12	46.53	47.93
16.25	9.60	15.16	20.73	26.29	31.85	33.24	34.63	36.02	37.41	38.81	40.20	41.59	42.98	44.37	45.76	47.15
16.50	9.27	14.77	20.27	25.77	31.27	32.64	34.02	35.39	36.77	38.14	39.51	40.89	42.26	43.64	45.01	46.39
16.75	8.96	14.39	19.83	25.26	30.70	32.06	33.42	34.77	36.13	37.49	38.85	40.21	41.57	42.93	44.29	45.65
17.00	8.65	14.03	19.40	24.77	30.15	31.49	32.83	34.18	35.52	36.86	38.21	39.55	40.89	42.24	43.58	44.92
17.25	8.36	13.67	18.98	24.30	29.61	30.94	32.26	33.59	34.92	36.25	37.58	38.91	40.23	41.56	42.89	44.22
17.50	8.07	13.33	18.58	23.83	29.09	30.40	31.71	33.03	34.34	35.65	36.97	38.28	39.59	40.91	42.22	43.53
17.75	7.80	13.00	18.19	23.38	28.58	29.88	31.18	32.47	33.77	35.07	36.37	37.67	38.97	40.27	41.56	42.86
18.00	7.54	12.67	17.81	22.95	28.08	29.37	30.65	31.94	33.22	34.51	35.79	37.07	38.36	39.64	40.93	42.21
18.25	7.28	12.36	17.44	22.52	27.60	28.87	30.14	31.41	32.68	33.95	35.22	36.49	37.76	39.03	40.31	41.58
18.50	7.04	12.06	17.09	22.11	27.14	28.39	29.65	30.91	32.16	33.42	34.67	35.93	37.19	38.44	39.70	40.96
18.75	6.80	11.77	16.74	21.71	26.68	27.92	29.17	30.41	31.65	32.90	34.14	35.38	36.62	37.87	39.11	40.35
19.00	6.57	11.49	16.40	21.32	26.24	27.47	28.70	29.93	31.16	32.39	33.62	34.84	36.07	37.30	38.53	39.76
20.00	5.73	10.44	15.16	19.87	24.58	25.76	26.94	28.12	29.30	30.48	31.65	32.83	34.01	35.19	36.37	37.55
25.00	2.92	6.80	10.69	14.57	18.45	19.42	20.39	21.37	22.34	23.31	24.28	25.25	26.22	27.19	28.16	29.13
30.00	1.51	4.79	8.08	11.36	14.64	15.46	16.28	17.10	17.93	18.75	19.57	20.39	21.21	22.03	22.85	23.67

Description: This table shows the yield to maturity of a bond purchased at the price shown in the index.

Example: The yield to maturity of a 6.75 %, 15 year bond at a price of 80.00 is 9.24 %.

COUPON RATE, %

PRICE	0.00%	1.00%	2.00%	3.00%	4.00%	4.25%	4.50%	4.75%	5.00%	5.25%	5.50%	5.75%	6.00%	6.25%	6.50%	6.75%
100	0.00	1.00	2.00	3.00	4.00	4.25	4.50	4.75	5.00	5.25	5.50	5.75	6.00	6.25	6.50	6.75
99	.06	1.07	2.07	3.08	4.08	4.34	4.59	4.84	5.09	5.34	5.59	5.85	6.10	6.35	6.60	6.85
98	.13	1.14	2.15	3.16	4.18	4.43	4.68	4.94	5.19	5.44	5.70	5.95	6.20	6.46	6.71	6.96
97	.20	1.21	2.23	3.25	4.27	4.52	4.78	5.03	5.29	5.54	5.80	6.05	6.31	6.56	6.82	7.07
96	.27	1.29	2.31	3.34	4.36	4.62	4.87	5.13	5.39	5.64	5.90	6.16	6.41	6.67	6.93	7.19
95	.34	1.36	2.39	3.42	4.46	4.71	4.97	5.23	5.49	5.75	6.01	6.26	6.52	6.78	7.04	7.30
94	.41	1.44	2.48	3.51	4.55	4.81	5.07	5.33	5.59	5.85	6.11	6.37	6.63	6.89	7.15	7.41
93	.48	1.52	2.56	3.60	4.65	4.91	5.17	5.43	5.70	5.96	6.22	6.48	6.74	7.01	7.27	7.53
92	.55	1.60	2.64	3.69	4.75	5.01	5.27	5.54	5.80	6.07	6.33	6.59	6.86	7.12	7.39	7.65
91	.62	1.68	2.73	3.79	4.85	5.11	5.38	5.64	5.91	6.17	6.44	6.71	6.97	7.24	7.51	7.77
90	.70	1.76	2.82	3.88	4.95	5.21	5.48	5.75	6.02	6.28	6.55	6.82	7.09	7.36	7.63	7.89
89	.77	1.84	2.91	3.98	5.05	5.32	5.59	5.86	6.13	6.40	6.67	6.94	7.21	7.48	7.75	8.02
88	.85	1.92	2.99	4.07	5.15	5.42	5.70	5.97	6.24	6.51	6.78	7.05	7.33	7.60	7.87	8.15
87	.93	2.00	3.08	4.17	5.26	5.53	5.81	6.08	6.35	6.63	6.90	7.17	7.45	7.72	8.00	8.27
86	1.00	2.09	3.18	4.27	5.37	5.64	5.92	6.19	6.47	6.74	7.02	7.30	7.57	7.85	8.13	8.40
85	1.08	2.17	3.27	4.37	5.47	5.75	6.03	6.31	6.58	6.86	7.14	7.42	7.70	7.98	8.26	8.54
84	1.16	2.26	3.36	4.47	5.58	5.86	6.14	6.42	6.70	6.98	7.26	7.55	7.83	8.11	8.39	8.67
83	1.24	2.35	3.46	4.57	5.70	5.98	6.26	6.54	6.82	7.11	7.39	7.67	7.96	8.24	8.52	8.81
82	1.32	2.44	3.55	4.68	5.81	6.09	6.38	6.66	6.95	7.23	7.52	7.80	8.09	8.38	8.66	8.95
81	1.40	2.53	3.65	4.79	5.92	6.21	6.50	6.78	7.07	7.36	7.65	7.93	8.22	8.51	8.80	9.09
80	1.49	2.62	3.75	4.89	6.04	6.33	6.62	6.91	7.20	7.49	7.78	8.07	8.36	8.65	8.94	9.24
79	1.57	2.71	3.85	5.00	6.16	6.45	6.74	7.03	7.33	7.62	7.91	8.20	8.50	8.79	9.09	9.38
78	1.66	2.80	3.95	5.11	6.28	6.57	6.87	7.16	7.46	7.75	8.05	8.34	8.64	8.94	9.23	9.53
77	1.75	2.90	4.06	5.23	6.40	6.70	7.00	7.29	7.59	7.89	8.19	8.48	8.78	9.08	9.38	9.68
76	1.83	2.99	4.16	5.34	6.53	6.83	7.13	7.43	7.73	8.03	8.33	8.63	8.93	9.23	9.54	9.84
75	1.92	3.09	4.27	5.46	6.66	6.96	7.26	7.56	7.86	8.17	8.47	8.77	9.08	9.39	9.69	10.00
74	2.01	3.19	4.38	5.58	6.79	7.09	7.39	7.70	8.00	8.31	8.62	8.92	9.23	9.54	9.85	10.16
73	2.10	3.29	4.49	5.70	6.92	7.22	7.53	7.84	8.15	8.46	8.77	9.08	9.39	9.70	10.01	10.32
72	2.20	3.39	4.60	5.82	7.05	7.36	7.67	7.98	8.29	8.60	8.92	9.23	9.54	9.86	10.18	10.49
71	2.29	3.50	4.71	5.94	7.19	7.50	7.81	8.13	8.44	8.76	9.07	9.39	9.71	10.02	10.34	10.66
70	2.39	3.60	4.83	6.07	7.33	7.64	7.96	8.27	8.59	8.91	9.23	9.55	9.87	10.19	10.51	10.84
69	2.48	3.71	4.95	6.20	7.47	7.78	8.10	8.42	8.75	9.07	9.39	9.71	10.04	10.36	10.69	11.02
68	2.58	3.82	5.07	6.33	7.61	7.93	8.25	8.58	8.90	9.23	9.55	9.88	10.21	10.54	10.87	11.20
67	2.68	3.93	5.19	6.47	7.76	8.08	8.41	8.74	9.06	9.39	9.72	10.05	10.38	10.72	11.05	11.38
66	2.78	4.04	5.31	6.60	7.91	8.23	8.56	8.90	9.23	9.56	9.89	10.23	10.56	10.90	11.24	11.57
65	2.89	4.15	5.44	6.74	8.06	8.39	8.72	9.06	9.39	9.73	10.07	10.41	10.75	11.09	11.43	11.77
64	2.99	4.27	5.57	6.88	8.21	8.55	8.89	9.23	9.56	9.90	10.25	10.59	10.93	11.28	11.62	11.97
63	3.10	4.39	5.70	7.03	8.37	8.71	9.05	9.40	9.74	10.08	10.43	10.77	11.12	11.47	11.82	12.17
62	3.21	4.51	5.83	7.17	8.54	8.88	9.22	9.57	9.92	10.27	10.61	10.97	11.32	11.67	12.03	12.38
61	3.32	4.63	5.97	7.32	8.70	9.05	9.40	9.75	10.10	10.45	10.81	11.16	11.52	11.88	12.23	12.59
60	3.43	4.76	6.11	7.48	8.87	9.22	9.58	9.93	10.29	10.64	11.00	11.36	11.72	12.08	12.45	12.81
59	3.54	4.88	6.25	7.63	9.04	9.40	9.76	10.12	10.48	10.84	11.20	11.57	11.93	12.30	12.67	13.04
58	3.66	5.01	6.39	7.79	9.22	9.58	9.94	10.31	10.67	11.04	11.41	11.78	12.15	12.52	12.89	13.27
57	3.78	5.15	6.54	7.96	9.40	9.77	10.13	10.50	10.87	11.24	11.62	11.99	12.37	12.75	13.13	13.51
56	3.90	5.28	6.69	8.12	9.59	9.96	10.33	10.70	11.08	11.45	11.83	12.21	12.59	12.98	13.36	13.75
55	4.02	5.42	6.84	8.29	9.78	10.15	10.53	10.91	11.29	11.67	12.05	12.44	12.83	13.22	13.61	14.00
54	4.15	5.56	7.00	8.47	9.97	10.35	10.73	11.12	11.50	11.89	12.28	12.67	13.07	13.46	13.86	14.26
53	4.27	5.70	7.16	8.65	10.17	10.56	10.94	11.33	11.73	12.12	12.52	12.91	13.31	13.71	14.12	14.52
52	4.40	5.85	7.32	8.83	10.38	10.77	11.16	11.56	11.95	12.35	12.76	13.16	13.56	13.97	14.38	14.79
51	4.53	5.99	7.49	9.02	10.59	10.98	11.38	11.78	12.19	12.59	13.00	13.41	13.83	14.24	14.66	15.08
50	4.67	6.15	7.66	9.21	10.80	11.21	11.61	12.02	12.43	12.84	13.26	13.67	14.09	14.52	14.94	15.37
49	4.81	6.30	7.84	9.41	11.02	11.43	11.85	12.26	12.68	13.10	13.52	13.94	14.37	14.80	15.23	15.66
48	4.95	6.46	8.02	9.61	11.25	11.67	12.09	12.51	12.93	13.36	13.79	14.22	14.66	15.09	15.53	15.97
47	5.09	6.63	8.20	9.82	11.49	11.91	12.34	12.77	13.20	13.63	14.07	14.51	14.95	15.40	15.84	16.29
46	5.24	6.79	8.39	10.04	11.73	12.16	12.59	13.03	13.47	13.91	14.36	14.81	15.26	15.71	16.17	16.62
45	5.39	6.96	8.59	10.26	11.98	12.42	12.86	13.30	13.75	14.20	14.66	15.11	15.57	16.03	16.50	16.97
44	5.54	7.14	8.79	10.49	12.24	12.68	13.13	13.59	14.04	14.50	14.96	15.43	15.90	16.37	16.85	17.32
43	5.70	7.32	8.99	10.72	12.50	12.96	13.42	13.88	14.34	14.81	15.28	15.76	16.24	16.72	17.20	17.69
42	5.86	7.51	9.20	10.96	12.78	13.24	13.71	14.18	14.65	15.13	15.61	16.10	16.59	17.08	17.58	18.08
41	6.03	7.70	9.42	11.21	13.06	13.54	14.01	14.49	14.98	15.47	15.96	16.45	16.95	17.46	17.97	18.48
40	6.20	7.89	9.65	11.47	13.36	13.84	14.33	14.82	15.31	15.81	16.32	16.82	17.34	17.85	18.37	18.89
39	6.37	8.09	9.88	11.74	13.66	14.16	14.65	15.16	15.66	16.17	16.69	17.21	17.73	18.26	18.79	19.33
35	7.12	8.96	10.89	12.90	15.01	15.55	16.10	16.65	17.21	17.78	18.35	18.92	19.50	20.09	20.68	21.28
30	8.18	10.22	12.37	14.65	17.06	17.69	18.32	18.96	19.61	20.26	20.93	21.60	22.28	22.96	23.66	24.36
25	9.45	11.75	14.22	16.88	19.73	20.48	21.24	22.01	22.79	23.58	24.39	25.21	26.03	26.87	27.72	28.58
20	11.02	13.70	16.65	19.90	23.48	24.42	25.39	26.37	27.38	28.40	29.44	30.50	31.57	32.66	33.76	34.88
15	13.05	16.35	20.13	24.48	29.42	30.75	32.11	33.50	34.92	36.37	37.85	39.35	40.87	42.41	43.97	45.54
10	15.95	20.46	26.08	33.05	41.33	43.56	45.84	48.17	50.52	52.91	55.32	57.75	60.20	62.65	65.12	67.59

BOND PRICE

Description: This table shows the price to pay for a bond at the yield rate. The yield is to maturity.

Example: The price of a 10.75 %, 15 year bond to yield 8 % to maturity is $ 123.78.

YIELD	7.00%	7.25%	7.50%	7.75%	8.00%	8.25%	8.50%	8.75%	9.00%	9.25%	9.50%	9.75%	10.00%	10.25%	10.50%	10.75%
0.00	205.00	208.75	212.50	216.25	220.00	223.75	227.50	231.25	235.00	238.75	242.50	246.25	250.00	253.75	257.50	261.25
1.00	183.38	186.86	190.33	193.80	197.28	200.75	204.23	207.70	211.18	214.65	218.12	221.60	225.07	228.55	232.02	235.50
2.00	164.52	167.75	170.97	174.20	177.42	180.65	183.88	187.10	190.33	193.55	196.78	200.00	203.23	206.46	209.68	212.91
3.00	148.03	151.03	154.04	157.04	160.04	163.04	166.04	169.05	172.05	175.05	178.05	181.05	184.06	187.06	190.06	193.06
4.00	133.59	136.39	139.19	141.99	144.79	147.59	150.39	153.19	155.99	158.79	161.59	164.39	167.19	169.99	172.79	175.59
4.25	130.27	133.02	135.78	138.53	141.28	144.03	146.78	149.54	152.29	155.04	157.79	160.54	163.30	166.05	168.80	171.55
4.50	127.06	129.76	132.47	135.17	137.88	140.58	143.29	146.00	148.70	151.41	154.11	156.82	159.52	162.23	164.94	167.64
4.75	123.94	126.60	129.26	131.93	134.59	137.25	139.91	142.57	145.23	147.89	150.55	153.21	155.87	158.53	161.19	163.85
5.00	120.93	123.55	126.16	128.78	131.40	134.01	136.63	139.24	141.86	144.48	147.09	149.71	152.33	154.94	157.56	160.17
5.25	118.01	120.59	123.16	125.73	128.31	130.88	133.45	136.02	138.60	141.17	143.74	146.32	148.89	151.46	154.04	156.61
5.50	115.19	117.72	120.25	122.78	125.31	127.84	130.37	132.91	135.44	137.97	140.50	143.03	145.56	148.09	150.62	153.15
5.75	112.45	114.94	117.43	119.92	122.41	124.90	127.39	129.88	132.37	134.86	137.35	139.84	142.33	144.82	147.31	149.80
6.00	109.80	112.25	114.70	117.15	119.60	122.05	124.50	126.95	129.40	131.85	134.30	136.75	139.20	141.65	144.10	146.55
6.25	107.23	109.64	112.05	114.47	116.88	119.29	121.70	124.11	126.52	128.93	131.34	133.75	136.16	138.57	140.99	143.40
6.50	104.75	107.12	109.49	111.86	114.24	116.61	118.98	121.35	123.73	126.10	128.47	130.85	133.22	135.59	137.96	140.34
6.75	102.34	104.67	107.01	109.34	111.68	114.01	116.35	118.68	121.02	123.35	125.69	128.03	130.36	132.70	135.03	137.37
7.00	100.00	102.30	104.60	106.90	109.20	111.50	113.79	116.09	118.39	120.69	122.99	125.29	127.59	129.89	132.19	134.49
7.25	97.74	100.00	102.26	104.53	106.79	109.05	111.32	113.58	115.84	118.11	120.37	122.63	124.90	127.16	129.42	131.69
7.50	95.54	97.77	100.00	102.23	104.46	106.69	108.91	111.14	113.37	115.60	117.83	120.06	122.29	124.52	126.74	128.97
7.75	93.42	95.61	97.81	100.00	102.19	104.39	106.58	108.78	110.97	113.17	115.36	117.56	119.75	121.95	124.14	126.34
8.00	91.35	93.52	95.68	97.84	100.00	102.16	104.32	106.48	108.65	110.81	112.97	115.13	117.29	119.45	121.62	123.78
8.25	89.35	91.48	93.61	95.74	97.87	100.00	102.13	104.26	106.39	108.52	110.65	112.77	114.90	117.03	119.16	121.29
8.50	87.42	89.51	91.61	93.71	95.81	97.90	100.00	102.10	104.19	106.29	108.39	110.49	112.58	114.68	116.78	118.88
8.75	85.54	87.60	89.67	91.73	93.80	95.87	97.93	100.00	102.07	104.13	106.20	108.27	110.33	112.40	114.46	116.53
9.00	83.71	85.75	87.78	89.82	91.86	93.89	95.93	97.96	100.00	102.04	104.07	106.11	108.14	110.18	112.22	114.25
9.25	81.94	83.95	85.95	87.96	89.97	91.97	93.98	95.99	97.99	100.00	102.01	104.01	106.02	108.03	110.03	112.04
9.50	80.22	82.20	84.18	86.16	88.13	90.11	92.09	94.07	96.04	98.02	100.00	101.98	103.96	105.93	107.91	109.89
9.75	78.56	80.51	82.46	84.41	86.36	88.30	90.25	92.20	94.15	96.10	98.05	100.00	101.95	103.90	105.85	107.80
10.00	76.94	78.86	80.78	82.71	84.63	86.55	88.47	90.39	92.31	94.24	96.16	98.08	100.00	101.92	103.84	105.76
10.25	75.37	77.27	79.16	81.06	82.95	84.84	86.74	88.63	90.53	92.42	94.32	96.21	98.11	100.00	101.89	103.79
10.50	73.85	75.72	77.58	79.45	81.32	83.19	85.06	86.92	88.79	90.66	92.53	94.40	96.26	98.13	100.00	101.87
10.75	72.37	74.21	76.05	77.90	79.74	81.58	83.42	85.26	87.11	88.95	90.79	92.63	94.47	96.32	98.16	100.00
11.00	70.93	72.75	74.57	76.38	78.20	80.02	81.83	83.65	85.47	87.28	89.10	90.92	92.73	94.55	96.37	98.18
11.25	69.54	71.33	73.12	74.91	76.71	78.50	80.29	82.08	83.87	85.66	87.46	89.25	91.04	92.83	94.62	96.42
11.50	68.18	69.95	71.72	73.49	75.25	77.02	78.79	80.56	82.32	84.09	85.86	87.63	89.39	91.16	92.93	94.70
11.75	66.87	68.61	70.35	72.10	73.84	75.59	77.33	79.07	80.82	82.56	84.31	86.05	87.79	89.54	91.28	93.02
12.00	65.59	67.31	69.03	70.75	72.47	74.19	75.91	77.63	79.35	81.07	82.79	84.51	86.24	87.96	89.68	91.40
12.25	64.35	66.04	67.74	69.44	71.14	72.83	74.53	76.23	77.93	79.63	81.32	83.02	84.72	86.42	88.12	89.81
12.50	63.14	64.81	66.49	68.16	69.84	71.52	73.19	74.87	76.54	78.22	79.89	81.57	83.24	84.92	86.60	88.27
12.75	61.96	63.62	65.27	66.93	68.58	70.23	71.89	73.54	75.19	76.85	78.50	80.16	81.81	83.46	85.12	86.77
13.00	60.82	62.46	64.09	65.72	67.35	68.99	70.62	72.25	73.88	75.51	77.15	78.78	80.41	82.04	83.68	85.31
13.25	59.72	61.33	62.94	64.55	66.16	67.77	69.38	70.99	72.61	74.22	75.83	77.44	79.05	80.66	82.27	83.89
13.50	58.64	60.23	61.82	63.41	65.00	66.59	68.18	69.77	71.36	72.95	74.55	76.14	77.73	79.32	80.91	82.50
13.75	57.59	59.16	60.73	62.30	63.87	65.44	67.01	68.58	70.15	71.73	73.30	74.87	76.44	78.01	79.58	81.15
14.00	56.57	58.12	59.67	61.22	62.77	64.32	65.88	67.43	68.98	70.53	72.08	73.63	75.18	76.73	78.28	79.84
14.25	55.58	57.11	58.64	60.17	61.70	63.24	64.77	66.30	67.83	69.36	70.89	72.43	73.96	75.49	77.02	78.55
14.50	54.61	56.12	57.64	59.15	60.66	62.18	63.69	65.20	66.71	68.23	69.74	71.25	72.77	74.28	75.79	77.31
14.75	53.67	55.17	56.66	58.16	59.65	61.14	62.64	64.13	65.63	67.12	68.62	70.11	71.61	73.10	74.59	76.09
15.00	52.76	54.23	55.71	57.19	58.66	60.14	61.62	63.09	64.57	66.05	67.52	69.00	70.47	71.95	73.43	74.90
15.25	51.87	53.33	54.79	56.24	57.70	59.16	60.62	62.08	63.54	65.00	66.45	67.91	69.37	70.83	72.29	73.75
15.50	51.00	52.44	53.89	55.33	56.77	58.21	59.65	61.09	62.53	63.97	65.41	66.86	68.30	69.74	71.18	72.62
15.75	50.16	51.58	53.01	54.43	55.86	57.28	58.70	60.13	61.55	62.98	64.40	65.82	67.25	68.67	70.10	71.52
16.00	49.34	50.75	52.15	53.56	54.97	56.38	57.78	59.19	60.60	62.00	63.41	64.82	66.23	67.63	69.04	70.45
16.25	48.54	49.93	51.32	52.71	54.10	55.49	56.89	58.28	59.67	61.06	62.45	63.84	65.23	66.62	68.01	69.40
16.50	47.76	49.14	50.51	51.89	53.26	54.64	56.01	57.39	58.76	60.13	61.51	62.88	64.26	65.63	67.01	68.38
16.75	47.00	48.36	49.72	51.08	52.44	53.80	55.16	56.52	57.88	59.23	60.59	61.95	63.31	64.67	66.03	67.39
17.00	46.27	47.61	48.95	50.30	51.64	52.98	54.33	55.67	57.01	58.36	59.70	61.04	62.39	63.73	65.07	66.42
17.25	45.55	46.87	48.20	49.53	50.86	52.19	53.51	54.84	56.17	57.50	58.83	60.16	61.48	62.81	64.14	65.47
17.50	44.84	46.16	47.47	48.78	50.10	51.41	52.72	54.04	55.35	56.66	57.98	59.29	60.60	61.92	63.23	64.54
17.75	44.16	45.46	46.76	48.06	49.36	50.65	51.95	53.25	54.55	55.85	57.15	58.45	59.74	61.04	62.34	63.64
18.00	43.49	44.78	46.06	47.35	48.63	49.92	51.20	52.48	53.77	55.05	56.34	57.62	58.91	60.19	61.47	62.76
18.25	42.85	44.12	45.39	46.66	47.93	49.20	50.47	51.74	53.01	54.28	55.55	56.82	58.09	59.36	60.63	61.90
18.50	42.21	43.47	44.72	45.98	47.24	48.49	49.75	51.01	52.26	53.52	54.77	56.03	57.29	58.54	59.80	61.06
18.75	41.59	42.84	44.08	45.32	46.56	47.81	49.05	50.29	51.54	52.78	54.02	55.26	56.51	57.75	58.99	60.23
19.00	40.99	42.22	43.45	44.68	45.91	47.14	48.37	49.60	50.83	52.06	53.29	54.51	55.74	56.97	58.20	59.43
20.00	38.73	39.90	41.08	42.26	43.44	44.62	45.80	46.97	48.15	49.33	50.51	51.69	52.87	54.04	55.22	56.40
25.00	30.10	31.07	32.04	33.01	33.99	34.96	35.93	36.90	37.87	38.84	39.81	40.78	41.75	42.72	43.69	44.66
30.00	24.49	25.31	26.13	26.95	27.77	28.59	29.42	30.24	31.06	31.88	32.70	33.52	34.34	35.16	35.98	36.80

Description: This table shows the yield to maturity of a bond purchased at the price shown in the index.

Example: The yield to maturity of a 10.75 %, 15 year bond at a price of 113.00 is 9.14 %.

COUPON RATE, %

PRICE	7.00%	7.25%	7.50%	7.75%	8.00%	8.25%	8.50%	8.75%	9.00%	9.25%	9.50%	9.75%	10.00%	10.25%	10.50%	10.75%
145	3.19	3.39	3.59	3.78	3.98	4.18	4.37	4.57	4.76	4.96	5.15	5.34	5.54	5.73	5.92	6.12
140	3.53	3.74	3.94	4.14	4.34	4.54	4.74	4.94	5.14	5.34	5.53	5.73	5.93	6.13	6.33	6.52
135	3.89	4.10	4.30	4.51	4.71	4.92	5.12	5.33	5.53	5.73	5.94	6.14	6.34	6.55	6.75	6.95
130	4.27	4.48	4.69	4.90	5.11	5.32	5.53	5.74	5.94	6.15	6.36	6.57	6.78	6.98	7.19	7.40
129	4.34	4.55	4.77	4.98	5.19	5.40	5.61	5.82	6.03	6.24	6.45	6.66	6.87	7.08	7.28	7.49
128	4.42	4.63	4.85	5.06	5.27	5.48	5.69	5.90	6.12	6.33	6.54	6.75	6.96	7.17	7.38	7.59
127	4.50	4.71	4.93	5.14	5.35	5.57	5.78	5.99	6.20	6.41	6.63	6.84	7.05	7.26	7.47	7.68
126	4.58	4.79	5.01	5.22	5.44	5.65	5.86	6.08	6.29	6.50	6.72	6.93	7.14	7.35	7.57	7.78
125	4.66	4.88	5.09	5.31	5.52	5.74	5.95	6.17	6.38	6.59	6.81	7.02	7.24	7.45	7.66	7.87
124	4.74	4.96	5.17	5.39	5.61	5.82	6.04	6.25	6.47	6.69	6.90	7.12	7.33	7.54	7.76	7.97
123	4.82	5.04	5.26	5.48	5.69	5.91	6.13	6.34	6.56	6.78	6.99	7.21	7.43	7.64	7.86	8.07
122	4.91	5.12	5.34	5.56	5.78	6.00	6.22	6.44	6.65	6.87	7.09	7.31	7.52	7.74	7.96	8.17
121	4.99	5.21	5.43	5.65	5.87	6.09	6.31	6.53	6.75	6.97	7.18	7.40	7.62	7.84	8.06	8.27
120	5.07	5.30	5.52	5.74	5.96	6.18	6.40	6.62	6.84	7.06	7.28	7.50	7.72	7.94	8.16	8.38
119	5.16	5.38	5.60	5.83	6.05	6.27	6.49	6.71	6.94	7.16	7.38	7.60	7.82	8.04	8.26	8.48
118	5.25	5.47	5.69	5.92	6.14	6.36	6.59	6.81	7.03	7.26	7.48	7.70	7.92	8.14	8.37	8.59
117	5.33	5.56	5.78	6.01	6.23	6.46	6.68	6.91	7.13	7.35	7.58	7.80	8.03	8.25	8.47	8.69
116	5.42	5.65	5.88	6.10	6.33	6.55	6.78	7.00	7.23	7.45	7.68	7.90	8.13	8.35	8.58	8.80
115	5.51	5.74	5.97	6.19	6.42	6.65	6.88	7.10	7.33	7.56	7.78	8.01	8.23	8.46	8.69	8.91
114	5.60	5.83	6.06	6.29	6.52	6.75	6.97	7.20	7.43	7.66	7.89	8.11	8.34	8.57	8.80	9.02
113	5.69	5.92	6.15	6.38	6.61	6.84	7.07	7.30	7.53	7.76	7.99	8.22	8.45	8.68	8.91	9.14
112	5.79	6.02	6.25	6.48	6.71	6.94	7.18	7.41	7.64	7.87	8.10	8.33	8.56	8.79	9.02	9.25
111	5.88	6.11	6.35	6.58	6.81	7.05	7.28	7.51	7.74	7.97	8.21	8.44	8.67	8.90	9.13	9.36
110	5.98	6.21	6.44	6.68	6.91	7.15	7.38	7.61	7.85	8.08	8.32	8.55	8.78	9.02	9.25	9.48
109	6.07	6.31	6.54	6.78	7.02	7.25	7.49	7.72	7.96	8.19	8.43	8.66	8.90	9.13	9.37	9.60
108	6.17	6.41	6.64	6.88	7.12	7.36	7.59	7.83	8.07	8.30	8.54	8.78	9.01	9.25	9.48	9.72
107	6.27	6.51	6.75	6.98	7.22	7.46	7.70	7.94	8.18	8.41	8.65	8.89	9.13	9.37	9.60	9.84
106	6.37	6.61	6.85	7.09	7.33	7.57	7.81	8.05	8.29	8.53	8.77	9.01	9.25	9.49	9.73	9.97
105	6.47	6.71	6.95	7.19	7.44	7.68	7.92	8.16	8.40	8.64	8.89	9.13	9.37	9.61	9.85	10.09
104	6.57	6.81	7.06	7.30	7.54	7.79	8.03	8.27	8.52	8.76	9.00	9.25	9.49	9.73	9.98	10.22
103	6.68	6.92	7.17	7.41	7.66	7.90	8.14	8.39	8.63	8.88	9.12	9.37	9.61	9.86	10.10	10.35
102	6.78	7.03	7.27	7.52	7.77	8.01	8.26	8.51	8.75	9.00	9.25	9.49	9.74	9.98	10.23	10.48
101	6.89	7.14	7.38	7.63	7.88	8.13	8.38	8.62	8.87	9.12	9.37	9.62	9.87	10.11	10.36	10.61
100	7.00	7.25	7.50	7.75	8.00	8.25	8.50	8.75	9.00	9.25	9.50	9.75	10.00	10.25	10.50	10.75
99	7.10	7.36	7.61	7.86	8.11	8.36	8.62	8.87	9.12	9.37	9.62	9.87	10.13	10.38	10.63	10.88
98	7.22	7.47	7.72	7.98	8.23	8.48	8.74	8.99	9.24	9.50	9.75	10.01	10.26	10.51	10.77	11.02
97	7.33	7.58	7.84	8.09	8.35	8.60	8.86	9.12	9.37	9.63	9.88	10.14	10.39	10.65	10.91	11.16
96	7.44	7.70	7.96	8.21	8.47	8.73	8.99	9.24	9.50	9.76	10.02	10.27	10.53	10.79	11.05	11.30
95	7.56	7.82	8.08	8.34	8.59	8.85	9.11	9.37	9.63	9.89	10.15	10.41	10.67	10.93	11.19	11.45
94	7.68	7.94	8.20	8.46	8.72	8.98	9.24	9.50	9.77	10.03	10.29	10.55	10.81	11.07	11.34	11.60
93	7.79	8.06	8.32	8.58	8.85	9.11	9.37	9.64	9.90	10.16	10.43	10.69	10.96	11.22	11.48	11.75
92	7.92	8.18	8.45	8.71	8.98	9.24	9.51	9.77	10.04	10.30	10.57	10.84	11.10	11.37	11.64	11.90
91	8.04	8.31	8.57	8.84	9.11	9.37	9.64	9.91	10.18	10.45	10.71	10.98	11.25	11.52	11.79	12.06
90	8.16	8.43	8.70	8.97	9.24	9.51	9.78	10.05	10.32	10.59	10.86	11.13	11.40	11.67	11.94	12.22
89	8.29	8.56	8.83	9.10	9.38	9.65	9.92	10.19	10.46	10.74	11.01	11.28	11.56	11.83	12.10	12.38
88	8.42	8.69	8.97	9.24	9.51	9.79	10.06	10.34	10.61	10.89	11.16	11.44	11.71	11.99	12.26	12.54
87	8.55	8.83	9.10	9.38	9.65	9.93	10.21	10.48	10.76	11.04	11.32	11.59	11.87	12.15	12.43	12.71
86	8.68	8.96	9.24	9.52	9.80	10.07	10.35	10.63	10.91	11.19	11.47	11.75	12.03	12.31	12.59	12.88
85	8.82	9.10	9.38	9.66	9.94	10.22	10.50	10.79	11.07	11.35	11.63	11.92	12.20	12.48	12.77	13.05
84	8.95	9.24	9.52	9.80	10.09	10.37	10.66	10.94	11.22	11.51	11.79	12.08	12.37	12.65	12.94	13.22
83	9.09	9.38	9.67	9.95	10.24	10.52	10.81	11.10	11.39	11.67	11.96	12.25	12.54	12.83	13.11	13.40
82	9.24	9.52	9.81	10.10	10.39	10.68	10.97	11.26	11.55	11.84	12.13	12.42	12.71	13.00	13.29	13.59
81	9.38	9.67	9.96	10.25	10.54	10.84	11.13	11.42	11.71	12.01	12.30	12.59	12.89	13.18	13.48	13.77
80	9.53	9.82	10.11	10.41	10.70	11.00	11.29	11.59	11.88	12.18	12.48	12.77	13.07	13.37	13.67	13.96
79	9.68	9.97	10.27	10.57	10.86	11.16	11.46	11.76	12.06	12.36	12.65	12.95	13.25	13.56	13.86	14.16
78	9.83	10.13	10.43	10.73	11.03	11.33	11.63	11.93	12.23	12.53	12.84	13.14	13.44	13.75	14.05	14.36
77	9.99	10.29	10.59	10.89	11.20	11.50	11.80	12.11	12.41	12.72	13.02	13.33	13.64	13.94	14.25	14.56
76	10.14	10.45	10.75	11.06	11.37	11.67	11.98	12.29	12.59	12.90	13.21	13.52	13.83	14.14	14.45	14.76
75	10.31	10.61	10.92	11.23	11.54	11.85	12.16	12.47	12.78	13.09	13.41	13.72	14.03	14.35	14.66	14.97
74	10.47	10.78	11.09	11.40	11.72	12.03	12.34	12.66	12.97	13.29	13.60	13.92	14.24	14.55	14.87	15.19
70	11.16	11.49	11.81	12.14	12.46	12.79	13.12	13.45	13.78	14.11	14.44	14.77	15.10	15.43	15.77	16.10
65	12.11	12.46	12.80	13.15	13.50	13.84	14.19	14.54	14.89	15.24	15.60	15.95	16.30	16.66	17.01	17.37
60	13.18	13.55	13.92	14.29	14.66	15.03	15.40	15.78	16.15	16.53	16.91	17.29	17.67	18.05	18.43	18.82
55	14.39	14.79	15.19	15.59	15.99	16.39	16.79	17.20	17.60	18.01	18.42	18.83	19.24	19.66	20.07	20.49
50	15.79	16.22	16.66	17.09	17.53	17.97	18.41	18.85	19.29	19.74	20.19	20.64	21.09	21.54	22.00	22.46
45	17.44	17.91	18.39	18.87	19.35	19.84	20.32	20.81	21.31	21.80	22.30	22.80	23.30	23.80	24.31	24.82
40	19.42	19.95	20.49	21.02	21.57	22.11	22.66	23.21	23.77	24.32	24.89	25.45	26.02	26.59	27.16	27.73
35	21.88	22.49	23.10	23.72	24.34	24.97	25.60	26.23	26.87	27.52	28.16	28.81	29.47	30.12	30.79	31.45

Description: This table shows the price to pay for a bond at the yield rate. The yield is to maturity.

Example: The price of a 15.00 %, 15 year bond to yield 8 % to maturity is $ 160.52.

COUPON RATE, %

YIELD	11.00%	11.25%	11.50%	11.75%	12.00%	12.25%	12.50%	12.75%	13.00%	13.25%	13.50%	13.75%	14.00%	14.25%	14.50%	15.00%
0.00	265.00	268.75	272.50	276.25	280.00	283.75	287.50	291.25	295.00	298.75	302.50	306.25	310.00	313.75	317.50	325.00
1.00	238.97	242.44	245.92	249.39	252.87	256.34	259.82	263.29	266.76	270.24	273.71	277.19	280.66	284.14	287.61	294.56
2.00	216.13	219.36	222.59	225.81	229.04	232.26	235.49	238.72	241.94	245.17	248.39	251.62	254.85	258.07	261.30	267.75
3.00	196.06	199.07	202.07	205.07	208.07	211.07	214.08	217.08	220.08	223.08	226.08	229.09	232.09	235.09	238.09	244.10
4.00	178.39	181.19	183.99	186.79	189.59	192.39	195.18	197.98	200.78	203.58	206.38	209.18	211.98	214.78	217.58	223.18
4.25	174.30	177.06	179.81	182.56	185.31	188.06	190.82	193.57	196.32	199.07	201.83	204.58	207.33	210.08	212.83	218.34
4.50	170.35	173.05	175.76	178.46	181.17	183.88	186.58	189.29	191.99	194.70	197.40	200.11	202.82	205.52	208.23	213.64
4.75	166.51	169.17	171.83	174.49	177.15	179.81	182.47	185.13	187.79	190.45	193.12	195.78	198.44	201.10	203.76	209.08
5.00	162.79	165.41	168.02	170.64	173.26	175.87	178.49	181.10	183.72	186.34	188.95	191.57	194.19	196.80	199.42	204.65
5.25	159.18	161.76	164.33	166.90	169.48	172.05	174.62	177.20	179.77	182.34	184.92	187.49	190.06	192.64	195.21	200.36
5.50	155.69	158.22	160.75	163.28	165.81	168.34	170.87	173.40	175.93	178.47	181.00	183.53	186.06	188.59	191.12	196.18
5.75	152.29	154.78	157.27	159.76	162.25	164.74	167.23	169.72	172.21	174.70	177.19	179.68	182.17	184.66	187.15	192.13
6.00	149.00	151.45	153.90	156.35	158.80	161.25	163.70	166.15	168.60	171.05	173.50	175.95	178.40	180.85	183.30	188.20
6.25	145.81	148.22	150.63	153.04	155.45	157.86	160.27	162.68	165.10	167.51	169.92	172.33	174.74	177.15	179.56	184.38
6.50	142.71	145.08	147.45	149.83	152.20	154.57	156.95	159.32	161.69	164.06	166.44	168.81	171.18	173.55	175.93	180.67
6.75	139.70	142.04	144.37	146.71	149.04	151.38	153.72	156.05	158.39	160.72	163.06	165.39	167.73	170.06	172.40	177.07
7.00	136.78	139.08	141.38	143.68	145.98	148.28	150.58	152.88	155.18	157.48	159.77	162.07	164.37	166.67	168.97	173.57
7.25	133.95	136.21	138.48	140.74	143.00	145.27	147.53	149.80	152.06	154.32	156.59	158.85	161.11	163.38	165.64	170.17
7.50	131.20	133.43	135.66	137.89	140.12	142.34	144.57	146.80	149.03	151.26	153.49	155.72	157.95	160.17	162.40	166.86
7.75	128.53	130.73	132.92	135.12	137.31	139.50	141.70	143.89	146.09	148.28	150.48	152.67	154.87	157.06	159.26	163.65
8.00	125.94	128.10	130.26	132.42	134.58	136.75	138.91	141.07	143.23	145.39	147.55	149.71	151.88	154.04	156.20	160.52
8.25	123.42	125.55	127.68	129.81	131.94	134.07	136.19	138.32	140.45	142.58	144.71	146.84	148.97	151.10	153.23	157.48
8.50	120.97	123.07	125.17	127.27	129.36	131.46	133.56	135.66	137.75	139.85	141.95	144.04	146.14	148.24	150.34	154.53
8.75	118.60	120.66	122.73	124.80	126.86	128.93	131.00	133.06	135.13	137.20	139.26	141.33	143.39	145.46	147.53	151.66
9.00	116.29	118.32	120.36	122.40	124.43	126.47	128.51	130.54	132.58	134.61	136.65	138.69	140.72	142.76	144.79	148.87
9.25	114.05	116.05	118.06	120.07	122.07	124.08	126.08	128.09	130.10	132.10	134.11	136.12	138.12	140.13	142.14	146.15
9.50	111.87	113.84	115.82	117.80	119.78	121.75	123.73	125.71	127.69	129.66	131.64	133.62	135.60	137.57	139.55	143.51
9.75	109.75	111.70	113.64	115.59	117.54	119.49	121.44	123.39	125.34	127.29	129.24	131.19	133.14	135.09	137.04	140.93
10.00	107.69	109.61	111.53	113.45	115.37	117.29	119.22	121.14	123.06	124.98	126.90	128.82	130.74	132.67	134.59	138.43
10.25	105.68	107.58	109.47	111.37	113.26	115.16	117.05	118.94	120.84	122.73	124.63	126.52	128.42	130.31	132.21	136.00
10.50	103.74	105.60	107.47	109.34	111.21	113.08	114.94	116.81	118.68	120.55	122.42	124.28	126.15	128.02	129.89	133.62
10.75	101.84	103.68	105.53	107.37	109.21	111.05	112.89	114.74	116.58	118.42	120.26	122.10	123.95	125.79	127.63	131.32
11.00	100.00	101.82	103.63	105.45	107.27	109.08	110.90	112.72	114.53	116.35	118.17	119.98	121.80	123.62	125.43	129.07
11.25	98.21	100.00	101.79	103.58	105.38	107.17	108.96	110.75	112.54	114.34	116.13	117.92	119.71	121.50	123.29	126.88
11.50	96.46	98.23	100.00	101.77	103.54	105.30	107.07	108.84	110.61	112.37	114.14	115.91	117.68	119.44	121.21	124.75
11.75	94.77	96.51	98.26	100.00	101.74	103.49	105.23	106.98	108.72	110.46	112.21	113.95	115.69	117.44	119.18	122.67
12.00	93.12	94.84	96.56	98.28	100.00	101.72	103.44	105.16	106.88	108.60	110.32	112.04	113.76	115.49	117.21	120.65
12.25	91.51	93.21	94.91	96.60	98.30	100.00	101.70	103.40	105.09	106.79	108.49	110.19	111.88	113.58	115.28	118.68
12.50	89.95	91.62	93.30	94.97	96.65	98.32	100.00	101.68	103.35	105.03	106.70	108.38	110.05	111.73	113.40	116.76
12.75	88.42	90.08	91.73	93.39	95.04	96.69	98.35	100.00	101.65	103.31	104.96	106.61	108.27	109.92	111.58	114.88
13.00	86.94	88.57	90.21	91.84	93.47	95.10	96.74	98.37	100.00	101.63	103.26	104.90	106.53	108.16	109.79	113.06
13.25	85.50	87.11	88.72	90.33	91.94	93.55	95.17	96.78	98.39	100.00	101.61	103.22	104.83	106.45	108.06	111.28
13.50	84.09	85.68	87.27	88.86	90.45	92.05	93.64	95.23	96.82	98.41	100.00	101.59	103.18	104.77	106.36	109.55
13.75	82.72	84.29	85.86	87.43	89.00	90.58	92.15	93.72	95.29	96.86	98.43	100.00	101.57	103.14	104.71	107.85
14.00	81.39	82.94	84.49	86.04	87.59	89.14	90.69	92.24	93.80	95.35	96.90	98.45	100.00	101.55	103.10	106.20
14.25	80.09	81.62	83.15	84.68	86.21	87.75	89.28	90.81	92.34	93.87	95.40	96.94	98.47	100.00	101.53	104.60
14.50	78.82	80.33	81.84	83.36	84.87	86.38	87.90	89.41	90.92	92.44	93.95	95.46	96.97	98.49	100.00	103.03
14.75	77.58	79.08	80.57	82.07	83.56	85.06	86.55	88.04	89.54	91.03	92.53	94.02	95.52	97.01	98.51	101.49
15.00	76.38	77.86	79.33	80.81	82.28	83.76	85.24	86.71	88.19	89.67	91.14	92.62	94.09	95.57	97.05	100.00
15.25	75.21	76.66	78.12	79.58	81.04	82.50	83.96	85.41	86.87	88.33	89.79	91.25	92.71	94.17	95.62	98.54
15.50	74.06	75.50	76.94	78.38	79.82	81.27	82.71	84.15	85.59	87.03	88.47	89.91	91.35	92.79	94.24	97.12
15.75	72.94	74.37	75.79	77.22	78.64	80.06	81.49	82.91	84.34	85.76	87.18	88.61	90.03	91.46	92.88	95.73
16.00	71.86	73.26	74.67	76.08	77.48	78.89	80.30	81.71	83.11	84.52	85.93	87.33	88.74	90.15	91.56	94.37
16.25	70.79	72.18	73.57	74.97	76.36	77.75	79.14	80.53	81.92	83.31	84.70	86.09	87.48	88.87	90.26	93.05
16.50	69.76	71.13	72.51	73.88	75.26	76.63	78.01	79.38	80.75	82.13	83.50	84.88	86.25	87.63	89.00	91.75
16.75	68.75	70.11	71.46	72.82	74.18	75.54	76.90	78.26	79.62	80.98	82.33	83.69	85.05	86.41	87.77	90.49
17.00	67.76	69.10	70.45	71.79	73.13	74.48	75.82	77.16	78.51	79.85	81.19	82.54	83.88	85.22	86.57	89.25
17.25	66.80	68.12	69.45	70.78	72.11	73.44	74.77	76.09	77.42	78.75	80.08	81.41	82.73	84.06	85.39	88.05
17.50	65.86	67.17	68.48	69.80	71.11	72.42	73.74	75.05	76.36	77.68	78.99	80.30	81.61	82.93	84.24	86.87
17.75	64.94	66.24	67.54	68.83	70.13	71.43	72.73	74.03	75.33	76.63	77.92	79.22	80.52	81.82	83.12	85.72
18.00	64.04	65.33	66.61	67.89	69.18	70.46	71.75	73.03	74.32	75.60	76.88	78.17	79.45	80.74	82.02	84.59
18.25	63.17	64.44	65.71	66.98	68.25	69.52	70.79	72.06	73.33	74.60	75.87	77.14	78.41	79.68	80.95	83.49
18.50	62.31	63.57	64.82	66.08	67.34	68.59	69.85	71.11	72.36	73.62	74.87	76.13	77.39	78.64	79.90	82.41
18.75	61.48	62.72	63.96	65.21	66.45	67.69	68.93	70.18	71.42	72.66	73.90	75.15	76.39	77.63	78.87	81.36
19.00	60.66	61.89	63.12	64.35	65.58	66.81	68.04	69.27	70.50	71.73	72.95	74.18	75.41	76.64	77.87	80.33
20.00	57.58	58.76	59.94	61.11	62.29	63.47	64.65	65.83	67.01	68.18	69.36	70.54	71.72	72.90	74.08	76.43
25.00	45.64	46.61	47.58	48.55	49.52	50.49	51.46	52.43	53.40	54.37	55.34	56.31	57.28	58.26	59.23	61.17
30.00	37.62	38.44	39.26	40.09	40.91	41.73	42.55	43.37	44.19	45.01	45.83	46.65	47.47	48.29	49.11	50.76

Description: This table shows the yield to maturity of a bond purchased at the price shown in the index.

Example: The yield to maturity of a 15.00 %, 15 year bond at a price of 117.00 is 12.46 %.

COUPON RATE, %

PRICE	11.00%	11.25%	11.50%	11.75%	12.00%	12.25%	12.50%	12.75%	13.00%	13.25%	13.50%	13.75%	14.00%	14.25%	14.50%	15.00%
190	3.32	3.49	3.65	3.81	3.97	4.13	4.29	4.45	4.61	4.77	4.93	5.09	5.25	5.41	5.56	5.88
185	3.61	3.77	3.94	4.10	4.26	4.43	4.59	4.75	4.92	5.08	5.24	5.40	5.56	5.72	5.88	6.20
180	3.90	4.07	4.23	4.40	4.57	4.73	4.90	5.06	5.23	5.40	5.56	5.72	5.89	6.05	6.22	6.54
175	4.20	4.37	4.54	4.71	4.88	5.05	5.22	5.39	5.56	5.73	5.89	6.06	6.23	6.39	6.56	6.89
170	4.52	4.69	4.86	5.04	5.21	5.38	5.55	5.73	5.90	6.07	6.24	6.41	6.58	6.75	6.92	7.26
165	4.85	5.02	5.20	5.38	5.55	5.73	5.90	6.08	6.25	6.43	6.60	6.77	6.95	7.12	7.29	7.64
160	5.19	5.37	5.55	5.73	5.91	6.09	6.27	6.44	6.62	6.80	6.98	7.15	7.33	7.51	7.69	8.04
155	5.54	5.73	5.91	6.10	6.28	6.46	6.64	6.83	7.01	7.19	7.37	7.55	7.73	7.91	8.10	8.45
150	5.92	6.11	6.29	6.48	6.67	6.86	7.04	7.23	7.41	7.60	7.79	7.97	8.16	8.34	8.52	8.89
145	6.31	6.50	6.69	6.89	7.08	7.27	7.46	7.65	7.84	8.03	8.22	8.41	8.60	8.79	8.98	9.35
140	6.72	6.92	7.11	7.31	7.51	7.70	7.90	8.09	8.29	8.48	8.68	8.87	9.06	9.26	9.45	9.84
135	7.15	7.35	7.55	7.76	7.96	8.16	8.36	8.56	8.76	8.96	9.16	9.36	9.55	9.75	9.95	10.35
130	7.61	7.81	8.02	8.23	8.43	8.64	8.84	9.05	9.25	9.46	9.67	9.87	10.07	10.28	10.48	10.89
125	8.09	8.30	8.51	8.72	8.94	9.15	9.36	9.57	9.78	9.99	10.20	10.41	10.62	10.84	11.05	11.46
123	8.29	8.50	8.72	8.93	9.15	9.36	9.57	9.79	10.00	10.22	10.43	10.64	10.85	11.07	11.28	11.70
122	8.39	8.61	8.82	9.04	9.25	9.47	9.68	9.90	10.11	10.33	10.54	10.76	10.97	11.19	11.40	11.83
121	8.49	8.71	8.93	9.14	9.36	9.58	9.79	10.01	10.23	10.44	10.66	10.87	11.09	11.31	11.52	11.95
120	8.60	8.82	9.03	9.25	9.47	9.69	9.91	10.12	10.34	10.56	10.78	10.99	11.21	11.43	11.64	12.08
119	8.70	8.92	9.14	9.36	9.58	9.80	10.02	10.24	10.46	10.68	10.89	11.11	11.33	11.55	11.77	12.20
118	8.81	9.03	9.25	9.47	9.69	9.91	10.13	10.35	10.58	10.80	11.02	11.24	11.45	11.67	11.89	12.33
117	8.92	9.14	9.36	9.58	9.81	10.03	10.25	10.47	10.69	10.92	11.14	11.36	11.58	11.80	12.02	12.46
116	9.03	9.25	9.47	9.70	9.92	10.15	10.37	10.59	10.82	11.04	11.26	11.48	11.71	11.93	12.15	12.60
115	9.14	9.36	9.59	9.81	10.04	10.26	10.49	10.71	10.94	11.16	11.39	11.61	11.83	12.06	12.28	12.73
114	9.25	9.48	9.70	9.93	10.16	10.38	10.61	10.84	11.06	11.29	11.51	11.74	11.96	12.19	12.41	12.87
113	9.36	9.59	9.82	10.05	10.28	10.50	10.73	10.96	11.19	11.41	11.64	11.87	12.10	12.32	12.55	13.00
112	9.48	9.71	9.94	10.17	10.40	10.63	10.86	11.09	11.31	11.54	11.77	12.00	12.23	12.46	12.69	13.14
111	9.60	9.83	10.06	10.29	10.52	10.75	10.98	11.21	11.44	11.67	11.90	12.13	12.36	12.60	12.83	13.28
110	9.71	9.95	10.18	10.41	10.65	10.88	11.11	11.34	11.57	11.81	12.04	12.27	12.50	12.73	12.97	13.43
109	9.83	10.07	10.30	10.54	10.77	11.01	11.24	11.47	11.71	11.94	12.17	12.41	12.64	12.88	13.11	13.57
108	9.96	10.19	10.43	10.66	10.90	11.14	11.37	11.61	11.84	12.08	12.31	12.55	12.78	13.02	13.25	13.72
107	10.08	10.32	10.56	10.79	11.03	11.27	11.50	11.74	11.98	12.22	12.45	12.69	12.93	13.16	13.40	13.87
106	10.21	10.44	10.68	10.92	11.16	11.40	11.64	11.88	12.12	12.36	12.60	12.83	13.07	13.31	13.55	14.03
105	10.33	10.57	10.81	11.05	11.30	11.54	11.78	12.02	12.26	12.50	12.74	12.98	13.22	13.46	13.70	14.18
104	10.46	10.70	10.95	11.19	11.43	11.67	11.92	12.16	12.40	12.64	12.89	13.13	13.37	13.61	13.85	14.34
103	10.59	10.84	11.08	11.32	11.57	11.81	12.06	12.30	12.55	12.79	13.03	13.28	13.52	13.77	14.01	14.50
102	10.72	10.97	11.22	11.46	11.71	11.96	12.20	12.45	12.69	12.94	13.19	13.43	13.68	13.92	14.17	14.66
101	10.86	11.11	11.35	11.60	11.85	12.10	12.35	12.60	12.84	13.09	13.34	13.59	13.84	14.08	14.33	14.83
100	11.00	11.25	11.50	11.75	12.00	12.25	12.50	12.75	13.00	13.25	13.50	13.75	14.00	14.25	14.50	15.00
99	11.13	11.39	11.64	11.89	12.14	12.39	12.65	12.90	13.15	13.40	13.65	13.91	14.16	14.41	14.66	15.17
98	11.27	11.53	11.78	12.04	12.29	12.54	12.80	13.05	13.31	13.56	13.81	14.07	14.32	14.58	14.83	15.34
97	11.42	11.67	11.93	12.19	12.44	12.70	12.95	13.21	13.47	13.72	13.98	14.23	14.49	14.75	15.00	15.52
96	11.56	11.82	12.08	12.34	12.59	12.85	13.11	13.37	13.63	13.89	14.14	14.40	14.66	14.92	15.18	15.70
95	11.71	11.97	12.23	12.49	12.75	13.01	13.27	13.53	13.79	14.05	14.31	14.57	14.84	15.10	15.36	15.88
94	11.86	12.12	12.39	12.65	12.91	13.17	13.43	13.70	13.96	14.22	14.49	14.75	15.01	15.27	15.54	16.06
93	12.01	12.28	12.54	12.81	13.07	13.34	13.60	13.87	14.13	14.40	14.66	14.93	15.19	15.46	15.72	16.25
92	12.17	12.43	12.70	12.97	13.24	13.50	13.77	14.04	14.30	14.57	14.84	15.11	15.37	15.64	15.91	16.45
91	12.33	12.59	12.86	13.13	13.40	13.67	13.94	14.21	14.48	14.75	15.02	15.29	15.56	15.83	16.10	16.64
90	12.49	12.76	13.03	13.30	13.57	13.84	14.12	14.39	14.66	14.93	15.21	15.48	15.75	16.02	16.30	16.84
89	12.65	12.92	13.20	13.47	13.75	14.02	14.29	14.57	14.84	15.12	15.39	15.67	15.94	16.22	16.50	17.05
88	12.82	13.09	13.37	13.65	13.92	14.20	14.48	14.75	15.03	15.31	15.59	15.86	16.14	16.42	16.70	17.25
87	12.98	13.26	13.54	13.82	14.10	14.38	14.66	14.94	15.22	15.50	15.78	16.06	16.34	16.62	16.90	17.47
86	13.16	13.44	13.72	14.00	14.28	14.57	14.85	15.13	15.41	15.70	15.98	16.26	16.55	16.83	17.11	17.68
85	13.33	13.62	13.90	14.19	14.47	14.76	15.04	15.33	15.61	15.90	16.18	16.47	16.76	17.04	17.33	17.90
84	13.51	13.80	14.09	14.37	14.66	14.95	15.24	15.52	15.81	16.10	16.39	16.68	16.97	17.26	17.55	18.13
83	13.69	13.98	14.27	14.56	14.85	15.14	15.44	15.73	16.02	16.31	16.60	16.89	17.19	17.48	17.77	18.36
82	13.88	14.17	14.46	14.76	15.05	15.35	15.64	15.93	16.23	16.52	16.82	17.11	17.41	17.70	18.00	18.59
81	14.07	14.36	14.66	14.96	15.25	15.55	15.85	16.14	16.44	16.74	17.04	17.34	17.63	17.93	18.23	18.83
80	14.26	14.56	14.86	15.16	15.46	15.76	16.06	16.36	16.66	16.96	17.26	17.56	17.87	18.17	18.47	19.08
79	14.46	14.76	15.06	15.37	15.67	15.97	16.28	16.58	16.88	17.19	17.49	17.80	18.10	18.41	18.71	19.33
78	14.66	14.97	15.27	15.58	15.88	16.19	16.50	16.80	17.11	17.42	17.73	18.04	18.34	18.65	18.96	19.58
77	14.87	15.17	15.48	15.79	16.10	16.41	16.72	17.03	17.34	17.66	17.97	18.28	18.59	18.90	19.22	19.84
76	15.08	15.39	15.70	16.01	16.33	16.64	16.95	17.27	17.58	17.90	18.21	18.53	18.84	19.16	19.48	20.11
75	15.29	15.60	15.92	16.24	16.55	16.87	17.19	17.51	17.83	18.14	18.46	18.78	19.10	19.42	19.74	20.39
74	15.51	15.83	16.15	16.47	16.79	17.11	17.43	17.75	18.07	18.40	18.72	19.04	19.37	19.69	20.02	20.67
73	15.73	16.06	16.38	16.70	17.03	17.35	17.68	18.00	18.33	18.66	18.98	19.31	19.64	19.97	20.30	20.95
70	16.44	16.77	17.11	17.44	17.78	18.12	18.45	18.79	19.13	19.47	19.81	20.15	20.49	20.83	21.18	21.86
65	17.73	18.09	18.44	18.80	19.16	19.53	19.89	20.25	20.61	20.98	21.34	21.71	22.07	22.44	22.80	23.54
60	19.20	19.59	19.97	20.36	20.75	21.14	21.53	21.92	22.31	22.70	23.10	23.49	23.89	24.28	24.68	25.47

Description: This table shows the price to pay for a bond at the yield rate. The yield is to maturity.

Example: The price of a 6.75 %, 16 year bond to yield 8 % to maturity is $ 88.83.

COUPON RATE, %

YIELD	0.00%	1.00%	2.00%	3.00%	4.00%	4.25%	4.50%	4.75%	5.00%	5.25%	5.50%	5.75%	6.00%	6.25%	6.50%	6.75%
0.00	100.00	116.00	132.00	148.00	164.00	168.00	172.00	176.00	180.00	184.00	188.00	192.00	196.00	200.00	204.00	208.00
1.00	85.25	100.00	114.75	129.50	144.25	147.94	151.63	155.32	159.01	162.69	166.38	170.07	173.76	177.45	181.13	184.82
2.00	72.73	86.37	100.00	113.63	127.27	130.68	134.09	137.50	140.90	144.31	147.72	151.13	154.54	157.95	161.36	164.77
3.00	62.10	74.73	87.37	100.00	112.63	115.79	118.95	122.11	125.27	128.43	131.58	134.74	137.90	141.06	144.22	147.38
4.00	53.06	64.80	76.53	88.27	100.00	102.93	105.87	108.80	111.73	114.67	117.60	120.53	123.47	126.40	129.34	132.27
4.25	51.02	62.55	74.07	85.60	97.12	100.00	102.88	105.76	108.64	111.52	114.40	117.29	120.17	123.05	125.93	128.81
4.50	49.07	60.38	71.70	83.02	94.34	97.17	100.00	102.83	105.66	108.49	111.32	114.15	116.98	119.81	122.64	125.47
4.75	47.18	58.30	69.42	80.54	91.66	94.44	97.22	100.00	102.78	105.56	108.34	111.12	113.90	116.68	119.46	122.24
5.00	45.38	56.30	67.23	78.15	89.08	91.81	94.54	97.27	100.00	102.73	105.46	108.19	110.92	113.66	116.39	119.12
5.25	43.64	54.38	65.11	75.85	86.58	89.27	91.95	94.63	97.32	100.00	102.68	105.37	108.05	110.73	113.42	116.10
5.50	41.97	52.52	63.07	73.62	84.17	86.81	89.45	92.09	94.72	97.36	100.00	102.64	105.28	107.91	110.55	113.19
5.75	40.37	50.74	61.11	71.48	81.85	84.44	87.04	89.63	92.22	94.81	97.41	100.00	102.59	105.19	107.78	110.37
6.00	38.83	49.03	59.22	69.42	79.61	82.16	84.71	87.26	89.81	92.35	94.90	97.45	100.00	102.55	105.10	107.65
6.25	37.36	47.38	57.40	67.42	77.45	79.95	82.46	84.97	87.47	89.98	92.48	94.99	97.49	100.00	102.51	105.01
6.50	35.94	45.79	55.65	65.50	75.36	77.82	80.29	82.75	85.22	87.68	90.14	92.61	95.07	97.54	100.00	102.46
6.75	34.57	44.26	53.96	63.65	73.34	75.77	78.19	80.61	83.04	85.46	87.88	90.31	92.73	95.15	97.58	100.00
7.00	33.26	42.79	52.33	61.86	71.40	73.78	76.16	78.55	80.93	83.31	85.70	88.08	90.47	92.85	95.23	97.62
7.25	32.00	41.38	50.76	60.14	69.52	71.86	74.21	76.55	78.90	81.24	83.59	85.93	88.28	90.62	92.97	95.31
7.50	30.79	40.02	49.24	58.47	67.70	70.01	72.32	74.62	76.93	79.24	81.54	83.85	86.16	88.46	90.77	93.08
7.75	29.62	38.70	47.79	56.87	65.95	68.22	70.49	72.76	75.03	77.30	79.57	81.84	84.11	86.38	88.65	90.92
8.00	28.51	37.44	46.38	55.32	64.25	66.49	68.72	70.96	73.19	75.42	77.66	79.89	82.13	84.36	86.59	88.83
8.25	27.43	36.23	45.02	53.82	62.62	64.81	67.01	69.21	71.41	73.61	75.81	78.01	80.21	82.41	84.61	86.81
8.50	26.40	35.06	43.72	52.37	61.03	63.20	65.36	67.53	69.69	71.86	74.02	76.19	78.35	80.52	82.68	84.85
8.75	25.40	33.93	42.45	50.98	59.51	61.64	63.77	65.90	68.03	70.16	72.29	74.42	76.56	78.69	80.82	82.95
9.00	24.45	32.84	41.24	49.63	58.03	60.13	62.22	64.32	66.42	68.52	70.62	72.72	74.82	76.92	79.01	81.11
9.25	23.53	31.80	40.07	48.33	56.60	58.67	60.73	62.80	64.87	66.93	69.00	71.07	73.13	75.20	77.27	79.33
9.50	22.65	30.79	38.93	47.08	55.22	57.25	59.29	61.33	63.36	65.40	67.43	69.47	71.50	73.54	75.57	77.61
9.75	21.80	29.82	37.84	45.86	53.88	55.89	57.89	59.90	61.90	63.91	65.91	67.92	69.92	71.93	73.93	75.94
10.00	20.99	28.89	36.79	44.69	52.59	54.57	56.54	58.52	60.49	62.47	64.44	66.42	68.39	70.37	72.35	74.32
10.25	20.20	27.99	35.77	43.56	51.34	53.29	55.24	57.18	59.13	61.07	63.02	64.97	66.91	68.86	70.81	72.75
10.50	19.45	27.12	34.79	42.46	50.13	52.05	53.97	55.89	57.81	59.72	61.64	63.56	65.48	67.40	69.31	71.23
10.75	18.72	26.28	33.85	41.41	48.97	50.86	52.75	54.64	56.53	58.42	60.31	62.20	64.09	65.98	67.87	69.76
11.00	18.03	25.48	32.93	40.38	47.84	49.70	51.56	53.42	55.29	57.15	59.01	60.88	62.74	64.60	66.47	68.33
11.25	17.36	24.70	32.05	39.39	46.74	48.58	50.41	52.25	54.09	55.92	57.76	59.60	61.43	63.27	65.11	66.94
11.50	16.71	23.95	31.20	38.44	45.68	47.49	49.30	51.11	52.92	54.73	56.55	58.36	60.17	61.98	63.79	65.60
11.75	16.09	23.23	30.37	37.52	44.66	46.44	48.23	50.01	51.80	53.58	55.37	57.15	58.94	60.72	62.51	64.29
12.00	15.50	22.54	29.58	36.62	43.66	45.42	47.18	48.95	50.71	52.47	54.23	55.99	57.75	59.51	61.27	63.03
12.25	14.92	21.87	28.81	35.76	42.70	44.44	46.18	47.91	49.65	51.38	53.12	54.86	56.59	58.33	60.07	61.80
12.50	14.37	21.22	28.07	34.92	41.77	43.48	45.20	46.91	48.62	50.33	52.05	53.76	55.47	57.19	58.90	60.61
12.75	13.84	20.60	27.36	34.11	40.87	42.56	44.25	45.94	47.63	49.32	51.01	52.70	54.39	56.08	57.76	59.45
13.00	13.33	20.00	26.66	33.33	40.00	41.66	43.33	45.00	46.66	48.33	50.00	51.66	53.33	55.00	56.66	58.33
13.25	12.84	19.42	25.99	32.57	39.15	40.80	42.44	44.09	45.73	47.37	49.02	50.66	52.31	53.95	55.60	57.24
13.50	12.37	18.86	25.35	31.84	38.33	39.95	41.58	43.20	44.82	46.45	48.07	49.69	51.31	52.94	54.56	56.18
13.75	11.91	18.32	24.72	31.13	37.54	39.14	40.74	42.34	43.94	45.55	47.15	48.75	50.35	51.95	53.55	55.15
14.00	11.47	17.80	24.12	30.44	36.77	38.35	39.93	41.51	43.09	44.67	46.25	47.83	49.41	50.99	52.58	54.16
14.25	11.05	17.30	23.54	29.78	36.02	37.58	39.14	40.70	42.26	43.82	45.38	46.94	48.50	50.07	51.63	53.19
14.50	10.65	16.81	22.97	29.13	35.30	36.84	38.38	39.92	41.46	43.00	44.54	46.08	47.62	49.16	50.70	52.24
14.75	10.26	16.34	22.43	28.51	34.60	36.12	37.64	39.16	40.68	42.20	43.72	45.24	46.76	48.28	49.81	51.33
15.00	9.88	15.89	21.90	27.91	33.91	35.42	36.92	38.42	39.92	41.42	42.93	44.43	45.93	47.43	48.93	50.44
15.25	9.52	15.46	21.39	27.32	33.25	34.74	36.22	37.70	39.19	40.67	42.15	43.64	45.12	46.60	48.09	49.57
15.50	9.18	15.04	20.90	26.75	32.61	34.08	35.54	37.01	38.47	39.94	41.40	42.87	44.33	45.80	47.26	48.73
15.75	8.84	14.63	20.42	26.21	31.99	33.44	34.89	36.33	37.78	39.23	40.67	42.12	43.57	45.02	46.46	47.91
16.00	8.52	14.24	19.96	25.67	31.39	32.82	34.25	35.68	37.11	38.54	39.97	41.40	42.83	44.25	45.68	47.11
16.25	8.21	13.86	19.51	25.16	30.80	32.22	33.63	35.04	36.45	37.87	39.28	40.69	42.10	43.51	44.93	46.34
16.50	7.91	13.49	19.07	24.66	30.24	31.63	33.03	34.42	35.82	37.21	38.61	40.00	41.40	42.79	44.19	45.58
16.75	7.63	13.14	18.66	24.17	29.69	31.06	32.44	33.82	35.20	36.58	37.96	39.34	40.71	42.09	43.47	44.85
17.00	7.35	12.80	18.25	23.70	29.15	30.51	31.87	33.24	34.60	35.96	37.32	38.69	40.05	41.41	42.77	44.14
17.25	7.08	12.47	17.86	23.24	28.63	29.98	31.32	32.67	34.02	35.36	36.71	38.06	39.40	40.75	42.10	43.44
17.50	6.83	12.15	17.48	22.80	28.12	29.46	30.79	32.12	33.45	34.78	36.11	37.44	38.77	40.10	41.43	42.77
17.75	6.58	11.84	17.11	22.37	27.63	28.95	30.26	31.58	32.90	34.21	35.53	36.84	38.16	39.48	40.79	42.11
18.00	6.34	11.55	16.75	21.95	27.16	28.46	29.76	31.06	32.36	33.66	34.96	36.26	37.56	38.86	40.16	41.46
18.25	6.12	11.26	16.40	21.55	26.69	27.98	29.27	30.55	31.84	33.12	34.41	35.70	36.98	38.27	39.55	40.84
18.50	5.90	10.98	16.07	21.16	26.24	27.51	28.79	30.06	31.33	32.60	33.87	35.14	36.42	37.69	38.96	40.23
18.75	5.68	10.71	15.74	20.77	25.80	27.06	28.32	29.58	30.83	32.09	33.35	34.61	35.86	37.12	38.38	39.64
19.00	5.48	10.45	15.43	20.40	25.38	26.62	27.87	29.11	30.35	31.60	32.84	34.08	35.33	36.57	37.82	39.06
20.00	4.74	9.50	14.26	19.03	23.79	24.98	26.17	27.36	28.55	29.74	30.93	32.12	33.32	34.51	35.70	36.89
25.00	2.31	6.22	10.12	14.03	17.94	18.92	19.89	20.87	21.85	22.82	23.80	24.78	25.75	26.73	27.71	28.68
30.00	1.14	4.44	7.73	11.03	14.32	15.15	15.97	16.79	17.62	18.44	19.27	20.09	20.91	21.74	22.56	23.39

Description: This table shows the yield to maturity of a bond purchased at the price shown in the index.

Example: The yield to maturity of a 6.75 %, 16 year bond at a price of 80.00 is 9.15 %.

COUPON RATE, %

PRICE	0.00%	1.00%	2.00%	3.00%	4.00%	4.25%	4.50%	4.75%	5.00%	5.25%	5.50%	5.75%	6.00%	6.25%	6.50%	6.75%
100	0.00	1.00	2.00	3.00	4.00	4.25	4.50	4.75	5.00	5.25	5.50	5.75	6.00	6.25	6.50	6.75
99	.06	1.06	2.07	3.07	4.08	4.33	4.58	4.84	5.09	5.34	5.59	5.84	6.09	6.35	6.60	6.85
98	.12	1.13	2.14	3.16	4.17	4.42	4.67	4.93	5.18	5.43	5.69	5.94	6.19	6.45	6.70	6.95
97	.19	1.20	2.22	3.24	4.26	4.51	4.77	5.02	5.28	5.53	5.79	6.04	6.30	6.55	6.81	7.06
96	.25	1.27	2.30	3.32	4.34	4.60	4.86	5.11	5.37	5.63	5.88	6.14	6.40	6.66	6.91	7.17
95	.32	1.34	2.37	3.40	4.43	4.69	4.95	5.21	5.47	5.73	5.99	6.24	6.50	6.76	7.02	7.28
94	.38	1.42	2.45	3.49	4.53	4.79	5.05	5.31	5.57	5.83	6.09	6.35	6.61	6.87	7.13	7.39
93	.45	1.49	2.53	3.57	4.62	4.88	5.14	5.40	5.67	5.93	6.19	6.45	6.72	6.98	7.24	7.50
92	.52	1.56	2.61	3.66	4.71	4.98	5.24	5.50	5.77	6.03	6.30	6.56	6.82	7.09	7.35	7.62
91	.59	1.64	2.69	3.75	4.81	5.07	5.34	5.60	5.87	6.14	6.40	6.67	6.94	7.20	7.47	7.74
90	.65	1.71	2.77	3.84	4.90	5.17	5.44	5.71	5.97	6.24	6.51	6.78	7.05	7.32	7.58	7.85
89	.72	1.79	2.86	3.93	5.00	5.27	5.54	5.81	6.08	6.35	6.62	6.89	7.16	7.43	7.70	7.97
88	.80	1.87	2.94	4.02	5.10	5.37	5.64	5.92	6.19	6.46	6.73	7.00	7.28	7.55	7.82	8.10
87	.87	1.94	3.03	4.11	5.20	5.48	5.75	6.02	6.30	6.57	6.85	7.12	7.39	7.67	7.95	8.22
86	.94	2.02	3.11	4.21	5.30	5.58	5.86	6.13	6.41	6.68	6.96	7.24	7.51	7.79	8.07	8.35
85	1.01	2.10	3.20	4.30	5.41	5.69	5.96	6.24	6.52	6.80	7.08	7.36	7.64	7.91	8.19	8.48
84	1.09	2.19	3.29	4.40	5.51	5.79	6.07	6.35	6.63	6.91	7.20	7.48	7.76	8.04	8.32	8.61
83	1.16	2.27	3.38	4.50	5.62	5.90	6.18	6.47	6.75	7.03	7.32	7.60	7.88	8.17	8.45	8.74
82	1.24	2.35	3.47	4.60	5.73	6.01	6.30	6.58	6.87	7.15	7.44	7.72	8.01	8.30	8.59	8.87
81	1.32	2.44	3.56	4.70	5.84	6.13	6.41	6.70	6.99	7.27	7.56	7.85	8.14	8.43	8.72	9.01
80	1.39	2.52	3.66	4.80	5.95	6.24	6.53	6.82	7.11	7.40	7.69	7.98	8.27	8.56	8.86	9.15
79	1.47	2.61	3.75	4.91	6.06	6.36	6.65	6.94	7.23	7.53	7.82	8.11	8.41	8.70	9.00	9.29
78	1.55	2.70	3.85	5.01	6.18	6.47	6.77	7.06	7.36	7.65	7.95	8.25	8.54	8.84	9.14	9.44
77	1.64	2.79	3.95	5.12	6.30	6.59	6.89	7.19	7.49	7.78	8.08	8.38	8.68	8.98	9.28	9.59
76	1.72	2.88	4.05	5.23	6.42	6.72	7.02	7.32	7.62	7.92	8.22	8.52	8.82	9.13	9.43	9.74
75	1.80	2.97	4.15	5.34	6.54	6.84	7.14	7.45	7.75	8.05	8.36	8.66	8.97	9.27	9.58	9.89
74	1.89	3.06	4.25	5.45	6.66	6.97	7.27	7.58	7.88	8.19	8.50	8.81	9.12	9.42	9.73	10.05
73	1.97	3.16	4.36	5.57	6.79	7.10	7.40	7.71	8.02	8.33	8.64	8.95	9.27	9.58	9.89	10.20
72	2.06	3.25	4.46	5.68	6.92	7.23	7.54	7.85	8.16	8.47	8.79	9.10	9.42	9.73	10.05	10.37
71	2.15	3.35	4.57	5.80	7.05	7.36	7.67	7.99	8.30	8.62	8.94	9.26	9.57	9.89	10.21	10.53
70	2.24	3.45	4.68	5.92	7.18	7.50	7.81	8.13	8.45	8.77	9.09	9.41	9.73	10.06	10.38	10.70
69	2.33	3.55	4.79	6.05	7.32	7.63	7.95	8.28	8.60	8.92	9.24	9.57	9.90	10.22	10.55	10.88
68	2.42	3.66	4.91	6.17	7.45	7.78	8.10	8.42	8.75	9.08	9.40	9.73	10.06	10.39	10.72	11.05
67	2.51	3.76	5.02	6.30	7.59	7.92	8.25	8.58	8.90	9.23	9.57	9.90	10.23	10.56	10.90	11.23
66	2.61	3.87	5.14	6.43	7.74	8.07	8.40	8.73	9.06	9.40	9.73	10.07	10.40	10.74	11.08	11.42
65	2.71	3.97	5.26	6.56	7.88	8.22	8.55	8.89	9.22	9.56	9.90	10.24	10.58	10.92	11.26	11.61
64	2.80	4.08	5.38	6.70	8.03	8.37	8.71	9.05	9.39	9.73	10.07	10.42	10.76	11.11	11.45	11.80
63	2.90	4.19	5.50	6.83	8.19	8.53	8.87	9.21	9.56	9.90	10.25	10.60	10.95	11.30	11.65	12.00
62	3.01	4.31	5.63	6.98	8.34	8.69	9.03	9.38	9.73	10.08	10.43	10.78	11.14	11.49	11.85	12.20
61	3.11	4.42	5.76	7.12	8.50	8.85	9.20	9.55	9.90	10.26	10.61	10.97	11.33	11.69	12.05	12.41
60	3.21	4.54	5.89	7.27	8.66	9.02	9.37	9.73	10.08	10.44	10.80	11.17	11.53	11.89	12.26	12.63
59	3.32	4.66	6.03	7.41	8.83	9.19	9.55	9.91	10.27	10.63	11.00	11.36	11.73	12.10	12.47	12.85
58	3.43	4.78	6.16	7.57	9.00	9.36	9.73	10.09	10.46	10.83	11.20	11.57	11.94	12.32	12.69	13.07
57	3.54	4.91	6.30	7.72	9.17	9.54	9.91	10.28	10.65	11.03	11.40	11.78	12.16	12.54	12.92	13.30
56	3.65	5.03	6.44	7.88	9.35	9.72	10.10	10.47	10.85	11.23	11.61	11.99	12.38	12.76	13.15	13.54
55	3.77	5.16	6.59	8.05	9.54	9.91	10.29	10.67	11.05	11.44	11.82	12.21	12.60	12.99	13.39	13.78
54	3.88	5.30	6.74	8.21	9.72	10.10	10.49	10.88	11.26	11.65	12.05	12.44	12.84	13.23	13.63	14.03
53	4.00	5.43	6.89	8.39	9.92	10.30	10.69	11.08	11.48	11.87	12.27	12.67	13.08	13.48	13.89	14.29
52	4.12	5.57	7.05	8.56	10.11	10.51	10.90	11.30	11.70	12.10	12.51	12.91	13.32	13.73	14.15	14.56
51	4.25	5.71	7.21	8.74	10.32	10.71	11.12	11.52	11.93	12.34	12.75	13.16	13.58	13.99	14.41	14.84
50	4.37	5.85	7.37	8.93	10.52	10.93	11.34	11.75	12.16	12.58	12.99	13.41	13.84	14.26	14.69	15.12
49	4.50	6.00	7.54	9.12	10.74	11.15	11.56	11.98	12.40	12.82	13.25	13.68	14.11	14.54	14.98	15.41
48	4.64	6.15	7.71	9.31	10.96	11.38	11.80	12.22	12.65	13.08	13.51	13.95	14.39	14.83	15.27	15.72
47	4.77	6.30	7.88	9.51	11.19	11.61	12.04	12.47	12.91	13.34	13.79	14.23	14.68	15.12	15.58	16.03
46	4.91	6.46	8.06	9.72	11.42	11.85	12.29	12.73	13.17	13.62	14.07	14.52	14.97	15.43	15.89	16.36
45	5.05	6.62	8.25	9.93	11.66	12.10	12.55	12.99	13.45	13.90	14.36	14.82	15.28	15.75	16.22	16.69
44	5.19	6.79	8.44	10.15	11.91	12.36	12.81	13.27	13.73	14.19	14.66	15.13	15.60	16.08	16.56	17.04
43	5.34	6.96	8.64	10.37	12.17	12.63	13.09	13.55	14.02	14.49	14.97	15.45	15.94	16.42	16.91	17.41
42	5.49	7.13	8.84	10.60	12.43	12.90	13.37	13.85	14.33	14.81	15.30	15.79	16.28	16.78	17.28	17.79
41	5.65	7.31	9.05	10.84	12.71	13.19	13.67	14.15	14.64	15.13	15.63	16.13	16.64	17.15	17.66	18.18
40	5.80	7.50	9.26	11.09	12.99	13.48	13.97	14.47	14.97	15.47	15.98	16.50	17.01	17.54	18.06	18.59
39	5.97	7.69	9.48	11.35	13.29	13.79	14.29	14.80	15.31	15.83	16.35	16.87	17.40	17.94	18.48	19.02
35	6.67	8.51	10.44	12.47	14.60	15.15	15.70	16.26	16.83	17.40	17.98	18.56	19.15	19.75	20.35	20.95
30	7.66	9.70	11.86	14.16	16.60	17.23	17.87	18.52	19.18	19.85	20.53	21.21	21.90	22.60	23.31	24.02
25	8.85	11.15	13.63	16.32	19.22	19.98	20.75	21.54	22.34	23.15	23.97	24.80	25.65	26.50	27.37	28.25
20	10.31	12.99	15.97	19.28	22.93	23.90	24.88	25.89	26.92	27.97	29.03	30.11	31.21	32.32	33.45	34.59
15	12.21	15.52	19.35	23.79	28.88	30.24	31.64	33.07	34.53	36.02	37.53	39.06	40.62	42.19	43.77	45.37
10	14.92	19.45	25.20	32.40	40.95	43.24	45.57	47.94	50.34	52.76	55.20	57.65	60.12	62.59	65.07	67.55

Description: This table shows the price to pay for a bond at the yield rate. The yield is to maturity.

Example: The price of a 10.75 %, 16 year bond to yield 8 % to maturity is $ 124.58.

COUPON RATE, %

YIELD	7.00%	7.25%	7.50%	7.75%	8.00%	8.25%	8.50%	8.75%	9.00%	9.25%	9.50%	9.75%	10.00%	10.25%	10.50%	10.75%
0.00	212.00	216.00	220.00	224.00	228.00	232.00	236.00	240.00	244.00	248.00	252.00	256.00	260.00	264.00	268.00	272.00
1.00	188.51	192.20	195.89	199.57	203.26	206.95	210.64	214.33	218.01	221.70	225.39	229.08	232.76	236.45	240.14	243.83
2.00	168.17	171.58	174.99	178.40	181.81	185.22	188.63	192.03	195.44	198.85	202.26	205.67	209.08	212.49	215.90	219.30
3.00	150.53	153.69	156.85	160.01	163.17	166.33	169.48	172.64	175.80	178.96	182.12	185.28	188.43	191.59	194.75	197.91
4.00	135.20	138.14	141.07	144.00	146.94	149.87	152.80	155.74	158.67	161.60	164.54	167.47	170.41	173.34	176.27	179.21
4.25	131.69	134.57	137.45	140.33	143.21	146.10	148.98	151.86	154.74	157.62	160.50	163.38	166.26	169.14	172.02	174.90
4.50	128.30	131.13	133.96	136.79	139.62	142.45	145.28	148.11	150.93	153.76	156.59	159.42	162.25	165.08	167.91	170.74
4.75	125.02	127.80	130.58	133.36	136.14	138.92	141.70	144.48	147.26	150.04	152.82	155.60	158.38	161.16	163.94	166.71
5.00	121.85	124.58	127.31	130.04	132.77	135.50	138.24	140.97	143.70	146.43	149.16	151.89	154.62	157.35	160.09	162.82
5.25	118.79	121.47	124.15	126.84	129.52	132.20	134.89	137.57	140.26	142.94	145.62	148.31	150.99	153.67	156.36	159.04
5.50	115.83	118.46	121.10	123.74	126.38	129.01	131.65	134.29	136.93	139.56	142.20	144.84	147.48	150.11	152.75	155.39
5.75	112.96	115.56	118.15	120.74	123.33	125.93	128.52	131.11	133.70	136.30	138.89	141.48	144.07	146.67	149.26	151.85
6.00	110.19	112.74	115.29	117.84	120.39	122.94	125.49	128.03	130.58	133.13	135.68	138.23	140.78	143.33	145.87	148.42
6.25	107.52	110.02	112.53	115.03	117.54	120.05	122.55	125.06	127.56	130.07	132.58	135.08	137.59	140.09	142.60	145.10
6.50	104.93	107.39	109.86	112.32	114.78	117.25	119.71	122.18	124.64	127.10	129.57	132.03	134.50	136.96	139.42	141.89
6.75	102.42	104.85	107.27	109.69	112.12	114.54	116.96	119.39	121.81	124.23	126.66	129.08	131.50	133.93	136.35	138.77
7.00	100.00	102.38	104.77	107.15	109.53	111.92	114.30	116.69	119.07	121.45	123.84	126.22	128.60	130.99	133.37	135.75
7.25	97.66	100.00	102.34	104.69	107.03	109.38	111.72	114.07	116.41	118.76	121.10	123.45	125.79	128.14	130.48	132.83
7.50	95.39	97.69	100.00	102.31	104.61	106.92	109.23	111.54	113.84	116.15	118.46	120.76	123.07	125.38	127.68	129.99
7.75	93.19	95.46	97.73	100.00	102.27	104.54	106.81	109.08	111.35	113.62	115.89	118.16	120.43	122.70	124.97	127.24
8.00	91.06	93.30	95.53	97.77	100.00	102.23	104.47	106.70	108.94	111.17	113.41	115.64	117.87	120.11	122.34	124.58
8.25	89.00	91.20	93.40	95.60	97.80	100.00	102.20	104.40	106.60	108.80	111.00	113.19	115.39	117.59	119.79	121.99
8.50	87.01	89.18	91.34	93.51	95.67	97.84	100.00	102.16	104.33	106.49	108.66	110.82	112.99	115.15	117.32	119.48
8.75	85.08	87.21	89.34	91.47	93.61	95.74	97.87	100.00	102.13	104.26	106.39	108.53	110.66	112.79	114.92	117.05
9.00	83.21	85.31	87.41	89.51	91.61	93.70	95.80	97.90	100.00	102.10	104.20	106.30	108.39	110.49	112.59	114.69
9.25	81.40	83.47	85.53	87.60	89.67	91.73	93.80	95.87	97.93	100.00	102.07	104.13	106.20	108.27	110.33	112.40
9.50	79.64	81.68	83.72	85.75	87.79	89.82	91.86	93.89	95.93	97.96	100.00	102.04	104.07	106.11	108.14	110.18
9.75	77.94	79.95	81.95	83.96	85.96	87.97	89.97	91.98	93.98	95.99	97.99	100.00	102.01	104.01	106.02	108.02
10.00	76.30	78.27	80.25	82.22	84.20	86.17	88.15	90.12	92.10	94.07	96.05	98.02	100.00	101.98	103.95	105.93
10.25	74.70	76.64	78.59	80.54	82.48	84.43	86.38	88.32	90.27	92.21	94.16	96.11	98.05	100.00	101.95	103.89
10.50	73.15	75.07	76.99	78.90	80.82	82.74	84.66	86.57	88.49	90.41	92.33	94.25	96.16	98.08	100.00	101.92
10.75	71.65	73.54	75.43	77.32	79.21	81.10	82.99	84.88	86.77	88.66	90.55	92.44	94.33	96.22	98.11	100.00
11.00	70.19	72.05	73.92	75.78	77.64	79.51	81.37	83.23	85.10	86.96	88.82	90.68	92.55	94.41	96.27	98.14
11.25	68.78	70.62	72.45	74.29	76.13	77.96	79.80	81.63	83.47	85.31	87.14	88.98	90.82	92.65	94.49	96.33
11.50	67.41	69.22	71.03	72.84	74.65	76.46	78.27	80.08	81.89	83.70	85.52	87.33	89.14	90.95	92.76	94.57
11.75	66.08	67.87	69.65	71.44	73.22	75.01	76.79	78.58	80.36	82.15	83.93	85.72	87.50	89.29	91.07	92.86
12.00	64.79	66.55	68.31	70.07	71.83	73.59	75.35	77.11	78.87	80.63	82.39	84.16	85.92	87.68	89.44	91.20
12.25	63.54	65.27	67.01	68.75	70.48	72.22	73.96	75.69	77.43	79.16	80.90	82.64	84.37	86.11	87.85	89.58
12.50	62.32	64.04	65.75	67.46	69.17	70.89	72.60	74.31	76.02	77.74	79.45	81.16	82.87	84.59	86.30	88.01
12.75	61.14	62.83	64.52	66.21	67.90	69.59	71.28	72.97	74.66	76.35	78.04	79.73	81.42	83.11	84.80	86.48
13.00	60.00	61.66	63.33	65.00	66.67	68.33	70.00	71.67	73.33	75.00	76.67	78.33	80.00	81.67	83.33	85.00
13.25	58.89	60.53	62.18	63.82	65.46	67.11	68.75	70.40	72.04	73.69	75.33	76.98	78.62	80.27	81.91	83.55
13.50	57.81	59.43	61.05	62.67	64.30	65.92	67.54	69.17	70.79	72.41	74.03	75.66	77.28	78.90	80.53	82.15
13.75	56.76	58.36	59.96	61.56	63.16	64.76	66.37	67.97	69.57	71.17	72.77	74.37	75.98	77.58	79.18	80.78
14.00	55.74	57.32	58.90	60.48	62.06	63.64	65.22	66.80	68.38	69.96	71.55	73.13	74.71	76.29	77.87	79.45
14.25	54.75	56.31	57.87	59.43	60.99	62.55	64.11	65.67	67.23	68.79	70.35	71.91	73.47	75.03	76.59	78.15
14.50	53.78	55.32	56.86	58.41	59.95	61.49	63.03	64.57	66.11	67.65	69.19	70.73	72.27	73.81	75.35	76.89
14.75	52.85	54.37	55.89	57.41	58.93	60.45	61.97	63.50	65.02	66.54	68.06	69.58	71.10	72.62	74.14	75.66
15.00	51.94	53.44	54.94	56.44	57.95	59.45	60.95	62.45	63.95	65.46	66.96	68.46	69.96	71.46	72.97	74.47
15.25	51.05	52.54	54.02	55.50	56.99	58.47	59.95	61.44	62.92	64.40	65.89	67.37	68.85	70.34	71.82	73.30
15.50	50.19	51.66	53.12	54.59	56.05	57.52	58.98	60.45	61.91	63.38	64.84	66.31	67.77	69.24	70.70	72.17
15.75	49.36	50.80	52.25	53.70	55.14	56.59	58.04	59.49	60.93	62.38	63.83	65.27	66.72	68.17	69.61	71.06
16.00	48.54	49.97	51.40	52.83	54.26	55.69	57.12	58.55	59.98	61.41	62.84	64.27	65.70	67.12	68.55	69.98
16.25	47.75	49.16	50.57	51.99	53.40	54.81	56.22	57.64	59.05	60.46	61.87	63.28	64.70	66.11	67.52	68.93
16.50	46.98	48.38	49.77	51.17	52.56	53.96	55.35	56.75	58.14	59.54	60.93	62.33	63.72	65.12	66.51	67.91
16.75	46.23	47.61	48.99	50.37	51.74	53.12	54.50	55.88	57.26	58.64	60.02	61.40	62.77	64.15	65.53	66.91
17.00	45.50	46.86	48.22	49.59	50.95	52.31	53.67	55.04	56.40	57.76	59.12	60.49	61.85	63.21	64.57	65.94
17.25	44.79	46.14	47.48	48.83	50.18	51.52	52.87	54.22	55.56	56.91	58.25	59.60	60.95	62.29	63.64	64.99
17.50	44.10	45.43	46.76	48.09	49.42	50.75	52.08	53.41	54.74	56.08	57.41	58.74	60.07	61.40	62.73	64.06
17.75	43.42	44.74	46.05	47.37	48.69	50.00	51.32	52.63	53.95	55.26	56.58	57.90	59.21	60.53	61.84	63.16
18.00	42.77	44.07	45.37	46.67	47.97	49.27	50.57	51.87	53.17	54.47	55.77	57.07	58.38	59.68	60.98	62.28
18.25	42.13	43.41	44.70	45.98	47.27	48.56	49.84	51.13	52.41	53.70	54.99	56.27	57.56	58.85	60.13	61.42
18.50	41.50	42.77	44.05	45.32	46.59	47.86	49.13	50.40	51.68	52.95	54.22	55.49	56.76	58.03	59.31	60.58
18.75	40.90	42.15	43.41	44.67	45.93	47.18	48.44	49.70	50.96	52.21	53.47	54.73	55.99	57.24	58.50	59.76
19.00	40.30	41.55	42.79	44.03	45.28	46.52	47.77	49.01	50.25	51.50	52.74	53.98	55.23	56.47	57.71	58.96
20.00	38.08	39.27	40.46	41.65	42.84	44.03	45.22	46.41	47.60	48.80	49.99	51.18	52.37	53.56	54.75	55.94
25.00	29.66	30.64	31.62	32.59	33.57	34.55	35.52	36.50	37.48	38.45	39.43	40.41	41.38	42.36	43.34	44.32
30.00	24.21	25.03	25.86	26.68	27.50	28.33	29.15	29.98	30.80	31.62	32.45	33.27	34.09	34.92	35.74	36.57

Description: This table shows the yield to maturity of a bond purchased at the price shown in the index.

Example: The yield to maturity of a 10.75 %, 16 year bond at a price of 111.00 is 9.40 %.

COUPON RATE, %

PRICE	7.00%	7.25%	7.50%	7.75%	8.00%	8.25%	8.50%	8.75%	9.00%	9.25%	9.50%	9.75%	10.00%	10.25%	10.50%	10.75%
155	2.73	2.92	3.11	3.29	3.48	3.67	3.86	4.04	4.23	4.41	4.60	4.78	4.97	5.15	5.34	5.52
150	3.03	3.22	3.41	3.60	3.80	3.99	4.18	4.37	4.56	4.75	4.94	5.13	5.31	5.50	5.69	5.88
145	3.34	3.54	3.73	3.93	4.12	4.32	4.51	4.71	4.90	5.10	5.29	5.48	5.68	5.87	6.06	6.25
140	3.67	3.87	4.07	4.27	4.47	4.67	4.87	5.07	5.26	5.46	5.66	5.86	6.06	6.25	6.45	6.65
135	4.01	4.21	4.42	4.62	4.83	5.03	5.24	5.44	5.64	5.85	6.05	6.25	6.45	6.66	6.86	7.06
130	4.37	4.58	4.79	5.00	5.21	5.42	5.63	5.83	6.04	6.25	6.46	6.67	6.87	7.08	7.29	7.49
125	4.75	4.96	5.18	5.39	5.61	5.82	6.04	6.25	6.46	6.68	6.89	7.10	7.32	7.53	7.74	7.95
124	4.82	5.04	5.26	5.47	5.69	5.91	6.12	6.34	6.55	6.77	6.98	7.19	7.41	7.62	7.84	8.05
123	4.90	5.12	5.34	5.56	5.77	5.99	6.21	6.42	6.64	6.85	7.07	7.29	7.50	7.72	7.93	8.15
122	4.98	5.20	5.42	5.64	5.86	6.08	6.29	6.51	6.73	6.95	7.16	7.38	7.60	7.81	8.03	8.24
121	5.06	5.28	5.50	5.72	5.94	6.16	6.38	6.60	6.82	7.04	7.25	7.47	7.69	7.91	8.13	8.34
120	5.14	5.37	5.59	5.81	6.03	6.25	6.47	6.69	6.91	7.13	7.35	7.57	7.79	8.01	8.22	8.44
119	5.23	5.45	5.67	5.89	6.12	6.34	6.56	6.78	7.00	7.22	7.44	7.66	7.88	8.10	8.32	8.54
118	5.31	5.53	5.76	5.98	6.20	6.43	6.65	6.87	7.09	7.32	7.54	7.76	7.98	8.20	8.43	8.65
117	5.39	5.62	5.84	6.07	6.29	6.52	6.74	6.97	7.19	7.41	7.64	7.86	8.08	8.31	8.53	8.75
116	5.48	5.71	5.93	6.16	6.38	6.61	6.83	7.06	7.28	7.51	7.73	7.96	8.18	8.41	8.63	8.86
115	5.57	5.79	6.02	6.25	6.48	6.70	6.93	7.16	7.38	7.61	7.83	8.06	8.29	8.51	8.74	8.96
114	5.65	5.88	6.11	6.34	6.57	6.80	7.02	7.25	7.48	7.71	7.93	8.16	8.39	8.62	8.84	9.07
113	5.74	5.97	6.20	6.43	6.66	6.89	7.12	7.35	7.58	7.81	8.04	8.27	8.49	8.72	8.95	9.18
112	5.83	6.06	6.29	6.53	6.76	6.99	7.22	7.45	7.68	7.91	8.14	8.37	8.60	8.83	9.06	9.29
111	5.92	6.15	6.39	6.62	6.85	7.08	7.32	7.55	7.78	8.01	8.24	8.48	8.71	8.94	9.17	9.40
110	6.01	6.25	6.48	6.72	6.95	7.18	7.42	7.65	7.88	8.12	8.35	8.58	8.82	9.05	9.28	9.52
109	6.11	6.34	6.58	6.81	7.05	7.28	7.52	7.75	7.99	8.22	8.46	8.69	8.93	9.16	9.40	9.63
108	6.20	6.44	6.67	6.91	7.15	7.38	7.62	7.86	8.09	8.33	8.57	8.80	9.04	9.28	9.51	9.75
107	6.29	6.53	6.77	7.01	7.25	7.49	7.73	7.96	8.20	8.44	8.68	8.92	9.15	9.39	9.63	9.87
106	6.39	6.63	6.87	7.11	7.35	7.59	7.83	8.07	8.31	8.55	8.79	9.03	9.27	9.51	9.75	9.99
105	6.49	6.73	6.97	7.21	7.45	7.70	7.94	8.18	8.42	8.66	8.90	9.14	9.39	9.63	9.87	10.11
104	6.59	6.83	7.07	7.32	7.56	7.80	8.05	8.29	8.53	8.77	9.02	9.26	9.50	9.75	9.99	10.23
103	6.69	6.93	7.18	7.42	7.67	7.91	8.16	8.40	8.65	8.89	9.13	9.38	9.62	9.87	10.11	10.36
102	6.79	7.03	7.28	7.53	7.77	8.02	8.27	8.51	8.76	9.01	9.25	9.50	9.75	9.99	10.24	10.48
101	6.89	7.14	7.39	7.64	7.88	8.13	8.38	8.63	8.88	9.12	9.37	9.62	9.87	10.12	10.37	10.61
100	7.00	7.25	7.50	7.75	8.00	8.25	8.50	8.75	9.00	9.25	9.50	9.75	10.00	10.25	10.50	10.75
99	7.10	7.35	7.60	7.86	8.11	8.36	8.61	8.86	9.12	9.37	9.62	9.87	10.12	10.37	10.63	10.88
98	7.21	7.46	7.71	7.97	8.22	8.48	8.73	8.98	9.24	9.49	9.74	10.00	10.25	10.51	10.76	11.01
97	7.32	7.57	7.83	8.08	8.34	8.59	8.85	9.10	9.36	9.62	9.87	10.13	10.38	10.64	10.90	11.15
96	7.43	7.68	7.94	8.20	8.46	8.71	8.97	9.23	9.49	9.74	10.00	10.26	10.52	10.77	11.03	11.29
95	7.54	7.80	8.06	8.32	8.58	8.83	9.09	9.35	9.61	9.87	10.13	10.39	10.65	10.91	11.17	11.43
94	7.65	7.91	8.17	8.44	8.70	8.96	9.22	9.48	9.74	10.00	10.27	10.53	10.79	11.05	11.32	11.58
93	7.77	8.03	8.29	8.56	8.82	9.08	9.35	9.61	9.87	10.14	10.40	10.67	10.93	11.20	11.46	11.72
92	7.88	8.15	8.41	8.68	8.95	9.21	9.48	9.74	10.01	10.27	10.54	10.81	11.07	11.34	11.61	11.87
91	8.00	8.27	8.54	8.80	9.07	9.34	9.61	9.88	10.14	10.41	10.68	10.95	11.22	11.49	11.76	12.03
90	8.12	8.39	8.66	8.93	9.20	9.47	9.74	10.01	10.28	10.55	10.82	11.09	11.37	11.64	11.91	12.18
89	8.25	8.52	8.79	9.06	9.33	9.61	9.88	10.15	10.42	10.70	10.97	11.24	11.52	11.79	12.06	12.34
88	8.37	8.64	8.92	9.19	9.47	9.74	10.02	10.29	10.57	10.84	11.12	11.39	11.67	11.94	12.22	12.50
87	8.50	8.77	9.05	9.33	9.60	9.88	10.16	10.43	10.71	10.99	11.27	11.55	11.82	12.10	12.38	12.66
86	8.62	8.90	9.18	9.46	9.74	10.02	10.30	10.58	10.86	11.14	11.42	11.70	11.98	12.26	12.54	12.83
85	8.76	9.04	9.32	9.60	9.88	10.16	10.44	10.73	11.01	11.29	11.58	11.86	12.14	12.43	12.71	12.99
84	8.89	9.17	9.46	9.74	10.02	10.31	10.59	10.88	11.16	11.45	11.73	12.02	12.31	12.59	12.88	13.17
83	9.02	9.31	9.60	9.88	10.17	10.46	10.74	11.03	11.32	11.61	11.90	12.18	12.47	12.76	13.05	13.34
82	9.16	9.45	9.74	10.03	10.32	10.61	10.90	11.19	11.48	11.77	12.06	12.35	12.64	12.94	13.23	13.52
81	9.30	9.59	9.88	10.18	10.47	10.76	11.05	11.35	11.64	11.93	12.23	12.52	12.82	13.11	13.41	13.70
80	9.44	9.74	10.03	10.33	10.62	10.92	11.21	11.51	11.81	12.10	12.40	12.70	12.99	13.29	13.59	13.89
79	9.59	9.89	10.18	10.48	10.78	11.08	11.37	11.67	11.97	12.27	12.57	12.87	13.18	13.48	13.78	14.08
78	9.74	10.04	10.34	10.64	10.94	11.24	11.54	11.84	12.15	12.45	12.75	13.06	13.36	13.66	13.97	14.28
77	9.89	10.19	10.49	10.80	11.10	11.40	11.71	12.01	12.32	12.63	12.93	13.24	13.55	13.86	14.16	14.47
76	10.04	10.35	10.65	10.96	11.27	11.57	11.88	12.19	12.50	12.81	13.12	13.43	13.74	14.05	14.36	14.68
75	10.20	10.51	10.82	11.12	11.44	11.75	12.06	12.37	12.68	12.99	13.31	13.62	13.94	14.25	14.57	14.88
74	10.36	10.67	10.98	11.29	11.61	11.92	12.24	12.55	12.87	13.18	13.50	13.82	14.14	14.46	14.77	15.09
73	10.52	10.83	11.15	11.47	11.78	12.10	12.42	12.74	13.06	13.38	13.70	14.02	14.34	14.66	14.99	15.31
70	11.03	11.35	11.68	12.01	12.34	12.67	12.99	13.32	13.66	13.99	14.32	14.65	14.99	15.32	15.66	15.99
65	11.95	12.30	12.65	12.99	13.34	13.69	14.04	14.40	14.75	15.10	15.46	15.81	16.17	16.53	16.88	17.24
60	12.99	13.36	13.74	14.11	14.48	14.86	15.23	15.61	15.99	16.37	16.75	17.13	17.51	17.90	18.28	18.67
55	14.18	14.58	14.98	15.38	15.79	16.19	16.60	17.01	17.42	17.83	18.24	18.66	19.07	19.49	19.91	20.33
50	15.55	15.99	16.42	16.86	17.30	17.75	18.19	18.64	19.09	19.54	19.99	20.44	20.90	21.36	21.82	22.28
45	17.17	17.65	18.13	18.62	19.10	19.59	20.09	20.58	21.08	21.58	22.09	22.59	23.10	23.61	24.12	24.63
40	19.13	19.66	20.20	20.75	21.30	21.85	22.41	22.97	23.53	24.09	24.66	25.23	25.81	26.38	26.96	27.55
35	21.57	22.18	22.80	23.43	24.06	24.70	25.34	25.98	26.63	27.28	27.94	28.60	29.26	29.93	30.60	31.27
30	24.74	25.47	26.21	26.95	27.70	28.45	29.21	29.97	30.74	31.52	32.29	33.08	33.86	34.65	35.44	36.24

Description: This table shows the price to pay for a bond at the yield rate. The yield is to maturity.

Example: The price of a 15.00 %, 16 year bond to yield 8 % to maturity is $ 162.56.

YIELD	11.00%	11.25%	11.50%	11.75%	12.00%	12.25%	12.50%	12.75%	13.00%	13.25%	13.50%	13.75%	14.00%	14.25%	14.50%	15.00%
0.00	276.00	280.00	284.00	288.00	292.00	296.00	300.00	304.00	308.00	312.00	316.00	320.00	324.00	328.00	332.00	340.00
1.00	247.52	251.20	254.89	258.58	262.27	265.96	269.64	273.33	277.02	280.71	284.40	288.08	291.77	295.46	299.15	306.52
2.00	222.71	226.12	229.53	232.94	236.35	239.76	243.17	246.57	249.98	253.39	256.80	260.21	263.62	267.03	270.43	277.25
3.00	201.07	204.23	207.39	210.54	213.70	216.86	220.02	223.18	226.34	229.49	232.65	235.81	238.97	242.13	245.29	251.60
4.00	182.14	185.07	188.01	190.94	193.87	196.81	199.74	202.67	205.61	208.54	211.47	214.41	217.34	220.28	223.21	229.08
4.25	177.79	180.67	183.55	186.43	189.31	192.19	195.07	197.95	200.83	203.71	206.60	209.48	212.36	215.24	218.12	223.88
4.50	173.57	176.40	179.23	182.06	184.89	187.72	190.55	193.38	196.21	199.04	201.87	204.70	207.53	210.36	213.19	218.85
4.75	169.49	172.27	175.05	177.83	180.61	183.39	186.17	188.95	191.73	194.51	197.29	200.07	202.85	205.63	208.41	213.97
5.00	165.55	168.28	171.01	173.74	176.47	179.20	181.93	184.67	187.40	190.13	192.86	195.59	198.32	201.05	203.78	209.25
5.25	161.73	164.41	167.09	169.78	172.46	175.14	177.83	180.51	183.20	185.88	188.56	191.25	193.93	196.61	199.30	204.67
5.50	158.03	160.66	163.30	165.94	168.58	171.21	173.85	176.49	179.13	181.76	184.40	187.04	189.68	192.31	194.95	200.23
5.75	154.44	157.04	159.63	162.22	164.81	167.41	170.00	172.59	175.18	177.78	180.37	182.96	185.55	188.15	190.74	195.92
6.00	150.97	153.52	156.07	158.62	161.17	163.71	166.26	168.81	171.36	173.91	176.46	179.01	181.56	184.10	186.65	191.75
6.25	147.61	150.12	152.62	155.13	157.63	160.14	162.64	165.15	167.66	170.16	172.67	175.17	177.68	180.19	182.69	187.70
6.50	144.35	146.82	149.28	151.74	154.21	156.67	159.14	161.60	164.06	166.53	168.99	171.46	173.92	176.39	178.85	183.78
6.75	141.20	143.62	146.04	148.47	150.89	153.31	155.74	158.16	160.58	163.01	165.43	167.85	170.28	172.70	175.12	179.97
7.00	138.14	140.52	142.90	145.29	147.67	150.06	152.44	154.82	157.21	159.59	161.97	164.36	166.74	169.12	171.51	176.28
7.25	135.17	137.52	139.86	142.21	144.55	146.90	149.24	151.59	153.93	156.28	158.62	160.97	163.31	165.66	168.00	172.69
7.50	132.30	134.61	136.91	139.22	141.53	143.83	146.14	148.45	150.76	153.06	155.37	157.68	159.98	162.29	164.60	169.21
7.75	129.51	131.78	134.05	136.32	138.59	140.86	143.13	145.40	147.67	149.94	152.21	154.48	156.75	159.02	161.30	165.84
8.00	126.81	129.04	131.28	133.51	135.75	137.98	140.22	142.45	144.68	146.92	149.15	151.39	153.62	155.85	158.09	162.56
8.25	124.19	126.39	128.59	130.79	132.99	135.19	137.38	139.58	141.78	143.98	146.18	148.38	150.58	152.78	154.98	159.37
8.50	121.65	123.81	125.98	128.14	130.31	132.47	134.64	136.80	138.97	141.13	143.30	145.46	147.63	149.79	151.95	156.28
8.75	119.18	121.31	123.44	125.58	127.71	129.84	131.97	134.10	136.23	138.36	140.49	142.63	144.76	146.89	149.02	153.28
9.00	116.79	118.89	120.99	123.08	125.18	127.28	129.38	131.48	133.58	135.68	137.78	139.87	141.97	144.07	146.17	150.37
9.25	114.47	116.53	118.60	120.67	122.73	124.80	126.87	128.93	131.00	133.07	135.13	137.20	139.27	141.33	143.40	147.53
9.50	112.21	114.25	116.28	118.32	120.36	122.39	124.43	126.46	128.50	130.53	132.57	134.60	136.64	138.67	140.71	144.78
9.75	110.03	112.03	114.04	116.04	118.05	120.05	122.06	124.06	126.07	128.07	130.08	132.08	134.09	136.09	138.10	142.11
10.00	107.90	109.88	111.85	113.83	115.80	117.78	119.75	121.73	123.70	125.68	127.65	129.63	131.61	133.58	135.56	139.51
10.25	105.84	107.79	109.73	111.68	113.62	115.57	117.52	119.46	121.41	123.36	125.30	127.25	129.19	131.14	133.09	136.98
10.50	103.84	105.75	107.67	109.59	111.51	113.43	115.34	117.26	119.18	121.10	123.01	124.93	126.85	128.77	130.69	134.52
10.75	101.89	103.78	105.67	107.56	109.45	111.34	113.23	115.12	117.01	118.90	120.79	122.68	124.57	126.46	128.35	132.13
11.00	100.00	101.86	103.73	105.59	107.45	109.32	111.18	113.04	114.90	116.77	118.63	120.49	122.36	124.22	126.08	129.81
11.25	98.16	100.00	101.84	103.67	105.51	107.35	109.18	111.02	112.86	114.69	116.53	118.37	120.20	122.04	123.87	127.55
11.50	96.38	98.19	100.00	101.81	103.62	105.43	107.24	109.05	110.86	112.67	114.48	116.30	118.11	119.92	121.73	125.35
11.75	94.64	96.43	98.21	100.00	101.79	103.57	105.36	107.14	108.93	110.71	112.50	114.28	116.07	117.85	119.64	123.21
12.00	92.96	94.72	96.48	98.24	100.00	101.76	103.52	105.28	107.04	108.80	110.56	112.32	114.08	115.84	117.61	121.13
12.25	91.32	93.05	94.79	96.53	98.26	100.00	101.74	103.47	105.21	106.95	108.68	110.42	112.15	113.89	115.63	119.10
12.50	89.72	91.44	93.15	94.86	96.57	98.29	100.00	101.71	103.43	105.14	106.85	108.56	110.28	111.99	113.70	117.13
12.75	88.17	89.86	91.55	93.24	94.93	96.62	98.31	100.00	101.69	103.38	105.07	106.76	108.45	110.14	111.83	115.20
13.00	86.67	88.33	90.00	91.67	93.33	95.00	96.67	98.33	100.00	101.67	103.33	105.00	106.67	108.33	110.00	113.33
13.25	85.20	86.84	88.49	90.13	91.78	93.42	95.07	96.71	98.36	100.00	101.64	103.29	104.93	106.58	108.22	111.51
13.50	83.77	85.39	87.02	88.64	90.26	91.89	93.51	95.13	96.75	98.38	100.00	101.62	103.25	104.87	106.49	109.74
13.75	82.38	83.98	85.59	87.19	88.79	90.39	91.99	93.59	95.20	96.80	98.40	100.00	101.60	103.20	104.80	108.01
14.00	81.03	82.61	84.19	85.77	87.35	88.93	90.52	92.10	93.68	95.26	96.84	98.42	100.00	101.58	103.16	106.32
14.25	79.71	81.27	82.83	84.40	85.96	87.52	89.08	90.64	92.20	93.76	95.32	96.88	98.44	100.00	101.56	104.68
14.50	78.43	79.97	81.51	83.05	84.59	86.14	87.68	89.22	90.76	92.30	93.84	95.38	96.92	98.46	100.00	103.08
14.75	77.18	78.71	80.23	81.75	83.27	84.79	86.31	87.83	89.35	90.87	92.39	93.92	95.44	96.96	98.48	101.52
15.00	75.97	77.47	78.97	80.47	81.98	83.48	84.98	86.48	87.98	89.49	90.99	92.49	93.99	95.49	97.00	100.00
15.25	74.79	76.27	77.75	79.23	80.72	82.20	83.68	85.17	86.65	88.13	89.62	91.10	92.58	94.07	95.55	98.52
15.50	73.63	75.10	76.56	78.03	79.49	80.96	82.42	83.89	85.35	86.82	88.28	89.75	91.21	92.68	94.14	97.07
15.75	72.51	73.95	75.40	76.85	78.30	79.74	81.19	82.64	84.08	85.53	86.98	88.42	89.87	91.32	92.77	95.66
16.00	71.41	72.84	74.27	75.70	77.13	78.56	79.99	81.42	82.85	84.28	85.71	87.14	88.57	89.99	91.42	94.28
16.25	70.34	71.76	73.17	74.58	75.99	77.41	78.82	80.23	81.64	83.05	84.47	85.88	87.29	88.70	90.11	92.94
16.50	69.30	70.70	72.09	73.49	74.89	76.28	77.68	79.07	80.47	81.86	83.26	84.65	86.05	87.44	88.84	91.63
16.75	68.29	69.67	71.05	72.43	73.80	75.18	76.56	77.94	79.32	80.70	82.08	83.46	84.83	86.21	87.59	90.35
17.00	67.30	68.66	70.02	71.39	72.75	74.11	75.47	76.84	78.20	79.56	80.92	82.29	83.65	85.01	86.37	89.10
17.25	66.33	67.68	69.03	70.37	71.72	73.07	74.41	75.76	77.11	78.45	79.80	81.15	82.49	83.84	85.19	87.88
17.50	65.39	66.72	68.06	69.39	70.72	72.05	73.38	74.71	76.04	77.37	78.70	80.03	81.37	82.70	84.03	86.69
17.75	64.47	65.79	67.11	68.42	69.74	71.05	72.37	73.68	75.00	76.32	77.63	78.95	80.26	81.58	82.90	85.53
18.00	63.58	64.88	66.18	67.48	68.78	70.08	71.38	72.68	73.98	75.29	76.59	77.89	79.19	80.49	81.79	84.39
18.25	62.70	63.99	65.28	66.56	67.85	69.13	70.42	71.71	72.99	74.28	75.56	76.85	78.14	79.42	80.71	83.28
18.50	61.85	63.12	64.39	65.66	66.94	68.21	69.48	70.75	72.02	73.29	74.57	75.84	77.11	78.38	79.65	82.20
18.75	61.02	62.27	63.53	64.79	66.05	67.30	68.56	69.82	71.08	72.33	73.59	74.85	76.11	77.36	78.62	81.14
19.00	60.20	61.45	62.69	63.93	65.18	66.42	67.66	68.91	70.15	71.40	72.64	73.88	75.13	76.37	77.61	80.10
20.00	57.13	58.32	59.51	60.70	61.89	63.09	64.28	65.47	66.66	67.85	69.04	70.23	71.42	72.61	73.80	76.18
25.00	45.29	46.27	47.25	48.22	49.20	50.18	51.15	52.13	53.11	54.08	55.06	56.04	57.02	57.99	58.97	60.92
30.00	37.39	38.21	39.04	39.86	40.69	41.51	42.33	43.16	43.98	44.80	45.63	46.45	47.28	48.10	48.92	50.57

Description: This table shows the yield to maturity of a bond purchased at the price shown in the index.

Example: The yield to maturity of a 15.00 %, 16 year bond at a price of 125.00 is 11.54 %.

PRICE	11.00%	11.25%	11.50%	11.75%	12.00%	12.25%	12.50%	12.75%	13.00%	13.25%	13.50%	13.75%	14.00%	14.25%	14.50%	15.00%
250	.90	1.04	1.18	1.31	1.45	1.59	1.72	1.86	1.99	2.13	2.26	2.40	2.53	2.66	2.80	3.06
240	1.28	1.42	1.57	1.71	1.85	1.99	2.12	2.26	2.40	2.54	2.68	2.81	2.95	3.09	3.22	3.49
230	1.69	1.83	1.98	2.12	2.26	2.40	2.55	2.69	2.83	2.97	3.11	3.25	3.39	3.53	3.67	3.95
220	2.11	2.26	2.41	2.56	2.70	2.85	3.00	3.14	3.29	3.43	3.58	3.72	3.86	4.01	4.15	4.44
210	2.57	2.72	2.87	3.02	3.17	3.32	3.47	3.62	3.77	3.92	4.07	4.22	4.37	4.51	4.66	4.95
200	3.05	3.20	3.36	3.52	3.67	3.83	3.98	4.14	4.29	4.44	4.60	4.75	4.90	5.05	5.21	5.51
195	3.30	3.46	3.62	3.78	3.93	4.09	4.25	4.41	4.56	4.72	4.87	5.03	5.18	5.34	5.49	5.80
190	3.56	3.72	3.89	4.05	4.21	4.37	4.53	4.69	4.84	5.00	5.16	5.32	5.48	5.63	5.79	6.10
185	3.84	4.00	4.16	4.33	4.49	4.65	4.81	4.98	5.14	5.30	5.46	5.62	5.78	5.94	6.10	6.42
180	4.12	4.28	4.45	4.62	4.78	4.95	5.11	5.28	5.44	5.60	5.77	5.93	6.09	6.26	6.42	6.74
175	4.41	4.58	4.75	4.92	5.09	5.25	5.42	5.59	5.76	5.92	6.09	6.26	6.42	6.59	6.75	7.08
170	4.71	4.89	5.06	5.23	5.40	5.57	5.74	5.92	6.09	6.26	6.43	6.60	6.76	6.93	7.10	7.44
165	5.03	5.21	5.38	5.56	5.73	5.91	6.08	6.26	6.43	6.60	6.78	6.95	7.12	7.29	7.47	7.81
160	5.36	5.54	5.72	5.90	6.08	6.25	6.43	6.61	6.79	6.96	7.14	7.32	7.49	7.67	7.85	8.20
155	5.71	5.89	6.07	6.25	6.44	6.62	6.80	6.98	7.16	7.34	7.52	7.70	7.88	8.06	8.24	8.60
150	6.07	6.25	6.44	6.63	6.81	7.00	7.19	7.37	7.56	7.74	7.93	8.11	8.29	8.48	8.66	9.03
145	6.44	6.64	6.83	7.02	7.21	7.40	7.59	7.78	7.97	8.16	8.35	8.54	8.72	8.91	9.10	9.47
140	6.84	7.04	7.23	7.43	7.62	7.82	8.01	8.21	8.40	8.60	8.79	8.98	9.18	9.37	9.56	9.95
135	7.26	7.46	7.66	7.86	8.06	8.26	8.46	8.66	8.86	9.06	9.26	9.46	9.65	9.85	10.05	10.45
130	7.70	7.91	8.11	8.32	8.52	8.73	8.93	9.14	9.34	9.55	9.75	9.96	10.16	10.36	10.57	10.97
125	8.17	8.38	8.59	8.80	9.01	9.22	9.44	9.65	9.86	10.07	10.28	10.49	10.70	10.91	11.12	11.54
120	8.66	8.88	9.10	9.32	9.53	9.75	9.97	10.19	10.40	10.62	10.84	11.05	11.27	11.49	11.70	12.13
115	9.19	9.41	9.64	9.86	10.09	10.31	10.54	10.76	10.98	11.21	11.43	11.66	11.88	12.10	12.33	12.77
113	9.41	9.63	9.86	10.09	10.32	10.55	10.77	11.00	11.23	11.45	11.68	11.91	12.13	12.36	12.59	13.04
112	9.52	9.75	9.98	10.21	10.44	10.67	10.89	11.12	11.35	11.58	11.81	12.04	12.27	12.49	12.72	13.18
111	9.63	9.86	10.09	10.33	10.56	10.79	11.02	11.25	11.48	11.71	11.94	12.17	12.40	12.63	12.86	13.32
110	9.75	9.98	10.21	10.45	10.68	10.91	11.14	11.37	11.61	11.84	12.07	12.30	12.53	12.76	13.00	13.46
109	9.86	10.10	10.33	10.57	10.80	11.03	11.27	11.50	11.74	11.97	12.20	12.44	12.67	12.90	13.13	13.60
108	9.98	10.22	10.45	10.69	10.93	11.16	11.40	11.63	11.87	12.10	12.34	12.57	12.81	13.04	13.28	13.75
107	10.10	10.34	10.58	10.82	11.05	11.29	11.53	11.76	12.00	12.24	12.47	12.71	12.95	13.18	13.42	13.89
106	10.23	10.46	10.70	10.94	11.18	11.42	11.66	11.90	12.14	12.37	12.61	12.85	13.09	13.33	13.57	14.04
105	10.35	10.59	10.83	11.07	11.31	11.55	11.79	12.03	12.27	12.51	12.75	13.00	13.24	13.48	13.72	14.20
104	10.47	10.72	10.96	11.20	11.44	11.69	11.93	12.17	12.41	12.66	12.90	13.14	13.38	13.62	13.87	14.35
103	10.60	10.85	11.09	11.33	11.58	11.82	12.07	12.31	12.56	12.80	13.04	13.29	13.53	13.78	14.02	14.51
102	10.73	10.98	11.22	11.47	11.72	11.96	12.21	12.45	12.70	12.95	13.19	13.44	13.68	13.93	14.18	14.67
101	10.86	11.11	11.36	11.61	11.85	12.10	12.35	12.60	12.85	13.09	13.34	13.59	13.84	14.09	14.33	14.83
100	11.00	11.25	11.50	11.75	12.00	12.25	12.50	12.75	13.00	13.25	13.50	13.75	14.00	14.25	14.50	15.00
99	11.13	11.38	11.63	11.89	12.14	12.39	12.64	12.89	13.15	13.40	13.65	13.90	14.15	14.41	14.66	15.16
98	11.27	11.52	11.78	12.03	12.28	12.54	12.79	13.05	13.30	13.55	13.81	14.06	14.32	14.57	14.83	15.33
97	11.41	11.66	11.92	12.18	12.43	12.69	12.94	13.20	13.46	13.71	13.97	14.23	14.48	14.74	14.99	15.51
96	11.55	11.81	12.07	12.32	12.58	12.84	13.10	13.36	13.62	13.87	14.13	14.39	14.65	14.91	15.17	15.68
95	11.69	11.95	12.21	12.47	12.73	12.99	13.26	13.52	13.78	14.04	14.30	14.56	14.82	15.08	15.34	15.86
94	11.84	12.10	12.36	12.63	12.89	13.15	13.42	13.68	13.94	14.20	14.47	14.73	14.99	15.26	15.52	16.05
93	11.99	12.25	12.52	12.78	13.05	13.31	13.58	13.84	14.11	14.37	14.64	14.90	15.17	15.44	15.70	16.23
92	12.14	12.41	12.67	12.94	13.21	13.48	13.74	14.01	14.28	14.55	14.81	15.08	15.35	15.62	15.89	16.42
91	12.29	12.56	12.83	13.10	13.37	13.64	13.91	14.18	14.45	14.72	14.99	15.26	15.53	15.80	16.08	16.62
90	12.45	12.72	12.99	13.27	13.54	13.81	14.08	14.36	14.63	14.90	15.17	15.45	15.72	15.99	16.27	16.81
89	12.61	12.89	13.16	13.43	13.71	13.98	14.26	14.53	14.81	15.08	15.36	15.64	15.91	16.19	16.46	17.02
88	12.77	13.05	13.33	13.60	13.88	14.16	14.44	14.71	14.99	15.27	15.55	15.83	16.11	16.38	16.66	17.22
87	12.94	13.22	13.50	13.78	14.06	14.34	14.62	14.90	15.18	15.46	15.74	16.02	16.30	16.58	16.87	17.43
86	13.11	13.39	13.67	13.95	14.24	14.52	14.80	15.09	15.37	15.65	15.94	16.22	16.50	16.79	17.07	17.64
85	13.28	13.56	13.85	14.13	14.42	14.71	14.99	15.28	15.56	15.85	16.14	16.42	16.71	17.00	17.28	17.86
84	13.45	13.74	14.03	14.32	14.61	14.89	15.18	15.47	15.76	16.05	16.34	16.63	16.92	17.21	17.50	18.08
83	13.63	13.92	14.21	14.51	14.80	15.09	15.38	15.67	15.96	16.26	16.55	16.84	17.13	17.43	17.72	18.31
82	13.82	14.11	14.40	14.70	14.99	15.29	15.58	15.87	16.17	16.47	16.76	17.06	17.35	17.65	17.95	18.54
81	14.00	14.30	14.59	14.89	15.19	15.49	15.78	16.08	16.38	16.68	16.98	17.28	17.58	17.88	18.18	18.78
80	14.19	14.49	14.79	15.09	15.39	15.69	15.99	16.29	16.60	16.90	17.20	17.50	17.81	18.11	18.41	19.02
79	14.38	14.69	14.99	15.29	15.60	15.90	16.21	16.51	16.82	17.12	17.43	17.73	18.04	18.35	18.65	19.27
78	14.58	14.89	15.19	15.50	15.81	16.12	16.42	16.73	17.04	17.35	17.66	17.97	18.28	18.59	18.90	19.52
77	14.78	15.09	15.40	15.71	16.02	16.33	16.65	16.96	17.27	17.58	17.90	18.21	18.52	18.84	19.15	19.78
76	14.99	15.30	15.62	15.93	16.24	16.56	16.87	17.19	17.50	17.82	18.14	18.45	18.77	19.09	19.41	20.04
75	15.20	15.52	15.83	16.15	16.47	16.79	17.11	17.43	17.75	18.07	18.39	18.71	19.03	19.35	19.67	20.32
74	15.41	15.73	16.06	16.38	16.70	17.02	17.34	17.67	17.99	18.32	18.64	18.96	19.29	19.62	19.94	20.59
73	15.63	15.96	16.28	16.61	16.94	17.26	17.59	17.92	18.24	18.57	18.90	19.23	19.56	19.89	20.22	20.88
70	16.33	16.66	17.00	17.34	17.68	18.02	18.36	18.70	19.04	19.38	19.72	20.06	20.40	20.75	21.09	21.78
65	17.60	17.96	18.32	18.68	19.05	19.41	19.77	20.14	20.50	20.87	21.24	21.60	21.97	22.34	22.71	23.45
60	19.06	19.45	19.84	20.23	20.62	21.01	21.40	21.80	22.19	22.59	22.98	23.38	23.78	24.17	24.57	25.37
55	20.75	21.17	21.59	22.02	22.44	22.87	23.30	23.73	24.16	24.59	25.02	25.46	25.89	26.32	26.76	27.63

Description: This table shows the price to pay for a bond at the yield rate. The yield is to maturity.

Example: The price of a 6.75 %, 17 year bond to yield 8 % to maturity is $ 88.49.

COUPON RATE, %

YIELD	0.00%	1.00%	2.00%	3.00%	4.00%	4.25%	4.50%	4.75%	5.00%	5.25%	5.50%	5.75%	6.00%	6.25%	6.50%	6.75%
0.00	100.00	117.00	134.00	151.00	168.00	172.25	176.50	180.75	185.00	189.25	193.50	197.75	202.00	206.25	210.50	214.75
1.00	84.40	100.00	115.60	131.20	146.79	150.69	154.59	158.49	162.39	166.29	170.19	174.09	177.99	181.89	185.79	189.69
2.00	71.30	85.65	100.00	114.35	128.70	132.29	135.88	139.47	143.05	146.64	150.23	153.82	157.41	160.99	164.58	168.17
3.00	60.28	73.52	86.76	100.00	113.24	116.55	119.86	123.17	126.48	129.79	133.10	136.41	139.72	143.03	146.34	149.65
4.00	51.00	63.25	75.50	87.75	100.00	103.06	106.12	109.19	112.25	115.31	118.37	121.44	124.50	127.56	130.62	133.69
4.25	48.92	60.94	72.96	84.98	97.00	100.00	103.00	106.01	109.01	112.02	115.02	118.03	121.03	124.04	127.04	130.05
4.50	46.93	58.72	70.52	82.31	94.10	97.05	100.00	102.95	105.90	108.85	111.79	114.74	117.69	120.64	123.59	126.54
4.75	45.02	56.59	68.17	79.74	91.32	94.21	97.11	100.00	102.89	105.79	108.68	111.57	114.47	117.36	120.26	123.15
5.00	43.19	54.55	65.91	77.28	88.64	91.48	94.32	97.16	100.00	102.84	105.68	108.52	111.36	114.20	117.04	119.88
5.25	41.44	52.59	63.75	74.90	86.06	88.85	91.63	94.42	97.21	100.00	102.79	105.58	108.37	111.15	113.94	116.73
5.50	39.76	50.71	61.66	72.62	83.57	86.31	89.05	91.79	94.52	97.26	100.00	102.74	105.48	108.21	110.95	113.69
5.75	38.15	48.90	59.66	70.42	81.18	83.86	86.55	89.24	91.93	94.62	97.31	100.00	102.69	105.38	108.07	110.76
6.00	36.60	47.17	57.74	68.30	78.87	81.51	84.15	86.79	89.43	92.08	94.72	97.36	100.00	102.64	105.28	107.92
6.25	35.13	45.51	55.89	66.27	76.65	79.24	81.84	84.43	87.03	89.62	92.22	94.81	97.41	100.00	102.59	105.19
6.50	33.71	43.91	54.11	64.30	74.50	77.05	79.60	82.15	84.70	87.25	89.80	92.35	94.90	97.45	100.00	102.55
6.75	32.35	42.37	52.39	62.42	72.44	74.94	77.45	79.96	82.46	84.97	87.47	89.98	92.48	94.99	97.49	100.00
7.00	31.05	40.90	50.75	60.60	70.45	72.91	75.37	77.84	80.30	82.76	85.22	87.69	90.15	92.61	95.07	97.54
7.25	29.80	39.48	49.16	58.85	68.53	70.95	73.37	75.79	78.21	80.63	83.05	85.48	87.90	90.32	92.74	95.16
7.50	28.60	38.12	47.64	57.16	66.68	69.06	71.44	73.82	76.20	78.58	80.96	83.34	85.72	88.10	90.48	92.86
7.75	27.46	36.82	46.18	55.54	64.90	67.24	69.58	71.92	74.26	76.60	78.94	81.28	83.62	85.96	88.30	90.64
8.00	26.36	35.56	44.77	53.97	63.18	65.48	67.78	70.08	72.38	74.68	76.99	79.29	81.59	83.89	86.19	88.49
8.25	25.30	34.36	43.41	52.46	61.52	63.78	66.05	68.31	70.57	72.84	75.10	77.36	79.63	81.89	84.15	86.42
8.50	24.29	33.20	42.10	51.01	59.92	62.14	64.37	66.60	68.82	71.05	73.28	75.51	77.73	79.96	82.19	84.41
8.75	23.32	32.08	40.85	49.61	58.37	60.56	62.76	64.95	67.14	69.33	71.52	73.71	75.90	78.09	80.28	82.47
9.00	22.39	31.01	39.64	48.26	56.88	59.04	61.19	63.35	65.51	67.66	69.82	71.97	74.13	76.29	78.44	80.60
9.25	21.50	29.98	38.47	46.96	55.44	57.57	59.69	61.81	63.93	66.05	68.17	70.30	72.42	74.54	76.66	78.78
9.50	20.64	29.00	37.35	45.70	54.06	56.14	58.23	60.32	62.41	64.50	66.59	68.67	70.76	72.85	74.94	77.03
9.75	19.82	28.05	36.27	44.49	52.72	54.77	56.83	58.88	60.94	62.99	65.05	67.11	69.16	71.22	73.27	75.33
10.00	19.04	27.13	35.23	43.32	51.42	53.45	55.47	57.49	59.52	61.54	63.57	65.59	67.61	69.64	71.66	73.69
10.25	18.28	26.25	34.23	42.20	50.17	52.16	54.16	56.15	58.14	60.14	62.13	64.12	66.12	68.11	70.10	72.10
10.50	17.56	25.41	33.26	41.11	48.96	50.93	52.89	54.85	56.82	58.78	60.74	62.70	64.67	66.63	68.59	70.56
10.75	16.86	24.60	32.33	40.06	47.80	49.73	51.66	53.60	55.53	57.46	59.40	61.33	63.26	65.20	67.13	69.07
11.00	16.20	23.81	31.43	39.05	46.67	48.58	50.48	52.38	54.29	56.19	58.10	60.00	61.91	63.81	65.72	67.62
11.25	15.56	23.06	30.57	38.08	45.58	47.46	49.33	51.21	53.09	54.96	56.84	58.72	60.59	62.47	64.35	66.22
11.50	14.94	22.34	29.74	37.13	44.53	46.38	48.23	50.08	51.92	53.77	55.62	57.47	59.32	61.17	63.02	64.87
11.75	14.36	21.64	28.93	36.22	43.51	45.33	47.16	48.98	50.80	52.62	54.44	56.27	58.09	59.91	61.73	63.56
12.00	13.79	20.98	28.16	35.34	42.53	44.32	46.12	47.92	49.71	51.51	53.30	55.10	56.90	58.69	60.49	62.28
12.25	13.25	20.33	27.41	34.49	41.58	43.35	45.12	46.89	48.66	50.43	52.20	53.97	55.74	57.51	59.28	61.05
12.50	12.73	19.71	26.69	33.67	40.66	42.40	44.15	45.89	47.64	49.38	51.13	52.87	54.62	56.36	58.11	59.86
12.75	12.23	19.11	26.00	32.88	39.77	41.49	43.21	44.93	46.65	48.37	50.09	51.81	53.53	55.25	56.98	58.70
13.00	11.75	18.54	25.33	32.12	38.91	40.60	42.30	44.00	45.69	47.39	49.09	50.78	52.48	54.18	55.88	57.57
13.25	11.29	17.99	24.68	31.38	38.07	39.75	41.42	43.09	44.77	46.44	48.11	49.79	51.46	53.14	54.81	56.48
13.50	10.85	17.46	24.06	30.66	37.27	38.92	40.57	42.22	43.87	45.52	47.17	48.82	50.47	52.12	53.77	55.43
13.75	10.43	16.94	23.46	29.97	36.49	38.11	39.74	41.37	43.00	44.63	46.26	47.89	49.51	51.14	52.77	54.40
14.00	10.02	16.45	22.88	29.30	35.73	37.34	38.94	40.55	42.16	43.76	45.37	46.98	48.58	50.19	51.80	53.40
14.25	9.63	15.97	22.32	28.66	35.00	36.58	38.17	39.75	41.34	42.93	44.51	46.10	47.68	49.27	50.85	52.44
14.50	9.26	15.52	21.77	28.03	34.29	35.85	37.42	38.98	40.55	42.11	43.68	45.24	46.81	48.37	49.94	51.50
14.75	8.90	15.07	21.25	27.43	33.60	35.15	36.69	38.24	39.78	41.32	42.87	44.41	45.96	47.50	49.04	50.59
15.00	8.55	14.65	20.75	26.84	32.94	34.46	35.99	37.51	39.04	40.56	42.08	43.61	45.13	46.66	48.18	49.70
15.25	8.22	14.24	20.26	26.28	32.29	33.80	35.30	36.81	38.31	39.82	41.32	42.83	44.33	45.84	47.34	48.84
15.50	7.90	13.85	19.79	25.73	31.67	33.16	34.64	36.13	37.61	39.10	40.58	42.07	43.55	45.04	46.52	48.01
15.75	7.60	13.46	19.33	25.20	31.07	32.53	34.00	35.47	36.93	38.40	39.87	41.33	42.80	44.27	45.73	47.20
16.00	7.30	13.10	18.89	24.68	30.48	31.93	33.38	34.82	36.27	37.72	39.17	40.62	42.07	43.51	44.96	46.41
16.25	7.02	12.74	18.47	24.19	29.91	31.34	32.77	34.20	35.63	37.06	38.49	39.92	41.35	42.78	44.21	45.64
16.50	6.75	12.40	18.06	23.71	29.36	30.77	32.18	33.60	35.01	36.42	37.83	39.25	40.66	42.07	43.49	44.90
16.75	6.49	12.08	17.66	23.24	28.82	30.22	31.61	33.01	34.41	35.80	37.20	38.59	39.99	41.38	42.78	44.17
17.00	6.24	11.76	17.27	22.79	28.30	29.68	31.06	32.44	33.82	35.20	36.58	37.95	39.33	40.71	42.09	43.47
17.25	6.00	11.45	16.90	22.35	27.80	29.16	30.52	31.89	33.25	34.61	35.97	37.34	38.70	40.06	41.42	42.78
17.50	5.77	11.16	16.54	21.93	27.31	28.66	30.00	31.35	32.70	34.04	35.39	36.73	38.08	39.43	40.77	42.12
17.75	5.55	10.87	16.19	21.51	26.84	28.17	29.50	30.83	32.16	33.49	34.82	36.15	37.48	38.81	40.14	41.47
18.00	5.34	10.60	15.86	21.12	26.38	27.69	29.00	30.32	31.63	32.95	34.26	35.58	36.89	38.21	39.52	40.84
18.25	5.14	10.33	15.53	20.73	25.93	27.23	28.53	29.83	31.13	32.43	33.72	35.02	36.32	37.62	38.92	40.22
18.50	4.94	10.08	15.22	20.35	25.49	26.78	28.06	29.35	30.63	31.92	33.20	34.49	35.77	37.05	38.34	39.62
18.75	4.75	9.83	14.91	19.99	25.07	26.34	27.61	28.88	30.15	31.42	32.69	33.96	35.23	36.50	37.77	39.04
19.00	4.57	9.59	14.62	19.64	24.66	25.92	27.17	28.43	29.68	30.94	32.19	33.45	34.71	35.96	37.22	38.47
20.00	3.91	8.72	13.52	18.33	23.13	24.33	25.53	26.73	27.94	29.14	30.34	31.54	32.74	33.94	35.14	36.34
25.00	1.82	5.75	9.68	13.60	17.53	18.51	19.49	20.48	21.46	22.44	23.42	24.40	25.39	26.37	27.35	28.33
30.00	.86	4.17	7.47	10.78	14.08	14.91	15.73	16.56	17.39	18.21	19.04	19.86	20.69	21.52	22.34	23.17

Description: This table shows the yield to maturity of a bond purchased at the price shown in the index.

Example: The yield to maturity of a 6.75 %, 17 year bond at a price of 80.00 is 9.08 %.

COUPON RATE, %

PRICE	0.00%	1.00%	2.00%	3.00%	4.00%	4.25%	4.50%	4.75%	5.00%	5.25%	5.50%	5.75%	6.00%	6.25%	6.50%	6.75%
100	0.00	1.00	2.00	3.00	4.00	4.25	4.50	4.75	5.00	5.25	5.50	5.75	6.00	6.25	6.50	6.75
99	.05	1.06	2.07	3.07	4.08	4.33	4.58	4.83	5.08	5.34	5.59	5.84	6.09	6.34	6.59	6.85
98	.11	1.12	2.14	3.15	4.16	4.41	4.67	4.92	5.17	5.43	5.68	5.93	6.19	6.44	6.69	6.95
97	.17	1.19	2.21	3.23	4.24	4.50	4.75	5.01	5.26	5.52	5.77	6.03	6.28	6.54	6.80	7.05
96	.24	1.26	2.28	3.30	4.33	4.59	4.84	5.10	5.36	5.61	5.87	6.13	6.38	6.64	6.90	7.16
95	.30	1.32	2.35	3.38	4.42	4.67	4.93	5.19	5.45	5.71	5.97	6.23	6.48	6.74	7.00	7.26
94	.36	1.39	2.43	3.47	4.50	4.76	5.02	5.28	5.54	5.81	6.07	6.33	6.59	6.85	7.11	7.37
93	.42	1.46	2.50	3.55	4.59	4.85	5.12	5.38	5.64	5.90	6.17	6.43	6.69	6.95	7.22	7.48
92	.49	1.53	2.58	3.63	4.68	4.95	5.21	5.47	5.74	6.00	6.27	6.53	6.80	7.06	7.33	7.59
91	.55	1.60	2.66	3.71	4.77	5.04	5.31	5.57	5.84	6.10	6.37	6.64	6.90	7.17	7.44	7.70
90	.62	1.67	2.73	3.80	4.87	5.13	5.40	5.67	5.94	6.21	6.47	6.74	7.01	7.28	7.55	7.82
89	.68	1.75	2.81	3.89	4.96	5.23	5.50	5.77	6.04	6.31	6.58	6.85	7.12	7.39	7.66	7.94
88	.75	1.82	2.89	3.97	5.06	5.33	5.60	5.87	6.14	6.42	6.69	6.96	7.23	7.51	7.78	8.05
87	.82	1.89	2.98	4.06	5.15	5.43	5.70	5.97	6.25	6.52	6.80	7.07	7.35	7.62	7.90	8.17
86	.88	1.97	3.06	4.15	5.25	5.53	5.80	6.08	6.35	6.63	6.91	7.18	7.46	7.74	8.02	8.30
85	.95	2.04	3.14	4.24	5.35	5.63	5.91	6.18	6.46	6.74	7.02	7.30	7.58	7.86	8.14	8.42
84	1.02	2.12	3.23	4.34	5.45	5.73	6.01	6.29	6.57	6.85	7.14	7.42	7.70	7.98	8.26	8.55
83	1.09	2.20	3.31	4.43	5.55	5.84	6.12	6.40	6.68	6.97	7.25	7.54	7.82	8.11	8.39	8.68
82	1.17	2.28	3.40	4.52	5.66	5.94	6.23	6.51	6.80	7.08	7.37	7.66	7.94	8.23	8.52	8.81
81	1.24	2.36	3.49	4.62	5.76	6.05	6.34	6.63	6.91	7.20	7.49	7.78	8.07	8.36	8.65	8.94
80	1.31	2.44	3.58	4.72	5.87	6.16	6.45	6.74	7.03	7.32	7.61	7.90	8.20	8.49	8.78	9.08
79	1.39	2.52	3.67	4.82	5.98	6.27	6.56	6.86	7.15	7.44	7.74	8.03	8.33	8.62	8.92	9.21
78	1.46	2.61	3.76	4.92	6.09	6.39	6.68	6.98	7.27	7.57	7.86	8.16	8.46	8.76	9.06	9.36
77	1.54	2.69	3.85	5.02	6.20	6.50	6.80	7.10	7.39	7.69	7.99	8.29	8.59	8.90	9.20	9.50
76	1.62	2.78	3.95	5.13	6.32	6.62	6.92	7.22	7.52	7.82	8.12	8.43	8.73	9.04	9.34	9.65
75	1.69	2.86	4.04	5.23	6.44	6.74	7.04	7.34	7.65	7.95	8.26	8.56	8.87	9.18	9.49	9.79
74	1.77	2.95	4.14	5.34	6.56	6.86	7.17	7.47	7.78	8.09	8.39	8.70	9.01	9.32	9.64	9.95
73	1.85	3.04	4.24	5.45	6.68	6.98	7.29	7.60	7.91	8.22	8.53	8.85	9.16	9.47	9.79	10.10
72	1.94	3.13	4.34	5.56	6.80	7.11	7.42	7.73	8.05	8.36	8.68	8.99	9.31	9.62	9.94	10.26
71	2.02	3.23	4.44	5.68	6.92	7.24	7.55	7.87	8.19	8.50	8.82	9.14	9.46	9.78	10.10	10.42
70	2.10	3.32	4.55	5.79	7.05	7.37	7.69	8.01	8.33	8.65	8.97	9.29	9.61	9.94	10.26	10.59
69	2.19	3.41	4.66	5.91	7.18	7.50	7.82	8.15	8.47	8.79	9.12	9.44	9.77	10.10	10.43	10.76
68	2.28	3.51	4.76	6.03	7.32	7.64	7.96	8.29	8.62	8.94	9.27	9.60	9.93	10.26	10.60	10.93
67	2.36	3.61	4.87	6.15	7.45	7.78	8.11	8.44	8.77	9.10	9.43	9.76	10.10	10.43	10.77	11.11
66	2.45	3.71	4.99	6.28	7.59	7.92	8.25	8.58	8.92	9.25	9.59	9.93	10.26	10.60	10.94	11.29
65	2.55	3.81	5.10	6.41	7.73	8.06	8.40	8.74	9.07	9.41	9.75	10.09	10.44	10.78	11.12	11.47
64	2.64	3.92	5.22	6.53	7.87	8.21	8.55	8.89	9.23	9.58	9.92	10.27	10.61	10.96	11.31	11.66
63	2.73	4.02	5.33	6.67	8.02	8.36	8.71	9.05	9.40	9.74	10.09	10.44	10.79	11.15	11.50	11.85
62	2.83	4.13	5.45	6.80	8.17	8.52	8.86	9.21	9.56	9.92	10.27	10.62	10.98	11.33	11.69	12.05
61	2.92	4.24	5.58	6.94	8.33	8.68	9.03	9.38	9.73	10.09	10.45	10.81	11.17	11.53	11.89	12.26
60	3.02	4.35	5.70	7.08	8.48	8.84	9.19	9.55	9.91	10.27	10.63	11.00	11.36	11.73	12.10	12.46
59	3.12	4.46	5.83	7.22	8.64	9.00	9.36	9.72	10.09	10.45	10.82	11.19	11.56	11.93	12.30	12.68
58	3.23	4.58	5.96	7.37	8.81	9.17	9.54	9.90	10.27	10.64	11.01	11.39	11.76	12.14	12.52	12.90
57	3.33	4.70	6.09	7.52	8.98	9.34	9.71	10.09	10.46	10.84	11.21	11.59	11.97	12.36	12.74	13.13
56	3.43	4.82	6.23	7.67	9.15	9.52	9.90	10.27	10.65	11.03	11.42	11.80	12.19	12.58	12.97	13.36
55	3.54	4.94	6.37	7.83	9.32	9.70	10.08	10.47	10.85	11.24	11.63	12.02	12.41	12.80	13.20	13.60
54	3.65	5.06	6.51	7.99	9.51	9.89	10.28	10.66	11.05	11.45	11.84	12.24	12.64	13.04	13.44	13.84
53	3.76	5.19	6.66	8.16	9.69	10.08	10.47	10.87	11.26	11.66	12.06	12.47	12.87	13.28	13.69	14.10
52	3.88	5.32	6.80	8.32	9.88	10.28	10.68	11.08	11.48	11.88	12.29	12.70	13.11	13.53	13.94	14.36
51	4.00	5.46	6.96	8.50	10.08	10.48	10.88	11.29	11.70	12.11	12.53	12.94	13.36	13.78	14.21	14.63
50	4.11	5.59	7.11	8.67	10.28	10.69	11.10	11.51	11.93	12.35	12.77	13.19	13.62	14.05	14.48	14.91
49	4.24	5.73	7.27	8.86	10.49	10.90	11.32	11.74	12.16	12.59	13.02	13.45	13.88	14.32	14.76	15.20
48	4.36	5.87	7.44	9.04	10.70	11.12	11.55	11.97	12.41	12.84	13.27	13.71	14.16	14.60	15.05	15.50
47	4.49	6.02	7.60	9.24	10.92	11.35	11.78	12.22	12.66	13.10	13.54	13.99	14.44	14.89	15.35	15.81
46	4.62	6.17	7.78	9.43	11.15	11.58	12.02	12.47	12.91	13.36	13.82	14.27	14.73	15.19	15.66	16.13
45	4.75	6.32	7.95	9.64	11.38	11.83	12.27	12.73	13.18	13.64	14.10	14.57	15.04	15.51	15.98	16.46
44	4.88	6.48	8.14	9.85	11.62	12.08	12.53	12.99	13.46	13.93	14.40	14.87	15.35	15.83	16.32	16.81
43	5.02	6.64	8.32	10.07	11.87	12.34	12.80	13.27	13.74	14.22	14.70	15.19	15.68	16.17	16.67	17.17
42	5.16	6.81	8.52	10.29	12.13	12.60	13.08	13.56	14.04	14.53	15.02	15.52	16.02	16.52	17.03	17.54
41	5.31	6.98	8.71	10.52	12.40	12.88	13.37	13.86	14.35	14.85	15.35	15.86	16.37	16.89	17.41	17.93
40	5.46	7.15	8.92	10.76	12.68	13.17	13.67	14.17	14.67	15.18	15.70	16.22	16.74	17.27	17.80	18.34
39	5.61	7.33	9.13	11.01	12.97	13.47	13.98	14.49	15.01	15.53	16.06	16.59	17.13	17.67	18.21	18.76
35	6.27	8.11	10.05	12.10	14.24	14.80	15.36	15.93	16.50	17.08	17.66	18.26	18.86	19.46	20.07	20.68
30	7.20	9.24	11.41	13.73	16.20	16.85	17.50	18.16	18.82	19.50	20.19	20.88	21.59	22.30	23.02	23.74
25	8.32	10.62	13.12	15.84	18.79	19.56	20.35	21.15	21.96	22.78	23.62	24.47	25.33	26.21	27.09	27.98
20	9.69	12.38	15.38	18.74	22.47	23.46	24.47	25.50	26.55	27.62	28.71	29.81	30.93	32.07	33.21	34.37
15	11.47	14.79	18.67	23.21	28.44	29.84	31.27	32.74	34.23	35.75	37.29	38.86	40.43	42.03	43.63	45.25
10	14.01	18.57	24.44	31.88	40.67	43.01	45.39	47.79	50.22	52.66	55.12	57.59	60.07	62.55	65.04	67.53

Description: This table shows the price to pay for a bond at the yield rate. The yield is to maturity.

Example: The price of a 10.75 %, 17 year bond to yield 8 % to maturity is $ 125.32.

COUPON RATE, %

YIELD	7.00%	7.25%	7.50%	7.75%	8.00%	8.25%	8.50%	8.75%	9.00%	9.25%	9.50%	9.75%	10.00%	10.25%	10.50%	10.75%
0.00	219.00	223.25	227.50	231.75	236.00	240.25	244.50	248.75	253.00	257.25	261.50	265.75	270.00	274.25	278.50	282.75
1.00	193.59	197.49	201.39	205.28	209.18	213.08	216.98	220.88	224.78	228.68	232.58	236.48	240.38	244.28	248.18	252.08
2.00	171.76	175.34	178.93	182.52	186.11	189.70	193.28	196.87	200.46	204.05	207.63	211.22	214.81	218.40	221.99	225.57
3.00	152.96	156.27	159.58	162.89	166.20	169.51	172.82	176.13	179.45	182.76	186.07	189.38	192.69	196.00	199.31	202.62
4.00	136.75	139.81	142.87	145.93	149.00	152.06	155.12	158.18	161.25	164.31	167.37	170.43	173.50	176.56	179.62	182.68
4.25	133.05	136.05	139.06	142.06	145.07	148.07	151.08	154.08	157.09	160.09	163.10	166.10	169.10	172.11	175.11	178.12
4.50	129.48	132.43	135.38	138.33	141.28	144.23	147.17	150.12	153.07	156.02	158.97	161.92	164.86	167.81	170.76	173.71
4.75	126.04	128.94	131.83	134.72	137.62	140.51	143.41	146.30	149.19	152.09	154.98	157.87	160.77	163.66	166.55	169.45
5.00	122.72	125.56	128.40	131.25	134.09	136.93	139.77	142.61	145.45	148.29	151.13	153.97	156.81	159.65	162.49	165.33
5.25	119.52	122.31	125.10	127.89	130.68	133.46	136.25	139.04	141.83	144.62	147.41	150.20	152.99	155.77	158.56	161.35
5.50	116.43	119.17	121.91	124.64	127.38	130.12	132.86	135.60	138.34	141.07	143.81	146.55	149.29	152.03	154.77	157.50
5.75	113.45	116.14	118.82	121.51	124.20	126.89	129.58	132.27	134.96	137.65	140.34	143.03	145.72	148.41	151.10	153.78
6.00	110.57	113.21	115.85	118.49	121.13	123.77	126.41	129.06	131.70	134.34	136.98	139.62	142.26	144.91	147.55	150.19
6.25	107.78	110.38	112.97	115.57	118.16	120.76	123.35	125.95	128.54	131.14	133.73	136.33	138.92	141.52	144.11	146.71
6.50	105.10	107.65	110.20	112.75	115.30	117.85	120.40	122.95	125.50	128.05	130.60	133.15	135.70	138.25	140.79	143.34
6.75	102.51	105.01	107.52	110.02	112.53	115.03	117.54	120.04	122.55	125.06	127.56	130.07	132.57	135.08	137.58	140.09
7.00	100.00	102.46	104.93	107.39	109.85	112.31	114.78	117.24	119.70	122.16	124.63	127.09	129.55	132.01	134.48	136.94
7.25	97.58	100.00	102.42	104.84	107.26	109.68	112.10	114.52	116.95	119.37	121.79	124.21	126.63	129.05	131.47	133.89
7.50	95.24	97.62	100.00	102.38	104.76	107.14	109.52	111.90	114.28	116.66	119.04	121.42	123.80	126.18	128.56	130.94
7.75	92.98	95.32	97.66	100.00	102.34	104.68	107.02	109.36	111.70	114.04	116.38	118.72	121.06	123.40	125.74	128.08
8.00	90.79	93.10	95.40	97.70	100.00	102.30	104.60	106.90	109.21	111.51	113.81	116.11	118.41	120.71	123.01	125.32
8.25	88.68	90.95	93.21	95.47	97.74	100.00	102.26	104.53	106.79	109.05	111.32	113.58	115.85	118.11	120.37	122.64
8.50	86.64	88.87	91.09	93.32	95.55	97.77	100.00	102.23	104.45	106.68	108.91	111.13	113.36	115.59	117.81	120.04
8.75	84.66	86.85	89.05	91.24	93.43	95.62	97.81	100.00	102.19	104.38	106.57	108.76	110.95	113.15	115.34	117.53
9.00	82.75	84.91	87.06	89.22	91.38	93.53	95.69	97.84	100.00	102.16	104.31	106.47	108.62	110.78	112.94	115.09
9.25	80.90	83.03	85.15	87.27	89.39	91.51	93.63	95.76	97.88	100.00	102.12	104.24	106.37	108.49	110.61	112.73
9.50	79.12	81.20	83.29	85.38	87.47	89.56	91.65	93.73	95.82	97.91	100.00	102.09	104.18	106.27	108.35	110.44
9.75	77.39	79.44	81.50	83.55	85.61	87.66	89.72	91.78	93.83	95.89	97.94	100.00	102.06	104.11	106.17	108.22
10.00	75.71	77.73	79.76	81.78	83.81	85.83	87.86	89.88	91.90	93.93	95.95	97.98	100.00	102.02	104.05	106.07
10.25	74.09	76.08	78.08	80.07	82.06	84.05	86.05	88.04	90.03	92.03	94.02	96.01	98.01	100.00	101.99	103.99
10.50	72.52	74.48	76.44	78.41	80.37	82.33	84.30	86.26	88.22	90.19	92.15	94.11	96.07	98.04	100.00	101.96
10.75	71.00	72.93	74.87	76.80	78.73	80.67	82.60	84.53	86.47	88.40	90.33	92.27	94.20	96.13	98.07	100.00
11.00	69.53	71.43	73.34	75.24	77.14	79.05	80.95	82.86	84.76	86.67	88.57	90.48	92.38	94.29	96.19	98.10
11.25	68.10	69.98	71.85	73.73	75.61	77.48	79.36	81.23	83.11	84.99	86.86	88.74	90.62	92.49	94.37	96.25
11.50	66.72	68.57	70.42	72.26	74.11	75.96	77.81	79.66	81.51	83.36	85.21	87.06	88.91	90.75	92.60	94.45
11.75	65.38	67.20	69.02	70.84	72.67	74.49	76.31	78.13	79.96	81.78	83.60	85.42	87.24	89.07	90.89	92.71
12.00	64.08	65.88	67.67	69.47	71.26	73.06	74.86	76.65	78.45	80.24	82.04	83.84	85.63	87.43	89.22	91.02
12.25	62.82	64.59	66.36	68.13	69.90	71.67	73.44	75.21	76.98	78.75	80.53	82.30	84.07	85.84	87.61	89.38
12.50	61.60	63.35	65.09	66.84	68.58	70.33	72.07	73.82	75.56	77.31	79.06	80.80	82.55	84.29	86.04	87.78
12.75	60.42	62.14	63.86	65.58	67.30	69.02	70.74	72.46	74.19	75.91	77.63	79.35	81.07	82.79	84.51	86.23
13.00	59.27	60.97	62.66	64.36	66.06	67.76	69.45	71.15	72.85	74.54	76.24	77.94	79.64	81.33	83.03	84.73
13.25	58.16	59.83	61.50	63.18	64.85	66.53	68.20	69.87	71.55	73.22	74.89	76.57	78.24	79.92	81.59	83.26
13.50	57.08	58.73	60.38	62.03	63.68	65.33	66.98	68.63	70.28	71.93	73.59	75.24	76.89	78.54	80.19	81.84
13.75	56.03	57.66	59.29	60.91	62.54	64.17	65.80	67.43	69.06	70.69	72.31	73.94	75.57	77.20	78.83	80.46
14.00	55.01	56.62	58.22	59.83	61.44	63.04	64.65	66.26	67.86	69.47	71.08	72.69	74.29	75.90	77.51	79.11
14.25	54.02	55.61	57.19	58.78	60.36	61.95	63.54	65.12	66.71	68.29	69.88	71.46	73.05	74.63	76.22	77.80
14.50	53.06	54.63	56.19	57.76	59.32	60.89	62.45	64.02	65.58	67.14	68.71	70.27	71.84	73.40	74.97	76.53
14.75	52.13	53.68	55.22	56.77	58.31	59.85	61.40	62.94	64.49	66.03	67.57	69.12	70.66	72.21	73.75	75.29
15.00	51.23	52.75	54.28	55.80	57.32	58.85	60.37	61.90	63.42	64.95	66.47	67.99	69.52	71.04	72.57	74.09
15.25	50.35	51.85	53.36	54.86	56.37	57.87	59.38	60.88	62.39	63.89	65.40	66.90	68.40	69.91	71.41	72.92
15.50	49.50	50.98	52.47	53.95	55.44	56.92	58.41	59.89	61.38	62.86	64.35	65.84	67.32	68.81	70.29	71.78
15.75	48.67	50.13	51.60	53.07	54.53	56.00	57.47	58.93	60.40	61.87	63.33	64.80	66.27	67.73	69.20	70.67
16.00	47.86	49.31	50.76	52.20	53.65	55.10	56.55	58.00	59.45	60.89	62.34	63.79	65.24	66.69	68.14	69.58
16.25	47.07	48.50	49.94	51.37	52.80	54.23	55.66	57.09	58.52	59.95	61.38	62.81	64.24	65.67	67.10	68.53
16.50	46.31	47.72	49.14	50.55	51.96	53.38	54.79	56.20	57.61	59.03	60.44	61.85	63.27	64.68	66.09	67.50
16.75	45.57	46.97	48.36	49.76	51.15	52.55	53.94	55.34	56.74	58.13	59.53	60.92	62.32	63.71	65.11	66.50
17.00	44.85	46.23	47.61	48.99	50.36	51.74	53.12	54.50	55.88	57.26	58.64	60.02	61.39	62.77	64.15	65.53
17.25	44.15	45.51	46.87	48.23	49.60	50.96	52.32	53.68	55.05	56.41	57.77	59.13	60.49	61.86	63.22	64.58
17.50	43.46	44.81	46.16	47.50	48.85	50.19	51.54	52.89	54.23	55.58	56.92	58.27	59.62	60.96	62.31	63.66
17.75	42.80	44.13	45.46	46.79	48.12	49.45	50.78	52.11	53.44	54.77	56.10	57.43	58.76	60.09	61.42	62.75
18.00	42.15	43.47	44.78	46.10	47.41	48.73	50.04	51.36	52.67	53.98	55.30	56.61	57.93	59.24	60.56	61.87
18.25	41.52	42.82	44.12	45.42	46.72	48.02	49.32	50.62	51.92	53.22	54.52	55.82	57.12	58.42	59.72	61.01
18.50	40.91	42.19	43.48	44.76	46.05	47.33	48.62	49.90	51.19	52.47	53.75	55.04	56.32	57.61	58.89	60.18
18.75	40.31	41.58	42.85	44.12	45.39	46.66	47.93	49.20	50.47	51.74	53.01	54.28	55.55	56.82	58.09	59.36
19.00	39.73	40.98	42.24	43.50	44.75	46.01	47.26	48.52	49.77	51.03	52.29	53.54	54.80	56.05	57.31	58.56
20.00	37.54	38.75	39.95	41.15	42.35	43.55	44.75	45.95	47.15	48.35	49.55	50.76	51.96	53.16	54.36	55.56
25.00	29.31	30.29	31.28	32.26	33.24	34.22	35.20	36.19	37.17	38.15	39.13	40.11	41.09	42.08	43.06	44.04
30.00	24.00	24.82	25.65	26.47	27.30	28.13	28.95	29.78	30.60	31.43	32.26	33.08	33.91	34.74	35.56	36.39

Description: This table shows the yield to maturity of a bond purchased at the price shown in the index.

Example: The yield to maturity of a 10.75 %, 17 year bond at a price of 111.00 is 9.43 %.

COUPON RATE, %

PRICE	7.00%	7.25%	7.50%	7.75%	8.00%	8.25%	8.50%	8.75%	9.00%	9.25%	9.50%	9.75%	10.00%	10.25%	10.50%	10.75%
155	2.88	3.07	3.26	3.44	3.63	3.82	4.00	4.19	4.37	4.56	4.74	4.93	5.11	5.30	5.48	5.66
150	3.17	3.36	3.55	3.74	3.93	4.12	4.31	4.50	4.69	4.88	5.07	5.26	5.45	5.63	5.82	6.01
145	3.47	3.66	3.86	4.05	4.25	4.44	4.64	4.83	5.03	5.22	5.41	5.60	5.80	5.99	6.18	6.37
140	3.78	3.98	4.18	4.38	4.58	4.78	4.98	5.18	5.37	5.57	5.77	5.97	6.16	6.36	6.56	6.75
135	4.11	4.32	4.52	4.73	4.93	5.13	5.34	5.54	5.74	5.94	6.15	6.35	6.55	6.75	6.95	7.15
130	4.46	4.67	4.88	5.09	5.30	5.50	5.71	5.92	6.13	6.34	6.54	6.75	6.96	7.16	7.37	7.58
125	4.82	5.04	5.25	5.47	5.68	5.90	6.11	6.32	6.54	6.75	6.96	7.18	7.39	7.60	7.81	8.02
124	4.90	5.11	5.33	5.55	5.76	5.98	6.19	6.41	6.62	6.84	7.05	7.26	7.48	7.69	7.90	8.12
123	4.97	5.19	5.41	5.63	5.84	6.06	6.27	6.49	6.71	6.92	7.14	7.35	7.57	7.78	8.00	8.21
122	5.05	5.27	5.49	5.71	5.92	6.14	6.36	6.58	6.79	7.01	7.23	7.44	7.66	7.87	8.09	8.31
121	5.13	5.35	5.57	5.79	6.01	6.22	6.44	6.66	6.88	7.10	7.32	7.53	7.75	7.97	8.18	8.40
120	5.21	5.43	5.65	5.87	6.09	6.31	6.53	6.75	6.97	7.19	7.41	7.63	7.84	8.06	8.28	8.50
119	5.29	5.51	5.73	5.95	6.17	6.40	6.62	6.84	7.06	7.28	7.50	7.72	7.94	8.16	8.38	8.60
118	5.37	5.59	5.81	6.04	6.26	6.48	6.70	6.93	7.15	7.37	7.59	7.81	8.03	8.26	8.48	8.70
117	5.45	5.67	5.90	6.12	6.35	6.57	6.79	7.02	7.24	7.46	7.69	7.91	8.13	8.35	8.58	8.80
116	5.53	5.76	5.98	6.21	6.43	6.66	6.88	7.11	7.33	7.56	7.78	8.01	8.23	8.45	8.68	8.90
115	5.61	5.84	6.07	6.29	6.52	6.75	6.97	7.20	7.43	7.65	7.88	8.10	8.33	8.55	8.78	9.00
114	5.70	5.93	6.15	6.38	6.61	6.84	7.07	7.29	7.52	7.75	7.98	8.20	8.43	8.66	8.88	9.11
113	5.78	6.01	6.24	6.47	6.70	6.93	7.16	7.39	7.62	7.85	8.08	8.30	8.53	8.76	8.99	9.22
112	5.87	6.10	6.33	6.56	6.79	7.02	7.25	7.49	7.72	7.95	8.18	8.41	8.64	8.87	9.09	9.32
111	5.96	6.19	6.42	6.65	6.89	7.12	7.35	7.58	7.81	8.05	8.28	8.51	8.74	8.97	9.20	9.43
110	6.05	6.28	6.51	6.75	6.98	7.21	7.45	7.68	7.91	8.15	8.38	8.61	8.85	9.08	9.31	9.54
109	6.13	6.37	6.61	6.84	7.08	7.31	7.55	7.78	8.02	8.25	8.49	8.72	8.95	9.19	9.42	9.66
108	6.23	6.46	6.70	6.94	7.17	7.41	7.65	7.88	8.12	8.36	8.59	8.83	9.06	9.30	9.53	9.77
107	6.32	6.56	6.79	7.03	7.27	7.51	7.75	7.99	8.22	8.46	8.70	8.94	9.17	9.41	9.65	9.89
106	6.41	6.65	6.89	7.13	7.37	7.61	7.85	8.09	8.33	8.57	8.81	9.05	9.29	9.53	9.76	10.00
105	6.50	6.75	6.99	7.23	7.47	7.71	7.95	8.19	8.44	8.68	8.92	9.16	9.40	9.64	9.88	10.12
104	6.60	6.84	7.09	7.33	7.57	7.82	8.06	8.30	8.54	8.79	9.03	9.27	9.52	9.76	10.00	10.24
103	6.70	6.94	7.19	7.43	7.68	7.92	8.17	8.41	8.65	8.90	9.14	9.39	9.63	9.88	10.12	10.37
102	6.79	7.04	7.29	7.53	7.78	8.03	8.27	8.52	8.77	9.01	9.26	9.51	9.75	10.00	10.24	10.49
101	6.89	7.14	7.39	7.64	7.89	8.14	8.38	8.63	8.88	9.13	9.38	9.62	9.87	10.12	10.37	10.62
100	7.00	7.25	7.50	7.75	8.00	8.25	8.50	8.75	9.00	9.25	9.50	9.75	10.00	10.25	10.50	10.75
99	7.10	7.35	7.60	7.85	8.10	8.36	8.61	8.86	9.11	9.36	9.62	9.87	10.12	10.37	10.62	10.88
98	7.20	7.45	7.71	7.96	8.22	8.47	8.72	8.98	9.23	9.48	9.74	9.99	10.25	10.50	10.75	11.01
97	7.31	7.56	7.82	8.07	8.33	8.58	8.84	9.10	9.35	9.61	9.86	10.12	10.37	10.63	10.89	11.14
96	7.41	7.67	7.93	8.19	8.44	8.70	8.96	9.22	9.47	9.73	9.99	10.25	10.50	10.76	11.02	11.28
95	7.52	7.78	8.04	8.30	8.56	8.82	9.08	9.34	9.60	9.86	10.12	10.38	10.64	10.90	11.16	11.42
94	7.63	7.89	8.15	8.42	8.68	8.94	9.20	9.46	9.72	9.99	10.25	10.51	10.77	11.03	11.30	11.56
93	7.74	8.01	8.27	8.53	8.80	9.06	9.32	9.59	9.85	10.12	10.38	10.64	10.91	11.17	11.44	11.70
92	7.86	8.12	8.39	8.65	8.92	9.18	9.45	9.72	9.98	10.25	10.52	10.78	11.05	11.32	11.58	11.85
91	7.97	8.24	8.51	8.77	9.04	9.31	9.58	9.85	10.11	10.38	10.65	10.92	11.19	11.46	11.73	12.00
90	8.09	8.36	8.63	8.90	9.17	9.44	9.71	9.98	10.25	10.52	10.79	11.06	11.33	11.61	11.88	12.15
89	8.21	8.48	8.75	9.02	9.30	9.57	9.84	10.11	10.39	10.66	10.93	11.21	11.48	11.76	12.03	12.30
88	8.33	8.60	8.88	9.15	9.43	9.70	9.98	10.25	10.53	10.80	11.08	11.35	11.63	11.91	12.18	12.46
87	8.45	8.73	9.00	9.28	9.56	9.83	10.11	10.39	10.67	10.95	11.22	11.50	11.78	12.06	12.34	12.62
86	8.58	8.85	9.13	9.41	9.69	9.97	10.25	10.53	10.81	11.09	11.37	11.66	11.94	12.22	12.50	12.78
85	8.70	8.98	9.26	9.55	9.83	10.11	10.39	10.68	10.96	11.24	11.53	11.81	12.10	12.38	12.66	12.95
84	8.83	9.11	9.40	9.68	9.97	10.25	10.54	10.82	11.11	11.40	11.68	11.97	12.26	12.54	12.83	13.12
83	8.96	9.25	9.54	9.82	10.11	10.40	10.69	10.97	11.26	11.55	11.84	12.13	12.42	12.71	13.00	13.29
82	9.10	9.38	9.67	9.96	10.25	10.54	10.84	11.13	11.42	11.71	12.00	12.29	12.59	12.88	13.17	13.47
81	9.23	9.52	9.82	10.11	10.40	10.69	10.99	11.28	11.58	11.87	12.17	12.46	12.76	13.05	13.35	13.65
80	9.37	9.66	9.96	10.26	10.55	10.85	11.14	11.44	11.74	12.04	12.33	12.63	12.93	13.23	13.53	13.83
79	9.51	9.81	10.11	10.40	10.70	11.00	11.30	11.60	11.90	12.20	12.50	12.81	13.11	13.41	13.71	14.02
78	9.66	9.96	10.26	10.56	10.86	11.16	11.46	11.77	12.07	12.37	12.68	12.98	13.29	13.59	13.90	14.21
77	9.80	10.11	10.41	10.71	11.02	11.32	11.63	11.94	12.24	12.55	12.86	13.17	13.47	13.78	14.09	14.40
76	9.95	10.26	10.56	10.87	11.18	11.49	11.80	12.11	12.42	12.73	13.04	13.35	13.66	13.98	14.29	14.60
75	10.10	10.41	10.72	11.03	11.35	11.66	11.97	12.28	12.60	12.91	13.23	13.54	13.86	14.17	14.49	14.81
74	10.26	10.57	10.89	11.20	11.51	11.83	12.15	12.46	12.78	13.10	13.42	13.73	14.05	14.37	14.69	15.01
73	10.42	10.73	11.05	11.37	11.69	12.01	12.33	12.65	12.97	13.29	13.61	13.93	14.25	14.58	14.90	15.23
70	10.91	11.24	11.57	11.90	12.23	12.56	12.89	13.22	13.55	13.89	14.22	14.55	14.89	15.22	15.56	15.90
65	11.82	12.16	12.51	12.86	13.21	13.57	13.92	14.27	14.63	14.98	15.34	15.70	16.05	16.41	16.77	17.13
60	12.84	13.21	13.58	13.96	14.33	14.71	15.09	15.47	15.85	16.23	16.61	17.00	17.39	17.77	18.16	18.55
55	14.00	14.40	14.80	15.21	15.61	16.02	16.43	16.85	17.26	17.67	18.09	18.51	18.93	19.35	19.77	20.19
50	15.35	15.78	16.23	16.67	17.11	17.56	18.01	18.46	18.91	19.37	19.83	20.28	20.74	21.21	21.67	22.14
45	16.94	17.43	17.91	18.40	18.90	19.39	19.89	20.39	20.90	21.40	21.91	22.42	22.93	23.45	23.97	24.49
40	18.88	19.42	19.97	20.52	21.08	21.64	22.20	22.77	23.34	23.91	24.48	25.06	25.64	26.23	26.81	27.40
35	21.30	21.93	22.56	23.20	23.84	24.48	25.13	25.78	26.44	27.10	27.77	28.43	29.10	29.78	30.46	31.13
30	24.48	25.22	25.96	26.72	27.48	28.24	29.01	29.79	30.57	31.35	32.14	32.93	33.72	34.52	35.32	36.13

Description: This table shows the price to pay for a bond at the yield rate. The yield is to maturity.

Example: The price of a 15.00 %, 17 year bond to yield 8 % to maturity is $ 164.44.

COUPON RATE, %

YIELD	11.00%	11.25%	11.50%	11.75%	12.00%	12.25%	12.50%	12.75%	13.00%	13.25%	13.50%	13.75%	14.00%	14.25%	14.50%	15.00%
0.00	287.00	291.25	295.50	299.75	304.00	308.25	312.50	316.75	321.00	325.25	329.50	333.75	338.00	342.25	346.50	355.00
1.00	255.98	259.88	263.78	267.68	271.58	275.47	279.37	283.27	287.17	291.07	294.97	298.87	302.77	306.67	310.57	318.37
2.00	229.16	232.75	236.34	239.93	243.51	247.10	250.69	254.28	257.86	261.45	265.04	268.63	272.22	275.80	279.39	286.57
3.00	205.93	209.24	212.55	215.86	219.17	222.48	225.79	229.10	232.41	235.72	239.03	242.34	245.65	248.96	252.27	258.89
4.00	185.75	188.81	191.87	194.93	197.99	201.06	204.12	207.18	210.24	213.31	216.37	219.43	222.49	225.56	228.62	234.74
4.25	181.12	184.13	187.13	190.14	193.14	196.15	199.15	202.15	205.16	208.16	211.17	214.17	217.18	220.18	223.19	229.20
4.50	176.66	179.61	182.55	185.50	188.45	191.40	194.35	197.30	200.24	203.19	206.14	209.09	212.04	214.99	217.93	223.83
4.75	172.34	175.24	178.13	181.02	183.92	186.81	189.70	192.60	195.49	198.39	201.28	204.17	207.07	209.96	212.85	218.64
5.00	168.17	171.01	173.85	176.69	179.53	182.37	185.21	188.05	190.90	193.74	196.58	199.42	202.26	205.10	207.94	213.62
5.25	164.14	166.93	169.72	172.51	175.29	178.08	180.87	183.66	186.45	189.24	192.03	194.82	197.60	200.39	203.18	208.76
5.50	160.24	162.98	165.72	168.46	171.20	173.93	176.67	179.41	182.15	184.89	187.63	190.36	193.10	195.84	198.58	204.06
5.75	156.47	159.16	161.85	164.54	167.23	169.92	172.61	175.30	177.99	180.68	183.37	186.06	188.75	191.43	194.12	199.50
6.00	152.83	155.47	158.11	160.75	163.40	166.04	168.68	171.32	173.96	176.60	179.24	181.89	184.53	187.17	189.81	195.09
6.25	149.30	151.90	154.49	157.09	159.68	162.28	164.87	167.47	170.06	172.66	175.25	177.85	180.44	183.04	185.63	190.82
6.50	145.89	148.44	150.99	153.54	156.09	158.64	161.19	163.74	166.29	168.84	171.39	173.94	176.49	179.04	181.59	186.69
6.75	142.59	145.10	147.61	150.11	152.62	155.12	157.63	160.13	162.64	165.14	167.65	170.16	172.66	175.17	177.67	182.68
7.00	139.40	141.86	144.33	146.79	149.25	151.71	154.18	156.64	159.10	161.56	164.03	166.49	168.95	171.41	173.88	178.80
7.25	136.31	138.73	141.15	143.57	145.99	148.41	150.84	153.26	155.68	158.10	160.52	162.94	165.36	167.78	170.20	175.04
7.50	133.32	135.70	138.08	140.46	142.84	145.22	147.60	149.98	152.36	154.74	157.12	159.50	161.88	164.26	166.64	171.40
7.75	130.42	132.76	135.10	137.44	139.78	142.12	144.46	146.80	149.14	151.48	153.82	156.16	158.50	160.84	163.18	167.86
8.00	127.62	129.92	132.22	134.52	136.82	139.12	141.43	143.73	146.03	148.33	150.63	152.93	155.23	157.53	159.84	164.44
8.25	124.90	127.16	129.43	131.69	133.95	136.22	138.48	140.75	143.01	145.27	147.54	149.80	152.06	154.33	156.59	161.12
8.50	122.27	124.49	126.72	128.95	131.18	133.40	135.63	137.86	140.08	142.31	144.54	146.76	148.99	151.22	153.44	157.90
8.75	119.72	121.91	124.10	126.29	128.48	130.67	132.86	135.05	137.24	139.44	141.63	143.82	146.01	148.20	150.39	154.77
9.00	117.25	119.40	121.56	123.71	125.87	128.03	130.18	132.34	134.49	136.65	138.81	140.96	143.12	145.27	147.43	151.74
9.25	114.85	116.97	119.10	121.22	123.34	125.46	127.58	129.70	131.83	133.95	136.07	138.19	140.31	142.43	144.56	148.80
9.50	112.53	114.62	116.71	118.80	120.88	122.97	125.06	127.15	129.24	131.33	133.41	135.50	137.59	139.68	141.77	145.94
9.75	110.28	112.34	114.39	116.45	118.50	120.56	122.61	124.67	126.73	128.78	130.84	132.89	134.95	137.01	139.06	143.17
10.00	108.10	110.12	112.14	114.17	116.19	118.22	120.24	122.27	124.29	126.31	128.34	130.36	132.39	134.41	136.43	140.48
10.25	105.98	107.97	109.97	111.96	113.95	115.95	117.94	119.93	121.92	123.92	125.91	127.90	129.90	131.89	133.88	137.87
10.50	103.93	105.89	107.85	109.81	111.78	113.74	115.70	117.67	119.63	121.59	123.56	125.52	127.48	129.44	131.41	135.33
10.75	101.93	103.87	105.80	107.73	109.67	111.60	113.53	115.47	117.40	119.33	121.27	123.20	125.13	127.07	129.00	132.87
11.00	100.00	101.90	103.81	105.71	107.62	109.52	111.43	113.33	115.24	117.14	119.05	120.95	122.86	124.76	126.66	130.47
11.25	98.12	100.00	101.88	103.75	105.63	107.51	109.38	111.26	113.14	115.01	116.89	118.77	120.64	122.52	124.39	128.15
11.50	96.30	98.15	100.00	101.85	103.70	105.55	107.40	109.25	111.09	112.94	114.79	116.64	118.49	120.34	122.19	125.89
11.75	94.53	96.36	98.18	100.00	101.82	103.64	105.47	107.29	109.11	110.93	112.76	114.58	116.40	118.22	120.04	123.69
12.00	92.82	94.61	96.41	98.20	100.00	101.80	103.59	105.39	107.18	108.98	110.78	112.57	114.37	116.16	117.96	121.55
12.25	91.15	92.92	94.69	96.46	98.23	100.00	101.77	103.54	105.31	107.08	108.85	110.62	112.39	114.16	115.93	119.47
12.50	89.53	91.27	93.02	94.76	96.51	98.25	100.00	101.75	103.49	105.24	106.98	108.73	110.47	112.22	113.96	117.45
12.75	87.95	89.67	91.40	93.12	94.84	96.56	98.28	100.00	101.72	103.44	105.16	106.88	108.60	110.33	112.05	115.49
13.00	86.42	88.12	89.82	91.51	93.21	94.91	96.61	98.30	100.00	101.70	103.39	105.09	106.79	108.49	110.18	113.58
13.25	84.94	86.61	88.28	89.96	91.63	93.31	94.98	96.65	98.33	100.00	101.67	103.35	105.02	106.69	108.37	111.72
13.50	83.49	85.14	86.79	88.44	90.09	91.75	93.40	95.05	96.70	98.35	100.00	101.65	103.30	104.95	106.60	109.91
13.75	82.09	83.71	85.34	86.97	88.60	90.23	91.86	93.49	95.11	96.74	98.37	100.00	101.63	103.26	104.89	108.14
14.00	80.72	82.33	83.93	85.54	87.15	88.75	90.36	91.97	93.57	95.18	96.79	98.39	100.00	101.61	103.21	106.43
14.25	79.39	80.98	82.56	84.15	85.73	87.32	88.90	90.49	92.07	93.66	95.24	96.83	98.41	100.00	101.59	104.76
14.50	78.10	79.66	81.23	82.79	84.35	85.92	87.48	89.05	90.61	92.18	93.74	95.31	96.87	98.44	100.00	103.13
14.75	76.84	78.38	79.93	81.47	83.01	84.56	86.10	87.65	89.19	90.74	92.28	93.82	95.37	96.91	98.46	101.54
15.00	75.61	77.14	78.66	80.19	81.71	83.23	84.76	86.28	87.81	89.33	90.86	92.38	93.90	95.43	96.95	100.00
15.25	74.42	75.93	77.43	78.94	80.44	81.95	83.45	84.95	86.46	87.96	89.47	90.97	92.48	93.98	95.49	98.50
15.50	73.26	74.75	76.23	77.72	79.20	80.69	82.17	83.66	85.15	86.63	88.12	89.60	91.09	92.57	94.06	97.03
15.75	72.13	73.60	75.07	76.53	78.00	79.47	80.93	82.40	83.87	85.33	86.80	88.27	89.73	91.20	92.67	95.60
16.00	71.03	72.48	73.93	75.38	76.83	78.27	79.72	81.17	82.62	84.07	85.52	86.96	88.41	89.86	91.31	94.21
16.25	69.96	71.39	72.82	74.25	75.68	77.11	78.54	79.97	81.40	82.83	84.27	85.70	87.13	88.56	89.99	92.85
16.50	68.92	70.33	71.74	73.16	74.57	75.98	77.39	78.81	80.22	81.63	83.05	84.46	85.87	87.28	88.70	91.52
16.75	67.90	69.30	70.69	72.09	73.48	74.88	76.27	77.67	79.07	80.46	81.86	83.25	84.65	86.04	87.44	90.23
17.00	66.91	68.29	69.67	71.05	72.42	73.80	75.18	76.56	77.94	79.32	80.70	82.08	83.45	84.83	86.21	88.97
17.25	65.94	67.31	68.67	70.03	71.39	72.75	74.12	75.48	76.84	78.20	79.57	80.93	82.29	83.65	85.02	87.74
17.50	65.00	66.35	67.69	69.04	70.39	71.73	73.08	74.42	75.77	77.12	78.46	79.81	81.15	82.50	83.85	86.54
17.75	64.08	65.41	66.74	68.07	69.40	70.73	72.06	73.39	74.73	76.06	77.39	78.72	80.05	81.38	82.71	85.37
18.00	63.19	64.50	65.82	67.13	68.45	69.76	71.08	72.39	73.71	75.02	76.33	77.65	78.96	80.28	81.59	84.22
18.25	62.31	63.61	64.91	66.21	67.51	68.81	70.11	71.41	72.71	74.01	75.31	76.61	77.91	79.21	80.51	83.11
18.50	61.46	62.75	64.03	65.32	66.60	67.88	69.17	70.45	71.74	73.02	74.31	75.59	76.88	78.16	79.45	82.02
18.75	60.63	61.90	63.17	64.44	65.71	66.98	68.25	69.52	70.79	72.06	73.33	74.60	75.87	77.14	78.41	80.95
19.00	59.82	61.07	62.33	63.59	64.84	66.10	67.35	68.61	69.86	71.12	72.38	73.63	74.89	76.14	77.40	79.91
20.00	56.76	57.96	59.16	60.36	61.57	62.77	63.97	65.17	66.37	67.57	68.77	69.97	71.17	72.38	73.58	75.98
25.00	45.02	46.00	46.98	47.97	48.95	49.93	50.91	51.89	52.88	53.86	54.84	55.82	56.80	57.78	58.77	60.73
30.00	37.21	38.04	38.87	39.69	40.52	41.34	42.17	43.00	43.82	44.65	45.47	46.30	47.13	47.95	48.78	50.43

Description: This table shows the yield to maturity of a bond purchased at the price shown in the index.

Example: The yield to maturity of a 15.00 %, 17 year bond at a price of 125.00 is 11.60 %.

COUPON RATE, %

PRICE	11.00%	11.25%	11.50%	11.75%	12.00%	12.25%	12.50%	12.75%	13.00%	13.25%	13.50%	13.75%	14.00%	14.25%	14.50%	15.00%
250	1.21	1.34	1.48	1.62	1.75	1.89	2.02	2.16	2.29	2.42	2.56	2.69	2.82	2.95	3.09	3.35
240	1.57	1.71	1.85	1.99	2.13	2.27	2.41	2.54	2.68	2.82	2.96	3.09	3.23	3.36	3.50	3.77
230	1.96	2.10	2.25	2.39	2.53	2.67	2.82	2.96	3.10	3.24	3.38	3.52	3.66	3.79	3.93	4.21
220	2.37	2.52	2.67	2.81	2.96	3.10	3.25	3.39	3.54	3.68	3.83	3.97	4.11	4.25	4.40	4.68
210	2.81	2.96	3.11	3.26	3.41	3.56	3.71	3.86	4.01	4.15	4.30	4.45	4.60	4.74	4.89	5.18
200	3.27	3.43	3.59	3.74	3.89	4.05	4.20	4.35	4.51	4.66	4.81	4.96	5.12	5.27	5.42	5.72
195	3.52	3.68	3.83	3.99	4.15	4.30	4.46	4.62	4.77	4.93	5.08	5.23	5.39	5.54	5.70	6.00
190	3.77	3.93	4.09	4.25	4.41	4.57	4.73	4.89	5.04	5.20	5.36	5.52	5.67	5.83	5.98	6.29
185	4.03	4.20	4.36	4.52	4.68	4.85	5.01	5.17	5.33	5.49	5.65	5.81	5.97	6.13	6.28	6.60
180	4.31	4.47	4.64	4.80	4.97	5.13	5.30	5.46	5.62	5.79	5.95	6.11	6.27	6.43	6.60	6.92
175	4.59	4.76	4.93	5.10	5.26	5.43	5.60	5.76	5.93	6.10	6.26	6.43	6.59	6.76	6.92	7.25
170	4.88	5.06	5.23	5.40	5.57	5.74	5.91	6.08	6.25	6.42	6.59	6.76	6.92	7.09	7.26	7.59
165	5.19	5.37	5.54	5.72	5.89	6.06	6.24	6.41	6.58	6.75	6.93	7.10	7.27	7.44	7.61	7.95
160	5.51	5.69	5.87	6.05	6.22	6.40	6.58	6.75	6.93	7.11	7.28	7.46	7.63	7.81	7.98	8.33
155	5.85	6.03	6.21	6.39	6.57	6.75	6.93	7.12	7.30	7.48	7.65	7.83	8.01	8.19	8.37	8.73
150	6.20	6.38	6.57	6.75	6.94	7.12	7.31	7.49	7.68	7.86	8.05	8.23	8.41	8.59	8.78	9.14
145	6.56	6.75	6.94	7.13	7.32	7.51	7.70	7.89	8.08	8.27	8.46	8.64	8.83	9.02	9.21	9.58
140	6.95	7.14	7.34	7.53	7.73	7.92	8.12	8.31	8.50	8.70	8.89	9.08	9.27	9.47	9.66	10.04
135	7.35	7.55	7.75	7.95	8.15	8.35	8.55	8.75	8.95	9.15	9.34	9.54	9.74	9.94	10.13	10.53
130	7.78	7.99	8.19	8.40	8.60	8.81	9.01	9.22	9.42	9.62	9.83	10.03	10.23	10.44	10.64	11.05
125	8.24	8.45	8.66	8.87	9.08	9.29	9.50	9.71	9.92	10.13	10.34	10.55	10.76	10.97	11.18	11.60
120	8.72	8.93	9.15	9.37	9.59	9.80	10.02	10.24	10.45	10.67	10.89	11.10	11.32	11.53	11.75	12.18
115	9.23	9.45	9.68	9.90	10.13	10.35	10.58	10.80	11.02	11.25	11.47	11.69	11.92	12.14	12.36	12.81
113	9.44	9.67	9.90	10.13	10.35	10.58	10.81	11.03	11.26	11.49	11.71	11.94	12.17	12.39	12.62	13.07
112	9.55	9.78	10.01	10.24	10.47	10.70	10.93	11.15	11.38	11.61	11.84	12.07	12.30	12.52	12.75	13.21
111	9.66	9.89	10.13	10.36	10.59	10.82	11.05	11.28	11.51	11.74	11.97	12.20	12.43	12.66	12.88	13.34
110	9.78	10.01	10.24	10.47	10.71	10.94	11.17	11.40	11.63	11.86	12.10	12.33	12.56	12.79	13.02	13.48
109	9.89	10.12	10.36	10.59	10.83	11.06	11.29	11.53	11.76	11.99	12.23	12.46	12.69	12.92	13.16	13.62
108	10.01	10.24	10.48	10.71	10.95	11.18	11.42	11.65	11.89	12.12	12.36	12.59	12.83	13.06	13.30	13.77
107	10.12	10.36	10.60	10.83	11.07	11.31	11.55	11.78	12.02	12.26	12.49	12.73	12.97	13.20	13.44	13.91
106	10.24	10.48	10.72	10.96	11.20	11.44	11.68	11.91	12.15	12.39	12.63	12.87	13.11	13.34	13.58	14.06
105	10.36	10.60	10.84	11.09	11.33	11.57	11.81	12.05	12.29	12.53	12.77	13.01	13.25	13.49	13.73	14.21
104	10.49	10.73	10.97	11.21	11.46	11.70	11.94	12.18	12.42	12.67	12.91	13.15	13.39	13.63	13.88	14.36
103	10.61	10.85	11.10	11.34	11.59	11.83	12.08	12.32	12.56	12.81	13.05	13.30	13.54	13.78	14.03	14.52
102	10.74	10.98	11.23	11.47	11.72	11.97	12.21	12.46	12.71	12.95	13.20	13.44	13.69	13.93	14.18	14.67
101	10.86	11.11	11.36	11.61	11.86	12.10	12.35	12.60	12.85	13.10	13.34	13.59	13.84	14.09	14.34	14.83
100	11.00	11.25	11.50	11.75	12.00	12.25	12.50	12.75	13.00	13.25	13.50	13.75	14.00	14.25	14.50	15.00
99	11.13	11.38	11.63	11.88	12.14	12.39	12.64	12.89	13.14	13.40	13.65	13.90	14.15	14.40	14.66	15.16
98	11.26	11.52	11.77	12.02	12.28	12.53	12.79	13.04	13.29	13.55	13.80	14.06	14.31	14.57	14.82	15.33
97	11.40	11.65	11.91	12.17	12.42	12.68	12.94	13.19	13.45	13.70	13.96	14.22	14.47	14.73	14.99	15.50
96	11.54	11.80	12.05	12.31	12.57	12.83	13.09	13.35	13.60	13.86	14.12	14.38	14.64	14.90	15.16	15.67
95	11.68	11.94	12.20	12.46	12.72	12.98	13.24	13.50	13.76	14.02	14.29	14.55	14.81	15.07	15.33	15.85
94	11.82	12.08	12.35	12.61	12.87	13.14	13.40	13.66	13.93	14.19	14.45	14.71	14.98	15.24	15.51	16.03
93	11.97	12.23	12.50	12.76	13.03	13.29	13.56	13.82	14.09	14.36	14.62	14.89	15.15	15.42	15.68	16.22
92	12.12	12.38	12.65	12.92	13.19	13.45	13.72	13.99	14.26	14.53	14.79	15.06	15.33	15.60	15.87	16.40
91	12.27	12.54	12.81	13.08	13.35	13.62	13.89	14.16	14.43	14.70	14.97	15.24	15.51	15.78	16.05	16.60
90	12.42	12.69	12.97	13.24	13.51	13.78	14.06	14.33	14.60	14.88	15.15	15.42	15.70	15.97	16.24	16.79
89	12.58	12.85	13.13	13.40	13.68	13.95	14.23	14.50	14.78	15.05	15.33	15.61	15.88	16.16	16.44	16.99
88	12.74	13.01	13.29	13.57	13.85	14.13	14.40	14.68	14.96	15.24	15.52	15.80	16.07	16.35	16.63	17.19
87	12.90	13.18	13.46	13.74	14.02	14.30	14.58	14.86	15.14	15.43	15.71	15.99	16.27	16.55	16.83	17.40
86	13.07	13.35	13.63	13.91	14.20	14.48	14.76	15.05	15.33	15.62	15.90	16.18	16.47	16.75	17.04	17.61
85	13.23	13.52	13.81	14.09	14.38	14.66	14.95	15.24	15.52	15.81	16.10	16.38	16.67	16.96	17.25	17.82
84	13.41	13.69	13.98	14.27	14.56	14.85	15.14	15.43	15.72	16.01	16.30	16.59	16.88	17.17	17.46	18.04
83	13.58	13.87	14.16	14.46	14.75	15.04	15.33	15.63	15.92	16.21	16.50	16.80	17.09	17.39	17.68	18.27
82	13.76	14.05	14.35	14.64	14.94	15.23	15.53	15.83	16.12	16.42	16.71	17.01	17.31	17.61	17.90	18.50
81	13.94	14.24	14.54	14.84	15.13	15.43	15.73	16.03	16.33	16.63	16.93	17.23	17.53	17.83	18.13	18.73
80	14.13	14.43	14.73	15.03	15.33	15.64	15.94	16.24	16.54	16.85	17.15	17.45	17.76	18.06	18.36	18.97
79	14.32	14.62	14.93	15.23	15.54	15.84	16.15	16.45	16.76	17.07	17.37	17.68	17.99	18.29	18.60	19.22
78	14.51	14.82	15.13	15.44	15.74	16.05	16.36	16.67	16.98	17.29	17.60	17.91	18.22	18.53	18.85	19.47
77	14.71	15.02	15.33	15.65	15.96	16.27	16.58	16.90	17.21	17.52	17.84	18.15	18.46	18.78	19.10	19.73
76	14.92	15.23	15.54	15.86	16.18	16.49	16.81	17.12	17.44	17.76	18.08	18.39	18.71	19.03	19.35	19.99
75	15.12	15.44	15.76	16.08	16.40	16.72	17.04	17.36	17.68	18.00	18.32	18.64	18.97	19.29	19.61	20.26
74	15.34	15.66	15.98	16.30	16.63	16.95	17.27	17.60	17.92	18.25	18.57	18.90	19.23	19.55	19.88	20.53
73	15.55	15.88	16.20	16.53	16.86	17.19	17.51	17.84	18.17	18.50	18.83	19.16	19.49	19.82	20.15	20.82
70	16.24	16.57	16.91	17.25	17.59	17.93	18.27	18.62	18.96	19.30	19.64	19.99	20.33	20.68	21.02	21.71
65	17.50	17.86	18.22	18.58	18.95	19.31	19.68	20.05	20.41	20.78	21.15	21.52	21.89	22.26	22.63	23.37
60	18.94	19.33	19.72	20.11	20.51	20.90	21.30	21.69	22.09	22.49	22.89	23.29	23.69	24.09	24.49	25.29
55	20.62	21.04	21.47	21.90	22.33	22.76	23.19	23.62	24.05	24.49	24.92	25.36	25.80	26.23	26.67	27.55

Description: This table shows the price to pay for a bond at the yield rate. The yield is to maturity.

Example: The price of a 6.75 %, 18 year bond to yield 8 % to maturity is $ 88.18.

							COUPON RATE, %									
YIELD	0.00%	1.00%	2.00%	3.00%	4.00%	4.25%	4.50%	4.75%	5.00%	5.25%	5.50%	5.75%	6.00%	6.25%	6.50%	6.75%
0.00	100.00	118.00	136.00	154.00	172.00	176.50	181.00	185.50	190.00	194.50	199.00	203.50	208.00	212.50	217.00	221.50
1.00	83.56	100.00	116.44	132.87	149.31	153.42	157.52	161.63	165.74	169.85	173.96	178.07	182.18	186.29	190.40	194.50
2.00	69.89	84.95	100.00	115.05	130.11	133.87	137.63	141.40	145.16	148.92	152.69	156.45	160.22	163.98	167.74	171.51
3.00	58.51	72.34	86.17	100.00	113.83	117.29	120.75	124.20	127.66	131.12	134.58	138.03	141.49	144.95	148.41	151.86
4.00	49.02	61.77	74.51	87.26	100.00	103.19	106.37	109.56	112.74	115.93	119.12	122.30	125.49	128.67	131.86	135.05
4.25	46.91	59.40	71.89	84.38	96.88	100.00	103.12	106.25	109.37	112.49	115.62	118.74	121.86	124.98	128.11	131.23
4.50	44.89	57.13	69.38	81.63	93.88	96.94	100.00	103.06	106.12	109.19	112.25	115.31	118.37	121.43	124.49	127.56
4.75	42.96	54.96	66.97	78.98	90.99	94.00	97.00	100.00	103.00	106.00	109.01	112.01	115.01	118.01	121.02	124.02
5.00	41.11	52.89	64.67	76.44	88.22	91.17	94.11	97.06	100.00	102.94	105.89	108.83	111.78	114.72	117.67	120.61
5.25	39.34	50.90	62.45	74.00	85.56	88.45	91.33	94.22	97.11	100.00	102.89	105.78	108.67	111.55	114.44	117.33
5.50	37.66	48.99	60.33	71.66	83.00	85.83	88.67	91.50	94.33	97.17	100.00	102.83	105.67	108.50	111.33	114.17
5.75	36.05	47.17	58.29	69.41	80.54	83.32	86.10	88.88	91.66	94.44	97.22	100.00	102.78	105.56	108.34	111.12
6.00	34.50	45.42	56.34	67.25	78.17	80.90	83.63	86.35	89.08	91.81	94.54	97.27	100.00	102.73	105.46	108.19
6.25	33.03	43.74	54.46	65.18	75.89	78.57	81.25	83.93	86.61	89.28	91.96	94.64	97.32	100.00	102.68	105.36
6.50	31.62	42.14	52.66	63.18	73.70	76.33	78.96	81.59	84.22	86.85	89.48	92.11	94.74	97.37	100.00	102.63
6.75	30.27	40.60	50.93	61.26	71.59	74.17	76.76	79.34	81.92	84.50	87.09	89.67	92.25	94.83	97.42	100.00
7.00	28.98	39.13	49.27	59.42	69.56	72.10	74.64	77.17	79.71	82.25	84.78	87.32	89.85	92.39	94.93	97.46
7.25	27.75	37.72	47.68	57.65	67.61	70.10	72.60	75.09	77.58	80.07	82.56	85.05	87.54	90.03	92.53	95.02
7.50	26.57	36.36	46.15	55.94	65.73	68.18	70.63	73.08	75.52	77.97	80.42	82.87	85.31	87.76	90.21	92.66
7.75	25.45	35.07	44.69	54.31	63.93	66.33	68.74	71.14	73.55	75.95	78.36	80.76	83.17	85.57	87.98	90.38
8.00	24.37	33.82	43.28	52.73	62.18	64.55	66.91	69.27	71.64	74.00	76.36	78.73	81.09	83.46	85.82	88.18
8.25	23.34	32.63	41.92	51.21	60.51	62.83	65.15	67.48	69.80	72.12	74.45	76.77	79.09	81.41	83.74	86.06
8.50	22.35	31.48	40.62	49.76	58.89	61.17	63.46	65.74	68.03	70.31	72.59	74.88	77.16	79.45	81.73	84.01
8.75	21.41	30.39	39.37	48.35	57.33	59.58	61.83	64.07	66.32	68.56	70.81	73.05	75.30	77.54	79.79	82.04
9.00	20.50	29.34	38.17	47.00	55.83	58.04	60.25	62.46	64.67	66.88	69.08	71.29	73.50	75.71	77.92	80.13
9.25	19.64	28.33	37.01	45.70	54.39	56.56	58.73	60.91	63.08	65.25	67.42	69.59	71.77	73.94	76.11	78.28
9.50	18.81	27.36	35.90	44.45	53.00	55.13	57.27	59.41	61.54	63.68	65.82	67.95	70.09	72.23	74.36	76.50
9.75	18.02	26.43	34.84	43.25	51.65	53.76	55.86	57.96	60.06	62.16	64.27	66.37	68.47	70.57	72.67	74.78
10.00	17.27	25.54	33.81	42.09	50.36	52.43	54.50	56.56	58.63	60.70	62.77	64.84	66.91	68.97	71.04	73.11
10.25	16.54	24.68	32.83	40.97	49.11	51.15	53.18	55.22	57.25	59.29	61.32	63.36	65.40	67.43	69.47	71.50
10.50	15.85	23.86	31.88	39.89	47.91	49.91	51.91	53.92	55.92	57.92	59.93	61.93	63.94	65.94	67.94	69.95
10.75	15.19	23.08	30.97	38.86	46.74	48.72	50.69	52.66	54.63	56.61	58.58	60.55	62.52	64.50	66.47	68.44
11.00	14.55	22.32	30.09	37.86	45.62	47.57	49.51	51.45	53.39	55.33	57.28	59.22	61.16	63.10	65.04	66.99
11.25	13.94	21.59	29.24	36.89	44.54	46.45	48.37	50.28	52.19	54.10	56.02	57.93	59.84	61.75	63.67	65.58
11.50	13.36	20.90	28.43	35.96	43.50	45.38	47.26	49.15	51.03	52.91	54.80	56.68	58.56	60.45	62.33	64.22
11.75	12.81	20.23	27.65	35.07	42.49	44.34	46.20	48.06	49.91	51.77	53.62	55.48	57.33	59.19	61.04	62.90
12.00	12.27	19.58	26.90	34.21	41.52	43.34	45.17	47.00	48.83	50.65	52.48	54.31	56.14	57.96	59.79	61.62
12.25	11.76	18.97	26.17	33.37	40.58	42.38	44.18	45.98	47.78	49.58	51.38	53.18	54.98	56.78	58.58	60.38
12.50	11.28	18.37	25.47	32.57	39.67	41.44	43.22	44.99	46.77	48.54	50.31	52.09	53.86	55.64	57.41	59.19
12.75	10.81	17.80	24.80	31.79	38.79	40.54	42.29	44.04	45.79	47.53	49.28	51.03	52.78	54.53	56.28	58.03
13.00	10.36	17.26	24.15	31.05	37.94	39.67	41.39	43.11	44.84	46.56	48.29	50.01	51.73	53.46	55.18	56.90
13.25	9.93	16.73	23.53	30.33	37.12	38.82	40.52	42.22	43.92	45.62	47.32	49.02	50.72	52.42	54.12	55.82
13.50	9.52	16.22	22.93	29.63	36.33	38.01	39.68	41.36	43.03	44.71	46.38	48.06	49.73	51.41	53.09	54.76
13.75	9.13	15.74	22.35	28.96	35.56	37.22	38.87	40.52	42.17	43.83	45.48	47.13	48.78	50.43	52.09	53.74
14.00	8.75	15.27	21.79	28.31	34.82	36.45	38.08	39.71	41.34	42.97	44.60	46.23	47.86	49.49	51.12	52.75
14.25	8.39	14.82	21.25	27.68	34.11	35.71	37.32	38.93	40.54	42.14	43.75	45.36	46.96	48.57	50.18	51.79
14.50	8.05	14.39	20.73	27.07	33.41	35.00	36.58	38.17	39.76	41.34	42.93	44.51	46.10	47.68	49.27	50.85
14.75	7.72	13.97	20.23	26.49	32.74	34.31	35.87	37.44	39.00	40.56	42.13	43.69	45.26	46.82	48.38	49.95
15.00	7.40	13.57	19.75	25.92	32.09	33.64	35.18	36.72	38.27	39.81	41.35	42.90	44.44	45.98	47.53	49.07
15.25	7.10	13.19	19.28	25.37	31.47	32.99	34.51	36.03	37.56	39.08	40.60	42.13	43.65	45.17	46.70	48.22
15.50	6.81	12.82	18.83	24.84	30.86	32.36	33.86	35.37	36.87	38.37	39.88	41.38	42.88	44.39	45.89	47.39
15.75	6.53	12.46	18.40	24.33	30.27	31.75	33.24	34.72	36.20	37.69	39.17	40.65	42.14	43.62	45.10	46.59
16.00	6.26	12.12	17.98	23.84	29.70	31.16	32.63	34.09	35.56	37.02	38.48	39.95	41.41	42.88	44.34	45.81
16.25	6.01	11.79	17.58	23.36	29.14	30.59	32.04	33.48	34.93	36.37	37.82	39.27	40.71	42.16	43.60	45.05
16.50	5.76	11.47	17.19	22.90	28.61	30.04	31.46	32.89	34.32	35.75	37.17	38.60	40.03	41.46	42.89	44.31
16.75	5.53	11.17	16.81	22.45	28.09	29.50	30.91	32.32	33.73	35.14	36.55	37.96	39.37	40.78	42.19	43.60
17.00	5.30	10.87	16.44	22.01	27.58	28.98	30.37	31.76	33.16	34.55	35.94	37.33	38.73	40.12	41.51	42.90
17.25	5.09	10.59	16.09	21.59	27.10	28.47	29.85	31.22	32.60	33.97	35.35	36.73	38.10	39.48	40.85	42.23
17.50	4.88	10.32	15.75	21.19	26.62	27.98	29.34	30.70	32.06	33.42	34.78	36.13	37.49	38.85	40.21	41.57
17.75	4.68	10.05	15.42	20.79	26.16	27.51	28.85	30.19	31.53	32.88	34.22	35.56	36.90	38.25	39.59	40.93
18.00	4.49	9.80	15.11	20.41	25.72	27.04	28.37	29.70	31.02	32.35	33.68	35.00	36.33	37.66	38.98	40.31
18.25	4.31	9.56	14.80	20.04	25.29	26.60	27.91	29.22	30.53	31.84	33.15	34.46	35.77	37.08	38.39	39.70
18.50	4.14	9.32	14.50	19.68	24.87	26.16	27.46	28.75	30.05	31.34	32.64	33.93	35.23	36.52	37.82	39.11
18.75	3.97	9.09	14.21	19.34	24.46	25.74	27.02	28.30	29.58	30.86	32.14	33.42	34.70	35.98	37.26	38.54
19.00	3.81	8.87	13.94	19.00	24.06	25.33	26.59	27.86	29.12	30.39	31.66	32.92	34.19	35.45	36.72	37.98
20.00	3.23	8.07	12.91	17.75	22.59	23.80	25.01	26.22	27.43	28.64	29.85	31.05	32.26	33.47	34.68	35.89
25.00	1.44	5.38	9.33	13.27	17.21	18.20	19.18	20.17	21.15	22.14	23.12	24.11	25.09	26.08	27.07	28.05
30.00	.65	3.96	7.28	10.59	13.90	14.73	15.56	16.38	17.21	18.04	18.87	19.69	20.52	21.35	22.18	23.01

Description: This table shows the yield to maturity of a bond purchased at the price shown in the index.

Example: The yield to maturity of a 6.75 %, 18 year bond at a price of 80.00 is 9.01 %.

COUPON RATE, %

PRICE	0.00%	1.00%	2.00%	3.00%	4.00%	4.25%	4.50%	4.75%	5.00%	5.25%	5.50%	5.75%	6.00%	6.25%	6.50%	6.75%
100	0.00	1.00	2.00	3.00	4.00	4.25	4.50	4.75	5.00	5.25	5.50	5.75	6.00	6.25	6.50	6.75
99	.05	1.06	2.06	3.07	4.07	4.33	4.58	4.83	5.08	5.33	5.58	5.84	6.09	6.34	6.59	6.84
98	.11	1.12	2.13	3.14	4.15	4.41	4.66	4.91	5.17	5.42	5.67	5.93	6.18	6.43	6.69	6.94
97	.16	1.18	2.20	3.22	4.23	4.49	4.74	5.00	5.25	5.51	5.77	6.02	6.28	6.53	6.79	7.04
96	.22	1.24	2.27	3.29	4.32	4.57	4.83	5.09	5.34	5.60	5.86	6.11	6.37	6.63	6.89	7.14
95	.28	1.31	2.34	3.37	4.40	4.66	4.92	5.18	5.43	5.69	5.95	6.21	6.47	6.73	6.99	7.25
94	.34	1.37	2.41	3.45	4.48	4.74	5.00	5.27	5.53	5.79	6.05	6.31	6.57	6.83	7.09	7.35
93	.40	1.44	2.48	3.52	4.57	4.83	5.09	5.36	5.62	5.88	6.14	6.41	6.67	6.93	7.19	7.46
92	.46	1.50	2.55	3.60	4.66	4.92	5.18	5.45	5.71	5.98	6.24	6.51	6.77	7.04	7.30	7.57
91	.52	1.57	2.63	3.68	4.74	5.01	5.28	5.54	5.81	6.07	6.34	6.61	6.87	7.14	7.41	7.68
90	.58	1.64	2.70	3.77	4.83	5.10	5.37	5.64	5.90	6.17	6.44	6.71	6.98	7.25	7.52	7.79
89	.64	1.71	2.78	3.85	4.92	5.19	5.46	5.73	6.00	6.27	6.54	6.82	7.09	7.36	7.63	7.90
88	.71	1.78	2.85	3.93	5.02	5.29	5.56	5.83	6.10	6.38	6.65	6.92	7.19	7.47	7.74	8.02
87	.77	1.85	2.93	4.02	5.11	5.38	5.66	5.93	6.20	6.48	6.75	7.03	7.31	7.58	7.86	8.13
86	.83	1.92	3.01	4.10	5.20	5.48	5.75	6.03	6.31	6.58	6.86	7.14	7.42	7.70	7.97	8.25
85	.90	1.99	3.09	4.19	5.30	5.58	5.85	6.13	6.41	6.69	6.97	7.25	7.53	7.81	8.09	8.37
84	.97	2.06	3.17	4.28	5.40	5.68	5.96	6.24	6.52	6.80	7.08	7.36	7.65	7.93	8.21	8.50
83	1.03	2.14	3.25	4.37	5.49	5.78	6.06	6.34	6.63	6.91	7.19	7.48	7.76	8.05	8.34	8.62
82	1.10	2.21	3.33	4.46	5.60	5.88	6.16	6.45	6.74	7.02	7.31	7.60	7.88	8.17	8.46	8.75
81	1.17	2.29	3.42	4.55	5.70	5.98	6.27	6.56	6.85	7.14	7.43	7.72	8.01	8.30	8.59	8.88
80	1.24	2.37	3.50	4.65	5.80	6.09	6.38	6.67	6.96	7.25	7.55	7.84	8.13	8.42	8.72	9.01
79	1.31	2.44	3.59	4.74	5.91	6.20	6.49	6.78	7.08	7.37	7.67	7.96	8.26	8.55	8.85	9.15
78	1.38	2.52	3.68	4.84	6.01	6.31	6.60	6.90	7.19	7.49	7.79	8.09	8.39	8.68	8.98	9.28
77	1.45	2.60	3.77	4.94	6.12	6.42	6.72	7.02	7.31	7.61	7.91	8.21	8.52	8.82	9.12	9.42
76	1.53	2.69	3.86	5.04	6.23	6.53	6.83	7.13	7.44	7.74	8.04	8.35	8.65	8.95	9.26	9.57
75	1.60	2.77	3.95	5.14	6.35	6.65	6.95	7.26	7.56	7.87	8.17	8.48	8.79	9.09	9.40	9.71
74	1.67	2.85	4.04	5.25	6.46	6.77	7.07	7.38	7.69	8.00	8.30	8.61	8.92	9.24	9.55	9.86
73	1.75	2.94	4.14	5.35	6.58	6.89	7.19	7.50	7.82	8.13	8.44	8.75	9.07	9.38	9.70	10.01
72	1.83	3.02	4.23	5.46	6.70	7.01	7.32	7.63	7.95	8.26	8.58	8.89	9.21	9.53	9.85	10.17
71	1.91	3.11	4.33	5.57	6.82	7.13	7.45	7.76	8.08	8.40	8.72	9.04	9.36	9.68	10.00	10.32
70	1.99	3.20	4.43	5.68	6.94	7.26	7.58	7.90	8.22	8.54	8.86	9.18	9.51	9.83	10.16	10.49
69	2.07	3.29	4.53	5.79	7.07	7.39	7.71	8.03	8.36	8.68	9.01	9.33	9.66	9.99	10.32	10.65
68	2.15	3.38	4.64	5.91	7.19	7.52	7.84	8.17	8.50	8.83	9.16	9.49	9.82	10.15	10.49	10.82
67	2.23	3.48	4.74	6.02	7.33	7.65	7.98	8.31	8.64	8.98	9.31	9.64	9.98	10.32	10.65	10.99
66	2.32	3.57	4.85	6.14	7.46	7.79	8.12	8.46	8.79	9.13	9.47	9.80	10.14	10.48	10.83	11.17
65	2.40	3.67	4.96	6.27	7.60	7.93	8.27	8.60	8.94	9.28	9.63	9.97	10.31	10.66	11.00	11.35
64	2.49	3.77	5.07	6.39	7.73	8.07	8.41	8.76	9.10	9.44	9.79	10.14	10.48	10.83	11.18	11.54
63	2.58	3.87	5.18	6.52	7.88	8.22	8.56	8.91	9.26	9.61	9.96	10.31	10.66	11.01	11.37	11.73
62	2.67	3.97	5.30	6.65	8.02	8.37	8.72	9.07	9.42	9.77	10.13	10.48	10.84	11.20	11.56	11.92
61	2.76	4.07	5.41	6.78	8.17	8.52	8.87	9.23	9.59	9.94	10.30	10.66	11.02	11.39	11.75	12.12
60	2.85	4.18	5.53	6.92	8.32	8.68	9.04	9.39	9.76	10.12	10.48	10.85	11.21	11.58	11.95	12.32
59	2.95	4.29	5.66	7.05	8.48	8.84	9.20	9.56	9.93	10.30	10.67	11.04	11.41	11.78	12.16	12.53
58	3.04	4.40	5.78	7.19	8.64	9.00	9.37	9.74	10.11	10.48	10.86	11.23	11.61	11.99	12.37	12.75
57	3.14	4.51	5.91	7.34	8.80	9.17	9.54	9.92	10.29	10.67	11.05	11.43	11.81	12.20	12.59	12.97
56	3.24	4.62	6.04	7.49	8.97	9.34	9.72	10.10	10.48	10.86	11.25	11.64	12.02	12.42	12.81	13.20
55	3.34	4.74	6.17	7.64	9.14	9.52	9.90	10.29	10.67	11.06	11.45	11.85	12.24	12.64	13.04	13.44
54	3.45	4.86	6.31	7.79	9.31	9.70	10.09	10.48	10.87	11.27	11.66	12.06	12.46	12.87	13.27	13.68
53	3.55	4.98	6.45	7.95	9.49	9.89	10.28	10.68	11.08	11.48	11.88	12.29	12.69	13.10	13.52	13.93
52	3.66	5.11	6.59	8.11	9.68	10.08	10.48	10.88	11.29	11.69	12.10	12.52	12.93	13.35	13.77	14.19
51	3.77	5.23	6.74	8.28	9.87	10.27	10.68	11.09	11.50	11.92	12.33	12.75	13.17	13.60	14.03	14.46
50	3.88	5.36	6.88	8.45	10.07	10.48	10.89	11.31	11.72	12.15	12.57	13.00	13.43	13.86	14.29	14.73
49	4.00	5.49	7.04	8.63	10.27	10.68	11.11	11.53	11.95	12.38	12.82	13.25	13.69	14.13	14.57	15.02
48	4.11	5.63	7.19	8.81	10.48	10.90	11.33	11.76	12.19	12.63	13.07	13.51	13.96	14.40	14.86	15.31
47	4.23	5.77	7.36	9.00	10.69	11.12	11.56	11.99	12.44	12.88	13.33	13.78	14.23	14.69	15.15	15.62
46	4.36	5.91	7.52	9.19	10.91	11.35	11.79	12.24	12.69	13.14	13.60	14.06	14.52	14.99	15.46	15.93
45	4.48	6.06	7.69	9.38	11.14	11.59	12.04	12.49	12.95	13.41	13.88	14.35	14.82	15.30	15.78	16.26
44	4.61	6.21	7.87	9.59	11.37	11.83	12.29	12.75	13.22	13.70	14.17	14.65	15.13	15.62	16.11	16.60
43	4.74	6.36	8.05	9.80	11.62	12.08	12.55	13.03	13.50	13.99	14.47	14.96	15.46	15.95	16.45	16.96
42	4.87	6.52	8.23	10.01	11.87	12.34	12.82	13.31	13.80	14.29	14.79	15.29	15.79	16.30	16.81	17.33
41	5.01	6.68	8.42	10.24	12.13	12.62	13.11	13.60	14.10	14.60	15.11	15.62	16.14	16.66	17.19	17.72
40	5.15	6.85	8.62	10.47	12.40	12.90	13.40	13.91	14.42	14.93	15.45	15.98	16.51	17.04	17.58	18.12
39	5.30	7.02	8.82	10.71	12.68	13.19	13.70	14.22	14.74	15.27	15.81	16.34	16.89	17.44	17.99	18.54
35	5.91	7.76	9.71	11.76	13.93	14.49	15.06	15.64	16.22	16.80	17.40	18.00	18.60	19.21	19.83	20.46
30	6.80	8.84	11.02	13.36	15.86	16.51	17.17	17.84	18.52	19.21	19.91	20.61	21.33	22.05	22.78	23.52
25	7.85	10.15	12.67	15.42	18.41	19.20	20.00	20.81	21.64	22.48	23.34	24.20	25.08	25.97	26.87	27.77
20	9.14	11.83	14.86	18.27	22.08	23.09	24.12	25.17	26.25	27.34	28.45	29.58	30.72	31.87	33.04	34.21
15	10.82	14.14	18.08	22.72	28.08	29.51	30.98	32.48	34.01	35.55	37.12	38.70	40.30	41.91	43.53	45.16
10	13.21	17.80	23.80	31.47	40.47	42.85	45.26	47.69	50.14	52.60	55.07	57.55	60.04	62.53	65.02	67.51

Description: This table shows the price to pay for a bond at the yield rate. The yield is to maturity.

Example: The price of a 10.75 %, 18 year bond to yield 8 % to maturity is $ 126.00.

COUPON RATE, %

YIELD	7.00%	7.25%	7.50%	7.75%	8.00%	8.25%	8.50%	8.75%	9.00%	9.25%	9.50%	9.75%	10.00%	10.25%	10.50%	10.75%
0.00	226.00	230.50	235.00	239.50	244.00	248.50	253.00	257.50	262.00	266.50	271.00	275.50	280.00	284.50	289.00	293.50
1.00	198.61	202.72	206.83	210.94	215.05	219.16	223.27	227.38	231.48	235.59	239.70	243.81	247.92	252.03	256.14	260.25
2.00	175.27	179.03	182.80	186.56	190.32	194.09	197.85	201.61	205.38	209.14	212.90	216.67	220.43	224.19	227.96	231.72
3.00	155.32	158.78	162.24	165.69	169.15	172.61	176.07	179.52	182.98	186.44	189.90	193.35	196.81	200.27	203.73	207.19
4.00	138.23	141.42	144.61	147.79	150.98	154.16	157.35	160.54	163.72	166.91	170.09	173.28	176.47	179.65	182.84	186.02
4.25	134.35	137.48	140.60	143.72	146.85	149.97	153.09	156.22	159.34	162.46	165.58	168.71	171.83	174.95	178.08	181.20
4.50	130.62	133.68	136.74	139.80	142.87	145.93	148.99	152.05	155.11	158.17	161.24	164.30	167.36	170.42	173.48	176.55
4.75	127.02	130.02	133.03	136.03	139.03	142.03	145.04	148.04	151.04	154.04	157.04	160.05	163.05	166.05	169.05	172.06
5.00	123.56	126.50	129.45	132.39	135.33	138.28	141.22	144.17	147.11	150.06	153.00	155.95	158.89	161.84	164.78	167.72
5.25	120.22	123.11	126.00	128.88	131.77	134.66	137.55	140.44	143.33	146.21	149.10	151.99	154.88	157.77	160.66	163.54
5.50	117.00	119.84	122.67	125.50	128.34	131.17	134.00	136.84	139.67	142.51	145.34	148.17	151.01	153.84	156.67	159.51
5.75	113.90	116.68	119.46	122.25	125.03	127.81	130.59	133.37	136.15	138.93	141.71	144.49	147.27	150.05	152.83	155.61
6.00	110.92	113.65	116.37	119.10	121.83	124.56	127.29	130.02	132.75	135.48	138.21	140.94	143.66	146.39	149.12	151.85
6.25	108.04	110.72	113.39	116.07	118.75	121.43	124.11	126.79	129.47	132.15	134.82	137.50	140.18	142.86	145.54	148.22
6.50	105.26	107.89	110.52	113.15	115.78	118.41	121.04	123.67	126.30	128.93	131.56	134.19	136.82	139.45	142.08	144.71
6.75	102.58	105.17	107.75	110.33	112.91	115.50	118.08	120.66	123.24	125.83	128.41	130.99	133.57	136.16	138.74	141.32
7.00	100.00	102.54	105.07	107.61	110.15	112.68	115.22	117.75	120.29	122.83	125.36	127.90	130.44	132.97	135.51	138.04
7.25	97.51	100.00	102.49	104.98	107.47	109.97	112.46	114.95	117.44	119.93	122.42	124.91	127.40	129.90	132.39	134.88
7.50	95.10	97.55	100.00	102.45	104.90	107.34	109.79	112.24	114.69	117.13	119.58	122.03	124.48	126.92	129.37	131.82
7.75	92.79	95.19	97.60	100.00	102.40	104.81	107.21	109.62	112.02	114.43	116.83	119.24	121.64	124.05	126.45	128.86
8.00	90.55	92.91	95.27	97.64	100.00	102.36	104.73	107.09	109.45	111.82	114.18	116.54	118.91	121.27	123.64	126.00
8.25	88.38	90.71	93.03	95.35	97.68	100.00	102.32	104.65	106.97	109.29	111.62	113.94	116.26	118.59	120.91	123.23
8.50	86.30	88.58	90.86	93.15	95.43	97.72	100.00	102.28	104.57	106.85	109.14	111.42	113.70	115.99	118.27	120.55
8.75	84.28	86.53	88.77	91.02	93.26	95.51	97.75	100.00	102.25	104.49	106.74	108.98	111.23	113.47	115.72	117.96
9.00	82.33	84.54	86.75	88.96	91.17	93.38	95.58	97.79	100.00	102.21	104.42	106.62	108.83	111.04	113.25	115.46
9.25	80.45	82.62	84.80	86.97	89.14	91.31	93.48	95.66	97.83	100.00	102.17	104.34	106.52	108.69	110.86	113.03
9.50	78.63	80.77	82.91	85.04	87.18	89.32	91.45	93.59	95.73	97.86	100.00	102.14	104.27	106.41	108.55	110.68
9.75	76.88	78.98	81.08	83.18	85.29	87.39	89.49	91.59	93.69	95.80	97.90	100.00	102.10	104.20	106.31	108.41
10.00	75.18	77.25	79.32	81.38	83.45	85.52	87.59	89.66	91.73	93.79	95.86	97.93	100.00	102.07	104.14	106.21
10.25	73.54	75.57	77.61	79.64	81.68	83.72	85.75	87.79	89.82	91.86	93.89	95.93	97.96	100.00	102.04	104.07
10.50	71.95	73.95	75.96	77.96	79.96	81.97	83.97	85.97	87.98	89.98	91.99	93.99	95.99	98.00	100.00	102.00
10.75	70.41	72.39	74.36	76.33	78.30	80.28	82.25	84.22	86.19	88.17	90.14	92.11	94.08	96.06	98.03	100.00
11.00	68.93	70.87	72.81	74.75	76.70	78.64	80.58	82.52	84.46	86.41	88.35	90.29	92.23	94.17	96.12	98.06
11.25	67.49	69.40	71.31	73.23	75.14	77.05	78.96	80.88	82.79	84.70	86.61	88.53	90.44	92.35	94.26	96.18
11.50	66.10	67.98	69.87	71.75	73.63	75.52	77.40	79.28	81.17	83.05	84.93	86.82	88.70	90.58	92.47	94.35
11.75	64.75	66.61	68.46	70.32	72.17	74.03	75.88	77.74	79.59	81.45	83.30	85.16	87.01	88.87	90.72	92.58
12.00	63.45	65.28	67.10	68.93	70.76	72.59	74.41	76.24	78.07	79.90	81.72	83.55	85.38	87.21	89.03	90.86
12.25	62.18	63.99	65.79	67.59	69.39	71.19	72.99	74.79	76.59	78.39	80.19	81.99	83.79	85.59	87.39	89.20
12.50	60.96	62.74	64.51	66.28	68.06	69.83	71.61	73.38	75.16	76.93	78.71	80.48	82.26	84.03	85.80	87.58
12.75	59.78	61.53	63.27	65.02	66.77	68.52	70.27	72.02	73.77	75.52	77.26	79.01	80.76	82.51	84.26	86.01
13.00	58.63	60.35	62.08	63.80	65.52	67.25	68.97	70.70	72.42	74.14	75.87	77.59	79.31	81.04	82.76	84.49
13.25	57.52	59.21	60.91	62.61	64.31	66.01	67.71	69.41	71.11	72.81	74.51	76.21	77.91	79.61	81.31	83.01
13.50	56.44	58.11	59.79	61.46	63.14	64.81	66.49	68.17	69.84	71.52	73.19	74.87	76.54	78.22	79.89	81.57
13.75	55.39	57.04	58.70	60.35	62.00	63.65	65.30	66.96	68.61	70.26	71.91	73.57	75.22	76.87	78.52	80.17
14.00	54.38	56.01	57.64	59.26	60.89	62.52	64.15	65.78	67.41	69.04	70.67	72.30	73.93	75.56	77.19	78.82
14.25	53.39	55.00	56.61	58.21	59.82	61.43	63.04	64.64	66.25	67.86	69.46	71.07	72.68	74.29	75.89	77.50
14.50	52.44	54.02	55.61	57.19	58.78	60.37	61.95	63.54	65.12	66.71	68.29	69.88	71.46	73.05	74.63	76.22
14.75	51.51	53.08	54.64	56.20	57.77	59.33	60.90	62.46	64.03	65.59	67.15	68.72	70.28	71.85	73.41	74.97
15.00	50.61	52.16	53.70	55.24	56.79	58.33	59.87	61.42	62.96	64.50	66.05	67.59	69.13	70.68	72.22	73.76
15.25	49.74	51.26	52.79	54.31	55.83	57.36	58.88	60.40	61.93	63.45	64.97	66.49	68.02	69.54	71.06	72.59
15.50	48.89	50.40	51.90	53.40	54.91	56.41	57.91	59.42	60.92	62.42	63.93	65.43	66.93	68.43	69.94	71.44
15.75	48.07	49.56	51.04	52.52	54.01	55.49	56.97	58.46	59.94	61.42	62.91	64.39	65.88	67.36	68.84	70.33
16.00	47.27	48.74	50.20	51.67	53.13	54.60	56.06	57.53	58.99	60.45	61.92	63.38	64.85	66.31	67.78	69.24
16.25	46.50	47.94	49.39	50.83	52.28	53.73	55.17	56.62	58.06	59.51	60.96	62.40	63.85	65.29	66.74	68.19
16.50	45.74	47.17	48.60	50.03	51.45	52.88	54.31	55.74	57.16	58.59	60.02	61.45	62.88	64.30	65.73	67.16
16.75	45.01	46.42	47.83	49.24	50.65	52.06	53.47	54.88	56.29	57.70	59.11	60.52	61.93	63.34	64.75	66.16
17.00	44.30	45.69	47.08	48.47	49.87	51.26	52.65	54.04	55.44	56.83	58.22	59.61	61.01	62.40	63.79	65.18
17.25	43.60	44.98	46.35	47.73	49.11	50.48	51.86	53.23	54.61	55.98	57.36	58.73	60.11	61.48	62.86	64.24
17.50	42.93	44.29	45.65	47.01	48.36	49.72	51.08	52.44	53.80	55.16	56.52	57.88	59.23	60.59	61.95	63.31
17.75	42.27	43.62	44.96	46.30	47.64	48.99	50.33	51.67	53.01	54.36	55.70	57.04	58.38	59.73	61.07	62.41
18.00	41.64	42.96	44.29	45.61	46.94	48.27	49.59	50.92	52.25	53.57	54.90	56.23	57.55	58.88	60.21	61.53
18.25	41.01	42.33	43.64	44.95	46.26	47.57	48.88	50.19	51.50	52.81	54.12	55.43	56.74	58.05	59.37	60.68
18.50	40.41	41.71	43.00	44.30	45.59	46.89	48.18	49.48	50.77	52.07	53.36	54.66	55.96	57.25	58.55	59.84
18.75	39.82	41.10	42.38	43.66	44.94	46.22	47.50	48.78	50.07	51.35	52.63	53.91	55.19	56.47	57.75	59.03
19.00	39.25	40.51	41.78	43.05	44.31	45.58	46.84	48.11	49.37	50.64	51.91	53.17	54.44	55.70	56.97	58.23
20.00	37.10	38.31	39.52	40.73	41.94	43.15	44.36	45.57	46.78	47.99	49.20	50.41	51.62	52.83	54.04	55.25
25.00	29.04	30.02	31.01	31.99	32.98	33.97	34.95	35.94	36.92	37.91	38.89	39.88	40.86	41.85	42.84	43.82
30.00	23.83	24.66	25.49	26.32	27.15	27.97	28.80	29.63	30.46	31.28	32.11	32.94	33.77	34.60	35.42	36.25

Description: This table shows the yield to maturity of a bond purchased at the price shown in the index.

Example: The yield to maturity of a 10.75 %, 18 year bond at a price of 111.00 is 9.46 %.

COUPON RATE, %

PRICE	7.00%	7.25%	7.50%	7.75%	8.00%	8.25%	8.50%	8.75%	9.00%	9.25%	9.50%	9.75%	10.00%	10.25%	10.50%	10.75%
155	3.01	3.20	3.39	3.57	3.76	3.95	4.13	4.32	4.50	4.69	4.87	5.05	5.24	5.42	5.60	5.79
150	3.29	3.48	3.67	3.86	4.05	4.24	4.43	4.62	4.81	5.00	5.19	5.37	5.56	5.75	5.94	6.12
145	3.58	3.78	3.97	4.17	4.36	4.55	4.75	4.94	5.13	5.33	5.52	5.71	5.90	6.09	6.28	6.47
140	3.88	4.08	4.28	4.48	4.68	4.88	5.08	5.27	5.47	5.67	5.87	6.06	6.26	6.45	6.65	6.84
135	4.20	4.41	4.61	4.81	5.02	5.22	5.42	5.63	5.83	6.03	6.23	6.43	6.63	6.83	7.04	7.24
130	4.54	4.75	4.96	5.16	5.37	5.58	5.79	6.00	6.20	6.41	6.62	6.82	7.03	7.24	7.44	7.65
125	4.89	5.10	5.32	5.53	5.75	5.96	6.17	6.39	6.60	6.81	7.03	7.24	7.45	7.66	7.87	8.08
124	4.96	5.18	5.39	5.61	5.82	6.04	6.25	6.47	6.68	6.90	7.11	7.32	7.54	7.75	7.96	8.17
123	5.04	5.25	5.47	5.69	5.90	6.12	6.33	6.55	6.77	6.98	7.20	7.41	7.62	7.84	8.05	8.27
122	5.11	5.33	5.55	5.76	5.98	6.20	6.42	6.63	6.85	7.07	7.28	7.50	7.71	7.93	8.14	8.36
121	5.19	5.40	5.62	5.84	6.06	6.28	6.50	6.72	6.93	7.15	7.37	7.59	7.80	8.02	8.24	8.45
120	5.26	5.48	5.70	5.92	6.14	6.36	6.58	6.80	7.02	7.24	7.46	7.68	7.89	8.11	8.33	8.55
119	5.34	5.56	5.78	6.00	6.22	6.45	6.67	6.89	7.11	7.33	7.55	7.77	7.99	8.21	8.43	8.64
118	5.42	5.64	5.86	6.08	6.31	6.53	6.75	6.97	7.20	7.42	7.64	7.86	8.08	8.30	8.52	8.74
117	5.50	5.72	5.94	6.17	6.39	6.61	6.84	7.06	7.28	7.51	7.73	7.95	8.17	8.40	8.62	8.84
116	5.57	5.80	6.03	6.25	6.48	6.70	6.93	7.15	7.37	7.60	7.82	8.05	8.27	8.49	8.72	8.94
115	5.66	5.88	6.11	6.34	6.56	6.79	7.01	7.24	7.47	7.69	7.92	8.14	8.37	8.59	8.82	9.04
114	5.74	5.97	6.19	6.42	6.65	6.88	7.10	7.33	7.56	7.79	8.01	8.24	8.47	8.69	8.92	9.14
113	5.82	6.05	6.28	6.51	6.74	6.97	7.20	7.42	7.65	7.88	8.11	8.34	8.57	8.79	9.02	9.25
112	5.90	6.13	6.37	6.60	6.83	7.06	7.29	7.52	7.75	7.98	8.21	8.44	8.67	8.90	9.12	9.35
111	5.99	6.22	6.45	6.68	6.92	7.15	7.38	7.61	7.84	8.08	8.31	8.54	8.77	9.00	9.23	9.46
110	6.07	6.31	6.54	6.77	7.01	7.24	7.48	7.71	7.94	8.17	8.41	8.64	8.87	9.10	9.34	9.57
109	6.16	6.40	6.63	6.87	7.10	7.34	7.57	7.81	8.04	8.27	8.51	8.74	8.98	9.21	9.45	9.68
108	6.25	6.49	6.72	6.96	7.20	7.43	7.67	7.90	8.14	8.38	8.61	8.85	9.08	9.32	9.56	9.79
107	6.34	6.58	6.81	7.05	7.29	7.53	7.77	8.00	8.24	8.48	8.72	8.95	9.19	9.43	9.67	9.90
106	6.43	6.67	6.91	7.15	7.39	7.63	7.87	8.11	8.34	8.58	8.82	9.06	9.30	9.54	9.78	10.02
105	6.52	6.76	7.00	7.24	7.48	7.73	7.97	8.21	8.45	8.69	8.93	9.17	9.41	9.65	9.89	10.14
104	6.61	6.85	7.10	7.34	7.58	7.83	8.07	8.31	8.56	8.80	9.04	9.28	9.53	9.77	10.01	10.25
103	6.71	6.95	7.20	7.44	7.68	7.93	8.17	8.42	8.66	8.91	9.15	9.40	9.64	9.88	10.13	10.37
102	6.80	7.05	7.29	7.54	7.79	8.03	8.28	8.53	8.77	9.02	9.26	9.51	9.76	10.00	10.25	10.50
101	6.90	7.15	7.39	7.64	7.89	8.14	8.39	8.63	8.88	9.13	9.38	9.63	9.88	10.12	10.37	10.62
100	7.00	7.25	7.50	7.75	8.00	8.25	8.50	8.75	9.00	9.25	9.50	9.75	10.00	10.25	10.50	10.75
99	7.09	7.35	7.60	7.85	8.10	8.35	8.61	8.86	9.11	9.36	9.61	9.86	10.12	10.37	10.62	10.87
98	7.19	7.45	7.70	7.96	8.21	8.46	8.72	8.97	9.22	9.48	9.73	9.99	10.24	10.49	10.75	11.00
97	7.30	7.55	7.81	8.06	8.32	8.58	8.83	9.09	9.34	9.60	9.85	10.11	10.37	10.62	10.88	11.13
96	7.40	7.66	7.92	8.17	8.43	8.69	8.95	9.20	9.46	9.72	9.98	10.24	10.49	10.75	11.01	11.27
95	7.51	7.77	8.02	8.28	8.54	8.80	9.06	9.32	9.58	9.84	10.10	10.36	10.62	10.88	11.14	11.41
94	7.61	7.87	8.14	8.40	8.66	8.92	9.18	9.44	9.71	9.97	10.23	10.49	10.76	11.02	11.28	11.54
93	7.72	7.98	8.25	8.51	8.78	9.04	9.30	9.57	9.83	10.10	10.36	10.63	10.89	11.16	11.42	11.68
92	7.83	8.10	8.36	8.63	8.89	9.16	9.43	9.69	9.96	10.23	10.49	10.76	11.03	11.29	11.56	11.83
91	7.94	8.21	8.48	8.75	9.02	9.28	9.55	9.82	10.09	10.36	10.63	10.90	11.17	11.44	11.70	11.97
90	8.06	8.33	8.60	8.87	9.14	9.41	9.68	9.95	10.22	10.49	10.76	11.04	11.31	11.58	11.85	12.12
89	8.17	8.45	8.72	8.99	9.26	9.54	9.81	10.08	10.36	10.63	10.90	11.18	11.45	11.73	12.00	12.27
88	8.29	8.56	8.84	9.11	9.39	9.66	9.94	10.22	10.49	10.77	11.04	11.32	11.60	11.87	12.15	12.43
87	8.41	8.69	8.96	9.24	9.52	9.80	10.07	10.35	10.63	10.91	11.19	11.47	11.75	12.03	12.31	12.59
86	8.53	8.81	9.09	9.37	9.65	9.93	10.21	10.49	10.77	11.05	11.34	11.62	11.90	12.18	12.46	12.75
85	8.65	8.94	9.22	9.50	9.78	10.07	10.35	10.63	10.92	11.20	11.48	11.77	12.05	12.34	12.62	12.91
84	8.78	9.06	9.35	9.63	9.92	10.21	10.49	10.78	11.06	11.35	11.64	11.92	12.21	12.50	12.79	13.08
83	8.91	9.20	9.48	9.77	10.06	10.35	10.63	10.92	11.21	11.50	11.79	12.08	12.37	12.66	12.95	13.25
82	9.04	9.33	9.62	9.91	10.20	10.49	10.78	11.07	11.37	11.66	11.95	12.24	12.54	12.83	13.12	13.42
81	9.17	9.46	9.76	10.05	10.34	10.64	10.93	11.23	11.52	11.82	12.11	12.41	12.70	13.00	13.30	13.60
80	9.31	9.60	9.90	10.19	10.49	10.79	11.08	11.38	11.68	11.98	12.28	12.58	12.88	13.18	13.48	13.78
79	9.44	9.74	10.04	10.34	10.64	10.94	11.24	11.54	11.84	12.14	12.44	12.75	13.05	13.35	13.66	13.96
78	9.58	9.89	10.19	10.49	10.79	11.09	11.40	11.70	12.01	12.31	12.62	12.92	13.23	13.54	13.84	14.15
77	9.73	10.03	10.34	10.64	10.95	11.25	11.56	11.87	12.17	12.48	12.79	13.10	13.41	13.72	14.03	14.34
76	9.87	10.18	10.49	10.80	11.11	11.42	11.73	12.04	12.35	12.66	12.97	13.28	13.60	13.91	14.22	14.54
75	10.02	10.33	10.64	10.96	11.27	11.58	11.89	12.21	12.52	12.84	13.15	13.47	13.79	14.10	14.42	14.74
74	10.17	10.49	10.80	11.12	11.43	11.75	12.07	12.38	12.70	13.02	13.34	13.66	13.98	14.30	14.62	14.95
73	10.33	10.65	10.96	11.28	11.60	11.92	12.24	12.56	12.89	13.21	13.53	13.86	14.18	14.50	14.83	15.16
70	10.81	11.14	11.47	11.80	12.13	12.46	12.80	13.13	13.46	13.80	14.13	14.47	14.81	15.14	15.48	15.82
65	11.70	12.05	12.40	12.75	13.10	13.46	13.81	14.17	14.52	14.88	15.24	15.60	15.96	16.32	16.68	17.04
60	12.70	13.07	13.45	13.82	14.20	14.58	14.96	15.35	15.73	16.11	16.50	16.89	17.28	17.67	18.06	18.45
55	13.84	14.25	14.65	15.06	15.47	15.88	16.29	16.71	17.13	17.54	17.96	18.38	18.81	19.23	19.66	20.08
50	15.17	15.61	16.06	16.50	16.95	17.40	17.86	18.31	18.77	19.23	19.69	20.15	20.62	21.08	21.55	22.02
45	16.75	17.24	17.73	18.22	18.72	19.22	19.73	20.23	20.74	21.25	21.77	22.28	22.80	23.32	23.84	24.37
40	18.67	19.22	19.77	20.33	20.90	21.46	22.03	22.60	23.18	23.76	24.34	24.92	25.51	26.10	26.69	27.28
35	21.09	21.72	22.36	23.00	23.65	24.30	24.96	25.62	26.29	26.96	27.63	28.30	28.98	29.66	30.35	31.03
30	24.26	25.01	25.77	26.53	27.30	28.08	28.86	29.64	30.43	31.22	32.02	32.82	33.62	34.43	35.23	36.04

Description: This table shows the price to pay for a bond at the yield rate. The yield is to maturity.

Example: The price of a 15.00 %, 18 year bond to yield 8 % to maturity is $ 166.18.

COUPON RATE, %

YIELD	11.00%	11.25%	11.50%	11.75%	12.00%	12.25%	12.50%	12.75%	13.00%	13.25%	13.50%	13.75%	14.00%	14.25%	14.50%	15.00%
0.00	298.00	302.50	307.00	311.50	316.00	320.50	325.00	329.50	334.00	338.50	343.00	347.50	352.00	356.50	361.00	370.00
1.00	264.36	268.46	272.57	276.68	280.79	284.90	289.01	293.12	297.23	301.33	305.44	309.55	313.66	317.77	321.88	330.10
2.00	235.48	239.25	243.01	246.77	250.54	254.30	258.06	261.83	265.59	269.35	273.12	276.88	280.65	284.41	288.17	295.70
3.00	210.64	214.10	217.56	221.02	224.47	227.93	231.39	234.85	238.30	241.76	245.22	248.68	252.13	255.59	259.05	265.96
4.00	189.21	192.40	195.58	198.77	201.96	205.14	208.33	211.51	214.70	217.89	221.07	224.26	227.44	230.63	233.82	240.19
4.25	184.32	187.45	190.57	193.69	196.82	199.94	203.06	206.18	209.31	212.43	215.55	218.68	221.80	224.92	228.05	234.29
4.50	179.61	182.67	185.73	188.79	191.85	194.92	197.98	201.04	204.10	207.16	210.23	213.29	216.35	219.41	222.47	228.60
4.75	175.06	178.06	181.06	184.07	187.07	190.07	193.07	196.07	199.08	202.08	205.08	208.08	211.09	214.09	217.09	223.10
5.00	170.67	173.61	176.56	179.50	182.45	185.39	188.34	191.28	194.23	197.17	200.11	203.06	206.00	208.95	211.89	217.78
5.25	166.43	169.32	172.21	175.10	177.99	180.87	183.76	186.65	189.54	192.43	195.32	198.20	201.09	203.98	206.87	212.65
5.50	162.34	165.18	168.01	170.84	173.68	176.51	179.34	182.18	185.01	187.85	190.68	193.51	196.35	199.18	202.01	207.68
5.75	158.39	161.17	163.95	166.74	169.52	172.30	175.08	177.86	180.64	183.42	186.20	188.98	191.76	194.54	197.32	202.88
6.00	154.58	157.31	160.04	162.77	165.50	168.23	170.95	173.68	176.41	179.14	181.87	184.60	187.33	190.06	192.79	198.25
6.25	150.90	153.58	156.26	158.93	161.61	164.29	166.97	169.65	172.33	175.01	177.69	180.37	183.04	185.72	188.40	193.76
6.50	147.34	149.97	152.60	155.23	157.86	160.49	163.12	165.75	168.38	171.01	173.64	176.27	178.90	181.53	184.16	189.42
6.75	143.90	146.49	149.07	151.65	154.23	156.82	159.40	161.98	164.56	167.15	169.73	172.31	174.89	177.48	180.06	185.22
7.00	140.58	143.12	145.65	148.19	150.73	153.26	155.80	158.34	160.87	163.41	165.94	168.48	171.02	173.55	176.09	181.16
7.25	137.37	139.86	142.35	144.84	147.34	149.83	152.32	154.81	157.30	159.79	162.28	164.78	167.27	169.76	172.25	177.23
7.50	134.27	136.71	139.16	141.61	144.06	146.50	148.95	151.40	153.85	156.29	158.74	161.19	163.64	166.08	168.53	173.43
7.75	131.26	133.67	136.07	138.48	140.88	143.29	145.69	148.10	150.50	152.91	155.31	157.72	160.12	162.53	164.93	169.74
8.00	128.36	130.73	133.09	135.45	137.82	140.18	142.54	144.91	147.27	149.63	152.00	154.36	156.72	159.09	161.45	166.18
8.25	125.55	127.88	130.20	132.52	134.85	137.17	139.49	141.82	144.14	146.46	148.79	151.11	153.43	155.76	158.08	162.73
8.50	122.84	125.12	127.41	129.69	131.97	134.26	136.54	138.83	141.11	143.39	145.68	147.96	150.24	152.53	154.81	159.38
8.75	120.21	122.46	124.70	126.95	129.19	131.44	133.68	135.93	138.17	140.42	142.67	144.91	147.16	149.40	151.65	156.14
9.00	117.67	119.87	122.08	124.29	126.50	128.71	130.92	133.12	135.33	137.54	139.75	141.96	144.17	146.37	148.58	153.00
9.25	115.20	117.38	119.55	121.72	123.89	126.06	128.23	130.41	132.58	134.75	136.92	139.09	141.27	143.44	145.61	149.95
9.50	112.82	114.96	117.09	119.23	121.37	123.50	125.64	127.77	129.91	132.05	134.18	136.32	138.46	140.59	142.73	147.00
9.75	110.51	112.61	114.71	116.82	118.92	121.02	123.12	125.22	127.33	129.43	131.53	133.63	135.73	137.84	139.94	144.14
10.00	108.27	110.34	112.41	114.48	116.55	118.62	120.68	122.75	124.82	126.89	128.96	131.03	133.09	135.16	137.23	141.37
10.25	106.11	108.14	110.18	112.21	114.25	116.28	118.32	120.36	122.39	124.43	126.46	128.50	130.53	132.57	134.60	138.68
10.50	104.01	106.01	108.01	110.02	112.02	114.03	116.03	118.03	120.04	122.04	124.04	126.05	128.05	130.05	132.06	136.06
10.75	101.97	103.94	105.92	107.89	109.86	111.83	113.81	115.78	117.75	119.72	121.70	123.67	125.64	127.61	129.59	133.53
11.00	100.00	101.94	103.88	105.83	107.77	109.71	111.65	113.59	115.54	117.48	119.42	121.36	123.30	125.25	127.19	131.07
11.25	98.09	100.00	101.91	103.82	105.74	107.65	109.56	111.47	113.39	115.30	117.21	119.12	121.04	122.95	124.86	128.69
11.50	96.23	98.12	100.00	101.88	103.77	105.65	107.53	109.42	111.30	113.18	115.07	116.95	118.83	120.72	122.60	126.37
11.75	94.43	96.29	98.14	100.00	101.86	103.71	105.57	107.42	109.28	111.13	112.99	114.84	116.70	118.55	120.41	124.12
12.00	92.69	94.52	96.34	98.17	100.00	101.83	103.66	105.48	107.31	109.14	110.97	112.79	114.62	116.45	118.28	121.93
12.25	91.00	92.80	94.60	96.40	98.20	100.00	101.80	103.60	105.40	107.20	109.00	110.80	112.61	114.41	116.21	119.81
12.50	89.35	91.13	92.90	94.68	96.45	98.23	100.00	101.77	103.55	105.32	107.10	108.87	110.65	112.42	114.20	117.74
12.75	87.76	89.51	91.26	93.00	94.75	96.50	98.25	100.00	101.75	103.50	105.25	107.00	108.74	110.49	112.24	115.74
13.00	86.21	87.93	89.66	91.38	93.10	94.83	96.55	98.28	100.00	101.72	103.45	105.17	106.90	108.62	110.34	113.79
13.25	84.71	86.40	88.10	89.80	91.50	93.20	94.90	96.60	98.30	100.00	101.70	103.40	105.10	106.80	108.50	111.90
13.50	83.24	84.92	86.60	88.27	89.95	91.62	93.30	94.97	96.65	98.32	100.00	101.68	103.35	105.03	106.70	110.05
13.75	81.83	83.48	85.13	86.78	88.43	90.09	91.74	93.39	95.04	96.70	98.35	100.00	101.65	103.30	104.96	108.26
14.00	80.45	82.08	83.71	85.34	86.96	88.59	90.22	91.85	93.48	95.11	96.74	98.37	100.00	101.63	103.26	106.52
14.25	79.11	80.71	82.32	83.93	85.54	87.14	88.75	90.36	91.96	93.57	95.18	96.79	98.39	100.00	101.61	104.82
14.50	77.80	79.39	80.98	82.56	84.15	85.73	87.32	88.90	90.49	92.07	93.66	95.24	96.83	98.41	100.00	103.17
14.75	76.54	78.10	79.67	81.23	82.79	84.36	85.92	87.49	89.05	90.62	92.18	93.74	95.31	96.87	98.44	101.56
15.00	75.31	76.85	78.39	79.94	81.48	83.02	84.57	86.11	87.65	89.20	90.74	92.28	93.83	95.37	96.91	100.00
15.25	74.11	75.63	77.16	78.68	80.20	81.72	83.25	84.77	86.29	87.82	89.34	90.86	92.39	93.91	95.43	98.48
15.50	72.94	74.45	75.95	77.45	78.96	80.46	81.96	83.47	84.97	86.47	87.98	89.48	90.98	92.48	93.99	96.99
15.75	71.81	73.29	74.78	76.26	77.75	79.23	80.71	82.20	83.68	85.16	86.65	88.13	89.61	91.10	92.58	95.55
16.00	70.71	72.17	73.64	75.10	76.57	78.03	79.49	80.96	82.42	83.89	85.35	86.82	88.28	89.75	91.21	94.14
16.25	69.63	71.08	72.53	73.97	75.42	76.86	78.31	79.76	81.20	82.65	84.09	85.54	86.99	88.43	89.88	92.77
16.50	68.59	70.02	71.44	72.87	74.30	75.73	77.15	78.58	80.01	81.44	82.87	84.29	85.72	87.15	88.58	91.43
16.75	67.57	68.98	70.39	71.80	73.21	74.62	76.03	77.44	78.85	80.26	81.67	83.08	84.49	85.90	87.31	90.13
17.00	66.58	67.97	69.36	70.76	72.15	73.54	74.93	76.33	77.72	79.11	80.50	81.90	83.29	84.68	86.07	88.86
17.25	65.61	66.99	68.36	69.74	71.11	72.49	73.86	75.24	76.62	77.99	79.37	80.74	82.12	83.49	84.87	87.62
17.50	64.67	66.03	67.39	68.75	70.11	71.46	72.82	74.18	75.54	76.90	78.26	79.62	80.98	82.34	83.69	86.41
17.75	63.75	65.10	66.44	67.78	69.12	70.47	71.81	73.15	74.49	75.84	77.18	78.52	79.86	81.21	82.55	85.23
18.00	62.86	64.19	65.51	66.84	68.16	69.49	70.82	72.14	73.47	74.80	76.12	77.45	78.78	80.10	81.43	84.08
18.25	61.99	63.30	64.61	65.92	67.23	68.54	69.85	71.16	72.47	73.78	75.10	76.41	77.72	79.03	80.34	82.96
18.50	61.14	62.43	63.73	65.02	66.32	67.61	68.91	70.21	71.50	72.80	74.09	75.39	76.68	77.98	79.27	81.86
18.75	60.31	61.59	62.87	64.15	65.43	66.71	67.99	69.27	70.55	71.83	73.11	74.39	75.67	76.95	78.23	80.79
19.00	59.50	60.77	62.03	63.30	64.56	65.83	67.09	68.36	69.62	70.89	72.16	73.42	74.69	75.95	77.22	79.75
20.00	56.46	57.67	58.87	60.08	61.29	62.50	63.71	64.92	66.13	67.34	68.55	69.76	70.97	72.18	73.39	75.81
25.00	44.81	45.79	46.78	47.76	48.75	49.73	50.72	51.71	52.69	53.68	54.66	55.65	56.63	57.62	58.61	60.58
30.00	37.08	37.91	38.74	39.56	40.39	41.22	42.05	42.88	43.70	44.53	45.36	46.19	47.01	47.84	48.67	50.33

Description: This table shows the yield to maturity of a bond purchased at the price shown in the index.

Example: The yield to maturity of a 15.00 %, 18 year bond at a price of 125.00 is 11.65 %.

COUPON RATE, %

PRICE	11.00%	11.25%	11.50%	11.75%	12.00%	12.25%	12.50%	12.75%	13.00%	13.25%	13.50%	13.75%	14.00%	14.25%	14.50%	15.00%
250	1.47	1.61	1.74	1.88	2.01	2.15	2.28	2.42	2.55	2.68	2.81	2.94	3.08	3.21	3.34	3.60
240	1.83	1.97	2.11	2.24	2.38	2.52	2.66	2.79	2.93	3.06	3.20	3.33	3.47	3.60	3.74	4.00
230	2.20	2.35	2.49	2.63	2.77	2.91	3.05	3.19	3.33	3.47	3.61	3.75	3.88	4.02	4.16	4.43
220	2.60	2.75	2.89	3.04	3.18	3.33	3.47	3.61	3.76	3.90	4.04	4.18	4.33	4.47	4.61	4.89
210	3.02	3.17	3.32	3.47	3.62	3.77	3.92	4.07	4.21	4.36	4.51	4.65	4.80	4.94	5.09	5.38
200	3.47	3.63	3.78	3.94	4.09	4.24	4.39	4.55	4.70	4.85	5.00	5.15	5.30	5.45	5.60	5.90
195	3.71	3.87	4.02	4.18	4.34	4.49	4.65	4.80	4.95	5.11	5.26	5.41	5.57	5.72	5.87	6.18
190	3.96	4.11	4.27	4.43	4.59	4.75	4.91	5.06	5.22	5.38	5.53	5.69	5.84	6.00	6.15	6.46
185	4.21	4.37	4.53	4.69	4.86	5.02	5.18	5.34	5.50	5.65	5.81	5.97	6.13	6.29	6.44	6.76
180	4.47	4.64	4.80	4.97	5.13	5.29	5.46	5.62	5.78	5.94	6.11	6.27	6.43	6.59	6.75	7.07
175	4.75	4.92	5.08	5.25	5.42	5.58	5.75	5.92	6.08	6.25	6.41	6.57	6.74	6.90	7.07	7.39
170	5.03	5.20	5.38	5.55	5.72	5.88	6.05	6.22	6.39	6.56	6.73	6.89	7.06	7.23	7.40	7.73
165	5.33	5.51	5.68	5.85	6.03	6.20	6.37	6.54	6.72	6.89	7.06	7.23	7.40	7.57	7.74	8.08
160	5.64	5.82	6.00	6.17	6.35	6.53	6.70	6.88	7.06	7.23	7.41	7.58	7.75	7.93	8.10	8.45
155	5.97	6.15	6.33	6.51	6.69	6.87	7.05	7.23	7.41	7.59	7.77	7.95	8.12	8.30	8.48	8.83
150	6.31	6.49	6.68	6.86	7.05	7.23	7.42	7.60	7.78	7.97	8.15	8.33	8.51	8.70	8.88	9.24
145	6.66	6.85	7.04	7.23	7.42	7.61	7.80	7.99	8.18	8.36	8.55	8.74	8.92	9.11	9.30	9.67
140	7.04	7.23	7.43	7.62	7.82	8.01	8.20	8.40	8.59	8.78	8.97	9.17	9.36	9.55	9.74	10.12
135	7.44	7.63	7.83	8.03	8.23	8.43	8.63	8.83	9.02	9.22	9.42	9.62	9.81	10.01	10.21	10.60
130	7.85	8.06	8.26	8.47	8.67	8.88	9.08	9.28	9.49	9.69	9.89	10.10	10.30	10.50	10.70	11.11
125	8.30	8.51	8.72	8.93	9.14	9.35	9.56	9.77	9.98	10.19	10.40	10.60	10.81	11.02	11.23	11.65
120	8.77	8.98	9.20	9.42	9.63	9.85	10.07	10.28	10.50	10.71	10.93	11.15	11.36	11.58	11.79	12.22
115	9.27	9.49	9.71	9.94	10.16	10.39	10.61	10.83	11.06	11.28	11.50	11.73	11.95	12.17	12.39	12.84
113	9.48	9.70	9.93	10.16	10.38	10.61	10.84	11.06	11.29	11.52	11.74	11.97	12.20	12.42	12.65	13.10
112	9.58	9.81	10.04	10.27	10.50	10.73	10.95	11.18	11.41	11.64	11.87	12.09	12.32	12.55	12.78	13.23
111	9.69	9.92	10.15	10.38	10.61	10.84	11.07	11.30	11.53	11.76	11.99	12.22	12.45	12.68	12.91	13.37
110	9.80	10.03	10.27	10.50	10.73	10.96	11.19	11.42	11.65	11.89	12.12	12.35	12.58	12.81	13.04	13.50
109	9.91	10.15	10.38	10.61	10.85	11.08	11.31	11.55	11.78	12.01	12.25	12.48	12.71	12.94	13.18	13.64
108	10.03	10.26	10.50	10.73	10.97	11.20	11.44	11.67	11.91	12.14	12.38	12.61	12.84	13.08	13.31	13.78
107	10.14	10.38	10.61	10.85	11.09	11.33	11.56	11.80	12.04	12.27	12.51	12.74	12.98	13.22	13.45	13.93
106	10.26	10.50	10.73	10.97	11.21	11.45	11.69	11.93	12.17	12.40	12.64	12.88	13.12	13.36	13.59	14.07
105	10.38	10.62	10.86	11.10	11.34	11.58	11.82	12.06	12.30	12.54	12.78	13.02	13.26	13.50	13.74	14.22
104	10.50	10.74	10.98	11.22	11.47	11.71	11.95	12.19	12.43	12.68	12.92	13.16	13.40	13.64	13.89	14.37
103	10.62	10.86	11.11	11.35	11.59	11.84	12.08	12.33	12.57	12.81	13.06	13.30	13.55	13.79	14.03	14.52
102	10.74	10.99	11.23	11.48	11.73	11.97	12.22	12.46	12.71	12.96	13.20	13.45	13.69	13.94	14.18	14.68
101	10.87	11.12	11.36	11.61	11.86	12.11	12.36	12.60	12.85	13.10	13.35	13.59	13.84	14.09	14.34	14.83
100	11.00	11.25	11.50	11.75	12.00	12.25	12.50	12.75	13.00	13.25	13.50	13.75	14.00	14.25	14.50	15.00
99	11.12	11.38	11.63	11.88	12.13	12.38	12.64	12.89	13.14	13.39	13.65	13.90	14.15	14.40	14.65	15.16
98	11.26	11.51	11.76	12.02	12.27	12.53	12.78	13.04	13.29	13.54	13.80	14.05	14.31	14.56	14.82	15.32
97	11.39	11.65	11.90	12.16	12.42	12.67	12.93	13.18	13.44	13.70	13.95	14.21	14.47	14.72	14.98	15.49
96	11.53	11.79	12.04	12.30	12.56	12.82	13.08	13.34	13.60	13.85	14.11	14.37	14.63	14.89	15.15	15.67
95	11.67	11.93	12.19	12.45	12.71	12.97	13.23	13.49	13.75	14.01	14.27	14.54	14.80	15.06	15.32	15.84
94	11.81	12.07	12.33	12.60	12.86	13.12	13.38	13.65	13.91	14.17	14.44	14.70	14.97	15.23	15.49	16.02
93	11.95	12.22	12.48	12.75	13.01	13.28	13.54	13.81	14.07	14.34	14.61	14.87	15.14	15.40	15.67	16.20
92	12.10	12.36	12.63	12.90	13.17	13.43	13.70	13.97	14.24	14.51	14.78	15.04	15.31	15.58	15.85	16.39
91	12.24	12.51	12.78	13.05	13.33	13.60	13.87	14.14	14.41	14.68	14.95	15.22	15.49	15.76	16.03	16.58
90	12.40	12.67	12.94	13.21	13.49	13.76	14.03	14.31	14.58	14.85	15.13	15.40	15.67	15.95	16.22	16.77
89	12.55	12.82	13.10	13.38	13.65	13.93	14.20	14.48	14.75	15.03	15.31	15.58	15.86	16.14	16.41	16.97
88	12.71	12.98	13.26	13.54	13.82	14.10	14.37	14.65	14.93	15.21	15.49	15.77	16.05	16.33	16.61	17.17
87	12.87	13.15	13.43	13.71	13.99	14.27	14.55	14.83	15.11	15.40	15.68	15.96	16.24	16.52	16.81	17.37
86	13.03	13.31	13.60	13.88	14.16	14.45	14.73	15.02	15.30	15.58	15.87	16.15	16.44	16.72	17.01	17.58
85	13.20	13.48	13.77	14.05	14.34	14.63	14.91	15.20	15.49	15.78	16.06	16.35	16.64	16.93	17.22	17.80
84	13.36	13.65	13.94	14.23	14.52	14.81	15.10	15.39	15.68	15.97	16.26	16.55	16.85	17.14	17.43	18.01
83	13.54	13.83	14.12	14.41	14.71	15.00	15.29	15.59	15.88	16.17	16.47	16.76	17.06	17.35	17.65	18.24
82	13.71	14.01	14.30	14.60	14.90	15.19	15.49	15.78	16.08	16.38	16.68	16.97	17.27	17.57	17.87	18.46
81	13.89	14.19	14.49	14.79	15.09	15.39	15.69	15.99	16.29	16.59	16.89	17.19	17.49	17.79	18.09	18.70
80	14.08	14.38	14.68	14.98	15.28	15.59	15.89	16.19	16.50	16.80	17.10	17.41	17.71	18.02	18.32	18.93
79	14.27	14.57	14.88	15.18	15.49	15.79	16.10	16.41	16.71	17.02	17.33	17.63	17.94	18.25	18.56	19.18
78	14.46	14.77	15.07	15.38	15.69	16.00	16.31	16.62	16.93	17.24	17.55	17.87	18.18	18.49	18.80	19.43
77	14.65	14.96	15.28	15.59	15.90	16.22	16.53	16.84	17.16	17.47	17.79	18.10	18.42	18.73	19.05	19.68
76	14.85	15.17	15.48	15.80	16.12	16.43	16.75	17.07	17.39	17.71	18.02	18.34	18.66	18.98	19.30	19.94
75	15.06	15.38	15.70	16.02	16.34	16.66	16.98	17.30	17.62	17.95	18.27	18.59	18.92	19.24	19.56	20.21
74	15.27	15.59	15.91	16.24	16.56	16.89	17.21	17.54	17.86	18.19	18.52	18.85	19.17	19.50	19.83	20.49
73	15.48	15.81	16.14	16.47	16.79	17.12	17.45	17.78	18.11	18.44	18.77	19.11	19.44	19.77	20.10	20.77
70	16.16	16.50	16.84	17.18	17.52	17.86	18.21	18.55	18.89	19.24	19.58	19.93	20.27	20.62	20.96	21.66
65	17.41	17.77	18.14	18.50	18.87	19.24	19.60	19.97	20.34	20.71	21.08	21.45	21.82	22.19	22.57	23.31
60	18.84	19.23	19.63	20.02	20.42	20.82	21.21	21.61	22.01	22.41	22.81	23.21	23.62	24.02	24.42	25.23
55	20.51	20.94	21.37	21.80	22.23	22.66	23.10	23.53	23.97	24.41	24.84	25.28	25.72	26.16	26.60	27.49

Description: This table shows the price to pay for a bond at the yield rate. The yield is to maturity.

Example: The price of a 6.75 %, 19 year bond to yield 8 % to maturity is $ 87.90.

COUPON RATE, %

YIELD	0.00%	1.00%	2.00%	3.00%	4.00%	4.25%	4.50%	4.75%	5.00%	5.25%	5.50%	5.75%	6.00%	6.25%	6.50%	6.75%
0.00	100.00	119.00	138.00	157.00	176.00	180.75	185.50	190.25	195.00	199.75	204.50	209.25	214.00	218.75	223.50	228.25
1.00	82.74	100.00	117.26	134.53	151.79	156.11	160.43	164.74	169.06	173.38	177.69	182.01	186.32	190.64	194.96	199.27
2.00	68.52	84.26	100.00	115.74	131.48	135.42	139.36	143.29	147.23	151.16	155.10	159.03	162.97	166.90	170.84	174.78
3.00	56.79	71.19	85.60	100.00	114.40	118.00	121.60	125.20	128.81	132.41	136.01	139.61	143.21	146.81	150.41	154.01
4.00	47.12	60.34	73.56	86.78	100.00	103.31	106.61	109.92	113.22	116.53	119.83	123.14	126.44	129.75	133.05	136.36
4.25	44.98	57.92	70.87	83.82	96.76	100.00	103.24	106.47	109.71	112.95	116.18	119.42	122.66	125.89	129.13	132.37
4.50	42.93	55.61	68.30	80.98	93.66	96.83	100.00	103.17	106.34	109.51	112.68	115.85	119.02	122.19	125.36	128.53
4.75	40.99	53.41	65.83	78.26	90.68	93.79	96.89	100.00	103.11	106.21	109.32	112.42	115.53	118.64	121.74	124.85
5.00	39.13	51.30	63.48	75.65	87.83	90.87	93.91	96.96	100.00	103.04	106.09	109.13	112.17	115.22	118.26	121.31
5.25	37.36	49.29	61.22	73.15	85.09	88.07	91.05	94.03	97.02	100.00	102.98	105.97	108.95	111.93	114.91	117.90
5.50	35.67	47.37	59.06	70.76	82.46	85.38	88.30	91.23	94.15	97.08	100.00	102.92	105.85	108.77	111.70	114.62
5.75	34.06	45.53	56.99	68.46	79.93	82.80	85.66	88.53	91.40	94.27	97.13	100.00	102.87	105.73	108.60	111.47
6.00	32.52	43.77	55.02	66.26	77.51	80.32	83.13	85.94	88.75	91.57	94.38	97.19	100.00	102.81	105.62	108.43
6.25	31.06	42.09	53.12	64.15	75.18	77.94	80.70	83.45	86.21	88.97	91.73	94.48	97.24	100.00	102.76	105.52
6.50	29.66	40.48	51.30	62.12	72.95	75.65	78.36	81.06	83.77	86.47	89.18	91.88	94.59	97.29	100.00	102.71
6.75	28.33	38.95	49.56	60.18	70.80	73.45	76.11	78.76	81.42	84.07	86.73	89.38	92.04	94.69	97.35	100.00
7.00	27.06	37.48	47.90	58.32	68.74	71.34	73.95	76.55	79.16	81.76	84.37	86.97	89.58	92.18	94.79	97.39
7.25	25.84	36.07	46.30	56.53	66.76	69.31	71.87	74.43	76.99	79.54	82.10	84.66	87.21	89.77	92.33	94.89
7.50	24.69	34.73	44.77	54.81	64.85	67.36	69.87	72.38	74.90	77.41	79.92	82.43	84.94	87.45	89.96	92.47
7.75	23.58	33.44	43.30	53.16	63.02	65.49	67.95	70.42	72.88	75.35	77.81	80.28	82.74	85.21	87.67	90.14
8.00	22.53	32.21	41.90	51.58	61.26	63.69	66.11	68.53	70.95	73.37	75.79	78.21	80.63	83.05	85.47	87.90
8.25	21.52	31.04	40.55	50.06	59.57	61.95	64.33	66.71	69.08	71.46	73.84	76.22	78.60	80.98	83.35	85.73
8.50	20.56	29.91	39.25	48.60	57.95	60.28	62.62	64.95	67.29	69.63	71.96	74.30	76.64	78.97	81.31	83.65
8.75	19.65	28.83	38.01	47.20	56.38	58.68	60.97	63.27	65.56	67.86	70.16	72.45	74.75	77.04	79.34	81.63
9.00	18.78	27.80	36.83	45.85	54.88	57.13	59.39	61.64	63.90	66.16	68.41	70.67	72.93	75.18	77.44	79.69
9.25	17.94	26.81	35.68	44.55	53.43	55.64	57.86	60.08	62.30	64.52	66.73	68.95	71.17	73.39	75.60	77.82
9.50	17.15	25.87	34.59	43.31	52.03	54.21	56.39	58.57	60.75	62.93	65.11	67.29	69.47	71.65	73.84	76.02
9.75	16.39	24.96	33.54	42.11	50.69	52.83	54.98	57.12	59.26	61.41	63.55	65.70	67.84	69.98	72.13	74.27
10.00	15.66	24.09	32.53	40.96	49.40	51.50	53.61	55.72	57.83	59.94	62.05	64.16	66.26	68.37	70.48	72.59
10.25	14.97	23.26	31.56	39.86	48.15	50.23	52.30	54.37	56.45	58.52	60.60	62.67	64.74	66.82	68.89	70.96
10.50	14.31	22.47	30.63	38.79	46.95	48.99	51.03	53.07	55.11	57.15	59.19	61.23	63.27	65.31	67.36	69.40
10.75	13.68	21.71	29.74	37.77	45.80	47.80	49.81	51.82	53.83	55.83	57.84	59.85	61.86	63.86	65.87	67.88
11.00	13.07	20.98	28.88	36.78	44.68	46.66	48.63	50.61	52.59	54.56	56.54	58.51	60.49	62.46	64.44	66.41
11.25	12.50	20.28	28.05	35.83	43.61	45.55	47.50	49.44	51.39	53.33	55.28	57.22	59.17	61.11	63.06	65.00
11.50	11.95	19.61	27.26	34.92	42.58	44.49	46.40	48.32	50.23	52.15	54.06	55.97	57.89	59.80	61.72	63.63
11.75	11.42	18.96	26.50	34.04	41.58	43.46	45.35	47.23	49.12	51.00	52.89	54.77	56.65	58.54	60.42	62.31
12.00	10.92	18.35	25.77	33.19	40.62	42.47	44.33	46.18	48.04	49.89	51.75	53.61	55.46	57.32	59.17	61.03
12.25	10.45	17.76	25.07	32.38	39.69	41.52	43.34	45.17	47.00	48.83	50.65	52.48	54.31	56.14	57.96	59.79
12.50	9.99	17.19	24.39	31.59	38.79	40.59	42.39	44.19	45.99	47.79	49.59	51.39	53.19	54.99	56.79	58.59
12.75	9.55	16.65	23.74	30.83	37.93	39.70	41.47	43.25	45.02	46.80	48.57	50.34	52.12	53.89	55.66	57.44
13.00	9.14	16.12	23.11	30.10	37.09	38.84	40.59	42.34	44.08	45.83	47.58	49.33	51.07	52.82	54.57	56.31
13.25	8.74	15.62	22.51	29.40	36.29	38.01	39.73	41.45	43.18	44.90	46.62	48.34	50.06	51.79	53.51	55.23
13.50	8.36	15.14	21.93	28.72	35.51	37.21	38.90	40.60	42.30	44.00	45.69	47.39	49.09	50.78	52.48	54.18
13.75	7.99	14.68	21.38	28.07	34.76	36.43	38.10	39.78	41.45	43.12	44.80	46.47	48.14	49.81	51.49	53.16
14.00	7.65	14.24	20.84	27.44	34.03	35.68	37.33	38.98	40.63	42.28	43.93	45.58	47.23	48.88	50.52	52.17
14.25	7.31	13.82	20.32	26.83	33.33	34.96	36.58	38.21	39.84	41.46	43.09	44.71	46.34	47.97	49.59	51.22
14.50	7.00	13.41	19.82	26.24	32.65	34.26	35.86	37.46	39.07	40.67	42.27	43.88	45.48	47.08	48.69	50.29
14.75	6.69	13.02	19.35	25.67	32.00	33.58	35.16	36.74	38.32	39.90	41.49	43.07	44.65	46.23	47.81	49.39
15.00	6.40	12.64	18.88	25.12	31.36	32.92	34.48	36.04	37.60	39.16	40.72	42.28	43.84	45.40	46.96	48.52
15.25	6.13	12.28	18.44	24.59	30.75	32.29	33.83	35.37	36.91	38.44	39.98	41.52	43.06	44.60	46.14	47.68
15.50	5.86	11.94	18.01	24.08	30.16	31.67	33.19	34.71	36.23	37.75	39.27	40.78	42.30	43.82	45.34	46.86
15.75	5.61	11.60	17.60	23.59	29.58	31.08	32.58	34.08	35.58	37.07	38.57	40.07	41.57	43.07	44.56	46.06
16.00	5.37	11.28	17.20	23.11	29.03	30.51	31.98	33.46	34.94	36.42	37.90	39.38	40.86	42.33	43.81	45.29
16.25	5.14	10.98	16.81	22.65	28.49	29.95	31.41	32.87	34.33	35.79	37.25	38.70	40.16	41.62	43.08	44.54
16.50	4.92	10.68	16.44	22.21	27.97	29.41	30.85	32.29	33.73	35.17	36.61	38.05	39.49	40.93	42.37	43.81
16.75	4.71	10.40	16.08	21.77	27.46	28.89	30.31	31.73	33.15	34.57	36.00	37.42	38.84	40.26	41.69	43.11
17.00	4.50	10.12	15.74	21.36	26.97	28.38	29.78	31.19	32.59	34.00	35.40	36.80	38.21	39.61	41.02	42.42
17.25	4.31	9.86	15.41	20.95	26.50	27.89	29.27	30.66	32.05	33.43	34.82	36.21	37.59	38.98	40.37	41.76
17.50	4.13	9.61	15.08	20.56	26.04	27.41	28.78	30.15	31.52	32.89	34.26	35.63	37.00	38.37	39.74	41.11
17.75	3.95	9.36	14.77	20.18	25.60	26.95	28.30	29.65	31.01	32.36	33.71	35.07	36.42	37.77	39.12	40.48
18.00	3.78	9.13	14.47	19.82	25.16	26.50	27.84	29.17	30.51	31.85	33.18	34.52	35.86	37.19	38.53	39.86
18.25	3.62	8.90	14.18	19.46	24.75	26.07	27.39	28.71	30.03	31.35	32.67	33.99	35.31	36.63	37.95	39.27
18.50	3.47	8.69	13.90	19.12	24.34	25.64	26.95	28.25	29.56	30.86	32.17	33.47	34.78	36.08	37.38	38.69
18.75	3.32	8.48	13.63	18.79	23.94	25.23	26.52	27.81	29.10	30.39	31.68	32.97	34.26	35.55	36.84	38.12
19.00	3.18	8.27	13.37	18.47	23.56	24.84	26.11	27.38	28.66	29.93	31.21	32.48	33.75	35.03	36.30	37.58
20.00	2.67	7.54	12.41	17.27	22.14	23.36	24.57	25.79	27.01	28.22	29.44	30.65	31.87	33.09	34.30	35.52
25.00	1.14	5.09	9.05	13.00	16.96	17.94	18.93	19.92	20.91	21.90	22.89	23.88	24.87	25.85	26.84	27.83
30.00	.49	3.81	7.13	10.44	13.76	14.59	15.42	16.25	17.08	17.91	18.74	19.57	20.39	21.22	22.05	22.88

Description: This table shows the yield to maturity of a bond purchased at the price shown in the index.

Example: The yield to maturity of a 6.75 %, 19 year bond at a price of 80.00 is 8.95 %.

COUPON RATE, %

PRICE	0.00%	1.00%	2.00%	3.00%	4.00%	4.25%	4.50%	4.75%	5.00%	5.25%	5.50%	5.75%	6.00%	6.25%	6.50%	6.75%
100	0.00	1.00	2.00	3.00	4.00	4.25	4.50	4.75	5.00	5.25	5.50	5.75	6.00	6.25	6.50	6.75
99	.05	1.05	2.06	3.06	4.07	4.32	4.57	4.83	5.08	5.33	5.58	5.83	6.08	6.34	6.59	6.84
98	.10	1.11	2.12	3.14	4.15	4.40	4.65	4.91	5.16	5.41	5.67	5.92	6.18	6.43	6.68	6.94
97	.16	1.17	2.19	3.21	4.23	4.48	4.74	4.99	5.25	5.50	5.76	6.01	6.27	6.52	6.78	7.03
96	.21	1.23	2.26	3.28	4.31	4.56	4.82	5.08	5.33	5.59	5.85	6.10	6.36	6.62	6.88	7.13
95	.27	1.29	2.32	3.35	4.39	4.64	4.90	5.16	5.42	5.68	5.94	6.20	6.46	6.71	6.97	7.23
94	.32	1.35	2.39	3.43	4.47	4.73	4.99	5.25	5.51	5.77	6.03	6.29	6.55	6.81	7.07	7.34
93	.38	1.42	2.46	3.50	4.55	4.81	5.07	5.34	5.60	5.86	6.12	6.39	6.65	6.91	7.18	7.44
92	.43	1.48	2.53	3.58	4.63	4.90	5.16	5.43	5.69	5.95	6.22	6.48	6.75	7.01	7.28	7.54
91	.49	1.54	2.60	3.66	4.72	4.98	5.25	5.52	5.78	6.05	6.32	6.58	6.85	7.12	7.38	7.65
90	.55	1.61	2.67	3.73	4.80	5.07	5.34	5.61	5.88	6.14	6.41	6.68	6.95	7.22	7.49	7.76
89	.61	1.67	2.74	3.81	4.89	5.16	5.43	5.70	5.97	6.24	6.51	6.78	7.06	7.33	7.60	7.87
88	.67	1.74	2.82	3.90	4.98	5.25	5.52	5.80	6.07	6.34	6.61	6.89	7.16	7.43	7.71	7.98
87	.73	1.81	2.89	3.98	5.07	5.34	5.62	5.89	6.17	6.44	6.72	6.99	7.27	7.54	7.82	8.10
86	.79	1.87	2.96	4.06	5.16	5.44	5.71	5.99	6.27	6.54	6.82	7.10	7.38	7.66	7.93	8.21
85	.85	1.94	3.04	4.14	5.25	5.53	5.81	6.09	6.37	6.65	6.93	7.21	7.49	7.77	8.05	8.33
84	.91	2.01	3.12	4.23	5.35	5.63	5.91	6.19	6.47	6.75	7.04	7.32	7.60	7.88	8.17	8.45
83	.98	2.08	3.20	4.32	5.44	5.73	6.01	6.29	6.58	6.86	7.14	7.43	7.72	8.00	8.29	8.57
82	1.04	2.16	3.28	4.40	5.54	5.82	6.11	6.40	6.68	6.97	7.26	7.54	7.83	8.12	8.41	8.70
81	1.11	2.23	3.36	4.49	5.64	5.93	6.21	6.50	6.79	7.08	7.37	7.66	7.95	8.24	8.53	8.83
80	1.17	2.30	3.44	4.58	5.74	6.03	6.32	6.61	6.90	7.19	7.49	7.78	8.07	8.37	8.66	8.95
79	1.24	2.38	3.52	4.68	5.84	6.13	6.43	6.72	7.01	7.31	7.60	7.90	8.19	8.49	8.79	9.22
78	1.31	2.45	3.61	4.77	5.94	6.24	6.53	6.83	7.13	7.42	7.72	8.02	8.32	8.62	8.92	9.22
77	1.38	2.53	3.69	4.86	6.05	6.35	6.64	6.94	7.24	7.54	7.84	8.15	8.45	8.75	9.05	9.36
76	1.44	2.61	3.78	4.96	6.16	6.46	6.76	7.06	7.36	7.66	7.97	8.27	8.58	8.88	9.19	9.50
75	1.51	2.68	3.87	5.06	6.26	6.57	6.87	7.18	7.48	7.79	8.10	8.40	8.71	9.02	9.33	9.64
74	1.59	2.76	3.96	5.16	6.38	6.68	6.99	7.30	7.61	7.91	8.22	8.53	8.85	9.16	9.47	9.78
73	1.66	2.85	4.05	5.26	6.49	6.80	7.11	7.42	7.73	8.04	8.36	8.67	8.98	9.30	9.62	9.93
72	1.73	2.93	4.14	5.36	6.60	6.92	7.23	7.54	7.86	8.17	8.49	8.81	9.13	9.44	9.76	10.08
71	1.81	3.01	4.23	5.47	6.72	7.04	7.35	7.67	7.99	8.31	8.63	8.95	9.27	9.59	9.92	10.24
70	1.88	3.10	4.33	5.58	6.84	7.16	7.48	7.80	8.12	8.44	8.77	9.09	9.42	9.74	10.07	10.40
69	1.96	3.18	4.43	5.69	6.96	7.28	7.61	7.93	8.26	8.58	8.91	9.24	9.57	9.90	10.23	10.56
68	2.04	3.27	4.52	5.80	7.09	7.41	7.74	8.07	8.40	8.72	9.06	9.39	9.72	10.05	10.39	10.72
67	2.11	3.36	4.63	5.91	7.21	7.54	7.87	8.20	8.54	8.87	9.20	9.54	9.88	10.22	10.55	10.89
66	2.19	3.45	4.73	6.03	7.34	7.68	8.01	8.34	8.68	9.02	9.36	9.70	10.04	10.38	10.72	11.07
65	2.28	3.54	4.83	6.14	7.48	7.81	8.15	8.49	8.83	9.17	9.51	9.86	10.20	10.55	10.90	11.24
64	2.36	3.64	4.94	6.26	7.61	7.95	8.29	8.64	8.98	9.33	9.67	10.02	10.37	10.72	11.07	11.43
63	2.44	3.73	5.05	6.39	7.75	8.09	8.44	8.79	9.13	9.48	9.84	10.19	10.54	10.90	11.26	11.61
62	2.53	3.83	5.16	6.51	7.89	8.24	8.59	8.94	9.29	9.65	10.00	10.36	10.72	11.08	11.44	11.80
61	2.61	3.93	5.27	6.64	8.03	8.39	8.74	9.10	9.45	9.81	10.17	10.54	10.90	11.27	11.63	12.00
60	2.70	4.03	5.39	6.77	8.18	8.54	8.90	9.26	9.62	9.98	10.35	10.72	11.09	11.46	11.83	12.20
59	2.79	4.13	5.50	6.90	8.33	8.69	9.06	9.42	9.79	10.16	10.53	10.90	11.28	11.65	12.03	12.41
58	2.88	4.24	5.62	7.04	8.49	8.85	9.22	9.59	9.96	10.34	10.72	11.09	11.47	11.85	12.24	12.62
57	2.98	4.34	5.74	7.18	8.64	9.02	9.39	9.77	10.14	10.52	10.91	11.29	11.67	12.06	12.45	12.84
56	3.07	4.45	5.87	7.32	8.81	9.18	9.56	9.94	10.33	10.71	11.10	11.49	11.88	12.27	12.67	13.07
55	3.17	4.56	6.00	7.47	8.97	9.36	9.74	10.13	10.52	10.91	11.30	11.70	12.09	12.49	12.90	13.30
54	3.26	4.68	6.13	7.62	9.14	9.53	9.92	10.32	10.71	11.11	11.51	11.91	12.31	12.72	13.13	13.54
53	3.36	4.79	6.26	7.77	9.32	9.71	10.11	10.51	10.91	11.31	11.72	12.13	12.54	12.95	13.37	13.79
52	3.47	4.91	6.40	7.93	9.50	9.90	10.30	10.71	11.12	11.53	11.94	12.35	12.77	13.19	13.62	14.04
51	3.57	5.03	6.54	8.09	9.69	10.09	10.50	10.91	11.33	11.75	12.17	12.59	13.01	13.44	13.87	14.30
50	3.68	5.16	6.68	8.26	9.88	10.29	10.71	11.12	11.55	11.97	12.40	12.83	13.26	13.70	14.13	14.58
49	3.78	5.28	6.83	8.43	10.07	10.49	10.92	11.34	11.77	12.20	12.64	13.08	13.52	13.96	14.41	14.86
48	3.90	5.41	6.98	8.60	10.28	10.70	11.13	11.57	12.00	12.44	12.89	13.33	13.78	14.24	14.69	15.15
47	4.01	5.54	7.13	8.78	10.48	10.92	11.36	11.80	12.24	12.69	13.14	13.60	14.06	14.52	14.98	15.45
46	4.12	5.68	7.29	8.97	10.70	11.14	11.59	12.04	12.49	12.95	13.41	13.88	14.34	14.81	15.29	15.77
45	4.24	5.82	7.46	9.16	10.92	11.37	11.83	12.29	12.75	13.22	13.69	14.16	14.64	15.12	15.60	16.09
44	4.36	5.96	7.62	9.36	11.15	11.61	12.08	12.55	13.02	13.49	13.97	14.46	14.95	15.44	15.93	16.43
43	4.49	6.11	7.80	9.56	11.39	11.86	12.33	12.81	13.29	13.78	14.27	14.77	15.26	15.77	16.27	16.78
42	4.61	6.26	7.98	9.77	11.64	12.12	12.60	13.09	13.58	14.08	14.58	15.09	15.60	16.11	16.63	17.15
41	4.74	6.41	8.16	9.99	11.89	12.38	12.88	13.38	13.88	14.39	14.90	15.42	15.94	16.47	17.00	17.54
40	4.88	6.57	8.35	10.21	12.16	12.66	13.17	13.68	14.19	14.71	15.24	15.77	16.31	16.85	17.39	17.94
39	5.01	6.74	8.55	10.45	12.44	12.95	13.47	13.99	14.52	15.05	15.59	16.13	16.68	17.24	17.80	18.36
35	5.60	7.44	9.40	11.47	13.66	14.23	14.80	15.38	15.97	16.57	17.17	17.77	18.39	19.01	19.63	20.27
30	6.43	8.47	10.67	13.03	15.56	16.22	16.89	17.57	18.26	18.96	19.67	20.38	21.11	21.84	22.58	23.33
25	7.43	9.73	12.27	15.05	18.09	18.89	19.71	20.53	21.38	22.23	23.10	23.98	24.87	25.77	26.69	27.61
20	8.65	11.35	14.41	17.87	21.75	22.78	23.83	24.91	26.00	27.12	28.25	29.39	30.55	31.72	32.90	34.09
15	10.23	13.57	17.56	22.31	27.79	29.26	30.76	32.28	33.83	35.41	36.99	38.60	40.21	41.84	43.47	45.11
10	12.49	17.11	23.25	31.15	40.33	42.74	45.17	47.62	50.09	52.56	55.04	57.53	60.02	62.51	65.01	67.51

Description: This table shows the price to pay for a bond at the yield rate. The yield is to maturity.

Example: The price of a 10.75 %, 19 year bond to yield 8 % to maturity is $ 126.63.

COUPON RATE, %

YIELD	7.00%	7.25%	7.50%	7.75%	8.00%	8.25%	8.50%	8.75%	9.00%	9.25%	9.50%	9.75%	10.00%	10.25%	10.50%	10.75%
0.00	233.00	237.75	242.50	247.25	252.00	256.75	261.50	266.25	271.00	275.75	280.50	285.25	290.00	294.75	299.50	304.25
1.00	203.59	207.91	212.22	216.54	220.85	225.17	229.49	233.80	238.12	242.44	246.75	251.07	255.38	259.70	264.02	268.33
2.00	178.71	182.65	186.58	190.52	194.45	198.39	202.33	206.26	210.20	214.13	218.07	222.00	225.94	229.87	233.81	237.75
3.00	157.61	161.21	164.81	168.41	172.01	175.61	179.21	182.81	186.42	190.02	193.62	197.22	200.82	204.42	208.02	211.62
4.00	139.66	142.97	146.27	149.58	152.88	156.19	159.49	162.80	166.10	169.41	172.71	176.02	179.32	182.63	185.93	189.24
4.25	135.60	138.84	142.08	145.31	148.55	151.79	155.02	158.26	161.50	164.73	167.97	171.21	174.44	177.68	180.92	184.15
4.50	131.70	134.87	138.04	141.21	144.39	147.56	150.73	153.90	157.07	160.24	163.41	166.58	169.75	172.92	176.09	179.26
4.75	127.95	131.06	134.17	137.27	140.38	143.48	146.59	149.70	152.80	155.91	159.01	162.12	165.23	168.33	171.44	174.54
5.00	124.35	127.39	130.44	133.48	136.52	139.57	142.61	145.65	148.70	151.74	154.78	157.83	160.87	163.92	166.96	170.00
5.25	120.88	123.86	126.85	129.83	132.81	135.80	138.78	141.76	144.74	147.73	150.71	153.69	156.68	159.66	162.64	165.63
5.50	117.54	120.47	123.39	126.32	129.24	132.17	135.09	138.01	140.94	143.86	146.79	149.71	152.63	155.56	158.48	161.41
5.75	114.34	117.20	120.07	122.94	125.80	128.67	131.54	134.40	137.27	140.14	143.01	145.87	148.74	151.61	154.47	157.34
6.00	111.25	114.06	116.87	119.68	122.49	125.30	128.12	130.93	133.74	136.55	139.36	142.17	144.98	147.80	150.61	153.42
6.25	108.27	111.03	113.79	116.55	119.30	122.06	124.82	127.58	130.33	133.09	135.85	138.61	141.37	144.12	146.88	149.64
6.50	105.41	108.12	110.82	113.53	116.23	118.94	121.64	124.35	127.05	129.76	132.46	135.17	137.88	140.58	143.29	145.99
6.75	102.65	105.31	107.96	110.62	113.27	115.93	118.58	121.24	123.89	126.55	129.20	131.85	134.51	137.16	139.82	142.47
7.00	100.00	102.61	105.21	107.82	110.42	113.03	115.63	118.24	120.84	123.45	126.05	128.66	131.26	133.87	136.47	139.08
7.25	97.44	100.00	102.56	105.11	107.67	110.23	112.79	115.34	117.90	120.46	123.01	125.57	128.13	130.69	133.24	135.80
7.50	94.98	97.49	100.00	102.51	105.02	107.53	110.04	112.55	115.06	117.57	120.08	122.59	125.10	127.62	130.13	132.64
7.75	92.60	95.07	97.53	100.00	102.47	104.93	107.40	109.86	112.33	114.79	117.26	119.72	122.19	124.65	127.12	129.58
8.00	90.32	92.74	95.16	97.58	100.00	102.42	104.84	107.26	109.68	112.10	114.53	116.95	119.37	121.79	124.21	126.63
8.25	88.11	90.49	92.87	95.24	97.62	100.00	102.38	104.76	107.13	109.51	111.89	114.27	116.65	119.02	121.40	123.78
8.50	85.98	88.32	90.65	92.99	95.33	97.66	100.00	102.34	104.67	107.01	109.35	111.68	114.02	116.35	118.69	121.03
8.75	83.93	86.23	88.52	90.82	93.11	95.41	97.70	100.00	102.30	104.59	106.89	109.18	111.48	113.77	116.07	118.37
9.00	81.95	84.21	86.46	88.72	90.98	93.23	95.49	97.74	100.00	102.26	104.51	106.77	109.02	111.28	113.54	115.79
9.25	80.04	82.26	84.48	86.69	88.91	91.13	93.35	95.56	97.78	100.00	102.22	104.44	106.65	108.87	111.09	113.31
9.50	78.20	80.38	82.56	84.74	86.92	89.10	91.28	93.46	95.64	97.82	100.00	102.18	104.36	106.54	108.72	110.90
9.75	76.42	78.56	80.70	82.85	84.99	87.14	89.28	91.42	93.57	95.71	97.86	100.00	102.14	104.29	106.43	108.58
10.00	74.70	76.81	78.92	81.02	83.13	85.24	87.35	89.46	91.57	93.67	95.78	97.89	100.00	102.11	104.22	106.33
10.25	73.04	75.11	77.19	79.26	81.33	83.41	85.48	87.56	89.63	91.70	93.78	95.85	97.93	100.00	102.07	104.15
10.50	71.44	73.48	75.52	77.56	79.60	81.64	83.68	85.72	87.76	89.80	91.84	93.88	95.92	97.96	100.00	102.04
10.75	69.89	71.89	73.90	75.91	77.92	79.92	81.93	83.94	85.95	87.95	89.96	91.97	93.98	95.98	97.99	100.00
11.00	68.39	70.37	72.34	74.32	76.29	78.27	80.24	82.22	84.20	86.17	88.15	90.12	92.10	94.07	96.05	98.02
11.25	66.94	68.89	70.83	72.78	74.72	76.67	78.61	80.56	82.50	84.44	86.39	88.33	90.28	92.22	94.17	96.11
11.50	65.55	67.46	69.37	71.29	73.20	75.12	77.03	78.94	80.86	82.77	84.69	86.60	88.52	90.43	92.34	94.26
11.75	64.19	66.08	67.96	69.85	71.73	73.62	75.50	77.39	79.27	81.15	83.04	84.92	86.81	88.69	90.58	92.46
12.00	62.88	64.74	66.60	68.45	70.31	72.16	74.02	75.88	77.73	79.59	81.44	83.30	85.15	87.01	88.87	90.72
12.25	61.62	63.45	65.27	67.10	68.93	70.76	72.59	74.41	76.24	78.07	79.90	81.72	83.55	85.38	87.21	89.03
12.50	60.39	62.20	64.00	65.80	67.60	69.40	71.20	73.00	74.80	76.60	78.40	80.20	82.00	83.80	85.60	87.40
12.75	59.21	60.98	62.76	64.53	66.30	68.08	69.85	71.62	73.40	75.17	76.94	78.72	80.49	82.27	84.04	85.81
13.00	58.06	59.81	61.56	63.30	65.05	66.80	68.55	70.29	72.04	73.79	75.54	77.28	79.03	80.78	82.53	84.27
13.25	56.95	58.67	60.40	62.12	63.84	65.56	67.28	69.00	70.73	72.45	74.17	75.89	77.61	79.34	81.06	82.78
13.50	55.88	57.57	59.27	60.97	62.66	64.36	66.06	67.76	69.45	71.15	72.85	74.54	76.24	77.94	79.63	81.33
13.75	54.83	56.51	58.18	59.85	61.52	63.20	64.87	66.54	68.22	69.89	71.56	73.23	74.91	76.58	78.25	79.93
14.00	53.82	55.47	57.12	58.77	60.42	62.07	63.72	65.37	67.02	68.67	70.31	71.96	73.61	75.26	76.91	78.56
14.25	52.84	54.47	56.10	57.72	59.35	60.97	62.60	64.23	65.85	67.48	69.10	70.73	72.36	73.98	75.61	77.23
14.50	51.89	53.50	55.10	56.71	58.31	59.91	61.52	63.12	64.72	66.33	67.93	69.53	71.14	72.74	74.34	75.95
14.75	50.97	52.56	54.14	55.72	57.30	58.88	60.46	62.04	63.63	65.21	66.79	68.37	69.95	71.53	73.12	74.70
15.00	50.08	51.64	53.20	54.76	56.32	57.88	59.44	61.00	62.56	64.12	65.68	67.24	68.80	70.36	71.92	73.48
15.25	49.22	50.76	52.29	53.83	55.37	56.91	58.45	59.99	61.53	63.07	64.61	66.14	67.68	69.22	70.76	72.30
15.50	48.38	49.89	51.41	52.93	54.45	55.97	57.49	59.00	60.52	62.04	63.56	65.08	66.60	68.11	69.63	71.15
15.75	47.56	49.06	50.56	52.06	53.55	55.05	56.55	58.05	59.55	61.05	62.54	64.04	65.54	67.04	68.54	70.04
16.00	46.77	48.25	49.73	51.21	52.68	54.16	55.64	57.12	58.60	60.08	61.56	63.03	64.51	65.99	67.47	68.95
16.25	46.00	47.46	48.92	50.38	51.84	53.30	54.76	56.22	57.68	59.14	60.60	62.06	63.51	64.97	66.43	67.89
16.50	45.26	46.70	48.14	49.58	51.02	52.46	53.90	55.34	56.78	58.22	59.66	61.10	62.54	63.98	65.42	66.87
16.75	44.53	45.95	47.38	48.80	50.22	51.64	53.06	54.49	55.91	57.33	58.75	60.18	61.60	63.02	64.44	65.86
17.00	43.83	45.23	46.64	48.04	49.44	50.85	52.25	53.66	55.06	56.47	57.87	59.27	60.68	62.08	63.49	64.89
17.25	43.14	44.53	45.92	47.30	48.69	50.08	51.46	52.85	54.24	55.62	57.01	58.40	59.78	61.17	62.56	63.94
17.50	42.48	43.85	45.22	46.59	47.95	49.32	50.69	52.06	53.43	54.80	56.17	57.54	58.91	60.28	61.65	63.02
17.75	41.83	43.18	44.54	45.89	47.24	48.59	49.95	51.30	52.65	54.00	55.36	56.71	58.06	59.42	60.77	62.12
18.00	41.20	42.54	43.87	45.21	46.55	47.88	49.22	50.55	51.89	53.23	54.56	55.90	57.24	58.57	59.91	61.25
18.25	40.59	41.91	43.23	44.55	45.87	47.19	48.51	49.83	51.15	52.47	53.79	55.11	56.43	57.75	59.07	60.39
18.50	39.99	41.30	42.60	43.91	45.21	46.52	47.82	49.12	50.43	51.73	53.04	54.34	55.65	56.95	58.26	59.56
18.75	39.41	40.70	41.99	43.28	44.57	45.86	47.15	48.44	49.73	51.02	52.30	53.59	54.88	56.17	57.46	58.75
19.00	38.85	40.12	41.40	42.67	43.95	45.22	46.49	47.77	49.04	50.32	51.59	52.86	54.14	55.41	56.69	57.96
20.00	36.74	37.95	39.17	40.39	41.60	42.82	44.04	45.25	46.47	47.69	48.90	50.12	51.34	52.55	53.77	54.99
25.00	28.82	29.81	30.80	31.79	32.77	33.76	34.75	35.74	36.73	37.72	38.71	39.69	40.68	41.67	42.66	43.65
30.00	23.71	24.54	25.37	26.20	27.03	27.86	28.69	29.52	30.35	31.17	32.00	32.83	33.66	34.49	35.32	36.15

Description: This table shows the yield to maturity of a bond purchased at the price shown in the index.

Example: The yield to maturity of a 10.75 %, 19 year bond at a price of 111.00 is 9.48 %.

PRICE	7.00%	7.25%	7.50%	7.75%	8.00%	8.25%	8.50%	8.75%	9.00%	9.25%	9.50%	9.75%	10.00%	10.25%	10.50%	10.75%
155	3.13	3.32	3.50	3.69	3.88	4.06	4.25	4.43	4.61	4.80	4.98	5.16	5.35	5.53	5.71	5.89
150	3.40	3.59	3.78	3.97	4.16	4.35	4.54	4.73	4.91	5.10	5.29	5.48	5.66	5.85	6.04	6.22
145	3.68	3.88	4.07	4.26	4.46	4.65	4.84	5.04	5.23	5.42	5.61	5.80	5.99	6.18	6.37	6.56
140	3.97	4.17	4.37	4.57	4.77	4.97	5.16	5.36	5.56	5.75	5.95	6.15	6.34	6.54	6.73	6.93
135	4.28	4.49	4.69	4.89	5.10	5.30	5.50	5.70	5.90	6.11	6.31	6.51	6.71	6.91	7.11	7.31
130	4.61	4.82	5.02	5.23	5.44	5.65	5.86	6.06	6.27	6.48	6.68	6.89	7.09	7.30	7.51	7.71
125	4.95	5.16	5.38	5.59	5.80	6.02	6.23	6.44	6.66	6.87	7.08	7.29	7.50	7.72	7.93	8.14
124	5.02	5.24	5.45	5.67	5.88	6.09	6.31	6.52	6.74	6.95	7.16	7.38	7.59	7.80	8.01	8.23
123	5.09	5.31	5.52	5.74	5.96	6.17	6.39	6.60	6.82	7.03	7.25	7.46	7.67	7.89	8.10	8.32
122	5.16	5.38	5.60	5.82	6.03	6.25	6.47	6.68	6.90	7.11	7.33	7.55	7.76	7.98	8.19	8.41
121	5.24	5.46	5.67	5.89	6.11	6.33	6.55	6.76	6.98	7.20	7.42	7.63	7.85	8.07	8.28	8.50
120	5.31	5.53	5.75	5.97	6.19	6.41	6.63	6.85	7.07	7.28	7.50	7.72	7.94	8.16	8.37	8.59
119	5.38	5.61	5.83	6.05	6.27	6.49	6.71	6.93	7.15	7.37	7.59	7.81	8.03	8.25	8.47	8.68
118	5.46	5.68	5.91	6.13	6.35	6.57	6.79	7.02	7.24	7.46	7.68	7.90	8.12	8.34	8.56	8.78
117	5.54	5.76	5.98	6.21	6.43	6.65	6.88	7.10	7.32	7.55	7.77	7.99	8.21	8.43	8.66	8.88
116	5.61	5.84	6.06	6.29	6.51	6.74	6.96	7.19	7.41	7.64	7.86	8.08	8.31	8.53	8.75	8.97
115	5.69	5.92	6.15	6.37	6.60	6.82	7.05	7.28	7.50	7.73	7.95	8.18	8.40	8.63	8.85	9.07
114	5.77	6.00	6.23	6.46	6.68	6.91	7.14	7.36	7.59	7.82	8.04	8.27	8.50	8.72	8.95	9.17
113	5.85	6.08	6.31	6.54	6.77	7.00	7.23	7.45	7.68	7.91	8.14	8.37	8.59	8.82	9.05	9.28
112	5.93	6.16	6.39	6.63	6.86	7.09	7.32	7.55	7.78	8.00	8.23	8.46	8.69	8.92	9.15	9.38
111	6.02	6.25	6.48	6.71	6.94	7.18	7.41	7.64	7.87	8.10	8.33	8.56	8.79	9.02	9.25	9.48
110	6.10	6.33	6.57	6.80	7.03	7.27	7.50	7.73	7.96	8.20	8.43	8.66	8.89	9.13	9.36	9.59
109	6.18	6.42	6.65	6.89	7.12	7.36	7.59	7.83	8.06	8.30	8.53	8.76	9.00	9.23	9.47	9.70
108	6.27	6.51	6.74	6.98	7.21	7.45	7.69	7.92	8.16	8.39	8.63	8.87	9.10	9.34	9.57	9.81
107	6.36	6.59	6.83	7.07	7.31	7.55	7.78	8.02	8.26	8.50	8.73	8.97	9.21	9.45	9.68	9.92
106	6.44	6.68	6.92	7.16	7.40	7.64	7.88	8.12	8.36	8.60	8.84	9.08	9.32	9.55	9.79	10.03
105	6.53	6.77	7.01	7.26	7.50	7.74	7.98	8.22	8.46	8.70	8.94	9.18	9.42	9.67	9.91	10.15
104	6.62	6.86	7.11	7.35	7.59	7.84	8.08	8.32	8.56	8.81	9.05	9.29	9.54	9.78	10.02	10.26
103	6.71	6.96	7.20	7.45	7.69	7.94	8.18	8.43	8.67	8.91	9.16	9.40	9.65	9.89	10.14	10.38
102	6.81	7.05	7.30	7.55	7.79	8.04	8.28	8.53	8.78	9.02	9.27	9.52	9.76	10.01	10.25	10.50
101	6.90	7.15	7.40	7.64	7.89	8.14	8.39	8.64	8.89	9.13	9.38	9.63	9.88	10.13	10.37	10.62
100	7.00	7.25	7.50	7.75	8.00	8.25	8.50	8.75	9.00	9.25	9.50	9.75	10.00	10.25	10.50	10.75
99	7.09	7.34	7.60	7.85	8.10	8.35	8.60	8.85	9.11	9.36	9.61	9.86	10.11	10.37	10.62	10.87
98	7.19	7.44	7.70	7.95	8.20	8.46	8.71	8.97	9.22	9.47	9.73	9.98	10.24	10.49	10.74	11.00
97	7.29	7.54	7.80	8.06	8.31	8.57	8.82	9.08	9.34	9.59	9.85	10.10	10.36	10.62	10.87	11.13
96	7.39	7.65	7.91	8.16	8.42	8.68	8.94	9.19	9.45	9.71	9.97	10.23	10.48	10.74	11.00	11.26
95	7.49	7.75	8.01	8.27	8.53	8.79	9.05	9.31	9.57	9.83	10.09	10.35	10.61	10.87	11.13	11.39
94	7.60	7.86	8.12	8.38	8.64	8.91	9.17	9.43	9.69	9.95	10.22	10.48	10.74	11.00	11.27	11.53
93	7.70	7.97	8.23	8.49	8.76	9.02	9.29	9.55	9.82	10.08	10.34	10.61	10.87	11.14	11.40	11.67
92	7.81	8.08	8.34	8.61	8.87	9.14	9.41	9.67	9.94	10.21	10.47	10.74	11.01	11.28	11.54	11.81
91	7.92	8.19	8.46	8.72	8.99	9.26	9.53	9.80	10.07	10.34	10.61	10.88	11.14	11.41	11.68	11.95
90	8.03	8.30	8.57	8.84	9.11	9.38	9.65	9.93	10.20	10.47	10.74	11.01	11.28	11.56	11.83	12.10
89	8.14	8.42	8.69	8.96	9.23	9.51	9.78	10.05	10.33	10.60	10.88	11.15	11.43	11.70	11.98	12.25
88	8.26	8.53	8.81	9.08	9.36	9.63	9.91	10.19	10.46	10.74	11.02	11.29	11.57	11.85	12.12	12.40
87	8.37	8.65	8.93	9.21	9.48	9.76	10.04	10.32	10.60	10.88	11.16	11.44	11.72	12.00	12.28	12.56
86	8.49	8.77	9.05	9.33	9.61	9.89	10.17	10.46	10.74	11.02	11.30	11.58	11.87	12.15	12.43	12.71
85	8.61	8.90	9.18	9.46	9.74	10.03	10.31	10.59	10.88	11.16	11.45	11.73	12.02	12.30	12.59	12.88
84	8.74	9.02	9.31	9.59	9.88	10.16	10.45	10.74	11.02	11.31	11.60	11.89	12.17	12.46	12.75	13.04
83	8.86	9.15	9.44	9.72	10.01	10.30	10.59	10.88	11.17	11.46	11.75	12.04	12.33	12.62	12.92	13.21
82	8.99	9.28	9.57	9.86	10.15	10.44	10.74	11.03	11.32	11.61	11.91	12.20	12.49	12.79	13.08	13.38
81	9.12	9.41	9.70	10.00	10.29	10.59	10.88	11.18	11.47	11.77	12.07	12.36	12.66	12.96	13.26	13.55
80	9.25	9.55	9.84	10.14	10.44	10.73	11.03	11.33	11.63	11.93	12.23	12.53	12.83	13.13	13.43	13.73
79	9.38	9.68	9.98	10.28	10.58	10.88	11.18	11.49	11.79	12.09	12.39	12.70	13.00	13.30	13.61	13.91
78	9.52	9.82	10.13	10.43	10.73	11.04	11.34	11.65	11.95	12.26	12.56	12.87	13.18	13.48	13.79	14.10
77	9.66	9.97	10.27	10.58	10.89	11.19	11.50	11.81	12.12	12.43	12.74	13.05	13.36	13.67	13.98	14.29
76	9.80	10.11	10.42	10.73	11.04	11.35	11.66	11.97	12.29	12.60	12.91	13.23	13.54	13.85	14.17	14.48
75	9.95	10.26	10.57	10.89	11.20	11.51	11.83	12.14	12.46	12.78	13.09	13.41	13.73	14.05	14.36	14.68
74	10.10	10.41	10.73	11.05	11.36	11.68	12.00	12.32	12.64	12.96	13.28	13.60	13.92	14.24	14.56	14.89
73	10.25	10.57	10.89	11.21	11.53	11.85	12.17	12.49	12.82	13.14	13.47	13.79	14.12	14.44	14.77	15.10
70	10.73	11.06	11.39	11.72	12.05	12.38	12.72	13.05	13.39	13.72	14.06	14.40	14.73	15.07	15.41	15.75
65	11.59	11.95	12.30	12.65	13.01	13.36	13.72	14.07	14.43	14.79	15.15	15.51	15.88	16.24	16.60	16.97
60	12.58	12.95	13.33	13.71	14.09	14.47	14.86	15.24	15.63	16.02	16.40	16.79	17.18	17.58	17.97	18.36
55	13.70	14.11	14.52	14.93	15.35	15.76	16.18	16.59	17.01	17.43	17.86	18.28	18.71	19.13	19.56	19.99
50	15.02	15.46	15.91	16.36	16.82	17.27	17.73	18.19	18.65	19.11	19.57	20.04	20.51	20.98	21.45	21.92
45	16.58	17.08	17.57	18.07	18.58	19.08	19.59	20.10	20.62	21.13	21.65	22.17	22.69	23.22	23.74	24.27
40	18.49	19.05	19.61	20.18	20.74	21.32	21.89	22.47	23.05	23.64	24.22	24.81	25.40	26.00	26.60	27.19
35	20.90	21.55	22.19	22.85	23.50	24.16	24.83	25.50	26.17	26.84	27.52	28.20	28.89	29.57	30.26	30.95
30	24.08	24.85	25.61	26.39	27.17	27.95	28.74	29.53	30.33	31.13	31.93	32.74	33.55	34.36	35.17	35.98

Description: This table shows the price to pay for a bond at the yield rate. The yield is to maturity.

Example: The price of a 15.00 %, 19 year bond to yield 8 % to maturity is $ 167.79.

COUPON RATE, %

YIELD	11.00%	11.25%	11.50%	11.75%	12.00%	12.25%	12.50%	12.75%	13.00%	13.25%	13.50%	13.75%	14.00%	14.25%	14.50%	15.00%
0.00	309.00	313.75	318.50	323.25	328.00	332.75	337.50	342.25	347.00	351.75	356.50	361.25	366.00	370.75	375.50	385.00
1.00	272.65	276.97	281.28	285.60	289.91	294.23	298.55	302.86	307.18	311.50	315.81	320.13	324.44	328.76	333.08	341.71
2.00	241.68	245.62	249.55	253.49	257.42	261.36	265.29	269.23	273.17	277.10	281.04	284.97	288.91	292.84	296.78	304.65
3.00	215.22	218.82	222.42	226.02	229.62	233.22	236.82	240.42	244.03	247.63	251.23	254.83	258.43	262.03	265.63	272.83
4.00	192.54	195.85	199.15	202.46	205.76	209.07	212.37	215.68	218.98	222.29	225.59	228.90	232.20	235.51	238.81	245.42
4.25	187.39	190.63	193.86	197.10	200.34	203.57	206.81	210.05	213.28	216.52	219.76	222.99	226.23	229.47	232.70	239.18
4.50	182.43	185.60	188.77	191.94	195.11	198.28	201.45	204.62	207.79	210.96	214.13	217.30	220.47	223.64	226.81	233.16
4.75	177.65	180.76	183.86	186.97	190.07	193.18	196.29	199.39	202.50	205.60	208.71	211.82	214.92	218.03	221.13	227.35
5.00	173.05	176.09	179.13	182.18	185.22	188.26	191.31	194.35	197.39	200.44	203.48	206.53	209.57	212.61	215.66	221.74
5.25	168.61	171.59	174.57	177.56	180.54	183.52	186.51	189.49	192.47	195.46	198.44	201.42	204.40	207.39	210.37	216.34
5.50	164.33	167.26	170.18	173.10	176.03	178.95	181.88	184.80	187.72	190.65	193.57	196.50	199.42	202.34	205.27	211.12
5.75	160.21	163.07	165.94	168.81	171.68	174.54	177.41	180.28	183.14	186.01	188.88	191.74	194.61	197.48	200.35	206.08
6.00	156.23	159.04	161.85	164.67	167.48	170.29	173.10	175.91	178.72	181.54	184.35	187.16	189.97	192.78	195.59	201.22
6.25	152.40	155.15	157.91	160.67	163.43	166.18	168.94	171.70	174.46	177.22	179.97	182.73	185.49	188.25	191.00	196.52
6.50	148.70	151.40	154.11	156.81	159.52	162.22	164.93	167.63	170.34	173.04	175.75	178.46	181.16	183.87	186.57	191.98
6.75	145.13	147.78	150.44	153.09	155.75	158.40	161.05	163.71	166.36	169.02	171.67	174.33	176.98	179.64	182.29	187.60
7.00	141.68	144.29	146.89	149.50	152.10	154.71	157.31	159.92	162.52	165.13	167.73	170.34	172.94	175.55	178.15	183.36
7.25	138.36	140.91	143.47	146.03	148.59	151.14	153.70	156.26	158.81	161.37	163.93	166.49	169.04	171.60	174.16	179.27
7.50	135.15	137.66	140.17	142.68	145.19	147.70	150.21	152.72	155.23	157.74	160.25	162.76	165.27	167.78	170.29	175.31
7.75	132.05	134.51	136.98	139.44	141.91	144.37	146.84	149.30	151.77	154.23	156.70	159.16	161.63	164.09	166.56	171.49
8.00	129.05	131.47	133.89	136.31	138.74	141.16	143.58	146.00	148.42	150.84	153.26	155.68	158.10	160.52	162.95	167.79
8.25	126.16	128.54	130.92	133.29	135.67	138.05	140.43	142.81	145.18	147.56	149.94	152.32	154.70	157.07	159.45	164.21
8.50	123.36	125.70	128.04	130.37	132.71	135.05	137.38	139.72	142.05	144.39	146.73	149.06	151.40	153.74	156.07	160.75
8.75	120.66	122.96	125.25	127.55	129.84	132.14	134.44	136.73	139.03	141.32	143.62	145.92	148.21	150.51	152.80	157.39
9.00	118.05	120.31	122.56	124.82	127.07	129.33	131.59	133.84	136.10	138.36	140.61	142.87	145.12	147.38	149.64	154.15
9.25	115.52	117.74	119.96	122.18	124.40	126.61	128.83	131.05	133.27	135.48	137.70	139.92	142.14	144.36	146.57	151.01
9.50	113.08	115.26	117.44	119.62	121.80	123.98	126.16	128.35	130.53	132.71	134.89	137.07	139.25	141.43	143.61	147.97
9.75	110.72	112.86	115.01	117.15	119.30	121.44	123.58	125.73	127.87	130.02	132.16	134.30	136.45	138.59	140.74	145.02
10.00	108.43	110.54	112.65	114.76	116.87	118.98	121.08	123.19	125.30	127.41	129.52	131.63	133.74	135.84	137.95	142.17
10.25	106.22	108.30	110.37	112.44	114.52	116.59	118.67	120.74	122.81	124.89	126.96	129.04	131.11	133.18	135.26	139.40
10.50	104.08	106.12	108.16	110.20	112.24	114.28	116.32	118.36	120.40	122.44	124.48	126.52	128.56	130.60	132.64	136.73
10.75	102.01	104.02	106.02	108.03	110.04	112.05	114.05	116.06	118.07	120.08	122.08	124.09	126.10	128.11	130.11	134.13
11.00	100.00	101.98	103.95	105.93	107.90	109.88	111.85	113.83	115.80	117.78	119.76	121.73	123.71	125.68	127.66	131.61
11.25	98.06	100.00	101.94	103.89	105.83	107.78	109.72	111.67	113.61	115.56	117.50	119.44	121.39	123.33	125.28	129.17
11.50	96.17	98.09	100.00	101.91	103.83	105.74	107.66	109.57	111.48	113.40	115.31	117.23	119.14	121.06	122.97	126.80
11.75	94.35	96.23	98.12	100.00	101.88	103.77	105.65	107.54	109.42	111.31	113.19	115.08	116.96	118.85	120.73	124.50
12.00	92.58	94.43	96.29	98.14	100.00	101.86	103.71	105.57	107.42	109.28	111.13	112.99	114.85	116.70	118.56	122.27
12.25	90.86	92.69	94.52	96.34	98.17	100.00	101.83	103.66	105.48	107.31	109.14	110.97	112.79	114.62	116.45	120.10
12.50	89.20	91.00	92.80	94.60	96.40	98.20	100.00	101.80	103.60	105.40	107.20	109.00	110.80	112.60	114.40	118.00
12.75	87.59	89.36	91.13	92.91	94.68	96.45	98.23	100.00	101.77	103.55	105.32	107.09	108.87	110.64	112.41	115.96
13.00	86.02	87.77	89.52	91.26	93.01	94.76	96.51	98.25	100.00	101.75	103.49	105.24	106.99	108.74	110.48	113.98
13.25	84.50	86.22	87.95	89.67	91.39	93.11	94.83	96.56	98.28	100.00	101.72	103.44	105.17	106.89	108.61	112.05
13.50	83.03	84.73	86.42	88.12	89.82	91.51	93.21	94.91	96.61	98.30	100.00	101.70	103.39	105.09	106.79	110.18
13.75	81.60	83.27	84.94	86.62	88.29	89.96	91.64	93.31	94.98	96.65	98.33	100.00	101.67	103.35	105.02	108.36
14.00	80.21	81.86	83.51	85.16	86.81	88.46	90.10	91.75	93.40	95.05	96.70	98.35	100.00	101.65	103.30	106.60
14.25	78.86	80.49	82.11	83.74	85.37	86.99	88.62	90.24	91.87	93.50	95.12	96.75	98.37	100.00	101.63	104.88
14.50	77.55	79.15	80.76	82.36	83.96	85.57	87.17	88.78	90.38	91.98	93.59	95.19	96.79	98.40	100.00	103.21
14.75	76.28	77.86	79.44	81.02	82.60	84.19	85.77	87.35	88.93	90.51	92.09	93.67	95.26	96.84	98.42	101.58
15.00	75.04	76.60	78.16	79.72	81.28	82.84	84.40	85.96	87.52	89.08	90.64	92.20	93.76	95.32	96.88	100.00
15.25	73.84	75.38	76.92	78.46	79.99	81.53	83.07	84.61	86.15	87.69	89.23	90.77	92.31	93.84	95.38	98.46
15.50	72.67	74.19	75.71	77.22	78.74	80.26	81.78	83.30	84.82	86.33	87.85	89.37	90.89	92.41	93.93	96.96
15.75	71.53	73.03	74.53	76.03	77.53	79.02	80.52	82.02	83.52	85.02	86.52	88.01	89.51	91.01	92.51	95.51
16.00	70.43	71.91	73.39	74.86	76.34	77.82	79.30	80.78	82.26	83.74	85.21	86.69	88.17	89.65	91.13	94.09
16.25	69.35	70.81	72.27	73.73	75.19	76.65	78.11	79.57	81.03	82.49	83.95	85.41	86.87	88.32	89.78	92.70
16.50	68.31	69.75	71.19	72.63	74.07	75.51	76.95	78.39	79.83	81.27	82.71	84.15	85.59	87.03	88.47	91.36
16.75	67.29	68.71	70.13	71.55	72.98	74.40	75.82	77.24	78.67	80.09	81.51	82.93	84.35	85.78	87.20	90.04
17.00	66.30	67.70	69.10	70.51	71.91	73.32	74.72	76.13	77.53	78.93	80.34	81.74	83.15	84.55	85.96	88.77
17.25	65.33	66.72	68.10	69.49	70.88	72.26	73.65	75.04	76.42	77.81	79.20	80.59	81.97	83.36	84.75	87.52
17.50	64.39	65.76	67.13	68.50	69.87	71.24	72.61	73.98	75.35	76.72	78.09	79.46	80.83	82.20	83.56	86.30
17.75	63.47	64.83	66.18	67.53	68.89	70.24	71.59	72.94	74.30	75.65	77.00	78.36	79.71	81.06	82.41	85.12
18.00	62.58	63.92	65.25	66.59	67.93	69.26	70.60	71.94	73.27	74.61	75.95	77.28	78.62	79.95	81.29	83.96
18.25	61.71	63.03	64.35	65.67	66.99	68.31	69.63	70.95	72.27	73.59	74.92	76.24	77.56	78.88	80.20	82.84
18.50	60.87	62.17	63.47	64.78	66.08	67.39	68.69	70.00	71.30	72.61	73.91	75.21	76.52	77.82	79.13	81.74
18.75	60.04	61.33	62.62	63.91	65.20	66.48	67.77	69.06	70.35	71.64	72.93	74.22	75.51	76.80	78.09	80.66
19.00	59.23	60.51	61.78	63.06	64.33	65.60	66.88	68.15	69.42	70.70	71.97	73.25	74.52	75.79	77.07	79.62
20.00	56.20	57.42	58.64	59.85	61.07	62.29	63.50	64.72	65.94	67.15	68.37	69.59	70.80	72.02	73.24	75.67
25.00	44.64	45.63	46.61	47.60	48.59	49.58	50.57	51.56	52.55	53.53	54.52	55.51	56.50	57.49	58.48	60.46
30.00	36.98	37.81	38.64	39.47	40.30	41.13	41.95	42.78	43.61	44.44	45.27	46.10	46.93	47.76	48.59	50.25

Description: This table shows the yield to maturity of a bond purchased at the price shown in the index.

Example: The yield to maturity of a 15.00 %, 19 year bond at a price of 125.00 is 11.69 %.

COUPON RATE, %

PRICE	11.00%	11.25%	11.50%	11.75%	12.00%	12.25%	12.50%	12.75%	13.00%	13.25%	13.50%	13.75%	14.00%	14.25%	14.50%	15.00%
250	1.71	1.85	1.98	2.11	2.25	2.38	2.51	2.65	2.78	2.91	3.04	3.17	3.30	3.43	3.56	3.82
240	2.05	2.19	2.33	2.47	2.60	2.74	2.88	3.01	3.15	3.28	3.41	3.55	3.68	3.81	3.95	4.21
230	2.42	2.56	2.70	2.84	2.98	3.12	3.26	3.40	3.54	3.67	3.81	3.95	4.09	4.22	4.36	4.63
220	2.80	2.95	3.09	3.24	3.38	3.52	3.67	3.81	3.95	4.09	4.23	4.38	4.52	4.66	4.80	5.07
210	3.21	3.36	3.51	3.66	3.81	3.95	4.10	4.25	4.39	4.54	4.68	4.83	4.97	5.12	5.26	5.55
200	3.65	3.80	3.96	4.11	4.26	4.41	4.56	4.72	4.87	5.02	5.17	5.32	5.47	5.61	5.76	6.06
195	3.88	4.03	4.19	4.35	4.50	4.65	4.81	4.96	5.12	5.27	5.42	5.57	5.72	5.88	6.03	6.33
190	4.12	4.28	4.43	4.59	4.75	4.91	5.06	5.22	5.37	5.53	5.68	5.84	5.99	6.15	6.30	6.61
185	4.36	4.53	4.69	4.85	5.01	5.17	5.33	5.48	5.64	5.80	5.96	6.12	6.27	6.43	6.59	6.90
180	4.62	4.78	4.95	5.11	5.27	5.44	5.60	5.76	5.92	6.08	6.24	6.40	6.56	6.72	6.88	7.20
175	4.89	5.05	5.22	5.39	5.55	5.72	5.88	6.05	6.21	6.38	6.54	6.70	6.87	7.03	7.19	7.52
170	5.17	5.34	5.51	5.67	5.84	6.01	6.18	6.35	6.52	6.68	6.85	7.02	7.18	7.35	7.51	7.84
165	5.46	5.63	5.80	5.97	6.15	6.32	6.49	6.66	6.83	7.00	7.17	7.34	7.51	7.68	7.85	8.19
160	5.76	5.93	6.11	6.29	6.46	6.64	6.81	6.99	7.16	7.34	7.51	7.69	7.86	8.03	8.21	8.55
155	6.07	6.26	6.44	6.62	6.80	6.97	7.15	7.33	7.51	7.69	7.87	8.05	8.22	8.40	8.58	8.93
150	6.41	6.59	6.78	6.96	7.14	7.33	7.51	7.69	7.88	8.06	8.24	8.42	8.60	8.78	8.97	9.33
145	6.75	6.94	7.13	7.32	7.51	7.70	7.88	8.07	8.26	8.45	8.63	8.82	9.01	9.19	9.38	9.75
140	7.12	7.31	7.51	7.70	7.89	8.09	8.28	8.47	8.66	8.86	9.05	9.24	9.43	9.62	9.81	10.19
135	7.51	7.71	7.90	8.10	8.30	8.50	8.70	8.89	9.09	9.29	9.48	9.68	9.88	10.07	10.27	10.66
130	7.91	8.12	8.32	8.53	8.73	8.93	9.14	9.34	9.54	9.75	9.95	10.15	10.35	10.55	10.76	11.16
125	8.35	8.56	8.77	8.98	9.19	9.40	9.61	9.82	10.02	10.23	10.44	10.65	10.86	11.07	11.27	11.69
120	8.81	9.02	9.24	9.46	9.67	9.89	10.11	10.32	10.54	10.75	10.97	11.18	11.40	11.61	11.83	12.26
115	9.30	9.52	9.75	9.97	10.19	10.42	10.64	10.86	11.09	11.31	11.53	11.75	11.98	12.20	12.42	12.87
113	9.50	9.73	9.96	10.18	10.41	10.64	10.86	11.09	11.32	11.54	11.77	11.99	12.22	12.45	12.67	13.12
112	9.61	9.84	10.07	10.29	10.52	10.75	10.98	11.21	11.43	11.66	11.89	12.12	12.34	12.57	12.80	13.25
111	9.71	9.95	10.18	10.41	10.63	10.86	11.09	11.32	11.55	11.78	12.01	12.24	12.47	12.70	12.93	13.38
110	9.82	10.05	10.29	10.52	10.75	10.98	11.21	11.44	11.67	11.91	12.14	12.37	12.60	12.83	13.06	13.52
109	9.93	10.17	10.40	10.63	10.87	11.10	11.33	11.56	11.80	12.03	12.26	12.50	12.73	12.96	13.19	13.66
108	10.04	10.28	10.51	10.75	10.98	11.22	11.45	11.69	11.92	12.16	12.39	12.63	12.86	13.09	13.33	13.80
107	10.16	10.39	10.63	10.87	11.10	11.34	11.58	11.81	12.05	12.29	12.52	12.76	12.99	13.23	13.47	13.94
106	10.27	10.51	10.75	10.99	11.22	11.46	11.70	11.94	12.18	12.42	12.65	12.89	13.13	13.37	13.61	14.08
105	10.39	10.63	10.87	11.11	11.35	11.59	11.83	12.07	12.31	12.55	12.79	13.03	13.27	13.51	13.75	14.23
104	10.50	10.75	10.99	11.23	11.47	11.72	11.96	12.20	12.44	12.68	12.93	13.17	13.41	13.65	13.89	14.38
103	10.62	10.87	11.11	11.36	11.60	11.84	12.09	12.33	12.58	12.82	13.06	13.31	13.55	13.80	14.04	14.53
102	10.75	10.99	11.24	11.48	11.73	11.98	12.22	12.47	12.71	12.96	13.21	13.45	13.70	13.94	14.19	14.68
101	10.87	11.12	11.37	11.61	11.86	12.11	12.36	12.61	12.85	13.10	13.35	13.60	13.84	14.09	14.34	14.84
100	11.00	11.25	11.50	11.75	12.00	12.25	12.50	12.75	13.00	13.25	13.50	13.75	14.00	14.25	14.50	15.00
99	11.12	11.37	11.63	11.88	12.13	12.38	12.64	12.89	13.14	13.39	13.64	13.90	14.15	14.40	14.65	15.16
98	11.25	11.51	11.76	12.01	12.27	12.52	12.78	13.03	13.29	13.54	13.79	14.05	14.30	14.56	14.81	15.32
97	11.38	11.64	11.90	12.15	12.41	12.67	12.92	13.18	13.44	13.69	13.95	14.21	14.46	14.72	14.98	15.49
96	11.52	11.78	12.04	12.29	12.55	12.81	13.07	13.33	13.59	13.85	14.11	14.36	14.62	14.88	15.14	15.66
95	11.65	11.92	12.18	12.44	12.70	12.96	13.22	13.48	13.74	14.00	14.26	14.53	14.79	15.05	15.31	15.83
94	11.79	12.06	12.32	12.58	12.85	13.11	13.37	13.64	13.90	14.16	14.43	14.69	14.95	15.22	15.48	16.01
93	11.93	12.20	12.47	12.73	13.00	13.26	13.53	13.79	14.06	14.33	14.59	14.86	15.12	15.39	15.66	16.19
92	12.08	12.35	12.61	12.88	13.15	13.42	13.69	13.95	14.22	14.49	14.76	15.03	15.30	15.57	15.84	16.37
91	12.22	12.49	12.77	13.04	13.31	13.58	13.85	14.12	14.39	14.66	14.93	15.20	15.48	15.75	16.02	16.56
90	12.37	12.65	12.92	13.19	13.47	13.74	14.01	14.29	14.56	14.83	15.11	15.38	15.66	15.93	16.20	16.75
89	12.53	12.80	13.08	13.35	13.63	13.90	14.18	14.46	14.73	15.01	15.29	15.56	15.84	16.12	16.39	16.95
88	12.68	12.96	13.24	13.51	13.79	14.07	14.35	14.63	14.91	15.19	15.47	15.75	16.03	16.31	16.59	17.15
87	12.84	13.12	13.40	13.68	13.96	14.24	14.53	14.81	15.09	15.37	15.65	15.94	16.22	16.50	16.78	17.35
86	13.00	13.28	13.57	13.85	14.13	14.42	14.70	14.99	15.27	15.56	15.84	16.13	16.41	16.70	16.99	17.56
85	13.16	13.45	13.74	14.02	14.31	14.60	14.88	15.17	15.46	15.75	16.04	16.33	16.61	16.90	17.19	17.77
84	13.33	13.62	13.91	14.20	14.49	14.78	15.07	15.36	15.65	15.94	16.23	16.53	16.82	17.11	17.40	17.99
83	13.50	13.79	14.09	14.38	14.67	14.97	15.26	15.55	15.85	16.14	16.44	16.73	17.03	17.32	17.62	18.21
82	13.67	13.97	14.27	14.56	14.86	15.15	15.45	15.75	16.05	16.34	16.64	16.94	17.24	17.54	17.84	18.43
81	13.85	14.15	14.45	14.75	15.05	15.35	15.65	15.95	16.25	16.55	16.85	17.15	17.46	17.76	18.06	18.67
80	14.03	14.34	14.64	14.94	15.24	15.55	15.85	16.16	16.46	16.76	17.07	17.37	17.68	17.98	18.29	18.90
79	14.22	14.52	14.83	15.14	15.44	15.75	16.06	16.36	16.67	16.98	17.29	17.60	17.91	18.22	18.53	19.15
78	14.41	14.72	15.03	15.34	15.65	15.96	16.27	16.58	16.89	17.20	17.51	17.83	18.14	18.45	18.77	19.39
77	14.60	14.92	15.23	15.54	15.86	16.17	16.48	16.80	17.11	17.43	17.75	18.06	18.38	18.70	19.01	19.65
76	14.80	15.12	15.43	15.75	16.07	16.39	16.70	17.02	17.34	17.66	17.98	18.30	18.62	18.94	19.26	19.91
75	15.00	15.32	15.64	15.97	16.29	16.61	16.93	17.25	17.58	17.90	18.22	18.55	18.87	19.20	19.52	20.17
74	15.21	15.54	15.86	16.18	16.51	16.84	17.16	17.49	17.82	18.14	18.47	18.80	19.13	19.46	19.79	20.45
73	15.42	15.75	16.08	16.41	16.74	17.07	17.40	17.73	18.06	18.39	18.73	19.06	19.39	19.73	20.06	20.73
70	16.09	16.43	16.78	17.12	17.46	17.81	18.15	18.49	18.84	19.18	19.53	19.88	20.22	20.57	20.92	21.61
65	17.33	17.70	18.07	18.43	18.80	19.17	19.54	19.91	20.28	20.65	21.02	21.40	21.77	22.14	22.52	23.27
60	18.76	19.15	19.55	19.95	20.35	20.74	21.14	21.55	21.95	22.35	22.75	23.16	23.56	23.96	24.37	25.18
55	20.42	20.85	21.29	21.72	22.15	22.59	23.03	23.46	23.90	24.34	24.78	25.22	25.67	26.11	26.55	27.44

BOND PRICE

Description: This table shows the price to pay for a bond at the yield rate. The yield is to maturity.

Example: The price of a 6.75 %, 20 year bond to yield 8 % to maturity is $ 87.63.

COUPON RATE, %

YIELD	0.00%	1.00%	2.00%	3.00%	4.00%	4.25%	4.50%	4.75%	5.00%	5.25%	5.50%	5.75%	6.00%	6.25%	6.50%	6.75%
0.00	100.00	120.00	140.00	160.00	180.00	185.00	190.00	195.00	200.00	205.00	210.00	215.00	220.00	225.00	230.00	235.00
1.00	81.91	100.00	118.09	136.17	154.26	158.78	163.30	167.82	172.34	176.87	181.39	185.91	190.43	194.95	199.47	204.00
2.00	67.17	83.58	100.00	116.42	132.83	136.94	141.04	145.15	149.25	153.36	157.46	161.57	165.67	169.77	173.88	177.98
3.00	55.13	70.08	85.04	100.00	114.96	118.70	122.44	126.18	129.92	133.66	137.39	141.13	144.87	148.61	152.35	156.09
4.00	45.29	58.97	72.64	86.32	100.00	103.42	106.84	110.26	113.68	117.10	120.52	123.94	127.36	130.77	134.19	137.61
4.25	43.12	56.51	69.89	83.27	96.65	100.00	103.35	106.69	110.04	113.38	116.73	120.07	123.42	126.77	130.11	133.46
4.50	41.06	54.16	67.26	80.35	93.45	96.73	100.00	103.27	106.55	109.82	113.10	116.37	119.65	122.92	126.19	129.47
4.75	39.11	51.93	64.75	77.57	90.39	93.59	96.80	100.00	103.20	106.41	109.61	112.82	116.02	119.23	122.43	125.64
5.00	37.24	49.79	62.35	74.90	87.45	90.59	93.72	96.86	100.00	103.14	106.28	109.41	112.55	115.69	118.83	121.96
5.25	35.47	47.76	60.05	72.34	84.64	87.71	90.78	93.85	96.93	100.00	103.07	106.15	109.22	112.29	115.36	118.44
5.50	33.79	45.82	57.86	69.90	81.94	84.95	87.96	90.97	93.98	96.99	100.00	103.01	106.02	109.03	112.04	115.05
5.75	32.18	43.98	55.77	67.57	79.36	82.31	85.26	88.21	91.15	94.10	97.05	100.00	102.95	105.90	108.85	111.79
6.00	30.66	42.21	53.77	65.33	76.89	79.77	82.66	85.55	88.44	91.33	94.22	97.11	100.00	102.89	105.78	108.67
6.25	29.20	40.53	51.86	63.19	74.51	77.35	80.18	83.01	85.84	88.67	91.50	94.34	97.17	100.00	102.83	105.66
6.50	27.82	38.93	50.03	61.14	72.24	75.02	77.79	80.57	83.34	86.12	88.90	91.67	94.45	97.22	100.00	102.78
6.75	26.51	37.40	48.28	59.17	70.06	72.78	75.50	78.22	80.95	83.67	86.39	89.11	91.83	94.56	97.28	100.00
7.00	25.26	35.93	46.61	57.29	67.97	70.64	73.31	75.98	78.64	81.31	83.98	86.65	89.32	91.99	94.66	97.33
7.25	24.07	34.54	45.01	55.49	65.96	68.58	71.20	73.82	76.43	79.05	81.67	84.29	86.91	89.53	92.14	94.76
7.50	22.93	33.21	43.48	53.76	64.04	66.60	69.17	71.74	74.31	76.88	79.45	82.02	84.59	87.16	89.72	92.29
7.75	21.86	31.94	42.02	52.10	62.19	64.71	67.23	69.75	72.27	74.79	77.31	79.83	82.35	84.88	87.40	89.92
8.00	20.83	30.73	40.62	50.52	60.41	62.89	65.36	67.84	70.31	72.78	75.26	77.73	80.21	82.68	85.16	87.63
8.25	19.85	29.57	39.28	49.00	58.71	61.14	63.57	66.00	68.43	70.86	73.28	75.71	78.14	80.57	83.00	85.43
8.50	18.92	28.46	38.00	47.54	57.08	59.46	61.85	64.23	66.61	69.00	71.38	73.77	76.15	78.54	80.92	83.31
8.75	18.04	27.40	36.77	46.14	55.51	57.85	60.19	62.53	64.87	67.21	69.56	71.90	74.24	76.58	78.92	81.27
9.00	17.19	26.39	35.59	44.80	54.00	56.30	58.60	60.90	63.20	65.50	67.80	70.10	72.40	74.70	77.00	79.30
9.25	16.39	25.43	34.47	43.51	52.55	54.81	57.07	59.32	61.58	63.84	66.10	68.36	70.62	72.88	75.14	77.40
9.50	15.63	24.51	33.39	42.27	51.15	53.37	55.59	57.81	60.03	62.25	64.47	66.69	68.91	71.14	73.36	75.58
9.75	14.90	23.63	32.35	41.08	49.81	51.99	54.18	56.36	58.54	60.72	62.90	65.09	67.27	69.45	71.63	73.81
10.00	14.20	22.78	31.36	39.94	48.52	50.67	52.81	54.96	57.10	59.25	61.39	63.54	65.68	67.83	69.97	72.12
10.25	13.54	21.98	30.41	38.85	47.28	49.39	51.50	53.61	55.72	57.83	59.94	62.04	64.15	66.26	68.37	70.48
10.50	12.92	21.21	29.50	37.80	46.09	48.16	50.24	52.31	54.38	56.46	58.53	60.60	62.68	64.75	66.83	68.90
10.75	12.32	20.47	28.63	36.79	44.94	46.98	49.02	51.06	53.10	55.14	57.18	59.22	61.26	63.30	65.33	67.37
11.00	11.75	19.77	27.79	35.82	43.84	45.84	47.85	49.86	51.86	53.87	55.87	57.88	59.88	61.89	63.90	65.90
11.25	11.20	19.10	26.99	34.88	42.78	44.75	46.72	48.70	50.67	52.64	54.61	56.59	58.56	60.53	62.51	64.48
11.50	10.69	18.45	26.22	33.98	41.75	43.69	45.63	47.58	49.52	51.46	53.40	55.34	57.28	59.23	61.17	63.11
11.75	10.19	17.84	25.48	33.12	40.76	42.68	44.59	46.50	48.41	50.32	52.23	54.14	56.05	57.96	59.87	61.78
12.00	9.72	17.25	24.77	32.29	39.81	41.70	43.58	45.46	47.34	49.22	51.10	52.98	54.86	56.74	58.62	60.50
12.25	9.27	16.68	24.09	31.49	38.90	40.75	42.60	44.45	46.31	48.16	50.01	51.86	53.71	55.56	57.41	59.27
12.50	8.85	16.14	23.43	30.72	38.02	39.84	41.66	43.49	45.31	47.13	48.95	50.78	52.60	54.42	56.25	58.07
12.75	8.44	15.62	22.80	29.98	37.17	38.96	40.76	42.55	44.35	46.14	47.94	49.73	51.53	53.32	55.12	56.91
13.00	8.05	15.13	22.20	29.27	36.35	38.11	39.88	41.65	43.42	45.19	46.95	48.72	50.49	52.26	54.03	55.80
13.25	7.68	14.65	21.62	28.59	35.55	37.30	39.04	40.78	42.52	44.26	46.00	47.75	49.49	51.23	52.97	54.71
13.50	7.33	14.20	21.06	27.93	34.79	36.51	38.22	39.94	41.65	43.37	45.09	46.80	48.52	50.23	51.95	53.67
13.75	7.00	13.76	20.53	27.29	34.05	35.74	37.43	39.13	40.82	42.51	44.20	45.89	47.58	49.27	50.96	52.65
14.00	6.68	13.34	20.01	26.68	33.34	35.01	36.67	38.34	40.01	41.67	43.34	45.01	46.67	48.34	50.01	51.67
14.25	6.37	12.94	19.51	26.08	32.65	34.30	35.94	37.58	39.22	40.87	42.51	44.15	45.80	47.44	49.08	50.72
14.50	6.08	12.56	19.04	25.51	31.99	33.61	35.23	36.85	38.47	40.09	41.71	43.33	44.95	46.56	48.18	49.80
14.75	5.81	12.19	18.58	24.96	31.35	32.95	34.54	36.14	37.74	39.33	40.93	42.53	44.12	45.72	47.32	48.91
15.00	5.54	11.84	18.14	24.43	30.73	32.31	33.88	35.45	37.03	38.60	40.18	41.75	43.33	44.90	46.47	48.05
15.25	5.29	11.50	17.71	23.92	30.13	31.68	33.24	34.79	36.34	37.90	39.45	41.00	42.55	44.11	45.66	47.21
15.50	5.05	11.18	17.30	23.43	29.55	31.08	32.62	34.15	35.68	37.21	38.74	40.27	41.80	43.34	44.87	46.40
15.75	4.82	10.86	16.91	22.95	28.99	30.50	32.02	33.53	35.04	36.55	38.06	39.57	41.08	42.59	44.10	45.61
16.00	4.60	10.57	16.53	22.49	28.45	29.94	31.43	32.92	34.41	35.91	37.40	38.89	40.38	41.87	43.36	44.85
16.25	4.39	10.28	16.16	22.05	27.93	29.40	30.87	32.34	33.81	35.28	36.75	38.22	39.70	41.17	42.64	44.11
16.50	4.20	10.00	15.81	21.62	27.42	28.87	30.32	31.78	33.23	34.68	36.13	37.58	39.03	40.49	41.94	43.39
16.75	4.01	9.74	15.47	21.20	26.93	28.36	29.80	31.23	32.66	34.09	35.53	36.96	38.39	39.83	41.26	42.69
17.00	3.83	9.48	15.14	20.80	26.46	27.87	29.28	30.70	32.11	33.53	34.94	36.36	37.77	39.18	40.60	42.01
17.25	3.65	9.24	14.82	20.41	26.00	27.39	28.79	30.18	31.58	32.98	34.37	35.77	37.17	38.56	39.96	41.35
17.50	3.49	9.00	14.52	20.03	25.55	26.93	28.31	29.69	31.06	32.44	33.82	35.20	36.58	37.96	39.34	40.72
17.75	3.33	8.78	14.23	19.67	25.12	26.48	27.84	29.20	30.56	31.92	33.29	34.65	36.01	37.37	38.73	40.09
18.00	3.18	8.56	13.94	19.32	24.70	26.04	27.39	28.73	30.08	31.42	32.77	34.11	35.46	36.80	38.15	39.49
18.25	3.04	8.35	13.67	18.98	24.29	25.62	26.95	28.28	29.61	30.93	32.26	33.59	34.92	36.25	37.57	38.90
18.50	2.90	8.15	13.40	18.65	23.90	25.21	26.52	27.83	29.15	30.46	31.77	33.08	34.40	35.71	37.02	38.33
18.75	2.78	7.96	13.15	18.33	23.52	24.81	26.11	27.41	28.70	30.00	31.29	32.59	33.89	35.18	36.48	37.78
19.00	2.65	7.77	12.90	18.02	23.15	24.43	25.71	26.99	28.27	29.55	30.83	32.11	33.39	34.67	35.95	37.24
20.00	2.21	7.10	11.99	16.88	21.77	22.99	24.21	25.43	26.66	27.88	29.10	30.32	31.55	32.77	33.99	35.21
25.00	.90	4.86	8.83	12.79	16.76	17.75	18.74	19.73	20.72	21.71	22.70	23.69	24.68	25.67	26.67	27.66
30.00	.37	3.69	7.02	10.34	13.66	14.49	15.32	16.15	16.98	17.81	18.64	19.47	20.30	21.13	21.96	22.79

Description: This table shows the yield to maturity of a bond purchased at the price shown in the index.

Example: The yield to maturity of a 6.75 %, 20 year bond at a price of 80.00 is 8.90 %.

COUPON RATE, %

PRICE	0.00%	1.00%	2.00%	3.00%	4.00%	4.25%	4.50%	4.75%	5.00%	5.25%	5.50%	5.75%	6.00%	6.25%	6.50%	6.75%
100	0.00	1.00	2.00	3.00	4.00	4.25	4.50	4.75	5.00	5.25	5.50	5.75	6.00	6.25	6.50	6.75
99	.05	1.05	2.06	3.06	4.07	4.32	4.57	4.82	5.08	5.33	5.58	5.83	6.08	6.33	6.59	6.84
98	.10	1.11	2.12	3.13	4.14	4.40	4.65	4.90	5.16	5.41	5.66	5.92	6.17	6.42	6.68	6.93
97	.15	1.16	2.18	3.20	4.22	4.47	4.73	4.98	5.24	5.49	5.75	6.00	6.26	6.52	6.77	7.03
96	.20	1.22	2.24	3.27	4.30	4.55	4.81	5.07	5.32	5.58	5.84	6.09	6.35	6.61	6.87	7.12
95	.25	1.28	2.31	3.34	4.37	4.63	4.89	5.15	5.41	5.67	5.93	6.18	6.44	6.70	6.96	7.22
94	.30	1.34	2.37	3.41	4.45	4.71	4.97	5.23	5.49	5.75	6.01	6.28	6.54	6.80	7.06	7.32
93	.36	1.40	2.44	3.48	4.53	4.79	5.06	5.32	5.58	5.84	6.11	6.37	6.63	6.90	7.16	7.42
92	.41	1.46	2.51	3.56	4.61	4.88	5.14	5.40	5.67	5.93	6.20	6.46	6.73	6.99	7.26	7.53
91	.47	1.52	2.57	3.63	4.69	4.96	5.23	5.49	5.76	6.03	6.29	6.56	6.83	7.09	7.36	7.63
90	.52	1.58	2.64	3.71	4.78	5.05	5.31	5.58	5.85	6.12	6.39	6.66	6.93	7.20	7.47	7.74
89	.58	1.64	2.71	3.78	4.86	5.13	5.40	5.67	5.94	6.21	6.48	6.76	7.03	7.30	7.57	7.84
88	.64	1.71	2.78	3.86	4.95	5.22	5.49	5.76	6.04	6.31	6.58	6.86	7.13	7.40	7.68	7.95
87	.69	1.77	2.85	3.94	5.03	5.31	5.58	5.86	6.13	6.41	6.68	6.96	7.24	7.51	7.79	8.07
86	.75	1.83	2.92	4.02	5.12	5.40	5.68	5.95	6.23	6.51	6.78	7.06	7.34	7.62	7.90	8.18
85	.81	1.90	3.00	4.10	5.21	5.49	5.77	6.05	6.33	6.61	6.89	7.17	7.45	7.73	8.01	8.29
84	.87	1.97	3.07	4.18	5.30	5.58	5.86	6.15	6.43	6.71	6.99	7.28	7.56	7.84	8.13	8.41
83	.93	2.03	3.15	4.27	5.40	5.68	5.96	6.25	6.53	6.81	7.10	7.39	7.67	7.96	8.24	8.53
82	.99	2.10	3.22	4.35	5.49	5.77	6.06	6.35	6.63	6.92	7.21	7.50	7.79	8.07	8.36	8.65
81	1.05	2.17	3.30	4.44	5.58	5.87	6.16	6.45	6.74	7.03	7.32	7.61	7.90	8.19	8.49	8.78
80	1.11	2.24	3.38	4.53	5.68	5.97	6.26	6.55	6.85	7.14	7.43	7.73	8.02	8.31	8.61	8.90
79	1.18	2.31	3.46	4.62	5.78	6.07	6.37	6.66	6.96	7.25	7.55	7.84	8.14	8.44	8.74	9.03
78	1.24	2.39	3.54	4.71	5.88	6.18	6.47	6.77	7.07	7.36	7.66	7.96	8.26	8.56	8.86	9.17
77	1.31	2.46	3.62	4.80	5.98	6.28	6.58	6.88	7.18	7.48	7.78	8.08	8.39	8.69	8.99	9.30
76	1.37	2.53	3.71	4.89	6.09	6.39	6.69	6.99	7.30	7.60	7.90	8.21	8.51	8.82	9.13	9.44
75	1.44	2.61	3.79	4.99	6.19	6.50	6.80	7.11	7.41	7.72	8.03	8.34	8.64	8.95	9.26	9.58
74	1.51	2.68	3.88	5.08	6.30	6.61	6.91	7.22	7.53	7.84	8.15	8.46	8.78	9.09	9.40	9.72
73	1.57	2.76	3.96	5.18	6.41	6.72	7.03	7.34	7.65	7.97	8.28	8.60	8.91	9.23	9.55	9.86
72	1.64	2.84	4.05	5.28	6.52	6.83	7.15	7.46	7.78	8.10	8.41	8.73	9.05	9.37	9.69	10.01
71	1.71	2.92	4.14	5.38	6.64	6.95	7.27	7.59	7.91	8.23	8.55	8.87	9.19	9.51	9.84	10.16
70	1.79	3.00	4.23	5.48	6.75	7.07	7.39	7.71	8.04	8.36	8.68	9.01	9.34	9.66	9.99	10.32
69	1.86	3.08	4.33	5.59	6.87	7.19	7.52	7.84	8.17	8.49	8.82	9.15	9.48	9.81	10.15	10.48
68	1.93	3.17	4.42	5.70	6.99	7.32	7.64	7.97	8.30	8.63	8.97	9.30	9.63	9.97	10.30	10.64
67	2.01	3.25	4.52	5.81	7.11	7.44	7.78	8.11	8.44	8.78	9.11	9.45	9.79	10.13	10.47	10.81
66	2.08	3.34	4.62	5.92	7.24	7.57	7.91	8.24	8.58	8.92	9.26	9.60	9.94	10.29	10.63	10.98
65	2.16	3.43	4.72	6.03	7.37	7.71	8.04	8.38	8.73	9.07	9.41	9.76	10.11	10.45	10.80	11.15
64	2.24	3.52	4.82	6.15	7.50	7.84	8.18	8.53	8.87	9.22	9.57	9.92	10.27	10.62	10.98	11.33
63	2.32	3.61	4.93	6.27	7.63	7.98	8.33	8.67	9.03	9.38	9.73	10.08	10.44	10.80	11.16	11.52
62	2.40	3.70	5.03	6.39	7.77	8.12	8.47	8.83	9.18	9.54	9.89	10.25	10.61	10.98	11.34	11.70
61	2.48	3.80	5.14	6.51	7.91	8.27	8.62	8.98	9.34	9.70	10.06	10.43	10.79	11.16	11.53	11.90
60	2.57	3.89	5.25	6.64	8.05	8.41	8.77	9.14	9.50	9.87	10.23	10.60	10.97	11.35	11.72	12.10
59	2.65	3.99	5.36	6.77	8.20	8.57	8.93	9.30	9.67	10.04	10.41	10.78	11.16	11.54	11.92	12.30
58	2.74	4.09	5.48	6.90	8.35	8.72	9.09	9.46	9.84	10.21	10.59	10.97	11.35	11.74	12.12	12.51
57	2.83	4.19	5.60	7.03	8.51	8.88	9.26	9.63	10.01	10.39	10.77	11.16	11.55	11.94	12.33	12.73
56	2.92	4.30	5.72	7.17	8.67	9.04	9.42	9.81	10.19	10.58	10.97	11.36	11.76	12.15	12.55	12.95
55	3.01	4.40	5.84	7.31	8.83	9.21	9.60	9.99	10.38	10.77	11.17	11.57	11.97	12.37	12.77	13.18
54	3.10	4.51	5.97	7.46	8.99	9.38	9.78	10.17	10.57	10.97	11.37	11.77	12.18	12.59	13.00	13.41
53	3.19	4.62	6.09	7.61	9.17	9.56	9.96	10.36	10.76	11.17	11.58	11.99	12.40	12.82	13.24	13.66
52	3.29	4.74	6.23	7.76	9.34	9.74	10.15	10.56	10.97	11.38	11.80	12.21	12.63	13.06	13.48	13.91
51	3.39	4.85	6.36	7.92	9.52	9.93	10.34	10.76	11.17	11.59	12.02	12.44	12.87	13.30	13.74	14.17
50	3.49	4.97	6.50	8.08	9.71	10.12	10.54	10.96	11.39	11.82	12.25	12.68	13.12	13.56	14.00	14.44
49	3.59	5.09	6.64	8.24	9.90	10.32	10.75	11.18	11.61	12.05	12.48	12.93	13.37	13.82	14.27	14.72
48	3.70	5.22	6.79	8.41	10.10	10.53	10.96	11.40	11.84	12.28	12.73	13.18	13.63	14.09	14.55	15.01
47	3.81	5.34	6.94	8.59	10.30	10.74	11.18	11.63	12.08	12.53	12.98	13.44	13.90	14.37	14.84	15.31
46	3.92	5.47	7.09	8.77	10.51	10.96	11.41	11.86	12.32	12.78	13.25	13.71	14.19	14.66	15.14	15.62
45	4.03	5.61	7.25	8.96	10.73	11.19	11.65	12.11	12.57	13.04	13.52	14.00	14.48	14.96	15.45	15.94
44	4.14	5.74	7.41	9.15	10.96	11.42	11.89	12.36	12.84	13.32	13.80	14.29	14.78	15.28	15.78	16.28
43	4.26	5.88	7.58	9.35	11.19	11.66	12.14	12.62	13.11	13.60	14.10	14.60	15.10	15.61	16.12	16.63
42	4.38	6.03	7.75	9.55	11.43	11.92	12.40	12.90	13.39	13.90	14.40	14.91	15.43	15.95	16.47	17.00
41	4.50	6.17	7.93	9.76	11.68	12.18	12.68	13.18	13.69	14.20	14.72	15.25	15.77	16.31	16.84	17.38
40	4.63	6.33	8.11	9.98	11.95	12.45	12.96	13.48	14.00	14.52	15.05	15.59	16.13	16.68	17.23	17.78
39	4.76	6.48	8.30	10.21	12.22	12.73	13.26	13.78	14.32	14.86	15.40	15.95	16.51	17.07	17.63	18.20
35	5.31	7.16	9.13	11.21	13.43	14.00	14.58	15.17	15.76	16.36	16.97	17.58	18.21	18.83	19.47	20.11
30	6.11	8.15	10.36	12.74	15.30	15.97	16.65	17.34	18.04	18.74	19.46	20.19	20.92	21.67	22.42	23.18
25	7.05	9.36	11.91	14.73	17.81	18.63	19.45	20.30	21.15	22.02	22.90	23.80	24.70	25.62	26.54	27.48
20	8.21	10.91	14.00	17.52	21.47	22.52	23.60	24.69	25.81	26.94	28.08	29.25	30.42	31.60	32.80	34.00
15	9.71	13.06	17.11	21.95	27.56	29.06	30.58	32.13	33.71	35.30	36.90	38.52	40.15	41.78	43.42	45.07
10	11.85	16.50	22.77	30.89	40.23	42.66	45.11	47.58	50.05	52.54	55.03	57.52	60.01	62.51	65.00	67.50

BOND PRICE

Description: This table shows the price to pay for a bond at the yield rate. The yield is to maturity.

Example: The price of a 10.75 %, 20 year bond to yield 8 % to maturity is $ 127.22.

YIELD	7.00%	7.25%	7.50%	7.75%	8.00%	8.25%	8.50%	8.75%	9.00%	9.25%	9.50%	9.75%	10.00%	10.25%	10.50%	10.75%
0.00	240.00	245.00	250.00	255.00	260.00	265.00	270.00	275.00	280.00	285.00	290.00	295.00	300.00	305.00	310.00	315.00
1.00	208.52	213.04	217.56	222.08	226.60	231.12	235.65	240.17	244.69	249.21	253.73	258.25	262.78	267.30	271.82	276.34
2.00	182.09	186.19	190.30	194.40	198.50	202.61	206.71	210.82	214.92	219.03	223.13	227.23	231.34	235.44	239.55	243.65
3.00	159.83	163.57	167.31	171.05	174.79	178.53	182.27	186.01	189.75	193.49	197.23	200.97	204.71	208.44	212.18	215.92
4.00	141.03	144.45	147.87	151.29	154.71	158.13	161.55	164.97	168.39	171.81	175.23	178.65	182.07	185.49	188.91	192.32
4.25	136.80	140.15	143.49	146.84	150.18	153.53	156.88	160.22	163.57	166.91	170.26	173.60	176.95	180.30	183.64	186.99
4.50	132.74	136.02	139.29	142.56	145.84	149.11	152.39	155.66	158.94	162.21	165.48	168.76	172.03	175.31	178.58	181.85
4.75	128.84	132.05	135.25	138.46	141.66	144.87	148.07	151.28	154.48	157.69	160.89	164.10	167.30	170.51	173.71	176.92
5.00	125.10	128.24	131.38	134.52	137.65	140.79	143.93	147.07	150.21	153.34	156.48	159.62	162.76	165.89	169.03	172.17
5.25	121.51	124.58	127.66	130.73	133.80	136.87	139.95	143.02	146.09	149.16	152.24	155.31	158.38	161.46	164.53	167.60
5.50	118.06	121.07	124.08	127.09	130.10	133.11	136.12	139.13	142.14	145.15	148.16	151.17	154.18	157.19	160.20	163.21
5.75	114.74	117.69	120.64	123.59	126.54	129.49	132.43	135.38	138.33	141.28	144.23	147.18	150.13	153.08	156.02	158.97
6.00	111.56	114.45	117.34	120.23	123.11	126.00	128.89	131.78	134.67	137.56	140.45	143.34	146.23	149.12	152.01	154.90
6.25	108.50	111.33	114.16	116.99	119.82	122.65	125.49	128.32	131.15	133.98	136.81	139.65	142.48	145.31	148.14	150.97
6.50	105.55	108.33	111.10	113.88	116.66	119.43	122.21	124.98	127.76	130.54	133.31	136.09	138.86	141.64	144.42	147.19
6.75	102.72	105.44	108.17	110.89	113.61	116.33	119.05	121.78	124.50	127.22	129.94	132.66	135.38	138.11	140.83	143.55
7.00	100.00	102.67	105.34	108.01	110.68	113.35	116.02	118.69	121.36	124.02	126.69	129.36	132.03	134.70	137.37	140.04
7.25	97.38	100.00	102.62	105.24	107.86	110.47	113.09	115.71	118.33	120.95	123.57	126.18	128.80	131.42	134.04	136.66
7.50	94.86	97.43	100.00	102.57	105.14	107.71	110.28	112.84	115.41	117.98	120.55	123.12	125.69	128.26	130.83	133.40
7.75	92.44	94.96	97.48	100.00	102.52	105.04	107.56	110.08	112.60	115.12	117.65	120.17	122.69	125.21	127.73	130.25
8.00	90.10	92.58	95.05	97.53	100.00	102.47	104.95	107.42	109.90	112.37	114.84	117.32	119.79	122.27	124.74	127.22
8.25	87.86	90.29	92.71	95.14	97.57	100.00	102.43	104.86	107.29	109.71	112.14	114.57	117.00	119.43	121.86	124.29
8.50	85.69	88.08	90.46	92.85	95.23	97.62	100.00	102.38	104.77	107.15	109.54	111.92	114.31	116.69	119.08	121.46
8.75	83.61	85.95	88.29	90.63	92.97	95.32	97.66	100.00	102.34	104.68	107.03	109.37	111.71	114.05	116.39	118.73
9.00	81.60	83.90	86.20	88.50	90.80	93.10	95.40	97.70	100.00	102.30	104.60	106.90	109.20	111.50	113.80	116.10
9.25	79.66	81.92	84.18	86.44	88.70	90.96	93.22	95.48	97.74	100.00	102.26	104.52	106.78	109.04	111.30	113.56
9.50	77.80	80.02	82.24	84.46	86.68	88.90	91.12	93.34	95.56	97.78	100.00	102.22	104.44	106.66	108.88	111.10
9.75	76.00	78.18	80.36	82.54	84.73	86.91	89.09	91.27	93.45	95.64	97.82	100.00	102.18	104.36	106.55	108.73
10.00	74.26	76.41	78.55	80.70	82.84	84.99	87.13	89.28	91.42	93.57	95.71	97.86	100.00	102.14	104.29	106.43
10.25	72.59	74.70	76.80	78.91	81.02	83.13	85.24	87.35	89.46	91.57	93.67	95.78	97.89	100.00	102.11	104.22
10.50	70.97	73.05	75.12	77.19	79.27	81.34	83.41	85.49	87.56	89.63	91.71	93.78	95.85	97.93	100.00	102.07
10.75	69.41	71.45	73.49	75.53	77.57	79.61	81.65	83.69	85.73	87.77	89.80	91.84	93.88	95.92	97.96	100.00
11.00	67.91	69.91	71.92	73.93	75.93	77.94	79.94	81.95	83.95	85.96	87.97	89.97	91.98	93.98	95.99	99.99
11.25	66.45	68.43	70.40	72.37	74.35	76.32	78.29	80.27	82.24	84.21	86.19	88.16	90.13	92.11	94.08	96.05
11.50	65.05	66.99	68.93	70.88	72.82	74.76	76.70	78.64	80.58	82.53	84.47	86.41	88.35	90.29	92.23	94.18
11.75	63.69	65.61	67.52	69.43	71.34	73.25	75.16	77.07	78.98	80.89	82.80	84.71	86.62	88.54	90.45	92.36
12.00	62.38	64.27	66.15	68.03	69.91	71.79	73.67	75.55	77.43	79.31	81.19	83.07	84.95	86.83	88.72	90.60
12.25	61.12	62.97	64.82	66.67	68.52	70.38	72.23	74.08	75.93	77.78	79.63	81.48	83.34	85.19	87.04	88.89
12.50	59.89	61.72	63.54	65.36	67.19	69.01	70.83	72.65	74.48	76.30	78.12	79.95	81.77	83.59	85.42	87.24
12.75	58.71	60.50	62.30	64.09	65.89	67.69	69.48	71.28	73.07	74.87	76.66	78.46	80.25	82.05	83.84	85.64
13.00	57.56	59.33	61.10	62.87	64.64	66.40	68.17	69.94	71.71	73.48	75.25	77.01	78.78	80.55	82.32	84.09
13.25	56.46	58.20	59.94	61.68	63.42	65.16	66.91	68.65	70.39	72.13	73.87	75.61	77.36	79.10	80.84	82.58
13.50	55.38	57.10	58.81	60.53	62.25	63.96	65.68	67.39	69.11	70.83	72.54	74.26	75.98	77.69	79.41	81.12
13.75	54.34	56.04	57.73	59.42	61.11	62.80	64.49	66.18	67.87	69.56	71.25	72.94	74.64	76.33	78.02	79.71
14.00	53.34	55.01	56.67	58.34	60.00	61.67	63.34	65.00	66.67	68.34	70.00	71.67	73.34	75.00	76.67	78.34
14.25	52.37	54.01	55.65	57.29	58.94	60.58	62.22	63.86	65.51	67.15	68.79	70.43	72.08	73.72	75.36	77.00
14.50	51.42	53.04	54.66	56.28	57.90	59.52	61.14	62.76	64.38	66.00	67.61	69.23	70.85	72.47	74.09	75.71
14.75	50.51	52.10	53.70	55.30	56.89	58.49	60.09	61.68	63.28	64.88	66.47	68.07	69.67	71.26	72.86	74.46
15.00	49.62	51.20	52.77	54.35	55.92	57.49	59.07	60.64	62.22	63.79	65.37	66.94	68.51	70.09	71.66	73.24
15.25	48.76	50.32	51.87	53.42	54.97	56.53	58.08	59.63	61.18	62.74	64.29	65.84	67.39	68.95	70.50	72.05
15.50	47.93	49.46	50.99	52.53	54.06	55.59	57.12	58.65	60.18	61.71	63.25	64.78	66.31	67.84	69.37	70.90
15.75	47.12	48.63	50.14	51.66	53.17	54.68	56.19	57.70	59.21	60.72	62.23	63.74	65.25	66.76	68.27	69.78
16.00	46.34	47.83	49.32	50.81	52.30	53.79	55.28	56.77	58.26	59.75	61.25	62.74	64.23	65.72	67.21	68.70
16.25	45.58	47.05	48.52	49.99	51.46	52.93	54.40	55.87	57.35	58.82	60.29	61.76	63.23	64.70	66.17	67.64
16.50	44.84	46.29	47.74	49.20	50.65	52.10	53.55	55.00	56.45	57.90	59.36	60.81	62.26	63.71	65.16	66.61
16.75	44.12	45.56	46.99	48.42	49.85	51.29	52.72	54.15	55.59	57.02	58.45	59.88	61.32	62.75	64.18	65.61
17.00	43.43	44.84	46.26	47.67	49.08	50.50	51.91	53.33	54.74	56.16	57.57	58.98	60.40	61.81	63.23	64.64
17.25	42.75	44.15	45.54	46.94	48.34	49.73	51.13	52.53	53.92	55.32	56.71	58.11	59.51	60.90	62.30	63.70
17.50	42.09	43.47	44.85	46.23	47.61	48.99	50.37	51.75	53.12	54.50	55.88	57.26	58.64	60.02	61.40	62.77
17.75	41.46	42.82	44.18	45.54	46.90	48.26	49.62	50.99	52.35	53.71	55.07	56.43	57.79	59.15	60.52	61.88
18.00	40.83	42.18	43.52	44.87	46.21	47.56	48.90	50.25	51.59	52.94	54.28	55.63	56.97	58.32	59.66	61.00
18.25	40.23	41.56	42.89	44.22	45.54	46.87	48.20	49.53	50.86	52.18	53.51	54.84	56.17	57.50	58.83	60.15
18.50	39.64	40.96	42.27	43.58	44.89	46.20	47.52	48.83	50.14	51.45	52.76	54.08	55.39	56.70	58.01	59.33
18.75	39.07	40.37	41.67	42.96	44.26	45.55	46.85	48.15	49.44	50.74	52.04	53.33	54.63	55.92	57.22	58.52
19.00	38.52	39.80	41.08	42.36	43.64	44.92	46.20	47.48	48.76	50.04	51.33	52.61	53.89	55.17	56.45	57.73
20.00	36.44	37.66	38.88	40.10	41.33	42.55	43.77	44.99	46.22	47.44	48.66	49.88	51.10	52.33	53.55	54.77
25.00	28.65	29.64	30.63	31.62	32.61	33.60	34.59	35.58	36.58	37.57	38.56	39.55	40.54	41.53	42.52	43.51
30.00	23.62	24.45	25.28	26.11	26.94	27.77	28.60	29.43	30.26	31.09	31.92	32.75	33.58	34.41	35.24	36.07

Description: This table shows the yield to maturity of a bond purchased at the price shown in the index.

Example: The yield to maturity of a 10.75 %, 20 year bond at a price of 111.00 is 9.51 %.

COUPON RATE, %

PRICE	7.00%	7.25%	7.50%	7.75%	8.00%	8.25%	8.50%	8.75%	9.00%	9.25%	9.50%	9.75%	10.00%	10.25%	10.50%	10.75%
155	3.24	3.42	3.61	3.79	3.98	4.16	4.35	4.53	4.72	4.90	5.08	5.26	5.45	5.63	5.81	5.99
150	3.50	3.69	3.88	4.07	4.26	4.44	4.63	4.82	5.01	5.19	5.38	5.57	5.75	5.94	6.12	6.31
145	3.77	3.96	4.16	4.35	4.54	4.74	4.93	5.12	5.31	5.50	5.70	5.89	6.08	6.27	6.46	6.64
140	4.06	4.25	4.45	4.65	4.85	5.04	5.24	5.44	5.63	5.83	6.03	6.22	6.42	6.61	6.80	7.00
135	4.35	4.56	4.76	4.96	5.17	5.37	5.57	5.77	5.97	6.17	6.37	6.57	6.77	6.97	7.17	7.37
130	4.67	4.88	5.09	5.29	5.50	5.71	5.92	6.12	6.33	6.53	6.74	6.95	7.15	7.36	7.56	7.77
125	5.00	5.22	5.43	5.64	5.86	6.07	6.28	6.49	6.71	6.92	7.13	7.34	7.55	7.76	7.97	8.18
124	5.07	5.29	5.50	5.72	5.93	6.14	6.36	6.57	6.78	7.00	7.21	7.42	7.63	7.85	8.06	8.27
123	5.14	5.36	5.57	5.79	6.00	6.22	6.43	6.65	6.86	7.08	7.29	7.50	7.72	7.93	8.14	8.36
122	5.21	5.43	5.64	5.86	6.08	6.30	6.51	6.73	6.94	7.16	7.37	7.59	7.80	8.02	8.23	8.45
121	5.28	5.50	5.72	5.94	6.15	6.37	6.59	6.81	7.02	7.24	7.46	7.67	7.89	8.11	8.32	8.54
120	5.35	5.57	5.79	6.01	6.23	6.45	6.67	6.89	7.11	7.32	7.54	7.76	7.98	8.19	8.41	8.63
119	5.43	5.65	5.87	6.09	6.31	6.53	6.75	6.97	7.19	7.41	7.63	7.85	8.07	8.28	8.50	8.72
118	5.50	5.72	5.94	6.17	6.39	6.61	6.83	7.05	7.27	7.49	7.71	7.93	8.15	8.37	8.59	8.81
117	5.57	5.80	6.02	6.24	6.47	6.69	6.91	7.14	7.36	7.58	7.80	8.02	8.25	8.47	8.69	8.91
116	5.65	5.87	6.10	6.32	6.55	6.77	7.00	7.22	7.44	7.67	7.89	8.11	8.34	8.56	8.78	9.00
115	5.73	5.95	6.18	6.40	6.63	6.86	7.08	7.31	7.53	7.76	7.98	8.21	8.43	8.65	8.88	9.10
114	5.80	6.03	6.26	6.49	6.71	6.94	7.17	7.39	7.62	7.85	8.07	8.30	8.52	8.75	8.98	9.20
113	5.88	6.11	6.34	6.57	6.80	7.02	7.25	7.48	7.71	7.94	8.16	8.39	8.62	8.85	9.07	9.30
112	5.96	6.19	6.42	6.65	6.88	7.11	7.34	7.57	7.80	8.03	8.26	8.49	8.72	8.95	9.17	9.40
111	6.04	6.27	6.50	6.74	6.97	7.20	7.43	7.66	7.89	8.12	8.35	8.58	8.81	9.05	9.28	9.51
110	6.12	6.35	6.59	6.82	7.05	7.29	7.52	7.75	7.99	8.22	8.45	8.68	8.91	9.15	9.38	9.61
109	6.20	6.44	6.67	6.91	7.14	7.38	7.61	7.85	8.08	8.31	8.55	8.78	9.02	9.25	9.48	9.72
108	6.29	6.52	6.76	7.00	7.23	7.47	7.70	7.94	8.18	8.41	8.65	8.88	9.12	9.35	9.59	9.82
107	6.37	6.61	6.85	7.08	7.32	7.56	7.80	8.04	8.27	8.51	8.75	8.98	9.22	9.46	9.70	9.93
106	6.46	6.70	6.94	7.18	7.41	7.65	7.89	8.13	8.37	8.61	8.85	9.09	9.33	9.57	9.80	10.04
105	6.54	6.78	7.03	7.27	7.51	7.75	7.99	8.23	8.47	8.71	8.95	9.19	9.43	9.67	9.92	10.16
104	6.63	6.87	7.12	7.36	7.60	7.85	8.09	8.33	8.57	8.82	9.06	9.30	9.54	9.79	10.03	10.27
103	6.72	6.96	7.21	7.45	7.70	7.94	8.19	8.43	8.68	8.92	9.16	9.41	9.65	9.90	10.14	10.39
102	6.81	7.06	7.30	7.55	7.80	8.04	8.29	8.53	8.78	9.03	9.27	9.52	9.77	10.01	10.26	10.50
101	6.90	7.15	7.40	7.65	7.89	8.14	8.39	8.64	8.89	9.14	9.38	9.63	9.88	10.13	10.38	10.62
100	7.00	7.25	7.50	7.75	8.00	8.25	8.50	8.75	9.00	9.25	9.50	9.75	10.00	10.25	10.50	10.75
99	7.09	7.34	7.59	7.84	8.10	8.35	8.60	8.85	9.10	9.36	9.61	9.86	10.11	10.36	10.62	10.87
98	7.19	7.44	7.69	7.95	8.20	8.45	8.71	8.96	9.22	9.47	9.72	9.98	10.23	10.49	10.74	10.99
97	7.28	7.54	7.79	8.05	8.31	8.56	8.82	9.07	9.33	9.58	9.84	10.10	10.35	10.61	10.87	11.12
96	7.38	7.64	7.90	8.15	8.41	8.67	8.93	9.19	9.44	9.70	9.96	10.22	10.48	10.74	10.99	11.25
95	7.48	7.74	8.00	8.26	8.52	8.78	9.04	9.30	9.56	9.82	10.08	10.34	10.60	10.86	11.12	11.38
94	7.58	7.84	8.11	8.37	8.63	8.89	9.15	9.42	9.68	9.94	10.20	10.47	10.73	10.99	11.26	11.52
93	7.69	7.95	8.21	8.48	8.74	9.01	9.27	9.54	9.80	10.06	10.33	10.59	10.86	11.12	11.39	11.66
92	7.79	8.06	8.32	8.59	8.86	9.12	9.39	9.66	9.92	10.19	10.46	10.72	10.99	11.26	11.53	11.80
91	7.90	8.17	8.43	8.70	8.97	9.24	9.51	9.78	10.05	10.32	10.59	10.86	11.13	11.40	11.67	11.94
90	8.01	8.28	8.55	8.82	9.09	9.36	9.63	9.90	10.17	10.45	10.72	10.99	11.26	11.54	11.81	12.08
89	8.12	8.39	8.66	8.94	9.21	9.48	9.76	10.03	10.30	10.58	10.85	11.13	11.40	11.68	11.95	12.23
88	8.23	8.50	8.78	9.05	9.33	9.61	9.88	10.16	10.44	10.71	10.99	11.27	11.55	11.82	12.10	12.38
87	8.34	8.62	8.90	9.18	9.45	9.73	10.01	10.29	10.57	10.85	11.13	11.41	11.69	11.97	12.25	12.53
86	8.46	8.74	9.02	9.30	9.58	9.86	10.14	10.43	10.71	10.99	11.27	11.55	11.84	12.12	12.40	12.69
85	8.58	8.86	9.14	9.43	9.71	9.99	10.28	10.56	10.85	11.13	11.42	11.70	11.99	12.27	12.56	12.85
84	8.70	8.98	9.27	9.55	9.84	10.13	10.41	10.70	10.99	11.28	11.56	11.85	12.14	12.43	12.72	13.01
83	8.82	9.11	9.40	9.68	9.97	10.26	10.55	10.84	11.13	11.42	11.71	12.01	12.30	12.59	12.88	13.17
82	8.94	9.23	9.53	9.82	10.11	10.40	10.69	10.99	11.28	11.57	11.87	12.16	12.46	12.75	13.05	13.34
81	9.07	9.36	9.66	9.95	10.25	10.54	10.84	11.13	11.43	11.73	12.03	12.32	12.62	12.92	13.22	13.52
80	9.20	9.50	9.79	10.09	10.39	10.69	10.99	11.29	11.59	11.89	12.19	12.49	12.79	13.09	13.39	13.69
79	9.33	9.63	9.93	10.23	10.53	10.84	11.14	11.44	11.74	12.05	12.35	12.65	12.96	13.26	13.57	13.87
78	9.47	9.77	10.07	10.38	10.68	10.99	11.29	11.60	11.90	12.21	12.52	12.82	13.13	13.44	13.75	14.06
77	9.60	9.91	10.22	10.52	10.83	11.14	11.45	11.76	12.07	12.38	12.69	13.00	13.31	13.62	13.93	14.25
76	9.74	10.05	10.36	10.67	10.98	11.30	11.61	11.92	12.23	12.55	12.86	13.18	13.49	13.81	14.12	14.44
75	9.89	10.20	10.51	10.83	11.14	11.46	11.77	12.09	12.40	12.72	13.04	13.36	13.68	14.00	14.32	14.64
74	10.03	10.35	10.67	10.98	11.30	11.62	11.94	12.26	12.58	12.90	13.22	13.54	13.87	14.19	14.51	14.84
73	10.18	10.50	10.82	11.14	11.46	11.79	12.11	12.43	12.76	13.08	13.41	13.73	14.06	14.39	14.72	15.04
70	10.65	10.98	11.31	11.65	11.98	12.31	12.65	12.98	13.32	13.66	14.00	14.33	14.67	15.01	15.35	15.70
65	11.50	11.86	12.21	12.57	12.92	13.28	13.64	14.00	14.36	14.72	15.08	15.44	15.81	16.17	16.54	16.90
60	12.47	12.85	13.23	13.61	14.00	14.38	14.77	15.15	15.54	15.93	16.32	16.71	17.11	17.50	17.89	18.29
55	13.59	14.00	14.41	14.82	15.24	15.66	16.07	16.50	16.92	17.34	17.77	18.19	18.62	19.05	19.48	19.91
50	14.89	15.34	15.79	16.24	16.70	17.16	17.62	18.08	18.54	19.01	19.48	19.95	20.42	20.89	21.37	21.85
45	16.44	16.94	17.44	17.95	18.45	18.96	19.48	19.99	20.51	21.03	21.55	22.08	22.60	23.13	23.66	24.19
40	18.34	18.91	19.47	20.04	20.62	21.20	21.78	22.36	22.95	23.54	24.13	24.72	25.32	25.92	26.52	27.12
35	20.75	21.40	22.06	22.72	23.38	24.05	24.72	25.39	26.07	26.75	27.44	28.12	28.81	29.50	30.20	30.89
30	23.94	24.71	25.49	26.27	27.06	27.85	28.65	29.45	30.25	31.05	31.86	32.67	33.49	34.30	35.12	35.94

Description: This table shows the price to pay for a bond at the yield rate. The yield is to maturity.

Example: The price of a 15.00 %, 20 year bond to yield 8 % to maturity is $ 169.27.

COUPON RATE, %

YIELD	11.00%	11.25%	11.50%	11.75%	12.00%	12.25%	12.50%	12.75%	13.00%	13.25%	13.50%	13.75%	14.00%	14.25%	14.50%	15.00%
0.00	320.00	325.00	330.00	335.00	340.00	345.00	350.00	355.00	360.00	365.00	370.00	375.00	380.00	385.00	390.00	400.00
1.00	280.86	285.38	289.90	294.43	298.95	303.47	307.99	312.51	317.03	321.55	326.08	330.60	335.12	339.64	344.16	353.21
2.00	247.76	251.86	255.96	260.07	264.17	268.28	272.38	276.49	280.59	284.70	288.80	292.90	297.01	301.11	305.22	313.43
3.00	219.66	223.40	227.14	230.88	234.62	238.36	242.10	245.84	249.58	253.32	257.06	260.80	264.54	268.28	272.02	279.50
4.00	195.74	199.16	202.58	206.00	209.42	212.84	216.26	219.68	223.10	226.52	229.94	233.36	236.78	240.20	243.62	250.46
4.25	190.33	193.68	197.02	200.37	203.72	207.06	210.41	213.75	217.10	220.44	223.79	227.13	230.48	233.83	237.17	243.86
4.50	185.13	188.40	191.68	194.95	198.23	201.50	204.77	208.05	211.32	214.60	217.87	221.15	224.42	227.69	230.97	243.86
4.75	180.12	183.33	186.53	189.74	192.94	196.15	199.35	202.56	205.76	208.97	212.17	215.38	218.58	221.79	224.99	231.40
5.00	175.31	178.45	181.58	184.72	187.86	191.00	194.14	197.27	200.41	203.55	206.69	209.82	212.96	216.10	219.24	225.51
5.25	170.67	173.75	176.82	179.89	182.97	186.04	189.11	192.18	195.26	198.33	201.40	204.48	207.55	210.62	213.69	219.84
5.50	166.21	169.22	172.23	175.24	178.25	181.26	184.27	187.28	190.29	193.30	196.31	199.32	202.33	205.34	208.35	214.37
5.75	161.92	164.87	167.82	170.77	173.72	176.66	179.61	182.56	185.51	188.46	191.41	194.36	197.30	200.25	203.20	209.10
6.00	157.79	160.68	163.57	166.45	169.34	172.23	175.12	178.01	180.90	183.79	186.68	189.57	192.46	195.35	198.24	204.02
6.25	153.81	156.64	159.47	162.30	165.13	167.96	170.80	173.63	176.46	179.29	182.12	184.96	187.79	190.62	193.45	199.11
6.50	149.97	152.75	155.52	158.30	161.07	163.85	166.63	169.40	172.18	174.95	177.73	180.51	183.28	186.06	188.83	194.39
6.75	146.27	148.99	151.72	154.44	157.16	159.88	162.60	165.33	168.05	170.77	173.49	176.21	178.94	181.66	184.38	189.82
7.00	142.71	145.38	148.05	150.72	153.39	156.06	158.73	161.40	164.07	166.73	169.40	172.07	174.74	177.41	180.08	185.42
7.25	139.28	141.89	144.51	147.13	149.75	152.37	154.99	157.60	160.22	162.84	165.46	168.08	170.70	173.31	175.93	181.17
7.50	135.96	138.53	141.10	143.67	146.24	148.81	151.38	153.95	156.52	159.08	161.65	164.22	166.79	169.36	171.93	177.07
7.75	132.77	135.29	137.81	140.33	142.85	145.37	147.90	150.42	152.94	155.46	157.98	160.50	163.02	165.54	168.06	173.10
8.00	129.69	132.16	134.64	137.11	139.59	142.06	144.53	147.01	149.48	151.96	154.43	156.90	159.38	161.85	164.33	169.27
8.25	126.72	129.14	131.57	134.00	136.43	138.86	141.29	143.72	146.15	148.57	151.00	153.43	155.86	158.29	160.72	165.58
8.50	123.85	126.23	128.62	131.00	133.39	135.77	138.15	140.54	142.92	145.31	147.69	150.08	152.46	154.85	157.23	162.00
8.75	121.08	123.42	125.76	128.10	130.44	132.79	135.13	137.47	139.81	142.15	144.49	146.84	149.18	151.52	153.86	158.55
9.00	118.40	120.70	123.00	125.30	127.60	129.90	132.20	134.50	136.80	139.10	141.40	143.70	146.00	148.30	150.60	155.20
9.25	115.82	118.08	120.34	122.60	124.86	127.12	129.38	131.64	133.90	136.16	138.42	140.68	142.93	145.19	147.45	151.97
9.50	113.32	115.54	117.76	119.98	122.20	124.42	126.64	128.86	131.09	133.31	135.53	137.75	139.97	142.19	144.41	148.85
9.75	110.91	113.09	115.27	117.46	119.64	121.82	124.00	126.19	128.37	130.55	132.73	134.91	137.10	139.28	141.46	145.82
10.00	108.58	110.72	112.87	115.01	117.16	119.30	121.45	123.59	125.74	127.88	130.03	132.17	134.32	136.46	138.61	142.90
10.25	106.33	108.43	110.54	112.65	114.76	116.87	118.98	121.09	123.20	125.30	127.41	129.52	131.63	133.74	135.85	140.06
10.50	104.15	106.22	108.29	110.37	112.44	114.51	116.59	118.66	120.73	122.81	124.88	126.95	129.03	131.10	133.17	137.32
10.75	102.04	104.08	106.12	108.16	110.20	112.23	114.27	116.31	118.35	120.39	122.43	124.47	126.51	128.55	130.59	134.67
11.00	100.00	102.01	104.01	106.02	108.02	110.03	112.03	114.04	116.05	118.05	120.06	122.06	124.07	126.07	128.08	132.09
11.25	98.03	100.00	101.97	103.95	105.92	107.89	109.87	111.84	113.81	115.79	117.76	119.73	121.71	123.68	125.65	129.60
11.50	96.12	98.06	100.00	101.94	103.88	105.82	107.77	109.71	111.65	113.59	115.53	117.47	119.42	121.36	123.30	127.18
11.75	94.27	96.18	98.09	100.00	101.91	103.82	105.73	107.64	109.55	111.46	113.38	115.29	117.20	119.11	121.02	124.84
12.00	92.48	94.36	96.24	98.12	100.00	101.88	103.76	105.64	107.52	109.40	111.28	113.17	115.05	116.93	118.81	122.57
12.25	90.74	92.59	94.45	96.30	98.15	100.00	101.85	103.70	105.55	107.41	109.26	111.11	112.96	114.81	116.66	120.37
12.50	89.06	90.88	92.71	94.53	96.35	98.18	100.00	101.82	103.65	105.47	107.29	109.12	110.94	112.76	114.58	118.23
12.75	87.43	89.23	91.02	92.82	94.61	96.41	98.20	100.00	101.80	103.59	105.39	107.18	108.98	110.77	112.57	116.16
13.00	85.85	87.62	89.39	91.16	92.93	94.70	96.46	98.23	100.00	101.77	103.54	105.30	107.07	108.84	110.61	114.15
13.25	84.32	86.07	87.81	89.55	91.29	93.03	94.77	96.52	98.26	100.00	101.74	103.48	105.23	106.97	108.71	112.19
13.50	82.84	84.56	86.27	87.99	89.70	91.42	93.14	94.85	96.57	98.28	100.00	101.72	103.43	105.15	106.86	110.30
13.75	81.40	83.09	84.78	86.47	88.16	89.85	91.55	93.24	94.93	96.62	98.31	100.00	101.69	103.38	105.07	108.45
14.00	80.00	81.67	83.34	85.00	86.67	88.33	90.00	91.67	93.33	95.00	96.67	98.33	100.00	101.67	103.33	106.67
14.25	78.65	80.29	81.93	83.57	85.22	86.86	88.50	90.14	91.79	93.43	95.07	96.71	98.36	100.00	101.64	104.93
14.50	77.33	78.95	80.57	82.19	83.81	85.43	87.05	88.67	90.28	91.90	93.52	95.14	96.76	98.38	100.00	103.24
14.75	76.05	77.65	79.25	80.84	82.44	84.03	85.63	87.23	88.82	90.42	92.02	93.61	95.21	96.81	98.40	101.60
15.00	74.81	76.39	77.96	79.53	81.11	82.68	84.26	85.83	87.41	88.98	90.55	92.13	93.70	95.28	96.85	100.00
15.25	73.61	75.16	76.71	78.26	79.82	81.37	82.92	84.47	86.03	87.58	89.13	90.68	92.24	93.79	95.34	98.45
15.50	72.43	73.97	75.50	77.03	78.56	80.09	81.62	83.15	84.69	86.22	87.75	89.28	90.81	92.34	93.87	96.94
15.75	71.30	72.81	74.32	75.83	77.34	78.85	80.36	81.87	83.38	84.89	86.40	87.91	89.42	90.94	92.45	95.47
16.00	70.19	71.68	73.17	74.66	76.15	77.64	79.13	80.62	82.11	83.60	85.09	86.58	88.08	89.57	91.06	94.04
16.25	69.11	70.58	72.05	73.52	75.00	76.47	77.94	79.41	80.88	82.35	83.82	85.29	86.76	88.23	89.70	92.65
16.50	68.07	69.52	70.97	72.42	73.87	75.32	76.77	78.23	79.68	81.13	82.58	84.03	85.48	86.94	88.39	91.29
16.75	67.05	68.48	69.91	71.35	72.78	74.21	75.64	77.08	78.51	79.94	81.37	82.81	84.24	85.67	87.11	89.97
17.00	66.06	67.47	68.89	70.30	71.71	73.13	74.54	75.96	77.37	78.79	80.20	81.61	83.03	84.44	85.86	88.69
17.25	65.09	66.49	67.88	69.28	70.68	72.07	73.47	74.87	76.26	77.66	79.06	80.45	81.85	83.24	84.64	87.43
17.50	64.15	65.53	66.91	68.29	69.67	71.05	72.43	73.80	75.18	76.56	77.94	79.32	80.70	82.08	83.46	86.21
17.75	63.24	64.60	65.96	67.32	68.69	70.05	71.41	72.77	74.13	75.49	76.85	78.22	79.58	80.94	82.30	85.02
18.00	62.35	63.69	65.04	66.38	67.73	69.07	70.42	71.76	73.11	74.45	75.80	77.14	78.49	79.83	81.17	83.86
18.25	61.48	62.81	64.14	65.47	66.79	68.12	69.45	70.78	72.11	73.44	74.76	76.09	77.42	78.75	80.08	82.73
18.50	60.64	61.95	63.26	64.57	65.89	67.20	68.51	69.82	71.13	72.45	73.76	75.07	76.38	77.69	79.01	81.63
18.75	59.81	61.11	62.41	63.70	65.00	66.30	67.59	68.89	70.18	71.48	72.78	74.07	75.37	76.67	77.96	80.56
19.00	59.01	60.29	61.57	62.85	64.13	65.42	66.70	67.98	69.26	70.54	71.82	73.10	74.38	75.66	76.94	79.51
20.00	55.99	57.22	58.44	59.66	60.88	62.11	63.33	64.55	65.77	67.00	68.22	69.44	70.66	71.89	73.11	75.55
25.00	44.50	45.49	46.49	47.48	48.47	49.46	50.45	51.44	52.43	53.42	54.41	55.40	56.40	57.39	58.38	60.36
30.00	36.90	37.73	38.56	39.39	40.22	41.05	41.88	42.71	43.54	44.38	45.21	46.04	46.87	47.70	48.53	50.19

Description: This table shows the yield to maturity of a bond purchased at the price shown in the index.

Example: The yield to maturity of a 15.00 %, 20 year bond at a price of 125.00 is 11.73 %.

COUPON RATE, %

PRICE	11.00%	11.25%	11.50%	11.75%	12.00%	12.25%	12.50%	12.75%	13.00%	13.25%	13.50%	13.75%	14.00%	14.25%	14.50%	15.00%
250	1.92	2.06	2.19	2.32	2.45	2.59	2.72	2.85	2.98	3.11	3.24	3.37	3.50	3.63	3.76	4.01
240	2.26	2.39	2.53	2.66	2.80	2.94	3.07	3.21	3.34	3.47	3.61	3.74	3.87	4.00	4.13	4.40
230	2.61	2.75	2.89	3.03	3.17	3.31	3.44	3.58	3.72	3.86	3.99	4.13	4.26	4.40	4.53	4.80
220	2.98	3.13	3.27	3.41	3.56	3.70	3.84	3.98	4.12	4.26	4.40	4.54	4.68	4.82	4.96	5.24
210	3.38	3.53	3.68	3.82	3.97	4.12	4.26	4.41	4.55	4.70	4.84	4.99	5.13	5.27	5.42	5.70
200	3.81	3.96	4.11	4.26	4.41	4.56	4.71	4.86	5.01	5.16	5.31	5.46	5.61	5.76	5.91	6.20
195	4.03	4.18	4.34	4.49	4.65	4.80	4.95	5.11	5.26	5.41	5.56	5.71	5.86	6.01	6.16	6.46
190	4.26	4.42	4.58	4.73	4.89	5.04	5.20	5.36	5.51	5.66	5.82	5.97	6.13	6.28	6.43	6.74
185	4.50	4.66	4.82	4.98	5.14	5.30	5.46	5.61	5.77	5.93	6.09	6.24	6.40	6.55	6.71	7.02
180	4.75	4.91	5.08	5.24	5.40	5.56	5.72	5.88	6.05	6.21	6.36	6.52	6.68	6.84	7.00	7.32
175	5.01	5.18	5.34	5.51	5.67	5.84	6.00	6.17	6.33	6.49	6.65	6.82	6.98	7.14	7.30	7.62
170	5.28	5.45	5.62	5.79	5.96	6.12	6.29	6.46	6.63	6.79	6.96	7.12	7.29	7.45	7.62	7.95
165	5.56	5.74	5.91	6.08	6.25	6.42	6.59	6.77	6.94	7.11	7.27	7.44	7.61	7.78	7.95	8.28
160	5.86	6.04	6.21	6.39	6.56	6.74	6.91	7.09	7.26	7.43	7.61	7.78	7.95	8.12	8.30	8.64
155	6.17	6.35	6.53	6.71	6.89	7.07	7.24	7.42	7.60	7.78	7.95	8.13	8.31	8.48	8.66	9.01
150	6.49	6.68	6.86	7.04	7.23	7.41	7.59	7.78	7.96	8.14	8.32	8.50	8.68	8.86	9.04	9.40
145	6.83	7.02	7.21	7.40	7.59	7.77	7.96	8.15	8.33	8.52	8.70	8.89	9.08	9.26	9.45	9.81
140	7.19	7.38	7.58	7.77	7.96	8.15	8.35	8.54	8.73	8.92	9.11	9.30	9.49	9.68	9.87	10.25
135	7.57	7.77	7.97	8.16	8.36	8.56	8.76	8.95	9.15	9.35	9.54	9.74	9.93	10.13	10.32	10.71
130	7.97	8.17	8.38	8.58	8.78	8.99	9.19	9.39	9.59	9.80	10.00	10.20	10.40	10.60	10.80	11.20
125	8.39	8.60	8.81	9.02	9.23	9.44	9.65	9.86	10.07	10.28	10.48	10.69	10.90	11.11	11.31	11.73
120	8.84	9.06	9.28	9.49	9.71	9.93	10.14	10.36	10.57	10.79	11.00	11.22	11.43	11.64	11.86	12.29
115	9.33	9.55	9.77	10.00	10.22	10.44	10.67	10.89	11.11	11.33	11.56	11.78	12.00	12.22	12.44	12.89
113	9.53	9.75	9.98	10.21	10.43	10.66	10.89	11.11	11.34	11.56	11.79	12.01	12.24	12.47	12.69	13.14
112	9.63	9.86	10.09	10.32	10.54	10.77	11.00	11.23	11.45	11.68	11.91	12.14	12.36	12.59	12.82	13.27
111	9.74	9.97	10.20	10.42	10.65	10.88	11.11	11.34	11.57	11.80	12.03	12.26	12.49	12.72	12.94	13.40
110	9.84	10.07	10.30	10.54	10.77	11.00	11.23	11.46	11.69	11.92	12.15	12.38	12.61	12.84	13.07	13.53
109	9.95	10.18	10.42	10.65	10.88	11.11	11.35	11.58	11.81	12.04	12.28	12.51	12.74	12.97	13.21	13.67
108	10.06	10.29	10.53	10.76	11.00	11.23	11.47	11.70	11.94	12.17	12.40	12.64	12.87	13.11	13.34	13.81
107	10.17	10.41	10.64	10.88	11.12	11.35	11.59	11.82	12.06	12.30	12.53	12.77	13.00	13.24	13.48	13.95
106	10.28	10.52	10.76	11.00	11.24	11.47	11.71	11.95	12.19	12.43	12.66	12.90	13.14	13.38	13.61	14.09
105	10.40	10.64	10.88	11.12	11.36	11.60	11.84	12.08	12.32	12.56	12.80	13.04	13.28	13.52	13.76	14.23
104	10.51	10.75	11.00	11.24	11.48	11.72	11.96	12.21	12.45	12.69	12.93	13.17	13.42	13.66	13.90	14.38
103	10.63	10.87	11.12	11.36	11.61	11.85	12.09	12.34	12.58	12.83	13.07	13.31	13.56	13.80	14.04	14.53
102	10.75	11.00	11.24	11.49	11.73	11.98	12.23	12.47	12.72	12.96	13.21	13.45	13.70	13.95	14.19	14.68
101	10.87	11.12	11.37	11.62	11.86	12.11	12.36	12.61	12.85	13.10	13.35	13.60	13.85	14.09	14.34	14.84
100	11.00	11.25	11.50	11.75	12.00	12.25	12.50	12.75	13.00	13.25	13.50	13.75	14.00	14.25	14.50	15.00
99	11.12	11.37	11.62	11.88	12.13	12.38	12.63	12.89	13.14	13.39	13.64	13.89	14.15	14.40	14.65	15.16
98	11.25	11.50	11.76	12.01	12.27	12.52	12.77	13.03	13.28	13.54	13.79	14.05	14.30	14.55	14.81	15.32
97	11.38	11.63	11.89	12.15	12.40	12.66	12.92	13.17	13.43	13.69	13.94	14.20	14.46	14.71	14.97	15.48
96	11.51	11.77	12.03	12.29	12.55	12.80	13.06	13.32	13.58	13.84	14.10	14.36	14.62	14.88	15.14	15.65
95	11.65	11.91	12.17	12.43	12.69	12.95	13.21	13.47	13.73	14.00	14.26	14.52	14.78	15.04	15.30	15.83
94	11.78	12.05	12.31	12.57	12.84	13.10	13.36	13.63	13.89	14.15	14.42	14.68	14.95	15.21	15.47	16.00
93	11.92	12.19	12.45	12.72	12.98	13.25	13.52	13.78	14.05	14.31	14.58	14.85	15.11	15.38	15.65	16.18
92	12.06	12.33	12.60	12.87	13.14	13.40	13.67	13.94	14.21	14.48	14.75	15.02	15.29	15.56	15.82	16.36
91	12.21	12.48	12.75	13.02	13.29	13.56	13.83	14.10	14.38	14.65	14.92	15.19	15.46	15.73	16.01	16.55
90	12.35	12.63	12.90	13.17	13.45	13.72	14.00	14.27	14.54	14.82	15.09	15.37	15.64	15.92	16.19	16.74
89	12.50	12.78	13.06	13.33	13.61	13.88	14.16	14.44	14.71	14.99	15.27	15.55	15.82	16.10	16.38	16.93
88	12.66	12.94	13.21	13.49	13.77	14.05	14.33	14.61	14.89	15.17	15.45	15.73	16.01	16.29	16.57	17.13
87	12.81	13.09	13.38	13.66	13.94	14.22	14.50	14.79	15.07	15.35	15.63	15.92	16.20	16.48	16.77	17.33
86	12.97	13.26	13.54	13.82	14.11	14.39	14.68	14.96	15.25	15.54	15.82	16.11	16.39	16.68	16.97	17.54
85	13.13	13.42	13.71	14.00	14.28	14.57	14.86	15.15	15.44	15.72	16.01	16.30	16.59	16.88	17.17	17.75
84	13.30	13.59	13.88	14.17	14.46	14.75	15.04	15.33	15.63	15.92	16.21	16.50	16.79	17.09	17.38	17.97
83	13.47	13.76	14.05	14.35	14.64	14.94	15.23	15.52	15.82	16.11	16.41	16.71	17.00	17.30	17.59	18.19
82	13.64	13.94	14.23	14.53	14.83	15.12	15.42	15.72	16.02	16.32	16.61	16.91	17.21	17.51	17.81	18.41
81	13.82	14.12	14.42	14.72	15.02	15.32	15.62	15.92	16.22	16.52	16.82	17.13	17.43	17.73	18.03	18.64
80	14.00	14.30	14.60	14.91	15.21	15.51	15.82	16.12	16.43	16.73	17.04	17.34	17.65	17.96	18.26	18.88
79	14.18	14.49	14.79	15.10	15.41	15.71	16.02	16.33	16.64	16.95	17.26	17.57	17.88	18.19	18.50	19.12
78	14.37	14.68	14.99	15.30	15.61	15.92	16.23	16.54	16.86	17.17	17.48	17.79	18.11	18.42	18.74	19.36
77	14.56	14.87	15.19	15.50	15.82	16.13	16.45	16.76	17.08	17.39	17.71	18.03	18.35	18.66	18.98	19.62
76	14.76	15.07	15.39	15.71	16.03	16.35	16.67	16.99	17.31	17.63	17.95	18.27	18.59	18.91	19.23	19.88
75	14.96	15.28	15.60	15.92	16.24	16.57	16.89	17.21	17.54	17.86	18.19	18.51	18.84	19.16	19.49	20.14
74	15.16	15.49	15.81	16.14	16.47	16.79	17.12	17.45	17.78	18.11	18.43	18.76	19.09	19.42	19.75	20.42
73	15.37	15.70	16.03	16.36	16.69	17.03	17.36	17.69	18.02	18.35	18.69	19.02	19.36	19.69	20.02	20.69
70	16.04	16.38	16.72	17.07	17.41	17.76	18.10	18.45	18.79	19.14	19.49	19.84	20.18	20.53	20.88	21.58
65	17.27	17.64	18.01	18.37	18.74	19.12	19.49	19.86	20.23	20.60	20.98	21.35	21.73	22.10	22.48	23.23
60	18.69	19.09	19.48	19.88	20.28	20.69	21.09	21.49	21.89	22.30	22.70	23.11	23.51	23.92	24.33	25.14
55	20.35	20.78	21.22	21.65	22.09	22.53	22.97	23.41	23.85	24.29	24.73	25.18	25.62	26.06	26.51	27.40

Description: This table shows the price to pay for a bond at the yield rate. The yield is to maturity.

Example: The price of a 6.75 %, 21 year bond to yield 8 % to maturity is $ 87.38.

COUPON RATE, %

YIELD	0.00%	1.00%	2.00%	3.00%	4.00%	4.25%	4.50%	4.75%	5.00%	5.25%	5.50%	5.75%	6.00%	6.25%	6.50%	6.75%
0.00	100.00	121.00	142.00	163.00	184.00	189.25	194.50	199.75	205.00	210.25	215.50	220.75	226.00	231.25	236.50	241.75
1.00	81.10	100.00	118.90	137.80	156.70	161.42	166.15	170.87	175.60	180.32	185.05	189.77	194.50	199.22	203.95	208.67
2.00	65.84	82.92	100.00	117.08	134.16	138.43	142.70	146.97	151.24	155.51	159.78	164.05	168.32	172.59	176.86	181.13
3.00	53.51	69.01	84.50	100.00	115.50	119.37	123.25	127.12	130.99	134.87	138.74	142.62	146.49	150.37	154.24	158.11
4.00	43.53	57.65	71.77	85.88	100.00	103.53	107.06	110.59	114.12	117.65	121.18	124.71	128.23	131.76	135.29	138.82
4.25	41.35	55.15	68.95	82.75	96.55	100.00	103.45	106.90	110.35	113.80	117.25	120.70	124.15	127.60	131.05	134.50
4.50	39.28	52.77	66.27	79.76	93.25	96.63	100.00	103.37	106.75	110.12	113.49	116.87	120.24	123.61	126.99	130.36
4.75	37.31	50.51	63.71	76.90	90.10	93.40	96.70	100.00	103.30	106.60	109.90	113.20	116.50	119.80	123.10	126.39
5.00	35.45	48.36	61.27	74.18	87.09	90.32	93.54	96.77	100.00	103.23	106.46	109.68	112.91	116.14	119.37	122.59
5.25	33.68	46.31	58.94	71.58	84.21	87.37	90.53	93.68	96.84	100.00	103.16	106.32	109.47	112.63	115.79	118.95
5.50	32.00	44.36	56.73	69.09	81.45	84.55	87.64	90.73	93.82	96.91	100.00	103.09	106.18	109.27	112.36	115.45
5.75	30.41	42.51	54.61	66.72	78.82	81.85	84.87	87.90	90.92	93.95	96.97	100.00	103.03	106.05	109.08	112.10
6.00	28.90	40.75	52.60	64.45	76.30	79.26	82.22	85.19	88.15	91.11	94.07	97.04	100.00	102.96	105.93	108.89
6.25	27.46	39.07	50.67	62.28	73.89	76.79	79.69	82.59	85.49	88.39	91.30	94.20	97.10	100.00	102.90	105.80
6.50	26.10	37.47	48.84	60.21	71.58	74.42	77.26	80.10	82.95	85.79	88.63	91.47	94.32	97.16	100.00	102.84
6.75	24.81	35.95	47.09	58.23	69.37	72.15	74.94	77.72	80.51	83.29	86.08	88.86	91.65	94.43	97.22	100.00
7.00	23.58	34.50	45.41	56.33	67.25	69.98	72.71	75.44	78.17	80.89	83.62	86.35	89.08	91.81	94.54	97.27
7.25	22.41	33.11	43.82	54.52	65.22	67.89	70.57	73.25	75.92	78.60	81.27	83.95	86.62	89.30	91.97	94.65
7.50	21.31	31.80	42.29	52.78	63.28	65.90	68.52	71.15	73.77	76.39	79.01	81.64	84.26	86.88	89.51	92.13
7.75	20.26	30.54	40.83	51.12	61.41	63.99	66.56	69.13	71.70	74.28	76.85	79.42	81.99	84.57	87.14	89.71
8.00	19.26	29.35	39.44	49.54	59.63	62.15	64.68	67.20	69.72	72.24	74.77	77.29	79.81	82.34	84.86	87.38
8.25	18.31	28.21	38.11	48.02	57.92	60.39	62.87	65.34	67.82	70.29	72.77	75.25	77.72	80.20	82.67	85.15
8.50	17.41	27.13	36.84	46.56	56.28	58.71	61.13	63.56	65.99	68.42	70.85	73.28	75.71	78.14	80.57	83.00
8.75	16.56	26.09	35.63	45.17	54.70	57.09	59.47	61.85	64.24	66.62	69.01	71.39	73.77	76.16	78.54	80.93
9.00	15.74	25.11	34.47	43.83	53.19	55.53	57.87	60.21	62.55	64.89	67.23	69.57	71.91	74.26	76.60	78.94
9.25	14.97	24.17	33.36	42.55	51.74	54.04	56.34	58.64	60.93	63.23	65.53	67.83	70.13	72.42	74.72	77.02
9.50	14.24	23.27	32.30	41.32	50.35	52.61	54.86	57.12	59.38	61.63	63.89	66.15	68.40	70.66	72.92	75.17
9.75	13.54	22.41	31.28	40.15	49.01	51.23	53.45	55.66	57.88	60.10	62.31	64.53	66.75	68.96	71.18	73.40
10.00	12.88	21.60	30.31	39.02	47.73	49.91	52.09	54.26	56.44	58.62	60.80	62.98	65.15	67.33	69.51	71.69
10.25	12.26	20.82	29.38	37.94	46.50	48.64	50.78	52.92	55.06	57.20	59.34	61.48	63.62	65.76	67.90	70.04
10.50	11.66	20.07	28.49	36.90	45.31	47.42	49.52	51.62	53.73	55.83	57.93	60.04	62.14	64.24	66.35	68.45
10.75	11.09	19.36	27.63	35.90	44.17	46.24	48.31	50.38	52.44	54.51	56.58	58.65	60.72	62.78	64.85	66.92
11.00	10.55	18.69	26.82	34.95	43.08	45.11	47.15	49.18	51.21	53.24	55.28	57.31	59.34	61.38	63.41	65.44
11.25	10.04	18.04	26.03	34.03	42.03	44.03	46.02	48.02	50.02	52.02	54.02	56.02	58.02	60.02	62.02	64.02
11.50	9.55	17.42	25.28	33.15	41.01	42.98	44.95	46.91	48.88	50.85	52.81	54.78	56.74	58.71	60.68	62.64
11.75	9.09	16.83	24.57	32.30	40.04	41.97	43.91	45.84	47.78	49.71	51.64	53.58	55.51	57.45	59.38	61.32
12.00	8.65	16.27	23.88	31.49	39.10	41.00	42.91	44.81	46.71	48.62	50.52	52.42	54.33	56.23	58.13	60.04
12.25	8.23	15.73	23.22	30.71	38.20	40.07	41.94	43.82	45.69	47.56	49.44	51.31	53.18	55.05	56.93	58.80
12.50	7.84	15.21	22.58	29.96	37.33	39.17	41.02	42.86	44.70	46.55	48.39	50.23	52.08	53.92	55.76	57.61
12.75	7.46	14.72	21.98	29.23	36.49	38.31	40.12	41.94	43.75	45.56	47.38	49.19	51.01	52.82	54.64	56.45
13.00	7.10	14.25	21.39	28.54	35.69	37.47	39.26	41.04	42.83	44.62	46.40	48.19	49.98	51.76	53.55	55.34
13.25	6.76	13.80	20.83	27.87	34.91	36.67	38.43	40.19	41.94	43.70	45.46	47.22	48.98	50.74	52.50	54.26
13.50	6.44	13.37	20.30	27.23	34.16	35.89	37.62	39.36	41.09	42.82	44.55	46.29	48.02	49.75	51.48	53.22
13.75	6.13	12.95	19.78	26.61	33.44	35.14	36.85	38.56	40.26	41.97	43.68	45.38	47.09	48.80	50.50	52.21
14.00	5.83	12.56	19.29	26.01	32.74	34.42	36.10	37.78	39.46	41.15	42.83	44.51	46.19	47.87	49.55	51.23
14.25	5.55	12.18	18.81	25.44	32.06	33.72	35.38	37.04	38.69	40.35	42.01	43.66	45.32	46.98	48.63	50.29
14.50	5.29	11.82	18.35	24.88	31.42	33.05	34.68	36.31	37.95	39.58	41.21	42.85	44.48	46.11	47.75	49.38
14.75	5.04	11.47	17.91	24.35	30.79	32.40	34.01	35.62	37.23	38.84	40.45	42.06	43.67	45.27	46.88	48.49
15.00	4.80	11.14	17.49	23.84	30.18	31.77	33.36	34.94	36.53	38.12	39.70	41.29	42.88	44.46	46.05	47.64
15.25	4.57	10.83	17.08	23.34	29.60	31.16	32.73	34.29	35.86	37.42	38.99	40.55	42.11	43.68	45.24	46.81
15.50	4.35	10.52	16.69	22.86	29.03	30.58	32.12	33.66	35.20	36.75	38.29	39.83	41.38	42.92	44.46	46.00
15.75	4.14	10.23	16.32	22.40	28.49	30.01	31.53	33.05	34.57	36.10	37.62	39.14	40.66	42.18	43.70	45.22
16.00	3.95	9.95	15.95	21.96	27.96	29.46	30.96	32.46	33.96	35.46	36.96	38.47	39.97	41.47	42.97	44.47
16.25	3.76	9.68	15.60	21.53	27.45	28.93	30.41	31.89	33.37	34.85	36.33	37.81	39.29	40.77	42.26	43.74
16.50	3.58	9.42	15.27	21.11	26.96	28.42	29.88	31.34	32.80	34.26	35.72	37.18	38.64	40.10	41.56	43.03
16.75	3.41	9.18	14.94	20.71	26.48	27.92	29.36	30.80	32.24	33.69	35.13	36.57	38.01	39.45	40.89	42.34
17.00	3.25	8.94	14.63	20.32	26.02	27.44	28.86	30.28	31.71	33.13	34.55	35.97	37.40	38.82	40.24	41.67
17.25	3.10	8.71	14.33	19.95	25.57	26.97	28.38	29.78	31.18	32.59	33.99	35.40	36.80	38.21	39.61	41.02
17.50	2.95	8.50	14.04	19.59	25.13	26.52	27.91	29.29	30.68	32.07	33.45	34.84	36.22	37.61	39.00	40.38
17.75	2.81	8.29	13.76	19.24	24.71	26.08	27.45	28.82	30.19	31.56	32.93	34.30	35.66	37.03	38.40	39.77
18.00	2.68	8.09	13.49	18.90	24.31	25.66	27.01	28.36	29.71	31.06	32.42	33.77	35.12	36.47	37.82	39.17
18.25	2.55	7.89	13.23	18.57	23.91	25.25	26.58	27.92	29.25	30.59	31.92	33.26	34.59	35.93	37.26	38.60
18.50	2.43	7.71	12.98	18.26	23.53	24.85	26.17	27.48	28.80	30.12	31.44	32.76	34.08	35.40	36.71	38.03
18.75	2.32	7.53	12.74	17.95	23.16	24.46	25.76	27.07	28.37	29.67	30.97	32.28	33.58	34.88	36.18	37.48
19.00	2.21	7.36	12.50	17.65	22.80	24.08	25.37	26.66	27.95	29.23	30.52	31.81	33.09	34.38	35.67	36.95
20.00	1.83	6.73	11.64	16.55	21.46	22.69	23.92	25.14	26.37	27.60	28.82	30.05	31.28	32.51	33.73	34.96
25.00	.71	4.68	8.65	12.63	16.60	17.59	18.58	19.58	20.57	21.56	22.55	23.55	24.54	25.53	26.53	27.52
30.00	.28	3.61	6.93	10.25	13.58	14.41	15.24	16.07	16.90	17.73	18.56	19.39	20.23	21.06	21.89	22.72

Description: This table shows the yield to maturity of a bond purchased at the price shown in the index.

Example: The yield to maturity of a 6.75 %, 21 year bond at a price of 80.00 is 8.86 %.

PRICE	0.00%	1.00%	2.00%	3.00%	4.00%	4.25%	4.50%	4.75%	5.00%	5.25%	5.50%	5.75%	6.00%	6.25%	6.50%	6.75%
100	0.00	1.00	2.00	3.00	4.00	4.25	4.50	4.75	5.00	5.25	5.50	5.75	6.00	6.25	6.50	6.75
99	.04	1.05	2.05	3.06	4.07	4.32	4.57	4.82	5.07	5.32	5.58	5.83	6.08	6.33	6.58	6.84
98	.09	1.10	2.11	3.13	4.14	4.39	4.65	4.90	5.15	5.41	5.66	5.91	6.17	6.42	6.67	6.93
97	.14	1.16	2.17	3.19	4.21	4.47	4.72	4.98	5.23	5.49	5.74	6.00	6.25	6.51	6.76	7.02
96	.19	1.21	2.23	3.26	4.29	4.54	4.80	5.06	5.31	5.57	5.83	6.09	6.34	6.60	6.86	7.11
95	.24	1.27	2.30	3.33	4.36	4.62	4.88	5.14	5.40	5.65	5.91	6.17	6.43	6.69	6.95	7.21
94	.29	1.32	2.36	3.40	4.44	4.70	4.96	5.22	5.48	5.74	6.00	6.26	6.52	6.79	7.05	7.31
93	.34	1.38	2.42	3.47	4.51	4.78	5.04	5.30	5.56	5.83	6.09	6.35	6.62	6.88	7.14	7.41
92	.39	1.44	2.49	3.54	4.59	4.86	5.12	5.39	5.65	5.92	6.18	6.45	6.71	6.98	7.24	7.51
91	.44	1.50	2.55	3.61	4.67	4.94	5.20	5.47	5.74	6.01	6.27	6.54	6.81	7.07	7.34	7.61
90	.50	1.56	2.62	3.68	4.75	5.02	5.29	5.56	5.83	6.10	6.37	6.63	6.90	7.17	7.44	7.71
89	.55	1.62	2.68	3.76	4.84	5.11	5.38	5.65	5.92	6.19	6.46	6.73	7.00	7.28	7.55	7.82
88	.60	1.68	2.75	3.83	4.92	5.19	5.46	5.74	6.01	6.28	6.56	6.83	7.10	7.38	7.65	7.93
87	.66	1.74	2.82	3.91	5.00	5.28	5.55	5.83	6.10	6.38	6.65	6.93	7.21	7.48	7.76	8.04
86	.71	1.80	2.89	3.99	5.09	5.36	5.64	5.92	6.20	6.47	6.75	7.03	7.31	7.59	7.87	8.15
85	.77	1.86	2.96	4.06	5.18	5.45	5.73	6.01	6.29	6.57	6.85	7.13	7.42	7.70	7.98	8.26
84	.83	1.93	3.03	4.14	5.26	5.54	5.83	6.11	6.39	6.67	6.96	7.24	7.52	7.81	8.09	8.38
83	.88	1.99	3.10	4.22	5.35	5.64	5.92	6.20	6.49	6.77	7.06	7.35	7.63	7.92	8.21	8.49
82	.94	2.06	3.18	4.31	5.44	5.73	6.02	6.30	6.59	6.88	7.17	7.46	7.74	8.03	8.32	8.61
81	1.00	2.12	3.25	4.39	5.54	5.83	6.11	6.40	6.69	6.98	7.27	7.57	7.86	8.15	8.44	8.74
80	1.06	2.19	3.33	4.47	5.63	5.92	6.21	6.51	6.80	7.09	7.38	7.68	7.97	8.27	8.56	8.86
79	1.12	2.26	3.40	4.56	5.73	6.02	6.31	6.61	6.90	7.20	7.50	7.79	8.09	8.39	8.69	8.99
78	1.18	2.33	3.48	4.65	5.83	6.12	6.42	6.72	7.01	7.31	7.61	7.91	8.21	8.51	8.81	9.12
77	1.24	2.40	3.56	4.74	5.92	6.22	6.52	6.82	7.12	7.43	7.73	8.03	8.33	8.64	8.94	9.25
76	1.31	2.47	3.64	4.83	6.03	6.33	6.63	6.93	7.24	7.54	7.85	8.15	8.46	8.77	9.07	9.38
75	1.37	2.54	3.72	4.92	6.13	6.43	6.74	7.04	7.35	7.66	7.97	8.28	8.59	8.90	9.21	9.52
74	1.43	2.61	3.80	5.01	6.23	6.54	6.85	7.16	7.47	7.78	8.09	8.40	8.72	9.03	9.34	9.66
73	1.50	2.69	3.89	5.11	6.34	6.65	6.96	7.27	7.59	7.90	8.22	8.53	8.85	9.17	9.48	9.80
72	1.57	2.76	3.97	5.20	6.45	6.76	7.08	7.39	7.71	8.03	8.34	8.66	8.98	9.30	9.63	9.95
71	1.63	2.84	4.06	5.30	6.56	6.88	7.19	7.51	7.83	8.15	8.48	8.80	9.12	9.45	9.77	10.10
70	1.70	2.92	4.15	5.40	6.67	6.99	7.31	7.64	7.96	8.28	8.61	8.94	9.26	9.59	9.92	10.25
69	1.77	3.00	4.24	5.50	6.79	7.11	7.44	7.76	8.09	8.42	8.75	9.08	9.41	9.74	10.07	10.41
68	1.84	3.08	4.33	5.61	6.90	7.23	7.56	7.89	8.22	8.55	8.89	9.22	9.56	9.89	10.23	10.57
67	1.91	3.16	4.43	5.71	7.02	7.36	7.69	8.02	8.36	8.69	9.03	9.37	9.71	10.05	10.39	10.73
66	1.98	3.24	4.52	5.82	7.15	7.48	7.82	8.16	8.49	8.83	9.18	9.52	9.86	10.21	10.55	10.90
65	2.06	3.33	4.62	5.93	7.27	7.61	7.95	8.29	8.64	8.98	9.32	9.67	10.02	10.37	10.72	11.07
64	2.13	3.41	4.72	6.05	7.40	7.74	8.09	8.43	8.78	9.13	9.48	9.83	10.18	10.54	10.89	11.25
63	2.21	3.50	4.82	6.16	7.53	7.88	8.23	8.58	8.93	9.28	9.64	9.99	10.35	10.71	11.07	11.43
62	2.28	3.59	4.92	6.28	7.67	8.02	8.37	8.72	9.08	9.44	9.80	10.16	10.52	10.88	11.25	11.61
61	2.36	3.68	5.02	6.40	7.80	8.16	8.51	8.87	9.23	9.60	9.96	10.33	10.69	11.06	11.43	11.81
60	2.44	3.77	5.13	6.52	7.94	8.30	8.66	9.03	9.39	9.76	10.13	10.50	10.87	11.25	11.62	12.00
59	2.52	3.86	5.24	6.65	8.09	8.45	8.82	9.19	9.56	9.93	10.30	10.68	11.06	11.44	11.82	12.20
58	2.61	3.96	5.35	6.77	8.23	8.60	8.97	9.35	9.72	10.10	10.48	10.86	11.25	11.63	12.02	12.41
57	2.69	4.06	5.46	6.91	8.38	8.76	9.14	9.52	9.90	10.28	10.67	11.05	11.44	11.84	12.23	12.63
56	2.78	4.16	5.58	7.04	8.54	8.92	9.30	9.69	10.07	10.46	10.86	11.25	11.65	12.04	12.44	12.85
55	2.86	4.26	5.70	7.18	8.70	9.08	9.47	9.86	10.26	10.65	11.05	11.45	11.85	12.26	12.66	13.07
54	2.95	4.36	5.82	7.32	8.86	9.25	9.65	10.04	10.44	10.84	11.25	11.66	12.07	12.48	12.89	13.31
53	3.04	4.47	5.94	7.46	9.03	9.43	9.83	10.23	10.64	11.04	11.46	11.87	12.29	12.70	13.12	13.55
52	3.13	4.58	6.07	7.61	9.20	9.60	10.01	10.42	10.83	11.25	11.67	12.09	12.51	12.94	13.37	13.80
51	3.23	4.69	6.20	7.76	9.38	9.79	10.20	10.62	11.04	11.46	11.89	12.32	12.75	13.18	13.62	14.06
50	3.32	4.80	6.34	7.92	9.56	9.98	10.40	10.82	11.25	11.68	12.11	12.55	12.99	13.43	13.88	14.32
49	3.42	4.92	6.47	8.08	9.75	10.17	10.60	11.03	11.47	11.91	12.35	12.79	13.24	13.69	14.14	14.60
48	3.52	5.04	6.61	8.25	9.94	10.37	10.81	11.25	11.69	12.14	12.59	13.04	13.50	13.96	14.42	14.89
47	3.62	5.16	6.76	8.42	10.14	10.58	11.03	11.48	11.93	12.38	12.84	13.30	13.77	14.24	14.71	15.19
46	3.73	5.28	6.91	8.59	10.35	10.80	11.25	11.71	12.17	12.63	13.10	13.57	14.05	14.53	15.01	15.50
45	3.83	5.41	7.06	8.78	10.56	11.02	11.48	11.95	12.42	12.89	13.37	13.85	14.34	14.83	15.32	15.82
44	3.94	5.54	7.22	8.96	10.78	11.25	11.72	12.20	12.68	13.16	13.65	14.14	14.64	15.14	15.65	16.15
43	4.05	5.68	7.38	9.16	11.01	11.49	11.97	12.46	12.95	13.44	13.94	14.45	14.96	15.47	15.98	16.50
42	4.17	5.82	7.54	9.36	11.25	11.74	12.23	12.73	13.23	13.74	14.25	14.76	15.28	15.81	16.34	16.87
41	4.29	5.96	7.72	9.56	11.50	12.00	12.50	13.01	13.52	14.04	14.56	15.09	15.63	16.16	16.70	17.25
40	4.41	6.10	7.89	9.78	11.76	12.26	12.78	13.30	13.83	14.36	14.89	15.44	15.98	16.53	17.09	17.65
39	4.53	6.26	8.08	10.00	12.02	12.54	13.07	13.61	14.14	14.69	15.24	15.80	16.36	16.92	17.49	18.07
35	5.06	6.91	8.88	10.98	13.21	13.79	14.38	14.97	15.58	16.18	16.80	17.42	18.05	18.69	19.33	19.97
30	5.81	7.86	10.08	12.48	15.07	15.75	16.44	17.13	17.84	18.56	19.29	20.03	20.77	21.52	22.28	23.05
25	6.71	9.02	11.59	14.44	17.57	18.40	19.24	20.10	20.96	21.85	22.74	23.65	24.57	25.49	26.43	27.37
20	7.81	10.52	13.64	17.21	21.24	22.31	23.40	24.51	25.65	26.79	27.96	29.13	30.32	31.52	32.72	33.93
15	9.24	12.60	16.70	21.65	27.37	28.90	30.45	32.02	33.61	35.21	36.83	38.46	40.10	41.74	43.39	45.05
10	11.27	15.95	22.37	30.68	40.16	42.61	45.08	47.55	50.03	52.52	55.01	57.51	60.00	62.50	65.00	67.50

Description: This table shows the price to pay for a bond at the yield rate. The yield is to maturity.

Example: The price of a 10.75 %, 21 year bond to yield 8 % to maturity is $ 127.76.

COUPON RATE, %

YIELD	7.00%	7.25%	7.50%	7.75%	8.00%	8.25%	8.50%	8.75%	9.00%	9.25%	9.50%	9.75%	10.00%	10.25%	10.50%	10.75%
0.00	247.00	252.25	257.50	262.75	268.00	273.25	278.50	283.75	289.00	294.25	299.50	304.75	310.00	315.25	320.50	325.75
1.00	213.39	218.12	222.84	227.57	232.29	237.02	241.74	246.47	251.19	255.92	260.64	265.37	270.09	274.82	279.54	284.27
2.00	185.40	189.67	193.93	198.20	202.47	206.74	211.01	215.28	219.55	223.82	228.09	232.36	236.63	240.90	245.17	249.44
3.00	161.99	165.86	169.74	173.61	177.49	181.36	185.23	189.11	192.98	196.86	200.73	204.60	208.48	212.35	216.23	220.10
4.00	142.35	145.88	149.41	152.94	156.47	160.00	163.53	167.06	170.59	174.12	177.65	181.18	184.70	188.23	191.76	195.29
4.25	137.95	141.40	144.85	148.30	151.75	155.20	158.65	162.10	165.55	169.00	172.45	175.90	179.35	182.80	186.25	189.70
4.50	133.73	137.11	140.48	143.86	147.23	150.60	153.98	157.35	160.72	164.10	167.47	170.84	174.22	177.59	180.96	184.34
4.75	129.69	132.99	136.29	139.59	142.89	146.19	149.49	152.79	156.09	159.39	162.69	165.99	169.29	172.59	175.88	179.18
5.00	125.82	129.05	132.28	135.50	138.73	141.96	145.19	148.41	151.64	154.87	158.10	161.32	164.55	167.78	171.01	174.23
5.25	122.11	125.26	128.42	131.58	134.74	137.90	141.06	144.21	147.37	150.53	153.69	156.85	160.00	163.16	166.32	169.48
5.50	118.55	121.64	124.73	127.82	130.91	134.00	137.09	140.18	143.27	146.36	149.45	152.54	155.64	158.73	161.82	164.91
5.75	115.13	118.15	121.18	124.21	127.23	130.26	133.28	136.31	139.33	142.36	145.39	148.41	151.44	154.46	157.49	160.51
6.00	111.85	114.81	117.78	120.74	123.70	126.66	129.63	132.59	135.55	138.51	141.48	144.44	147.40	150.37	153.33	156.29
6.25	108.70	111.61	114.51	117.41	120.31	123.21	126.11	129.02	131.92	134.82	137.72	140.62	143.52	146.43	149.33	152.23
6.50	105.68	108.53	111.37	114.21	117.05	119.90	122.74	125.58	128.42	131.27	134.11	136.95	139.79	142.64	145.48	148.32
6.75	102.78	105.57	108.35	111.14	113.92	116.71	119.49	122.28	125.06	127.85	130.63	133.42	136.20	138.99	141.77	144.56
7.00	100.00	102.73	105.46	108.19	110.92	113.65	116.38	119.11	121.83	124.56	127.29	130.02	132.75	135.48	138.21	140.94
7.25	97.32	100.00	102.68	105.35	108.03	110.70	113.38	116.05	118.73	121.40	124.08	126.75	129.43	132.11	134.78	137.46
7.50	94.75	97.38	100.00	102.62	105.25	107.87	110.49	113.12	115.74	118.36	120.99	123.61	126.23	128.85	131.48	134.10
7.75	92.28	94.86	97.43	100.00	102.57	105.14	107.72	110.29	112.86	115.43	118.01	120.58	123.15	125.72	128.30	130.87
8.00	89.91	92.43	94.95	97.48	100.00	102.52	105.05	107.57	110.09	112.62	115.14	117.66	120.19	122.71	125.23	127.76
8.25	87.62	90.10	92.57	95.05	97.52	100.00	102.48	104.95	107.43	109.90	112.38	114.85	117.33	119.80	122.28	124.75
8.50	85.43	87.85	90.28	92.71	95.14	97.57	100.00	102.43	104.86	107.29	109.72	112.15	114.57	117.00	119.43	121.86
8.75	83.31	85.70	88.08	90.46	92.85	95.23	97.62	100.00	102.38	104.77	107.15	109.54	111.92	114.30	116.69	119.07
9.00	81.28	83.62	85.96	88.30	90.64	92.98	95.32	97.66	100.00	102.34	104.68	107.02	109.36	111.70	114.04	116.38
9.25	79.32	81.62	83.91	86.21	88.51	90.81	93.11	95.40	97.70	100.00	102.30	104.60	106.89	109.19	111.49	113.79
9.50	77.43	79.69	81.95	84.20	86.46	88.72	90.97	93.23	95.49	97.74	100.00	102.26	104.51	106.77	109.03	111.28
9.75	75.62	77.83	80.05	82.27	84.48	86.70	88.92	91.13	93.35	95.57	97.78	100.00	102.22	104.43	106.65	108.87
10.00	73.87	76.04	78.22	80.40	82.58	84.75	86.93	89.11	91.29	93.47	95.64	97.82	100.00	102.18	104.36	106.53
10.25	72.18	74.32	76.46	78.60	80.74	82.88	85.02	87.16	89.30	91.44	93.58	95.72	97.86	100.00	102.14	104.28
10.50	70.55	72.66	74.76	76.86	78.97	81.07	83.17	85.28	87.38	89.48	91.59	93.69	95.79	97.90	100.00	102.10
10.75	68.99	71.05	73.12	75.19	77.26	79.32	81.39	83.46	85.53	87.59	89.66	91.73	93.80	95.86	97.93	100.00
11.00	67.47	69.51	71.54	73.57	75.61	77.64	79.67	81.70	83.74	85.77	87.80	89.84	91.87	93.90	95.93	97.97
11.25	66.02	68.01	70.01	72.01	74.01	76.01	78.01	80.01	82.01	84.01	86.01	88.01	90.00	92.00	94.00	96.00
11.50	64.61	66.57	68.54	70.51	72.47	74.44	76.41	78.37	80.34	82.30	84.27	86.24	88.20	90.17	92.14	94.10
11.75	63.25	65.18	67.12	69.05	70.99	72.92	74.86	76.79	78.72	80.66	82.59	84.53	86.46	88.39	90.33	92.26
12.00	61.94	63.84	65.74	67.65	69.55	71.45	73.36	75.26	77.16	79.07	80.97	82.87	84.78	86.68	88.58	90.48
12.25	60.67	62.54	64.42	66.29	68.16	70.04	71.91	73.78	75.65	77.53	79.40	81.27	83.15	85.02	86.89	88.76
12.50	59.45	61.29	63.14	64.98	66.82	68.66	70.51	72.35	74.19	76.04	77.88	79.72	81.57	83.41	85.25	87.10
12.75	58.27	60.08	61.90	63.71	65.52	67.34	69.15	70.97	72.78	74.60	76.41	78.23	80.04	81.85	83.67	85.48
13.00	57.12	58.91	60.70	62.48	64.27	66.06	67.84	69.63	71.42	73.20	74.99	76.78	78.56	80.35	82.13	83.92
13.25	56.02	57.78	59.54	61.30	63.06	64.81	66.57	68.33	70.09	71.85	73.61	75.37	77.13	78.89	80.65	82.41
13.50	54.95	56.68	58.42	60.15	61.88	63.61	65.35	67.08	68.81	70.54	72.28	74.01	75.74	77.48	79.21	80.94
13.75	53.92	55.62	57.33	59.04	60.74	62.45	64.16	65.86	67.57	69.28	70.98	72.69	74.40	76.10	77.81	79.52
14.00	52.92	54.60	56.28	57.96	59.64	61.32	63.01	64.69	66.37	68.05	69.73	71.41	73.10	74.78	76.46	78.14
14.25	51.95	53.61	55.26	56.92	58.58	60.23	61.89	63.55	65.20	66.86	68.52	70.17	71.83	73.49	75.15	76.80
14.50	51.01	52.64	54.28	55.91	57.54	59.18	60.81	62.44	64.07	65.71	67.34	68.97	70.61	72.24	73.87	75.51
14.75	50.10	51.71	53.32	54.93	56.54	58.15	59.76	61.37	62.98	64.59	66.20	67.81	69.42	71.03	72.64	74.25
15.00	49.22	50.81	52.40	53.98	55.57	57.16	58.74	60.33	61.92	63.50	65.09	66.68	68.27	69.85	71.44	73.03
15.25	48.37	49.94	51.50	53.07	54.63	56.19	57.76	59.32	60.89	62.45	64.02	65.58	67.15	68.71	70.28	71.84
15.50	47.55	49.09	50.63	52.17	53.72	55.26	56.80	58.35	59.89	61.43	62.97	64.52	66.06	67.60	69.15	70.69
15.75	46.75	48.27	49.79	51.31	52.83	54.35	55.88	57.40	58.92	60.44	61.96	63.48	65.00	66.53	68.05	69.57
16.00	45.97	47.47	48.97	50.47	51.97	53.47	54.97	56.48	57.98	59.48	60.98	62.48	63.98	65.48	66.98	68.48
16.25	45.22	46.70	48.18	49.66	51.14	52.62	54.10	55.58	57.06	58.54	60.02	61.50	62.98	64.46	65.95	67.43
16.50	44.49	45.95	47.41	48.87	50.33	51.79	53.25	54.71	56.17	57.63	59.10	60.56	62.02	63.48	64.94	66.40
16.75	43.78	45.22	46.66	48.10	49.54	50.99	52.43	53.87	55.31	56.75	58.19	59.63	61.08	62.52	63.96	65.40
17.00	43.09	44.51	45.93	47.36	48.78	50.20	51.63	53.05	54.47	55.89	57.32	58.74	60.16	61.58	63.01	64.43
17.25	42.42	43.82	45.23	46.63	48.04	49.44	50.85	52.25	53.66	55.06	56.46	57.87	59.27	60.68	62.08	63.49
17.50	41.77	43.16	44.54	45.93	47.32	48.70	50.09	51.48	52.86	54.25	55.63	57.02	58.41	59.79	61.18	62.57
17.75	41.14	42.51	43.88	45.25	46.62	47.98	49.35	50.72	52.09	53.46	54.83	56.20	57.57	58.93	60.30	61.67
18.00	40.53	41.88	43.23	44.58	45.93	47.28	48.64	49.99	51.34	52.69	54.04	55.39	56.75	58.10	59.45	60.80
18.25	39.93	41.27	42.60	43.94	45.27	46.60	47.94	49.27	50.61	51.94	53.28	54.61	55.95	57.28	58.62	59.95
18.50	39.35	40.67	41.99	43.31	44.62	45.94	47.26	48.58	49.90	51.22	52.54	53.85	55.17	56.49	57.81	59.13
18.75	38.79	40.09	41.39	42.69	44.00	45.30	46.60	47.90	49.21	50.51	51.81	53.11	54.42	55.72	57.02	58.32
19.00	38.24	39.53	40.81	42.10	43.39	44.67	45.96	47.25	48.53	49.82	51.11	52.39	53.68	54.97	56.25	57.54
20.00	36.19	37.41	38.64	39.87	41.10	42.32	43.55	44.78	46.00	47.23	48.46	49.69	50.91	52.14	53.37	54.59
25.00	28.51	29.50	30.50	31.49	32.48	33.48	34.47	35.46	36.45	37.45	38.44	39.43	40.43	41.42	42.41	43.41
30.00	23.55	24.38	25.21	26.04	26.87	27.70	28.54	29.37	30.20	31.03	31.86	32.69	33.52	34.35	35.18	36.01

Description: This table shows the yield to maturity of a bond purchased at the price shown in the index.

Example: The yield to maturity of a 10.75 %, 21 year bond at a price of 111.00 is 9.52 %.

COUPON RATE, %

PRICE	7.00%	7.25%	7.50%	7.75%	8.00%	8.25%	8.50%	8.75%	9.00%	9.25%	9.50%	9.75%	10.00%	10.25%	10.50%	10.75%
165	2.86	3.03	3.21	3.39	3.57	3.75	3.92	4.10	4.27	4.45	4.62	4.80	4.97	5.14	5.32	5.49
160	3.09	3.27	3.45	3.63	3.81	3.99	4.17	4.35	4.53	4.71	4.89	5.07	5.25	5.42	5.60	5.77
155	3.33	3.52	3.70	3.89	4.07	4.26	4.44	4.62	4.81	4.99	5.17	5.35	5.53	5.71	5.89	6.07
150	3.58	3.77	3.96	4.15	4.34	4.53	4.72	4.90	5.09	5.28	5.46	5.65	5.83	6.02	6.20	6.39
145	3.85	4.04	4.24	4.43	4.62	4.81	5.01	5.20	5.39	5.58	5.77	5.96	6.15	6.34	6.53	6.72
140	4.13	4.33	4.52	4.72	4.92	5.11	5.31	5.51	5.70	5.90	6.09	6.29	6.48	6.67	6.87	7.06
135	4.42	4.62	4.82	5.03	5.23	5.43	5.63	5.83	6.03	6.23	6.43	6.63	6.83	7.03	7.23	7.43
130	4.73	4.93	5.14	5.35	5.56	5.76	5.97	6.18	6.38	6.59	6.79	7.00	7.20	7.41	7.61	7.81
125	5.05	5.26	5.48	5.69	5.90	6.11	6.33	6.54	6.75	6.96	7.17	7.38	7.59	7.80	8.01	8.22
122	5.25	5.47	5.69	5.90	6.12	6.34	6.55	6.77	6.98	7.20	7.41	7.63	7.84	8.06	8.27	8.48
121	5.32	5.54	5.76	5.98	6.19	6.41	6.63	6.84	7.06	7.28	7.49	7.71	7.93	8.14	8.36	8.57
120	5.39	5.61	5.83	6.05	6.27	6.49	6.71	6.92	7.14	7.36	7.58	7.79	8.01	8.23	8.44	8.66
119	5.46	5.68	5.90	6.12	6.34	6.56	6.78	7.00	7.22	7.44	7.66	7.88	8.10	8.32	8.53	8.75
118	5.53	5.76	5.98	6.20	6.42	6.64	6.86	7.08	7.31	7.53	7.75	7.97	8.19	8.40	8.62	8.84
117	5.61	5.83	6.05	6.28	6.50	6.72	6.94	7.17	7.39	7.61	7.83	8.05	8.27	8.50	8.72	8.94
116	5.68	5.91	6.13	6.35	6.58	6.80	7.03	7.25	7.47	7.70	7.92	8.14	8.36	8.59	8.81	9.03
115	5.75	5.98	6.21	6.43	6.66	6.88	7.11	7.33	7.56	7.78	8.01	8.23	8.46	8.68	8.90	9.13
114	5.83	6.06	6.28	6.51	6.74	6.97	7.19	7.42	7.64	7.87	8.10	8.32	8.55	8.77	9.00	9.22
113	5.91	6.14	6.36	6.59	6.82	7.05	7.28	7.51	7.73	7.96	8.19	8.42	8.64	8.87	9.10	9.32
112	5.98	6.21	6.44	6.67	6.90	7.13	7.36	7.59	7.82	8.05	8.28	8.51	8.74	8.97	9.19	9.42
111	6.06	6.29	6.53	6.76	6.99	7.22	7.45	7.68	7.91	8.14	8.37	8.60	8.83	9.06	9.29	9.52
110	6.14	6.37	6.61	6.84	7.07	7.31	7.54	7.77	8.00	8.24	8.47	8.70	8.93	9.16	9.40	9.63
109	6.22	6.46	6.69	6.93	7.16	7.39	7.63	7.86	8.10	8.33	8.56	8.80	9.03	9.26	9.50	9.73
108	6.30	6.54	6.78	7.01	7.25	7.48	7.72	7.95	8.19	8.43	8.66	8.90	9.13	9.37	9.60	9.84
107	6.38	6.62	6.86	7.10	7.34	7.57	7.81	8.05	8.29	8.52	8.76	9.00	9.23	9.47	9.71	9.94
106	6.47	6.71	6.95	7.19	7.43	7.67	7.90	8.14	8.38	8.62	8.86	9.10	9.34	9.58	9.81	10.05
105	6.55	6.79	7.04	7.28	7.52	7.76	8.00	8.24	8.48	8.72	8.96	9.20	9.44	9.68	9.92	10.16
104	6.64	6.88	7.12	7.37	7.61	7.85	8.10	8.34	8.58	8.82	9.07	9.31	9.55	9.79	10.03	10.28
103	6.73	6.97	7.22	7.46	7.70	7.95	8.19	8.44	8.68	8.93	9.17	9.41	9.66	9.90	10.15	10.39
102	6.81	7.06	7.31	7.55	7.80	8.05	8.29	8.54	8.78	9.03	9.28	9.52	9.77	10.02	10.26	10.51
101	6.90	7.15	7.40	7.65	7.90	8.14	8.39	8.64	8.89	9.14	9.39	9.63	9.88	10.13	10.38	10.63
100	7.00	7.25	7.50	7.75	8.00	8.25	8.50	8.75	9.00	9.25	9.50	9.75	10.00	10.25	10.50	10.75
99	7.09	7.34	7.59	7.84	8.09	8.35	8.60	8.85	9.10	9.35	9.61	9.86	10.11	10.36	10.61	10.87
98	7.18	7.43	7.69	7.94	8.20	8.45	8.70	8.96	9.21	9.47	9.72	9.97	10.23	10.48	10.74	10.99
97	7.28	7.53	7.79	8.04	8.30	8.56	8.81	9.07	9.32	9.58	9.84	10.09	10.35	10.60	10.86	11.12
96	7.37	7.63	7.89	8.15	8.40	8.66	8.92	9.18	9.44	9.69	9.95	10.21	10.47	10.73	10.99	11.25
95	7.47	7.73	7.99	8.25	8.51	8.77	9.03	9.29	9.55	9.81	10.07	10.33	10.59	10.85	11.11	11.38
94	7.57	7.83	8.09	8.36	8.62	8.88	9.14	9.41	9.67	9.93	10.19	10.46	10.72	10.98	11.25	11.51
93	7.67	7.94	8.20	8.46	8.73	8.99	9.26	9.52	9.79	10.05	10.32	10.58	10.85	11.11	11.38	11.64
92	7.77	8.04	8.31	8.57	8.84	9.11	9.37	9.64	9.91	10.17	10.44	10.71	10.98	11.25	11.51	11.78
91	7.88	8.15	8.42	8.68	8.95	9.22	9.49	9.76	10.03	10.30	10.57	10.84	11.11	11.38	11.65	11.92
90	7.99	8.26	8.53	8.80	9.07	9.34	9.61	9.88	10.16	10.43	10.70	10.97	11.25	11.52	11.79	12.06
89	8.09	8.37	8.64	8.91	9.19	9.46	9.73	10.01	10.28	10.56	10.83	11.11	11.38	11.66	11.93	12.21
88	8.20	8.48	8.75	9.03	9.31	9.58	9.86	10.14	10.41	10.69	10.97	11.25	11.52	11.80	12.08	12.36
87	8.31	8.59	8.87	9.15	9.43	9.71	9.99	10.27	10.55	10.83	11.11	11.39	11.67	11.95	12.23	12.51
86	8.43	8.71	8.99	9.27	9.55	9.83	10.12	10.40	10.68	10.96	11.25	11.53	11.81	12.10	12.38	12.66
85	8.54	8.83	9.11	9.39	9.68	9.96	10.25	10.53	10.82	11.10	11.39	11.67	11.96	12.25	12.53	12.82
84	8.66	8.95	9.23	9.52	9.81	10.09	10.38	10.67	10.96	11.25	11.53	11.82	12.11	12.40	12.69	12.98
83	8.78	9.07	9.36	9.65	9.94	10.23	10.52	10.81	11.10	11.39	11.68	11.98	12.27	12.56	12.85	13.15
82	8.91	9.20	9.49	9.78	10.07	10.37	10.66	10.95	11.25	11.54	11.84	12.13	12.43	12.72	13.02	13.31
81	9.03	9.32	9.62	9.91	10.21	10.50	10.80	11.10	11.39	11.69	11.99	12.29	12.59	12.89	13.19	13.48
80	9.16	9.45	9.75	10.05	10.35	10.65	10.95	11.25	11.55	11.85	12.15	12.45	12.75	13.05	13.36	13.66
79	9.29	9.59	9.89	10.19	10.49	10.79	11.09	11.40	11.70	12.01	12.31	12.61	12.92	13.23	13.53	13.84
78	9.42	9.72	10.03	10.33	10.64	10.94	11.25	11.55	11.86	12.17	12.48	12.78	13.09	13.40	13.71	14.02
77	9.55	9.86	10.17	10.47	10.78	11.09	11.40	11.71	12.02	12.33	12.64	12.96	13.27	13.58	13.89	14.21
76	9.69	10.00	10.31	10.62	10.93	11.25	11.56	11.87	12.19	12.50	12.82	13.13	13.45	13.76	14.08	14.40
75	9.83	10.15	10.46	10.77	11.09	11.40	11.72	12.04	12.36	12.67	12.99	13.31	13.63	13.95	14.27	14.59
74	9.98	10.29	10.61	10.93	11.25	11.57	11.89	12.21	12.53	12.85	13.17	13.50	13.82	14.14	14.47	14.79
73	10.12	10.44	10.76	11.09	11.41	11.73	12.06	12.38	12.71	13.03	13.36	13.69	14.01	14.34	14.67	15.00
70	10.58	10.91	11.25	11.58	11.92	12.25	12.59	12.92	13.26	13.60	13.94	14.28	14.62	14.96	15.31	15.65
65	11.42	11.78	12.13	12.49	12.85	13.21	13.57	13.93	14.29	14.65	15.02	15.38	15.75	16.11	16.48	16.85
60	12.38	12.76	13.14	13.53	13.91	14.30	14.69	15.08	15.47	15.86	16.25	16.65	17.04	17.44	17.83	18.23
55	13.48	13.90	14.31	14.73	15.15	15.57	15.99	16.41	16.84	17.26	17.69	18.12	18.55	18.98	19.42	19.85
50	14.77	15.23	15.68	16.14	16.60	17.06	17.52	17.99	18.46	18.93	19.40	19.87	20.35	20.82	21.30	21.78
45	16.32	16.82	17.33	17.84	18.35	18.86	19.38	19.90	20.42	20.95	21.47	22.00	22.53	23.06	23.60	24.13
40	18.22	18.78	19.36	19.93	20.51	21.10	21.68	22.27	22.86	23.46	24.05	24.65	25.25	25.86	26.46	27.07
35	20.63	21.28	21.94	22.61	23.28	23.95	24.63	25.31	26.00	26.68	27.37	28.06	28.76	29.45	30.15	30.85
30	23.82	24.60	25.39	26.18	26.97	27.77	28.57	29.38	30.19	31.00	31.81	32.63	33.45	34.27	35.09	35.91

Description: This table shows the price to pay for a bond at the yield rate. The yield is to maturity.

Example: The price of a 15.00 %, 21 year bond to yield 8 % to maturity is $ 170.65.

COUPON RATE, %

YIELD	11.00%	11.25%	11.50%	11.75%	12.00%	12.25%	12.50%	12.75%	13.00%	13.25%	13.50%	13.75%	14.00%	14.25%	14.50%	15.00%
0.00	331.00	336.25	341.50	346.75	352.00	357.25	362.50	367.75	373.00	378.25	383.50	388.75	394.00	399.25	404.50	415.00
1.00	288.99	293.72	298.44	303.17	307.89	312.62	317.34	322.07	326.79	331.51	336.24	340.96	345.69	350.41	355.14	364.59
2.00	253.71	257.98	262.25	266.52	270.79	275.06	279.33	283.60	287.87	292.14	296.41	300.68	304.95	309.22	313.49	322.03
3.00	223.98	227.85	231.72	235.60	239.47	243.35	247.22	251.10	254.97	258.84	262.72	266.59	270.47	274.34	278.22	285.96
4.00	198.82	202.35	205.88	209.41	212.94	216.47	220.00	223.53	227.06	230.59	234.12	237.64	241.17	244.70	248.23	255.29
4.25	193.15	196.60	200.05	203.50	206.95	210.40	213.85	217.30	220.75	224.20	227.65	231.10	234.55	238.01	241.46	248.36
4.50	187.71	191.08	194.46	197.83	201.20	204.58	207.95	211.33	214.70	218.07	221.45	224.82	228.19	231.57	234.94	241.69
4.75	182.48	185.78	189.08	192.38	195.68	198.98	202.28	205.58	208.88	212.18	215.48	218.78	222.08	225.37	228.67	235.27
5.00	177.46	180.69	183.92	187.14	190.37	193.60	196.83	200.05	203.28	206.51	209.74	212.97	216.19	219.42	222.65	229.10
5.25	172.64	175.79	178.95	182.11	185.27	188.43	191.59	194.74	197.90	201.06	204.22	207.38	210.53	213.69	216.85	223.17
5.50	168.00	171.09	174.18	177.27	180.36	183.45	186.54	189.64	192.73	195.82	198.91	202.00	205.09	208.18	211.27	217.45
5.75	163.54	166.57	169.59	172.62	175.64	178.67	181.70	184.72	187.75	190.77	193.80	196.82	199.85	202.88	205.90	211.95
6.00	159.25	162.22	165.18	168.14	171.10	174.07	177.03	179.99	182.95	185.92	188.88	191.84	194.81	197.77	200.73	206.66
6.25	155.13	158.03	160.93	163.83	166.74	169.64	172.54	175.44	178.34	181.24	184.15	187.05	189.95	192.85	195.75	201.55
6.50	151.16	154.00	156.85	159.69	162.53	165.37	168.22	171.06	173.90	176.74	179.59	182.43	185.27	188.11	190.96	196.64
6.75	147.34	150.13	152.91	155.70	158.48	161.27	164.05	166.84	169.62	172.41	175.19	177.98	180.76	183.55	186.33	191.90
7.00	143.67	146.40	149.13	151.86	154.59	157.32	160.05	162.78	165.50	168.23	170.96	173.69	176.42	179.15	181.88	187.34
7.25	140.13	142.81	145.48	148.16	150.83	153.51	156.18	158.86	161.53	164.21	166.89	169.56	172.24	174.91	177.59	182.94
7.50	136.72	139.35	141.97	144.59	147.22	149.84	152.46	155.09	157.71	160.33	162.96	165.58	168.20	170.82	173.45	178.69
7.75	133.44	136.01	138.59	141.16	143.73	146.30	148.88	151.45	154.02	156.59	159.17	161.74	164.31	166.88	169.46	174.60
8.00	130.28	132.80	135.32	137.85	140.37	142.89	145.42	147.94	150.46	152.99	155.51	158.03	160.56	163.08	165.60	170.65
8.25	127.23	129.71	132.18	134.66	137.13	139.61	142.08	144.56	147.03	149.51	151.98	154.46	156.94	159.41	161.89	166.84
8.50	124.29	126.72	129.15	131.58	134.01	136.44	138.87	141.29	143.72	146.15	148.58	151.01	153.44	155.87	158.30	163.16
8.75	121.46	123.84	126.23	128.61	130.99	133.38	135.76	138.15	140.53	142.91	145.30	147.68	150.07	152.45	154.83	159.60
9.00	118.72	121.06	123.40	125.74	128.09	130.43	132.77	135.11	137.45	139.79	142.13	144.47	146.81	149.15	151.49	156.17
9.25	116.09	118.38	120.68	122.98	125.28	127.58	129.87	132.17	134.47	136.77	139.07	141.36	143.66	145.96	148.26	152.85
9.50	113.54	115.80	118.05	120.31	122.57	124.83	127.08	129.34	131.60	133.85	136.11	138.37	140.62	142.88	145.14	149.65
9.75	111.08	113.30	115.52	117.73	119.95	122.17	124.38	126.60	128.82	131.04	133.25	135.47	137.69	139.90	142.12	146.55
10.00	108.71	110.89	113.07	115.25	117.42	119.60	121.78	123.96	126.13	128.31	130.49	132.67	134.85	137.02	139.20	143.56
10.25	106.42	108.56	110.70	112.84	114.98	117.12	119.26	121.40	123.54	125.68	127.82	129.96	132.10	134.24	136.38	140.66
10.50	104.21	106.31	108.41	110.52	112.62	114.72	116.83	118.93	121.03	123.14	125.24	127.34	129.45	131.55	133.65	137.86
10.75	102.07	104.14	106.20	108.27	110.34	112.41	114.47	116.54	118.61	120.68	122.74	124.81	126.88	128.95	131.01	135.15
11.00	100.00	102.03	104.07	106.10	108.13	110.16	112.20	114.23	116.26	118.30	120.33	122.36	124.39	126.43	128.46	132.53
11.25	98.00	100.00	102.00	104.00	106.00	108.00	110.00	111.99	113.99	115.99	117.99	119.99	121.99	123.99	125.99	129.99
11.50	96.07	98.03	100.00	101.97	103.93	105.90	107.86	109.83	111.80	113.76	115.73	117.70	119.66	121.63	123.59	127.53
11.75	94.20	96.13	98.07	100.00	101.93	103.87	105.80	107.74	109.67	111.61	113.54	115.47	117.41	119.34	121.28	125.14
12.00	92.39	94.29	96.19	98.10	100.00	101.90	103.81	105.71	107.61	109.52	111.42	113.32	115.22	117.13	119.03	122.84
12.25	90.64	92.51	94.38	96.25	98.13	100.00	101.87	103.75	105.62	107.49	109.36	111.24	113.11	114.98	116.85	120.60
12.50	88.94	90.78	92.63	94.47	96.31	98.16	100.00	101.84	103.69	105.53	107.37	109.22	111.06	112.90	114.75	118.43
12.75	87.30	89.11	90.93	92.74	94.56	96.37	98.19	100.00	101.81	103.63	105.44	107.26	109.07	110.89	112.70	116.33
13.00	85.71	87.49	89.28	91.07	92.85	94.64	96.43	98.21	100.00	101.79	103.57	105.36	107.15	108.93	110.72	114.29
13.25	84.17	85.93	87.69	89.44	91.20	92.96	94.72	96.48	98.24	100.00	101.76	103.52	105.28	107.04	108.80	112.31
13.50	82.67	84.41	86.14	87.87	89.60	91.34	93.07	94.80	96.53	98.27	100.00	101.73	103.47	105.20	106.93	110.40
13.75	81.23	82.93	84.64	86.35	88.05	89.76	91.47	93.17	94.88	96.59	98.29	100.00	101.71	103.41	105.12	108.53
14.00	79.82	81.50	83.18	84.87	86.55	88.23	89.91	91.59	93.27	94.96	96.64	98.32	100.00	101.68	103.36	106.73
14.25	78.46	80.12	81.77	83.43	85.09	86.74	88.40	90.06	91.72	93.37	95.03	96.69	98.34	100.00	101.66	104.97
14.50	77.14	78.77	80.40	82.04	83.67	85.30	86.94	88.57	90.20	91.84	93.47	95.10	96.73	98.37	100.00	103.27
14.75	75.86	77.47	79.08	80.69	82.29	83.90	85.51	87.12	88.73	90.34	91.95	93.56	95.17	96.78	98.39	101.61
15.00	74.61	76.20	77.79	79.37	80.96	82.55	84.13	85.72	87.31	88.89	90.48	92.07	93.65	95.24	96.83	100.00
15.25	73.40	74.97	76.53	78.10	79.66	81.23	82.79	84.36	85.92	87.48	89.05	90.61	92.18	93.74	95.31	98.44
15.50	72.23	73.77	75.32	76.86	78.40	79.94	81.49	83.03	84.57	86.12	87.66	89.20	90.74	92.29	93.83	96.91
15.75	71.09	72.61	74.13	75.66	77.18	78.70	80.22	81.74	83.26	84.78	86.31	87.83	89.35	90.87	92.39	95.44
16.00	69.98	71.48	72.98	74.49	75.99	77.49	78.99	80.49	81.99	83.49	84.99	86.49	87.99	89.49	90.99	94.00
16.25	68.91	70.39	71.87	73.35	74.83	76.31	77.79	79.27	80.75	82.23	83.71	85.19	86.67	88.15	89.64	92.60
16.50	67.86	69.32	70.78	72.24	73.70	75.16	76.63	78.09	79.55	81.01	82.47	83.93	85.39	86.85	88.31	91.23
16.75	66.84	68.28	69.73	71.17	72.61	74.05	75.49	76.93	78.38	79.82	81.26	82.70	84.14	85.58	87.03	89.91
17.00	65.85	67.28	68.70	70.12	71.54	72.97	74.39	75.81	77.24	78.66	80.08	81.50	82.93	84.35	85.77	88.62
17.25	64.89	66.29	67.70	69.10	70.51	71.91	73.32	74.72	76.13	77.53	78.93	80.34	81.74	83.15	84.55	87.36
17.50	63.95	65.34	66.73	68.11	69.50	70.89	72.27	73.66	75.04	76.43	77.82	79.20	80.59	81.98	83.36	86.14
17.75	63.04	64.41	65.78	67.15	68.52	69.89	71.25	72.62	73.99	75.36	76.73	78.10	79.47	80.84	82.21	84.94
18.00	62.15	63.50	64.86	66.21	67.56	68.91	70.26	71.61	72.97	74.32	75.67	77.02	78.37	79.72	81.08	83.78
18.25	61.29	62.62	63.96	65.29	66.63	67.96	69.30	70.63	71.97	73.30	74.64	75.97	77.31	78.64	79.98	82.65
18.50	60.45	61.76	63.08	64.40	65.72	67.04	68.36	69.68	70.99	72.31	73.63	74.95	76.27	77.59	78.90	81.54
18.75	59.63	60.93	62.23	63.53	64.84	66.14	67.44	68.74	70.04	71.35	72.65	73.95	75.25	76.56	77.86	80.46
19.00	58.83	60.11	61.40	62.69	63.97	65.26	66.55	67.83	69.12	70.41	71.69	72.98	74.27	75.55	76.84	79.41
20.00	55.82	57.05	58.28	59.50	60.73	61.96	63.18	64.41	65.64	66.87	68.09	69.32	70.55	71.77	73.00	75.46
25.00	44.40	45.39	46.38	47.38	48.37	49.36	50.36	51.35	52.34	53.33	54.33	55.32	56.31	57.31	58.30	60.28
30.00	36.85	37.68	38.51	39.34	40.17	41.00	41.83	42.66	43.49	44.32	45.16	45.99	46.82	47.65	48.48	50.14

Description: This table shows the yield to maturity of a bond purchased at the price shown in the index.

Example: The yield to maturity of a 15.00 %, 21 year bond at a price of 125.00 is 11.76 %.

COUPON RATE, %

PRICE	11.00%	11.25%	11.50%	11.75%	12.00%	12.25%	12.50%	12.75%	13.00%	13.25%	13.50%	13.75%	14.00%	14.25%	14.50%	15.00%
250	2.11	2.24	2.38	2.51	2.64	2.77	2.90	3.03	3.16	3.29	3.42	3.55	3.68	3.80	3.93	4.18
240	2.44	2.57	2.71	2.84	2.98	3.11	3.24	3.38	3.51	3.64	3.78	3.91	4.04	4.17	4.30	4.56
230	2.78	2.92	3.06	3.20	3.33	3.47	3.61	3.75	3.88	4.02	4.15	4.29	4.42	4.56	4.69	4.96
220	3.14	3.29	3.43	3.57	3.71	3.85	3.99	4.14	4.28	4.42	4.55	4.69	4.83	4.97	5.11	5.38
210	3.53	3.68	3.82	3.97	4.12	4.26	4.41	4.55	4.70	4.84	4.98	5.13	5.27	5.41	5.55	5.84
200	3.94	4.10	4.25	4.40	4.55	4.70	4.85	5.00	5.15	5.29	5.44	5.59	5.74	5.88	6.03	6.32
195	4.16	4.32	4.47	4.62	4.78	4.93	5.08	5.23	5.38	5.53	5.69	5.84	5.99	6.13	6.28	6.58
190	4.39	4.55	4.70	4.86	5.01	5.17	5.32	5.48	5.63	5.78	5.94	6.09	6.24	6.39	6.55	6.85
185	4.62	4.78	4.94	5.10	5.26	5.42	5.57	5.73	5.89	6.04	6.20	6.35	6.51	6.66	6.82	7.13
180	4.87	5.03	5.19	5.35	5.51	5.67	5.83	5.99	6.15	6.31	6.47	6.63	6.79	6.95	7.10	7.42
175	5.12	5.29	5.45	5.62	5.78	5.94	6.11	6.27	6.43	6.59	6.76	6.92	7.08	7.24	7.40	7.72
170	5.39	5.55	5.72	5.89	6.06	6.22	6.39	6.56	6.72	6.89	7.05	7.22	7.38	7.55	7.71	8.04
165	5.66	5.83	6.01	6.18	6.35	6.52	6.69	6.86	7.03	7.20	7.36	7.53	7.70	7.87	8.03	8.37
160	5.95	6.13	6.30	6.48	6.65	6.82	7.00	7.17	7.34	7.52	7.69	7.86	8.03	8.20	8.38	8.72
155	6.25	6.43	6.61	6.79	6.97	7.15	7.32	7.50	7.68	7.85	8.03	8.21	8.38	8.56	8.73	9.08
150	6.57	6.75	6.94	7.12	7.30	7.48	7.67	7.85	8.03	8.21	8.39	8.57	8.75	8.93	9.11	9.47
145	6.90	7.09	7.28	7.47	7.65	7.84	8.03	8.21	8.40	8.58	8.77	8.95	9.14	9.32	9.51	9.87
140	7.25	7.45	7.64	7.83	8.02	8.21	8.41	8.60	8.79	8.98	9.17	9.36	9.55	9.74	9.93	10.30
135	7.63	7.82	8.02	8.22	8.41	8.61	8.81	9.00	9.20	9.40	9.59	9.79	9.98	10.18	10.37	10.76
130	8.02	8.22	8.42	8.63	8.83	9.03	9.23	9.44	9.64	9.84	10.04	10.24	10.44	10.64	10.84	11.24
125	8.43	8.64	8.85	9.06	9.27	9.48	9.69	9.90	10.10	10.31	10.52	10.73	10.93	11.14	11.35	11.76
120	8.88	9.09	9.31	9.52	9.74	9.96	10.17	10.39	10.60	10.82	11.03	11.24	11.46	11.67	11.89	12.31
115	9.35	9.57	9.80	10.02	10.24	10.47	10.69	10.91	11.13	11.36	11.58	11.80	12.02	12.24	12.46	12.91
113	9.55	9.78	10.00	10.23	10.45	10.68	10.91	11.13	11.36	11.58	11.81	12.03	12.26	12.48	12.71	13.16
112	9.65	9.88	10.11	10.33	10.56	10.79	11.02	11.24	11.47	11.70	11.93	12.15	12.38	12.61	12.83	13.29
111	9.75	9.98	10.21	10.44	10.67	10.90	11.13	11.36	11.59	11.82	12.05	12.27	12.50	12.73	12.96	13.42
110	9.86	10.09	10.32	10.55	10.78	11.01	11.24	11.48	11.71	11.94	12.17	12.40	12.63	12.86	13.09	13.55
109	9.96	10.20	10.43	10.66	10.90	11.13	11.36	11.59	11.83	12.06	12.29	12.52	12.75	12.99	13.22	13.68
108	10.07	10.31	10.54	10.78	11.01	11.24	11.48	11.71	11.95	12.18	12.42	12.65	12.88	13.12	13.35	13.82
107	10.18	10.42	10.65	10.89	11.13	11.36	11.60	11.83	12.07	12.31	12.54	12.78	13.01	13.25	13.49	13.96
106	10.29	10.53	10.77	11.01	11.24	11.48	11.72	11.96	12.20	12.43	12.67	12.91	13.15	13.39	13.62	14.10
105	10.40	10.64	10.88	11.12	11.36	11.60	11.84	12.08	12.32	12.56	12.80	13.04	13.28	13.52	13.76	14.24
104	10.52	10.76	11.00	11.24	11.49	11.73	11.97	12.21	12.45	12.70	12.94	13.18	13.42	13.66	13.90	14.39
103	10.63	10.88	11.12	11.37	11.61	11.85	12.10	12.34	12.59	12.83	13.07	13.32	13.56	13.80	14.05	14.53
102	10.75	11.00	11.24	11.49	11.74	11.98	12.23	12.47	12.72	12.97	13.21	13.46	13.70	13.95	14.19	14.69
101	10.87	11.12	11.37	11.62	11.86	12.11	12.36	12.61	12.86	13.10	13.35	13.60	13.85	14.10	14.34	14.84
100	11.00	11.25	11.50	11.75	12.00	12.25	12.50	12.75	13.00	13.25	13.50	13.75	14.00	14.25	14.50	15.00
99	11.12	11.37	11.62	11.88	12.13	12.38	12.63	12.88	13.14	13.39	13.64	13.89	14.15	14.40	14.65	15.15
98	11.25	11.50	11.75	12.01	12.26	12.52	12.77	13.03	13.28	13.53	13.79	14.04	14.30	14.55	14.81	15.32
97	11.37	11.63	11.89	12.14	12.40	12.66	12.91	13.17	13.43	13.68	13.94	14.20	14.45	14.71	14.97	15.48
96	11.50	11.76	12.02	12.28	12.54	12.80	13.06	13.32	13.57	13.83	14.09	14.35	14.61	14.87	15.13	15.65
95	11.64	11.90	12.16	12.42	12.68	12.94	13.20	13.47	13.73	13.99	14.25	14.51	14.77	15.03	15.30	15.82
94	11.77	12.04	12.30	12.56	12.83	13.09	13.35	13.62	13.88	14.14	14.41	14.67	14.94	15.20	15.47	15.99
93	11.91	12.18	12.44	12.71	12.97	13.24	13.51	13.77	14.04	14.30	14.57	14.84	15.10	15.37	15.64	16.17
92	12.05	12.32	12.59	12.85	13.12	13.39	13.66	13.93	14.20	14.47	14.74	15.01	15.28	15.55	15.81	16.35
91	12.19	12.46	12.73	13.01	13.28	13.55	13.82	14.09	14.36	14.63	14.91	15.18	15.45	15.72	15.99	16.54
90	12.34	12.61	12.88	13.16	13.43	13.71	13.98	14.25	14.53	14.80	15.08	15.35	15.63	15.90	16.18	16.73
89	12.49	12.76	13.04	13.31	13.59	13.87	14.14	14.42	14.70	14.98	15.25	15.53	15.81	16.09	16.36	16.92
88	12.64	12.92	13.20	13.47	13.75	14.03	14.31	14.59	14.87	15.15	15.43	15.71	15.99	16.27	16.56	17.12
87	12.79	13.07	13.35	13.64	13.92	14.20	14.48	14.77	15.05	15.33	15.62	15.90	16.18	16.47	16.75	17.32
86	12.95	13.23	13.52	13.80	14.09	14.37	14.66	14.94	15.23	15.52	15.80	16.09	16.38	16.66	16.95	17.52
85	13.11	13.40	13.68	13.97	14.26	14.55	14.84	15.13	15.41	15.70	15.99	16.28	16.57	16.86	17.15	17.73
84	13.27	13.56	13.85	14.14	14.44	14.73	15.02	15.31	15.60	15.90	16.19	16.48	16.77	17.07	17.36	17.95
83	13.44	13.73	14.03	14.32	14.62	14.91	15.21	15.50	15.80	16.09	16.39	16.68	16.98	17.28	17.57	18.17
82	13.61	13.91	14.20	14.50	14.80	15.10	15.40	15.69	15.99	16.29	16.59	16.89	17.19	17.49	17.79	18.39
81	13.78	14.08	14.39	14.69	14.99	15.29	15.59	15.89	16.19	16.50	16.80	17.10	17.41	17.71	18.01	18.62
80	13.96	14.27	14.57	14.87	15.18	15.48	15.79	16.09	16.40	16.71	17.01	17.32	17.63	17.93	18.24	18.85
79	14.14	14.45	14.76	15.07	15.38	15.68	15.99	16.30	16.61	16.92	17.23	17.54	17.85	18.16	18.47	19.09
78	14.33	14.64	14.95	15.26	15.58	15.89	16.20	16.51	16.83	17.14	17.45	17.77	18.08	18.40	18.71	19.34
77	14.52	14.84	15.15	15.47	15.78	16.10	16.41	16.73	17.05	17.36	17.68	18.00	18.32	18.64	18.96	19.59
76	14.72	15.03	15.35	15.67	15.99	16.31	16.63	16.95	17.27	17.59	17.92	18.24	18.56	18.88	19.21	19.85
75	14.92	15.24	15.56	15.88	16.21	16.53	16.86	17.18	17.51	17.83	18.16	18.48	18.81	19.14	19.46	20.12
74	15.12	15.45	15.77	16.10	16.43	16.76	17.09	17.41	17.74	18.07	18.40	18.73	19.06	19.39	19.73	20.39
73	15.33	15.66	15.99	16.32	16.66	16.99	17.32	17.65	17.99	18.32	18.66	18.99	19.32	19.66	20.00	20.67
70	15.99	16.34	16.68	17.02	17.37	17.72	18.06	18.41	18.76	19.10	19.45	19.80	20.15	20.50	20.85	21.55
65	17.22	17.59	17.96	18.33	18.70	19.07	19.44	19.82	20.19	20.56	20.94	21.31	21.69	22.07	22.44	23.20
60	18.63	19.03	19.43	19.83	20.23	20.64	21.04	21.45	21.85	22.26	22.66	23.07	23.48	23.89	24.29	25.11
55	20.29	20.72	21.16	21.60	22.04	22.48	22.92	23.36	23.81	24.25	24.69	25.14	25.58	26.03	26.48	27.37

Description: This table shows the price to pay for a bond at the yield rate. The yield is to maturity.

Example: The price of a 6.75 %, 22 year bond to yield 8 % to maturity is $ 87.16.

							COUPON RATE, %									
YIELD	0.00%	1.00%	2.00%	3.00%	4.00%	4.25%	4.50%	4.75%	5.00%	5.25%	5.50%	5.75%	6.00%	6.25%	6.50%	6.75%
0.00	100.00	122.00	144.00	166.00	188.00	193.50	199.00	204.50	210.00	215.50	221.00	226.50	232.00	237.50	243.00	248.50
1.00	80.30	100.00	119.70	139.41	159.11	164.04	168.96	173.89	178.82	183.74	188.67	193.59	198.52	203.45	208.37	213.30
2.00	64.54	82.27	100.00	117.73	135.46	139.89	144.32	148.75	153.18	157.62	162.05	166.48	170.91	175.34	179.77	184.21
3.00	51.94	67.96	83.98	100.00	116.02	120.03	124.03	128.04	132.04	136.05	140.05	144.06	148.06	152.07	156.07	160.08
4.00	41.84	56.38	70.92	85.46	100.00	103.63	107.27	110.90	114.54	118.17	121.81	125.44	129.08	132.71	136.35	139.98
4.25	39.65	53.85	68.05	82.25	96.45	100.00	103.55	107.10	110.65	114.20	117.75	121.30	124.85	128.40	131.95	135.50
4.50	37.57	51.44	65.32	79.19	93.06	96.53	100.00	103.47	106.94	110.41	113.87	117.34	120.81	124.28	127.75	131.22
4.75	35.60	49.16	62.72	76.27	89.83	93.22	96.61	100.00	103.39	106.78	110.17	113.56	116.95	120.34	123.73	127.12
5.00	33.74	46.99	60.24	73.50	86.75	90.06	93.37	96.69	100.00	103.31	106.63	109.94	113.25	116.56	119.88	123.19
5.25	31.98	44.94	57.89	70.85	83.80	87.04	90.28	93.52	96.76	100.00	103.24	106.48	109.72	112.96	116.20	119.43
5.50	30.31	42.98	55.65	68.32	80.99	84.16	87.33	90.50	93.66	96.83	100.00	103.17	106.34	109.50	112.67	115.84
5.75	28.73	41.13	53.52	65.92	78.31	81.41	84.51	87.61	90.70	93.80	96.90	100.00	103.10	106.20	109.30	112.39
6.00	27.24	39.36	51.49	63.62	75.75	78.78	81.81	84.84	87.87	90.90	93.94	96.97	100.00	103.03	106.06	109.10
6.25	25.82	37.69	49.56	61.43	73.30	76.26	79.23	82.20	85.16	88.13	91.10	94.07	97.03	100.00	102.97	105.93
6.50	24.48	36.10	47.72	59.34	70.95	73.86	76.76	79.67	82.57	85.48	88.38	91.29	94.19	97.10	100.00	102.90
6.75	23.21	34.59	45.96	57.34	68.72	71.56	74.40	77.25	80.09	82.94	85.78	88.62	91.47	94.31	97.16	100.00
7.00	22.01	33.15	44.29	55.43	66.58	69.36	72.15	74.93	77.72	80.50	83.29	86.07	88.86	91.64	94.43	97.21
7.25	20.87	31.79	42.70	53.61	64.53	67.26	69.99	72.71	75.44	78.17	80.90	83.63	86.36	89.09	91.81	94.54
7.50	19.79	30.49	41.18	51.88	62.57	65.24	67.92	70.59	73.26	75.94	78.61	81.29	83.96	86.63	89.31	91.98
7.75	18.77	29.25	39.73	50.22	60.70	63.32	65.94	68.56	71.18	73.80	76.42	79.04	81.66	84.28	86.90	89.52
8.00	17.80	28.08	38.35	48.63	58.90	61.47	64.04	66.61	69.18	71.75	74.31	76.88	79.45	82.02	84.59	87.16
8.25	16.89	26.96	37.04	47.11	57.18	59.70	62.22	64.74	67.26	69.78	72.30	74.81	77.33	79.85	82.37	84.89
8.50	16.02	25.90	35.78	45.66	55.54	58.01	60.48	62.95	65.42	67.89	70.36	72.83	75.30	77.77	80.24	82.71
8.75	15.20	24.89	34.58	44.27	53.96	56.39	58.81	61.23	63.66	66.08	68.50	70.92	73.35	75.77	78.19	80.62
9.00	14.42	23.93	33.44	42.94	52.45	54.83	57.21	59.59	61.96	64.34	66.72	69.10	71.47	73.85	76.23	78.60
9.25	13.68	23.01	32.34	41.67	51.01	53.34	55.67	58.01	60.34	62.67	65.00	67.34	69.67	72.00	74.34	76.67
9.50	12.98	22.14	31.30	40.46	49.62	51.91	54.20	56.49	58.78	61.07	63.36	65.65	67.94	70.23	72.52	74.81
9.75	12.31	21.31	30.30	39.29	48.29	50.54	52.78	55.03	57.28	59.53	61.78	64.03	66.27	68.52	70.77	73.02
10.00	11.69	20.52	29.35	38.18	47.01	49.22	51.43	53.64	55.84	58.05	60.26	62.47	64.67	66.88	69.09	71.30
10.25	11.09	19.76	28.44	37.11	45.79	47.96	50.12	52.29	54.46	56.63	58.80	60.97	63.13	65.30	67.47	69.64
10.50	10.53	19.05	27.57	36.09	44.61	46.74	48.87	51.00	53.13	55.26	57.39	59.52	61.65	63.78	65.91	68.04
10.75	9.99	18.36	26.74	35.11	43.48	45.58	47.67	49.76	51.85	53.95	56.04	58.13	60.23	62.32	64.41	66.51
11.00	9.48	17.71	25.94	34.17	42.40	44.45	46.51	48.57	50.63	52.68	54.74	56.80	58.86	60.91	62.97	65.03
11.25	9.00	17.09	25.18	33.27	41.36	43.38	45.40	47.42	49.44	51.47	53.49	55.51	57.53	59.56	61.58	63.60
11.50	8.54	16.50	24.45	32.40	40.35	42.34	44.33	46.32	48.31	50.30	52.28	54.27	56.26	58.25	60.24	62.22
11.75	8.11	15.93	23.75	31.57	39.39	41.35	43.30	45.26	47.21	49.17	51.12	53.08	55.03	56.99	58.94	60.90
12.00	7.70	15.39	23.08	30.78	38.47	40.39	42.31	44.24	46.16	48.08	50.00	51.93	53.85	55.77	57.70	59.62
12.25	7.31	14.88	22.44	30.01	37.58	39.47	41.36	43.25	45.14	47.04	48.93	50.82	52.71	54.60	56.49	58.38
12.50	6.94	14.39	21.83	29.28	36.72	38.58	40.44	42.30	44.17	46.03	47.89	49.75	51.61	53.47	55.33	57.19
12.75	6.59	13.92	21.24	28.57	35.90	37.73	39.56	41.39	43.22	45.05	46.89	48.72	50.55	52.38	54.21	56.04
13.00	6.26	13.47	20.68	27.89	35.10	36.91	38.71	40.51	42.31	44.12	45.92	47.72	49.52	51.33	53.13	54.93
13.25	5.95	13.04	20.14	27.24	34.34	36.11	37.89	39.66	41.44	43.21	44.99	46.76	48.54	50.31	52.09	53.86
13.50	5.65	12.64	19.63	26.61	33.60	35.35	37.10	38.85	40.59	42.34	44.09	45.83	47.58	49.33	51.08	52.82
13.75	5.36	12.25	19.13	26.01	32.89	34.61	36.34	38.06	39.78	41.50	43.22	44.94	46.66	48.38	50.10	51.82
14.00	5.09	11.87	18.65	25.43	32.21	33.91	35.60	37.29	38.99	40.68	42.38	44.07	45.77	47.46	49.16	50.85
14.25	4.84	11.52	18.20	24.87	31.55	33.22	34.89	36.56	38.23	39.90	41.57	43.24	44.91	46.58	48.25	49.92
14.50	4.60	11.18	17.76	24.34	30.92	32.56	34.21	35.85	37.49	39.14	40.78	42.43	44.07	45.72	47.36	49.01
14.75	4.37	10.85	17.33	23.82	30.30	31.92	33.54	35.16	36.79	38.41	40.03	41.65	43.27	44.89	46.51	48.13
15.00	4.15	10.54	16.93	23.32	29.71	31.31	32.90	34.50	36.10	37.70	39.29	40.89	42.49	44.09	45.68	47.28
15.25	3.94	10.24	16.54	22.84	29.14	30.71	32.29	33.86	35.44	37.01	38.59	40.16	41.74	43.31	44.89	46.46
15.50	3.75	9.96	16.17	22.38	28.59	30.14	31.69	33.24	34.80	36.35	37.90	39.45	41.01	42.56	44.11	45.66
15.75	3.56	9.68	15.81	21.93	28.05	29.58	31.11	32.65	34.18	35.71	37.24	38.77	40.30	41.83	43.36	44.89
16.00	3.38	9.42	15.46	21.50	27.54	29.05	30.56	32.07	33.58	35.09	36.60	38.10	39.61	41.12	42.63	44.14
16.25	3.22	9.17	15.13	21.08	27.04	28.53	30.02	31.51	33.00	34.48	35.97	37.46	38.95	40.44	41.93	43.42
16.50	3.06	8.93	14.81	20.68	26.56	28.03	29.50	30.96	32.43	33.90	35.37	36.84	38.31	39.78	41.25	42.71
16.75	2.90	8.70	14.50	20.30	26.09	27.54	28.99	30.44	31.89	33.34	34.79	36.24	37.69	39.13	40.58	42.03
17.00	2.76	8.48	14.20	19.92	25.64	27.07	28.50	29.93	31.36	32.79	34.22	35.65	37.08	38.51	39.94	41.37
17.25	2.62	8.27	13.91	19.56	25.20	26.62	28.03	29.44	30.85	32.26	33.67	35.08	36.49	37.91	39.32	40.73
17.50	2.50	8.07	13.64	19.21	24.78	26.17	27.57	28.96	30.35	31.75	33.14	34.53	35.93	37.32	38.71	40.10
17.75	2.37	7.87	13.37	18.87	24.37	25.75	27.12	28.50	29.87	31.25	32.62	34.00	35.37	36.75	38.12	39.50
18.00	2.26	7.69	13.12	18.55	23.98	25.33	26.69	28.05	29.41	30.76	32.12	33.48	34.84	36.19	37.55	38.91
18.25	2.14	7.51	12.87	18.23	23.59	24.93	26.27	27.61	28.95	30.29	31.64	32.98	34.32	35.66	37.00	38.34
18.50	2.04	7.33	12.63	17.92	23.22	24.54	25.87	27.19	28.52	29.84	31.16	32.49	33.81	35.13	36.46	37.78
18.75	1.94	7.17	12.40	17.63	22.86	24.17	25.47	26.78	28.09	29.40	30.70	32.01	33.32	34.63	35.93	37.24
19.00	1.84	7.01	12.18	17.34	22.51	23.80	25.09	26.38	27.67	28.97	30.26	31.55	32.84	34.13	35.42	36.72
20.00	1.51	6.43	11.36	16.28	21.21	22.44	23.67	24.90	26.13	27.36	28.59	29.83	31.06	32.29	33.52	34.75
25.00	.56	4.54	8.52	12.49	16.47	17.47	18.46	19.45	20.45	21.44	22.44	23.43	24.43	25.42	26.42	27.41
30.00	.21	3.54	6.87	10.19	13.52	14.35	15.18	16.01	16.84	17.68	18.51	19.34	20.17	21.00	21.83	22.67

Description: This table shows the yield to maturity of a bond purchased at the price shown in the index.

Example: The yield to maturity of a 6.75 %, 22 year bond at a price of 80.00 is 8.82 %.

COUPON RATE, %

PRICE	0.00%	1.00%	2.00%	3.00%	4.00%	4.25%	4.50%	4.75%	5.00%	5.25%	5.50%	5.75%	6.00%	6.25%	6.50%	6.75%
100	0.00	1.00	2.00	3.00	4.00	4.25	4.50	4.75	5.00	5.25	5.50	5.75	6.00	6.25	6.50	6.75
99	.04	1.05	2.05	3.06	4.06	4.32	4.57	4.82	5.07	5.32	5.57	5.83	6.08	6.33	6.58	6.83
98	.09	1.10	2.11	3.12	4.13	4.39	4.64	4.89	5.15	5.40	5.66	5.91	6.16	6.42	6.67	6.92
97	.13	1.15	2.17	3.19	4.21	4.46	4.72	4.97	5.23	5.48	5.74	5.99	6.25	6.50	6.76	7.01
96	.18	1.20	2.23	3.25	4.28	4.53	4.79	5.05	5.31	5.56	5.82	6.08	6.33	6.59	6.85	7.11
95	.23	1.26	2.29	3.32	4.35	4.61	4.87	5.13	5.39	5.64	5.90	6.16	6.42	6.68	6.94	7.20
94	.28	1.31	2.35	3.38	4.42	4.69	4.95	5.21	5.47	5.73	5.99	6.25	6.51	6.77	7.04	7.30
93	.33	1.36	2.41	3.45	4.50	4.76	5.02	5.29	5.55	5.81	6.08	6.34	6.60	6.87	7.13	7.39
92	.37	1.42	2.47	3.52	4.58	4.84	5.10	5.37	5.63	5.90	6.16	6.43	6.70	6.96	7.23	7.49
91	.42	1.48	2.53	3.59	4.65	4.92	5.19	5.45	5.72	5.99	6.25	6.52	6.79	7.06	7.33	7.59
90	.47	1.53	2.59	3.66	4.73	5.00	5.27	5.54	5.81	6.08	6.34	6.61	6.88	7.15	7.42	7.70
89	.53	1.59	2.66	3.73	4.81	5.08	5.35	5.62	5.89	6.17	6.44	6.71	6.98	7.25	7.53	7.80
88	.58	1.65	2.72	3.81	4.89	5.16	5.44	5.71	5.98	6.26	6.53	6.81	7.08	7.35	7.63	7.90
87	.63	1.71	2.79	3.88	4.97	5.25	5.52	5.80	6.07	6.35	6.63	6.90	7.18	7.46	7.73	8.01
86	.68	1.77	2.86	3.95	5.06	5.33	5.61	5.89	6.17	6.44	6.72	7.00	7.28	7.56	7.84	8.12
85	.74	1.83	2.92	4.03	5.14	5.42	5.70	5.98	6.26	6.54	6.82	7.10	7.39	7.67	7.95	8.23
84	.79	1.89	2.99	4.11	5.23	5.51	5.79	6.07	6.36	6.64	6.92	7.21	7.49	7.78	8.06	8.35
83	.84	1.95	3.06	4.19	5.32	5.60	5.88	6.17	6.45	6.74	7.02	7.31	7.60	7.89	8.17	8.46
82	.90	2.01	3.13	4.26	5.40	5.69	5.98	6.26	6.55	6.84	7.13	7.42	7.71	8.00	8.29	8.58
81	.96	2.08	3.21	4.35	5.49	5.78	6.07	6.36	6.65	6.94	7.23	7.53	7.82	8.11	8.40	8.70
80	1.01	2.14	3.28	4.43	5.59	5.88	6.17	6.46	6.75	7.05	7.34	7.64	7.93	8.23	8.52	8.82
79	1.07	2.21	3.35	4.51	5.68	5.97	6.27	6.56	6.86	7.15	7.45	7.75	8.05	8.35	8.65	8.95
78	1.13	2.27	3.43	4.60	5.77	6.07	6.37	6.67	6.96	7.26	7.56	7.86	8.17	8.47	8.77	9.07
77	1.19	2.34	3.50	4.68	5.87	6.17	6.47	6.77	7.07	7.37	7.68	7.98	8.29	8.59	8.90	9.20
76	1.25	2.41	3.58	4.77	5.97	6.27	6.57	6.88	7.18	7.49	7.79	8.10	8.41	8.72	9.02	9.33
75	1.31	2.48	3.66	4.86	6.07	6.37	6.68	6.99	7.29	7.60	7.91	8.22	8.53	8.84	9.16	9.47
74	1.37	2.55	3.74	4.95	6.17	6.48	6.79	7.10	7.41	7.72	8.03	8.35	8.66	8.98	9.29	9.61
73	1.43	2.62	3.82	5.04	6.28	6.59	6.90	7.21	7.53	7.84	8.16	8.47	8.79	9.11	9.43	9.75
72	1.49	2.69	3.90	5.13	6.38	6.70	7.01	7.33	7.65	7.96	8.28	8.60	8.92	9.25	9.57	9.89
71	1.56	2.76	3.99	5.23	6.49	6.81	7.13	7.45	7.77	8.09	8.41	8.73	9.06	9.39	9.71	10.04
70	1.62	2.84	4.07	5.33	6.60	6.92	7.24	7.57	7.89	8.22	8.54	8.87	9.20	9.53	9.86	10.19
69	1.69	2.91	4.16	5.43	6.71	7.04	7.36	7.69	8.02	8.35	8.68	9.01	9.34	9.67	10.01	10.34
68	1.76	2.99	4.25	5.53	6.83	7.16	7.48	7.82	8.15	8.48	8.81	9.15	9.49	9.82	10.16	10.50
67	1.82	3.07	4.34	5.63	6.94	7.28	7.61	7.94	8.28	8.62	8.95	9.29	9.63	9.98	10.32	10.66
66	1.89	3.15	4.43	5.74	7.06	7.40	7.74	8.08	8.42	8.76	9.10	9.44	9.79	10.13	10.48	10.83
65	1.96	3.23	4.52	5.84	7.19	7.53	7.87	8.21	8.55	8.90	9.25	9.59	9.94	10.29	10.65	11.00
64	2.03	3.31	4.62	5.95	7.31	7.66	8.00	8.35	8.70	9.05	9.40	9.75	10.10	10.46	10.82	11.17
63	2.11	3.40	4.72	6.06	7.44	7.79	8.14	8.49	8.84	9.20	9.55	9.91	10.27	10.63	10.99	11.35
62	2.18	3.48	4.82	6.18	7.57	7.92	8.28	8.63	8.99	9.35	9.71	10.07	10.44	10.80	11.17	11.54
61	2.25	3.57	4.92	6.30	7.70	8.06	8.42	8.78	9.14	9.51	9.87	10.24	10.61	10.98	11.35	11.73
60	2.33	3.66	5.02	6.41	7.84	8.20	8.57	8.93	9.30	9.67	10.04	10.41	10.79	11.16	11.54	11.92
59	2.41	3.75	5.13	6.54	7.98	8.35	8.72	9.09	9.46	9.83	10.21	10.59	10.97	11.35	11.73	12.12
58	2.49	3.84	5.23	6.66	8.12	8.50	8.87	9.25	9.62	10.00	10.39	10.77	11.16	11.54	11.93	12.32
57	2.57	3.94	5.34	6.79	8.27	8.65	9.03	9.41	9.79	10.18	10.57	10.96	11.35	11.74	12.14	12.54
56	2.65	4.03	5.46	6.92	8.42	8.81	9.19	9.58	9.97	10.36	10.75	11.15	11.55	11.95	12.35	12.75
55	2.73	4.13	5.57	7.05	8.58	8.97	9.36	9.75	10.15	10.54	10.94	11.35	11.75	12.16	12.57	12.98
54	2.82	4.23	5.69	7.19	8.74	9.13	9.53	9.93	10.33	10.73	11.14	11.55	11.96	12.38	12.79	13.21
53	2.90	4.33	5.81	7.33	8.90	9.30	9.71	10.11	10.52	10.93	11.35	11.76	12.18	12.60	13.03	13.45
52	2.99	4.44	5.93	7.48	9.07	9.48	9.89	10.30	10.72	11.13	11.56	11.98	12.41	12.83	13.27	13.70
51	3.08	4.54	6.06	7.63	9.25	9.66	10.08	10.50	10.92	11.34	11.77	12.20	12.64	13.07	13.51	13.96
50	3.17	4.65	6.19	7.78	9.43	9.85	10.27	10.70	11.13	11.56	12.00	12.44	12.88	13.32	13.77	14.22
49	3.26	4.76	6.32	7.94	9.61	10.04	10.47	10.90	11.34	11.78	12.23	12.68	13.13	13.58	14.04	14.50
48	3.36	4.88	6.46	8.10	9.80	10.24	10.68	11.12	11.56	12.01	12.47	12.92	13.38	13.85	14.31	14.78
47	3.46	4.99	6.60	8.26	10.00	10.44	10.89	11.34	11.79	12.25	12.72	13.18	13.65	14.12	14.60	15.08
46	3.56	5.11	6.74	8.44	10.20	10.65	11.11	11.57	12.03	12.50	12.97	13.45	13.93	14.41	14.90	15.39
45	3.66	5.24	6.89	8.61	10.41	10.87	11.34	11.81	12.28	12.76	13.24	13.73	14.22	14.71	15.21	15.71
44	3.76	5.36	7.04	8.80	10.63	11.10	11.57	12.05	12.54	13.03	13.52	14.02	14.52	15.02	15.53	16.04
43	3.87	5.49	7.20	8.98	10.85	11.34	11.82	12.31	12.81	13.31	13.81	14.32	14.83	15.35	15.87	16.39
42	3.98	5.63	7.36	9.18	11.09	11.58	12.08	12.58	13.08	13.59	14.11	14.63	15.16	15.69	16.22	16.76
41	4.09	5.76	7.53	9.38	11.33	11.83	12.34	12.86	13.37	13.90	14.43	14.96	15.50	16.04	16.59	17.14
40	4.20	5.90	7.70	9.59	11.59	12.10	12.62	13.14	13.68	14.21	14.75	15.30	15.85	16.41	16.97	17.54
39	4.32	6.05	7.88	9.81	11.85	12.38	12.91	13.45	13.99	14.54	15.10	15.66	16.23	16.80	17.37	17.96
35	4.82	6.68	8.66	10.77	13.03	13.61	14.21	14.81	15.41	16.03	16.65	17.28	17.92	18.56	19.21	19.86
30	5.54	7.59	9.82	12.25	14.87	15.56	16.25	16.96	17.68	18.41	19.14	19.89	20.64	21.40	22.17	22.95
25	6.40	8.72	11.31	14.19	17.37	18.20	19.06	19.92	20.81	21.70	22.61	23.53	24.46	25.39	26.34	27.29
20	7.45	10.17	13.31	16.94	21.04	22.13	23.24	24.37	25.52	26.68	27.86	29.04	30.24	31.45	32.66	33.88
15	8.81	12.18	16.34	21.40	27.23	28.77	30.34	31.93	33.54	35.16	36.79	38.42	40.07	41.72	43.37	45.03
10	10.74	15.46	22.02	30.53	40.11	42.57	45.05	47.53	50.02	52.51	55.01	57.50	60.00	62.50	65.00	67.50

Description: This table shows the price to pay for a bond at the yield rate. The yield is to maturity.

Example: The price of a 10.75 %, 22 year bond to yield 8 % to maturity is $ 128.25.

COUPON RATE, %

YIELD	7.00%	7.25%	7.50%	7.75%	8.00%	8.25%	8.50%	8.75%	9.00%	9.25%	9.50%	9.75%	10.00%	10.25%	10.50%	10.75%
0.00	254.00	259.50	265.00	270.50	276.00	281.50	287.00	292.50	298.00	303.50	309.00	314.50	320.00	325.50	331.00	336.50
1.00	218.22	223.15	228.08	233.00	237.93	242.85	247.78	252.71	257.63	262.56	267.48	272.41	277.34	282.26	287.19	292.12
2.00	188.64	193.07	197.50	201.93	206.37	210.80	215.23	219.66	224.09	228.53	232.96	237.39	241.82	246.25	250.69	255.12
3.00	164.08	168.09	172.09	176.10	180.10	184.11	188.11	192.12	196.12	200.13	204.13	208.14	212.14	216.15	220.15	224.16
4.00	143.62	147.25	150.89	154.52	158.16	161.79	165.43	169.06	172.70	176.33	179.97	183.60	187.24	190.87	194.51	198.14
4.25	139.05	142.60	146.15	149.70	153.25	156.80	160.35	163.91	167.46	171.01	174.56	178.11	181.66	185.21	188.76	192.31
4.50	134.68	138.15	141.62	145.09	148.56	152.03	155.50	158.97	162.43	165.90	169.37	172.84	176.31	179.77	183.24	186.71
4.75	130.50	133.89	137.28	140.67	144.06	147.45	150.84	154.23	157.62	161.01	164.40	167.79	171.18	174.57	177.96	181.35
5.00	126.50	129.82	133.13	136.44	139.76	143.07	146.38	149.69	153.01	156.32	159.63	162.95	166.26	169.57	172.89	176.20
5.25	122.67	125.91	129.15	132.39	135.63	138.87	142.11	145.35	148.59	151.83	155.06	158.30	161.54	164.78	168.02	171.26
5.50	119.01	122.17	125.34	128.51	131.68	134.84	138.01	141.18	144.35	147.52	150.68	153.85	157.02	160.19	163.35	166.52
5.75	115.49	118.59	121.69	124.79	127.89	130.99	134.08	137.18	140.28	143.38	146.48	149.58	152.68	155.77	158.87	161.97
6.00	112.13	115.16	118.19	121.22	124.25	127.29	130.32	133.35	136.38	139.41	142.44	145.48	148.51	151.54	154.57	157.60
6.25	108.90	111.87	114.84	117.80	120.77	123.74	126.70	129.67	132.64	135.61	138.57	141.54	144.51	147.47	150.44	153.41
6.50	105.81	108.71	111.62	114.52	117.43	120.33	123.24	126.14	129.05	131.95	134.85	137.76	140.66	143.57	146.47	149.38
6.75	102.84	105.69	108.53	111.38	114.22	117.06	119.91	122.75	125.60	128.44	131.28	134.13	136.97	139.82	142.66	145.50
7.00	100.00	102.79	105.57	108.36	111.14	113.93	116.71	119.50	122.28	125.07	127.85	130.64	133.42	136.21	138.99	141.78
7.25	97.27	100.00	102.73	105.46	108.19	110.91	113.64	116.37	119.10	121.83	124.56	127.29	130.01	132.74	135.47	138.20
7.50	94.65	97.33	100.00	102.67	105.35	108.02	110.69	113.37	116.04	118.71	121.39	124.06	126.74	129.41	132.08	134.76
7.75	92.14	94.76	97.38	100.00	102.62	105.24	107.86	110.48	113.10	115.72	118.34	120.96	123.58	126.20	128.82	131.44
8.00	89.73	92.29	94.86	97.43	100.00	102.57	105.14	107.71	110.27	112.84	115.41	117.98	120.55	123.12	125.69	128.25
8.25	87.41	89.93	92.44	94.96	97.48	100.00	102.52	105.04	107.56	110.07	112.59	115.11	117.63	120.15	122.67	125.19
8.50	85.18	87.65	90.12	92.59	95.06	97.53	100.00	102.47	104.94	107.41	109.88	112.35	114.82	117.29	119.76	122.23
8.75	83.04	85.46	87.89	90.31	92.73	95.15	97.58	100.00	102.42	104.85	107.27	109.69	112.11	114.54	116.96	119.38
9.00	80.98	83.36	85.74	88.11	90.49	92.87	95.25	97.62	100.00	102.38	104.75	107.13	109.51	111.89	114.26	116.64
9.25	79.00	81.34	83.67	86.00	88.33	90.67	93.00	95.33	97.67	100.00	102.33	104.67	107.00	109.33	111.67	114.00
9.50	77.10	79.39	81.68	83.97	86.26	88.55	90.84	93.13	95.42	97.71	100.00	102.29	104.58	106.87	109.16	111.45
9.75	75.27	77.52	79.76	82.01	84.26	86.51	88.76	91.01	93.25	95.50	97.75	100.00	102.25	104.50	106.75	108.99
10.00	73.51	75.71	77.92	80.13	82.34	84.55	86.75	88.96	91.17	93.38	95.58	97.79	100.00	102.21	104.42	106.62
10.25	71.81	73.98	76.15	78.31	80.48	82.65	84.82	86.99	89.16	91.33	93.49	95.66	97.83	100.00	102.17	104.34
10.50	70.18	72.31	74.44	76.57	78.70	80.83	82.96	85.09	87.22	89.35	91.48	93.61	95.74	97.87	100.00	102.13
10.75	68.60	70.69	72.79	74.88	76.97	79.07	81.16	83.25	85.35	87.44	89.53	91.63	93.72	95.81	97.91	100.00
11.00	67.08	69.14	71.20	73.26	75.31	77.37	79.43	81.48	83.54	85.60	87.66	89.71	91.77	93.83	95.89	97.94
11.25	65.62	67.64	69.67	71.69	73.71	75.73	77.76	79.78	81.80	83.82	85.84	87.87	89.89	91.91	93.93	95.96
11.50	64.21	66.20	68.19	70.18	72.17	74.15	76.14	78.13	80.12	82.11	84.09	86.08	88.07	90.06	92.05	94.04
11.75	62.85	64.81	66.76	68.72	70.67	72.63	74.58	76.54	78.49	80.45	82.40	84.36	86.31	88.27	90.22	92.18
12.00	61.54	63.46	65.39	67.31	69.23	71.16	73.08	75.00	76.93	78.85	80.77	82.69	84.62	86.54	88.46	90.39
12.25	60.28	62.17	64.06	65.95	67.84	69.73	71.63	73.52	75.41	77.30	79.19	81.08	82.98	84.87	86.76	88.65
12.50	59.05	60.92	62.78	64.64	66.50	68.36	70.22	72.08	73.94	75.81	77.67	79.53	81.39	83.25	85.11	86.97
12.75	57.88	59.71	61.54	63.37	65.20	67.03	68.86	70.70	72.53	74.36	76.19	78.02	79.85	81.68	83.52	85.35
13.00	56.74	58.54	60.34	62.14	63.95	65.75	67.55	69.35	71.16	72.96	74.76	76.57	78.37	80.17	81.97	83.78
13.25	55.63	57.41	59.18	60.96	62.73	64.51	66.28	68.06	69.83	71.61	73.38	75.16	76.93	78.70	80.48	82.25
13.50	54.57	56.32	58.07	59.81	61.56	63.31	65.05	66.80	68.55	70.30	72.04	73.79	75.54	77.29	79.03	80.78
13.75	53.54	55.26	56.98	58.70	60.42	62.15	63.87	65.59	67.31	69.03	70.75	72.47	74.19	75.91	77.63	79.35
14.00	52.55	54.24	55.94	57.63	59.33	61.02	62.72	64.41	66.11	67.80	69.49	71.19	72.88	74.58	76.27	77.97
14.25	51.59	53.25	54.92	56.59	58.26	59.93	61.60	63.27	64.94	66.61	68.28	69.95	71.62	73.29	74.96	76.63
14.50	50.65	52.30	53.94	55.59	57.23	58.88	60.52	62.17	63.81	65.46	67.10	68.75	70.39	72.04	73.68	75.33
14.75	49.75	51.37	52.99	54.62	56.24	57.86	59.48	61.10	62.72	64.34	65.96	67.58	69.20	70.82	72.44	74.07
15.00	48.88	50.48	52.07	53.67	55.27	56.87	58.46	60.06	61.66	63.26	64.85	66.45	68.05	69.65	71.24	72.84
15.25	48.03	49.61	51.18	52.76	54.33	55.91	57.48	59.06	60.63	62.21	63.78	65.36	66.93	68.51	70.08	71.66
15.50	47.22	48.77	50.32	51.87	53.43	54.98	56.53	58.08	59.64	61.19	62.74	64.29	65.85	67.40	68.95	70.50
15.75	46.42	47.95	49.48	51.01	52.55	54.08	55.61	57.14	58.67	60.20	61.73	63.26	64.79	66.32	67.85	69.38
16.00	45.65	47.16	48.67	50.18	51.69	53.20	54.71	56.22	57.73	59.24	60.75	62.26	63.77	65.28	66.79	68.30
16.25	44.91	46.40	47.89	49.37	50.86	52.35	53.84	55.33	56.82	58.31	59.80	61.29	62.78	64.26	65.75	67.24
16.50	44.18	45.65	47.12	48.59	50.06	51.53	53.00	54.47	55.93	57.40	58.87	60.34	61.81	63.28	64.75	66.22
16.75	43.48	44.93	46.38	47.83	49.28	50.73	52.18	53.63	55.08	56.52	57.97	59.42	60.87	62.32	63.77	65.22
17.00	42.80	44.23	45.66	47.09	48.52	49.95	51.38	52.81	54.24	55.67	57.10	58.53	59.96	61.39	62.82	64.25
17.25	42.14	43.55	44.96	46.37	47.78	49.20	50.61	52.02	53.43	54.84	56.25	57.66	59.07	60.49	61.90	63.31
17.50	41.50	42.89	44.28	45.68	47.07	48.46	49.85	51.25	52.64	54.03	55.43	56.82	58.21	59.61	61.00	62.39
17.75	40.87	42.25	43.62	45.00	46.37	47.75	49.12	50.50	51.87	53.25	54.62	56.00	57.37	58.75	60.12	61.50
18.00	40.27	41.62	42.98	44.34	45.70	47.06	48.41	49.77	51.13	52.49	53.84	55.20	56.56	57.92	59.27	60.63
18.25	39.68	41.02	42.36	43.70	45.04	46.38	47.72	49.06	50.40	51.74	53.08	54.42	55.76	57.10	58.44	59.79
18.50	39.11	40.43	41.75	43.08	44.40	45.72	47.05	48.37	49.70	51.02	52.34	53.67	54.99	56.31	57.64	58.96
18.75	38.55	39.86	41.16	42.47	43.78	45.09	46.39	47.70	49.01	50.32	51.62	52.93	54.24	55.55	56.85	58.16
19.00	38.01	39.30	40.59	41.88	43.17	44.46	45.76	47.05	48.34	49.63	50.92	52.21	53.51	54.80	56.09	57.38
20.00	35.98	37.21	38.44	39.67	40.91	42.14	43.37	44.60	45.83	47.06	48.29	49.52	50.75	51.99	53.22	54.45
25.00	28.40	29.40	30.39	31.39	32.38	33.38	34.37	35.36	36.36	37.35	38.35	39.34	40.34	41.33	42.33	43.32
30.00	23.50	24.33	25.16	25.99	26.82	27.65	28.49	29.32	30.15	30.98	31.81	32.64	33.48	34.31	35.14	35.97

Description: This table shows the yield to maturity of a bond purchased at the price shown in the index.

Example: The yield to maturity of a 10.75 %, 22 year bond at a price of 111.00 is 9.54 %.

						COUPON RATE, %									
PRICE	7.00%	7.25%	7.50%	7.75%	8.00%	8.25%	8.50%	8.75%	9.00%	9.25%	9.50%	9.75%	10.00%	10.25%	10.50%	10.75%
165	2.95	3.13	3.31	3.49	3.66	3.84	4.02	4.19	4.37	4.54	4.71	4.89	5.06	5.23	5.41	5.58
160	3.18	3.36	3.54	3.72	3.90	4.08	4.26	4.44	4.62	4.80	4.98	5.15	5.33	5.51	5.68	5.86
155	3.42	3.60	3.79	3.97	4.15	4.34	4.52	4.70	4.89	5.07	5.25	5.43	5.61	5.79	5.97	6.15
150	3.66	3.85	4.04	4.23	4.42	4.60	4.79	4.98	5.16	5.35	5.53	5.72	5.90	6.09	6.27	6.46
145	3.92	4.11	4.31	4.50	4.69	4.88	5.07	5.27	5.46	5.65	5.84	6.02	6.21	6.40	6.59	6.78
140	4.19	4.39	4.59	4.78	4.98	5.18	5.37	5.57	5.76	5.96	6.15	6.35	6.54	6.73	6.93	7.12
135	4.48	4.68	4.88	5.08	5.28	5.49	5.69	5.89	6.09	6.29	6.49	6.68	6.88	7.08	7.28	7.48
130	4.78	4.98	5.19	5.40	5.60	5.81	6.02	6.22	6.43	6.63	6.84	7.04	7.25	7.45	7.65	7.86
125	5.09	5.31	5.52	5.73	5.94	6.15	6.37	6.58	6.79	7.00	7.21	7.42	7.63	7.84	8.05	8.26
122	5.29	5.51	5.72	5.94	6.16	6.37	6.59	6.80	7.02	7.23	7.45	7.66	7.87	8.09	8.30	8.51
121	5.36	5.58	5.79	6.01	6.23	6.45	6.66	6.88	7.09	7.31	7.53	7.74	7.96	8.17	8.39	8.60
120	5.43	5.65	5.86	6.08	6.30	6.52	6.74	6.96	7.17	7.39	7.61	7.82	8.04	8.26	8.47	8.69
119	5.50	5.72	5.94	6.16	6.38	6.60	6.82	7.03	7.25	7.47	7.69	7.91	8.13	8.34	8.56	8.78
118	5.57	5.79	6.01	6.23	6.45	6.67	6.89	7.11	7.33	7.55	7.77	7.99	8.21	8.43	8.65	8.87
117	5.64	5.86	6.08	6.31	6.53	6.75	6.97	7.19	7.42	7.64	7.86	8.08	8.30	8.52	8.74	8.96
116	5.71	5.93	6.16	6.38	6.60	6.83	7.05	7.28	7.50	7.72	7.94	8.17	8.39	8.61	8.83	9.05
115	5.78	6.01	6.23	6.46	6.68	6.91	7.13	7.36	7.58	7.81	8.03	8.25	8.48	8.70	8.93	9.15
114	5.85	6.08	6.31	6.54	6.76	6.99	7.22	7.44	7.67	7.89	8.12	8.34	8.57	8.79	9.02	9.24
113	5.93	6.16	6.39	6.61	6.84	7.07	7.30	7.53	7.75	7.98	8.21	8.44	8.66	8.89	9.12	9.34
112	6.00	6.23	6.46	6.69	6.92	7.15	7.38	7.61	7.84	8.07	8.30	8.53	8.76	8.98	9.21	9.44
111	6.08	6.31	6.54	6.78	7.01	7.24	7.47	7.70	7.93	8.16	8.39	8.62	8.85	9.08	9.31	9.54
110	6.16	6.39	6.62	6.86	7.09	7.32	7.56	7.79	8.02	8.25	8.48	8.72	8.95	9.18	9.41	9.64
109	6.24	6.47	6.71	6.94	7.18	7.41	7.64	7.88	8.11	8.34	8.58	8.81	9.04	9.28	9.51	9.74
108	6.32	6.55	6.79	7.03	7.26	7.50	7.73	7.97	8.20	8.44	8.67	8.91	9.14	9.38	9.61	9.85
107	6.40	6.64	6.87	7.11	7.35	7.59	7.82	8.06	8.30	8.53	8.77	9.01	9.24	9.48	9.72	9.95
106	6.48	6.72	6.96	7.20	7.44	7.68	7.91	8.15	8.39	8.63	8.87	9.11	9.35	9.59	9.82	10.06
105	6.56	6.80	7.04	7.29	7.53	7.77	8.01	8.25	8.49	8.73	8.97	9.21	9.45	9.69	9.93	10.17
104	6.65	6.89	7.13	7.37	7.62	7.86	8.10	8.34	8.59	8.83	9.07	9.31	9.56	9.80	10.04	10.28
103	6.73	6.98	7.22	7.47	7.71	7.95	8.20	8.44	8.69	8.93	9.18	9.42	9.66	9.91	10.15	10.40
102	6.82	7.06	7.31	7.56	7.80	8.05	8.30	8.54	8.79	9.03	9.28	9.53	9.77	10.02	10.26	10.51
101	6.91	7.15	7.40	7.65	7.90	8.15	8.39	8.64	8.89	9.14	9.39	9.63	9.88	10.13	10.38	10.63
100	7.00	7.25	7.50	7.75	8.00	8.25	8.50	8.75	9.00	9.25	9.50	9.75	10.00	10.25	10.50	10.75
99	7.09	7.34	7.59	7.84	8.09	8.35	8.60	8.85	9.10	9.35	9.61	9.86	10.11	10.36	10.61	10.87
98	7.18	7.43	7.68	7.94	8.19	8.45	8.70	8.95	9.21	9.46	9.72	9.97	10.23	10.48	10.73	10.99
97	7.27	7.53	7.78	8.04	8.29	8.55	8.81	9.06	9.32	9.57	9.83	10.09	10.34	10.60	10.86	11.11
96	7.37	7.62	7.88	8.14	8.40	8.65	8.91	9.17	9.43	9.69	9.95	10.20	10.46	10.72	10.98	11.24
95	7.46	7.72	7.98	8.24	8.50	8.76	9.02	9.28	9.54	9.80	10.06	10.32	10.59	10.85	11.11	11.37
94	7.56	7.82	8.08	8.35	8.61	8.87	9.13	9.40	9.66	9.92	10.18	10.45	10.71	10.97	11.24	11.50
93	7.66	7.92	8.19	8.45	8.72	8.98	9.25	9.51	9.78	10.04	10.31	10.57	10.84	11.10	11.37	11.63
92	7.76	8.03	8.29	8.56	8.83	9.09	9.36	9.63	9.89	10.16	10.43	10.70	10.97	11.23	11.50	11.77
91	7.86	8.13	8.40	8.67	8.94	9.21	9.48	9.75	10.02	10.29	10.56	10.83	11.10	11.37	11.64	11.91
90	7.97	8.24	8.51	8.78	9.05	9.32	9.59	9.87	10.14	10.41	10.68	10.96	11.23	11.50	11.78	12.05
89	8.07	8.35	8.62	8.89	9.17	9.44	9.72	9.99	10.26	10.54	10.82	11.09	11.37	11.64	11.92	12.19
88	8.18	8.46	8.73	9.01	9.28	9.56	9.84	10.12	10.39	10.67	10.95	11.23	11.50	11.78	12.06	12.34
87	8.29	8.57	8.85	9.13	9.40	9.68	9.96	10.24	10.52	10.80	11.08	11.37	11.65	11.93	12.21	12.49
86	8.40	8.68	8.96	9.25	9.53	9.81	10.09	10.37	10.66	10.94	11.22	11.51	11.79	12.07	12.36	12.64
85	8.52	8.80	9.08	9.37	9.65	9.94	10.22	10.51	10.79	11.08	11.36	11.65	11.94	12.22	12.51	12.80
84	8.63	8.92	9.20	9.49	9.78	10.07	10.35	10.64	10.93	11.22	11.51	11.80	12.09	12.38	12.67	12.96
83	8.75	9.04	9.33	9.62	9.91	10.20	10.49	10.78	11.07	11.36	11.66	11.95	12.24	12.53	12.83	13.12
82	8.87	9.16	9.45	9.75	10.04	10.33	10.63	10.92	11.22	11.51	11.81	12.10	12.40	12.69	12.99	13.29
81	8.99	9.29	9.58	9.88	10.17	10.47	10.77	11.07	11.36	11.66	11.96	12.26	12.56	12.86	13.16	13.46
80	9.12	9.42	9.71	10.01	10.31	10.61	10.91	11.21	11.51	11.81	12.12	12.42	12.72	13.02	13.33	13.63
79	9.25	9.55	9.85	10.15	10.45	10.75	11.06	11.36	11.67	11.97	12.28	12.58	12.89	13.19	13.50	13.81
78	9.38	9.68	9.98	10.29	10.60	10.90	11.21	11.52	11.82	12.13	12.44	12.75	13.06	13.37	13.68	13.99
77	9.51	9.82	10.12	10.43	10.74	11.05	11.36	11.67	11.98	12.29	12.61	12.92	13.23	13.55	13.86	14.17
76	9.64	9.95	10.27	10.58	10.89	11.20	11.52	11.83	12.15	12.46	12.78	13.09	13.41	13.73	14.05	14.36
75	9.78	10.10	10.41	10.73	11.04	11.36	11.68	12.00	12.31	12.63	12.95	13.27	13.59	13.92	14.24	14.56
74	9.92	10.24	10.56	10.88	11.20	11.52	11.84	12.16	12.49	12.81	13.13	13.46	13.78	14.11	14.43	14.76
73	10.07	10.39	10.71	11.04	11.36	11.68	12.01	12.33	12.66	12.99	13.32	13.64	13.97	14.30	14.63	14.96
70	10.52	10.86	11.19	11.52	11.86	12.20	12.54	12.87	13.21	13.55	13.89	14.23	14.58	14.92	15.26	15.61
65	11.35	11.71	12.07	12.43	12.78	13.14	13.51	13.87	14.23	14.60	14.96	15.33	15.70	16.06	16.43	16.80
60	12.30	12.68	13.07	13.45	13.84	14.23	14.62	15.01	15.40	15.80	16.19	16.59	16.98	17.38	17.78	18.18
55	13.39	13.81	14.23	14.65	15.07	15.49	15.91	16.34	16.77	17.20	17.63	18.06	18.49	18.93	19.36	19.80
50	14.68	15.13	15.59	16.05	16.51	16.98	17.45	17.92	18.39	18.86	19.33	19.81	20.29	20.77	21.25	21.73
45	16.21	16.72	17.23	17.74	18.26	18.78	19.30	19.82	20.35	20.88	21.41	21.94	22.47	23.01	23.54	24.08
40	18.11	18.68	19.26	19.84	20.43	21.01	21.60	22.20	22.79	23.39	23.99	24.60	25.20	25.81	26.41	27.02
35	20.52	21.18	21.85	22.52	23.20	23.88	24.56	25.25	25.94	26.63	27.32	28.02	28.71	29.41	30.11	30.81
30	23.73	24.52	25.31	26.11	26.91	27.71	28.52	29.33	30.14	30.96	31.77	32.59	33.42	34.24	35.06	35.89

Description: This table shows the price to pay for a bond at the yield rate. The yield is to maturity.

Example: The price of a 15.00 %, 22 year bond to yield 8 % to maturity is $ 171.92.

COUPON RATE, %

YIELD	11.00%	11.25%	11.50%	11.75%	12.00%	12.25%	12.50%	12.75%	13.00%	13.25%	13.50%	13.75%	14.00%	14.25%	14.50%	15.00%
0.00	342.00	347.50	353.00	358.50	364.00	369.50	375.00	380.50	386.00	391.50	397.00	402.50	408.00	413.50	419.00	430.00
1.00	297.04	301.97	306.89	311.82	316.75	321.67	326.60	331.52	336.45	341.38	346.30	351.23	356.15	361.08	366.01	375.86
2.00	259.55	263.98	268.41	272.85	277.28	281.71	286.14	290.57	295.00	299.44	303.87	308.30	312.73	317.16	321.60	330.46
3.00	228.16	232.17	236.17	240.18	244.18	248.19	252.19	256.20	260.20	264.21	268.21	272.22	276.22	280.23	284.23	292.24
4.00	201.78	205.41	209.05	212.68	216.32	219.95	223.59	227.22	230.86	234.49	238.13	241.76	245.40	249.03	252.67	259.94
4.25	195.86	199.41	202.96	206.51	210.06	213.61	217.16	220.71	224.26	227.81	231.36	234.91	238.46	242.01	245.56	252.66
4.50	190.18	193.65	197.12	200.59	204.05	207.52	210.99	214.46	217.93	221.40	224.86	228.33	231.80	235.27	238.74	245.68
4.75	184.73	188.12	191.51	194.90	198.29	201.68	205.07	208.46	211.85	215.24	218.63	222.02	225.41	228.80	232.19	238.97
5.00	179.51	182.82	186.14	189.45	192.76	196.08	199.39	202.70	206.02	209.33	212.64	215.95	219.27	222.58	225.89	232.52
5.25	174.50	177.74	180.98	184.22	187.46	190.70	193.93	197.17	200.41	203.65	206.89	210.13	213.37	216.61	219.85	226.33
5.50	169.69	172.86	176.02	179.19	182.36	185.53	188.70	191.86	195.03	198.20	201.37	204.53	207.70	210.87	214.04	220.37
5.75	165.07	168.17	171.27	174.37	177.47	180.56	183.66	186.76	189.86	192.96	196.06	199.16	202.25	205.35	208.45	214.65
6.00	160.64	163.67	166.70	169.73	172.76	175.79	178.83	181.86	184.89	187.92	190.95	193.99	197.02	200.05	203.08	209.14
6.25	156.38	159.34	162.31	165.28	168.24	171.21	174.18	177.15	180.11	183.08	186.05	189.01	191.98	194.95	197.92	203.85
6.50	152.28	155.19	158.09	161.00	163.90	166.80	169.71	172.61	175.52	178.42	181.33	184.23	187.14	190.04	192.95	198.76
6.75	148.35	151.19	154.04	156.88	159.72	162.57	165.41	168.26	171.10	173.94	176.79	179.63	182.48	185.32	188.16	193.85
7.00	144.57	147.35	150.14	152.92	155.71	158.49	161.28	164.06	166.85	169.63	172.42	175.20	177.99	180.78	183.56	189.13
7.25	140.93	143.66	146.39	149.11	151.84	154.57	157.30	160.03	162.76	165.49	168.21	170.94	173.67	176.40	179.13	184.59
7.50	137.43	140.10	142.78	145.45	148.12	150.80	153.47	156.14	158.82	161.49	164.17	166.84	169.51	172.19	174.86	180.21
7.75	134.06	136.68	139.30	141.92	144.54	147.16	149.78	152.41	155.03	157.65	160.27	162.89	165.51	168.13	170.75	175.99
8.00	130.82	133.39	135.96	138.53	141.10	143.67	146.23	148.80	151.37	153.94	156.51	159.08	161.65	164.22	166.78	171.92
8.25	127.70	130.22	132.74	135.26	137.78	140.30	142.82	145.33	147.85	150.37	152.89	155.41	157.93	160.45	162.96	168.00
8.50	124.70	127.17	129.64	132.11	134.58	137.05	139.52	141.99	144.46	146.93	149.40	151.87	154.34	156.81	159.28	164.22
8.75	121.81	124.23	126.65	129.08	131.50	133.92	136.34	138.77	141.19	143.61	146.04	148.46	150.88	153.30	155.73	160.57
9.00	119.02	121.40	123.77	126.15	128.53	130.90	133.28	135.66	138.04	140.41	142.79	145.17	147.55	149.92	152.30	157.06
9.25	116.33	118.66	121.00	123.33	125.66	128.00	130.33	132.66	135.00	137.33	139.66	141.99	144.33	146.66	148.99	153.66
9.50	113.74	116.03	118.32	120.61	122.90	125.19	127.48	129.77	132.06	134.35	136.64	138.93	141.22	143.51	145.80	150.38
9.75	111.24	113.49	115.74	117.99	120.24	122.48	124.73	126.98	129.23	131.48	133.73	135.97	138.22	140.47	142.72	147.22
10.00	108.83	111.04	113.25	115.45	117.66	119.87	122.08	124.29	126.49	128.70	130.91	133.12	135.33	137.53	139.74	144.16
10.25	106.51	108.67	110.84	113.01	115.18	117.35	119.52	121.69	123.85	126.02	128.19	130.36	132.53	134.70	136.87	141.20
10.50	104.26	106.39	108.52	110.65	112.78	114.91	117.04	119.17	121.30	123.43	125.56	127.69	129.82	131.96	134.09	138.35
10.75	102.09	104.19	106.28	108.37	110.47	112.56	114.65	116.75	118.84	120.93	123.03	125.12	127.21	129.31	131.40	135.59
11.00	100.00	102.06	104.11	106.17	108.23	110.29	112.34	114.40	116.46	118.52	120.57	122.63	124.69	126.74	128.80	132.92
11.25	97.98	100.00	102.02	104.04	106.07	108.09	110.11	112.13	114.16	116.18	118.20	120.22	122.24	124.27	126.29	130.33
11.50	96.02	98.01	100.00	101.99	103.98	105.96	107.95	109.94	111.93	113.92	115.91	117.89	119.88	121.87	123.86	127.83
11.75	94.13	96.09	98.04	100.00	101.96	103.91	105.87	107.82	109.78	111.73	113.69	115.64	117.60	119.55	121.51	125.42
12.00	92.31	94.23	96.15	98.08	100.00	101.92	103.85	105.77	107.69	109.61	111.54	113.46	115.38	117.31	119.23	123.07
12.25	90.54	92.43	94.33	96.22	98.11	100.00	101.89	103.78	105.67	107.57	109.46	111.35	113.24	115.13	117.02	120.81
12.50	88.83	90.69	92.56	94.42	96.28	98.14	100.00	101.86	103.72	105.58	107.44	109.31	111.17	113.03	114.89	118.61
12.75	87.18	89.01	90.84	92.67	94.51	96.34	98.17	100.00	101.83	103.66	105.49	107.33	109.16	110.99	112.82	116.48
13.00	85.58	87.38	89.18	90.99	92.79	94.59	96.39	98.20	100.00	101.80	103.61	105.41	107.21	109.01	110.82	114.42
13.25	84.03	85.80	87.58	89.35	91.13	92.90	94.68	96.45	98.23	100.00	101.77	103.55	105.32	107.10	108.87	112.42
13.50	82.53	84.27	86.02	87.77	89.52	91.26	93.01	94.76	96.51	98.25	100.00	101.75	103.49	105.24	106.99	110.48
13.75	81.07	82.79	84.51	86.23	87.96	89.68	91.40	93.12	94.84	96.56	98.28	100.00	101.72	103.44	105.16	108.60
14.00	79.66	81.36	83.05	84.75	86.44	88.14	89.83	91.53	93.22	94.92	96.61	98.31	100.00	101.69	103.39	106.78
14.25	78.30	79.97	81.64	83.31	84.97	86.64	88.31	89.98	91.65	93.32	94.99	96.66	98.33	100.00	101.67	105.01
14.50	76.97	78.62	80.26	81.91	83.55	85.20	86.84	88.49	90.13	91.78	93.42	95.07	96.71	98.36	100.00	103.29
14.75	75.69	77.31	78.93	80.55	82.17	83.79	85.41	87.03	88.65	90.27	91.90	93.52	95.14	96.76	98.38	101.62
15.00	74.44	76.04	77.63	79.23	80.83	82.43	84.02	85.62	87.22	88.82	90.41	92.01	93.61	95.21	96.80	100.00
15.25	73.23	74.80	76.38	77.95	79.53	81.10	82.68	84.25	85.83	87.40	88.98	90.55	92.13	93.70	95.28	98.43
15.50	72.06	73.61	75.16	76.71	78.27	79.82	81.37	82.92	84.48	86.03	87.58	89.13	90.69	92.24	93.79	96.90
15.75	70.92	72.45	73.98	75.51	77.04	78.57	80.10	81.63	83.16	84.69	86.22	87.75	89.28	90.82	92.35	95.41
16.00	69.81	71.32	72.83	74.34	75.85	77.36	78.87	80.37	81.88	83.39	84.90	86.41	87.92	89.43	90.94	93.96
16.25	68.73	70.22	71.71	73.20	74.69	76.18	77.67	79.15	80.64	82.13	83.62	85.11	86.60	88.09	89.58	92.56
16.50	67.69	69.15	70.62	72.09	73.56	75.03	76.50	77.97	79.44	80.90	82.37	83.84	85.31	86.78	88.25	91.19
16.75	66.67	68.12	69.57	71.02	72.47	73.91	75.36	76.81	78.26	79.71	81.16	82.61	84.06	85.51	86.96	89.86
17.00	65.68	67.11	68.54	69.97	71.40	72.83	74.26	75.69	77.12	78.55	79.98	81.41	82.84	84.27	85.70	88.56
17.25	64.72	66.13	67.54	68.95	70.36	71.78	73.19	74.60	76.01	77.42	78.83	80.24	81.65	83.07	84.48	87.30
17.50	63.78	65.18	66.57	67.96	69.36	70.75	72.14	73.53	74.93	76.32	77.71	79.11	80.50	81.89	83.28	86.07
17.75	62.87	64.25	65.62	67.00	68.37	69.75	71.12	72.50	73.87	75.25	76.62	78.00	79.37	80.75	82.12	84.87
18.00	61.99	63.35	64.70	66.06	67.42	68.78	70.13	71.49	72.85	74.21	75.56	76.92	78.28	79.64	80.99	83.71
18.25	61.13	62.47	63.81	65.15	66.49	67.83	69.17	70.51	71.85	73.19	74.53	75.87	77.21	78.55	79.89	82.57
18.50	60.29	61.61	62.93	64.26	65.58	66.91	68.23	69.55	70.88	72.20	73.52	74.85	76.17	77.50	78.82	81.47
18.75	59.47	60.78	62.08	63.39	64.70	66.01	67.31	68.62	69.93	71.24	72.54	73.85	75.16	76.47	77.77	80.39
19.00	58.67	59.96	61.25	62.55	63.84	65.13	66.42	67.71	69.00	70.29	71.59	72.88	74.17	75.46	76.75	79.34
20.00	55.68	56.91	58.14	59.37	60.60	61.83	63.07	64.30	65.53	66.76	67.99	69.22	70.45	71.68	72.92	75.38
25.00	44.31	45.31	46.30	47.30	48.29	49.29	50.28	51.28	52.27	53.26	54.26	55.25	56.25	57.24	58.24	60.22
30.00	36.80	37.63	38.46	39.30	40.13	40.96	41.79	42.62	43.45	44.29	45.12	45.95	46.78	47.61	48.44	50.11

Description: This table shows the yield to maturity of a bond purchased at the price shown in the index.

Example: The yield to maturity of a 15.00 %, 22 year bond at a price of 125.00 is 11.79 %.

COUPON RATE, %

PRICE	11.00%	11.25%	11.50%	11.75%	12.00%	12.25%	12.50%	12.75%	13.00%	13.25%	13.50%	13.75%	14.00%	14.25%	14.50%	15.00%
250	2.28	2.41	2.54	2.68	2.81	2.94	3.07	3.20	3.32	3.45	3.58	3.71	3.83	3.96	4.09	4.34
240	2.60	2.73	2.87	3.00	3.13	3.27	3.40	3.53	3.67	3.80	3.93	4.06	4.19	4.32	4.45	4.71
230	2.93	3.07	3.21	3.35	3.48	3.62	3.76	3.89	4.03	4.16	4.30	4.43	4.56	4.70	4.83	5.10
220	3.29	3.43	3.57	3.71	3.85	3.99	4.13	4.27	4.41	4.55	4.69	4.83	4.96	5.10	5.24	5.51
210	3.66	3.81	3.96	4.10	4.25	4.39	4.54	4.68	4.82	4.97	5.11	5.25	5.39	5.53	5.67	5.96
200	4.07	4.22	4.37	4.52	4.67	4.82	4.97	5.12	5.26	5.41	5.56	5.71	5.85	6.00	6.14	6.43
195	4.28	4.44	4.59	4.74	4.89	5.04	5.20	5.35	5.50	5.65	5.80	5.95	6.09	6.24	6.39	6.69
190	4.50	4.66	4.81	4.97	5.12	5.28	5.43	5.59	5.74	5.89	6.04	6.19	6.35	6.50	6.65	6.95
185	4.73	4.89	5.05	5.21	5.36	5.52	5.68	5.83	5.99	6.14	6.30	6.45	6.61	6.76	6.92	7.22
180	4.97	5.13	5.29	5.45	5.61	5.77	5.93	6.09	6.25	6.41	6.57	6.72	6.88	7.04	7.20	7.51
175	5.22	5.38	5.55	5.71	5.87	6.04	6.20	6.36	6.52	6.69	6.85	7.01	7.17	7.33	7.49	7.80
170	5.48	5.65	5.81	5.98	6.15	6.31	6.48	6.64	6.81	6.97	7.14	7.30	7.47	7.63	7.79	8.12
165	5.75	5.92	6.09	6.26	6.43	6.60	6.77	6.94	7.11	7.27	7.44	7.61	7.78	7.94	8.11	8.44
160	6.03	6.21	6.38	6.55	6.73	6.90	7.07	7.25	7.42	7.59	7.76	7.93	8.10	8.28	8.45	8.79
155	6.33	6.51	6.68	6.86	7.04	7.22	7.39	7.57	7.75	7.92	8.10	8.27	8.45	8.62	8.80	9.15
150	6.64	6.82	7.00	7.19	7.37	7.55	7.73	7.91	8.09	8.27	8.45	8.63	8.81	8.99	9.17	9.52
145	6.97	7.15	7.34	7.53	7.71	7.90	8.08	8.27	8.45	8.64	8.82	9.01	9.19	9.38	9.56	9.93
140	7.31	7.50	7.69	7.89	8.08	8.27	8.46	8.65	8.84	9.03	9.22	9.41	9.60	9.78	9.97	10.35
135	7.67	7.87	8.07	8.27	8.46	8.66	8.85	9.05	9.24	9.44	9.63	9.83	10.02	10.22	10.41	10.80
130	8.06	8.26	8.47	8.67	8.87	9.07	9.27	9.47	9.68	9.88	10.08	10.28	10.48	10.68	10.88	11.28
125	8.47	8.68	8.89	9.10	9.30	9.51	9.72	9.93	10.14	10.34	10.55	10.76	10.96	11.17	11.38	11.79
120	8.91	9.12	9.34	9.55	9.77	9.98	10.20	10.41	10.63	10.84	11.05	11.27	11.48	11.70	11.91	12.34
115	9.37	9.60	9.82	10.04	10.26	10.49	10.71	10.93	11.15	11.37	11.60	11.82	12.04	12.26	12.48	12.92
113	9.57	9.79	10.02	10.25	10.47	10.70	10.92	11.15	11.37	11.60	11.82	12.05	12.27	12.50	12.72	13.17
112	9.67	9.90	10.12	10.35	10.58	10.81	11.03	11.26	11.49	11.71	11.94	12.17	12.39	12.62	12.85	13.30
111	9.77	10.00	10.23	10.46	10.69	10.92	11.14	11.37	11.60	11.83	12.06	12.29	12.52	12.74	12.97	13.43
110	9.87	10.10	10.33	10.57	10.80	11.03	11.26	11.49	11.72	11.95	12.18	12.41	12.64	12.87	13.10	13.56
109	9.98	10.21	10.44	10.68	10.91	11.14	11.37	11.60	11.84	12.07	12.30	12.53	12.76	13.00	13.23	13.69
108	10.08	10.32	10.55	10.79	11.02	11.26	11.49	11.72	11.96	12.19	12.43	12.66	12.89	13.13	13.36	13.83
107	10.19	10.43	10.66	10.90	11.14	11.37	11.61	11.84	12.08	12.32	12.55	12.79	13.02	13.26	13.49	13.96
106	10.30	10.54	10.78	11.01	11.25	11.49	11.73	11.97	12.20	12.44	12.68	12.92	13.15	13.39	13.63	14.10
105	10.41	10.65	10.89	11.13	11.37	11.61	11.85	12.09	12.33	12.57	12.81	13.05	13.29	13.53	13.77	14.25
104	10.52	10.77	11.01	11.25	11.49	11.73	11.98	12.22	12.46	12.70	12.94	13.18	13.43	13.67	13.91	14.39
103	10.64	10.88	11.13	11.37	11.61	11.86	12.10	12.35	12.59	12.83	13.08	13.32	13.56	13.81	14.05	14.54
102	10.76	11.00	11.25	11.49	11.74	11.99	12.23	12.48	12.72	12.97	13.21	13.46	13.71	13.95	14.20	14.69
101	10.87	11.12	11.37	11.62	11.87	12.11	12.36	12.61	12.86	13.11	13.35	13.60	13.85	14.10	14.34	14.84
100	11.00	11.25	11.50	11.75	12.00	12.25	12.50	12.75	13.00	13.25	13.50	13.75	14.00	14.25	14.50	15.00
99	11.12	11.37	11.62	11.87	12.13	12.38	12.63	12.88	13.13	13.39	13.64	13.89	14.14	14.40	14.65	15.15
98	11.24	11.50	11.75	12.01	12.26	12.51	12.77	13.02	13.28	13.53	13.79	14.04	14.30	14.55	14.80	15.31
97	11.37	11.63	11.88	12.14	12.40	12.65	12.91	13.17	13.42	13.68	13.94	14.19	14.45	14.71	14.96	15.48
96	11.50	11.76	12.02	12.27	12.53	12.79	13.05	13.31	13.57	13.83	14.09	14.35	14.61	14.87	15.13	15.64
95	11.63	11.89	12.15	12.41	12.67	12.94	13.20	13.46	13.72	13.98	14.24	14.51	14.77	15.03	15.29	15.81
94	11.76	12.03	12.29	12.55	12.82	13.08	13.35	13.61	13.87	14.14	14.40	14.67	14.93	15.19	15.46	15.99
93	11.90	12.17	12.43	12.70	12.96	13.23	13.50	13.76	14.03	14.30	14.56	14.83	15.10	15.36	15.63	16.17
92	12.04	12.31	12.58	12.84	13.11	13.38	13.65	13.92	14.19	14.46	14.73	15.00	15.27	15.54	15.81	16.35
91	12.18	12.45	12.72	12.99	13.26	13.54	13.81	14.08	14.35	14.62	14.90	15.17	15.44	15.71	15.98	16.53
90	12.32	12.60	12.87	13.14	13.42	13.69	13.97	14.24	14.52	14.79	15.07	15.34	15.62	15.89	16.17	16.72
89	12.47	12.75	13.02	13.30	13.58	13.85	14.13	14.41	14.69	14.96	15.24	15.52	15.80	16.07	16.35	16.91
88	12.62	12.90	13.18	13.46	13.74	14.02	14.30	14.58	14.86	15.14	15.42	15.70	15.98	16.26	16.54	17.11
87	12.77	13.05	13.34	13.62	13.90	14.18	14.47	14.75	15.03	15.32	15.60	15.88	16.17	16.45	16.74	17.31
86	12.93	13.21	13.50	13.78	14.07	14.36	14.64	14.93	15.21	15.50	15.79	16.07	16.36	16.65	16.93	17.51
85	13.09	13.38	13.66	13.95	14.24	14.53	14.82	15.11	15.40	15.69	15.98	16.27	16.56	16.85	17.14	17.72
84	13.25	13.54	13.83	14.12	14.42	14.71	15.00	15.29	15.58	15.88	16.17	16.46	16.76	17.05	17.34	17.93
83	13.42	13.71	14.00	14.30	14.59	14.89	15.18	15.48	15.78	16.07	16.37	16.67	16.96	17.26	17.56	18.15
82	13.58	13.88	14.18	14.48	14.78	15.07	15.37	15.67	15.97	16.27	16.57	16.87	17.17	17.47	17.77	18.37
81	13.76	14.06	14.36	14.66	14.96	15.26	15.57	15.87	16.17	16.48	16.78	17.08	17.39	17.69	17.99	18.60
80	13.93	14.24	14.54	14.85	15.15	15.46	15.76	16.07	16.38	16.68	16.99	17.30	17.61	17.91	18.22	18.84
79	14.12	14.42	14.73	15.04	15.35	15.66	15.97	16.28	16.59	16.90	17.21	17.52	17.83	18.14	18.45	19.08
78	14.30	14.61	14.92	15.24	15.55	15.86	16.17	16.49	16.80	17.12	17.43	17.74	18.06	18.37	18.69	19.32
77	14.49	14.80	15.12	15.44	15.75	16.07	16.39	16.70	17.02	17.34	17.66	17.98	18.30	18.61	18.93	19.57
76	14.68	15.00	15.32	15.64	15.96	16.28	16.60	16.93	17.25	17.57	17.89	18.21	18.54	18.86	19.18	19.83
75	14.88	15.20	15.53	15.85	16.18	16.50	16.83	17.15	17.48	17.80	18.13	18.46	18.78	19.11	19.44	20.10
74	15.09	15.41	15.74	16.07	16.40	16.73	17.06	17.38	17.71	18.05	18.38	18.71	19.04	19.37	19.70	20.37
73	15.29	15.62	15.96	16.29	16.62	16.96	17.29	17.62	17.96	18.29	18.63	18.96	19.30	19.64	19.97	20.65
70	15.95	16.30	16.64	16.99	17.33	17.68	18.03	18.38	18.73	19.07	19.42	19.77	20.12	20.47	20.82	21.53
65	17.17	17.54	17.91	18.29	18.66	19.03	19.41	19.78	20.16	20.53	20.91	21.28	21.66	22.04	22.42	23.17
60	18.58	18.98	19.39	19.79	20.19	20.60	21.00	21.41	21.82	22.22	22.63	23.04	23.45	23.86	24.27	25.09
55	20.24	20.68	21.12	21.56	22.00	22.44	22.88	23.33	23.77	24.22	24.66	25.11	25.56	26.00	26.45	27.35

Description: This table shows the price to pay for a bond at the yield rate. The yield is to maturity.

Example: The price of a 6.75 %, 23 year bond to yield 8 % to maturity is $ 86.95.

COUPON RATE, %

YIELD	0.00%	1.00%	2.00%	3.00%	4.00%	4.25%	4.50%	4.75%	5.00%	5.25%	5.50%	5.75%	6.00%	6.25%	6.50%	6.75%
0.00	100.00	123.00	146.00	169.00	192.00	197.75	203.50	209.25	215.00	220.75	226.50	232.25	238.00	243.75	249.50	255.25
1.00	79.50	100.00	120.50	141.00	161.50	166.63	171.75	176.88	182.00	187.13	192.25	197.38	202.51	207.63	212.76	217.88
2.00	63.27	81.64	100.00	118.36	136.73	141.32	145.91	150.50	155.09	159.68	164.27	168.86	173.45	178.05	182.64	187.23
3.00	50.42	66.94	83.47	100.00	116.53	120.66	124.79	128.92	133.06	137.19	141.32	145.45	149.58	153.72	157.85	161.98
4.00	40.22	55.16	70.11	85.05	100.00	103.74	107.47	111.21	114.95	118.68	122.42	126.16	129.89	133.63	137.37	141.10
4.25	38.01	52.60	67.18	81.77	96.35	100.00	103.65	107.29	110.94	114.59	118.23	121.88	125.52	129.17	132.82	136.46
4.50	35.93	50.17	64.41	78.64	92.88	96.44	100.00	103.56	107.12	110.68	114.24	117.80	121.36	124.92	128.47	132.03
4.75	33.97	47.87	61.77	75.67	89.57	93.05	96.52	100.00	103.48	106.95	110.43	113.90	117.38	120.85	124.33	127.80
5.00	32.11	45.69	59.27	72.85	86.42	89.82	93.21	96.61	100.00	103.39	106.79	110.18	113.58	116.97	120.37	123.76
5.25	30.36	43.63	56.89	70.16	83.42	86.74	90.05	93.37	96.68	100.00	103.32	106.63	109.95	113.26	116.58	119.90
5.50	28.71	41.67	54.63	67.60	80.56	83.80	87.04	90.28	93.52	96.76	100.00	103.24	106.48	109.72	112.96	116.20
5.75	27.15	39.82	52.49	65.16	77.83	81.00	84.16	87.33	90.50	93.67	96.83	100.00	103.17	106.33	109.50	112.67
6.00	25.67	38.06	50.45	62.84	75.22	78.32	81.42	84.52	87.61	90.71	93.81	96.90	100.00	103.10	106.19	109.29
6.25	24.28	36.40	48.51	60.63	72.74	75.77	78.80	81.83	84.86	87.88	90.91	93.94	96.97	100.00	103.03	106.06
6.50	22.96	34.82	46.67	58.52	70.37	73.33	76.30	79.26	82.22	85.19	88.15	91.11	94.07	97.04	100.00	102.96
6.75	21.72	33.32	44.91	56.51	68.11	71.01	73.91	76.81	79.71	82.60	85.50	88.40	91.30	94.20	97.10	100.00
7.00	20.55	31.90	43.25	54.60	65.95	68.79	71.62	74.46	77.30	80.14	82.97	85.81	88.65	91.49	94.32	97.16
7.25	19.44	30.55	41.66	52.77	63.89	66.66	69.44	72.22	75.00	77.78	80.55	83.33	86.11	88.89	91.67	94.44
7.50	18.39	29.27	40.15	51.03	61.91	64.64	67.36	70.08	72.80	75.52	78.24	80.96	83.68	86.40	89.12	91.84
7.75	17.40	28.06	38.71	49.37	60.03	62.70	65.36	68.02	70.69	73.35	76.02	78.68	81.35	84.01	86.68	89.34
8.00	16.46	26.90	37.35	47.79	58.23	60.84	63.45	66.06	68.67	71.28	73.89	76.50	79.12	81.73	84.34	86.95
8.25	15.58	25.81	36.04	46.28	56.51	59.07	61.63	64.18	66.74	69.30	71.86	74.42	76.98	79.53	82.09	84.65
8.50	14.74	24.77	34.80	44.83	54.86	57.37	59.88	62.39	64.89	67.40	69.91	72.42	74.92	77.43	79.94	82.45
8.75	13.95	23.78	33.62	43.45	53.29	55.75	58.20	60.66	63.12	65.58	68.04	70.50	72.96	75.41	77.87	80.33
9.00	13.20	22.85	32.49	42.13	51.78	54.19	56.60	59.01	61.42	63.83	66.25	68.66	71.07	73.48	75.89	78.30
9.25	12.50	21.96	31.42	40.88	50.34	52.70	55.07	57.43	59.80	62.16	64.53	66.89	69.26	71.62	73.99	76.35
9.50	11.83	21.11	30.39	39.67	48.95	51.27	53.59	55.91	58.23	60.55	62.87	65.20	67.52	69.84	72.16	74.48
9.75	11.20	20.30	29.41	38.52	47.63	49.91	52.18	54.46	56.74	59.01	61.29	63.57	65.84	68.12	70.40	72.68
10.00	10.60	19.54	28.48	37.42	46.36	48.59	50.83	53.06	55.30	57.53	59.77	62.00	64.24	66.47	68.71	70.94
10.25	10.04	18.81	27.59	36.37	45.14	47.34	49.53	51.73	53.92	56.11	58.31	60.50	62.70	64.89	67.09	69.28
10.50	9.50	18.12	26.74	35.36	43.98	46.13	48.29	50.44	52.60	54.75	56.91	59.06	61.21	63.37	65.52	67.68
10.75	9.00	17.46	25.93	34.39	42.86	44.97	47.09	49.21	51.32	53.44	55.56	57.67	59.79	61.91	64.02	66.14
11.00	8.52	16.84	25.15	33.47	41.78	43.86	45.94	48.02	50.10	52.18	54.26	56.34	58.42	60.50	62.58	64.66
11.25	8.07	16.24	24.41	32.58	40.75	42.80	44.84	46.88	48.93	50.97	53.01	55.06	57.10	59.14	61.18	63.23
11.50	7.64	15.67	23.70	31.73	39.77	41.77	43.78	45.79	47.80	49.80	51.81	53.82	55.83	57.84	59.84	61.85
11.75	7.24	15.13	23.03	30.92	38.82	40.79	42.76	44.74	46.71	48.68	50.66	52.63	54.60	56.58	58.55	60.53
12.00	6.85	14.62	22.38	30.14	37.90	39.84	41.78	43.72	45.66	47.61	49.55	51.49	53.43	55.37	57.31	59.25
12.25	6.49	14.13	21.76	29.39	37.03	38.93	40.84	42.75	44.66	46.57	48.48	50.38	52.29	54.20	56.11	58.02
12.50	6.15	13.66	21.17	28.67	36.18	38.06	39.94	41.81	43.69	45.57	47.44	49.32	51.20	53.07	54.95	56.83
12.75	5.83	13.21	20.60	27.98	35.37	37.22	39.06	40.91	42.76	44.60	46.45	48.30	50.14	51.99	53.84	55.68
13.00	5.52	12.79	20.06	27.32	34.59	36.41	38.22	40.04	41.86	43.68	45.49	47.31	49.13	50.94	52.76	54.58
13.25	5.23	12.38	19.53	26.69	33.84	35.63	37.42	39.20	40.99	42.78	44.57	46.36	48.14	49.93	51.72	53.51
13.50	4.96	12.00	19.04	26.08	33.12	34.88	36.64	38.40	40.16	41.92	43.68	45.44	47.20	48.96	50.72	52.48
13.75	4.70	11.63	18.56	25.49	32.42	34.15	35.89	37.62	39.35	41.08	42.82	44.55	46.28	48.02	49.75	51.48
14.00	4.45	11.27	18.10	24.92	31.75	33.46	35.16	36.87	38.57	40.28	41.99	43.69	45.40	47.11	48.81	50.52
14.25	4.22	10.94	17.66	24.38	31.10	32.78	34.46	36.14	37.83	39.51	41.19	42.87	44.55	46.23	47.91	49.59
14.50	4.00	10.62	17.24	23.86	30.48	32.14	33.79	35.45	37.10	38.76	40.41	42.07	43.72	45.38	47.03	48.69
14.75	3.79	10.31	16.83	23.36	29.88	31.51	33.14	34.77	36.40	38.03	39.66	41.29	42.93	44.56	46.19	47.82
15.00	3.59	10.02	16.45	22.87	29.30	30.91	32.51	34.12	35.73	37.33	38.94	40.55	42.15	43.76	45.37	46.98
15.25	3.40	9.74	16.07	22.41	28.74	30.32	31.91	33.49	35.07	36.66	38.24	39.83	41.41	42.99	44.58	46.16
15.50	3.23	9.47	15.71	21.96	28.20	29.76	31.32	32.88	34.44	36.00	37.57	39.13	40.69	42.25	43.81	45.37
15.75	3.06	9.21	15.37	21.52	27.68	29.22	30.76	32.30	33.83	35.37	36.91	38.45	39.99	41.53	43.07	44.61
16.00	2.90	8.97	15.04	21.11	27.18	28.69	30.21	31.73	33.24	34.76	36.28	37.80	39.31	40.83	42.35	43.86
16.25	2.75	8.74	14.72	20.70	26.69	28.18	29.68	31.18	32.67	34.17	35.67	37.16	38.66	40.15	41.65	43.15
16.50	2.61	8.51	14.41	20.32	26.22	27.69	29.17	30.65	32.12	33.60	35.07	36.55	38.02	39.50	40.97	42.45
16.75	2.47	8.30	14.12	19.94	25.76	27.22	28.67	30.13	31.59	33.04	34.50	35.95	37.41	38.86	40.32	41.78
17.00	2.35	8.09	13.83	19.58	25.32	26.76	28.20	29.63	31.07	32.50	33.94	35.38	36.81	38.25	39.68	41.12
17.25	2.22	7.89	13.56	19.23	24.90	26.31	27.73	29.15	30.57	31.98	33.40	34.82	36.23	37.65	39.07	40.48
17.50	2.11	7.70	13.30	18.89	24.48	25.88	27.28	28.68	30.08	31.48	32.88	34.27	35.67	37.07	38.47	39.87
17.75	2.00	7.52	13.04	18.56	24.09	25.47	26.85	28.23	29.61	30.99	32.37	33.75	35.13	36.51	37.89	39.27
18.00	1.90	7.35	12.80	18.25	23.70	25.06	26.42	27.79	29.15	30.51	31.87	33.24	34.60	35.96	37.32	38.69
18.25	1.80	7.18	12.56	17.94	23.32	24.67	26.01	27.36	28.70	30.05	31.40	32.74	34.09	35.43	36.78	38.12
18.50	1.71	7.02	12.33	17.65	22.96	24.29	25.62	26.95	28.27	29.60	30.93	32.26	33.59	34.92	36.24	37.57
18.75	1.62	6.87	12.11	17.36	22.61	23.92	25.23	26.54	27.86	29.17	30.48	31.79	33.10	34.41	35.73	37.04
19.00	1.54	6.72	11.90	17.08	22.27	23.56	24.86	26.15	27.45	28.74	30.04	31.34	32.63	33.93	35.22	36.52
20.00	1.25	6.18	11.12	16.06	21.00	22.23	23.47	24.70	25.94	27.17	28.40	29.64	30.87	32.11	33.34	34.58
25.00	.44	4.43	8.41	12.39	16.37	17.37	18.36	19.36	20.35	21.35	22.35	23.34	24.34	25.33	26.33	27.32
30.00	.16	3.49	6.82	10.15	13.47	14.31	15.14	15.97	16.80	17.63	18.47	19.30	20.13	20.96	21.79	22.63

Description: This table shows the yield to maturity of a bond purchased at the price shown in the index.

Example: The yield to maturity of a 6.75 %, 23 year bond at a price of 80.00 is 8.79 %.

PRICE	0.00%	1.00%	2.00%	3.00%	4.00%	4.25%	4.50%	4.75%	5.00%	5.25%	5.50%	5.75%	6.00%	6.25%	6.50%	6.75%
100	0.00	1.00	2.00	3.00	4.00	4.25	4.50	4.75	5.00	5.25	5.50	5.75	6.00	6.25	6.50	6.75
99	.04	1.04	2.05	3.06	4.06	4.31	4.57	4.82	5.07	5.32	5.57	5.82	6.08	6.33	6.58	6.83
98	.08	1.09	2.11	3.12	4.13	4.38	4.64	4.89	5.14	5.40	5.65	5.91	6.16	6.41	6.67	6.92
97	.13	1.14	2.16	3.18	4.20	4.45	4.71	4.97	5.22	5.48	5.73	5.99	6.24	6.50	6.75	7.01
96	.17	1.19	2.22	3.24	4.27	4.53	4.78	5.04	5.30	5.56	5.81	6.07	6.33	6.59	6.84	7.10
95	.22	1.25	2.28	3.31	4.34	4.60	4.86	5.12	5.38	5.64	5.90	6.15	6.41	6.67	6.93	7.19
94	.26	1.30	2.33	3.37	4.41	4.67	4.93	5.20	5.46	5.72	5.98	6.24	6.50	6.76	7.02	7.29
93	.31	1.35	2.39	3.44	4.49	4.75	5.01	5.27	5.54	5.80	6.06	6.33	6.59	6.85	7.12	7.38
92	.36	1.40	2.45	3.50	4.56	4.82	5.09	5.35	5.62	5.88	6.15	6.42	6.68	6.95	7.21	7.48
91	.41	1.46	2.51	3.57	4.64	4.90	5.17	5.44	5.70	5.97	6.24	6.51	6.77	7.04	7.31	7.58
90	.45	1.51	2.57	3.64	4.71	4.98	5.25	5.52	5.79	6.06	6.33	6.60	6.87	7.14	7.41	7.68
89	.50	1.57	2.64	3.71	4.79	5.06	5.33	5.60	5.87	6.14	6.42	6.69	6.96	7.23	7.51	7.78
88	.55	1.62	2.70	3.78	4.87	5.14	5.41	5.69	5.96	6.23	6.51	6.78	7.06	7.33	7.61	7.88
87	.60	1.68	2.76	3.85	4.95	5.22	5.50	5.77	6.05	6.33	6.60	6.88	7.16	7.43	7.71	7.99
86	.65	1.74	2.83	3.93	5.03	5.31	5.58	5.86	6.14	6.42	6.70	6.98	7.26	7.54	7.82	8.10
85	.70	1.79	2.89	4.00	5.11	5.39	5.67	5.95	6.23	6.51	6.79	7.08	7.36	7.64	7.92	8.21
84	.75	1.85	2.96	4.07	5.20	5.48	5.76	6.04	6.33	6.61	6.89	7.18	7.46	7.75	8.03	8.32
83	.81	1.91	3.03	4.15	5.28	5.56	5.85	6.13	6.42	6.71	6.99	7.28	7.57	7.85	8.14	8.43
82	.86	1.97	3.10	4.23	5.37	5.65	5.94	6.23	6.52	6.81	7.09	7.38	7.67	7.96	8.26	8.55
81	.91	2.03	3.16	4.31	5.46	5.74	6.03	6.32	6.62	6.91	7.20	7.49	7.78	8.08	8.37	8.66
80	.97	2.10	3.24	4.38	5.55	5.84	6.13	6.42	6.72	7.01	7.30	7.60	7.89	8.19	8.49	8.79
79	1.02	2.16	3.31	4.47	5.64	5.93	6.23	6.52	6.82	7.11	7.41	7.71	8.01	8.31	8.61	8.91
78	1.08	2.22	3.38	4.55	5.73	6.03	6.32	6.62	6.92	7.22	7.52	7.82	8.12	8.43	8.73	9.03
77	1.13	2.29	3.45	4.63	5.82	6.12	6.42	6.72	7.03	7.33	7.63	7.94	8.24	8.55	8.85	9.16
76	1.19	2.35	3.53	4.72	5.92	6.22	6.53	6.83	7.13	7.44	7.75	8.05	8.36	8.67	8.98	9.29
75	1.25	2.42	3.60	4.80	6.02	6.32	6.63	6.94	7.24	7.55	7.86	8.17	8.49	8.80	9.11	9.42
74	1.31	2.49	3.68	4.89	6.12	6.43	6.74	7.05	7.36	7.67	7.98	8.30	8.61	8.93	9.24	9.56
73	1.37	2.56	3.76	4.98	6.22	6.53	6.84	7.16	7.47	7.79	8.10	8.42	8.74	9.06	9.38	9.70
72	1.43	2.63	3.84	5.07	6.32	6.64	6.95	7.27	7.59	7.91	8.23	8.55	8.87	9.19	9.52	9.84
71	1.49	2.70	3.92	5.17	6.43	6.75	7.07	7.39	7.71	8.03	8.35	8.68	9.00	9.33	9.66	9.99
70	1.55	2.77	4.00	5.26	6.54	6.86	7.18	7.50	7.83	8.16	8.48	8.81	9.14	9.47	9.80	10.14
69	1.61	2.84	4.09	5.36	6.65	6.97	7.30	7.62	7.95	8.28	8.62	8.95	9.28	9.62	9.95	10.29
68	1.68	2.92	4.17	5.45	6.76	7.09	7.42	7.75	8.08	8.41	8.75	9.09	9.42	9.76	10.10	10.44
67	1.74	2.99	4.26	5.55	6.87	7.20	7.54	7.87	8.21	8.55	8.89	9.23	9.57	9.91	10.26	10.60
66	1.81	3.07	4.35	5.66	6.99	7.33	7.66	8.00	8.34	8.69	9.03	9.38	9.72	10.07	10.42	10.77
65	1.88	3.15	4.44	5.76	7.11	7.45	7.79	8.14	8.48	8.83	9.17	9.52	9.88	10.23	10.58	10.94
64	1.94	3.23	4.53	5.87	7.23	7.58	7.92	8.27	8.62	8.97	9.32	9.68	10.03	10.39	10.75	11.11
63	2.01	3.31	4.63	5.98	7.36	7.71	8.06	8.41	8.76	9.12	9.48	9.83	10.20	10.56	10.92	11.29
62	2.08	3.39	4.72	6.09	7.48	7.84	8.19	8.55	8.91	9.27	9.63	10.00	10.36	10.73	11.10	11.47
61	2.16	3.47	4.82	6.20	7.62	7.97	8.33	8.70	9.06	9.42	9.79	10.16	10.53	10.90	11.28	11.65
60	2.23	3.56	4.92	6.32	7.75	8.11	8.48	8.84	9.21	9.58	9.96	10.33	10.71	11.09	11.47	11.85
59	2.30	3.64	5.02	6.44	7.89	8.25	8.62	9.00	9.37	9.75	10.13	10.51	10.89	11.27	11.66	12.04
58	2.38	3.73	5.13	6.56	8.03	8.40	8.78	9.15	9.53	9.92	10.30	10.69	11.07	11.46	11.85	12.25
57	2.45	3.82	5.23	6.68	8.17	8.55	8.93	9.31	9.70	10.09	10.48	10.87	11.26	11.66	12.06	12.46
56	2.53	3.92	5.34	6.81	8.32	8.71	9.09	9.48	9.87	10.27	10.66	11.06	11.46	11.86	12.27	12.67
55	2.61	4.01	5.45	6.94	8.47	8.86	9.26	9.65	10.05	10.45	10.85	11.26	11.66	12.07	12.48	12.90
54	2.69	4.11	5.57	7.08	8.63	9.03	9.42	9.83	10.23	10.64	11.05	11.46	11.87	12.29	12.71	13.13
53	2.77	4.20	5.68	7.21	8.79	9.19	9.60	10.01	10.42	10.83	11.25	11.67	12.09	12.51	12.94	13.37
52	2.86	4.31	5.80	7.35	8.96	9.37	9.78	10.19	10.61	11.03	11.46	11.88	12.31	12.74	13.18	13.61
51	2.94	4.41	5.93	7.50	9.13	9.54	9.96	10.39	10.81	11.24	11.67	12.10	12.54	12.98	13.42	13.87
50	3.03	4.51	6.05	7.65	9.30	9.73	10.15	10.58	11.02	11.45	11.89	12.33	12.78	13.23	13.68	14.13
49	3.12	4.62	6.18	7.80	9.49	9.92	10.35	10.79	11.23	11.67	12.12	12.57	13.03	13.48	13.94	14.41
48	3.21	4.73	6.31	7.96	9.67	10.11	10.55	11.00	11.45	11.90	12.36	12.82	13.28	13.75	14.22	14.69
47	3.30	4.84	6.45	8.12	9.87	10.31	10.76	11.22	11.68	12.14	12.61	13.08	13.55	14.02	14.50	14.99
46	3.40	4.96	6.59	8.29	10.07	10.52	10.98	11.45	11.91	12.39	12.86	13.34	13.82	14.31	14.80	15.29
45	3.50	5.08	6.73	8.47	10.28	10.74	11.21	11.68	12.16	12.64	13.13	13.62	14.11	14.61	15.11	15.62
44	3.60	5.20	6.88	8.64	10.49	10.96	11.44	11.93	12.41	12.91	13.40	13.90	14.41	14.92	15.43	15.95
43	3.70	5.32	7.03	8.83	10.71	11.20	11.69	12.18	12.68	13.18	13.69	14.20	14.72	15.24	15.77	16.30
42	3.80	5.45	7.19	9.02	10.94	11.44	11.94	12.44	12.95	13.47	13.99	14.52	15.05	15.58	16.12	16.66
41	3.91	5.58	7.35	9.22	11.18	11.69	12.20	12.72	13.24	13.77	14.30	14.84	15.39	15.93	16.49	17.04
40	4.02	5.72	7.52	9.43	11.43	11.95	12.48	13.01	13.54	14.08	14.63	15.18	15.74	16.30	16.87	17.44
39	4.13	5.86	7.69	9.64	11.70	12.23	12.76	13.31	13.86	14.41	14.97	15.54	16.11	16.69	17.27	17.86
35	4.61	6.47	8.45	10.59	12.86	13.45	14.05	14.66	15.27	15.90	16.53	17.16	17.80	18.45	19.11	19.77
30	5.30	7.35	9.59	12.04	14.69	15.39	16.09	16.81	17.54	18.27	19.02	19.77	20.54	21.30	22.08	22.86
25	6.11	8.44	11.05	13.96	17.18	18.03	18.90	19.78	20.67	21.58	22.50	23.43	24.37	25.31	26.27	27.23
20	7.12	9.84	13.02	16.70	20.87	21.98	23.10	24.25	25.41	26.59	27.78	28.98	30.18	31.40	32.62	33.85
15	8.42	11.81	16.02	21.18	27.11	28.67	30.26	31.86	33.48	35.11	36.75	38.40	40.05	41.70	43.36	45.02
10	10.26	15.01	21.71	30.40	40.08	42.55	45.03	47.52	50.01	52.51	55.00	57.50	60.00	62.50	65.00	67.50

Description: This table shows the price to pay for a bond at the yield rate. The yield is to maturity.

Example: The price of a 10.75 %, 23 year bond to yield 8 % to maturity is $ 128.72.

COUPON RATE, %

YIELD	7.00%	7.25%	7.50%	7.75%	8.00%	8.25%	8.50%	8.75%	9.00%	9.25%	9.50%	9.75%	10.00%	10.25%	10.50%	10.75%
0.00	261.00	266.75	272.50	278.25	284.00	289.75	295.50	301.25	307.00	312.75	318.50	324.25	330.00	335.75	341.50	347.25
1.00	223.01	228.13	233.26	238.38	243.51	248.63	253.76	258.88	264.01	269.13	274.26	279.38	284.51	289.64	294.76	299.89
2.00	191.82	196.41	201.00	205.59	210.18	214.77	219.36	223.95	228.55	233.14	237.73	242.32	246.91	251.50	256.09	260.68
3.00	166.11	170.25	174.38	178.51	182.64	186.77	190.91	195.04	199.17	203.30	207.43	211.57	215.70	219.83	223.96	228.09
4.00	144.84	148.58	152.31	156.05	159.78	163.52	167.26	170.99	174.73	178.47	182.20	185.94	189.68	193.41	197.15	200.89
4.25	140.11	143.76	147.40	151.05	154.69	158.34	161.99	165.63	169.28	172.93	176.57	180.22	183.87	187.51	191.16	194.80
4.50	135.59	139.15	142.71	146.27	149.83	153.39	156.95	160.51	164.07	167.63	171.19	174.75	178.30	181.86	185.42	188.98
4.75	131.28	134.75	138.23	141.70	145.18	148.65	152.13	155.61	159.08	162.56	166.03	169.51	172.98	176.46	179.93	183.41
5.00	127.15	130.55	133.94	137.34	140.73	144.13	147.52	150.91	154.31	157.70	161.10	164.49	167.89	171.28	174.67	178.07
5.25	123.21	126.53	129.84	133.16	136.48	139.79	143.11	146.42	149.74	153.06	156.37	159.69	163.00	166.32	169.64	172.95
5.50	119.44	122.68	125.92	129.16	132.40	135.64	138.89	142.13	145.37	148.61	151.85	155.09	158.33	161.57	164.81	168.05
5.75	115.84	119.00	122.17	125.34	128.51	131.67	134.84	138.01	141.18	144.34	147.51	150.68	153.85	157.01	160.18	163.35
6.00	112.39	115.48	118.58	121.68	124.78	127.87	130.97	134.07	137.16	140.26	143.36	146.45	149.55	152.65	155.74	158.84
6.25	109.09	112.12	115.14	118.17	121.20	124.23	127.26	130.29	133.32	136.35	139.37	142.40	145.43	148.46	151.49	154.52
6.50	105.93	108.89	111.85	114.81	117.78	120.74	123.70	126.67	129.63	132.59	135.55	138.52	141.48	144.44	147.41	150.37
6.75	102.90	105.80	108.70	111.60	114.50	117.40	120.29	123.19	126.09	128.99	131.89	134.79	137.69	140.59	143.49	146.39
7.00	100.00	102.84	105.68	108.51	111.35	114.19	117.03	119.86	122.70	125.54	128.38	131.21	134.05	136.89	139.73	142.56
7.25	97.22	100.00	102.78	105.56	108.33	111.11	113.89	116.67	119.45	122.22	125.00	127.78	130.56	133.34	136.11	138.89
7.50	94.56	97.28	100.00	102.72	105.44	108.16	110.88	113.60	116.32	119.04	121.76	124.48	127.20	129.92	132.64	135.36
7.75	92.01	94.67	97.34	100.00	102.66	105.33	107.99	110.66	113.32	115.99	118.65	121.32	123.98	126.65	129.31	131.98
8.00	89.56	92.17	94.78	97.39	100.00	102.61	105.22	107.83	110.44	113.05	115.66	118.27	120.88	123.50	126.11	128.72
8.25	87.21	89.77	92.33	94.88	97.44	100.00	102.56	105.12	107.67	110.23	112.79	115.35	117.91	120.47	123.02	125.58
8.50	84.95	87.46	89.97	92.48	94.98	97.49	100.00	102.51	105.02	107.52	110.03	112.54	115.05	117.55	120.06	122.57
8.75	82.79	85.25	87.71	90.17	92.62	95.08	97.54	100.00	102.46	104.92	107.38	109.83	112.29	114.75	117.21	119.67
9.00	80.71	83.12	85.53	87.94	90.36	92.77	95.18	97.59	100.00	102.41	104.82	107.23	109.64	112.06	114.47	116.88
9.25	78.72	81.08	83.45	85.81	88.18	90.54	92.91	95.27	97.64	100.00	102.36	104.73	107.09	109.46	111.82	114.19
9.50	76.80	79.12	81.44	83.76	86.08	88.40	90.72	93.04	95.36	97.68	100.00	102.32	104.64	106.96	109.28	111.60
9.75	74.95	77.23	79.51	81.78	84.06	86.34	88.61	90.89	93.17	95.45	97.72	100.00	102.28	104.55	106.83	109.11
10.00	73.18	75.41	77.65	79.88	82.12	84.35	86.59	88.82	91.06	93.29	95.53	97.76	100.00	102.24	104.47	106.71
10.25	71.47	73.67	75.86	78.06	80.25	82.45	84.64	86.83	89.03	91.22	93.42	95.61	97.81	100.00	102.19	104.39
10.50	69.83	71.99	74.14	76.30	78.45	80.61	82.76	84.92	87.07	89.23	91.38	93.54	95.69	97.85	100.00	102.15
10.75	68.25	70.37	72.49	74.60	76.72	78.84	80.95	83.07	85.19	87.30	89.42	91.53	93.65	95.77	97.88	100.00
11.00	66.73	68.81	70.89	72.97	75.05	77.13	79.21	81.29	83.37	85.45	87.53	89.60	91.68	93.76	95.84	97.92
11.25	65.27	67.31	69.36	71.40	73.44	75.48	77.53	79.57	81.61	83.66	85.70	87.74	89.79	91.83	93.87	95.91
11.50	63.86	65.87	67.87	69.88	71.89	73.90	75.91	77.91	79.92	81.93	83.94	85.95	87.95	89.96	91.97	93.98
11.75	62.50	64.47	66.45	68.42	70.39	72.37	74.34	76.32	78.29	80.26	82.24	84.21	86.18	88.16	90.13	92.11
12.00	61.19	63.13	65.07	67.01	68.95	70.89	72.83	74.77	76.71	78.65	80.59	82.54	84.48	86.42	88.36	90.30
12.25	59.93	61.83	63.74	65.65	67.56	69.47	71.38	73.28	75.19	77.10	79.01	80.92	82.83	84.73	86.64	88.55
12.50	58.71	60.58	62.46	64.34	66.21	68.09	69.97	71.84	73.72	75.60	77.48	79.35	81.23	83.11	84.98	86.86
12.75	57.53	59.38	61.22	63.07	64.92	66.76	68.61	70.46	72.30	74.15	75.99	77.84	79.69	81.53	83.38	85.23
13.00	56.39	58.21	60.03	61.84	63.66	65.48	67.30	69.11	70.93	72.75	74.56	76.38	78.20	80.01	81.83	83.65
13.25	55.30	57.09	58.87	60.66	62.45	64.24	66.03	67.81	69.60	71.39	73.18	74.97	76.75	78.54	80.33	82.12
13.50	54.24	56.00	57.76	59.52	61.28	63.04	64.80	66.56	68.32	70.08	71.84	73.60	75.36	77.12	78.88	80.64
13.75	53.21	54.95	56.68	58.41	60.15	61.88	63.61	65.34	67.08	68.81	70.54	72.28	74.01	75.74	77.47	79.21
14.00	52.22	53.93	55.64	57.34	59.05	60.76	62.46	64.17	65.87	67.58	69.29	70.99	72.70	74.41	76.11	77.82
14.25	51.27	52.95	54.63	56.31	57.99	59.67	61.35	63.03	64.71	66.39	68.07	69.75	71.43	73.11	74.79	76.47
14.50	50.34	52.00	53.65	55.31	56.96	58.62	60.27	61.93	63.59	65.24	66.90	68.55	70.21	71.86	73.52	75.17
14.75	49.45	51.08	52.71	54.34	55.97	57.60	59.23	60.86	62.49	64.12	65.76	67.39	69.02	70.65	72.28	73.91
15.00	48.58	50.19	51.80	53.40	55.01	56.62	58.22	59.83	61.44	63.04	64.65	66.26	67.86	69.47	71.08	72.68
15.25	47.74	49.33	50.91	52.49	54.08	55.66	57.24	58.83	60.41	62.00	63.58	65.16	66.75	68.33	69.91	71.50
15.50	46.93	48.49	50.05	51.61	53.17	54.74	56.30	57.86	59.42	60.98	62.54	64.10	65.66	67.22	68.78	70.34
15.75	46.14	47.68	49.22	50.76	52.30	53.84	55.38	56.92	58.45	59.99	61.53	63.07	64.61	66.15	67.69	69.23
16.00	45.38	46.90	48.42	49.93	51.45	52.97	54.48	56.00	57.52	59.04	60.55	62.07	63.59	65.10	66.62	68.14
16.25	44.64	46.14	47.63	49.13	50.63	52.12	53.62	55.12	56.61	58.11	59.60	61.10	62.60	64.09	65.59	67.08
16.50	43.93	45.40	46.88	48.35	49.83	51.30	52.78	54.26	55.73	57.21	58.68	60.16	61.63	63.11	64.58	66.06
16.75	43.23	44.69	46.14	47.60	49.05	50.51	51.96	53.42	54.88	56.33	57.79	59.24	60.70	62.15	63.61	65.07
17.00	42.56	43.99	45.43	46.86	48.30	49.74	51.17	52.61	54.04	55.48	56.92	58.35	59.79	61.23	62.66	64.10
17.25	41.90	43.32	44.74	46.15	47.57	48.99	50.40	51.82	53.24	54.65	56.07	57.49	58.91	60.32	61.74	63.16
17.50	41.27	42.66	44.06	45.46	46.86	48.26	49.66	51.05	52.45	53.85	55.25	56.65	58.05	59.45	60.84	62.24
17.75	40.65	42.03	43.41	44.79	46.17	47.55	48.93	50.31	51.69	53.07	54.45	55.83	57.21	58.59	59.97	61.35
18.00	40.05	41.41	42.77	44.14	45.50	46.86	48.22	49.59	50.95	52.31	53.67	55.04	56.40	57.76	59.12	60.49
18.25	39.47	40.81	42.16	43.50	44.85	46.19	47.54	48.88	50.23	51.57	52.92	54.26	55.61	56.95	58.30	59.64
18.50	38.90	40.23	41.56	42.88	44.21	45.54	46.87	48.20	49.53	50.85	52.18	53.51	54.84	56.17	57.50	58.82
18.75	38.35	39.66	40.97	42.28	43.60	44.91	46.22	47.53	48.84	50.15	51.47	52.78	54.09	55.40	56.71	58.02
19.00	37.81	39.11	40.40	41.70	43.00	44.29	45.59	46.88	48.18	49.47	50.77	52.06	53.36	54.66	55.95	57.25
20.00	35.81	37.05	38.28	39.51	40.75	41.98	43.22	44.45	45.69	46.92	48.15	49.39	50.62	51.86	53.09	54.33
25.00	28.32	29.31	30.31	31.31	32.30	33.30	34.29	35.29	36.28	37.28	38.28	39.27	40.27	41.26	42.26	43.25
30.00	23.46	24.29	25.12	25.95	26.79	27.62	28.45	29.28	30.11	30.94	31.78	32.61	33.44	34.27	35.10	35.94

Description: This table shows the yield to maturity of a bond purchased at the price shown in the index.

Example: The yield to maturity of a 10.75 %, 23 year bond at a price of 111.00 is 9.55 %.

COUPON RATE, %

PRICE	7.00%	7.25%	7.50%	7.75%	8.00%	8.25%	8.50%	8.75%	9.00%	9.25%	9.50%	9.75%	10.00%	10.25%	10.50%	10.75%
165	3.04	3.22	3.40	3.57	3.75	3.93	4.10	4.28	4.45	4.62	4.80	4.97	5.14	5.31	5.48	5.66
160	3.26	3.44	3.63	3.81	3.98	4.16	4.34	4.52	4.70	4.88	5.05	5.23	5.40	5.58	5.76	5.93
155	3.49	3.68	3.86	4.05	4.23	4.41	4.59	4.78	4.96	5.14	5.32	5.50	5.68	5.86	6.04	6.22
150	3.73	3.92	4.11	4.30	4.49	4.67	4.86	5.05	5.23	5.42	5.60	5.78	5.97	6.15	6.34	6.52
145	3.99	4.18	4.37	4.56	4.75	4.95	5.14	5.33	5.52	5.71	5.89	6.08	6.27	6.46	6.65	6.83
140	4.25	4.45	4.64	4.84	5.04	5.23	5.43	5.62	5.82	6.01	6.21	6.40	6.59	6.78	6.98	7.17
135	4.53	4.73	4.93	5.13	5.33	5.53	5.74	5.93	6.13	6.33	6.53	6.73	6.93	7.13	7.32	7.52
130	4.82	5.03	5.24	5.44	5.65	5.85	6.06	6.26	6.47	6.67	6.88	7.08	7.29	7.49	7.69	7.90
125	5.13	5.34	5.56	5.77	5.98	6.19	6.40	6.61	6.82	7.03	7.25	7.46	7.66	7.87	8.08	8.29
122	5.32	5.54	5.76	5.97	6.19	6.40	6.62	6.83	7.05	7.26	7.48	7.69	7.90	8.12	8.33	8.54
121	5.39	5.61	5.83	6.04	6.26	6.48	6.69	6.91	7.12	7.34	7.56	7.77	7.99	8.20	8.41	8.63
120	5.46	5.68	5.89	6.11	6.33	6.55	6.77	6.98	7.20	7.42	7.64	7.85	8.07	8.28	8.50	8.72
119	5.53	5.75	5.97	6.19	6.40	6.62	6.84	7.06	7.28	7.50	7.72	7.93	8.15	8.37	8.59	8.80
118	5.59	5.82	6.04	6.26	6.48	6.70	6.92	7.14	7.36	7.58	7.80	8.02	8.24	8.46	8.67	8.89
117	5.66	5.89	6.11	6.33	6.55	6.78	7.00	7.22	7.44	7.66	7.88	8.10	8.32	8.54	8.76	8.98
116	5.73	5.96	6.18	6.41	6.63	6.85	7.08	7.30	7.52	7.74	7.97	8.19	8.41	8.63	8.85	9.08
115	5.80	6.03	6.26	6.48	6.71	6.93	7.16	7.38	7.60	7.83	8.05	8.28	8.50	8.72	8.95	9.17
114	5.88	6.10	6.33	6.56	6.78	7.01	7.24	7.46	7.69	7.91	8.14	8.36	8.59	8.81	9.04	9.26
113	5.95	6.18	6.41	6.63	6.86	7.09	7.32	7.55	7.77	8.00	8.23	8.45	8.68	8.91	9.13	9.36
112	6.02	6.25	6.48	6.71	6.94	7.17	7.40	7.63	7.86	8.09	8.32	8.54	8.77	9.00	9.23	9.46
111	6.10	6.33	6.56	6.79	7.02	7.25	7.48	7.72	7.95	8.18	8.41	8.64	8.87	9.10	9.33	9.55
110	6.17	6.41	6.64	6.87	7.11	7.34	7.57	7.80	8.03	8.27	8.50	8.73	8.96	9.19	9.42	9.65
109	6.25	6.49	6.72	6.95	7.19	7.42	7.66	7.89	8.12	8.36	8.59	8.82	9.06	9.29	9.52	9.76
108	6.33	6.57	6.80	7.04	7.27	7.51	7.74	7.98	8.22	8.45	8.69	8.92	9.16	9.39	9.62	9.86
107	6.41	6.65	6.88	7.12	7.36	7.60	7.83	8.07	8.31	8.54	8.78	9.02	9.25	9.49	9.73	9.96
106	6.49	6.73	6.97	7.21	7.45	7.68	7.92	8.16	8.40	8.64	8.88	9.12	9.36	9.59	9.83	10.07
105	6.57	6.81	7.05	7.29	7.53	7.77	8.02	8.26	8.50	8.74	8.98	9.22	9.46	9.70	9.94	10.18
104	6.65	6.90	7.14	7.38	7.62	7.87	8.11	8.35	8.59	8.84	9.08	9.32	9.56	9.80	10.05	10.29
103	6.74	6.98	7.23	7.47	7.71	7.96	8.20	8.45	8.69	8.94	9.18	9.42	9.67	9.91	10.16	10.40
102	6.82	7.07	7.31	7.56	7.81	8.05	8.30	8.54	8.79	9.04	9.28	9.53	9.77	10.02	10.27	10.51
101	6.91	7.16	7.40	7.65	7.90	8.15	8.40	8.64	8.89	9.14	9.39	9.64	9.88	10.13	10.38	10.63
100	7.00	7.25	7.50	7.75	8.00	8.25	8.50	8.75	9.00	9.25	9.50	9.75	10.00	10.25	10.50	10.75
99	7.08	7.34	7.59	7.84	8.09	8.34	8.60	8.85	9.10	9.35	9.60	9.86	10.11	10.36	10.61	10.86
98	7.17	7.43	7.68	7.94	8.19	8.44	8.70	8.95	9.21	9.46	9.71	9.97	10.22	10.48	10.73	10.99
97	7.27	7.52	7.78	8.03	8.29	8.55	8.80	9.06	9.31	9.57	9.83	10.08	10.34	10.60	10.85	11.11
96	7.36	7.62	7.87	8.13	8.39	8.65	8.91	9.17	9.42	9.68	9.94	10.20	10.46	10.72	10.98	11.23
95	7.45	7.71	7.97	8.23	8.49	8.75	9.01	9.27	9.54	9.80	10.06	10.32	10.58	10.84	11.10	11.36
94	7.55	7.81	8.07	8.34	8.60	8.86	9.12	9.39	9.65	9.91	10.18	10.44	10.70	10.96	11.23	11.49
93	7.65	7.91	8.18	8.44	8.70	8.97	9.23	9.50	9.76	10.03	10.30	10.56	10.83	11.09	11.36	11.62
92	7.75	8.01	8.28	8.55	8.81	9.08	9.35	9.61	9.88	10.15	10.42	10.69	10.95	11.22	11.49	11.76
91	7.85	8.12	8.38	8.65	8.92	9.19	9.46	9.73	10.00	10.27	10.54	10.81	11.08	11.35	11.63	11.90
90	7.95	8.22	8.49	8.76	9.04	9.31	9.58	9.85	10.12	10.40	10.67	10.94	11.22	11.49	11.76	12.04
89	8.05	8.33	8.60	8.87	9.15	9.42	9.70	9.97	10.25	10.52	10.80	11.08	11.35	11.63	11.90	12.18
88	8.16	8.44	8.71	8.99	9.27	9.54	9.82	10.10	10.38	10.65	10.93	11.21	11.49	11.77	12.05	12.33
87	8.27	8.55	8.83	9.10	9.38	9.66	9.94	10.22	10.50	10.79	11.07	11.35	11.63	11.91	12.19	12.47
86	8.38	8.66	8.94	9.22	9.50	9.79	10.07	10.35	10.64	10.92	11.20	11.49	11.77	12.06	12.34	12.63
85	8.49	8.77	9.06	9.34	9.63	9.91	10.20	10.48	10.77	11.06	11.34	11.63	11.92	12.20	12.49	12.78
84	8.60	8.89	9.18	9.46	9.75	10.04	10.33	10.62	10.91	11.20	11.49	11.78	12.07	12.36	12.65	12.94
83	8.72	9.01	9.30	9.59	9.88	10.17	10.46	10.75	11.05	11.34	11.63	11.92	12.22	12.51	12.81	13.10
82	8.84	9.13	9.42	9.72	10.01	10.30	10.60	10.89	11.19	11.48	11.78	12.08	12.37	12.67	12.97	13.26
81	8.96	9.26	9.55	9.85	10.14	10.44	10.74	11.04	11.33	11.63	11.93	12.23	12.53	12.83	13.13	13.43
80	9.08	9.38	9.68	9.98	10.28	10.58	10.88	11.18	11.48	11.79	12.09	12.39	12.69	13.00	13.30	13.61
79	9.21	9.51	9.81	10.11	10.42	10.72	11.03	11.33	11.64	11.94	12.25	12.55	12.86	13.17	13.47	13.78
78	9.34	9.64	9.95	10.25	10.56	10.87	11.17	11.48	11.79	12.10	12.41	12.72	13.03	13.34	13.65	13.96
77	9.47	9.78	10.08	10.39	10.70	11.01	11.33	11.64	11.95	12.26	12.57	12.89	13.20	13.52	13.83	14.15
76	9.60	9.91	10.23	10.54	10.85	11.17	11.48	11.80	12.11	12.43	12.74	13.06	13.38	13.70	14.02	14.34
75	9.74	10.05	10.37	10.69	11.00	11.32	11.64	11.96	12.28	12.60	12.92	13.24	13.56	13.88	14.21	14.53
74	9.88	10.20	10.52	10.84	11.16	11.48	11.80	12.12	12.45	12.77	13.10	13.42	13.75	14.07	14.40	14.73
73	10.02	10.34	10.67	10.99	11.32	11.64	11.97	12.29	12.62	12.95	13.28	13.61	13.94	14.27	14.60	14.93
70	10.47	10.80	11.14	11.48	11.81	12.15	12.49	12.83	13.17	13.51	13.85	14.19	14.54	14.88	15.23	15.57
65	11.29	11.65	12.01	12.37	12.73	13.09	13.45	13.82	14.18	14.55	15.74	15.28	15.65	16.02	16.39	16.76
60	12.23	12.61	13.00	13.39	13.78	14.17	14.56	14.95	15.35	15.74	16.14	16.54	16.94	17.34	17.74	18.14
55	13.31	13.73	14.15	14.57	15.00	15.42	15.85	16.28	16.71	17.14	17.57	18.01	18.44	18.88	19.32	19.76
50	14.59	15.05	15.51	15.97	16.44	16.91	17.38	17.85	18.33	18.80	19.28	19.76	20.24	20.72	21.20	21.69
45	16.12	16.63	17.15	17.67	18.19	18.71	19.23	19.76	20.29	20.82	21.35	21.89	22.43	22.96	23.50	24.04
40	18.02	18.59	19.18	19.76	20.35	20.94	21.54	22.14	22.74	23.34	23.94	24.55	25.16	25.77	26.38	26.99
35	20.43	21.10	21.77	22.45	23.13	23.82	24.51	25.20	25.89	26.58	27.28	27.98	28.68	29.38	30.08	30.79
30	23.65	24.45	25.24	26.05	26.85	27.66	28.47	29.29	30.11	30.93	31.75	32.57	33.39	34.22	35.04	35.87

Description: This table shows the price to pay for a bond at the yield rate. The yield is to maturity.

Example: The price of a 15.00 %, 23 year bond to yield 8 % to maturity is $ 173.10.

COUPON RATE, %

YIELD	11.00%	11.25%	11.50%	11.75%	12.00%	12.25%	12.50%	12.75%	13.00%	13.25%	13.50%	13.75%	14.00%	14.25%	14.50%	15.00%
0.00	353.00	358.75	364.50	370.25	376.00	381.75	387.50	393.25	399.00	404.75	410.50	416.25	422.00	427.75	433.50	445.00
1.00	305.01	310.14	315.26	320.39	325.51	330.64	335.76	340.89	346.01	351.14	356.26	361.39	366.51	371.64	376.76	387.02
2.00	265.27	269.86	274.45	279.05	283.64	288.23	292.82	297.41	302.00	306.59	311.18	315.77	320.36	324.95	329.55	338.73
3.00	232.23	236.36	240.49	244.62	248.75	252.89	257.02	261.15	265.28	269.41	273.55	277.68	281.81	285.94	290.07	298.34
4.00	204.62	208.36	212.10	215.83	219.57	223.31	227.04	230.78	234.52	238.25	241.99	245.73	249.46	253.20	256.93	264.41
4.25	198.45	202.10	205.74	209.39	213.04	216.68	220.33	223.98	227.62	231.27	234.91	238.56	242.21	245.85	249.50	256.79
4.50	192.54	196.10	199.66	203.22	206.78	210.34	213.90	217.46	221.02	224.58	228.14	231.69	235.25	238.81	242.37	249.49
4.75	186.88	190.36	193.83	197.31	200.78	204.26	207.74	211.21	214.69	218.16	221.64	225.11	228.59	232.06	235.54	242.49
5.00	181.46	184.86	188.25	191.65	195.04	198.43	201.83	205.22	208.62	212.01	215.41	218.80	222.19	225.59	228.98	235.77
5.25	176.27	179.58	182.90	186.22	189.53	192.85	196.16	199.48	202.80	206.11	209.43	212.74	216.06	219.38	222.69	229.32
5.50	171.29	174.53	177.77	181.01	184.25	187.49	190.73	193.97	197.21	200.45	203.69	206.93	210.18	213.42	216.66	223.14
5.75	166.52	169.68	172.85	176.02	179.19	182.35	185.52	188.69	191.86	195.02	198.19	201.36	204.53	207.69	210.86	217.20
6.00	161.94	165.04	168.13	171.23	174.33	177.42	180.52	183.62	186.71	189.81	192.91	196.00	199.10	202.20	205.30	211.49
6.25	157.55	160.58	163.60	166.63	169.66	172.69	175.72	178.75	181.78	184.81	187.83	190.86	193.89	196.92	199.95	206.01
6.50	153.33	156.30	159.26	162.22	165.18	168.15	171.11	174.07	177.04	180.00	182.96	185.92	188.89	191.85	194.81	200.74
6.75	149.29	152.19	155.09	157.98	160.88	163.78	166.68	169.58	172.48	175.38	178.28	181.18	184.08	186.98	189.88	195.67
7.00	145.40	148.24	151.08	153.91	156.75	159.59	162.43	165.27	168.10	170.94	173.78	176.62	179.45	182.29	185.13	190.80
7.25	141.67	144.45	147.23	150.00	152.78	155.56	158.34	161.12	163.89	166.67	169.45	172.23	175.01	177.78	180.56	186.12
7.50	138.09	140.81	143.53	146.25	148.97	151.69	154.41	157.13	159.85	162.57	165.29	168.01	170.73	173.45	176.17	181.61
7.75	134.64	137.30	139.97	142.63	145.30	147.96	150.63	153.29	155.96	158.62	161.29	163.95	166.62	169.28	171.94	177.27
8.00	131.33	133.94	136.55	139.16	141.77	144.38	146.99	149.60	152.21	154.82	157.43	160.04	162.65	165.26	167.88	173.10
8.25	128.14	130.70	133.26	135.82	138.37	140.93	143.49	146.05	148.61	151.17	153.72	156.28	158.84	161.40	163.96	169.07
8.50	125.08	127.58	130.09	132.60	135.11	137.61	140.12	142.63	145.14	147.65	150.15	152.66	155.17	157.68	160.18	165.20
8.75	122.13	124.59	127.04	129.50	131.96	134.42	136.88	139.34	141.80	144.25	146.71	149.17	151.63	154.09	156.55	161.46
9.00	119.29	121.70	124.11	126.52	128.93	131.34	133.75	136.17	138.58	140.99	143.40	145.81	148.22	150.63	153.04	157.87
9.25	116.55	118.92	121.28	123.65	126.01	128.38	130.74	133.11	135.47	137.84	140.20	142.57	144.93	147.30	149.66	154.39
9.50	113.92	116.24	118.56	120.88	123.20	125.52	127.84	130.16	132.48	134.80	137.13	139.45	141.77	144.09	146.41	151.05
9.75	111.39	113.66	115.94	118.22	120.49	122.77	125.05	127.32	129.60	131.88	134.16	136.43	138.71	140.99	143.26	147.82
10.00	108.94	111.18	113.41	115.65	117.88	120.12	122.35	124.59	126.82	129.06	131.29	133.53	135.76	138.00	140.23	144.70
10.25	106.58	108.78	110.97	113.17	115.36	117.55	119.75	121.94	124.14	126.33	128.53	130.72	132.91	135.11	137.30	141.69
10.50	104.31	106.46	108.62	110.77	112.93	115.08	117.24	119.39	121.55	123.70	125.86	128.01	130.17	132.32	134.48	138.79
10.75	102.12	104.23	106.35	108.47	110.58	112.70	114.81	116.93	119.05	121.16	123.28	125.40	127.51	129.63	131.75	135.98
11.00	100.00	102.08	104.16	106.24	108.32	110.40	112.47	114.55	116.63	118.71	120.79	122.87	124.95	127.03	129.11	133.27
11.25	97.96	100.00	102.04	104.09	106.13	108.17	110.21	112.26	114.30	116.34	118.39	120.43	122.47	124.52	126.56	130.64
11.50	95.98	97.99	100.00	102.01	104.02	106.02	108.03	110.04	112.05	114.05	116.06	118.07	120.08	122.09	124.09	128.11
11.75	94.08	96.05	98.03	100.00	101.97	103.95	105.92	107.89	109.87	111.84	113.82	115.79	117.76	119.74	121.71	125.66
12.00	92.24	94.18	96.12	98.06	100.00	101.94	103.88	105.82	107.76	109.70	111.64	113.58	115.52	117.46	119.41	123.29
12.25	90.46	92.37	94.28	96.18	98.09	100.00	101.91	103.82	105.72	107.63	109.54	111.45	113.36	115.27	117.17	120.99
12.50	88.74	90.61	92.49	94.37	96.25	98.12	100.00	101.88	103.75	105.63	107.51	109.39	111.26	113.14	115.02	118.77
12.75	87.07	88.92	90.77	92.61	94.46	96.31	98.15	100.00	101.85	103.69	105.54	107.39	109.23	111.08	112.93	116.62
13.00	85.46	87.28	89.10	90.92	92.73	94.55	96.37	98.18	100.00	101.82	103.63	105.45	107.27	109.08	110.90	114.54
13.25	83.91	85.70	87.48	89.27	91.06	92.85	94.64	96.42	98.21	100.00	101.79	103.58	105.36	107.15	108.94	112.52
13.50	82.40	84.16	85.92	87.68	89.44	91.20	92.96	94.72	96.48	98.24	100.00	101.76	103.52	105.28	107.04	110.56
13.75	80.94	82.67	84.40	86.14	87.87	89.60	91.34	93.07	94.80	96.53	98.27	100.00	101.73	103.47	105.20	108.66
14.00	79.52	81.23	82.94	84.64	86.35	88.06	89.76	91.47	93.17	94.88	96.59	98.29	100.00	101.71	103.41	106.83
14.25	78.15	79.84	81.52	83.20	84.88	86.56	88.24	89.92	91.60	93.28	94.96	96.64	98.32	100.00	101.68	105.04
14.50	76.83	78.48	80.14	81.79	83.45	85.10	86.76	88.41	90.07	91.72	93.38	95.03	96.69	98.34	100.00	103.31
14.75	75.54	77.17	78.80	80.43	82.06	83.69	85.32	86.95	88.59	90.22	91.85	93.48	95.11	96.74	98.37	101.63
15.00	74.29	75.90	77.50	79.11	80.72	82.33	83.93	85.54	87.15	88.75	90.36	91.97	93.57	95.18	96.79	100.00
15.25	73.08	74.66	76.25	77.83	79.41	81.00	82.58	84.16	85.75	87.33	88.92	90.50	92.08	93.67	95.25	98.42
15.50	71.90	73.47	75.03	76.59	78.15	79.71	81.27	82.83	84.39	85.95	87.51	89.07	90.63	92.20	93.76	96.88
15.75	70.76	72.30	73.84	75.38	76.92	78.46	80.00	81.54	83.07	84.61	86.15	87.69	89.23	90.77	92.31	95.38
16.00	69.66	71.17	72.69	74.21	75.73	77.24	78.76	80.28	81.79	83.31	84.83	86.35	87.86	89.38	90.90	93.93
16.25	68.58	70.08	71.57	73.07	74.57	76.06	77.56	79.05	80.55	82.05	83.54	85.04	86.53	88.03	89.53	92.52
16.50	67.54	69.01	70.49	71.96	73.44	74.91	76.39	77.87	79.34	80.82	82.29	83.77	85.24	86.72	88.19	91.15
16.75	66.52	67.98	69.43	70.89	72.34	73.80	75.25	76.71	78.17	79.62	81.08	82.53	83.99	85.44	86.90	89.81
17.00	65.53	66.97	68.41	69.84	71.28	72.71	74.15	75.59	77.02	78.46	79.89	81.33	82.77	84.20	85.64	88.51
17.25	64.57	65.99	67.41	68.83	70.24	71.66	73.08	74.49	75.91	77.33	78.74	80.16	81.58	83.00	84.41	87.25
17.50	63.64	65.04	66.44	67.84	69.23	70.63	72.03	73.43	74.83	76.23	77.63	79.02	80.42	81.82	83.22	86.02
17.75	62.73	64.11	65.49	66.87	68.25	69.63	71.01	72.39	73.77	75.16	76.54	77.92	79.30	80.68	82.06	84.82
18.00	61.85	63.21	64.57	65.94	67.30	68.66	70.02	71.39	72.75	74.11	75.47	76.84	78.20	79.56	80.92	83.65
18.25	60.99	62.33	63.68	65.02	66.37	67.72	69.06	70.41	71.75	73.10	74.44	75.79	77.13	78.48	79.82	82.51
18.50	60.15	61.48	62.81	64.14	65.47	66.79	68.12	69.45	70.78	72.11	73.43	74.76	76.09	77.42	78.75	81.40
18.75	59.34	60.65	61.96	63.27	64.58	65.90	67.21	68.52	69.83	71.14	72.45	73.77	75.08	76.39	77.70	80.32
19.00	58.54	59.84	61.13	62.43	63.72	65.02	66.32	67.61	68.91	70.20	71.50	72.79	74.09	75.38	76.68	79.27
20.00	55.56	56.80	58.03	59.26	60.50	61.73	62.97	64.20	65.44	66.67	67.91	69.14	70.37	71.61	72.84	75.31
25.00	44.25	45.24	46.24	47.24	48.23	49.23	50.22	51.22	52.21	53.21	54.20	55.20	56.20	57.19	58.19	60.18
30.00	36.77	37.60	38.43	39.26	40.10	40.93	41.76	42.59	43.42	44.26	45.09	45.92	46.75	47.58	48.42	50.08

BOND YIELD

Description: This table shows the yield to maturity of a bond purchased at the price shown in the index.

Example: The yield to maturity of a 15.00 %, 23 year bond at a price of 125.00 is 11.81 %.

COUPON RATE, %

PRICE	11.00%	11.25%	11.50%	11.75%	12.00%	12.25%	12.50%	12.75%	13.00%	13.25%	13.50%	13.75%	14.00%	14.25%	14.50%	15.00%
250	2.43	2.57	2.70	2.83	2.96	3.09	3.21	3.34	3.47	3.60	3.72	3.85	3.98	4.10	4.23	4.48
240	2.74	2.88	3.01	3.14	3.28	3.41	3.54	3.67	3.80	3.93	4.06	4.19	4.32	4.45	4.58	4.84
230	3.07	3.21	3.34	3.48	3.62	3.75	3.89	4.02	4.16	4.29	4.43	4.56	4.69	4.82	4.96	5.22
220	3.42	3.56	3.70	3.84	3.98	4.12	4.26	4.40	4.53	4.67	4.81	4.95	5.08	5.22	5.36	5.63
210	3.79	3.93	4.08	4.22	4.36	4.51	4.65	4.79	4.94	5.08	5.22	5.36	5.50	5.64	5.78	6.06
200	4.18	4.33	4.48	4.63	4.78	4.93	5.07	5.22	5.37	5.52	5.66	5.81	5.95	6.10	6.24	6.53
195	4.39	4.54	4.69	4.85	5.00	5.15	5.30	5.45	5.60	5.75	5.89	6.04	6.19	6.34	6.49	6.78
190	4.61	4.76	4.92	5.07	5.22	5.38	5.53	5.68	5.83	5.99	6.14	6.29	6.44	6.59	6.74	7.04
185	4.83	4.99	5.15	5.30	5.46	5.61	5.77	5.93	6.08	6.24	6.39	6.54	6.70	6.85	7.00	7.31
180	5.06	5.22	5.39	5.54	5.70	5.86	6.02	6.18	6.34	6.49	6.65	6.81	6.96	7.12	7.28	7.59
175	5.31	5.47	5.63	5.80	5.96	6.12	6.28	6.44	6.61	6.77	6.93	7.09	7.25	7.40	7.56	7.88
170	5.56	5.73	5.89	6.06	6.23	6.39	6.56	6.72	6.89	7.05	7.21	7.38	7.54	7.70	7.86	8.19
165	5.83	6.00	6.17	6.34	6.51	6.67	6.84	7.01	7.18	7.35	7.51	7.68	7.85	8.01	8.18	8.51
160	6.10	6.28	6.45	6.62	6.80	6.97	7.14	7.31	7.49	7.66	7.83	8.00	8.17	8.34	8.51	8.85
155	6.39	6.57	6.75	6.93	7.10	7.28	7.46	7.63	7.81	7.98	8.16	8.33	8.51	8.68	8.85	9.20
150	6.70	6.88	7.06	7.25	7.43	7.61	7.79	7.97	8.15	8.33	8.51	8.68	8.86	9.04	9.22	9.58
145	7.02	7.21	7.39	7.58	7.77	7.95	8.14	8.32	8.51	8.69	8.87	9.06	9.24	9.42	9.61	9.97
140	7.36	7.55	7.74	7.93	8.12	8.31	8.50	8.69	8.88	9.07	9.26	9.45	9.64	9.83	10.01	10.39
135	7.72	7.92	8.11	8.31	8.50	8.70	8.89	9.09	9.28	9.48	9.67	9.87	10.06	10.25	10.45	10.83
130	8.10	8.30	8.50	8.70	8.91	9.11	9.31	9.51	9.71	9.91	10.11	10.31	10.51	10.71	10.91	11.31
125	8.50	8.71	8.92	9.13	9.33	9.54	9.75	9.96	10.16	10.37	10.58	10.78	10.99	11.20	11.40	11.81
120	8.93	9.15	9.36	9.58	9.79	10.01	10.22	10.43	10.65	10.86	11.08	11.29	11.50	11.72	11.93	12.36
115	9.39	9.61	9.84	10.06	10.28	10.50	10.73	10.95	11.17	11.39	11.61	11.83	12.05	12.28	12.50	12.94
113	9.58	9.81	10.04	10.26	10.49	10.71	10.94	11.16	11.39	11.61	11.84	12.06	12.29	12.51	12.74	13.18
112	9.68	9.91	10.14	10.37	10.59	10.82	11.05	11.27	11.50	11.73	11.95	12.18	12.41	12.63	12.86	13.31
111	9.78	10.01	10.24	10.47	10.70	10.93	11.16	11.39	11.61	11.84	12.07	12.30	12.53	12.75	12.98	13.44
110	9.89	10.12	10.35	10.58	10.81	11.04	11.27	11.50	11.73	11.96	12.19	12.42	12.65	12.88	13.11	13.57
109	9.99	10.22	10.45	10.69	10.92	11.15	11.38	11.62	11.85	12.08	12.31	12.54	12.77	13.01	13.24	13.70
108	10.09	10.33	10.56	10.80	11.03	11.26	11.50	11.73	11.97	12.20	12.43	12.67	12.90	13.13	13.37	13.83
107	10.20	10.44	10.67	10.91	11.14	11.38	11.62	11.85	12.09	12.32	12.56	12.79	13.03	13.27	13.50	13.97
106	10.31	10.55	10.78	11.02	11.26	11.50	11.74	11.97	12.21	12.45	12.69	12.92	13.16	13.40	13.64	14.11
105	10.42	10.66	10.90	11.14	11.38	11.62	11.86	12.10	12.34	12.58	12.81	13.05	13.29	13.53	13.77	14.25
104	10.53	10.77	11.01	11.26	11.50	11.74	11.98	12.22	12.46	12.70	12.95	13.19	13.43	13.67	13.91	14.39
103	10.64	10.89	11.13	11.37	11.62	11.86	12.11	12.35	12.59	12.84	13.08	13.32	13.57	13.81	14.05	14.54
102	10.76	11.00	11.25	11.50	11.74	11.99	12.23	12.48	12.72	12.97	13.22	13.46	13.71	13.95	14.20	14.69
101	10.88	11.12	11.37	11.62	11.87	12.12	12.36	12.61	12.86	13.11	13.35	13.60	13.85	14.10	14.35	14.84
100	11.00	11.25	11.50	11.75	12.00	12.25	12.50	12.75	13.00	13.25	13.50	13.75	14.00	14.25	14.50	15.00
99	11.12	11.37	11.62	11.87	12.12	12.38	12.63	12.88	13.13	13.39	13.64	13.89	14.14	14.40	14.65	15.15
98	11.24	11.49	11.75	12.00	12.26	12.51	12.77	13.02	13.28	13.53	13.78	14.04	14.29	14.55	14.80	15.31
97	11.37	11.62	11.88	12.14	12.39	12.65	12.91	13.16	13.42	13.68	13.93	14.19	14.45	14.70	14.96	15.47
96	11.49	11.75	12.01	12.27	12.53	12.79	13.05	13.31	13.57	13.82	14.08	14.34	14.60	14.86	15.12	15.64
95	11.62	11.88	12.15	12.41	12.67	12.93	13.19	13.45	13.72	13.98	14.24	14.50	14.76	15.02	15.29	15.81
94	11.76	12.02	12.28	12.55	12.81	13.07	13.34	13.60	13.87	14.13	14.40	14.66	14.92	15.19	15.45	15.98
93	11.89	12.16	12.42	12.69	12.96	13.22	13.49	13.76	14.02	14.29	14.56	14.82	15.09	15.36	15.62	16.16
92	12.03	12.30	12.57	12.83	13.10	13.37	13.64	13.91	14.18	14.45	14.72	14.99	15.26	15.53	15.80	16.34
91	12.17	12.44	12.71	12.98	13.25	13.53	13.80	14.07	14.34	14.61	14.89	15.16	15.43	15.70	15.98	16.52
90	12.31	12.58	12.86	13.13	13.41	13.68	13.96	14.23	14.51	14.78	15.06	15.33	15.61	15.88	16.16	16.71
89	12.46	12.73	13.01	13.29	13.56	13.84	14.12	14.40	14.67	14.95	15.23	15.51	15.79	16.06	16.34	16.90
88	12.60	12.88	13.16	13.44	13.72	14.00	14.28	14.57	14.85	15.13	15.41	15.69	15.97	16.25	16.53	17.10
87	12.76	13.04	13.32	13.60	13.89	14.17	14.45	14.74	15.02	15.30	15.59	15.87	16.16	16.44	16.73	17.29
86	12.91	13.20	13.48	13.77	14.05	14.34	14.63	14.91	15.20	15.49	15.77	16.06	16.35	16.64	16.92	17.50
85	13.07	13.36	13.65	13.93	14.22	14.51	14.80	15.09	15.38	15.67	15.96	16.25	16.54	16.83	17.12	17.71
84	13.23	13.52	13.81	14.11	14.40	14.69	14.98	15.28	15.57	15.86	16.16	16.45	16.74	17.04	17.33	17.92
83	13.39	13.69	13.98	14.28	14.57	14.87	15.17	15.46	15.76	16.06	16.35	16.65	16.95	17.24	17.54	18.14
82	13.56	13.86	14.16	14.46	14.76	15.06	15.35	15.65	15.95	16.25	16.55	16.85	17.16	17.46	17.76	18.36
81	13.73	14.04	14.34	14.64	14.94	15.24	15.55	15.85	16.15	16.46	16.76	17.07	17.37	17.67	17.98	18.59
80	13.91	14.22	14.52	14.83	15.13	15.44	15.74	16.05	16.36	16.67	16.97	17.28	17.59	17.90	18.20	18.82
79	14.09	14.40	14.71	15.02	15.33	15.64	15.95	16.26	16.57	16.88	17.19	17.50	17.81	18.12	18.44	19.06
78	14.27	14.59	14.90	15.21	15.52	15.84	16.15	16.47	16.78	17.10	17.41	17.73	18.04	18.36	18.67	19.31
77	14.46	14.78	15.09	15.41	15.73	16.05	16.36	16.68	17.00	17.32	17.64	17.96	18.28	18.60	18.92	19.56
76	14.65	14.97	15.29	15.62	15.94	16.26	16.58	16.90	17.22	17.55	17.87	18.19	18.52	18.84	19.17	19.81
75	14.85	15.18	15.50	15.83	16.15	16.48	16.80	17.13	17.45	17.78	18.11	18.44	18.76	19.09	19.42	20.08
74	15.05	15.38	15.71	16.04	16.37	16.70	17.03	17.36	17.69	18.02	18.35	18.69	19.02	19.35	19.68	20.35
73	15.26	15.59	15.93	16.26	16.59	16.93	17.26	17.60	17.93	18.27	18.61	18.94	19.28	19.61	19.95	20.63
70	15.92	16.26	16.61	16.96	17.30	17.65	18.00	18.35	18.70	19.05	19.40	19.75	20.10	20.45	20.80	21.51
65	17.13	17.51	17.88	18.25	18.63	19.00	19.38	19.75	20.13	20.50	20.88	21.26	21.64	22.02	22.39	23.15
60	18.54	18.94	19.35	19.75	20.16	20.57	20.97	21.38	21.79	22.20	22.61	23.01	23.42	23.83	24.25	25.07
55	20.20	20.64	21.08	21.52	21.96	22.41	22.85	23.30	23.74	24.19	24.64	25.08	25.53	25.98	26.43	27.33

BOND PRICE

Description: This table shows the price to pay for a bond at the yield rate. The yield is to maturity.

Example: The price of a 6.75 %, 24 year bond to yield 8 % to maturity is $ 86.75.

COUPON RATE, %

YIELD	0.00%	1.00%	2.00%	3.00%	4.00%	4.25%	4.50%	4.75%	5.00%	5.25%	5.50%	5.75%	6.00%	6.25%	6.50%	6.75%
0.00	100.00	124.00	148.00	172.00	196.00	202.00	208.00	214.00	220.00	226.00	232.00	238.00	244.00	250.00	256.00	262.00
1.00	78.71	100.00	121.29	142.58	163.87	169.19	174.52	179.84	185.16	190.48	195.81	201.13	206.45	211.77	217.10	222.42
2.00	62.03	81.01	100.00	118.99	137.97	142.72	147.47	152.21	156.96	161.71	166.45	171.20	175.95	180.69	185.44	190.19
3.00	48.94	65.96	82.98	100.00	117.02	121.28	125.53	129.79	134.04	138.30	142.55	146.81	151.06	155.32	159.57	163.83
4.00	38.65	53.99	69.33	84.66	100.00	103.83	107.67	111.50	115.34	119.17	123.00	126.84	130.67	134.51	138.34	142.18
4.25	36.45	51.40	66.35	81.31	96.26	100.00	103.74	107.48	111.22	114.95	118.69	122.43	126.17	129.91	133.65	137.38
4.50	34.37	48.95	63.54	78.12	92.71	96.35	100.00	103.65	107.29	110.94	114.58	118.23	121.88	125.52	129.17	132.82
4.75	32.41	46.64	60.87	75.10	89.33	92.89	96.44	100.00	103.56	107.11	110.67	114.23	117.79	121.34	124.90	128.46
5.00	30.57	44.45	58.34	72.23	86.11	89.59	93.06	96.53	100.00	103.47	106.94	110.41	113.89	117.36	120.83	124.30
5.25	28.83	42.39	55.94	69.50	83.05	86.44	89.83	93.22	96.61	100.00	103.39	106.78	110.17	113.56	116.95	120.33
5.50	27.19	40.43	53.67	66.91	80.14	83.45	86.76	90.07	93.38	96.69	100.00	103.31	106.62	109.93	113.24	116.55
5.75	25.65	38.58	51.51	64.44	77.37	80.60	83.84	87.07	90.30	93.53	96.77	100.00	103.23	106.47	109.70	112.93
6.00	24.20	36.83	49.47	62.10	74.73	77.89	81.05	84.21	87.37	90.52	93.68	96.84	100.00	103.16	106.32	109.48
6.25	22.83	35.18	47.53	59.87	72.22	75.31	78.39	81.48	84.57	87.65	90.74	93.83	96.91	100.00	103.09	106.17
6.50	21.54	33.61	45.68	57.75	69.82	72.84	75.86	78.88	81.89	84.91	87.93	90.95	93.96	96.98	100.00	103.02
6.75	20.33	32.13	43.93	55.74	67.54	70.49	73.44	76.39	79.34	82.29	85.25	88.20	91.15	94.10	97.05	100.00
7.00	19.18	30.73	42.27	53.82	65.36	68.25	71.14	74.02	76.91	79.80	82.68	85.57	88.45	91.34	94.23	97.11
7.25	18.10	29.40	40.69	51.99	63.29	66.11	68.93	71.76	74.58	77.41	80.23	83.06	85.88	88.70	91.53	94.35
7.50	17.08	28.14	39.19	50.25	61.31	64.07	66.83	69.60	72.36	75.12	77.89	80.65	83.42	86.18	88.94	91.71
7.75	16.12	26.95	37.77	48.59	59.41	62.12	64.83	67.53	70.24	72.94	75.65	78.35	81.06	83.77	86.47	89.18
8.00	15.22	25.82	36.41	47.01	57.61	60.26	62.91	65.56	68.21	70.86	73.51	76.16	78.80	81.45	84.10	86.75
8.25	14.37	24.75	35.13	45.51	55.89	58.48	61.08	63.67	66.27	68.86	71.46	74.05	76.65	79.24	81.84	84.43
8.50	13.56	23.73	33.90	44.07	54.24	56.78	59.32	61.87	64.41	66.95	69.49	72.04	74.58	77.12	79.66	82.20
8.75	12.80	22.77	32.74	42.70	52.67	55.16	57.65	60.14	62.63	65.12	67.61	70.10	72.60	75.09	77.58	80.07
9.00	12.09	21.86	31.63	41.39	51.16	53.60	56.04	58.49	60.93	63.37	65.81	68.25	70.70	73.14	75.58	78.02
9.25	11.42	20.99	30.57	40.15	49.72	52.12	54.51	56.90	59.30	61.69	64.09	66.48	68.88	71.27	73.66	76.06
9.50	10.78	20.17	29.56	38.95	48.35	50.69	53.04	55.39	57.74	60.09	62.43	64.78	67.13	69.48	71.83	74.17
9.75	10.18	19.39	28.60	37.82	47.03	49.33	51.64	53.94	56.24	58.54	60.85	63.15	65.45	67.76	70.06	72.36
10.00	9.61	18.65	27.69	36.73	45.77	48.03	50.29	52.55	54.81	57.07	59.33	61.59	63.85	66.11	68.36	70.62
10.25	9.08	17.95	26.82	35.69	44.56	46.78	49.00	51.21	53.43	55.65	57.87	60.08	62.30	64.52	66.74	68.95
10.50	8.58	17.28	25.99	34.70	43.40	45.58	47.76	49.94	52.11	54.29	56.47	58.64	60.82	63.00	65.17	67.35
10.75	8.10	16.65	25.20	33.75	42.30	44.43	46.57	48.71	50.85	52.98	55.12	57.26	59.39	61.53	63.67	65.81
11.00	7.65	16.05	24.44	32.84	41.23	43.33	45.43	47.53	49.63	51.73	53.83	55.93	58.02	60.12	62.22	64.32
11.25	7.23	15.48	23.72	31.97	40.22	42.28	44.34	46.40	48.46	50.52	52.58	54.65	56.71	58.77	60.83	62.89
11.50	6.83	14.93	23.04	31.14	39.24	41.26	43.29	45.31	47.34	49.37	51.39	53.42	55.44	57.47	59.49	61.52
11.75	6.46	14.42	22.38	30.34	38.30	40.29	42.28	44.27	46.26	48.25	50.24	52.23	54.22	56.21	58.20	60.19
12.00	6.10	13.92	21.75	29.57	37.40	39.36	41.31	43.27	45.22	47.18	49.14	51.09	53.05	55.01	56.96	58.92
12.25	5.76	13.46	21.15	28.84	36.54	38.46	40.38	42.30	44.23	46.15	48.07	50.00	51.92	53.84	55.77	57.69
12.50	5.45	13.01	20.58	28.14	35.70	37.60	39.49	41.38	43.27	45.16	47.05	48.94	50.83	52.72	54.61	56.51
12.75	5.15	12.59	20.03	27.47	34.91	36.77	38.63	40.49	42.35	44.21	46.06	47.92	49.78	51.64	53.50	55.36
13.00	4.87	12.18	19.50	26.82	34.14	35.97	37.80	39.63	41.46	43.29	45.12	46.94	48.77	50.60	52.43	54.26
13.25	4.60	11.80	19.00	26.20	33.40	35.20	37.00	38.80	40.60	42.40	44.20	46.00	47.80	49.60	51.40	53.20
13.50	4.35	11.43	18.52	25.60	32.69	34.46	36.23	38.00	39.77	41.55	43.32	45.09	46.86	48.63	50.40	52.17
13.75	4.11	11.08	18.06	25.03	32.01	33.75	35.49	37.24	38.98	40.72	42.47	44.21	45.95	47.70	49.44	51.18
14.00	3.89	10.75	17.62	24.48	31.35	33.06	34.78	36.50	38.21	39.93	41.65	43.36	45.08	46.79	48.51	50.23
14.25	3.67	10.43	17.19	23.95	30.71	32.40	34.09	35.78	37.47	39.16	40.85	42.54	44.23	45.92	47.61	49.30
14.50	3.47	10.13	16.79	23.45	30.10	31.77	33.43	35.10	36.76	38.42	40.09	41.75	43.42	45.08	46.74	48.41
14.75	3.29	9.84	16.40	22.96	29.51	31.15	32.79	34.43	36.07	37.71	39.35	40.99	42.63	44.27	45.91	47.54
15.00	3.11	9.57	16.03	22.49	28.95	30.56	32.18	33.79	35.40	37.02	38.63	40.25	41.86	43.48	45.09	46.71
15.25	2.94	9.30	15.67	22.03	28.40	29.99	31.58	33.17	34.76	36.35	37.94	39.54	41.13	42.72	44.31	45.90
15.50	2.78	9.05	15.32	21.60	27.87	29.44	31.00	32.57	34.14	35.71	37.28	38.85	40.41	41.98	43.55	45.12
15.75	2.63	8.81	14.99	21.18	27.36	28.90	30.45	31.99	33.54	35.09	36.63	38.18	39.72	41.27	42.81	44.36
16.00	2.49	8.58	14.68	20.77	26.87	28.39	29.91	31.44	32.96	34.48	36.01	37.53	39.05	40.58	42.10	43.63
16.25	2.35	8.36	14.37	20.38	26.39	27.89	29.39	30.90	32.40	33.90	35.40	36.90	38.41	39.91	41.41	42.91
16.50	2.23	8.15	14.08	20.00	25.93	27.41	28.89	30.37	31.85	33.34	34.82	36.30	37.78	39.26	40.74	42.22
16.75	2.11	7.95	13.79	19.64	25.48	26.94	28.41	29.87	31.33	32.79	34.25	35.71	37.17	38.63	40.09	41.56
17.00	1.99	7.76	13.52	19.29	25.05	26.49	27.94	29.38	30.82	32.26	33.70	35.14	36.58	38.02	39.47	40.91
17.25	1.89	7.57	13.26	18.95	24.64	26.06	27.48	28.90	30.32	31.75	33.17	34.59	36.01	37.43	38.86	40.28
17.50	1.78	7.40	13.01	18.62	24.23	25.64	27.04	28.44	29.85	31.25	32.65	34.05	35.46	36.86	38.26	39.67
17.75	1.69	7.23	12.77	18.30	23.84	25.23	26.61	28.00	29.38	30.77	32.15	33.54	34.92	36.31	37.69	39.07
18.00	1.60	7.06	12.53	18.00	23.46	24.83	26.20	27.57	28.93	30.30	31.67	33.03	34.40	35.77	37.13	38.50
18.25	1.51	6.91	12.31	17.70	23.10	24.45	25.80	27.15	28.50	29.84	31.19	32.54	33.89	35.24	36.59	37.94
18.50	1.43	6.76	12.09	17.42	22.74	24.08	25.41	26.74	28.07	29.40	30.74	32.07	33.40	34.73	36.06	37.40
18.75	1.35	6.62	11.88	17.14	22.40	23.71	25.03	26.35	27.66	28.98	30.29	31.61	32.92	34.24	35.55	36.87
19.00	1.28	6.48	11.67	16.87	22.07	23.36	24.66	25.96	27.26	28.56	29.86	31.16	32.46	33.76	35.05	36.35
20.00	1.03	5.98	10.93	15.88	20.82	22.06	23.30	24.54	25.77	27.01	28.25	29.48	30.72	31.96	33.20	34.43
25.00	.35	4.34	8.32	12.31	16.29	17.29	18.29	19.28	20.28	21.28	22.27	23.27	24.27	25.26	26.26	27.26
30.00	.12	3.45	6.78	10.11	13.44	14.27	15.10	15.94	16.77	17.60	18.43	19.27	20.10	20.93	21.76	22.59

Description: This table shows the yield to maturity of a bond purchased at the price shown in the index.

Example: The yield to maturity of a 6.75 %, 24 year bond at a price of 80.00 is 8.75 %.

PRICE	0.00%	1.00%	2.00%	3.00%	4.00%	4.25%	4.50%	4.75%	5.00%	5.25%	5.50%	5.75%	6.00%	6.25%	6.50%	6.75%
								COUPON RATE, %								
100	0.00	1.00	2.00	3.00	4.00	4.25	4.50	4.75	5.00	5.25	5.50	5.75	6.00	6.25	6.50	6.75
99	.04	1.04	2.05	3.05	4.06	4.31	4.56	4.82	5.07	5.32	5.57	5.82	6.07	6.33	6.58	6.83
98	.08	1.09	2.10	3.11	4.13	4.38	4.63	4.89	5.14	5.39	5.65	5.90	6.16	6.41	6.66	6.92
97	.12	1.14	2.16	3.17	4.19	4.45	4.71	4.96	5.22	5.47	5.73	5.98	6.24	6.49	6.75	7.01
96	.17	1.19	2.21	3.24	4.26	4.52	4.78	5.03	5.29	5.55	5.81	6.06	6.32	6.58	6.84	7.09
95	.21	1.24	2.27	3.30	4.33	4.59	4.85	5.11	5.37	5.63	5.89	6.15	6.41	6.67	6.93	7.19
94	.25	1.29	2.32	3.36	4.40	4.66	4.92	5.19	5.45	5.71	5.97	6.23	6.49	6.75	7.02	7.28
93	.30	1.34	2.38	3.43	4.47	4.74	5.00	5.26	5.53	5.79	6.05	6.32	6.58	6.84	7.11	7.37
92	.34	1.39	2.44	3.49	4.55	4.81	5.08	5.34	5.61	5.87	6.14	6.40	6.67	6.93	7.20	7.47
91	.39	1.44	2.50	3.56	4.62	4.89	5.15	5.42	5.69	5.95	6.22	6.49	6.76	7.03	7.30	7.56
90	.43	1.49	2.56	3.62	4.69	4.96	5.23	5.50	5.77	6.04	6.31	6.58	6.85	7.12	7.39	7.66
89	.48	1.55	2.62	3.69	4.77	5.04	5.31	5.58	5.85	6.13	6.40	6.67	6.94	7.22	7.49	7.76
88	.53	1.60	2.68	3.76	4.85	5.12	5.39	5.67	5.94	6.21	6.49	6.76	7.04	7.31	7.59	7.87
87	.58	1.65	2.74	3.83	4.92	5.20	5.48	5.75	6.03	6.30	6.58	6.86	7.13	7.41	7.69	7.97
86	.62	1.71	2.80	3.90	5.00	5.28	5.56	5.84	6.12	6.39	6.67	6.95	7.23	7.51	7.79	8.07
85	.67	1.76	2.86	3.97	5.08	5.36	5.64	5.92	6.21	6.49	6.77	7.05	7.33	7.62	7.90	8.18
84	.72	1.82	2.93	4.04	5.17	5.45	5.73	6.01	6.30	6.58	6.87	7.15	7.43	7.72	8.01	8.29
83	.77	1.88	2.99	4.12	5.25	5.53	5.82	6.10	6.39	6.68	6.96	7.25	7.54	7.83	8.12	8.40
82	.82	1.94	3.06	4.19	5.33	5.62	5.91	6.20	6.48	6.77	7.06	7.35	7.64	7.94	8.23	8.52
81	.87	2.00	3.13	4.27	5.42	5.71	6.00	6.29	6.58	6.87	7.17	7.46	7.75	8.05	8.34	8.63
80	.93	2.06	3.20	4.35	5.51	5.80	6.09	6.39	6.68	6.97	7.27	7.56	7.86	8.16	8.46	8.75
79	.98	2.12	3.26	4.42	5.60	5.89	6.19	6.48	6.78	7.08	7.38	7.67	7.97	8.27	8.57	8.87
78	1.03	2.18	3.33	4.50	5.69	5.98	6.28	6.58	6.88	7.18	7.48	7.78	8.09	8.39	8.69	9.00
77	1.09	2.24	3.41	4.59	5.78	6.08	6.38	6.68	6.99	7.29	7.59	7.90	8.20	8.51	8.82	9.12
76	1.14	2.30	3.48	4.67	5.87	6.18	6.48	6.79	7.09	7.40	7.71	8.01	8.32	8.63	8.94	9.25
75	1.20	2.37	3.55	4.75	5.97	6.28	6.58	6.89	7.20	7.51	7.82	8.13	8.44	8.76	9.07	9.38
74	1.25	2.43	3.63	4.84	6.07	6.38	6.69	7.00	7.31	7.62	7.94	8.25	8.57	8.88	9.20	9.52
73	1.31	2.50	3.70	4.93	6.17	6.48	6.79	7.11	7.42	7.74	8.06	8.37	8.69	9.01	9.33	9.66
72	1.37	2.57	3.78	5.02	6.27	6.58	6.90	7.22	7.54	7.86	8.18	8.50	8.82	9.15	9.47	9.80
71	1.43	2.63	3.86	5.11	6.37	6.69	7.01	7.33	7.65	7.98	8.30	8.63	8.95	9.28	9.61	9.94
70	1.49	2.70	3.94	5.20	6.48	6.80	7.12	7.45	7.77	8.10	8.43	8.76	9.09	9.42	9.75	10.09
69	1.55	2.77	4.02	5.29	6.58	6.91	7.24	7.57	7.90	8.23	8.56	8.89	9.23	9.56	9.90	10.24
68	1.61	2.85	4.10	5.39	6.69	7.02	7.35	7.69	8.02	8.36	8.69	9.03	9.37	9.71	10.05	10.39
67	1.67	2.92	4.19	5.49	6.81	7.14	7.47	7.81	8.15	8.49	8.83	9.17	9.51	9.86	10.20	10.55
66	1.73	2.99	4.28	5.59	6.92	7.26	7.60	7.94	8.28	8.62	8.97	9.31	9.66	10.01	10.36	10.71
65	1.80	3.07	4.36	5.69	7.04	7.38	7.72	8.07	8.41	8.76	9.11	9.46	9.81	10.17	10.52	10.88
64	1.86	3.14	4.45	5.79	7.16	7.50	7.85	8.20	8.55	8.90	9.26	9.61	9.97	10.33	10.69	11.05
63	1.93	3.22	4.54	5.90	7.28	7.63	7.98	8.34	8.69	9.05	9.41	9.77	10.13	10.49	10.86	11.23
62	2.00	3.30	4.64	6.01	7.41	7.76	8.12	8.48	8.84	9.20	9.56	9.93	10.30	10.66	11.03	11.41
61	2.07	3.38	4.73	6.12	7.53	7.89	8.26	8.62	8.98	9.35	9.72	10.09	10.46	10.84	11.21	11.59
60	2.13	3.46	4.83	6.23	7.67	8.03	8.40	8.77	9.14	9.51	9.88	10.26	10.64	11.02	11.40	11.78
59	2.21	3.55	4.93	6.35	7.80	8.17	8.54	8.92	9.29	9.67	10.05	10.43	10.82	11.20	11.59	11.98
58	2.28	3.63	5.03	6.47	7.94	8.31	8.69	9.07	9.45	9.84	10.22	10.61	11.00	11.39	11.79	12.18
57	2.35	3.72	5.13	6.59	8.08	8.46	8.84	9.23	9.62	10.01	10.40	10.79	11.19	11.59	11.99	12.39
56	2.43	3.81	5.24	6.71	8.23	8.61	9.00	9.39	9.79	10.18	10.58	10.98	11.38	11.79	12.20	12.60
55	2.50	3.90	5.35	6.84	8.38	8.77	9.16	9.56	9.96	10.36	10.77	11.17	11.58	12.00	12.41	12.83
54	2.58	3.99	5.46	6.97	8.53	8.93	9.33	9.73	10.14	10.55	10.96	11.38	11.79	12.21	12.63	13.06
53	2.66	4.09	5.57	7.11	8.69	9.10	9.50	9.91	10.33	10.74	11.16	11.58	12.01	12.43	12.86	13.29
52	2.74	4.19	5.69	7.24	8.85	9.27	9.68	10.10	10.52	10.94	11.37	11.80	12.23	12.66	13.10	13.54
51	2.82	4.28	5.81	7.39	9.02	9.44	9.86	10.29	10.71	11.14	11.58	12.02	12.46	12.90	13.34	13.79
50	2.90	4.39	5.93	7.53	9.20	9.62	10.05	10.48	10.92	11.36	11.80	12.24	12.69	13.14	13.60	14.06
49	2.99	4.49	6.05	7.68	9.37	9.81	10.24	10.68	11.13	11.58	12.03	12.48	12.94	13.40	13.86	14.33
48	3.08	4.60	6.18	7.84	9.56	10.00	10.45	10.89	11.35	11.80	12.26	12.73	13.19	13.66	14.14	14.61
47	3.17	4.71	6.31	8.00	9.75	10.20	10.65	11.11	11.57	12.04	12.51	12.98	13.46	13.94	14.42	14.91
46	3.26	4.82	6.45	8.16	9.95	10.41	10.87	11.34	11.81	12.28	12.76	13.25	13.73	14.22	14.72	15.21
45	3.35	4.93	6.59	8.33	10.15	10.62	11.09	11.57	12.05	12.54	13.03	13.52	14.02	14.52	15.02	15.53
44	3.45	5.05	6.74	8.51	10.37	10.84	11.32	11.81	12.30	12.80	13.30	13.81	14.32	14.83	15.35	15.87
43	3.54	5.17	6.88	8.69	10.59	11.07	11.57	12.06	12.57	13.07	13.59	14.10	14.63	15.15	15.68	16.21
42	3.64	5.29	7.04	8.88	10.81	11.31	11.82	12.33	12.84	13.36	13.89	14.42	14.95	15.49	16.03	16.58
41	3.74	5.42	7.20	9.07	11.05	11.56	12.08	12.60	13.13	13.66	14.20	14.74	15.29	15.84	16.40	16.96
40	3.85	5.55	7.36	9.27	11.30	11.82	12.35	12.89	13.43	13.97	14.52	15.08	15.64	16.21	16.78	17.36
39	3.96	5.69	7.53	9.49	11.56	12.09	12.64	13.18	13.74	14.30	14.87	15.44	16.02	16.60	17.19	17.78
35	4.42	6.27	8.27	10.42	12.72	13.31	13.92	14.53	15.15	15.78	16.42	17.06	17.71	18.36	19.02	19.69
30	5.08	7.13	9.38	11.85	14.54	15.24	15.95	16.68	17.41	18.16	18.91	19.67	20.45	21.22	22.01	22.80
25	5.86	8.18	10.81	13.76	17.03	17.89	18.77	19.66	20.56	21.48	22.41	23.35	24.29	25.25	26.21	27.18
20	6.81	9.55	12.76	16.50	20.73	21.85	22.99	24.15	25.33	26.51	27.71	28.92	30.14	31.36	32.59	33.82
15	8.06	11.46	15.74	20.99	27.01	28.59	30.20	31.81	33.44	35.08	36.73	38.38	40.03	41.69	43.35	45.01
10	9.82	14.61	21.46	30.31	40.05	42.53	45.02	47.51	50.01	52.50	55.00	57.50	60.00	62.50	65.00	67.50

Description: This table shows the price to pay for a bond at the yield rate. The yield is to maturity.

Example: The price of a 10.75 %, 24 year bond to yield 8 % to maturity is $ 129.14.

COUPON RATE, %

YIELD	7.00%	7.25%	7.50%	7.75%	8.00%	8.25%	8.50%	8.75%	9.00%	9.25%	9.50%	9.75%	10.00%	10.25%	10.50%	10.75%
0.00	268.00	274.00	280.00	286.00	292.00	298.00	304.00	310.00	316.00	322.00	328.00	334.00	340.00	346.00	352.00	358.00
1.00	227.74	233.06	238.39	243.71	249.03	254.35	259.68	265.00	270.32	275.64	280.97	286.29	291.61	296.93	302.26	307.58
2.00	194.93	199.68	204.43	209.18	213.92	218.67	223.42	228.16	232.91	237.66	242.40	247.15	251.90	256.64	261.39	266.14
3.00	168.09	172.34	176.60	180.85	185.11	189.36	193.62	197.87	202.13	206.38	210.64	214.89	219.15	223.40	227.66	231.91
4.00	146.01	149.84	153.68	157.51	161.35	165.18	169.01	172.85	176.68	180.52	184.35	188.19	192.02	195.85	199.69	203.52
4.25	141.12	144.86	148.60	152.34	156.08	159.81	163.55	167.29	171.03	174.77	178.51	182.25	185.98	189.72	193.46	197.20
4.50	136.46	140.11	143.75	147.40	151.05	154.69	158.34	161.99	165.63	169.28	172.92	176.57	180.22	183.86	187.51	191.15
4.75	132.02	135.57	139.13	142.69	146.25	149.80	153.36	156.92	160.47	164.03	167.59	171.15	174.70	178.26	181.82	185.38
5.00	127.77	131.24	134.72	138.19	141.66	145.13	148.60	152.07	155.55	159.02	162.49	165.96	169.43	172.90	176.38	179.85
5.25	123.72	127.11	130.50	133.89	137.28	140.67	144.06	147.45	150.84	154.22	157.61	161.00	164.39	167.78	171.17	174.56
5.50	119.86	123.17	126.47	129.78	133.09	136.40	139.71	143.02	146.33	149.64	152.95	156.26	159.57	162.88	166.19	169.50
5.75	116.16	119.40	122.63	125.86	129.09	132.33	135.56	138.79	142.02	145.26	148.49	151.72	154.95	158.19	161.42	164.65
6.00	112.63	115.79	118.95	122.11	125.27	128.43	131.58	134.74	137.90	141.06	144.22	147.38	150.53	153.69	156.85	160.01
6.25	109.26	112.35	115.43	118.52	121.61	124.69	127.78	130.87	133.95	137.04	140.13	143.21	146.30	149.39	152.47	155.56
6.50	106.04	109.05	112.07	115.09	118.11	121.12	124.14	127.16	130.18	133.19	136.21	139.23	142.25	145.26	148.28	151.30
6.75	102.95	105.90	108.85	111.80	114.75	117.71	120.66	123.61	126.56	129.51	132.46	135.41	138.36	141.31	144.26	147.21
7.00	100.00	102.89	105.77	108.66	111.55	114.43	117.32	120.20	123.09	125.98	128.86	131.75	134.64	137.52	140.41	143.30
7.25	97.18	100.00	102.82	105.65	108.47	111.30	114.12	116.94	119.77	122.59	125.42	128.24	131.07	133.89	136.71	139.54
7.50	94.47	97.24	100.00	102.76	105.53	108.29	111.06	113.82	116.58	119.35	122.11	124.88	127.64	130.40	133.17	135.93
7.75	91.88	94.59	97.29	100.00	102.71	105.41	108.12	110.82	113.53	116.23	118.94	121.65	124.35	127.06	129.76	132.47
8.00	89.40	92.05	94.70	97.35	100.00	102.65	105.30	107.95	110.60	113.25	115.90	118.55	121.20	123.84	126.49	129.14
8.25	87.03	89.62	92.22	94.81	97.41	100.00	102.59	105.19	107.78	110.38	112.97	115.57	118.16	120.76	123.35	125.95
8.50	84.75	87.29	89.83	92.37	94.92	97.46	100.00	102.54	105.08	107.63	110.17	112.71	115.25	117.80	120.34	122.88
8.75	82.56	85.05	87.54	90.03	92.53	95.02	97.51	100.00	102.49	104.98	107.47	109.97	112.46	114.95	117.44	119.93
9.00	80.46	82.91	85.35	87.79	90.23	92.67	95.12	97.56	100.00	102.44	104.88	107.33	109.77	112.21	114.65	117.09
9.25	78.45	80.85	83.24	85.63	88.03	90.42	92.82	95.21	97.61	100.00	102.39	104.79	107.18	109.58	111.97	114.37
9.50	76.52	78.87	81.22	83.56	85.91	88.26	90.61	92.96	95.30	97.65	100.00	102.35	104.70	107.04	109.39	111.74
9.75	74.67	76.97	79.27	81.58	83.88	86.18	88.48	90.79	93.09	95.39	97.70	100.00	102.30	104.61	106.91	109.21
10.00	72.88	75.14	77.40	79.66	81.92	84.18	86.44	88.70	90.96	93.22	95.48	97.74	100.00	102.26	104.52	106.78
10.25	71.17	73.39	75.61	77.82	80.04	82.26	84.48	86.69	88.91	91.13	93.35	95.56	97.78	100.00	102.22	104.44
10.50	69.53	71.70	73.88	76.06	78.23	80.41	82.59	84.76	86.94	89.12	91.29	93.47	95.65	97.82	100.00	102.18
10.75	67.94	70.08	72.22	74.35	76.49	78.63	80.77	82.90	85.04	87.18	89.31	91.45	93.59	95.73	97.86	100.00
11.00	66.42	68.52	70.62	72.72	74.81	76.91	79.01	81.11	83.21	85.31	87.41	89.51	91.60	93.70	95.80	97.90
11.25	64.95	67.02	69.08	71.14	73.20	75.26	77.32	79.38	81.45	83.51	85.57	87.63	89.69	91.75	93.82	95.88
11.50	63.54	65.57	67.59	69.62	71.64	73.67	75.70	77.72	79.75	81.77	83.80	85.82	87.85	89.87	91.90	93.92
11.75	62.18	64.17	66.16	68.15	70.15	72.14	74.13	76.12	78.11	80.10	82.09	84.08	86.07	88.06	90.05	92.04
12.00	60.87	62.83	64.79	66.74	68.70	70.66	72.61	74.57	76.52	78.48	80.44	82.39	84.35	86.31	88.26	90.22
12.25	59.61	61.54	63.46	65.38	67.31	69.23	71.15	73.08	75.00	76.92	78.85	80.77	82.69	84.61	86.54	88.46
12.50	58.40	60.29	62.18	64.07	65.96	67.85	69.74	71.63	73.53	75.42	77.31	79.20	81.09	82.98	84.87	86.76
12.75	57.22	59.08	60.94	62.80	64.66	66.52	68.38	70.24	72.10	73.96	75.82	77.68	79.54	81.40	83.26	85.12
13.00	56.09	57.92	59.75	61.58	63.41	65.24	67.07	68.90	70.73	72.56	74.39	76.22	78.05	79.88	81.71	83.53
13.25	55.00	56.80	58.60	60.40	62.20	64.00	65.80	67.60	69.40	71.20	73.00	74.80	76.60	78.40	80.20	82.00
13.50	53.95	55.72	57.49	59.26	61.03	62.80	64.57	66.34	68.12	69.89	71.66	73.43	75.20	76.97	78.74	80.52
13.75	52.93	54.67	56.41	58.16	59.90	61.64	63.39	65.13	66.87	68.62	70.36	72.11	73.85	75.59	77.34	79.08
14.00	51.94	53.66	55.38	57.09	58.81	60.52	62.24	63.96	65.67	67.39	69.11	70.82	72.54	74.26	75.97	77.69
14.25	50.99	52.68	54.37	56.06	57.75	59.44	61.13	62.82	64.51	66.20	67.89	69.58	71.27	72.96	74.65	76.34
14.50	50.07	51.74	53.40	55.07	56.73	58.39	60.06	61.72	63.39	65.05	66.72	68.38	70.04	71.71	73.37	75.04
14.75	49.18	50.82	52.46	54.10	55.74	57.38	59.02	60.66	62.30	63.94	65.58	67.22	68.85	70.49	72.13	73.77
15.00	48.32	49.94	51.55	53.17	54.78	56.40	58.01	59.63	61.24	62.86	64.47	66.09	67.70	69.32	70.93	72.55
15.25	47.49	49.08	50.67	52.26	53.86	55.45	57.04	58.63	60.22	61.81	63.40	64.99	66.59	68.18	69.77	71.36
15.50	46.69	48.25	49.82	51.39	52.96	54.53	56.09	57.66	59.23	60.80	62.37	63.93	65.50	67.07	68.64	70.21
15.75	45.91	47.45	49.00	50.54	52.09	53.63	55.18	56.72	58.27	59.82	61.36	62.91	64.45	66.00	67.54	69.09
16.00	45.15	46.67	48.20	49.72	51.24	52.77	54.29	55.81	57.34	58.86	60.39	61.91	63.43	64.96	66.48	68.00
16.25	44.42	45.92	47.42	48.92	50.43	51.93	53.43	54.93	56.43	57.94	59.44	60.94	62.44	63.95	65.45	66.95
16.50	43.71	45.19	46.67	48.15	49.63	51.11	52.59	54.08	55.56	57.04	58.52	60.00	61.48	62.96	64.45	65.93
16.75	43.02	44.48	45.94	47.40	48.86	50.32	51.78	53.24	54.71	56.17	57.63	59.09	60.55	62.01	63.47	64.93
17.00	42.35	43.79	45.23	46.67	48.11	49.55	51.00	52.44	53.88	55.32	56.76	58.20	59.64	61.09	62.53	63.97
17.25	41.70	43.12	44.54	45.97	47.39	48.81	50.23	51.65	53.08	54.50	55.92	57.34	58.76	60.19	61.61	63.03
17.50	41.07	42.47	43.88	45.28	46.68	48.09	49.49	50.89	52.30	53.70	55.10	56.50	57.91	59.31	60.71	62.12
17.75	40.46	41.84	43.23	44.61	46.00	47.38	48.77	50.15	51.54	52.92	54.31	55.69	57.08	58.46	59.84	61.23
18.00	39.87	41.23	42.60	43.97	45.33	46.70	48.07	49.43	50.80	52.17	53.53	54.90	56.27	57.63	59.00	60.37
18.25	39.29	40.64	41.99	43.34	44.68	46.03	47.38	48.73	50.08	51.43	52.78	54.13	55.48	56.83	58.18	59.53
18.50	38.73	40.06	41.39	42.72	44.06	45.39	46.72	48.05	49.38	50.72	52.05	53.38	54.71	56.04	57.38	58.71
18.75	38.18	39.50	40.81	42.13	43.44	44.76	46.07	47.39	48.70	50.02	51.34	52.65	53.97	55.28	56.60	57.91
19.00	37.65	38.95	40.25	41.55	42.85	44.15	45.45	46.74	48.04	49.34	50.64	51.94	53.24	54.54	55.84	57.14
20.00	35.67	36.91	38.14	39.38	40.62	41.86	43.09	44.33	45.57	46.80	48.04	49.28	50.52	51.75	52.99	54.23
25.00	28.25	29.25	30.25	31.24	32.24	33.23	34.23	35.23	36.22	37.22	38.22	39.21	40.21	41.21	42.20	43.20
30.00	23.43	24.26	25.09	25.92	26.76	27.59	28.42	29.25	30.09	30.92	31.75	32.58	33.41	34.25	35.08	35.91

Description: This table shows the yield to maturity of a bond purchased at the price shown in the index.

Example: The yield to maturity of a 10.75 %, 24 year bond at a price of 111.00 is 9.57 %.

COUPON RATE, %

PRICE	7.00%	7.25%	7.50%	7.75%	8.00%	8.25%	8.50%	8.75%	9.00%	9.25%	9.50%	9.75%	10.00%	10.25%	10.50%	10.75%
165	3.12	3.30	3.48	3.65	3.83	4.00	4.18	4.35	4.53	4.70	4.87	5.04	5.21	5.39	5.56	5.73
160	3.34	3.52	3.70	3.88	4.06	4.24	4.41	4.59	4.77	4.95	5.12	5.30	5.47	5.65	5.82	6.00
155	3.56	3.75	3.93	4.11	4.30	4.48	4.66	4.84	5.02	5.20	5.38	5.56	5.74	5.92	6.10	6.28
150	3.80	3.99	4.17	4.36	4.55	4.73	4.92	5.11	5.29	5.47	5.66	5.84	6.03	6.21	6.39	6.57
145	4.05	4.24	4.43	4.62	4.81	5.00	5.19	5.38	5.57	5.76	5.95	6.14	6.32	6.51	6.70	6.89
140	4.30	4.50	4.70	4.89	5.09	5.28	5.48	5.67	5.87	6.06	6.25	6.45	6.64	6.83	7.02	7.21
135	4.58	4.78	4.98	5.18	5.38	5.58	5.78	5.98	6.18	6.38	6.57	6.77	6.97	7.17	7.36	7.56
130	4.86	5.07	5.28	5.48	5.69	5.89	6.10	6.30	6.51	6.71	6.91	7.12	7.32	7.52	7.73	7.93
125	5.16	5.38	5.59	5.80	6.01	6.22	6.44	6.65	6.86	7.07	7.28	7.49	7.69	7.90	8.11	8.32
122	5.35	5.57	5.79	6.00	6.22	6.43	6.65	6.86	7.08	7.29	7.50	7.72	7.93	8.14	8.36	8.57
121	5.42	5.64	5.85	6.07	6.29	6.50	6.72	6.94	7.15	7.37	7.58	7.80	8.01	8.23	8.44	8.65
120	5.49	5.70	5.92	6.14	6.36	6.58	6.79	7.01	7.23	7.44	7.66	7.88	8.09	8.31	8.52	8.74
119	5.55	5.77	5.99	6.21	6.43	6.65	6.87	7.09	7.30	7.52	7.74	7.96	8.18	8.39	8.61	8.83
118	5.62	5.84	6.06	6.28	6.50	6.72	6.94	7.16	7.38	7.60	7.82	8.04	8.26	8.48	8.70	8.91
117	5.69	5.91	6.13	6.35	6.58	6.80	7.02	7.24	7.46	7.68	7.90	8.12	8.34	8.56	8.78	9.00
116	5.76	5.98	6.20	6.43	6.65	6.87	7.10	7.32	7.54	7.76	7.99	8.21	8.43	8.65	8.87	9.09
115	5.83	6.05	6.28	6.50	6.73	6.95	7.18	7.40	7.62	7.85	8.07	8.29	8.52	8.74	8.96	9.19
114	5.90	6.12	6.35	6.58	6.80	7.03	7.25	7.48	7.71	7.93	8.16	8.38	8.61	8.83	9.05	9.28
113	5.97	6.20	6.42	6.65	6.88	7.11	7.34	7.56	7.79	8.02	8.24	8.47	8.70	8.92	9.15	9.37
112	6.04	6.27	6.50	6.73	6.96	7.19	7.42	7.65	7.87	8.10	8.33	8.56	8.79	9.01	9.24	9.47
111	6.11	6.35	6.58	6.81	7.04	7.27	7.50	7.73	7.96	8.19	8.42	8.65	8.88	9.11	9.34	9.57
110	6.19	6.42	6.65	6.89	7.12	7.35	7.58	7.82	8.05	8.28	8.51	8.74	8.97	9.20	9.44	9.67
109	6.26	6.50	6.73	6.97	7.20	7.44	7.67	7.90	8.14	8.37	8.60	8.84	9.07	9.30	9.53	9.77
108	6.34	6.58	6.81	7.05	7.28	7.52	7.76	7.99	8.23	8.46	8.70	8.93	9.16	9.40	9.63	9.87
107	6.42	6.66	6.89	7.13	7.37	7.61	7.84	8.08	8.32	8.55	8.79	9.03	9.26	9.50	9.74	9.97
106	6.50	6.74	6.98	7.22	7.45	7.69	7.93	8.17	8.41	8.65	8.89	9.12	9.36	9.60	9.84	10.08
105	6.58	6.82	7.06	7.30	7.54	7.78	8.02	8.26	8.50	8.74	8.98	9.22	9.46	9.70	9.94	10.18
104	6.66	6.90	7.14	7.39	7.63	7.87	8.11	8.36	8.60	8.84	9.08	9.32	9.57	9.81	10.05	10.29
103	6.74	6.99	7.23	7.47	7.72	7.96	8.21	8.45	8.70	8.94	9.18	9.43	9.67	9.92	10.16	10.40
102	6.82	7.07	7.32	7.56	7.81	8.06	8.30	8.55	8.79	9.04	9.29	9.53	9.78	10.02	10.27	10.51
101	6.91	7.16	7.41	7.65	7.90	8.15	8.40	8.65	8.89	9.14	9.39	9.64	9.89	10.13	10.38	10.63
100	7.00	7.25	7.50	7.75	8.00	8.25	8.50	8.75	9.00	9.25	9.50	9.75	10.00	10.25	10.50	10.75
99	7.08	7.33	7.59	7.84	8.09	8.34	8.59	8.85	9.10	9.35	9.60	9.85	10.11	10.36	10.61	10.86
98	7.17	7.42	7.68	7.93	8.19	8.44	8.69	8.95	9.20	9.46	9.71	9.97	10.22	10.47	10.73	10.98
97	7.26	7.52	7.77	8.03	8.28	8.54	8.80	9.05	9.31	9.57	9.82	10.08	10.34	10.59	10.85	11.11
96	7.35	7.61	7.87	8.13	8.38	8.64	8.90	9.16	9.42	9.68	9.94	10.19	10.45	10.71	10.97	11.23
95	7.45	7.71	7.97	8.23	8.49	8.75	9.01	9.27	9.53	9.79	10.05	10.31	10.57	10.83	11.09	11.36
94	7.54	7.80	8.06	8.33	8.59	8.85	9.12	9.38	9.64	9.90	10.17	10.43	10.69	10.96	11.22	11.49
93	7.64	7.90	8.16	8.43	8.69	8.96	9.22	9.49	9.76	10.02	10.29	10.55	10.82	11.08	11.35	11.62
92	7.73	8.00	8.27	8.53	8.80	9.07	9.34	9.60	9.87	10.14	10.41	10.68	10.94	11.21	11.48	11.75
91	7.83	8.10	8.37	8.64	8.91	9.18	9.45	9.72	9.99	10.26	10.53	10.80	11.07	11.34	11.62	11.89
90	7.93	8.21	8.48	8.75	9.02	9.29	9.57	9.84	10.11	10.38	10.66	10.93	11.20	11.48	11.75	12.03
89	8.04	8.31	8.58	8.86	9.13	9.41	9.68	9.96	10.23	10.51	10.79	11.06	11.34	11.61	11.89	12.17
88	8.14	8.42	8.69	8.97	9.25	9.53	9.80	10.08	10.36	10.64	10.92	11.20	11.47	11.75	12.03	12.31
87	8.25	8.53	8.81	9.09	9.37	9.65	9.93	10.21	10.49	10.77	11.05	11.33	11.61	11.89	12.18	12.46
86	8.36	8.64	8.92	9.20	9.48	9.77	10.05	10.33	10.62	10.90	11.19	11.47	11.75	12.04	12.32	12.61
85	8.47	8.75	9.04	9.32	9.61	9.89	10.18	10.46	10.75	11.04	11.32	11.61	11.90	12.19	12.48	12.76
84	8.58	8.87	9.15	9.44	9.73	10.02	10.31	10.60	10.89	11.18	11.47	11.76	12.05	12.34	12.63	12.92
83	8.69	8.98	9.27	9.56	9.86	10.15	10.44	10.73	11.02	11.32	11.61	11.90	12.20	12.49	12.79	13.08
82	8.81	9.10	9.40	9.69	9.98	10.28	10.57	10.87	11.17	11.46	11.76	12.05	12.35	12.65	12.95	13.25
81	8.93	9.23	9.52	9.82	10.12	10.41	10.71	11.01	11.31	11.61	11.91	12.21	12.51	12.81	13.11	13.41
80	9.05	9.35	9.65	9.95	10.25	10.55	10.85	11.15	11.46	11.76	12.06	12.37	12.67	12.97	13.28	13.58
79	9.18	9.48	9.78	10.08	10.39	10.69	11.00	11.30	11.61	11.91	12.22	12.53	12.83	13.14	13.45	13.76
78	9.30	9.61	9.91	10.22	10.53	10.84	11.14	11.45	11.76	12.07	12.38	12.69	13.00	13.31	13.63	13.94
77	9.43	9.74	10.05	10.36	10.67	10.98	11.29	11.61	11.92	12.23	12.55	12.86	13.18	13.49	13.81	14.12
76	9.56	9.88	10.19	10.50	10.82	11.13	11.45	11.76	12.08	12.40	12.71	13.03	13.35	13.67	13.99	14.31
75	9.70	10.02	10.33	10.65	10.97	11.29	11.60	11.92	12.24	12.57	12.89	13.21	13.53	13.85	14.18	14.50
74	9.84	10.16	10.48	10.80	11.12	11.44	11.77	12.09	12.41	12.74	13.06	13.39	13.72	14.04	14.37	14.70
73	9.98	10.30	10.63	10.95	11.28	11.60	11.93	12.26	12.59	12.92	13.25	13.58	13.91	14.24	14.57	14.90
70	10.42	10.76	11.09	11.43	11.77	12.11	12.45	12.79	13.13	13.47	13.82	14.16	14.50	14.85	15.19	15.54
65	11.24	11.60	11.96	12.32	12.68	13.04	13.41	13.77	14.14	14.51	14.87	15.24	15.61	15.98	16.36	16.73
60	12.17	12.55	12.94	13.33	13.72	14.12	14.51	14.90	15.30	15.70	16.10	16.50	16.90	17.30	17.70	18.10
55	13.25	13.67	14.09	14.51	14.94	15.37	15.79	16.23	16.66	17.09	17.53	17.96	18.40	18.84	19.28	19.72
50	14.52	14.98	15.44	15.91	16.38	16.85	17.32	17.80	18.27	18.75	19.23	19.71	20.20	20.68	21.17	21.65
45	16.05	16.56	17.08	17.60	18.12	18.65	19.18	19.71	20.24	20.77	21.31	21.85	22.39	22.93	23.47	24.01
40	17.94	18.52	19.11	19.70	20.29	20.89	21.49	22.09	22.69	23.30	23.90	24.51	25.12	25.74	26.35	26.96
35	20.36	21.03	21.71	22.39	23.08	23.77	24.46	25.15	25.85	26.55	27.25	27.95	28.65	29.36	30.06	30.77
30	23.59	24.39	25.19	26.00	26.81	27.62	28.44	29.26	30.08	30.90	31.72	32.55	33.38	34.20	35.03	35.86

BOND PRICE

Description: This table shows the price to pay for a bond at the yield rate. The yield is to maturity.

Example: The price of a 15.00 %, 24 year bond to yield 8 % to maturity is $ 174.18.

COUPON RATE, %

YIELD	11.00%	11.25%	11.50%	11.75%	12.00%	12.25%	12.50%	12.75%	13.00%	13.25%	13.50%	13.75%	14.00%	14.25%	14.50%	15.00%
0.00	364.00	370.00	376.00	382.00	388.00	394.00	400.00	406.00	412.00	418.00	424.00	430.00	436.00	442.00	448.00	460.00
1.00	312.90	318.22	323.55	328.87	334.19	339.51	344.84	350.16	355.48	360.80	366.13	371.45	376.77	382.09	387.42	398.06
2.00	270.88	275.63	280.38	285.12	289.87	294.62	299.36	304.11	308.86	313.60	318.35	323.10	327.84	332.59	337.34	346.83
3.00	236.17	240.43	244.68	248.94	253.19	257.45	261.70	265.96	270.21	274.47	278.72	282.98	287.23	291.49	295.74	304.26
4.00	207.36	211.19	215.02	218.86	222.69	226.53	230.36	234.19	238.03	241.86	245.70	249.53	253.37	257.20	261.03	268.70
4.25	200.94	204.68	208.41	212.15	215.89	219.63	223.37	227.11	230.84	234.58	238.32	242.06	245.80	249.54	253.28	260.75
4.50	194.80	198.45	202.09	205.74	209.39	213.03	216.68	220.32	223.97	227.62	231.26	234.91	238.56	242.20	245.85	253.14
4.75	188.93	192.49	196.05	199.60	203.16	206.72	210.28	213.83	217.39	220.95	224.51	228.06	231.62	235.18	238.74	245.85
5.00	183.32	186.79	190.26	193.73	197.21	200.68	204.15	207.62	211.09	214.56	218.04	221.51	224.98	228.45	231.92	238.87
5.25	177.95	181.34	184.73	188.11	191.50	194.89	198.28	201.67	205.06	208.45	211.84	215.23	218.62	222.01	225.39	232.17
5.50	172.81	176.12	179.42	182.73	186.04	189.35	192.66	195.97	199.28	202.59	205.90	209.21	212.52	215.83	219.14	225.76
5.75	167.88	171.12	174.35	177.58	180.81	184.05	187.28	190.51	193.74	196.98	200.21	203.44	206.67	209.91	213.14	219.60
6.00	163.17	166.33	169.48	172.64	175.80	178.96	182.12	185.28	188.43	191.59	194.75	197.91	201.07	204.23	207.38	213.70
6.25	158.65	161.73	164.82	167.91	171.00	174.08	177.17	180.26	183.34	186.43	189.52	192.60	195.69	198.78	201.86	208.04
6.50	154.32	157.34	160.35	163.37	166.39	169.41	172.42	175.44	178.46	181.48	184.49	187.51	190.53	193.55	196.56	202.60
6.75	150.17	153.12	156.07	159.02	161.97	164.92	167.87	170.82	173.77	176.72	179.67	182.62	185.58	188.53	191.48	197.38
7.00	146.18	149.07	151.96	154.84	157.73	160.61	163.50	166.39	169.27	172.16	175.05	177.93	180.82	183.71	186.59	192.36
7.25	142.36	145.19	148.01	150.83	153.66	156.48	159.31	162.13	164.95	167.78	170.60	173.43	176.25	179.07	181.90	187.55
7.50	138.69	141.46	144.22	146.99	149.75	152.51	155.28	158.04	160.81	163.57	166.33	169.10	171.86	174.63	177.39	182.92
7.75	135.17	137.88	140.59	143.29	146.00	148.70	151.41	154.11	156.82	159.52	162.23	164.94	167.64	170.35	173.05	178.46
8.00	131.79	134.44	137.09	139.74	142.39	145.04	147.69	150.34	152.99	155.64	158.29	160.94	163.59	166.23	168.88	174.18
8.25	128.54	131.14	133.73	136.33	138.92	141.52	144.11	146.71	149.30	151.90	154.49	157.09	159.68	162.28	164.87	170.06
8.50	125.42	127.96	130.51	133.05	135.59	138.13	140.68	143.22	145.76	148.30	150.85	153.39	155.93	158.47	161.01	166.10
8.75	122.42	124.91	127.40	129.90	132.39	134.88	137.37	139.86	142.35	144.84	147.33	149.83	152.32	154.81	157.30	162.28
9.00	119.54	121.98	124.42	126.86	129.30	131.75	134.19	136.63	139.07	141.51	143.96	146.40	148.84	151.28	153.72	158.61
9.25	116.76	119.15	121.55	123.94	126.34	128.73	131.12	133.52	135.91	138.31	140.70	143.10	145.49	147.88	150.28	155.07
9.50	114.09	116.44	118.78	121.13	123.48	125.83	128.17	130.52	132.87	135.22	137.57	139.91	142.26	144.61	146.96	151.65
9.75	111.52	113.82	116.12	118.42	120.73	123.03	125.33	127.64	129.94	132.24	134.55	136.85	139.15	141.46	143.76	148.36
10.00	109.04	111.30	113.56	115.82	108.08	120.34	122.60	124.86	127.12	129.38	131.64	133.89	136.15	138.41	140.67	145.19
10.25	106.65	108.87	111.09	113.31	115.52	117.74	119.96	122.18	124.39	126.61	128.83	131.05	133.26	135.48	137.70	142.13
10.50	104.35	106.53	108.71	110.88	113.06	115.24	117.41	119.59	121.77	123.94	126.12	128.30	130.47	132.65	134.83	139.18
10.75	102.14	104.27	106.41	108.55	110.69	112.82	114.96	117.10	119.23	121.37	123.51	125.65	127.78	129.92	132.06	136.33
11.00	100.00	102.10	104.20	106.30	108.40	110.49	112.59	114.69	116.79	118.89	120.99	123.09	125.19	127.28	129.38	133.58
11.25	97.94	100.00	102.06	104.12	106.18	108.25	110.31	112.37	114.43	116.49	118.55	120.62	122.68	124.74	126.80	130.92
11.50	95.95	97.97	100.00	102.03	104.05	106.08	108.10	110.13	112.15	114.18	116.20	118.23	120.25	122.28	124.30	128.36
11.75	94.03	96.02	98.01	100.00	101.99	103.98	105.97	107.96	109.95	111.94	113.93	115.92	117.91	119.90	121.89	125.87
12.00	92.17	94.13	96.09	98.04	100.00	101.96	103.91	105.87	107.83	109.78	111.74	113.69	115.65	117.61	119.56	123.48
12.25	90.38	92.31	94.23	96.15	98.08	100.00	101.92	103.85	105.77	107.69	109.62	111.54	113.46	115.39	117.31	121.15
12.50	88.65	90.54	92.44	94.33	96.22	98.11	100.00	101.89	103.78	105.67	107.56	109.46	111.35	113.24	115.13	118.91
12.75	86.98	88.84	90.70	92.56	94.42	96.28	98.14	100.00	101.86	103.72	105.58	107.44	109.30	111.16	113.02	116.74
13.00	85.36	87.19	89.02	90.85	92.68	94.51	96.34	98.17	100.00	101.83	103.66	105.49	107.32	109.15	110.98	114.64
13.25	83.80	85.60	87.40	89.20	91.00	92.80	94.60	96.40	98.20	100.00	101.80	103.60	105.40	107.20	109.00	112.60
13.50	82.29	84.06	85.83	87.60	89.37	91.14	92.91	94.69	96.46	98.23	100.00	101.77	103.54	105.31	107.09	110.63
13.75	80.82	82.57	84.31	86.05	87.80	89.54	91.28	93.03	94.77	96.51	98.26	100.00	101.74	103.49	105.23	108.72
14.00	79.40	81.12	82.84	84.55	86.27	87.99	89.70	91.42	93.13	94.85	96.57	98.28	100.00	101.72	103.43	106.87
14.25	78.03	79.72	81.41	83.10	84.79	86.48	88.17	89.86	91.55	93.24	94.93	96.62	98.31	100.00	101.69	105.07
14.50	76.70	78.37	80.03	81.69	83.36	85.02	86.69	88.35	90.01	91.68	93.34	95.01	96.67	98.34	100.00	103.33
14.75	75.41	77.05	78.69	80.33	81.97	83.61	85.25	86.89	88.53	90.16	91.80	93.44	95.08	96.72	98.36	101.64
15.00	74.16	75.78	77.39	79.01	80.62	82.24	83.85	85.47	87.08	88.70	90.31	91.93	93.54	95.16	96.77	100.00
15.25	72.95	74.54	76.13	77.72	79.31	80.91	82.50	84.09	85.68	87.27	88.86	90.45	92.04	93.64	95.23	98.41
15.50	71.77	73.34	74.91	76.48	78.05	79.62	81.18	82.75	84.32	85.89	87.46	89.02	90.59	92.16	93.73	96.86
15.75	70.63	72.18	73.73	75.27	76.82	78.36	79.91	81.45	83.00	84.54	86.09	87.64	89.18	90.73	92.27	95.36
16.00	69.53	71.05	72.57	74.10	75.62	77.15	78.67	80.19	81.72	83.24	84.76	86.29	87.81	89.33	90.86	93.91
16.25	68.45	69.95	71.46	72.96	74.46	75.96	77.47	78.97	80.47	81.97	83.48	84.98	86.48	87.98	89.48	92.49
16.50	67.41	68.89	70.37	71.85	73.33	74.82	76.30	77.78	79.26	80.74	82.22	83.70	85.19	86.67	88.15	91.11
16.75	66.39	67.86	69.32	70.78	72.24	73.70	75.16	76.62	78.08	79.54	81.01	82.47	83.93	85.39	86.85	89.77
17.00	65.41	66.85	68.29	69.73	71.17	72.62	74.06	75.50	76.94	78.38	79.82	81.26	82.70	84.15	85.59	88.47
17.25	64.45	65.87	67.30	68.72	70.14	71.56	72.98	74.40	75.83	77.25	78.67	80.09	81.51	82.94	84.36	87.20
17.50	63.52	64.92	66.33	67.73	69.13	70.54	71.94	73.34	74.74	76.15	77.55	78.95	80.36	81.76	83.16	85.97
17.75	62.61	64.00	65.38	66.77	68.15	69.54	70.92	72.31	73.69	75.08	76.46	77.85	79.23	80.61	82.00	84.77
18.00	61.73	63.10	64.47	65.83	67.20	68.57	69.93	71.30	72.67	74.03	75.40	76.77	78.13	79.50	80.87	83.60
18.25	60.87	62.22	63.57	64.92	66.27	67.62	68.97	70.32	71.67	73.02	74.37	75.72	77.06	78.41	79.76	82.46
18.50	60.04	61.37	62.70	64.04	65.37	66.70	68.03	69.36	70.70	72.03	73.36	74.69	76.02	77.36	78.69	81.35
18.75	59.23	60.54	61.86	63.17	64.49	65.80	67.12	68.43	69.75	71.06	72.38	73.69	75.01	76.33	77.64	80.27
19.00	58.43	59.73	61.03	62.33	63.63	64.93	66.23	67.53	68.83	70.13	71.42	72.72	74.02	75.32	76.62	79.22
20.00	55.46	56.70	57.94	59.18	60.41	61.65	62.89	64.12	65.36	66.60	67.83	69.07	70.31	71.55	72.78	75.26
25.00	44.20	45.19	46.19	47.19	48.18	49.18	50.18	51.17	52.17	53.16	54.16	55.16	56.15	57.15	58.15	60.14
30.00	36.74	37.58	38.41	39.24	40.07	40.91	41.74	42.57	43.40	44.23	45.07	45.90	46.73	47.56	48.40	50.06

Description: This table shows the yield to maturity of a bond purchased at the price shown in the index.

Example: The yield to maturity of a 15.00 %, 24 year bond at a price of 125.00 is 11.84 %.

COUPON RATE, %

PRICE	11.00%	11.25%	11.50%	11.75%	12.00%	12.25%	12.50%	12.75%	13.00%	13.25%	13.50%	13.75%	14.00%	14.25%	14.50%	15.00%
250	2.57	2.70	2.83	2.96	3.09	3.22	3.35	3.47	3.60	3.73	3.85	3.98	4.10	4.23	4.35	4.60
240	2.87	3.01	3.14	3.27	3.41	3.54	3.67	3.80	3.93	4.06	4.19	4.32	4.44	4.57	4.70	4.95
230	3.19	3.33	3.47	3.60	3.74	3.87	4.01	4.14	4.28	4.41	4.54	4.67	4.81	4.94	5.07	5.33
220	3.53	3.67	3.81	3.95	4.09	4.23	4.37	4.51	4.64	4.78	4.92	5.05	5.19	5.33	5.46	5.73
210	3.90	4.04	4.18	4.33	4.47	4.61	4.76	4.90	5.04	5.18	5.32	5.46	5.60	5.74	5.88	6.16
200	4.28	4.43	4.58	4.73	4.88	5.02	5.17	5.32	5.46	5.61	5.75	5.90	6.04	6.19	6.33	6.62
195	4.49	4.64	4.79	4.94	5.09	5.24	5.39	5.54	5.69	5.84	5.98	6.13	6.28	6.42	6.57	6.86
190	4.70	4.85	5.01	5.16	5.31	5.47	5.62	5.77	5.92	6.07	6.22	6.37	6.52	6.67	6.82	7.12
185	4.92	5.08	5.23	5.39	5.54	5.70	5.85	6.01	6.16	6.32	6.47	6.62	6.77	6.93	7.08	7.38
180	5.15	5.31	5.47	5.63	5.78	5.94	6.10	6.26	6.41	6.57	6.73	6.88	7.04	7.19	7.35	7.66
175	5.39	5.55	5.71	5.87	6.04	6.20	6.36	6.52	6.68	6.84	7.00	7.16	7.32	7.47	7.63	7.95
170	5.64	5.80	5.97	6.13	6.30	6.46	6.63	6.79	6.95	7.12	7.28	7.44	7.60	7.77	7.93	8.25
165	5.90	6.07	6.24	6.40	6.57	6.74	6.91	7.08	7.24	7.41	7.58	7.74	7.91	8.07	8.24	8.57
160	6.17	6.34	6.52	6.69	6.86	7.03	7.20	7.37	7.54	7.72	7.89	8.05	8.22	8.39	8.56	8.90
155	6.45	6.63	6.81	6.99	7.16	7.34	7.51	7.69	7.86	8.04	8.21	8.38	8.56	8.73	8.90	9.25
150	6.76	6.94	7.12	7.30	7.48	7.66	7.84	8.02	8.20	8.38	8.55	8.73	8.91	9.09	9.27	9.62
145	7.07	7.26	7.44	7.63	7.81	8.00	8.18	8.37	8.55	8.73	8.92	9.10	9.28	9.46	9.65	10.01
140	7.40	7.60	7.79	7.98	8.17	8.36	8.55	8.73	8.92	9.11	9.30	9.49	9.68	9.86	10.05	10.42
135	7.76	7.95	8.15	8.35	8.54	8.74	8.93	9.12	9.32	9.51	9.71	9.90	10.09	10.29	10.48	10.86
130	8.13	8.33	8.54	8.74	8.94	9.14	9.34	9.54	9.74	9.94	10.14	10.34	10.54	10.74	10.94	11.33
125	8.53	8.74	8.95	9.15	9.36	9.57	9.78	9.98	10.19	10.39	10.60	10.81	11.01	11.22	11.42	11.84
120	8.95	9.17	9.38	9.60	9.81	10.03	10.24	10.45	10.67	10.88	11.10	11.31	11.52	11.73	11.95	12.37
115	9.41	9.63	9.85	10.08	10.30	10.52	10.74	10.96	11.18	11.41	11.63	11.85	12.07	12.29	12.51	12.95
113	9.60	9.83	10.05	10.28	10.50	10.73	10.95	11.18	11.40	11.63	11.85	12.07	12.30	12.52	12.75	13.20
112	9.70	9.92	10.15	10.38	10.61	10.83	11.06	11.29	11.51	11.74	11.96	12.19	12.42	12.64	12.87	13.32
111	9.80	10.03	10.25	10.48	10.71	10.94	11.17	11.40	11.62	11.85	12.08	12.31	12.54	12.76	12.99	13.45
110	9.90	10.13	10.36	10.59	10.82	11.05	11.28	11.51	11.74	11.97	12.20	12.43	12.66	12.89	13.12	13.58
109	10.00	10.23	10.46	10.70	10.93	11.16	11.39	11.62	11.86	12.09	12.32	12.55	12.78	13.01	13.25	13.71
108	10.10	10.34	10.57	10.81	11.04	11.27	11.51	11.74	11.97	12.21	12.44	12.57	12.80	13.04	13.27	13.51	13.84
107	10.21	10.44	10.68	10.92	11.15	11.39	11.62	11.86	12.09	12.33	12.57	12.80	13.04	13.27	13.51	13.98
106	10.32	10.55	10.79	11.03	11.27	11.50	11.74	11.98	12.22	12.45	12.69	12.93	13.17	13.40	13.64	14.11
105	10.42	10.66	10.90	11.14	11.38	11.62	11.86	12.10	12.34	12.58	12.82	13.06	13.30	13.54	13.78	14.25
104	10.53	10.78	11.02	11.26	11.50	11.74	11.98	12.23	12.47	12.71	12.95	13.19	13.43	13.67	13.92	14.40
103	10.65	10.89	11.13	11.38	11.62	11.87	12.11	12.35	12.60	12.84	13.08	13.33	13.57	13.81	14.06	14.54
102	10.76	11.01	11.25	11.50	11.74	11.99	12.24	12.48	12.73	12.97	13.22	13.46	13.71	13.95	14.20	14.69
101	10.88	11.12	11.37	11.62	11.87	12.12	12.36	12.61	12.86	13.11	13.36	13.60	13.85	14.10	14.35	14.84
100	11.00	11.25	11.50	11.75	12.00	12.25	12.50	12.75	13.00	13.25	13.50	13.75	14.00	14.25	14.50	15.00
99	11.12	11.37	11.62	11.87	12.12	12.38	12.63	12.88	13.13	13.39	13.64	13.89	14.14	14.39	14.65	15.15
98	11.24	11.49	11.75	12.00	12.26	12.51	12.76	13.02	13.27	13.53	13.78	14.04	14.29	14.55	14.80	15.31
97	11.36	11.62	11.88	12.13	12.39	12.65	12.90	13.16	13.42	13.67	13.93	14.19	14.44	14.70	14.96	15.47
96	11.49	11.75	12.01	12.27	12.52	12.78	13.04	13.30	13.56	13.82	14.08	14.34	14.60	14.86	15.12	15.64
95	11.62	11.88	12.14	12.40	12.66	12.93	13.19	13.45	13.71	13.97	14.23	14.50	14.76	15.02	15.28	15.81
94	11.75	12.01	12.28	12.54	12.80	13.07	13.33	13.60	13.86	14.13	14.39	14.66	14.92	15.18	15.45	15.98
93	11.88	12.15	12.42	12.68	12.95	13.22	13.48	13.75	14.02	14.28	14.55	14.82	15.08	15.35	15.62	16.15
92	12.02	12.29	12.56	12.83	13.10	13.36	13.63	13.90	14.17	14.44	14.71	14.98	15.25	15.52	15.79	16.33
91	12.16	12.43	12.70	12.97	13.25	13.52	13.79	14.06	14.33	14.61	14.88	15.15	15.42	15.70	15.97	16.52
90	12.30	12.57	12.85	13.12	13.40	13.67	13.95	14.22	14.50	14.77	15.05	15.32	15.60	15.87	16.15	16.70
89	12.44	12.72	13.00	13.28	13.55	13.83	14.11	14.39	14.66	14.94	15.22	15.50	15.78	16.06	16.33	16.89
88	12.59	12.87	13.15	13.43	13.71	13.99	14.27	14.55	14.84	15.12	15.40	15.68	15.96	16.24	16.52	17.09
87	12.74	13.02	13.31	13.59	13.87	14.16	14.44	14.73	15.01	15.29	15.58	15.86	16.15	16.43	16.72	17.29
86	12.90	13.18	13.47	13.75	14.04	14.33	14.61	14.90	15.19	15.47	15.76	16.05	16.34	16.62	16.91	17.49
85	13.05	13.34	13.63	13.92	14.21	14.50	14.79	15.08	15.37	15.66	15.95	16.24	16.53	16.82	17.11	17.70
84	13.21	13.50	13.80	14.09	14.38	14.67	14.97	15.26	15.55	15.85	16.14	16.44	16.73	17.02	17.32	17.91
83	13.38	13.67	13.97	14.26	14.56	14.85	15.15	15.45	15.74	16.04	16.34	16.64	16.93	17.23	17.53	18.13
82	13.54	13.84	14.14	14.44	14.74	15.04	15.34	15.64	15.94	16.24	16.54	16.84	17.14	17.44	17.74	18.35
81	13.71	14.02	14.32	14.62	14.92	15.23	15.53	15.83	16.14	16.44	16.75	17.05	17.36	17.66	17.97	18.58
80	13.89	14.19	14.50	14.81	15.11	15.42	15.73	16.03	16.34	16.65	16.96	17.27	17.57	17.88	18.19	18.81
79	14.07	14.38	14.69	15.00	15.31	15.62	15.93	16.24	16.55	16.86	17.17	17.48	17.80	18.11	18.42	19.05
78	14.25	14.56	14.88	15.19	15.50	15.82	16.13	16.45	16.76	17.08	17.39	17.71	18.03	18.34	18.66	19.29
77	14.44	14.75	15.07	15.39	15.71	16.03	16.34	16.66	16.98	17.30	17.62	17.94	18.26	18.58	18.90	19.54
76	14.63	14.95	15.27	15.59	15.92	16.24	16.56	16.88	17.21	17.53	17.85	18.18	18.50	18.83	19.15	19.80
75	14.83	15.15	15.48	15.80	16.13	16.45	16.78	17.11	17.44	17.76	18.09	18.42	18.75	19.08	19.41	20.06
74	15.03	15.36	15.69	16.02	16.35	16.68	17.01	17.34	17.67	18.00	18.34	18.67	19.00	19.33	19.67	20.33
73	15.23	15.57	15.90	16.24	16.57	16.91	17.24	17.58	17.91	18.25	18.59	18.92	19.26	19.60	19.94	20.61
70	15.89	16.23	16.58	16.93	17.28	17.63	17.98	18.33	18.68	19.03	19.38	19.73	20.08	20.43	20.79	21.49
65	17.10	17.47	17.85	18.22	18.60	18.97	19.35	19.73	20.11	20.48	20.86	21.24	21.62	22.00	22.38	23.14
60	18.51	18.91	19.32	19.72	20.13	20.54	20.95	21.36	21.76	22.17	22.58	22.99	23.41	23.82	24.23	25.05
55	20.16	20.60	21.05	21.49	21.94	22.38	22.83	23.27	23.72	24.17	24.62	25.07	25.52	25.96	26.41	27.32

Description: This table shows the price to pay for a bond at the yield rate. The yield is to maturity.

Example: The price of a 6.75 %, 25 year bond to yield 8 % to maturity is $ 86.57.

YIELD	0.00%	1.00%	2.00%	3.00%	4.00%	4.25%	4.50%	4.75%	5.00%	5.25%	5.50%	5.75%	6.00%	6.25%	6.50%	6.75%
0.00	100.00	125.00	150.00	175.00	200.00	206.25	212.50	218.75	225.00	231.25	237.50	243.75	250.00	256.25	262.50	268.75
1.00	77.93	100.00	122.07	144.14	166.21	171.73	177.25	182.77	188.29	193.80	199.32	204.84	210.36	215.87	221.39	226.91
2.00	60.80	80.40	100.00	119.60	139.20	144.10	149.00	153.89	158.79	163.69	168.59	173.49	178.39	183.29	188.19	193.09
3.00	47.50	65.00	82.50	100.00	117.50	121.87	126.25	130.62	135.00	139.37	143.75	148.12	152.50	156.87	161.25	165.62
4.00	37.15	52.86	68.58	84.29	100.00	103.93	107.86	111.78	115.71	119.64	123.57	127.50	131.42	135.35	139.28	143.21
4.25	34.95	50.25	65.56	80.87	96.17	100.00	103.83	107.65	111.48	115.31	119.13	122.96	126.79	130.61	134.44	138.27
4.50	32.87	47.79	62.71	77.62	92.54	96.27	100.00	103.73	107.46	111.19	114.92	118.65	122.38	126.11	129.83	133.56
4.75	30.92	45.47	60.01	74.55	89.09	92.73	96.36	100.00	103.64	107.27	110.91	114.54	118.18	121.81	125.45	129.08
5.00	29.09	43.28	57.46	71.64	85.82	89.36	92.91	96.45	100.00	103.55	107.09	110.64	114.18	117.73	121.27	124.82
5.25	27.37	41.21	55.04	68.87	82.71	86.17	89.62	93.08	96.54	100.00	103.46	106.92	110.38	113.83	117.29	120.75
5.50	25.76	39.26	52.75	66.25	79.75	83.13	86.50	89.88	93.25	96.63	100.00	103.37	106.75	110.12	113.50	116.87
5.75	24.24	37.41	50.59	63.77	76.94	80.24	83.53	86.82	90.12	93.41	96.71	100.00	103.29	106.59	109.88	113.18
6.00	22.81	35.68	48.54	61.41	74.27	77.49	80.70	83.92	87.14	90.35	93.57	96.78	100.00	103.22	106.43	109.65
6.25	21.47	34.03	46.60	59.16	71.73	74.87	78.01	81.15	84.29	87.43	90.58	93.72	96.86	100.00	103.14	106.28
6.50	20.21	32.48	44.76	57.03	69.31	72.38	75.45	78.52	81.59	84.66	87.72	90.79	93.86	96.93	100.00	103.07
6.75	19.02	31.02	43.01	55.01	67.01	70.01	73.01	76.01	79.01	82.00	85.00	88.00	91.00	94.00	97.00	100.00
7.00	17.91	29.63	41.36	53.09	64.82	67.75	70.68	73.61	76.54	79.48	82.41	85.34	88.27	91.20	94.14	97.07
7.25	16.86	28.32	39.79	51.26	62.73	65.60	68.46	71.33	74.20	77.06	79.93	82.80	85.66	88.53	91.40	94.27
7.50	15.87	27.09	38.31	49.52	60.74	63.54	66.35	69.15	71.96	74.76	77.57	80.37	83.17	85.98	88.78	91.59
7.75	14.94	25.92	36.89	47.87	58.84	61.59	64.33	67.07	69.82	72.56	75.31	78.05	80.79	83.54	86.28	89.02
8.00	14.07	24.81	35.55	46.29	57.04	59.72	62.41	65.09	67.78	70.46	73.15	75.83	78.52	81.20	83.89	86.57
8.25	13.25	23.77	34.28	44.80	55.31	57.94	60.57	63.20	65.83	68.45	71.08	73.71	76.34	78.97	81.60	84.23
8.50	12.48	22.78	33.07	43.37	53.67	56.24	58.81	61.39	63.96	66.54	69.11	71.68	74.26	76.83	79.41	81.98
8.75	11.75	21.84	31.92	42.01	52.09	54.62	57.14	59.66	62.18	64.70	67.22	69.74	72.27	74.79	77.31	79.83
9.00	11.07	20.95	30.83	40.71	50.59	53.07	55.54	58.01	60.48	62.95	65.42	67.89	70.36	72.83	75.30	77.77
9.25	10.43	20.11	29.80	39.48	49.16	51.58	54.00	56.42	58.85	61.27	63.69	66.11	68.53	70.95	73.37	75.79
9.50	9.82	19.32	28.81	38.30	47.79	50.17	52.54	54.91	57.29	59.66	62.03	64.40	66.78	69.15	71.52	73.90
9.75	9.26	18.56	27.87	37.18	46.48	48.81	51.14	53.46	55.79	58.12	60.44	62.77	65.10	67.43	69.75	72.08
10.00	8.72	17.85	26.98	36.10	45.23	47.51	49.80	52.08	54.36	56.64	58.92	61.21	63.49	65.77	68.05	70.33
10.25	8.22	17.17	26.13	35.08	44.03	46.27	48.51	50.75	52.99	55.23	57.47	59.70	61.94	64.18	66.42	68.66
10.50	7.74	16.53	25.32	34.10	42.89	45.08	47.28	49.48	51.67	53.87	56.07	58.26	60.46	62.66	64.85	67.05
10.75	7.30	15.92	24.54	33.17	41.79	43.95	46.11	48.26	50.41	52.57	54.73	56.88	59.04	61.19	63.35	65.51
11.00	6.88	15.34	23.81	32.27	40.74	42.86	44.97	47.09	49.21	51.32	53.44	55.55	57.67	59.79	61.90	64.02
11.25	6.48	14.79	23.11	31.42	39.73	41.81	43.89	45.97	48.05	50.12	52.20	54.28	56.36	58.44	60.51	62.59
11.50	6.11	14.27	22.44	30.60	38.77	40.81	42.85	44.89	46.93	48.97	51.01	53.05	55.10	57.14	59.18	61.22
11.75	5.76	13.78	21.80	29.82	37.84	39.85	41.85	43.86	45.86	47.87	49.87	51.88	53.88	55.89	57.89	59.90
12.00	5.43	13.31	21.19	29.07	36.95	38.92	40.89	42.86	44.83	46.80	48.77	50.74	52.71	54.68	56.65	58.63
12.25	5.12	12.86	20.61	28.35	36.10	38.04	39.97	41.91	43.85	45.78	47.72	49.65	51.59	53.53	55.46	57.40
12.50	4.83	12.44	20.05	27.67	35.28	37.18	39.09	40.99	42.90	44.80	46.70	48.61	50.51	52.41	54.32	56.22
12.75	4.55	12.04	19.52	27.01	34.50	36.37	38.24	40.11	41.98	43.85	45.72	47.60	49.47	51.34	53.21	55.08
13.00	4.29	11.65	19.02	26.38	33.74	35.58	37.42	39.26	41.10	42.94	44.78	46.62	48.46	50.30	52.15	53.99
13.25	4.05	11.29	18.53	25.77	33.01	34.82	36.63	38.44	40.26	42.07	43.88	45.69	47.50	49.31	51.12	52.93
13.50	3.82	10.94	18.07	25.19	32.31	34.10	35.88	37.66	39.44	41.22	43.00	44.78	46.56	48.35	50.13	51.91
13.75	3.60	10.61	17.62	24.63	31.64	33.40	35.15	36.90	38.65	40.41	42.16	43.91	45.66	47.42	49.17	50.92
14.00	3.39	10.30	17.20	24.10	31.00	32.72	34.45	36.17	37.90	39.62	41.35	43.07	44.80	46.52	48.25	49.97
14.25	3.20	10.00	16.79	23.58	30.37	32.07	33.77	35.47	37.17	38.86	40.56	42.26	43.96	45.66	47.36	49.05
14.50	3.02	9.71	16.40	23.09	29.77	31.45	33.12	34.79	36.46	38.13	39.81	41.48	43.15	44.82	46.49	48.17
14.75	2.85	9.44	16.02	22.61	29.20	30.84	32.49	34.14	35.78	37.43	39.08	40.72	42.37	44.02	45.66	47.31
15.00	2.69	9.18	15.66	22.15	28.64	30.26	31.88	33.50	35.13	36.75	38.37	39.99	41.61	43.24	44.86	46.48
15.25	2.54	8.93	15.32	21.71	28.10	29.70	31.30	32.89	34.49	36.09	37.69	39.29	40.88	42.48	44.08	45.68
15.50	2.39	8.69	14.99	21.29	27.58	29.16	30.73	32.31	33.88	35.45	37.03	38.60	40.18	41.75	43.33	44.90
15.75	2.26	8.46	14.67	20.88	27.08	28.63	30.19	31.74	33.29	34.84	36.39	37.94	39.49	41.05	42.60	44.15
16.00	2.13	8.25	14.37	20.48	26.60	28.13	29.66	31.19	32.72	34.25	35.77	37.30	38.83	40.36	41.89	43.42
16.25	2.01	8.04	14.07	20.10	26.13	27.64	29.15	30.65	32.16	33.67	35.18	36.68	38.19	39.70	41.21	42.71
16.50	1.90	7.84	13.79	19.74	25.68	27.17	28.65	30.14	31.63	33.11	34.60	36.09	37.57	39.06	40.55	42.03
16.75	1.79	7.66	13.52	19.38	25.25	26.71	28.18	29.64	31.11	32.57	34.04	35.51	36.97	38.44	39.90	41.37
17.00	1.69	7.48	13.26	19.04	24.82	26.27	27.72	29.16	30.61	32.05	33.50	34.94	36.39	37.83	39.28	40.73
17.25	1.60	7.30	13.01	18.71	24.42	25.84	27.27	28.69	30.12	31.55	32.97	34.40	35.82	37.25	38.68	40.10
17.50	1.51	7.14	12.76	18.39	24.02	25.43	26.83	28.24	29.65	31.06	32.46	33.87	35.28	36.68	38.09	39.50
17.75	1.42	6.98	12.53	18.08	23.64	25.03	26.42	27.80	29.19	30.58	31.97	33.36	34.75	36.13	37.52	38.91
18.00	1.34	6.83	12.31	17.79	23.27	24.64	26.01	27.38	28.75	30.12	31.49	32.86	34.23	35.60	36.97	38.34
18.25	1.27	6.68	12.09	17.50	22.91	24.26	25.61	26.97	28.32	29.67	31.02	32.38	33.73	35.08	36.43	37.79
18.50	1.20	6.54	11.88	17.22	22.56	23.90	25.23	26.57	27.90	29.24	30.57	31.91	33.24	34.58	35.91	37.25
18.75	1.13	6.41	11.68	16.95	22.22	23.54	24.86	26.18	27.50	28.82	30.13	31.45	32.77	34.09	35.41	36.72
19.00	1.07	6.28	11.48	16.69	21.90	23.20	24.50	25.80	27.10	28.41	29.71	31.01	32.31	33.61	34.91	36.22
20.00	.85	5.81	10.77	15.72	20.68	21.92	23.16	24.40	25.64	26.88	28.12	29.36	30.60	31.84	33.08	34.31
25.00	.28	4.27	8.25	12.24	16.23	17.23	18.23	19.22	20.22	21.22	22.22	23.21	24.21	25.21	26.20	27.20
30.00	.09	3.42	6.75	10.08	13.41	14.25	15.08	15.91	16.74	17.58	18.41	19.24	20.07	20.91	21.74	22.57

BOND YIELD

Description: This table shows the yield to maturity of a bond purchased at the price shown in the index.

Example: The yield to maturity of a 6.75 %, 25 year bond at a price of 80.00 is 8.72 %.

COUPON RATE, %

PRICE	0.00%	1.00%	2.00%	3.00%	4.00%	4.25%	4.50%	4.75%	5.00%	5.25%	5.50%	5.75%	6.00%	6.25%	6.50%	6.75%
100	0.00	1.00	2.00	3.00	4.00	4.25	4.50	4.75	5.00	5.25	5.50	5.75	6.00	6.25	6.50	6.75
99	.04	1.04	2.05	3.05	4.06	4.31	4.56	4.81	5.07	5.32	5.57	5.82	6.07	6.33	6.58	6.83
98	.08	1.09	2.10	3.11	4.12	4.38	4.63	4.88	5.14	5.39	5.65	5.90	6.15	6.41	6.66	6.91
97	.12	1.13	2.15	3.17	4.19	4.45	4.70	4.96	5.21	5.47	5.72	5.98	6.23	6.49	6.75	7.00
96	.16	1.18	2.20	3.23	4.26	4.51	4.77	5.03	5.29	5.54	5.80	6.06	6.32	6.57	6.83	7.09
95	.20	1.23	2.26	3.29	4.32	4.58	4.84	5.10	5.36	5.62	5.88	6.14	6.40	6.66	6.92	7.18
94	.24	1.28	2.31	3.35	4.39	4.65	4.91	5.18	5.44	5.70	5.96	6.22	6.48	6.75	7.01	7.27
93	.29	1.33	2.37	3.41	4.46	4.73	4.99	5.25	5.51	5.78	6.04	6.31	6.57	6.83	7.10	7.36
92	.33	1.37	2.42	3.48	4.53	4.80	5.06	5.33	5.59	5.86	6.12	6.39	6.66	6.92	7.19	7.46
91	.37	1.42	2.48	3.54	4.61	4.87	5.14	5.41	5.67	5.94	6.21	6.48	6.75	7.01	7.28	7.55
90	.42	1.48	2.54	3.61	4.68	4.95	5.22	5.49	5.75	6.02	6.29	6.56	6.84	7.11	7.38	7.65
89	.46	1.53	2.60	3.67	4.75	5.02	5.29	5.57	5.84	6.11	6.38	6.65	6.93	7.20	7.47	7.75
88	.51	1.58	2.66	3.74	4.83	5.10	5.37	5.65	5.92	6.20	6.47	6.75	7.02	7.30	7.57	7.85
87	.55	1.63	2.72	3.81	4.90	5.18	5.45	5.73	6.01	6.28	6.56	6.84	7.12	7.39	7.67	7.95
86	.60	1.68	2.78	3.87	4.98	5.26	5.54	5.81	6.09	6.37	6.65	6.93	7.21	7.49	7.77	8.06
85	.65	1.74	2.84	3.94	5.06	5.34	5.62	5.90	6.18	6.46	6.75	7.03	7.31	7.59	7.88	8.16
84	.69	1.79	2.90	4.02	5.14	5.42	5.70	5.99	6.27	6.56	6.84	7.13	7.41	7.70	7.98	8.27
83	.74	1.85	2.96	4.09	5.22	5.51	5.79	6.08	6.36	6.65	6.94	7.22	7.51	7.80	8.09	8.38
82	.79	1.90	3.03	4.16	5.30	5.59	5.88	6.17	6.46	6.75	7.04	7.33	7.62	7.91	8.20	8.49
81	.84	1.96	3.09	4.23	5.39	5.68	5.97	6.26	6.55	6.84	7.14	7.43	7.72	8.02	8.31	8.61
80	.89	2.02	3.16	4.31	5.47	5.77	6.06	6.35	6.65	6.94	7.24	7.53	7.83	8.13	8.43	8.72
79	.94	2.08	3.23	4.39	5.56	5.86	6.15	6.45	6.75	7.04	7.34	7.64	7.94	8.24	8.54	8.84
78	.99	2.14	3.29	4.47	5.65	5.95	6.25	6.55	6.85	7.15	7.45	7.75	8.05	8.36	8.66	8.97
77	1.04	2.20	3.36	4.54	5.74	6.04	6.34	6.64	6.95	7.25	7.56	7.86	8.17	8.48	8.78	9.09
76	1.10	2.26	3.43	4.63	5.83	6.14	6.44	6.75	7.05	7.36	7.67	7.98	8.29	8.60	8.91	9.22
75	1.15	2.32	3.51	4.71	5.93	6.23	6.54	6.85	7.16	7.47	7.78	8.09	8.40	8.72	9.03	9.35
74	1.20	2.38	3.58	4.79	6.02	6.33	6.64	6.95	7.27	7.58	7.89	8.21	8.53	8.84	9.16	9.48
73	1.26	2.45	3.65	4.88	6.12	6.43	6.75	7.06	7.38	7.69	8.01	8.33	8.65	8.97	9.29	9.62
72	1.31	2.51	3.73	4.96	6.22	6.53	6.85	7.17	7.49	7.81	8.13	8.46	8.78	9.10	9.43	9.76
71	1.37	2.58	3.80	5.05	6.32	6.64	6.96	7.28	7.61	7.93	8.26	8.58	8.91	9.24	9.57	9.90
70	1.43	2.64	3.88	5.14	6.42	6.75	7.07	7.40	7.72	8.05	8.38	8.71	9.04	9.38	9.71	10.04
69	1.48	2.71	3.96	5.23	6.53	6.86	7.18	7.51	7.84	8.18	8.51	8.84	9.18	9.52	9.85	10.19
68	1.54	2.78	4.04	5.33	6.64	6.97	7.30	7.63	7.97	8.30	8.64	8.98	9.32	9.66	10.00	10.35
67	1.60	2.85	4.12	5.42	6.75	7.08	7.42	7.75	8.09	8.43	8.78	9.12	9.46	9.81	10.16	10.50
66	1.66	2.92	4.21	5.52	6.86	7.20	7.54	7.88	8.22	8.57	8.91	9.26	9.61	9.96	10.31	10.66
65	1.73	3.00	4.29	5.62	6.97	7.32	7.66	8.01	8.35	8.70	9.05	9.41	9.76	10.11	10.47	10.83
64	1.79	3.07	4.38	5.72	7.09	7.44	7.79	8.14	8.49	8.84	9.20	9.56	9.91	10.27	10.64	11.00
63	1.85	3.14	4.47	5.82	7.21	7.56	7.92	8.27	8.63	8.99	9.35	9.71	10.07	10.44	10.80	11.17
62	1.92	3.22	4.56	5.93	7.34	7.69	8.05	8.41	8.77	9.13	9.50	9.87	10.24	10.61	10.98	11.35
61	1.98	3.30	4.65	6.04	7.46	7.82	8.19	8.55	8.92	9.29	9.66	10.03	10.40	10.78	11.16	11.54
60	2.05	3.38	4.75	6.15	7.59	7.96	8.32	8.69	9.07	9.44	9.82	10.20	10.57	10.96	11.34	11.73
59	2.12	3.46	4.84	6.26	7.72	8.09	8.47	8.84	9.22	9.60	9.98	10.37	10.75	11.14	11.53	11.92
58	2.19	3.54	4.94	6.38	7.86	8.24	8.61	9.00	9.38	9.76	10.15	10.54	10.93	11.33	11.72	12.12
57	2.26	3.63	5.04	6.50	8.00	8.38	8.77	9.15	9.54	9.93	10.33	10.72	11.12	11.52	11.92	12.33
56	2.33	3.71	5.14	6.62	8.14	8.53	8.92	9.31	9.71	10.11	10.51	10.91	11.31	11.72	12.13	12.54
55	2.40	3.80	5.25	6.75	8.29	8.68	9.08	9.48	9.88	10.29	10.69	11.10	11.51	11.93	12.34	12.76
54	2.48	3.89	5.36	6.87	8.44	8.84	9.25	9.65	10.06	10.47	10.88	11.30	11.72	12.14	12.57	12.99
53	2.55	3.98	5.47	7.01	8.60	9.01	9.42	9.83	10.24	10.66	11.08	11.51	11.93	12.36	12.79	13.23
52	2.63	4.08	5.58	7.14	8.76	9.17	9.59	10.01	10.43	10.86	11.29	11.72	12.15	12.59	13.03	13.47
51	2.71	4.17	5.70	7.28	8.93	9.35	9.77	10.20	10.63	11.06	11.50	11.94	12.38	12.83	13.27	13.73
50	2.79	4.27	5.82	7.43	9.10	9.53	9.96	10.39	10.83	11.27	11.72	12.16	12.62	13.07	13.53	13.99
49	2.87	4.37	5.94	7.57	9.27	9.71	10.15	10.59	11.04	11.49	11.94	12.40	12.86	13.32	13.79	14.26
48	2.95	4.47	6.06	7.72	9.46	9.90	10.35	10.80	11.25	11.71	12.18	12.64	13.11	13.59	14.06	14.54
47	3.04	4.58	6.19	7.88	9.65	10.10	10.55	11.01	11.48	11.95	12.42	12.90	13.38	13.86	14.35	14.84
46	3.13	4.69	6.32	8.04	9.84	10.30	10.77	11.24	11.71	12.19	12.67	13.16	13.65	14.14	14.64	15.14
45	3.21	4.80	6.46	8.21	10.04	10.51	10.99	11.47	11.95	12.44	12.94	13.43	13.94	14.44	14.95	15.46
44	3.31	4.91	6.60	8.38	10.25	10.73	11.22	11.71	12.21	12.71	13.21	13.72	14.23	14.75	15.27	15.80
43	3.40	5.03	6.75	8.56	10.47	10.96	11.46	11.96	12.47	12.98	13.50	14.02	14.54	15.07	15.61	16.14
42	3.50	5.15	6.90	8.75	10.70	11.20	11.71	12.22	12.74	13.26	13.79	14.33	14.87	15.41	15.96	16.51
41	3.59	5.27	7.05	8.94	10.93	11.45	11.97	12.49	13.02	13.56	14.10	14.65	15.20	15.76	16.32	16.89
40	3.69	5.40	7.21	9.14	11.18	11.70	12.24	12.78	13.32	13.87	14.43	14.99	15.56	16.13	16.71	17.29
39	3.80	5.53	7.38	9.35	11.43	11.97	12.52	13.07	13.63	14.20	14.77	15.35	15.93	16.52	17.11	17.71
35	4.24	6.10	8.10	10.27	12.58	13.19	13.80	14.42	15.04	15.68	16.32	16.97	17.62	18.29	18.95	19.62
30	4.87	6.93	9.19	11.69	14.40	15.11	15.83	16.56	17.31	18.06	18.82	19.59	20.37	21.15	21.94	22.74
25	5.62	7.95	10.60	13.58	16.89	17.76	18.65	19.55	20.47	21.40	22.33	23.28	24.23	25.20	26.16	27.14
20	6.54	9.28	12.52	16.31	20.61	21.75	22.90	24.07	25.26	26.46	27.67	28.88	30.10	31.33	32.56	33.80
15	7.73	11.15	15.49	20.83	26.94	28.53	30.15	31.77	33.41	35.06	36.71	38.36	40.02	41.68	43.34	45.01
10	9.42	14.24	21.23	30.23	40.03	42.52	45.01	47.51	50.00	52.50	55.00	57.50	60.00	62.50	65.00	67.50

Description: This table shows the price to pay for a bond at the yield rate. The yield is to maturity.

Example: The price of a 10.75 %, 25 year bond to yield 8 % to maturity is $ 129.54.

COUPON RATE, %

YIELD	7.00%	7.25%	7.50%	7.75%	8.00%	8.25%	8.50%	8.75%	9.00%	9.25%	9.50%	9.75%	10.00%	10.25%	10.50%	10.75%
0.00	275.00	281.25	287.50	293.75	300.00	306.25	312.50	318.75	325.00	331.25	337.50	343.75	350.00	356.25	362.50	368.75
1.00	232.43	237.95	243.46	248.98	254.50	260.02	265.54	271.05	276.57	282.09	287.61	293.12	298.64	304.16	309.68	315.20
2.00	197.99	202.89	207.79	212.69	217.59	222.49	227.39	232.29	237.19	242.09	246.99	251.88	256.78	261.68	266.58	271.48
3.00	170.00	174.37	178.75	183.12	187.50	191.87	196.25	200.62	205.00	209.37	213.75	218.12	222.50	226.87	231.25	235.62
4.00	147.14	151.06	154.99	158.92	162.85	166.78	170.70	174.63	178.56	182.49	186.41	190.34	194.27	198.20	202.13	206.05
4.25	142.09	145.92	149.75	153.57	157.40	161.23	165.05	168.88	172.71	176.53	180.36	184.19	188.01	191.84	195.67	199.49
4.50	137.29	141.02	144.75	148.48	152.21	155.94	159.67	163.40	167.13	170.86	174.59	178.32	182.04	185.77	189.50	193.23
4.75	132.72	136.36	139.99	143.63	147.26	150.90	154.53	158.17	161.80	165.44	169.08	172.71	176.35	179.98	183.62	187.25
5.00	128.36	131.91	135.45	139.00	142.54	146.09	149.63	153.18	156.72	160.27	163.82	167.36	170.91	174.45	178.00	181.54
5.25	124.21	127.67	131.13	134.58	138.04	141.50	144.96	148.42	151.88	155.33	158.79	162.25	165.71	169.17	172.63	176.08
5.50	120.25	123.62	127.00	130.37	133.75	137.12	140.50	143.87	147.25	150.62	153.99	157.37	160.74	164.12	167.49	170.87
5.75	116.47	119.76	123.06	126.35	129.65	132.94	136.23	139.53	142.82	146.12	149.41	152.70	156.00	159.29	162.59	165.88
6.00	112.86	116.08	119.30	122.51	125.73	128.95	132.16	135.38	138.59	141.81	145.03	148.24	151.46	154.68	157.89	161.11
6.25	109.42	112.57	115.71	118.85	121.99	125.13	128.27	131.41	134.55	137.70	140.84	143.98	147.12	150.26	153.40	156.54
6.50	106.14	109.21	112.28	115.34	118.41	121.48	124.55	127.62	130.69	133.76	136.83	139.90	142.97	146.03	149.10	152.17
6.75	103.00	106.00	109.00	112.00	115.00	118.00	120.99	123.99	126.99	129.99	132.99	135.99	138.99	141.99	144.99	147.99
7.00	100.00	102.93	105.86	108.80	111.73	114.66	117.59	120.52	123.46	126.39	129.32	132.25	135.18	138.12	141.05	143.98
7.25	97.13	100.00	102.87	105.73	108.60	111.47	114.34	117.20	120.07	122.94	125.80	128.67	131.54	134.40	137.27	140.14
7.50	94.39	97.20	100.00	102.80	105.61	108.41	111.22	114.02	116.83	119.63	122.43	125.24	128.04	130.85	133.65	136.46
7.75	91.77	94.51	97.26	100.00	102.74	105.49	108.23	110.98	113.72	116.46	119.21	121.95	124.69	127.44	130.18	132.93
8.00	89.26	91.94	94.63	97.31	100.00	102.69	105.37	108.06	110.74	113.43	116.11	118.80	121.48	124.17	126.85	129.54
8.25	86.86	89.48	92.11	94.74	97.37	100.00	102.63	105.26	107.89	110.52	113.14	115.77	118.40	121.03	123.66	126.29
8.50	84.56	87.13	89.70	92.28	94.85	97.43	100.00	102.57	105.15	107.72	110.30	112.87	115.44	118.02	120.59	123.17
8.75	82.35	84.87	87.39	89.91	92.44	94.96	97.48	100.00	102.52	105.04	107.56	110.09	112.61	115.13	117.65	120.17
9.00	80.24	82.71	85.18	87.65	90.12	92.59	95.06	97.53	100.00	102.47	104.94	107.41	109.88	112.35	114.82	117.29
9.25	78.21	80.63	83.05	85.47	87.90	90.32	92.74	95.16	97.58	100.00	102.42	104.84	107.26	109.68	112.10	114.53
9.50	76.27	78.64	81.02	83.39	85.76	88.13	90.51	92.88	95.25	97.63	100.00	102.37	104.75	107.12	109.49	111.87
9.75	74.41	76.73	79.06	81.39	83.71	86.04	88.37	90.69	93.02	95.35	97.67	100.00	102.33	104.65	106.98	109.31
10.00	72.62	74.90	77.18	79.46	81.74	84.03	86.31	88.59	90.87	93.15	95.44	97.72	100.00	102.28	104.56	106.85
10.25	70.90	73.14	75.38	77.61	79.85	82.09	84.33	86.57	88.81	91.05	93.28	95.52	97.76	100.00	102.24	104.48
10.50	69.25	71.44	73.64	75.84	78.03	80.23	82.43	84.62	86.82	89.02	91.21	93.41	95.61	97.80	100.00	102.20
10.75	67.66	69.82	71.97	74.13	76.29	78.44	80.60	82.75	84.91	87.06	89.22	91.38	93.53	95.69	97.84	100.00
11.00	66.14	68.25	70.37	72.49	74.60	76.72	78.84	80.95	83.07	85.18	87.30	89.42	91.53	93.65	95.77	97.88
11.25	64.67	66.75	68.83	70.91	72.98	75.06	77.14	79.22	81.30	83.37	85.45	87.53	89.61	91.69	93.77	95.84
11.50	63.26	65.30	67.34	69.38	71.42	73.47	75.51	77.55	79.59	81.63	83.67	85.71	87.75	89.79	91.84	93.88
11.75	61.90	63.91	65.91	67.92	69.92	71.93	73.93	75.94	77.94	79.95	81.95	83.96	85.96	87.97	89.97	91.98
12.00	60.60	62.57	64.54	66.51	68.48	70.45	72.42	74.39	76.36	78.33	80.30	82.27	84.24	86.21	88.18	90.15
12.25	59.34	61.27	63.21	65.15	67.08	69.02	70.95	72.89	74.83	76.76	78.70	80.64	82.57	84.51	86.45	88.38
12.50	58.12	60.03	61.93	63.83	65.74	67.64	69.54	71.45	73.35	75.25	77.16	79.06	80.97	82.87	84.77	86.68
12.75	56.95	58.83	60.70	62.57	64.44	66.31	68.18	70.05	71.93	73.80	75.67	77.54	79.41	81.28	83.16	85.03
13.00	55.83	57.67	59.51	61.35	63.19	65.03	66.87	68.71	70.55	72.39	74.23	76.07	77.91	79.75	81.59	83.43
13.25	54.74	56.55	58.36	60.17	61.98	63.79	65.60	67.41	69.22	71.03	72.84	74.65	76.46	78.27	80.09	81.90
13.50	53.69	55.47	57.25	59.03	60.81	62.60	64.38	66.16	67.94	69.72	71.50	73.28	75.06	76.84	78.63	80.41
13.75	52.68	54.43	56.18	57.93	59.69	61.44	63.19	64.95	66.70	68.45	70.20	71.96	73.71	75.46	77.21	78.97
14.00	51.70	53.42	55.15	56.87	58.60	60.32	62.05	63.77	65.50	67.22	68.95	70.67	72.40	74.12	75.85	77.57
14.25	50.75	52.45	54.15	55.85	57.54	59.24	60.94	62.64	64.34	66.04	67.73	69.43	71.13	72.83	74.53	76.23
14.50	49.84	51.51	53.18	54.85	56.53	58.20	59.87	61.54	63.21	64.89	66.56	68.23	69.90	71.58	73.25	74.92
14.75	48.96	50.60	52.25	53.89	55.54	57.19	58.83	60.48	62.13	63.77	65.42	67.07	68.71	70.36	72.01	73.65
15.00	48.10	49.72	51.34	52.97	54.59	56.21	57.83	59.45	61.08	62.70	64.32	65.94	67.56	69.18	70.81	72.43
15.25	47.27	48.87	50.47	52.07	53.67	55.26	56.86	58.46	60.06	61.65	63.25	64.85	66.45	68.04	69.64	71.24
15.50	46.47	48.05	49.62	51.20	52.77	54.35	55.92	57.49	59.07	60.64	62.22	63.79	65.37	66.94	68.51	70.09
15.75	45.70	47.25	48.80	50.35	51.91	53.46	55.01	56.56	58.11	59.66	61.21	62.77	64.32	65.87	67.42	68.97
16.00	44.95	46.48	48.01	49.54	51.07	52.60	54.12	55.65	57.18	58.71	60.24	61.77	63.30	64.83	66.36	67.89
16.25	44.22	45.73	47.24	48.74	50.25	51.76	53.27	54.77	56.28	57.79	59.30	60.80	62.31	63.82	65.33	66.83
16.50	43.52	45.00	46.49	47.98	49.46	50.95	52.44	53.92	55.41	56.90	58.38	59.87	61.35	62.84	64.33	65.81
16.75	42.83	44.30	45.77	47.23	48.70	50.16	51.63	53.10	54.56	56.03	57.49	58.96	60.42	61.89	63.36	64.82
17.00	42.17	43.62	45.06	46.51	47.95	49.40	50.85	52.29	53.74	55.18	56.63	58.07	59.52	60.97	62.41	63.86
17.25	41.53	42.96	44.38	45.81	47.23	48.66	50.09	51.51	52.94	54.36	55.79	57.22	58.64	60.07	61.49	62.92
17.50	40.91	42.31	43.72	45.13	46.53	47.94	49.35	50.75	52.16	53.57	54.98	56.38	57.79	59.20	60.60	62.01
17.75	40.30	41.69	43.08	44.46	45.85	47.24	48.63	50.02	51.41	52.79	54.18	55.57	56.96	58.35	59.74	61.13
18.00	39.71	41.08	42.45	43.82	45.19	46.56	47.93	49.30	50.67	52.04	53.41	54.78	56.15	57.52	58.89	60.26
18.25	39.14	40.49	41.84	43.20	44.55	45.90	47.25	48.61	49.96	51.31	52.66	54.02	55.37	56.72	58.07	59.43
18.50	38.58	39.92	41.25	42.59	43.92	45.26	46.59	47.93	49.26	50.60	51.93	53.27	54.61	55.94	57.28	58.61
18.75	38.04	39.36	40.68	42.00	43.32	44.63	45.95	47.27	48.59	49.91	51.23	52.54	53.86	55.18	56.50	57.82
19.00	37.52	38.82	40.12	41.42	42.72	44.03	45.33	46.63	47.93	49.23	50.53	51.84	53.14	54.44	55.74	57.04
20.00	35.55	36.79	38.03	39.27	40.51	41.75	42.99	44.23	45.47	46.71	47.95	49.19	50.43	51.67	52.90	54.14
25.00	28.20	29.20	30.19	31.19	32.19	33.19	34.18	35.18	36.18	37.17	38.17	39.17	40.17	41.16	42.16	43.16
30.00	23.40	24.24	25.07	25.90	26.73	27.57	28.40	29.23	30.06	30.90	31.73	32.56	33.39	34.23	35.06	35.89

Description: This table shows the yield to maturity of a bond purchased at the price shown in the index.

Example: The yield to maturity of a 10.75 %, 25 year bond at a price of 111.00 is 9.58 %.

COUPON RATE, %

PRICE	7.00%	7.25%	7.50%	7.75%	8.00%	8.25%	8.50%	8.75%	9.00%	9.25%	9.50%	9.75%	10.00%	10.25%	10.50%	10.75%
165	3.20	3.37	3.55	3.72	3.90	4.07	4.25	4.42	4.59	4.77	4.94	5.11	5.28	5.45	5.62	5.79
160	3.41	3.59	3.77	3.95	4.12	4.30	4.48	4.66	4.83	5.01	5.18	5.36	5.53	5.71	5.88	6.05
155	3.63	3.81	3.99	4.18	4.36	4.54	4.72	4.90	5.08	5.26	5.44	5.62	5.80	5.98	6.15	6.33
150	3.86	4.05	4.23	4.42	4.61	4.79	4.98	5.16	5.34	5.53	5.71	5.90	6.08	6.26	6.44	6.62
145	4.10	4.29	4.48	4.67	4.86	5.05	5.24	5.43	5.62	5.81	6.00	6.18	6.37	6.56	6.74	6.93
140	4.35	4.55	4.74	4.94	5.13	5.33	5.52	5.72	5.91	6.10	6.30	6.49	6.68	6.87	7.06	7.25
135	4.62	4.82	5.02	5.22	5.42	5.62	5.82	6.02	6.22	6.41	6.61	6.81	7.01	7.20	7.40	7.60
130	4.90	5.11	5.31	5.52	5.72	5.93	6.13	6.34	6.54	6.74	6.95	7.15	7.35	7.56	7.76	7.96
125	5.20	5.41	5.62	5.83	6.04	6.25	6.46	6.67	6.88	7.09	7.30	7.51	7.72	7.93	8.14	8.35
122	5.38	5.60	5.81	6.03	6.24	6.46	6.67	6.89	7.10	7.31	7.53	7.74	7.95	8.17	8.38	8.59
121	5.45	5.66	5.88	6.10	6.31	6.53	6.74	6.96	7.18	7.39	7.60	7.82	8.03	8.25	8.46	8.67
120	5.51	5.73	5.95	6.17	6.38	6.60	6.82	7.03	7.25	7.47	7.68	7.90	8.11	8.33	8.54	8.76
119	5.58	5.80	6.02	6.23	6.45	6.67	6.89	7.11	7.33	7.54	7.76	7.98	8.20	8.41	8.63	8.85
118	5.64	5.86	6.08	6.30	6.52	6.74	6.96	7.18	7.40	7.62	7.84	8.06	8.28	8.50	8.71	8.93
117	5.71	5.93	6.15	6.38	6.60	6.82	7.04	7.26	7.48	7.70	7.92	8.14	8.36	8.58	8.80	9.02
116	5.78	6.00	6.22	6.45	6.67	6.89	7.12	7.34	7.56	7.78	8.00	8.23	8.45	8.67	8.89	9.11
115	5.85	6.07	6.30	6.52	6.74	6.97	7.19	7.42	7.64	7.86	8.09	8.31	8.53	8.76	8.98	9.20
114	5.92	6.14	6.37	6.59	6.82	7.05	7.27	7.50	7.72	7.95	8.17	8.40	8.62	8.85	9.07	9.29
113	5.99	6.21	6.44	6.67	6.90	7.12	7.35	7.58	7.80	8.03	8.26	8.48	8.71	8.94	9.16	9.39
112	6.06	6.29	6.52	6.74	6.97	7.20	7.43	7.66	7.89	8.12	8.34	8.57	8.80	9.03	9.25	9.48
111	6.13	6.36	6.59	6.82	7.05	7.28	7.51	7.74	7.97	8.20	8.43	8.66	8.89	9.12	9.35	9.58
110	6.20	6.43	6.67	6.90	7.13	7.36	7.60	7.83	8.06	8.29	8.52	8.75	8.98	9.21	9.45	9.68
109	6.28	6.51	6.74	6.98	7.21	7.45	7.68	7.91	8.15	8.38	8.61	8.85	9.08	9.31	9.54	9.78
108	6.35	6.59	6.82	7.06	7.29	7.53	7.76	8.00	8.23	8.47	8.70	8.94	9.17	9.41	9.64	9.88
107	6.43	6.67	6.90	7.14	7.38	7.61	7.85	8.09	8.32	8.56	8.80	9.03	9.27	9.51	9.74	9.98
106	6.51	6.74	6.98	7.22	7.46	7.70	7.94	8.18	8.42	8.65	8.89	9.13	9.37	9.61	9.85	10.08
105	6.58	6.83	7.07	7.31	7.55	7.79	8.03	8.27	8.51	8.75	8.99	9.23	9.47	9.71	9.95	10.19
104	6.66	6.91	7.15	7.39	7.63	7.88	8.12	8.36	8.60	8.85	9.09	9.33	9.57	9.81	10.05	10.30
103	6.74	6.99	7.23	7.48	7.72	7.97	8.21	8.45	8.70	8.94	9.19	9.43	9.67	9.92	10.16	10.41
102	6.83	7.07	7.32	7.57	7.81	8.06	8.30	8.55	8.80	9.04	9.29	9.53	9.78	10.03	10.27	10.52
101	6.91	7.16	7.41	7.65	7.90	8.15	8.40	8.65	8.89	9.14	9.39	9.64	9.89	10.13	10.38	10.63
100	7.00	7.25	7.50	7.75	8.00	8.25	8.50	8.75	9.00	9.25	9.50	9.75	10.00	10.25	10.50	10.75
99	7.08	7.33	7.58	7.84	8.09	8.34	8.59	8.84	9.10	9.35	9.60	9.85	10.11	10.36	10.61	10.86
98	7.17	7.42	7.68	7.93	8.18	8.44	8.69	8.95	9.20	9.46	9.71	9.96	10.22	10.47	10.73	10.98
97	7.26	7.51	7.77	8.03	8.28	8.54	8.79	9.05	9.31	9.56	9.82	10.08	10.33	10.59	10.85	11.10
96	7.35	7.61	7.86	8.12	8.38	8.64	8.90	9.16	9.41	9.67	9.93	10.19	10.45	10.71	10.97	11.23
95	7.44	7.70	7.96	8.22	8.48	8.74	9.00	9.26	9.52	9.78	10.04	10.31	10.57	10.83	11.09	11.35
94	7.53	7.79	8.06	8.32	8.58	8.84	9.11	9.37	9.63	9.90	10.16	10.42	10.69	10.95	11.22	11.48
93	7.63	7.89	8.16	8.42	8.69	8.95	9.22	9.48	9.75	10.01	10.28	10.54	10.81	11.08	11.34	11.61
92	7.72	7.99	8.26	8.52	8.79	9.06	9.33	9.59	9.86	10.13	10.40	10.67	10.94	11.20	11.47	11.74
91	7.82	8.09	8.36	8.63	8.90	9.17	9.44	9.71	9.98	10.25	10.52	10.79	11.06	11.33	11.61	11.88
90	7.92	8.19	8.46	8.74	9.01	9.28	9.55	9.83	10.10	10.37	10.65	10.92	11.19	11.47	11.74	12.02
89	8.02	8.30	8.57	8.84	9.12	9.39	9.67	9.95	10.22	10.50	10.77	11.05	11.33	11.60	11.88	12.16
88	8.12	8.40	8.68	8.96	9.23	9.51	9.79	10.07	10.35	10.62	10.90	11.18	11.46	11.74	12.02	12.30
87	8.23	8.51	8.79	9.07	9.35	9.63	9.91	10.19	10.47	10.75	11.04	11.32	11.60	11.88	12.16	12.45
86	8.34	8.62	8.90	9.18	9.47	9.75	10.03	10.32	10.60	10.89	11.17	11.45	11.74	12.03	12.31	12.60
85	8.45	8.73	9.02	9.30	9.59	9.87	10.16	10.45	10.73	11.02	11.31	11.60	11.88	12.17	12.46	12.75
84	8.56	8.84	9.13	9.42	9.71	10.00	10.29	10.58	10.87	11.16	11.45	11.74	12.03	12.32	12.61	12.91
83	8.67	8.96	9.25	9.54	9.83	10.13	10.42	10.71	11.00	11.30	11.59	11.89	12.18	12.47	12.77	13.06
82	8.79	9.08	9.37	9.67	9.96	10.26	10.55	10.85	11.14	11.44	11.74	12.04	12.33	12.63	12.93	13.23
81	8.90	9.20	9.50	9.79	10.09	10.39	10.69	10.99	11.29	11.59	11.89	12.19	12.49	12.79	13.09	13.39
80	9.02	9.32	9.62	9.92	10.23	10.53	10.83	11.13	11.43	11.74	12.04	12.34	12.65	12.95	13.26	13.56
79	9.15	9.45	9.75	10.06	10.36	10.67	10.97	11.28	11.58	11.89	12.20	12.50	12.81	13.12	13.43	13.74
78	9.27	9.58	9.88	10.19	10.50	10.81	11.12	11.43	11.74	12.05	12.36	12.67	12.98	13.29	13.60	13.92
77	9.40	9.71	10.02	10.33	10.64	10.95	11.27	11.58	11.89	12.21	12.52	12.84	13.15	13.47	13.78	14.10
76	9.53	9.84	10.16	10.47	10.79	11.10	11.42	11.74	12.05	12.37	12.69	13.01	13.33	13.65	13.97	14.29
75	9.66	9.98	10.30	10.62	10.94	11.25	11.57	11.90	12.22	12.54	12.86	13.18	13.51	13.83	14.15	14.48
74	9.80	10.12	10.44	10.76	11.09	11.41	11.73	12.06	12.38	12.71	13.04	13.36	13.69	14.02	14.35	14.68
73	9.94	10.26	10.59	10.92	11.24	11.57	11.90	12.23	12.56	12.89	13.22	13.55	13.88	14.21	14.54	14.88
70	10.38	10.72	11.05	11.39	11.73	12.07	12.41	12.76	13.10	13.44	13.78	14.13	14.47	14.82	15.17	15.51
65	11.19	11.55	11.91	12.27	12.64	13.00	13.37	13.73	14.10	14.47	14.84	15.21	15.58	15.95	16.33	16.70
60	12.11	12.50	12.89	13.28	13.67	14.07	14.46	14.86	15.26	15.66	16.06	16.46	16.86	17.26	17.67	18.07
55	13.18	13.61	14.03	14.46	14.89	15.32	15.75	16.18	16.61	17.05	17.49	17.93	18.36	18.81	19.25	19.69
50	14.45	14.92	15.38	15.85	16.32	16.80	17.27	17.75	18.23	18.71	19.19	19.68	20.16	20.65	21.14	21.62
45	15.98	16.50	17.02	17.54	18.07	18.60	19.13	19.66	20.20	20.73	21.27	21.81	22.35	22.90	23.44	23.99
40	17.87	18.46	19.05	19.64	20.24	20.84	21.44	22.05	22.65	23.26	23.87	24.48	25.10	25.71	26.33	26.94
35	20.30	20.98	21.66	22.35	23.04	23.73	24.42	25.12	25.82	26.52	27.22	27.93	28.63	29.34	30.05	30.75
30	23.54	24.34	25.15	25.96	26.78	27.60	28.41	29.24	30.06	30.88	31.71	32.54	33.36	34.19	35.02	35.85

Description: This table shows the price to pay for a bond at the yield rate. The yield is to maturity.

Example: The price of a 15.00 %, 25 year bond to yield 8 % to maturity is $ 175.19.

COUPON RATE, %

YIELD	11.00%	11.25%	11.50%	11.75%	12.00%	12.25%	12.50%	12.75%	13.00%	13.25%	13.50%	13.75%	14.00%	14.25%	14.50%	15.00%
0.00	375.00	381.25	387.50	393.75	400.00	406.25	412.50	418.75	425.00	431.25	437.50	443.75	450.00	456.25	462.50	475.00
1.00	320.71	326.23	331.75	337.27	342.79	348.30	353.82	359.34	364.86	370.37	375.89	381.41	386.93	392.45	397.96	409.00
2.00	276.38	281.28	286.18	291.08	295.98	300.88	305.78	310.68	315.58	320.48	325.38	330.28	335.18	340.08	344.98	354.77
3.00	240.00	244.37	248.75	253.12	257.50	261.87	266.25	270.62	275.00	279.37	283.75	288.12	292.50	296.87	301.25	310.00
4.00	209.98	213.91	217.84	221.77	225.69	229.62	233.55	237.48	241.41	245.33	249.26	253.19	257.12	261.05	264.97	272.83
4.25	203.32	207.15	210.97	214.80	218.63	222.45	226.28	230.11	233.93	237.76	241.59	245.41	249.24	253.07	256.90	264.55
4.50	196.96	200.69	204.42	208.15	211.88	215.61	219.34	223.07	226.80	230.53	234.25	237.98	241.71	245.44	249.17	256.63
4.75	190.89	194.52	198.16	201.80	205.43	209.07	212.70	216.34	219.97	223.61	227.24	230.88	234.52	238.15	241.79	249.06
5.00	185.09	188.63	192.18	195.72	199.27	202.81	206.36	209.90	213.45	216.99	220.54	224.09	227.63	231.18	234.72	241.81
5.25	179.54	183.00	186.46	189.92	193.38	196.83	200.29	203.75	207.21	210.67	214.13	217.58	221.04	224.50	227.96	234.88
5.50	174.24	177.62	180.99	184.37	187.74	191.12	194.49	197.86	201.24	204.61	207.99	211.36	214.74	218.11	221.49	228.24
5.75	169.17	172.47	175.76	179.06	182.35	185.64	188.94	192.23	195.53	198.82	202.11	205.41	208.70	212.00	215.29	221.88
6.00	164.32	167.54	170.76	173.97	177.19	180.41	183.62	186.84	190.05	193.27	196.49	199.70	202.92	206.14	209.35	215.78
6.25	159.68	162.83	165.97	169.11	172.25	175.39	178.53	181.67	184.81	187.96	191.10	194.24	197.38	200.52	203.66	209.94
6.50	155.24	158.31	161.38	164.45	167.52	170.59	173.66	176.72	179.79	182.86	185.93	189.00	192.07	195.14	198.21	204.34
6.75	150.99	153.99	156.99	159.98	162.98	165.98	168.98	171.98	174.98	177.98	180.98	183.98	186.98	189.98	192.98	198.97
7.00	146.91	149.84	152.78	155.71	158.64	161.57	164.50	167.43	170.37	173.30	176.23	179.16	182.09	185.03	187.96	193.82
7.25	143.01	145.87	148.74	151.61	154.47	157.34	160.21	163.07	165.94	168.81	171.68	174.54	177.41	180.28	183.14	188.88
7.50	139.26	142.06	144.87	147.67	150.48	153.28	156.09	158.89	161.69	164.50	167.30	170.11	172.91	175.72	178.52	184.13
7.75	135.67	138.41	141.16	143.90	146.64	149.39	152.13	154.88	157.62	160.36	163.11	165.85	168.59	171.34	174.08	179.57
8.00	132.22	134.91	137.59	140.28	142.96	145.65	148.33	151.02	153.71	156.39	159.08	161.76	164.45	167.13	169.82	175.19
8.25	128.92	131.55	134.17	136.80	139.43	142.06	144.69	147.32	149.95	152.58	155.20	157.83	160.46	163.09	165.72	170.98
8.50	125.74	128.32	130.89	133.46	136.04	138.61	141.19	143.76	146.33	148.91	151.48	154.06	156.63	159.21	161.78	166.93
8.75	122.69	125.21	127.73	130.26	132.78	135.30	137.82	140.34	142.86	145.38	147.91	150.43	152.95	155.47	157.99	163.03
9.00	119.76	122.23	124.70	127.17	129.64	132.11	134.58	137.05	139.52	141.99	144.46	146.93	149.41	151.88	154.35	159.29
9.25	116.95	119.37	121.79	124.21	126.63	129.05	131.47	133.89	136.31	138.73	141.15	143.58	146.00	148.42	150.84	155.68
9.50	114.24	116.61	118.98	121.36	123.73	126.10	128.48	130.85	133.22	135.60	137.97	140.34	142.71	145.09	147.46	152.21
9.75	111.63	113.96	116.29	118.61	120.94	123.27	125.59	127.92	130.25	132.57	134.90	137.23	139.56	141.88	144.21	148.86
10.00	109.13	111.41	113.69	115.97	118.26	120.54	122.82	125.10	127.38	129.67	131.95	134.23	136.51	138.79	141.08	145.64
10.25	106.72	108.95	111.19	113.43	115.67	117.91	120.15	122.39	124.62	126.86	129.10	131.34	133.58	135.82	138.06	142.53
10.50	104.39	106.59	108.79	110.98	113.18	115.38	117.57	119.77	121.97	124.16	126.36	128.56	130.75	132.95	135.15	139.54
10.75	102.16	104.31	106.47	108.62	110.78	112.94	115.09	117.25	119.40	121.56	123.71	125.87	128.03	130.18	132.34	136.65
11.00	100.00	102.12	104.23	106.35	108.47	110.58	112.70	114.82	116.93	119.05	121.16	123.28	125.40	127.51	129.63	133.86
11.25	97.92	100.00	102.08	104.16	106.23	108.31	110.39	112.47	114.55	116.63	118.70	120.78	122.86	124.94	127.02	131.17
11.50	95.92	97.96	100.00	102.04	104.08	106.12	108.16	110.21	112.25	114.29	116.33	118.37	120.41	122.45	124.49	128.58
11.75	93.98	95.99	97.99	100.00	102.01	104.01	106.02	108.02	110.03	112.03	114.04	116.04	118.05	120.05	122.06	126.07
12.00	92.12	94.09	96.06	98.03	100.00	101.97	103.94	105.91	107.88	109.85	111.82	113.79	115.76	117.73	119.70	123.64
12.25	90.32	92.25	94.19	96.13	98.06	100.00	101.94	103.87	105.81	107.75	109.68	111.62	113.55	115.49	117.43	121.30
12.50	88.58	90.48	92.39	94.29	96.19	98.10	100.00	101.90	103.81	105.71	107.61	109.52	111.42	113.32	115.23	119.03
12.75	86.90	88.77	90.64	92.51	94.39	96.26	98.13	100.00	101.87	103.74	105.61	107.49	109.36	111.23	113.10	116.84
13.00	85.28	87.12	88.96	90.80	92.64	94.48	96.32	98.16	100.00	101.84	103.68	105.52	107.36	109.20	111.04	114.72
13.25	83.71	85.52	87.33	89.14	90.95	92.76	94.57	96.38	98.19	100.00	101.81	103.62	105.43	107.24	109.05	112.67
13.50	82.19	83.97	85.75	87.53	89.31	91.09	92.88	94.66	96.44	98.22	100.00	101.78	103.56	105.34	107.12	110.69
13.75	80.72	82.47	84.23	85.98	87.73	89.48	91.24	92.99	94.74	96.49	98.25	100.00	101.75	103.51	105.26	108.76
14.00	79.30	81.02	82.75	84.47	86.20	87.92	89.65	91.37	93.10	94.82	96.55	98.27	100.00	101.73	103.45	106.90
14.25	77.92	79.62	81.32	83.02	84.72	86.41	88.11	89.81	91.51	93.21	94.91	96.60	98.30	100.00	101.70	105.09
14.50	76.59	78.26	79.94	81.61	83.28	84.95	86.62	88.30	89.97	91.64	93.31	94.98	96.66	98.33	100.00	103.34
14.75	75.30	76.95	78.59	80.24	81.89	83.53	85.18	86.83	88.47	90.12	91.77	93.41	95.06	96.71	98.35	101.65
15.00	74.05	75.67	77.29	78.92	80.54	82.16	83.78	85.40	87.03	88.65	90.27	91.89	93.51	95.13	96.76	100.00
15.25	72.84	74.44	76.03	77.63	79.23	80.83	82.42	84.02	85.62	87.22	88.82	90.41	92.01	93.61	95.21	98.40
15.50	71.66	73.24	74.81	76.39	77.96	79.53	81.11	82.68	84.26	85.83	87.41	88.98	90.55	92.13	93.70	96.85
15.75	70.52	72.07	73.63	75.18	76.73	78.28	79.83	81.38	82.93	84.49	86.04	87.59	89.14	90.69	92.24	95.35
16.00	69.42	70.95	72.47	74.00	75.53	77.06	78.59	80.12	81.65	83.18	84.71	86.24	87.77	89.30	90.82	93.88
16.25	68.34	69.85	71.36	72.86	74.37	75.88	77.39	78.89	80.40	81.91	83.42	84.92	86.43	87.94	89.45	92.46
16.50	67.30	68.79	70.27	71.76	73.25	74.73	76.22	77.70	79.19	80.68	82.16	83.65	85.14	86.62	88.11	91.08
16.75	66.29	67.75	69.22	70.68	72.15	73.62	75.08	76.55	78.01	79.48	80.94	82.41	83.88	85.34	86.81	89.74
17.00	65.30	66.75	68.19	69.64	71.09	72.53	73.98	75.42	76.87	78.31	79.76	81.21	82.65	84.10	85.54	88.43
17.25	64.35	65.77	67.20	68.63	70.05	71.48	72.90	74.33	75.76	77.18	78.61	80.03	81.46	82.89	84.31	87.16
17.50	63.42	64.82	66.23	67.64	69.05	70.45	71.86	73.27	74.67	76.08	77.49	78.89	80.30	81.71	83.12	85.93
17.75	62.51	63.90	65.29	66.68	68.07	69.46	70.84	72.23	73.62	75.01	76.40	77.79	79.17	80.56	81.95	84.73
18.00	61.63	63.00	64.37	65.74	67.11	68.49	69.86	71.23	72.60	73.97	75.34	76.71	78.08	79.45	80.82	83.56
18.25	60.78	62.13	63.48	64.84	66.19	67.54	68.89	70.25	71.60	72.95	74.30	75.66	77.01	78.36	79.71	82.42
18.50	59.95	61.28	62.62	63.95	65.29	66.62	67.96	69.29	70.63	71.96	73.30	74.63	75.97	77.30	78.64	81.31
18.75	59.13	60.45	61.77	63.09	64.41	65.73	67.04	68.36	69.68	71.00	72.32	73.64	74.95	76.27	77.59	80.23
19.00	58.35	59.65	60.95	62.25	63.55	64.85	66.16	67.46	68.76	70.06	71.36	72.66	73.97	75.27	76.57	79.17
20.00	55.38	56.62	57.86	59.10	60.34	61.58	62.82	64.06	65.30	66.54	67.78	69.02	70.26	71.49	72.73	75.21
25.00	44.16	45.15	46.15	47.15	48.14	49.14	50.14	51.14	52.13	53.13	54.13	55.12	56.12	57.12	58.12	60.11
30.00	36.73	37.56	38.39	39.22	40.06	40.89	41.72	42.55	43.39	44.22	45.05	45.88	46.72	47.55	48.38	50.05

Description: This table shows the yield to maturity of a bond purchased at the price shown in the index.

Example: The yield to maturity of a 15.00 %, 25 year bond at a price of 125.00 is 11.85 %.

COUPON RATE, %

PRICE	11.00%	11.25%	11.50%	11.75%	12.00%	12.25%	12.50%	12.75%	13.00%	13.25%	13.50%	13.75%	14.00%	14.25%	14.50%	15.00%
250	2.70	2.83	2.96	3.09	3.21	3.34	3.47	3.59	3.72	3.85	3.97	4.10	4.22	4.34	4.47	4.71
240	2.99	3.13	3.26	3.39	3.52	3.65	3.78	3.91	4.04	4.17	4.30	4.43	4.55	4.68	4.81	5.06
230	3.31	3.44	3.58	3.71	3.85	3.98	4.12	4.25	4.38	4.51	4.65	4.78	4.91	5.04	5.17	5.43
220	3.64	3.78	3.92	4.06	4.20	4.33	4.47	4.61	4.74	4.88	5.02	5.15	5.29	5.42	5.55	5.82
210	3.99	4.14	4.28	4.42	4.57	4.71	4.85	4.99	5.13	5.27	5.41	5.55	5.69	5.83	5.97	6.24
200	4.37	4.52	4.67	4.82	4.96	5.11	5.26	5.40	5.55	5.69	5.84	5.98	6.13	6.27	6.41	6.70
195	4.57	4.73	4.88	5.03	5.17	5.32	5.47	5.62	5.77	5.92	6.06	6.21	6.36	6.50	6.65	6.94
190	4.78	4.94	5.09	5.24	5.39	5.55	5.70	5.85	6.00	6.15	6.30	6.45	6.60	6.74	6.89	7.19
185	5.00	5.15	5.31	5.47	5.62	5.78	5.93	6.08	6.24	6.39	6.54	6.69	6.85	7.00	7.15	7.45
180	5.22	5.38	5.54	5.70	5.86	6.01	6.17	6.33	6.48	6.64	6.80	6.95	7.11	7.26	7.41	7.72
175	5.46	5.62	5.78	5.94	6.10	6.26	6.42	6.58	6.74	6.90	7.06	7.22	7.38	7.54	7.69	8.01
170	5.70	5.87	6.03	6.20	6.36	6.53	6.69	6.85	7.02	7.18	7.34	7.50	7.66	7.82	7.98	8.30
165	5.96	6.13	6.30	6.46	6.63	6.80	6.97	7.13	7.30	7.47	7.63	7.80	7.96	8.13	8.29	8.62
160	6.23	6.40	6.57	6.74	6.92	7.09	7.26	7.43	7.60	7.77	7.94	8.11	8.27	8.44	8.61	8.95
155	6.51	6.69	6.86	7.04	7.21	7.39	7.56	7.74	7.91	8.08	8.26	8.43	8.60	8.78	8.95	9.29
150	6.80	6.99	7.17	7.35	7.53	7.71	7.88	8.06	8.24	8.42	8.60	8.78	8.95	9.13	9.31	9.66
145	7.12	7.30	7.49	7.67	7.86	8.04	8.22	8.41	8.59	8.77	8.96	9.14	9.32	9.50	9.68	10.05
140	7.44	7.64	7.83	8.01	8.20	8.39	8.58	8.77	8.96	9.15	9.33	9.52	9.71	9.90	10.08	10.46
135	7.79	7.99	8.18	8.38	8.57	8.77	8.96	9.16	9.35	9.54	9.74	9.93	10.12	10.32	10.51	10.89
130	8.16	8.36	8.56	8.77	8.97	9.17	9.37	9.57	9.77	9.97	10.17	10.36	10.56	10.76	10.96	11.36
125	8.55	8.76	8.97	9.18	9.38	9.59	9.80	10.00	10.21	10.42	10.62	10.83	11.03	11.24	11.44	11.85
120	8.97	9.19	9.40	9.62	9.83	10.05	10.26	10.47	10.69	10.90	11.11	11.33	11.54	11.75	11.96	12.39
115	9.42	9.65	9.87	10.09	10.31	10.53	10.75	10.98	11.20	11.42	11.64	11.86	12.08	12.30	12.52	12.96
113	9.61	9.84	10.06	10.29	10.51	10.74	10.96	11.19	11.41	11.64	11.86	12.09	12.31	12.53	12.76	13.20
112	9.71	9.94	10.16	10.39	10.62	10.84	11.07	11.30	11.52	11.75	11.97	12.20	12.43	12.65	12.88	13.33
111	9.81	10.04	10.26	10.49	10.72	10.95	11.18	11.41	11.63	11.86	12.09	12.32	12.55	12.77	13.00	13.46
110	9.91	10.14	10.37	10.60	10.83	11.06	11.29	11.52	11.75	11.98	12.21	12.44	12.67	12.90	13.12	13.58
109	10.01	10.24	10.47	10.70	10.94	11.17	11.40	11.63	11.86	12.10	12.33	12.56	12.79	13.02	13.25	13.71
108	10.11	10.34	10.58	10.81	11.05	11.28	11.51	11.75	11.98	12.21	12.45	12.68	12.91	13.15	13.38	13.85
107	10.22	10.45	10.69	10.92	11.16	11.39	11.63	11.86	12.10	12.34	12.57	12.81	13.04	13.28	13.51	13.98
106	10.32	10.56	10.80	11.03	11.27	11.51	11.75	11.98	12.22	12.46	12.70	12.93	13.17	13.41	13.64	14.12
105	10.43	10.67	10.91	11.15	11.39	11.63	11.87	12.11	12.35	12.58	12.82	13.06	13.30	13.54	13.78	14.26
104	10.54	10.78	11.02	11.26	11.50	11.75	11.99	12.23	12.47	12.71	12.95	13.19	13.44	13.68	13.92	14.40
103	10.65	10.89	11.14	11.38	11.62	11.87	12.11	12.35	12.60	12.84	13.09	13.33	13.57	13.82	14.06	14.55
102	10.76	11.01	11.25	11.50	11.75	11.99	12.24	12.48	12.73	12.97	13.22	13.46	13.71	13.96	14.20	14.69
101	10.88	11.13	11.37	11.62	11.87	12.12	12.36	12.61	12.86	13.11	13.36	13.60	13.85	14.10	14.35	14.84
100	11.00	11.25	11.50	11.75	12.00	12.25	12.50	12.75	13.00	13.25	13.50	13.75	14.00	14.25	14.50	15.00
99	11.11	11.37	11.62	11.87	12.12	12.38	12.63	12.88	13.13	13.38	13.64	13.89	14.14	14.39	14.65	15.15
98	11.24	11.49	11.74	12.00	12.25	12.51	12.76	13.02	13.27	13.53	13.78	14.04	14.29	14.54	14.80	15.31
97	11.36	11.62	11.87	12.13	12.39	12.64	12.90	13.16	13.41	13.67	13.93	14.19	14.44	14.70	14.96	15.47
96	11.48	11.74	12.00	12.26	12.52	12.78	13.04	13.30	13.56	13.82	14.08	14.34	14.60	14.86	15.12	15.64
95	11.61	11.87	12.14	12.40	12.66	12.92	13.18	13.44	13.71	13.97	14.23	14.49	14.75	15.02	15.28	15.80
94	11.74	12.01	12.27	12.54	12.80	13.06	13.33	13.59	13.86	14.12	14.39	14.65	14.92	15.18	15.45	15.97
93	11.88	12.14	12.41	12.68	12.94	13.21	13.48	13.74	14.01	14.28	14.54	14.81	15.08	15.35	15.61	16.15
92	12.01	12.28	12.55	12.82	13.09	13.36	13.63	13.90	14.17	14.44	14.71	14.98	15.25	15.52	15.79	16.33
91	12.15	12.42	12.69	12.97	13.24	13.51	13.78	14.05	14.33	14.60	14.87	15.14	15.42	15.69	15.96	16.51
90	12.29	12.56	12.84	13.11	13.39	13.66	13.94	14.21	14.49	14.77	15.04	15.32	15.59	15.87	16.14	16.70
89	12.43	12.71	12.99	13.27	13.54	13.82	14.10	14.38	14.66	14.93	15.21	15.49	15.77	16.05	16.33	16.89
88	12.58	12.86	13.14	13.42	13.70	13.98	14.26	14.54	14.83	15.11	15.39	15.67	15.95	16.23	16.52	17.08
87	12.73	13.01	13.30	13.58	13.86	14.15	14.43	14.72	15.00	15.28	15.57	15.85	16.14	16.42	16.71	17.28
86	12.88	13.17	13.45	13.74	14.03	14.32	14.60	14.89	15.18	15.46	15.75	16.04	16.33	16.62	16.90	17.48
85	13.04	13.33	13.62	13.91	14.20	14.49	14.78	15.07	15.36	15.65	15.94	16.23	16.52	16.81	17.10	17.69
84	13.20	13.49	13.78	14.08	14.37	14.66	14.96	15.25	15.54	15.84	16.13	16.43	16.72	17.01	17.31	17.90
83	13.36	13.66	13.95	14.25	14.54	14.84	15.14	15.44	15.73	16.03	16.33	16.63	16.92	17.22	17.52	18.12
82	13.53	13.83	14.13	14.42	14.72	15.02	15.32	15.63	15.93	16.23	16.53	16.83	17.13	17.43	17.73	18.34
81	13.70	14.00	14.30	14.61	14.91	15.21	15.52	15.82	16.12	16.43	16.73	17.04	17.34	17.65	17.95	18.57
80	13.87	14.18	14.48	14.79	15.10	15.40	15.71	16.02	16.33	16.64	16.94	17.25	17.56	17.87	18.18	18.80
79	14.05	14.36	14.67	14.98	15.29	15.60	15.91	16.22	16.54	16.85	17.16	17.47	17.78	18.10	18.41	19.04
78	14.23	14.54	14.86	15.17	15.49	15.80	16.12	16.43	16.75	17.06	17.38	17.70	18.01	18.33	18.65	19.28
77	14.42	14.73	15.05	15.37	15.69	16.01	16.33	16.65	16.97	17.29	17.61	17.93	18.25	18.57	18.89	19.53
76	14.61	14.93	15.25	15.57	15.90	16.22	16.54	16.87	17.19	17.51	17.84	18.16	18.49	18.81	19.14	19.79
75	14.80	15.13	15.46	15.78	16.11	16.44	16.76	17.09	17.42	17.75	18.08	18.40	18.73	19.06	19.39	20.05
74	15.01	15.34	15.67	16.00	16.33	16.66	16.99	17.32	17.65	17.99	18.32	18.65	18.99	19.32	19.65	20.32
73	15.21	15.55	15.88	16.21	16.55	16.89	17.22	17.56	17.90	18.23	18.57	18.91	19.25	19.58	19.92	20.60
70	15.86	16.21	16.56	16.91	17.26	17.61	17.96	18.31	18.66	19.01	19.36	19.72	20.07	20.42	20.77	21.48
65	17.07	17.45	17.82	18.20	18.58	18.95	19.33	19.71	20.09	20.46	20.84	21.22	21.60	21.98	22.36	23.12
60	18.48	18.88	19.29	19.70	20.11	20.52	20.93	21.34	21.75	22.16	22.57	22.98	23.39	23.80	24.22	25.04
55	20.13	20.58	21.02	21.47	21.91	22.36	22.81	23.25	23.70	24.15	24.60	25.05	25.50	25.95	26.40	27.30

Description: This table shows the price to pay for a bond at the yield rate. The yield is to maturity.

Example: The price of a 6.75 %, 26 year bond to yield 8 % to maturity is $ 86.41.

COUPON RATE, %

YIELD	0.00%	1.00%	2.00%	3.00%	4.00%	4.25%	4.50%	4.75%	5.00%	5.25%	5.50%	5.75%	6.00%	6.25%	6.50%	6.75%
0.00	100.00	126.00	152.00	178.00	204.00	210.50	217.00	223.50	230.00	236.50	243.00	249.50	256.00	262.50	269.00	275.50
1.00	77.16	100.00	122.84	145.69	168.53	174.25	179.96	185.67	191.38	197.09	202.80	208.51	214.22	219.94	225.65	231.36
2.00	59.61	79.80	100.00	120.20	140.39	145.44	150.49	155.54	160.59	165.64	170.69	175.74	180.79	185.84	190.89	195.94
3.00	46.11	64.07	82.04	100.00	117.96	122.46	126.95	131.44	135.93	140.42	144.91	149.40	153.89	158.38	162.88	167.37
4.00	35.71	51.78	67.86	83.93	100.00	104.02	108.04	112.05	116.07	120.09	124.11	128.13	132.14	136.16	140.18	144.20
4.25	33.51	49.15	64.80	80.44	96.09	100.00	103.91	107.82	111.73	115.65	119.56	123.47	127.38	131.29	135.20	139.11
4.50	31.44	46.68	61.91	77.15	92.38	96.19	100.00	103.81	107.62	111.43	115.24	119.04	122.85	126.66	130.47	134.28
4.75	29.51	44.35	59.19	74.03	88.87	92.58	96.29	100.00	103.71	107.42	111.13	114.84	118.55	122.26	125.97	129.68
5.00	27.69	42.15	56.62	71.08	85.54	89.15	92.77	96.38	100.00	103.62	107.23	110.85	114.46	118.08	121.69	125.31
5.25	25.99	40.09	54.19	68.28	82.38	85.90	89.43	92.95	96.48	100.00	103.52	107.05	110.57	114.10	117.62	121.15
5.50	24.40	38.14	51.89	65.64	79.38	82.82	86.25	89.69	93.13	96.56	100.00	103.44	106.87	110.31	113.75	117.18
5.75	22.90	36.31	49.72	63.13	76.54	79.89	83.24	86.59	89.94	93.30	96.65	100.00	103.35	106.70	110.06	113.41
6.00	21.50	34.58	47.67	60.75	73.83	77.10	80.38	83.65	86.92	90.19	93.46	96.73	100.00	103.27	106.54	109.81
6.25	20.19	32.96	45.73	58.50	71.27	74.46	77.65	80.84	84.04	87.23	90.42	93.61	96.81	100.00	103.19	106.39
6.50	18.95	31.42	43.89	56.36	68.83	71.95	75.06	78.18	81.30	84.41	87.53	90.65	93.77	96.88	100.00	103.12
6.75	17.80	29.98	42.15	54.33	66.51	69.56	72.60	75.64	78.69	81.73	84.78	87.82	90.87	93.91	96.96	100.00
7.00	16.71	28.61	40.51	52.41	64.31	67.28	70.26	73.23	76.20	79.18	82.15	85.13	88.10	91.08	94.05	97.03
7.25	15.70	27.33	38.95	50.58	62.21	65.12	68.02	70.93	73.84	76.74	79.65	82.56	85.47	88.37	91.28	94.19
7.50	14.74	26.11	37.48	48.85	60.21	63.06	65.90	68.74	71.58	74.42	77.27	80.11	82.95	85.79	88.63	91.47
7.75	13.85	24.97	36.08	47.20	58.31	61.09	63.87	66.65	69.43	72.21	74.99	77.77	80.55	83.33	86.10	88.88
8.00	13.01	23.88	34.76	45.63	56.50	59.22	61.94	64.66	67.38	70.10	72.82	75.53	78.25	80.97	83.69	86.41
8.25	12.22	22.86	33.50	44.14	54.78	57.44	60.10	62.76	65.42	68.08	70.74	73.40	76.06	78.72	81.38	84.04
8.50	11.48	21.90	32.31	42.72	53.14	55.74	58.34	60.95	63.55	66.16	68.76	71.36	73.97	76.57	79.17	81.78
8.75	10.79	20.98	31.18	41.38	51.57	54.12	56.67	59.22	61.77	64.32	66.86	69.41	71.96	74.51	77.06	79.61
9.00	10.14	20.12	30.11	40.09	50.08	52.57	55.07	57.57	60.06	62.56	65.05	67.55	70.05	72.54	75.04	77.53
9.25	9.53	19.31	29.09	38.87	48.65	51.10	53.54	55.99	58.43	60.88	63.32	65.77	68.21	70.66	73.10	75.55
9.50	8.95	18.54	28.12	37.70	47.29	49.68	52.08	54.48	56.87	59.27	61.66	64.06	66.46	68.85	71.25	73.64
9.75	8.42	17.81	27.20	36.60	45.99	48.34	50.69	53.03	55.38	57.73	60.08	62.43	64.78	67.12	69.47	71.82
10.00	7.91	17.12	26.33	35.54	44.75	47.05	49.35	51.65	53.95	56.26	58.56	60.86	63.16	65.47	67.77	70.07
10.25	7.44	16.47	25.50	34.53	43.56	45.82	48.07	50.33	52.59	54.85	57.10	59.36	61.62	63.88	66.13	68.39
10.50	6.99	15.85	24.71	33.56	42.42	44.64	46.85	49.07	51.28	53.49	55.71	57.92	60.14	62.35	64.57	66.78
10.75	6.57	15.26	23.95	32.64	41.34	43.51	45.68	47.85	50.03	52.20	54.37	56.54	58.72	60.89	63.06	65.24
11.00	6.18	14.71	23.24	31.77	40.30	42.43	44.56	46.69	48.82	50.96	53.09	55.22	57.35	59.49	61.62	63.75
11.25	5.81	14.18	22.55	30.93	39.30	41.39	43.49	45.58	47.67	49.77	51.86	53.95	56.04	58.14	60.23	62.32
11.50	5.46	13.68	21.90	30.12	38.35	40.40	42.46	44.51	46.57	48.62	50.68	52.73	54.79	56.84	58.90	60.95
11.75	5.14	13.21	21.28	29.36	37.43	39.45	41.47	43.49	45.50	47.52	49.54	51.56	53.58	55.60	57.61	59.63
12.00	4.83	12.76	20.69	28.62	36.55	38.54	40.52	42.50	44.49	46.47	48.45	50.43	52.42	54.40	56.38	58.36
12.25	4.54	12.34	20.13	27.92	35.71	37.66	39.61	41.56	43.51	45.45	47.40	49.35	51.30	53.25	55.19	57.14
12.50	4.27	11.93	19.59	27.25	34.91	36.82	38.74	40.65	42.56	44.48	46.39	48.31	50.22	52.14	54.05	55.97
12.75	4.02	11.55	19.08	26.60	34.13	36.01	37.90	39.78	41.66	43.54	45.42	47.31	49.19	51.07	52.95	54.83
13.00	3.78	11.18	18.59	25.99	33.39	35.24	37.09	38.94	40.79	42.64	44.49	46.34	48.19	50.04	51.89	53.74
13.25	3.56	10.84	18.12	25.39	32.67	34.49	36.31	38.13	39.95	41.77	43.59	45.41	47.23	49.05	50.87	52.69
13.50	3.35	10.51	17.67	24.83	31.99	33.78	35.57	37.36	39.15	40.94	42.73	44.51	46.30	48.09	49.88	51.67
13.75	3.15	10.19	17.24	24.28	31.33	33.09	34.85	36.61	38.37	40.13	41.89	43.65	45.41	47.17	48.93	50.70
14.00	2.97	9.90	16.83	23.76	30.69	32.42	34.15	35.89	37.62	39.35	41.09	42.82	44.55	46.28	48.02	49.75
14.25	2.79	9.61	16.43	23.26	30.08	31.78	33.49	35.19	36.90	38.60	40.31	42.02	43.72	45.43	47.13	48.84
14.50	2.63	9.34	16.06	22.77	29.49	31.17	32.85	34.52	36.20	37.88	39.56	41.24	42.92	44.60	46.28	47.96
14.75	2.47	9.08	15.70	22.31	28.92	30.57	32.23	33.88	35.53	37.19	38.84	40.49	42.14	43.80	45.45	47.10
15.00	2.33	8.84	15.35	21.86	28.37	30.00	31.63	33.26	34.88	36.51	38.14	39.77	41.40	43.02	44.65	46.28
15.25	2.19	8.60	15.02	21.43	27.85	29.45	31.05	32.66	34.26	35.86	37.47	39.07	40.67	42.28	43.88	45.48
15.50	2.06	8.38	14.70	21.02	27.34	28.92	30.50	32.08	33.65	35.23	36.81	38.39	39.97	41.55	43.13	44.71
15.75	1.94	8.17	14.39	20.62	26.85	28.40	29.96	31.51	33.07	34.63	36.18	37.74	39.30	40.85	42.41	43.97
16.00	1.83	7.96	14.10	20.24	26.37	27.90	29.44	30.97	32.51	34.04	35.57	37.11	38.64	40.18	41.71	43.24
16.25	1.72	7.77	13.82	19.87	25.91	27.42	28.94	30.45	31.96	33.47	34.98	36.50	38.01	39.52	41.03	42.54
16.50	1.62	7.58	13.55	19.51	25.47	26.96	28.45	29.94	31.43	32.92	34.41	35.90	37.40	38.89	40.38	41.87
16.75	1.53	7.41	13.28	19.16	25.04	26.51	27.98	29.45	30.92	32.39	33.86	35.33	36.80	38.27	39.74	41.21
17.00	1.44	7.24	13.03	18.83	24.63	26.08	27.53	28.98	30.43	31.88	33.33	34.77	36.22	37.67	39.12	40.57
17.25	1.35	7.07	12.79	18.51	24.23	25.66	27.09	28.52	29.95	31.38	32.81	34.24	35.67	37.10	38.53	39.95
17.50	1.28	6.92	12.56	18.20	23.84	25.25	26.66	28.07	29.48	30.89	32.30	33.71	35.12	36.53	37.94	39.35
17.75	1.20	6.77	12.33	17.90	23.47	24.86	26.25	27.64	29.03	30.42	31.82	33.21	34.60	35.99	37.38	38.77
18.00	1.13	6.62	12.12	17.61	23.10	24.48	25.85	27.22	28.60	29.97	31.34	32.71	34.09	35.46	36.83	38.21
18.25	1.07	6.49	11.91	17.33	22.75	24.11	25.46	26.82	28.17	29.53	30.88	32.24	33.59	34.95	36.30	37.66
18.50	1.00	6.36	11.71	17.06	22.41	23.75	25.08	26.42	27.76	29.10	30.44	31.77	33.11	34.45	35.79	37.12
18.75	.95	6.23	11.51	16.80	22.08	23.40	24.72	26.04	27.36	28.68	30.00	31.32	32.64	33.96	35.29	36.61
19.00	.89	6.11	11.32	16.54	21.76	23.06	24.37	25.67	26.97	28.28	29.58	30.89	32.19	33.49	34.80	36.10
20.00	.70	5.67	10.63	15.60	20.56	21.80	23.05	24.29	25.53	26.77	28.01	29.25	30.49	31.73	32.98	34.22
25.00	.22	4.21	8.20	12.19	16.18	17.18	18.18	19.18	20.18	21.17	22.17	23.17	24.17	25.16	26.16	27.16
30.00	.07	3.40	6.73	10.06	13.39	14.23	15.06	15.89	16.72	17.56	18.39	19.22	20.06	20.89	21.72	22.55

Description: This table shows the yield to maturity of a bond purchased at the price shown in the index.

Example: The yield to maturity of a 6.75 %, 26 year bond at a price of 80.00 is 8.70 %.

COUPON RATE, %

PRICE	0.00%	1.00%	2.00%	3.00%	4.00%	4.25%	4.50%	4.75%	5.00%	5.25%	5.50%	5.75%	6.00%	6.25%	6.50%	6.75%
100	0.00	1.00	2.00	3.00	4.00	4.25	4.50	4.75	5.00	5.25	5.50	5.75	6.00	6.25	6.50	6.75
99	.03	1.04	2.04	3.05	4.06	4.31	4.56	4.81	5.06	5.32	5.57	5.82	6.07	6.32	6.58	6.83
98	.07	1.08	2.10	3.11	4.12	4.37	4.63	4.88	5.14	5.39	5.64	5.90	6.15	6.40	6.66	6.91
97	.11	1.13	2.15	3.17	4.19	4.44	4.70	4.95	5.21	5.46	5.72	5.97	6.23	6.49	6.74	7.00
96	.15	1.17	2.20	3.22	4.25	4.51	4.77	5.02	5.28	5.54	5.79	6.05	6.31	6.57	6.83	7.08
95	.19	1.22	2.25	3.28	4.32	4.58	4.84	5.09	5.35	5.61	5.87	6.13	6.39	6.65	6.91	7.17
94	.23	1.27	2.30	3.34	4.38	4.65	4.91	5.17	5.43	5.69	5.95	6.21	6.48	6.74	7.00	7.26
93	.27	1.31	2.36	3.40	4.45	4.72	4.98	5.24	5.50	5.77	6.03	6.30	6.56	6.82	7.09	7.35
92	.32	1.36	2.41	3.46	4.52	4.79	5.05	5.32	5.58	5.85	6.11	6.38	6.65	6.91	7.18	7.45
91	.36	1.41	2.47	3.53	4.59	4.86	5.13	5.39	5.66	5.93	6.20	6.46	6.73	7.00	7.27	7.54
90	.40	1.46	2.52	3.59	4.66	4.93	5.20	5.47	5.74	6.01	6.28	6.55	6.82	7.09	7.36	7.64
89	.44	1.51	2.58	3.65	4.74	5.01	5.28	5.55	5.82	6.09	6.37	6.64	6.91	7.19	7.46	7.73
88	.49	1.56	2.64	3.72	4.81	5.08	5.36	5.63	5.90	6.18	6.45	6.73	7.00	7.28	7.56	7.83
87	.53	1.61	2.69	3.79	4.88	5.16	5.44	5.71	5.99	6.26	6.54	6.82	7.10	7.38	7.66	7.93
86	.58	1.66	2.75	3.85	4.96	5.24	5.52	5.79	6.07	6.35	6.63	6.91	7.19	7.47	7.76	8.04
85	.62	1.71	2.81	3.92	5.04	5.32	5.60	5.88	6.16	6.44	6.72	7.01	7.29	7.57	7.86	8.14
84	.67	1.77	2.87	3.99	5.12	5.40	5.68	5.96	6.25	6.53	6.82	7.10	7.39	7.68	7.96	8.25
83	.71	1.82	2.93	4.06	5.19	5.48	5.77	6.05	6.34	6.63	6.91	7.20	7.49	7.78	8.07	8.36
82	.76	1.87	3.00	4.13	5.28	5.56	5.85	6.14	6.43	6.72	7.01	7.30	7.59	7.88	8.18	8.47
81	.81	1.93	3.06	4.20	5.36	5.65	5.94	6.23	6.52	6.82	7.11	7.40	7.70	7.99	8.29	8.58
80	.86	1.98	3.12	4.28	5.44	5.74	6.03	6.32	6.62	6.91	7.21	7.51	7.80	8.10	8.40	8.70
79	.90	2.04	3.19	4.35	5.53	5.82	6.12	6.42	6.71	7.01	7.31	7.61	7.91	8.21	8.52	8.82
78	.95	2.10	3.26	4.43	5.61	5.91	6.21	6.51	6.81	7.11	7.42	7.72	8.02	8.33	8.63	8.94
77	1.00	2.16	3.32	4.51	5.70	6.00	6.31	6.61	6.91	7.22	7.52	7.83	8.14	8.44	8.75	9.06
76	1.05	2.21	3.39	4.59	5.79	6.10	6.40	6.71	7.02	7.32	7.63	7.94	8.25	8.56	8.87	9.19
75	1.10	2.27	3.46	4.67	5.89	6.19	6.50	6.81	7.12	7.43	7.74	8.06	8.37	8.68	9.00	9.32
74	1.16	2.34	3.53	4.75	5.98	6.29	6.60	6.91	7.23	7.54	7.86	8.17	8.49	8.81	9.13	9.45
73	1.21	2.40	3.60	4.83	6.07	6.39	6.70	7.02	7.34	7.65	7.97	8.29	8.61	8.94	9.26	9.58
72	1.26	2.46	3.68	4.92	6.17	6.49	6.81	7.13	7.45	7.77	8.09	8.42	8.74	9.07	9.39	9.72
71	1.32	2.52	3.75	5.00	6.27	6.59	6.91	7.24	7.56	7.89	8.21	8.54	8.87	9.20	9.53	9.86
70	1.37	2.59	3.83	5.09	6.37	6.70	7.02	7.35	7.68	8.01	8.34	8.67	9.00	9.33	9.67	10.01
69	1.43	2.65	3.90	5.18	6.48	6.80	7.13	7.46	7.80	8.13	8.46	8.80	9.14	9.47	9.81	10.15
68	1.48	2.72	3.98	5.27	6.58	6.91	7.25	7.58	7.92	8.26	8.59	8.93	9.27	9.62	9.96	10.31
67	1.54	2.79	4.06	5.36	6.69	7.03	7.36	7.70	8.04	8.38	8.73	9.07	9.42	9.76	10.11	10.46
66	1.60	2.86	4.14	5.46	6.80	7.14	7.48	7.83	8.17	8.52	8.86	9.21	9.56	9.91	10.27	10.62
65	1.66	2.93	4.23	5.56	6.91	7.26	7.60	7.95	8.30	8.65	9.00	9.36	9.71	10.07	10.42	10.78
64	1.72	3.00	4.31	5.66	7.03	7.38	7.73	8.08	8.43	8.79	9.15	9.50	9.86	10.23	10.59	10.95
63	1.78	3.07	4.40	5.76	7.15	7.50	7.86	8.21	8.57	8.93	9.29	9.66	10.02	10.39	10.76	11.13
62	1.84	3.15	4.49	5.86	7.27	7.63	7.99	8.35	8.71	9.08	9.44	9.81	10.18	10.55	10.93	11.30
61	1.91	3.22	4.58	5.97	7.40	7.76	8.12	8.49	8.86	9.23	9.60	9.97	10.35	10.73	11.11	11.49
60	1.97	3.30	4.67	6.08	7.52	7.89	8.26	8.63	9.00	9.38	9.76	10.14	10.52	10.90	11.29	11.67
59	2.03	3.38	4.76	6.19	7.65	8.03	8.40	8.78	9.16	9.54	9.92	10.31	10.69	11.08	11.48	11.87
58	2.10	3.46	4.86	6.30	7.79	8.17	8.55	8.93	9.31	9.70	10.09	10.48	10.88	11.27	11.67	12.07
57	2.17	3.54	4.96	6.42	7.93	8.31	8.69	9.08	9.47	9.87	10.26	10.66	11.06	11.46	11.87	12.27
56	2.24	3.62	5.06	6.54	8.07	8.46	8.85	9.24	9.64	10.04	10.44	10.85	11.25	11.66	12.07	12.49
55	2.31	3.71	5.16	6.66	8.21	8.61	9.01	9.41	9.81	10.22	10.63	11.04	11.45	11.87	12.29	12.71
54	2.38	3.80	5.26	6.79	8.36	8.76	9.17	9.58	9.99	10.40	10.82	11.24	11.66	12.08	12.51	12.94
53	2.45	3.88	5.37	6.92	8.52	8.92	9.34	9.75	10.17	10.59	11.01	11.44	11.87	12.30	12.73	13.17
52	2.53	3.98	5.48	7.05	8.68	9.09	9.51	9.93	10.36	10.78	11.22	11.65	12.09	12.53	12.97	13.41
51	2.60	4.07	5.60	7.19	8.84	9.26	9.69	10.12	10.55	10.99	11.43	11.87	12.31	12.76	13.21	13.67
50	2.68	4.16	5.71	7.33	9.01	9.44	9.87	10.31	10.75	11.19	11.64	12.09	12.55	13.01	13.47	13.93
49	2.76	4.26	5.83	7.47	9.18	9.62	10.06	10.51	10.96	11.41	11.87	12.33	12.79	13.26	13.73	14.20
48	2.84	4.36	5.95	7.62	9.36	9.81	10.26	10.71	11.17	11.64	12.10	12.57	13.04	13.52	14.00	14.48
47	2.92	4.46	6.08	7.78	9.55	10.00	10.46	10.93	11.40	11.87	12.34	12.82	13.31	13.79	14.28	14.78
46	3.00	4.57	6.21	7.93	9.74	10.21	10.68	11.15	11.63	12.11	12.60	13.09	13.58	14.08	14.58	15.08
45	3.09	4.67	6.34	8.10	9.94	10.42	10.90	11.38	11.87	12.36	12.86	13.36	13.86	14.37	14.88	15.40
44	3.18	4.78	6.48	8.27	10.15	10.63	11.12	11.62	12.12	12.62	13.13	13.64	14.16	14.68	15.21	15.73
43	3.27	4.90	6.62	8.45	10.37	10.86	11.36	11.87	12.38	12.89	13.41	13.94	14.47	15.00	15.54	16.08
42	3.36	5.01	6.77	8.63	10.59	11.10	11.61	12.13	12.65	13.18	13.71	14.25	14.79	15.34	15.89	16.45
41	3.45	5.13	6.92	8.82	10.82	11.34	11.87	12.40	12.93	13.48	14.02	14.57	15.13	15.69	16.26	16.83
40	3.55	5.26	7.08	9.01	11.07	11.60	12.14	12.68	13.23	13.79	14.35	14.91	15.49	16.06	16.64	17.23
39	3.65	5.38	7.24	9.22	11.32	11.87	12.42	12.98	13.54	14.11	14.69	15.27	15.86	16.45	17.05	17.65
35	4.07	5.93	7.95	10.13	12.47	13.07	13.69	14.32	14.95	15.59	16.24	16.89	17.55	18.22	18.89	19.57
30	4.68	6.74	9.02	11.53	14.28	15.00	15.73	16.47	17.22	17.98	18.75	19.52	20.31	21.10	21.89	22.69
25	5.40	7.74	10.40	13.42	16.77	17.65	18.55	19.46	20.39	21.33	22.27	23.23	24.19	25.15	26.13	27.10
20	6.28	9.03	12.30	16.15	20.51	21.66	22.83	24.01	25.21	26.41	27.63	28.85	30.08	31.31	32.55	33.79
15	7.43	10.86	15.26	20.70	26.88	28.49	30.11	31.75	33.39	35.04	36.69	38.35	40.01	41.67	43.34	45.00
10	9.05	13.91	21.04	30.18	40.02	42.51	45.01	47.50	50.00	52.50	55.00	57.50	60.00	62.50	65.00	67.50

Description: This table shows the price to pay for a bond at the yield rate. The yield is to maturity.

Example: The price of a 10.75 %, 26 year bond to yield 8 % to maturity is $ 129.90.

YIELD	7.00%	7.25%	7.50%	7.75%	8.00%	8.25%	COUPON RATE, % 8.50%	8.75%	9.00%	9.25%	9.50%	9.75%	10.00%	10.25%	10.50%	10.75%
0.00	282.00	288.50	295.00	301.50	308.00	314.50	321.00	327.50	334.00	340.50	347.00	353.50	360.00	366.50	373.00	379.50
1.00	237.07	242.78	248.49	254.20	259.91	265.63	271.34	277.05	282.76	288.47	294.18	299.89	305.60	311.32	317.03	322.74
2.00	200.99	206.03	211.08	216.13	221.18	226.23	231.28	236.33	241.38	246.43	251.48	256.53	261.58	266.63	271.68	276.72
3.00	171.86	176.35	180.84	185.33	189.82	194.31	198.80	203.30	207.79	212.28	216.77	221.26	225.75	230.24	234.73	239.22
4.00	148.22	152.24	156.25	160.27	164.29	168.31	172.33	176.34	180.36	184.38	188.40	192.42	196.43	200.45	204.47	208.49
4.25	143.03	146.94	150.85	154.76	158.67	162.58	166.49	170.40	174.32	178.23	182.14	186.05	189.96	193.87	197.78	201.70
4.50	138.09	141.90	145.71	149.51	153.32	157.13	160.94	164.75	168.56	172.37	176.18	179.98	183.79	187.60	191.41	195.22
4.75	133.39	137.10	140.81	144.52	148.23	151.94	155.65	159.36	163.07	166.78	170.49	174.20	177.91	181.62	185.33	189.04
5.00	128.92	132.54	136.15	139.77	143.38	147.00	150.62	154.23	157.85	161.46	165.08	168.69	172.31	175.92	179.54	183.15
5.25	124.67	128.19	131.72	135.24	138.77	142.29	145.81	149.34	152.86	156.39	159.91	163.44	166.96	170.48	174.01	177.53
5.50	120.62	124.06	127.49	130.93	134.36	137.80	141.24	144.67	148.11	151.55	154.98	158.42	161.86	165.29	168.73	172.17
5.75	116.76	120.11	123.46	126.82	130.17	133.52	136.87	140.22	143.58	146.93	150.28	153.63	156.98	160.34	163.69	167.04
6.00	113.08	116.35	119.62	122.90	126.17	129.44	132.71	135.98	139.25	142.52	145.79	149.06	152.33	155.60	158.87	162.14
6.25	109.58	112.77	115.96	119.16	122.35	125.54	128.73	131.93	135.12	138.31	141.50	144.70	147.89	151.08	154.27	157.47
6.50	106.23	109.35	112.47	115.59	118.70	121.82	124.94	128.05	131.17	134.29	137.41	140.52	143.64	146.76	149.87	152.99
6.75	103.04	106.09	109.13	112.18	115.22	118.27	121.31	124.36	127.40	130.44	133.49	136.53	139.58	142.62	145.67	148.71
7.00	100.00	102.97	105.95	108.92	111.90	114.87	117.85	120.82	123.80	126.77	129.74	132.72	135.69	138.67	141.64	144.62
7.25	97.09	100.00	102.91	105.81	108.72	111.63	114.53	117.44	120.35	123.26	126.16	129.07	131.98	134.88	137.79	140.70
7.50	94.32	97.16	100.00	102.84	105.68	108.53	111.37	114.21	117.05	119.89	122.73	125.58	128.42	131.26	134.10	136.94
7.75	91.66	94.44	97.22	100.00	102.78	105.56	108.34	111.12	113.90	116.67	119.45	122.23	125.01	127.79	130.57	133.35
8.00	89.13	91.84	94.56	97.28	100.00	102.72	105.44	108.16	110.87	113.59	116.31	119.03	121.75	124.47	127.18	129.90
8.25	86.70	89.36	92.02	94.68	97.34	100.00	102.66	105.32	107.98	110.64	113.30	115.96	118.62	121.28	123.94	126.60
8.50	84.38	86.98	89.59	92.19	94.79	97.40	100.00	102.60	105.21	107.81	110.41	113.02	115.62	118.22	120.83	123.43
8.75	82.16	84.71	87.26	89.80	92.35	94.90	97.45	100.00	102.55	105.10	107.65	110.20	112.74	115.29	117.84	120.39
9.00	80.03	82.53	85.02	87.52	90.02	92.51	95.01	97.50	100.00	102.50	104.99	107.49	109.98	112.48	114.98	117.47
9.25	77.99	80.44	82.88	85.33	87.77	90.22	92.66	95.11	97.55	100.00	102.45	104.89	107.34	109.78	112.23	114.67
9.50	76.04	78.44	80.83	83.23	85.62	88.02	90.42	92.81	95.21	97.60	100.00	102.40	104.79	107.19	109.58	111.98
9.75	74.17	76.52	78.87	81.21	83.56	85.91	88.26	90.61	92.96	95.30	97.65	100.00	102.35	104.70	107.04	109.39
10.00	72.37	74.68	76.98	79.28	81.58	83.88	86.19	88.49	90.79	93.09	95.40	97.70	100.00	102.30	104.60	106.91
10.25	70.65	72.91	75.17	77.42	79.68	81.94	84.20	86.45	88.71	90.97	93.23	95.48	97.74	100.00	102.26	104.52
10.50	69.00	71.21	73.43	75.64	77.85	80.07	82.28	84.50	86.71	88.93	91.14	93.36	95.57	97.79	100.00	102.21
10.75	67.41	69.58	71.75	73.93	76.10	78.27	80.45	82.62	84.79	86.96	89.14	91.31	93.48	95.65	97.83	100.00
11.00	65.88	68.02	70.15	72.28	74.41	76.54	78.68	80.81	82.94	85.07	87.21	89.34	91.47	93.60	95.74	97.87
11.25	64.42	66.51	68.60	70.70	72.79	74.88	76.98	79.07	81.16	83.26	85.35	87.44	89.53	91.63	93.72	95.81
11.50	63.01	65.06	67.12	69.17	71.23	73.28	75.34	77.39	79.45	81.50	83.56	85.61	87.67	89.72	91.78	93.83
11.75	61.65	63.67	65.69	67.71	69.72	71.74	73.76	75.78	77.80	79.82	81.83	83.85	85.87	87.89	89.91	91.93
12.00	60.35	62.33	64.31	66.29	68.28	70.26	72.24	74.23	76.21	78.19	80.17	82.16	84.14	86.12	88.10	90.09
12.25	59.09	61.04	62.99	64.93	66.88	68.83	70.78	72.73	74.68	76.62	78.57	80.52	82.47	84.42	86.36	88.31
12.50	57.88	59.80	61.71	63.62	65.54	67.45	69.37	71.28	73.20	75.11	77.03	78.94	80.85	82.77	84.68	86.60
12.75	56.72	58.60	60.48	62.36	64.24	66.13	68.01	69.89	71.77	73.65	75.53	77.42	79.30	81.18	83.06	84.94
13.00	55.59	57.44	59.29	61.14	62.99	64.84	66.69	68.54	70.39	72.25	74.10	75.95	77.80	79.65	81.50	83.35
13.25	54.51	56.33	58.15	59.97	61.79	63.61	65.43	67.25	69.07	70.89	72.71	74.53	76.34	78.16	79.98	81.80
13.50	53.46	55.25	57.04	58.83	60.62	62.41	64.20	65.99	67.78	69.57	71.36	73.15	74.94	76.73	78.52	80.31
13.75	52.46	54.22	55.98	57.74	59.50	61.26	63.02	64.78	66.54	68.30	70.06	71.83	73.59	75.35	77.11	78.87
14.00	51.48	53.22	54.95	56.68	58.41	60.15	61.88	63.61	65.34	67.08	68.81	70.54	72.28	74.01	75.74	77.47
14.25	50.54	52.25	53.95	55.66	57.36	59.07	60.78	62.48	64.19	65.89	67.60	69.30	71.01	72.71	74.42	76.12
14.50	49.63	51.31	52.99	54.67	56.35	58.03	59.71	61.39	63.07	64.74	66.42	68.10	69.78	71.46	73.14	74.82
14.75	48.76	50.41	52.06	53.72	55.37	57.02	58.67	60.33	61.98	63.63	65.29	66.94	68.59	70.25	71.90	73.55
15.00	47.91	49.54	51.16	52.79	54.42	56.05	57.67	59.30	60.93	62.56	64.19	65.81	67.44	69.07	70.70	72.33
15.25	47.09	48.69	50.29	51.90	53.50	55.10	56.71	58.31	59.91	61.52	63.12	64.72	66.33	67.93	69.53	71.14
15.50	46.29	47.87	49.45	51.03	52.61	54.19	55.77	57.35	58.93	60.51	62.09	63.67	65.25	66.83	68.41	69.99
15.75	45.52	47.08	48.64	50.19	51.75	53.31	54.86	56.42	57.97	59.53	61.09	62.64	64.20	65.76	67.31	68.87
16.00	44.78	46.31	47.85	49.38	50.91	52.45	53.98	55.52	57.05	58.58	60.12	61.65	63.19	64.72	66.25	67.79
16.25	44.06	45.57	47.08	48.59	50.10	51.62	53.13	54.64	56.15	57.66	59.18	60.69	62.20	63.71	65.22	66.74
16.50	43.36	44.85	46.34	47.83	49.32	50.81	52.30	53.79	55.28	56.77	58.26	59.75	61.24	62.74	64.23	65.72
16.75	42.68	44.15	45.62	47.09	48.56	50.03	51.50	52.97	54.44	55.91	57.38	58.85	60.32	61.79	63.26	64.73
17.00	42.02	43.47	44.92	46.37	47.82	49.27	50.72	52.17	53.62	55.07	56.52	57.97	59.42	60.86	62.31	63.76
17.25	41.38	42.81	44.24	45.67	47.10	48.53	49.96	51.39	52.82	54.25	55.68	57.11	58.54	59.97	61.40	62.83
17.50	40.77	42.18	43.59	45.00	46.41	47.82	49.23	50.64	52.05	53.46	54.87	56.28	57.69	59.10	60.51	61.92
17.75	40.16	41.56	42.95	44.34	45.73	47.12	48.51	49.91	51.30	52.69	54.08	55.47	56.86	58.25	59.65	61.04
18.00	39.58	40.95	42.33	43.70	45.07	46.45	47.82	49.19	50.57	51.94	53.31	54.69	56.06	57.43	58.80	60.18
18.25	39.01	40.37	41.72	43.08	44.43	45.79	47.15	48.50	49.86	51.21	52.57	53.92	55.28	56.63	57.99	59.34
18.50	38.46	39.80	41.14	42.48	43.81	45.15	46.49	47.83	49.16	50.50	51.84	53.18	54.52	55.85	57.19	58.53
18.75	37.93	39.25	40.57	41.89	43.21	44.53	45.85	47.17	48.49	49.81	51.13	52.45	53.78	55.10	56.42	57.74
19.00	37.41	38.71	40.01	41.32	42.62	43.93	45.23	46.53	47.84	49.14	50.45	51.75	53.05	54.36	55.66	56.97
20.00	35.46	36.70	37.94	39.18	40.42	41.66	42.90	44.15	45.39	46.63	47.87	49.11	50.35	51.59	52.83	54.08
25.00	28.16	29.16	30.15	31.15	32.15	33.15	34.14	35.14	36.14	37.14	38.14	39.13	40.13	41.13	42.13	43.12
30.00	23.39	24.22	25.05	25.89	26.72	27.55	28.38	29.22	30.05	30.88	31.71	32.55	33.38	34.21	35.05	35.88

Description: This table shows the yield to maturity of a bond purchased at the price shown in the index.

Example: The yield to maturity of a 10.75 %, 26 year bond at a price of 111.00 is 9.59 %.

COUPON RATE, %

PRICE	7.00%	7.25%	7.50%	7.75%	8.00%	8.25%	8.50%	8.75%	9.00%	9.25%	9.50%	9.75%	10.00%	10.25%	10.50%	10.75%
175	2.88	3.05	3.21	3.38	3.55	3.72	3.88	4.05	4.22	4.38	4.55	4.71	4.87	5.04	5.20	5.36
170	3.07	3.24	3.41	3.58	3.75	3.92	4.09	4.26	4.43	4.60	4.77	4.93	5.10	5.27	5.43	5.60
165	3.26	3.44	3.62	3.79	3.96	4.14	4.31	4.48	4.66	4.83	5.00	5.17	5.34	5.51	5.68	5.85
160	3.47	3.65	3.83	4.01	4.18	4.36	4.54	4.71	4.89	5.07	5.24	5.41	5.59	5.76	5.94	6.11
155	3.69	3.87	4.05	4.23	4.42	4.60	4.78	4.96	5.14	5.32	5.49	5.67	5.85	6.03	6.20	6.38
150	3.91	4.10	4.29	4.47	4.66	4.84	5.03	5.21	5.39	5.58	5.76	5.94	6.12	6.31	6.49	6.67
145	4.15	4.34	4.53	4.72	4.91	5.10	5.29	5.48	5.67	5.85	6.04	6.23	6.41	6.60	6.79	6.97
140	4.40	4.59	4.79	4.98	5.18	5.37	5.56	5.76	5.95	6.14	6.34	6.53	6.72	6.91	7.10	7.29
135	4.66	4.86	5.06	5.26	5.46	5.66	5.86	6.05	6.25	6.45	6.65	6.84	7.04	7.24	7.43	7.63
130	4.93	5.14	5.35	5.55	5.76	5.96	6.16	6.37	6.57	6.77	6.98	7.18	7.38	7.58	7.79	7.99
125	5.23	5.44	5.65	5.86	6.07	6.28	6.49	6.70	6.91	7.12	7.33	7.54	7.75	7.95	8.16	8.37
120	5.53	5.75	5.97	6.19	6.40	6.62	6.84	7.05	7.27	7.49	7.70	7.92	8.13	8.35	8.56	8.78
119	5.60	5.82	6.04	6.26	6.47	6.69	6.91	7.13	7.35	7.56	7.78	8.00	8.21	8.43	8.65	8.86
118	5.66	5.88	6.10	6.32	6.54	6.76	6.98	7.20	7.42	7.64	7.86	8.08	8.30	8.51	8.73	8.95
117	5.73	5.95	6.17	6.39	6.62	6.84	7.06	7.28	7.50	7.72	7.94	8.16	8.38	8.60	8.82	9.04
116	5.80	6.02	6.24	6.47	6.69	6.91	7.13	7.36	7.58	7.80	8.02	8.24	8.46	8.68	8.90	9.13
115	5.86	6.09	6.31	6.54	6.76	6.99	7.21	7.43	7.66	7.88	8.10	8.33	8.55	8.77	8.99	9.22
114	5.93	6.16	6.38	6.61	6.84	7.06	7.29	7.51	7.74	7.96	8.19	8.41	8.63	8.86	9.08	9.31
113	6.00	6.23	6.46	6.68	6.91	7.14	7.36	7.59	7.82	8.04	8.27	8.50	8.72	8.95	9.17	9.40
112	6.07	6.30	6.53	6.76	6.99	7.22	7.44	7.67	7.90	8.13	8.36	8.58	8.81	9.04	9.27	9.49
111	6.14	6.37	6.60	6.83	7.06	7.29	7.52	7.75	7.98	8.21	8.44	8.67	8.90	9.13	9.36	9.59
110	6.21	6.45	6.68	6.91	7.14	7.37	7.61	7.84	8.07	8.30	8.53	8.76	8.99	9.22	9.45	9.69
109	6.29	6.52	6.76	6.99	7.22	7.46	7.69	7.92	8.16	8.39	8.62	8.85	9.09	9.32	9.55	9.78
108	6.36	6.60	6.83	7.07	7.30	7.54	7.77	8.01	8.24	8.48	8.71	8.95	9.18	9.42	9.65	9.88
107	6.44	6.67	6.91	7.15	7.39	7.62	7.86	8.10	8.33	8.57	8.80	9.04	9.28	9.51	9.75	9.99
106	6.51	6.75	6.99	7.23	7.47	7.71	7.95	8.18	8.42	8.66	8.90	9.14	9.38	9.61	9.85	10.09
105	6.59	6.83	7.07	7.31	7.55	7.79	8.03	8.27	8.51	8.75	8.99	9.23	9.47	9.71	9.95	10.19
104	6.67	6.91	7.15	7.40	7.64	7.88	8.12	8.37	8.61	8.85	9.09	9.33	9.57	9.82	10.06	10.30
103	6.75	6.99	7.24	7.48	7.73	7.97	8.21	8.46	8.70	8.95	9.19	9.43	9.68	9.92	10.16	10.41
102	6.83	7.08	7.32	7.57	7.81	8.06	8.31	8.55	8.80	9.04	9.29	9.54	9.78	10.03	10.27	10.52
101	6.91	7.16	7.41	7.66	7.90	8.15	8.40	8.65	8.90	9.14	9.39	9.64	9.89	10.14	10.38	10.63
100	7.00	7.25	7.50	7.75	8.00	8.25	8.50	8.75	9.00	9.25	9.50	9.75	10.00	10.25	10.50	10.75
99	7.08	7.33	7.58	7.84	8.09	8.34	8.59	8.84	9.10	9.35	9.60	9.85	10.10	10.36	10.61	10.86
98	7.17	7.42	7.67	7.93	8.18	8.44	8.69	8.94	9.20	9.45	9.71	9.96	10.22	10.47	10.72	10.98
97	7.25	7.51	7.77	8.02	8.28	8.53	8.79	9.05	9.30	9.56	9.82	10.07	10.33	10.59	10.84	11.10
96	7.34	7.60	7.86	8.12	8.38	8.63	8.89	9.15	9.41	9.67	9.93	10.19	10.44	10.70	10.96	11.22
95	7.43	7.69	7.95	8.21	8.47	8.74	9.00	9.26	9.52	9.78	10.04	10.30	10.56	10.82	11.09	11.35
94	7.52	7.79	8.05	8.31	8.58	8.84	9.10	9.36	9.63	9.89	10.15	10.42	10.68	10.95	11.21	11.47
93	7.62	7.88	8.15	8.41	8.68	8.94	9.21	9.47	9.74	10.01	10.27	10.54	10.80	11.07	11.34	11.60
92	7.71	7.98	8.25	8.51	8.78	9.05	9.32	9.59	9.85	10.12	10.39	10.66	10.93	11.20	11.47	11.74
91	7.81	8.08	8.35	8.62	8.89	9.16	9.43	9.70	9.97	10.24	10.51	10.78	11.05	11.33	11.60	11.87
90	7.91	8.18	8.45	8.72	9.00	9.27	9.54	9.82	10.09	10.36	10.64	10.91	11.18	11.46	11.73	12.01
89	8.01	8.28	8.56	8.83	9.11	9.38	9.66	9.93	10.21	10.49	10.76	11.04	11.32	11.59	11.87	12.15
88	8.11	8.39	8.66	8.94	9.22	9.50	9.78	10.05	10.33	10.61	10.89	11.17	11.45	11.73	12.01	12.29
87	8.21	8.49	8.77	9.05	9.33	9.61	9.90	10.18	10.46	10.74	11.02	11.30	11.59	11.87	12.15	12.44
86	8.32	8.60	8.88	9.17	9.45	9.73	10.02	10.30	10.59	10.87	11.16	11.44	11.73	12.01	12.30	12.58
85	8.43	8.71	9.00	9.28	9.57	9.86	10.14	10.43	10.72	11.00	11.29	11.58	11.87	12.16	12.45	12.74
84	8.54	8.82	9.11	9.40	9.69	9.98	10.27	10.56	10.85	11.14	11.43	11.72	12.02	12.31	12.60	12.89
83	8.65	8.94	9.23	9.52	9.81	10.11	10.40	10.69	10.99	11.28	11.58	11.87	12.16	12.46	12.75	13.05
82	8.76	9.06	9.35	9.65	9.94	10.24	10.53	10.83	11.13	11.42	11.72	12.02	12.32	12.61	12.91	13.21
81	8.88	9.18	9.47	9.77	10.07	10.37	10.67	10.97	11.27	11.57	11.87	12.17	12.47	12.77	13.08	13.38
80	9.00	9.30	9.60	9.90	10.20	10.50	10.81	11.11	11.41	11.72	12.02	12.33	12.63	12.94	13.24	13.55
79	9.12	9.42	9.73	10.03	10.34	10.64	10.95	11.26	11.56	11.87	12.18	12.49	12.79	13.10	13.41	13.72
78	9.24	9.55	9.86	10.17	10.47	10.78	11.09	11.40	11.71	12.02	12.34	12.65	12.96	13.27	13.59	13.90
77	9.37	9.68	9.99	10.30	10.62	10.93	11.24	11.56	11.87	12.18	12.50	12.81	13.13	13.45	13.76	14.08
76	9.50	9.81	10.13	10.44	10.76	11.08	11.39	11.71	12.03	12.35	12.67	12.99	13.31	13.63	13.95	14.27
75	9.63	9.95	10.27	10.59	10.91	11.23	11.55	11.87	12.19	12.51	12.84	13.16	13.48	13.81	14.13	14.46
74	9.77	10.09	10.41	10.73	11.06	11.38	11.71	12.03	12.36	12.68	13.01	13.34	13.67	14.00	14.33	14.66
73	9.91	10.23	10.56	10.88	11.21	11.54	11.87	12.20	12.53	12.86	13.19	13.52	13.86	14.19	14.52	14.86
70	10.34	10.68	11.02	11.36	11.70	12.04	12.38	12.72	13.07	13.41	13.76	14.10	14.45	14.80	15.14	15.49
65	11.14	11.51	11.87	12.23	12.60	12.96	13.33	13.70	14.07	14.44	14.81	15.18	15.55	15.93	16.30	16.68
60	12.06	12.45	12.84	13.24	13.63	14.03	14.43	14.82	15.22	15.62	16.03	16.43	16.83	17.24	17.64	18.05
55	13.13	13.56	13.98	14.41	14.84	15.27	15.71	16.14	16.58	17.02	17.45	17.89	18.34	18.78	19.22	19.66
50	14.39	14.86	15.33	15.80	16.28	16.75	17.23	17.71	18.19	18.68	19.16	19.65	20.13	20.62	21.11	21.60
45	15.92	16.44	16.97	17.49	18.02	18.56	19.09	19.63	20.16	20.70	21.24	21.79	22.33	22.87	23.42	23.97
40	17.81	18.41	19.00	19.60	20.20	20.80	21.41	22.02	22.62	23.24	23.85	24.46	25.08	25.69	26.31	26.93
35	20.25	20.93	21.62	22.31	23.00	23.70	24.39	25.09	25.80	26.50	27.20	27.91	28.62	29.33	30.03	30.74
30	23.50	24.31	25.12	25.94	26.75	27.57	28.39	29.22	30.04	30.87	31.70	32.53	33.35	34.18	35.01	35.84

Description: This table shows the price to pay for a bond at the yield rate. The yield is to maturity.

Example: The price of a 15.00 %, 26 year bond to yield 8 % to maturity is $ 176.12.

COUPON RATE, %

YIELD	11.00%	11.25%	11.50%	11.75%	12.00%	12.25%	12.50%	12.75%	13.00%	13.25%	13.50%	13.75%	14.00%	14.25%	14.50%	15.00%
0.00	386.00	392.50	399.00	405.50	412.00	418.50	425.00	431.50	438.00	444.50	451.00	457.50	464.00	470.50	477.00	490.00
1.00	328.45	334.16	339.87	345.58	351.29	357.00	362.72	368.43	374.14	379.85	385.56	391.27	396.98	402.69	408.41	419.83
2.00	281.77	286.82	291.87	296.92	301.97	307.02	312.07	317.12	322.17	327.22	332.27	337.32	342.37	347.41	352.46	362.56
3.00	243.71	248.21	252.70	257.19	261.68	266.17	270.66	275.15	279.64	284.13	288.63	293.12	297.61	302.10	306.59	315.57
4.00	212.51	216.53	220.54	224.56	228.58	232.60	236.62	240.63	244.65	248.67	252.69	256.71	260.72	264.74	268.76	276.80
4.25	205.61	209.52	213.43	217.34	221.25	225.16	229.08	232.99	236.90	240.81	244.72	248.63	252.54	256.45	260.37	268.19
4.50	199.03	202.84	206.65	210.45	214.26	218.07	221.88	225.69	229.50	233.31	237.12	240.93	244.73	248.54	252.35	259.97
4.75	192.75	196.46	200.18	203.89	207.60	211.31	215.02	218.73	222.44	226.15	229.86	233.57	237.28	240.99	244.70	252.12
5.00	186.77	190.38	194.00	197.62	201.23	204.85	208.46	212.08	215.69	219.31	222.92	226.54	230.15	233.77	237.38	244.62
5.25	181.06	184.58	188.11	191.63	195.15	198.68	202.20	205.73	209.25	212.77	216.30	219.82	223.35	226.87	230.40	237.44
5.50	175.60	179.04	182.48	185.91	189.35	192.78	196.22	199.66	203.09	206.53	209.97	213.40	216.84	220.28	223.71	230.59
5.75	170.39	173.75	177.10	180.45	183.80	187.15	190.51	193.86	197.21	200.56	203.91	207.27	210.62	213.97	217.32	224.03
6.00	165.42	168.69	171.96	175.23	178.50	181.77	185.04	188.31	191.58	194.85	198.12	201.39	204.66	207.94	211.21	217.75
6.25	160.66	163.85	167.04	170.24	173.43	176.62	179.81	183.01	186.20	189.39	192.58	195.78	198.97	202.16	205.35	211.74
6.50	156.11	159.23	162.34	165.46	168.58	171.69	174.81	177.93	181.05	184.16	187.28	190.40	193.51	196.63	199.75	205.98
6.75	151.76	154.80	157.85	160.89	163.93	166.98	170.02	173.07	176.11	179.16	182.20	185.25	188.29	191.33	194.38	200.47
7.00	147.59	150.57	153.54	156.51	159.49	162.46	165.44	168.41	171.39	174.36	177.34	180.31	183.29	186.26	189.23	195.18
7.25	143.60	146.51	149.42	152.33	155.23	158.14	161.05	163.95	166.86	169.77	172.67	175.58	178.49	181.40	184.30	190.12
7.50	139.79	142.63	145.47	148.31	151.15	154.00	156.84	159.68	162.52	165.36	168.20	171.05	173.89	176.73	179.57	185.26
7.75	136.13	138.91	141.69	144.46	147.24	150.02	152.80	155.58	158.36	161.14	163.92	166.70	169.48	172.26	175.03	180.59
8.00	132.62	135.34	138.06	140.78	143.50	146.21	148.93	151.65	154.37	157.09	159.81	162.52	165.24	167.96	170.68	176.12
8.25	129.26	131.92	134.58	137.24	139.90	142.56	145.22	147.88	150.54	153.20	155.86	158.52	161.18	163.84	166.50	171.82
8.50	126.03	128.64	131.24	133.84	136.45	139.05	141.66	144.26	146.86	149.47	152.07	154.67	157.28	159.88	162.48	167.69
8.75	122.94	125.49	128.04	130.59	133.14	135.68	138.23	140.78	143.33	145.88	148.43	150.98	153.53	156.08	158.62	163.72
9.00	119.97	122.47	124.96	127.46	129.95	132.45	134.95	137.44	139.94	142.43	144.93	147.43	149.92	152.42	154.92	159.91
9.25	117.12	119.56	122.01	124.45	126.90	129.34	131.79	134.23	136.68	139.12	141.57	144.01	146.46	148.90	151.35	156.24
9.50	114.38	116.77	119.17	121.56	123.96	126.36	128.75	131.15	133.54	135.94	138.34	140.73	143.13	145.52	147.92	152.71
9.75	111.74	114.09	116.44	118.79	121.13	123.48	125.83	128.18	130.53	132.88	135.22	137.57	139.92	142.27	144.62	149.31
10.00	109.21	111.51	113.81	116.12	118.42	120.72	123.02	125.32	127.63	129.93	132.23	134.53	136.84	139.14	141.44	146.05
10.25	106.77	109.03	111.29	113.55	115.80	118.06	120.32	122.58	124.83	127.09	129.35	131.61	133.87	136.12	138.38	142.90
10.50	104.43	106.64	108.86	111.07	113.29	115.50	117.72	119.93	122.15	124.36	126.57	128.79	131.00	133.22	135.43	139.86
10.75	102.17	104.35	106.52	108.69	110.86	113.04	115.21	117.38	119.55	121.73	123.90	126.07	128.25	130.42	132.59	136.94
11.00	100.00	102.13	104.26	106.40	108.53	110.66	112.79	114.93	117.06	119.19	121.32	123.46	125.59	127.72	129.85	134.12
11.25	97.91	100.00	102.09	104.19	106.28	108.37	110.47	112.56	114.65	116.74	118.84	120.93	123.02	125.12	127.21	131.40
11.50	95.89	97.94	100.00	102.06	104.11	106.17	108.22	110.28	112.33	114.39	116.44	118.50	120.55	122.61	124.66	128.77
11.75	93.94	95.96	97.98	100.00	102.02	104.04	106.06	108.07	110.09	112.11	114.13	116.15	118.17	120.18	122.20	126.24
12.00	92.07	94.05	96.03	98.02	100.00	101.98	103.97	105.95	107.93	109.91	111.90	113.88	115.86	117.84	119.83	123.79
12.25	90.26	92.21	94.16	96.10	98.05	100.00	101.95	103.90	105.84	107.79	109.74	111.69	113.64	115.58	117.53	121.43
12.50	88.51	90.43	92.34	94.26	96.17	98.09	100.00	101.91	103.83	105.74	107.66	109.57	111.49	113.40	115.32	119.15
12.75	86.83	88.71	90.59	92.47	94.35	96.24	98.12	100.00	101.88	103.76	105.65	107.53	109.41	111.29	113.17	116.94
13.00	85.20	87.05	88.90	90.75	92.60	94.45	96.30	98.15	100.00	101.85	103.70	105.55	107.40	109.25	111.10	114.80
13.25	83.62	85.44	87.26	89.08	90.90	92.72	94.54	96.36	98.18	100.00	101.82	103.64	105.46	107.28	109.10	112.74
13.50	82.10	83.89	85.68	87.47	89.26	91.05	92.84	94.63	96.42	98.21	100.00	101.79	103.58	105.37	107.16	110.74
13.75	80.63	82.39	84.15	85.91	87.67	89.43	91.20	92.96	94.72	96.48	98.24	100.00	101.76	103.52	105.28	108.80
14.00	79.21	80.94	82.67	84.41	86.14	87.87	89.60	91.34	93.07	94.80	96.53	98.27	100.00	101.73	103.47	106.93
14.25	77.83	79.53	81.24	82.95	84.65	86.36	88.06	89.77	91.47	93.18	94.88	96.59	98.29	100.00	101.71	105.12
14.50	76.50	78.17	79.85	81.53	83.21	84.89	86.57	88.25	89.93	91.61	93.28	94.96	96.64	98.32	100.00	103.36
14.75	75.20	76.86	78.51	80.16	81.82	83.47	85.12	86.78	88.43	90.08	91.73	93.39	95.04	96.69	98.35	101.65
15.00	73.95	75.58	77.21	78.84	80.47	82.09	83.72	85.35	86.98	88.60	90.23	91.86	93.49	95.12	96.74	100.00
15.25	72.74	74.35	75.95	77.55	79.16	80.76	82.36	83.97	85.57	87.17	88.78	90.38	91.98	93.59	95.19	98.40
15.50	71.57	73.15	74.73	76.31	77.88	79.46	81.04	82.62	84.20	85.78	87.36	88.94	90.52	92.10	93.68	96.84
15.75	70.43	71.98	73.54	75.10	76.65	78.21	79.77	81.32	82.88	84.44	85.99	87.55	89.10	90.66	92.22	95.33
16.00	69.32	70.86	72.39	73.92	75.46	76.99	78.52	80.06	81.59	83.13	84.66	86.19	87.73	89.26	90.80	93.86
16.25	68.25	69.76	71.27	72.78	74.30	75.81	77.32	78.83	80.34	81.86	83.37	84.88	86.39	87.90	89.42	92.44
16.50	67.21	68.70	70.19	71.68	73.17	74.66	76.15	77.64	79.13	80.62	82.11	83.60	85.09	86.58	88.08	91.06
16.75	66.20	67.67	69.14	70.60	72.07	73.54	75.01	76.48	77.95	79.42	80.89	82.36	83.83	85.30	86.77	89.71
17.00	65.21	66.66	68.11	69.56	71.01	72.46	73.91	75.36	76.81	78.26	79.71	81.16	82.61	84.06	85.51	88.40
17.25	64.26	65.69	67.12	68.55	69.98	71.41	72.84	74.27	75.70	77.13	78.56	79.98	81.41	82.84	84.27	87.13
17.50	63.33	64.74	66.15	67.56	68.97	70.38	71.79	73.20	74.61	76.02	77.43	78.84	80.26	81.67	83.08	85.90
17.75	62.43	63.82	65.21	66.60	67.99	69.39	70.78	72.17	73.56	74.95	76.34	77.74	79.13	80.52	81.91	84.69
18.00	61.55	62.92	64.30	65.67	67.04	68.42	69.79	71.16	72.54	73.91	75.28	76.66	78.03	79.40	80.78	83.52
18.25	60.70	62.05	63.41	64.76	66.12	67.47	68.83	70.18	71.54	72.89	74.25	75.61	76.96	78.32	79.67	82.38
18.50	59.87	61.20	62.54	63.88	65.22	66.56	67.89	69.23	70.57	71.91	73.24	74.58	75.92	77.26	78.60	81.27
18.75	59.06	60.38	61.70	63.02	64.34	65.66	66.98	68.30	69.62	70.94	72.27	73.59	74.91	76.23	77.55	80.19
19.00	58.27	59.57	60.88	62.18	63.49	64.79	66.09	67.40	68.70	70.01	71.31	72.61	73.92	75.22	76.53	79.14
20.00	55.32	56.56	57.80	59.04	60.28	61.52	62.76	64.01	65.25	66.49	67.73	68.97	70.21	71.45	72.69	75.18
25.00	44.12	45.12	46.12	47.12	48.11	49.11	50.11	51.11	52.11	53.10	54.10	55.10	56.10	57.09	58.09	60.09
30.00	36.71	37.54	38.38	39.21	40.04	40.87	41.71	42.54	43.37	44.21	45.04	45.87	46.70	47.54	48.37	50.03

Description: This table shows the yield to maturity of a bond purchased at the price shown in the index.

Example: The yield to maturity of a 15.00 %, 26 year bond at a price of 125.00 is 11.87 %.

PRICE	11.00%	11.25%	11.50%	11.75%	12.00%	12.25%	12.50%	12.75%	13.00%	13.25%	13.50%	13.75%	14.00%	14.25%	14.50%	15.00%
250	2.82	2.94	3.07	3.20	3.33	3.45	3.58	3.70	3.83	3.95	4.08	4.20	4.33	4.45	4.57	4.81
240	3.10	3.24	3.37	3.50	3.63	3.76	3.89	4.02	4.14	4.27	4.40	4.53	4.65	4.78	4.90	5.15
230	3.41	3.55	3.68	3.81	3.95	4.08	4.21	4.35	4.48	4.61	4.74	4.87	5.00	5.13	5.26	5.52
220	3.74	3.88	4.01	4.15	4.29	4.43	4.56	4.70	4.83	4.97	5.10	5.24	5.37	5.51	5.64	5.90
210	4.08	4.23	4.37	4.51	4.65	4.79	4.94	5.08	5.22	5.35	5.49	5.63	5.77	5.91	6.05	6.32
200	4.46	4.60	4.75	4.90	5.04	5.19	5.34	5.48	5.63	5.77	5.91	6.06	6.20	6.34	6.48	6.77
195	4.65	4.80	4.95	5.10	5.25	5.40	5.55	5.69	5.84	5.99	6.13	6.28	6.43	6.57	6.72	7.00
190	4.86	5.01	5.16	5.32	5.47	5.62	5.77	5.92	6.07	6.22	6.37	6.51	6.66	6.81	6.96	7.25
185	5.07	5.23	5.38	5.54	5.69	5.84	6.00	6.15	6.30	6.45	6.61	6.76	6.91	7.06	7.21	7.51
180	5.29	5.45	5.61	5.77	5.92	6.08	6.24	6.39	6.55	6.70	6.86	7.01	7.17	7.32	7.47	7.78
175	5.52	5.68	5.85	6.01	6.17	6.33	6.49	6.64	6.80	6.96	7.12	7.28	7.43	7.59	7.75	8.06
170	5.76	5.93	6.09	6.26	6.42	6.58	6.75	6.91	7.07	7.23	7.39	7.55	7.71	7.88	8.03	8.35
165	6.02	6.18	6.35	6.52	6.69	6.85	7.02	7.19	7.35	7.52	7.68	7.85	8.01	8.17	8.34	8.66
160	6.28	6.45	6.62	6.79	6.97	7.14	7.31	7.48	7.65	7.81	7.98	8.15	8.32	8.49	8.65	8.99
155	6.56	6.73	6.91	7.08	7.26	7.43	7.61	7.78	7.95	8.13	8.30	8.47	8.65	8.82	8.99	9.33
150	6.85	7.03	7.21	7.39	7.57	7.75	7.92	8.10	8.28	8.46	8.64	8.81	8.99	9.17	9.34	9.69
145	7.16	7.34	7.53	7.71	7.89	8.08	8.26	8.44	8.63	8.81	8.99	9.17	9.35	9.53	9.72	10.08
140	7.48	7.67	7.86	8.05	8.24	8.43	8.61	8.80	8.99	9.18	9.37	9.55	9.74	9.93	10.11	10.48
135	7.82	8.02	8.21	8.41	8.60	8.80	8.99	9.18	9.38	9.57	9.76	9.96	10.15	10.34	10.53	10.92
130	8.19	8.39	8.59	8.79	8.99	9.19	9.39	9.59	9.79	9.99	10.19	10.39	10.58	10.78	10.98	11.38
125	8.58	8.78	8.99	9.20	9.41	9.61	9.82	10.02	10.23	10.44	10.64	10.85	11.05	11.26	11.46	11.87
120	8.99	9.21	9.42	9.63	9.85	10.06	10.28	10.49	10.70	10.91	11.13	11.34	11.55	11.76	11.98	12.40
115	9.44	9.66	9.88	10.10	10.32	10.55	10.77	10.99	11.21	11.43	11.65	11.87	12.09	12.31	12.53	12.97
113	9.62	9.85	10.07	10.30	10.52	10.75	10.97	11.20	11.42	11.65	11.87	12.09	12.32	12.54	12.77	13.21
112	9.72	9.95	10.17	10.40	10.63	10.85	11.08	11.31	11.53	11.76	11.98	12.21	12.43	12.66	12.89	13.34
111	9.82	10.05	10.27	10.50	10.73	10.96	11.19	11.41	11.64	11.87	12.10	12.33	12.55	12.78	13.01	13.46
110	9.92	10.15	10.38	10.61	10.84	11.07	11.30	11.53	11.76	11.98	12.21	12.44	12.67	12.90	13.13	13.59
109	10.02	10.25	10.48	10.71	10.94	11.18	11.41	11.64	11.87	12.10	12.33	12.56	12.80	13.03	13.26	13.72
108	10.12	10.35	10.59	10.82	11.05	11.29	11.52	11.75	11.99	12.22	12.45	12.69	12.92	13.15	13.39	13.85
107	10.22	10.46	10.69	10.93	11.16	11.40	11.63	11.87	12.11	12.34	12.58	12.81	13.05	13.28	13.52	13.99
106	10.33	10.56	10.80	11.04	11.28	11.51	11.75	11.99	12.23	12.46	12.70	12.94	13.17	13.41	13.65	14.12
105	10.43	10.67	10.91	11.15	11.39	11.63	11.87	12.11	12.35	12.59	12.83	13.07	13.31	13.54	13.78	14.26
104	10.54	10.78	11.02	11.27	11.51	11.75	11.99	12.23	12.47	12.71	12.96	13.20	13.44	13.68	13.92	14.40
103	10.65	10.90	11.14	11.38	11.63	11.87	12.11	12.36	12.60	12.84	13.09	13.33	13.57	13.82	14.06	14.55
102	10.76	11.01	11.26	11.50	11.75	11.99	12.24	12.48	12.73	12.98	13.22	13.47	13.71	13.96	14.20	14.69
101	10.88	11.13	11.37	11.62	11.87	12.12	12.37	12.61	12.86	13.11	13.36	13.60	13.85	14.10	14.35	14.84
100	11.00	11.25	11.50	11.75	12.00	12.25	12.50	12.75	13.00	13.25	13.50	13.75	14.00	14.25	14.50	15.00
99	11.11	11.37	11.62	11.87	12.12	12.37	12.63	12.88	13.13	13.38	13.64	13.89	14.14	14.39	14.65	15.15
98	11.23	11.49	11.74	12.00	12.25	12.51	12.76	13.02	13.27	13.52	13.78	14.03	14.29	14.54	14.80	15.31
97	11.36	11.61	11.87	12.13	12.38	12.64	12.90	13.15	13.41	13.67	13.93	14.18	14.44	14.70	14.95	15.47
96	11.48	11.74	12.00	12.26	12.52	12.78	13.04	13.30	13.56	13.82	14.08	14.33	14.59	14.85	15.11	15.63
95	11.61	11.87	12.13	12.39	12.66	12.92	13.18	13.44	13.70	13.97	14.23	14.49	14.75	15.01	15.28	15.80
94	11.74	12.00	12.27	12.53	12.79	13.06	13.32	13.59	13.85	14.12	14.38	14.65	14.91	15.18	15.44	15.97
93	11.87	12.14	12.40	12.67	12.94	13.20	13.47	13.74	14.01	14.27	14.54	14.81	15.08	15.34	15.61	16.15
92	12.00	12.27	12.54	12.81	13.08	13.35	13.62	13.89	14.16	14.43	14.70	14.97	15.24	15.51	15.78	16.32
91	12.14	12.41	12.69	12.96	13.23	13.50	13.78	14.05	14.32	14.59	14.87	15.14	15.41	15.69	15.96	16.51
90	12.28	12.56	12.83	13.11	13.38	13.66	13.93	14.21	14.48	14.76	15.03	15.31	15.59	15.86	16.14	16.69
89	12.42	12.70	12.98	13.26	13.54	13.81	14.09	14.37	14.65	14.93	15.21	15.48	15.76	16.04	16.32	16.88
88	12.57	12.85	13.13	13.41	13.69	13.97	14.26	14.54	14.82	15.10	15.38	15.66	15.95	16.23	16.51	17.07
87	12.72	13.00	13.29	13.57	13.85	14.14	14.42	14.71	14.99	15.28	15.56	15.85	16.13	16.42	16.70	17.27
86	12.87	13.16	13.44	13.73	14.02	14.31	14.59	14.88	15.17	15.46	15.74	16.03	16.32	16.61	16.90	17.47
85	13.03	13.32	13.61	13.90	14.19	14.48	14.77	15.06	15.35	15.64	15.93	16.22	16.51	16.81	17.10	17.68
84	13.18	13.48	13.77	14.06	14.36	14.65	14.94	15.24	15.53	15.83	16.12	16.42	16.71	17.01	17.30	17.89
83	13.35	13.64	13.94	14.24	14.53	14.83	15.13	15.42	15.72	16.02	16.32	16.62	16.91	17.21	17.51	18.11
82	13.51	13.81	14.11	14.41	14.71	15.01	15.31	15.61	15.92	16.22	16.52	16.82	17.12	17.42	17.73	18.33
81	13.68	13.98	14.29	14.59	14.90	15.20	15.50	15.81	16.11	16.42	16.72	17.03	17.33	17.64	17.95	18.56
80	13.85	14.16	14.47	14.78	15.08	15.39	15.70	16.01	16.32	16.62	16.93	17.24	17.55	17.86	18.17	18.79
79	14.03	14.34	14.65	14.96	15.28	15.59	15.90	16.21	16.52	16.84	17.15	17.46	17.77	18.09	18.40	19.03
78	14.21	14.53	14.84	15.16	15.47	15.79	16.10	16.42	16.74	17.05	17.37	17.68	18.00	18.32	18.64	19.27
77	14.40	14.72	15.04	15.35	15.67	15.99	16.31	16.63	16.95	17.27	17.59	17.91	18.24	18.56	18.88	19.52
76	14.59	14.91	15.23	15.56	15.88	16.20	16.53	16.85	17.18	17.50	17.83	18.15	18.48	18.80	19.13	19.78
75	14.79	15.11	15.44	15.77	16.09	16.42	16.75	17.08	17.40	17.73	18.06	18.39	18.72	19.05	19.38	20.04
74	14.99	15.32	15.65	15.98	16.31	16.64	16.97	17.31	17.64	17.97	18.31	18.64	18.97	19.31	19.64	20.31
73	15.19	15.53	15.86	16.20	16.53	16.87	17.21	17.54	17.88	18.22	18.56	18.90	19.23	19.57	19.91	20.59
70	15.84	16.19	16.54	16.89	17.24	17.59	17.94	18.29	18.64	19.00	19.35	19.70	20.06	20.41	20.76	21.47
65	17.05	17.43	17.80	18.18	18.56	18.93	19.31	19.69	20.07	20.45	20.83	21.21	21.59	21.97	22.35	23.11
60	18.45	18.86	19.27	19.68	20.09	20.50	20.91	21.32	21.73	22.14	22.55	22.97	23.38	23.79	24.20	25.03
55	20.11	20.55	21.00	21.45	21.89	22.34	22.79	23.24	23.69	24.14	24.59	25.04	25.49	25.94	26.39	27.30

Description: This table shows the price to pay for a bond at the yield rate. The yield is to maturity.

Example: The price of a 6.75 %, 27 year bond to yield 8 % to maturity is $ 86.25.

COUPON RATE, %

YIELD	0.00%	1.00%	2.00%	3.00%	4.00%	4.25%	4.50%	4.75%	5.00%	5.25%	5.50%	5.75%	6.00%	6.25%	6.50%	6.75%
0.00	100.00	127.00	154.00	181.00	208.00	214.75	221.50	228.25	235.00	241.75	248.50	255.25	262.00	268.75	275.50	282.25
1.00	76.39	100.00	123.61	147.22	170.83	176.73	182.64	188.54	194.44	200.35	206.25	212.15	218.05	223.96	229.86	235.76
2.00	58.43	79.22	100.00	120.78	141.57	146.76	151.96	157.16	162.35	167.55	172.75	177.94	183.14	188.33	193.53	198.73
3.00	44.75	63.17	81.58	100.00	118.42	123.02	127.62	132.23	136.83	141.43	146.04	150.64	155.25	159.85	164.45	169.06
4.00	34.32	50.74	67.16	83.58	100.00	104.10	108.21	112.31	116.42	120.52	124.63	128.73	132.84	136.94	141.05	145.15
4.25	32.13	48.10	64.07	80.04	96.01	100.00	103.99	107.99	111.98	115.97	119.96	123.96	127.95	131.94	135.93	139.93
4.50	30.07	45.61	61.15	76.69	92.23	96.12	100.00	103.88	107.77	111.65	115.54	119.42	123.31	127.19	131.08	134.96
4.75	28.15	43.28	58.40	73.53	88.66	92.44	96.22	100.00	103.78	107.56	111.34	115.13	118.91	122.69	126.47	130.25
5.00	26.36	41.09	55.81	70.54	85.27	88.95	92.64	96.32	100.00	103.68	107.36	111.05	114.73	118.41	122.09	125.77
5.25	24.68	39.03	53.37	67.72	82.07	85.65	89.24	92.83	96.41	100.00	103.59	107.17	110.76	114.35	117.93	121.52
5.50	23.11	37.09	51.07	65.05	79.03	82.52	86.02	89.51	93.01	96.50	100.00	103.50	106.99	110.49	113.98	117.48
5.75	21.64	35.27	48.90	62.52	76.15	79.56	82.97	86.37	89.78	93.19	96.59	100.00	103.41	106.81	110.22	113.63
6.00	20.27	33.56	46.84	60.13	73.42	76.74	80.07	83.39	86.71	90.03	93.36	96.68	100.00	103.32	106.64	109.97
6.25	18.98	31.95	44.91	57.87	70.83	74.07	77.32	80.56	83.80	87.04	90.28	93.52	96.76	100.00	103.24	106.48
6.50	17.78	30.43	43.08	55.73	68.38	71.54	74.70	77.86	81.03	84.19	87.35	90.51	93.68	96.84	100.00	103.16
6.75	16.66	29.00	41.35	53.70	66.04	69.13	72.22	75.31	78.39	81.48	84.57	87.65	90.74	93.83	96.91	100.00
7.00	15.60	27.66	39.72	51.77	63.83	66.84	69.86	72.87	75.89	78.90	81.92	84.93	87.94	90.96	93.97	96.99
7.25	14.62	26.40	38.17	49.95	61.73	64.67	67.61	70.56	73.50	76.45	79.39	82.33	85.28	88.22	91.17	94.11
7.50	13.70	25.20	36.71	48.22	59.73	62.60	65.48	68.36	71.23	74.11	76.99	79.86	82.74	85.62	88.49	91.37
7.75	12.84	24.08	35.33	46.58	57.82	60.64	63.45	66.26	69.07	71.88	74.69	77.51	80.32	83.13	85.94	88.75
8.00	12.03	23.02	34.02	45.02	56.01	58.76	61.51	64.26	67.01	69.76	72.51	75.26	78.01	80.76	83.51	86.25
8.25	11.27	22.03	32.78	43.54	54.29	56.98	59.67	62.36	65.05	67.74	70.42	73.11	75.80	78.49	81.18	83.87
8.50	10.57	21.09	31.61	42.13	52.65	55.28	57.91	60.54	63.17	65.80	68.43	71.07	73.70	76.33	78.96	81.59
8.75	9.90	20.20	30.50	40.79	51.09	53.66	56.24	58.81	61.39	63.96	66.54	69.11	71.68	74.26	76.83	79.41
9.00	9.28	19.36	29.44	39.52	49.60	52.12	54.64	57.16	59.68	62.20	64.72	67.24	69.76	72.28	74.80	77.32
9.25	8.70	18.57	28.44	38.31	48.18	50.65	53.12	55.59	58.05	60.52	62.99	65.46	67.92	70.39	72.86	75.33
9.50	8.16	17.83	27.49	37.16	46.83	49.25	51.66	54.08	56.50	58.91	61.33	63.75	66.16	68.58	71.00	73.41
9.75	7.65	17.12	26.59	36.07	45.54	47.91	50.27	52.64	55.01	57.38	59.75	62.11	64.48	66.85	69.22	71.58
10.00	7.17	16.46	25.74	35.02	44.30	46.63	48.95	51.27	53.59	55.91	58.23	60.55	62.87	65.19	67.51	69.83
10.25	6.73	15.83	24.93	34.03	43.13	45.40	47.68	49.95	52.23	54.50	56.78	59.05	61.33	63.60	65.88	68.15
10.50	6.31	15.23	24.16	33.08	42.00	44.23	46.46	48.69	50.92	53.15	55.39	57.62	59.85	62.08	64.31	66.54
10.75	5.92	14.67	23.42	32.17	40.93	43.11	45.30	47.49	49.68	51.86	54.05	56.24	58.43	60.62	62.80	64.99
11.00	5.55	14.14	22.72	31.31	39.90	42.04	44.19	46.34	48.48	50.63	52.78	54.92	57.07	59.22	61.36	63.51
11.25	5.21	13.63	22.06	30.49	38.91	41.02	43.12	45.23	47.34	49.44	51.55	53.66	55.76	57.87	59.98	62.08
11.50	4.88	13.16	21.43	29.70	37.97	40.04	42.10	44.17	46.24	48.31	50.37	52.44	54.51	56.58	58.65	60.71
11.75	4.58	12.70	20.82	28.94	37.07	39.10	41.13	43.16	45.19	47.22	49.25	51.28	53.31	55.34	57.37	59.40
12.00	4.30	12.28	20.25	28.23	36.20	38.19	40.19	42.18	44.18	46.17	48.16	50.16	52.15	54.14	56.14	58.13
12.25	4.04	11.87	19.70	27.54	35.37	37.33	39.29	41.25	43.20	45.16	47.12	49.08	51.04	53.00	54.96	56.91
12.50	3.79	11.48	19.18	26.88	34.57	36.50	38.42	40.35	42.27	44.20	46.12	48.04	49.97	51.89	53.82	55.74
12.75	3.55	11.12	18.68	26.25	33.81	35.70	37.59	39.48	41.38	43.27	45.16	47.05	48.94	50.83	52.72	54.61
13.00	3.34	10.77	18.21	25.64	33.08	34.94	36.80	38.66	40.51	42.37	44.23	46.09	47.95	49.81	51.67	53.53
13.25	3.13	10.44	17.75	25.06	32.37	34.20	36.03	37.86	39.69	41.51	43.34	45.17	47.00	48.82	50.65	52.48
13.50	2.94	10.13	17.32	24.51	31.70	33.49	35.29	37.09	38.89	40.68	42.48	44.28	46.08	47.87	49.67	51.47
13.75	2.76	9.83	16.90	23.97	31.05	32.82	34.58	36.35	38.12	39.89	41.66	43.42	45.19	46.96	48.73	50.50
14.00	2.59	9.55	16.51	23.46	30.42	32.16	33.90	35.64	37.38	39.12	40.86	42.60	44.34	46.08	47.82	49.56
14.25	2.43	9.28	16.13	22.97	29.82	31.53	33.24	34.95	36.67	38.38	40.09	41.80	43.51	45.22	46.94	48.65
14.50	2.28	9.02	15.76	22.50	29.24	30.92	32.61	34.29	35.98	37.66	39.35	41.03	42.72	44.40	46.09	47.77
14.75	2.14	8.78	15.41	22.05	28.68	30.34	32.00	33.66	35.32	36.97	38.63	40.29	41.95	43.61	45.27	46.93
15.00	2.01	8.55	15.08	21.61	28.14	29.78	31.41	33.04	34.68	36.31	37.94	39.57	41.21	42.84	44.47	46.11
15.25	1.89	8.32	14.76	21.19	27.62	29.23	30.84	32.45	34.06	35.67	37.27	38.88	40.49	42.10	43.71	45.32
15.50	1.78	8.11	14.45	20.79	27.12	28.71	30.29	31.88	33.46	35.05	36.63	38.21	39.80	41.38	42.97	44.55
15.75	1.67	7.91	14.15	20.40	26.64	28.20	29.76	31.32	32.88	34.45	36.01	37.57	39.13	40.69	42.25	43.81
16.00	1.57	7.72	13.87	20.02	26.18	27.71	29.25	30.79	32.33	33.87	35.40	36.94	38.48	40.02	41.56	43.09
16.25	1.47	7.54	13.60	19.66	25.73	27.24	28.76	30.27	31.79	33.30	34.82	36.34	37.85	39.37	40.88	42.40
16.50	1.38	7.36	13.34	19.31	25.29	26.78	28.28	29.77	31.27	32.76	34.26	35.75	37.24	38.74	40.23	41.73
16.75	1.30	7.19	13.08	18.98	24.87	26.34	27.82	29.29	30.76	32.24	33.71	35.18	36.66	38.13	39.60	41.07
17.00	1.22	7.03	12.84	18.65	24.46	25.92	27.37	28.82	30.27	31.73	33.18	34.63	36.08	37.54	38.99	40.44
17.25	1.15	6.88	12.61	18.34	24.07	25.50	26.94	28.37	29.80	31.23	32.67	34.10	35.53	36.96	38.40	39.83
17.50	1.08	6.73	12.38	18.04	23.69	25.10	26.52	27.93	29.34	30.75	32.17	33.58	34.99	36.41	37.82	39.23
17.75	1.01	6.59	12.17	17.74	23.32	24.71	26.11	27.50	28.90	30.29	31.69	33.08	34.47	35.87	37.26	38.66
18.00	.95	6.46	11.96	17.46	22.96	24.34	25.71	27.09	28.47	29.84	31.22	32.59	33.97	35.34	36.72	38.10
18.25	.90	6.33	11.76	17.19	22.62	23.97	25.33	26.69	28.05	29.41	30.76	32.12	33.48	34.84	36.19	37.55
18.50	.84	6.20	11.56	16.92	22.28	23.62	24.96	26.30	27.64	28.98	30.32	31.66	33.00	34.34	35.68	37.02
18.75	.79	6.08	11.37	16.66	21.96	23.28	24.60	25.92	27.25	28.57	29.89	31.22	32.54	33.86	35.18	36.51
19.00	.74	5.97	11.19	16.42	21.64	22.95	24.25	25.56	26.86	28.17	29.48	30.78	32.09	33.39	34.70	36.01
20.00	.58	5.55	10.52	15.49	20.47	21.71	22.95	24.19	25.44	26.68	27.92	29.16	30.41	31.65	32.89	34.14
25.00	.17	4.17	8.16	12.15	16.15	17.14	18.14	19.14	20.14	21.14	22.13	23.13	24.13	25.13	26.13	27.13
30.00	.05	3.38	6.72	10.05	13.38	14.21	15.04	15.88	16.71	17.54	18.38	19.21	20.04	20.88	21.71	22.54

Description: This table shows the yield to maturity of a bond purchased at the price shown in the index.

Example: The yield to maturity of a 6.75 %, 27 year bond at a price of 80.00 is 8.68 %.

PRICE	0.00%	1.00%	2.00%	3.00%	4.00%	4.25%	4.50%	4.75%	5.00%	5.25%	5.50%	5.75%	6.00%	6.25%	6.50%	6.75%
100	0.00	1.00	2.00	3.00	4.00	4.25	4.50	4.75	5.00	5.25	5.50	5.75	6.00	6.25	6.50	6.75
99	.03	1.04	2.04	3.05	4.06	4.31	4.56	4.81	5.06	5.32	5.57	5.82	6.07	6.32	6.57	6.83
98	.07	1.08	2.09	3.11	4.12	4.37	4.63	4.88	5.13	5.39	5.64	5.89	6.15	6.40	6.66	6.91
97	.11	1.12	2.14	3.16	4.18	4.44	4.69	4.95	5.20	5.46	5.71	5.97	6.23	6.48	6.74	6.99
96	.15	1.17	2.19	3.22	4.25	4.50	4.76	5.02	5.27	5.53	5.79	6.05	6.31	6.56	6.82	7.08
95	.19	1.21	2.24	3.28	4.31	4.57	4.83	5.09	5.35	5.61	5.87	6.13	6.39	6.65	6.91	7.17
94	.22	1.26	2.29	3.33	4.38	4.64	4.90	5.16	5.42	5.68	5.94	6.21	6.47	6.73	6.99	7.25
93	.26	1.30	2.35	3.39	4.44	4.71	4.97	5.23	5.50	5.76	6.02	6.29	6.55	6.82	7.08	7.34
92	.30	1.35	2.40	3.45	4.51	4.78	5.04	5.31	5.57	5.84	6.10	6.37	6.64	6.90	7.17	7.44
91	.34	1.40	2.45	3.51	4.58	4.85	5.11	5.38	5.65	5.92	6.19	6.45	6.72	6.99	7.26	7.53
90	.39	1.44	2.51	3.58	4.65	4.92	5.19	5.46	5.73	6.00	6.27	6.54	6.81	7.08	7.35	7.62
89	.43	1.49	2.56	3.64	4.72	4.99	5.26	5.54	5.81	6.08	6.35	6.63	6.90	7.17	7.45	7.72
88	.47	1.54	2.62	3.70	4.79	5.07	5.34	5.61	5.89	6.16	6.44	6.71	6.99	7.27	7.54	7.82
87	.51	1.59	2.67	3.77	4.87	5.14	5.42	5.69	5.97	6.25	6.53	6.80	7.08	7.36	7.64	7.92
86	.55	1.64	2.73	3.83	4.94	5.22	5.50	5.78	6.05	6.33	6.61	6.90	7.18	7.46	7.74	8.02
85	.60	1.69	2.79	3.90	5.02	5.30	5.58	5.86	6.14	6.42	6.71	6.99	7.27	7.56	7.84	8.12
84	.64	1.74	2.85	3.97	5.09	5.38	5.66	5.94	6.23	6.51	6.80	7.08	7.37	7.66	7.94	8.23
83	.69	1.79	2.91	4.04	5.17	5.46	5.74	6.03	6.32	6.60	6.89	7.18	7.47	7.76	8.05	8.34
82	.73	1.84	2.97	4.10	5.25	5.54	5.83	6.12	6.41	6.70	6.99	7.28	7.57	7.86	8.16	8.45
81	.78	1.90	3.03	4.18	5.33	5.62	5.91	6.20	6.50	6.79	7.08	7.38	7.67	7.97	8.26	8.56
80	.82	1.95	3.09	4.25	5.41	5.71	6.00	6.30	6.59	6.89	7.18	7.48	7.78	8.08	8.38	8.68
79	.87	2.01	3.16	4.32	5.50	5.79	6.09	6.39	6.69	6.99	7.28	7.59	7.89	8.19	8.49	8.79
78	.92	2.06	3.22	4.40	5.58	5.88	6.18	6.48	6.78	7.09	7.39	7.69	8.00	8.30	8.61	8.91
77	.97	2.12	3.29	4.47	5.67	5.97	6.27	6.58	6.88	7.19	7.49	7.80	8.11	8.42	8.72	9.03
76	1.01	2.18	3.35	4.55	5.76	6.06	6.37	6.68	6.98	7.29	7.60	7.91	8.22	8.53	8.85	9.16
75	1.06	2.23	3.42	4.63	5.85	6.16	6.47	6.78	7.09	7.40	7.71	8.02	8.34	8.65	8.97	9.29
74	1.11	2.29	3.49	4.71	5.94	6.25	6.56	6.88	7.19	7.51	7.82	8.14	8.46	8.78	9.10	9.42
73	1.16	2.35	3.56	4.79	6.03	6.35	6.66	6.98	7.30	7.62	7.94	8.26	8.58	8.90	9.23	9.55
72	1.22	2.41	3.63	4.87	6.13	6.45	6.77	7.09	7.41	7.73	8.05	8.38	8.70	9.03	9.36	9.69
71	1.27	2.47	3.70	4.96	6.23	6.55	6.87	7.20	7.52	7.85	8.17	8.50	8.83	9.16	9.49	9.83
70	1.32	2.54	3.78	5.04	6.33	6.65	6.98	7.31	7.64	7.97	8.30	8.63	8.96	9.30	9.63	9.97
69	1.37	2.60	3.85	5.13	6.43	6.76	7.09	7.42	7.75	8.09	8.42	8.76	9.10	9.44	9.78	10.12
68	1.43	2.67	3.93	5.22	6.53	6.87	7.20	7.54	7.87	8.21	8.55	8.89	9.23	9.58	9.92	10.27
67	1.48	2.73	4.01	5.31	6.64	6.98	7.32	7.66	8.00	8.34	8.68	9.03	9.37	9.72	10.07	10.42
66	1.54	2.80	4.09	5.40	6.75	7.09	7.43	7.78	8.12	8.47	8.82	9.17	9.52	9.87	10.23	10.58
65	1.60	2.87	4.17	5.50	6.86	7.21	7.55	7.90	8.25	8.60	8.96	9.31	9.67	10.02	10.38	10.74
64	1.65	2.94	4.25	5.60	6.98	7.32	7.68	8.03	8.38	8.74	9.10	9.46	9.82	10.18	10.55	10.91
63	1.71	3.01	4.33	5.70	7.09	7.45	7.80	8.16	8.52	8.88	9.24	9.61	9.97	10.34	10.71	11.08
62	1.77	3.08	4.42	5.80	7.21	7.57	7.93	8.29	8.66	9.02	9.39	9.76	10.13	10.51	10.88	11.26
61	1.83	3.15	4.51	5.90	7.33	7.70	8.06	8.43	8.80	9.17	9.55	9.92	10.30	10.68	11.06	11.44
60	1.90	3.23	4.60	6.01	7.46	7.83	8.20	8.57	8.95	9.32	9.70	10.09	10.47	10.85	11.24	11.63
59	1.96	3.30	4.69	6.12	7.59	7.96	8.34	8.72	9.10	9.48	9.87	10.25	10.64	11.03	11.43	11.82
58	2.02	3.38	4.78	6.23	7.72	8.10	8.48	8.87	9.25	9.64	10.03	10.43	10.82	11.22	11.62	12.02
57	2.09	3.46	4.88	6.34	7.86	8.24	8.63	9.02	9.41	9.81	10.21	10.61	11.01	11.41	11.82	12.23
56	2.15	3.54	4.98	6.46	8.00	8.39	8.78	9.18	9.58	9.98	10.38	10.79	11.20	11.61	12.02	12.44
55	2.22	3.62	5.08	6.58	8.14	8.54	8.94	9.34	9.75	10.16	10.57	10.98	11.40	11.81	12.24	12.66
54	2.29	3.71	5.18	6.71	8.29	8.69	9.10	9.51	9.92	10.34	10.76	11.18	11.60	12.03	12.45	12.88
53	2.36	3.79	5.28	6.83	8.44	8.85	9.26	9.68	10.10	10.52	10.95	11.38	11.81	12.24	12.68	13.12
52	2.43	3.88	5.39	6.96	8.60	9.02	9.44	9.86	10.29	10.72	11.15	11.59	12.03	12.47	12.92	13.36
51	2.50	3.97	5.50	7.10	8.76	9.18	9.61	10.04	10.48	10.92	11.36	11.81	12.25	12.70	13.16	13.61
50	2.58	4.06	5.62	7.24	8.93	9.36	9.80	10.24	10.68	11.13	11.58	12.03	12.49	12.95	13.41	13.88
49	2.65	4.16	5.73	7.38	9.10	9.54	9.98	10.43	10.89	11.34	11.80	12.26	12.73	13.20	13.67	14.15
48	2.73	4.25	5.85	7.53	9.28	9.73	10.18	10.64	11.10	11.56	12.03	12.51	12.98	13.46	13.94	14.43
47	2.81	4.35	5.98	7.68	9.46	9.92	10.38	10.85	11.32	11.80	12.27	12.76	13.24	13.73	14.23	14.72
46	2.89	4.45	6.10	7.84	9.65	10.12	10.59	11.07	11.55	12.04	12.53	13.02	13.52	14.02	14.52	15.03
45	2.97	4.56	6.23	8.00	9.85	10.33	10.81	11.30	11.79	12.29	12.79	13.29	13.80	14.31	14.83	15.35
44	3.06	4.67	6.37	8.17	10.06	10.55	11.04	11.54	12.04	12.55	13.06	13.58	14.10	14.62	15.15	15.68
43	3.15	4.78	6.51	8.34	10.27	10.77	11.27	11.78	12.30	12.82	13.34	13.87	14.41	14.94	15.48	16.03
42	3.23	4.89	6.65	8.52	10.50	11.01	11.52	12.04	12.57	13.10	13.64	14.18	14.73	15.28	15.83	16.39
41	3.32	5.01	6.80	8.71	10.73	11.25	11.78	12.31	12.85	13.40	13.95	14.51	15.07	15.63	16.20	16.77
40	3.42	5.12	6.95	8.90	10.97	11.50	12.05	12.59	13.15	13.71	14.27	14.85	15.42	16.00	16.59	17.17
39	3.51	5.25	7.11	9.10	11.22	11.77	12.33	12.89	13.46	14.03	14.62	15.20	15.79	16.39	16.99	17.60
35	3.92	5.78	7.81	10.00	12.36	12.97	13.60	14.23	14.87	15.51	16.17	16.83	17.49	18.16	18.84	19.52
30	4.50	6.57	8.86	11.40	14.17	14.89	15.63	16.38	17.14	17.91	18.68	19.46	20.25	21.05	21.85	22.66
25	5.20	7.54	10.22	13.27	16.67	17.56	18.47	19.39	20.32	21.27	22.22	23.18	24.15	25.12	26.10	27.08
20	6.05	8.80	12.11	16.01	20.43	21.59	22.77	23.96	25.16	26.38	27.60	28.83	30.06	31.29	32.53	33.77
15	7.15	10.60	15.06	20.59	26.83	28.45	30.08	31.73	33.37	35.03	36.69	38.35	40.01	41.67	43.33	45.00
10	8.71	13.60	20.88	30.13	40.01	42.51	45.00	47.50	50.00	52.50	55.00	57.50	60.00	62.50	65.00	67.50

Description: This table shows the price to pay for a bond at the yield rate. The yield is to maturity.

Example: The price of a 10.75 %, 27 year bond to yield 8 % to maturity is $ 130.24.

COUPON RATE, %

YIELD	7.00%	7.25%	7.50%	7.75%	8.00%	8.25%	8.50%	8.75%	9.00%	9.25%	9.50%	9.75%	10.00%	10.25%	10.50%	10.75%
0.00	289.00	295.75	302.50	309.25	316.00	322.75	329.50	336.25	343.00	349.75	356.50	363.25	370.00	376.75	383.50	390.25
1.00	241.66	247.57	253.47	259.37	265.27	271.18	277.08	282.98	288.89	294.79	300.69	306.59	312.50	318.40	324.30	330.20
2.00	203.92	209.12	214.31	219.51	224.71	229.90	235.10	240.29	245.49	250.69	255.88	261.08	266.27	271.47	276.67	281.86
3.00	173.66	178.26	182.87	187.47	192.08	196.68	201.28	205.89	210.49	215.10	219.70	224.30	228.91	233.51	238.11	242.72
4.00	149.26	153.36	157.47	161.57	165.68	169.78	173.89	177.99	182.10	186.20	190.31	194.41	198.51	202.62	206.72	210.83
4.25	143.92	147.91	151.90	155.90	159.89	163.88	167.87	171.87	175.86	179.85	183.84	187.84	191.83	195.82	199.81	203.81
4.50	138.85	142.73	146.62	150.50	154.39	158.27	162.16	166.04	169.93	173.81	177.70	181.58	185.47	189.35	193.24	197.12
4.75	134.03	137.81	141.60	145.38	149.16	152.94	156.72	160.50	164.28	168.07	171.85	175.63	179.41	183.19	186.97	190.75
5.00	129.46	133.14	136.82	140.50	144.19	147.87	151.55	155.23	158.91	162.60	166.28	169.96	173.64	177.32	181.01	184.69
5.25	125.11	128.69	132.28	135.87	139.45	143.04	146.63	150.21	153.80	157.39	160.97	164.56	168.15	171.73	175.32	178.91
5.50	120.97	124.47	127.96	131.46	134.95	138.45	141.94	145.44	148.93	152.43	155.92	159.42	162.91	166.41	169.90	173.40
5.75	117.03	120.44	123.85	127.26	130.66	134.07	137.48	140.88	144.29	147.70	151.10	154.51	157.92	161.32	164.73	168.14
6.00	113.29	116.61	119.93	123.26	126.58	129.90	133.22	136.54	139.87	143.19	146.51	149.83	153.16	156.48	159.80	163.12
6.25	109.72	112.96	116.20	119.44	122.68	125.93	129.17	132.41	135.65	138.89	142.13	145.37	148.61	151.85	155.09	158.33
6.50	106.32	109.49	112.65	115.81	118.97	122.14	125.30	128.46	131.62	134.79	137.95	141.11	144.27	147.43	150.60	153.76
6.75	103.09	106.17	109.26	112.35	115.43	118.52	121.61	124.69	127.78	130.87	133.96	137.04	140.13	143.22	146.30	149.39
7.00	100.00	103.01	106.03	109.04	112.06	115.07	118.08	121.10	124.11	127.13	130.14	133.16	136.17	139.18	142.20	145.21
7.25	97.06	100.00	102.94	105.89	108.83	111.78	114.72	117.67	120.61	123.55	126.50	129.44	132.39	135.33	138.27	141.22
7.50	94.25	97.12	100.00	102.88	105.75	108.63	111.51	114.38	117.26	120.14	123.01	125.89	128.77	131.64	134.52	137.40
7.75	91.56	94.38	97.19	100.00	102.81	105.62	108.44	111.25	114.06	116.87	119.68	122.49	125.31	128.12	130.93	133.74
8.00	89.00	91.75	94.50	97.25	100.00	102.75	105.50	108.25	111.00	113.75	116.49	119.24	121.99	124.74	127.49	130.24
8.25	86.56	89.25	91.93	94.62	97.31	100.00	102.69	105.38	108.07	110.75	113.44	116.13	118.82	121.51	124.20	126.89
8.50	84.22	86.85	89.48	92.11	94.74	97.37	100.00	102.63	105.26	107.89	110.52	113.15	115.78	118.41	121.04	123.67
8.75	81.98	84.55	87.13	89.70	92.28	94.85	97.43	100.00	102.57	105.15	107.72	110.30	112.87	115.45	118.02	120.59
9.00	79.84	82.36	84.88	87.40	89.92	92.44	94.96	97.48	100.00	102.52	105.04	107.56	110.08	112.60	115.12	117.64
9.25	77.79	80.26	82.73	85.20	87.66	90.13	92.60	95.07	97.53	100.00	102.47	104.93	107.40	109.87	112.34	114.80
9.50	75.83	78.25	80.67	83.08	85.50	87.92	90.33	92.75	95.17	97.58	100.00	102.42	104.83	107.25	109.67	112.08
9.75	73.95	76.32	78.69	81.06	83.42	85.79	88.16	90.53	92.90	95.26	97.63	100.00	102.37	104.74	107.10	109.47
10.00	72.15	74.47	76.79	79.11	81.43	83.76	86.08	88.40	90.72	93.04	95.36	97.68	100.00	102.32	104.64	106.96
10.25	70.43	72.70	74.98	77.25	79.53	81.80	84.08	86.35	88.63	90.90	93.18	95.45	97.73	100.00	102.27	104.55
10.50	68.77	71.00	73.23	75.46	77.69	79.92	82.15	84.38	86.62	88.85	91.08	93.31	95.54	97.77	100.00	102.23
10.75	67.18	69.37	71.56	73.74	75.93	78.12	80.31	82.50	84.68	86.87	89.06	91.25	93.44	95.62	97.81	100.00
11.00	65.65	67.80	69.95	72.09	74.24	76.39	78.53	80.68	82.83	84.97	87.12	89.27	91.41	93.56	95.71	97.85
11.25	64.19	66.30	68.40	70.51	72.62	74.72	76.83	78.93	81.04	83.15	85.25	87.36	89.47	91.57	93.68	95.79
11.50	62.78	64.85	66.92	68.98	71.05	73.12	75.19	77.26	79.32	81.39	83.46	85.53	87.59	89.66	91.73	93.80
11.75	61.43	63.46	65.49	67.52	69.55	71.58	73.61	75.64	77.67	79.70	81.73	83.76	85.79	87.82	89.85	91.88
12.00	60.13	62.12	64.11	66.11	68.10	70.09	72.09	74.08	76.08	78.07	80.06	82.06	84.05	86.04	88.04	90.03
12.25	58.87	60.83	62.79	64.75	66.71	68.66	70.62	72.58	74.54	76.50	78.46	80.42	82.37	84.33	86.29	88.25
12.50	57.67	59.59	61.51	63.44	65.36	67.29	69.21	71.14	73.06	74.98	76.91	78.83	80.76	82.68	84.61	86.53
12.75	56.50	58.40	60.29	62.18	64.07	65.96	67.85	69.74	71.63	73.52	75.42	77.31	79.20	81.09	82.98	84.87
13.00	55.39	57.24	59.10	60.96	62.82	64.68	66.54	68.40	70.26	72.12	73.97	75.83	77.69	79.55	81.41	83.27
13.25	54.31	56.13	57.96	59.79	61.62	63.45	65.27	67.10	68.93	70.76	72.58	74.41	76.24	78.07	79.90	81.72
13.50	53.27	55.06	56.86	58.66	60.46	62.25	64.05	65.85	67.65	69.44	71.24	73.04	74.84	76.63	78.43	80.23
13.75	52.26	54.03	55.80	57.57	59.34	61.10	62.87	64.64	66.41	68.18	69.94	71.71	73.48	75.25	77.02	78.78
14.00	51.29	53.03	54.77	56.51	58.25	59.99	61.73	63.47	65.21	66.95	68.69	70.43	72.17	73.91	75.65	77.39
14.25	50.36	52.07	53.78	55.50	57.21	58.92	60.63	62.34	64.05	65.77	67.48	69.19	70.90	72.61	74.32	76.04
14.50	49.46	51.14	52.83	54.51	56.20	57.88	59.57	61.25	62.94	64.62	66.30	67.99	69.67	71.36	73.04	74.73
14.75	48.58	50.24	51.90	53.56	55.22	56.88	58.54	60.19	61.85	63.51	65.17	66.83	68.49	70.15	71.80	73.46
15.00	47.74	49.37	51.01	52.64	54.27	55.91	57.54	59.17	60.81	62.44	64.07	65.70	67.34	68.97	70.60	72.24
15.25	46.92	48.53	50.14	51.75	53.36	54.97	56.57	58.18	59.79	61.40	63.01	64.62	66.22	67.83	69.44	71.05
15.50	46.14	47.72	49.30	50.89	52.47	54.06	55.64	57.23	58.81	60.39	61.98	63.56	65.15	66.73	68.31	69.90
15.75	45.37	46.93	48.49	50.05	51.61	53.18	54.74	56.30	57.86	59.42	60.98	62.54	64.10	65.66	67.22	68.78
16.00	44.63	46.17	47.71	49.25	50.78	52.32	53.86	55.40	56.94	58.47	60.01	61.55	63.09	64.63	66.16	67.70
16.25	43.91	45.43	46.95	48.46	49.98	51.49	53.01	54.53	56.04	57.56	59.07	60.59	62.10	63.62	65.14	66.65
16.50	43.22	44.71	46.21	47.70	49.20	50.69	52.19	53.68	55.17	56.67	58.16	59.66	61.15	62.65	64.14	65.63
16.75	42.55	44.02	45.49	46.97	48.44	49.91	51.39	52.86	54.33	55.81	57.28	58.75	60.23	61.70	63.17	64.64
17.00	41.89	43.35	44.80	46.25	47.71	49.16	50.61	52.06	53.52	54.97	56.42	57.87	59.33	60.78	62.23	63.68
17.25	41.26	42.69	44.13	45.56	46.99	48.42	49.86	51.29	52.72	54.15	55.59	57.02	58.45	59.89	61.32	62.75
17.50	40.65	42.06	43.47	44.89	46.30	47.71	49.13	50.54	51.95	53.37	54.78	56.19	57.61	59.02	60.43	61.84
17.75	40.05	41.44	42.84	44.23	45.63	47.02	48.42	49.81	51.20	52.60	53.99	55.39	56.78	58.17	59.57	60.96
18.00	39.47	40.85	42.22	43.60	44.97	46.35	47.73	49.10	50.48	51.85	53.23	54.60	55.98	57.35	58.73	60.11
18.25	38.91	40.27	41.62	42.98	44.34	45.70	47.05	48.41	49.77	51.13	52.48	53.84	55.20	56.56	57.91	59.27
18.50	38.36	39.70	41.04	42.38	43.72	45.06	46.40	47.74	49.08	50.42	51.76	53.10	54.44	55.78	57.12	58.46
18.75	37.83	39.15	40.47	41.80	43.12	44.44	45.77	47.09	48.41	49.73	51.06	52.38	53.70	55.03	56.35	57.67
19.00	37.31	38.62	39.92	41.23	42.54	43.84	45.15	46.45	47.76	49.07	50.37	51.68	52.98	54.29	55.60	56.90
20.00	35.38	36.62	37.86	39.11	40.35	41.59	42.83	44.08	45.32	46.56	47.81	49.05	50.29	51.53	52.78	54.02
25.00	28.12	29.12	30.12	31.12	32.12	33.12	34.11	35.11	36.11	37.11	38.11	39.11	40.10	41.10	42.10	43.10
30.00	23.37	24.21	25.04	25.87	26.71	27.54	28.37	29.20	30.04	30.87	31.70	32.54	33.37	34.20	35.03	35.87

Description: This table shows the yield to maturity of a bond purchased at the price shown in the index.

Example: The yield to maturity of a 10.75 %, 27 year bond at a price of 111.00 is 9.60 %.

PRICE	COUPON RATE, %															
	7.00%	7.25%	7.50%	7.75%	8.00%	8.25%	8.50%	8.75%	9.00%	9.25%	9.50%	9.75%	10.00%	10.25%	10.50%	10.75%
175	2.95	3.11	3.28	3.45	3.62	3.78	3.95	4.12	4.28	4.44	4.61	4.77	4.94	5.10	5.26	5.42
170	3.13	3.30	3.48	3.65	3.82	3.99	4.16	4.32	4.49	4.66	4.83	4.99	5.16	5.33	5.49	5.66
165	3.33	3.50	3.68	3.85	4.02	4.20	4.37	4.54	4.71	4.88	5.05	5.22	5.39	5.56	5.73	5.90
160	3.53	3.71	3.89	4.06	4.24	4.42	4.59	4.77	4.94	5.12	5.29	5.47	5.64	5.81	5.98	6.16
155	3.74	3.92	4.10	4.29	4.47	4.65	4.83	5.01	5.19	5.36	5.54	5.72	5.90	6.07	6.25	6.43
150	3.96	4.15	4.33	4.52	4.70	4.89	5.07	5.26	5.44	5.62	5.80	5.99	6.17	6.35	6.53	6.71
145	4.19	4.38	4.57	4.76	4.95	5.14	5.33	5.52	5.71	5.89	6.08	6.27	6.45	6.64	6.82	7.01
140	4.44	4.63	4.83	5.02	5.22	5.41	5.60	5.79	5.99	6.18	6.37	6.56	6.75	6.94	7.13	7.32
135	4.69	4.89	5.09	5.29	5.49	5.69	5.89	6.09	6.28	6.48	6.68	6.87	7.07	7.27	7.46	7.66
130	4.96	5.17	5.38	5.58	5.78	5.99	6.19	6.40	6.60	6.80	7.00	7.21	7.41	7.61	7.81	8.01
125	5.25	5.46	5.67	5.88	6.09	6.30	6.51	6.72	6.93	7.14	7.35	7.56	7.77	7.98	8.18	8.39
120	5.56	5.77	5.99	6.21	6.42	6.64	6.86	7.07	7.29	7.51	7.72	7.94	8.15	8.37	8.58	8.79
119	5.62	5.84	6.06	6.27	6.49	6.71	6.93	7.15	7.36	7.58	7.80	8.01	8.23	8.45	8.66	8.88
118	5.68	5.90	6.12	6.34	6.56	6.78	7.00	7.22	7.44	7.66	7.88	8.09	8.31	8.53	8.75	8.96
117	5.75	5.97	6.19	6.41	6.63	6.85	7.07	7.29	7.51	7.73	7.95	8.17	8.39	8.61	8.83	9.05
116	5.81	6.04	6.26	6.48	6.70	6.93	7.15	7.37	7.59	7.81	8.03	8.26	8.48	8.70	8.92	9.14
115	5.88	6.10	6.33	6.55	6.78	7.00	7.22	7.45	7.67	7.89	8.12	8.34	8.56	8.78	9.01	9.23
114	5.95	6.17	6.40	6.62	6.85	7.08	7.30	7.52	7.75	7.97	8.20	8.42	8.65	8.87	9.09	9.32
113	6.01	6.24	6.47	6.70	6.92	7.15	7.38	7.60	7.83	8.06	8.28	8.51	8.73	8.96	9.18	9.41
112	6.08	6.31	6.54	6.77	7.00	7.23	7.46	7.68	7.91	8.14	8.37	8.59	8.82	9.05	9.28	9.50
111	6.15	6.38	6.62	6.85	7.08	7.31	7.54	7.77	7.99	8.22	8.45	8.68	8.91	9.14	9.37	9.60
110	6.23	6.46	6.69	6.92	7.15	7.38	7.62	7.85	8.08	8.31	8.54	8.77	9.00	9.23	9.46	9.69
109	6.30	6.53	6.76	7.00	7.23	7.47	7.70	7.93	8.16	8.40	8.63	8.86	9.09	9.33	9.56	9.79
108	6.37	6.61	6.84	7.08	7.31	7.55	7.78	8.02	8.25	8.49	8.72	8.95	9.19	9.42	9.66	9.89
107	6.44	6.68	6.92	7.16	7.39	7.63	7.87	8.10	8.34	8.58	8.81	9.05	9.28	9.52	9.76	9.99
106	6.52	6.76	7.00	7.24	7.47	7.71	7.95	8.19	8.43	8.67	8.90	9.14	9.38	9.62	9.86	10.09
105	6.60	6.84	7.08	7.32	7.56	7.80	8.04	8.28	8.52	8.76	9.00	9.24	9.48	9.72	9.96	10.20
104	6.67	6.92	7.16	7.40	7.64	7.88	8.13	8.37	8.61	8.85	9.09	9.34	9.58	9.82	10.06	10.30
103	6.75	7.00	7.24	7.48	7.73	7.97	8.22	8.46	8.70	8.95	9.19	9.44	9.68	9.92	10.17	10.41
102	6.83	7.08	7.32	7.57	7.82	8.06	8.31	8.55	8.80	9.05	9.29	9.54	9.78	10.03	10.27	10.52
101	6.91	7.16	7.41	7.66	7.90	8.15	8.40	8.65	8.90	9.14	9.39	9.64	9.89	10.14	10.38	10.63
100	7.00	7.25	7.50	7.75	8.00	8.25	8.50	8.75	9.00	9.25	9.50	9.75	10.00	10.25	10.50	10.75
99	7.08	7.33	7.58	7.83	8.09	8.34	8.59	8.84	9.10	9.35	9.60	9.85	10.10	10.36	10.61	10.86
98	7.16	7.42	7.67	7.93	8.18	8.43	8.69	8.94	9.20	9.45	9.71	9.96	10.21	10.47	10.72	10.98
97	7.25	7.51	7.76	8.02	8.27	8.53	8.79	9.04	9.30	9.56	9.81	10.07	10.33	10.58	10.84	11.10
96	7.34	7.60	7.85	8.11	8.37	8.63	8.89	9.15	9.41	9.66	9.92	10.18	10.44	10.70	10.96	11.22
95	7.43	7.69	7.95	8.21	8.47	8.73	8.99	9.25	9.51	9.77	10.04	10.30	10.56	10.82	11.08	11.34
94	7.52	7.78	8.04	8.31	8.57	8.83	9.10	9.36	9.62	9.89	10.15	10.41	10.68	10.94	11.20	11.47
93	7.61	7.87	8.14	8.41	8.67	8.94	9.20	9.47	9.73	10.00	10.27	10.53	10.80	11.06	11.33	11.60
92	7.70	7.97	8.24	8.51	8.77	9.04	9.31	9.58	9.85	10.12	10.38	10.65	10.92	11.19	11.46	11.73
91	7.80	8.07	8.34	8.61	8.88	9.15	9.42	9.69	9.96	10.23	10.50	10.78	11.05	11.32	11.59	11.86
90	7.90	8.17	8.44	8.71	8.99	9.26	9.53	9.81	10.08	10.35	10.63	10.90	11.18	11.45	11.72	12.00
89	8.00	8.27	8.55	8.82	9.10	9.37	9.65	9.92	10.20	10.48	10.75	11.03	11.31	11.58	11.86	12.14
88	8.10	8.37	8.65	8.93	9.21	9.49	9.76	10.04	10.32	10.60	10.88	11.16	11.44	11.72	12.00	12.28
87	8.20	8.48	8.76	9.04	9.32	9.60	9.88	10.16	10.45	10.73	11.01	11.29	11.58	11.86	12.14	12.43
86	8.30	8.59	8.87	9.15	9.44	9.72	10.00	10.29	10.57	10.86	11.14	11.43	11.72	12.00	12.29	12.57
85	8.41	8.70	8.98	9.27	9.55	9.84	10.13	10.42	10.70	10.99	11.28	11.57	11.86	12.15	12.44	12.73
84	8.52	8.81	9.10	9.39	9.67	9.96	10.25	10.55	10.84	11.13	11.42	11.71	12.00	12.29	12.59	12.88
83	8.63	8.92	9.21	9.50	9.80	10.09	10.38	10.68	10.97	11.27	11.56	11.86	12.15	12.45	12.74	13.04
82	8.74	9.04	9.33	9.63	9.92	10.22	10.52	10.81	11.11	11.41	11.71	12.00	12.30	12.60	12.90	13.20
81	8.86	9.16	9.45	9.75	10.05	10.35	10.65	10.95	11.25	11.55	11.85	12.15	12.46	12.76	13.06	13.36
80	8.98	9.28	9.58	9.88	10.18	10.48	10.79	11.09	11.40	11.70	12.00	12.31	12.62	12.92	13.23	13.53
79	9.10	9.40	9.70	10.01	10.32	10.62	10.93	11.24	11.54	11.85	12.16	12.47	12.78	13.09	13.40	13.71
78	9.22	9.53	9.83	10.14	10.45	10.76	11.07	11.38	11.69	12.01	12.32	12.63	12.94	13.26	13.57	13.88
77	9.34	9.66	9.97	10.28	10.59	10.91	11.22	11.53	11.85	12.16	12.48	12.80	13.11	13.43	13.75	14.07
76	9.47	9.79	10.10	10.42	10.74	11.05	11.37	11.69	12.01	12.33	12.65	12.97	13.29	13.61	13.93	14.25
75	9.60	9.92	10.24	10.56	10.88	11.20	11.52	11.85	12.17	12.49	12.82	13.14	13.47	13.79	14.12	14.44
74	9.74	10.06	10.38	10.71	11.03	11.36	11.68	12.01	12.34	12.66	12.99	13.32	13.65	13.98	14.31	14.64
73	9.88	10.20	10.53	10.86	11.18	11.51	11.84	12.17	12.51	12.84	13.17	13.50	13.84	14.17	14.50	14.84
70	10.31	10.65	10.99	11.33	11.67	12.01	12.35	12.70	13.04	13.39	13.73	14.08	14.43	14.78	15.12	15.47
65	11.11	11.47	11.83	12.20	12.56	12.93	13.30	13.67	14.04	14.41	14.78	15.16	15.53	15.90	16.28	16.65
60	12.02	12.41	12.80	13.20	13.60	13.99	14.39	14.79	15.19	15.60	16.00	16.40	16.81	17.21	17.62	18.03
55	13.08	13.51	13.94	14.37	14.80	15.24	15.67	16.11	16.55	16.99	17.43	17.87	18.31	18.75	19.20	19.64
50	14.34	14.81	15.29	15.76	16.24	16.72	17.20	17.68	18.16	18.65	19.13	19.62	20.11	20.60	21.09	21.58
45	15.87	16.39	16.92	17.45	17.98	18.52	19.06	19.59	20.13	20.68	21.22	21.76	22.31	22.85	23.40	23.95
40	17.77	18.36	18.96	19.56	20.16	20.77	21.38	21.99	22.60	23.21	23.83	24.44	25.06	25.68	26.30	26.91
35	20.20	20.89	21.58	22.28	22.97	23.67	24.37	25.07	25.78	26.48	27.19	27.90	28.61	29.31	30.02	30.73
30	23.47	24.28	25.09	25.91	26.73	27.56	28.38	29.21	30.03	30.86	31.69	32.52	33.35	34.18	35.01	35.84

Description: This table shows the price to pay for a bond at the yield rate. The yield is to maturity.

Example: The price of a 15.00 %, 27 year bond to yield 8 % to maturity is $ 176.98.

COUPON RATE, %

YIELD	11.00%	11.25%	11.50%	11.75%	12.00%	12.25%	12.50%	12.75%	13.00%	13.25%	13.50%	13.75%	14.00%	14.25%	14.50%	15.00%
0.00	397.00	403.75	410.50	417.25	424.00	430.75	437.50	444.25	451.00	457.75	464.50	471.25	478.00	484.75	491.50	505.00
1.00	336.11	342.01	347.91	353.81	359.72	365.62	371.52	377.43	383.33	389.23	395.13	401.04	406.94	412.84	418.74	430.55
2.00	287.06	292.26	297.45	302.65	307.84	313.04	318.24	323.43	328.63	333.82	339.02	344.22	349.41	354.61	359.80	370.20
3.00	247.32	251.93	256.53	261.13	265.74	270.34	274.95	279.55	284.15	288.76	293.36	297.96	302.57	307.17	311.78	320.98
4.00	214.93	219.04	223.14	227.25	231.35	235.46	239.56	243.67	247.77	251.88	255.98	260.09	264.19	268.30	272.40	280.61
4.25	207.80	211.79	215.78	219.78	223.77	227.76	231.75	235.74	239.74	243.73	247.72	251.72	255.71	259.70	263.69	271.68
4.50	201.01	204.89	208.77	212.66	216.54	220.43	224.31	228.20	232.08	235.97	239.85	243.74	247.62	251.51	255.39	263.16
4.75	194.54	198.32	202.10	205.88	209.66	213.44	217.22	221.01	224.79	228.57	232.35	236.13	239.91	243.69	247.47	255.04
5.00	188.37	192.05	195.73	199.42	203.10	206.78	210.46	214.15	217.83	221.51	225.19	228.87	232.56	236.24	239.92	247.28
5.25	182.49	186.08	189.67	193.25	196.84	200.43	204.01	207.60	211.19	214.77	218.36	221.95	225.53	229.12	232.71	239.88
5.50	176.89	180.39	183.88	187.38	190.87	194.37	197.86	201.36	204.85	208.35	211.84	215.34	218.83	222.33	225.82	232.81
5.75	171.55	174.95	178.36	181.77	185.17	188.58	191.99	195.39	198.80	202.21	205.61	209.02	212.43	215.84	219.24	226.06
6.00	166.44	169.77	173.09	176.41	179.73	183.06	186.38	189.70	193.02	196.34	199.67	202.99	206.31	209.63	212.96	219.60
6.25	161.57	164.81	168.05	171.30	174.54	177.78	181.02	184.26	187.50	190.74	193.98	197.22	200.46	203.70	206.94	213.42
6.50	156.92	160.08	163.25	166.41	169.57	172.73	175.90	179.06	182.22	185.38	188.54	191.71	194.87	198.03	201.19	207.52
6.75	152.48	155.56	158.65	161.74	164.82	167.91	171.00	174.08	177.17	180.26	183.34	186.43	189.52	192.60	195.69	201.87
7.00	148.23	151.24	154.25	157.27	160.28	163.30	166.31	169.33	172.34	175.35	178.37	181.38	184.40	187.41	190.42	196.45
7.25	144.16	147.11	150.05	153.00	155.94	158.88	161.83	164.77	167.72	170.66	173.60	176.55	179.49	182.44	185.38	191.27
7.50	140.27	143.15	146.03	148.90	151.78	154.66	157.53	160.41	163.29	166.17	169.04	171.92	174.80	177.67	180.55	186.30
7.75	136.55	139.36	142.18	144.99	147.80	150.61	153.42	156.24	159.05	161.86	164.67	167.48	170.29	173.11	175.92	181.54
8.00	132.99	135.74	138.49	141.24	143.99	146.74	149.48	152.23	154.98	157.73	160.48	163.23	165.98	168.73	171.48	176.98
8.25	129.58	132.26	134.95	137.64	140.33	143.02	145.71	148.40	151.09	153.77	156.46	159.15	161.84	164.53	167.22	172.60
8.50	126.30	128.93	131.57	134.20	136.83	139.46	142.09	144.72	147.35	149.98	152.61	155.24	157.87	160.50	163.13	168.39
8.75	123.17	125.74	128.32	130.89	133.46	136.04	138.61	141.19	143.76	146.34	148.91	151.48	154.06	156.63	159.21	164.35
9.00	120.16	122.68	125.20	127.72	130.24	132.76	135.28	137.80	140.32	142.84	145.36	147.88	150.40	152.92	155.44	160.48
9.25	117.27	119.74	122.21	124.67	127.14	129.61	132.08	134.54	137.01	139.48	141.95	144.41	146.88	149.35	151.82	156.75
9.50	114.50	116.92	119.33	121.75	124.17	126.59	129.00	131.42	133.84	136.25	138.67	141.09	143.50	145.92	148.34	153.17
9.75	111.84	114.21	116.58	118.94	121.31	123.68	126.05	128.42	130.78	133.15	135.52	137.89	140.25	142.62	144.99	149.73
10.00	109.28	111.60	113.92	116.24	118.57	120.89	123.21	125.53	127.85	130.17	132.49	134.81	137.13	139.45	141.77	146.41
10.25	106.82	109.10	111.37	113.65	115.92	118.20	120.47	122.75	125.02	127.30	129.57	131.85	134.12	136.40	138.67	143.22
10.50	104.46	106.69	108.92	111.15	113.38	115.62	117.85	120.08	122.31	124.54	126.77	129.00	131.23	133.46	135.69	140.15
10.75	102.19	104.38	106.56	108.75	110.94	113.13	115.32	117.50	119.69	121.88	124.07	126.26	128.44	130.63	132.82	137.20
11.00	100.00	102.15	104.29	106.44	108.59	110.73	112.88	115.03	117.17	119.32	121.47	123.61	125.76	127.91	130.05	134.35
11.25	97.89	100.00	102.11	104.21	106.32	108.43	110.53	112.64	114.75	116.85	118.96	121.07	123.17	125.28	127.38	131.60
11.50	95.86	97.93	100.00	102.07	104.14	106.20	108.27	110.34	112.41	114.47	116.54	118.61	120.68	122.74	124.81	128.95
11.75	93.91	95.94	97.97	100.00	102.03	104.06	106.09	108.12	110.15	112.18	114.21	116.24	118.27	120.30	122.33	126.39
12.00	92.03	94.02	96.01	98.01	100.00	101.99	103.99	105.98	107.97	109.97	111.96	113.96	115.95	117.94	119.94	123.92
12.25	90.21	92.17	94.12	96.08	98.04	100.00	101.96	103.92	105.88	107.83	109.79	111.75	113.71	115.67	117.63	121.54
12.50	88.45	90.38	92.30	94.23	96.15	98.08	100.00	101.92	103.85	105.77	107.70	109.62	111.55	113.47	115.39	119.24
12.75	86.76	88.65	90.54	92.44	94.33	96.22	98.11	100.00	101.89	103.78	105.67	107.56	109.46	111.35	113.24	117.02
13.00	85.13	86.99	88.85	90.71	92.56	94.42	96.28	98.14	100.00	101.86	103.72	105.58	107.44	109.29	111.15	114.87
13.25	83.55	85.38	87.21	89.03	90.86	92.69	94.52	96.34	98.17	100.00	101.83	103.66	105.48	107.31	109.14	112.79
13.50	82.03	83.82	85.62	87.42	89.22	91.01	92.81	94.61	96.41	98.20	100.00	101.80	103.59	105.39	107.19	110.78
13.75	80.55	82.32	84.09	85.86	87.62	89.39	91.16	92.93	94.70	96.46	98.23	100.00	101.77	103.54	105.30	108.84
14.00	79.13	80.87	82.61	84.34	86.08	87.82	89.56	91.30	93.04	94.78	96.52	98.26	100.00	101.74	103.48	106.96
14.25	77.75	79.46	81.17	82.88	84.59	86.31	88.02	89.73	91.44	93.15	94.86	96.58	98.29	100.00	101.71	105.14
14.50	76.41	78.10	79.78	81.47	83.15	84.84	86.52	88.21	89.89	91.58	93.26	94.95	96.63	98.32	100.00	103.37
14.75	75.12	76.78	78.44	80.10	81.76	83.41	85.07	86.73	88.39	90.05	91.71	93.37	95.02	96.68	98.34	101.66
15.00	73.87	75.50	77.14	78.77	80.40	82.04	83.67	85.30	86.94	88.57	90.20	91.83	93.47	95.10	96.73	100.00
15.25	72.66	74.27	75.87	77.48	79.09	80.70	82.31	83.92	85.52	87.13	88.74	90.35	91.96	93.57	95.17	98.39
15.50	71.48	73.07	74.65	76.24	77.82	79.40	80.99	82.57	84.16	85.74	87.33	88.91	90.49	92.08	93.66	96.83
15.75	70.34	71.91	73.47	75.03	76.59	78.15	79.71	81.27	82.83	84.39	85.95	87.51	89.07	90.64	92.20	95.32
16.00	69.24	70.78	72.32	73.85	75.39	76.93	78.47	80.01	81.54	83.08	84.62	86.16	87.70	89.23	90.77	93.85
16.25	68.17	69.68	71.20	72.72	74.23	75.75	77.26	78.78	80.29	81.81	83.33	84.84	86.36	87.87	89.39	92.42
16.50	67.13	68.62	70.12	71.61	73.10	74.60	76.09	77.59	79.08	80.58	82.07	83.56	85.06	86.55	88.05	91.03
16.75	66.12	67.59	69.06	70.54	72.01	73.48	74.96	76.43	77.90	79.38	80.85	82.32	83.80	85.27	86.74	89.69
17.00	65.14	66.59	68.04	69.49	70.95	72.40	73.85	75.31	76.76	78.21	79.66	81.12	82.57	84.02	85.47	88.38
17.25	64.18	65.62	67.05	68.48	69.91	71.35	72.78	74.21	75.65	77.08	78.51	79.94	81.38	82.81	84.24	87.11
17.50	63.26	64.67	66.08	67.50	68.91	70.32	71.74	73.15	74.56	75.98	77.39	78.80	80.22	81.63	83.04	85.87
17.75	62.36	63.75	65.15	66.54	67.93	69.33	70.72	72.12	73.51	74.90	76.30	77.69	79.09	80.48	81.88	84.66
18.00	61.48	62.86	64.23	65.61	66.98	68.36	69.74	71.11	72.49	73.86	75.24	76.61	77.99	79.37	80.74	83.49
18.25	60.63	61.99	63.34	64.70	66.06	67.42	68.78	70.13	71.49	72.85	74.21	75.56	76.92	78.28	79.64	82.35
18.50	59.80	61.14	62.48	63.82	65.16	66.50	67.84	69.18	70.52	71.86	73.20	74.54	75.88	77.22	78.56	81.24
18.75	58.99	60.32	61.64	62.96	64.28	65.61	66.93	68.25	69.58	70.90	72.22	73.54	74.87	76.19	77.51	80.16
19.00	58.21	59.51	60.82	62.13	63.43	64.74	66.04	67.35	68.66	69.96	71.27	72.57	73.88	75.19	76.49	79.10
20.00	55.26	56.50	57.75	58.99	60.23	61.48	62.72	63.96	65.20	66.45	67.69	68.93	70.17	71.42	72.66	75.15
25.00	44.10	45.10	46.09	47.09	48.09	49.09	50.09	51.08	52.08	53.08	54.08	55.08	56.08	57.07	58.07	60.07
30.00	36.70	37.53	38.37	39.20	40.03	40.86	41.70	42.53	43.36	44.20	45.03	45.86	46.69	47.53	48.36	50.03

Description: This table shows the yield to maturity of a bond purchased at the price shown in the index.

Example: The yield to maturity of a 15.00 %, 27 year bond at a price of 125.00 is 11.88 %.

COUPON RATE, %

PRICE	11.00%	11.25%	11.50%	11.75%	12.00%	12.25%	12.50%	12.75%	13.00%	13.25%	13.50%	13.75%	14.00%	14.25%	14.50%	15.00%
250	2.92	3.05	3.18	3.30	3.43	3.55	3.68	3.80	3.93	4.05	4.17	4.30	4.42	4.54	4.66	4.91
240	3.20	3.33	3.47	3.59	3.72	3.85	3.98	4.11	4.24	4.36	4.49	4.62	4.74	4.87	4.99	5.24
230	3.50	3.64	3.77	3.91	4.04	4.17	4.30	4.43	4.57	4.70	4.83	4.96	5.08	5.21	5.34	5.60
220	3.82	3.96	4.10	4.24	4.37	4.51	4.65	4.78	4.92	5.05	5.18	5.32	5.45	5.58	5.72	5.98
210	4.17	4.31	4.45	4.59	4.73	4.87	5.01	5.15	5.29	5.43	5.57	5.71	5.84	5.98	6.12	6.39
200	4.53	4.68	4.83	4.97	5.12	5.26	5.41	5.55	5.69	5.84	5.98	6.12	6.27	6.41	6.55	6.83
195	4.73	4.88	5.02	5.17	5.32	5.47	5.62	5.76	5.91	6.05	6.20	6.34	6.49	6.63	6.78	7.06
190	4.93	5.08	5.23	5.38	5.53	5.68	5.83	5.98	6.13	6.28	6.43	6.57	6.72	6.87	7.02	7.31
185	5.14	5.29	5.45	5.60	5.75	5.91	6.06	6.21	6.36	6.51	6.66	6.81	6.96	7.11	7.26	7.56
180	5.35	5.51	5.67	5.83	5.98	6.14	6.29	6.45	6.60	6.76	6.91	7.07	7.22	7.37	7.52	7.83
175	5.58	5.74	5.90	6.06	6.22	6.38	6.54	6.70	6.86	7.01	7.17	7.33	7.48	7.64	7.80	8.11
170	5.82	5.98	6.15	6.31	6.47	6.64	6.80	6.96	7.12	7.28	7.44	7.60	7.76	7.92	8.08	8.40
165	6.07	6.24	6.40	6.57	6.74	6.90	7.07	7.23	7.40	7.56	7.73	7.89	8.05	8.22	8.38	8.70
160	6.33	6.50	6.67	6.84	7.01	7.18	7.35	7.52	7.69	7.86	8.02	8.19	8.36	8.53	8.69	9.03
155	6.60	6.78	6.95	7.13	7.30	7.47	7.65	7.82	7.99	8.17	8.34	8.51	8.68	8.85	9.02	9.37
150	6.89	7.07	7.25	7.43	7.61	7.78	7.96	8.14	8.32	8.49	8.67	8.85	9.02	9.20	9.37	9.72
145	7.19	7.38	7.56	7.74	7.93	8.11	8.29	8.48	8.66	8.84	9.02	9.20	9.38	9.56	9.74	10.10
140	7.51	7.70	7.89	8.08	8.27	8.46	8.64	8.83	9.02	9.21	9.39	9.58	9.77	9.95	10.14	10.51
135	7.85	8.05	8.24	8.44	8.63	8.82	9.02	9.21	9.40	9.59	9.79	9.98	10.17	10.36	10.55	10.94
130	8.21	8.41	8.61	8.81	9.01	9.21	9.41	9.61	9.81	10.01	10.21	10.41	10.60	10.80	11.00	11.39
125	8.60	8.80	9.01	9.22	9.42	9.63	9.84	10.04	10.25	10.45	10.66	10.86	11.07	11.27	11.48	11.88
120	9.01	9.22	9.44	9.65	9.86	10.08	10.29	10.50	10.72	10.93	11.14	11.35	11.56	11.78	11.99	12.41
115	9.45	9.67	9.89	10.11	10.33	10.56	10.78	11.00	11.22	11.44	11.66	11.88	12.10	12.32	12.54	12.98
113	9.63	9.86	10.08	10.31	10.53	10.76	10.98	11.21	11.43	11.65	11.88	12.10	12.33	12.55	12.77	13.22
112	9.73	9.96	10.18	10.41	10.64	10.86	11.09	11.31	11.54	11.77	11.99	12.22	12.44	12.67	12.89	13.34
111	9.83	10.05	10.28	10.51	10.74	10.97	11.19	11.42	11.65	11.88	12.10	12.33	12.56	12.79	13.01	13.47
110	9.92	10.15	10.38	10.61	10.84	11.07	11.30	11.53	11.76	11.99	12.22	12.45	12.68	12.91	13.14	13.59
109	10.02	10.26	10.49	10.72	10.95	11.18	11.41	11.64	11.88	12.11	12.34	12.57	12.80	13.03	13.26	13.72
108	10.12	10.36	10.59	10.83	11.06	11.29	11.53	11.76	11.99	12.23	12.46	12.69	12.92	13.16	13.39	13.86
107	10.23	10.46	10.70	10.93	11.17	11.40	11.64	11.87	12.11	12.35	12.58	12.82	13.05	13.28	13.52	13.99
106	10.33	10.57	10.81	11.04	11.28	11.52	11.76	11.99	12.23	12.47	12.70	12.94	13.18	13.41	13.65	14.13
105	10.44	10.68	10.92	11.16	11.39	11.63	11.87	12.11	12.35	12.59	12.83	13.07	13.31	13.55	13.79	14.26
104	10.54	10.79	11.03	11.27	11.51	11.75	11.99	12.23	12.48	12.72	12.96	13.20	13.44	13.68	13.92	14.40
103	10.65	10.90	11.14	11.39	11.63	11.87	12.12	12.36	12.60	12.85	13.09	13.33	13.58	13.82	14.06	14.55
102	10.77	11.01	11.26	11.50	11.75	11.99	12.24	12.49	12.73	12.98	13.22	13.47	13.71	13.96	14.20	14.69
101	10.88	11.13	11.38	11.62	11.87	12.12	12.37	12.61	12.86	13.11	13.36	13.60	13.85	14.10	14.35	14.84
100	11.00	11.25	11.50	11.75	12.00	12.25	12.50	12.75	13.00	13.25	13.50	13.75	14.00	14.25	14.50	15.00
99	11.11	11.36	11.62	11.87	12.12	12.37	12.63	12.88	13.13	13.38	13.64	13.89	14.14	14.39	14.64	15.15
98	11.23	11.49	11.74	12.00	12.25	12.51	12.76	13.01	13.27	13.52	13.78	14.03	14.29	14.54	14.80	15.31
97	11.35	11.61	11.87	12.12	12.38	12.64	12.90	13.15	13.41	13.67	13.92	14.18	14.44	14.70	14.95	15.47
96	11.48	11.74	12.00	12.26	12.52	12.77	13.03	13.29	13.55	13.81	14.07	14.33	14.59	14.85	15.11	15.63
95	11.60	11.87	12.13	12.39	12.65	12.91	13.18	13.44	13.70	13.96	14.22	14.49	14.75	15.01	15.27	15.80
94	11.73	12.00	12.26	12.53	12.79	13.06	13.32	13.58	13.85	14.11	14.38	14.64	14.91	15.17	15.44	15.97
93	11.86	12.13	12.40	12.67	12.93	13.20	13.47	13.73	14.00	14.27	14.54	14.80	15.07	15.34	15.61	16.14
92	12.00	12.27	12.54	12.81	13.08	13.35	13.62	13.89	14.16	14.43	14.70	14.97	15.24	15.51	15.78	16.32
91	12.13	12.41	12.68	12.95	13.22	13.50	13.77	14.04	14.32	14.59	14.86	15.13	15.41	15.68	15.95	16.50
90	12.27	12.55	12.82	13.10	13.37	13.65	13.93	14.20	14.48	14.75	15.03	15.31	15.58	15.86	16.13	16.69
89	12.42	12.69	12.97	13.25	13.53	13.81	14.09	14.36	14.64	14.92	15.20	15.48	15.76	16.04	16.32	16.88
88	12.56	12.84	13.12	13.40	13.69	13.97	14.25	14.53	14.81	15.09	15.38	15.66	15.94	16.22	16.50	17.07
87	12.71	12.99	13.28	13.56	13.85	14.13	14.41	14.70	14.98	15.27	15.55	15.84	16.12	16.41	16.69	17.27
86	12.86	13.15	13.43	13.72	14.01	14.30	14.58	14.87	15.16	15.45	15.74	16.02	16.31	16.60	16.89	17.47
85	13.02	13.31	13.60	13.89	14.18	14.47	14.76	15.05	15.34	15.63	15.92	16.21	16.51	16.80	17.09	17.67
84	13.17	13.47	13.76	14.05	14.35	14.64	14.94	15.23	15.52	15.82	16.11	16.41	16.70	17.00	17.29	17.89
83	13.33	13.63	13.93	14.22	14.52	14.82	15.12	15.41	15.71	16.01	16.31	16.61	16.91	17.21	17.50	18.10
82	13.50	13.80	14.10	14.40	14.70	15.00	15.30	15.60	15.91	16.21	16.51	16.71	17.02	17.42	17.72	18.32
81	13.67	13.97	14.28	14.58	14.88	15.19	15.49	15.80	16.10	16.41	16.71	17.02	17.33	17.63	17.94	18.55
80	13.84	14.15	14.46	14.76	15.07	15.38	15.69	16.00	16.31	16.61	16.92	17.23	17.54	17.85	18.16	18.78
79	14.02	14.33	14.64	14.95	15.26	15.57	15.89	16.20	16.51	16.82	17.14	17.45	17.76	18.08	18.39	19.02
78	14.20	14.51	14.83	15.14	15.46	15.78	16.09	16.41	16.72	17.04	17.36	17.68	17.99	18.31	18.63	19.26
77	14.38	14.70	15.02	15.34	15.66	15.98	16.30	16.62	16.94	17.26	17.58	17.90	18.23	18.55	18.87	19.51
76	14.57	14.90	15.22	15.54	15.87	16.19	16.52	16.84	17.16	17.49	17.81	18.14	18.47	18.79	19.12	19.77
75	14.77	15.10	15.42	15.75	16.08	16.41	16.74	17.06	17.39	17.72	18.05	18.38	18.71	19.04	19.37	20.03
74	14.97	15.30	15.63	15.96	16.30	16.63	16.96	17.29	17.63	17.96	18.30	18.63	18.96	19.30	19.63	20.30
73	15.17	15.51	15.85	16.18	16.52	16.86	17.19	17.53	17.87	18.21	18.55	18.88	19.22	19.56	19.90	20.58
70	15.82	16.17	16.52	16.87	17.22	17.58	17.93	18.28	18.63	18.98	19.34	19.69	20.04	20.40	20.75	21.46
65	17.03	17.41	17.78	18.16	18.54	18.92	19.30	19.68	20.06	20.44	20.82	21.20	21.58	21.96	22.34	23.11
60	18.43	18.84	19.25	19.66	20.07	20.48	20.89	21.31	21.72	22.13	22.54	22.96	23.37	23.78	24.20	25.02
55	20.09	20.54	20.98	21.43	21.88	22.33	22.78	23.23	23.68	24.13	24.58	25.03	25.48	25.93	26.39	27.29

Description: This table shows the price to pay for a bond at the yield rate. The yield is to maturity.

Example: The price of a 6.75 %, 28 year bond to yield 8 % to maturity is $ 86.11.

COUPON RATE, %

YIELD	0.00%	1.00%	2.00%	3.00%	4.00%	4.25%	4.50%	4.75%	5.00%	5.25%	5.50%	5.75%	6.00%	6.25%	6.50%	6.75%
0.00	100.00	128.00	156.00	184.00	212.00	219.00	226.00	233.00	240.00	247.00	254.00	261.00	268.00	275.00	282.00	289.00
1.00	75.63	100.00	124.37	148.74	173.11	179.20	185.29	191.38	197.48	203.57	209.66	215.75	221.84	227.94	234.03	240.12
2.00	57.28	78.64	100.00	121.36	142.72	148.06	153.40	158.74	164.08	169.42	174.76	180.10	185.44	190.78	196.12	201.46
3.00	43.44	62.29	81.15	100.00	118.85	123.57	128.28	132.99	137.71	142.42	147.13	151.85	156.56	161.27	165.99	170.70
4.00	32.99	49.74	66.50	83.25	100.00	104.19	108.38	112.56	116.75	120.94	125.13	129.32	133.50	137.69	141.88	146.07
4.25	30.80	47.09	63.37	79.65	95.93	100.00	104.07	108.14	112.21	116.28	120.35	124.42	128.49	132.56	136.63	140.70
4.50	28.76	44.59	60.42	76.25	92.08	96.04	100.00	103.96	107.92	111.87	115.83	119.79	123.75	127.70	131.66	135.62
4.75	26.86	42.26	57.66	73.05	88.45	92.30	96.15	100.00	103.85	107.70	111.55	115.40	119.25	123.10	126.95	130.79
5.00	25.09	40.07	55.05	70.04	85.02	88.76	92.51	96.25	100.00	103.75	107.49	111.24	114.98	118.73	122.47	126.22
5.25	23.43	38.02	52.60	67.19	81.77	85.42	89.06	92.71	96.35	100.00	103.65	107.29	110.94	114.58	118.23	121.88
5.50	21.89	36.09	50.29	64.49	78.70	82.25	85.80	89.35	92.90	96.45	100.00	103.55	107.10	110.65	114.20	117.75
5.75	20.45	34.28	48.12	61.95	75.79	79.25	82.71	86.16	89.62	93.08	96.54	100.00	103.46	106.92	110.38	113.84
6.00	19.10	32.59	46.07	59.55	73.03	76.41	79.78	83.15	86.52	89.89	93.26	96.63	100.00	103.37	106.74	110.11
6.25	17.85	30.99	44.14	57.28	70.43	73.71	77.00	80.28	83.57	86.86	90.14	93.43	96.71	100.00	103.29	106.57
6.50	16.68	29.50	42.32	55.13	67.95	71.16	74.36	77.57	80.77	83.98	87.18	90.39	93.59	96.80	100.00	103.20
6.75	15.59	28.09	40.60	53.10	65.61	68.74	71.86	74.99	78.11	81.24	84.37	87.49	90.62	93.75	96.87	100.00
7.00	14.57	26.77	38.98	51.18	63.39	66.44	69.49	72.54	75.59	78.64	81.69	84.74	87.80	90.85	93.90	96.95
7.25	13.61	25.53	37.44	49.36	61.28	64.25	67.23	70.21	73.19	76.17	79.15	82.13	85.11	88.08	91.06	94.04
7.50	12.73	24.36	36.00	47.64	59.27	62.18	65.09	68.00	70.91	73.82	76.73	79.64	82.55	85.45	88.36	91.27
7.75	11.90	23.26	34.63	46.00	57.37	60.21	63.05	65.90	68.74	71.58	74.42	77.26	80.11	82.95	85.79	88.63
8.00	11.12	22.23	33.34	44.45	55.56	58.34	61.12	63.89	66.67	69.45	72.23	75.00	77.78	80.56	83.34	86.11
8.25	10.40	21.26	32.12	42.98	53.84	56.56	59.27	61.99	64.70	67.42	70.13	72.85	75.56	78.28	80.99	83.71
8.50	9.72	20.34	30.96	41.58	52.21	54.86	57.52	60.17	62.83	65.48	68.14	70.79	73.45	76.10	78.76	81.41
8.75	9.09	19.48	29.87	40.26	50.65	53.25	55.84	58.44	61.04	63.64	66.23	68.83	71.43	74.03	76.62	79.22
9.00	8.50	18.67	28.83	39.00	49.17	51.71	54.25	56.79	59.33	61.88	64.42	66.96	69.50	72.04	74.58	77.13
9.25	7.95	17.90	27.85	37.80	47.76	50.24	52.73	55.22	57.71	60.19	62.68	65.17	67.66	70.15	72.63	75.12
9.50	7.44	17.18	26.92	36.67	46.41	48.85	51.28	53.72	56.15	58.59	61.03	63.46	65.90	68.33	70.77	73.21
9.75	6.96	16.50	26.04	35.59	45.13	47.51	49.90	52.29	54.67	57.06	59.44	61.83	64.21	66.60	68.99	71.37
10.00	6.51	15.86	25.21	34.56	43.90	46.24	48.58	50.92	53.25	55.59	57.93	60.27	62.60	64.94	67.28	69.61
10.25	6.09	15.25	24.41	33.57	42.74	45.03	47.32	49.61	51.90	54.19	56.48	58.77	61.06	63.35	65.64	67.93
10.50	5.70	14.68	23.66	32.64	41.62	43.87	46.11	48.36	50.60	52.85	55.09	57.34	59.58	61.83	64.07	66.32
10.75	5.33	14.14	22.94	31.75	40.56	42.76	44.96	47.16	49.36	51.56	53.77	55.97	58.17	60.37	62.57	64.77
11.00	4.99	13.62	22.26	30.90	39.54	41.70	43.86	46.02	48.17	50.33	52.49	54.65	56.81	58.97	61.13	63.29
11.25	4.67	13.14	21.62	30.09	38.56	40.68	42.80	44.92	47.04	49.16	51.27	53.39	55.51	57.63	59.75	61.87
11.50	4.37	12.68	21.00	29.32	37.63	39.71	41.79	43.87	45.95	48.03	50.11	52.18	54.26	56.34	58.42	60.50
11.75	4.09	12.25	20.41	28.58	36.74	38.78	40.82	42.86	44.90	46.94	48.98	51.02	53.06	55.11	57.15	59.19
12.00	3.83	11.84	19.86	27.87	35.88	37.89	39.89	41.90	43.90	45.90	47.91	49.91	51.91	53.92	55.92	57.92
12.25	3.58	11.45	19.32	27.20	35.07	37.03	39.00	40.97	42.94	44.90	46.87	48.84	50.81	52.78	54.74	56.71
12.50	3.35	11.09	18.82	26.55	34.28	36.21	38.15	40.08	42.01	43.95	45.88	47.81	49.74	51.68	53.61	55.54
12.75	3.14	10.74	18.33	25.93	33.53	35.43	37.33	39.23	41.12	43.02	44.92	46.82	48.72	50.62	52.52	54.42
13.00	2.94	10.41	17.87	25.34	32.80	34.67	36.54	38.40	40.27	42.14	44.00	45.87	47.74	49.60	51.47	53.34
13.25	2.75	10.09	17.43	24.77	32.11	33.95	35.78	37.62	39.45	41.29	43.12	44.95	46.79	48.62	50.46	52.29
13.50	2.58	9.80	17.01	24.23	31.44	33.25	35.05	36.86	38.66	40.46	42.27	44.07	45.88	47.68	49.49	51.29
13.75	2.42	9.51	16.61	23.71	30.80	32.58	34.35	36.13	37.90	39.67	41.45	43.22	45.00	46.77	48.55	50.32
14.00	2.26	9.24	16.22	23.21	30.19	31.93	33.68	35.42	37.17	38.91	40.66	42.40	44.15	45.90	47.64	49.39
14.25	2.12	8.99	15.86	22.73	29.59	31.31	33.03	34.75	36.46	38.18	39.90	41.61	43.33	45.05	46.77	48.48
14.50	1.98	8.74	15.50	22.26	29.02	30.71	32.40	34.09	35.78	37.47	39.16	40.85	42.54	44.23	45.92	47.61
14.75	1.86	8.51	15.17	21.82	28.47	30.14	31.80	33.46	35.13	36.79	38.45	40.12	41.78	43.44	45.11	46.77
15.00	1.74	8.29	14.84	21.39	27.94	29.58	31.22	32.86	34.49	36.13	37.77	39.41	41.05	42.68	44.32	45.96
15.25	1.63	8.08	14.53	20.98	27.43	29.05	30.66	32.27	33.88	35.50	37.11	38.72	40.33	41.95	43.56	45.17
15.50	1.53	7.88	14.24	20.59	26.94	28.53	30.12	31.71	33.29	34.88	36.47	38.06	39.65	41.24	42.82	44.41
15.75	1.43	7.69	13.95	20.21	26.47	28.03	29.60	31.16	32.72	34.29	35.85	37.42	38.98	40.55	42.11	43.68
16.00	1.34	7.51	13.68	19.84	26.01	27.55	29.09	30.63	32.17	33.72	35.26	36.80	38.34	39.88	41.42	42.96
16.25	1.26	7.34	13.41	19.49	25.56	27.08	28.60	30.12	31.64	33.16	34.68	36.20	37.72	39.24	40.76	42.27
16.50	1.18	7.17	13.16	19.15	25.14	26.63	28.13	29.63	31.13	32.62	34.12	35.62	37.11	38.61	40.11	41.61
16.75	1.11	7.01	12.91	18.82	24.72	26.20	27.67	29.15	30.63	32.10	33.58	35.06	36.53	38.01	39.48	40.96
17.00	1.04	6.86	12.68	18.50	24.32	25.78	27.23	28.69	30.14	31.60	33.05	34.51	35.97	37.42	38.88	40.33
17.25	.97	6.71	12.45	18.19	23.94	25.37	26.81	28.24	29.68	31.11	32.55	33.98	35.42	36.85	38.29	39.72
17.50	.91	6.57	12.24	17.90	23.56	24.98	26.39	27.81	29.22	30.64	32.05	33.47	34.88	36.30	37.72	39.13
17.75	.86	6.44	12.03	17.61	23.20	24.59	25.99	27.39	28.78	30.18	31.58	32.97	34.37	35.77	37.16	38.56
18.00	.80	6.31	11.82	17.33	22.85	24.22	25.60	26.98	28.36	29.73	31.11	32.49	33.87	35.25	36.62	38.00
18.25	.75	6.19	11.63	17.07	22.51	23.86	25.22	26.58	27.94	29.30	30.66	32.02	33.38	34.74	36.10	37.46
18.50	.71	6.07	11.44	16.81	22.17	23.52	24.86	26.20	27.54	28.88	30.23	31.57	32.91	34.25	35.59	36.93
18.75	.66	5.96	11.26	16.56	21.85	23.18	24.50	25.83	27.15	28.48	29.80	31.13	32.45	33.77	35.10	36.42
19.00	.62	5.85	11.08	16.31	21.54	22.85	24.16	25.47	26.77	28.08	29.39	30.70	32.00	33.31	34.62	35.93
20.00	.48	5.46	10.43	15.41	20.38	21.63	22.87	24.12	25.36	26.60	27.85	29.09	30.34	31.58	32.82	34.07
25.00	.14	4.13	8.13	12.12	16.11	17.11	18.11	19.11	20.11	21.11	22.11	23.11	24.10	25.10	26.10	27.10
30.00	.04	3.37	6.70	10.04	13.37	14.20	15.03	15.87	16.70	17.53	18.37	19.20	20.03	20.86	21.70	22.53

Description: This table shows the yield to maturity of a bond purchased at the price shown in the index.

Example: The yield to maturity of a 6.75 %, 28 year bond at a price of 80.00 is 8.65 %.

COUPON RATE, %

PRICE	0.00%	1.00%	2.00%	3.00%	4.00%	4.25%	4.50%	4.75%	5.00%	5.25%	5.50%	5.75%	6.00%	6.25%	6.50%	6.75%
100	0.00	1.00	2.00	3.00	4.00	4.25	4.50	4.75	5.00	5.25	5.50	5.75	6.00	6.25	6.50	6.75
99	.03	1.04	2.04	3.05	4.06	4.31	4.56	4.81	5.06	5.31	5.57	5.82	6.07	6.32	6.57	6.83
98	.07	1.08	2.09	3.10	4.12	4.37	4.62	4.88	5.13	5.38	5.64	5.89	6.15	6.40	6.65	6.91
97	.10	1.12	2.14	3.16	4.18	4.43	4.69	4.94	5.20	5.46	5.71	5.97	6.22	6.48	6.73	6.99
96	.14	1.16	2.19	3.21	4.24	4.50	4.76	5.01	5.27	5.53	5.79	6.04	6.30	6.56	6.82	7.08
95	.18	1.21	2.24	3.27	4.30	4.56	4.82	5.08	5.34	5.60	5.86	6.12	6.38	6.64	6.90	7.16
94	.22	1.25	2.29	3.33	4.37	4.63	4.89	5.15	5.41	5.68	5.94	6.20	6.46	6.72	6.99	7.25
93	.25	1.29	2.34	3.38	4.43	4.70	4.96	5.22	5.49	5.75	6.02	6.28	6.54	6.81	7.07	7.34
92	.29	1.34	2.39	3.44	4.50	4.77	5.03	5.30	5.56	5.83	6.09	6.36	6.63	6.89	7.16	7.43
91	.33	1.38	2.44	3.50	4.57	4.84	5.10	5.37	5.64	5.91	6.17	6.44	6.71	6.98	7.25	7.52
90	.37	1.43	2.49	3.56	4.64	4.91	5.18	5.45	5.72	5.99	6.26	6.53	6.80	7.07	7.34	7.61
89	.41	1.48	2.55	3.62	4.71	4.98	5.25	5.52	5.79	6.07	6.34	6.61	6.89	7.16	7.43	7.71
88	.45	1.52	2.60	3.69	4.78	5.05	5.32	5.60	5.87	6.15	6.42	6.70	6.98	7.25	7.53	7.81
87	.49	1.57	2.66	3.75	4.85	5.12	5.40	5.68	5.96	6.23	6.51	6.79	7.07	7.35	7.63	7.91
86	.53	1.62	2.71	3.81	4.92	5.20	5.48	5.76	6.04	6.32	6.60	6.88	7.16	7.44	7.72	8.01
85	.58	1.67	2.77	3.88	5.00	5.28	5.56	5.84	6.12	6.40	6.69	6.97	7.26	7.54	7.82	8.11
84	.62	1.72	2.83	3.94	5.07	5.36	5.64	5.92	6.21	6.49	6.78	7.06	7.35	7.64	7.93	8.21
83	.66	1.77	2.88	4.01	5.15	5.43	5.72	6.01	6.29	6.58	6.87	7.16	7.45	7.74	8.03	8.32
82	.71	1.82	2.94	4.08	5.23	5.52	5.80	6.09	6.38	6.67	6.97	7.26	7.55	7.84	8.14	8.43
81	.75	1.87	3.00	4.15	5.31	5.60	5.89	6.18	6.47	6.77	7.06	7.36	7.65	7.95	8.24	8.54
80	.79	1.92	3.06	4.22	5.39	5.68	5.98	6.27	6.57	6.86	7.16	7.46	7.76	8.06	8.35	8.65
79	.84	1.98	3.13	4.29	5.47	5.77	6.06	6.36	6.66	6.96	7.26	7.56	7.86	8.16	8.47	8.77
78	.88	2.03	3.19	4.36	5.55	5.85	6.15	6.45	6.76	7.06	7.36	7.67	7.97	8.28	8.58	8.89
77	.93	2.08	3.25	4.44	5.64	5.94	6.24	6.55	6.85	7.16	7.47	7.77	8.08	8.39	8.70	9.01
76	.98	2.14	3.32	4.51	5.73	6.03	6.34	6.65	6.95	7.26	7.57	7.88	8.19	8.51	8.82	9.13
75	1.03	2.20	3.38	4.59	5.82	6.12	6.43	6.74	7.06	7.37	7.68	8.00	8.31	8.63	8.94	9.26
74	1.07	2.25	3.45	4.67	5.91	6.22	6.53	6.84	7.16	7.48	7.79	8.11	8.43	8.75	9.07	9.39
73	1.12	2.31	3.52	4.75	6.00	6.31	6.63	6.95	7.27	7.58	7.91	8.23	8.55	8.87	9.20	9.52
72	1.17	2.37	3.59	4.83	6.09	6.41	6.73	7.05	7.37	7.70	8.02	8.35	8.67	9.00	9.33	9.66
71	1.22	2.43	3.66	4.91	6.19	6.51	6.83	7.16	7.48	7.81	8.14	8.47	8.80	9.13	9.46	9.80
70	1.27	2.49	3.73	5.00	6.29	6.61	6.94	7.27	7.60	7.93	8.26	8.59	8.93	9.26	9.60	9.94
69	1.32	2.55	3.81	5.08	6.39	6.72	7.05	7.38	7.71	8.05	8.39	8.72	9.06	9.40	9.74	10.09
68	1.38	2.62	3.88	5.17	6.49	6.82	7.16	7.49	7.83	8.17	8.51	8.85	9.20	9.54	9.89	10.23
67	1.43	2.68	3.96	5.26	6.60	6.93	7.27	7.61	7.95	8.30	8.64	8.99	9.34	9.69	10.04	10.39
66	1.48	2.74	4.03	5.35	6.70	7.04	7.39	7.73	8.08	8.43	8.78	9.13	9.48	9.83	10.19	10.55
65	1.54	2.81	4.11	5.45	6.81	7.16	7.51	7.86	8.21	8.56	8.91	9.27	9.63	9.99	10.35	10.71
64	1.60	2.88	4.19	5.54	6.92	7.27	7.63	7.98	8.34	8.69	9.05	9.42	9.78	10.14	10.51	10.87
63	1.65	2.95	4.28	5.64	7.04	7.39	7.75	8.11	8.47	8.83	9.20	9.56	9.93	10.30	10.67	11.05
62	1.71	3.02	4.36	5.74	7.16	7.52	7.88	8.24	8.61	8.98	9.35	9.72	10.09	10.47	10.84	11.22
61	1.77	3.09	4.44	5.84	7.28	7.64	8.01	8.38	8.75	9.12	9.50	9.88	10.26	10.64	11.02	11.40
60	1.83	3.16	4.53	5.95	7.40	7.77	8.14	8.52	8.90	9.27	9.66	10.04	10.42	10.81	11.20	11.59
59	1.89	3.23	4.62	6.05	7.53	7.91	8.28	8.66	9.05	9.43	9.82	10.21	10.60	10.99	11.38	11.78
58	1.95	3.31	4.71	6.16	7.66	8.04	8.42	8.81	9.20	9.59	9.98	10.38	10.78	11.18	11.58	11.98
57	2.01	3.39	4.81	6.28	7.79	8.18	8.57	8.96	9.36	9.75	10.15	10.56	10.96	11.37	11.77	12.18
56	2.08	3.46	4.90	6.39	7.93	8.33	8.72	9.12	9.52	9.92	10.33	10.74	11.15	11.56	11.98	12.40
55	2.14	3.54	5.00	6.51	8.08	8.47	8.88	9.28	9.69	10.10	10.51	10.93	11.35	11.77	12.19	12.61
54	2.21	3.63	5.10	6.63	8.22	8.63	9.04	9.45	9.86	10.28	10.70	11.12	11.55	11.98	12.41	12.84
53	2.28	3.71	5.20	6.76	8.37	8.78	9.20	9.62	10.04	10.47	10.89	11.33	11.76	12.20	12.63	13.07
52	2.34	3.79	5.31	6.89	8.53	8.95	9.37	9.80	10.23	10.66	11.09	11.53	11.98	12.42	12.87	13.32
51	2.41	3.88	5.42	7.02	8.69	9.11	9.55	9.98	10.42	10.86	11.30	11.75	12.20	12.65	13.11	13.57
50	2.49	3.97	5.53	7.16	8.85	9.29	9.73	10.17	10.62	11.06	11.52	11.97	12.43	12.90	13.36	13.83
49	2.56	4.06	5.64	7.30	9.02	9.47	9.91	10.37	10.82	11.28	11.74	12.21	12.68	13.15	13.62	14.10
48	2.63	4.16	5.76	7.44	9.20	9.65	10.11	10.57	11.03	11.50	11.97	12.45	12.93	13.41	13.89	14.38
47	2.71	4.25	5.88	7.59	9.38	9.84	10.31	10.78	11.25	11.73	12.21	12.70	13.19	13.68	14.18	14.68
46	2.79	4.35	6.00	7.75	9.57	10.04	10.52	11.00	11.48	11.97	12.46	12.96	13.46	13.96	14.47	14.98
45	2.87	4.45	6.13	7.90	9.77	10.25	10.74	11.23	11.72	12.22	12.72	13.23	13.74	14.26	14.78	15.30
44	2.95	4.56	6.26	8.07	9.98	10.47	10.96	11.46	11.97	12.48	13.00	13.52	14.04	14.57	15.10	15.63
43	3.03	4.66	6.40	8.24	10.19	10.69	11.20	11.71	12.23	12.75	13.28	13.81	14.35	14.89	15.43	15.98
42	3.12	4.77	6.54	8.42	10.41	10.92	11.44	11.97	12.50	13.03	13.58	14.12	14.67	15.23	15.79	16.35
41	3.20	4.89	6.69	8.60	10.64	11.17	11.70	12.24	12.78	13.33	13.89	14.45	15.01	15.58	16.15	16.73
40	3.29	5.00	6.84	8.80	10.88	11.42	11.97	12.52	13.08	13.64	14.21	14.79	15.37	15.95	16.54	17.13
39	3.39	5.12	6.99	9.00	11.13	11.68	12.25	12.81	13.39	13.97	14.55	15.14	15.74	16.34	16.94	17.55
35	3.78	5.64	7.68	9.89	12.27	12.89	13.51	14.15	14.79	15.45	16.11	16.77	17.44	18.12	18.80	19.48
30	4.34	6.41	8.71	11.27	14.07	14.81	15.55	16.31	17.07	17.85	18.63	19.42	20.21	21.01	21.82	22.63
25	5.01	7.36	10.06	13.14	16.58	17.48	18.40	19.33	20.27	21.22	22.18	23.15	24.12	25.10	26.08	27.06
20	5.83	8.59	11.93	15.89	20.35	21.53	22.72	23.92	25.13	26.35	27.57	28.81	30.04	31.28	32.52	33.77
15	6.89	10.35	14.87	20.49	26.79	28.42	30.06	31.71	33.36	35.02	36.68	38.34	40.00	41.67	43.33	45.00
10	8.39	13.32	20.74	30.10	40.01	42.50	45.00	47.50	50.00	52.50	55.00	57.50	60.00	62.50	65.00	67.50

Description: This table shows the price to pay for a bond at the yield rate. The yield is to maturity.

Example: The price of a 10.75 %, 28 year bond to yield 8 % to maturity is $ 130.55.

COUPON RATE, %

YIELD	7.00%	7.25%	7.50%	7.75%	8.00%	8.25%	8.50%	8.75%	9.00%	9.25%	9.50%	9.75%	10.00%	10.25%	10.50%	10.75%
0.00	296.00	303.00	310.00	317.00	324.00	331.00	338.00	345.00	352.00	359.00	366.00	373.00	380.00	387.00	394.00	401.00
1.00	246.21	252.31	258.40	264.49	270.58	276.67	282.77	288.86	294.95	301.04	307.14	313.23	319.32	325.41	331.50	337.60
2.00	206.80	212.14	217.48	222.82	228.16	233.50	238.84	244.18	249.52	254.86	260.20	265.54	270.88	276.22	281.56	286.90
3.00	175.41	180.12	184.84	189.55	194.26	198.98	203.69	208.40	213.12	217.83	222.54	227.26	231.97	236.68	241.40	246.11
4.00	150.26	154.45	158.63	162.82	167.01	171.20	175.39	179.57	183.76	187.95	192.14	196.33	200.51	204.70	208.89	213.08
4.25	144.77	148.84	152.91	156.99	161.06	165.13	169.20	173.27	177.34	181.41	185.48	189.55	193.62	197.69	201.76	205.83
4.50	139.58	143.53	147.49	151.45	155.41	159.36	163.32	167.28	171.24	175.19	179.15	183.11	187.07	191.02	194.98	198.94
4.75	134.64	138.49	142.34	146.19	150.04	153.89	157.74	161.59	165.44	169.29	173.14	176.99	180.84	184.69	188.54	192.38
5.00	129.96	133.71	137.46	141.20	144.95	148.69	152.44	156.18	159.93	163.68	167.42	171.17	174.91	178.66	182.40	186.15
5.25	125.52	129.17	132.81	136.46	140.11	143.75	147.40	151.04	154.69	158.34	161.98	165.63	169.28	172.92	176.57	180.21
5.50	121.30	124.85	128.40	131.95	135.51	139.06	142.61	146.16	149.71	153.26	156.81	160.36	163.91	167.46	171.01	174.56
5.75	117.29	120.75	124.21	127.67	131.13	134.59	138.05	141.51	144.96	148.42	151.88	155.34	158.80	162.26	165.72	169.18
6.00	113.48	116.85	120.22	123.59	126.97	130.34	133.71	137.08	140.45	143.82	147.19	150.56	153.93	157.30	160.67	164.04
6.25	109.86	113.14	116.43	119.72	123.00	126.29	129.57	132.86	136.15	139.43	142.72	146.00	149.29	152.58	155.86	159.15
6.50	106.41	109.61	112.82	116.02	119.23	122.43	125.64	128.84	132.05	135.25	138.46	141.66	144.87	148.07	151.27	154.48
6.75	103.13	106.25	109.38	112.51	115.63	118.76	121.89	125.01	128.14	131.26	134.39	137.52	140.64	143.77	146.90	150.02
7.00	100.00	103.05	106.10	109.15	112.20	115.26	118.31	121.36	124.41	127.46	130.51	133.56	136.61	139.67	142.72	145.77
7.25	97.02	100.00	102.98	105.96	108.94	111.92	114.89	117.87	120.85	123.83	126.81	129.79	132.77	135.75	138.72	141.70
7.50	94.18	97.09	100.00	102.91	105.82	108.73	111.64	114.55	117.45	120.36	123.27	126.18	129.09	132.00	134.91	137.82
7.75	91.47	94.32	97.16	100.00	102.84	105.68	108.53	111.37	114.21	117.05	119.89	122.74	125.58	128.42	131.26	134.10
8.00	88.89	91.67	94.45	97.22	100.00	102.78	105.55	108.33	111.11	113.89	116.66	119.44	122.22	125.00	127.77	130.55
8.25	86.42	89.14	91.85	94.57	97.28	100.00	102.72	105.43	108.15	110.86	113.58	116.29	119.01	121.72	124.44	127.15
8.50	84.07	86.72	89.38	92.03	94.69	97.34	100.00	102.66	105.31	107.97	110.62	113.28	115.93	118.59	121.24	123.90
8.75	81.82	84.42	87.01	89.61	92.21	94.81	97.40	100.00	102.60	105.19	107.79	110.39	112.99	115.58	118.18	120.78
9.00	79.67	82.21	84.75	87.29	89.83	92.38	94.92	97.46	100.00	102.54	105.08	107.62	110.17	112.71	115.25	117.79
9.25	77.61	80.10	82.59	85.07	87.56	90.05	92.54	95.02	97.51	100.00	102.49	104.98	107.46	109.95	112.44	114.93
9.50	75.64	78.08	80.51	82.95	85.38	87.82	90.26	92.69	95.13	97.56	100.00	102.44	104.87	107.31	109.74	112.18
9.75	73.76	76.14	78.53	80.91	83.30	85.69	88.07	90.46	92.84	95.23	97.61	100.00	102.39	104.77	107.16	109.54
10.00	71.95	74.29	76.63	78.96	81.30	83.64	85.98	88.31	90.65	92.99	95.33	97.66	100.00	102.34	104.67	107.01
10.25	70.22	72.51	74.80	77.09	79.39	81.68	83.97	86.26	88.55	90.84	93.13	95.42	97.71	100.00	102.29	104.58
10.50	68.57	70.81	73.06	75.30	77.55	79.79	82.04	84.28	86.53	88.77	91.02	93.26	95.51	97.75	100.00	102.25
10.75	66.98	69.18	71.38	73.58	75.78	77.98	80.19	82.39	84.59	86.79	88.99	91.19	93.40	95.60	97.80	100.00
11.00	65.45	67.61	69.77	71.93	74.09	76.25	78.41	80.57	82.72	84.88	87.04	89.20	91.36	93.52	95.68	97.84
11.25	63.99	66.10	68.22	70.34	72.46	74.58	76.70	78.81	80.93	83.05	85.17	87.29	89.41	91.53	93.64	95.76
11.50	62.58	64.66	66.74	68.82	70.89	72.97	75.05	77.13	79.21	81.29	83.37	85.45	87.53	89.61	91.68	93.76
11.75	61.23	63.27	65.31	67.35	69.39	71.43	73.47	75.51	77.55	79.59	81.63	83.67	85.72	87.76	89.80	91.84
12.00	59.93	61.93	63.94	65.94	67.94	69.95	71.95	73.95	75.96	77.96	79.96	81.97	83.97	85.97	87.98	89.98
12.25	58.68	60.65	62.61	64.58	66.55	68.52	70.48	72.45	74.42	76.39	78.36	80.32	82.29	84.26	86.23	88.19
12.50	57.48	59.41	61.34	63.27	65.21	67.14	69.07	71.01	72.94	74.87	76.80	78.74	80.67	82.60	84.54	86.47
12.75	56.32	58.22	60.12	62.02	63.92	65.81	67.71	69.61	71.51	73.41	75.31	77.21	79.11	81.01	82.91	84.81
13.00	55.20	57.07	58.94	60.80	62.67	64.54	66.40	68.27	70.14	72.00	73.87	75.74	77.60	79.47	81.33	83.20
13.25	54.13	55.96	57.80	59.63	61.47	63.30	65.14	66.97	68.81	70.64	72.48	74.31	76.15	77.98	79.82	81.65
13.50	53.09	54.90	56.70	58.51	60.31	62.11	63.92	65.72	67.53	69.33	71.13	72.94	74.74	76.55	78.35	80.15
13.75	52.09	53.87	55.64	57.42	59.19	60.97	62.74	64.51	66.29	68.06	69.84	71.61	73.39	75.16	76.93	78.71
14.00	51.13	52.88	54.62	56.37	58.11	59.86	61.60	63.35	65.09	66.84	68.58	70.33	72.07	73.82	75.57	77.31
14.25	50.20	51.92	53.64	55.35	57.07	58.79	60.50	62.22	63.94	65.66	67.37	69.09	70.81	72.52	74.24	75.96
14.50	49.30	50.99	52.68	54.37	56.06	57.75	59.44	61.13	62.82	64.51	66.20	67.89	69.58	71.27	72.96	74.65
14.75	48.43	50.10	51.76	53.42	55.09	56.75	58.42	60.08	61.74	63.41	65.07	66.73	68.40	70.06	71.72	73.39
15.00	47.60	49.23	50.87	52.51	54.15	55.78	57.42	59.06	60.70	62.33	63.97	65.61	67.25	68.89	70.52	72.16
15.25	46.78	48.40	50.01	51.62	53.24	54.85	56.46	58.07	59.69	61.30	62.91	64.52	66.14	67.75	69.36	70.97
15.50	46.00	47.59	49.18	50.76	52.35	53.94	55.53	57.12	58.71	60.29	61.88	63.47	65.06	66.65	68.24	69.82
15.75	45.24	46.81	48.37	49.93	51.50	53.06	54.63	56.19	57.76	59.32	60.89	62.45	64.02	65.58	67.14	68.71
16.00	44.51	46.05	47.59	49.13	50.67	52.21	53.75	55.30	56.84	58.38	59.92	61.46	63.00	64.55	66.09	67.63
16.25	43.79	45.31	46.83	48.35	49.87	51.39	52.91	54.43	55.95	57.47	58.98	60.50	62.02	63.54	65.06	66.58
16.50	43.10	44.60	46.10	47.60	49.09	50.59	52.09	53.58	55.08	56.58	58.08	59.57	61.07	62.57	64.07	65.56
16.75	42.44	43.91	45.39	46.86	48.34	49.82	51.29	52.77	54.24	55.72	57.20	58.67	60.15	61.62	63.10	64.58
17.00	41.79	43.24	44.70	46.15	47.61	49.06	50.52	51.97	53.43	54.88	56.34	57.80	59.25	60.71	62.16	63.62
17.25	41.16	42.59	44.03	45.46	46.90	48.33	49.77	51.20	52.64	54.07	55.51	56.94	58.38	59.81	61.25	62.69
17.50	40.55	41.96	43.38	44.79	46.21	47.62	49.04	50.46	51.87	53.29	54.70	56.12	57.53	58.95	60.36	61.78
17.75	39.95	41.35	42.75	44.14	45.54	46.94	48.33	49.73	51.13	52.52	53.92	55.31	56.71	58.11	59.50	60.90
18.00	39.38	40.76	42.13	43.51	44.89	46.27	47.65	49.02	50.40	51.78	53.16	54.53	55.91	57.29	58.67	60.05
18.25	38.82	40.18	41.54	42.90	44.26	45.62	46.98	48.34	49.70	51.06	52.42	53.77	55.13	56.49	57.85	59.21
18.50	38.28	39.62	40.96	42.30	43.64	44.99	46.33	47.67	49.01	50.35	51.69	53.04	54.38	55.72	57.06	58.40
18.75	37.75	39.07	40.40	41.72	43.05	44.37	45.70	47.02	48.34	49.67	50.99	52.32	53.64	54.97	56.29	57.62
19.00	37.23	38.54	39.85	41.16	42.46	43.77	45.08	46.39	47.70	49.00	50.31	51.62	52.93	54.23	55.54	56.85
20.00	35.31	36.56	37.80	39.04	40.29	41.53	42.78	44.02	45.26	46.51	47.75	49.00	50.24	51.48	52.73	53.97
25.00	28.10	29.10	30.10	31.09	32.09	33.09	34.09	35.09	36.09	37.09	38.08	39.08	40.08	41.08	42.08	43.08
30.00	23.36	24.20	25.03	25.86	26.70	27.53	28.36	29.19	30.03	30.86	31.69	32.53	33.36	34.19	35.03	35.86

Description: This table shows the yield to maturity of a bond purchased at the price shown in the index.

Example: The yield to maturity of a 10.75 %, 28 year bond at a price of 111.00 is 9.61 %.

COUPON RATE, %

PRICE	7.00%	7.25%	7.50%	7.75%	8.00%	8.25%	8.50%	8.75%	9.00%	9.25%	9.50%	9.75%	10.00%	10.25%	10.50%	10.75%
175	3.01	3.18	3.35	3.51	3.68	3.84	4.01	4.17	4.34	4.50	4.67	4.83	4.99	5.15	5.31	5.48
170	3.19	3.36	3.53	3.70	3.87	4.04	4.21	4.38	4.55	4.71	4.88	5.05	5.21	5.38	5.54	5.71
165	3.38	3.56	3.73	3.90	4.08	4.25	4.42	4.59	4.76	4.93	5.10	5.27	5.44	5.61	5.78	5.95
160	3.58	3.76	3.94	4.11	4.29	4.47	4.64	4.82	4.99	5.17	5.34	5.51	5.69	5.86	6.03	6.20
155	3.79	3.97	4.15	4.33	4.51	4.69	4.87	5.05	5.23	5.41	5.59	5.76	5.94	6.12	6.29	6.47
150	4.01	4.19	4.38	4.56	4.75	4.93	5.11	5.30	5.48	5.66	5.84	6.03	6.21	6.39	6.57	6.75
145	4.23	4.42	4.61	4.80	4.99	5.18	5.37	5.56	5.74	5.93	6.12	6.30	6.49	6.67	6.86	7.04
140	4.47	4.67	4.86	5.06	5.25	5.44	5.64	5.83	6.02	6.21	6.40	6.59	6.78	6.97	7.16	7.35
135	4.73	4.93	5.13	5.32	5.52	5.72	5.92	6.12	6.31	6.51	6.71	6.90	7.10	7.29	7.49	7.68
130	4.99	5.20	5.40	5.61	5.81	6.02	6.22	6.42	6.62	6.83	7.03	7.23	7.43	7.63	7.83	8.03
125	5.28	5.49	5.70	5.91	6.12	6.33	6.54	6.75	6.95	7.16	7.37	7.58	7.79	7.99	8.20	8.41
120	5.57	5.79	6.01	6.23	6.44	6.66	6.88	7.09	7.31	7.52	7.74	7.95	8.17	8.38	8.60	8.81
119	5.64	5.86	6.07	6.29	6.51	6.73	6.95	7.16	7.38	7.60	7.81	8.03	8.25	8.46	8.68	8.89
118	5.70	5.92	6.14	6.36	6.58	6.80	7.02	7.24	7.45	7.67	7.89	8.11	8.33	8.54	8.76	8.98
117	5.76	5.99	6.21	6.43	6.65	6.87	7.09	7.31	7.53	7.75	7.97	8.19	8.41	8.63	8.84	9.06
116	5.83	6.05	6.27	6.50	6.72	6.94	7.16	7.38	7.61	7.83	8.05	8.27	8.49	8.71	8.93	9.15
115	5.89	6.12	6.34	6.57	6.79	7.01	7.24	7.46	7.68	7.91	8.13	8.35	8.57	8.79	9.02	9.24
114	5.96	6.19	6.41	6.64	6.86	7.09	7.31	7.54	7.76	7.99	8.21	8.43	8.66	8.88	9.10	9.33
113	6.03	6.25	6.48	6.71	6.94	7.16	7.39	7.62	7.84	8.07	8.29	8.52	8.74	8.97	9.19	9.42
112	6.10	6.32	6.55	6.78	7.01	7.24	7.47	7.69	7.92	8.15	8.38	8.60	8.83	9.06	9.29	9.51
111	6.16	6.40	6.63	6.86	7.09	7.32	7.55	7.77	8.00	8.23	8.46	8.69	8.92	9.15	9.38	9.61
110	6.23	6.47	6.70	6.93	7.16	7.39	7.63	7.86	8.09	8.32	8.55	8.78	9.01	9.24	9.47	9.70
109	6.31	6.54	6.77	7.01	7.24	7.47	7.71	7.94	8.17	8.40	8.64	8.87	9.10	9.33	9.57	9.80
108	6.38	6.61	6.85	7.08	7.32	7.55	7.79	8.02	8.26	8.49	8.73	8.96	9.19	9.43	9.66	9.90
107	6.45	6.69	6.93	7.16	7.40	7.64	7.87	8.11	8.34	8.58	8.82	9.05	9.29	9.52	9.76	10.00
106	6.53	6.76	7.00	7.24	7.48	7.72	7.96	8.20	8.43	8.67	8.91	9.15	9.38	9.62	9.86	10.10
105	6.60	6.84	7.08	7.32	7.56	7.80	8.04	8.28	8.52	8.76	9.00	9.24	9.48	9.72	9.96	10.20
104	6.68	6.92	7.16	7.40	7.65	7.89	8.13	8.37	8.61	8.86	9.10	9.34	9.58	9.82	10.06	10.31
103	6.75	7.00	7.24	7.49	7.73	7.98	8.22	8.46	8.71	8.95	9.19	9.44	9.68	9.93	10.17	10.41
102	6.83	7.08	7.33	7.57	7.82	8.06	8.31	8.56	8.80	9.05	9.29	9.54	9.78	10.03	10.28	10.52
101	6.91	7.16	7.41	7.66	7.91	8.15	8.40	8.65	8.90	9.15	9.39	9.64	9.89	10.14	10.38	10.63
100	7.00	7.25	7.50	7.75	8.00	8.25	8.50	8.75	9.00	9.25	9.50	9.75	10.00	10.25	10.50	10.75
99	7.08	7.33	7.58	7.83	8.09	8.34	8.59	8.84	9.09	9.35	9.60	9.85	10.10	10.36	10.61	10.86
98	7.16	7.42	7.67	7.92	8.18	8.43	8.69	8.94	9.20	9.45	9.70	9.96	10.21	10.47	10.72	10.98
97	7.25	7.50	7.76	8.02	8.27	8.53	8.78	9.04	9.30	9.55	9.81	10.07	10.32	10.58	10.84	11.10
96	7.33	7.59	7.85	8.11	8.37	8.63	8.88	9.14	9.40	9.66	9.92	10.18	10.44	10.70	10.96	11.22
95	7.42	7.68	7.94	8.20	8.46	8.73	8.99	9.25	9.51	9.77	10.03	10.29	10.55	10.82	11.08	11.34
94	7.51	7.77	8.04	8.30	8.56	8.83	9.09	9.35	9.62	9.88	10.14	10.41	10.67	10.94	11.20	11.46
93	7.60	7.87	8.13	8.40	8.66	8.93	9.20	9.46	9.73	9.99	10.26	10.53	10.79	11.06	11.33	11.59
92	7.70	7.96	8.23	8.50	8.77	9.03	9.30	9.57	9.84	10.11	10.38	10.65	10.92	11.18	11.45	11.72
91	7.79	8.06	8.33	8.60	8.87	9.14	9.41	9.68	9.95	10.23	10.50	10.77	11.04	11.31	11.58	11.86
90	7.89	8.16	8.43	8.70	8.98	9.25	9.52	9.80	10.07	10.35	10.62	10.89	11.17	11.44	11.72	11.99
89	7.98	8.26	8.53	8.81	9.09	9.36	9.64	9.91	10.19	10.47	10.74	11.02	11.30	11.58	11.85	12.13
88	8.08	8.36	8.64	8.92	9.20	9.47	9.75	10.03	10.31	10.59	10.87	11.15	11.43	11.71	11.99	12.27
87	8.19	8.47	8.75	9.03	9.31	9.59	9.87	10.15	10.44	10.72	11.00	11.28	11.57	11.85	12.13	12.42
86	8.29	8.57	8.86	9.14	9.42	9.71	9.99	10.28	10.56	10.85	11.13	11.42	11.71	11.99	12.28	12.56
85	8.39	8.68	8.97	9.25	9.54	9.83	10.12	10.40	10.69	10.98	11.27	11.56	11.85	12.14	12.43	12.72
84	8.50	8.79	9.08	9.37	9.66	9.95	10.24	10.53	10.82	11.11	11.41	11.70	11.99	12.28	12.58	12.87
83	8.61	8.90	9.20	9.49	9.78	10.08	10.37	10.66	10.96	11.25	11.55	11.84	12.14	12.43	12.73	13.03
82	8.72	9.02	9.31	9.61	9.91	10.20	10.50	10.80	11.10	11.39	11.69	11.99	12.29	12.59	12.89	13.19
81	8.84	9.14	9.44	9.73	10.03	10.33	10.63	10.93	11.24	11.54	11.84	12.14	12.44	12.75	13.05	13.35
80	8.96	9.26	9.56	9.86	10.16	10.47	10.77	11.07	11.38	11.68	11.99	12.30	12.60	12.91	13.21	13.52
79	9.07	9.38	9.68	9.99	10.30	10.60	10.91	11.22	11.53	11.83	12.14	12.45	12.76	13.07	13.38	13.69
78	9.20	9.50	9.81	10.12	10.43	10.74	11.05	11.36	11.68	11.99	12.30	12.61	12.93	13.24	13.56	13.87
77	9.32	9.63	9.95	10.26	10.57	10.89	11.20	11.51	11.83	12.15	12.46	12.78	13.10	13.42	13.73	14.05
76	9.45	9.76	10.08	10.40	10.71	11.03	11.35	11.67	11.99	12.31	12.63	12.95	13.27	13.59	13.91	14.24
75	9.58	9.90	10.22	10.54	10.86	11.18	11.50	11.83	12.15	12.47	12.80	13.12	13.45	13.77	14.10	14.43
74	9.71	10.04	10.36	10.68	11.01	11.33	11.66	11.99	12.31	12.64	12.97	13.30	13.63	13.96	14.29	14.62
73	9.85	10.18	10.50	10.83	11.16	11.49	11.82	12.15	12.48	12.82	13.15	13.48	13.82	14.15	14.49	14.82
70	10.28	10.62	10.96	11.30	11.64	11.99	12.33	12.67	13.02	13.37	13.71	14.06	14.41	14.76	15.11	15.46
65	11.07	11.43	11.80	12.17	12.53	12.90	13.27	13.64	14.01	14.39	14.76	15.13	15.51	15.88	16.26	16.64
60	11.98	12.37	12.77	13.17	13.56	13.96	14.36	14.76	15.17	15.57	15.97	16.38	16.79	17.19	17.60	18.01
55	13.04	13.47	13.90	14.33	14.77	15.20	15.64	16.08	16.52	16.96	17.40	17.85	18.29	18.73	19.18	19.63
50	14.30	14.77	15.25	15.73	16.20	16.68	17.17	17.65	18.14	18.62	19.11	19.60	20.09	20.58	21.07	21.56
45	15.83	16.35	16.88	17.42	17.95	18.49	19.03	19.57	20.11	20.65	21.20	21.74	22.29	22.84	23.39	23.94
40	17.73	18.32	18.93	19.53	20.14	20.74	21.35	21.97	22.58	23.19	23.81	24.43	25.05	25.66	26.28	26.90
35	20.17	20.86	21.55	22.25	22.95	23.65	24.35	25.06	25.76	26.47	27.18	27.89	28.60	29.31	30.02	30.73
30	23.44	24.25	25.07	25.89	26.72	27.54	28.37	29.19	30.02	30.85	31.68	32.51	33.34	34.17	35.00	35.84

Description: This table shows the price to pay for a bond at the yield rate. The yield is to maturity.

Example: The price of a 15.00 %, 28 year bond to yield 8 % to maturity is $ 177.77.

COUPON RATE, %

YIELD	11.00%	11.25%	11.50%	11.75%	12.00%	12.25%	12.50%	12.75%	13.00%	13.25%	13.50%	13.75%	14.00%	14.25%	14.50%	15.00%
0.00	408.00	415.00	422.00	429.00	436.00	443.00	450.00	457.00	464.00	471.00	478.00	485.00	492.00	499.00	506.00	520.00
1.00	343.69	349.78	355.87	361.97	368.06	374.15	380.24	386.33	392.43	398.52	404.61	410.70	416.80	422.89	428.98	441.16
2.00	292.24	297.58	302.92	308.26	313.60	318.94	324.28	329.62	334.96	340.30	345.64	350.98	356.32	361.66	367.00	377.68
3.00	250.82	255.54	260.25	264.96	269.68	274.39	279.10	283.82	288.53	293.24	297.96	302.67	307.38	312.10	316.81	326.24
4.00	217.27	221.45	225.64	229.83	234.02	238.21	242.39	246.58	250.77	254.96	259.15	263.34	267.52	271.71	275.90	284.28
4.25	209.90	213.97	218.04	222.11	226.18	230.25	234.32	238.39	242.46	246.53	250.60	254.67	258.74	262.81	266.88	275.03
4.50	202.90	206.85	210.81	214.77	218.73	222.68	226.64	230.60	234.56	238.51	242.47	246.43	250.39	254.34	258.30	266.22
4.75	196.23	200.08	203.93	207.78	211.63	215.48	219.33	223.18	227.03	230.88	234.73	238.58	242.43	246.28	250.13	257.82
5.00	189.89	193.64	197.39	201.13	204.88	208.62	212.37	216.11	219.86	223.61	227.35	231.10	234.84	238.59	242.33	249.82
5.25	183.86	187.51	191.15	194.80	198.44	202.09	205.74	209.38	213.03	216.67	220.32	223.97	227.61	231.26	234.90	242.20
5.50	178.11	181.66	185.21	188.76	192.31	195.86	199.41	202.97	206.52	210.07	213.62	217.17	220.72	224.27	227.82	234.92
5.75	172.63	176.09	179.55	183.01	186.47	189.93	193.39	196.85	200.30	203.76	207.22	210.68	214.14	217.60	221.06	227.98
6.00	167.41	170.78	174.16	177.53	180.90	184.27	187.64	191.01	194.38	197.75	201.12	204.49	207.86	211.23	214.60	221.34
6.25	162.43	165.72	169.01	172.29	175.58	178.86	182.15	185.44	188.72	192.01	195.29	198.58	201.87	205.15	208.44	215.01
6.50	157.68	160.89	164.09	167.30	170.50	173.71	176.91	180.12	183.32	186.53	189.73	192.94	196.14	199.34	202.55	208.96
6.75	153.15	156.28	159.40	162.53	165.66	168.78	171.91	175.03	178.16	181.29	184.41	187.54	190.67	193.79	196.92	203.17
7.00	148.82	151.87	154.92	157.97	161.02	164.08	167.13	170.18	173.23	176.28	179.33	182.38	185.43	188.49	191.54	197.64
7.25	144.68	147.66	150.64	153.62	156.60	159.58	162.56	165.53	168.51	171.49	174.47	177.45	180.43	183.41	186.39	192.34
7.50	140.73	143.64	146.55	149.46	152.36	155.27	158.18	161.09	164.00	166.91	169.82	172.73	175.64	178.55	181.46	187.27
7.75	136.95	139.79	142.63	145.47	148.32	151.16	154.00	156.84	159.68	162.53	165.37	168.21	171.05	173.89	176.74	182.42
8.00	133.33	136.11	138.88	141.66	144.44	147.22	149.99	152.77	155.55	158.33	161.10	163.88	166.66	169.44	172.21	177.77
8.25	129.87	132.58	135.30	138.01	140.73	143.44	146.16	148.87	151.59	154.30	157.02	159.74	162.45	165.17	167.88	173.31
8.50	126.55	129.21	131.86	134.52	137.17	139.83	142.48	145.14	147.79	150.45	153.10	155.76	158.42	161.07	163.73	169.04
8.75	123.38	125.97	128.57	131.17	133.77	136.36	138.96	141.56	144.16	146.75	149.35	151.95	154.55	157.14	159.74	164.94
9.00	120.33	122.87	125.42	127.96	130.50	133.04	135.58	138.12	140.67	143.21	145.75	148.29	150.83	153.37	155.92	161.00
9.25	117.41	119.90	122.39	124.88	127.37	129.85	132.34	134.83	137.32	139.81	142.29	144.78	147.27	149.76	152.24	157.22
9.50	114.62	117.05	119.49	121.92	124.36	126.79	129.23	131.67	134.10	136.54	138.97	141.41	143.85	146.28	148.72	153.59
9.75	111.93	114.31	116.70	119.09	121.47	123.86	126.24	128.63	131.01	133.40	135.79	138.17	140.56	142.94	145.33	150.10
10.00	109.35	111.69	114.02	116.36	118.70	121.04	123.37	125.71	128.05	130.39	132.72	135.06	137.40	139.73	142.07	146.75
10.25	106.87	109.16	111.45	113.74	116.03	118.32	120.61	122.91	125.20	127.49	129.78	132.07	134.36	136.65	138.94	143.52
10.50	104.49	106.74	108.98	111.23	113.47	115.72	117.96	120.21	122.45	124.70	126.94	129.19	131.43	133.68	135.93	140.42
10.75	102.20	104.40	106.60	108.81	111.01	113.21	115.41	117.61	119.81	122.02	124.22	126.42	128.62	130.82	133.02	137.43
11.00	100.00	102.16	104.32	106.48	108.64	110.80	112.96	115.12	117.28	119.43	121.59	123.75	125.91	128.07	130.23	134.55
11.25	97.88	100.00	102.12	104.24	106.36	108.47	110.59	112.71	114.83	116.95	119.07	121.19	123.30	125.42	127.54	131.78
11.50	95.84	97.92	100.00	102.08	104.16	106.24	108.32	110.39	112.47	114.55	116.63	118.71	120.79	122.87	124.95	129.11
11.75	93.88	95.92	97.96	100.00	102.04	104.08	106.12	108.16	110.20	112.24	114.28	116.33	118.37	120.41	122.45	126.53
12.00	91.99	93.99	95.99	98.00	100.00	102.00	104.01	106.01	108.01	110.02	112.02	114.03	116.03	118.03	120.04	124.04
12.25	90.16	92.13	94.10	96.06	98.03	100.00	101.97	103.94	105.90	107.87	109.84	111.81	113.77	115.74	117.71	121.64
12.50	88.40	90.34	92.27	94.20	96.13	98.07	100.00	101.93	103.87	105.80	107.73	109.66	111.60	113.53	115.46	119.33
12.75	86.71	88.60	90.50	92.40	94.30	96.20	98.10	100.00	101.90	103.80	105.70	107.60	109.50	111.40	113.29	117.09
13.00	85.07	86.93	88.80	90.67	92.53	94.40	96.27	98.13	100.00	101.87	103.73	105.60	107.47	109.33	111.20	114.93
13.25	83.49	85.32	87.16	88.99	90.83	92.66	94.50	96.33	98.17	100.00	101.83	103.67	105.50	107.34	109.17	112.84
13.50	81.96	83.76	85.57	87.37	89.18	90.98	92.78	94.59	96.39	98.20	100.00	101.80	103.61	105.41	107.22	110.82
13.75	80.48	82.26	84.03	85.81	87.58	89.35	91.13	92.90	94.68	96.45	98.23	100.00	101.77	103.55	105.32	108.87
14.00	79.06	80.80	82.55	84.29	86.04	87.78	89.53	91.27	93.02	94.76	96.51	98.25	100.00	101.75	103.49	106.98
14.25	77.68	79.39	81.11	82.83	84.55	86.26	87.98	89.70	91.41	93.13	94.85	96.57	98.28	100.00	101.72	105.15
14.50	76.34	78.03	79.72	81.41	83.10	84.79	86.48	88.17	89.86	91.55	93.24	94.93	96.62	98.31	100.00	103.38
14.75	75.05	76.71	78.38	80.04	81.70	83.37	85.03	86.69	88.36	90.02	91.68	93.35	95.01	96.67	98.34	101.66
15.00	73.80	75.44	77.07	78.71	80.35	81.99	83.62	85.26	86.90	88.54	90.17	91.81	93.45	95.09	96.72	100.00
15.25	72.59	74.20	75.81	77.42	79.04	80.65	82.26	83.87	85.49	87.10	88.71	90.32	91.94	93.55	95.16	98.39
15.50	71.41	73.00	74.59	76.18	77.76	79.35	80.94	82.53	84.12	85.71	87.29	88.88	90.47	92.06	93.65	96.82
15.75	70.27	71.84	73.40	74.97	76.53	78.10	79.66	81.23	82.79	84.35	85.92	87.48	89.05	90.61	92.18	95.31
16.00	69.17	70.71	72.25	73.79	75.34	76.88	78.42	79.96	81.50	83.04	84.58	86.13	87.67	89.21	90.75	93.83
16.25	68.10	69.62	71.14	72.66	74.18	75.69	77.21	78.73	80.25	81.77	83.29	84.81	86.33	87.85	89.37	92.40
16.50	67.06	68.56	70.05	71.55	73.05	74.55	76.04	77.54	79.04	80.54	82.03	83.53	85.03	86.52	88.02	91.02
16.75	66.05	67.53	69.00	70.48	71.96	73.43	74.91	76.38	77.86	79.34	80.81	82.29	83.76	85.24	86.72	89.67
17.00	65.07	66.53	67.98	69.44	70.89	72.35	73.80	75.26	76.71	78.17	79.63	81.08	82.54	83.99	85.45	88.36
17.25	64.12	65.56	66.99	68.43	69.86	71.30	72.73	74.17	75.60	77.04	78.47	79.91	81.34	82.78	84.21	87.08
17.50	63.20	64.61	66.03	67.44	68.86	70.27	71.69	73.10	74.52	75.94	77.35	78.77	80.18	81.60	83.01	85.84
17.75	62.30	63.69	65.09	66.49	67.88	69.28	70.68	72.07	73.47	74.86	76.26	77.66	79.05	80.45	81.85	84.64
18.00	61.42	62.80	64.18	65.56	66.93	68.31	69.69	71.07	72.44	73.82	75.20	76.58	77.96	79.33	80.71	83.47
18.25	60.57	61.93	63.29	64.65	66.01	67.37	68.73	70.09	71.45	72.81	74.17	75.53	76.89	78.25	79.61	82.33
18.50	59.75	61.09	62.43	63.77	65.11	66.45	67.80	69.14	70.48	71.82	73.16	74.51	75.85	77.19	78.53	81.21
18.75	58.94	60.26	61.59	62.91	64.24	65.56	66.89	68.21	69.54	70.86	72.19	73.51	74.83	76.16	77.48	80.13
19.00	58.16	59.46	60.77	62.08	63.39	64.69	66.00	67.31	68.62	69.92	71.23	72.54	73.85	75.16	76.46	79.08
20.00	55.22	56.46	57.70	58.95	60.19	61.44	62.68	63.92	65.17	66.41	67.66	68.90	70.14	71.39	72.63	75.12
25.00	44.08	45.08	46.07	47.07	48.07	49.07	50.07	51.07	52.07	53.06	54.06	55.06	56.06	57.06	58.06	60.05
30.00	36.69	37.52	38.36	39.19	40.02	40.86	41.69	42.52	43.36	44.19	45.02	45.85	46.69	47.52	48.35	50.02

Description: This table shows the yield to maturity of a bond purchased at the price shown in the index.

Example: The yield to maturity of a 15.00 %, 28 year bond at a price of 125.00 is 11.90 %.

COUPON RATE, %

PRICE	11.00%	11.25%	11.50%	11.75%	12.00%	12.25%	12.50%	12.75%	13.00%	13.25%	13.50%	13.75%	14.00%	14.25%	14.50%	15.00%
250	3.02	3.14	3.27	3.40	3.52	3.65	3.77	3.89	4.02	4.14	4.26	4.39	4.51	4.63	4.75	4.99
240	3.30	3.43	3.55	3.68	3.81	3.94	4.07	4.19	4.32	4.45	4.57	4.70	4.82	4.95	5.07	5.32
230	3.59	3.72	3.86	3.99	4.12	4.25	4.38	4.51	4.64	4.77	4.90	5.03	5.16	5.29	5.42	5.67
220	3.91	4.04	4.18	4.32	4.45	4.59	4.72	4.86	4.99	5.12	5.26	5.39	5.52	5.65	5.79	6.05
210	4.24	4.38	4.52	4.66	4.80	4.94	5.08	5.22	5.36	5.50	5.63	5.77	5.91	6.04	6.18	6.45
200	4.60	4.75	4.89	5.04	5.18	5.33	5.47	5.61	5.76	5.90	6.04	6.18	6.33	6.47	6.61	6.89
195	4.79	4.94	5.09	5.24	5.38	5.53	5.68	5.82	5.97	6.11	6.26	6.40	6.55	6.69	6.83	7.12
190	4.99	5.14	5.29	5.44	5.59	5.74	5.89	6.04	6.19	6.34	6.48	6.63	6.78	6.92	7.07	7.36
185	5.20	5.35	5.50	5.66	5.81	5.96	6.11	6.27	6.42	6.57	6.72	6.87	7.02	7.17	7.31	7.61
180	5.41	5.57	5.72	5.88	6.04	6.19	6.35	6.50	6.65	6.81	6.96	7.11	7.27	7.42	7.57	7.87
175	5.64	5.80	5.96	6.11	6.27	6.43	6.59	6.75	6.90	7.06	7.22	7.37	7.53	7.68	7.84	8.15
170	5.87	6.03	6.20	6.36	6.52	6.68	6.84	7.00	7.16	7.33	7.49	7.64	7.80	7.96	8.12	8.44
165	6.11	6.28	6.45	6.61	6.78	6.94	7.11	7.27	7.44	7.60	7.77	7.93	8.09	8.25	8.42	8.74
160	6.37	6.54	6.71	6.88	7.05	7.22	7.39	7.56	7.73	7.89	8.06	8.23	8.40	8.56	8.73	9.06
155	6.64	6.82	6.99	7.16	7.34	7.51	7.68	7.86	8.03	8.20	8.37	8.54	8.72	8.89	9.06	9.40
150	6.93	7.10	7.28	7.46	7.64	7.82	7.99	8.17	8.35	8.52	8.70	8.88	9.05	9.23	9.40	9.75
145	7.23	7.41	7.59	7.78	7.96	8.14	8.32	8.50	8.69	8.87	9.05	9.23	9.41	9.59	9.77	10.13
140	7.54	7.73	7.92	8.11	8.30	8.48	8.67	8.86	9.04	9.23	9.42	9.60	9.79	9.97	10.16	10.53
135	7.88	8.07	8.27	8.46	8.65	8.85	9.04	9.23	9.42	9.62	9.81	10.00	10.19	10.38	10.57	10.96
130	8.24	8.44	8.64	8.83	9.03	9.23	9.43	9.63	9.83	10.03	10.23	10.42	10.62	10.82	11.02	11.41
125	8.62	8.82	9.03	9.23	9.44	9.65	9.85	10.06	10.26	10.47	10.67	10.88	11.08	11.29	11.49	11.90
120	9.02	9.24	9.45	9.66	9.88	10.09	10.30	10.51	10.73	10.94	11.15	11.36	11.58	11.79	12.00	12.42
115	9.46	9.68	9.90	10.12	10.34	10.57	10.79	11.01	11.23	11.45	11.67	11.89	12.11	12.33	12.55	12.99
113	9.64	9.87	10.09	10.32	10.54	10.77	10.99	11.21	11.44	11.66	11.89	12.11	12.33	12.56	12.78	13.23
112	9.74	9.96	10.19	10.42	10.64	10.87	11.10	11.32	11.55	11.77	12.00	12.22	12.45	12.67	12.90	13.35
111	9.83	10.06	10.29	10.52	10.75	10.97	11.20	11.43	11.66	11.88	12.11	12.34	12.57	12.79	13.02	13.47
110	9.93	10.16	10.39	10.62	10.85	11.08	11.31	11.54	11.77	12.00	12.23	12.46	12.68	12.91	13.14	13.60
109	10.03	10.26	10.49	10.72	10.96	11.19	11.42	11.65	11.88	12.11	12.34	12.57	12.81	13.04	13.27	13.73
108	10.13	10.36	10.60	10.83	11.06	11.30	11.53	11.76	12.00	12.23	12.46	12.70	12.93	13.16	13.39	13.86
107	10.23	10.47	10.70	10.94	11.17	11.41	11.64	11.88	12.11	12.35	12.58	12.82	13.05	13.29	13.52	13.99
106	10.34	10.57	10.81	11.05	11.28	11.52	11.76	12.00	12.23	12.47	12.71	12.94	13.18	13.42	13.65	14.13
105	10.44	10.68	10.92	11.16	11.40	11.64	11.88	12.12	12.35	12.59	12.83	13.07	13.31	13.55	13.79	14.27
104	10.55	10.79	11.03	11.27	11.51	11.75	12.00	12.24	12.48	12.72	12.96	13.20	13.44	13.68	13.92	14.41
103	10.66	10.90	11.14	11.39	11.63	11.87	12.12	12.36	12.60	12.85	13.09	13.33	13.58	13.82	14.06	14.55
102	10.77	11.01	11.26	11.50	11.75	12.00	12.24	12.49	12.73	12.98	13.22	13.47	13.71	13.96	14.20	14.70
101	10.88	11.13	11.38	11.62	11.87	12.12	12.37	12.61	12.86	13.11	13.36	13.61	13.85	14.10	14.35	14.84
100	11.00	11.25	11.50	11.75	12.00	12.25	12.50	12.75	13.00	13.25	13.50	13.75	14.00	14.25	14.50	15.00
99	11.11	11.36	11.62	11.87	12.12	12.37	12.63	12.88	13.13	13.38	13.63	13.89	14.14	14.39	14.64	15.15
98	11.23	11.49	11.74	11.99	12.25	12.50	12.76	13.01	13.27	13.52	13.78	14.03	14.29	14.54	14.80	15.31
97	11.35	11.61	11.87	12.12	12.38	12.64	12.89	13.15	13.41	13.67	13.92	14.18	14.44	14.69	14.95	15.47
96	11.48	11.73	11.99	12.25	12.51	12.77	13.03	13.29	13.55	13.81	14.07	14.33	14.59	14.85	15.11	15.63
95	11.60	11.86	12.12	12.39	12.65	12.91	13.17	13.44	13.70	13.96	14.22	14.48	14.75	15.01	15.27	15.80
94	11.73	11.99	12.26	12.52	12.79	13.05	13.32	13.58	13.85	14.11	14.38	14.64	14.91	15.17	15.44	15.97
93	11.86	12.13	12.39	12.66	12.93	13.20	13.46	13.73	14.00	14.27	14.53	14.80	15.07	15.34	15.60	16.14
92	11.99	12.26	12.53	12.80	13.07	13.34	13.61	13.88	14.15	14.42	14.69	14.96	15.23	15.51	15.78	16.32
91	12.13	12.40	12.67	12.95	13.22	13.49	13.76	14.04	14.31	14.58	14.86	15.13	15.40	15.68	15.95	16.50
90	12.27	12.54	12.82	13.09	13.37	13.64	13.92	14.20	14.47	14.75	15.02	15.30	15.58	15.85	16.13	16.68
89	12.41	12.69	12.97	13.24	13.52	13.80	14.08	14.36	14.64	14.92	15.20	15.47	15.75	16.03	16.31	16.87
88	12.55	12.83	13.12	13.40	13.68	13.96	14.24	14.52	14.81	15.09	15.37	15.65	15.93	16.22	16.50	17.06
87	12.70	12.99	13.27	13.55	13.84	14.12	14.41	14.69	14.98	15.26	15.55	15.83	16.12	16.40	16.69	17.26
86	12.85	13.14	13.43	13.71	14.00	14.29	14.58	14.87	15.15	15.44	15.73	16.02	16.31	16.60	16.89	17.46
85	13.01	13.30	13.59	13.88	14.17	14.46	14.75	15.04	15.33	15.62	15.92	16.21	16.50	16.79	17.08	17.67
84	13.16	13.46	13.75	14.04	14.34	14.63	14.93	15.22	15.52	15.81	16.11	16.40	16.70	16.99	17.29	17.88
83	13.32	13.62	13.92	14.22	14.51	14.81	15.11	15.41	15.70	16.00	16.30	16.60	16.90	17.20	17.50	18.10
82	13.49	13.79	14.09	14.39	14.69	14.99	15.29	15.60	15.90	16.20	16.50	16.80	17.11	17.41	17.71	18.32
81	13.66	13.96	14.26	14.57	14.87	15.18	15.48	15.79	16.09	16.40	16.71	17.01	17.32	17.62	17.93	18.54
80	13.83	14.14	14.44	14.75	15.06	15.37	15.68	15.99	16.30	16.61	16.92	17.23	17.53	17.85	18.16	18.78
79	14.01	14.32	14.63	14.94	15.25	15.56	15.88	16.19	16.50	16.82	17.13	17.44	17.76	18.07	18.39	19.01
78	14.19	14.50	14.82	15.13	15.45	15.76	16.08	16.40	16.71	17.03	17.35	17.67	17.98	18.30	18.62	19.26
77	14.37	14.69	15.01	15.33	15.65	15.97	16.29	16.61	16.93	17.25	17.57	17.90	18.22	18.54	18.86	19.51
76	14.56	14.88	15.21	15.53	15.86	16.18	16.50	16.83	17.15	17.48	17.81	18.13	18.46	18.78	19.11	19.76
75	14.75	15.08	15.41	15.74	16.07	16.40	16.72	17.05	17.38	17.71	18.04	18.37	18.70	19.03	19.37	20.03
74	14.95	15.29	15.62	15.95	16.28	16.62	16.95	17.28	17.62	17.95	18.29	18.62	18.96	19.29	19.63	20.30
73	15.16	15.50	15.83	16.17	16.51	16.84	17.18	17.52	17.86	18.20	18.54	18.88	19.22	19.55	19.89	20.57
70	15.81	16.16	16.51	16.86	17.21	17.56	17.92	18.27	18.62	18.97	19.33	19.68	20.04	20.39	20.74	21.45
65	17.01	17.39	17.77	18.15	18.53	18.91	19.29	19.67	20.05	20.43	20.81	21.19	21.57	21.95	22.33	23.10
60	18.42	18.83	19.24	19.65	20.06	20.47	20.88	21.29	21.71	22.12	22.53	22.95	23.36	23.77	24.19	25.02
55	20.07	20.52	20.97	21.42	21.87	22.32	22.77	23.22	23.67	24.12	24.57	25.02	25.47	25.93	26.38	27.29

Description: This table shows the price to pay for a bond at the yield rate. The yield is to maturity.

Example: The price of a 6.75 %, 29 year bond to yield 8 % to maturity is $ 85.98.

COUPON RATE, %

YIELD	0.00%	1.00%	2.00%	3.00%	4.00%	4.25%	4.50%	4.75%	5.00%	5.25%	5.50%	5.75%	6.00%	6.25%	6.50%	6.75%
0.00	100.00	129.00	158.00	187.00	216.00	223.25	230.50	237.75	245.00	252.25	259.50	266.75	274.00	281.25	288.50	295.75
1.00	74.88	100.00	125.12	150.24	175.36	181.64	187.92	194.20	200.48	206.76	213.04	219.32	225.60	231.88	238.16	244.44
2.00	56.15	78.08	100.00	121.92	143.85	149.33	154.81	160.29	165.77	171.25	176.74	182.22	187.70	193.18	198.66	204.14
3.00	42.17	61.44	80.72	100.00	119.28	124.10	128.92	133.74	138.56	143.37	148.19	153.01	157.83	162.65	167.47	172.29
4.00	31.71	48.78	65.85	82.93	100.00	104.27	108.54	112.80	117.07	121.34	125.61	129.88	134.15	138.41	142.68	146.95
4.25	29.54	46.12	62.70	79.28	95.86	100.00	104.14	108.29	112.43	116.58	120.72	124.87	129.01	133.16	137.30	141.45
4.50	27.51	43.62	59.73	75.84	91.95	95.97	100.00	104.03	108.05	112.08	116.11	120.14	124.16	128.19	132.22	136.24
4.75	25.63	41.29	56.94	72.60	88.26	92.17	96.09	100.00	103.91	107.83	111.74	115.66	119.57	123.49	127.40	131.31
5.00	23.88	39.10	54.33	69.55	84.78	88.58	92.39	96.19	100.00	103.81	107.61	111.42	115.22	119.03	122.84	126.64
5.25	22.25	37.06	51.87	66.68	81.49	85.19	88.89	92.60	96.30	100.00	103.70	107.40	111.11	114.81	118.51	122.21
5.50	20.73	35.14	49.56	63.97	78.38	81.98	85.59	89.19	92.79	96.40	100.00	103.60	107.21	110.81	114.41	118.02
5.75	19.32	33.35	47.38	61.41	75.45	78.95	82.46	85.97	89.48	92.98	96.49	100.00	103.51	107.02	110.52	114.03
6.00	18.01	31.67	45.34	59.00	72.67	76.09	79.50	82.92	86.33	89.75	93.17	96.58	100.00	103.42	106.83	110.25
6.25	16.78	30.10	43.41	56.73	70.04	73.37	76.70	80.03	83.36	86.69	90.01	93.34	96.67	100.00	103.33	106.66
6.50	15.65	28.62	41.60	54.58	67.56	70.80	74.04	77.29	80.53	83.78	87.02	90.27	93.51	96.76	100.00	103.24
6.75	14.58	27.24	39.89	52.55	65.20	68.36	71.53	74.69	77.86	81.02	84.18	87.35	90.51	93.67	96.84	100.00
7.00	13.60	25.94	38.28	50.63	62.97	66.06	69.14	72.23	75.31	78.40	81.49	84.57	87.66	90.74	93.83	96.91
7.25	12.68	24.72	36.77	48.81	60.86	63.87	66.88	69.89	72.90	75.91	78.92	81.93	84.94	87.96	90.97	93.98
7.50	11.82	23.58	35.34	47.09	58.85	61.79	64.73	67.67	70.61	73.55	76.49	79.43	82.36	85.30	88.24	91.18
7.75	11.02	22.51	33.99	45.47	56.95	59.82	62.69	65.56	68.43	71.30	74.17	77.04	79.91	82.78	85.65	88.52
8.00	10.28	21.50	32.71	43.93	55.14	57.94	60.75	63.55	66.36	69.16	71.96	74.77	77.57	80.37	83.18	85.98
8.25	9.59	20.55	31.51	42.47	53.43	56.16	58.90	61.64	64.38	67.12	69.86	72.60	75.34	78.08	80.82	83.56
8.50	8.95	19.66	30.37	41.08	51.79	54.47	57.15	59.83	62.51	65.18	67.86	70.54	73.22	75.90	78.58	81.25
8.75	8.34	18.82	29.29	39.77	50.24	52.86	55.48	58.10	60.72	63.34	65.96	68.58	71.19	73.81	76.43	79.05
9.00	7.78	18.03	28.28	38.52	48.77	51.33	53.89	56.45	59.02	61.58	64.14	66.70	69.26	71.82	74.38	76.95
9.25	7.26	17.29	27.31	37.34	47.37	49.87	52.38	54.88	57.39	59.90	62.40	64.91	67.42	69.92	72.43	74.94
9.50	6.78	16.59	26.40	36.22	46.03	48.48	50.94	53.39	55.84	58.30	60.75	63.20	65.65	68.11	70.56	73.01
9.75	6.32	15.93	25.54	35.15	44.76	47.16	49.56	51.96	54.36	56.77	59.17	61.57	63.97	66.37	68.77	71.18
10.00	5.90	15.31	24.72	34.13	43.54	45.89	48.25	50.60	52.95	55.30	57.66	60.01	62.36	64.71	67.07	69.42
10.25	5.51	14.73	23.95	33.16	42.38	44.69	46.99	49.30	51.60	53.91	56.21	58.52	60.82	63.13	65.43	67.73
10.50	5.14	14.18	23.21	32.24	41.28	43.54	45.80	48.05	50.31	52.57	54.83	57.09	59.35	61.61	63.86	66.12
10.75	4.80	13.66	22.51	31.37	40.22	42.44	44.65	46.86	49.08	51.29	53.51	55.72	57.93	60.15	62.36	64.58
11.00	4.48	13.16	21.85	30.53	39.22	41.39	43.56	45.73	47.90	50.07	52.24	54.41	56.58	58.75	60.92	63.09
11.25	4.18	12.70	21.22	29.73	38.25	40.38	42.51	44.64	46.77	48.90	51.03	53.16	55.29	57.41	59.54	61.67
11.50	3.91	12.26	20.62	28.97	37.33	39.42	41.51	43.60	45.69	47.78	49.86	51.95	54.04	56.13	58.22	60.31
11.75	3.65	11.85	20.05	28.25	36.45	38.50	40.55	42.60	44.65	46.70	48.75	50.80	52.85	54.90	56.95	59.00
12.00	3.41	11.46	19.51	27.55	35.60	37.62	39.63	41.64	43.65	45.67	47.68	49.69	51.70	53.72	55.73	57.74
12.25	3.18	11.08	18.99	26.89	34.80	36.77	38.75	40.72	42.70	44.67	46.65	48.63	50.60	52.58	54.55	56.53
12.50	2.97	10.73	18.50	26.26	34.02	35.96	37.90	39.84	41.78	43.72	45.66	47.60	49.54	51.49	53.43	55.37
12.75	2.78	10.40	18.03	25.65	33.28	35.18	37.09	39.00	40.90	42.81	44.72	46.62	48.53	50.43	52.34	54.25
13.00	2.59	10.09	17.58	25.07	32.56	34.44	36.31	38.18	40.06	41.93	43.80	45.68	47.55	49.42	51.30	53.17
13.25	2.42	9.79	17.15	24.52	31.88	33.72	35.56	37.40	39.24	41.08	42.93	44.77	46.61	48.45	50.29	52.13
13.50	2.26	9.50	16.74	23.98	31.22	33.03	34.84	36.65	38.46	40.27	42.08	43.89	45.70	47.51	49.32	51.13
13.75	2.11	9.23	16.35	23.47	30.59	32.37	34.15	35.93	37.71	39.49	41.27	43.05	44.83	46.61	48.39	50.17
14.00	1.98	8.98	15.98	22.98	29.98	31.73	33.48	35.23	36.98	38.73	40.49	42.24	43.99	45.74	47.49	49.24
14.25	1.85	8.73	15.62	22.51	29.40	31.12	32.84	34.56	36.29	38.01	39.73	41.45	43.17	44.90	46.62	48.34
14.50	1.73	8.50	15.28	22.06	28.84	30.53	32.22	33.92	35.61	37.31	39.00	40.70	42.39	44.09	45.78	47.47
14.75	1.61	8.28	14.95	21.62	28.29	29.96	31.63	33.30	34.96	36.63	38.30	39.97	41.63	43.30	44.97	46.64
15.00	1.51	8.07	14.64	21.21	27.77	29.41	31.06	32.70	34.34	35.98	37.62	39.26	40.90	42.55	44.19	45.83
15.25	1.41	7.87	14.34	20.80	27.27	28.89	30.50	32.12	33.73	35.35	36.97	38.58	40.20	41.82	43.43	45.05
15.50	1.32	7.68	14.05	20.42	26.78	28.38	29.97	31.56	33.15	34.74	36.33	37.93	39.52	41.11	42.70	44.29
15.75	1.23	7.50	13.77	20.04	26.32	27.88	29.45	31.02	32.59	34.15	35.72	37.29	38.86	40.43	41.99	43.56
16.00	1.15	7.33	13.51	19.69	25.86	27.41	28.95	30.50	32.04	33.59	35.13	36.68	38.22	39.76	41.31	42.85
16.25	1.08	7.16	13.25	19.34	25.43	26.95	28.47	29.99	31.51	33.04	34.56	36.08	37.60	39.12	40.65	42.17
16.50	1.01	7.01	13.01	19.01	25.01	26.51	28.01	29.51	31.01	32.51	34.00	35.50	37.00	38.50	40.00	41.50
16.75	.94	6.86	12.77	18.68	24.60	26.08	27.55	29.03	30.51	31.99	33.47	34.95	36.43	37.90	39.38	40.86
17.00	.88	6.71	12.54	18.37	24.20	25.66	27.12	28.58	30.03	31.49	32.95	34.41	35.86	37.32	38.78	40.24
17.25	.82	6.57	12.32	18.07	23.82	25.26	26.70	28.13	29.57	31.01	32.45	33.88	35.32	36.76	38.19	39.63
17.50	.77	6.44	12.11	17.78	23.45	24.87	26.29	27.70	29.12	30.54	31.96	33.37	34.79	36.21	37.63	39.05
17.75	.72	6.31	11.91	17.50	23.09	24.49	25.89	27.29	28.69	30.09	31.48	32.88	34.28	35.68	37.08	38.48
18.00	.67	6.19	11.71	17.23	22.75	24.13	25.51	26.89	28.27	29.64	31.02	32.40	33.78	35.16	36.54	37.92
18.25	.63	6.08	11.52	16.97	22.41	23.77	25.13	26.49	27.86	29.22	30.58	31.94	33.30	34.66	36.02	37.38
18.50	.59	5.96	11.34	16.71	22.08	23.43	24.77	26.11	27.46	28.80	30.14	31.49	32.83	34.18	35.52	36.86
18.75	.55	5.86	11.16	16.46	21.77	23.09	24.42	25.75	27.07	28.40	29.72	31.05	32.38	33.70	35.03	36.35
19.00	.52	5.75	10.99	16.23	21.46	22.77	24.08	25.39	26.70	28.01	29.32	30.62	31.93	33.24	34.55	35.86
20.00	.40	5.38	10.36	15.34	20.32	21.56	22.81	24.05	25.30	26.54	27.79	29.03	30.28	31.52	32.77	34.01
25.00	.11	4.10	8.10	12.09	16.09	17.09	18.09	19.09	20.09	21.09	22.08	23.08	24.08	25.08	26.08	27.08
30.00	.03	3.36	6.69	10.03	13.36	14.19	15.03	15.86	16.69	17.52	18.36	19.19	20.02	20.86	21.69	22.52

Description: This table shows the yield to maturity of a bond purchased at the price shown in the index.

Example: The yield to maturity of a 6.75 %, 29 year bond at a price of 80.00 is 8.64 %.

COUPON RATE, %

PRICE	0.00%	1.00%	2.00%	3.00%	4.00%	4.25%	4.50%	4.75%	5.00%	5.25%	5.50%	5.75%	6.00%	6.25%	6.50%	6.75%
100	0.00	1.00	2.00	3.00	4.00	4.25	4.50	4.75	5.00	5.25	5.50	5.75	6.00	6.25	6.50	6.75
99	.03	1.04	2.04	3.05	4.05	4.31	4.56	4.81	5.06	5.31	5.56	5.82	6.07	6.32	6.57	6.82
98	.06	1.08	2.09	3.10	4.11	4.37	4.62	4.87	5.13	5.38	5.64	5.89	6.14	6.40	6.65	6.91
97	.10	1.12	2.13	3.15	4.17	4.43	4.69	4.94	5.20	5.45	5.71	5.96	6.22	6.48	6.73	6.99
96	.14	1.16	2.18	3.21	4.24	4.49	4.75	5.01	5.27	5.52	5.78	6.04	6.30	6.56	6.81	7.07
95	.17	1.20	2.23	3.26	4.30	4.56	4.82	5.08	5.34	5.60	5.86	6.12	6.38	6.64	6.90	7.16
94	.21	1.24	2.28	3.32	4.36	4.62	4.88	5.15	5.41	5.67	5.93	6.19	6.46	6.72	6.98	7.24
93	.25	1.29	2.33	3.38	4.43	4.69	4.95	5.22	5.48	5.74	6.01	6.27	6.54	6.80	7.07	7.33
92	.28	1.33	2.38	3.43	4.49	4.76	5.02	5.29	5.55	5.82	6.09	6.35	6.62	6.89	7.15	7.42
91	.32	1.37	2.43	3.49	4.56	4.83	5.09	5.36	5.63	5.90	6.17	6.43	6.70	6.97	7.24	7.51
90	.36	1.42	2.48	3.55	4.63	4.89	5.16	5.43	5.70	5.98	6.25	6.52	6.79	7.06	7.33	7.60
89	.40	1.46	2.53	3.61	4.69	4.97	5.24	5.51	5.78	6.06	6.33	6.60	6.88	7.15	7.42	7.70
88	.44	1.51	2.59	3.67	4.76	5.04	5.31	5.59	5.86	6.14	6.41	6.69	6.96	7.24	7.52	7.80
87	.48	1.55	2.64	3.73	4.83	5.11	5.39	5.66	5.94	6.22	6.50	6.78	7.05	7.33	7.61	7.89
86	.52	1.60	2.69	3.80	4.91	5.18	5.46	5.74	6.02	6.30	6.58	6.86	7.15	7.43	7.71	7.99
85	.56	1.65	2.75	3.86	4.98	5.26	5.54	5.82	6.11	6.39	6.67	6.96	7.24	7.52	7.81	8.09
84	.60	1.70	2.81	3.92	5.05	5.34	5.62	5.90	6.19	6.48	6.76	7.05	7.34	7.62	7.91	8.20
83	.64	1.74	2.86	3.99	5.13	5.41	5.70	5.99	6.28	6.56	6.85	7.14	7.43	7.72	8.01	8.30
82	.68	1.79	2.92	4.06	5.21	5.49	5.78	6.07	6.36	6.65	6.95	7.24	7.53	7.82	8.12	8.41
81	.72	1.84	2.98	4.13	5.28	5.57	5.87	6.16	6.45	6.75	7.04	7.34	7.63	7.93	8.23	8.52
80	.77	1.90	3.04	4.19	5.36	5.66	5.95	6.25	6.54	6.84	7.14	7.44	7.74	8.04	8.34	8.64
79	.81	1.95	3.10	4.26	5.44	5.74	6.04	6.34	6.64	6.94	7.24	7.54	7.84	8.14	8.45	8.75
78	.85	2.00	3.16	4.34	5.53	5.83	6.13	6.43	6.73	7.03	7.34	7.64	7.95	8.25	8.56	8.87
77	.90	2.05	3.22	4.41	5.61	5.91	6.22	6.52	6.83	7.13	7.44	7.75	8.06	8.37	8.68	8.99
76	.94	2.11	3.29	4.48	5.70	6.00	6.31	6.62	6.93	7.24	7.55	7.86	8.17	8.48	8.80	9.11
75	.99	2.16	3.35	4.56	5.78	6.09	6.40	6.71	7.03	7.34	7.65	7.97	8.28	8.60	8.92	9.24
74	1.04	2.22	3.42	4.64	5.87	6.19	6.50	6.81	7.13	7.45	7.76	8.08	8.40	8.72	9.04	9.37
73	1.08	2.27	3.48	4.71	5.96	6.28	6.60	6.92	7.23	7.55	7.88	8.20	8.52	8.85	9.17	9.50
72	1.13	2.33	3.55	4.79	6.06	6.38	6.70	7.02	7.34	7.67	7.99	8.32	8.64	8.97	9.30	9.63
71	1.18	2.39	3.62	4.87	6.15	6.48	6.80	7.12	7.45	7.78	8.11	8.44	8.77	9.10	9.44	9.77
70	1.23	2.45	3.69	4.96	6.25	6.58	6.90	7.23	7.56	7.90	8.23	8.56	8.90	9.23	9.57	9.91
69	1.28	2.51	3.76	5.04	6.35	6.68	7.01	7.34	7.68	8.01	8.35	8.69	9.03	9.37	9.71	10.06
68	1.33	2.57	3.83	5.13	6.45	6.78	7.12	7.46	7.80	8.14	8.48	8.82	9.16	9.51	9.86	10.20
67	1.38	2.63	3.91	5.22	6.55	6.89	7.23	7.57	7.92	8.26	8.61	8.95	9.30	9.65	10.00	10.36
66	1.43	2.69	3.98	5.31	6.66	7.00	7.35	7.69	8.04	8.39	8.74	9.09	9.45	9.80	10.16	10.51
65	1.49	2.76	4.06	5.40	6.77	7.11	7.46	7.81	8.17	8.52	8.88	9.23	9.59	9.95	10.31	10.68
64	1.54	2.82	4.14	5.49	6.88	7.23	7.58	7.94	8.30	8.65	9.01	9.38	9.74	10.11	10.47	10.84
63	1.59	2.89	4.22	5.59	6.99	7.35	7.71	8.07	8.43	8.79	9.16	9.53	9.89	10.27	10.64	11.01
62	1.65	2.96	4.30	5.69	7.11	7.47	7.83	8.20	8.56	8.93	9.30	9.68	10.05	10.43	10.81	11.19
61	1.71	3.03	4.39	5.79	7.23	7.59	7.96	8.33	8.70	9.08	9.46	9.83	10.22	10.60	10.98	11.37
60	1.76	3.10	4.47	5.89	7.35	7.72	8.09	8.47	8.85	9.23	9.61	10.00	10.38	10.77	11.16	11.55
59	1.82	3.17	4.56	6.00	7.48	7.85	8.23	8.61	9.00	9.38	9.77	10.16	10.56	10.95	11.35	11.74
58	1.88	3.24	4.65	6.10	7.61	7.99	8.37	8.76	9.15	9.54	9.94	10.33	10.73	11.13	11.54	11.94
57	1.94	3.32	4.74	6.21	7.74	8.13	8.52	8.91	9.31	9.71	10.11	10.51	10.92	11.32	11.73	12.15
56	2.00	3.39	4.83	6.33	7.87	8.27	8.67	9.07	9.47	9.87	10.28	10.69	11.11	11.52	11.94	12.36
55	2.07	3.47	4.93	6.44	8.02	8.42	8.82	9.23	9.64	10.05	10.46	10.88	11.30	11.72	12.15	12.58
54	2.13	3.55	5.03	6.56	8.16	8.57	8.98	9.39	9.81	10.23	10.65	11.08	11.50	11.93	12.37	12.80
53	2.20	3.63	5.13	6.69	8.31	8.72	9.14	9.56	9.99	10.41	10.84	11.28	11.71	12.15	12.59	13.04
52	2.26	3.71	5.23	6.81	8.46	8.88	9.31	9.74	10.17	10.61	11.04	11.49	11.93	12.38	12.83	13.28
51	2.33	3.80	5.34	6.95	8.62	9.05	9.48	9.92	10.36	10.80	11.25	11.70	12.15	12.61	13.07	13.53
50	2.40	3.89	5.45	7.08	8.79	9.22	9.66	10.11	10.56	11.01	11.47	11.92	12.39	12.85	13.32	13.79
49	2.47	3.98	5.56	7.22	8.96	9.40	9.85	10.30	10.76	11.22	11.69	12.16	12.63	13.10	13.58	14.06
48	2.54	4.07	5.67	7.36	9.13	9.58	10.04	10.51	10.97	11.44	11.92	12.40	12.88	13.36	13.85	14.34
47	2.62	4.16	5.79	7.51	9.31	9.78	10.24	10.72	11.19	11.67	12.16	12.65	13.14	13.64	14.13	14.64
46	2.69	4.26	5.91	7.66	9.50	9.97	10.45	10.93	11.42	11.91	12.41	12.91	13.41	13.92	14.43	14.94
45	2.77	4.35	6.04	7.82	9.70	10.18	10.67	11.16	11.66	12.16	12.67	13.18	13.70	14.21	14.74	15.26
44	2.85	4.46	6.17	7.98	9.90	10.39	10.89	11.40	11.91	12.42	12.94	13.46	13.99	14.52	15.06	15.59
43	2.93	4.56	6.30	8.15	10.11	10.62	11.13	11.64	12.17	12.69	13.22	13.76	14.30	14.84	15.39	15.94
42	3.01	4.67	6.44	8.33	10.33	10.85	11.37	11.90	12.43	12.97	13.52	14.07	14.62	15.18	15.74	16.31
41	3.09	4.78	6.58	8.51	10.56	11.09	11.63	12.17	12.72	13.27	13.83	14.39	14.96	15.53	16.11	16.69
40	3.18	4.89	6.73	8.70	10.80	11.34	11.89	12.45	13.01	13.58	14.15	14.73	15.32	15.91	16.50	17.09
39	3.27	5.01	6.88	8.90	11.05	11.61	12.17	12.74	13.32	13.91	14.50	15.09	15.69	16.29	16.90	17.51
35	3.65	5.51	7.56	9.78	12.12	12.81	13.44	14.08	14.73	15.39	16.05	16.72	17.40	18.08	18.76	19.45
30	4.19	6.26	8.58	11.16	13.99	14.73	15.48	16.24	17.01	17.79	18.58	19.37	20.17	20.98	21.79	22.60
25	4.83	7.19	9.91	13.03	16.50	17.41	18.34	19.27	20.22	21.18	22.15	23.12	24.09	25.07	26.06	27.05
20	5.62	8.40	11.77	15.78	20.29	21.48	22.67	23.88	25.10	26.33	27.56	28.79	30.03	31.27	32.52	33.76
15	6.64	10.13	14.71	20.41	26.77	28.40	30.05	31.70	33.35	35.01	36.67	38.34	40.00	41.67	43.33	45.00
10	8.09	13.07	20.62	30.08	40.00	42.50	45.00	47.50	50.00	52.50	55.00	57.50	60.00	62.50	65.00	67.50

Description: This table shows the price to pay for a bond at the yield rate. The yield is to maturity.

Example: The price of a 10.75 %, 29 year bond to yield 8 % to maturity is $ 130.84.

COUPON RATE, %

YIELD	7.00%	7.25%	7.50%	7.75%	8.00%	8.25%	8.50%	8.75%	9.00%	9.25%	9.50%	9.75%	10.00%	10.25%	10.50%	10.75%
0.00	303.00	310.25	317.50	324.75	332.00	339.25	346.50	353.75	361.00	368.25	375.50	382.75	390.00	397.25	404.50	411.75
1.00	250.72	257.00	263.28	269.56	275.84	282.12	288.40	294.68	300.96	307.24	313.52	319.80	326.08	332.36	338.64	344.92
2.00	209.62	215.10	220.58	226.06	231.55	237.03	242.51	247.99	253.47	258.95	264.43	269.91	275.39	280.88	286.36	291.84
3.00	177.11	181.93	186.75	191.57	196.39	201.21	206.03	210.85	215.67	220.49	225.31	230.12	234.94	239.76	244.58	249.40
4.00	151.22	155.49	159.75	164.02	168.29	172.56	176.83	181.09	185.36	189.63	193.90	198.17	202.44	206.70	210.97	215.24
4.25	145.59	149.74	153.88	158.03	162.17	166.32	170.46	174.61	178.75	182.90	187.04	191.19	195.33	199.48	203.62	207.77
4.50	140.27	144.30	148.33	152.35	156.38	160.41	164.43	168.46	172.49	176.51	180.54	184.57	188.60	192.62	196.65	200.68
4.75	135.23	139.14	143.06	146.97	150.88	154.80	158.71	162.63	166.54	170.46	174.37	178.28	182.20	186.11	190.03	193.94
5.00	130.45	134.25	138.06	141.87	145.67	149.48	153.28	157.09	160.90	164.70	168.51	172.31	176.12	179.93	183.73	187.54
5.25	125.92	129.62	133.32	137.02	140.73	144.43	148.13	151.83	155.54	159.24	162.94	166.64	170.35	174.05	177.75	181.45
5.50	121.62	125.22	128.82	132.43	136.03	139.63	143.24	146.84	150.44	154.05	157.65	161.25	164.86	168.46	172.06	175.66
5.75	117.54	121.05	124.55	128.06	131.57	135.08	138.59	142.09	145.60	149.11	152.62	156.12	159.63	163.14	166.65	170.16
6.00	113.67	117.08	120.50	123.91	127.33	130.75	134.16	137.58	141.00	144.41	147.83	151.25	154.66	158.08	161.49	164.91
6.25	109.99	113.31	116.64	119.97	123.30	126.63	129.96	133.29	136.62	139.94	143.27	146.60	149.93	153.26	156.59	159.92
6.50	106.49	109.73	112.98	116.22	119.47	122.71	125.96	129.20	132.44	135.69	138.93	142.18	145.42	148.67	151.91	155.16
6.75	103.16	106.33	109.49	112.65	115.82	118.98	122.14	125.31	128.47	131.64	134.80	137.96	141.13	144.29	147.45	150.62
7.00	100.00	103.09	106.17	109.26	112.34	115.43	118.51	121.60	124.69	127.77	130.86	133.94	137.03	140.12	143.20	146.29
7.25	96.99	100.00	103.01	106.02	109.03	112.04	115.06	118.07	121.08	124.09	127.10	130.11	133.12	136.13	139.14	142.16
7.50	94.12	97.06	100.00	102.94	105.88	108.82	111.76	114.70	117.64	120.57	123.51	126.45	129.39	132.33	135.27	138.21
7.75	91.39	94.26	97.13	100.00	102.87	105.74	108.61	111.48	114.35	117.22	120.09	122.96	125.83	128.70	131.57	134.44
8.00	88.79	91.59	94.39	97.20	100.00	102.80	105.61	108.41	111.21	114.02	116.82	119.63	122.43	125.23	128.04	130.84
8.25	86.30	89.04	91.78	94.52	97.26	100.00	102.74	105.48	108.22	110.96	113.70	116.44	119.18	121.92	124.66	127.40
8.50	83.93	86.61	89.29	91.97	94.64	97.32	100.00	102.68	105.36	108.03	110.71	113.39	116.07	118.75	121.42	124.10
8.75	81.67	84.29	86.91	89.53	92.14	94.76	97.38	100.00	102.62	105.24	107.86	110.47	113.09	115.71	118.33	120.95
9.00	79.51	82.07	84.63	87.19	89.75	92.32	94.88	97.44	100.00	102.56	105.12	107.68	110.25	112.81	115.37	117.93
9.25	77.44	79.95	82.46	84.96	87.47	89.97	92.48	94.99	97.49	100.00	102.51	105.01	107.52	110.03	112.53	115.04
9.50	75.47	77.92	80.37	82.83	85.28	87.73	90.19	92.64	95.09	97.55	100.00	102.45	104.91	107.36	109.81	112.27
9.75	73.58	75.98	78.38	80.78	83.19	85.59	87.99	90.39	92.79	95.20	97.60	100.00	102.40	104.80	107.21	109.61
10.00	71.77	74.12	76.48	78.83	81.18	83.53	85.89	88.24	90.59	92.94	95.30	97.65	100.00	102.35	104.70	107.06
10.25	70.04	72.34	74.65	76.95	79.26	81.56	83.87	86.17	88.48	90.78	93.09	95.39	97.70	100.00	102.30	104.61
10.50	68.38	70.64	72.90	75.16	77.41	79.67	81.93	84.19	86.45	88.71	90.97	93.22	95.48	97.74	100.00	102.26
10.75	66.79	69.00	71.22	73.43	75.65	77.86	80.07	82.29	84.50	86.72	88.93	91.14	93.36	95.57	97.79	100.00
11.00	65.27	67.44	69.61	71.78	73.95	76.12	78.29	80.46	82.63	84.80	86.97	89.15	91.32	93.49	95.66	97.83
11.25	63.80	65.93	68.06	70.19	72.32	74.45	76.58	78.71	80.84	82.97	85.10	87.22	89.35	91.48	93.61	95.74
11.50	62.40	64.49	66.58	68.67	70.75	72.84	74.93	77.02	79.11	81.20	83.29	85.38	87.47	89.56	91.64	93.73
11.75	61.05	63.10	65.15	67.20	69.25	71.30	73.35	75.40	77.45	79.50	81.55	83.60	85.65	87.70	89.75	91.80
12.00	59.75	61.76	63.78	65.79	67.80	69.81	71.83	73.84	75.85	77.86	79.88	81.89	83.90	85.91	87.93	89.94
12.25	58.51	60.48	62.46	64.43	66.41	68.39	70.36	72.34	74.31	76.29	78.27	80.24	82.22	84.19	86.17	88.14
12.50	57.31	59.25	61.19	63.13	65.07	67.01	68.95	70.89	72.83	74.77	76.71	78.65	80.59	82.53	84.48	86.42
12.75	56.15	58.06	59.97	61.87	63.78	65.69	67.59	69.50	71.40	73.31	75.22	77.12	79.03	80.94	82.84	84.75
13.00	55.04	56.92	58.79	60.66	62.54	64.41	66.28	68.16	70.03	71.90	73.77	75.65	77.52	79.39	81.27	83.14
13.25	53.97	55.81	57.65	59.50	61.34	63.18	65.02	66.86	68.70	70.54	72.38	74.22	76.07	77.91	79.75	81.59
13.50	52.94	54.75	56.56	58.37	60.18	61.99	63.80	65.61	67.42	69.23	71.04	72.85	74.66	76.47	78.28	80.09
13.75	51.95	53.73	55.51	57.29	59.07	60.85	62.63	64.41	66.18	67.96	69.74	71.52	73.30	75.08	76.86	78.64
14.00	50.99	52.74	54.49	56.24	57.99	59.74	61.49	63.24	64.99	66.74	68.49	70.24	71.99	73.74	75.49	77.24
14.25	50.06	51.78	53.51	55.23	56.95	58.67	60.39	62.12	63.84	65.56	67.28	69.00	70.73	72.45	74.17	75.89
14.50	49.17	50.86	52.56	54.25	55.95	57.64	59.33	61.03	62.72	64.42	66.11	67.81	69.50	71.20	72.89	74.58
14.75	48.31	49.97	51.64	53.31	54.98	56.64	58.31	59.98	61.65	63.31	64.98	66.65	68.32	69.98	71.65	73.32
15.00	47.47	49.11	50.75	52.40	54.04	55.68	57.32	58.96	60.60	62.24	63.89	65.53	67.17	68.81	70.45	72.09
15.25	46.66	48.28	49.90	51.51	53.13	54.75	56.36	57.98	59.59	61.21	62.83	64.44	66.06	67.68	69.29	70.91
15.50	45.88	47.48	49.07	50.66	52.25	53.84	55.43	57.03	58.62	60.21	61.80	63.39	64.98	66.58	68.17	69.76
15.75	45.13	46.70	48.26	49.83	51.40	52.97	54.54	56.10	57.67	59.24	60.81	62.37	63.94	65.51	67.08	68.65
16.00	44.40	45.94	47.49	49.03	50.58	52.12	53.66	55.21	56.75	58.30	59.84	61.39	62.93	64.48	66.02	67.57
16.25	43.69	45.21	46.73	48.26	49.78	51.30	52.82	54.34	55.87	57.39	58.91	60.43	61.95	63.47	65.00	66.52
16.50	43.00	44.50	46.00	47.50	49.00	50.50	52.00	53.50	55.00	56.50	58.00	59.50	61.00	62.50	64.00	65.50
16.75	42.34	43.82	45.30	46.77	48.25	49.73	51.21	52.69	54.17	55.65	57.12	58.60	60.08	61.56	63.04	64.52
17.00	41.69	43.15	44.61	46.07	47.53	48.98	50.44	51.90	53.36	54.81	56.27	57.73	59.19	60.64	62.10	63.56
17.25	41.07	42.51	43.94	45.38	46.82	48.26	49.69	51.13	52.57	54.01	55.44	56.88	58.32	59.75	61.19	62.63
17.50	40.46	41.88	43.30	44.72	46.13	47.55	48.97	50.39	51.80	53.22	54.64	56.06	57.47	58.89	60.31	61.73
17.75	39.87	41.27	42.67	44.07	45.47	46.86	48.26	49.66	51.06	52.46	53.86	55.25	56.65	58.05	59.45	60.85
18.00	39.30	40.68	42.06	43.44	44.82	46.20	47.58	48.96	50.34	51.72	53.10	54.48	55.86	57.24	58.61	59.99
18.25	38.75	40.11	41.47	42.83	44.19	45.55	46.91	48.27	49.64	51.00	52.36	53.72	55.08	56.44	57.80	59.16
18.50	38.21	39.55	40.89	42.24	43.58	44.92	46.27	47.61	48.95	50.30	51.64	52.98	54.33	55.67	57.01	58.36
18.75	37.68	39.01	40.33	41.66	42.98	44.31	45.64	46.96	48.29	49.61	50.94	52.27	53.59	54.92	56.24	57.57
19.00	37.17	38.48	39.79	41.10	42.40	43.71	45.02	46.33	47.64	48.95	50.26	51.57	52.88	54.19	55.49	56.80
20.00	35.26	36.50	37.75	38.99	40.24	41.48	42.73	43.97	45.22	46.46	47.71	48.95	50.20	51.44	52.69	53.93
25.00	28.08	29.08	30.08	31.07	32.07	33.07	34.07	35.07	36.07	37.07	38.07	39.07	40.06	41.06	42.06	43.06
30.00	23.36	24.19	25.02	25.86	26.69	27.52	28.35	29.19	30.02	30.85	31.69	32.52	33.35	34.19	35.02	35.85

Description: This table shows the yield to maturity of a bond purchased at the price shown in the index.

Example: The yield to maturity of a 10.75 %, 29 year bond at a price of 111.00 is 9.61 %.

							COUPON	RATE, %								
PRICE	7.00%	7.25%	7.50%	7.75%	8.00%	8.25%	8.50%	8.75%	9.00%	9.25%	9.50%	9.75%	10.00%	10.25%	10.50%	10.75%
175	3.07	3.24	3.40	3.57	3.74	3.90	4.07	4.23	4.39	4.56	4.72	4.88	5.04	5.20	5.36	5.52
170	3.25	3.42	3.59	3.76	3.93	4.10	4.26	4.43	4.60	4.76	4.93	5.10	5.26	5.42	5.59	5.75
165	3.44	3.61	3.78	3.96	4.13	4.30	4.47	4.64	4.81	4.98	5.15	5.32	5.49	5.66	5.82	5.99
160	3.63	3.81	3.98	4.16	4.34	4.51	4.69	4.86	5.04	5.21	5.38	5.55	5.73	5.90	6.07	6.24
155	3.83	4.02	4.20	4.38	4.56	4.74	4.91	5.09	5.27	5.45	5.63	5.80	5.98	6.15	6.33	6.50
150	4.05	4.23	4.42	4.60	4.79	4.97	5.15	5.34	5.52	5.70	5.88	6.06	6.24	6.42	6.60	6.78
145	4.27	4.46	4.65	4.84	5.03	5.22	5.40	5.59	5.78	5.96	6.15	6.33	6.52	6.70	6.89	7.07
140	4.51	4.70	4.90	5.09	5.28	5.48	5.67	5.86	6.05	6.24	6.43	6.62	6.81	7.00	7.19	7.38
135	4.76	4.96	5.15	5.35	5.55	5.75	5.95	6.14	6.34	6.54	6.73	6.93	7.12	7.32	7.51	7.71
130	5.02	5.22	5.43	5.63	5.84	6.04	6.24	6.45	6.65	6.85	7.05	7.25	7.45	7.65	7.85	8.06
125	5.30	5.51	5.72	5.93	6.14	6.35	6.56	6.77	6.97	7.18	7.39	7.60	7.81	8.01	8.22	8.43
120	5.59	5.81	6.03	6.24	6.46	6.68	6.89	7.11	7.32	7.54	7.75	7.97	8.18	8.39	8.61	8.82
119	5.65	5.87	6.09	6.31	6.53	6.74	6.96	7.18	7.39	7.61	7.83	8.04	8.26	8.47	8.69	8.91
118	5.72	5.94	6.16	6.37	6.59	6.81	7.03	7.25	7.47	7.69	7.90	8.12	8.34	8.56	8.77	8.99
117	5.78	6.00	6.22	6.44	6.66	6.88	7.10	7.32	7.54	7.76	7.98	8.20	8.42	8.64	8.86	9.07
116	5.84	6.07	6.29	6.51	6.73	6.95	7.18	7.40	7.62	7.84	8.06	8.28	8.50	8.72	8.94	9.16
115	5.91	6.13	6.36	6.58	6.80	7.03	7.25	7.47	7.69	7.92	8.14	8.36	8.58	8.81	9.03	9.25
114	5.97	6.20	6.42	6.65	6.87	7.10	7.32	7.55	7.77	8.00	8.22	8.44	8.67	8.89	9.11	9.34
113	6.04	6.27	6.49	6.72	6.95	7.17	7.40	7.63	7.85	8.08	8.30	8.53	8.75	8.98	9.20	9.43
112	6.11	6.34	6.56	6.79	7.02	7.25	7.48	7.70	7.93	8.16	8.39	8.61	8.84	9.07	9.29	9.52
111	6.17	6.41	6.64	6.87	7.10	7.32	7.55	7.78	8.01	8.24	8.47	8.70	8.93	9.16	9.38	9.61
110	6.24	6.48	6.71	6.94	7.17	7.40	7.63	7.86	8.10	8.33	8.56	8.79	9.02	9.25	9.48	9.71
109	6.31	6.55	6.78	7.01	7.25	7.48	7.71	7.95	8.18	8.41	8.64	8.88	9.11	9.34	9.57	9.80
108	6.39	6.62	6.86	7.09	7.33	7.56	7.79	8.03	8.26	8.50	8.73	8.97	9.20	9.43	9.67	9.90
107	6.46	6.69	6.93	7.17	7.40	7.64	7.88	8.11	8.35	8.59	8.82	9.06	9.29	9.53	9.77	10.00
106	6.53	6.77	7.01	7.25	7.49	7.72	7.96	8.20	8.44	8.68	8.91	9.15	9.39	9.63	9.86	10.10
105	6.61	6.85	7.09	7.33	7.57	7.81	8.05	8.29	8.53	8.77	9.01	9.25	9.49	9.73	9.96	10.20
104	6.68	6.92	7.17	7.41	7.65	7.89	8.13	8.38	8.62	8.86	9.10	9.34	9.58	9.83	10.07	10.31
103	6.76	7.00	7.25	7.49	7.73	7.98	8.22	8.47	8.71	8.95	9.20	9.44	9.68	9.93	10.17	10.42
102	6.84	7.08	7.33	7.57	7.82	8.07	8.31	8.56	8.80	9.05	9.29	9.54	9.79	10.03	10.28	10.52
101	6.91	7.16	7.41	7.66	7.91	8.15	8.40	8.65	8.90	9.15	9.39	9.64	9.89	10.14	10.39	10.63
100	7.00	7.25	7.50	7.75	8.00	8.25	8.50	8.75	9.00	9.25	9.50	9.75	10.00	10.25	10.50	10.75
99	7.08	7.33	7.58	7.83	8.08	8.34	8.59	8.84	9.09	9.35	9.60	9.85	10.10	10.35	10.61	10.86
98	7.16	7.41	7.67	7.92	8.18	8.43	8.68	8.94	9.19	9.45	9.70	9.96	10.21	10.47	10.72	10.97
97	7.24	7.50	7.76	8.01	8.27	8.53	8.78	9.04	9.30	9.55	9.81	10.07	10.32	10.58	10.84	11.09
96	7.33	7.59	7.85	8.11	8.36	8.62	8.88	9.14	9.40	9.66	9.92	10.18	10.44	10.69	10.95	11.21
95	7.42	7.68	7.94	8.20	8.46	8.72	8.98	9.24	9.50	9.77	10.03	10.29	10.55	10.81	11.07	11.34
94	7.51	7.77	8.03	8.30	8.56	8.82	9.09	9.35	9.61	9.88	10.14	10.40	10.67	10.93	11.20	11.46
93	7.60	7.86	8.13	8.39	8.66	8.92	9.19	9.46	9.72	9.99	10.25	10.52	10.79	11.05	11.32	11.59
92	7.69	7.96	8.22	8.49	8.76	9.03	9.30	9.57	9.83	10.10	10.37	10.64	10.91	11.18	11.45	11.72
91	7.78	8.05	8.32	8.59	8.86	9.13	9.41	9.68	9.95	10.22	10.49	10.76	11.03	11.31	11.58	11.85
90	7.88	8.15	8.42	8.70	8.97	9.24	9.52	9.79	10.06	10.34	10.61	10.89	11.16	11.44	11.71	11.99
89	7.97	8.25	8.52	8.80	9.08	9.35	9.63	9.91	10.18	10.46	10.74	11.01	11.29	11.57	11.85	12.12
88	8.07	8.35	8.63	8.91	9.19	9.46	9.74	10.02	10.30	10.58	10.86	11.14	11.42	11.70	11.98	12.27
87	8.17	8.45	8.73	9.02	9.30	9.58	9.86	10.14	10.43	10.71	10.99	11.27	11.56	11.84	12.13	12.41
86	8.28	8.56	8.84	9.13	9.41	9.70	9.98	10.27	10.55	10.84	11.12	11.41	11.70	11.98	12.27	12.56
85	8.38	8.67	8.95	9.24	9.53	9.82	10.10	10.39	10.68	10.97	11.26	11.55	11.84	12.13	12.42	12.71
84	8.49	8.78	9.07	9.36	9.65	9.94	10.23	10.52	10.81	11.10	11.40	11.69	11.98	12.27	12.57	12.86
83	8.60	8.89	9.18	9.47	9.77	10.06	10.36	10.65	10.95	11.24	11.54	11.83	12.13	12.42	12.72	13.02
82	8.71	9.00	9.30	9.59	9.89	10.19	10.49	10.78	11.08	11.38	11.68	11.98	12.28	12.58	12.88	13.18
81	8.82	9.12	9.42	9.72	10.02	10.32	10.62	10.92	11.22	11.52	11.83	12.13	12.43	12.73	13.04	13.34
80	8.94	9.24	9.54	9.84	10.15	10.45	10.76	11.06	11.36	11.67	11.98	12.28	12.59	12.90	13.20	13.51
79	9.06	9.36	9.67	9.97	10.28	10.59	10.89	11.20	11.51	11.82	12.13	12.44	12.75	13.06	13.37	13.68
78	9.18	9.49	9.79	10.10	10.41	10.73	11.04	11.35	11.66	11.97	12.29	12.60	12.91	13.23	13.54	13.86
77	9.30	9.61	9.93	10.24	10.55	10.87	11.18	11.50	11.81	12.13	12.45	12.77	13.08	13.40	13.72	14.04
76	9.43	9.74	10.06	10.38	10.69	11.01	11.33	11.65	11.97	12.29	12.61	12.93	13.26	13.58	13.90	14.22
75	9.56	9.88	10.20	10.52	10.84	11.16	11.48	11.81	12.13	12.46	12.78	13.11	13.43	13.76	14.09	14.41
74	9.69	10.01	10.34	10.66	10.99	11.31	11.64	11.97	12.30	12.63	12.96	13.29	13.62	13.95	14.28	14.61
73	9.82	10.15	10.48	10.81	11.14	11.47	11.80	12.13	12.47	12.80	13.13	13.47	13.80	14.14	14.47	14.81
70	10.25	10.59	10.93	11.28	11.62	11.96	12.31	12.65	13.00	13.35	13.70	14.04	14.39	14.74	15.09	15.44
65	11.04	11.41	11.77	12.14	12.51	12.88	13.25	13.62	13.99	14.37	14.74	15.12	15.49	15.87	16.24	16.62
60	11.95	12.34	12.74	13.14	13.54	13.94	14.34	14.74	15.14	15.55	15.95	16.36	16.77	17.18	17.58	17.99
55	13.00	13.44	13.87	14.30	14.74	15.18	15.61	16.05	16.50	16.94	17.38	17.83	18.27	18.72	19.16	19.61
50	14.26	14.74	15.21	15.69	16.17	16.66	17.14	17.63	18.11	18.60	19.09	19.58	20.07	20.57	21.06	21.55
45	15.79	16.32	16.85	17.39	17.92	18.46	19.00	19.55	20.09	20.64	21.18	21.73	22.28	22.83	23.38	23.93
40	17.69	18.29	18.90	19.50	20.11	20.72	21.33	21.95	22.56	23.18	23.80	24.42	25.04	25.66	26.28	26.90
35	20.14	20.83	21.53	22.23	22.93	23.63	24.34	25.04	25.75	26.46	27.17	27.88	28.59	29.30	30.01	30.72
30	23.42	24.24	25.06	25.88	26.71	27.53	28.36	29.19	30.02	30.85	31.68	32.51	33.34	34.17	35.00	35.83

Description: This table shows the price to pay for a bond at the yield rate. The yield is to maturity.

Example: The price of a 15.00 %, 29 year bond to yield 8 % to maturity is $ 178.50.

COUPON RATE, %

YIELD	11.00%	11.25%	11.50%	11.75%	12.00%	12.25%	12.50%	12.75%	13.00%	13.25%	13.50%	13.75%	14.00%	14.25%	14.50%	15.00%
0.00	419.00	426.25	433.50	440.75	448.00	455.25	462.50	469.75	477.00	484.25	491.50	498.75	506.00	513.25	520.50	535.00
1.00	351.20	357.48	363.76	370.04	376.32	382.59	388.87	395.15	401.43	407.71	413.99	420.27	426.55	432.83	439.11	451.67
2.00	297.32	302.80	308.28	313.76	319.24	324.72	330.21	335.69	341.17	346.65	352.13	357.61	363.09	368.57	374.05	385.02
3.00	254.22	259.04	263.86	268.68	273.50	278.32	283.14	287.96	292.78	297.60	302.42	307.24	312.06	316.87	321.69	331.33
4.00	219.51	223.78	228.04	232.31	236.58	240.85	245.12	249.39	253.65	257.92	262.19	266.46	270.73	274.99	279.26	287.80
4.25	211.91	216.06	220.20	224.35	228.49	232.64	236.78	240.93	245.07	249.22	253.36	257.51	261.65	265.80	269.94	278.23
4.50	204.70	208.73	212.76	216.79	220.81	224.84	228.87	232.89	236.92	240.95	244.98	249.00	253.03	257.06	261.08	269.14
4.75	197.85	201.77	205.68	209.60	213.51	217.43	221.34	225.25	229.17	233.08	237.00	240.91	244.83	248.74	252.65	260.48
5.00	191.35	195.15	198.96	202.76	206.57	210.38	214.18	217.99	221.79	225.60	229.41	233.21	237.02	240.82	244.63	252.24
5.25	185.16	188.86	192.56	196.26	199.97	203.67	207.37	211.07	214.77	218.48	222.18	225.88	229.58	233.29	236.99	244.39
5.50	179.27	182.87	186.47	190.08	193.68	197.28	200.89	204.49	208.09	211.69	215.30	218.90	222.50	226.11	229.71	236.92
5.75	173.66	177.17	180.68	184.19	187.69	191.20	194.71	198.22	201.73	205.23	208.74	212.25	215.76	219.26	222.77	229.79
6.00	168.33	171.74	175.16	178.58	181.99	185.41	188.83	192.24	195.66	199.07	202.49	205.91	209.32	212.74	216.16	222.99
6.25	163.24	166.57	169.90	173.23	176.56	179.89	183.22	186.54	189.87	193.20	196.53	199.86	203.19	206.52	209.85	216.50
6.50	158.40	161.64	164.89	168.13	171.38	174.62	177.87	181.11	184.35	187.60	190.84	194.09	197.33	200.58	203.82	210.31
6.75	153.78	156.94	160.11	163.27	166.43	169.60	172.76	175.92	179.09	182.25	185.42	188.58	191.74	194.91	198.07	204.40
7.00	149.37	152.46	155.54	158.63	161.72	164.80	167.89	170.97	174.06	177.15	180.23	183.32	186.40	189.49	192.57	198.75
7.25	145.17	148.18	151.19	154.20	157.21	160.22	163.23	166.24	169.26	172.27	175.28	178.29	181.30	184.31	187.32	193.34
7.50	141.15	144.09	147.03	149.97	152.91	155.85	158.79	161.72	164.66	167.60	170.54	173.48	176.42	179.36	182.30	188.18
7.75	137.31	140.18	143.05	145.92	148.79	151.66	154.53	157.40	160.27	163.14	166.01	168.88	171.75	174.62	177.49	183.24
8.00	133.64	136.45	139.25	142.06	144.86	147.66	150.47	153.27	156.07	158.88	161.68	164.49	167.29	170.09	172.90	178.50
8.25	130.14	132.88	135.62	138.36	141.10	143.84	146.57	149.31	152.05	154.79	157.53	160.27	163.01	165.75	168.49	173.97
8.50	126.78	129.46	132.14	134.82	137.49	140.17	142.85	145.53	148.21	150.88	153.56	156.24	158.92	161.60	164.27	169.63
8.75	123.57	126.19	128.81	131.42	134.04	136.66	139.28	141.90	144.52	147.14	149.76	152.37	154.99	157.61	160.23	165.47
9.00	120.49	123.05	125.62	128.18	130.74	133.30	135.86	138.42	140.98	143.55	146.11	148.67	151.23	153.79	156.35	161.48
9.25	117.54	120.05	122.56	125.06	127.57	130.08	132.58	135.09	137.60	140.10	142.61	145.12	147.62	150.13	152.63	157.65
9.50	114.72	117.17	119.63	122.08	124.53	126.99	129.44	131.89	134.35	136.80	139.25	141.70	144.16	146.61	149.06	153.97
9.75	112.01	114.41	116.81	119.22	121.62	124.02	126.42	128.82	131.23	133.63	136.03	138.43	140.83	143.23	145.64	150.44
10.00	109.41	111.76	114.11	116.47	118.82	121.17	123.52	125.88	128.23	130.58	132.93	135.29	137.64	139.99	142.34	147.05
10.25	106.91	109.22	111.52	113.83	116.13	118.44	120.74	123.05	125.35	127.66	129.96	132.27	134.57	136.87	139.18	143.79
10.50	104.52	106.78	109.03	111.29	113.55	115.81	118.07	120.33	122.59	124.84	127.10	129.36	131.62	133.88	136.14	140.65
10.75	102.21	104.43	106.64	108.86	111.07	113.28	115.50	117.71	119.93	122.14	124.35	126.57	128.78	131.00	133.21	137.64
11.00	100.00	102.17	104.34	106.51	108.68	110.85	113.03	115.20	117.37	119.54	121.71	123.88	126.05	128.22	130.39	134.73
11.25	97.87	100.00	102.13	104.26	106.39	108.52	110.65	112.78	114.90	117.03	119.16	121.29	123.42	125.55	127.68	131.94
11.50	95.82	97.91	100.00	102.09	104.18	106.27	108.36	110.44	112.53	114.62	116.71	118.80	120.89	122.98	125.07	129.25
11.75	93.85	95.90	97.95	100.00	102.05	104.10	106.15	108.20	110.25	112.30	114.35	116.40	118.45	120.50	122.55	126.65
12.00	91.95	93.96	95.98	97.99	100.00	102.01	104.02	106.04	108.05	110.06	112.07	114.09	116.10	118.11	120.12	124.15
12.25	90.12	92.10	94.07	96.05	98.02	100.00	101.98	103.95	105.93	107.90	109.88	111.86	113.83	115.81	117.78	121.73
12.50	88.36	90.30	92.24	94.18	96.12	98.06	100.00	101.94	103.88	105.82	107.76	109.70	111.64	113.58	115.52	119.41
12.75	86.66	88.56	90.47	92.37	94.28	96.19	98.09	100.00	101.91	103.81	105.72	107.63	109.53	111.44	113.34	117.16
13.00	85.01	86.89	88.76	90.63	92.51	94.38	96.25	98.13	100.00	101.87	103.75	105.62	107.49	109.37	111.24	114.99
13.25	83.43	85.27	87.11	88.95	90.79	92.64	94.48	96.32	98.16	100.00	101.84	103.68	105.52	107.36	109.21	112.89
13.50	81.90	83.71	85.52	87.33	89.14	90.95	92.76	94.57	96.38	98.19	100.00	101.81	103.62	105.43	107.24	110.86
13.75	80.42	82.20	83.98	85.76	87.54	89.32	91.10	92.88	94.66	96.44	98.22	100.00	101.78	103.56	105.34	108.90
14.00	78.99	80.75	82.50	84.25	86.00	87.75	89.50	91.25	93.00	94.75	96.50	98.25	100.00	101.75	103.50	107.00
14.25	77.61	79.34	81.06	82.78	84.50	86.22	87.95	89.67	91.39	93.11	94.83	96.56	98.28	100.00	101.72	105.17
14.50	76.28	77.97	79.67	81.36	83.06	84.75	86.44	88.14	89.83	91.53	93.22	94.92	96.61	98.31	100.00	103.39
14.75	74.99	76.65	78.32	79.99	81.66	83.32	84.99	86.66	88.33	89.99	91.66	93.33	95.00	96.66	98.33	101.67
15.00	73.74	75.38	77.02	78.66	80.30	81.94	83.58	85.23	86.87	88.51	90.15	91.79	93.43	95.08	96.72	100.00
15.25	72.52	74.14	75.76	77.37	78.99	80.61	82.22	83.84	85.45	87.07	88.69	90.30	91.92	93.54	95.15	98.38
15.50	71.35	72.94	74.53	76.13	77.72	79.31	80.90	82.49	84.08	85.68	87.27	88.86	90.45	92.04	93.63	96.82
15.75	70.21	71.78	73.35	74.92	76.48	78.05	79.62	81.19	82.75	84.32	85.89	87.46	89.03	90.59	92.16	95.30
16.00	69.11	70.65	72.20	73.74	75.29	76.83	78.38	79.92	81.47	83.01	84.55	86.10	87.64	89.19	90.73	93.82
16.25	68.04	69.56	71.08	72.61	74.13	75.65	77.17	78.69	80.22	81.74	83.26	84.78	86.30	87.82	89.35	92.39
16.50	67.00	68.50	70.00	71.50	73.00	74.50	76.00	77.50	79.00	80.50	82.00	83.50	85.00	86.50	88.00	91.00
16.75	66.00	67.47	68.95	70.43	71.91	73.39	74.87	76.34	77.82	79.30	80.78	82.26	83.74	85.22	86.69	89.65
17.00	65.02	66.47	67.93	69.39	70.85	72.31	73.76	75.22	76.68	78.14	79.59	81.05	82.51	83.97	85.42	88.34
17.25	64.07	65.50	66.94	68.38	69.82	71.25	72.69	74.13	75.57	77.00	78.44	79.88	81.31	82.75	84.19	87.06
17.50	63.14	64.56	65.98	67.40	68.81	70.23	71.65	73.07	74.48	75.90	77.32	78.74	80.15	81.57	82.99	85.82
17.75	62.25	63.64	65.04	66.44	67.84	69.24	70.64	72.03	73.43	74.83	76.23	77.63	79.03	80.42	81.82	84.62
18.00	61.37	62.75	64.13	65.51	66.89	68.27	69.65	71.03	72.41	73.79	75.17	76.55	77.93	79.31	80.69	83.45
18.25	60.52	61.89	63.25	64.61	65.97	67.33	68.69	70.05	71.41	72.78	74.14	75.50	76.86	78.22	79.58	82.30
18.50	59.70	61.04	62.39	63.73	65.07	66.42	67.76	69.10	70.45	71.79	73.13	74.48	75.82	77.16	78.51	81.19
18.75	58.90	60.22	61.55	62.87	64.20	65.53	66.85	68.18	69.50	70.83	72.15	73.48	74.81	76.13	77.46	80.11
19.00	58.11	59.42	60.73	62.04	63.35	64.66	65.97	67.28	68.58	69.89	71.20	72.51	73.82	75.13	76.44	79.06
20.00	55.18	56.42	57.67	58.91	60.16	61.40	62.65	63.89	65.14	66.38	67.63	68.87	70.12	71.36	72.61	75.10
25.00	44.06	45.06	46.06	47.06	48.06	49.06	50.05	51.05	52.05	53.05	54.05	55.05	56.05	57.05	58.05	60.04
30.00	36.69	37.52	38.35	39.19	40.02	40.85	41.68	42.52	43.35	44.18	45.02	45.85	46.68	47.52	48.35	50.02

Description: This table shows the yield to maturity of a bond purchased at the price shown in the index.

Example: The yield to maturity of a 15.00 %, 29 year bond at a price of 125.00 is 11.91 %.

COUPON RATE, %

PRICE	11.00%	11.25%	11.50%	11.75%	12.00%	12.25%	12.50%	12.75%	13.00%	13.25%	13.50%	13.75%	14.00%	14.25%	14.50%	15.00%
250	3.11	3.23	3.36	3.48	3.61	3.73	3.85	3.98	4.10	4.22	4.34	4.47	4.59	4.71	4.83	5.07
240	3.38	3.51	3.64	3.77	3.89	4.02	4.15	4.27	4.40	4.52	4.65	4.77	4.90	5.02	5.15	5.39
230	3.67	3.80	3.93	4.07	4.20	4.33	4.46	4.59	4.72	4.85	4.97	5.10	5.23	5.36	5.48	5.74
220	3.98	4.12	4.25	4.39	4.52	4.66	4.79	4.92	5.06	5.19	5.32	5.45	5.59	5.72	5.85	6.11
210	4.31	4.45	4.59	4.73	4.87	5.01	5.15	5.28	5.42	5.56	5.70	5.83	5.97	6.10	6.24	6.51
200	4.67	4.81	4.96	5.10	5.24	5.39	5.53	5.67	5.81	5.96	6.10	6.24	6.38	6.52	6.66	6.94
195	4.85	5.00	5.15	5.30	5.44	5.59	5.73	5.88	6.02	6.17	6.31	6.45	6.60	6.74	6.88	7.17
190	5.05	5.20	5.35	5.50	5.65	5.80	5.94	6.09	6.24	6.39	6.53	6.68	6.83	6.97	7.12	7.41
185	5.25	5.40	5.56	5.71	5.86	6.01	6.16	6.31	6.47	6.62	6.76	6.91	7.06	7.21	7.36	7.65
180	5.46	5.62	5.78	5.93	6.09	6.24	6.39	6.55	6.70	6.85	7.01	7.16	7.31	7.46	7.61	7.91
175	5.68	5.84	6.00	6.16	6.32	6.48	6.63	6.79	6.95	7.10	7.26	7.41	7.57	7.72	7.88	8.19
170	5.92	6.08	6.24	6.40	6.56	6.72	6.89	7.05	7.21	7.37	7.52	7.68	7.84	8.00	8.16	8.47
165	6.16	6.32	6.49	6.65	6.82	6.98	7.15	7.31	7.48	7.64	7.80	7.97	8.13	8.29	8.45	8.77
160	6.41	6.58	6.75	6.92	7.09	7.26	7.43	7.59	7.76	7.93	8.10	8.26	8.43	8.59	8.76	9.09
155	6.68	6.85	7.03	7.20	7.37	7.54	7.72	7.89	8.06	8.23	8.40	8.57	8.74	8.91	9.08	9.42
150	6.96	7.14	7.32	7.49	7.67	7.85	8.02	8.20	8.38	8.55	8.73	8.90	9.08	9.25	9.43	9.78
145	7.26	7.44	7.62	7.80	7.99	8.17	8.35	8.53	8.71	8.89	9.07	9.25	9.43	9.61	9.79	10.15
140	7.57	7.76	7.94	8.13	8.32	8.51	8.69	8.88	9.07	9.25	9.44	9.62	9.81	9.99	10.18	10.55
135	7.90	8.10	8.29	8.48	8.67	8.87	9.06	9.25	9.44	9.64	9.83	10.02	10.21	10.40	10.59	10.97
130	8.25	8.45	8.65	8.85	9.05	9.25	9.45	9.65	9.85	10.04	10.24	10.44	10.64	10.83	11.03	11.42
125	8.63	8.84	9.04	9.25	9.46	9.66	9.87	10.07	10.28	10.48	10.69	10.89	11.09	11.30	11.50	11.91
120	9.04	9.25	9.46	9.68	9.89	10.10	10.31	10.53	10.74	10.95	11.16	11.37	11.59	11.80	12.01	12.43
115	9.47	9.69	9.91	10.13	10.35	10.57	10.79	11.01	11.24	11.46	11.68	11.90	12.12	12.33	12.55	12.99
113	9.65	9.88	10.10	10.33	10.55	10.77	11.00	11.22	11.45	11.67	11.89	12.12	12.34	12.56	12.79	13.23
112	9.75	9.97	10.20	10.42	10.65	10.88	11.10	11.33	11.55	11.78	12.00	12.23	12.45	12.68	12.90	13.35
111	9.84	10.07	10.30	10.52	10.75	10.98	11.21	11.43	11.66	11.89	12.12	12.34	12.57	12.80	13.02	13.48
110	9.94	10.17	10.40	10.63	10.86	11.09	11.31	11.54	11.77	12.00	12.23	12.46	12.69	12.92	13.15	13.60
109	10.04	10.27	10.50	10.73	10.96	11.19	11.42	11.65	11.89	12.12	12.35	12.58	12.81	13.04	13.27	13.73
108	10.13	10.37	10.60	10.84	11.07	11.30	11.53	11.77	12.00	12.23	12.47	12.70	12.93	13.16	13.40	13.86
107	10.24	10.47	10.71	10.94	11.18	11.41	11.65	11.88	12.12	12.35	12.59	12.82	13.06	13.29	13.53	14.00
106	10.34	10.58	10.81	11.05	11.29	11.53	11.76	12.00	12.24	12.47	12.71	12.95	13.18	13.42	13.66	14.13
105	10.44	10.68	10.92	11.16	11.40	11.64	11.88	12.12	12.36	12.60	12.84	13.07	13.31	13.55	13.79	14.27
104	10.55	10.79	11.03	11.27	11.52	11.76	12.00	12.24	12.48	12.72	12.96	13.20	13.44	13.69	13.93	14.41
103	10.66	10.90	11.15	11.39	11.63	11.88	12.12	12.36	12.61	12.85	13.09	13.34	13.58	13.82	14.06	14.55
102	10.77	11.01	11.26	11.51	11.75	12.00	12.24	12.49	12.73	12.98	13.22	13.47	13.71	13.96	14.21	14.70
101	10.88	11.13	11.38	11.62	11.87	12.12	12.37	12.62	12.86	13.11	13.36	13.61	13.85	14.10	14.35	14.84
100	11.00	11.25	11.50	11.75	12.00	12.25	12.50	12.75	13.00	13.25	13.50	13.75	14.00	14.25	14.50	15.00
99	11.11	11.36	11.62	11.87	12.12	12.37	12.63	12.88	13.13	13.38	13.63	13.89	14.14	14.39	14.64	15.15
98	11.23	11.48	11.74	11.99	12.25	12.50	12.76	13.01	13.27	13.52	13.78	14.03	14.29	14.54	14.80	15.31
97	11.35	11.61	11.86	12.12	12.38	12.64	12.89	13.15	13.41	13.66	13.92	14.18	14.44	14.69	14.95	15.47
96	11.47	11.73	11.99	12.25	12.51	12.77	13.03	13.29	13.55	13.81	14.07	14.33	14.59	14.85	15.11	15.63
95	11.60	11.86	12.12	12.38	12.65	12.91	13.17	13.43	13.70	13.96	14.22	14.48	14.74	15.01	15.27	15.79
94	11.73	11.99	12.25	12.52	12.78	13.05	13.31	13.58	13.84	14.11	14.37	14.64	14.90	15.17	15.43	15.96
93	11.86	12.12	12.39	12.66	12.92	13.19	13.46	13.73	13.99	14.26	14.53	14.80	15.07	15.33	15.60	16.14
92	11.99	12.26	12.53	12.80	13.07	13.34	13.61	13.88	14.15	14.42	14.69	14.96	15.23	15.50	15.77	16.31
91	12.12	12.40	12.67	12.94	13.21	13.49	13.76	14.03	14.31	14.58	14.85	15.13	15.40	15.67	15.95	16.50
90	12.26	12.54	12.81	13.09	13.36	13.64	13.92	14.19	14.47	14.74	15.02	15.30	15.57	15.85	16.13	16.68
89	12.40	12.68	12.96	13.24	13.52	13.80	14.07	14.35	14.63	14.91	15.19	15.47	15.75	16.03	16.31	16.87
88	12.55	12.83	13.11	13.39	13.67	13.95	14.24	14.52	14.80	15.08	15.36	15.65	15.93	16.21	16.50	17.06
87	12.69	12.98	13.26	13.55	13.83	14.12	14.40	14.69	14.97	15.26	15.54	15.83	16.11	16.40	16.69	17.26
86	12.84	13.13	13.42	13.71	13.99	14.28	14.57	14.86	15.15	15.44	15.72	16.01	16.30	16.59	16.88	17.46
85	13.00	13.29	13.58	13.87	14.16	14.45	14.74	15.04	15.33	15.62	15.91	16.20	16.50	16.79	17.08	17.67
84	13.15	13.45	13.74	14.04	14.33	14.63	14.92	15.22	15.51	15.81	16.10	16.40	16.69	16.99	17.28	17.88
83	13.31	13.61	13.91	14.21	14.50	14.80	15.10	15.40	15.70	16.00	16.30	16.59	16.89	17.19	17.49	18.09
82	13.48	13.78	14.08	14.38	14.68	14.98	15.29	15.59	15.89	16.19	16.50	16.80	17.10	17.40	17.71	18.31
81	13.65	13.95	14.26	14.56	14.87	15.17	15.48	15.78	16.09	16.39	16.70	17.01	17.31	17.62	17.93	18.54
80	13.82	14.13	14.43	14.74	15.05	15.36	15.67	15.98	16.29	16.60	16.91	17.22	17.53	17.84	18.15	18.77
79	13.99	14.31	14.62	14.93	15.24	15.56	15.87	16.18	16.50	16.81	17.12	17.44	17.75	18.07	18.38	19.01
78	14.17	14.49	14.81	15.12	15.44	15.76	16.07	16.39	16.71	17.02	17.34	17.66	17.98	18.30	18.62	19.25
77	14.36	14.68	15.00	15.32	15.64	15.96	16.28	16.60	16.92	17.25	17.57	17.89	18.21	18.53	18.86	19.50
76	14.55	14.87	15.20	15.52	15.85	16.17	16.50	16.82	17.15	17.47	17.80	18.12	18.45	18.78	19.10	19.76
75	14.74	15.07	15.40	15.73	16.06	16.39	16.72	17.04	17.37	17.71	18.04	18.37	18.70	19.03	19.36	20.02
74	14.94	15.27	15.61	15.94	16.27	16.61	16.94	17.27	17.61	17.94	18.28	18.61	18.95	19.28	19.62	20.29
73	15.15	15.48	15.82	16.16	16.50	16.83	17.17	17.51	17.85	18.19	18.53	18.87	19.21	19.55	19.89	20.57
70	15.79	16.14	16.50	16.85	17.20	17.55	17.91	18.26	18.61	18.97	19.32	19.67	20.03	20.38	20.74	21.45
65	17.00	17.38	17.76	18.14	18.52	18.90	19.28	19.66	20.04	20.42	20.80	21.18	21.56	21.95	22.33	23.09
60	18.40	18.81	19.22	19.64	20.05	20.46	20.87	21.29	21.70	22.11	22.53	22.94	23.35	23.77	24.18	25.01
55	20.06	20.51	20.96	21.41	21.86	22.31	22.76	23.21	23.66	24.11	24.56	25.02	25.47	25.92	26.38	27.28

BOND PRICE

Description: This table shows the price to pay for a bond at the yield rate. The yield is to maturity.

Example: The price of a 6.75 %, 30 year bond to yield 8 % to maturity is $ 85.86.

COUPON RATE, %

YIELD	0.00%	1.00%	2.00%	3.00%	4.00%	4.25%	4.50%	4.75%	5.00%	5.25%	5.50%	5.75%	6.00%	6.25%	6.50%	6.75%
0.00	100.00	130.00	160.00	190.00	220.00	227.50	235.00	242.50	250.00	257.50	265.00	272.50	280.00	287.50	295.00	302.50
1.00	74.14	100.00	125.86	151.73	177.59	184.05	190.52	196.99	203.45	209.92	216.38	222.85	229.31	235.78	242.25	248.71
2.00	55.04	77.52	100.00	122.48	144.96	150.57	156.19	161.81	167.43	173.05	178.67	184.29	189.91	195.53	201.15	206.77
3.00	40.93	60.62	80.31	100.00	119.69	124.61	129.54	134.46	139.38	144.30	149.23	154.15	159.07	163.99	168.92	173.84
4.00	30.48	47.86	65.24	82.62	100.00	104.35	108.69	113.04	117.38	121.73	126.07	130.42	134.76	139.11	143.45	147.80
4.25	28.32	45.19	62.05	78.92	95.78	100.00	104.22	108.43	112.65	116.87	121.08	125.30	129.52	133.73	137.95	142.17
4.50	26.31	42.69	59.06	75.44	91.81	95.91	100.00	104.09	108.19	112.28	116.37	120.47	124.56	128.66	132.75	136.84
4.75	24.45	40.36	56.26	72.17	88.07	92.05	96.02	100.00	103.98	107.95	111.93	115.90	119.88	123.86	127.83	131.81
5.00	22.73	38.18	53.64	69.09	84.55	88.41	92.27	96.14	100.00	103.86	107.73	111.59	115.45	119.32	123.18	127.05
5.25	21.13	36.15	51.17	66.20	81.22	84.98	88.73	92.49	96.24	100.00	103.76	107.51	111.27	115.02	118.78	122.54
5.50	19.64	34.25	48.86	63.47	78.08	81.74	85.39	89.04	92.69	96.35	100.00	103.65	107.31	110.96	114.61	118.26
5.75	18.26	32.47	46.69	60.91	75.12	78.68	82.23	85.78	89.34	92.89	96.45	100.00	103.55	107.11	110.66	114.22
6.00	16.97	30.81	44.65	58.49	72.32	75.78	79.24	82.70	86.16	89.62	93.08	96.54	100.00	103.46	106.92	110.38
6.25	15.78	29.26	42.73	56.21	69.68	73.05	76.42	79.79	83.16	86.53	89.89	93.26	96.63	100.00	103.37	106.74
6.50	14.68	27.80	40.93	54.06	67.18	70.46	73.75	77.03	80.31	83.59	86.87	90.15	93.44	96.72	100.00	103.28
6.75	13.65	26.44	39.23	52.03	64.82	68.02	71.22	74.41	77.61	80.81	84.01	87.21	90.41	93.60	96.80	100.00
7.00	12.69	25.17	37.64	50.11	62.58	65.70	68.82	71.94	75.06	78.17	81.29	84.41	87.53	90.65	93.76	96.88
7.25	11.81	23.97	36.14	48.30	60.47	63.51	66.55	69.59	72.63	75.67	78.71	81.75	84.79	87.84	90.88	93.92
7.50	10.98	22.85	34.72	46.59	58.46	61.43	64.39	67.36	70.33	73.29	76.26	79.23	82.20	85.16	88.13	91.10
7.75	10.22	21.80	33.39	44.97	56.56	59.45	62.35	65.25	68.14	71.04	73.93	76.83	79.73	82.62	85.52	88.42
8.00	9.51	20.82	32.13	43.44	54.75	57.58	60.41	63.24	66.06	68.89	71.72	74.55	77.38	80.20	83.03	85.86
8.25	8.85	19.89	30.94	41.99	53.04	55.80	58.57	61.33	64.09	66.85	69.62	72.38	75.14	77.90	80.66	83.43
8.50	8.23	19.03	29.82	40.62	51.42	54.12	56.81	59.51	62.21	64.91	67.61	70.31	73.01	75.71	78.41	81.11
8.75	7.66	18.21	28.77	39.32	49.87	52.51	55.15	57.79	60.43	63.06	65.70	68.34	70.98	73.62	76.26	78.89
9.00	7.13	17.45	27.77	38.09	48.40	50.98	53.56	56.14	58.72	61.30	63.88	66.46	69.04	71.62	74.20	76.78
9.25	6.64	16.73	26.82	36.92	47.01	49.53	52.06	54.58	57.10	59.63	62.15	64.67	67.20	69.72	72.24	74.77
9.50	6.18	16.05	25.93	35.81	45.68	48.15	50.62	53.09	55.56	58.03	60.50	62.96	65.43	67.90	70.37	72.84
9.75	5.75	15.42	25.08	34.75	44.42	46.83	49.25	51.67	54.08	56.50	58.92	61.33	63.75	66.17	68.58	71.00
10.00	5.35	14.82	24.28	33.75	43.21	45.58	47.94	50.31	52.68	55.04	57.41	59.78	62.14	64.51	66.87	69.24
10.25	4.98	14.25	23.52	32.79	42.06	44.38	46.70	49.02	51.33	53.65	55.97	58.29	60.60	62.92	65.24	67.56
10.50	4.64	13.72	22.81	31.89	40.97	43.24	45.51	47.78	50.05	52.32	54.59	56.86	59.13	61.40	63.67	65.94
10.75	4.32	13.22	22.12	31.02	39.92	42.15	44.37	46.60	48.82	51.05	53.27	55.50	57.72	59.95	62.17	64.40
11.00	4.03	12.75	21.48	30.20	38.93	41.11	43.29	45.47	47.65	49.83	52.01	54.19	56.38	58.56	60.74	62.92
11.25	3.75	12.31	20.86	29.42	37.97	40.11	42.25	44.39	46.53	48.67	50.81	52.94	55.08	57.22	59.36	61.50
11.50	3.49	11.88	20.28	28.67	37.06	39.16	41.26	43.35	45.45	47.55	49.65	51.75	53.84	55.94	58.04	60.14
11.75	3.25	11.49	19.72	27.95	36.19	38.25	40.31	42.36	44.42	46.48	48.54	50.60	52.66	54.71	56.77	58.83
12.00	3.03	11.11	19.19	27.27	35.35	37.37	39.39	41.41	43.44	45.46	47.48	49.50	51.52	53.54	55.56	57.58
12.25	2.82	10.76	18.69	26.62	34.56	36.54	38.52	40.50	42.49	44.47	46.45	48.44	50.42	52.40	54.39	56.37
12.50	2.63	10.42	18.21	26.00	33.79	35.74	37.68	39.63	41.58	43.53	45.47	47.42	49.37	51.32	53.26	55.21
12.75	2.45	10.10	17.75	25.40	33.06	34.97	36.88	38.79	40.71	42.62	44.53	46.44	48.36	50.27	52.18	54.10
13.00	2.29	9.80	17.32	24.84	32.35	34.23	36.11	37.99	39.87	41.75	43.63	45.51	47.38	49.26	51.14	53.02
13.25	2.13	9.52	16.90	24.29	31.68	33.52	35.37	37.22	39.06	40.91	42.76	44.60	46.45	48.30	50.14	51.99
13.50	1.99	9.25	16.51	23.77	31.03	32.84	34.66	36.47	38.29	40.10	41.92	43.73	45.55	47.36	49.18	50.99
13.75	1.85	8.99	16.13	23.27	30.40	32.19	33.97	35.76	37.54	39.33	41.11	42.90	44.68	46.46	48.25	50.03
14.00	1.73	8.75	15.76	22.78	29.80	31.56	33.31	35.07	36.82	38.58	40.33	42.09	43.84	45.60	47.35	49.11
14.25	1.61	8.51	15.42	22.32	29.23	30.95	32.68	34.41	36.13	37.86	39.58	41.31	43.04	44.76	46.49	48.22
14.50	1.50	8.29	15.09	21.88	28.67	30.37	32.07	33.77	35.47	37.16	38.86	40.56	42.26	43.96	45.66	47.35
14.75	1.40	8.08	14.77	21.45	28.14	29.81	31.48	33.15	34.82	36.49	38.17	39.84	41.51	43.18	44.85	46.52
15.00	1.30	7.88	14.46	21.04	27.62	29.27	30.91	32.56	34.20	35.85	37.49	39.14	40.78	42.43	44.07	45.72
15.25	1.22	7.69	14.17	20.65	27.13	28.75	30.37	31.99	33.60	35.22	36.84	38.46	40.08	41.70	43.32	44.94
15.50	1.13	7.51	13.89	20.27	26.65	28.24	29.84	31.43	33.03	34.62	36.22	37.81	39.41	41.00	42.59	44.19
15.75	1.06	7.34	13.62	19.90	26.19	27.76	29.33	30.90	32.47	34.04	35.61	37.18	38.75	40.32	41.89	43.46
16.00	.99	7.18	13.36	19.55	25.74	27.29	28.83	30.38	31.93	33.48	35.02	36.57	38.12	39.66	41.21	42.76
16.25	.92	7.02	13.12	19.21	25.31	26.83	28.36	29.88	31.41	32.93	34.46	35.98	37.50	39.03	40.55	42.08
16.50	.86	6.87	12.88	18.89	24.89	26.40	27.90	29.40	30.90	32.40	33.91	35.41	36.91	38.41	39.91	41.42
16.75	.80	6.72	12.65	18.57	24.49	25.97	27.45	28.93	30.41	31.89	33.37	34.86	36.34	37.82	39.30	40.78
17.00	.75	6.59	12.43	18.26	24.10	25.56	27.02	28.48	29.94	31.40	32.86	34.32	35.78	37.24	38.70	40.16
17.25	.70	6.46	12.21	17.97	23.72	25.16	26.60	28.04	29.48	30.92	32.36	33.80	35.24	36.68	38.12	39.56
17.50	.65	6.33	12.01	17.68	23.36	24.78	26.20	27.62	29.04	30.46	31.88	33.29	34.71	36.13	37.55	38.97
17.75	.61	6.21	11.81	17.41	23.01	24.41	25.81	27.21	28.61	30.01	31.41	32.81	34.21	35.61	37.01	38.41
18.00	.57	6.09	11.62	17.14	22.66	24.05	25.43	26.81	28.19	29.57	30.95	32.33	33.71	35.09	36.47	37.86
18.25	.53	5.98	11.43	16.88	22.33	23.69	25.06	26.42	27.78	29.14	30.51	31.87	33.23	34.60	35.96	37.32
18.50	.50	5.87	11.25	16.63	22.01	23.35	24.70	26.04	27.39	28.73	30.08	31.42	32.77	34.11	35.46	36.80
18.75	.46	5.77	11.08	16.39	21.70	23.02	24.35	25.68	27.01	28.33	29.66	30.99	32.31	33.64	34.97	36.30
19.00	.43	5.67	10.91	16.15	21.39	22.70	24.01	25.32	26.63	27.94	29.25	30.56	31.87	33.18	34.49	35.80
20.00	.33	5.31	10.30	15.28	20.26	21.51	22.75	24.00	25.25	26.49	27.74	28.98	30.23	31.48	32.72	33.97
25.00	.09	4.08	8.08	12.08	16.07	17.07	18.07	19.07	20.07	21.07	22.07	23.07	24.06	25.06	26.06	27.06
30.00	.02	3.36	6.69	10.02	13.35	14.19	15.02	15.85	16.69	17.52	18.35	19.19	20.02	20.85	21.68	22.52

Description: This table shows the yield to maturity of a bond purchased at the price shown in the index.

Example: The yield to maturity of a 6.75 %, 30 year bond at a price of 80.00 is 8.62 %.

COUPON RATE, %

PRICE	0.00%	1.00%	2.00%	3.00%	4.00%	4.25%	4.50%	4.75%	5.00%	5.25%	5.50%	5.75%	6.00%	6.25%	6.50%	6.75%
100	0.00	1.00	2.00	3.00	4.00	4.25	4.50	4.75	5.00	5.25	5.50	5.75	6.00	6.25	6.50	6.75
99	.03	1.03	2.04	3.05	4.05	4.30	4.56	4.81	5.06	5.31	5.56	5.82	6.07	6.32	6.57	6.82
98	.06	1.07	2.09	3.10	4.11	4.37	4.62	4.87	5.13	5.38	5.63	5.89	6.14	6.40	6.65	6.90
97	.10	1.11	2.13	3.15	4.17	4.43	4.68	4.94	5.19	5.45	5.71	5.96	6.22	6.47	6.73	6.99
96	.13	1.15	2.18	3.20	4.23	4.49	4.75	5.00	5.26	5.52	5.78	6.04	6.29	6.55	6.81	7.07
95	.17	1.19	2.22	3.26	4.29	4.55	4.81	5.07	5.33	5.59	5.85	6.11	6.37	6.63	6.89	7.15
94	.20	1.24	2.27	3.31	4.36	4.62	4.88	5.14	5.40	5.66	5.93	6.19	6.45	6.71	6.98	7.24
93	.24	1.28	2.32	3.37	4.42	4.68	4.95	5.21	5.47	5.74	6.00	6.27	6.53	6.79	7.06	7.33
92	.27	1.32	2.37	3.42	4.48	4.75	5.01	5.28	5.55	5.81	6.08	6.34	6.61	6.88	7.15	7.41
91	.31	1.36	2.42	3.48	4.55	4.82	5.08	5.35	5.62	5.89	6.16	6.43	6.69	6.96	7.23	7.50
90	.35	1.40	2.47	3.54	4.61	4.88	5.15	5.42	5.69	5.97	6.24	6.51	6.78	7.05	7.32	7.60
89	.38	1.45	2.52	3.60	4.68	4.95	5.23	5.50	5.77	6.04	6.32	6.59	6.87	7.14	7.41	7.69
88	.42	1.49	2.57	3.66	4.75	5.02	5.30	5.57	5.85	6.12	6.40	6.68	6.95	7.23	7.51	7.78
87	.46	1.54	2.62	3.72	4.82	5.10	5.37	5.65	5.93	6.21	6.48	6.76	7.04	7.32	7.60	7.88
86	.50	1.58	2.68	3.78	4.89	5.17	5.45	5.73	6.01	6.29	6.57	6.85	7.13	7.42	7.70	7.98
85	.54	1.63	2.73	3.84	4.96	5.24	5.53	5.81	6.09	6.37	6.66	6.94	7.23	7.51	7.80	8.08
84	.58	1.68	2.79	3.91	5.04	5.32	5.60	5.89	6.17	6.46	6.75	7.03	7.32	7.61	7.90	8.18
83	.62	1.72	2.84	3.97	5.11	5.40	5.68	5.97	6.26	6.55	6.84	7.13	7.42	7.71	8.00	8.29
82	.66	1.77	2.90	4.04	5.19	5.47	5.76	6.05	6.34	6.64	6.93	7.22	7.51	7.81	8.10	8.40
81	.70	1.82	2.96	4.10	5.26	5.55	5.85	6.14	6.43	6.73	7.02	7.32	7.61	7.91	8.21	8.51
80	.74	1.87	3.01	4.17	5.34	5.64	5.93	6.23	6.52	6.82	7.12	7.42	7.72	8.02	8.32	8.62
79	.78	1.92	3.07	4.24	5.42	5.72	6.02	6.31	6.61	6.92	7.22	7.52	7.82	8.12	8.43	8.73
78	.82	1.97	3.13	4.31	5.50	5.80	6.10	6.41	6.71	7.01	7.32	7.62	7.93	8.23	8.54	8.85
77	.87	2.02	3.19	4.38	5.58	5.89	6.19	6.50	6.80	7.11	7.42	7.73	8.04	8.35	8.66	8.97
76	.91	2.07	3.25	4.45	5.67	5.98	6.28	6.59	6.90	7.21	7.52	7.83	8.15	8.46	8.78	9.09
75	.96	2.13	3.32	4.53	5.76	6.07	6.38	6.69	7.00	7.31	7.63	7.94	8.26	8.58	8.90	9.22
74	1.00	2.18	3.38	4.60	5.84	6.16	6.47	6.79	7.10	7.42	7.74	8.06	8.38	8.70	9.02	9.34
73	1.05	2.24	3.45	4.68	5.93	6.25	6.57	6.89	7.21	7.53	7.85	8.17	8.50	8.82	9.15	9.47
72	1.09	2.29	3.51	4.76	6.02	6.34	6.67	6.99	7.31	7.64	7.96	8.29	8.62	8.95	9.28	9.61
71	1.14	2.35	3.58	4.84	6.12	6.44	6.77	7.09	7.42	7.75	8.08	8.41	8.74	9.08	9.41	9.75
70	1.19	2.41	3.65	4.92	6.21	6.54	6.87	7.20	7.53	7.86	8.20	8.53	8.87	9.21	9.55	9.89
69	1.24	2.46	3.72	5.00	6.31	6.64	6.98	7.31	7.65	7.98	8.32	8.66	9.00	9.34	9.69	10.03
68	1.28	2.52	3.79	5.09	6.41	6.75	7.08	7.42	7.76	8.10	8.45	8.79	9.13	9.48	9.83	10.18
67	1.33	2.58	3.86	5.17	6.51	6.85	7.19	7.54	7.88	8.23	8.57	8.92	9.27	9.62	9.98	10.33
66	1.38	2.65	3.94	5.26	6.62	6.96	7.31	7.65	8.00	8.35	8.71	9.06	9.41	9.77	10.13	10.49
65	1.44	2.71	4.01	5.35	6.73	7.07	7.42	7.77	8.13	8.48	8.84	9.20	9.56	9.92	10.28	10.65
64	1.49	2.77	4.09	5.45	6.84	7.19	7.54	7.90	8.26	8.62	8.98	9.34	9.71	10.07	10.44	10.81
63	1.54	2.84	4.17	5.54	6.95	7.30	7.66	8.03	8.39	8.75	9.12	9.49	9.86	10.23	10.61	10.98
62	1.59	2.90	4.25	5.64	7.06	7.42	7.79	8.16	8.52	8.89	9.27	9.64	10.02	10.40	10.77	11.16
61	1.65	2.97	4.33	5.74	7.18	7.55	7.92	8.29	8.66	9.04	9.42	9.80	10.18	10.56	10.95	11.34
60	1.71	3.04	4.41	5.84	7.30	7.67	8.05	8.43	8.81	9.19	9.57	9.96	10.35	10.74	11.13	11.52
59	1.76	3.11	4.50	5.94	7.43	7.80	8.18	8.57	8.95	9.34	9.73	10.12	10.52	10.91	11.31	11.71
58	1.82	3.18	4.59	6.05	7.55	7.94	8.32	8.71	9.11	9.50	9.90	10.29	10.70	11.10	11.50	11.91
57	1.88	3.25	4.68	6.16	7.69	8.08	8.47	8.86	9.26	9.66	10.06	10.47	10.88	11.29	11.70	12.11
56	1.94	3.33	4.77	6.27	7.82	8.22	8.62	9.02	9.42	9.83	10.24	10.65	11.07	11.48	11.90	12.32
55	2.00	3.40	4.86	6.38	7.96	8.36	8.77	9.18	9.59	10.00	10.42	10.84	11.26	11.69	12.11	12.54
54	2.06	3.48	4.96	6.50	8.10	8.51	8.93	9.34	9.76	10.18	10.61	11.03	11.46	11.90	12.33	12.77
53	2.12	3.56	5.06	6.62	8.25	8.67	9.09	9.51	9.94	10.37	10.80	11.23	11.67	12.11	12.56	13.00
52	2.19	3.64	5.16	6.75	8.40	8.83	9.25	9.69	10.12	10.56	11.00	11.44	11.89	12.34	12.79	13.24
51	2.25	3.72	5.26	6.88	8.56	8.99	9.43	9.87	10.31	10.75	11.20	11.66	12.11	12.57	13.03	13.49
50	2.32	3.81	5.37	7.01	8.72	9.16	9.61	10.05	10.51	10.96	11.42	11.88	12.34	12.81	13.28	13.75
49	2.39	3.89	5.48	7.15	8.89	9.34	9.79	10.25	10.71	11.17	11.64	12.11	12.59	13.06	13.54	14.02
48	2.46	3.98	5.59	7.29	9.07	9.52	9.98	10.45	10.92	11.39	11.87	12.35	12.84	13.32	13.81	14.31
47	2.53	4.07	5.71	7.43	9.25	9.71	10.18	10.66	11.14	11.62	12.11	12.60	13.10	13.59	14.10	14.60
46	2.60	4.17	5.83	7.58	9.43	9.91	10.39	10.88	11.37	11.86	12.36	12.86	13.37	13.88	14.39	14.91
45	2.67	4.26	5.95	7.74	9.63	10.11	10.61	11.10	11.60	12.11	12.62	13.13	13.65	14.17	14.70	15.23
44	2.75	4.36	6.08	7.90	9.83	10.33	10.83	11.34	11.85	12.37	12.89	13.42	13.95	14.48	15.02	15.56
43	2.83	4.46	6.21	8.07	10.04	10.55	11.06	11.58	12.11	12.64	13.17	13.71	14.26	14.80	15.35	15.91
42	2.91	4.57	6.34	8.24	10.26	10.78	11.31	11.84	12.38	12.92	13.47	14.02	14.58	15.14	15.71	16.27
41	2.99	4.67	6.48	8.42	10.49	11.02	11.56	12.11	12.66	13.22	13.78	14.35	14.92	15.49	16.07	16.66
40	3.07	4.79	6.63	8.61	10.73	11.27	11.83	12.39	12.96	13.53	14.11	14.69	15.27	15.87	16.46	17.06
39	3.16	4.90	6.78	8.81	10.98	11.54	12.11	12.68	13.26	13.85	14.45	15.05	15.65	16.26	16.87	17.48
35	3.53	5.39	7.44	9.68	12.10	12.73	13.37	14.02	14.68	15.34	16.01	16.68	17.36	18.04	18.73	19.42
30	4.05	6.12	8.45	11.06	13.91	14.66	15.42	16.19	16.96	17.75	18.54	19.34	20.14	20.95	21.77	22.58
25	4.67	7.03	9.77	12.92	16.43	17.35	18.28	19.23	20.18	21.15	22.12	23.09	24.07	25.06	26.05	27.04
20	5.43	8.22	11.62	15.68	20.24	21.44	22.64	23.86	25.08	26.31	27.54	28.78	30.02	31.27	32.51	33.76
15	6.42	9.92	14.56	20.34	26.74	28.38	30.03	31.69	33.35	35.01	36.67	38.33	40.00	41.66	43.33	45.00
10	7.82	12.83	20.52	30.06	40.00	42.50	45.00	47.50	50.00	52.50	55.00	57.50	60.00	62.50	65.00	67.50

BOND PRICE

Description: This table shows the price to pay for a bond at the yield rate. The yield is to maturity.

Example: The price of a 10.75 %, 30 year bond to yield 8 % to maturity is $ 131.11.

							COUPON RATE, %									
YIELD	7.00%	7.25%	7.50%	7.75%	8.00%	8.25%	8.50%	8.75%	9.00%	9.25%	9.50%	9.75%	10.00%	10.25%	10.50%	10.75%
0.00	310.00	317.50	325.00	332.50	340.00	347.50	355.00	362.50	370.00	377.50	385.00	392.50	400.00	407.50	415.00	422.50
1.00	255.18	261.64	268.11	274.57	281.04	287.51	293.97	300.44	306.90	313.37	319.83	326.30	332.77	339.23	345.70	352.16
2.00	212.39	218.01	223.63	229.25	234.87	240.48	246.10	251.72	257.34	262.96	268.58	274.20	279.82	285.44	291.06	296.68
3.00	178.76	183.68	188.61	193.53	198.45	203.37	208.30	213.22	218.14	223.06	227.99	232.91	237.83	242.75	247.68	252.60
4.00	152.14	156.49	160.83	165.18	169.52	173.87	178.21	182.56	186.90	191.25	195.59	199.94	204.28	208.63	212.97	217.32
4.25	146.38	150.60	154.81	159.03	163.25	167.46	171.68	175.90	180.11	184.33	188.55	192.76	196.98	201.20	205.41	209.63
4.50	140.94	145.03	149.12	153.22	157.31	161.40	165.50	169.59	173.69	177.78	181.87	185.97	190.06	194.15	198.25	202.34
4.75	135.78	139.76	143.74	147.71	151.69	155.66	159.64	163.62	167.59	171.57	175.55	179.52	183.50	187.47	191.45	195.43
5.00	130.91	134.77	138.64	142.50	146.36	150.23	154.09	157.95	161.82	165.68	169.54	173.41	177.27	181.14	185.00	188.86
5.25	126.29	130.05	133.80	137.56	141.32	145.07	148.83	152.58	156.34	160.09	163.85	167.61	171.36	175.12	178.87	182.63
5.50	121.92	125.57	129.22	132.88	136.53	140.18	143.83	147.49	151.14	154.79	158.45	162.10	165.75	169.40	173.06	176.71
5.75	117.77	121.32	124.88	128.43	131.99	135.54	139.09	142.65	146.20	149.76	153.31	156.87	160.42	163.97	167.53	171.08
6.00	113.84	117.30	120.76	124.22	127.68	131.14	134.59	138.05	141.51	144.97	148.43	151.89	155.35	158.81	162.27	165.73
6.25	110.11	113.47	116.84	120.21	123.58	126.95	130.32	133.69	137.06	140.42	143.79	147.16	150.53	153.90	157.27	160.64
6.50	106.56	109.85	113.13	116.41	119.69	122.97	126.25	129.54	132.82	136.10	139.38	142.66	145.94	149.23	152.51	155.79
6.75	103.20	106.40	109.59	112.79	115.99	119.19	122.39	125.59	128.78	131.98	135.18	138.38	141.58	144.78	147.97	151.17
7.00	100.00	103.12	106.24	109.35	112.47	115.59	118.71	121.83	124.94	128.06	131.18	134.30	137.42	140.54	143.65	146.77
7.25	96.96	100.00	103.04	106.08	109.12	112.16	115.21	118.25	121.29	124.33	127.37	130.41	133.45	136.49	139.53	142.58
7.50	94.07	97.03	100.00	102.97	105.93	108.90	111.87	114.84	117.80	120.77	123.74	126.71	129.67	132.64	135.61	138.57
7.75	91.31	94.21	97.10	100.00	102.90	105.79	108.69	111.58	114.48	117.38	120.27	123.17	126.07	128.96	131.86	134.75
8.00	88.69	91.52	94.34	97.17	100.00	102.83	105.66	108.48	111.31	114.14	116.97	119.80	122.62	125.45	128.28	131.11
8.25	86.19	88.95	91.71	94.48	97.24	100.00	102.76	105.52	108.29	111.05	113.81	116.57	119.34	122.10	124.86	127.62
8.50	83.81	86.50	89.20	91.90	94.60	97.30	100.00	102.70	105.40	108.10	110.80	113.50	116.19	118.89	121.59	124.29
8.75	81.53	84.17	86.81	89.45	92.09	94.72	97.36	100.00	102.64	105.28	107.91	110.55	113.19	115.83	118.47	121.11
9.00	79.36	81.94	84.52	87.10	89.68	92.26	94.84	97.42	100.00	102.58	105.16	107.74	110.32	112.90	115.48	118.06
9.25	77.29	79.81	82.34	84.86	87.38	89.91	92.43	94.95	97.48	100.00	102.52	105.05	107.57	110.09	112.62	115.14
9.50	75.31	77.78	80.25	82.72	85.19	87.65	90.12	92.59	95.06	97.53	100.00	102.47	104.94	107.41	109.88	112.35
9.75	73.42	75.83	78.25	80.67	83.08	85.50	87.92	90.33	92.75	95.17	97.58	100.00	102.42	104.83	107.25	109.67
10.00	71.61	73.97	76.34	78.70	81.07	83.44	85.80	88.17	90.54	92.90	95.27	97.63	100.00	102.37	104.73	107.10
10.25	69.87	72.19	74.51	76.83	79.14	81.46	83.78	86.10	88.41	90.73	93.05	95.37	97.68	100.00	102.32	104.63
10.50	68.21	70.48	72.75	75.03	77.30	79.57	81.84	84.11	86.38	88.65	90.92	93.19	95.46	97.73	100.00	102.27
10.75	66.62	68.85	71.07	73.30	75.52	77.75	79.97	82.20	84.42	86.65	88.87	91.10	93.32	95.55	97.77	100.00
11.00	65.10	67.28	69.46	71.64	73.83	76.01	78.19	80.37	82.55	84.73	86.91	89.09	91.28	93.46	95.64	97.82
11.25	63.64	65.78	67.92	70.06	72.19	74.33	76.47	78.61	80.75	82.89	85.03	87.17	89.31	91.44	93.58	95.72
11.50	62.24	64.33	66.43	68.53	70.63	72.73	74.82	76.92	79.02	81.12	83.22	85.31	87.41	89.51	91.61	93.71
11.75	60.89	62.95	65.01	67.07	69.12	71.18	73.24	75.30	77.36	79.42	81.47	83.53	85.59	87.65	89.71	91.77
12.00	59.60	61.62	63.64	65.66	67.68	69.70	71.72	73.74	75.76	77.78	79.80	81.82	83.84	85.86	87.88	89.90
12.25	58.35	60.34	62.32	64.30	66.29	68.27	70.25	72.24	74.22	76.20	78.19	80.17	82.15	84.13	86.12	88.10
12.50	57.16	59.11	61.05	63.00	64.95	66.89	68.84	70.79	72.74	74.68	76.63	78.58	80.53	82.47	84.42	86.37
12.75	56.01	57.92	59.83	61.75	63.66	65.57	67.48	69.40	71.31	73.22	75.13	77.05	78.96	80.87	82.79	84.70
13.00	54.90	56.78	58.66	60.54	62.42	64.30	66.18	68.05	69.93	71.81	73.69	75.57	77.45	79.33	81.21	83.09
13.25	53.84	55.68	57.53	59.37	61.22	63.07	64.91	66.76	68.61	70.45	72.30	74.15	75.99	77.84	79.69	81.53
13.50	52.81	54.62	56.44	58.25	60.07	61.88	63.70	65.51	67.33	69.14	70.96	72.77	74.59	76.40	78.22	80.03
13.75	51.82	53.60	55.39	57.17	58.96	60.74	62.52	64.31	66.09	67.88	69.66	71.45	73.23	75.02	76.80	78.59
14.00	50.86	52.62	54.37	56.13	57.88	59.64	61.39	63.15	64.90	66.66	68.41	70.17	71.92	73.68	75.43	77.19
14.25	49.94	51.67	53.39	55.12	56.85	58.57	60.30	62.02	63.75	65.48	67.20	68.93	70.66	72.38	74.11	75.83
14.50	49.05	50.75	52.45	54.15	55.84	57.54	59.24	60.94	62.64	64.34	66.03	67.73	69.43	71.13	72.83	74.53
14.75	48.19	49.86	51.54	53.21	54.88	56.55	58.22	59.89	61.56	63.23	64.90	66.58	68.25	69.92	71.59	73.26
15.00	47.36	49.01	50.65	52.30	53.94	55.59	57.23	58.88	60.52	62.17	63.81	65.46	67.10	68.75	70.39	72.04
15.25	46.56	48.18	49.80	51.42	53.04	54.66	56.28	57.90	59.52	61.13	62.75	64.37	65.99	67.61	69.23	70.85
15.50	45.78	47.38	48.97	50.57	52.16	53.76	55.35	56.95	58.54	60.14	61.73	63.32	64.92	66.51	68.11	69.70
15.75	45.03	46.60	48.17	49.74	51.31	52.89	54.46	56.03	57.60	59.17	60.74	62.31	63.88	65.45	67.02	68.59
16.00	44.31	45.85	47.40	48.95	50.49	52.04	53.59	55.13	56.68	58.23	59.78	61.32	62.87	64.42	65.96	67.51
16.25	43.60	45.13	46.65	48.17	49.70	51.22	52.75	54.27	55.80	57.32	58.84	60.37	61.89	63.42	64.94	66.47
16.50	42.92	44.42	45.92	47.43	48.93	50.43	51.93	53.43	54.94	56.44	57.94	59.44	60.94	62.45	63.95	65.45
16.75	42.26	43.74	45.22	46.70	48.18	49.66	51.14	52.62	54.10	55.58	57.06	58.54	60.02	61.51	62.99	64.47
17.00	41.62	43.08	44.54	46.00	47.46	48.91	50.37	51.83	53.29	54.75	56.21	57.67	59.13	60.59	62.05	63.51
17.25	40.99	42.43	43.87	45.31	46.75	48.19	49.63	51.07	52.51	53.95	55.39	56.83	58.26	59.70	61.14	62.58
17.50	40.39	41.81	43.23	44.65	46.07	47.49	48.91	50.33	51.75	53.16	54.58	56.00	57.42	58.84	60.26	61.68
17.75	39.81	41.21	42.60	44.00	45.40	46.80	48.20	49.60	51.00	52.40	53.80	55.20	56.60	58.00	59.40	60.80
18.00	39.24	40.62	42.00	43.38	44.76	46.14	47.52	48.90	50.28	51.67	53.05	54.43	55.81	57.19	58.57	59.95
18.25	38.68	40.05	41.41	42.77	44.13	45.50	46.86	48.22	49.58	50.95	52.31	53.67	55.03	56.40	57.76	59.12
18.50	38.15	39.49	40.83	42.18	43.52	44.87	46.21	47.56	48.90	50.25	51.59	52.94	54.28	55.63	56.97	58.32
18.75	37.62	38.95	40.28	41.60	42.93	44.26	45.59	46.91	48.24	49.57	50.89	52.22	53.55	54.88	56.20	57.53
19.00	37.11	38.42	39.73	41.05	42.36	43.67	44.98	46.29	47.60	48.91	50.22	51.53	52.84	54.15	55.46	56.77
20.00	35.21	36.46	37.71	38.95	40.20	41.44	42.69	43.93	45.18	46.43	47.67	48.92	50.16	51.41	52.66	53.90
25.00	28.06	29.06	30.06	31.06	32.06	33.06	34.06	35.06	36.05	37.05	38.05	39.05	40.05	41.05	42.05	43.05
30.00	23.35	24.18	25.02	25.85	26.68	27.52	28.35	29.18	30.02	30.85	31.68	32.52	33.35	34.18	35.01	35.85

Description: This table shows the yield to maturity of a bond purchased at the price shown in the index.

Example: The yield to maturity of a 10.75 %, 30 year bond at a price of 111.00 is 9.62 %.

PRICE	7.00%	7.25%	7.50%	7.75%	8.00%	8.25%	8.50%	8.75%	9.00%	9.25%	9.50%	9.75%	10.00%	10.25%	10.50%	10.75%
175	3.12	3.29	3.46	3.62	3.79	3.95	4.12	4.28	4.44	4.61	4.77	4.93	5.09	5.25	5.41	5.57
170	3.30	3.47	3.64	3.81	3.98	4.14	4.31	4.48	4.64	4.81	4.98	5.14	5.30	5.47	5.63	5.79
165	3.48	3.66	3.83	4.00	4.17	4.35	4.52	4.69	4.86	5.02	5.19	5.36	5.53	5.70	5.86	6.03
160	3.68	3.85	4.03	4.20	4.38	4.55	4.73	4.90	5.08	5.25	5.42	5.59	5.77	5.94	6.11	6.28
155	3.88	4.06	4.24	4.42	4.60	4.77	4.95	5.13	5.31	5.48	5.66	5.84	6.01	6.19	6.36	6.54
150	4.09	4.27	4.46	4.64	4.82	5.01	5.19	5.37	5.55	5.73	5.91	6.09	6.27	6.45	6.63	6.81
145	4.31	4.50	4.69	4.87	5.06	5.25	5.44	5.62	5.81	5.99	6.18	6.36	6.55	6.73	6.92	7.10
140	4.54	4.73	4.93	5.12	5.31	5.50	5.70	5.89	6.08	6.27	6.46	6.65	6.84	7.03	7.22	7.40
135	4.78	4.98	5.18	5.38	5.58	5.78	5.97	6.17	6.36	6.56	6.76	6.95	7.15	7.34	7.53	7.73
130	5.04	5.25	5.45	5.66	5.86	6.06	6.26	6.47	6.67	6.87	7.07	7.27	7.47	7.67	7.87	8.07
125	5.32	5.53	5.74	5.95	6.16	6.37	6.57	6.78	6.99	7.20	7.41	7.61	7.82	8.03	8.23	8.44
120	5.61	5.83	6.04	6.26	6.47	6.69	6.91	7.12	7.34	7.55	7.77	7.98	8.19	8.41	8.62	8.83
119	5.67	5.89	6.11	6.32	6.54	6.76	6.97	7.19	7.41	7.62	7.84	8.06	8.27	8.49	8.70	8.92
118	5.73	5.95	6.17	6.39	6.61	6.83	7.04	7.26	7.48	7.70	7.92	8.13	8.35	8.57	8.78	9.00
117	5.79	6.01	6.23	6.46	6.68	6.90	7.12	7.34	7.55	7.77	7.99	8.21	8.43	8.65	8.87	9.08
116	5.86	6.08	6.30	6.52	6.74	6.97	7.19	7.41	7.63	7.85	8.07	8.29	8.51	8.73	8.95	9.17
115	5.92	6.14	6.37	6.59	6.81	7.04	7.26	7.48	7.71	7.93	8.15	8.37	8.59	8.81	9.04	9.26
114	5.98	6.21	6.44	6.66	6.88	7.11	7.33	7.56	7.78	8.01	8.23	8.45	8.68	8.90	9.12	9.35
113	6.05	6.28	6.50	6.73	6.96	7.18	7.41	7.63	7.86	8.09	8.31	8.54	8.76	8.99	9.21	9.44
112	6.12	6.35	6.57	6.80	7.03	7.26	7.48	7.71	7.94	8.17	8.39	8.62	8.85	9.07	9.30	9.53
111	6.18	6.41	6.64	6.87	7.10	7.33	7.56	7.79	8.02	8.25	8.48	8.71	8.93	9.16	9.39	9.62
110	6.25	6.48	6.72	6.95	7.18	7.41	7.64	7.87	8.10	8.33	8.56	8.79	9.02	9.25	9.48	9.71
109	6.32	6.56	6.79	7.02	7.25	7.49	7.72	7.95	8.19	8.42	8.65	8.88	9.11	9.35	9.58	9.81
108	6.39	6.63	6.86	7.10	7.33	7.57	7.80	8.04	8.27	8.50	8.74	8.97	9.21	9.44	9.67	9.91
107	6.46	6.70	6.94	7.17	7.41	7.65	7.88	8.12	8.35	8.59	8.83	9.06	9.30	9.53	9.77	10.00
106	6.54	6.77	7.01	7.25	7.49	7.73	7.97	8.20	8.44	8.68	8.92	9.16	9.39	9.63	9.87	10.11
105	6.61	6.85	7.09	7.33	7.57	7.81	8.05	8.29	8.53	8.77	9.01	9.25	9.49	9.73	9.97	10.21
104	6.68	6.93	7.17	7.41	7.65	7.89	8.14	8.38	8.62	8.86	9.10	9.35	9.59	9.83	10.07	10.31
103	6.76	7.00	7.25	7.49	7.74	7.98	8.22	8.47	8.71	8.96	9.20	9.44	9.69	9.93	10.17	10.42
102	6.84	7.08	7.33	7.58	7.82	8.07	8.31	8.56	8.80	9.05	9.30	9.54	9.79	10.03	10.28	10.52
101	6.92	7.16	7.41	7.66	7.91	8.16	8.40	8.65	8.90	9.15	9.39	9.64	9.89	10.14	10.39	10.63
100	7.00	7.25	7.50	7.75	8.00	8.25	8.50	8.75	9.00	9.25	9.50	9.75	10.00	10.25	10.50	10.75
99	7.08	7.33	7.58	7.83	8.08	8.34	8.59	8.84	9.09	9.34	9.60	9.85	10.10	10.35	10.61	10.86
98	7.16	7.41	7.67	7.92	8.17	8.43	8.68	8.94	9.19	9.45	9.70	9.96	10.21	10.46	10.72	10.97
97	7.24	7.50	7.75	8.01	8.27	8.52	8.78	9.04	9.29	9.55	9.81	10.06	10.32	10.58	10.83	11.09
96	7.33	7.58	7.84	8.10	8.36	8.62	8.88	9.14	9.40	9.66	9.91	10.17	10.43	10.69	10.95	11.21
95	7.41	7.67	7.93	8.20	8.46	8.72	8.98	9.24	9.50	9.76	10.02	10.29	10.55	10.81	11.07	11.33
94	7.50	7.76	8.03	8.29	8.55	8.82	9.08	9.34	9.61	9.87	10.14	10.40	10.66	10.93	11.19	11.46
93	7.59	7.86	8.12	8.39	8.65	8.92	9.18	9.45	9.72	9.98	10.25	10.52	10.78	11.05	11.32	11.58
92	7.68	7.95	8.22	8.49	8.75	9.02	9.29	9.56	9.83	10.10	10.37	10.64	10.91	11.17	11.44	11.71
91	7.77	8.04	8.31	8.59	8.86	9.13	9.40	9.67	9.94	10.21	10.49	10.76	11.03	11.30	11.57	11.85
90	7.87	8.14	8.41	8.69	8.96	9.23	9.51	9.78	10.06	10.33	10.61	10.88	11.16	11.43	11.71	11.98
89	7.96	8.24	8.52	8.79	9.07	9.34	9.62	9.90	10.17	10.45	10.73	11.01	11.28	11.56	11.84	12.12
88	8.06	8.34	8.62	8.90	9.18	9.46	9.74	10.02	10.29	10.57	10.86	11.14	11.42	11.70	11.98	12.26
87	8.16	8.44	8.72	9.01	9.29	9.57	9.85	10.13	10.42	10.70	10.98	11.27	11.55	11.83	12.12	12.40
86	8.26	8.55	8.83	9.12	9.40	9.69	9.97	10.26	10.54	10.83	11.11	11.40	11.69	11.97	12.26	12.55
85	8.37	8.65	8.94	9.23	9.52	9.80	10.09	10.38	10.67	10.96	11.25	11.54	11.83	12.12	12.41	12.70
84	8.47	8.76	9.05	9.34	9.63	9.93	10.22	10.51	10.80	11.09	11.39	11.68	11.97	12.26	12.56	12.85
83	8.58	8.87	9.17	9.46	9.76	10.05	10.34	10.64	10.93	11.23	11.53	11.82	12.12	12.41	12.71	13.01
82	8.69	8.99	9.28	9.58	9.88	10.18	10.47	10.77	11.07	11.37	11.67	11.97	12.27	12.57	12.87	13.17
81	8.81	9.10	9.40	9.70	10.00	10.30	10.61	10.91	11.21	11.51	11.81	12.12	12.42	12.72	13.03	13.33
80	8.92	9.22	9.53	9.83	10.13	10.44	10.74	11.05	11.35	11.66	11.96	12.27	12.58	12.89	13.19	13.50
79	9.04	9.34	9.65	9.96	10.26	10.57	10.88	11.19	11.50	11.81	12.12	12.43	12.74	13.05	13.36	13.67
78	9.16	9.47	9.78	10.09	10.40	10.71	11.02	11.33	11.65	11.96	12.27	12.59	12.90	13.22	13.53	13.85
77	9.28	9.59	9.91	10.22	10.54	10.85	11.17	11.48	11.80	12.12	12.43	12.75	13.07	13.39	13.71	14.03
76	9.41	9.72	10.04	10.36	10.68	11.00	11.32	11.64	11.96	12.28	12.60	12.92	13.24	13.57	13.89	14.21
75	9.54	9.86	10.18	10.50	10.82	11.14	11.47	11.79	12.12	12.44	12.77	13.09	13.42	13.75	14.08	14.40
74	9.67	9.99	10.32	10.64	10.97	11.30	11.62	11.95	12.28	12.61	12.94	13.27	13.60	13.93	14.27	14.60
73	9.80	10.13	10.46	10.79	11.12	11.45	11.78	12.12	12.45	12.78	13.12	13.45	13.79	14.12	14.46	14.80
70	10.23	10.57	10.91	11.25	11.60	11.94	12.29	12.64	12.98	13.33	13.68	14.03	14.38	14.73	15.08	15.43
65	11.01	11.38	11.75	12.12	12.49	12.86	13.23	13.60	13.97	14.35	14.72	15.10	15.48	15.85	16.23	16.61
60	11.92	12.31	12.71	13.11	13.51	13.91	14.31	14.72	15.12	15.53	15.94	16.34	16.75	17.16	17.57	17.98
55	12.97	13.40	13.84	14.28	14.71	15.15	15.59	16.03	16.48	16.92	17.36	17.81	18.26	18.70	19.15	19.60
50	14.23	14.71	15.19	15.67	16.15	16.63	17.12	17.61	18.10	18.59	19.08	19.57	20.06	20.55	21.05	21.54
45	15.76	16.29	16.82	17.36	17.90	18.44	18.98	19.53	20.07	20.62	21.17	21.72	22.27	22.82	23.37	23.92
40	17.66	18.27	18.87	19.48	20.09	20.70	21.32	21.93	22.55	23.17	23.79	24.41	25.03	25.65	26.27	26.89
35	20.11	20.81	21.51	22.21	22.92	23.62	24.33	25.03	25.74	26.45	27.16	27.87	28.58	29.30	30.01	30.72
30	23.40	24.22	25.04	25.87	26.70	27.52	28.35	29.18	30.01	30.84	31.67	32.50	33.34	34.17	35.00	35.83

BOND PRICE

Description: This table shows the price to pay for a bond at the yield rate. The yield is to maturity.

Example: The price of a 15.00 %, 30 year bond to yield 8 % to maturity is $ 179.18.

COUPON RATE, %

YIELD	11.00%	11.25%	11.50%	11.75%	12.00%	12.25%	12.50%	12.75%	13.00%	13.25%	13.50%	13.75%	14.00%	14.25%	14.50%	15.00%
0.00	430.00	437.50	445.00	452.50	460.00	467.50	475.00	482.50	490.00	497.50	505.00	512.50	520.00	527.50	535.00	550.00
1.00	358.63	365.09	371.56	378.02	384.49	390.96	397.42	403.89	410.35	416.82	423.28	429.75	436.22	442.68	449.15	462.08
2.00	302.30	307.92	313.54	319.16	324.78	330.39	336.01	341.63	347.25	352.87	358.49	364.11	369.73	375.35	380.97	392.21
3.00	257.52	262.44	267.37	272.29	277.21	282.13	287.06	291.98	296.90	301.82	306.75	311.67	316.59	321.51	326.44	336.28
4.00	221.66	226.01	230.35	234.70	239.04	243.39	247.73	252.08	256.42	260.77	265.11	269.46	273.80	278.15	282.49	291.18
4.25	213.85	218.06	222.28	226.50	230.71	234.93	239.15	243.36	247.58	251.80	256.01	260.23	264.44	268.66	272.88	281.31
4.50	206.43	210.53	214.62	218.71	222.81	226.90	231.00	235.09	239.18	243.28	247.37	251.46	255.56	259.65	263.74	271.93
4.75	199.40	203.38	207.35	211.33	215.31	219.28	223.26	227.23	231.21	235.19	239.16	243.14	247.11	251.09	255.07	263.02
5.00	192.73	196.59	200.45	204.32	208.18	212.04	215.91	219.77	223.63	227.50	231.36	235.23	239.09	242.95	246.82	254.54
5.25	186.39	190.14	193.90	197.65	201.41	205.17	208.92	212.68	216.43	220.19	223.95	227.70	231.46	235.21	238.97	246.48
5.50	180.36	184.02	187.67	191.32	194.97	198.63	202.28	205.93	209.58	213.24	216.89	220.54	224.20	227.85	231.50	238.81
5.75	174.64	178.19	181.74	185.30	188.85	192.41	195.96	199.51	203.07	206.62	210.18	213.73	217.28	220.84	224.39	231.50
6.00	169.19	172.65	176.11	179.57	183.03	186.49	189.95	193.41	196.86	200.32	203.78	207.24	210.70	214.16	217.62	224.54
6.25	164.01	167.37	170.74	174.11	177.48	180.85	184.22	187.59	190.96	194.32	197.69	201.06	204.43	207.80	211.17	217.91
6.50	159.07	162.35	165.63	168.92	172.20	175.48	178.76	182.04	185.32	188.61	191.89	195.17	198.45	201.73	205.01	211.58
6.75	154.37	157.57	160.77	163.96	167.16	170.36	173.56	176.76	179.96	183.15	186.35	189.55	192.75	195.95	199.14	205.54
7.00	149.89	153.01	156.13	159.24	162.36	165.48	168.60	171.72	174.83	177.95	181.07	184.19	187.31	190.42	193.54	199.78
7.25	145.62	148.66	151.70	154.74	157.78	160.82	163.86	166.91	169.95	172.99	176.03	179.07	182.11	185.15	188.19	194.28
7.50	141.54	144.51	147.48	150.44	153.41	156.38	159.34	162.31	165.28	168.25	171.21	174.18	177.15	180.12	183.08	189.02
7.75	137.65	140.55	143.44	146.34	149.24	152.13	155.03	157.92	160.82	163.72	166.61	169.51	172.41	175.30	178.20	183.99
8.00	133.94	136.76	139.59	142.42	145.25	148.07	150.90	153.73	156.56	159.39	162.21	165.04	167.87	170.70	173.53	179.18
8.25	130.38	133.15	135.91	138.67	141.43	144.20	146.96	149.72	152.48	155.25	158.01	160.77	163.53	166.29	169.06	174.58
8.50	126.99	129.69	132.39	135.09	137.79	140.49	143.19	145.88	148.58	151.28	153.98	156.68	159.38	162.08	164.78	170.18
8.75	123.74	126.38	129.02	131.66	134.30	136.94	139.57	142.21	144.85	147.49	150.13	152.77	155.40	158.04	160.68	165.96
9.00	120.64	123.22	125.80	128.38	130.96	133.54	136.12	138.70	141.28	143.86	146.44	149.02	151.60	154.17	156.75	161.91
9.25	117.66	120.19	122.71	125.23	127.76	130.28	132.80	135.33	137.85	140.37	142.90	145.42	147.94	150.47	152.99	158.04
9.50	114.81	117.28	119.75	122.22	124.69	127.16	129.63	132.10	134.57	137.04	139.50	141.97	144.44	146.91	149.38	154.32
9.75	112.08	114.50	116.92	119.33	121.75	124.17	126.58	129.00	131.42	133.83	136.25	138.67	141.08	143.50	145.92	150.75
10.00	109.46	111.83	114.20	116.56	118.93	121.30	123.66	126.03	128.39	130.76	133.13	135.49	137.86	140.22	142.59	147.32
10.25	106.95	109.27	111.59	113.90	116.22	118.54	120.86	123.17	125.49	127.81	130.13	132.44	134.76	137.08	139.40	144.03
10.50	104.54	106.81	109.08	111.35	113.62	115.89	118.16	120.43	122.70	124.97	127.25	129.52	131.79	134.06	136.33	140.87
10.75	102.23	104.45	106.68	108.90	111.13	113.35	115.58	117.80	120.03	122.25	124.48	126.70	128.93	131.15	133.38	137.83
11.00	100.00	102.18	104.36	106.54	108.72	110.91	113.09	115.27	117.45	119.63	121.81	123.99	126.17	128.36	130.54	134.90
11.25	97.86	100.00	102.14	104.28	106.42	108.56	110.69	112.83	114.97	117.11	119.25	121.39	123.53	125.67	127.81	132.08
11.50	95.80	97.90	100.00	102.10	104.20	106.29	108.39	110.49	112.59	114.69	116.78	118.88	120.98	123.08	125.18	129.37
11.75	93.82	95.88	97.94	100.00	102.06	104.12	106.18	108.23	110.29	112.35	114.41	116.47	118.53	120.58	122.64	126.76
12.00	91.92	93.94	95.96	97.98	100.00	102.02	104.04	106.06	108.08	110.10	112.12	114.14	116.16	118.18	120.20	124.24
12.25	90.08	92.07	94.05	96.03	98.02	100.00	101.98	103.97	105.95	107.93	109.92	111.90	113.88	115.87	117.85	121.81
12.50	88.32	90.26	92.21	94.16	96.11	98.05	100.00	101.95	103.89	105.84	107.79	109.74	111.68	113.63	115.58	119.47
12.75	86.61	88.52	90.44	92.35	94.26	96.17	98.09	100.00	101.91	103.83	105.74	107.65	109.56	111.48	113.39	117.21
13.00	84.97	86.85	88.73	90.60	92.48	94.36	96.24	98.12	100.00	101.88	103.76	105.64	107.52	109.40	111.27	115.03
13.25	83.38	85.23	87.07	88.92	90.77	92.61	94.46	96.31	98.15	100.00	101.85	103.69	105.54	107.39	109.23	112.93
13.50	81.85	83.66	85.48	87.29	89.11	90.92	92.74	94.55	96.37	98.18	100.00	101.82	103.63	105.45	107.26	110.89
13.75	80.37	82.15	83.94	85.72	87.51	89.29	91.08	92.86	94.65	96.43	98.22	100.00	101.78	103.57	105.35	108.92
14.00	78.94	80.70	82.45	84.21	85.96	87.72	89.47	91.23	92.98	94.74	96.49	98.25	100.00	101.75	103.51	107.02
14.25	77.56	79.29	81.01	82.74	84.46	86.19	87.92	89.64	91.37	93.10	94.82	96.55	98.27	100.00	101.73	105.18
14.50	76.22	77.92	79.62	81.32	83.02	84.72	86.41	88.11	89.81	91.51	93.21	94.91	96.60	98.30	100.00	103.40
14.75	74.93	76.60	78.27	79.95	81.62	83.29	84.96	86.63	88.30	89.97	91.64	93.32	94.99	96.66	98.33	101.67
15.00	73.68	75.33	76.97	78.62	80.26	81.91	83.55	85.20	86.84	88.49	90.13	91.78	93.42	95.07	96.71	100.00
15.25	72.47	74.09	75.71	77.33	78.95	80.57	82.19	83.81	85.43	87.04	88.66	90.28	91.90	93.52	95.14	98.38
15.50	71.30	72.89	74.49	76.08	77.68	79.27	80.86	82.46	84.05	85.65	87.24	88.84	90.43	92.03	93.62	96.81
15.75	70.16	71.73	73.30	74.87	76.44	78.01	79.58	81.15	82.72	84.30	85.87	87.44	89.01	90.58	92.15	95.29
16.00	69.06	70.61	72.15	73.70	75.25	76.79	78.34	79.89	81.44	82.98	84.53	86.08	87.62	89.17	90.72	93.81
16.25	67.99	69.51	71.04	72.56	74.09	75.61	77.14	78.66	80.18	81.71	83.23	84.76	86.28	87.81	89.33	92.38
16.50	66.95	68.46	69.96	71.46	72.96	74.46	75.97	77.47	78.97	80.47	81.97	83.48	84.98	86.48	87.98	90.99
16.75	65.95	67.43	68.91	70.39	71.87	73.35	74.83	76.31	77.79	79.27	80.75	82.23	83.71	85.19	86.67	89.64
17.00	64.97	66.43	67.89	69.35	70.81	72.27	73.73	75.19	76.65	78.11	79.57	81.03	82.49	83.94	85.40	88.32
17.25	64.02	65.46	66.90	68.34	69.78	71.22	72.66	74.10	75.53	76.97	78.41	79.85	81.29	82.73	84.17	87.05
17.50	63.10	64.52	65.94	67.36	68.78	70.20	71.61	73.03	74.45	75.87	77.29	78.71	80.13	81.55	82.97	85.81
17.75	62.20	63.60	65.00	66.40	67.80	69.20	70.60	72.00	73.40	74.80	76.20	77.60	79.00	80.40	81.80	84.60
18.00	61.33	62.71	64.09	65.48	66.86	68.24	69.62	71.00	72.38	73.76	75.14	76.52	77.90	79.29	80.67	83.43
18.25	60.48	61.85	63.21	64.57	65.94	67.30	68.66	70.02	71.39	72.75	74.11	75.47	76.84	78.20	79.56	82.29
18.50	59.66	61.00	62.35	63.69	65.04	66.38	67.73	69.07	70.42	71.76	73.11	74.45	75.80	77.14	78.49	81.17
18.75	58.86	60.18	61.51	62.84	64.17	65.49	66.82	68.15	69.48	70.80	72.13	73.46	74.78	76.11	77.44	80.09
19.00	58.08	59.39	60.70	62.01	63.32	64.63	65.94	67.25	68.56	69.87	71.18	72.49	73.80	75.11	76.42	79.04
20.00	55.15	56.39	57.64	58.89	60.13	61.38	62.62	63.87	65.11	66.36	67.61	68.85	70.10	71.34	72.59	75.08
25.00	44.05	45.05	46.05	47.05	48.04	49.04	50.04	51.04	52.04	53.04	54.04	55.04	56.04	57.04	58.04	60.03
30.00	36.68	37.51	38.35	39.18	40.01	40.85	41.68	42.51	43.35	44.18	45.01	45.85	46.68	47.51	48.35	50.01

Description: This table shows the yield to maturity of a bond purchased at the price shown in the index.

Example: The yield to maturity of a 15.00 %, 30 year bond at a price of 125.00 is 11.92 %.

COUPON RATE, %

PRICE	11.00%	11.25%	11.50%	11.75%	12.00%	12.25%	12.50%	12.75%	13.00%	13.25%	13.50%	13.75%	14.00%	14.25%	14.50%	15.00%
250	3.19	3.31	3.44	3.56	3.69	3.81	3.93	4.05	4.18	4.30	4.42	4.54	4.66	4.78	4.90	5.13
240	3.46	3.58	3.71	3.84	3.97	4.09	4.22	4.35	4.47	4.59	4.72	4.84	4.97	5.09	5.21	5.46
230	3.74	3.87	4.01	4.14	4.27	4.40	4.53	4.66	4.78	4.91	5.04	5.17	5.29	5.42	5.55	5.80
220	4.05	4.18	4.32	4.45	4.59	4.72	4.85	4.99	5.12	5.25	5.38	5.51	5.65	5.78	5.91	6.16
210	4.37	4.51	4.65	4.79	4.93	5.07	5.21	5.34	5.48	5.62	5.75	5.89	6.02	6.16	6.29	6.56
200	4.72	4.87	5.01	5.16	5.30	5.44	5.58	5.73	5.87	6.01	6.15	6.29	6.43	6.57	6.71	6.99
195	4.91	5.06	5.20	5.35	5.49	5.64	5.78	5.93	6.07	6.22	6.36	6.50	6.64	6.79	6.93	7.21
190	5.10	5.25	5.40	5.55	5.70	5.85	5.99	6.14	6.29	6.43	6.58	6.72	6.87	7.01	7.16	7.45
185	5.30	5.45	5.61	5.76	5.91	6.06	6.21	6.36	6.51	6.66	6.81	6.96	7.10	7.25	7.40	7.69
180	5.51	5.67	5.82	5.98	6.13	6.28	6.44	6.59	6.74	6.90	7.05	7.20	7.35	7.50	7.65	7.95
175	5.73	5.89	6.05	6.20	6.36	6.52	6.67	6.83	6.99	7.14	7.30	7.45	7.61	7.76	7.91	8.22
170	5.96	6.12	6.28	6.44	6.60	6.76	6.92	7.08	7.24	7.40	7.56	7.72	7.88	8.03	8.19	8.51
165	6.20	6.36	6.53	6.69	6.86	7.02	7.18	7.35	7.51	7.67	7.84	8.00	8.16	8.32	8.48	8.80
160	6.45	6.62	6.79	6.95	7.12	7.29	7.46	7.63	7.79	7.96	8.13	8.29	8.46	8.62	8.79	9.12
155	6.71	6.88	7.06	7.23	7.40	7.57	7.75	7.92	8.09	8.26	8.43	8.60	8.77	8.94	9.11	9.45
150	6.99	7.17	7.34	7.52	7.70	7.87	8.05	8.23	8.40	8.58	8.75	8.93	9.10	9.28	9.45	9.80
145	7.28	7.46	7.65	7.83	8.01	8.19	8.37	8.55	8.73	8.92	9.10	9.27	9.45	9.63	9.81	10.17
140	7.59	7.78	7.97	8.16	8.34	8.53	8.71	8.90	9.09	9.27	9.46	9.64	9.83	10.01	10.20	10.57
135	7.92	8.12	8.31	8.50	8.69	8.89	9.08	9.27	9.46	9.65	9.84	10.03	10.23	10.42	10.61	10.99
130	8.27	8.47	8.67	8.87	9.07	9.27	9.47	9.66	9.86	10.06	10.26	10.45	10.65	10.85	11.04	11.44
125	8.65	8.85	9.06	9.26	9.47	9.67	9.88	10.08	10.29	10.49	10.70	10.90	11.10	11.31	11.51	11.92
120	9.05	9.26	9.47	9.69	9.90	10.11	10.32	10.54	10.75	10.96	11.17	11.38	11.59	11.80	12.02	12.44
115	9.48	9.70	9.92	10.14	10.36	10.58	10.80	11.02	11.24	11.46	11.68	11.90	12.12	12.34	12.56	13.00
113	9.66	9.88	10.11	10.33	10.56	10.78	11.00	11.23	11.45	11.67	11.90	12.12	12.34	12.57	12.79	13.24
112	9.75	9.98	10.20	10.43	10.66	10.88	11.11	11.33	11.56	11.78	12.01	12.23	12.46	12.68	12.91	13.36
111	9.85	10.07	10.30	10.53	10.76	10.99	11.21	11.44	11.67	11.89	12.12	12.35	12.57	12.80	13.03	13.48
110	9.94	10.17	10.40	10.63	10.86	11.09	11.32	11.55	11.78	12.01	12.24	12.46	12.69	12.92	13.15	13.61
109	10.04	10.27	10.50	10.73	10.97	11.20	11.43	11.66	11.89	12.12	12.35	12.58	12.81	13.04	13.27	13.74
108	10.14	10.37	10.61	10.84	11.07	11.31	11.54	11.77	12.00	12.24	12.47	12.70	12.94	13.17	13.40	13.87
107	10.24	10.48	10.71	10.95	11.18	11.42	11.65	11.89	12.12	12.36	12.59	12.82	13.06	13.29	13.53	14.00
106	10.34	10.58	10.82	11.05	11.29	11.53	11.77	12.00	12.24	12.48	12.71	12.95	13.19	13.42	13.66	14.13
105	10.45	10.69	10.93	11.16	11.40	11.64	11.88	12.12	12.36	12.60	12.84	13.08	13.31	13.55	13.79	14.27
104	10.55	10.79	11.04	11.28	11.52	11.76	12.00	12.24	12.48	12.72	12.96	13.20	13.45	13.69	13.93	14.41
103	10.66	10.90	11.15	11.39	11.63	11.88	12.12	12.36	12.61	12.85	13.09	13.34	13.58	13.82	14.07	14.55
102	10.77	11.02	11.26	11.51	11.75	12.00	12.24	12.49	12.73	12.98	13.22	13.47	13.72	13.96	14.21	14.70
101	10.88	11.13	11.38	11.62	11.87	12.12	12.37	12.62	12.86	13.11	13.36	13.61	13.85	14.10	14.35	14.84
100	11.00	11.25	11.50	11.75	12.00	12.25	12.50	12.75	13.00	13.25	13.50	13.75	14.00	14.25	14.50	15.00
99	11.11	11.36	11.62	11.87	12.12	12.37	12.62	12.88	13.13	13.38	13.63	13.89	14.14	14.39	14.64	15.15
98	11.23	11.48	11.74	11.99	12.25	12.50	12.76	13.01	13.27	13.52	13.78	14.03	14.29	14.54	14.80	15.30
97	11.35	11.61	11.86	12.12	12.38	12.63	12.89	13.15	13.41	13.66	13.92	14.18	14.43	14.69	14.95	15.46
96	11.47	11.73	11.99	12.25	12.51	12.77	13.03	13.29	13.55	13.81	14.07	14.33	14.59	14.85	15.11	15.63
95	11.60	11.86	12.12	12.38	12.64	12.91	13.17	13.43	13.69	13.96	14.22	14.48	14.74	15.01	15.27	15.79
94	11.72	11.99	12.25	12.52	12.78	13.05	13.31	13.58	13.84	14.11	14.37	14.64	14.90	15.17	15.43	15.96
93	11.85	12.12	12.39	12.65	12.92	13.19	13.46	13.72	13.99	14.26	14.53	14.80	15.06	15.33	15.60	16.14
92	11.98	12.25	12.52	12.79	13.06	13.33	13.61	13.88	14.15	14.42	14.69	14.96	15.23	15.50	15.77	16.31
91	12.12	12.39	12.66	12.94	13.21	13.48	13.76	14.03	14.30	14.58	14.85	15.12	15.40	15.67	15.95	16.49
90	12.26	12.53	12.81	13.08	13.36	13.64	13.91	14.19	14.46	14.74	15.02	15.29	15.57	15.85	16.12	16.68
89	12.40	12.68	12.95	13.23	13.51	13.79	14.07	14.35	14.63	14.91	15.19	15.47	15.75	16.03	16.31	16.87
88	12.54	12.82	13.10	13.39	13.67	13.95	14.23	14.51	14.80	15.08	15.36	15.64	15.93	16.21	16.49	17.06
87	12.69	12.97	13.26	13.54	13.83	14.11	14.40	14.68	14.97	15.25	15.54	15.82	16.11	16.40	16.68	17.25
86	12.84	13.12	13.41	13.70	13.99	14.28	14.57	14.85	15.14	15.43	15.72	16.01	16.30	16.59	16.88	17.46
85	12.99	13.28	13.57	13.86	14.15	14.45	14.74	15.03	15.32	15.61	15.91	16.20	16.49	16.78	17.08	17.66
84	13.15	13.44	13.73	14.03	14.32	14.62	14.91	15.21	15.51	15.80	16.10	16.39	16.69	16.98	17.28	17.87
83	13.31	13.60	13.90	14.20	14.50	14.80	15.10	15.39	15.69	15.99	16.29	16.59	16.89	17.19	17.49	18.09
82	13.47	13.77	14.07	14.37	14.68	14.98	15.28	15.58	15.88	16.19	16.49	16.79	17.10	17.40	17.70	18.31
81	13.64	13.94	14.25	14.55	14.86	15.16	15.47	15.78	16.08	16.39	16.69	17.00	17.31	17.61	17.92	18.53
80	13.81	14.12	14.43	14.73	15.04	15.35	15.66	15.97	16.28	16.59	16.90	17.21	17.52	17.83	18.14	18.77
79	13.98	14.30	14.61	14.92	15.23	15.55	15.86	16.18	16.49	16.80	17.12	17.43	17.75	18.06	18.37	19.00
78	14.16	14.48	14.80	15.11	15.43	15.75	16.06	16.38	16.70	17.02	17.34	17.65	17.97	18.29	18.61	19.25
77	14.35	14.67	14.99	15.31	15.63	15.95	16.27	16.60	16.92	17.24	17.56	17.88	18.21	18.53	18.85	19.50
76	14.54	14.86	15.19	15.51	15.84	16.16	16.49	16.81	17.14	17.47	17.79	18.12	18.45	18.77	19.10	19.75
75	14.73	15.06	15.39	15.72	16.05	16.38	16.71	17.04	17.37	17.70	18.03	18.36	18.69	19.02	19.35	20.02
74	14.93	15.26	15.60	15.93	16.26	16.60	16.93	17.27	17.60	17.94	18.27	18.61	18.94	19.28	19.61	20.29
73	15.13	15.47	15.81	16.15	16.49	16.83	17.16	17.50	17.84	18.18	18.52	18.86	19.20	19.54	19.88	20.56
70	15.78	16.13	16.49	16.84	17.19	17.54	17.90	18.25	18.60	18.96	19.31	19.67	20.02	20.38	20.73	21.44
65	16.99	17.37	17.75	18.13	18.51	18.89	19.27	19.65	20.03	20.41	20.79	21.18	21.56	21.94	22.32	23.09
60	18.39	18.80	19.21	19.63	20.04	20.45	20.86	21.28	21.69	22.11	22.52	22.93	23.35	23.76	24.18	25.01
55	20.05	20.50	20.95	21.40	21.85	22.30	22.75	23.20	23.66	24.11	24.56	25.01	25.47	25.92	26.37	27.28

Description: This table shows the current yield of a bond purchased at the price shown in the index.

Example: The current yield of a 6.75 % bond at a price of 104.00 is 6.49 %.

PRICE	0.00%	1.00%	2.00%	3.00%	4.00%	4.25%	4.50%	4.75%	5.00%	5.25%	5.50%	5.75%	6.00%	6.25%	6.50%	6.75%
140	0.00	.71	1.43	2.14	2.86	3.04	3.21	3.39	3.57	3.75	3.93	4.11	4.29	4.46	4.64	4.82
135	0.00	.74	1.48	2.22	2.96	3.15	3.33	3.52	3.70	3.89	4.07	4.26	4.44	4.63	4.81	5.00
130	0.00	.77	1.54	2.31	3.08	3.27	3.46	3.65	3.85	4.04	4.23	4.42	4.62	4.81	5.00	5.19
125	0.00	.80	1.60	2.40	3.20	3.40	3.60	3.80	4.00	4.20	4.40	4.60	4.80	5.00	5.20	5.40
120	0.00	.83	1.67	2.50	3.33	3.54	3.75	3.96	4.17	4.38	4.58	4.79	5.00	5.21	5.42	5.63
119	0.00	.84	1.68	2.52	3.36	3.57	3.78	3.99	4.20	4.41	4.62	4.83	5.04	5.25	5.46	5.67
118	0.00	.85	1.69	2.54	3.39	3.60	3.81	4.03	4.24	4.45	4.66	4.87	5.08	5.30	5.51	5.72
117	0.00	.85	1.71	2.56	3.42	3.63	3.85	4.06	4.27	4.49	4.70	4.91	5.13	5.34	5.56	5.77
116	0.00	.86	1.72	2.59	3.45	3.66	3.88	4.09	4.31	4.53	4.74	4.96	5.17	5.39	5.60	5.82
115	0.00	.87	1.74	2.61	3.48	3.70	3.91	4.13	4.35	4.57	4.78	5.00	5.22	5.43	5.65	5.87
114	0.00	.88	1.75	2.63	3.51	3.73	3.95	4.17	4.39	4.61	4.82	5.04	5.26	5.48	5.70	5.92
113	0.00	.88	1.77	2.65	3.54	3.76	3.98	4.20	4.42	4.65	4.87	5.09	5.31	5.53	5.75	5.97
112	0.00	.89	1.79	2.68	3.57	3.79	4.02	4.24	4.46	4.69	4.91	5.13	5.36	5.58	5.80	6.03
111	0.00	.90	1.80	2.70	3.60	3.83	4.05	4.28	4.50	4.73	4.95	5.18	5.41	5.63	5.86	6.08
110	0.00	.91	1.82	2.73	3.64	3.86	4.09	4.32	4.55	4.77	5.00	5.23	5.45	5.68	5.91	6.14
109	0.00	.92	1.83	2.75	3.67	3.90	4.13	4.36	4.59	4.82	5.05	5.28	5.50	5.73	5.96	6.19
108	0.00	.93	1.85	2.78	3.70	3.94	4.17	4.40	4.63	4.86	5.09	5.32	5.56	5.79	6.02	6.25
107	0.00	.93	1.87	2.80	3.74	3.97	4.21	4.44	4.67	4.91	5.14	5.37	5.61	5.84	6.07	6.31
106	0.00	.94	1.89	2.83	3.77	4.01	4.25	4.48	4.72	4.95	5.19	5.42	5.66	5.90	6.13	6.37
105	0.00	.95	1.90	2.86	3.81	4.05	4.29	4.52	4.76	5.00	5.24	5.48	5.71	5.95	6.19	6.43
104	0.00	.96	1.92	2.88	3.85	4.09	4.33	4.57	4.81	5.05	5.29	5.53	5.77	6.01	6.25	6.49
103.75	0.00	.96	1.93	2.89	3.86	4.10	4.34	4.58	4.82	5.06	5.30	5.54	5.78	6.02	6.27	6.51
103.50	0.00	.97	1.93	2.90	3.86	4.11	4.35	4.59	4.83	5.07	5.31	5.56	5.80	6.04	6.28	6.52
103.25	0.00	.97	1.94	2.91	3.87	4.12	4.36	4.60	4.84	5.08	5.33	5.57	5.81	6.05	6.30	6.54
103.00	0.00	.97	1.94	2.91	3.88	4.13	4.37	4.61	4.85	5.10	5.34	5.58	5.83	6.07	6.31	6.55
102.75	0.00	.97	1.95	2.92	3.89	4.14	4.38	4.62	4.87	5.11	5.35	5.60	5.84	6.08	6.33	6.57
102.50	0.00	.98	1.95	2.93	3.90	4.15	4.39	4.63	4.88	5.12	5.37	5.61	5.85	6.10	6.34	6.59
102.25	0.00	.98	1.96	2.93	3.91	4.16	4.40	4.65	4.89	5.13	5.38	5.62	5.87	6.11	6.36	6.60
102.00	0.00	.98	1.96	2.94	3.92	4.17	4.41	4.66	4.90	5.15	5.39	5.64	5.88	6.13	6.37	6.62
101.75	0.00	.98	1.97	2.95	3.93	4.18	4.42	4.67	4.91	5.16	5.41	5.65	5.90	6.14	6.39	6.63
101.50	0.00	.99	1.97	2.96	3.94	4.19	4.43	4.68	4.93	5.17	5.42	5.67	5.91	6.16	6.40	6.65
101.25	0.00	.99	1.98	2.96	3.95	4.20	4.44	4.69	4.94	5.19	5.43	5.68	5.93	6.17	6.42	6.67
101.00	0.00	.99	1.98	2.97	3.96	4.21	4.46	4.70	4.95	5.20	5.45	5.69	5.94	6.19	6.44	6.68
100.75	0.00	.99	1.99	2.98	3.97	4.22	4.47	4.71	4.96	5.21	5.46	5.71	5.96	6.20	6.45	6.70
100.50	0.00	1.00	1.99	2.99	3.98	4.23	4.48	4.73	4.98	5.22	5.47	5.72	5.97	6.22	6.47	6.72
100.25	0.00	1.00	2.00	2.99	3.99	4.24	4.49	4.74	4.99	5.24	5.49	5.74	5.99	6.23	6.48	6.73
100.00	0.00	1.00	2.00	3.00	4.00	4.25	4.50	4.75	5.00	5.25	5.50	5.75	6.00	6.25	6.50	6.75
99.75	0.00	1.00	2.01	3.01	4.01	4.26	4.51	4.76	5.01	5.26	5.51	5.76	6.02	6.27	6.52	6.77
99.50	0.00	1.01	2.01	3.02	4.02	4.27	4.52	4.77	5.03	5.28	5.53	5.78	6.03	6.28	6.53	6.78
99.25	0.00	1.01	2.02	3.02	4.03	4.28	4.53	4.79	5.04	5.29	5.54	5.79	6.05	6.30	6.55	6.80
99.00	0.00	1.01	2.02	3.03	4.04	4.29	4.55	4.80	5.05	5.30	5.56	5.81	6.06	6.31	6.57	6.82
98.75	0.00	1.01	2.03	3.04	4.05	4.30	4.56	4.81	5.06	5.32	5.57	5.82	6.08	6.33	6.58	6.84
98.50	0.00	1.02	2.03	3.05	4.06	4.31	4.57	4.82	5.08	5.33	5.58	5.84	6.09	6.35	6.60	6.85
98.25	0.00	1.02	2.04	3.05	4.07	4.33	4.58	4.83	5.09	5.34	5.60	5.85	6.11	6.36	6.62	6.87
98.00	0.00	1.02	2.04	3.06	4.08	4.34	4.59	4.85	5.10	5.36	5.61	5.87	6.12	6.38	6.63	6.89
97.75	0.00	1.02	2.05	3.07	4.09	4.35	4.60	4.86	5.12	5.37	5.63	5.88	6.14	6.39	6.65	6.91
97.50	0.00	1.03	2.05	3.08	4.10	4.36	4.62	4.87	5.13	5.38	5.64	5.90	6.15	6.41	6.67	6.92
97.25	0.00	1.03	2.06	3.08	4.11	4.37	4.63	4.88	5.14	5.40	5.66	5.91	6.17	6.43	6.68	6.94
97	0.00	1.03	2.06	3.09	4.12	4.38	4.64	4.90	5.15	5.41	5.67	5.93	6.19	6.44	6.70	6.96
96	0.00	1.04	2.08	3.13	4.17	4.43	4.69	4.95	5.21	5.47	5.73	5.99	6.25	6.51	6.77	7.03
95	0.00	1.05	2.11	3.16	4.21	4.47	4.74	5.00	5.26	5.53	5.79	6.05	6.32	6.58	6.84	7.11
94	0.00	1.06	2.13	3.19	4.26	4.52	4.79	5.05	5.32	5.59	5.85	6.12	6.38	6.65	6.91	7.18
93	0.00	1.08	2.15	3.23	4.30	4.57	4.84	5.11	5.38	5.65	5.91	6.18	6.45	6.72	6.99	7.26
92	0.00	1.09	2.17	3.26	4.35	4.62	4.89	5.16	5.43	5.71	5.98	6.25	6.52	6.79	7.07	7.34
91	0.00	1.10	2.20	3.30	4.40	4.67	4.95	5.22	5.49	5.77	6.04	6.32	6.59	6.87	7.14	7.42
90	0.00	1.11	2.22	3.33	4.44	4.72	5.00	5.28	5.56	5.83	6.11	6.39	6.67	6.94	7.22	7.50
89	0.00	1.12	2.25	3.37	4.49	4.78	5.06	5.34	5.62	5.90	6.18	6.46	6.74	7.02	7.30	7.58
88	0.00	1.14	2.27	3.41	4.55	4.83	5.11	5.40	5.68	5.97	6.25	6.53	6.82	7.10	7.39	7.67
87	0.00	1.15	2.30	3.45	4.60	4.89	5.17	5.46	5.75	6.03	6.32	6.61	6.90	7.18	7.47	7.76
86	0.00	1.16	2.33	3.49	4.65	4.94	5.23	5.52	5.81	6.10	6.40	6.69	6.98	7.27	7.56	7.85
85	0.00	1.18	2.35	3.53	4.71	5.00	5.29	5.59	5.88	6.18	6.47	6.76	7.06	7.35	7.65	7.94
80	0.00	1.25	2.50	3.75	5.00	5.31	5.63	5.94	6.25	6.56	6.88	7.19	7.50	7.81	8.13	8.44
75	0.00	1.33	2.67	4.00	5.33	5.67	6.00	6.33	6.67	7.00	7.33	7.67	8.00	8.33	8.67	9.00
70	0.00	1.43	2.86	4.29	5.71	6.07	6.43	6.79	7.14	7.50	7.86	8.21	8.57	8.93	9.29	9.64
65	0.00	1.54	3.08	4.62	6.15	6.54	6.92	7.31	7.69	8.08	8.46	8.85	9.23	9.62	10.00	10.38
60	0.00	1.67	3.33	5.00	6.67	7.08	7.50	7.92	8.33	8.75	9.17	9.58	10.00	10.42	10.83	11.25
55	0.00	1.82	3.64	5.45	7.27	7.73	8.18	8.64	9.09	9.55	10.00	10.45	10.91	11.36	11.82	12.27
50	0.00	2.00	4.00	6.00	8.00	8.50	9.00	9.50	10.00	10.50	11.00	11.50	12.00	12.50	13.00	13.50

BOND YIELD

CURRENT YIELD

Description: This table shows the current yield of a bond purchased at the price shown in the index.

Example: The current yield of a 10.75 % bond at a price of 104.00 is 10.34 %.

							COUPON RATE, %									
PRICE	**7.00%**	**7.25%**	**7.50%**	**7.75%**	**8.00%**	**8.25%**	**8.50%**	**8.75%**	**9.00%**	**9.25%**	**9.50%**	**9.75%**	**10.00%**	**10.25%**	**10.50%**	**10.75%**
140	5.00	5.18	5.36	5.54	5.71	5.89	6.07	6.25	6.43	6.61	6.79	6.96	7.14	7.32	7.50	7.68
135	5.19	5.37	5.56	5.74	5.93	6.11	6.30	6.48	6.67	6.85	7.04	7.22	7.41	7.59	7.78	7.96
130	5.38	5.58	5.77	5.96	6.15	6.35	6.54	6.73	6.92	7.12	7.31	7.50	7.69	7.88	8.08	8.27
125	5.60	5.80	6.00	6.20	6.40	6.60	6.80	7.00	7.20	7.40	7.60	7.80	8.00	8.20	8.40	8.60
120	5.83	6.04	6.25	6.46	6.67	6.88	7.08	7.29	7.50	7.71	7.92	8.13	8.33	8.54	8.75	8.96
119	5.88	6.09	6.30	6.51	6.72	6.93	7.14	7.35	7.56	7.77	7.98	8.19	8.40	8.61	8.82	9.03
118	5.93	6.14	6.36	6.57	6.78	6.99	7.20	7.42	7.63	7.84	8.05	8.26	8.47	8.69	8.90	9.11
117	5.98	6.20	6.41	6.62	6.84	7.05	7.26	7.48	7.69	7.91	8.12	8.33	8.55	8.76	8.97	9.19
116	6.03	6.25	6.47	6.68	6.90	7.11	7.33	7.54	7.76	7.97	8.19	8.41	8.62	8.84	9.05	9.27
115	6.09	6.30	6.52	6.74	6.96	7.17	7.39	7.61	7.83	8.04	8.26	8.48	8.70	8.91	9.13	9.35
114	6.14	6.36	6.58	6.80	7.02	7.24	7.46	7.68	7.89	8.11	8.33	8.55	8.77	8.99	9.21	9.43
113	6.19	6.42	6.64	6.86	7.08	7.30	7.52	7.74	7.96	8.19	8.41	8.63	8.85	9.07	9.29	9.51
112	6.25	6.47	6.70	6.92	7.14	7.37	7.59	7.81	8.04	8.26	8.48	8.71	8.93	9.15	9.38	9.60
111	6.31	6.53	6.76	6.98	7.21	7.43	7.66	7.88	8.11	8.33	8.56	8.78	9.01	9.23	9.46	9.68
110	6.36	6.59	6.82	7.05	7.27	7.50	7.73	7.95	8.18	8.41	8.64	8.86	9.09	9.32	9.55	9.77
109	6.42	6.65	6.88	7.11	7.34	7.57	7.80	8.03	8.26	8.49	8.72	8.94	9.17	9.40	9.63	9.86
108	6.48	6.71	6.94	7.18	7.41	7.64	7.87	8.10	8.33	8.56	8.80	9.03	9.26	9.49	9.72	9.95
107	6.54	6.78	7.01	7.24	7.48	7.71	7.94	8.18	8.41	8.64	8.88	9.11	9.35	9.58	9.81	10.05
106	6.60	6.84	7.08	7.31	7.55	7.78	8.02	8.25	8.49	8.73	8.96	9.20	9.43	9.67	9.91	10.14
105	6.67	6.90	7.14	7.38	7.62	7.86	8.10	8.33	8.57	8.81	9.05	9.29	9.52	9.76	10.00	10.24
104	6.73	6.97	7.21	7.45	7.69	7.93	8.17	8.41	8.65	8.89	9.13	9.38	9.62	9.86	10.10	10.34
103.75	6.75	6.99	7.23	7.47	7.71	7.95	8.19	8.43	8.67	8.92	9.16	9.40	9.64	9.88	10.12	10.36
103.50	6.76	7.00	7.25	7.49	7.73	7.97	8.21	8.45	8.70	8.94	9.18	9.42	9.66	9.90	10.14	10.39
103.25	6.78	7.02	7.26	7.51	7.75	7.99	8.23	8.47	8.72	8.96	9.20	9.44	9.69	9.93	10.17	10.41
103.00	6.80	7.04	7.28	7.52	7.77	8.01	8.25	8.50	8.74	8.98	9.22	9.47	9.71	9.95	10.19	10.44
102.75	6.81	7.06	7.30	7.54	7.79	8.03	8.27	8.52	8.76	9.00	9.25	9.49	9.73	9.98	10.22	10.46
102.50	6.83	7.07	7.32	7.56	7.80	8.05	8.29	8.54	8.78	9.02	9.27	9.51	9.76	10.00	10.24	10.49
102.25	6.85	7.09	7.33	7.58	7.82	8.07	8.31	8.56	8.80	9.05	9.29	9.54	9.78	10.02	10.27	10.51
102.00	6.86	7.11	7.35	7.60	7.84	8.09	8.33	8.58	8.82	9.07	9.31	9.56	9.80	10.05	10.29	10.54
101.75	6.88	7.13	7.37	7.62	7.86	8.11	8.35	8.60	8.85	9.09	9.34	9.58	9.83	10.07	10.32	10.57
101.50	6.90	7.14	7.39	7.64	7.88	8.13	8.37	8.62	8.87	9.11	9.36	9.61	9.85	10.10	10.34	10.59
101.25	6.91	7.16	7.41	7.65	7.90	8.15	8.40	8.64	8.89	9.14	9.38	9.63	9.88	10.12	10.37	10.62
101.00	6.93	7.18	7.43	7.67	7.92	8.17	8.42	8.66	8.91	9.16	9.41	9.65	9.90	10.15	10.40	10.64
100.75	6.95	7.20	7.44	7.69	7.94	8.19	8.44	8.68	8.93	9.18	9.43	9.68	9.93	10.17	10.42	10.67
100.50	6.97	7.21	7.46	7.71	7.96	8.21	8.46	8.71	8.96	9.20	9.45	9.70	9.95	10.20	10.45	10.70
100.25	6.98	7.23	7.48	7.73	7.98	8.23	8.48	8.73	8.98	9.23	9.48	9.73	9.98	10.22	10.47	10.72
100.00	7.00	7.25	7.50	7.75	8.00	8.25	8.50	8.75	9.00	9.25	9.50	9.75	10.00	10.25	10.50	10.75
99.75	7.02	7.27	7.52	7.77	8.02	8.27	8.52	8.77	9.02	9.27	9.52	9.77	10.03	10.28	10.53	10.78
99.50	7.04	7.29	7.54	7.79	8.04	8.29	8.54	8.79	9.05	9.30	9.55	9.80	10.05	10.30	10.55	10.80
99.25	7.05	7.30	7.56	7.81	8.06	8.31	8.56	8.82	9.07	9.32	9.57	9.82	10.08	10.33	10.58	10.83
99.00	7.07	7.32	7.58	7.83	8.08	8.33	8.59	8.84	9.09	9.34	9.60	9.85	10.10	10.35	10.61	10.86
98.75	7.09	7.34	7.59	7.85	8.10	8.35	8.61	8.86	9.11	9.37	9.62	9.87	10.13	10.38	10.63	10.89
98.50	7.11	7.36	7.61	7.87	8.12	8.38	8.63	8.88	9.14	9.39	9.64	9.90	10.15	10.41	10.66	10.91
98.25	7.12	7.38	7.63	7.89	8.14	8.40	8.65	8.91	9.16	9.41	9.67	9.92	10.18	10.43	10.69	10.94
98.00	7.14	7.40	7.65	7.91	8.16	8.42	8.67	8.93	9.18	9.44	9.69	9.95	10.20	10.46	10.71	10.97
97.75	7.16	7.42	7.67	7.93	8.18	8.44	8.70	8.95	9.21	9.46	9.72	9.97	10.23	10.49	10.74	11.00
97.50	7.18	7.44	7.69	7.95	8.21	8.46	8.72	8.97	9.23	9.49	9.74	10.00	10.26	10.51	10.77	11.03
97.25	7.20	7.46	7.71	7.97	8.23	8.48	8.74	9.00	9.25	9.51	9.77	10.03	10.28	10.54	10.80	11.05
97	7.22	7.47	7.73	7.99	8.25	8.51	8.76	9.02	9.28	9.54	9.79	10.05	10.31	10.57	10.82	11.08
96	7.29	7.55	7.81	8.07	8.33	8.59	8.85	9.11	9.38	9.64	9.90	10.16	10.42	10.68	10.94	11.20
95	7.37	7.63	7.89	8.16	8.42	8.68	8.95	9.21	9.47	9.74	10.00	10.26	10.53	10.79	11.05	11.32
94	7.45	7.71	7.98	8.24	8.51	8.78	9.04	9.31	9.57	9.84	10.11	10.37	10.64	10.90	11.17	11.44
93	7.53	7.80	8.06	8.33	8.60	8.87	9.14	9.41	9.68	9.95	10.22	10.48	10.75	11.02	11.29	11.56
92	7.61	7.88	8.15	8.42	8.70	8.97	9.24	9.51	9.78	10.05	10.33	10.60	10.87	11.14	11.41	11.68
91	7.69	7.97	8.24	8.52	8.79	9.07	9.34	9.62	9.89	10.16	10.44	10.71	10.99	11.26	11.54	11.81
90	7.78	8.06	8.33	8.61	8.89	9.17	9.44	9.72	10.00	10.28	10.56	10.83	11.11	11.39	11.67	11.94
89	7.87	8.15	8.43	8.71	8.99	9.27	9.55	9.83	10.11	10.39	10.67	10.96	11.24	11.52	11.80	12.08
88	7.95	8.24	8.52	8.81	9.09	9.38	9.66	9.94	10.23	10.51	10.80	11.08	11.36	11.65	11.93	12.22
87	8.05	8.33	8.62	8.91	9.20	9.48	9.77	10.06	10.34	10.63	10.92	11.21	11.49	11.78	12.07	12.36
86	8.14	8.43	8.72	9.01	9.30	9.59	9.88	10.17	10.47	10.76	11.05	11.34	11.63	11.92	12.21	12.50
85	8.24	8.53	8.82	9.12	9.41	9.71	10.00	10.29	10.59	10.88	11.18	11.47	11.76	12.06	12.35	12.65
80	8.75	9.06	9.38	9.69	10.00	10.31	10.62	10.94	11.25	11.56	11.88	12.19	12.50	12.81	13.13	13.44
75	9.33	9.67	10.00	10.33	10.67	11.00	11.33	11.67	12.00	12.33	12.67	13.00	13.33	13.67	14.00	14.33
70	10.00	10.36	10.71	11.07	11.43	11.79	12.14	12.50	12.86	13.21	13.57	13.93	14.29	14.64	15.00	15.36
65	10.77	11.15	11.54	11.92	12.31	12.69	13.08	13.46	13.85	14.23	14.62	15.00	15.38	15.77	16.15	16.54
60	11.67	12.08	12.50	12.92	13.33	13.75	14.17	14.58	15.00	15.42	15.83	16.25	16.67	17.08	17.50	17.92
55	12.73	13.18	13.64	14.09	14.55	15.00	15.45	15.91	16.36	16.82	17.27	17.73	18.18	18.64	19.09	19.55
50	14.00	14.50	15.00	15.50	16.00	16.50	17.00	17.50	18.00	18.50	19.00	19.50	20.00	20.50	21.00	21.50

BOND YIELD

Description: This table shows the current yield of a bond purchased at the price shown in the index.

Example: The current yield of a 15.00 % bond at a price of 104.00 is 14.42 %.

PRICE	11.00%	11.25%	11.50%	11.75%	12.00%	12.25%	12.50%	12.75%	13.00%	13.25%	13.50%	13.75%	14.00%	14.25%	14.50%	15.00%
140	7.86	8.04	8.21	8.39	8.57	8.75	8.93	9.11	9.29	9.46	9.64	9.82	10.00	10.18	10.36	10.71
135	8.15	8.33	8.52	8.70	8.89	9.07	9.26	9.44	9.63	9.81	10.00	10.19	10.37	10.56	10.74	11.11
130	8.46	8.65	8.85	9.04	9.23	9.42	9.62	9.81	10.00	10.19	10.38	10.58	10.77	10.96	11.15	11.54
125	8.80	9.00	9.20	9.40	9.60	9.80	10.00	10.20	10.40	10.60	10.80	11.00	11.20	11.40	11.60	12.00
120	9.17	9.38	9.58	9.79	10.00	10.21	10.42	10.62	10.83	11.04	11.25	11.46	11.67	11.88	12.08	12.50
119	9.24	9.45	9.66	9.87	10.08	10.29	10.50	10.71	10.92	11.13	11.34	11.55	11.76	11.97	12.18	12.61
118	9.32	9.53	9.75	9.96	10.17	10.38	10.59	10.81	11.02	11.23	11.44	11.65	11.86	12.08	12.29	12.71
117	9.40	9.62	9.83	10.04	10.26	10.47	10.68	10.90	11.11	11.32	11.54	11.75	11.97	12.18	12.39	12.82
116	9.48	9.70	9.91	10.13	10.34	10.56	10.78	10.99	11.21	11.42	11.64	11.85	12.07	12.28	12.50	12.93
115	9.57	9.78	10.00	10.22	10.43	10.65	10.87	11.09	11.30	11.52	11.74	11.96	12.17	12.39	12.61	13.04
114	9.65	9.87	10.09	10.31	10.53	10.75	10.96	11.18	11.40	11.62	11.84	12.06	12.28	12.50	12.72	13.16
113	9.73	9.96	10.18	10.40	10.62	10.84	11.06	11.28	11.50	11.73	11.95	12.17	12.39	12.61	12.83	13.27
112	9.82	10.04	10.27	10.49	10.71	10.94	11.16	11.38	11.61	11.83	12.05	12.28	12.50	12.72	12.95	13.39
111	9.91	10.14	10.36	10.59	10.81	11.04	11.26	11.49	11.71	11.94	12.16	12.39	12.61	12.84	13.06	13.51
110	10.00	10.23	10.45	10.68	10.91	11.14	11.36	11.59	11.82	12.05	12.27	12.50	12.73	12.95	13.18	13.64
109	10.09	10.32	10.55	10.78	11.01	11.24	11.47	11.70	11.93	12.16	12.39	12.61	12.84	13.07	13.30	13.76
108	10.19	10.42	10.65	10.88	11.11	11.34	11.57	11.81	12.04	12.27	12.50	12.73	12.96	13.19	13.43	13.89
107	10.28	10.51	10.75	10.98	11.21	11.45	11.68	11.92	12.15	12.38	12.62	12.85	13.08	13.32	13.55	14.02
106	10.38	10.61	10.85	11.08	11.32	11.56	11.79	12.03	12.26	12.50	12.74	12.97	13.21	13.44	13.68	14.15
105	10.48	10.71	10.95	11.19	11.43	11.67	11.90	12.14	12.38	12.62	12.86	13.10	13.33	13.57	13.81	14.29
104	10.58	10.82	11.06	11.30	11.54	11.78	12.02	12.26	12.50	12.74	12.98	13.22	13.46	13.70	13.94	14.42
103.75	10.60	10.84	11.08	11.33	11.57	11.81	12.05	12.29	12.53	12.77	13.01	13.25	13.49	13.73	13.98	14.46
103.50	10.63	10.87	11.11	11.35	11.59	11.84	12.08	12.32	12.56	12.80	13.04	13.29	13.53	13.77	14.01	14.49
103.25	10.65	10.90	11.14	11.38	11.62	11.86	12.11	12.35	12.59	12.83	13.08	13.32	13.56	13.80	14.04	14.53
103.00	10.68	10.92	11.17	11.41	11.65	11.89	12.14	12.38	12.62	12.86	13.11	13.35	13.59	13.83	14.08	14.56
102.75	10.71	10.95	11.19	11.44	11.68	11.92	12.17	12.41	12.65	12.90	13.14	13.38	13.63	13.87	14.11	14.60
102.50	10.73	10.98	11.22	11.46	11.71	11.95	12.20	12.44	12.68	12.93	13.17	13.41	13.66	13.90	14.15	14.63
102.25	10.76	11.00	11.25	11.49	11.74	11.98	12.22	12.47	12.71	12.96	13.20	13.45	13.69	13.94	14.18	14.67
102.00	10.78	11.03	11.27	11.52	11.76	12.01	12.25	12.50	12.75	12.99	13.24	13.48	13.73	13.97	14.22	14.71
101.75	10.81	11.06	11.30	11.55	11.79	12.04	12.29	12.53	12.78	13.02	13.27	13.51	13.76	14.00	14.25	14.74
101.50	10.84	11.08	11.33	11.58	11.82	12.07	12.32	12.56	12.81	13.05	13.30	13.55	13.79	14.04	14.29	14.78
101.25	10.86	11.11	11.36	11.60	11.85	12.10	12.35	12.59	12.84	13.09	13.33	13.58	13.83	14.07	14.32	14.81
101.00	10.89	11.14	11.39	11.63	11.88	12.13	12.38	12.62	12.87	13.12	13.37	13.61	13.86	14.11	14.36	14.85
100.75	10.92	11.17	11.41	11.66	11.91	12.16	12.41	12.66	12.90	13.15	13.40	13.65	13.90	14.14	14.39	14.89
100.50	10.95	11.19	11.44	11.69	11.94	12.19	12.44	12.69	12.94	13.18	13.43	13.68	13.93	14.18	14.43	14.93
100.25	10.97	11.22	11.47	11.72	11.97	12.22	12.47	12.72	12.97	13.22	13.47	13.72	13.97	14.21	14.46	14.96
100.00	11.00	11.25	11.50	11.75	12.00	12.25	12.50	12.75	13.00	13.25	13.50	13.75	14.00	14.25	14.50	15.00
99.75	11.03	11.28	11.53	11.78	12.03	12.28	12.53	12.78	13.03	13.28	13.53	13.78	14.04	14.29	14.54	15.04
99.50	11.06	11.31	11.56	11.81	12.06	12.31	12.56	12.81	13.07	13.32	13.57	13.82	14.07	14.32	14.57	15.08
99.25	11.08	11.34	11.59	11.84	12.09	12.34	12.59	12.85	13.10	13.35	13.60	13.85	14.11	14.36	14.61	15.11
99.00	11.11	11.36	11.62	11.87	12.12	12.37	12.63	12.88	13.13	13.38	13.64	13.89	14.14	14.39	14.65	15.15
98.75	11.14	11.39	11.65	11.90	12.15	12.41	12.66	12.91	13.16	13.42	13.67	13.92	14.18	14.43	14.68	15.19
98.50	11.17	11.42	11.68	11.93	12.18	12.44	12.69	12.94	13.20	13.45	13.71	13.96	14.21	14.47	14.72	15.23
98.25	11.20	11.45	11.70	11.96	12.21	12.47	12.72	12.98	13.23	13.49	13.74	13.99	14.25	14.50	14.76	15.27
98.00	11.22	11.48	11.73	11.99	12.24	12.50	12.76	13.01	13.27	13.52	13.78	14.03	14.29	14.54	14.80	15.31
97.75	11.25	11.51	11.76	12.02	12.28	12.53	12.79	13.04	13.30	13.55	13.81	14.07	14.32	14.58	14.83	15.35
97.50	11.28	11.54	11.79	12.05	12.31	12.56	12.82	13.08	13.33	13.59	13.85	14.10	14.36	14.62	14.87	15.38
97.25	11.31	11.57	11.83	12.08	12.34	12.60	12.85	13.11	13.37	13.62	13.88	14.14	14.40	14.65	14.91	15.42
97	11.34	11.60	11.86	12.11	12.37	12.63	12.89	13.14	13.40	13.66	13.92	14.18	14.43	14.69	14.95	15.46
96	11.46	11.72	11.98	12.24	12.50	12.76	13.02	13.28	13.54	13.80	14.06	14.32	14.58	14.84	15.10	15.63
95	11.58	11.84	12.11	12.37	12.63	12.89	13.16	13.42	13.68	13.95	14.21	14.47	14.74	15.00	15.26	15.79
94	11.70	11.97	12.23	12.50	12.77	13.03	13.30	13.56	13.83	14.10	14.36	14.63	14.89	15.16	15.43	15.96
93	11.83	12.10	12.37	12.63	12.90	13.17	13.44	13.71	13.98	14.25	14.52	14.78	15.05	15.32	15.59	16.13
92	11.96	12.23	12.50	12.77	13.04	13.32	13.59	13.86	14.13	14.40	14.67	14.95	15.22	15.49	15.76	16.30
91	12.09	12.36	12.64	12.91	13.19	13.46	13.74	14.01	14.29	14.56	14.84	15.11	15.38	15.66	15.93	16.48
90	12.22	12.50	12.78	13.06	13.33	13.61	13.89	14.17	14.44	14.72	15.00	15.28	15.56	15.83	16.11	16.67
89	12.36	12.64	12.92	13.20	13.48	13.76	14.04	14.33	14.61	14.89	15.17	15.45	15.73	16.01	16.29	16.85
88	12.50	12.78	13.07	13.35	13.64	13.92	14.20	14.49	14.77	15.06	15.34	15.63	15.91	16.19	16.48	17.05
87	12.64	12.93	13.22	13.51	13.79	14.08	14.37	14.66	14.94	15.23	15.52	15.80	16.09	16.38	16.67	17.24
86	12.79	13.08	13.37	13.66	13.95	14.24	14.53	14.83	15.12	15.41	15.70	15.99	16.28	16.57	16.86	17.44
85	12.94	13.24	13.53	13.82	14.12	14.41	14.71	15.00	15.29	15.59	15.88	16.18	16.47	16.76	17.06	17.65
80	13.75	14.06	14.37	14.69	15.00	15.31	15.63	15.94	16.25	16.56	16.88	17.19	17.50	17.81	18.12	18.75
75	14.67	15.00	15.33	15.67	16.00	16.33	16.67	17.00	17.33	17.67	18.00	18.33	18.67	19.00	19.33	20.00
70	15.71	16.07	16.43	16.79	17.14	17.50	17.86	18.21	18.57	18.93	19.29	19.64	20.00	20.36	20.71	21.43
65	16.92	17.31	17.69	18.08	18.46	18.85	19.23	19.62	20.00	20.38	20.77	21.15	21.54	21.92	22.31	23.08
60	18.33	18.75	19.17	19.58	20.00	20.42	20.83	21.25	21.67	22.08	22.50	22.92	23.33	23.75	24.17	25.00
55	20.00	20.45	20.91	21.36	21.82	22.27	22.73	23.18	23.64	24.09	24.55	25.00	25.45	25.91	26.36	27.27
50	22.00	22.50	23.00	23.50	24.00	24.50	25.00	25.50	26.00	26.50	27.00	27.50	28.00	28.50	29.00	30.00

Calculating an Interest Rate

Calculating a rate from the amount, term, and payment of a loan is not a simple matter. Finding a rate is an indirect process.

If the term is an even year such as 1, 2, 5, or 30 years, then the finance charge per 100 can be determined and the rate can be found in the APR Scan table. Alternatively, the payment per $1 can be determined, and the rate found in the Compound Interest and Annuity table or the Installment Loan Payment tables. In a table, the rate may be found either exactly or by interpolation.

If the rate cannot be found in the tables, or if a rate to more than 2 decimal places is required, then a formula and process must be used to find the rate. The formula computes an approximate rate, and the process is one of iteration.

By Iteration. The formula in this iterative process will calculate the interest rate for a regular loan that is amortized by regular payments over the term. If anything about the loan is irregular, such as an odd first payment period, a change of payment, or a balance outstanding at the end of the term, then this process will not work. Another process must be used, called the incremental process, which is described later in this Appendix.

An iterative process is a sequence of program steps performed over and over again. The steps are the formula that solves for an approximate rate. When the difference between 2 successive rates is so small as to be without significance, then the last approximate rate is considered to be the desired rate. The process starts with an initial rate and continues until the test for termination is satisfied.

The formula for calculating an initial rate is:

$$i_0 = \frac{\text{Payment}}{\text{Original principal}}$$

where:

i_0 = initial value of rate per period, k = 0
k = number of iterations
n = term in periods

The formula for computing a subsequent rate is:

$$i_{k+1} = \frac{\text{Payment}}{\text{Original principal}} \times \left(1 - \frac{1}{(1 + i_k)^n}\right)$$

i_{k+1} = Subsequent rate per period

Using this formula, the rate calculation is repeated until the difference between 2 successive rates is a very small number such that the last 2 rates are considered for practical purposes to be the same.

Example: The interest rate on a loan of $1,000 amortized over 5 years by a monthly payment of $21.25 is 10.01%. The initial rate and the first 3 iterations of the formula are shown here:

$$i_0 = \frac{21.25}{1,000} = .02125$$

$$i_1 = .02125 \times (1 - (1 \div (1 + .02125)^{60}))$$
$$= .015\ 232\ 241$$

$$i_2 = .02125 \times (1 - (1 \div (1 + .015232241)^{60}))$$
$$= .012\ 671\ 036$$

$$i_3 = .02125 \times (1 - (1 \div (1 + .012671036)^{60}))$$
$$= .011\ 267\ 125$$

The iterations are repeated until $i_k - i_k + 1 < .0000001$.

The difference between 2 successive rates must be less than 1 in the seventh decimal place. The number of iterations varies with the term. For 1 year, the process stops after 153 iterations. For 5 years, there are 37 iterations; for 20 years, there are 21 iterations.

A BASIC computer program that will do these calculations is provided on page A-3.

By Increment. When there are irregular payments to amortize a loan, when payments are skipped or there is a balance at the end of the term, or when the rate generally is implicit in the right-hand side of an equation (such as in a bond yield or a prepaid mortgage yield), then the rate can be calculated by an incremental process.

There are 2 parts to the process: First, there is the formula used for calculation; and second, there is the incremental process to calculate the interest rate.

The formula computes the present worth of the future payments at an interest rate. The variables of the formula are an amount, or present value; a rate; a term in periods; and a balance, or future value. The formula is stated as:

$$\text{Amount} = P_1 V^1 + P_2 V^2 + P_3 V^3 + \cdots + P_n V^n + BV^n$$

where:

$P_1, P_2, P_3, \cdots, P_n$ = payments

B = balance outstanding at end of term

$V^1, V^2, V^3, \cdots, V^n$ = Present Worth of 1, for each period of the term of n periods

This formula is the most basic of all present worth formulas. Virtually every problem concerning amount, rate, term, and

CALCULATING AN INTEREST RATE

payment where 3 are known and 1 is unknown can be solved by this equation.

The basic present worth formula is modified for the calculation of yields for mortgages, prepayment mortgages, and bonds, using the incremental process, as follows:

The mortgage formula is:

$$\text{Price} = \text{Payment} \times A_{\overline{n}|}$$

The prepayment mortgage formula is:

$$\text{Price} = \text{Payment} \times A_{\overline{n}|} + \text{Balance} \times V^n$$

The bond formula is:

$$\text{Price} = (\text{Coupon} \div 2) \times A_{\overline{n}|} + \text{Principal} \times V^n$$

The Coupon Issue Yield Equivalent formula for a Treasury bill, 183 to 364 days, is:

$$100 = \text{Price} \times (1 + \frac{i}{2}) \times \left(1 + (\frac{2n - 365}{365}) \times \frac{i}{2}\right)$$

The incremental process is very simple. The initial rate is always 0%; the next rate is 10%. If 10% is low, the next rate is 20%. If 20% is high, the process backs down to 10% and starts up again in increments of 1% until the rate is too high. The process then backs down by 1% and starts up again in incre-

ments of .1%, and so on. For a final rate of 16.21%, the incremental rates are: 0, 10, 20, 10%; 11, 12, 13, 14, 15, 16, 17, 16%; 16.1, 16.2, 16.3, 16.2%; 16.21, 16.22, 16.21%.

The program arrives at a rate by several steps. At each rate, a present worth is computed. The result is subtracted from the original amount. If the difference is negative, the rate is increased by the increment. If the difference is positive, the rate backs down; the rate is then decreased by the increment; the increment is divided by 10, and the process continued. Another present worth is computed and tested against the amount. The process continues until the difference between the computed present worth and the amount is zero.

A BASIC computer program that will do these calculations is provided on page A-3.

A Word of Caution. The iteration program has no intelligence. If, in the example, a payment of 2.125 instead of 21.25 is input, the program will compute a rate of .000028%.

The increment program also has no intelligence, but in a different manner. When an incorrect number is input, this program may compute an incorrect negative rate. The amount, term and payment should be checked for reasonableness before the process begins. All this is by way of saying that computing an interest rate is not a simple matter.

Calculating an Interest Rate by Iteration

```
10    ! CALCULATE RATE BY ITERATION
20    !
30    DISP "AMOUNT";
40    INPUT Amt
50    DISP "TERM,YRS";
60    INPUT Years
70    DISP "PAYMENT";
80    INPUT Payt
90    PRINT
100   PRINT "         CALCULATE RATE FOR"
110   PRINT "    AMOUNT    TERM,YRS    PAYMENT"
120   PRINT USING A;Amt,Years,Payt
130 A:IMAGE 10D,9D,10D.2D
140   PRINT
150   PRINT "        PROCESS OF ITEREATION"
160   PRINT
170   PRINT " #    RATE     DELTA  MONTHLY RATE"
180   !
190   B=Years*12   ! TERM IN MONTHS
200   Ctr=0
210   I3=Payt/Amt
220   I2=Payt/Amt  ! INITIAL RATE
230   !
240 ! *** LOOP
250   I1=I3*(1-(1/(1+I2)^B))
260   Rate=I1*12*100
270   Delta=I2-I1
280   I2=I1
290   !
300   Ctr=Ctr+1
310   PRINT USING F;Ctr,Rate,Delta,I1
320 F:IMAGE 3D,3D.6D,2D.7D,3D.6D
330   !
340   If Delta>.0000001 THEN 250
350   !
360   PRINT
370   Rt=Rate
380   IF Rt>=0 THEN 400
390   PRINT "RATE IS NEGATIVE"
400   PRINT "RATE IS ",Rate;"%"
410   END
```

```
         CALCULATE RATE FOR
   AMOUNT    TERM,YRS    PAYMENT
     1000        5        21.25

     PROCESS OF ITEREATION

 #    RATE     DELTA  MONTHLY RATE
 1 18.278690  .0060178   .015232
 2 15.205243  .0025612   .012671
 3 13.520550  .0014039   .011267

34 10.006722  .0000002   .008339
35 10.006556  .0000001   .008339
36 10.006429  .0000001   .008339
37 10.006331  .0000001   .008339

RATE IS   10.0063305931 %
```

Calculating an Interest Rate by Increments

```
10    ! CALCULATE RATE BY INCREMENTS
20    !
30    DISP "AMOUNT";
40    INPUT Amt
50    DISP "TERM,YRS";
60    INPUT Years
70    DISP "PAYMENT";
80    INPUT Payt
90    PRINT
100   PRINT "         CALCULATE RATE FOR"
110   PRINT "    AMOUNT    TERM,YRS    PAYMENT"
120   PRINT USING A;Amt,Years,Payt
130 A: IMAGE 10D,9D,10D.2D
140   PRINT
150   PRINT "     PROCESS OF INCREMENTATION"
160   PRINT
170   PRINT " #   RATE    TAMT     DELTA    INC"
180   !
190   Rate=Rate0   ! INITIAL RATE
200   Inc=10.00    ! INITIAL INCREMENT
210   B=Years*12   ! TERM IN MONTHS
220   Ctr=0        ! COUNTER
230   !
240 ! *** CALCULATE PRESENT WORTH
250   D1=Rate/100/12    ! MONTHLY INTEREST FACTOR
260   B=Years*12        ! TERM IN MONTHS
270   D3=(1+D1)^B       ! (1+I)^N
280   D4=1/D3           ! PRESENT WORTH OF 1, V^N
290   IF D1<>0 THEN 320 ! IF RATE=0
300   D5=B
310   GOTO 330
320   D5=(1-D4)/D1      ! PRES WORTH OF 1 PER PRD
330   Tamt=Payt*D5      ! TRIAL AMOUNT
340   !
350   Delta=Amt-Tamt
360   Delta=Delta*10000
370   Delta=INT(Delta)
380   Delta=Delta/10000
390   !
400   Ctr=Ctr+1
410   PRINT USING F;Ctr,Rate,Tamt,Delta,Inc
420 F:IMAGE 3D,3D.3D,6D.2D,6D.2D,3D.3D
430   !
440   IF Delta<=0 THEN
450      Rate=Rate+Inc
460      GOTO 250
470   ELSE
480      Rate=Rate-Inc
490      Inc=Inc/10
500      IF Inc<.001 THEN 540
510      GOTO 250
520   END IF
530   !
540   PRINT
550   Rt=Rate
560   IF Rt>=0 THEN 580
570   PRINT "RATE IS NEGATIVE"
580   PRINT "RATE IS ",Rate;"%"
590 END
```

```
         CALCULATE RATE FOR
   AMOUNT    TERM,YRS    PAYMENT
     1000        5        21.25

     PROCESS OF INCREMENTATION

 #   RATE    TAMT     DELTA    INC
 1  0.000  1275.00  -275.00 10.000
 2 10.000  1000.14     -.14 10.000
 3 20.000   802.07   197.93 10.000

14 10.004  1000.05     -.05   .001
15 10.005  1000.02     -.02   .001
16 10.006  1000.00    -0.00   .001
17 10.007   999.98     .02   .001

RATE IS   10.006 %
```

Index

[References are to page numbers.]

Numbers

0% bond, 27-1.2
e, the number 2.71828, 15-1.2
Rule of 72, years for money to double, 15-1.2
Rule of 78, rebate and earning, 21-1.1

A

Actuarial method, v, 22-1.1
Actuarial Rebate and Earnings, 22-1.1
Add on, 8-1.5
Amortization, v, 5-1.1
   Bond, 27-1.1
   Mortgage, 25-1.1
   Prepayment mortgage, 26-1.1
Amount of 1, 8-1.2
Amount of 1 Per Period, 8-1.3
Annual add on rate, 8-1.5
APR Scan Table, 19-1.1
Annual Percentage Rate, v, 8-1.2, 20-1.1
   Biweekly, 19-1.1
   Monthly, 19-1.1
   Semimonthly, 19-1.1
   Weekly, 19-1.1
Annuity, 8-1.1
Annuity payment, 8-1.1
Average life of mortgage, 5-1.2

B

Balloon payment, 8-1.2
Bank discount, 24-1.1
Bills, Treasury, 24-1.1
Bond, 27-1.1

C

Calendar, 16-1.2
Callable bond, 27-1.2
Calculating an Interest Rate, A-1
   Increment, A-1
   Iteration, A-1
Compensating Balance, 13-1.1
Compound interest
   Annual, 8-1.2, 15-1.2, 16-1.2
   Continuous, 15-1.2
   Daily, 12-1.1, 15-1.2, 16-1.2
   Monthly, 8-1.2, 15-1.2, 16-1.2
   Quarterly, 8-1.2, 15-1.2, 16-1.2
   Semiannual, 8-1.2, 15-1.2, 16-1.2
Compound Interest and Annuity, 8-1.1
Constant Annual Percent, 1-1.1, 8-1.5
Construction Loan, 14-1.1
Coupon Issue Yield Equivalent, 24-1.1
Current yield, 27-1.2

D

Daily Compound Interest on $100, 12-1.1
Daily Rebate, 23-1.1
Day, a, 10-1.1
Days Between Dates, 10-1.1
Days, exact, 10-1.1
Days in a period, 10-1.1
Days, months and, 10-1.1
Days of the Year, 9-1.1
Debt Service, 2-1.1
Deposits for savings growth
   Annual, 16-1.1
   Monthly, 16-1.1
   Quarterly, 16-1.1
   Semiannual, 16-1.1
   Weekly, 16-1.1
Direct reduction loan schedule, 5-1.1
Discount, 11-1.2
   Bank, 24-1.1
   Bond, 27-1.2
   Mortgage, 25-1.1
   Prepayment mortgage, 26-1.1
Discounted cash flow, 8-1.6
Discount Price, 24-1.1
Double your money, 15-1.2

E

e, the number 2.71828, 15-1.2
Earning
   Actuarial, 22-1.1
   Rule of 78, 21-1.1
Effective rate, v, 8-1.2, 15-1.2
Elements of a financial transaction, 8-1.1
Equivalent yield, discount, 24-1.1
Extension of tables, 8-1.5

INDEX

[References are to page numbers.]

F

Finance charge, 18-1.1
Find a payment, vi

G

Growth of one, 15-1.1
Growth, Savings, 16-1.1

I

Installment Loan Payments, 18-1.1
Interest, 11-1.1
    Annual compound, 15-1.2, 16-1.2
    Bank, 11-1.2, 15-1.2
    Compound, 8-1.3, 11-1.1, 12-1.1, 15-1.2, 16-1.2
    Continuous compound, 15-1.2
    Daily compound, 15-1.2, 16-1.2
    Discount, 11-1.2
    Exact day, 11-1.2
    Factor, 11-1.1
    Monthly compound, 15-1.2, 16-1.2
    Ordinary, 11-1.2
    Quarterly compound, 15-1.2, 16-1.2
    Semiannual compound, 15-1.2, 16-1.2
    Simple, 8-1.3, 11-1.1, 11-1.2, 15-1.2, 16-1.1

L

Lease Payments, 20-1.1

M

Makeham's formula, 8-1.5
Minimum charge, 21-1.1, 22-1.1
Monthly rebate and earnings, rule of 78, 22-1.1
Mortgage
    Discount, 25-1.1
    Loan schedule, 5-1.1
    Payment, v
    Premium, 25-1.1
    Prepayment, 26-1.1
    Price, 25-1.1
    Yield, 25-1.1

N

Net present value, 8-1.6
Nominal Rate, v, 8-1.2, 15-1.2

P

Par
    Bond, 27-1.1
    Mortgage, 25-1.1
    Prepayment mortgage, 26-1.1
Payment, v
    In advance, 1-1.1, 8-1.7
    In advance with balance, 8-1.7
    In arrears, 1-1.1
    Biweekly, 18-1.1
    Irregular, 8-1.6
    Monthly, 18-1.1
    Semimonthly, 18-1.1
    Weekly, 18-1.1
Percent Paid Off, 4-1.1
Period, 8-1.2, 15-1.2
Periodic interest factor, 8-1.2
Periodic payment to amortize 1, 8-1.5
Points, 3-1.1, 6-1.1, 14-1.1
Premium
    Bond, 27-1.2
    Mortgage, 25-1.1
Prepayment Mortgage, 26-1.1
Present Worth of 1, 8-1.4
Present Worth of 1 Per Period, 8-1.4
Price
    Bond, 27-1.1
    Discount, 24-1.1
    Mortgage, 25-1.1
    Prepayment mortgage, 26-1.1

R

Rate
    Adjusted annual, 15-1.2
    Effective, 8-1.2, 15-1.2
    Nominal, 8-1.2, 15-1.2
Rebate
    Actuarial, 22-1.1
    Daily, 23-1.1
    Rule of 78, 21-1.1
Residual, 20-1.1
Rule of 72, years for money to double, 15-1.2
Rule of 78, rebate and earning, 21-1.1

S

Savings and deposits, 8-1.2
Savings and Withdrawal, 17-1.1
Savings Growth, 16-1.1
Scan Table, 7-1.1
Simple Interest on $100, 11-1.1
Sinking fund, 8-1.4
Sum of the digits, 21-1.2

[References are to page numbers.]

T

Time factor, 10-1.1, 11-1.1
Total Interest, 3-1.1, 8-1.5
Treasury bills, 24-1.1
Truth in lending, v
Two accounts method, 8-1.5

U

United States rule, v

W

Weekly deposits, 16-1.1
Weekly payments, 18-1.1
Withdrawal, 17-1.1

Y

Year, 9-1.1, 10-1.1
Yield
    Bond, 27-1.2
    Current, 27-1.2
    Discount equivalent, 24-1.1
    Mortgage, 25-1.1
    Prepayment mortgage, 26-1.1